Who'sWho of American Women®

Biographical Titles Currently Published by Marquis Who's Who

Who's Who in America
Who's Who in America Junior & Senior High School Version
Who Was Who in America
  Historical Volume (1607–1896)
  Volume I (1897–1942)
  Volume II (1943–1950)
  Volume III (1951–1960)
  Volume IV (1961–1968)
  Volume V (1969–1973)
  Volume VI (1974–1976)
  Volume VII (1977–1981)
  Volume VIII (1982–1985)
  Volume IX (1985–1989)
  Volume X (1989–1993)
  Index Volume (1607–1993)
Who's Who in the World
Who's Who in the East
Who's Who in the Midwest
Who's Who in the South and Southwest
Who's Who in the West
Who's Who in American Education
Who's Who in American Law
Who's Who in American Nursing
Who's Who of American Women
Who's Who of Emerging Leaders in America
Who's Who in Finance and Industry
Who's Who in Science and Engineering
Index to Marquis Who's Who Publications
The *Official* ABMS Directory of Board Certified Medical Specialists

Who's Who of American Women

1995~1996

19th Edition

MARQUIS Who's Who™
A REED REFERENCE PUBLISHING COMPANY

121 Chanlon Road
New Providence, NJ 07974 U.S.A.

Marquis Who's Who
Who's Who of American Women ®

Vice President, Production—Directories	Dean Hollister
Editorial Director	Paul Canning
Senior Managing Editor	Fred M. Marks
Managing Editor	Lisa Weissbard

Editorial

Senior Editor	Christina F. Moxley
Associate Editor	Kristin Anna Eckes
Assistant Editors	Hazel C. Conner
	Roger N. Generazzo
	Lisa A. Heft
	Jacqueline M. Lewis
	Eileen McGuinness
	Matthew O'Connell
	Stephanie A. Palenque
	Josh Samber
	Rebecca Sultzbaugh

Editorial Services

Manager	Nadine Hovan
Supervisors	Debra Krom
	Mary Lyn K. Sodano
Coordinator	Anne Marie C. Calcagno

Editorial Support

Manager	Sharon L. Gonzalez
Staff	J. Hector Gonzalez

Mail Processing

Manager	Kara A. Seitz
Staff	Shawn Johnston
	Cheryl A. Rodriguez
	Jill S. Terbell
	Scott Van Houten

Database Operations

Supervisor	Ren Reiner

Research

Researcher	Connie Harbison

Support Services

Assistant	Jeanne Danzig

Reed Reference Publishing

Chief Operating Officer Andrew W. Meyer **Senior Vice President, Database Publishing** Peter E. Simon
Senior Vice President, Marketing Stanley Walker **Senior Vice President, Sales** Edward J. Roycroft
Vice President & Publisher Sandra S. Barnes

Table of Contents

Preface

In 1958, Marquis Who's Who published the first edition of *Who's Who of American Women*. Since that time there has been an increasing interest and need for the biographical data of successful American women.

Many of the Biographees in the premier edition were volunteer workers involved in civic, religious, and club activities. This, the nineteenth edition, features Biographees in a broader range of endeavors and varying levels of responsibility. Listed in this volume are outstanding women from the fields of business, education, government, law, medicine, the performing and visual arts, the sciences, and many more.

The Marquis researchers have drawn on a wide range of sources in identifying listees: newspapers, magazines, trade publications, professional association rosters, and nominations by current Biographees, among others, were consulted in the preparation of the more than 30,000 sketches found in this edition. The result is a wealth of personal and professional biographical facts concerning women in virtually every important field of endeavor.

To supplement the efforts of Marquis researchers, and to ensure comprehensive coverage of important professionals, members of the distinguished Board of Advisors have nominated outstanding individuals in their own geographic regions or professional fields for inclusion in this volume.

As in all Marquis Who's Who biographical volumes, the principle of current reference value determines selection of Biographees. Reference interest is based either on position of responsibility or noteworthy achievement. In the editorial evaluation that resulted in the ultimate selection of the names in this directory, an individual's desire to be listed was not sufficient reason for inclusion.

The nineteenth edition of *Who's Who of American Women* continues the tradition of excellence established in 1899 with the publication of the first edition of *Who's Who in America*. Each candidate is invited to submit biographical data about her life and professional career. Submitted information is reviewed by the Marquis editorial staff before being written in sketch form, and a prepublication proof of the composed sketch is sent to potential Biographees for verification. Every verified sketch returned by a candidate and accepted by the editorial staff is written in the final Marquis Who's Who format. This process ensures a high degree of accuracy.

In the event that an individual of significant reference interest fails to submit biographical data, the Marquis staff compiles the needed information through independent research. Brief key information is provided in the sketches of selected individuals, new to this edition, who did not submit data. Such sketches are denoted by an asterisk.

Marquis Who's Who editors exercise the utmost care in preparing each biographical sketch for publication. Occasionally, however, errors do appear. Users of this directory are requested to notify the publisher of any errors found so that corrections can be made in a subsequent edition.

Board of Advisors

Marquis Who's Who gratefully acknowledges the following distinguished individuals who have made themselves available for review, evaluation, and general comment with regard to the publication of the nineteenth edition of *Who's Who of American Women*. The advisors have enhanced the reference value of this edition by the nomination of outstanding individuals for inclusion. However, the Board of Advisors, either collectively or individually, is in no way responsible for the final selection of names appearing in this volume, nor does the Board of Advisors bear responsibility for the accuracy or comprehensiveness of the biographical information or other material contained herein.

Standards of Admission

The foremost consideration in selecting Biographees for *Who's Who of American Women* is the extent of an individual's reference interest. Such reference interest is judged on either of two factors: (1) the position of responsibility held, or (2) the level of achievement attained by the individual.

Admissions based on the factor of position include:

High-level federal officials

Specified elected and appointed state officials

Mayors of major cities

Principal officers of selected businesses

Outstanding educators from major universities and colleges

Principal figures of cultural and artistic institutions

Heads of major women's organizations

Recipients of major awards and honors

Members of selected honorary organizations

Other women chosen because of incumbency or membership

Admission for individual achievement is based on qualitative criteria. To be selected, a person must have attained conspicuous achievement.

Key to Information

[1] **CHAMBERS, ELIZABETH BATES,** [2] lawyer; [3] b. Mitchell, S.D., July 19, 1940; [4] d. Oscar William and Judith (Strait) Bates; [5] m. Richard T. Chambers, Dec. 11, 1967; [6] children: Christopher Dwight, Mary Beth. [7] BA, U. Okla., 1962, MA, 1967; JD, Rice U., 1970. [8] Bar: Tex. 1970, S.D. 1973, U.S. Dist. Ct. S.D. 1982, U.S. Supreme Ct. 1982. [9] Assoc. Newman, Calvin & Swain, Houston, 1967-73, ptnr., 1973-74; ptnr. Hadley, Ellis, Chambers & Gonzalez, Amarillo, Tex., 1974-78; sole practice, Rapid City, S.D., 1978-82; ptnr. Chambers & Costner, Rapid City, 1982-85, sr. ptnr., 1985—; [10] lectr. Black Hills State Coll., Spearfish, S.D., 1987; mem. Gov.'s Task Force on Constl. Revision, Pierre, S.D., 1988—; bd. dirs. Custer Nat. Bank. [11] Contbr. articles to profl. jours. [12] Trustee The Grove Sch., Rapid City, 1982—; active Pennington County United Way. [13] Served with WAC, 1962-63. [14] Named Outstanding Woman of Yr., Amarillo C. of C., 1975; Lincoln Found. grantee, 1980. [15] Mem. ABA, S.D. Bar Assn., S.D. Assn. Def. Counsel, Pennington County Bar Assn., World Wildlife Fedn., Rushmore Hills Country Club, Noontime Club, Order Eastern Star. [16] Democrat. [17] Lutheran. [18] Home: 527 Woodbine Way Rapid City SD 57702 [19] Office: Chambers & Costner 964 N Omaha St Rapid City SD 57701

KEY

[1]	Name
[2]	Occupation
[3]	Vital statistics
[4]	Parents
[5]	Marriage
[6]	Children
[7]	Education
[8]	Professional certifications
[9]	Career
[10]	Career related
[11]	Writings and creative works
[12]	Civic and political activities
[13]	Military
[14]	Awards and fellowships
[15]	Professional and association memberships, clubs and lodges
[16]	Political affiliation
[17]	Religion
[18]	Home address
[19]	Office address

Table of Abbreviations

The following abbreviations and symbols are frequently used in this book.

*An asterisk following a sketch indicates that it was researched by the Marquis Who's Who editorial staff and has not been verified by the Biographee.

A Associate (used with academic degrees only)
AA, A.A. Associate in Arts, Associate of Arts
AAAL American Academy of Arts and Letters
AAAS American Association for the Advancement of Science
AACD American Association for Counseling and Development
AACN American Association of Critical Care Nurses
AAHA American Academy of Health Administrators
AAHP American Association of Hospital Planners
AAHPERD American Alliance for Health, Physical Education, Recreation, and Dance
AAS Associate of Applied Science
AASL American Association of School Librarians
AASPA American Association of School Personnel Administrators
AAU Amateur Athletic Union
AAUP American Association of University Professors
AAUW American Association of University Women
AB, A.B. Arts, Bachelor of
AB Alberta
ABA American Bar Association
ABC American Broadcasting Company
AC Air Corps
acad. academy, academic
acct. accountant
acctg. accounting
ACDA Arms Control and Disarmament Agency
ACHA American College of Hospital Administrators
ACLS Advanced Cardiac Life Support
ACLU American Civil Liberties Union
ACOG American College of Ob-Gyn
ACP American College of Physicians
ACS American College of Surgeons
ADA American Dental Association
a.d.c. aide-de-camp
adj. adjunct, adjutant
adj. gen. adjutant general
adm. admiral
adminstr. administrator
adminstrn. administration
adminstrv. administrative
ADN Associate's Degree in Nursing
ADP Automatic Data Processing
adv. advocate, advisory
advt. advertising
AE, A.E. Agricultural Engineer
A.E. and P. Ambassador Extraordinary and Plenipotentiary

AEC Atomic Energy Commission
aero. aeronautical, aeronautic
aerodyn. aerodynamic
AFB Air Force Base
AFL-CIO American Federation of Labor and Congress of Industrial Organizations
AFTRA American Federation of TV and Radio Artists
AFSCME American Federation of State, County and Municipal Employees
agr. agriculture
agrl. agricultural
agt. agent
AGVA American Guild of Variety Artists
agy. agency
A&I Agricultural and Industrial
AIA American Institute of Architects
AIAA American Institute of Aeronautics and Astronautics
AIChE American Institute of Chemical Engineers
AICPA American Institute of Certified Public Accountants
AID Agency for International Development
AIDS Acquired Immune Deficiency Syndrome
AIEE American Institute of Electrical Engineers
AIM American Institute of Management
AIME American Institute of Mining, Metallurgy, and Petroleum Engineers
AK Alaska
AL Alabama
ALA American Library Association
Ala. Alabama
alt. alternate
Alta. Alberta
A&M Agricultural and Mechanical
AM, A.M. Arts, Master of
Am. American, America
AMA American Medical Association
amb. ambassador
A.M.E. African Methodist Episcopal
Amtrak National Railroad Passenger Corporation
AMVETS American Veterans of World War II, Korea, Vietnam
ANA American Nurses Association
anat. anatomical
ANCC American Nurses Credentialing Center
ann. annual
ANTA American National Theatre and Academy
anthrop. anthropological
AP Associated Press
APA American Psychological Association
APGA American Personnel Guidance Association
APHA American Public Health Association
APO Army Post Office
apptd. appointed
Apr. April
apt. apartment
AR Arkansas

ARC American Red Cross
arch. architect
archeol. archeological
archtl. architectural
Ariz. Arizona
Ark. Arkansas
ArtsD, ArtsD. Arts, Doctor of
arty. artillery
AS American Samoa
AS Associate in Science
ASCAP American Society of Composers, Authors and Publishers
ASCD Association for Supervision and Curriculum Development
ASCE American Society of Civil Engineers
ASHRAE American Society of Heating, Refrigeration, and Air Conditioning Engineers
ASME American Society of Mechanical Engineers
ASNSA American Society for Nursing Service Administrators
ASPA American Society for Public Administration
ASPCA American Society for the Prevention of Cruelty to Animals
assn. association
assoc. associate
asst. assistant
ASTD American Society for Training and Development
ASTM American Society for Testing and Materials
astron. astronomical
astrophys. astrophysical
ATLA Association of Trial Lawyers of America
ATSC Air Technical Service Command
AT&T American Telephone & Telegraph Company
atty. attorney
Aug. August
AUS Army of the United States
aux. auxiliary
Ave. Avenue
AVMA American Veterinary Medical Association
AZ Arizona
AWHONN Association of Women's Health Obstetric and Neonatal Nurses

B. Bachelor
b. born
BA, B.A. Bachelor of Arts
BAgr, B.Agr. Bachelor of Agriculture
Balt. Baltimore
Bapt. Baptist
BArch, B.Arch. Bachelor of Architecture
BAS, B.A.S. Bachelor of Agricultural Science
BBA, B.B.A. Bachelor of Business Administration
BBB Better Business Bureau
BBC British Broadcasting Corporation
BC, B.C. British Columbia

BCE, B.C.E. Bachelor of Civil Engineering
BChir, B.Chir. Bachelor of Surgery
BCL, B.C.L. Bachelor of Civil Law
BCLS Basic Cardiac Life Support
BCS, B.C.S. Bachelor of Commercial Science
BD, B.D. Bachelor of Divinity
bd. board
BE, B.E. Bachelor of Education
BEE, B.E.E. Bachelor of Electrical
   Engineering
BFA, B.F.A. Bachelor of Fine Arts
bibl. biblical
bibliog. bibliographical
biog. biographical
biol. biological
BJ, B.J. Bachelor of Journalism
Bklyn. Brooklyn
BL, B.L. Bachelor of Letters
bldg. building
BLS, B.L.S. Bachelor of Library Science
BLS Basic Life Support
Blvd. Boulevard
BMI Broadcast Music, Inc.
BMW Bavarian Motor Works (Bayerische
   Motoren Werke)
bn. battalion
B.&O.R.R. Baltimore & Ohio Railroad
bot. botanical
BPE, B.P.E. Bachelor of Physical Education
BPhil, B.Phil. Bachelor of Philosophy
br. branch
BRE, B.R.E. Bachelor of Religious
   Education
brig. gen. brigadier general
Brit. British, Brittanica
Bros. Brothers
BS, B.S. Bachelor of Science
BSA, B.S.A. Bachelor of Agricultural Science
BSBA Bachelor of Science in Business
   Administration
BSChemE Bachelor of Science in Chemical
   Engineering
BSD, B.S.D. Bachelor of Didactic Science
BSEE Bachelor of Science in Electrical
   Engineering
BSN Bachelor of Science in Nursing
BST, B.S.T. Bachelor of Sacred Theology
BTh, B.Th. Bachelor of Theology
bull. bulletin
bur. bureau
bus. business
B.W.I. British West Indies

CA California
CAA Civil Aeronautics Administration
CAB Civil Aeronautics Board
CAD-CAM Computer Aided Design-
   Computer Aided Model
Calif. California
C.Am. Central America
Can. Canada, Canadian
CAP Civil Air Patrol
capt. captain
cardiol. cardiological

cardiovasc. cardiovascular
CARE Cooperative American Relief
   Everywhere
Cath. Catholic
cav. cavalry
CBC Canadian Broadcasting Company
CBI China, Burma, India Theatre of
   Operations
CBS Columbia Broadcasting Company
C.C. Community College
CCC Commodity Credit Corporation
CCNY City College of New York
CCRN Critical Care Registered Nurse
CCU Cardiac Care Unit
CD Civil Defense
CE, C.E. Corps of Engineers, Civil Engineer
CEN Certified Emergency Nurse
CENTO Central Treaty Organization
CEO chief executive officer
CERN European Organization of Nuclear
   Research
cert. certificate, certification, certified
CETA Comprehensive Employment Training
   Act
CFA Chartered Financial Analyst
CFL Canadian Football League
CFO chief financial officer
CFP Certified Financial Planner
ch. church
ChD, Ch.D. Doctor of Chemistry
chem. chemical
ChemE, Chem.E. Chemical Engineer
ChFC Chartered Financial Consultant
Chgo. Chicago
chirurg. chirurgical
chmn. chairman
chpt. chapter
CIA Central Intelligence Agency
Cin. Cincinnati
cir. circle, circuit
CLE Continuing Legal Education
Cleve. Cleveland
climatol. climatological
clin. clinical
clk. clerk
C.L.U. Chartered Life Underwriter
CM, C.M. Master in Surgery
CM Northern Mariana Islands
CMA Certified Medical Assistant
cmty. community
CNA Certified Nurse's Aide
CNOR Certified Nurse (Operating Room)
C.&N.W.Ry. Chicago & North Western
   Railway
CO Colorado
Co. Company
COF Catholic Order of Foresters
C. of C. Chamber of Commerce
col. colonel
coll. college
Colo. Colorado
com. committee
comd. commanded
comdg. commanding

comdr. commander
comdt. commandant
comm. communications
commd. commissioned
comml. commercial
commn. commission
commr. commissioner
compt. comptroller
condr. conductor
Conf. Conference
Congl. Congregational, Congressional
Conglist. Congregationalist
Conn. Connecticut
cons. consultant, consulting
consol. consolidated
constl. constitutional
constn. constitution
constrn. construction
contbd. contributed
contbg. contributing
contbn. contribution
contbr. contributor
contr. controller
Conv. Convention
COO chief operating officer
coop. cooperative
coord. coordinator
CORDS Civil Operations and
   Revolutionary Development Support
CORE Congress of Racial Equality
corp. corporation, corporate
corr. correspondent, corresponding,
   correspondence
C.&O.Ry. Chesapeake & Ohio Railway
coun. council
CPA Certified Public Accountant
CPCU Chartered Property and Casualty
   Underwriter
CPH, C.P.H. Certificate of Public Health
cpl. corporal
CPR Cardio-Pulmonary Resuscitation
C.P.Ry. Canadian Pacific Railway
CRT Cathode Ray Terminal
C.S. Christian Science
CSB, C.S.B. Bachelor of Christian Science
C.S.C. Civil Service Commission
CT Connecticut
ct. court
ctr. center
ctrl. central
CWS Chemical Warfare Service
C.Z. Canal Zone

D. Doctor
d. daughter
DAgr, D.Agr. Doctor of Agriculture
DAR Daughters of the American Revolution
dau. daughter
DAV Disabled American Veterans
DC, D.C. District of Columbia
DCL, D.C.L. Doctor of Civil Law
DCS, D.C.S. Doctor of Commercial Science
DD, D.D. Doctor of Divinity
DDS, D.D.S. Doctor of Dental Surgery

DE Delaware
Dec. December
dec. deceased
def. defense
Del. Delaware
del. delegate, delegation
Dem. Democrat, Democratic
DEng, D.Eng. Doctor of Engineering
denom. denomination, denominational
dep. deputy
dept. department
dermatol. dermatological
desc. descendant
devel. development, developmental
DFA, D.F.A. Doctor of Fine Arts
D.F.C. Distinguished Flying Cross
DHL, D.H.L. Doctor of Hebrew Literature
dir. director
dist. district
distbg. distributing
distbn. distribution
distbr. distributor
disting. distinguished
div. division, divinity, divorce
DLitt, D.Litt. Doctor of Literature
DMD, D.M.D. Doctor of Dental Medicine
DMS, D.M.S. Doctor of Medical Science
DO, D.O. Doctor of Osteopathy
docs. documents
DON Director of Nursing
DPH, D.P.H. Diploma in Public Health
DPhil, D.Phil. Doctor of Philosophy
D.R. Daughters of the Revolution
Dr. Drive, Doctor
DRE, D.R.E. Doctor of Religious Education
DrPH, Dr.P.H. Doctor of Public Health, Doctor of Public Hygiene
D.S.C. Distinguished Service Cross
DSc, D.Sc. Doctor of Science
DSChemE Doctor of Science in Chemical Engineering
D.S.M. Distinguished Service Medal
DST, D.S.T. Doctor of Sacred Theology
DTM, D.T.M. Doctor of Tropical Medicine
DVM, D.V.M. Doctor of Veterinary Medicine
DVS, D.V.S. Doctor of Veterinary Surgery

E, E. East
ea. eastern
E. and P. Extraordinary and Plenipotentiary
Eccles. Ecclesiastical
ecol. ecological
econ. economic
ECOSOC Economic and Social Council (of the UN)
ED, E.D. Doctor of Engineering
ed. educated
EdB, Ed.B. Bachelor of Education
EdD, Ed.D. Doctor of Education
edit. edition
editl. editorial
EdM, Ed.M. Master of Education
edn. education
ednl. educational

EDP Electronic Data Processing
EdS, Ed.S. Specialist in Education
EE, E.E. Electrical Engineer
E.E. and M.P. Envoy Extraordinary and Minister Plenipotentiary
EEC European Economic Community
EEG Electroencephalogram
EEO Equal Employment Opportunity
EEOC Equal Employment Opportunity Commission
E.Ger. German Democratic Republic
EKG Electrocardiogram
elec. electrical
electrochem. electrochemical
electrophys. electrophysical
elem. elementary
EM, E.M. Engineer of Mines
EMT Emergency Medical Technician
ency. encyclopedia
Eng. England
engr. engineer
engring. engineering
entomol. entomological
environ. environmental
EPA Environmental Protection Agency
epidemiol. epidemiological
Episc. Episcopalian
ERA Equal Rights Amendment
ERDA Energy Research and Development Administration
ESEA Elementary and Secondary Education Act
ESL English as Second Language
ESPN Entertainment and Sports Programming Network
ESSA Environmental Science Services Administration
ethnol. ethnological
ETO European Theatre of Operations
Evang. Evangelical
exam. examination, examining
Exch. Exchange
exec. executive
exhbn. exhibition
expdn. expedition
expn. exposition
expt. experiment
exptl. experimental
Expy. Expressway
Ext. Extension

F.A. Field Artillery
FAA Federal Aviation Administration
FAO Food and Agriculture Organization (of the UN)
FBA Federal Bar Association
FBI Federal Bureau of Investigation
FCA Farm Credit Administration
FCC Federal Communications Commission
FCDA Federal Civil Defense Administration
FDA Food and Drug Administration
FDIA Federal Deposit Insurance Administration
FDIC Federal Deposit Insurance Corporation

FE, F.E. Forest Engineer
FEA Federal Energy Administration
Feb. February
fed. federal
fedn. federation
FERC Federal Energy Regulatory Commission
fgn. foreign
FHA Federal Housing Administration
fin. financial, finance
FL Florida
Fl. Floor
Fla. Florida
FMC Federal Maritime Commission
FNP Family Nurse Practitioner
FOA Foreign Operations Administration
found. foundation
FPC Federal Power Commission
FPO Fleet Post Office
frat. fraternity
FRS Federal Reserve System
FSA Federal Security Agency
Ft. Fort
FTC Federal Trade Commission
Fwy. Freeway

G-1 (or other number) Division of General Staff
GA, Ga. Georgia
GAO General Accounting Office
gastroent. gastroenterological
GATE Gifted and Talented Educators
GATT General Agreement on Tariffs and Trade
GE General Electric Company
gen. general
geneal. genealogical
geod. geodetic
geog. geographic, geographical
geol. geological
geophys. geophysical
geriat. geriatrics
gerontol. gerontological
G.H.Q. General Headquarters
GM General Motors Corporation
GMAC General Motors Acceptance Corporation
G.N.Ry. Great Northern Railway
gov. governor
govt. government
govtl. governmental
GPO Government Printing Office
grad. graduate, graduated
GSA General Services Administration
Gt. Great
GTE General Telephone and Electric Company
GU Guam
gynecol. gynecological

HBO Home Box Office
hdqs. headquarters
HEW Department of Health, Education and Welfare

HHD, H.H.D. Doctor of Humanities
HHFA Housing and Home Finance Agency
HHS Department of Health and Human Services
HI Hawaii
hist. historical, historic
HM, H.M. Master of Humanities
HMO Health Maintenance Organization
homeo. homeopathic
hon. honorary, honorable
Ho. of Dels. House of Delegates
Ho. of Reps. House of Representatives
hort. horticultural
hosp. hospital
H.S. High School
HUD Department of Housing and Urban Development
Hwy. Highway
hydrog. hydrographic

IA Iowa
IAEA International Atomic Energy Agency
IATSE International Alliance of Theatrical and Stage Employees and Moving Picture Operators of the United States and Canada
IBM International Business Machines Corporation
IBRD International Bank for Reconstruction and Development
ICA International Cooperation Administration
ICC Interstate Commerce Commission
ICCE International Council for Computers in Education
ICU Intensive Care Unit
ID Idaho
IEEE Institute of Electrical and Electronics Engineers
IFC International Finance Corporation
IGY International Geophysical Year
IL Illinois
Ill. Illinois
illus. illustrated
ILO International Labor Organization
IMF International Monetary Fund
IN Indiana
Inc. Incorporated
Ind. Indiana
ind. independent
Indpls. Indianapolis
indsl. industrial
inf. infantry
info. information
ins. insurance
insp. inspector
insp. gen. inspector general
inst. institute
instl. institutional
instn. institution
instr. instructor
instrn. instruction
instrnl. instructional
internat. international
intro. introduction

IRE Institute of Radio Engineers
IRS Internal Revenue Service
ITT International Telephone & Telegraph Corporation

JAG Judge Advocate General
JAGC Judge Advocate General Corps
Jan. January
Jaycees Junior Chamber of Commerce
JB, J.B. Jurum Baccalaureus
JCB, J.C.B. Juris Canoni Baccalaureus
JCD, J.C.D. Juris Canonici Doctor, Juris Civilis Doctor
JCL, J.C.L. Juris Canonici Licentiatus
JD, J.D. Juris Doctor
jg. junior grade
jour. journal
jr. junior
JSD, J.S.D. Juris Scientiae Doctor
JUD, J.U.D. Juris Utriusque Doctor
jud. judicial

Kans. Kansas
K.C. Knights of Columbus
K.P. Knights of Pythias
KS Kansas
K.T. Knight Templar
KY, Ky. Kentucky

LA, La. Louisiana
L.A. Los Angeles
lab. laboratory
L.Am. Latin America
lang. language
laryngol. laryngological
LB Labrador
LDS Latter Day Saints
LDS Church Church of Jesus Christ of Latter Day Saints
lectr. lecturer
legis. legislation, legislative
LHD, L.H.D. Doctor of Humane Letters
L.I. Long Island
libr. librarian, library
lic. licensed, license
L.I.R.R. Long Island Railroad
lit. literature
litig. litigation
LittB, Litt.B. Bachelor of Letters
LittD, Litt.D. Doctor of Letters
LLB, LL.B. Bachelor of Laws
LLD, L.L.D. Doctor of Laws
LLM, L.L.M. Master of Laws
Ln. Lane
L.&N.R.R. Louisville & Nashville Railroad
LPGA Ladies Professional Golf Association
LPN Licensed Practical Nurse
LS, L.S. Library Science (in degree)
lt. lieutenant
Ltd. Limited
Luth. Lutheran
LWV League of Women Voters

M. Master
m. married

MA, M.A. Master of Arts
MA Massachusetts
MADD Mothers Against Drunk Driving
mag. magazine
MAgr, M.Agr. Master of Agriculture
maj. major
Man. Manitoba
Mar. March
MArch, M.Arch. Master in Architecture
Mass. Massachusetts
math. mathematics, mathematical
MATS Military Air Transport Service
MB, M.B. Bachelor of Medicine
MB Manitoba
MBA, M.B.A. Master of Business Administration
MBS Mutual Broadcasting System
M.C. Medical Corps
MCE, M.C.E. Master of Civil Engineering
mcht. merchant
mcpl. municipal
MCS, M.C.S. Master of Commercial Science
MD, M.D. Doctor of Medicine
MD, Md. Maryland
MDiv Master of Divinity
MDip, M.Dip. Master in Diplomacy
mdse. merchandise
MDV, M.D.V. Doctor of Veterinary Medicine
ME, M.E. Mechanical Engineer
ME Maine
M.E.Ch. Methodist Episcopal Church
mech. mechanical
MEd., M.Ed. Master of Education
med. medical
MEE, M.E.E. Master of Electrical Engineering
mem. member
meml. memorial
merc. mercantile
met. metropolitan
metall. metallurgical
MetE, Met.E. Metallurgical Engineer
meteorol. meteorological
Meth. Methodist
Mex. Mexico
MF, M.F. Master of Forestry
MFA, M.F.A. Master of Fine Arts
mfg. manufacturing
mfr. manufacturer
mgmt. management
mgr. manager
MHA, M.H.A. Master of Hospital Administration
M.I. Military Intelligence
MI Michigan
Mich. Michigan
micros. microscopic, microscopical
mid. middle
mil. military
Milw. Milwaukee
Min. Minister
mineral. mineralogical
Minn. Minnesota
MIS Management Information Systems

Miss. Mississippi
MIT Massachusetts Institute of Technology
mktg. marketing
ML, M.L. Master of Laws
MLA Modern Language Association
M.L.D. Magister Legnum Diplomatic
MLitt, M.Litt. Master of Literature, Master of Letters
MLS, M.L.S. Master of Library Science
MME, M.M.E. Master of Mechanical Engineering
MN Minnesota
mng. managing
MO, Mo. Missouri
moblzn. mobilization
Mont. Montana
MP Northern Mariana Islands
M.P. Member of Parliament
MPA Master of Public Administration
MPE, M.P.E. Master of Physical Education
MPH, M.P.H. Master of Public Health
MPhil, M.Phil. Master of Philosophy
MPL, M.P.L. Master of Patent Law
Mpls. Minneapolis
MRE, M.R.E. Master of Religious Education
MRI Magnetic Resonance Imaging
MS, M.S. Master of Science
MS, Ms. Mississippi
MSc, M.Sc. Master of Science
MSChemE Master of Science in Chemical Engineering
MSEE Master of Science in Electrical Engineering
MSF, M.S.F. Master of Science of Forestry
MSN Master of Science in Nursing
MST, M.S.T. Master of Sacred Theology
MSW, M.S.W. Master of Social Work
MT Montana
Mt. Mount
MTO Mediterranean Theatre of Operation
MTV Music Television
mus. museum, musical
MusB, Mus.B. Bachelor of Music
MusD, Mus.D. Doctor of Music
MusM, Mus.M. Master of Music
mut. mutual
MVP Most Valuable Player
mycol. mycological

N. North
NAACOG Nurses Association of the American College of Obstetricians and Gynecologists
NAACP National Association for the Advancement of Colored People
NACA National Advisory Committee for Aeronautics
NACDL National Association of Criminal Defense Lawyers
NACU National Association of Colleges and Universities
NAD National Academy of Design
NAE National Academy of Engineering, National Association of Educators

NAESP National Association of Elementary School Principals
NAFE National Association of Female Executives
N.Am. North America
NAM National Association of Manufacturers
NAMH National Association for Mental Health
NAPA National Association of Performing Artists
NARAS National Academy of Recording Arts and Sciences
NAREB National Association of Real Estate Boards
NARS National Archives and Record Service
NAS National Academy of Sciences
NASA National Aeronautics and Space Administration
NASP National Association of School Psychologists
NASW National Association of Social Workers
nat. national
NATAS National Academy of Television Arts and Sciences
NATO North Atlantic Treaty Organization
NATOUSA North African Theatre of Operations, United States Army
nav. navigation
NB, N.B. New Brunswick
NBA National Basketball Association
NBC National Broadcasting Company
NC, N.C. North Carolina
NCAA National College Athletic Association
NCCJ National Conference of Christians and Jews
ND, N.D. North Dakota
NDEA National Defense Education Act
NE Nebraska
NE, N.E. Northeast
NEA National Education Association
Nebr. Nebraska
NEH National Endowment for Humanities
neurol. neurological
Nev. Nevada
NF Newfoundland
NFL National Football League
Nfld. Newfoundland
NG National Guard
NH, N.H. New Hampshire
NHL National Hockey League
NIH National Institutes of Health
NIMH National Institute of Mental Health
NJ, N.J. New Jersey
NLRB National Labor Relations Board
NM New Mexico
N.Mex. New Mexico
No. Northern
NOAA National Oceanographic and Atmospheric Administration
NORAD North America Air Defense
Nov. November
NOW National Organization for Women
N.P.Ry. Northern Pacific Railway
nr. near

NRA National Rifle Association
NRC National Research Council
NS, N.S. Nova Scotia
NSC National Security Council
NSF National Science Foundation
NSTA National Science Teachers Association
NSW New South Wales
N.T. New Testament
NT Northwest Territories
nuc. nuclear
numis. numismatic
NV Nevada
NW, N.W. Northwest
N.W.T. Northwest Territories
NY, N.Y. New York
N.Y.C. New York City
NYU New York University
N.Z. New Zealand

OAS Organization of American States
ob-gyn obstetrics-gynecology
obs. observatory
obstet. obstetrical
occupl. occupational
oceanog. oceanographic
Oct. October
OD, O.D. Doctor of Optometry
OECD Organization for Economic Cooperation and Development
OEEC Organization of European Economic Cooperation
OEO Office of Economic Opportunity
ofcl. official
OH Ohio
OK Oklahoma
Okla. Oklahoma
ON Ontario
Ont. Ontario
oper. operating
ophthal. ophthalmological
ops. operations
OR Oregon
orch. orchestra
Oreg. Oregon
orgn. organization
orgnl. organizational
ornithol. ornithological
orthop. orthopedic
OSHA Occupational Safety and Health Administration
OSRD Office of Scientific Research and Development
OSS Office of Strategic Services
osteo. osteopathic
otol. otological
otolaryn. otolaryngological

PA, Pa. Pennsylvania
P.A. Professional Association
paleontol. paleontological
path. pathological
PBS Public Broadcasting System
P.C. Professional Corporation
PE Prince Edward Island
pediat. pediatrics

P.E.I. Prince Edward Island
PEN Poets, Playwrights, Editors, Essayists and Novelists (international association)
penol. penological
P.E.O. women's organization (full name not disclosed)
pers. personnel
pfc. private first class
PGA Professional Golfers' Association of America
PHA Public Housing Administration
pharm. pharmaceutical
PharmD, Pharm.D. Doctor of Pharmacy
PharmM, Pharm.M. Master of Pharmacy
PhB, Ph.B. Bachelor of Philosophy
PhD, Ph.D. Doctor of Philosophy
PhDChemE Doctor of Science in Chemical Engineering
PhM, Ph.M. Master of Philosophy
Phila. Philadelphia
philharm. philharmonic
philol. philological
philos. philosophical
photog. photographic
phys. physical
physiol. physiological
Pitts. Pittsburgh
Pk. Park
Pky. Parkway
Pl. Place
P.&L.E.R.R. Pittsburgh & Lake Erie Railroad
Plz. Plaza
PNP Pediatric Nurse Practitioner
P.O. Post Office
PO Box Post Office Box
polit. political
poly. polytechnic, polytechnical
PQ Province of Quebec
PR, P.R. Puerto Rico
prep. preparatory
pres. president
Presbyn. Presbyterian
presdl. presidential
prin. principal
procs. proceedings
prod. produced (play production)
prodn. production
prodr. producer
prof. professor
profl. professional
prog. progressive
propr. proprietor
pros. atty. prosecuting attorney
pro tem. pro tempore
PSRO Professional Services Review Organization
psychiat. psychiatric
psychol. psychological
PTA Parent-Teachers Association
ptnr. partner
PTO Pacific Theatre of Operations, Parent Teacher Organization
pub. publisher, publishing, published
pub. public

publ. publication
pvt. private

quar. quarterly
qm. quartermaster
Q.M.C. Quartermaster Corps
Que. Quebec

radiol. radiological
RAF Royal Air Force
RCA Radio Corporation of America
RCAF Royal Canadian Air Force
RD Rural Delivery
Rd. Road
R&D Research & Development
REA Rural Electrification Administration
rec. recording
ref. reformed
regt. regiment
regtl. regimental
rehab. rehabilitation
rels. relations
Rep. Republican
rep. representative
Res. Reserve
ret. retired
Rev. Reverend
rev. review, revised
RFC Reconstruction Finance Corporation
RFD Rural Free Delivery
rhinol. rhinological
RI, R.I. Rhode Island
RISD Rhode Island School of Design
Rlwy. Railway
Rm. Room
RN, R.N. Registered Nurse
roentgenol. roentgenological
ROTC Reserve Officers Training Corps
RR Rural Route
R.R. Railroad
rsch. research
rschr. researcher
Rt. Route

S. South
s. son
SAC Strategic Air Command
SAG Screen Actors Guild
SALT Strategic Arms Limitation Talks
S.Am. South America
san. sanitary
SAR Sons of the American Revolution
Sask. Saskatchewan
savs. savings
SB, S.B. Bachelor of Science
SBA Small Business Administration
SC, S.C. South Carolina
SCAP Supreme Command Allies Pacific
ScB, Sc.B. Bachelor of Science
SCD, S.C.D. Doctor of Commercial Science
ScD, Sc.D. Doctor of Science
sch. school
sci. science, scientific
SCLC Southern Christian Leadership Conference

SCV Sons of Confederate Veterans
SD, S.D. South Dakota
SE, S.E. Southeast
SEATO Southeast Asia Treaty Organization
SEC Securities and Exchange Commission
sec. secretary
sect. section
seismol. seismological
sem. seminary
Sept. September
s.g. senior grade
sgt. sergeant
SHAEF Supreme Headquarters Allied Expeditionary Forces
SHAPE Supreme Headquarters Allied Powers in Europe
S.I. Staten Island
S.J. Society of Jesus (Jesuit)
SJD Scientiae Juridicae Doctor
SK Saskatchewan
SM, S.M. Master of Science
SNP Society of Nursing Professionals
So. Southern
soc. society
sociol. sociological
S.P.Co. Southern Pacific Company
spkr. speaker
spl. special
splty. specialty
Sq. Square
S.R. Sons of the Revolution
sr. senior
SS Steamship
SSS Selective Service System
St. Saint, Street
sta. station
stats. statistics
statis. statistical
STB, S.T.B. Bachelor of Sacred Theology
stblzn. stabilization
STD, S.T.D. Doctor of Sacred Theology
std. standard
Ste. Suite
subs. subsidiary
SUNY State University of New York
supr. supervisor
supt. superintendent
surg. surgical
svc. service
SW, S.W. Southwest
sys. system

TAPPI Technical Association of the Pulp and Paper Industry
tb. tuberculosis
tchg. teaching
tchr. teacher
tech. technical, technology
technol. technological
tel. telephone
Tel. & Tel. Telephone & Telegraph
telecom. telecommunications
temp. temporary
Tenn. Tennessee
Ter. Territory

Ter. Terrace
TESOL Teachers of English to Speakers of Other Languages
Tex. Texas
ThD, Th.D. Doctor of Theology
theol. theological
ThM, Th.M. Master of Theology
TN Tennessee
tng. training
topog. topographical
trans. transaction, transferred
transl. translation, translated
transp. transportation
treas. treasurer
TT Trust Territory
TV television
TVA Tennessee Valley Authority
TWA Trans World Airlines
twp. township
TX Texas
typog. typographical

U. University
UAW United Auto Workers
UCLA University of California at Los Angeles
UDC United Daughters of the Confederacy
U.K. United Kingdom
UN United Nations
UNESCO United Nations Educational, Scientific and Cultural Organization
UNICEF United Nations International Children's Emergency Fund
univ. university
UNRRA United Nations Relief and Rehabilitation Administration
UPI United Press International

U.P.R.R. United Pacific Railroad
urol. urological
U.S. United States
U.S.A. United States of America
USAAF United States Army Air Force
USAF United States Air Force
USAFR United States Air Force Reserve
USAR United States Army Reserve
USCG United States Coast Guard
USCGR United States Coast Guard Reserve
USES United States Employment Service
USIA United States Information Agency
USMC United States Marine Corps
USMCR United States Marine Corps Reserve
USN United States Navy
USNG United States National Guard
USNR United States Naval Reserve
USO United Service Organizations
USPHS United States Public Health Service
USS United States Ship
USSR Union of the Soviet Socialist Republics
USTA United States Tennis Association
USV United States Volunteers
UT Utah

VA Veterans Administration
VA, Va. Virginia
vet. veteran, veterinary
VFW Veterans of Foreign Wars
VI, V.I. Virgin Islands
vice pres. vice president
vis. visiting
VISTA Volunteers in Service to America
VITA Volunteers in Technical Assistance
vocat. vocational
vol. volunteer, volume
v.p. vice president
vs. versus

VT, Vt. Vermont

W, W. West
WA Washington (state)
WAC Women's Army Corps
Wash. Washington (state)
WATS Wide Area Telecommunications Service
WAVES Women's Reserve, US Naval Reserve
WCTU Women's Christian Temperance Union
we. western
W. Ger. Germany, Federal Republic of
WHO World Health Organization
WI Wisconsin
W.I. West Indies
Wis. Wisconsin
WSB Wage Stabilization Board
WV West Virginia
W.Va. West Virginia
WWI World War I
WWII World War II
WY Wyoming
Wyo. Wyoming

YK Yukon Territory
YMCA Young Men's Christian Association
YMHA Young Men's Hebrew Association
YM & YWHA Young Men's and Young Women's Hebrew Association
yr. year
YT, Y.T. Yukon Territory
YWCA Young Women's Christian Association

zool. zoological

Alphabetical Practices

Names are arranged alphabetically according to the surnames, and under identical surnames according to the first given name. If both surname and first given name are identical, names are arranged alphabetically according to the second given name.

Surnames beginning with De, Des, Du, however capitalized or spaced, are recorded with the prefix preceding the surname and arranged alphabetically under the letter D.

Surnames beginning with Mac and Mc are arranged alphabetically under M.

Surnames beginning with Saint or St. appear after names that begin Sains, and are arranged according to the second part of the name, e.g. St. Clair before Saint Dennis.

Surnames beginning with Van, Von, or von are arranged alphabetically under the letter V.

Compound surnames are arranged according to the first member of the compound.

Many hyphenated Arabic names begin Al-, El-, or al-. These names are alphabetized according to each Biographee's designation of last name. Thus Al-Bahar, Neta may be listed either under Al- or under Bahar, depending on the preference of the listee.

Also, Arabic names have a variety of possible spellings when transposed to English. Spelling of these names is always based on the practice of the Biographee. Some Biographees use a Western form of word order, while others prefer the Arabic word sequence.

Similarly, Asian names may have no comma between family and given names, but some Biographees have chosen to add the comma. In each case, punctuation follows the preference of the Biographee.

Parentheses used in connection with a name indicate which part of the full name is usually deleted in common usage. Hence Chambers, E(lizabeth) Anne indicates that the usual form of the given name is E. Anne. In such a case, the parentheses are ignored in alphabetizing and the name would be arranged as Chambers, Elizabeth Anne. However, if the name is recorded Chambers, (Elizabeth) Anne, signifying that the entire name Elizabeth is not commonly used, the alphabetizing would be arranged as though the name were Chambers, Anne. If an entire middle or last name is enclosed in parentheses, that portion of the name is used in the alphabetical arrangement. Hence Chambers, Elizabeth (Anne) would be arranged as Chambers, Elizabeth Anne.

Where more than one spelling, word order, or name of an individual is frequently encountered, the sketch has been entered under the form preferred by the Biographee, with cross-references under alternate forms.

Who's Who of American Women®

Biographies

AALUND, PEGGY MACHELL STANLEY, nurse, educator; b. Quonset Point, R.I., Nov. 4, 1951; d. Reginald Montague and Nancy (Heberton) Machell; m. Tony Ray Aalund; children: Robert, Rebecca, Rex, Troy. BSN with honors, U. Tex. Sch. Nursing, Galveston, 1974, MSN with highest honors, 1975. RN, Tex.; cert. childbirth educator. Pediatric nurse John Sealy Hosp., Galveston, 1974; nurse educator U. Tex. Sch. Nursing, 1976-77; pediatric nurse Humble (Tex.) Pediatric Assn., 1977-80; childbirth educator N.E. Med. Ctr., Humble, 1981-83; owner, childbirth educator Prepared Childbirth: A Shared Beginning, Humble, 1983-85; nurse educator North Harris County Coll., Houston, 1985—; mother and baby nurse Northeast Med. Ctr. Hosp., Humble, Tex., 1992—. Vol. 3H Community Ctr., Humble, 1981; Sunday sch. tchr. St. Martha's Cath. Ch., Kingwood, Tex., 1988-92; speaker to health classes Humble Ind. Sch. Dist., 1980—. Winner Tchr. Excellence award, 1994. Mem. Sigma Theta Tau. Home: 3431 Tree Ln Humble TX 77339

AARON, BETSY, journalist; b. N.Y.C., Nov. 11, 1938; d. Bertram Henry and Evelyn (Horner) Siegeltuch; m. Richard Threlkeld, 1983. BA, Am. U., 1960. Researcher, writer, field producer, reporter, corr. ABC News, Washington, N.Y.C., Chgo., 1960-76; network corr. CBS News, Atlanta, N.Y.C., 1976-80; corr. CBS News, N.Y.C., 1988—; network corr. NBC Mag., NBC News, N.Y.C., 1980-82; Nightline corr. ABC News, N.Y.C., 1980-84; corr. World News Tonight ABC News, 1985-88; corr. CBS Evening News, N.Y.C., 1989-91, CBS Sunday Morning, 1991-93. Mem. Amnesty Internat. (dep. exec. dir. comms. 1995).

AARON, CYNTHIA G., judge; b. Mpls., May 3, 1957; d. Allen Harold and Barbara Lois (Perlman) A.; m. Craig D. Higgs, May 15, 1993. Student, Brandeis U., 1975-77; BA with honors and distinction, Stanford U., 1979; JD cum laude, Harvard U., 1984. Bar: Calif. 1984, U.S. Dist. Ct. (so. dist.) Calif. 1984, U.S. Ct. Appeals (9th cir.) 1984, U.S. Dist. Ct. (no. dist.) Calif. 1986, U.S. Dist. Ct. (ctrl. dist.) Calif. 1988, U.S. Supreme Ct. 1991. Law clerk Topel & Goodman, San Francisco, 1982; rsch. asst. law sch. Harvard U., 1982-83; law clerk Coblentz, Cahen, McCabe & Breyer, San Francisco, 1983; trial atty. Fed. Defenders San Diego, Inc., 1984-88; ptnr. Aaron & Cortez, 1988-94; U.S. magistrate judge U.S. Dist. Ct. (so. dist.) Calif., San Diego, 1994—; guest instr. law sch. U. San Diego, 1988-90; instr. pacific regional program Nat. Inst. for Trial Advocacy, 1988-91, instr. deposition skills workshop, 1993;adj. prof. Calif. We. Sch. Law, San Diego, 1990-93; instr., critiquer baskic trial skills workshop Continuing Edn. Bar, San Diego, 1991; instr. advocacy trial skills acad. Inst. for Criminal Def., San Diego, 1992-94; adj. prof. law sch. U. San Diego, 1993. Mem. Nat. Assn. Women Judges, Lawyers Club San Diego, U.J.F. Downtown Breakfast Club, City Club San Diego. Office: US Dist Ct (So Dist) Calif Edward J Scwartz US Courthouse 940 Front St Rm E San Diego CA 92101*

AARON, LYNN, dancer; b. Gainesville, Ga., 1962; d. Jimmye and Tommy A.; m. Jeffrey Neeck, 1992. Studied with Diane Callahan; student, Sch. Am. Ballet. Dancer Feld Ballets/NY, N.Y.C., 1987-93, leading ballerina, 1993—. Performed in dances including Embraced Waltzes, Savage Glance, 1991, Endsong, 1991, Ah, Scarlatti, Hadji, 1992, MRI, many others. Office: Feld Ballet/NY Wien Ctr for Dance & Theater 890 Broadway 8th Fl New York NY 10003*

AARON, SHIRLEY MAE, tax consultant; b. Covington, La., Feb. 28, 1935; d. Morgan and Pearl (Jenkins) King; m. Richard L. King, Feb. 16, 1952 (div. Feb. 1965); children: Deborah, Richard, Roberta, Keely; m. Michael A. Aaron, Nov. 27, 1976 (dec. July 1987). Adminstrv. asst. South Central Bell, Covington, La., 1954-62; acct. Brown & Root, Inc., Houston, 1962-75; timekeeper Alyeska Pipeline Co., Fairbanks, Alaska, 1975-77; adminstrv. asst. Boeing Co., Seattle, 1979-93; pres. Aaron Enterprises, Seattle, 1977—; owner Gabriel's Dinner Club, La., 1993—. Contbr.: Who's Cooking What in America by Phyllis Hanes, 1993. Bd. dirs. Burien 146 Homeowners Assn., Seattle, 1979—, pres., 1980-83. Mem. NAFE. Avocation: singing, art. Home: 131 Gerard St Mandeville LA 70448-5808

AARONS-HOLDER, CHARMAINE MICHELE, lawyer; b. Kingston, Jamaica, Jan. 24, 1959; came to U.S., 1982; d. Alan Oswald and Berly-Mae Aarons; m. Lisle Anthony Holder, 1982. LLB honors, U. W.I., Barbados, 1980; Cert. Legal Edn., Norman Manley Law Sch., Kingston, 1982; JD cum laude, U. Houston, 1987. Bar: Barbados 1982, Tex. 1987, U.S. Dist. Ct. (so. dist.) Tex. 1988. Participating assoc. Fulbright & Jaworski, Houston, 1987-94; atty. Wickliff & Hall, Houston, 1994—. Co-editor, co-author: The Texas Environmental Law Handbook, 1989, 2nd edit., 1990, 3rd edit., 1993. Mem. ABA, Tex. Bar Assn., Houston Bar Assn., Houston Young Lawyers Assn. (chair hunger relief com. 1994—), Tex. Young Lawyers Assn., Order of Coif, Order of Barons. Democrat. Home: 2314 Loyanne Dr Spring TX 77373-6240 Office: Wickliff & Hall 1000 Louisiana St Houston TX 77002

ABAJIAN, WENDY ELISSE, writer, producer, educator; b. Selma, Calif., Mar. 16, 1955; d. Mesik Nishon and Blanche Peggy (Emerzian) A. AA, Kings River Community Coll., 1975; BA, Calif. State U., Fresno, 1978; MS, U. So. Calif., 1981, EdD, 1986. Instr., tchr. various sch. dists., Burbank, Fresno & L.A., Calif., 1981—; free-lance writer various corps., Los Angeles area, 1984—; pres., ind. producer Abhawk Prodns., Inc., Long Beach, Calif., 1986-91; ind. writer/producer for TV, cable and video, 1991—; cons. multi-media projects. Contbr. articles to profl. jours. Active Rep. Nat. Com., Washington, 1983—, Statue of Liberty Ellis Island Found., 1984—, Women Appointees Coun., Sacramento, 1988-93, Burbank Ctr. for Retarded; gubernatorial appointee to adv. bd. Lanterman State Hosp., 1986-93; gubernatorial appointee to bd. dirs. Protection and Advocacy, Inc., 1990-93. Mem. Ednl. Grad. Orgn., Am. Film Inst., Farm Bur. Fedn., Film Adv. Bd., Nat. Com. Prevention Child Abuse, U.S. Com. for UN Devel. Fund for Women, World Affairs Coun. Armenian. Apostolic.

ABANTO, MARINA NIEVES, industrial microbiologist; b. Cin., May 19, 1960; d. Bruno Napoleon and Modestina (Seta) A. BS, Xavier U., Cin., 1982; MS, U. Cin., 1985. Grad. teaching asst. U. Cin., 1983-85; rsch. asst. U. Cin. Med. Ctr., 1985-87; sr. microbiologist Cin. Milacron Products, 1987—. Contbr. articles to profl. jours.; patentee in field. Bd. dirs. Cin. Inter-Ethnic Coun., 1992—. Xavier U. Presdl. scholar, 1978, DaVinci Univ. Club scholar, 1978, U. Cin. grad. asst., 1983, U. Cin. Rsch. Coun. summer fellow, 1984. Mem. DaVinci Univ. Club (v.p. 1989-91, pres. 1991—). Office: Cin Milacron Products 4701 Marburg Ave Cincinnati OH 45209-1025

ABARBANELL, GAYOLA HAVENS, financial planner; b. Chgo., Oct. 21, 1939; d. Leonard Milton and Lillian Love (Leviten) Havens; m. Burton J. Abarbanell, June 1, 1965 (div. 1972); children: Jeffrey J. and Dena Reddick Lamb. Student, UCLA, 1975; student, San Joaquin Coll. Law, 1976-77. Cert. fin. planner; lic. real estate rep., Calif.; lic. life ins. broker, Calif., Wash., Nev., N.Y., Ill.; lic. securities broker. Postal clk. Van Nuys, Calif., 1966-69; regional mgr. Niagara Cyclo Massage, Fresno, Calif., 1969-72; owner, mgr. AD Enterprises, Fresno, 1970-72; agt., field supr. Equitable of Iowa, Fresno, 1972-73; rep. Ciba Pharms., Fresno, 1973-75; owner, operator Creativity Unltd., Fresno, 1975-76; registered fin. advisor Univ. Securities Corp., L.A., 1976-83, Fin. Network Investment Corp., L.A., 1983—; lectr. seminars for civic orgns.; mem. adv. bd. Fin. Network, Torrance, Calif., 1985-88. Co-author: Guidelines to Feminist Consciousness Raising, 1985. Mem. bus. adv. bd. of 2d careers. Recipient award Women in Ins., 1972. Mem. Bus. and Profl. Assn., L.A. Internat. Assn. Fin. Planners (bd. dirs. 1993-94), Inst. Cert. Fin. Planners, So. Calif. Socially Responsible Investment Profls., ACLU, NOW (nat. consciousness raising coord. 1975-76), Gay Acad. Union, Nat. Gay Task Force, Culver City C. of C., Internat. Assn. Fin. Planners, Social Investment Forum, Rotary (founding mem. L.A. Westside Sunrise Club sgt. at arms 1990-91, community svc. chair 1991-94, v.p. 1992-93, found. chair 1993-94). Democrat. Jewish. Home: 57124 Mono Wind Way North Fork CA 93643-9797 Office: Fin Network Investment Corp 5625 Green Valley Cir Apt 103 Culver City CA 90230-7120

ABATO, F. ROZANN, federal government administrator, nurse; b. Morrilton, Ark., Dec. 23, 1946; d. Vernon James Morris and Naomi Ruth (Williams) Hampton; m. Cosimo Carl Abato, May 28, 1983 (div. 1989). RN, Bapt. Hosp. Sch. Nursing, 1967. Hosp. staff nurse, 1967-68, surg. nurse for pvt. physicians, 1968-74, state health planning, 1974-76; program analyst Medicaid and Medicare Health Care Financing Adminstrn., Washington and Balt., 1976-81, staff dir. task force for regulatory relief, 1981-82, dir. Office Regulations Mgmt., 1982-86, dir. Office Exec. Ops., 1986-90, dep. dir. Medicaid bur., 1990—. Recipient Superior Svc. award Dept. Health and Human Svcs., 1988. Presbyterian. Home: 10 E Lee St Baltimore MD 21202 Office: Health Care Financing Adminstrn 6325 Security Blvd Rm 200 Baltimore MD 21207

ABBOTT, FRANCES ELIZABETH DOWDLE, journalist, civic worker; b. Rome, Ga., Mar. 21, 1924; d. John Wesley and Lucille Elizabeth (Field) Dowdle; m. Jackson Miles Abbott, May 15, 1948; children: Medora Frances, David Field, Elizabeth Stockton, Robert Jackson; m. Archibald W. Lyon, Oct. 15, 1993. Student, Draughon's Bus. Coll., Columbia, S.C.. Feature writer Mt. Vernon corr. Alexandria Gazette, Va., 1967-75; libr., rsch. assoc. Gadsby's Tavern Mus., Alexandria, 1977—. Chmn. ann. George Washington Birthnight Ball, Mt. Vernon, 1974-82; sec. George Washington 250th Birthday Celebration Commn., 1979-82; chmn. publicity Waynewood Woman's Club, Waynewood Citizens Assn.; treas. Mt. Vernon Citizens Assn., 1967-82; dist. chmn. Mt. Vernon March of Dimes, 1960-62; sec. Waynewood Sch. PTA, 1962-64; tchr. 1st aid Girl Scouts U.S., 1964-65; den mother Cub Scouts, 1966; registrar DAR, 1968-77; chmn. publicity Mt. Vernon Women's Rep. Club, 1955; mem. steering com. Neighborhood Friends of Hist. Mt. Vernon, 1988-92. Named Mrs. Waynewood by Community Vote, 1969. Mem. Audubon Naturalist Soc., Nat. Trust Hist. Preservation. Episcopalian. Home: 9110 Belvoir Woods Pky J-414 Fort Belvoir VA 22060 Office: 134 N Royal St Alexandria VA 22314-3226

ABBOTT, GAIL EOLINE, nurse practitioner; b. Cherry Point, N.C., Dec. 18, 1948; d. Ralph G. Morse Jr. and Florence Ethel (Newkerk) Morse; m. Don V. Mahaffey, June 12, 1966 (div. 1972); children: Susan, JoAnn; m. Arthur J. Abbott, Dec. 7, 1976. ASN, Miami (Fla.)-Dade C.C., 1974; student, Fla. Intenrat. U., 1974-75, BSN, 1991; MSN, U. Miami, 1993. Advanced registered nurse practitioner, cert. specialist. Staff nurse, surg.-obgyn units North Miami (Fla.) Gen. Hosp., 1974-76; staff nurse med-surg. unit Palmetto Gen. Hosp., Hialeah, Fla., 1976, Charlotte (N.C.) Meml. Hosp., 1976-77; staff nurse endocrine unit Parkway Gen. Hosp., North Miami Beach, Fla., 1977-79; head nurse endocrine unit Pembroke Pines (Fla.) Gen. Hosp., 1979-80; head nurse med-surg. unit Internat. Hosp., Miami, 1980-82; asst. head nurse endocrine unit Lee Meml. Hosp., Fort Myers, Fla., 1982-84; staff nurse and head nurse CCU Miami Heart Inst., Miami Beach, 1984-89; staff nurse CCU North Shore Med. Ctr., Miami, Fla., 1989-93; family nurse practitioner Camillus Health Concern, Miami, 1993—. Vol. Women in Distress, Broward County, 1990. Mem. ANA, AACN, Fla. Nurses Assn., Union County (Ga.) Jaycetts (past pres., treas.), Phi Lambda Beta, Sigma Theta Tau (Beta Tau chpt.). Home: 11370 Wayne Dr Cooper City FL 33026-3737

ABBOTT, GAYLE ELIZABETH, human resources consultant; b. Cleve., July 7, 1954; d. Olcott Rutherford and Eleanor Francis (Norley) A.; 1 child, Elizabeth Laura. BA, Am. U., 1976; MBA, Loyola Coll., Balt., 1983. Cert. sr. profl. in human resources, compensation profl. Personnel mgmt. specialist Food and Drug Adminstrn., Washington, 1975-77; personnel mgr. Computer Network Corp., Washington, 1977-78; dir. human resources STSC, Inc., Rockville, Md., 1978-84; compensation cons. Comm. Satellite Corp., Washington, 1984-85; pres., founder HURECO, Inc. (formerly Human Resource Solutions), Fairfax, Va., 1985—; lectr., adj. faculty Marymount U., Arlington, Va., 1990—; speaker profl. assns. and confs. Coauthor: Deflecting Workplace Violence; contbr. articles to profl. jours. Chmn. pers. com. Lewinsville Presbyn. Ch., 1987-91. Recipient Lodestar award Am. U., 1992. Mem. AAUW (bd. rec. sec. 1987, v.p. membership 1988-89), Soc. for Human Resource Mgmt. (dir. Va. state coun. 1991), No. Va. Soc. for Human Resource Mgmt. (legis. rep. 1987-88, v.p. programs 1988, pres. 1989-90, dir. 1991-93, Disting. Leadership award 1991), Am. U. Alumni Assn. (v.p. 1988-90, pres. 1990-92, bd. dirs. 1993—). Presbyterian. Office: HURECO Inc 3603 Chain Bridge Rd Ste B Fairfax VA 22030-3244

ABBOTT, MARY ELAINE, photographer, lecturer, researcher; b. LaGrange, Ill., Apr. 23, 1922; d. Vergil and Goldie (Wright) Schwarzkopf; m. Harry Edward Abbott, Oct. 8, 1949; children: John Edward, Jane Ann. BA in English, Psychology, U. Iowa, 1944. With child welfare dept. Montgomery County Children's Home, Dayton, Ohio, 1944-47, Mich. Children's Inst., Ann Arbor, 1947-49; photographer, lectr., researcher, 1978—; researcher, lectr. in field. Documentary photography for regional history books, mags., calendars and brochures; commd. Taft Sculpture, Sculpture Jackson County; artistic dir. James Agee's Knoxville Summer 1915 with Jackson Symphony Orch.; Claire Allen Architecture for Mich. State Hist. Soc.; commd. by Jackson Historic Dist. Commn. and State Hist. Soc., Mich. Dance Assn.; hist. dist. commn. advisor Dance for the Handicapped, Savs. and Loan "40 Doors", Amitech, Jackson Alliance of Businessmen; works hung in various exhbns. and juried shows; photographs in many pvt., pub. and bus. collections; permanent commissions: Ella Sharp Mus., Jackson Symphony, St. Paul's Episcopal Ch., Carnegie Libr., others. Mem. Jr. League, Jackson Chorale, Nat. Trust for Hist. Preservation; panel participant on creative process Ella Sharp Mus.; advisor Jackson Hist. Commn. Lorado Taft Scholarship; tchr. Gt. Books, U. Chgo.; participant in enrichment for advanced children, also others; participant Save Outdoor Sculpture for Nat. Inst. Conservation Cultural Property, Smithsonian Instn. Recipient photography award Our Town Exhibit, Ella Sharp Mus., Hist. Trinity Ch., Detroit, Cert. of Honor, Spl. Recognitions Excellence Luth. Ctr. Assn.; Lorado Taft scholar. Mem. Internat. Platform Assn. (arts adv. bd., photography award, Juror's Choice in art exhibit, Inner Cir. Merit award 1993, 2d prize for photography 1994), Log Cabin Soc. Mich., Nat. Mus. Women in Arts, Arts Midwest, Kappa Alpha Theta. Republican. Episcopalian. Home and Office: 721 Oakridge Dr Jackson MI 49203-3914

ABBOTT, PATTI MARIE, middle school educator; b. Lewistown, Mont., Mar. 15, 1942; d. Vernal Hall and Marquerite (Cowen) A. BS, Ea. Mont. Coll., 1963, MS, 1968; postgrad. in adminstrn., Mont. State U., 1980. Tchr. Sch. Dist. No. 1, Glendive, Mont., 1964; tchr. Billings (Mont.) Pub. Schs., 1964—, pub. rels. rep., 1983-87. Contbr. articles to profl. jours. Resource person Girl Scouts U.S., Billings, 1973—, cadet leader, 1976-79; resource person Campfire Girls, Billings, 1978—; vol. Heart Fund, Am. Cancer Soc., Birth Defects Found., 1976—; v.p. Sweet Adelines, Billings, 1981-83. Named Tchr. of Yr., Masonic Order, Billings, 1985, 86. Mem. NEA, ASCD, AAUW (sec. Billings chpt. 1985-87, scholar 1987, essay chairperson 1992-93), Am. Bus. Women's Assn. (pres. Billings chpt. 1980-82, Woman of Yr. award 1980), Harmony Club (pres. 1986-87), Rebeccas, Eagles, Alpha Delta Kappa (mem. internat. exec. bd., grand historian, grand v.p. 1983-87, grand pres. 1993—). Home: 701 Torch Dr Billings MT 59102-5925 Office: Lewis and Clark Jr High 1315 Lewis Ave Billings MT 59102-4237

ABBOTT, REBECCA PHILLIPS, museum director; b. Giessen, Germany, Jan. 10, 1950; d. Charles Leonard and Janet Alice (Praeger) Phillips. BA, Emory and Henry Coll., 1973; postgrad., Georgetown U., 1975, Am. U., 1982-88. Asst. to assoc. univ. registrar Am. U., Washington, 1974-77, assoc. univ. registrar, 1977-81, assoc. dir. adminstrv. computing, 1981-84, dir. adminstrv. computing, 1984-88; dir. membership Nat. Mus. of Women in the Arts, Washington, 1988-89, dir., 1989—; fine arts photographer. Photographs exhibited in solo and group exhbns. Mem. Am. Assn. Mus. Office: National Museum of Women in Arts 1250 New York Ave NW Washington DC 20005-3920

ABBOTT, REGINA A., neurodiagnostic technologist, consultant, business owner; b. Haverhill, Mass., Mar. 5, 1950; d. Frank A. and Ann (Drelick) A. Student, Pierce Bus. Sch., Boston, 1967-70, Seizure Unit Children's Hosp. Med. Ctr. Sch. EEG Tech., Boston, 1970-71. Registered technologist. Tech. dir. electrodiagnostic labs. Salem Hosp., 1972-76; lab. dir. neurophysiology Tufts U. New Eng. Med. Ctr., Boston, 1976-78; clin. instr. EEG program Laboure Coll., Boston, 1977-81; adminstrv. dir. dept. Neurology Mt. Auburn Hosp., Cambridge, Mass., 1978-81; tech. dir. clin. neurophysiology Drs. Diagnostic Service, Virginia Beach, Va.; tech. dir. neurodiagnostic ctr. Portsmouth Psychiatric Ctr., 1981-87; founder, pres., owner Commonwealth Neurodiagnostic Services, Inc., 1986—; co-dir. continuing edn. program EEG tech., Boston, 1977-78; mem. adv. com. sch. neurodiagnostic tech. Laboure Coll., 1977-81, sch. EEG Tech. Children's Hosp. Med. Ctr., Boston, 1980-81; assoc. examiner Am. Bd. Registration of Electroencephalographic Technologists, 1977-83; mem. guest faculty Oxford Medilog Co., 1986; cons. Nihon Kohden America, 1981-83; cons., educator Teca Corp., Pleasantville, N.Y., 1981-87; allied health profl. staff mem. Virginia Beach Gen. Hosp., Humana Hosp. Bayside, Virginia Beach. Contbr. articles to profl. jours. EIL scholar, Poland/USSR, 1970; recipient Internat. Woman of Yr. award in bus. and sci., 1993-94, Woman of Yr. award, 1993. Mem. NAFE, Am. Soc. Electroneurodiagnostic Technologists, New England Soc. EEG Technologists (bd. dirs., sec., tng. and edn. com., faculty tng. and edn.), Epilepsy Soc. of Mass. Office: Commonwealth Neurodiagnostic Svcs Inc 400 Biltmore Ct Virginia Beach VA 23454-3459

ABBOTT, SUSAN ALICIA, elementary education educator; b. Easton, Pa., July 8, 1947; d. Solomon and Edith Mae (Cooper) Bergstein; m. William Walter Wood, Aug. 28, 1971 (div. Mar. 1976); m. Karl Richard Abbott, Feb. 19, 1977; 1 child, Tracie Ellen. BA in Psychology, Pa. State U., 1969; MS in Edn., Nazareth Coll. of Rochester, N.Y., 1976. Cert. nursery/elem. and spl. edn. tchr., N.Y. Tchr. Penn Yan (N.Y.) Cen. Schs., 1970; learning disabilities tchr. Wayne-Finger Lakes Bd. Coop. Schs., Stanley, N.Y., 1970-79; spl. edn. tchr. Victor (N.Y.) Cen. Schs., 1979—; tchr. rep. com. on handicapped Com. Spl. Edn., Victor, 1987-91, coord. grades 4-6, 1991-94, chmn. grades 5-6, 1991-93. Bd. dirs. Genesee Valley Orch. and Chorus; active First Universalist Ch., Sta. WXXI, pub TV, Rochester, 1978—; leader Girl Scouts U.S.A., Fairport, N.Y., 1987-90; chmn. publicity program Seneca Zool. Soc., Rochester, 1974-77, bd. dirs., 1975-78, mem. 1982—. Mem. ASCD, Coun. Exceptional Children (div. learning disabilities), Am. Fedn. Tchrs., Nature Conservancy, Whale Adoption Project, Internat. Assn. Children and Adults with Learning Disabilities, N.Y. State Assn. Learning Disabilities, N.Y. State United Tchrs., Monroe County Learning Disabilities Assn., Greenpeace, Rochester Mus. Sci. Ctr., Pa. State U. Alumni Assn., Habitat for Humanity, Fairport PTSA, Nat. Coun. Tchrs. Math., Victor PTSA, Victor Tchrs. Assn., AAUW, Psi Chi. Home: 58 Alina St Fairport NY 14450-2843 Office: Victor Cen Schs 953 High St Victor NY 14564-1167

ABDELLAH, FAYE GLENN, retired public health service executive; b. N.Y.C., Mar. 13; d. H.B. and Margaret (Glenn) A. BS in Teaching, Columbia U., 1945, MA in Teaching, 1947, EdD, 1955; LLD (hon.), Case Western Res. U., 1967, Rutgers U., 1973; DSc (hon.), U. Akron, 1978, Cath. U. Am., 1981, Monmouth Coll., 1982, Ea. Mich U., 1987, U. Bridgeport, 1987, Georgetown U., 1989; D Pub. Svc. (hon.), Am. U., 1987; LHD (hon.), Georgetown U., 1989, U. S.C., 1991; D Pub. Svc., U. S.C., 1991. RN. Commd. officer USPHS, Rockville, Md., 1949, advanced through grades to rear adm., 1970, asst. surgeon gen., chief nurse officer, 1970-87, dep. surgeon gen., 1981-89, chief nursing edn. br., div. nursing, 1949-59; surgeon gen. USPHS, 1989; chief rsch. grants br. Bur. Health Manpower Edn., NIH, HEW, Rockville, 1959-69; dir. Office Rsch. Tng. Nat. Ctr. for Health Svcs. R & D, Health Svcs. Mental Health Adminstrn., Rockville, 1969; acting dep. dir. Nat. Ctr. for Health Svcs. R & D, Rockville, 1971, Bur. Health Svcs. Rsch. and Evaluation, Health Resources Adminstrn., Rockville, 1973; dir. Office Long-Term Care, Office Asst. Sec. for Health, HEW, Rockville, 1973-80; exec. dir. grad. sch. nursing uniformed svcs., acting dean U. Health Scis., Bethesda, Md., 1993—; exec. dir., acting dean; prof. nursing, Emily Smith chair U. S.C., Columbia, 1990-91; dean Grad. Sch. Nursing, Uniformed Srvs. U. Health Scis., 1993—. Author: Effect of Nurse Staffing on Satisfactions with Nursing Care, 1959, Patient Centered Approaches to Nursing, 1960, Better Patient Care Through Nursing Research, 1965, 2d edit., 1979, 3d edit., 1986, Intensive Care, Concepts and Practices for Clinical Nurse Specialists, 1969, New Directions in Patient Centered Nursing, 1972, Preparing Nursing Research for the 21st Century, 1994; contbr. articles to profl. jours. Recipient Mary Adelaide Nutting award, 1983, hon. recognition ANA, 1986, Oustanding Leadership award U. Pa., 1987, 99, Disting. Svc. award, 1973-89, Surgeon Gen.'s medal and medallion, 1989, Allied-Signal Achievement award in aging, 1989, Gustav O. Lienhard award Inst. Medicine, NAS, 1992. Fellow Am. Acad. Nursing (charter, past v.p., pres.); mem. Am. Psychol. Assn., AAAS, Assn. Mil. Surgeons U.S., Sigma Theta Tau (Disting. Rsch. Fellow award 1989), Phi Lambda Theta. Home: 3713 Chanel Rd Annandale VA 22003-2024

ABDUL, CORINNA GAY, software engineer, consultant; b. Honolulu, Aug. 10, 1961; d. Daniel Lawrence and Katherine Yoshie (Kanada) A. BS in Computer Sci., U. Hawaii, 1984. With computer support for adminstrv. and fiscal svcs. U. Hawaii, Honolulu, 1982-84; mem. tech. staff II test systems and software engr. dept. of Space & Tech. Group TRW Inc., Redondo Beach, Calif., 1985-89; systems software engr. II, Sierra On-Line, Inc., Oakhurst, Calif., 1989-90; sr. programmer, analyst Decision Rsch. Corp., Honolulu, 1990-92; computer cons. Honolulu, 1992-94, Wailuku, Hawaii, 1994—. Home: 856 West Kaena Pl Wailuku HI 96793

ABDUL, PAULA (JULIE), singer, dancer, choreographer; b. L.A., June 19, 1963; d. Harry and Lorraine A.; m. Emilio Estevez, Apr. 29, 1992. Student, Calif. State Univ., Northridge; studied tap, jazz with Joe Tramine, the Bella Lewitzky Co. Laker Girls cheerleader, choreographer L.A. Lakers basketball team; choreography for Jacksons singing group, Janet Jackson, ZZ Top, Arnold Schwarzenegger, Tom Hanks, The Tracey Ullman Show, others. Albums: Forever Your Girl, 1988, Shut Up and Dance, 1990, Spellbound, 1991; choreographer films The Running Man, 1987, Coming to America, 1988, The Karate Kid Part III, 1989, She's Out of Control, 1989. Recipient Soul Train award, Am. Video Arts award choreographer of yr., Nat. Acad. Video Arts and Scis., 1987, Emmy award best choreography for the Tracy Ullman Show, 1988-89, MTV award best female video, best dance video, best choreography in a video, best editing in a video for hit Straight Up, 1989.

Office: Third Rail Entertainment Tri-Star Bldg 10202 W Washington Ave # 26 Culver City CA 90232*

ABEL, ANNE ELIZABETH SUTHERLAND, pediatrician; b. Milw., June 16, 1945; d. David Hollingsworth and Mildred June (Nees) Sutherland; m. Francis Lee Abel; 1 child, Jonathan Earl. BA, Pasadena Coll., 1967; MS, Ind. U., Indpls., 1969, MD, 1973. Diplomate Am. Bd. Pediatrics. Resident in pediat. Meth. Hosp., Indpls., 1973-75; chief resident in pediat. Richland Meml. Hosp., Columbia, S.C., 1975-76; pediatrician Moncrief Army Hosp., Ft. Jackson, S.C., 1976-80; child and adolescent psychiatry fellow William S. Hall Psychiat. Inst., Columbia, 1981, 82-83, U. B.C.-Vancouver Gen. Hosp., 1982; pvt. practice Columbia, S.C., 1983—; pediatrician Children's Rehabilitative Svcs., Orangeburg, S.C., 1984-91, 92—; chief med. sect. Columbia Area Mental Health Ctr., 1987-92; assoc. prof. neuropsychiatry and behavioral sci. U. S.C., Columbia, 1992—; cons. behavioral pediatrics Epworth Children's Home, Columbia, 1983-86, 90—; mem. med. adv. com., children's health rehabilitative svcs. S.C. Dept. Health & Environ. Control, Columbia, 1986-92, mem. maternal and child health adv. com., 1989-91; behavioral/devel. pediatrician Orangeburg Health Dept., 1994—. Contbr. articles to profl. jours. Mem. S.C. Gov.'s Youth Unemployment Coun., Columbia, 1987. Recipient Alumni award Pasadena Coll., 1977, Vol. of Yr. award Mayor's Com. Employment Handicapped, 1988; grantee Ctr. Family Soc., U. S.C., 1993—. Fellow Am. Acad. Pediatrics; mem. AMA, Am. Acad. Cerebral Palsy and Devel. Medicine, Am. Profl. Soc. on Abuse of Children, S.C. Med. Assn., S.C. Pediatric Soc., Columbia Med. Soc. Office: 1 Harbison Way Ste 108 Columbia SC 29212

ABEL, DAWNA MICHELLE, personnel executive, consultant; b. Chgo., Aug. 29, 1966; d. Charles Lynn and Dawna Bell (Gooch) A. BA in Psychology, Emory U., 1987. Cert. pers. cons. Pers. recruiter D.H.R.G. Inc., Atlanta, 1988-90, mgr., 1990-91; owner, v.p. ops. Bus. Profl. Group, Inc., Atlanta, 1991—; owner, CFO Diversified Human Resources, Inc., Atlanta, 1994—. Co-author: Job Search '94, 1994. Mem. NOW (mem. com. 1993—, v.p. action Atlanta chpt.), Ga. Assn. Pers. Svcs. Democrat. Home: 107 Powell Cv Decatur GA 30030-2900 Office: Bus Profl Group Inc 3490 Piedmont Rd NE Atlanta GA 30305-1743

ABEL, ELIZABETH A., dermatologist; b. Hartford, Conn., Mar. 16, 1940; d. Frederick A. and Rose (Borovicka) A.; m. Barton Lane; children: Barton, Geoffrey, Suzanne. Student, Colby-Sawyer Coll., 1957-60; BS, Wash. Hosp. Ctr. Sch. Med. Tech., 1961, U. Md., 1965; MD cum laude, U. Md., 1967. Diplomate Am. Bd. Dermatology. Intern San Francisco Gen. Hosp., 1967-68; resident, fellow in oncology U. Calif. Med. Ctr., San Francisco, 1968-69; resident in dermatology NYU Med. Ctr., 1969-72, USPHS research trainee in dermatology, 1972-73; dep. chief dept. dermatology USPHS Hosp., S.I., N.Y., 1973-74; instr. clin. dermatology Columbia U. Coll. Physicians and Surgeons, N.Y.C., 1974-75; instr. clin. dermatology Stanford (Calif.) U. Sch. Medicine, 1975-77, clin. asst. prof. dermatology, 1977-82, asst. prof. dermatology, 1982-90, clin. assoc. prof., 1990—; asst. editor Jour. Am. Acad. Dermatology; mem. med. adv. bd. The Nat. Psoriasis Found. Contbr. articles to sci. jours. Mellon Found. fellow, 1983, 87. Fellow Am. Acad. Dermatology; mem. N.Am. Clin. Dermatologic Soc., Soc. Investigative Dermatology, San Francisco Dermatologic Soc., Internat. Soc. Dermatology Surgery, Dermatology Found., Pacific Dermatologic Assn., Women's Dermatologic Soc., Alpha Omega Alpha. Episcopalian. Office: 525 South Dr Ste 115 Mountain View CA 94040

ABEL, MARY, state legislator; m. Richard Abel; 1 child, Jason. BS, MSJ, Ohio U. Mem. Ohio Ho. of Reps., 1989—. Mem. adv. coun. exec. programs Capitol U.; bd. dirs. Big Bros.-Big Sisters. Mem. AAUW, LWV, Indsl. Rels. Rsch. Assn., Inst. Local Govt. Adminstrn. and Rural Devel. (mem. adv. com.), Delta Kappa Gamma. Democrat. Home: 48 Strathmore Blvd Athens OH 45701 Office: OH Ho of Reps State House Columbus OH 43215*

ABEL, MARY ELLEN KATHRYN, quality control executive, chemist; b. Cleve., Nov. 3, 1949; d. Arthur L. and Dorothy Virginia (DeLura) Jaklic; m. Burton E. Abel, June 22, 1990; 2 stepchildren: Stephanie, Russell E.; 1 child, Matthew Anthony. A.A. with honors Lakeland Community Coll., 1985, BS in Chem. magna cum laude, Lake Erie Coll., Painesville, Ohio, 1991. Lab technician W.S. Tyler, Inc., Cleve., 1969-71, C-E Tyler, Cleve., 1974-76; quality control mgr., environ. coord, Morton Salt, Painesville, Ohio, 1977—. Treas. com. mem. Boy Scouts Am., 1988-90, sr. mem. explorer scouts marksmanship post, 1987-90, sec. local com., 1987-90; mem. Lake County Indsl. Community Awareness Emergency Response Adv. Panel, 1987-90. Mem. NAFE, Am. Chem. Soc, Gold Wing Road Riders Assn. Republican. Roman Catholic. Avocations: traveling, photography, tutoring math. Home: 391 Manhattan Pky Painesville OH 44077-5024 Office: Morton Salt Divsn Morton Internat Inc PO Box 428 Grand River OH 44045-0428

ABEL, MILLICENT HOPE, psychology educator; b. New Castle, Ind., Aug. 16, 1949; d. Ray Chalmers and Velma Mary-Margaret (Cole) Williams; m. E. Malcolm Abel II, Apr. 16, 1968; children: Kristina, E. Malcolm III, E. Daniel. BA, Ind. U. S.E., New Albany, 1979; MA, U. Louisville, 1982, PhD, 1988. Lectr. U. Louisville, 1983-92, asst. rsch. scientist, 1989-92; asst. prof. psychology Western Carolina U., Cullowhee, N.C., 1992—; lectr. Ind. U. S.E., 1984-88; rsch. psychologist U.S. Army Rsch. Inst., Ft. Knox, Ky., 1985-89; tech. cons. S.E. Regional Ctr. for Drug-free Schs. and Communities, Louisville, 1991-92; cons., mem. rsch. com. Seven Counties Svcs., Inc., Louisville, 1991-92. Contbr. articles to profl. jours. Mem. Coalition for Homeless, Louisville, 1990-92; presenter Ky. Gov.'s Conf. on Alcohol and Other Drug Abuse, Louisville, 1991. With USMC, 1967-68. Grantee Ky. Cabinet for Human Resources, 1989-91, Nat. Inst. for Alcohol Abuse and Alcoholism, 1989-91, Metro United Way, 1990, Office Substance Abuse Prevention, 1991-92. Mem. APA, AAUP, Southeastern Psychol. Assn. Office: Western Carolina U Dept Psychology Cullowhee NC 28723

ABEL HOROWITZ, MICHELLE SUSAN, advertising executive; b. Detroit, Mar. 31, 1950; d. Martin Louis and Phyllis (Berkowitz) A.; m. H. Jay Abel Horowitz, July 11, 1976; children—Jordan Michael, Stefanie Jennifer. Student Goucher Coll., 1967-70; B.A. in Econs., U. Mich., 1971; postgrad. in econs. U. Calif.-San Diego, 1973; M.A. in Econs., U. Detroit, 1974-76. Planning group supr. Hill Holliday Connors, Cosmopolus, Mass., 1976-78; econ. analyst Data Resources, Boston, 1978-79; v.p., media dir. Barkley & Evergreen, Southfield, Mich., 1979-80; v.p., dir. mktg. and media Yaffe/Berline, Southfield, Mich., 1980-82; exec. v.p., ptnr., corp. treas. Berline Group, Birmingham, Mich., 1982—; instr. Oakland U., Rochester, Mich., 1982; trustee, chairperson mktg. com. Harbinger Dance Co., Farmington, Mich., 1983—. Named Advt. Woman of Yr., Women's Ad Club Detroit, 1982. Mem. Adcraft Club Detroit, Women in Communications. Democrat. Jewish. Office: The Berline Group 31600 Telegraph Rd #100 Birmingham MI 48010-3439

ABELL, JAN MARY, architect; b. Chgo.; d. Philip and Dolores (Krumdick) Meisterheim. BArch, Ohio U., 1969. Registered architect, N.Y., Fla. Architect apprentice Verster, Djikstra, Cannegieter, Amsterdam, The Netherlands, 1970-72, Stevens, Bertin, O'Connell, Rochester, N.Y., 1972-76; architect McElvy, Jennewein Stefany, Howard, Tampa, Fla., 1976-79; prin., owner Abell Garcia Partnership Architects, Tampa, 1980—; adj. faculty mem. U. South Fla., Tampa, 1989-93; guest critic U. Fla., Gainesville, 1990, 92; lectr. in field. Prin works include B.C. Graham Elem. Sch. (Outstanding Preservation Project award), Leiman Wilson House (Gt. Am. Home award Nat. Trust for Hist. Preservation, Outstanding Preservation Project award Hillsborough County Planning Commn.), Edson Keith Estate, Sarasota, Fla. (Fla. Preservation award), Founder's House, Koreshan State Hist. Park, Estero, Fla. (Outstanding award for Restoration, Fla. Trust for Hist. Preservation); exhbns. include Women in Architecture, Washington, 1987, Fla./Caribbean Arch., San Juan, P.R. Recipient numerous awards for architecture, 1979—, Women of Achievement award Bus. and Profl. Women's Assn., 1982, Leadership Fla., 1990. Fellow AIA (juror Broward County chpt. Honor awards 1990, Nat. AIA Honor awards 1993, Nat. Com. on Design co-chmn. publs., Medal of Honor Fla. Cen. chpt. 1990), AIA Fla. Assn. (Comty. Svc. award 1979). Office: Abell Garcia Architects 2201 Dekle Ave Tampa FL 33606

ABELL, LYNN MARIE, chemist; b. Buffalo, N.Y., Dec. 26, 1958; d. Donald Eugene and Geraldine (Sivori) A. BS, Carnegie-Mellon U., 1981; PhD in Organic Chemistry, U. Wis., 1987. Postdoctoral fellow NIH/Pa. State U., State College, Pa., 1987-90; rsch. biochemist DuPont Agrl. Products, Wilmington, Del., 1990—. Contbr. articles to profl. jours.; patentee in field. Mem. Am. Chem. Soc., Delaware Valley Enzymology Club (treas., co-chair 1991—). Office: Dupont Agrl Products PO Box 30 Newark DE 19714

ABELLA, MARISELA CARLOTA, business executive; b. Havana, Cuba, Feb. 5, 1943; d. Carlos and Angela (Acosta) A.; m. Alberto Herrera Nogueira, Apr. 6, 1968 (div. Apr. 1986); 1 child, Carlos Alberto Herrera Abella. Asst. to v.p. and gen. mgr. bonding dept. Manuel San Juan (P.R.) Co. Inc., 1962-64; asst. corp. sec. and exec. sec. to pres. and stockholder Interstate Gen. Corp., Hato Rey, P.R., 1964-72, corp. sec. and pvt. sec. to corp. pres., 1972-79; sec.-treas., dir. A. H. Enterprises Inc., Caparra Heights, P.R., 1979-86; v.p., sec., bd. dirs. El Viajero Inc.; bd. dirs. A. H. Enterprises Inc., San Juan; pres. Marisela Abella Mktg. and Selling Promotional Items and Ideas, Caparra Heights, 1986—. Roman Catholic. Clubs: Caribe Hilton Swimming and Tennis, Barry U. Alumnae Assn. Home: 909 Borinquen Towers 2 Caparra Heights PR 00920 Office: PO Box 10510 Caparra Heights San Juan PR 00922-0510

ABENDROTH, JULIE DAWN, marketing executive; b. Amarillo, Tex., July 11, 1960; d. Larry Dean and Dawn Newell (Boyles) Cooper m. Russell C. Abendroth, Oct. 19, 1991. AA, Tex. State Tech. Inst., 1981; BA, West Tex. State U., 1988. Graphic artist Tex. State Tech. Inst., Amarillo, 1986-88; tng. specialist Naylor Industries, Houston, 1989-90; mktg. dir. Coastal Flow Measurement, Houston, 1990-94; mktg. mgr. the Americas Courtaulds Coatings Internat., Houston, 1994—; cons. Energy Control Products, Pasadena, Tex., 1993. Vol. Habitat for Humanity, Houston, 1993. Mem. Am. Mktg. Assn., Advt. Fedn. Home: 3325 Westview La Porte TX 77571

ABERCROMBIE, CHARLOTTE MANNING, reading specialist, supervisor; b. Swampscott, Mass., Oct. 25, 1915; d. Fredric Wilbur and Mary Sayer (Delano) Manning; m. Alexander Vaughan Abercrombie, Oct. 17, 1937; children: Lois A. Street, Paul M., David M., Lucia A. Harvilchuck. BA, Marietta Coll., 1937; MA, Columbia U., 1974, EdD, 1976. Cert. tchr. R.I., Wash., Wis., N.J.; cert. reading specialist, supr. N.J. Tchr. elem. schs. Tacoma (Wash.) Pub. Schs., 1958-62, Warwick (R.I.) Pub. Schs., 1957; tchr., reading specialist Milw. Pub. Schs., 1966-69; elem. tchr. and reading specialist, supr. East Orange (N.J.) Pub. Schs., 1969-79; dir. Fla. Ctr. for Philosophy of Children, Pensacola, 1994—. Mem. Nat. Assn. Congregational Chs. (exec. com. 1980-84). Mem. AAUW (v.p. Marco Island, Fla. chpt. 1988-89, bd. dirs. State of Fla. 1990, bd. dirs. Pensacola br. Coll. Univ., 1992). Repulican. Home: 10100 Hillview Rd Apt 616 Pensacola FL 32514

ABERNATHY, MARCIA E., nursing administrator; b. Phila., June 9; d. Edwin Carles and Armena (Palouian) A. AS in Nursing, So. Coll., 1967, BSN, 1981; MSN in Adult Health, U. Ala., 1985. RN, Tenn. Program dir. geropsych unit Parkridge Hosp., Chattanooga; med.-surg. staff nurse Erlanger Med. Ctr., Chattanooga, emergency room nurse surg. ICU, gerontology nurse, mem. TPN/IV teams, med.-surg. nurse mgr.; nurse mgr., med., surg. TPN/IV teams; geriatric med. care/program dir. Sr. Life Ctr., Parkridge Med. Ctr., Chattanooga. Mem. ANA (coun. gerontol. nursing, cert. gerontol. nurse, clin. specialist in gerontol. nursing), Tenn. Nurses Assn., Nurses House, Inc., Chattanooga Civil War Roundtable, Sigma Theta Tau. Home: 114 Narragansette Ave Chattanooga TN 37415-2623

ABERNATHY, MARGARET DENNY, elementary school educator; b. Durham, N.C., Aug. 23, 1948; d. John Howard and Myrtle Ruth (Lunsford) Denny; divorced; children: Guenevere Anjanette, Chadwick Sean. BS in Spanish, Appalachian State U., 1970; BS in Early Childhood Edn., Brenau Coll., 1976; postgrad., N.C. Cen. U., 1981-83. Cert. tchr. Spanish, 7-12, early childhood edn., K-4, N.C. Tchr. Spanish/English North Wilkes High Sch., Hays, N.C., 1970-71; tchr. coll.-level basic English Army Edn. Ctr. Lang. Sch., Fort Bragg, N.C., 1972; tchr. Spanish/English North Hall High Sch., Gainesville, Ga., 1976-77; Title 1 1st-grade tchr. Hall County Schs., Gainesville, 1978-79; tchr. asst. Durham (N.C.) County Schs., 1979-86, tchr. third grade, 1986—, team leader 3d grade, 1991-93. Mem. PTA, Durham, 1979—; pianist, Sunday Sch. tchr., adminstr. bd., others, Rougemont (N.C.) United Meth. Ch., 1979—; helper, den mother Boy Scouts of Am., Durham, 1984-85, 87—; v.p. United Meth. Women. Mem. NEA, N.C. Assn. Educators, Durham Assn. Educators, Christian Bus. and Profl. Women (Stonecroft Durham chpt.). Democrat. Home: 12507 Roxboro Rd Rougemont NC 27572 Office: Easley Elem Sch/Durham Pub Schs 302 Lebanon Cir Durham NC 27712-2644

ABERNATHY, VICKI MARIE, nurse; b. L.A., Feb. 14, 1949; d. James David and Margaret Helen (Quider) Abernathy; m. Dirk Klaus Ernst Wiese, Aug. 15, 1968 (div. 1973); 1 child, Zoe Erde. Student, U. Calif., Riverside, 1966-67, L.A. City Coll., 1968-69; AA in Nursing, Riverside City Coll., 1971-74. RN, Calif.; cert. med.-surg. nurse; cert. ACLS. Staff nurse Riverside (Calif.) County Hosp., 1974, Oceanside (Calif.) Community Hosp., 1974-76; with Scripps Hosp., Encinitas, Calif., 1976—, ambulatory surgery unit coord., 1981-93, staff nurse short stay unit, 1994—. Mem. ACLU, Calif. Nurses Assn., San Diego Zool. Soc. Democrat.

ABERNETHY, DEBORAH BENSON, personnel placement firm executive; b. Dalton, Ga., Mar. 4, 1953; d. James Henry and Robbie (Broome) Benson; m. James Elon Abernethy (div.); children—Lauren Marisa, Matthew Elon. B.S.H.E., U. Ga., 1974, Ed.M., 1983. Cert. tchr. home econs., Ga. Tchr. Paulding County High Sch., Dallas, 1974-80; personnel recruiter Premier Personnel, Atlanta, 1980-81; pres. Career Blazers, Inc., Atlanta, 1981-86; owner, pres. Corp. Career Cons., 1986—; co-owner sales & design Simply Kitchens, 1994—. Editor U. Ga. Yearbook, 1974. Mem. Atlanta C. of C., Am. Water Ski Assn. (asst. judge, asst. scorer 1978-80), Ga. Water Ski Fedn. (historian 1978-81), Phi Upsilon Omicron. Episcopalian. Avocations: collecting antiques; water and snow skiing; scuba diving. Home: 468 W Paces Ferry Rd NW Atlanta GA 30327-2306 Office: Corp Career Cons Inc 1266 W Paces Ferry Rd NW Atlanta GA 30327-2306

ABERNETHY, IRENE MARGARET, county official; b. Ord, Nebr., Mar. 28, 1924; d. Glen Dayton and Margaret Lillian (Jones) Auble; m. Don R. Abernethy, Aug. 8, 1954 (dec. Nov. 1980); children: Jill Adele Abernethy Johnson, Ted Verne. BA cum laude, Hastings Coll., 1946; postgrad., U. Nebr., 1950-53. Tchr. Ord High Sch., 1946-50, Scottsbluff (Nebr.) High Sch., 1950-55, Grand Island (Nebr.) Sr. High Sch., 1961-62; mem. Hall County Bd. Suprs., Grand Island, 1979—, chair, 1984, 95. Vice chair Hall County Rep. Ctrl. Com., Grand Island, 1971-73; chair campaign Congresswoman Virginia Smith for Hall County, 1974-80; sr. v.p. Nebr. Rep. Founders Day, Lincoln, 1981; chair Gov.'s Juv. Justice Adv. Group, Lincoln, 1981-91; mem. Nebr. Commn. on Law Enforcement and Criminal Justice, Lincoln, 1970-91; bd. dirs. Head Start, 1979—, Hall County Leadership Tomorrow, 1990-94, Indsl. Found., 1991, College Park, 1991—, Community Help Ctr., 1991—, Family Violence Coalition, 1993—, Midland Area Agy. on Aging, 1993-95; adv. com. Region III Mental Health Adv. Bd.; active Nat. Coalition State Juvenile Justice Adv. Groups, 1988-91, Partners in Community Planning, 1994—, Grand Island Area Edn. 2000; mem. task force on needs Heartland United Way. Named Woman of Yr. Grand Island Ind., 1980, Bus. and Profl. Women, Grand Island, 1980, Beta Sigma Phi, 1982, Nebr. chpt. NASW, 1983; recipient Svc. to Mankind award Sertoma, 1983-84, Recognition award PTA, 1988, Outstanding Community Svc. award Rotary, 1985. Mem. LWV (local pres. 1962-64, state bd. dirs. 1965-69), YWCA (local pres. 1974-75, Woman of Distinction 1988), AAUW (local pres. 1986-88, state bd. dirs. 1970-71), nebr. Assn. County Ofcls. (pres. 1985), Assn. Child Abuse Prevention, Grand Island Area C. of C. (bd. dirs. 1992-95), Philanthropic Ednl. Orgn. (local pres. 1970-71), Woodland Gold Club Ladies Assn. (champion 1961, 63, 64, local pres. 1963), Riverside Gold Club (champion 1969), Pi Lambda Theta. Republican. Methodist. Home: 707 S Blaine St Grand Island NE 68803-6146 Office: Hall County Adminstrn 121 S Pine St Grand Island NE 68801-6076

ABID, ANN B., art librarian; b. St. Louis, Mar. 17, 1942; d. Clarence Frederick and Luella (Niehaus) Bartelsmeyer; m. Amor Abid (div. 1969); children: Rod, Kady; m. Cleon R. Yohe, Aug. 10, 1974 (div.); m. Roldo S. Bartimole, Feb. 1, 1991. Cert. in Librarianship, Washington U., St. Louis, 1976. Asst. to libr. St. Louis Art Mus., 1963-68, libr., 1968-85; head libr. Cleve. Mus. Art, 1985—; vis. com. univ. librs. Case We. Res.U., 1987-90, co-chairperson, 1990. Co-author: Documents of Surrealism, 1918-1942, 1981; contbr. articles to profl. jours. Grantee Mo. Coun. Arts, 1978, Mo. Com. Humanities, 1980, Nat. Hist. Pubs. and Records Commn., 1981, Reinberger Found., 1987. Mem. ALA, Art Librs. Soc. N.Am. (Ohio and nat. chpts., chairperson Mus.-Type-of-Libr. group 1979-81, chair New Orleans 1980, nominating com. 1980, 84, Wittenborn awards com. 1981, 90, v.p., pres. elect 1987-88, pres. 1988-89, past pres. 1989-90, chairperson N.Am. art libr. resources com. 1991-93, search com. new exec. dir. 1993-94, presenter numerous papers), Soc. Am. Archivists, Midwest Mus. Conf. (co-chairperson program com. ann. meeting 1982), Spl. Librs. Assn. Office: Cleve Mus of Art 11150 East Blvd Cleveland OH 44106-1711

ABISH, CECILE, artist; b. N.Y.C.; m. Walter Abish. B.F.A., Bklyn. Coll., 1953. Instr. art Queens Coll.; vis. artist U. Mass, Amherst, Cooper Union, Harvard U. Solo exhbns. include Newark Coll. Engring., 1968, Inst. Contemporary Art, Boston, 1974, U. Md., 1975, Alessandra Gallery, N.Y.C., 1977, Wright State U., Dayton, Ohio, 1978, Carpenter Ctr., Cambridge, Mass., 1979, Anderson Gallery, Va. Commonwealth U., Richmond, 1981, SUNY-Stony-Brook, 1982, Ctr. for Creative Photography, Tucson, 1984; group exhbns: Detroit Inst. Art, 1969, Aldrich Mus. Art, 1971, 10 Bleecker St., N.Y.C., 1972, Lakeview Ctr. Arts, Peoria. Ill., 1972, Bykert Gallery, N.Y.C., 1971-74, Michael Walls Gallery, N.Y.C., 1975, Fine Arts Bldg. Gallery, N.Y.C., 1976, Mus. Modern Art, N.Y.C., 1976, Hudson River Mus., 1979, Atlanta Arts Festival, 1980, New Mus., N.Y.C, 1980, 81, Kuntsgebaude, Stuttgart, Fed. Republic Germany, 1981, Long Beach (Calif.) Mus., 1983, Edith C. Blum Art Inst., Bard Coll., Annandale-on-Hudson, N.Y., 1984, Mus. Modern Kunst, Vienna, Austria, 1985, U. R.I., Kingston, 1985, Art Défense Galleries, Paris, 1993, Architektur Zentrum, Vienna, 1993, Artists Space, N.Y.C., 1994, Islip Art Mus., N.Y., 1995; numerous commns.; represented in permanent collections; published photo works: Firsthand, 1978, Chinese Crossing, 1986, 99: The New Meaning, 1990. Nat. Endowment Arts fellow, 1975, 77, 80; CAPS fellow, 1975. Mem. Coll. Art Assn. Office: Cooper Station 4th Ave PO Box 485 New York NY 10003-5204

ABLES, NANCY BUMSTEAD, sales executive; b. Galesburg, Ill., Mar. 9, 1948; d. Charles Heath Bumstead and Thelma Delta (Hughes) McDonald; m. Laurence Clifton Greenwold, June 4, 1966 (div. Feb. 1987); children: Laurie J. Greenwold Campos, Charles Howard Greenwold; m. David Stephen Ables, Mar. 15, 1987. With, Knox Coll., 1965-69. Assembler printed circuit bd. Astro Internat. Corp., League City, Tex., 1987, spare parts sales mgr., 1987—; printed circuit bd. assembler Gadget Electronics, Pasadena, Tex., 1986—, v.p., 1987—. Chmn. Environ. Commn., Park Forest South, Ill., 1971-74; v.p. Balmoral Elem. P.T.O., Crete, Ill., 1980-81, pres., 1981-83; campaign mgr. J. Gustafson Sch. Bd. mem., Crete, 1980. Home: 9800 Hollock St Apt 1009 Houston TX 77075-1833 Office: Astro Internat Corp 100 Park Ave League City TX 77573-2446

ABRAHAM, JANICE MENKE, college treasurer; b. Pitts., May 12, 1957; m. Kim Abraham; 1 child, Lena. BA in Internat. Rels., Am. U., Washington, 1979; MBA, U. Pa., 1982. Staff asst. Nat. Assn. Coll. and Univ. Bus. Officers, Washington, 1979-80; asst. treas. Morgan Guaranty Trust, N.Y.C., 1982-85; asst. dir. bus. mgmt., residential life Cornell U., Ithaca, N.Y., 1985-86, sr. adminstr. nutritional scis., 1986-87, exec. dir. Theory Ctr., 1987-89; treas., CFO Whitman Coll., Walla Walla, Wash., 1989—; speaker in field. Bd. dirs. Project Read, Walla Walla, 1992—, Team Walla Walla; program chair Main St. Found., Walla Walla. Mem. Western Assn. Coll. and Univ. Bus. Officers (profl. devel. com. 1990-93, host com. 1992, ann. meeting chair 1993-94, 1st v.p. 1994-95, pres. 1995-96), Nat. Assn. Coll. and Univ. Bus. Officers (editorial bd. 1991—). Office: Whitman Coll 345 Boyer Ave Walla Walla WA 99362

ABRAHAMSON, SHIRLEY SCHLANGER, state supreme court justice; b. N.Y.C., Dec. 17, 1933; d. Leo and Ceil (Sauerteig) Schlanger; m. Seymour Abrahamson, Aug. 26, 1953; 1 son, Daniel Nathan. AB, NYU, 1953; JD, Ind. U., 1956; SJD, U. Wis., 1962. Bar: Ind. 1956, N.Y. 1961, Wis. 1962. Asst. dir. Legis. Drafting Research Fund, Columbia U. Law Sch., 1957-60; since practiced in Madison, Wis., 1962-76; mem. firm LaFollette, Sinykin, Anderson & Abrahamson, 1962-76; justice Supreme Ct. Wis., Madison, 1976—; prof. U. Wis. Sch. Law, 1966-92; bd. visitors Ind. U. Sch. Law, 1972—, U. Miami Sch. Law, 1982—, U. Chgo. Law Sch., 1988-92, Brigham Young U. Sch. Law, 1986-88, Northwestern U. Law Sch., 1989—; chmn. Wis. Rhodes Scholarship Com., 1992—; chair nat. adv. com. on court-adjudicated and court-ordered health Care George Washington U. Ctr. for Health Policy, Washington, 1993—. Editor: Constitutions of the United States (National and State) 2 vols, 1962. Mem. study group program of rsch., mental health and the law John D. and Catherine T. MacArthur Found., 1988—; mem. coun. fund for rsch. on dispute resolution Ford Found., 1987-91; bd. dirs. Wis. Civil Liberties Union, 1968-72. Mem. ABA (coun., sect. of legal edn. and admissions to the bar 1976-86, mem. commn. on undergrad. edn. in law and the humanities 1978-79, standing com. on pub. edn. 1991—, mem. commn. on acccess to justice/2000 1993—, mem. adv. bd. Ctrl. and East European law initiative 1994—), Wis. Bar Assn., Dane County Bar Assn., 7th Cir. Bar Assn., Nat. Assn. Women Judge, Am. Law Inst. (coun. 1985—), Order of Coif, Phi Beta Kappa. Home: 2012 Waunona Way Madison WI 53713-1616 Office: Wis Supreme Ct PO Box 1688 Madison WI 53701-1688

ABRAHM, JANET LEE, hematologist, oncologist, educator; b. San Francisco, Mar. 14, 1949; d. Paul Milton and Helen Lesser Abrahm; m. David Rytman Slavitt, Apr. 16, 1978. Student, U. Calif., Berkeley, 1969; BA, U. Calif., San Francisco, 1970, MD, 1973. Diplomate Am. Bd. Internal Medicine. Intern and resident medicine Mass. Gen. Hosp., Boston, 1973-75, hematology fellow, 1975-76; chief resident medicine Moffitt Hosp. U. Calif., San Francisco, 1976-77; hematology/oncology fellow Hosp. U. Pa., Phila., 1977-80; postdoctoral fellow medicine U. Pa., Phila., 1977-78, postdoctoral trainee medicine, 1977-80, asst. prof. medicine, 1980-86; asst. prof. medicine Hosp. U. Pa. and VA Med. Ctr., Phila., 1986-89, assoc. prof. medicine, 1989—; attending physician Hosp. U. Pa., Phila., 1980-93; staff physician Phila. VA Med. Ctr., 1982—, dir. Hematology/Oncology Clinic, 1983-94, chief hematology and oncology sect., 1984-94, med. oncologist Hospice Consultation Team, 1993—, chief med. svc., 1994—; chmn. adv. com. Cancer Care VA Dist. 4, 1987-90; sec. subspecialty bd. hematology Am. Bd. Internal Medicine, 1987-92; vis. asst. prof. medicine Med. Coll. Pa., 1988—; adj. asst. prof. clin. pharmacy Phila. Coll. Pharmacy and Sci., 1988—; mem. tech. adv. group Cancer Care Region 1, 1990—; med. oncology cons. cancer pain consultation panel Ctr. for Continuing Edn. U. Pa. Sch. Nursing, 1990—; med. sec. subspecialty edn. program subcom. subspecialty bd. hematology Am. Bd. Internal Medicine, 1993—; lectr. Med. Coll. Pa., 1989, 93, Sch. Medicine U. Va., 1989, Conf. on Cancer VA Region 2, Durham, N.C., 1989, Sacred Heart Hosp., Chester, Pa., 1991, Albert Einstein Hosp., Phila., 1991, Mt. Zion Med. Ctr. U. Calif., San Francisco, 1992, Women in Medicine, Phila., 1993, Pa. Hosp., 1993, Sacred Heart Hosp., Allentown, Pa., 1993, Med. Coll. Pa., Phila., 1993, Mercy Hosp., Wilkes-Barre, Pa., 1993, Wilkes-Barre VA Hosp., 1993, Delaware Valley Geriatrics Soc., King of Prussia, Pa., 1993, Am. Cancer Soc. MCP, Phila., 1993, Family Practice Group Bryn Mawr (Pa.) Hosp., 1994, Pa. Cancer Control Program, Phila., 1994, Hospice Conf. Phila. VA Med. Ctr., 1994, Washington VA Med. Ctr., 1994, Phila. Corp. for Aging, 1994. Author: (with others) Handbook of Experimental Pharmacology, 1980, Vivo and In Vitro Erythropoiesis: The Friend System, 1980, Clinical Care of the Terminal Patient, 1982, Yearbook of Medicine, 1984, Yearbook of Cancer, 1984, Vitamins and Cancer - Human Cancer Prevention by Vitamins and Micronutrients, 1985, Biological Regulation of Cell Proliferation, vol. 34, 1986, Hematology: Basic Principles and Practice, 1990, 94, Internal Medicine for Dentistry, 2d edit., 1990; contbr. (booklets) Caring for the Terminally Ill Patient at Home - A Guide for Family Caregivers, 1986, Caring for the Cancer Patient at Home - A Guide for Patients and Families, 1986; reviewer JAMA, Cancer, Archives Internal Medicine, Annals Internal Medicine, Jour. Cancer Edn., Resident and Staff Physician; contbr. numerous articles to profl. jours. Vol. lectr. Am. Soc. Pain Control in Cancer Patients; mem. edn. com. Greater Phila. Pain Soc., 1993. Recipient Manual award Merck, 1973; Fife Medicine scholar, 1973. Fellow ACP (lectr. Pa. chpt. 1994); mem. Am. Soc. Hematology, Am. Fedn. Clin. Rsch., Am. Soc. Clin. Hypnosis, Am. Soc. Clin. Oncology, Am. Assn. Cancer Edn. (program com. 1993), Am. Pain Soc., Phi Beta Kappa, Alpha Omega Alpha. Home: 523 S 41st St Philadelphia PA 19104 Office: Phila VA

Med Ctr Hematology/Oncology Sect 9 West University and Woodland Aves Philadelphia PA 19104

ABRAM, PRUDENCE BEATTY, federal judge; b. Kingston, R.I., Nov. 19, 1942; d. Kenneth Orion and Mary Catharine (Carter) Beatty; 1 child, Andrea Beatty. B.A., U. Mich., 1964, J.D. cum laude, 1968. Bar: Mich. 1969, N.Y. 1971, U.S. Dist. Ct. for so. dist. N.Y. 1972, U.S. Dist. Ct. for eastern dist. N.Y. 1972, U.S. Ct. Appeals for 2d circuit 1972, U.S. Supreme Ct. 1979. Assoc. firm Breed Abbott & Morgan, N.Y.C., 1970-72, Weil Gotshal & Manges, N.Y.C., 1972-78, Krause, Hirsch & Gross, N.Y.C., 1978-79; ptnr. firm Stroock & Stroock & Lavan, N.Y.C., 1980-82; judge U.S. Bankruptcy Ct. (so. dist.) N.Y., N.Y.C., 1982—. Mem. ABA. Office: US Bankruptcy Ct US Custom House One Bowling Green 6th Fl New York NY 10004-1408*

ABRAMOWICZ, JANET, painter, print-maker; b. N.Y.C.; children: Alex, Anna. Student, Art Students League, 1948-50, Columbia U., 1948-50; BFA, Accademia di Belle Arti, Bologna, Italy, 1952, MFA, 1953. Instr. dept. art and architecture U. Ill., 1955-57, Sch. Worcester, Mass., 1957-58; sr. lectr. fine arts Harvard U., Cambridge, Mass., 1971-91; former lectr. on spl. exhibits Mus. Fine Arts, Boston; vis. artist Am. Acad. Rome, 1984, 85, 94; advisor Calcografia Nazionale, Rome, 1989-90; hon. fellow Accademia Clementina, Bologna, Italy, 1990—. Contbg. editor: Opera Grafiche di Morandi, 1990; contbr. articles to profl. jours. Sr. Fulbright fellow, 1977-79, 89, Rockefeller Found., 1989—, Am. Coun. Learned Socs. fellow, 1990, John Simon Guggenheim fellow, 1992. Democrat.

ABRAMS, BARBARA, nutritionist, educator. BS in Nutrition and Dietetics, Simmons Coll., 1974; MPH in Nutrition, U. Calif., Berkeley, 1975, MS in Epidemiology, 1983, DrPH in Nutrition, 1985. Registered dietitian. Dietetic intern U. Calif., Berkeley, 1975; rsch. asst. Calif. Assn. for Maternal and Child Health, San Francisco, 1975-76; rsch. nutritionist dept. nutritional scis. U. Calif.-Berkeley and Kaiser Found. Rsch. Inst., Oakland, 1976-78; lectr., clin. nutritionist U. Calif., San Francisco, 1978-86; lectr. womens health care project dept. community medicine Stanford (Calif.) U., 1981-85; asst. prof. pub. health nutrition dept. social & adminstrv. health scis. U. Calif., Berkeley, 1985—; asst. prof. dept. obstetrics, gynecology & reproductive scis. U. Calif., San Francisco, 1986—; assoc. prof. Sch. Pub. Health, U. Calif., Berkeley; mem numerous coms. U. Calif., Berkeley; cons. nutritionist Berkeley Obstetrics, Gynecology and Infertility Group, 1975-91; cons. Senate Select Com. on Nutrition and Human Needs, Dietary Goals, 1978, Calif. Dept. Health Svcs. Cancer Prevention Project, 1986—, Calif. Dept. Health Svcs. Maternal Nutrition during Pregnancy and Lactation Manual Task Force, 1987-90, Weight Watchers Internat., Jericho, N.Y., 1988-89; epidemiologist nat. growth & health study U. Calif., Berkeley, 1986-88; reviewer Nat. Ctr. for Health Svcs., 1985, U. Wash. Fred Hutchinson Cancer Ctr., Seattle, 1987, Calif. Dept. Health Svcs./Nat. Cancer Inst., 1987, Calif. Dept. Health Svcs. Children's Food Guide, 1988; invited participant doctoral tng. workshop in pub. health nutrition Assn. Faculties of Grad. Programs in Pub. Health Nutrition, Washington, 1987; mem. com. on nutritional status during pregnancy and lactation NAS Inst. Medicine Food and Nutrition Bd., 1988—, mem. subcom. for clin. application guide, 1990—; mem. expert panel on weight gain during pregnancy U. Minn. Sch. Pub. Health, Mpls., 1988, mem. com. Nutritional Status Pregnancy Lactation, Inst. Medicine, Nat. Acad. Scis., 1988-92; lectr. in field; reviewer Am. Jour. Epidemiology, Obstetrics and Gynecology, Am. Jour. Health Promotion, Jour. Nutrition Edn. Author book revs., reports; contbr. numerous articles to profl. jours., chpts. to books. Mem. task force on reimbursement for patient edn. svcs. for pregnant diabetic mothers Calif. Dept. Health Svcs., 1985; cons. community substance abuse svcs. San Francisco City and County/Tri County Pregnancy and Addiction Project, 1985; mem. smoking & pregnancy steering com. Am. Lung Assn., Alameda County, Calif., 1985-86. Regents fellow U. Calif., Berkeley, 1985, Jr. Faculty fellow, 1988; March of Dimes fellow U. N.C., Chapel Hill, 1982;. Mem. APHA, Am. Dietetic Assn., Soc. for Epidemiol. Rsch., Soc. for Nutrition Edn. (program chair pub. health div. ann. meeting 1981, chair major session & mem. local arrangements com. ann. meeting 1987), Am. Inst. Nutrition, Am. Soc. Clin. Nutrition, Calif. Perinatal Assn. (coordinating coun. 1980). Office: U Calif Sch Pub Health 426 Warren Hall Berkeley CA 94720

ABRAMS, FRANCES ELISE, psychotherapist; b. Balt., Aug. 21, 1947; d. Julius and Sylvia (Astor) Kovitz; m. Roger Ian Abrams, June 1, 1969; children: Jason Harris, Seth Douglas. BS, Boston U., 1969; MS, Nova U., Ft. Lauderdale, Fla., 1991. Tchr. 3d grade Lexington (Mass.) Pub. Schs.; tchr. 5th grade English Portland (Maine) Pub. Schs.; psychotherapist in pvt. practice Plantation, Fla.; counselor and advisor Rutgers U., Newark. Mem. ACA. Home: 379 Thornden St South Orange NJ 07079

ABRAMS, LINDA, public relations executive. BS, Syracuse U. Promotion mgr. CBS Records, Arista Records, 1980-85; acct. supr. Lucker & Co., 1985-86; acct. supr. Ruder, Finn & Rotman, 1986-88, dir. pub. rels., sr. acct. mgr., 1988-89; sr. acct. supr. Ruder Finn, 1989-90, v.p., 1990-93; dir. affiliate mktg., 1993—. Office: MTV 1515 Broadway New York NY 10036

ABRAMS, ROBERTA BUSKY, hospital administrator, nurse; b. Bklyn., Feb. 16, 1937; d. Albert H. and Gladys Busky; m. Robert L. Abrams, June 28, 1959 (div. 1977); children: Susan Abrams Federman, David B. BSN, U. Rochester, 1959; MA, Fairfield U., 1977. Asst. head nurse Jewish Hosp., Bklyn., 1959-60; instr. medicine/surgery Bklyn. Hosp., 1960-62, U. Rochester, N.Y., 1963-64; instr. ob-gyn Malden (Mass.) Hosp. Sch. Nursing, 1965-66; instr. prospective parents ARC, San Rafael, Calif., 1968-69; instr. ob-gyn SUNY, Farmingdale, 1970-71; instr. maternal/child health Stamford (Conn.) Hosp., 1971-75; clinician maternal/child health Lawrence Hosp., Bronxville, N.Y., 1975-78; asst. prof. nursing Ohio Wesleyan U., Delaware, 1981-84; dir. Elizabeth Blackwell Hosp. at Riverside Meth., Columbus, Ohio, 1978-86; dir. nursing Henry Ford Hosp., Detroit, 1986-87, assoc. adminstr. nursing, 1988-92; cons. Henry Ford Health Systems, Detroit, 1993—; cons. maternal/child nursing currents Ross Labs., 1984-94; cons. women's children's health Henry Ford Health Systems, 1993-94, cons. at large, 1994—; state coord. maternal/child health 1st Am. Home Care; lectr. in field. Contbr. articles to profl. jours. Mem. NAACOG (vice-chmn. Ohio chpt. 1984-87), Am. Soc. Psychoprophylaxsis, Greater Detroit Orgn. Nurses Execs., LWV, Sigma Theta Tau. Home and Office: 32478 Dunford Rd Farmington Hills MI 48334

ABRAMS, ROSALIE SILBER, state agency official; b. Balt.; d. Isaac and Dora (Rodbell) Silber. R.N., Sinai Hosp.; postgrad., Columbia U.; BS, Johns Hopkins U., 1963, MA in Polit. Sci.; 1 child, Elizabeth Joan. Public health nurse, USNR, 1945-46; bus. mgr. Sequoia Med. Group, Calif., 1946-47; asst. bus. mgr. Silber's Bakery, Balt., 1947-53; mem. Md. Ho. of Dels., 1967-70; mem. Md. Senate, 1970-83, majority leader, 1978-82; chmn. Dem. Party of Md., 1978-83, chmn. fin. com., 1982-83; dir. Office on Aging, State of Md., 1983—, chair dept. human resources, dept. health and mental hygiene, trans., housing and community devel., econ. and employment devel., Interagency Com., 1984—; host Outlook TV show, 1983-90; guest lectr., witness before congl. coms. Platform com. on nat. health care Dem. Nat. Com., 1979—; chmn. Md. Humane Practices Commn., 1978-83, mem., 1971-74; mem. New Coalition, 1979-83, State-Fed. Assembly Com. on Human Resources, 1977-83, Md. Comprehensive Health Planning Agency, 1972-75, Md. Commn. on Status of Women, 1968— , Am. Jewish Com.; bd. dirs. Sinai Hosp., Balt., 1973—, Balt. Jewish Coun., Cross Country Improvement Assn., 1969—, Fifth Dist. Reform Democrats, 1967—; chmn. legis. com. Balt. Area Coun. on Alcoholism, 1973-75; mem. adv. bd. long term care project U. Md., Balt., 1986; mem. Md. Adv. Com. for Adult and Community Svcs., 1984; mem. nat. adv. bd. Pre-Retirement Edn. Planning, 1986—; mem. State Adv. Coun. on Nutrition, 1988—;bd. dir. Sinai Hosp., 1973—; special trustee Sheppard-Pratt Hosp., 1992—. With Nurse Corps USN, 1944-46. Recipient Louise Waterman Wise Community Svc. award, 1969, award Am. Acad. Comprehensive Health Planning, 1971, Balt. News Am. award, Women of Distinction in Medicine, 1971, traffic safety award, Safety First Club of Md., 1971, Ann London Scott Meml. award for legis. excellence, Md. Chpt. NOW, 1975, Md. Nurses Assn., 1975, svc. award Balt. Area Coun. on Alcoholism, 1975; named to Md. Women's Hall of Fame, Md. Commn. for Women and Women Legislators of Md. Gen. Assembly, 1994, numerous others. Mem. AARP, Md. Order Women Legislators (pres., 1973-75), Nat. Conf. State Legislatures (human resources and urban affairs steering com. 1977-83), Nat. Legis. Conf. (human resources task force, intergovt. rels. com. 1975-83), Md. Gerontol. Assn. (bd. dirs. 1984—), Nat. Fedn. Dem. Women, Am. Jewish Congress, Am. Soc. on Aging, Md. Gerontological Assn. Home: 66 Olmstead Green Ct Baltimore MD 21210-1508 Office: Md Office on Aging 301 W Preston St Rm 1007 Baltimore MD 21201-2305

ABRAMS, SYLVIA FLECK, religious studies educator; b. Buffalo, Apr. 5, 1942; d. Abraham and Ann (Hanf) Fleck; m. Ronald M. Abrams, June 30, 1963; children—Ruth, Sharon. BA magna cum laude, Western Res. U., 1963, MA, 1964, PhD, 1988; BHL, Cleve. Coll. Jewish Studies, 1976, MHL, 1983; postgrad. U. Haifa, 1975, Yad Va Shem Summer Inst., Hebrew U., 1983. Hebrew tchr. The Temple, 1959-77, Hebrew coord., 1973-77; tchr. Beachwood High Sch., 1964-66; tchr. Hebrew and social studies Agnon Sch., Cleve., 1975-77, social studies resource tchr., 1976-77; ednl. dir. Temple Emanu El, Cleve., 1977-85; asst. dir. Cleve. Bur. Jewish Edn., 1985-92, acting exec. v.p., 1993-94, , exec. dir. ednl. svcs. Jewish Edn. Ctr. Cleve., 1994—; chmn. ednl. dirs. coun. Cleve. Bd. Jewish Edn., 1982-85. Appointed to Ohio Coun. Holocaust Edn., 1986. Recipient Elbert J. Benton award Western Res. U., 1963; Fred and Rose Rosenwasser Bible award Coll. Jewish Studies, 1974; Emmanuel Gamoran Meml. Curriculum award Nat. Assn. Temple Educator, 1978; Samuel Lipson Meml. award Coll. Jewish Studies, 1981 Bingham fellow Case Western Res. U., 1984-86. Mem. ASCD, Nat. Assn. Temple Educators (bd. dirs. 1984-88), Coun. Jewish Edn. (bd. dirs. 1991—), Coalition for Alternative in Jewish Edn. (bd. mem. at large 1989-93), Union Am. Hebrew Congregations (Israel curriculum task force), Cleve. Bur. Jewish Edn. (chmn. ednl. dirs. coun. 1982-85), Nat. Coun. Jewish Women (life), Phi Beta Kappa. Jewish. Club: Hadassah (life). Editor: You and Your Schools, 1972. Office: Jewish Edn Ctr of Cleve 2030 S Taylor Rd Cleveland OH 44118-2699

ABRAMS, VIVIEN, artist; b. Cleve.. BFA, Carnegie-Mellon U.; MFA, Instituto Allende, San Miguel de Allende, Mex. Art tchr. Biblioteca Publica, San Miguel de Allende, Mex., 1969, Cleve. Mus. Art, 1971-72; instr. watercolor Dept. Commumity Svcs., Cleveland Heights, Univ. Heights, Ohio, 1974; instr. drawing Cuyahoga C.C., Cleve., 1974; design instr. Manhattanville Coll., Purchase, N.Y., 1985-86; artist-in-residence Bennington (Vt.) Coll., 1980; vis. artist in painting SUNY, Purchase, N.Y., 1983; lectr. in field. One-woman shows include Akron (Ohio) Art Inst., 1976, The New Gallery Contemporary Art, Cleve., 1977, 80, Luise Ross Gallery, N.Y.C., 1984, Coup de Grâce Gallery, N.Y.C., 1992, 100 Church Street, N.Y.C., 1992, Lisa Stern Gallery, Mountainville, N.Y., 1993, Lycian Ctr. Galleries, Sugarloaf, N.Y., 1994; selected group exhbns. include Butler Inst. Am. Art, Ohio, 1976, 77, Cleve. Mus. Art, 1976, 77, 79, 81, 84 (1st Prize in Painting 1981), Akron Inst. Art, 1977, Harbourfront Gallery, Toronto, 1978, Marilyn Pearl Gallery, N.Y.C., 1978, 82, Phoenix Mus. Art, 1979, Soho Ctr. Visual Artists, N.Y.C., 1979, Washingtion Sq. East Galleries, N.Y.C., 1980, Little Rock (Ark.) Art Mus., 1982, Steven Rosenberg Gallery, N.Y.C., 1983, Ericson Gallery, N.Y.C., 1983, Sculpture Ctr., N.Y.C., 1983, A.I.R. Gallery, N.Y.C., 1983, Aldrich Mus. Contemporary Art, Ridgefield, Conn., 1984, 86, 92, Luise Ross Gallery, 1984, Mus. of the Hudson Highlands, N.Y., 1985, City Gallery, N.Y.C., 1987, Squibb Gallery, Princeton, N.J., 1988, Cleve. Inst. Art, 1988, Mansfield Art Ctr., Ohio, 1989, OIA Salon, N.Y.C., 1991, Middletown Art Ctr., 1994 (Oil/Acrylic award 1994), Dietrich Contemporary Arts, N.Y.C., 1994, Cleve. Ctr. for Contemporary Art, 1994, Mansfield (Ohio) Art Ctr., 1995; permanent collections include Cleve. Found., Cleve. Art Assn., The Currier Gallery Art, Home Ins. Co., We. Electric, J.P. Morgan & Co., Continental Corp., Progressive Ins. Co., Nat. City Bank Cleve., Sohio, Walter & Samuels, Inc., Columbus Mus. Arts & Scis., Cleve. Mus. Art, Aldrich Mus. Contemporary Art; commns. include AT&T Longlines. Mem. fellows exec. com. MacDowell Colony, 1982-85. Cleve. Found. grantee, 1976, Athena Found. grantee, 1984; Hand Follow Found. fellow, 1983, fellow MacDowell Colony, Peterborough, N.H., 1979, 81, 85; recipient 1st prize Cleve. Mus. Art 62nd May Show, 1981, award Middletown Art Ctr., 1994; named to Shaker Heights H.S. Hall of Fame, 1994. Office: 11 Worth St New York NY 10013-2922 also: 196 Mountain Rd Cornwall On Hudson NY 12520-1803

ABRAMSON, ELAINE SANDRA, graphic designer, crafts artist; b. Cleve., Aug. 27, 1942; d. Norman Morris and Ruth Leah (Glassman) Splaver; m. Martin Stanley Abramson, May 27, 1977; children: Deborah Sue, Mitchell Lee. Hebrew tchr. cert. Hyam Greenberg Inst., Jerusalem, 1960-61; cert. in appraising fine and decorative arts NYU, 1990, Cleve. Inst. Art, 1954-64, 90, NYU, 1990; BS in Edn., Kent State U., 1964. Illustrator Ednl. Research Council, Cleve., 1964-65; tchr. art Cleve. Bd. Edn., 1965-67; pres., owner A & A (formerly Create-A-Craft), Ft. Worth, 1967—; author, spkr. affects of copyright law and politics on the artist, 1991—; founding artist, publicity designer Sassy Cat, Chagrin Falls, Ohio, 1967-71; adviser Women's Am. ORT Collection, Houston, 1983-84; designer Golden Gourmet dolls, Hobby Industries Am., Dallas, 1981, 85; intern, columnist Appraisers Assn. Am., 1990; cons. appraising and decorative arts for copyright law. Group shows of illustration, soft crafts, toys, enamelling include: Cleve. Mus. Art, 1964, Cleve. Inst. Art, 1964-71, Towson Courthouse Art Exhibit, Md., 1972-77; one-woman shows include: Kent State U., 1963-64, Central Nat. Bank Cleve., 1961-66; Md. Pub. TV Arts Exhibits, 1972-77, Tex. State Artist Competition. Designer, inventor, creator craft kits, toys, games, 1967—; author: (syndicated column) Appraisals by Abramson, (cartoons) Rojo the Red Lobster, The Golden Gourmets, Those Characters From Cowtown, 1991; editor, art dir. Art Forum, 1991—; creator, lic. Those Characters from Cowtown (recipient citation Tex. Ho. Reps. 1987, Tex. Senate Proclamation, 3 Mayor of Fort Worth Proclamations incl. Proclamation First Woman State Artist of Tex., 1993, numerous letters, used to stimulate Tex. tourism 1988-91, used in Richards for Gov. campaign 1990, used in state artist competition and other art work)). Advisor Jr. Achievement, Fort Worth. Named Internat. Woman of the Yr. England, 1994; nominee First Woman State Artist, 1988-91, now State Artist Tex., 1993-94, Tex. Women Hall of Fame, 1989-91, Guinness Book of Records, 1991, Practicing Law Inst. scholar, 1992, Internat. Woman of Yr. Art, 1994 Mem. Soc. Craft Designers (in Dallas Showcase of Designers 1985), Md. Art League (bd. dirs., workshop chmn.), Graphic Artists Guild (bd. dirs. 1991-94, editor Art Forum 1990-94), Cartoonists Guild, Am. Crafts Coun., Nat. Enamelists Guild, Am. Mus. Natural History, Nat. Geographic Soc., Smithsonian Instn., Nat. Assn. Self-Employed, Orgn. for Enforcement of Child Support, Internat. Historic Preservation Soc., Composers, Tex. Accts., Lawyers for Arts, Graphic Artists Guild (founder Tex. chpt. 1991), Authors & Artists of Am., Nat. League Advt. Agys., Am. Film Inst., Nat. Writers Club, Nat. Mus. Women in the Arts, Tex. Accts. and Lawyers for the Arts (cons. for lawyers on copyrights and appraising fine and decorative arts, 1991—), Bus. Profl. Women's Found., Delegation for Friendship among Women Writers' Workshop, Dallas Soc. Illustrators, Soc. Children's Book Writers and Illustrators, Nat. League of Am. Pen Women, Advt. Club Ft. Worth, Am. Advt. Fedn., Graphic Artists Guild (founder Tex. -at-large chpt. 1991, first chpt. dir., sr. adv.), Zonta. Jewish. Avocations: sewing, painting, reading, travel. Office: A & A PO Box 330008 Fort Worth TX 76163-0008

ABRAMSON, SARA JANE, radiologist, educator; b. New Orleans, La., May 12, 1945; m. Walter Squire; children: Harrison, Russell, Zachary, Andrew. BA, Sarah Lawrence Coll., 1967; postgrad., Tulane U., 1967-69; MD, Mt. Sinai Sch. Medicine, 1971. Intern in pediatrics Mt. Sinai Hosp., N.Y.C., 1971-72, resident in pediatrics, 1972-73; resident in radiology St. Luke's Children's Mercy Hosp., Kansas City, Mo., 1973-76; asst. prof. radiology U. Mo., 1976-79, Harvard U. Med. Sch., Cambridge, Mass., 1979-81; fellow in pediatric radiology Children's Hosp., Boston, 1979-81; asst. prof. radiology Columbia Coll. Physicians & Surgeons, N.Y.C., 1981-88, assoc. prof. radiology, 1988-93; assoc. attending radiologist Babies Hosp. Columbia Presbyn. Med. Ctr., N.Y.C., 1981-93, dep. dir. Div. Pediatric Radiology, 1992-93; assoc. prof. radiology Med. Coll. Cornell U., Ithaca, N.Y., 1993—; assoc. attending radiologist, assoc. mem. Mem. Sloan-Kettering Cancer Ctr. Mem. Hosp., N.Y.C., 1993—; apptd. to radiology elective program Columbia U. Med. Sch., N.Y.C., 1981-93, radiology residency program reevaluation, 1984-93, affirmative action com., 1987-90, program coord. affiliated hosps. teaching program, 1991-93, med. student advisor, 1991-93; mem. faculty coun. Columbia U., 1987-93; mem. resident selection com. Columbia-Presbyn. Med. Ctr., N.Y.C., 1985-93, quality assurance com., 1987-91, practice rev. com., 1991-93; cons. in pediatric radiology Blythedale Children's Hosp., 1982—, Bet Israel Hosp., N.Y.C., 1983—, Harlem Hosp., N.Y.C., 1983—, N.Y. Foundling Hosp., 1988—, Lenox Hill Hosp., 1990—, Morristown Meml. Hosp., 1990—; lectr., presenter in field. Contbr. over 40 articles to profl. jours., chpts. to books. Mem. AMA, Am. Coll. Radiology (del. N.Y. chpt. 1991—, alt. del. 1984-91), Soc. for Pediatric Radiology, Radiology Soc. N.Am., European Soc. for Pediatric Radiology, Soc. Thoracic Radiology, Am. Assn. Ultrasound in Medicine, Am. Assn. Women in Radiology, N.Y. Roentgen Soc. (sec.-treas. 1991—, moderator, pediatric program chair spring conf. 1991, guest lectr. spring conf. 1990), Nat. Children's Cancer Study Group, Caffey Soc., Neuhauser Soc., Kirkpatrick Soc. Office: Sloan-Kettering Cancer Ctr 1175 York Ave New York NY 10021

ABREU, SUE HUDSON, physician, army officer; b. Indpls., May 24, 1956; d. M.B. Hudson and Wilma (Jones) Hudson Black. B.S. in Engring., Purdue U., 1978; M.D., Uniformed Services U., 1982. Grad. U.S. Army Command & Gen. Staff Coll, 1988, Armed Forces Staff Coll., 1990. Commd. 2d lt. U.S. Army, 1978, advanced to lt. col., 1993; intern Walter Reed Army Med. Ctr., Washington, 1982-83, resident in diagnostic radiology, 1983-85, fellow in nuclear medicine, 1985-87, staff nuclear medicine physician, 1987-88, med. research fellow, 1988-89; chief Nuclear Medicine Svc., 1990—; chief Dept. Radiology Womack Army Med. Ctr., Ft. Bragg, N.C., 1991-92. Fellow Am. Coll. Nuclear Physicians; mem. Am. Coll. Radiology, Soc. Nuclear Medicine, Am. Coll. Nuclear Physicians, Soc. Women Engrs., U.S. Parachute Assn., Tau Beta Pi, Omicron Delta Kappa, Phi Kappa Phi. Avocations: calligraphy, parachuting. Home: 459 Saddlebred Ln Raeford NC 28376-9075 Office: Nuclear Medicine Clinic Womack Army Med Ctr Fort Bragg NC 28307

ABSHER, JANET S., banker; b. Fairfield, Ala., July 17, 1955; d. Farris R. and Martha L. (Edmonds) A. BS in Acctg., U. Ala., 1976. Cert. internal auditor. Auditor AmSouth Bank, Birmingham, Ala., 1976-78; sr. auditor Fed. Res. Bank, Birmingham, 1978-81; supervising auditor Fed. Res. Bank, Atlanta, 1981, mgr. auditing, 1981-83, mgr. acctg., 1983-85, mgr. electronic payments, 1985-88; assoc. product mgr. Electronic Funds Transfer Fed. Res. System, Atlanta, 1989—; instr. Fed. Res. Audit Tng., various U.S. cities, 1981-85. Mem. Young Careers, Atlanta, 1985, Atlanta Landmarks, 1986, Smithsonian Instn., Washington, Zoo Atlanta, 1987, Atlanta Bot. Gardens, 1988, High Mus. Art, Hist. Preservation Soc. Mem. Inst. Internal Auditors (gov. 1980—, instr. Atlanta chpt. 1983), Am. Inst. Bankers and Acctg. Instrs., Atlanta History Ctr., Swan House Doscent. Republican. Baptist. Home: 3100 Randolph Rd Atlanta GA 30345-9999 Office: Fed Res Bank Atlanta 104 Marietta St NW Atlanta GA 30303-2706

ABT, SYLVIA HEDY, dentist; b. Chgo., Oct. 7, 1957; d. Wendel Peter and Hedi Lucie (Wieder) A. Student, Loyola U., Chgo., 1975-77; cert. dental hygiene, Loyola U., Maywood, Ill., 1979, DDS, 1983. Registered dental hygienist. Dental asst. Office Dr. Baran and Dr. O'Neill, DDS, Chgo., 1977-78; dental hygienist Drs. Spiro, Sudakoff, Kadens, Weidman, DDS, Skokie, Ill., 1979-83, Dr. Laudando, DiFranco, Rosemont, Ill., 1980-83; gen. practice dentistry Chgo., 1983—. Vol. Community Health Rotations, VA Hosps., grammar schs., convalescent ctrs., mental health ctrs., Maywood, Ill. and Chgo., 1978-82. Recipient 1st Pl. award St. Apollonia Art Show Loyola U., 1982. Mem. ADA, Ill. Dental Soc., Chgo. Dental Soc., Loyola Dental Alumni Assn. (golf outing registration chmn. 1987, awards in golf and tennis 1987), Ill. Dentists 99th Club (legis. interest com.), Psi Omega (historian, editor Kappa chpt.). Office: 6509 W Higgins Ave Chicago IL 60656-2204

ABUDULMAJID, IMAN See IMAN

ABU-LUGHOD, JANET LIPPMAN, sociologist, educator; b. Newark, Aug. 3, 1928; d. Irving O. and Tessie Lippman; m. Ibrahim Abu-Lughod, Dec. 8, 1951 (div. 1992); children: Lila, Mariam, Deena, Jawad. BA, U. Chgo., 1947, MA, 1950; PhD (NSF fellow), U. Mass., 1966. Dir. research Am. Soc. Planning Ofcls., 1950-52; sociologist-cons. Am. Council to Improve Our Neighborhoods, 1953-57; asst. prof. sociology Am. U., Cairo, 1958-60, Smith Coll., 1963-66; assoc. prof. Northwestern U., Evanston, Ill., 1967-71; prof. sociology, urban affairs Northwestern U., 1971-87, dir. comparative urban studies program, 1974-77, dir. urban studies program, 1984-87; prof. sociology Grad. Faculty The New Sch. for Social Research, N.Y.C., 1986—; dir. Rsch. Ctr. on Lower Manhattan, N.Y.C., 1988-91, chmn. dept. of sociology, 1990-92; cons. UN, 1971—, UNESCO, 1979-80. Author: (with Nelson Foote, others) Housing Choices and Constraints, 1960, Cairo-1001 Years of the City Victorious, 1971, (with Richard Hay, Jr.) Third World Urbanization, 1977, Rabat: Urban Apartheid in Morocco, 1980, Before European Hegemony, 1989, Changing Cities, 1991, From Urban Village to East Village, 1994; contbr. chpts. to books, articles, revs. to profl. jours.; also monographs. Radcliffe Inst. scholar, 1963-64; Ford Faculty fellow, 1971-72, Guggenheim fellow, 1976-77, NEH fellow, 1977-78, ACLS fellow, 1994; Getty Sr. scholar, 1994-96. Mem. Internat. Sociol. Assn., Am. Sociol. Assn. (governing coun. 1994—), Social Sci. History Assn., Chgo. Coun. on Fgn. Rels. (dir. 1973-76), Social Sci. Rsch. Coun. (com. on Near East 1973-75.), Phi Beta Kappa. Office: New Sch for Social Rsch Grad Faculty 64 University Pl New York NY 10003-4520

ABZUG, BELLA SAVITZKY, lawyer, former congresswoman; b. N.Y.C., July 24, 1920; d. Emanuel and Esther Savitzky; m. Maurice M. Abzug, June 4, 1944 (dec.); children: Eve Gail, Isobel Jo. B.A., Hunter Coll., 1942; LL.B., Columbia U., 1947; hon. degree, Hunter Coll., Hobart Coll., Manhattanville Coll. Bar: N.Y. 1947. Private law practice in N.Y.C., 1944-70, 1980—; legislative dir. Women Strike for Peace, 1961-70; mem. 92d Congress from 19th Dist. N.Y., 1970-72, 93d-94th Congresses from 20th Dist. N.Y., 1972-76; presiding officer Nat. Commn. on Observance of Internat. Women's Year, 1977; presided Nat. Women's Conf., Houston, 1977; co-chmn. Pres.'s Nat. Adv. Com. for Women, 1978; cable news commentator; speaker numerous coll. campuses; Congl. advisor to U.S. Del. to UN Conf. on the Decade for Women, Mexico City, 1975; fellow Inst. Politics, John F. Kennedy Sch. Govt., Harvard U., 1987; founder Nat. Women's Polit. Caucus; co-chair Women's Environment & Devel. Org., 1991; presided over World Women's Congress for a Healthy Planet, 1991; mem. Internat. Facilitating Com. of Nongovtl. Orgns. and Ind. Sectors, UN Conf. on Environment and Devel., Brazil, 1992; sr. adv. to UNCED sec. gen. for UN Conf. on Environment & Devel., 1992. Editor: Columbia Law Rev.; author: Bella! Ms. Abzug Goes to Washington, 1972, Gender Gap: Bella Abzug's Guide to Political Power for American Women, 1984. Apptd. chair of Commn. on Status of Women by Mayor Dinkins, 1992. Mem. Women Strike for Peace, Nat. Urban League, NOW, Nat. Women's Polit. Caucus, ACLU, Women U.S.A. (pres.), UN Assn. U.S., Ams. for Democratic Action (v.p.), Am. Jewish Congress, Women's Environment & Devel. Orgn. (co-chair). *

ACE, KATHERINE, artist; b. Chgo., Jan. 31, 1953; d. Karl Peak and Evelyn (Schmitt) Zerfoss; m. Brian Corbett, Apr. 25, 1987 (div. 1980); m. Mark Ace, Dec. 10, 1983; 1 child, Corinna. BA cum laude, Knox Coll., 1975. Artist various galleries including Acanthus Gallery, Portland; illustrator, 1979—; Provider cover illustration for Body Types, 1993, Healing the Feminine, 1994; illustrator Women of the American West, Native American series, 1983-92; numerous other illustrations for publs.; recipient comms. in field; collections held by AT&T, Ambac Corp., N.Y.C., Children's Hosp., Oakland, Calif., Corestates Fin. of Phila. Bank, Dieber, Lazar, Stroup, MDPA, Fla., DuPont Pvt. Collection, Fla., Herman Goelitz Corp., Fairfield, Calif., Temple Sinai, Oakland. Solo shows and two-person exhbns. include: Maude Kerns Art Ctr., 1995, Cultural Forum U. Oreg., Eugene, 1995, Oreg. Sch. Arts and Crafts, 1994, Grants Pass Mus. Art, 1994, Pacific U., Oreg., 1995, Paccar Corp., Seattle, Wash., 1994, Shoreline Coll., Seattle, 1993, Stanford U., Palo Alto, Calif., 1993, U. Portland, 1993, So. Oreg. State Coll./The OtherArt Gallery, Ashland, 1992, Martin Chasin Curator, Bridgeport, Conn., 1992, Portland City Hall, 1991, Conv. Plaza Bldg, San Francisco, 1989; numerous group exhbns. including Eastwick Gallery, Chgo., 1993, Calyx Art Show, Corvallis, Oreg., 1993, Parliament of World's Religions, Chgo, 1993, others. Recipient numerous awards in field including Northwest Poets and Artists Calendar runner-up, Bainbridge Island, Wash., 1994, 95, second place Spirit Echoes Gallery, Austin, Tex., 1992, 1st pla. Invitational Christmas competition, Sacramento Mag., 1987, third pla. Grumbacher Gold Medallion award Batavia Soc. Artists 3rd Ann. Nat. Exhbn., Calif., 1985, second Best of Show award Corsicana Ann. Nat. Juried Exhbn., 1985, numerous others. Home and Office: 4017 SW 41st Pl Portland OR 97221-3704

ACERS, PATSY PIERCE, financial seminars company executive; b. Muskogee, Okla., Mar. 10, 1933; d. Claude James and Clara B. (Chaney) Pierce;

m. Thomas Edward Acers, Apr. 9, 1955 (div. Feb. 1980); children: Alison Ann, Angela Lynn, Ann Pierce, Ashley French. BA, U. Okla., 1955. Tchr. Oklahoma City Pub. Schs., 1955-58; dir. spl. events Am. Cancer Soc., 1980-86, dir. legacies and planned giving, 1983-86; ins. agt. life and health Conn. Mut., Oklahoma City, 1986-90; pres., owner Bag Lady Fin. Svcs., Inc., Oklahoma City, 1987—. Developer slide seminars: Do You Really Want to Be a Bag Lady, 1987, The Bag Lady Returns With Who Do You Trust, 1991, There Is Financial Life for Singles, 1989. Mem. Women Life Underwriters (pres. 1989-90), High Noon Profl. Women (pres. 1990-91), Women's Exec. Network (pres. 1988-89), Million Dollar Round Table, Am. Bus. Women's Assn., Okla. Spkrs. Assn., Nat. Spkrs. Assn., Nat. Leaders Club. Methodist. Avocations: aerobics, movies, canoeing, camping. Home: 1413 Sims Edmond OK 73013 Office: Bag Lady Fin Seminars Inc PO Box 20213 Oklahoma City OK 73156

ACHESON, AMY J., lawyer; b. Pitts., July 16, 1963; d. Willard Phillips and Patricia Louise (Marshall) A. BA, Haverford Coll., 1984; JD cum laude, U. S.C., 1987. Bar: Pa. 1987, U.S. Dist. Ct. (we. dist.) Pa. 1987, U.S. Ct. Appeals (10th cir.) 1989, U.S. Ct. Appeals (3d cir.) 1988, U.S. Ct. Appeals (4th cir.) 1993. Assoc. Reed, Smith, Shaw & McClay, Pitts., 1987—. Mem. S.C. Law Rev., 1985-87. Fin. officer Ret. Sr. Vol. Program Allegheny County, Pitts., 1990-91; treas. Parents League for Emotional Adjustments, Pitts., 1990-91; mem. adv. bd. Pa. Dept. Correction, Community Svc. Ctr. No. 1, Pitts., 1990—; bd. mgrs. The Woodwell, Pitts., 1992—. Mem. ABA (jud. adminstrn. div. com., chmn. subcom. on discipline of fed. judges, 1990-91), Pa. Bar Assn., Allegheny County Bar Assn. (young lawyers sect. coun. 1990-91), Order of the Coif, Order of the Wig and Robe. Office: Reed Smith Shaw & McClay 435 6th Ave Pittsburgh PA 15219

ACHESON, BARBARA FISHER, real estate broker, small business owner; b. Mpls., Dec. 13, 1946; d. Wallace Chandler Fisher and Barbara Jane Zaiser; m. Richard Barclay, June 13, 1976 (div. 1987); m. Edward Paul Acheson, Jan. 15, 1989 (dec. Jan. 1992). BA in English, U. Calif., Santa Barbara, 1976. Lic. real estate broker, Calif. Owner, broker Del Sol Properties, Idyllwild, Calif., 1989—. Mem. DAR, Nat. Assn. Realtors, Calif. Assn. Realtors, Idyllwild Bd. Realtors, Soc. Mayflower Descendants in State of Calif. Office: Del Sol Properties PO Box 70 54585 A N Circle Dr Idyllwild CA 92549

ACHESON, LOUISE SEYMOUR, physician, educator; b. Assiut, Egypt, Jan. 12, 1953; d. Willard Phillips and Patricia Louise (Marshall) A.; m. Robert Louis Ruff, Apr. 26, 1980; children: Elizabeth, Emily. BA in Chemistry, Oberlin Coll., 1972; MD, Harvard Med. Sch., 1976; MS in Family Medicine, Case Western Res. U., 1987. Diplomate Am. Bd. Family Practice. Resident in family practice U. Wash. Affiliated Hosps., Seattle, 1976-79; pvt. practice Seattle, 1980-84; asst. prof. family medicine Case Western Res. U., Cleve., 1984—; cons. Am. Bd. Family Practice, Lexington, Ky., 1990—; med. dir. teen pregnancy program Cleve. Free Clinic, 1993—. Assoc. editor Archives of Family Medicine, 1993—; contbr. articles to profl. jours. Mem. adv. bd. Middlefield (Ohio) Amish Birth Ctr., 1989—; trustee Nursing Health Ctr., Cleve., 1993—. Ohio Acad. Family Physicians Found. grantee, 1991-92. Mem. AMA, Am. Acad. Family Physicians, Am. Med. Women's Assn., Soc. Tchrs. Family Medicine, N.Am. Primary Care Interest Group, Physicians for Social Responsibility. Office: Case Western Res U Sch Medicine 2074 Abington Rd Cleveland OH 44106

ACKER, VIRGINIA MARGARET, nursing educator; b. Madison, Wis., Aug. 11, 1946; d. Paul Peter and Lucille (Klein) A. Diploma in Nursing, St. Mary's Med. Ctr., Madison, 1972; BS in Nursing, Incarnate Work Coll., San Antonio, 1976; MS in Health Professions, S.W. Tex. State U., 1980; postgrad., U. Tex., 1992-93. RN, Wis., Tex. Staff nurse St. Mary's Hosp., Milw., 1972-73, Kenosha Meml. Hosp., Wis., 1973-74, S.W. Tex. Meth. Hosp., San Antonio, 1974-75, Met. Gen. Hosp., San Antonio, 1975-76; instr. Bapt. Meml. Hosp. System Sch. Nursing, San Antonio, 1976-83; dir. nursing Meml. Hosp., Gonzales, Tex., 1983-84; instr., dir. nursing Victoria Coll., Cuero, Tex., 1984-86; dir. nursing Rocky Knoll Health Care Facility, Plymouth, Wis., 1986-87, Unicare Health Facilities, Milw., 1987-88; coord. nursing edn. St. Nicholas Hosp., Sheboygan, Wis., 1989-90; instr. U. Wis., Oshkosh, 1990-92, St. David's Hosp., Austin, Tex., 1992—. Roman Catholic. Avocations: cross-stiching, reading, camping, fishing. Home: 2103 Four Oaks Ln Austin TX 78704

ACKERLY, RAE WICKES, substance abuse and family counselor; b. White Plains, N.Y., Dec. 15, 1930; d. William Wirt and Blanche Elizabeth (Gilbert) Wickes; m. Peter John Callahan, May 3, 1954 (div.); children: Carolyn Gilbert Callahan Carroll, Peter John Jr., William Wickes; m. Dana Clay Ackerly, Feb. 16, 1974; stepchildren: Dana Tartell Ackerly, Richard Whitlock, Mary Myers, James Clay. BA, Mt. Holyoke Coll., 1953; postgrad., Colby (Maine Coll.), 1977, New Eng. Inst. Alcohol Studies, 1977-78, Westchester Inst. Coun./Psycho, 1978-80, Ctr. for Family Learning, New Rochelle, N.Y., 1981-82. Cert. alcoholism counselor. Staff pers. dept. Reader's Digest, 1953-54; asst. to chief of gastroenterology U. Pa. Hosp., Phila., 1954-56; fashion cons. The Whitney Shop, 1965-75; staff inpatient div. Norwal Hosp. Alcohol Rehab. Program, 1979-80; pres., chmn. vols. TAACT, Inc., 1979-83; pvt. practice substance abuse counseling New Canaan, Conn., 1985—; founder, pres., exec. dir., clin. cons. and tng. supr. New Canaan CARES, Inc., 1983—; lectr. in field. Author, editor Community Cares newsletter, 1984; contbr. articles to profl. jours. Exec. com. bd. dirs. Silver Hill Hosp., New Canaan, 1984—, New Canaan YMCA, Waveny Care Ctr., Dept. of Children and Youth Svcs. Regional Adv. Coun. of State of Conn.; mem. New Canaan Cmty. Coun.; mem. choir and children's Christmas pageant, dir. First Presbyn. Ch., New Canaan; campaign com. Bd. Edn., New Canaan; 1st selectman Town of New Canaan. Recipient J.C. Penney Award for Outstanding Vol. Svc., 1982, 83, Founders' award New Canaan CARES, 1992. Mem. Nat. Fedn. Parents for Drug Free Youth, The Profl. Collaborative, New Canaan Field Club (admissions com.), Country Club of New Canaan, Conn. Fedn. Alcohol and Drug Abuse Counselors. Republican. Presbyterian.

ACKERLY, WENDY SAUNDERS, aeronautic engineer, systems analyst; b. Chgo., July 23, 1960; d. Robert S. Jr. and Linda Ackerly. BS in Atmospheric Sci., U. Calif., Davis, 1982; postgrad., U. Nev., Reno, 1985. Programmer U. Calif, Davis, 1982-83; cons. software Tesco, Sacramento, 1983; software engr. Bently Nev. Corp., Minden, Nev., 1984-85; mgr. computer scis. Jensen Electric Co., Reno, 1985-86; software engr. Jensen Electric Co., Cameron Park, Calif., 1986-89; sr. engr. Aerojet, Sacramento, 1989—; sec.-treas. Kerry King Constrn. Co., Inc., 1991—. Pres. Four Springs Homeowners Assn., 1993—. Mem. Nat. Space Soc., Am. Meteorol. Soc., Planetary Soc., U.S. Tennis Assn., Calif. Aggie Alumni Assn. Republican. Office: Aerojet PO Box 13222 Sacramento CA 95813-6000

ACKERMAN, DORIS, university development officer; b. Somerville, N.J., Dec. 19, 1958; d. Robert Manton and Doris (Pellegrini) A. AB magna cum laude, Colgate U., 1981; MS summa cum laude, New Sch. for Social Rsch., 1990. Rsch. asst. Russell Sage Found., N.Y.C., 1984-87, publs. assoc., 1987-90; dir. devel. and pub. rels. N.J. Ctr. for Visual Arts, Summit, N.J., 1990-93; dir. corp. and found. rels. Montclair State U., Upper Montclair, N.J., 1993—. AT&T Found. grantee New Sch. for Social Rsch., 1988-89. Mem. Lit. Vols. Am. (instr. 1992—). Roman Catholic. Office: Montclair State U Upper Montclair NJ 07043

ACKERMAN, ELLEN LINDA, civil engineer; b. N.Y.C., Nov. 20, 1956. BSCE, Rensselaer Poly. Inst., 1978. Registered profl. engr., N.Y. Field engr. Consol. Rail Corp., Phila., 1978-82; assoc. engr. Consol. Edison, N.Y.C., 1982-86; project mgr. United Parcel Svc., Inc., N.Y.C., 1986-92, regional environ. coord., 1992—. Mem. ASCE, Rensselaer Poly. Inst. Players. Jewish.

ACKERMAN, HELEN PAGE, librarian, educator; b. Evanston, Ill., June 30, 1912; d. John Bernard and Florence Page. B.A., Agnes Scott Coll., Decatur, Ga., 1933; B.L.S., U. N.C., 1940. Cataloger Columbia Theol. Sem., 1942-43; post librarian U.S. Army, Aberdeen Proving Ground, Md., 1943-45; asst. librarian Union Theol. Sem., Richmond, Va., 1945-49; reference librarian UCLA, 1949-54, asst. univ. librarian, 1954-65, asso. univ. librarian, 1965-73, univ. librarian, 1973-77, prof. Sch. Info. and Library Sci., 1973-77, 82, 83; vis. prof. Sch. Librarianship, U. Calif., Berkeley, 1978, 80. Recipient Disting. Alumni award U. N.C., 1973; award of distinction in library sci. UCLA Alumnae Assn., 1977, Disting. Career Citation Assn. Coll. and Rsch. Librs., 1989. Mem. Am., Calif. library assns., AAUW (Status of Women award 1973), Council on Library Resources (bd. dirs. 1975-90). Home: 310 20th St Santa Monica CA 90402-2414

ACKERMAN, HELEN RUTH PENNER, psychologist; b. N.Y.C., Mar. 5, 1939; d. Isaac and Sylvia (Katz) Penner; m. Ross A. Ackerman, 1960; children: Eric, Ruth. B.A., Hofstra U., 1960; M.A., George Washington U., 1962; Ed.D., U. Md., 1967. Lic. psychologist, Fla., Md., New Hampshire. Psychiat. technician U. Md. Psychiat. Inst., Balt., 1960; psychology extern Springfield State Hosp., Sykesville, Md., 1961; tchr. Army Edn. Ctr., Bad Kissingen, W. Ger., 1961-63, lectr. U. Md. Schweinfurt Ctr., 1962-63; research psychologist Johns Hopkins U., Balt., 1965; asst. prof. Anne Arundel Community Coll., Arnold Md., 1968; psychologist Balt. County pub. schs., 1966-68, Mills Sch., Fort Lauderdale, Fla., 1968-69; cons. Hosp. Mgmt. and Planning Assocs., Miami, 1968-75; pvt. practice psychology, Ft. Lauderdale, 1975—; Md. psychol. cons. for Md. residents in Fla. institutions, 1979-83; psychol cons. Broward County (Fla.) pub. schs., 1980-83. U. Md. fellow, 1964-65. Trustee Ft. Lauderdale Am. Lung Assn.; active numerous Plantation (Fla.) civic orgns., local Jewish community affairs, local sch. support groups. Mem. Am. Psychol. Assn. Contbr. numerous articles to profl. jours. Home: 5921 Almond Ter Fort Lauderdale FL 33317-2501 Office: 1020 SW 40th Ave Plantation FL 33317

ACKERMAN, JOYCE SHOHET, psychologist; b. Boston, Aug. 3, 1950; d. Robert and Jeanne (Prager) Shohet; m. Alan Harvey Ackerman, Dec. 27, 1970; children: Laura, Rachel. BS in Spl. Edn. and Elem. Edn., Boston U., 1971; MS in Edn., Lesley Coll., 1974; EdD in Counseling Psychology, U. No. Colo., 1981. Lic. psychologist, Colo.; cert. elem. tchr.; cert. tchr. grades K-12 emotionally disturbed, learning disabled and retarded. Intern Somerville (Mass.) Mental Health Clinic, 1971; learning disabilities specialist Somerville (Mass.) Pub. Schs., 1972; tchr. emotionally disturbed children Dedham (Mass.) Pub. Schs., 1972-74; edn. specialist, counselor Rough Rock (Ariz.) Demonstration Sch., 1975; chairperson dept. edn. and behavioral scis. Navajo C.C., Tsaile, Ariz., 1975-78; pvt. practice in psychology Greeley, Colo., 1981—; adj. faculty in edn. and psychology Curry Coll., 1972, U. N.Mex., 1975, Aims C.C., Greeley, 1980-87; psychologist subcontractor Vietnam Vets. Counseling Program VA, 1983-86; provider, coord. mental health svcs. Peak Health Care, Greeley, Colo., 1986-89; cons. psychologist Progressive Care Rehab. Ctr., Greeley, 1986—, Family Recovery Ctr., North Colo. Med. Ctr., Greeley, 1986-89; head injury treatment team North Colo. Med. Ctr., Greeley, 1989-92, others. Bd. mem. Scott Elem. Sch. Adv. Bd., Greeley, 1982-85; mem. Women's Polit. Caucus, Greeley, 1983-87. Mem. APA, Colo. Psychol. Assn. (bd. mem. 1987-90, Pres.'s award 1989), Colo. Women Psychologists. Jewish. Office: 1750 25th Ave Greeley CO 80631

ACKERMAN, LINDA DIANE, manufacturing executive; b. Portland, Oreg., May 4, 1964; d. David Gilbert and Diane (Sause) A. BA in Econs., U. Wash., 1991. Office mgr. Hawaii Wood Preserving Co., Kahului, 1984-85, v.p., 1987—; with inventory control dept. Monarch Bldg. Supply, Kahului, 1986-87. Adminstrv. asst. I Have A Fream Program, Kahului, 1990-91; mem. area com. Spl. Olympics Maui County. 1993; unified softball coach Spl. Olympics, 1994—. Mem. Am. Wood Preservers Assn., Chi Omega (pres. Phi chpt. 1985). Republican. Mem. Christian Ch. Home: 43 Nonohe Pl Paia HI 96779 Office: Hawaii Wood Preserving Co 356 Hanakai St Kahului HI 96732-2407

ACKERMAN, LOUISE MAGAW, civic worker, writer; b. Topeka, July 9, 1904; d. William Glenn and Anna Mary (Shaler) Magaw; BS, Kans. State U., 1926; MA, U. Nebr., 1942; m. Grant Albert Ackerman, Dec. 27, 1926; children—Edward Shaler, Anita Louise. Free lance writer, 1930—. Mem. Nat. Soc. Daus. Colonial Wars (nat. pres. 1977-80), Daus. Am. Colonists (regent Nebr. 1970-72), DAR (past v.p. gen.), Americans of Armorial Ancestry (sec. 1976-82), Nat. Huguenot Soc. (2d v.p. 1977-81), Nebr. Writers Guild (past sec.-treas.), Nat. League Am. Pen Women, Colonial Lords in Am., Nat. Gavel Soc., Soc. Descs. of Founders of Hartford, Conn., Phi Kappa Phi. Republican. Club: Nat. Writers. Lodge: Order Eastern Star. Home: 6315 O St Rm 509 Lincoln NE 68510-2238

ACKERMANN, BARBARA BOGEL, counselor; b. Bay Shore, N.Y., Nov. 16, 1940; d. Charles Henry Jurgens and Marjorie (Stevens) Bogel; children: Erika, Stefan. BS in Polit. Sci., Ursinus Coll., 1962; MS in Counseling Edn., L.I. U., 1978, profl. diploma in counseling, 1982, postgrad. Lic. sch. adminstr., N.Y. Child protective worker Suffolk County (N.Y.) Social Svc., 1962-65; med. social worker St. Joseph's Hosp., Syracuse, N.Y., 1965-69; child protective worker Tallahassee (Fla.) Social Svc., 1967-68; RSVP coord. Suffolk County Ret. Sr. Vol. Program, 1975; sch. counselor Hampton Bays (N.Y.) H.S., 1978-86; guidance dir., counselor Southold (N.Y.) H.S., 1986—; treas. Human Understanding and Growth Seminars, Laurel, N.Y., 1987-89, bd. dirs., 1984-90. Alt. committeewoman Southold Town Rep. Com., 1976-83; deacon Presbyn. Ch., Mattituck, N.Y., 1977—. Mem. East End Counselors Assn. (pres. 1982, bd. dirs. 1979—), L.I. Counselors Ann. Conf. (co-chairperson 1985, 94), N.Y. State Assn. for Counseling and Devel. (v.p. 1983-85, North Atlantic region rep. 1985-87), Am. Sch. Counselor Assn., N.Y. State Sch. Counselors Assn. (dist. gov. 1989-92), Rotary (bd. dirs.). Home: Azalea Rd # 330 Mattituck NY 11952-1951 Office: Southold High Sch Oaklawn Ave Southold NY 11971-1701

ACKERMAN-REENTS, MARY ALICE, educational administrator, family mediator/trainer; b. Lincoln, Nebr., Dec. 27, 1947; d. James Nils and Jean Caroline (Doty) Ackerman; m. James William Reents, Nov. 23, 1990; 1 child, Nils Peter. BA, Macalester Coll., St. Paul, 1970; postgrad., Harvard U., 1989; Cert., Mediation Ctr., St. Paul, 1992. Admissions counselor Macalister Coll., St. Paul, 1970-73, asst. dir. admissions, 1973-74, assoc. dir. admissions, 1974-75, dir. admissions, officer, 1975-79, dean of students, 1979-91; assoc. Erickson Mediation Inst., Mpls., 1992; family mediator Linden Ctr., St. Paul, 1993; v.p. for external affairs Shattuck-St. Mary's Sch., Faribault, Minn., 1994—, also bd. dirs.; bd. dirs. Coop. Solutions Mediation. Chmn. edn./schs. com. Ramsey County Family Violence Initiative, St. Paul, 1991—; mem. Ramsey County Child Welfare Budget Com., St. Paul, 1992; reader Truman Scholarship, Coca-Cola Found Scholarship Com., 1989-92; mem. nominating com. Camp Fire Boys/Girls, St. Paul, 1990—. Recipient Vol. Svc. award Channel 11/TV, Mpls., Leadership Recognition award St. Paul YWCA. Mem. Acad. of Family Mediators, St. Paul U. Club, PEO. Dem. Farm Labor Party. United Ch. of Christ. Home: 1725 Wellesley Ave Saint Paul MN 55105-2009 Office: Shattuck-St Marys Sch 1000 Shumway Ave Faribault MN 55021

ACKERSON, LYNN M., researcher; b. Feb. 19, 1957. BS in Math., U. Puget Sound, 1979; MS in Biomed. Engring., Case Western Res. U., 1983; PhD in Biometrics, U. Colo., 1988. Biomed. engr. VA Med. Ctr., Cleve., 1982-85; data mgr. Nat. Ctr. Am. Indian and Alaska Native Mental Health Rsch., U. Colo., Denver, 1986-88, rsch. assoc., 1989—, profl. rsch. asst. dept. biometrics, 1989—. U. Colo. Health Scis. Ctr. fellow, 1986-87. Mem. Am. Statis. Assn., Biometric Soc., Mathematical Assn. Am., Phi Kappa Phi. Office: U Colo Dept Biometrics 4200 E 9th Ave Denver CO 80262-0001

ACORD-SKELTON, BARBARA BURROWS, counselor, educator, artist; b. L.A., Dec. 26, 1928; d. Harry and Sophia (Dittman) Burrows; m. Benjamin Raddatz, June 11, 1949 (div. Dec. 1970); children: Randolph, Marjorie, Thomas, Deborah; m. William A. Acord, Feb. 26, 1974 (dec.); m. Gerald Skelton, 1989. AA, Riverside City Coll., 1956; BA, Calif. State U., San Bernardino, 1970; MA, Pacific Oaks Coll., 1974; postgrad., Claremont Coll., 1976-91. Lic. marriage, family and child counselor, Calif., 1974. Dir. pvt. nursery sch. Headstart, Riverside, Calif., 1964-66; career devel., coord. Riverside County Head Start and Corono Norco Sch. Dist., Riverside, 1966-72; instr. Chaffey Community Coll., Alta Loma, Calif., 1971-82; class room coord., family counselor Casa Colina Hosp., Pomona, Calif., 1973-79; counselor LaVerne (Calif.) Ctr. for Edn. Counseling, 1976-82; social worker III San Andreas Regional Ctr., Salinas, Calif., 1984-87; pvt. practice family and individual counseling Medford, 1987-92; cons. Pomona U. Sch. Dist., Calif., 1973-80, San Gabriel Valley Regional Ctr., Covina, Calif., 1976-82, Nat. Council Alcoholism, Covina, 1980-82; instr. U. LaVerne, 1976-82. Author: On Learning and Growing, 1974; co-author: Parent Advocacy Training, 1977, Creative Competency, 1978. Vol. Day Springs Hospice, Medford, 1987—; bd. dirs. Gold Coast Arab Horse Assn., Santa Clara County, Calif., 1983-85. Riverside County Headstart scholar, 1967, Ednl. Profl. Devel. Act scholar, 1971-74. Mem. Am. Assn. Marriage and Family Therapists, Calif. Assn. Marriage and Family Therapists, Upper Rogue Art Assn., Arab Horse Assn. (So. Oreg. bd. dirs. 1988, pres. 1989), Women Artists Cascades Mountains, Region III Arab Horse Assn. (bd. dirs. 1983-85), GRA, WSO, WACM. Home: 13856 Weowna Way White City OR 97503-9572

ACOSTA, SILVIA, elementary education educator; b. Aberdeen, Md., July 10, 1960; d. Julio Barnhardt and Rosa Elvira (Escudero) A.; m. Gregg Martin Bendian, Aug. 6, 1994. BA, Mich. State U., 1982; MSE in Edn., CUNY, S.I., 1992. Bilingual tchr. Lansing (Mich.) Pub. Schs., 1981-83, Alhambra (Calif.) Pub. Schs., 1983-87, Linden (N.J.) Pub. Schs., 1994; tchr. S.I. (N.Y.) Acad., 1980-90, The Collegiate Sch., N.Y.C., 1990-94. Active Cmty. Theatre at Tenafly, N.J., 1994—. Multicultural Curriculum Devel. grantee DeWitt-Wallace/Readers Digest, 1993. Mem. NEA, Assn. Tchrs. Ind. Schs. (sch. rep. 1992-94).

ACTON, EMELINE, lawyer; b. Bryn Athyn, Pa., July 13, 1955; d. John Thomas Acton and Barbara (Barnitz) Larsen; m. Michael Scott Maher, May 24, 1981; children: Richard Alexander Acton-Maher, Christopher Nicholas Acton-Maher. BA, New Coll of U. So. Fla., 1978; JD, Stetson U., 1980. Bar: Fla. 1980, U.S. Dist. Ct. (mid. dist.) Fla. 1981, U.S. Ct. Appeals (11th cir.) 1983, U.S. Supreme Ct. 1985. Rsch. clk. 2d dist. Ct. Appeals, State of Fla., Lakeland, 1980-82; asst. county atty. Hillsborough County Atty's. Office, Tampa, 1982-87, chief asst. county atty., 1987-90, county atty., 1990—. Mem. Fla. Assn. County Attys. (pres. 1994—), Hillsborough County Bar Assn. (bd. dirs. 1988-93, sec. 1993-94, treas. 1994—), Hillsborough Assn. Women Lawyers (pres. 1987-88), Leadership Tampa Alumni (bd. dirs. 1995—), Athena Soc. Office: Office County Atty County Ctr 27th Fl 601 E Kennedy Blvd Tampa FL 33602-4910

ACTON, PATRICIA NASSIF (LADY ACTON), lawyer, educator; b. Cedar Rapids, Iowa, June 7, 1949; d. M. Morey and Barbara (Lindsey) Nassif; m. Richard Gerald Lyon Dalberg Acton (Lord Acton), Mar. 19, 1988. B.A. in history with highest distinction, U. Iowa, 1971, J.D. with high distinction, 1974. Admitted to Iowa bar, 1974; assoc. atty. Simmons, Perrine, Albright & Ellwood, Cedar Rapids, 1974-78; sole practice, Cedar Rapids 1978-80; Bigelow teaching fellow, lectr. law U. Chgo. Law Sch., 1980-81; vis. assoc. prof. Coll. Law, U. Iowa, 1981-84, clin. assoc. prof., 1984-85, clin. prof., 1985—; vis. prof. U. Fla. Coll. Law, 1985; bd. dir. London Law Consortium. Mem. ABA, Iowa Bar Assn., Order of Coif, Phi Beta Kappa. Author: Invasion of Privacy: The Cross Creek Trial of Marjorie Kinnan Rawlings, 1988, Entertainment Law, 2nd edit. 1992; editor notes and comments The Iowa Law Rev. 1973-74; contbr. articles to profl. jours. and books on lit. and entertainment law. Office: U Iowa College of Law Iowa City IA 52242

ADAIR, JACQUELINE PRITNER, psychotherapist, hypnotherapist; b. Whittington, Tex., Jan. 14, 1936; d. Ural Dick and Ina Alene (Singleton) Adair; m. Calvin L. Pritner, Sept. 3, 1954 (div. Mar. 1983); children: Christopher P., Juliet P. BS, Ill. State U., 1972, MS, 1978. Sec. to office mgr. P&G, Kansas City, Kans., 1957-59; rsch. asst. Nat. Assn. County Officers, Washington, 1960; tchr. English Univ. High Sch., Normal, Ill., 1972-73; clin. program mgr. McLean County Ctr. for Human Svcs., Bloomington, 1978-83; tchr. English Cen. Cath. High Sch., Bloomington, Ill., 1974-75; clin. psychologist Perth (W, Australia) Psychiat. Clinic, 1984-87, Victoria Health Dept., Ballarat, Victoria, Australia, 1987-88; staff counselor Ill. State U., Normal, Ill., 1990-93; psychotherapist pvt. practice Normal, 1990—; cons. Dept. Children and Family Svcs., Bloomington, Ill., 1990-94. Bd. dirs. Am. Cancer Soc., Mc Lean County, Ill., 1993-94. Mem. Am. Psychol. Assn. (assoc.), Am. Acad. Psychotherapists. Home and Office: 213 Eisenhower Dr # A Bloomington IL 61701-2024

ADAIR-VERBAIS, TRUDY MAY, early childhood educator; b. Ogden, Utah, June 11, 1954; d. Ned Allain and Marcia Edine (Bacchus) Adair; m. Henry R. Verbais, Jan. 29, 1977; children: Melissa J., Meghan Elena. BA, U. Ariz., 1977. Cert. early childhood tchr., supr., cert. C.C. instr. Cons. Santa Barbara (Calif.) County Edn. Office, 1977, tchr., 1978-83, program specialist, 1983-85, 1983-85, asst. coord., 1986-88, coord., 1989-94, program dir., 1994—; instr. Calif. State U., Long Beach, 1992, Santa Barbara C.C., 1981; coord. U. Calif., Santa Barbara, 1989; owner, dir. Kid's Club, Santa Barbara, 1981-84; presenter in field. Author: Opening the Door: Serving Children with Special Needs in Child Care, 1993. Founder, dir. Holiday Cheer Project, Santa Barbara, 1981—; chair Santa Barbara County Health Tng. Consortium, 1989—; instr. ARC, 1990—; chair Santa Barbara County Child Care Planning Coun., 1991—, Program Improvement Consortium, 1994—. Nat. Def. scholarship U. Ariz., 1974, 75; recipient Cert. of Recognition Santa Barbara Industry Edn. Coun., 1992, Exemplary Leadership award Santa Barbara County Child Care Planning Coun., 1991. Mem. Nat. Assn. for the Edn. of Young Children, Tri-Counties Assn. for the Edn. of Young Children (chair membership 1981-83), Alternative Payment Program Assn., Calif. Child Care Adminstrn. Assn., Family Day Care Assn. Office: Santa Barbara County Edn Office PO Box 6307 Santa Barbara CA 93160-6307

ADAMO, EVELYN FELEPPA, psychologist; b. Mt. Vernon, N.Y., Aug. 18, 1936; d. Alfred Edward and Anna Evelyn (Foresti) Feleppa; m. Ido Adamo, June 20, 1964; children: Sonya, Alisa. BS, Boston U., 1958; MA, Fordham U., 1961, PhD, 1965. Lic. psychologist, Md., D.C. Psychologist Douglas Hosp., Montreal, Can., 1964-65, C. T. Perkins Hosp., Jessup, Mo., 1965-80; ind. practice psychologist Laurel and Bowie, Md., 1969—; psychologist Prince Georges County Bur. Mental Health, Cheverly, Md., 1970-73; cons. Divsn. Rehab. Svcs., Balt., 1980—, Job Corps, Woodland Job Corps, Laurel, 1983-85, Social Security Adminstrn., Office of Med. Evaluation, Balt., 1986—, Juvenile Svcs. Adminstrn., Howard County, Md., 1990-92. Contbr. articles to profl. jours. Fellow Md. Psychol. Assn.; mem. APA, Ea. Psychol. Assn., Sigma Xi. Home: 10901 Balantre Ln Potomac MD 20854 Office: Laurel Bowie Psychol Ctr 8381 Cherry Ln Laurel MD 20707-4832

ADAMOVICH, SHIRLEY GRAY, retired librarian, state official; b. Pepperell, Mass., May 8, 1927; d. Willard Ellsworth and Carrie (Shattuck) Gray; m. Frank Walter Adamovich, Aug. 31, 1960; children: Carrie Rose, Elizabeth Maude. BA, U. N.H., 1954; MS, Simmons Coll., Boston, 1955; LittD, New Eng. Coll., 1991. Cons. Vt. State Libr ., Montpelier, 1955-58; head cataloger Bentley Coll., Boston, 1958-60; tchr. U. N.H. System, Durham, 1965-79; asst. state librarian N.H. State Libr., Concord, 1979-81; state librarian N.H. State Library, Concord, 1981-85; commr. cultural affairs N.H. Dept. Cultural Affairs, Concord, 1985-92. Editor: A Reader in Library Technology, 1975, The Road Taken, 1989. Served in USAF, 1949-53. Mem. ALA, Nat. Commn. Librs. and Info. Scis., New Eng. Libr. Assn., N.H. Libr. Assn.

ADAMS, ALGALEE POOL, college dean, art educator; b. Columbia, Mo., Nov. 6, 1919; d. William I. and Anna Ethelene (Dunning) Pool; 1 dau., Judith Dean Adams. B.S. in Art and English, U. Mo., 1941, M.A. in Art, 1951; Ed.D. in Fine Arts and Art Edn, Pa. State U., 1960; postgrad., Inst. Adminstrv. Adavancement for Women, U. Mich., Inst. Ednl. Mgmt., Harvard U. Tchr. art Cuba (Mo.) High Sch., 1941-42, Hickman High Sch., Columbia, 1942-43; art specialist elementary schs. St. Joseph, Mo., 1943-45; tchr. art St. Clair (Mo.) High Sch., 1946-49; pub. sch. art supr. Webb City, Mo., 1949-51; instr. dept. of art St. Cloud (Minn.) State Coll., 1951-58, asst. prof., 1958-60, assoc. prof., 1960-63, prof., 1963-64, chmn. dept. art, 1959-64; prof. art edn. Mass. Coll. Art, Boston, 1964-77; also chmn. div. of edn. Mass. Coll. Art, 1967-70, dir. tchr. placement, 1964-70, dir. grad. programs in edn., 1970-77; chmn. grad. council, 1970-74; dean Firelands Coll. Bowling Green State U., Huron, Ohio, 1977-85; owner Adams Miniature Fiber Arts, Columbia, Mo., 1989; liaison with bus. and industry; mem. gov.'s adv. commn. on edn. in arts, 1958, 67; asso. dir. Project Renewal Mass. State Coll. System, 1974-76; art curriculum cons. to numerous pub. schs. in, Minn., 1951-64; art cons. to Minn. Ins. Info. Center, 1960-62; chmn. Eastern Arts Student Conf., N.Y.C., 1968; participant Internat. Conf., Notre Dame U., 1968; field reader HEW, 1966-70. Vol. tutor state literacy program; docent Detroit Inst. Arts. Recipient Distinguished Alumni award U. Mo., 1968, Artisan status award Internat. Guild. Miniature Artisans, 1991. Mem. Nat. Art Edn. Assn. (faculty adviser 1965-69, chmn. student conf. 1969, seminar chmn. conf. 1967, speaker nat. conv. 1961, 66, 67, life mem.),

AAUW, Mass. State Coll. Assn., Eastern Arts Assn. (speaker conv. 1966), Sigma Pi Alpha, Phi Delta Kappa, Delta Phi Delta, Kappa Pi, Delta Kappa Gamma. Club: Zonta. Home: 2604 Grant Ln Columbia MO 65203-0652

ADAMS, ALICE, writer; b. Fredericksburg, Va., Aug. 14, 1926; d. Nicholson Barney and Agatha Erskine (Boyd) A.; 1 son, Peter Adams Linenthal. A.B., Radcliffe Coll., 1946. Author: (novels) Careless Love, 1966, Families and Survivors, 1975, Listening to Bilie, 1978, Rich Rewards, 1980, Superior Women, 1984, Second Chances, 1988, Caroline's Daughters, 1991, Almost Perfect, 1993; (short story collections) Beautiful Girl, 1979, To See You Again, 1982, Return Trips, 1985, After You've Gone, 1989, (travel) Mexico: Some Travels and Travellers There, 1991; editor; Best American Short Stories, 1991; contbr. short stories to New Yorker mag., others. Recipient Best Am. Short Stories award, 1976, 92, O. Henry awards, 1971-82, 84-95, Acad. and Inst. award in lit. Am. Acad. and Inst. of Arts and Letters, 1992; grantee NEA, 1976; Guggenheim fellow, 1978-79. Mem. PEN. Democratic Socialist. Office: Alfred A Knopf Inc Press Rels 201 E 50th St New York NY 10022-7703

ADAMS, ALICE, sculptor; b. N.Y.C., Nov. 16, 1930; d. Charles P. and Loretto G. (Tobin) A.; m. William D. Gordy, Feb. 7, 1969; 1 dau., Katherine Adams Gordy. Student, Adelphi Coll., 1948-50; BFA, Columbia U., 1953; postgrad. (French Govt. fellow), 1953-54; postgrad. Fulbright Travel grantee, L'Ecole Nat d'Art Decoratif, Aubusson, France, 1953-54. Lectr. Manhattanville Coll., Purchase, N.Y., 1960-79; instr. sculpture Sch. Visual Arts, 1980-87. One-woman shows N.Y.C., 1972, 74, 75, Hal Bromm Gallery, N.Y.C., 1979, 80; group shows include Whitney Mus. Am. Art, N.Y.C., 1971, 73, Indpls. Mus. Art, 1974, Nassau County Mus. Fine Arts, Roslyn, N.Y., 1977, Wave Hill, Riverdale, N.Y., 1979, Mus. Modern Art, N.Y.C., 1984; represented in permanent collections Weatherspoon Gallery U. N.C., Greensboro, U. Nebr., Everson Mus., Syracuse, N.Y., Haags Gemetemuseum, The Hague, Netherlands, Edwin I. Ulrich Mus., Wichita, Kans.; pub. commissions include Bot. Garden, Toledo, Ohio, Design Team Seattle Transit Project, St. Louis Metro-Link Project, Midland Metro, Birmingham, Eng., Port Authority of N.Y. and N.J., Thomas Jefferson U., Phila., N.Y.C. Bd. Edn., State of Conn., Denver Internat. Airport. Creative Artists Pub. Service grantee, 1973-74, 76-77; Nat. Endowment for Arts Artists grantee, 1978-79; Guggenheim fellow, 1981-82. Home: 3370 Fort Independence St Bronx NY 10463-4502

ADAMS, ARLENE PUGH, real estate company executive; b. N.Y.C., Dec. 23, 1927; d. Raymond Travis and Mary Elizabeth (Warner) Pugh; m. Byron Korth Adams, Sept. 15, 1951 (div. June 1972); children: Pamela, Chip, Cynthia, Suzanne, John W., Mark W. BS, Russell Sage Coll., 1949. Cert. residential broker. Dress buyer Specialty Stores Assocs., N.Y.C., 1949-52; real estate salesman The Dalzell Co. and Allsopp Realtors, Short Hills, N.J., 1972-77; br. mgr. Burgdorff Realtors, Inc., Short Hills, 1977-93; v.p. Burgdorff Realtors, Inc., Murray Hill, N.J., 1993—; mem. pres. adv. bd. Burgdorff Realtors, Inc., Short Hills, 1990. Named Realtor of Yr. Bd. Realtors Oranges and Maplewood, 1982. Fellow Grad. Realtors Inst.; mem. N.J. Assn. Realtors. Republican. Roman Catholic. Office: Burgdorff Realtors Inc 545 Millburn Ave Short Hills NJ 07078-2553

ADAMS, BARBARA, English language educator, poet, writer; b. N.Y.C., Mar. 23, 1932; d. David S. Block and Helen (Taxter) Block Tyler; m. Elwood Adams, June 6, 1952 (dec. 1993); children: Steven, Amy, Anne, Samuel. BS, SUNY-New Paltz, 1962, MA, 1970; PhD, NYU, 1981. Adj. instr. Orange County C.C., Middletown, N.Y., 1970-77; grad. asst. NYU, N.Y.C., 1974-77; adj. lectr. SUNY-Albany, 1977-81; instr. Mt. St.Mary Coll., Newburgh, N.Y., 1980-81; asst. prof. SUNY-Cobleskill, 1981-83; adj. assoc. prof. Pace U., N.Y.C., 1983-84, prof. English, 1984—, dir. bus. communications, 1984—; poet in residence Cape Cod Writers' Conf., 1988. Author: Double Solitaire, 1982, The Enemy Self: The Poetry & Criticism of Laura Riding, 1990, Hapax legomena, 1990; contbr. poems, stories, articles to various mags. and jours. Recipient 1st prize for poetry NYU and Acad. Am. Poets, 1975; Penfield fellow NYU, 1977. Mem. MLA, PEN, Poetry Soc. Am., Assn. Bus. Communication, Poets and Writers. Home: 57 Coach Ln Newburgh NY 12550-3818 Office: Pace U Pace Plz New York NY 10038

ADAMS, BEEJAY (MEREDITH ELISABETH JANE J. ADAMS), sales executive; b. Jefferson Banks, Mo., June 9, 1920; d. Alden Humphrey and Louise Marion (Banta) Seabury; m. Merlin Francis Adams, July 10, 1948 (dec. 1977); children; S(tephen) Kent, Mark Francis. AB, Bradley U., 1942. Svc. editor Peoria (Ill.) Jour. Star, 1942-46; women's program dir. Sta. WEEK-AM, Peoria, 1946-47; on air personality Sta. KSD-AM, St. Louis, 1948; lectr. Sch. Assembly Svc., Chgo., 1948-49; pres. M.F. Adams, Inc., Quincy, Ill., 1977-85; commodities broker Quincy, 1985-87; pres. MarKent, Inc., Quincy, 1975—; sec., treas. Miss. Belle Distbn. Co., Inc., Quincy, 1976—, v.p., treas., 1979—. Active Quincy Svc. League, 1949-57, local polit. campaigns, co-chmn. local presdl. campaigns, 1952-77; founder, past pres. Quincy Jr. Theatre, 1953-78; charter mem. Quincy Community Theatre; co-chmn. coll. fund drive Quincy Coll., 1988, chmn. 1989. Mem. Quincy C. of C., Adams County Red Cross Bd., Sales and Mktg. Execs. Club, Quincy Art Club, Atlantis Study Club, Quincy Country Club, Phi Beta Phi. Episcopalian. Home: 2303 Jersey St Quincy IL 62301-4343 Office: Miss Belle Distbn Co Inc PO Box 768 Quincy IL 62306-0768

ADAMS, BETH FORD, interior designer; b. Montgomery, Ala., Oct. 23, 1959; d. Schuyler Colfax and Nancy Joe Eubank; 1 child, Jennifer Marie. B. of Interior Design, Auburn U., 1983. Sr. comml. interior designer PH & J. Architects, Montgomery, Ala., 1986—. Mem. Am. Soc. Interior Designers, Inst. Bus. Designers. Home: 4045 Johnstown Dr Montgomery AL 36109-2409 Office: PH&J Architects Inc 807 S Mcdonough St Montgomery AL 36104-5054

ADAMS, BETT YATES, newspaper publisher; b. Lawton, Okla., Oct. 22, 1942; d. Lawden Henry and Bessie Louise (Cooper) Yates; m. Louis M. Perez, Mar. 22, 1969 (div. 1980); 1 child, Christian M.; m. Dixon D. Adams, Aug. 10, 1985. BA, Fla. State U., 1963; MA, Ea. Washington U., 1967; PhD, U. Fla., 1972. Coll. instr. Sante Fe Community Coll., and U. Fla., 1972-73, Fla. So. Coll., Lakeland, 1976-78; tchr. Alachua County Schs., Gainesville, Fla., 1973-74; edn. and tng. coordinator Shands Teaching Hosp., Gainesville, 1974-75; journalism coordinator Polk County Schs., Gainesville, 1976-78; with N.Y. Times Regional Newspaper Group, 1979-91; publ. News-Leader N.Y. Times Regional Newspaper Group, Fernandina Beach, Fla., 1983-91; editor Atencion San Miguel, Mexico, 1992—; vis. prof. journalism U. Fla., 1983-85; cons. assoc. Am. Press Inst., Reston, Va., 1986. Contbr. articles to profl. jours. and chpts. to books. Mem. adv. bd. Nassau County Vol. Ctr., 1985-91; bd. trustees, Florida Community Coll., Jacksonville, 1990-91, Pennsacola Jr. Coll., Fla, 1991-93. Newspaper Fund grantee, 1978; 1st woman publisher of N.Y. Times Regional Newspaper. Mem. Fernandina Beach C. of C. (bd. dirs. 1983-91), Nassau Assn. Good Govt. (bd. dirs. 1986-91), Nassau County Com. of 100 (sec. 1984-86), Fla. Press Assn. (bd. dirs. 1988), Nat. Newspaper Assn., Leadership Fla., Class VI. Republic. Roman Catholic. Home: PO Box 2348 Pensacola FL 32513-2348 Office: ReFugio Sur # 13, G70 San Miguel de Allende Mexico

ADAMS, BETTY K., state official; b. Shelbyville, Tenn., Apr. 4, 1946; d. Arthur and Katherine Gray (Cortner) Keeling; m. Fred L. Heltsley (div.); children: Amanda Gray, Andrew Fredrick; m. Clinton R. Adams (div.); 1 child, Allyson Alia. BA, Vanderbilt U., 1968; MS, Mid. Tenn. State U.; JD, Nashville Sch. of Law, 1985. Tchr. Highland Rim Sch., Tullahoma, Tenn., 1968-74; field rsch. cons. Tenn. Commn. on Children and Youth, Nashville, 1974-80; exec. sec. Tenn. Coun. Juvenile and Family Ct. Judges, Nashville, 1980-85; asst. dist. atty. Davidson County Dist. Atty. Office, Nashville, 1985-88; commr. designee Tenn. Dept. Youth Devel., Nashville, 1988-89, commr., 1989—; adj. faculty mem. Mid. Tenn. State U., Murfreesboro, 1989-94; cons. Nat. Inst. Corrections, Longmont, Colo., 1992-94. Recipient Disting. Svc. award Tenn. Coun. Juvenile and Family Ct. Judges, 1986, Tenn. Youth Svcs. award Southeastern Network of Youth and Family Svcs., 1989, Pres.'s award for Juvenile Justice Tenn. Juvenile Ct. Svcs. Assn., 1989, 93. Mem. Am. Correctional Assn. (bd. govs. 1990-94, exec. com. 1992-94, cons. 1993), Y-CAP (bd. dirs. 1988-93, adv. bd. 1993-94), Coun. Juvenile Correctional Adminstrs. (v.p. 1993-94). Methodist. Home: 5401 Eulala Dr Nashville TN 37211-6114 Office: Tenn Dept Youth Devel 710 James Robertson Pky Fl 9 Nashville TN 37219-1219

ADAMS, BEVERLY JOSEPHINE, data processing specialist; b. Kansas City, Kans., Nov. 29, 1951; d. Cecil and Eula Laverne (Lynch) Brown; m. Theodore Lavern Adams, Sept. 20, 1969; children: Theodore Lavern Jr., Terry Levar, Traveon LeVar. AA in Data Processing, Kansas City Kans. Community Coll., 1980; BS in Mgmt. and Computers, Park Coll., Parkville, Mo., 1986; postgrad., Rockhurst Coll.; MA, Webster U., 1991. Sr. data processor AT&T, Kansas City, Mo., 1984-86, computer programmer, 1987—; prof. devel. facilitator tng. orgn. AT&T, 1991; lectr. in field. Editor: (newspaper) Courier, 1969, (newsletter) Kansas City Link, 1987. Cons. Youth of Am., Kansas City, 1983; mem. Kansas City Chiefs Football, 1968-72, Coalition Labor Union Women, Washington, 1984, AFL-CIO City Labor Council, Kansas City, 1984; dir. ch. adult and youth choir, Kansas City, 1982—. Recipient Outstanding Community Svcs. award AT&T Techs., 1984; named one of Outstanding Young Women of Am., 1981. Mem. NAFE, Alliance AT&T Employees (chairperson 1987, treas. 1988-89, regional dir.), Profl. Women's Fedn., Young People's Willing Workers, Alpha Kappa Alpha (exec. bd., philacter), Gamma Mu Gamma (program chmn. 1985). Republican. Pentacostal. Clubs: Wecomo (svcs. award 1983), Young Adults Action (bd. dirs., Leadership award 1980), YWCA (Kansas City). Home: 2635 N 22nd St Kansas City KS 66104-4514 Office: AT&T Comms 2121 E 63rd St Kansas City MO 64130-3440

ADAMS, BONNIE JEAN, psychologist; b. Morristown, N.J., July 14, 1961; d. Lenroy F. and Barbara J. (Lizdas) A. Student, Moravian Coll., 1979-81; BA, Fairleigh Dickinson U., Madison, N.J., 1985; MA, Fairleigh Dickinson U., Teaneck, N.J., 1989, PhD, 1990. Lic. psychologist, N.J. Intern U. of Medicine and Dentistry, Newark, 1989-90; psychologist juvenile evaluation and treatment svcs. Morristown (N.J.) Meml. Hosp., 1990—; psychologist Ctr. for Psychol. Svcs., Hackensack, N.J., 1993—. Contbr. articles to profl. jours. Mem. APA, N.J. Psychol. Assn. Office: Jets #6 Morristown Meml 100 Madison Ave Morristown NJ 07962

ADAMS, CAROL CHRISPINA, lawyer; b. Saint George's, Grenada, Dec. 5, 1963; d. Ewart and Veronica (Hamilton) A. BA in Polit. Sci, UCLA, 1985; JD, U. Md., 1989. Law clk. to the Hon. J. William Hinkel U.S. Cir. Ct. Balt. County, Md., 1989-90; asst. pub. defender Public Defender Office, State Md., 1990—. Mem. ABA. Office: Office Pub Defender 500 Virginia Ave Baltimore MD 21204

ADAMS, CAROLINE JEANETTE H., writer; b. Dallas, June 15, 1951; d. Bill Gene and Anita N. (Murrah) Hickey. BFA, So. Meth. U., 1973. Media buyer Jim Leslie & Assocs., Dallas, 1973; continuity dir. Sta. KZEW-FM, Dallas, 1973-75; adminstrv. asst. Neiman-Marcus Co., Dallas, 1975-77; exec. sec. Harris Data Communications, Dallas, 1978-80; mgr. classified sales ADWEEK/Southwest mag., Dallas, 1980-91; freelance copywriter, editor, proofreader, 1992—. Editor, writer Dallas Advt. League newsletter, 1987-89. Mem. Press Club Dallas (editor bulletin 1993). Methodist. Avocations: travel, antiques, collecting soundtrack and rare record albums, restoring classic automobiles.

ADAMS, CHERYL ANN, legal assistant; b. Georgetown, Guyana, Nov. 14, 1955; came to U.S., 1981; d. Joseph Lewellyn and Elsa Agatha (Gill) A.; divorced; 1 child, Kirk U. Cumberbatch. BS, U. Md., 1991; postgrad., Johns Hopkins U., 1993—. Supr. Guyana Nat. Coop. Bank, Georgetown, 1975-81; rsch. asst. EF Hutton, N.Y.C., 1982-85; adminstrv. asst. Merrill Lynch, N.Y.C., 1985-86; exec. asst. Skadden, Arps, et al, Washington, 1986—. Mem. Loan Star Toastmasters (rotating functionary 1994—), Alpha Sigma Lambda. Congregational.

ADAMS, CHRISTINE BEATE LIEBER, psychiatrist, educator; b. Greensboro, N.C., June 20, 1949; d. Paul Lieber Adams and Marjorie Pinckney (Quackenbos) Ould; 1 child, Justin McKendree Adams-Tucker. Student, Agnes Scott Coll., 1967-69; BA in English Lit. with honors, U. Fla., 1971, MD, 1976. Diplomate Am. Bd. Psychiatry and Neurology (examiner 1985), Am. Bd. Child Psychiatry (examiner 1984, 91), Nat. Bd. Med. Examiners. Resident in gen. psychiatry U. Louisville Sch. Medicine, 1976-78, fellow in child psychiatry, 1978-80, asst. clin. prof. dept. psychiatry and behavioral scis., 1981—, attending psychiatrist consultation-liaison svc., 1992, 93; pvt. practice, Louisville, 1980—; med. advisor Social Security Adminstrn., HHS, Louisville, 1986—; child psychiatry cons. Seven Counties Svcs., Ky. Dept. Human Resources, 1989,, 93; physician advisor Healthcare Rev. Corp., Louisville, 1993—; reviewer Am. Jour. Psychiatry, 1983—; cons. So. Ind. Mental Health and Guidance Ctr., Jeffersonville, 1981-83, U. Fla., 1982; presenter in field. Contbr. articles to med. jours., chpts. to books. Bd. dirs. Gainesville (Fla.) Women's Health Ctr., 1973-75; mem. Jefferson County (Ky.) Juvenile Justice Commn., 1982-86. Recipient award Nat. Psychiat. Endowment Fund, 1980. Fellow Am. Acad. Child and Adolescent Psychiatry (com. on rights and legal matters 1984-92); mem. Am. Psychiat. Assn. (mem. com. family violence and child sexual abuse 1987-94), Am. Orthopsychiat. Assn., Am. Acad. Psychiatry and Law, Nat. Com. for Prevention Child Abuse, Ky. Psychiat. Assn., Ky. Acad. Child Psychiatry (sec.-treas. 1980-81, pres.-elect 1981-82, pres. 1982-83). Office: Med Arts Bldg Ste 3364 1169 Eastern Pky Louisville KY 40217

ADAMS, CHRISTINE HANSON, advertising executive; b. Hackensack, N.J., May 24, 1950; d. Kenwood Alwin and Doris (Rogers) Hanson; m. L. Ashby Adams III, June 1, 1974 (div. Aug. 1993). BA, Lafayette Coll., 1972; MBA, Duke U., 1979. Med. sales rep. Hoffman-LaRoche, Nutley, N.J., 1972-75; sr. market rsch. analyst Burroughs Wellcome Co., Research Triangle Park, N.C., 1976-77, product planner, 1978; dir. market research Sterling Drug Inc., N.Y.C., 1979-81; group product mgr. Pfizer Inc., N.Y.C., 1981-83; account supr. Kallir Philips Ross Inc., N.Y.C., 1983, v.p., account group supr., 1984-86; v.p., account supr. Baxter Gurian and Mazzei Inc., Beverly Hills, Calif., 1987-89, account group v.p., 1990-91, sr. v.p. account group, supr., 1991-94, sr. v.p. mgmt. supr., 1994—; sr. v.p., group acct. dir. Kallir Philips Ross Inc, N.Y., 1994—; cons. advt. Wellness Community, Santa Monica, Calif., 1988-92. Active membership com. St. Michael's Episcopal Ch., Studio City, Calif., 1987-93, altar guild, 1988-93, tchr. Sunday sch., 1990-91. Named Young Career Woman Bus. Profl. Women's Assn., Chapel Hill, N.C., 1978. Mem. Med. Mktg. Assn., Am. Hosp. Assn., Am. Soc. Hosp. Mktg. and Pub. Rels., Am. Mgmt. Assn. Republican. Home: 129 Phelps Ave Englewood NJ 07631 Office: Kallir Philips Ross Inc 333 E 38th St New York NY 10016

ADAMS, CYNTHIA ANN, nursing administrator; b. Duluth, Minn., Apr. 11, 1956; d. Arthur Raymond and Joyce Kathleen (Bonneville) Mattson; m. Timothy Lee Adams, Nov. 9, 1985; 1 child, Michael Stephen. BSN cum laude, Azusa Pacific U., 1978. RN, Ariz. Team leader spinal cord injury unit Casa Colina Rehab. Hosp., Pomona, Calif., 1978-79; staff nurse, lead nurse orthopedic/neurology unit Portland (Oreg.) Adventist Med. Ctr., 1979-83; office nurse North Pacific Orthopedics, Portland, 1980-81; instr. Maricopa Skill Ctr., Phoenix, 1983-87; sales rep. Reed and Carnrick Pharm. Co., Phoenix, 1987-90; dir. nursing FHP Healthcare, Phoenix, 1990-93; coord. disaster action team Portland unit ARC, 1981-82. Author: New, Once-A-Day Levatol: Penbutolol Sulfate 20 mg., 1990, Dilatrate-SR (Isosorbide dinitrate) 40 mg; The One that Measures Up in Clinical Documentation, 1990. Mem. Am. Acad. Ambulatory Nursing Adminstrn., Nat. League for Nursing, Ariz. Nurses' Assn. Home: 3632 W Kesler Ln Chandler AZ 85226

ADAMS, CYNTHIA D., health sciences educator; b. Detroit, Sept. 10, 1946; d. Walter Norbert Tokarz and Eugenia W. (Czastkiewicz) Tokarz; m. Charles Richard Adams, Feb. 18, 1978; children—Erik, Jessica, Kerensa. B.S., Wayne State U., 1968, Ed.D., 1973; M.A., Eastern Mich. U., 1970. Instr., Wayne State U., Detroit, 1970-71; chief technologist, ednl. coordinator Detroit Macomb Hosp. Assn., 1971-74; dir., asst. prof. health adminstrn. program Mercy Coll., Detroit, 1974-76; assoc. prof., chmn. dept. med. tech. Univ. of Health Scis., Chgo. Med. Sch., North Chicago, Ill., 1976-80, prof., dean, 1980—; dir. workshops Profl. Seminars Cons., N.Y.C., 1985—. Contbr. articles to profl. jours. Mem. adv. bd. Coll. Lake County, Grayslake, Ill., 1979-84; sci. fair judge Ill. Jr. Acad. Sci., 1980—; adv. bd. Lake County Urban League, Waukegan, Ill., 1980—; yearbook advisor Lake Bluff Jr. High Sch., Ill., 1983—; adv. bd. Lake County YWCA, Waukegan, 1984—. Recipient Cert. of Achievement for Outstanding Women in Edn., YWCA, Lake County, 1983, 84. Mem. Am. Assn. Allied Health Professionals, Am. Soc. Med. Technologists (cert. Omicron Sigma award 1980), Am. Soc. Clin. Pathologists (dir. workshops 1976—), Am. Soc. Allied Health Profls. (chmn. women's interest sect. 1984—), Am. Midwest Assn. Allied Health Deans, Ill. Med. Technology Assn. (chmn. sci. assembly 1979-80), Chgo. Soc. Med. Technologists (co-chmn. by-laws com. 1984-85, bd. dirs., 1984—). Home: 340 E Scranton Ave Lake Bluff IL 60044-2534 Office: The Univ of Health Scis Sch Of Related Health North Chicago IL 60064

ADAMS, DARLENE AGNES, educator, library media specialist; b. Prague, Okla., Aug. 23, 1952; d. Carney and Bertha Ellen (Capps) A. AS, Murray State Coll., 1972; BA, East Ctrl. State Coll., 1974, MEd, 1978. Tchr., libr. Carney Pub. Schs., 1974-75, Paden (Okla.) Pub. Schs., 1975—; staff devel com. Paden Pub. Schs., 1985-90, curriculum guidelines com., 1985—, career counseling com., 1990—, gifted and talented com., 1993—, sponsor jr. and sr. class plays and proms. Pres. The Chem. People, Paden, 1983—; sponsor Beta Club, 1990-91. Mem. ALA, NEA, Okla. Library Assn., Okla. Edn. Assn., Smithsonian, Phi Theta Kappa. Republican. Pentacostal. Home: RR 1 Box 82 Paden OK 74860-9766 Office: Paden Pub Schs PO Box 370 Paden OK 74860-0370

ADAMS, DAWN LORRAINE, technology consultant, designer, developer; b. Charlotte, Mich., Aug. 19, 1956; d. Edwin Keith and Jacqueline Lorraine (Rhines) A. BS in Geology, Western Mich. U., 1974-77; student, U. Conn., 1981-83, U. N.C., Greensboro, 1990-91, Boise State U., 1993-94. Sr. cons. Anderson Cons., Hartford, Conn., 1984-89; prin. Computeach, Kernersville, N.C., 1989-92; pres. TechKnowledegy Inc., Kernersville, N.C., 1993—; solution provider Microsoft, Redmond, Wash., 1992—. Chpt. v.p. Am. Bus. Women's Assn., Kernersville, 1989-90. Named Vendor of Yr. Digital Equipment Corp., Maynard, Mass., 1992. Mem. ASTD (chpt. v.p.), Nat. Soc. Performance and Instrn., Assn. for Computer Tng. and Support, Data Processing Mgrs. Assn. (chpt. v.p.), Soc. Applied Learning and Tech. Republican. Office: TechKnowledgy Inc 107 Edgedale Ct Kernersville NC 27284-3329

ADAMS, DIANNE F., bank executive; b. Tracy, Calif., Nov. 9, 1956; d. George M. and Faye D. (Klatt) Hanlon; m. Larry A. Adams, May 16, 1978; children: Tiesha Eileen, Jeanice Vonda, Lawrence Alan, Robert Welcome. AS in Liberal Arts, Modesto Jr. Coll., 1978; BSBA, U. Phoenix, 1991. Owner, pres. Adams Express Bookkeeping and Tax Svcs., Stockton, Calif., 1979—; bookkeeper EMAC, Inc., Oakland, Calif., 1982-83, sr. acct., 1983-84, office mgr., 1984-85; controller OFWHC, Inc., Oakland, 1985-85, CFO acct., 1986-89; acting CFO VNA, Stanislaus, Calif., 1989; sr. acct. Tracy (Calif.) Fed. Bank, 1991-92, fin. analyst, 1992-94, mgr. fin. and planning, 1994—; bd. dirs. LL & R Gems, Ms. Petite, Inc., WCFHP Inc.; contracted sr. acct. Calif. Youth Soccer League, Pleasanton, 1989-91, Sta. KPIX, Livermore, Calif., 1989-91, R. Zaballos & Sons Constrn., Hayward, Calif., 1989-91, Stone Bros. Inc., Stockton, 1989-91, Lodi (Calif.) Meml. Hosp., 1989-91. Leader youths and adults Enterprise 4H Club, Escalon, Calif., 1976-78; tchr. teen and adult Sunday Sch., Saron Luth. Ch., Escalon, 1976-92; coach tee ball, mr. sr. boys team, v.p., sec., Montezuma Little League, Stocton Calif., 1992-93. Mem. NAFE (pres., founder Bay Area Networkers 1985-86), Nat. Assn. Tax Cons., Am. Bus. Womens Assn. (bd. dirs. 1981-86, sec., historian, membership com. Oakdale chpt.), Inst. Mgmt. Accts. (membership com. 1991—). Republican. Office: Tracy Fed Bank PO Box 389 1003 Central Ave Tracy CA 95378

ADAMS, DORIS CRUZ, art educator; b. Santa Cruz, Calif., June 17, 1921; d. Edward C. and Emma Anna (Blome) Cruz; m. Edmund Burke Adams, Apr. 18, 1943; children: Michael Edward, Stephen Anthony. BA, U. Calif., Santa Barbara, 1945; MA, Calif. State Northridge, 1965. Art tchr. Burroughs Jr. High Burbank Unified Sch. Dist., Burbank, Calif., 1945-47; art tchr. Jordan Jr. High Burbank Unified Sch. Dist., Burbank, 1950-65, art tchr. Burroughs Evening Sch., 1950-60; art tchr. Burbank High Sch., 1965-77, Burbank (Calif.) Unified Sch. Dist., Monarch Beach, Calif., 1978—; art tchr. Burbank Evening Sch., 1947-77; watercolor workshop leader North Hollywood, Calif., 1973, Glendale, Calif., 1973, France, 1986, Hawaii, 1987, Mexico, 1992, others; curriculum developer Burbank Unified Sch. dist., 1945-47, 65-70; newsletter coord. Niguel Shores Community Assn., Monarch Beach, 1988—. Illustrator: (books) Greek Songs, Elementary Administration, Supervision, Look and See, 1950-57; author: (classroom manuals) Painting, Stitchery, Ceramics, Jewelry, Silk Screen, 1965-70; painter. Mem. steering coms. Dana Point (Calif.) Cultural Commn., 1992-93; mem., past pres. Niguel Art Assn., Dana Point, 1978—; mem. Sand Dollars, Dana Point, 1992—; mem. planning com. for Ann. Whale Parade, Dana Point, 1992—. Recipient Community Svc. award Niguel Shores Community Assn., Monarch Beach, 1989, numerous ribbons and medals for watercolor paintings. Mem. Nat. Watercolor Soc., Dana Point Arts Coun., Laguna Art Mus., Delta Kappa Gamma (pres.).

ADAMS, ELAINE, art agent, publicist; b. L.A., Sept. 15, 1960; d. Mikhael Nikitovich Periev-Shelby and Emma (Davidian) Shelby; m. Peter Seitz Adams, Mar. 12, 1990. B in Econs. and Math., U. So. Calif., L.A., 1982. Stock broker Crowell, Weedon & Co., L.A., 1983-89; art agt., artist rep. Peter Adams Studio, Pasadena, Calif., 1990—; publicity chmn. Calif. Art Club, Pasadena, 1993. Editor Calif. Art Club newsletter, 1994—. Assoc. trustee Pacific Asia Mus., Pasadena, 1993, chmn. Festival of the Autumn Moon, 1994; bd. dirs. Pasadena Symphony, 1994. Republican. Russian Orthodox. Office: Peter Adams Studio and Pub Rels for Fine Art 949 Linda Vista Ave Pasadena CA 91103

ADAMS, ELAINE PARKER, college president. BA in Spanish Edn., Xavier U., 1961; MS in Libr. Sci., La. State U., 1966; PhD in Libr. Sci., U. So. Calif., 1973. Cert. learning resources specialist. Dist. catalog libr. Grossmont Union High Sch. Dist., La Mesa, Calif., 1971; mid. sch. libr. Upper St. Clair (Pa.) Sch. Dist., 1972-73; vis. asst. prof. U. Md., College Park, 1973; media specialist U. So. Calif., L.A., 1974-75; coord. Learning Resources Ctr. Tex. So. U., Houston, 1976-80; supr. libr. svcs. and tech. tng. Getty Oil Rsch. Ctr., Houston, 1980-83; assoc. v.p. acad. svcs. and planning Prairie View (Tex.) A&M U., 1983-85, v.p. student affairs, 1985-89; asst. commr. Edn. Opportunity Planning Tex. Higher Edn. Coordinating Bd., Austin, 1989-91; pres. N.E. Coll. Houston C.C. System, 1991—; lectr. Sch. Profl. Edn. U. Houston-Clear Lake, summers 1977-79; planner Honors Coll. Prairie View A&M U., 1983-84, user coord. bldg. cons. libr., 1984-88; cons. Libr./Pharmacy Addition Xavier U., New Orleans, 1988-93; evaluator Mid States Assn. Commn. on Higher Edn., Phila., 1988—, So. Assn. Colls. and Schs., 1991—. Co-editor: Media and the Young Adult, 1981; contbr. articles to profl. jours. Trustee Xavier U., 1990—, Lon Morris Coll., 1993-94, Houston Pl. Preservation, 1993—; mem. ACE Commn. on Leadership Devel., 1994-96. Fellow U. So.. Calif., 1968-71; scholar Xavier U., 1957-61, AT&T scholar Harvard U. Inst. for Edn. Mgmt., Cambridge, Mass., 1989. Mem. ALA, Am. Assn. C.C.s, Nat. Assn. Student Pers. Adminstrs. (editl. bd. 1988-90), Am. Assn. for Higher Edn. (Black Caucus exec. bd. 1990—), Nat. Assn. Women in Edn., Nat. Coalition of 100 Black Women (bd. dirs. Houston chpt., Makeda award 1993), Xavier Univ. Alumni Assn. (nat. pres. 1990-91, Alumna of Yr.). Office: NE Coll Houston C C Sys PO Box 7849 Houston TX 77270-7849

ADAMS, ELIZABETH HERRINGTON, banker; b. Tulsa, May 25, 1947; d. James Dillon and Helen (Allderdice) Herrington; m. Phillip Hollis Hackney, Mar. 5, 1977 (dec. Jan. 1990); m. Keith R. Adams, Sept. 4, 1993. Student, No. Ariz. U., 1965-67, 68-69. With Coldwater (Kans.) Nat. Bank, summers 1964-67; with The Ariz. Bank, Phoenix, 1969, Flagstaff, 1970-71; asst. cashier The Wilmore (Kans.) State Bank, 1972—; asst. cashier The Coldwater Nat. Bank, 1974-83, cashier, ops. officer, 1984—; dir. The Coldwater Nat. Bank, 1972—, The Wilmore State Bank, 1970—. Bd. dirs. Pioneer Lodge Nursing Home, Coldwater, 1984-89; mem. sch. site coun., 1993-94; life mem. Girl Scouts, chmn. Neighborhood Cookie Drive, 1991—; bd. dirs., mem. strategic planning com. Wheatbelt Area Girl Scout Coun., 1994—; elder 1st Presbyn. Ch., Coldwater. Mem. Fin. Women Internat., Community Bankers Assn. Kans. (membership com. 1991—, INPAC com. 1992—), Kans. Ind. Bankers (gen. svcs. com. 1986-87), PEO, Alpha Omicron Pi. Republican. Office: Coldwater Nat Bank PO Box 726 Coldwater KS 67029-0726

ADAMS, EVE MAYO, psychologist; b. Huntington, W. Va., July 19, 1961; d. Dan Boyd and Mary Calista (Newhard) A. BA, Ohio Wesleyan U., 1983; MA, Ohio State U., 1985, PhD, 1988. Lic. psychologist, Ohio. Psychology intern Ohio State U., Columbus, 1987-88; counseling psychologist U. Akron, Ohio, 1988-93; acting tng. dir. U. Akron, 1994; adj. asst. prof. counseling and ednl. psychology N.Mex. State U., Las Cruces, 1994—. Contbr. articles to profl. jours. Mem. ACA, APA, Am. Coll. Pers. Assn. (mem. directorate 1988-94, trainer).

ADAMS, FLORENCE MARIE, computer scientist; b. N.Y.C., May 18, 1932; d. Francis Joseph and Florence Marie (White) O'Neill; m. Donald L. Adams, Aug. 25, 1962 (div. Apr. 1967); children: David Garrick, Samuel Theodore. BA in Math., Hunter Coll., 1955. Advanced math., programmer N.Am. Aviation-Rocketdyne, Canoga Park, Calif., 1956; asst. mgr. computer ctr. Geo. Buck, N.Y.C., 1956-63; mgr. computer ctr. J.K. Lasser, N.Y.C., 1965-75; computer coord. Dennis Yarmouth Reg. Sch. Dist., South Yarmouth, Mass., 1981-84; programmer Vis. Nurse Assn. Boston, 1978-81, supr. data processing, 1989—. Author: I Took a Hammer to My Hand, 1973, Mushy Eggs, 1973, Catch a Sunbeam, 1978, Build Your Own Baby Furniture, 1980.

ADAMS, FRANCES GRANT, II, lawyer; b. Wheeling, W.Va., Nov. 30, 1955; d. Jack Richard and Frances Irene (Grant) A. BA, W.Va. U., 1976, JD, 1979; MA, Webster U., 1983. Bar: W.Va. 1979, U.S. Dist. Ct. (so. dist.) W.Va. 1979, U.S. Ct. Mil. Appeals 1979, U.S. Supreme Ct. 1988, D.C. 1989. Asst. staff judge advocate armament div. USAF, Eglin AFB, Fla., 1979-82; dep. staff judge advocate USAF, Keflavik, Iceland, 1982-83; staff judge advocate 71st Air Base Group USAF, Vance AFB, Okla., 1984-86; chief gen. torts sect. claims and tort litigation staff hdqrs. USAF, Washington, 1986-88; chief mgmt. and analysis br. claims and tort litigation div. Air Force Legal Svcs. Agy., Washington, 1988-92, sr. tort atty. tort claims and litigation div., 1992—. Program chmn. Pentagon chpt. Fed. Bar Assn., 1989-90. Mem. DAR (chmn. procedures manual W.Va. chpt. 1989-92), Magna Carta Dames, Ancient and Honorable Arty. Co., Air Force Assn. (life), Ret. Officers Assn. (life).

ADAMS, JANE, actress. Diploma, Julliard Sch. performances include (Broadway) An Inspector Calls (Antoinette Perry award 1994), I Hate Hamlet, The Crucible (off-Broadway) The Nice and the Nasty, Psychoneurotic Phantasies, Mutterschaft (regional) Careless Love, Our Town, Love Diatribe, The Glass Menagerie (T.V.) The Rising Sun, Family Ties (film) Vital Signs, Light Sleeper, Mrs. Parker and the Roundtable, I Love Trouble, Father of the Bride II. Office: ICM 8942 Wilshire Blvd Beverly Hills CA 90211*

ADAMS, JANNA HOUSTON, psychotherapist, educator; b. Odessa, Tex., May 3, 1958; d. Billy Jack and Thelma Louise (Henley) Houston; divorced; children: Kelly Sky, Mindy Summer, Cy Houston. BS, U. North Tex., 1980; MA, Adams State Coll., 1992. Cert. seconday edn. counselor. Speech and drama instr. Hoehne (Colo.) Sch. Dist. Re-3, 1980-82, music instr., 1985-88; speech and drama instr. Trinidad (Colo.) State Jr. Coll., 1988-89, instr., 1992-94; counselor Trinidad (Colo.) High Sch., 1992—; pvt. practice Trinidad, 1992-94; crisis evaluator Spanish Peaks Mental Health, Trinidad, 1994; counselor John Mall H.S., Walsenburg, Colo., 1994—; counselor Crisis Intervention Team, Trinidad, 1992—. Youth instr. Faith Christian Fellowship, Trinidad, 1988-91, music instr., 1989-91; organizer, leader Parents for Better Edn., Aguilar, Colo., 1990-91. Mem. ACA, Am. Sch. Counselors Assn., Colo. Counseling Assn., Colo. Sch. Counselors Assn., Philanthropic Edn. Orgn. Democrat. Home: PO Box 883 Walsenburg CO 81089 Office: 355 Pine St Walsenburg CO 81089

ADAMS, JEAN RUTH, entomologist; b. Edgewater Park, N.J., Aug. 17, 1928; d. Herbert Raymond and Gertrude Gladys (Budd) A. BS, Rutgers U., 1950, PhD (Trubeck fellow), 1962. Registered profl. entomologist. Lab. technician Rohm & Haas Co., Bristol, Pa., 1951-57; postdoctoral fellow U. Pa., Phila., 1961-62; rsch. entomologist U.S. Dept. Agr., Agr. Rsch. Ctr., Beltville, Md., 1962—; cons. insect pathology, electron microscopy. Mem. nominating com. D.C. Bapt. Conv., 1977-79, dir. Acteens, Mission Youth Orgn., D.C. Bapt. Conv., 1972-87, 88—, Sunday sch. tchr. 1st Bapt. Ch., Hyattsville, Md., 1962—, chmn. Christian edn. bd., 1973-74, mem. nominating com., 1974-77, mem. bd. missions, 1977-80, ch. treas., 1973-74, mem. choir, 1979—, diaconate, 1980-86, 90—, vice chmn., 1981-82, chmn., 1982-91, trustee Bapt. Home, 1982-91, sec., 1985-91; trustee Sunday sch. bd. SBC, 1991—. Mem. editorial bd. Jour. of Invertebrate Pathology, 1986-89. Mem. Am. Registered Profl. Entomologists (bd. dirs. Chesapeake chpt. 1989—, pres. 1991-93), Electron Microscopy Soc. Am. (chmn. sci. exhibits ann. meeting 1982), Entomol. Soc. Am., Am. Soc. for Cell Biology, Soc. for Invertebrate Pathology (sec. 1982-84), Washington Soc. for Electron Microscopy (coun. 1976-83, sec.-treas. 1976-78, 80-82), Washington Entomol. Soc., Md. Entomol. Soc., Sigma Xi, Sigma Delta Epsilon. Editor: Atlas of Invertebrate Viruses, 1991, Insect Potpourri: Adventures in Entomology, 1992; contbr. articles to profl. jours. Home: 6004 41st Ave Hyattsville MD 20782-3058 Office: US Dept Agr Agr Rsch Ctr Bldg 011A W Insect Biocontrol Lab Rm 214 Beltsville MD 20705

ADAMS, JO-ANN MARIE, data processing consultant; b. L.A., May 27, 1949; d. Joseph John and Georgia S. (Wein) A.; AA, Pasadena City Coll., 1968; BA, Pomona Coll., 1970; MA, Calif. State U., L.A., 1971; MBA, Pacific Luth. U., 1983; cert. in Telecomm. and Info. Resource Mgmt., U. Hawaii, 1993; postgrad. Santa Clara U., 1993—. Secondary tchr. South Pasadena (Calif.) Unified Schs., 1970-71; appraiser Riverside County (Calif.) Assessor's Office, 1972-74; systems and procedures analyst Riverside County Data Processing Dept., 1974-76, supervising systems analyst, 1976-79; systems analyst computer Boeing Computer Svcs. Co., Seattle, 1979-81; sr. systems analyst Thurston County Central Svcs., Olympia, Wash., 1981-83, data processing systems mgr., 1983-84; data processing systems engr. IBM Corp., 1984-87; realtor-assoc., Dower Realty, 1987-92; corp. sales rep. UniGlobe Met. Travel, 1988-89; project mgr. Servco Pacific, 1989-90, Scott Software Systems, 1990-91; systems analyst Dept. Atty. Gen., 1991-93; cons. in field, 1993—; instr. Riverside City Coll., 1977-79. Chairperson legis. task force Riverside/San Bernardino chpt. NOW, 1975-76, chpt. co-chairperson, 1978; mem. ethics com. Calif. NOW Inc., 1978; alt. del. Calif Dem. Caucus, 1978. Mem. NAFE, Pomona Coll. Alumni Assn. Home: 18415 Purdue Dr Saratoga CA 95070-4712

ADAMS, JOANNE CASS, packaging engineer; b. London, July 29, 1964; came to U.S., 1964; d. John G. Cass and Marian (Roughead) Schafer. BS in Packaging, Mich. State U., 1987; MBA, Pa. State U., 1991. Engr. The Duro Bag, Florence, Ky., 1987-88, Supelco, Belleforte, Pa., 1988-91, The Upjohn Co., Kalamazoo, Mich., 1991—. Mem. Inst. Packaging Profls. (v.p. adminstrn. West Mich. chpt.). Office: The Upjohn Co 7171 Portage Rd Kalamazoo MI 49001

ADAMS, JULIE KAREN, clinical psychologist; b. Portland, Oreg., Dec. 12, 1955; d. Allen Hays and Susanna Angelina (Meyers) A. B degree, Willamette U., 1977; M degree, Ctrl. Wash. U., 1982; cert. in bus. adminstrn., U. Wash., 1986; D degree, Pacific U., 1992. Cert. counselor, sch. psychologist, Wash. Sch. psychologist Highline Sch. Dist., Seattle, 1987-90; psychology intern Elmcrest Psychiat. Hosp., Portland, Conn., 1990, clinician, 1991; rsch. asst. Yale U., New Haven, Conn., 1991; clinician Advanced Clin. Svcs., Seattle, 1991-93; postdoctoral fellow U. Wash., Seattle, 1991-93; acad. counselor Johns Hopkins U., Balt., 1993; behavior intervention specialist Edmonds (Wash.) Sch. Dist., 1993-94, Marysville Sch. Dist., Marysville, Wash., 1994—; guest spkr., instr. U. Washington, Assn. Sch. Adminstrs., Wash., Assn. Sch. Psychologists, Wash., Edmonds Sch. Psychologists, Pacific U., U. Oreg., APA, Portland and L.A., 1989—. Contbr. articles to profl. jours. Mem. tng. com., kids week com., nursing home com., pub. policy com. Jr. League of Seattle, 1988—; health care researcher Wash. State Legis., Olympia, 1993; campaigner Bush for Pres., Seattle, 1988, 92; rsch. asst. to state senator Oreg. State Legis., Salem, 1985; press page nat. conv. Rep. Nat. Com., Detroit, 1980; student grad. v.p., faculty rep. com. Pacific U. Sch. of Profl. Psychology, 1989-90. Mem. APA (health psychology com. student rep. 1992-93), Wash. Psychol. Assn., Willamette U. Alumni Assn. (bd. dirs. (1983-88), Vols. for Outdoor Wash. (bd. dirs. 1986-87), City Club of Seattle (membership com. 1986-88), Psi Chi, Beta Alpha Gamma. Home: 1038 NE 125th Seattle WA 98125

ADAMS, KAREN ELAINE, preschool administrator; b. San Diego, Nov. 8, 1960; d. Billy Joe and Betty Joy (Crutchfield) A.; children: Christopher Vaughan, Peter Vaughan, Lesley Vaughan, Pegeen Adams. BS in Human Devel., U. Calif., Davis, 1983. Cert. tchr., Calif. Tchr. Discovery Presch., Davis, 1979-80; tchr., dir. Milpitas (Calif.) Parents Presch., 1984; day care owner Karen n' Kids Daycare, San Jose, Calif., 1985-88; sr. staff San Jose Family Camp, Groveland, Calif., 1993—; tchr., dir. Eastside Parents Participating Nursery Sch., San Jose, 1988—; adv. bd. Bay Area Parent Mag., Los Gatos, Calif., 1992-93; cons., and lectr. in field. Inventor in field. Validator Nat. Acad. Early Childhood Programs, 1993-95. Recipient Nat. 1st Place award for disability equipment for dolls, 1993. Mem. Nat. Assn. for the Edn. Young Children, Nat. Parenting Instrs. Assn., Calif. Coun. Partent Participating Nursery Schs., Parent Cooperative Preschs. Internat., Santa Clara County Child Care Coalition, Helping After Neonatal Death, Coun. for Exceptional Children. Democrat. Home: 1933 Quiet Cir San Jose CA 95132-3538 Office: Eastside Parents Participating Nursery Sch 935 Piedmont Rd San Jose CA 95132-2820

ADAMS, KRISTI KAY, association executive; b. St. Paul, Jan. 26, 1971; d. Fred James Adams and Valjeanne Rose Matson. BA, U. Minn., 1995. Mem. nat. bd. YWCA of the U.S.A., N.Y.C., chairwoman nat. student coun., 1992-94. Bd. dirs. U. Minn. YWCA, 1990-93. Mem. Democratic Farm Labor Party. Home: 72 Clarence Ave SE Minneapolis MN 55414-3528

ADAMS, LAURA ANN, critical care nurse; b. Thibodaux, La., Mar. 17, 1960; d. John Anthony Sr. and M. Elma Theresa (Dufrene) A. AD, Nicholls State U., Thibodaux, 1981, BSN, 1988. RNC, La.; cert. neonatal intensive care. Staff nurse Med. Force Internat., Inc., New Orleans, 1989—, TravCorps Nursing Agy., Malden, Mass., 1991—, South La. Med. Ctr. (now Leonard J. Chabert Med. Ctr.), Houma, 1981-89, 90—, Earl K. Long Med. Ctr., Baton Rouge, 1992—. Mem. AWHONN, Nat. Assn. Neonatal Nurses, La. Assn. Neonatal Nurses, Nat. Legaue of Nurses. Home: PO Box 356 Cut Off LA 70345-0356

ADAMS, LINETTE M., principal. Prin. Benjamin Banneker High Sch., Washington. Recipient Blue Ribbon Sch. award U.S. Dept. Edn., 1990-92. Office: Benjamin Banneker High Sch 800 Euclid St NW Washington DC 20001-2296

ADAMS, LORRAINE, reporter. BA in English, Princeton U., 1981, MA in English, 1982. With The Concord (N.H.) Monitor, 1983, 84, The Dallas Morning News; now projects reporter The Washington Post. Recipient Pulitzer Prize for investigative reporting, 1992. Office: Washington Post 1150 15th St NW Washington DC 20071

ADAMS, LYNN, speech-language pathologist, educator; b. Coral Gables, Fla., Nov. 12, 1957; d. William A. and Georgia (Bonus) A. BS, Fla. State U, 1979, MS, 1980; PhD, U. Tenn., 1993. Speech pathologist Montgomery County Schs., Troy, N.C., 1980-84, Devel. Evaluation Ctr., Wadesboro, N.C., 1984-87; dir. Wadesboro Speech & Hearing Ctr., 1986-87; clin. supr. U. Tenn., Knoxville, 1988-92; asst. prof. S.W. Mo. State U., 1993—; cons. Project Access, Springfield, Mo., 1994—. Recipient Outstanding Svc. award Interdisciplinary Coun., 1987. Mem. Am. Speech and Hearing Assn., Mo. Speech and Hearing Assn., Autism Soc. Am. Democrat. Episcopalian. Home: 3371 B East Sunset St Springfield MO 65804 Office: SW Mo State U Dept Comm Disorders 901 S National Ave Springfield MO 65804-0027

ADAMS, MARGARET BERNICE, retired museum official; b. Toronto, Ont., Can., Apr. 29, 1936; came to U.S., 1948, naturalized, 1952; d. Robert Russell and Kathleen Olive (Buffin) A.; m. Alberto Enrique Sánchez-Quiñonez, Nov. 30, 1956 (div. 1960). AA, Monterey Peninsula Coll., 1969; BA, San Jose State U., 1971; MA, U. Utah, 1972. Curator ethnic arts Civic Art Gallery, San Jose, 1971; staff asst. Utah Mus. Fine Arts, Salt Lake City, 1972; lectr./curator Coll. Seven, U. Calif., Santa Cruz, 1972-74; part-time educator Cabrillo Coll., Aptos, Calif., 1973, Monterey Peninsula Coll., 1973-84; dir. U.S. Army Mus., Presidio of Monterey, 1974-83; chief. mus. br. Ft. Ord Mil. Complex, 1983-88; Guest curator Am. Indian arts Monterey Peninsula Mus. Art, 1975-88. Author: Indian Tribes of North America and Chronology of World Events in Prehistoric Pueblo Times, 1975, Historic Old Monterey, 1976; cntbg. editor Indian Am., (exhibit catalogue) Writing on the Wall: WWII Patriotic Posters, 1987; contbr. articles to jours. Mem. native Am. adv. panel AAAS, Washington, 1972-78; mem. rev. and adv. com. Project Media, Nat. Indian Edn. Assn., Mpls., 1973-78; working mem. Program for Tng. Am. Indian Counsellors in Alcoholism Counselling and Rehab. Programs, 1972-74; mem. hist. adv. com. Montery County Bd. Suprs., 1987-89. Grad. fellow, dean's scholar U. Utah, 1972; dean's scholar Monterey (Calif.) Peninsula Coll., 1969, San Jose (Calif.) State U., 1971. Mem. Am. Anthrop. Assn., Am. Assn. Museums, Soc. for Applied Anthropology, Soc. Am. Archeology, Am. Ethnol. Soc., Nat., Calif., Indian edn. assns. Home: 1000 Pacific Grove Ln # 7 Pacific Grove CA 93950-3838

ADAMS, NANCY ANN, school system administrator; b. Syracuse, N.Y., Mar. 20, 1932; d. Percival William Normand and Marion Vivian (Arnold) Taylor; m. Walter Adams, June 19, 1959 (div. 1970); children: Norman, Laurie. BEd, U. Miami, Coral Gables, 1957; MEd, Fla. Atlantic U., 1969; PhD, U. Wyoming, 1981. Cert. tchr., Fla. Tchr. Broward County Schs., Ft. Lauderdale, Fla., 1957-62, rsch. asst., 1969-73, counselor high sch. srs., 1973-79, counselor adults, 1980-81, coord. adult program, 1981-93. Mem. Fla. Adminstrs. Adult Edn. (vce chmn. 1984-86), Adult and Community Educators of Fla. (bd. dirs. 1988-94), Am. Assn. Adult and Continuing Edn., Fla. Sch. Counselor Assn. (v.p. 1987), Adult and Community Educators of Fla. (chmn. adminstr.'s affiliate). Republican. Home: 800 NW 6th Terr Boca Raton FL 33486 Office: 700 NE 56th Ste Oakland Park FL 33334

ADAMS, NANCY R., nurse, military officer. BSN, Cornell U., N.Y. Hosp. Sch. Nursing; MSN, Cath. U. Am.; grad., Command and Gen. Staff Coll., U.S. Army War Coll. Commd. Nurse Corps, U.S. Army, 1968, advanced through grades to brig. gen.; chief nurse Army Regional Med. Ctr., Frankfurt, Germany; nursing adminstr. various locations; nurse consultant to U.S. Surgeon Gen.; now chief, Nurse Corps, asst. surgeon gen., comdr. Ctr. for Health Promotion and Preventive Medicine, U.S. Army; now Army Nurse Corps Office of Chief, Surgeon Gen. U.S. Army. Author textbooks; contbr. articles to profl. jours. Fellow Am. Acad. Nursing; mem. ANA, Assn. Mil. Surgeons of U.S., Am. Orgn. Nurse Execs., Sigma Theta Tau. Office: Army Nurse Corp Office of Chief 5111 Leesburg Pike Skyline 5 Falls Church VA 22041

ADAMS, NORMA AUER, painter; b. Sacramento, Calif., Dec. 22, 1939; d. Walter George and Florence Madelyne (Rohrer) Auer; m. Rodney Hollis Adams, May 26, 1962 (div. Dec. 1979); children: Anne-Marie Elizabeth, Philip John, Randall Robert; m. Stephen Peter de Jong, June 14, 1981; 1 child, Deborah Lyn de Jong. BA in Art, Stanford U., 1961. Represented by Reece Gallery, N.Y.C. Exhbns. include Triton Mus., Calif., 1978, The Gallery, Spartanburg, S.C., 1978, Birmingham Mus. Art, 1978, 80, Asheville Mus., N.C., 1978, Los Robles Gallery, Palo Alto, Calif., 1979, La. Watercolor Soc., 1980, Pitts. Watercolor Soc., 1980, 81, Rahr-West Mus., Wis., 1980, The Art Works Gallery, Sacramento, 1980, 82, Artists' Coop. Gallery, San Francisco, 1980, Bay Arts Exhbns., Calif., 1980, Salmagundi Club, N.Y.C., 1980, Springville Mus., Utah, 1980, Burpee Mus., Ill., 1981, Gallery of World Art, Newton Upper Falls, Mass., 1982, Arts Exclusive Gallery, Simsbury, Conn., 1982, 83, 84, 85,, Reece Galleries, N.Y.C., 1986, 89, So. Alleghenies Mus. Art, Pa., 1987; represented in numerous pub. and pvt. collections. Recipient Gehner Watercolor award Nat. Assn. Women Artists, 1978, Greenville Artists Guild award, 1978. Home: 1102 La Grange St Chestnut Hill MA 02167

ADAMS, PAMELA MCGEE, marketing professional; b. Ft. Monmouth, N.J., Jan. 10, 1956; d. William Clyde Jr. and Cornelia Scott (Cree) McGee. BSBA, Oral Roberts U., 1978. Mktg. rep. archtl. bldg products divsn. Armstrong World Industries, Mpls., 1979-81; sr. mktg. rep. Armstrong World Industries, Dallas, 1981-83, nat. accounts rep., 1983-84; asst. regional mgr. Armstrong World Industries, Phila., 1984-86; asst. mktg. mgr. Armstrong World Industries, Lancaster, Pa., 1986-88; regional mgr. Armstrong World Industries, Balt., 1988-93; mktg. mgr. comml. walls Armstrong-Bldg Prodn. Ops., Lancaster, 1993-94, mktg. mgr. Pacific Rim, 1994; regional area sales mgr. Armstrong-Bldg. Prodn. divsn., Orange City, Calif., 1994—. Corporate campaign chair United Way, Lancaster, 1987; vol. Doing Something, Washington, 1990-93; bd. dirs. Child Abuse Prevention Commn. of Ctrl. Pa., Lancaster, 1993—. Republican. Office: Armstrong World Industries PO Box 3001 313 W Liberty St Lancaster PA 17604

ADAMS, PATSY RUTH, elementary physical education educator; b. East St Louis, Ill., July 2, 1938; d. William Russel Sr. and Iva (Langston) A. BS in Edn., Ill. State U., Normal, 1960; MS in Edn., So. Ill. U., 1974. Registered tchr. phys. edn., elem. edn., ednl. adminstrn., Ill. Phys. edn. tchr. Woodstock (Ill.) Community High Sch., 1960-61, Westmer Sch. Dist., Joy, Ill., 1961-62, Alton (Ill.) Sch. Dist., 1962-63; field hockey coach So. Ill. U., Edwardsville, 1974; phys. edn. educator East Alton (Ill.) Sch. Dist., 1963-94; field hockey and basketball umpire, referee for high schs., colls. and clubs, Ill. and Mo., 1958-83; also worked as swimming instr. and waterfront dir. Photographer for suburban newspapers and pub. books. Vol. Cahokia Mounds Historic Site, Collinsville, Ill., 1991-93, Sr. Olympics and Elderhostel, Edwardsville, 1991, 93. Recipient Helen Manley award Mo. Assn. Health, Phys. Edn., Recreation and Dance, 1990; Kappa Delta Epsilon scholar Ill. State U., 1959. Mem. AAHPERD (commendation 1977), NEA (life), AAUW, U.S. Field Hocky Assn. (life), Women's Phys. Edn. Club of St. Louis (v.p., sec. 1968-70), St. Louis Bd. Women Ofcls. (chair 1967-68), Kappa Delta Pi, Sigma Phi Omega. Presbyterian.

ADAMS, PHOEBE-LOU, journalist; b. Hartford, Conn., Dec. 18, 1918; d. Harold Irving and Alice (Burlingame) A. A.B. cum laude, Radcliffe Coll., 1939. Reporter Hartford Courant, 1942-45; with editorial staff Atlantic Monthly, Boston, 1945—. Author: A Rough Map of Greece, 1965. also: The Atlantic 745 Boylston St Boston MA 02116

ADAMS, PHYLLIS LOUISE, travel agent; b. East Liverpool, Ohio, Jan. 17, 1957; d. Anthony Aloysius and Alberta Elma (Stefl) Scelp; m. Harry Thomas Adams, Nov. 10, 1979; 1 child, Kara Alyssa. AS, C.C. of Beaver County, 1977. Cert. travel counselor. Sec. Stone and Webster Engring. Corp., Shippingport, Pa., 1977-78, Wheeling Pitts. Steel, Steubenville, Ohio, 1978-80; travel agent Auto Club of S.W. Ohio, Steubenville, 1980-81, Jacobson T. Travel, Shenandoah, Iowa, 1982-83; travel agent Maryville (Mo.) Travel Agy., 1983-92, cert. travel counselor, 1992—. Mem. P.E.O., Today Civic Women. Office: Maryville Travel Agy 119 N Main St Maryville MO 64468-1622

ADAMS, REBECCA A., taxation analyst; b. Poteau, Okla., Mar. 8, 1959; d. Ronald and Rosalie J. Garner; m. Randall David Adams, Dec. 29, 1979; children: Ronald, Lauren, Amelia. A in Bus., Ea. Okla. State, 1978; BS in Fin., U. Ctrl. Okla., 1981, MBA in Fin., 1985. Acct. capitol improvement Okla. Dept. Corrections, Oklahoma City, 1980-81; tax auditor oil and gas divsn. Okla. Tax Commn., Oklahoma City, 1981-84, tax assessment and equalization analyst, 1984—; chmn. rsch. com. Midwestern States Conf. Unit Valuation Stds., Denver, 1990—. Active Rep. League Voters, 1988—; tchr. Sunday sch. Ch. Religious Sci., Oklahoma City, 1990-91; leader Cub Scouts, Edmond, Okla., 1993—. Mem. Internat. Assn. Assessing Officers (cert. advanced appraiser accredited). Home: 1508 Colony Ct Edmond OK 73003

ADAMS, ROSE ANN, social service administrator; b. McHenry, Ill., Apr. 4, 1952; d. Clemens Jacob and Marguerite Elizabeth (Freund) A. BS in Edn., Ill. State U., 1974; MEd, U. Ark., 1979. Supt., exec. dir. Clinton County Children's Services, Wilmington, Ohio, 1979-81; dir. ednl. and adult svcs. Bost Human Devel. Svcs., Ft. Smith, Ark., 1981-87; adminstrv. officer Cen. Ark. Devel. Coun., Benton, 1987; adminstrv. officer, interim Head Start dir., dir. resource devel. Community Orgn. Poverty Elimination Pulaski, Lonoke Counties, Little Rock, 1987-93; exec. dir. So. Early Childhood Assn., 1993-94; cons. Earl Moore and Assocs., Little Rock, 1994—. Active Welfare Adv. Bd., Clinton County, 1979-81, Home Econs. Extension Svcs. Adv. Com., 1979-81, adv. bd. U. Ark. Women's Ctr., 1979; coord. White House Conf. on Families, 1980; mem. Task Force Child Abuse, 1985; trustee Multiple Sclerosis Soc., Ark.; bd. dirs. Morris Found.; chair Ark. Health Promotion Coalition; vice-chair Pulaski County Local Planning Group; chair Ark. Com. on Women's Concerns; charter mem. Am. Lung Assn. of Ark. Aux.; adv. com. Ark. Mentors; v.p. Ark. Single Parent Scholarship Fund. Named one of Outstanding Young Women of Am., 1982. Mem. Am. Bus. Women's Assn. (Woman of Yr. Avant Garde chpt. 1992). Home: Sonata Trail #1 Little Rock AR 72205 Office: Earl Moore and Assocs 300 S Spring # 612 Little Rock AR 72201

ADAMS, SALLYANN KELLY, chiropractor; b. Omaha, Aug. 28, 1952; d. Paul Samuel and Sally Mae (Hayman) Kelly; m. Larry Leon Adams, Dec. 27, 1985; children: Laurie, Ryan, Mica, Kelly, Sarah, Paul, Levi, Jana, Benjamin, Samuel. D. of Chiropractic, Palmer Coll., 1976; AA, Parkland Coll., Champaign, Ill., 1977. Bd. cert. chiropractic orthopedist. Dir. Moore Chiropractic Family Ctr., Danville, Ill., 1977-84; assoc. Barrow Chriopractic Ctr., Hattiesburg, Miss., 1984-86; owner, pres. Adams Chiropractic, Gautier, Miss., 1986—; mem. Miss. State Bd. Chiropractic Examiners, 1992—. Mem. NAFE, Miss. Assn. Chiropractors (chmn. worker's comp PPO 1990-91, Spl. Recognition award 1990, Achievement award 1991, Clinician of Yr. 1993), Am. Bus. Women's Assn. (Spl. Recognition 1991), Am. Chiropractic Assn. Latter Day Saints. Office: Adams Chiropractic 1408 Hwy 90 Gautier MS 39553-5449

ADAMS, SHARRON ANN EMANUEL, business owner, educator; b. Norman, Okla., Sept. 29, 1939; d. Norbit Thomas Emanuel and Theda Belle (Halford) Smethers; m. Jeffrey Inglis Adams, Mar. 21, 1970; children: Adrian H. Inglis, Julia Alison. BS in Edn. cum laude, Abilene Christian U., 1961; MA, Mich. State U., 1972. Tchr. Wichita (Kans.) Pub. Schs., 1961-63, Orlando (Fla.) Pub. Schs., 1963-64; educator U.S. Dept. Def. Schs., Europe, 1964-75, Santa Fe Pub. Schs., 1978-90; v.p. Jeffrey Adams Antiques, Inc., Santa Fe, 1981-91, Carefree, Ariz., 1991—; adj. faculty Prescott (Ariz.) Coll., 1994—. Co-author: A Critical Guide to Dining Out in Santa Fe, 1987. Capt. CAP aux. USAF, 1986-91, comdr. Santa Fe Composite Squadron, 1989-91. Mem. NOW, Carefree/Cave Creek C. of C. (bd. dirs. 1993, v.p. 1994), Kappa Delta Pi, Sigma Tau Delta. Democrat. Unitarian Universalist. Office: Jeffrey Adams Antiques Inc PO Box 3155 Carefree AZ 85377

ADAMS, SUMMER NANETTE, insurance adjuster, neuromuscular therapist; b. Battle Creek, Mich., Apr. 22, 1954; d. Alfred Francis and Lyndall Ann (Herroon) A. AS, Palm Beach Jr. Coll., 1976; postgrad., Fla. State U., 1971, Sch. of Holistic Massage, 1986. Lic. massage therapist, lic. nutritional counselor. Dispatcher, teletype operator North Palm Beach (Fla.) Police Dept., 1972-74; crime records technician II Fla. Dept. Law Enforcement, Tallahassee, Fla., 1974-77; intelligence analyst State Atty.'s Office, Ft. Lauderdale, Fla., 1977-80; salesperson Ft. Lauderdale, 1980-85; sales mgr. Burdines, Plantation, Fla., 1985-86; therapist Ft. Lauderdale, 1986-92; ins. adjuster Simsol Ins. Svcs., Orlando, Fla., 1992—; therapist U.S. Swim Team, Ft. Lauderdale, Fla. Home: 1017 Merien Ct Oviedo FL 32765

ADAMS, VICTORIA ELEANOR, retired realty company executive; b. San Francisco, Feb. 8, 1941; d. George Mulford and Sarah Louise (Dearborn) A.; m. Gene M. Richardson, 1965 (div. 1972); 1 child, Raymond; m. Franklin Carlisle Boosman, 1972 (div. 1990); 1 child, Eric; m. Harold Glen Kirchner, Mar. 14, 1992. AA, Palomar Coll., 1976; BBA summa cum laude, Nat. U., 1978. Sales adminstr. Evergreen Internat. Airlines, McMinnville, Oreg., 1983; corp. adminstr. N.N. Jaeschke, Inc., San Diego, 1984—; adminstrv. mgr. Tomlinson Agy., Inc., Spokane, Wash., 1980-86; v.p. Champion Realty Inc., Spokane, 1987-93; pub. dir. Champion Pubs., 1987-93; ret., 1993. Editor: Bravura, 1976; (text) Science Among Us, 1965, Principles in Action Newsletter, 1992—; author: No More than 4 Ingredients Cookbook, 1994; designer Astrology game, 1974. Contbr. articles to profl. jours. Solicitor, Am. Heart Assn., 1985. Recipient Cert. Real Estate Sales Achievment, 1978, 1982, 85, 86, 88, 89, 91; Cert. Outstanding Contbn. to Real Estate Edn., 1980. Avocations: writing, ednl. rsch., fishing, camping, traveling. Home: 6110 Pleasant Ridge Rd Apt 3433 Arlington TX 76016

ADAMSON, JANE NAN, elementary school educator; b. Amarillo, Tex., Feb. 5, 1931; d. Carl W. and Lydie O. (Martin) Ray; 1 child, Dave R. Student, Amarillo Coll., Richland Coll. Univ. Dallas, North Tex. State U.; BS, West Tex. State U., Canyon, 1953; MEd, East Tex. State U., Commerce, 1975; diploma, Inst. Children's Lit., 1991; cert., Bur. Edn. and Rsch.,

1995. Cert. elem. tchr., Tex.; lic. real estate salesman. Tchr. Dallas Ind. Sch. Dist. Mem. Alliance of Dallas Educators, Navy League U.S.

ADAMSON, MARY ANNE, geographer, systems engineer; b. Berkeley, Calif., June 25, 1954; d. Arthur Frank and Frances Isobel (Key) A.; m. Richard John Harrington, Sept. 20, 1974. BA with highest honors and great distinction U. Calif., Berkeley, 1975, MA, 1976, postgrad., 1976-78. Cert. tchr. earth scis., Calif.; cert. cave rescue ops. and mgmt., Calif.; lic. emergency med. technician, Contra Costa (Calif.) County, 1983. Teaching asst. dept. geography U. Calif., Berkeley, 1976; geographer, environ. and fgn. area analyst Lawrence Livermore Nat. Lab., Livermore, Calif., 1978-83, cons., 1983-86; systems engr. ESL, Sunnyvale, Calif., 1986-90; rsch. analyst, rsch. devel. and analysis P.G. & E., San Francisco, 1990-93; admin. asst. Internal Audit Dept., 1993—. Contbr. articles to profl. jours. With USNR, 1983—, lt. comdr., 1993—. Recipient Navy Achievement medal, 1992. Staff mem. ARC/Am. Trauma Soc/Sierra Club Urgent Care and Mountain Medicine seminars, 1983—. Asst. editor Vulcan's Voice, 1982. Mem. Assn. Am. Geographers (life), Assn. Pacific Coast Geographers, Nat. Speleol. Soc. (geology, geography sects., sec., editor newsletter Diablo Grotto chpt. 1982-86), Toastmasters Internat. Club (adminstrv. v.p. Blue Monday Club 1991), Sierra Club (life), Nature Conservancy (life), U. Calif. Alumnae Assn., Phi Beta Kappa. Home: 4603 Lakewood St Pleasanton CA 94588-4342 Office: PG&E Internal Auditing 50 Fremont St San Francisco CA 94106-0001

ADAMS-ROBINSON, BRENETIA, human resource management professional/consultant; b. Havana, Fla., Aug. 24, 1960; d. James Alphonza and Maggie Mae (Jenkins) Adams; m. Jeffrey Lee Robinson Sr., Aug. 23, 1980; children: Shaketia Jovan, Jeffrey Lee Jr. BS, U. Md., 1992; MBA, Ala. A&M U. Inventory specialist Kingsmill on the James Restaurant, Williamsburg, Va., 1985; supply technician 2d Coscom, Nellingen, Germany, 1986-87; pers. asst. Stuttgart (Germany) Civilian Personnel Office, 1987-91; community support officer Family Support Div., Stuttgart, 1991-92; personnel recruitment mgr. Martek Inc., Huntsville, Ala., 1992-93; customer svc. rep. Goldstar Am. Inc., Huntsville, 1993—; career counselor; motivational spkr.; sml. bus. entrepreneur. Author, illustrator, editor (newsletter) The Stuttgart Review, 1991-92; author, illustrator various booklets. Founding chairperson Black Employment Program, Stuttgart, 1989; founding pres. Hist. Arts Theatre and Mus. Assn., 1994—; sec., asst. Sunday Sch. Program. Mem. PTO, Ala. Businesswomen's Assn., Nat. Assn. of Self-Employed, Zeta Phi Beta Inc. Democrat. Home: 4602 Blue Haven Dr NW Huntsville AL 35810-1812

ADAMS-ZIMMERMAN, DONNA RAE, maternal-child nurse specialist; b. Arkansas City, Kans., Dec. 28, 1951; d. David Earl and Marilyn Thelma (Henderson) Adams; m. Don Parker Zimmerman, Oct. 28, 1979; children: Jenny, Don Jr., Lindsay. BA in Edn. with honors, Wichita State U., 1974, BSN with honors, 1976, MSN with honors, 1991. Staff nurse NICU Wesley Med. Ctr., Wichita, Kans., 1976, relief charge, rec. nurse, 1976, charge nurse PICU, 1976-82, ob-gyn. edn. coord., 1982-83; staff nurse postpartum/wellbaby HCA/Wesley Med. Ctr., Wichita, 1984-89; nursing faculty Butler County C.C., El Dorado, Kans., 1987—, staff devel./nursing faculty maternal/child and gerontology mgmt., 1989-92; advanced med. surg. nursing and nursing mgmt., 1993—. Mem. Walnut Valley Univserv Adminstrv. Bd., 1994—, membership commr., 1994—; mem. KNEA First Women's Leadership Cadre of Kans., 1994—. Mem. Butler County C.C. Edn. Assn. (v.p. 1992-93, state rep. assembly mem. 1990—, win-win negotiator 1992, 93, lead negotiatior 1994-95, pres. 1993-94), Sigma Theta Tau. Home: 14300 Timber Lake Rd Wichita KS 67230-9110 Office: Butler County Community Coll 901 S Haverhill Rd Wichita KS 67042-9989

ADATO, PERRY MILLER, documentary producer, director, writer; b. Yonkers, N.Y.; d. Perry and Ida (Block) Miller; m. Neil M. Adato, Sept. 11, 1955; children: Laurie, Michelle. Student, Marshalov Sch. Drama, N.Y.C., New Sch. Social Research; L.H.D. hon., Ill. Wesleyan U., 1984. Film research coordinator CBS-TV, N.Y.C., 1959-64, producer, 1964; assoc. producer NET (became WNET Thirteen, Pub. Broadcasting System 1972, N.Y.C., 1964-68, producer dir., 1968-91; lectr. Fairfield U., Conn., 1974-75; exec. prod. Alvin H. Perlmutter Inc./Ind. Prodn. Fund, 1992—; guest lectr. on film Harvard U., Columbia U., NYU, Yale U., others, 1970—; mem. film award jury Am. Film Inst., Beverly Hills, Calif., 1974; judge film award Creative Artists Pub. Svc., N.Y.C., 1976; fist chmn. UN Women in the Arts Film Com., 1976-77; pres. jury Montreal Internat. Film Festival, 1990; mem. jury Pompidou Ctr., Paris Internat. Festival of Films on Art, 1994. Producer, dir.: (TV documentary films) Dylan Thomas: The World I Breathe, 1968 (Emmy award for outstanding achievement in cultural documentary 1968), Gertrude Stein: When This You See, Remember Me, 1970 (Montreal Festival Diplome d'Excellence 1970, Am. Film Festival Blue Ribbon award 1970, 2 Emmy nominations for outstanding direction and outstanding achievement in cultural documentary 1971), The Great Radio Comedians, 1972 (Am. Film Festival Red Ribbon award 1975), An Eames Celebration: Several Worlds of Charles and Ray Eames, 1973 (Chgo. Internat. Film Festival Silver Hugo award 1973, Am. Film Festival Red Ribbon award 1973), Mary Cassatt: Impressionist From Philadelphia, 1974 (Women in Communications Clarion award 1974), Georgia O'Keeffe, 1977 (Dirs. Guild Am. award for documentary achievement 1977-1st woman to receive any Dirs. Guild Am. award, NCCJ Christopher award 1978, Com. for Internat. Events Golden Eagle award 1978, Women in Communications Clarion award 1978, Alfred I. DuPont/Columbia U. citation 1978), Frankenthaler: Toward a New Climate, 1978 (Am. Film Festival Blue Ribbon award in fine arts 1979), Picasso: A Painter's Diary, 1980 (Dirs. Guild Am. award for directorial achievement in TV documentary 1980, Alfred I. DuPont/Columbia U. award for excellence in broadcast journalism 1980, Com. for Internat. Events Golden Eagle award 1980, Am. Film Festival Blue Ribbon award in fine arts 1980, Montreal Internat. Festival of Films on Art First prize for Best Biography of an Artist 1981), Carl Sandburg: Echoes and Silences, 1982 (Women in Communications Matrix award 1982, American Women in Radio and TV (Pinnacle award for TV documentary 1982), Dirs. Guild Am. award for achievement in TV documentary 1983), Eugene O'Neill: A Glory of Ghosts, 1984-85, Broadcast, 1986 (Most Outstanding Achievement in TV Documentary award Dirs. Guild Am. 1986, Spl. Jury award San Francisco Film Festival 1985, Internat. Film and TV Festival of N.Y. Silver medal 1986); exec. producer (9-hour TV series): Art of the Western World, 1985-89; producer, dir., writer: A White Garment of Churches, 1989 (Clarion award 1990, Silver Plaque award Chgo. Internat. Film Festival 1990, Silver Cindy award 1990); exec. prodr. 3 part series Asian Art, 1990-94; prodr., dir. Great Tales in Asian Art, 1993-94; writer Dream Journeys-Nature in East Asian Art, 1994. Hon. bd. dirs. Weston-Westport (Conn.) Arts Coun., 1981-89. Poynter fellow Yale U., 1976; grantee Nat. Endowment for the Arts, 1977-78, 93, NEH, 1980, 83, 91, 93; Calhoun Coll. Fellow Yale U., 1993; subject special tribute, Montreal Internat. Art Film Festival, 1990. Mem. NATAS, Dirs. Guild Am., Writers Guild Am., Women in Communications, N.Y. Women in Film and TV.

ADCOCK, ELIZABETH, controller; b. Heidelburg, Fed. Republic Germany, May 14, 1955; came to U.S., 1958; d. O.T. and Rebecca F. (Kinzer) A. BA in Math., Cameron U., 1976; postgrad., Okla. State U., 1976-79; MBA, Oklahoma City U., 1985. Bookkeeper, sec. Mercer Tackle Co., Lawton, Okla., 1973-76; bookkeeper Tau Beta Sigma-Kappa Kappa Psi Nat. Office, Stillwater, Okla., 1976-78; cashier dept. fin. aid Oklahoma State U., Stillwater, 1977-79; sect. mgr. prodn. Goodyear Tire & Rubber Co., Lawton, Okla., 1979-83, cost acct., 1983-87; asst. plant contr. Goodyear Tire & Rubber Co., Gadsden, Ala., 1987-92, plant contr., 1992—; cons. Jr. Achievement Project Bus., 1994—, Noccalula Civitan Club. Dir. children's choir First United Meth. Ch., Rainbow City, Ala., 1990—; team walk chmn., asst. chair North Ala. chpt., br. bd. dirs. Dixie div. March of Dimes, Anniston, Ala., 1993—; treas., mem. exec. bd. Child Advocacy Ctr., Gadsden, 1993—. Mem. Inst. Mgmt. Accts., Tau Beta Sigma (life). Office: Goodyear Tire & Rubber Co 922 E Meighan Blvd Gadsden AL 35903-1922

ADCOCK, MELODEE ANN, dialysis nurse; b. Troy, N.Y., July 9, 1948; d. Robert Uri and Anna Belle (Ruddy) Brookins; m. John Adcock, Mar. 5, 1983. Diploma, Ann May Sch. of Nursing, 1970; student, Monmouth Coll., 1967-68, Seton Hall U., 1990-92. Cert. nephrology nurse. Evening charge nurse med./surg. unit Jersey Shore Med. Ctr., 1970-77, 78-81, evening nursing supr. med./surg. unit, 1977-78, staff nurse home tng. peritoneal dialysis, 1981-90, asst. nurse mgr. dialysis, 1990, nurse mgr. dialysis, 1990—. Mem. ANA, Am. Nephrology Nurses Assn., N.J. State Nurses Assn., Am. Kidney Found., Acad. Med./Surg. Nursing (charter).

ADCOCK, MURIEL W., special education educator; b. Chgo.. BA, U. Calif. Sonoma State, Rohnert Park, 1979. Cert. spl. edn. tchr., Calif., Montessori spl. edn. tchr. Tchr. The Concordia Sch., Concord, Calif., 1980-85; tchr., cons. Tenderloin Community Children's Ctr., San Francisco, 1985-86; adminstr. Assn. Montessori Internat.-USA, San Francisco, 1988, tchr., advisor, 1989—; course asst. Montessori Spl. Edn. Inst., San Francisco, 1985-87, tchr. spl. edn., 1990, tchr. cons., 1991—, rschr. 1992—. Contbr. articles to profl. jour. Sec. Internat. Forum World Affairs Coun., San Francisco, 1990—, program chair, 1993—. Mem. ASCD, Coun. for Exceptional Children, Nat. Assn. Edn. Young Children, Am. Prthopsychiat. Assn., Am. Assn. Mental Retardation, Assn. Montessori Internat., N.Am. Montessori Tchrs. Assn., Assn. Childhood Edn. Internat., Smithsonian Assocs. N.Y. Acad. Scis., Nat. Geog. Soc., Elmwood Inst., Menninger Found. Office: PO Box 424519 San Francisco CA 94142-4519

ADDINGTON, DEBORAH ANN, tax accountant, foundation executive; b. Phoenix, Aug. 25, 1949; d. Zachary Taylor Jr. and Rose Mary (Pierce) A.; m. Richard James Wright, May 10, 1970 (div. Aug. 1975); 1 child, George Jerome Wright. BS, Ariz. State U., 1978, postgrad. Store comptr. Montgomery Ward, Long Beach, Calif., 1978-79; tax auditor City of Phoenix, 1979-80; corp. sec. Ariz. Radio Comms., Inc., Phoenix, 1980-92; founder, CEO, pub. policy analyst and advocate Advocacy Unltd. Found., Glendale, Ariz., 1987—; tax acct. AAA Abacus Tax Svc., Glendale, 1990—. Author more than 5,000 letters and pub. policy statements to polit. dignitaries and pub. ofcls., 1987—. Fellow Internat. Biog. Assn. (Internat. Woman of Yr. 1993); mem. Am. Biog. Soc. (rsch. bd. advisors, Disting. Leadership award 1993), Soil and Water Conservation Soc., Nat. Wildlife Fedn. (hon. leader), Union of Concerned Scientists, Zero Population Growth. Republican. Jewish. Office: Advocacy Unltd Found 7102 N 43rd Ave Apt 307 Glendale AZ 85301-2926

ADDIS, DEBORAH JANE, management consultant; b. Rahway, N.J., Jan. 29, 1950; d. Emmanuel and Stella (Oles) Addis; m. James Eldin Reed, Apr. 14, 1983. BA, Bowling Green State U., 1972; MA in Orgn., Mgmt. and Pub. Policy, Lesley Coll., Cambridge, Mass., 1992. Cert. mgmt. cons. Pub. info. officer Dept. Transp., State of Ohio, 1972-73; dir. pub. info. and edn. Dept. Commerce, State of Ohio, 1973-75; press sec. Atty. Gen., State of Ohio, 1975-77; dep. press sec. Office of Gov., Commonwealth of Mass., Boston, 1978-79; sr. account exec. Miller Communications, Boston, 1979-80; v.p., prin. Addis & Reed Cons., Inc., Boston, 1981-91, pres., 1992—; founder, pres. Asbestos Victims Campaign, Boston, 1987—; adj. faculty Lesley Coll. Grad. Sch., 1992—. Author monograph and articles, congl. testimony. Bd. govs. Women's City Club of Boston, 1982-85; mem. Ohio Task Force on Domestic Violence, Columbus, 1976. Mem. ABA, Assn. Mgmt. Cons. (v.p. 1985-89), Inst. Mgmt. Cons., Harvard Club of Boston. Democrat. Unitarian. Home: 25 Holly Ln Chestnut Hill MA 02167 Office: Addis & Reed Cons Inc PO Box 85 Chestnut Hill MA 02167

ADDIS, SARA ALLEN, franchise executive; b. El Paso, Tex., May 15, 1930; d. Waldo Rufus and Cordelia Dean (Kerr) Allen; m. Bobby Joe Addis, June 5, 1949; children: Craig Dell, Alan Blake, Neil Clark, Sara Kathleen. Sec. to adminstr. Southwestern Gen. Hosp., El Paso, 1948-49; sec. to dir. of personnel U. Tex., El Paso, 1964-65; pres., founder Sara Care Franchise Corp., El Paso, 1978—; chmn. bd. Sara Care Inc., 1988—. Named Small Bus. Person of Yr., Small Bus. Adminstrn., 1986, 87. Mem. Internat. Franchise Assn., Nat. Fedn. Ind. Businesses, Presidents Assn. Am. Mgmt. Assn., El Paso Better Bus. Bur., El Paso C. of C., Assn. Pioneer Women. (Entrepreneur of Yr.), Bus. and Profl. Women El Paso (Small Bus. Person of Yr. 1983, 85, 86, 87), Exec. Forum, Profl. Women's Network U. Tex. El Paso. Republican. Club: Lower Valley Women's. Lodge: Order Eastern Star. Avocations: oil painting, music, travel. Home: 8417 Parkland Dr El Paso TX 79925-2637 Office: Sara Care Franchise Corp 1612 N Lee Trevino Dr Ste A El Paso TX 79936-5104

ADDISON, ANITA LOUISE, health services planner, clinic official; b. L.A., Aug. 9, 1953; d. Edward Thurman and Carolyn Elizabeth (Boddie) A. BA in Sociology, Stanford U., 1975; M City Planning, U. Calif., Berkeley, 1978, MPH, 1979. Planning analyst Spanish Speaking Unity Coun., Oakland, Calif., 1979-81, sr. planner, 1981-82, program devel. dir., 1988-89; planner William F. Ryan Community Health Ctr., N.Y.C., 1982-86, dir. planning and devel., 1986-88; dir. planning and devel. La Clinica de la Raza, Oakland, 1989—. Bd. dirs. Support Svcs. for Srs., Hayward, Calif., 1989-90. Scholar State of Calif., 1971-75. Mem. NOW, Am. Pub. Health Assn., Nat. Women's Health Network, Planned Parenthood, Sierra Club, Soka Gakkai Internat.-USA, Stanford U. Alumni Assn. Democrat. Buddhist. Office: La Clinica de la Raza 1515 Fruitvale Ave Oakland CA 94601-2355

ADDISON, BRENDA ANN RATHEL, physician's assistant, nurse; b. Bainbridge, Ga., May 31, 1952; d. James Buck and Ruby Lee (Hutto) Rathel; m. Toby Addison, July 2, 1972; children: Benjamin Mark, Lori Suzanne. ADN, Darton Coll., 1972; BSN, Albany State Coll., 1984, MSN, 1989. RN, Ga.; registered physician's asst., pub. mgr. Dir., physician's asst. Rentz Clinic, Colquitt, Ga., 1972-77; dir. Jinks Sch. Nursing, Colquitt, 1977-87, Miller County Health Ctr., Colquitt, 1987—; bd. dirs. SOWEGA-CHI, Albany, Ga.; coord. Mktg. Pub. Rels. Work Group Health Dist. 8/2, Albany, 1983—. Editor: (newsletter) S.W. Health Connection, 1994; composer gospel and country songs, 1986—; weekly columnist for 2 newspapers, 1990—. Mem. Ga. Assn. Physicians Assts., Women's Aglow Fellowship Area Bd. S.W. Ga. (v.p. outreach). Office: Miller County Health Ctr 250 W Pine St Colquitt GA 31737

ADDISON, MARY JANE, civic worker; b. Beaumont, Tex.; d. Henry Davis and Corinne (Carter) Pond; m. Eugene Morse Addison, Mar. 10, 1946; children: Eugene Morse, Paul Davis. RN, Jefferson Davis Sch. Nursing, 1945; student, U. Houston, U. Tex., U. Tenn. Mem. choir First Bapt. Ch.; den mother Cub Scouts, 6 years, recipient Den Mothers award, 1961; pres. Huntsville (Tex.) PTA, 1955-56, v.p. dist. bd., 1956-57, state life mem. PTA, 1967; pres. Women's Missionary Union, First Bapt. Ch., 1965-68, also Sunday Sch. tchr.; chmn. heritage com. Mayor's Bicentennial Com., 1974-76; chmn. bd. dirs. city beautification com. Tex. Sesquicentennial Celebration, 1982-86; pres. Woman's Forum, 1973-74, Tex. Fedn. Womens Clubs, 1972-74, 80-81, named Woman of Year, 1974; charter and life mem. Hosp. Aux., pres., 1971-72; pres. Walker County Cancer Soc., 1983-84; bd. dirs. Cultural Arts Ctr., 71-72; chmn. bd. dirs. Sam Houston Meml. Mus. 1983-87; bd. dirs. Walker County Hist. Commn.; mem., dir., sponsor Community Choir; mem. mayors com. Bicentennial of the Constn. of U.S. Celebration, 1987—. Decorated Grand Priory of Am. Order St. John of Jerusalem, dame Knights Hospitaller; recipient Cert. of Commendation, Heritage Com., 1980, 81. Mem. Daus. Republic of Tex. (pres. Houston chpt. 1970-75, 79-81, registrar 1975—, state rec. sec. gen. 1973-75, state 1st v.p. gen. 1975-77, pres. gen. 1977-79 library bd. 1981-83, Alamo bd. 1983-85, 87-89), DAR (regent Mary Martin Elmore Scott chpt. 1972-74, 82-86, state chmn. 1991-94), Daus. Am. Colonists (regent Capt. John Utie chpt., state corr. sec. 1977-79, state rec. sec. 1983-85, state 1st vice regent 1985-87, regent 1987-89), UDC (dist. rec. sec. 1974-76, dist. chmn. 1981-83, state div. historian 1984-86, pres. chpt. 1983-85, 88—, Jefferson Davis medal), Colonial Dames Am. (pres. chpt. VIII 1989-91), Dames of Ct. of Honor, Tex. Hist. Found. (chpt. regent 1987-89, dir., cert. of commendation 1980, 81, mem. state heritage com.), Walker County Geneal. Soc., San Jacinto Mus. History Assn., Washington-on-the-Brazos State Park Assn., Lone Star Drama Hist. Assn. (state adv. bd.), Am., Tex. (pres. 38th Dist. 1977-83) nurses assns., AMA, Tri-County (past pres.) med. auxs., Tex. Acad. Family Physicians (charter; state parliamentarian 1983-84), Beautify Tex. Council, Nat. Soc. Magna Charta Dames (state sec. 1988—), Daus. War of 1812, Colonial Dames of XVII Century (organizing regent 1988—). Clubs: Garden (past pres. chmn. city beautification com.), Univ. Women Sam Houston State U. (charter).

ADDISS, SUSAN SILLIMAN, state government administrator; b. New Haven, Apr. 3, 1931; d. Thomas North Tracy and Susan Silliman (Bennett) Pearson; m. James M. Addiss, Apr. 21, 1956 (div. July 1967); children: Justus Joseph, Susan Silliman. BA, Smith Coll., 1951; MPH, M. Urban Studies, Yale U., 1969. Health educator New Haven Health Dept., 1969-72; health dir. Naugatuck Valley Health Dist., Ansonia, Conn., 1972-76; health planning bur. chief Conn. Dept. Health Svcs., Hartford, Conn., 1976-85; health dir. Quinnipiack Valley Health Dist., Hamden, Conn., 1985-91; health commr. Conn. Dept. of Pub. Health and Addiction Svcs., Hartford, 1991—; lectr. Dept. of Epidemiology & Pub. Health, Yale Univ., 1970—, Univ. Conn. Health Ctr., Farmington, 1978—; asst. clin. prof. Yale Sch. of Nursing, 1988—. Mem. APHA (pres. 1984), Conn. Pub. Health Assn. (pres. 1985-87, C.E.A. Winslow award 1994), Nat. Assn. for Pub. Health Policy (treas. 1978-93), Quota Club Internat. (New Haven), Phi Beta Kappa. Office: Conn Dept Pub Health & Addiction Svcs 150 Washington St Hartford CT 06106-4476

ADDY, JAN ARLENE, clinical nurse, educator; b. Balt., Apr. 16, 1951; d. James Anderson and June Annette (Windsor) Briggle; m. Rick Edward Addy, Feb. 26, 1988; children: Brittany Anissa, Richard Michael. AA in Nursing, Essex Community Coll., Balt., 1972; BSN, U. San Francisco, 1976; MS, U. Md., Balt., 1979; postgrad., Nova Southeastern U. Cert. pub. health sch. nurse. Sr. staff nurse Francis Scott Key Med. Ctr., Balt., 1980-87; clin. instr. Harford Community Coll., Bel Air, Md., 1987-88; primary nurse and nurse educator U. Md., Balt., 1987—; asst. prof. Baltimore City C.C., 1994—; adj. faculty Catonsville C.C., 1994; instr. jr. students St. Joseph's Hosp. Sch. Nursing, Towson, Md., 1979-80; clin. instr., skills instr. Essex C.C., 1978-79; mem. U. Md. Med. Systems Partnership Program, Frederick Douglas H.S. Contbr. articles to profl. jours. Mem. ASCD, Nat. Soc. Trauma Nurses, Nat. Nursing Staff Devel. Orgn., Emergency Nurses Assn., C.A.R.E., Sigma Theta Tau (program com. Pi chpt.).

ADEKSON, MARY OLUFUNMILAYO, therapist; b. Ogbomoso, Nigeria; came to U.S., 1988; d. Gabriel and Deborah Williams; children: Adedayo, Babatunde. BA in English and Am. Lit., Brandeis U., 1975; MEd in Guidance and Counseling, Obafemi Awolowo U., Ile-Ife, Nigeria, 1987; PhD, Ohio U., 1995. English tchr. Cen. Sch. Bd., Ibadan, Nigeria, 1976-88; acting prin. Abe Tech. Coll., Ibadan, 1978; coord. guidance svcs. Min. Edn., Ile-Ife, 1984-88; part-time lectr. Obafemi Awolowo U., Ile-Ife, 1986-88; vice prin. Olubuse Meml. High Sch., Ile-Ife, 1987-88; grad. asst. Ohio U., Athens, 1988-91; vol. contract worker, trainer Careline, Tri-County Mental Health Ctr., Athens, 1988-92; vol. My Sister's Place, Athens, 1989, Good Works Athens, 1989, Montgomery County Hotline, 1994; contract worker Tri County Activity Ctr., Athens, 1989-92, therapist II Woodland Ctr., Gallipolis, Ohio, 1991-92; part-time lectr. U. Md., 1993, coord. tutorial svcs.; dir. Christian Book Ctr., Ile-Ife; vol., part-time counselor DWI program Prince George's County Health Dept., Hyattsville, Md. Vol. Montgomery County Police Dept.; mem. Alcohol and Other Drug Abuse Adv. Coun., Montgomery County, Md.; mem. adv. com. Germantown (Md.) Libr.; mem. Gaithersburg (Md.) City Adv. Com.; chmn. bd. dirs. Faith Enterprises, Germantown. Recipient Gold medal West African Athletic Assn., 1965; Internat. Peace scholar P.E.O., 1990-91, Wien Internat. scholar Brandeis U., 1973-75. Mem. ACA, Am. Mental Health Counselors Assn. Network on Children and Teens (membership chair 1991-92, chair 1993—), Am. Assn. Counseling and Devel. (award for internat. grad. students 1990), Counseling Assn. Nigeria (planning com. 1986), Am. Rehab. Counselors Assn., Am. Mental Health Counseling Assn., Assn. Multicultural Counseling and Devel., Oyo State Assn. Guidance Counselors (chmn. Oranmiyan local govt. area 1986-88), Chi Sigma Iota (program coord. 1990).

ADELEKAN, PATRICIA ANN, school administrator; b. Columbus, Ohio, Mar. 13, 1942; d. Arthur H. and Betty Jane Isbell; children: Adebola, Adetokunbo, Aderemi, Adegboyega. BA, Ohio State U., 1966; MA, U. San Francisco, 1975; PhD, U. Ibadan, 1983. Cert. coll. adminstr., secondary tchr. Tchr. various schs., Hartford, Conn. and Oakland, Calif., 1968-75; v.p. Lagos State Coll. Edn., Nigeria, 1976-80; dept. head Ogun State Poly. U., Nigeria, 1980-84; rsch. specialist Sacramento City (Calif.) Unified Sch. Dist., 1985-87; lectr. Sierra Coll., Rocklin, Calif., 1988-89; founder, pres. Youth-on-the-Move, Inc., Sacramento, 1986—; cons. Gifted and Talented Edn., Sacramento, 1985-86; columnist Sacramento Observer, 1987—; founder Am. Heritage Prep. Acad. and Family Learning Ctr., 1992, Youth-on-the-Move, Inc. Educators' Hall of Fame, 1993. Author: Hall of Fame Educators, 1993, Multicultural Educators, 1994; prodr. Youth Talk, a live youth radio program, 1993; editor numerous articles; contbr. articles to profl. jours.; pub./editor Youth on the News, monthly newspaper, 1989—. V.p. YWCA, Sacramento, 1988-89; commr. County Children's Commn., Sacremento, 1989—; mem. Leadership Sacramento, 1988-89; program coord. World Exch., 1991—; chairperson Juneteenth Art & Music Festival, 1992. Recipient Cert. of Recognition award, assemblyman Norman Waters, 1981, Proclamation award City of Sacramento Mayor, 1989, Plaque of Achievement award, 1989, Love and Help Children award, Luminary of the Yr. award Coors, 1992, over 25 awards and honors, 1992—. Mem. Calif. Tchr.'s Assn., Nat. Assn. French Tchrs., Nat. Mensa Soc., AAUW (chair edn. com.), NAFE, Phi Delta Kappa. Home: 1131 26th Ave Sacramento CA 95822-1841

ADELMAN, IRMA GLICMAN, economics educator; b. Cernowitz, Rumania, Mar. 14, 1930; came to U.S., 1949, naturalized, 1955; d. Jacob Max and Raissa (Ettinger) Glicman; m. Frank L. Adelman, Aug. 16, 1950 (div. 1979); 1 son, Alexander. BS, U. Calif., Berkeley, 1950, MA, 1951, PhD, 1955. Teaching assoc. U. Calif., Berkeley, 1955-56; instr. U. Calif., 1956-57, lectr. with rank asst. prof., 1957-58; vis. asst. prof. Mills Coll., 1958-59; acting asst. prof. Stanford, 1959-61, asst. prof., 1961-62; assoc. prof. Johns Hopkins, Balt., 1962-65; prof. econs. Northwestern U., Evanston, Ill., 1966-72, U. Md., 1972-78; prof. econs. and agrl. econs. U. Calif. at Berkeley, 1979-94; prof. emeritus, 1994—; cons. divsn. indsl. devel. UN, 1962-63, AID U.S. Dept. State, Washington, 1963-72, World Bank, 1968—, ILD, Geneva, 1973—. Author: Theories of Economic Growth and Development, 1961, Institutions and Development Strategies: Selected Essays of Irma Adelman Volume I, 1994, Dynamics and Income Distribution: Selected Essays of Irma Adelman Volume II, 1994, Selected Essays (in Spanish), 1994, (with A. Pepelasis and L. Mears) Economic Development: Analysis and Case Studies, 1961, (with Eric Thorbecke) The Theory and Design of Economic Development, 1966, (with C.T. Morris) Society, Politics and Economic Development—A Quantitative Approach, 1967, Practical Approaches to Development Planning-Korea's Second Five Year Plan, 1969, (with C.T. Morris) Economic Development and Social Equity in Developing Countries, 1973, (with Sherman Robinson) Planning for Income Distribution, 1977-78, (with C. T. Morris) Comparative Patterns of Economic Growth, 1850-1914, 1987. Fellow Center Advanced Study Behavioral Scis., 1970-71. Fellow Am. Acad. Arts and Scis., Econometric Soc., Royal Soc. Encouragement Arts, Mfgs. & Commerce; mem. Am. Econ. Assn. (mem. exec. com., v.p. 1969-71), Social Sci. Rsch. Coun. (exec. com.). Office: Univ Calif Dept Agr & Natural Resources Berkeley CA 94720-3310

ADELMAN, MERLE, marketing professional; b. Boston, May 15, 1958; d. George and Sondra (Cohen) A.; m. Douglas Everett (div. Feb. 1991). BA in Econs., Dartmouth Coll., 1980. Mktg. exec. Digital Equipment Corp., Marlboro, Mass., 1980-81, M/A Com OSI, Bedford, Mass., 1981-82; account exec. Compugraphic Corp., Wilmington, Mass., 1983-86; mktg. exec. Symbolics Inc., Cambridge, Mass., 1986-87; account supr. Hill and Knowlton, Waltham, Mass., 1987-88; mktg. staff mgr. Hewlett-Packard Co., Waltham, 1988—. Mem. Med. Mktg. Assn., Combined Jewish Philanthropies (vol. 1991—), Appalachian Mountain Club, League Am. Wheelman, Dartmouth Alumni Fund, Mosaic Outdoor Club. Democrat. Home: C12 Scotty Hollow Dr North Chelmsford MA 01863-1224 Office: Hewlett-Packard Co 3000 Minuteman Rd Andover MA 01810

ADELMAN, PAMELA BERNICE KOZOLL, education educator; b. Milw., Dec. 26, 1945; d. Harry and Rebecca (Sharp) Kozoll; m. Steven H. Adelman, June 30, 1968; children: David, Robert. BS, U. Wis., Madison, 1967; MA, Northwestern U., 1972, PhD, 1982. Cert. tchr., Ill. Tchr. Peckham Jr. High Sch., Milw., 1967-68, Fairview Sch., Skokie, Ill., 1968-70; learning disabilities specialist Sch. Dist 28, Northbrook, Ill., 1971-77; instr., rsch. asst. Northwestern U., Evanston, Ill., 1977-80; lectr., asst. prof., then assoc. prof. Barat Coll., Lake Forest, Ill., 1977-90, prof. edn., 1990—, dir. learning opportunities program, 1985—; cons. Deerfield (Ill.) Pub. Schs., 1986-90; proposal reviewer State of N.J., Trenton, 1986-87; mem. Pres.'s Com. on Hiring of Disabled, 1990; mem. higher edn. adv. coun. State of Ill.; presenter at profl. confs. Co-author: Learning Disabilities, Graduate School, and Careers, 1990; co-editor: Success for College Students with Learning

Disabilities, 1993; consulting editor Learning Disabilities Focus, 1989—, Jour. Developmental Edn., 1990—, Jour. of Postsecondary Edn. and Disabilities, 1991-93; contbr. articles to ednl. publs. Chair Sch. Dist. 107 Caucus, Highland Park, Ill., 1982; bd. dirs. Jewish Children's Bur., Chgo., 1985—, pres., 1994—. Paul A. Witty fellow Northwestern U., 1978-80; grantee Lloyd A. Fry Found., 1985-86, Kraft Corp., Chgo., 1989, McDonald's Corp., Chgo., 1986. Mem. Coun. Exceptional Children, Learning Disabilities Assn. Am., Coun. Learning Disabilities, Orton Dyslexia Soc., Internat. Reading Assn., Assn. on Higher Edn. and Disabilities, Internat. Acad. for Rsch. in Learning Disabilities. Office: Barat Coll 700 E Westleigh Rd Lake Forest IL 60045-3263

ADELMAN, YVETTE MARIE, accountant; b. St. Cloud, Minn., Apr. 19, 1960; d. John Arthur and Donna Marie Apolonia (Packert) A. Grad., St. Cloud Tech. Coll., 1980; postgrad., Met. State U. Contr., cost acct. Palmer Printing, St. Cloud, Minn., 1979-83; credit mgr. May Printing, St. Cloud, 1983-84; sr. cost acct., computer sys. adminstr. Nahan Printing, St. Cloud, 1984-91; cost acct. Coborn's/DBC Foods, St. Cloud, 1992—; pvt. practice Sauk Rapids, Minn., 1990—. Mem. Inst. Mgmt. Accts. (v.p. 1985-89, 90-91, bd. dirs. 1982-85, 89-90, 92-93, pres. 1991-92, treas. 1993-94. Roman Catholic. Home: 2670 10th Ave NE Sauk Rapids MN 56379 Office: Coborn's/DBC Foods PO Box 6146 1445 East Hwy 23 Saint Cloud MN 56302-6146

ADELSON, MARGERY J(EAN), psychologist, educator; b. N.Y.C., Jan. 10, 1945; d. Emanuel George and Greta (Weingartner) Gross; m. Joseph Bernard Adelson, May 24, 1981; children: Eric Daniel, David Seth, Gretchen Diana. AB summa cum laude, U. Rochester, 1966; PhD, U. Mich., 1971. Lic. psychologist, Mich. Clin. psychologist U. Mich., Ann Arbor, 1971—; pvt. practice psychology Ann Arbor, 1971—. Mem. Am. Psychol. Assn., Phi Beta Kappa. Home: 3743 Meadow Ln Saline MI 48176-9554 Office: U Mich Psychol Clinic 1027 E Huron St Ann Arbor MI 48109-0001 also: 609 E Liberty St Ann Arbor MI 48104

ADENIRAN, DIXIE DARLENE, library administrator; b. L.A., May 26, 1943; d. Alfred and Madge (Clare) Harvey. BA, U. Calif., Santa Barbara, 1965; MA, Mich. State U., 1968; MLS, U. Mich., 1970. Libr. Free Libr. of Phila., 1970-72, Coll. Sci. and Tech., Port Harcourt, Nigeria, 1972-73; libr. Ventura (Calif.) County Libr. Svcs. Agy., 1974-79, libr. dir., 1979—. Pres. Ventura County Master Chorale and Opera Assn., 1985. Mem. ALA, Calif. Libr. Assn. (assembly 1994—), Calif. County Librs. Assn. (pres. 1988), Soroptimists (pres. Ventura club 1984). Home: 5548 Rainier St Ventura CA 93003-1135 Office: Ventura County Libr Svcs 4274 Telegraph Rd Ventura CA 93003-3706

ADER, DEBORAH N., psychologist, medical educator; b. Rochester, N.Y., May 17, 1958; d. Robert and Gayle (Simon) A. BA, Tufts U., 1979; MA, U. Colo., 1985, PhD, 1988. Postdoctoral fellowship U. Fla. Health Sci. Ctr., Gainesville, Fla., 1988-91; rsch. coord. Faculty Devel. Ctr., Waco, Tex., 1991-93; asst. prof. psychiatry, med. and clin. psychology Uniformed Svcs. U. Bethesda (Md.) Health Scis., 1994—. Mem. editorial bd.: Health Psychology, 1991-93; contbr. articles to profl. jours. Literacy vol. Gainesville, Fla., 1989; bd. com. mem. United Way Waco, Tex., 1992-93. Mem. Am. Psychological Assn., Soc. Behavioral Medicine. Office: Uniformed Svcs U Health Scis Dept Psychiatry 400 Jones Bridge Rd Bethesda MD 20814

ADERHOLD, LOUISE KATHRYN, art educator; b. St. Johns, Mich., Jan. 4, 1941; d. Robert Gerald and Mabel Louise (Waidelich) Harris; m. Bruce Alan Aderhold, June 20, 1964; children: Amy, Bryan. BS, U. Wis., 1963, postgrad., 1963, 88, 92-93. Cert. art tchr., Wis. Elem. art tchr. Port Washington (Wis.) Pub. Sch., 1963-66; art tchr. West DePere (Wis.) H.S., 1966-68; substitute art tchr. Sauk Prairie Schs., Sauk City, Wis., 1968, mid. sch. art tchr., 1969-70; owner Carousel Gift Store, Baraboo, Wis., 1974-87; substitute tchr. Baraboo (Wis.) Pub. Schs., 1990—; art tchr. Madison Area Tech. Coll., Portage, Wis., 1991-92, U. Wis., Oxford Prison Camp, 1992. Exhbn. Bradley Gallery, Thiensville, Wis., 1963. Mem. adminstrv. bd. Emanuel Ch. Sch. Bd., also libr., tchr., 1968—; illustrator art projects Baraboo Jaycees, 1968-69, v.p., 1969-70; v.p., treas. Baraboo (Wis.) Newcomers Orgn., 1968-70; mem. adv. bd. St. Clare Hosp., 1980-85, pres., 1985; mem. adv. bd. Baraboo Sauk County-U. Wis., 1982-91; pres. adv. bd. U. Wis., Sauk County, 1989-91, bd. visitors, 1992; active Friends of the Campus, 1992-95, Baraboo Theatre Guild, 1994-95. Mem. AAUW (v.p. 1988-91, pres. 1992-94, 5 Star Br. award 1994), Wis. Calligraphers Guild, Sauk County Art Assn. Home: 1520 Oak St Baraboo WI 53913

ADICK, SHEILA MARIE, sales and marketing executive; b. Dover, Del., Oct. 14, 1964. BA, Marquette U., 1987, MBA, 1994. Adminstrv. asst. Mercurio Homes, Cin., 1987-88; mktg. specialist Enerpac, Milw., 1988-90; mktg. analyst Emerpac, Milw., 1990-91, svc. tech., 1991-92, territory mgr., 1992—. Active Jr. League, Milw., 1989—. Home: 4602 N 71st St Milwaukee WI 53218-4851 Office: Enerpac 13000 W Silver Spring Dr Butler WI 53007-1093

ADICKES, SANDRA ELAINE, English language educator, writer; b. N.Y.C., July 14, 1933; d. August Ernst and Edythe Louise (Oberschlake) A.; 1 child, Delores, Sept. 16, 1966. BA, Douglass Coll., 1954; MA, CUNY, 1964; PhD, N.Y.U., 1977. Asst. registrar N.Y.U., 1954-55; sec. McCann Erickson, J. Walter Thompson Cos., N.Y.C., 1955-60; English tchr. N.Y.C. Bd. Edn., 1960-70, 1980-88; instr. edn. N.Y.C. Tech. Coll., 1970-72; asst. prof. English S.I. Community Coll., N.Y.C., 1972-77; dir. project chance Bklyn. Coll., 1977-80; from assoc. prof. to prof. English Winona State U., Minn., 1988—; cons. Antioch Coll. N.Y.C., 1970; guest tutor London U., 1979. Author: The Social Quest, 1991, Legends of Good Women, 1992; editor: By A Woman Writt, 1973; contbr. articles to profl. jours. Co-founder Tchrs'. Freedom Sch. Project, Miss., 1963-64, Tchrs'. Com. for Peace Vietnam, 1965-66. Named Woman of Yr. Nat. Assn. Negro Bus. Profl. Women, N.J., 1966. Mem. MLA, Am. Studies Assn. Democrat. Home: 621 E 3rd St Winona MN 55987-4226 Office: Winona State U Dept English Winona MN 55987

ADILETTA, DEBRA JEAN OLSON, business analyst consultant; b. Gloucester, Mass., Oct. 1, 1959; d. Melvin Porter Jr. and Ruth Margaret (Dahlmer) Olson; m. Mark Anthony Adiletta, Aug. 25, 1984; children: Christopher Michael, Nicole Brianna, Mark Andrew. BA, Coll. of Holy Cross, Worcester, Mass., 1981; MBA, U. Rochester, 1986. Systems analyst Eastman Kodak Co., Rochester, N.Y., 1981-85, infosystems specialist, 1985-86, personal computer area mgr., 1986-87, bus. analyst cons., 1987—. seminar instr., Rochester, 1987. Fin. advisor Sts. Peter and Paul Ch., Rochester, 1985-86; div. chairperson United Way, Rochester, 1987. Mem. Assn. Systems Mgmt., Holy Cross Alumni Assn. (class agt. 1981—, sec. 1983-84, treas. 1984-88, v.p. 1988-90, pres. 1990-91, bd. dirs. 1992—). Office: Eastman Kodak Co 343 State St Rochester NY 14650-0001

ADKERSON, DONYA LYNN, psychotherapist; b. Mattoon, Ill., Oct. 5, 1959; d. Edwin Dwayne and Sonya Jeanne (Abernathie) Adkerson; m. George Anthony Ferguson, May 20, 1990; 1 child, Tiana Jo Berry. MA, So. Ill. U., Edwardsville, 1983. Outpatient dir. Children's Ctr. for Behavioral Devel., Centerville, Ill., 1983-90; pvt. practice psychotherapy Evaluation & Therapy Svc., Edwardsville, 1991-92; dir. Alternatives Counseling, Inc., 1993—; cons. St. Louis City Juvenile Ct., 1991-94, Covenant Children's Home, 1991-93. Co-author: Adult Sexual Offender Assessment Packet, 1994. Pres. Ill. Network for Mgmt. Abusive Sexuality, 1991; mem. Adolescent Perpetrator Network, 1987—; exec. bd. Arts League Players Theatre, Edwardsville, 1986—; chmn. Metro-East Task Force on Sexual Offenders. Mem. APA, ACA, Assn. for Treatment of Sex Abusers (clin. mem.; exec. bd. 1994—). Office: Alternatives Counseling 1 Mark Twain Plz Edwardsville IL 62025

ADKINS, BETTY A., state legislator; b. Mpls., June 4, 1934; d. John Edward and Barbara (Graff) Whalen; m. Wally Adkins, 1956; children—Patrick, Susan, Michael, Kathleen, Caroline, Nancy. Student North Hennepin Community Coll.; student U. Minn., 1952-53. Formerly dep. clk. Otsego Twp., vice chmn. Wright County Bd. Adjustment, Minn.; mem. Minn. Senate, St. Paul, 1982—. Formerly chmn. Wright County Democratic-Farmer-Labor Party. Home: 1655 Kadler Ave NE Saint Michael MN 55376-9287 Office: State Senate State Capital Saint Paul MN 55155 also: 550 Central Ave E Saint Michael MN 55376-9522*

ADKINS, JACQUELINE ANN, art educator; b. Decatur, Ill., July 31, 1945; d. Gerard B. and Eloise F. (Scott) Douin; 1 child, Craig Vincent Adkins. BEd, Eastern Ill. U., 1967, MEd, 1971. Cert. art tchr. K-12, Ga. Art tchr. 7-12 grades Marshall (Ill.) Sch. Dist., 1967-69; art tchr. 1-6 grades Charleston (Ill.) Sch. Dist., 1970-75, elem. tchr., 1975-77, art tchr. 7-8 grades, 1977-87; art tchr. 9-12 grades Marietta (Ga.) Sch. Dist., 1987—; recruiter Marietta City Schs., 1990-91, incentive pay co., 1992-93; supr. student tchrs. Charleston Schs., 1982-84; supr. participants Marietta High Sch., 1991-92. Mem. Marietta/Cobb Mus. of Art, High Mus. of Art; vol. Piedmont Arts Festival, Atlanta, Peachtree Rd. Race, Atlanta. Mem. NEA, Nat. Art Edn. Assn. (Southeastern Secondary Art Tchr. of Yr., 1993-94), Ga. Art Edn. Assn. (treas. 1993—, Ga. Secondary Art Tchr. of Yr. 1992-93), Marietta Edn. Assn. (co-v.p. 1990—), Epsilon Sigma Alpha, Phi Delta Kappa. Roman Catholic. Home: 1692 Grist Mill Dr Marietta GA 30062 Office: Marietta High Sch 121 Winn St Marietta GA 30064

ADKINS, JEANNE M., state legislator; b. North Platte, Nebr., May 2, 1949. BA, U. Nebr. Journalist; mem. Colo. Ho. of Reps., chairwoman judiciary com., vice-chairwoman legal svcs. com., mem. fin. com., regional air quality control coun., state edn. accountability commn. Founding sec. Douglas County Econ. Devel. Coun., bd. dirs., 1988. Fellow Vanderbilt U. Govt., Gates fellow JFK Sch. Govt. State/Local Program, Toll fellow. Mem. Am. Soc. Newspaper Editors, Soc. Profl. Journalists, Suburban Newspaper Assn. Republican. Baptist. Home: 6505 E Alcorn Ave Parker CO 80134-8003 also: 8102 E Windwood Way Parker CO 80134-6344 Office: Office of State Senate State Capital Denver CO 80203*

ADKINS, ROSANNE BROWN, speech and language pathologist, myofunctional therapist; b. Norfolk, Va., Jan. 10, 1944; d. Melvin Dillard and Mattye Marie (Cox) Brown; BS, U. Ga., 1968, MEd, 1971; m. Steve Bunker, Aug. 24, 1962 (div.); children: Steve, Amy Bunker Patterson; m. Jon Adkins, May 27, 1988. Speech pathologist Barrow County Schs., Winder, Ga., 1968-69, Madison County Schs., Danielsville, Ga., 1969-70, Hall County Schs., Gainesville, Ga., 1971-72, Hope Haven Sch. for Retarded Children, Athens, Ga., 1972-73, Buford (Ga.) City Schs., 1973-75, Duval County Bd. Pub. Instrn., Jacksonville, Fla., 1975-79, Orange County Pub. Schs., Orlando, Fla., 1979—. Sallie Maude Jones scholar, U. Ga., 1966-68; USPHS grad. fellow, 1970-71. Mem. Am. Speech-Lang.-Hearing Assn. (cert. of clin. competence), Fla. Lang. Speech and Hearing Assn. Delta Zeta, Zeta Phi Eta, Kappa Delta Pi, Phi Kappa Phi. Mem. Disciples of Christ. Clubs: Order Amaranth (past Royal Matron), Ladies of the Elks. Editor, Speakeasy, Speech and Language Newsletter, 1982—. Home: 2997 Carlsbad Ct Oviedo FL 32765 Office: Orange County Sch System 434 N Tampa Ave Orlando FL 32805-1220

ADKINS-OVERTON, BETTY JEAN, foundation administrator; b. Jacksonville, Fla., Oct. 10, 1949; d. Henry and Miriam (Gordon) Crawford; children from previous marriage: Joseph Alonzo III, Jermaine Lamar; m. Eugene Adkins, Apr. 24, 1992. BA in English, Tenn. State U., 1970, MA in English, 1974; PhD in English, Vanderbilt U., 1980; student Inst. Ednl. Mgmt., Harvard U., 1990. Reporter Race Rels. Reporter Mag., Nashville, 1970-71; tchr. Met. Nashville Sch. System, 1971-72; instr., project dir. Tenn. State U., Nashville, 1972-76; asst. prof. Nashville State Tech. Inst., 1976-78, Fisk U., Nashville, 1978-83; assoc. dean. grad. sch. U. Ark., Little Rock, 1983-85, dean grad. sch., 1985-91; program dir. Kellogg Found., Battle Creek, Mich., 1991—; asst. dir. Kellogg Nat. Fellowship Program, Battle Creek, Mich., 1991-94; coord. higher edn. programs Kellogg Found., Battle Creek, 1994—; instr. U. Tenn., Nashville, 1976-82; dir. rsch. sponsored programs, U. Ark., 1986-88; bd. dirs. Sci. and Info. Liason Office, 1984—. Bd. dirs. Ark. Sci. and Technology Authority, Little Rock, 1989—, Women's Project, 1986—, Ark. Pub. Policy Panel, 1988—, No. Bank Women's Adv. Bd., 1988—, Nashville Panel, 1974-83, Cen. Ark. Libr. Sys., 1990—, Ark. Coun. of Nat. Conf. Christians and Jews, Inc., 1990—, Bread for the World, 1990—; mem. commn. on edn. credits & credentials Am. Coun. on Edn., 1989—; chair Bi-Racial Adv. Com. Little Rock Sch. Dist., 1987—. Am. Coun. Edn. fellow, 1981-82, W.K. Kellogg Found. fellow, 1988—. Mem. Nat. Coun. Tchrs. of English, Coun. Grad. Schs., Coun. So. Grad. Schs., Women Color United Against Domestic Violence (pres.), An. Assn. High Edn., Rotary, Alpha Kappa Alpha. Democrat. Roman Catholic. Office: W K Kellogg Found One Michigan Ave E Battle Creek MI 49017

ADLER, BARBARA ANN, social worker, consultant; b. Chgo., July 6, 1938; d. Joe and Sarah (Kesselman) Moret; widowed; 1 child, Karyn A. AA with honors, Lake Mich. Coll., 1976; BA cum laude, Western Mich. U., 1978, MSW, 1981. Cert. social worker, Mich.; lic. marriage and family therapist. Dir. Coll. Vocat. Edn. Rasmussen Bus. Coll., St. Paul; pres. The Fashion Mart, Inc., South Haven, Mich.; dir. Coll. Vocat. Edn. Mich. Dunes Correctional Facility, 1985-87; pvt. practice South Haven; adj. faculty Southwestern Mich. Coll., Dowagiac, Mich., Lake Mich. Coll., Benton Harbor, Mich. Active Citizen Amb. Program-Law Enforcement Adminstrn. Delegation, Shanghai and Manila, 1987, China, 1987, 88; citizen amb. to Russia, 1990; mem. City Coun., South Haven, 1993—. Recipient award of Appreciation, Commendation Dept. Social Svc. State of Mich., 1979, hon. fellowship Office Substance Abuse Western Mich. U. Mem. NASW, Internat. Soc. Prevention Child Abuse, Am. Assn. Marriage and Family Therapists, Am. Soc. Criminology, Mich. League for Human Svcs. (chair S.W. Mich. Total Living Ctrs.). Home: 38 Lake Shore Dr South Haven MI 49090-1131

ADLER, JUDITH ANN, planner; b. Stoughton, Wis., Jan. 3, 1944; d. Rollin and Edna Jeanne (Grubel) Hansen; m. Dennis Lee Adler, Aug. 27, 1966; 1 child, Eric Michael. BA in Internat. Rels., U. Wis., 1966, MS in Urban and Regional Planning, 1975. Prin. planner County of Rock, Janesville, Wis., 1975-79; assoc. planner, asst. to community devel. dir. City of Janesville, 1979—, acting community devel. dir., 1986-87; mem. cmty. adv. coun. Bank One, Janesville, 1991—. Co-author: Evansville Architectural Survey and Preservation Plan, 1976. Named Woman of Distinction, Janesville YWCA, 1994. Mem. LWV-Janesville (pres. 1975-77), AAUW (treas. Janesville br. 1993-95), Am. Planning Assn. (planning and women div. treas. 1982-86), Internat. Fedn. for Housing and Planning, Wis. Trust for Historic Preservation (Historic Preservation award 1989), State Hist. Soc. Wis., Rock County Hist. Soc. Home: 320 Oakland Ave Janesville WI 53545 Office: City of Janesville 18 N Jackson St Janesville WI 53545

ADLER, LOUISE DECARL, bankruptcy judge; b. 1945. BA, Chatham Coll., Pitts.; JD, Loyola U., Chgo. Bar: Ill., 1970, Calif., 1972. Staff atty. Chgo. Title and Trust Co., 1970-71; practicing atty. San Diego, 1972-84; standing trustee in bankruptcy Bankruptcy Ct. for So. Dist. Calif., 1974-79; judge bankruptcy Bankruptcy Ct. for So. Dist. Calif., San Diego, 1984—. Mem. editorial bd. Calif. Bankruptcy Jour., 1991-92. Bd. dirs. San Diego County Bankruptcy Forum, 1990-93. Mem. San Diego County Bar Assn. (chair bus. law study sect. 1979, fed. ct. com. 1983-84), Lawyers Club of San Diego (bd. dirs. 1972-73, treas. 1972-75, sec. 1972-74, v.p. 1974-75), San Diego Bankruptcy Forum (bd. dirs. 1989-92), Nat. Conf. Bankruptcy Judges (bd. dirs. 1989-91, sec. 1992-93, v.p. 1993-94, pres. 1994-95). Office: US Bankruptcy Ct 325 W F St San Diego CA 92101-6017

ADLER, MARGOT SUSANNA, journalist, radio producer; b. Little Rock, Apr. 16, 1946; d. Kurt Alfred and Freyda (Nacque) A. B.A., U. Calif.-Berkeley, 1968, M.S., Columbia U., 1970. Newscaster Sta. WBAI-FM, N.Y.C., 1968-71, host talk show, 1972—; chief Washington bur. Pacifica News Service Network, 1971-72; reporter, producer All Things Considered, Morning Edit., Nat. Pub. Radio, N.Y.C., 1978—; instr. radio communications Goddard Coll., Plainfield, Vt., 1977; instr. religion and ecology Inst. for Social Ecology, Vt., 1986-93. Author: Drawing Down the Moon, 1979. Co-producer, dir. (radio drama) War Day, 1985. Contbr. articles to jours. Nieman fellow Harvard Univ., 1982. Mem. Phi Beta Kappa. Avocations: swimming; running; bird watching. Home: 333 Central Park W New York NY 10025-7145 Office: Nat Pub Radio 801 2nd Ave Ste 701 New York NY 10017

ADLER, NADIA C., lawyer; b. Salford, Lancashire, Eng., Feb. 26, 1945; came to U.S., 1948; d. David Colin and Rose (Bolton) Cohen; m. David Jonathan Adler, Mar. 13, 1977 (div. 1992). BA, CCNY, 1966; JD, N.Y.U., 1973. Bar: N.Y. 1974, U.S. Dist. Ct. (so. and ea. dists.) N.Y. 1974, U.S. Ct. Appeals (2d cir.) 1975, U.S. Supreme Ct. 1983. Assoc. Rosenman Colin Freund Lewis & Cohen and predecessor firms, N.Y.C., 1973-82; ptnr. Rosenman & Colin, N.Y.C., 1983-87; v.p., gen. counsel Montefiore Med. Ctr., N.Y.C., 1987-89, sr. v.p., gen. counsel, 1989—; Mem. legal adv. com., legal and regulatory com. Greater N.Y. Hosp. Assn., N.Y.C., 1987—; mem. bioethics task force, subcoms. on patient decision making, reproductive techs. and physician-assisted suicide, commn. women's equality Am. Jewish Congress, N.Y.C., 1989—. Bd. dirs. Berkeley-in-Scarsdale (N.Y.) Assn., 1989-91; v.p., bd. dirs. Rosecliff Homeowners Assn., Briarcliff, N.Y., 1994—. Mem. ABA (mem. forum on health care), Assn. of Bar of City of N.Y., Am. Acad. Hosp. Attys., Am. Hosp. Assn., Nat. Health Lawyers Assn. Democrat. Office: Montefiore Med Ctr 111 E 210th St Bronx NY 10467-2401

ADLER, NAOMI SAMUEL, real estate counselor; b. N.Y.C., Sept. 30, 1931; d. Jacob Alexander and Madeline Samuel; m. Gerson Adler, Aug. 1, 1950; children: Don A., Samson Y., Nathan Tzvi, Eliyohu, Hillel M., Ezra, William Martin Selman, Zahava Sara. Student, 1945-50, John Carroll U., 1980-82. Real estate agt. B.O.D. Milliken, Cleveland Heights, Ohio, 1981-82, The Kenny Co., University Heights, Ohio, 1982-84, Century 21 Crysler-Kenny, Cleve., 1984-90; gen. mgr. Fialkoff Bungalow Colony Real Estate, Monticello, N.Y., 1981—; real estate counselor HKS Realty, Inc., Shaker Heights, Ohio, 1993—; real estate counselor Realty One, Lyndhurst, Ohio, 1990-93. Bd. dirs. Monticello Bungalow Assn., Bur. Jewish Edn., Jewish Community Fedn. Cleve.; child adv. Jewish Children's Foster Family, Jewish Day Nursery, Shaker Heights, 1970-93, Traditional Fund, Jewish Welfare; mem. loan com. Hebrew Free Loan Assn., sec., 1992—, treas., 1989-90, bd. dirs., 1972—; past pres. Shomre Shabbas Sisterhood, 1978-82, N'shei Agudah Women, 1990-92, Hebrew Acad., Cleve., 1972-75, Union Orthodox Jewish Congregations, 1975-77, Mosdos Ohr Hatora Sch., 1977-80. Named Woman of Valor, Hebrew Acad., Woman of Yr., Beth Jacob High Sch. of Denver. Mem. Grad. Realtors Inst., Cleve. Area Bd. Realtors (RPAC com.), Nat. Assn. Parliamentarians. Home: 3595 Severn Rd Cleveland Hts OH 44118-1999 Office: HKS Realty Inc 3645 Warrensville Center Rd Shaker Hts OH 44122-5203

ADLER, PEGGY See ROBOHM, PEGGY ADLER

ADOLF, MAUREEN EMMERT, insurance executive, lobbyist; b. Buffalo, Apr. 10, 1955; d. John George and Mary Ann (Brown) Emmert; m. Jay Adolf; 1 child, Kate; stepchildren: Peter, James. BA in Psychol. and Polit. Sci., SUNY, Buffalo, 1977. Legis. analyst N.Y. State Assembly, Albany, 1978-81; asst. v.p. govt. rels. Marine Midlane Bank, N.Y.C., 1981-83; v.p. govt. rels. Prudential Ins., Newark, 1983—. Mem. Fin. Women's Assn., Am. Coun. Life Ins. (legis. com. 1993-94). Democrat. Roman Catholic. Office: Prudential Ins Co 751 Broad St Newark NJ 07102-3777

ADOLPH, MARY ROSENQUIST, financial executive; b. Springfield, Mass., Oct. 7, 1949; d. Jesse Woodson and Doris May (Marquette) Rosenquist; m. Earl Anthony Soares, Mar. 18, 1972 (div. 1982); m. Joseph Edward Adolph, Oct. 3, 1986. Student San Domenico Sch., 1966-68, Dominican Coll., San Rafael, 1967-69, Calif., San Francisco Conservatory of Music, 1968-70; A.A., Coll. of Marin, 1969. Asst. v.p. Western Travelers Life Ins. Co./Putnam Fin. Services, San Rafael, 1970-80; v.p. Unimarc, Ltd., Novato, Calif., 1980-83; v.p. mktg. Western States Monetary Planning Services, Inc., Newhall, Calif., 1983-88; asst. to pres. Fed. Inventory Wholesale, Inc., 1988-90; v.p. E.W. Richardson & Assocs. Inc., Newhall, Calif., 1991-94; dir. ops. Tri Telic Inc., Santa Rosa, Calif., 1994—. Prodr. Radio Talk Show Financial Information, 1994—. Mem. exec. com. San Marin Valley Homeowners Assn., 1979-81. Mem. Internat. Assn. Fin. Planners, Life Underwriters Assn. Democrat. Roman Catholic. Home: 1676 Guerneville Rd Santa Rosa CA 95401 Office: Tri Telic Inc 555 Fifth St Ste 320 Santa Rosa CA 95401

ADREON, BEATRICE MARIE RICE, pharmacology executive; b. Huntington, W.Va., July 23, 1929; d. Lloyd Emerson and Beatrice (Odell) Rice; student Mary Washington Coll., 1947-49; B.S. in Pharmacy, Med. Coll. Va., 1952; M.A. in Spl. Studies and Women's Studies, George Washington U., 1976; m. Harry Barnes Adreon, Jr., Dec. 27, 1952. Summer vol. worker pharmacies De Paul Hosp., Norfolk, Va., 1949, U.S. Marine Hosp., Norfolk, 1950; pharmacist Washington Clinic, 1954-71; counselor George Washington U., 1976-77, cons. gerontology health scis. dept., 1977—; cons. medicine control traffic patterns nursing homes Cross & Adreon, Washington, 1962-87; founder, pres. Pharmacy Counseling Services, Inc., 1978—. Instr. advanced first aid ARC, 1952—, civil def. instr., 1952—; vol. Spanish Edn. Devel. Center, Washington, 1972; mem. Arlington (Va.) Community Services Bd., 1980-83; chmn. com. substance abuse. Recipient Arnold and Marie Schwartz award in pharmacy, 1980. Mem. Acad. Pharmacy Practice and Mgmt., Am. Pharm. Assn., Va. Pharm. Assn., Potomac Pharmacists Assn., Am. Inst. History of Pharmacy, Nat. Council Patient Info. and Edn. (task force pub. info.), Panhellenic Assn., Kappa Epsilon. Episcopalian (mem. bishop's com. neighborhood services 1967-69, chmn. services for aged div. 1967-69). Contbr. articles in field to profl. jours. Home: 4524 19th Rd N Arlington VA 22207-2352 Office: Pharmacy Counseling Svcs Inc 950 N Glebe Rd # 140 Arlington VA 22203-1824

ADRI (ADRIENNE STECKLING), fashion designer; b. St. Joseph, Mo.. Ed., Sch. Fine Arts, Washington U., St. Louis, Parson Sch. Design. With B.H. Wragge; owner, pres. Adri Studio, Ltd., N.Y.C., 1983—; with Claire McCardell in 2-person showing, Innovative Contemporary Fashion, Smithsonian Instn., Washington, 1971. Recipient Coty award, 1982, Internat. Best Five award, Tokyo, 1986. Office: Adri 143 W 20th St New York NY 10011-3630

ADRIANCE, ANNE ALTMAIER, advertising executive, consultant; b. Marshall Islands, Aug. 13, 1957; d. Donald Worth and Frances Winchester (Walker) Altmaier; m. Matthew Edwin Adriance, Sept. 12, 1987; children: Samuel, Edwin. BA, Princeton U., 1979. Media planner Benton & Bowless, N.Y.C., 1979-80; asst. account exec. Dancer Fitzgerald Sample, N.Y.C., 1980-81, account exec., 1981-84, account supr., 1984-87; sr. v.p., mgmt. supr. DFS/Saatchi & Saatchi Advt., N.Y.C., 1987-90; mgmt. dir., sr. v.p. Saatchi & Saatchi Advt., N.Y.C., 1990—. Cons. Ashoka, N.Y.C., 1986-90; mem. leadership bd. Nat. Found. for Advancement in Arts, N.Y.C., 1988-92; founding mem. Boat Rockers, N.Y.C., 1992. Office: Saatchi & Saatchi 375 Hudson St New York NY 10014-3620*

ADRIANOPOLI, BARBARA CATHERINE, librarian; b. Ft. Dodge, Iowa, Jan. 27, 1943; d. Daniel Joseph and Mary Dolores (Coleman) Hogan; m. Carl David Adrianopoli, June 28, 1968; children: Carlin, Laurie. BS, Mundeline Coll., 1966; M.L.S., Rosary Coll., 1975. Tchr., Father Bertrand High Sch., Memphis, 1966-68; caseworker Dept. Pub. Aid Chgo., 1968; tchr. North Chicago Jr. High Sch. (Ill.), 1968-70, Austin Middle Sch., Chgo., 1970-73; libr. Barrington Pub. Libr. (Ill.), 1976-79, Schaumburg Twp. Dist. Library (Ill.), 1979—; adv. com. N. Suburban/Suburban Library Systems, LaGrange, Ill., 1981-84 . Contbr. articles to jours. Mem. Com. Schaumburg Twp. Disabled, 1981—; historian Village of Hoffman Estates, 1986—; mem. Sch. Dist. 54-Citizens Adv. Com., Schaumburg, 1983-86, Hoffman Estates Sister Cities, 1988—; advisor Boy Scout Am. handicapped badge, Schaumburg Twp., 1981—; co-chair Dist. 54 study group on low achievers, 1988-89, Hoffman Estates rep. Nat. Orgn. on Disability, 1990-93,; bd. dirs. Children's Mus. and Imaginasium, 1990-93. Grantee Sears Community Project for Literacy. Mem. ALA, NOW, Ill. Libr. Assn., Polit. Majority, Common Cause. Democrat. Roman Catholic. Home: 1105 Kingsdale Rd Schaumburg IL 60194-2378 Office: Schaumburg Twp Pub Libr 32 W Library Ln Schaumburg IL 60194-3421

AELION, C. MARJORIE, educator. BS summa cum laude, U. Mass., 1980; MSCE, MIT, 1983; PhD, U. N.C., 1988. Park ranger Nat. Park Svc., Cape Cod Nat. Seashore, South Wellfleet, Mass., 1976-78; biologist resource assessment divsn. NAt. Marine Fisheries, Woods Hole, Mass., 1978-84; rsch. asst. MIT, Cambridge, Mass., 1981-83, U. Mass., Amherst, 1983-84; rsch. asst. U. N.C., Chapel Hill, 1986-88, teaching asst., 1987; hydrologist U.S. Geol. Survey, Water Resources Divsn., Columbia, S.C., 1988-91, faculty mem., 1991—; asst. prof. dept. environ. health scis. U. S.C., Columbia, 1991—; presenter in field. contbr. articles to profl. jours. Fulbright-Hayes scholar, 1980-81; Bd. Govs.' fellow U. N.C., 1984-86, Dissertation fellow, 1988, NSF fellow, 1993; grantee U.S. EPA, 1991-93, Hazardous Waste Mgmt. Rsch. Fund, 1991-94, Nat. Geographic Soc., 1992, S.C. Dept. Health and Environ. Control and Hazardous Waste Mgmt. Rsch. Fund, 1992-94, U. S.C., 1993-94, NSF, 1993—; recipient Grad. Student Travel award U. N.C., 1988. Mem. Am. Chem. Soc., Am. Soc. Microbiology, Soc. Women Engrs., Soc. Environ. Toxicology and Chemistry, Water Environ. Fedn., Phi Kappa Phi. Office: U SC Environ Health Scis Dept Columbia SC 29208

AERY, SHAILA ROSALIE, state educational administrator; b. Tulsa, Dec. 4, 1938; d. Silas Cleveland and Billie (Brewer) A. B.S., U. Okla., 1964; M.S., Okla. State U., 1972, Ed.D., 1975. Spl. asst., chancellor Okla. Regents for Higher Edn., Oklahoma City, 1977; spl. asst., chancellor U. Mo., Columbia, 1978-80, asst. provost acad. affairs, 1980-81; dep. commr. higher edn. State of Mo., Jefferson City, 1981, commr., 1982-89; sec. higher edn., Md., 1989—; dir. Mo. Higher Edn. Loan Authority, St. Louis, 1982-89; commr. Edn. Commn. of the States, Denver, 1983—, (Nat. Steering Com., nat. treas. 1993—); mem. exec. bd. State Higher Edn. Officers, Denver, 1983—, So. Regionals Edn. Bd., 1990—. Contbr. articles to profl. jours. Mem. AAUW, Women Execs. in State Govt. (bd. dirs.). Democrat. Episcopalian. Office: Md Higher Edn Commn 16 Francis St Annapolis MD 21401-1733

AFFLECK, JULIE KARLEEN, accountant; b. Upland, Calif., Dec. 23, 1944; d. Karl W. and Juliette O. (Oppegaard) Hall; m. William J. Affleck, Aug. 29, 1964; children: Stephen, Tamara. BS in Bus., U. Colo., 1967; MBA, U. Denver, 1972. CPA, Colo. Cost acct. IBM, Boulder, Colo., 1967-71; audit supr. Ernst & Young, Denver, 1972-79, Rosemary E. Weiss & Co., Denver, 1979-80; ptnr. Affleck, Melaragno, Gilman & Co., Denver, 1980—; tchr. Colo. Soc. CPA's., U. Denver; dir., corp. sec. Better-Way Electric, Inc. Treas., bd. dirs. Bal Swan Children's Ctr. for Handicapped, Broomfield, Colo. Mem. Am. Inst. CPA's., Colo. Soc. CPA's., Am. Soc. Women Accts. (pres. chpt. 1980-81), Nat. Assn. Women Bus. Owners (treas., dir., pres. 1988-89). Republican. Lutheran. Home: 1270 Elmwood Ct Broomfield CO 80020

AFRIAT, CYDNEY IRIS, nurse midwife, medical sonographer; b. Newark, May 3, 1951; d. Donald S. and B. Patricia Afriat; m. Jack Menihan; stepchildren: Courtney, Christopher. BSN, U. Pitts., 1973; CNM, U. So. Calif., 1981; MSN, Calif. State U., L.A., 1986. Registered diagnostic med. sonographer. Staff nurse, perinatal rsch. assoc. Cedars-Sinai Med. Ctr., L.A., 1973-77; perinatal nurse specialist Corometrics Med. Systems, Inc., Newport Beach, Calif., 1977-79; perinatal cons. Perinatal Prodns., Calif., 1980-90, R.I., 1990—; nurse midwife L.A. County, U. So. Calif. Med. Ctr., Kaiser Permanente, 1982-83; pvt. practice Monterey, Calif., 1983-89; nurse midwife Women and Infants' Hosp., Providence, R.I., 1990—; asst. clin. prof. U. R.I. Sch. Nursing; clin. tchg. assoc. Brown U. Sch. Medicine. Author: Electronic Fetal Monitoring, 1989; mem. editl. rev. bd. Jour. Perinatal/Neonatal Nursing and JOGMM, 1989—; contbr. articles to profl. jours. Active Humane Soc. U.S. Mem. Assn. Women's Health, Obstetric and Neonatal Nursing, Soc. Diagnostic Med. Sonographers, Am. Coll. Nurse Midwives. Jewish. Home: 240 Foddering Farm Rd Narragansett RI 02882-4306 Office: Women and Infants Hosp 101 Dudley St Providence RI 02905-2401

AFTOORA, PATRICIA JOAN, transportation executive; b. Cleve., Jan. 2, 1940; d. Joseph Patrick and Frances Dolores (Fabis) Hunady; m. Albert B. Aftoora, Feb. 17, 1989; 1 child, Christopher Hunady; stepchildren: Melissa, Matthew, Richard. Student, Fenn Coll., Cleve., 1957-59, UCLA, 1959-61, John Carroll U., Cleve., 1961-63. Various positions Chesapeake and Ohio Ry. Co., Balt. and Ohio R.R. Co., Cleve., 1962-73; asst. corp. sec. Chessie System, Inc., Cleve., 1973-79; dept. corp. sec. Chessie System Inc. and Affiliates, Cleve., 1979-80; corp. sec. Chesapeake and Ohio Ry. Co., Balt. and Ohio R.R. Co., Cleve., 1980-87, CSX Transp. Inc., Balt., 1986-87; asst. v.p., asst. corp. sec. CSX Corp., Richmond, Va., 1987-89, v.p., corp. sec., from 1989; now v.p., corp. sec. CSX Transp., Inc., Jacksonville, Fla. Mem. Am. Soc. Corp. Secs. Inc., Nat. Assn. Records Mgrs. and Adminstrs. Home: 1211 Creekview Way Ponte Vedra Beach FL 32082 Office: CSX Transp Inc 500 Water St Jacksonville FL 32202

AGABIAN, NINA MARTHA, molecular biologist, biochemist, educator, parasitologist; b. July 16, 1945. BA, Adelphi U., 1966, MS in Biology, 1968; PhD in Molecular Biology, Albert Einstein Coll. Medicine, 1971. Teaching asst. dept. biology Adelphi U., Garden City, N.Y., 1966-68; rsch. fellow dept. molecular biology Albert Einstein Coll. Medicine, Bronx, N.Y., 1968-71; asst. prof. biochemistry Sch. Medicine, U. Wash., Seattle, 1973-78, assoc. prof., 1978-83, prof., 1983-84; prof. biomed. and environ. health scis. Sch. Pub. Health U. Calif., Berkeley, 1984—; prof. pharm. chemistry, dir. intercampus program molecular parasitology U. Calif., San Francisco and Berkeley, 1986—; bd. dirs. Drug and Vaccine Devel. Corp., 1986—; appt. mem. sci. and tech. adv. com. of UNDP/World Bank/WHO Spl. Program for Rsch. & Tng. in Tropical Diseases, 1993-96; mem. study sect. NIH; mem. expert adv. panel on parasite diseases WHO, 1994. Mem. editorial adv. bd. Parasitology Today, 1985-91; mem editorial bd. Jour. Bacteriology, 1978-80. Recipient Burroughs Wellcome award for molecular parasitology, 1984-89; Guggenheim Meml. fellow, 1979-80, NIH rsch. fellow, 1968-71, 71-73. Fellow AAAS; mem. Am. Soc. Biol. Chemists, Tri Beta. Office: U of Calif San Francisco Laurel Heights PO Box 1204 San Francisco CA 94143-0001

AGARD, EMMA ESTORNEL, psychotherapist; b. Bronx, N.Y.. BA, Queens Coll.; MSW, Fordham U., 1962; cert. in Psychoanalytic Psychotherapy, Tng. Inst. for Mental Health, 1979; cert. in Child and Adolescent Psychotherapy, Postgrad. Ctr. for Mental Health, 1982. Supr. social work Foster Care Div., N.Y.C., 1968-72; asst. dir. Henry St. Settlement Urban Family Ctr., N.Y.C., 1972-74; tng. analyst, sr. supr. Tng. Inst. for Mental Health, N.Y.C., 1974—; pvt. practice psychotherapist N.Y.C., 1974—; lectr. social work Columbia U., N.Y.C., 1977-90; adj. asst. prof. NYU, 1978-80; field instr. N.Y.C. Housing Authority, 1974-80; dist. dir., cons. Am. Consultation Ctrs., Bklyn. and N.Y.C., 1985—, dir. Park Slope br. Mem. Albemarle-Kenmore Neighborhood Assn., Bklyn., 1974—, dir. Park Slope br. Fellow N.Y. State Soc. Clin. Social Work Psychotherapists (pres. Bklyn. chpt. 1988-91); mem. Profl. Soc. Tng. Inst. for Mental Health (sec.), Nat. Assn. Social Workers (diplomate), Acad. Cert. Social Workers, Nat. Coalition 100 Black Women, Delta Sigma Theta. Address: 221 E 21st St Brooklyn NY 11226

AGEE, NELLE HULME, art history educator; b. Memphis, May 22, 1940; d. John Eulice and Nelle (Ray) Hulme; m. Bob R. Agee, June 7, 1958; children: Denise, Robyn. Student Memphis State U., 1971-72; BA, Union U., Jackson, Tenn., 1978; postgrad. Seminole Okla. Coll., 1982, Okla. Bapt. U., 1984; MEd Cen. State U., Edmond, Okla., 1989. Cert. tchr. art, history, Ky., Tenn., Okla. Offices services supr. So. Bapt. Theol. Sem., Louisville, 1961-64; kindergarten tchr. Shively Heights Bapt. Ch., Louisville, 1965-70; editorial asst. Little Publs., agrl. mags., Memphis, 1973-75; tchr. art Humboldt High Sch., Tenn., 1978-82; vis. artist-in-schs. Tenn. Arts Commn., Nashville, 1978, 81, 82; adj. prof. art history Seminole Coll., Okla., 1985-86, 87, 89; instr. art Okla. Baptist U., 1989, asst. prof. art and edn., 1989—; frequent speaker art orgns., ch. groups; tchr. art workshops Humboldt City Sch. system; tchr. Cultural Arts Day Camp, Jackson, Tenn., 1982; nat. pres. ministers' wives conf. So. Bapt. Conv., 1987-88; vol. Mabee-Gerrer Mus., Shawnee. Exhibited art in various shows. Bd. dirs. Robert Dotson Found., Mabee-Gerrer Mus., Family Resource Ctr. 1993—; active Salvation Army Aux., Shawnee; v.p. Union U. Woman's Club, 1976-77, pres., 1978. Recipient Disting. Classroom Tchr. award Tenn. Edn. Assn., 1982. Mem. Univ. Alliance, Okla Bapt. U., Goals 2000, Delta Kappa Gamma, Alpha Delta Kappa. Democrat. Baptist. Avocations: stained glass, pottery making, travel. Home: 616 University Pky Shawnee OK 74801-1711

AGLER, VICKIE LYN, state legislator; b. St. Joseph, Mo., July 14, 1946; d. Harry Ernest and Fern Dorothy (Hart) Kerr; m. Rex Duane Agler, June 7, 1968; children: Kristen Michelle, Stephanie Dianne. Assoc. degree, Mo. Western Jr. Coll., St. Joseph, 1966; BS in Edn., U. Mo., 1968. Secondary sch. tchr. Topeka (Kans.) Pub. Sch., 1968-70; paralegal Dan Moran, Atty. at Law, Huntsville, Ala., 1970-76; stained glass artist Agler's Arts & Glass, Littleton, Colo., 1980-86; planning commr. Jefferson Co. Planning Commn., Littleton, 1983-87; staff asst. Congressman Joel Hefley, Littleton, 1987-90; state rep. Colo. Gen. Assembly, Denver, 1990—; coun. mem., v.p. Arapahoe C.C. Coun., 1989-92. Mem. Colo. Fedn. Rep. Women, Littleton, Am. Legis. Exchange Coun., Washington, So. Jefferson County Rep. Club, Littleton, Rep. Leadership Program, Colo.; dir. Foothills Found. Bd.; bd. mem., legis. liaison Chatfield P.T.S.A., 1989-92; del., v.p. Coun. Homeowners for Planned Environment, 1984-89. Named Woman of Yr., Sentinal Newspaper, Jefferson County, Colo., 1984, Outstanding Legislator, Colo. Counties, 1992. Mem. West C. of C. (Community Svc. award 1992), Beta Sigma Phi. Methodist. Home: 10289 W Burgundy Ave Littleton CO 80127-5532 Office: Colo Gen Assembly State Capital Denver CO 80203*

AGNEW, MIRIAM NELWYN, retired secondary school educator; b. Henderson, Ky., Oct. 4, 1901; d. William Walter and Lila Rene (Cooper) A. AB, Oxford (Ohio) Coll. for Women, 1924; MA, U. Denver, 1937; postgrad., U. Ky., 1926, U. Chgo., 1928. Tchr. English Barret Manual Tng. High Sch., Henderson, 1924-25; tchr. English Chanute (Kans.) High Sch., 1925-27, Ashland (Ky.) High Sch., 1927-44, Bosse High Sch., Evansville, Ind., 1944-67; head English dept. Ashland High Sch., 1940-44. Sunday sch. tchr. 1st United Meth. Ch., Henderson, 1944-67, 72-93. Mem. Evansville Ret. Tchr. Orgn., Ind. State Tchr. Assn., NEA, AAUW. Democrat. Home: 900 S Main St Henderson KY 42420-3948

AGONIA, BARBARA ANN, emeritus English language educator, communications consultant; b. St. Louis, June 11, 1934; d. Robert Lewis and Suzanne (Carter) Klinefelter; m. Robert James Agonia, Mar. 25, 1972. Student, U. Exeter, Devon, Eng., 1954-55; BA, Hanover Coll., 1957; MA, U. Nev., Las Vegas, 1971; postgrad., U. Nev., Reno, 1983-84. Tchr. Carrollton (Ill.) Community Unit High Sch., 1955-56, 59-61, White Hall (Ill.) Community Unit High Sch., 1957-59; tchr., chmn. dept. English ROVA Community Unit High Sch., Oneida, Ill., 1961-69; prof. English Clark County Community Coll., North Las Vegas, Nev., 1971-89, chmn. dept., 1972-75, 87-89, dir. re-entry ctr., 1980-83; interim v.p. acad. affairs Clark County C.C., North Las Vegas, Nev., 1994-95; speaker in field, Ind., Ill., Nev., Eng., 1952—. Author poems. Vol. Opportunity Village, Las Vegas, Nev., 1985—; bd. dirs. Friends of Nev. Wilderness, Las Vegas, 1985—, Community Action Against Rape. Mem. Western Lit. Assn. (Golden award 1984), Shakespeare Assn. Am., Coll. Conf. Composition and Communication (exec. com.), Nev. State Edn. Assn. (exec. bd. 1975-79), League United Latin Am. Citizens (nat. parliamentarian 1978-82), Internat. Platform Assn., Soroptimist Internat. (parliamentarian Las Vegas 1984—, pres.-elect 1986-87, pres. 1987-88, Women Helping Women award 1983, Woman of Distinction 1986, dist. dir. 1994—), Order of Eastern Star (Worthy Matron 1960-61). Methodist. Home and Office: 3411 Frontier St Las Vegas NV 89102-8158

AGRESTI, MIRIAM MONELL, psychologist; b. N.Y.C., Mar. 23, 1926; d. James McCloud and Marion Henrietta (Zippel) Monell; B.S., Queens Coll., 1947; M.A. in Sci. Edn., Columbia U., 1949; Ph.D. in Clin. Psychology, Yeshiva U., 1976; postgrad. Ackerman Inst. Family Therapy, 1977-81, L.I. Jewish Hosp. Human Sexuality Center; children—Robert, Carol. Psychology intern Creedmoor Psychiat. Center, Queens, N.Y., 1963-64, family therapist, 1964-69; psychologist Northeast Nassau Psychiat. Center, Kings Park, N.Y., 1969-72; adminstrv. dir. Friendship House Day Hosp., Glen Cove, N.Y., 1972-74; psychologist and team leader Central Islip (N.Y.) Psychiat. Center, 1974-75; tchr., coordinator family therapy program Pilgrim Psychiat. Center, West Brentwood, N.Y., 1976-80; pvt. practice psychotherapy, 1977—; pres. Nassau County Med. Ctr., 1990—. co-dir. L.I. Family Inst., 1976-79; cons. family therapy Cath. Charities, 1979, St. Vincent's Hall, 1979, Nassau County Mental Health Assn., 1980; adj. faculty Sch. Edn., C.W. Post Coll., L.I. U., 1972, CUNY, 1978-80, St. John's U., 1983, Hofstra U., 1985-88. Exec. dir. movie/videotape Beware the Gaps in Medical Care for Older People (1st prize Am. Film Festival). Lic. psychologist, N.Y. Diplomate Am. Bd. Family Psychology (pres. 1984-85). Fellow Am. Orthopsychiat. Assn., Internat. Council Sex Edn. and Parenthood of Am. U.; mem. Am. Psychol. Assn., N.Y. State Psychol. Assn., Nassau County Psychol. Assn., Suffolk County Psychol. Assn., Am. Assn. for Marriage and Family Therapy (pres. L.I. chpt. 1981-83), Am. Orthopsychiat. Assn., Pi Lambda Theta. Unitarian. Address: 11 Wren Dr Woodbury NY 11797-3212

AGUILAR, ISABEL (CHAVELA), counselor, university official; b. Calexico, Calif., Nov. 5, 1936; d. Silbestre Macias Badajós and Petra (Soria) Badajós; m. Ruben Aguilar, Apr. 7, 1956; children: Ruben Anthony, John Xavier. AA, Imperial Valley Coll.; BA in Art, San Diego State U., MS in Counseling. Credentialed cmty. coll. counselor, adminstr., instr., pers. worker, Calif. Admissions and records officer Imperial Valley Campus, San Diego State U., Calexico, 1972-77; admissions officer San Diego State U.-Imperial Valley Campus, Calexico, 1977-80, admissions counselor and vet., 1980-83, outreach coordinator, counselor, alumni dir., scholarship coordinator,campus staff senator disabled students services, student info. coordinator, student life advisor, new student orientation coord., 1978-93; supr. high schs., student intern counselors, 1987-93; outreach coordinator for local area, campus staff chair, coordinator ann. Women's Non-traditional Conf. for High Sch. Women, 15 years. San Diego State U.-Imperial Valley Campus, Calexico, 1987-93; campus liaison Imperial Valley Coll., Imperial, Calif., 1980—. Sec. Tirado for County Supr., Dist. One polit. campaign, 1993-94; chmn. City Beautification Com., Calexico, 1980-93; past chmn. Affirmative Action Adv. Cons. to Bd. of Suprs., El Centro, 1983-92; trustee self-sufficiency adv. bd. Imperial Valley Housing Authority; trustee, v.p. Calexico Ednl. Found.; bd. dirs. Calexico Neighborhood House; commr. City of Calexico Sister Cities, 1993—. Recipient San Diego State U. Annual Alumna award, 1980; Delta Kappa Gamma scholar, 1978; named SER-Hispanic Woman of Yr., 1991. Mem. Advocated for Women in Academia, Imperial Valley Guidance Assn. (sec. 1985-90), Raza Advocates for Calif. Higher Edn., Western Assn. Ednl. Opportunity Pers., Hispanic Assn. Colls. and Univs., Soroptimists (pres. Calexico club 1983-84, v.p. 1982-83, sec. 1984-85, publicity mgr. 1981-82, alt. del. 1985-86). Democrat. Roman Catholic. Home: 814 Rockwood Ave Calexico CA 92231-2438 Office: San Diego State U Imperial Valley 720 Heber Ave Calexico CA 92231-2480

AGUILAR, SANDRA MATILDE, counselor, educator; b. Mar. 14, 1950; d. Juan Blas and Rita (Mejia) A. B degree, Nat. Louis U., 1976, postgrad., 1993—; M in Spl. Edn., Northeastern U., 1984; M in Guidance and Counseling, Chgo. State U., 1990. Cert. tchr., Ill.; cert. guidance counselor, Ill. Bilingual tchr. Chgo. Bd. Edn., 1976-80, bilingual coord., 1980-87, bilingual and spl. edn. tchr., 1989-90, sch. counselor, 1990—, spl. edn. case mgmt., 1991. Del. Logan Sq. Neighborhood Assn., Chgo., 1990; v.p. PTA, Chgo., 1978-81. Recipient Recognition award PTA, 1979. Mem. Am. Counseling Assn. (Humanitarian Care award 1992), Chgo. Guidance Counselor Assn. Home: 5825 N Whipple St Chicago IL 60641

AGUIRRE, LINDA G., state legislator; b. Flagstaff, Ariz., July 12, 1951; m. John Aguirre; children: Eric, Stephanie. BA, Ariz. State U., 1978. Educator; mem. Ariz. Ho. of Reps., mem. banking and ins., human svcs. and transp. coms. Active Ariz. Sch. Bd., Nat. Sch. Bd., Nat. Hispanic Sch. Bd., Ariz. Citizens Edn. Mem. South Mountain C. of C. Democrat. Office: Ariz House of Reps State Capitol Phoenix AZ 85007*

AGUT, BEVERLEE R., accountant; b. Kansas City, Mo., Mar. 26, 1956; d. Lester Roy and Mary Lee (Spence) Reynolds; m. John Phillip Agut, Sept. 16, 1989; 1 child, Erin Ashlee. AS, Cen. Mo. State U., 1976; BS in Bus. Adminstrn., Rockhurst Coll., 1986. CMA. Various clerical pos. Mo. Pub. Svc., Kansas City, 1976-85, sr. rate analyst, 1985-88; mgr. acctg. Kans. Pub. Svc., Lawrence, 1988—. Mem. NAFE, Am. Bus. Women's Assn. (sec. 1989—), Inst. Mgmt. Accts. Democrat. Office: Kansas Pub Svc 110 East 9th St Lawrence KS 66044

AHERN, ARLEEN FLEMING, retired librarian; b. Mt. Harris, Colo., Oct. 15, 1922; d. John R. and Josephine (Vidmar) Fleming; m. George Irving Ahern Jr., June 14, 1944; 1 child, George Irving. BA, U. Utah, 1943; MA, U. Denver, 1962; postgrad. U. Colo., 1967. Library asst. Army Air Force Library, Salt Lake City, 1943-44; library asst. Colo. Women's Coll. Library (now U. Denver/CWC Campus), 1952-60, acquisitions librarian, 1960—, rep. Adult Edn. Council Denver, 1960-90, reference librarian Penrose Library, WEC librarian, assoc. prof. librarianship through 1987, U. Denver Penrose Libr.; prof. emeritus, U. Denver; retired. Committeewoman, Republican Com., Denver, 1958-59; vol., Opera Colo. Guild, Denver Lyric Opera, U. Denver Women's Libr. Assn., bd. dirs., 1992-93, Samaritan House Guild, Jeanne Jugan (Little Sisters Poor) Aux., Colo. Symphony Guild, Cinema Study Club Colo., Carson Brierly Dance Libr., bd. dirs. Mem. AAUP, ALA, Mountain Plains Library Assn., Colo. (1st v.p., pres. 1969-70, dir. 1971—), Library Assn., Altrusa Club of Denver (2d v.p. 1968-69, dir. 1971-74, 76, 78), Soc. Am. Archivists, Mountain Plains Adult Edn. Assn., Denver Botanic Gardens. Home: 746 Monaco Pky Denver CO 80220-6041

AHERN, JUDITH ANNE, artist; b. Sydney, NSW, Australia, Sept. 26, 1961; came to U.S., 1988; d. Walter and Shirley (Perry) A. BFA, U. Sydney, 1983; BA in Studio Art, Sydney Coll. Arts, 1984, Grad. Diploma in Photography, 1985; MA in Studio Art, NYU, 1992. Photographer Festival of Sydney, 1986, Panache Mag., Sydney, 1986-87, No. Herald/Sydney Morning Herald, 1987; asst. dir. Burden Gallery Aperture Found., N.Y.C., 1991; tchr. photomedia dept. Canberra Inst. Art, Australia, 1993; photographer N.Y. office Sydney Morning Herald, 1994; tchr. No. Territory U., Australia, 1994; tchr. introductory and intermediate photography Australian Ctr. Photography, Sydney, 1987-88. One-woman shows include Art Gallery NSW, Australia, 1984, Images Gallery, Sydney, 1984, 85, Avago Gallery, Sydney, 1984, 338 Pitt St. Gallery, 1985, Span Gallery, Sydney, 1986, Woodstock Country Music Festival, 1986, Longyard Hotel, Tamworth, Australia, 1986, First Draft, Sydney, 1987, King St. Gallery, Sydney, 1987, Port Lincoln Town Hall, Whyalla Mid. Back Theatre, Ceduna Town Hall, Berri Town Hall, Barmera Town Hall, Port Pirie Town Hall, Riddoch Art Gallery, Naracoorte Regional Art Gallery, Adelaide Exptl. Art Found., Tamworth Regional Art Gallery, 1988, Australian Ctr. Photography, 1988, 1990, Canberra Inst. Art, 1993, No. Territory Univ. Gallery, 1994; exhibited in group shows at Sydney Trade Union Club, 1983, Sydney Coll. Arts, 1983, Art Unit, Sydney, 1984, Images Gallery, 1984, 85, Glebe Town Hall, Sydney, 1985, The Performance Space, Sydney, 1985, Australian Ctr. Photography, 1985, Pier 2, Sydney, 1986, Art Gallery NSW, 1988, 89, Australian Nat. Gallery, Canberra, 1988, Mus. Contemporary Art, Brisbane, 1989, South Australian Sch. Art, Adelaide, 1989, New Eng. Regional Art Mus., Armidale, 1989, U. Tasmania, 1989, Nat. Gallery Victoria, Melbourne, 1989, Gardener Ctr., Brighton, 1989, Chisenhale Gallery, London, 1989, Drew Gallery, Canterbury, Kent, 1989, First Draft (West), Sydney, 1990, Baracaldine Workers Heritage Ctr., Cloncurry Regional Art Gallery, Myers Gallery, Brisbane, Broken Hill Art Gallery, Longreach Cultural Ctr., Dolby Arts Ctr., Moree Art Gallery, Redcliffe Entertainment Ctr., Rockhampton Regional Art Gallery, Gladstone Regional Art Gallery, Mc Wharters Art Space, Brisbane, Warkwick Regional Art Gallery, Circulo De Bellos Artes, Madrid, Drill Hall Gallery, ACT, Albury Regional Art Gallery, Campelltown City Art Gallery, Moree Plains Gallery, Ivan Dougherty Gallery, 1991, Bathurst Regional Art Gallery, Tamworth City Gallery, Dooley Le Cappellaine Gallery, N.Y.C., 1991, 92, Port Authority N.Y., N.Y.C., 1991, 80 Washington Sq. East Galleries, N.Y.C., 1992, U. St. Louis, 1992, Canberra Inst. Art, 1993, No. Territory Univ. Gallery, 1994; represented in collections Australian Nat. Gallery, Australian Nat. Libr., NYU, Mitchell Libr., Tamworth Regional Art Gallery; author: Darwin-A Contemporary Portrait, 1994.

AHERN, MARGARET ANN, nun, nursing educator; b. Manchester, N.H., Nov. 23, 1931; d. Timothy Joseph and Helen Bridget (Kearns) Ahern. Diploma, Sacred Heart Hosp. Sch. Nursing, 1952; BSN, Mt. St. Mary Coll., 1957; MSN, Cath. U. Am., 1965. Entered Sisters of Mercy, Roman Cath. Ch., 1953. Staff nurse Sacred Heart Hosp., Manchester, 1954-57, oper. rm. supr., 1957-62, med.-surg. nursing instr., 1962-66, dir. Sch. Nursing, 1966-75; dir. Sch. Nursing Cath. Med. Ctr., Manchester, 1975-79, dir. dept. edn. and mem. sr. mgmt., 1979-87; pres. Cath. Med. Ctr. Networks, Inc., Manchester, 1987-94; mng. dir. Optima Health Systems, Inc., Manchester, N.H., 1994—. Contbr. articles to profl. jours. Chmn. bd. dirs. Health Edn. Consortium, 1977-89; bd. dirs. Vis. Nurse Assn., 1981-87; adv. bd. Hesser Coll., 1980—, N.H. Vocat.-Tech. Coll., 1979-87; mem. United Health Systems Agy., 1977-83; mem. adv. council on continuing edn. St. Anselm Coll., 1978-89; mem. gen. chpt. Sisters of Mercy, 1968-70, 79-81, chmn. fin. bd., 1981-86, chmn. Bd. Consolidation and Arbitration, 1981-86, 1991—. Recipient Disting. Women Leaders award YWCA, 1986, Pres's. award Fidelity Health Alliance, 1992. Mem. ANA, N.H. Nurses Assn., Nat. League for Nursing, New Eng. Cath. Hosp. Assn., N.H. Heart Assn., Sigma Theta Tau (Leadership Recognition award Epsilon Tau chpt. 1989, Disting. Leaders award 1989). Democrat. Roman Catholic. Home: 647 Amoskeag Pl Manchester NH 03101 Office: Cath Med Ctr Network 77 Pearl St Manchester NH 03101-1464

AHERNS, PAMELA BENGSON, state legislator; b. Portland, Oreg., Nov. 15, 1945; 1 child, Melissa Ann. Student, Ea. Wash. State U. Mem. Idaho Ho. of Reps., 1983—; with equipment rental bus. Active Boise State Found. Named to Hall of Fame, Idaho Rep. Party. Mem. Idaho Hosp. Assn. (dir. polit. activities), Idaho Rep. Women's Fedn. (pres. 1983—). Republican. Presbyterian. Home: 2854 S Swallowtail Ln Boise ID 83706-6138 Office: Idaho House of Reps State Capitol Boise ID 83720*

AHL, JANYCE BARNWELL, historian, writer, retired educator; b. St. Augustine, Fla., Oct. 13, 1911; d. Carlos Drew and Martha Rebecca (Adams) A. BS in English and Biology, Fla. Southern Coll., Lakeland, Fla., 1939. Tchr., sci. Lake Wales Jr. High, Fla. Author: Early History of Lake Wales Woman's Club, 1989, Crown Jewel of the Highlands: Lake Wales, Florida, 1983, Early History of the Lake Wales Cemetery, 1984; co-author Late History of the First Presbyterian Church of Lake Wales Florida, 1989. Donated proceeds from book to Lake Wales Libr. Assn., 1983—; mem. Prayer and Care Group, Sunday Afternoon Circle, Lakes Wales Hist. Soc. (life mem.), Lake Wales Mus. and Culture Ctr., Polk County Hist. Soc., Friends of Bok Tower, Polk County Hist. Commn., 1992—; campaigned for Gov. Lawton Chiles; fin. com. Chiles/Mackay Campaign, 1990, 94; guest spkr. various schs., civic and social orgns. Named Pioneer of the Yr. City of Lake Wales, 1979, Citizen of the Yr. Lake Wales Masonic Lodge, 1990; recipient key to the City of Lake Wales, 1979; Gold pin Woman's Soc., 1982, Lifetime Achievement award Polk County Sch. Bd., 1992. Mem. Am. Legion Aux. (pres. 1988, 89), Polk County Ret. Tchrs. Assn., Fla. Ret. Educators Assn., Nat. Edn. Assn., AARP Nat. Ret. Tchrs. Assn., Lake Wales Democratic Club. Democrat. Presbyterian.

AHLAN-LIDO, CAROLEE GLORIA, commodities trader; b. Beverly, Mass., Oct. 16, 1947; d. Terrence Joseph and Edith Gloria (Swanson) Tavis; m. David Fosdahl, Mar. 24, 1974 (div.); 1 child, Heather Linea; m. Yuri Dadov, Nov. 26, 1986; m. Zion Ahlan, Nov. 13, 1989. Promotion asst. Ft. Lauderdale (Fla.) News, 1966-67; prodn. supr. Real Estate Computer Svcs., Pompano Beach, Fla., 1969-72; asst. graphics Fla. Living Mag., Ft. Lauderdale, 1972-75; supr. computer dept. Commerce Clearing House, Pompano Beach, 1980-82; dispatch asst. State Farm Ins., Ft. Lauderdale, 1982-86; ops. mgr. Norstar Brokerage, Ft. Lauderdale, 1986; asst. mgr. Prestige Investments, Ft. Lauderdale, 1986-87; office mgr. Berk Constrn., Ft. Lauderdale, 1987; asst. trader Multivest Inc., Ft. Lauderdale, 1987—; office mgr., coord. govt. contract printing and silkscreener Impressions Group, 1988—; owner/operator Sabra Restaurant, Ft. Lauderdale, 1988-92; rep. Iams Pet Food, 1988-93; mgr. Fla. Bldg. Inspections, Inc., Hollywood, Fla., 1993—; rep., mktg. coord. Science Diet Pet Food, Miami, 1993—. Author numerous poems. Mem. Internat. Platform Assn., Nat. Orgn. of Poetry for Women, Forresters. Democrat. Lutheran. Home: 1243 SW 37th Ave #1 Fort Lauderdale FL 33312

AHLGREN, MADELYN, state legislator; b. Manchester, N.H., Feb. 6, 1915; m. Adler R. (dec.); 3 children. BA, U. N.H., 1936; attended, Northeastern, Wesleyan, U. N.H. Del. Dem. Nat. Convention, 1988; treas. Ward 4 Dem. Com., 1991—; Dem. presdl. elector, 1988. Mem. N.H. Ret. Tchrs., Manchester Hist. Assn., Manchester Ret. Tchrs., Manchester Women's Club, ADK Tchr's Sorority. Roman Catholic. Office: NH Ho of Reps State Capitol Concord NH 03301*

AHLRICHS, NANCY SURRATT, marketing professional; b. Harrisburg, Pa., Oct. 13, 1952; d. Joe Free and Mary Alice (Norris) Surratt; m. Karl J. Ahlrichs, Sept. 10, 1983. BA in Anthropology, Purdue U., 1974, MS in Phys. Anthropology, 1976. With dept. prodn. Steuben Printing Co., Angola, Ind., 1977-78; project specialist A.B. Dick Co., Chgo., 1978-81, sr. instructional designer, 1981-82; mgr. tng. and devel. Equitable Relocation Mgmt. Corp., Chgo. and Orlando, 1982-83; v.p. Todd Persons Communications, Inc., Orlando, 1984-87, Gary Bitner Pub. Rels., Orlando, 1987-89; v.p. client svcs. Right Assocs., San Diego, 1989-90; v.p. profl. svcs. Right Assocs., Indpls., 1992-94; mktg. cons., entrepreneur Indpls., 1994—. Producer videotape: The Big Push, 1983; author/ghost writer over 50 mag. and trade jour. articles; writer, producer, dir. over 50 corp. videotapes. Vol. Steve Goldsmith for Mayor, Indpls., 1991; major gifts chmn. Am. Heart Assn., San Diego, 1990-91. Recipient Pres.'s award Cen. Fla. Zool. Soc., 1988. Mem. Kiwanis Indpls. (mktg. com., chmn. downtown program 1994-95, numerous other coms. 1994-95), Phi Kappa Phi. Democrat. Lutheran. Office: 6160 N Meridian St Indianapolis IN 46280

AHLSWEDE, JILL MARIE, mental health therapist; b. Milw., June 29, 1966; d. Jon Peter and Audrey Ann (Gall) A. BS, U. Wis., Oshkosh, 1988; MA, DePaul U., 1993. Children's counselor Waukesha (Wis.) County Human Svcs., 1988-89; residential coord. Creative Cmty. Living Sys., Milw., 1988-89; mental health counselor Lake County Health Dept., Waukegan, Ill., 1989-94; dir. counseling Northwestern Bus. Coll., Chgo., 1994—. Vol. Big Sister, United Way, Gurnee, Ill., 1994. Mem. Am. Counseling Assn., Am. Coll. Pers. Assn., Kappa Delta Pi, Alpha Lambda Delta, Psi Chi. Roman Catholic. Home: 2318 N Southport Ave Chicago IL 60614

AHMES, ELIZABETH ANNE, physical therapist; b. Flushing, N.Y., Nov. 7, 1950; d. Edward John and Ladislava (Olszewska) Mentel; m. Richard Francis Ahmes, Dec. 1, 1972; children: Brian, Laura. BS in Physical Therapy, Columbia U., 1972; MA, Adelphi U., 1976; cert. in bus. adminstrn., Hofstra U. and Cornell U., 1979. Lic. phys. therapist, N.Y., N.J., Fla.; cert. sch. phys. therapist, N.J. Phys. therapist Nassau County Med. Ctr., East Meadow, N.Y., 1972-73; sr. staff phys. therapist North Shore Univ. Hosp., Manhasset, N.Y., 1973-79; chief phys. therapist Kings Park (N.Y.) Hosp., 1979-80; dir. rehab. svcs. West Hudson Hosp., Kearny, N.J., 1980-87; sch. phys. therapist Millburn (N.J.) Regional Day Sch., 1987-88, Orange County (Fla.) Schs., 1989—; pvt. practice Seminole County Schs., Fla., 1990—; clin. dir. (Fla.) Sundance Rehab. Corp., 1994—. HEW traineeship, Washington, 1971-72. Mem. Am. Phys. Therapy Assn. (past recording sec. L.I. chpt.), Jr. League (sustainer 1987—). Republican. Roman Catholic. Home: 421 Wild Oak Cir Longwood FL 32779-3357

AHRENS, VIRGINIA ROSE, early childhood educator; b. Grinnell, Iowa, Oct. 22, 1934; d. Hilliard Hayes and Eldora Virginia (Rickard) Turner; m. Richard Glenn Ahrens, Sept. 4, 1955; children: Michael, Steven, Robert. Student, Ottawa U., 1953-56; BS in Elem. Edn., Drury Coll., 1976; ME in Elem. Edn., Southwest Mo. State U., 1983; degree in Edn. Spl., U. Mo., Columbia, 1992. Lead tchr. Bethany Nursery Sch., Rochester, Minn., 1967-69; ins. agt. Ahrens Ins., Marshfield, Mo., 1978—; tchr. elem. sch. Marshfield R-1 Schs., 1976—; pres. bd. dirs. Marshfield Child Devel. Ctr., 1994. Bd. dirs., pres.-elect Local County Bd. Am. Heart Assn., Webster, County, Mo., 1994. Arria Murto scholar, 1987; Steven Morgan Ferman Meml. grantee, 1985. Mem. AAUW (past pres. 1990-94), Mo. State Tchrs. Assn. (local pres. 1976-94), Internat. Reading Assn. (bd. dirs. 1993-95), PEO, Phi Delta Kappa, Delta Kappa Gamma. Methodist. Office: Marshfield Hubble Elem PO Box B Marshfield MO 65706-0921

AHUJA, INDRA, accountant, financial planner; b. New Delhi, Jan. 17, 1950; came to U.S., 1979; children: Deep S., Gitika. BSc, Delhi U., 1969, MSC, 1973, BEd, 1975; MBA, Calif. State U., San Bernardino, 1991. H.s. tchr. Salwan Pub. Schs., New Delhi, 1975-79; acctg. mgr. Sunkist Growers, Ontario, Calif., 1980—. Fellow NAFE; mem. Am. Prodn. and Inventory Control Soc. (v.p. fin. 1992-94). Home: 2121 Caroline Dr Ontario CA 91764 Office: Sunkist Growers 760 E Sunkist St Ontario CA 91761

AHWINONA, CYNTHIA A., legislative consultant; b. Nome, Alaska, Dec. 12, 1952; d. Jacob and Hannah (Anagick) A. Student, U. Alaska, 1972-83, U. Alaska, Anchorage, 1988. With Green Constrn. Co., 1973-76; mem. staff Senator Mike Gravel, 1976-80, Rep. Don Young, 1980-87; regional planner, with pub. rels. Bering Sea Fishermen's Assn., Anchorage, 1988-89; cons. Native Affairs Ho. Com. Natural Resources. Mem. Nat. Conf. State Socs. (regional dir. 1994), Alaska State Soc. (bd. dirs.). Office: O'Neill House Office Bldg Rm 522 Washington DC 20515*

AIELLO, ELIZABETH ANN, public relations liaison; b. Pitts., Apr. 10, 1922; d. Edward Aloysius and Sarah Marie (Short) Maroney; m. William Peter Aiello, June 4, 1946 (dec. Nov. 1989); children: David Robert, Beverly Ann Aiello Reecer. BA, Chatham Coll., 1943; MA, St. John's Coll., Santa Fe, N.Mex., 1969; postgrad., U. N.Mex., 1970—. Cert. tchr. elem./secondary English, history, social studies, govt., civics. Secondary instr. history Moon Twp. Schs., Coraopolis, Pa., 1943-44; secondary instr. English, Latin Blawnox (Pa.) Schs., 1944-49; elementary instr. upper primary Los Alamos (N.Mex.) Schs., 1949-59, secondary instr. advanced placement English/history, 1959-82; chair English dept. U. N.Mex., Los Alamos, 1982-90, head humanities div., 1986-90, dir. reentry program for women in sci., 1984-89, dir. reentry program for Native Am./Hispanic students, 1987-90; ednl. pub. rels. liaison Los Alamos Nat. Lab., 1984—; Great Books discussion groups coord. No. N.Mex., 1992—; adv. bd. N.Mex. Women in Sci., Santa Fe, 1980-84, Los Alamos Women in Sci., 1984-90; Fulbright teaching fellow U.S. Dept. Edn., Washington, 1971-72. Author: Perigrinations at Pokesdown, 1974, Consumation and Other Poems, 1984, New Hope for Dying Muse, 1986, Perceptions and Reality, 1991, Perceptions I-IV. Phoebe Brashear Soc. scholar, Pitts., 1939-43; Am. Hist. Soc.-NEH joint fellow, 1976, William Robertson Coe fellow, 1981; rsch. grantee AAUW, 1982, Carl Perkins grantee N.Mex. Dept. Vocat.-Tech. Edn., 1986-90; named Outstanding N.Mex. History Tchr., DAR, 1976, One of 80 Women to Watch in 80's, N.Mex. Women's Polit. Caucus, 1980; recipient N.Mex. Women at Work award Nat. Coun. Working Women and Minority Affairs, Washington, 1975, Gov.'s award Gov. N.Mex., N.Mex. Commn. Status of Women, 1986, 89. Mem. NEA, AAUW (div. adv. bd. 1985-90, nat. adv. bd. 1985-89, June B. West fellow N.Mex. div. 1969, Grace Braker Wilson award 1990), Los Alamos Nat. Edn. Assn. (adv. bd., pres. 1975-80), Delta Kappa Gamma. Office: Los Alamos Nat Lab Box 1663 MS C330 Los Alamos NM 87545

AIGNER, EMILY BURKE, lay worker; b. Henrico, Va., Oct. 28, 1920; d. William Lyne and Susie Emily (Willson) Burke; m. Louis Cottrell Aigner, Nov. 27, 1936; children: Lyne, Betty, D. Muriel (dec.), Willson, Norman, William, Randolph, Dorothy. Cert. in Bible, U. Richmond, 1969; postgrad., So. Bapt. Seminary Extension, Nashville, 1987, Va. Commonwealth U., 1981; Diploma in Bible, Liberty Home Bible Inst., 1992. Deacon Four Mile Creek Bapt. Ch., Richmond, Va., 1972—, trustee, 1991, dir. Woman's Missionary Union, 1986-94, treas., 1984-89, dir. Sunday sch., 1969-78, 84-85, 1989-93; acctg. tech., 1959-80. Producer Dial-A-Devotion for pub. by telephone, 1978-85. Solicitor ARC, Henrico County, 1947-49, United Givers' Fund, Henrico County, 1945-48; sec.-treas. soliciting funds Bible Edn. in Varina Sch., 1946-49; singer Bellwood Choir, Chesterfield County, Va., 1965-70; telephone counselor Richmond Contact, 1980-82, Am. Cancer Soc., Richmond, 1980-82; program chmn. Varina (Va.) Home Demonstration Club, 1950-53; vol. worker Vol. Visitor Program Capital Area on Aging, 1983—; vol. patient rep. Richmond Meml. Hosp., 1994; jail min. Richmond City Jail, 1973—. Mem. Gideons Internat. (sec. Va. aux. 1977-80, 82-84, new plan rep. 1981, 85, 91, 94, zone leader 1988-89, 90-91, state cabinet rep. 1989-90, pres. Richmond N.E. Camp 1976-78, sec.-treas. 1980-82, 93, scripture sec. 1973-75, 87-89, chmn. Va. state widows com. 1993—), Alpha Phi Sigma. Home: 9717 Varina Rd Richmond VA 23231-8428

AIKEN, BETSY ANN, management consultant; b. Pitts., Oct. 2, 1954; d. William Morris and Nancy Jane (Skinner) A.; m. Jeffrey Stephen Kelly, May 15, 1982 (div.); 1 child, Maureen Elizabeth; m. Arvind Gangadhar Paranjpe, Apr. 23, 1994. BA, U. Pitts., 1975, MBA, 1976. Mgr. quality assurance Hamill Mfg. Co., Trafford, Pa., 1976-83; chief adminstr. Municipality of Murrysville, Pa., 1990-93; v.p. Dynamic Leadership Co., Pitts., 1993—. Mem. Toastmasters. Home: 4106 Hilty Rd Export PA 15632-1606

AIKEN, DOROTHY LOUISE, educator; b. Washington, Apr. 27, 1924; d. Willard Ross and Gertrude (Rucker) Snyder; m. William David Aiken, May 22, 1948 (dec. 1988); children: Katherine Aiken Schwartz, Mary Aiken Fishback, Sally Aiken Fitterer, Jerome. BS, George Washington U., 1946; postgrad., Wash. State U., 1946-47. Teaching fellow Wash. State U., Pullman, 1946-47; tchr. secondary sch. D.C. Schs., Washington, 1947-50; tchr. Sunnyside (Wash.) Sch. Dist. 201, 1962-80. Sec. vestry Holy Trinity Ch., 1968-70; staff Evergreen Girls State, 1972-81; Dem. precinct committeeman, Sunnyside, 1980-86; mem. com. Margaret Rayburn Legislator campaign, Grandview, Wash., 1990; vice chair Yakima Valley C.C., 1994-95, trustee; trustee Assn. Cmty. and Tech. Colls., mem. conf. com., 1992; co-producer Valley Mus. Comedy Co. Prodns., 1989-91; chmn. Hospice Light Up a Life, 1991; vol., program head ARC. Mem. Am. Legion Aux. (pres. 1974-76, meritorious svc. citation 1983, 88), Nouvella Federated Women's Club (2d v.p. 1984-86), Women's Golf Assn. (pres.). Episcopalian. Home: 1241 Sunset Pl Sunnyside WA 98944-1720

AIKEN, LINDA HARMAN, nurse, sociologist, educator; b. Roanoke, Va., July 29, 1943; d. William Jordan and Betty Philips (Warner) Harman; children: June Elizabeth, Alan James. BSN, U. Fla., 1964, M in Nursing, 1966; PhD in Sociology, U. Tex., 1973. Nurse Med. Ctr. U. Fla., Gainesville, 1964-65, instr. coll. nursing, 1966-67; instr. sch. of nursing U. Mo., Columbia, 1967-70, clin. nurse specialist sch. of nursing, 1967-70; program officer Robert Wood Johnson Found., Princeton, N.J., 1974-76, dir. rsch., 1976-79, asst. v.p., 1979-81, v.p., 1981-87; trustee prof. nursing and sociology U. Pa., Phila., 1988—; dir. Ctr. for Health Svcs. and Policy Rsch. U. Pa.; rsch. assoc. population studies ctr. U. Pa.; mem. Sec. Health and Human Svcs. Commn. on Nursing, 1988, Pres. Clinton's Nat. Health Care Reform Task Force, 1993; commr. Physician Payment Rev. Commn. nat. adv. coun. U.S. Agy. for Health Care Care Policy and Rsch. Author: Health Policy and Nursing Practice, 1981, Nursing in the 1980s, 1982, Applications of Social Science to Clinical Medicine and Health Policy, 1986, Evaluation Studies Rev. Ann., 1985, Charting Nursing's Future, 1991; assoc. editor Jour. Health and Social Behavior, 1979-81, Transaction Soc., 1985—; mem. editorial bd. Evaluation Quar., 1979-80, Med. Care, 1983—; contbr. articles to profl. jours. Mem. Adv. Council Social Security, 1982-83. Recipient Joint Secretarial commendation U.S. Dept. Health and Human Services and HUD, 1987; NIH Nurse Scientist fellow, 1970-73. Mem. ANA (Jessie M. Scott award 1984), Inst. Medicine, Nat. Acad. Scis., Nat. Acad. Social Ins., Am. Acad. Nursing (pres. 1979-80), Am. Sociol. Assn. (chair med. sociology sect. 1983-84), Sociol. Rsch. Assn., Coun. Nurse Rschrs. (Nurse Scientist of Yr. 1991), Sigma Theta Tau, Phi Kappa Phi. Home: 2209 Lombard St Philadelphia PA 19146 Office: U Pa 420 Service Dr Philadelphia PA 19104-6020

AIKENS, AMY ANNE BURGESS, emergency department nurse; b. Flint, Mich., Dec. 11, 1966; d. Daniel Charles and Rita Louise (Adams) Burgess. Student, Drury Coll., 1984-85; diploma, Burge Sch. Nursing, 1987; BA in Healthcare & Philosophy with honor, Stephens Coll., 1994. CEN; cert. ACLS instr., PALS provider. Staff nurse, charge nurse intensive/coronary care unit Delta Regional Med. Ctr., Greenville, Miss., 1987-88, staff nurse emergency rm., 1988-89, charge nurse emergency rm., 1989; RN treatment rm. Kings Daus. Hosp., Greenville, 1989-90; RN Kodiak Island (Alaska) Hosp., 1991; RN emergency room Breech Med. Ctr., Lebanon, Mo., 1992; RN emergency rm. Burdette Tomlin Meml. Hosp., Cape May Courthouse, N.J., 1992—, mem. biomed. ethics com., 1993—; cons. Smith, Hutcheson & Dunbar, St. Robert, Mo., 1992. RN Health Fairs King Daus. Hosp., 1990; walker March of Dimes Walkathon, Greenville, 1990; active Greene County Disaster Drill, Springfield, Mo., 1986; vol. Peterson Elem. Sch., Kodiak, 1991. Mem. Mo. Nurses Assn., Emergency Nurses Assn. Roman Catholic.

AIKENS, JOAN DEACON, government official; b. Lansdowne, Pa.; d. Robert Wallace and Bessie (Crook) Deacon; m. Donald R. Aikens (div.); 1 son, Donald R. B.A., Ursinus Coll., 1950, LL.D. (hon.), 1979. Fashion cons. Park Ave. Shop, Swarthmore, Pa., 1971-73; v.p. Lew Hodges Communications, Inc., Valley Forge, Pa., 1974-75; mem. Fed. Election Commn., Washington, 1975—, vice chmn., 1977-78, 85, 91, chmn., 1978-79, 85-86, 92, now commr.; Chmn. women's div. Washington conf. Republican Nat. Com., 1966; hospitality chmn. Pa. del. Rep. Nat. Conf., 1968, alt.-at-large, 1972; bd. dirs. Nat. Fedn. Rep. Women, 1972-75; active Pa. Council Rep. Women, 1960-74, pres., 1972-74; co-chmn. Women for McCorkle-Williams, Pa. Rep. State Com., 1970; mem. exec. com. Pa. Rep. State Com., 1972-74, elected mem., 1974; vice chmn. Citizens for Nixon-Agnew, Delaware County (Pa.) Rep. Party, 1968, Com. to Re-Elect the Pres., 1972; precinct committeewoman Swarthmore (Pa.) Rep. Party, 1960-75; pres. Swarthmore Council Rep. Women, 1970-72; chmn. various campaigns Swarthmore Rep. Hdqrs., 1960-74. Active Swarthmore Presbyn. Ch., 1955-64; bd. dirs. Women's Assn., 1956-60; active Riddle Meml. Hosp., Delaware County, Pa., 1958-74; pres. Women's Bd. Asso. Auxs., 1970-72; mem. Women's bd. Women's Med. Coll., Phila., 1978-91. Mem. Exec. Women in Govt. (pres. 1989-91), Washington Host Lions Club (King lion 1993-94). Office: Fed Election Commn 999 E St NW Washington DC 20463-0002

AIKMAN, ELFLORA ANNA, senior citizens center administrator; b. Marion, Ill., July 21, 1929; d. John Frederick and Elsa Flora (Weber) Kaeser; m. Samuel Vick Aikman, Dec. 24, 1949; children: Vicki Ann Aikman Kaeser, Vance J., Valerie Sue Aikman Moore, Samuel Vick III. Student, So. Ill. U., 1949, John A. Logan Coll., 1970, 80, 87; cert. food handler, John A. Logan Coll., 1984. Numerous positions, 1947-67; sec. Color-Craft Products, Detroit, 1967-69; admitting clk. Marion Meml. Hosp., 1969-70, appointed to task force, 1989—; co-owner, office mgr., decorating cons. House of Color, Marion, 1970-79; sec., bookkeeper, receptionist Mitchell-Hughes Funeral Home, Marion, 1979-80; receptionist Meredith Funeral Home, Marion, 1980—; exec. dir. Marion Sr. Citizens Ctr., 1981—; columnist Marion Daily Republican, 1984—; columnist, contbr. Sr. World, 1987—; producer program Sta. WGGH, 1989—. Editor monthly newsletter The Yodler, 1984—; co-designer, decorator Meredith Funeral Home; decorator Marion Meml. Hosp. Chapel, 1971, 77; columnist, contbr. newspaper Old Friends, 1989—. Organist, jr. choir dir. St. Clair, Mo., 1958-63; organist, jr. choir organizer, sr. choir organizer Trinity Episcopal Ch., Mt. Vernon, Ill., 1964-67; choir mem. United Ch. Christ, Plymouth, Mich., 1967-69; organist Myers Funeral Home, Mt. Vernon, 1964-67; com. mem. Girl Scouts Am., Mt. Vernon, 1964-67, PTA, St. Clair, Mo., 1960-63; pack officer Boy Scouts Am., Mt. Vernon, 1964-67; home rm. mother, St. Clair, Mo., Mt. Vernon, 1958-67; chmn. Vols. to Arts, Mt. Vernon, Ill., 1966-67; library asst. Plymouth (Mich.) Mid. Sch., 1968-69; com. mem. Williamson County (Ill.) Sesquicentennial Celebration, 1989; mem. Marion Meml. Hosp. Aux., 1980—, Hearts Helping Heart, Marion, 1987—; asst. organist and choir mem., Sunday sch. tchr. Zion United Ch. of Christ, Marion, mem. numerous other ch. coms.; mem. So. Ill. Easter Seal Soc., 1987. Recipient Svc. Plaque Marion Recreation Dept. Bd., 1983. Mem. Marion C. of C. (com. 1988), Beta Sigma Phi. Home: 516 S Market St Marion IL 62959 Office: Marion Sr Citizens Ctr 507 W Main St Marion IL 62959-2437

AIKMAN, ROSALIE H., state legislator. Mem. Maine Ho. of Reps., mem. utilities and labor coms. Republican. Home: PO Box 420 Poland ME 04273 Office: Maine State Senate State Capital Augusta ME 04333*

AILLONI-CHARAS, MIRIAM CLARA, interior designer, consultant; b. Veere, The Netherlands, July 31, 1935; came to U.S., 1958; d. Maurits and Elzina (De Groot) Taytelbaum; m. Dan Ailloni-Charas, Oct. 8, 1957; children: Ethan Benjamin, Orrin, Adam. Degree in Interiors, Pratt Inst., 1962; BSc, SUNY, Albany, 1978. Interior designer S.J. Miller Assocs., N.Y.C., 1960-63; interior design cons. Rye Brook, N.Y., 1963-88, 90—; exec. v.p. Contract 2000 Inc., Port Chester, N.Y., 1988-90. Treas. Temple Guild, Congregation Emanu-El, Rye, N.Y., 1979-88, co-chair, 1988—, trustee, 1986-92. Recipient Cert. of Merit, U.S. Jaycees, 1962, March of Dimes, 1989, 91. Mem. Am. Soc. Interior Designers, Allied Bd. Trade, Westchester Assn. Women Bus. Owners (bd. dirs. 1988-93), Nat. Trust for Historic Preservation, Westchester C. of C. (area devel. coun. 1988-90). Home and Office: 23 Woodland Dr Rye Brook NY 10573-1797

AINSWORTH, ELAINE MARIE, occupational therapist; b. Jamestown, N.Y., July 24, 1948; d. Ralph Marion and Martha Elaine (Dunn) Sorenson; m. Stephen Marshall Ainsworth, Jan. 17, 1970 (div. Aug. 1973). BS in Edn., Edinboro State Coll., 1971; MS in Occupational Therapy, Columbia U., 1975. Mem. occupational therapy staff Warren (Pa.) State Hosp., 1975-77, chief occupational therapy staff, 1977; mem. occupational therapy staff Sheppard & Enoch Pratt Hosp., Towson, Md., 1978; pvt. practice Allentown, Pa., 1981-82; chief occupational therapy dept. Community Hosp. of Lancaster, Pa., 1982-86; asst. prof. Elizabethtown (Pa.) Coll., 1986-88; chief occupational therapy dept. Lebanon (Pa.) VA Med. Ctr., 1989-90; owner Elaine Ainsworth & Assocs., Lancaster, 1991—; cons. Mental Health Mgmt., Alexandria, Va., 1985, Stairways Agy., Erie, Pa., 1976, Hamot Med. Ctr., Erie, 1976, W.C.A. Hosp., Jamestown, N.Y., 1976; allied health liaison Parkinson Support Group, Lancaster, 1983-86. Author: (with others) Core Curriculum for Home Health Care Nursing, 1993. Treas., bd. dirs. Orgn. for Responsible Care of Animals, Lancaster, 1988. Recipient scholarship Commonwealth of Pa., 1973-75. Mem. Am. Occupational Therapy Assn., Pa. Occupational Therapy Assn. (chair nominating com. 1980-81, chair program com. state conf. 1982). Office: 245 Butler Ave Ste 304 Lancaster PA 17601

AINSWORTH, HARRIET CRAWFORD, journalist, public relations consultant; b. Columbus, Ohio, Nov. 27, 1914; d. Harry Hoskins and Pansy Lucy (Graham) Crawford; m. J. Gordon Ainsworth, Oct. 6, 1945; children: J. Gordon Jr., Adeline Ainsworth Forrest. BA, Ohio Wesleyan U., 1934; postgrad., Columbia U. Sch. Journalism, 1934-35, Gonzaga U., 1940, Calif. Coll. Arts and Crafts, 1968; life adult edn.-C.C. tchg. credential, U. Calif., Berkeley, 1967. Reporter Portland Oregonian, 1936-37; ind. pub. rels. writer, 1937-42; fgn. corr. Oakland Tribune, Indpls. Star, Japan, China, The Philippines, 1946; pub. info. dir. Am. Cancer Soc., Contra Costa County, Calif., 1958-89; cons. Calif. divsn. Am. Cancer Soc., 1965-77; pres. Ainsworth-Powell Pub. Rels., 1965-77; v.p. Corp. Identity Assocs., Orinda, Calif., 1968—; columnist (Sunbeams), feature writer Contra Costa Sun, Contra Costa Times, 1990—. Co-author: The Road Back, 1968; contbr. articles to profl. jours., newspaper columns. Mem. Citizen's Recreation Commn., dist. 6, Orinda, 1974-79; founder, pres. Orinda Found., 1975; chmn. spl. events Calif. Shakespeare Festival Amphitheater campaign, 1988-92. Lt. comdr. USNR, 1942-58. Named Orinda Citizen of Yr., 1976; recipient Plaque and Resolution Commendation Recreation Dist. 6, Orinda, 1979, Recognition award Plaque Pres. U.S. People-to-People Sports Com. Mem. San Francisco Pub. Rels. Round Table, Contra Costa Press Club, East Bay Women's Press Club (pres.), Orinda Country Club, Orindawoods Tennis Club, Orinda Tennis Club, Kappa Alpha Theta (co-founder Diablo Valley chpt.).

AINSWORTH, KRISTINE M., critical care nurse; b. Manchester, N.H., Jan. 10, 1959; d. Harry P. and Adoree Thomasina (Cote) A. BSN, St. Anselm Coll., 1981; student, U. Mass. Cert. CCRN. Staff nurse Elliot Hosp., Manchester, 1984—. Mem. AACN (past pres. So. N.H. chpt.), Sigma Theta Tau.

AIREY-WILSON, VERONICA ESTELLE, insurance agent, councilwoman; came to U.S., 1962; BA magna cum laude, Ithaca Coll., 1976; postgrad., Hartford Grad. Ctr., 1980. Claim rep. Aetna Life & Casualty Co., Hartford, Conn., 1976-78, personnel mgr., 1978-80, cons., 1980-82, mgr., 1982-84; owner, operator VerJen Creative Fashions, Hartford, 1984-91; ins. agt., owner Allstate Ins. Co., West Hartford, Conn., 1990—; councilwoman City of Hartford, 1993—; mgmt. trainee AIM Exec. Program, L.I., N.Y., 1979; cons. career devel. workshops Aetna Life & Casualty Co., 1979-82; chair Econ. Devel. Com.; co chair Hartford Mktg. Collaborative; dir. Hartford Downtown Coun. 1994—. Bd. dirs. Riverfront Recapture, Hartford, 1990-93; chair fundraising My Sister's Pl., 1990—, bd. dirs. 1992—; v.p. Say Yes To Edn., 1992—; 1st female pres. West Indian Social Club, 1989-90; bd. dirs., chair fundraising West Indian Found., 1989-93. Named Businesswoman of Yr., Iota Phi Lambda, Hartford, 1986; recipient Achievement in Excellence award Air Jamaica, 1989, ofcl. citation City of Hartford, 1989. Mem. Ind. United Order Mechanics (founder Rose of Sharon chpt. 1), Coalition 100 Black Women (treas. 1989-90). Republican. Episcopalian. Home: 16 Chatham St Hartford CT 06112 Office: Allstate Ins 345 N Main St West Hartford CT 06117

AITA, WENDY FAYE, clinical psychologist; b. Atlantic City, Nov. 2, 1965; d. Charles Y. and Catherine M. (Devine) McKelvey; m. Derek P. Aita, Feb. 8, 1992. BA, Oglethorpe U., 1987; MA, Fairleigh Dickinson U., 1989, PhD, 1991. Lic. psychologist, N.J. Rehab. counselor Rehab. Specialists, Glen Rock, N.J., 1988-90; intern Friends Hosp., Phila., 1990-91; behaviorist Rolling Hill Hosp., Phila., 1991-92; clin. dir. Therapeutic Alternatives, Mt. Holly, N.J., 1991-92; psychologist in pvt. practice Lumberton, N.J., 1992—; adj. prof. Burlington County Coll., Pemberton, N.J., 1993—, Stockton State Coll., Pomona, N.J., 1993—, Rowan State Coll., Glassboro, N.J., 1993—; group leader Women's Opportunity Ctr., Moorestown, N.J. Contbr. articles to profl. jours. Mem. APA, N.J. Psychol. Assn. Roman Catholic. Office: 693 Main St Lumberton NJ 08048

AITCHISON, ANNE CATHERINE, environmental activist; b. Pontiac, Mich., Dec. 27, 1939; d. Willard Francis and Elizabeth (Smith) Speer; m. Robert Terrington Aitchison, Aug. 10, 1963; children: Hannah, Guy, Will. MusB, U. Mich., 1963, MusM, 1965. Chair Naperville (Ill.) Area Recycling Ctr., 1980-89, exec. dir., 1989-93; exec. dir. Sun Shares, Durham, N.C., 1994—; mem. Citizen's Solid Waste Adv. Com., Will County, Ill., 1989-90, Task Force on Solid Waste, Ill., 1989-90, Task Force on Degradable Plastic, Ill., 1990-91, Mayor's Adv. Com. on Plastic Recycling, Chgo., 1990, Solid Waste Adv. Com., Durham, N.C., 1994—, Chmn.'s Environ. Com., DuPage County, 1993. Co-author: Resource Recycling, 1991, Environmental Policy for DuPage County, 1993. Founding mem. Naperville Chamber Winds, 1981-93; dir. DuPage Environ. Awareness Ctr., 1987-93; mem. Chmn.'s Environ. Commn., DuPage County, 1992-93; mem. Durham County Solid Waste Adv. Bd., 1994—; bd. dirs. Durham Symphony, 1994—. Named Individual Recycler of Yr. Keep Am. Beautiful, 1987, Outstanding Woman Leader YWCA, 1988. Mem. Ill. Recycling Assn. (co-pres. 1987-90, founding dir. 1980—, Pied Piper of Recycling 1989), Women in Waste, Ill. Environ. Coun. (bd. dirs. 1989-90), LWV (bd. dirs. Naperville chpt. 1977-93), Kiwanis (Disting. Svc. award 1987). Office: Sun Shares Inc 1215 S Briggs Ave # 100 Durham NC 27703

AIZEN, RACHEL K., clinical psychologist; b. Tel-Aviv, Israel; d. Aron and Jochewed L. Klotz; m. Icek Aizen; children: Ron, Elie, Jonathan. MA, U. Ill., 1968, PhD, 1970; postgrad. in clin. psychology, U. Mass., 1980-83. Lic. psychologist, Mass.; nat. cert. sch. psychologist. Asst. prof. Tel-Aviv U., 1972-73; psychologist Northampton (Mass.) State Hosp., 1971-72; clin. psychologist Amherst (Mass.) Sch. System, 1974—; pvt. practice, 1974—; intern VA Med. Ctr., Northampton, 1982-83; clin. psychologist Shieba Med. Ctr., Israel, 1985-86; fellow in neuropsychology Mass. Mental Health Hosp., Boston, 1987-88; cons. psychologist Mass. Rehab., 1974—, various local agys. and cts. Cons. editor The Am. Psychologist, 1974; co-author: Psychological Counseling: Principles, Strategies and Intervention, 1990; contbr. articles to profl. jours. With Israeli Air Force, 1960-62. Mem. APA (divsn. clin. and psychoanalysis), NEA, Nat. Assn. Sch. Psychologists. Office: 48 N Pleasant St Ste 204 Amherst MA 01002-1740

AJELLO, EDITH H., state legislator; b. Apr. 26, 1944; d. Kenneth Aaron and Rozella Christina (Ewoldt) Hanover; m. Arnold Bendixen Ajello, 1968; children: Linell, Aaron. BA, Bucknell U., 1966. Store mgr. V George Rustigian Rugs, Inc., 1981-93; interim exec. dir. Providence Schs., 1993—; mem. R.I. Ho. of Reps., 1993—. Democrat. Office: RI Ho of Reps State House Providence RI 02903*

AKABAS, SHEILA HELENE, social work educator; b. N.Y.C., Apr. 24, 1931; d. Louis Arnold and Lillian (Lefrak) Epstein; BS, Cornell U., 1951; PhD, NYU, 1970; m. Aaron Louis Akabas, Sept. 27, 1953; children: Myles, Seth, Miriam. Assoc. dir. Just One Break, 1953-55; rsch. dir. mental health rehab. program Amalgamated Clothing & Textile Workers Union, 1963-71; rsch. dir. Ctr. for Social Policy and Practice in the Workplace, Columbia U., N.Y.C., 1971-76, dir., 1976—, prof. Sch. Social Work, 1975—; adv. bd. Work in Am. Inst., 1988—, N.Y. State Sch. Indsl. Labor Rels., Cornell U., 1989—, chair, 1992-93, 93-94; dir. Mcpl. Employees Legal Svcs., 1973-83. Bd. dirs. Westchester Symphony Orch., 1965-80; mem. Pres.'s Com. Employment of Persons with Disabilities, 1975—, chair med. and ins. com. NIMH Manpower Demonstration Rev. Com., 1980-85, exec. com. NIMH Manpower Demonstration Rev. Com., 1994—, Cornell U. Coun., 1971-86, 1988-92; bd. dirs. Internat. Com. on Occupational Mental Health, 1982-86, 94—; mem. adv. bd. Menninger Found. Rehab. Inst., 1984-88; mem. tech. adv. com. Dole Found., 1984—, chair, 1992—; mem. adv. bd. Washington Bus. Group on Health Inst. Rehab. and Disability Mgmt., 1985—; editorial advisor Employee Assistance, 1988—; mem. editorial bd. Jour. Disability Policy Studies, 1988—; mem. adv. workplace policy panel Nat. Inst. Drug Abuse, 1990—; fund rep. Cornell U. Class Assn.; active Temple B'nai Jeshurum, N.Y.C. Switzer fellow, 1980; recipient Research in Rehab. award, 1982, Rehab. Project of Yr. award NRA, 1992; World Rehab. Fund fellow, 1983, 88; HHS grantee; NIMH grantee; Nat. Inst. Disability and Rehab.

Research grantee, U.S. Dept. Edn. grantee, 1985—. Nat. Inst. on Drug Abuse grantee, others. Mem. Council Social Work Edn. Club: Hadassah (N.Y.C.). Co-author: Mental Health Care in the World of Work, 1973, Disability Management, 1992; co-editor: Work, Workers & Work Organizations, 1982, Work and Well-Being, 1993; guest editor Practice Digest issue, 1982; contbr. articles to jours. Office: Columbia U Ctr Social Policy in Workplace 622 W 113th St New York NY 10025-7982

AKE, MARY KATHERINE, librarian, educator; b. East Chicago, Ind., Mar. 2, 1930; d. William Henry and Elsbeth Marguerite (Lenehan) Weichsel; m. John W. Ake, May 22, 1955 (div. May 1981); children: J. David, Katherine Mary. BA, Youngstown State U., 1952; MS, Carnegie Mellon U., 1953. Cert. tchr. Libr. Pub. Library Youngstown And Mahoning County, Ohio, 1953-55; libr., media specialist Littleton (Colo.) Pub. Schs., 1974-93, ret., 1993. Author: (with others) Touchstones, 1985, Writers for Children, 1987, The Phoenix Award, 1993. Founder Friends of the Library/Mus., 1964; served on numerous county, city, recreational, Littleton, sch. coms., 1962-75. Mem. Am. Assn. Sch. Librs., Children's Lit. Assn. (bd. dirs. 1979-83), Colo. Ednl. Media Assn., AAUW (founder local chpt. 1963), Dr. Watson's Neglected Patients Club (co-founder, chief surgeon 1988-89). Republican. Presbyterian. Home: 1351 Northcrest Dr Highlnds Rnch CO 80126-2504

AKERS, DEBORAH ROWLEY, lawyer; b. Troy, N.Y., Apr. 27, 1949; d. Samuel Lansing and Audrey (Relyea) Rowley. AB, Washington U., St. Louis, 1971; JD, Cleve. State U., 1976. Bar: Ohio 1976. Assoc. Wm. F. Manlove Co., L.P.A.; ptnr. Manlove, Manlove, Rowley & Fuhry, Chagrin Falls, Ohio, 1976-79; pvt. practice Avon Lake, Ohio, 1979-84; assoc. Schwarzwald, Robiner, Wolf & Rock, L.P.A., Cleve., 1984-88; prin. Wolf & Akers, L.P.A., Cleve., 1988—; mem. faculty Ohio CLE Inst., 1985-87, 89-93, Ohio Supreme Ct. Jud. Coll. Teleconf., 1991. Co-author: Disqualification, Family Advocate, vol. 9, #3, 1987; mem. editorial bd. The Domestic Rels. Jour. of Ohio. Trial referee Medina County Ct. of Common Pleas, 1983-84; mem. Profl. Edn. systems, 1990-91; appointee 9th Ohio Appellate Dist. Jud. Conf., 1991, Bench Bar Conf., 1990, 94, Ohio Jud. Conf. Fellow Am. Acad. Matrimonial Lawyers; mem. ABA (family law sect., property divsn. com. 1992-95, litigation sect., participant Advanced Family Law Advocacy Inst. 1987, faculty 1992-95, chair 1994, family law sect., family law sect. ann. meeting compendium 1990, family law ethics, vice-chmn. 1990-91), Ohio State Bar Assn. (family law com. vice chair 1992-93, chair, 1994—, chmn. legis. drafting subcom. 1989-93, del. coun. of dels. 1990—, spl com. child support collection and enforcement, 1992—), Cuyahoga County Bar Assn. (chmn. family law com. 1992-93, trustee 1986-87, mem. grievance com., faculty Trial Advocacy Inst. 1988-89, co-chair 1990-91, chair 1993), Cleve. Bar Assn. (chmn. family law sect.1989-90, profl. ethics com. 1986-93), Medina County Bar Assn. (lectr. 1983, 84, 87), Ohio Family Law Inst., Akron Bar Assn., Wayne County Bar Assn, Geauga County Bar Assn. Episcopalian. Office: 1515 East Ohio Bldg 1717 E 9th St Cleveland OH 44114-2802

AKINS, ELLEN, writer; b. South Bend, Ind., July 21; d. Edward L. and Mary L. (Swingendorf) A.; m. Stephen Denker, July 21, 1990. BA, U. So. Calif., 1981; MA, Johns Hopkins U., 1983. Teaching fellow Johns Hopkins U., Balt., Md., 1982-83; advtg. dir. U. Notre Dame Press, Ind., 1983-85; promotions mgr. U. Chgo. Press, 1985-88. Author: Home Movie, 1988 (Whiting Writer's award Mrs. Giles Whiting Found. 1989), Little Woman, 1990, World Like a Knife, 1991, Public Life, 1993. Ed Moses grantee U. So. Calif., 1981, grantee NEA, 1988, Ingram Merrill Found., 1989; recipient McGinnis prize Southwest Review, 1985, Acad. award Lit. Am. Acad. of Arts and Letters, 1993. Office: Charlotte Sheedy Lit Agy 611 Broadway # 428 New York NY 10012-2608 also: Star Route PO Box 1 Cornucopia WI 54827*

AKINS, LISA ANNE, financial analyst; b. Lincoln, Nebr., Sept. 13, 1961; d. Duane Burge and Arlene Luella (Maahs) Ketelhut; m. Robert Jordan Akins Jr., May 21, 1993. BS in Bus., U. Nebr., 1983; MBA, U. Denver, 1988. CFA. Tax analyst Nebr. Dept. Revenue, Lincoln, 1984-85; tax agt. Union Pacific Corp., Broomfield, Colo., 1985-86, sr. tax agt., 1986-88, asst. mgr. valuation rsch., 1988-91, mgr. valuation rsch., 1991—. Mem. Nat. Assn. R.R. Tax Reps., Nat. Assn. R.R. and Pub. Utility Tax Reps., Denver Soc. Security Analysts, Western States Assn. Tax Reps. Home: 1569 48th St Boulder CO 80303-1127 Office: Union Pacific Corp 350 Interlocken Blvd Ste 350 Broomfield CO 80021

AKIYAMA, CAROL LYNN, motion picture industry executive; b. Chgo., Dec. 5, 1946; d. Makio M. Akiyama and Mary (Uyeda) Maruyama; m. Peter Richard Bierstedt, Aug. 23, 1980. BA magna cum laude, U. So. Calif., 1968, JD, 1971. Bar: Calif. Atty. NLRB, Los Angeles, 1971-75, ABC-TV, Hollywood, Calif., 1975-79, So. Calif. Edison, Rosemead, 1980-81; asst. gen. atty. CBS Inc., Los Angeles, 1981-82; sr. v.p. Alliance of Motion Picture and TV Producers, Sherman Oaks, Calif., 1982-88; ind. producer and writer TV and motion pictures Rancho Palos Verdes, 1988—. Mem. Los Angeles County Bar Assn. (chmn. labor law sect. 1981-82, exec. com. 1975-85), Phi Kappa Phi, Phi Beta Kappa.

AKIYOSHI, TOSHIKO, jazz composer, pianist; b. Ryoyo, Manchuria, Dec. 12, 1929; d. Tatsuro and Shigeko (Hiraike) A.; m. Charlie Mariano, 1959 (div.); m. Lewis Tabackin, Nov. 3, 1969; 1 child, Michiru Mariano. Grad., Berklee Coll. Music, Boston. Founder, pianist, trio, 1953-70; appeared throughout U.S., Europe, Japan, founder, leader, composer-arranger, Toshiko Akiyoshi/Lew Tabackin Big Band, 1972-83, ToshikoAkiyoshi Jazz Orchestra, 1983—; albums include Long Yellow Road, 1976 (named Best Jazz Album of Yr., Stereo Rev.), Insights, 1978, Notorious Tourist from the East, 1978, Farewell to Mingus, 1980, European Memoirs, 1984, Top of the Gate, 1986, Finesse, 1987, Interlude, 1987, Remembering Bud, 1990, Wishing Peace, 1991, The Toshiko Akiyoshi/Lew Tabackin Big Band, 1991; Live at Birdland 1960-61, with The Charlie Mariano Quintet, 1992, Live at Carnegie Hall, 1992. Named Best Arranger, Best Band by Downbeat Poll, 1978, 79, Best Arranger, 1989.Ellis Island Medal of Honor, National Ethnic Coalition of Organizations, 1986. Address: Sony Music Entertainment 550 Madison Ave New York NY 10022*

ALAFOUZO, ANTONIA, marketing professional; b. Cairo, Egypt, Oct. 13, 1952; came to U.S., 1982; d. Pano Antony and Agni-Maria (Ranos) A.; m. Thomas D'Ambola Jr., May 29, 1988; 1 child. BSC in Econs., Brunel U., London, 1975; Diploma in Econs. and Politics, Oxford (Eng.) U., 1977, M of Philosophy, PhD, 1980. Staff reporter The Economist, London, 1973-75, contbg. writer, 1975-82; communications exec. Rubenstein, Wolfson Co., N.Y.C., 1982-87; founder, pres. Markcom Ltd., N.Y.C., 1987—; contbg. writer Fin. Report, London, 1975-82; cons. writer Fin. Times, London, 1980-82; cons. communications and econs. World Gold Council, N.Y.C., 1982—. Contbr. reports to fin. publs. Mem. Inst. Journalism Internat., Oxford Union Soc. Office: Markcom Ltd 277 Broadway New York NY 10007

ALAKSZAY, MARGARET KERN, elementry school educator, small business owner; b. Akron, Ohio, Dec. 4, 1931; d. Peter and Helen (Farkas) Kern; m. Joseph Julius Alakszay, June 23, 1956; children: Joann Lydia, James Kern. BS in Edn., U. Akron, 1953. Cert. elem. sch. tchr. (life), Calif. Tchr. grades 5 and 6 Akron (Ohio) Pub. Schs., 1952-56; tchr. grade 5 Compton (Calif.) Schs., 1956-57; tchr. grades 3 and 5 Covina (Calif.) Unified Sch. Dist., 1957-63; tchr. grades 4 and 6 Pomona (Calif.) Unified Sch. Dist., 1963-71; tchr. grades 4 and 5 Lakeport (Calif.) Unified Sch. Dist., 1972—; mem. Terrace Sch. Site Coun., Lakeport, 1989-91, Children's Coun., Lakeport, 1991-93; master tchr. Lakeport Unified Sch. Dist., 1992. Mem. Lake County Libr. Adv. Bd., 1988-89, founder Friends of Libr., 1989; sec. Lake County Dem. Cen. Com., 1990. Mem. AAUW (v.p. Pomona, 1959, pres., founder, Lake County, 1980), Calif. Tchrs. Assn. (congressional contact 1990-93, Redwood svc. ctr. steering com., state coun. 1986-93), Lake County Tchrs. Assn. (chmn. 1986-93), Lakeport Tchrs. Assn. (pres. 1985-93), Am. Assn. Retired Persons (legis. contact 1980-93), Delta Kappa Gamma (legis. chmn. 1990-93). Home: 1030 Boggs Ln Lakeport CA 95453-3008 Office: Terrace Sch 250 Lange St Lakeport CA 95453-3230

ALBA, BENNY, artist; b. Columbus, Ohio, May 7, 1949; d. Louis Peter and Marjorie Helen (Post) Benua. BA in Psychology, U. Mich., 1982. artist-in-residence St. Charles Boy's Pres. Sch., Columbus, 1982-85; represented by numerous cons., Calif., Fla., Ill., Tex., Md., N.J., N.Y., Va., Mass.; lectr. Columbus Cultural Arts Ctr., 1983, 84, 93; presenter workshops in field. One woman shows include Columbus Cultural Arts Ctr., 1993, Apprentice Alliance, San Francisco, 1994, Las Vegas (Nev.) Mus., 1994, Artist TV Access, San Francisco, 1994, Western Wyo. Coll., Rock Springs, 1994, A Gallery in the Clock Tower, San Francisco, 1994, Ctr. for Psy. Studies, Albany, Calif., 1994, Idyllwild (Calif.) Sch. Music and Art, 1995; exhibited in group shows at Davis (Calif.) Art Ctr., 1993, Kunst für Begegnungen, Munich, 1993, Ednl. Testing Svc., Emeryville, Calif., 1993-94, Diablo (Calif.) Valley Coll. Gallery, 1994; represented in Nat. Mus. Women in Arts, Ark. A Ctr., Little Rock, U. Mich. Mus. Art, Kalamazoo (Mich.) Inst. Arts, Greenpeace, Ulli Wachter (Germany), others. Recipient Lenore Miles award North Platte Valley Art Gallery, 1991, Body of Work award Women Artists, A Celebration, 1990, Merit award San Francisco Women Artist Gallery, 1986. Mem. Women's Caucus for Art (bd. dirs. No. Calif. 1991-94, sec. 1991, 92). Studio: 4400 Market St Oakland CA 94608-3424

ALBAGLI, LOUISE MARTHA, psychologist; b. Queens, N.Y., Jan. 15, 1954; d. Meyer Nathan and Leah (Bleier) Greenberg; m. Eli S. Albagli, July 31, 1977. BA in Psychology summa cum laude, CUNY, 1976; D of Clin. Psychology, Rutgers U., 1983. Clin. psychology intern Postgrad. Ctr. Mental Health, N.Y.C., 1980-81; staff psychologist Queens County Neuropsychiat. Inst., Jackson Heights, N.Y., 1981-83, Bklyn. Community Counseling Ctr., 1981-84; sr. clin. psychologist Richard Hall Community Mental Health Ctr., Bridgewater, N.J., 1984-86; pvt. practice specializing in women's reproductive health issues cen. N.J., 1985—; adj. faculty mem. Rutgers U., 1990—. Mem. Nat. Register Health Care Providers, Am. Psychol. Assn., N.J. Psychol. Assn. (com. inter-profl. rels.), Internat. Childbirth Edn. Assn., RESOLVE, Raritans, Phi Beta Kappa.

ALBAND, LINDA ANN, small business owner; b. Portland, Oreg., Apr. 30, 1948; d. John and Jean (Whitlock) A. AAS in Computer Tech., North Seattle C.C., 1985; BA in Tech. & Profl. Writing summa cum laude, San Francisco State U., 1994. Mgr. REP Bookcenter and Press, Portland, Oreg., 1970-73; program mgr. microcomputer program North Seattle C.C., 1985-88; owner, operator Linda Alband Bookseller, San Francisco and Oakland, Calif., 1988—; personal asst., rschr. to author Randy Shilts, San Francisco, 1988-94; rschr., grant writer Woman Vision Video Prodns., 1994—; rschr. in field. Editor, fact checker Conduct Unbecoming, 1990-94. Oreg. organizer, mem. nat. steering com. Vietnam Vets Against War, 1970-73; co-founder, bd. dirs. Bay Area Mil. Studies Group, San Francisco, 1974-80; video project developer, prodr. San Francisco Bay Area Book Festival, 1992—; organizer, prodr. Randy Shilts Pub. Meml., Glide Meml., San Francisco, 1994; active Calif. Laywers for Arts, San Francisco Bay Area Book Coun., San Francisco Cinema League. Mem. Nat. Writers Union, Media Alliance, Film Arts Found., Bay Area Video Coalition. Home and Office: 1327 45th Ave # 4 San Francisco CA 94122

ALBANESE, ELLEN LOUISE, newspaper editor; b. Cohasset, Mass., Sept. 17, 1949; d. Francis Joseph and Louise (Whittredge) A.; m. William P. Landers, Oct. 23, 1971; children: Abby Jean, Tracy Ellen. Cert., Sorbonne U., Paris, 1970; BA in Sociology and French, Tufts U., 1971; MS in Pub. Rels., Boston U., 1975. Editor MIT Press, Cambridge, 1971-73; publicity dir. Cahners Books, Boston, 1973-75; pub. rels. dir. Ea. Mass. and R.I. dists. Weight Watchers, Attleboro, Mass., 1976-78; editor The Country GAZETTE, Franklin, Mass., 1980-92; editor-in-chief Norfolk Newspaper Co., Franklin, 1992—. Publicity chair Women's Success Network, Franklin, 1986-88; leader Girl Scouts U.S.A., Franklin, 1988-89; mem. community coun. Dean Jr. Coll., Franklin, 1989—. Recipient 1st pl. column writing award N.Eng. Press Assn., Boston, 1987. Mem. Internat. Soc. Weekly Newspaper Editors (bd. dirs., pres. 1993-94, Golden Dozen award 1986, 94, Golden Quill award 1987), Am. Press Inst. (mem. Weekly Adv. Track), Mass. Press Assn. (treas. 1986-88, pres. 1989, 1st Place in Editl. Writing award 1994), Phi Beta Kappa. Office: Norfolk Newspaper Co PO Box 612 Franklin MA 02038

ALBAUM, JEAN STIRLING, psychologist, educator; b. Beijing, China, Jan. 11, 1932; came to U.S., 1936; d. Richard Henry and Emma Bowyer (Lueders) Ritter; m. B. Taylor Stirling, Aug. 15, 1953 (div. 1965); 1 child, Christopher Taylor Stirling; m. Joseph H. Albaum; stepchildren: Thomas Gary, Lauren Jean. BA, Beloit (Wis.) Coll., 1953; MS, Danbury (Conn.) State U., 1964, U. La Verne, Calif., 1983; PhD, Claremont (Calif.) Grad. Sch., 1985. Lic. ednl. psychologist, Calif. Spl. edn. tchr. Charter Oak (Calif.) Sch. Dist., 1966-80; psychologist, coord. elem. counseling Claremont Sch. Dist., 1980—; pvt. practice ednl. psychologist Encino, Calif., 1987—; clin. supr. Marriage, Family and Child Counselor Interns, Claremont, 1987—; part-time lectr. U. La Verne, 1988—; oral commr. Bd. Behavioral Sci. Examiners, Sacramento, 1989—. Contbr. articles to profl. jours. Hostess L.A. World Affairs Coun., 1980—; pres. Woodley Homeowner's Assn., Encino, 1986-89. Grantee Durfee Found., 1986, 92. Mem. Am. Psychol. Assn., Calif. Assn. Marriage, Family and Child Therapists, Calif. Assn. Lic. Ednl. Psychologists. Office: Edn Ctr 2080 N Mountain Ave Claremont CA 91711-2643

ALBERG, MILDRED FREED, film and television producer, writer; b. Montreal, Que., Can., Jan. 15, 1921; d. Harry and Florence (Goldstein) Freed; m. Somer Alberg, Jan. 28, 1940 (dec.). Grad., high sch. Assoc. producer N.Y.C. Radio, 1940-43; writer radio shows AFL-CIO Community Services Com., N.Y.C., 1944-46; dir. info. CARE, Inc., N.Y.C., 1947-51; lectr. univs. Producer: Hallmark Hall of Fame, N.Y.C., 1953-60; TV series Our Am. Heritage, assoc. with Am. Heritage mag., N.Y.C., 1961-62; Broadway show Little Moon of Alban, 1961; (films) Hot Millions, 1968, M.G.M.; film series on Bibl. archaeology, ABC-TV, 1972-75; producer, co-dir., co-writer: PBS documentary The Royal Archives of Ebla, 1981; contbr. articles, N.Y. Post. Trustee Am. Schs. Oriental Research, Albright Inst. Archaeol. Research; bd. dirs. Holy Land Conservation Fund. Recipient numerous awrds for radio, TV and film prodns.; NEH grantee, 1978-80. Mem. Writers Guild-East, Nat. Acad TV Arts and Scis. (past gov.). Home: 3333 NE 34th St #801 Fort Lauderdale FL 33308

ALBERGA, ALTA WHEAT, artist; b. Ala.; d. James Richard and Leila Savannah (Sullivan) Wheat; B.A., M.A., Wichita State U., 1954; B.F.A., Washington U., St. Louis, 1961; M.F.A., U. Ill., 1964; m. Alvyn Clyde Alberga, Dec. 3, 1930. Mem. faculty Wichita (Kans.) State U., 1955-56, Webster Coll., St. Louis, 1969. art tchr. Ossining (N.Y.) High Sch., 1968; asst. prof., head visual arts Presbyn. Coll., Clinton, S.C., 1969-74; pvt. art tchr., Greenville, S.C., 1972—; substitute tchr. Greenville County Schs.; tchr. painting Tempo Gallery Sch., Greenville, 1974—, Greenville County Mus. Sch., 1975—, Tryon (N.C.) Fine Arts Ctr., 1986 (merit award 1987); tchr. Tri-County Tech. Coll., Pendleton, S.C., 1975. One-woman shows include Greenville County Mus., 1979, Greenville Artists Guild Gallery, 1979, 83, Wichita State U., 1954, St. Louis Artists Guild, 1956, N.C. State U., 1965, 66, Met. Arts Council, Greenville, 1980, 83, 85, Tryon Fine Arts Ctr., 1988, S.C. State U., 1992, 93; exhibited in group shows at Pickens County Mus., 1979, 88-89, Internation, Washington, 1981-82, Greenville Artists Guild, 1982, 88, Art/7, Washington, 1983, N.C. Univ., Charlotte invitational, 1989, Furman U. Women's Show, 1989, S.C. State U., 1992, Upstate Visual Arts, 1993, S.C. State U., 1993, Rolling Green Gallery, 1993, Internationale Grafiek Biennale, Maastricht, the Netherlands, 1993, S.C. Watercolor Soc., 1994; represented in permanent collections S.C. State Mus., Columbia, S.C. Arts Commn., Pickens County Mus.; represented in pvt. collections; bd. dirs. Greenville Artists Guild, 1977-79, pres., 1985; bd. dirs. Guild Gallery, 1978, Guild Greenville Symphony, 1989-90. Recipient Richard K. Weil award St. Louis Mus., 1957; Purchase prize S.C. Arts Commn., 1972; Merritt award Greenville Mus., 1986, Pickens County Mus., 1987, 88; Cash award S.C. Water Color Assn. Mem. Artists Equity (pres. St. Louis chpt. 1962), Internat. Platform Assn. (life), Art Students League (life), Guild Greenville Artists (pres. 1984-85), S.C. Artists Guild, Southeastern Council Printmakers, Greenville Symphony Guild, Mus. Assn. (invited), Kappa Pi, Kappa Delta Pi. Democrat. Home: 11 Overton Dr Greenville SC 29609-2612

ALBERS, JO-ANN HUFF, journalism educator; b. Cain's Store, Ky., Jan. 3, 1938; d. Vertreese Henry and Olowene (Brown) Huff; m. Henry Hall Albers; children: Stephen G., H. William. BA, Miami U., Oxford, Ohio, 1959; MEd, Xavier U., Cin., 1962. Specialist tech. info. GE, Evendale, Ohio, 1959; supr. traffic Sta. WCPO subs. Scripps Howard, Cin., 1959-60; editing, writing positions The Cin. Enquirer, 1960-81; pub., editor Sturgis (Mich.) Jour., 1981-82, Pub. Opinion, Chambersburg, Pa., 1982-86; gen. news exec. Gannett. Co. Inc., Arlington, Va., 1986-87; head journalism dept. Western Ky. U., Bowling Green, 1987—. Recipient Noel Ross Strader award Coll. Media Advisers, 1988, Bingham Freedom of Info. award Ky. Press Assn., 1989; Poynter teaching fellow, 1988. Mem. Women in Comm. (pres. 1974-75, rep. to accrediting coun. on edn. in journalism/mass comm. 1980—, Nat. Headliner award 1979), Assn. Schs. Journalism and Mass Comm. (pres. 1993-94), Kiwanis. Mem. Church of Christ. Office: Western Ky U Gordon Wilson Hall Bowling Green KY 42101

ALBERS, LUCIA BERTA, land developer; b. Guatemala, Feb. 10, 1943; d. Jose Luis De Leon Polanco and Maria Marta (Vasquez) De Leon; m. Ray Cisneros, Nov. 2, 1968 (div. 1972); 1 child, Elizabeth Ann Albers Cisneros; m. Monte Dean Albers, June 12, 1974; 1 child, Monte Roberto. Grad. in Acctg., Sacred Heart, Guatemala, 1963; student in Econs., San Carlos, Guatemala, 1964; student, Diablo Valley Coll., 1975, 76. Chief acct. Discovery Bay, Byron, Calif., 1971-76; asst. fin. dir. City of Pittsburg, Calif., 1976-78; corporate contr. Conco Cement, Concord, Calif., 1981-90; land developer Contra Costa County, Calif., 1990—. Mem. adv. coun. City of Byron, Calif., 1991-94; dir. Ctr. for New Ams., Concord, 1994—. Mem. Nat. Assn. Accts., Nat. Assn. Exec. Women, Nat. Assn. Women, Mex.-Am. Polit. Assn. Home: 9601 Deer Valley Rd Brentwood CA 94513

ALBERT, CHRISTINE LYNNETTE, accountant; b. Stillman Valley, Ill., May 21, 1965; d. Charles Ralph and June Ruth (Freeman) Peterson; m. James Howard Albert, May 28, 1988. AAS in Bus., Rock Valley Coll., 1986; BS in Acctg., Rockford Coll., 1992. CPA, Ill. Bookkeeper, supr. Harwood Aviation, Inc., Rockford, Ill., 1984-86; comml. lending credit analyst Bank One 1st Nat. Bank, Rockford, 1986-92; acct. Ringdahl's, Inc., Rockford, 1992—. Student mem. Coast Guard Aux., Ill., 1994; fundraiser Chgo. Children's Hosp., 1992-94. Mem. Ill. CPA Soc., Inst. Mgmt. Accts. (bd. dirs.), Golf League (treas.). Home: 7170 S Main Rd Rockford IL 61102

ALBERT, JANYCE LOUISE, business educator, banker; b. Toledo, July 27, 1932; d. Howard C. and Glenola Mae (Masters) Blessing; m. John R. Albert, Aug. 7, 1954; children: John R., James H. Student Ohio Wesleyan U., 1949-51; BA, Mich. State U., 1953; MS, Iowa State U., 1980. Asst. pers. mgr./tng. supr. Sears, Roebuck & Co., Toledo, 1953-56; tchr. adult edn. Tenafly Pub. Schs. (N.J.), 1966-70; pers. officer, tng. officer, tng. and edn. mgr. Iowa Dept. Transp., Ames, 1974-77; coll. recruiting coord. Rockwell Internat., Cedar Rapids, Iowa, 1977-79, engrng. adminstrn. mgr., 1979-80; employee rels. and job evaluation analyst Phillips Petroleum Co., Bartlesville, Okla., 1980-81; v.p., dir. pers. Rep. Bancorp, Tulsa, 1981-83; sr. v.p. and dir. human resources First Nat. Bank, Rockford, Ill., 1983-94; dir. bus. divsn. Rock Valley Coll., Rockford, 1994—; advisor to Nat. Profl. Secs. Assn. Pres. bd. dirs. Rocvale Children's Home., 1991-94; v.p. bd. dirs. United Way of Ames, 1976-77; mem. employee svc. comm., Rockford Pub. Schs., 1988-92; bd. dirs. Rockford Human Resources Community Action Program, Womenspace Ctr., 1993—; sec. bd. dirs. Rockford Symphony Orch., 1993—; chairperson legis. com., Rockford State Job Svcs. Office; chairperson Rockford State of Ill. Job Svcs. Employers Coun., 1990—; publicity chmn. Tenafly 300th Ann. Celebration, 1969; mem. task force Rockford Bd. Educators, 1993—; mem. gala com. Janet Wattles Mental Health Ctr., 1990; bd. deacons Presbyn. Ch., Ames, 1972-75; mem. adv. coun. Rockford YWCA, bd. dirs., 1986; co-chmn. YWCA Leader Luncheon, 1985; advisor Rockford chpt. ARC; mem. Mayor's Task Force for Rockford Project Self-Sufficiency, chmn. adv. coun., 1991; chairperson info. and referral task force United Way of Rockford, 1994; bd. dirs. Rockford Symphony Orch., sec. bd., 1994—; dir. bus. divsn. Rock Valley Coll., Rockford, Ill. Pres.'s scholar, 1951-53; recipient YWCA Kate O'Connor award for Women in Labor Force 1984, Athena award Rockford C. of C., 1991. Mem. Rockford Network (past chairperson 1985, pres. 1986), Rockford C. of C. (transp. com., human resources com., leadership program 1989, pres. club 1992—), Rockford Pers. Assn. (co-chmn. programs 1985-86, adv. coun.), Am. Soc. Pers. Adminstrn., Rockford Pers. Assn., Employee Benefits Assn. No. Ill. (membership chmn.), Rockford Coun. Affordable Health Care, Womenspace (bd. dirs. 1993—, sec. 1994—), Rockford Personal and Profl. Power Coalition, P.E.O., Rockford Panhellenic Coun. (sec. 1992-93, treas. 1993—, Woman of Yr. award 1994), World Trade Coun. (bd. dirs. 1994—, chairperson info. referral svc. task force), Sigma Epsilon, Alpha Gamma Delta, Phi Kappa Phi. Home: 5587 Thunderidge Dr Rockford IL 61107-1756 Office: Rock Valley Coll Bus Divsn 3301 N Mulford Rd Rockford IL 61114-4499

ALBERT, JUDITH FLORENCE, doll and plush designer, inventor; b. Rockville Center, N.Y., Sept. 30, 1938; d. Ernest A. and Florence Ruth (Ott) Carman; m. Joseph P. Paruolo, Sept. 3, 1961 (div. Feb. 1975); m. I. Arthur Albert, Mar. 21, 1975; stepchildren: Ronda Kornfeld, Ross Albert. AAS, Fashion Inst. of Tech., 1958; student, L.I. U. Designer Arranbee Doll Corp., Hicksville, N.Y., 1958, Valentine Doll Corp., Bklyn., 1958-59; designer to dir. Ideal Toy Corp., Hollis, N.Y., 1959-81; pres. Alberts Design Co. Inc., Oyster Bay, N.Y., 1981—; design cons. Galoob Toy Corp., South San Francisco, 1990-92, Tyco Toys Inc., Mt. Laurel, N.J., 1988—, Direct Connect Inc., 1991-92, Ideal Viewmaster Corp., 1987-88, Roseart Industries, Inc., Orange, N.J., 1993—. Designer Cabbage Patch Dolls, 1982-86, Ideal Nursery, 1988—, Furskin Bears, Rub A Dub Dolly, Crissy Doll, Betsy Wetsy, Baby Bubbles, Tiffany Taylor, Tuesday Taylor, Tiny Tears, Shirley Temple, 1974, Flatsy, Whoopsie, Tammy, Jody, Thumbelina, Maxi, Magic Bottle Baby and Pets, Baby Face, Baby Feels So Real, The Little Raggedies Babies, Magic Feeding Baby, Baby Giggles 'N Go, Kewpie Dolls, Xuxa, others; inventor Snuggles, 1979, Karen and her Magic Carriage, 1980, Pretty Curls, 1980, My Bottle Baby, 1980, Cabbage Patch Poseables, 1983, Cabbage Patch Corn Silk Hair, 1984, Puffalumps, 1985; co-inventor Dress-n-Dazzle, 1986, Honeycombs Dolls, 1986, Twinkling Thumbelina, 1991. Mem. Mill River Club, Art Student LEague, The Art Now Alliance, Visual Art Alliance L.I. Lutheran. Home and Office: Sea View Dr Mill Neck NY 11765

ALBERTINI, NANCY LIBERIS, language educator; b. Worcester, Mass., Dec. 27, 1949; d. Adolph William and Jeannette Marie (Cournoyer) L.; 1 child, Jonathan Robert. BA, Worcester State Coll., 1971; MA, Clark U., 1986. cert. fgn. lang. tchr., Mass. Asst. dir. planning and program devel. U. Mass. Med. Sch., Worcester, 1972-73; tchr. Spanish Worcester East Middle Sch., 1971-72; tchr. Spanish and English Doherty H.S., Worcester, 1973-74; tchr. ESL Keefe Tech., Framingham, Mass., 1980-82; asst. dir. campus ctr. Fitchburg State Coll., Mass., 1988-89; tchr. Spanish Ashland (Mass.) H.S., 1974-94, dir. student activities, 1990—. chair min. rels. com. First Unitarian Universalist Soc. Franklin (Mass.), 1988-94; score keeper Franklin Youth Basketball, 1989-94; mem. Ashland Boosters, 1989-94. Mem. NOW, Nat. Educators Assn., Mass. Tchrs. Assn., Ashland Educators Assn., Worcester Art Mus. Democrat. Office: Ashland High Sch 70 W Union St Ashland MA 01721

ALBERTS, CELIA ANNE, lawyer; b. Denver, May 3, 1953; d. Robert Edward and Barbara Ellen (Wedge) A. BA in French, U. Colo., 1975, JD, 1979; LLM in Taxation, U. Denver, 1984. Bar: Colo. 1979, U.S. Dist. Ct. Colo. 1979, U.S. Ct. Appeals (10th cir.) 1979. Assoc. Dietze, Davis & Porter, Boulder, Colo., 1979-82; sole practice Boulder, 1983-84; assoc. George, Davies and Assocs., Denver, 1984-86, Loser, Davies, Magoon & Fitzgerald, Denver, 1986-87; sole practice Denver, 1987-89; v.p., sr. counsel Merrill Lynch, Denver, 1989—. Mem. ABA (tax div., real estate div., corp. div.), Colo. Bar Assn. (tax div.), Denver Bar Assn. (tax, corp., real estate, estate/probate div.), Greater Denver Tax Counsel's Assn., Alliance of Profl. Women. Club: Toastmasters. Home: 237 S Lamb Ln Golden CO 80401-9426 Office: Merrill Lynch Legal Advisory 3840 S Wadsworth Blvd Denver CO 80235

ALBERT-SHERIDAN, LENORE LUANN, legal research fellow; b. Coldwater, Mich.; d. Samuel George and Carol Louise (Huttenen) Albert; m. James Christopher Sheridan, Feb. 23, 1990. AA in Liberal Arts, Long Beach City Coll.; BA in Econs., Calif. State U., Long Beach, 1992; postgrad., U. of the Pacific, 1994—. Asst. purchasing agt., supr. warehouse assembly, head inventory control Neill Aircraft Co., Long Beach, 1987-89; head inventory control/regional purchasing & receiving supr. Internat. Paper, Inc., L.A., 1989-91; fin./gen. ledger acct. Port of Long Beach, 1991-92; corp. acct. Weber Aircraft Inc., Fullerton, Calif., 1993; fin. analyst Sizzler Internat., L.A., 1993; rsch. fellow McGeorge Sch. Law, Sacramento, Calif., 1994—;

participant Nat. Inst. Judicial Hearsay Study, McGeorge/U. Calif.-Davis, Sacramento, 1994; tutor minority bus. program Calif. State U., Long Beach, 1992. Back stage mgr. San Pedro (Calif.) Theatre Performing Arts, 1987. Mem. ABA (internat. law and antitrust sects.), Inst. Managerial Accts., Phi Alpha Delta., Phi Alpha Delta (Clair Eagle chpt. alumni com. 1994-95). Lutheran. Home: 2701 Corabel Ln # 70 Sacramento CA 95821

ALBERTSON, SUSAN L., retired federal government official; b. Washington, Dec. 3, 1929; d. J. Mark and Alice (Myers) A. BS, Purdue U., 1952; postgrad. in internat. rels., George Washington U., 1956-58. Numerous profl. positions CIA, Washington, 1952-88; ret., 1988. Republican.

ALBRECHT, BEVERLY JEAN, special education educator; b. Dixon, Ill., Sept. 8, 1936; d. Harold Ivan Foster and Grace Gertrude Tracy Freed; m. Marvin Blackert Albrecht, Aug. 13, 1960; children: Bradley K., Brent D., Kimberly S. Albrecht Schluns. BS, Manchester Coll., North Manchester, Ind., 1958; MS, No. Ill. U., 1978. Cert. in elem. edn., educable mentally handicapped, learning disabled, supervision and early childhood edn., Ill. Kindergarten tchr. Sch. Dist. 300, Carpentersville, Ill, 1958-60; thcr. 5th grade Sch. Dist. 5, Sterling, Ill., 1960-61, 64-65, kindergarten tchr., 1962-64, substitute tchr., 1965-71; dir. nursery sch. Sterling YWCA, 1971-75; program dir. Ctr. for Human Devel., Sterling, 1975-76; family advocate Ill. Dept. Child and Family Svcs., Rock Falls, 1977-78; learning disablities and behavior disorders spl. edn. tchr. Sch. Dist. 289, Mendota, Ill., 1978-84, devel. pre-sch. tchr., 1984-89; clinician, case mgr., family preservation Sinnissippi Ctrs. Inc., Sterling, 1989—; replication specialist PEECH project U. Ill., Champaign, 1985-88; supervisory faculty Ill. State U., Normal, 1983-85, Ill. Valley C.C., Oglesby 1985-89. Host family Rock River Valley Internat. Fellowships, Sterling, 1975-92; chair coun. on edn. United Meth. Ch., Rock Falls, 1973-75, supt., tchr. ch. sch., 1968-88. Spl. Edn. fellow Ill. Office of Pub. Instrn., 1966; name grant honoree United Meth. Women, Rock Falls. Mem. NEA, Ill. Edn. Assn., Coun. for Exceptional Children. Republican. Home: 3254 Mineral Springs Rd Sterling IL 61081-4107

ALBRECHT, CAROL HEATH, artist, educator; b. Lafayette, Ind., May 26, 1921; d. Donald Leroy and Zula Elpha (Whicker) Heath; m. Edward Mathews Albrecht, May 25, 1944; children: Lynn, Catherine. Grad. high sch., Lafayette, Ind. Sec. U.S. Maritime Commn., San Francisco, 1941-44; mem. faculty art dept. Pensacola (Fla.) Jr. Coll., 1984-86, Eastern Shore Fine Arts Acad., Fairhope, Ala., 1986-91; presenter workshops in field, including oriental brush painting workshop/seminar, Sarasota, Fla., Clearwater, Fla., Pensacola. One-woman shows include Maison Le Cel, Ft. Walton Beach, Fla., 1976, 77, Whiting Gallery, Fairhope, 1989, Estate Gallery, Pensacola, 1991, Elliott Mus., Stuart, Fla., 1983; group shows include Fla. Watercolor Soc., Tallahassee, 1982, Pensacola Mus. Art, 1983-93, Sumi-e Soc. Am., Washington, 1982-94, Fla. Gulf Coast Art Ctr., Belleair, 1983, Asheville (N.C.) Mus. Art, 1983, Yosemite (Calif.) Renaissance Nat. Art Exhibit, 1987. Recipient purchase award Elliot Mus., 1983. Mem. Sumi-e Soc. Am. (pres. White Lotus chpt., Best in Show award 1990, Grumbacher gold medal 1991, Winsor-Newton award 1992, Sarasota chpt. award 1993, Shaffer award for brush mastery 1994, Reba Dickerson Hill Meml. award 1994). Home and Studio: 2026 Copley Dr Pensacola FL 32503-3349

ALBRECHT, KAY MONTGOMERY, primary school educator, consultant, child advocate; b. Lafayette, La., Jan. 29, 1949; d. Michael H. and Imogene (McCallum) M.; m. Larry Steven Albrecht, June 23, 1973. BA, U. Southwestern La., 1970; MS in Child Devel., U. Tenn., 1972, PhD in Family Studies, 1984. Head Start coordinator U. Tenn., Knoxville, 1972-75; instr. Incarnate Word Coll., San Antonio, 1976-77; instr. Southwest Tex. State U., San Marcos, 1977-80; tng. dir. Daybridge Learning Ctrs., Houston, 1984-85, v.p., 1985-86; v.p. Child Care Mgmt. Assocs., 1986-90, sr. ptnr., 1990-92; founder Hearts Home Early Learning Ctrs., Inc., 1986—; sr. ptnr. Innovations in Early Childhood Edn., 1992—; cons. Adminstrn. for Children, Youth and Families, HHS, Washington, 1982-83, Binney & Smith (author Crayola Creativity Program), Mervyn's, Angeles Toys, Houston Ind. Sch. Dist., Houston Mayor's Office; adv. bd. Nat. Acad. Early Childhood Programs, validator, commr., 1989—, 1986-91; scholarship chmn. Parrish Sch. Bd., 1990-93. Author staff orientation manual and consumer curriculum guide, 1980, 85, quality assurance manual for child care ctrs., 1987, School-Age Child Care Manual, Infant-Toddler Child Care Manual, Crayola Creativity Program Manual, Developmentally Appropriate Practice in School-Age Child Care, 1991, 2nd edit., 1993; contbg. editor Child Care Information Exchange mag.; contbr. Pre-K Today/Scholastic mag. Mem. Hayes County Child Welfare Bd. San Marcos, 1979-81, Houston Com. for Pvt. Sector Initiatives Child Care Com.; vol. Initiatives for Children, 1988-90; coord. Child Care Am. Campaign, 1988; pres. bd. dirs. Big Bros.-Big Sisters, Knoxville, 1981-83; vol. cons. Head Start, San Marcos and Knoxville, 1978-84; mem. com. Mayor's Task Force on Children, Houston, 1985; cons. Brown & Root Inc., Vinsin & Elkins, Baker & Botts, Table Toys Inc., 1982-83. Recipient Woman of Excellence award Houston Fedn. Profl. Women, 1993. Mem. Am. Home Econs. Assn. (section treas. 1984-86, project Home Safe Nat. Adv. bd. 1988-93), Nat. Assn. for Edn. Young Children, Nat. Council Family Relations, Nat. Acad. Early Childhood Programs (adv. bd. 1987-91), Houston Assn. Edn. Young Children (bd. dirs. 1984-86, 91—, Child Care Am. coordinator 1988, Educator of Yr. award 1993), Internat. Council on Women's Health Issues (bd. dirs. 1987-90). Democrat. Methodist. Avocations: water skiing, hiking, cooking, wild flower identification. Office: Innovations in Early Childhood Edn 1307 S Voss Rd Houston TX 77057

ALBRECHT, PATRICIA LOUISE, psychologist; b. Cleve., Oct. 26, 1957; d. Nicholas and Elizabeth (Hrovat) Sudar; m. Kurt William Albrecht, May 28, 1994. BSSW, Ohio State U., 1979; MA, No. Ariz. U., 1989. Cert. sch. psychologist, Ariz., 1990; nat. cert. sch. psychologist, 1991. Asst. dir. activities Rosemont Sch., Columbus, Ohio, 1979-81; youth specialist Youth Evaluation and Treatment Ctr., Phoenix, 1981-82; recreation supr. New Found., Phoenix, 1982-83; researcher Bald Eagles U.S. Forest Svc./Fish and Wildlife, Phoenix, 1983-87; student advisor NAU, Flagstaff, Ariz., 1987-88; grad. asst. No. Ariz. U., Flagstaff, 1988-89; sch. psychometrist Kingman (Ariz.) Elem. Dist., 1989-90, sch. psychologist, 1990-92; sch. psychologist No. Ariz. U., 1992—. Mem. Nat. Assn. Sch. Psychology, Ariz. Assn. Sch. Psychology (no. regl. dir. 1993-95). Office: No Ariz U PO Box 5630 Flagstaff AZ 86011

ALBRIGHT, ANNAROSE M., secondary school educator; b. Norton, Va., May 8, 1944; d. Joseph Paul and Dorothy Mae (Woody) Cooch; m. William J. Albright, Mar. 28, 1975; children: Angela Rose, Marisa Rose. BS in Edn., Millersville (Pa.) U., 1965; MS in Edn., Temple U., 1968. Cert. English and history tchr., supr., Pa. Tchr. Lancaster County Sch. Dist., New Holland, Pa., 1965-67, Lancaster (Pa.) Sch. Dist., 1967-70, Conestoga Valley Sch. Dist., Lancaster, Pa., 1970-84; supr. English dept. Hempfield Sch. Dist., Landisville, Pa., 1984-91. Chairperson Christian edn. adv. com. St. John Neumann Cath. Ch., tchr., catechist; mem. pub. policy com. YWCA, Pa. Recipient journalistic recognition from local and state edn. assns. Mem. AAUW (chair local chpt. pub. policy com.), ASCD, Nat. Coun. Tchrs. English (hospitality com. 1990), Conf. on English Leadership (program com. 1991), Pa. Coun. Tchrs. English, Landis Valley Mus. Assn. (chmn. Christmas program, bd. dirs.), Mission Hills Civic Assn. Home: 2636 Breezewood Dr Lancaster PA 17601-4804

ALBRIGHT, DEBORAH ELAINE, emergency physician; b. Springfield, Ill., May 21, 1958; d. Jacob Eugene and Josephine (Ciotti) A.; m. William Ray Dudleston, Dec. 29, 1978; 1 child, Victoria Josephine. AA, Springfield Coll., 1978; BS, U. Ill., 1980; MD, So. Ill. U., 1984. Diplomate Am. Bd. Pediatrics, Am. Bd. Internal Medicine. Lab. asst. dept. microbiology Sch. Medicine So. Ill. U., Springfield, 1977-78; resident in internal medicine, pediatrics So. Ill. U. Affiliated Hosps., Springfield, 1984-88; emergency rm. physician St. Vincent's Hosp., Taylorville, Ill., 1987-88, Abraham Lincoln Meml. Hosp., Lincoln, Ill., 1988; pediatrician locum tenens Dr. Anthony Agatucci, Springfield, 1988, Dr. Ann Pearson, Springfield, 1988; staff physician dept. emergency medicine St. John's Hosp., Springfield, 1988—; clin. asst. prof. dept. pediatrics Sch. Medicine So. Ill. U., 1988—; part-time staff physician McFarland Mental Health Ctr., Springfield, 1990, State Ill. Dept. Disability Svcs., Springfield, 1991—. Mem. St. Aloysius Parish, Springfield, 1958—; vol. dept. radiology Mercy Hosp., Champaign, Ill., 1980; vol. Roman Cultural Women's Aux., Springfield, 1985—, Camp CoCo, Springfield, 1988-90; sponsor Sta. WILL, Springfield, 1987-91, Children's Miracle Network Telethon, Springfield, 1988—, Springfield Symphony Orch., 1992—. Fellow Am. Acad. Pediatrics; mem. Am. Coll. Physicians, Am. Acad. Pediatrics, Am. Coll. Emergency Physicians, Phi Theta Kappa, Alpha Epsilon Delta. Republican. Home: 2125 Shabbona Dr Springfield IL 62702-1338

ALBRIGHT, DIANNE ELIZABETH, counselor, educator; b. Phila., Dec. 20, 1944; d. William Henry Walters and Eleanor Florence (Astfalk) Walters Schmidt; m. Paul Robert Albright, June 1966 (div. Sept. 1973); children: Cherie Lynnette, Lisa Renee. BMus, Ea. Nazarene Coll., 1967; postgrad., Rivier Coll., 1978-79; MEd, Plymouth State U., 1990; PhD, Ohio U., 1994. Cert. tchr. music K-12, elem. K-6, guidance counselor, N.H., Mass., Conn.; lic. profl. clin. counselor, Ohio. Social worker Mass. Dept. Welfare, Dedham, 1968-70; sustitute tchr. Braintree/Quincy (Mass.) Pub. Schs., 1970-77; music tchr. Nashua (N.H.) Pub. Schs., 1976-80, classroom tchr., 1980-90; clin. counselor Backus Hosp., Norwich, Conn., 1990-91; sch. counselor Plainfield (Conn.) Pub. Schs., 1990-91; instr. Ohio U., Athens, 1991-94; asst. prof., coord. counselor edn. Cen. Mo. State U., 1994—; ednl. cons. IBM, Bedford, N.H., 1983-84; rsch. asst. NASA Mascot Project, Ohio U. Athens, 1992-93. Author: (booklet) Am. Counseling Assn., 1993; contbr. articles to profl. jours. Recipient scholarship, grad. assoc. Ohio U., Athens, 1991-94, fellowship Chi Sigma Iota, Balt., 1992. Mem. Am. Counseling Assn., Ohio Counseling Assn. (membership com., Columbus chpt. 1993-94), Assn. for Humanistic Edn. and Devel. (editorial asst. 1992-94, sec. elect 1993-94, sec. 1994-95, editorial bd. 1994—), Mo. Counseling Assn., Internat. Assn. Marriage, Family Counselors, Assn. for Counselor Edn. and Supervision, Am. Sch. Counselors Assn., Phi Delta Kappa, Phi Kappa Phi, Chi Sigma Iota (assoc. editor 1993—, pres. Alpha chpt. Ohio U. 1992-93, Outstanding Chpt. award 1993). Home: 116 S Main St # 5 Warrensburg MO 64093 Office: Central Mo State Univ Dept Pysch Warrensburg MO 64093

ALBRIGHT, DOROTHY JANE, sales and marketing executive; b. Charlotte, N.C., Sept. 16, 1945; d. George Franklin and Dorothy (Severs) A.; m. James Rolens Millikan, Apr. 22, 1989. Student Queens Coll., Charlotte, N.C., 1963-66. Mgr. sales and mktg. J.M. Garner Devel., Atlanta, 1978-82; account exec. sales and mktg. Bryant Lithographing, Atlanta, 1982-83; sr. account mgr. sales and mktg. COMPACK-Comprehensive Packaging, Atlanta, 1983-85; sales and mktg. mgr. Brock, Green & Assocs., Atlanta, 1985-86; owner Albright and Assocs. Mktg. Services, Atlanta, 1986—. Bd. dirs. High Mus. Art, Atlanta, 1981-85. Mem. Am. Mktg. Assn. (bd. dirs. Atlanta chpt. 1983-84, sec. 1984-85, v.p. 1986-88, pres-elect 1988-89, pres. 1989-90, v.p. profl. chpt. divsn., 1994—, Inst. Packaging Profls. (adv. bd. Atlanta chpt.). Republican. Episcopalian.

ALBRIGHT, ELAINE MCCLAY, dean; b. Waterville, Maine, Aug. 21, 1946. BS, U. Maine, 1968; MLS, U. Ill., 1969. Head Ill. sect. interlibr. loan U. Ill. Libr., Urbana, 1969-75, coord. reference & rsch. ctr., 1975-77; exec. dir. Lincoln Trails Libr. System, Champaign, Ill., 1977-83; dir. librs. U. Maine, Orono, 1983—, dean cultural affairs & librs., 1991—; interim dir. the Hudson Mus. U. Maine, 1989-91; vis. lectr. Grad. Sch. Libr. Sci. U. Ill., 1969-83. Bd. dirs. Maine Libr. Commn. Bd., Augusta, 1991—. Sr. fellow UCLA, 1989. Mem. Rotary. Office: U Maine 5729 Fogler Libr Orono ME 04469

ALBRIGHT, MADELEINE KORBEL, diplomat, political scientist; b. Prague, Czechoslovakia, May 15, 1937; d. Josef and Anna (Speeglova) Korbel; m. Joseph Medill Patterson Albright, June 11, 1959 (div. 1983); children: Anne Korbel, Alice Patterson, Katharine Medill. B.A. with honors, Wellesley Coll., 1959; M.A., Columbia U., 1968; cert., Russian Inst., 1968, Ph.D., 1976. Washington coord. Maine for Muskie, 1975-76; chief legis. asst. to U.S. Senator Muskie, 1976-78; mem. staff NSC, 1978-81; fellow Woodrow Wilson Internat. Ctr. for Scholars, Washington, 1981-82; Donner prof. internat. affairs, dir. women in fgn. service Sch. Fgn. Service Georgetown U., 1982-93, sr. fellow in Soviet and Eastern European Affairs Ctr. for Strategic and Internat. Studies,, 1981; fgn. policy coord. Mondale for Pres. campaign, 1984, to Geraldine A. Ferraro, 1984; vice chmn. Nat. Dem. Inst. for Internat. Affairs, Washington, 1984-93; perm. rep. of the U.S. UN, N.Y.C., 1993—. Author: Poland: The Role of the Press in Political Change, 1983; contbr. articles to profl. jours., chpts. to books. Bd. dirs. Beauvoir Sch., Washington, 1968-76, chmn., 1978-83; trustee Black Student Fund, 1969-78, 82-93, Democratic Forum, 1976-78, Williams Coll., 1978-82, Wellesley Coll., 1983-89; mem. exec. com. D.C. Citizens for Better Pub. Edn., 1975-76; bd. dirs. Washington Urban League, 1982-84, Atlantic Council, 1984-93, Ctr. for Nat. Policy, 1985-93, Chatham House Fedn., 1986-88; sr. fgn. policy advisor Dukakis for Pres. Campaign, 1988. Mem. Council Fgn. Relations, Am. Polit. Sci. Assn., Czeckoslovak Soc. Arts and Scis. Am., Atlantic Council U.S. (dir.), Am. Assn. for Advancement Slavic Studies. Office: US Mission to the UN 799 United Nations Plz New York NY 10017-3505*

ALBRIGHT, OLGA DENISE, human resources executive; b. Chgo., Aug. 1, 1964; d. Billy Joe Albright and Olga Iris Quinones Tichenor. BS in Supervision, Purdue U., Hammond, Ind., 1988; MS in Human Resources Mgmt./Devel., Nat. Louis U., Evanston, Ill., 1991. Pers. sec. Cozzi Iron & Metal, Chgo., 1988-89, pers. adminstr., 1989, corp. recruiter, 1990, human resources mgr., 1991—. Interviewing trainer Jewish Vocat. Svc., Chgo., 1988—. Mem. Soc. Human Resources Mgmt. Office: Cozzi Iron & Metal Inc 2500 S Paulina St Chicago IL 60608

ALBUQUERQUE, LITA, artist; b. Santa Monica, Calif., Jan. 3, 1946; d. Mauriceo Yaeche and Ferida (Hayat) A.; m. Carey P. Peck, Jan., 1990; 1 child, Christopher; children from previous marriage: Isabelle, Jasmine. B.A. cum laude, UCLA, 1968; student, Otis Art Inst., 1971-72. Tchr. Claremont Grad. Coll., U. Calif., Santa Barbara, Otis/Parsons Sch., Los Angeles; vis. artist Chgo. Art Inst., 1984, San Francisco Art Inst., 1987; tchr. grad. seminars Ariz. State U., 1984, Otis/Parsons, Los Angeles, 1985, 86, San Francisco Art Inst., 1985; workshops include Idyllwild (Calif.) Sch. Music and Arts, 1986, 87; participated as juror for Los Angeles County Mus. Art, 1974, Menlo Park (Calif.) Coll., 1978, San Francisco Art Fest., 1983, Calif. State U., Northridge, 1985; grad. advisor Art Ctr. Coll. of Design, Pasadena, Calif., 1979-90. One-woman exhibitions include Univ. Arts Mus., U. Calif., Santa Barbara, 1978, Janus Gallery, Los Angeles, 1979, 81, 82, Marianne Deson Gallery, Chgo., 1980, 84, Lerner-Heller Gallery, N.Y.C., 1981, Robert Cronin, Inc., Houston, 1982, Loyola Marymount U., Los Angeles, 1984, Saxon-Lee Gallery, Los Angeles, 1986, Works Gallery, Costa Mesa, 1991, 93, Haines Gallery, San Francisco, 1992; group exhibits include Smithsonian Inst., 1981, San Francisco Mus. Modern Art, 1982, Mus. Contemporary Art, Los Angeles, 1983, Los Angeles Design Ctr., 1984, San Francisco Art Inst., 1985, U.S. Embassy, Helsinki, Finland, 1986, Fresno (Calif.) Arts Ctr. and Mus., 1987, Wright Art Gallery, UCLA, 1987; environ. works include Beneath the Black Polished Granite are a series of Ten Subterranean Islands Each One Floating on a Copper Plate, Security Pacific Plaza, Los Angeles, 1983, Rock and Pigment Installation, Mojave Desert, Calif., 1978, Sleeping Beauty, 1986, Forbidden City, 1983, Tangency Horizon, Santa Monica, Calif., 1986; represented in permanent collections Vesti Trust Internat., Boston, Times-Mirror Corp., N.Y.C., AT&T, N.Y.C., Sohio Corp., Cleve., Frederick Weisman Corp., Los Angeles, Palm Springs (Calif.) Desert Mus., Newport Harbor Mus., Newport Beach, Calif., Los Angeles County Mus. Art; film work includes Heartbreakers, 1983, The Other Lover, 1985, Out On A Limb, 1986. Nat. Endowment Arts fellow, 1975; NEA Art in Pub. Places grantee, 1983, 84; named Woman of Yr., Palm Springs Mus. Art, 1985; awarded Retrospective Fellows Contemporary Art Santa Monica Mus. Art, 1990. Studio: Annex Gallery 453 6th Ave San Diego CA 92101*

ALCIVAR-WARREN, ACACIA ATENAYS, veterinarian, educator; b. Chone, Ecuador, June 6, 1952; came to U.S., 1980; d. Gonzalo A. and Doryhs De la O (Arteaga) Alcivar; m. William B. Warren, June 25, 1988. DVM, U. Guayaquil, Ecuador, 1978; MS, Iowa State U., 1983, PhD, 1987. Vet. clinician Clinica Veterinaria Miraflores, Guayaquil, 1979-80; rsch. asst. Iowa State U., Ames, 1980-87; rsch. assoc. biology dept. Tufts U., Medford, Mass., 1987-90; postdoctoral fellow Roche Inst. Molecular Biology, Nutley, N.J., 1990-91; asst. prof. Tufts U. Sch. Vet. Medicine, Grafton, Mass., 1991—. Fulbright scholar Fulbright Commn., 1980-83, OAS fellow, Washington, 1983-85; recipient Internat. Peace Scholarship Fund award Internat. chpt. PEO, Switzerland. Mem. AAAS, Soc. Devel. Biology, Soc. Study Reprodn., Internat. Embryo Transfer Soc., N.Y. Acad. Scis. Democrat. Roman Catholic. Office: Tufts U Sch Vet Med 200 Westboro Rd North Grafton MA 01536

ALCON, SONJA LEE DE BEY GEBHARDT RYAN, medical social worker; b. Orange City, Iowa, Aug. 2, 1937; d. Albert Lee Gerard and Clarice Victoria (Brown) deBey; m. Richard J. Gebhardt, June 6, 1959; children: Russell, Cheryl, Kurt Gebhardt Ryan; m. George W. Ryan, Dec. 28, 1968; 1 dau., Alanna (dec.); m. David E. Alcon, July 20, 1985. C BA, Western Md. Coll., 1959; MSW, U. Md., 1973. Caseworker, Springfield State Hosp., Sykesville, Md., 1959-61; dir. social work dept. Hanover (Pa.) Gen. Hosp., 1966—; clin. assoc. prof. sch. social work and social planning U. Md., 1987—; cons. Golden Age Nursing Home, Hanover, 1973-76, Carlisle (Pa.) Hosp., 1974-78, Hanover Vis. Nurse Assn., 1977-83, emergency svcs. Mental Health Clinic, 1972; chmn. profl. adv. com. Vis. Nurse Assn. of Hanover and Spring Grove, Inc., 1986-89; mem. social work adv. coun. Western Md. Coll., 1979, 80. Bd. dirs. Hospice of York, 1980-82, Hanover chpt. ARC, 1976-79, Adams-Hanover Mental Health, 1973-76; pres. Human Svcs. Orgn., 1980, v.p., 1985-86; mem. adv. coun. Hanover Hospice, 1982-85; treas. Hanover Community Progress Com., 1976-80; mem. Adams-Hanover Sheltered Workshop Com., 1968-70; bd. dirs. Hanover Community Players, 1974-77, sec., 1982; organizer local chpt. Make Today Count and Preemie Parent Support Group, 1979; initiator Children's Cardiac Fund, 1979; mem. Hanover Oratorio Soc., 1964-85, adv. bd. United Cerebral Palsy South Cen. Pa., 1989-90; active YWCA, 1979-84; co-organizer Adams-Hanover chpt. Compassionate Friends, 1983; mem. vestry All Saints Episcopal Ch., 1973-74, 76-79, 83-86, vestry sec., 1975, diocesan del. Central Pa., 1978, 80-86, mem. altar guild, 1968-86, treas. ch. women, 1979-83; life mem. Hanover Gen. Hosp. Aux.; mem. adv. coun. Parents Anonymous, 1976-79, 85-92; adminstr. Hanover Gen. Hosp. Spl. Needs Fund, 1986—; co-facilitator I Can Cope classes Am. Cancer Soc., 1989-92; active Cmty. Needs Coalition, 1990—, South Ctrl. Pa. Orgn./Time Donation Coalition, 1994—. Recipient York Daily Record Exceptional Citizen award, 1979, Spl. Recognition cert. Col. Richard McAllister chpt. DAR, 1980; finalist YWCA Salute to Women, 1986, 87. Mem. Nat. Assn. Social Workers, Acad. Cert. Social Workers, Ea. Pa. Soc. Hosp. Social Workers, Am. Hosp. Assn. Soc. Hosp. Social Work Dirs., Cen. Pa. Hosp. Social Workers (treas. 1981-85, v.p. 1987, pres. 1988), Hosp. Assn. of Pa. Soc. for Hosp. Social Work Dirs., U. Md. Alumni Assn. (bd. dirs. 1983), Order Eastern Star (worthy matron 1985-86), Order of Amaranth (royal patron 1988-89, line officer 1992—), Order of the White Shrine of Jerusalem (worthy high priestess 1994-95), Social Order of Beauceant, Commandery Ladies Aux. (pres. 1989-90), Elks Aux. (v.p. local club 1986-88). Home: RD # 3 Spring Grove PA 17362 Office: Hanover Gen Hosp 300 Highland Ave Hanover PA 17331-2214

ALCORN, CATHERINE SUE, air traffic controller; b. Topeka, June 23, 1958; d. Richard Dean and Elizabeth Ann (Hafner) Chartier; m. Paul Burton Frantz, Oct. 18, 1980 (div. Oct. 1984); m. Larry David Alcorn, Sept. 3, 1992. Lic. air traffic control tower operator, radar and ltd. aviation weather observer. Air traffic contr. FAA, Juneau, Alaska, 1982-85; air traffic contr. FAA, Anchorage, 1985—, meeting facilitor, 1992—, mem. regional steering com. air traffic divsn., 1992—, co-facilitator investment in excellence program, 1993-94. sec. Thunderbird Heights Homeowners Assn., Chugiak, Alaska, 1992-94, pres., 1995. Mem. Nat. Air Traffic Contrs. Assn. (pres. Merrill local 1987-90, nat. legis. action com. 1987-89, pres. Anchorage local 1992-94, nat. constn. com. 1994, campaign chmn. Alaska region 1994, alt. Alaska region v.p. 1994—), Profl. Women Contrs., Alaska Airedale Terrier Club (treas. 1989—). Home: 24743 Teal Loop Chugiak AK 99567

ALCORN, KAREN ZEFTING HOGAN, art educator; b. Hartford, Conn., Sept. 29, 1949; d. Edward C. and Doris V. (Anderson) Zefting; m. Wendell R. Alcorn, Apr. 12, 1985. BS, Skidmore Coll., 1971; MFA, Boston U., 1976. Secondary art tchr. Scituate (Mass.) High Sch., 1971-73, Milton (Mass.) High Sch., 1973-79; engr. VEDA, Inc., Arlington, Va., 1979-80; analyst Info. Spectrum, Inc., Arlington, Va., 1980-82, Pacer Systems, Inc., Arlington, Va., 1982-84; dir. ops., mgr. tng. program Starmark Corp., Arlington, Va., 1984; sr. systems analyst VSE Corp., Arlington, Va., 1984-85; analyst, tech. writer Allen Corp., Las Vegas, 1987-88; recreational svcs. instr. Naval Air Sta., Corpus Christi, Tex., 1985-87; instr. Newport (R.I.) Art Mus., 1989-92; mem. faculty Western Nev. C.C., 1989; youth drawing instr. North Tahoe Recreation and Parks, Tahoe City, Calif., 1992—; dir. Artward Bound, 1994. Exhbns. include Skidmore Coll., 1970, 71, Boston U., 1975, Newport Art Mus., 1990, 91, Naval War Coll. Mus., 1989, 90, 91, Newport Art Mus. Artists Guild, 1991, 92, Artruckee, Truckee, Calif., Pogans's Northshore Gallery, Tahoe City, Tahoe Forest Hospital Corridor Gallery, Truckee, The Upstairs Gallery, Truckee, 1993, Fisher Gallery, Newport, 1992, Officer's Club Naval Edn. and Tng. Ctr., Newport, 1992. Mem. Sierra Artists Network, North Tahoe Fine Arts Coun., Arts for the Schs., AAUW. Home: PO Box 5385 Tahoe City CA 96145

ALDAVE, BARBARA BADER, law educator, lawyer; b. Tacoma, Dec. 28, 1938; d. Fred A. and Patricia W. (Burns) Bader; m. Ralph Theodore Aldave, Apr. 2, 1966; children—Anna Marie, Anthony John. B.S., Stanford U., 1960; J.D., U. Calif.-Berkeley, 1966. Bar: Oreg. 1966, Tex. 1982. Assoc. law firm Eugene, Oreg., 1967-70; asst. prof. U. Oreg., 1970-73; vis. prof. U. Calif., Berkeley, 1973-74; from vis. prof. to prof. U. Tex., Austin, 1974-89, co-holder James R. Dougherty chair for faculty excellence, 1981-82, Piper prof., 1982, Joe A. Worsham centennial prof., 1984-89, Liddell, Sapp, Zivley, Hill and LaBoon prof. banking financial and comml. law, 1989; dean sch. law St. Mary's U., San Antonio, 1989—; vis. prof. Northeastern U., 1985-88. Pres. NETWORK, 1985-89; chair Gender Bias Task Force of Supreme Ct. Tex., 1991—; bd. dirs. San Antonio Community Law Ctr., Partnership for Hope, Tex. Resource Ctr., Lawyers' Com. for Civil Rights Under Law of Tex., Bexar County Women's Ctr., Common Cause, Mex. Am. Legal Def. and Ednl. Fund. Recipient Teaching Excellence award U. Tex. Student Bar Assn., 1976, appreciation awards Thurgood Marshall Legal Soc. of U. Tex., 1979, 81, 85, 87, Teaching Excellence award Chicano Law Students Assn. of U. Tex., 1984, Hermine Tobolowsky award Women's Law Caucus of U. Tex., 1985, ethics award Kugle, Stewart, Dent & Frederick, 1988, Leadership award Women's Law Assn. St. Mary's U., 1989, Ann. Inspirational award Women's Advocacy Project, 1989, Appreciation award San Antonio Black Lawyers Assn., 1990, Spl. Recognition award Nat. Conv. Nat. Lawyers Guild, 1990, Spirit of the American Woman award J. C. Penny Co., 1992, Sarah T. Hughes award Women and the law sect. State Bar Tex., 1994. Mem. ABA (com. on corp. laws sect., banking and bus. law 1982-88), Bexar County Women's Bar Assn. (Belva Lockwood Outstanding Lawyer award 1991), San Antonio Bar Assn., Nat. Lawyers Guild, William S. Sessions Inn of Ct., World Affaris Coun. San Antonio, Harlan Soc., Tex. Women's Forum, Stanford U. Alumni Assn., Order of Coif, Phi Delta Phi, Iota Sigma Pi, Omicron Delta Kappa, Delta Theta Phi (Outstanding Law Prof. award St. Mary's U. chpt. 1990, 91). Roman Catholic. Home: 323 W Woodlawn Ave San Antonio TX 78212-3312 Office: St Mary's U 1 Camino Santa Maria St San Antonio TX 78228-5433

ALDEA, PATRICIA, architect; b. Bucharest, Romania, Mar. 18, 1947; came to U.S., 1976; d. Dan Jasmin Negreanu and Sonia (Friedgant) Philip-Negreanu; m. Val O. Aldea, Feb. 17, 1971; 1 child, Donna-Dana. MArch, Ion Mincu, Bucharest, 1970. Registered architect, N.Y. Architect, project. mgr. The Landmark Preservation Inst., Bucharest, 1971-76; architect Edward Durell Stone Assn., N.Y.C., 1977-79; assoc. architect, project mgr. Alan Lapidus P.C., N.Y.C., 1980—. Columnist Contemporanul art jour., 1969-73. Hist. landmarks study fellow Internationes Fed. Republic of Germany, 1974. Office: Alan Lapidus PC 1841 Broadway New York NY 10023

ALDEN, BARBARA GAYLE, nursing home administrator; b. Millinocket, Maine, May 6, 1935; d. Donald Bennett and Pearle Beatrice (Parsons) Lesuer; m. Frederick Emrich Alden, Mar. 29, 1986. BS in Pharmacy, Mass. Coll. of Pharmacy, 1957. Registered pharmacist; lic. adminstr. Staff pharmacist Peter Bent Brigham Hosp., Boston, 1957-64; chief pharmacist Franklin Med. Ctr., Greenfield, Mass., 1964-69; staff pharmacist Ind. U. Med. Ctr., Indpls., 1969-70; infection control officer Franklin Med. Ctr., Greenfield, Mass., 1970-78; asst. adminstr. Franklin Nursing Hom, Greenfield, 1978—; cons. pharmacist Franklin Nursing Home, Greenfield, 1977-84, Poet Seat Nursing Home, Greenfield, 1978-79. Pres. Quota Club of Franklin County, 1990-91. Fellow Am. Coll. of Health Care Adminstrs.; mem. Order

Eastern Star. Office: Franklin Nursing Home 329 Conway St Greenfield MA 01301

ALDEN, STACIA, board game manufacturing company executive; b. St. Louis, June 16, 1945; d. Henry J. and Mildred (Judkins) Ballas; m. Harvey A. Alden, Sept. 28, 1963 (div. Jan. 1979); children—Brian Gerald, Michael Todd. Pres., owner S. Alden Inc., Kansas City, Mo., 1980—. Patentee Beverly Hills Game, The Plaza, The Golden Triangle, L.V. The Game, N.Y.C. The Big Apple, Australia, The Land Down Under, Elvis, The Game, Les Miserables, We The People. Sec., v.p. Boy Scouts Am., 1976-83; pres., v.p. PTA, 1976-83. Mem. Mchts. Assn. (v.p. 1979-82), Econ. Devel. Com. (exec. com. 1979-81).

ALDER, ALTHEA ALICE, marketing service agency executive; b. Wilmore, Kans., Jan. 4, 1933; d. Lloyd Lewis and Margaret Mae (Baldwin) A.; student Ft. Hays State U., 1952-55. Owner, operator 2 beauty shops, 1961-67; quality control mgr., supr. women Solo Cup Co., 1967-70; v.p. purchasing, prodn. and premiums William A. Robinson, Inc., Northbrook, Ill., 1970-79; pres. A-three Services Agy., Ltd., Northbrook, Ill., 1980—, Lake Forest Tng. Salon, Ltd., 1979-80. With U.S. Army, 1956-61, Japan, France. Decorated Army Commendation medal. Mem. Promotion Mktg. Assn. Am., Am. Legion, Order of Eastern Star. Home: 1116 Greenwood Ave Deerfield IL 60015-2901 Office: A-three Services 3125 Commercial Ave Northbrook IL 60062-1905

ALDER, GAIL CECELIA, medical record administrator; b. Grosse Pointe Farms, Mich., Sept. 9, 1944; d. John Joseph and Lydia Marie (Doom) A. BS, Mercy Coll., Detroit, 1966; MA, Cen. Mich. U., 1984. Registered record adminstr., 1966. Asst. dir. med. records Mt. Carmel Mercy Hosp., Detroit, 1966-71; dir. med. record svs. Providence Hosp., Southfield, Mich., 1971-88; pres. Alder Assocs., Inc., Farmington Hills, Mich., 1988—; cons. Georgian N.W. Extended Care Facility, Detroit, 1969-72, McNamara Hosp., Warren, Mich., 1973-75; cons. to med. record profession, 1969—; instr. directed practice Mercy Coll., 1971-88; instr. directed practice Schoolcraft Community Coll., Livonia, Mich., 1971-88, mem. adv. bd., 1973—; assoc. prof. Oakland Community Coll., Farmington Hills, 1975-76; guest lectr. Wayne State U. Sch. Pharmacy, Detroit, 1980. Mem. Oakland County Comprehensive Health Planning Coun., 1977-83; mem. adv. com. Mich. Cancer Found., 1978-88; chmn. Oakland Health Edn. Program, Rochester, Mich., 1980-81. Mem. Am. Med. Record Assn., Mich. Med. Record Assn. (pres. 1985-86, bd. dirs. 1986-87), Southeastern Mich. Med. Record Assn. (pres. 1977-78, bd. dirs. 1978-79), NAFE. Republican. Roman Catholic. Office: 35526 Grand River Ave Ste 350 Farmington MI 48335-3120

ALDERDICE, CYNTHIA LOU, artist; b. Des Moines, Mar. 16, 1932; d. Charles Lloyd and Marion Maxine (Hinn) Sandahl; m. Lee Edward Alderdice, Jan. 30, 1954; children: Cheryl Lynn, Kirk Bryan. BA, U. Tex., 1957. Pres. Am. Art Assocs., Inc., Bethesda, Md., 1966-92; v.p. Am. Art Make-A-Frame, Inc., Rockville, Md., 1972—; v.p., bd. dirs. Pyramid Atlantic, Inc., Riverdale, Md., 1994—; com. mem. Jewelry from Walters Art Gallery and Zucker Family Collection, 1987, Greek Gold from Beenaki Mus., 1991; com. mem. tarnished vistas Hist. Annapolis, Md., 1988. Exhibited in group shows Mus. Contemporary Art, Chamalieres, France, 1991, Walters Art Gallery, Balt., 1991, Internat. Monetary Fund Collection, Washington, Freddie Mac's COllection Honoring Washington Artists; permanent collections incl. Musee d'Art Contemporain of Chamalieres, France, Artist Book Collection Balt. Mus. Art, Touchstone Gallery, Washington, 1993, Md. Fedn. Art, 1991. Recipient individual artist award Md. Arts Coun., 1992. Mem. Md. Fedn. Art (pres., bd. dirs. 1985-87), Md. Printmakers, So. Graphics Art Coun., Washington Guild Goldsmiths, Friends Cardinal Gallery (hon.). Studio: Annapolis Bus Pk 2104 Renard Ct Annapolis MD 21401

ALDERMAN, MINNIS AMELIA, psychologist, educator, small business owner; b. Douglas, Ga., Oct. 14, 1928; d. Louis Cleveland Sr. and Minnis Amelia (Wooten) A. AB in Music, Speech and Drama, Ga. State Coll., Milledgeville, 1949; MA in Supervision and Counseling Psychology, Murray State U., 1960; postgrad. Columbia Pacific U., 1987—. Tchr. music Lake County Sch. Dist., Umatilla, Fla., 1949-50; instr. vocal and instrumental music, dir. band, orch. and choral Fulton County Sch. Dist., Atlanta, 1950-54; instr. English, speech, debate, vocal and instrumental music, dir. drama, band, choral and orch. Elko County Sch. Dist., Wells, Nev., 1954-59; tchr. English and social studies Christian County Sch. Dist., Hopkinsville, Ky., 1960; instr. psychology, counselor critic prof. Murray (Ky.) State U., 1961-63, U. Nev., Reno, 1963-67; owner Minisizer Exercising Salon, Ely, Nev., 1969-71, Knit Knook, Ely, 1969—, Minimimeo, Ely, 1969—, Gift Gamut, Ely, 1977—; prof. dept. fine arts Wassuk Coll., Ely, 1986-91, assoc. dean, 1986-87, dean, 1987-90; counselor White Pine County Sch. Dist., Ely, 1960-68; dir. Child and Family Ctr., Ely Indian Tribe, 1988-93, Family and Community Ctr., Ely Shoshone Indian Tribe, 1988-93; adv. Ely Shoshone Tribal Youth Coun., 1990-93, Budge Stanton Meml. Scholarship, 1991-93, Budge Stanton Meml. Living Mus. and Cultural Ctr., 1991-93; fin. aid contracting officer Ely Shoshone Tribe, 1990-93; supr. testing Ednl. Testing Svc., Princeton, N.J., 1960-68, Am. Coll. Testing Program, Iowa, 1960-68, U. Nev., Reno, 1960-68; chmn. bd. White Pine Sch. Dist. Employees Fed. Credit Union, Ely, 1961-69; psychologist mental hygiene div. Nev. Pers., Ely, 1969-75, dept. employment security, 1975-80; sec.-treas. bd. dirs. Gt. Basin Enterprises, Ely, 1969-71; speaker at confs. Author various news articles, feature stories, pamphlets, handbooks and grants in field. Pvt. instr. piano, violin, voice and organ, Ely, 1981—; bd. dirs. band Sacred Heart Sch., Ely, 1982—; mem. Gov.'s Mental Health State Commn., 1963-65, Ely Shoshone Tribal Youth Camp, 1991-92, Elys Shoshone Tribal Unity Conf., 1991-92, Tribal Parenting Skills Coord., 1991; bd. dirs. White Pine County Sch. Employees Fed. Credit Union, 1961-68, pres., 1963-68; 2d v.p. White Pine Community Concert Assn., 1965-67, pres., 1967, 85—, treas., 1975-79, dr. chmn., 1981-85; chmn. of bd., 1984; bd. dirs. White Pine chpt. ARC, 1978-82; mem. Nev. Hwy. Safety Leaders Bd., 1979-82; mem. Gov.'s Commn. on Status Women, 1968-74, Gov.'s Nevada State Juvenile Justice Adv. Commn., 1992-94, White Pine Overall Econ. Devel. Plan Coun., 1992-94; sec.-treas. White Pine Rehab. Tng. Ctr. for Retarded Persons, 1973-75; mem. Gov.'s Commn. on Hwy. Safety, 1979-81, Gov's. Juvenile Justice Program; sec.-treas. White Pine County Juvenile Problems Cabinet, 1994—; dir. Ret. Sr. Vol. Program, 1973-74; vice chmn. Gt. Basin Health Coun., 1973-75, Home Extension Adv. Bd., 1977-80; sec.-treas. Great Basin chpt. Nev. Employees Assn.; bd. dirs. United Way, 1970-76; vice chmn. White Pine Coun. on Alcoholism and Drug Abuse, 1975-76, chmn., 1976-77; grants author 3 yrs. Indian Child Welfare Act, originator Community Tng. Ctr. for Retarded People, 1972, Ret. Sr. Vol. Program, 1974, Nutrition Program for Sr. Citizens, 1974, Sr. Citizens Ctr., 1974, Home Repairs for Sr. Citizens, 1974, Sr. Citizens Home Assistance Program, 1977, Creative Crafters Assns., 1976, Inst. Current World Affairs, 1989, Victims of Crime, 1990-92; bd. dirs. Family coalition, 1990-92, Sacred Heart Parochial Sch., 1982—, dir. band, 1982—; candidate for diaconal ministry, 1982-93; dir. White Pine Community Choir, 1962—, Ely Meth. Ch. Choir, 1960-84; choir dir., organist Sacred Heart Ch., 1984—. Precinct reporter ABC News 1966; speaker U.S. Atty. Gen. Conf. Bringing Nev. Together; bd. dirs. White Pine Juvenile Cabinet, 1993—. Recipient Recognition rose Alpha Chi State Delta Kappa Gamma, 1994. Fellow Am. Coll. Musicians, Nat. Guild Piano Tchrs.; mem. NEA (life), UDC, n. Ind. Bus. (dist. chair 1971-85, nat. guardian coun. 1985—, state guardian coun. 1987—), AAUW (pres. Wells br. 1957-58, pres. White Pine br. 1965-66, 86-87, 89-91, 93—, bd. dirs. 1965-87, rep. edn. 1965-67, implementation chair 1967-69, area advisor 1969-73, 89-91), Nat. Fedn. Bus. and Profl. Women (1st v.p. Ely chpt. 1965-66, pres. Ely chpt. 1966-68, 74-76, 85—, bd. dirs. Nev. chpt. 1966—, 1st v.p. Nev. Fedn. 1970-71, pres. Nev. chpt. 1972-73, nat. bd. dirs. 1972-73), White Pine County Mental Health Assn. (pres. 1960-63, 78—), Mensa (supr. testing 1965—), Delta Kappa Gamma (br. pres. 1968-72, 94—, state bd. 1967—, chpt. parliamentarian 1974-78, state 1st v.p. 1967-69, state pres. 1969-71, nat. bd. 1969-71, state parliamentarian 1971-73), White Pine Knife and Fork Club (1st v.p. 1969-70, pres. 1970-71, bd. dirs. 1979—), Soc. Descendants of Knights of Most Noble Order of Garter, Nat. Soc. Magna Charta Dames. Home: 945 Ave H PO Box 150457 East Ely NV 89315-0457 Office: 1280 Avenue F East Ely NV 89301-2511

ALDERSON, GLORIA FRANCES DALE, rehabilitation specialist; b. Rainelle, W.Va., May 11, 1945; d. Orval Rupert and Juanita Rose (Nelson) Dale; m. Grayson Raines Alderson, June 3, 1964; children: John Grayson, James Leslie, Kathy LeDawn. ADN, U. Charleston; BS, W.Va. U. DON Charleston Area Med. Ctr., Charleston, 1977-84; head nurse Eye & Ear Clinic, Charleston, 1981-84; owner, operator ABZ Nursing, Kanawha County, W.Va., 1983-87; rehab. specialist W.Va., 1983—; bd. dirs. Profl. and Social Com. on Nursing. Bd. dirs. Urban Politics Symposium, Charleston, 1978; election campaign mgr. Rep. Party, Charleston. Scholarship Bd. Regents, 1974-77. Mem. AAUW, Am. Rehab. Profls., Ea. Star. Home: 1089 Highland Dr Saint Albans WV 25177-3675 Office: Ind Rehab Specialist 1089 Highland Dr Saint Albans WV 25177-3675

ALDERSON, KAREN ANN, librarian; b. Caledonia, Minn., Aug. 2, 1947; d. Merle Richard and Zelda Edna (Gray) A. BA, Upper Iowa U., 1968; MA, U. Denver, 1979. Lic. pvt. investigator. Libr. North Linn Community Sch. Dist., Coggon, Iowa, 1968-79; cataloger, acquisitions libr. Coll. of St. Mary, Omaha, 1982; tech. svcs., information libr. Mason City (Iowa) Pub. Libr., 1982-86; free-lance libr. Marion, Iowa, 1986—. Indexer: After Hours Manual for Information and Referral, 1987. Del. Iowa Gov.'s pre-White House Conf. on Libr. and Info. Svcs., 1991. Named Find-A-Fellow Campaign winner AAUW Ednl. Found., 1988, 89; named Profl. Women's Network Woman of Yr., 1992. Mem. ALA, NEA (various local chpt. offices), AAUW (br. newsletter editor, 1985-86, 88-90), Cedar Rapids Area C. of C., Profl. Women's Network, Iowa Libr. Assn., Iowa Assn. Pvt. Investigators, Alpha Delta Kappa (various local chpt. offices). Office: 1164 44th St Ste 2 Marion IA 52302-6508

ALDERSON, MARGARET NORTHROP, arts administrator, educator, artist; b. Washington, Nov. 28, 1936; d. Vernon D. and Margaret (Lloyd) Northrop; m. Donald Marr Alderson, Jr., June 4, 1955; children: Donald Marr III, Barbara Lynn Hennesy, Brian, Graham. Student George Washington U., 1954-55; A.A., Monterey Peninsula Jr. Coll., 1962. Staff, tchr. Galerie Jaclande, Springfield, Va. 1972-73; artist/tchr. Studio 7, Torpedo Factory Art Ctr., Alexandria, 1974—, dir. ctr., 1979-85; tchr. Fairfax County Recreation, 1972-73, Art League Schs., Alexandria, 1978—, ann. Feb. workshop, Accapulco, Mex., 1985—, English Painting Workshop, 1989, 90, 91, 93, 95, Santa Fe Workshop, 1991, 92, 95, Provence, France Workshop, 1995; cons. in field; project supr. City of Alexandria for Torpedo Factory Art Ctr., 1978-83; ptnr. Soho Hubris Art Gallery (N.Y.), 1977-78; pres. Touchstone Gallery, Washington. One woman shows include Way Up Gallery, Livermore, Calif., 1971, Lynchburg Coll. (Va.), 1978, Farm House Gallery, Rehobeth, Del., 1979, Art League Gallery, Alexandria, Va., 1980, 86, 93, Lyceum Mus., Alexandria, 1987, Alexandria Mus., 1987-88, William Ris Gallery, Stone Harbor, N.J., 1988, Touchstone Gallery, Washington, 1992, 94; exhibited in group shows at Art League Gallery, Alexandria, 1972—, Lynchburg (Va.) Coll., 1978, Montgomery (Ala.) Mus., 1980, Art Barn, 1989, Moscow-Washington Art Exch. Exhibit Internat., Moscow, 1990, Washington, 1991; represented in permanent collections Texaco, Inc., Phillip Morse Collection, United Va. Bank, CSX Corp., Fannie Mae Corp., Acacia Fin. Group, Office U.S. Atty. Gen., Office of Ins. Gen. EPA, Aerospace Corp., Texaco Corp. Festival chmn. City Festival Cultural Arts, Livermore, Calif., 1971; bd. dirs., Cultural Alliance Greater Washington, 1982—; bd. dirs. Torpedo Factory Art Ctr., 1978—; mem. Partners for Liveable Places, 1979—; mem. Catherine Llorilard Wolfe Art Soc.; pres. Touchstone Art Coop. Recipient Md. found. award Balt. watercolor regional annual, 1989, Elgie and David Ject Kay award Audubon Artists annual, 1989, 1st Place Awards in Watercolor, Art League, 1975, 76, 77, 82, 84-85, also numerous purchase awards, Jane Morton Norman award Ky. Nat. Watercolor Show, 1986, Adrirondack Nat. Watercolor Show, 1987, 3d award Catherine Lorillard Show, N.Y.C., 1987, Albert Ehringer award, 1989, Holbein award Mid Atlantic Watercolor Regional show, 1992, Purchase award d'Arches Paper Co., Knickerbocker Exhibit, Best in Show award Deland Mus. Art, 1993, Catherine Lovell award, 1993; nominated Woman of Yr. Alexandria C. of C., 1992, 93; travel show include Chrysler Mus. Biennial, 1988, Audubon Artists Nat. Show, 1989 (Elsie & Davis Ject Key award 1989), Balt. Regional Watercolor Annual, 1989 (Md. Found. award 1989). Mem. Fed. Nat. Mortgage Assn., Va. Watercolor Soc. (pres. 1982, 1st place awards ann. exhibit 1980, 82, excellence award 1989, 94), Potomac Valley Watercolorists (pres. 1978), Torpedo Factory Artists Assn. (pres. 1977-78), Springfield Art Guild (pres. 1977), Artists Equity, Am. Council on Arts, Am. Watercolor Soc., Am. Council of Univ. and Community Arts Ctrs., Phila. Watercolor Club, Watercolor West, Soc. Layerists Multi-Media, Va. Watercolor Soc., Am. Profl. Artist's League, Am. Mgmt. Assn., Nat. Hist. Trust, Ga. Watercolor Soc., Miss. Watercolor Soc., La. Watercolor Soc., Ky. Watercolor Soc., Catherine Llorilard Wolfe Club. Republican. Home: 2204 Windsor Rd Alexandria VA 22307-1018 Studio: Torpedo Factory Art Ctr 105 N Union St # 7 Alexandria VA 22314-3217

ALDOUS, JOAN, sociology educator. BS, Kans. State U., 1948; MA, U. Tex., 1949; PhD, U. Minn., 1963. With U. Notre Dame, Ind., 1976—, now William R. Kenan Jr. prof. sociology; mem. adv. coun. Coll. Human Ecol. Cornell U., 1987-92. Recipient Ernest W. Burgess award, 1988. Mem. Nat. Coun. Family Rels. (pres. 1986), Am. Sociol. Assn. (mem. coun. 1990-93). Office: U of Notre Dame Dept Of Sociology Notre Dame IN 46556

ALDREDGE, THEONI VACHLIOTIS, costume designer; b. Athens, Greece, Aug. 22, 1932; d. Gen. Athanasios and Meropi (Gregoriades) Vachliotis; m. Thomas E. Aldredge, Dec. 10, 1953. Student, Am. Sch., Athens, 1949-53, Goodman Theatre, Chgo.; LHD, De Paul U., 1985. Mem. design staff Goodman Theatre, 1951-53; head designer N.Y. Shakespeare Festival, 1962—. Designer numerous Broadway and off Broadway shows, ballet, opera, TV spls.; films include Girl of the Night, You're a Big Boy Now, No Way To Treat a Lady, Uptight, Last Summer, I Never Sang for My Father, Promise at Dawn, The Great Gatsby (Brit. Motion Picture Acad. award 1976), Network, The Cheap Detective, The Fury, The Eyes of Laura Mars (Acad. Sci. Fiction Films award), The Champ, Semi-Tough, The Rose, Monsignor, Annie, Ghostbusters, Moonstruck, We're No Angels, Stanley and Iris, Other People's Money, Night and the City, Addams Family Values, Milk Money; Broadway shows include A Chorus Line (Theatre World award 1976), Annie (Tony award 1977), Barnum (Tony award 1979), Dream Girls, Woman of the Year, Onward Victoria, La Cage Aux Folles (Tony award 1984), 42nd Street, A Little Family Business, Merlin, Private Lives, The Corn Is Green, The Rink, Blithe Spirit, Chess, Gypsy (1989 revival), Oh, Kay, The Secret Garden, Nick and Nora, High Rollers, Putting it Together, Annie Warbucks, The Flowering Peach, "EFX" MGM Grand. Recipient Obie award for Disting. Svc. to Off-Broadway Theatre Village Voice, Maharam award for Peer Gynt, N.Y.C. Liberty medal, 1986, numerous Drama Desk and Critic awards; inducted into Theatre Hall of Fame. Mem. United Scenic Artists, Costume Designers Guild, Acad. Motion Picture Arts Scis. (Oscar award Great Gatsby 1975). Office: 350 W 50th St New York NY 10019-6668

ALDRICH, ANN, federal judge; b. Providence, June 28, 1927; d. Allie C. and Ethel M. (Carrier) A.; m. Chester Aldrich, 1960 (dec.); children: Martin, William; children by previous marriage: James, Allen; m. John H. McAllister III, 1986. BA cum laude, Columbia U., 1948; LLB cum laude, NYU, 1950, LLM, 1964, JSD, 1967. Bar: D.C. bar, N.Y. bar 1952, Conn. bar 1966, Ohio bar 1973, Supreme Ct. bar 1956. Research asst. to mem. faculty N.Y. U. Sch. Law; atty. IBRD, 1952; atty., rsch. asst. Samuel Nakasian, Esq., Washington, 1952-53; mem. gen. counsel's staff FCC, Washington, 1953-60; U.S. del. to Internat. Radio Conf., Geneva, 1959; practicing atty. Darien, Conn., 1961-68; asso. prof. law Cleve. State U., 1968-71, prof., 1971-80; judge U.S. Dist. Ct. (no. dist.) Ohio, Cleveland, 1980—; bd. govs. Citizens' Communications Center, Inc., Washington; mem. litigation com.; guest lectr. Calif. Inst. Tech., Pasadena, summer 1971. Mem. Fed. Bar Assn., Nat. Assn. of Women Judges, Fed. Communications Bar Assn., Fed. Judge Assn. Episcopalian. Office: US Dist Ct 212 US Courthouse 201 Superior Ave E Cleveland OH 44114-1203*

ALDRICH, NANCY ARMSTRONG, psychotherapist, clinical social worker; b. Taylorville, Ill., Oct. 4, 1925; d. Guy L. and Alice Irene (Hicks) Armstrong; m. Paul Harwood Aldrich, Sept. 30, 1949; children: Gregory Paul, Mark Douglas, Alice Ann Aldrich White, Ruth Lynne Aldrich Sammis. AB with highest honors, U. Ill., 1947, BS in Chemistry, 1948, MS in Chemistry, 1949; MSS, Bryn Mawr Coll., 1986. Lic. clin. social worker, Del., Pa. Parole bd. mem. State of Del., Dover, 1970-74; instr. continuing edn. U. Del., Newark, 1976-78, program specialist, 1978-83; founder Acad. Lifelong Learning; v.p. Aldrich Assocs. Inc., Landenberg, Pa., 1983—, psychotherapist, 1987—; psychotherapist Family Community Service Del. County, Media, Pa., 1986, Tressler Ctr. for Human Growth, Wilmington, Del., 1987-93; clin. affiliate Personal Performance Cons., 1990—, Acorn, 1990—, CMG Health, 1991—, Achievement and Guidance, 1991—, Inst. for Human Resources, 1992—, Green Spring Health Mgmt., 1993—, employee assistance program DuPont, 1992—, Champus, 1988—, HAI/Aetna, 1994—, Value Behavioral Health, 1994—; coord. human resources devel. program Tressler Ctr. for Human Growth, 1983-84. Pres. YWCA New Castle County, Wilmington, 1974-76; mem. Statewide Health Coordinating Coun., Del., 1978-79; bd. dirs., com. mem. United Way Del., Wilmington, 1975-84; trustee Unitarian Universalist House, Phila., 1992-94. Mem. NASW, AAUW (pres. Wilmington br. 1968-70, nat. resolutions com. 1971-72, fellowship gift named in her honor 1970), Del. Soc. Lic. Clin. Social Workers (pres. 1990-91), Del. Gerontol. Soc., Mental Health Assn. Del., Internat. Soc. Bioenergetic Analysis, Phi Beta Kappa, Phi Kappa Phi, Iota Sigma Pi. Office: 625 Chambers Rock Rd Landenberg PA 19350-1041

ALDRICH, PATRICIA ANNE RICHARDSON, retired magazine editor; b. St. Paul, Apr. 6, 1926; d. James Calvin and Anna Catherine (Eskra) Richardson; m. Edwin Chauncey Aldrich, July 31, 1948; 1 son, Mason Calvin. Student, Stout Inst., 1944-45; BS in Journalism; scholar, Northwestern U., 1948. Editor Child's World News, The Child's World, Inc., Chgo., 1952-57; assoc. editor Home Life mag. Advt. Div., Inc., Chgo., 1957-71, editor, 1971-90, ret., 1990; pres. Aldrich Enterprises, Inc., Chgo. Mem. steering com., publicity chmn. Evanston Urban League, 1961-64. Democrat.

ALEANDRI, EMELISE FRANCESCA, producer, director, television personality, actress; b. Riva del Garda, Italy; d. John Baptist and Elodia (Lutterotti) A. AB in French, Coll. of New Rochelle, N.Y.; MA in Theater, Hunter Coll., N.Y.C., 1975; MPhil in Theater, CUNY, 1976, PhD in Theater, 1983. Drama instr. N.Y.C. Tech. Coll., Bklyn., Hunter Coll., N.Y.C., Borough of Manhattan C.C., N.Y.C., Bennington (Vt.) Coll., NYU, N.Y.C., 1977-78; dir. Ctr. Italian-Am. Studies, Bklyn. Coll., 1984-87; producer Italics Mag. Show CUNY-TV, N.Y.C., 1987—. Actress (TV) Loving, Our Family Honor, Internal Affairs, Tattingers, Eischeid, Donohue, Nurse, MTV, Another World, Equalizer, Mathnet, Law and Order, America's Most Wanted, (films) Crooklyn, Godfather III, My New Gun, Age of Innocence, Teenage Mutant Ninja Turtles, Cookie, Married to the Mob, Moonstruck, Jumping Jack Flash, Car 54, Turk 182, All That Jazz, Ft. Apache, John and Yoko, Raging Bull, Danger Adrift, Regarding Henry, The World According to Garp, King of the Gypsies, Night of the Juggler, Defiance, Willie and Phil, Rooftops; author: Italian-American Theatre, 1983, host (TV show) Italics; appeared in numerous plays, concerts, operas; translator various plays from Italian to English; contbr. articles on theater to profl. jours. Recipient N.Y. State Hist. award; NEA grantee Bklyn. Coll., CUNY, Ctr. for Italian-Am. Studies, Bklyn. Coll., Recreation Assn. for Handicapped, Milan, InterCities Performing Arts, N.J. Mem. AGVA, AFTRA, SAG, Actors Equity Assn., Dramatists Guild, Soc. Stage Dirs. and Choreographers, Italian Actors Union, Am. Italian Hist. Assn., Folk Theatre Co. Office: Italian-Am Inst 25 W 43d St Ste 1000 New York NY 10036-7406

ALEFF, ANDREA LEE (ANDY ALEFF), newspaper editor; b. Sheboygan, Wis., Oct. 2, 1946; d. Howard Joseph and Phyllis Leanne (Perkins) A.; m. David L. Nelson, Apr. 18, 1970 (div. 1981); 1 child, Andrew. AA, Christian Coll., Columbia, Mo., 1965; BJ, U. Mo., 1967. Reporter AP, N.Y.C., 1967-68, Chgo. Tribune, 1968-69, Sta. WTVJ-TV, Miami, Fla., 1969-70, Sta. WLS-TV, Chgo., 1970-73; instr. journalism Northwestern U., Evanston, Ill., 1975-76; dir. advt. and pub. rels. Expn. Corp. Am., Coral Gables, Fla., 1979-81; shoreline editor Sun-Sentinel, Ft. Lauderdale, Fla., 1981-84, assoc. editor, 1984-94, spl. projects mgr., 1995—. Mem. Am. Soc. Newspaper Editors, Navy League of the U.S., Ocean Watch. Episcopalian. Home: 3064 NE 49th St Fort Lauderdale FL 33308-4915 Office: Sun-Sentinel 200 E Las Olas Blvd Fort Lauderdale FL 33301-2248

ALEMAN, ARCILA, principal; b. Pomona, Calif., Jan. 13, 1947; d. Fernando and Ruth (Godoy) Lopez; m. Frank Aleman, July 15, 1967; children: Brian Frank, Dayna Sueli. AA, Chaffey Jr. Coll., Alta Loma, Calif., 1966; BA in Spanish, Calif. State U., San Bernardino, 1971; BA in Edn., LaVerne (Calif.) U., 1976, MA in Bilingual Edn., 1978. Tchr. Alta Loma (Calif.) Sch. Dist., 1977-84, asst. prin., 1984-88, prin., 1988—. Bd. dirs. Vis. Nurses Assn., Pomona, 1988-92. Recipient VIP award Carnelian Sch. PTA, 1988. Mem. West End Adminstrs., It's Elem. Alliance. Democrat. Ch. of the Nazarene. Office: Alta Loma Elementary Sch 7085 Amethyst Alta Loma CA 91701

ALEMAN, MINDY R., advertising and public relations executive, freelance writer and columnist; b. N.Y.C., Nov. 23, 1950; d. Lionel and Jocelyn (Cohen) Luskin; m. Gary Aleman, Aug. 27, 1983. BA, U. Akron, 1972, MA, 1975. Instr. speech U. Akron, 1973-83; car salesperson Dave Towell Cadillac, Akron, 1977-79, mgr. fin. and ins., 1979; account exec., pub. rels. dir. Loos, Edwards & Sexauer, Akron, 1980-82; mktg. svcs. coord. Century Products, Stow, Ohio, 1982-83; mgr. advt., pub. rels. Century Products, Gerber Furniture Group, Stow, 1983-86, Macedonia, Ohio, 1986-89; dir. rsch. and promotion Akron Beacon Jour., 1989—; instr. commn. U. Akron, 1975—. Playwright Danny's Choice, 1972; weekly columnist Ready or Not Sunday Beacon Mag., 1991—. Mem. Internat. Newspaper Mktg. Assn. (various awards 1989-93), Am. Mktg. Assn., Newspaper Assn. Am., Pub. Rels. Soc. Am. (accredited), Akron Advt. Club (various awards 1983-94). Office: Akron Beacon Jour Rsch and Promotion Dept PO Box 640 44 E Exchange St Akron OH 44309-0640

ALESCHUS, JUSTINE LAWRENCE, real estate broker; b. New Brunswick, N.J., Aug. 13, 1925; d. Walter and Mildred Lawrence; student Rutgers U.; m. John Aleschus, Jan. 23, 1949; children: Verdene Jan, Janine Kimberley, Joanna Lauren. Dept. sec. Am. Baptist Home Mission Soc., N.Y.C., 1947-49; claims examiner Republic Ins. Co., Dallas, 1950-52; broker Damon Homes, L.I., 1960-72; exclusive broker estate of Kenneth H. Leeds, L.I., 1980-90; pres. Justine Aleschus Real Estate, 1975—. Past-pres. Nassau-Suffolk Coun. of Hosp. Aux., 1981-82; hon. mem. aux. of St. John's Episcopal Hosp., Smithtown, N.Y., past pres., hosp. adv. bd.; past pres. L.I. Coalition for Sensible Growth, Inc.; mem. exec. bd. dirs. Suffolk County coun. Boy Scouts Am.; mem. adv. bd. Suffolk County coun. Girl Scouts U.S. Mem. Suffolk County Real Estate Bd. (v.p., past pres., treas.), L.I. Builders Inst. (bd. dirs.), L.I. Mid-Suffolk Businessmen's Assn. (past pres.), Roundtable Eastern L.I., Smithtown Bus. and Profl. Women's Network, New L.I. Partnership, L.I. Econ. Summit Coord. Coun., S.C. Women's Bus. Enterprise Coalition, Sky Island Club (gov.). Republican. Lutheran. Office: PO Box 267 Smithtown NY 11787

ALESIO, VENA BETH, music educator; b. Libertyville, Ill., Feb. 15, 1954; d. Marvin Charles Genuchi and Mary Kathleen (Wiggs) Stephens; m. Thomas Andrew Alesio, Sept. 3, 1983. BMus, Tex. Tech U., 1976, PhD, 1989; MMus, U. Nebr., 1978. Grad. asst. dept. music U. Nebr., Lincoln, 1976-78, Tex. Tech U., Lubbock, 1979, 82-83, 85; piano and voice tchr. Lincoln, 1985-87; instr. dept. music Southeast C.C., Beatrice, Nebr., 1987—, asst. program chair humanities divsn., 1992—. Bd. dirs. Beatrice Area Arts Coun., 1991-92; participant Nat. Inst. for Leadership Devel., 1991; speaker, presenter Nat. Leadership 2000 Conf., 1991. Recipient Burlington No. Faculty Achievement award, 1989. Mem. Am. Assn. Women in Community Colls., Coll. Music Soc., Nebr. Music Educators Assn., Music Educators Nat. Conf., Mu Phi Epsilon, Pi Beta Lambda, Phi Kappa Phi, Alpha Lambda Delta. Office: Southeast CC Rte 2 Box 35A Beatrice NE 68310

ALEWEL, TERESA FINE, university director; b. Mexico, Mo., Aug. 11, 1962; d. James Bruce and Geraldine Ann (Jarboe) Fine; m. Randy Allen Alewel, May 4, 1984; children: Paige Marie, Austin Allen, Kayla Anise. B of Ednl. Studies, U. Mo., 1984; MS, Cen. Mo. State U., 1990. Pers. cons. E.J. Ross & Assocs., Kansas City, Mo., 1984-85; adminstrv. asst. Cen. Mo. State U., Warrensburg, 1986, asst. dir., 1986-88, acting dir., 1988-90, dir., 1990—. Exec. bd. dirs. Totally Country Products Inc., 1986—; grad. Community Leadership & Involvement Mean a Better Community, 1992, program com., 1993; active Warrensburg PTA. Recipient Hon. Recruiter award U.S. Army Recruiting, 1987, scholarship Mgmt. Inst., U. Richmond, Va., 1993; named Outstanding Young Women in Am., 1988. Mem. Assn. Sch., Coll. and Univ. Staffing, Midwest Coll. Placement Assn. (com. 1987-

92), Coll. Placement Coun., Human Resource Mgmt. Assn., Ctrl. Mo. State Univs. Pres.'s Soc., Warrensburg C. of C., U. Mo. Alumni Assn., Mo. Army Nat. Guard Women's Aux., Alpha Gamma Delta (chpt. advisor 1987-88, rush advisor 1986-88, faculty advisor 1988—). Republican. Roman Catholic. Home: 343 NE 51st Warrensburg MO 64093 Office: Cen Mo State U Union 302 Warrensburg MO 64093

ALEX, IRIS S., architect; b. N.Y.C., July 12, 1926; d. Joseph J. and Lillian (Langsam) Steinmuller; m. William Alex, June 21, 1950 (div. July 1961). BA, Bklyn. Coll., 1947; BA in Architecture, Chgo. Inst. Design, 1950. Lic. architect, N.Y. Job capt. Skidmore, Owings & Merrill, N.Y.C., 1956-69; nat. bldg. cons. YWCA of the U.S.A. Nat. Bd., N.Y.C., 1970-81; devel. adminstr. N.Y. State Facilities Devel. Corp., N.Y.C., 1981-94; ret., 1994. Author: (2 vols.) A Building Manual for the YWCA, 1979. Active Community Bd. # 1, Manhattan, 1971-91; trustee Beekman-Downtown Hosp., 1976-82. Fellow AIA.

ALEXANDER, ALPHA V., association executive; b. Nashville, June 9, 1954; d. Rufus S. and Alpha Omega (Goins) A. BA, The Coll. of Wooster, 1976; MA, Temple U., 1978, PhD, 1981. Asst. athletic dir. Temple U., Phila., 1980-81, athletic dir. for women, 1981-83; dir. cmty. projects Women's Sports Found., San Francisco, 1984-85; dir. health promotion svcs. YWCA San Francisco, 1985-87; dir. health promotion and sports YWCA of U.S.A., N.Y.C., 1987—; bd. dirs. U.S. Olympic Com., co-chairwoman mem. svcs., 1993—. Author: Black Women in Sports, 1981; exec. prodr. videos It's a Shot, 1991, It's a Hit, 1992, Amazing Grace, 1993. Mem. chancellor sex equity com. N.Y.C. Pub. Schs., 1987—; bd. dirs. Covenant House, N.Y.C., 1988—, Peter Westbrook Found., Black Women Sports Found., 1992—, v.p. Recipient Nancy Rehm Ann. Meml. award Ft. Wayne's Women's Bur., 1990, Pride award Ethnic Minority Girls & Sport, 1991, Susan B. Anthony award NOW, 1993; named to Sport Hall of Fame, The Coll. of Wooster, 1993. Mem. African-Am. Athletic Assn. (pres. 1992—, bd. dirs.), Phipps. Presbyterian. Office: YWCA of USA 726 Broadway 5th fl New York NY 10003

ALEXANDER, BARBARA BOSCH, librarian; b. Maryville, Mo., Dec. 5, 1944. BS in English and Journalism, N.W. Mo. State U., 1982, MA in English, 1986; MSLS, N. Tex. State U., 1986. Reference libr. humanities Sterling C. Evans Library, Tex. A&M U., College Station, 1987, microtext reference libr., 1988-89, reference libr. documents divsn., 1990, interim head to head documents and maps, 1990-92; head gen. reference and documents Milner Library, Ill. State U., Normal, 1992—; instr. humanities Tex. A&M U., 1988-90; mem., chair numerous coms. Sterling C. Evans Libr., Milner Libr.; participant Snowbird Leadership Inst., 1990, chair 1st ann. reunion com. 1991; also various workshops and seminars; mem. publicity com. Tex. Conf. on Librs. and Info. Sci., 1989-90; mem. info. svcs. com. Houston Area Rsch. Consortium, 1989; rschr., presenter in field. Co-editor: Guide to the Microform Collections in the Sterling C. Evans Library, 3d edit., 1989; editor Analyzing Reference Tools: Thirty-two Commonly Used Indexes in the Sterling C. Evans Library, Texas A&M University, 1989; contbr., reviewer articles to profl. publs.; columnist NMRT Newsletter, 1990-91. Area coord. Campus Charity Drive, Sterling C. Evans Library, 1990. Grantee Tex. A&M U., 1989, 91, Tex. Libr. Assn., 1990; Tex. Library Assn. scholar, 1985; recipient Outstanding New Libr. award Tex. Library Assn. Jr. Mem. Round Table, 1990. Mem. ALA (membership promotion and relations 1987-88, chair 1989-90, various coms. Jr. Mem. Round Table, intern reference and adult svcs. divsn. 1988-90, mem. 1989-91, vice chair, chair libr. adminstrn. mgmt. assn. 1994—), Ill. Libr. Assn. (nominating com. Govt. Documents Round Table 1993-94, mgr.-elect, mgr. govt. documents round table 1994—), Ill. State U. Women's Assn., Ill. State U. Univ. Club. Office: Ill State U Campus Box 8900 Normal IL 61790-8900

ALEXANDER, BARBARA LEAH SHAPIRO, clinical social worker; b. St. Louis, May 6, 1943; d. Harold Albert and Dorothy Miriam (Leifer) Shapiro; m. Richard E. Alexander. B in Music Edn., Washington U., St. Louis, 1964; postgrad., U. Ill., 1964-66; MSW, Smith Coll., 1970; postgrad., Inst. Psychoanalysis, Chgo., 1971-73, grad., child therapy program, 1976-80; cert. therapist Sex Dysfunction Clinic, Loyola U., Chgo., 1975. Diplomate in Clin. Social Work. Research asst., NIMH grantee Smith Coll., 1968-70; probation officer Juvenile Ct. Cook County, Chgo., 1966-68, 70; therapist Madden Mental Health Center, Hines, Ill., 1970-72; supr., therapist, field instr. U. Chgo., U. Ill. Grad. Schs. Social Work; therapist Pritzker Children's Hosp., Chgo., 1972-82; therapist, cons., also pvt. practice, 1973—; pres. On Good Authority; instr. tng. and advanced tng. Effectiveness Tng. Assocs., Chgo., 1974; instr. psychology Northeastern U., Chgo., 1975; intern Divorce Conciliation Service, Circuit Ct. Cook County, 1976-77. Contbr. articles to profl. jours. Bd. dirs., Grant Park Concerts Soc.; sec. Art Resources in Teaching. Recipient Sterling Achievement award Mu Phi Epsilon, 1964. Mem. Nat. Fed. Soc. for Clin. Social Work (chmn. 20th ann. conf., exec. bd.), Ill. Soc. Clin. Social Work (pres. 1986-90, bd. dirs., chmn. services to mems. com., dir. pvt. practitioners' referral service), Assn. Child Psychotherapists, Amateur Chamber Music Players Assn., Jewish Geneal. Soc., Smith Coll. Alumni Assn. (bd. dirs.). Democrat. Home and Office: 6 Horizon Ln Galena IL 61036

ALEXANDER, BARBARA TOLL, investment banker; b. Little Rock, Dec. 18, 1948; d. Lawrence Jesser and Geraldine Best (Proctor) Toll; m. Lawrence Allen Alexander, Jan. 25, 1969 (div. 1980); m. Thomas Beveridge Stiles, II, Mar. 7, 1981; stepchildren: Thomas B. Stiles III, Jonathan E. Stiles. BS, U. Ark., 1969, MS, 1970. Asst. v.p. Wachovia Bank & Trust Co., Winston-Salem, N.C., 1972-77; security analyst Investors Diversified Services, Mpls., 1977-78; 1st v.p. Smith Barney Inc., N.Y.C., 1978-84; mng. dir. Salomon Bros., N.Y.C., 1984-91, Dillon Read & Co., 1992—; vice chmn. policy adv. bd. Joint Ctr. for Housing Studies of Harvard U.; mem. N.Y. adv. bd. Enterprise Found; bd. dir. Covenant House; chmn. audit com. Covenant House. Presbyterian. Home: 18 Tuttle Ave Spring Lake NJ 07762-1564 Office: Dillon Read & Co Inc 535 Madison Ave New York NY 10022-4212

ALEXANDER, CHERYL LEE, executive search and consulting firm executive; b. Mpls., Feb. 22, 1946; d. Wallace Einar and Dorothy Florence (Abrahamson) Arneson; m. Douglas Joel Hawkinson, Mar. 5, 1966; children: Tamara Lee, Alexander Lowell. Student, Gustavus Adolphus Coll., 1964-66, Nan Yang U., Singapore, 1971; BA summa cum laude, U. Minn., 1972. Pers. recruiter Nat. Recruiters, Mpls., 1972; pres. Alexander Recruiters, Mpls., 1973-79, Alexander Cos., (formerly Alexander Recruiters), Mpls., 1979—; former dir. Micro Application Systems, Inc., Proto Circuits, Inc.; active U.S. Sec. Energy Adv. Bd., 1994—, Task Force on Strategic Energy Rsch. and Devel.; lectr. numerous univs. Author: Up The Typewriter, 1977; Transition Management, 1980; contbg. author: The New Entrepreneurs: Visionaries for the 21st Century, 1994; subject of interviews by profl. jours, TV and radio. Advisor Hennepin County Pvt. Industry Council, Mpls., 1981-83; mem. St. Paul Set-Aside Adv. Com., 1981-82, Mpls. Tech. Enterprise Ctr., 1984—; bd. dirs. Continuum Center, advisor Discovery of Self Project, participant White House Conf. on Small Bus., 1980; judge Internat. Sci. and Engring. Fair, 1980; bd. dirs. Children's Communication Exchange, 1981-82. Mem. World Bus. Acad.,Womens Fund Speakers Bureau, 100 Mentor, Soc. Women Engrs. (founder, bd. dirs., sec.), Assn. Women in Computing (founder, bd. dirs., v.p. 1978-79), Nat. Assn. Women Bus. Owners (founder, bd. dirs. v.p., nat. sec. 1978-81). Avocations: tennis, public speaking, skiing, sailing. Office: Alexander Cos 3205 Casco Cir Wayzata MN 55391-9717

ALEXANDER, CONSTANCE JOY (CONNIE ALEXANDER), sculptor; b. Hillsboro, Ohio, Oct. 13, 1939; d. Laurence Adair and Martha Ellen (Hill-Overman) Lucas; m. Anfred Agee Alexander, June 6, 1959; children: Troy Arthur, Andrea Ellen. Grad., Cin. Art Acad., 1962; postgrad., Atlanta Coll. of Art, 1977. represented by Miller Gallery Cin., also various galleries in Ga. and Fla. Exhibited in group exhibitions at Southeastern Artists Ga. Jubilee Festival (1st in sculpture award 1974), Southeastern Arts & Crafts Festival, Macon (Ga.) Colisuem, 1977 (1st in sculpture), World's Fair, Knoxville, Tenn., 1982, David Schaeffer Gallery, Alpharetta, Ga., 1988-93, Ga. Marble Festival, Jasper, 1989 (1st place award), Ariel Gallery, Soho, N.Y., 1989 (award of excellence), 90, 45th Ann. Pen & Brush Sculpture Exhbn., Soho, N.Y., 1991 (Excalibur Bronze Sculpture Foundry award), Ariel Gallery, Soho, 1989-91, Tim Verstegen's The Dutch Framer Gallery, Canton, Ga., 1989-93, Artistic Frames & Gallery, Jasper, Ga., 1991-93, Buckhead Trinity Arts Group, Atlanta, Ga., 1994, Gallery 300, Atlanta, 1994; represented in permanent collections Cin. Pub. Libr., Ga. Inst. Tech., Atlanta, Hartsfield Internat. Airport, North Dekalb Coll., Coca-Cola Internat. Hdqs. Mem. Soc. of Friends. Home: PO Box 67 Canton GA 30114 Office: Trinity Arts Group 315 E Paces Ferry Rd Atlanta GA 30305

ALEXANDER, CRYSTAL CZARNECKI, financial analyst; b. Tacoma, Wash., Nov. 30, 1957; d. Stefan Frederick and Vivian Jean (Scribner) Czarnecki; m. Kenneth Sidney Alexander, Aug. 21, 1982; 1 child, Glenn. BA in Polit. Sci., U. Wash., 1978, MPA in Fin./Urban Affairs, 1980. Budget examiner State of N.Y., Albany, 1980-82; sr. budget analyst City of Seattle, 1983-86; budget & audit mgr. City of Beverly Hills, Calif., 1986-93; city internal auditor City of Redondo Beach, Calif., 1994—. Commr., chairperson Civil Svc. Commn., Culver City, Calif., 1992—; mem. Econ. Devel. Adv. Com., Culver City, 1993—; mem., subcom. chair Pub. Fin. Adv. Com., Culver City, 1990-92. Recipient Disting. Budget Presentation award Govt. Fin. Officers Assn. N.Am., Beverly Hills, 1987, 88, 89, 90, 91. Mem. Calif. Soc. Mcpl. Fin. Officers. Democrat. Roman Catholic. Office: City Redondo Beach 415 Diamond St Redondo Beach CA 90277

ALEXANDER, CYNTHIA ELIZABETH, state agency advisor; b. Houston, Aug. 23, 1949; d. Thomas P. and Bettye Alexander; children: Sloan Speck, Harrison Speck. BA in Mktg., U. Tex., 1970; MBA, Boston U., 1974. Analyst budget and policy Tex. Legis. Budget Bd., Austin, 1975-78; v.p. Lawrence W. Speck & Assocs., Austin, 1983-88; sr. advisor policy and budget Office of Tex. Gov., Austin, 1988-90; dir. adminstrn. and fin. State Preservation Bd., Austin, 1990-91; sr. advisor budget and policy Office Comptr. Pub. Accounts, Tex. Performance Rev., Austin, 1992—.

ALEXANDER, DIANE MARIE, telemarketing and sales executive; b. Clinton, Okla., Aug. 31, 1945; d. Edwin Michael Jr. and Gloria Louise (McCray) Drass; m. Larry Edward Allen, Dec. 18, 1965 (div. Aug. 1972); children: Larry Dean, Lynn Edward; m. Nicol Brandon Alexander, June 28, 1980 (div. Jan. 1988); children: Danielle Nicole, Derek Brandon. Student, Lindenwood Coll., 1963-64, Abilene Christian Coll., 1964-65. Cert. neurolinguistic programming practitioner, 1989, cert. customer svc. exec. Telesales rep. GTE Corp., Irving, Tex., 1974-77, dist. telesales mgr., 1977-78; v.p. Brandon and Assocs., Inc., Grand Prairie, Tex., 1980-81; v.p. TeleMktg. Enterprises, Inc., Grand Prairie, 1982-88, pres., owner, 1988—; v.p. mktg. Barakel Corp., Arlington, Tex., 1981-82; lectr. in field; cons., tchr. Internat. Aviation and Travel Acad./Frontier Airlines, Arlington, Tex., 1983-84. Author: Advanced Communications Technology, 1980, Telemarketing Series, 1982-87, Professional TeleAppointments, 1985; contbr. articles to profl. jours. Jr. Achievement scholar Lindenwood Coll., 1963. Mem. Am. Soc. Tng. and Devel., Internat. Customer Svc. Assn. (conv. speaker Nashville chpt. 1989). Republican. Episcopalian.

ALEXANDER, EDNA M. DEVEAUX, elementary education educator; d. Richard and Eva (Musgrove) DeVeaux. BBA, Fla. A & M U., 1943; BS in Elem. Edn., Fla. A&M U., 1948; MS in Supervision and Adminstrn., U. Pa., 1954; cert., U. Madrid, 1961; postgrad., Dade Jr. Coll., U. Miami. Sec. Dunbar Elem. Sch., 1943-46, tchr., 194-55; tchr. Orchard Villa Elem., 1959-66; prin. A. L. Lewis Elem. Sch., 1955-57; reading specialist North Cen. Dist., 1966-69; tchr. L. C. Evans Elem. Sch., 1969-71; first black woman newscaster in Miami, Sta. WBAY, 1948. V.p. Fla. Council on Human Relations Dade County, Coun. for Internat. Visitors Greater Miami; past pres. Episcopal Churchwomen of Christ Ch., Miami; bd. dirs. YWCA; vice chmn. Community Action Agy. Dade County; chmn. Dade County Minimum Housing Appeals Bd.; active Vol. Unltd. Project Nat. Coun. Negro Women; sponsor Am. Jr. Red Cross, Girl Scouts U.S.; trustee Fla. Internat. U. Found., 1974-79. Mem. AAUW (life, Edna M. DeVeaux Alexander fellowship named in her honor Miami br.), NEA (life), LWV, Fla. Edn. Assn., Classroom Tchrs. Assn., Dade County Edn. Assn. (chmn. pub. rels. com.), Dade County Reading Assn., Assn. for Childhood Edn., Internat. Reading Tchr. Assn., U. Pa. Alumni Assn., Alpha Kappa Alpha. Home: 805 Blue Gill Rd PO Box 26063 Jacksonville FL 32218

ALEXANDER, ELIZABETH FAYE TUTOR, nursing educator; b. Pontotoc, Miss., Oct. 27, 1940; d. Vearl Arlis and Rozelle Lavonia (Walls) Tutor; m. Kenneth Barber Alexander, Aug. 9, 1959; children: Kenneth Barber, Sherrie Alexander Williams. ADN, John C. Calhoun Community Coll., 1976. Cert. Red Cross instr. Dir. nursing asst. course Nash Community Coll., Rocky Mount, N.C.; supr. newborn nursery Florence (S.C.) Gen. Hosp.; dialysis nurse VA, Salem, Va.; instr. Nash Community Coll., Rocky Mt., N.C.

ALEXANDER, ERIKA DUTSCHKE, statistician; b. Cleve., May 15, 1969; d. Gerald Herman and Cynthia Anne (Fleming) Dutschke; m. Jon Drew Alexander, Aug. 11, 1990. BS in Applied Math. Sci., Tex. A&M U., 1990, MS in Stats., 1991; postgrad., U. North Tex., 1993—. Instr. stats. Tex. A&M U., College Station, 1990-91; prodn. mgmt. trainee E-Sys., Inc., Greenville, Tex., 1991-92; statistician IRS, Dallas, 1992—; statis. cons. Am. Cyanimid, Tex. A&M U., College Station, 1991. Author: (tech. jour.) IRS Rsch. Bull., 1994. Comty. svcs. scholar YMCA, 1986-90; Lechner fellow Tex. A&M U., 1986-90. Mem. Am. Statis. Assn., Delta Delta Delta (acad. scholar 1987-88), Phi Eta Sigma.

ALEXANDER, JANE, arts endowment administrator, actress, producer; b. Boston, Oct. 28, 1939; d. Thomas Bartlett and Ruth (Pearson) Quigley; m. Robert Alexander, July 23, 1962 (div. 1969); 1 child, Jason; m. Edwin Sherin, Mar. 29, 1975. Student, Sarah Lawrence Coll., 1957-59, U. Edinburgh, 1959-60; LHD, Wilson Coll., 1984; DFA (hon.), The Julliard Sch., 1994, N.C. Sch. Arts, 1994. Ind. TV, film and theatrical actress, 1962—; chmn. Nat. Endowment for Arts, Washington, 1993—; guest artist in residence Okla. Arts Inst., 1982, tchr. adult theatre workshop, 1984, 91, tchr. master class, 1990; mem. adv. bd. Nat. Wildlife Art Mus., hon. group, 1992—; mem. adv. bd. Women for a Meaningful Summit, 1985-90, The Acting Co., 1980-93, The Video Project, 1990-93, Nat. Stroke Assn., 1984-91, Women's Action for New Directions, 1981-90, N.Y. Zool. Soc./Wildlife Conservation Soc., 1985-93. Author: (with Greta Jacobs) The Bluefish Cookbook, 4 edits., 1979-92; translator: (with Sam Engelstad) The Master Builder (Henrik Ibsen), 1978; appeared in prodns.: Charles Playhouse Boston, 1964-65, Arena Stage, Washington, 1965-68, 70—, Am. Shakespeare Festival; plays include Major Barbara, Mourning Becomes Electra, Merry Wives of Windsor, Stratford, Conn., summers 1971-72; Broadway prodns. include The Great White Hope, 1968-69 (Tony award 1969, Drama Desk award, Theatre World award), 6 Rms Riv Vu, 1972-73 (Tony nomination), Find Your Way Home, 1974 (Tony nomination), Hamlet, 1975, The Heiress, 1976, First Monday in October, 1978 (Tony nomination), Goodbye Fidel, 1980, Monday After the Miracle, 1982, Night of the Iguana, 1988, Shadowlands, 1990-91, The Visit, 1992 (Tony nomination), The Sisters Rosensweig, 1993 (Drama Desk award 1992-93, Tony award nomination, Obie award 1993); also appeared in plays The Time of Your Life, Present Laughter, 1975, The Master Builder, 1977, Losing Time, 1980, Antony and Cleopatra, 1981, Hedda Gabler, 1981, Old Times, 1984, Approaching Zanzibar, 1989, Mystery of the Rose Bouquet, 1989; appeared in films The Great White Hope, 1970 (Acad. award nomination), A Gunfight, 1970, The New Centurions, 1972, All the President's Men, 1976 (Acad. award nomination), The Betsy, 1978, Kramer vs. Kramer, 1979 (Acad. award nomination), Brubaker, 1980, Night Crossing, 1981, Testament, 1983 (Acad. award nomination), City Heat, 1984, Sweet Country, 1986, Square Dance, 1987, Glory, 1989; appeared in TV films Welcome Home Johny Bristol, 1971, Miracle on 34th Street, 1973, Death Be Not Proud, 1974, This Was the West That Was, 1974, Eleanor and Franklin, 1976 (Emmy nomination), Eleanor and Franklin: The White House Years, 1977 (Emmy nomination, TV Critics Circle award), Lovey, 1977, A Question of Love, 1978, Playing for Time, 1980 (Emmy award 1980), Calamity Jane: The Diary of a Frontier Woman, 1981, Dear Liar, 1981, Kennedy's Children, 1981, In the Custody of Strangers, 1982, When She Says No, 1983, Mountainview, 1989, Daughter of the Streets, 1990, A Marriage: Georgia O'Keeffe and Alfred Stieglitz, 1991; appeared in TV spls. A Circle of Children, 1977, Blood and Orchids, 1986, Calamity Jane, 1984 (Emmy nomination), Malice in Wonderland, 1985 (Emmy nomination), In Love and War, 1987, Open Admissions, 1988, A Friendship in Vienna, 1988, Stay the Night, 1992. Recipient Achievement in Dramatic Arts award St. Botolph Club, 1979, Israel Cultural award, 1982, Western Heritage Wrangler award, 1985, Helen Caldicott Leadership award, 1984, Living Legacy award Women's Internat. Ctr., San Diego, 1988, Environ. Leadership award Eco-Expo, 1991, Muse award N.Y. Women in Film, 1993, Torch of Hope award 1992, Lectureship award NIH, 1994, Houseman award The Acting Co., 1994, medal UCLA, 1994, Helen Hayes award Am. Express Tribute, 1994, Women of Achievement award Anti-Defamation League, 1994. Mem. AFTRA, SAG, Actors Equity Assn., Acad. Motion Picture Arts and Scis., Actors Fund. Office: Nat Endowment for Arts Nancy Hanks Bldg 1100 Pennsylvania Ave NW Washington DC 20506

ALEXANDER, JANICE HOEHNER, physician, educator; b. Detroit; d. Robert Paul and Leafy Edna (Phillips) Hoehner; m. Michael Alexander; children: Jason, Janelle Collins. BSN, Wayne State U., 1971, MD, 1979. Resident in family practice, emergency rm. Providence Hosp., Southfield, Mich., 1980-86; resident in ob-gyn. Saginaw (Mich.) Gen. Hosp., 1986-88; staff surgeon ob-gyn. Columbia and St. Joseph Hosps., Milw., 1988—; clin. instr. Mich. State U., Lansing, 1986-88, Med. Coll. Wis., Milw., 1988—; physician, tchr. Women's Med. Internat. People to People, Russia, Latvia, Lithuania, 1993. Instr. CPR ARC, Milw., 1991—. Fellow AAFP; mem. ACOG, AMA, AFS, SLS, MGynS, Milw. Med. Soc., Wis. Med. Soc. Office: 2025 E Newport Ste 129 Milwaukee WI 53211

ALEXANDER, JOYCE LONDON, judge. BA, Howard Univ., D.C.; JD, New Eng. Law Sch., 1972; LLD, Northeastern Univ., New Eng. Law Sch., Bridgewater State Coll. Staff atty. Greater Boston Legal Assistance Project, 1972-74; legal counsel Youth Activities Commn., Boston, 1974-76; gen. counsel Mass. Bd. of Higher Edn., 1976-79; magistrate judge U.S. Dist. Ct. (Mass. dist.), 1st circuit, Boston, 1979—; asst. prof. Tufts Univ., 1974-75; legal editor WBZ-TV, Boston, 1978-79. Trustee Boys & Girls Club of Greater Boston. Recipient Martin Luther King Jr. Drum Major for Justice award So. Christian Leadership Conf., 1985, Raymond Pace Alexander award Nat. Bar Assn.; named Outstanding Young Leader of Mass. Boston Jaycees, 1980. Mem. Am. Judicature Soc., Nat. Bar Assn., Nat. Coun. of U.S. Magistrate, Mass. Black Judges Conf., Urban League of Ea. Mass. (co-founder, pres. emeritus), World Peace Through Law Conf., Orgn. of Black Airline Pilots. Office: John W McCormack Courthouse 90 Devonshire St Rm 707 Boston MA 02109*

ALEXANDER, JOYCE MARY, illustrator; b. Pepin, Wis., Mar. 31, 1927; d. Colonel and Martha (Varnum) Yochem; m. Don Tocher, June 27, 1955 (div. 1962); m. Dorsey Potter Alexander, Nov. 1, 1963. Student, Coll. Arts and Crafts, 1946, Acad. of Art, 1961-62. Co-founder, owner Turtle's Quill Scriptorium Publishers, Berkeley, Calif., 1963—. Author: Thaddeus, 1972, Happy Bird Day, 1980; illustrator numerous books including: Soil and Plant Analysis, A Practical Guide for the Home Gardener, 1963, California Farm and Ranch Law, 1967, Chinatown, A Legend of Old Cannery Row, 1968, The Sea: Excerpts from Herman Melville, 1970, Of Mice, 1970, David: Psalm Twenty-Four, 1970, Shakespeare: Selected Sonnets, 1974, The Blue-Jay Yarn, 1975, Psalm One Hundred Four, 1978, Messiah: Choruses from Handel's Messiah, 1985, A Flurry of Angels, Angels in Literature, 1986, Eleven Poems by Emily Dickinson, A Packet of Rhymes, 1989, Psalm 8 (A Nature Psalm), 1991, Poems, Emily Dickinson, 1992, Comfort Me With Apples, 1993; work represented in permanent collections Hunt Botan. Libr. at Carnegie-Mellon U. Republican. Office: Turtle's Quill Scriptorium PO Box 643 Mendocino CA 95460-0643

ALEXANDER, JUDITH ANNE, secondary school educator, counselor; b. Evanston, Ill., July 20, 1945; d. David Allen and Mary Virginia (Ewing) Burns; m. Franklyn Alexander, Aug. 17, 1974. BA in English, Mundelein Coll., 1968; MA in English, Northeastern Ill. U., 1975, MA in Counseling, 1988. Cert. tchr. grades 6-12, Ill. Tchr. English St. Scholastica High Sch., Chgo., 1969-71, Mother Guerin High Sch., River Grove, Ill., 1974-79; English dept. chair St. Scholastica High Sch., Chgo., 1979-88, guidance dept. chair, 1988—. Author: (short story) The Silent Drum, 1968. Named to Classical Inst., NEH, Tufts U., 1983, Shakespeare Inst., NEH, U. Md., 1984. Mem. Am. Counseling Assn., Nat. Assn. Coll. Admission Counselors, Ill. Assn. Coll. Admission Counselors, Kappa Gamma Pi Honor Sorority. Roman Catholic. Office: Saint Scholastica High Sch 7416 N Ridge Blvd Chicago IL 60645

ALEXANDER, KATHARINE VIOLET, lawyer; b. N.Y.C., Nov. 19, 1934; d. George Clifford and Violet (Jambor) Sziklai; m. George Jonathon Alexander, Sept. 6, 1958; children: Susan Katina, George J. II. Student, Smith Coll., Geneva, 1954-55; BA, Goucher Coll., 1956; JD, U. Pa., 1959; student specialized courses, U. Santa Clara, 1974-76. Bar: Calif. 1974, U.S. Dist. Ct. (no. dist.) Calif. 1974, U.S. Ct. Appeals (9th cir.) 1974; cert. criminal lawyer Calif. State Bar Bd. Legal Specialization. Research dir., adminstr. Am. Bar Found., Chgo., 1959-60; lectr. law San Jose (Calif.) State U., 1972-74; sr. atty. Santa Clara County, San Jose, 1974—. Editor: Mentally Disabled and the Law, 1961; contbg. author: The Aged and the Need for Surrogate Management, 1969-70, Jury Instructions on Medical Issues, 1965-67. Community rep. Office Econ. Opportunity Com., Syracuse, N.Y., 1969-70. Mem. ABA (active various coms.), AAUW, Food and Wine Inst., Calif. Bar Assn., Santa Clara County Bar Assn. (trustee 1981-82), Calif. Attys. for Criminal Justice (bd. govs. 1988-92), Calif. Pub. Def. Assn., Jr. League. Presbyterian. Home: 11600 Summit Wood Ct Los Altos Hls CA 94022-4500 Office: County Govt Ctr West Wing 70 W Hedding St San Jose CA 95110

ALEXANDER, KATHLEEN DENISE, medical, surgical nurse; b. Kansas City, Mo., Feb. 2, 1963; d. Irwin Eugene and Carolyn Sue (Fortune) A. Diploma, Bapt. Sch. Nursing, Memphis, 1985. Cert. BLS. Staff RN Bapt. Meml. Hosp., Memphis, 1985-87; contract RN Largo (Fla.) Med. Hosp., 1988, New Hanover, Wilmington, N.C., 1988; PRN Bapt. Mem. Hosp., Memphis, 1988; contract RN Mother Francis, Tyler, Tex., 1989, Burdette Tomlin Hosp., Sea Isle City, N.J., 1989, Dominquez Hosp., Compton, Calif., 1990, St. Vincent Hosp., L.A., 1990; staff RN Bapt. Meml. Desoto, Southaven, Miss., 1990—. Mem. Nat. Assn. Orthopedic Nurses. Home: 6365 Riverbirch Rd Walls MS 38680

ALEXANDER, LENORA COLE, business executive, educator; b. Buffalo, Mar. 9, 1935; d. John L. and Susie (Stamper) Cole; m. T.M. Alexander Sr., June 22, 1976. BS, SUNY, Buffalo, 1957, MEd, 1969, PhD, 1974. Lic. elem. tchr., elem. sch. prin. Tchr. pub. schs. Chgo. and Lancaster, N.Y., 1957-68; v.p. student life Am. U., Washington, 1974-77; v.p. student affairs U. D.C., 1978-81; dir. Women's Bur. Dept. Labor, Washington, 1981-86; Commonwealth prof. George Mason U., Fairfax, Va., 1986-88; pres. LCA and Assocs., Inc., Washington, 1986—; cons. div. student affairs U. Calif. Irvine, 1971, CCNY, 1972, Temple U., 1973; advisor regional and city planning colloquium U. Pa., 1973; panel on selection fellow HEW, 1976-77; cons. advanced instrl. devel. program Dillard U., 1977-81; mem. mayor's blue ribbon panel on reorgn. Dept. Human Resources, Washington, 1977; mem. selection com. fellows program Am. Council on Edn., 1982; lectr. in field. Author tech. reports for U.S. Govt. Printing Office. Trustee Wider Opportunities for Women, 1975-77; del. Internat. Commn. on Status Women, 1982, Columbia, 1983, Women in World Prep. Conf., 1983; apptd. del. Decade for Women in World Conf., UN, Vienna, Austria, 1984, Kenya, 1986; U.S. rep. on role women on economy Orgn. Econ. Devel., Paris, 1982-86; mem. adv. com. on women vets VA, 1983; participant Jerusalem Internat. Forum, Am.-Israel Friendship League, 1986; mem. D.C. Bd. Elections and Ethics, 1986-88, Def. Adv. Com. On Women in Mil., def. adv. com. Women in the Svc., 1989—; bd. dirs. Legal Aid Soc., Washington, 1975-77, D.C. Rental Accommodations Commn., 1978-79, McAuley Inst., Silver Spring, Va., 1987—; pres. bd. dirs. Found. for Exceptional Children, Reston, Va., 1987—. SUNY grad. fellow, 1968; recipient Disting. Alumnus award SUNY-Buffalo, 1983, Pauline Weeden Maloney award in nat. trends and Services The Links, Phila., 1984, Disting. Service Citation Nat. MBA Assn., 1984, Outstanding Woman award DC chpt. Federally Employed Women, Washington, 1984, Outstanding Polit. Achievement award Nat. Assn. Minortiy Polit. Women, 1985, Outstanding Career Woman award women's activities com. Alpha Phi Alpha, Washington, 1986, Woman of Achievement award Women's City Club Cleve., 1986. Mem. Delta Sigma Theta. Republican. Home and Office: 3020 Brandywine St NW Washington DC 20008-2140

ALEXANDER, LINDA K., adult education educator; b. Cleve., July 31, 1949; d. Robert E. and Evelyn E. (Sullivan) Schreiner; m. Michael F. Alexander, Aug. 29, 1971 (div. May 1994); children: Christa, Heidi, Jared. BS in Edn., Bowling Green State U., 1971. Tchr. pre-sch. Day Care Ctr.-Cmty. Nursery Sch., London, Ohio, 1975-78; substitute tchr. London City Schs.,

1974-78; tchr. London Adult Basic Edn., 1978—, dir., 1989—. Mem. recreation com. London City Recreation Coun., 1989—, London Correctional Instn., 1988—. Recipient Dirs. Cmty. Svc. award Tecumseh Consortium, 1988-89. Fellow Literacy Coun. Republican. Roman Catholic. Home: 179 N Main St London OH 43140-1143 Office: London ABLE 60 S Walnut St London OH 43140-1246

ALEXANDER, LYNN See MARGULIS, LYNN

ALEXANDER, MARGARET ALICE, psychologist, researcher; b. Adrian, Mich., Dec. 8, 1947; d. Howard Wright and Mary Alice (Nace) A. BA, Earlham Coll., 1970; MA, NYU, 1977, PhD, 1984. Lic. psychologist, Wis. Intake screener Ct. Employment Project, N.Y.C., 1971-74; intern, extern Ednl. Alliance Settlement House, N.Y.C., 1976-79; conf. planner Sch. Indsl. and Labor Rels. Cornell U., N.Y.C., 1980-82; mem. mental health staff Del. Dept. Corrections, Smyrna, 1983-90; clin. dir. Wis. Sex Offender Treatment Program Wis. Dept. Corrections, Oshkosh, 1990—; cons. N.J. Adult Diagnostic and Treatment Ctr., Avenel, 1988-90; cons. on conflict resolution Unitarian Universalist Ch., Chgo., 1993—; v.p. Wis. Sex Offender Treatment Network, Madison, 1993—. Pres. Fox Valley Unitarian Universalist Fellowship, Appleton, Wis., 1994-96. Mem. APA, Assn. for the Treatment of Sexual Abusers (clin.). Office: Wis Dept Corrections PO Box 3530 Oshkosh WI 54903-3530

ALEXANDER, MARIE BAILEY, family economist, consulting editor; b. Chattanooga, Sept. 2, 1913; d. Claude Esmond and Elsie Blanche (Peterson) Bailey; m. Theron Alexander, Aug. 29, 1936; children: Thomas T., Mary E. BS, Maryville (Tenn.) Coll., 1935; postgrad., Fla. State U., 1950-51. Mktg. cons. Gas & Electric Co., Chattanooga, 1935; tchr. North High Sch., Chattanooga, 1935-36; cons. editor Iowa City, Iowa, 1957-65, Phila., 1966-86, Menlo Park, Calif., 1987—. Deacon, Valley Presbyn. Ch., Portola Valley, Calif., 1989-90. Mem. AAUW (co-chmn. internat. rels. sect. Menlo-Atherton br. 1987-89, chmn. 1989—, mem. lit. group 1986—, bd. dirs. 1987—), P.E.O. (del. regional bd. Calif. 1988-89, pres. chpt. E 1979-81). Democrat. Home: 350 Sharon Park Dr Apt 3C Menlo Park CA 94025-6810

ALEXANDER, MARJORIE ANNE, artist, hand papermaker, consultant; b. Chgo., Apr. 16, 1928; d. Alexander and Nancy Rebecca (Cordrey) Roberts; m. Harold Harman Alexander, June 13, 1948; children: Jeffrey C., Cassandra J., Peter B., Timothy C., Patrick J. Student, Wilson Jr. Coll., 1946-47; MFA in Painting, U. Ill., 1968, MA in Art Edn., 1972. cert. tchr. K-12: Ill., Minn. Graphic artist Barry Martin Studio, Rumson, N.J., 1963-65; instr. painting, drawing U. YMCA, Champaign, Ill., 1968-72; teaching asst. U. Ill., Urbana, 1968-72, rsch. assoc., 1972-76; instr. art Champaign High Sch., 1973-75, Urbana High Sch., 1976-80, Concordia Acad., St. Paul, Minn., 1982-84, U. Minn., Mpls., 1984-87; design, housing and apparel artist in residence U. Minn., St. Paul, 1984-88; craft cons. and educator tech. asstance program USAID, OAS, U. Minn., Kingston, Jamaica, 1986—; design cons. J.A.M. Corp., Mpls., 1988—; tech. cons. OAS, Kingston, 1990-91, Blandin Found. grantee, Minn., 1989—; rsch. and product devel. agrl. utilization rsch. inst., 1992—; tech. cons. Zabbaleen Paper Project, Assn. for the Protection of the Environment, Cairo, Egypt, 1993—. Works have appeared in over 20 solo shows, 1960—, over 17 invitational shows nationally and internationally, 1985—; co-author (book): Selected Papers, 1994; contbr. articles to profl. jours. Vestry mem. St. John's Episcopal Ch., Champaign, 1975-78, St. Matthew's Episcopal Ch., St. Paul, 1989—. Recipient Celebrity award Minn. State Fair, 1984, book First award 1986, Honorable mention 3rd Onn/Off Paper Nat., Wis., 1984; grantee Blandin Found. U. Minn., 1989-90, OAS, 1990-91, Agrl. Utilization Rsch. Inst. grantee, 1992—. Mem. Nat. League Am. Penwomen (Minn. art chair 1990-94, state v.p. 1994—), Internat. Assn. Hand Papermakers and Paper Artists, Friends of Dard Hunter Paper Mus. (com. chair 1990—). Episcopalian. Home: Graybridge 3251 Fernwood St Arden Hills MN 55112

ALEXANDER, MARTHA SUE, librarian; b. Washington, June 8, 1945; d. Lyle Thomas and Helen (Goodwin) Alexander; m. David Henry Bowman, June 11, 1965 (div. 1982); 1 child, Elaine. B.A., U. Md., 1967; M.S. in Library Sci., Cath. U. Am., 1969. Librarian U. Md., College Park, 1969-72, head acquisitions, 1973-75; asst. univ. librarian George Washington U., Washington, 1975-78, assoc. univ. librarian, 1978-82; univ. librarian U. Louisville, 1983-90; dir. libraries U. Mo., Columbia, 1990—; chmn. bd. dirs. SOLINET (Southeastern Library Network), 1987-88. Coord. U. Louisville United Way, 1987; bd. dirs. Mo. Libr. Network Corp., 1990—. Mem. ALA (chmn. poster sessions 1983-85, co-chmn. nat. conf. in Cin. 1989), Am. Assn. Higher Edn., Athletic Assn. U. Louisville (vice chmn., bd. dirs. 1989-90), D.C. Library Assn. (pres. 1981-82), Women Acad. Libr. Dirs. Exch. Network. Episcopalian. Home: 100 Mumford Dr Columbia MO 65203-0226 Office: Univ Mo Columbia-Ellis Libr Columbia MO 65201

ALEXANDER, MARY ELSIE, lawyer; b. Chgo., Nov. 16, 1947; d. Theron and Marie (Bailey) A.; m. Lyman Saunders Faulkner, Jr., Dec. 1, 1984; 1 child, Michelle. BA, U. Iowa, 1969; MPH, U. Calif.-Berkeley, 1975; JD, U. Santa Clara, 1982. Bar: Calif. 1982, U.S. Dist. Ct. (no. dist.) Calif. 1982, U.S. ct. Appeals (9th cir.) 1982. Rschr., U. Cin., 1969-74; dept. dir., sr. environ. health scientist Stanford Rsch. Inst., Menlo Park, Calif., 1975-80; cons. Alexander Assocs., Ambler, Pa., 1980-82; assoc. Caputo, Liccardo Rossi Sturges & McNeil, San Jose, Calif., 1982-84; assoc. Cartwright, Slobodin, Bokelman, et al, San Francisco, 1984-88, ptnr., 1988—. Com. mem. Cancer Soc., San Jose, 1983; elder Valley Presbyn. Ch., Portola Valley, 1987-90; active Am. Heart Assn., Santa Clara County. Named one of top 10 Trail Lawyers San Francisco Bay Area, San Francisco Chronicle, 1990. Nat. Inst. Occpational Safety and Health scholar U. Calif., Berkeley, 1975. Mem. ABA, Assn. Trial Lawyers Am. (state del.), Calif. Trial Lawyers Assn. (PAC bd. 1989—, parliamentarian 1991, v.p. 1992, chair mem. com., editor Forum), San Francisco Trial Lawyers Assn., Trial Lawyers for Pub. Justice, Calif. Women Lawyers, Am. Indsl. Hygiene Assn. (bd. dirs. 1979-81, treas. 1977-79), Nat. Assn. Advancement of Sci., Santa Clara Trial Lawyers Assn. (bd. dirs. 1983-84). Democrat. Office: Cartwright Slobodin Bokelman 101 California St Fl 26 San Francisco CA 94111-5802

ALEXANDER, MARY MILDRED, religious organization administrator; b. Little Rock, Jan. 11, 1939; d. John Fred and Mildred (Waters) A. Student, U. So. Calif., Princeton Theol. Sem., Columbia U. Founder, executive Okla. Found. Advancement Christian Edn. Inc., Oklahoma City, 1991—; founder, exec. Okla. Bible Learning Ctr., Oklahoma City, 1992—; past model, featured in Glamour Mag. Sr. editor Our America Program, L.A; writer TV scripts Sunset Portals, Hollywood, Calif.; co-writer TV scripts Mississippi Fury, Jackson, Miss., Beverly Hillbillies; patentee salad chopper, perfume dispenser, others. Found. exec. Okla. Released Time Religious Edn., Oklahoma City, 1994—; active ARC, March of Dimes, Salvation Army, Hosp. Guild, YWCA. Recipient Hon. award Nat. Go to Ch. Orgn., L.A., award Calif. Press Women, L.A. Mem. Petroleum Club (Oklahoma City). Democrat. Presbyterian. Avocations: music, piano, golf, swimming. Office: Okla Bible Learning Ctr 6488 Avondale Dr Ste 153 Oklahoma City OK 73116

ALEXANDER, MICHELE YERMACK, educator; b. Pitts., Sept. 16, 1947; d. Michael and Bernadette (Vogel) Yermack; m. Michael Allen Alexander, Aug. 14, 1971; children: Alexia Michele, Aaron Michael, Adam Mikhail. BS in Biology, George Mason U., 1969; MA in Sci. Edn., Ohio State U., 1975, postgrad., 1975-79. Cert. sci. tchr., Va., Ohio, Pa. 8th grade sci. tchr. Fred M. Lynn Mid. Sch., Woodbridge, Va., 1969-71; 7th grade sci. tchr. Orange (Va.) Intermediate Sch., 1971-72; sci.-biology tchr. Groveport (Ohio) Madison High Sch., 1972-77; biology tchr. Sewickley (Pa.) Acad., 1980-87; substitute tchr. Corpus Christi Sch., Wilmington, Del., 1991-92, full-time sci. tchr., sci. coord., 1993—; quality monitor Stream Watch of Del., Hockessin, 1989—. Editor: Energy Activities for the Classroom, 1976. Mem. Sewickley Watershed Assn., 1980-87; nature guide Sewickley Nature Guides, 1980-87; bd. dirs. Conservation Consultants, Sewickley, 1980-87; sec. Bon Ayre Civic Assn., Hockessin, 1981-88, treas., 1988-89; co-leader Girl Scouts U.S., Wilmington, 1989-90; mem. St. Mary of the Assumption Parish Coun., Hockessin, 1990-93. Mem. Nat. Sci. Tchrs.' Assn., Corpus Christi Home and Sch. Assn. (bd. dirs., v.p. 1989-91, pres.-elect 1991-92, pres. 1992-93), Del. Nature Soc., Phi Delta Kappa. Roman Catholic. Home: 803 Ciderbrook Rd Hockessin DE 19707-1325

ALEXANDER, MONICA MARY HARRIET, laboratory technician; b. Manama, Bahrain, May 4, 1942; came to U.S., 1967; d. Emidio Simplicio and Sabina Isabela (De-Rego) Simoes; divorced; children: Robert, Mark. Student, Midland Tech. Inst., U. S.C., 1978, Dale Carnegie Inst., 1980. Receiver/contr. Carolina Eastman Kodak, Columbia, S.C., 1972-87, lab. fiber analyst, 1987-90; environ. lab. analyst Eastman Chem. Co., Columbia, 1990—. Vol. Floyd Spence campaign Rep. Party, Columbia, 1985, Bob Dole campaign, Columbia, 1988; vol. Lexington County Hosp., West Columbia, S.C., 1993. Mem. NAFE, NOW. Roman Catholic.

ALEXANDER, PATRICIA ROSS, administrative assistant; b. Blue Ridge, Ga., May 19, 1955; d. Ernest B. and Sara P. (Williams) Ross; m. Robert W. Alexander, Jr., June 24, 1978; children: Sarah E., Robert R. AA, Young Harris (Ga.) Coll., 1975; BA, North Ga. Coll., 1978, postgrad.; postgrad., Emory U. Fiber artist Morganton, Ga.; clk., postmaster relief U.S. Postal Svc., Mineral Bluff, Ga., 1987—; adminstrv. asst. Indsl. Strength Art, Morganton. Contbr. articles to publs. Recipient cert. of Appreciation and Pride in Performance Gold medal, U.S. Postal Svc., 1992; grantee Ga. Coun. for Arts, 1984, NSF, 1979. Mem. NAPUS, So. Highlands Handicraft Guild, Ga. Mountain Crafts (bd. dirs. 1981-84), Copper Basin/Fannin C. of C., Blue Ridge Mountains Arts Assn. (v.p. 1979-80, coord. 1980-81, bd. dirs. 1993—), Basket Weavers Guild Ga., Fannin County Heritage Found., Fannin County Tree League (bd. dirs. 1993-95), Ga. Pub. TV Leadership Cir. Baptist. Home: PO Box 599 Morganton GA 30560-0599 Office: Us Post Ofc Mineral Bluff GA 30559

ALEXANDER, SUSAN HORTON, choral director; b. Rapid City, S.D., Oct. 4, 1949; d. Wallace Dale and Dorothy Ellen (Morgan) Horton; m. Thomas N. Alexander, June 20, 1970 (div. Apr. 1981); children: Sandra Kathleen, Robert Wade. BS, Radford Coll., 1971. Tchr., choral dir. Fairfax (Va.) County Pub. Schs., 1971—; music dir., organist Fairfax Bapt. Ch., 1974-81; tchr. piano pvt. practice, Centreville, Va., 1990—; choral clinician, adjudicator pvt. practice, Centreville, 1991—; curriculum devel. gifted & talented Fairfax County, 1984, 85, 88, 89, 92. Mem. Fairfax Choral Soc., 1990-92, Robert Shaw Festival Chorus, 1992, 94, 95. Mem. Am. Choral Dirs. Assn., Va. Choral Dirs. Assn. (sec. 1984—), Va. Music Educators Assn. (dist. chair 1983—), Music Educators Nat. Conf. Mem. LDS Ch. Home: 14437 Golden Oak Rd Centreville VA 22020 Office: Fairfax High Sch 3500 Old Lee Hwy Fairfax VA 22030

ALEXANDER, VERA, dean, marine science educator; b. Budapest, Hungary, Oct. 26, 1932; came to U.S., 1950; d. Paul and Irene Alexander; div.; children: Graham Alexander Dugdale, Elizabeth Alexander. BA in Zoology, U. Wis., 1955, MS in Zoology, 1962; PhD in Marine Sci., U. Alaska, 1965. From asst. prof. to assoc. prof. marine sci. U. Alaska, Fairbanks, 1965-74, prof., 1974—, dean Coll. Environ. Scis., 1977-78, 80-81, dir. Inst. Marine Sci., 1979-93, acting dean Sch. Fisheries and Ocean Scis., 1987-89, dean, 1989—; mem. adv. com. Office Health and Environ. Rsch. U.S. Dept. Energy, Washington, 1987-90; vice chmn. Arctic Ocean Scis. Bd., 1988-89; mem. adv. com. to Ocean Scis. divsn. NSF, 1980-84, chairperson adv. com., 1983-84; mem. com. to evaluate outer continental shelf environ. assessment program Minerals Mgmt. Svc., Bd. Environ. Sci. and Tech. NRC, 1987-91, mem. com. on geophys. and environ. Data, 1993—; U.S. del. to North Pacific Marine Sci. Orgn. Editor: Marine Biological Systems of the Far North (W.L. Rey), 1989. Sec. Fairbanks Light Opera Theatre Bd., 1987-88; chairwoman Rhodes Scholar Selection Com., Ak., 1986—. Research grantee U. Alaska. Fellow AAAS, Arctic Inst. N.Am., Explorers Club (sec., treas. Alaska/Yukon chpt. 1987-89, 91—, pres. 1990-91); mem. Am. Soc. Limnology and Oceanography, Am. Geophysical Union, Oceanography Soc., Rotary. Office: PO Box 80650 Fairbanks AK 99708-0650 also: U Alaska PO Box 707220 Fairbanks AK 99775

ALEXANDER-MINTER, RAE, cultural center director; d. Raymond Pace and Sadie Tanner (Mossell) Alexander; m. Thomas K. Minter, Jan. 29, 1971. BS in Journalism and Polit. Theory, Boston U., 1965; MS in Early Childhood/Child Devel., Bank St. Coll. Edn., 1973; EdD in Edn. and Anthropology, U. Pa., 1981. Program specialist Sch. Dist. of Phila., 1970-72; project dir., prin. investigator U. Pa., Phila., 1972-77; sr. rsch. assoc. Nat. Inst. Edn., Washington, 1977-79; rsch. scientist Hawthorne Sch./Hawthorne Ctr. for Study of Lang., Washington, 1979-82; dir. rsch. and devel. Opportunities Industrialization Ctr. of N.Y., N.Y.C., 1982-84; scholar-in-residence Studio Mus. in Harlem, N.Y.C., 1986-89; sr. cons. Phila. Mus. Art, 1986-89; dir. pub. programs and edn. N.Y. Hist. Soc., N.Y.C., 1989-92; dir. Paul Robeson Cultural Ctr. Rutgers U., Piscataway, N.J., 1993—; adj. lectr. Bronx C. C., CUNY, N.Y.C., 1986-87; adj. asst. prof. Marymount Manhattan Coll., N.Y.C., 1983-84; lectr. in field; presenter radio and TV programs. Editor: Young and Black in America, 1970 and other publs. in field. Commr. N.Y. City Landmarks Preservation Commn., bd. chmn. Lehman Coll. Art Gallery, CUNY; bd. dirs. Wave Hill; standing com. N.Y. City Bd. Edn.; bd. dirs. med. Coll. of Pa. Black Women Physicians' Archives; adv. bd. Doing Art Together, others. Grantee in field from various sources, including Cleveland H. Dodge Found., N.Y. State Coun. on Arts, The Ford Found., U.S. Dept. Labor, Bicentennial Commn. of Pa. with The Rockfeller Found. and William Penn Found., and others. Fellow Am. Anthropol. Assn., Inst. for Edn. Leadership.

ALEXANDRE, KRISTIN KUHNS, public relations executive; b. Dayton, Ohio, July 15, 1948; d. James Edward and Faith (Colgan) Kuhns; m. Dick Gerrity (div. 1984); m. DeWitt Loomis Alexandre; children: James Andrew, Cynthia Lenox Banles. BA, Sweet Briar, 1968. Editor C.I.T. Finance Corp., N.Y.C., 1970-73; newscaster Channel 5 News, N.Y.C., 1973-74, Channel 13 News, N.Y.C., 1974-75; editor Champion Internat., N.Y.C., 1975-76; copy editor House Beautiful, N.Y.C., 1975-76; pub. rels. officer Economic Devel. Adminstrn. Puerto Rico, N.Y.C., 1976-80; pres. Kristin Alexandre Pub. Rels., N.Y.C., 1980—. Mem. New York Jr. League. Home: PO Box 367 Far Hills NJ 07931-0367

ALEXIOU, MARGARET BEATRICE, Greek studies educator; b. Birmingham, England, Mar. 25, 1939; d. George Derwent and Katharine Fraser (Stewart) Thomson; m. Christos Dimitriou Alexiou, July 14, 1961 (div. 1981); children: Dimitris George, Pavlos Michael. BA with honors, U. Cambridge, Eng., 1961, MA, 1964, PhD, 1967. Lectr. in Byzantine and Modern Greek U. Birmingham, 1964-76, sr. lectr., 1976-85; George Seferis prof. Modern Greek Studies Harvard U., Cambridge, Mass., 1986—. Author: The Ritual Lament, 1974; editor: (book) The Text and Its Margins, 1985; mem. editorial bd. Byzantine and Modern Greek Studies, 1976-85, Jour. Modern Greek Studies, 1986—; contbr. articles to profl. jours. Mem. Modern Greek Studies Assn. (mem. exec. com. 1986—), Newnham Coll. Alumni (assoc.). Office: Harvard U Dept Modern Greek Studies 319 Boylston Hall Cambridge MA 02138-6502

ALEXIS, CHRISTINA-JEAN, administrator; b. N.Y.C., Oct. 3, 1953; d. John Alexis and Matilda Dobratz. BA in Econs. and History, Iona Coll., 1976. Adminstrv. claim examiner, mgr. litigation support N.Y.C. Transit Authority Dept., Bklyn., 1981—; claim agt. Staten Island (N.Y.) Rapid Transit Operating Authority, 1985—. Recipient Disting. Svc. medal N.Y.C. Transit Authority, 1990, Cert. of Merit, 1989. Mem. Nat. R.R. Hist. Soc., Astron. Soc. Pacific, Royal Astron. Soc. Can., Balt. & Ohio R.R. Mus., Balt. & Ohio R.R. Hist. Soc. Office: NYC Transit Authority 130 Livingston St Brooklyn NY 11201

ALEXIS, RUPERTA, judge, lawyer; b. New Orleans, Jan. 19, 1953; d. Rupert Maylon and Celestine Verone (Nelson) A.; m. Napoleon Caldwell, Sept. 25, 1976; 1 child, Sekou Rashad Caldwell. BA, CUNY, 1974; JD, U. Puget Sound, 1981. Bar: Wash. 1982. Staff atty. Puget Sound Legal Assistance Found., Tacoma, 1981-83; adminstrv. law judge Office Adminstrv. Hearings, Seattle, 1983-90; dep. hearing examiner Office Hearing Examiner, Seattle, 1990-94; U.S. adminstrv. judge Office of Hearings and Appeals, Dallas, 1994—; arbitrator Wash. Arbitration and Mediation Svc., Seattle, 1988-94, King County Superior Ct., Seattle, 1989—; instr. Seattle Ctr. C.C., 1990-94; co-chair sub-com. Minority and Justice Commn., 1993-94; chair Bar Assn. Jud. Evaluation Com., 1992-94. Chair Paula Marcus/Odessa Brown Clinic, Seattle, 1992-94; sec. Seattle-Mombasa Sister City Assn., Seattle, 1993; v.p., bd. dirs. Seattle Emergency Housing Svc., 1993-94. Named Reginald Heber Smith Community Lawyer, Legal Svcs. Corp., Tacoma, 1981-83. Office: Office of Hearings and Appeals 10830 N Central Expwy Ste 480 Dallas TX 75231

ALEXOPOULOS, HELENE, ballet dancer; b. Chgo.. Studies with Maria Tallchief, Chgo.; student, Sch. Am. Ballet, N.Y.C., 1977—. Mem. corps de ballet N.Y.C. Ballet, 1978-84, soloist, 1984-89, prin. dancer, 1989—. created roles in Jerome Robbins' Glass Pieces, Antique Epigraphs, William Forsythe's Behind the China Dogs, 1988, Ib Andersen's Baroque Variations, 1988; performed in N.Y.C. Ballet's Balanchine Celebration, 1993; TV appearances include Dance in America, Live from Studio 8-H. Office: NYC Ballet Inc NY State Theater Lincoln Ctr Plz New York NY 10023*

ALFARO, CORDELIA ANN, quality assurance professional, nurse; b. Clear Lake, Wis., Jan. 26, 1938; d. Frank Ray Kuhn and Blanche Rachael (Lee) Nelson; m. Donald Arthur Weier, Mar. 1, 1958 (div. 1975); children: Daniel, Timothy, Jane, David, Kristin; m. Ciro Alfaro, May 5, 1982. RN, Hamline U., 1960; AD, Mass. Bay Community Coll., 1978; BA, Wellesley Coll., 1980; M in Liberal Arts, Harvard U., 1984. Nurse Midway Hosp., St. Paul, 1960-63, 64; ob-gyn. nurse Miller Hosp., St. Paul, 1964-69; nurse, supr. Monadnok Hosp., Peterborough, N.H., 1969-71; clin. coord. urban health clinics ABCD-Anti Poverty Orgn., Boston, 1986-88; quality assesement coord. Middlesex County Hosp., Waltham, Mass., 1988-93; CQI nursing coord. St. Elizabeth's Med. Ctr., Brighten, Mass., 1993—; Mem. Internat. Com. Family Planning, Nat. Assn. Family Planning, Local Family Planning Orgn., 1986-89. Com. mem. for resettlement of polit. refuges, Peace Luth. Ch., Wayland, Mass., 1976-79. Mem. AAUW, Nat. Assn. Healthcare Quality, Mass. Nurses Assn. Democrat.

ALFELD, BEVERLY ELLEN SCHOONMAKER, author, artist, educator, civic volunteer; b. Kingston, N.Y., Dec. 28, 1946; d. Donald LeFevre and Doris (Pine) Schoonmaker; children: Kimberly, Timothy. BA, SUNY, Cortland, 1968; MA, No. Ill. U., 1972, MFA, 1974. Lic. tchr., adminstr., Ill. Tchr. B.O.C.E.S., Truxton, N.Y., 1968-69, Streator (Ill.) High Sch., 1970-71; instr. No. Ill. U., DeKalb, 1976, Dist. 200 Schs., Woodstock, Ill., 1971-88; instr. weaving McHenry County C.C., 1973, 74, 76, quilting and applique, 1977, 78; instr. weaving, textile printing No. Ill. U., 1976; instr. macrame Harper Rainey Coll., Schaumburg, Ill., 1976; instr. quilting and applique Lake County C.C., 1977, 79; ins. agt. Woodmen Accident and Life, 1977-79; lectr. in field. Author poems. Foster parent Ctrl. Bapt. Home, Lake Villa, Ill., 1982-83; vol. Luths. for Life, Pregnancy Counseling Ctr., Palatine, Ill., 1983-88; fundraiser R.J. Meml. Fund, Children's Meml. Hosp., Chgo., 1986-94. Mem. DAR, Am. Field Svc., Ill. Art Edn. Assn., Ill. Women Adminstrs., Omicron Delta Kappa. Episcopalian. Office: PO Box 76 Accord NY 12404-0076

ALFIERI, LISA GWYNETH, ballet dancer, teacher; b. Mount Holly, N.J., Mar. 25, 1967; d. Donal John and Susan Elizabeth (Hocter) A. Scholarship student Pa. Ballet, Phila., 1982-85; from soloist to prin. Cleve. San Jose Ballet, 1985—; dancer New Steps, Cleve., 1990, Jackson (Miss.) Internat. Ballet Competition, 1990, Cain Park "Ohio Artists", Cleveland Heights, Ohio, 1991; tchr. Cleve. City Dance, 1991, West Dance Ctr., Lakewood, Ohio, 1991. Home: 12943 Clifton Blvd Cleveland OH 44107-1573 also: Cleve San Jose Ballet 1 Playhouse Sq Ste 330 1375 Euclid Ave Cleveland OH 44115*

ALFORD, DOLORES IDA M., nursing consultant; b. New Orleans, Sept. 13, 1928; d. Theodore Henry and Dolores Marie (Guerrero) Marsh; m. John Herbert Alford, Apr. 4, 1958. Diploma, Charity Hosp. Sch. Nursing, 1951; BS in Nursing Edn., La. State U., 1957; MSN, U. Tex., 1961; PhD, Columbia Pacific U., 1989. Cons. Tex. Dept. of Health, Austin, 1969-70; ind. cons. gerontic nursing Dallas, 1970—. Contbr. articles to profl. jours. Mem. ANA (site visitor accreditation unit), Tex. Nurses Assn. (vice chmn. gerontol. conf. group, coord. manpower project), Sigma Theta Tau. Home: 3184 Lockmoor Ln Dallas TX 75220-1630

ALFORD, JOAN FRANZ, entrepreneur; b. St. Louis, Sept. 16, 1940; d. Henry Reisch and Florence Mary (Shaughnessy) Franz; m. Charles Hebert Alford, Dec. 28, 1978; stepchildren: Terry, David, Paul. BS, St. Louis U., 1962; postgrad. Consortium of State U., Calif., 1975-77; MBA, Pepperdine U., 1987, postgrad., Fielding Inst., 1988—. Head user svcs. Lawrence Berkeley Lab., Calif., 1977-78, head software support and devel. Computer Ctr., 1978-82, dep. head, 1980-81; regional site analyst mgr. Cray Rsch., Inc., Pleasanton, Calif., 1982-83; owner, pres. Innovative Leadership, Oakland, Calif., 1983-91; realtor, assoc. Mason-McDuffie Real Estate, Inc., 1991—; bd. dirs. East Bay Regional Data, Inc., Oakland Multiple Listing Svc., also treas., 1994—; co-chair computer user com. OAR, 1992-93, chair, 1993-94; bd. dirs. Oakland's Multiple Listing Svc., treas., 1994—. Contbr. articles to profl. jours. Bd. dirs., sec. Vol. Ctrs. of Alameda County, 1985, chair nominating com., 1990-91, pres. bd. dirs., 1991—, Oakland Multiple Listing Svc., 1994—, treas. 1994; campaign mem. Marge Gibson for County Supr., Oakland, 1984; pres. bd. dirs. Vol. Ctrs. Alameda City, 1991-92; mem. Oakland Piedmont Rep. Orgn., Alameda County Apt. Owners Assn., 1982. Mem. Assn. Computing Machinery, Spl. Interest Group on Computer Pers. Rsch. (past chmn.), Nat. Assn. Realtors, Calif. Assn. Realtors, Oakland Assn. Realtors, Internat. Platform Assn., Small Owners for Fair Treatment. Republican. Clubs: Claremont Pool and Tennis, Lakeview, San Francisco Opera Guild. Avocations: swimming, skiing, opera, horseback riding, gardening. Home: 2605 Beaconsfield Pl Piedmont CA 94611-2501 Office: Mason McDuffie Real Estate Inc 342 Highland Ave Piedmont CA 94611

ALFORD, PAULA N., federal agency administrator; b. Monterey, Calif., Nov. 18, 1952; d. Paul and Thelma Nuschke; m. James K. Alford; 1 child, Karen Louise. BA, Scripps Coll., 1974; MPA, George Washington U., 1978. Fed. rels. assoc. Adv. Commn. Intergovernmental Rels., 1979-81; dir. fed. legislation and regulations Nat. Assn. Towns and Twps., 1982-86; cons. hazardous materials transp. and environ. issues, 1986-88; dir. external affairs Monitored Retrievable Storage Rev. Commn., 1988-89, Nuclear Waste Tech. Rev. Bd., Arlington, Va. Author various publs. in field. Mem. Pi Alpha Alpha. Office: Nuclear Waste Tech Review Bd 1100 Wilson Blvd Arlington VA 22209*

ALFORD, SYLVIA ELENA, human resources executive; b. Coral Gables, Fla., Nov. 22, 1954; d. Peter and Norma (Viera) Guarisco; m. Randall Lynn Alford, Aug. 27, 1983; 1 child, Pace Mercer. BS, Samford U., 1976. Asst. in personnel Fla. Dept. Banking and Fin., Tallahassee, 1978-80; dir. Fla. Realtors Polit. Action Com., Tallahassee, 1980-83; adminstrv. asst. Marine Resources Council East Cen. Fla., Melbourne, 1984-85; spl. asst. Brevard County Bd. of County Commrs., Melbourne, 1985-88; pers./EEO officer Brevard County Bd. County Commrs., Melbourne, Fla., 1988—. Coord. Fla. senatorial campaigns, Leon and Brevard Counties, 1976, 84; vol. coord. Haven for Children Inc., Satellite Beach, 1987-88; bd. dirs. Jr. League South Brevard, Melbourne, 1986-88, 93-94, Brevard County chpt. ARC, 1987-89; mem. distbn. bd. United Way Brevard County, 1986-87; chmn. community coun. com. Fla. Inst. Tech., Melbourne, 1988—; mem. lang. com. Space Coast Coun. Internat. Visitors, Melbourne, 1986-88. Mem. South Brevard Profl. Women's Network, Fla.-Colombia Ptnrs. (mem. bus. and industry com. 1984-85), Am. Bus. Women's Assn., Am. Assn. U. Women (v.p. 1986-87, parliamentarian 1987-88, recording sec. 1988—), Toastmasters (v.p. 1986-88), Circulo Cultural Hispano (treas. 1984-88) Rotary Ann, Phi Chi Theta. Republican. Southern Baptist. Home: 917 Plymouth Ct NE Palm Bay FL 32905-4563 Office: Brevard County Bd County Commrs 2725 St Johns St Melbourne FL 32940-6605

AL-HASHIMI, IBTISAM, oral scientist, educator; b. Karbala, Iraq; d. Hadi A. and Rabab H. Al-H. B Dental Sci., Sch. Dentistry, Baghdad, 1973; MS, SUNY, Buffalo, 1985, PhD, 1989. Diplomate in Oral Surgery. Registrar Sch. Dentistry, Baghdad, 1975-81; postdoctoral assoc. SUNY, Buffalo, 1984-88, asst. prof., 1988-89; asst. prof. U. Pacific, San Francisco, 1989-90; dir. stomatology lab. Baylor Coll. Dentistry, Dallas, 1991—, dir. salivery dysfunction clinic, 1992—; adv. com. mem. SS Found. (we. N.Y. chpt.) Buffalo, 1985-89, Dallas-Ft. Worth chpt., 1992—, mem. med. adv. bd. Author: Proceeding of the Second Dows Symposium, 1987; contbr. articles to profl. jours. Mem. AAAS, Am. Assn. Dental Schs., Internat. Assn. Dental Schs., Salivary Rsch. Group, N.Y. Acad. Scis., Platform Assn., Sigma Xi. Office: Baylor Coll Dentistry 3302 Gaston Ave Dallas TX 75246-2013

ALICE, MARY (MARY ALICE SMITH), actress; b. Indianola, Miss., Dec. 3, 1941; d. Sam and Ozelar (Jurnakin) Smith. BE, Chgo. State U.; studied with Lloyd Richards, Negro Ensemble Co., N.Y.C. Sch. tchr. Chgo. Theater debut Purlie Victorious, Chgo.; off-Broadway debut Trials of Brother Jero and the StrongBreed, Greenwich Mews Theatre, 1967; Broadway debut No Place to Be Somebody, Morosco Theatre, 1971; other N.Y.C. appearances include A Rat's Mass, 1969, The Duplex, 1972, Miss Julie, 1973, House Party, 1973, Black Sunlight, 1974, Terraces, 1974, Heaven and Hell's Agreement, 1974, In the Deepest Part of Sleep, 1974, Cockfight, 1977, Nongogo, 1978 (Obie award Village Voice 1979), Julius Caesar, N.Y. Shakespeare Festival, 1979 (Obie award Village Voice 1979), Player #9, Spell #7, N.Y. Shakespeare Festival, 1979, Zooman and the Sign, 1980, Glasshouse, 1984, Take Me Along, 1984, Fences, Goodman Theatre, Chgo., 1986, 46th St. Theatre, N.Y.C., 1987 (Antoinette Perry award for best featured actress in a play, Drama Desk award 1987), The Shadow Box, 1994; other theater appearances include Open Admissions, Long Wharf Theatre, New Haven, 1982, A Raisin in the Sun, Yale Repertory Theatre, 1984; film debut The Education of Sonny Carson, 1974; other film appearances include Sparkle, 1976, Teachers, 1984, Brat Street, 1984, To Sleep With Anger, 1990, Awakenings, 1990, Bonfire of the Vanities, 1990, A Perfect World, 1992, Life with Mikey, 1993, The Inkwell, 1994; appeared in TV films The Sty of the Blind Pig, 1974, Just an Old Sweet Song, 1976, This Man Stands Alone, 1979, Joshua's World, 1980, The Color of Friendship, 1981, The Killing Floor, 1984, Concealed Burmies, 1984, Charlotte Forten's Mission: Experiment on Freedom, 1984, The Women of Brewster Place, 1989, Laurel Avenue, 1993, The Mother, 1994, The Vernon Johns Story, 1994; TV series include: Sanford and Son, 1972, A Different World, 1988-89, I'll Fly Away (Emmy Award, Outstanding Supporting Actress in a Drama Series, 1993), 1991-1993. Mem. AFTRA, SAG, Actors' Equity Assn. Office: Ambrosio/Mortimer and Assocs Inc 9150 Wilshire Blvd Ste 175 Beverly Hills CA 90212*

ALIM, MARILYN PRYCE, management consultant and school administrator; b. L.A., Oct. 10, 1941; d. Edward Lyons and Woodia (Smith) Pryce; m. Skunder Boghossian (div. 1970); children: Aida, Edward; m. Khalil Abdel Alim; children: Camille, Melanie, Khalilah. Student, U. Paris, Paris, 1961; BA, Spelman Coll., 1963; postgrad., L'ecole du Cinema Francais, Paris, 1964; MBA, Nova Southeastern U., 1993. Pub. relations officer Ethiopian Tourist Orgn., Addis Ababa, 1966-68; dir. pub. relations Spelman Coll., Atlanta, 1968-69; internat. programs adminstr. Tuskegee (Ala.) U., 1981-91; French instr. Booker T. Washington High Sch., Tuskegee, 1991-93; acctg. ops. mgr. Macon County Bd. Edn., 1993—; founder, dir. A.M. Players, Washington, 1979-82; cons. Montgomery (Ala.) Media; cross-cultural coord. Ctrl. Am. Peace Scholarship, Tuskegee U., 1986-89. Producer: (videos) French for Francophones, 1983; writer, producer (musical) Oh, Freedom!, 1980; producer: (TV series) The African Connection, 1989, (documentaries) Cen. Am. Peace Scholarship at Tuskegee, 1986. Vol. French instr. Clara Muhammad Sch., Washington, 1979-82. Named Merrill scholar, Spelman Coll., Atlanta, 1961-67. Mem. Southeastern Assn. Sch. Bus. Ofcls., Ala. Assn. Sch. Bus. Ofcls., Assn. Internat. Educators, Assn. of MBA Execs., Nat. Black MBA Assn. Inc. Democrat. Home: 1508 Logan St Tuskegee Institute AL 36088-2212 Office: 3608 Martin Luther King Hwy Tuskegee AL 36083

ALKIRE, BETTY JO, artist, commercial real estate broker, marketing consultant; b. Kansas City, Mo., June 20, 1942; d. Robert Emmitt and Gladys Faye (Craigg) Sharp; m. Daniel Wayne Hedrick, Nov. 15, 1958 (div.); children—Diane Laurie, Lisa Kay, Brett, Darin, Julie; m. William Edgar Alkire, Sept. 23, 1975. Tchr. art Independence Adult Edn., Mo., 1967—; portrait artist Silver Dollar City Nat. Crafts Festival, 1971—; owner, operator portrait artist's concession Kansas City Worlds of Fun, 1972—; tchr. pvt. art classes, 1970—; tchr., lectr. mktg. art U. Mo. Extension Program, 1982—; cons. mktg. and life-planning for artists; broker and cons. comml. investment real estate. Contbr. articles in field to various mags. Mem. Mo. Arts Council, Table Rock Art Guild, Independent Profl. Artists Assn. (pres. 1980—). Methodist. Clubs: Rockaway Beach Ladies, Rockaway Beach Booster (Mo.). Avocations: local art and history, antiques, real estate. Home: Historic Taneywood Rockaway Beach MO 65740

ALKON, ELLEN SKILLEN, physician; b. Los Angeles, Apr. 10, 1936; d. Emil Bogen and Jane (Skillen) Rost; m. Paul Kent Alkon, Aug. 30, 1957; children: Katherine Ellen, Cynthia Jane, Margaret Elaine. BA, Stanford U., 1955; MD, U. Chgo., 1961; MPH, U. Calif., Berkeley, 1968. Diplomate Nat. Bd. Med. Examiners, Am. Bd. Pediatrics, Am. Bd. Preventive Medicine in Pub. Health. Chief sch. health Anne Arundel County Health Dept., Annapolis, Md., 1970-71; practice medicine specializing in pediatrics Mpls. Health Dept., 1971-73, dir. MCH, 1973-75, commr. health, 1975-80; chief preventive and pub. health Coastal Region of Los Angeles County Dept. Health Services, 1980-81; chief pub. health West Area Los Angeles County Dept. Health Services, 1981-85; acting med. dir. pub. health Los Angeles County Dept. Health, 1986-87, med. dir. pub. health, 1987-93; med. dir. Coastal Cluster Health Ctrs. L.A. County Dept. Health Svcs., 1993—; adj. prof. UCLA Sch. Pub. Health, 1981—; adminstr. vis. nurses service, Mpls., 1975-80. Fellow Am. Coll. Preventive Medicine, Am. Acad. Pediatrics; mem. So. Calif. Pub. Health Assn. (pres. 1985-86), Minn. Pub. Health Assn. (pres. 1978-79), Am. Pub. Health Assn., Calif. Conf. Local Health Officers (pres. 1990-91), Delta Omega. Office: Long Beach Comprehensive Health Ctr 1333 Chestnut Ave Long Beach CA 90813-2944

ALLAMONG, BETTY D., academic administrator; b. Morgantown, W.Va., Apr. 8, 1935; d. Lonnie R. and Jessie R. (Hoffman) Davis; m. Joseph K. Allamong, Sept. 12, 1954; 1 child, John Bradley. BS, W.Va. U., 1961, MA, 1964, PhD, 1971; student, Inst. for Ednl. Mgmt. Harvard U., 1984. Instr. biology Morgantown High Sch., W.Va., 1961-67; instr. edn. W.Va. U., Morgantown, 1965-67, instr. biology, 1967-72; asst. to full prof. Ball State U., Muncie, Ind., 1972-87, assoc. dean, scis. and humanities, 1981-86, acting dean, scis. and humanities, 1986-87; provost and v.p. acad. affairs Bloomsburg U., Pa., 1987-92; mem. Ind. Corp. for Sci. & Tech., 1983-87. Co-author: Energy for Life, 1976; author numerous lab. manuals; contbr. articles to profl.jours. Mem. Ind. Corp. Sci. & Tech., 1983-87. Recipient Women of Achievement edn. award Women in Comms. Inc., Muncie, 1981. Mem. Muncie-Del. County C. of C. (various coms.), AAAS, NSF (rev. Panel), Am. Soc. Plant Physiologists (midwest div.), Ind. Coll. Biology Tchrs. Assn., Sigma Xi; fellow Ind. Acad. Sci. Home: PO Box 577 Dellslow WV 26531-0577

ALLAN, ANN GOULD, library science educator; b. Youngstown, Ohio, Jan. 9, 1940; d. Charles Howard and Florilla (Tibbets) Gould; m. Aug. 17, 1963; children: Jennifer, Katherine, Matthew. BA, U. Mich., 1962; MLS, Simmons Coll., Boston, 1963; PhD in Libr. and Info Sci., Case Western Res. U., 1976. Bibliographer law sch. libr. U. Mich., Ann Arbor, 1963-64; bibliographer acquisitions dept. grad. libr. U. Mich., 1963-65; asst. head acquisitions Kent State U., Ohio, 1966-68; asst. univ. libr. Bierce Libr. U. Akron, Ohio, 1968-71; assoc. prof. libr. sci. Kent (Ohio) State U., 1975-93; prof. emeritus, libr. cons., 1993—; adv. com. State Libr. Catalog Com. for CD-ROM statewide catalog, Columbus, 1989. Contbr. articles to profl. jours.. Bd. dirs. Planned Parenthood of Medina-Summit-Portage Counties, Akron, 1988-90. Mem. Acad. Libr. Assn. Ohio (pres. 1982-82, Disting. Svc. award 1993), ALA, Assn. for Libr. and Info. Sci. Edn., Ohio Libr. Assn. (chmn. rsch. com. 1986-88), Jr. League, Garden Club Am. Home: 219 Ely Rd Akron OH 44313-4449

ALLAN, MARJORIE LEE GRIERSON, women's health nurse practitioner; b. Detroit, Jan. 28, 1956; d. Ralph Brooks and Mary Constance (Thurlow) Grierson; m. Paul Bradley Allan, Oct. 21, 1991. BSN, U. Ariz., 1978; MSN, Oreg. Health Scis. U., 1986. cert. HIV counselor and tester. Staff nurse Tucson Med. Ctr., Ariz., 1979; asst. head nurse Tucson Med. Ctr., 1980; staff nurse, transport team nurse Oreg. Health Scis. U., Portland, 1981-86; DON, nurse practitioner Sault Ste Marie Tribe of Chippewa Indians, Mich., 1986-89; nurse practitioner Coos County Health Dept., North Bend, Oreg., 1986; commdr. USPHS, Fairbank, 1986—; maternal-child health coord. nurse practitioner Tanana Chiefs Conf., Fairbanks, AK, 1989—; counselor and tester HIV State of Alaska, 1989—, State of Mich., 1986-89; guest lectr. Lake Superior State U., 1987-89. Mem. prodn. team (video) Healthy Choices-Sexual Wellness, 1992. vol. Planned Parenthood of So. Ariz., 1975-77, Chippewa County Health Fair, 1988-89, Alaska Helath Fair, 1990-93, United Methodist Youth Fellowship, 1994. Mem. Assn. Women's Health, Obstetric and Neonatal Nurses, Sigma Theta Tau. Methodist. Office: Chief Andrew Isaac Health Care Ctr 1638 Cowles St Fairbanks AK 99701

ALLARD, LINDA MARIE, fashion designer; b. Akron, Ohio, May 27, 1940; d. Carroll Preston and Zella Viola (Indoe) A. BFA, Kent State U., 1962, LHD (hon.), 1992. Designer Ellen Tracy, N.Y.C., 1962—; design critic Fashion Inst. Tech., N.Y.C.; vis. prof. Internat. Acad. Merchandising and Design, Chgo. Author: Absolutely Delicious cookbook, 1994. Bd. dirs. N. Y. adv. bd. Kent State U.; bd. dirs. Kent State U. Found. Bd. Recipient Dallas Fashion award Dallas Apparel Mart, 1986, 87, 94. Mem. Fashion Group Internat., Inc. (past bd. dirs.), Coun. Fashion Designers Am. Office: Ellen Tracy 575 7th Ave New York NY 10018

ALLARD, NANCI A., state legislator; b. Portland, Maine, Feb. 9, 1946. Student, U. N.H. Adminstrv. asst. Conway Village Fire Dist.; mem. N.H. State Senate, mem. pub. works com. Past selectman, mem. mcpl. budget com. Town of Conway. Mem. N.H. State Grange (dep. state master), Elmwood Grange # 314 (master, lectr.). Home: PO Box 31 Conway NH 03818-0031 Office: NH State Senate State Capitol Concord NH 03301*

ALLBEE, SANDRA MOLL, real estate broker; b. Reading, Pa., July 15, 1947; d. Charles Lewars and Isabel May (Ackerman) Frederici; m. Thomas J. Allbee, Oct. 18, 1975 (div. 1987). Exec. sec. Hamburg (Pa.) State Sch. and Hosp., 1965-73; regional mgr. Am. Bus. Service Corp., Newport Beach, Calif., 1973-78; v.p. T.A.S.A., Inc., Long Beach, Calif., 1978-86; realtor Very Important Properties, Inc., Rolling Hills Estates, Calif., 1986-90, Re/Max Palos Verdes Realty, Rolling Hills Estates, Calif., 1990—. Bd. dirs., v.p. Nat. Coun. on Alcoholism, Torrance, Calif., 1987; pres. Rollingwood Homeowners Assn., Rolling Hills Estates, Calif., 1985-92. Mem. Palos Verdes Rep. Women's Club (bd. dirs. 1989-94). Office: Re/Max Palos Verdes Realty 4030 Palos Verdes Dr N Ste 104 Rllng Hls Est CA 90274-2526

ALLBRIGHT, KARAN ELIZABETH, psychologist, consultant; b. Oklahoma City, Okla., Jan. 28, 1948; d. Jack Gahnal and Irma Lolene (Keesee) A. BA, Oklahoma City U., 1970, MAT, 1972; PhD, U. So. Miss., 1981. Cert. sch. psychologist, psychometrist; lic. psychologist, Okla., Ark. Psychol. technician Donald J. Bertoch, Ph.D., Oklahoma City, 1973-76; asst. adminstr. Parents' Assistance Ctr., Oklahoma City, 1976-77; psychology intern Burwell Psycho-ednl. Ctr., Carrollton, Ga., 1980-81; staff psychologist Griffin Area Psychoednl. Ctr., Ga., 1981-85; clinic dir. Sequoyah County Guidance Clinic, Sallisaw, Okla., 1985-88; psychologist Baker Psychiatric Clinic, Ft. Smith, Ark., 1988-90; cons. Harbor View Mercy Hosp., 1988-90, Bethany Hosp. Pavilion, 1992—; pvt. practice, Oklahoma City, 1990—; lectr. various orgns.; bd. dirs. workshops. Mem. Task Force to Prevent Child Abuse, Fayette County, Ga., 1984-85, Task Force on Family Violence, Spalding County, Ga., 1983-85; cons. Family Alliance (Parents Anonymous) Sequoyah County, Okla., 1985-88; assoc. bd. dirs. Lyric Theatre. Named Outstanding Young Women in Am., 1980. Mem. APA, Southeastern Psychol. Assn., Nat. Assn. Sch. Psychologists (cert. sch. psychologist), Okla. Psychol. Assn., Play Therapy Assn., Nat. Assn. Health Svc. Providers in Psychology, Psi Chi, Delta Zeta (chpt. dir. 1970-72). Democrat. Presbyterian. Home: 3941 NW 44th St Oklahoma City OK 73112-2517 Office: Northwest Mental Health Assocs 3832 N Meridian Ave Oklahoma City OK 73112-2820

ALLEE, NANCY JANE, reference librarian; b. Greencastle, Ind.; d. Walter L. and Peggy J. (Matlock) A. BA, DePauw U., 1985; MLS, Ind. U., 1986; MPH, U. Okla., 1994. Reference libr. Northeastern State U., Tahlequah, Okla., 1987—; presenter in field. Reviewer (video reviews) Video Rating Guide for Libraries, 1990—. Actress Tahlequah Community Playhouse, 1988— (Best Actress 1988); bd. dirs. Arts Coun. Tahlequah, 1992-93, Habitat for Humanity, 1993-94. Mem. ALA, APHA, MLA, Acad. Health Info. Profls., Assn. Visual Sci. Librs., Phi Beta Kappa, Phi Delta Kappa (sec. Tahlequah chpt. 1988-89, pres. 1989-90). Office: John Vaughan Libr Northeastern State U Tahlequah OK 74464

ALLEMAN, AURELIA RUSHTON (LEA ALLEMAN), business executive; b. Fortville, Ind., Sept. 30, 1928; d. Frank M. and Mary M. (Davis) Rushton; m. Zachary T. Bunch, June 5, 1950; children: Zachary Taylor, Tanja Flame, Freeman Enmeier, Olivia Cutcher; m. Ralph J. Alleman, May 7, 1973; children: Stephanie Miller, Bruce, Mark. Student Fortville, Ind. pub. schs. Owner, pres. Be Wise, Inc., Indpls., 1956-62, Miracles Happen, Inc., 1963-67, 20th Century Computer Matching, 1965-73; v.p. Dip-Er-Do Plane Co., Fort Lee, N.J., 1976-77; adminstr. Mgmt. Cleaning Controls, Inc., Chgo., 1981-84; 1st v.p. Am. Indsl. Cleaning Co., Inc., Chgo., 1986-87, exec. v.p. 1987—; dir. ASQ Clubs; chmn. Lee Parker Enterprises, Inc. Mem. LVW, Am. Bus. Women (ednl. com. mem., 1973-74). Author: How to Happily Kiss the Singles Scene Goodbye, 1979. Home: 5100 N Marine Dr Chicago IL 60640-3274 Office: Berman Sales Co Inc 1728 S Michigan Ave Chicago IL 60616-1283 also: Am Indsl Cleaning Co Inc 1730 W Belmont Ave Chicago IL 60657

ALLEMANN, SABINA, ballet dancer; b. Bern, Switzerland. Student, Nat. Ballet Sch., Toronto, Ont., Can., 1971-80. With Nat. Ballet Can., 1980-89, 2d soloist, 1982-84, 1st soloist, 1984-88, prin. dancer, 1988-89; prin. guest artist San Francisco Ballet Co., 1988-89, prin. dancer, 1989—; Performed in Toronto's Internat. Festival, 1984; in Reykjavik Arts Festival, Iceland, 1990. Repertoire includes (with San Francisco Ballet) The Sleeping Beauty, Swan Lake, Con Brio, Valses Poeticos, Menuetto, Reflections of Saint Joan, Handel -- A Celebration, Le Quattro Stagioni, Forevermore, La pavane Rouge, Tagore, Dark Elegies, Filling Station, La fille mal gardée, Job, The End, Nutcracker, Rodeo, Serenade, Symphony in C, Glinka Pas de Trois, The Four Temperaments, Who Cares?, Pulcinella, Seeing Stars, Connotations; (with other companies) Napoli, Symphony in C, The Four Temperaments, Serenade, La Bayadere, Act II, Alice, The Merry Widow, Les Sylphides, La Ronde; appeared in film Onegin, 1986. Office: San Francisco Ballet 455 Franklin St San Francisco CA 94102-4471*

ALLEN, ALICE, public relations and marketing executive; b. N.Y.C., May 31, 1943; d. C. Edmonds and Helen (McCreery) A.; 1 child, Helen. Student, Conn. Coll., 1961. Sr. v.p. Alice Allen, Inc., N.Y.C., 1970-83, Robert Marston, N.Y.C., 1983-84, Cunningham & Walsh, N.Y.C., 1984-86, Carl Byoir (acquired by Hill & Knowlton), N.Y.C., 1986, Hill & Knowlton, N.Y.C., 1986-88; pres., owner Allen Comms. Group, Inc., N.Y.C., 1988—. Bd. dirs. Family Dynamics, N.Y.C., 1976-78, Veritas, 1980-85; v.p. Junior League, N.Y.C., 1975-76; mem. adv. bd. Enterprise Found., 1992—; mem. Women's Media Group. Mem. Women in Comms., Assn. Book Travelers, Publicity Club of N.Y., Pub. Rels.Soc. Am., Pub. Publicity Assn. (pres. 1969-71). Home: 320 E 72nd St New York NY 10021-4769 Office: Allen Comms Group Inc 770 Lexington Ave New York NY 10021-8165

ALLEN, ALICE CATHERINE TOWSLEY, public relations professional, writer, consultant; b. N.Y.C., July 26, 1924; d. George Everett and Alice Sophia (Kunkeli) Goldsmith; m. Harold Dulmage Towsley, Jan. 4, 1940 (div. 1942); m. Charles Kissam Allen, Jan. 20, 1973. Student, U. Hawaii, 1941-42. Writer Honolulu Advertiser, 1942-47; advt. mgr. Paterson Morning Call, Paterson, N.J., 1949-52; publ. cons. N.Y. (N.Y.C.) Herald Tribune, 1953; assoc. editor Mayfair, Travel, Fashion mags., N.Y.C., 1953-54; pub. editor Assoc. Jr. Leagues, Inc., N.Y.C., 1954-59; editor, asst. pub. Doctor's Wife mag., N.Y.C., 1959-65; pub. relations dir., editor Am. Field Svc. Internat., N.Y.C., 1967-72; free-lance writer, pub. cons. N.Y.C., 1973—. Recipient award for outstanding copy promotion Blood Bank Hawaii, 1944, Golden Poet award World of Poetry, 1989, Editor's Choice award for Outstanding Achievement, Nat. Libr. of Poetry, 1994. Mem. Overseas Press Club Am., ASCAP. Republican. Home and Office: 325 E 41st St New York NY 10017-5955

ALLEN, ANN CHASE, art history educator, consultant; b. Hanover, N.H., Sept. 26, 1934; d. Thelbert Alger and Madeline Elizabeth (Kendall) Chase; m. Jonathan Allen, Oct. 29, 1960; children: Jay, Douglas. BA in English Lit., U. N.H., 1956; MA in Art History, Boston U., 1988. Art gallery speaker Davis Mus. & Cultural Ctr., Wellesley (Mass.) Coll., 1972—; adj. lectr. Mus. Fine Arts, Boston, 1991—; assoc. curator MIT Mus., Cambridge, 1988-89. Home: 10 Hampshire St Newton MA 02165-2946

ALLEN, ANNA MARIE, financial executive; b. Ft. Scott, Kans., Aug. 3, 1955; d. Harold Laverne and Dorothy Arlene Kirk; m. John Leroy Allen, Sept. 18, 1982. AA, Johnson County C.C., Overland Park, Kans., 1976; BSBA in Fin., Pittsburg (Kans.) State U., 1979; student, Ohio State U., 1993—. CPA, Kans. Asst. teller supr. Kans. Nat. Bank & Trust, Prairie Village, 1975-77; bookkeeper Foodtown, Pittsburg, 1978-79; sr. v.p. tax GRA, Inc., Merriam, Kans., 1979-89, also bd. dirs.; sr. cons. Grant Thornton, Wichita, Kans., 1989-91; mgr. fin. ops. Legent Corp. (formerly Goal Systems Internat., Inc.), Columbus, Ohio, 1991-94; internat. treasury supr. CompuServe Inc., Columbus, 1994—. Mem. com. bd. Kansas City (Mo.) Ballet Guild, 1985-89; mem. Jr. League Kansas City, Wichita Jr. League, Columbus Jr. League; charter mem. Women's Resource Ctr. Johnson County, bd. dirs., 1986-89. Mem. AICPA, AAUW (bd. dirs. Shawnee Mission, Kans. chpt. 1979-89), Cen. Exch., Ctrl. Ohio Treasury Mgmt. Assn., Am. Legion Aux., Sawmill Athletic Club, Phi Kappa Phi, Delta Mu Delta. Baptist.

ALLEN, BARBARA, state legislator. Atty.; mem. Kans. Ho. of Reps. Republican. Home: 8136 Rosewood Dr Shawnee Mission KS 66208-5008 Office: Kans State Senate State Capital Topeka KS 66612*

ALLEN, BEATRICE, music educator, pianist; b. N.Y.C., June 30, 1917; d. Samuel and Rose (Krell) Hyman; m. Eugene Murray Allen, Jan. 23, 1937; children: Marlene Allen Galzin, Julian Lewis. Student NYU, 1933-36; diploma (scholar), Inst. Musical Arts, N.Y.C., 1939, postgrad. (scholar), 1939-40; diploma (fellow, letter commendation), Juilliard Grad. Sch., N.Y.C., 1943; BA magna cum laude Cedar Crest Coll., 1980. Mem. faculty prep. div. Juilliard Sch. Music, 1957-69, Moravian Coll., 1967-68, Northampton County Area Community Coll., 1968-70, Manhattan Sch. Music, 1969-89; mem. founding faculty Community Music Sch., Allentown, Pa., 1982—; artist-in-residence, condr. Tchrs. Workshop, Antioch Coll., Yellow Springs, Ohio, 1966; Bach lectr., recitals various univs.; concert appearances Town Hall, N.Y.C., Chautauqua, N.Y., others. Winner N.J. Artists contest, 1936. Mem. Music Tchrs. Nat. Assn. (program chmn. Lehigh Valley chpt. 1981-82), Pa. Music Tchrs. Assn. Address: 2100 Main St Bethlehem PA 18017-3752

ALLEN, BELLE, management consulting firm executive, communications company executive; b. Chgo.; d. Isaac and Clara (Friedman) A. AD in Edn., U. Chgo. Cert. conf. mgr. Internat. Inst. Conf. Planning and Mgmt., 1989. Cons., v.p., treas., dir. William Karp Cons. Co. Inc., Chgo., 1961-79, chmn. bd., pres., treas., 1979—; pres. Belle Allen Comms., Chgo., 1961—; reporter/writer CCA Press Svc., 1990—; v.p., treas., bd. dirs. Cultural Arts Survey Inc., Chgo., 1965-79; cons., bd. dirs. Am. Diversified Rsch. Corp., Chgo., 1967-70; v.p., sec., bd. dirs. Mgmt. Performance Systems Inc., 1976-77; cons. City Club Chgo., 1962-65, Ill. Commn. on Tech. Progress, 1965-67; mem. Ill. Gov.'s Grievance Panel for State Employees, 1979—; mem. grievance panel Ill. Dept. Transp., 1985—; mem. adv. governing bd. Ill. Coalition on Employment of Women, 1980-88; spl. program advisor President's Project Partnership, 1980-88; mem. consumer adv. coun. FRS, 1979-82; reporter CCA Press Svc., 1990—; panel mem. Free Press vs. Fair Trial Nat. Ctr. Freedom of Info. Studies Loyola U. Law Sch., 1993, mem. planning com. Freedom of Info. awards, 1993; conf. chair The Swedish Inst. Press Ethics: How to Handle, 1993. Editor: Operations Research and the Management of Mental Health Systems, 1968; contbr. articles to profl. jours. Mem. campaign staff Adlai E. Stevenson II, 1952, 56, John F. Kennedy, 1960; founding mem. women's bd. United Cerebral Palsy Assn., Chgo., 1954, bd. dirs., 1954-58; pres. Dem. Fedn. Ill., 1958-61; pres. conf. staff Eleanor Roosevelt, 1960; mem. Welfare Pub. Rels. Forum, 1960-61; bd. dirs., mem. exec. com., chmn. pub. rels. com. Regional Ballet Ensemble, Chgo., 1961-63; bd. dirs. Soc. Chgo. Strings, 1963-64; mem. Ind. Dem. Coalition, 1968-69; bd. dirs. Citizens for Polit. Change, 1969; campaign mgr. aldermanic election 42d ward Chgo. City Coun., 1969; mem. selection com. Robert Aragon Scholarship, 1991. Recipient Outstanding Svc. award United Cerebral Palsy Assn., Chgo., 1954, 55, Chgo. Lighthouse for Blind, 1986, Spl. Comms. award The White House, 1961, cert. of appreciation Ill. Dept. Human Rights, 1985, Internat. Assn. Ofcl. Human Rights Agys., 1985; selected as reference source Am. Bicentennial Rsch. Inst. Libr. Human Resources, 1973; named Hon. Citizen, City of Alexandria, Va., 1985. Mem. AAAS, NOW, AAAU, Am. Assn. Univ. Women, Affirmative Action Assn. (bd. dirs. 1981-85, chmn. mem. and programs com. 1981-85, pres. 1983—), Fashion Group (bd. dirs. 1981-83, chmn. Restrospective View of An Hist. Decade 1960-70, editor The Bull. 1981), Indsl. Rels. Rsch. Assn. (bd. dirs., chmn. personnel placement com. 1960-61), Sarah Siddons Soc., Soc. Personnel Adminstrs., Women's Equity Action League, Nat. Assn. Inter-Group Rels. Ofcls. (nat. conf. program 1959), Publicity Club Chgo. (chmn. inter-city rels. com. 1960-61, Disting. Svc. award 1968), Ill. C. of C. (community rels. com., alt. mem. labor rels. com. 1971-74), Chgo. C. of C. and Industry (merit employment com. 1961-63), Internat. Press Club Chgo. (charter 1992—, bd. dirs. 1992—), Chgo. Press Club (chmn. women's activities 1969-71), U. Chgo. Club of Met. Chgo. (program com. 1993—, chair summer quarter programs 1994), Soc. Profl. Journalists (Chgo. Headline Club 1992—, regional conf. planning com. 1993, co-chair Peter Lisagor awards 1993, program com. 1992—). Office: 111 E Chestnut St Chicago IL 60611

ALLEN, BESSIE MALVINA, music educator, church organist; b. LaKemp, Okla., Oct. 14, 1918; d. Percy J. and Mary Allen (Hagler) Gheen; m. Edgar Charles Allen, Aug. 29, 1940 (dec. May 1981); children: Stanley Charles, Stephen Wayne. BA in English, Tex. Woman's U., 1939; MA in Music, W. Tex. State U., 1970. Cert. secondary edn. Tchr. English Balko (Okla.) High Sch. and Jr. High Sch., 1939-40; pvt. practice Phillips, Tex., 1950-85; tchr. music Frank Phillips Coll., Borger, Tex., 1960-63, 65-73, 76-85; pvt. practice Borger, 1986—; organist First Bapt. Ch., Borger, 1947-65, Faith Covenant Ch.-Ind., Borger, 1970-81, First Christian Ch., Borger, 1981-82, Faith Covenant Ch., Borger, 1982—. Active Nat. Rep. Senatorial Com., Washington, 1988-91. Recipient Presdl. Order of Merit, Nat. Rep. Senatorial Com., 1991; McCulley Organ scholar, W. Tex. State U., Canyon, 1969. Mem. Music Tchrs. Nat. Assn., Tex. Fedn. Music Clubs, Amarillo Music Tchrs. Assn., Borger Music Club. Home and Office: 221 Inverness St Borger TX 79007-8215

ALLEN, BETTY (MRS. RITTEN EDWARD LEE, III), mezzo-soprano; b. Campbell, Ohio, Mar. 17, 1930; d. James Corr and Dora Catherine (Mitchell) A.; m. Ritten Edward Lee, III, Oct. 17, 1953; children: Anthony Edward, Juliana Catherine. Student, Wilberforce U., 1944-46; certificate, Hartford Sch. Music, 1953; pupil voice, Sarah Peck More, Zinka Milanov, Paul Ulanowsky, Carolina Segrera Holden; LHD (hon.), Wittenberg U., 1971; MusD (hon.), Union Coll., 1981; DFA (hon.), Adelphi U., 1990, Bklyn. Coll., 1991; LittD (hon.), Clark U., 1993; MusD (hon.), New Sch. Social Rsch., 1994. Faculty Phila. Mus. Acad., 1979, Manhattan Sch. Music, 1971, N.C. Sch. Arts, 1978-87; tchr. master classes Inst. Teatro Colon, 1985-86, Curtis Inst. Music, 1987—; exec. dir. Harlem Sch. Arts, 1979, now pres.; vis. faculty Sibelius Akademie, Helsinki, Finland, 1976; mem. adv. bd. music panel Amherst Coll.; mem. music panel N.Y. State Council of the Arts, Dept. State Office Cultural Presentations, Nat. Endowment Arts.; bd. dirs. Arts Alliance, Karl Weigl Found., Diller-Quaile Sch. Music, U.S. Com. for UNICEF, Manhattan Sch. Music, Theatre Devel. Fund, Children's Storefront; mem. adv. bd. Bloomingdale House of Music; bd. vis. artists Boston U.; bd. dirs., mem. exec. com. Carnegie Hall, Nat. Found. for Advancement in the Arts; bd. dirs. Chamber Music Soc. of Lincoln Ctr., N.Y.C. Housing Authority Orch., Independent Sch. Orch., N.Y.C. Opera CO., Joy in Singing, Arts & Bus. Coun.; mem. Mayor's adv. commn. Cultural Affairs. Appeared as soloist: Leonard Bernstein's Jeremiah Symphony, Tanglewood, 1951, Virgil Thomson's Four Saints in Three Acts, N.Y.C. and Paris, 1952, N.Y.C. Light Opera Co., 1954; recitalist, also soloist with major symphonies on tours including ANTA-State Dept. tours, Europe, N. Africa, Caribbean, Can., U.S., S.Am., Far East, 1954-, S.Am. tour, 1968, Bellas Artes Opera, Mexico City, 1970; recital debut, Town Hall, N.Y.C., 1958, ofcl. debuts, London, Berlin, 1958, formal opera debut, Teatro Colon, Buenos Aires, Argentina, 1964; U.S. opera debut San Francisco Opera, 1966; N.Y.C. opera debut, 1973, Mini-Met. debut, 1973; Broadway debut in Treemonisha, 1975; opened new civic theaters in San Jose, Calif., and Regina, Sask., Can., concert hall, Lyndon Baines Johnson Library, Austin,

Tex., 1971; artist-in-residence, Phila. Opera Co.; appeared with Caramoor Music Festival, summer 1965, 71, Cin. May Festival, 1972, Santa Fe Opera, 1972, 75, Canadian Opera Co., Winnipeg, Man., 1972, 77, Washington Opera Co., 1971, Tanglewood Festival, 1951, 52, 53, 67, 74, Oslo, The Hague, Montreal, Kansas City, Houston and Santa Fe operas, 1975, Saratoga Festival, 1975, Casals Festival, 1967, 68, 69, 76, Helsinki Festival, 1976, Marlboro Festival, 1967-74, numerous radio and TV performances, U.S., Can., Mex., Eng., Germany, Scandinavia; rec. artist, London, Vox, Capitol, Odeon-Pathe, Decca, Deutsche Grammophon, Columbia Records, RCA Victor records; represented U.S. in Cultural Olympics, Mexico City. Recipient Marian Anderson award, 1953-54, Nat. Music League Mgmt. award, 1953, 52 St Am. Festival Duke Ellington Meml. award, 1989, Bowery award Bowery Bank, 1989, Harlem Sch. of the Arts award Harlem Sch. and Isaac Stern, 1990, Womans Day Celebration award St. Thomas Episcopal Ch., 1990, St. Thomas Ch. award St. Thomas Catholic Ch., 1990, Men's Day Celebration award St. Paul's Ch., 1990, Martell House of Segram award Avery Fisher Hall, 1990; named Best Singer of Season Critics' Circle, Argentina and Chile, 1959, Best Singer of Season Critics' Circle, Uruguay, 1961; Martha Baird Rockefeller Aid to Music grantee, 1953, 58; John Hay Whitney fellow, 1953-54; Ford Found. concert soloist grantee, 1963-64. Mem. NAACP, Urban League, Hartford Mus. Club (life), Am. Guild Mus. Artists, Actors Equity, AFTRA, Silvermine Guild Artists, Jeunesses Musicales, Gioventu Musicale, Student Sangverein Trondheim, Unitarian-Universalist Women's Fedn., Nat. Negro Musicians Assn. (life), Concert Artists Guild, Met. Opera Guild, Amherst Glee Club(hon. life), Union Coll. Glee Club (hon. life), Met. Mus. Art, Mus. Modern Art, Am. Mus. Natural History, Sigma Alpha Iota (hon.). Unitarian-Universalist. Clubs: Cosmopolitan, Second. Office: Harlem Sch of Arts 645 St Nicholas Ave New York NY 10030-1098*

ALLEN, BONNIE LYNN, pension actuary; b. L.A., Oct. 2, 1957; d. David and Lucille M. (Scott) A. B.A. summa cum laude, UCLA, 1979. Math. tutor, L.A., 1971—; reader math. dept. UCLA, 1977-79; pension actuary Martin E. Segal Co., L.A., 1980-92. Author short stories and poetry. Active mentor program UCLA Alumni Assn., 1978-79, bd. dirs. Westside Bruins. Mem. Math. Assn. Am., Am. Math. Soc., L.A. Film Tchrs'. Assn., Acad. Sci. Fiction, Fantasy and Horror Films, UCLA Alumni Assn. (life), Westside Bruin Club (bd. dirs.), L.A. Actuarial Club, Phi Beta Kappa.

ALLEN, CATHERINE MACDONALD, artist, communications company executive; b. Winchester, Va., Aug. 8, 1949; d. Douglas Brooke and Nancy Grey (Stevens) A.; m. Howard Goodman, Aug. 24, 1980; children: Aaron, Michael. BA with gen. honors, Am. U., 1971; MFA in Painting, Boston U., 1976. Grad. asst., instr. printmaking Boston U., 1975-76; mem. faculty Mt. Wachusett C.C., Gardner, Mass., 1977-79, Coll. of New Rochelle, 1980-81; dir. core program N.Y. Feminist Art Inst., N.Y.C., 1980-81, bd. dirs., 1980-89, dir. spl. events, 1980-82, dir. visual artists exch., 1983, 87; lectr. Calif. State U., Long Beach, 1991; CEO, Goodman Comm. West, Calabasas, Calif., 1991—. One-woman shows include SOHO 20 Gallery, N.Y.C., 1985, 86, 89; 2-person show John Jay Coll., CUNY, 1994; 3-person show Wade Gallery, L.A., 1990; exhibited in group shows, including Ny Carlsberg Mus., Copenhagen, 1980, Smithsonian Instn., Washington, 1981, Everson Mus., Syracuse, N.Y., 1984, South Bay Contemporary Mus. Art, Torrance, Calif., 1992, L.A. Festival, 1993; represented in permanent collections South Bay Contemporary Mus. Art, Nat. Mus. Women in Arts Libr., Boston U., also corps. Yaddo fellow, 1982, fellow Hand Hollow Found., 1983, Nat. Endowment for Arts, 1989-90. Mem. Coll. Art Assn., Women's Caucus for Art. Home and Studio: 27061 Esward Dr Calabasas CA 91301

ALLEN, CHERI, legislative staff director; b. Washington, Feb. 14, 1953. BA in Psychology, U. Md., 1983. Program asst. gen. revenue sharing U.S. Dept. Treas., 1972-81; customer svc. rep. City of North Miami Beach, Fla., 1984-87; computer applications asst., statistician Congl. Rsch. Svc., 1987-89; exec. dir. Sen. Rep. Policy Com., 1991—. Office: Sen Rep Policy Com 347 Senate Russell Office Bldg Washington DC 20510*

ALLEN, DEBORAH COLLEEN, state legislator; b. Denver, Jan. 25, 1950; d. Anton Jr. and Esther Ochs; m. Bob Allen; 1 child, Dallas. Student, Aurora C.C. Jr. acct. Am. TV & Comm.; bus mgr. Deer Trail Pub. Schs., sch. bus driver; data entry clk. United Banking Svcs.; caretaker Evergreen Cemetery; owner, mgr. Custom Data Sys. Specialists, Aurora, 1979—; mem. Colo. Ho. of Reps., 1992—, mem. various coms., 1993—. Former sec., vice chmn., chmn. Arapahoe County Rep. Party; past pres. Aurora Rep. Forum; active Arapahoe County Chmn.'s Cir.; block capt. Am. Cancer Soc., Am. Arthritis Found. Recipient 5 Yr. Award as Leathercraft Instr., 4-H. Mem. Nat. Fedn. Rep. Women, Colo. Fedn. Rep. Women, South Metro C. of C., Colo. Rep. 250 Club, Arapahoe Rep. Men's Club. Republican. Home: 923 S Ouray St Aurora CO 80017-3152 Office: Colo House of Reps State Capitol Denver CO 80203*

ALLEN, DIANA D., insurance agent, author; b. Dallas, Nov. 26, 1945; d. William S. and Pearl P. (Sessions) Dandridge; m. Edwin Richard Allen, Dec. 23, 1966; children: Reagan, Ryan. BS, U. Ark., 1967. Tchr. elem. sch. Lincoln/McKinley Sch., Enid, Okla., 1967-72; real estate agent House of Hough Agy., Enid, 1972-75; ins. agent Dick Allen Ins. Co., Inc., Enid, 1990—. Author: Gourmet: The Quick and Easy Way, 1992. Asst. pack master, den leader Boy Scouts Am., Glenwood Sch., Enid, 1981-85; sustaining chmn. Jr. Welfare League, Enid, 1979, 94; head Parent of Okla. Tiger Football Parents Orgn., Columbia, Mo., 1994—; bd. dirs. Arts and Humanities Coun., Enid, 1994—; mem. Rep. Women's Club; tchr. Bible and Sunday Sch.; sponsor Bravettes Pep Club, 1993-95; pres. Enid High Sch. Parent Tchr. Student Assn., 1993-94, parliamentarian, 1994-95. Mem. PEO (pres. 1987-88), DAR, Ladies Shrine (v.p. 1970), Oakwood Ladies Golf Assn. (v.p. 1992-93), Bravettes Pep Club (sponsor 1994—), PTA (pres. 1993-94), Kappa Alpha Theta (alumni pres. 1969, 85). Baptist. Home: 1614 Quailwood Dr Enid OK 73703

ALLEN, DORIS, state legislator; b. Mo., May 26, 1936. Student, U. Wyo., Long Beach C.C., Golden West Coll. Lic. real estate agent. Mem. Calif. State Assembly, 1982—, mem. various coms.; mem. Calif. Planning Coun. Mental Health Master Plan, 1990. Active Orange County Commn. Status Women, Met. Water Dist. Speakers' Bur., West Orange County Consortium Spl. Edn.; founder, dir. Orange County Bus-Bloc, 1978; mem. adv. bd. Casa de Bienvenidos; bd. dirs. Coastline C.C. Found., Huntington Beach Conf. and Visitors Bur.; trustee Huntington Beach Union High Sch., 1976-81, pres., 1980. Recipient Spl. Recognition, Calif. Assn. Work Experience Educators, 1987, Nat. Coalition Marine Conservation, 1987, 90, Soc. Preservation Bighorn Sheep, 1988, Calif. Spl. Edn. Local Planning Area Adminstrs., 1989, Order of Jassid, Sierra Pacific Flyfisher, 1988, Project Workability award State Dept. Edn., 1988, Conservation award Internat. Game Fish Assn., 1992; named Legislator of Yr., Sportsmen's Coun. Ctrl. Calif., 1986, Calif. Bus. Educators Assn., 1987, 91, Calif. Indsl. and Tech. Edn. Assn., Inc., 1989, Pacific region Nat. Coalition Marine Conservation, 1989, Pub. Ofcl. of Yr., Orange County chpt. Am. Soc. Pub. Adminstrn., 1987, Woman of Distinction, Westminster Soroptimist Internat., 1987, Personality of Yr., Hunting and Fishing News, 1989, Nat. Legislator of Yr., Am. Fishing Tackle Mfrs. Assn., 1991. Mem. Am. Bus. Women's Assn., Calif. Elected Women;s Assn. Edn. and Rsch., L.A. Rod and Reel Club (hon.). Office: 16052 Beach Blvd Ste 160 Huntington Beach CA 92647-3808*

ALLEN, DOROTHEA, secondary education educator; b. Rockaway, N.J., Apr. 30, 1919; d. Harrison Engleman and Caroline (Tierney) A. AB, Montclair (N.J.) U., 1941, MA, 1949. Cert. secondary, sci., math. tchr., counselor, supr., prin., N.J. Tchr. sci. and math. Denville (N.J.) Jr. High Sch., 1942-46; tchr. sci. Boonton (N.J.) High Sch., 1946—, supr. sci. dept., 1978—; lab. technician Drew Chem. Corp., Boonton, 1942-47; tech. asst. Bell Telecommunications Lab., Whippany, N.J., 1956; rsch. scientist Warner Lambert Rsch. Inst., Morris Plains, N.J., 1959-62; tchr. sci. enrichment Boonton Summer Sch., 1963-85; curriculum developer Morris County Vo-cat.-Tech. Sch., Denville, 1987; conf. program presenter, 1978, 85; project evaluator sci. fairs, N.J., 1970—; program evaluator Mid. States Assn., 1973, 79; facilitator Ptnrs. in Edn. Program; spkr., promoter Media Ctr. Open House; cons., reviewer Am. Biol. Tchr. mag., 1975—; com. mem. Sch. Articulation Program, Boonton Schs., 1991—; spkr., resource person Career Confs.; sponsor Student Showcase of Excellence in Sci., 1990—; faculty sponsor, mentor h.s. students, 1966—; mentor Alt. Rt. Program Tchrs., N.J. Author: Research Projects/High School Biology, 1971, Biology Teacher's Desk Book, 1979, Science Activities for Every Month of the Year, 1981, Science Demonstrations for Elementary Classrooms, 1988, Science Experiments on File, 1989, Hands-On Science, 1991, More Science Experiments on File, 1991; contbr. numerous articles to profl. jours. Organizer Am. Dental Health Clinic, Boonton, 1968-72; mem. career com. N.J. div. Theobald Smith Soc., 1975-76; fund raiser Am. Hemophilia Found., Rockaway, N.J., 1985—; cons. Community Mid. Sch. Planning Com., Boonton, 1988-90. Recipient citation Boonton Bd. Edn., 1972, Spotlight award, 1980-86, Tchr. of Yr. award 1984, 90; Outstanding Biology Tchr. award Nat. Assn. Biology Tchrs., 1972, Outstanding Sci. Tchr. award Rsch. Assn. N.Am., 1980, 86, Disting. Citizen's award Town of Rockaway, 1984, Gov.'s and Edn. award N.J. Dept. Edn., 1984, Morris County Tchr. of Yr. award, 1990, Predl. award NSF, 1984, Cert. of honor State of N.J., 1985,. Mem. NEA, ASCD, NSTA, Nat. Assn. Secondary Sch. Prins., Assn. Presdl. Award Winners in Sci. Tchg., N.J. Edn. Assn., N.J. Prins. and Suprs. Assn., N.J. Acad. Alliance for Math. and Sci., N.J. Dept. Edn. Exec. Acad., Morris Area Sci. Alliance. Home: 115 Jackson Ave Rockaway NJ 07866-3039

ALLEN, EDNA LOUISE, physical education educator; b. Dallas, June 2, 1940; d. Abner and Hattie Mae (Barker) A.; m. Curry C. Hill, Dec. 5, 1964 (div.). BS, Prairie View A&M U., 1963. Tchr. phys. edn. Dallas Ind. Sch. Dist., 1963—. Recipient Outstanding Leadership Edn. award, 1990-91, Outstanding Svc. Edn. award, 1990-91. Mem. Alliance Dallas Educators, Dallas Assn. Phys. Edn., Dance and Recreation, Nat. Assn. Negro Bus. and Profl. Women's Clubs Inc. (life), South Ctrl. Bus. and Profl. Women's Clubs (rec. sec. 1980), Dallas Met. Bus. and Profl. Women's Clubs (pres. 1992, Outstanding Leadership award 1982), Delta Sigma Theta (Violets and Roses orgn. met. Dallas Alumnae chpt.). Democrat. Baptist. Home: 1317 Fern Glen Trail Dallas TX 75241 Office: Rufus C Burleson Elem Sch Dallas Ind Sch Dist 6300 Elam Rd Dallas TX 75217

ALLEN, ELIZABETH MARESCA, marketing executive; b. Red Bank, N.J., Jan. 4, 1958; d. Paul William Michael and Roberta Gertrude (Abbes) Maresca. Student, Brookdale Community Coll., 1976-77; A Bus. Adminstrn., Tidewater C.C., 1988; student, Va. Wesleyan Coll., 1994—. Systems analyst Methods Research Corp., Farmingdale, N.J., 1977-79; div. mgr. Abacus Bus. Svcs., Inc., Virginia Beach, Va., 1979—. Bd. dirs. Arthritis Found., Norfolk, Va., 1986-90; v.p. Charlestowne Civic League, Virginia Beach, 1983-84, Plantation Lakes Homeowners Assn., Chesapeake, Va., 1992—; advisor Commonwealth Coll., Norfolk, 1984-91; del. Va. Rep. Conv., 1993—. Mem. Women's Network Hampton Roads (publicity chmn. 1988-91, chmn. publicity for Job Fair 1989), Hampton Roads C. of C. (com. chmn. 1985, 88), Williamsburg Area C. of C. (exhibit chmn. 1987). Republican. Roman Catholic. Office: Abacus Bus Svcs Inc 5620 Va Beach Blvd Virginia Beach VA 23462-5631

ALLEN, FLORENCE JEAN, hospital radiology administrator; b. Malone, N.Y., Feb. 20, 1940; d. Milton Wilson and Florence Irene (Fish) A.; 1 child, Brent D. Diploma in radiol. tech., X-Ray Guild, 1961; student, Russell State U., 1989. Registered sonographer; lic. radiol. technologist. Radiol. technologist Children's Hosp., Albany, N.Y., 1963-69, Albany Meml. Hosp., 1970-73; adminstr. Cesar Wong med. office, Troy, N.Y., 1973-75; radiol. technologist, mgr./adminstr. med. imaging Bellevue-The Woman's Hosp., Schenectady, N.Y., 1976—; adminstr., cons. N.E. Diagnostic Imaging Cons., Rexford, N.Y., 1986-88. Mem. Am. Healthcare Radiology Adminstrs., Am. Soc. Radiol. Technologists, Am. Registry Diagnostic Med. Sonographers. Home: 17 Ronald Dr Poestenkill NY 12140-2109 Office: Bellevue Woman's Hosp 2210 Troy Rd Schenectady NY 12309-4725

ALLEN, FRANCES ELIZABETH, computer scientist; b. Peru, N.Y., Aug. 4, 1932; d. John Abram and Ruth Genevieve (Downs) A. BS, State U. N.Y., Albany, 1954; MA, U. Mich., 1957; DSc (hon.), U. Alta., 1991. Fellow IBM Research Lab., Yorktown Heights, N.Y., 1957—; adj. assoc. prof. N.Y. U., 1970-72; mem. computer sci. adv. bd. NSF, 1972-75, cons., 1975-78; lectr. Chinese Acad. Scis., 1973, 77; IEEE disting. visitor, 1973-74; cons. prof. Stanford U., 1977-78; chancellor's disting. vis. lectr., U. Calif., Berkeley, 1988-89. IBM Corp. fellow, 1989. Fellow IEEE, Am. Acad. Arts and Scis., Assn. Computing Machinery (nat. lectr. 1972-73); mem. NAE, Programming Sys. and Langs. (Paper award 1976). Home: Finney Farm Croton On Hudson NY 10520 Office: IBM Corp PO Box 704 Yorktown Heights NY 10598-0704

ALLEN, FRANCES MICHAEL, publisher; b. Charlotte, N.C., Apr. 7, 1939; d. Thomas Wilcox and Lola Frances (Horne) A.; m. Joseph Taylor Lisenbee, Feb. 24, 1955 (div. 1957); 1 child, Leslie Autice. Abilene (Tex.) Christian Coll., 1954-56, Chico (Calif.) State U., 1957-59. Art dir. B&E Publs., L.A., 1963-65; editor B&E Publs., 1969-70; art dir. Tiburon Corp., Chgo., 1970-75; founder, editor Boxers, Internat., L.A., 1970-76; editor The Hound's Tale, 1974, Saints, Incorp., 1974-76; founder, editor Setters, Incorp., Costa Mesa, Calif., 1975-85; founder, owner Michael Enterprises, Midway City, Calif., 1976—; editor Am. Cocker Rev., Midway City, 1980-81; editor, publisher, ptnr. Am. Cocker Mag., 1981—; editor, co-publisher Sporting Life, 1991—. Author: The American Cocker Book, 1989; editor The Sporting Life, 1991—; illustrator: The First Five Years, 1970, The Aftercare of the Ear, 1975, The Shenn Simplicity Collection, 1976, The Miniature Pinscher, 1967; prin. works include mag. and book covers for USA, most widely published show dog artist world wide, past 15 yrs. Recipient Dog World Award Top Producer, 5 times, 1966-88, numerous 1st awards in art fairs. Mem. Dog Writers Assn. Am. Republican. Mem. Ch. of Christ. Home and Office: 14531 Jefferson St Midway City CA 92655-1030

ALLEN, GAIL A., pediatrics educator; b. Nashville, May 5, 1960; d. Harvey H. Allen and Simona Atkins. BA in Biology, Oberlin Coll., 1982; MD, East Carolina U., 1986. Intern, then resident in pediatrics U. Md. Hosp., Balt., 1989-92; fellow Oakland (Calif.) Children's Hosp., 1992; asst. prof. pediatrics Wyler Children's Hosp., U. Chgo., 1992—. Office: Wyler Childrens Hosp U Chgo 5841 S Maryland Ave MC-1051 Chicago IL 60637

ALLEN, GLORIA ANN, realtor; b. Paterson, N.J., May 1, 1940; d. Victor and Anna (Nagorny) Borovoy; m. Byron Paul Allen, July 7, 1964 (div. Jan. 1986); children: Andreya Monica, Sarah Patricia. Student, Cir. in Sq. Acting Sch., N.Y.C., 1963-64; MA, Johns Hopkins U., 1962; MBA, Golden Gate U., 1986. Lic. real estate broker, Calif. Tchr. Elem. Sch., East Rutherford, N.J., 1963; social worker Bur. Child Welfare City of N.Y., 1964-68; social worker Dept. Social Svcs. City and County San Francisco, 1968-78; property mgr. San Francisco, 1981-91; broker assoc. Ritchie and Ritchie, San Francisco, 1992, Evans Pacific Realtor, San Francisco, 1993-94, Frank Howard Allen Realtors, San Francisco, 1994—. Fin. com. mem. St. Mary's Cathedral, San Francisco, 1993—. Mem. Nat. Assn. Realtors, Nat. Network Comml. Real Estate Women (chief fin. officer 1987-89, co-chair facilities Nat. Conv. 1993), San Francisco Assn. Realtors. Democrat. Office: Frank Howard Allen Realtors 1700 California St San Francisco CA 94109

ALLEN, JANET LOUISE, school system administrator; b. Cleve., Nov. 17, 1935; d. W. Paul and Clara (Townhill) A.; m. H. Paul Koepke, June 15, 1957 (div. 1978); children: Scott Paul, Sheryl Louise. BS, Syracuse U., 1957; MA, Wayne State U., 1971, PhD, 1976; postgrad., Ea. Mich. U., 1982, Wayne State U., 1989. Tchr. Grand Rapids, Mich., 1967-69; tchr. Birmingham (Mich.) Pub. Schs., 1969-77, dir. gifted edn., 1977-79; prin. Bingham Farms Sch., Birmingham, 1979-80; dept. head Derby Mid. Sch., Birmingham, 1980-81; prin. Twin Beach Sch., Walled Lake, Mich., 1981-87; dep. supt. Jackson (Mich.) Pub. Schs., 1988-90; supt. Three Rivers (Mich.) Community Schs., 1990—; adj. prof. Mich. State U., East Lansing, 1979-81, Eastern Mich. U., Ypsilanti, 11990, Western Mich. U., Kalamazoo, 1994. Contbr. articles to profl. jours. Apptd. mem. Three Rivers Indsl. Authority; mem. Three Rivers Family Coun., 1992—, Three Rivers Human Rels. Commn., 1992—. IDEA fellow Inst. Devel. Ednl. Activities, Appleton, Wis., 1992, 1994. Mem. Am. Assn. Sch. Adminstrs. (del. nat. conv. 1991—), Mich. Assn. Sch. Adminstrs. (chmn. ednl. leadership 1992-93, exec. bd. 1993—), St. Joseph County Supt. Assn. (pres. 1991-93), Three Rivers C. of C., Rotary, Players, Phi Delta Kappa (pres. 1984-85). Home: 605 Tulip Ln Three Rivers MI 49093 Office: Three Rivers Community Schs 1008 8th St Three Rivers MI 49093

ALLEN, JANICE FAYE CLEMENT, nursing adminstrator; b. Norfolk, Nebr., Aug. 19, 1946; d. Allen Edward and Hilda Bernice (Stange) Reeves; m. Roger Allen Clement, Oct. 6, 1968 (dec. July 1974).; m. August H. Allen, Sept. 17, 1988. RN, Meth. Sch. Nursing, Omaha, 1967; BS in Nursing, magna cum laude, Creighton U., 1978; MS in Nursing, U. Nebr., 1981; cert. in nursing adminstrn. With Meth. Hosp., 1967-68, 72-83, asst. head nurse, 1974-77, staff devel. nurse, 1977-81, dir. staff adminstrv. services, 1981-83; pub. health nurse Wichita-Sedgwick County Health Dept., Wichita, Kans., 1970-72; dir. nursing Meth. Med. Ctr., St. Joseph, Mo., 1983-84, Broadlawns Med. Ctr., Des Moines, 1984-93; dir. staff mgmt./infection control Ea. N.Mex. Med. Ctr., Roswell, 1993—; adj. clin. faculty nursing Drake U. Nursing, Des Moines, 1986-93, mem. adv. bd., 1984-93, Cen. Campus Practical Nursing, 1984-93; mem. adv. bd. Des Moines Area Community Coll. Dist., 1987—, Des Moines Area C.C. Nursing Bd., 1987-93, Grandview Coll., 1988-93; bd. dirs. Vis. Nurse Svcs., 1988-93. Mem. Am. Nurses Assn., Am. Orgn. Nurse Execs., N.Mex. Nurses Assn., Cen. Iowa Nursing Leadership Conf. (pres. 1985), Colloquium Nursing Leaders Cen. Iowa, Iowa League for Nursing (treas. 1987-89, pres. 1989), Iowa Orgn. Nurse Execs. (treas. 1987, sec. 1989, pres.-elect 1993), Assn. Infection Control and Epidemiology, Sigma Theta Tau (pres. Zeta Chi chpt. 1990-92). Democrat. Presbyterian. Avocations: flying, sewing, golf, walking, reading. Home: 3201 Allison Dr Roswell NM 88201 Office: Ea NMex Med Ctr 405 W Country Club Blvd Roswell NM 88201

ALLEN, JANICE MANNING, nurse, office manager, actress, model; b. Evanston, Ill., May 29, 1953; d. Paul John and Claudia Stroman (White) Mandabach; m. George Whitaker Allen, Apr. 26, 1980. Student, Syracuse U., 1971-72; BSN, Tex. Christian U., 1976. Nurse oper. rm., circulating nurse oper. rm. Northwestern Meml. Hosp., Chgo., 1976-78; model and actress Chgo., 1978-86, 94—; nurse, office mgr. George W. Allen, MD, Chgo., 1986—. Mem. Carlton Club, Sand Creek Country Club. Republican. Methodist. Home: 1503 Sand Creek Dr S Chesterton IN 46304 Office: George W Allen MD 150 E Huron Chicago IL 60611

ALLEN, JEANNIE LAIYEE, consultant; b. Kowloon, Hong Kong, Apr. 15, 1956; d. Chungho and Mailan Choi; m. Darrel L. Allen, July 29, 1978; 1 child, Isak. BBA, U. Hawaii, 1976. CPA. Sr. acct. Syntex Chems., Inc., Boulder, Colo., 1978-81; staff acct. McGladrey, Hendrickson & Co. CPA, Denver, 1981-83; budget analyst GTE Northwest, Everett, Wash., 1984-88; controller Union Tank Works Mfg., Seattle, 1988-89; asst. fin. mgr. City of Indpls./Dept. Met. Devel., 1989-90; bd. dirs. Am. States Employee Federal Credit Union, Indpls. Officer Eagle Nest Property Owners Assn., Indpls., 1993. Recipient Bronze award Edinburg Award Scheme, Hong Kong, 1971. Mem. Inst. Mgmt. Accts. (bd. dirs. 1991-93). Home: 7701 White Dove Dr Indianapolis IN 46256-1705

ALLEN, JOAN, actress; b. Rochelle, Ill., Aug. 20, 1956. Student, Ea. Ill. U., No. Ill. U. Founding mem. Steppenwolf Theatre Co., Chgo.; theater appearances include (debut) And A Nightingale Sang, N.Y.C. (Clarence Derwent award, Drama Desk award, Outer Critics Circle award 1984), Steppenwolf Theatre Co., also Hartford, 1983, The Marriage of Bette and Boo, N.Y. Shakespeare Festival, 1986, Burn This! (Tony awrd 1988) Mark Taper Forum, L.A., also N.Y.C., 1987, The Heidi Chronicles, N.Y.C., 1988, 89; film appearances include Compromising Positions, 1985, Peggy Sue Got Married, 1986, Manhunter, 1986, In Country, 1989, Tucker: The Man and His Dream, 1988, Ethan Fromme, 1993, Searching for Bobbie Fischer, 1993, Josh and S.A.M., 1993; TV appearances include miniseries Evergreen, 1985, All My sons, Am. Playhouse, PBS, 1987, Robert Frost, Voices and Visions, PBS, 1988, TV film The Room Upstairs, 1987, Without Warning: The James Brady Story, 1991. Office: Internat Creative Mgmt care Bill Mann 40 W 57th St New York NY 10019-4001*

ALLEN, JOYCE SMITH, librarian; b. Englewood, N.J., Aug. 1, 1939; d. Harold Willard and Mary Elizabeth Smith; m. Jim Frank Allen, Mar. 1974 (div. 1982); 1 child, Shani Jamilla. BA, Howard U., 1961; MLS, Atlanta U., 1966; cert. in advanced studies, U. Ill., 1974. Reference librarian Howard U., Washington, 1966-73; mgr. libr. Meth. Hosp. Ind., Indpls., 1974-94; libr. Aenon Bible Coll., Indpls., 1994—; instr. Lake Area Health Edn. Ctr. (Vets. Affairs Med. Ctr.), 1994—; instr. Ind. Vocat. Tech. Coll., 1979, 85, Med. Library Assn., 1982—, Martin Ctr. Coll., Indpls., 1983-84. Author career materials. Vol. Indpls. Police Dept. Libr., 1977, Children's Mus., Indpls., 1987-88. Recipient Minority Bus. and Profl. Achiever award Ctr. for Leadership Devel., Indpls., 1981, Central Ind. Area Libr. Svcs. Authority cert. of Excellence, 1990. Mem. ALA, Internat. Tng. In Comm., Ch. and Synagogue Libr. Assn. (pres. 1992-93), Med. Libr. Assn., Coun. on Libr. Technicians, Spl. Librs. Assn., Indpls. Interdenominational Ch. Users' Assn. Democrat. Home: 3815 N Bolton Ave Indianapolis IN 46226-4826 Office: Aenon Bible Coll 3939 N Meadows Dr Indianapolis IN 46205

ALLEN, JUDITH MARLER, realtor; b. Cleveland, Tenn., Nov. 19, 1938; d. Thomas James and Hazel (Wilson) Marler; m. Larry Dean Allen, July 27, 1963; children: Ann Katherine, Gregory Marler. BA, Tulane U., 1960. Tchr. Long Beach (Calif.) Sch. Dist., 1960-63, Glenview (Ill.) Schs., 1963-64; realtor Coldwell Banker Hamilton & Williams, Cleveland, Tenn., 1989—. Mem. Nat. Bd. Realtors, Tenn. Bd. Realtors, Cleveland Bd. Realtors (membership chmn. 1993—). Republican. Methodist. Office: Coldwell Banker Hamilton & Williams 1340 25th St NW Cleveland TN 37311-3615

ALLEN, JUDITH MARTHA, nursing administrator, career officer; b. Syracuse, N.Y., Feb. 4, 1942; d. Bernard J. and Genevieve R. (Greene) Arndt; m. Anthony S. Allen, Nov. 1984. Diploma, Champlain Valley Sch. Nursing, Plattsburg, N.Y., 1964; BSN, D'Youville Coll., 1974; postgrad., U. N.C., 1976; MS, U. San Francisco, 1984. Cert. cardiovascular nurse clinician; CPR instr. trainer; CCM. Head nurse CCU Millard Fillmore Hosp., Buffalo, 1974-80; commd. officer U.S. Army, 1976, advanced through grades to lt. col., 1986; chief surg. nursing Ireland Army Community Hosp., Ft. Knox, Ky., 1985-87, chief nursing edn. and staff devel., 1987-88; clin. coord. ICU, CCU, asst. chief spl. projects officer Letterman Army Med. Ctr., San Francisco, 1980-85, head nurse post operative cardiovascular/neurosurg. unit, 1988-89, asst. chief nursing edn., staff devel. svc., 1989-91, asst. chief evenings/nights, 1991-92, asst. quality improvement nurse, 1992, chief nursing adminstrn., days, med. surg. sect. chief, 1992-94; rev. coord. State Indsl. Ins. Sys. Utilization State Indsl. Ins. Sys. Universal Health Netwrok, Sparks, Nev., 1994—; speaker in field. Contbr. articles to profl. jours. Lt. col. Nev. State NG. Mem. AACCN, Nev. State Nurses Assn. Home: PO Box 1026 Virginia City NV 89440 Office: 2345 E Prater Way Sparks NV 89434

ALLEN, JUDITH RUTH, elementary school educator, staff developer; b. Potsdam, N.Y., July 8, 1943; d. Gordon Harold and Ruth Elizabeth (Smith) A. BS, SUNY, Potsdam, 1966; MA in History, Political, Coll. of St. Rose, Albany, 1974. Tchr. Tchr. So. Colonie Central Schs., Albany, N.Y., 1966—; del. N.Y. State United Tchrs., Albany, 1971—, Am. Fedn. Tchrs., Washington, 1974, 75, 80, 84, NEA, Washington, 1974, 75; local site coord. Ednl. Rsch. and Dissemination Program, 1989—; presenter in field. Author: Geography Curriculum Guide, 1978, Computer Curriculum Guide, 1983, Elementary Schools: The Forgotten Corner, 1990; contbr. Vibrations, 1989—. Lobbyist N.Y. State United Tchrs., Albany, 1977—, Chairperson S. Colonie Tchrs. Polit. Action, Albany, 1979-87; active Capital Dist. Coun. for Social Studies. Nominated Tchr. of the Year S. Colonie Bd. of Edn., Albany, 1983. Mem. ASCD, Nat. Coun. Tchrs. Math., Internat. Assn. for Study Cooperation in Edn., N.Y. State Geographic Alliance, Am. Ednl. Rsch. Assn., So. Colonie Tchrs. Assn. (sec. 1971-75, v.p. 1993—), N.Y. State United Tchrs. Am. Fedn. Tchrs., Nat. Geographic Soc. (tchr. cons. 1993—), N.Y. State PTA, Schola Cantorum, Ancient Order of Hibernians. Democrat. Roman Catholic. Home: 109 Beverwyck Dr Apt 10 Guilderland NY 12084-9678 Office: South Colonie Ctrl Schs 329 Sand Creek Rd Albany NY 12205-2928

ALLEN, KAREN ALFSTAD, management consultant; b. Wichita, Kans., Nov. 21, 1942; d. Harold Daniel and Myrtle (Creach) Keefer; m. Richard Allen, Dec. 16, 1962 (dec. 1994). AS, Oreg. Inst. of Tech., L.A., 1964; AA, Pasadena City, 1973; BS,, Calif. State U., Pasadena City, 1974. Adminstra. asst. Transamerica, Los Angeles, 1974-75; v.p. Calif. Fed., Los Angeles, 1975-86; mgmt. cons. Coopers & Lybrand, Los Angeles, 1986-90; mgr. large accounts J.D. Edwards, Denver, 1990-92; v.p. Insecon Computer Sys., Encino, Calif., 1992—. Bd. dirs. Polit. Action Com. Calif. Fed., L.A., 1984-86, Arcadia Arts Coun., 1993—; vol. Youth Motivation Task Force, L.A., 1982-

86. Recipient Honors Calif. State U., Los Angeles, 1974. Mem. Nat. Trust for Historic Preservation, Internat. Facility Mgmt., So. Calif. Emergency Assn., NAFE, NOW, U. Club L.A. Democrat. Home: 1632 Hyland Ave Arcadia CA 91006 Office: Insecon 16027 Ventura Blvd Encino CA 91436

ALLEN, KAREN JANE, actress; b. Carrollton, Ill., Oct. 5, 1951; d. Carroll Thompson and Patricia (Howell) A. Student, George Washington U., 1974-76. Mem. Washington Theatre Lab., 1973-77. Appeared in films The Whidjit-Maker, 1977, National Lampoon's Animal House, 1978, The Wanderers, 1979, Manhattan, 1979, A Small Circle of Friends, 1979, Cruising, 1979, Raiders of the Lost Ark, 1981, Shoot The Moon, 1981, Split Image, 1981, Strange Invaders, 1983, Until September, 1984, Starman, 1984, The End of the Line, 1986, The Glass Menagerie, 1987, Backfire, 1987, Scrooged, 1988, Animal Behavior, 1989, Sweet Talker, 1991, Malcolm X, 1992, Secret Places of the Heart, Confidence, Exile, The Sandlot, 1993, King of the Hill, 1993, Ghost in the Machine, 1994; TV films Lovey: A Circle of Children, Part II, 1978, East of Eden, 1980, Secret Weapon, 1990, Challenge, 1990, Rapture, 1993, Voyage, 1993; TV series Knots Landing, 1979, The Road Home, 1994; Broadway debut as Helen Keller in Monday After the Miracle, 1982; other stage appearances include Two For the Seesaw, 1981, Monday After The Miracle, Actors Studio (N.Y.C.), Kennedy Ctr. (Washington), (Theatre World award 1983), Tennessee Williams: A Celebration, Williamstown Theatre Festival, 1982, Extremities, West Side Arts Theatre, N.Y.C., 1983, The Glass Menagerie, Williamstown Theatre Festival, 1985, Longwharf Theatre, New Haven, Ct., 1986, The Miracle Worker, Roundabout Theatre, N.Y.C., 1987, Beautiful Bodies, The Whole Theatre, 1987, As You Like It, Mount Theatre, 1988, The Country Girl, Roundabout Theatre, N.Y.C., 1990-91. Mem. Screen Actors Guild, Actor's Equity Assn. Office: The Gersh Agy 232 N Canon Dr Beverly Hills CA 90210*

ALLEN, KATHERINE SPICER, writer, former chemist; b. Plainfield, N.J., Apr. 29, 1919; d. Arthur Joseph and Linda Varner (Morrison) Spicer; m. Carl Holley Allen, Sept. 24, 1943; children: Carl Holly Jr., David Randolph, Katherine Allen Fehn, Linda Ruth Allen. BA, U. Del., 1942. Libr. asst. State Libr., Dover, Del., summers 1936-41; typist U. Del., Newark, 1940-42; chemist Esso Rsch. Divsn., Bayway and Elizabeth, N.J., 1942-46; analyst Azoplate Corp., Murray Hill, N.J., 1963-67; enumerator U.S. Census Bur., Somerset County, N.J., 1980, 90; contbg. writer Bernardsville (N.J.) News, 1982—. Co-author: A History of the Presbyterian Church of Liberty Corner, 1937-1987, 1987, (booklet) Christian Education Goals and Objectives, 1991, (with others) Past and Present Lives of New Jersey Women, 1990. Mem. Bernards Twp. Local Assistance Bd., 1972—, sec., 1974-89, chmn., 1990; mem. Bernards Twp. Mcpl. Alliance, 1992—; mem. Somerset County Rep. Com., 1972-93; mem. personnel com. Mcpls. Com. Bernards Twp., 1990-93; mem. comm. com. Am. Cancer Soc., 1990—, vol. Reach to Recovery, 1985—, Somerset County coord. programs, 1987-89; ordained elder Presbyn Ch. U.S.A., 1980; mem. justice for women com. Elizabeth Presbytery, 1988—, mem. comm. com., 1992—, commr. to Synod of N.E., 1991, 92-93, mem. media com. 1988-90, mem. nominating com. 1987-92, vice chairperson 1990-92, mem. search com. for assoc. exec. 1993; pres. Liberty Corner Presbyn. Ch. Women's Assn., 1973, 74, 84, ch. sch. tchr., 1952-81, ruling elder, 1980-82, chmn. ch. and soc. com. 1980-82; dir. Ch. Women United Somerset County, 1979-81; state chmn. Ecumenical Action, 1982-83. Named Somerset County Reach to Recovery Vol. of Yr., Am. Cancer Soc., 1991; recipient svc. pins. Mem. N.J. Press Women (various awards for articles written in Bernardsville News), AAUW, Bernard Twp. Mcpl. Alliance. Home: 218 Lurline Dr Basking Ridge NJ 07920

ALLEN, LEATRICE DELORICE, psychologist; b. Chgo., July 15, 1948; d. Burt and Mildred Floy (Taylor) Hawkins; m. Allen Moore, Jr., July 30, 1965 (div. Oct. 1975); children: Chandra, Valarie, Allen; m. Armstead Allen, May 11, 1978 (div. May 1987). AA in Bus. Edn., Olive Harvey Coll., Chgo., 1975; BA in Psychology cum laude, Chgo. State U., 1977; M.Clin. Psychology, Roosevelt U., 1980; MA in Health Care Adminstrn., Coll. St. Francis, Joliet, Ill., 1993. Clk., U.S. Post Office, Chgo., 1967-72; clin. therapist Bobby Wright Mental Health Ctr., Chgo., 1979-80; clin. therapist Community Mental Health Council, Chgo., 1980-83, assoc. dir., 1983—; cons. Edgewater Mental Health, Chgo., 1984—, Project Pride, Chgo., 1985—; victim services coordinator Community Mental Health Council, Chgo., 1986-87; mgr. youth family services Mile Square Health Ctr., Chgo., 1987-88; coord. Evang. Health Systems, Oakbrook, Ill., 1988-93; adminstr. Human Enrichment Devel. Assn., Hazel Crest, Ill., 1993—. Scholar Chgo. State U., 1976, Roosevelt U., 1978; fellow Menninger Found., 1985. Mem. Am. Profl. Soc. on Abuse of Children, Nat. Orgn. for Victim Assistance, Ill. Coalition Against Sexual Assault (del. 1985—), Soc. Traumatic Stress Studies (treatment innovations task force), Chgo. Sexual Assault Svcs. Network (vice-chair, bd. dirs.), Chgo. Coun. Fgn. Rels. Avocations: aerobics, reading, theatre, dining.

ALLEN, LEILANI ELEANOR, data processing executive; b. Rudesheim, Rhein, Fed. Republic Germany, Nov. 27, 1949; d. John Kaleiapu and Ilse Eva (Ritter) A. BA, San Francisco State U., 1971, MA, 1973; PhD, U. Conn., 1978. Sr. analyst VISA, U.S.A., San Mateo, Calif., 1978-81; asst. gen. mgr. Inst. for Info. Mgmt., Sunnyvale, Calif., 1981-85; pres. Knowledge Consortium, Oakland, Calif., 1985-87; sr. cons. Amdahl Corp., Sunnyvale, 1987-88; v.p. Aon Corp., Chgo., 1988-91; sr. v.p. PNC Mortgage Corp., Vernon Hills, Ill., 1991—; chmn. No Cal Computer Measurement Group, San Francisco, 1982-84. Co-author: Management Handbook of Info. Center and End User Computer, 1987, Strategic Planning for Info. Systems, 1987 (survey), Tech Tales cartoon; editor: Executive Perspectives on Info Systems, 1985; contbr. articles to profl. jours.; columnist Software mag. Mem. NAFE (chair MBA tech. com.), Mensa, Mortgage Bankers Assn. (chair technology com.). Office: PNC Mortgage Corp 440 North Fairway Vernon Hills IL 60061

ALLEN, LOIS ARLENE HEIGHT (MRS. JAMES PIERPONT ALLEN), musician; b. Kenton, Ohio, Sept. 2, 1932; d. Robert Harold and Frances (Sims) Height; B.S., Ohio State U., 1954, M.A., 1958; m. James Pierpont Allen, June 14, 1953; children: Daniel Pierpont, Carole Elizabeth. Tchr. jr. and sr. high music, Upper Arlington High Sch., Columbus, O., 1954-56; high sch. music supr., Westerville, Ohio, 1956-67; tchr. music Ohio State U. Sch., 1957-59; pvt. tchr. music, Columbus, 1960—; exec. dir. Battelle Scholars Program Trust Fund, 1983-86; ch. organist, choir dir. Mountview Bapt. Ch., Upper Arlington, Ohio, 1960-77; ednl. radio interviewer WOSU, 1970, 71, 72. Mem. Project Hope, Central Ohio, 1967-73; mem. sustaining bd. Maryhaven House for Alcoholic Women, 1969-73, 1st v.p.; mem. women's bd. Columbus Symphony, 1965-79, 1991, 92, 93, 94, bd. dirs., chmn. youth council, 1965-68, pres.-elect. women's assn., 1973, chmn. edn. com., 1991—, pres., 1974-76; v.p. Am. Symphony Orch. League, 1987-88; organist, choir master The Ch. of St. Edwards, 1990-92; chmn. juried art competition Central Ohio Arts Festival, 1969, 70, chmn. fine and applied arts, 1971, gen. chmn. of festival, 1972; area chmn. United Appeals Franklin County, 1966-68, Heart drive, 1968-85; pres. Ohio State U. Soc. Friends Sch. Music, 1977-78; trustee Columbus Symphony Orch., 1973-81, Opera/Columbus, 1981-85; v.p. women's guild Opera/Columbus, 1986-94, pres., 1987-88; mem. vol. coun. Am. Symphony Orch. League, 1981—, v.p., 1983-84, mem. exec. com., 1986-88, mem. artistic affairs com., 1987-89, pres. 1987-88; organist, choir dir. North Congregational Ch., 1979-85; area leader Rep. party, 1966-68; mem. Mayor's Award Coun. Com., 1981-84; active Connexions, Columbus Literacy Coun.; bd. dirs. Ohio Theatre Shop, 1992—, Women's Bd. Columbus Mus. Art, 1991—. Mem. Am. Guild Organists, Choristers Guild Am., Fedn. Am. Bapt. Musicians, Center Sci. and Industry, Ohio State Hist. Soc., Ohio Orgn. Orchs. (treas. 1976-79, sec. 1979-82), Nat. Trust U.S.A., Tau Beta Sigma, Delta Omicron, Kappa Delta (Central Ohio Woman of Yr. 1970). Mem. Order Eastern Star, White Shrine of Jerusalem. Clubs: Ohio State U. Alumnae of Franklin County (pres. 1962-64, 71-72). Home: 3355 Somerford Rd Columbus OH 43221-1436

ALLEN, LOUISE, writer, educator; b. Alliance, Ohio, Sept. 21, 1910; d. Earl Wayne and Ella Celesta (Goodall) Allerton; m. Benjamin Yukl, June 27, 1936; children: Katherine Anne Yukl Johnston, Kenneth Allen, Richard Lee, Margaret Louise Yukl Border. Student, Cleve. Coll. Western Res. U., 1963, Lakeland Community Coll., 1981-84. Co-founder Sch. Writing, Cleve., 1961-62; founder, dir. Allen Writers' Agy., Wickliffe, Ohio, 1963-84; editorial assoc. criticism service Writer's Digest mag., 1967-69; instr. Cuyahoga Community Coll., 1965-81, Lakeland Community Coll., Mentor, Ohio, 1973-81, Scottsdale Community Coll., 1984-88; writer. Author: (poems) Confetti, 1987; contbr. articles to mags. Mem. Mensa, Assn. Mundial de Mujures Periodistas y Escritoras, Women in Communications, Nat. League Am. Pen Women, DAR, Shore Writers Club (founder), Euclid Three Arts Club, Women's City Club (Cleve.). Republican. Congregationalist. Address: 2609 W Southern Ave Lot 11 Tempe AZ 85282-4208

ALLEN, LOUISE KITCHIN, tennis player; b. Durham, N.C., Jan. 7, 1962; d. Burwell Algernon and Mary Louise (Lineberger) A. BS, Trinity U.; postgrad., U. Tex. Profl. tennis player Women's Tennis Assn., St. Petersburg, Fla., 1984—; mem. tournament com. Women's Tennis Assn., 1989-92. Vol. AIDS Resource Ctr., San Antonio, 1994—; tennis coord. Spl. Olympics, Conn., 1986, 87. Mem. NOW, U.S. Tennis Assn. Democrat. Home: 3201 Duval Rd #737 Austin TX 78759

ALLEN, MARIE BARONI, operations manager; b. Brockton, Mass., Jan. 9, 1944; d. Peter Joseph and Mary Katherine (Sheehan) Baroni; m. James Grant Allen, Jan. 2, 1977. BS, State Coll. Bridgewater, 1965; MS in Chemistry, U. Notre Dame, 1971; CAS Mgmt., Radcliffe Coll., 1989. Educator Whitman (Mass.)-Hanson Regional High Sch., 1965-68; educator Needham (Mass.) High Sch., 1968-76, dept. adminstr., 1976-80; lab. mgr. Moleculon Rsch. Co., Cambridge, Mass., 1980-83; ops. mgr. Moleculon Biotech. Inc., Cambridge, Mass., 1983-88; cons. Allen Assocs., Newton, Mass., 1988-89; dir. ops. Genzyme Corp., Cambridge, 1990—. Pres. Newton (Mass.) Choral Soc., 1986-88; bd. mem. Fund for the Arts in Newton, Mass., 1987-88. Grantee NSF, U. Notre Dame, 1969, 70, 71. Mem. Am. Soc. Quality Control, Am. Chem. Soc., Internat. Soc. Pharmaceutical Engrs., Regulatory Affairs Profl. Soc. Office: Genzyme Corp One Kendall Sq Cambridge MA 02139-1562

ALLEN, MARILYN MYERS POOL, theater director, video producer; b. Fresno, Calif., Nov. 2, 1934; d. Laurence B. and Asa (Griggs) Myers; B.A., Stanford U., 1955, postgrad., 1955-56; postgrad. U. Tex., 1957-60, West Tex. State U. summers 1962, 63, Odessa Coll., 1987-88; m. Joseph Harold Pool, Dec. 28, 1955; children—Pamela Elizabeth, Victoria Anne, Catherine Marcia; m. Neal R. Allen, Apr. 1982. Pvt. tchr. drama, speech, acting, directing, speech correction, Amarillo, Tex., 1960-82, Midland, Tex., 1982—; free-lance radio and TV actress; asst. mng. dir. Amarillo Little Theatre, 1964-66, mng. dir., 1966-68; mng. dir. Horseshoe Players, touring profl. theater, 1969-73; actress, multi-media prodn. Palo Duro Canyon, 1971; dir. touring children's theatre, 1978-79 guest actress in Medea, Amarillo Coll., 1981; guest reciter Amarillo Symphony, 1972, Midland-Odessa Symphony, 1984. Pres. Tex. Non-Profit Theatres, 1972-74, 75-77, bd. dirs., 1988-91; 1st v.p. High Plains Center for Performing Arts, 1969-73; adv. mem. dept. fine arts Amarillo Coll., 1980-82. Adv. mem. Tex. Constnl. Revision Commn., 1973-75; mem. adv. council U. Tex. Coll. Fine Arts, 1969-72; community adv. com. for women Amarillo Coll., 1975-79; conv. program com. Am. Theatre Assn., 1978, program participant 1978-80, bd. dirs., 1980-83; bd. dirs. Amarillo Found. Health and Sci. Edn., 1976-82, program v.p., 1979-81; bd. dirs. Domestic Violence Council, 1979-82, March of Dimes, 1979-81, Tex. Panhandle Heritage Found., 1964-82, Friends of Fine Arts, W. Tex. State U., 1980-82, Amarillo Pub. Library, 1980-82, Amarillo Symphony, 1981-82; publicity chmn. Midland Community Theatre, 1984-87, bd. govs., 1986-92, sec., 1987-88, v.p., 1988-92; mem. Mus. of S.W., Midland Arts Assembly; bd. dirs. Midland County Rep. Women, Ways and Means Ch., 1991, 1st v.p., 1992, publicity chair, 1994; cultural exchange del. from Midland, Tex., to Dong Ying, China, 1993. Recipient cert. of appreciation Woman of Year, Amarillo Bus. and Profl. Women's Club, 1966; Best Actress award for Hedda Gabler role Amarillo Little Theatre 1965, Best Dir. award for Rashomon, 1967, 1st Pl. award for video special Tex. Press Conf., 1988, 1st Pl. award for news Tex. Press Conf., 1989, Disting. Svc. award Tex. Non-Profit Theatres, 1992, Vol. award Midland Arts Assembly, 1992; named Amarillo Woman of Yr., Beta Sigma Phi, 1980, Broadcaster of the Yr., Rocky Mountain Press Conf., 1988, Hamhock of Yr., Midland Community Theatre, 1992, Outstanding Svc. award Midland Arts Assembly, 1992; Travel fellow AAUW, 1973, 78. Fellow Am. Assn. Community Theatre (dir. 1969-72, 82-84, v.p. planning and devel. 1985-87, co-chair MidlAACT/festival, 1995); mem. USTA (sr. women's team sect. winner 1993, 94), S.W. Theatre Conf. (dir. 1973-76, 82-84, exec. com. 1982-84, Disting. Svc. award 1985), Tex. Theatre Council (dir. 1974-78, exec. com., pres. 1975-76), AAUW (br. pres. 1973-75, state chmn. cultural interests 1975-77, 86-88, state program v.p. 1977-79, state bd. dirs. 1984-88, program v.p. Midland 1988-89), Episc. Ch. Women (program v.p. Midland 1988-89), DAR (chpt. chaplain 1971-75, historian 1975-77), C. of C. (fine arts council), U.S. Judo Assn., Symphony Guild, Amarillo Art Assn., Midland Symphony Guild (arrangements chmn. 1983-84), Act IX, Amarillo Law Wives Club (pres. 1976-77), Midland Law Wives, Hamhocks (v.p. 1985-86).

ALLEN, MARY LOUISE HOOK, physical education educator; b. Ironwood, Mich., July 18, 1930; d. Frank Eugene and Elsie Clara (Schneider) Hook; m. Dale Sanson Allen, June 30, 1955; children: Jack Eugene, Bradley Arthur. BS in Phys. Edn. cum laude, U. Mich., 1951; MA in Phys. Edn., U. Minn., 1970, postgrad., 1987—. Life teaching cert., coaching lic., Minn. Secondary edn. tchr. New Trier Twp. High Sch., Winnetka, Ill., 1951-55, Richfield (Minn.) Sch. Dist., 1955-59; teaching assoc. U. Minn., Mpls., 1969-70; part-time lectr. U. Minn., 1985-86; tchr. Bloomington (Minn.) Sch. Dist., 1961-85; adj. prof. Concordia Coll., St. Paul, Minn., 1987-92; officiator U.S. Synchro Minn. Assn., Minn. State High Sch. League, Pan-Am. Trials Swimming Co-Chair, others; past officiating bd. chmn. North Shore (Winnetka) Basketball/Volleyball, Ill. State Basketball com., others. Co-author: Soccer/Speedball Rule Book - Creative Game, 1952. Mem. Atonement Luth. Ch., Bloomington, 1956—; worker Dem. Party, Bloomington, 1988—; dir. Synchronized Swimming Camp, 1980-87. Recipient numerous athletic awards. Mem. AAHPERD (mem. com. 1949—), Minn. Assn. Health, Phys. Edn., Recreation and Dance (sec. 1982-83, pres.-elect 1984, pres. 1985, past pres. 1986, conv. chmn. 1984, 86, student confs. 1988-92), Synchronized Swim Coaches Assn. (state chmn. 1980-82), Athletic Fedn. Coll. Women (chmn. nat. conv. 1951), Phi Beta Kappa, Phi Kappa Phi, Mortarboard, Pi Lambda Theta, others. Home: 10312 Wentworth Ave Bloomington MN 55420-5249

ALLEN, MARYON PITTMAN, former senator, journalist, lecturer, interior and clothing designer; b. Meridian, Miss., Nov. 30, 1925; d. John D. and Tellie (Chism) Pittman; m. Joshua Sanford Mullins, Jr., Oct. 17, 1946 (div. Jan. 1959); children: Joshua Sanford III, John Pittman, Maryon Foster; m. James Browning Allen, Aug. 7, 1964 (dec. June 1978). Student, U. Ala., 1944-47, Internat. Inst. Interior Design, 1970. Office mgr. for Dr. Alston Callahan, Birmingham, Ala., 1959-60; bus. mgr. psychiat. clinic U. Ala. Med. Center, Birmingham, 1960-61; life underwriter Protective Life Ins. Co., Birmingham, 1961-62; women's editor Sun Newspapers, Birmingham, 1962-64; v.p., ptnr. Pittman family cos., J.D. Pittman Partnership Co., J.D. Pittman Tractor Co., Emerald Valley Corp., Mountain Lake Farms, Inc., Birmingham; mem. U.S. Senate (succeeding late husband James B. Allen), 1978; dir. pub. rels. and advt. C.G. Sloan & Co. Auction House, Washington, 1981; feature writer Birmingham News, 1964; writer syndicated column Reflections of a News Hen, Washington, 1969-78; feature writer, columnist Maryon Allen's Washington, Washington Post, 1979-81; columnist McCall's Needlework Mag., 1993—; owner The Maryon Allen Co. Cliff House (Restoration/Design), Birmingham. Contbg. editor So. Accents Mag., 1976-78. Mem. Ladies of U.S. Senate unit ARC, Former Mems. of Congress, Ala. Hist. Commn., Blair House Fine Arts Commn.; charter mem. Birmingham Com. of 100 for Women; trustee Children's Fresh Air Farm; trustee, deacon, elder Ind. Presbyn. Ch., Birmingham; Democratic Presdl. elector, Ala., 1968. Recipient 1st place award for best original column Ala. Press Assn., 1962, 63, also various press state and nat. awards for typography, fashion writing, food pages, also several awards during Senate service; sponsor, U.S. Navy Nuclear submarine, U.S.S. Birmingham, S.S.N. 695, launched Newport News, Va., 1977, commissioned 1978. Mem. Nat. Press Club, 1925 F Street Club, 91st Congress Club, Congl. Club, Birmingham Country Club. Home: Cliff House 3215 Cliff Rd S Birmingham AL 35205-1405

ALLEN, NANCY SCHUSTER, librarian; b. Buffalo, Jan. 10, 1948; d. Joseph E. and Margaret (Cormack) Schuster; m. Richard R. Allen, Sept. 2, 1967; children: Seth Cormack, Emily Margaret, Laura Jean. BA, U. Rochester, 1971, MA in Art History, 1973; MLS, Rutgers U., 1973. Asst. librarian Mus. Fine Arts, Boston, 1975-76, chief librarian, 1976—; reference librarian Medford Pub. Library, Mass., 1973-75; lectr. Grad. Sch. Libr. and Info. Scis., Simmons Coll., Boston, 1984—; mem. preservation adv. group Rsch. Librs. Group, 1993—; mem. Aga Kahn project libr. rev. com., 1992. Mem. art history scholarly adv. com. and joint task force Commn. on Preservation and Access, 1990-92. Mem. Art Libr. Soc. N.Am. (chmn. 1983-84), Soc. Am. Archivists, Rsch. Librs. Info. Network (chmn. art and arch. program com. 1985-88, preservation adv. coun. 1993—), Internat. Fedn. Librs. (sect. art librs., fin. officer 1985-89), Fenway Librs. Online (v.p. 1987-89, pres. 1989-91). Office: Hunt Meml Libr Mus Fine Art Boston 465 Huntington Ave Boston MA 02115-5519

ALLEN, PATRICIA J., library director, professor; b. McLean County, Ky., Nov. 10, 1941; d. Richard Louis and Helen (Hancock) Jones; m. Jerry M. Mize, Mar. 19, 1960 (div. 1978); children: Martin P., Elizabeth M. Atherton; m. Lawrence A. Allen, Nov. 24, 1983 (div. 1985). Student, Murray (Ky.) State U., 1959-60; BA, Ky. Wesleyan Coll., 1962; MA, Western Ky. U., 1974; MLS, U. Ky., 1982; postgrad., U. N.C., 1983-84. Librarian pub. elem. schs. Daviess County, Ky., 1963-70; media specialist pub. elem., mid. and high schs. McLean County, Ky., 1970-78; head pub. svcs., assoc. prof. library sci. Ky. Wesleyan Coll., Owensboro, 1978-83; asst. dir. Evansville (Ind.) Vanderburgh County Pub. Library, 1985-89; dir. Carmel (Ind.) Clay Pub. Library, 1989-91, Sanibel (Fla.) Pub. Libr., 1991—; mem. adj. faculty Western Ky. U., Bowling Green, 1977-78, Ind. U., Bloomington, 1988; workshop presenter Nursing Home Activities Dirs. Assn., Owensboro, Ky., 1981; cons. Ky. Dept. for Libraries and Archives, Frankfort, 1982, Purchase (Ky.) Regional Library System, Murray, 1983, Henderson (Ky.) Community Coll. Library, 1988. Editor: handbook Emergency Handbook, 1987, Circulation Policies and Procedures, 1988; contbr. articles to profl. jours. Pres. Ret. Sr. Vol. Program Adv. Coun., Evansville, 1986-88; bd. dirs. Evansville Goodwill Industries, 1987-89. Caroline M. Hewins scholar U. Ky., 1982, Margaret Ellen Kalp scholar U. N.C., 1983-84. Mem. ALA, Ky. Libr. Assn., Fla. Libr. Assn., Pub. Libr. Assn., Libr. Adminstrs. and Mgrs. Assn., P.E.O., Altrusa Club (bd dirs. Evansville chpt. 1988, treas. Hamilton County chpt. 1990-91), Tales and Scales (pres. Evansville chpt. 1986), Beta Phi Mu. Democrat. Baptist. Office: Sanibel Pub Libr 770 Dunlop Rd Sanibel FL 33957-4016

ALLEN, PEGGY GETTS, administrative assistant, grievance clerk; b. Peoria, Ill., Apr. 20, 1953; d. W.W. and Mary Adeline (Hepperly) Getts; m. William Glynn Allen Jr., Mar. 28, 1981. BA, McMurry U., 1975; MLS, U. No. Tex., 1976. Cataloger libr. Sam Houston State U., Huntsville, Tex., 1976; cataloger reference libr. Meth. House, Nashville, 1977; clk. McMurry U., Abilene, Tex., 1977-78; clk. I Abilene State Sch., 1978-82, libr. I, 1982-90, ckl. II, 1991—; staff West Tex. Utilities, Abilene, 1990-91. Mem. Abilene Area Libr. Assn. (sec.-treas. 1987-88), Parliamentarians (sec. 1986-91), Toastmasters (area gov. 1987-88, 91-92, div. gov. 1988-89, sec.-treas. 1988-92). Baptist. Home: 3826 Jester Cir Abilene TX 79606-3234

ALLEN, ROBERTA JANE, social worker; b. Billings, Mont., July 8, 1954; d. Nat and Jane Leone (Barker) A.; m. Steven J. Dawes, Dec. 20, 1986. BSW with honors, U. Mont., 1975; MSW, Portland State U., 1982. Cert. social worker. Social worker Fergus County Welfare, Lewistown, Mont., 1975-80, Denver Dept. Social Svcs., 1983-84; dir. community svcs. Nat. MS Soc., Denver, 1984-87; social worker Adams County Sch. Dist. 50, Westminster, Colo., 1987—. Mem. Nat. Asns. Social Workers. Home: 3085 E Hinsdale Ave Littleton CO 80120

ALLEN, SANDRA NAIR, cooking educator; b. Bauru, Brazil, May 28, 1933; came to U.S., 1963; d. Germano and Leonor M. (Ribeiro) DeCampos; m. John Lowell Allen, Dec. 20, 1969. Home econs. tchr. Santa Catarina DeMessina, São Paulo, Brazil, 1954-61; restaurant mgr. Hotel Esmeralda, São Paulo, 1961-63; cooking tchr. adult edn. Monmouth County, Ocean Twp., N.J., 1979; cooking tchr. D. Crosby Ross Sch., Santa Barbara, Calif., 1980-82, Santa Barbara (Calif.) Cooking Sch., 1981-83; cooking tchr. adult edn. Danbury (Conn.) High Sch., 1984-90; cooking tchr. Peter Kump's Cooking Sch., N.Y.C., 1985-91, New Sch. for Social Rsch., N.Y.C., 1986—, Sandy's Brazilian and Continental Cuisine, Oxford, Conn., 1990—; pres., CEO S.B. & C.C., Inc., 1994—; cons. Elizabeth Schneider (writer), N.Y.C., 1986. Judge, Conn. Dept. Agr. Pie Bake, Brookfield, 1991-92, Kraft's Salad Dressing Contest, Bethlehem, Conn., 1991; v.p. NYACT, 1994—. Mem. Internat. Assn. Culinary Profls. (chmn. Conn. regional meeting 1989, cert. culinary profl.), Conn. Woman's Culinary Assn., N.Y. Assn. Cooking Tchrs. (bd. dirs. 1991-92), James Beard Found. (cons. 1991). Home and Office: Sandy's Brazilian and Continental Cuisine 222 Maple Tree Hill Rd Oxford CT 06478

ALLEN, SARAH DUNGEY, editor; b. Dayton, Ohio, July 22, 1942; d. Arthur Bertram and Lucretia M. (Nash) Dungey; child from previous marriage: Michael Uman; m. Marshall B. Allen; 1 child, Sebastian. Student, New Sch. for Social Rsch., 1962-64. Editorial assoc., publicity dir. Grove Press, Inc., N.Y.C., 1970-79; sr. editor Playboy Paperbacks, N.Y.C., 1979-81, Berkley Pub., N.Y.C., 1982-85; exec. editor Consumer Reports Books, Yonkers, N.Y., 1985-94, Rights Unltd., N.Y.C., 1994—.

ALLEN, SARAH GARDNER, wildlife ecologist; b. Morristown, N.J., Aug. 12, 1951; d. Richard Donovan and Janet (Brown) A. BS, U. Calif., Berkeley, 1976, MS, 1988, PhD, 1994. Biologist, rsch. assoc. Point Reyes Bird Obs., Stinson Beach, Calif., 1976-82, staff biologist, 1982-88, rsch. assoc., 1988—; grad. asst. State Lands Commn., Sacramento, Calif., 1989-91, U. Calif., Berkeley, 1991-93; ecologist Nat. Park Svc., San Francisco, 1993—; mem. sci. adv. bd. Marine Mammal Ctr., Sausalito, Calif., 1984—. Mem. Am. Soc. Photogrametry and Remote Sensing (award North chpt. 1988), Soc. Marine Mammalogy, Wildlife Soc., Soc. Conservation Biology, Pacific Seabird Group. Office: Nat Park Svc 600 Harrison St Ste 600 San Francisco CA 94907

ALLEN, THERESA OHOTNICKY, neurobiologist, consultant; b. Torrington, Conn., Apr. 27, 1948; d. Frank Richard and Helen Theresa (Drozdenko) Ohotnicky; m. Thomas Atherton Allen, Aug. 12, 1972; children: Melanie Atherton, Abigail Baldwin. BA, U. Conn., 1970; MS, Villanova U., 1975; PhD, Duke U., 1978; cert. in bus. adminstrn., U. Pa., 1983. Realtor. Rsch. assoc. U. Pa., Phila., 1981-83; sci. dir. Drexel U., Phila., 1983-84; cons. on neurobiology to sci.-oriented cos., 1984—. Contbr. articles to profl. jours., also chpts. to books. Bd. dirs. Gladwyne (Pa.) Libr. League, 1986—, Athena Inst. for Women's Wellness, Haverford, Pa., 1989-93; trustee Gladwyne Libr., 1988—, pres., 1991-93; com. chmn. Jr. League Phila., 1989-90. Fellow Inst. Neurol. Scis., U. Pa., 1978-80, NIH, 1980-81. Mem. Phila. Skating Club, Humane Soc., Phi Beta Kappa. Episcopalian. Home: 1433 Waverly Rd Gladwyne PA 19035-1224 Office: 336 Conshohockew State Rd Gladwyne PA 19035

ALLEN, VICKI LYNETTE, physical education educator; b. Denver, Oct. 27, 1952; d. Donald Joseph and Jacqueline (Jones) Roth; m. Robert Craig Allen, Aug. 14, 1976; children: Jeffrey, Gregory, Stacy. BA magna cum laude, Calif. State U., Northridge, 1974; MEd summa cum laude, U. Nev., Las Vegas, 1987. Cert. tchr., Nev. Tchr. phys. edn., jr. varsity basketball coach Beverly Hills (Calif.) Unified Sch. Dist., 1975-78; tchr. secondary phys. edn. Clark County Sch. Dist., Las Vegas, 1978-89, elementary tchr. phys. edn., 1989—, basketball coach, 1988-89; adj. instr. U. Nev., Las Vegas, 1993—; mem. phys. fitness task force Clark County Sch. Dist., 1990-91, integrated curriculum task force, 1992-93; mem. Nev. State Dept. Edn. com. to set stds. for phys. edn. tchr. licensure, 1993; presenter workshops, 1990-94. Author phys. fitness and multicultural games publs. Coach Nev. State Youth Soccer Orgn., Las Vegas, 1988-91, Am. Youth Soccer Orgn., 1992; eucharistic minister St. Thomas More Cath. Ch., Las Vegas, 1991—, core leader for youth group, 1994-95. Jr. League Nev. grantee, 1991. Mem. NEA, AAHPERD, Nev. Alliance Health, Phys. Edn., Recreation and Dance (membership chair 1993-94, v.p. elect 1994-95), Phi Kappa Phi. Office: Whitney Elem Sch 5005 Keenan St Las Vegas NV 89122

ALLEN, VICKY, business development technical specialist; b. Springfield, Pa., May 27, 1957; d. James Joseph and Ann Marie (Cifone) Cattafesta; m. James Francis DeLeone, Aug. 11, 1979 (div. 1982); m. Dennis Ronald Allen, June 30, 1990. BBA in Computer Sci., Temple U., 1979. Quality assurance Burroughs Corp., Downingtown, Pa., 1977, software QA, 1978, systems analyst, 1979-81; program analyst Crocker Internal Systems, San Jose, Calif., 1981-83; sr. systems analyst Avantek, Inc., Santa Clara, Calif., 1983-84; bus. devel. tech. specialist Micro Focus, Palo Alto, Calif., 1984—; programmer cons. Fin. Group, Palo Alto, 1985-86. Active Sierra Club. Mem. Phi Sigma Sigma (sec. 1978-79). Democrat. Roman Catholic. Office: Micro Focus 2465 E Bayshore Rd Ste 400 Palo Alto CA 94303-3205

ALLEN-CLAIBORNE, JOYCE G., clinical and educational psychologist; b. Columbus, Ga., Feb. 23 1948; d. Homer W. Jr. and Berneda C. Allen; B.A. cum laude, Spelman Coll., 1970; M.A., U. Pitts., 1972, Ph.D. (NIMH pub. health fellow, 1972-74), 1975; m. Andrew J. Claiborne, Nov. 20, 1976 (dec.); 1 child, Jomo Abd-Allah Kenyatta Claiborne. Teaching fellow U. Pitts., 1972, research assoc., 1975-77; clin. psychologist Hillcrest Children's Center, Washington, 1977-78; pvt. practice clin. psychology, Washington, 1980-90; psychologist, Region D, D.C. Pub. Schs., Washington, 1979-90; adj. prof. Union Grad. Sch., Clin., 1980-83; mem. rev. bd. Nat. Register Health Service Providers in Psychology, 1987-90; psychologist Dougherty County Sch. System, 1990—. Adv. bd. St. Anselm's Abbey Day Camp, Washington. Mem. APA, Assn. Black Psychologists, Delta Sigma Theta. Baptist. Home: 601 Freemont St Albany GA 31707-4507 Office: PO Box 1470 Albany GA 31702-1470

ALLENDER, NANCY G., corporate turnaround specialist, commercial print broker; b. Eugene, Oreg., May 30, 1957; d. Marvin Loren and Leslie Marie (Ramsey) A. BS in Adminstrn., Oreg. State U., 1979; postgrad., Ariz. State U., 1979, Rockhurst U., Kansas City, Mo., 1983. Asst. gen. mgr./player-coach Dallas Diamonds, Women's Basketball League, 1979-80; circulation asst. Dallas Cowboys, NFL, 1979-82; season ticket mgr., asst. mktg. dir. Kansas City (Mo.) Kings, NBA, 1982-84; sales mgr. Northwest Web, Eugene, Oreg., 1984-86; pres., owner NGA & Assocs., Portland, Oreg., 1986-90; turnaround workout cons. Hamstreet and Co., 1990—; asst. coach Women's Pro-Am Summer League, Garland, Tex., 1979-80; basketball coach NBA Summer/Winter Youth Prog., Kansas City, 1982-83. Big sister Y-Round Table Big Bro./Sister, Corvallis, 1975-79; track ofcl. Spl. Olympics, Tempe, Ariz., 1979; bd. vols. Scottish Rite Hosp. for Crippled Children, Dallas, 1981; coordinator Autistic Soc. for Children, Dallas, 1979-82; active Teensand Co. Theater Prodn. Planned Parenthood, 1994; participant animal assistance therapy Oreg. Humane Soc., 1994. Recipient Tex. Disting. Svcs. award, State of Tex., 1981. Mem. NAFE, NOW, Nat. Abortion Rights Action League, Oreg. State U. Alumni Assn., Kappa Alpha Theta (Panhellenic del.), Sigma Chi, Delta Chi. Republican. Office: NGA & Associates PO Box 987 Lake Oswego OR 97034-0109

ALLEN-HAYNES, LEETTA MARIE, researcher, educator, consultant; b. New Orleans, Aug. 24, 1945; d. Charles Edward and Elizabeth (Thomas) Allen; m. Vernon E. Haynes, Jr. (div. 1993). BA in Sociology, U. New Orleans, 1973; MA in Counseling, Xavier U., 1987; PhD in Edn. Adminstrn., U. New Orleans, 1993. Lic. prof. mental health counselor. Dir. Head Start Ctr., New Orleans, 1971-79, Orleans Parish Truancy Ctr., New Orleans, 1979-89; cons., auditor La. Dept. Health and Hosps., New Orleans, 1989-91; rsch. assoc. U. New Orleans, 1991—; adj. faculty U. New Orleans, 1991-94; asst. prof. So. U., Baton Rouge, 1994—; grad. rep. at rsch. seminar Danforth Found., Balt., 1991-94. Chairperson bd. youth svcs. Kingsley House, Inc., New Orleans, 1989-91. Invited to Tesity U.S. Hous Subcom. on Edn., Washington, 1992. Mem. AACD, AAUW, ASCD, NEA, Am. Ednl. Rsch. Assn., Phi Delta Kappa. Democrat. Roman Catholic. Home: PO Box 871603 New Orleans LA 70187-1603

ALLEN-LOMARO, YVETTE MARIE, coordinator student activities; b. Morristown, N.J., Aug. 29, 1966; d. Kenard William and Jean Marie (Shema) A.; m. Todd Andrew Lomaro, Oct. 21, 1989. BA, Rutgers U., 1988, postgrad., 1994—. Dir. student activities Coll. St. Elizabeth, Convent Station, N.J., 1988-91; asst. coord. student activities Rutgers Coll., New Brunswick, N.J., 1991-92, coord. student activities, 1992—; co-founder, co-pres. Rutgers Higher Edn. Assn. Rutgers Univ., New Brunswick; grants com. Rutgers U., 1992—; edn. chair Assn. Coll. Unions Internat., 1991. Mem. Phi Delta Kappa (coord. sec. 1994). Democrat. Roman Catholic. Home: 9 Broadview Dr Newton NJ 07860-6106 Office: Rutgers Coll 613 George St New Brunswick NJ 08901-1176

ALLENSTEIN, GLORIA GOMEZ, technical writer, consultant; b. Denver, Nov. 26, 1945; d. Cecelio and Ursula (Ortiz) Gomez; m. Felix Martinez, Sept. 10, 1965 (div. 1965); m. Myron Allenstein, Mar. 24, 1973; children: Solomon, Christie, Rose, Angel. BA, Jacksonville State U., 1986, postgrad., 1992. Caseworker Denver Gen. Health Hosps., 1966-73; therapist C.E.D. Mental Health Ctr., Gadsden, Ala., 1973-76; exec. dir. C.E.D. Regional Alcoholism Coun., Gadsden, 1976-94; pres. Ramah House Inc., Gadsden, 1987-93; devel. dir. Christian Counseling Ctr., Gadsden, 1990-94; owner Antonio's Italian Ristorante, Gadsden, 1993—; bd. mem. The Love Ctr. for Homeless, Gadsden, 1990-94, The Young Life Com., Gadsden, 1988-91; grants writer Gadsden Pub. Sch. Bd., 1989—. Candidate Ala. Ho. of Reps. from dist. 26, 1986, 90; grad. Leadership Ala., 1992; active United Givers-Red Feather Club, Gadsden, 1990—, City Inc., 1991-92, Fighting Back Quest for Excellence Com.; bd. dirs. Rosa Young Sch. Mem. Etowah County C. of C. (mem. econ. com.). Democrat. Lutheran. Home: 510 S 10th St Gadsden AL 35901-9999 Office: Ramah House Inc 141 S 9th St Gadsden AL 35901-3645

ALLENSWORTH, DOROTHY ALICE, education foundation administrator; b. Willoughby, Ohio, Aug. 12, 1907; d. William and Effie Alice (Minthorn) Etzensperger; m. Carl Allensworth, Jan. 12, 1944; children: Stephen Edward, Robert Minthorn. BA, Smith Coll., Northampton, Mass., 1929; MA, Western Res. U., 1935. Various positions, 1935-41; program dir. Cleve. Festival of Freedom, 1939-41; costume designer Shrine Circus, Cleve., 1941, 49th St. Circus, Rockefeller Ctr., N.Y.C., 1942, Shubert Costume Co., N.Y.C., 1942-44; co-producer Cedarhurst (N.Y.C) Summer Theatre, 1943; costumer Chgo. Ice Circus, 1944; dir. neighborhood youth corps Westchester Community Opportunity Program, U.S. Dept. Labor, Westchester County, N.Y., 1965-68; founder, exec. dir. Coll. Careers Fund of Westchester, Westchester County, 1967-91. Co-author: The Complete Play Production Handbook, 1973; co-author (play) Interurban, 1947-48. Pres. Rye Neck Sch. Dist. Community Coun., Mamaroneck, N.Y., 1953-57; mem., co-founder recreation coun. Village of Mamaroneck, 1957-59, chmn. recreation commn., 1960-65; co-founder Village Fours pre-school program for 4-yr. olds. Recipient Award for Improving Human Rels., B'nai B'rith Tri-Town chpt., Larchmont, Mamaroneck, Harrison, N.Y., 1967, Woman of Achievement award Westchester County, 1975, Jesse Hill Meml. award Ionic 108 lodge Prince Hall Masons, Westchester County, 1977, Onward and Upward award New Rochelle (N.Y.) Urban League, 1978, Humanitarian award United Bapt. Deacon's Union and Deaconess' Aux., Westchester County, 1979, Disting. Alumna medal Smith Coll., 1980, citation Gov. of N.Y., 1989, Edn. for the Poor award Westchester County, 1991, Award for Educating Poor Minority Youth Westchester Clubmen, 1991, State Senator Suzi Oppenheimer award for edn., 1991, Congresswoman Nita Lowey spl. award for dedication to the poor, 1991. Mem. Westchester Coun. on Crime and Delinquency (bd. dirs.), Westchester Coalition for Legal Abortion (bd. dirs.), Westchester Alliance for Juvenile and Criminal Justice (Marjorie Johnson Margolis award 1985). Home: 220 S Barry Ave Mamaroneck NY 10543-4103

ALLER, MARGO FRIEDEL, astronomer; b. Springfield, Ill., Aug. 27, 1938; d. Jules and Claire (Cornick) Friedel; m. Hugh Duncan Aller, Aug. 17, 1963; 1 child, Monique Christine. BA, Vassar Coll., 1960; postgrad., Harvard U., 1961-62; MS, U. Mich., 1964, PhD, 1969. Mathematician programmer Smithsonian Astrophys. Obs., Cambridge, Mass., 1960-62; rsch. assoc. U. Mich., Ann Arbor, 1970-76, assoc. rsch. scientist, 1976-85, rsch. scientist, 1985—; mem. users' com. Nat. Radio Astronomy Observatory, 1984-86. Mem. Am. Astron. Soc., Internat. Astron. Union, Sigma Xi. Office: U Mich Dept Astronomy 817 Dennison Bldg Ann Arbor MI 48109-1090

ALLEY, KIRSTIE, actress; b. Wichita, Kans., Jan. 12, 1955; m. Parker Stevenson; 1 child, William True. Student, U. Kans., Kans. State U. Actress: (stage prodns.) Cat on a Hot Tin Roof, Answers; (feature films) Star Trek II: The Wrath of Khan, 1982, Blind Date, 1984, Champions, 1984, Runaway, 1984, Summer School, 1987, Shoot to Kill, 1988, Look Who's Talking, 1989, Daddy's Home, 1989, One More Chance, 1990, Madhouse, 1990, Sibling Rivalry, 1990, Look Who's Talking Too, 1990, Look Who's Talking Now, 1993; (TV mini-series) North and South Book I, 1985, North and South, Book II, 1986; (TV movies) Sins of the Past, 1984, A Bunny's Tale, 1984, The Prince of Bel Air, 1985, Stark: Mirror Image, 1986, Infidelity, 1987, David's Mother, 1994 (Emmy award, Lead Actress - Special, 1994); (TV series) Masquerade, 1984-85, Cheers, 1987-1993 (Emmy award as Outstanding Lead Actress in a Comedy Series 1991). Office: Met Travel Agy 4526 Wilshire Blvd Los Angeles CA 90010*

ALLEYNE, BARBARA CHRISTINA, retail executive; b. Bridgetown, Barbados; d. Percival and Chriscilda (Mullin) Bennett; 1 child, Eric. AA, Elizabeth Seton Coll., Yonkers, N.Y., 1978; BA in English, Marymount Coll., Tarrytown, 1981. With Barbados Local Govt., 1959-61, Community Svc. Soc., N.Y.C., 1962-64; exec. sec. YMCA of Greater N.Y., N.Y.C., 1964-72; adminstrv. asst. Ford Found., N.Y.C., 1972-86, Texaco Inc., White Plains, N.Y., 1975-86; contbns. asst. Texaco Found. of Texaco Inc., White Plains, 1987-90; pres., owner Flick City, Inc., White Plains, 1986—; v.p. Texaco Forum, 1988, pres., 1989. Vol. YMCA Greater N.Y.; founder, bd. dirs. Greenburgh 4-H Club, N.Y., 1978-80. Recipient Outstanding Svc. award YMCA Greater N.Y., 1970. Mem. Eta Phi Beta. Home: 24 Manitou Trl White Plains NY 10603-3020

ALLIGOOD, ELIZABETH H., special education educator; b. W. Palm Beach, Fla., Dec. 7, 1931; d. Hubert Victor and Ethel Ruth (Palmer) Hiers; m. Jesse LeRoy Alligood, Aug. 24, 1952; children: Stephen Leon, Larry Lamar, Miriam Ruth, Julia Ann, Carol Beth. AA, Norman Coll., 1951; BS in Edn., Valdosta State, 1978; postgrad., Columbus Coll., 1987, 92. Cert. tchr., Ga. Resource educator Irwin County Bd. Edn., Ocilla, Ga., 1969-71; dir. Sunny Dale Tng. Ctr., Ocilla, Ga., 1971-78, Green Oaks Tng. Ctr., Moultrie, Ga., 1978-81; tchr. Calhoun County Bd. Edn., Edison, Ga., 1978; cons. Am. Heart Assn., Columbus, Ga., 1984-86; tchr. Thomas County Bd. Edn., Thomasville, Ga., 1987-89, Muscogee County Bd. Edn., Columbus, 1989-94, Colquitt County Bd. Edn., Moultrie, Ga., 1994—; founder Sunny Dale Tng. Ctr., 1969; mem. adv. bd. Columbus Specialized Preschool, 1985. Chairperson W. Ga. area Mental Health Adv. Coun., Columbus, 1986-87. Named to Honors Day, Sunny Dale Tng. Ctr., 1992. Mem. Civitan, Assn. Retarded Citizens Ga. (bd. dirs. at large 1977-78, state sec. 1980-81,), Ga. Assn. Educators. Democrat. Baptist.

ALLISON, ANNE MARIE, librarian; b. Oak Park, Ill., Oct. 3, 1931; d. Gerald Patrick and Anna Evelyn (Beam) Myers; m. James Dixon Alison, Aug. 28, 1954; children: Mark, Mary, Clare, Ruth, Edward. BA in French, St. Mary of the Woods Coll., 1951; postgrad., U. Fribourg, 1952-53; MLS, Rosary Coll., 1968. Asst. libr. Triton Coll., River Grove, Ill., 1967-68; asst. libr. tech. svcs. Moraine Valley Community Coll., Palos Hills, Ill., 1968-69; dir. learning resources, head libr. Coll. Lake County, Grayslake, Ill., 1969-71; asst. head catalog dept. Kent (Ohio) State U. Librs., 1971-73, head processing dept., 1973-79, asst. dir. libr. svcs., 1979-81; acting dir. Fla. Atlantic U. Libr., Boca Raton, 1980-81; asst. dir., head tech. svcs. Wayne State U. Librs., Detroit, 1981-83; dir. librs. U. Cen. Fla., Orlando, 1983—; past chair, bd. dirs. Fla. Extension Libr., Tampa; bd. dirs. Ctr. for Libr. Automation, Gainesville, Fla., Cen. Fla. Holocaust Meml. Resource Ctr., Orlando. Editor: OCLC: A National Library Network, 1979; contbr. articles to profl. jours. Arbitrator alternative dispute resolution program Better Bus. Bur. Cen. Fla., Maitland, 1985—; active Friends Winter Park Pub. Libr., Friends of Orlando Pub. Libr. Recognized for Outstanding Leadership in Edn. Cen. Fla. Ednl. Consortium for Women, 1990. Mem. ALA (chair profl. ethics com.), Fla. Libr. Assn., Fla. Assn. Coll. and Rsch. Librs. (pres. bd. dirs.). Office: U Cen Fla PO Box 25000 Orlando FL 32816

ALLISON, BRENDA KAYE, special education educator; b. Clover, S.C., Dec. 19, 1952; d. Waddell and Georgia Elois (McDaniel) A. BA, Johnson C. Smith U., 1975; MEd, Coppin State Coll., 1978. Cert. educator, Md. Diagnostic/prescriptive tchr. Balt. City Pub. Schs., 1978-82, resource tchr., 1982-88, spl. edn. tchr., 1988-90; spl. edn. tchr. Balt. County Pub. Schs., Towson, Md., 1990-92, Balt., 1992—; GED testing proctor Md. State Dept. Edn., Balt., 1988—; home/hosp. tutor Balt. County Pub. Schs., 1991—. With USAF, 1990-91; with Md. Air N.G., 1991—. Mem. Balt. County Tchrs. Assn., Nat. Tchrs. Assn. Democrat. Methodist. Home: 1421 Druid Hill Ave Baltimore MD 21217-3423

ALLISON, DONNA M. (DONNA MAUGHAN), critical care nurse; b. Doylestown, Pa., Apr. 20, 1965; d. James H. and Elsie A. (Haubeck) Maughan; m. Scott D. Allison, July 21, 1990; children: Heather M., Scott D. Jr. BSN cum laude, U. Pa., 1987. Staff nurse pediatric ICU A. I. duPont Inst., Wilmington, Del.; staff nurse neo-natal ICU Hosp. of U. of Pa., Phila.; staff nurse Children's Seashore House, Phila.; staff nurse adult ICU/trauma unit Brandywine Hosp., Caln, Pa.; nurse neonatal ICU Riddle Hosp., Pa. Mem. Nat. Assn. Neo Natal Nurses.

ALLISON, ELISABETH KOVACS, information company executive; b. Lorain, Ohio, Sept. 6, 1946; d. Emery and Helen (Loose) Kovacs; m. Graham T. Allison. BA, Harvard U., 1967, PhD in Bus. Econs., 1972. Lectr. bus. sch. Harvard U., Boston, 1972-73; asst. prof. econs. Harvard U., Cambridge, Mass., 1974-77, assoc. prof. econ., 1977-80; sr. economist DRI, Lexington, Mass., 1980-83, mgr. electronic pub., 1983-85; dir. acquisitions McGraw-Hill Pub., N.Y.C., 1985-86, v.p. acquisitions, 1987-88, sr. v.p. devel., 1989—; dir. New Perspectives Fund EuroPacific Fund; bd. dirs. New Perspectives Fund, Euro Pacific. Contbr. numerous articles to profl. jours. Mem. Am. Econ. Assn., Phi Beta Kappa. Clubs: Harvard (Boston and N.Y.). Home: 69 Pinehurst Rd Belmont MA 02178-1502

ALLISON, JOAN KELLY, music educator, pianist; b. Denison, Iowa, Jan. 25, 1935; d. Ivan Martin and Esther Cecelia (Newborg) K.; m. Guy Hendrick Allison, July 25, 1954 (div. Apr. 1973); children: David, Dana, Douglas, Diane. MusB, St. Louis Inst. of Music, 1955; MusM, So. Meth. U., 1976. Korrepetitor Corpus Christi (Tex.) Symphony, 1963-85; staff pianist Am. Inst. Mus. Studies, Graz, Austria, 1974-89; prof. Del Mar Coll., Corpus Christi, 1976—; adj. prof. Del Mar Coll., 1959-75, Corpus Christi State U., 1978-93, Tex. A&M U., Corpus Christi, 1993—; program dir. Corpus Christi Chamber Music Soc., 1986—; piano chmn. Corpus Christi Young Artists' Competition, 1987—; chmn. Del Mar Coll. Student Programs Com., 1986-88, 91-92, 94-95; chmn. radio commn., S.Tex. Pub. Broadcasting Svc., Corpus Christi, 1987-88; asst. mus. dir. Little Theater, Corpus Christi, 1970-74; judge, Houston Symphony Auditions, 1988, S.C. Young Artist Competition, Columbia, 1990; freelance accompanist, 1955—, adjudicator, 1960—; v.p. united fac., Del Mar Coll., 1986-88; pianist with Del Mar Trio, 1965-95, Young Audiences, Inc., 1975-83; recital tours in U.S., Mex., Austria, 1954-88. Piano soloist, St. Louis Symphony, 1956, 57, Bach Festival Orch., St. Louis, 1955, Corpus Christi Symphony; recipient Artist Presentation award, Artist Presentation Soc., St. Louis, 1956. Co-chmn. Mayor's Com. on Recycling, Corpus Christi, 1989-91; bd. dirs. Corpus Christi Symphony; adv. bd. Corpus Christi Concert Ballet. Mem. Music Tchrs. Nat. Assn., Tex. Music Tchrs. Assn., Corpus Christi Music Tchrs. Assn., Liszt Soc. Home: 4709 Curtis Clark Dr Corpus Christi TX 78411-4801 Office: Del Mar Coll Baldwin & Ayers Corpus Christi TX 78404

ALLISON, JOAN LACEY, educational administrator, consultant; b. Munhall, Pa., Aug. 23, 1949; d. John Joseph and Margaret (Bamford) Lacey; divorced; 1 child, Kevin John. BS in Speech and Lang. Psychology, U. Pitts., 1972, MEd in Early Childhood Edn., 1973; postgrad., DePaul U., NYU, 1980, Fla. State U., 1984. Fellow U. Pa.; tchr. DuPage/West Cook Spl. Edn. Coop., Lombard, Ill., 1973-77, ednl. cons., 1977-78, dir. low incidence summer, 1978—, adminstr. instrnl. programs, 1988—; contractual cons. Ill. Deaf Blind Svc. Ctr., Glen Ellyn, 1982-86; instr. No. Ill. U., DeKalb, 1988; mem. Blue Ribbon Com. for Persons with Disabilities, 1994. Author: (tng. manual) Illinois College of Optometry Low Vision, 1985; presenter in field. Pres. Ill. Vision Leadership Coun., 1984-86, sec.-treas., 1982-84, program chair statewide conf., 1983, 84; trainer Midwest Regional Deaf-Blind Ctr., East Lansing, Mich., 1985, 86; credit com. mem. DuPage Schs. Credit Union, Wheaton, Ill., 1982-85; nat. ad hoc com. Am Found. for Blind, N.Y.C., 1984; vol. coord. Lowe's Syndrome Assn., Chgo., 1988; mem. adv. com. Ill. State Bd. Edn., 1978, 88, hearing officer, 1989—. Recipient Jane Landis award, 1994; U.S. Office Edn. fellow, Pitts., 1973; Calif. State U. fellow, Northridge, 1978. Mem. ASCD, Ill. Adminstrs. Spl. Edn., Coun. for Exceptional Children. Home: 1522 Huntleigh Dr Wheaton IL 60187 Office: DuPage/West Cook Regional Spl Edn Assn 1500 S Grace St Lombard IL 60148

ALLISON, MARY DONZETTA, cosmetologist; b. Carnegie, Okla., Dec. 31, 1955; d. Billy Joe and Sadie Viola Williams; m. Mark Wayne Landers, Feb. 13, 1978 (div. 1988); children: Christina Lynn, Christopher Michael, Crystal Diane; m. Terry Wayne Allison, Oct. 15, 1988. Cosmetology cert., Arleen's Beauty, Clinton, Okla., 1992. Cert. cosmetologist Okla. State Bd. Cosmetology. Nurse's aide Clinton Regional Hosp., Clinton, 1979-80; waitress Park Inn, Clinton, 1987-90; census taker 1990 census Fed. Govt., Okla., 1989-90; caretaker of elderly Clinton, 1990-92; cosmetologist The Vintage Salon, Clinton, 1992—; owner, operator The Hair Express of Cordell, Cordell, Okla., 1994—. Office: The Hair Express of Cordell 119 E Main St Cordell OK 73632

ALLISON, MERITA ANN, state legislator. Mem. S.C. Ho. of Reps., 1993—; spl. program coord. Springs Indust-Lyman Complex. Republican. Office: SC House of Reps State House Columbia SC 29211*

ALLISON, TOMILEA, mayor; b. Madera, Calif., Mar. 28, 1934; d. John and Edna (Archer) Radosevich; m. James Allison, 1958; children: Devon, Leigh. B.A. in Sociology, Occidental Coll., 1955; postgrad. Fresno State Coll., 1956. City council mem. City of Bloomington, Ind., 1977-82, mayor, 1983—; pres. Ind. Assn. Cities and Towns, 1994. Active Citizens for Good Govt., Bloomington, 1960-65, Community Progress Council, 1980-85. Mem. LWV, Bloomington C. of C. Recipient Russell G. Lloyd Dist. Svc. award. Democrat. Home: 1127 E First St Bloomington IN 47402 Office: 220 E 3rd St Bloomington IN 47401-0100

ALLMAN, MARGO HUTZ, sculptor, painter; b. N.Y.C., Feb. 23, 1933; d. Werner H. and Avis (Newcomb) Hutz; student Smith Coll., 1950-51, Moore Coll. Art, 1952-54, Hans Hofmann Sch. Art, 1953, U. Del., 1967-70; m. William B. Allman, Feb. 19, 1954; children—Avis Louise, David Drue. One-person shows include: Wallingford (Pa.) Art Center, 1964, Windham Coll., 1974, Bloomsburg State Coll., 1976, 77, Moore Coll. Art, 1979, Marian Locks Gallery, Phila., 1984, West Chester U., Pa., 1994; group shows include: Phila. Art Alliance, 1954, Del. Art Museum, Wilmington, 1958 (Ann. Show Drawing prize), 65, 67, Print Club, Phila., 1959, U. Del., 1977, Del. State Arts Council, Wilmington, 1981, C. Grimaldis Gallery, Balt., 1983, Art in Form Gallery, Karlsruhe, W.Ger., Contemporary Women Artists of Phila., 1986-87, Del. Art Mus., 1993; represented in permanent collections, including: Del. Mus., Phila. Mus.; works include: Ferro Cement Sculpture, Tidewater Pub. Co., Centerville, Md., 1975, Crocheted Sculpture of Herculon, Hercules Inc., Wilmington, 1975. Bd. dirs. Robert Small Dance Co., N.Y.C., 1979-80. Recipient Mildred Boericke prize Print Club, Phila., 1958, Landscape prize Wilmington Trust Bank, 1969. Mem. Moore Coll. Art Alumnae Assn., Del. Center Contemporary Arts, Del. Art Mus., Nat. Mus. Women in the Arts (charter mem.). Unitarian. Home: 202 State Rd West Grove PA 19390-8906

ALLMAND, LINDA F(AITH), library director; b. Port Arthur, Tex., Jan. 31, 1937; d. Clifton James and Jewel Etoile (Smith) A. BA, North Tex. State U., 1960; MA, U. Denver, 1962. Clerical asst. Gates Meml. Libr., 1953-55; libr. asst. Houston Pub. Libr., 1955-58; children's libr. Denver Pub. Libr., 1960-63; children's coord. Anaheim Pub. Libr., Calif., 1963-65; br. mgr. Dallas Pub. Libr, 1965-71, chief br. svcs., 1971-81; dir. Ft. Worth Pub. Libr., 1981—; instr. North Tex. State U., Denton, 1967—; instr. Dallas County C.C., 1981; bldg. cons. Dallas Pub. Libr., 1974-80, Hurst Pub. Libr., 1977-78, Jacksonville (Tex.) Pub. Libr., 1976-79, Carrollton Pub. Libr., 1979-81, Haltom (Tex.) City Pub. Libr., 1984, Iowa Park (Tex.) Pub. Libr., 1985, S.W. Regional Libr., Ft. Worth, 1987. Author: 1981-2000, Ft. Worth Public Library—Facilities and Long-Range Planning Study, 1982; contbr. chpts. to books, articles to profl. jours. Bd. dirs. City of Dallas Credit Union, 1973-81, Sr. Citizen's Ctrs., Inc., 1982; com. chmn. Goals for Dallas, 1967-69; mem. Forum Ft. Worth, 1983. Pilot Club of Port Arthur scholar, 1954, Libr. Binding Inst. scholar, 1958; recipient Disting. Alumnus award North Tex. State U., 1983, Leadership Ft. Worth, 1982-83; named Tarrant County Newsmaker of the Yr., 1984, Outstanding Leader, Ft. Worth Star Telegram, 1989, Outstanding Woman of the Yr., Mayor's Commn. on Status of Women, 1989, North Tex. Pub. Adminstr. of the Yr., 1990. Mem. ALA, AAUP, AAUW, Tex. Libr. Assn. (pres. pub. libr. divsn. 1980-81, chmn. planning com. 1982-84, pres.-elect 1985-86, pres. 1986-87, Libr. of Yr. award 1985, North Tex. Pub. Adminstr. of Yr. award 1990), Tarrant Regional Librs. Assn., Am. Mgmt. Assn., Dallas County Librs. Assn. (pres. 1968-69), Downtown Ft. Worth (mem. edn. info. task force 1992-93), Freedom to Read Found., Ft. Worth C. of C. (bd. dirs. 1993—), Rotary, Sister Cities, Inc., Ft. Worth Pub. Libr. Found. Home: 701 Timberview Ct N Fort Worth TX 76112-1715 Office: Fort Worth Pub Libr 300 Taylor St Fort Worth TX 76102-7309

ALLMARAS, LORRAINE, state legislator; m. John Allmaras; 3 children. Former tchr., former twp. clk.; mem. N.D. Ho. of Reps. Active County Commn. Mem. Am. Legion Aux. Democrat. Roman Catholic. Home: R R 1 Box 82 New Rockford ND 58356 Office: ND Ho of Reps State Capitol Bismarck ND 58505*

ALLMON, REBECCA LEA, marketing executive; b. San Antonio, Apr. 18, 1956; d. Jack Dale and Dorothy Ruth (Norris) A. BS in Bus., Trinity U., San Antonio, 1980; BS in Journalism/Broadcasting/Film, 1980. News anchor, producer Sta. KTBC-TV, Austin, Tex., 1980-82; pub. rels. dir. Topletz Devel. Co., Austin, 1982-86; pub. rels. account exec. DBG&H Unltd., Inc., Austin and Houston, 1986-88; chief media rels. Tex. Dept. Commerce, Austin, 1988-89; dir. mktg. communications Cycle Sat, Inc., Forest City, Iowa, 1990-93; dir. corp. comm. Expeditors Internat., Seattle, 1993—. Bd. dirs. Big Bros./Big Sisters, Austin, 1987-88, mem. Leadership Iowa Class of 1991, Des Moines, mktg. adv. com. Iowa Dept. Econ. Devel., Des Moines, 1990-93, adv. com. Hospice of Forest City, 1991-93; mem. Des Moines Symphony Guild, 1991-93, Austin Symphony League, 1984-89,. Named Outstanding Woman in Tex. Govt., State of Tex., 1989. Mem. Am. Mktg. Assn. Republican. Office: Expeditors Inernat. 19119 16th Ave S Seattle WA 98188

ALLOGGIAMENTO, NANCY THOMAS, advertising agency executive, consultant, business owner; b. Palos Park, Ill., May 23, 1937; d. Warren Arthur and Ruth Elizabeth (Martin) Thomas; m. Alberto Alloggiamento, Dec. 19, 1965. Student, U. Ill., 1955-57. Media asst. Lennen & Newell Advt., N.Y.C., 1960-64; v.p. media Jameson Advt., N.Y.C., 1964-72; v.p., dir. account services Waterman, Getz, Niedelman Advt., N.Y.C., 1972-77; v.p., account supr. DKG Advt., N.Y.C., 1977-78, deGarmo Advt., N.Y.C., 1978-80, D'Arcy, MacManus & Masius, N.Y.C., 1980-82; pres. NTA & Co., N.Y.C., 1982-83, NTA/An Ogilvy & Mather Co., N.Y.C., 1983—; pres., chief exec. officer Sussman & Sugar/Ogilvy & Mather, N.Y.C., 1985—; pres. NA Communications, N.Y.C., 1983—. Home: 60 Sutton Pl S New York NY 10022-4168 Office: Sussman & Sugar/Ogilvy & Mather 221 W 41st St New York NY 10036-7208

ALLOTTA, JOANNE MARY, elementary education educator; b. Bklyn., Dec. 8, 1962; d. Joseph and Adela (Castagna) A.; m. Edward James Cirminiello, Mar. 23, 1991. BA, St. Joseph's Coll., 1984; MS in Edn., Bklyn. Coll., 1987; postgrad., 1987-88. Cert. tchr., N.Y. Tchr. Holy Family Sch., Bklyn., 1984-85, Pub. Sch. 97, Bklyn., 1985—; curriculum writer dist. 21 N.Y.C., 1991—; mem. sch. guidance and discipline com., 1987-89, com. for sch. improvement, 1988-89; mem. United Fedn. Tchrs. Consultation Com., 1990-91; cooperating tchr. Xavierian H.S. Sr. Involvement Program, 1991-92; participant Dist. 21 Multi-cultural Fair, 1991-94, mem. S.M.A.R.T. com., 1991-94, chair curriculum sub-com., mem. pupil pers. com., 1991—; workshop presenter, curriculum writer Dist. 21, Bklyn., 1992—; reviewer N.Y.C. Bd. Edn., Bklyn., 1992; task force Dist. 21 N.Y. Ptnrship for Statewide Systems Change, 1993—; recording sec. Mainstream Com., 1994—; chmn. Compact for Learning Achieves Successful Schs. com., 1994—; presenter papers in field. Active Pub. Sch. 97 PTA, 1985—; fund raiser St. Jude's Children's Hosp., 1990-94. Recipient Tchr. of Yr. award Phi Delta Kappa, 1994. Mem. ASCD, Am. Fedn. Tchrs., United Fedn. Tchrs., N.Y. State of United Tchrs., Kappa Delta Pi. Roman Catholic. Office: PS 97 1855 Stillwell Ave Brooklyn NY 11223-2439

ALLRED, GLADEEN BURRIS, gerontological counselor; b. Oklahoma City, June 12, 1942; d. Edward Cansler and Gladys Opal (Toler) Burris; m. Larry Dean Allred, July 16, 1966; children: Lance Burris Allred, Brett Buris Allred. BS, Okla. State U., 1964; MA, Tulsa U., 1971; EdD, Okla. State U., 1985. Cert. gerontol. counselor. Tchr. English dept. Cleveland Jr. High Sch., Tulsa, Okla., 1964-65, North Denver (Colo.) High Sch., 1965-67; substitute tchr. Tulsa Pub. Sch. System, 1968-69; dir. care ministries First United Meth. Ch., Stillwater, Okla., 1989-94; program coord. Sr. Day Treatment, Willow View Mental Health Sys., 1994—; adj. prof. Okla. State U., Stillwater, 1986—; counselor Life Adult Day Care Ctr., Stillwater, 1992—; host, radio show Sta. KSPI-AM, Stillwater, 1992—; advisor Sigma Phi Omega, 1991—, Mortor Bd., 1986-88, Pi Beta Phi Sorority, 1983-85. Contbr. articles to profl. jours. Pres. bd. dirs. LIFE, Inc., Stillwater, 1983—; chair Gerontology Grad. faculty Okla. State U., 1993—. Mem. ACA, LWV, Am. Soc. on Aging (nat. conf. presenter 1992, 93), S.W. Soc. on Aging, Lions Club (pres. 1992-93), Delta Kappa Gamma. Democrat. Office: Okla State U 202 N Murray Hall Stillwater OK 74078

ALLRED, GLORIA RACHEL, lawyer; b. Phila., July 3, 1941; d. Morris and Stella Bloom; m. William Allred (div. Oct. 1987); 1 child, Lisa. BA, U. Pa., 1963; MA, NYU, 1966; JD, Loyola U., L.A., 1974; JD (hon.), U. West Los Angeles, 1981. Bar: Calif. 1975, U.S. Dist. Ct. (cen. dist.) Calif. 1975, U.S. Ct. Appeals (9th cir.) 1976, U.S. Supreme Ct. 1979. Ptnr. Allred, Maroko, Goldberg & Ribakoff (now Allred, Maroko & Goldberg), L.A., 1976—. Contbr. articles to profl. jours. Pres. Women's Equal Rights Legal Def. and Edn. Fund, L.A., 1978—, Women's Movement Inc., L.A. Recipient Commendation award L.A. Bd. Suprs., 1986, Mayor of L.A., 1986, Pub. Svc. award Nat. Assn. Fed. Investigators, 1986, Vol. Action award Pres. of U.S., 1986. Mem. ABA, Calif. Bar Assn., Nat. Assn. Women Lawyers, Calif. Women Lawyers Assn., Women Lawyers L.A. Assn., Friars (Beverly Hills, Calif.), Magic Castle Club (Hollywood, Calif.). Office: Allred Maroko & Goldberg 6300 Wilshire Blvd Ste 1500 Los Angeles CA 90048-5217*

ALLRED, RITA REED, artist; b. Davenport, Iowa, Apr. 12, 1935; d. Edward Platt and Delia Marie (Quinn) Reed; m. Glenn Charles Scott, June 9, 1956 (div. Nov. 1977); children: Sheryl Marie, Laura Ann; m. Robert Yates Allred, Dec. 9, 1977. Student Marycrest Coll., Davenport, 1953-56; BS in Art Edn., Drake U., 1958. Art tchr. Fayetteville City Schs., N.C., 1961-64, Charlotte-Mecklenburg Schs., N.C., 1967-71; cons., project dir. PCA Internat., Matthews, N.C., 1981; artist, art cons., dir. workshops, 1976—; civilian artist USCG, 1981—; instr. portrait painting Cen. Piedmont Community Coll., 1986—; instr. drawing and painting Mint Mus. Art, 1991—; courtroom sketch artist WBTV, 1991—; adj. prof. art Gardner-Webb U., Boiling Springs, N.C., 1993—; painter in oils; recent commns. include paintings for U.S. Army, USCG, portraits for ABCO Industries, U.S. Naval Inst. Service Head Portrait Series, NASA Art Team; pres. Willow Reed Studios, 1986-90. Bd. dirs. Internat. House, Charlotte, 1985-86; mem. Sister Cities Com., Charlotte, 1984-85. Recipient George Gray award USCG, 1983. Democrat. Mem. Cedarwood Country Club. Avocation: golf. Home and Studio: 7217 Quail Meadow Ln Charlotte NC 28210-5124 Office: Willow Reed Studios 7217 Quail Meadow Ln Charlotte NC 28210-5124

ALLRED, SUSAN CREAGER, lawyer; b. Ogden, Utah, Jan. 25, 1954; d. Theron Benjamin and Janith (Whittemore) Creager; m. John Franklin Allred, Dec. 12, 1992. BA, Weber State U., 1974; JD, U. Utah, 1977. Bar: Utah 1977. Prosecutor Salt Lake County, 1977-80; assoc. gen. counsel Utah State Legislature, Salt Lake City, 1980—. Vol. state dir. Am. Field Svc. Student Exch. Programs, Salt Lake City, 1986—; mem. Utah Symphony Guild, Salt Lake City, 1986—; pres. Community Animal Welfare Soc., Salt Lake City, 1993—. Mem. Utah State Bar Assn., Salt Lake County Bar Assn. Office: Legis Rsch & Gen Counsel 436 Utah State Capitol Salt Lake City UT 84114

ALLYN, AUDRIE GAIL, controller; b. Pasadena, Calif., Dec. 12, 1956; d. Burton Charles and Mildred Virginia (Barnett) A.; m. William Lipton Gannon, July 31, 1982 (div. Nov. 1989). BA, Humboldt State U., 1981; M in Acctg., U. Mont., 1994. Libr. clk. Coll. of the Redwoods, Eureka, Calif., 1983-86; libr. info. specialist U. N.Mex., Albuquerque, 1986-90; libr. technician Sonoma County Libr., Santa Rosa, Calif., 1990-94; grad. asst. U. Mont., Missoula, 1993; contr. The Sterling Group, Missoula, 1994—. Mem. Inst. Mgmt. Accts.

ALLYN, DEANE C., opera company executive; married. Student, Peabody Conservatory. With Sarasota Opera Assn., 1976—, exec. dir., 1986-89, mng. dir., 1989—; bd. dirs. Sarasota Opera Assn. (pres. 1981); mem. Planning Com., Opera Am. Office: Sarasota Opera Assn Sarasota Opera House 61 N Pineapple Ave Sarasota FL 34236*

ALMAN, EMILY ARNOW, sociologist, lawyer; b. N.Y.C., Jan. 20, 1922; d. Joseph Michael and Cecilia (Greenstone) Arnow; B.A., Hunter Coll., 1948; Ph.D., New Sch. for Social Research, 1963; J.D., Rutgers U., Newark, 1977; m. David Alman, Aug. 1, 1940; children: Michelle Alman Harrison, Jennifer Alman Michaels. Bar: N.J. 1978, U.S. Supreme Ct. 1987. Probation officer, N.Y.C., 1945-48; assoc. prof. sociology Douglass Coll. Rutgers U., Newark, 1960-86, prof. emeritus, 1986—; sr. ptnr. Alman & Michaels, Highland Park, N.J., 1978—. Candidate for mayor, City of East Brunswick, 1972; chmn. Concerned Citizens of East Brunswick, 1970-78; pres. bd. trustees Concerned Citizens Environ. Fund., East Brunswick, 1977-78. Mem. ABA (com. family law) N.J. Bar Assn. (bd. dirs. legal svcs), Middlesex County Bar Assn. (Ann. Aldona Appleton award women lawyers sect. 1990, Ann. Svc. to Families award 1993), Am. Sociol. Assn., Assn. Fed. Bar State of N.J., Assn. Trial Lawyers Am., Trial Lawyers Assn. Middlesex County, Law and Soc. Assn., Am. Judicature Soc., Nat. Assn. Women Lawyers, N.J. Assn. Women Lawyers, ACLU, AAUP, Women Helping Women. Author: Ride The Long Night, 1963; screenplay, The Ninety-First Day, 1963. Home: 611 S Park Ave Highland Park NJ 08904-2928

ALMEIDA, EVELYN, retired elementary educator; b. Fall River, Mass., Nov. 21, 1924; d. Amelia (Enos) Almeida. BS in Edn., Bridgewater State Coll., 1946; postgrad., R.I. Coll., 1950's, Bridgewater State Coll., 1970's. Cert. elem. tchr., Mass. Elem. tchr. Swansea (Mass.) Sch. Dept., 1946-94; dir. elem. sch., glee club and drama dir. Luther and Stevens, Swansea, 1948-68; tchr. Brown Sch., Swansea, 1968—; English as second lang. tchr. Fall River Diocesan Clergy, 1970—. Contbr. articles to profl. publs. Sec., treas. parish socs., St. Michael's Ch., Fall River, 1953-67, also pres., fundraising, dir. activities, parish sec. 1945-67, co-chairman golden jubilee Catholic Charities, sec., lector, 1986—, choir mem., tchr. spl. needs children Christian Doctrine Class; fundraiser Assn. for Devel. of Cath. U. of Portugal, Fall River, 1982—; bd. dirs. Swansea PTA, 1946-94; cons. Sch. Coun. Assn., Swansea, 1990-93; mem. Fall River Hist. Soc., 1990—; corr. sec. North End. Community Devel. Assn., Fall River, 1987—; bd. dirs. ednl. com. St. Michael's Fall River Credit Union, 1950's; instr. Fall River Playground, 1940's. Recipient Commonwealth of Mass. Ho. of Reps. citation, 1991, Classroom Excellence citation State House, Boston, Bristol County Commrs. of Mass. citation, Town of Swansea, Mass., proclamation, Hon. Mayor Town of Fall River, Mass., citation, PTO Brown Sch. citation, Outstanding Tchg. citation City Coun. Fall River. Mem. AAUW (edn. role group 1970's), NEA, Mass. Tchrs. Assn., Swansea Educators Assn., Portuguese Am. Fedn. (sec. 1987-90, bd. dirs. 1990-93, 94—, Advancement of Portugese Culture citation), Portuguese Am. Hist. Found. of Fall River (founding mem. bd. dirs. 1991—), Coimbra U. Club (corr. sec.), Cath. Woman's Club (mem. bd., registrat, scholarship com.), Arts Unltd., Bristol County Ret. Tchrs. Assn. of Mass., Friends of Fall River Pub. Libr., Bridgewater Coll. Alumni Assn., Sacred Heart Acad. Alumni Assn., Delta Kappa Gamma. Roman Catholic.

ALMES, JUNE, retired education educator, librarian; b. Pitts., Feb. 14, 1934; d. Donald John Rowbottom and Marie Catherine (Linz) Douglas; widowed; children: Lawrence John, Douglas Alan. BS in Edn., Ind. U. of Pa., 1955; MLS, U. Pitts., 1969. Tchr. Shippensburg (Pa.) Area High Sch., 1964-68; assoc. prof. Lock Haven (Pa.) U., 1971-94; ret., 1990; instr. Changsha U. Electric Power, Hunan, China, 1989-90, 95. Trustee Ross Pub. Libr., Lock Haven, 1975-88, community story programs, 1973-86; tutor Clinton City Literacy Found., Lock Haven, 1979. Mem. Am. Assn. Sch. Librs., Pa. Assn. Sch. Librs., ACLU, Phi Kappa Phi, Phi Delta Kappa. Democrat. Home: 227 Hillside Dr Lock Haven PA 17745-1731

ALMOND, LYNNE SUSAN, healthcare recruiter; b. Warwick, R.I., Sept. 6, 1957; d. George William and Beatrice (Houghton) A. Cert. personnel cons. Mgr. Positions Inc., Boston, 1981-91; corp. recruiter New Medico, Lynn, Mass., 1991-92; recruiter Heath Tour, North Andover, Mass., 1992-93; dir. recruitment Sundance Rehab., East Berlin, Conn., 1993—. Home and Office: Sundance Rehab 31 Warren St Newburyport MA 01950

ALMOND, NANCY ELIZABETH, gifted/talented education educator; b. Florence, Ala., Sept. 4, 1953; d. Lawrence H. and Ann Cullom (Arthur) A. BS, U. North Ala., 1974, MA, 1976; Gifted Cert., U. Ala., Tuscaloosa, 1979. Cert. in elem. edn., early childhood edn., gifted and talented edn., Ala. Sec. Muscle Shoals (Ala.) Schs., 1974; sales clk. Rogers Dept. Store, Florence, Ala., 1974; tchr. Muscle Shoals City Schs., 1975—; treas. Odyssey of the Mind, Tuscaloosa, Ala., 1988-93. Recipient Keller Key U. North Ala., 1974. Mem. NEA, Ala. Edn. Assn., Muscle Shoals Edn. Assn., Soc. Ind. Pioneers, DAR, United Daus. of Confederacy (pres. 1987-89, treas. 1990-94), U.S. Daus. of War of 1812, Daus. of Union Vets. of Civil War. Methodist. Home: 812 Davison Ave Muscle Shoals AL 35661 Office: Muscle Shoals Bd Edn PO Box 2730 Muscle Shoals AL 35661

ALMORE-RANDLE, ALLIE LOUISE, special education educator; b. Jackson, Miss., Apr. 20; d. Thomas Carl and Theressa Ruth (Garrett) Almore; m. Olton Charles Randle, Sr., Aug. 3, 1974. BA, Tougaloo (Miss.) Coll., 1951; MS in Edn., U. So. Calif., L.A., 1971. Recreation leader Pasadena (Calif.) Dept. Recreation, 1954-56; demonstration tchr. Pasadena Unified Schs., 1956-63; cons. spl. edn. Temple City (Calif.) Sch. Dist., 1967; supr. tchr. edn. U. Calif., Riverside, 1971; tchr. spl. edn. Pasadena Unified Sch. Dist., 1955-70, dept. chair spl. edn. Pasadena High Sch., 1972—; also adminstrv. asst. Pasadena High Sch., 1993—; supr. Evelyn Frieden Ctr., U. So. Calif., L.A., 1970; mem. Coun. Exceptional Children, 1993—. Organizer Northwest Project, Camp Fire Girls, Pasadena, 1963; leader Big Sister Program, YWCA, Pasadena, 1966; organizer, dir. March on The Boys' Club, the Portrait of a Boy, 1966; pub. souvenir jours. Women's Missionary Soc., AME Ch., State of Wash. to Mo.; mem. NAACP, Ch. Women United, Afro-Am. Quilters L.A. Recipient Cert. of Merit, Pasadena City Coll., 1963, Outstanding Achievement award Nat. Coun. Negro Women, Pasadena, 1965, Earnest Thompson Seton award Campfire Girls, Pasadena, 1968, Spl. Recognition, Outstanding Community Svc. award The Tuesday Morning Club, 1967, Dedicated Svc. award AME Ch., 1983, Educator of Excellence award Rotary Club of Pasadena, 1993, Edn. award Altadena NAACP, 1994; named Tchr. of Yr., Pasadena Masonic Bodies, 1967, Woman of the Yr. for Community Svc. and Edn., Zeta Phi Beta, 1992; grad. fellow U. So. Calif., L.A., 1970. Mem. NAACP (bd. mem., chmn. ch. workers com. 1955-63, Fight for Freedom award West Coast region 1957, NAACP Edn. award Altadena, Calif. chpt. 1994), ASCD, Calif. Tchrs. Assn., Nat. Coun. Negro Women, Phi Delta Gamma (hospitality chair 1971—), Alpha Kappa Alpha (membership com.), Phi Delta Phi (founder, organizer 1961). Democrat. Mem. AME Ch. Home: 1710 La Cresta Dr Pasadena CA 91103-1261

ALOFF, MINDY, writer; b. Phila., Dec. 20, 1947; d. Jacob and Selma (Album) A.; m. Martin Steven Cohen, June 16, 1968; 1 child, Ariel Nikiya. AB in English, Vassar Coll., 1969; MA in English, SUNY, Buffalo, 1972. Asst. prof. English U. Portland, Oreg., 1973-75; editor Encore Mag. of the Arts, Portland, 1977-80, Vassar Quar., Poughkeepsie, N.Y., 1980-88; free-lance writer Bklyn., 1988—; coord. Portland Poetry Festival, 1974-75. Author (poems) Night Lights, 1979; author essays and revs. theatrical dancing and lit. for New Yorker mag., New Republic mag., Nation mag., Threepenny Rev., Dance mag., N.Y. Times Book Rev., ann. Ency. Britannica, others. Mem. urgent action com. Amnesty Internat. Recipient Whiting Writers award Mrs. Giles Whiting Found., N.Y.C., 1987; Woodrow Wilson Found. fellow, 1969, Woodburn fellow SUNY-Buffalo, 1972, Am. Dance Festival Dance Critics Inst. fellow, New London, Conn., 1977, John Simon Guggenheim Meml. Found. fellow, 1990. Mem. Dance Critics Assn. (pres. 1984-85), Nat. Book Critics Circle (bd. dirs. 1988-91), Phi Beta Kappa.

ALOISI, CAROL ANN, marketing executive; b. Plainfield, N.J., Nov. 29, 1953; d. Edward Charles and Evelyn Helen (Nowhark) Schaffernoth; m. Michael Francis Aloisi, Jan. 20, 1979. BA, Rutgers the State U., 1979; MBA, Rutgers the State U., Newark, 1991. Mgr. employment Bamberger's/Macy's, Newark, 1975-78; pers. adminstr. John Wiley & Sons., N.Y.C., 1978-79, corp. pers. mgr., 1979-81; mgr. pers. adminstrn. Ortho Diagnostic Sys., Inc., N.Y.C., 1981-82, mgr. employee rels., 1982-83, dir. employee rels., 1984-85, nat. account exec., 1985-87, product mgr., 1987-89; dir. mktg. Ortho Diagnostic Sys., Inc., Raritan, N.J., 1989-92; gen. mgr. Ortho Diagnostic Systems Inc., Raritan, N.J., 1992-93; pres. Career Mgmt. Cons., Inc., Bound Brook, N.J., 1994—. Recipient Tribute to Women in Industry award YWCA/TWIN of Cen. N.J., 1987. Mem. Tribute to Women in Industry, BioMed Mktg. Assn., Internat. Assn. Career Mgmt. Profls. Office: Career Mgmt Cons Inc 20 W Maple Ave Bound Brook NJ 08805

ALPER, BARBARA JEANNE, library director; b. Phila., Nov. 3, 1946; d. Edward David and Dorothy (Eligator) A.; m. Alan McCormick (div.); m. Edmond C. Fursa, Feb. 22, 1982. AB, George Washington U., 1968; MLS, Columbia U., 1972. Info. asst. N.Y. Pub. Libr., N.Y.C., 1969-72, libr., 1972-78, sr. libr., 1978-81, libr. III, 1981-85, asst. chief econ. and pub. affairs div., 1985-89; asst. dir. Ridgewood (N.J.) Pub. Libr., 1989-92; dir. Sidney Silverman Libr. Bergen C.C., Paramus, N.J., 1992—. Mem. ALA, N.J. Libr. Assn. Home: 22 Rosewood Ter Bloomfield NJ 07003-3607 Office: Bergen CC 400 Paramus Rd Paramus NJ 07652

ALPERIN, GOLDIE GREEN, consulting librarian, lawyer; b. Des Moines, Aug. 16, 1905; d. Morris and Bessie (Miliwer) Green; LL.B., Drake U., 1927; m. Moses Alperin, Dec. 25, 1930 (dec. 1950); children—Herschel Burton, Judith Miriam. Admitted to Iowa bar, 1927, U.S. Supreme Ct. bar, 1959; practice in Des Moines, 1927-30; law librarian Chgo. Bar. Assn., 1951-63; dir. Def. Information Office, Chgo., 1963-65; librarian book selections Northwestern U. Law Sch. Library, 1966-72; ret., 1972. Named one of 20 rep. U.S. women lawyers of various phases practice Women's Adjustment Bd., London, Eng., 1957; One of Outstanding Women of Am. Bicentennial, Austin (Tex.) Bicentennial Com., 1976; cert. religious sch. tchr. Bd. Jewish Edn., Chgo., 1951. Mem. Am. (sec. 1960-65), Chgo. (past exec. bd., editor 1958-59) assns. law libraries, Nat. Assn. Women Lawyers (regional) dir. 1960-64). Jewish religion. Asst. editor Women Lawyers Jour., 1961-67, exec. bd., 1961-67. Home: 3100 N Lake Shore Dr Apt 1512 Chicago IL 60657-4953

ALPERN, LINDA LEE WEVODAU, health agency administrator; b. Harrisburg, Pa., July 16, 1949; d. William Irvin Wevodau and Maretia Christine (Mills) Staley; m. Neil Stephen Alpern, Apr. 12, 1985; 1 child, Philip Wevodau. BS in Edn., Shippensburg (Pa.) U., 1971. Unit program coord. Pa. Div. Am. Cancer Soc., Harrisburg, 1973-75, unit exec. dir., 1975-76, div. svc. dir., 1976-81; div. med. affairs dir. Pa. Div. Am. Cancer Soc., Hershey, 1981-83; div. crusade dir. Md. Div. Am. Cancer Soc., Balt., 1983-87, div. v.p. for field ops., 1988, div. dep., exec. v.p. ops., 1988—. Bd. dirs., sec. Community Assn. Democrat. Methodist. Home: 4108 Colonial Rd Baltimore MD 21208-6042

ALPERN, MILDRED, history educator, consultant; b. Boston, Sept. 10, 1931; d. Samuel and Mary (Poncewicz) Rosoff; m. Hale Nissen Alpern, Aug. 27, 1954; children—Merry, Spenser. BA, Boston U., 1953; MA summa cum laude, Columbia U., 1966. Cert. tchr. social studies. Tchr. history Spring Valley (N.Y.) Sr. High Sch., 1966—; adj. instr. Rockland Community Coll., Suffern, N.Y., 1973-76; instr. Manhattan Coll., Riverdale, N.Y., summers 1983, 84, 85, 87, LaSalle U., summer 1988, Columbia U. Tchrs. Coll., 1988; mem. advanced placement European history test devel. com., Coll. Bd. 1979-82, chmn. 1982-86, mem. Coll. Bd. history and social scis. adv. com., 1983-85, chmn., 1985-88, chmn. acad. adv. coun., 1987-89, middle states regional assembly, 1993—; master tchr. summer inst. Sarah Lawrence Coll., Bronxville, N.Y., 1984; mem. faculty Coll. Bd. Project Equality Inst., 1986, 87; adj. instr. econs. Syracuse U., 1988—. Co-editor (history column) Am. Hist. Assn. Perspectives, 1982-88; co-author (teaching guide) Household and Kin, 1981; author: Longman's Guide to the Advanced Placement European History Examination, 1993; contbr. articles to profl. publs. Recipient award for contbns. in edn. Rockland County Women's Network, 1984, Tchr. of Yr. award Jr. Achievement, 1989, 90; Finalist N.Y. State Tchr. of Yr., 1988; Fulbright Commn. study grantee, Italy, 1980, NEH grantee Tufts U., 1983. Mem. Orgn. Am. Historians (chmn. teaching div. 1982-83), Am. Hist. Assn. (teaching div.), Phi Beta Kappa, Pi Gamma Mu. Democrat. Home: 13 Cragmere Rd Suffern NY 10901-7515 Office: Spring Valley Sr High Sch RR 59 Spring Valley NY 10977

ALPERT, ANN SHARON, insurance claims examiner; b. Indpls., Feb. 24, 1938; d. Oscar and Adele Alpert. BS in Edn., Ind. U., 1959. Tchr. Indpls. Pub. Schs., 1959-60; libr. George Fry & Assocs., Chgo., 1960-62, DeLeuw, Cather & Co., Chgo., 1962-65, Arthur Young & Co., CPAs, Chgo., 1965-74; statis. asst. Sargent & Lundy, Chgo., 1974-81, computer liaison agt., 1981-83, tech. editor, 1983-87; sales assoc. Jewelmaster, Inc., Chgo., 1987-88; claims processor Benefit Trust Life Ins. Co., 1988-90; claims examiner Ft. Dearborn Life Ins. Co., 1990-91, sr. claims examiner, 1991—. Mem. Chgo. Claims Assn., Women in Workers' Compensation.

ALPERT, CAROLINE EVELYN, nurse; b. Bklyn., June 18, 1926; d. Harry Noah and Anna Fanny (Walfish) Spalter; m. Meyer Alpert, Jan. 21, 1951; children: Robert, Linda, Mark, David, Steven. Diploma, Jewish Hosp. Bklyn., 1947; AAS in Human Services, Westchester Community Coll., 1988. RN, N.Y. Staff nurse Jewish Hosp. Bklyn., 1947-51, 53, Burbank Hosp., Fitchburg, Mass., 1952-53; radiation therapy staff nurse Roswell Park Meml. Hosp., Buffalo, 1953-54; substitute sch. nurse Westchester County Schs., N.Y., 1974-85; sch. nurse Yonkers (N.Y.) Bd. Edn., 1985—; nurse Westchester Summer Day Camp, Mamaroneck, N.Y., summers, 1976-86. Mem. Jewish Hosp. Bklyn. Alumni Assn. (life). Democrat. Home: 80 Avondale Rd Yonkers NY 10710-2021

ALPERT, DEIRDRE WHITTLETON, state legislator; b. N.Y.C., Oct. 6, 1945; d. Harry Mark and Dorothy (Lehn) Whittleton; m. Michael Edward Alpert, Jan. 1, 1964; children: Lehn, Kristin, Alison. Student, Pomona Coll., 1963-65; LLD (hon.), Western Am. U., 1994. Mem. from 78th dist. Calif. State Assembly, Sacramento, 1990—; chairwoman Women's Legislators Caucus, Sacramento, 1993; active Calif. Tourism Commn., Sacramento, 1990—, Calif. Libr. Allocations Bd., Sacramento, 1993—. dist. rep., troop leader Girl Scouts Am., San Diego, 1977-83; spl. advocate Voices for Children, San Diego, 1982-90; mem. bd. Solana Beach (Calif.) Sch. Bd., 1983-90, also pres.; pres. beach and county guild United Cerebral Palsy, San Diego, 1986. Recipient Legis. award Calif. Regional Occupation Program, 1991-92, Am. Acad. Pediats., 1991-92, San Diego Psychol. Assn., 1993-94, Commitment to Children award Calif. Assn. for Edn. of Young Children, 1991-92, Legis. Commendation award Nat. Assn. for Yr.-Round Edn., 1991-92, State Commn. on Status of Women, 1993-94; named Friend of Yr., Children's PKU Network, 1991-92, Woman of Yr., Nat. Women's Polit. Caucus San Diego, 1991-92, Orgn. for Rehab. through Tng., 1993-94, Legislator of Yr., Am. Electronics Assn., 1991-92, 1993-94, Calif. Sch.-Age Consortium, 1993-94, Women of Distinction, Soropimists Internat. of La Jolla, 1993-94, Assemblymember of Yr., Calif. Assn. Edn. Young Children, 1993-94. Mem. Charter 100 of San Diego, Calif. Elected Women's Assn. for Edn. and Rsch. (v.p. 1994—). Democrat. Mem. Congregation Ch. Office: 1350 Front St Ste 6013 San Diego CA 92101

ALPERT-GILLIS, LINDA JAYNE, clinical psychologist; b. Quincy, Mass., Nov. 12, 1959; d. Edwin and Joyce Eleanor (Zucker) Alpert; m. Stephen Michael Gillis, June 2, 1985; 1 child, Sarah Elizabeth. ScB magna cum laude, Brown U., 1982; MA, U. Rochester, 1985, PhD, 1987. Lic. psychology, N.Y. Clin. assoc. psychology U. Rochester (N.Y) Dept. Psychology Ctr. for Community Study, 1986-87; sr. instr. psychiatry U. Rochester Sch. Medicine & Dentistry Dept. Psychiatry, 1987-88; asst. prof. psychiatry and pediatrics U. Rochester Sch. Medicine & Dentistry, 1988-94, assoc. prof. psychiatry and pediatrics, 1994—; asst. dir. children of divorce intervention program U. Rochester, 1986-89; cons. single-parent family project Western Monroe Mental Health Ctr., 1984-86, Noyes Meml. Hosp., Dansville, N.Y., 1988-94. Contbr. articles to profl. jours.; co-author (curricula) Interventions for Children of Divorce. Mem. Am. Psychol. Assn., N.Y. State Psychol. Assn., Rochester Area Assn. Clin. Psychologists, Genesee Valley Psychol. Assn., Phi Beta Kappa, Sigma Xi. Office: U Rochester Med Ctr 300 Crittenden Blvd Rochester NY 14642-0001

ALSOP, DANIELLE RAE, environmental scientist, engineer; b. Fontana, Calif., Jan. 11, 1970; d. William Ernest and Shirley Ann (Peterson) Dorrington. Degree in environ. systems tech., Cornell U., 1992. Intern Dept. Regulatory Assurance, Waste Isolation Plant Westinghouse, Carlsbad, N.Mex., summer 1990; computer operator Cornell Info. Technologies, Ithaca, N.Y., 1990-92; asst. mgr. Student Agys., Inc., Ithaca, N.Y., fall 1992; rsch. asst. soil, crop and atmospheric scis. Cornell U., Ithaca, N.Y., fall 1992; tech. writer Cornell Waste Mgmt. Inst., Ithaca, N.Y., 1992; environ. engr. Resource Applications, Inc., Burke, Va., 1993—; region II coord. resource applications EPA, Burke, 1993, Computer Aided Mgmt. of Emergency Ops. instr., 1993. Recipient Rowing Champion award Nat. Scholastic Rowing Assn., 1988. Mem. NAFE. Home: 3515 Forestdale Ave Woodbridge VA 22193

ALSOP, MARIN, conductor; d. LaMar and Ruth A. Student, Yale Univ., Julliard Sch. Debut with Symphony Space, N.Y.C., 1984; founder, artistic dir. Concordia Chamber Orchestra, N.Y.C., 1984—; asst. condr. Richmond Symphony, Va., 1987; music dir. Eugene Symphony Orchestra, Oreg., 1989—, Long Island Philharmonic, N.Y, 1990-94; principal condr. Colorado Symphony Orchestra, Denver, 1993—; guest condr. San Francisco Symphony Orchestra, Boston Pops, Los Angeles Philharmonic Orchestra, 1991, City Ballet Orchestra, 1992; dir. Cabrillo Music Festival, Calif., 1991—; concertmaster Northeastern Pennsylvania Philharmonic, Scranton; founder, mem. String Fever (swing band), 1980—. Recipient Koussevitzky Conducting prize Tanglewood Music Festival, 1988. Office: Colorado Symphony Orchestra Boettcher Concert Hall 1031 13 St Denver CO 80204*

ALSTON, LELA, state senator; b. Phoenix, June 26, 1942; d. Virgil Lee and Frances Mae Koonse Mulkey; B.S., U. Ariz., 1967; M.S., Ariz. State U., 1971; children—Brenda Susan, Charles William. Tchr. high sch., 1968—; mem. Ariz. State Senate, 1977—. Named Disting. Citizen, U. Ariz. Alumni Assn., 1978. Mem. NEA, Ariz. Edn. Assn., Am. Home Econs. Assn., Ariz. Home Econs. Assn., Am. Vocat. Assn. Methodist. Office: Ariz State Sen State Capitol Phoenix AZ 85007-2812

ALSWORTH, LINDA RAE, helicopter pilot; b. Trenton, N.J., Oct. 7, 1955; d. Raymond and Odette (Amelin) Walukiewicz; m. Wayne C. Alsworth, Sr., Aug. 2, 1988; 1 child, Rae Lynn Sculerati. Pvt. pilot degree, 1976, instrument airplane degree, comml. pilot degree, multiengine land degree, 1987, flight instr. airplane degree, comml. helicopter degree, 1988. Lic. comml. pilot. Air traffic controller FAA Flight Svc. Sta., King Salmon, Alaska, 1985-88; pres., helicopter pilot Rotor Air Alaska, Inc., Soldotna, Alaska, 1988—. Mem. Whirlygirls, Ninety-Nines, Exptl. Aircraft Assn., Aircraft Owners and Pilots Assn. Home and Office: Rotor Air Alaska Inc PO Box 1290 Soldotna AK 99669-1290

ALT, BETTY L., sociology educator; b. Walsenburg, Colo., Nov. 12, 1931; d. Cecil R. and Mary M. (Giordano) Sowers; m. William E. Alt, June 19, 1960; 1 child, Eden Jeanette Alt Murrie. BA, Colo. Coll., 1960; MA, NE Mo. State U., 1968. Instr. sociology Indian Hills Community Coll., Centerville, Iowa, 1965-70; dept. chmn. Middlesex Community Coll., Bedford, Mass., 1971-75; instr. sociology Auburn U., Montgomery, 1975-76; div. chmn. Tidewater Community Coll., Virginia Beach, Va., 1976-80; program coord. Pikes Peak Community Coll., Woomera, Australia, 1980-83; instr. sociology Hawaii Pacific Coll., Honolulu, 1983-86, U. Md., Okinawa, Japan, 1987-88, Christopher Newport Coll., Newport News, Va., 1988-89, U. Colo., Colorado Springs, 1989—. Co-author: Uncle Sam's Brides, 1990, Campfollowing: A History of the Military Wife, 1991, Weeping Violins: The Gypsy Tragedy in Europe, 1995. Mem. AAUW, AAUP, Pen Women, N.E. Mo. State U. Alumni Assn. (bd. dirs. 1993—). Home: 2460 I-25 North Pueblo CO 81008-1745 Office: U Colo Austin Bluff Pky Colorado Springs CO 80918-3915

ALTAMURA, CARMELA ELIZABETH, concert artist, philanthropist; b. San Piero Patti, Sicily, Italy, Apr. 7, 1939; d. Salvatore and Mary (Butto) Bucceri; m. Leonard John Altamura, Apr. 15, 1938; children: Christina Chiara Maria, Leonard Anthony. Student, Caldwell Coll., 1957-59; artistic diploma, Giuseppe Verdi Conservatory, Milan, 1964. Founder, dir. Altamura Sch. Fine and Performing Arts, Union City, N.J., 1972-84, Inter-Cities Performing Arts, Inc., Union City, 1984—; founder, dir. adjudicator Enrico Caruso Internat. Voice Competition, U.S.A., Union City, 1988—; concert artist U.S., Europe, Middle East; recording artist Jericho Label & Olympia Arts, Ltd., N.Y.C., 1984-90; adjudicator Enrico Caruso Internat. Voice Composition, N.Y.C., 1988—; lectr. seminars Wagner Coll., Staten Island, N.Y., 1989—. Appeared as solo artist in numerous halls including Weill Hall at Carnegie Hall, Merkin Concert Hall, Tully Hall at Lincoln Ctr., Town Hall, Marymount Concert Hall, Symphony Hall, Newark, N.J., War Meml. Bldg., Trenton, N.J., Teatro dei Filodrammatici, Milan, Piccolo Teatro di Strehler, Milan, Ambroseaum Concert Hall, Milan, Teatro Ducale, Parma, Italy, Teatro Fraschini di Pavia, Italy, Teatro Communale di Bologna, Teatro G. Rossini, Pesaro, Italy and various others; bd. editors La Follia cultural Pub., 1990-91, Il Ponte, 1990-91; commd. bronze sculpture of Giulietta Simionato by Domenico Mazzone for Met. Opera Founder's Hall, Fanfare for the Americas orchestral work commd. from composer Rodrigo Henao and performed at Carnegie Hall Gala Salute to Italy and the Americas, 1991; performed in quincentennial celebrations Carlo Felice Opera House, Genoa, Italy, 1992; creator, author, researcher, narrator, interpreter Commemorative Concert on the Life of Christopher Columbus; prodr. 5th Altamura/Enrico Caruso Internat. Voice Competition, pres. jury. Concert series founder, dir. Fomento Cultural Orgn., Union City, 1984-86; founder, dir. Italian Cultural Soc. of St. Peter's Coll., Jersey City, 1986-87; mem. Leonardo Da Vinci Cultural Soc. Recipient Gold medal Fano Opera Festival, William Matthew Sullivan Found. award, Barga Opera Festival, Cert. of Recognition as "Better World Builder" Italian Am. Hist. Soc., 1991, recipient award 1992. Mem. Nat. Orgn. Italian Am. Women, Nat. Italian Am. Found. Democrat. Roman Catholic.

ALTEKRUSE, JOAN MORRISSEY, retired preventive medicine educator; b. Cohoes, N.Y., Nov. 15, 1928; d. William T. Dee and Agnes Kay (Fitzgerald) Morrissey; m. Ernest B. Altekruse, Dec. 17, 1950; children—Philip, Clifford, Lisa, Janice, Charles, Sean, Lowell, Patrick, E. Caitlin. AB, Vassar Coll., N.Y., 1949; MD, Stanford U., Calif., 1960; MPH, Harvard U., Cambridge, 1965; DPH, U. Calif., Berkeley, 1973. Lic. physician, S.C. Cons., program dir. Calif. State Health Dept., 1966-69; mem. faculty U. Heidelberg, Fed. Republic Germany, 1970-72; med. dir. regional office Fla. State Health Dept., 1972-75; prof., dir. health adminstrn. Sch. Pub. Health, U. S.C., Columbia, 1975-77; prof. preventive medicine Univ. S.C. Sch. of Medicine, Columbia, 1975-94, chmn. dept., 1979-89, disting. prof. emerita, 1994—; fellow, assoc. dir. Irish Peace Inst., U. Limerick, Ireland, 1990—; vis. scholar Ctr. for Rsch. in Disease Prevention, Stanford U., 1992; Women in Medicine liaison officer Assn. Am. Med. Colls. Mem. editorial bd. Family and Community Health Jour., Jour. Community Health; editorial adv. bd. VA Practitioner. Alumni councillor Harvard Sch. Pub. Health; docent, vol. bd. mem. Hunter Mus. Am. Art, Chattanooga. Lt. USMC, 1949-51; sr. surgeon USPHS, 1960-64. Recipient Adminstrn. award Women in Higher Edn., 1989, Achievement award S.C. Commn. on Women, 1990, Ann. award, 1991; WHO travel fellow, Eng., 1974; grantee NIH, NCI, Ctr. for Disease Control, pvt. founds. Fellow Assn. Tchrs. Preventive Medicine; mem. Am. Bd. Preventive Medicine (trustee 1984—), Am. Bd. Med. Specialties (del. 1990-93), Am. Heart Assn. (S.C. affiliate pres. 1986, agenda planning com. 1987-89, women and minorities leadership com. 1989—, Lifetime Achievement award 1992), Nat. Bd. Med. Examiners (comprehensive test com. 1986-92), Am. Women's Med. Assn. Democrat. Catholic.

ALTENHOFEN, JANE ELLEN, federal agency administrator, auditor; b. Seneca, Kans., Sept. 4, 1952; d. Justin Leo and Marva Mae (Sextro) A.; m. John Dean Arnette, Sept. 12, 1975 (div. Mar. 1978). BBA cum laude, Wichita (Kans.) State U., 1973; MPA, Am. U., 1982; cert., Inst. Internal Auditors, 1986. Auditor U.S. Gen. Acctg. Office, Kansas City, Kans., 1974-76, Honolulu, 1976-80, Washington, 1980-84; auditor Fed. Emergency Mgmt. Agy., Washington, 1984-89; insp. gen. U.S. Internat. Trade Commn., Washington, 1989—. Mem. Adopt a Grandparent Program, Wichita, 1973; vol. reading course work to blind students, Wichita, 1973; vol. Vis. Nurse Assn., Washington, 1986—; host, traveler, Wash. area rep. SERVAS, 1987—; commr. Adv. Neighborhood Commn., Washington, 1986-89; troop leader Girl Scouts U.S., Washington, 1983-85. Mem. Inst. Internal Auditors, Mid-Atlantic Intergovtl. Audit Forum, Assn. Govt. Accounts, Toastmasters (sgt.-at-arms Washington chpt. 1973), Phi Kappa Phi, Pi Alpha Pi. Home: 507 2nd St SE Washington DC 20003-1928 Office: US Internat Trade Commn 500 E St NW Ste 220 Washington DC 20436-0003*

ALTER, ELEANOR BREITEL, lawyer; b. N.Y.C., Nov. 10, 1938; d. Charles David and Jeanne (Hollander) Breitel; children: Richard B. Zabel, David B. Zabel. BA with honors, U. Mich., 1960; postgrad., Harvard U., 1960-61; LLB, Columbia U., 1964. Bar: N.Y. 1965. Atty., office of gen. counsel, ins. dept. State of N.Y., 1964-66; assoc. Miller & Carlson, N.Y.C., 1966-68, Marshall, Bratter, Greene, Allison & Tucker, N.Y.C., 1968-74; mem. firm Marshall, Bratter, Greene, Allison & Tucker, 1974-82, Rosenman & Colin, 1982—; fellow U. Chgo. Law Sch., 1988; adj. prof. law NYU Sch. Law, 1983-87; vis. prof. law U. Chgo., 1990-91, 93; lectr. in field. Editorial bd.: N.Y. Law Jour. Contbr. articles to profl. jours. Trustee Lawyers' Fund for Client Protection of the State of N.Y., 1983—, chmn., 1985—; bd. visitors U. Chgo. Law Sch., 1984-87. Mem. ABA, Am. Law Inst., N.Y. State Bar Assn., Assn. of Bar of City of N.Y. (libr. com. 1978-80, com. on matrimonial law 1977-81, 87-88, judiciary com. 1981-84, 94, 95, exec. com. 1988-92), Am. Acad. Matrimonial Lawyers. Office: Rosenman & Colin 575 Madison Ave New York NY 10022-2511

ALTER, MELANIE S., jewelry designer, interior designer, print maker; b. La Salle, Ill., Dec. 14, 1937; d. Harry Emlyn and Thelma Celia (Klein) Rose; m. John May (dec. Feb., 1963); m. Milton Alter (div. July, 1976); children: Craig, Meridee, Joel. BFA, U. Wis., 1959. Staff designer W.J. Sloane, Beverly Hills, Calif., 1959-61; print maker Chgo., Indpls, 1963-65; owner, designer Melanie Interiors, Indpls., 1965-70, Melanie Collection, Albuquerque, New Mex., 1977—; instr. in designing, stringing, identifying beads through community orgns. Jewelry designer, exhibiting in shows worldwide, including de Young Mus., San Francisco, also Saks Fifth Ave, Nordstrom's; author art column Jewish Post, 1967-69. Bd. mem. So. Shore Commn., Chogo., 1963-65; founder frst art, music programs in Indpls. schs. 1967-69; docent Maxwell Mus. Anthropology, Albuquerque, New Mex., 1976-78; mem. Humane Soc. Albuquerque, 1976—. Recipient Interior of Yr. award GE, 1970. Mem. New Mex. Bead Soc. (founder, first pres., bd. dirs.), Albuquerque United Artists (bd. dirs.). Home and Office: 12105 Bermuda Dr NE Albuquerque NM 87111-2857

ALTER, SHIRLEY JACOBS, jewelry store owner; b. Beaumont, Tex., June 23, 1929; d. Morris Louis and Helen (Dow) Jacobs; m. Nelson Tobias Alter, June 12, 1949; children: Dennis, Keith, Brian, Wendy. Student, U. Tex., Austin, 1950. Owner Gem Jewelry Co., Beaumont, 1950—. Pres. Nat. Coun. Jewish Women, Beaumont, 1965, 66, Sisterhood of Temple Emanuel, Beaumont, 1967, 68, Buckner Bapt. Benevolence Aux., Beaumont, 1970-72; bd. dirs. Temple Emanuel, pres. elect, 1994-96, pres. 1996-98; active Beaumont Music Commn., 1990; founder Beaumont Reach to Recovery, 1973; trustee Art Mus. S.E. Tex., Beaumont Heritage Soc.; mem. adv. bd. Bapt. Hosp., 1989—. Democrat. Office: Gem Jewelry Co 795 N 11th St Beaumont TX 77702-1501

ALTFEST, KAREN CAPLAN, financial planning executive; b. Mont., Que., Can.; d. Philip and Betty (Gamer) Caplan; m. Lewis Jay Altfest; children: Ellen Wendy, Andrew Gamer. Tchr.'s diploma, McGill U.; BA cum laude, Hunter Coll., 1970, MA, 1972; PhD, CUNY, 1979. CFP, N.Y. V.p. L. J. Altfest & Co., Inc., N.Y.C., 1985—; dir. fin. planning program New Sch. for Social Rsch., N.Y.C., 1989—; dir. CFP program Pace U., White Plains, N.Y., 1988-90. Author: Robert Owen, 1978; co-author: Lew Altfest Answers Almost All Your Questions about Money, 1992; contbr. articles to fin. jours. Founding chmn. Yorkville Common Pantry, N.Y.C., 1980-84; v.p. PS 6 PTA, N.Y.C., 1991-92; bd. dirs. Temple Shaaray Tefila. Recipient Community Svc. award Temple Shaaray Tefila, N.Y.C., 1985. Mem. Nat. Assn. Women Bus. Owners (bd. dirs., chmn. FOCUS 1993-95), Assn. for Can. Studies in U.S., Assn. for Women's Econ. Devel., Inst. CFP (bd. dirs. N.Y. chpt. 1994—), Nat. Assn. Personal Fin. Advisors (chair Northeast-Mid Atlantic Conf., 1995, CUNY PhD Alumni Assn. (v.p. 1982-84), Fin. Women's Assn., Phi Alpha Theta. Office: L J Altfest & Co Inc Penthouse 140 William St New York NY 10038-3800

ALTMAN, ADELE ROSENHAIN, radiologist; b. Tel Aviv, Israel, June 4, 1924; came to U.S., 1933, naturalized, 1939; d. Bruno and Salla (Silberzweig) Rosenhain; m. Emmett Altman, Sept. 3, 1944; children: Brian R., Alan L., Karen D. Diplomate Am. Bd. Radiology. Intern Queens Gen. Hosp., N.Y.C., 1949-51; resident Hosp. for Joint Diseases, N.Y.C., 1951-52, Roosevelt Hosp., N.Y.C., 1955-57; clin. instr. radiology Downstate Med. Ctr., SUNY, Bklyn., 1957-61; asst. prof. radiology N.Y. Med. Coll., N.Y.C., 1961-65, assoc. prof., 1965-68; assoc. prof. radiology U. Okla. Health Sci. Ctr., Oklahoma City, 1968-78; assoc. prof. dept. radiology U. N.Mex. Sch. Medicine, Albuquerque, 1978-85. Author: Radiology of the Respiratory System: A Basic Review, 1978; contbr. articles to profl. jours. Fellow Am. Coll. Angiology, N.Y. Acad. Medicine; mem. Am. Coll. Radiology, Am. Roentgen Ray Soc., Assn. Univ. Radiologists, Radiol. Soc. N.Am., B'nai B'rith Anti-Defamation League (bd. dirs. N.Mex. state bd.), Hadassah Club.

ALTMAN, ANNEMARIE, controller; b. Zurich, Switzerland, Nov. 27, 1943; came to U.S., 1965; d. Eduard and Marie (Reich) Nunlist; widowed. BS, Bentley Coll., Waltham, Mass., 1979. Retail Bus. Cert., Zurich. Contr. Dytron, Inc., Waltham, 1974-79, Coulter Biomed. div. Coulter Electronics, Concord, Mass., 1979-84; subs. contr. Avery Dennison Corp. (formerly Dennison Corp.), Framingham, Mass., 1984-85, mgr. fin., internat., 1985-86, group contr., 1987-91; contr. N.Am. Instron Corp., Canton, Mass., 1991—. Vol. Mass. Audubon Soc., Sharon. Mem. Fin. Execs. Inst. Office: Instron Corp 100 Royall St Canton MA 02021

ALTMAN, EILEEN SHEA, psychotherapist; b. N.Y.C.; m. Michael Altman, Jan. 15, 1977. Cert., N.Y. Sch. for Psychoanalysis and Psychotherapy, 1984; MSW, Fordham U., 1980. Lic./ cert. social worker; bd. cert. diplomate clin. social work. Psychotherapist, psychoanalyst pvt. practice, N.Y.C., 1980—; mem. Grad. N.Y. Sch. for Psychoanalysis and Psychotherapy. Mem. NASW, Internat. Acad. Behavioral Medicine Counseling and Psychotherapy, Register Clin. Social Workers. Office: 37 Candlestick Ct Warwick NY 10990

ALTMAN, ELLEN, librarian, educator; b. Pitts., Jan. 1, 1936; d. William and Catherine (Wall) Conley. AB, Duquesne U., 1957; MLS, Rutgers U., 1965, PhD, 1971. Instr., asst research prof. Rutgers U., 1965-67, 70-72; asst. prof. U. Ky., 1972-73, U. Toronto, 1974-76; assoc. prof. Ind. U., 1976-79; prof. Grad. Library Sch., U. Ariz., Tucson, 1979—; cons. various research orgns., state libraries. Author: Performance Measures in Pub. Libraries, 1973, A Data Gathering and Instructional Manual for Performance Measures in Public Libraries, 1976, Local Public Library Administration, 1980; editor Pub. Librs., 1992—. Fulbright-Hayes sr. lectr., 1978. Mem. ALA, AAUP. Office: 1515 E 1st St Tucson AZ 85719-4505

ALTON, ANN LESLIE, judge, lawyer, educator; b. Pipestone, Minn., Sept. 10, 1945; d. Howard Robert, Jr. and Camilla Ann (DeMong) A.; m. Gerald Russell Freeman Sr.; children: Brady Michael Alton Freeman, Matthew Alton Freeman (dec.). BA Smith Coll., 1967; JD U. Minn., 1970; postgrad. Nat. Jud. Coll., U. Nev., 1989. Bar: Minn. 1970, U.S. Dist. Ct. Minn. 1972, U.S. Supreme Ct. 1981. Apptd. gen. jurisdiction state trial ct. judge civil and criminal jurisdiction Dist. Ct., 4th Jud. Dist., Hennepin County, Minn., 1989—, elected, 1990—, vice chair adminstrv. com., 1989—; asst. county atty. Hennepin County, Mpls., 1970-89, felony prosecutor, criminal div., 1970-75, acting chief citizen protection div., 1975-76, chief citizen protection/econ. crime div., 1976-79, chief econ. crime unit, 1979-85, sr. atty. civil div. handling labor and employment law, 1985-89; instr. Hamline U. Law Sch., St. Paul, 1973-76; adj. prof. law William Mitchell Coll. Law, St. Paul, 1977—; adj. prof. U. Minn. Law Sch., 1978-82; lectr. in field, 1970—; sr. faculty Minn. Advocacy Inst., Minn. Continuing Legal Edn., 1988—; mem. faculty Nat. Inst. Trial Advocacy, U. Notre Dame Law Sch., 1989—, asst. team leader North Cen. Regional Jury Trial Advocacy Course, 1991—; sr. critiquing judge Jud. Trial Skills Training Program Minn. Supreme Ct. Continuing Edn. Program for State Cts., 1993—; mem. faculty intensive trial advocacy program Widener U. Sch. of Law, Wilmington, Del., 1993—; bd. dirs. Pan-O-Gold Realty Co., 1986-89, Alton Realty Co., 1986-89. Vice-chmn. bd. dirs. Minn. Program on Victims of Sexual Assault, 1974-76; bd. dirs. Physician's Health Plan (now Allina), Health Maintenance Orgn., 1976-80, exec. com. 1977-80; mem. legal drug abuse subcom. Gov. Minn. Adv. Com. Drug Abuse, 1972-74; bd. visitors U. Minn. Law Sch., 1979-85; mem. child abuse project coordinating com. Hennepin County Med. Soc., 1982-83, chmn. corp., labor, ins. subcom. 1982. Mem. ABA (jud. adminstrn. div.), Minn. Bar Assn. (criminal law, labor and employment law, civil litigation sects.), Hennepin County Bar Assn. (ethics com. 1973-76, criminal law com. 1973—, vice chmn. 1979-80, 83-84, unauthorized practice law com. 1977-78, individual rights and responsibilities com. 1977-78, labor and employment law com. 1985—, civil litigation com. 1985—), Minn. Dist. Judges Assn. (benefits com. 1991—, mem. program and edn. com., 1993—), Nat. Assn. Women Judges, Minn. Women Lawyers, U. Minn. Law Sch. Alumni Assn. (bd. dirs. 1979-85). Author articles, pamphlet, manual. Office: 1251C Hennepin County Govt Ctr Minneapolis MN 55487-0001

ALTSCHUL, B J, public relations counselor; b. Norfolk, Va., Jan. 28, 1948; d. Lemuel and Sylva (Behr) A. Student, Goucher Coll., 1965-67; BA, U. South Fla., 1970, postgrad., 1980-84. Reporter St. Petersburg Times, Fla., 1973-74; dir. pub. rels. Valkyrie Press, Inc., St. Petersburg, 1974-77; founding editor Bay Life, Clearwater, Fla., 1977-79, Tampa Bay Monthly, Clearwater, 1977-79; mng. editor Fla. Tourist News, Tampa and Orlando, 1981; founder Capital Communications of Tampa, 1981, since owner, prin., name changed to b j Altschul & Assocs., 1985—; mgr. editorial and info. svcs. Va. Port Authority, Norfolk, 1985-88; dir. pub. rels. Va. Dept. Agr. and Consumer Svcs., Richmond, 1988-93; adj. faculty Old Dominion U., Norfolk, 1986-88, U. Richmond, 1990—. Author: Cracker Cookin' & Other Favorites, 1984; editor: The Underground Gourmet, 1983; contbg. author: Virginia: A Commonwealth Comes of Age, 1988. Bd. dirs. Pinellas County Big Bros.-Big Sisters, 1980-82, Fla. Folklore Soc., 1984-85. Grant rev. panelist Fla. Fine Arts Coun., 1981. Mem. Fla. Motion Picture and TV Assn. (treas. 1976-78), Hampton Rds. C. of C. (co-chmn. pub. rels. Internat. Azalea Festival 1986, chmn. publs. 1987), Va. Conf. on World Trade (chmn. pub. relations com.), Downtown Norfolk Devel. Corp. (chmn. urban living com.), Mensa, Pub. Rels. Soc. Am. (chmn. Mid-Atlantic Dist. 1988, chmn. govt. sect. 1989, bd. dirs. accreditation chmn. Old Dominion chpt. 1988—), Va. State Agy. Pub. Affairs Assn. (pres. 1990), Forum Agriculture and Consumer Topics (founder, chmn. 1992). Avocations: sailing, classical music, folk music, jazz. Office: b j Altschul & Assocs 2226 Rockwater Terr Richmond VA 23233-3622

ALTWEGG, PATRICIA ANN, college program director; b. Alva, Okla., Oct. 17, 1945; d. Karl H. and Sarah A. (Dillard) S.; m. H. Robert Altwegg; 1 child, Kristin. BS in Bus. Edn., Kans. State U., 1967, MS in Curriculum and Instrn., 1975, PhD, 1980. Instr. bus. Chapman (Kans.) High Sch., 1967-71, Miltonvale (Kans.) High Sch., 1971-73, Miltonvale Wesleyan Coll., 1971-72; instr. bus. tech. Cloud County C.C., Concordia, Kans., 1975-78, dept. head travel tourism mgmt., 1980-93, dir. Career Assistance Ctr., 1991—, chair dept. of aviation, 1991-93; Apptd. to Kansas Tourism Comsn., 1993. Mem. Am. Bus. Women's Assn., Am. Hotel and Motel Assn., Am. Soc. Assn. Execs., Univ. Aviation Assn., Kans. Aerospace Commn., Concordia Area C. of C., Coll. Placement Coun., Coun. on Hotel-Restaurant and Instl. Edn., Coop. Edn. Assn., Kans. Assn. Career Svcs. and Employment, Kans. Lodging Assn., Resort and Comml. Recreation Assn., Soc. Travel-Tourism Educators, Southwest Placement Assn., Travel Industry Assn. Kans., Rebecca Lodge, PEO, Delta Kappa Gamma. Office: Cloud County C C PO Box 1002 Concordia KS 66901-1002

ALUMBAUGH, JOANN MCCALLA, magazine editor; b. Ann Arbor, Mich., Sept. 16, 1952; d. William Samuel and Jean Arliss (Guy) McCalla; m. Lyle Ray Alumbaugh, Apr. 30, 1974; children: Brent William, Brandon Jess, Brooke Louise. BA, Ea. Mich. U., 1974. Cert. elem. tch., Mich. Assoc. editor Chester White Swine Record Assn., Rochester, Ind., 1974-77; prodn. editor United Duroc Swine Registry, Peoria, Ill., 1977-79; dir., pres. Nat. Assn. Swine Records, Macomb, Ill., 1979-82; free-lance writer, artist Ill. and Nat. Specific Pathogen Free Assn., Ind. producers, Good Hope, Emden, Ill., 1982-85; editor The Hog Producer, Farm Progress Publs., Urbandale, Iowa, 1985—; coord. Master Farm Homemaker Program, Pub. div. Cap Cities ABC, West Des Moines, 1985—, Family Living Program, Farm Progress Show, 1985—; mem. U.S. Agrl. Export Devel. Coun., Washington, 1979-82, apptd. mem. Blue Ribbon Com. on Agr., 1980-81. Contbr. numerous articles to profl. jours. Precinct chmn. Rep. Party, Linden, Iowa, 1988; mem. Keep Improving Dist. Schs., Panora, Iowa, 1990-91; v.p. Sunday sch. com. Sunset Circle, United Meth. Ch., Linden, 1990-91; pres. PTA, Panorama Schs., Panora, 1993-94. Mem. Am. Agrl. Editors Assn. (Outstanding Young Women Am. award 1988, chmn. dist. svc. com. 1991, co-chmn. Info-Expo com. 1994—), U.S. Animal Health Assn. (pseudorabies, identification coms. 1989—), Farm Found., Iowa Pork Producers Assn. (legis. com. 1990—, hon. master pork producer), Nat. Pork Producers Coun. (product devel. com. 1980-81), McDonough County and Ill. Porkettes (county pres. 1978-79, Bellleringer award 1979), Guthrie County Pork Prodrs. Home: 2644 Amarillo Ave Linden IA 50146-8029 Office: Farm Progress Publs/Wallaces Farmer 6200 Aurora Ave Ste 609E Urbandale IA 50322-2838

ALVAREZ, MERCEDES, advertising executive; b. Havana, Cuba; d. José Manuel and Teresita (Rionda) A. BBA, U. Miami, 1963; postgrad., Manhattanville Coll., Purchase, N.Y., 1964. Sr. rsch. analyst J. Walter Thompson, N.Y.C., 1966-78; v.p. rsch. dir. Isidore, Lefkowitz & Elgort, N.Y.C., 1978-79, Bozell & Jacobs, N.Y.C., 1979-85; sr. v.p. assoc. rsch. dir., rsch. dir. Latin Am. BBDO, Inc., N.Y.C., 1985—; sec., treas. Rsch. Dirs. Coun., 1979-80, Communications Rsch. Coun., 1988-89, pres., 1989—. Mem. Am. Mktg. Assn. (Effie Judge, 1978-85). Office: BBDO NY 1285 Avenue Of The Americas New York NY 10019-6028

ALVAREZ, NORMA L., interpreter, translator; b. Holguin, Oriente, Cuba, June 15, 1961; d. Natalio A. Alvarez and Norma C. Gómez; m. Joseph P. Parker, Oct. 9, 1988. BA, U. P.R., 1984; MA, Monterey Inst. of Internat., Studies, 1987. Cert. Calif. ct. interpreter; federally cert. interpreter. Editoral asst. Hampton-Brown Co., Carmel, Calif., 1988; freelance translator, 1988—; freelance intrepreter various, Calif. and Fla., 1988—; adj. prof. Fla. A&M U., Tallahassee, 1993-94, Monterey (Calif.) Inst. Internat. Studies, 1989—. Co-author: The Interpreter's Edge Turbo Supplement, 1993. Recipient French Consulate award for Acad. Excellence in Freng Lang. and Lit., U. P.R., 1984. Mem. Calif. Ct. Interpreters Assn. (guest speaker 1992), Am. Translators Assn. (accreditation Spanish), No. Calif. Translators Assn., Nat. Assn. Jud. Interpreters and Translators. Home and Office: 43 Brigantine Ct Saint Augustine FL 32084 also: PO Box 191074 San Juan PR 00919-1074

ALVAREZ-GAUTNEY, JACQUELINE, financial analyst; b. Miami, July 1, 1962; d. Lino and Raquel (Rodriguez) Alvarez; m. Scott Eric Gautney, June 27, 1992. BBA in Acctg., U. Miami, 1983, M of Profl. Acctg., 1984. CPA, Fla. From staff acct. to sr. acct. Deloitte & Touche, Miami, 1984-88; fin. analyst Ryder Truck Rental, Miami, 1988-89; from rsch. acct. to sr. product evaluation analyst Fla. Power & Light Co., Miami, 1989-93, sr. product evaluation analyst, 1993—. Active City of South Miami (Fla.) Trust Fund, 1993—. Mem. AICPA, Fla. Inst. CPAs, U. Miami Sch. Bus. Alumni Assn. (dir. 1992—). Home: 7850 SW 67th Ct Miami FL 33143-4519

ALVINO, GLORIA DORA, motivational speaker, writer, medical researcher; b. Revere, Mass., June 27, 1931; d. Alfonso and Mary (Scotti) A. Student, Boston U., 1949-51; BS in Pharmacy, Mass. Coll. Pharmacy and Allied Health Scis., 1955; MS in Health and Human Svcs., Columbia Pacific U., 1992. Registered pharmacist, Mass. Pharmacy mgr., 1955-59; owner Med. Ctr. Surg. Supply, Medi-Rents, Med. Ctr. Fitting Svc., Boston, 1959-94; founder, pres. Heart to Heart Assoc., Inc., Brookline, Mass., 1992—; guest lectr. in field. Producer TV series: Heart to Heart on Health Issues. Fellow Am. Coll. Apothecaries; mem. Sierra Club, NOW, Audubon Soc., Health Industry Distbn. Assn., Am. Pharm. Assn. Avocations: horseback riding, writing, reading, sketching, gardening. Home: 32 Clark Rd Brookline MA 02146-6030

AMADIO, BARI ANN, metal fabrication executive, former nurse; b. Phila., Mar. 26, 1949; d. Fred Deutscher and Celena (Lusky) Garber; m. Peter Colby Amadio, June 24, 1973; children: P. Grant, Jamie Blair. BA in Psychology, U. Miami, 1970; diploma in Nursing, Thomas Jefferson U., 1973, Johnston-Willis Sch. Nursing, 1974; BS in Nursing, Northeastern U., 1977; MS in Nursing, Boston U., 1978; JD, U. Bridgeport, 1983. Faculty Johnston-Willis Sch. Nursing, Richmond, Va., 1974-75; staff, charge nurse Mass. Gen. Hosp., Boston, 1975-78; faculty New Eng. Deaconess, Boston, 1978-80, Lankenau Hosp. Sch. of Nursing, Phila., 1980-81; pres. Original Metals, Inc., Phila., 1985—, also bd. dirs.; owner Silver Carousel Antiques, Rochester, Minn. Treas. Women's Assn. Minn. Orch., Rochester, 1986-87, pres., 1987-89, life advisor, 1989—, editor newsnotes, 1985-87; mem. mayor's coms. All Am. City Award Com., Rochester, 1984-88, Entertainment League, Rochester, 1987-88; bd. dirs. Rochester Civic League, 1988-94, pres.-elect, 1990-91, pres., 1991-92; pres. Rochester Friends of Mpls. Inst. Arts, 1989-90, Folwell PTA, 1990-91; state liaison Gateway, 1990-91; bd. dirs. Rochester Civic Theatre, 1993—, v.p., 1994—. Mem. Am. Soc. Law and Medicine, Zumbro Valley Med. Soc. Aux. (Rochester, fin. chmn. 1986-90, treas. 1988-90), NAFE, Nat. Assn. Food Equipment Mfrs., Friends of Mayowood, Phi Alpha Delta, Sigma Theta Tau.

AMADO, HONEY KESSLER, lawyer; b. Bklyn., July 20, 1949; d. Bernard and Mildred Kessler; m. Ralph Albert Amado, Oct. 24, 1976; children: Jessica Reina, Micah Solomon, Gabrielle Beth. BA in Polit. Sci., Calif. State Coll., Long Beach, 1971; JD, Western State U., Fullerton, Calif., 1976. Bar: Calif. 1977, U.S. Dist. Ct. (ctrl. dist.) Calif. 1981, U.S. Ct. Appeals (9th cir.) 1981, U.S. Supreme Ct. 1994. Assoc. Law Offices of Jack M. Lasky, Beverly Hills, Calif., 1977-78; pvt. practice Beverly Hills, Calif., 1978—; lectr. in field. Contbr. articles to profl. jours. Me. Com. Concerned Lawyers for Soviet Jewry, 1979-90; bd. dirs. Jewish Nat. Fund, L.A., 1990—, bd. dirs. Sephardic Temple Tifereth Israel, 1991-94, Am. Jewish Congress, Jewish Feminist Ctr., 1992—; co-chair A.J. Congress Feminist Ctr., 1994—; mem. Commn. on Soviet Jewry of Jewish Fedn. Coun. Greater L.A., 1977-83, chmn., 1979-81, commn. on edn., 1982-83, cmty. rels. com., 1979-83. Mem. Calif. Women Lawyers (bd. govs. 1988-90, 1st v.p. 1989-90, jud. evaluations co-chair 1988-90), San Fernando Valley Bar Assn. (family law mediators and arbitrators planel 1983-94, judge pro-tem panel 1987-94), Beverly Hills Bar Assn. (family law mediators panel 1985-94), L.A. County Bar Assn. (family law sect., appellate cts. com. 1987—, chmn. subcom. to examine reorgn. Calif. Supreme Ct. 1990-94, judge pro tem panel 1985—, appellate jud. evaluations com. 1989—), Calif. State Bar. Democrat. Jewish. Office: 261 S Wetherly Dr Beverly Hills CA 90211

AMADOR, TAMERA DIANE, nursing director; b. Pueblo, Colo., Dec. 27, 1958; d. Scott and Jessie Marie (Mirelez) Chadwick; m. Arthur Amador, Apr. 5, 1979 (div. Jan. 1983); 1 child, Sophia Lorraine. Diploma, L.A. County Sch. Nursing, 1985; BSN, Calif. State U., Long Beach, 1989; JD, Loyola Law Sch., 1994. Bar: Calif. 1994; RN; cert. pub. health nurse, Calif., respiratory therapist, emergency nurse, nurse administrator. From staff nurse to nurse dir. Dept. Emergency Medicine L.A. County and U. So. Calif. Med. Ctr., 1985—; legal extern L.A. City Atty's Office, 1994—; instr. Am. Heart Assn., 1991—; cons. Harrington, Foxx, Dubrow & Canter, L.A., 1992. 2d lt. USAR, 1987-95. Mem. Am. Assn. Nurse Attys., Emergency Nurses Assn. Republican. Office: LA County USC Med Ctr 1200 N State St Rm 1060 R Los Angeles CA 90033

AMAFITANO, LELIA, curator. BFA, Calif. Inst. Arts, 1974; MFA, Art Inst. Chgo., 1978. Instr. Albany Inst. History and Art, Albany, 1979; dir., curator Rathbone Gallery Russell Stage/Jr. Coll. Albany, 1983-86; curator Stux Gallery, Boston & N.Y.C., 1986-87; curator, dir. exhbns. & vis. artists programs Sch. Mus. Fine Arts, Boston, 1986—; vis. artist Art Resources Open Women, Schenectady, N.Y., 1978; adj. prof. fine arts divsn. Russell Stage/Jr. Coll. Albany, 1980-86; lectr. in field. Contbr., editor numerous catalogues. Home: 441 Shawmut Ave Boston MA 02118 Office: Sch Mus Fine Art 230 The Fenway Boston MA 02115-5534

AMALONG, SALLY LOUISE, small business owner; b. Pitts., Nov. 4, 1947; d. James E. and Phyllis M. (Frank) Davis; m. Gerald L. Amalong, Jan. 14, 1967 (div. May 1989); children: Julie A., Laurie M. Student, Asbury Coll., Wilmore, Ky., 1965, U. Pitts., 1968-69; AAS, Westmoreland County C.C., Youngwood, Pa., 1993. Sr. rep., acctg. clk. Sears, Roebuck and Co., Greensburg, Pa., 1978-85; owner, operator The Gown Salon-Sally Jack's,

Export, Pa., 1987—; dir. bridal and prom shows, 1987—; initiator, dir. bridal seminars, Delmont, Pa., 1990. Mem. choir Laurel Highlands Ch. of God, 1991—, also mem. power team. Mem. Phi Theta Kappa. Republican. Office: The Gown Salon-Sally Jack's 5127 Old William Penn Hwy Export PA 15632-9348

AMANN, JUDITH JAY, small business owner; b. Kansas City, Kans., Apr. 23, 1938; d. Neville Norwood and Mary Margaret (Abercrombie) Cobb; m. Carl W. Amann; 1 child, Wesley Neville. Owner Ace Hi Kennel, Choctaw, Okla., 1964-72, Jay Amann Antiques, Houston, 1975—; reporter Collectors Jour. and Antique Week, 1990—. Mem. Paper & Advt. Club Am., Pen Club of Houston, Perfume & Scent Bottle Collectors Club. Home and Office: 5300 N Braeswood Blvd # 373 Houston TX 77096-3307

AMANTIA, JACQUELIN BOULANGER, visual artist; b. Pawhuska, Okla., June 14, 1957; d. Edward Eugene and Frances Rose (Frye) Boulanger; m. Samuel Andrew Amantia, Nov. 28, 1981. BA magna cum laude, Fla. State U., 1991, MFA, 1994. Exhibited art in shows including Space 67, 1988, Fla. State U. Art Students League, 1989, 92, 93, Fla. State U. Ctr. for Profl. Devel., 1989, Tallahassee City Hall, 1989, 93. Recipient fellowship Fla. State U., 1992-93, various awards for art. Mem. Adoptive Families Am., Fla. State U. Alumni Assn., Osage Indian Tribe. Democrat. Roman Catholic. Home: 2814 Vann Cir Tallahassee FL 32312-2745

AMARI, KATHRYN JANE, elementary education educator; b. Sopris, Colo.; d. Thomas S. and Catherine (Ossola) Parker; m. Carl Leo Amari Sr., July 27, 1957; children: Jayne Amari Graham, Carl Leo Amari Jr. AA, Trinidad State Jr. Coll., 1951; BA, Western State Coll., 1954. Cert. tchr., Colo. Tchr. Valdez (Colo.) Elem. Sch., 1951-54, Trinidad (Colo.) Pub. Sch. Dist. #1, 1954—; mem. lang. curriculum com., sch. improvement com. Contbr. articles to profl. mags. Mem. PTA, Trinidad, 1954-91. Mem. AAUW, Trinidad Edn. Assn. (sec. 1958-59), Colo. Edn. Assn. (rep. 1954-64), Trinidad State Jr. Coll. Alumni, Delta Kappa Gamma, Beta Sigma Phi. Democrat. Roman Catholic. Home: 307 S Spruce St Trinidad CO 81082-3536 Office: Park St Sch 612 Park St Trinidad CO 81082-2307

AMATO, CAMILLE JEAN, manufacturing executive; b. N.Y.C., Aug. 6, 1942; d. William and Mary Carmela (Lombardi) Tuorto; m. Thomas Amato, June 1, 1963; children—Dawn, Thomas. Assoc. Sci., SUNY-Albany, 1981, B.S., 1983; B.S., Empire State Coll., 1983, M. Bus. and Policy, 1986. Lic. realtor, notary, N.Y. Controller, owner Island Marine Inc., Bellmore, N.Y., 1977—; account mgr. L.I. Luth. Assn., Brookville, N.Y., 1983-84, Borden Inc. Chem., Glen Cove, N.Y., 1984-85; real estate agt. N. of 25A R.E. Inc., Locust Valley, N.Y., 1986—; owner, v.p. Penn Yan (N.Y.) Marine Mfg. Inc., 1986—; pres., owner Camille Properties, Inc., Penn Yan, 1986—; pres. Pendragon Co., 1991—; cons. various areas. Cons. sub-com. edn. and safety N.Y. State Senate, 1976-77. Mem. Nat. Assn. Female Execs. Roman Catholic. Avocation: classical piano. Home: Woodstock Manor Muttontown Oyster Bay NY 11771

AMATO, CAROL JOY, writer, anthropologist; b. Portland, Oreg., Apr. 9, 1944; d. Sam Lawrence and Lena Dorothy (Dindia) A.; m. Neville Stanley Motts, Aug. 26, 1967 (div. 1978); children: Tracy, Damon. BA, U. Portland, 1966; MA, Calif. State U., 1986. Freelance writer, Westminster, Calif., 1969—; human factor cons. Design Sci. Corp., L.A., 1979—; dir. software documentation Trans-Ed Communications, Westminster, 1980-84, pres. Advanced Profl. Software, Inc., Westminster, 1984-86, Systems Rsch. Analysis, Inc., Westminster, 1986—. Author: The Earth, 1992, Astronomy, 1992, The Human Body, 1992, Inventions, 1992, Inside Out: The Wonders of Modern Technologies Explained, 1992, 50 Nifty Science Fair Projects, 1993, The Super Science Project Book, 1994, The World's Easiest Guide to Using the APA, 1994; editor, Cultural Futuristics, 1975-80, numerous articles and short stories; participant in numerous radio and TV interviews. Sec. bd. dirs. Am. Space Meml. Found., L.A., 1986-87; bd. dirs. Orange County Acad. Decathalon, 1986-94. Mem. Ind. Writers of So. Calif. (bd. dirs. Orange County sect. 1986-93), Profl. Writers Orange County (bd. dirs. 1993—), Writers' Club of Whittier, Inc., Internat. Pen. Home: 10151 Heather Ct Westminster CA 92683-5754

AMATO, ISABELLA ANTONIA, real estate executive; b. Noto, Italy, July 17, 1942; d. Raimondo and Giuseppa (Pinna) Sesta; m. Vincent Amato; children: Alice, Claudine. Acctg. diploma, Inst. Tech. and Commerce, 1962. V.p., dir. Thomas F. Seay & Assocs., Chgo., 1977-81; treas. Seay & Thomas Inc., Chgo., 1979-81; CFO Group One Investments, Chgo., 1981—; exec. v.p., registered prin. First Group Securities, Ltd., Chgo., 1983—. Vol. translator Altrusa Lang. Bank, Chgo., 1980-86; v.p. Jr. Woman Club, Elk Grove Village, Ill., 1977; chairperson Atty. Exec. Forum, Chgo., 1985. Mem. Nat. Assn. Securities Dealers (prin.), Nat. Assn. Realtors (comml. investment, specialist real estate securities Real Estate Securities and Syndication Inst. 1987), Chgo. Real Estate Bd., Real Estate Fin. Forum, Altrusa Profl. Woman (treas. Chgo. club 1984-85). Office: Group One Investments 77 W Washington St Ste 1005 Chicago IL 60602-2858

AMATOS, BARBARA HANSEN, accounting executive; b. Toledo, Aug. 30, 1944; d. John Richard and Irene Emily (Greunke) Hansen; m. James David Mokren, Sept. 12, 1964 (div. Feb. 1974); children: Frederic Hansen Mokren, Jennifer Joy Mokren; m. David Michael Amatos, Dec. 27, 1975; 1 stepchild, Anthony Steven. Student, Capital U., 1962-64, Cen. Mich. U., 1965-66; BBA, Franklin U., 1979. CPA, Ohio; cert. fraud examiner. Account clk. Buckeye Mart, Columbus, Ohio, 1971-73, SCOA Industries Inc., Columbus, 1973-75; payroll mgr. City of Columbus Auditor's Office, 1975-86; mgmt. adv. cons. State of Ohio Auditor's Office, Columbus, 1986-87, acctg. mgr., 1987—; ptnr. McGuiness Amatos Properties, Amatos & Amatos, CPA's. Mem. AICPA, Am. Woman's Soc. CPAs, Assn. Govt. Accts. (pres. 1993-94, exec. com. 1989-90, emerging issues task force), Govt. Fin. Officers Assn. (spl. rev. com.), Assn. Cert. Fraud Examiners. Office: Auditor State of Ohio 88 E Broad St Columbus OH 43215-3506

AMAZON, ELIZABETH GANNON, retired elementary education educator, civic worker; b. Cambridge, N.Y., Sept. 29, 1912; d. John Joseph and Mary Camilla (McGowan) Gannon; m. Maurice D. Amazon (dec. May 1967); children: Mary Alyce, David, Maureen, Sheila, Dana, Jennifer, Rosemary. BS in Edn., SUNY, Albany, 1941; grad., SUNY, Oneonta, 1935; student, Skidmore Coll., 1933-34. Elem. tchr. pub. schs., Cambridge, 1932-34, Easton, N.Y., 1936-41; tchr. English, John Bigsbee Jr. High Sch., Schenectady, 1941-46; elem. tchr. pub. schs., Nott Terrace, N.Y., 1959-60, South Colonie, N.Y., 1961-81; ret., 1981. Sr. citizen rep. Schenectady County, 1991; vol. Schenectady Mus.; active Sunnyview Aux., Glendale Home Aux., St. Clare's Aux.; health chair Legis. Forum; intake worker Inner City Ministry; mem. Friends of Libr., Lady of Fatima Sr. Citizen Group, St. Helen's Sr. Citizen Group; v.p. Youth over Fifty, Ea. Pkwy. Meth. Ch.; active numerous other orgns. Named Woman of Vision, 1990. Mem. AAUW (study groups), Am. Assn. Ret. Persons (past sec., v.p., chmn.), Cath. Daus. Am. (past regent), Ea. Zone Ret. Tchrs. Assn., Schenectady County Ret. Tchrs. Assn. (past pres.), SUNY-Oneonta Alumni Assn. (past Capital Dist. pres.), Schenectady Women's Club (pres.), Schenectady Hist. Aux. (bd. dirs., v.p., pres.), Niskayuna Garden Club (v.p., bd. dirs., com. mem.), Ladies of Charity (v.p. 1993—), Christ Child, Faith and Light. Democrat. Home: 1160 Keyes Ave Niskayuna NY 12309

AMBOR, MICHELE MARIE, nurse practitioner; b. Buffalo, N.Y., Oct. 30, 1960; d. Stephen Raymond Ambor and Carolyn Marie (Paulson) Santi. BSN, D'Youville Coll., 1981; MS, SUNY, Buffalo, 1985. Cert. nurse practitioner, N.Y., NCC. ICU nursery nurse Children's Hosp., Buffalo, 1981-86, ob/gyn nurse practitioner, 1986-88; ob/gyn nurse practitioner Buffalo Gen. Hosp., 1986—, Health Care Plan, Buffalo, 1988—; adj. clin. faculty SUNY, Buffalo, 1986—, D'Youville Coll., Buffalo, 1994; speaker Progressive Woman's Svcs., Buffalo, 1993—. Exam writer NAACOG, 1990. Speaker March of Dimes, Buffalo, 1992—; vol. World Univ. Games, Buffalo, 1993. Recipient Citizenship award DAR, Buffalo, 1977. Mem. Lederhosen Ski Club (sec. 1988-90, Skier of the Yr. 1990, 2nd v.p. 1992-94), NAACOG (chmn. 1991-94), N.Y. State Perinatal Task Force, N.Y. State Coalition of Nurse Practitioners, Sigma Theta Tau. Republican. Office: Buffalo Gen Hosp 100 High St Buffalo NY 14203

AMBROSE, DONETTA W., federal judge; b. 1945. BA, Duquesne U., 1967, JD cum laude, 1970. Law clerk to Hon. Louis L. Manderino Commonwealth Ct. Pa., 1970-71, Supreme Ct. Pa., 1972; asst. atty. gen. Pa. Dept. Justice, 1972-74; pvt. practice atty. Ambrose & Ambrose, Kensington, Pa., 1974-81; asst. dist. atty. Westmoreland County, Pa., 1977-81; judge Ct. Common Pleas Westmoreland County, 1982-93, U.S. Dist. Ct. (we. dist.) Pa., Pitts., 1994—; resident advisor Duquesne U., 1967-70. Scholar Pa. Conf. State Trial Judges, 1992, State Justice Inst., 1993. Mem. ABA, Nat. Assn. Women Judges, Am. Judicature Soc., Pa. Bar Assn., Women's Bar Assn. Western Pa., Pa. Conf. State Trial Judges (sec. 1992-93), Westmoreland County Bar Assn., Italian Sons and Daus. Am., William Penn Fraternal Assn., New Kensington Women's Club, Delta Kappa Gamma. Office: 620 US Post Office & Courthouse 7th Ave Grant Pittsburgh PA 15219*

AMBRUS, CLARA MARIA, physician; b. Rome, Dec. 28, 1924; came to U.S., 1949, naturalized, 1955; d. Anthony and Charlotte (Schneider) Bayer; m. Julian Lawrence Ambrus, Feb. 17, 1945; children—Madeline Ambrus Lillie, Peter, Julian, Linda, Steven, Katherine Ambrus-Cheney, Charles. Student, U. Budapest (Hungary), 1943-47; M.D., U. Zurich, Switzerland, 1949; postgrad., U. Paris, 1949; Ph.D., Jefferson Med. Coll., 1955. Diplomate: Am. Bd. Clin. Chemists. Research asst. Inst. Histology, Embryology and Biology U. Budapest, 1943-45; demonstrator in pharmacology U. Budapest Med. Sch., 1946-47; asst. dept. pharmacology U. Zurich Med. Sch., 1947-49; asst. dept. therapeutic chemistry and virology Inst. Pasteur, Paris, 1949; asst. prof. pharmacology Phila. Coll. Pharmacy and Sci., 1950-52, asso. prof., 1952-55; research asso. Roswell Park Meml. Inst., Buffalo, 1955-58; sr. cancer research scientist Roswell Park Meml. Inst., 1958-64, asso. scientist, 1964-69, prin. cancer research scientist, 1969-85; prof. pharmacology State U. N.Y.; prof. pharmacology Buffalo Med. and Grad. Schs., 1955—, asso. prof. pediatrics, 1955-76, prof. pediatrics, 1976, research prof. ob-gyn, 1983—; chmn., CEO Hemex Inc., 1984—. Contbr. articles to med. and sci. jours. Trustee Nichols Sch., Buffalo, Community Music Sch. Named Outstanding Woman of Western N.Y. Community Adv. Council, SUNY, Buffalo, 1980. Fellow ACP, Internat. Soc. Hematology; mem. Am. Soc. Pharmacology and Exptl. Therapeutics, Am. Soc. Cancer Rsch., Am. Fedn. Clin. Rsch., Am. Physiol. Soc., Am. Soc. Hematology, Buffalo Acad. Medicine, Am. Med. Women's Assn., Clarksburg Country Club, Saturn Club, Garrett Club, Sigma Xi. Home: 143 Windsor Ave Buffalo NY 14209-1020 also: West Hill Farm Boston NY 14025 Office: Buffalo Gen Hosp 100 High St Buffalo NY 14203-1154

AMEEN, MARY DIPIETRO, civil engineer, lawyer; b. Newark, Sept. 22, 1954; d. Diego David and Catherine Ann (Nealon) Di Pietro; m. Ramsey M. Ameen, June 17, 1983; children: Alexander David, Amber Claire. BE, Stevens Inst. Tech., Hoboken, N.J., 1976; MS in Civil Engring., N.J. Inst. Tech., Newark, 1982; MS in Mgmt., Stevens Inst. Tech., 1987; JD, Rutgers U., 1993. Bar: N.J. 1993, Pa., 1993; registered profl. engr., N.J. Engr. Exxon Rsch. & Engring., Florham Park, N.J., 1976-78, Vollmer Assocs., N.Y.C., 1979-80; traffic engr. N.J. Highway Authority, Woodbridge, 1980-86, asst. chief engr., 1986—; Mem. program com. N.J. Bus., Industry & Sci. Edn. Coun., Hoboken, 1992—. Mem. ABA, ASCE, Nat. Soc. Profl. Engrs., Inst. Transp. Engrs., Stevens Women Engrs. Network. Office: NJ Hwy Authority PO Box 5050 Woodbridge NJ 07095

AMELING, ELLY, soprano; b. Rotterdam, The Netherlands, Feb. 8, 1933; d. Dirk and Aleida (Zikking) A.; m. Arnold W. Belder, Nov. 6, 1964. Student, Conservatory of Music, The Hague, Netherlands; hon. degree, U.B.C., Vancouver, Can., Westminster Choir Coll., Princeton, N.J. Debut, Victoria Hall, Geneva, Switzerland; numerous solo recitals, also with orchs. throughout world; rec. artist, Philips, CBS, Decca London, EMI Angel, RCA, ODeon, Harmonia Mundi, Peters Internat., Etcetera, Hyperion and Vanguard records. Decorated Order Oranje Nassau, The Netherlands; recipient Preis der Deutschen Schallplattenkritik; Grand prix du Disque, Edison prize, Stereo Review Record Yr. award. Office: care Sheldon Soffer Mgmt 130 W 56th St New York NY 10019-3818

AMELL, DIANA MARIE, customer service administrator; b. Plattsburgh, N.Y., May 21, 1952; d. Clarence Elmer and Ruth Virginia (O'Connell) Duquette; 1 child, Marcelle Lynn. A in Humanities, Clinton C.C., Plattsburgh, N.Y., 1972; student, SUNY, Plattsburgh, 1982-87, Regents Coll., 1994—. Pers. asst. Georgia-Pacific Corp., Plattsburgh, 1973-85, asst. prodn. control mgr., 1985-87; allocation and inventory control mgr. Georgia-Pacific Corp., Atlanta, 1987-90, customer svc. mgr., 1993—, nat. customer svc. mgr., 1993—. Mem. NAFE, Coun. Logistics Mgmt. Home: 4815 Hunters Trace Powder Springs GA 30073 Office: Georgia-Pacific Corp 233 Peachtree St Atlanta GA 30303

AMENDOLA, MARY ROSE, mental retardation services professional; b. Monongahela, Pa., May 21, 1956; d. Joseph and Carmen Cosima (Battilana) A. BA, Waynesburg Coll., 1978; cert. reality therapy, S.W. Area Regional Tng. Coun., Greensburg, Pa., 1978; student, California (Pa.) State Coll., 1980. Cert. athletic coach, Pa. Counselor Try Again Homes, Waynesburg, Pa., 1978; mental retardation aide Western Ctr. Dept. Pub. Welfare, Canonsburg, Pa., 1978-80, therapeutic recreation aide, 1980-86, residential svcs. aide supr., 1986-87, residential svcs. worker, 1987-89; residential svcs. supr. Qualified Mental Retardation Profl., Canonsburg, 1989—; sr. exec. Quorum Internat., Ltd., 1994—. Mem. Defenders of Wildlife, Washington, People for the Ethical Treatment of Animals, Washington. Mem. Phi Sigma Sigma, Theta Chi. Democrat. Roman Catholic. Home: 158 Terrace Dr Monongahela PA 15063

AMENDT, MARILYN JOAN, personnel director; b. Marshalltown, Iowa, June 21, 1928; d. Floyd Wilford and Helen Mary (Scheid) Peterson; m. Virgil E. Amendt, Sept. 4, 1949 (div. Aug. 1971); children: Gregory F., Scott R., Brad A. AA, Stephens Coll., Columbia, Mo., 1948; postgrad., U. Mich., 1978, U. Wis., Superior, 1980-83. Cert. personnel mgr. Office mgr. S&O Products, Inc., Marshalltown, Iowa, 1961-71; life underwriter Lincoln Liberty Life Ins. Co., Marshalltown, Iowa, 1971-72; retail store mgr. Amy's Fashions, Marshalltown, Iowa, 1972-74, Maurices, Inc., Marshalltown, Iowa, 1974-76; corp. personnel dir. Maurices, Inc., Duluth, Minn., 1976-84; sr. v.p., dir. human resources Ohrbach's, Inc., N.Y.C., 1984-87; dir. personnel adminstrn. AMCENA Corp., N.Y.C., 1970-91; pres., owner Success Strategies, Des Moines, 1992—; lectr. U. Wis, Superior, 1981-82, U. Minn., Duluth, 1981-82. Founder, pres., bd. dirs. Mid-Iowa Sheltered Workshop, Marshalltown, 1968-76; mem. Hostess com. Duluth (Minn.) Day Luncheon, 1983; keynote speaker Am. Bus. Women's Day, Mpls. and Duluth, 1984, 85, 86, 90. Mem. Am. Bus. Women's Assn. (dist. v.p. 1982, nat. v.p. 1983, nat. pres. 1984, woman of the yr. 1978), Am. Soc. Exec. and Profl. Women. Home: 2233 Country Club Blvd Des Moines IA 50325-8602

AMERO, JANE ADAMS, state legislator; b. Rumford, Maine, Aug. 6, 1941; d. William Anthony and Evangeline Jean (McInnis) Adams; m. Gerald M. Amero, Sept. 4, 1961; children: Scott Martin, Brett Douglas, Melanie Jane. BA, Cornell U., 1963. Tchr. South Portland (Maine) Sch. Dist., 1965-67; mem. Cape Elizabeth (Maine) Sch. Bd., 1975-81, Maine Bd. Edn., Augusta, 1987—; chmn. Maine Bd. Edn., 1989—; mem. Maine Senate; mem. Maine Coalition for Excellence in Edn., 1990—, Sci. Literacy Commn., Augusta, 1990—, Commn. to Evaluate Tech. Coll. System, Augusta, 1990-91; mem. 3 sch. funding task forces, Augusta, 1987, 88, 90-91. Me. coun. Town of Cape Elizabeth, 1982—, chmn., 1987; mem., pres. Catherine Morrill Day Nursery, Portland, 1981-87; mem. Commn. on Restructuring State Govt., Augusta, 1991—; corporator Maine Med. Ctr., Portland, 1989—; active Vol. Lawyers Project, Portland, 1984-90; mem. Ptnrs. for Progress in Portland Leadership Initiative, 1990—. Recipient Svc. Above Self award Rotary Clubs, Cape Elizabeth, South Portland, 1991. Mem. Nat. Assn. State Bds. Edn. (nat. study com. parent and community involvement in schs. 1989), Maine Mcpl. Assn., Nat. League Cities, Maine Assn. Ptnrs. in Edn. (bd. dirs. 1988—), LWV (Emily Farley award Portland 1989), Phi Beta Kappa, Phi Kappa Phi. Republican. Home: 444 Old Ocean House Rd Cape Eliz ME 04107-2625 Office: Maine State Senate State Capitol Augusta ME 04330*

AMES, JULIE ANN, bank officer; b. Huntington, N.Y., Mar. 4, 1959; d. James Paul and Bonnie Jean (Laing) Hektner; m. Christopher Conlan Ames, May 9, 1992. BA, U. Va., 1981; MPA, Harvard U., 1991; grad., Ecole Nat. Adminstrn., Paris, 1991. Sr. policy analyst Fed. Res. Bd., Washington, 1981-92; fin. svcs. dir. Fed. Res. Bank, Jacksonville, Fla., 1992-94; acting dir. pub. policy connect program U. Calif. San Diego, La Jolla, Calif., 1994—. Bd. dirs. Arlington (Va.) Met. Chorus, 1982-91, Hospice of N.E. Fla., Jacksonville, 1993-94. Mem. Women in Govt. Rels., Women in Internat. Security, Harvard Club of the First Coast. Roman Catholic. Office: U Calif San Diego La Jolla CA 92092

AMEY, RAE, television and video developer, producer; b. Shreveport, La., Sept. 26, 1947; d. Bruce Harold and Genevieve (Amey) Gentry; m. John E. Scarborough, Dec. 18, 1971 (div. Nov. 1979). Student, La. State U., 1968-70, U. Houston, 1972-74; BA in Liberal Arts, Antioch U., 1985; grad., U. So. Calif., 1988—. Freelance photographer Calif., 1973—; adminstrn. coord. Y.E.S. Inc., Sta. KCET-TV, L.A., 1980-83; freelande ednl. TV writer, cons. L.A., 1983-84; asst. to pres. prodn. So. Calif. Consortium, Cypress, 1984, project mgr., dir. devel., project dir. The Human Condition, 1985-87; v.p. devel. and outreach The California Channel, L.A., 1990-92, project dir., 1991, 92; pres. Video Nexus, L.A., 1987—. Editor TV guide book, 1985; photography exhbns. include: Contemporary Art Mus., Houston, 1973, Galveston (Tex.) Arts Ctr., 1975, Cameravision Gallery, L.A.,1980, Aloft, Pasadena, 1989. Co-founder Harbor Arts Alliance; mem., bd. dirs. African Am. Arts Coun.; founder, chair, bd. dirs. CIVICS, 1993—; advisor Congress on Racial Equality. Ellen Torgenson Shaw scholar Annenberg Sch. Communications, U. So. Calif., 1989. Mem. Women in Communications (bd. dirs., v.p. campus svcs. 1987-88, exec. v.p. 1988-89, bd. dirs. scholarship and edn. fund L.A. chpt.). Democrat. Home: 255 S Grand Ave Apt 1914 Los Angeles CA 90012-6010 Office: 255 S Grand Ave #2201 Los Angeles CA 90012-6010

AMIDEI, NANCY JEAN, social service agency executive, writer, media commentator; b. Lake Forest, Ill., Mar. 27, 1942; d. Natale and Dema (Capitani) A. B.S. in Humanities, Loyola U., Chgo., 1963; M.S.W., U. Mich., 1968. Vol., Peace Corps, Nigeria, 1964-65; mem. staff, then staff dir. U.S. Senate Com. on Nutrition and Human Needs, Washington, 1969-72; dep. asst. sec. HEW, Washington, 1977-79; dir. Food Research Action Ctr., Washington, 1980-84; weekly columnist; Washington corr. Commonweal Mag.; commentator All Things Considered program Nat. Pub. Radio, 1985; vis. prof. Sch. Social Work, U. Mich., Ann Arbor, 1985, Sch. Social Work, Catholic U., Washington, 1986-89; assoc. dir. Ctr. Policy and Practise Rsch., Sch. Social Work U. Wash., 1992—. Co-author: Protest, Politics and Prosperity: Black Americans and White Institutions, 1940-75, 1978; prin. author: Hunger in the Eighties: A Primer, 1984; author: So You Want to Make a Difference, 1992; also numerous articles. Commn. mem. Hunger Watch, N.Y. State, 1983; mem. adv. bd. Project Vote; bd. dirs. OMB Watch. Recipient Disting. Alumni award U. Mich. Sch. Social Work, 1984, Spl. Achievement award Kenny and Marianne Rogers Hunger Awards, 1984; alumna in residence U. Mich. Alumnae Assn., 1985. Mem. Nat. Assn. Social Workers, Nat. Anti-Hunger Coalition.

AMIDON, KATHLEEN ANN, aerospace executive; b. Springfield, Vt., Oct. 11, 1963; d. David Michael and Janice Ann (Mahoney) A. BS in Math., Va. Polytechnic Inst., 1985. Group leader attitude and pointing NASA Johnson Space Ctr., Houston, 1989-94, attitude and pointing specialist, 1985-94; exec. NASA Hdqs., Washington, 1994—. Mem. Mus. Fine Arts, Houston, 1993-94, L'Alliance Française, Houston, 1993-94. Roman Catholic. Home: 3700 1st Road South Arlington VA 22204 Office: NASA Hdqs Washington DC 20546

AMISS, BARBARA JEAN, accountant; b. Ft. Wayne, Ind., Nov. 11, 1944; d. John Lester and Virginia May (Little) Smith; m. Stephen Karl Amiss, Nov. 14, 1964 (div. May 1973); 1 child, David C. Student, Internat. Bus. Coll., 1962-64, Manchester Coll., 1979. Bookkeeper, asst. to sec.-treas. The Heckman Bindery, Inc., North Manchester, Ind., 1964-66, data processing ops. supr., 1966-70, acct., asst. to contr., 1970—. Author: Simon Baker Family Genealogy, 1987. Treas., bd. dirs. Big Bros.-Big Sisters-Wabash, 1990-94; active Manchester Symphony Soc., North Manchester, 1994; precinct clk. Rep. Party, Servia, Ind., 1994. Mem. Inst. Mgmt. Accts., Ind. Bus. & Profl. Women's Found. (sec.-treas.), Ohio State Geneal. Soc., Manchester Hist. Soc., Ind. Fedn. Bus. & Profl. Women's Club, Inc. (state pres. 1989-90), Ea. Star (Ivy chpt.), Kappa, Kappa, Kappa, Inc. Republican. Methodist. Home: 654 E-1000 N North Manchester IN 46962 Office: The Heckman Bindery Inc 1010 N Sycamore St North Manchester IN 46962

AMMAN, E(LIZABETH) JEAN, university official; b. Hoyleton, Ill., July 13, 1941; d. James Kerr and Marie Fern (Schnake) White; m. Douglas Dorrance Amman, Aug. 12, 1962; children: Mark, Kirk, Jill, Drew, Gwen. BA in English, Ill. Wesleyan U., 1963; MA in English, U. Cin., 1975. Cert. tchr., Ill. Tchr. lang. arts John Greer Jr. High Sch., Hoopeston, Ill., 1963-64, Pleasant Hill Sch., East Peoria, Ill., 1966-67; tchr. English, chmn. Am. studies Anderson Sr. High Sch., Cin., 1967-69; instr. English, No. Mich. U., Marquette, 1976-82; instr. English, Ball State U., Muncie, Ind., 1982-86, adminstrv. intern, 1983-84, asst. to chmn. dept., 1984-86, adminstrv. asst., 1986, asst. to provost, coord. provost's lecture series, 1986—, exec. sec. student and campus life coun., 1986—. Editor: Provost's Lecture Series: Perspectives on Culture and Society, Vol. I, 1988, Vol. II, 1991, The Associator, 1983-86. Mem. choir College Ave. Meth. Ch., Muncie, 1989—; fundraiser Delaware County Coalition for Literacy, 1989, 90; flutist Muncie Sinfonietta Orch., 1989—, Am.'s Hometown Band, 1991—. Recipient recognition Black Student Assn., Ball State U., 1988, cert. of svc. for minority student devel., 1990, 91, 92. Mem. AAUW (corr. sec. Muncie chpt. 1993—), Ind. Coll. English Assn. (editor, exec. bd. 1983-86), P.E.O. (pres. Muncie 1985-87), Sigma Alpha Iota (v.p. 1993-94, pres. 1994—), Kappa Delta (Ind. Kappa Delta of Yr. 1994, advisor 1992—). Democrat. Home: 4305 Castleton Ct Muncie IN 47304 Office: Ball State U 2000 W University Ave Muncie IN 47306

AMMANN, LILLIAN ANN NICHOLSON, interior landscape executive; b. Pearsall, Tex., June 20, 1946; d. Harvey Franklin and Annie Laura (Matthews) Nicholson; m. Jack Jordan Ammann Jr., May 31, 1967; 1 child, William Erik. BA magna cum laude, Southwestern U., 1968. Mgr. inventory Kelly AFB, San Antonio, 1967-70; employment counselor Tex. Employment Commn., San Antonio, 1970-75; owner, operator Lillie's Lovely Little Gardens, San Antonio, 1975-77; owner, operator Lillie's Interior Landscapes, San Antonio, 1980-82, pres., 1983—; sec. Jack Ammann Inc., 1983-87; pres. Lillie's & Sherry's Plants & Pottery, San Antonio, 1977-80. Author: Lillie's Lovely Little Gardening Book, 1976. Mem. Women in Bus. (past pres.), San Antonio Interior Landscape Assn. (founder, 1st pres.), Associated Landscape Contractors of Am. (cert. interior landscape profl.), North San Antonio C. of C, San Antonio Bldg. Owners & Mgrs. Assn. Episcopalian. Home: 603 Mauze Dr San Antonio TX 78216-3711 Office: Lillie's Interior Landscapes 17585 Blanco Rd # 16-1 San Antonio TX 78232-1037

AMMAR, MARTI FARHA, activist; b. Wichita, Kans., Nov. 30, 1954; d. Philip Farah and Gloria May (Eddie) Farha; m. Alex David Ammar, Aug. 21, 1976; children: Alex Shafeek, Chad Philip. BA in Govt. and Near Eastern Studies, Mills Coll., Oakland, Calif., 1976. pres. Women's Studies Community Coun. Bd. Del. Dem. Nat. Conf., Atlanta, 1988, precinct commiteewoman; pres. bd. dirs. Don J. Allen Meml. Huntington's Disease Clinic, 1988-92; pres. Save Lebanon, Inc., Washington, 1988—; mem. bd. Women's Studies Cmty. Coun., 1993—, Wesley Med. Rsch. Inst., 1993—; advisor Israel/PLO Peace Accord, 1993—. NEH youth grantee in humanities, 1977-79, Thomas J. Watson fellow, 1976; recipient Women of Achievement Matrix award Women in Comm., Wichita profl. chpt. 1993; nominee for Women's Rights Star of Yr. award, 1994. Office: 345 N Belmont St Wichita KS 67208-3808

AMMONS, CAROL HAMRICK, psychologist, editor; b. Tampa, Fla., Feb. 22, 1927; d. Joe Fred and B. Carolyn (Patton) Hamrick; m. Robert Bruce Ammons, Aug. 26, 1949; children: Carl, Bruce, Douglas, Beth, Richard, Stephanie, Glenyss. BA, Hariette Sophie Newcomb Coll. for Women, 1947; MA, Tulane U., 1949; PhD, U. Ky., 1955. Lectr. U. Louisville, 1949-55; pvt. practice cons. psychologist Louisville, 1949—. Co-editor Perceptual and Motor Skills, 1949—, Psychol. Reports, 1955—; contbr. numerous articles to profl. jours. Grantee U. Ky., Lexington, 1952-54, Tulane U., New Orleans, 1947-49. Mem. AAAS, Am. Psychol. Assn., Internat. Coun. Psychologists (sec. 1965-68), Sigma Xi. Home: 411 Keith Ave Missoula MT 59801-4110 Office: PO Box 9229 Missoula MT 59807-9229

AMNEUS, D. A., English language educator; b. Beverly, Mass., Oct. 15, 1919; d. Nils A. and Harriet S. (Anchersen) Amneus; divorced; children: Paul, Pamela. AB, U. Calif. Berkeley, 1941; MA, U. So. Calif., 1947, PhD, 1953. From asst. prof. to prof. Calif. State U., L.A., 1950-86, prof. emeritus, 1986—; pub. Primrose Press, Alhambra, Calif. Author: Back to Patriarchy, 1979, The Mystery of Macbeth, 1983, The Three Othellos, 1986, The Garbage Generation, 1990; contbr. articles to profl. jours. Mem. NOW. Republican. Home: 2131 S Primrose Ave Alhambra CA 91803-3834 Office: Calif State U English Dept 5151 State University Dr Los Angeles CA 90032-4221

AMON, CAROL BAGLEY, federal judge; b. 1946. BS, Coll. William and Mary, 1968; JD, U. Va., 1971. Bar: Va. 1971, D.C. 1972, N.Y. 1980. Staff atty. Communications Satellite Corp., Washington, 1971-73; trial atty. U.S. Dept. Justice, Washington, 1973-74; asst. U.S. atty. Ea. Dist. N.Y., 1974-86, U.S. magistrate, 1986-90, dist. ct. judge, 1990—. Recipient John Marshall award U.S. Dept. Justice, 1983. Mem. ABA, Assn. of Bar of City of N.Y., Va. State Bar Assn., D.C. Bar Assn. Office: US District Court US Courthouse 225 Cadman Plz E Brooklyn NY 11201-1876 also: US Dist Ct Uniondale Ave At Hemps Uniondale NY 11553*

AMONSON, JOHANNE LESLIE, barrister, solicitor; b. Edmonton, Alta., Can., Mar. 28, 1949; d. Leslie Earl and Trudy Johanna (Fritz) A.; married, Mar. 6, 1981; 1 child: Matthew Charles Arthur. BA, U. Oreg., 1970; LLB, U. Alta., 1977. Bar: Alta. 1978. Assoc. Weeks Joyce, Edmonton, 1978-85; ptnr. Peterson Ross, Edmonton, 1985-89, McLennan Ross, Edmonton, 1989—; appointed Queen's Counsel Lt. Gov. of Alberta, 1992; appointee fed. jud. appointments com. Province of Alberta, 1991-93; mem. Atty. Gen. Alberta Surrogate Rules Amendment Project; panel chmn. Legal Edn. Soc. Alberta; tchr., lectr. on legal edn. tchr. Bavarian Ministry of Edn., Germany, 1972-73; sessional lectr. U. Alberta Law Sch., 1987, 88. Exhbns. registrar Glenbow Mus. Calgary, 1973-74. Named to Dean's List, U. Ore., 1969-70, U. Alta. Law Rev., 1975-77; recipient of fgn. student scholarship, U. Ore., 1967-70. Mem. Law Soc. Alta. (mentor), Can. Bar Assn. (panelist, nat. coun. and provincial exec. com., coord. no. sects., past chair wills and trusts sect.), Edmonton Bar Assn., Internat. Commn. Jurists, Can. Tax Found. (surrogate rules com.). Conservative. Lutheran. Office: McLennan Ross, POB 12040 12220 Stony Plain Rd, Edmonton, AB Canada T5J 3L2

AMOR, GAIL E., long-term care facility consultant; b. S.I., N.Y., Feb. 27, 1949; d. William J. and Jacqueline E. (Johnson) Howard; m. Manuel Amor Jr., Feb. 1, 1981; children: Debra Porcelli, David Porcelli, Nisa Amor-Stein, Toyanna Stapleton, Delton Amor. AASN, Ocean County Coll., 1983; BSN, Monmouth Coll., 1985; MSN, Seton Hall U., 1986; postgrad., U. Pa. Cons. N.J. Dept. Health, Trenton; co-owner, co-dir. Elder Resources, Inc., Lakewood, N.J.; pres., owner Care Perspectives, Lakewood; mem. adj. faculty Grad. Sch. Nursing Seton Hall U., South Orange, N.J. Mem. ANA, N.J. State Nurses Assn., Gerontological Soc. Am., Sigma Theta Tau. Home: 88 Shady Lane Dr Lakewood NJ 08701-2350

AMORNMARN, LINA, chemist; b. Bangkok; came to U.S., 1981; BS in Chemistry, Chulalongkorn U., Bangkok, 1978; MS in Chemistry, Fairleigh Dickinson U., 1985; AAS in Computer with high honors, County Coll. Morris, 1990. Chemist YKK Zipper Co., Ltd., Bangkok, 1978-81, Atlantic Industries Inc., Nutley, N.J., 1985-88, York Labs., Whippany, N.J., 1988-89; co-op computer Sandoz Pharm., East Hanover, N.J., 1987-88; asst. sci. Hoffmann La-Roche, Nutley, N.J., 1989-91, asst. supr., 1990-93, assoc. scientist pharm. quality control, 1991—. Mem. Am. Chem. Soc., Alpha Beta Gamma. Home: 360 Park Rd Parsippany NJ 07054-1737 Office: Hoffmann La-Roche 340 Kingsland St Nutley NJ 07110-1150

AMOROSO, MARIE DOROTHY, retired medical technologist; b. Phila., Jan. 16, 1924; d. Salvatore and Clorinda (Gaudio) A. Med. Lab. Tech., Hahnemann Hosp., Phila., 1943; postgrad., Temple U., Phila., 1945-48, U. Pa., Phila., 1947-48, 1950. Registered EEG Technologist; cert. registered EEG Technologist. EEG technician Hahnemann Med. Coll., Phila., 1943-53, Phila. Gen. Hosp., 1953-62; histology technician Temple Med. Coll. Temple U., Phila., 1962-63; allergy technician Harry Rogers, M.D., Phila., 1963; EEG technologist Haverford (Pa.) State Hosp., 1963-85, Irvin M. Gerson, MD, Haverford, 1985-88; EEG technologist to pvt. physician Haverford State Hosp., 1985-88; ret., 1988; instr. EEG Osteopathic Med. Ctr. Sch. Allied Health, Phila., 1978-85. Editor: The Eastern Breeze, 1977-79; contbr. articles to profl. jours.; patentee in field. Mem. Am. Soc. Electroneurodiagnostic Technologists Inc., Western Soc. Electrodiagnostic Technologists, So. Soc. Electroneurodiagnostic Technologists Inc., Ea. Soc. EEG and Neurodiagnostic Technicians Assn. (sec. 1977-79), Phila. Regional EEG Technicians Assn. (exec. bd. dirs. 1967, sec. 1969), Ctrl. Soc. Electroneurodiagnostic Technologists, Ea. Assn. Electroencephalographers (subscriber). Home: 477 Brookfield Rd Drexel Hill PA 19026-1107

AMOS, BETTY GILES, restaurant company executive, accountant; b. Lebanon, Mo., July 18, 1941; d. Clarence Edgar and Clara Mae (Gann) Giles; m. E.L. Amos, Sept. 18, 1959 (div. Oct. 1965); 1 child, Jeffrey Lee; m. Thomas R. Righetti, Jan. 2, 1983. BBA magna cum laude, U. Miami, Coral Gables, Fla., 1973, MBA, 1976; D of Bus. Adminstrn. honoris causa, Johnson & Wales U., 1990. CPA, Fla. Sec. City of Lebanon, 1959-63; dept. head Empire Gas Co., Lebanon, 1963-68; fin. analyst asst. Biscayne Assocs., Ltd., Miami, Fla., 1968-73; investment mgr. Universal Restaurants Inc., Miami, 1973-77; pvt. practice accountant, investment mgr. Miami, 1977-83; pres. The Abkey Cos., Miami, 1983—; founder, bd. dirs. Mega Bank, Miami; adv. com., Fuddruckers, Inc., Boston (named Franchisee of the Yr. 1988, 89, 91); mem. bd. dirs. Humane Soc. Greater Miami, 1993—, pres. 1994—; pres. coun. U. Miami, 1994—. Trustee Miami Project, 1986-89, United Fund of Dade County, 1992—; pres. Humane Soc. Greater Miami, 1994—, bd. dirs., 1993—; mem. pres. coun. U. Miami, 1994—, mem. founder's soc., 1994—. Recipient Philip J. Romano Founders award, 1988. Mem. AICPA, Fla. Inst. CPAs, Am. Women's Soc. CPAs, Coconut Grove C. of C. (trustee 1988—), Nat. Assn. Women Bus. Owners. Republican. Roman Catholic. Home: 13724 SW 92d Ct Miami FL 33176 Office: The Abkey Cos 3444 48 Main Hwy 3d Floor PO Box 330927 Coconut Grove FL 33233-0927

AMOS, TORI, singer, musician; d. Edison and Mary Ellen A. Student, Peabody Conservatory. Albums: Y Kant Tori Read, 1988, Little Earthquakes, 1992, Under the Pink, 1994 (Grammy nomination, Best Alternative Music Performance, 1995). Office: Atlantic Records 75 Rockefeller Plz New York NY 10019-6907*

AMOUR, JAN'ETTE ALICE, pet center owner; b. Elgin, Ill., July 2, 1957; d. Peter Jack and Gertrude Marie (Fruedenberg) Buniatian. Student, Elgin C.C., 1980-82, 85, 93. Lic. med. technician, Ill.; lic. ins. agt., Ill., ordained minister Ministry of Salvation Ch., 1985. Groomer's asst. Bohanna Dog Salon, Elgin, Ill., 1969-74; owner Amour Dog Salon, Elgin, 1975-90; gen. contractor Rehabs., Elgin, 1985—; fin. cons. Primerica, De Kalb, Ill., 1987—; owner Hi I.Q. Kennels, Sycamore, Ill., 1988—, Amour Pet Ctr., Elgin, 1991—. Vol. employer Donation Ctr. for Larry Jones Ministries for Feed the Children Programs, 1985—. mem. Ill. Agrl. Assn., Assn. for Rsch. and Enlightenment, Theosophical Soc., Nat. Fedn. Ind. Bus., Internat. Platform Assn., Ill. Great Dane Club, Pet Industry Assn. Republican. Office: Amour Pet Ctr 901 N Liberty St Elgin IL 60120-3020

AMPOLA, MARY G., pediatrician, geneticist; b. Syracuse, N.Y., Nov. 2, 1934; d. Mariangelo and Filomena (Albahese) Giambattista; m. Vincent G. Ampola, Aug. 7, 1966; children: Leanna, David. BA cum laude, Syracuse U., 1956; MD, SUNY, Syracuse, 1960. Diplomate Am. Bd. Pediatrics. Intern George Washington Univ. Hosp., Washington, 1960-61; pediatric resident Children's Nat. Med. Ctr., Washington, 1961-63, chief resident in pediatrics, 1963-64; genetics fellow Children's Hosp. Med. Ctr., Boston, 1964-66; metabolic diseases fellow Mass. Gen. Hosp., Boston, 1966-67; cytogeneticist New Eng. Med. Ctr., Boston, 1967-69, dir. pediatric amino acid lab., 1969—, pediatrician, 1969—, acting chief clin. genetics divsn. dept. pediatrics, 1989—; from asst. to assoc. prof. pediatrics New Eng. Med. Ctr./Tufts U. Sch. Medicine, Boston, 1967-92, prof., 1992—; chmn. PL-1 selection com. dept. pediatrics New Eng. Med. Ctr., 1975-81, chmn. residency com., 1981-87, mem. residency com. 1987—, bd. dirs. Ctr. Children Spl. Needs, 1990—, mem. hosp. quality assurance com., 1982-92; mem. curriculum com., various others sch. medicine Tufts U., 1981—. Editor: Early Detection and Management of Inborn Errors, 1976; author: Metabolic Diseases in Pediatric Practice, 1982; contbr. chpts. to books and articles to profl. jours. Named Alumna of Yr., SUNY Coll. Medicine, 1980. Fellow Am. Acad. Pediatrics (sect. genetics); mem. Am. Soc. Human Genetics, New Eng. Pediatric Soc. (sec.-treas. 1993—), Soc. Inherited Metabolic Disorders, Soc. Study Inborn Errors Metabolism, Phi Beta Kappa. Republican. Office: New Eng Med Ctr 750 Washington St Boston MA 02111-1854

AMSDEN, LUCIA LANDON, consultant; b. Kansas City, Mo., Nov. 9, 1941; d. Barney Williams; m. Timothy L. Amsden; children: Timothy, Matthew. BS in Edn., U. Mo., 1962; MSW, U. Kans., 1980. Cert. clin. social worker. Family therapist Crittenton Ctr., Kansas City, 1981-83; orgnl. cons. MBL Group, Kansas City, 1987-90; human rels. counselor Lucia W. Landon & Assocs., Kansas City, 1983-87; instr. Webster U., Kansas City, 1989; presenter seminars to assns. and corps. on Energy in the 90's: The Balancing Act; orgnl. cons. on teambuilding. Author: (curriculum/video series) The Empowering Series, 1989, (parenting curriculum) Blue Ribbon Parenting, 1987, The Energy Recharge Card, 1993; contbr. articles to profl. jours. Bd. dirs. Mid-Am. Assistance Coalition, Kansas City, 1989-94; prin. Family to Family Project for Homeless Families. Mem. NASW, Am. Tng. and Devel. Assn., Greater Kansas City C. of C., Cen. Exch. Office: 8301 State Line Ste 202 Kansas City MO 64114

AMSTER, LINDA EVELYN, newspaper executive, consultant; b. N.Y.C., May 21, 1938; d. Abraham and Belle Shirley (Levine) Meyerson; m. Robert L. Amster, Feb. 18, 1961 (dec. Feb. 1974). B.A., U. Mich., 1960; M.L.S., Columbia U., 1968. Tchr. English Stamford High Sch., Conn., 1961-63; research librarian The Detroit News, 1965-67; research librarian The N.Y. Times, N.Y.C., 1967-69, supr. news research, 1969-74, news research mgr., 1974—; bd. dirs. Council for Career Planning, N.Y.C., 1982—. Contbr. articles to books, N.Y. Times and other publs. Mem. Spl. libraries Assn. Club: Coffee House. Home: 336 Central Park W New York NY 10025-7111 Office: The NY Times 229 W 43rd St New York NY 10036-3913

AMSTERDAM, SUSAN MARTHA, arts administrator; b. N.Y.C., Jan. 16, 1940; d. Nathan and Harriett (Wasserman) London; m. Marvin J. Amsterdam, Aug. 19, 1962; children: Deborah, Bonnie. BA in English, NYU, 1961, MA in Edn., 1962. Cert. elem. tchr. English. Elem. sch. tchr. Pub. Sch. System, N.Y.C., 1962-64; tchr. Pub. Sch. System, Bergen County, N.J., 1974-78; instr. English Essex Coll. of Bus., Newark, N.J., 1978-82; chairperson English dept. First Sch. of Careers, Passaic Park, N.J., 1982-89; adj. instr. English Berkeley Coll. of Bus., Waldwick, N.J., 1990-93; Young People's Theatre coord. Passaic County Cultural and Heritage Coun., Paterson, N.J., 1994—; book reviewer, lectr. librs. and orgns., 1974—. Author, editor newsletters. Chairperson Kasschau Meml. Shell Com., Ridgewood, N.J., 1987-90; bd. dirs. Temple Israel, Hadassah, PTA, Jewish Family Svc., Ridgewood, 1973—, others. Mem. Nat. Coun. of Tchrs. of English.

AMTOFT-NIELSEN, JOAN THERESA, physician, educator, researcher; b. Reading, Pa., Jan. 31, 1940; children: Andre Christian, Nikolaj Johan, Anja. BS, Kutztown (Pa.) State U., 1960; MD, Ansalt U. Munchen, Fed. Republic Germany, 1965; DC, Nat. Coll., 1968; MD, U. Copenhagen, 1978; postgrad., Harvard U., 1989-90, 91. Regional dir. Pa. Acad. Sci., Reading, 1961; intern Cook County Hosp., Chgo., 1966-68; clin. instr. U. Copenhagen, 1975-80; proctor N.C. Coalition Health, Durham, 1985-87; founder, cons. Triangle PMS Ctr., Cary, N.C., 1987—, also bd. dirs. Contbr. articles to profl. jours. Bd. dirs. shelter St. Francis Ho., Chapel Hill, N.C., 1989—; bd. dirs., grant coordinator N.C. Coalition Chs., Raleigh; v.p. Danish Red Cross, 1975-80; cons. physician Handicapped Encounter in Christ, Raleigh, 1984-87. NSF grantee, 1961; recipient award Sardoni Found., 1964, Walter Morris Found., 1957, Community Svc. award K.C., 1989. Mem. Am. Acad. Holistic Physicians, European Acad. Preventative Medicine, AAUW (v.p. Raleigh chpt. 1987—), NAFE, Scandinavian Club. Republican. Roman Catholic. Home: 218 Rosebrooks Dr Cary NC 27513-3609

AMUNDSEN, JOANNE ELAINE, speech pathologist; b. Chgo., Mar. 30, 1954; d. Alvin Norman and Elaine June (Thompson) A. BA, U. Mich., 1975; MA, Cen. Mich. U., 1976, San Diego State U., 1981. Speech pathologist No. Trails Edn. Agy., Clear Lake, Iowa, 1976-78, San Diego City Schs., 1978—; pvt. practice speech pathology San Diego, 1980—. Exhibited in group shows at Midsummer Award Show, San Diego Art Inst., 1986, Pt. Loma Art and Design Ctr. Dem. vol., San Diego. Mem. Am. Speech and Hearing Assn. (cert. clin. competence), Calif. Speech and Hearing Assn., Nat. Tchrs. Assn., Calif. Tchrs. Assn., Humane Soc., Pastel Soc. San Diego, Am. Diabetes Assn., Walkabout Internat., Amnesty Internat., Sierra Club, Smithsonian Assocs., U. Mich. Alumni Club. Lutheran. Office: Lang Speech Hearing Whittier Ctr 3401 Clairemont Dr Rm 25 San Diego CA 92117-5975

ANABLE, SHAHIN HORMOZI, medical technologist; b. Kermanshah, Iran, Mar. 15, 1945; came to U.S., 1964; d. Abbas and Moneer (Gholestani) Hormozi; m. Leonard Joseph Anable, Jan. 1, 1983; children: Abbas-John Leonard, Nicolas-John Leonard. BS, Ariz. State U., 1969. Tech. rep. Abbott Labs, Phoenix, 1973-80; TV cooking tchr. Bahai Faith, Phoenix, 1980; med. technologist Phoenix Bapt. Hosp., 1980-82, Ft. Ord Hosp., Salinas, Calif., 1983-85, Natividad Med. Ctr., Salinas, 1989—; translator Abbott Labs, Kermanshah, 1974. Sec. Local Spiritual Assembly, 1992. Recipient scholarship Ariz. State U., 1965-69. Mem. AAUW (pres. 1982, mentor 1990—, named gift 1992). Home: 13445 Paseo Terrano Salinas CA 93908

ANAPLE, ELSIE MAE, medical, surgical and geriatrics nurse; b. Urbana, Ohio, Apr. 22, 1932; d. Marion N. and Mae Irene (Newell) Bodey; div.; children: Glenn, Gretchen, Gloria, Giselle, Gregory, Gordon, Gary. BSN, Ohio State U., 1955. Cert. med.-surg. nurse. Night supr. Shriner's Burn Inst., Cin., 1971-73; clin. instr. med.-surg. Deaconess Hosp. Sch. Nursing, Cin., 1973-75; staff nurse Good Samaritan Hosp., Cin., Our Lady of Mercy Hosp., Fairfield, Ohio; clin. nurse, staff nurse Univ. Hosp.-U. Cin., asst. head nurse med. unit, 1992; part-time nurse Mercy Hosp., Fairfield. Mem. ARC Cin. chpt., Our Lady of the Rosary Ch. Mem. ANA, Ohio Nurses Assn., S.W. Ohio Dist. Nurses Assn.

ANARGYROS, NEDRA HARRISON, cytotechnologist; b. N.Y.C., Dec. 3, 1915; d. Leverette Roland and Florence Martha (Pickard) Harrison; student Emerson Coll., 1936; cert. in cytology U. Calif., San Francisco, 1957; m. Spero Drosos Anargyros, Oct. 21, 1940 (div. 1969). Supr. cytology San Francisco Gen. Hosp., 1957-88; ret. 1988. Mem. Am. Soc. Clin. Pathologists (affiliate mem.), Am. Soc. for Cytotech. (affiliate mem., cert. cytologist), Women Flyers of Am., DAR (past regent, 1990-91, 1st vice regent La Puerta de Ora chpt., San Francisco), Nat. Soc. Colonial Dames of Am. in Calif., Huguenot Soc. of Calif. Republican. Christian Scientist. Club: Presidents of Mercer U. (Macon, Ga.). Home: 2503 Clay St San Francisco CA 94115-1810 also: 1400 Geary Blvd Apt 5N San Francisco CA 94109-6561

ANAS, JULIANNE KAY, administrative laboratory director; b. Detroit, Oct. 31, 1941; d. Theodore John and Lorraine (Comment) Knechtges; m. Donald Cartwright, Jan. 25, 1965 (div. June 1968); m. Daniel James Anas, Jan. 6, 1979. BS, Ea. Mich. U., 1969; MA, Cen. Mich. U., 1978. Cert. specialist in chemistry and med. tech. Am Soc. Clin. Pathologists. Med. technologist W.A. Foote Hosp., Jackson, Mich., 1962-63; med. technologist PCHA Annapolis Hosp., Wayne, Mich., 1964-65, supr. spl. chemistry and nuclear medicine, 1969-71; med. technologist Herrick Hosp., Tecumseh, Mich., 1965, Emma L. Bixby Hosp., Adrian, Mich., 1965-68; asst. clin. chemist Peoples Community Hosp. Authority, Wayne, 1971-81; adminstrv. lab. dir. Metro Med. Group Health Alliance Plan Henry Ford Health System, Detroit, 1981—; adv. panel Medicalab Observor mag., 1988—. Contbr. articles to profl. publs. Mem. Am. Soc. Med. Tech. (bd. dirs. Mich. sect. 1972-73, pres. Detroit sect. 1972), Hosp. Lab. Mgrs. Assn. (membership chmn. 1984, 85, 90), Detroit Soc. Med. Technologists (Med. Technologist of Yr. 1975), Am. Assn. Clin. Chemists (nominations chair Mich. sect. 1992), Founders Art Inst. Republican. Home: 30774 Bobrich St Livonia MI 48152-3410

ANASTASI, ANNE (MRS. JOHN PORTER FOLEY, JR.), psychology educator; b. N.Y.C., Dec. 19, 1908; d. Anthony and Theresa (Gaudiosi) A.; m. John Porter Foley, Jr., July 26, 1933. A.B., Barnard Coll., 1928; Ph.D., Columbia U., 1930; Litt.D. (hon.), U. Windsor, Can., 1967; Sc.D. (hon.), Cedar Crest Coll., 1971, La Salle Coll., 1979, Fordham U., 1979; Paed.D. (hon.), Villanova U., 1971. Instr. psychology Barnard Coll., N.Y.C., 1930-39; asst. prof., chmn. dept. Queens Coll., N.Y.C., 1939-46; assoc. prof. psychology Fordham U., N.Y.C., 1947-51; prof. Fordham U., 1951-79, prof. emeritus, 1979—, chmn. dept. psychology, 1968-74; mem. NRC, 1952-55; pres. Am. Psychol. Found., 1965-67. Author: Differential Psychology, 1937, rev. edit., 1949, 58, Psychological Testing, 1954, 6th edit., 1988, Fields of Applied Psychology, 1964, 2d edit., 1979; also articles in field.; editor: Individual Differences, 1965, Testing Problems in Perspective, 1966; Contributions to Differential Psychology, 1982. Recipient award for disting. svc. to measurement Ednl. Testing Svc., 1977, award disting. contbns. to rsch. Am. Ednl. Rsch. Assn., 1983, Gold medal Am. Psychol. Found., 1984, Nat. medal of Sci., 1987; James McKeen Cattell fellow Am. PSychol. Soc., 1993. Mem. APA (rec. sec. 1952-55, pres. divsn. gen. psychology 1956-57, bd. dirs. 1956-59, 68-70, pres. divsn. evaluation and measurement 1965-66, pres. 1971-72, Disting. Sci. award 1981, E.L. Thorndike medal divsn. ednl. psychology 1984, Lifetime Contbn. award 1994), Ea. Psychol. Assn. (pres. 1946-47, bd. dirs. 1948-50), Psychonomic Soc., Phi Beta Kappa, Sigma Xi.

ANASTOLE, DOROTHY JEAN, electronics company executive; b. Akron, Ohio, Mar. 26, 1932; d. Leonard L. and Helen (Sagedy) Dice; children: Kally, Dennis, Christopher. Student, De Anza Jr. Coll., Cupertino, Calif., 1969. Various secretarial positions in mfg., 1969-75; office mgr. Sci. Devices Co., Mountain View, Calif., 1975-76; exec. adminstrv. sec. corp. office Cezar Industries, Palo Alto, Calif., 1976-77; office and personnel mgr. AM Bruning Co., Mountain View, 1977-81; dir. employee relations Consol. Micrographics, Mountain View, 1981-83; personnel mgmt. cons., 1983-84; mgr. adminstrn./employee relations Mitsubishi Electronics Am., Inc., Sunnyvale, Calif., 1984-89, sr. mgr., 1989-91, corp. v.p., 1991—. Bd. dirs. Agnew State Hosp., San Jose, Calif., 1966-72, div. chmn. program mentally retarded, 1966-72, staff tutor, 1966-72; bd. dirs. Project Hired, Sunnyvale, 1991-93. Recipient Scv. award Agnew State Hosp., 1972. Office: Mitsubishi Electronics Am 1050 E Arques Ave Sunnyvale CA 94086-4601

ANASTOS, ROSEMARY PARK, retired educator; b. Andover, Mass., 1907. AB, Radcliffe Coll., 1928, AM, 1929; PhD, U. Cologne, Germany, 1934; 25 hon. degrees, Yale U., Columbia U., NYU, Brown U., Syracuse U., U. Notre Dame, Claremont Coll., U. Pa., Oberlin Coll., others. Prof. German, acad. dean Conn. Coll., New London, 1943-47, pres., 1947-62; pres. Barnard Coll., dean Columbia U., 1962-67; vice-chancellor UCLA, 1967-70, prof. higher edn. Grad. Sch. Edn., 1967-74, prof. emeritus, 1974—, prof. on recall, 1974-75; pres. United Chpts. Phi Beta Kappa, 1970-73. Author: Das Bild Richard Wagner's Tristan und Isolde, 1935, two textbooks; articles in field; contbg. editor Change mag. Trustee Mt. St. Mary's Coll., L.A.; former chmn. bd. visitors Def. Intelligence Coll., U.S. Dept. Def.; former trustee Robert Coll., Istanbul, Turkey, New Sch. for Social Rsch., N.Y., Danforth Found., U. Hartford, Scripps Coll., Marlborough Sch., U. Notre Dame, Carnegie Found. for Advancement of Teaching; former mem. adv. coun. and chmn. rsch. com. NEH; former mem. adv. coun. Fund for Improvement of Post-secondary Edn.; former dir. Am. Coun. on Edn. Recipient Woman of Yr. award L.A. Times, 1967, Radcliffe Coll. Alumnae award, 1974, medal U.S. Dept. Def. Fellow Am. Acad. Arts and Scis. Home: 10501 Wilshire Blvd Apt 2101 Los Angeles CA 90024-6330

ANAWALT, PATRICIA RIEFF, anthropologist; b. Ripon, Calif., Mar. 10, 1924; d. Edmund Lee and Anita Esto (Capps) Rieff; m. Richard Lee Anawalt, June 8, 1945; children: David, Katherine Anawalt Arnoldi, Harmon Fred. BA in Anthropology, UCLA, 1957, MA in Anthropology, 1971, PhD in Anthropology, 1975. Cons. curator costumes and textiles Mus. Cultural History UCLA, 1975-90, dir. Ctr. for Study Regional Dress, Fowler Mus. Cultural History, 1990—; trustee S.W. Mus., L.A., 1978-92; rsch. assoc. UCLA Inst. Archaeology, 1994—, San Diego Mus. of Man, 1981—; traveling lectr. Archaeol. Inst. Am., U.S., Can.,a 1975-86, 94-95, Pres.'s Lectureship, 1993-94, trustee, 1983—; cons. Nat. Geog. Soc., 1980-82, Denver Mus. Natural History, 1992-93; apptd. by U.S. Pres. to Cultural Property Adv. Com., Washington, 1984-93; fieldwork Guatemala, 1961, 70, 72, Spain, 1975, Sierra Norte de Puebla, Mex., 1983, 85, 88, 89, 91. Author: Indian Clothing Before Cortés: Mesoamerican Costumes from the Codices, 1981, paperback edit., 1990; co-author: The Codex Mendoza, 4 vols., 1992 (winner Archaeol. Inst. Am. 1994 James Wiseman Book award). Adv. com Textile Mus., Washington, 1983-87. Recipient NEH grant, J. Paul Getty Found. grant, Nat. Geog. Soc. grants, 1983, 85, 88, 89, 91, Guggenheim fellowship, 1988-89. Fellow Am. Anthrop. Assn., L.A. County Mus. Natural History; mem. Centre Internat. D'Etude Des Textiles Anciens, Am. Ethnol. Soc., Soc. Am. Archaeology, Soc. Women Geographers (Outstanding Achievement award 1993), Textile Soc. Am. (bd. dirs. 1992—, co-coord. 1994 biennial symposium), Pres.'s Patrons Cir. L.A. County Mus. Art, AIA So. Calif. Soc. (pres. 1986-89, v.p. 1983-86, sec. 1979-83), Archaeol. Inst. Am. (trustee 1983—). Office: Fowler Mus Cultural History Ctr Study Of Regional Dress Los Angeles CA 90024-1549

ANCHIE, TOBY LEVINE, health facility administrator; b. New Haven, Conn., Jan. 21, 1944; d. Solomon and Mary (Karlins) Levine; children: Michael D. Anchie, Robert P. Anchie. BSN, U. of Conn., 1966; MA in Edn. magna cum laude, Nor. Ariz. U., 1984. RN Ariz., Conn. Coord. spl. projects, nurse coord., adult day hosp. Barrow Neurol. Inst. of St. Joseph's Hosp. and Med. Ctr., Phoenix, 1984-87, mgr., 1985-92; mgr. adminstrv. and support svcs., neuroscis. Barrow Neurol. Inst. of St. Joseph's Hosp. and Med. Ctr., 1992-94; mgr. clin. rsch., 1994—; cons.; presenter in field; mem. faculty U. Phoenix; adv. bd. Myasthenia Gravis Assn. Contbr. articles to profl. jours., chpts. Mem. NAFE, Assn. Rehab. Nurses, Am. Assn. Neurosci. Nurses (bd. dirs., pres.), Am. Bd. Neurosci. Nursing (bd. dirs.), World Fedn. Neurosci. Nurses, Ariz. Head Injury Found. (adv. bd.), Ariz. Assn. Neurosci. Nurses. Home: 3112 S Los Feliz Dr Tempe AZ 85282-2854

ANCKER-JOHNSON, BETSY, physicist, engineer, retired automotive company executive; b. St. Louis, Apr. 29, 1927; d. Clinton James and Fern (Lalan) A.; m. Harold Hunt Johnson, Mar. 15, 1958; children: Ruth P. Johnson, David H. Johnson, Paul A. Johnson, Marti H. Johnson. B.A. in Physics with high honors (Pendleton scholar), Wellesley Coll., 1949; Ph.D. magna cum laude, U. Tuebingen, Germany, 1953; D.Sc. (hon.), Poly. Inst. N.Y., 1979, Trinity Coll., 1981, U. So. Calif., 1984, Alverno Coll., 1984; LL.D. (hon.), Bates Coll., 1980. Instr., jr. research physicist U. Calif., Berkeley, 1953-54; physicist Sylvania Microwave Physics Lab., 1956-58; mem. tech. staff RCA Labs., 1958-61; research specialist Boeing Co., 1961-70, exec., 1970-73; asst. sec. U.S. Dept. Commerce for Sci. and Tech., 1973-77; dir. phys. research Argonne Nat. Lab., Ill., 1977-79; v.p. environ. activities staff GM, Warren, Mich., 1979-92; affiliate prof. elec. engring. U. Wash, 1961-73; bd. dirs. Gen. Mills; mem. Energy Rsch. Adv. Bd., adv. com. on inertial confinement fusion Dept. Energy, 1993—, U.S. Safety Rev. Panel NSF, 1987-88, Sci. and Tech. Coun. of Inland Steel Industries, 1991—; bd. dirs. Enterprise Devel., Inc., 1992—; mem. adv. com. Rowan Sch. Engring., 1993—. Author of 80 sci. papers; patentee in field. Mem. staff Inter-Varsity Christian Fellowship, 1954-56; mem. vis. com. elec. and computer divsn. MIT, U.S. Dept. Def. Sci. Bd.; mem. adv. bd. Stanford U. Sch. Engring., Fla. State U., Fla. A&M U., Congl. Caucus for Sci. and Tech.; trustee Wellesley Coll., 1971-77; chair bd. dirs. World Environ. Ctr., 1988-93, dir., 1988—. AAUW fellow, 1950-51; Horton Hollowell fellow, 1951-52; NSF grantee, 1967-72. Fellow AAAS, IEEE, Am. Phys. Soc. (councillor-at-large 1973-76); mem. NRC (bd. engring. edn. 1991—, com. on women in sci. and engring. 1990—, office sci. and engring. pers. adv. com. 1993—), Nat. Acad. Engring., Air Pollution Control Assn., Soc. Automotive Engrs. (bd. dirs. 1979-81), Phi Beta Kappa, Sigma Xi. Home: 222 Harbour Dr Apt 311 Naples FL 33940-4087

ANCRUM, CHERYL DENISE, dentist; b. Bklyn., Sept. 28, 1958; d. Ida Jackson. BA in Psychology, Harvard U., Cambridge, 1980; DDS, Columbia U., N.Y., 1986, MPH, 1989. Dentist. Credit analyst Hartford (Conn.) Nat. Bank, 1980-81; statistical coding instr./analyst Aetna Ins. Co., Hartford,

Conn., 1981-82; dental asst. Gouverneur Hosp., N.Y.C., 1983; clk. typist Columbia Presbyn. Med. Ctr., N.Y.C., 1984-86; gen. practice resident Beth Israel Med. Ctr., N.Y.C., 1986-87; dental attending Montefiore Med. Ctr., Bronx, 1987-90; rsch. assoc./dentist North Central Bronx Hosp., 1989-90; dental dir. Manhattan Men's Ho. of Detention, N.Y.C., 1989—; dental extern N. Central Bronx. Hosp., 1985-86. Vol. St. John Episc. Hosp., Bklyn., 1974-75, Mt. Auburn Hosp., Cambridge, 1978, Harlem Hosp., N.Y.C., 1987-88; health adv. Harvard U., Cambridge, 1977-80; active Sutton for Mayor Campaign, Bklyn., 1977; mem. Girl Scouts U.S., Bklyn., 1969-75, Operation PUSH, Hartford, 1981-82, Hartford Black Women Network, 1980-82, Kuumba Singers, Harvard U., 1977-80, New Temple Singers, Cambridge, 1977-80; mem. tape commn. Bridge St. A.M.E. Ch., Bklyn., 1987-88; fin. sec. Flower Guild, Allen A.M.E. Church, Queens, 1994—; bd. dirs. F.I.S.H. of Uniondale, 1991—. Recipient scholarship A Better Chance, 1973-76, Am. Fund for Dental Health, 1982-84, Clark Found., 1983-86, selected profl. fellowship AAUW, 1985-86, Letter of Commendation, Columbia U., 1983, Applewhite award, 1986, William Bailey Dunning award, 1986, Lester R. Cain Pathology prize, 1986; named to Outstanding Young Women of Am., 1983. Mem. ADA, N.Y. State Dental Soc., Acad. of Gen. Dentistry, Am. Assn. of Pub. Health Dentistry, Am. Profl. Practice Assn., Delta Sigma Theta. Democrat. Mem. African Methodist Episcopal Ch. Home: 1043 Tulsa St Uniondale NY 11553-1615

ANCUTA, KATHLEEN MADELINE, financial executive; b. Kineley AFB, St. George, Bermuda, Sept. 7, 1953; (parents Am. citizens); d. Daniel Philip and Beatrice Madeline (Murphy) Allen; m. Len Ancuta, Jan. 29, 1977; 1 child, Leonard Daniel. BS, Ramapo Coll., 1975; MBA, Fairleigh Dickenson U., 1981. Acct. Merrill Lynch Pierce Fenner & Smith, N.Y.C., 1976-77, fin. analyst, acctg. supr., 1977-78; asst. mgr. Young & Rubicam Inc., N.Y.C., 1978-79, fin. mgr., 1979-82, asst. contr., 1982-84, v.p., 1984-86, dir. compensation and equity, 1984-91, sr. v.p., 1986-91, sr. v.p. corp. fin., 1991—. Named to Acad. Women Achievers, YWCA, N.Y.C., 1987. Mem. NAFE, Am. Mgmt. Assn., Fin. Execs. Inst. Republican. Roman Catholic. Home: 457 Shadyside Rd Ramsey NJ 07446-1732 Office: Young & Rubicam Inc 285 Madison Ave New York NY 10017-6486

ANDERER, SUSAN ECKER, clinical psychologist, school psychologist; b. Plattsburgh, N.Y., May 29, 1965; d. Malcolm Lewis and Elaine Joan (Weissman) Ecker; m. Stephen John Anderer, Jan. 4, 1992. BA cum laude, Cornell U., 1987; D of Psychology, Widener U., 1992. Cert. sch. psychologist, Pa.; lic. psychologist, Pa., Del. Instr. Manor Jr. Coll., Jenkintown, Pa., 1988; psychology trainee The Eye Inst., Phila., 1989-90, sch. psychologist, 1990-92; psychology intern Albert Einstein Med. Ctr., Phila., 1990-91; assoc. Ctr. Psychol. Svcs., Ardmore, Pa., 1991—; cons. Rockford Ctr., Newark, Del., 1992—; instr. U. Pa., Phila., 1993—; adj. clin. faculty Widener U., Chester, Pa., 1993—. Mem. APA, Pa. Psychol. Assn., Nat. Assn. Sch. Psychologists, Soc. Personality Assessment. Office: Ctr for Psychol Svcs 125 Coulter Ave Ardmore PA 19003-2426

ANDERHUB, BETH MARIE, medical educator; b. St. Louis, Feb. 7, 1953; d. Anthony Pierre and Eleanor (Corich) A. A in Applied Sci., Forest Park C.C., St. Louis, 1974; BS in Radiologic Tech., U. Mo., 1975; MEd, St. Louis U., 1989, postgrad., 1989—. Cert. radiologic tech., nuclear medicine, abdominal sonography, ob-gyn sonography. Nuclear medicine and ultrasound technician VA Hosp., St. Louis, 1976-79; ultrasound technologist, sr. sonographer Deaconess Hosp., St. Louis, 1979-82, chief sonographer, 1982-83; assoc. prof., dir. ultrasound program St. Louis C.C., 1983—; chmn. accreditation com. Ultrasound Program, Englewood, Colo., 1990—; v.p. Commn. on Accreditation for Allied Health Program, 1994—; lectr., presenter programs in field confs., symposia, colls., univs. Author: Manual on Abdominal Sonography, 1983, General Sonography, 1994; contbr. articles to profl. jours. Fellow Soc. Diagnostic Med. Sonographers (chmn. edn. com. 1984-86, contbg. editor Jour. Diagnostic Med. Sonography 1984-89, bd. dirs. 1986-89, v.p. 1989-91, pres.-elect 1991-93, pres. 1993—, treas. ednl. found. 1988-91, other coms.), Am. Soc. Radiologic Technologists (bd. dirs. 1982-85, task force modality del. roles 1988-89, rep. sonography summit 1988, chmn. ultrsound com. 1980, 82-85, others); mem. Am. Inst. Ultrasound in Medicine, Mo. Soc. Radiologic Technologists (pres. 1979-80, pres. 4th dist. 1978-79). Home: 12449 Dawn Hill Dr Maryland Heights MO 63043 Office: St Louis C C 5600 Oakland Ave Saint Louis MO 63110

ANDERS, CAMILLE SHEPHARD, mission development representative; b. Meridian, Miss., Dec. 28, 1938; m. Dan Raney Anders, Sept. 3, 1994; children: Christel Camille Funk, Lisa Leah Funk Nied, Melanie Maria Funk Futch, Wendi Wanita Funk. BA, U. Miss., 1960; Lang. Cert., Yale Inst. Far Ea. Langs., 1962. Speech pathologist Quincy (Mass.) City Schs., 1960-61; lay ednl. missionary Gen. Bd. Global Ministries, Un. Meth. Ch., Kapit and Sibu, Sarawak, Malaysia, 1962-71; sec. Gen. Bd. Global Ministries, Un. Meth. Ch., Atlanta, 1976-84, mission educator, 1985, southeastern mission devel. field rep., 1986-94; mem., organizer U.S.-China Peoples Friendship Assn., Atlanta, 1974—; leader mission edn. workshops. Author (study book guide) 10 Sessions for 3d-4th Grade, 1989, (study book guide) Winds Across China, 1985 (study, program) God, Our World, and Me, 1989, Leader's Guide to Ecumenical Mission Study on China/Hong Kong, 1995; contbr. articles to publs. Democrat. Home: 3216 Prince William Dr Fairfax VA 22031

ANDERS, CLAUDIA DEE, occupational therapist; b. Buffalo, May 2, 1951; d. Walter Gregory and Helen (Cedizlo) A.; (div. 1983); 1 child, Andrew T. Kiko. BS in Occupational Therapy (high honors), Va. Commonwealth U., 1973; postgrad., Ashland (Ohio) Coll., 1984, Walsh (Ohio) Coll., 1985, Kent (Ohio) State U., 1988, 89, Colo. State U., 1991, 92. Lic. occupational therapist, Ohio; bd. cert. pediatric occupational therapist. With Children's Rehab. Ctr., Warren, Ohio, 1974-76; mem. transdisciplinary team Goodwill Rehab. Ctr., Canton, Ohio, 1976-78; pvt. practice, 1978-83; with Timken Mercy Med. Ctr., Canton, 1978-83; occupational therapist adult tng. team Stark County Bd. Mental Retardation, Canton, 1983-85; developer occupational therapy svcs. Stark County Local Schs., 1985-87; occupational therapist Lakewood (Ohio) City Schs., 1987-91, Elyria (Ohio) City Schs., 1991-93; occupational therapist/supr. pediatric div. Rehab. Svcs., Cleve., 1991-93; pvt. practice rehab. svcs. Berea, Ohio, 1993—; Medina County Achievement Ctr. Vol. Nat. Park Svc., Cleve. Metroparks; sec. Rocky River Trailsiders. A. D. Williams scholar Va. Commonwealth U., 1972, 73. Mem. Am. Occupational Therapy Assn., Ohio Occupational Therapy Assn., Coun. for Exceptional Children, NDT, Inc. Home and Office: 237 Kraft St Berea OH 44017-1448

ANDERSEN, FRANCES ELIZABETH GOLD, religious leadership educator; b. Hot Springs, Ark., Feb. 11, 1916; d. Benjamin Knox and Pearl Scott (Smith) Gold; m. Robert Thomas Andersen, June 27, 1942; children: Nancy Ruth (Mrs. Bernd Neumann), Robert Thomas. BA, UCLA, 1936, sec. teaching credential, 1937. Tchr. math. L.A. City Schs., 1937-42, 46-48; faculty Ariz. State Coll., Tempe, 1943-45; mem. nat. bd. missions United Meth. Ch., 1940-44; dir. Christian edn. 1st Presbyn. Ch., Phoenix, 1943-45, Trinity Meth. ch., L.A., 1953-55, 1st Bapt. Ch., Lakewood, Calif., 1955-57; dir. Christian edn. Grace Bapt. Ch., Riverside, 1958-83, chmn. nursery sch. bd., 1969-83; mem. nat. bd. Bible sch. and youth Bapt. Gen. Conf., 1966-71; coord. leadership tng. insts. Greater L.A. Sunday Sch. Assn., 1956-80; exec. dir. San Bernardino-Riverside Sunday Sch. Assn., 1959—; prin. Riverside Christian Sch., 1985-87, bd. dirs., 1985—; mem. Christian edn. bd. S.W. Bapt. Conf., 1956-59, 63-66, 72-75, 80-83; bd. dirs. GLASS, 1956—; dir. Women's guild, Calif. Bapt. Coll., Riverside, 1983—. Author: How to Organize Area Leadership Training Institutes, 1964. Pres. Univ. Jr. High Sch., PTA, Riverside, 1963-64, Poly High Sch., PTA, 1965-67; life mem. PTA. Named Grace Bapt. Mother of Yr., 1981. Mem. Sons of Norway, Alpha Delta Chi (nat. pres. 1950-51, exec. sec. 1952-54), Pi Mu Epsilon. Home: 1787 Prince Albert Dr Riverside CA 92507-5852

ANDERSEN, JO ANN, broker; b. Proctorville, Ohio, Dec. 17, 1934; d. Lee Roy and Pauline (Faulkner) Smith; m. Milton V. Andersen, Dec. 29, 1965 (dec. 1988); children: Debra, Jr., Stacy. Student, Huntington (W.Va.) Sch. Bus., 1952. Sec. Hensley Ins. Agy., Huntington, W.Va., 1953-55; office mgr. Sidney Sheritz, Atty., Detroit, 1955-60; med. sec. Gallipolis (Ohio) State Inst., 1960-63; office mgr. ACR Industries, Roseville, Mich., 1963-67; owner, pres. Beaute Shops & Merle Norman Cosmetic Studio, Roseville, 1967-77; broker sales person Re/Max Realty, Marco Island, Fla., 1981-90; owner, pres. JJA Assoc. Inc., Marco Island, 1990—. Mem. YMCA, Marco Island Assoc. Realtors (Outstanding Svc. award 1989, Appreciation award 1989), Women's Coun. Realtors (pres. 1987-88, Woman of Yr. 1988, Leadership award 1987), Marco Island Tax Payers Assn., Marco Island Beach Assn., C. of C. Office: JAA Associates Inc PO Box 1100 Marco Island FL 33969

ANDERSEN, MARIANNE SINGER, clinical psychologist; b. Baden nr. Vienna, Austria; came to U.S., 1940, naturalized, 1946; d. Richard L. and Jolanthe (Garda) Singer; 1 son, Richard Esten. BA, CUNY, 1950, MA, 1974; PhD, Fla. Inst. Tech., 1980. Rsch. assoc. Inst. for Rsch. in Hypnosis, N.Y.C., 1974-76, fellow in clin. hypnosis, 1976, dir. seminars, 1978-82, dir. edn., 1982—; psychotherapist specializing in hypnotherapy Morton Prince Ctr. for Hypnotherapy, 1976—, dir. weight control clinic, 1980—, dir. clin. services, 1981-82; dir. adminstrn. Internat. Grad. U., N.Y.C., 1974-77; pvt. practice psychotherapy, 1977—; adminstrv. coordinator Internat. Grad. Sch. Behavior Sci., Fla. Inst. Tech., 1978; co-dir. The Melbourne Group, 1983—; lectr. hypnosis and hypnotherapy to mental and phys. health profls., 1977—. Author: (with Louis Savary) Passages: A Guide for Pilgrims of the Mind, 1972; rsch. on treatment obesity with hypnotherapy; book editor specializing in psychology and psychiatry including W.W. Norton Co., Sterling Pub. Co., E.P. Dutton Co., 1950-71. Fellow Soc. for Clin. and Exptl. Hypnosis; mem. Internat. Soc. for Clin. and Exptl. Hypnosis, Am. Psychol. Assn., N.Y. Acad. Scis. Home: 60 W 57th St New York NY 10019

ANDERSEN, RHODA M. (RANDY ANDERSEN), association executive, educator; b. Howard, S.D., July 3, 1922; d. Charley and Eva (Thom) A. BS in Recreation and Leisure Studies, Calif. State U., San Jose, 1949; MA in Adminstrn. Non-Profit Agys., Lindenwood U., 1977. Dir. svc. club U.S. Army Spl. Svcs., Germany and France, 1949-53; dir. YWCA divsn. USO, Memphis, Hollywood, Phoenix, Paris, Greece, 1953-60; nat. program dir. YWCA divsn. USO, N.Y.C., 1960-63; exec. dir. Vol. Ctr., L.A., 1963-70; western regional dir. Vol. Nat. Ctr., 1970-74; prof. leisure studies classes Calif. State U., Long Beach., 1974-94; ret., 1994. Author: Answers: Questions Volunteer Managers Ask, 1974. Sgt. USMC, 1943-46. Mem. Dirs. Vols. in Agys. (founder 1967). Home: 21436 Via Straits Ln Huntington Beach CA 92646-7530

ANDERSON, ALLAMAY EUDORIS, health educator, home economist; b. N.Y.C., July 18, 1933; d. John Samuel and Charlotte Jane (Harrigan) Richardson; B.A., Queens Coll., CUNY, 1975; profl. mgmt. cert. Adelphi U., 1978; M.S. in Edn., Fordham U., 1984; m. Edgar Leopold Anderson, Jr., Apr. 14, 1957; 1 son, David Lancelot. Mem. staff sch. food service, dietitian Bd. Edn., N.Y.C., 1968-88; tchr. home and career skills Louis Armstrong Middle Sch., 1988; spl. edn. tchr. Manhattan High Sch., N.Y.C., 1989—, coord AIDS resource, 1995; profl. devel. cons., N.Y.C., 1978—; ptnr. Masiba Bldg. Corp., Corona, N.Y., 1975-82; adj. lectr. home econs. Queens Coll., 1987; owner AEA Devel. Svc., 1987—. Devel. coord. League for Better Community Life, Inc., 1977; treas. exec. bd., 1970-76; officer N.Y.C. Community Devel. Agy., 1980-83; mem. Kwanzaa Adv. Com. (P.R.) Urban Coalition, 1983, L.I. # 28 Episcopal Cursillo, 1991; vestry mem. youth ministries Grace Episcopalian Ch., 1982-85; mem. NAACP. Recipient Elmcor Community Svc. award Elmcor Youth and Adult Activities, Inc., 1989. Mem. United Fedn. Tchrs. N.Y.C., Nat. Soc. Fund Raising Execs., Langston Hughes Libr. Action Com. (bd. dirs. 1987—, treas. 1989), Queens Coll. Home Econs. Alumni Assn. (v.p., chmn. bylaws com. 1982), Phi Delta Kappa. Office: 10013 34th Ave Flushing NY 11368-1052

ANDERSON, ANDREA ELLEN, healthcare administrator; b. N.Y.C.; d. Percy S. and Anna Mae (Helms) Holmes; children: Leslie Blake, Kimberly Lenore. Profl. RN, Jewish Hosp. Sch. Nursing, 1960; student, Columbia U., N.Y.C., 1961, L.I. U., Southampton Campus, 1967; BA, Southwestern U., Tuscon, 1982. RN, N.Y. RN Suffolk County Dept. Health, Riverhead, N.Y., 1964-77; outreach dir. Children's Medicaid Program Suffolk County Dept. Social Svcs., Hauppauge, N.Y., 1978-86; dir. Child/Teen Health Plan Suffolk County Dept. Social Svcs., Hauppauge, 1986-88, outreach coord. Perinatal Rotation Plan, 1988—; adv. com. mem. N.Y. State Child/Teen Health Plan Leadership Group, Albany, 1986—; speaker N.Y. State Pub. Welfare Assn., Inc., Albany, 1991; mem. Community Rev. Team of Suffolk County Health Dept., Hauppaud, 1991—. Contbr. articles to profl. jours. Active Profl. Women in Govt., Suffolk County, 1981—, Suffolk County Martin Luther King Jr. Commn., Hauppauge, 1992—, Goodwill AME Zion Ch., Riverhead. Recipient achievement award Nat. Assn. Counties, Washington, 1986, 87, 88, 90, Diana Dolgin Nurse of Yr. award March of Dimes, Woodbury, N.Y., 1992. Mem. NAACP (life), Nat. Assn. Nurses, Suffolk County Assn. Nurses, Perinatal Coalition of Suffolk County, Suffolk Coalition to Prevent Alcohol and Drug Dependency, Inc.; Suffolk Network on Adolescent Pregnancy, Inc., Suffolk County Child Care Coun., Jewish Hosp. Bklyn. Alumni Assn. Home: 64 Feller Dr Central Islip NY 11722 Office: Suffolk County Dept Social Svcs PO Box 2000 - Equipark Hauppauge NY 11788

ANDERSON, ANN, state legislator; b. Yakima, Wash., 1952; married Eric Anderson; 1 child, Cori. Former tchr., mem. Wash. State Senate, majority whip. Republican. Home: 2718 McLeod Rd Bellingham WA 98225 Office: Senate House 205 Institutions Bldg Olympia WA 98504-0001*

ANDERSON, ANNELISE GRAEBNER, economist; b. Oklahoma City, Nov. 19, 1938; d. Elmer and Dorothy (Zilisch) Graebner; m. Martin Anderson, Sept. 25, 1965. B.A., Wellesley Coll., 1960; M.A., Columbia U., 1965, Ph.D., 1974. Assoc. editor McKinsey and Co., Inc., 1963-65; researcher Nixon Campaign Staff, 1968-69; project mgr. Dept. Justice, 1970-71; from asst. prof. bus. adminstrn. to assoc. prof. Calif. State U.-Hayward, 1975-80; sr. policy adviser Reagan Presdl. campaign and transition, Washington, 1980; assoc. dir. econs. and govt. Office Mgmt. and Budget, Washington, 1981-83; sr. rsch. fellow Hoover Instn., Stanford U., Calif., 1983—, assoc. dir., 1989-90; mem. Nat. Sci. Bd., 1985-90; Author: The Business of Organized Crime: A Cosa Nostra Family, 1979, Illegal Aliens and Employer Sanctions: Solving the Wrong Problem, 1986, The Ruble Problem: A Competitive Solution, 1992; co-editor: Thinking About America: The United States in the 1990's, 1988; contbr. articles to profl. jours., chpts. to books. Mem. bd. overseers Rand/UCLA Ctr. for Soviet Studies, L.A., 1987-91. Mem. Am. Econ. Assn., Western Econ. Assn., Beta Gamma Sigma. Office: Stanford U Hoover Institute Stanford CA 94305

ANDERSON, AVERY HUNTER, glass artist; b. Detroit, Jan. 22, 1945; d. Duncan and Patricia Ann (Adams) Hunter; m. Peter L. Anderson, Jan. 16, 1981. Student, Worcester (Mass.) Ctr. Crafts, 1988, Camp Colton Glass Sch., Colton, Oreg., 1989. Owner Anderson Glass Works, North Grafton, Mass., 1985—. Exhibited as featured artist at Artisans Gallery, Boone, N.C., 1991, Opus 5 Gallery, Eugene, Oreg., 1992, High Springs (Fla.) Gallery, 1993—; artist fused glass: Fish Images, A Competition, 1990, Nat. Juried Exhbn. of Contemporary Crafts, 1990; artist sandblast etched glass: Arts Worcester Biennial Juried Exhbn., 1993, Archtl. Art/Glass Light Show, 1993—. Mem. Worcester Ctr. for Crafts, Stained Glass Assn. of Am., Internat. Guild of Glass Artists (bd. dirs., vice chmn.), ArtsWorcester, Am. Craft Coun., Pilchuck Soc.

ANDERSON, BARBARA ELIZABETH, social worker; b. East Orange, N.J., May 23, 1952; d. David Preston and Irene Elizabeth (Thompson) A. BA, Ashland (Ohio) Coll., 1974. Ct. clk. Morris County Dist. Ct. Courthouse, Morristown, N.J., 1974-76; social svc. aide N.J. Div. Youth & Family Svcs., Flemington, N.J., 1976-78, social worker II, 1978-85, family svc. specialist I, 1985—; facilitator, liaison N.J. Child Assault Prevention, 1986—. Democrat. Roman Catholic. Home: 10 Ramsey Rd Lebanon NJ 08833-4346 Office: Div Youth & Family Svcs 84 Park Ave Flemington NJ 08822-1127

ANDERSON, BETTY KAY, guidance counselor; b. Sioux City, Iowa, Oct. 31, 1940; d. George Fred and Dorothy Pearl (Bailey) Stading; m. Dean Merle Anderson, June 15, 1963; children: Gary Dean, Larry Lee. BS in Home Econs., U. Nebr., 1964; MS in Edn., Wayne State U., 1988. Cert. tchr., Nebr., vocat. homemaker, guidance counselor. Tchr. home econs. Sioux City Pub. Schs., 1964-65; tchr. vocat. home econs. Newcastle (Nebr.) Pub. Sch., 1971-74; tchr. vocat. home econs. South Sioux City (Nebr.) Community Schs., 1974-89, guidance counselor, 1989—; advisor Future Homemakers of Am., South Sioux City, 1980-84. Leader 4-H Clubs, Dakota County, Nebr., 1973-85; sec., mem. ch. coun. Salem Luth. Ch., Ponca, Nebr., 1978-81, 88-91. Mem. ACA, NEA, Nebr. State Edn. Assn., Nebr. Counseling Assn., South Sioux City Edn. Assn. (pres. 1993—), Siouxland Home Econs. Club. Democrat. Office: South Sioux City Jr High 3625 G St South Sioux City NE 68776

ANDERSON, CARLA, photographer, educator; b. Phila., Oct. 20, 1943; d. Edward Carl and Reba (Kleinboard) Pintzuk. BFA in Photography, Ctr. for Creative Studies, Detroit, 1976; MFA, Cranbrook Acad. Art, Bloomfield Hills, Mich., 1978; student, Mich. Art Workshops, 1983-86; MA in Edn., Wayne State U., 1988. Med. photographer dept. pathology Harper Hosp., Detroit, 1971-73; adj. instr. photography art dept. Henry Ford C.C., Dearborn, Mich., 1977-87; project photographer Preservation Wayne, Detroit, 1984-85; asst. Balthazar Korab archtl. photographer, Troy, Mich., 1984-85; archtl. photographer Nat. Park Svc., State of Mich., City of Detroit, 1985—; lab. technician Dept. Photgraphy, Ctr. for Creative Studies, Detroit, 1978-81; vis. lectr. dept. art Wayne State U., Detroit, 1980, dept. art Eastern Mich. U., Ypsilanti, Mich., 1983-84, Lianong Normal U., Dalian, Peoples Republic of China,1986; photog. cons. Nat. Automotive Archives, Detroit Pub. LIbr., 1985, adj. instr. dept. art Eastern Mich. U., Ypsilanti, 1986, Ctr. for Creative Studies, Detroit, 1988-90; vis. artist Eastern Mich. U., Ypsilanti, 1983, Wayne State U., Detroit, 1984, Western Mich. U., Kalamazoo, 1985; lectr. Midwest Regional Conf. U. Wis., Green Bay, 1982. Selected exhibitions include Arts and Crafts, 1976, Contemporary Photographs, 1983, Detroit Inst. of Arts, Works on Paper, 1979, Present Tense/Photography, 1986, Detroit Focus Gallery, Untitled, Saginaw (Mich.) Art Mus., 1978, Untitled Calvin Coolidge, Grand Rapids, Mich., 1979, The Blixt Gallery, Ann Arbor, 1980, Michigan Artists Exhibition, U. Mich., Ann Arbor, 1981, Photography and Tiger Stadium, The Michigan Gallery, Detroit, 1984, Autosuggestions, Detroit Artists Market, 1985, The Aetna Inst. Gallery, 1985, Detroit Focus Gallery, 1986, Ctr. Gallery, Detroit, 1992, Cranbrook Acad. Art Mus., Bloomfield Hills, Mich., 1992, and others. Kate Carter Residency fellow Maine Photographic Workshops, 1994; grantee Mich. Coun. for the Arts. Mem. Friends of Photography, Coll. Art Assn., Soc. for Contemporary Photography, Mich. Friends of Photography, Toledo Friends of Photography. Home: 4828 Commonwealth Detroit MI 48208

ANDERSON, CAROL LEE, communications executive; b. Sharon, Pa., Nov. 5, 1943; d. James W. and Charlene Helen (Lang) Thomas; m. Duane A. Anderson, Dec. 16, 1978; children: Mark Powell, Steve Anderson. Student, Youngstown (Ohio) State U., 1961, Pa. State U., Sharon, 1964. Field mgr. Welcome Wagon Internat., Memphis, 1975-78; dir. Merrill Chase Gallery, Naperville, Ill., 1978-80; br. mgr. CONTEL/Executone, Burr Ridge, Ill., 1980-84; major mkt. account exec. Ill. Bell Comm., Westbrook, 1984-90; strategic account exec. govt. accounts Ameritech Custom Bus., Westbrook, Ill., 1990-93, account mgr. fed., mil. and civilian, 1993—. Mem. Internat. Orgn. Women in Telecommunications, Delta Chi Epsilon. Home: 213 Pfaff Dr Frankfort IL 60423-1624 Office: Ameritech Custom Bus Two Westbrook Corp Westchester IL 60154

ANDERSON, CAROL PATRICIA, chemistry educator; b. Bluefield, W.Va., May 19, 1946; d. Carroll Curtis and Naomi Bessie (Bowles) A.; m. James Brent Anderson, Sept. 9, 1978. BS, Concord Coll., Athens, W.Va., 1968; PhD, U. Tenn., 1973. Post-doctoral instr. U. Conn., Storrs, 1973-75, asst. prof., 1975-80, assoc. prof., 1980—, co-dir. Marine Environ. Analysis Labs. Svc., 1990—; cons. R&D USCG, 1976-90. Contbr. articles to profl. jours. Mem. Am. Chem. Soc., Nat. Sci. Tchrs. Assn., New Eng. Chemistry Tchrs. Assn. Episcopalian. Home: 143 Pequot Ave Mystic CT 06355-1728 Office: U Conn Avery Point Groton CT 06340

ANDERSON, CAROL SUE, mayor; b. Tucson, Feb. 2, 1942; m. Stuart L. Anderson; 3 children. Student, Mohave C.C., 1978-84, U. Ariz., 1960-63. Sec., receptionist Mohave County Coop. Extension Svc., U. Ariz., 1982-85; sec., receptionist Allstate Ins. Agy., Kingman, 1985-86, ins. agt., 1986-88; owner, bus. ptrn. Stockton Hill Nursery, Kingman, 1985-87; gen. ptnr. Western Landscape Mgmt., Phoenix, 1988-93; ptnr. Willows Ranch Partnership, 1969—; mayor City of Kingman, 1984-86, 88-90, 90-92, 92-94, 94-96, coun. mem., 1984-88, vice mayor, 1986-88; appointed Commerce and Econ. Devel. Commn., 1992-94, Ariz. Water Adv. Bd., 1991—, chmn. 1993—, Nat. League of Cities-Energy, Environ. and Natural Resources com., 1991—, Rump, Group II and III, 1988-89, Mcpl. Utilities Commn., Coun. Liaison; mem. Univ. Ariz. Coop. Extension Svc. Adv. Bd., 1975—, sec. to bd. 1976-89. Pres. League of Ariz. Cities and Towns, 1990-92; exec. com. mem., 1985—, fin. and nominating coms., 1989, v.p., 1988-90; founding chmn. Am. Heart Assn., 1989—; bd. dirs. Ariz. Acad. Town Hall, 1986-88, mem., 1986—; sec. Ariz. Rural Water Assn., 1990-91, v.p., 1989-90, pres., 1991-92; founding com. Kingman Area Town Hall, 1987; bd. dirs. Ariz. Hwys. Users Conf., 1989—; exec. bd. Agri-Bus. Coun. of Ariz., 1979-80; mem. Reps. Women's Assn., 1982—; vol. cert. dental asst. ARC. Recipient Disting. Citizen award Univ. Ariz. Alumni Assn., 1986. Mem. Order of Eastern Star, Soroptimists Internat. (Kingman chpt.), Cattlemen's Assn. (various coms.), Cowbelle Orgn. (various coms.). Office: City of Kingman 310 N 4th St Kingman AZ 86401-5890

ANDERSON, CAROLE ANN, nursing educator; b. Chgo., Feb. 21, 1938; d. Robert and Marian (Harrity) Irving; m. Clark Anderson, Feb. 14, 1973; 1 child, Julie. Diploma, St. Francis Hosp., 1958; BS, U. Colo., 1962, MS, 1963, PhD, 1977. Group psychotherapist Dept. Vocat. Rehab., Denver, 1963-72; psychotherapist Prof. Psychiatry and Guidance Clinic, Denver, 1970-71; asst. prof., chmn. nursing sch. U. Colo., Denver, 1971-75; therapist, coordinator The Genessee Mental Health, Rochester, N.Y., 1977-78; assoc. dean U. Rochester, N.Y., 1978-86; dean, prof. coll. of nursing Ohio State U., Columbus, 1986—; lectr. nursing sch. U. Colo., Denver, 1970-71; prin. investigator biomed. rsch. support grant, 1986-93, clin. rsch. facilitation grant, 1981-82; program dir. profl. nurse traineeship, 1978-86, advanced nurse tng. grant, 1982-85. Author: (with others) Women as Victims, 1986, Violence Toward Women, 1982, Substance Abuse of Women, 1982; editor Nursing Outlook, 1993—. Pres., bd. dirs. Health Assn., Rochester, 1984-86; mem. north sub area council Finger Lakes Health Systems Agy., 1983-86, longrange planning com., 1981-82; mem. Columbus Bd. Health; dir. Netcare Mental Health Ctr. Am. Acad. Nursing fellow. Mem. ANA, Am. Sociol. Assn., Ohio Nurses Assn., Am. Assn. Colls. Nursing (bd. dirs. 1992-94, pres.-elect 1994—), Sigma Theta Tau. Home: 406 W 6th Ave Columbus OH 43201-3137 Office: Ohio State U Coll Nursing 1585 Neil Ave Columbus OH 43210-1216

ANDERSON, CAROLYN JOYCE, business development executive; b. Mishawaka, Ind., Mar. 14, 1947; d. Ebon Clayton and Maxine Ruth (Haag) Angel; m. Thomas Anderson (dec.); children: Charmien, Andrew, Paul. BS in Bus., Ind. U., 1978. CPA, Ind. Staff acct. Holdeman, Fulmer and Chiddister CPA's, Elkhart, Ind., 1974-78; comml. lender Midwest Commerce Bank, Elkhart, 1978-81; corp. controller Bivouac Industries, Inc., Vandalia, Mich., 1981-84; exec. dir. Small Bus. Devel. Ctr., South Bend, Ind., 1984—; developer, implementer Michiana Investment Network, 1986—, The Emerging Bus. Forum, 1992—. Bd. dirs. Davenport Coll., Grand Rapids, Mich., 1986-94, The Montessori Acad., South Bend, 1994—; Ind. state judge Blue Chip Enterprise Initiative, 1990—; chmn. Small Bus. Week awards, 1993—; co-chair Women's Econ. Summit St. Mary's Coll., Notre Dame, Ind., 1993. Mem. Planned Parenthood (treas. 1987-90, pres. 1991-92), Kiwanis (sec. 1988-91, Disting. Svc. award 1989). Methodist. Office: Small Bus Devel Ctr 300 N Michigan St South Bend IN 46601-1226

ANDERSON, CATHERINE M., consulting company executive; b. N.Y.C., Feb. 28, 1937; d. Edward Charles and Elizabeth (O'Shea) McElligott; m. Robert Brown Anderson, June 22, 1963; children: Mark Robert, Jennifer Elizabeth. BA, Douglass Coll., 1959; MA, Rutgers U., 1960. Staff asst. to pres. Chatham Coll., Pitts., 1960-61; instr. urban studies ctr. Rutgers U., New Brunswick, N.J., 1961-63; prin. urban renewal coord. City of Cleve., Cleve., 1963-64; regional admissions counselor Am. Inst. Fgn. Study, Pitts., 1964-74; chief planner, mgr. emergency ops. ctr. Allegheny County Govt., Pitts., 1975-79; dir. accreditation svcs. Energy Cons., Inc., Pitts., 1981-83; pub. involvement cons. Pitts., 1983—. Contbr. articles to profl. jours. Committeewoman Mt. Lebanon (Pa.) Mcpl. Dem. Com., 1970-85; active United Way Allegheny County, Pitts., mem. rev. com., 1980—, chmn. rev. com., 1986-89; bd. dirs. Mt. Lebanon Nature Conservancy, v.p., 1985-88, pres., 1988-92; bd. dirs. Conservation Cons. Inc., v.p., 1983-92, pres.,

1992—; bd. dirs. Pitts. chpt. Women's Transp. Seminar, v.p., 1992-94, pres. 1994—; bd. dirs. Exec. Women's Coun. Greater Pitts., v.p., 1986-88; bd. dirs. Carnegie-Mellon U. Art Gallery, 1986-89. Recipient Robert L. Wells award Mt. Lebanon Nature Conservancy, 1991, Outstanding Svc. award Exec. Women's Coun., 1988; Eagleton Inst. Politics grad. fellow Rutgers U., 1960. Mem. Exec. Women's Coun. (charter mem., v.p., 1987-88, Outstanding Svc. award 1988), Women's Transp. Seminar (v.p. 1992-94, pres. 94—), Women's Press Club Pitts. Home and Office: 2061 Outlook Dr Upper Saint Clair PA 15241

ANDERSON, CELIA M., biochemist, researcher, association executive; b. Phenix City, Ala., Jan. 24, 1949; d. Leroy and Celia (Tolliver) A. BA in Biology, Caldwell Coll., 1972. Scientist Hoffmann LaRoche, Inc., Nutley, N.J., 1973—. Author: (with others) Advancement in Experimental Medicine and Biology, 1990; contbr. numerous sci. articles to profl. jours. Pres. bd. dirs. YWCA Passaic/Clifton, N.J., 1992—. Mem. NAACP, Inflammatory Rsch. Assn., Concern Women Roche, Sigma Xi. Baptist. Office: YWCA Passaic/Clifton 114 Prospect St Passaic NJ 07055-4927

ANDERSON, CLAIRE W., computer gifted and talented educator; b. Albuquerque, May 22, 1930; d. Wentworth Henry and Clara Lea (Magruder) Corley; m. William James Young (div.); children: Gayle L. Mirkin, D. Young, Sherry B. Butler; m. Wallace L. Anderson. Student in Engring., U. Miss., 1946; BA, Rice U., 1951, postgrad., 1993; MEd, U. Houston, 1962, postgrad., 1963; postgrad., Carnegie Mellon U., Tex. A&M, 1992. Cert. elem. and secondary tchr., early childhood, exceptional children tchr., Tex. Tchr. Golfcrest Elem. Shc., Houston, 1959-60, Montrose, Poe Elem. Sch., Houston, 1960-62, St. Mark's Private Sch., Houston, 1962-63; substitute teaching Spring Branch Ind. Sch. Dist., Houston, 1965-68; tchr. Meml. Hall, Houston, 1968-73; instr. English, math. Internat. Hispanic U., Houston, 1971-74; tchr. Dogan Elem. Sch., Houston, 1971-74, Lanier Mid. Sch., Houston, 1974-79, High Sch. Health Profl., Houston, 1979-90, Clifton Mid. Sch., Houston, 1990-91, Jesse H. Jones Sr. High Sch., Houston, 1992—; adj. tutoring David Livingston and Assoc., Houston, 1960-65; instr. Internat. Hispanic U., Houston, 1971-74, Houston C.C., 1984—, Internat. Ednl. Comm. Ctr., High Point, N.C., 1990, Houston C.C. Sys., 1991; invited judge Kiev, Ukraine Math. and Sci. Competitions, 1989; facilitator Tex. Coun. of Women Sch. Execs. Summer Conf., 1994—; active The Rice/HISD Sch. Writing Project; acad. sponsor secondary edn. svc. and sci. clubs. Pres. bd. dirs. Women for Justice, 1990-94; active Houston Photography Ctr., Mus. Fine Arts, Houston Health Objectives 2000, Children's Mus.; coord. study and enrichment tutoring program, 1994. Recipient Tex. award for Excellence in Tchg. and Outstanding Svc. to the Cmty., 1994; scholar Precalculus Design Team, Dow Jones scholar Pa. State, Advance Placement scholar Tex. A&M, Woodrow Wilson; grantee NSF, Impact II. Mem. IEEE, Nat. Coun. Tchrs. Math., Nat. Coun. Tchrs. English, Am. Acoustic Soc., Assn. Calculating Machinery, Assn. for Early Childhood Edn. (internat. chairperson), Tex. Assn. Edn. Tech., Tex. Computers Educators Assn., N.Y. Acad. Sci., Internat. Coun. Computers in Edn., Phi Delta Kappa. Office: 7414 St Lo Rd Houston TX 77033

ANDERSON, CONSTANCE MYERS, retired association executive; b. N.Y.C., May 19, 1898; d. Howard Gillespie and Antoinette (Darwood) Myers; m. Arthur Forrest Anderson, May 30, 1925 (dec.); children: Constance Anderson Tate, Forrest Gillespie (dec.). BA, Vassar Coll., 1919. V.p., chmn. ctrl. br., hon. bd. dirs. YWCA, N.Y.C.; mem. nat. bd. dirs. YWCA U.S.A., 1936-75, pres. nat. bd. dirs., 1946-52, mem. various coms.; mem. exec. com. World YWCA. Former v.p., bd. dirs. U.S. Com. UNICEF; past mem., chmn. Com. Corr.; former mem. bd. deacons Riverside Ch.; past bd. dirs. USO. Recipient Ambassador award YWCA of the U.S.A., 1993.

ANDERSON, DARLA R., lawyer; b. Orlando, Fla., June 9, 1957; d. M.H. and Dawn R. (Stout) A.; life ptnr. Richard A. Kallan. BA, U. Nev., 1978; JD, U. San Diego, 1981. Bar: Nev., Calif. Assoc. Rogers, Monsey, Woodbury, Bran & Baggrem, Las Vegas, 1981-83, Capello & Foley, Santa Barbara, Calif., 1987-88; asst. gen. counsel State Indsl. Ins. Sys., Las Vegas, 1983-86; corporate atty. Mintor Corp., Santa Barbara, 1988—; lectr. Santa Barbara Adult Edn., 1992—; instr. intelletual property law U. La Verne, Encino, Calif., 1993-94. Bd. dirs. Nev. Temporary Assistance for Dem. Crisis, Las Vegas, 1984-85; founding mem. Nev. for Hart, Las Vegas, 1984; mem. credential std. com. Dem. Nat. Com., Washington, 1984; tutor Adult Literacy Program, Santa Barbara, 1991—; active Calif. Lawyers for Arts, 1993—. Mem. ABA, Santa Barbara County Bar Assn. (bd. dirs. 1993-94), Santa Barbara Women Lawyers Assn. (mem. com.). Home: 560 Ricardo Ave Santa Barbara CA 93109 Office: Mentor Corp 5425 Hollister Ave Santa Barbara CA 93110

ANDERSON, DEBORAH ANN, marketing professional; b. New Brunswick, N.J., Feb. 25, 1963; d. Marlin Richard and Martha (Sabol) A. BA in Women's Studies and Econs., Douglass Coll., 1986; MA in Internat. Rels., Fordham U., 1989. Accts. payable rep. White Consolidates Ind., Edison, N.J., 1988-89; ops. staff, asst. br. mgr. Intercommunity Bank, Springfield, N.J., 1989-90; trust acct. adminstr. Bankers Trust Co., Jersey City, 1990-91; data collections mktg. rschr., supr. Maritz Mktg. Rsch., Somerset, N.J., 1991-92; telemarketing mgr. Sales Solutions, New Brunswick, N.J., 1991-93; pres., cons., owner Future Waves Telemarketing, Highland Park, N.J., 1993—. Mem. Le Tip Internat. (v.p. 1994), Middlesex County C. of C., Douglass Coll. Alumni Assn., Fordham Alumni Assn. Home and Office: 22B Bartle Ct Highland Park NJ 08904

ANDERSON, DENICE ANNA, editor; b. Detroit, Nov. 11, 1947; d. Carl Magnus and Geraldine Elizabeth (Willer) A. BA in Journalism, Mich. State U., 1970. Copy editor/reporter The State News, East Lansing, Mich., 1965-70; reporter/copy editor/photographer The Tecumseh (Mich.) Herald, 1966-68; copy editor/entertainment editor The State Jour., Lansing, Mich., 1970-76; freelance writer State Jour./Lansing Mag., 1977-79; freelance corr. Collier's Year Book, N.Y.C., 1977-79; copy editor, proofreader Booz, Allen & Hamilton, N.Y.C., 1980-81, Rogers & Wells, N.Y.C., 1981-83, Advanced Therapeutic Communications, N.Y.C., 1983-84; freelance editor N.Y.C., Santa Fe, 1984—. Contbr. articles to profl. jours. Bd. dirs., sec. March of Dimes, Lansing, 1972-76; vol./writer Polio Info. Ctr., N.Y.C., 1984-88; vol. Vol. Involvement Svcs., Santa Fe, N.M., 1989—. Mem. Editorial Freelancers Assn. Lutheran. Home: Shadowridge Apts 941 Calle Mejia Apt 304 Santa Fe NM 87501

ANDERSON, DOROTHY FISHER, social worker, psychotherapist; b. Funchal, Madeira, May 31, 1924; d. Lewis Mann Anker and Edna (Gilbert) Fisher (adoptive father David Henry Fisher); m. Theodore W. Anderson, July 8, 1950; children: Robert Lewis, Janet Anderson Yang, Jeanne Elizabeth. BA, Queens Coll., Flushing, N.Y., 1945; AM, U. Chgo., 1947. Diplomate Am. Bd. Examiners in Clin. Social Work; lic. clin. social worker, Calif.; registered cert. social worker, N.Y.;. Intern Cook County (Ill.) Bur. Pub. Welfare, Chgo., 1945-46, Ill. Neuropsychiat. Inst., Chgo., 1946; clin. caseworker, Neurol. Inst. Presbyn. Hosp., N.Y.C., 1947; therapist, Mental Hygiene Clinic VA, N.Y.C., 1947-50; therapist, Child Guidance Clinic Pub. Elem. Sch. 42, N.Y.C., 1950-53; social worker, counselor Cedarhurst (N.Y.) Family Service Agy., 1954-55; psychotherapist, counselor Family Service of the Midpeninsula, Palo Alto, Calif., 1971-73, 79-86, George Hexter, M.D., Inc., 1972-83; clin. social worker Tavistock Clinic, London, 1974-75, El Camino Hosp., Mountain View, Calif., 1979; pvt. practice clin. social work, 1978-92, ret., 1992; cons. Human Resource Services, Sunnyvale, Calif., 1981-86. Hannah G. Solomon scholar U. Chgo., 1945-46; Commonwealth fellow U. Chgo., 1946-47. Fellow Soc. Clin. Social Work (Continuing Edn. Recognition award 1980-83); mem. Nat. Assn. Social Workers (diplomate in clin. social work).

ANDERSON, ELIZABETH CARMAL (BETTE ANDERSON), librarian, freelance writer; b. Henagar, Ala., Jan. 20, 1925; d. Buren Martin and Evelyn Vashtie (Keys) Farr; m. G. Kenneth Anderson, Aug. 23, 1947; 1 child, Merrill Clinton. BA in English, Wayne State U., 1946, MA in English, 1955, MLS, 1966. Cert. secondary edn. and library sci tchr., Mich. Copywriter Mich. Bell Tel. Co., Detroit, 1947-52; sch. libr. Bloomfield Hills (Mich.) Schs., 1964-68; libr. coord., media cons. West Bloomfield Schs., 1968-86; reference libr. Newport Beach (Calif.) Libr., 1988—; instr. adult edn. West Bloomfield Schs., 1975; instr. part-time Oakland Community Coll., Farmington, Mich., 1980. Mem. Laguna Canyon Conservancy, Laguna Beach, Calif., 1988—; vice chmn. Laguna Beach Cable TV Com., 1988, Laguna North Community Assn. U. Mich. grant, 1979. Mem. NEA (v.p. West Bloomfield chpt. 1985, union rep. 1986—), AAUW (ofcl. photographer 1988-90), LWV (pub. rels. dir. Orange Coast 1990-92), Common Cause, Los Angeles County Art Mus., Detroit Inst. Art, Laguna Art Mus., Newport Harbor Art Mus. Democrat. Presbyterian. Home: 611 High Dr Laguna Beach CA 92651-1555 Office: Newport Beach Ctrl 1000 Avocado Newport Beach CA 92660-6301

ANDERSON, ELIZABETH SECOR, philosopher, educator; b. Boston, Dec. 5, 1959. BA in Philosophy, Swarthmore Coll., 1981; AM in Philosophy, Harvard U., 1984, PhD in Philosophy, 1987. Instr. philosophy Swarthmore (Pa.) Coll., 1985-86; asst. prof. philosophy U. Mich., Ann Arbor, 1987-93, assoc. prof. philosophy and women's studies, 1993—, Arthur F. Thurnau prof., 1994. Author: Value in Ethics and Economics, 1993; contbr. articles to profl. jours. Inst. for Humanities fellow U. Mich., 1989-90. Mem. Am. Philos. Assn., Soc. for Analytic Feminism. Office: Univ Mich Dept Philosophy Ann Arbor MI 48109

ANDERSON, ELIZABETH SHERMAN, personnel consultant; b. Cin., Sept. 28, 1954; d. Roger Talbot and Ruth (Thieman) Sherman; m. John Richard Anderson, Aug. 26, 1977 (div. 1982); 1 child, Erika Elizabeth. BFA, So. Meth. U., 1976; MA, Stephen F. Austin U., 1977. Ceet. tchr. all levels, sr. account mgr. Pers. cons. OM5-Divsn. Mgmt. Recruiters Internat., Atlanta, 1986—. Home: 1273 N Druid Hills Atlanta GA 30319 Office: OM5 400 Colony Sq # 1001 Atlanta GA 30361

ANDERSON, ELLEN RUTH, state senator; b. Gary, Ind., Nov. 25, 1959; d. John Ernest Anderson and Marion Jane (Reeves) Martin. BA in History, Carleton Coll., 1982; JD, U. Minn., 1986. Bar: Minn., 1987, U.S. Dist. Ct. Minn. 1988. Jud. law clk. Minn. Ct. Appeals, St. Paul, 1987-88; atty. Hennepin County Pub. Defender, Mpls., 1988-91; staff atty. Minn. Edn. Assn., St. Paul, 1991-92; state senator State of Minn., St. Paul, 1993—. Democrat. Office: State of Minn G27 State Capitol Saint Paul MN 55155-1002*

ANDERSON, ETHEL AVARA, retired retail executive; b. Meridian, Miss.; d. Thomas Franklin and Annie Ethel (Jones) Avara.; m. Theron Young Anderson, Aug. 2, 1940 (dec. Aug. 1964); 1 child, Brenda Anderson Jackson. Grad. high sch., Meridian. Mem. exec. bd., sec. United Way of Meridian, Industries for Developmentally Disabled, Meridian, 1984-93, Lauderdale Assn. Retarded Children, Meridian, 1983-91; mem. exec. bd. Lauderdale County Mental Health, 1991, 92, 93, v.p., 1993-94; bd. dirs. 1st Ladies Civitan of Meridian, 1980-93. Mem. Meridian C. of C. (liaison 1985-87), Xi Gamma, Beta Sigma Phi (life). Methodist. Home: 3400 20th St Meridian MS 39301-2834

ANDERSON, FRANCES SWEM, nuclear medical technologist; b. Grand Rapids, Mich., Nov. 27, 1913; d. Frank Oscar and Carrie (Strang) Swem; m. Clarence A.F. Anderson, Apr. 9, 1934; children: Robert Curtis, Clarelyn Christine (Mrs. Roger L. Schmelling), Stanley Herbert. Student, Muskegon Sch. Bus., 1959-60; cert., Muskegon Community Coll., 1964; cert. adult edn. computer course, Fruitport Cmty. Schs., 1992. Registered nuclear med. technologist Am. Registry Radiol. Technologists. X-ray file clk., film librarian Hackley Hosp., Muskegon, Mich., 1957-59, radioisotope technologist and sec., 1959-65; nuclear med. technologist Butler Meml. Hosp., Muskegon Heights, Mich., 1966-70; nuclear med. technologist Mercy Hosp., Muskegon, 1970-79, ret., 1979. Mem. Muskegon Civic A Capella choir, 1932-39; mem. Mother-Tchr. Singers, PTA, Muskegon, 1941-48, treas. 1944-48; with Muskegon Civic Opera Assn., 1950-51, office vol. Alive '88 Crusade, mem. com. for 60th High Sch. class reunion. Soc. Nuclear Medicine Cert. nuclear medicine technologist Soc. Nuclear Medicine; active Forest Park Covenant Ch., mem. choir 1953-79, 83—, choir pres. 1992, 93, choir sec. 1963-69, Sunday sch. tchr. 1954-75, supt. Sunday sch. 1975-78, sec. and treas. Sunday sch. 1981-86, chmn. master planning coun., 1982, coord. centennial com. to 1981, ch. sec. 1982-84, 87, 91, registrar vacation Bible sch., 1988-89, 90, 91, sec. Sunday Sch. 1991, 92, 93, 94, mem. Sunday Sch. support team, sec., 1993; co-chmn. Jackson Hill Old Timers Reunion, 1982, 83, 85. Mem. Am. Registry Radiologic Technologists. Home: 5757 Sternberg Rd Fruitport MI 49415-9740

ANDERSON, GAIL CHRISTINE, school counselor; b. La Junta, Colo., June 23, 1951; d. Roy H. and Erlene A. (Lundahl) Hughes; m. Kenny L. Anderson, Sept. 4, 1972; children: Clinton, Clay. BA, So. Colo. State Coll., 1973; MA, Adams State Coll., 1989. Cht. I math. tchr. Crowley County Schs., Ordway, Colo., 1981-82, jr. high math. instr., 1982-88, elem.-jr. high sch. counselor, 1988-93, jr. high-sr. high sch. counselor, 1993—. Mem. ACA, Am. Sch. Counselors Assn. Home: 10335 County Lane 5 Olney Springs CO 81062-9770 Office: Crowley County Sch Dist 602 Main St Ordway CO 81063-1001

ANDERSON, GERALDINE LOUISE, laboratory scientist; b. Mpls., July 7, 1941; d. George M. and Viola Julia-Mary (Abel) Havrilla; m. Henry Clifford Anderson, May 21, 1966; children: Bruce Henry, Julie Lynne. BS, U. Minn., 1963. Med. technologist Swedish Hosp., Mpls., 1963-68; hematology supr. Glenwood Hills Hosp. lab., Golden Valley, Minn., 1968-70; assoc. scientist dept. pediatrics U. Minn. Hosps., Mpls., 1970-74; instr. health occupations and med. lab. asst. Suburban Hennepin County Area Vocat. Tech. Ctr., Brooklyn Park, Minn., 1974-81, 92—, St. Paul Tech. Vocat. Inst., 1978-81; rsch. med. technologist Miller Hosp., St. Paul, 1975-78; rsch. assoc. Children's and United Hosps., St. Paul, 1979-88; sr. lab. analyst Cascade Med. Inc., Eden Prairie, Minn., 1989-90; lab. mgr. VA Med. Ctr., Mpls., 1990; technical support scientist INCSTAR Corp., 1990-94; mem. reg. affairs com. Medtronic Neurological, Mpls., 1995—; mem. health occupations adv. com. Hennepin Tech. Ctrs., 1975-90, chairperson, 1978-79; mem. hematology slide edn. rev. bd. Am. Soc. Hematology, 1976—; mem. flow cytometry and clin. chemistry quality control subcoms. Nat. Com. for Clin. Lab. Standards, 1988-92; cons. FCM Specialists, 1989—. Mem. rev. bd. Clin. Lab. Sci., 1990-91, The Learning Laboratorian Series 1991; contbr. and presenter In Svc. Rev. in Clin. Lab. Sci., audio taped study program for ASMT, 1992; contbr. articles to profl. jours. Mem. Med. Lab. Tech. Polit. Action Com., 1978—; charter orgns. rep. troop #534 Boy Scouts Am., Viking Coun., 1988-90; resource person lab. careers Robbinsdale Sch. Dist., Minn., 1970-79; del. Crest View Home Assn., 1981—; mem. sci. and math. subcom. Minn. High Tech. Council, 1983-88, mem. Women Scientists Speakers Bur., 1989-92.Recipient svc. awards and honors Omicron Sigma. Mem. AAAS, AAUW, NAFE (Twin Cities network), Am. Med. Writers Assn., Women in Com. Inc., Assn. Clin. Pharmacology, Soc. Tech. Comm., Nat. Assn. Women Cons., Inc., Minn. Emerging Med. Orgns., Minn. Soc. Med. Tech. (sec. 1969-71), Am. Soc. Profl. and Exec. Women, Am. Soc. Clin. Lab. Sci. (del. to ann. meetings 1972—, chmn. hematology sci. assembly 1977-79, nomination com. 1979-81, bd. dirs. 1985-88), Twin City Hosp. Assn. (speakers bur. 1968-70), Assn. Women in Sci., World Future Soc., Minn. Med. Tech. Alumni, Am. Soc. Hematology, Internat. Soc. Analytical Cytology, Great Lakes Internat. Flow Cytometry Assn. (charter mem. 1992), Sigma Delta Epsilon (corr. sec. Xi chpt. 1980-82, pres. 1982-84, membership com. 1990-92, nat. nominations chair 1991-92, nat. v.p. 1992-93, nat. pres.-elect 1993-94, nat. pres. 1994-95), Alpha Mu Tau. Lutheran. Office: Medtronic Neurol Divsn Mail Stop N225 800 53d Ave NE Minneapolis MN 55421

ANDERSON, HOLLY GEIS, medical clinic executive, radio personality; b. Waukesha, Wis., Oct. 23, 1946; d. Henry H. and Hulda (Sebroff) Geis; m. Richard Kent Anderson, June 6, 1969. BA, Azusa Pacific U., 1970. CEO Oak Tree Antiques, San Gabriel, Calif., 1975-82; pres., founder, CEO Premenstrual Syndrome Treatment Clinic, Arcadia, Calif., 1982—, Hormonal Treatment Ctrs., Inc., Arcadia, 1992-94; lectr. radio and TV shows, L.A.; on-air radio personality Women's Clinic with Holly Anderson, 1990—. Author: What Every Woman Needs to Know About PMS (audio cassette), 1987, The PMS Treatment Program (video cassette), 1989, PMS Talk (audio cassette), 1989. Mem. NAFE, The Dalton Soc. Republican. Office: PMS Treatment Clinic 150 N Santa Anita Ave Ste 755 Arcadia CA 91006-3113

ANDERSON, IRIS ANITA, retired educator; b. Forks, Wash., Aug. 18, 1930; d. James Adolphus and Alma Elizabeth (Haase) Gilbreath; m. Donald Rene Anderson, 1951; children: Karen Christine, Susan Adele, Gayle Lynne, Brian Dale. BA in Teaching, U. Wash., 1969; MA in English, Seattle U., 1972. Cert. English tchr., adminstr., Calif. Tchr. Issaquah (Wash.) Sr. High Sch., 1969-77, L.A. Sr. High Sch., 1977-79. Nutrition vol. Santa Monica (Calif.) Hosp. Aux., Jules Stein Eye Inst., L.A.; mem. Desert Beautiful, Palm Springs Panhellenic; mem. Rancho Mirage Reps. W-Key activities scholar U. Wash. Mem. NEA, DAR (vice-regent Palm Springs, 1st vice-regent Cahuilla chpt.), AAUW, LWV, Wash. Speech Assn., Nat. Thespians, Bob Hope Cultural Ctr., Palm Springs Press Women, Coachella Valley Hist. Soc., Palm Desert Womens Club, Calif. Ret. Tchrs. Assn., CPA Wives Club, Desert Celebrities, Rancho Mirage Womens Club, Round Table West, World Affairs Coun. Republican.

ANDERSON, ISABEL, artist, educator; b. N.Y.C., Apr. 10, 1931; d. William and Mary Elizabeth (Doerr) Smith; m. Hugh Riddell Anderson, Feb. 4, 1955 (div. Jan. 1968); m. William Anthony Dietz, Apr. 29, 1978. Student, Art Students' League, 1951-52; BA, Antioch Coll., 1954; postgrad., UCLA, 1956; MFA, State U. of Iowa, 1956. Cert. h.s. tchr., Calif. C.C. standard teaching credential, instr. credential. Stained glass artist Paul L. Phillips Studio, Altadena, Calif., 1960-64, Roger Daricarrerre Studio, L.A., 1965-66; h.s. art tchr. L.A. Unified Sch. Dist., 1967-76; instr. art Glendale (Calif.) C.C., 1979-80; asst. prof. screen printing Pasadena (Calif.) City Coll., 1980-90; artist, writer, 1990—; invited spkr., panelist in field. Exhbns., prints, drawings, paintings, 1965—; represented in permanent collections Boston Coll. Art, Home Savs. and Loan, Antioch Coll., Pasadena City Coll., Kerala State U., India, Hanover Bank, L.A.; contbr. articles and art revs. to profl. jours. Recipient Award of Merit 11th All-City Art Exhbn., 1963, Purchase award State Coll. Art, 1963, Spl. award Inland XII Art Exhbn., 1981, James Jones Purchae award Ink & Clay Exhbn. Calif. Poly., 1982. Mem. L.A. Printmaking Soc. (sec. 1978-79, newsletter editor 1978-79), Screen Printing Assn. Internat. (2 seminar grants 1985, 88), Women's Caucus for Art, SITE, L.A. Contemporary Exhbns., Beyond Baroque Found., Wednesday Poetry Workshop. Office: 1564 Talmadge St Los Angeles CA 90027

ANDERSON, JACQUELINE, community health nurse; b. Fayetteville, Tenn., June 22, 1943; d. Roy T. Smith and Lucile Horton Smith-Holt; m. Grady F. Anderson Jr., Apr. 17, 1965; children: Traci D., Grady Eric. BS, SUNY, Plattsburgh, 1964; MA, Columbia U., 1976. Sch. nurse-tchr. East Ramapo Sch. Dist., Spring Valley, N.Y., 1964-75; staff nurse F.D.R. VA Hosp., Montrose, N.Y., 1976-77, community health nurse coord., 1977—. Mem. health adv. bd. ARC, Nyack, N.Y., 1989-93; mem. nursing adv. bd. Hudson Valley chpt., Am. Lung Assn., White Plains, N.Y., 1986-88; fin. sec. Rockland Negro Scholarship Fund, Nanuet, N.Y., 1973—; trustee East Ramapo Sch. Bd., 1987—; epic facilitator Effective Parenting Info. for Children, Spring Valley, 1991—. Recipient Humanitarian award Town of Ramapo, 1991, Hands and Heart award VA, 1985, 40 and 8 award Am. Legion, 1991. Mem. ANA, Nurses Orgn. of VA, Dist. 17 Nurses Assn., N.Y. State Nurses Assn., Am. Assn. Continuity of Care. Democrat. Home: 65 N Pascack Rd Nanuet NY 10954 Office: FDR VA Hosp Bldg 1 Rm 26 Montrose NY 10548

ANDERSON, JANE A., scriptwriter. TV series include: Raising Miranda, 1988, The Wonder Years, 1989; TV movies include: The Positively True Adventures of the Alleged Texas Cheerleader-Murdering Mom, 1992 (Emmy award outstanding individual achievement in writing in a miniseries or special); film: It Could Happen to You; plays: The Baby Dance, Food and Shelter, Hotel Oubliette, Lynette at 3 A.M. Office: c/o Martin Gage The Gage Group 9255 Sunset Blvd Ste 515 Los Angeles CA 90069

ANDERSON, JANE LOUISE BLAIR, librarian, horse breeder, poet; b. Wilkinsburg, Pa., Nov. 6, 1948; d. Francis Preston and Mary Louise (Maxwell) Blair; m. Russell Karl Anderson Jr., Apr. 20, 1973; children: Christina Lynn, Melissa Jane. BS in Edn., Clarion State Coll., 1971; MS in Library Sci., Duquesne U., 1974. Cert. pub. librarian, Pa. Substitute tchr. Wilkinsburg Schs., 1971, tchr. Head Start, 1971; librarian Franklin Regional Schs., Murrysville, Pa., 1971—; breeder quarter horses, Fenelton, Pa., 1978—; owner, operator Fern Valley Farm Boarding Kennels. Contbr. poems to various anthologies. Vol. mem. Rescue 5 Ambulance, Murrysville, 1974-76, Medic I ambulance, 1976-78; sec. Franklin Area REACT, 1976-78; first aid instr. ARC, Murrysville, 1975-80; instr. CPR, Am. Heart Assn., Westmoreland County, 1976-80; vol. worker with deaf, 1978-83; vol. United Cerebral Palsey, Butler, Pa., 1981—. Mem. Westmoreland County Library Assn. (pres.), Pa. Sch. Libr. Assn. (presentor regional workshops 1989, 90, speaker 1989, adv. coun. 1992), SHARE Westmoreland Access Pa. Libr. Consortium, Am. Quarter Horse Assn., Western Pa. Quarter Horse Assn., Butler County C. of C., Am. Boarding Kennel Assn. Home: Fern Valley Farm PO Box 12 Fenelton PA 16034-0012 Office: 3200 School Rd Murrysville PA 15668

ANDERSON, JANET ALM, librarian; b. Lafayette, Ind., Dec. 20, 1952; d. Charles Henry and Lenore Elaine Alm; m. Jay Allan Anderson, May 21, 1983. BS, Bemidji State U., 1975; MA in Folklore, Western Ky. U., 1981, MSLS in Libr. Sci., 1982; PhD in Recreation Resources Mgmt., Utah State U., 1994. Cert. elem. tchr., sch. libr. and media specialist. Storyteller, puppeteer North Country Arts Coun., Bemidji, Minn., 1975-76; head children's libr. Bemidji State U., 1976-77; mid. sch. libr. Custer County Sch. Dist., Miles City, Mont., 1977-79; tchr. of gifted and talented Custer County Sch. Dist., Miles City, 1979-80; folklore archivist Western Ky. U., Bowling Green, 1981-83; head children's and young adults' svcs. Bowling Green Pub. Libr., 1983-85; head of serials Utah State U., Logan, 1986-91, campus svcs. libr., 1991—, chmn. adv. bd. Women's Ctr., 1988-92; adj. instr. Miles Community Coll., 1978-80; cons. to various Am. outdoor museums; speaker Utah Endowment for the Humanities Speakers Bur., Salt Lake City, 1987-90. Author: Old Fred, 1972, A Taste of Kentucky, 1986 (Ky. State Book Fair award), Bounty, 1990; (with others) Advances in Serials Management, Vol. 3, 1989, Vendors and Library Acquistions, 1991; contbr. to Ency. of Am. Popular Beliefs and Superstitions, articles on folklore, librarianship and museology to mags. and periodicals; delivered radio and TV presentations on folklore and librarianship. Co-founder and past pres. Rosebud chpt. Nat. Audubon Soc., Miles City, Mont., 1978-80; invited author Ky. State Book Fair, 1986, Utah Arts Festival, 1991. Recipient Exhibit and Program Grant Nat. Endowment for the Arts, Bowling Green, Ky., 1984-85. Mem. ALA, Utah Libr. Assn., N.Am. Serials Interest Group, Mt.-Plains Libr. Assn., Consortium of Utah Women in Higher Edn. (campus coord. 1989-91), Bridgerland Bus. and Profl. Women (bd. dirs., pub. chairperson Logan chpt. 1986-90), Ky. Coun. on Archives, Am. Folklore Soc., Utah Folklore Soc., Assn. Living Hist. Farms and Agrl. Mus., Visitor Studies Assn., Am. Assn. Mus., Assn. Coll. and Rsch. Librs. Democrat. Lutheran. Home: 1090 S 400 E Providence UT 84332-9461 Office: Utah State U Merrill Libr Logan UT 84322-3000

ANDERSON, JANET ANN, city official; b. Franklin, N.C., Oct. 13, 1957; d. Turner Cleveland and Annie Lou (Waldroop) A. AAS in Acctg., Southwestern C.C., Sylva, N.C., 1977; BS in Bus. Adminstrn., Western Carolina U., 1987. CPA, N.C.; cert. mcpl. clk. Asst. town clk. Town of Franklin, N.C., 1977-88, town clk., 1988—. Mem. AICPAs, N.C. Assn. CPAs, Internat. Inst. Mcpl. Clks., N.C. Govt. Investment Assn., N.C. Assn. Mcpl. Clks. Office: Town of Franklin 70 W Main St Franklin NC 28734

ANDERSON, JANICE GWENDOLYN, accountant; b. Dalton, Ga., Feb. 24, 1955; d. Ernest B. and Evelyn Irene (DuVall) A. Cert., Sears Extension Inst., 1984; student, Fgn. Svc. Inst., 1987—; AS in BA cum laude, Dalton Coll., 1993. Customer svc. rep., cashier Sears, Roebuck & Co., Dalton, 1984; acctg. mgr. Southeastern Coatings, Dalton, 1986-87; accounts receivable clk. Aladdin Mills, Inc., Dalton, 1988-90; head bookkeeper Skinner Furniture Co., Dalton, 1990-94. Contbr. short stories to profl. publs. Mem. Acad. Polit. Sci., N.Y.C., 1993-94; Ctr. for Study of the Presidency, N.Y.C., 1993-94. Mem. NAFE, Am. Inst. Profl. Bookkeepers, Assn. Interactive Mgmt. (v.p. 1993, treas. Collegiate chpt. 1993, Leadership award 1993), Phi Theta Kappa. Home: PO Box 1713 Dalton GA 30722-1713

ANDERSON, JANICE SCOTT, health care administrator; b. Magnolia, Miss., Apr. 22, 1949; d. Stafford and Mable (Holden) Scott; m. Willie James Anderson, (div. Jan. 1976); children: James Patrick, Christopher Scott. BA, Millsaps Coll., 1970; MA, U. Wis., 1972, MA, 1974, PhD, 1981. Writer, City Milw., 1975-76; news analyst WISN-AM, Milw., 1974-76; staff cons. Office

Mayor, Milw., 1976-84; pres., chief exec. officer Health Reach HMO, Milw., 1984—. Columnist, The Bus. Jour., 1985—, Milw. Community Jour., 1983—. Pres., founder Reach for the Stars, Milw., 1985; mem. Sojourner Truth House; pres.-elect Milw. Mental Health Assn.; bd. dirs. Leukemia Soc. Wis., United Cerebral Palsy, Goals for Greater Milw.-2000, Girl Scouts Am.-Milw. Mem. Am. Mgmt. Assn., Am. Med. Care and Rev. Assn., Wis. HMO Assn., Speech Communication Assn. Am., Milw. Press Club. Office: Health Reach HMO 2266 N Prospect Ave Suite 612 Milwaukee WI 53202

ANDERSON, JENNIFER KOLDE, training specialist; b. Loveland, Ohio, July 28, 1966; d. Richard Raymond and Mary Kay (Nimersheim) Kolde; m. Derrick B. Anderson, July 21, 1990; children: Brennen Michael, Dorrian Joseph, Garrison John. BA, Miami U., 1988; M of Labor & Human Resources, Ohio State U., 1992. Asst. mgr. Ames Dept. Stores, Ashland, Ky., 1988; personnel analyst City of Columbus (Ohio) Civil Svc. Commn., 1989-93; training specialist Columbus Divsn. of Water, 1993—; mem. com. Am.'s with disabilities City of Columbus, 1992—. Chair Oper. Feed, Columbus, 1989, 91; trainer Girl Scouts Am., 1989— (Outstanding Vol. 1990, Leadership Devel. award 1990, Outstanding Leader award 1990). Mem. ASTD, Nat. Mgmt. Assn. (cert. mgr., sec. 1994—). Office: Columbus Divsn of Water 910 Dublin Rd Columbus OH 43215

ANDERSON, JOAN WELLIN FREED, communications executive, consultant, freelance journalist, writer; b. Shreveport, La., Aug. 18, 1945; d. Cyril and Rose (Friedman) F.; m. Steven G. Rapfogel, 1966 (div. 1984); children: Lisa L., Robert B.; m. J. Warren Anderson, July 21, 1984 (div. 1991). BA in Gen. Studies, Tex. Christian U. Freelance reporter Sta. KERA-TV, Dallas, 1979-80, Fort Worth Star-Telegram, 1980-83, Fort Worth bur. Dallas Morning News, 1980-82; pub. relations coordinator Amon Carter Mus., Fort Worth, 1982; med. writer Tex. Coll. Osteo. Medicine, Fort Worth, 1982-85; freelance writer, 1985-87; producer video programs for pub. access cable channel, Ft. Worth, 1987-90; community programming coord. cable TV channel City/Video-45, Ft. Worth, 1988-90, chair; v.p. corp. comms. & health svcs. Comm. Osteo. Health System of Tex., 1990—; co-owner, playwright, actress Catered Theater, Character Acts. Bd. dirs. Am. Cancer Soc., 1982-84, Am. Heart Assn. 1993-94, Leadership Texas Class 1993, active Cancer Hotline, Community Programming Adv. Coun.; facilitator for fair housing edn. and info. for Community Housing Resource Bd., Ft. Worth; bd. dirs. Women's Haven of Tarrant County (Tex.) Inc., 1987-88, chmn. community relations com., 1988, Dispute Resolutions Svcs. Tarrant County (bd. dirs., chmn. community rels. 1989-90); mem. Court Apptd. Spl. Adv. for Foster Children, 1986-88. Mem. Women in Communications, Inc. (past dir.), Internat. Assn. Bus. Communicators, Soc. for Theatrical Artists' Guidance and Enhancement, Advt. Club, Sigma Delta Chi. Author: children's book Diggy Armadillo Goes to the Rodeo; playwright: 1-800-4ADVICE, 1994; contbr. articles to popular mags. Office: Osteopathic Health System of Tex 3715 Camp Bowie Fort Worth TX 76102

ANDERSON, JOLENE SLOVER, small business owner, publishing executive, consultant; b. Tulare, Calif.; James P. Sr., and Helen B. (Walters) Slover; m. Douglas R. Anderson, June 14, 1975; 1 child by previous marriage, Sabrina Jo. Student, Victor Valley Coll., Riverside City Coll. Model Connor Sch. Modeling, Fresno, Calif., 1955-65; actress M. Kosloff Studios, Hollywood, Calif., 1965; nat. sales mgr. Armed Services Publs., Hollywood, Calif., 1966-68; pres., dir. Sullivan Publs., Inc., Riverside, Calif., 1970-82; pres., chief exec. officer Heritage House Publs., Riverside, 1983-84; pres. Jolene S. Anderson Pub. Cons., Inc., Riverside, 1987—; bd. dirs. Riverside County Econ. Devel. Coun. Co-comdr. March AFB, Riverside Tourists and Conv.; mem. YWCA, City of Riverside Cultural Heritage Bd., Yr. 2000 Com., 1988, Riverside County Philharm. Bd., Temecula-Murrieta Econ. Devel. Corp. Named Woman of Achievement YWCA, 1989, Humanitarian of Yr. Rotary, 1990. Mem. Riverside Downtown Assn., Sun City/Menifee Valley C. of C., Greater Riverside C. of C., Temecula Valley C. of C., Temecula Valley Econ. Devel. Corp., Soroptimists (Riverside chpt.). Office: PO Box 800 Riverside CA 92502-0800

ANDERSON, JUDITH ANNE, academic administrator; b. Little Falls, Minn., June 23, 1943; d. Thomas Martin and Elda Rose Ethel (Klapel) McDonnell; m. Gene Wesley Anderson, Aug. 12, 1961 (div. 1993); children: Jeffery Thomas, Gregory Carl, Joel Michael, Julie Ann. AA, Cambridge (Minn.) Anoka-Ramsey C.C., 1982; BA, Met. State U., St. Paul, 1987; MS, Cardinal Stritch Coll., Milw., 1990. Bookkeeper Peoples State Bank, Cambridge, 1971-77; bus. mgr. Cambridge Anoka-Ramsey C.C., 1979-90; ednl. coord. Barnes Bus. Coll., Denver, 1991-92, dir., 1992—; cons. for low-income families U. Minn. Extension Dept., Isanti County, 1987-90. Treas. Govt. Maple Ridge Twp., Isanti County, Minn., 1978-91; chmn. United Charities Dr., Maple Ridge Twp., 1980-85, Jefferson County Ext. Adv. Bd., 1994—. Named State Vol. Gov. of Minn., 1987, 88, 89, 90. Mem. AAUW (Denver), Muskies Inc., Women for Fishing, Hunting and Wildlife, Lady Ducks, Nat. Outdoors Women, Phi Theta Kappa (Alpha Minn. chpt.). Republican. Mem. Covenant Ch. Home: 6836 S Everett Ct Littleton CO 80123-4023

ANDERSON, JUDITH MARY, investment marketing professional; b. Norwood, Mass., Nov. 27, 1961; d. Leonard and Ruth Patricia (Silvestri) A. BA magna cum laude, Emmanuel Coll., 1983. Telephone inquiry operator Boston Fin. Svcs., Quincy, Mass., 1983-84; telephone inquiry operator The Colonial Group, Boston, 1984, account specialist, 1985, supr. dealer priority ctr., 1986, mgr. account specialists, 1987, mem. CTRAN project team, 1988, compliance adminstr., 1989-91, asst. v.p., asst. dir. qualified plan sales, 1991—. Mem. fiscal and monetary rev. com. Walpole, Mass., 1986. Mem. Kappa Gamma Pi. Roman Catholic. Office: Colonial Investment Svcs 1 Financial Ctr Boston MA 02111-2621

ANDERSON, KATHLEEN CALLAHAN, lawyer; b. Milw., May 26, 1953; d. Edgar Fred and Sally Ann (Conley) Callahan; m. Christopher P. Anderson, June 27, 1987. BA, Marquette U., 1975; MBA, U. Calif., 1989, JD, 1978. Assoc. Jackson Tufts Cole Block (formerly Petty Andrews Tufts & Jackson), San Francisco, 1978-83; v.p., gen. counsel, sec. We. Community, Walnut Creek, Calif., 1983-85, ACA Joe, San Francisco, 1986-88, Esprit, San Francisco, 1988—. Bd. dirs., gen. counsel Leadership Calif., 1989-95. Mem. ABA (gov. bd. franchising forum 1992—). Home: 524 Dalewood Dr Orinda CA 94563 Office: Esprit 900 Minnesota St San Francisco CA 94107

ANDERSON, KATHLEEN GAY, mediator, hearing officer, arbitrator, educator; b. Cin., July 27, 1950; d. Harold B. and Trudi L. (Chambers) Briggs; m. J.R. Carr, July 4, 1988; 1 child, Jesse J. Anderson. Student, U. Cin., 1971-72, Antioch Coll., 1973-74; cert., Nat. Jud. Coll., U. Nev., Reno, 1987, Inst. Applied Law, 1987, Acad. Family Mediators, 1991. Cert. Am. Arbitration Assn., Lemmon Mediation Inst. Paralegal Lauer & Lauer, Santa Fe, 1976-79, Wilkinson, Cragun & Barker, Anchorage, 1981-82; employment law paralegal specialist Hughes, Thorsness, Gantz, Powell & Brundin, Anchorage, 1983-91; investigator, mediator Alaska State Commn. Human Rights, 1992-93; mediator, arbitrator The Arbitration Group, Anchorage, 1987—; hearing officer Municipality of Anchorage, 1993—; State of Alaska, 1994—; mem. faculty Nat. Jud. Coll., U. Nev., Reno, 1988-89; adj. prof. U. Alaska, Anchorage, 1985—, Alaska Pacific U., 1990—, Chapman U., 1990; mem. Alaska Supreme Ct. Mediation Task Force, 1991; adv. com. Am. Arbitration Assn. for Alaska, 1994—; trainer mediation svcs. pvt. profit and nonprofit groups, pub. groups, U.S. mil., state and fed. govt. Author, editor: Professional Responsibility Handbook for Legal Assistants and Paralegals, 1986; contbr. articles to profl. jours. Lectr. Alaska Bar Assn., 1989—, NLRB, Anchorage, 1986, Alaska Assn. Bus. and Profl. Women, 1988—, Coun. on Edn. and Mgmt., 1993—, Small Bus. Devel. Coun., various employers and bus. groups. Mem. Soc. Profls. in Dispute Resolution, Nat. Assn. Mediation in Edn., Nat. Fedn. Paralegal Assn. (edn. task force coord. 1988-89, adminstrv. v.p. 1988-91), Conflict Resolution Ctr. Internat., Acad. Family Mediators (cert., practitioner mem.), Alaska Bar Assn. (employment, alt. dispute resolution, family law sects.), Bus. and Profl. Women, Alaska Dispute Settlement Assn. (v.p. 1992-93). Home: PO Box 100098 Anchorage AK 99510-0098 Office: PO Box 240783 Anchorage AK 99524-0783

ANDERSON, KATHRYN DUNCAN, surgeon; b. Ashton-Under-Lyne, Lancashire, Eng., Mar. 14, 1939; came to U.S., 1961; m. French Anderson, June 24, 1961. BA, Cambridge (Eng.) U., 1961, MA, 1964; MD, Harvard U., 1964. Diplomate Am. Bd. Surgery. Intern in pediat. Children's Hosp., Boston, 1964-65; resident in surgery Georgetown U. Hosp., Washington, 1965-69, chief resident in surgery, 1969-70, attending surgeon, 1972-74, vice chmn. surgery, 1984-92; chief resident in pediat. surgery Children's Hosp., Washington, 1970-72, sr. attending surgeon, 1974-84; surgeon-in-chief Children's Hosp., L.A., 1992—; prof. surgery U. So. Calif. Fellow ACS (sec. 1992—), Am. Acad. Pediatrics (sec. surg. sect. 1982-85, chmn. 1985-86), Am. Pediatric Surg. Assn. (sec. 1988-91); Am. Surg. Assn., Soc. Univ. Surgeons. Office: Children's Hosp 4650 Sunset Blvd Los Angeles CA 90027

ANDERSON, KIM ELIZABETH, health and fitness organization executive; b. Canton, OH, Oct. 29, 1960; d. Doyle Edward and Joan Elizabeth (Mayeros) Parcell; m. Mark Alan Anderson, Aug. 22, 1981; children: Kyle Edward, Nathan Alan. BA, Mount Union Coll., 1983. Cert. high sch. phys. edn. and bus. edn. tchr. Fitness instr. Scandinavian Health Spa, Canton, 1983-84, Goodyear Tire and Rubber, Akron, Ohio, 1984-86; youth sports dir. Canton YMCA, 1984-86; pres., owner IKEN Enterprises, Alliance, Ohio, 1987-94; adult fitness dir. Louisville (Ohio) YMCA, 1994—; instr. step aerobics Alliance YMCA, 1990-93; women's soccer coach Alliance High Sch., 1993-94. Mem. adv. bd. Am. Cancer Soc., Alliance, 1989-91, Ohio Edison Consumer Panel, Alliance, 1987-92; publicity chmn. Centennial Celebration Com., Alliance, 1989—; instr. ARC, Alliance, 1990-94; bd. dirs. Carnation Festival, Alliance, 1989-92; chmn. kick-off parade, 1990, 91; publicity chmn. Alliance Community Hosp. follies, 1991; div. I coach Alliance Community Youth Soccer Club, 1992, 93, 94; bd. dirs., asst. treas. Liberty Elem. Sch. PTO, 1992-93. Mem. Alliance Jaycees (bd. dirs. 1986-87, v.p. 1987-90, Outstanding Community Project award 1986, Jaycee of Yr. award, 1987, Thoams CaSale award, 1989), Alliance C. of C. (bd. dirs., ways and means com. women's div., membership com. retail svc. div. 1991). Republican. Methodist. Office: Louisville YMCA 1421 S Nickel Plate Louisville OH 44641

ANDERSON, LEA E., lawyer; b. Clarksburg, W.Va., May 25, 1954; d. Jackson Lawler and Barbara Jean (Sanford) A.; m. Templeton Smith Jr., Aug. 22, 1980; children: Templeton Smith III, Suzanne Lea Smith. BA, W.Va. U., 1976, JD, 1979. Bar: W.Va. 1979, U.S. Dist. Ct. (so. dist.) W.Va. 1979, Pa. 1981, U.S. Supreme Ct. 1982. Assoc. Bowles, McDavid, Graff & Love, Charleston, W.Va., 1979-80; assoc. Goehring, Rutter & Boehm, Pitts., 1980-84, ptnr., 1984-89, mem., 1990—, sec., 1993—; mem. credit com. Alcobar Fed. Credit Union, 1985-87, mem. supervisory com., 1981; mem. vis. com. W.Va. Coll. Law, 1986-89. Vol. March of Dimes, 1986, neighborhood coord., 1987-91; chmn. fundraising com. Southminster Nursery Sch., 1989; chmn. Windy Ridge, 1991-93; mem. Performing Arts for Children, South, 1991-94, v.p., membership com., 1993-94; mem. bd. deacons Southminster Presbyn. Ch., Mt. Lebanon, Pa., 1990-93, session mem., elder, trustee, 1993—, vice chmn. bd. deacons, 1993. Mem. W.Va. Bar Assn., Pa. Bar Assn., Allegheny County Bar Assn. (chmn. edn. com. of young lawyers 1983-84, treas. 1984-85, mem. rules com. family law sect. 1993-94), Child Study Club of Mt. Lebanon (pres. 1989-91), Phi Beta Kappa, Phi Kappa Phi, Phi Delta Phi. Republican. Office: Goehring Rutter & Boehm 1424 Frick Bldg 437 Grant Ave Pittsburgh PA 15219

ANDERSON, LINDA (LYNN ANDERSON), radio executive; b. Detroit, Dec. 24; d. Robert A. and Lucille A. Tower; children: Kierstyn R. Anderson, Gretchen N. Anderson. BA in Bus., Mich. State U., 1968; postgrad., UCLA, 1968-70. Cert. radio mktg. cons. Tchr. pub. schs. L.A. and Chgo., 1968-70; mgr. display ads Frontier Publs., 1970-71; broadcaster Sta. WVVX, Chgo., 1971-72; account exec. Metromedia Radio, Sta. WDHF, Chgo., 1972-76; v.p. sales Metro Radio Sales Metromedia Radio, L.A., 1976-79; sr. account exec. RKO Radio/Sta. KHJ, L.A., 1979-80; with Gannett Radio/Sta. KIIS AM-FM, L.A., 1980-90, v.p. sales, 1984-85, v.p., sta. mgr., 1986, v.p., gen. mgr., 1986-87, pres., 1987-90; exec. v.p. mktg. and sales worldwide Radio Express, L.A., 1991—. Mem. bd. visitors Southwestern Coll. Law, Los Angeles, 1987. Recipient Jim Dunkan awards 1987, 88; named Gen. Mgr. Yr. Poe Music Survey, 1989. Mem. Nat. Assn. Broadcasters (steering com. 1987—), Am. Women Radio & TV (Broadcaster of Yr. 1990), Hollywood Radio & TV Soc. (IBA awards chair), Hollywood Arts Com. (bd. dirs. 1986—), So. Calif. Broadcasters Assn. (sec. 1989, bd. dirs. 1986—), Hollywood Women's Polit. Com., Hollywood C. of C. (spl. events com. 1987—). Clubs: Los Angeles Ad; Calif. Yacht; Santa Monica Yacht. Office: Radio Express Los Angeles CA 90068-1366

ANDERSON, LINDA D., psychologist; b. Beaver Falls, Pa.; d. Addison S. and Elizabeth W. Anderson. BS in Elem. Edn., Ind. U. Pa., 1969, MEd in Elem. Edn., 1970, diploma in sch. psychology, 1973; diploma in supr. sch. psychol. svcs., Millersville U. Pa., 1978. Grad. asst. Ind. U. Pa., 1969-70; tchr. elem. edn. Ind. Area Sch. Dist., 1969-74; psychologist, case mgr. Lincoln Intermediate Unit # 12, New Oxford, Pa., 1964-76, 78-81; psychologist Camp Hill (Pa.) Sch. Dist., 1978-81; instr. Community Coll. Allegheny County, Pitts., 1982; psychologist D.T. Watson Rehab. Hosp., Leetsdale, Pa., 1982, Allegheny Intermediate Unit, Pitts., 1982-83, PACE Sch., Pitts., 1983-85; psychologist pre-sch. Westmoreland Intermediate Unit # 7, Greensburg, Pa., 1985—; writer presch. guidelines Pa. Dept. Edn., Harrisburg, 1990. Bd. dirs. presch. 1st Presbyn. Ch., Greensburg, 1989-91. Mem. NEA, APA, Pa. Interagency Coordinating Coun. (Early Intervention Personnel Preparation Com. 1992—), Pa. Psychol. Assn. (past pres. sch. div., bd. dirs.), Nat. Assn. Sch. Psychologist, Assn. Sch. Psychologists Pa. (regional del., state bd. dirs. 1979-82, 88-90, recipient Outstanding Sch. Psychologist of the Yr. award 1991-92), Pa. State Edn. Assn., Coun. Exceptional Children, Pediatric Psychology Soc., Nat. Tourette Syndrome Assn., Pa. Tourette Syndrome Assn. (sec./treas., bd. dirs. 1984-92), Zelienople Hist. Soc. (life), Harmony Hist. Assn. (life), Western Pa. Geneaol. Soc., Nat. Cory Soc. (sec.), 99th Inf. Divsn. Checkerboard (assoc.), Kappa Delta Pi. Home: PO Box 447 Greensburg PA 15601-0447 Office: Westmoreland Intermediate Unit RD # 12 Box 205 Donohue Rd Greensburg PA 15601

ANDERSON, LINDA LEE, oncology nurse; b. Alpena, Mich., May 10, 1957; d. Roy James and Celia Jeanette (Swartzinski) A. ADN, Lake Superior State U., Sault Ste. Marie, Mich., 1977; BSN, Wayne State U., 1980; MS, U. Mich., 1988. Oncology cert. nurse, Oncology Nursing Certification Corp. Staff nurse Alpena Gen. Hosp., 1977-79, U. Mich. Med. Ctr., Ann Arbor, 1980-81, Catherine McAuley Health Ctr., Ann Arbor, 1981-89; case mgr. Harper Hosp., Detroit Med. Ctr., Detroit, 1989-91; clin. nurse specialist McLaren Regional Med. Ctr., Flint, Mich., 1991-93; case mgr. Harper Hosp., Detroit Med. Ctr., Detroit, 1993—. Mem. ANA, Oncology Nursing Soc. (sec. Detroit chpt. 1994—), Ann Arbor Ski Club, Ann Arbor Bicycle Touring Soc., Am. Youth Hostels. Democrat. Roman Catholic. Home: 21455 Green Hill Rd Apt 182 Farmington Hills MI 48335 Office: Harper Hosp 3990 John R Detroit MI 48201

ANDERSON, LISA ANNE, oncology and hematology nurse; b. Crowley, La., Oct. 2, 1960; d. Jefferson Davis and Peggy Jean (Phillips) A. BS in Nursing, Med. Coll. Ga., Augusta, 1984. Cert. oncology nurse. Nursing asst. burn unit Talmadge Mem. Hosp., Augusta, 1982-84; staff nurse oncology Cobb Hosp. and Med. Ctr., Austell, Ga., 1984-88; staff nurse gastrointestinal lab. Cobb Gen. Hosp., Austell, 1988-92; nurse oncology, hematology St. Joseph's Hosp., Atlanta, 1992-93; staff nurse hematology and oncology St. John Hosp., Nassau Bay, Tex., 1993-94; preoperative assessment nurse Cobb Hosp., Austell, Ga., 1994—. Lt. Nurse Corps, USNR, 1990—. Mem. Clin. Oncology Assn. Ga., Oncology Nurses Soc., Naval Res. Assn. (v.p. jr. officers), Navy League, Naval Order U.S. Home: 1003 Augusta Dr Marietta GA 30067-8208

ANDERSON, LISA MARIE, religious organization executive; b. Vallejo, Calif., Feb. 18, 1964; d. Jerome William Dotter and Hisako Ueno McCarty; m. Steven Gail Anderson, aug. 1, 1987; 1 child, Mikayla Iame'. BBA in Acctg., Pacific Luth. U., Tacoma, Wash., 1986. Acct. Arthur Anderson, Seattle, 1986; bank examiner FDIC, San Francisco, 1986-89; control system analyst PACCAR, Bellevue, Wash., 1989-91; contr. Presbyn. Ministries, Inc., Seattle, 1990, CFO, 1990—; pvt. practice acctg. mem. NAFE, Nat. Soc. Pub. Accts. Office: Presbyterian Ministries 16300 Christensen Rd Ste 203 Seattle WA 98188-3418

ANDERSON, LORNA KATHRYN, government official; b. Harrisonville, Mo., May 9, 1942; d. Loran Francis and Mary Louise (Russell) Honley; m. Thomas Jerald Anderson, Mar. 5, 1962; children: Jerome William, Benjamin Joseph. Student, Cen. Mo. State U., 1960-62, postgrad., 1976-79; BA summa cum laude, U. No. Colo., 1972, postgrad., 1972; MPA, U. Mo., Kansas City, 1989. Dep. Cass County Recorder of Deeds, Harrisonville, 1966-68; coordinator abstract dept. Stewart Title Co., Greeley, Colo., 1972-73; benefit authorizer Social Security Adminstrn., Kansas City, Mo., 1973-77, recovery reviewer, 1977-80, claims authorizer, 1980-88, asst. module mgr. Mid-Am. Program Svc. Ctr., 1988-93, staff asst., 1993-94, module mgr., 1994—; asst. coordinator women's issues Local 1336 Am. Fedn. Govt. Employees, Kansas City, 1985-88. Mem. Community Coll. Support com., Blue Springs, Mo., 1984; dist. chmn. Am. Cancer Soc., Independence, Mo., 1982; committeewoman Dem. Ctrl. Com., Weld County, Colo., 1972; pres. Dem. Women's Club, Harrisonville, 1968; bd. dirs. 5th Congl. Dist. Dem. Women's Club, Kansas City, 1968. Mem. AAUW (v.p. Independence br. 1981-83, pres. 1983-85), Mensa, Mo. Fedn. Wome's Clubs, Sigma Sigma Sigma. Democrat. Home: 3924 Crackerneck Rd Independence MO 64055-3925 Office: Social Security Adminstrn Mid-Am Program Svc Ctr 601 E 12th St Kansas City MO 64106-2808

ANDERSON, MARCIA KAY, physical education educator; b. Waterloo, Iowa, Oct. 21, 1950; d. Amos Theodore and Barbara Louise (Gravatt) A. BS, Upper Iowa Coll., 1972; MS, Ind. U., 1980; PhD, U. Iowa, 1991. Lic. athletic trainer, Mass. Tchr. phys. edn., coach Jessup (Iowa) Community Schs., 1972-73, North Fayette Community Schs., West Union, Iowa, 1973-78; instr. sports emergency care Ind. U., Bloomington, 1979-80; prof. phys. edn., dir. athletic tng. program Bridgewater (Mass.) State Coll., 1981—, mem. president's coun. on women's issues, 1990—; textbook cons., reviewer Times Mirror/Mosby Coll. Pub., St. Louis, 1984-91; women's athletic trainer U.S. Tennis Assn., N.Y.C., 1985-88. Author: Instructor's Manual for Modern Principles in Athletic Training, 1986, 7th edit., 1990, Sports Injury Management, 1995; contbg. author: Essentials in Athletic Training, 1991, Current Issues in Athletic Training, 1995. Mem. statewide comprehensive injury prevention program Mass. Dept. Health, 1985-88; chmn. affirmative action coun. Mass. State Coll., 1986-88. Recipient Disting. Svc. award in edn. Bridgewater State Coll., 1987, profl. devel. grantee, 1984, 85, 90. Mem. AAHPERD, Nat. Athletic Trainers Assn. (cert.), Mass. AAHPERD (exec. com. 1992—, sports medicine cons. 1992—, Honor award 1993), Ea. Athletic Trainers, Athletic Trainers Mass. (spkr.'s bur. 1983—, treas. 1985-86), Mass. State Coll. Assn. (v.p. and grievance officer 1993—), Women's Inst. Sport and Edn. Found. (chair exec. bd. 1993—). Democrat. Office: Bridgewater State Coll Park Ave Bridgewater MA 02325

ANDERSON, MARGARET ALLYN, carpet showroom manager; b. Meeker, Okla., Aug. 1, 1922; d. Edgar Allen and Maggie May (Smith) Martin; m. Ralph Carlos Huffman, Dec. 23, 1939 (div. Dec. 1954); children: Ronald Carlos, Darrell Duane; m. Walter Monroe Anderson, June 4, 1956. Student, San Antonio Jr. Coll., 1950-51. Clk. stenographer Sinclair Oil Co., Tulsa, 1947-48; clk. stenographer to sec. U.S. Govt. Civil Svc., San Antonio, 1948-55, Wiesbaden, Germany, 1956, Denver, 1956-57, Boise, Idaho, 1957-64; co-owner, sec./treas. Anthane, Inc., Boise, Idaho, 1964-87; co-owner, showroom mgr., sec. Anthane, Inc., San Francisco, 1987—. Mem. Am. Bus. Womens Assn. Democrat. Mem. Christian Ch. Office: Anthane Inc 6 S Linden Ave # 10 South San Francisco CA 94080-6408

ANDERSON, MARILYN JOAN, guidance director; b. Denver, Oct. 21, 1935; d. Richard Walter and Dorothy Lela (Clark) Whinnerah; m. Edwin Knowles Anderson, Feb. 12, 1961; children: Kevin Knowles, Cynthia Elizabeth Anderson Schouker. BA, U. Colo., 1958; MA, San Jose State U., 1968. Cert. pupil pers. svcs. grades K-14, Calif.; cert. secondary tchr. life time credential, Calif.; cert. counselor, Va. Tchr. grade 8 M.H. Stanley Intermediate, Lafayette, Calif., 1958-61; sch. psychologist Monroe County, Fla., 1968-69; adjustment counselor Rogers High Sch., Newport, R.I., 1969-70; psychol. examiner Windward Oahu Sch. Dist., Kaneohe, Hawaii, 1970-75; ednl. diagnostician Tri-Svcs. Ctr. for Learning Disabled Student, Chevy Chase, Md., 1978-79; tchr. grades 2 & 3 Shirley Lantham Elem. Sch., Atsugi, Japan, 1980-82; dir. rsch. Tri-Svcs. Ctr., Chevy Chase, 1983-84; counseling psychologist Family Svcs. Ctr./NATO Base, Keflavik, Iceland, 1985-86; guidance dir. George Mason Middle & High Sch., Falls Church, Va., 1987—. Mem. NEA, Va. Tchrs. Orgn., Nat. Assn. Coll. Admissions Counselors, Potomac and Cheseapeke Assn. Coll. Admissions Counselors, Am. Counselors Assn., Va. Counselors Assn., Falls Church Tchrs. Assn. Office: George Mason High Sch 7124 Leesburg Pike Falls Church VA 22043-2364

ANDERSON, MARTHA ALENE, safety and security executive; b. Monessen, Pa., June 15, 1945; d. Jesse Lee and Helen Frances (Daugherty) Cain; m. James O. Anderson, Sept. 9, 1966; 1 child, Heather Linn. BS in Biology, U. Calif. of Pa., 1967. Rsch. asst. W.Va. U., Morgantown, 1967-72; tchr. Hokkaido Internat. Sch., Sapporo, Japan, 1972-73; research asst. Pa. State U., 1974-75, Trudeau Inst., 1975-76; research assoc. U. Ariz., Tucson, 1976-80; mgr. chem. waste Dept. Risk Mgmt., U. Ariz., Tucson, 1980-81, asst. dir., 1981-85, dir., 1985-87; dir. environ. health and safety Thomas Jefferson U., Phila., 1987-90, asst. v.p. for safety and security, 1990—; chmn. Phila. Local Emergency Planning Com. Named Woman of Yr., Tucson Bus. and Profl. Women, 1985, Woman on Move, Tucson YWCA, 1985. Mem. Am. Soc. Hosp. Engrs., Bus. and Profl. Women, Campus Safety Assn. Avocations: Japanese literature, sewing. Office: Thomas Jefferson U Edison 1630 Philadelphia PA 19107-5233

ANDERSON, MARTHA ANN, laboratory coordinator; b. Panama City, Fla., Jan. 21, 1950; d. James Harvey and Mallie Alice (Wright) Cothran; m. Robert Charles Peterson, May 30, 1968 (div. 1987); children: Jeffrey Alvin Peterson, Laura Ann Peterson. Attended, Owen Brown Cardiac Ultrasound, 1986, 91, 94, St. Joseph Heart Inst., Tampa, Fla., 1990, Hewlett Packard Ultrasound, Atlanta, 1993. Cardiovascular tech. Univ. Med. Ctr., Montgomery, Ala., 1979-82, East Montgomery (Ala.) Med. Ctr., 1986-94; chief EEG tech. Ala. Neurol. Clinic, Montgomery, 1982-85; coord. physiologic lab. Am. Mobile Imaging, Montgomery, 1994—. Mem. Am. Soc. Electroencephalographic Techs., Am. Cardiol. Techs. Assn., Ala. Electroencephalographic Soc. Democrat. Mem. Ch. of Christ. Home: 3632 Honeysuckle Rd Montgomery AL 36109

ANDERSON, MARTHA JEAN, media specialist; b. Greenville, S.C., May 15, 1946; d. Benjamin Mason and Gladys (Harling) A. BS, Appalachian State U., Boone, N.C., 1968; M.Librarianship, Emory U., Atlanta, 1974, D.A.S.L., 1983. Libr. Arlington Schs., Atlanta, 1968-70, Archer Public High Sch., Atlanta, 1970-74; media specialist Woodmont High Sch. Greenville County Sch. Dist., Piedmont, S.C., 1974-76; media specialist Berea High Sch. Greenville County Sch. Dist., Greenville, S.C., 1976-80; media specialist Hillcrest High Sch. Greenville County Sch. Dist., Simpsonville, S.C., 1980—. Recipient Citation award S.C. Occupational Info. Coord. Com., 1988. Mem. NEA, S.C. Assn. Sch. Librs., S.C. Edn. Assn., Greenville County Edn. Assn., Rotary, Iowa Alpha Delta Kappa (historian 1978-80, 88-90, 92-94, v.p. 1980-82, pres. 1982-84, 94-96, sgt.-at-arms 1990-92). Methodist. Home: 537 Harrison Bridge Rd Simpsonville SC 29680-7004 Office: Hillcrest High Sch 3665 S Industrial Dr Simpsonville SC 29681-9171

ANDERSON, MARY HELEN STEED, volunteer; b. Pitts., July 24, 1914; d. Arthur Whitten and Helen Vincent (McKee) Steed; m. Townsend Canfield Anderson, Apr. 03, 1939 (dec. Feb. 1987). AB in Speech, Miami U., Oxford, Ohio, 1936. Elder Merritt Island Presbyn. Ch., mem. permanent jud. com. Fla. Synod, mem. com. on ministry St. Johns Presbytery, 1972-80; sustainer Jr. League, Cocoa-Titusville, 1974—; mem. bd. Brevard Symphony Orch., 1988-90; vice chmn. adv. bd. Salvation Army, Cocoa, Fla., 1978—; chmn. adv. bd. Domestic Violence Shelter, Cocoa, 1988—; bd. past pres. Brevard Parliamentary Law Unit, 1981-82, 88-89, Ctrl. Brevard Guild, Brevard Symphony, 1978-90; pres. Brevard Mus. Guild, 1990-92, 94—. Named Woman of Yr. Panhellenic and Orlando Sentinel, 1971, Citizen of Yr. Kiwanis Club of Merritt Island, 1981, Historic Woman of Brevard, Brevard Cultural Alliance, 1991. Mem. AAUW (bd. dirs. 1974—), Merritt Island Woman's Club (past pres. 1969-70, 87-88, Woman of Achievement 1989), Phi Beta Kappa. Home: 55 Alhambra Dr Merritt Island FL 32952-5029

ANDERSON, MARY JANE, public library director; b. Des Moines, Jan. 23, 1935; d. William Kenneth and Margaret Louise (Snider) McPherson; m. Charles Robert Anderson, Oct. 21, 1965 (div. Oct. 24, 1989); 1 child, Mary Margaret. B.A. in Edn., U. Fla., 1957; MLS, Fla. State U., 1963. Elem. sch. librarian Dade County Schs., Miami, Fla., 1957-61; children's/young adult librarian Santa Fe Regional Library, Gainesville, Fla., 1961-63; br. librarian Jacksonville (Fla.) Pub. Library, 1963-64, chief of children's services, 1964-66, head of circulation, 1966-67; pub. library cons. Fla. State Library, Tallahassee, 1967-70; dir. tech. processing St. Mary's Coll. of Md., St. Mary's City, 1970-72; coordinator children's services Balt. County Pub. Library, Towson, Md., 1972-73; exec. dir. young adult services div. ALA, Chgo., 1973-75, exec. dir. assn. for library service to children, 1973-82; pres. Answers Unltd., Inc., Deerfield, Ill., 1982-92; dir. Wilmington (Ill.) Pub. Libr., 1993—; instr. and cons. in field; part-time faculty No. Ill. U., 1985-86, Nat. Coll. Edn., Evanston, Ill., 1989; head youth svcs. Waukegan (Ill.) Pub. Libr., 1988-93; mem. exec. com. U.S. sect. Internat. Bd. on Books for Young People, 1973-82; mem. adv. bd. Reading Rainbow, TV series, 1981-84; mem. sch. bd. Avoca Sch. Dist. 37, 1985-87; mem. ALSC Newbery Medal Com., 1991. Editor: Top of the News, 1971-73, Fla. State Library Newsletter, 1967-70, Nor'Easter (North Suburban Library System Newsletter), 1984-88; contbr. articles to profl. jours. Bd. dirs. Child Devel. Assocs. Consortium, 1975-83, Coalition for Children and Youth, 1978-80; mem. exec. bd. NSLS Youth Librs., 1991-93, Diocesan Coun. Episcopal Diocese Chgo., 1988-94, Standing Com., 1994—. Mem. ALA (coun. 1992—), Ill. Library Assn., Rotary (sec./treas. Island City chpt. 1994—), Beta Phi Mu, Sigma Kappa. Episcopalian. Office: Wilmington Pub Libr 201 S Kankakee St Wilmington IL 60481-1338

ANDERSON, MARY LOU, educator; b. Mt. Pleasant, Iowa, Aug. 29, 1949; d. Carl Marion and Hazel Lucile (Mitchell) A. BS in Edn., Northeast Mo. State U., 1971, MS in Elem. Guidance, 1974. Cert. elem. tchr., Mo. Elem. tchr. Waynesville pub. schs., Mo., 1971-73, Hannibal pub. schs., Mo., 1973-79, Bel Ridge Elem. Sch., St. Louis, 1979-86; counselor Bel Ridge Elem. Sch., 1986-87, Lincoln Elem. Sch., 1987-91, Sappington Elem. Sch., 1991—; ERA cons. ERAm., Washington, 1980-81, NEA, Washington, 1980-82; state conf. workshop leader NEA, 1979-83; co-founder, chmn. Mo. NEA Women's Caucus, 1975-78. Pres. Mo. ERA Coalition, 1980-82; pres. Polit. Action Com. St. Louis Women's Polit. Caucus, 1984-85, endorsement com. chair, 1987; campaign worker Mo. Dem. Orgn., 1982—; leader parenting workshop, 1990—; supt. goal setting task force Normandy Sch. Dist., 1988-89; mem. Conf. on Edn.; trustee Mo. Pub. Sch. Retirement System, 1992—. Mem. NEA (LEAST discipline cons. 1981—, Lorna Bottger Polit. Action award 1982, facilitator beginning tchr. network 1991—), ACLU, ASCD, ACA, Mo. Edn. Assn., St. Louis Suburban Tchrs. Assn. (bd. dirs. 1983-87), Normandy Tchrs. Assn. (chmn. pub. rels. com. 1980-81, chmn. profl. rights and responsibilities com. 1981-83, chmn. instrn. and profl. devel. com. 1987-89, negotians com. 1985-89), Mo. Sch. Counselors Assn., St. Louis Suburban Counselors Assn., Confluence (St. Louis chpt., pub. edn., econ. devel. com. 1990-91), Phi Delta Kappa (sec. 1990-91, v.p. programs 1991-92, membership 1992-93). Mem. United Ch. of Christ. Avocations: playing piano, aerobics, reading, plays and movies. Home: 4497 Pershing Ave Apt 107 Saint Louis MO 63108-2527 Office: Sappington Elem Sch 11011 Gravois Rd Saint Louis MO 63126-3601

ANDERSON, MARY LUCILLE, lawyer; b. Houston, July 23, 1967; d. William Leland and Carol Ann (Casseb) A. BA, Washington & Lee U., 1989, postgrad. in law, 1992—; cert., N.Y. Studio Sch., 1992. Legal asst. White and Case, N.Y.C., 1989-92; rsch. asst. Washington & Lee Sch. of Law, Lexington, Va., 1993. Choir mem. St. Patrick's Ch., Lexington, 1993-94, St. Patrick's Cathedral, N.Y., 1989. Mem. Kappa Alpha Theta (scholarship chmn. 1989), Phi Beta Kappa, Phi Eta Sigma. Roman Catholic.

ANDERSON, MARY SEXTON GRAYSON, school counselor, consultant; b. Saltville, Va., Apr. 17, 1921; d. John Tate and Nannie Lou (Altice) Grayson; m. Francis Sidney Anderson, Jr., July 12, 1944; children: Patricia Josephine, Maude Ellen, Mary Sidney. BA in Edn., Radford (Va.) Coll., 1942; MEd, Ga. State U., 1970, EdS, 1972. Nat. cert. counselor; lic. profl. counselor, Ga.; ordained ruling elder Presbyn. Ch., 1976. Tchr. Bristol (Va.) Sch. Bd., 1942-44, The Napsonian Sch., Atlanta, 1944-45, Newton County Sch. Bd., Porterdale, Ga., 1950-52, 56-57, The Westminster Schs., Inc., Atlanta, 1960-68; counselor, psychometrist The Westminster Schs., Inc., 1968-90; cons. Decatur, Ga., 1990—; missionary, tchr. The Presbyn. Ch., Lavras, Brazil, 1945-47; sec., v.p., pres. Secondary Sch. Rsch. Program, Inc., Boston, 1971-80; bd. judges Columbia Scholastic Press Assn., 1969-87. Contbr. articles to profl. jours. Recipient Columbia Gold Key award Columbia Scholastic Press Assn., N.Y.C., 1973, Disting. Svc. in Ind. Edn. award GAIS, Atlanta, 1985. Mem. ACA, Assn. Psychol. Type, Am. Sch. Counselors Assn., Leafmore-Creek Park Community Club.

ANDERSON, MARY THERESA, investment manager; b. Flushing, N.Y., Mar. 30, 1945; d. William John and Loretta (Lent) Donovan; m. Anders Franklin Anderson, Oct. 4, 1964; children: Krista J., A. Erik. BS magna cum laude, So. Oreg. State Coll., 1981. Dir. sales and mktg. Riverside Conf. Ctr., Grants Pass, Oreg., 1981-82; sales mgr. Ashland (Oreg.) Hills Inn, 1982-84; fin. cons. Prudential Ins. Co., Portland, Oreg., 1984-87; investment counselor Vancouver (Wash.) Fed. Savs. Bank, 1987-89; fin. svcs. counselor United Brokerage Svcs. Inc., Lawrenceville, N.J., 1990; fin. svcs. assoc. United Jersey Bank, Hackensack, N.J., 1990-92, asst. v.p., mgr., 1992—; cons. Pegnato Cons. Group Internat., Nutley, N.J., 1993—. Vol. Josephine County Welfare Office, Grants Pass. Named Most Valuable Producer Mktg. One Inc., 1988. Mem. NAFE, Nat. Life Underwriters Assn.

ANDERSON, MURIEL, guitarist, composer; b. Downers Grove, Ill., June 17, 1960; d. Thomas Theodore and Andrea Mae (Jacobson) Anderson; m. Michael V. Kurtz, June 17, 1984. B.Music, DePaul U., Chgo., 1982. Guitarist, co-founder Wildwood Pickers Bluegrass Band, Chgo., 1976-82; guitarist Old Town Jazz Ensemble, Chgo., 1977-79; guitarist, co-founder Chgo. Guitar Duo, Elmhurst, Ill., 1982-90; touring artist Towers Entertainment, Nashville, 1992—; prodr. Glenn Yarbrough CD for Folk Era Records, 1994; instr. guitar Joliet (Ill.) Jr. Coll., 1990-91, Coll. of DuPage, Glen Ellyn, Ill., 1989-91, Old Town Sch. of Folk Music, Chgo., 1979-92, Wheaton (Ill.) Coll., 1992—, Elmhurst Coll., 1993—; performer/educator Internat. Music Found., Chgo., 1983—. Author: (instrnl. book) Chord Constellations, 1991, (book/CD/video) Building Guitar Arrangements from the Ground Up, 1993; columnist Acoustic Performer mag., 1991-92, Acoustic Guitar mag., 1993—, Classical Guitar mag., 1993, Fingerstyle Guitar mag., 1994—; recording artist (CD/cassette) Hometown Live!, Heartstrings, Arioso From Paris; composer title track for albums: Ultra Violet, Read My Heart to Me, Say Hello to a Friend. Gibson Guitars artist-clinician. DePaul Competitive scholar, Galvin Scholarship Fund, 1976. Mem. Am. Fedn. Musicians, ASCAP. Soc. Friends. Office: Muriel Anderson/CGD Music PO Box 168 Elmhurst IL 60126-0168

ANDERSON, NANCI LOUISE, computer analyst; b. Lynchburg, Va., Sept. 21, 1944; d. Ashby Littleton and Louise Elvin (Kirby) Marsh; 1 child, Toni Lynn Nelson. AAS in Computer Sci., Ctrl. Tex. Coll., 1983, AAS in Microcomputer Tech., 1985. Real estate salesperson Blake Isley Real Estate, Lynchburg, Va., 1974; sec. U.S. Army, Germany, 1975-80; office mgr. Am. Solar Energy Soc., Killeen, Tex., 1981-82; programmer BDM, West Fort Hood, Tex., 1982-87; analyst, programmer PRC, Inc., West Fort Hood, Tex., 1987—. Mem. Clipper User's Group. Home: 101 S Twin Creek Dr Apt 2001 Killeen TX 76543 Office: PRC Inc Texcom Data Ctr W Fort Hood TX 76544

ANDERSON, NANCY ANN, real estate company executive; b. St. Louis, July 22, 1953; d. Lawrence E. and Maryanne (Borgmann) Page; m. David L. Anderson, May 10, 1985 (div. May 1990). Grad. high sch., Chesterfield, Mo. Sec. City & Vill. Tax Office, Bridgeton, Mo., 1971-72; instr., mgr. Mademoiselle Fitness Club, Creve Coeur, Mo., 1972-74; manicurist Nails by Farrar, Frontenac, Mo., 1974-76; sales assoc. Carl Stifel Real Estate, Chesterfield, 1976-80, Gundaker Better Homes & Gardens, St. Charles, Mo., 1980-86; asst. mgr. Gundaker Better Homes & Gardens, St. Peters, Mo., 1986-87; dir. career devel. Gundaker Better Homes & Gardens, Maryland Hts., Mo., 1987—; master class faculty, speaker Better Homes & Gardens R.E., Des Moines, 1990-93. Ill. Grad. Realty Inst. faculty Ill. Assn. Realtors, 1992. Mem. Nat. Assn. Realtors, Am. Speakers Assn., St. Charles County Bd. Realtors (Realtor Assoc. of Yr. 1984). Republican. Home: 1610 Forest Hills Dr Saint Charles MO 63303-3504 Office: Gundaker Better Homes & Gardens 2458 Old Dorsett Rd Ste 300 Maryland Hts MO 63043-2423

ANDERSON, NANCY DIXON, librarian; b. Clarkesville, Ga., Oct. 7, 1938; d. Sherman Allen and Willie Mae (Black) Dixon; m. David Morris Anderson, Nov. 23, 1958 (div. June 1978); children: Wendy, Laurie, David Jr. BS in Mid. Grades Edn., Brenau Coll., 1981; MEd in Ednl. Media, U. Ga., 1985. Asst. prof. humanities, libr. Brenau Coll., Gainesville, Ga., 1979-87; also acad. tutor Learning Disability Ctr., 1985-87; head libr. Hightower Libr. Gordon Coll., Barnesville, Ga., 1987—. Children's ch. dir. 1st Presbyn. Ch., Gainesville, 1983-87; v.p. Friends of Libr., Barnesville/Lamar County, 1991; pres. Newcomers Club, Gainesville, 1974, Phoenix Soc., Ga. Fedn. Women's Club, Gainesville, 1978; pub. chmn. Barnesville Women's League, 1992-94; pres. Barnesville Garden Club, 1992; mem. Community Svcs. Bd., Barnesville, 1994—. Mem. Ga. Libr. Assn., Ctr. Ga. Associated Librs. Consortium (pres. 1992-93). Home: 236 Harrell Cir Barnesville GA 30204 Office: Gordon Coll Hightower Libr 419 College Dr Barnesville GA 30204

ANDERSON, NANCY ELAINE, home economics educator; b. Chgo., Feb. 11, 1941; d. Ralph Daniel and Ruth Louise (Johanson) A. BS, So. Ill. U., 1963; postgrad., Mich. State U., 1966-67; Cert. of Advanced Grad. Studies, Am. Internat. Coll., 1994; MEd, Springfield Coll., 1980. Cert. tchr., Mass. Tchr. home econs. and spl. edn. Hennepin (Ill.) Sch., 1963-65; tchr. home econs. East Jordan (Mich.) Sch., 1965-67, Tech. High Sch., Springfield, Mass., 1967-68, Chicopee (Mass.) High Sch., 1968—; tchr. adult edn. Bobbin Shop Fabric Store, South Hadley, Mass., 1982-94. Mem. nat. edn. bd. Covenant Ch. Women's Group, Chgo., 1986-89; edn. bd. Springfield Covenant Ch., 1970-73, mission bd., 1981-87, fin. bd., 1987-90. Mem. NEA, Mass. Edn. Assn., Chicopee Edn. Assn. Home: 113 Fuller Rd Chicopee MA 01020-3726 Office: Chicopee High Sch 650 Front St Chicopee MA 01013-3198

ANDERSON, NANCY MARIE GREENWOOD, special education educator; b. Roanoke, Va., Aug. 19, 1944; d. John Reese and Alice T. (Powell) Greenwood; m. Samuel Edward Anderson, Apr. 30, 1960; children: Sheryl L. Anderson Wicklund, Samuel Edward Jr., Donna M. BS, SUNY, Auburn, 1988; postgrad., SUNY, Oswego, 1989-90, SUNY, Geneseo, 1991-92. Cert. spl. edn., elem. edn. K-6, N.Y. Libr., dir. Wolcott (N.Y.) Civic Free Libr., 1977-89; spl. edn. tchr. North Rose Wolcott Mid. Sch., 1990—. Mem. Nat. Fedn. Bus. and Profl. Women (chair issues mgmt. 1990), N.Y. State Assn. Tchrs. Handicapped, Rose Bus. and Profl. Womens Club (pres. 1993—), Oswego Reading Coun., Whole Lang. Tchrs. Assn., Coun. for Exceptional Children. Home: 14640 Lake St Sterling NY 13156-9533 Office: North Rose Wolcott Mid Sch New Hartford St Wolcott NY 14590

ANDERSON, PAMELA O., legislative staff member, lawyer; b. Phila., Jan. 13, 1963; d. Kenneth Richard and Priscilla (Barrett) A. BA, Purdue U., 1985; JD, Seton Hall U., 1990. Mgmt. trainee Mellon-PSFS, Phila., 1985-86; legal asst. Office of Atty. Gen., Trenton, N.J., 1986-87; law clk. McCarter & English, Newark, 1988-89; summer assoc. Hill Wallack, Princeton, N.J., 1989; law sec. Judge McGann - Chancery Div., Freehold, N.J., 1990-91; rsch. assoc. N.J. Senate, Trenton, 1992—. Vol. Willingboro (N.J.) Reps., 1991—, Burlington County (N.J.) Reps., 1991—. Mem. ABA, Nat. Bar Assn., N.J. Bar Assn., Phi Alpha Delta. Home: 28 Hepburn Ln Willingboro NJ 08046 Office: New Jersey Senate CN 099 State House Trenton NJ 08625

ANDERSON, PATRICIA FRANCIS, librarian; b. Ames, Iowa, Oct. 20, 1956; d. Arthur Raymond and Rose Ann (Cooper) Anderson; m. Patrick Henry Veninga, Apr. 27, 1991; 2 children: Zera Esther Ruth Anderson, Luke Robert Morris Veninga. BS, Iowa State U., 1979; M in Info. and Libr. Sci., U. Mich., 1987. Libr. assoc. Engring Librs. U. Mich., Ann Arbor, 1985-87; media libr. Galter Health Sci. Libr. Northwestern U., Chgo., 1987—. Recipient Wallace H. Bonk award U. Mich., 1987, Beta Phi Mu Essay award, 1987. Mem. Am. Soc. for Info. Sci. (Nat. Student Paper award 1986), Health Scis. Comms. Assn. (biomed. librs. interest group sec. 1992-93), Med. Libr. Assn. (Rittenhouse award 1989), Feminist Writers Guild (bd. dirs. 1990-93, newsletter editor 1990—). Democrat. Roman Catholic. Office: Northwestern U Galter Libr 303 E Chicago Ave Chicago IL 60611-3008

ANDERSON, PAULINE HARRIET, library consultant; b. Broadalbin, N.Y., Nov. 27, 1918; d. Donald and Bertha (Brooks) A. BA, Keuka Coll., 1939; BLS, NYU, 1943. Libr. Abbot Acad., Andover, Mass., 1945-50; dir. Andrew Mellon Libr. Choate Rosemary Hall, Wallingford, Conn., 1950-73, sch. libr. cons., 1963—, dir. of ednl. devel., 1973-83, holder of the Leinbach chair, 1981-83; pres. bd. mgrs. Wallingford Pub. Libr., 1979-82. Author: The Library in the Independent School, 1968, Library Media Leadership in Academic Secondary Schools, 1985, Planning School Library Media Facilities, 1990; contbr. articles to profl. jours. Archivist First Presbyn. Ch., Broadalbin, 1983—; mem. Kennyetto Hist. Soc., Broadalbin, 1987—; sec. bd. dirs. Amsterdam (N.Y.) Free Pub. Libr., 1991—. Braitmayer fellow Nat. Assn. Ind. Schs., 1966-67. Mem. ALA, AAUW, Assn. Ind. Sch. Librs., Internat. Sch. Libr. Assn., Soc. Sch. Librs. Internat., N.Y. State Libr. Assn., English Speaking Union. Home: 71 N Main St Broadalbin NY 12025

ANDERSON, PEGGY REES, accountant; b. Casper, Wyo., Sept. 8, 1958; d. John William and Pauline Marie (Harris) Rees; m. Steven R. Anderson, May 26, 1984 (div. Sept. 1990). BS in Acctg. with honors, U. Wyo., 1980. CPA. Audit staff to sr. Price Watershouse, Denver, 1980-84; asst. contr. to contr. Am. Investments, Denver, 1984-88; cons. ADI Residential, Denver, 1988-89; contr., treas. Plante Properties, Inc., Denver, 1989-92; acctg. mgr. Woodward-Clyde Group, Inc., Denver, 1992—. Recipient diving scholarship U. Wyo., 1976-77, 77-78. Mem. Colo. Soc. CPAs. Roman Catholic. Office: Woodward-Clyde Group Inc 4582 S Ulster St # 600 Denver CO 80237

ANDERSON, PHILLIPA LOIS, lawyer, clothing store owner; b. Charleston, S.C., Sept. 21, 1951; d. Louis Pierce and Sarah Lee (Johnson) A. BA, Newcomb Coll., Tulane U., 1973; JD, George Washington U., 1976. Bar: S.C. 1976. Atty. Westinghouse Hanford Corp., Richland, Wash., 1976-78; contract analyst Westinghouse Electric Corp., Pitts., 1978-80; staff atty. Gen. Svcs. Adminstrn. Bd. Contract Appeals, Washington, 1980-82; sr. trial atty. Office of Gen. Counsel, Dept. Vet. Affairs, Washington, 1982-88, dep. asst. gen. counsel, 1988—; owner phillipa's, African-Inspired Fashions, 1991—; lectr. Dept. Justice, Legal Edn. Inst., Washington, 1989—. Featured designer 17th and 18th Ann. Congl. Black Caucus Spouses Fashion Shows, Essence mag. Bd. dirs. D.C.-Dakar Capital Cities Friendship Coun., Washington, 1993-94. Mem. ABA (vice chair constrn. claims com. pub. contract law sect. 1994—), Bd. Contract Appeals Bar Assn., Am. Arbitration Assn. (panel of arbitrators 1994—). Democrat. Mem. African Methodist Episcopal Ch. Home: 320 14th Pl NE Washington DC 20002 Office: Dept Vets Affairs Office of Gen Counsel 810 Vermont Ave NW Washington DC 20420

ANDERSON, RACHAEL KELLER, library administrator; b. N.Y.C., Jan. 15, 1938; d. Harry and Sarah Keller; m. Alexander M. Goldstein (dec.); m. Paul J. Anderson; 1 child, Rebecca. A.B., Barnard Coll., 1959; M.S., Columbia U., 1960. Librarian CCNY, 1960-62; librarian Mt. Sinai Med. Ctr., N.Y.C., 1964-73, dir. library, 1973-79; dir. Health Scis Libr. Columbia U., N.Y.C., 1979-91, acting v.p., univ. libr., 1982; dir. Ariz. Health Scis. Libr., U. Ariz., Tucson, 1991—; bd. dirs. Med. Library Ctr. of N.Y., N.Y.C., 1983-91; mem. biomed. library rev. com. Nat. Library Medicine, Bethesda, Md., 1984-88, chmn., 1987-88; mem. bd. regents Nat. Libr. Medicine, 1990-94, chmn., 1993-94. Contbr. articles to profl. jours. Mem. Med. Library Assn. (bd. dirs. 1983-86), Assn. Acad. Health Scis. Library Dirs. (bd. dirs. 1983-86, pres. 1991-92). Office: Ariz Health Scis Libr 1501 N Campbell Ave Tucson AZ 85724-0001

ANDERSON, ROBERTA JOAN See MITCHELL, JONI

ANDERSON, ROSE MARIE FILLIPIH, dietitian; b. Pitts., Mar. 26, 1966; d. Jacob Anthony Jr. and Rose Marie (Paladino) Fillipih; m. Gregg Quinn Anderson, June 8, 1991. BS in Dietetics, Seton Hill Coll., 1988; postgrad., Chgo. Med. Sch., 1993-95. Registered dietitian. Clin. dietitian Trident Regional Med. Ctr., Charleston, S.C., 1988-90, cardiac rehabilitation dietitian, 1990—. Editor: (newsletter) Beat Goes On, 1990-94; Co-author: Johnson & Wales Cookbook, 1991; contbr. articles to local newspaper. Mem. Am. Heart Assn. (bd. dirs., nutrition chair 1990—), S.C. Dietetic Assn., Low Country Nutrition Coun. (sec. 1991-94), Charleston-Trident Dietetic Assn., Mended Hearts (hosp. rep. 1991—, Red Rose award 1993). Roman Catholic. Home: 3 Fitzroy Dr Charleston SC 29414-7331 Office: Trident Regional Med Ctr 9330 Medical Plaza Dr Charleston SC 29406-9195

ANDERSON, RUTH CARRINGTON, retired secondary school educator; b. Lake Hopatcong, N.J., Jan. 7, 1915; d. Harry Porter and Mary Lamberetta (Cook) Carrington; m. Lee Silas Anderson, Nov. 9, 1942 (dec. Dec. 1972); children: Lawrence Lee, Lynette G. Anderson Esposito, Leslie Carl. BA in English, Iowa State Tchrs. Coll., 1938; MS in Edn. and English, Western Ill. U., 1970; postgrad., U. Iowa, 1954, U. Ill., 1958. Cert. elem. tchr., Ill. Tchr. rural schs. Henry County, Ill., 1933-36; jr. high sch. tchr. Woodhull (Ill.) Grade Sch., 1936-42; interviewer U.S. Employment Svc., Galesburg, Ill., 1942-44; English, lit. and govt. tchr. Geneseo (Ill.) Jr. High Sch., 1952-76; ret., 1976; speaker in field; sr. svcs. planning com. Hammond Henry Hosp., Geneseo, Ill., 1992-93; co-chmn. tchr. welfare com. Geneseo Community Unit Dist. 228, 1975-76. Mem. Western Ill. Sr. Advocacy Coun., Kewanee, Ill., 1988-94, Rock Island Sr. Coun., 1988-94, Henry County Farm Bur.; pres Henry County Sr. Advocacy Coun., Geneseo, 1987-94, chmn. pub. info. meetings and programs, 1987-94, moderator Ill. legis. candidate forum, 1992; sec.-treas. Andover, Ill. Sr. Citizens, 1989—; mem. Henry County Sr. Citizens Bd., Kewanee, 1993—; del. to Ill. Conf. on Aging, Springfield, 1990; bd. dirs. Augustana Luth. Ch., Andover, 1989-95, chmn. congl. learning com.; edn. chmn. Augustana Luth. Ch. Women, 1985, mem. peace circle, 1965—; pianist United Meth. Ch., Woodhull, 1931-42; active Evang. Luth. Ch. Women. Mem. DAR, Ill. Ret. Tchrs. Assn. (life, legis. com. 1989-92), Am. Assn. Ret. Persons, Nat. Ret. Tchrs. Assn., Andover Hist. Assn. (life), Am. Legion Aux. (1st v.p. 1979—, pres. 1976-79), U. No. Iowa Alumni Assn., We. Ill. U. Alumni Assn., Kappa Delta Pi, Sigma Tau Delta. Home: PO Box 137 507 5th St Andover IL 61233-0137

ANDERSON, RUTH LUCILLE, interior designer, educator, artist; b. Cyprus Hills, N.Y.; d. Arthur Albert and Marie Rose (Weston) Buehler; grad. N.Y. Sch. Applied Design for Women (Pratt Inst.), N.Y. Sch. Interior Design; B.A., Adelphi U., 1979, M.A., 1981, postgrad. NYU, Nat. Acad. Sch. Fine Arts, 1987; m. Gunnar Bohlin Anderson, June 22, 1946; children: Anna Kristine Kornblatt, Deborah Val. Fabric cons. F. Schumacher & Co., N.Y.C., 1954-60; sr. interior designer W&J Sloane, N.Y.C., 1960-83; adj. assoc. prof. Nassau Community Coll., 1979—, Adelphi U., 1980; instr. Hofstra U., 1990—; mem. faculty Parson (New Sch.), 1980-81; lectr. in field. Mem. Nat. Trust for Historic Preservation. Recipient Spl. participation award Open Door Program N.Y.C.; named Partner in Edn. N.Y.C. Pub. Schs., 1991-92. Mem. Am. Soc. Interior Designers (profl. mem. 1976), Internat. Furnishings and Design Assn., Internat. Platform Assn. Paintings and sculptures exhibited at W&J Sloane, Cold Spring Harbor, Oyster Bat Cove, Adelphi U. and 75 Varick St., N.Y.C., Garden City and Cold Spring Harbor Gallery, 1993. Home: 127 2nd St Garden City NY 11530-5929

ANDERSON, SANDRA FLORENCE, publishing executive; b. Chgo., Sept. 23, 1948; d. Theodore Budnik and Florence (Lehman) Eggert. BS in Edn., No. Ill. U., 1971; MBA with honors, Lake Forest Coll., 1989. Programmer Allstate Ins. Co., Northbrook, Ill., 1972-74; programming supr. Allstate Ins. Co., Northbrook, 1974-75; bus. systems analyst Abbott Labs., N. Chgo., Ill., 1975-78; credit support mgr. Trans Union Credit Info. Co., Chgo., 1978-79, product mgr., 1979-82; cons., pvt. practice Chgo., 1982-84; mgr. order completion Scott, Foresman & Co., Glenview, Ill., 1984-85; dir. customer support svcs. Scott, Foresman & Co., Glenview, 1985-88, dir. planning, client svcs., 1988-92; prin. bus. cons.-sales Landis & Gyr Powers, Buffalo Grove, Ill., 1993—. Mem. fin. bd. St. Edna's Ch., Arlington Heights, Ill. Mem. Internat. Customer Svcs. Assn., Sales Automation Assn., Am. Soc. Quality Control. Office: Landis & Gyr Powers 1000 Deerfield Pkwy Buffalo Grove IL 60089

ANDERSON, SANDRA M., manufacturing executive; b. Houston, May 1, 1943; d. Vincent Theodore Marek and Marie (Seppa) Morris; m. Michael G. Weiss, Feb. 20, 1983; children from a previous marriage: James C., Jennifer Anderson McGuire, Tracey Anderson Meinecke. BS in Acctg. and Fin., U. Tex., Dallas, 1977. CPA, Tex. Fin. analyst Collins Radio/Rockwell Internat., Dallas, 1977; corp. internal auditor RSR Corp., Dallas, 1977-80, mgr. internal audit, 1980-83, mgr. corp. acctg., 1983-85, corp. contr., 1985-92, v.p., CFO, 1992—. Block capt., chair com. Lake Highlands Sq. Homeowners Assn., Dallas, 1991-92, chmn. new residents, 1993-94. Mem. AICPA, Tex. Soc. CPA, Inst. Mgmt. Accts. (coun. contr.), U. Tex. Dallas Alumni Assn. (vol. 1983—, mem. exec. com. bd. 1994—, treas. 1995—). Office: RSR Corp 2777 Stemmons Fwy Ste 1800 Dallas TX 75207

ANDERSON, SHARON ANNE, gas company executive, financial reporting manager; d. DeWayne C. and Edith (Walker) A. BSBA, U. Tulsa, 1977. CPA, Okla. With Okla. Natural Gas Co., Tulsa, 1965—, asst. mgr. corp. responsibility and community affairs, 1979-80, asst. mgr. fin. reporting, 1980-83, mgr. fin. reporting, 1983—. Mem. Skiatook Reservoir Authority, Tulsa, 1980-84. Mem. AICPA, Okla. Soc. CPA's, LWV (pres. Met. Tulsa chpt. 1991-92, treas. Okla. 1990-93), Toastmasters. Office: Okla Natural Gas Co 100 W 5th St Tulsa OK 74103-4240

ANDERSON, SHERRY RUTH, psychologist; b. Phila., Nov. 25, 1942; d. Milton and Frances (Shotz) A; m. Paul H. Ray. BA, Goucher Coll., 1964; MA, U. Toronto, 1966, PhD, 1970. Lic. psychologist. Head psychol. rsch. Clarke Inst. of Psychiatry, Toronto, 1969-80; asst. to assoc. prof. dept. psychiatry U. Toronto Med. Sch., 1969-80; producer, host CJRT, CKEY, CBC Radio, 1980-83; pvt. practice psychology San Rafael, Mountain View, Calif., 1989—; cons. Nat. Inst. Mental Health, 1976-80. Author: Crazy Talk, 1980, The Feminine Face of God, 1991. Founder, bd. chair Women's Counseling and Referral Svc., Toronto, 1975-80; bd. dirs. Rape Crisis Ctr., 1977-78, Three Mountain Found., Lone/Pine, Calif., 1982-83. Home and Office: 242 Locust Ave San Rafael CA 94901-2241

ANDERSON, SUSAN STUEBING, business equipment company executive; b. Cin., Nov. 7, 1951; d. Edward Norman and Ruth Marcella Stuebing; m. Randall Anderson, 1988. B.A., Western Ky. U., 1973, M.A., 1975. Legis. aide U.S. Ho. of Reps., 1975-80; legis. cons. Harvard U., 1981; spl. asst. Nat. Telecommunications and Info. Adminstrn.-U.S. Dept. Commerce, Washington, 1981, dept. asst. sec., 1982-85, acting asst. sec. for communications and info., 1983; dir. Computer and Bus. Equipment Mfrs. Assn., Washington, 1985-86; mgr. govt. affairs Xerox Corp., Washington, 1987-92; mgr. Office of the Corp. Sec., Stamford, Conn., 1992—; U.S. rep. Gen. Assembley-Atlantic Treaty Assn., Funchal, Madeira, 1980. Presbyterian. Office: Xerox Corp 800 Long Ridge Rd Stamford CT 06904

ANDERSON, TERESA DIANE, health education educator; b. Mobile, Ala., Nov. 16, 1953; d. Clarence Neal and Hanna (Janke) A. BS in Med. Tech., U. South Ala., 1976; Specialist in Blood Bank Tech., Alton Ochsner Med. Found., New Orleans, 1979. Cert. med. tech., transfusion medicine specialist. Blood bank tech. Providence Hosp., Mobile, 1976-78; blood bank techl and SBB student Alton Ochsner Med. Found., New Orleans, 1978-79, dir. program for specialist in blood bank tech., 1981—, dir. blood bank quality assessment and edn., 1992—; blood bank tech. Tex. Children's Hosp., Houston, 1979-80, The Meth. Hosp., Houston, 1980-81. Contbg. author: Neonatal Testing and Component Therapy, 1984, A Grass Roots Approach to Blood Banking, 1985, Transfusion Therapy From Donor to Patient, 1992: author: (manual) Blood Transfusion Manual, 1987. EdZOOcator Audubon Zoo, New Orleans, 1982—; vol. Ochsner Healthcare Facility/The World's Fair, New Orleans, 1984. Vol. of Month, City of New Orleans, 1987. Mem. Am. Assn. Blood Banks, South Cen. Assn. Blood Banks (Larry L. Trow Edn. award 1990), Am. Soc. Med. Tech., La. State Soc. Med. Tech., Greater New Orleans Antibody Club (sec., pres. 1983-86), Friends of Audubon Zoo. Home: 6965 Argonne Blvd New Orleans LA 70124

ANDERSON, VALERIE LEE, educator; b. Worcester, Mass., Dec. 9, 1955; d. John Willard and Shirley Anne (Enman) A. BS summa cum laude, Worcester State Coll., 1977, MEd summa cum laude, 1983, postgrad., 1987; EdD, Calif. Coast U., 1992. Cert. elem. tchr., prin., supt., Mass. Tchr. elem. grades Worcester Pub. Schs., 1977-80; resource tchr. high sch. Northbridge Pub. Schs., Whitinsville, Mass., 1980-81; supr. grade sch. programs Kindercare Learning Ctrs., Inc., Westboro, Mass., 1981-83; reading tchr. Millbury (Mass.) Pub. Schs., 1983-87, 89—, tchr. 3rd grade, 1987-88, tchr. 1st grade, 1988-89. Mem. Internat. Reading Assn., Mass. Reading Assn., Cen. Mass. Reading Coun. (rec. sec. 1985-87, 92-93, pres. 1993—), Kappa delta Pi (treas.). Methodist. Home: 11 Ash St Spencer MA 01562-2246

ANDERSON, VERNA LAVELL, secretarial service professional; b. Franklin, Tex., Mar. 28, 1933; d. Edd and Pallie Mae (Kizzee) Ballard; m. Robert Lee Mills Sr., Apr. 27, 1957 (div. Feb. 1964); 1 child, Robert Lee Jr.; m. Clarence Anderson, Oct. 14, 1968. BS in Bus. Edn., Tex. So. U., 1957, MS in Adminstrn. and Supervision, 1967. Tchr. Houston (Tex.) Ind. Sch. Dist., 1959-80; owner Andersons Secretarial Svc., Houston, 1983—; mem. tutorial staff Gethsemane Bapt. Ch., Houston, 1983-85; co-sponsor spl. edn. program, 1991-93; typist Houston-Harris County Ret. Tchrs. Assn. Ann. Yearbook, 1991-92. Editor Block Club newsletter. Mem. Pleasantville Civic League, Houston, 1980-93, Pleasantville Block Club, Houston, 1985-93; mem. affirmative action divsn. City of Houston for Minority and Women in Bus.; mem. Parents of Retarded of Tex., Nat. Psoraiss Found.; mem. Houston Edn. Bd., asst. sec. Named Outstanding Elem. Tchr. of Am., 1975; recipient Cert. of Appreciation Houston Ind. Sch. Dist., Cert. of Merit, Bd. Dirs. Houston Ind. Sch. Affirmation Action Program for Minority and Women in Bus. Mem. Am. Assn. Ret. Persons. Home and Office: 8645 Fannette St Houston TX 77029-3322

ANDERSON, VIOLET HENSON, artist, educator; b. June 8, 1931; m. Charles A. Anderson, 1953. Grad., U. Tenn., Knoxville. Tchr. art Oak Ridge (Tenn.) Sch. System, 1953-54, Andrew Jackson Elem. Sch., Nashville, 1969-79; originator, dir. Andrew Jackson Art Show, Old Hickory, Tenn., 1972-79. One-woman shows include Nashville Bd. Edn., 1972, Cookeville (Tenn.) Art Ctr., 1972, Tenn. Art Gallery, 1983, 88, Brentwood (Tenn.) Libr., 1991; exhibited in group shows at Falls Creek Falls State Park, Tenn., 1984, 86, Castner Knott Art Festival, Nashville, 1983-89, 90, Downtown Arts Gallery, Nashville, 1989, Dogwood Art Festival, Knoxville, 1993, 94, 95, Summer Lights Art Festival, Nashville, 1989, 92, 93, 94; also 1928 paintings and prints in pvt. and pub. collections in 38 states and 9 fgn. countries; work featured in Nashville Banner, Chattanooga Free Press, Knoxville News Sentinel, others. Named Golden Poet, World of Poetry, 1989-92; included in Best Poems of 90s and Disting. Poets of Am., 1993 Nat. Libr. Poetry, Best Poems of 95, Nat. Libr. Poetry, 1995. Mem. Tenn. Watercolor Soc., Tenn. Art League (past officer), Friends of Tenn. Art League (bd. dirs., 1st v.p.), Cumberland Art Soc., Tenn. Artists Assn., Artists Guild, Hendersonville, Nat. Women's Caucus for Art, Mid. Tenn. Com., Nat. Mus. of Women in the Arts (charter mem., slides and photos in libr. archives), Knoxville Arts Coun., Donelson-Hermitage C. of C., Stones River Woman's Club, Internat. Soc. Poets (charter mem.), Delta Zeta (past province alumnae dir.), Alpha Delta Kappa.

ANDERSON-CARMIN, CHERYL KAY, orthodontics educator; b. Osceola, Wis., Aug. 28, 1956; d. Darrell Duane and Barbara Carolyn (Paulson) Peterson; m. Paul Bradley Anderson, Aug. 12, 1978 (div. June 1986); m. Jonathan A. Carmin, Dec. 31, 1995. AA, Normandale C.C., Bloomington, Minn., 1977; BS, U. Minn., 1985, DDS, 1986; cert. in advanced grad. studies, Boston U., 1990. Intern Sch. Dental Medicine Harvard U., Boston, 1986-87; pvt. practice, Boston, 1988-90; rsch. fellow U. Tex. S.W. Med. Sch., Dallas, 1990-91, asst. prof. orthodontics, dir. orthodontics, 1991—. Bd. dirs. Life Enhancement for People, Dallas, 1993-94; sec. ch. coun. Shepherd of Life Luth. Ch., Arlington, Tex., 1993-94. Mem. ADA, Am. Assn. Orthodontists, Am. Cleft Palate Assn. Office: U Tex SW Med Sch 5323 Harry Hines Blvd Dallas TX 75235-9031

ANDERSON-KUKUK, KARIN LOUISE, administrator; b. Eldorado, Ill., Nov. 8, 1963; d. Russell Eugene and Inez Marie (Carls) A.; m. Randall Howard Cox, Nov. 14, 1987 (div. June 1993); m. James Donald, Dec. 8, 1993; stepchildren: Josh, Jason, Jamie, James. Student, Southeastern Ill. Coll., 1981-83, Western U., 1986—. Adminstrv. asst., chief fin. officer Cass. County Health Dept., Virginia, Ill., 1983-87; sec. Eldorado (Ill.) Sch. Dist., 1988-90; owner, mgr. Office Connection, Eldorado, 1990—. Active Reps. of Cass County, 1985. Lutheran. Home and office: 1425 Perkins Rd Eldorado IL 62930

ANDERSON-MANN, SHELLEY N., institutional review specialist; b. Cleve., Jan. 21, 1964; d. William Henry and Frances Louise (Anderson) Mann. AS in Computer Sci., El Centro, 1990, AA in Acctg., 1990; BS in Sociology, Paul Quinn Coll., 1992, BSBA, 1992; MSI in Interdisciplinary Study, Dallas Bapt. U.-U. Tex., Arlington, 1993. Youth supr. City of Dallas Park and Recreation, 1979-87; instnl. rev. officer U.S. Dept. Edn., 1979-87; acct. asst. Dallas County Sheriff Adult Probation Dept., Dallas, 1984-89; claims asst. Social Security Adminstrn., Dallas, 1989—; founder Shelley Anderson-Mann Computer Ctr., Paul Quinn Coll., 1992. Author: DQB Procedural Manual, 1991 (Yes award 1991), EPA Archive Manual, 1991 (Promotion award 1991). Mem. exec. bd., vol. City of Dallas Parks and Recreation; vol. Youth Village Criminal Justice, Dallas Ind. Sch. Dist., Dallas County Juvenile Assn., Youth in Action, Dallas. Recipient commendation Dallas Police Dept., 1988, Dept. of Treasury, 1988, award City of Dallas Vol. of the Dallas, 1989, Am. Disting. Women, 1990, Bronze medal for gymnastics. Mem. NAFE, NOW, Am. Mgmt. Assn. (1st place 1991), Liberty U. Charter, Student Free Enterprise (1st place 1991), Distributive Edn. Club (1st place 1991), Internat. Platform Assn. Democrat. Baptist. Home: PO Box 41247 Dallas TX 75241-0247

ANDERSON-RANDLE, VEL (RANDI), education specialist; b. Colt, Ark., Aug. 14, 1952; d. Leo and Joanna (Burrow) Anderson; m. Bobby G. Randle, May 19, 1984 (div. Aug. 1986); 1 child. BS, Lane Coll., 1974; MEd, U. Miss., 1976, U. Miss., 1978. Tchr. South Panola Consold. Schs., Batesville, Miss., 1975-77; adult basic edn. North Miss. Retardation Ctr., Oxford, Miss., 1977-78; ednl. specialist Memphis City Schs. System, 1979-87, tchr. spl. edn., 1979-87; ednl. specialist St. Francis Hosp., Memphis, 1987-93; instrnl. specialist Supt.'s Intervention/Prevention Com. San Francisco Unified Sch. Dist., 1994—. Mem. LWV, NOW, NAFE, ABWA (pub. rels. 1987—). Roman Catholic. Home: PO Box 5380 San Mateo CA 94402-0380

ANDERT-SCHMIDT, DARLENE MARY, management consultant and trainer; b. Milw., Mar. 7, 1954; d. Howard G. and Mary L. (Kutcher) Andert; m. Thomas F. Schmidt, Apr. 12, 1975; children: Trevor, Gavin. BA in Bus. Mgmt. and Communications, Alverno Coll., Milw., 1983; M in Adminstrn., Cen. Mich. U., 1993. Cert. fin. mgr.; cert. mgmt. cons. Group spl. events coord. Sears Roebuck & Co., Milw., 1968-76; pres., owner Dance in Exercise, Inc., Milw., 1980-85; security sales Prudential Bache and The Equitable, Milw., 1985-86; stockbroker Merrill Lynch, Ft. Myers, Fla., 1986-89; trainer, cons. Bus. & Industry Svcs., Ft. Myers, 1989; pres. mgmt. Concepts Mgmt., Cape Coral, Fla., 1989—; pres. mgmt. Concepts Mgmt., Cape Coral, Fla. Author: Diversity at Work, 1994. Trustee Lee County Electric Coop., Inc., 1994—. Mem. ASTD, Inst. Mgmt. Cons. (cert.). Office: PO Box 150904 Cape Coral FL 33915

ANDRAU, MAYA HEDDA, physical therapist; b. Digboi, Assam, India, Apr. 15, 1936; came to U.S., 1946; d. William Henry and Klara Irén Judit (Sima) Andrau; married, Sept. 1971 (div. July 1989); children: Francis Meher Traver, Darwin Meher Traver. BS in Phys. Therapy, Columbia U., 1958; MA in Social Anthropology, NYU, 1966. Lamaze cert. childbirth educator; lic. and registered phys. therapist. Phy. therapist Beekman-Downtown Hosp., N.Y.C., 1959-60; physiotherapist Stamford (Conn.) Hosp., 1963-64, Benedictine Hosp., Kingston, N.Y., 1966-69; pvt. practice in phys. therapy and lamaze Woodstock, N.Y., 1968-71; chief phy. therapist No. Duchess Hosp., Rhinebeck, N.Y., 1970-71; phy. therapist Waccamaw Pub. Health Dist., S.C. Dept. Health, Myrtle Beach, 1982-84; pain clinic specialist Pain Therapy Ctr. of Columbia (S.C.), Richland Meml. Hosp., 1986-87; phy. therapist Comprehensive Med. Rehab. Ctr., Conway, S.C., 1988-92; phys. therapist, instr. conditioning program Pawleys Island (S.C.) Wellness Inst., 1993; phys. therapist Total Care, Inc., 1993—; instr. phys. conditioning and therapeutic exercise courses, 1980—. Instr. Conditioning Program, Health Focus Brief for TV, 1990. Mem. Meher Spiritual Ctr., Inc., Alpha Kappa Delta. Follower of Avatar Meher Baba.

ANDRE, PAMELA Q. J., library director; b. Lewiston, Maine, Sept. 29, 1942; d. Charles Custer and Wilma (Hall) Quimby; m. Ronald E. Jensen, Dec. 26, 1966 (div. 1971); children: Stacy, Jaylyn; m. James Roch Andre, Mar. 3, 1973; 1 child, Brett. BA, U. N.H., 1964; MLS, U. Md., 1969. Computer programm U.S. Navy Dept., Washington, 1964-66; computer systems analyst Libr. Congress, Washington, 1968-81, asst. chief MARC editorial div., 1981-84; assoc. dir. for automation Nat. Agrl. Libr., USDA, Beltsville, Md., 1984-94, dir., 1994—; cons. UN FAO Hdqrs., Rome, 1989, Egyptian Nat. Agrl. Libr., Cairo, 1990. Mem. editorial bd. Libr. Hi Tech, 1989—, Internet Rsch.: Electronic Networking Applications and Policy, 1991—, Microcomputers for Information Management, 1993—; contbr. articles to jours. in field. Recipient Superior Svc. award USDA, 1990. Mem. ALA, IAALD. Office: US Delt Agriculture Nat Agrl Libr 10301 Baltimore Ave Beltsville MD 20705-2326

ANDREA, ELMA WILLIAMS, retail executive; b. Carroll County, Va.; d. Preston and Macy (Goad) Williams; m. Mario I. Andrea, Nov. 29, 1986; AB with spl. honors, George Washington U., 1953; MA in Public Adminstrn., Am. U., 1961. Asst. program dir., asst. dir. ops. WTOP, CBS-Radio and TV, 1947-51; mem. pub. relations staff George Washington U., 1951-52; registrar Washington Sch. for Secs., 1953; exec. sec. Joint Econ. Com. of U.S. Congress, 1956-59; legis. info. specialist NEA, Washington, 1960-84; asst. mgr. Gem Tree Jewelry Store, Bethesda, Md., 1984—. Bd. dirs. Edn. Assocs. Fed. Credit Union, 1973-83, pres., 1975-77; bd. dirs. Met. Area Credit Union Mgmt. Assn., 1977-82, sec., 1977-82; bd. dirs. Kenwood Beach (Md.) Citizens Assn., 1981-84. Recipient Alumni Service award George Washington U., 1970. Mem. AAUW (br. publicity chmn. 1956-59), NEA (life), Columbian Women George Washington U. (pres. 1965-67), George Washington U. Alumni Assn. (dir. 1965-67, 69-70), Edn. Writers Assn., The Jamestowne Soc., Daughter of the Am. Revolution, Gemological Inst. Am., Women's Joint Congl. Com. (chmn. 1974-76), Am. News Women's Club, Nat. Dem. Club, Twentieth Century Club, Nat. Woman's Party, Md. Free State Doll Study Club (v.p. 1993-94), United Fedn. Doll Clubs, Woman's Nat. Dem. Club, Phi Delta Gamma (chpt. pres. 1973-74, nat. conv. chmn. 1980, nat. treas. 1980-84, nat. pres. 1984-86 , trustee 1980-86, nat. bylaws 1986-92), Pi Sigma Alpha. Address: Il Bel Tramonto White Sands MD 20657

ANDREA, MARTHA MARY, art educator, artist/designer; b. Grand Rapids, Mich., Dec. 13, 1952. BFA, Colo. State U., 1975; MFA, W.Va. U., 1978. Prof. art, chair dept. fine & performing arts Colby-Sawyer Coll., New London, N.H., 1978—; designer Mesa Internat., Elkins, N.H., 1990—. Artist in intaglio/mixed media/collage/painting. Recipient artist grant N.H. State Coun. on Arts. Home: PO Box 1515 New London NH 03257

ANDREASEN, NANCY COOVER, psychiatrist, educator; d. John A. Sr. and Pauline G. Coover; children: Robin, Susan. BA summa cum laude, U. Nebr., 1958, PhD, 1963; MA, Radcliffe Coll., 1959; MD, U. Iowa, 1970. Instr. English Nebr. Wesleyan Coll., 1960-61, U. Nebr., Lincoln, 1962-63; asst. prof. English U. Iowa, Iowa City, 1963-66; resident U. Iowa, 1970-73; asst. prof. psychiatry U. Iowa, Iowa City, 1973-77, assoc. prof., 1977-81, Andrew H. Woods prof. psychiatry, 1981—, dir. Mental Health Clin. Rsch. Ctr., 1987—; sr. cons. Northwick Pk. Hosp., London, 1983; acad. visitor Maudsley Hosp., London, 1986. Author: The Broken Brain, 1984, Introductory Psychiatry Textbook, 1991; editor: Can Schizophrenia be Localized to the Brain?, 1986, Brain Imaging: Applications in Psychiatry, 1988; book forum editor: Am. Jour. Psychiatry, 1988—, dep. editor, 1989-93, editor, 1993—. Woodrow Wilson fellow, 1958-59, Fulbright fellow Oxford U., London, 1959-60. Fellow Royal Coll. Physicians Surgeons Can. (hon.), Am. Psychiat. Assn., Am. Coll. Neuropharmacologists; mem. Am. Psychopathol. Assn. (pres. 1989-90), Inst. of Medicine of NAS. Office: U Iowa Hosps & Clinics 200 Hawkins Dr Iowa City IA 52242-1009

ANDRÉ BLOCK, JANET EILEEN, women's issues consultant; b. Lowville, N.Y., May 19, 1951; d. William Joseph and Vesta Helen (Powers) André; m. Zenas Block. BS, U. Ga., 1973; MS, Ind. U., 1975. Traveling cons. Sigma Kappa Sorority, Indpls., 1973-74; ednl. assoc. N.Y. State Edn. Dept., Albany, N.Y., 1975-80; assoc. dir. career devel. NYU Grad. Bus. Sch., N.Y.C., 1980-84; prin. The Hay Group, N.Y.C., 1984-86; v.p. Drexel, Burham, Lambert, N.Y.C., 1986-90, Catalyst, N.Y.C., 1990-92; cons. women's issues Salisbury, Conn., 1992—. Bus. outreach com. Ms. Found. for Women, N.Y.C., 1989—; bd. dirs. Berkshire Taconic Cmty. Found., Salisbury, 1990—, Women's Emergency Svcs., Salisbury, 1995—. Home: PO Box 758 Salisbury CT 06068-0758

ANDRES, AVIS HAZEL, artist; b. Mpls., Feb. 26, 1928; d. Vurnen L. and Frances (Ness) Johnson; m. Richard Andres, Feb. 10, 1951; children: Mark, Peter, Max, Claire. Cert., Cleve. Sch. of Art, 1950. Freelance portrait artist, 1948—. Artist numerous commd. portraits. Recipent 1st prize for portrait Cleve. Mus. of Art, 1948, 1st prize for oil painting Canton Inst. of Art. Mem. Women in the Arts, Cleve. Inst. Art Alumni, Cleve. Mus. Art. Home: 1525 Prospect Hudson OH 44236

ANDRES, MARIE LORRAINE, rehabilitation case coordinator; b. Peoria, Ill., June 28, 1963; d. Jack William and Dolores (Campen) A. BA, Bradley U., 1984, MA, 1987. Psychotherapist Inst. Physical Medicine Rehab., Peoria, Ill., 1986-87, Psychol. Assocs., Peoria, 1988; cognitive rehab. therapist St. Vincent/New Hope, Indpls., 1988-89; cognitive rehab. therapist Rehab. Achievement Ctr., Wheeling, Ill., 1989-93, case coord., 1994—. Vol. Evanston (Ill.) North Shore Masters, 1989-93, BE-HIVE, Evanston, 1993—. Mem. APA, Ill. Head Injury Assn., Nat. Head Injury Assn. Office: Rehab Achievement Ctr 5150 Capitol Dr Wheeling IL 60090

ANDRESS, CHARLOTTE FRANCES, retired social work executive; b. Birmingham, Ala., Apr. 22, 1910; d. Francis Samuel and Tommie (Daniel) A.; B.S., Birmingham-So. Coll., 1932; A.M. in Social Service Adminstrn., U. Chgo., 1943. Asst. dir. Girl Scouts U.S., Birmingham, 1932-35, exec. dir., Nashville, 1935-41; instr. Loyola U., Chgo., 1942-45; dir. U.S.O., Augusta, Ga., 1945-48; asst. dir. YWCA, Chgo., 1948-50, exec. dir., St. Louis, 1950-53; dir. group work, youth svcs. Fedn. Protestant Welfare Agys., N.Y.C., 1953-59; exec. dir. Inwood House, N.Y.C., 1959-82, exec. dir. emerita, 1982—. Chmn. adv. bd. Jefferson Park Center, 1959-65; nat. camp com. Camp Fire Girls, 1959-68; bd. dir. Social Work Vocat. Bur., 1961-66, Trail Blazer Camps, 1957-83, chmn. personnel com., 1982-83; mem. Camp Sharparoon com. N.Y.C. Mission Soc., 1960-76, mem. personnel com., 1962-66; active adv. bd. social welfare Meth. Ch., 1958-63; mem. United Meth. Bd. Missions, 1964-72; bd. dir. Bethel Meth. Home, 1965-72, sec. bd., 1966-72; women's com. Japan Internat. Christian U. Found., 1969-88, exec. com., 1983-88; adv. bd. Isabella Thoburn Coll., 1967-75; chmn. nat. com. Wesleyan Service Guild, 1970-72; trustee Christ United Meth. Ch., 1975-84; trustee Martha Mertz Found., 1979—, sec., 1981—, v.p., 1983—; bd. United Meth. City Soc., 1980-86. Named Disting. Alumna Birmingham So. Coll., 1981; recipient Spl. Recognition award Trail Blazer Camp, 1989. Cert. social worker, N.Y. Mem. Nat. Assn. Social Workers (sec. bd. N.Y.C. chpt. 1958-60, chmn. personnel standards and practices 1960-69, 73-74), Acad. Cert. Social Workers, Nat. Conf. on Social Welfare, Bethany Deaconess Soc. (bd. dir. 1971-93, sec. 1974-76, pres. 1976-93), Internat. Conf. Social Welfare, N.Y. Deaconess Assn. (bd. dir. 1969-93, sec. 1971-93), Soc. Women Geographers, Gamma Phi Beta. Democrat. Club: Cosmopolitan. Home: 3030 Park Ave Bridgeport CT 06604-1138

ANDRESS, KATHRYN MARIE, pharmacist; b. Niskayuna, N.Y., Apr. 8, 1963; d. Otto George and Marlene Ann (Cooper) A. BS in Pharmacy, Albany Coll. Pharmacy, 1986. Registered pharmacist. Supervising pharmacist Brooks Drugs, Albany, 1986-88; pharmacist Fays Drugs, Glenville, N.Y., 1988-93, Am. Assn. Ret. Persons, Schenectady, N.Y., 1993—.

ANDRESS, LUCRETIA ANN KING, health care exectutive; b. Durham, N.C., May 10, 1942; d. James Thomas and Gladys Virginia (Burgamy) King; m. Wayne Edward Andress, Aug. 26, 1961 (div. June 1979); children: Kevin Edward Andress, Jason Thomas Andress. BSBA, Tampa Coll., 1994. Br. mgr. Trust Co. Bank, Atlanta, 1974-81; dir. lending coord. Barnett Bank of Polk County, Fla., 1981-89; br. mgr. First Fla. Bank, Polk County, 1989-91; mktg. dir. Olsten Healthcare Svcs., Lakeland, Fla., 1991-93; field devel. rep. First Am. Home Care, Winter Haven, Fla., 1994—; bd. dir. Polk County Assn. for Handicapped Citizens, Inc., Lakeland, Olsten Healthcare, Lakeland. Bd. dirs. Am. Heart Assn., Lakeland, Ret. Sr. Vol. Program, Lakeland, Spouse Abuse Coun., Polk County, Resource Ctr. for Women, Polk County; mem. Polk Hardy Highland AIDS Svc. and Edn., client svcs. com.; mem. Polk County Aging Svcs., Polk County Cmty. Svcs. Coun., United Way of Ctrl. Fla., Sr. Orphans of Polk County; host task force Lakeland Ch., of Commerce. Recipient Membership award United Way of Ctrl. Fla., 1991. Mem. Sertoma, C. of C., Winter Haven C. of C. (amb.). Democrat. Episcopalian. Home: 865 S Oakwood Loop Bartow FL 33830-7042

ANDREW, KAREN JEAN, social worker; b. Sioux City, Iowa, Jan. 25, 1955; d. Malcolm W. and Beverly Ann (Toner) Brodie; m. Michael Kirk Andrew, June 12, 1976; children: Emilee Jean, Ellyn Marie, Robert Glenn. BS in Child Devel., Iowa State U., 1977; postgrad., Drake U., 1981-91. Cert. in handicapped edn. Svc. worker Mainstream Living, Ames, Iowa, 1976-77; Washington County HeadStart coord. HaCap Community Action Agy., Cedar Rapids, Iowa, 1981-87; social worker, child protection and adoption specialist State of Iowa, Washington, 1987—. Active YWCA, Washington, 1986-89, pres., 1988-89. Mem. AAUW (edn. chair, pres. 1988-89, membership co-chair 1992-94). Roman Catholic. Home: 523 W Washington St Washington IA 52353-1639

ANDREWS, ALICE FRENCH, neonatologist educator; b. Alma, Mich., June 22, 1948; d. Lloyd Henry and Gladys (Schneider) French; m. Charles Andrew Andrews, July 15, 1972; children: Rebecca Kirstin, Kimberly Rose. BA, Messiah Coll., 1970; MD, U. Mich., 1974. Asst. prof. pediatrics U. Mich., Ann Arbor, 1983-85; with staff Macha Hospital, Zambia, 1986-88; neonatologist Blodgett Meml. Med. Ctr., Grand Rapids Neonatology, Grand Rapids, Mich., 1988—. Contbr. articles to profl. jours. Mem. Brethren in Christ Ch. Office: Grand Rapids Neonatology 1840 Wealthy SE Grand Rapids MI 49506

ANDREWS, BARBARA PARKER, librarian; b. Nantucket, Mass., Mar. 18, 1918; d. James S. and Elizabeth H. (Parker) A.; B.S., Simmons Coll., 1944. Cataloguer, U. Cin. Library, 1944-46; with descriptive cataloguing div. Library of Congress, Washington, 1946-65, adminstrv. asst., 1950-63, research asst., 1963-65; librarian Nantucket Atheneum, 1965-92, libr. emerita, 1992—. Mem. ALA, Nantucket Hist. Assn., Maria Mitchell Assn. Home: 1 E York St Nantucket MA 02554-3816 Office: Nantucket Atheneum India St Nantucket MA 02554

ANDREWS, BETHLEHEM KOTTES, research chemist; b. New Orleans, Sept. 18, 1936; d. George Leonidas and Anna Mercedes (Russell) Kottes; B.A. with honors in Chemistry, Newcomb Coll., Tulane U., 1957; m. William Edward Andrews, May 9, 1959 (dec.); children—Sharon Leslie, Keith Edward. Chemist wash wear investigation, So. Regional Research Center, Sci. and Edn. Adminstrn., Dept. Agr., New Orleans, 1958-63, research chemist wash wear investigation, cotton textile chemistry lab., 1968-70, research chemist spl. products research, cotton textile chemistry lab., 1976-83, sr. research chemist cotton chem. reactions research, 1983-85, lead scientist textile finishing chemistry research, 1985—; scientist-supr. Grace King High Sch. Lab. Tech. Tng. Program; U.S. del. ISO Meeting on Textiles, 1984—, head U.S. Delegation, 1992. Recipient outstanding professionalism citation New Orleans Fedn. Businessman's Assn., 1977, Disting. Service award in med./sci. category, 1983, named Women of Yr. award in profl. category, 1978; recipient Profl. Excellence award Ita Sigma Pi, 1990, Miles award Cotton Found., 1991, Tech. Transfer award USDA-ARS, 1992; La. Heart Assn. grantee, 1957. Mem. Am. Chem. Soc., Am. Assn. Textile Chemists and Colorists (v.p. 1990, 91, exec. com. on research, Olney medal 1992), Fiber Soc., Phi Beta Kappa, Sigma Xi, Phi Mu. Democrat. Greek Orthodox. Clubs: P.E.O., Southern Yacht. Contbr. chpts. to books, articles to sci. jours.; patentee. Office: So Regional Rsch Ctr 1100 Robert E Lee Blvd New Orleans LA 70124

ANDREWS, GLORIA MAXINE, fundraiser; b. Cleve., Feb. 23, 1927; d. George Charles and Isabel Maxine (Bryden) Sternad; m. J. Melvin Andrews, July 15, 1950; children: Charles Melvin, Scott Michael, Countess Judith De Maleissye Melun. Student, San Miguel de Allende, Mex., 1947, Queen's U., Kingston, Ont., Can., 1948; BFA, Ohio Wesleyan U., 1949. Pres., trustee Lake County (Ohio) Hist. Soc., 1965-85; trustee Old Mentor (Ohio) Found., 1970's, Lawnfield Civic Com., 1988—; v.p. bd. trustees Western Res. Hist. Soc., Cleve., 1980; hist. tour guide Lantern Ct. Holden Arboretum, Lake County, 1970—, bd. dirs., 1989; pres. adv. com. Lake Erie Coll., Plainesville, Ohio, 1980-87, Lakeland Coll. Found.; foreman Lake County Grand Jury, 1969. Recipient Liberty Bell award Lake County Bar Assn., 1980. Republican. Episcopalian. Home and Office: Echo Hill 8188 Garfield Rd Mentor OH 44060-5931

ANDREWS, JESSICA LOUISE, performing arts company executive; b. London, Oct. 7, 1943. Grad. h.s. Mng. dir. Ind. Repertory Theatre, Hartford Stage Co., The Shakespeare Theatre, Washington; dir. theatre divsn. FEDAPT; cons. Nat. Endowment for Arts Advancement Program-Round II, Bush Found., St. Paul; dir., site reporter Nat. Endowment for Arts Theater Program; reader Fund for New Plays; guest faculty Ind. U., Purdue U. Indpls., theatre seminar Miami U., Ohio; guest lectr. Yale Sch. Drama; mem. numerous panels including Mich. Coun. on Arts theatre panel, Nat. Theatre Artist Residency Program panel, Arts Devel. and Challenge panels Ohio Arts Coun., chair theatre adv. panel N.Y. State Coun. Arts; mem. exec. com. League of Resident Theatres; mem. exec. coun. Arts Coun. for Arts, Greater Rochester, Ind. Arts Commn.; mem. N.J. Arts Coun.; Lila Wallace-Reader's Digest Resident Theatre Initiative. Recipient Ohio Theatre Alliance award for Outstanding Achievement in Theatre. Office: 141 12th St NE # 7 Washington DC 20002

ANDREWS, JUDITH ANN, social worker; b. Jackson, Mich., June 17, 1950; d. Burdette Wesley and Annabel (Shafer) A. AA in Bus. Mgmt., Jackson C.C., Mich.; BGS, U. Mich., 1982, MSW, 1984, postgrad.; postgrad., Wayne State U., Eastern Mich. U. Cert. social worker Mich., sch. social worker Mich. Social work intern Ann Arbor VA Med. Ctr., Mich., 1984; therapist Catholic Social Svcs., Adrian, Mich., 1985-86; psychiatric social worker St. Vincent Med. Ctr., Toledo, Ohio, 1986-87; contractual therapist Ann Arbor Inst., Inc, 1987-89, Huron Valley Consultation Ctr., Ann Arbor, 1989-90; mental health therapist Community Care Svcs., Belleville, Mich., 1987-92; pvt. practice Ann Arbor, 1989-92, Ypsilanti, Mich., 1992—. Vol. counselor SOS Crisis Ctr. Ypsilanti, Mich., 1980-82. Mem. Nat. Assn. Social Workers, Nat. Assn. Mentally Ill, Women in Bus., Acad. Cert. Social Workers, Soc. for the Advancement of Psychoanalysis,Mich. Psychoanalytic Inst., Detroit Inst. of Arts Founders Soc., Optimist Club of Ann Arbor.

ANDREWS, JUDY COKER, electronics company executive; b. Hot Springs, Ark., Dec. 19, 1940; d. Leon G. and Bobbie (Randles) Coker; m. William Campbell Andrews, June 27, 1961; children: Alan Campbell Andrews, Theresa Lee Andrews Mills. BSE, Henderson State U., 1961; MEd, U. N.C., 1973. Instr. math. High Point (N.C.) Coll., 1973, Greensboro (N.C.) Pub. Schs., 1974, Richland Coll., Dallas, 1974-78; systems analyst J.C. Penney Co., Dallas, 1978-80; systems analyst Texas Instruments, Dallas, 1980-83, info. ctr. mgr., 1983-85, customer svc. mgr., 1986-90, bus. devel. mgr., 1990-92; acct. mgr. Telecom Sys., Tex. Instruments, Dallas, 1993—. Inventor: system and method for securing cellular telephone access through a cellular telephone network using voice verification (pat. pending). Adult advisor Explorer Post 444, Boy Scouts Am., Richardson, Tex., 1980-82. U. N.C. fellow, 1971-73. Mem. Assn. for Systems Mgmt. (chpt. pres. 1984-85, chair internat. ann. conf. 1989, chair internat. corp. ptnr. com. 1992, Disting. Svc. award 1992). Office: Texas Instruments 6550 Chase Oaks Blvd Plano TX 75023

ANDREWS, JULIE, actress, singer; b. Walton-on-Thames, Eng., Oct. 1, 1935; d. Edward C. and Barbara Wells; m. Tony Walton, May 10, 1959 (div.); 1 dau., Emma; m. Blake Edwards, 1969. Studied with pvt. tutors, studied voice with Mme. Stiles-Allen. Debut as singer, Hippodrome, London, 1947; appeared in pantomime Cinderella, London, 1953; appearences include (Broadway prodns.) The Boy Friend, N.Y.C., 1954, My Fair Lady, 1956-60 (N.Y. Drama Critics award 1956), Camelot, 1960-62, Putting It Together, 1993, Victor/Victoria, 1995; films include Mary Poppins, 1964 (Acad. award for Best Actress 1964), The Americanization of Emily, 1964, Torn Curtain, 1966, The Sound of Music, 1966, Hawaii, 1966, Thoroughly Modern Millie, 1967, Star!, 1968, Darling Lili, 1970, The Tamarind Seed, 1973, 10, 1979, Little Miss Marker, 1980, S.O.B, 1981, Victor/Victoria, 1982, The Man Who Loved Women, 1983, That's Life!, 1986, Duet For One, 1986, A Fine Romance, 1992; TV debut in High Tor, 1956; star TV series The Julie Andrews Hour, 1972-73 (Emmy award for Best Variety Series), Julie, 1992; also spls.; TV movies include Our Sons, 1991; author: (as Julie Edwards): Mandy, 1971, The Last of the Really Great Whangdoodles, 1974; recs.: The King and I, 1992. Recipient Golden Globe award Hollywood Fgn. Press Assn., 1964, 65; named World Film Favorite (female), 1967. *

ANDREWS, JULIE ANN, sales operations manager; b. St. Charles, Ill., Apr. 6, 1960; d. Joseph Peter and Carol Marie (Oksas) Fabrizius; m. Jeffrey Lee Andrews, June 2, 1989; children: Lawrence J., Annalee M. BS in Bus., Ea. Ill U., 1982. Acct. exec. Fidelity Investments, Chgo., 1983-87; sales ops. mgr. Amoco Oil CO., Boca Raton, Fla., 1986—. Home and Office: 399 NE 3d St Boca Raton FL 33432

ANDREWS, LAUREEN E., foundation administrator; b. Seneca Falls, N.Y., July 28, 1954; d. Lawrence J. and Anita (Schmidt) A.; m. Craig T. Scherer, Oct. 4, 1983; children: Casey Alena, Lindsey Adele. BA, George Washington U., 1976; MA in Law and Diplomacy, Fletcher Sch. Law and Diplomacy, Mass., 1978. Lobbyist, editor League of Women Votersof the U.S.A., Washington, 1978-80; dir. internat. rels. League of Women Voters Edn. Fund, Washington, 1980-85; dep. dir. def. budget project Ctr. Budget & Policy Priorities, Washington, 1985—. Editor: (legis. newsletter) Report from the Hill, 1978-80. Mem. Phi Beta Kappa. Office: Def Budget Project 777 N Capitol St NE Ste 710 Washington DC 20002-4239

ANDREWS, LAVONE D., architect; b. Beaumont, Tex., Sept. 18, 1912; d. Charles and Lavone (Lowman) Dickensheets; m. Mark Edwin Andrews, July 23, 1948; 1 son, Mark Edwin III. Student, Miss Hamlin's Sch., San Francisco, Marlborough Sch., L.A.; AB, Rice Inst., 1933, BS in Architecture, 1934. Assoc. with outstanding architects in Southwest, 1934-37; opened own office Houston, 1937-41; architect firm Anderson, Clayton & Co. (cotton firm), 1941-51; v.p. Ancon Oil & Gas, Inc. Also pvt. work, museum in, Washington, Naval Hist. Found. & Health Center, schs. for City of Houston. Trustee Mus. Fine Arts in Houston; mem. YWCA World Service Council. Selected as 3d of the 10 outstanding women architects in Am. Archtl. Record, 1947. Fellow AIA, Royal Inst. Architects Ireland; mem. Pallas Athene Lit. Soc. of Rice Inst., Colony Club (N.Y.C.), Houston Club, River Oaks Country Club, Garden of Houston Club, Bayou Club, Garden of Am. Club. Episcopalian. Home: 2121 Kirby Dr # 109 Houston TX 77019 also (summer): Knappague Castle, County Clare Ireland Office: Lavone Dickensheets Andrews 2001 Kirby Dr Ste 805 Houston TX 77019-6033

ANDREWS, MARY ANN, nursing services director; b. Geneva, N.Y., Apr. 3, 1928; d. Joseph John and Catherine (Gillotte) Yannotti; m. Donald R. Andrews Sr., Mar. 28, 1947 (dec. 1989); children: Donald Jr., Michael J., Thomas C., Maryrose Arimoto. AA in Nursing, De Anza Coll., 1975; BA in Health Sci. Adminstrn., St. Mary's Coll., Morega, Calif., 1982; MPA in Health Sci. Adminstrn., U. San Francisco, 1988; Mgmt. Cert., San Jose State U., 1987. RN; cert. direct staff devel. Pharmacy Corp. Am. Asst. head nurse San Jose (Calif.) Health Ctr., 1975-82; shift supr. San Benito Hosp. Dist., Hollister, Calif., 1982-86, AMI Community Hosp., Santa Cruz, Calif., 1986-88; dir. nursing svcs. Care West Enterprises Inc., Watsonville, Calif., 1988-91; dir. nursing Hillhaven Corp., San Jose, 1991-92, Guardian Corp., San Jose, 1992-93; dir. staff devel. Empress Convalescent Hosp., San Jose, 1994—. Roman Catholic. Home: 1406 Alma Ter San Jose CA 95125

ANDREWS, ROWENA, public relations executive; b. Chattanooga, Dec. 31, 1944; d. Mose Porter and Waudie Tarvin; married, 1966 (div. 1971); 1 child, Elizabeth Paige Andrews. BA in Journalism, U. Ga., 1974. Info. specialist NASA-Cosmic, Athens, Ga., 1967-74; pub. rels. and photography freelancer Chattanooga, 1974-76; comm. specialist Providence Life Ins., Chattanooga, 1976-78; dir. pub. info. Aid United Givers, L.A., 1978-80; corp. comm. mgr. Informatics Gen. Corp., Woodland Hills, Calif., 1980-81; dir. pub. rels. Candle Corp., L.A., 1981-83; pub. rels. cons. Andrews Pub. Rels., Newnan, Ga., 1983—. Mem. Internat. Pub. Rels. Assn. Home and Office: Andrews PR 45 Ebenezer Dr Newnan GA 30265

ANDREWS, SALLY MAY, healthcare administrator; b. Westfield, Mass., Feb. 29, 1956; d. Roger N. and Dorothy M. (Goodhind) A. Student, U. Conn., 1974-76; BA, Simmons Coll., Boston, 1978; MBA, Boston U., 1986. Payroll clk. Children's Hosp., Boston, 1978-79, asst. payroll supr., 1979-81, staff analyst dept. medicine, 1981-83, asst. adminstr. dept. medicine, 1983-86, adminstr. dept. medicine, 1986—. Bd. overseers Lasell Coll., Newton, Mass. Mem. Am. Mgmt. Assn., Adminstrs. of Internal Medicine, Assn. Adminstrs. in Acad. Pediatrics. Congregationalist. Office: Children's Hosp Dept Medicine 300 Longwood Ave Boston MA 02115-5737

ANDREWS, SHIRLEY ANN, retail executive; b. Dora, Mo., Dec. 28, 1945; d. Olen Franklin Fish and Edna (Collins) Conley; m. Bill Andrews, Apr. 11, 1970 (div. 1982); children: Kevin, Billy, Kristen. Grad. high sch., St. Joseph, Mo. Office mgr. R.F. Dickson Co., Inc., Downey, Calif., 1966-73; owner, pres. Turner's Outdoorsman (formerly Andrews Sporting Goods), Orange, Calif., 1971-88, Chino, Calif., 1988—. Office: Turner's Outdoorsman 12615 Colony Ct Chino CA 91710-2975

ANDREWS, THEODORA ANNE, retired librarian, educator; b. Carroll County, Ind., Oct. 14, 1921; d. Harry Floyd and Margaret Grace (Walter) Ulrey; B.S. with distinction, Purdue U., 1953; M.S., U. Ill., 1955; m. Robert William Andrews, July 18, 1940 (div. 1946); 1 son, Martin Harry. Asst. reference libr. Purdue U., West Lafayette, Ind., 1955-56, pharmacy libr., instr., 1956-60, pharmacy libr., asst. prof., 1960-65, pharmacy libr. an, assoc. prof. libr. sci., 1965-71, prof. libr. sci., pharmacy libr., 1971-79, prof. libr. sci., pharmacy, nursing and health scis. libr., 1979-90, prof. libr. sci., spl. bibliographer, 1991-92, prof. emerita of libr. sci., 1992—. Mem. Purdue Women's Caucus, 1973—, v.p., 1975-76, pres., 1976-77; mem. Internat. Women's Yr. Regional Planning Com., 1977; del. Ind. Gov.'s Conf. Librs. and Info. Svcs., 1978. U. Ill. grad. fellow, 1954-55. Mem. Spl. Libr. Assn. (John H. Moriarty award Ind. chpt. 1972), ALA, Med. Libr. Assn., AAUP, Am. Assn. Colls. Pharmacy, Kappa Delta Pi, Delta Rho Kappa. Baptist. Author: A Bibliography of the Socioeconomic Aspects of Medicine, 1975; A Bibliography of Drug Abuse Including Alcohol and Tobacco, 1977; A Bibliography of Drug Abuse, Supplement 1977-1980, 1981; Bibliography on Herbs, Herbal Remedies and Natural Foods, 1982; Substance Abuse Materials for School Libraries, an Annotated Bibliography, 1985; Guide to the Literature of Pharmacy and the Pharmaceutical Sciences, 1986; sect. editor Advances in Alcohol and Substance Abuse, 1981-92; contbr. articles to profl. jours. Office: Purdue U Sch Pharmacy West Lafayette IN 47907

ANDROS, HAZEL LAVERNE (BRISSETTE ANDROS), prevention education educator; b. St. Louis, Sept. 25, 1939; d. Louis Albert and Catherine Virginia (Gonzalas) Brissette; divorced; 1 child, Wendy Gay; m. Nicholas James Andros, Nov. 3, 1962; 1 child, James Nicholas II. AA, Rend Lake Coll., 1976; BS, So. Ill. U., 1979, MS, 1981, PhD, 1994. Office mgr. Tractor Supply Co., Bloomington, Ill., 1969-70; sec. Ill. State U., Normal, 1970-73; office mgr. Wit and Wisdom, Benton, Ill., 1978; intern So. Ill. U., Carbondale, 1978, instr., 1979-80, office mgr., 1980-83; tchr., coord. Benton High Sch., 1984-89; instr. J.A. Logan Coll., Carterville, Ill., 1989-91; rsch. asst. So. Ill. U., Carbondale, 1991-92; ext. instr. bus. edn., adult edn., violence prevention U. Ill., Vienna, 1993—. Pres. Benton Youth Bd., 1984—, Benton Dist. Libr. Bd., 1987—, Benton Airport Bd., 1991-93. Mem. Ill. Women Adminstrs., Ill. Bus. Edn. Assn. (affiliate pres. 1987-88), Bus. and Profl. Women's Assn. (chmn. pub. rels. Benton chpt., legis. chair 1989—). Democrat. Methodist. Home: 532 E Main St Benton IL 62812-2521 Office: U Ill Coop Ext Svc PO Box 158 208 E Main Vienna IL 62995-0158

ANDRUS, DOROTHY MARIE, retired association executive; b. Columbus, Ohio, Nov. 22, 1918; d. Earl Clay and Marie Francis (Fisher) A. Student, George Williams Coll., 1944-46; BBA, U. Chgo., 1949; postgrad., NYU, 1963-64. Bus. mgr. nat. bd. dirs. YWCA U.S.A., Chgo., 1942-52; asst. to exec. dir. YWCA Cleve., 1952-56, dir. pub. rels., 1956-58; asst. exec. dir. Nat. YWCA Retirement Fund, N.Y.C., 1958-65, exec. dir., 1965-81; ret., 1981; chair seminar retirement planning for women Wharton Sch. Fin., Phila. Nat. Bank, 1975; chair Ch. Pensions Conf., 1976. Recipient Cert. of Appreciation, County of L.A., 1992. Mem. LWV (bd. dirs. 1986-93, v.p. 1986-93, Cert. of Appreciation 1993), NOW, Nat. Hemlock Soc. (local co-chair 1983-85). Democrat. Mem. United Ch. of Christ Congregationa. Home: 603 Harrison Ave Claremont CA 91711-4537

ANDRUS, THERESA KESTER, photojournalist, communications specialist; b. Manchester, Iowa, Aug. 2, 1953; d. Francis Alfred and Mary Veronica (Keegan) Kester; m. Douglas Burton Andrus, Dec. 23, 1978; children: Ian, Ross. AA in Applied Arts, Hawkeye Inst. Tech., 1975; BS summa cum laude, St. Cloud State U., 1992. Chief photographer Larson Publs., Osseo, Minn., 1978-86; reporter, photographer Monticello (Minn.) Times, 1992-94; comm. dir. Maple Lake (Minn.) Pub. Schs., 1994—; mem. Cmty. Care Adv. Bd., 1993—. Photographer: (books) Full Circle Five, 1984, A Sampler of Women, 1984, Full Circle Seven, 1986. Ctrl. Minn. Mother's March chairperson March of Dimes, St. Cloud, 1988, Porch Light Night chairperson, 1988-91; gen. coord. for Centennial Playground, Maple Lake (Minn.) Schs., 1989-90; mem. Blandin Cmty. Leadership Program, 1991-92; co-chairperson Irish Summer Fest, Maple Lake, 1992; mem. sch. bd. Maple Lake Schs., 1992-94. Recipient Maple Lake (Minn.) Disting. Svc. award, 1990, Mpls. Aquatennial Assn. Commodore's award, 1993, numerous state and nat. awards for photojournalism, 1980-95. Mem. Maple Lake (Minn.) Jaycees (v.p. for pub. rels. 1989-91, pres. 1991-92, chair bd., sec. 1993—, Jaycee of Yr. 1990). Office: Maple Lake Pub Schs 200 State Hwy 55 E Maple Lake MN 55358

ANDRUZZI, ELLEN ADAMSON, nurse, marital and family therapist; b. Colon, Panama, Dec. 15, 1917; d. Charles and Annie Isabel (Grinder) Adamson; m. Francis Victor Andruzzi, May 28, 1941; children: Barbara F., Francis C., Judith E., Antonette T., John J. BS in Pub. Health Nursing, Cath. U. Am., 1947, MS in Nursing, 1951. Cert. clin. specialist, psychiat. nurse. Pub. health nurse Washington Health Dept., 1942-44; instr. psychiat. nursing St. Elizabeth's Hosp., Washington, 1948-57; dir. nursing Glenn Dale Hosp., Md., 1961-67; chief mental health nurse dept. human resources D.C. Govt., 1967-73; cons. NIMH, HHS, Rockville, Md., 1973-81; marital and family therapist TA Assocs., Camp Springs, Md., 1973-94; assoc. GWITA, Rockville, 1975-79; instr. Charles County C.C., LaPlata, Md., 1976-78, Prince George Community Coll., Largo, Md., 1973-81; assoc. Ctr. for Study of Human Systems, Chevy Chase, Md., 1976-94; nurse psychotherapist pvt. practice. Author chpts. in books. Dist. co-capt. Prince Georgians for Glendening, Prince George County, Md., 1985-86; chmn. plan devel. com. So. Md. Health Systems Agy., Clinton, 1984-89, sec. governing body, 1978-80; chmn. Mental Health Adv. Com. Prince George County, Cheverly, Md., 1983-85; mem. Blue Ribbon Commn. on Health, Prince George's County, 1991-92; mem. Commn. Health, Prince George's County, 1992-94; mem. health com. and voter reporter League Women Voters. Recipient Disting. Nurse award St. Elizabeths Hosp., 1985, Paula Hamburger Vol. award Mental Health Assn. Md., 1985, Recognition of Service award Md. Nurses Assn., 1983, Prince Georgian of the Yr. award, 1994, Vol. award Prince George's County, 1995. Fellow Am. Acad. Nursing, Am. Orthopsychiat. Assn.; mem. Internat. Transactional Analysis Assn. (clin.), Am. Nurses Assn., World Fedn. for Mental Health, Am. Assn. for Marriage and Family Therapy (clin.), Nat. Mental Health Assn. (v.p. 1984-87, bd. dirs. 1982-87), Mental Health Assn. Prince George County (pres. 1974-76, 87-88, Vol. of Yr. award 1993), Sigma Theta Tau (Kappa chpt., Excellence in Nursing award 1984). Democrat. Roman Catholic. Avocations: theatre, ballet, swimming, foreign travel.

ANDRZEJAK-ANDRE, MARILYN KATHLEEN, electronics company official; b. Detroit, Sept. 19, 1960; d. Serge and Pauline Mary (Pawlas) A. Cert., Wayne County Community Coll., Detroit, 1980, Golden Gate U., 1983; student, Ga. State U., 1987—. Prodn. mgr. Prudential Bldg. Maintenance Co., Detroit, 1978-82; sales rep. SP Communications Sprint, Birmingham, Mich., 1981-82; sales supr. Communications Sprint, Birmingham, Mich., 1982; dist. sales mgr. GTE Sprint Communications, Birmingham, 1982-85; regional sales mgr. U.S. Sprint Communications, Sacramento, 1985-87; prin. Integrated Mktg. Solutions, N.Y.C., 1992—; project mgr. SONY Corp. Am., Park Ridge, N.J., 1993—; cons. in field. Mem. Am. Mgmt. Assn., Am. Telemktg. Assn. Jewish. Office: SONY Corp Am Md 3 D 3D # 2 Park Ridge NJ 07656

ANGEL, E. STEPHANIE, management consultant; b. San Antonio, Sept. 9, 1947; d. Robert William and Roselle (Bartlett) Cribley; m. Robert Howard Angel II, June 7, 1969 (div. 1977); 1 child, Ryan; m. James Isaac Van Liere, Aug. 11, 1981. BS in Edn. and English, Fla. State U., 1969, MS in Edn. and English, 1975. Trainer, instr. Levin Assocs., Fla. State U., Leon Country Schs., Tallahassee, 1970-79; bus. devel. mgr. Wayne H. Coloney Co., Tallahassee, 1979-80; sr. devel. rep. nat. accounts Fla. Dept. Commerce, Tallahassee, 1980-83; tng. program designer USAID, Washington, 1983; program developer Coopers & Lybrand, Washington, 1984-87, SRI Internat., Arlington, Va., 1987-89; founder, pres. Devel. Consortium, 1983-89; ptnr. Decision Processes Internat., Westport, Conn., 1990—. Office: Decision Processes Internat 10 Bay St Westport CT 06880

ANGELASTRO, JANE ELLEN, staff manager; b. N.Y.C., May 14, 1942; d. George Christian and Edna Frances (Byrnes) Schofield; m. Michael Angelo Angelastro, Jan. 21, 1967; children: Terese, Pat George, Karen. BS, Coll. of Mt. St. Vincent, 1964; MLS, L.I. U., 1985. Biochemist Merck Inst., Rahway, N.J., 1964-67; sr. libr. asst. L.I. Univ. Grad. Sch., Sparkill, N.Y., 1981-85; library dir. Halcon Rsch. div. Tex. Ea. Corp., Montvale, N.J., 1985-86; supr. AT&T Tech. Info. Ctr., White Plains, N.Y., 1986-91; asst. mgr. publicity univ. rels. and coll. recruiting AT&T, Morristown, N.J., 1991—. Officer various town and ch. youth orgns., Nanuet, 1975-85. Mem. Soc. Women Engrs. (corp. mem. conf. bd.), Southwest Placement Assn. Home: 6 Constitution Ct Montville NJ 07045-9152 Office: AT&T Univ Rels/Coll Recruiting 100 Southgate Pky Morristown NJ 07960-6441

ANGEL DAVIS, MARIA KATRINA, association director; b. Clayton, Mo., June 8, 1968; d. Ronald Ray and Shirley Jolene (Long) Angel; m. Dennis Merton Davis II, May 8, 1993. BA in History, N.E. Mo. State U., 1990; MA in Pub. History, Sangamon State U., 1992. Pub. info. officer Ill. Police Tng. Bd., Springfield, Ill., 1990-92; cultural resource planner St. Louis Devel. Corp., 1992-94; exec. dir. S.W. Garden Neighborhood Assn., St. Louis, 1994—. Bd. dirs. Christmas in April, St. Louis, 1994—; active Girl Scout Coun. Greater Sports Night, 1974—, Forest Park Master Plan Com., St. Louis, 1994. Mem. Nat. Trust Hist. Preservation, Nat. Coun. Pub. History, Am. Assn. State and Local History, Phi Alpha Theta. Office: SW Garden Neighborhood Assn 4950 Southwest Ave Saint Louis MO 63110

ANGELINE, SUSAN ANN, emergency nurse; b. Wilmington, Del., Mar. 10, 1964; d. Richard Louis and Carolyn Lorraine (Burns) Stafford; m. Alfred Paul Angeline, Nov. 6, 1987. LPN, Del Castle Tech. High Sch., 1982; BSN, U. Del., 1986; MSN in Burn, Emergency & Trauma Nursing, Widener U., 1991. Cert. instr. BLS, emergency nurse, PALS. LPN staff nurse Millcroft Retirement Home, Newark, Del., 1984-85; LPN staff nurse Christiana Hosp., Newark, 1985-86, RN staff nurse, 1986-88, RN staff nurse emergency dept., 1988—; asst. nurse mgr. emergency dept. Med. Ctr. of Del.; instr. ACLS, BLS, PALS provider, trauma nursing core provider Emergency Nurses Assn.; rschr. (with others) Do Staff Nurses Who Participate in Continuing Edn. Prefer Self-Directed or Other-Directed Methods of Learning?. Mem. Del. Nurses Assn., Emergency Nurses Assn., U. Del. Alumni Assn., Toastmasters, Sigma Theta Tau. Democrat. Roman Catholic. Home: 4 Ashleaf Ct Hockessin DE 19707 Office: Med Ctr of Del 501 W 14th St Wilmington DE 19899

ANGELINI, DIANE JEAN, nursing administrator; b. Leominster, Mass., June 18, 1948; d. Paul Peter and Anne Jean (Amorosi) A.; m. David Peter DeStefano, June 8, 1986. BSN, Fitchburg State Coll., 1971; M. Nursing, U. Pitts., 1973; cert. nurse midwife, SUNY, Bklyn., 1976; EdD, Boston U., 1992. Cert. nursing adminstrn., ANA. Asst. clin. prof. UCLA Sch. Nursing, 1977-78; staff nurse-midwife L.A. County-U. So. Calif. Med. Ctr., L.A., 1976-77, dir. nurse-midwifery svc., ednl. dir., 1978-81; clin. dir. nursing for obstetrics Danbury (Conn.) Hosp., 1982; pvt. practice nurse-midwifery Thomas M. Hanson MD, PC (affiliated with Yale-New Haven), 1983-85; asst. nursing dir. ob-gyn./neonatal nursing Brigham and Women's Hosp., Boston, 1985-90; dir. nursing edn. and devel., dir. nurse-midwifery sect. Women and Infants' Hosp., Providence, 1990—; clin. asst. prof. Brown U. Sch. of Medicine; cons., adv. editor for perinatal nursing Aspen Publs., 1986-89. Co-editor: Case Studies in Perinatal Nursing, 1992, Perinatal-Neonatal Nursing: A Clinical Handbook, 1986; editor Jour. of Perinatal-Neonatal Nursing, 1986—; contbr. articles to profl. jours. Recipient Books of the Yr. award Am. Jour. Nursing, 1986. Mem. Am. Coll. Nurse-Midwives (CNM), Am. Orgn. Nurse Execs., Nat. Nursing Staff Devel. Orgn., Sigma Theta Tau (Rsch. award Delta Upsilon chpt. 1991), Phi Delta Kappa. Home: 155 Adirondack Dr East Greenwich RI 02818 Office: Women and Infants' Hosp 101 Dudley St Providence RI 02905

ANGELL, KARLA MICHELLE, school counselor; b. Columbus, Ohio, July 4, 1963; d. Norman Dean and Patricia Jean (Kelly) A. BJ, U. Ariz., 1985; MEd, Coll. of Idaho, 1990. Lic. profl. counselor, Idaho; cert. K-12 sch. counselor, Idaho. Copy editor The Idaho Statesman, Boise, 1986-89; office mgr. Boise Care Unit, 1990-91; sch. counselor Boise Sch. Dist., 1991-92; sch. counselor McMillan Elem. Sch., Meridian Sch. Dist., Boise, 1992—; chem. dependency counselor Comp Care, Nampa, Idaho, 1991—; group facilitator, program coord. Touchstone Ctr., Boise, 1990-92; co-facilitator parent edn. classes Meridian Sch. Dist., 1993—. Tchr. religious edn. St. Paul's Cath. Ch., Boise, 1987-89. Recipient 1st place for headline writing Idaho Press Club, 1987, 2d place for headline writing Pacific N.W. Excellence in Journalism Competition, 1987. Mem. ACA, Am. Sch. Counseling Assn., Idaho Counseling Assn., Idaho Sch. Counseling Assn., Phi Beta Kappa. Office: McMillan Elem Sch 10901 McMillan Rd Boise ID 83713

ANGELL, M(ARY) FAITH, federal magistrate judge; b. Buffalo, May 7, 1938; d. San S. and Marie B. (Caboni) A.; m. Kenneth F. Carobus, Oct. 27, 1973; children: Andrew M. Carobus, Alexander P. Carobus. AB, Mt. Holyoke Coll., 1959; MSS, Bryn Mawr Coll., 1965; JD, Temple U., 1971. Bar: Pa. 1971, U.S. Dist. Ct. (ea. dist) Pa. 1971, U.S. Ct. Appeals (3rd cir.) Pa. 1974, U.S. Supreme Ct. 1979; Acad. Cert. Social Workers. Dir. social work, vol. svcs. Wills Eye Hosp., Phila., 1961-64, 65-69; dir. soc. work dept. juvenile divsn. Defender Assoc., Phila., 1969-71; asst. dist. atty. City of Phila., 1971-72; asst. atty. gen. Commonwealth of Pa., Phila., 1972-74, deputy atty. gen., 1974-78; regional counsel ICC, Phila., 1978-80, regional dir., 1980-88; administrv. law judge Social Security Administrn., Phila., 1988-90; U.S. magistrate judge Ea. Dist. Pa., Phila., 1990—; adj. prof. Temple Law Sch., Phila., 1976-94, clin. instr., 1973-76. Federal trustee Defender Assn. Phila., 1985-90; bd. dirs. Child Welfare Adv. Bd., Phila., 1984-90, Federal Cts. 200 Adv. Bd., Phila., 1987-88, Phila. Woman's Network, 1986-88. Recipient Sr. Exec. Svc. award U.S. Govt., 1980. Mem. NASW, Nat. Assn. Women Judges, Fed. Magistrate Judges Assn., Fed. Bar Assn. (chair exec. com., pres. 1990-92, recognition 1992), Phila. Bar Assn. (chmn. com. 1976-77), Temple Am. Inn of Cts. (master 1993—, co-chair commn. on gender for 3rd cir. task force on equal treatment in the cts. 1994—). Office: US District Court 4316 US Courthouse 601 Market St Philadelphia PA 19106

ANGELO, MARGARET IDA, stockbroker; b. Elizabeth, N.J., June 21, 1960; d. Ernest James and Margaret P. (Falcetano) A. BA in History, Seton Hall U., 1982. Sr. option prin., asst. v.p., correspondent liaison Richardson Greenshields Securities Inc., N.Y.C., 1984—. Mem. Met. Mus. Art, N.Y.C., 1986—, Mus. of Natural History, N.Y.C., 1986—. Mem. Securities Traders Assn., Phi Alpha Theta. Roman Catholic. Office: Richardson Greenshields 4 World Trade Ctr New York NY 10048-0204

ANGELOU, MAYA, author; b. St. Louis, Apr. 4, 1928; d. Bailey and Vivian (Baxter) Johnson; 1 son, Guy Johnson. Studied dance with, Pearl Primus, N.Y.C.; hon. degrees, Smith Coll., 1975, Mills Coll., 1975, Lawrence U., 1976. Taught modern dance The Rome Opera House and Hambina Theatre, Tel Aviv; writer-in-residence U. Kans.-Lawrence, 1970; disting. vis. prof. Wake Forest U., 1974, Wichita State U., 1974, Calif. State U.-Sacramento, 1974; apptd. mem. Am. Revolution Bicentennial Council by Pres. Ford, 1975-76; 1st Reynolds prof. Am. Studies, Wake Forest U. since 1981, a lifetime appointment. Author: I Know Why the Caged Bird Sings, 1970, Just Give Me A Cool Drink of Water 'Fore I Die, 1971, Gather Georgia, 1972, Gather Together in My Name, 1974, Oh Pray My Wings Are Gonna Fit Me Well, 1975, Singin' and Swingin' and Gettin' Merry Like Christmas, 1976, And Still I Rise, 1978, The Heart of a Woman, 1981, Shaker, Why Don't You Sing?, 1983, All God's Children Need Traveling Shoes, 1986, Now Sheba Sings the Song, 1987, I Shall Not Be Moved, 1990, On the Pulse of Morning: The Inaugural Poem, 1992, Lessons in Living, 1993, Wouldn't Take Nothing for My Journey Now, 1993, My Painted House, My Friendly Chicken, and Me, 1994; producer: Moon on a Rainbow Shawl, 1988 (by Errol John); appeared on TV in The Richard Pryor Special, author and producer Three Way Choice, Afro-American in the Arts (Golden Eagle award), in ltd. series Roots; appeared in revue Cabaret for Freedom and The Blacks (Obie award) with Godfrey Cambridge; adapted Ajax for Mark Taper Forum in L.A.; librettist, lyricist and composer And Still I Rise, 1976; wrote and presented Trying to Make it Home, 1988; writer for Oprah Winfrey's Harpo Prodns.; poetry writer for film Poetic Justice, 1993; also numerous appearances on network and local talk shows; articles, short stories, poems to Black Scholar, Chgo. Daily News, Cosmopolitan, Harper's Bazaar, Life Mag., Redbook, Sunday N.Y. Times, others. Mem. adv. bd. Women's Prison Assn.; No. Coord. So. Christian Leadership Conf.; apptd. by Pres. Ford to Bicentennal Commn., by Pres. Carter to Nat. Commn. on Observance of Internat. Women's Yr. Named Woman of Yr. in Communications, 1976; Ladies Home Jour. Top 100 Most Influential Women, 1983, The Matrix award, 1983, The North Carolina Award in Literature, 1987; named 1st Reynolds prof. Wake Forest U., 1981, a lifetime appointment, Woman of the Yr. Essence Mag., 1992, Disting. Woman of N.C., 1992; recipient Horatio Alger award, 1992; Grammy award, Best Spoken Word or Non-Traditional Album, 1994 (for recording of "On the Pulse of the Morning). Mem. AFTRA, Dirs. Guild Am., Equity, Harlem Writers Guild, Am. Film Inst. (trustee). Office: care Dave La Camera Lordly and Dame Inc 51 Church St Boston MA 02116

ANGERS, JOANN MARIE, religious education director, nurse; b. Bay City, Mich., May 19, 1944; d. Virgil H. and Marie Veronica (Nowak) Goyett; m. Theodore Leibert Angers, Feb. 6, 1965; children: Theodore Allen, Toni Marie, Terry Michael, Troy, Theresa, Tammy, Timothy. Grad., Bay City Sch. Nursing, 1964; postgrad., St. Mary's Coll., Orchard Lake, Mich., Lansing (Mich.) Community Coll.; BA in Human Resources, Spring Arbor Coll., 1994—. Lic. nurse, Mich.; cert. catechist, Mich., 1977. Nurse Bay Osteopathic Hosp., Bay City, 1964-65, physician's office, Lansing, 1966, nursing home, Lansing, 1968; coord. religious edn. Immaculate Heart of Mary, Lansing, 1968-84, dir. religious edn., 1984—; master catechist, speaker Diocese Lansing, 1968—; mem. diocesan team determining AIDS policy, Lansing, 1990. Author: My Beginning Mass Book, 1978, Meeting the Forgiving Jesus, 1984; (filmstrip) Celebrating Sunday with God's Family, 1981, (video) Amanda Goes to Mass, 1991; contbr. articles to religious publs. Tutor, Reading Coalition of Lansing. Recipient Dedicated Svc. award Diocese of Lansing, 1969-89, Pastor's Religious Edn. Award Immaculate Heart of Mary Parish, 1982, Pius X award Diocese of Lansing, 1983, Vol. Svc. award Lansing Sch. Dist., 1985-90, Children's Reading Round Table award, 1985. Mem. Profl. Pastoral Mins. Assn., Nat. Cath. Ednl. Assn. Home: 310 E Miller Rd Lansing MI 48911-5641

ANGIER, NATALIE MARIE, science journalist; b. N.Y.C., Feb. 16, 1958; d. Keith and Adele Bernice (Rosenthal) A.; m. Richard Steven Weiss, July 27, 1991. Student, U. Mich., 1974-76; BA, Barnard Coll., 1978. Staff writer Discover Mag., N.Y.C., 1980-83, Time Mag., N.Y.C., 1984-86; editor Savvy Mag., N.Y.C., 1983-84; journalism educator NYU, N.Y.C., 1987-89; became reporter N.Y. Times, N.Y.C., 1990; now science correspondent N.Y. Times, Washington. Author: Natural Obsessions, 1988. Recipient Pulitzer prize for beat reporting, 1991, Journalism award GM Ind. Bd., 1991, Lewis Thomas award Marine Biol. Labs., 1990, Journalism award AAAS, 1992, Disting. Alumna award Barnard Coll., 1993. Mem. Nat. Assn. Sci. Writers. Office: NY Times Washington Bureau 1627 I St NW 7th Fl Washington DC 20006*

ANGLE, MARGARET SUSAN, lawyer; b. Lincoln, Nebr., Feb. 20, 1948; d. John Charles and Catherine (Sellers) A. BA with distinction in Polit. Sci., U. Wis., Madison, 1970, MA in Scandinavian Studies (scholarship, NDEA fellow), 1972, JD cum laude, 1976. Bar: Wis. 1977, Minn. 1978. Law clk., Madison, Mpls., Chgo., 1974-76; law clk. U.S. Dist. Ct., Mpls., 1977-78; mem. firm Faegre & Bensen, Mpls., 1978-84; sr. atty., asst. gen. counsel, asst. sec. Nat. Car Rental System, Inc., Mpls., 1984-90; corp. sec. Car-Temps; chief exec. officer Angle & Assocs., Ltd., Eagan, Minn., 1990—, clients include Avis, Budget, Hertz, Nat. Car Rental Cos., 1990—. Note and comment editor U. Wis. Law Rev.; contbr. articles to profl. publs. Mem. ABA, Am. Car Rental Assn. (bd. dirs. 1987-90), Minn. Bar Assn., Wis. Bar Assn.,

Hennepin County Bar Assn., Alternative Dispute Resolution Com., Order of Coif. Home: 4340 Fox Ridge Ct Saint Paul MN 55122-2257 Office: Angle & Assocs Ltd 1971 Seneca Rd Ste C Eagan MN 55122-1039

ANGLEMYER, ROMA KATHLEEN, elementary school educator; b. Wakarusa, Ind., Sept. 17, 1932; d. Wayne Douglas and Evelyn Virginia (Weldy) Wyman; m. Keith Alois Anglemyer, June 10, 1956; children: Debra Anglemyer McNally, Linda Anglemyer Stolley. BE, Goshen (Ind.) Coll., 1955; MA, St. Mary's Coll., Notre Dame, Ind., 1966. Lic. real estate rep. Tchr. Bremen (Ind.) Pub. Sch., 1955-59; tchr. Wa-Nee Schs., Nappanee, Ind., 1960-93, instr. enrichment classes, 1984-86; mem. adj. faculty, instr. Bethel Coll., Mishawaka, Inc., 1993; instr. mentally handicapped Concord Schs., Elkhart, Ind., 1967; instrl. asst. Coll. of the Gifted and Talented, Ind. U., Bloomington, 1984, Kids-on-Campus, Goshen Coll., 1985. Contbr. curriculum Wa-Nee Ind. History, 1980-86. Sponsor Wakarusa 4-H Clubs Elkhart County, 1974-76; pres. Progressive Homemakers, Elkhart County, 1984-85, Searchlight Club; sch. rep. Wa-Nee Sch. Reorgn. 25th Anniversary, Nappanee, 1987; mem. steering com. Gifted and Talented Program Wa-Nee, Nappanee, 1985-86, mem. curriculum devel. team for gifted and talented Elkhart Schs., 1984-86; mem. curriculum com. Wa-Nee Drug Awareness program, 1988—. Mem. NEA, Ind. State Tchrs. Assn., Wa-Nee Tchrs. Assn. (exec. mem. 1984-85), Wakarusa Tchrs. Assn. (pres. 1981-82), Wa-Nee Tchrs. Exec. Com., Elkhart Country Reading Assn., Hoosier Assn. Sci. Tchrs., Inc., Pi Lambda Theta (membership chmn. No. Ind. 1985-87, pres. 1987-89, del., sec. Great Lakes Region II 1988-90, del. Biennial Coun. 1987, award com. 1987-89). Home: RR 1 Wakarusa IN 46573-9801

ANGOVE, DAWN ANNYCE, academic administrator; b. Gainesville, Tex., June 12, 1956; d. R. Wayne and June V. (Amoroso) Williams; m. R. Ray Angove, Jul. 31, 1982; 1 child, Tyler William. BS, Univ. North Tex., 1977, MEd, 1982, EdD, 1989. Cert. tchr., Tex. First grade tchr. Lake Dallas (Tex.) Ind. Sch. Dist., 1977-84, asst. middle sch. prin., 1984-85; elem. prin. Argyle (Tex.) Ind. Sch. Dist., 1985-88; elem. prin. Lake Dallas (Tex.) Sch. Dist., 1988-89, asst. supt., 1989—. Mem. ASCD, Tex. Assn. Sch. Adminstrs., Phi Delta Kappa, Phi Kappa Phi. Home: 1408 Hidden Oaks Cir Denton TX 76205 Office: Lake Dallas ISD PO Box 548 Lake Dallas TX 75065

ANGUIANO, LUPE, business executive; b. La Junta, Colo., Mar. 12, 1929; d. Jose and Rosario (Gonzalez) A. Student, Ventura (Calif.) Jr. Coll., 1948, Victory Noll Jr. Coll., Huntington, Ind., 1949-52, Marymount Coll., Palos Verdes, Calif., 1958-59, Calif. State U., L.A., 1965-67; M.A., Antioch-Putney-Yellow Springs, Ohio, 1978. S.W. regional dir. NAACP Legal Def. and Ednl. Fund, L.A., 1965-69; civil rights specialist HEW, Washington, 1969-73; S.W. regional dir. Nat. Coun. Cath. Bishops, Region X, San Antonio, 1973-77; pres. Nat. Women's Employment and Edn., Inc., L.A., 1979-91; pres., cons. Lupe Anguiano & Assocs., 1981—; cons. Tex. Dept. Human Resources, Dept. Labor, Women's Bur.; proposal reader U.S. Office Edn.-Women's Equity Act; mem. Tex. Adv. Coun. on Tech.-Vocat. Edn. Calif. del. White House Conf. on Status Mexican-Ams. in U.S., 1967; founding mem. policy coun. Nat. Women's Polit. Caucus, from 1971; Tex. and nat. del. Internat. Women's Year, 1976-77; chmn. Nat. Women's Polit. Caucus Welfare Reform Task Force, from 1977; co-chmn. Nat. Peace Acad. Campaign, 1977-81; founder, bd. dirs. Nat. Chicana Found., Inc., 1971-78; bd. dirs. Calif. Coun. Children and Youth, 1967, Rio Grande Fedn. Chicano Health Ctrs., S.W. Rural States, 1974-76, Women's Lobby, Washington, 1974-77, Rural Am. Women, Washington, from 1978, Small Bus. Coun. Greater San Antonio; mem. Pres.'s Coun. on Pvt. Sector Initiatives, 1983. Recipient Community award Coalition Mexican-Am. Orgns., 1967, Outstanding Svc. award Washington, 1968, Thanksgiving award Boys' Club, 1976, Outstanding Svc. award Tex. Women's Polit. Caucus, 1977, Liberty Bell award San Antonio Young Lawyers, 1981, Vista award for exceptional svc. to end poverty, 1980, Headliner award San Antonio Women in Communications, 1978, Woman of Yr. award Tex. Women's Polit. Caucus, 1978, Pres.'s Vol. Action award 1983, Leadership award Nat. Network Hispanic Women, 1989; named Outstanding Woman of Yr., L.A. County, 1972, Woman of the 80s Ms. mag., 1980; Nat. Pres.'s award Nat. Image, Inc., 1981, Wonder Woman Found. award, 1982, Pres.' Vol. Action award 1983, Adv. of Yr. San Antonio SBA, 1984; selected Am. 100 Most Important Women, Ladies Home Jour., 1988, 89; featured in CBS TV series An Am. Portrait, 1985, Leadership award Nat. Network Hispanic Women, 1989. Mem. Assn. Female Execs., Pres.'s Assn., Am. Mgmt. Assn. Republican. Roman Catholic. Author: (with others) U.S. Bilingual Education Act, 1967, Texas A.F.D.C. Employment and Education Act, 1977; manuals Women's Employment and Education Model Program.

ANJUR, SOWMYA SRIRAM, biologist, zoologist, biochemist, research scientist, educator; b. Ahmadi, Kuwait, Oct. 4, 1962; came to U.S. 1987; d. V.S. Krishna and Saraswathi (Venkitachalam) Moorthi; m. Sriram Padmanabhan Anjur, Aug. 22, 1991. BS in Biochemistry, Madras U., India, 1982; MS in Biochemistry, Bharathar U., India, 1984, MPhil in Biochemistry/Microbiology, 1986; PhD, Iowa State U., 1992. Biochemist ICCU, Modern Hosp., Salem, India, 1983-84; biochemist R&D Symbiotic Labs, Madras, India, 1984-85; chemistry lectr OCF High Sch., Madras, India, 1985-86; asst. prof. biochemistry Kongunadu Arts & Scis. Coll., Coimbatore, India, 1987; teaching asst. biology/zoology Iowa State U., Ames, 1987-92; lectr. U. Wis., Oshkosh, 1992; rsch. scientist Kimberly-Clark Corp., Neenah, Wis., 1993—; dietary cons. Hosp. Bd. Nutrition, Coimbatore, India, 1978-82; wastewater treatment cons. U. Madras, 1985-87, microbiology cons., 1984-86. Choreographer/performer solo Indian dance fundraisers: Bharathanatyam, 1979-82 (Best Dancer 1980, 81); dir. drama troupe: The Funsters, 1978-80. Group leader Nat. Adult Edn. Program, India, 1978-84; mgr. Nat. Svc. Scheme, India, 1978-84; team leader Community Social Svc. Projects, India, 1978-84; chief fundraiser Solo Bharathanatyam, 1979-82. Recipient Gold medal for proficiency Bharathiar U., India, 1984. Mem. IEEE, Soc. Engrs. in Medicine and Biology, Iowa Acad. Sci., Am. Soc. Animal Sci., Am. Dairy Sci. Assn., Soc. of Biol. Chemists (India), Am. Mensa, Gamma Sigma Delta. Home: 624 E Capitol Dr Appleton WI 54911-1209

ANNE, LOIS, artist, educator; b. Buffalo, Oct. 15, 1950; d. Raymond Stephen and Elizabeth Anne (White) Ignaczak. BFA, Alfred (N.Y.) U., 1972. Working and exhibiting artist, 1972—; arts program coord. Coastal Workshop, Camden, Maine, 1989—; tchr. privately, in pub. schs., galleries, museums and univs., 1968—. Exhibited in shows at Albright-Knox Art Gallery,1975, U. Maine at Augusta, 1977, 78, 86, 89, Wm. A. Farnsworth Art Mus., Rockland, Maine, 1980, Maine Coast Artists Gallery, Rockport, 1979, 81, 83, 90, 91, Portland (Maine) Sch. Art, 1981, 83, U. Maine at Orono, 1982, Fine Art Ctr., Taos, N.Mex., 1985, Waterville (Maine) Gallery Fine Arts, 1986, Ogunquit (Maine) Art Ctr., 1990, 94, Maine Crafts Assn., Deer Isle, 1990-94, Bensons Fibre & Wood, Camden, 1993, 94, White House, Washington, 1993, others. Mem. Maine Crafts Assn., Union of Maine Visual Artists (newsletter editor 1986-87), Mid Coast Graphic Artists Network. Studio: 407 Main St Rockland ME 04841

ANNENBERG, MARCIA, artist; b. N.Y.C., BA, CCNY, 1972; MA, NYU, 1982. Curator Color Now, N.Y.C., 1987; one-woman shows include Rockland Ctr. Holocaust Studies, 1995. Winner nat. contest Limner Gallery, 1993. Home: 148 W 68th St New York NY 10023-5803

ANNESE, BETSY JANE, public relations executive; b. Scranton, Pa., Sept. 26, 1949; d. Frank Nicholas and Ruth Elizabeth (Pillow) A. BA in Journalism, U. S.C., 1971. Reporter The (Columbia, S.C.) State, 1971-73, The (Anderson, S.C.) Ind., 1973-74; mgr. pub. rels Bigelow Carpets, Inc., Greenville, S.C., 1974-80; from sr. pub. rels. rep. to v.p. pub. affairs R. J. Reynolds Tobacco Co., Winston-Salem, N.C., 1980-94; v.p., deputy external rels. R.J. Reynolds Tobacco Internat. Inc. Bd. dirs. Family Svc., Inc., Winston-Salem, 1990—, Multiple Sclerosis Soc., Winston-Salem, 1990—, Horizons Residential Care, Inc., Winston-Salem, 1991-93, Winston-Salem Urban League, 1993—. Mem. Twin City Club (bd. dirs. 1989-93), Piedmont Club, Forsyth Country Club, Wild Dunes Beach and Racquet Club, Ad 2 Club (hon.). Office: RJ Reynolds Tobacco Internat Inc PO Box 2959 Winston Salem NC 27102-2959

ANNS, ARLENE EISERMAN, publishing company executive; b. Pearl River, N.Y.; d. Frederick Joel and Anna (Behnke) E.; student Bergen Jr. Coll., 1946-48; BS, Utah State U., 1950; postgrad. Traphagen Sch. Design, 1957, NYU, 1958, Hunter Coll., 1959-60. Rsch. and promotion asst. Archtl. Record, N.Y.C., 1952-56; asst. rsch. dir. Esquire Mag., N.Y.C., 1956-62; rsch. mgr. Am. Machinist, publ. McGraw-Hill, Inc., N.Y.C., 1962-67, mktg. svc. mgr., 1967-69, 1969-71, sales mgr., 1976-77, dir. mktg., 1977-78; v.p. mktg. svcs. Morgan-Grampian, Inc., N.Y.C., 1971-72; mktg. dir. Family Health & Diversion mag., 1972-74; dist. sales mgr. Postgrad. Medicine, 1974-76; advt. sales mgr. Contemporary Ob/Gyn, 1976-78; dir. profl. devel., 1978-80; pub. graduating engr. and dir. mktg. Aviation Week Group, 1980-90; pub. World Aviation Directory; dir. communications Aviation Week Group, 1990-92; v.p., Phase, Ltd., 1993—. Mem. Am. Mktg. Assn., Pharm. Advt. Club, Advt. Women N.Y., Advt. Club N.Y., Sales Exec. Club, Employment Mgmt. Assn., Am. Soc. Pers. Adminstrs., Nat. Orgn. Disability, Internat. Platform Assn., Coll. Placement Coun., Wings Club, Dir. Assn., Pi Sigma Alpha. Home: 2824 Brianwood Ct Quinton VA 23141-1616

ANOFF, JEAN SCHOENSTADT, advertising specialty company executive; b. Chgo., Sept. 25, 1937; d. Arthur H. and Gwendolyn M. (Straus) Schoenstadt; m. Philip R. Anoff, July 16, 1964; children: Carol Marie Jennings, Donald William, Cathy Jane. Student, Pomona Coll., Clairmont, Calif.; BA, U. Mich., 1959. Cert. Master Advt. Specialist, 1988. Legal sec. Chgo., 1958-60; v.p. H. Schoenstadt & Sons, Inc., Chgo., 1960-64; pres. Sesco, Inc., Charlotte, N.C., 1975—. Leader Jewish Family Service Task Force on Sustance Abuse, Charlotte, 1987; vol. Sr. Women's Group, Charlotte, 1987; pres. B'nai B'rith Women, Charlotte, 1970; v.p. Temple Beth'El, 1968; bd. dirs., charter mem. Temple Beth Shalom, 1971-76, Jewish Community Ctr., 1977-78; neighborhood chairperson Hornet's Nest coun. Girl Scouts of U.S., Charlotte, 1972, neighborhood cookie chair, troop leader, 1973; v.p. Young Dems., Chgo., 1958; chair Mecklenburg County (N.C.) Women's Commn. Adv. Bd., 1991-93; bd. dirs., treas. Cmty. Works, 1992—; chair bd. trustees Charlotte Summit Ho., 1994. Recipient Clio award, 1981, 82, 83, Community Service award, B'nai B'rith Internat., 1979. Mem. NAFE (charter, bd. dirs. Queen's Crown chpt. 1989, sec.-treas. 1990, hostess-chair women's commn. equality day com. 1990), Nat. Assn. Commn. for Women (sec. 1994—), Specialty Advt. Assn. Internat. (CAS/MAS alumni 1968, distbrs. com. 1991), Carolinas Assn. Advt. Specialists (mem. chmn., bd. dirs. 1992—, treas. 1995), Charlotte C. of C. (spl. events com. 1988, entertainment com. spring bus. fair 1989, chair excellence in customer svc. com. 1990, criteria com. for direct link program 1990, sec. super bd. of enterprisers 1990, edn. com. 1992—, svc. award 1989, finalist woman entrepreneur of yr. award small bus. div. 1990), Women Bus. Owners (charter, chair scholarship com. 1985-86, historian, photographer 1987-90, chair blueprint directory, 1989, bd. dirs. 1989, finalist bus. woman of yr. award 1991), Charlotte Women's Bus. Owners. Club: Women's Variety of Ill. (pres. 1962-64). Home: 1635 Cavendish Ct Charlotte NC 28211-3943 Office: Sesco Inc 5212 Monroe Rd Charlotte NC 28205-7859

ANSHAW, CAROL, writer; b. Grosse Pointe Station, Mich., Mar. 22, 1946; d. Henry G. and Virginia (Anshaw) Stanley; m. Charles J. White III, Mar. 15, 1969. BA, Mich. State U., 1968. Book reviewer, Voice Literary Supplement. Author: They Do It All With Mirrors, 1978, Aquamarine, 1992. Tutor Literacy Council of Chgo., 1989—. Recipient Nat. Book Critics Circle citation for excellence in reviewing, 1989. Mem. Nat. Book Critics Cir., Nat. Writers Council. Democrat. Office: 3959 N Lincoln Ave Rm 595 Chicago IL 60613-2433

ANSHEN, RUTH NANDA, philosopher, author; b. Plymouth, Mass., 1914. Lectr in philosophy and morality numerous univs., U.S.A., Europe, Near and Middle East; founder Anshen Seminars on Nature of Man, Columbia U.; chmn. Nature of Man seminar Columbia U., N.Y.C.; vis. philosopher Div. Sch., Harvard U., 1940-58; lectr. in field. Author: The Reality of the Devil: Evil in Man, 1980, Anatomy of Evil, 1991, Biography of an Idea, 1990, Morals, Equals, Manners, 1992, The Mystery of Consciousness A Prescription for Human Survival, 1994; founder, editor (series) World Perspectives, 54 vols., Religious Perspectives, 27 vols., 1939-50, Credo Perspectives, 22 vols., 1957-60, Perspectives in Humanism, 1951-55, Science of Culture Series, 1935-48, Tree of Life Series, 1940-41, Convergence, 5 vols., 1937-40; writer, lectr. worldwide. Founder Anshen Transdisciplinary Lectureships in Art, Sci. and Philosophy of Culture, Frick Collection, N.Y.C. Fellow Royal Soc. Arts of London; mem. Am. Philos. Assn., History of Sci. Soc., Internat. Philos. Soc., Metaphys. Soc. Am. Address: 50 E 77th St New York NY 10021-1836

ANSLEY, JUDITH A., legislative staff member; b. Somerville, Mass., Feb. 25, 1958; d. Emilio J. and Gilda C. (Piccoli) Scalesse. BA summa cum laude, Tufts U., 1979; MA, Fletcher Sch. Law and Diplomacy, 1980. Rsch. asst. Congl. Rsch. Svc. Libr. Congress, 1980-83; mem. profl. staff Senate Com. Armed Svcs., 1983-93, Senate Select Com. Intelligence, 1993—. Mem. Phi Beta Kappa. Office: Select Com on Intelligence Hart Senate Office Bldg Rm 211 Washington DC 20510*

ANSON, MARY GWYN, rehabilitation center executive; b. Cordell, Okla., Mar. 19, 1938; d. Hugh Rutherford and Rena Maye (Bonham) Maxwell; m. Brooke Bowen Anson, Dec. 22, 1957 (div. 1961); 1 child, Michael William. BA, Morningside Coll., 1962; postgrad., U. Iowa, 1968, Marycrest Coll., 1969, Tex. Tech U., 1978-81, East Cen. U., 1978-85, Okla. U., 1985-90. Social worker Cass County Pub. Welfare, Plattsmouth, Nebr., 1962-65, Denver County Pub. Welfare, Denver, 1965-66; protective service worker Logan (Iowa) County Welfare, 1966-67; supr. Scott County Welfare, Davenport, Iowa, 1968-72; psychiatric therapist Texarkana Mental Health Ctr., Tex., 1972-74; supr. protective services Tex. Dept. Pub. Welfare, Paris, 1974-76; pvt. counselor Paris, 1976-77; cons. Okla. Assn. for Retarded Citizens, Oklahoma City, 1977-81, exec. dir., 1981-82; chief exec. officer EpiCenter, Inc., 1982—; founder, cons. Youth Hotline, Davenport, Iowa, 1969; cons. in field. Spl. foster parent Iowa Child Welfare Service, 1967-68, Tex. Child Welfare Services, 1975-76; mem. Consumer Adv. Bd., Vocat. Rehab. Services, Oklahoma City, 1984-88, pres., 1985; pres. Client Assistance Program Adv. Bd., Oklahoma City, 1986—; bd. dirs. Gov. Adv. Bd. on Handicapped Concerns, Oklahoma City, 1983—; chaplain Oklahoma City Pilot Club, 1984—; del. Dem. State Conv., 1968. Mem. Am. Assn. on Mental Deficieny, Nat. Conf. Execs. of Assns. for Retarded Citizens, Nat. Assn. Developmental Disabilities Mgrs., Okla. Assn. Workshops and Community Residential Facilities. Democrat. Methodist. Lodges: P.E.O., Order Eastern Star. Office: EpiCenter Inc 7001 Berkley Ave Oklahoma City OK 73116-4503

ANSORGE, IONA MARIE, retired real estate agent, musician; b. Nov. 3, 1927; d. Edgar B. and Marie Louise (Bleeke) Bohn; m. Edwin James Ansorge, Sept. 13, 1949; children: Richard, Michelle. BA, Valparaiso U., 1949; cert. teaching, Drake U., 1964; MA, U. Iowa, 1976. Min. of music Our Savior Luth. Ch., Des Moines, 1949-63; tchr. Johnston (Iowa) High Sch., 1964-75; instr. Iowa Meth. Sch. Nursing, Des Moines, 1978-87; owner, pres. Bed and Breakfast in Iowa, Ltd., 1982-86; realtor Better Homes and Gardens First Realty, Des Moines, 1986-92. Pres. Des Moines Jaycee-ettes; fundraiser Des Moines Zoo; founder Messiah Luth. Ch., Des Moines, 1978; started Iowa Bed and Breakfast Industry, 1982; owner, pres. Bed and Breakfast in Iowa, Ltd.; mem. Faith Luth. Ch. Mem. LWV, AAUW, Des Moines Bd. Realtors, Women's Coun. Realtors, Realtor's Million Dollar Club, Jaycee-ettes (pres. Des Moines chpt. 1957-58), Valparaiso U. Guild (charter mem. Des Moines chpt.). Home: 7104 Franklin Ave Windsor Heights IA 50322-5850

ANSPACH, JUDITH FORD, law librarian, law educator; b. Akron, Ohio, Oct. 29, 1940; m. Stephen Fredrick Anspach, Apr. 10, 1963; 1 child, Erich Stephen. BS in Edn., Kent State U., 1962, MLS, 1977; JD, Miss. Coll., 1983. Pub. svcs. librarian Miss. Coll. Law Library, Jackson, 1978-84; assoc. law librarian Law Library, U. Conn., Hartford, 1984-89; assoc. prof., dir. library svcs. Thomas M. Cooley Law Sch., Lansing, Mich., 1989-93; assoc. prof., dir. U. N.Mex. Law Sch., Albuquerque, 1993—; paralegal instr. U. Miss., Jackson, 1983. Mem. Am. Assn. Law Librs. (chmn. scholarship com. 1988-89, publs. rev. com. 1993-95), Mich. Assn. Law Librs. (v.p. 1991-92, pres. 1992-93), Ohio Regional Assn. Law Librs., Govt. Documents Roundtable Conn. (chmn. 1988-89). Episcopalian. Office: U NMex Sch Law Libr 1117 Stanford Dr NE Albuquerque NM 87106-3721

ANTES, ANN ELIZABETH, stock brokerage executive; b. Somers Point, N.J., July 30, 1965; d. Charles Francis and Elizabeth (Feustel) Bonadio; m. James P. Antes, June 17, 1989. BA, U. Denver, 1987. Asst. mgr. The Boston Co., 1987-90, ops. officer, 1990-93; asst. v.p. Lehman Bros., Boston, 1993—. Mem. Delta Gamma. Republican. Lutheran.

ANTHOLT, SHARRON G., artist, educator; b. Santa Rosa, Calif., July 5, 1944; d. Kenneth and Carol (Wright) Gowans; m. Charles Anthoct; 1 child, Sandra. BFA, Calif. State U., Hayward, 1971; MFA, San Francisco Art Inst., 1973. Asst. instr. painting San Francisco Art Inst., 1972-73; lectr. No. Va. C.C., Alexandria, Va., 1976-89, Montgomery Coll., Rockville, Md., 1985-86, Marymount U., Arlington, Va., 1989-90, U. Md., College Park, 1993-94; lectr. George Mason U., Fairfax, Va., 1986-94, asst. prof., 1994—; artist-in-residence The MacDowell Colony, Peterborough, N.H., 1984, Yaddo, Saratoga Springs, N.Y., 1989, Va. Ctr. for Creative Arts, Sweet Briar, Va., 1992, 93. One-woman shows include Washington Project for Arts, Washington, 1976, Gallery 10, Washington, 1978, 83, 86, Salve Regina Gallery, Washington, 1982, Foundry Gallery, Washington, 1984, Md. Art Place, Balt., 1984, 93, Blue Mountain Gallery, N.Y.C., 1986, India Internat. Ctr., New Delhi, India, 1988, Franz Bader Gallery, Washington, 1988, 90, Anton Gallery, Washington, 1992, 94; group shows include Foundry Gallery, 1976, Washington Woman's Art Ctr., 1977, Dimmock Gallery, Washington, 1977, Washington Project for Arts, 1977, 78, 88, Gallery 10, 83, 85, Art Barn Gallery, Washington, 1984, Winston Gallery, Washington, 1988, Anton Gallery, 90, 91, 92, 93, 94, Tretyakov Gallery, Moscow, 1990, Carnegie Libr., Washington, 1991, Chemould Gallery, Calcutta, India, 1992, Japan Info. and Culture Ctr., Washington, 1993, Emerson Gallery, McLean, Va., 1993, Clair Spitler Gallery, Ann Arbor, Mich., 1994, many others. Artist grantee D.C. Commn. on Arts, 1990, 92; recipient Fellowship award Morris and Gwendolyn Cafritz Found., 1991. Mem. AAUW, Coll. Art Assn., Washington Project for Arts. Office: George Mason U Art Dept Fairfax VA 22030-4444

ANTHONY, CAROL A., judge; b. 1953. Student, Trinity Univ., 1971-73; BA, Univ. of Ark., Fayetteville, 1976; JD, Univ. of Ark. Sch. of Law, 1979. Law clk. to Hon. Marian Penix, 1979-80, law clk. to Hon. Oren Harris, 1981-84; with Compton, Prewett, Thomas & Hickey, 1984—; magistrate judge U.S. Dist. Ct. (Ark. we. dist.), 8th circuit, El Dorado, 1987—; instr. Southern Ark. Univ. Mem. Ark. Bar Assn., Am. Trial Lawyers Assn., Ark. Trial Lawyers. Office: US Dist Ct 423 N Washington El Dorado AR 71730*

ANTHONY, KATHRYN HARRIET, architecture educator; b. N.Y.C., Sept. 11, 1955; d. Harry Antoniades and Anne (Skoufis) A.; m. Barry Daniel Riccio, May 24, 1980. AB in Psychology, U. Calif., Berkeley, 1976, PhD in Architecture, 1981. Rsch. promotion Kaplan/McLaughlin/Diaz Architects and Planners, San Francisco, 1980-81; vis. lectr. U. Calif., Berkeley, 1980-81, 82-83, San Francisco State U., 1981; assoc. prof. Calif. State Poly. U., Pomona, 1981-84; asst. prof. U. Ill., Urbana-Champaign, 1984-89, assoc. prof., 1989—, chair bldg. rsch. coun., 1994—; guest lectr. numerous orgns., colls. and univs.; mem. numerous comms. Coll. of Fine and Applied Arts, Sch. Architecture, Housing Rsch. and Devel. Program, Dept. Landscape Architecture. Author: Design Juries on Trial: The Renaissance of the Design Studio, 1991; co-editor Jour. Archtl. Edn. 47:1, 1993; mem. editl. bd. Jour. Archtl. and Planning Rsch., 1989—, Jour Archtl. Edn., 1990—, Environ. and Behavior Jour., 1991—; reviewer Landscape Jour., 1990; contbr. articles to profl. jours. Recipient Creative Achievement award Assn. Collegiate Sch. Architecture, 1992, grant U.S. Army C.E.R.L., 1993, grant U. Ill., 1984, 87, 92, 93, grant Graham Found., 1989-91, 93-95, grant Decatur Housing Authority, 1988, grant Upgrade Cos., Peoria, Ill., 1987, grant Nat. Endowment for Arts, 1986-87, grant L.A. County Community Devel. Commn., 1984, grant Calif. State U. and Colls., 1982, 83, summer grant U. Calif., Berkeley, 1980. Mem. AIA (Champaign Urbana sect.), Environ. Design Rsch. Assn. (bd. dirs. 1989-92, treas. 1990-92, co-editor Coming of Age: Proceedings of 21st Ann. Conf. 1990), Chgo. Women in Architecture, Women in Info. Tech. and Scholarship. Home: 309 W Pennsylvania Ave Urbana IL 61801-4918 Office: Univ Ill Sch Architecture 600 E Lorado Taft Dr Champaign IL 61820-6922

ANTHONY, SHEILA F., federal official; b. Hope, Ark., Nov. 8, 1940; m. Beryl F. Anthony; children: Alison, Lauren. BA, U. Ark., 1962; JD, Am. U., 1984. Bar: Ark. 1985, D.C. 1985, U.S. Ct. Appeals (D.C. cir.) 1987, U.S. Supreme Ct. 1992. Tchr. Ark. Pub. Schs., 1962-63, 74-76; with Dow, Lohnes & Albertson, Washington, 1985-93; asst. atty. gen. Dept. of Justice, Washington, 1993—. Del. Dem. Nat. Conv., 19890; justice of the peace Union County, Ark., 1969; trustee South Ark. U., 1971-75, Wash. Ctr. Seminars and Acad. Internships, 1993—. Office: Dept of Justice 3900 Macomb St NW Washington DC 20016*

ANTHONY, SONJA RICKS, child nutrition supervisor; b. Alexandria, La., Sept. 5, 1961; d. Joe Willie and Edwina Helen (Glover) Ricks; m. Leonard Levert Anthony, Dec. 29, 1984. BS, Grambling (La.) State U., 1982; MS, Iowa State U., 1984. Store clk. Family Grocery Store, Colfax, La., 1976-79; resident asst. Grambling State U., 1981; grad. asst. dept. hotel/restaurant, institutional mgmt. Iowa State U., Ames, 1982-84; dietary mgr. U. Ala. Hosp., Birmingham, 1985-90; supr. child nutrition Jefferson County Bd. Edn., Birmingham, 1990—. Mem. Am. Sch. Food Svcs. Assn. (cert.), Am. Dietetics Assn., Ala. Assn. Child Nutrition Program Suprs. (state sec. 1993-94, state pres. elect 1994-95), Ala. Sch. Food Svc. Assn., Ala. Coun. Sch. Adminstrn. and Supervision. Democrat. Baptist. Office: Jefferson County Bd Edn 2100 18th St S Homewood AL 35209

ANTHONY, SUSAN MAE, entrepreneur; b. Elmhurst, Ill., Oct. 11, 1959; d. Neil Jack and Shirley Mae (Deckard) A.; m. Mark Stephan Rogers, Jan. 28, 1989 (div. May 1993); 1 child, Ryan James Rogers. Student, Edison C.C., 1977-82; AS, Internat. Corr. Sch., 1982. Clk. Lee County Elec. Coop., North Ft. Myers, Fla., 1975-78, apprentice journeyman, 1978-82; spl. agt. Northwestern Mut. Life, Ft. Myers, Fla., 1982-86; broker rep. Paul Revere Ins. Co., Ft. Myers, 1986-88; owner Anthony Ins. Svcs., Ft. Myers, 1982-92; co-owner Soil Plus, Ft. Myers, 1988-92; pres. Crews Sanitation Co., Ft. Myers, 1993—; owner Anthony Contracting Svcs., Ft. Myers, 1992—. Author: (guidebook) Guide and Checklist for Starting a Small Business, 1993. Founder, organizer New Directions, Am. Cancer Soc., Ft. Myers, 1986-88, crusade chmn., bd. officer, 1986-88; organizer, chmn. Interfaith Vol. Caregivers Project, Ft. Myers, 1993—; founder, chmn. Elder Abuse Task Force, Ft. Myers, 1993—; elder abuse prevention coord. Area Agy. on Aging of S.W. Fla., Ft. Myers, 1993—; mem. steering com. for minority task force Horizon Coun. on Econ. Devel., Ft. Myers, 1991-93; active Fla. and Nat. Women's Polit. Caucus, 1991—. Mem. NRA, Fla. Septic Tank Assn., Fla. Restaurant Assn., Ft. Myers Womens Network (steering com., bd. dirs. 1984—). Republican. Home: PO Box 2031 Fort Myers FL 33902-2031 Office: Crews Sanitation Co PO Box 27 Fort Myers FL 33902-0027

ANTHONY-PEREZ, BOBBIE COTTON MURPHY, psychology educator, researcher; b. Macon, Ga., Nov. 15, 1923; d. Solomon Richard and Maude Alice (Lockett) Cotton; m. William Anthony, Aug. 22, 1959 (dec.); 1 child, Freida; m. Andrew Silviano Perez, June 20, 1979. B.S., DePaul U., 1953, M.S., 1954; M.S., U. Ill., 1959; Ph.D., U. Chgo., 1967; M.A., DePaul, 1975. Tchr. Chgo. Pub. Schs., 1954-68; math. cons. U. Chgo., 1965; prof. Chgo. State U., 1968—, coord. Black Studies Program, 1982-83; with psychol. svcs. Chgo. Pub. Schs., 1971-72; rsch. coord. Urban Affairs Inst., Howard U., Washington, 1978; coordinator Higher Edn. Careers Counseling Campus Ministry, Ingleside Whitfield Parish, 1978-84; coord. Black Studies Chgo. State U., 1990-94. V.p. Community Affairs Chatham Bus. Assn., 1981-85, asst. sec., 1985-86, sec., 1986-87, directory com., 1987, 88; bus. relations chmn. Chatham Avalon Park Community Coun., 1984—; bd. dirs. United Meth. Found. at U. Chgo., 1980-84, Community Mental Health Council, Inc., 1979-83; pub. edn. chairperson Chatham Avalon Unit Am. Cancer Soc., 1977-88, 90—, pub. info. chairperson, 1988-94; pres. Aux. Chgo. Chpt. Tuskeegee Airmen, Inc., 1994. NSF fellow, 1957, 58, 59; recipient numerous awards religious, civic and ednl. instns. and assns. Mem. Am. Psychol. Assn., Internat. Assn. Applied Psychology, Internat. Assn. Cross-Cultural Psychology, Internat. Assn. Ednl. and Vocat. Guidance, Assn. Black Psychologists (pres. elect Chgo. chpt.), Chgo. Psychol. Assn., Nat. Council Tchrs. Math., Am. Ednl. Research Assn., Midwest Ednl. Research Assn., Am. Soc. Clin. Hypnosis, Midwestern Psychol. Assn.

Methodist. Contbr. numerous articles to profl. jours. Office: Chgo State U Dept Psychology 9500 S King Dr Chicago IL 60628-1502

ANTICH, ROSE ANN, state legislator. Student, Hammond Bus. Coll., Ind. U. N.W. Radio and TV personality, lectr., astrologist; mem. Ind. State Senate from 4th dist., 1990—. Democrat. Roman Catholic. Home: 5401 Lincoln St Merrillville IN 46410 Office: Ind State House 200 W Washington St Indianapolis IN 46204-2785

ANTILLA, SUSAN, journalist; b. New Rochelle, N.Y., May 18, 1954; d. Oscar E. Antilla and Gloria (Jennings) Claudet; m. James Harlan Burdsall, Sept. 26, 1981 (div. Nov. 1995). BA, Manhattanville Coll., 1976; MA, NYU, 1981. Reporter Dun's Bus. Month, N.Y.C., 1978-81, asst. editor, 1981-82; contbg. editor Working Woman Mag., N.Y.C., 1980-86; fin. bur. chief Balt. Sun., N.Y.C., 1985-86; stock market reporter USA Today, N.Y.C., 1982-85, chief Money bur., columnist, 1986-92; columnist, reporter N.Y. Times, 1992—; guest lectr. Marymount Manhattan Coll., 1984, 85; guest lectr. NYU, 1985, adj. prof., 1987-88. Contbr. Savvy mag., 1986-88, also articles to other mags. and profl. jours. Cons. Girls Club Am., N.Y.C., 1983. Mem. N.Y. Fin. Writers Assn. Office: NY Times 229 W 43rd St New York NY 10036-3913

ANTOINE, GRETA JANE, freelance writer and storyteller; b. Depauville, N.Y., Mar. 5, 1934; d. Joseph Lavina and Flora Alberta (Darou) LaRose; m. Stanley Antoine. Diploma, E. Jordan High Sch., Mich., 1972. Project dir. Title V-A Jordan (Mich.) Pub. Schs., 1980-89; exec. dir. Anishinabe Inter-Tribal Coun., E. Jordan, 1980-89, Odawa Bear Clan Coun., E. Jordan, 1989-94; cons. Mich. Sch. System, 1980—; freelance writer and storyteller of Native Am. legends from oral history, also culture, traditions and spiritual values; women's traditional dancer Bear Clan/Odawa Tribe. Councilman, City Council, E. Jordan, 1982-84; bd. dirs. Am. Indian Dem. Mem. Odawa Bear Clan Coun. (clan mother). Home: 6185 Behling Rd East Jordan MI 49727-9746

ANTONACCI, LORI (LORETTA MARIE ANTONACCI), marketing executive, consultant; b. Riverton, Ill., Mar. 31, 1947; d. Antonio and Gena Marie A. BA, Bradley U., 1969. Broadcast copywriter Sta. WIRL-TV, Peoria, Ill., 1969; communications specialist Walgreen Co., Chgo., 1970-72; creative supr. Nat. Assn. Realtors, Chgo., 1973; creative dir., producer Steve Sohmer, Inc., N.Y.C., 1974-77; owner, exec. producer Antonacci Prodns., N.Y.C., 1977-79; promotion specialist Ziff-Davis Publs., 1979-80; promotion mgr. Psychology Today, 1980-81; pres. Antonacci & Assocs., N.Y.C., 1982—; adj. prof. Gallatin div. NYU, 1986—. Bd. advisors Wildcare, Inc., Artists Talk on Art, Inc.; founder Artists Talk on Art Panel series, 1974. Recipient Golden Eagle award CINE, 1976; award U.S. Indsl. Film Festival, 1977; CEBA award, 1979; Bronze medal Internat. Film and TV Festival N.Y., 1979. Mem. Advt. Women N.Y. (profl. devel. com. 1983-85, program com. 1986-90, chmn. speakers bur. 1988-90, chmn. pub. policy com. 1991—), Women in Comm., Am. Women in Radio and TV, Women's City Club of N.Y. (v.p. devel. 1994—), N.Y. Women's Agenda (founding mem. 1992—, v.p. events 1993—). Address: 15 E 10th St New York NY 10003

ANTONUCCI, TONI CLAUDETTE, psychology educator; b. Bklyn., Sept. 9, 1948; d. Santino and Dorothy A.; m. James S. Jackson; children: Ariana, Kendra. BA, Hunter Coll., 1969; MA, Wayne State U., 1972, PhD, 1973. Asst. prof. psychology Syracuse (N.Y.) U., 1973-77; postdoctoral NIMH fellow U. Mich., Ann Arbor, 1977-79, lectr. in psychology, 1979, asst. prof. Family Practice Med. Sch., 1979-88, assoc. prof. Family Practice, 1988—, prof. psychology, 1991—; asst. rsch. sci. Inst. Social Rsch. U. Mich., 1979-82, assoc. rsch. sci., 1982-90, rsch. sci., 1990—; adj. assoc. prof. psychology U. Mich., 1982-90; vis. scholar Inst. Nat. de la Sante et de la Recherche Medicale, Paris, 1992-94; sr. internat. fellow Fogarty Sr. Internat. Ctr., Washington, 1992-94. Mem. editl. bd. Devel. Psychology and Revue d'epidemiolgie et de sante publique epidemiology, 1993; author chpts. to books; contbr. articles to profl. jours. Fellow APA, Am. Psychol. Soc., Gerontol. Soc. Am. (v.p. 1991-92, chair BSS awards com. 1993-94); mem. Internat. Soc. Study of Behavioral Devel., Soc. Rsch. in Child Devel. Office: Inst Social Rsch 426 Thompson St Ann Arbor MI 48106-1248

ANTOUN, DEETTA ARDITH, graphic arts marketing consultant; b. Meadville, Pa., Oct. 8, 1948; d. James LeRoy and DeLeeo Ellen (Peterson) Riordan; m. Frederic George Antoun, Jr., Apr. 19, 1969; children: Vanessa Marie, Frederic George III. Student, Wilson Coll., Chambersburg, Pa., 1986-87; BS in Edn. summa cum laude, Shippensburg (Pa.) U., 1990. Cert. in elem. edn., environ. edn., Pa. Circulation and subscription sales The Paxton Herald, Harrisburg, Pa., 1972-83; fitness instr. Chambersburg (Pa.) YMCA, 1985-87; substitute tchr. Waynesboro (Pa.) Area Sch. Dist., 1991-92, Chambersburg Area Sch. Dist., 1991-92; graphics arts mktg. cons. Chambersburg, 1992—; asst. dir. legis. affairs Govt. Printing Office Contractors Coalition, Chambersburg, 1992—; fund raiser for various Senatorial and Congl. candidates, 1992—. Artist, working in oils and acrylics. Coord., vol. Ctrl. Pa. Lung Assn., Franklin County, 1984-87; fundraiser Chambersburg Area YMCA. Mem. Chambersburg Art Alliance, Pa. Alliance for Environ. Edn., Wildlife Conservation Soc., Kappa Delta Pi. Home: 4857 Letterkenny Rd W Chambersburg PA 17201-8789

ANZALONE, FILIPPA ELIZABETH, law librarian; b. Cambridge, Mass., Sept. 27, 1953; d. Gaspar Edward and Patricia Alice (O'Connell) Marullo; m. Antonio Anzalone, Oct. 30, 1983; children: Patricia, Lucia. AB, Smith Coll., 1975; SM, Simmons Coll., 1977; JD, Suffolk U., 1985. Bar: Mass. 1985, U.S. Dist. Ct. Mass. 1986. Br. libr. Medford (Mass.) Pub. Libr., 1975-76, children's libr., 1976-78; br. dir. Cambridge (Mass.) Pub. Libr., 1978-80; rsch. libr. Dike, Bronstein, Roberts, Cushman and Pfund, Boston, 1980-81; dir. law libr. Bingham, Dana & Gould, Boston, 1981-91; dir. info. and access svcs. Sch. Law Northeastern U., Boston, 1991-93, dir. law libr., 1993—; book reviewer Legal Info. Alert. Mem. Am. Assn. Law Librs. (chair coun. chpt. pres. 1993-94), Assn. Boston Law Librs. (pres. 1989-90), Law Librs. New Eng. (pres. 1992-93). Roman Catholic. Office: Northeastern U Sch Law 400 Huntington Ave Boston MA 02115-5098

APEL, SUSAN BETH, law educator; b. Pitts., Jan. 17, 1953; d. Robert Albert and Shirley Ann (Holmes) A. BA, Pa. State U., 1974; JD, Northeastern U., 1977. Staff atty. Keystone Legal Svcs., Huntingdon, Pa., 1977-80; co-dir. Keystone Legal Svcs., Huntingdon, 1980-82; clin. prof. law Vt. Law Sch., South Royalton, 1982-87, assoc. prof. law, 1987-91, prof. law, 1991—, asst. dir. gen. practice program, 1987—; Amicus brief U.S. Supreme Ct., Washington, 1989; expert testimony Vt. Legis., 1990, 91; organizer Inns of Ct., Vt., 1994; presenter in field. Contbr. articles to profl. jours. Mem. Gender Bias Task Force, Vt., 1992-94. Recipient citation and incorporation U.S. Senate Judiciary Com., Washington, 1989, citation Vt. Supreme Ct., 1991. Home: PO Box 171 Wilder VT 05088-0171 Office: Vt Law Sch PO Box 96 South Royalton VT 05068-0096

APEL-BRUEGGEMAN, MYRNA L., entrepreneur; b. Cleve., July 19, 1942; d. Melvin Arthur and Merle Ruth (Hoffman) Rehlender; children: Timothy, Kristen, Michelle, Kim, Mellissa; m. Earl L. Brueggeman, May 7, 1994. BS in Edn., Kent State U., 1965, M. in Edn. Counseling, 1987. Cert. tchr., Ohio; lic. minister, Ohio. Owner, mgr. real estate investments Kent, Ohio; owner, founder IHS Counseling Ctr., Ravenna, Ohio; owner, mgr. Winning Edge, Kent, Ohio; founder, pres. IHS Sch. Personal Devel., Ravenna, Ohio; owner IHS Bookstore; co-owner Chapel on the Lakes. Mem. NAFE, Ohio Manufactured Housing Assn. (pres. We. Res. chpt.), Internat. Soc. Profl. Hypnotists, Sigma Epsilon, Chi Sigma Iota.

APELIAN, VIRGINIA MATOSIAN, psychologist, assertiveness training instructor, lecturer, consultant; b. Yoghun-Oluk, Turkey, Dec. 3, 1934; came to U.S., 1950; d. Hagop M. and Christina (Atamian) Matosian; m. Henry M. Apelian, Apr. 4, 1959; children: Arminée, Gregory, Christopher and David (twins). AA in Liberal Arts, Union County Coll., 1973; BA in Psychology, Douglass Coll., Rutgers U., 1975. From clk. to v.p. N.J. Bank & Trust Co., Paterson, N.J., 1955-59; freelance artist, 1966—; adminstrv. aide dist. 22 N.J. State Assembly, Clark, Trenton, N.J., 1976-78; elected councilwoman Township Coun., Clark, 1978; office supr. Electronic Corp. Am., Springfield, N.J., 1979-81; pres. Township Council, Clark, 1979-82; dir. sr. citizens group Union County Dept. Parks, Clark, 1983-84; coord. youth programming Cen. Presbyn. Ch., Summit, N.J., 1984-85; tchr., cons. Union County Adult Edn. System, Clark, 1975-87; psychologist, assertiveness trainer, lectr. Union County Coll., Cranford, N.J., 1987—; elected to bd. govs. Union County Coll., 1992; mem. Juvenile Conf. Com., Clark, N.J., 1983-86, 90-94, chair, 1990-94, N.J. Coun. for the Social Studies, 1990-94; lectr. in field. Co-editor The Presbyn., 1987-90; contbr. articles to profl. jours. Apptd. mem. Ethnic Adv. Coun., State of N.J., 1992—; tchr. Christian edn. various Presbyn. chs., Clark and Paterson, 1955-91; mem., tchr., budget and evangelism com. mem., pulpit nominating com., mediator counselor, chmn. mission and Christian edn. coms. Osceloa Presbyn. Ch., Clark; Christian edn. commr. Fanwood (N.J.) Presbyn. Ch.; liaison Elizabeth Presbytery and Armenian Missionary Assn. Am. for Armenian Earthquake Relief Fund of Dec. 1988 Catastrophe; co-chair Heart Fund Drive, Clark, 1977; chair and coord. cancer crusade Am. Cancer Soc., Clark, 1978; legis. com., chair local pub. schs. and high schs., Clark, 1975-80; lectr. on drug abuse at local schs., Clark, 1975-80; lectr. on human rights issues; mem. pub. rels. coord., lectr. fund raiser Mayor's Com. on Drug Abuse, Clark, 1973-80; mem. Clark Little League Aux., 1970-80; mem., research chair environ. health bd. Union County, 1983-84, consumer affairs bd., 1980-84; mem., sec. Union County Juvenile Adv. Bd., Elizabeth Superior Ct., 1983-86, 90—, elected chair, 1990-94; trustee Clark Pub. Libr. Bd., 1988-89; commr. Christian edn. dept. Fanwood (N.J.) Presbyn. Ch.; bd. govs. Union County Coll. Recipient spl. plaque Mayor and Twp. Coun., Clark, 1982, Disting. Alumna award Union County Coll. 1983, C.C. Excellence award N.J. Coun. of County Colls., 1994; named in N.J. State Assembly resolution for disting. svc. to community, 1964, honored at Union County Coll's. 60th anniversary for svc. to community and profession, 1994. Mem. Profl. Women's Assn. (spl. cert. recognition 1988), N.J. Assn. for Elected Women Ofcls. (charter, treas., 1st v.p.), Armenian Relief Soc. (adv. bd. dirs. 1955—, sec. 1955-60, pres. 1960-70, Gold Pin, 1985), N.J. Coun. for the Social Studies, Gov.'s Ethnic Adv. Coun. N.J. Clark Hist. Soc. (cultural programs 1980—, pres. 1993-94), Union County Coll. Alumni Assn. (pres. 1993-95), Clark Rep. Club (v.p. 1970-75, pres. 1976-82). Republican. Presbyterian. Home: 85 Rutgers Rd Clark NJ 07066-2729

APGAR, BARBARA SUE, physician, educator; b. Guthrie, Okla., Oct. 4, 1943; d. Wallace Duke and Gloria Jayne (Glover) McMillin; 1 child, Larisa Ann. BA in Biology, Loretto Heights Coll., 1965; MS in Anatomy, U. Mich., 1968; MD, Tex. Tech. Med. Sch., 1976. Diplomate Am. Bd. Family Practice, Am. Bd. Med. Examiners. Rsch. asst. Parke Davis, Ann Arbor, Mich., 1965-66, Aerospace Med. Labs Wright-Patterson AFB, Ohio, 1968-70; instr. anatomy dept. Tex. Tech. U. Med. Sch., Lubbock, 1972-74, resident in family practice, 1976-79, clin. asst. prof., 1980-83; physician The Pavilion, Lubbock, 1981-83; sr. physician, dir. gynecology clinic U. Mich., 1983-86, instr. dept. family practice, 1984-89, med. dir. Briarwood Health Ctr., 1986—, also mem. steering com. for ambulatory care, asst. prof. dept. family practice, 1989-93, assoc. prof Dept Family Practice, 1993—; dir. women's health, 1989—, asst. residency dir. dept. family practice, 1991—; mem. staff Meth. Hosp., St. Mary of the Plains Hosp., U. Mich. Hosp.; mem. med. exec. com. dept. of family practice U. Mich. Editl. reviewer Jour. Family Practice, 1991—; assoc. editor: American Family Physician, 1993; editorial bd., co-editor primary care series Female Patient. Mem. adv. bd. Lubbock chpt. March of Dimes, 1972-74. Recipient Upjohn Achievement award, 1976, Psychiatry Achievement award, 1976; Soroptimist Internat. grantee, 1978-79, U. Mich. Dept. Family Practice Resident Teaching award, 1985, 87, 88, 89, 91; fellow Mich. State U., 1989-90. Mem. Am. Acad. Family Practice (task force on clin. policy 1991, mem. faculty procedural skills), Lubbock County Med. Soc., Tex. Med. Assn., Mich. Acad. Family Practice (perinatal com. 1987—), Soc. of Tchrs. of Family Medicine, Am. Soc. Colposcopy and Cervical Pathology (task force on resident edn., mem. com. on colposcopy recognition award), Alpha Omega Alpha. Democrat. Home: 883 Scio Meadows Dr Ann Arbor MI 48103 Office: U Mich Family Practice Dept 775 S Main St Chelsea MI 48118-1370

APGAR, CASSANDRA HANCOCK, healthcare facility administrator, nurse; b. Bradford, Pa.; d. John R. Hancock and Helen M. Mack; m. Richard W. Apgar; children: Suzanne, John, Richard, Heather, Rebecca, Rollin, Byron, Meghan, Holly. Diploma, West Pa. Hosp. Sch. Nursing, Pitts., 1971; BSN magna cum laude, York Coll. of Pa., 1987; MSN, Widener U., 1988; MBA, York Coll., 1992. CEN; cert. nursing adminstr.-advanced, clin. specialist in med.-surg. nursing, TNCC instr. Staff and charge nurse burn unit West Pa. Hosp., Pitts., 1971; staff/charge nurse emergency, oper. rm. and critical care Canonsburg (Pa.) Gen. Hosp., 1971-73; staff and charge nurse nursery St. Clair Meml. Hosp., Pitts., 1973-75; staff/charge nurse emergency, med.-surg. and critical care Meml. Hosp., York, Pa., 1975-80; staff and charge nurse post partum York (Pa.) Hosp., 1980-82; staff/charge nurse emergency dept., med.-surg. Sinai Hosp., Balt., 1981-86; dir. trauma svcs. York (Pa.) Hosp., 1989—; part time staff nurse Carroll County Gen. Hosp., Westminster, Md., 1991-94; adj. faculty Widener Univ. Grad. Sch. Nursing, Chester, Pa., 1990-91, 94; ad hoc nursing standards com. mem. Pa. Trauma Systems Found., Mechanicsburg, Pa., 1991-93. Mem. AACN, Am. Trauma Soc., Soc. Trauma Nurses, Emerg. Nurses Assn., York Coll. of Pa. Sr. Honor Soc., Pa. Trauma Systems Found. (mem. standards com. 1993—), Hosp. Assn. of Pa. (mem. exec. com. sect. for accredited trauma ctrs. 1993—). Office: York Hosp Trauma Svcs 1001 S George St York PA 17403-3676

APODACA, FELICE ANNE, financial analyst; b. L.A., Mar. 2, 1948; d. Gilbert V. and Helen R. (Commander) A.; m. Jack Brian, Apr. 23, 1994. BA, UCLA, 1970. MIS fin. analyst Warner Bros., Burbank, Calif., 1973—. Home: 10824 Pickford Way Culver City CA 90230-4936 Office: Warner Bros 4000 Warner Blvd Bldg 131 Burbank CA 91522-0002

APPEL, ANTOINETTE RUTH, neuropsychologist; b. N.Y.C., Mar. 31, 1943; d. Leon S. and Augusta (Marienberg) A. B.A., U. Vt., 1964; M.A., Mt. Holyoke Coll., 1965; postgrad., Yeshiva U., 1965-66, Hofstra U., 1966; Ph.D., CUNY, 1972. Diplomate Am. Bd. Profl. Neuropsychology. Instr. C.W. Post Coll., Greenvale, N.Y., 1968-69; lectr., instr. Queens Coll., Flushing, N.Y., 1970-71; fellow in neurology, instr. ophthalmology Mt. Sinai Sch. Medicine, N.Y.C., 1971-74; adj. asst. prof. St. Francis Coll., Bklyn., 1974; asst. prof. dept. psychology So. Ill. U. Sch. Medicine, Carbondale, 1974-76; USPHS intern Conn. Valley Hosp., Middletown, Conn., 1976-77; asst. prof., asst. project coordinator dept. psychiatry Nat. Alcohol Research Ctr., U. Conn. Health Ctr., Farmington, 1977-79; neuropsychologist, asst. prof. program in medicine Brown U., Providence, 1979-82; adj. asst. prof. psychology U. R.I., Kingston and Providence, 1979-83; pvt. practice psychology, 1981-83; dir. Neuropsychol. Assessment and Treatment Ctr., Ctr. for Neuropsychology Services, Ft. Lauderdale, 1983-90, So. Inst. Forensic Neuropsychology, 1990—; invited speaker NATO Neuropsychology Congress, 1980, Internat. Council Psychology, 1980, 22 Internat. Congress of Psychology, 1980; cons. Narco Bio-systems, 1974-75; cons. to commr. mental health State of Conn., 1978-79. Bd. dirs. Sojourner House, 1979-80, Combined Hosp. Alcoholism Program, 1978, Hartford Interval House, 1978. Served with WAC, 1963. CUNY fellow, 1972; recipient Hartford Salute award, 1979; USPHS tng. fellow, 1966-67, NIMH predoctoral fellow 1967-70. Mem. Am. Psychol. Assn. (mem. exec. bd.), Assn. Women in Psychology (mem. steering com.), Eastern Psychol. Assn. (chmn. 1980 conv.), Conn. Psychol. Assn. (council 1978-79), R.I. Psychol. Assn., N.Y. Acad. Scis., Sigma Xi, Psi Chi. Home: 6622 Racquet Club Dr Fort Lauderdale FL 33319-5026 Office: 1392 N University Dr Plantation FL 33322

APPEL, DANEÉ LACHELL, financial analyst; b. Belleville, Ill., Feb. 10, 1963; d. Aaron Ivan and Naomi Louise (Edwards) Hollon; m. Robert Charles Appel Jr., Oct. 10, 1987. BBA, Evangel, 1985. Acct. Computerland of So. Ill., Fairview Heights, 1985-87; bank examiner Fed. Reserve Bank St. Louis, 1987-91, auditor, 1991-93, fin. analyst, 1993—; ind. skin care cons. Mary Kay Cosmetics, Dallas, 1991—; aerobics instr. various health clubs, Fairview Heights, 1982—. Home: 6 Primrose Ln Fairview Hts IL 62208-2439

APPELBAUM, ANN H., lawyer; b. Decatur, Ill., Oct. 31, 1948; d. Irving and Cecelia (Hecht) A.; m. Neal Borovitz, July 4, 1982; children: Abby, Jeremy. BA, Barnard Coll., 1970; JD, Boston U., 1973. Bar: N.Y., U.S. Dist. Ct. (so. dist.) N.Y., U.S. Ct. Appeals (2nd cir.), U.S. Supreme Ct. Assoc. Hart & Hume, N.Y.C., 1974-76, Warshaw, Burstein, N.Y.C., 1976-80; counsel Jewish Theol. Sem. & Jewish Mus., N.Y.C., 1980—. Sec. Solomon Schechter Day Sch., N.J., 1992—. Mem. Nat. Assn. Coll. & Univ. Attys. Office: The Jewish Museum 1109 Fifth Ave New York NY 10125

APPELBAUM, JUDITH PILPEL, editor, consultant, educator; b. N.Y.C., Sept. 26, 1939; d. Robert Cecil and Harriet Florence (Fleischl) Pilpel; m. Alan Appelbaum, Apr. 16, 1961; children: Lynn Stephanie, Alexander Eric. BA with honors Vassar Coll., 1960. Editor, Harper's Mag., N.Y.C., 1960-74; mng. editor Harper's Weekly, 1974-76; sr. cons. Atlas World Press Rev., 1977; mng. editor Pubs. Weekly, 1978-81; founder Sensible Solutions, Inc., 1979; contbg. editor Publishers Weekly, 1981-82; columnist N.Y. Times Book Rev., 1982-84; mng. dir. Sensible Solutions, Inc., 1984—; assoc. dir. Ctr. for Book Rsch., U. Scranton, 1985-88; book rev. editor Publishing Research Quar., 1984-86, editor in chief, 1986-88, cons. editor, 1988—; contbg. editor Small Press mag. 1991—; mem. faculty Pub. Inst. of U. Denver, 1981—, CUNY edn. in pub. program, 1982—; editorial adv. Book Industry Study Group Publs., 1980—; mem. stats. com. Book Industry Study Group, 1984—; adv. bd. Coordinating Coun. Lit. Mags., 1980-84, PEN Ctr. USA West, 1988-90. Mem. Authors Guild, Women's Media Group (bull. editor 1990-92), PEN, Com. Small Mag./Press Editors & Pubs., Pubs. Mktg. Assn. (bd. dirs. 1990-92). Author: How to Get Happily Published, 1978, 4th edit., 1992; co-author: The Writer's Workbook: A Full and Friendly Guide to Boosting Your Book's Soles, 1991; editor: (with Tony Jones and Gwyneth Cravens) The Big Picture: A Wraparound Book, 1976; The Question of Size in the Book Industry Today, 1978; Getting a Line on Backlist, 1979; Paperback Primacy, 1981; Small Publisher Power, 1982. Office: Sensible Solutions Inc 271 Madison Ave Ste 1007 New York NY 10016-1001

APPELBAUM, MICHELLE GELLMAN, family nurse practitioner; b. Monticello, N.Y.; d. Emanuel and Sally Gellman; m. Joel Appelbaum, June 8, 1980; 1 child, Edward. BA in English, SUNY, Binghamton, 1977; MS, Pace U., N.Y. Med. Coll., 1980; cert. FNP, Pace U., 1980. Cert. family nurse practitioner. Nursing supr. Wellness Home Care, Liberty, N.Y., 1986-89; family nurse practitioner Sullivan Diagnostic Treatment Ctr., Harris, N.Y., 1989—; instr., cons. phys. assessment in employment and ednl. settings; adj. instr. nursing div. Sullivan County Community Coll., Loch Shelorake, N.Y., 1988; 1st nurse practitioner med. staff Community Gen. Hosp., Harris. Developer parent aide program for high risk families, Sullivan County. Mem. ANA, N.Y. State Coalition Nurse Practitioenrs (pub. rels. com.), Nat. Assn. Pediatric Nurse Practitioners, Sigma Theta Tau.

APPELHOF, RUTH STEVENS, museum director, curator, art historian; b. Washington, Feb. 14, 1945. BFA in Painting and Art History, Syracuse U., 1965, MA in Art History, 1974, MPhil, 1980, PhD in Humanities, 1988. Assoc. prof. art SUNY, Cayuga Coll., Auburn, 1971-80, gallery dir., 1977-79; asst. prof. museology grad. divsn. Sch. Art Coll. Visual and Performing Arts, Syracuse (N.Y.) U., 1981-84; curator exhbns. Lowe Art Gallery, Syracuse, 1981-84; curator painting, sculpture and graphic arts Birmingham (Ala.) Mus. Art, 1984-89; exec. dir. Art Mus. Western Va. (formerly Roanoke (Va.) Mus. Fine Arts), 1989-94; dir. Minn. Mus. Am. Art, St. Paul, 1994—; adj. prof. art dept. U. Ala., Birmingham, 1984-89; lectr. in field. Exhbns. curated include: Margaret Bourke-White, Syracuse, 1983, The New Figure, Birmingham, 1985, The Expressionist Landscape, Birmingham, 1988, Looking South, Birmingham, 1988, The Commonwealth, Roanoke, 1990, Bill Dunlap, Roanoke, 1992, Hunt Slonem, 1993, Fritz Bultman, Roanoke, 1994. Chair Mus. and the Artist, AAM, 1993; mem. bd. continuing edn. U. Va. Fellow Whitney Mus. Am. Art, N.Y.C., 1980-81. Mem. Am. Assn. Mus., Va. Assn. Mus., Coll. Art Assn., Women's Caucus Art, Roanoke Valley-Va. Tech. Adv. Coun. Office: Minnesota Mus Am Art Landmark Ctr 75 W 5th St Saint Paul MN 55102-1480

APPELL, CLARA TAUBMAN, marital and family therapist, consultant; b. N.Y.C., July 31, 1921; d. Max and Yetta (Schuber) Taubman; m. Morey L. Appell, Sept. 16, 1942 (dec. June 1976); children: Laurie, Randy Johnson, Glenn, Jodie, Jonathan. BSc, Ohio State U., 1942, MA, 1946; EdD, Columbia U., 1959; postgrad., Ackerman Inst. Family Therapy, N.Y.C., 1971-73. Cert. marital/family therapist, Conn. Coord. child devel. and family life edn. Greenwich (Conn.) Health Assn., 1969-71; co-dir. family life ctr. N.Y. Soc. for Ethical Culture, N.Y.C., 1972-73; marital and family therapist in pvt. practice Greenwich, 1971—; cons. in human devel. Morey L. Appell Human Rels. Found., Greenwich, 1978—; lectr. in human devel. U. Conn., Stamford, 1982-83; psychol. cons. Hospice, Stamford, 1981-82; adj. prof. Queens Coll., CUNY, Flushing, 1975-79; cons. relationship series filmstrips MacLean Hunter Media Inc., Stamford, 1979-80; radio host Family Talk program WGCH-AM Radio, Greenwich, 1973-80; cons. Conn. State Dept. Edn., Hartford, 1968-69. Author: (with M. Appell) We Are Six, 1959; co-author, editor Glenn Learns to Read, 2d edit., 1987; editor: John Dewey-Pattern for Adventuring, 1988. Mem. adv. bd. Mothering Ctr., Greenwich, 1979—, Camp Sunbeam, Greenwich, 1989—; mem. adv. com. diversity Greenwich Pub. Schs., 1993-94. Grad. fellow Ohio State U., 1945-46; Title XX grantee U. Conn., 1979. Fellow Am. Orthopsychiat. Assn.; mem. APA, Am. Assn. for Marriage and Family Therapy (Conn. program chair 1978), Internat. Coun. Psychologists, Nat. Coun. on Family Rels., Soc. for Rsch. in Child Devel. (emerita). Democrat. Jewish. Home: 145 Old Church Rd Greenwich CT 06830-4861 Office: Morey L Appell Human Rels Found 145 Old Church Rd Greenwich CT 06830-4861

APPERSON, JEAN, psychologist; b. Durham, N.C., June 8, 1934; d. James Harry and Dorothy Elizabeth (Johnson) Apperson; m. Calvin Adams Pope, Mar. 23, 1956 (div. 1967); 1 child, Richard Allan. BA, U. S. Fla., 1966; MA, Mich. State U., 1970, PhD, 1973. Cert. in psychoanalysis Mich. Psychoanalytic Coun., 1990. Teaching asst. Mich. State U., E. Lansing, 1968-69; psychiatric technician St. Lawrence Community Mental Health Ctr., Lansing, Mich., 1968-69; psychology intern St. Lawrence Community Mental Health Ctr., 1969-71, Mich. State U. Counseling Ctr., 1971-73; clin. psychologist U. Mich. Counseling Ctr., Ann Arbor, 1973-81; pvt. practice psychology and psychoanalysis Ann Arbor, 1974—; mem., chmn. Mich. Bd. Psychology, Lansing, 1984-91. Contbr. articles to profl. jours.; cons. editor Am. Psychol. Assn. Catalog of Selected Documents, 1975-80. USPHS grantee, 1969-70; NIMH grantee, 1970-71. Fellow Mich. Psychol. Assn. (chmn. women's issues com. 1981-83); mem. APA (com. on sci. and profl. ethics and conduct 1977-80), Mich. Soc. Psychoanalytic Psychology (treas. 1982-86), Mich. Psychoanalytic Coun. (teaching and supervising analyst, mem. at large 1991-93, tng. com. 1992—, pres.-elect 1993-95), Assn. for Advancement Psychology, Am. Women in Psychology, Mich. Women Psychologists. Democrat. Unitarian. Home: 7224 Chelsea Manchester Rd Manchester MI 48158 Office: 555 E William St Apt 23E Ann Arbor MI 48104-2428

APPLE, DAINA DRAVNIEKS, government agency official; b. Latvia, Latvia, July 6, 1944; came to U.S., 1951; d. Albins Dravnieks and Alina A. (Bergs) Zelmenis; divorced; 1 child, Almira Moronne; m. Martin A. Apple, Sept. 2, 1986. BSc, U. Calif., Berkeley, 1977, MA, 1980. Economist USDA Pacific S.W. Rsch., Berkeley, 1976-85; mgr. regional land use appeals USDA Forest Svc., San Francisco, 1986-88, program analysis officer, engrng., 1988-90; asst. regulatory officer USDA Forest Svc., 1990—. Author: Public Involvement in the Forest Service-Methodologies, 1977, Public Involvement, Selected Abstracts for Natural Resource Managers, 1979, The Management of Policy and Direction in the Forest Service, 1982, An Analysis of the Forest Service Human Resource Management Program, 1984, Organization Design-Abstracts for Natural Resources Users, 1985; contbg. editor Jour. of Women in Natural Resources. Mem. Am. Forestry Assn., Assn. Women in Sci., Soc. Am. Foresters (sec. nat. capital chpt.), Am. Latvian Assn. (bd. dirs.), Phi Beta Kappa Assocs. (nat. sec. 1985-88, pres. No. Calif. chpt. 1982-84, 1st v.p. 1981), Sigma Xi. Office: USDA Forest Svc Info Sys and Tech Staff PO Box 96090 Washington DC 20090-6090

APPLEBY, JOYCE OLDHAM, historian; b. Omaha, Apr. 9, 1929; d. Junius G. and Edith (Cash) Oldham; children: Ann Lansburgh Caylor, Mark Lansburgh, Frank Bell Appleby. B.A., Stanford U., 1950; M.A., U. Calif., Santa Barbara, 1959; Ph.D., Claremont Grad. Sch., 1966. With Mademoiselle mag., 1950-52; asst. prof. history San Diego State U., 1967-70, asso. prof., 1970-73; prof. history, asso. dean Coll. Arts and Letters, 1973-75, prof., 1976-81; vis. asso. prof. U. Calif., Irvine, 1975-76; vis. prof. UCLA, 1978-79, prof. history, 1981—; vis. fellow St. Catherine's Coll., U. Oxford,

1983; Harmsworth prof. Am. History, U. Oxford, 1990-91; Bd. fellows Claremont Grad. Sch. and U. Center, 1970-73. Author: Economic Thought and Ideology in Seventeenth-Century England, 1978, Capitalism and a New Social Order, 1983, Liberalism and Republicanism in the Historical Imagination, 1992; co-author: Telling the Truth About History, 1994; contbr. articles to profl. jours.; mem. bd. editors Democracy, 1980-83, William and Mary Quar., 1980-83, 18th Century Studies, 1982-87, Ency. Am. Polit. History, Am. Hist. Rev., 1988—, Jour. Interdisciplinary History, 1989—, The Papers of Thomas Jefferson, 1988—, The Adams Papers, 1990—; mem. adv. bd. Am. Nat. Biography. Mem. Am. Acad. Arts and Scis., Am. Philos. Soc., Smithsonian Inst. (coun.), Am. Hist. Assn. (coun.), Orgn. Am. Historians (pres.), Inst. Early Am. History and Culture (coun. 1980-86, chmn. coun. 1983-86). Home: 615 Westholme Ave Los Angeles CA 90024-3209 Office: UCLA Dept History Los Angeles CA 90024

APPLEMAN, MARJORIE (M. H. APPLEMAN), playwright, educator, poet; b. Ft. Wayne, Ind.; d. Theodore E. and Martha C. (Rathert) Haberkorn; m. Philip Appleman. BA, Northwestern U.; MA, Ind. U.; degré supérieur, U. Sorbonne, Paris. Lectr. in French and English Ind. U., 1960-72; asst. prof. English, playwriting NYU, 1976-86; lectr. in English and playwriting Columbia U., N.Y.C., 1977-80; mem. playwrights unit Circle Repertory Co., N.Y.C., 1978—. Author: (plays) Nice Place You Have Here, 1971, The Best Is Yet to Be, 1975, The Bedroom, 1978, Seduction Duet, 1982, Fox-Trot by the Bay, 1982, The Commuter, 1982, Thirty-Nine Seconds and Counting, 1983, Space, 1983, Intermission, 1985, Penelope's Odyssey, 1986, The Country House, 1988, Seduction Triangle, 1988, On the Edge, 1989, Happy New Year, 1990, Fox-Trot on Gardiner's Bay, 1991-92, Love Puzzles, 1992, Secrets, 1993, The Black Staircase, 1994, (poetry) Against Time, 1994. Recipient Eugene O'Neill award Nat. Playwrights Conf., 1979, Double Image Short Play award Samuel French, Inc., 1981, 12th Ann. Playwriting award Jacksonville U., 1982, New Play Contest award John Drew Theatre, 1987; Hartford Found. fellow. Mem. PEN (membership com. Am. Ctr. 1980—), Dramatists Guild, Author's League Am., Acad. Am. Poets, Women's Project and Prodns., League Profl. Theatre Women (bd. dirs. 1989—). Home: PO Box 39 Sagaponack NY 11962-0039

APREA, SHARON MARTIN, merchandiser; b. Portsmouth, Va., July 17, 1956; d. Addison Berkley and Nancy Carolyn (Kiser) M.; m. Marc Angelo Aprea, Dec. 24, 1985. AS in Bus. Adminstrn., Va. Intermont, 1976; BSBA, Va. Tech., 1978. Ill. regional sales rep. Broyhill Furniture, Lenoir, N.C., 1979-82; sales mgr., acct. rep. Economon & Assocs., Dallas, 1982-87; nat. sales dir. Cavendish Furnitures, Dallas, Ipswich, England, 1987-88; accessories buyer J.C. Penney, Portfolio, Dallas, 1988-90, Breuners, Pleasant Hill, Calif., 1991-92; with Schnadig Internat. Corp., Chgo., Calif., 1992—. Columnist profl. mag., 1990—. Campaign rep. Judge Superior Ct., Rep. party, Dallas, 1990. Mem. Ill. Home Furnishings Reps. Assn. (treas. 1980-82), Internat. Trade Club (com. leader 1985-88), Southwest Trade Commn. (assoc. mem. 1982-85), Cimarron Club (dir. programs 1986-87, 1st v.p. and social chmn. 1987-88, pres. 1988-90), 500, Inc. (organizing com. mem. 1988-90). Republican. Baptist. Home: 171 Tomlinson Dr Folsom CA 95630

APUZZO, GLORIA ISABEL, accountant; b. N.Y.C., Jan. 9, 1935; d. Joseph and Emanuella Nellie (Vespo) Incremona; m. Nicholas Francis Apuzzo, Dec. 8, 1957; children: Angela Marie Apuzzo Bogholtz, Nicholas Joseph. AAS with honors, Dutchess Community Coll., 1971; student, SUNY, New Paltz, 1980. Bookkeeper, acct. Storm King Sch., Cornwall-On-Hudson, N.Y., 1972-80; jr. acct. Newburgh (N.Y.) Bd. Edn., 1980-94. Lector Our Lady of Fatima Ch., Plattekill, N.Y., 1978—; mem. Cath. Daughters of Am. Ct. Patricia #195, Newburgh, 1990—. Democrat. Roman Catholic. Home: Platekill-Ardonia Rd PO Box 670 Plattekill NY 12568 Office: Newburgh Bd Edn 124 Grand St Newburgh NY 12550-4615

AQUINO-RIVERSO, DENISE, mental health nurse; b. N.Y.C., June 6, 1951; d. Joseph and Frances (DioGuardi) A.; m. Vincent G. Riverso, Feb. 14, 1989. ADN, SUNY, Farmingdale, 1986. Staff nurse N.Y. Hosp./ Cornell West Div., White Plains, N.Y.; oper. room nurse Jack D. Weiler Hosp. Albert Einstein Sch. Med., Bronx, N.Y.; residence RN Westchester Assn. for Retarded Citizens, White Plains, N.Y. Mem. ANA, N.Y. State Nurses Assn. Home: 7 Sentry Pl # 1D Scarsdale NY 10583-2526

ARAGON, WENDY MARIE RUBIO, accountant, tax preparer; b. San Diego, June 19, 1965; d. Remigio Brozo and Wenifreda (Rubio) Aragon; m. Anthony Charles Mills, June 19, 1993. B in Acctg., U. San Diego, 1993. Adminstrv. asst. CWA, San Diego, 1985-87; customer svc. rep. San Diego Trust-Savings, 1989-91; staff acct. Bank of Am., San Diego, 1993—. Mem. Filipino Dems. of San Diego County. Mem. Inst. Mgmt. Accts., Asian Bus. Assn., Delta Sigma Pi. Democrat. Roman Catholic. Office: Security Pacific Fin Svcs 10089 Willow Creek Rd San Diego CA 92131

ARANDA, MARY KATHRYN, state legislator; b. Nassawadox, Va., Sept. 28, 1945; d. John McCallister and Frances Esther (Mausteller) Copper; m. Ronald William Meyer, Dec. 28, 1965 (dec. June 1966); m. Rembert Aranda, Feb. 4, 1973; 1 child, Olivia Kathryn. BA, Goucher Coll., 1969. Jr. planner Balt. Regional Planning Coun., 1968-71; asst. planner edn. sect. N.Y.C. Dept. City Planning, 1971-74, assoc. dir. edn. and social svcs. sect., 1974-76; rep. Gen. Ct. State of N.H., Concord, 1993—. Commr. Derry House and Revel. Authority, 1985—, treas., 1986-87, vice chmn., 1987-90, chmn., 1990—; incorporator Alexander-Eastman Found., Derry and Concord, 1993—; mem. Derry Planning Bd., 1984-88; mem. fiscal adv. com. Derry Coop. Sch. Dist., 1986-89. Republican. Home: 24 Redfield Cir Derry NH 03038-4839 Office: Dowling Assocs 60 Crystal Ave Derry NH 03038-1710

ARASON, LEESHA KAYE, director of corporate sales; b. Anaheim, Calif., Apr. 16, 1961; d. Lawrence Sigadur and Gayel Barbara (Bergh) A. AA in Comm., Orange Coast Coll., Costa Mesa, Calif., 1981; BA in Sociology, Calif. State U., Fullerton, 1984. Profl. singer Profile (Band), So. Calif, 1982-86; program coord. Imperial Health Spa, Fullerton, Calif., 1986-89; prodn. mgr. Pacific Amphitheatre, Nederlander, Costa Mesa, Calif., 1989-93; dir. of corp. sales Blockbuster Pavilion, Pace Mgmt., Devore, Calif., 1993. Mem. Childrens Fund, San Bernardino (Calif.), 1993, Orange County Young Reps., 1990-92; foster "parent" Samoyed (dogs) Rescue, Orange, Calif., 1993. Mem. San Bernardino C. of C. Democrat. Office: Blockbuster Pavilion 2575 Glen Helen Pky Devore CA 92407-1539

ARBEITER, JOAN, artist, educator; b. N.Y.C., May 8, 1937; d. David and Winifred Arden (Lembke) Berman; m. Jay David Arbeiter, June 15, 1958 (div. May 1990); children: Lisa Arbeiter Kroschke, Gail Arbeiter Goldstein. BA, CUNY, 1959; MFA, Pratt Inst., 1981. Lic. art tchr., N.Y., N.J. Tchr. N.Y.C. Sch. Sys. Bd. Edn., 1959-63; dir. Joan Arbeiter Studio Sch., Metuchen, N.J., 1976-90; instr. art, coord. founds. Ducret Sch. Art, Plainfield, N.J., 1978—, instr. art history, 1981—, instr. art appreciation, 1983—; juror various art orgns., N.J., 1981—; cons. Ednl. Testing Svc., Princeton, N.J., 1988; curator traveling art exhibit Age As a Work of Art,, Plainfield, Boston, N.Y.C., 1985-86; artist-in-residence area librs. Artists League Ctrl. N.J., 1989; presenter paper, slides Coll. Art Assn. Conf., San Antonio, 1995. One-woman shows Ceres Gallery, N.Y.C., 1985, 87, 89, 93, Wagner Coll., S.I., N.Y., 1992, Douglass Coll. Ctr., New Brunswick, N.J., 1992, Stony Brook-Millstone Watershead Assn. Gallery, Pennington, N.J., 1991; exhibited in group shows at Everhardt Gallery, Basking Ridge, N.J., 1993—, Artsphere Gallery, N.Y.C., 1994, MS Found., N.Y.C., 1995, Krasdale Corp. Gallery, Bronx, N.Y., 1995; represented in permanent collections at Fairmount Chem., Newark, CSR Group Architects and Builders-Leon Cohen, Nutley, N.J., also pvt. collections. Recipient 1st place all media award Metuchen Cultural Arts Commn. Art Exhbn., 1988, best in show award Artists League Ctrl. N.J., 1989; grantee Vt. Studio Colony, 1987. Mem. Coll. Art Assn., Women's Caucus for Art, Alpha Beta Kappa. Studio: 41 Victory Ct Metuchen NJ 08840

ARBELBIDE, CINDY LEA, victim advocate, librarian, educator; b. Stockton, Calif., Aug. 4, 1949; d. Garrett Walter and Fern Mable (Lea) A. AA in History, Santa Barbara City Coll., Calif., 1969; BS in Health & Phys. Edn., Oreg. State U., 1972; M in Libr. Sci., Emporia State U., 1980; cert., Nat. Crisis Response Team Tng. Inst., 1991. Tchr. Petersburg (Ala.) Sch. System, 1972-73, Santa Barbara (Calif.) Sch. System, 1973-74, Linn Benton Community Coll., Oreg. State U., Albany, Corvallis, 1974-75, Can. Acad., Kobe, Japan, 1975-76; tchr., libr. Wichita (Kans.) Pub. Schs., 1976-81; mgr. Geol. Info. Libr., Dallas, 1982-84; coord., cons. North Tex. Libr. System, Ft. Worth, 1984-86; dir. libr., rsch. svcs. Nat. Victim Ctr., Ft. Worth, 1986-91; dir. tng., coord. tng. all insts. Nat. Orgn. for Victim Assistance, Washington, 1991—; cons. Inst. Child Adv., Clearwater, Fla., 1990—, Nat. Sch. Safety Ctr., Encino, Calif., 1989, Ala. Ednl. Assn, Mobile, 1990, Nat. Community Response Team, N.J., Tex., 1992, FBI Washington, 1994. Author: Librarian's Planning Handbook, 1986, National Library Resource Project on Crime Victimization, 1988, 1989, Child Safety Curriculum Standards, 1989. Crisis counselor Ft. Worth Rape Crisis Ctr., 1989—, com. elderly NOVA, 1990. Named Woman of the Month Ladies Home Jour., 1973; recipient Yellow Rose of Tex. award Gov. Tex., 1992, Outstanding Contbn. letter U.S. Army, 1993, Recognition and Appreciation cert. Concerns of Police Survivors, 1994. Mem. ALA, Am. Assn. Law Librs., Spl. Librs. Assn. (chairperson catalog com., 1990-91, chairperson Social Sci. Div. Roundtable Health and Human Svcs. 1990), Nat. Victim Ctr., Am. Women's Self Def. Assn., Tex. Libr. Assn. (vice chairperson div. spl. librs. 1987-88, chairperson 1988-89), Assn. Threat Assessment Profls., Critical Incident Stress Debriefing Soc. Internat. Assn. Trauma Counselors, Nat. Cmty. Crisis Response Team. Office: NOVA 1757 Park Rd NW Washington DC 20010-2101

ARBIT, BERYL ELLEN, legal assistant; b. L.A., Aug. 16, 1949; d. Harry A. and Norma K. (Michelson) A. BA, UCLA, 1970. From legal asst. to sr. legal asst. O'Melveny & Myers, L.A., 1977—; guest lectr. atty. asst. tng. program UCLA, 1991. Mem. UCLA Atty. Asst. Alumni Assn. (bd. dirs. 1980-82), Alpha Omicron Pi (treas. West L.A. alumnae chpt. 1993—), Nu Lambda (corp. bd. pres. 1978-80, chpt. adv. 1976-78). Office: O'Melveny & Myers 400 S Hope St Los Angeles CA 90071

ARBITELL, MICHELLE RENEÉ, clinical psychologist; b. Trenton, N.J., Oct. 24, 1962; d. John A. and Adele M. (Klama) A. BA, Lehigh U., 1984; MA, Indiana U. of Pa., 1986, D Psychology, 1988. Lic. psychologist, Pa.; cert. counselor Office Vocat. Rehab. Clin. pscyhology intern Geisinger Med. Ctr., Danville, Pa., 1987-88; dir. behavioral medicine and neuropsychology HealthSouth Rehab. Hosp., 1988—; adv. bd. mem. Blair County Pain Support Groups, Altoona, 1988—; pvt. practice psychology, cons., Altoona, State College, Pa., 1991-94; invited lectr. Pa. State U., University Park, 1991—; presenter in field. Author: (with others) On Spouse Abuse..., 1985; (with others) Bulimics' Perceptions..., 1991. Mem. APA, NAFE, Nat. Acad. Neuropsychology, Pa. Psychol. Assn., Soc. Behavioral Medicine, Phi Beta Kappa, Psi Chi (v.p./sec. 1980-84). Office: HealthSouth Rehab Hosp Altoona Valley View Blvd Altoona PA 16602

ARCESI-DOZIER, BEVERLY ANN, former small business owner; b. Ocala, Fla., Mar. 1, 1959; d. Harry Beecher and Linda Marie (Hancock) Clarkson; m. Luciano Humberto Giovanni Arcesi, July 8, 1937 (dec. 1987); children: Luciana, Giancarlo, Marina Elena; m. Howard Ronald Dozier, Nov. 24, 1989; 1 child, Christian Ronald. Student, Stetson U., Deland, Fla., 1993—. Receptionist N.Am. Realty Corp., Miami, 1975-76; file clk. Anthony Abraham Chevrolet, Miami, 1976-77; dept. head warranty claim dept. Milano Imported Motors, Inc., Miami, 1977-79; dept. head acctg. Maurice Jay Kutner, Miami, 1979-80; sec. to controller Omni Internat. Hotel, Miami, 1980-81; pres. Italian Tile Imports, Inc., Ocala, Fla., 1985-89, chmn. bd., chief exec. officer, 1987-89. Active Ocala Royal Dames for Cancer Rsch., 1988, 89, 90, Heart of Ocala Debutante Soc., 1989. Mem. Italian Trade Commn., Marion County Builders Assn., Mid-State Builders Assn., Marion County C. of C., Ocala Breakfast Club, Caritas Club (pres. 1976-77), Phi Theta Kappa. Republican. Presbyterian. Home and Office: 2525 SE 67th Street Rd Ocala FL 34480-6213

ARCH, GAIL THELMA, international business educator; b. Boston, July 16, 1952; d. Joseph Sherrard and Thelma Mathilde (Terkelsen) A.; m. George Nichols Vorys, July 31, 1977 (div. Feb. 1987); 1 child, George Christian. BA, Wheaton Coll., 1974; MA, Ohio State U., 1980, PhD, 1991. Grad. rsch. assoc. Ohio State U., Columbus, 1986-91; asst. prof. U. Houston, 1991—, acad. fellow Inst. for Diversity and Cross-Cultural Mgmt., 1991—; bd. gov. coun. Inst. for Bus. Ethics and Pub. Issues, Houston, 1991—. Contbr. articles to profl. jours. Recipient Greenwood award Houston City Coun., 1993; grantee Inst. Turkish Studies, 1991; bus. and econs. fellow Dept. Edn., 1992. Mem. Internat. Indsl. Rels. Rsch. Assn., Indsl. Rels. Rsch. Assn. (exec. bd. dirs. 1992—), Global Future Found. (treas. 1993), Internat. Design for Extreme Environments Assn. (treas. 1993), Acad. Internat. Bus., Acad. Mgmt., Phi Beta Kappa, Phi Kappa Phi. Home: 3435 Westheimer Rd Apt 1106 Houston TX 77027-5347 Office: U Houston 4800 Calhoun Rd Houston TX 77204-6283

ARCHABAL, NINA M(ARCHETTI), historical society director; b. Long Branch, N.J., Apr. 11, 1940; d. John William and Santina Matilda (Giuffre) Marchetti; m. John William Archabal, Aug. 8, 1964; 1 child, John Fidel. BA in Music History cum laude, Radcliffe Coll., 1962; MAT in Music History, Harvard U., 1963; PhD in Music History, U. Minn., 1979. Asst. dir. humanities art mus. U. Minn., Mpls., 1975-77; asst. supr. edn. div. Minn. Hist. Soc., St. Paul, 1977-78, dep. dir. for program mgmt., 1978-86, acting dir., 1986-87, dir., 1987—. Trustee, bd. dirs. Am. Folklife Ctr., Libr. of Congress, 1989—; bd. dirs. N.W. Area Found., St. Paul Acad. and Summit Sch.; v.p. Friends of St. Paul Pub. Libr., 1983-93. NDEA fellow U. Minn., 1969-72, U. Minn. grad. fellow, 1974-75. Mem. Am. Assn. State and Local History (sec. 1986-88), Am. Assn. Mus. (v.p. 1991-94, chair of bd. 1994—). Office: Minn Hist Soc 345 Kellogg Blvd W Saint Paul MN 55102-1903

ARCHER, ANNE, actress; b. L.A., Aug. 25, 1949; d. John and Marjorie (Lord) A.; m. Terry Jastrow; children: Thomas, Jeffrey. Appearances include (theatre) A Couple White Chicks Sitting Around Talking, 1981, Les Liaisons Dangeruses, 1988, (films) The Honkers, 1972, Cancel My Reservation, 1972, The All-American Boy, 1973, Trackdown, 1976, Lifeguard, 1976, Paradise Valley, 1978, Good Guys Wear Black, 1978, Raise the Titanic, 1980, Hero At Large, 1980, Green Ice, 1981, Waltz Across Texas, 1983, Too Scared to Scream, 1985, The Naked Face, 1985, The Check Is in the Mail, 1985, Fatal Attraction, 1987 (Golden Globe nominee 1987, Acad. award nominee 1988), Love at Large, 1990, Narrow Margin, 1990, Eminent Domain, 1991, Patroit Games, 1992, Body of Evidence, 1993, Short Cuts, 1993, Clear and Present Danger, 1994; (TV series) Bob and Carol and Ted and Alice, 1973, The Family Tree, 1983, Falcon Crest, 1985, (TV movies) The Blue Knight, 1973, The Mark of Zorro, 1974, The Log of the Black Pearl, 1975, A Matter of Wife...and Death, 1976, The Dark Side of Innocence, 1976, Seventh Avenue, 1977, The Pirate, 1978, The Sky's No Limit, 184, A Different Affair, 1987, A Leap of Faith, 1988, The Last of His Tribe, 1992, Nails, 1992, Jane's House, 1994, Because Mommy Works, 1994. *

ARCHER, MARY JANE, state agency administrator; b. Oakland, Calif., Aug. 23, 1949; d. Doris Marlene (Howard) Wood; m. Bradley Eugene Archer; Nov. 10, 1984. BS in Acctg., Calif. State U., Hayward, 1971, MBA in Acctg., 1977. Auditor Calif. State Controller's Office, Sacramento, 1972-81, supr., 1981-84, asst. div. chief, 1984-90; acting div. chief, 1990—. Tutor Sacramento Literacy Ctr. Mem. Calif. Assn. Mgmt. Republican. Office: Calif State Contr's Office Div Tax Adminstrn PO Box 942850 Ofc Sacramento CA 94250-0001

ARCHER, RITA KWIATKOWSKI, safety engineer; b. Wilkes-Barre, Pa., Apr. 8, 1963; d. Frank and Alice (Iwanowski) Kwiatkowski; m. Stuart Kieth Archer, June 20, 1987; 2 children: Christopher Alexander, Nathan Andrew. BS in Chem. Engring., Pa. State U., 1985; MBA, La. Tech., 1989. Contract engr. Trey Corp., Vivian, La., 1992-94; safety specialist environmental concerns Naval Air Warfare Ctr., Warminster, Pa., 1994—. Capt. USAF, 1985-91. Roman Catholic. Home: 31 Cypress Dr Eastampton Township NJ 08060

ARCHER, VIVIAN THOMAS, educational administrator; b. West Orange, N.J., July 27, 1939; d. Daniel and Etta Mae (Johnson) Thomas; B.A., Kean Coll., 1961; M.Ed., U. D.C., 1972; postgrad. U. So. Calif., 1978-80; EdD, U. Mass., 1990; m. Carl Edward Archer, July 16, 1961; children: Carla Evette Mitchell, Crystal Evonne. Tchr., Richmond (Va.) Pub. Schs., 1961-64; tchr. Washington Pub. Schs., 1964-71, math. resource tchr., 1971-74, asst. dir. math. Response to Ednl. Needs project, 1974-78, acting asst. prin., 1978-80, elem. supr., 1980-90, field supr. ESEA Title I programs, 1981-82, instructional supr. ECIA Chpt. 1, 1982-90, acting prin., 1985-86, asst. prin., 1990—, adminstrv. practitioner LEAD, 1991-92. Pres. Leckie PTA, Washington, 1971-73, chairperson bd., 1974-79, v.p., 1981-83; mem. Anacostia Community Sch. Bd., 1980-83; mem. fin. com. Covenant Baptist Ch., 1981—; bd. dirs. Area D Mental Health Ctr., 1985—; mentor, trainer Springfield Leadership Devel. Program, 1992; fellow Inst. for Ednl. Leadership, 1990-91, Inst. for Devel. Ednl. Activities, 1992. Mem. D.C. Council Tchrs. Math., Nat. Council Tchrs. Math., Council Basic Edn., Council Sch. Officers, D.C. Council Staff Devel., Nat. Assn. Supervision and Curriculum Devel., D.C. Assn. Supervision and Curriculum Devel. (program co-chairperson 1982-83, pres.-elect 1984, pres. 1985), Internat. Reading Assn., Nat. Congress Parents and Tchrs. Assn., Nat. Assn. Black Sch. Educators, Assn. Tchr. Educators, Nat. Assn. Elem. Sch. Prins., Am. Assn. Sch. Adminstrs., Nat. Assn. Disadvantaged Children, AAUW, Delta Sigma Theta. Democrat. Home: 50 Brandywine St SW Washington DC 20032-1309 Office: Martin Luther King Jr ES 6th and Alabama Ave SE Washington DC 20032

ARCHER-SMITH, STEPHANIE DEE, health facility administrator; b. Wash., Sept. 29, 1962; d. Joe Dee and Angela Rose (Fahey) Archer; m. Andrew Blair Smith, Apr. 27, 1991. BS, U. Md., 1985; MS, U. Balt., 1994. Tchr. Holy Spirit Mid. Sch., Balt., 1985-86; counselor Villa Maria Resdl. Treatment Ctr., Timonium, Md., 1986-89; child life coord. Mt. Wash. Pediatric Hosp., Balt., 1989-94; mental health therapist North Balt. Cmty. Mental Health Clinic & Children's Svc., 1994—; employee trainer, program developer Mt. Wash. Pediatric Hosp., 1989-94. Mem. NOW, Psi Chi. Home: 1428 W 37th St Baltimore MD 21211 Office: N Balt Cmty Mental Health Clinic & Childrens Svc 1708 W Rogers Ave Baltimore MD 21209

ARCHIBALD, CLAUDIA JANE, parapsychologist, consultant; b. Atlanta, Nov. 14, 1939; d. Claud Bernard and Doris Evelyn (Linch) A. B in Psychology, Georgia State U., 1962; BTh., Emory U., 1964; DD, Stanton Coll., 1969. Pvt. practice psycho-spiritual counselor Atlanta, 1960—; minister Nat. Spiritualist Assn., Atlanta, 1969-72; parapsychologist Ctr. for Life, Atlanta, 1985-86; parapsychologist Inst. of Metaphysical Inquiry, Atlanta, 1980—, also bd. dirs., founder, 1980—. Author: (book) Quantitative Symbolism, 1980, short stories; dir. Phoenix Dance Unltd., 1984-90; choregrapher (dance) Phoenix Rising, 1985. Vol. Aid Atlanta, 1987-89. Recipient City Grant award Bur. Cultural Affairs, Atlanta, 1985, 86. Mem. Am. Psychical Rsch. Assn., Soc. Metaphysicians (corr. Eng. chpt.), Am. Assn. Parapsychology, Nat. Assn. Alcoholism and Drug Abuse Counselors, Ga. Addiction Counselors' Assn., N.Am. Ballet Assn., Nat. Leather Assn., Echoes of the People, Native Am. Orgn., Sun Dancer. Home: 2638 Valmar Dr Atlanta GA 30340-1945

ARCHIBALD, GAIL ARDELY, assistant principal; b. Chgo., July 8, 1951; d. Eddie Lee and Ida (Morgan) A. BS in Edn., Chgo. State U., 1972, MA in Edn. Adminstrn., 1994; MA in Inner City, Northeastern U., 1977. Cert. tchr., Ill. Elem. tchr. Chgo. Bd. Edn., 1972-75, social studies tchr., 1975-94, asst. prin., 1994—; social studies chairperson Chgo. Bd. Edn., 1993-94. Libr. trustee Bellwood (Ill.) Libr., 1991—, bd. treas., 1991-94, trustee, 1991—. Democrat. Methodist. Home: 306 Hyde Park Ave Bellwood IL 60104

ARCHIBALD, JEANNE S., lawyer; b. Jan. 30, 1951; d. George R. Stokes and Eleanore (Moran) L.; m. Thomas P. Archibald, Aug. 19, 1972; children: Charles Edward. BA, SUNY, Stony Brook, 1973; JD, Georgetown U., 1977. D.C. bar: 1977. Staff asst. House Com. on Ways and Means, 1975-77, profl. staff mem., 1977-80; assoc. gen. counsel, chmn. sect. 301 com. U.S. Trade Rep., 1980-86; dep. asst. gen. counsel internat. affairs Dept. of Treasury, 1986-88; dep. gen. counsel Dept. of Treasury, 1988-90, gen. counsel, 1990-93; ptnr. Hogan & Hartson, Washington, 1993—. Office: Hogan & Hartson Columbia Sq 555 13th St NW Washington DC 20004-1109

ARCIERI, SANDY LEE, professional collector, researcher; b. Chgo., July 23, 1955; d. Adam Eugene and Marie Prudence (Worek) Prucznal; m. Dennis James Arcieri, July 22, 1979. BA in Math. and Edn., St. Xavier Coll., Chgo., 1977. Tchr. math. St. Peter and St. Paul Schs., Chgo., 1977-79; pvt. math. tutor, 1979-83, collector Jean Harlow personal effects, 1971—. Contbg. rschr. Life at the Marmont, 1987, Mayer and Thalberg: The Make-Believe Saints, 1988, Deadly Illusions, 1990, Bombshell, 1993. Roman Catholic. Home: 9530 S Clifton Park Ave Evergreen Park IL 60642-2131

ARCORI, ANNE EILEEN, program management professional; b. Detroit, Jan. 8, 1959; d. Thomas Charles and Eileen B. (Cody) Fischer; m. Frank Marino Arcori, Dec. 1, 1986 (div. Nov. 1991). A of Indsl. Mgmt., Chrysler U.; BS in Mgmt. and Supervision magna cum laude, Ctrl. Mich. U., 1993. Engring. records/specifications clk. Gen. Dynamics Land Systems, Inc., 1977-81, engring. change coord., 1981-83, engring. document control supr., 1983-84, prodn. planning specialist, 1984-90, material planning specialist, 1992-94; process leader Ford Motor Corp. Electronics Tech. Ctr., Dearborn, Mich., 1994—. Mem. NAFE, APICS, Nat. Mgmt. Assn., Toastmasters Internat. (sec. 1991). Home: 31721 Verona Circle Beverly Hills CA 48025

ARDEN, SHERRY W., publishing company executive; b. N.Y.C., Oct. 18, 1930; d. Abraham and Rose (Bellak) Waretnick; m. Hal Marc Arden (div. 1974); children: Doren, Cathy; m. George Bellak, Oct. 20, 1979. Student, Columbia U. Publicity dir. Coward-McCann, N.Y.C., 1965-67; producer Allan Foshko Assoc., ABC-TV, N.Y.C., 1967-68; sr. v.p., pub. William Morrow & Co., N.Y.C., 1968-85; pres., pub. William Morrow & Co., 1985-89; owner Sherry W. Arden Lit. Agy., 1990—. Mem. Assn. Am. Pubs. (dir.). Club: Pubs. Lunch.

ARDINE, DONNA MARIE, retail executive; b. Pitts., Oct. 25, 1965; d. Eugene A. and Rosanna C. (Carlini) A. BS in Mktg., Pa. State U., 1988. Buyer's asst. May Co. Dept. Stores, Rochester, N.Y., 1988-90; dept. mgr. May Co./Lord & Taylor, Phila., 1990; regional distbr. Ltd., Inc., Ltd. Express, Columbus, Ohio, 1990-91; distbn. mgr. Ltd. Express, Columbus, Ohio, 1991-92; mgr. testing Ltd., Bath & Body Wks., Columbus, Ohio, 1993, merchandise planner, 1993—. Mem. NOW. Home: 1376 Mentor Dr Westerville OH 43081-4649

ARDIS, SUSAN BARBER, librarian, educator; b. Holly, Mich., Feb. 21, 1947; d. Raymond Walker and Joan Violet (Grove) Barber; m. Thomas John Ardis, Aug. 18, 1968; children: Jessica, Andrew. BA, U. Mich., 1968, AMLS, 1969. Head natural sci. libr. U. Mich., Ann Arbor, 1969-78; head reference Rosenberg Libr., Galveston, Tex., 1978-79; head Engring. Libr. U. Tex., Austin, 1979—. Author: An Introduction to Patent Searching, 1991, Electrical Electronic Engineering Information Sources, 1987, Toward the Electronic Library, 1994; contbr. articles to profl. jours. Mem. Spl. Librs. Assn., Am. Soc. Engring. Edn. Office: U Tex Austin Engring Libr Gen Librs ECJ 1.300 Austin TX 78713-7330

ARDISON, LINDA G., author, writing educator; b. Ft. Smith, Ark., Apr. 11, 1940; d. Bill Eugene and Mildred M. (Fry) Tanner; m. Gary Winship Ardison, June 10, 1962; children: Amy Roberts, Elizabeth Winship, Matthew Tanner. AA, Stephens Coll., 1960; student, Middlebury Coll., 1960-61; postgrad., Bread Loaf Sch. of English, 1960; BA, U. Ark., 1962. Adminstrv. asst. Wachovia Nat. Bank, Winston-Salem, N.C., 1962-63; English tchr. Wiley Jr. High Sch., Winston-Salem, 1963-64; writing instr. York Coll. of Pa., 1984—; vis. poet York Country Day Sch., 1986, instr. poetry workshop, 1993. Editor Standard lit. mag., 1959-60; asst. editor Keystone News, 1980-82; contbr. articles, poems, plays, short stories to jours. Bd. dirs. York County med. Soc. Aux., York, 1978-80; mem. Jr. League of York, 1974-75; adult educator Living Word Community Ch., York, 1980—; bd. dirs. Human Life Svcs., York, 1989-92. Recipient 3d place for fiction in annual coll. contest The Atlantic Monthly, 1960; Bread Loaf scholar The Atlantic Monthly, 1960; Pa. Arts Coun. fellowship grantee, 1990-91. Mem. York County Med. Soc. Aux., Pa. Med. Soc. Aux. Republican. Home: 260 School St York PA 17402-9543 Office: York Coll of Pa Country Club Rd York PA 17404

ARDOLF, CONNIE RENEE, interior designer; b. Glencoe, Minn., Jan. 9, 1949; d. Leonard Edward and Eleanore Gertrude (Goranowski) A. Lic. cosmetologist, Red Carpet, Mpls., 1969; interior design diploma, Dakota County Tech. Coll., Rosemount, Minn., 1992. Cosmetologist Kut and Kurl

Beauty Salon, Winsted, Minn., 1969-70, Bernadines Beauty Salon, Mpls., 1970-73, Betty's Artcraft, Mpls., 1973-76, Beauty Spot Hairstyles, Mpls., 1976-93; merchandising asst. window treatments J.C. Penney, Minnetonka, Minn., 1993—. Photography book: Train Bum, 1992, The Stealing of Mona Lisa, 1993.

AREEN, JUDITH CAROL, law educator; b. Chgo., Aug. 2, 1944; d. Gordon Eric and Pauline Jeanette (Payberg) A.; m. Richard M. Cooper, Feb. 17, 1979; children—Benjamin Eric, Jonathan Gordon. AB, Cornell U., 1966; JD, Yale U., 1969. Bar: Mass. 1970, D.C. 1972. Program planner for higher edn. Mayor's Office City of N.Y., 1969-70; dir. edn. voucher study Ctr. for Study Pub. Policy, Cambridge, Mass., 1970-72; mem. faculty Georgetown U., Washington, 1971—, assoc. prof. law, 1972-76, prof., 1976—, prof. community and family medicine, 1980-89, assoc. dean Law Ctr., 1984-87; dean, exec. v.p. for law affairs Georgetown U, Washington, 1989—; gen. counsel, coord. domestic reorgn. Office of Mgmt. and Budget, Washington, 1977-80; spl. counsel White House Task Force on Regulatory Reform, Washington, 1978-80; cons. NIH, 1984; cons. NRC, 1985, mem. com. film badge dosimetry; bd. dirs. MCI. Author: Youth Service Agencies, 1977, Cases and Materials on Family Law, 1978, 3d edit., 1992; co-author: Education Vouchers, 1970, Cases and Materials on Law, Science and Medicine, 1984. Mem. Def. Adv. Com. Women In Svcs., Washington, 1979-82. Woodrow Wilson Internat. Ctr. for Scholars fellow, 1988-89, Kennedy Inst. Ethics Sr. Rsch. fellow, Washington, 1982—. Mem. ABA, D.C. Bar Assn., Am. Law Inst. Office: Georgetown U Law Ctr 1507 Isherwood St NE # 1 Washington DC 20002-5564

AREGLADO, NANCY, elementary education educator, consultant; b. Boston, Dec. 10, 1946; d. William Vincent and Julia Marie (Dierkes) Hyland; m. Ronald James Areglado, Aug. 24, 1968; children: Kristin Holly, Kimberly Anne, Julie Lynn. BS, Boston State Coll., 1968; MEd, U. Mass., 1982. Tchr. Quincy (Mass.) Pub. Schs., 1968-70; lang. specialist Mass. Migrant Edn. Program, Holyoke, 1981-83; spl. edn. tutor Greenfield (Mass.) Sch. Dept., 1984; tchr. North Adams (Mass.) Pub. Schs., 1986-89, early childhood coord., 1987-89; adj. instr. North Adams State Coll., 1988-89; pvt. practice whole lang. cons. pvt. practice integrated lang. arts con., Mass., 1987—; 1st grade tchr. Village Sch., West Stockbridge, Mass., 1989-90; whole lang. coord. Berkshire Hills Schs., Stockbridge, 1990; reading specialist Fairfax County Pub. Schs., 1990—. Co-author: Portfolios in the Classroom: A Teacher's Sourcebook. Co-organizer Cambodia Assistance Dr., Franklin County, Mass., 1979; bd. dirs. Big Bros./Big Sisters Assn., Greenfield, Mass., 1975-85. Recipient Exemplary Svc. award Big Bros./Big Sisters, 1976, Celebrate Literacy award, Berkshire Reading Coun., 1990. Mem. Whole Lang. Tchrs. Assn. (networking chair Berkshires 1987-89, mem. Whole Lang. Umbrella 1986—), Nat. Coun. Tchrs. English, Internat. Reading Assn., Phi Delta Kappa. Democrat. Roman Catholic. Home: 11107 Robert Carter Rd Fairfax VA 22039 Office: Reading Ctr Rolling Valley Sch Fairfax County Pub Schs Springfield VA 22152

AREKAPUDI, VIJAYALAKSHMI, obstetrician-gynecologist; b. Davajigudem, Andhra Pradesh, India, Sept. 28, 1948; came to U.S., 1974; d. Subba Rao and Ramatulasamma (Ravi) Gondi; m. Bapu P. Arekapudi, May 5, 1974; children: Smitha, Swathi. MB, BChir, Guntur Med. Coll., Andhra Pradesh, India, 1970; DGO, Coll. Physicians and Surgeons Bombay, 1973. Intern Ill. Masonic Med. Ctr., Chgo., 1975-76, resident in ob-gyn., 1976-79, jr. attending staff, 1979-82, assoc. attending staff, 1982-84, attending physician, 1985—; group practice Lake Shore Med. Assocs., Ltd., Chgo., 1979—, sec., treas., 1981—; mem. med. staff, mem. exec. com. Ill. Masonic Med. Ctr., 1994—. Fellow ACOG. Democrat. Hindu. Office: Lake Shore Med Assocs Ltd 2734 N Lincoln Ave Chicago IL 60614-1321

ARENA, KELLI, news correspondent; b. Bklyn., N.Y., Dec. 17, 1963; d. Melvin Mullins and Mary Ann (Scafa) Tracy. BFA, NYU, 1985. Prodr. various shows CNN, N.Y.C., 1985-89, prodr. spl. reports, 1988-89, line prodr., 1989-90, supervising prodr., 1990-92; exec. prodr. CNN, London, 1992; news editor CNN, N.Y.C., 1992-93, reporter, anchor, 1993—. Youth dir. St. George's Ch., N.Y.C., 1989-93. Recipient Peabody award U. Ga., 1987, Cable Ace award, 1987, Gold award Houston Internat. Film Festival, 1987; named Topten Fin. Journalist Jour. Fin. Reporting, 1989-92. Mem. Soc. Am. Bus. Editors and Writers, Internat. Womens Media Found., N.Y. Fin. Writers Assn. Office: CNN Bus News 5 Penn Plz 20th Fl New York NY 10001

ARENA, MARY HELEN, lay worker; b. Pensacola, Fla., Dec. 12, 1951; d. Richard Joseph and Mary Eileen (Adams) Owens; m. Augustine Anthony Arena, Aug. 23, 1975; children: Andrew, Philip, Thomas, Katherine. Diploma, Berkeley Bus. Sch., White Plains, N.Y., 1971; student, Westchester Community Coll., White Plains, N.Y., 1975-76. Catechist St. Columbanus Parish, Peekskill, N.Y., 1979—; founder, facilitator Parish Mothers and Preschoolers Group, Peekskill, 1981-90; coord. St. Columbanus N.Y. Archdiocesan Synod Efforts, Peekskill; mem. N.Y. Archdiocesan Pastoral Coun., N.Y.C., 1985-90, No. Westchester/Putnam Vicariate Coun., Mahopac, N.Y., 1983-90; chmn. St. Colombanus Parish Coun., 1990-93, catechist/coord. RCIA program, 1990—. mem. St. Colombanus choir, 1963-89, bible study group, 1983—. Leader Taconic Girl Scout Coun., Mahopac, 1970-73. Republican. Home: 14 Mountain View Rd Putnam Valley NY 10579-2016

AREND, SHARON GAIL, historian, archivist; b. Mt. Clemens, Mich., Aug. 22, 1938; d. Paul William Long and Patricia Ann (King) Lickteig; m. Pierre Leon Arend, May 28, 1966; children: Pierre Andre, Patrice Sharon. BFA, Ctr. for Creative Study, 1981; MA, Wayne State U., 1991. Writer, lectr. Detroit Inst. of Arts, 1985-88; graphic designer City of Sterling Heights, Mich., 1986-89; co. historian, archivist Little Caesar Enterprises, Inc. Detroit Red Wings, Detroit Tigers, Fox Theatre, 1989—. Bd. dirs. state adv. bd. Nat. Hist. Publs. and Records Commn., Lansing, Mich., 1992-95; chair Sterling Heights Cultural Commn., 1985—. Named Patron of the Arts, Macomb Arts Coun., 1991; grad. profl. scholar Wayne State U., 1984-85. Mem. Soc. Am. Archivists, Preservation Wayne. Home: 37145 Alper Dr Sterling Heights MI 48312 Office: Little Caesar Enterprises 2211 Woodward Ave Detroit MI 48201

ARENT, LORENE LUCILLE, retired secondary education educator; b. Gordon, Nebr., Aug. 6, 1927; d. Phillip Clarence and Louise Linda (Jones) A. BA, Wayne State Coll., 1949; MA, No. U. of Colo., 1956. Cert. tchr., Nebr. Home econs., English tchr. Oakdale (Nebr.) Pub. Schs., 1949-51, Rising City (Nebr.) Pub. Schs., 1951-52; home econs. and geography tchr. Wisner (Nebr.) Pub. Schs., 1952-53; home econs. and English tchr. Wausa (Nebr.) Pub. Schs., 1954-91, ret., 1991. Treas. Congl. United Ch. of Christ Women's Fellowship; sec. Bd. Christian Edn. Mem. NEA, Nebr. State Edn. Assn., Am. Home Econs. Assn., Wausa Edn. Assn. (treas., pres.), Am. Vocat. Assn. (asst. grand warden 1983), Order of Eastern Star (worthy matron 1983-84), Delta Kappa Gamma (treas. 1984-90), Sigma Tau Delta (Pi Beta chpt. 1948), Pi Gamma Mu. Republican. Congregationalist. Home: HC 65 Box 170 Ainsworth NE 69210-9443

ARETZ, TONYA MARIE, lawyer; b. Lafayette, Ind., Nov. 6, 1959; d. Donald T. and Ruth M. (Crone) A. BA, Ind. U., 1982; JD, U. Dayton, 1985. Police officer Ind. U. Police Dept., Bloomington, 1980-82; law clk. to presiding justice Montgomery County Common Pleas Ct., Dayton, Ohio, 1984-85; dep. atty. gen. State of Ind., Indpls., 1986-95; assoc. Stephenson Daly Morow and Kurnik, 1995—. Named one of Outstanding Young Women Am., 1983. Mem. ABA (liaison 1984-85), Ind. Bar Assn., Phi Delta Phi. Republican. Roman Catholic. Home: 940 Green Meadows Dr Plainfield IN 46158-9231 Office: 8902 N Meridian St Ste 205 Indianapolis IN 46260-5307

AREVALO, DIANE CHRISTINE, computer systems analyst; b. Manila, Sept. 16, 1966; came to U.S., 1983; d. Jose and Naida Arevalo Tempongko. BS in Computer Sci., U. Calif., Irvine, 1988. Programmer/analyst I Eaton Corp., Costa Mesa, Calif., 1988-89, programmer/analyst II, 1989-92, systems analyst, 1992—; systems designer, cons. Dr. Hanahan Family Dentistry, L.A., 1992-93. Republican. Roman Catholic. Home: 2624 E Andover Ave Fullerton CA 92631-1490

ARGRETT, LORETTA COLLINS, attorney general, educator; b. Carlisle, Miss., Oct. 7, 1937; d. Joseph Daniel and Katie Marie (Jones) C.; m. James H. Argrett Jr., Mar. 28, 1959 (div.); children: Lisa Argrett Ahmad, Brian E.; m. Vantile E. Whitfield, May 29, 1993. BS cum laude, Howard U., 1958; student, Technische Hochschule, Zurich, Switzerland, 1958; postgrad., Howard U., 1966-67, George Washington U., 1968; JD, Harvard U., 1976. Bar: D.C. Ct. Appeals 1976, U.S. Dist. Ct. D.C. 1977, U.S. Ct. Appeals D.C. 1977, U.S. Tax Ct. 1977. Chemist NIH, 1958-59, 59-61; tchr. Duval County Bd. Instrn., Fla., 1961-62; chemist Hazleton Labs., Reston, Va., 1965-66, FDA, 1966-68; chemist, supr. lab. Walter Reed Army Inst. of Rsch., 1968-73; summer assoc. Mahoney, Hadlow, Chambers & Adams, Jacksonville, Fla., summer 1975; summer assoc. Arent, Fox, Kintner, Plotkin & Kahn, Washington, summer 1975, assoc., 1976-78; assoc. Stroock & Stroock & Lavan, Washington, 1978-79; legis. atty. Joint Com. on Taxation U.S. Congress, 1979-81; ptnr. Wald, Harkrader & Ross, Washington, 1981-86; pvt. practice Washington, 1986; assoc. prof., then prof. Sch. Law, Howard U., Washington, 1986—; sec. bd. meetings Opportunity Funding Corp., 1984—; adj. prof. Georgetown Law Ctr., Washington Coll. Law, 1986-88, Am. U., 1988; mem. vis. com. Harvard Law Sch., 1987-93; appointed mem. adv. com. grad. tax program U. Balt. Law Sch., 1986—; mem. spl. com. on gender D.C. Cir. Task Force on Gender, Race and Ethnic Bias, 1992—; mem. adv. com. for grad. Contbr. articles to profl. jours. Bd. trustees Free the Children Trust; bd. dirs. Jubilee Enterprise of Greater Washington, Inc.; adv. bd. Jubilee Support Alliance; mem. NAACP, Pub. Defender Svc. of D.C. Lucy Moten fellow, 1958. Fellow Am. Bar Found.; mem. ABA (sect. on taxation, chair task force capital cost recovery 1985, vice chair com. womena and minorities 1993—, lobbyist), Nat. Bar Assn., Washington Bar Assn., D.C. Bar Assn. (mem. atty. client arbitration bd. 1984-90, legal ethics com. 1993—), Sigma Xi (assoc.), Beta Kappa Chi, Harvard Law Sch. Alumni Assn. Office: Howard U Sch of Law Dept Justice 2900 Van Ness St NW Washington DC 20008

ARGUN, FATIMA HATICE, international consultant, specialist. BA in Polit. Sci. and Internat. Studies, U. Tex., 1983; Cert. de Langue Francaise, U. Paris-Sorbonne, 1983; MPA, U. Tex., 1985. With Office of the U.S. Trade Rep., Washington, 1986; freelance writer Internat. Reports, N.Y.C., 1986-87; dir. internat. trade Competitive Enterprise Inst., Washington, 1987-88; campaign liaison George Bush for President and Bush-Quayle '88 campaigns, Washington, 1987-88; coord. transition office contacts Office of the Pres.-Elect, Washington, 1988-89; confidential asst. to dir. internat. trade Minority Bus. Devel. Agy. U.S. Dept. Commerce, Washington, 1989-91; legis. fellow U.S. Sen. Arlen Specter, Washington, 1991-92; confidential adv. to chmn. U.S. Merit Systems Protection Bd., Washington, 1992—. Co-author: U.S. Trade with Newly Industrializing Countries. Mem. Women in Internat. Trade (charter, bd. dirs., spl. events chmn. 1987-88), World Affairs Coun. Washington, Fgn. Policy Assn. N.Y., Gt. Decisions Fgn. Policy Discussion Group, Washington Internat. Trade Assn., Tex. State Soc., Am. Friends of Turkey, LBJ Sch. Alumni Assn. (v.p. 1989—), Les Compagnons (France). Republican.

ARJONA, SANDRA KATHERINE, medical librarian, knowledge and software engineer; b. Pitts., May 27, 1947; d. Angelo William and Mary Louise (Kredick) Fabbozzi; m. Saturnino Arjona, May 22, 1976 (div.). BA in Liberal Arts and Edn. cum laude, Carlow Coll., Pitts., 1969; MLS, U. Pitts., 1985. Exec. asst. to mgr. purchasing dept. Comml. DVP, S.A., Barcelona, Spain, 1972-74; exec. asst. to pres. CINSA, Barcelona, 1974-75; editorial asst., adminstrv. sec. Children's Hosp. Pitts., 1976-79, info. processing specialist, 1980-83, mgr. info. systems ear, nose and throat dept., 1983-85; dir. med. libr. Health Info. and Resource Ctr. St. Margaret Meml. Hosp., Pitts., 1986-91; editorial processing mgr. Annals of Otology, Rhinology and Laryngology, St. Louis, 1984-86; mng. editor W.B. Saunders Co., Phila., 1985-87, assoc. editor, 1983; editorial coord. Year Book Med. Pubs., Chgo., 1986-87; editorial cons. Gower Med. Pub. Ltd., N.Y.C., 1987; coord., dir. workshops and seminars. Translator English to Spanish, Rainbow Fgn. Lang. Series, 1987, Tracheotomy, 1986, A Colour Atlas of Clinical Conditions in Paedodontics, 1979, Spanish to English Clinical Visual Schemes in Rheumatology, 1987, Atlas of Perinatology, 1982. Mem. Am. Assn. for Med. Systems and Informatics, Am. Med. Writers Assn. (pres. Ohio Valley chpt. 1984-86, del. to nat. bd. dirs. 1984-86, mem.-at-large exec. com. 1985-86, chmn. pub. rels. 1985-86), Armed Forces Communication and Electronics Assn., Assn. for Computing Machinery, Internat. Tech. Inst., IEEE Computer Soc., World Future Soc., Beta Phi Mu, Lambda Iota Tau. Home and Office: 843 Geyer Rd Pittsburgh PA 15212-1125

ARLINGHAUS, SANDRA JUDITH LACH, mathematical geographer, educator; b. Elmira, N.Y., Apr. 18, 1943; d. Donald Frederick and Alma Elizabeth (Satorius) Lach; m. William Charles Arlinghaus, Sept. 3, 1966; 1 child, William Edward. AB in Math., Vassar Coll., 1964; postgrad., U. Chgo., 1964-66, U. Toronto, Ont., Can., 1966-67, Wayne State U., 1968-70; MA in Geography, Wayne State U., 1976; PhD in Geography, U. Mich., 1977. Vis. instr. math. U. Ill., Chgo., 1966; vis. asst. prof. geography Ohio State U., Columbus, 1977-78, lectr. math., 1978-79; lectr. math. Loyola U., Chgo., 1979-81, asst. prof. math., 1981-82; lectr. math. and geography U. Mich., Dearborn and Ann Arbor, 1982-83; founding dir. Inst. Math. Geography, Ann Arbor, 1985—; adj. prof. math. geography, population-environment dynamics Sch. Natural Resources and Environment U. Mich.; guest lectr. U. Mich., Ann Arbor, 1983, 90-93, U. Chgo., 1979, 87, U. Calif., 1979, Syracuse U., 1991, U. No. Iowa, 1991; cons. U. Mich. Transp. Rsch. inst., 1985-86, Coll. Architecture, 1985-86, Coll. Edn., 1992; cons. Cmty. Svcs. Found., 1993—. Author: Down the Mail Tubes: The Pressured Postal Era, 1853-1984, Essays on Mathematical Geography, 1986, Essays on Mathematical Geography-II, 1987, An Atlas of Steiner Networks, 1989, Essays on Mathematical Geography-III, 1991 ; co-author: Population-Environment Dynamics, Sectors in Transition, 1992, Mathematical Geography and Global Art, 1986, Environmental Effects on Bus Durability, 1990, Fractals in Geography, 1993; founder, editor, co-author electronic jour. Solstice, 1990—; author, editor-in-chief Practical Handbook of Curve Fitting, 1994; co-author, editor-in-chief Practical Handbook of Digital Mapping: Terms and Concepts, 1994; editor internat. monograph series; reviewer Mathematical Reviews, 1992—; contbr. articles, book reviews to profl. jours. in fields of geography, psychology, math., biology, history, philately; founder, editor, co-author: Image Interactive Atlases, Image Game Series, Image Discussion Papers. Bd. dirs., membership chmn. Bromley Homeowners Assn., Ann Arbor, 1989-93, pres., 1990—; bd. dirs. World Jr. Bridge Championships, Ann Arbor, 1990-91, Dolfins Inc, 1993-95; head Neighborhood Watch, Bromley Sub-Divsn., 1994—; artist math. Awareness Week, Lawrence Tech. U., 1988—. Fellow Am. Geog. Soc. (rep. seach com. for curator of collection in Golda Meir Libr. U. Wis.-Milw Libr. 1993-94); mem. AAAS, Am. Math. Soc., Math. Assn. Am., Assn. Am. Geographers, N.Y. Acad. Scis., Engring. Soc. Detroit, Regional Sci. Assn., Tex. User's Group, Am. Biog. Inst. (nat. mem. adv. coun. 1992—), Internat. Biog. Ctr. (Cambridge, Eng.) (hon. mem. adv. coun. 1992—). Office: Inst Math Geography 2790 Briarcliff St Ann Arbor MI 48105-1429 also: Sch Natural Resources U Mich Ann Arbor MI 48109

ARLOW, BARBARA, educator; b. N.Y.C., Mar. 25, 1937; d. Hyman and Shevie (Fine) Berland; m. Robert Arlow, Dec. 18, 1956 (div. 1969); m. Gerald E. Pease, Aug. 14, 1992. BA in Edn., Bklyn. Coll., 1957; MS in Edn., U. of the City of N.Y., 1961; postgrad., Chapman Coll., 1973-75. Cert. tchr., cert. adminstr., Calif. Elem. tchr. N.Y.C. Schs., 1958-62; elem. tchr. La Cañada (Calif.) Unified Schs., 1963-82, sci. tchr., 1982-88, math tchr., 1988-89, social sci. tchr., 1989-91, sci. tchr., 1991—; project RISE-LA facilitator UCLA, 1983-86; sci. curriculum writer La Cañada Sch. Dist., 1985-86; sci. cons. Inglewood (Calif.) Unified Sch. Dist., 1988, Monrovia (Calif.) Sch. Dist., 1987. Sci. rsch. scholarship UCLA, France, 1986, Am. History scholarship Freedoms Found., 1988; recipient Hon. Svc. award Calif. Congress PTA, 1987. Mem. Calif. Tchrs. Assn. (steering com., state coun. rep., WHO 1981, 91), La Cañada Tchrs. Assn. (pres., negotiations chair, treas., Tchr. of Yr. 1994-95). Office: La Canada Unified Sch Dist 5025 Palm Dr La Canada CA 91011

ARMACOST, MARY-LINDA SORBER MERRIAM, educational administrator; b. Jeannette, Pa., May 31, 1943; d. Everett Sylvester Calvin and Madeleine (Case) Sorber; m. E. William Merriam, Dec. 13, 1969 (div. 1975); m. Peter H. Armacost, July 10, 1993. Student, Grove City Coll., 1961-63; BA, Pa. State U., 1963-65, MA, 1965-67, PhD, 1967-70; HHD (hon.), Carroll Coll., 1991; LLD (hon.), Wilson Coll., 1994. Rsch. assoc. Pa. State U., University Park, 1970-72; asst. prof. speech Emerson Coll., Boston, 1972-79, dir. continuing edn., 1974-77, spl. asst. to pres., 1977-78, v.p. adminstrn., 1978-79; asst. to pres. Boston U., 1979-81; pres. Wilson Coll., Chambersburg, Pa., 1981-91, Moore Coll. Art and Design, Phila., 1991-93; sr. fellow Office of Women in Higher Edn. Am. Coun. on Edn., 1994—; cons. Govt. Edn. and Secondary Edn. Act Title III, Alameda County, Calif., 1968. Bd. dirs. Sta. WITF, Inc., Harrisburg, Pa., 1982-91, chmn. bd. dirs., 1988-91; bd. dirs. Chambersburg Hosp., 1984-89, vice chmn. bd. dirs., 1987-89; bd. dirs. Sta. WHYY-FM-TV, Phila., 1992-93, Boston Zool. Soc., 1980-81, Arts Boston, 1979-81, Scotland Sch. Vets. Children, Pa., 1984-90; mem. exec. com. Found. for Ind. Colls., 1989-91; pres. Chambersburg Area Coun. Arts, 1988-90; chmn. higher edn. com. Gen. Assembly Presbyn. Ch., 1987-90; elder Falling Spring Presbyn. Ch., 1988-90. Recipient Disting. Alumna award Pa. State U., 1984, Disting. Dau. of Pa., 1986, Athena award Chambersburg C. of C., 1988, Outstanding Alumnae award Sch. Dist. Jeannette, 1991. Fellow Women Higher Edn. (sr.); mem. NATAS (bd. govs. New Eng. chpt. 1980-81), AAUW, Am. Coun. Edn. (commn. on women 1992-93, fellow 1977-78), Speech Comm. Assn., Pa. Assn. Colls. and Univs. (exec. com. 1984-90), Assn. Presbyn. Colls. and Univs. (exec. com. 1983-88, pres. 1986-87), Am. Assn. Higher Edn., Nat. Soc. Arts and Letters, Forum for Exec. Women, Phi Kappa Phi, Rho Tau Sigma, Phi Delta Kappa.

ARMAGOST, ELSA GAFVERT, retired computer industry communications consultant; b. Duluth, Minn.; d. Axel Justus and Martina Emelia (Magnuson) Gafvert; m. Byron William Armagost, Dec. 8, 1945; children: David Byron, Laura Martina. Grad. with honors, Duluth Jr. Coll., 1936; BJ, U. Minn., 1938, postgrad. in pub. rels., bus. mgmt. and computer tech., 1965-81; PhD in Computer Commn. Cons. Sci. (hon.), Internat. U. Found. Freelance editor, Duluth, 1939-42; procedure editor and analyst U.S. Steel, Duluth, 1942-45; fashion advt. staff Dayton Co., Mpls., 1945-48; systems applications and documentation mgr. Control Data Corp., Mpls., 1969-74, promotion specialist, mktg. editor, 1974-76, corp. staff coord. info. on edn., 1976-78; instr. comm., publ. specialist, 1978-79; commn. cons. peripheral products group, 1979-83; industry comm. cons., 1983-88, ret., 1988; mem. steering com. U.S. Senatorial Bus. Adv. Bd., 1962-68; mem. U.S. Congrl. Adv. Bd., 1958-62. V.p. Sewickley (Pa.) Valley Hosp. Aux.; bd. dirs. Sewickley Valley Mental Health Coun., LWV Pitts.; bd. dirs. publicity chmn. Sacred Arts Expo; mem. World Affairs Coun. radio program, Pitts. Recipient Medal of Merit Rep. Presdl. Task Force. Mem. AAUW (1st v.p. Caracas, Venezuela), Women in Communication (bd. dir. job mart), Marsh Pk. Condominium Assn. (bd. mem.), Toastmasters (Comm. award 1984), N. Ctrl. Deming Mgmt. Forum, Ctr. of the Am. Expt., Internat. Platform Assn., Friends of Mpls. Inst. Art., Walker Art Inst., Ceridian Corp. Retirees Assn. (bd. dirs.), Minn. Alumni Assn. (life), Am. Swedish Inst., Internat. Soc. Newspaper Editors, Phi Beta Nat. Profl. Arts Frat., Internat. Bible Study Fellowship. Nominated for Alumni NOtable Achievement, U. Minn., 1995. Home and Office: 9500 Collegeview Rd # 312 Minneapolis MN 55437-2148

ARMAO, ROSEMARY C., journalist, educator; b. Troy, N.Y., Oct. 12, 1950; d. Guy James and Theresa (Stellato) A.; m. Francis Joseph Liuzzi, Aug. 29, 1971; children: Francisco Liuzzi, Guy Michael Liuzzi, Marco Liuzzi. BA, Syracuse U., 1972; MA, Ohio State U., 1981. Reporter Knickerbocker News, Albany, N.Y., 1972-75, UPI, Cleve. and Albany, 1975-82; bur. mgr. UPI, Youngstown, Ohio, 1982-84; reporter Cleve. Plain Dealer, 1984-87; reporter Virginian-Pilot Newspaper, Norfolk, Va., 1987-90, Portsmouth city editor, 1990-91, edn. editor, 1991-94; exec. dir. Investigative Reporters & Editors, Inc., Columbia, Mo., 1994—; assoc. prof. Sch. Journalism U. Mo., 1994—. columnist family issues Virginian Pilot, 1991-94; contbr. articles, book revs. newspapers, mags. Newhouse scholar Syracuse U., 1972; David Hudson fellow Case Western Reserve U., Cleve., 1983-84, Knight Ctr. for Specialized Journalism fellow U. Md., 1992, Poynter Inst. fellow for investigative reporting, St. Petersburg, Fla., 1992. Mem. Nat. Press Women (awards 1978, 79), Edn. Writers Assn. (reporting award 1994), Coun. Pres. (exec. com.), Journalism and Women's Symposium. Home: 1901 E Walnut St Columbia MO 65201 Office: IRE 100 Neff Hall Columbia MO 65211

ARMAS, JENNIFER VILLAREAL, nurse; b. Manila, July 27, 1967; (parents Am. citizens); d. Ferdinand and Erlinda (Villareal) A. AS in Nursing, Chattanooga State Tech. Community Coll., 1989; student, Ellsworth Aviation Sch., 1990—. RN, Tenn. Pediatric emergency rm. nurse Erlanger Med. Ctr., Chattanooga, 1990—; nurse hematology/oncology unit Egleston Children's Hosp. at Emory U., Atlanta, 1993—. Vol. Riverbend, Chattanooga, 1990; vol. nurse Chattanooga Sports Clinic, 1990—. Mem. ANA, Emergency Nurses Assn., Chattanooga Jaycees.

ARMISTEAD, KATHERINE KELLY (MRS. THOMAS B. ARMISTEAD, III), travel consultant, interior designer, civic worker; b. Pitts., Apr. 14, 1926; d. Joseph Anthony and Katherine Arnold (Manning) Kelly; grad. Finch Jr. Coll., 1946; m. Thomas Boyd Armistead, III, Nov. 29, 1952; children: Katherine Kelly (Mrs. W. Michael Roark), Thomas Boyd IV. Editor news Sta. WOR, N.Y.C., 1946-51; with Dumont TV, 1951-52; editor Social Service Rev., 1956-57; interior designer, L.A., 1963—; travel cons. Gilner Internat. Travels, Beverly Hills, Calif., 1980—. Editorial bd. Previews Mag., 1984-87. Pres. Jrs. Social Svc.,L.A., 1962-64; nat. chpt. chmn. Associated Alumnae of Sacred Heart, 1960-66; pres. Las Floristas, 1967-68; pres. L.A. Orphanage Guild, 1969-70; coord. Jr. Mannequin Assisteens, Assistance League So. Calif., 1971-72; pres. docent coun. L.A. County Mus. Art, 1976-77, pres. decorative arts council, 1977-80, chmn. Am. antiques conf., 1979-81, mem. costume coun., mem. past pres.' coun., 1981—, mem. capital gifts campaign com.; bd. dirs. L.A. Orphanage Guild, 1970—; Cert. travel cons. Recipient Eve award Assistance League So. Calif. Mem. Am. Soc. Travel Agts., Inst. Cert. Travel Agts. (cert.), Equestrian Order of the Holy Sepulchre of Jerusalem. Republican. Roman Catholic. Clubs: Birnam Wood Golf (Santa Barbara, Calif.), Bel Air Garden.

ARMITAGE, ELISABETH CALDWELL, management consultant; b. Phila., Apr. 15, 1963; d. Robert Bruce and Constance Lynn (Barbour) A. BS, Cornell U., 1985; MBA in Strategic Mgmt. with honors, U. Pa., 1993. Asst. treas. Morgan Shareholders Svcs., N.Y.C., 1985-89; asst. v.p. First Chgo. Trust Co. of N.Y., N.Y.C., 1989-92, Bankers Trust Co., N.Y.C., 1992; cons. Andersen Consulting, N.Y.C., 1993—. Coord. Say Yes to Edn., U. Pa., Phila., 1992-93, interviewer, 1993; alumni interviewer Cornell U., 1985-93. Home: 409 Washington St # 398 Hoboken NJ 07030-2603 Office: Andersen Consulting 1345 Avenue Of The Americas New York NY 10105-0032

ARMITAGE, KAROLE, dancer, choreographer; b. Madison, Wis., Mar. 3, 1954. Studied, N.C. Sch. of the Arts, with Bill Evans, U. Utah, 1971-72. Dancer Geneva (Switzerland) Opera Ballet, 1973-75, Merce Cunningham Dance Co., 1976-81; free-lance choreographer, artistic dir. The Armitage Ballet (formerly Armitage Dance Co.), N.Y.C., 1981—. Choreographer Ne, 1978, Do We Could 1979, Veritige, 1980, Drastic-Classicism, 1981, It Happened at Club Bombay Cinema, 1981, Slaughter on MacDougal Street, 1981, Paradise, version 1, 1981, The Last Gone Dance, 1983, Paradise, version 2, 1983, A Real Gone Dance, 1983, (with Rosella Hightower) The Nutcracker, 1983, Tasmanian Devil, 1984, GV-10, 1984, The Water Duets, 1985, The Mollino Room, 1985, The Elizabethan Phrasing of the Late Albert Ayler, 1986, The Tarnished Angels, 1987, Les Stances a Sophie, 1987, Duck Dances, 1988, Kammerdisco, 1988, GoGo Ballerina, 1988, Contempt, 1989, Forty Guns, 1990, Dancing Zappa, 1990, Jack and Betty, 1990, The Marmot Quickstep, 1991, Renegade Dance Wave, 1991, Overboard, 1991, Segunda Piel, 1992, Happy Birthday Rossini, 1992, Hucksters of the Soul, 1993, I Had A Dream. 1993, Hovering at the Edge of Chaos, 1994, Tattoo and Tutu, 1994, The Dog Is Us, 1994, The Return of Rasputin, 1994; (dance for TV) Parafango, 1983, Ex-Romance, 1984; (arts program) The South Bank Show, 1985; (feature films) Without You, I'm Nothing, 1989, Chain of Desire, 1991, Search and Destroy, 1994; (videoclips) Love School for the Dyvinals, 1990, Vogue for Madonna, 1991, In The Closet for Michael Jackson, 1992; (world tours) Milli Vanilli, 1990, Madonna's Blonde Ambition, 1991, The Dyvinals, 1991; (videoclips for feature film) Kuffs, 1990; writer, dir., choreographer (feature film) Hall of Mirrors, 1992. Guggenheim fellow, 1986. Office: Armitage Found 3 N Moore Ste 4 New York NY 10013

ARMOCIDA, PATRICIA ANNE, managed health care official; b. Portland, Maine, July 29, 1956; d. Gerald Arthur and Aileen Patricia (Malone) Faneuf; m. William Joseph Armocida, June 21, 1986. BS, Purdue U., 1980; MBA, Boston U., 1983. RN, Mass. Staff nurse New Eng. Med. Ctr., Boston, 1980-81, Mass. Gen. Hosp., Boston, 1981; cons. Deloitte, Haskins & Sells, Boston, 1981, Health Data Inst., Boston, 1981-82; cons. Blue Cross/Blue Shield Assn., Chgo., 1983, asst. to the pres., 1983-85; mgr. health svcs. Blue Cross/Blue Shield Ill., 1985-86, dir. HMO, dir. utilization mgmt., 1987-90; v.p. mktg. Health Mgmt. Strategies, Alexandria, Va., 1990-91; dir. med. mgmt. Blue Cross and Blue Shield of the Nat. Capital Area, Washington, 1991-92; pres. Health Dimensions, Inc., Seattle, 1992—; lectr. George Washington U., 1991-93. Vol. Sr. Citizens Ctr., Chgo., 1987; vol. instr. Handicapped Riders, Chgo., 1986; mem. rev. com. Nat. Inst. Drug Abuse Project; campaign vol. United Way, Chgo., 1988. Boston U. scholar, 1983; recipient Leadership award YWCA and Blue Cross/Blue Shield, 1988. Mem. Am. Peer Rev. Assn., Am. Care Rev. Assn., Women Employee Benefits Assn. Roman Catholic.

ARMSTEAD, MARCIA BEVERLY, business owner, consultant; b. Jamaica, W.I., June 23, 1948; came to U.S., 1960; d. James Henry and Iris May (Dixon) Townsend; m. Eugene Armstead Sr., Dec. 14, 1969 (dec. Jan. 1993); children: Eugene Jr., Jonathan Keith. Clk., typist Met. Life Ins. Co., N.Y.C., 1966-70; sec. RKO Radio Rep., N.Y.C., 1970-71; pub. rels. sec. Oakwood Coll., Huntsville, Ala., 1971-76; exec. office sec. Adventist Health Systems/North, Hinsdale, Ill., 1978-82, Adventist Health Systems/Sunbelt, Orlando, Fla., 1982-84; customer svc. rep. FDIC, Orlando, Fla., 1984—; pres., self-esteem cons., CEO, freelance writer newsletter Complete Woman/Man Seminars Corp., Orlando, Fla., 1991—. Contbr. Job Watch Mag., 1992; writer, producer: (videotape) Tech. Employee Tng., 1990. Mem. NAFE, Am. Diabetic Assn. Office: Complete Woman/Man Seminars PO Box 77674 Atlanta GA 30357-1674

ARMSTEAD, TRESSA MADDUX, secondary school educator; b. Pecos, Tex., Apr. 23, 1949; d. Obie Eugene and Nell (Simpson) Maddux; m. Karl Frank Armstead, June 8, 1974; children: Stephen Kristopher, Tiffany Julene. BS, Sul Ross State U., 1970; MA, Eastern New Mex. U., 1977. Cert. secondary tchr., Tex. Educator Boyd (Tex.) Ind. Sch. Dist.; grad. asst. Eastern N.Mex. U., Portales; tchr. Pecos (Tex.)-Barstow-Toyah Ind. Sch. Dist., Midland (Tex.) Ind. Sch. Dist. Mem. Tex. Classroom Tchrs. Assn., Nat. Coun. Tchrs. English, Tex. Joint Coun. Tchrs. English, Delta Kappa Gamma.

ARMSTRONG, ANNE LEGENDRE (MRS. TOBIN ARMSTRONG), former ambassador, corporate director; b. New Orleans, Dec. 27, 1927; d. Armant and Olive (Martindale) Legendre; m. Tobin Armstrong, Apr. 12, 1950; children: John Barclay, Katharine A. Idsal, Sarita A. Hixon, Tobin and James L. (twins). BA in English, Vassar Coll., 1949. Co-chmn. Rep. Nat. Com., 1971-73; del. Rep. Nat. Conv., 1964-84; counsellor to U.S. Pres., 1973-74; U.S. amb. to Gt. Britain and No. Ireland, London, Gt. Britain, No. Ireland, 1976-77; chmn. adv. bd. Ctr. for Strategic and Internat. Studies (formerly affiliated with Georgetown U.), 1981-87, chmn. bd. trustees, 1987—; chmn. Pres.'s Fgn. Intelligence Adv. Bd., 1981-90; commn. on Integrated Long Term Strategy, 1987; pres. Nat. Thanksgiving Commn., 1986-94; bd. dirs. GM Corp., Halliburton Co., Boise Cascade Corp., Am. Express Co., Glaxo Holdings. Bd. regents Smithsonian Instn., 1978-94, emeritus, 1994; bd. overseers Hoover Instn., 1978—; co-chmn. Reagan-Bush Campaign, 1980. Recipient Rep. Woman of Yr. award, 1979, Texan of Yr. award, 1981, Presdl. Medal of Freedom award, 1987, Golden Plate award Am. Acad. Achievement, 1989; named to Tex. Women's Hall of Fame, 1986. Mem. English-Speaking Union (chmn. 1978-80), Coun. Fgn. Rels., Tex. Women's Alliance (chmn. 1985-89, chmn. emeritus), Am. Assocs. of Royal Acad. Trust (trustee 1985—), Phi Beta Kappa. Clubs: Alfalfa Club, Washington, F St. (Washington).

ARMSTRONG, CAROLYN ANN, health care agency director; b. Platteville, Wis., Feb. 10, 1938; d. William Henry and Mary Emily (Kaiser) Hartlip; m. Robert B. Armstrong, July 25, 1964; children: Robert Jr., William. BS, U. Wis., Platteville, 1960; MPA, L.I. U., 1993. Cert. secondary educator, Wis. Tchr. Wauwatosa (Wis.) Bd. Edn., 1960-64, Jacksonville (Fla.) Bd. Edn., 1965-66, Valley Stream (N.Y.) Bd. Edn., 1966-68, S. Hunt (N.Y.) Bd. Edn., 1968-69; personnel dir. Health Svc. at Home, Inc., Huntington, N.Y., 1982-87; dir. Health Svc. at Home, Inc., Commack, N.Y., 1987—; speaker for corp. giving United Way, Melville, N.Y., 1983-91; cons., instr. L.I. U., Southampton, N.Y., 1991-93; cons. in health field. Bd. dirs. Southdown PTA Inter Coun., Huntington, 1975-81, Vis. Homemaker Svc., Huntington, 1979-81. Recipient Svc. award AAUW, 1986, United Way of L.I., 1985, Rotary Club, 1991. Mem. AAUW (pres. 1973-75), NAFE, L.I. Assn., Home Care Assn. of N.Y., N.Y. State Assn. HealthCare Providers, Am. Mgmt. Assn., Brookhaven Meml. Hosp. Home Care. Roman Catholic. Office: Health Svc at Home Inc 2171 Jericho Tpke Commack NY 11725-2900

ARMSTRONG, DEANNA FRANCES, engineer; b. Winchester, Va., July 14, 1962; d. Gerald Francis and Reta Marie (Wyatt) A. AS in Mech. Engring. Tech., W.Va. Inst. Tech., 1982, AS in Elec. Engring. Tech. cum laude, 1983, BS in Electronics Engring. Tech. cum laude, 1984. Student engring. asst. Monongahela Power Co., Elkins, W.Va., summers 1980-83; machine shop lab. asst. W.Va. Inst. Tech., Montgomery, 1982-83, acad. asst., 1983-84; engring. technician Monongahela Power Co., Elkins, 1984—; competition judge Vocat. and Indsl. Club. Am., Elkins, 1985—; mem. Partnership in Edn. Com. Corr. Monongahela News, 1993—. Mem. adv. coun. Randolph County Vocat. Tech. Ctr., Partnership in Edn. Com.; vol. Mountain State Forest Festival. Mem. Elkins Jr. C. of C., Alpha Chi Nat. Honor Soc. Republican. Home: 508 Center St Elkins WV 26241-3729 Office: Monongahela Power Co US Rte 215 & 250 Elkins WV 26241

ARMSTRONG, DONNA MORE, insurance agent; b. Amboy, Minn., June 6, 1929; d. Harold Sargent and Grace Catherine (Sloan) More; m. Warner J. (Bill) Armstrong, Aug. 28, 1948; children: Mary Jo, Royce S., Thomas, Lisa. Grad. high sch., Mapleton, Minn. Bookkeeper Stanton Motors, Mapleton, 1946-49; clk. Brecht Drug, Minn. Lake, 1959-62; ins. agt. M&M Ins., Minn. Lake, 1962-83; ins. agy. mgr. Minn. Lake Agy., Inc., 1983—. Bd. dirs. Faribault County Human Svcs., Blue Earth, Minn., 1960-67; mem. adv. bd. Tri-County Human Svcs., Blue Earth, 1967-70; mem. City Coun., Minn. Lake, 1974-78; bd. dirs. Mapleton Cmty. Home, 1976-80. Mem. Mankato Area Assn. Ins. Women (charter, pres. 1987-89, treas. 1989-93), Nat. Assn. Ins. Women (state dir.-elect Minn. chpt. 1993-94), Am. Legion Aux. (treas. 1992—), Gen. Fedn. Women's Club, Minn. Lake Cmty. Club (pres.-sec. 1983—). Democrat. Roman Catholic. Home: 650 4th Ave SW Wells MN 56097-1334

ARMSTRONG, JANE BOTSFORD, sculptor; b. Buffalo; d. Samuel Booth and Edith (Pursel) Botsford; m. Robert Thexton Armstrong, July 3, 1960. Student, Middlebury Coll., 1939-40, Pratt Inst., 1940-41, Art Students' League, 1962-64. One-man shows Frank Rehn Gallery, N.Y.C., 1971, 73, 75, 77, Columbus (Ohio) Gallery Fine Arts, 1972, Columbia (S.C.) Mus. Art, 1975, New Britain (Conn.) Mus. Am. Art, 1972, Johnson Gallery, Middlebury Coll., 1973, Mary Duke Biddle Gallery for Blind N.C. Mus. Art, 1974, J.B. Speed Art Mus., Louisville, 1975, Buffalo State U., 1975, Marjorie Parr Gallery, London, 1976, Ark. Art Center, 1977, Dallas Mus. Fine Art, 1978, Wichita (Kans.) Art Mus., 1978, 82, Wadsworth Atheneum, 1979, Foster Harmon Gallery Am. Art, 1979, 81, 92, Washington County (Md.) Mus. Fine Arts, Hagerstown, 1979, Chautauqua (N.Y.) Nat. Exhbn. Am. Art, 1980, Southeastern Center Contemporary Art, Winston-Salem, N.C., 1980, Rollins Coll., Winter Park, Fla., 1981, The Sculpture Center, N.Y.C., 1981, Sid Deutsch Gallery, N.Y.C., 1983, Boca Raton Mus. (Fla.), 1983, Burchfield Ctr., Buffalo, 1985, Glass Art Gallery, Toronto, 1985, Schiller-Wapner Galleries, N.Y.C., 1987, St. Gaudens Gallery, St. Gaudens Nat. Hist. Site, 1988, Middlebury Coll., Vt., 1988, Grand Cen. Art Galleries, N.Y.C., 1989; exhibited in USIA group exhbn., Europe, 1975-76, Artists of Am., Denver, 1981, 82, 83, 84, 85, 86, 87, 88, 90 (U.S. Art mag. award 1990), 91, 92, 93, 94; represented in numerous acad., indsl., pub. and pvt. collections. Recipient Pauline Law prize Allied Artists Am., 1969, 70, Porton award, 1981, Gold medal, 1976, Ralph Fabri medal of honor, 1978, Chaim Gross Found. award, 1980, Helen Apen Oehler Meml. award, 1988, Meiselman award, 1993, cert. merit NAD, 1973, Coun. Am. Artists' Socs. prize Nat. Sculpture Soc., 1973, gold medal of honor Knickerbocker Artists, 1986, Elliott Lisking Meml. award, 1991, Alumni Achievement award Middlebury Coll., 1993. Fellow Nat. Sculpture Soc. (Bronze medal 1976, 88, Tallix Foundry award 1985, Percival Dietsch prize 1986); mem. Nat. Arts Club (Gold medal 1968, 69, 71, Best in Show 1973, Edith W. MacGuire award 1975, Plaque of Honor 1977, Alexander Saltzman award 1983, Exhbn. Com. award 1990), Audubon Artists (Medal of Honor 1972, Vincent Glinsky Meml. award 1992, Gold medal 1994), Sculptors Guild, Allied Artists Am., Nat. Assn. Women Artists (Charles N. Whinston Meml. prize 1973, Anonymous Meml. prize 1979, Elizabeth S. Blake prize 1980, Amelia Peabody award 1986, Freelander-Sawyer Meml. award 1993). Home and Studio: Dorset Hill Rd Rural Rt Box 684 East Dorset VT 05253

ARMSTRONG, KAREN, religious studies educator, writer. Grad., Oxford Univ. Tchr. Leo Baeck Coll. for the Study of Judaism, London. Author: 10 books including Through the Narrow Gate, Muhammad: Western Attempt to Understand Islam, Gospel According to Woman: Christianity of the Sex War in the West, English Mystics: Of the Fourteenth Century, Holy War: The Crusade's and Their Impact on Today's World, End of Silence: Women and Priesthood, Visions of God: Four Medieval Mystics and Their Writings, A History of God: The Four Thousand Year Quest of Judaism, Christianity and Islam, 1993, Jerusalem, 1996. Mem. Assn. Muslim Social Sciences (hon.). Office: Leo Baeck Inst, 4 Devonshire St, London W1N 2BH, England*

ARMSTRONG, KAREN LEE, special education educator; b. Schenectady, N.Y., Dec. 6, 1941; d. William James and Rita Mae (Peabody) Safford; m. John Edward Armstrong, July 14, 1962; 1 child, Lori Ellen. BA in English, SUNY, Albany, 1963, MS in Spl. Edn., 1986. Tchr. English Ballston Lake High Sch., Burnt Hills, N.Y., 1963-66; tchr. spl. edn. Oak Hill Sch., Scotia, N.Y., 1975-88, Schenectady City Schs., 1988—; chair spl. edn. curriculum com., lead tng. sessions Schenectady Schs., 1988—, chmn. 1993-94; mem. spl. edn. del. People's Rep. China, 1993. Founder Schenectady br. Amnesty Internat., 1990. Mem. Coun. for Exceptional Children, Coun. for Children with Behavioral Disorders (regional rep. N.Y. state chpt.). Sufi. Home: 642 Swaggertown Rd Scotia NY 12302

ARMSTRONG, LEONA MAY BOTTRELL, counselor; b. Rochester, Ill., Aug. 14, 1930; d. Vernon Sampson Bottrell and Leonia Ruth (Meeks) Cooper; m. Bryce G. Armstrong, June 11, 1950 (div. 1975); children: Steven Lee, Rebecca Sue, Paul Bryce, Brian Mark, Kevin John. BS, Ind. Ctrl. U., 1952; MS, U. Wis., 1967. Tchr. Dayton, Ohio, 1952-55; sch. counselor Oshkosh, Verona, Wis., 1967-72, West Allis Schs., Milw., 1972-88; pvt. practice as astrologer and counselor West Allis, Milw., Wis., 1988—; Reiki master Reiki Healers Internat., 1992; guest spkr. in area of parapsychology and metaphysics U. Minn., U., Wis., Milw., other schs.; spkr. World Peace Program, Milw., 1987. Ecumenical spkr. United Ch. Women, 1966. Named one of Outstanding Personalities in Midwest, 1968. Mem. Nat. Coun. for Geocosmic Rsch. Home and Office: 2706 S 112th St Milwaukee WI 53227-3023

ARMSTRONG, LESLIE ANN CRONKHITE, educational visual arts specialist, graphic artist; b. Pendleton, Oreg., Apr. 29, 1954; d. Jackson Edward and Ann Marie (Bogovich) Cronkhite; m. Robert John Armstrong, June 21, 1980; children: Lindsay, Cailey, Stacey. BA in Edn., BFA in Art, Ea. Wash. U., 1977; postgrad., Seattle U., 1983. Tour guide Ford Motor Co., Expo 74, Spokane, Wash., 1973-74; tchr. art, coach Kennedy High Sch., Seattle, 1977-84; art specialist Kent (Wash.) Sch. Dist., 1989—; co-owner Rosewood Farms Art Loft, Kent, Wash., 1993—; freelance graphic artist; guest tchr. AG Petunia Art Works, Seattle, 1992. Exhibited in group show Bellevue (Wash.) Arts Festival, 1992, 93; illustrator: Our Best to Your, 1981, Kite Flight, 1986. Mem. U.S. Equestrian Campaign Team. Grantee King County Arts Commn., 1991. Mem. Nat. Art Edn. Assn., Kappa Alpha Theta. Roman Catholic. Home: 13836 SE 237th Pl Kent WA 98042

ARMSTRONG, MARGARET COURY, small business owner; b. Las Vegas, Nev., July 6, 1937; d. Isidore John and Mona Craine Coury; m. Edwin Guy Armstrong Jr., June 3, 1961; children: Edwin Coury, Robert James. Student, U. N.Mex, 1954-57, Tobe Coburn, 1959. Buyer Sanger-Harris, Dallas, 1960-65; bookkeeper Armstrong/Coury Ins., Farmington, N.Mex., 1973-85; sec., treas. Armstrong, Inc. (formerly Armstrong/Coury Ins.), Farmington, 1986—, Valley Constrn. & Devel., Farmington, 1974—; owner M's Ladies Apparel, Farmington, 1988—. Sec. N.Mex. Amateur Baseball Congress, 1978-91; bd. dirs. San Juan Econ. Devel. Svc., 1991, Farmington Conv. and Visitors Bur., 1991; mem. Sacred Heart Sch. Bd., 1976-79, rec. sec., 1977-79; com. mem. Gov.'s Immunization Bd., 1978; v.p. Title I Dist. Parent Adv. Com., 1977. Named Amateur Baseball Woman of Yr. Oscar Mayer, 1987, Regional Woman of Yr. Am. Amateur Baseball Congress, 1991. Mem. N.Mex. Fedn. Women's Clubs (pres. 1988-90), Farmington Women's Club (pres. 1973, 90-91), Farmington Redcoats Goodwill Ambs., Gen. Fedn. Women's Clubs (South Ctrl. region sec./treas., regional SOAR chmn. 1992-94), Gen. Fedn. Women's Clubs Home Life Econs. (div. chmn.), Downtown Merchants (sec. 1991), Farmington C. of C. (bd. dirs. 1981-91, v.p. 1988, pres. elect 1989, pres. 1990), Gen. Fedn. Women's Clubs (South Ctrl. region sec./treas. 1992, v.p. 1993, pres. 1994—), San Juan Plz. Merchants Assn. (sec. 1993). Democrat. Roman Catholic. Home: 5310 Hallmarc Dr Farmington NM 87402-5108 Office: M's Ladies Apparel 3030 W Main St Farmington NM 87401-6242

ARMSTRONG, MARTHA SUSAN, accountant, educator; b. Harrisonburg, Va., Dec. 28, 1954; d. Harry Lee and Elizabeth (Roller) Anderson; m. Marvin Edward Armstrong, May 27, 1978; children: Nathaniel Roller, Andrew Michael. BBA cum laude, Bridgewater Coll., 1977; MS in Acctg., U. Va., 1985. CPA, Va. Asst. dir. of fin. aid Bridgewater (Va.) Coll., 1978-81, asst. prof. acctg. and bus. adminstrn., 1981—; staff acct. Morris & Sprinkel CPA's, Harrisonburg, 1985—; cons. acctg. edn. WLR Foods, Hinton, 1990—. Deacon Bridgewater Presbyn. Ch., 1982-85, v.p. Women of the Ch., 1983-85, asst. ch. treas., 1990—; concert bell ringer Harrisonburg 1st Presbyn. Ch., 1987-91, asst. treas., 1990—; treas. Dayton Nursery Sch., 1991-94. Named one of Outstanding Young Women Am., 1986. Mem. AICPA, Va. Soc. CPAs. Home: RR 1 Box 177 Harrisonburg VA 22801-9801 Office: Bridgewater Coll Bridgewater VA 22812

ARMSTRONG, MARY OGDEN, artist, graphic designer; b. Homeworth, Ohio, Sept. 30, 1933; d. Clarence George and Elsie Augusta (Kraun) Ogden; m. John Herbert Armstrong, June 7, 1958; children: Michael David, Jennifer H. Armstrong Park. BFA, Akron Art Inst., 1955; student, Cleve. Inst. Art, 1966, 69, Lakeland C.C., Kirtland, Ohio, 1989. Artist Cmty. Graphics, Cleve., 1955-57, Wise Advt., Cleve., 1957-58, Epstein Design, Cleve., 1959-61, Epstein & Szilagyi Design, Cleve., 1963-64, 69-70; freelance artist Cleve., 1962—; part-time artist Mktg. Comm., Willoughby, Ohio, 1977-84, Coyle & Assocs., Hudson, Ohio, 1978-91; part-time graphic artist, coord. Fine Arts Assn., Willoughby, 1975-95. Illustrator: (book) Going Home, 1979, So You Are Going to Have an Operation, 1985, revised, 1993, Loves Goes on Forever, 1990, So You Are Going to Have a Heart Operation, 1993. Vol. Coun. Human Rels., Cleve., 1980-89, Lake Farmpark, Lake County Met. Parks, Kirtland, Ohio, 1991-93. Recipient Merit award Cleve. Mus. Art, 1956, Advt. Excellence award Art Dirs. Club, 1957, Artistic Excellence award JCC, 1968-69, 75. Mem. Lake County Profl. Communicators (art judge 1993-94), Ohio Designers/Craftsmen. Home: 7451 Euclid-Chardon Rd Kirtland OH 44094 Office: Fine Arts Assn 38660 Mentor Ave Willoughby OH 44094

ARMSTRONG, SAUNDRA BROWN, federal judge; b. Oakland, Calif., Mar. 23, 1947; d. Coolidge Logan and Pauline Marquette (Bearden) Brown; m. George Walter Armstrong, Apr. 18, 1982. B.A., Calif. State U.-Fresno, 1969; J.D., U. San Francisco, 1977. Bar: Calif. 1977, U.S. Supreme Ct. 1984. Policewoman Oakland Police Dept., 1970-77; prosecutor, dep. dist. atty. Alameda County Dist. Atty., Oakland, 1978-79, 80-82; staff atty. Calif. Legis. Assembly Com. on Criminal Justice, Sacramento, 1979-80; trial atty. Dept. Justice, Washington, 1982-83; vice chmn. U.S. Consumer Product Safety Commn., Washington, 1984-86; commr. U.S. Parole Commn., Washington, 1986-89; judge Alameda Superior Ct., 1989-91, U.S. Dist. Ct. (no. dist.) Calif., San Francisco, 1991—. Recipient commendation Calif. Assembly, 1980. Mem. Nat. Bar Assn., ABA, Calif. Bar Assn., Charles Houston Bar Assn., Black C. of C., Phi Alpha Delta. Democrat. Baptist. Office: US Dist Ct 450 Golden Gate Ave Rm 17-6618 PO Box 36060 San Francisco CA 94102*

ARNDT, CARMEN GLORIA, educator; b. N.Y.C., Mar. 29, 1942; d. Charles Joseph and Pura María (Rios) A. BA in Spanish, Pace U., 1968; MA in Spanish, NYU, 1970; profl. diploma, Fordham U., 1975. Lic. asst. prin., prin. Simultaneous translator UN, N.Y.C., 1968; instr. Marymount Manhattan Coll., N.Y.C., 1968-70; tchr. Bd. Edn., N.Y.C., 1970—, dir. Bilingual Comprehensive High Sch., 1975-78; chairperson sch. based mgmt./shared decision com. L.D. Brandeis High Sch., N.Y.C., 1990—; asst. prin. L.D. Brandeis H.S., N.Y.C., 1984; interim acting asst. prin., 1994, coord. coop. tech./trades, 1993-94; chairperson restructuring com. Bd. Edn., N.Y.C., 1990—; bd. dirs. First N.Y.C. Comprehensive Bilingual Program, 1975-79; adj. faculty Fordham U., N.Y.C., 1972-75, City Coll., N.Y.C., 1985—. Author: Conversational Spanish, 1975, Native Language Art K-8, 1975; contbr. articles to profl. jours. Electioneer, Dem. Party, N.Y.C. Mem. P.R. Edn. Assn. (chairperson-mentor 1988, del.), United Fedn. Tchr. (del. 1985-88), State Assn. Bilingual Edn., Am. Assn. Tchrs. of Spanish and Portuguese, Assn. Suprs. Curriculum Devel., Phi Beta Kappa. Roman Catholic. Home: 110 W 90th St Apt 4C New York NY 10024-1209 Office: 145 W 84th St New York NY 10024-4603

ARNDT, DIANNE JOY, artist, photographer; b. Springfield, Mass., Dec. 20, 1939; d. Samuel Vincent and Carrie Lillian Annino. Student, Art Students League, 1965-71; BFA with honors in Painting, Pratt Inst., 1974; postgrad., Columbia U., 1979-86; MFA, Hunter Coll., 1981; m. Joseph Vincent Bower, June 16, 1979; 1 child by previous marriage, Christabelle Nita Arndt. Photojournalist, photo cons. to mags. and bus., N.Y.C., 1978—; assoc. editor McGraw-Hill World, N.Y.C., 1987-94; artist, filmmaker, 1962—; recent exhbns. include Am. Cultural Ctr., U.S., New Delhi and Bombay, 1987, Bathurst Arms Installation, Eng., 1987, Camden Arts, London, 1987, Nat. Inst. of Archtl. Edn., 1988, Phillip Morris Traveling Photo Exhibit, 1988, Centennial Libr. Gallery, Isca Graphics, Edmonton, Alta., Can., 1988, Nat. Inst. Archtl. Edn., 1988, N.Y. Sci. & Tech. Gallery, N.Y., USSR, 1989, Mercer Gallery, 1989, Circolo Pickwick, Alessandria, Italy, 1989, Clocktower Gallery, N.Y., 1989, Alijira Gallery, Newark, 1990, Food Stamp Gallery, 1990, Phila. Art Alliance Exhibit, 1990, P.S.I. & Blum Helman Gallery, 1989-90, Franklin Furnace, 1991, New Sch. Gallery, 1991, Emerging Collector, 1991, Modern Age, 1992, Balt. Mus. Industry, 1992, Aaron Davis Hall, 1992, N.Y. City Coll., Orgn. Ind. Artists Salon Show, N.Y.C., 1994, Alijira Gallery, Newark, 1994, UN, 1994, Phila. Art Alliance, Phila., 1995, Columbia U., 1995. Mem. Am. Soc. Media Photographers (bd. dirs.), Am. Soc. Picture Profls., Am. Soc. Mag. Photographers (bd. dirs.), Profl. Women Photographers, Working Press Nation.

ARNDT, JOAN MARIE, media specialist, educator; b. Stillwater, Minn., Sept. 7, 1945; d. Harriet Joan (Richert) A. BA, Coll. of St. Catherine, St. Paul, 1967; MA, U. Minn., 1970, degree in media specialty, 1973. Cert. librarian, elem. educator. Media generalist, librarian Roseville (Minn.) Area Schs., 1967—; instr. continuing edn. Hamline U., St. Paul, 1981—; guest lectr. U. Wis., Eau Claire, 1985, Coll. St. Thomas, St. Paul, Upper Mississippi Media Conf., 1988; book reviewer U. Minn., Mpls., 1988—, Five Owls, Mpls., 1988—; workshop cons. Columbia Hts. Sch., Mpls., Osseo Pub. Schs. Program chairperson Norwegian Explorers subs. Sherlock Holmes Club. Mem. ALA, Am. Assn. Sch. Librs., Minn. Edn. Media Orgn., Minn. Reading Assn., Am. Fedn. Tchrs., Minn. Fedn. Tchrs., Friends of Ramsey County Libr. Kerlan Collection. Lutheran. Home: 5730 Donegal Dr Shoreview MN 55126-4798 Office: Cen Park Media Ctr 535 County Road B2 W Roseville MN 55113-3519

ARNEST, BARBARA MAURIN, editor; b. Fergus Falls, Minn., Sept. 2, 1923; d. John J. and Susan E. (Hotchkiss) Maurin; m. Bernard P. Arnest, June 5, 1948 (dec. Aug. 1986); children: Paul G. Arnest, Lisa Arnest Mondori, Mark B. Arnest. BA in Journalism, U. Minn., 1978. Edn. reporter Mpls. Tribune, 1945-46; publicity dir. Minn. Soc. for Crippled Children and Adults, Inc., Mpls., 1946-48; editor coll. mag. The Colo. Coll., Colorado Springs, 1960-75; scholarly editor Colorado Springs, 1975—. Editor: Van Briggle Pottery: The Early Years, 1975, A Quiet Work: One Hundred Years of the W.E.S., 1990. Boardman Robinson retrospective com. Colo. Springs Fine Arts Ctr., 1989—. Recipient Atlantic award Am. Alumni Coun., 1970. Mem. ACLU, Woman's Ednl. Soc. of Colo. Coll. (sec. 1990-92, pres. 1992-94, treas. 1994—), Amnesty Internat., Colorado Spring Fine Arts Ctr., Mortar Bd., Phi Beta Kappa, Theta Sigma Phi, Pi Gamma Mu, Gamma Phi Beta. Democrat.

ARNETT, LOUISE EVA, information records management executive; b. Cin., Sept. 8, 1945; d. Matthew Michael John Waldeck and Edith Louise (Reinholz) Driskell; m. Daniel L. Arnett, May 1, 1965; children: Matthew, Michael, John. Student, U. Cin., 1978-82, Thomas More, 1986—. Teller mgr. Tri State Savs., Cin., 1963-69; owner, operator Arnett's Hobby and Craft Shop, Inc., Erlanger, Ky., 1969-75; evening mgr. Wileswood Country Store, Greater Cin. Airport, Ky., 1975-78; records mgr. Federated Department Stores, Inc., Cin., 1978—. Commr. Tiger Cubs, Boy Scouts Am., Greater Cin., 1980-82; vol. Cin.'s 200th Birthday, 1988, Kenton County (Ky.) 150th Birthday, 1990; campaigner Kenton County Sch. Bd., 1987; booster Dixie Band, Ft. Mitchell, Ky., 1986; vol. Tall Stacks, 1988, 92, 95, United Way and Cmty. Chest Greater Cin., 1994—, mem. corp. voluntarism coun., spl. projects liaison, 1994-95; vol. Cmty. Care Day, Nat. Vol. Week for the Elderly. Named for Meritorious Svc., Boy Scouts Am., 1979; recipient Order of the Heart, Boy Scouts Am., 1978. Mem. Assn. Records Mgrs. and Adminstrs. Inc. (program chmn. 1980-81, treas. 1981-82, sec. 1982-83, v.p. 1983-84, pres. 1984-85, bd. dirs. Cin. chpt. 1986-92, chmn. bd. Cin. chpt. 1985, Membershp award 1982, Mem. of Yr. 1980). Republican. Office: Federated Dept Stores Inc 7 W 7th St Cincinnati OH 45202-2424

ARNOFF, ALISA BETH, lawyer; b. Chgo., Oct. 28, 1962; d. Harold and Yvonne (Yarmat) A. BA cum laude, Loyola U. Chgo., 1984; JD, Loyola U. Chgo. Sch. Law, 1988. Bar: Ill. 1988, U.S. Dist. Ct. (no. dist. Ill.) 1988, U.S. Ct. Appeals (11th cir., 7th cir.) 1990. Jud. law clk. to Joan B. Gottschall U.S. Dist. Ct., Chgo., 1988-89; litigation assoc. Rosenthal and Schanfield, Chgo., 1989-91; employment law assoc. Borovsky & Erlich, Chgo., 1991; founding ptnr. Scalambrino & Arnoff, Chgo., 1992—; pro bono svcs. provided to St. Mary's Svcs., Arlington Heights, Ill., Deborah's Place, Chgo., Crohn's & Colitis Found. of Am., Inc., N.Y.C. Trustee Greater Ill. Carol Fisher chpt. Crohn's & Colitis Found. Am., Inc., 1993—, nat. bd., 1994—, Race Setter Walk com., 1993, bowl-a-thon co-chairperson, 1993-94; dir. High Ridge YMCA, Chgo. Mem. ABA (labor and employment law, litigation, law practice mgmt. sects.), Ill. State Bar Assn. (labor and employment law sect. coun. 1993—, co-editor newsletter 1993—, sec. 1994—, litigation sect.), Chgo. Bar Assn. (labor and employment law com., chairperson dept. labor liaison subcom. 1992—, young lawyers div. labor and employment law com., core planning com. 1992—), NAFE. Office: Scalambrino & Arnoff 30 N LaSalle St Ste 3500 Chicago IL 60602

ARNOLD, ANNIE BAKER, accountant; b. Kirbyville, Tex., Aug. 6, 1929; d. Lloyd H. Baker and Lillian S. Freeman; m. Ralph L. Arnold, Jr., July 14, 1948; children: Ralph III, Susan A. AA, Lamar Coll., Beaumont, Tex., 1948; BS in Bus. Adminstrn., Calif. State U., Fresno, 1984. Cert. mgmt. acct. Mgr. Fresno (Calif.) Dental Group, 1971-72; acctg. mgr. Fred S. James, Fresno, 1975-79, Vendo Co., Fresno, 1980-84; sr. acct. Legacy VNA, Portland, Oreg., 1984—. Charter pres. Dental Group Mgmt. Assn., Fresno, 1971-72. Mem. Health Care Fin. Mgmt. Assn., Inst. Mgmt. Accts. Home: 4215 NE 130th Pl Portland OR 97230-1415

ARNOLD, BARBARA EILEEN, state legislator; b. N. Adams, Mass., Aug. 3, 1924; d. Lester Flemming and Sarah (Van Hagen) Smith; m. William E. Arnold, Dec. 5, 1946; children: Wynn, Jeffrey, Gayle, Christopher. B.A. in Psychology, U. Mass.; postgrad. Keene State Coll. Spl. Edn. Clinic tchr. Keene State Coll., N.H., 1964-67; spl. edn. tchr. Easter Seal Rehab. Ctr., Manchester, N.H., 1967-74; state legislator N.H., 1982-95, now Republican floor leader Ho. of Reps., 1989—; mem. N.H. Coun. Vocat. Tech. Edn., 1986—; mem. Ways and Means com., vice chmn., 1992—; mem. State and Fed. Rels. commn.; chmn. Manchester Rep. Del.; Del. Bd. dirs. ARC, 1975—, chmn. bd. dirs., 1977-80; Manchester campaign chmn. Warren Rudman for U.S. Senate, 1980, 86, Gov. Judd Gregg for U.S. Senate, 1992; chair Manchester Rep. Com., 1993—; sec. N.E. State Coun. Vocational

Edn.; mem. adv. bd. Greater Manchester Federated Women's Club; mem. adv. coun. adult rehab Easter Seal Soc., N.H., 1990—; mem. vestry, registered lay leader, mem. diocesan commns., del. gen. conv. Episcopal Ch.; mem. com. for children, families, social svcs. on the Nat. Conf. of State Legislatures; state adv. com. Vocat. Child Care Programs; chmn. Manchester Rep. Com., 1992—. Recipient Norris Colton Republican of Yr. award, 1989. Mem. Kappa Kappa Gamma. Address: 374 Pickering St Manchester NH 03104

ARNOLD, BARBARA JEANNE, librarian; b. N.Y.C., Sept. 21, 1950; d. George Nelson and Jeanne Katherine (Lawless) Cornell; m. Stephen Louis Arnold, Jan. 19, 1974. AB in English and History, Marquette U., 1972; MLS, U. Wis., 1973. Cert. of profl. devel. in libr. mgmt. Project asst. Waukesha (Wis.) Pub. Libr., 1974; LTE librarian Wis. Dept. Natural Resources, 1974-75; specialist U. Wis. Steenbock Meml. Libr., Madison, 1975-78; Marine Adv. Svcs. specialist U. Wis. Extension Sea Grant, Madison, 1978-82; ad hoc adminstrv. aide Madison Pub. Libr., 1982; program coord. U. Wis. Extension Communication Programs, Madison, 1982-85; specialist in social sci. rsch. U. Wis., Madison, 1984-85; admissions and placement advisor Sch. Libr. and Info. Studies U. Wis.-Madison, 1985-93, sr. acad. advisor, 1993—; mem. oral interview panel City of Madison Pers., 1987; libr. devel. cons. Internat. Crane Found., Baraboo, Wis., 1989—; bibliog. searching Nash & Zullo Prodns., Inc., Palm Beach, Fla., 1989; mem. adv. com. U. Wis.-Madison Continuing Edn. Svcs., 1989; elected acad. staff profl. devel. com. U. Wis.-Madison, 1994—. Contbr. articles to profl. jours.; writer for newsletters and guides. Bd. dirs. Friends of Madison Pub. Libr., 1985—; mem. sec. alumni rels. coun. U. Wis.-Madison, 1992. Mem. Wis. Libr. Assn. (past chmn. Spl. Librs.), Spl. Librs. Assn. (Wis. chpt., chair profl. devel. com. 1991-93, mem. profl. devel. com. 1993—, chair nominations com. 1993-94). Office: U Wis-Madison SLIS 600 N Park St Madison WI 53706-1403

ARNOLD, CAROLE ANNE WALCUTT, nurse; b. Paris, Ky., Apr. 29, 1954; d. Hardin Owsley and Cecele Christine (Smith) Walcutt; m. Richard Wood Arnold, Feb. 22, 1976; children: Richard Wood Jr., John Walcutt. AD in Nursing, Midway Coll., 1975; BSN summa cum laude, St. Joseph's Coll., 1992. Staff nurse, evening supr. U. Ky. Med. Ctr., Lexington, 1976-77; office mgr. Arnold, M.D., Cynthiana, Ky., 1977—; obstetric nurse Humana Corp., Lexington, 1983—. Dir. Woman's Missionary Union, 1982-87, Cynthiana Bapt. Ch., 1982-89, tchr. Sunday sch., 1978-92, mem. choir, 1978-92; mem. Harrison County Fine Arts Council, 1980-92; mem. Ky. Heritage Woman's Mus., Inc. Recipient Woman of Achievement award YMCA, 1982; named to hon. order Ky. Cols., 1986-87; fellow U. Ky. Mem. Midway Coll. Alumni Assn. (named Miss Midway Coll. 1975, Disting. Alumnae award, 1989), Ky. Nurse's Assn., Am. Nurse's Assn., Ky. Hist. Soc., Blue Grass Trust, The Hereditary Register of the U.S., Daus. of 1812 (rec. sec. River Raisin chpt. 1989—; 1st v.p. 1988-90, 2d v.p. 1990-92, rec. sec.), Sovereign Soc., Phi Theta Kappa. Democrat. Clubs: DAR (KSDAR state corresponding sec. east cen. division, nat. vice chmn. scholarships 1992—; def. chmn. 1979-81, Good Citizenship award 1975, 1st alt. nat. conv. 1980, Ky. State Page 1987-89, Nat. Congl. Page 1987-89, Nat. Personal Page to Pres. Gen., 1990, nat. vice-chair east cen. div. pages, state program chmn. 1987—, sch. chmn. 1987—, nat. page 1988-89, nat. choir 1987-89, nat. del. 1988, corr. sec. 1989—, Ky. outstanding jr. mem.), Harrison County Women's Club (fine arts chmn. 1978-80, 1st v.p. 1981-83), Colonial Dames (mem. 17th century nat. outstanding young Woman of Yr. 1990-91, nat. chmn. Jr. membership, state officer, Ky. state corresponding sec. 1990-92, Sarah Morgan Boone chpt., 1st. v.p., state nat. def. chair., chaplain, state page 1988, nat. congl. page 1989), chmn. membership com. 1988—), Family of Bruce Soc. in Am., Owsley Family Soc. of Am. (recipient merit award 1987), Sovereign Colonial Soc., Ams. Royal Descent, Harrison Hosp. Aux. (pres. 1979-80), Daus. Colonial Wars, Ky chpt., Order St. Andrew of Jerusalem, Magna charta Dames, Colonial Order of Crown in Am., Soc. Washington's Army Valley Forge. Home: 116 Culpepper Dr Cynthiana KY 41031-9348 Office: 300 E Pleasant St Cynthiana KY 41031-1699

ARNOLD, CAROLE WALTERS, art education educator; b. Washington, June 30, 1951; d. Donald and Babette (Rothchild) Walters; m. Robert Lloyd Arnold, July 29, 1973; 1 child, Leah Carole. BAE, Ohio State U., 1973, MA, 1989. Art tchr. St. Joseph Acad., Columbus, Ohio, 1972-75; artist in schs. Greater Columbus Arts Coun., 1976-77; art tchr. St. Joseph Montessori Sch., Columbus, 1977-82, Dublin (Ohio) City Schs., 1984—. Recipient Excellence in Edn. award Dublin C. of C., 1991; Dublin City Schs. grantee, 1990. Mem. Nat. Art Edn. Assn., Ohio Art Edn. Assn. Home: 289 Odessa Ln Dublin OH 43017-1330 Office: Riverside Elem Sch 3260 Riverside Green Dr Dublin OH 43017-1671

ARNOLD, CLAIRE GROEMLING, administrator; b. Chgo., Dec. 1, 1962; d. Robert Max and Dorothy Irene (Messerschmidt) Groemling; m. Daniel Lee Arnold, June 23, 1990; 1 child, Christopher Alan. BS in Health Adminstrn., We. Ky. U., 1985; MBA, U. Louisville, 1989. Profl. rels. rep. Met Life Healthcare Network, Louisville, 1988-89; network devel. specialist Humana Inc., Louisville, 1989-90; program coord. U. Louisville Sch. Medicine, 1990-93, program mgr., 1993—. Contbr. articles to profl. jours. Bd. dirs. Goals for Greater Louisville, 1992, The Louisville Orch. Bd., Jr. League of Louisville, 1994. Mem. Am. Coll. Healthcare Execs., Ky. Soc. Hosp. Planning and Mktg., Acad. for Health Svcs. Mktg. (pres. 1993-94), Discover the Louisville Orch. (sec. 1989-91, chmn. 1992-93), Western Ky. U. Alumni Assn., Phi Mu (pres. 1991-93). Democrat. Presbyterian. Office: U Louisville Sch Medicine James G Brown Cancer Ctr 529 S Jackson St Louisville KY 40202-1621

ARNOLD, DEBORRAH ANN, human services director; b. Elkins, W.Va., June 1, 1950; d. Lawrence Arnold and Sybil Dumire. ADN, Broome Community Coll., 1977; BSN, SUNY, Syracuse, 1987, MSN, 1987. Cert. clin. nurse specialist. Community health nurse Broome County Health Dept., Binghamton, N.Y., 1977-81, supr. home health aides, 1981-82, coord. employee health svcs., 1982-86; dir. profl. svcs. Kimberly Quality Care, Binghamton, N.Y., 1987-91; div. dir. clin. svcs. Kimberly Quality Care, Vestal, N.Y., 1991-93; quality assurance mgr. Olsten Kimberly Quality Care, Vestal, N.Y., 1993—. Mem. N.Y. Nurses Assn. (dist. 5).

ARNOLD, ELIZABETH MARIE, social worker; b. Waterville, Maine, June 17, 1962; d. Willard Bailey and Joan (Williams) A. BS, U. Maine, 1984; MSW, Boston U., 1988. Lic. ind. clin. social worker. Tchr. Waterville (Maine) Pub. Schs., 1984-86; social worker Mass. Eye and Ear Infirmary, Boston, 1988—. Author: (book chpt.) Principals and Practice of Ophthalmology, 1993. Bd. dirs., clk. Women, Inc., Boston, 1991—. Mem. NASW, NOW (bd. dirs., v.p. Boston chpt. 1989—). Democrat. Episcopalian. Home: 19 Andrew Rd Swampscott MA 01907 Office: Mass Eye and Ear Infirmary 243 Charles St Boston MA 02114

ARNOLD, JANET NINA, health care consultant; b. Poughkeepsie, N.Y., Apr. 23, 1933; d. Paul Dudley and Pauline Katherine (Board) Bartram; AB, Vassar Coll., 1955; postgrad. Sch. Med. Tech., Albany Med. Center, 1955-56; MS, Vassar Coll., 1963; MHSM, Webster Coll., 1981; m. Robert William Arnold, Dec. 19, 1954; children: Paul Dudley, Janet Elizabeth. Research asst., med. technologist H. Aird Boswell, M.D., Troy, N.Y., 1956-59; teaching supr., adminstrv. cons. Vassar Bros. Hosp., Poughkeepsie, N.Y., 1959-69; adv. to med. lab., lectr. med. mycology Vassar Coll., Poughkeepsie, 1961-66; asst. adminstr., lab. mgr. Boulder (Colo.) Meml. Hosp., 1975-80; cons. hosp. planning Mercy Med. Center, Denver, 1981-82; clin. lab. dir./adminstr. Humana, 1982-85, cons. health care mgmt., 1982-85; with MRI, 1985—, ptnr., 1988; pres. Arnold and Assocs., 1992—; ptnr. InterExec (divsn. MRI), 1994—; acad./adminstrv. cons. U. Guam, Vassar Coll., Boulder Community Hosp., Humana Int., 1990—, others. Sec., bd. dirs. Sanitas Fed. Credit Union, 1977-78, pres., 1979-82; teaching fellow Vassar Coll., 1961-63, unrestricted fund chmn., 1989—. Contbr. NMC, 1988—. NSF research fellow, 1960-62. Mem. Am. Acad. Microbiology, Soc. for Gen. Microbiology, Am. Soc. Med. Technologists, Colo. Public Health Assn., Med. Mycological Soc. of the Ams. Republican. Episcopalian. Asso. editor Am. Jour. Med. Tech., 1980-88; contbr. articles to profl. jours. Home: 4195 Chippewa Dr Boulder CO 80303-3610

ARNOLD, JEAN ANN, health science facility administrator; b. Coronado, Calif., Nov. 17, 1948; d. Scott Crittenden Daubin and Barbara Jean (Spooner) Annowada; m. Lonnie Lea Arnold, July 14, 1973; children: Danielle Louise and Casey Jean (twins). Student, Santa Barbara City Coll., Calif., 1966-67, U. Wyo., Laramie, 1968-69, Weber State U. Registered Technol., LIc. Technol., Calif., Wash. Staff technol. x-ray Mt. Auburn Hosp., Cambridge, Mass., 1971-72, Victor Valley Hosp., Victorville, Calif., 1972-74, Fairfield Hosp., Calif., 1974-76; chief technol. Oakridge Med. Group, Roseville, Calif., 1976-78; staff technol. radiation therapy U. Cancer Ctr., U. Hosp., Seattle, 1979-84; staff technol. Providence Med. Ctr., Seattle, 1984; relief technol. UCSD Med. Ctr., San Diego, 1984-85; staff technol. Scripps Meml. Hosp., La Jolla, Calif., 1984-87, dir. radiation oncology, 1987—; clin. coord., instr. San Diego Radiation Therapy Tech. Edn. Program. Producer Video, Occpl. Radiation Safety 1988. Mem. Soc. for Radiation Oncology Adminstrs., Calif. Soc. Radiologic Technologists, Am. Soc. Radiologic Technologists, Am. Registry Radiologic Technologists (job analysis adv. com., radiation therapy exam. com., item writer Therapy Tech.). Republican. Baptist. Office: Scripps Meml Hosp 9888 Genesee Ave La Jolla CA 92037-1276

ARNOLD, KIM MARIE, communications engineer; b. Freeport, N.Y., Oct. 1, 1963; d. Edward William and Diane Renee (Milbauer) A. BA in Polit. Sci., Manhattanville Coll., Purchase, N.Y., 1985. Customer svc. specialist MCI Telecomms., Ryebrook, N.Y., 1985-87, tech. staff asst., 1987-88; database tech. specialist MCI Telecomms., Reston, Va., 1988-90, database group leader, 1990-91, engr. I, 1991-92; mgr. network engrng. Cleartel Comms., Washington, 1992—; mem. Carrier Liason Com. Adhoc 800 Database Com., Washington, 1993—. Pub. com. Citizens Against the Stadium-2, Laurel, Md., 1993—. Roman Catholic. Office: Cleartel Communications 1232 22nd St NW Washington DC 20037-1201

ARNOLD, LESLIE BISGER, educational specialist; b. Cheyenne, Wyo., Aug. 26, 1956; d. Fred Bennett and Natalie Sylvia (Cohen) B.; m. Kevin Durkin Arnold, July 6, 1980. BS in Spl. Edn. cum laude, Old Dominion U., 1978, MS in Edn. cum laude, 1984. Cert. spl. educator, emotionally disturbed, mentally retarded, presch. handicapped, severly and profoundly handicapped. Tchr. multiple handicapped Virginia Beach (Va.) Pub. Schs., 1978-81; tchr. autistic Southeastern Coop. Ednl. Programs, Norfolk, Va., 1981-82; tchr. emotionally disturbed/mentally retarded Norfolk Pub. Schs., 1983-86, tchr. specialist, 1986-89, ednl. diagnostician, 1989-90, liaison program mgr., 1990—; mental health worker Tidewater Psychiat. Inst., Virginia Beach, 1985-86; curriculum coord. CHANCE program Old Dominion U., Norfolk, 1986-91; ednl. cons. St. Croix, V.I., 1991; speaker in field. Author: Behavioral Disorders, 1987, Developmental Skills Attainment Sequence Guide, 1989, ERIC-CEC, 1991, Programming for Behaviorally Disordered Adolescents, 1991, CHIME (Clearinghouse for Immigrant Education), 1993. Active PTA. Recipient Sch. Bell award Norfolk Pub. Sch. Bd., 1989, 91, 94; Nat. Found. for Improvement of Edn. grantee, 1992. Mem. NEA, Tidewater Soc. for Autistic Children (pres. 1980-82), Coun. for Exceptional Children, Autism Soc. Am., Nat. Alliance for Mentally Ill, Assn. Retarded Citizens, Optimists Internat. Home: 1884 Wolfsnare Rd Virginia Beach VA 23454-3542

ARNOLD, LINDA GAYLE, human resources executive; b. Columbia, Mo., Aug. 26, 1947; d. Lahmon Emery and Mary Lee (Bennett) Wren; m. Jerry Earl Arnold, Mar. 11, 1965; children: Lesley Arnold Siegfried, Bryce Jefferson. Student, U. Mo., Kansas City, 1965-66. Pricing coord. Gateway Sporting Goods, Kansas City, Mo., 1967-69; legal sec. Tull & Mayse, Columbia, Mo., 1969-74; profit sharing adminstr. McGraw-Edison, Columbia, Mo., 1978-81; dir. pers. Toastmaster Inc., Columbia, Mo., 1981-87, v.p. human resources, 1987—, corp. sec., 1992—. Bd. dirs. Columbia Area United Way, Advent Enterprises; bd. dirs. Mo. Women's Coun., 1993-95; mem. adv. bd. dept. consumer and family econs. U. Mo. Mem. Soc. for Human Resource Mgmt. (Cen. Mo. chpt.), Women's Network (past pres.), Columbia C. of C., Greater Mo. Alumnae Assn., Mo. Found. Women's Resources (bd. dirs., v.p.). Baptist. Office: Toastmaster Inc 1801 N Stadium Blvd Columbia MO 65202-1330

ARNOLD, NANCY NAKAMURA, consultant, mediator; b. Hilo, Hawaii, Dec. 14, 1949; m. Roy Noel Arnold, July 24, 1982. BA with distinction, U. Hawaii, 1972; postgrad., Columbia U., 1973, U. Hawaii, 1974-75; JD, George Washington U., 1985. Tng. cons. Honolulu, 1972-75; program dir., officer, editor APA, Washington, 1975-87; health policy cons. Washington, 1987-88; mediator Fairfax County (Va.) Dept. Consumer Affairs, 1988-92; mental health therapist Fairfax Falls Ch. Community Svcs. Bd., Annandale, Va., 1992—; legal asst. Gallaudet U., Washington, 1984; legal fellow George Washington U., 1985; cons. Nat. AIDS Network, Washington, 1987; symposium panel mem. APA, Washington, 1986. Expert rev. panelist: (book) AIDS Information Resources Directory, 1988. Mem. Am. Soc. on Aging., Phi Beta Kappa. Home: 3954 Mountain Rd Haymarket VA 22069-1716

ARNOLD, ROXANNE, post anesthesia nurse, educator; b. Connellsville, Pa.; d. Tyree Franklin Sr. and Reva Gayle (Thieler) A. AAS, Gloucester County Coll., 1983; BSN, Widener U., 1989. RN, Fla.; cert. critical care nurse; cert. emergency nurse; cert. trauma nurse, BLS-instr., BLS-provider, ACLS provider. Staff devel. instr., nursing supr., cardiac care nurse Meth. Hosp., Phila., 1982-89; emergency nurse Underwood Meml. Hosp., Woodbury, N.J., 1988-89; critical care nurse Jupiter (Fla.) Hosp., 1989-91; emergency clin. nurse III Indian River Meml. Hosp., Vero Beach, Fla., 1990-92; EMT/paramedic instr. Indian River Community Coll., Ft. Pierce, Fla., 1990-92; emergency asst. nurse mgr. Holmes Regional Med. Ctr., Melbourne, Fla., 1992-94; post anesthesia clin. nurse III Indian River Meml. Hosp., Vero Beach, Fla., 1994—. Mem. Am. Soc. Post Anesthesia Nurses, Am. Assn. Critical Care Nurses, Emergency Nurses Assn., Sigma Theta Tau, Eta Beta. Home: 1309 B Peppertree Trl Fort Pierce FL 34950

ARNOLD, SANDRA PETERSON, non-profit research service company executive; b. L.A., Apr. 18, 1936; d. Kenneth T. and Yolanda Cecilia (Chiapetta) Peterson; m. Lawrence John Arnold, Jan. 4, 1964; children: EricaLynn Tobin, Lauren Arnold. BA, Immaculate Heart Coll., 1958. Mem. profl. & tech. tng. staff System Devel. Corp., Santa Monica, Calif., 1960-65; mgr. documentation Digitek Corp., L.A., 1965-69; v.p. devel., ops. and engrng. Computer Scis. Corp., El Segundo, Calif., 1969-84; v.p., gen. mgr. nat. accts. Automatic Data Processing, Inc., Clifton, N.J., 1984-93; v.p. corp. affairs The Population Coun., N.Y., 1994—. Pres. Aux. of the Silverhill Found., 1987-90. Mem. AAUW. Home: PO Box 1207 New Canaan CT 06840 Office: The Population Coun 1 Dag Hammarskjold Plz New York NY 10017

ARNOLD, SANDRA RUTH KOUNS, healthcare marketing executive; b. Cleburne, Tex., Jan. 20, 1941; d. Wyatt Allen and Ethel Louise (Gandillon) Kouns; m. William Patrick Arnold, Feb. 27, 1960; children: Allyson Arnold House, Lynn Ann Workman. Student, Hill Coll., Cleburne, Tex., 1975, 78, 79, Richland Coll., Dallas, 1986. Lic. realtor, Tex. With Howell's Dept. Store, Cleburne, 1959-64; decorator Baileys Home Improvements, Cleburne, 1971-77; realtor Red Carpet and Holliday Assocs., Cleburne, 1979-94; pub./patient rels. Meml. Hosp., Cleburne, 1982-86; mktg./patient rels. staff Walls Regional Hosp., Cleburne, 1986; mktg. mgr. Harris Meth. Health System, Ft. Worth, 1986-88; mktg./physician recruiting mgr. Kimbro Med. Ctr., Cleburne, 1988-92; v.p. A&A Plastic Co., 1969—; vocalist weddings, theaters, and chs., Cleburne, 1959—. Contbr. articles to profl. jours. Coord. Area Alzheimer Support Group, Cleburne, 1984; active St. Mark Meth. Ch., Cleburne; coord., cons. Adopt-A-Sch./Cleburne Schs., 1984—; mem. actress Carnegie Theater; active Johnson County Hist. Commn., PTA. Named one of Outstanding Women of S.W., 1979. Mem. Cleburne C. of C. (dir. 1991-93), Women's Forum, Heritage Assembly (charter), Beta Sigma Phi (pres., Woman of Yr. 1963, 81). Home and Office: PO Box 63 Cleburne TX 76033-0063

ARNOLD, SHEILA, former state legislator; b. N.Y.C., Jan. 15, 1929; d. Michael and Eileen (Lynch) Keddy; coll. courses; m. George Longan Arnold, Nov. 12, 1960; 1 child, Peter; 1 child by previous marriage, Michael C. Young; stepchildren: Drew, George Longan, Joe. Mem. Wyo. Ho. of Reps., 1978-93, mem. Laramie Regional Airport Bd . Former mem., sec. Wyo. Land Use Adv. Coms.; past pres. Dem. Women's Club, Laramie; past vice chmn. Albany County Dem. Party, now chmn.; past mem. Dem. State Com.; mem. adv. bd. Wyo. Home Health Care; former mem. Nat. Conf. State Legislatures Com. on Fiscal Affairs and Oversight Com. Recipient Spl. Recognition award from Developmentally Disabled Citizens of Wyo., 1985. Mem. Laramie Area C. of C. (pres. 1982; Top Hand award 1977), LWV (Laramie bd. dirs. 1993-94), Internat. Platform Assn., Faculty Women's Club (past pres.), VFW Ladies Aux. (sr. v.p. Post 2221), Zonta, Laramie Women's Club.

ARNOLD, TONI LAVALLE, engineering specialist; b. N.Y.C., Nov. 29, 1947; d. Aldo Peter and Margaret E. (Tessitore) Lavalle; m. Asbury Rembert Arnold, July 26, 1975. Student, Marymount Coll., 1965-67. Electro-mech. drafter PRD Electronics, Syosset, N.Y., 1973-74; electro-mech. designer/drafter Cadre Corp., Atlanta, 1974-79; EDA libr. resource mgr. Harris Corp., Palm Bay, Fla., 1982—. Stained glass artist represented in galleries in Fla., N.Y. Vol., leader Camp Fire Sunshine Coun., Lakeland, Fla., 1984-87, bd. dirs., 1993—; mem. Brevard County Dem. Exec. Com., 1993—, chair environ. com., 1994—; vol. south Brevard Habitat for Humanity. Recipient scholarship N.Y. State Bd. Regents, 1964, Blue Ribbon award Camp Fire Nat., Kansas City, 1985. Democrat. Home: 1670 Heartwellville St NW Palm Bay FL 32907-9999 Office: Harris Corp Govt Com Divsn PO Box 91000 Melbourne FL 32902-3001

ARNOLD-BIAGIOLI, BEVERLY JEAN, clinical nurse specialist; b. Kansas City, Mo., Jan. 3, 1953; d. Glen K. and Barbara Jean (Hall) Arnold; m. John A. Biagioli, June 12, 1981. BSN, William Jewell Coll., 1975; MN, U. Kans., 1989. Staff nurse, charge nurse pediatrics Independence (Mo.) Regional Health Ctr., 1975-76; pediatrics office charge nurse Drs. Van Biber, Pugh and Goertz, 1976-77; staff nurse, charge nurse, acting head nurse Kans. U. Med. Ctr., 1977-79; employment rep., nurse recruiter St. Joseph Health Ctr., 1979-84, nursing supr., 1984-90; emergency rm. staff nurse, nursing supr. Children's Mercy Hosp., Kansas City, 1988—, clin. specialist in child protection, 1988—; speaker to groups on domestic violence, battered women, date rape, rape crisis, and child phys. and sexual abuse. Bd. dirs. Hope House, Inc., Independence, 1991—, vol., 1987-91; bd. dirs. Domestic Violence Network, Kansas City, 1991—; mem. Jackson County Child Sexual Abuse Task Force. Named Vol. of Yr. Hope House, Inc., 1989. Mem. ANA, Mo. Nurses Assn., Am. Profl. Soc. for Abused Children, Nursing Network Violence Against Women, Mo. Safe Network, Internat. Assn. Forensic Nursing, Sigma Theta Tau. Office: Childrens Mercy Hosp 2401 Gillham Rd Kansas City MO 64108-4698

ARNOLD HUBERT, NANCY KAY, writer; b. Kalamazoo, Mich., May 9, 1951; d. Byron Lyle and Ada (Doorlag) Arnold; m. Louis Scott Hubert, May 5, 1989. BFA in Painting, Western Mich. U., 1983, postgrad., 1985-86. Writer Advanced Systems & Designs, Inc., Farmington Hills, Mich., 1987-89; pres., owner TechWrite, Kalamazoo, 1989—. Author: (poetry) Tetragonal Pyramids, 1982; exhibited in group shows, Kalamazoo, 1983, Western Mich. U., 1982, 85. Mem. NAFE, Humane Farming Assn. Am. People for Ethical Treatment of Animals. Libertarian. Office: 3857 Wolf Dr Kalamazoo MI 49009

ARNONE, MARY GRACE, radiology technologist; b. Bronx, N.Y., Dec. 28, 1961; d. Anthony Rocco and Mary Helen (Doring) A. AA, Acad. Health Sci., U.S. Army, 1982. Lic. radiologist Hawaii, N.J., Fla., N.Y., lic. mammographer, N.Y. Radiology technologist, 1986-90, Our Lady of Mercy Hosp., Yonkers, N.Y., 1988—. With U.S. Army, 1982-86. Democrat. Lutheran. Office: Our Lady of Mercy Hosp PO Box 3 Yonkers NY 10701

ARNOT-HEANEY, SUSAN EILEEN, cosmetics executive; b. East Orange, N.J., Aug. 10, 1957; d. Robert B. and Mae (Cockcroft) A.; m. Kevin Barry Heaney, Mar. 28, 1992. BA, Coll. William and Mary, 1979; postgrad., Cambridge U., 1977; cert., NYU, 1979. Promotion asst. Viking Press/Penguin Books, N.Y.C., 1979-82; mgr. promotion Rizzoli Internat. Publs., N.Y.C., 1982-83; mgr. advt. promotion USA Today, N.Y.C., 1983-85; promotion dir. 50 Plus mag., N.Y.C., 1985-88, In Fashion mag., N.Y.C., 1988-89; mktg. svcs. mgr. TAXI mag., N.Y.C., 1989-90; dir. pub. rels. and spl. events Elizabeth Arden, N.Y.C., 1990—; career adv. Coll. William and Mary, 1980—. Writer/editor quar.: (newsletter) 50 Plus Market Update, 1985-88. Vol. cook, fundraiser Cathedral Soup Kitchen, St. John the Divine Cathedral, 1983-85; vol. Women in Need Image Workshops, 1990-94; mem. nat. leadership com. Save the Children Fedn., 1993—. Recipient Best of N.Y. Addy award for advt., 1986. Mem. Cosmetic, Toiletries and Fragrance Assn. (chair pub. rels. com., ex officio bd. dirs. 1994—), Cosmetic Exec. Women, Women in Communications Inc. (chpt. publicity com. 1985-86, fin. com. 1986-87, spl. events com. 1986-87), NOW, Fashion Group Internat., William and Mary Alumni Soc. (chpt. pres. 1986-90, exec. bd. 1983-86, 90-92), AAUW (chpt. corr. sec. 1983-86, chair com. on women's work 1984-86), Mcpl. Art Soc. Methodist. Avocations: travel, music, theater, reading, art collecting, film. Home: 230 W 107th St Apt 2C New York NY 10025-3041

ARNOTT, ELLEN MARIE, medical case management executive; b. Berwyn, Ill., Apr. 28, 1945; d. Howard Thomas and Catherine Marie (Stauber) Simon; m. John Michael Arnott, Dec. 16, 1967; children: John Michael II, Michelle Marie. BSN, Seton Hall U., 1981; MA, Tex. Woman's U., 1991. Cert. occupational health nurse, case mgr. Staff nurse oncology, med.-surgery, ICU, CCU, recovery, 1981-83, community health nurse, 1982-83; disability health nurse AT&T, 1983-84; mgr. health svcs. Lone Star Gas Co., 1985-86, Abbott Labs., 1986-88; corp. nursing supr. J.C. Penney, 1988-89; pres. Arnott & Assocs., Roanoke, Tex., 1989—, 1992—; wellness cons.; cons. health fair; occupational health mgmt. cons.; workers compensation case mgmt. cons. CPR instr. trainer Am. Heart Assn.; vol. and facilitator SBE and smoking cessation Am. Cancer Soc.; CPR instr. to community; first aid vol.; local rescue squad vol.; mem. edn. com., skin cancer com. Am. Cancer Soc. Recipient Tex. State Achievement award for excellence in occupational health, 1990; named one of the Great One-Hundred Nurses of 1991, Dallas/Ft. Worth. Mem. Am. Assn. Occupational Health Nurses, Nat. Assn. Women Bus. Owners, Case Mgmt. Soc. Am., Tex. Assn. Occupational Health Nurses (fin. com. 1989-90, v.p. 1989-91), Dallas Tex. Assn. Occupational Health Nurses (hospitality com. 1985, edn. com. 1986-87, dir.-newsletter editor 1987, v.p. 1988-90, pres. 1991-93), ANA, Tex. Nurses Assn., Omicron Delta Epsilon. Roman Catholic. Office: Arnott & Assocs Inc 115 E Worth Ste C Grapevine TX 76051

AROCHO, CATHLEEN HALL, accountant; b. Fredericksburg, Va., Oct. 10, 1956; d. Edward Preston and Catherine Isabelle (Crim) Hall; m. Hector J. Arocho, Nov. 29, 1980 (div. Aug. 1990); children: Mackenzie C., Hector J. Jr. BS, Va. Poly. Inst. and State U., 1979, M Accountancy, 1993. CPA, Va. Tchr.'s aide Fairfax County Schs., Alexandria, Va., 1980; dir. Hartwood House, Alexandria, 1980-82; recreation specialist U.S. Army Corps Engrs., Saudi Arabia, 1982-84; recreation therapist Leader Nursing & Rehab., Harrisburg, Pa., 1987-90; program mgr. New Directions, Harrisburg, 1990-91; staff acct. Durham's Bus. Svc., Blacksburg, Va., 1992; grad. asst. Va. Poly. Inst. and State U., Blacksburg, 1992-93; staff acct. Ernst & Young, LLP, Balt., 1993—; tax preparer H&R Block, Harrisburg, 1988, 89, 91; treas., bd.dirs. Court Apptd. Spl. Advocate Program, 1994-97. Pres., dist. sec.-treas. Cir. K, Blacksburg, 1976-79; vol. Va. Golden Olympics, Blacksburg, 1992, Md. Spl. Olympics, 1994, coach Youth Basketball, Lutherville, Md., 1995. Mem. AICPA, MACPA, Inst. Cert. Mgmt. Accts. Methodist. Office: Ernst & Young LLP One North Charles Baltimore MD 21093

AROMIN, MERCEDES FUNG, portfolio manager, investment advisor, consultant; b. Kowloon, Hong Kong, Dec. 1, 1956; came to U.S., 1974; d. Remigio N. and Josephine (Fung) A. BS in Bus. Adminstrn., U. Tenn., Knoxville, 1978; MBA, Ga. State U., 1989. Mgr. Ramada Inn, Scottsburg, Ind., 1978; asst. mgr. York Steak House, Nashville, 1978-80; asst. terminal mgr. Greyhound Lines Inc., Atlanta, 1980-84; staff asst. The Coca-Cola Co., Atlanta, 1985-87; staff asst. Coca-Cola Enterprises Inc., Atlanta, 1987-89, shareholder rels. mgr., 1989-92; pres., CEO MFA Fin. Asset Mgmt., Atlanta, 1992—; sec.-treas. Coca-Cola Enterprises Inc. Employee Nonpartisan Com. for Good Govt., Atlanta, 1989-91. William Way scholar, 1976, Alcoa Found. scholar, 1977. Mem. Atlanta Investment Group (founder, chief fin. officer 1990, exec. com., adv. com.), Ga. State U. MBA Alumni Group (charter). Roman Catholic. Office: 2040 Carmel Bascomb Rd Woodstock GA 30188-3545

ARON, EVE GLICKA SERENSON, personal care industry executive; b. N.Y.C., Sept. 5, 1937; d. Max and Edith (Gitelson) Serenson; m. Joel Edward Aron, Dec. 13, 1964; children: Jennifer, Joshua, Eric. BS, CCNY, 1958; MS, Yeshiva U., 1960; MBA with honors, Iona Coll., 1985. Med. technician Albert Einstein Coll. Medicine, Bronx, N.Y., 1959-60; chemist Strasenburgh labs., Belleville, N.J., 1961-63, Roche Labs., Nutley, N.J., 1963-67; sr. chemist Pantene Labs. div. Roche, Nutley, 1967-69; mgr. R&D Combe Inc., White Plains, N.Y., 1978-85, assoc. dir. R&D, 1985—. Contbr. articles and book revs. to profl. jours. Tutor Literacy Vols. of Am. mem. NOW, Am. Chem. Soc., Soc. Cosmetic Chemists (sec. Conn. chpt. 1989-90, chair 1992, hospitality/membership chair Conn. chpt. 1994-95, chpt. advisor 1993). Home: 470 Park Ave Rye NY 10580-1213 Office: Combe Inc 1101 Westchester Ave White Plains NY 10604-3503

ARONOW, JANI ALLISON, public relations executive; b. N.Y.C., Aug. 9, 1957; d. William and Audrey (Lipsky) A. BA in Journalism, Pub. Rels., Ohio State U., 1979. Pub. rels. asst. Union Am. Hebrew Congregations, N.Y.C., 1980-81; asst. pub. rels. dir. Pub. Rels. Soc. Am., N.Y.C., 1981-83; sr. v.p., group mgr. Ketchum Pub. Rels., N.Y.C., 1983-91—; pres. Aronow and Pollock Communications, Inc., N.Y.C., 1991—. Recipient Gold Leaf award, Food Mktg. Inst/Family Circle mag., 1988, Best award, Nat. Agr. Mktg. Assn., 1988, Golden Circle cert., Am. Soc. Assn. Execs., 1988, Excellence in Advt. award, AMA, 1989. Mem. Pub. Rels. Soc. Am. (Silver Anvil award 1988, 94), N.Y. Pub. Rels. Soc. (publicity com. chmn. 1985, honors and awards com. 1989), Ohio State Alumni Club. Office: Aronow & Pollock Comms Inc 3d Flr 524 Broadway New York NY 10012

ARONSON, DANA LYNNE, public relations executive; b. Newark, Nov. 12, 1960; d. Stephen Earl and Lila Muriel (Seletsky) A. BS, Boston U., 1982. Asst. acct. exec. Doremus & Co., N.Y.C., 1982-84; sr. acct. exec. Manning Selvage & Lee, N.Y.C., 1984-85; mgr. pub. rels. United Media, N.Y.C., 1985-91; v.p. pub. rels. Am. Diabetes Assn., Somerset, N.J., 1991-94, v.p. programs, 1994—. Recipient Silver Anvil award Pub. Rels. Soc., 1988. Office: Am Diabetes Assn 200 Cottontail Ln Somerset NJ 08873

ARONSON, ESTHER LEAH, association administrator, psychotherapist; b. Bklyn., Sept. 8, 1941; d. Nathan and Nellie (Borack) A.; m. Joel Allen Bernstein, Sept. 8, 1967 (div. 1978). BA, Bklyn. Coll., 1965; MA, New Sch. for Social Rsch., N.Y.C., 1982; MSW, NYU, 1984, postgrad., 1985—. Lic. social worker, N.Y. Resource cons. N.Y.C. Human Resources Adminstrn., 1965-82; counselor Fordham-Tremont Community Mental Health Ctr., Bronx, 1982-83, South Beach Psychiat. Ctr., Bklyn., 1983-84; social worker Alfred Adler Clinic, N.Y.C., 1984-85; pvt. practice clin. social work psychotherapist N.Y.C., 1986—; program developer Emanu-El Midtown YM-YWHA, N.Y.C., 1987-88, dir. ret. adult div., 1988—; lectr. Am. Mus. Natural History, N.Y.C., 1978. Contbr. articles to profl. jours. Mem. Am. Orthopsychiat. Assn., Inc., N.Y. State Soc. Clin. Social Work Psychotherapists, Inc., Soc. for Pub. Health Edn., NAFE, Phi Delta Kappa, Kappa Delta Pi. Home: 2 Fifth Ave Apt 31 New York NY 10011

ARONSON, HELENE ESTELLE, nurse, family counselor; b. L.A., June 21, 1945; d. Robert H. and Celia C. (Cooperman) Pittler. BS in Pub. Health Nursing, San Francisco State U., 1970; postgrad., Loyola Marymount U., L.A., 1984—. RN, Calif. Childbirth education instr. Cedars Sinai Med. Ctr., L.A., 1980-81, Brotman Meml. Hosp., L.A., 1981-82; head nurse Cancer Detection Ctr., L.A., 1981-89, nurse, 1991—; trainee therapist L.A. Free Clinic, 1990—; mental health worker Psychiat. Inst. Century City Hosp., 1992-93, Brotman Med. Ctr., Culver City, 1994. Vol. fundraiser City of Hope Med. Ctr., Duarte, Calif., 1972-75. Mem. Calif. Assn. Marriage, Child and Family Counselors, Psi Chi.

ARONSON, LUANN MARIE, actress; b. Ithaca, N.Y., Nov. 18, 1964; d. Arthur Lawrence and Marilyn Ann (Lundeen) A. BA, Ithaca Coll., 1986; MusM, Southern Meth. U., Dallas, 1988. Mem. C.W. Post Summer Opera, N.Y., 1987, Music Theatre North, Potsdam, N.Y., 1989, 90, Graeat Buffalo Opera, Buffalo, N.Y., 1990; mem. nat. tour Gateway Playhouse, 1991, mem. far east tour, 1992; mem. Andrew Lloyd Webber's Sydmonton Festival, London, Eng., 1992; featured soloist Music of Andrew Lloyde Webber, Radio City Music Hall, N.Y.C., 1992. Appearances on broadway include Phantom of the Opera as Christine, N.Y.C., 1992—. Recipient Outstanding Young Alimni award Ithaca Coll. Allumni Assn., 1994; Blossom Music Festival scholar, 1988, Tanglewood Summer Music Festival scholar, 1986. Mem. Actor's Equity Assn.

ARONSON, REBECCA, designer; b. Lima, Ohio, Oct. 17, 1941; d. Walter Gilbert Everett and Marian Marciel (Evans) Pearce; m. Niels R. Keiper, Dec. 23, 1968 (div. Apr. 1975); m. Douglas Ira Battenberg, May 19, 1979. Student, Bowling Green (Ohio) State U., 1959-61. Pvt. sec. Chem. Abstracts, Columbus, Ohio, 1961-63; flight attendant Am. Airlines, Chgo., Washington, 1963-69; booking agt. Nat. Concert Bur., Lawrence, Kans., 1969-72; owner The Village Jewel, Columbus and Cin., 1972-75; territory rep. Reynolds Metals Co., Columbus, 1973-75; project coord. Holland & Lyons, Inc., Washington, 1976-78; dir. mktg. Mid. States Constrn., Rockville, Md., 1978-79; asst. dir. condominium devel. Charles E. Smith Cos., Arlington, Va., 1980-81; pres., designer Aronson Enterprises, Inc., Shepherdstown, W.Va., 1982—. Dir. Edn. Foundry Meth. Ch., Washington, 1978-81, trustee, 1988, 89, chmn. fin. com., 1989; rep. Real Estate Developers Task Force, Washington, 1981. Mem. NAFE, Assn. for Rsch. and Elightenment, An Toiseach (leader), Am. Comunn Uisge Beatha . Home and Office: Aronson Enterprises Box 2182 The Carriage House High St Shepherdstown WV 25443

ARONSON, VIRGINIA RUTH, music educator, conductor; b. Glens Falls, N.Y., May 31, 1931; d. Irving Milton and Florence Estelle (Orcutt) Falkenbury; m. Andrew Thomas Murphy, June 12, 1955 (div. 1970); children: Marion Elizabeth, Katherine Annette, Patricia Lynn, Andrew Thomas; m. Chester Samuel Aronson, July 21, 1984 (dec. 1992). BA, Colby Coll., Waterville, 1953; Music Cert., U. Pacific, Stockton, 1955; MM, Westminster Choir, Princeton, 1977; ORFF cert., Conn. Cen. State Coll., Hartford, 1987; Kindermusik cert., Westminster Choir Coll., 1989, 90, 94. Classroom tchr. Wash. Sch., Stockton, Calif., 1955-56, Bellemeade Sch., Richmond, Va., 1956-57; bookstore mgr. Union Theol. Sem., Richmond, 1958-60; adminstrv. sec. Wash. Cathedral, Wash., 1970-73; product mgr. Mr. Rogers Neighborhood, Princeton, N.J., 1973-74; music tchr. The Hun Sch., 1975-77, Millstone Sch., N.J., 1978-89; pvt. music tchr., 1989—; dir. music St. John's Luth. Ch., Morrisville, Pa., 1990-92; dir. Colbyettes, Waterville, 1952-53; pres. Glee Club Colby Coll., 1952-53. Arranger: Songs of the Rain, 1952, Thank God I'm Old, 1985; composer Early in the Morn, 1940. Soprano Peace Odyssey Chorus, 1988; laborer World Coun. Chs., France, 1952; recreation dir. Am. Friends Svc. Com., Rapid City, 1951; seminar leader World Coun. Chs., N.Y.C., 1948; music dir. Unitarian Ch., Princeton, 1980-90. Mem. Unitarian Universalist Musicians Network (chmn. profl. concerns com. 1987-89), Am. Orff Schulwerk Assn. (v.p. ctrl. N.J. chpt. 1989-91), Am. Choral Dirs. Assn., Music Edn. Nat. Conf., N.J. Edn. Assn., Princeton Ski Club, Princeton Pro Musica (sight singing tchr. 1993—), Westminster Alumni Choir. Democrat. Home: 66 Sycamore Ln Skillman NJ 08558-2013

ARORA, SHIRLEY LEASE, Spanish language educator; b. Youngstown, Ohio, June 3, 1930; d. Leland J. and Ruth (Brice) Lease; m. Harbans L. Arora; children: David, Alan. BA, Stanford U., 1950, MA, 1951; PhD, UCLA, 1962. Asst. prof. Spanish UCLA, 1962-70, assoc. prof., 1970-76, prof., 1976—, chmn. dept., 1981-91. Author: What Then, Raman, 1960 (Charles W. Follett award, Jane Addams award 1960), The Left-Handed Chank, 1966, Proverbial Comparisons in Ricardo Palma's Tradiciones peruanas, 1966, Proverbial Comparisons and Related Expressions in Spanish, 1977. Mem. MLA, Am. Folklore Soc., Calif. Folklore Soc. (v.p. 1983-85), Internat. Soc. for Folk Narrative Rsch., Internat. Soc. for Contemporary Legend Rsch., Asociacion Internacional de Hispanistas, Instituto Internacional de Literatura Iberoamericana. Office: UCLA Dept Spanish & Portuguese 5310 Rolfe Hall Los Angeles CA 90024-1532

AROSIO, CHARLYNE MARY, school librarian; b. Gilroy, Calif., Jan. 6, 1938; d. Charles Joseph and Annie Rose (Olivieri) A. BA, San Francisco State, 1960; student in Libr./Media Studies, U. Ariz., Tempe, 1969, U. Nev., 1974; MA in Computer Edn., Fresno Pacific Coll., 1989; cert. in paralegal studies, U. Nev., 1992. Cert. media specialist. Tchr. Washoe County Sch. Dist., Reno, 1961—, media specialist, 1970—; tchr. Truckee Meadow Coll., Reno, 1989—; libr. cons. Washoe County Sch. Dist., Reno, 1980—. Named Tchr. of Month Greater Reno C. of C., 1977; recipient Dedicated Performance award Washoe County Tchrs. Assn., 1980. Mem. AAUW (sec. parlimentarian 1989—), Am. Libr. Assn., Nev. Assn. Sch. Libr. (pres. 1980-81), No. Nev. Tchrs. English (bd. dirs.), Phi Kappa. Home: 3510 Yosemite Pl Reno NV 89503-3839

AROVA, SONIA, artistic director, ballet educator; b. Sofia, Bulgaria; came to U.S., 1954; d. Albert and Rene (Melamedoff) Errio; m. Thor Sutowski, Mar. 11, 1965; 1 child, Ariane. Grad. Fine Arts Sch., Paris, 1940, Eng., 1944. Ballerina Internat. Ballet, London, 1944-47, Rambert Ballet, London, 1947-50, Royal Ballet, London, 1962-63, Festival Ballet, London, 1950-54, Ballet deChamps-Elysees, Paris, 1958-60, Am. Ballet Theater, N.Y.C., 1954-58, Ballet Russe, 1960-62; artistic dir. Nat. Ballet, Oslo, 1964-70, Hamburg Ballet, Fed. Republic Germany, 1970-71; co-dir. San Diego Ballet, 1971-75; dir. State of Ala. Ballet, Ballet South, Birmingham, 1981—, instr. Sch. Fine Arts, 1975—; guest tchr. Australian Ballet, 1993, 94, Bayerische Staatsballet, Munich, Germany, 1994. Recipient World Championship of Dance award Ballet Jury, Paris, 1939; decorated knight of First Order, King Olav of Norway, 1971.

ARP LOTTER, DONNA, investor, venture capitalist; b. Henrietta, Tex., Dec. 17, 1950; d. T.S. Jr. and Coy Lee (Howard) Grimsley; m. Bruce D. Lotter, Feb. 18, 1984; children: Brandon, Collin. BS, Midwestern State U., 1975, M in Counseling, 1979. Sales rep. Burroughs-Wellcome Co., Fort Worth, Tex., 1978-79; sales mgr. Procter & Gamble Co., Dallas, 1979-84; pres. Arp-Lotter Investments, Colleyville, Tex., 1984—; prin. DBL Investments, Inc.; sec., officer KCB Corp., Inc. Trustee Baylor Hosp., Grapevine, Tex., 1991; bd. dirs. Am. Cancer Soc.; bd. govs. N.E. Arts Coun. Hardin scholar Midwestern State U., 1975. Mem. Bus. Profl. Womens Club, Nat. Assn. Women Bus. Owners, Colleyville C. of C. (pres. 1995). Republican. Methodist.

ARQUETTE, ROSANNA, actress; b. N.Y.C., Aug. 10, 1959; d. Lewis and Mardi Arquette; m. John Sidel, Dec. 1993. Actress: (TV films) Having Babies II, 1978, Dark Secret of Harvest Home, Zuma Beach, The Executioner's Song, 1982, In the Deep Woods, 1992 (films) S.O.B., 1981, Baby it's You, 1983, Desperately Seeking Susan, 1985, After Hours, 1985, Silverado, 1985, The Aviator, 1985, 8 Million Ways To Die, 1986, Nobody's Fool, 1986, The Big Blue, 1988, New York Stories, 1989, The Linguini Incident, 1992, Fathers and Sons, 1992, Nowhere to Run, 1993, Pulp Fiction, 1994, Search and Destroy, 1995. Office: Internat Creative Mgt 8942 Whilshire Blvd Beverly Hills CA 90211*

ARRANTS, LETHA F., retired association executive; b. Feb. 9, 1917; d. Charles H. and Varieta Mary (Mavis) A. BS, Miami U., Oxford, Ohio, 1939; M of Social Scis., Case Western Res. U., 1950. Dir. teens YWCA, Beloit, Wis., 1942-45, Reading, Pa., 1945-48; dir. teen camp YWCA, Akron, Ohio, 1950-57; exec dir. YWCA, Lima, Ohio, 1957-65; br. exec. YWCA, Cleve., 1965-72; pers. cons. YWCA of U.S.A., N.Y.C., 1973-82, part-time cons., 1982—. Mem. sch. screening bd. Parma (Ohio) Sch. Dist., 1970; trainer vols. Sonnenberg Gardens, Canandaigua, N.Y., 1990-94, pres. vols., 1991-93; vol. supr. Cmty. Kitchens, Canandaigua. Named Vol. of Yr. Welcome Wagon, Canandaigua, N.Y., 1987. Mem. AAUW (historian), Soroptimists (pres. Lima chpt. 1962). Democrat. Home: 208 Buffalo St Canandaigua NY 14424-1014

ARRATHOON, LEIGH ADELAIDE, medievalist, editor, writer; b. N.Y.C., Nov. 30, 1942; d. Henry and Peggy Adelaide (Weed) A.; m. Raymond Arrathoon, June 10, 1967. Cours de Vacances at U. de Genève, Lausanne, Lille at Boulogne, 1961-63; AB in French and Spanish, Hunter Coll., 1963; MA in French, Stanford U., 1966, MA in Spanish, 1968; MA in Medieval French Lit., Princeton U., 1975, PhD in Medieval French Lit., 1975. With UN Secretariat, N.Y.C., 1963-64; teaching asst., Stanford U., 1964-66; tchr. Spanish and French, Convent of Sacred Heart, Menlo Park, Calif., 1966-67; asst. prof. Spanish, Rider Coll., Trenton, N.J., 1970-71; pub. editor-in-chief Solaris Press, Troy, Idaho, 1975-80, Rochester, Mich., 1980-86; pres. Solaris Press II, 1986—, advt. and mktg. cons. A.D. Images, Inc., 1986—; v.p. John J. Davio, Rochester, Mich. Scholar, Centre d'Art Dramatique, 1957. Mem. MLA, Medieval Acad. Am., Courtly Lit. Soc., Sigma Delta Pi, Alpha Gamma Delta. Contbg. editor: The Craft of Fiction: Essays in Medieval Poetics, 1984; editor, translator The Lady of Vergi, 1984; contbg. editor: Chaucer and the Craft of Fiction, 1986; contbg. numerous fictional short stories; editor: South Hill Gazette (weekly periodical). Office: PO Box 547 Rochester MI 48307

ARRIGO, ANTOINETTE, counseling; b. Bayonne, N.J., Apr. 22, 1930; d. Vincent and Rose (Bernardo) Butera; m. Paul Magarelli, Oct. 3, 1948 (dec. July 1964); children: Maria, Paul, Rosanne; m. Anthony J. Arrigo, Feb. 11, 1974. BA Elem. Edn., Jersey City State Coll.; MA in Counseling, Seton Hall U.; PhD, Ariz. State U. Cert. sch. psychologist. Elem. tchr. Union Ave Sch., Hazlet, N.J., 1969-72; instr. disabled vets Seton Hall U., South Orange, N.J., 1969-72; intern W. Orange (N.J.) Family Svcs. Clinic, 1971; exec. dir. Community Drug Program, Hudson County/Bayonne, N.J., 1972-74; cons. Ariz. Dept. Corrections, Phoenix, 1974-75; cons./instr. Devereaux Day Sch., Scottsdale, Ariz., 1975-77; cons. Saguaro High Sch., Scottsdale, 1975-77; tchng. asst. Ariz. State U., Tempe, 1980-94; pvt. practice Scottsdale, 1980—; exec. dir. Hudson County Cmty. Drug Program, Bayonne, 1972-74; cons. Ariz. Dept. Corrections, 1974-75; cons., instr. Elder Hostel and Franciscan Renewal Ctr., Scottsdale, 1980-93. Author publs. in field. Named Woman of Achievement, Hudson County, N.J., 1973. Mem. APA, Inst. Logtherapy, Ariz. State U. Alumni Assn., Phi Delta Kappa, Kappa Delta Pi. Democrat. Roman Catholic. Home: 12282 E Palomino Rd Scottsdale AZ 85259

ARRINGTON, DOROTHY ANITA COLLINS, retired real estate broker; b. Laurel, Miss., Sept. 9, 1922; d. Jeff Clay and Maude Eula (Sudduth) Collins; m. Robert Newton Arrington, Oct. 27, 1956; children: Robert William, Cynthia Anne Arrington Morris. AA, Jones County Jr. Coll., 1941; student, U. Ala., 1942-43. Assoc. realtor Town & Country Village Realtors, Houston, 1970-72, McGuirt & Co., Realtors, Houston, 1974-77, 79-81, Duffy & LaRoe, Realtors, Houston, 1978-79; owner-broker Dotty Arrington, Realtors, Houston, 1972-74; asst. sales mgr. Realmco, Inc., Houston, 1977-78; pres. Dotty Arrington, Inc., Houston, 1981-89, ret., 1989; adult tchr. Bethel Bible Series. Mem. Daus of the King, Delphians. Republican. Episcopalian.

ARRINGTON, HARRIET ANN, historian, biographer, writer; b. Salt Lake City, June 22, 1924; d. Lyman Merrill and Myrtle (Swainston) Horne; m. Frederick C. Sorensen, Dec. 22, 1943 (div. Dec. 1954); children: Annette S. Rogers, Frederick Christian, Heidi S. Swinton; m. Gordon B. Moody, July 26, 1958 (div. Aug. 1963); 1 child, Stephen Horne; m. Leonard James Arrington, Nov. 19, 1983. BS in Edn., U. Utah, 1957. Cert. tchr., Utah, Ga. Supr. surg. secs. Latter-day Sts. Hosp., Salt Lake City, 1954-58; tchr. Salt Lake City Schs., 1954-57, Glynn County Schs., Brunswick, Ga., 1958-59; from med. sec. to office mgr. Dr. Horne, Salt Lake City, 1962-83; tchr. Carden Sch., Salt Lake City, 1973-74, women's history rschr., tchr.; mem. Utah Women's Legis. Coun.; co-establisher Arrington Archives, Utah Stae U. Author: Heritage of Faith, 1988; contbr. articles to profl. jours. and confs. Dist. chmn. Utah Rep. Com., 1972-76; mem. art com. Salt Lake City Bd. Edn.; chmn. art exhibit Utah Women's Conf., 1986-87; active LDS Women's Relief Soc.; chmn. Utah Women Artists' Exhbn., AAUW, Utah divsn., 1986-87. Recipient Vol. Action award Utah Women Artists' Exhbn., 1987, resolution of appreciation Utah Arts Coun., 1989. Mem. AAUW (Utah state cultural refinement chmn., cert. of appreciation 1988), DAR (Utah Am. history chmn.), Old Main Soc. Utah State U., Chi Omega (past pres. alumni chpt.). Home and Office: 2236 S 2200 E Salt Lake City UT 84109-1135

ARRINGTON, KAREN KEMP, marketing executive; b. Salisbury, Md., Feb. 11, 1953; d. Robert George and Laverne (Briggs) Kemp; m. Daniel Richard Arrington III, Dec. 19, 1981; children: Daniel Richard IV, James William. BS, Iowa State U., 1975; MEd, Salisbury State U., 1979. Dir. horticultural project Chesapeake Rehab. Ctr., Easton, Md., 1975-76; mgr. greenhouses Bountiful Ridge Nurseries, Inc., Princess Anne, Md., 1976-77; instr. horticulture Dorchester Bd. Edn., Cambridge, Md., 1978-80, Fredrick (Md.) Bd. Edn., 1980-87; instr. agronomy Frederick Community Coll., 1985; treas. Kemp's Ltd., Inc., Martinsburg, W.Va., 1985-87; pres. Kemp's Ltd., Inc., Mt. Airy, Md., 1987-94; mgr. U.S. retail sales Kord Products, Ltd., Brampton, Ont., Can., 1995—; keynote speaker Vocat. Counseling Orgn., Md., 1980-88; cons. retail and comml. mktg. groups, 1977-91; dir. Russian-Georgian Rose Project, Tblissi, 1993. Editor newsletter The Spreader, 1990; featured narrator documentary Our Land, Our Future, 1980 (Gold award 1980); exhibitor Assn. Nurserymen, Balt. and King of Prussia, Pa., 1986-91. Coach 4-H, FFA, NJHA, and other youth orgns., Md., 1977-91; state chair Soil Conservation Poster Competition, Md., 1990-91; judge horticulture county fairs, state and nat. 4-H and FFA activities, 1977-91. Named Conservation Tchr. of Yr., State Soil and Water Conservation Svc., Annapolis, Md., 1984, Outstanding Young Co-Operator, Md. and Va. Coop., Lancaster, Pa., 1988. Mem. DAR, Md. Greenhouse Growers Assn., New Market Grange, Md. Hist. Soc., Hackers Creek Hist. Soc., Somerset Pa. Hist. Soc. Home and Office: Kemp's Ltd Inc 44 E 3d St Frederick MD 21701

ARRON, JUDITH HAGERTY, concert hall executive; b. Seattle, Dec. 8, 1942; d. Richard Graydon and Bernice Sarah (Lund) Hagerty; m. Ronald David Arron, Aug. 31, 1968; children: Joseph Richard, Edward Daniel. MusB, U. Puget Sound, 1964. Mem. spl. projects staff Am. Symphony Orch. League, Washington, 1964-69; research specialist youth concert study U.S. Office Edn., Washington, 1967; dir. regional and ednl. programs Cin. Symphony, 1969-76, mgr., 1976-86; exec. dir. Carnegie Hall, N.Y.C., 1986—; cons., panelist Ky. Arts Council, Frankfort, 1970—; panelist Ohio Arts Council, Columbus, 1970-80; career devel. council Wilmington (Ohio) Coll., 1980-85; mentoring council Coll. Mt. St. Joseph, Cin., 1985-87. chmn. Lay adv. com. U. Colo. Health Sci. Ctr. Bone Marrow Transplant program, 1992—; bd. dirs. Leukemia Soc. Southwest Ohio, Cin., 1985; vice chair Music for Life Benefit, N.Y.C., 1987, adv. com. 1990, 93. Recipient Arts Adminstr. of Yr. award Arts Mgmt. News Svc., 1992. Mem. Am. Symphony Orch. League, Internat. Soc. Performing Arts Adminstrs. Office: Carnegie Hall Corp 881 7th Ave New York NY 10019-3210*

ARSHT, LESLYE ALENE, public relations executive; b. St. Louis, June 28, 1945; d. Raymond I. and Martorie (Meyer) A. BA, U. Houston, 1968. With pres. news summary The White House, Washington, 1968-72; pub. affairs officer U.S. EPA, Washington, 1972-75; mgr. pub. rels. Union Carbide Corp., Washington, 1975-79; mgr. corp. communications Cabot Corp., Boston, 1979-83, dir. pub. affairs, 1983-86; deputy asst. to the pres., deputy press sec. The White House, 1987-89; assoc. vice chancellor news and pub. affairs Vanderbilt U., Nashville, 1989-91; counselor to the sec. of edn., dir. communications U.S. Dept. Edn., Washington, 1991-92; pres. Coalition for Goals 2000, Washington, 1992—; cons. Arsht & Co., Boston, 1986. Class mem. Leadership Nashville, 1990-91. Recipient 1990 Gold Key award Pub. Rels. News, 1990, TWIN award YWCA, Boston, 1986, Matrix award Women in Communications, Yankee chpt., 1982; named Communication of Yr. IABC, Yankee chpt., 1981. Republican. Jewish. Home: 2324 N Edgewood St Arlington VA 22201-4319 Office: Coalition for Goals 2000 Sch Edn Human Devel George Washington U Washington DC 20052

ARSIC, ANTOINETTE, publishing executive, editor; b. Tuscaloosa, Ala., Oct. 11, 1960; d. Velimir and Elinor (Brannen) A. BSBA, Old Dominion U., 1984. Long range planner, writer M. Rosenblatt & Son, Inc., Virginia Beach, Va., 1984-87; pub. rels. rep. Am. Club, Inc., Gordonsville, Va., 1988-90; pub., editor Double A Pub., Inc., Gordonsville, 1990—. Pub., editor (mag.) Virginia Country Life, 1990—. Theatre prodr. Four County Players, 1993-95; mem. bd. adminstrv. coun. First United Meth. Ch., Gordonsville, 1994. Named to Achievement 100 Club, Am. Edn. Inst., 1989. Office: Double A Pub Inc Virginia Country Life PO Box 427 Gordonsville VA 22942

ARTAUD-WILD, SABINE MARIE, research dietitian; b. Marseille, France, Jan. 25, 1928; came to U.S., 1953; d. Charles Marie and Jane Virginie (Millaud) Artaud; m. John B. Wild; children: Anne Wild Mozell, Phillip Charles, Paul James. BS in Pharmacy, U. Aix-Marseille, 1950, BS in Dietetic, 1958. Lic. dietitian; registered Am. Dietetic Assn. Pharmacist Ciotat, France, 1950-52; rsch. dietitian Inst. Gustave Roussy, Villejuif, France, 1952-53; adminstrv. dietitian Children's Hosp., Iowa City, 1954-55; cons. dietitian Weight Mgmt., Portland, Oreg., 1985-94, Health Mgmt. Resources, Portland, 1987-91; rsch. dietitian Lipid Atherosclerosis Oreg. Health Scis. U.-Lab., Portland, 1977-92. Editor: Simply Nutritious, 1985; contbr. articles to profl. jours. Pres. Reed Coll. Women Com., Portland, 1974-75; docent Portland Art Mus., 1971-77, Oreg. Hist. Soc., Portland, 1976-78; sec. Alliance Francaise, Portland, 1986; mem. City Club of Portland, 1983—; mem. program com., archivist, historian Native Am. Art Coun. Portland Art Mus., 1992—; mem. house of dels. Am. Dietetic Assn., 1992—. Mem. Oreg. Dietetic Assn. (pres. 1989-90, newsletter editor 1986-87, historian 1992, career guidance 1985). Home: 2309 SW 1st Ave # 545 Portland OR 97201 Office: Oreg Health Scis U 3181 SW Sam Jackson Park Rd Portland OR 97201-3011

ARTHUR, BEATRICE, actress; b. N.Y.C., May 13, 1926; d. Philip and Rebecca Frankel; m. Gene Saks, May 28, 1950 (div.); 2 sons. Student, Blackstone Coll., also Franklin Inst. Sci. and Arts; student acting with, Erwin Piscator, Dramatic Workshop, New Sch. Social Research. Theatrical appearances include: Lysistrata, 1947, Dog Beneath the Skin, 1947, Gas, 1947, Yerma, 1947, No Exit, 1948, The Taming of the Shrew, 1948, Six Characters in Search of An Author, 1948, The Owl and the Pussycat, 1948, Le Bourgeois Gentilhomme, 1949, Yes Is for a Very Young Man, 1949, Creditors, 1949, Heartbreak House, 1949, Three Penny Opera, 1954, 55, Shoestring Revue, 1955, Seventh Heaven, 1955, The Ziegfield Follies, 1956, What's The Rush?, summer 1956, Mistress of the Inn, 1957, Nature's Way, 1957, Ulysses in Nightown, 1958, Chic, 1959, Gay Divorcee, 1960, A Matter of Position, 1962, Mame, 1966 (Tony award best supporting mus. actress), Fiddler on the Roof, 1964; stock appearances with Fiddler on the Roof, Circle Theatre, Atlantic City, summer 1951, State Fair Music Hall, Dallas, 1953, Music Circus, Lambertville, N.J., 1953, resident commedienne, Tamiment (Pa.) Theatre, 1953; numerous TV and nightclub appearances, 1948—; motion picture appearances That Kind of Woman, 1959; Lovers and Other Strangers, 1970, Mame, 1974, History of the World Part I, 1981, Stranger Things, 1995; TV movie: My First Love, 1988; TV appearances include All in the Family, 1971, leading role in TV series Maude, 1972-78 (Emmy award for Best Actress in a Comedy Series 1977), The Golden Girls, 1985-92 (Emmy award for Best Actress in a Comedy Series 1988), The Beatrice Arthur Spl., TV series 30 Years of TV Comedy's Greatest Hits. Mem. Artists Equity Assn., Screen Actors Guild, AFTRA. *

ARTHUR, BRENDA KAY, financial consultant; b. Charleston, W.Va., May 28, 1951; d. Earl Washington and Martena (Miller) A. BA in Sociology, W.Va. U., 1972; MS in Edn., U. Dayton, 1975. Lic. ins. rep., Calif., Ariz. Field underwriter N.Y. Life Ins. Co., Long Beach, Calif., 1981-85; registered rep. N.Y. Life Securities Corp., Long Beach, Calif., 1984-85; fin. planner CIGNA Individual Fin. Services Corp., Irvine, Calif., 1985-87; registered rep. CIGNA Securities, Irvine, 1985-87; fin. cons., planner MKA Fin. Svcs., Inc., Newport Beach, Calif., 1987—; registered rep. Southmark Securities, 1987; registered broker, dealer Corp. Benefit Securities, Inc., Mission Viejo, Calif., 1988—. Mem. ARC, Santa Ana, Calif. 1982—; mem. Adam Walsh Resource Ctr., Orange County, planned giving com. Named Distinguished West Virginian, gov. W.Va., 1986. Mem. Nat. Assn. Life Underwriters, Orange County Charitable Giving Council, Planned Giving Roundtable Los Angeles, Orange County Planned Giving Com., Internat. Assn. Fin. Planning. Lodge: Zonta Internat. (v.p. 1985-86, bd. dirs. 1986—). Home: 1737 N Oak Knolls Dr Anaheim CA 92807-1303 Office: MKA Fin Svcs Inc 1101 Quail St Newport Beach CA 92660-2740

ARTHUR, JEWELL KATHLEEN, dental hygienist; b. Bloomington, Ind., Apr. 12, 1947; d. Gerald E. and Wilma Kathleen (McDonald) Beyers; m. Leland Stanley Arthur, Sept. 21, 1968; children: Sherri Kay, Brian Lee. AS in Dental Hygiene, Ind. U., 1968. Lic./registered dental hygienist. Infection control mgr., dental hygienist Office Dr. Thomas Watkins, DDS, Bloomington, Ind., 1990—; speaker and presenter in field. Vice-chmn. precinct Rep. Com., Batholomew, 1987—; chmn. Batholomew Consolidated Sch. Aids Com., Columbus, 1988—; vice chair City of Columbus Bd. Zoning Appeals, 1989-93, Bartholomew County Pers. Adminstrn. Com., 1993—; councilwoman Batholomew County Coun., Columbus, Ind., 1993—;. Mem. Am. Assn. Ret. Persons, Am. Dental Hygienists Assn. (liaison 1989—, Disting. Svc. award 1994), Ind. Dental Hygienists Assn. (pres. 1986-87, del. 1991—, Comty. Svc. award 1991, Outstanding Dental Hygienists of Yr. award 1991), Ind. Pub. Health Assn. (chair legislation 1986-89), Driftwood Valley Dental Hygienists Assn. (trustee 1989-91), Assn. Ind. Counties, DAR-Joseph Hart, Order Eastern Star. Republican. Methodist. Home: 1800 Clover Ct Columbus IN 47203

ARTL, KAREN ANN, business owner; b. Bainbridge, N.Y., July 4, 1950; d. Douglas Robert and Beverly Florence (Schofell) Moore; m. Robert Edward Gurney, June 15, 1969 (div. June 1981); children: Douglas Albert Gurney, Rebecca Susan Gurney; m. Jeffrey Joseph Artl, Nov. 8, 1986; 1 child, Grace Beverly. BA in Edn., SUNY Coll. at Oneonta, 1972; MA in Reading and Edn., Cleve. State U., 1981. Tchr. reading Independence (Ohio) Mid. Sch., 1979-81; sr. editor Am. Greetings Corp., Cleve., 1981-87; mem. adj. faculty Lorain Community Coll., Cleve., 1987-89; owner WordsWorth Studio, Inc., Rocky River, Ohio, 1989-93; owner, pres. WordsWorth Studio, Inc.; conf. speaker, trainer, cons. Social Expression Industry. Author: (biog. textbook) M. Washington, etc., 1991, (children's book) I'm Me and You're Not, 1991; concept developer Guy Gilchrist Prodns., 1992, inspirational plaque line for Christian market; editor CR Gibson/Gift Books, 1993, Gibson Greetings, 1993. Vol. Am. Cancer Soc., Cleve., 1991. Mem. AAUW, NAFE, Greeting Card Assn., Greeting Card Creative Network, Soc. Children's Book Writers. Lutheran. Home and Office: WordsWorth Studio Inc 7260 Capri Way # 9 Maineville OH 45039

ARVIEW, KATHLEEN YVONNE, geriatrics nurse; b. Tucson, Dec. 31, 1957; d. Merwin Lawrence and Betty Alice (Damrau) Saxe; m. Arthur Ray Arview, Mar. 18, 1986 (div. Feb. 1992); 1 child, Bettina Raye. Lic. vocat. nurse, Howard County Jr. Coll., 1989. Cert. BLS instr.; cert. nurse aide instr. Nurse Scenic Mountain Med. Ctr. Hosp., Big Spring, Tex., 1989-91, Mt. View Lodge, Big Spring, 1991-92; staff devel. coord. Manor Park, Midland, Tex., 1993; treatment nurse Stanton (Tex.) Care Ctr., 1993-94; coord. infection control, quality assurance com. Mt. View Lodge, Big Spring, 1991-92; instr. BSL. Comdr. DAV Aux., Big Spring, 1986-87; asst. leader Girl Scout U.S. Home: # 212 3814 Holiday Hill Rd Midland TX 79707

ARZOUMANIAN, LINDA LEE, educational consultant, curriculum specialist; b. Madison, Wis., Apr. 29, 1942; d. James Arthur Luck and Rosemary M. (Peacock) Engstrom; m. Youri Feridoon Arzoumanian, Oct. 7, 1967; children: Stephan, Aaron. BS, Stout State U., Menomonie, Wis., 1964; MEd, Ohio U., Athens, 1969; EdD, Nova U., 1994. Cert. tchr. vocat., secondary, community coll., Ariz. Residence hall asst. Ohio U., Athens, 1965-67; quality control supr. Advalloy, Inc., Palo Alto, Calif., 1967; tchr. adult edn. Eau Claire (Wis.) Pub. Sch., 1964-65; patient svc. dietitian Camden Clark Meml. Hosp., Parkersburg, W.Va., 1970; adminstr. pre-sch. Fishkill (N.Y.) Meth. Nursery Sch., 1976-84; substitute tchr. Tucson Unified Sch. Dist., 1987, cons., early childhood ednl. curriculum specialist, 1988-93; instr. Prescott Coll., 1991-92, Ctrl. Ariz. Coll., 1990—; tchr. pre-sch. Tanque Verde Luth. Presch., Tucson, 1988-89; dist. moderator Sch. Community Partnership Coun., Tucson, 1988-90; dir. child and family svcs., program mgmt. CODAC, Behavioral Health Svcs. of Pima County, Inc., Tucson, 1990—; mem. supts. adv. cabinet Tucson Unified Sch. Dist., 1988-89, mem. curriculum and instrn. coun., 1989-90, spl. edn. pre-sch. adv. com., 1989-91, info. tech. bond rev. com., 1989—, sex edn. curriculum adv. com., core curriculum com., 1988-90, 2000 com., 1988-89; nat. child devel. assoc. adv./field adv., nat. child devel. assoc. rep. Nat. Assn. for Edn. of Young Children; grantswriter Comstock Found.; validator early childhood programs for Nat. Acad. Early Childhood Programs. Mem. Dutchess County Child Devel. Com., Poughkeepsie, N.Y., 1979-81; advancement chmn. troop 1968 Boy Scouts Am., Tucson, 1986, com. person troop 194, 1986-89; mem. joint com. on site based decision making Tucson Unified Sch. Dist./Tucson Edn. Assn., 1989—; active Armenian Cultural Soc.; early childhood edn. adv. com. Ctrl. Ariz. Coll.; life mem. Ariz. PTA. Mem. AAUW, ASCD, NAFE, Assn. Childhood Edn. Internat., World Future Soc., Nat. Assn. Edn. Young Children, So. Ariz. Child Care Assn. Family Resource Coalition, Tucson Assn. Edn. Young Children. Home: 8230 E Ridgebrook Dr Tucson AZ 85715-2442 Office: 333 W Ft Lowell #219 Tucson AZ 85705

ASAAD, KOLLEEN JOYCE, special education educator; b. West Union, Iowa, July 13, 1941; d. Leonard Henry and Catherine Adelade (Bishop) Anfinson; children: Todd, Robin, Tara, Jason. BA in Elem. Edn., Upper Iowa U., 1961; MA in Spl. Edn. and Adminstrn., U. Cin., 1973. Elem. tchr. Fredericksburg (Iowa) Elem. Sch., 1961-62, Tyler Sch., Cedar Rapids, Iowa, 1962-64, Oasis Sch., 29 Palms, Calif., 1964-69, Longfellow Sch., Waterloo, Iowa, 1969-70; spl. edn. tchr. Fairview Sch., Cin., 1970-77; learning disabilities tchr. Lincoln Sch., Portsmouth, Ohio, 1977-78; dir. spl. edn. Vermilion Assn. for Spl. Edn., Danville, Ill., 1978-94; dir. edn. Swann Spl. Care Ctr., Champaign, Ill., 1994-95; mem. Govtl. Rels. Com., Ill. Coun. for Exceptional Children, Jacksonville, Ill., 1992. Bd. mem. Crosspoints, Danville, Catlin Music Boosters, pres.; active Catlin Athletic Boosters. Named Best Adminstr., Regional Supt. of Schs., 1991. Mem. Coun. for Exceptional Children, Coun. for Adminstrs. of Spl. Edn., Ill. Adminstrs. of Spl. Edn., Assn. for Persons with Severe Handicaps, Exec. Club. Lutheran. Home: 122 Mapleleaf Dr Catlin IL 61817-9646 Office: Swann Spl Care Ctr 109 Kenwood Rd Champaign IL 61821

ASADORIAN, DIANA C., electrical engineer; b. Leninakan, Armenia, June 16, 1950; came to U.S., 1975; d. Eduard and Vartuhi (Seraidarian) Martirosyan; m. William R. Asadorian, July 22, 1978; 1 child, Ronald E. M in Electromech. Engring. Elec. Motors, Polytech. Inst., Odessa, USSR, 1972. Elect. engr. Odessa Cable Plant, 1972-75; draftsman Leviton Co., Bklyn., 1976-77; from engring. asst. to design engr. engring. and devel. CBS, N.Y.C., 1977-86, assoc. dir. engring. lab., 1986-89, dir. engring. lab. and drafting. engring. and devel., 1989-90, dir. tech. tng. and documentation engring., 1990—. Mem. Soc. Motion Picture and TV Engring., Am. Soc. Tng. Dir. Republican. Armenian Orthodox. Office: CBS 524 W 57th St New York NY 10019-2902

ASAKAWA, TAKAKO, dancer, dance teacher; b. Toyko, Feb. 23, 1939; came to U.S., 1962; d. Kamenosuke and Chiaki Asakawa. Student, Tokyo schs., 1962-91. Pron. dancer Martha Graham Dance Co., N.Y.C., 1962-76, 81—; dancer Alvin Ailey, 1968-69, Pearl Lang, 1967, Lar Lubovitch, 1974-80; guest tchr. at Martha Graham Sch., Juilliard Sch.; co.-founder Asakawalker Dance Co. Performer Bell Telephone Hours, L.A., 1970; performed as Eliza, The King and I. Named Legendary Woman of Am., St. Vincent's Hosp., 1975; recipient Tokyo Shinbun Dace award 1950-62. Mem. Am. Guild Musical Artists. Home and Office: 257 Central Park W New York NY 10024-4103*

ASARE, KAREN MICHELLE GILLIAM, reading and English educator; b. Bklyn., Jan. 21; d. James Henry and Frances (Walker) Gilliam; m. William Kofi, May 4, 1977; 1 child, Anton William Kwaku Asare Jr. BA, Hunter Coll., 1976, MS in Edn., 1979. Cert. tchr., N.Y. state. Tchr. Women's Prison Assn., N.Y., 1977-78, St. Augustine's Sch. of the Arts, Bronx, N.Y., 1978—, Ednl. Opportunity Ctr. of SUNY, 1989—. Mem. NAACP, Nat. Coun. Tchrs. English, Reading Reform Found., Nat. Cath. Edn. Assn., Profl. Staff Congress, Sigma Gamma Rho-Delta Nu Sigma. Office: Saint Augustine's Sch Arts 1176 Franklin Ave Bronx NY 10456

ASCHOFF, LORRAINE MARIE, computer information scientist; b. N.Y.C., Feb. 14, 1950; d. Edward William and Marie Louise (Marshall) A.; m. John Morgan Roquemore III, Feb. 23, 1973 (div. June 1976). BA in Art History, U. Fla., 1971; MBA in Fin., NYU, 1984, advanced profl. cert. in computer applications and info. systems, 1988. Sales rep. VIP Fabrics, N.Y.C., 1978-81; asst. to v.p. mktg. RAM Data, N.Y.C., 1981-82; sales agt. Equitable Life Assurance Soc., N.Y.C., 1982; programmer/analyst Drexel Burnham Lambert, N.Y.C., 1984-86, sr. programmer/analyst, 1986-88, project leader, 1988-89, project mgr., asst. v.p., 1989-90; project mgr. retail banking svcs. application architecture Chem. Banking Corp. (formerly Mfrs. Hanover Trust), N.Y.C., 1990-91, officer, 1991—. Clin. assoc. Suicide and Crisis Prevention Ctr., Gainesville, Fla., 1972; mem. pres.'s coun. U. Fla., 1992—; vol. fundraiser Walk Am. program March of Dimes. Mem. Mensa, L.I. Alumni Assn., Phi Beta Kappa (sec. 1985-87, pres. 1987-93), Alpha Lambda Delta. Democrat. Home: Apt A-8 64-85 Saunders St Rego Park NY 11374 Office: Chem Banking Corp 4 New York Plaza New York NY 10004

ASCONE, TERESA PALMER, artist, educator; b. Cortland, N.Y., Nov. 1, 1945; d. Lawrence Henry and Bernice Rosella (Holcomb) Palmer; m. Michael Wayne Ascone, Oct. 15, 1965 (div. Jan. 1995); 1 child, Michael Palmer. Student, Alaska Meth. U., Alaska Pacific U., U. Alaska. Painter/tchr. Alaska Pacific U., Anchorage, 1989-91, U. Alaska, 1992; pvt. tchr. watercolor Anchorage, 1992—; owner Alaskan Portfolio, 1981—; tchr. U. Alaska, Anchorage, 1992—. Juried shows include Alaska State Fair, 1979-80, Fur Rendezvous Juried Show, 1979, 80, All Alaska Juried Show, 1981, 84, 85, 90, Alaska Watercolor Soc. juried show, 1981, 83, 85, 86, 87, 88, 89, 90, 91, April in Paris juried exhibit at Capt. Cook Hotel, 1982, 83, 84, 87, Featured Artist, 1986, Watercolor Fairbanks, 1989, Women Artist of West 1st Ann. Internat. Show, 1990; one women shows include Anchorage Mcpl. Librs., 1980, 82, NBA Heritage Libr., 1986, Alaska Pacific U., 1989, Chitose City Hall, Chitose, Hokkaido, Japan, 1990; represented in permanent collection Alaska Pacific U.; cover artist Arctic Horizons Mag., 1986, Alaska Horizons Mag., 1986; subject of TV spl., 1988; developer original design, manufacture & mktg. The Ultimate Palette, 1993; author: We're All Artists: Watercolor for Everyone, 1994; editor, publisher Hot Press Mag., 1994. Mcpl. commr. Anchorage Sister Cities Commn., 1991-93. Recipient Vol. of Yr. Caverly Sr. Ctr., 1986, various art show awards to date; works chosen as ofcl. gifts to cities of Inchon, Korea and Magadan, Russia from city of Anchorage. Mem. Alaska Watercolor Soc. (v.p. 1983), Alaska Artists Guild, N.W. Watercolor Soc.

ASH, DOROTHY MATTHEWS, civic worker; b. Dresden, Germany, Nov. 10, 1918; came to U.S., 1924; d. Kurt Horst and Ana (Sekes) Matthesius; m. Harry A. Ash, Apr. 13, 1941 (dec. June 1981); children: Fredrick Curtis, Dorothea Ash Linklater. Dancer, 1933-40; treas. Inheritance Abstractors Inc., Chgo., 1949-70; reporter Miami (Fla.) Sun Post, 1983; reporter, columnist Social Mag., Miami, 1984—; chmn. Miss Universe Pageant, 1983-85; cruise chmn. Miami U., 1984, mem. Pres.'s Club, 1983. Pres. Big Bros. and Big Sisters, 1982-83; founding mem. World Sch. of Arts, 1985—; founding and bd. mem. Cancer Link Rsch., 1990; mem. Bd. Animal Welfare; active Project: Newborn, Am. Cancer Soc., March of Dimes, chmn. quest for the best, 1988-92, winner gourmet gala, 1988, Children's Resource, Erase Diabetes, founding and bd. mem. 1990, Cerebral Palsy Found., Theatre Arts League, Linda Ray Infant Ctr., Miami City Ballet, Am. ballet; bd. dirs. Greater Miami Opera, 1975—; pub. rels. vol. Miami Heart Inst., 1988—; com. mem. Miami Beach (Fla.) Beautification Program, 1984; mem. bd. Miami Mayor's Ad Hoc Com., 1984; mem. com. Challenger Seven Meml., 1988; active Cousteau Coun.; numerous others. Named Woman of Yr., Big Bros. and Big Sisters, Miami, 1981, Best Dressed, Am. Cancer Soc., 1981, Outstanding Humanitarian and Civic Leader, Mayor City of Miami, 1985, Woman of the Yr., Project: New Born, 1985, Miss Charity, Biscayne Bay Hosp., 1986, Queen of Hearts, Miami Children's Hosp., 1988; recipient Shining Star award Bon Secours Hosp., 1993, Patron Recognition award Mia Heart Rsch. Inst., 1993. Mem. Miami Internat. Press Club. Home: 10245 Collins Ave Bal Harbour FL 33154 also (summer): 330 W Diversey Pky Chicago IL 60657

ASH, ERIN MCNERNEY, educator, case worker; b. Bradford, Pa., Jan. 21, 1953; d. Edward Augustine and Alice Frances (Hane) McNerney; m. Emil John Ash, June 11, 1976; children: Emilia Anne, Anna Elizabeth, Aaron Edward. BA, St. Bonaventure U., 1974, MS in edn., 1991. Owner, operator Family Tree Toys, Olean, N.Y., 1983-87; educator, program developer Parent Edn. Program, Inc., Olean, N.Y., 1988-91; caseworker dept. social svcs. Cattaragus County, Olean, N.Y., 1989—; cons. C-H Healthcare Ltd., Olean, 1987; part-time faculty Jamestown C.C., Olean, 1990; evaluator Parent Edn. Program, Inc., 1991; bd. dirs. Olean Child Devel. Ctr. Group facilitator Effective Parenting Info. for Children, Olean, 1988-90. Mem. APA (affiliate), Am. Counseling Assn. (prof. mem.), Am. Mental Health Counselors Assn., N.Y. Assn. Edn. Young Children (exec. com. 1988-89), Assn. for Measurement and Evaluation in Counseling and Devel., Cattaragus Allegany Assn. for Edn. of Young Children (v.p. 1989-90), Ctr. Family Unity (adv. bd.). Republican. Roman Catholic. Home: 121 S Barry St Olean NY 14760-3626 Office: Cattaragus County Dept Social Svcs 1701 Lincoln Ave Olean NY 14760-1121

ASH, MARY KAY WAGNER, cosmetics company executive; b. Hot Wells, Tex., May 12; d. Edward Alexander and Lula Vember (Hastings) Wagner; m. Melville Jerome Ash, Jan. 6, 1966 (dec.); children: Marylyn Theard (dec.), Ben Rogers, Richard Rogers. Student, U. Houston, 1942-43. Mgr. Stanley Home Products, Houston, 1939-52; nat. tng. dir. World Gift Co., Dallas, 1952-63; founder, chmn. emeritus Mary Kay Cosmetics, Dallas, 1963—; speaker to various orgns. Bd. dirs. Horatio Alger Assn.; chmn. bldg. fund. Prestonwood Bapt. Ch., Dallas; hon. chmn. Tex. Breast Screening Project, Am. Cancer Soc. Office: Mary Kay Cosmetics Inc 8787 N Stemmons Fwy Dallas TX 75247-3713

ASH, SHARON KAYE, real estate company executive; b. Altus, Ark., July 21, 1943; d. William Clyde and Odus Marie (Drew) Cline; m. J.W. Ash, June 1, 1966 (div. Oct. 1978); 1 child, Brian Edward. B.S., S.W. Mo. State U., 1985; grad. Realtor Inst.; cert. residential specialist. Lic. real estate broker, Mo. Personal lines asst. Squibb Ins., Springfield, Mo., 1967-69; bookkeeper Hood-Rich, Architects and Engrs., Springfield, 1969-89; owner Ash Computer Service, Springfield, 1985—; owner, broker Ash Real Estate, Springfield, 1985—; dir. Multilist Svc. Mem. Womens Coun. Realtors (past pres. Springfield chpt., Member of Yr. 1993), Mo. Assn. Realtors, Nat. Assn. Realtors, Springfield Area C. of C., Million Dollar Sales Club (life mem.), Multi Million Dollar Club. Democrat. Episcopalian. Avocations: golf, boating, reading, collecting clowns, jogging. Home: PO Box 10585 Springfield MO 65808-0585 Office: Ash Real Estate 1340 W Battlefield St Ste 114 Springfield MO 65807-4102

ASH, TERRY ANN, computer information systems specialist; b. Indpls., May 9, 1957; d. Jack Livingston and Betty L. (Pavey) Morris; 1 child, Phebe May. Student in secretarial studies, Sullivan Coll., 1975-76; student in acctg., Ind. U., 1980, Ind. Voc-Tech Coll., 1981-82; student, Ctrl. Ariz. Coll., 1985-86. Project leader, programmer, cost acct. Talley Def. Systems, Mesa, Ariz., 1982-88; computer cons. AGS Genasys (Nynex) Corp., Mountainside, N.J., 1989; programmer analyst Ferranti Internat. Def. Systems, Lancaster, Pa., 1989-90; user support specialist, programmer analyst Polaris, Inc., Falls Church, Va., 1990; software cons. Wesson, Taylor, Wells & Assocs., Inc., Charlotte, N.C., 1990-92; analyst programmer IV divsn. pub. assistance sys. ops. Dept. Health and Social Svcs., State of Alaska, Anchorage, 1993—. Nominated Internat. Woman of Yr., 1991, 92, 93, 94; selected World Intellectual, 1993. Mem. NAFE. Baptist. Office: Alaska Dept Health & Social Svcs Divsn Pub Assistance-Systems Ops PO Box 240249 Anchorage AK 99524

ASHBROOK, MARILYN WISSINGER, artist; b. Worthington, Ohio, Nov. 25, 1930; d. Herbert John and Susanna Catherine (Wright) Wissinger; m. John Roland Ashbrook, Sept. 19, 1953; children: Lucy Ashbrook Sloan, Donald Duncan, Carol Ashbrook Bapty. BFA, Ohio Wesleyan U., 1952; MLS, Drexel U., 1968; postgrad., Pa. Acad. Fine Arts, 1976-79; studied with Tom Gaughan, Fleisher Art Meml.; studied with Jim Lueders, Pa. Acad. Fine Arts.; studied with Fran Lachman, Community Arts Ctr., Wallingford, Pa.; student, York Acad. Arts, York, Pa., Toledo Mus. of Art, Ohio, Carnegie Inst., Pitts. Staff artist, display dept. Macy's Dept. Store, Toledo, 1952-53; tchr. silk screen York (Pa.) Acad. Arts, 1954-55; rsch. libr. Elwyn (Pa.) Inst., 1968-73, JEVS, Phila., 1973-81; freelance painter Media, Pa., 1981—; tchr. Fleisher Art Meml., Phila., 1991; lectr. in field. One woman shows include Fleisher Art Meml., 1983, Cafe Gallery, Burlington, N.J., 1986, Baker St. Gallery, Media, Pa., 1987, Widener U. Art Mus., Chester, Pa., 1989, Ohio Wesleyan U., Delaware, Ohio, 1989, Axis Fine Art, Wilmington, Delware, 1992, Port of History Mus., 1993; exibited in group shows at Cheltenham Art Ctr., 1980, 83, 85, Widener U., Pa., 1985, Delaware Women's Conf., 1985, 86, Plum Gallery, Paoli, Pa. 1985, 86, 87, 88, 89, 90, 92, 93, 94, Baker Street Gallery, 1985, 86, Phila. Mus. Sales and Rentals, 1985, 86, 87, 88, 89, 91, 92, 93, Delaware Art Mus, 1991, 93, Pa. State U., 1991, 92, U. Delaware, 1991, Gloucester County Coll., 1992, Am. Artist Gallery, Devon, Pa., 1994, ArtSouth, Pa., 1989, 93, 94, Axis Fine Art, Delaware, 1994, Roger LaPelle Gallery, Pa., 1987, 88, 89, 90, 92, 93, 94, Three Rivers Art Festival, Pa, 1994 and many others. Bd. dirs. Artists Equity Assn., Phila., 1981-89; mem. Rose Valley Sch. Bd., Moylan, Pa., 1972-73; ch. br. officer Unitarian Universalist Ch., Media, 1973-75. Mem. Beta Phi Mu. Democrat. Unitarian. Home: 135 Glen Riddle Rd Media PA 19063

ASHBY, NORMA RAE BEATTY, journalist, beauty consultant, Mont., Dec. 27, 1935; d. Raymond Wesley Beatty and Ella Mae (Lamb) Beatty Watson Mehmke; m. Shirley Carter Ashby, Sept. 5, 1964; children—Ann, Tony. BA, U. Mont., Missoula, 1957. Reporter, Helena Ind. Record, 1953-56; picture dept. Life mag., N.Y.C., 1957-58; picture researcher MD Med. Newsmag., N.Y.C., 1959-61; producer, hostess TV Show Today in Mont., Sta. KRTV, Great Falls, 1962-85; editor Noon News, Sta. KRTV, 1985-88, beauty cons. Mary Kay Cosmetics, Inc., 1988—; freelance journalist, 1988—. Author: What Is A Montanan?, 1971, Montana Woman, 1977, Montanans, 1982, scriptwriter: Last Chance Gulch, 1964, Gentle Giants, 1969, Our Latch-string is Out, 1979, Paris Gibson, 1983, Martha, Pioneer Woman, 1984, Great Falls Centennial, 1984, First Ladies of Montana, 1986, Anuka, Montana's Island Home, 1986, North American Indian Days, 1987, Missiles of October, 1987, (co-author) Symbols of Montana, 1989. Mem. First Presbyn. Ch.; co-chmn. Cascade County Bicentennial Com., Great Falls, 1974-76; founder, chmn. C.M. Russell Auction, Great Falls, 1979; bd. dirs. Mont. Physicians Service, Helena, 1980-87; co-chmn. Great Falls Centennial Com., 1982-84; Festivals chmn. Cascade Coounty 89ers, 1987-89; coord. Mont. Statewide BellRinging Project, 1989; chair Mont. Jefferson awards; pres. Cascade County Mental Health Assn., 1980-82; bd. dirs. Cascade County Hist. Soc., 1987-91, Mental Health Assn. Mont., also editor; coord. Mont. Statehood Centennial Bell Award, 1990—. Co-host Children's Miracle Network Telethon, 1989—. Recipient TV Program of Yr. award Greater Mont. Found. 1982-88, Communication and Leadership award Mont. Toastmasters Internat., 1983, Preservation award Cascade County Hist. Soc., 1994; named Tribune Most Influential Woman in Great Falls, 1984, hon. mem. Blackfeet Tribe Blackfeet Reservation, Browning, Mont., 1981, Mont. TV Broadcaster Yr., 1985. Mem. Women in Communications (founder, pres. Great Falls, Mont. chpt. 1988-90), Great Falls Advt. Fedn. (dir., Silver medal 1980, Scriver Bronze medal 1993), AWRT (founder, pres. Mt. Big Sky chpt. 1967, recipient cert. of commendation 1982). Club: PEO, Broadcast Pioneers.

ASHBY, ROSEMARY GILLESPY, college president; b. Farnham, Surrey, Eng., May 16, 1940; came to U.S. 1967; d. Robert Dymock and Margaret Lois (Gillespy) Watson; m. John Hallam Ashby, June 17, 1967. B.A., U. Capetown, S. Africa, 1960; B.A., Cambridge U., 1963, M.A., 1967, M.Litt., 1972. Head resident Radcliffe Coll., Cambridge, Mass., 1968-70, asst. dir. career planning, 1969-70; dir. residence, instr. French Pine Manor Coll., Chestnut Hill, Mass., 1970-71, dean students, 1971-75, acting pres., 1975-76, pres., 1976—; pvt. tutor Sao Paulo, Brazil, 1963-65; teaching asst. U. Capetown, 1959-60; panelist N.E. Assn. Schs. and Colls., Boston, 1983, Nat. Assn. Ind. Schs., Boston, 1985. Author chpt. in book. Adv. bd. Keimei Fund for Internat. Edn., N.Y.C., 1978—. Nat. Endowment of Humanities fellow, 1984. Mem. Mass. Commn. on Post-secondary Edn., Assn. Am. Colls. (exec. com. 1977-78), Assn. Ind. Colls. and Univs. in Mass. (exec. com. 1977-80, 89-92), Women's Coll. Coalition (exec. com. 1985-88), Am. Inst. Fgn. Study (bd. acad. advisors 1986—), New England Bd. Higher Edn. (Mass. delegate 1993—), Rassias Found. (bd. overseers 1993—). Home: 41 Crafts Rd Chestnut Hill MA 02167-1823 Office: Pine Manor Coll Office of the President 400 Heath St Chestnut Hill MA 02167-2332

ASHBY, TERI HELENA, lawyer; b. Albuquerque, Sept. 29, 1948; d. Delbert and Geraldine (Evans) Johnson; m. Marvin Rodney Ashby, July 1971 (div. 1982); 1 child, Erin. BA, U. N.Mex., 1970; JD, U. San Francisco, 1984. Bar: Calif. 1984. Tchr. So. San Francisco Unified Sch. Dist., 1970-83; rsch. atty. Superior Ct. of Santa Clara, San Jose, Calif., 1984-85; assoc. Kaplan, Russin, Vecchi & Eytan, San Francisco, 1985-88, Holtzman, Wise & Shepard, Palo Alto, Calif., 1988-89; counsel, sr. counsel Bank of Am., San Francisco, 1989—. Office: Bank of Am Legal Dept 555 California St San Francisco CA 94104

ASHCRAFT, VIRGINIA CARSON, financial analyst; b. Tegucigalpa, Honduras, Mar. 12, 1949; came to U.S., 1951; d. Howard William and Nelda Ellen Ashcraft; m. John Willard Everitt, Sept. 24, 1977; children: John Willard Davis, Eric Jeffers. B cum laude, Smith Coll., Northampton, Mass., 1971; MBA with distinction, Stern Sch. Bus., N.Y.C., 1979. Chartered fin. analyst. V.p. Morgan Guaranty Trust Co., N.Y.C., 1971-82; cons. David Jeffery Assocs., Ft. Lee, N.J., 1982-90; pres. Profl. Learning Resources, Brookhaven, N.Y., 1990—. Co-author: Tools and Techniques for Private Business, 1987. Treas. Christ Episcopal Ch., Bellport, N.Y., 1988-89; budget adv. com. South County Sch. Dist., Bellport, 1992. Mem. Am. Inst. CFA, Beta Gamma Sigma. Office: Profl Learning Resources 56 Bay Rd Brookhaven NY 11719-9741

ASHDOWN, MARIE MATRANGA (MRS. CECIL SPANTON ASHDOWN, JR.), writer, lecturer; b. Mobile, Ala.; d. Dominic and Ave (Mallon) Matranga; m. Cecil Spanton Ashdown Jr., Feb. 8, 1958; children: Cecil Spanton III, Charles Coster; children by previous marriage: John Stephen Gartman, Vivian Marie Gartman. Student, Maryville Coll. Sacred Heart; student, Springhill Coll. Feature artist, women's program dir. daily program Sta. WALA, WALA-TV, Mobile, 1953-58; v.p., dir. Met. Opera Guild, N.Y.C., 1970-78, opera instr. in-svc. program, 1970-80; opera instr. in-svc. program Marymont Coll., N.Y.C., 1979-85; exec. dir. Musicians Emergency Fund, Inc., N.Y.C., 1985—; cons. No. Ill. U. Coll. of Visual and Performing Arts, 1985—; lectr. in field. Author: Opera Collectables, 1979, contbr. articles to profl. jours. Recipient Extraordinary Service award March of Dimes, 1958, Medal of Appreciation award Harvard Bus. Sch. Club N.Y.C., 1974, Cert. Appreciation, Kiwanis Internat., 1975, Arts Excellence award N.J. State Opera, 1986. Mem. AAUW, Successful Meetings Directory, Nat. Inst. Social Scis., Com. for U.S.-China Rels. Home: 25 Sutton Pl S Apt 16K New York NY 10022-2456 Office: Musicians Emergency Fund Inc 820 2nd Ave Ste 203 New York NY 10017-4504

ASHE, KATHY RAE, educator; b. Bismarck, N.D., Oct. 24, 1950; d. Raymond Charles and Virginia Ann (Mason) Lynch; m. Barth Eugene Olson, Aug. 11, 1973; 1 child, William Raymond; m. Fredrick A. Ashe, Aug. 5, 1994. BS, U. N.D., 1972; MS in Spl. Edn., U. N.D., 1987. Cert. elem. tchr. with spl. edn. credential, N.D. Instr., Grafton State Sch., N.D., 1972-74; tchr. spl. edn. Grand Forks Sch. Dist., N.D., 1974—; bd. dirs. Agassiz Enterprises; mem. RAD com. Valley Jr. High; mem. transition governing bd., Region IV. Bd. dirs. Assn. Retarded Citizens, Devel. Homes, Inc., N.D. Sch. Blind Found.; spl. needs recreation program Grand Forks Park Bd., 1973-76; mem. Spl. Olympics Area Mgmt. Team, 1984—. Named N.D. Tchr. of Yr., Coun. of Chief State Sch. Officers, 1981. Mem. AAUW, Delta Kappa Gamma (sec. 1984-86, pres. 1990-94), Alpha Phi (alumni pres. 1984-86, 90-91), Pi Lambda Theta., Phi Delta Kappa. Republican. Roman Catholic. Avocations: sporting events, civic work, cross stitch, bowling. Home: 3208 Walnut St Grand Forks ND 58201-7665

ASHE, MAUDE LLEWELLYN, home economics educator; b. Bakersfield, Calif., Feb. 9, 1908; d. Richard Samuel and Marguerite J. (Loudon) A. AB, U. Calif., 1928; MS, Oreg. State U., Corvallis, 1944; postgrad., San Jose (Calif.) State Coll., 1936-38, Stanford U., 1948. Cert. tchr., Calif. Instr. in home econs. Oreg. State U., 1943; assoc. prof. home econs. San Jose State U., 1944-73, emeritus prof. home econs., 1973—. Author: Finding West Country Ancestors, 1939. Mem. Santa Clara County Fair Assn., San Jose, 1968; v.p. Kern Genealogy Soc., Bakersfield, Calif., 1986. Mem. AAUW (sec., chmn. San Jose chpt. 1978), Calif. Ret. Tchr.'s Assn., Calif. Ret. State Employees, Emeritus Faculty Assn., Nat. Trust for Hist. Preservation, Family Assn. of Austin, Geer Family Assn., Calif. Home Econs. Assn. (chmn. com. San Francisco chpt. 1965, state advisor to student clubs No. Calif. area 1966), Imperial Valley Gem and Mineral Soc. (charter), Phi Upsilon Omicron. Democrat. Home: 2601 Century Dr Bakersfield CA 93306-1511

ASHEN, YVON LONGRIE, painter; b. Milw., Apr. 11, 1947; d. Milton P. and Helen (Pfankuch) Longrie; m. Johann Aschenbrenner, Jr., June 6, 1969. BFA, U. Wis., 1990. Curator exhibitions Appleton (Wis.) Art Ctr., 1993-94; cons. Peltz Gallery, Milw., 1992-93. Solo exhibitions include Allen Priebe Gallery, Oshkosh, 1990, U. Wis., Oshkosh, 1990; exhibited in group shows at U. Wis., Madison, 1988, Wustum Mus. Fine Art, Racine, Wis., 1991, Neville Mus., Green Bay, Wis., 1991, 92, 93, 95, Secura, Appleton,

1991, 92, 93, Peltz Gallery, Milw., 1991, 92, 93, 94, Uhlig Gallery, Milw., 1991, 92, 93, 94, River Edge Galleries, Mishicot, Mis., 1992, 93, 94, 95, Capitol Civic Ctr., Manitowoc, Wis., 1992, Appleton Art Ctr., 1992, 94, Art Works Galley, Green Bay, 1992, 93, 94, 95, Lazzaro Signature Gallery, Stoughton, Wis., 1992, 93, 94, Uhlein-Peters Gallery, Milw., 1993, Anderson Art Ctr., Kenosha, Wis., 1994, U. Alaska, 1994, 8th St. Gallery, Albuquerque, N. Mex., 1994, EMU Gallery, Eugene, Oreg., 1994, Western Kentucky U., Bowling Green, 1994, Capitol Arts Ctr., Bowling Green, 1994, U. Va., Charlottesville, 1994, Hot Weather Gallery, Charlottesville, 1994, U. Oregon, Eugene, 1994, St. Mary-of-the-Woods (Ind.) Coll., 1995, San Francisco Art Inst., 1995, David Adler Cultural Ctr., Libertyville, Ill., 1995. Recipient Nat. Juror's awards, Wis. Painters and Sculptors award 1992; U. Wis. grantee, 1989-90. Mem. Wis. Painters and Sculptors. Home and Studio: 6705 State Road 175 Oshkosh WI 54901-9142

ASHER, BETTY TURNER, academic administrator; b. Booneville, Ky., Oct. 19, 1944. BA, Ea. Ky. U.; MA, Western Ky. U.; EdD, U. Cin. Sr. assoc. vice provost U. Cin., 1978-80; assoc. vice chancellor acad. affairs Minn. State U. System, 1981-82; v.p. student affairs Ariz. State U., Tempe, 1982-89; pres. U. S.D., Vermillion, 1989—. Office: U of SD Office of the President 414 E Clark St Vermillion SD 57069-2390

ASHER, DONNA THOMPSON, psychiatric-mental health nurse; b. Kansas City, Mo., Aug. 29, 1933; d. William Volker and Frances Ellen (Todd) Thompson; 1 child, Janet Asher McKinney. LPN, Kansas City Area Vo-Tech. Sch., Kans., 1989; student, Ft. Scott C.C., Paola, Kans., 1992—, Sanford-Brown Coll., 1994. Lab. technician, chemistry lab. Greater Balt. Med. Ctr., rsch. asst., endocrinology and biochemistry lab. technician; practical nurse adult psychiat. unit U. Kans., Kansas City, 1989-91, Kans. State Sch. for the Blind, Kansas City, 1991—; mem. alumni adv. bd. Kansas City Area Vo-Tech. Sch., 1990—. Home: 5315 W 95th Ter Shawnee Mission KS 66207-3209

ASHFORD, EVELYN, track and field athlete; m. Ray Washington; 1 child, Rana. Student, UCLA. Track and field athlete, 1976—. Competed in 1976 Olympics; winner 2 Gold medals, 1984 Olympics (Women's 100 Meters, Women's 4x100-Meter); winner Gold medal, 1988 Olympics (Women's 4x100-Meter); recipient Flo Hyman award Women's Sport Found., 1989; winner Gold medal, 1992 Olympics, Barcelona, Spain (4x100-Meter). Address: 818 Plantation Ln Walnut CA 91789*

ASHFORD, ROSALIND MARY, advertising and marketing executive; b. Worcester, Eng., Oct. 8, 1954; came to U.S, 1978; d. Raymond Henry Joseph and Eileen Mary (Churchill) A. Cert. edn. with distinction, Madeley Coll., Staffordshire, Eng., 1976; BEd with honors, U. Keele, Eng., 1977. Lic. pilot. Promotional dir. Woodstock (N.Y.) Playhouse, 1979-82; dir. mktg. Bardavon 1869 Opera House, Poughkeepsie, N.Y., 1982-84, Pepsico Summerfare and Performing Arts Ctr. SUNY, Purchase, 1984-85, Hipp Waters, Inc., Greenwich, Conn., 1985-87; pres. Ashford Co., Poughkeepsie, N.Y., 1987—, The British Accent, Poughkeepsie, 1991—; cons. Bronx (N.Y.) Coun. on Arts, 1986—, Schoharie County Arts Coun., Cobleskill, N.Y., 1987—, East End Arts Coun., Riverhead, N.Y., 1987—. Contbr. articles to newspapers. Tutor Literacy Vols. Am., White Plains, 1987—. Mem. Actors Equity Assn., AAUW. Anglican. Office: 18 W Lake St Poughkeepsie NY 12601-1302

ASHHURST, ANNA WAYNE, educator; b. Phila., Jan. 5, 1933; d. Astley Paston Cooper and Anne Pauline (Campbell) Ashhurst; m. Ronald G. Gerber, July 22, 1978. AB, Vassar Coll., 1954; MA, Middlebury Coll., 1956; PhD, U. Pitts., 1967. English tchr. Internat. Inst. Spain, Madrid, 1954-56; asst. prof. Juniata Coll., Huntingdon, Pa., 1961-63; asst. prof. Spanish dept. Franklin and Marshall Coll., Lancaster, Pa., 1968-74, acting chmn. Spanish dept., 1972, convenor, fgn. lang. council, 1972-74; assoc. prof. dept. modern fgn. langs. U. Mo., St. Louis, 1974-78. Author: La literatura hispano-americana en la crítica española, 1980. Mem. Welcome Wagon of Lancaster, Pa., 1968-70, 71-74. Fulbright-Hays grantee, Colombia, S.Am., summer 1963; Ford Humanities fellow, summer 1970; Mellon fellow, 1970-71. Mem. AAUW (pres. Ferguson-Florissant br. 1989-91, chmn. St. Louis area interbranch coun. 1992-94, chair environ. task force Mo. 1992—), Internat. Inst. in Spain, Instituto Internacional de Literatura Iberoamericana, Am. Assn. Tchrs. Spanish & Portuguese. Home: 2105 Barcelona Dr Florissant MO 63033-2805

ASHKIN, ROBERTA ELLEN, lawyer; b. N.Y.C., July 1, 1953; d. Sidney and Beverly Ashkin. BA magna cum laude, Hofstra U., 1975; JD, St. John's U., N.Y.C., 1978. Bar: N.Y., 1979, U.S. Dist. Ct. (ea. and so. dists.), 1980. Program dir. Sta. WVHC-FM, N.Y.C., 1974-75; assoc. editor Matthew Bender, N.Y.C., 1975-79; assoc. Morris & Duffy, N.Y.C., 1979-81, Lipsig, Sullivan & Liapakis, N.Y.C., 1981-84, Julien & Schlesinger, P.C., N.Y.C., 1984-89; adminstrv. law judge N.Y.C. Dept. Transp., 1988-92; ptnr. Trolman & Glaser, P.C., N.Y.C., 1991—. Chmn. bd. Actor's Classical Troupe, 1987-89. Mem. N.Y. State Bar Assn., Assn. Trial Lawyers Am., N.Y. Trial Lawyers Assn., Phi Beta Kappa.

ASHLEY, DARLENE JOY, psychologist; b. N.Y.C., Oct. 29, 1945; d. George Geiger and Ann Debra (Bernstein) Munzer; m. Joseph Michael O'Brien, Sept. 23, 1974 (div. June 1981); 1 child, Sundara Amber; m. Roy William Fagan, Aug. 16, 1991. BA with honors, Antioch Coll., 1966; MA, NYU, 1973; PhD, Calif. Grad. Sch. Family Psychology, San Rafael, 1987. Lic. clin. psychologist, Hawaii, Calif.; Diplomate Am. Bd. Med. Psychotherapists; lic. marriage, family and child counselor, Calif.; cert. Calif. Community Coll. instr., biofeedback therapist. Psychology instr. Coll. of the Redwoods, 1977-82, North Am. Coll., San Rafael, 1980; cons., psychol. examiner Hawaii Bd. Edn., Hilo, 1982; psychology lectr. U. Hawaii, Hilo and Manoa (Honolulu), 1982—; predoctoral clin. psychology intern Redwood Ctr., Berkeley, Calif., 1983-85; pvt. practice psychotherapy, San Rafael and Berkeley, 1985-87; pvt. practice psychology, Darlene Ashley, PhD and Assocs., Kailua Kona, Hawaii, 1988—; workshop presenter, 1977—; instr. psychology Coll. of Redwoods, Ft. Bragg, Calif., 1978-82; presenter Sta. KMPO, Caspar, Calif., Sta. KKON, Kealakekua, Hawaii. Author: Voluntary Controls Training Handbook, 1982; author: (cassette) Deep Relaxation, 1983. Proponent House bill pertaining to psychologists, 1988; com. Rep. Virginia Isbell's Fundraiser, Kailua-Kona, 1988—. Recipient rsch. grant NSF, Mus. Natural History, N.Y.C., 1965, NIMH, NYU, 1968-70, fellowship NIMH, 1969, Outstanding Rsch. award Biofeedback Soc. Calif., 1987. Mem. Am. Psychol. Assn., Assn. Applied Psychophysiology and Biofeedback, Hawaii Psychol. Assn., Biofeedback/Behavioral Medicine Soc. of Hawaii, NAFE. Office: 75-5744 Alii Dr Ste 237 Kailua Kona HI 96740-1740

ASHLEY, ELIZABETH, actress; b. Ocala, Fla., Aug. 30, 1941; d. Arthur Kingman and Lucille (Ayer) Cole; m. George Peppard (div.); 1 son, Christian Moore; m. James Michael McCarthy. Student ballet with, Tatiana Semenova; student, La. State U., 1957-58; grad., Neighborhood Playhouse, N.Y.C., 1961. Apptd. Pres.'s council 1st Nat. Council on the Arts, 1965-69; dir. Am. Film Inst., 1968-72. Appeared on Broadway in The Highest Tree, 1961, Take Her, She's Mine, 1962, Barefoot in the Park, 1963; motion pictures include The Carpet Baggers, 1963, Ship of Fools, 1964, The Third Day, 1965, Marriage of a Young Stockbroker, 1971, Paperback Hero, 1974, Golden Needles, 1974, Rancho Deluxe, 1975, 92 in the Shade, 1976, The Great Scout and Cathouse Thursday, 1976, Coma, 1978, Windows, 1980, Paternity, 1981, Lookin' to Get Out, 1982, Split Image, 1982, Dragnet, 1987, Dangerous Curves, 1987, Vampire's Kiss, 1989; TV work includes (series) Evening Shade, CBS, 1990-94; TV movies include When Michael Calls, 1972, Second Chance, 1972, The Heist, 1972, Your Money or Your Wife, 1972, The War Between the Tates, 1977, Svengali, 1983, Stage Coach, 1986, He's Fired, She's Hired, Warm Hearts, Cold Feet, The Two Mrs. Grenvilles, Orleans (series), The Rope; stage appearances include The Enchanted, Washington, 1973, The Skin of Our Teeth, Washington, Broadway, 1975, Cat on a Hot Tin Roof, Stratford, Conn. and Broadway, 1974, Agnes of God; author: Postcards from the Road, 1978. Recipient Antoinette Perry award, 1962. Mem. Actors Equity, Screen Actors Guild, AFTRA. Office: Duva-Flack Assoc Inc 200 W 57th St Ste 1407 New York NY 10019*

ASHLEY, ELLA JANE (ELLA JANE RADER), medical technologist; b. Dewitt, Ark., Mar. 6, 1941; d. Clayton Ervin and Emma Mae (Coleman) Funderburk; m. Albert Ashley, Sept. 27, 1957 (div. Nov. 1962); 1 child, Cynthia Gayle. Student, Westark Community Coll. Cert. clin. lab. technologist, clin. lab. scientist. Lab. asst. U. Ark. Med. Ctr., Little Rock, 1966-67; lab. technician II Ark. State Hosp., Little Rock, 1967-68; staff technologist Cooper Clinic, Ft. Smith, Ark., 1969-71; asst. chief technologist Nat. Health Labs (formerly Bioassay/Am. Biomed.) div. Revlon, Ft. Smith, 1972—; mem. profl. adv. panel Med. Lab. Observer, 1976—. research in lithium carbonate. Mem. Am. Soc. Med. Technology. Lutheran. Home: 1310 S Houston St Fort Smith AR 72901-7271 Office: Nat Health Labs 500 Lexington Ave Fort Smith AR 72901-4641

ASHLEY, HEATHER RENEE, chemical research analyst; b. Woodstock, Va., Nov. 23, 1969; d. William Lee and Sylvia Chapman (Bashaw) Pearson; m. Michael Harmon Ashley Jr., Sept. 17, 1967. BA in English, Mary Baldwin Coll., 1991. Cert. secondary edn. tchr. English. V.p. Ashley's Svc. and Maintenance, Toms Brook, Va., 1991—; sr. lab technician Woodstock (Va.) Internal Medicine, 1992—; chm. rsch. analyst Miles Diagnostics, Middletown, Va., 1993—. Vol. Literacy Vol. of Am., Woodstock/Staunton, 1990—; coord. Mary Baldwin Coll. Tutoring Program, Staunton, 1990-91. Mem. Mary Baldwin Coll. Alumnae Orgn. Presbyterian. Home: RR 1 Box 319A Toms Brook VA 22660-9733

ASHLEY, LADELL CAROL, transportation executive; b. Monterey Park, Calif., Aug. 27, 1962; d. Bernard Eugene and Barbara Marie (Roksa) A. Diploma, Rosemead (Calif.) H.S., 1980. Firefighter Calif. Conservation Corps, Klamath, 1980-81; foreperson, deckhand Sterling Seafoods, Sitka, Alaska, 1982-84; deckhand Glacier Bay Lodge, Seattle, 1984; relief capt., chief mate Exploration Cruise lines, Seattle, 1985-88; relief capt. Pacific N.W. Explorer, Prince William Sound, Alaska, 1989; capt. Yachts Around, Seattle, 1990, YachtShip CruiseLines, Seattle, 1991-94; capt. Americas Cup Races, San Diego, 1992, Alaska Sea Charters, Valdez, Alaska, 1989. Democrat. Roman Catholic. Avocations: travel, photography, prose, recreational athletics.

ASHLEY, LYNN, educator, consultant, administrator; b. Rock Island, Ill., Nov. 18, 1920; d. Francis Ford and Cleo Marguerite (Monahan) Haynes; m. Edward Messenger Ashley, Aug. 16, 1946; children: Edward Jr., Ann Rice, Rebecca Pocisk, William. BS in Social Psychology, Union Inst., Cin., 1978; MEd., U. Cin., 1979, EdD, 1985. Clk. Lumberman's Mutual Casualty Co., Chgo., 1940-43; account asst. Quaker Oats Co., Chgo., 1941-43; riveter Douglas Aircraft Co., Chgo., 1943-44; organizer, dir. Forest Park Youth Ctr., Forest Park, Ohio, 1967-73; staffing coord. Presbytery of Cin., 1973-78; grad. teaching asst. U. Cin., 1978-84; adminstr. Nat. Corrective Tng. Inst., Cin., 1979—; mem. adj. faculty Union Inst., 1986—; cons. Hamilton County Probation Dept., Warren County Juvenile Ct., Cin., 1987—; field rep. Women in Mil. Svc. for Am.; trainer, cons. Allen County Juvenile Ct. Councilwoman City of Forest Park, 1981-85, organizer community rels. com., 1983; organizer, bd. dirs. Community Youth Ctr., Forest Park, 1967-70; mem. Cin.-Harare, Zimbabwe Sister Cities Assn., 1989—; mem. Ohio Gov.'s Adv. Com. on Women Vets., 1993—. With WAC, 1944-46. Recipient In Recognition award Forest Park City Coun., 1985, In Appreciation award Union Inst., 1987, Recognition award AMVETS, U. Cin., 1993. Mem. Am. Counseling Assn., Nat. Assn. Corrective Tng. Affiliations (pres. 1987—), Women's Vet. Assn., Assn. Family and Conciliation Cts. Office: Nat Corrective Tng Inst 811 Hanson Dr Cincinnati OH 45240-1921

ASHLEY, MARY ELLEN, library assistant, newsletter editor; b. Duluth, Minn., Mar. 24, 1942; d. Leo B. and Mae C. (Johnson) Hansen; m. Roger P. Ashley, Dec. 29, 1964; children: Ellen, Rhoda. BA, Carleton Coll., 1964. Libr. asst. Stanford U., Palo Alto, Calif., 1965-70; instrnl. aide Palo Alto Unified Sch. Dist., 1986-90; libr. asst. J.L. Stanford Mid. Sch., Palo Alto, 1990—. Campaign mgr. Alan Davis for Sch. Bd., Palo Alto, 1982; campaign treas. Debbie Mytels for Sch. Bd., Palo Alto, 1986, Julie Jerome for Sch. Bd., Palo Alto, 1988. Mem. AAUW (br. pres. 1986-87, local editor 1988-92, Calif. state newsletter editor 1992-94, Top State Newsletter in Nation award 1993), Neighbors Abroad (Sister Cities Internat. affiliate bd. dirs., newsletter editor 1987-92, pres. 1989-90), Daus. of Norway (treas. 1992-94). Democrat. Lutheran. Home: 3114 Cowper St Palo Alto CA 94306

ASHLEY, MERRILL, ballerina; b. St. Paul; m. Kibbe Fitzpatrick. Student, Sch. Am. Ballet. Joined N.Y.C. Ballet, 1967, prin. dancer, 1977—. Created prin. roles in Balanchine's Ballo della Regina and Ballade, Jerome Robbins' Four Chambers Works, Robbins'/Tharp's Brahms/Handel, Peter Martins' Barber Violin Concerto, Fearful Symmetries, The Sleeping Beauty; TV appearances include roles in Emeralds, Four Temperaments, Divertimento #15, Ballo della Regina, Bournonville Divertissements, Midsummer Night's Dream and Barber Violin Concerto for Dance in America (PBS); also appeared on PBS Gala of Stars, 1980, 82, 84; author: Dancing for Balanchine, 1984. Recipient Dance Mag. award, 1987. Office: care NYC Ballet Inc Lincoln Center Pla New York NY 10023

ASHLEY, SHARON ANITA, pediatric anesthesiologist; b. Goulds, Fla., Dec. 28, 1948; d. John H. Ashley and Johnnie Mae (Everett) Ashley-Mitchell; m. Clifford K. Sessions, Sept. 1977 (div. 1985); children: Cecili, Nicole, Erika. BA, Lincoln U., 1970; postgrad., Pomona Coll., 1971; MD, Hahnemann Med. Sch., Phila., 1976. Diplomate Am. Bd. Pain Mgmt., Am. Bd. Anesthesiologists. Intern pediatrics Martin Luther King Hosp., L.A., 1976-77, resident pediatrics, 1977-78, resident anesthesiology, 1978-81, mem. staff, 1981—. Named Outstanding Tchr. of Yr., King Drew Med. Ctr., Dept. Anesthesia, 1989, Outstanding Faculty of Yr., 1991. Mem. Am. Soc. Anesthesiologists, Calif. Med. Assn., L.A. County Med. Soc., Soc. Regional Anesthesia, Soc. Pediatric Anesthesia. Democrat. Baptist. Office: Martin Luther King Hosp 12021 Wilmington Ave Los Angeles CA 90059-3019

ASHLEY, THOMEA ANN, surgical nurse; b. Bethpage, N.Y., May 19, 1957; d. George Harry and Mary (Liakos) Margaritis; m. Richard Noel Ashley, Jan. 21, 1984; children: Michael George, Evan Richard. BSN, Wagner Coll., 1979; MSN, Molloy Coll., 1994. Staff nurse operating room St. Vincent's Hosp., N.Y.C., 1980-83; nurse cardio-thoracic unit North Shore U. Hosp., Manhasset, N.Y., 1983-88; sr. clin. coord. North Shore U. Hosp., Manhasset, 1990-93; clinical instr. Molloy Coll., 1994—. Mem. AORN (cert. oper. room nurse), Sigma Theta Tau. Mem. Greek Orthodox Ch. Home: 25 Sherwood Gate Oyster Bay NY 11771

ASHLEY-FRIDIE, BEVERLY FAYE, school system administrator; b. Houston, Dec. 6, 1957; d. Fred Lee and Naomi (Stallworth) Ashley; m. David H. Fridie II, June 21, 1986. BS in Edn., U. Houston Ctrl., 1980, MS in Instrnl. Tech., 1987; MEd in Adminstrn., The Citadel, 1991. Cert. elem., early childhood, kindergarten tchr., supervision, mid-mgmt., psychologist, Tex. Tchr. Ft. Bend Ind. Schs., Houston, 1984-86, Charleston (S.C.) Sch. Dist., 1987-90; computer specialist N.Y.C. Pub. Schs., 1990-92; supr. instrnl. tech. Edinburg (Tex.) Sch. Dist., 1992—; mem. adv. com. Tex. Edn. Agy., Austin, 1992—. Named Tchr. of Yr., N.Y.C. Schs., 1990, Charleston County Schs., 1991. Mem. Tex. ASCD, Nat. Sch. Bd. Assn., Tex. Computer Edn. Agy., Tex. Edn. Ctr. for Tech., NAACP (1st v.p. Tex. 1993—). Home: 4123 Michael Blvd Edinburg TX 78539

ASHMEAD, ALLEZ MORRILL, speech-hearing-language pathologist, orofacial myologist, consultant; b. Provo, Utah, Dec. 18, 1916; d. Laban Rupert and Zella May (Miller) M.; m. Harvey H. Ashmead, 1940; children: Harve DeWayne, Sheryl Mae Harames, Zeltha Janeel Henderson, Emma Allez Broadfoot. BS, Utah State U., 1938; MS summa cum laude, U. Utah, 1952, PhD summa cum laude, 1970; postgrad., Idaho State U., Oreg. State Coll., U. Denver, U. Utah, Brigham Young U., Utah State U., U. Washington, U. No. Colo. Cert. secondary edn., remedial reading, spl. edn., learning disabilities; cert. ASHA clin. competence speech pathology and audiology; profl. cert. in orofacial myology. Tchr. pub. schs. Utah, Idaho, 1938-43; speech and hearing pathologist Bushnell Hosp., Brigham City, Utah, 1943-45; sr. speech correctionist Utah State Dept. Health, Salt Lake City, 1945-52; dir. speech and hearing dept. Davis County Sch. Dist., Farmington, Utah, 1952-65; clin., field supr. U. Utah, Salt Lake City, 1965-70, 75-78; speech pathologist Box Elder Sch. Dist., Brigham City, 1970-75, 78-84; teaching specialist Brigham Young U., Provo, 1970-73; speech pathologist Primary Children's Med. Ctr., Salt Lake City, 1975-77; pvt. practice speech pathology and orofacial myology, 1970-88; del. USSR Profl. Speech Pathology seminar, 1984, 86; participant numerous internat. seminars. Author: Physical Facilities for Handicapped Children, 1957, A Guide for Training Public School Speech and Hearing Clinicians, 1965, A Guide for Public School Speech Hearing Programs, 1959, Impact of Orofacial Myofunctional Treatment on Orthodontic Correction, 1982, Meeting Needs of Handicapped Children, 1975, Relationship of Trace Minerals to Disease, 1972, Macro and Trace Minerals in Human Metabolism, 1971, Electromotive Potential Differences Between Stutterers and Non-stutterers, 1970, Learning Disability, An Educational Adventure, 1969, New Horizons in Special Education, 1969, Developing Speech and Language in the Exceptional Child, 1961, Parent Teacher Guidance in Primary Stuttering, 1951, numerous others; contbr. research articles to profl. jours. Student Placement chair Am. Field Service, Kaysville, Utah, 1962-66; ednl. del. Women's State Legis. Council, Salt Lake City, 1958-70; chairwoman fund raising Utah Symphony Orch., Salt Lake City, 1970-71; sec., treas. Utah chpt. U.S. Council for Exceptional Children, 1958-62, membership com. chair, 1962-66, program com. chair, 1966-68. Recipient Scholarship award for Higher Edn. U. Utah, Salt Lake City, 1969; Delta Kappa Gamma scholar, 1968; rsch. grantee Utah Dept. Edn., 1962. Mem. NEA, Utah Ednl. Assn., Am. Speech, Lang. Hearing Assn. (life, continuing edn. com. 1985, Ace award for Continuing Edn. 1984), Western Speech Assn., Internat. Assn. Orofacial Myology (life, bd. examiners, Sci. Contribution award 1982), Utah Speech, Hearing and Lang. Assn. (life, sec., treas. 1956-60), AAUW (Utah state bd. chair status of women 1959-62, Kaysville br. 1957-60, bd. dirs. Kaysville-Davis br. 1987-92, chair internat. rels. 1987-91, chair cultural interests Kaysville-Davis br. 1991-92), Delta Kappa Gamma (state scholarship award 1968, del. Woman's State Legis. Coun. 1958-70, profl. affairs chair 1963-67, tchr. of yr. award 1978), AAUW (bd. dirs. internat. rels. Kaysvile-Davis br., 1988-91), Sigma Alpha Eta, Theta Alpha Phi, Psi Chi, Zeta Phi Eta, Phi Kappa Phi. Republican. Mormon. Lodges: Daus. Utah Pioneers (parlimentarian Kaysville chpt. 1980-92, historian 1975-80, lesson leader 1992—), Soroptimist Internat. (charter mem. 1954, bd. dirs. 1954-56, pres. Davis County chpt. 1965-69, treas. 1956-54, Rocky Mountain regional bd. dirs. 1965-70, community service award 1968, pub. service award 1970). Home: 719 E Center St Kaysville UT 84037-2138

ASHMEAD, LOUISA HARRAL, lawyer, assistant district attorney; b. Merion, Pa., Sept. 22, 1957; d. John Jr. and Ann (Harnwell) A. Student, Bryn Mawr Coll., 1975-77; BA, Haverford Coll., 1979; JD, Temple U., 1984. Legal intern Hon. Theodore O. Rogers, Commonwealth Ct., West Chester, Pa., 1982; law clk. Montgomery, McCracken, Walker & Rhoads, Phila., 1983; assoc. Ominsky, Joseph & Welsh, P.C., Phila., 1984-86; asst. dist. atty. Phila. Dist. Atty.'s Office, 1986—. Mem. staff Temple Law Rev., 1982-84. Mem. Pa. Dist. Atty.'s Assn., Haverford Coll. Alumni Assn. (exec. com. 1979-84). Office: Phila Dist Atty's Office 1421 Arch St Philadelphia PA 19102-1507

ASHTON, BETSY FINLEY, broadcast journalist, author, lecturer; b. Wilkes-Barre, Pa., May 13, 1944; d. Charles Leonard Hancock Jones and Margaretta Betty (Hart) Jones Layton; m. Arthur Benner Ashton, Nov. 5, 1966 (div. 1972); m. Robert Clarke Freed, May 18, 1974 (div. 1981); m. Jacob B. Underhill III, Oct. 17, 1987. BA, Am. U., 1966, postgrad. in fine arts, 1969-71; student in painting, Corcoran Sch. Art, 1968. Tchr. art Fairfax County (Va.) Pub. Schs., 1967-70; reporter, anchor Sta. WWDC, Washington, 1972-73, Sta. WMAL-AM-FM, Washington, 1973-75; corr. Sta. WTTG-TV, Washington, 1975-76, Sta. WJLA-TV, Washington, 1976-82; consumer corr. CBS News and Sta. WCBS-TV, N.Y.C., 1982-86; sr. corr. Today's Bus., 1986-87; personal fin. contbr. CBS Morning Program, 1987, Lifetime Cable TV, 1988—; anchor FNN Money Talk, 1989; bd. dirs. Lowell E. Mellett Fund for a Free and Responsible Press, Washington, 1979-82; courtroom artist numerous trials, Washington, 1978-81. Reporter TV news report Caffeine, 1981 (AAUW award 1982); reporter spot news 6 P.M. News, 1979 (Emmy award); author: Betsy Ashton's Guide to Living on Your Own, 1988. Concert master of ceremonies Beethoven Soc., Washington, 1979-82. Recipient Laurel award Columbia Journalism Rev., 1984, Outstanding Alumna award Am. U., 1985, Outstanding Media award Am. U., 1986, Best Consumer Journalism citation Nat. Press Club, 1983. Mem. Soc. Profl. Journalists (pres. N.Y. chpt. 1994—, Washington chpt. 1980-81, bd. dirs. N.Y. chpt. 1989—), Alpha Chi Omega (v.p. chpt. 1964-66). Episcopalian.

ASHTON, JEAN WILLOUGHBY, library director; b. Detroit, Mar. 1, 1938; d. Gerald Woodrow and Dorothy (McEwen) Willoughby; m. Robert William Ashton, Mar. 30, 1960; children: Katherine, Susanna, Emily, Isabel. BA, U. Mich., 1959; MA, Radcliffe Coll., 1961; PhD, Columbia U., 1970; MLS, Rutgers U., 1985. Lectr. Fisk U., Nashville, 1962-64; asst. prof. English L.I. U., Bklyn., 1969-73; reference libr. N.Y. Hist. Soc., N.Y.C., 1984-87, assoc. libr. pub. svcs., 1987-89, acting libr., 1989-90, dir. libr., 1990-93; dir. rare books and manuscripts libr. Columbia U., N.Y.C., 1993—; vis. lectr. N.Y. area Colls., 1976-80; lectr. N.Y. Coun. for the Humanities, 1988-92; coord. Comm. for Resources in N.Y. History, 1987-90. Author: (book) Harriet Beecher Stowe: A Reference Guide, 1976; contbr. articles to N.Y. Times, Am. Lit. Realism, Prospects, Magill's Lit. Ann., New Bklyn., Imprint, Biblion, RQ. Vol. BAM Theater Co., Bklyn., 1980-81; mem. bd. govs. Rsch. Librs. Group, 1989-91; mem. Metro Adminstrv. Svcs. Com., 1990-92. Recipient Avery Hopwood Writing award U. Mich., 1959; Woodrow Wilson fellow Woodrow Wilson Found., 1959; faculty scholar Columbia U., 1966-67. Mem. ALA, Am. Printing History Assn., Bibliog. Soc. Am., Soc. History Authorship, Readership and Pub. Librs., The Grolier Club. Home: 574 4th St Brooklyn NY 11215 Office: Rare Book and Manuscript Libr Columbia U 535 E 114th St New York NY 10027

ASHTON, SISTER MARY MADONNA, healthcare administrator; b. St. Paul; d. Avon B. and Ruth (Fehring) A. B.A., St. Catherine's Coll., St. Paul, 1944; MSW, St. Louis U., 1946; M.H.A., U. Minn., 1958. Joined Congregation Sisters of St. Joseph of Carondelet, Roman Cath. Ch., 1946. Dir. med. social service dept. St. Joseph's Hosp., St. Paul, 1949-56; dir. outpatient dept. St. Mary's Hosp., Mpls., 1958-59; asst. adminstr. St. Mary's Hosp., 1959-62, adminstr., 1962-68, exec. v.p., 1968-72, pres., 1972-82; commr. health State of Minn., 1983-91; pres. Carondelet LifeCare Ministries, St. Paul, 1991—; dir. Nat. City Bank, Mpls., St. Catherine's Coll., St. Paul; mem. bd. scientific counselors Nat. Cancer Inst. Recipient Sabra Hamilton award Program in Hosp. Adminstrn. U. Minn., 1958; Minn. Health Citizen of Yr. award, 1977, Gaylord Anderson Leadership award, 1988; Bush summer fellow Harvard Sch. Bus., 1976. Fellow Am. Coll. Healthcare Execs.; mem. Nat. Catholic Health Assn. (sec.), Assn. State Territorial health Officers (sec.-treas.). Home: 5101 W 70th St Apt 120 Minneapolis MN 55439-2105 Office: Carondelet LifeCare 1884 Randolph Ave Saint Paul MN 55105

ASHTON-COOMBS, TAMARAH M., learning disabilities specialist, consultant; b. Toledo, Dec. 5, 1961; d. Harold Leroy and Patricia Marie (Casto) Ashton; m. John G. Coombs, Feb. 11, 1989; 1 child, Rebecca Marie. MusB, Western Mich. U., 1984; MS, San Diego State U., 1988, MA, 1990, postgrad., 1990. Cert. tchr., Calif. Tchr. spl. edn., counselor Lincoln High Sch., San Diego, 1988-89; learning disabilities specialist San Diego State U., 1989-90, instr. dept. of spl. edn., 1992—; pvt. practice ednl. cons., San Diego, 1990—; rsch. asst. doctoral program edn. San Diego State U., 1990-93. Mem. Assn. Ednl. Therapists (profl.), Coun. for Exceptional Children (profl.), Phi Kappa Phi, Pi Lambda Theta (sec. 1990-92, v.p. 1992-93, pres. 1993-94). Home and Office: 4689 49th St San Diego CA 92115-3240

ASKEY, THELMA J., legislative staff member; b. Lakehurst, N.J.. BA, Tenn. Tech. U., 1970; postgrad., George Washington U., Am. U. Press asst. Rep. John Duncan, 1972-74; editor The Nat. Rsch. Coun. Marine Bd., 1974-76; asst. minority trade counsel Ho. Com. Ways and Means, 1976-79, minority trade counsel, 1979—. Office: 1106 Longworth House Office Bldg Washington DC 20515*

ASKOV, EUNICE MAY, education educator; b. St. Louis, Nov. 20, 1940; d. David Hull and Marjorie Jane (Gutgsell) Nicholson; m. Warren Hopkins Askov, Jan. 22, 1967; children: David, Karen. BA in English, Denison U., 1962; MA in English, U. Wis., 1966, PhD in Curriculum and Instrn., 1969. English and reading tchr. Rich Twp. High Sch., Park Forest, Ill., 1962-64; reading svc. reading specialist U. Wis., Madison, 1965-66, project asst. Wis. R & D Ctr. for Cognitive Learning, 1966-67, rsch. assoc., 1969-72, lectr. dept. curriculum and instrn., 1968-69; coord. adult basic edn. programs U. Wis. Extension, 1966-67; remedial reading specialist Lincoln Jr. High Sch.,

Madison, 1966; adult basic edn. tchr. Madison Vocat., Tech. and Adult Schs., 1967-68; asst. prof. elem. edn. Minn. State U., Bemidji, 1972-74; assoc. prof. Pa. State U., University Park, 1974-79, prof., 1980—; presenter seminars on adult edn., Germany, 1986, 93; cons., speaker in field; mem. editorial bd. Jour. Ednl. Rsch., Adult Basic Edn., Am. Reading Forum Yearbook; mem. steering com. Adult Literacy and Tech.; memory and cognitive processes program reviewer NSF; mem. panel nat. work group on cancer and literacy Nat. Cancer Inst.; workshop leader Pa. Right to Read; organizer, coord. Pa. State Coalition for Adult Literacy; mem. adv. coun. Pa. State Libr. Workplace. Contbr. articles to profl. publs. Mem. celebration com. Pa., Yes!, 1990; mem. Pa. task force Project Literacy U.S.; adv. mem. goal 5 task force Pa. 2000. Fulbright sr. scholar, 1983; Literacy Leader fellow Nat. Inst. for Literacy, 1994-95. Mem. ASCD, Am. Assn. Adult and Continuing Edn. (chair, mem. various coms., bd. dirs.), Am. Edn. Rsch. Assn., Nat. Reading Conf. (chair, organizer symposia), Nat. Clearinghouse Literary Edn. (adv. bd.), Internat. Reading Assn. (chair, mem. various coms.), Keystone State Reading Assn. (mem. adult lit. com., chair rsch. com., pres. disabled reader spl. interest coun. Pa.), Mid-State Literacy Coun. (bd. dirs., pers. com., long range planning com.), Mid-State Reading Coun. (pres.), Nat. Coun. Tchrs. English, Pa. Assn. Adult and Continuing Edn., Phi Beta Kappa, Phi Delta Kappa. Democrat. Methodist. Office: Pa State U Inst for Study Adult Lit 204 Calder Way Ste 209 University Park PA 16801-4756

ASLAKSON, SARAH, artist; b. N.Y.C., Aug. 23, 1947; d. David A. and Edith (Silver) Wiesen; m. David Lee Aslakson, Sept. 1, 1968. BS, U. Wis., 1969, MSLS, 1970. Exhbns. include Bone and Joint Surgery Assn., Madison, Wis., 1982, Wustum Mus. Fine Arts, Racine, Wis., 1982, Valperine Gallery, Madison, 1986-93, Katie Gingrass Gallery, Milw., 1986, 88-95, Art Resources, St. Paul, Minn., 1989, 92-94, Banaker Gallery, Walnut Creek, Calif., 1987, MB Perine Gallery, Madison, 1993-95, Edgewood Orchard Gallery, Fish Creek, Wis., 1992, West Bend (Wis.) Mus. Fine Arts, 1990, 92, Jan Cicero Gallery, Chgo., 1992-93, Kornbluth Gallery, Fairlawn, N.J., 1992—, Cary Gallery, Rochester, Mich., Hadley Sch. Blind Invitational, Chgo., 1993, Wis. Acad. Arts and Scis., 1994, U. Wis., Platteville, 1995; permanent collections include: City of Milw., Swiss Colony, Minn. Dept. Revenue, Mpls., City of Milw. Visitors Ctr., Paine Art Ctr., Oshkosh, Wis., numerous others.

ASLINGER, ALLISON MARIE, engineer; b. Chattanooga, Sept. 18, 1962; d. Wayne Eugene and Dorothy Alyne (Wilson) A. Grad., U. Tenn., 1985; postgrad., U. Wis., 1994—. Mech. engr. U.S. Army Tank-Automotive Command, 1987-90; test engr. GM Truck and Bus, Milford, Mich., 1990-93; sr. product engr. GM N.Am. Truck Platform, Janesville, Wis., 1993—. Mem. Janesville Newcomer's Club (pres. 1994—), Janesville Women's Club. Office: GM NAm Truck Platform 1000 Industrial Ave Janesville WI 53547

ASTER, RUTH MARIE RHYDDERCH, business owner; b. Cleve., Aug. 15, 1939; d. Roy William and Ruth Marie (Teckmeyer) Rhydderch; m. Ferdinand Aster, Nov. 23, 1963; children: Anneliese Ruth Aster Wilt, Christian Josef Roy. Student, Cooper Sch. Art, 1956-57; BS, Kent State U., 1962. Art tchr. North Olmsted (Ohio) Jr. and High Sch., 1962; art dept. chmn. Andrews Sch. for Girls, Willoughby, Ohio, 1963-64; co-owner, treas. Aster Cabinet Shop, Chesterland, Ohio, 1963—; co-owner, v.p., treas. Ferdl Aster Ski Sch., Chesterland, 1964—; owner, v.p., sec., treas. Ferdl Aster Ski Shop, Chesterland, 1972—; owner, v.p., advt. designer, fashion buyer, tour advisor Ferdl Aster Sport Ctr., Chesterland, 1985—; chmn. region IV U.S. Ski Assn., Colorado Springs, Colo., 1980-84, Alpine ofcl., 1983-88; ski racing coach U.S. Ski Coaches Assn., Park City, Utah, 1980-89; adv. bd. First County Bank, Chesterland, 1992—; adv. coun. U.S. Postal Svc., Chesterland, 1993—. Exhibited paintings and photographs to various shows, 1963-93. Creator blind ski program Cleve. (Ohio) Sight Ctr., 1969; pres., trustee Chesterland (Ohio) Hist. Found., 1986—; chair, vice chair, commr. Chester Twp. Zoning Com., Chesterland, 1987—; friend Friends of Geauga West Libr., 1989—. Mem. Chesterland C. of C. (pres., v.p., treas., trustee, Bus. Person of Yr. 1993), Community Improvement Corp. Geauga County (re-orgn. com., nominating com., trustee), North Ea. Ohio Ski Retailers Assn. (bd. mem. 1987—), Kent State U. (life mem.), Silver Reunion Com. (bd. mem., v.p.). Lutheran. Office: Ferdl Aster Ski Shop 8330 Mayfield Rd Chesterland OH 44026-2520

ASTOR, BROOKE, foundation administrator, philanthropist, writer; b. Portsmouth, N.H.; d. John Henry and Mabel (Howard) Russell; m. Vincent Astor. LLD (hon.), Columbia U., 1971, Brown U., 1980; LHD (hon.), Fordham U., 1980, NYU, 1986; PhD in Biomed. Sci. (honoris causa), Rockefeller U., 1986. Pres., trustee Astor Home for Children; trustee Hist. Hudson Valley, Marconi Internat. Fellowship; trustee and hon. chmn., mem. devel. com., mem. exec. com. N.Y. Pub. Libr., N.Y.C.; life trustee, mem. conservation com. N.Y. Zool. Soc.; trustee emeritus, mem. coun. of fellows Pierpont Morgan Libr.; trustee emeritus, chmn. vis. com. dept. Asian art, mem. acquisitions com., exec. com. ex officio Met. Mus. Art, N.Y.C.; life trustee Rockefeller U. Author: Patchwork Child, 1962, rev. edit., 1993, The Bluebird Is at Home, 1965, Footprints, 1980, The Last Blossom on the Plum Tree, 1986; feature editor: House and Garden, 1946-56, cons. editor, 1956-93. Mem. N.Y. State Pk. Commn., 1967-69. Decorated dame Venerable Order of St. John of Jerusalem; recipient Anniversary medal Astor, Lenox and Tilden Founds. of N.Y. Pub. Libr., 1961, award Sisters of Good Shepherd and Children of Madonna Heights Sch. for Girls, 1963, Client Award cert. N.Y. State Assn. Architects, 1964, award Pk. Assn. N.Y.C. Inc., 1965, Honor award HUD, 1966, cert. of appreciation City of N.Y., 1967, Albert S. Bard Merit award City Club N.Y., 1967, Award of Honor, Women's Aux. N.Y. chpt. AIA, 1968, Rector's award St. Phillip's Ch., 1968, Michael Friedsam medal Archtl. League N.Y., 1968, award Brotherhood-In-Action, Inc., 1968, Outstanding Contbn. award Am. Soc. Landscape Architects, 1968, Spirit of Achievement award Albert Einstein Coll. Medicine, Yeshiva U., 1969, Good Samaritan award P. Ballentine & Sons, 1969, Good Samaritan award Prospect Block Civic Assn., 1969, Disting. Svc. award N.Y. region Rotary, 1970, YWCA honor, 1970, Housing award N.Y. Met. chpt. Nat. Assn. Housing and Redevel. Officials, 1971, $24 award Mus. City of N.Y., award N.Y. Pub. Libr., 1972, Albert Gallatin medal NYU, 1972, spl. citation AIA, 1973, Medal of Merit award Lotos Club, 1973, commendation Neighborhood Com. for the Asphalt Green, 1975, commendation ARCS Found., 1976, Pres.'s medal Mcpl. Art Soc. N.Y., 1976, Gold Medal award N.Y. Zool. Soc., 1978, Elizabeth Seton Humanitarian award N.Y. Foundling Hosp., 1978, Little Apple award Met. Mus. Art, Little Apple award Morgan Library, Little Apple award N.Y. Public Library, Little Apple award N.Y. Zool. Soc., Little Apple award Rockefeller U., Little Apple award South St. Seaport and Sta. WNET-TV/Channel 13, 1978, New Yorker for N.Y. award Citizens Com. for N.Y.C., 1980, 1st Myer Myers Cultural award City of N.Y., award Citizens Housing and Planning Coun., 1980, Bishop's Cross, Diocese of N.Y., 1980, Forsythia award Bklyn. Bot. Garden, 1981, award Pks. Coun., 1981, Woman of Conscience award Appeal of Conscience Found., 1981, commendation Lower Manhattan Cultural Coun., 1984, Disting. New Yorkers award Bowery Savs. Bank, 1984, Gov.'s Arts award State of N.Y., 1985, Am. Acad. and Inst. Arts and Letters award, 1986, Marconi Internat. Fellowship Coun. award, 1986, landmark plaque and medallion N.Y. Landmarks Preservation Found., 1987, Gold medal St. Nicholas Soc., N.Y.C., 1987, Fashion Industry award Coun. of Fashion Designers Am., 1988, Presdl. Citizen's medal Pres. Reagan, 1988, Nat. Medal of Arts, Nat. Endowment for the Arts, 1988, World Monuments Fund The Hadrian award, 1991, annual humanitarian award ARC of Greater N.Y., 1993, Eleanor Roosevelt medallion City of N.Y., 1993, 8th Annual Town & Country Most Generous American award, The Hearst Corp. and Hearst Mags., 1993, The Mayor's award of Honor and Culture, City of N.Y., 1993, 10th Annual Humanitarian award N.Y., 1993, Richard Rodgers award for Disting. Svc., Profl. Children's Sch., 1994, Scroll of Honor, N.Y. coun. Navy League of U.S., 1994; Brooke Astor Day proclaimed by Mayor of N.Y.C., March 5, 1992. Fellow Am. Acad. Arts and Scis.; mem. Mcpl. Art Soc. N.Y., Pilgrims U.S., Venerable Order St. John of Jerusalem (dame), The Century Assn., Colony Club, Knickerbocker Club, N.Y. Yacht Club, Sleepy Hollow Country Club. Office: The Vincent Astor Found 405 Park Ave New York NY 10022-4405

ASWAD, BETSY (BETSY BECKER), writer; b. Binghamton, N.Y., Feb. 10, 1939; d. George Marrinan and Jane (Sprout) Becker; m. Richard N. Aswad, Sept. 22, 1962; children: Jem, Kristin. B.A.in English with honors, Harpur Coll., Binghamton; M.A., SUNY, Binghamton, 1965, Ph.D. with distinction, 1973. Mem. film editing staff Sta. WNBF-TV, Binghamton, 1957; apprentice So. Tier Playhouse, summers 1957, 58; asst. editor Link Log, 1962-63; from teaching asst. to instr. English SUNY, Binghamton, 1963-74, mem. adj. faculty, 1974-83, fellow Coll.-in-the Woods, 1973. Author: Winds of the Old Days (Edgar Allan Poe spl. award Mystery Writers Am.), 1980, paperback edit., 1983; Family Passions, 1985. Sec., Friends of Binghamton Pub. Libr., 1977-78; vol. Probe, Binghamton Gen. Hosp., 1978-79, Meals on Wheels, 1979-82, St. Mary's Soup Kitchen, 1983—, Binghamton Downtown Forum, 1986—. Mem. Women's Nat. Book Assn. (hon. 1986). Home: 201 Deyo Hill Rd Johnson City NY 13790

ATAMIAN, SUSAN, nurse; b. Cambridge, Mass., Sept. 14, 1950; d. Raymond H. and Alice (Chakerian) A. BA, Simmons Coll., Boston, 1972; postgrad., Simmons Coll., 1991—. RN, Mass.; cert, infection control. Staff nurse Mass. Gen. Hosp., Boston, 1972-74, pvt. duty nurse, 1975-76, staff nurse, 1976-77; rsch. asst. III U. Cinn. Hosp., 1980-81; rsch. study nurse Mass. Gen. Hosp., Boston, 1977-80, instr. nursing, 1982-84, sr. rsch. study nurse, 1984-87, dir. clin. rsch. nurse group, 1985-90, infection control nurse, 1988-90; infection control nurse clinician Mass. Gen. Hosp., Boston, 1990-92; staff nurse Kimberly Nurses, Orange, Calif., 1982; coord., clin. rsch., vascular surg. div. Mass. Gen. Hosp., 1992—; cons. nutrition and liver diseases, McGaw Labs., Santa Ana, Calif., 1980-81; chmn. faculty devel. libr. com. Shepard Gill Sch., Boston, 1983-84; mem. rsch. nurses forum, Mass. Gen. Hosp., 1992—. Class agt. 1972 Simmons Coll., 1972, 86—, mem. com. alumnae fund, 1987-89, reunion com., 1990—, com. on classes, 1991-92, class of 1972 reunion fund chair, 1991-92. Mem. ANA, Mass. Nurses Assn., Am. Nurses Found. Century Club, Assn. Practitioners Infection Control, Soc. for Vascular Nursing, Rsch. Nurses Forum Mass. Gen. Hosp., Simmons Coll. Nursing Honor Soc., Simmons Club Boston (bd. dirs. 1988-90, v.p. 1990-92, co-chmn. boutique 1992-94, nominating com. 1994—), Sigma Theta Tau. Mem. Armenian Apostolic Ch. Office: Mass Gen Hosp Wang Acc Ste 458 Boston MA 02114

ATCHESON, SUE HART, business educator; b. Dubuque, Iowa, Apr. 12; d. Oscar Raymond and Anna (Cook) Hart; m. Walter Clark Atcheson (div.); children: Christine A. Hischar, Moffet Zoe, Claye Williams. BBA, Mich. State U.; MBA, Calif. State Poly. U., Pomona, 1973. Cert. tchr. and adminstr. Instr. Mt. San Antonio Coll., Walnut, Calif., 1968-90; bd. dirs. faculty assn. Mt. San Antonio Coll.; mem. acad. senate Mt. San Antonio Coll.; originator vol. income tax assistance Mt. San Antonio Coll.; speaker in field. Author: Fractions and Equations on Your Own, 1975. Speaker Howard Ruff Nat. Conv., San Diego, 1983, Mike DeFalco Numismatics Seminar, Claremont, Calif., 1986; charter mem. Internat. Commn. on Monetary and Econ. Reform; panelist infrastructure funding reform, Freeport, Ill., 1989. Mem. Community Concert Assn. of Inland Empire (bd. dirs.), Scripps Coll. Fine Arts Found.

ATCHISON, JANE ELLA NABORS, French language educator; b. Meridian, Miss., Sept. 24, 1940; d. Ben Frank and Verba Ann (Huey) N.; m. James William David Atchison, June 23, 1962; children: Heather Elizabeth, Laura Jane Atchison Pittman, Phillip Daniels. BA in French, Agnes Scott Coll., 1962; MA in Secondary Counseling, La. Tech. U., 1993. La. Class A Secondary French tchr. cert. Jr. high French tchr. Guy B. Phillips Jr. H.S., Chapel Hill, N.C., 1962-65; secondary French tchr. Lincoln Parish Sch. Bd., Ruston, La., 1984-89, 90—, Cedar Creek Sch., Ruston, La., 1989-90; advisor, founder Simsboro (La.) H.S. French Club, 1984—, founder Nat. Honor Soc. chpt., 1985; tour organizer, head tchr. Am. Coun. Internat. Studies, Boston, 1986—. Founder, past bd. pres. Ruston YMCA, 1978; vestry mem., sec. Grace Episcopal Ch., Monroe, La., 1990-92, choir mem.; fund-raising co-chmn. Agnes Scott Coll., Decatur, Ga., 1990-93; mem. bishop's sch. Western Diocese of Episcopal Ch. of La., Alexandria, 1993—. Mem. Ouachita Parish Med. Aux., Société d'Honneur Francaise, Pi Delta Phi. Office: Simsboro Sch Box 118 1 Tiger Ln Simsboro LA 71275

ATHANS, SISTER MARY CHRISTINE, church history educator; b. Joliet, Ill., Apr. 7, 1932; d. Christophil Nicholas and Mary Elizabeth (Anderson) A. BS in Humanities, Loyola U., Chgo., 1954; MA in History, Cath. U. Am., 1966; MA in Theology, U. San Francisco, 1975; Licentiate in Sacred Theology, Jesuit Sch. Theology, Berkeley, Calif., 1982; PhD in Hist. Theology, Grad. Theol. Union, Berkeley, Calif., 1982. Joined Sisters of Charity of Blessed Virgin Mary, Roman Cath. Ch., 1955. Exec. dir. N. Phoenix Corp. Ministry, 1970-76; asst. acad. dean/dean students Sch. Theology, Claremont, Calif., 1979-80; adj. faculty U. San Francisco and U. Santa Clara, 1980-82; asst. prof. religious studies U. Ill., Urbana-Champaign, 1982-84; assoc. prof. ch. history The St. Paul Sem. Sch. of Div., U. St. Thomas, St. Paul, 1984—; mem. numerous religious and civic bds. and commns. Author: The Coughlin-Fahey Connection: Father Charles E. Coughlin, Father Denis Fahey C.S.Sp., and Religious Anti-Semitism in the United States, 1938-54, 1991; co-editor: In Service of the Church; contbr. articles to profl. jours. bd. dirs. Minn. Interreligious Com., Mpls.; trustee Mundelein Coll., Chgo., 1984-87, Grad. Theol. Union, Berkeley, 1978-79. Recipient Humanitarian of Yr. award B'nai B'rith, Phoenix, 1974, Sisterhood award, Nat. Conf. Christians and Jews, 1994; named fellow Inst. for Ecumenical and Cultural Rsch., 1990. Mem. Am. Acad. Religion, Am. Cath. Hist. Assn., Cath. Theol. Soc. Am., U.S. Cath. Hist. Soc., Phi Alpha Theta. Democrat. Office: U St Thomas Sch Div 2260 Summit Ave Saint Paul MN 55105-1094

ATHANSON, MARY CATHERYNE, elementary school principal. Prin. Marjorie Kinnan Rawlings Elem. Sch., Pinellas Park, Fla. Office: Marjorie Kinnan Rawlings Elem Sch 6505 68th St Pinellas Park FL 34665-4946

ATHEY, BARBARA JEANNE, environmental engineer, safety professional; b. Austin, Minn., Jan. 21, 1944; d. George Lewis and Evelyn (Bruback) Savides; m. Robert Wayne Athey, Aug. 29, 1964; children: Geoffrey, Paul, John Robert, Jason Benjamin. BA, U. Tex., 1983, MS, 1986. Indsl. pretreatment coord. City of Sherman, Tex., 1979-84; environ. engr. Texas Instruments, Sherman, 1984-87; environ. cons. Profl. Svc. Industries, Lawrence (Kans.), N.Y.C., 1987-90; safety specialist NYU, 1990-93; chief health & safety officer MTA Bridges & Tunnels, N.Y.C., 1993—. Mem. Am. Soc. Safety Engrs., Women's Transp. Seminar. Republican. Office: MTA Bridges & Tunnels 10 Columbus Cir 18th Fl New York NY 10019

ATIL, ESIN, Islamic art historian, researcher; b. Istanbul, Turkey, June 11, 1938; came to U.S., 1956; d. Dogan and Layika (Hilmi) Aka; m. Taskin Atil, Sept. 10, 1959. BA, Am. Coll. for Girls, Istanbul, 1956, Western Coll. for Women, Oxford, Ohio, 1958; MA, U. Mich., 1960, PhD, 1969; PhD (hon.), Bosporus U., Istanbul, Turkey, Karadeniz U., Trabzon, Turkey. Asst. in Turkish lang. dept. Nr. Ea. langs. and lits. U. Mich., Ann Arbor, 1960-61, teaching fellow dept. history art, 1967-68; rsch. libr. Tippetts-Abbott-McCarthy-Stratton, N.Y.C., 1961-63; curator Queens Coll., N.Y.C., 1963-66; curator Islamic art Freer Gallery Art, Washington, 1970-85; guest curator Nat. Gallery Art, Washington, 1985-87; head exhbns. programs and collection mgmt. Arthur M. Sackler Gallery and Freer Gallery Art, Washington, 1987-89, historian Islamic art, 1989—; mem. adv. com. Islamic Teaching Materials Project, Am. Coun. Learned Socs., 1977-80; transls. panel NEH, 1978; mem. master jury The Aga Khan Award for Architecture, 1989, adv. coun. Textile Mus., 1991—; lectr. in field. Author: Exhibition of 2500 Years of Persian Art, 1971, Ceramics from the World of Islam, 1973, Turkish Art of the Ottoman Period, 1973, Art of the Arab World, 1975, (with John A. Pope and Josephine Knapp) Oriental Ceramics, the World's Greatest Collections: Freer Gallery of Art, 1975, The Brush of Masters: Drawings from Iran and India, 1978, Renaissance of Islam: Art of Mamluks, 1981, Kalila wa Dimma: Fables from a Fourteenth-Century Arabic Manuscript, 1981, Islamic Metalwork in the Freer Gallery of Art, 1985, Süleymanname: The Illustrated History of Süleyman, 1986, The Age of Sultan Süleyman the Magnificent, 1987; editor: Islamic Art and Patronage: Treasures from Kuwait, 1990; editor, contbr.: Turkish Art, 1980; translator, editor: Islamic Miniature Painting: Topkapi Palace Museum, 1979, Anatolian Civilizations: Seljuk and Ottoman Art, 1983; translator: Turkish Miniature Painting, 1974; mem. editorial bd. Ars Orientalis, 1970-85, Muqarnas, 1981—, Bull. Asia Inst., 1982—; contbr. articles to profl. jours.; curator exhbns. Mamluk art rsch. grantee Smithsonian Instn., 1977-81; recipient Fulbright Islamic Civilization Rsch. award, 1982-83, Grand award Republic of Turkey, 1987, TURK-93 award Found. Turkish Culture, 1988, Fulbright Rsch. award, 1992-93; Smithsonian Inst. scholar, 1991-92. Mem. Am. Turkish Assn. Washington (bd. dirs. 1971-78), Asia Soc. (adv. coun. 1975-92), Mid. East Studies Assn. (bd. dirs. 1976-78), Smithsonian Instn. (steering com., fgn. currency adv. coun. 1977-79), Inst. Turkis Studies (assoc. mem. adv. bd. 1983-85). Office: Arthur M Sackler Gallery Freer Gallery Art Smithsonian Instn Washington DC 20560

ATKINS, KAREN MELINDA, dean; b. Mayo, S.C., Nov. 22, 1938; d. Benjamin Calvin and Hazel Middleton (Turner) Bonner; m. Donald Eugene Atkins, Dec. 21, 1958; children: Donald Kyle, Scarlet Melinda. BA in Biology, Converse Coll., 1965, MA in Teaching, 1972; EdD, Nova U., 1980. Lab. technologist Spartanburg (S.C.) Regional Med. Ctr., 1958-60; med. technologist Williamsburg (Va.) Community Hosp., 1961-62, Spartanburg Regional Med. Ctr., 1963-65; teaching supr. Spartanburg Regional MEd. Ctr., Sch. Med. Tech., 1965-68; instr. Spartanburg Tech. Coll., 1968, dean health scis., 1968-85, 87-94; retail, wholesale, fundraising exec., 1994—; dean instrn. Spartanburg Tech. Coll., 1985-87; on-site evaluator So. Assn. Colls. and Schs., Atlanta, 1972-93, Nat. Accreditating Agy. Clin. Lab. Scis., Chgo., 1965-75; presenter, cons. in field. Contbr. tech. papers to profl. pubs. 1st woman vice chair Spartanburg County Health Planning Commn., 1978-82, 1st woman chair, 1982-86. Mem. Nat. Network Health Career, Nat. Alliance Invitational Edn., S.C. Tech. Educators Assn. (finalist Outstanding Tech. Educator of Yr. 1979, finalist Outstanding Adminstr. of Yr. 1986). Baptist. Home: 309 Corn Mill Rd Cowpens SC 29330 Office: Branch Bargains Inc 3500 Chesnee Hwy Chesnee SC 29323

ATKINS, LYNN TARRIS, counselor, therapist; b. N.Y.C., Oct. 17, 1940; d. James Harrington and Tharice Alexine (Holz) Coleman; m. Leonard Neil Atkins, Apr. 9, 1965; 1 child, Diane Tracy. AA in Human Svcs., Saddleback Coll., 1962; BA in Bus. Adminstrn., Ind. U., 1962. Lic. real estate salesperson, Calif., real estate broker, Ind. Sales rep. V.C. Sales, Inc., Chgo., 1970-75; sales and mktg. rep. Coleman Prodns., Phoenix, Ariz., 1975-83; real estate sales agt. Orange Tree Realty, Orange, Calif., 1985—; counselor intern recovery svcs. St. Joseph's Hosp., Orange, 1986; counselor intern Starting Point, Costa Mesa, Calif., 1987; case mgr., group facilitator/leader Nat. Coun. Alcoholism, Sch. Ten Inc., Nat. Traffic Safety Inst., Orange County, Calif., 1990—; acting program dir., family and after care therapist Bellflower (Calif.) Dr. Hosp.-Janet Greeson's A Place for Us, 1990—; counselor Avalon Treatment Programs, Rosemead, Calif., 1993—. Cert. Achievement Alcohol and Drug Studies, Saddleback Coll., 1990, Cert. Achievement Human Svcs., 1990. Mem. B'nai Brith Women (Cert. of Honor), United Jewish Appeal, Nat. Assn. Alcoholism and Drug Abuse Counselors,Nat. Assn. Realtors, Calif. Assn. Alcoholism and Drug Abuse Counselors (cert.), Calif. Drinking Driving Treatment Programs (cert.), Calif. Assn. Realtors, East Orange County Bd. Realtors (RAD steering com.), Orange County Substance Abuse Prevention Network (membership com., treas.), Toughlove Internat. (Appreciation award, clinician). Home: 5126 E Stacey Lee Ln Orange CA 92667-3206

ATKINS, TERESA ANNE EANES, water and sewage plant manager; b. Roanoke, Va., Sept. 3, 1963; d. Bobby Frank and June Phyllis (McGee) Eanes; m. Landon Dean Atkins, Apr. 7, 1984. AS in Environ. Sci., Ferrum (Va.) Coll., 1984. Lic. operator class IV, Va. Lab. technician Ferrum (Va.) Coll., 1986-87; computer operator Erath Veneer, Rocky Mount, Va., 1987-89; lab. technician Ferrum Water and Sewerage Authority, Ferrum, 1989-93, plant mgr., 1993—; supr. Ferrum Coll. Internship Program, 1993. Mem. Va. Rural Water Assn. Home: PO Box 136A Ferrum VA 24088 Office: Ferrum Water & Sewage PO Box 40 St Rte 864 Ferrum VA 24088

ATKINSON, BARBARA ANN, internist; b. Grand Rapids, Mich., Mar. 22, 1942; d. Kenneth Wendell and Marion (Burton) Atkinson. BS, Mich. State U., 1964; degree in med. tech., St. Luke's Hosp. Sch. Med. Tech., Saginaw, Mich., 1965; MA in Health Care Edn., Cen. Mich. U., 1978; D Osteopathic Medicine, Mich. State U., 1988. Diplomate Am. Bd. Osteopathy. From med. tech. to microbiology supr. tech. St. Luke's Hosp., Saginaw, 1965-73; from rsch. microbiologist to assoc. microbiologist Bronx (N.Y.) Lebanon Hosp. Ctr., 1973-83; intern Flint (Mich.) Osteopathic Hosp., 1988-89, resident internal medicine, 1989-91; fellow in infectious diseases U. Tex. Health Sci. Ctr., San Antonio, 1991-94; asst. prof. dept. medicine U. North Tex. Health Sci. Ctr., Ft. Worth, 1994—. Mem. DAR, Am. soc. Microbiology, Am. Osteo. Assn., Infectious Diseases Soc. Am., Cranial Acad., Nat. Registry Microbiologists, Beta Sigma Phi (v.p. Chi chpt. Saginaw, Mich. 1971-72, pres. 1972-73, treas. Xi Gamma chpt. N.Y.C. 1975-76, v.p. 1976-77, pres. 1978-79, v.p. Xi Phi Theta chpt. San Antonio 1993-94). Home: 3409 Riveroad Ct Apt 2005 Fort Worth TX 76116 Office: U North Tex Health Sci Ctr Dept Medicine 3500 Camp Bowie Blvd Fort Worth TX 76107

ATKINSON, CLAUDENE DOUGLAS, writer; b. Wichita Falls, Tex., Nov. 17, 1928; d. Walter Claud Jr. and Eula Marguerite (Fletcher) Douglas; married; 1 child, Mark Douglas. BA, U. Houston, 1951; MA, Calif. State U., 1959. Cert. adminstr., counselor, supr., tchr., Tex., Calif. Tchr. English Brazosport Pub. Schs., Lake Jackson, Tex., 1948-51, 54-55; counselor, chair English dept. Houston Pub. Schs., 1955-57, 67-70, Bellflower Pub. Schs., Lakewood, Calif., 1958-63; counselor, instr. Long Beach (Calif.) City Coll., 1965-66; cons. English Houston Pub. Schs., 1970-71; chair humanities divsn. Houston C.C., 1971-77, TV writer, presenter, 1975-77; freelance writer Houston and Ingram, Tex., 1978—; vis. prof. writing Nat. Coll. Edn., Evanston, Ill., 1979; staff leading woman Alley Theatre, Houston, 1955-57; comms. cons. Byrum Assocs., Houston, 1978-79; speaker conv. Tex. Coun. Tchrs. of English, 1968; presenter conf. Nat. Coun. Tchrs. of English, Las Vegas, Nev., 1971. Field editor lang. textbooks, 1972-77; women's editor: Daily Facts Rev., 1954; contbr. articles to profl. jours. Speaker on women's issues, racial equality and lit. various civic, profl. and religious groups, Houston, Long Beach, Honolulu, 1942—; comm. chair United Meth. Ch. Recipient Best Original Short Story award S.W. Writers Conf., 1976, Original Poetry award S.W. Writers Conf., 1977. Mem. AAUW. Home and Office: PO Box 1350 Ingram TX 78025-1350

ATKINSON, DENISE STEFFE, engineer; b. Vermillion, S.D., Nov. 13, 1961; d. Dirl Hane Sr. and Shirley Gertrude (Larsen) S.; m. William Henry Atkinson Jr., Jan. 18, 1985; children: Ariel Jesmine, Sapphire Aurora. Student, Chadron (Nebr.) State, 1979-82, Roosevelt Univ., Honolulu, 1985-87. Comm. tech. Lockheed, Sunnyvale, Calif., 1987-90; sr. engr. Martin Marietta, Sunnyvale, 1990-94, Loral FSC, Gaithersburg, Md., 1994—; owner Atkinson Tax and Scholarship Svc., Frederick, Md., 1993—. With U.S. Army, 1982-87. Mem. NAFE. Home: 5306 Regal Ct Frederick MD 21701

ATKINSON, HOLLY GAIL, physician, journalist, author, lecturer; b. Detroit, Oct. 20, 1952. BA in Biology magna cum laude, Colgate U., 1974; MD, U. Rochester, 1978; MS in Journalism, Columbia U., 1981. Diplomate Nat. Med. Bds. Intern in internal medicine Strong Meml. Hosp., Rochester, N.Y., 1978-79; rschr. Walter Cronkite's Universe show CBS News, N.Y.C., 1981-82; med. reporter CBS Morning News, N.Y.C., 1982-83; on-air co-host Bodywatch health show PBS, 1983-88; contbg. editor and health columnist New Woman mag., 1983-88; on-air corr., med. editor Lifetime Med. TV, 1985-89, sr. v.p. programming and med. affairs, 1989-93; assoc. editor Journal Watch, 1986-90; med. corr. Today Show NBC News, N.Y.C., 1991-94; exec. v.p. Reuters Health, N.Y.C., 1994—; editor Health News, 1994—; mem. trustee's com. U. Rochester, 1983-90. Author: Women and Fatigue, 1986. Vol. nat. and local level Am. Heart Assn., 1984-91; bd. dirs., chairperson Nat. Comms. Com., 1987-91. Commd. officer USPHS, 1979-80. Recipient Young Achievers award Nat. Coun. of Women, 1986. Phi Beta Kappa. Office: Reuters Health Info Svc 825 8th Ave New York NY 10019-7416

ATKINSON, LOUISE CECILIA, telecommunications executive; b. Cleve., Dec. 19, 1954; d. Cleatus J. Jr. and Rose Mary (DiRenzo) Oxenreiter; m. William Duffy Atkinson, Nov. 27, 1992. BEd, So. Meth. U., 1977; MBA, U. Denver, 1979. Ops. supr. long lines AT&T, San Francisco, 1980, acct. exec. long lines, 1981-83, staff mgr. long lines, 1987-89, nat. acct. mgr. long lines, 1983-86; dist. mgr. ops., lead negotiator large accts. AT&T, Bridgewater, N.J., 1990-91; br. mbr. comml. market AT&T, Chgo., 1991-92; dir. compensation comml. market AT&T, Short Hills, N.J., 1992-94, dir. sales response ctr., 1994-95; gen. mgr. global svcs. AT&T, Seattle, 1995—; exec. dean bus. dirs. series AT&T, 1993. Vol. Devon Horse Show, March of Dimes; bd. dirs. U. Denver; trustee New Brunswick Ballet. Republican.

Home: 2155 Fox Creek Rd Berwyn PA 19312 Office: 700 5th Ave Ste 1708 Seattle WA 98104

ATKINSON, REGINA ELIZABETH, medical social worker; b. New Haven, May 13, 1952; d. Samuel and Virginia Louise Griffin. BA, U. Conn., Storrs, 1974; MSW, Atlanta U., 1978. Social work intern Atlanta Residential Manpower Center, 1976-77, Grady Meml. Hosp., Atlanta, 1977-78; med. social worker, hosp. coordinator USPHS, Atlanta, Palm Beach County (Fla.) Health Dept., West Palm Beach, 1978-81; dir. social services Glades Gen. Hosp., Belle Glade, Fla., 1981—; instr. Palm Beach Jr. Coll.; participant various work shops, task forces. Vice pres. Community Action Council South Bay, 1978-79. Whitney Young fellow, 1977; USPHS scholar, 1977. Mem. NAFE, NAACP, Am. Hosp. Assn. (soc. for social work adminstrn. in health care), Soc. Hosp. Social Work Dirs., Assn. State and Territorial Pub. Health Social Workers, Nat. Assn. Black Social Workers, Nat. Assn. Social Workers, Fla. Soc. for Hosp. Social Work Dirs. (adminstrn. in health care), Glades Area Assn. for Retarded Citizens. Home: 525 1/2 SW 10th St Belle Glade FL 33430-3712 Office: 1201 S Main St Belle Glade FL 33430-4911

ATKINSON, SUSAN D., producing artistic director, theatrical consultant; b. Phila., May 23, 1944; d. Joseph A. and Josephine (Mierley) Davis; m. Robert Atkinson, 1971 (div. 1986). BA, Juniata Coll., 1966; postgrad., San Francisco State Coll., 1968-69, U. Calif., Berkeley, 1968-69. Dir. Am. Conservatory Theatre, San Francisco, 1967-72; guest dir. Berkeley Repertory Theatre Co., 1968-69; dir. Marin Shakespeare Festival, Marin County, Calif., 1968-69; producing artistic dir. Repertory Theatre Co. Bucks County, Doylestown, Pa., 1980-86, Bristol (Pa.) Riverside Theatre, 1986—; guest dir. Grove Shakespeare Festival, 1992. Bd. dirs. Pa. Coun. on the Arts, Harrisburg, Pa., 1989—. Mem. Soc. Stage Dirs. and Choreographers (cert.). Office: Bristol Riverside Theatre PO Box 1250 Bristol PA 19007-1250

ATKINSON, VALERIE JO, writer, system administrator; b. Pasadena, Tex.; d. Vernon Thurman and Mildred Kay (Heaton) A. BA, U. Tex., 1981; postgrad., Universidad de Salamanca, Spain, 1983; cert., Southwest Tex. State U., San Marcos, 1985; postgrad., City U. London, 1987. Coord. State Bar Tex., Austin, 1988-90, chair publs. com., 1989-90, adminstr., 1991—; system adminstr. First Tex. Lawyer's Bulletin Bd. Svcs., 1993—. Author: Texas Pocket Part (accompanies the Law of Real Property), 1993, Paralegal Guide to Intellectual Property, 1994, Legal Research Via Internet, 1995; extra (films) Blank Check, Without Consent, Texas Justice. Mem. ABA (assoc. exec. mem., patent, trademark and copyright law, internat. law sects., newsletter com.).

ATLAS, LIANE WIENER, writer, publishing company executive; b. N.Y.C.; d. Louis and Frances (Ferne) Wiener; m. Martin Atlas, Mar. 5, 1944; children: Stephen Terry, Jeffrey L. AB, Vassar Coll., 1943; postgrad., Johns Hopkins U., 1953-55. Cert. fin. planner. Fgn. affairs officer Dept. State, Washington, 1962-68; sr. economist U.S. Commerce Dept., Washington, 1968-75, U.S. Treasury Dept., Washington, 1975-79, Riggs Nat. Bank, Washington, 1980-82; v.p. Fintapes Inc., Washington, 1984-87, pres., 1987-95; mem. U.S. delegation UN Econ. Orgns., N.Y.C., Geneva, 1963, 64, 68, 79. Author: Middle East Financial Institutions, 1977, (audio cassettes) What Every Wife Should Know, 1986, rev., 1992, Financial Planning for Divorce, rev. edit. 1992; freelance writer Changing Times and other mags., 1982-87. Treas. Entertaining People/Washington Home, 1986-90; treas. Smithsonian Craft Show, 1993—. Fellow in econs. Johns Hopkins U., Balt., 1954-55; recipient Cert. of Appreciation U.S. Treasury Dept., Washington, 1977. Mem. NAFE, Inst. CFPs, Smithsonian Women's Com., Am. Econ. Assn., Washingotn Ind. Writers, City Tavern Club, Vassar Club. Home: 2254 48th St NW Washington DC 20007-1035

ATLAS, NANCY FRIEDMAN, lawyer, mediator, arbitrator; b. N.Y.C., May 20, 1949. BS, Tufts U., 1971; JD, NYU, 1974. Bar: N.Y. 1975, U.S. Dist. Ct. (so. and ea. dists.) N.Y. 1975, U.S. Ct. Appeals (2nd cir.) 1975, U.S. Dist. Ct. (so. dist.) Tex. 1982, U.S. Ct. Appeals (5th cir.) 1982, U.S. Dist. Ct. (no. dist.) Tex. 1989. Law clerk to Hon. Dudley B. Bonsal U.S. Dist Ct. (so. dist.) N.Y., 1974-76; assoc. Webster & Sheffield, 1977-78; asst. U.S. atty. So. Dist. N.Y., 1979-82; shareholder Sheinfeld, Maley & Kay, P.C., Houston, 1982—, dir., 1994-95; lectr. numerous programs CLE. Mng. editor NYU Annual Survey Am. Law, 1973-74; contbr. numerous articles to profl. jours. Chair Tex. Higher Edn. Coord. Bd., 1992—; mem. Tex. Coun. Workforce and Econ. Competitiveness, 1993—. Fellow ABA Found., State Bar Tex., Houston Bar Assn.; mem. ABA (co-chair ADR com. litigation sect. 1994—, bus. and litigation joint task force on bankruptcy practice 1994—), Fed. Bar Assn. (trustee), Houston Bar Found., Phi Beta Kappa. Office: Sheinfeld Maley & Kay 3700 First City Ctr 1001 Fannin St Houston TX 77002-6706

ATLEE, DEBBIE GAYLE, sales consultant, nurse; b. Oklahoma City, Jan. 8, 1955; d. Harold Phillip and Ella Ruth (Birks) A. BS in Nursing, U. Okla., 1977. Registered nurse, Okla.; cert. diabetes educator. Team leader ob-gyn Bapt. Med. Ctr. of Okla., Oklahoma City, 1977-80, asst. clin. supr. urology, 1980-81, nursing educator, diabetes educator, 1981-84; sales specialist Boehringer Mannheim Diagnostics, Inc., Indpls., 1984—; mem. regional piloting adv. group Nat. Diabetes Adv. Bd., Oklahoma City, 1984-85. Named Outstanding Bus. Woman, Bus. and Profl. Women, Capitol Hill chpt., 1981, Salesperson of Yr., 1987; recipient Outstanding Sales Achievement award, 1985, 87, 90, 91. Mem. Am. Diabetes Assn. (exec. bd. Met. chpt. 1985—, pres. 1987), Am. Assn. Diabetes Educators, Western Okla. Diabetes Educators (pres. 1984, Outstanding Service and Dedication award 1984, chpt. service award 1985, chpt. edn. award 1984), Nat. Bd. Cert. Diabetes Educator, U.S. Power Squadron (bd. dirs. Oklahoma City 1984, 87), U. Okla. Alumni Assn. (life). Republican. Roman Catholic. Avocations: sailing, photography, gardening, music. Home and Office: 1008 NW 14th St Oklahoma City OK 73106-6604

ATNIP, LINDA, writer; b. Sewanee, Tenn., Feb. 9, 1949; d. Herman Louis and Frances Louise (Hawkins) A. BS, Fla. State U., 1971. Actress Am. Internat. Pictures, Beverly Hills, Calif., 1973; mktg. svcs. mgr. Leisure Village, Camarillo, Calif., 1976-77; sales promotion mgr. Brentwood Pub., L.A., 1977-79; account exec. Performing Arts mag., Beverly Hills, 1979-80; coord. advt. and promotion KNBC-TV, Burbank, Calif., 1980-82; unit publicist Columbia Pictures TV, Burbank, 1982-85; publicist RAP Comms., L.A., 1985-88; entertainment editor New Orleans Mag., 1988-90; pub. Words of Light Prodns., L.A., 1990—; news reporter WPTV, Palm Beach, Fla., 1971-73. Author/performer: (poetry album) When the Heart Sings, 1990; author: (children's book) The Magic Garden, 1992; columnist (music review) Alternatives, New Orleans, 1989-94; prodr./host: (TV show) When the Heart Sings, 1992-94. Performance grantee for one-woman show "The Dream Voyage," City of L.A. Cultural Affairs Dept., Barnsdall Art Park, Hollywood, Calif., 1992. Mem. Publicists Guild of Am., Screen Actors Guild, Fla. State U. Alumni Assn., Fla. Theatre Connection, Internat. Assn. of Transformative Artists. Office: Words of Light Prodns PO Box 39597 Los Angeles CA 90039-0597

ATON, MARY FREDERICKA LAWHON, librarian, retired; b. Arkansas City, Kans., Oct. 2, 1930; d. Fred Ralph and Ethel Alice (Richardson) Lawhon; m. Harry Bruncho Cordes, Aug. 28, 1951 (div. July 1973); children: Frederick Richard, Michael Steven; m. Bert Benton Aton, Jan. 20, 1979. Student, Ark. City Jr. Coll., 1948-50; postgrad., Kans. State U., 1950-51; BS in Informational Media, Millersville State Coll., 1965-75; postgrad., Towson U., 1980. Law librarian York (Pa.) County Law Library, 1975-76; elem. librarian Franklin Elem. Sch., York, Pa., 1976-78; asst. librarian Petroleum Reference Group, Washington, 1980-81, Foster Assocs., Washington; substitute tchr. Fairfax County Schs., Springfield, Va., 1982-83; proprietor Antique Shop, York, Pa., 1983; sales clk. Bloomingdale's, McLean, Va., 1983-84; asst. librarian Dickstein, Shapiro and Morin, Washington, 1984-85; law librarian Prince William County Law Libr., Manassas, Va., 1986-92; ret., 1992. Fellow mem. Am. Assn. Law Libraries, (So. Eastern chpt.), Law Librarians' Soc. Wash. Republican.

ATOOLI, CHERYL ANN, electrical engineer; b. San Diego, Feb. 7, 1959; d. Joseph Hilry and Ardean (Skinner) Guillory; m. Mark Wallace, June 19, 1982 (div. Mar. 1984); m. Jimmy Atooli, Mar. 15, 1984; children: Jamal, Jameela, Jasmine. BSEE, San Diego State U., 1992. Electronic technician Wavetek, San Diego, 1980-81, Gen. Atomic, San Diego, 1981-84; nuclear technician San Onofre (Calif.) Power Plant, 1984-85; elec. engr. Cubic Corp., San Diego, 1992, Solar Turbines, San Diego, 1992—; speaker Math. Enhancement Orgn., San Diego, 1992-93. Vol. St. Rita's Ch. Bazaars, San Diego, 1984—. Republican. Roman Catholic. Home: 6632 Cielo Dr San Diego CA 92114-5729 Office: Solar Turbines 9250 Sky Park Ct San Diego CA 92123-5398

ATOR, SUSAN MARIE, resort manager; b. Pittsfield, Ill., Dec. 17, 1950; d. Gerald W. and Fern L. (Melton) Dimmitt; m. Charles G. Cooper, July 5, 1971 (dec. June 1973); 1 child, Jeramy D. Student, John Wood C.C., Pittsfield, Ill., 1984. Cert. hospitality supr. Legal sec. Dray, Madison & Thomson, Cheyenne, Wyo., 1980-83, McNiff & Patton, Cheyenne, 1985-86; exec. sec. Boeing Aerospace, F.E. Warren AFB, Wyo., 1986-89; mgr. Wagon Wheel Village, Jackson Hole, Wyo., 1989—. Mem. NAFE, Nat. Tour Assn., Am. Hotel Assn., Dancers Workshop. Office: Wagon Wheel Village PO Box 525 Jackson WY 83001-0525

ATSUMI, IKUKO, management school administrator, educator; b. Nagoya, Japan, May 28, 1940; came to U.S., 1980; d. Zenzo Kato and Kaoru Atsumi. BA, Aoyama-Gakuin U., Tokyo, 1964, MA, 1970, PhD equivalent, 1976. Tenured assoc. prof. Aoyama-Gakuin U., Tokyo, 1970-82; founder, pres. Feminist Mag., Tokyo, 1977-80; rsch. fellow Radcliffe and Harvard U., Cambridge, Mass., 1982-83; founder, pres. Intercultural Bus. Ctr., Inc., Framingham, Mass., 1983—; guest writer U.S. State Dept./Internat. Writers' Workshop, Iowa City, 1975. Author: Sales Success in Asia, 10 vols., 1995; author, co-editor (with Kenneth Rexroth, anthology): Women Poets of Japan, 1977; author essay. Bd. advisor Worcester (Mass.) Poly. Inst. Sch. Mgmt., 1991—; founder Pacific Rim Bus. Coun., 1994. Fellow Am. Coun. Learned Socs., 1980-81; rsch. grantee Ella Lyman Cabot Trust, 1983. Office: Intercultural Bus Ctr Inc Framingham Office Park Ste 103 1661 Worcester Rd Framingham MA 01701-5401

ATTAYA, BARBARA ELAINE, sales executive and trainer; b. New Orleans, May 11, 1963; d. Moses and Barbara Jean (Campbell) A. Student, La. State U., 1981, U. New Orleans, 1982-83. Lic. life ins. salesperson; registered securities sales rep. Teller Dixie Savs. (now Oak Tree), Metairie, La., 1983-84; customer svc. rep. Dixie Savs., Metairie, La., 1984-86; customer svc. rep. Dixie Savs., Baton Rouge, 1986, tng. instr., 1987-89; account exec. Landmark Fin. Svcs., Shreveport, La., 1989-91; nat. tng. instr. Fin. Horizons Distributors, Columbus, Ohio, 1991-92; dir. tng. IFS Fin. Svcs., Cin., 1992-93, dir. tng. and comms., 1993—. Republican. Baptist. Home: 3438 Shaw Ave Cincinnati OH 45208

ATTEBERY, SANDRA TOOTHAKER, clinical nurse specialist; b. Ft. Hood, Tex., Apr. 2, 1951; d. Raymond David and Connie Ruth (Roberts) Toothaker; m. Larry G. Smith, May 27, 1972 (div. 1981); m. Bruce W. Attebery, Aug. 21, 1987; 1 child, Matthew Glenn Smith. BSN cum laude, Okla. Bapt. U., 1973; cert Nat. Cancer Inst., Hillcrest Med. Ctr., Tulsa, 1977; MS Community Health Nursing, U. Okla., 1981; postgrad. Enterostomal Therapy Nursing, Abbott-Northwestern, Mpls., 1989. RN, Okla., Tex. Nurse clinician Shawnee (Okla.) Med. Ctr. Hosp., 1977-82; head nurse City of Faith Med. Rsch. Ctr., Tulsa, 1982-84, clin. nurse specialist, 1984; nurse team supr. VA Outpatient Clinic, Tulsa, 1985-87, clin. nurse, 1987-88; clin. nurse specialist St. Vincent's Hosp. and Health Ctr., Billings, Mont., 1988-89, Bapt. Med. Ctr. Okla., Oklahoma City, 1990-91; coord. Oncology Clinic St. John's Regional Med. Ctr., Joplin, Mo., 1991-93; clin. nurse specialist oncology Tex. Cancer Ctr. at Brackenridge, Austin, 1993—; staff nurse St. John's Regional Med. Ctr., Joplin, 1991-93; presentations and speaker in field. Mem. Am. Cancer Soc., Oncology Nurses' Soc., Sigma Theta Tau. Southern Baptist. Office: Tex Cancer Ctr Brackenridge 601 E 15th St Austin TX 78701-1930

ATTEBURY, JANICE MARIE, accountant; b. Sterling, Ill., Sept. 8, 1954; d. Carl Edwin and Eileen Marie (Gilley) McDonald; m. Rudy Joe Attebury, July 8, 1972 (div. 1977); 1 child, Nicole Marie. Student, Okaloosa Walton Jr. Coll., Fort Walton Beach, Fla., Sauk Valley Coll., Dixon, Ill., Houston Community Coll.; BSBA in Acctg., Calif. U. for Advanced Studies, 1990; grad., Rhema Bible Tng. Ctr., 1992. Office mgr. Diamond Jim Enterprises, 1973-74; mgr. data processing dept. Sterling High Sch., 1974-75; bookkeeper 3-G Care Mgmt., Inc., 1977-78, office mgr., 1978-81; staff acct. Jerry T. Paul, CPA, 1982-84; staff acct. Lindgren, Callihan, Van Osdol and Co., Ltd., 1984-85, jr. acct., 1985-89; mgr. Riverside Cemetery, Sterling, 1989-90; pvt. practice J.M. Attebury Acctg. & Bookkeeping Svc., 1989-90, A & E Acctg., Sterling, Ill., 1990—. Mem. corp. bd. dirs., CEO Abiding Word Christian Ctr., Sterling, 1985-94, fin. adminstr., 1985-94; tng. coord. Omega C.G. Ltd., 1994—; mem. corp. bd. Twin City Crists Pregnancy Ctr., Sterling, 1988-90. Mem. NAFE, Nat. Soc. Pub. Accts., Nat. Soc. of Tax Profls. Republican. Mem. Charismatic Ch. Office: 409 4th Ave Sterling IL 61081

ATTEE, JOYCE VALERIE JUNGCLAS, artist; b. Cin., Apr. 4, 1926; d. LeRoy Francis and Clara Marie (Becker) Jungclas; B.A., Rollins Coll., 1948; postgrad. U. Cin., 1952, 54, Art Acad. Cin., 1962-64, Edgecliff Coll., 1967; m. William Robert Attee III, Oct. 25, 1952; children: Robin Wilson, Wendy Ann. One-man shows include Loring Andrews Rattermann Gallery, 1964, Town Club, 1966, 69, 72, 75, 78, 81, 82, 83, 84, 90, Jr. League Office, 1975, Court Gallery, 1969, Bissingers', 1970, 76, Cin. Nature Ctr., 1974, 78, Cin. Country Day Sch., 1974; group shows include Town Club Cin., 1984, Bissinger's, 1984, Cin. Art Mus., 1962, Zoo Arts Festival, 1961, 62, 66, Town Club Cin., 1973-75, 77-79, 80-84, 85, Palm Beach (Fla.) Galleries, 1974, Showcase of Arts, 1976, Ursuline Ctr., 1976, Court Galleries, 1977, Indian Hill Artists, 1957-76, 82, 83, regional and local shows Nat. League Am. Pen Women, 77, 78, also nat. biennial art exhibit, 1970, Nat. Bicentennial Show, Washington, 1976, James H. Barker Gallery, Palm Beach, Fla., 1979, 80, 81, 82, Nantucket, 1982, Cin. Women's Club Show, 1979, Cin. Nature Ctr., 1983, Kimberton (Pa.) Gallery, 1988-89; represented in permanent collections: Bissingers, Cin. Recipient 1st prize in still life or flowers Cin. Womans Art Club, 1965, 69; Marjorie Ewell Meml. award, 1975. Mem. Nat. League Am. Pen Women (past pres. Cin. br., past state art chmn. 1st prize graphics 1975), Women's Art Club Cin. (past v.p.), Jr. League Cin., Jr. League Garden Circle (pres. 1974-75, speaker on flower paintings 1990). Episcopalian. Clubs: Town, University, Indian Hill, Cin. Woman's. Author: Elbey Jay, 1964. Home: 8050 Indian Hill Rd Cincinnati OH 45243-3908

ATTKISSON, SHARYL T., news correspondent, writer; b. St. Petersburg, Fla., Jan. 26, 1961; d. Robert F. Thompson and Judith Jon (Starr) Crist; m. James H. Attkisson, Feb. 18, 1984. BS in Broadcast Journalism, U. Fla., 1982. Reporter, prodr. Sta. WTVX-TV, Ft. Pierce, Fla., 1982-85; reporter Sta. WBNS-TV, Columbus, Ohio, 1985-86, Sta. WTVT-TV, Tampa, Fla., 1986-90; anchor, corr. Cable News Network, Atlanta, 1990-93, CBS News, N.Y.C., 1993-94; corr. CBS News Washington, 1995—; mem. adv. bd. Coll. Journalism, U. Fla., Gainesville, 1994—. Author: Unreliable Sources, 1993. Recipient First Pl. TV Reporting Communicator's award Fla. Agribusiness Inst., 1983, 1st Place award Mature Media Nat. Awards, 1993, Bronze Medal award, Mature Media Nat. awards, 1994, First Place Sports Reporting award Sigma Delta Chi, 1990. Office: CBS News Washington 2020 M St NW Washington DC 20036

ATWATER, JULIE DEMERS, critical care nurse; b. Santa Maria, Calif., Aug. 29, 1945; d. Julian G. and Luella M. (Drown) Demers; m. Roy Michael Atwater, Jan. 29, 1977; children: Michael J. Kawecki, Joel M. LPN, Fanny Allen Sch. for Practical Nursing, Winooski, Vt., 1967; ADN, Weber State Coll., Ogden, Utah, 1982, BS in Allied Health, 1987, BSN, 1989. Lic. practical nurse, Vt., Mass., N.H.; RN, Utah. Practical nurse Brattleboro (Vt.) Meml. Hosp.; practical nurse ICU, Cooley Dickerson Hosp., Northampton, Mass., Cheshire Meml. Hosp., Keene, N.H.; clin. nurse ICU/CCU Evanston (Wyo.) Regional Hosp., 1978-87; critical care nurse ladder IV McKay Dee Hosp., Ogden, Utah, 1987-92, clinical head nurse ICU, 1990-94; com. mem. ICU and Heart Right Group, mem. ICU adv. com. and critical care re-eingring. com. Mem. AACN, No. Utah AACN, Utah Nurses Assn., Utah Orgn. Nurse Execs. Home: 3191 S 3500 W Hooper UT 84315-9624

ATWOOD, CAROL ANN, healthcare executive; b. Artesia, N.Mex., Sept. 26, 1945. BS in Phys. Therapy, U. Okla., 1967; MA in Healthcare Adminstrn., George Washington U., 1976. Staff phys. therapist St. Anthony Hosp., Oklahoma City, 1967-70; dir. rehab. svcs. U. Ky., Lexington, 1970-74; adminstrv. resident Thomas Jefferson U. Hosp., Phila., 1975-76; adminstr. Kaider-Permanente, Cleve. Med. Ctr., 1976-81; sr. assoc. adminstr. Cedars-Sinai Med. Ctr., L.A., 1981-91; sr. v.p. corp. svcs. Meth. Hosps. Dallas, 1991—. Fellow Am. Coll. Healthcare Execs.; mem. Am. Phys. Therapy Assn., Healthcare Adminstrs. Assn. Northeast Ohio, Healthcare Execs. So. Calif., Hosp. Coun. So. Calif., Women in Health Adminstrn., Dallas Ft. Worth Hosp. Coun., C. of C., Rotary, Phi Beta Kappa. Office: So Calif Health Care Systems 1300 E Green St Pasadena CA 91106

ATWOOD, COLLEEN, costume designer. Films include: Firstborn, 1984, Out of the Darkness, 1985 (TV movie), Bring on the Night, 1985, Manhunter, 1986, Critical Condition, 1987, Someone to Watch Over Me, 1987, The Pick-Up Artist, 1987, Torch Song Trilogy, 1988, Married to the Mob, 1988, Fresh Horses, 1988, For Keeps, 1988, Hider in the House, 1989, The Handmaid's Tale, 1989, Joe Verses the Volcano, 1990, Edward Scissorhands, 1990, Silence of the Lambs, 1991, Rush, 1991, Lorenzo's Oil, 1992, Love Field, 1992, Philadelphia, 1993, Born Yesterday, 1993, Cabin Boy, 1994, Wyatt Earp, 1994, Ed Wood, 1994, Little Women, 1994 (Acad. award nom., Best Costume Design). Office: IATSE 1515 Broadway New York NY 10023*

ATWOOD, DIANA FIELD, business owner, innkeeper; b. Rochester, N.Y., Nov. 3, 1946; d. Edwin Havens and Barbara (Field) A.; m. Kenneth Durant Milne, June 10, 1967 (div. Apr. 1982); m. Howard Samuel Tooker, May 5, 1985. BA, Skidmore Coll., 1968. Owner, innkeeper Old Lyme (Conn.) Inn, 1976—; bd. dirs. Maritime Bank & Trust, Essex, Conn.; incorporator Lawrence Meml. Hosp., New London, Conn., 1990—. Trustee Conn. River Mus., Essex, 1976—, pres., 1989-94, chmn., 1994—; trustee Lyme Hist. Soc., Old Lyme, 1985-87, Lyme Acad. Fine Arts, Old Lyme, 1982—, treas., 1992—; vice chmn. Mystic Coast Travel and Leisure Coun., 1992-94, chmn. 1994—; dir. The Nature Conservancy (Conn. Chpt.1994—); adv. bd. Norwich Navigators, 1995—. Mem. Nat. Restaurant Assn., Conn. Restaurant Assn. (bd. dirs. 1991-93), Prof. Assn. Innkeepers, Master Chef's Inst., Gray Gables Croquet Club (founder), U.S. Croquet Assn. (mktg. com.). Republican. Presbyterian. Home: 12 Tantummaheag Rd Old Lyme CT 06371-1137 Office: Old Lyme Inn Inc 85 Lyme St # 787 Old Lyme CT 06371-2336

ATWOOD, HOLLYE STOLZ, lawyer; b. St. Louis, Dec. 25, 1945; d. Robert George and Elise (Sauselle) Stolz; m. Frederick Howard Atwood III, Aug. 12, 1978; children: Katherine Stolz, Jonathan Robert. BA, Washington U., St. Louis, 1968; JD, Washington U., 1973. Bar: Mo. 1973. Jr. ptnr. Bryan Cave, St. Louis, 1973-82, ptnr., 1983—. Bd. dirs. St. Louis council Girl Scouts U.S., 1976-86; trustee John Burroughs Sch., St. Louis, 1983-86. Mem. ABA, Met. St. Louis Bar Assn., Washington U. Law Sch. Alumni Assn. (pres. 1983-84). Club: Noonday (St. Louis) (bd. govs. 1983-86). Office: Bryan Cave 1 Metropolitan Sq 211 N Broadway Saint Louis MO 63102-2110*

ATWOOD, MARGARET ELEANOR, author; b. Ottawa, Ont., Can., Nov. 18, 1939; d. Carl Edmund and Margaret Dorothy (Killam) A. BA, U. Toronto, 1961; AM, Radcliffe Coll., 1962; postgrad., Harvard U., 1962-63, 65-67; LittD (hon.), Trent U., 1973, Concordia U., 1980, Smith Coll., Northampton, Mass., 1982, U. Toronto, 1983, U. Waterloo, 1985, U. Guelph, 1985, Mt. Holyoke Coll., 1985, Victoria Coll., 1987, Univ. de Montréal, 1991; LLD (hon.), Queen's U., 1974. Lectr. in English U. B.C., 1964-65, Sir George Williams U., 1967-68, U. Alta., 1969-70; asst. prof. English York U., Toronto, 1971-72; writer-in-residence U. Toronto, 1972-73, U. Ala., Tuscaloosa, 1985; Berg Chair NYU, 1986; writer-in-residence Macquarie U., Australia, 1987, Trinity U., San Antonio, 1989. Author: (poetry) Double Persephone, 1961, The Circle Game, 1967, The Animals in That Country, 1968, The Journals of Susanna Moodie, 1970, Procedures for Underground, 1970, Power Politics, 1973, Poems for Voices, 1970, You Are Happy, 1975, Selected Poems, 1976 (Am. edit. 1978), Selected Poems, 1966-84, Margaret Atwood Poems, 1965-75, 1990, Two-Headed Poems, 1978, True Stories, 1981, Interlunar, 1984, Selected Poems II, 1986; (novels) The Edible Woman, 1969 (Am. edit. 1970), Surfacing, 1972 (Am. edit. 1973), Lady Oracle, 1976, Life Before Man, 1979, Bodily Harm, 1981, The Handmaid's Tale, 1985, Cat's Eye, 1988 (City Toronto Book award 1989, Coles Book of the Yr. 1989, Can. Booksellers Assn. Author of Yr. 1989, Book of Yr. award Found. for Advancement of Can. Letters, Periodical Marketers Can., 1989, Torgi Talking Book award 1989), The Robber Bride, 1993 (award for Fiction Can. Authors Assn. 1993, Trillium award for Excellence in Ont. Writing 1993, Regional Commonwealth Lit. award); (short stories) Dancing Girls, 1977, Bluebeard's Egg, 1983, Murder in the Dark, 1983, Wilderness Tips, 1991 (Trillium award 1992, Book of Yr. award Periodical Marketers of Can., 1992), Good Bones, 1992; (juvenile) Up in the Tree, 1978, Anna's Pet, 1980, For the Birds, 1990; (non-fiction) Survival: A Thematic Guide to Canadian Literature, 1972, Second Words: Selected Critical Prose, 1982; (TV scripts) The Servant Girl, Can. Broadcasting Co., 1974—, (with Peter Pearson) Heaven on Earth, Can. Broadcasting Co., 1986; editor: (with Shannon Ravenal) The Best American Short Stories 1989; contbr. poems, short stories, revs. and articles to scholarly jours. and consumer mags. Recipient E.J. Pratt medal, 1961, Pres.'s medal U. Western Ont., 1965, YWCA Women of Distinction award, Gov. Gen.'s award, 1966, 1st pl. Centennial Commn. Poetry Competition, 1967, Union Poetry prize Chicago, 1969, Bess Hoskins prize of Poetry Chicago, 1974, City of Toronto Book award, 1977, Can. Booksellers Assn. award, 1977, award for short fiction Periodical Distbr. Can., 1977, St. Lawrence award for Fiction, 1978, Radcliffe Grad. medal, 1980, Molson award, 1981, Internat. Writer's prize Welsh Arts Council, 1982, Book of Yr. award Periodical Distbrs. of Can. and Found. for Advancement Can. Letters, 1983, Los Angeles Times Fiction award, 1986, Gov. Gen.'s Lit. award, 1986, Ida Nudel Humanitarian award, 1986, Toronto Arts award, 1986, Arthur C. Clarke award for Best Sci. Fiction, 1987, shortlisted for Ritz Hemingway prize, Paris, 1987, Commonwealth Lit. Prize regional award, 1987, 94, Silver medal for Best Article of Yr. Council for Advancement and Support of Edn., 1987, Nat. Mag. award 1st prize, 1988, Sunday Times award for literary excellence, YWCA Women of Distinction award 1988, Centennial medal Harvard U., 1990, John Hughes prize Welsh Devel. Bd., 1992, Commemorative medal 125th Anniversary of Can. Confedn., 1992; Guggenheim fellow, 1981; decorated companion Order of Can., 1981, Order of Ont., 1990; named Woman of Yr. Ms. Mag., 1986, Humanist of Yr., 1987, Chevalier de l'Ordre des Arts et des Lettres, 1994. Fellow Royal Soc. of Can., Am. Acad. Arts and Scis. (fgn. hon. lit. mem. 1988). Address: care Oxford U Press, 70 Wynford Dr, Don Mills, ON Canada M3C 1J9

ATWOOD, MARY SANFORD, writer; b. Mt. Pleasant, Mich., Jan. 27, 1935; d. Burton Jay and Lillian Belle (Sampson) Sanford; B.S., U. Miami, 1957; m. John C. Atwood, III, Mar. 23, 1957. Author: A Taste of India, 1969. Mem. San Francisco/N. Peninsula Opera Action, Hillsborough-Burlingame Newcomers, Suicide Prevention and Crisis Center, DeYoung Art Mus., Internat. Hospitality Center, Peninsula Symphony, San Francisco Art Mus., World Affairs Council, Mills Hosp. Assos. Mem. AAUW, Suicide Prevention Aux. Republican. Club: St. Francis Yacht. Office: 40 Knightwood Ln Hillsborough CA 94010-6132

ATWOOD, MERTHEL LURETTA, neurology staff nurse; b. Lincoln, Nebr., June 18, 1945; d. Lloyd Oswald and Edith Margaret (Cook) Barnes; m. Wayne Dean Vorhies, Aug. 1, 1965 (div. Aug. 1979); children: Sondra Renae Brickell, Steve Allen Vorhies; m. Mark Lindsay Atwood, Mar. 30, 1986. BS, Union Coll., 1967; BA, Augustana Coll., 1989. RN, N.H. Staff RN McKennan Hosp., Sioux Falls, S.D., 1989-90, Sioux Valley Hosp., 1990-91, Dartmouth-Hitchcock Med. Ctr., Lebanon, N.H., 1991—. Adventist. Home: 14 Lakeside Apts Enfield NH 03748 Office: Dartmouth-Hitchcock Med Ctr One Medical Ctr Dr Lebanon NH 03756

AU, MARY LEE, school system administrator; b. West Chester, Pa., June 17, 1931; d. James and Lou Shee (Fong) Lee; m. Markley Lee Au, June 24, 1956. BS in Elem. Edn., West Chester State U., 1953; MA in Elem. Edn., George Washington U., 1968; student, U. So. Calif., 1975-76. Cert. elem. and middle sch. adminstr., Md. Tchr. West Chester Sch. Dist., 1953-59, Marple Newton, Pa., 1959-62, Montgomery County Pub. Sch., Md., 1962-68; asst. prin. Roling Terr. Elem. Sch., Tacoma Park, Md., 1989-91; acting asst. prin. Wyngate Elem. Sch., Bethesda, Md., 1990-91; acting prin. Oakland Terr. Elem. Sch., Kensington, Md., 1991, asst. prin., 1991—; mem. undergrad. affairs com., mem. curriculum devel. Am. U., Washington, 1968-79; adv. multicultural curriculum devel. U. So. Calif., 1977; tchr. certification advisor to Md. state supt. Md. State Dept. Edn.; pres., dir. L.A. Assocs. Cons. for Human Resources, 1977—; coord. tchr. tng. ctr. Am. U./ Montgomery County (Md.) Pub. Schs.; pers. recruiter Montgomery County Pub. Schs. Author: Chronology of Asian Pacific American History, 1979-94. Named one of the Women of the 80's, Ms. Mag., Asian-Chinese Am. historian "Write Women Back Into History" project by Nat. Women's Project. Mem. ASCD, Nat. Assn. Elem. Sch. Prins., NAACP, Md. Assn. Elem. Sch. Adminstrs., Asian Pacific Am. Heritage Coun. (co-founder 1979—, nat. treas. 1990-91), Orgn. Chinese Ams. (nat. pres. 1980, v.p. ednl., social, and cultural program 1975), Actors Guild. Baptist. Home: 8800 Fox Hills Trail Potomac MD 20854 Office: Montgomery County Pub Schs 850 Hungerford Dr Rockville MD 20850

AUBREY, SHERILYN SUE, elementary school educator; b. Louisville, Nov. 7, 1951; d. Sheridan and Alice (Rivera) A. BA in Edn., U. Ky., 1974; MA in Edn., Murray State U., 1979. Cert. elem. tchr., Ky. Primary tchr. Hopkins County Bd. Edn., Madisonville, Ky., 1975—; mem. coun. site-base com. Grapevine Sch., Madisonville, 1991—. Mem. NEA, Ky. Edn. Assn., Hopkins County Edn. Assn. (rep. 1986-90), Alpha Delta Kappa (chair altruistic com. Omicron chpt. 1988-91). Baptist. Home: 501 E Morehead St Central City KY 42330 Office: Grapevine Sch Hayes Ave Madisonville KY 42431-3296

AUBRY, LINDA KAY, human resources professional; b. Marinette, Wis., Mar. 5, 1950; d. James T. and Katherine A. (Pape) Comins; m. Robert J. Aubry, Aug. 24, 1968. Student, Waukesha County Tech. Coll., Pewaukee, Wis., 1980-85, Bus. Sch. U. Wis., 1980-85. With Envirex Inc., Waukesha, Wis., 1968—, mgr. human resources, 1987-88, dir. human resources, 1988-94, v.p. human resources, 1994—. Adv. mem. Women's Ctr., 1983-93, Waukesha County Tech. Coll., 1980-93; bd. dirs. YWCA, Waukesha, 1986-89, Assn. of Retarded Citizens, Waukesha, 1988. Mem. Soc. Human Resources Mgmt. Home: PO Box 1604 Waukesha WI 53187-1604

AUDIA, CHRISTINA, librarian; b. Carolina, W.Va., July 6, 1941; d. John and Roze (Horvath) A. B.S. in Edn., Wayne State U., 1967, M.S. in L.S., 1969. Cert. librarian, Mich. Chief libr. original cataloging dept. Detroit Pub. Libr., 1980-89, bibliographic database mgr., 1989—; specialist for monograph cataloging Mich. Libr. Consortium, 1987-89; mem. Dalnet Database Standards Com., 1989—. Mem. ALA. Office: Detroit Pub Libr Bibliographic Database Mgmt 5201 Woodward Ave Detroit MI 48202-4093

AUEL, JEAN MARIE, author; b. Chgo., Feb. 18, 1936; d. Neil Solomon and Martha Amelia (Wirtanen) Untinen; m. Ray Bernard Auel, Mar. 19, 1954; children: RaeAnn Marie, Karen Jean, Lenore Jerica, Kendall Poul, Marshall Philip. MBA, U. Portland, 1976, LittD (hon.), 1984; HHD (hon.), U. Maine, 1986; LHD (hon.), Mt. Vernon Coll., 1986. Office and tech. positions, then tech. writer, credit mgr. Tektronix, Inc., Beaverton, Oreg., 1964-76. Author: The Clan of the Cave Bear, 1980 (Friends of Lit. award 1980, finalist Best First Novel Nat. Book Awards 1980), The Valley of Horses, 1982, The Mammoth Hunters, 1985, The Plains of Passage, 1990 (Waldo award Waldenbooks 1990, Persie award WIN/WIN 1990). Bd. dirs. Oreg. Mus. Sci. and Industry, 1993—; hon. campaign chair Oreg. Coun. for Humanities, 1991; speaker, fund raiser various charitable and ednl. orgns. Recipient Excellence in Writing award Pacific N.W. Booksellers Assn., 1980, award Scandinavian Kaleidoscope of Art and Life, 1982, Bronze Sculpture award Publieksprijs voor het Nederlandse Boek, 1990, Silver Trowel award Sacramento Archeol. Soc., 1990, contbn. award Dept. Interior/Soc. for Am. Archaeology, 1990, Nat. Zoo award, Centennial medal Smithsonian Instn., 1990, Golden Plate award Am. Acad. Achievement, 1986. Mem. PEN, Authors Guild, Willamette Writers (life), Oreg. Writers Colony (charter mem.), Internat. Women's Forum (bd. dirs. 1985-93), Mensa (hon. v.p. 1990—). Office: Jean V Naggar Lit Agy 217 E 75th St New York NY 10021-2902

AUERBACH, JAN, nursing educator; b. Corsicana, Tex., Jan. 16, 1954; d. Donal Lewis and Marzie Pearl (Holloway) A.; m. Michael Don Lee (div.); 1 child, Tamra Rene Lee. Diploma in vocational nursing, Navarro Coll., 1975, A in Gen. Edn., 1977; ADN, El Centro C.C., Dallas, 1979; BSN, U. Tex., 1982, MSN, 1986. RN, Tex.; cert. EMT, paramedic, basic life support instr., advanced cardiac life support. Operating rm. asst. Med. Arts Clinic, Corsicana, Tex., 1975-77; staff and relief charge nurse Navarro County Hosp., Corsicana, 1979-82; staff nurse Parkland Hosp., Dallas, 1982-83; clin. nursing instr. El Centro Coll., Dallas, 1984; grad. tchg. asst. U. Tex., Arlington, 1985; emergency med. svc. tchg. asst. U. Tex. Health Sci. Ctr., Dallas, 1985-87; emergency med. svc. specialist Trinity Hosp., Carrollton, Tex., 1987; instr. health care scis. U. Tex. S.W. Med. Ctr., Dallas, 1987-90, asst. prof., paramedic tng. coord., 1990—; active NME Emergency Svcs. Mktg. Com., 1987, Clin. Evaluation Criteria Devel. Com., 1992; mem. EMS skills com. Tex. Dept. Health, 1990-92; mem. exch. park com. S.W. Sch. Allied Health Scis. Chairperson, 1992; site evaluator The Joint Rev. Com. on Ednl. Programs for EMT-Paramedic, 1993-94. Author (books); contbr. articles to profl. jours. Recipient EMS Educator award Tex. Dept. Health, 1989. Mem. Nat. Assn. EMTs, Tex. Soc. Allied Health Profls., Tex. Assn. EMTs, Emergency Nurses Assn. Home: 4228 Cuesta Irving TX 75038

AUERBACK, SANDRA JEAN, social worker; b. San Francisco, Feb. 21, 1946; d. Alfred and Molly Loy (Friedman) A. BA, U. Calif., Berkeley, 1967; MSW, Hunter Sch. Social Work, 1972. Diplomate clin. social work. Clin. social worker Jewish Family Services, Bklyn., 1972-73; clin. social worker Jewish Family Services, Hackensack, N.J., 1973-78; pvt. practice psychotherapy San Francisco, 1978—; dir. intake adult day care Jewish Home for the Aged, San Francisco, 1979-91. Mem. NASW (cert., bd. dirs. Bay Area Referral Svc. 1983-87, chmn. referral svc. 1984-87, state practice com. 1987-91, regional treas. 1989-91, rep. to Calif. Coun. Psychiatry, Psychology, Social Work and Nursing, 1987—, chmn. 1989, 93, v.p. cmty. svcs. 1991-93, chair Calif. polit. action com. 1993—), Am. Group Psychotherapy Assn., Mental Health Assn. San Francisco (trustee 1987—). Home: 1100 Gough St Apt 8C San Francisco CA 94109-6639 Office: 450 Sutter St San Francisco CA 94108-4206

AUFDENKAMP, JO ANN, librarian; b. Springfield, Ill, Mar. 22, 1926; d. Erwin C. and Johanna (Ostermeier) A.; B.A., MacMurray Coll. for Women, 1945; B.L.S., U. Ill., 1946; postgrad. U. Chgo., 1964-66; J.D., John Marshall Law Sch., 1976. Asst. libr. Commerce Libr. U. Ill., 1946-48; libr. Fed. Res. Bank of Chgo., 1948-80; adminstr. info. services legal dept. Lincoln Nat. Life Ins. Co., Ft. Wayne, Ind., 1980-81; asst. trust officer Central Trust and Savs. Bank, Geneseo, Ill., 1981-83; practice law, 1983-84; cons. Ill. Valley Libr. System, 1984-87, Harvey (Ill.) Pub. Libr., 1987-89; libr. Bus. and Econs. Libr. No. Ill. U., De Kalb, 1989—; with Office Nat. Planning, Liberia, 1963. Mem. ALA, Spl. Libraries Assn., Ill. Library Assn. Republican. Lutheran. Home: 350 Miller Ave De Kalb IL 60115-2310 Office: No Ill U Libr De Kalb IL 60115-2868

AUGHINBAUGH, PATRICIA BARTLEY, librarian; b. Youngstown, Ohio, July 13, 1950; d. William Wesley and Isabelle Agnes (Durso) Bartley; 1 child, Ian Robert Aughinbaugh. BA, U. Pitts., 1972, MLS, 1978. Learning resource ctr. coord. Sch. Health Related Professions, U. Pitts., 1972-73; ref. asst. Hillman Libr., U. Pitts., 1974-76, bibliographic control unit asst., 1977-79; retrospective conversion coord. Centre County Libr. & Hist. Mus., Bellefonte, Pa., 1982-83; cataloger and instr. libr. sci. Pasquerilla Libr. St. Francis Coll., Loretto, Pa., 1983-86, dir. libr., 1986—; pres. Pitts. Regional Libr. Ctr., 1988-89, 91-92, trustee, 1986-92. Adv. bd. Diocese of Altoona/Johnstown, Hollidaysburg, Pa., 1989—; facilitator New Hope Support Group for Div. and Separated, Ebensburg, Pa., 1989-93. Mem. Cambria County Hist. Soc. (exec. bd. 1992—), Beta Phi Mu. Republican. Roman Catholic. Office: St Francis Coll Loretto PA 15940

AUGUR, MARILYN HUSSMAN, distribution executive; b. Texarkana, Ark., Aug. 23, 1938; d. Walter E. and Betty (Palmer) H.; m. James M. Augur, Dec. 29, 1962; children: Margaret M. Hancock, Elizabeth H., Ann Louise. BA, U. N.C., 1960; MBA, So. Meth. U., 1989. Pres. N. Tex. Mountain Valley Water, Irving, 1989—; bd. dirs. Camden News Pub. Co., Little Rock. Trustee Hussman Found., Little Rock, 1991—, U. Tex. Southwestern Med. Found., 1993—, Nat. Jewish Hosp., 1993—, Marilyn Augur Found., Dallas, 1991—; bd. dirs. Baylor Health Systems Found., 1992—, chmn., 1995; bd. dirs. Dallas Summer Musicals, So. Meth. U., 1992—, exec. com., 1992—, Tate lecture series, 1994; mem Tex. Bus. Hall of Fame, 1992—, exec. com., 1994; mem. Dallas Citizens Coun., 1994, exec. com., 1995; mem. Dallas County Cmty. Coll. Dist. Found., Dallas Helps, 1994; chmn. bd. dirs. and exec. com. Baylor Hosp. Found. Mem. Dallas Country Club, Crescent Club, Dallas Women's Club, Beta Gamma Sigma. Episcopalian. Office: N Tex Mountain Valley Water 3132 Iron Ridge St Dallas TX 75247

AUGUSTIN, KATHRYN MARY, financial advisor; b. Milw., Apr. 6, 1946; d. John Norbert and Berwyn (Burke) Augustin; m. Peter E. McAlpine, June 14, 1969 (div. 1984). BA, U. Mich., 1967, MBA, 1973. Sr. profit forecaster Ford Motor Co., Dearborn, Mich., 1973-77; asst. treas., asst. sec. RP Scherer Corp., Troy, Mich., 1977-81; lectr. bus. Wayne State U., Detroit, 1981-83; investment advisor A.G. Edwards, Bloomfield, Mich., 1983-85, Merrill Lynch, Rochester, Mich., 1985, First of Mich., Troy, 1992—; owner, fin. advisor August & Assocs., Lake Orion, Mich., 1985-92; part-time faculty Oakland U., Rochester, 1982-84, Walsh Coll., Troy, Mich. author/leader seminars in field; contbr. articles to profl. jours. Co-founder Mich. Libertarian Party. Mem. Nat. Assn. Accts. (cert.), Risk Assurance Mgmt. Soc., Orion Area C. of C. (bd. dirs. 1986-92). Libertarian Party. Office: First of Michigan 1719 W Big Beaver Rd Troy MI 48084-3510

AUGUSTINE, KATHY MARIE, state legislator, primary school educator; b. L.A., Calif., May 29, 1956; d. Philip Blase and Katherine Alice (Thompson) A.; m. Charles Francis Augustine, July 22, 1988; children: Andrea, Greg, Larry, Dallas. AB, Occidental Coll., 1977; MPA, Calif. State U., Long Beach, 1983. Flight attendant Continental Airlines, Houston, 1978-83; crew scheduler Delta Airlines, L.A., 1983-88; tchr. Diocese of Reno/Las Vegas, 1990-92; mem. Nev. Legislature, 1992-94, Nev. Senate, 1995—. Mem. Active Rep. Women's Club, Las Vegas, Nev., 1992-93. Recipient Achievement award Bank of Am., Calif., 1974, Achievement Medallion Am. Legion, 1974, Congressional Internship grantee, Washington, 1975. Mem. AAUP (v.p. programs), Am. Legislative Exchg. Coun. (transportation com.), Nat. Conf. of State Legislators (arts & tourism com.), Nev. Dance Theater Guild, Jr. League of Las Vegas (sr. legis. rep.), Clark County Panhellenic Assn. (treas.), Italian-Am. Club of Las Vegas, Women Legislator's Lobby. Republican. Roman Catholic. Home: 1400 Maria Elena Dr Las Vegas NV 89104*

AUKOFER, CLARE ELIZABETH, university official; b. Milw., June 1, 1949; d. Herbert Anselm and Wanda Mary (Kaminski) A. BFA, U. Wis., Milw., 1972. Assoc. dir. comm. Ford's Theatre, Washington, 1973-74; assoc. editor Am. Rifleman mag., Washington, 1974-77; sr. comm. specialist GE, Rockville, Md., 1977-81; program mgr. comm. and edn. GE, Charlottesville, Va., 1981-83; editor HELIX, dir. comm. U. Va. Health Scis. Ctr., Charlottesville, 1984—; adv. bd., adj. faculty U. Va. Continuing Edn. Pub. Program, 1994—; theatre critic Charlottesville Daily Progress, 1981—. Chmn. arts com. 1st Night Va., Charlottesville, 1989-91; del. Charlottesville Dem. Caucus, 1991; participant Leadership Charlottesville, 1992. Mem. Coun. for Advancement and Support Edn. (16 gold, silver or bronze medals for HELIX 1984-92), Va. Assn. for Printing, Publs. and Pub. Rels. Profls. (pres. 1990-92, pres. emeritus 1992—). Office: U Va Health Scis Ctr PO Box 224 Charlottesville VA 22902-0224

AULER, ANGELA CRUZ, banker; b. Rio de Janeiro, Aug. 21, 1949; came to U.S., 1988; d. Homero and Maria Magdalena (Cruz) A. Diplome superieur, Universite de Nancy, Rio de Janeiro, 1971; BA in Econs., Fed. U., Rio de Janeiro, 1978; student, Loyola U., Chgo., 1982. Cert. tchr. of English, Rio de Janeiro. Tchr. pub. and pvt. schs., Rio de Janeiro, 1968-73; English, Portuguese translator Motor Union Ins. Co., Rio de Janeiro, 1972-73; fgn. trade dept. clk. Banco do Brasil S.A., Rio de Janeiro, 1973-78, dir.'s staff advisor, 1978-85; trainee in internat. banking Banco do Brasil S.A., Chgo., 1982; advisor v.p.'s staff internat. banking Banco do Brasil S.A., Rio de Janeiro, 1985-87; mgr. trainee Banco do Brasil S.A., London, 1988; rep. Banco do Brasil S.A., Chgo., 1988—. Mem. Soc. of Ex-students in Great Britain, Instituto dos Economistas do Rio de Janeiro, Ptnrs. of The Americas, Pan Am. Coun. of Chgo. Roman Catholic. Office: Banco Do Brasil SA 2 N La Salle St Ste 2005 Chicago IL 60602-3801

AUMACK, SHIRLEY JEAN, financial planner, tax consultant; b. Newark, May 17, 1949; d. Herbert O. and Edythe V. (England) Marlatt; m. Kenneth J. Aumack, Oct. 25, 1969; children: Douglas, Steven. BA in Econs., Wilson Coll., 1971. Cert. fin. planner, enrolled agt.; registered investment advisor. Account exec. N.J. Bell Telephone, Scotch Plains, N.J., 1972-76; ptnr., ind. contr. Personal Mgmt. and Planning Inc., Matawan, N.J., 1982-90; pvt. practice fin. planner Fair Haven, 1990—; instr. fin. planning Monmouth County Pk. System, Lincroft, N.J., 1991, Rutgers U., 1993, 94. Pres. Performing Arts Soc., Rumson Fair-Haven Regional High Sch., 1992-94. Mem. Internat. Assn. for Fin. Planning (seminar speaker 1990), Nat. Assn. Enrolled Agts., N.J. Assn. Pub. Accts., Accreditation Coun. for Accountancy and Taxation (tax advisor). Office: 21 Cedar Ave # E Fair Haven NJ 07704 also: 2 Ethel Rd Ste 201A Edison NJ 08817

AUNE, DEBRA BJURQUIST, lawyer; b. Rochester, Minn., June 13, 1956; d. Alton Herbert and Violet Lucille (Dutcher) Bjurquist; m. Gary ReMine, June 6, 1981 (div. June 1993); children: Jessica Bjurquist ReMine, Melissa Bjurquist ReMine; m. David Aune, Jan. 1, 1995. BA, Augsburg Coll., 1978; JD, Hamline U., 1981. Bar: Minn. 1981. Assoc. Hvistendahl & Moersch, Northfield, Minn., 1981-82; adjuster Federated Ins. Cos., Owatonna, 1982-84; advanced life markets advisor Federated Life Ins. Co., Owatonna, 1984-87; mktg. svcs. advisor Federated Ins. Cos., 1987-89, 2d v.p., corp. legal counsel, 1989-92, v.p. gen. counsel, 1992—. Mem. Hamline Law Rev., 1979-80. Pres. Owatonna Ins. Women, 1983-84; charter commr. City of Owatonna, 1992—. Mem. ABA, Minn. State Bar Assn., 5th Dist. Bar Assn., Steele County Bar Assn. (sec. 1986-87, v.p. 1987-88, pres. 1988-89), Assn. Life Ins. Counsel, Alliance Am. Insurers (legal com. 1989—). Lutheran. Office: Federated Ins Cos 121 E Park Sq Owatonna MN 55060-3046

AURICHIO, ALICIA GRACE, marketing professional; b. Queens, N.Y., Feb. 17, 1957; d. Dominic Thomas and Eda Gloria (Lavoti) A. BA, Hamilton Coll., 1979; MBA, Columbia U., 1986. Field cons. asst. Am. Field Svc., N.Y.C., 1979-80; editorial asst. Van Nostrand Reinhold Co., N.Y.C., 1980-82, product mgr., 1982-85; mem. faculty NYU, N.Y.C., 1988-90; mgr. mktg. Prentice Hall, Englewood Cliffs, N.J., 1990-94. Home: 827 President St Brooklyn NY 11215-1405 Office: Prentice Hall RR 9 # W Englewd Clfs NJ 07632

AURILIA, CHRISTINE MARIE, administrative assistant; b. Bklyn., Mar. 23, 1962; d. Anthony Neil and Christina Mary (Chernega) A. BA in Journalism, Rutgers U., 1984. Editorial asst. Marvel Entertainment Group, N.Y.C., 1985-87, adminstrv. asst., 1987—. Sponsor Futures for Children, Albuquerque, 1988; active Am. Friends of the Royal Shakespeare Co., London, 1985, Amnesty Internat., 1990, Oxfam Am., 1991, Greenpeace, 1991; supporter Colonial Williamsburg Found., 1994. Office: Marvel Entertainment Group 387 Park Ave S New York NY 10016-8810

AUSBURN, LYNNA JOYCE, curriculum developer, technical education specialist, consultant; b. Austin, Tex., July 18, 1944; d. Richard F. and Mary Joyce (Aab) Burt; m. Floyd B. Ausburn, July 30, 1966. BS, U. Tulsa, 1966, MA, 1970; PhD, U. Okla., 1976. English and drama tchr. John Marshall High Sch., Oklahoma City, 1966-67; English and speech tchr. West Jr. High Sch., Muskogee, Okla., 1967-70; lang. arts tchr. Muskogee High Sch., 1970-73; grad. teaching asst. clin. instrnl. media and devel. Coll. Edn., U. Okla., 1974-76; edn. svcs. coord. Swinburne Coll. of Tech. and Further Edn., Melbourne, Australia, 1976-84; head planning and rsch. Frankston Coll. Tech. and Further Edn., Melbourne, 1984-89; curriculum devel. coord. Okla. Dept. Vocat. and Tech. Edn., Stillwater, 1990—; sessional lectr. Monash U., Melbourne, 1976-83, external PhD thesis examiner 1980-84; sessional lectr. State Coll. Victoria, Melbourne, 1980-81; rsch. cons., program Vocat. Orientation Ctr., Royal Melbourne Inst. Tech., 1979; vis. researcher Papua New Guinea U. Tech., Lae, 1980; cons., instr., Colombo Plan Staff Coll., Singapore, 1983, Australian Devel. Assistance Bur., Dept. Fgn. Affairs, Bangladesh, 1985, Regional Edn. Ctr. Sci. & Math., Penang, Malaysia, 1986, 88; sr. researcher USAF, 1977-79, Nat. Ctr. Rsch. and Devel., Adelaide, 1983-84; presenter, cons. UNESCO Workshop on Tech. Edn., Colombo, Sri Lanka, 1995; spkr. in field. Co-author Evaluation Basics for Instructional Methods and Materials, 1981, Instructional Development Skills for Teaching, 1985; contbr. articles to profl. publs., chpt. to book. Recipient Hon. Mention article award Writer's Digest Nat. Competition, 1991, 92; award-winning photographer, 1990-94. Mem. Australian Coll. Edn., Okla. Vocat. Assn., Am. Vocat. Assn., Okla. Vocat. Instrnl. Materials (state advisor 1992—), Soc. for Tech. Comms., Phi Delta Kappa. Republican. Home: RR 3 Box 47 Cleveland OK 74020-9505 Office: Okla Dept Vocat & Tech Edn 1500 W 7th Ave Stillwater OK 74074-4398

AUSLAND, THOMASINE, controller; b. Seattle, Apr. 29, 1941. BA, City Univ., Seattle, 1982. CPA, Wash. V.p. Omnwest, Inc., Seattle, 1972-80; controller The Steinhaver Group, Seattle, 1980-82, Doug Fox Travel, Inc., Seattle, 1982-89, Gene Juarez Salons, Inc., Seattle, 1989—; instr. City U., Seattle, 1986-88. Treas. A. Dunn Guild/Mary Hill Mus., 1993—. Mem. Nat. Assn. Accts. Office: Gene Juarez Salons Inc 1661 E Olive Way Seattle WA 98102-5645

AUSTEN, SHELLI, actress; b. Tulsa, Sept. 8, 1954; m. Fred Chris Sorenson, Dec. 31, 1984 (div. Oct. 1988); 1 child, Kristen Amara. BA, U. Calif., Santa Barbara, 1974. With various improvisational acting troupes, 1974-80; news dir. Sta. KMVI, Maui, Hawaii, 1980-83; v.p. Bill Baker Advt., Honolulu, 1983-85; advt. dir. Ground Swell Mag., Haleiwa, 1985-87; prodr., reporter, anchor Sta. KHVH, Honolulu, 1987-92; dir. adv. Beachcomber Mag., 1992-93; disc jockey Sta. KGY, Olympia, Wash., 1994—; reporter Alameda (Calif.) Times Star, 1994—; media cons. Rep. Party of Hawaii, Honolulu, 1987—; reporter Alameda Times Star, Alameda, Calif.; actress Starlight Theatre, Pasadena Playhouse, Altarina Playhouse. Contbr. articles to profl. jours. Media coord. Merimed found., Honolulu, 1988; del. Rep. Party, Honolulu, 1989, mem. presdl. task force, Honolulu, 1989-90. Episcopalian. Home: 849 Cedar St Alameda CA 94501

AUSTER, CAROL JEAN, sociology educator; b. Bloomington, Ind., Mar. 2, 1954; d. Donald and Nancy Eileen (Ross) A.; m. Neil George Gussman, Aug. 23, 1986; children: Lauren Jean, Lisa Amy. AB in Social Rels., Colgate U., 1976; MA in Sociology, Princeton U., 1979, PhD in Sociology, 1984. Instr. sociology Franklin and Marshall Coll., Lancaster, Pa., 1981-84, asst. prof., 1984-88, assoc. prof., 1988—, acting chair dept., 1982-83, chair dept., 1988-91; NSF rsch. assoc. N.H. Coll., Manchester, 1974, Hampshire Coll., Amherst, Mass., 1975; cons. dept. planning Lancaster (Pa.) Gen. Hosp., 1984—. Contbr. articles, revs. to profl. jours. N.Y. State Regents scholar Colgate U., 1976, Princeton U. fellow, 1977-80; Rockefeller Found. grantee U. Ill., 1979-80, Alfred P. Sloan Found. grantee, 1993-95. Mem. AAUP (dist. VII rep. to nat. coun. 1986-89, com. F. on confs. 1986-92, memberships grants com. 1987-89, 2d v.p. 1990-92, chair com. B. on ethics 1994—), Am. Sociol. Assn. (com. on employment 1994—), Soc. for Study Social Problems, Sociologists for Women in Society, Ea. Sociol. Soc., So. Sociol. Soc. Office: Franklin and Marshall Coll Dept Sociology Lancaster PA 17604

AUSTIN, ANN SHEREE, lawyer; b. Tyler, Tex., Aug. 25, 1960; d. George Patrick and Mary Jean (Brookshire) A. BA cum laude, U. Houston, 1983; JD, South Tex. Coll., 1987. Bar: Tex. 1987, U.S. Dist. Ct. (no. dist.) Tex. 1988, U.S. Ct. Appeals (5th cir.) 1989, U.S. Dist. Ct. (we. dist.) Tex. 1990, U.S. Ct. Appeals (D.C. cir.) 1992, U.S. Supreme Ct. 1992, U.S. Dist Ct. (ea. dist.) Tex. 1993. With First City Ops. Ctr., Houston, 1980-85; law clk. Lipstet, Singer, Hirsch & Wagner, Houston, 1985-86, Pizzitola, Hinton & Sussman, Houston, 1986-87; briefing atty. Hon. Hal M. Lattimore Ct. Appeals, 2d Jud. Dist., Ft. Worth, 1987-88; assoc. Cantey & Hanger, Ft. Worth, 1988-92, Cantey & Hanger, L.L.P., Dallas, 1992-93, Smith, Ralston & Russell, Dallas, 1993-94, Russell, Austin & Henschel, Dallas, 1994—; tchr. Project Outreach State Bar of Tex., 1992. Chpt. editor: Cases and Materials on Civil Procedure, 1987. Mem. Ft. Worth Hist. Preservation Soc., com. mem., 1992; fundraiser Nat. Com. Prevention Child Abuse, 1988—, Women's Haven. Mem. Tex. Young Lawyers Assn. (women in the profession com. 1992—, profl. ethics and grievance awareness com. 1992—, jud. review com. 1990), Dallas Bar Assn. (jud. com. 1993—), Dallas Assn. Young Lawyers, Dallas Women's Bar Assn., Ft. Worth Tarrant County Young Lawyers Assn. (treas., 1989-90, dir. 1989, judge Teen Ct., co-chair Adopt-A-Sch. program), Tarrant County Women's Bar Assn., 5th Cir. Fed. Bar Assn., Am. Inns of Ct. Methodist. Office: Russell Austin & Henschel 302 N Market Ste 501 Dallas TX 75202

AUSTIN, BERIT SYNNOVE, small business owner, warehouse assistant; b. Oslo, Norway, July 22, 1938; came to U.S., 1957; d. Johan Andreas and Astrid (Bjerke) Irgens; m. William Paul Austin, Dec. 22, 1961 (div. 1978); children: Lisa Christine, Paul Erik, Ivar Jon. AA, Saddleback Coll., 1984, AS, 1988. Accounts payable clk. Dynatech Corp., Santa Ana, Calif., 1976-78; accounts payable acct., jr. buyer/Kardex Brunswick Corp., Costa Mesa, Calif., 1978-81; fin. clk. Fluor Corp., Irvine, Calif., 1981-84; warehouse asst. Saddleback Coll., Mission Viejo, Calif., 1984—; owner, cons. Home Prescription, Lake Elsinore, Calif., Mission Viejo, 1984—. Mem. NAFE, Calif. Assn. Sch. Bus. Officials, San Juan Capistrano Hist. Soc., Sierra Country Club, Sons of Norway Fraternal Internat. Soc. (historian 1972, publicity dir. 1973, asst. soc. dir. 1974, social dir. 1992, cultural dir. 1994). Republican. Lutheran. Home: PO Box 4013 Mission Viejo CA 92690 Office: Home Prescription PO Box 4013 San Juan Capistrano CA 92690-4013

AUSTIN, DIANA PAYNE, elementary educator; b. Lafayette, Ind., Oct. 1, 1946; d. William Vorhees and Sarah Louise (Willard) Payne; m. Benjamin Lee Austin, Apr. 3, 1970 (div. 1990); children: Benjamin Lee Jr., Bretton T. BS, Ind. U., 1968, MEd, 1969. Primary tchr. Valparaiso (Ind.) Community Schs., 1968-69, tchr., 1969—. Mem. NEA, Ind. State Tchrs. Assn., Internat. Orgn. Women Pilots (internat. student pilot chmn. 1988-90), The 99s (student pilot chmn. north ctrl. sect. 1988-90,chmn. Ind. Dunes chpt. 1988-90), Valparaiso Tchrs. Assn. (sec. 1979-80), Exptl. Aircraft Assn., Aircraft Owners and Pilots Assn., Jaycees (v.p. 1971-79, award 1979), Tri Kappa, Alpha Omicron Pi (sec. 1967-68). Republican. Presbyterian. Home: 211 Weblos Tr Valparaiso IN 46383-5341

AUSTIN, JUDY ESSARY, scriptwriter; b. Jackson, Tenn., Apr. 7, 1948; d. Hershel Dee and Elizabeth Sue (Rhodes) Essary; m. James Michael Austin, July 4, 1965; children: James Allan Austin, Julia Ann Austin Patterson. AS, DeKalb Coll., 1988; BA in Communications and Journalism, Mercer U., 1989. Retail mgr. Bankers Note, Atlanta, 1980-84, Le Chocolat Elegant, Atlanta, 1984-85; student asst. student affairs DeKalb Coll., Dunwoody, Ga., 1987-88; asst. art dir. Sportime, Atlanta, 1990-92; writer, prodr. CAMA, Atlanta, 1993-94; freelance scriptwriter Atlanta, 1994-95; bd. dirs. Second Wind Orgn., Dekalb Coll., Dunwoody, 1987-88. Scholar Am. Bus. Womens Assn., 1987. Mem. Women in Communications, NAFE, Phi Kappa Phi. Home: 3133 Raymond Dr Atlanta GA 30340-1826

AUSTIN, PAGE INSLEY, lawyer; b. Balt., May 1, 1942; d. John Webb and Sallie Byrd (Massey) Insley. BA in Philosophy, Valparaiso U., 1962; MA in Philosophy, Washington U., St. Louis, 1963; postgrad., Yale U., 1963-66; JD, U. Tex., 1977. Bar: Tex. 1977, U.S. Dist. Ct. (so. dist.) Tex. 1978, U.S. Ct. Appeals (10th cir.) 1980, U.S. Ct. Appeals (5th cir.) 1981, U.S. Supreme Ct. 1986. Instr. Yale U., New Haven, 1966-67, U. Houston, 1967-73; assoc. Vinson & Elkins, Houston, 1977-84, ptnr., 1984—; adj. prof. U. Tex., 1986-87. Mem. ABA, Tex. Bar Assn., Houston Bar Assn., Am. Law Inst., Order of Coif, Chancellors. Home: 2706 Glen Haven Blvd Houston TX 77025-2102 Office: Vinson & Elkins 2500 First City Tower 1001 Fannin Houston TX 77002

AUSTIN, RAE NOLA, mental health nurse; b. Enid, Okla., Feb. 14, 1937; d. George Raymond and Vivian Luicille (Park) Bradford; m. Paul Eugene Throndson, June 28, 1953 (dec. Dec. 1975); children: Paula Rae Throndson, Loretta Gail Throndson; m. Lynn Charles Austin, June 6, 1983; 1 child, Charlene. Diploma, N.W. Tex. Hosp. Sch. Nursing, Amarillo, 1979; BSN, West Tex. State U., 1982. Cert. nurse adminstr., ANCC. Staff nurse Prowers Med. Ctr., Lamar, Colo., 1979-80; instr. nursing Otero Jr. Coll., La Junta, Colo., 1982-83; staff nurse Fort Lyon (Colo.) VA Med. Ctr., 1980-81, 83-84, head nurse, 1985-92, instr. nursing edn., 1992—. Mem. ANA, Rebekah Lodge. Republican. Home: 1505 S 11th St Lamar CO 81052 Office: Fort Lyon VA Med Ctr Bldg 19 Fort Lyon CO 81038

AUSTIN, RHEA COCHRAN, librarian, information specialist; b. Dallas, July 6, 1938; d. William Rhea and Dorothy (Shaw) Cochran; m. Richard Stephen Austin, Aug. 21, 1965; children: Patricia Louise. BA, So. Meth. U., 1959, MA, 1961; MS, Cath. U. Am., 1982. Teaching asst. So. Meth. U., Dallas, 1959-60; tchr. Dallas Ind. Sch. Dist., 1960-61, Highland Park Ind. Sch. Dist., Dallas, 1961-64; asst. prof. Centenary Coll. La., Shreveport, 1964-65; adminstrv. aide Overseas Edn. Fund of LWV, Washington, 1969; librarian ISC Inc., Vienna, Va., 1984-85, corp. librarian OAO Corp., Greenbelt, Md., 1985-87; info. specialist Pub. Tech. Inc., Washington, 1987-90. Mem. home econs. adv. com. Arlington County Pub. Schs., 1983—. NDEA grantee, 1961, 62. Mem. D.C. Library Assn., Special Librs. Assn., Am. Soc. for Info. Scientists, Phi Beta Kappa, Pi Delta Phi, Alpha Lambda Delta. Episcopalian. Home: 4848 27th St N Arlington VA 22207-2708 Office: Nathan Assocs Inc 2101 Wilson Blvd Ste 1200 Arlington VA 22201-3062

AUSTIN, SHARON ROHR, nurse; b. Columbus, Ohio, Dec. 25, 1938; d. Lovell Wilson and Marie Evelyn (Kashner) Rohr; m. Ross Edwin Austin, Aug. 25, 1962; children: Elizabeth, Victoria. BSN, Ohio State U., 1961. Sch. nurse Columbus (Ohio) Bd. Edn., 1962-66, Christina Sch. Dist., Newark, Del., 1980—. Mem. AAUW, DAR, Del. Sch. Nurses Assn., Del. State Edn. Assn. Republican. Office: Newark High Sch E Del Ave Newark DE 19711

AUSTIN, SIGRID LINNEVOLD, counselor; b. Madison, Wis., Aug. 15, 1939; d. Bernhard Olaf Johann and Agnes Elizabeth (Spiva) Linnevold; m. William Jerome Austin, May 16, 1962; children: Christopher Peter, Douglas Patrick, Colin Michael. BA, Barnard Coll., 1961; MS, Va. Commonwealth U., 1986. Lic. profl. counselor. Sr. counselor Peninsula Hosp., Hampton, Va., 1986-88; counselor Williamsburg (Va.) Ctr. for Therapy, 1988—; counselor outreach program Williamsburg Hosp., 1988—; counselor eating disorder program Williamsburg Hosp. Outreach, 1993; crisis counselor William & Mary Police Dept., 1993—; adj. faculty Va. Commonwealth U., Richmond, 1988-90. Asst. editor: (newsletter) The Addiction Letter, 1986-89; contbr. articles to profl. jours. Bd. dirs. Surry County Soc. Prevention of Cruelty to Animals, Surry, Va., 1993; active Nat. Trust Hist. Preservation, Washington, 1992-93, Nat. Conservancy, 1992-93. Scholar Sch. Pub. Affairs, Va. Commonwealth U., 1986. Mem. Internat. Assn. Eating Disorders, Nat. Assn. Alcohol and Drug Abuse, Va. Assn. Alcohol and Drug Abuse, Va. Mental Health Assn., Va. Assn. Clin. Counselors, Obsessive Compulsive Found., Phi Kappa Phi. Democrat. Lutheran. Office: Williamsburg Ctr Therapy Ste 2 217 MC Laws Circle Williamsburg VA 23185

AUSTIN, SUSAN REBECCA, librarian, writer, storyteller; b. Harrisburg, Pa., Jan. 23, 1945; d. Paul Leighty and Margaret Erna (Keim) A. BS in Library Edn., Kutztown (Pa.) State U., 1966; MS in Library Sci., Villanova (Pa.) U., 1967; MEd, Temple U., 1971; PhD, U. Pa., 1989. Cataloger, instr. West Chester (Pa.) State U., 1967-69; libr., media coord. St. James/Msgr. Bonner High Sch., Chester and Drexel Hill, Pa., 1969-72, 73-76; librarian elem. div. Am. Sch. in London, 1972-73; asst. prof. Appalachian State U., Boone, N.C., 1976-78; librarian Upper Darby (Pa.) High Sch., 1980-81; asst. prof. Kutztown State U., 1981-82; learning materials specialist Sabold Elem. Sch., Springfield, Pa., 1984—; freelance storyteller, 1980—. Contbr. articles to profl. jours. Mem. NEA, Pa. State Edn. Assn., Nat. Assn. for the Preservation and Perpetuation of Storytelling. Republican. Methodist. Home: 3701 Columbia Court Way Newtown Square PA 19073-1064 Office: Sabold Elem Sch Thomson Ave & Baltimore Springfield PA 19064

AUST-KEEFER, MARY BETH, library administrator; b. Cleve., Mar. 9, 1958; d. Donald and Mary Lee (Hepner) Aust; m. Steven H. Keefer, Feb. 13, 1981. BA in History, Kent State U., 1979, MLS, 1980. Libr. asst. Kent (Ohio) State U. Music Libr., 1975-79; asst. Kent State U. Archives/Spl. Collections, 1979-80; libr. dir. Blackfeet Community Coll., Browning, Mont., 1981-84; head libr. Edison State Community Coll., Piqua, Ohio, 1984-87, dir. libr. and audiovisual svcs., 1987—, affirmative action officer, 1991—; cons. Blackfeet Indian Tribe, Browning, 1982-84; info. distbn. coord. Blackfeet Indian Tribe Media, Browning, 1983-84; facilitator Am. Indian Higher Edn. Consortium, Rapid City, S.D., 1983; presenter League of Innovation, 1994. Chair Edison Nat. Issues Forum, Piqua, 1990-92; coord. Shelby County (Ohio) -Librs. Learning for Life, 1988; mem. Summer Pub. Policy Inst., Oxford, Ohio, 1990, 91. Recipient Nat. Inst. for Leadership Development award, 1992. Mem. ALA, AAUW, Ohio Libr. Assn., Southwestern Ohio Coun. for Higher Edn. (vice chair libr. div. 1990-91), Beta Phi Mu.

AUTERI, ROSE MARY PATTI, school system administrator; b. N.Y.C., June 6, 1928; d. Francesco and Stefana (Patti) A. BS, Hunter Coll., 1950; MA, Columbia U., 1962; EdD, Nova-Southeastern U., 1975; postdoctoral, Columbia U., 1976-77. Tchr. Howell Rd Sch., Valley Stream, N.Y., 1951-58, asst. prin., 1958-64; prin. Centennial Ave Sch., Roosevelt, N.Y., 1964-69, Northside Sch., Levittown, N.Y., 1969-83, Abbey Ln. Sch., Levittown, 1983-89; adminstr. in charge elem. schs. Levittown Pub. Schs., 1989-90; prin. Abbey Ln. Sch., Levittown, 1990—. Recipient Disting. Prin. award State of N.Y., 1988, 89, Disting. Svc. award Nat. PTA; named Italian Am. Woman of Yr., 1990. Mem. Am. Assn. Sch. Adminstrs., Nat. Assn. Elem. Sch. Prins., Nat. Assn. Supervision and Curriculum Devel., Nassau County Elem. Prins. Assn. (pres.), L.I. Assn. Supervision and Curriculum Devel. (bd. dirs.), N.Y. State Assn. Devel., Am. Assn. Electroencephalographic Technologists, Am.-Italian Hist. Assn. (sec. 1988—, pres., editor L.I. regional chpt.). Home: 1816 Thomas St Merrick NY 11566-2652 Office: Levittown Pub Schs Abbey Ln Levittown NY 11756

AVAKIAN, LAURA ANN, hospital administrator; b. DeSoto, Mo., July 6, 1945; d. Edward Ernest and Elizabeth (Gamel) McClary; m. Stephen Avakian, Dec. 30, 1969. BA, U. Mo., 1967; MA, Northwestern U., 1968. Instr. Sacramento (Calif.) State Coll., 1968-69; English tchr. Hathaway Brown Sch., Cleve., 1969-73; pers. profl. Huron Rd. Hosp., Cleve., 1974-76, dir. human resources, 1978-80; dir. employment Cleve. Clinic Found., 1976-78; v.p. human resources Beth Israel Hosp., Boston, 1980—. Assoc. editor Yearbook of Healthcare Management, 1990, 91, 92, 93. Mem. Mayor's Commn. on Comparable Worth, Boston, 1989-90. Mem. Am. Soc. Healthcare Human Resources Adminstrn. (bd. dirs. 1989-93, Pres. Leadership award 1989, Literature award 1992, pres. 1994—), Soc. Human Resource Mgmt., Mass. Health Care Human Resources Assn. (pres. 1987-88). Office: Beth Israel Hosp 330 Brookline Ave Boston MA 02215-5491

AVALLONE, CHARLENE SHERMAN, humanities educator; b. Glens Falls, N.Y., Apr. 29, 1949; d. William Morris and Mary Angeline (Brayman) Sherman; 1 child, Nathan Avallone; m. Robert S. Hughes Jr., May 25, 1987. BA, Coll. of St. Rose, 1971; MA, SUNY, Binghamton, 1973, PhD, 1982. Asst. prof. English U. Hawaii, Honolulu, 1981-85; asst. prof. English U. Notre Dame (Ind.), 1985-92, exec. chair gender studies, 1990-91. Contbr. articles to profl. jours. Grantee Lilly Endowment, 1988; fellow Newberry Libr., 1983; humanities scholar NEH, 1982, 84. Mem. MLA, Nat. Women's Studies Assn.

AVANT, TRACY WRIGHT, artist; b. Fort Dix, N.J., 1960. Studied with various artists, 1988-94. conductor workshops. One-woman shows include Coppini Gallery, 1992, The Longhorn Gallery, 1993, Ceci's Gallery Fine Art, Bryan, Tex., 1994, Briarcrest Country Club, 1994; exhibited in group shows Dilley Civic Ctr., F.J. Avant Meml. Park, Dilley, Tex, 1987-88, Artbeat, San Antonio, 1992, Coppini Gallery, San Antonio, 1993, Joe Freeman Coliseum, San Antonio, 1988-93, La Villita Assembly Hall, San Antonio, 1993, Richardson (Tex.) Pub. Libr., 1993, 95, Bridge Gallery, N.Y.C., 1993, Irving (Tex.) Art Ctr., 1993, J.R. Mooney Gallery, San Antonio, 1993, 94, St. Edwards U., Austin, Tex., 1993, Palette and Chisel Gallery, Chgo., 1993, 94, Gwendolyn's Gallery, Colo., 1993, 94, D Art Gallery, Dallas, 1994, Scottsdale (Ariz.) Artist's Sch., 1994, 95, Ceci's Gallery Fine Art, 1994, Carol's at the Hitching Post, 1994, Mae S. Bruce Libr., Santa Fe, Tex., 1994, 95, Deposit Guaranty Salon Internat., Jackson, Miss., 1994, Bosque County Conservatory, Clifton, Tex., 1994, Nanette Richardson Gallery, San Antonio, 1994 (Judge's Choice award 1994), Thomas Gilcrease Mus., 1994, Nat. Soc. Artists, 1995, Pasadena (Tex.) Art League, 1995, and numerous others; represented in permanent collections Wyoming Gallery, Jackson, Tex. Trails Gallery, San Antonio, Love Tex. Gallery, San Antonio, Carol's at the Hitching Post, Canyon Lake, Tex., Triple C Gallery, Devine, Tex., Phil Isley Inc., Tex., Normangee State Bank, Tex., Ocean Wash USA, Tex., pvt. individuals. Mem. Am. Soc. Classical Realists, Nat. Soc. Artists, Nat. Wildlife Art Mus. Assn., Allied Artists Am., Oil Painters Am., Cowboy Artists Am. Mus. Assn., Tex. Watercolor Soc., Houston Civil Arts Assn., Artists and Craftsmen Assn. Dallas, Palette and Chisel Acad. Fine Art Chgo., Austin Palette Club, Scottsdale Artist Sch., New Braunfels Art League, Coppini Acad. Fine Art, Knickerbocker Artist Assocs.

AVERETT-SHORT, GENEVA EVELYN, college administrator; b. Boston, Mar. 12, 1938; d. William Pinkney and Geneva Zepplyn (Stepp) A.; m. Roger Inman Blackwell, Dec. 19, 1959 (div. 1975); children: Thomas, LaVerne, Constance; m. Floyd J. Short Jr., July 3, 1984. BA in Social Sci., Bennett Coll., Greensboro, N.C., 1958; EdM, SUNY, Buffalo, 1972; paralegal cert., Prince George's C.C., Largo, Md., 1994. Social caseworker Erie County Dept. Pub. Welfare, Buffalo, 1958-59; substitute tchr. Buffalo Bd. Edn., 1959-60; employment inteviewer N.Y. Dept. Labor, Div. Employment, Buffalo, 1967-69; admissions counselor SUNY, Buffalo, 1969-72; assoc. dean students U. Utah, Salt Lake City, 1972-74; coordinator counseling svcs. Ednl. Devel. Prog., SUNY, Fredonia, 1974-77; acting dir. Ednl. Devel. Prog., SUNY, 1976-77; substitute tchr. Greensboro (N.C.) pub. schs., 1977-78; prog. asst. D.C. Dept. Human Svcs. Commn. on Pub. Health, 1978-89; assessment counselor, coord. Prince George's Community Coll., Largo, Md., 1989-94; cons. in field. Active in past various charitable orgns. Mem. Nat. Alumnae Assn. Bennett Coll., Pierians, Inc. (pres. D.C. chpt. 1992-94). Democrat. Episcopalian. Address: Apt 102 11845 Royal Palm Blvd Coral Springs FL 33065

AVERSA, DOLORES SEJDA, educational administrator; b. Phila., Mar. 26, 1932; d. Martin Benjamin and Mary Elizabeth (Esposito) Sejda; BA, Chestnut Hill Coll., 1953; m. Zefferino A. Aversa, May 3, 1958; children: Dolores Elizabeth, Jeffrey Martin, Linda Maria. Owner, Personal Rep. and Pub. Rels., Phila., 1965-68; ednl. cons. Franklin Sch. Sci. and Arts, Phila., 1968-72; pres., owner, dir. Martin Sch. of Bus., Inc., Phila., 1972—; file reader, cons. for ct. reporting and travel tng. Southwestern Pub. Co., 1990; mem. ednl. planning com. Ravenhill Acad., Phila., 1975-76. Active Phila. Mus. of Art, Phila. Drama Guild. Mem. Nat. Bus. Edn. Assn., Pa. Bus. Edn. Assn., Am. Bus. Law Assn., Pa. Sch. Counselors Assn., Am.-Italy Soc., Am. Soc. Travel Agts. (sec. Del. Valley chpt., edn. chmn. Del. Valley chpt.), Phila. Hist. Soc., World Affairs Coun. Phila., Hist. Soc. Pa., Phila. Orch. Mem. ASTA (sch. div., nat. educators com.), Chestnut Hill Coll. Alumnae Assn. Roman Catholic. Home: 2111 Locust St Philadelphia PA 19103-4802 Office: 2417 Welsh Rd Philadelphia PA 19114-2213

AVERY, CHRISTINE ANN, pediatrician; b. Bklyn., Mar. 30, 1951; d. Basil Steven and Mary P. Goerner; m. Hernry Jakob Wachtendorf, June 7, 1973; 1 child, Henry James. BS summa cum laude, U. Houston, 1972; MD, U. Tex. Health Sci. Ctr., 1976. Resident in pediatrics U. Tex. Health Sci. Ctr., San Antonio, 1976-79, asst. clin. prof. pediatrics and otorhinolaryngology; dir. Otitis Media Study Ctr., NIH, San Antonio, 1980-87, asst. prof. pediatrics Cornell Med. Ctr., 1987-89; assoc. dir. anti-inflammatory/pulmonary clin. rsch. pharm. div. Ciba-Geigy Corp., Summit, N.J., 1989-93, assoc. dir. cardiovascular clin. rsch. pharm. divsn., 1994—. Contbr. articles to profl. jours. Recipient Physician Recognition award, 1979, 82, 85. Republican. Roman Catholic. Office: Ciba-Geigy Corp Pharm Div 556 Morris Ave DEV-3081 Summit NJ 07901-1330

AVERY, MARGARET, make-up artist, singer; b. Lorain, Ohio, July 20, 1951; d. Joseph Raymond and Margaret Mae (Meszes) Nagy; m. Jim Avery; (div. 1981). Makeup artist Cinandre Salon, N.Y.C., 1975-77, freelance mags., commls., video, N.Y.C., 1977-90; freelance make-up artist, 1977-94; singer N.Y.C., 1985-94, Jan Wallmans, Trocadero, Angry Squire, Eighty Eights, Duplex, The Supper Club, N.Y.C.; spokesperson Complex 15 (moisturizer) Nat'l 1989, Schering Lab. Media (TV-Radio Press); vol. worker for Diana Vreeland, Met. Mus. of Art, N.Y.C., 1980-83. Makeup work for various mags. including Vogue, Self, Glamour, Mademoiselle, Harper's Bazaar, Elle, Bride's, Cosmopolitan, New Woman, Mirabella, New York, New York Times Mag., German Vogue, French Vogue, Italian Vogue, Harper's Queen, Brit. Vogue, Lears; makeup work for various notables including Goldie Hawn, Isabella Rosellini, Brooke Shields, Shari Belafonte, Paulina, Tracy Pollan, Nicolette Sheridan, Donna Dixon, Virginia Madsen, Dustin Hoffman, Victoria Principal, Lori Singer, Twyla Tharpe, Joanna Pacula, Barbara Bush, (photographers) Helmut Newton, Richard Avedon, Irving Penn, Denis Piel, Eric Boman, Deborah Turbeville, Andrea Blanche, Susan Shacter, Lord Snowdon, Al Pacino. Democrat. Roman Catholic. Office: Streeters 146 E 56th St 2d Fl New York NY 10022

AVERY, MARY ELLEN, pediatrician, educator; b. Camden, N.J., May 6, 1927; d. William Clarence and Mary (Miller) A. AB, Wheaton Coll., Norton, Mass., 1948, DSc (hon.), 1974; MD, Johns Hopkins U., 1952; DSc (hon.), Trinity Coll., 1976, U. Mich., 1975, Med. Coll. Pa., 1976, Albany Med. Coll., 1977, Med. Coll. Wis., 1978, Radcliffe Coll., 1978; MA (hon.), Harvard U., 1974; LHD (hon.), Emmanuel Coll., 1979, Northeastern U., 1981, Russell Sage Coll., 1983, Meml. U., Newfoundland, 1993. Intern Johns Hopkins Hosp., 1953-54, resident, 1954-57; research fellow in pediatrics Boston, 1957-59, Balt., 1959-69; assoc. prof. pediatrics Johns Hopkins U., 1964-69; prof., chmn. dept. pediatrics McGill U. Med. Sch., 1969-74; prof. pediatrics Harvard U., 1974—; physician-in-chief Montreal Children's Hosp., 1969-74, Children's Hosp. Med. Center, Boston, 1974-85; mem. Med. Rsch. Coun. Can.; mem. study sect. NIH, 1968-71, 84-88. Author: The Lung and Its Disorders in the Newborn Infant, 4th edit., 1981, (with A. Schaffer) Diseases of the Newborn, 1971, 6th edit. (with H.W. Taeusch and R. Ballard), 1991; (with G. Litwack) Born Early, 1984; author, editor: (with L. First) Pediatric Medicine, 1988, 2nd edit., 1994; also articles; mem. editorial bd. Pediatrics, 1965-71, Am. Rev. Respiratory Diseases, 1969-73, Am. Jour. Physiology, 1967-73, Jour. Pediatrics, 1974-84, Medicine, 1985, Johns Hopkins Med. Jour., 1978-82, Clin. and Investigative Critical Care Medicine, 1990, New Eng. Jour. Medicine, 1990. Trustee Wheaton Coll. (1965-85), Radcliffe Coll., Johns Hopkins U., 1982-88. Recipient Mead Johnson award in pediatric rsch., 1968, Trudeau medal Am. Thoracic Soc., 1984, Nat. Medal of Sci. NSF, 1991; Markle scholar in med. scis., 1961-66. Fellow AAAS (dir. 1989), NAS, Internat. Pediatric Assn. (standing com. 1986-89), Am. Acad. Pediatrics, Am. Acad. Arts and Scis., Royal Coll. Physicians and Surgeons Can.; mem. Can. Pediatric Soc., Am. Physiol. Soc., Soc. Pediatric Rsch. (pres. 1972-73), Brit. Pediatric Assn. (hon.), Inst. Medicine (coun. 1987), Am. Pediatric Soc. (pres. 1990), Phi Beta Kappa, Alpha Omega Alpha. Office: 221 Longwood Ave Boston MA 02115-5817

AVILES, YVETTE MARIE, human resources specialist; b. N.Y.C., Oct. 29, 1966; d. Gilbert Anthony and Zaida Luz (Alers) A. BA in Psychology, LaSalle U., 1988; postgrad., Fairleigh Dickson Univ., 1992—. Asst. mgr. Consumer Value Stores, Teaneck, N.J., 1988-89; sr. unit supr. Covenant House, N.Y.C., 1989; human resource recruiter Republic Nat. Bank, N.Y.C., 1990—. Mem. NAFE. Home: 164 Ft Lee Rd Teaneck NJ 07666-3901 Office: Butler TG/G Com 110 Summit Ave Montvaig NJ 07645

AVOLIO, WENDY FREEDMAN, speech and language pathologist; b. Phila., Feb. 24, 1953; d. Harold Stanley and Phyllis Maxine (Broodno) Freedman; m. Michael Howard Strauss, Aug. 31, 1975 (div. 1981); children: Nicole Erin, Mallary Blair; m. Mark Richard Avolio, Mar. 24, 1985. BS, Bradley U., 1973; MA, No. Ill. U., 1975. Speech-lang. pathologist Bartlett (Ill.) Sch. Dist., 1975-76, Proviso Area for Exceptional Children, Maywood, Ill., 1976-77, Cen. Reading and Speech Clinic, Mt. Prospect, Ill., 1977-78, Tucson Unified Sch. Dist., 1978-79, Handmaker Jewish Geriatric Ctr., Tucson, 1981; mgr. speech-lang. therapy program Dept. Econ. Security/Div. Devel. Disabilities, Tucson, 1981-86, So. Ariz. Spl. Edn. Coop., Vail, 1986-92, Amphitheater Sch. Dist., 1992—; cons. speech-lang. Parent Support Group, Tucson, 1981-87, Ariz. Adv. Com. For Deaf-Blind, Tucson, 1983-87; lang. cons. Community Outreach Program for Deaf, Tucson, 1983. Active youth and children com. Jewish Comty. Ctr., Tucson, 1986-88, Tucson Classics, 1989—; bd. dirs. Tucson Residence Found., 1993—. Mem. Am. Speech Lang. and Hearing Assn. (cert.), Ariz. Speech and Lang. Assn. Home: 3532 N Fiesta Del Sol Tucson AZ 85715-2013 Office: 701 W Wetmore Tucson AZ 85705

AVRAHAM, REGINA, retired secondary education educator; b. Ludenscheid, Germany, Aug. 15, 1935; Came to U.S., 1937.; d. Joseph and Feiga (Press) Artman; m. Josef Esa Abraham, Mar. 12, 1962; children: Randi Beth, Jesse Richard. BS, City Coll., N.Y.C., 1955. Elem. tchr. N.Y. Bd. Edn., 1955-63; tchr. N.Y. Bd. Edn., Bklyn., 1963-91; sci. and health magnet tchr. Bd. Edn., N.Y., 1987-91. Author: Our Founding Sisters, 1976, Readings in Life Science, 1986, Readings in Physical Science, 1986, The Downside of Drugs, 1988, Substance Abuse Treatment and Prevention, 1988, The Circulation System, 1989, The Digestive System, 1989, The Reproductive System, 1989; contbg. editor Tchr. Ctrs. Consortium, 1989. Woodrow Wilson fellow, 1989; named Tchr. of Yr., Bklyn. Sch. Bd., 1987. Mem. United Fed. Tchrs. Democratic. Home: 2218 Avenue P Brooklyn NY 11229-1508

AVRAM, HENRIETTE DAVIDSON, librarian, government official; b. N.Y.C., Oct. 7, 1919; d. Joseph and Rhea (Olsho) Davidson; m. Herbert Mois Avram, Aug. 23, 1941; children: Lloyd, Marcie, Jay. Student, CUNY, George Washington U.; ScD (hon.), So. Ill. U., 1977; DLitt (hon.), Rochester Inst. Tech., 1991; DSc (hon.), U. Ill., 1993. Systems analyst, methods analyst, programmer Nat. Security Agy., 1952-59; systems analyst Am. Rsch. Bur., 1959-61, Datatrol Corp., 1961-65; supervisory info. systems specialist Libr. of Congress, Washington, 1965-67, asst. coord. info. systems, 1967-70, chief MARC Devel. Office, 1970-76, dir. Network Devel. Office, 1976-80, dir. processing systems, network and automation planning, 1980-83, asst. libr. for processing svcs., 1983-89, assoc. libr. Collection Svcs., 1989-92; ret. Libr. Congress, 1992; chmn. network adv. com. Libr. of Congress, Washington, 1981-92, chmn. emerita network adv. com., 1992—; chair subcom. 2 sectional com. Z39 Am. Nat. Standards Inst., 1966-80 (recipient Meritorious Svc. award, 1992); chair RECON Working Task Force, 1968-73, Internat. Relations Round Table, 1986-87; chair subcom. 4 working group 1 on character sets Internat. Orgn. for Standardization, 1971-80; lectr. dept. library sci. Cath. U. Am., Washington, 1973—, mem. strategies for 80's com. Sch. Library and Info. Sci., 1980-81; mem. Com. for Coordination of Nat. Bibliog. Control, 1976-79, Linked Systems Project Policy Com., 1985-91; mem. steering com. MARC Internat. Network Study, 1975-90; bd. visitors Library and Learning Resources Com., 1980—; mem. internat. standards coordinating com. Info. Systems Standards Bd., 1983-86; del. to U.S. nat. com. UNESCO/Gen. Info. Program, 1983; chair internat. relations com. Nat. Info. Standards Orgn., 1983-92. Bd. editors: Jour. Library Automation, 1970-72; contbr. articles to profl. jours. Recipient Superior Svc. award Libr. of Congress, 1968, Margaret Mann citation, 1971, Fed. Woman's award, 1974, Achievement award ALA/Libr. Info. Tech. Assn., 1980, Meritorious Svc. award ANSI, 1992, Disting. Exec. Svc. award Fed. Govt., 1990; co-recipient Rsch. Libr. of Yr. award Assn. Coll. and Rsch. Libr. Acad., 1979. Fellow Internat. Fedn. Libr. Assns. and Instns. (chair working group on content designators 1972-77, chair profl. bd. 1979-81, mem. program mgmt. com. 1983-90, mem. exec. bd. 1983-87, 1st v.p. 1985-87); mem. ALA (bd. dirs., past pres. info sci. and automation div., John Ames Humphrey Forest Press award 1990, Melvil Dewey award 1981, Lippincott award 1988), Am. Soc. Info. Sci. (spl. interest group on libr. automation and networks 1965), Spl. Librs. Assn. (Recognition award 1990), Assn. Libr. and Info. Sci. Edn., Assn. Bibliog. Agys. Gt. Britain, Australia, Can. and U.S. (del. 1977—). Home: 1776 Elton Rd Silver Spring MD 20903-1701 Office: Libr of Congress Washington DC 20540

AWALT, MARILENE KAY, principal; b. Mineral Wells, Tex., Mar. 20, 1942; d. Pat O. T. and Mary Lee (Curry) Morse; children: Stacy (dec.), Bradley. B.S., Tex. Wesleyan Coll., 1966; M.S. in Edn., Baylor U., 1972; Ph.D., George Peabody Coll., Vanderbilt U., 1988. Cert. tchr., prin., supr. Elem. tchr. San Antonio Pub. Schs., 1966, LaVega Pub. Schs., Waco, Tex., 1966-68; with reading clinic Baylor U., Waco, 1969-70; tchr. reading Franklin Spl. Schs. (Tenn.), 1970-71, first grade tchr., 1971-80, asst. prin., 1980-84, prin., 1984-90; prin. Moore Elem. Sch., Franklin, 1990—. Mem. adv. council for tchr. cert. and edn. Tenn. State Sch. Bd., 1977-86; adminstr. career level III State of Tenn., 1987—. Tenn. spl. scholar, 1983-84. Named Tenn. Elem. Prin. of Yr., 1994. Mem. ASCD (bd. dirs. 1992—, exec. coun. 1995—), Mid. Tenn. Coun. Internat. Reading Assn., Internat. Reading Assn., Tenn. Assn. Supervision and Curriculum Devel. (pres. 1986-87, 92-93, exec. sec. 1993—), Tenn. Bd. of Examiners for State for Approval of Tchr. Edn., Delta Kappa Gamma (pres. Rho chpt.). Baptist. Co-author Religious Christian Day Sch. Curriculum, 1978; author: Study Book for 6-8 Year Olds, 1980; chmn. for revision elem. cert. State of Tenn. Office: Moore Elem Sch 1061 Lewisburg Pike Franklin TN 37064-6727

AXELROD, BERNADETTE BONNER, television director, producer; b. Honolulu, Hawaii, Mar. 7, 1963; d. Horace Teddlie and Florence Ayson (Suyat) B. Student, Loyola Marymount U., 1981-82; BS in Broadcast Journalism, U. Ill., 1985. Prodn. asst. Sta. KITV-TV (ABC), Honolulu, 1984; studio technician Sta. WCIA-TV (CBS), Champaign, Ill., 1984; teaching asst. U. Ill., Champaign, 1984-85; programming coord. People's Choice TV, Rantoul, Ill., 1985; dir., tech. dir. Sta. WICS-TV (NBC), Springfield, Ill., 1985-89; producer, dir. Sta. KPLR-TV, St. Louis, 1989-90, Sta. WFLD-TV, Chgo., 1990—; prodr. Children's Miracle Network Telethon, Springfield, 1988-89, dir., St. Louis, 1990; speaker St. Louis Sch. Partnership Program, 1990, U. Ill., Champaign, 1994; dir. Fox News Chgo., 1990; prodr., dir. A Sleek Preview, 1993, Bumper to Bumper, 1994. Recipient 3 Midwest Emmy award nominations, 1993, 2 nominations, 1994. Mem. NATAS, Dirs. Guild Am. (coun. mem. 1994—), Dir. Guild Am. (East/Midwest coun. mem.), Kappa Tau Alpha, Phi Kappa Phi. Roman Catholic. Office: Sta WFLD Fox 32 444 N Michigan Ave Ste 2000 Chicago IL 60611-3902

AXELROD, LEAH JOY, tour company executive; b. Milw., Sept. 7, 1929; d. Harry J. and Helen Janet (Ackerman) Mandelker; m. Leslie Robert Axelrod, Mar. 10, 1951; children: David Jay, Craig Lewis, Harry Besser, Garrick Paul, Bradley Neal, Nell Anne. BS, U. Wis., 1951. Creative drama specialist Highland Park Parks & Recreation Dept., Ill., 1962-82; program specialist Pub. Libr., Highland Park, 1972-82; ednl. cons. Bd. Jewish Edn., Chgo., 1973-80; children's edn. specialist Jewish Community Ctr., Chgo., 1975-82; tour cons. My Kind of Town Tours, Highland Park, 1975-79, pres., 1979—; co-owner Tours at the Mart, 1992—. Editor: Highland Park: All American City, 1976. Co-author: Highland Park By Foot or By Frame, 1980; Highland Park: American Suburb, 1982. Bd. dirs. Midwest Fedn. Temple Sisterhoods, 1975-79, Midwest Zionist Youth Commn.; pres. B'nai Torah Sisterhood, 1982-84; founding mem., v.p. Highland Park Hist. Soc., pres. 1987-94, past pres., 1994—; bd. dirs. Ill. State Hist. Soc., 1989—; founder, bd. dirs. Chgo. Jewish Hist. Soc.; mem. exec. com. Apple Tree Theatre Co., mem. at large, mem. adv. bd.; active Highland Park Historic Preservation Commn. Mem. Nat. Assn. Women Bus. Owners, Am. Theatre Assn., Ill. Theatre Assn. (dir. creative dramatics 1977-79), Hadassah Club (Highland Park chpt.), Chgo. Area Women's History Conf. Bd., Coun. for Ill. History, North Shore Sr. Ctr. (assoc. bd. mem.) Home: 2100 Linden Ave Highland Park IL 60035-2516 Office: My Kind of Town Tours Inc PO Box 924 Highland Park IL 60035-0924

AXNER, CAROL CHRISTIE, elementary school educator; b. Altoona, Pa., Feb. 6, 1947; d. Robert Walter and Emilie Elizabeth (Boehling) Christie; m. Gerald Frederick Axner II, July 11, 1970. BS in Elem. Edn., Valparaiso U., 1969; MAT, Manhattanville Coll., 1973. Cert. tchr., N.Y. Tchr. St. John's Luth. Sch., Glendale, N.Y., 1969-70, Ossining (N.Y.) Union Free Sch. Dist., 1970—; asst. dir. No. Westchester-Putnam Tchr. Ctr., North Salem, N.Y., 1988-91; dir. Ossining Staff Devel. Ctr., 1992—; mem. N.Y. State Task Force on Tchr. Ctrs., Albany, 1992—. Mem. ASCD, Ossining Tchrs. Assn., N.Y. State United Tchrs. (del. 1982—), AFT (del. 1981—), Nat. Staff Devel. Coun. Home: 24 Coventry Circle Mahopac NY 10541 Office: Ossining Staff Devel Ctr Claremont School Ossining NY 10562

AXTELL-KOCH, AMY ANN, therapist; b. Livingston, N.J., Apr. 14, 1965; d. William Bicket and Adeline Patricia (Resciniti) Axtell; m. Douglas John Koch, Oct. 30, 1993. BA in Psychology, U. Ariz., 1987, MA in Counseling and Guidance, 1991. Cert. eating disorder specialist. Visitation supr. Child Protective Svcs., Tucson, Ariz., 1989-90; psychotherapist Desert Hills Counseling, Tucson, 1991—; lectr. on eating disorders U. Ariz., 1991-94. Mem. Ariz. Counselors Assn., Internat. Assn. Eating Disorder Profls., So. Ariz. Task Force Against Domestic Violence. Democrat. Office: Desert Hills Counseling 2002 W Anklam Tucson AZ 85745

AXTHELM, M. BONNIE, advertising executive. Pres., CEO, bd. dirs. Media Networks, Inc., Stamford, Conn. Office: Media Networks Inc 1 Station Pl Stamford CT 06902*

AYACH, MARY See HOLDEN, MARY

AYALA, ROWENA WINIFRED, principal; b. Detroit; d. Reginald Peter Ayala, Sept. 17, 1955; children: Kevin, Terrence, Peter, Kathryn, Gail, Gladys. BS, Mich. State U., 1955; MEd, Marygrove Coll., 1972; EdD, Wayne State U., 1977. Tchr. Cass Tech. High Sch., Detroit, 1967-75; jr. adminstrv. asst. Detroit Pub. Schs., 1975-80; prin. Crockett Adult Edn. & Career Ctr., Detroit, 1980—; bd. dirs. Crockett Tech. High Sch., Detroit, 1980—. Mem. Jack and Jill Am., Detroit, Great Lakes chpt. of the Links, Inc.; bd. dirs. Barat Human Svcs., Detroit. Recipient Disting. Svc. award Mich. Black Coll. Alumni Assn., 1987, Achievement award Booker T. Washington Assn., 1990. Mem. NAACP (life), Am. Vocat. Assn., Mich. Assn. Secondary Sch. Prins., Mich. Assn. Health Occupation (hon. life), Orgn. Sch. Adminstrs. and Suprs., Met. Area Svc. Orgn., Alpha Kappa Alpha, Phi Delta Kappa. Roman Catholic. Home: 19444 Parkside Rd Detroit MI 48221 Office: Crockett Tech High Sch 571 Mack Ave Detroit MI 48201-2137

AYCOCK, ALICE, artist; b. Harrisburg, Pa., 1946; d. Jesse N. and Alyce F. (Haskins) A. B.A., Douglass Coll., 1968; M.A., Hunter Coll., 1971. Tchr. Hunter Coll., N.Y.C., 1972-73; asst. prof. Hunter Coll., 1982-85, Sch. Visual Arts, 1977-78, 79-82, 91-92; dir. grad. sculpture studies Yale U., 1988-92; vis. tchr. sculpture Princeton U., spring 1979. One-woman exhbns. include, 112 Green St. Gallery, N.Y.C., 1974, 77, Williams Coll. Mus. Art, 1974, Studies for a Town, projects room Mus. Modern Art, N.Y.C., 1977-78, Portland (Oreg.) Center Visual Arts, 1978, How to Catch and Manufacture Ghosts; The Machine that Makes the World, John Weber Gallery, N.Y.C., 1978, 79, U. R.I., 1978, Project entitled "The Angels Continue Turning the Wheels of the Universe Despite their Ugly Souls...", Salvatore Ala, Milan, Italy, 1978, Projects for PCA 4 at Phila. Coll. Art, 1978, Cranbrook Acad. Art, Bloomfield Hills, Mich., 1978, Projects and Proposals at Muhlenberg Coll., Allentown, Pa., 1979, Explanation, An, of Spring and the Weight of Air, Contemporary Art Center, Cin., 1979, San Francisco Art Inst., 1979, Protetch-McIntosh Gallery, Washington, 1979, U. Mass., Amherst, 1979, Inst. Art and Urban Resources, Long Island City, 1980, Ghosts, U. Calif.-Irvine, 1980, Protetch-McIntosh Gallery, Washington, 1980, The Game of Fliers, Washington Public Arts, (D.C.), 1980, The Large Scale Dis/Integration of Micro-Electronic Memories, Battery Park City Landfill, N.Y.C., 1980, Collected Ghost Stories from the Workhouse, U. South Fla., Tampa, 1980, The Savage Sparkler, State U. Plattsburgh, N.Y., 1981, A Theory for Universal Causality (Time/Creation Machines), Lawrence Oliver Gallery, Phila., 1982, (outdoor work) The Miraculating Machine in the Garden (Tower of the Winds), Douglass Coll., New Brunswick, N.J., 1982, The Nets of Soloman, Phase II, Mus. Contemporary Art, Chgo., 1983, The Thousand and One Nights in the Mansion of Bliss, Protetch McNeil Gallery, N.Y.C., 1983, (outdoor work) The Solar Wind, Roanoke Coll., Salem, Va., 1983, The Thousand and One Nights in the Mansion of Bliss., Wurttembergischer Kunstverein, Stuttgart, W. Ger., 1983, Salisbury State Coll., Md., 1984, Serpentine Gallery, London, 1985, Sheldon Meml. Art Gallery, Lincoln, Nebr., 1985, Graz, Austria, 1985, Three-Fold Manifestations, N.Y.C., 1987, Kansas city (Mo.) Art Inst., 1987, Galerie Walter Storms, Fed. Republic Germany, 1987, Kunstforum, Fed. Republic Germany, 1987, SUNY Coll., Buffalo, 1988, John Weber Gallery, N.Y.C., 1988, 90, City Gallery Contemporary Art, Raleigh, N.C., 1989, Atlantic Arts Ctr., 1989, Storm King Art Ctr., Mountainville, N.Y., 1990, Yoshiaki Inove Gallery, Osaka, Japan, 1990, Galerie Grita Insam, Vienna, Austria, 1991, John Weber Gallery, N.Y.C., 1993, Sean Kelley Studio, Kansas City, 1993; outdoor works include Maze, New Kingston, Pa., 1972, Low Bldg. with Dirt Roof, New Kensington, 1973, Williams Coll. Project, 1974, Simple Network of Underground Wells and Tunnels, Far Hills, N.J., 1975, Circular Bldg. with Narrow Ledges for Walking, Silver Springs, 1976, Wooden Shacks on Stilts with Platform, Hartford Art Sch., Conn., 1976, The Beginnings of a Complex, Kassel, W. Ger., 1977, Artpark, Lewiston, N.Y., 1977, On the Eve of the Indsl. Revolution, Bloomfield Hills, 1978, Bushnami Sculpture Pk., nr. Houston, 1986, Carmeier Sculpture Pk., St. Louis, 1986, Central Pk. South, N.Y.C., 1987, Kunstforum, Munich, Germany, 1987, Western Wash. U., Bellingham, 1987, SUNY, Buffalo, 1988, Estate of J. Orton Jr., La Jolla, Calif., 1989, Abington Art Ctr., Jenkintown, Pa., 1990, U. Mich., Ann Arbor, 1991, project New 107th Police Precinct, N.Y.C., 1992, project U. Nebr. Med. Ctr., Omaha, 1993; group exhbns. since 1971 include Documenta 6, Kassel, W. Ger., 1977, Venice Biennial, Italy, 1978, The Angels Continue Turning the Wheels of the Universe: Part II, Stedelijk Mus., Amsterdam, 1978, Whitney Biennial, Whitney Mus. Am. Art., N.Y.C., 1978, 79, 81; Ft. Worth Art Mus., 1980, Machineworks, Inst. Contemporary Art, U. Pa., Phila., 1981, Hoodo (Laura) Vertical and Horizontal Cross Sections of the Ether Wind, Hirshhorn Mus. and Sculpture Garden, Washington, 1981, 84, Past-Present-Future, Wurttembergischer Kunstverein, Stuttgart, Ger., 1982, Nets of Solomon (permanent installations), Fattoria de Celle, Pistoria, Italy, 1982, The Leonardo Swirl II, Middelheim, Antwerp, Belgium, 1983, Houston Festival for Arts, Texas, 1984, Société des Expositions, Brussels, 1984-85, Environmental and Sculpture Exhbn., Lake Biwa, Japan, 1984, Contemporary Sculpture Exhbn., Toledo Mus. Art, 1984, Modern Machines, Whitney Mus., N.Y.C., 1985, Resource and Response, Sheldon Meml. Art Gallery, Lincoln, Nebr., 1985, John Weber Gallery, New York, 1986-88, 91, La Jolla Mus. Contemporary Art, Calif., 1986, Sitings Threefold Manifestation, Tel Aviv Mus., 1986, Documenta 8, 1987, Kunstmuseum, Luzern, Switzerland, 1987, Hudson River Mus., Yonkers, N.Y., 1988, Jack Shainman Gallery, N.Y., 1988, Cin. Art Mus., 1988, Santa Barbara (Calif.) Mus., 1990, CEAAC, Strasbourg, France, 1990, Storm King Art Center, Mountainville, N.Y., 1991, Mus. fur Moderne Kunst, Berlin, 1991-92, Chgo. Cultural Ctr., 1993; contbr. articles to profl. jours. Grantee CAPS, 1976, CUNY, 1983; fellow Nat. Endowment Arts, 1975, 80, 86. Office: care John Weber Gallery 142 Greene St New York NY 10012-3236*

AYCOCK, PAMELA GAYLE, assistant underwriter; b. Kenansville, N.C., July 22, 1961; d. Herbert Carol and Judith Ann (Thigpen) A. Assoc. Bus. Adminstrn., James Sprunt Community Coll., 1990; student, N.C. State U., 1979-80. Cert. ins. svc. rep., profl. ins. woman; lic. ins. agt. Adminstrv. specialist Brown & Root, Inc., Bay City, Tex., 1980-81, Houston, 1981-83; litigation supr. Brown & Root, U.S.A., Houston, 1983-85; underwriting asst. Interstate Casualty Ins., Kinston, N.C., 1985-89; account exec. SIA Group, Jacksonville, N.C., 1989—. Author: East Duplin Boosters Club Athletic Program, 1987, 88. Mem. com. Wallace (N.C.) Area Cancer Fund, 1990. Mem. NAFE, DAR (award 1979), Am. Soc. Quality Control (charter Gulf Coast sect., sec. 1980-81, chmn. publicity 1980-82), Onslow Assn. Ins. Profls. (membership com. 1991-93, Cystic Fibrosis chmn. 1991-92), N.C. Assn. Ins. Women (bd. dirs. 1990—, publicity chmn. 1991-92, membership chmn. 1992-93, by-laws chmn. 1993-94, state v.p. 1992-93, state pres.-elect 1993-94, state pres. 1994-95). Democrat. Baptist. Home: 1100 Cypress Creek Wallace NC 28466-9412

AYDELOTTE, MYRTLE KITCHELL, nursing administrator, educator, consultant; b. Van Meter, Iowa, May 31, 1917; d. John J. and Larava Josephine (Gutshall) Kitchell; m. William O. Aydelotte, June 22, 1956; children—Marie Elizabeth, Jeannette Farley. B.S., U. Minn., 1939, M.A., 1947, Ph.D., 1955; postgrad., Columbia U. Tchrs. Coll., summer 1948. Head nurse Charles T. Miller Hosp., St. Paul, 1939-41; surg. teaching St. Mary's Hosp. Sch. Nursing, Mpls., 1941-42; instr. U. Minn., 1945-49; dir., dean State U. Iowa Coll. Nursing, 1949-57, prof., 1957-62; assoc. chief nurse VA Hosp. Rsch. for Nursing, Iowa City, 1963-64, chief nursing rsch., 1964-65; prof. U. Iowa Coll. Nursing, 1964-76, 82-88; exec. dir. Am. Nurses Assn., 1977-81; dir. nursing U. Iowa Hosps. and Clinics, 1968-76; mem. sci. adv. bd. Ctr. for Health Rsch. Wayne State U., 1972-76, Inst. Medicine, 1973—; cons. U. Minn., 1970, 82, 90, U. Rochester, 1971, U. Mich., 1970, 73, U. Colo., 1970-71, U. Hawaii, 1972-73, Ariz. State U., 1972, U. Nebr., 1972-73. Contbr. articles to profl. jours.; editorial bd.: Nursing Forum, 1969-72, Jour. Nursing Adminstrn, 1971. Mem., v.p. Iowa City Library Bd., 1961-67; mem. Johnson County Bd. Health, 1967-70; mem. adv. com. on family living courses Iowa City Bd. Edn., 1970-72. Served with Army Nurse Corps, 1942-46. Mem. Am. Nurses Assn., Am. Hosp. Assn., Am. Acad. Nursing, Sigma Theta Tau (research com. 1968-72). Home: 201 N 1st Ave Apt 308 Iowa City IA 52245

AYERS, ANNE LOUISE, education services specialist; b. Albuquerque, Oct. 22, 1948; d. F. Ernest and Gladys Marguerite (Miles) A. BA, U. Kans., 1970; MEd, Seattle Pacific U., 1971. Staff cons. in student devel. Cen. Wash. State U., Ellensburg, 1971-72; dir. Aerospace Def. Command Resident Edn. Ctrs. for N.D. and Mont. Chapman Coll., Orange, Calif., 1972-74; instr. psychology Hampton (Va.) U., 1973-75; edn. svc. specialist Gen. Ednl. Devel. Ctr., Fort Monroe, Va., 1975-77; edn. specialist U.S. Army Transp. Sch., Ft. Eustis, Va., 1977-79, Nat. Mine Health and Safety Acad., Beckley, W.Va., 1979-89; edn. svcs. specialist NASA Hdqrs., Washington, 1989—; pres. Appalachian Love Arts, Martinsburg, W.Va., 1983—. Inventor decorative pen/thermometer holder/corsage, psychedelic jewelry process. Mem. Women in Aerospace, W.Va. Coun. Inventors, Am. Ednl. Rsch. Assn., Nat. Assn. Womens Deans Adminstrn. and Counselors, Internat. Platform Soc., Alumnus of Growing Vision (Century in Edn. award). Methodist. Home: 3021 Tanbridge St Martinsburg WV 25401-2914 Office: NASA Hdqrs Code FET 300 E St NW Washington DC 20546-0001

AYOTTE, STACY SINSKIE, accountant; b. Heidelburg, Germany, Aug. 11, 1959; (parents Am. citizens); d. Dale Edward and Marilyn Ella (White) Sinskie; m. Michael Anthony Ayotte, June 21, 1985; 1 child, Chad Vincent. BS summa cum laude, U. Southern Maine, 1981. Cert. mgmt. acct. Desk auditor Blue Cross Blue Shield of Maine, South Portland, 1981, auditor, 1981-86, sr. auditor, 1986-88, acctg. mgr., 1988—. Mem. Inst. Mgmt. Accts. (dir. manusripts 1992-93, dir. student activities 1993-94, sec. 1994), Phi Kappa Phi. Republican. Roman Catholic. Office: Blue Cross Blue Shield of Maine 2 Gannett Dr South Portland ME 04106

AYRAULT, EVELYN WEST, psychologist, writer; b. Buffalo, Mar. 3, 1922; d. John and Evelyn (West) A.; BS, Fla. State Coll. for Women, 1945; MA, U. Chgo., 1947. Chief psychologist, asst. prin. Crippled Children's Sch., Jamestown, N.D., 1947-48; psychologist, tchr. spl. edn. dept. Sharon (Pa.) Public Schs., 1948-50; chief psychologist, instr. Med. Coll. Va., Richmond, 1950-52; pvt. practice, psychology N.Y.C., 1952-68; clin. psychologist, Erie, Pa., 1968—; dir. psychol. services United Cerebral Palsy Assn., Miami, Fla., 1952-54, Erie County (Pa.) Crippled Children's Soc., 1968-78; mem. med. staff HealthSouth Great Lakes Rehab. Hosp., Erie, Pa., 1986—; psychol. cons. Shriners Hosp. for Crippled Children, Erie. Mem. Am. Pa. psychol. assns., Council for Exceptional Children, Psi Chi. Author: Take Step, 1963; You Can Raise Your Handicapped Child, 1964; Helping the Handicapped Teenager Mature, 1971; Growing Up Handicapped, 1978; Sex, Love, and the Physically Handicapped, 1981. Home: 10054 Law Rd North East PA 16428-3750

AYRES, JANICE RUTH, social service executive; b. Idaho Falls, Idaho, Jan. 23, 1930; d. Low Ray and Frances Mae (Salem) Mason; m. Thomas Woodrow Ayres, Nov. 27, 1953 (dec. 1966); 1 child, Thomas Woodrow Jr. (dec.). MBA, U. So. Calif., 1952, M in Mass Comms., 1953. Asst. mktg. dir. Disneyland, Inc., Anaheim, Calif., 1954-59; gen. mgr. Tamasha Town & Country Club, Anaheim, Calif., 1959-65; dir. mktg. Am. Heart Assn., Santa Ana, Calif., 1966-69; state exec. dir. Nev. Assn. Mental Health, Las Vegas, 1969-71; exec. dir. Clark Co. Easter Seal Treatment Ctr., Las Vegas, 1971-73; mktg. dir., fin devel. officer So. Nev. Drug Abuse Coun., Las Vegas, 1973-74; exec. dir. Nev. Assn. Retarded Citizens, Las Vegas, 1974-75; assoc., cons. Don Luke & Assocs., Phoenix, 1976-77; program dir. Inter-Tribal Coun. Nev., Reno, 1977-79; exec. dir. Ret. Sr. Vol. Program, Carson City, Nev., 1979—; conductor workshops in field. Elected to bd. suprs. Carson City, Nev., 1992—; commr. Carson City Parks and Recreation, 1993—; apptd. to gen. obligation bond com., Carson City; apptd. to N.W. Assn. for Transit Svcs., also legis. chair; bd. dirs. Nev. Dept. Transp., 1993; commr. V&TRR Commn., 1993; apptd. Nat. Cmty. Svc. Commn., 1994. Named Woman of Distinction, Soroptimist Club, 1988, Outstanding Dir. of Excellence, Gov. State of Nev., 1989, Outstanding Dir., Vol. Action Ctr., J.C. Penney Co.; named to Western Fairs Assn. Hall of Fame for outstanding contbns. to the fair industry, 1995. Mem. AAUW, Am. Mgmt. Assn. (bd. dirs.), Am. Mktg. Assn., Internat. Platform Assn., Nat. Pub. Rels. Soc. Am. (chpt. pres.), Women Radio & TV, Nat. Soc. Fund Raising Execs., Nev. Fair & Rodeo Assn. (pres.), Nev. Assn. Transit Svcs. (bd. dirs., legis. chmn). Home: 1624 Karin Dr Carson City NV 89706-2626 Office: Ret Sr Vol Program 801 N Division St Carson City NV 89703-3925

AYRES, JAYNE LYNN ANKRUM, community health nurse; b. Reed City, Mich., Oct. 12, 1944; d. Quinten Wayne and Marshia Agetha (Crum) Ankrum; m. Ronald Francis Ayres, Apr. 16, 1977; children: Linda, Michele, Julie. ADN, Manatee C.C., Bradenton, Fla., 1975. RN, Fla., Ga. Staff nurse med.-surg., cardiac, oncology and float team Sarasota (Fla.) Meml. Hosp., 1975-77; nursing supr. Upjohn Healthcare Svcs., Sarasota, 1981-85; staff nurse Devereux Found., Kennesaw, Ga., 1986-89; staff nurse, supr. Vis. Nurse Health Sys., Metro, Atlanta, 1989—. Vol. ARC, M.U.S.T. Ministries Health Clinic for Homeless. Mem. Am. Legion (hon.), Fla. Nurses Assn. (hon.), Beta Sigma Phi.

AYRES, MARY ELLEN, government official; b. Spokane, Wash., June 23, 1924; d. Frank H. and Marion (Kellogg) A. Student, U. Wash., 1942-43; B.A., Stanford U., 1946; postgrad., Am. U., 1960. With Henry von Morpurgo, Advt., 1946-47; reporter Wenatchee Daily World, Wash., 1947-50, Washington Post, 1951-52; with U.S. Fgn. Service, Dept. State, 1950-51; mem. editorial staff Changing Times, 1952-61; editor Family Guide, Kiplinger Washington Editors, 1958-61, Bur. Labor Stats., Manpower Adminstrn., U.S. Dept. Labor, 1962-67; pub. info. specialist Bur. Indian Affairs, U.S. Dept. Interior, 1967-75; writer-editor Bur. Labor Stats., 1975—; tchr. newsletter class Dept. Agriculture Grad. Sch., 1975-89, editing style and technique class, 1987-89; past treas. Govt. Info. Orgn. Mem. publicity com. Nat. Capitol YWCA, 1982-83; dir. Wenatchee High Sch. Scholarship Found., 1988—. Mem. Nat. Assn. Govt. Communicators (founding treas., dir. 1975-80, 89-91, chmn. Blue Pencil Contest 1987, nat. capital chpt. treas. 1989), Am. News Women's Club, Am. Econ. Assn., Stanford U. Alumnae Assn., Kappa Kappa Gamma. Episcopalian. Club: Nat. Press (Washington). Home: 2400 Virginia Ave NW Apt C802 Washington DC 20037-2656 Office: Bur Labor Stats 2 Mass Ave NE Washington DC 20212-0001

AZARYAN, ANAHIT VAZGENOVNA, biochemist, researcher; b. Yerevan, Armenia, Jan. 9, 1950; came to U.S., 1991; d. Vazgen Kh. and Dazy T. (Mirzoyan) A.; m. David B. Akopian, Jan. 30, 1981; 1 Child, Tigran. MD, Med. Sch., Yerevan, 1972; PhD, Inst. Molecular Biology, Moscow, 1979; Dr. Sc., Inst. Biochemistry, Yerevan, 1988. Prin. investigator Inst. Biochemistry, Yerevan, 1980-84, head proteolysis group, 1984-90; rsch. program vis. scientist Nat. Inst. Child Health and Human Devel./NIH, Bethesda, Md., 1991; rsch. assoc. dept. biochemistry Uniformed Svcs. U. Health Scis., Bethesda, 1992-94, sr. rsch. assoc. dept. pharmacology, 1994—. Author: Brain Peptide Hydrolases and Their Biological Functions, 1989; contbr. articles to Jour. Biol. Chem., Neurochem. Rsch., Jour. Neurosci. Rsch., others. Recipient fellowship Martin Luther U., Halle, Germany, 1983, fellowship N. Kline Inst. Psychiat. Rsch., N.Y.C., 1988, Travel award Internat. Soc. Neurochem.-FIDIA, Washington, 1991; Fogarty Internat. Ctr. Rsch. fellow, 1991. Mem. Internat. Soc. for Neurochemistry, European Soc. for Neurochemistry, Am. Soc. for Neuroscience, N.Y. Acad. Scis. Office: USPHS Dept Pharmacology 4301 Jones Bridge Rd Bethesda MD 20814

AZCUENAGA, MARY LAURIE, government official; b. Council, Idaho, July 25, 1945. AB, Stanford U., 1967; JD, U. Chgo., 1973. Atty. FTC, Washington, 1973-75, asst. to gen. counsel, 1975-76, staff atty. San Francisco regional office, 1977-80, asst. regional dir., 1980-81, asst. to exec. dir., 1981-82, litigation atty. Office of Gen. Counsel, 1982, asst. gen. counsel for legal counsel, 1983-84, commr., Washington, 1984—; mem. Adminstrv. Conf. of the U.S., 1990—. Trustee Food and Drug Law Inst., 1990—. Office: FTC 6th & Pennsylvania Ave NW Washington DC 20580-0002

AZÍOS, BLANCA STELLA, pediatrician, medical administrator, educator; b. Laredo, Tex., July 3, 1940; d. Enrique Luis and Blanca Stella (Zuniga) A. BA, U. St. Thomas, 1961; MD, U. Tex., 1965. Diplomate Am. Bd. Pediats. Intern in pediats. John Sealy Hosp., Galveston, Tex., 1965-66, resident in pediats., 1966-68; pediatrician Clinic of the Southwest, Houston, 1968-72, Southwest Pediat. Assn., Houston, 1972-94; asst. prof. Coll. Medicine, Baylor U., Houston, 1994—; med. dir. Harris County Cmty. Health Clinic, Houston, 1994—; attending pediatrician Harris County Hosp. Dist., Houston, 1994—; chief pediats. Meml. Hosp. Southwest, Houston, 1970-72, 84-91; pres., med. dir. Southwest Pediat. Assocs., Houston. 1979-94; attending physician Tex. Children's Hosp., Meth. Hosp., Hermann Hosp., Women's Hosp., Meml. Hosp., St. Luke's Hosp., Park Plz. Hosp. Fellow Am. Acad. Pediats.; mem. Tex. Pediatrician Soc., Harris County Med. Soc., Houston Pediat. Soc. Roman Catholic. Home: 10802 Vickijohn Ct Houston TX 77071 Office: Baylor U Dept Cmty Medicine One Baylor Plz Rm 650E Houston TX 77030

AZRACK, JOAN M., judge; b. 1951. BS, Rutgers Univ., N.J., 1974; JD, N.Y. Law Sch., 1979. With U.S. Dept. of Justice, 1979-81, U.S. Attorney's Office (N.Y. ea. dist.), 1982-90; magistrate judge U.S. Dist. Ct. (N.Y. ea. dist.), 2nd circuit, Brooklyn, 1991—. Office: US District Court 225 Cadman Plz East Rm 333 Brooklyn NY 11201-1876*

AZZARONE, CAROL ANN, advertising executive; b. Jersey City, Aug. 1, 1946; d. Paul Buglione and Catherine (DellaFave) LicCalsi; m. Dominick L. Azzarone, May 13, 1967 (div. 1989); children: Anthony Paul, Kathryn Ann. AA, Bergen Community Coll., 1982; BA, Ramapo Coll., 1984. Editorial asst. McGraw-Hill, Inc., N.Y.C., 1964-69; real estate agt. Auburn Realty, Inc., Bergenfield, N.J., 1975-80, Weichert Realty, Morris Plains, N.J., 1975—; pub. rels. coord. Ridgefield (N.J.) Bd. Edn., 1982-84; mktg. dir. Spa Lady Corp., Fairfax, Va., 1984-86, Newson Fitness, Morristown, N.J., 1986-88; creative dir. Publ. Corp., Morristown, 1988-90; advt. dir. RonTon Advt., Union, N.J., 1990—; advt. cons. Gianni Disegnatore, West Caldwell, N.J., 1991-92. Editor (newsletters) Ridgefield Sch. News, 1982-84, Cliffside Park Sch. News, 1984-85, The Grapevine, 1985-86. Mem. NOW, 1989—. N.J. Bell scholar N.J. Bell Corp., 1980, Bergen Community Coll. Alumni scholar, 1981. Mem. Advt./Pub. Rels. Assn., N.J. Advt. Club, Phi Theta Kappa. Democrat. Roman Catholic. Office: Ronton Advt 2285 Rte 22 W Union NJ 07083

BAAS, JACQUELYNN, art historian, museum administrator; b. Grand Rapids, Mich., Feb. 14, 1948. BA in History of Art, Mich. State U.; Ph.D. in History of Art, U. Mich. Registrar U. Mich. Mus. Art, Ann Arbor, 1974-78, asst. dir., 1978-82; editor Bull. Museums of Art and Archaeology, U. Mich., 1976-82; chief curator Hood Mus. Art, Dartmouth Coll., Hanover, N.H., 1982-84, dir., 1985-89; dir. Univ. Art Mus. and Pacific Film Archive, Berkeley, Calif., 1989—. Contbr. articles to jours. and catalogues. NEH fellow, 1972-73; Nat. Endowment Arts fellow, 1973-74, 87-88. Mem. Coll. Art Assn. Am., Print Council Am., Am. Assn. Museums, Assn. Art Mus. Dirs.. Office: Univ Art Mus and Pacific Film Archive 2625 Durant Ave Berkeley CA 94704-1710

BABA, MARIETTA LYNN, business anthropologist; b. Flint, Mich., Nov. 9, 1949; d. David and Lillian (Joseph) Baba; m. David Smokler, Feb. 14, 1977 (div. 1982); 1 child, Alexia Baba Smokler; m. Ronald Delon Glotta, June 23, 1990. BA with highest distinction, Wayne State U., 1971, MA in Anthropology, 1973, PhD in Phys. Anthropology, 1975; MBAMich. State U., 1994. Asst. prof. sci. and tech. Wayne State U., Detroit, Mich., 1975-80, assoc. prof. anthropology, 1980-88, prof., 1988—, spl. asst. to pres., 1980-82, econ. devel. officer, 1982-83, asst. provost, 1983-85; assoc. provost, 1985—, dir. Internat. Programs and Interim Assoc. Dean of Grad. Sch., 1988-89, assoc. dean grad. sch., 1989-90, acting chair Dept. Anthropology, 1990-92; program dir. transformations to quality orgns. program, dir. social, behav. and econ. scis. NSF, 1994—; founder, corp. officer Applied Rsch. Teams Mich., Inc., Detroit, Intelligent Techs., Inc., Detroit; evolution researcher Wayne State U., 1975-82; cons. GM Rsch. Labs., 1988-92, Electronic Data Systems, 1990—, McKinsey Global Inst., 1991; rsch. contractor GM/EDS, 1990—; program dir. Social Behaviorial and Econ. Scis. Nat. Sci. Found., 1994—. with USAF, SBIR, 1992—; lectr. nat. and internat. symposia, profl. confs. Contbr. numerous papers and abstracts to tech. jours; patentee in field. Bd. dirs. City-Univ. Consortium, Detroit, 1980-83; v.p. Neighborhood Svc. Orgn., Detroit, 1980-85; mem. State Rsch. Fund Feasibility Rev. Panel, 1982-94; mem. adv. panel on tech., innovation and U.S. trade U.S. Congl. Office Tech. Assessment, 1990-91, mem. panel on electronic enterprise, 1993-94; active Leadership Detroit Class IV, 1982-83; dir. Mich. Tech. Coun. (SE div.), 1984-85. Job Partnership Tng. Act grantee, 1981-90; NSF grantee, 1982, 84-85. Adv. editor for orgnl. anthropology American Anthropologist, 1990-93; Issued letters patent for method to map joint ventures and maps produced thereby. Fellow Am. Anthrop. Assn. (bd. dirs. 1986-88, exec. com. 1986-88, del. to the Internat. Union Anthrop. and Ethnol. Sci. 1990-94, chair global commn. anthropology, 1993—), Nat. Assn. Practice Anthropology (pres. 1986-88), Soc. Applied Anthropology, Phi Beta Kappa, Sigma Xi (Morton Fried award, 1991), Beta Gamma Sigma. Office: Wayne State U 137 Mackenzie Hall Detroit MI 48202

BABB, ROBERTA J., educational administrator; b. East Chicago, Ill., Jan. 5, 1944; d. Joseph A. and Katherine Phillips; m. Donald L. Babb, July 30, 1966; children: Sasha M., Holly S. BS in Edn., Ind. U., 1966; postgrad., De Paul U. Tchr. East Chicago Pub. Schs., Hammond (Ind.) Pub. Schs.; head tchr. The Lab Sch., Washington; co-founder, dir. Creme de le Creme, Houston. Scholar Ind. U., PTA.

BABBAGE, JOAN DOROTHY, journalist; b. Montclair, N.J., Jan. 10, 1926; d. Laurence Washburn and Dorothy A. (Davenport) Babbage; m. Vernon H. Ellsworth, Mar. 6, 1971. B.A. in English, Mt. Holyoke Coll., 1948; postgrad. Art Students League, New Sch. for Social Research. Publicist Paramount Internat. Films, N.Y.C., 1952-58; reporter Newark News, 1960-67, food editor, 1967-72; feature writer, reporter Star-Ledger, Newark, 1972—. Author: (with others) Past and Present Lives of New Jersey Women, 1990; contbr. bus. articles to New Jersey Business mag., articles to Official Dog mag. Operator rescue orgn. SaintSaver, N.J., N.Y., Pa.; v.p. jr. group Women's Nat. Republican Club, N.Y.C., 1955. Recipient recommendation award N.J. br. Humane Soc. U.S., PICA Club N.J. award, 1980, Community Media award Assn. Retarded Citizens, Morris County Unit, N.J., 1987, Willard H. Allen Agrl. Communications Media award, N.J. Agrl. Soc., 1988, Communicator of Yr. award N.J. Dept. Agriculture, 1990. Appeared on NBC-TV to demonstrate dog tng. Home: Washington St Montclair NJ 07042-4522 Office: Star-Ledger Court St Newark NJ 07101

BABBITT, HARRIET C., federal official; b. Charleston, W.Va., Nov. 13, 1947; d. Henry Bradbury II and Harriet (Edmunds) Coons; m. Bruce Babbitt, Aug. 9, 1969; children: Christopher E., Thomas J. Student, U. Madrid, 1967-68; BA in Spanish, Ariz. State U., 1969, JD, 1972. Bar: Ariz. 1972. Law clk. to Hon. Jack D.H. Hayes Ariz. Supreme Ct.; tchr. Ariz. State U.; atty. Robbins & Green, Phoenix, 1974-93; U.S. permanent rep. Orgn. Am. States, Dept. State, Washington, 1993—; bd. dirs. Citibank, Ariz. Mem. adv. bd. Bus. Jour.; contbr. articles to profl. jours. and newspapers. Mem. delegation to monitor elections in Nicaragua, 1990; mem. Medal of Peace adv. panel U.S. Inst. Peace, 1992; co-chairwoman Women for Clinton-Gore, Ariz.; active Coun. for Am. Land Conservancy; mem. bd. sponsors Planned Parenthood Ctrl. and No. Ariz.; bd. dirs. Nat. Dem. Inst. Internat. Affairs, Alan Guttmacher Inst. Mem. Chpt. 100 Ariz. (founding mem.), Internat. Women's Forum (founding mem. Ariz. chpt.). Office: Dept of State 2201 C St NW Rm 6494 Washington DC 20520*

BABBITT, KATHY JEAN, public relations executive, marketing executive, consultant; b. Westfield, N.Y., Oct. 9, 1950; d. Clarence Randy and Boots (Florence Porter) Johnson; m. David Clair Babbitt, Feb. 14, 1970; children: Jeannette, Kimberly, Dione. Student, Lancaster (Pa.) Coll. of Bible, 1968-69; grad., Moody Bible Inst. Evang. Sch., 1972-74, East Tenn. State U., 1975, Ecole de Commerce, Neuchatel, Switzerland, 1977, U. Neuchatel, 1978, Austin C. C., 1989. Missionary Mission Aviation Fellowship, Zaire, 1978-81; comml. artist Christian Printing Svc., Anaheim, Calif., 1981; newscaster Sta. KABN Radio, Big Lake, Ark., 1983-84; owner Babbitt and Assocs. Mktg. and Pub. Rels., Palmer, Alaska, 1984-86, Flowery Branch, Ga., 1986-88, Austin, Tex., 1988-91, Claypool, Ind., 1991—; cons. in field; lectr. in life mgmt.; instr. writing courses. Author: Habits of the Heart, 1990 (1st pl. award 1991); editor: Downscaling, 46510, 1993 (1st pl. Nat. award 1993), Downscaling; Simplify and Enrich Your Lifestyle, 1993 (1st pl. Nat. award 1993); host talk show, 1995. Missionary Mission Aviation Fellowship, Zaire, Africa, 1978-81; promotional designer Edna Devries for State Senate, Palmer, 1984; campaign mgr. Al Strawn for Borough Mayor, Palmer, 1984-85; organizer youth employment opportunities, 1985. Recipient 1st Pl. award for pub. affairs Pub. Rels. Soc. Am., 1985, 1st Pl. award for speaking Toastmasters, 1985, 15 awards plus Sweepstakes award Alaska Press Women, 1986, 7 1st Pl., 3 2nd, 1 3rd Pl. award Women's Press Club Ind., 1994. Mem. Tex. Press Women (1st pl. Gym brochure 1989, publrs. resource group brochure 1990), Nat. Fedn. Press Women. (3rd Pl. pub. affairs 1986, 4-color brochure 1994, 1st Pl. 2-color brochure, 1988, nat.

award 1993). Republican. Evangelical. Home and Office: 8782 S Fisherman Cove Claypool IN 46510-9801

BABCOCK, BARBARA ALLEN, lawyer, educator; b. Washington, July 6, 1938; d. Henry Allen and Doris Lenore (Moses) B.; m. Thomas C. Grey, Aug. 19, 1979. AB, U. Pa., 1960; LLB, Yale U., 1963. Bar: Md. 1963, D.C. 1964, JD (hon.), U. San Diego 1983, U. Puget Sound, 1988. Law clk. U.S. Ct. Appeals D.C., 1963; assoc. Edward Bennett Williams, 1964-66; staff atty. Legal Aid Agy., Washington, 1966-68; dir. Pub. Defender Svc. (formerly Legal Aid Agy.), 1968-72; assoc. prof. Stanford U., 1972-77, prof., 1977—; asst. atty. gen. U.S. Dept. Justice, 1977-79. Ernest W. McFarland Prof. Law, 1986—. Democrat. Author: (with others) Sex Discrimination and The Law, 1975; (with Carrington) Civil Procedure, 1977; contbr. articles to profl. jours. Home: 835 Mayfield Ave Palo Alto CA 94305-1052 Office: Stanford U Sch Law Stanford CA 94305

BABCOCK, JANICE BEATRICE, health care coordinator; b. Milw., June 2, 1942; d. Delbert Martin and Constance Josephine (Dworschack) B. BS in Med. Tech., Marquette U., 1964; MA in Healthcare Mgmt. and Supervision, Cen. Mich. U., 1975. Registered med. technologist and microbiologist., clin. lab. scientist, epidemiologist; cert. bioanalytical lab. mgr. Intern St. Luke's Hosp., Milw., 1963-64; microbiologist St. Michael's Hosp., Milw., 1964-65; supr. clin. lab. svc. VA Regional Office, Milw., 1965-66; hosp. epidemiologist VA Ctr., Milw., 1966-74, supr. anaerobic microbiology and rsch. lab., 1974-78, adminstrv. officer, chief med. tech., 1978-83, quality assurance coord., 1983-86, asst. to chief of staff profl. svcs., 1986-92; coord. constrn. vet. affairs outpatient clinic VHA Med. Ctr., Milw., 1992-94; coord. Coop. Adminstrv. Support Unit (CASU) VHA Nat. Ctr. for Cost Containment, Milw., 1993-94; health sys. specialist managed care/primary care VHA Managed Care, Milw., 1994—; lectr. Marquette U., 1966-86, U. Wis., 1966-86, Med. Coll. Wis., 1966-86. Contbr. numerous articles to profl. jours. Rec. sec. Wis. Svc. League, 1989-92, corr. sec., 1991. Recipient Wood VA Fed. Woman's award, 1975, Profl. Achievement award Lab. World jour., 1981, Disting. Alumni award Cen. Mich. U., 1986. Fellow Royal Soc. Health, Am. Acad. Med. Adminstrs. (Wis. state Dir. of the Yr. award 1989, Diplomate 1989, mem. editorial bd. Exec. jour. 1987—, editor 1994, regional dir. 1992—, mem. fed. exec. coun. 1994—); mem. Internat. Acad. Healthcare Mgmt., Internat. Soc. of Tech. Assessment in Health Care, Am. Soc. Microbiology, Am. Coll. Healthcare Execs., Am. Soc. Med. Tech. (Nat. Sci. Creativity award 1974, Nat. Microbiology Sci. Achievement award 1978, Mem. of the Yr. award 1979, Profl. Achievement Lectureship award 1981, French Lectureship award 1983), Assn. for Health Svcs. Rsch., Assn. Marquette U. Women (bd. dirs. 1987-93, v.p., sec.), Assn. Mil. Surgeons U.S. (lifetime), Nat. Assn. Med. Staff Svcs. (mem. editorial bd. Overview Jour. 1990-93), Wis. Assn. Med. Staff Svcs., Wis. Hosp. Assn., Fed. Execs. Assn. (Milw. 1983—), Alpha Mu Tau (pres. 1984-85), Alpha Delta Theta, Sigma Iota Epsilon, Alpha Delta Pi (Alumni Honor award 1979). Home: 6839 Blanchard St Milwaukee WI 53213-2853 Office: VHA Med Ctr 5000 W National Ave Milwaukee WI 53295-0002

BABLADELIS, GEORGIA, retired psychology educator; b. Manistique, Mich., Jan. 30, 1931; d. Alexander and Panayota Babladelis. BA, U. Mich., 1953; MA, U. Calif., Berkeley, 1957; PhD, U. Colo., 1960. Sr. clin. psychologist Guidance Clinic, Ala. County Probation Dept., 1960-63; prof. psychology Calif. State U., Hayward, 1963-94, prof. emerita, 1994—; cons. Calif. Sch. Profl. Psychology, Berkeley, 1979—; U.S. dir. rsch. UNESCO, 1979; lectr. in field. Author: The Study of Personality, 1985; co-author: The Shaping of Personality, 1967; editor Psychology of Women Quar., 1974-82, Computer Users Newsletter, 1984-87; contbr. articles to profl. jours. Chosen One of 100 Outstanding Women in Psychology, Divsn. 35 APA, 1992; grantee USPHS, NIMH, NSF, others, 1969-79. Fellow APA, The Psychology of Women Soc. (divsn. 35), The Soc. for Study of Sotical Issues (divsn. 9).

BABRAUCKAS, THERESA LOUISE, computer engineer; b. Chardon, Ohio, Nov. 25, 1965; d. Frank Michael Benyo and Bonnie Louise (Gardner) McGimpsey; m. Robert Joseph Babrauckas, Aug. 20, 1988. BS, Kent State U., 1988; MS, Case Western Res. U., 1994. Lab. technician Liquid Crystal Inst., Kent, Ohio, 1985-88; jr. physicist Bicron Corp., Newbury, Ohio, 1987-89; computer engr. NASA Lewis Rsch. Ctr., Cleve., 1989—; exemplar, sci. tutor Ohio Acad. Sci., Columbus, 1990—. Office: NASA Lewis Rsch Ctr 21000 Brookpark Rd # 11 Cleveland OH 44135-3127

BABYLON, DEBRA SUE, artist, educator; b. Findlay, Ohio, Feb. 26, 1956; d. Charles C. Hatfield and June Ilene (Cramer) Anderson. BFA magna cum laude, Bowling Green State U., 1979, MFA in Painting, 1981. Rsch. asst. grad. sch. Bowling Green State U. Sch. Art, 1979-80, grad. teaching asst., 1980-81, instr., 1981-85; instr. Toledo (Ohio) Mus. Art, 1981-85; adj. prof. Mesa C.C., San Diego, 1988-90, San Diego City Coll., 1990—, U. San Diego, 1990—; juror San Diego Art Inst. Exhbn., 1991, 94. Exhibited in group shows at San Diego Art Inst., 1987, 90, 93, San Bernardino County (Calif.) Mus., 1993, Butler Inst. Am. Art, Youngstown, Ohio, 1993, Art of Calif. Mag. Discovery Awards Competition, 1993; represented in permanent collections at Gallery Yolanda, Chgo., Barrett Galleries, Toledo, Rosenthal Gallery, Chgo., Malton Gallery, Cin., The Aesthetics Collection Gallery, San Diego; also pvy. collections. Recipient 2d Place of Show Ft. Wayne Regional, 1982, 1st Pl. 2D Ann. Lima Area Art Exhbn., 1983, 1st Pl. Fine Arts Exhbn. Ohio State Fair, 1983, 1st Pl. and Roulet medal for excellence Toledo Area Artists' Exhbn., 1984, Best of Show Lima Area Art Exhbn., 1985, Silver award 1993 Discovery awards. Office: San Diego City Coll 1313 12th Ave San Diego CA 92101

BACA, POLLY, state senator; b. La Salle, Colo., Feb. 13, 1941; B.A. in Polit. Sci., Colo. State U., 1962; postgrad. Am. U., 1966-67; children—Monica, Mike. Editorial asst. dept. research and edn. Internat. Brotherhood Pulp, Sulphite and Paper Mill Workers, AFL-CIO, Washington, 1962-65; editor Airline News mag., legis. aide Brotherhood Ry. and Airline Clks., AFL-CIO, Washington, 1966-67; public info. officer Interagy. Com. on Mexican-Ams., The White House, Washington, 1967-68; nat. dep. dir. Viva Kennedy div. Nat. Robert F. Kennedy for Pres. Campaign, Washington, 1968; dir. research services and info. Nat. Council of La Raza, Phoenix, 1968-70; dir. div. Spanish-speaking affairs, spl. asst. to chmn. Dem. Nat. Com., Washington, 1971-72; dir., pres. Bronze Publs., Inc., Denver, 1972-74; mem. Colo. Ho. of Reps., 1975-78, chmn. Dem. caucus, 1977-78, vice chmn. house rules com., 1975-76; mem. Colo. Senate, 1979—; dir. Fed. Home Loan Bank, Topeka, 1979—; mem. nat. adv. council Fed. Savs. and Loan Assns., 1980-81. Mem. exec. com., state sec. Colo. Young Dems., 1960-62; del. or alt. Nat. Dem. Conv., 1974, 76, 78, 80, co-chmn., 1980, 84; Dem. nat. committeewoman from Colo., 1973—; vice chmn. procedures and rules com. Dem. Nat. Com., 1978, mem. compliance rev. com., 1979-80, mem. exec. com., 1977—, vice chmn., 1981—; chmn. Colo. del. to Nat. Dem. Mid-Term Conf., 1978; Rocky Mountain states coordinator Carter/Mondale Presdl. Campaign, 1979; Dem. candidate for U.S. Congress from 4th Dist. of Colo., 1980; mem. Adams County Dem. Central Com., 1973—, Colo. Dem. Exec. Com., 1973—; participant Camp David Domestic Summit, 1979; participant Am. Council Young Polit. Leaders legis. del. to USSR, 1978; mem. policyholders' adv. council Div. State Compensation Ins. Fund, 1975—; trustee St. Mary's Acad., Labor's Community Agy., 1973—; bd. dirs. La Unidad Broadcasting Corp., 1980—, Nat. Inst. for Socio-Econ. Research, 1979—; mem. nat. steering com. Hispanic/Black Dem. Coalition, 1978—, Hispanic Am. Dems., 1978—; mem. nat. adv. bd. Nat. Women's Polit. Caucus, 1978—; mem. Nat. Overseas Edn. Fund of LWV, 1980—; mem. sec.'s adv. com. on rights and responsibilities of women HEW, 1979-81; mem. Colo. Gov.'s Commn. on Public Telecommunications, 1980—, Nat. Women's Employment and Edn., Inc.; mem. adv. bd. Nat. Inst. for Women of Color; participant German Marshall Fund and European Coop. Fund. fgn. policy seminar, Brussels, 1981. Recipient Outstanding Service in State Govt. award Adams County Fiesta Day Com., 1979; cert. of appreciation Colo. Migrant Council, 1979; Salute to Women award Big Sisters of Colo., Inc., 1979; named One of 10 Women of Future, Ladies Home Jour., 1979, One of 80 Women To Watch in '80s, MS mag., 1980, One of 20 New Dem. Faces for '80s, Newsweek mag., 1980. Office: Dem Nat Com 430 S Capitol St SE Washington DC 20003-4024*

BACALL, LAUREN, actress; b. N.Y.C., Sept. 16, 1924; d. William and Natalie (Bacall) Perske; m. Humphrey Bogart, May 21, 1945 (dec. 1957); children: Stephen, Leslie; m. Jason Robards, July 1961 (div.); 1 son, Sam. Student pub. schs., Am. Acad. Dramatic Art. Actress in Broadway plays Franklin Street, 1942, Goodbye Charlie, 1959; motion picture actress, 1944—, film appearances include To Have and Have Not, 1944, The Big Sleep, 1944, Confidential Agent, 1945, Dark Passage, 1947, Key Largo, 1948, Young Man With a Horn, 1949, Bright Leaf, 1950, How To Marry a Millionaire, 1953, Woman's World, 1954, The Cobweb, Blood Alley, 1955, Written on the Wind, 1956, Designing Woman, 1957, The Gift of Love, 1958, Flame Over India, 1959, Sex and the Single Girl, 1965, Harper, 1966, Murder on the Orient Express, 1974, The Shootist, 1976, Health, 1980, The Fan, 1981, Tree of Hands, 1987, Appointment With Death, 1987, Mr. North, 1988, Misery, 1990, A Star for Two, 1991, All I Want for Christmas, 1991, Ready to Wear (Prêt-à-Porter), 1994; appeared in Broadway play Cactus Flower, 1966-68, Applause, 1969-71 (Sarah Siddons award 1975); also road co., 1971-72, London co., 1972-73 (recipient Tony award for best actress in a musical 1970); Broadway play Woman of the Year, 1981 (recipient Tony award for best actress in a musical 1981, Sarah Siddons award 1983); TV spl. The Paris Collections, 1968, Applause, 1973, A Commercial Break (Happy Endings), 1975; TV movies: Perfect Gentlemen, 1978, Dinner at Eight, 1989, The Portrait, 1992, A Foreign Field, 1993; author: Lauren Bacall By Myself, 1978, Now, 1994. Recipient Am. Acad. Dramatic Arts award for achievement, 1963, Standard award London Evening, 1973, Nat. Book award, 1979. Office: care Johnnie Planco William Morris Agy 1350 Ave Of The Americas New York NY 10019-4701*

BACHER, JUDITH ST. GEORGE, executive search consultant; b. New Rochelle, N.Y., July 14, 1946; d. Thomas A. and Rose-Marie (Martocci) Baiocchi; B.S., Georgetown U., 1968; M.L.S., Columbia U., 1971; m. Albert Bacher, Jan. 2, 1972; 1 son, Alexander Michael. Researcher, Time mag., N.Y.C., 1968-71; librarian Mus. Modern Art, N.Y.C., 1971-72; cons. Informaco Inc., N.Y.C., 1972-74, Booz-Allen & Hamilton, N.Y.C., 1974-79; prin. Nordeman Grimm/MBA Resources, N.Y.C., 1979—; mem. White House Adv. Com. on Personnel, Exec. Office of Pres., 1979-81; co-founder Research Roundtable, pres. 1981-83. Mem. Assn. of Exec. Search Cons. (N.E. region chair 1994—), Phi Beta Kappa. Office: Nordeman Grimm Inc 717 Fifth Ave New York NY 10022-8101

BACHER, ROSALIE WRIDE, educational administrator; b. L.A., May 25, 1925; d. Homer M. and Reine (Rogers) Wride; m. Archie O. Bacher, Jr., Mar. 30, 1963. AB, Occidental Coll., 1947, MA, 1949. Tchr. English, Latin, history David Starr Jordan High Sch., Long Beach, Calif., 1949-55, counselor, 1955-65; counselor Lakewood (Calif.) Sr. High Sch., Long Beach, 1965-66; rsch. asst., counselor Poly. High Sch., Long Beach, 1966-67; counselor, office occupational preparation, vocat. guidance sect. Long Beach Unified School Dist., Long Beach, 1967-68; vice prin. Washington Jr. High Sch., Long Beach, 1968-70; asst. prin. Lakewood Sr. High Sch., Long Beach, spring 1970; vice prin. Marshall Jr. High Sch., Long Beach, 1981-87, 1981-87; vice prin. Lindbergh Jr. High Sch., Long Beach, 1987—; counselor Millikan High Sch., Calif., 1988—, Hill Jr. High Sch., Calif., 1988-89; ret. Hill Jr. High Sch., 1989; chmn. vocat. guidance steering com. Long Beach Unified Sch. Dist., 1963—. V.p. Palos Verdes Woman's Club, 1993—, philanthropy com., garden tour chmn.; docent coun. sec. Palos Verdes Art Ctr., 1991—; leader TOPS CA 471, 1992-93. Mem. AAUW, Long Beach Pers. and Guidance Assn. (dir. 1958-60), Long Beach Sch. Counselors Assn. (sec. high sch. segment 1963-64), Phi Beta Kappa, Delta Kappa Gamma (pres., area dir. Delta Psi chpt., Calif. profl. affairs com. chmn. 1972-74), Phi Delta Gamma (pres. chpt. 1977-78, 87-90, nat. chmn. bylaws com. 1980-91, 87-90, nat. conv. com. 1987-88, nat. nominating com. 1989), Pi Lambda Theta (pres. chpt. 1974-76, v.p. So. Calif. coun. 1974-76, sec. 1991—), Phi Delta Kappa (sec. Long Beach chpt. 1977-80). Home: 265 Rocky Point Rd Palos Verdes Estates CA 90274-2621 also: 17721 Misty Ln Huntington Beach CA 92649

BACHMAN, CAROL CHRISTINE, trust company executive; b. Buffalo, Jan. 20, 1959; d. Christian George and Joan Marie (Fincel) B. Student, Grad. Inst. Internat. Study, 1979-80; AB, Smith Coll., 1981; grad., New Eng. Sch. Banking, 1987. Trust asst. BayBank Middlesex, Burlington, Mass., 1984-85, sr. trust asst., 1985-87, trust adminstr., 1987, trust officer, 1987-88; estate settlement specialist Bank of Boston, 1988-90, system cons., 1990, mgr. adminstrv. support svcs., asst. v.p., 1990—. Roman Catholic. Home: 58 Circuit Ave Waterbury CT 06708-2160 Office: Bank of Boston 81 W Main St Waterbury CT 06702-2006

BACHMANN, KAREN C., public relations executive. Grad., U. N.C. With pub. rels. RJR Nabisco; dir. pub. rels. Del Monte Foods; owner KCB Comm.; mgr. corporate comm. Levi Strauss & Co., San Francisco, 1992-93, sr. mgr. corporate comm., 1993—. Recipient Golden Quill awards (3) IABC. Office: Levi Strauss & Co 1155 Battery St San Francisco CA 94111*

BACHRACH, EVE ELIZABETH, lawyer; b. Oakland, Calif., July 3, 1951; d. Howard Lloyd and Shirley Faye (Lichterman) B. AB cum laude, Boston U., 1972; JD with honors, George Washington U., 1976. Bar: D.C. 1976, U.S. Dist. Ct. D.C. 1976, U.S. Ct. Appeals (D.C. cir.) 1976. Assoc. Stein, Mitchell & Mezines, Washington, 1976-79; assoc. gen. counsel Cosmetic, Toiletry, and Fragrance Assn., Washington, 1979-85; v.p., assoc. gen. counsel, corp. sec. Nonprescription Drug Mfrs. Assn., Washington, 1985—; guest lectr. Am. U., Washington, 1986—, George Washington Nat. Law Ctr., Washington, 1986—, Cath. U. Law Sch., 1988—. Author, Editor: Small Business Resource Manual, 1984. Vol. lawyer Legal Counsel for the Elderly, Washington, 1978—. Mem. ABA (food and drug com., antitrust sect., adminstrv. law sect.), D.C. Bar Assn., Women's Bar Assn. D.C., Fed. Bar Assn. (chmn. food and drug com. 1986-90), Food and Drug Law Inst. (chmn. writing awards com. 1982-88, vice chmn. 1987-89, chmn. 1990, editorial adv. bd. Food Drug Law Jour.). Office: Nonprescription Drug Mfrs Assn 1150 Connecticut Ave NW Washington DC 20036-4104

BACHRACH, LYNN S., rehabilitation company executive; b. N.Y.C., Feb. 26, 1951; d. Jesse Silberstein and Nancy (Cohen) Sawyer. BA, Antioch Coll., 1973. Saleswoman Dunhill Greater Phila., 1974-76, Meloy Labs., Phila., 1976-78, Physio Control, Phila., 1978-80, Datamedix, Phila., 1980-82; sr. v.p. C.P. Rehab. Corp. Midlantic, Phila., 1982-87; sr. v.p. sales and mktg., pres. C.P. Rehab. Corp., N.Y.C., 1987-89; pres. The Cardiac Rehab. Co. and Clin. Rsch. Group, Phila., 1989—. Mem. Drug Info. Assn., Assn. Clin. Pharmacology, Tech. Coun. Greater Phila., Am. Assn. Cardiovascular and Pulmonary Rehab., Tri-State Soc. for Cardiovascular and Pulmonary Rehab. Jewish. Office: The Cardiac Rhab Co PO Box 127 Haverford PA 19041-0127

BACHRACH, NANCY, advertising executive; b. Providence, Jan. 29, 1948; d. David and Maida Horovitz. BA magna cum laude, Conn. Coll. for Women, 1969; MA with honors, Brandeis U., 1973, PhD, 1975. Assoc. dir. Grey France, Paris, 1980-84; sr. v.p., account mgmt. Grey Advt., N.Y.C., 1985-91, exec. v.p., 1992—. Author: The Irrefutability of Skepticism, 1975. Bd. dirs. Nat. Ctr. for Learning Disabilities, N.Y.C., 1992—. Named one of 100 Best and Brightest Women, Advt. Age, 1988; named to Acad. Women Achievers, 1992. Office: Grey Advt Inc 777 3rd Ave New York NY 10017

BACHTEL, ANN ELIZABETH, educational consultant, researcher, educator; b. Winnipeg, Man., Can., Dec. 12, 1928; d. John Wills and Margaret Agnes (Gray) Macleod; m. Richard Earl Bachtel, Dec. 19, 1947 (dec.); children: Margaret Ann, John Macleod, Bradley Wills; m. Louis Philip Nash, June 30, 1978 (div. 1987). AB, Occidental Coll., 1947; MA, Calif. State U.-L.A., 1976; PhD, U. So. Calif., 1988. Cert. life tchr., adminstr., Calif. Elem. tchr. pub. and pvt. schs. in Calif., 1947-50, 64-77; dir. Emergency Sch. Aid Act program, spl. projects, spl. arts State of Calif., 1977-80; leader, mem. program rev. team Calif. State Dept. Edn., 1981-85; cons. Pasadena Unified Sch. Dist., 1981-86; teaching asst., adj. prof. U. So. Calif.; cons. sch. dists., state depts. internat. edn.; presenter workshops/seminars; mem. legis. task forces. Chmn. resource allocation com. City of Pasadena, 1982-90, Pasadena-Mishima (Japan) Sister Cities Internat. Com., 1983-87; asst. chair Pasadena-Jarvenpaa, Finland, 1990-92, chair, 1992-95; mem. L.A. World Affairs Coun., Bonita Unified Sch. Dist. Curriculum Coun., 1990-93, Dist. Task Force Fine Arts, 1990-93, Dist. Task Force Tech., 1990-93, Dist. Handwriting Task Force, 1993; active Pasadena Hist. Soc., Pasadena Philharm. Com., Women's Com. Pasadena Symphony Assn.; deacon Pasadena Presbyn. Ch., 1989-92. Emergency Sch. Aid Act grantee, 1977-81. Named to Hall of Fame Bonita Unified Sch. Dist., 1990-91. Mem. World Coun. Gifted and Talented Children, Internat. Soc. Edn. Through Art, Nat. Art Educators Assn. (dels. assembly 1988-92), Clan MacLeod Soc. (bd. dirs. So. Calif. chpt.), Phi Delta Kappa, Kappa Delta Pi, Pi Lambda Theta (Ella Victoria Dobbs Nat. Rsch. award 1989, pres. L.A. chpt. 1991-95, nat. rsch. awards com. 1989-91, chair 1991-95, co-pres. region V 1993-95), Outstanding Pi Lambda Thetan in region V 1993-95), Assistance League of Pasadena. Contbr. articles to publs.; writer/editor: Arts for the Gifted and Talented, 1981; author Nat. Directory of Programs for Artistically Gifted and Talented Students, K-12.

BACKER, GRACIA YANCEY, state legislator; b. Jefferson City, Mo., Jan. 25, 1950; m. F. Mike Backer; 1 child, Justin. Student, S.W. Mo. State Coll. Mem. Mo. Ho. of Reps., 1983—. Active NAACP. Democrat. Baptist. Home: RR 2 Box 281 New Bloomfield MO 65063 Office: Mo Ho of Reps State Capitol Jefferson City MO 65101*

BACKES, JOAN, artist; b. Milw., Jan. 31, 1950; d. Gilbert Frances and Jeanne (Vogt) B.; m. Thomas Deeg Sills, June 14, 1975; children: Joseph Backes Sills, Elizabeth Backes Sills. BA, U. Iowa, 1972; MA, U. Mo., 1983; MFA, Northwestern U., Evanston, Ill., 1985. Adjunct asst. prof. U. Mo., Kansas City, 1985-88; instr. Kansas City Art Inst., 1988-94; vis. prof. U. Chile, Santiago, 1994-95; resident artist Aberdeen Art Mus., Scotland, 1986-87, Nat. Gallery, Reykjavik, Iceland, 1989, Edward Munch Studio Ekely, Olso, Norway, 1991, Yellowstone (Wyo.) Nat. Park, 1992. One-man shows include Aberdeen Art Mus., Scotland, 1987, Hafnarborg Art Mus., Iceland, 1991, Dorry Gates Gallery, Kansas City, 1988, 90, 94; exhibited in group show at Chgo. Art Inst., Chgo., 1990; represented in collections at Nelson-Atkins Mus., Kansas City, Aberdeen Art Mus., Scotland, Hafnarborg Art Mus., Iceland, Wustum Mus. Fine Arts, Racine, Wis. Grantee Kans. Arts Commn./NEA, 1986, 92, Am.-Scandinavian Found., N.Y., 1991; Fulbright scholar 1994-95. Mem. Coll. Art Assn., Kansas City Artists Coalition, Phi Kappa Phi. Office: PO Box 87069 South Dartmouth MA 02748

BACKMAN, MARGARET ESTHER, psychologist; b. Johnstown, Pa.; d. Peter Louis and Helen (McNulty) B. AB, Barnard Coll., 1960; MA, Columbia U., 1961, PhD, 1970; postdoctoral cert. clin. psychology, NYU, 1980-83. Cert. clin. psychologist. Dir. research Internat. Ctr. for Disabled, N.Y.C., 1973-78; dir. program devel. services, exec. dir. personnel devel. Coll. Bd., N.Y.C., 1978-80; clin. asst. prof. NYU Med. Ctr., N.Y.C., 1985—; psychologist health services dept. Barnard Coll., N.Y.C., 1985—; pvt. practice clin. psychologist N.Y.C., 1980—; with panel on testing handicapped people Nat. Acad. Scis., Washington, 1979-81, adv. council research and tng. ctr. U. Wis.-Stout, Menomenie, 1976-82. Author: The Psychology of the Physically Ill Patient, 1989, Choosing a Therapist, 1994. Postdoctoral fellow Cancer Rehab. Med. Ctr. NYU, 1984-85. Mem. Am. Psychological Assn., Nat. Rehab. Assn. Office: 30 E 40th St Suite 902 New York NY 10016

BACKUS, JAN, state legislator; b. Norristown, Pa., July 30, 1947; m. Robert Backus; 3 children. Student, U. Vt., U. Adelaide, South Australia, Kilkenny Tech. Coll., South Australia. Mem. Vt. State Senate, 1989—. Home: 11 Chapin St Brattleboro VT 05301-2802 Office: Vt State Senate State Capitol Montpelier VT 05602*

BACKUS, MARCIA ELLEN, lawyer; b. Melrose, Mass., Sept. 8, 1954; d. Milo Morlan and Barbara (Cairns) B.; m. Robert M. Roach Jr., June 14, 1986. BA, U. Tex., 1976, JD, 1983. Assoc. Vinson & Elkins, Houston, 1983-90, ptnr., 1991—. Mem. ABA, State Bar Tex., Houston Bar Assn. Office: Vinson & Elkins 1101 Fannin St Ste 3300 Houston TX 77002-6910

BACON, A(DELAIDE) SMOKI, public relations consultant; b. Brookline, Mass., Jan. 29, 1928; d. Alfred Leon and Ruth Dorothy (Burns) Ginepra; m. Edwin Conant Bacon, May 11, 1957 (dec. July 1974); children: Brooks Conant, Hilary Conant; m. Richard Francis Concannon, Oct. 13, 1979. Student, Art Inst. Boston, 1947; grad., Jackson Von Ladau Sch. Design, Boston, 1951. Pub. rels. cons. Boston, 1968—; pres. Bacon-Concannon Assocs., Boston, 1979—; dir. craftsmobiles Summerthing Program, Boston, 1968-73; dir. exhibits Citifair, Boston, 1974; dir. Victorian exhibits Bicentennial Boston 200, 1975, dir. spl. events, 1976; cons. spl. events. Inst. Contemporary Art, 1977-78, Boston Tea Party Ship, 1978-79; fundraiser Mass. Assn. Mental Health, 1979; dir. promotions Met. Ctr., 1979; coord. grand finale celebration Boston Jubilee 350, 1979-80; coord. Elliot Norton Awards, 1983; pub. rels. Dyansen Gallery, Boston, 1987-88, French Speaking League, 1987; cons. spl. events Jordan Marsh, 1987; fundraiser, pub. rels. Boston Philharmonic, 1988; coord. 30th anniversary celebration Charles Playhouse, 1988; fundraiser Elliot Norton Awards, 1989; coord. benefit New Eng. Premiere of film Glory Afro-Am. Mus., 1990; pub. rels. cons. Boston Chamber Music Soc., 1990; pub. rels. Paul Sorota Gallery of Fine Arts, 1990-91; fundraising cons. Internat. Inst., 1991; pub. rels., fundraiser Brookline H.S. Sesquicentennial Celebration, 1992-93; co-host radio show Celebrity Time, 1980—; guest lectr. Boston U. Sch. Pub. Rels., 1979, ARC, 1987, Radcliffe Coll. 4'0'Clock Forums, 1989; contbg. editor Design Times Mag. Social calendar editor Boston Tab Newspaper, 1987-90. Candidate Dem. State Rep., Mass., 1980; Bastile Day chmn. French Libr. Boston, 1994—; local adv. com. Nat. Trust for Historic Preservation; bd. dirs. Boston Lit. Hour; host parents com. Harvard Coll.; bd. dirs. Mugar Libr., Spl. Collections, 1994—; vis. com. Mus. Fine Arts, Eqyptian Dept., 1994—; bd. trustees Boston Arts Festival, 1960-63; bd. dirs., treas. Samaritans, Boston, 1974-84; art auction chairperson WGBH-Pub. Radio-TV, Boston, 1969-70; bd. dirs. Urban League Ea. Mass., Boston, 1975-85; former mem. numerous civic coms. Recipient Woman of Great Achievement award Cambridge Young Women's Assn., 1991; named One of Boston's 100 Female Leaders, Boston Mag., 1980; Guest of Honor, Womens' City Club Ann. Dinner Dance, 1979. Democrat. Home: 9 Fairfield St Boston MA 02116 Office: Bacon Concannon Assocs 9 Fairfield St Boston MA 02116

BACON, CAROLINE SHARFMAN, commercial paper credit analyst; b. Ann Arbor, Mich., Aug. 27, 1942; d. Mahlon Samuel and Mary Patricia (Potter) Sharp; m. William Lee Sharfman, Sept. 5, 1964 (div. 1985); m. James Edmund Bacon, Nov. 4, 1989. BA with distinction, U. Mich., 1964; MBA, Columbia U., 1975. Assoc. Goldman, Sachs & Co., N.Y.C., 1975-80, v.p., 1980-83; v.p. Goldman Sachs Money Markets Inc., N.Y.C., 1983-90; sr. cons. investor rels. Burson-Marsteller, 1991—; mng. dir. Johnnie D. Johnson & Co. Investor Rels., N.Y.C., 1992—. Mem. Phi Beta Kappa, Phi Sigma Iota, Beta Gamma Sigma. Episcopalian.

BACON, MARTHA BRANTLEY, small business owner; b. Wrightsville, Ga., Apr. 20, 1938; d. William Riley and Susie Mae (Colston) B.; m. Albert Sidney Bacon, Jr., Aug. 3, 1958; children: Albert Sidney, III, Gregory Riley. BS, Ga. So., Statesboro, 1959; Post Grad., U. Va., Charlottesville, 1978-80, Adrian Hall Interior Design, Savannah, Ga., 1984. Lic. real estate broker, Ga., Va. Tchr. Chatham Bd. Edn., Savannah, Ga., 1961; co-owner mgr. Two Kentucky Fried Chicken Restaurants, Charlottesville, Va., 1967-80; real estate broker Real Estate III, Charlottesville, Va., 1978-83, Landmark Realty, Statesboro, Ga.; tree farmer Johnson Co., Ga., 1980—; mgr., co-owner Restaurant, 1987-92; co-owner Plunderosa Antiques and Collectibles, Brooklet, Ga., 1993—; v.p. Bd. Realtors Statesboro Ga. 1985; regional franchise agt., owner Ice Cream Churn of South Ga. Chmn. Jaycettes Gov. Columbus, Ga., 1962; vol. First Bapt. Ch. Pers. Com., Charlottesville, 1978, U. Va. Hosp., 1980-83; com. mem. Athletic Hall of Fame Ga. So. U.; mem. Ga. Forestry Stewardship, 1991—. Recipient Outstanding Sales award Real Estate III Co. Charlottesville 1980; named Outstanding Jaycette 1961, Jaycettes Gov. Columbus, 1962. Mem. AAUW, Charlottesville Restaurant Assn., Westchester Garden Club, Ga. Restaurant Assn., Ga. So. Univ. Alumni Bd., Ga. So. Symphony Guild, Ga. So. Univ. Athletic Boosters Club, Pilot Club, Evergeen Garden Club, Ga. (v.p.), Optimist (Stateboro essay chmn.),. Baptist. Home: 30 Golf Club Cir Statesboro GA 30458-9163

BACON, VICKY LEE, lighting services executive; b. Oregon City, Oreg., Mar. 25, 1950; d. Herbert Kenneth and Lorean Betty (Boltz) Rushford; m. Dennis M. Bacon, Aug. 7, 1971; 1 child, Randene Tess. Student, Portland Community Coll., 1974-75, Mt. Hood Community Coll., 1976, Portland State Coll., 1979. With All Electric Constrn., Milwaukie, Oreg., 1968-70, Lighting Maintenance Co., Portland, Oreg., 1970-78; svc. mgr. GTE Sylvania Lighting Svcs., Portland, 1978-80, br. mgr., 1980-83; div. mgr. Christenson

Electric Co. Inc., Portland, 1983-90, v.p. mktg. and lighting svcs., 1990-91, v.p. svc. ops. and mktg., 1991—. Mem. Illuminating Engring. Soc., Nat. Assn. Lighting Maintenance Contractors. Office: Christenson Electric Co Inc 111 SW Columbia St Ste 480 Portland OR 97201-5886

BACON-MORAN, COLLEEN ELIZABETH, physical therapist; b. Providence, July 16, 1959; d. John Edward and Nancy Ann (Lomax) Bacon; m. Daniel R. Moran, Sept. 26, 1986; 1 child, Patrick Edward. BS in Phys. Therapy, Boston U., 1983; cert. in neurodevel. treatment approach, adult hemiplegia, Spaulding Hosp., Boston, 1986, cert. craniosacral therapy I, 1992, cert. craniosacral therapy II, 1993. Registered phys. therapist. Staff phys. therapist Vanderbilt Rehab. Ctr., Newport (R.I.) Hosp., 1983-90, ctr. coord. for clin. edn., 1988-90; sr. staff phys. therapist Cranston (R.I.) Gen. Hosp.-Osteo., 1991-92; staff phys. therapist acute inpatient/home care Kent County Meml. Hosp., Warwick, R.I., 1993—. Mem. Neurodevel. Treatment Assn. Home: 25 Ingersoll Ave Warwick RI 02886 Office: Kent County Meml Hosp Tollgate Rd Warwick RI 02886

BADDOUR, ANNE BRIDGE, aviatrix; b. Royal Oak, Mich.; d. William George and Esther Rose (Pfiester) Bridge; m. Raymond F. Baddour, Sept. 25, 1954; children: Cynthia Anne, Frederick Raymond, Jean Bridge. Student, Detroit Bus. Sch., 1948-50. Stewardess Eastern Airlines, Boston, 1952-54; instr. aero. Powers Sch., Boston, 1958; co-pilot, flight attendant Raytheon Co., Bedford, Mass., 1958-63; flight dispatcher, ferry Pilot Comerford Flight Sch., Bedford, 1974-76; adminstrv. asst., ferry pilot Jenney Beachcraft, Bedford, 1976; mgr., pilot Balt. Airways, Inc., Bedford, 1976-77; pilot Lincoln Lab. Flight Test Facility MIT, Lexington, 1977—; aviation cons., corp. pilot Energy Resources, Inc., Cambridge, Mass., 1974-84; holder World Class speed records for single-engine aircraft; Boston to Goose Bay, Labrador, 1985, Boston to Reykjavik, Iceland, 1985, Portland, Maine to Goose Bay, 1985, Portland to Reykjavik, 1985, Goose Bay to Reykjavik, 1985; records for twin-engine aircraft: Sept Isles to Goose Bay, 1988, Mont Joll to Goose Bay, 1988, Presque Isle to Goose Bay, 1988, Millinocket to Goose Bay, 1988, Bedford to Goose Bay, 1988, Goose Bay to Narssassrag, Greenland, 1988, Narssassrag to Klevelevic, Iceland, 1988, Narssassrag to Reykjavik, 1988, Bedford to Narssassrag, 1988, Millinochet to Narssassrag, 1988, Presque Isle to Narssassrag, 1988, Bedford to St. John, 1991, Bedford to Charlottetown, 1991, Charlottetown to Kennebunk, 1991, Charlottetown to Portsmouth, 1991, Muncton to Bedford, 1991, St. John, to Kennebunk, 1991, St. John to Bedford, 1991. Bd. dirs. Cambridge Opera, 1977-79; mem. campaign coun. Mus. Transp., Boston; mem. coun. assocs. French Libr. in Boston; commr. Commonwealth of Mass., Mass. Aero. Commn., 1979-83; chmn. regional adv. coun. FAA, 1984-88; trustee bd. adminstrn. Amelia Earhart Birthplace Mus., 1992-93. Winner trophy Phila. Transcontinental Air Race, 1954, New Eng. Air Race, 1957, Clifford B. Harmon trophy Internat. Aviatrix, 1988; recipient Spl. Recognition award FAA, 1990; honoree Internat. Aviation Forest of Friendship, Atchison, Kans., 1991; named Pilot of the Year, New Eng. sect. Internat. Women Pilots Orgn./The Ninety-Nines, Inc., 1992. Mem. Fedn. Aeronautique Internat., Nat. Aero. Assn., Ninety-Nines (New Eng. Safety trophy 1986), Aero Club New Eng. (v.p., dir. 1978—), Aircraft Owners Pilots Assn., Nat. Pilots Assn., U.S. Sea Plane Pilots Assn., Assn. Women Transcontinental Air Race, Bostonian Soc., English Speaking Union, Soc. Exptl. Test Pilots, Friends of Switzerland, French Ctr. Libr. Club, Belmont Hill Club, St. Botolph Club. Republican. Episcopalian. Office: MIT Lincoln Lab 244 Wood St Lexington MA 02173-6499

BADEL, JULIE, lawyer; b. Chgo., Sept. 14, 1946; d. Charles and Saima (Hyrkas) B.; m. Craig B. Feldpausch, Feb. 3, 1968 (dec. Dec. 1986). Student, Knox Coll., 1963-65; BA, Columbia Coll., Chgo., 1967; JD, DePaul U., 1977. Bar: Ill. 1977, U.S. Dist. Ct. (no. dist.) Ill. 1977, U.S. Ct. Appeals (7th and D.C. cirs.) 1981, U.S. Supreme Ct. 1985, U.S. Dist. Ct. (ea. dist.) Mich. 1989. Hearings referee State of Ill., Chgo., 1974-78; assoc. Cohn, Lambert, Ryan & Schneider, Chgo., 1978-80; assoc. McDermott, Will & Emery, Chgo., 1980-84, ptnr., 1985—; legal counsel, mem. adv. bd. Health Evaluation Referral Svc. Chgo., 1980-89; bd. dirs. Alternatives, Inc., Chgo. chpt. Asthma and Allergy Found., 1993-94, Glenwood Sch. for Boys. Author: Hospital Restructuring: Employment Law Pitfalls, 1985; editor DePaul U. Law Rev., 1976-77. Mem. ABA, Columbia Coll. Alumni Assn. (1st v.p., bd. dirs. 1981-86), Pi Gamma Mu. Office: McDermott Will & Emery 227 W Monroe St Chicago IL 60606-5016

BADENHOP, SHARON LYNN, psychologist, educator, entrepreneur; b. Roswell, N.Mex., Feb. 21, 1946; d. Charles Theodore and Anna (Burke) B.; B.A. in Ednl. Psychology, SUNY-Oneonta, 1967, M.S., 1969, M.S. in Counselor Edn., 1971. Cert. mental health adminstr. Tchr., Gilbertsville (N.Y.) Central Sch., 1968-70; guidance counselor Delaware Acad., Delhi, N.Y., 1970-71; instr. SUNY-Oneonta, 1971-75; prof. SUNY-Delhi, 1974-75; psychol. case worker United Cerebral Palsy Assn., 1977-78; psychologist in psychogeratrics Rochester (N.Y.) Psychiat. Center, 1979, dir. edn. and tng. dept., 1979-81, psychologist, 1981—; instr. U. Rochester, 1978-91, Rochester Inst. Tech., 1981-83, 92—; psychologist Securecare, 1985-91; founder, pres. USA East Assocs., Inc., 1991—. Bd. dir. East House. Lic. guidance counselor, N.Y. State; cert. mental health adminstr.; cert. tchr. grades 1-6, N.Y. State, GEMS cons. Mem. NAFE, Am. Psychol. Assn., Clin. Sociology Assn., Soc. Internat. Devel. (mem. com. fgn. rels.), Assn. Mental Health Adminstrs., Rochester Profl. Cons. Network. Home and Office: 18 Hollingham Rise Fairport NY 14450-1609

BADGER, BRENDA JOYCE, counselor; b. Camden, Ark., May 10, 1950; d. Woodrow Alexander and Lizzie Mae (Frazier) Hildreth; m. Rickey Thomas Jackson, June 22, 1970 (div. 1981); children: Kreya Shawn Jackson, Keith Woodrow Jackson; m. David William Badger, Feb. 27, 1982. BS, Wayne State U., 1982, MA, 1987. Lic. counselor, Mich. Counselor Huron Valley Prision, Detroit, 1986, Lawrence Tech. U., Southfield, Mich., 1992—; disaster counselor, instr. ARC, 1992—; founder, dir. edn. Spirit, Ambition, Vigor, Enthusiasm, Detroit, 1986—, pres., 1988-94, polit. contact person, 1989—. Editor: The Community Informant, 1989—, columnist, 1990—; host TV program Did You Know?, 1990—; curator mus. exhibit, 1993; creator, poet coloring book, 1991; composer, lyricist gospel and jazz songs. Candidate Detroit Bd. Edn., 1990; mem. Juvenile/Teen & Violence Com., 1982. Recipient Strong Achiever award WJLB-FM Radio, 1991. Mem. ACA, Am. Coll. Counseling Assn., Assn. Marriage and Family Counselors. Democrat. Baptist. Office: Spirit Ambition Vibor Enthusiasm PO Box 32169 Detroit MI 48232

BADGER, SALLY ANN, mechanical engineer; b. Tulsa, Feb. 13, 1965; d. Jack Frank and Glenda Dell (Hampton) B. BS, U. Tulsa, 1987. Assoc. mech. engr. Kerr McGee Refining Corp., Wynnewood, Okla., 1989-93, mech. engr., 1993—. Mem. Am. Assn. Cost Engrs., Arbuckle Assn. Girls in Action (dir.). Republican. Baptist. Office: Kerr McGee Refining Corp 906 S Powell Wynnewood OK 73098

BADGER, SANDRA RAE, health and physical education educator; b. Pueblo, Colo., Nov. 2, 1946; d. William Harvey and Iva Alberta (Belveal) Allenbach; m. Graeme B. Badger, Oct. 9, 1972; 1 child, Jack Edward. BA in Phys. Edn., U. So. Colo., Pueblo, 1969; MA in Arts and Humanities, Colo. Coll., 1979; postgrad., Adams State U., Alamosa, Colo., 1980-91. Cert. tchr., secondary endorsement in health and phys. edn., Colo. Head women's swimming coach Mitchell High Sch., Doherty High Sch., Colorado Springs, Colo., 1969-90; head dept. Health Edn. Doherty High Sch., 1979—; trainer student asst. program CARE, Colorado Springs, 1983—; trainer drug edn. U.S. Swim Olympic Tng. Ctr., Colorado Springs, 1988-89; trainer in track and field, Colorado Springs, 1989, 91; cons. Assocs. in Recovery Therapy, 1989—; speaker in field. Author, editor: Student Assistant Training Manual, 1983-94. Bd. dirs. ARC, Colorado Springs, 1990—, sec., 1991—, mem. health and safety com., 1990-94; mem. comprehensive health adv. com. Dept. Edn., State of Colo., Denver, 1991. Recipient Svc. award ARC, 1985, Coach of Yr. award Gazette Telegraph, 1979, 84, CARE award State of Colo., 1988, others; Gamesfield grantee, 1985; Nat. Coun. on Alcoholism grantee, 1990. Mem. NEA, Colorado Springs Edn. Assn. Office: Doherty High Sch 4515 Barnes Rd Colorado Springs CO 80917-1599

BAER, CARLA KRISTINE, systems engineer; b. Twin Falls, Idaho, Apr. 9, 1955; d. Willis Carlton and Ella Kristine (Jansen) McCauley) Smith; m. Howard Stephen Baer, Apr. 12, 1981 (div. Nov. 1992); children: Christopher, Stephanie. BA, Pacific Luth. U., 1977; MA, Webster U., 1979. Fin. analyst NCR Corp., Wichita, Kans.; instr. Troy State U., Oslo, Norway, 1983-85; project mgr. Esso Norge A.S., Oslo, 1985-88, Fin. Techs., Herndon, Va., 1988-89; assoc. Perot Systems, Auburn Hills, Mich., 1989—; ind. auditor U.S. Govt. activities, Oslo, 1985-88; v.p. Ohio Am. Sch. Adv.Com., Oslo, 1983-84. Campaign chmn. NCR Corp. United Way, Wichita, 1982; capt. Ladies Team Am. Allied Forces No. Europe, Kolsas, Norway, 1986. Capt. USAF, 1977-81. Decorated Meritorious Svc. medal. Mem. NAFE. Office: Perot Systems Mail Stop 2B01 3800 Hamlin Rd Auburn Hills MI 48326

BAERMANN, DONNA LEE ROTH, property executive, retired insurance analyst; b. Carroll, Iowa, Apr. 28, 1939; d. Omer H. and Mae Lavina (Larson) Real; m. Edwin Ralph Baermann, Jr., July 8, 1961; children: Beth, Bryan, Cynthia. BS, Mt. Mercy Coll., 1973; student Iowa State U.-Ames, 1957-61. Cert. profl. ins. woman; fellow Life Mgmt. Inst. Ins. agt. Lutheran Mut. Ins. Co., Cedar Rapids, Iowa, 1973; home economist Iowa-Ill. Gas & Electric Co., Cedar Rapids, Iowa, 1973-77; supr. premium collection Life Investors Ins. Co. (now Aegon USA), Cedar Rapids, 1978-83, methods and procedures analyst, 1987-94, sr. supr. policy svc., 1987-84; v.p. bd. dirs. Roth & Assocs., Roth Farms, Roth Inc. & Readymix, Roth Apts. Inc., 1988-90; pres. bd. dirs. Roth & Assocs., Roth Farms, Roth, Inc., Roth Readymix, Roth Apts. Inc., 1990—; pres., CEO Roth Apt. Corp., 1990—, Baerman Apts Inc., 1992—; mem. telecom. study group com. 1982-83, mem. productivity task force, 1984-94. Mem. Internat. Platform Assn., Citizens Com. for Persons with Disabilities, Nat. Assn. Ins. Women, Nat. Mgmt. Assn. (bd. dirs. Cedar Rapids chpt.), DAR, Knights of Malta (named Damsel of Ancient Order of St. John, N.Y.C.), Chi Omega. Republican. Presbyterian. Home: 361 Willshire Ct NE Cedar Rapids IA 52402-6922

BAEUMLER, BRENDA KAY, project design mechanical engineer; b. Ft. Wayne, Ind., May 4, 1966; d. Larry Wayne and Sharon Irene (Wooldridge) Wellman; m. Roger Wayne Baeumler, Mar. 7, 1987. Cert. in drafting, Purdue U., 1986, A in Mech. Drafting Design Tech., 1988, A in Mech. Engring. Tech., 1989, BS in Mech. Engring. Tech., 1993. Draftsman DeKalb County Surveyor's Office, Auburn, Ind., 1984-85; detail drafter Fruehauf Corp., Ft. Wayne, 1985-86, ITT Aerospace/Optical, Ft. Wayne, 1986-89; project design engr. Navistar, Ft. Wayne, 1989—. Mem. Am. Soc. Mech. Engrs., Soc. Automotive Engrs. Home: 18217 Old US Highway 30 Monroeville IN 46773-9629 Office: Navistar 2911 Meyer Rd Fort Wayne IN 46803-2993

BAEZ, JOAN CHANDOS, folk singer; b. S.I., N.Y., Jan. 9, 1941; d. Albert V. and Joan (Bridge) B.; m. David Victor Harris, Mar. 1968 (div. 1973); 1 son, Gabriel Earl. Appeared in coffeehouses, Gate of Horn, Chgo., 1958, Ballad Room, Club 47, 1958-68, Newport (R.I.) Folk Festival, 1959-69, 85, 87, 90, 92, 93, extended tours to colls. and concert halls, 1960s, appeared Town Hall and Carnegie Hall, 1962, 67, 68, U.S. tours, 1970—, concert tours in Japan, 1966, 82, Europe, 1970-73, 80, 83-84, 87-90, 93, Australia, 1985; rec. artist for Vanguard Records, 1960-72, A&M, 1973-76, Portrait Records, 1977-80, Gold Castle Records, 1986-89, Virgin Records, 1990-93, European record albums, 1981, 83; awarded 8 gold albums, 1 gold single; albums include Play Me Backwards, 1992, Rare, Live & Classic (box set), 1993; author: Joan Baez Songbook, 1964, (biography) Daybreak, 1968, (with David Harris) Coming Out, 1971, And a Voice to Sing With, 1987, (songbook) And Then I Wrote, 1979. Extensive TV appearances and speaking tours U.S. and Can. for anti-militarism, 1967-68; visit to Dem. Republic of Vietnam, 1972, visit to war torn Bosnia-Herzegovina, 1993; founder, v.p. Inst. for Study Nonviolence (now Resource Ctr. for Nonviolence, Santa Cruz, Calif.), Palo Alto, Calif., 1965; mem. nat. adv. coun. Amnesty Internat., 1974-92; founder, pres. Humanitas/Internat. Human Rights Com., 1979-92; condr. fact-finding mission to refugee camps, S.E. Asia, Oct. 1979; began refusing payment of war taxes, 1964; arrested for civil disobedience opposing draft, Oct., Dec., 1967. Office: care Diamonds and Rust Prodns PO Box 1026 Menlo Park CA 94026-1026

BAGALIO, JOAN BEVERLY, state agency administrator; b. Barre, Vt., Sept. 25, 1934; d. Clarence George and Rachel Isabelle (Beckman) Gould; m. Paul A. Bagalio, June 13, 1953; children: Grace, Paul, Jr., Dino, Tony, Sabrina. Grad. high sch., Barre. Legal sec. Law Office Rice & Knosher, Montpelier, Vt., 1982-86; adminstrv. asst. Vt. Rep. State Com., Montpelier, 1986-88; Congl. aide Congressman Peter Smith, Montpelier, 1989-91; pub. info. officer Gov. Richard Snellin, Montpelier, 1991, Gov. Howard Dean, Montpelier, 1991—. Home: PO Box 746 Montpelier VT 05601

BAGAN-PROCHELO, BARBARA ELLEN, psychotherapist; b. Sioux City, Iowa, Jan. 15, 1939; d. Elmer Emanuel and Minerva Lucille (Henry) Bagan; divorced; children: L. Charles, Joseph, Gary, Michael, Thomas, Mari Jo. BA in Psychology/Art, Buena Vista Coll., 1981; MA in Art Therapy, Ariz. Inst. Art Therapy, 1983; PhD in Psychology, Walden U., 1986. Registered art therapist; cert. sandplay therapist; cert. substance abuse counselor; cert. sex therapist. Family programs coord. Phoenix Gen. Hosp., 1983-86; pvt. practice therapist C.A.R.E. Assocs., Scottsdale, Ariz., 1986-89, Psychol. Counseling Svcs., Scottsdale, 189—; adj. faculty Ottawa U. Phoenix, 1990—; trainer, tchr. of therapists Ludwig Tng. Inst., Phoenix, 1991—; cons. Draw From Within, Inc., Scottsdale, 1990—. Author: Draw from Within, 1990, (with others) Sexual Addiction: Case Studies and Treatment, 1994. Fellow Am. Bd. Sexology (clin., diplomate); mem. Am. Psychol. Assn., Am. Art Therapy Assn. (registered), Internat. Soc. of Sandplay Therapists (cert.), Ariz. Bd. of Alcohol and Drug Counselors (cert.). Office: Psychol Counseling Svcs 7530 E Angus Dr Scottsdale AZ 85251

BAGEANT, MARTHA DYER, volunteer; b. Seattle, Apr. 19, 1906; Republican. Mem. United Ch. of Christ.; d. Harry Cheney and Florence Annette (Whedon) Dyer; m. Kenneth Edmond Bageant, June 2, 1928; children; Susan Weilhoefer, Judith Driscoll. BS, Wash. State U., 1928. Leader Girl Scouts of Am., Baldwin, L.I., N.Y., 1942, badge leader; officer Jr. High Sch. PTA, L.I. Pan Hellenic; Mem. N.Y. City Theatre Guild, N.Y.C., 1950—; student Mus. and Art Study. Active Marco Island Civic Assn., 1971—, Marco Island Taxpayers Assn., 1975—; counselor Campfire Girls, Yakima, Wash.; alt. del. Rep. Convention, Fla., 1992. Mem. AAUW, DAR, Marco Island Residents Beach Club, Pi Beta Phi. Republican. Home: 848 Chestnut Ct Marco FL 33937-2312

BAGGETT, HARRIETTE LANE, family planning counselor; b. St. Louis, Aug. 2, 1922; d. James Purcell and Sallie Atwood (Bodley) Lane; m. Billy Baggett, Nov. 23, 1949 (div. Oct. 1976); children: Sarah Bodley, William Brown, Mary Lane, Teresa Lee, Harriet Lane. AB, Maryville Coll., St. Louis, 1942; MS, St. Louis U., 1949; MDiv, Christ Sem.-Seminex, 1981. Rsch. asst. biochemistry St. Louis U. Dental Sch., 1947-51, Harvard U. Sch. Dental Medicine, Boston, 1954-57, U. N.C. Med. Sch., Chapel Hill, 1959, 61; mem. staff homeless shelter St. Louis Cath. Worker Community, 1978-90; pastoral and ednl. asst. Visitation Cath. Ch., St. Louis, 1981-83; cons. Reproductive Health Svcs., St. Louis, 1987-91; nat. core commr. Women's Ordination Conf., Fairfax, Va., 1984-87; convenor St. Louis Caths. for Choice, St. Louis, 1987-93; chaplain's asst. VA Hosp. St. Louis and Truman Hosp., St. Louis, 1978-80. Author: (pamphlet) Our Sunday Visitor, 1962. Bd. dirs. YWCA, Charleston, S.C., 1974-75, Mo. Religious Coalition for Abortion Rights, St. Louis, 1987-93, LWV, Charleston, 1970-73; local activist Caths. for Free Choice, 1985—. Scholar AAUW, 1963. Mem. NOW (charter). Democrat. Home: 3201 Miccosukee Rd Apt 25-C Tallahassee FL 32308-5531

BAGGETT, KAREN GARAVENTA, state agency administrator; b. Reno, Nev., Nov. 3, 1948; d. Louis J. and Nieves C. (Marcuerquiaga) Garaventa; m. Stephan W. Lehman, Oct. 23, 1971 (div. June 1977); 1 child, Brandi A.; m. Rex T. Baggett, Jan. 1, 1984. B degree, U. Nev., 1971. Nat. accounts sec., br. mgr.'s sec. First Nat. Bank, Reno, 1968-71; math. tchr. Washoe County Sch. Dist., Reno, 1971-78; sec., legis. aide Senate Paul Laxalt U.S. Senate, Washington, 1978-81; rural counties rep. Senator Paul Laxalt U.S. Senate, Reno and Carson City, 1981-87; exec. dir. Nev. Water Resources Assn., Reno, 1987-89; pub. affairs officer Toiyabe Nat. Forest, Reno, 1989-93; dep. dir. Commn. on Econ. Devel., Carson City, 1993—. Dir., points sec. yearbook advisor Nev. State H.S. Rodeo Assn., 1992-94; past mem. ctrl. com. Douglas Rep. Com., Gardnerville, Nev., 1981-85; pres. ad. bd. U. Nev.-Reno Desert Rsch. Inst. of Water Resources, 1989-93; charter bd. dirs. Western Nev. Clean Com., Reno, 1992-93. Mem. Nev. Water Resources Assn. (pres. bd. dirs. 1989-93), , Nev. Econ. Devel. Assn., Carson Douglas Med. Alliance (legis. com.). Republican. Roman Catholic. Office: Commn on Econ Devel 5151 S Carson St Carson City NV 89710

BAGGISH, JOY, actress, costume designer; b. Hartford, Conn., July 1, 1950; d. Samuel and Stefania (Wojcek) B. MS, Fla. State U., 1973; BFA, U. Conn., 1972. Freelance designer L.A., 1981-93; legal asst. Viacom Prodns., Universal City, Calif., 1985-86; supr. bus. affairs Showtime Networks Inc., Universal City, 1987-94; costumer Middlesex Coll., Edison, N.J., 1975-79, U. Nev., 1979-80; costumer and visiting prof., U. Wis., 1980-81. Appeared (films) Best Defense, 1985, An American Summer, 1989, Whore, 1990, (tv series) Divorce Court, 1987, Superior Court, 1988, Freddie's Nightmare, 1990, (commls.) Clusters, 1989, VW, 1989, Chevrolet, 1989, Toshiba, 1990; spokesperson (comml.) Jasco Dept. Stores, 1991—; designer for Nutmeg Summer Playhouse, 1972, Asolo State Theatre, 1972, PBS series Saga on Aging, 1980. Civilian superfund RAB apptd. Long Beach Naval Sta./Shipyard, 1994-96. Mem. AFTRA, SAG, Actors Equity Assn., Am. Women in Radio and Television, Costume Soc. of Victoria & Albert Mus., Actresses Helping Actresses,. Home: 7890 E Spring St # 2-0 Long Beach CA 90815-1636 Office: Showtime Networks Inc 10 Universal City Plz Universal Cty CA 91608-1009

BAGLEY, AMY L., state legislator; b. Portsmouth, N.H., Apr. 23, 1971; d. Paul David and Micheleen Gail (Mahoney) B. BA in Polit. Sci. cum laude, Emmanuel Coll., 1990-91; BA in Polit. Sci., Keene State Coll., 1991-94. Cons. Dick Swett for Congress, Bow, N.H., 1992; state representative N.H. State Ho. of Reps., Concord, 1993—. Vol. Clinton N.H. Primary Campaign, Manchester, N.H., 1991-92. Challenge scholar Keene State Coll., Keene, N.H., 1993-94. Mem. Nat. Order Women Legislators, 1993—. Democrat. Office: NH Ho of Reps State House Concord NH 03301*

BAGLEY, CONSTANCE ELIZABETH, lawyer, educator; b. Tucson, Dec. 18, 1952; d. Robert Porter Smith and Joanne Snow-Smith. AB in Polit. Sci. with distinction, with honors, Stanford U., 1974; JD magna cum laude, Harvard U., 1977. Bar: Calif. 1978, N.Y. 1978. Tchg. fellow Harvard U., 1975-77; assoc. Webster & Sheffield, N.Y.C., 1977-78, Heller, Ehrman, White & McAuliffe, San Francisco, 1978-79; assoc. McCutchen, Doyle, Brown & Enersen, San Francisco, 1979-84, ptnr., 1984-90; lectr. bus. law Stanford (Calif.) U., 1988-90, lectr. mgmt., 1990-91, lectr. law and mgmt., 1991—; also lectr. Stanford Exec. Program, lectr. exec. program for growing cos.; bd. dirs. Alegre Enterprises, Inc.; mem. corp. practice series adv. bd. Bur. Nat. Affairs, 1984—; mem. faculty adv. bd. Stanford Jour. Law, Bus. and Fin., 1994—; lectr., mem. planning com. Calif. Continuing Edn. of Bar, L.A. and San Francisco, 1983, 85-87; lectr. So. Area Conf., Silverado, 1988, Young Pres. Orgn. Internat. U. for Pres., Hong Kong, 1988. Author: Mergers, Acquisitions and Tender Offers, 1983, Proxy Contests and Corporate Control, 1990, Managers and the Legal Environment: Strategies for the 21st Century, 1991, 2d edit., 1995; co-author: Negotiated Acquisitions, 1992, Cutting Edge Cases in the Legal Environment of Business, 1993. Vestry mem. Trinity Episcopal Ch., San Francisco, 1984-85; vol. Moffit Hosp. U. Calif., San Francisco, 1983-84. Mem. ABA, Acad. Legal Studies in Bus., Stanford Faculty Club (bd. dirs.), Phi Beta Kappa. Republican. Office: Stanford U Grad Sch Bus Stanford CA 94305-5015

BAGLEY, EDYTHE SCOTT, theater arts educator; b. Marion, Ala., Dec. 13, 1924; d. Obie and Bernice (McMurry) Scott; m. Arthur Moten Bagley, June 5, 1954; 1 child, Arturo Scott. BEd, Ohio State U., 1949; MA in English, Columbia U., 1954; MFA in Theater Arts, Boston U., 1965. Instr. Elizabeth City (N.C.) State Coll., 1953-56; asst. prof. Albany (Ga.) State Coll., 1956-57, A&T U., Greensboro, N.C., 1957-58, Norfolk (Va.) State Coll., 1963-65; assoc. prof. theater Cheyney (Pa.) U., 1971—, also chair dept. theater arts; cons. in black theater Mich. State U., East Lansing, 1969-71. Dir. numerous coll. prodns., 1968-71. Spl. asst. to Coretta Scott King, Martin Luther King, Jr. Ctr. for Nonviolent Social Change, Atlanta. Mem. NAACP, AAUW, Nat. Coun. Negro Women, Theater Assn. Pa., The Links Inc. (chair com. on arts 1972-80), Womens Internat. League for Peace and Freedom, The Pa. Martin Luther King Jr. Assn. for Nonviolence (bd. dirs.), The Martin Luther King Jr. Ctr. for Nonviolent Soc. Change (bd. dirs.). Home: 2 Derry Dr Cheyney PA 19319 Office: Cheyney U Cheyney PA 19319

BAGSBY, N. DIONNE, county commissioner, speech pathologist; b. Phoenix, Ill., Mar. 16, 1936; d. Paul William and Ann Della (Wicks) Phillips; children: Dionne Ann, James Tipkins. BS, Ill. Wesleyan, 1958; MA, Tex. Christian U., 1985. Cert. speech pathologist. Service rep. Ill. Bell, Chgo., 1958-59; social worker Ill. Dept. of Human Service, Chgo., 1959-60; teacher, speech pathologist pub. schs. Ill., Tex. and Ark., 1960-85, 86-88; community liaison State Senator Hugh Parmer, Ft. Worth, 1985-86; commr. Tarrant County, Tex., 1988—. Named Exec. Woman of Yr., Zonta, Ft. Worth, 1988, Trailblazer of Yr., Greater Ft. Worth Area Negro Bus. and Profl. Women's Club, 1989; recipient Cert. of Recognition, Better Influence Assn., Ft. Worth, 1989. Mem. Links (pres. Ft. Worth chpt. 1989—), Smart Set, Omega Psi Phi (named Citizen of Yr. 1989), Phi Delta Kappa (Eminent Women award, 1988). Methodist. Office: Office County Commrs 100 E Weatherford St Fort Worth TX 76196-0609

BAGSTAD, KRISTIN KIM, clinical nurse specialist; b. Salina, Kans., Nov. 11, 1954; d. Richard William and Barbara Bee (Billings) Fry; m. Brian D. Bagstad. Diploma in Nursing, St. Francis Hosp. Sch. Nursing, Wichita, Kans., 1975; BSN, Pitts. State U., 1979; MSN, U. Kans. Med. Ctr., 1987. Staff nurse St. Francis Hosp., Wichita, Kans., 1975-76, charge nurse, 1976-78; staff nurse St. Joseph's Hosp., Kansas City, 1979-80; staff nurse Wesley Med. Ctr., Kansas City, Mo., 1981, charge nurse, 1981-82; nurse clin. Prime Health, Kansas City, 1982-87; clin. nurse specialist Children's Mercy Hosp., Kansas City, 1987—; mem. affiliate faculty U. Mo., Kansas City, 1988—; mem. family adv. bd. Am. Lung Assn., Kansas City, 1987—, mem. program com., 1992; coord. Asthma Camp Western Mo., 1987—. Author, researcher: Erikson's Developmental Milestones in Relation to a Chronic Immune Deficiency Syndrome, 1992; contbr. articles to profl. jours. Vol. nurse Turner House Children's Clinic, Kansas City, Kans., 1991-92, bd. dirs. Turner House, 1992—. Mem. ANA, Mo. Nurses Assn., Am. Acad. Allergy/Immunology, Immunology Nurses Soc., Sigma Theta Tau. Episcopalian. Office: Children's Mercy Hospital 2401 Gillham Rd Kansas City MO 64108-4698

BAHARESTANI, MONA MYLENE, clinical nurse specialist/adult nurse practitioner. BSN summa cum laude, East Tenn. State U., 1984; MSN summa cum laude, Hunter Coll., 1986; PhD summa cum laude, Adelphi U., 1993. RN, N.Y., Tenn.; cert. in enterostomal therapy; cert. adult nurse practitioner. Med.-surg. nurse Boulevard Hosp., Long Island City, N.Y., 1984-85, Flushing (N.Y.) Hosp. and Med. Ctr., 1985-86; clin. nurse specialist enterostomal therapy L.I. Jewish Med. Ctr., New Hyde, N.Y., 1986—; faculty continuing edn. Queensborough Community Coll., Bayside, N.Y., 1990—; lectr. Knoll Pharms., Whippany, N.J., 1991—. Mem. L.I. Ostomy Assn. (profl. advisor New Hyde Park chpt. 1986—), Wound, Ostomy and Continence Nurse's Soc., Alpha Lambda Delta, Phi Kappa Phi, Gamma Beta Phi, Sigma Theta Tau (rsch. award 1992). Office: LI Jewish Med Ctr New Hyde Park NY 11040

BAHNER, SUE (FLORENCE SUZANNA BAHNER), radio broadcasting executive; b. Phila.; d. William and Florence (Quinlivan) McElwee; m. David S. Bahner; children—Suzanna Elizabeth, Carol Aileen. Grad. Columbia Bus. Coll., 1950. Various exec. sec. positions, 1954-74; office mgr. Sta. WYRD, Syracuse, N.Y., 1974, gen. mgr., 1974-80; gen. mgr. Sta. WWWG-AM, Rochester, N.Y., 1980-93; gen. mgr. WDCW, Syracuse, N.Y., 1993—; pres. The Cornerstone Group, 1986—. Bd. dirs. Rescue Mission, Syracuse; active Eastern Hills Bible Ch. Mem. Greater Syracuse Assn. Evangelicals (treas. 1993—), Nat. Religious Broadcasters (pres. ea. chpt. 1984—, bd. dirs. 1983—, 2nd. v.p., 1992—). Office: WDCW 1022 Willis Ave Syracuse NY 13204

BAHR, BEVERLY KATHERINE, critical care nurse; b. St. Louis, Oct. 23, 1950; d. Leeds Brown and Ruth Katherine (Purzner) Berridge; m. Robert John Bahr, Jan. 12, 1980; children: Kris, Zach, Gabe. Diploma, Luth. Hosp. Sch. Nursing, St. Louis, 1971; BA, Stephens Coll., Columbia, Mo., 1975; BSN, St. Mary of the Plains, Dodge City, Kans., 1988; MS, Okla. U.,

1993. CCRN, Cert. ACLS, ACLS instr. Staff nurse ICU Boone County Hosp., Columbia, Mo., 1971-73; staff nurse dialysis U. Mo. Med. Ctr., Columbia, 1973-74; staff nurse ICU/Critical Care Unit U. Mo. Med. Ctr./Boone County, Columbia, 1974-76; staff devel. coord. U. Mo. Med. Ctr., Columbia, 1976, head nurse cardiac cath lab., 1977-79; instr. Stephens Coll., Columbia, 1975-76; asst. head nurse med. ICU/Critical Care Unit Parkland Hosp., Dallas, 1977-78; head nurse cardiac rehab. Placentia (Calif.) Linda Hosp., 1980-82; staff nurse ICU Stillwater (Okla.) Hosp., 1986-90; staff nurse ICU float pool Okla. Meml. Hosp., Oklahoma City, 1989-92, transplant program mgr., coord., 1992-93, clin. nurse specialist, 1993-95, critical care instr., 1994—; cons. Early Autumn Residential Care Home, Stillwater, 1991—; ACLS instr. Am. Heart Assn., Oklahoma City, 1988—; class alumni reporter Luth. Hosp. Sch. Nursing Alumni Assn., Stillwater, 1988, 92, 95. Instr. Sunday Sch., midweek sch. Zion Luth. Ch., Stillwater, 1985—, chmn. bd. edn.; pres. Vet. Wives Aux., Stillwater, 1986-87. Mem. AACN (pres. Ctrl. Mo. chpt. 1975), Grad. Nurse Assn. (sec. 1992), Toastmasters, Sigma Theta Tau. Republican. Home: 1119 Oakridge Dr Stillwater OK 74074-1111

BAHR, LAUREN S., publishing company executive; b. New Brunswick, N.J., July 3, 1944; d. Simon A. and Rosalind J. (Cabot) B. Student, U. Grenoble, France, 1964; B.A. (Branstrom scholar); MA, U. Mich., 1966. Asst. editor New Horizons Pubs., Inc., Chgo., 1967, Scholastic Mags., Inc., N.Y.C., 1968-71; supervising editor Houghton Mifflin Co., Boston, 1971; product devel. editor Appleton-Century-Crofts, N.Y.C., 1972-74; sponsoring editor McGraw-Hill, Inc., N.Y.C., 1974-75; editor Today's Sec. mag., 1975-77; sr. editor Media Systems Corp., N.Y.C., 1978; sr. editor coll. dept. CBS Coll. Pub., N.Y.C., 1978-82, mktg. mgr. fgn. langs., dir. mktg. adminstrn., 1982-83; dir. devel. Coll. div. Harper & Row, N.Y.C., 1983-86, dir. mktg. coll. div., 1986-88, pub. cons., 1988-91; v.p., editorial dir. P.F. Collier, Inc., N.Y.C., 1991—. Democrat. Jewish. Home: 444 E 82d St New York NY 10028

BAHRE, JEANNETTE, educational consultant; b. Darby, Pa., Dec. 28, 1948; d. Paul Florent and Jeanne (Shangraw) Gibson; m. Stephen Alan Bahre, May 14, 1974; children: Kimberly, Christian, Rachael. BA, Merrimack Coll., 1970; MEd, U. Ariz., 1979. Cert. experienced tchr., N.H.; cert. English tchr., Mass. Tchr., 1970—; libr. St. Augustine Sch., Andover, Mass., 1980-83; Beverly (Mass.) Sch. for Deaf, 1988-89; instr. No. Essex C.C., Haverhill, Mass., 1982-84, libr. evening svc., 1986-88; tchr., advisor Linton Hall Sch., Bristow, Va., 1985-86; lectr. George Mason U., Fairfax, Va., 1985-86; tchr., tutor Even Start: Family Lit. Project, Amesbury, Mass., 1990-93;, 1970—. Editor Four Winds Lit. Jours., 1992, 93, 94. Active master tchr.'s program Archdiocese of Boston, Aquinas Coll., 1991-92. Grantee NEH, 1988. Mem. AAUW, N. Eng. Libr. Assn., Sartre Soc. N.Am., N.H. Humanities Coun. Home: 25 Elizabeth St Amesbury MA 01913

BAIK-KROMALIC, SUE S., metallurgical engineer; b. Seoul, Korea, June 21, 1965; came to U.S., 1968; d. Boo Sung Baik and Katherine Kim; m. Joseph Jay Kromalic, Dec. 14, 1991. BS in Metallurgical Engring., Ohio State U., Columbus, 1990. Project engr. Cummins Engine Co., Columbus, Ind, 1988-89; engring. staff, materials testing and devel. engr. Honda Am. Mfg., Inc., East Liberty, Ohio, 1990-92; trainer problem solving Honda Am., Inc., East Liberty, Ohio, 1992-93, new model project engr., 1993-94, leader tech. devel., 1994; prodn. planning operations, 1994—; guest speaker Ohio State U., Columbus, 1991—. mem. ASM Internat. (awards chmn. 1992-94, sec. 1994, chpt. task force 1993-94, membership devel. com. 1994-97, treas. 1994—, chpt. coun. 1994-97). Roman Catholic. Office: Honda of Am Mfg Inc 11000 State Route 347 East Liberty OH 43319-9407

BAIL, DOLORES JEAN, association executive; b. Dunbar, W.Va., July 17, 1934; d. George Mancil and Lana (Bell) Walker; m. Franklin Delano Bail, June 5, 1954; children: Jeffrey Walker, Melody Alyce. Student, U. Akron, Ohio, 1957, 78, 79, U. Md., 1985; BA, W.Va. U., 1991. Adult program dir. Cleve. YWCA, 1966-74; br. exec. Akron YWCA, 1974-78; exec. dir. Alliance (Ohio) YWCA, 1978-79, YWCA Annapolis (Md.) and Anne Arundel County, 1979—. Treas. Coun. Community Svcs., 1986-88, v.p. 1988-89; bd. dirs. United Way Partnership, 1987—, campaign coord., 1993; pres. Coun. Vol. Coords., Annapolis, 1991—; appointee Gov.'s Vol. Coun., Md., 1984—, Human Rels. Commn., 1991—. Recipient Brenda Kopro award Coun. Cmty. Svc., Anne Arundel County, 1989, Mgmt. Distinction award United Way Ctrl. Md., 1990, award of exec. excellence Nat. Assn. YWCA Execs., L.A., 1994. Mem. Nat. Assn. YWCA Execs., 21st Century Club, Zonta (adv., past pres.). Democrat. United Ch. of Christ. Office: YWCA of Annapolis & Anne Arundel County 1517 Ritchie Hwy Ste 201 Arnold MD 21012-2461

BAILEY, ANGELA JANE, graphics design company executive; b. Norman, Okla., Nov. 20, 1961; d. Wilbur Edgar and Mary Jane (Hill) Carter; m. Timothy William Bailey, Mar. 3, 1984; children: Amber Christine, Emily Jane, Christopher William. Student, No. Va. Community Coll., Woodbridge, Va. Office mgr. Inter-Assocs., Inc., Rosslyn, Va., 1980-84; asst. to dir. pub. rels. Mary Washington Hosp., Fredericksburg, Va., 1985; adminstrv. asst. Gen. Nutrition Ctr., Fredericksburg, 1986-87; pres., chief exec. officer ABCreations, Inc., Fredericksburg, 1987—; graphics cons. Spotsylvania County Litter Control, 1988—. Photographer Rappahannock Mag., 1990; editor (newsletter) Quar. Perspectives, 1988—. Speaker Olde Towne Fredericksburg Bus. Bldg. Blocks, 1989; rep. Mary Washington Coll. Career Svcs., 1990; graphics coord. Fredericksburg Area United Way, 1991. Recipient Red Triangle award Rappahannock Area YMCA, 1991, Community Svc. award, 1992, Svc. award Spotsylvania County Litter Control, 1989-92, Award of Excellence, Excellence in Print Communications, 1990, 1st Pl. award, 1990. Mem. C. of C. (com. mem.), Fredericksburg Area Pub. Rels. Soc., Va. Women in Bus., Rappahannock Area YMCA. Office: AB-Creations Inc 1261 Dockside Dr Lutz FL 33549

BAILEY, ANN V., federal agency administrator. BA, Goucher Coll., 1959. Libr. USIA, 1959-61, staff asst., 1961-66; corr. asst. Office Edn. HEW, 1966-68, chief of commr.'s corr. staff, 1968-74; com. mgmt. officer Office Asst. Sec. Intergovtl. and Interagy. Affairs Dept. Edn., Washington, 1974—; acting dir. Goals 2000 Initiative Svc., 1993. Office: Office Asst Sec Intergovtl & Interagy Affairs US Dept Edn Rm 3057 400 Maryland Ave SW Washington DC 20202-3571*

BAILEY, CYNTHIA LEE, chemical company official; b. Bloomfield, Iowa, Oct. 21, 1956; d. A.G. and E. Marilee (Hargrove) Fredrickson. BA in Econs., U. Iowa, 1979. Acctg. clk. Le Febure, Cedar Rapids, Iowa, 1980-82, mfg. scheduler, 1982-85; inventory analyst Paulwels Transformer, Washington, Mo., 1986-89; mfg. scheduler Mallinckrodt Co., St. Louis, 1989—. Mem. Step Up St. Louis. Mem. Am. Prodn. and Inventory Control Soc. (treas. Cedar Rapids 1986, sec. St. Louis 1991—).

BAILEY, DEENA TAMARA, health care administrator; b. Haifa, Israel, June 13, 1947; came to U.S., 1960; d. Fred Ephraim and Devora (Glaser) Mansbacher; m. Wayne W. Bailey, Apr. 4, 1970 (div. 1977); 1 child, Devora Elyse. BS in Health Sci., U. Redlands, 1989; MHA, U. So. Calif., 1994. Mgr. dept. surgery Cedars-Sinai Med. Ctr., L.A., 1980-87; mgr. cardiovascular intervention ctr. Cedars-Sinai Med. Ctr., 1988-93; dir. Cardiology Mgmt. Svcs., 1993-94; adminstrv. resident UniHealth, Burbank, Calif., 1994—. Mem. Health Care Execs. So. Calif., Women in Health Adminstrn. (pres. 1993), Am. Coll. Cardiovascular Adminstrs. (regional dir. 1990-92), Am. Acad. Med. Adminstrs., Am. Coll. Health Care Execs. (assoc.), Soc. Cardiovascular Mgmt., Med. Group Mgmt. Assn., Healthcare Forum. Democrat. Jewish.

BAILEY, DONNA NAOMI ELIZABETH, academic project coordinator; b. Groton, Conn., Apr. 5, 1966; d. Robert Jerome Sr. and Christine Emaline (Reitz) Bailey. BS, U. Vt., 1988. Ednl. asst. Burlington (Vt.) Pub. Schs., 1989-90; polit. cons. Sanders For Congress, Vt., 1990, 92, Clavelle for Mayor, Burlington, 1991, Save James Bay, Burlington, 1991; mem. staff Progressive Vt. Alliance, 1992; tchr. adult basic edn. Vt. Inst. for Self-Reliance, Chittenden County, Vt., 1993; coord. homeless literacy project Vt. Inst. for Self-Reliance, ChiHenden County, Vt., 1993—. City councilor City of Burlington, 1992-94. Mem. YMCA, Vt. Pub. Interest Rsch. Group, Outright Vt., Burlington Community Land Trust, Planned Parenthood Pro Choice, Phi Alpha Delta. Home: RD 1 Box 3955 Bristol VT 05443

BAILEY, EXINE MARGARET ANDERSON, soprano, educator; b. Cottonwood, Minn., Jan. 4, 1922; d. Joseph Leonard and Exine Pearl (Robertson) Anderson; m. Arthur Albert Bailey, May 5, 1956. B.S., U. Minn., 1944; M.A., Columbia U., 1945; profl. diploma, 1951. Instr. Columbia U., 1947-51; faculty U. Oreg., Eugene, 1951—, prof. voice, 1966-87, coordinator voice instrn., 1969-87, prof. emeritus, 1987—; faculty dir. Salzburg, Austria, summer 1968, Europe, summer 1976; vis prof., head vocal instrn. Columbia U., summers 1952, 59; condr. master classes for singers, developer summer program study for high sch. solo singers, U. Oreg. Sch. Music, 1988—. Profl. singer, N.Y.C.; appearances with NBC, ABC symphonies; solo artist appearing with Portland and Eugene (Oreg.) Symphonies, other groups in Wash., Calif., Mont., Idaho, also in concert; contbr. articles, book revs. to various mags. Del. fine arts program to Ea. Europe, People to People Internat. Mission to Russia for 1990. Recipient Young Artist award N.Y.C. Singing Tchrs., 1945, Music Fedn. Club (N.Y.C.) hon. award, 1951; Kathryn Long scholar Met. Opera, 1945. Mem. Nat. Assn. Tchrs. Singing (lt. gov. 1968-72), Oreg. Music Tchrs. Assn (pres. 1974-76), Music Tchrs. Nat. Assn. (nat. voice chmn. high sch. activities 1970-74, nat. chmn. voice 1973-75, 81-85, NW chmn. collegiate activities and artists competition 1978-80, editorial com. Am. Music Tchr. jour. 1987-89), AAUP, Internat. Platform Assn., Kappa Delta Pi, Sigma Alpha Iota, Pi Kappa Lambda. Home: 17 Westbrook Way Eugene OR 97405-2074 Office: U Oreg Sch Music Eugene OR 97403

BAILEY, GRACE DANIEL, retired secondary school educator; b. Wilson, N.C., Dec. 7, 1927; d. James Clenon and Ella Mae (West) Daniel; m. Hubert Jesse Bailey, Apr. 27, 1951; 1 child, Vicky Lynette Bailey Freeman. BS in Bus. Edn. and English, East Carolina U., 1950, MAE in Guidance and Counseling, 1966. Tchr. bus. edn., English Apex (N.C.) High Sch., 1950-51; tchr. bus. edn. Atlantic Christian Coll., Wilson, N.C., summer 1951; tchr. bus. edn., English Lucama (N.C.) High Sch., 1951-53, 1956-75, tchr. bus. edn., counselor, 1975-77, counselor, 1977-78; counselor Hunt High Sch., Wilson, 1978-79, counselor, dept. chair, 1979-86; ret., 1986. Sec. adv. com. Community Manpower and Tng., Wilson, 1973-74; organizer Wilson Community Coun., 1973-74; sec. Wilson County Humane Soc., 1978; edn. com. Am. Cancer Soc., Wilson, 1987-88. Recipient award Am. Legion, Wilson, 1986; grantee Wilson County Mental Health Assn., 1964. Mem. AAUW, N.C. Assn. of Educators (treas. Wilson county chpt. 1974-75), Wilson County Guidance Pers. Assn. (organizer, 1st pres. 1966-67), Wilson Women's Club (co-chair comm. com. 1993-94), Delta Kappa Gamma (v.p. Gamma Mu chpt. 1986-88, pres. 1988-90). Methodist. Home: 4021 US Highway 117 Wilson NC 27893-0916

BAILEY, JOAN WEISENFELD, education educator; b. Bklyn., Oct. 20, 1959; d. Bernard and Barbara A. (George) Weisenfeld; m. Lawrence H. Bailey, June 29, 1984. BA, Hunter Coll., 1980; PhD, Grad. Sch./Univ. Ctr. of N.Y., 1988. Rsch. asst. The Grad. Sch./Univ. Ctr. of N.Y., 1983-86; assoc. prof. Jersey City (N.Y.) State Coll., 1988—; adj. lectr. Queen's Coll., Flushing, N.Y., 1983-84; reviewer Harcourt, Brace & Jovanovich, Dallas, Harper Collins, N.Y.C. Contbr. articles to profl. jours.; editorial bd. Jersey City State Coll. publ., 1993—. Tchng. fellow Grad. Sch./Univ. Ctr. of N.Y., 1983-84, acad. fellow 1982-83. Mem. APA (Minority fellow 1986-88). Home: 600 First St #5 Hoboken NJ 07030 Office: Jersey City State Coll 2039 Kennedy Blvd Jersey City NJ 07305

BAILEY, JOSELYN ELIZABETH, physician; b. Pine Bluff, Ark.; d. Joseph Alexander and Angeline Elaine (Davis) B.; B.Mus., Manhattanville Coll., 1952; M.Music Edn., Manhattan Sch. Music, 1954; M.D., Howard U., 1971. Straight med. intern Huntington Meml. Hosp., Pasadena, Calif., 1971-72, resident, 1972-74; fell in nephrology Wadsworth VA Hosp., Los Angeles, 1975-77; practice medicine specializing in internal medicine and nephrology, Torrance, Calif.; assoc. staff Torrance Meml., South Bay; active Little Company of Mary hosps.; attending staff Harbor Gen. Hosp.; clin. faculty Dept. Medicine, UCLA; active staff Bay Harbor Hosp., trustee, 1982—.

BAILEY, KATHERINE CHRISTINE, artist, writer; b. Glendale, Calif., Dec. 1, 1952; d. Carl Leonard and Anna Alice (Dzamka) Abrahamson; m. David Francis Bailey, Sept. 27, 1975. BA, Calif. State U., L.A., 1974, MA, 1975; PhD, U. N.Mex., 1982. Exhbns. include Miniature Painters Sculptors & Gravers Soc., Washington, Oil Pastel Assn., N.Y.C., Mont. Miniature Art Soc. Internat., many others; author: (novel) Brush With Death; also numerous short stories. Recipient hon. mention in mixed media category Nat. Western Small Painting Show, Bosque Art Gallery, N.Mex., 1985, 2d pl. award in pastels, 1986, Cert. of Merit award 4th Ann. Holiday Exhbn. of Oil Pastel Assn., 1994; tuition fellow U. N.Mex., 1977; Alpha Gamma Sigma scholar, 1972. Mem. Oil Pastel Assn., Nat. Mus. Women in Arts, Mont. Miniature Art Soc., Phi Kappa Phi, Alpha Gamma Sigma. Home and Studio: PO Box 301 Daggett CA 92327-0301

BAILEY, KRISTEN, legal assistant; b. Davenport, Iowa, Jan. 5, 1952; d. Donald Ray and Alta Llewellyn (Mandler) B. AS, Mo. So. State Coll., 1974; cert. paralegal studies, Rockhurst Coll., 1978. Legal sec. Ralph E. Baird, Lawyer, Joplin, Mo., 1972-75; legal asst. Benny J. Harding, Atty. at Law, Kansas City, Mo., 1976-87, Polsinelli, White, Vardeman & Shalton, Kansas City, 1988—; speaker in field. Vol. Heartland's Sch. Riding, Overland Park, Kans., 1988—; mem. Friends of the Zoo, Kansas City Mus. Assn. Winner Ark. and Iowa state championships, 3-gaited Pleasure Horse, Am. Saddlebred Pleasure Horse Assn., 1981; named Kansas City Legal Sec. of Yr., 1979. Mem. Assn. Trial Lawyers Am. (paralegal mem. 1993—), Kansas City Assn. Legal Assts. (bd. dirs. 1993-94), Kansas City Legal Sec. Assn. (bd. dirs. 1977-89, 92-93, pres. 1979-81, life mem.), Mid-Am. Saddle Horse Club (sec. 1981-83). Republican. Methodist. Office: Polsinelli White Vardeman & Shalton 700 W 47th St Ste 1000 Kansas City MO 64112-1805

BAILEY, LINDA RAE, realtor; b. Indpls., Apr. 20, 1949; d. Simon Leopold and Jeanne Sylvia (Spitalny) Ackerman; m. Richard C. Abrams, Aug. 30, 1968 (div. Apr. 1973); 1 child, Sheri Dawn; m. Dale Alfred Bailey, June 23, 1984. Cert. Residential Specialist, Grad. Realtor Inst. Broker, owner Metro Brokers Rosener Realty, Englewood, Colo., 1977-79; broker assoc. Re/Max Assoc., Englewood, Colo., 1979-81; property mgr. asst. R.J. Fulscher Co., Denver, 1981-84; broker assoc. Coldwell Banker Curry, Carthage, Mo., 1985-88, Lawson & Wilson BH&G, Carthage, Mo., 1988—; pres. Carthage Bd. Realtors, 1993—, treas., 1986-88. Dist. v.p. Mo. Assn. Realtors, Columbia, 1988-92; pres. Community Theatre S.W. Mo., Carthage, 1993, sec., 1992, v.p., 1990-91. Named Realtor of Yr. Carthage Assn. Realtors, 1987, 93; recipient Sally Ann award for best actress CTSM, 1984, 92, Presdl. award excellence Mo. Assn. Realtors, 1987. Mem. RS Coun. Mo. (sec. 1993—). Democrat. Jewish. Home: Rt 1 Box 177 Carthage MO 64836 Office: Lawson & Wilson BH&G 2425 Fairlawn Dr Carthage MO 64836-3517

BAILEY, LOIS MARIAN ADAMS, artist; b. Mahanoy City, Pa., Aug. 21, 1927; d. Raymond William and H. Marian (Jones) Adams; m. John Davis Bailey, Aug. 20, 1949 (div. 1966). Student, Frankford Hosp. Sch. Nursing, Phila., 1948, Art Students League, N.Y.C., 1969-70; AAS, Parsons Sch. Design, 1982; student, New Sch., N.Y.C. RN. Mem. Composers, Authors and Artists of Am., Nat. Mus. Women in Arts, Beaux Arts Soc. (sec. 1993). Buddhist. Home: 220 W 19th St 2-A New York NY 10011

BAILEY, LUCILLE MARIE, English language and women's studies educator; b. Bellefontaine, Ohio, Jan. 18, 1945; d. Clifford Harm and Anna Marie (Wright) B. BA, Ohio No. U., 1966; MA, Miami U., Oxford, Ohio, 1972; PhD, Ball State U., 1991. Tchr. English various high schs., Ohio, 1966-70; grad. asst. Miami U., 1970-72; substitute tchr. Chgo. City Schs., 1972-74; instr. No. Ill. U., DeKalb, 1974-77; dir. Mut. Ground Women's Shelter, Aurora, Ill., 1978-79; social worker Community Action Program, New Castle, Ind., 1979-81; instr. Ball State U., Muncie, Ind., 1981-87; lectr. Berea (Ky.) Coll., 1987-89; asst. prof. English, chair women's studies Ind. U. at Kokomo, 1989—. Mem. MLA (del. assembly 1987-90), NOW (state sec., planning com. for nat. conf. 1982), Linguistic Soc. Am., Am. Dialect Soc., Midwest MLA (sec., chair applied linguistics sect. 1991-93), Nat. Women's Studies Assn., North Ctr. Women's Studies Assn. (treas. 1990—), Women's Caucus for Modern Langs., Orgn. for Study of Comm., Lang. and Gender. Christian Scientist.

BAILEY, MARIANNE THERESE, human resources specialist; b. Evanston, Ill., Dec. 26, 1949; d. Eugene Thomas and Marguerite O'Brien B. Student, Sorbonne, Paris, 1970, San Francisco Coll. Women, 1967-69; BA, Barat Coll. of Sacred Heart, 1971; cert., U. Paris, Sorbonne, 1972; ancien élève, Ecole du Louvre, Paris, 1973-74. Tchr. 2d and 3d grade Marymount Internat. Sch., Neuilly, France, 1971-72; dir. Ctr. Audio Visuel des Langues, Enghien, France, 1973-76; pre-sch. dir. P.L. Child Care Ctrs., Glenview, Ill., 1976-81; with dept. def. civilian Child Support Svcs., Ft. Sheridan, Ill., 1981-82; dir. tng. and spl. events N.W. Mcpl. Conf., Mt. Prospect, Ill., 1982-84; exec. dir. PRC Paratransit Svcs., Park Ridge, Ill., 1984—. V.p. N.W. suburban chpt. Citizens with Disabilities; lobbyist disabled and sr. citizens State of Ill.; treas. Wheeling Twp. Reps., 1986—; pres. N.W. Suburban Coun. for Cmty. Svcs., 1989-91; v.p. Twp. Officials Ill. Disabled Advocacy, 1985-90, pres., 1990—; active Chgo. Area Transp. Study, 1984—, PACE-ADA Adv. Com., 1990—, Sage Sr. Advocacy Group, 1990—; mem. Twp. Officials of Cook County. Mem. AAUW, ALTRUSA, Am. Pub. Transit Assn., Am. Pub. Works Assn., Ill. Paratransit Assn. (bd. dirs., sec. 1987-91), Ill. Alliance Info. & Referral, Cmty. Transp. Assn. Am. (state del.), Lions Club (v.p. 1990-92, pres. 1992-93, Lion of the Yr. 1991-92, mem. bd. dirs. 1988-94, dist. diabetes awareness chmn. 1991-93), Pi Delta Phi. Roman Catholic. Home: 200 N Arlington Heights Rd # 501 Arlington Heights IL 60004 Office: PRC Paratransit Svcs 1700 Ballard Rd Park Ridge IL 60068

BAILEY, MARY BEATRICE, nursing information systems director; b. Pitts., Dec. 24, 1933; d. Harry Chantler and Beatrice Iseli (Koenig) B. Diploma in Nursing, Allegheny Gen. Hosp., Pitts., 1956; BSNE, Chatham Coll., Pitts., 1956; MSN, Duke U., Durham, 1967. Cert. nursing adminstr., advanced. Staff nurse, head nurse, nursing supr. Allegheny Gen. Hosp., Pittsburgh, 1956-60; nursing instr. pediatrics Duke U. Sch. Nursing, Durham, N.C., 1960-61; nursing instr. med. surg Rex Hosp. Sch. Nursing, Raleigh, N.C., 1962-63; nursing supr. Rex Hosp., Raleigh, 1964-71, patient care coord., 1972-86, clin. dir., 1987, dir. nursing info. system, 1987—. Author: The Role of the Mother with her Hospitalized Child, 1966. Vol. RN open door clinic, Raleigh, 1987-88; mem. N.C. United for Equal Rights Amendment, Raleigh, N.C. Coalition for Choice; elected N.C. Bd. of Nursing, 1991-93, 94—. Named to The Great 100 N.C. Nurses, 1992. Mem. NOW, N.C. Coun. Women's Orgns., N.C. League for Nursing, N.C. Nurses Assn. (treas. 1977-79), Great 100 (charter treas. 1989), Zonta Club of Raleigh (charter treas.). Democrat. Episcopalian. Home: 311 Furches St Raleigh NC 27607-4015 Office: Rex Hosp 4420 Lake Boone Trl Raleigh NC 27607-6599

BAILEY, MISSY P., credit manager; b. Chgo., Jan. 11, 1954; d. Philip Arthur and Nancy (Fox) Watson; m. Larry Dean Bailey, July 11, 1977 (div. 1979). Student, Ariz. State U., 1978. Clk. Ford Motor Credit, Chgo., 1978-80; supr. customer svc. Ford Motor Credit, Glendale and Orange, Calif., 1980-87; dealer acct. mgr. Ford Motor Credit, St. Louis, 1987-89; regional fin. specialist Ford Motor Credit, Detroit, 1989-91; br. mgr. Ford Motor Credit, Fargo, N.D., 1991-94, Rosemont, Ill., 1994—. Supporter ASPCA, N.Y.C. Republican. Office: Ford Motor Credit 9700 Higgins Rd # 720 Rosemont IL 60018

BAILEY, NAILA CELESTE, immunologist; b. Teheran, Iran, Mar. 7, 1958; came to U.S., 1976; d. George and Tatiana (Gribanos) Naayem; m. Timothy Silleck Bailey, June 9, 1984; 1 child, Alexander Stephen. BS, U. Fla., 1979; MS, N.Y. Med. Coll., 1985; PhD, CUNY, 1991. Rsch. tech. The Population Coun., N.Y.C., 1980-82, Cornell Univ. Med. Sch., N.Y.C., 1982-83; science specialist Alcohol Rsch., Bronx, N.Y., 1985-86; postdoctoral fellow U. Calif., San Diego, 1991—. Editor, prohost: The Newsletter for Biotechnology Insight and Investment, 1992—; contbr. articles to profl. jours. Basic Equal Opportunity grantee, 1977-79; recipient Nat. Kidney Found., 1992-94, Nat. Rsch. Svc. award NIH, 1994—. Mem. Am. Assn. Immunologists.

BAILEY, NANCY JOYCE, educator; b. Detroit, May 9, 1942; d. Thomas Hill and Margaret (McGrath) Rainey; m. Carl John Bailey, June 12, 1963; 1 child, John. BA, Vanderbilt U., 1960; postgrad., U. Mex., 1957, U. Santa Clara, 1975, George Washington U., 1979-80. Cert. early childhood edn. tchr., early childhood specialist. Hostess Brentwood (Tenn.) Country Club, 1960; adminstrv. aide U.S. Senate, Washington, 1966; sec. U.S. Ho. of Reps., Washington, 1971-74; tchr. D.C. Pub. Schs., 1961—; bd. dirs. Cabvin Internat. Corp.; rep. Washington Tchrs. Union, 1982-94; founder David Lipscomb U., Nashville, 1988; participant Internat. Tchr. Exch. Program, Korea, 1994. Keyperson United Way campaign, Washington, 1974-93; docent The White House, Exec. Office of the Pres., Washington, 1987—; vol. First Lady's Corr., The White House, Washington, 1990—, Social Sec.'s Office, East Wing, 1993, Office of First Lady, 1993; coord. Presdl. Youth Vol. Day, 1993; mem. Nat. Trust for Historic Preservation, 1990—, Friendship Force of Nat. Capital Area, 1993—, People to People Internat. of Nat. Capital Area, 1993—; adv. bd. New Visions for Child Care, Inc., 1993—; chairperson Local Schools Restructuring Team, 1992-93; participant Internat. Tchr. Exchange Program, Korea, 1994; mem. exec. com. YWCA Internat. Fair, Washington, 1994. Recipient Internat. Cooperation award Am. Fgn. Study Program, Am. Study Program, 1984-86, Am. Student Ednl. Travel. Mem. Delta Group (coun. 1989-91), Am. Fedn. Tchrs., Internat. Reading Assn. Home: 10729 Deborah Dr Potomac MD 20854-2714 Office: LaSalle Sch Riggs Rd Madison St NE Washington DC 20011

BAILEY, PATRICIA PRICE, lawyer, former government official; b. Ft. Smith, Ark., June 20, 1937; m. Douglas L. Bailey; 2 children. BA in History cum laude, Lindenwood Coll., 1959; MA in Internat. Affairs, Tufts U., 1960; JD summa cum laude, Am. U., 1976. Bar: D.C., U.S. Ct. Appeals (D.C. cir.), U.S. Ct. Appeals (8th cir.), U.S. Supreme Ct. Editor, rsch. analyst Bur. of Intelligence and Rsch., U.S. Dept. State, 1960-61; exec. asst. Bur. for Latin Am., then asst. to dep. coordinator Alliance for Progress, AID, 1961-66; advisor fgn. affairs Rep. F. Bradford Morse, 1967-68; legal asst. Office of Counsel to Pres. in White House, 1976; spl. asst. to asst. atty. gen. U.S. Dept. Justice, 1977-79; exec. asst. to gen. counsel U.S. Merit systems Protection Bd., 1979; commr. FTC, Washington, 1979-88; ptnr., Squire, Sanders & Dempsey, Washington, 1989—; bd. dirs. Arbella Mut. Ins. Co.; bd. dirs., trustee Avdel PLC; mem. adv. com. Impact of Women in Pub. Office Rutgers U. Eagleton Inst. Politics. Contbr. articles to profl. jours. Bd. dirs. The Washington Ctr., 1987-89, Women's Legal Def. Fund, 1982-83, Lindenwood Coll., Found. for Women's Resources; mem. Dean's Adv. Coun. Washington Coll. Law of Am. U.; mem. Spl. Commn. to Rev. Honor System and Honor Code at West Point, 1988. Recipient Spl. Recognition award Nat. Assn. Attys. Gen., 1987, Philip Hart Pub. Svc. award Consumer Fedn. Am., 1985. Mem. Women's Bar Assn. of D.C. (bd. dirs. 1981-83, bd. dirs. Women's Bar Assn. Found. 1981-85, named Woman Lawyer of Yr., 1988). Office: Squire Sanders & Dempsey PO Box 407 1201 Pennsylvania Ave NW Washington DC 20044*

BAILEY, RITA MARIA, investment advisor, psychologist; b. Frankfurt, Germany, June 10, 1949; came to U.S., 1957; d. Ludwig and Gertrude (Cierniak) Fleischmann; m. William W. Bailey, Feb. 17, 1974; children: Anne Christine, Cynthia Patricia. BS in Psychology, Austin Peay U., 1975, MA in Psychology, 1977, postgrad., 1977-79. Cert. counselor, Tenn. Editor U.S. Army Spl. Warfare Inst., Ft. Bragg, N.C., 1967-74, edn. officer, 1979-82; edn. officer Augsburg (Germany) Cmty. Ctr., 1982-85; pvt. practice counseling Leavenworth, Kans., 1985-90; pvt. practice investments, 1990—; sr. investment advisor pvt. orgns., Washington, 1991—. Author: Extroversion and Introversion, 1978, Special Warfare Training Plan, 1981; author, editor tng. manual Foreign Small Arms, 1982. Dir. Energy Conservation Campaign, Clarksville, 1976; founder, dir. Women's Support Ctr., Leavenworth, 1986. Mem. Nat. Assn. Investors, Alpha Mu Gamma. Roman Catholic.

BAILEY, SALLY DOROTHY, drama therapist, playwright; b. Pitts., Dec. 31, 1954; d. John Lemon and Sally Lee (Dietrich) B. Student, Allegheny Coll., 1972-73; BFA summa cum laude, U. Tex., 1976; MFA, Trinity U., 1981. Apprentice Houston Stage Equipment, 1977-78; journeyman Dallas Theater Ctr., 1978-81; office mgr. NORCOSTCO/Tex. Costume, Dallas, 1981-83; asst. mng. dir. TheatreVa., Richmond, 1983-85; asst. to artistic dir.

Shakespeare Theatre at the Folger, Washington, 1985-87; tchr. drama Fillmore Arts Ctr., Washington, 1988-94; drama specialist Hartwood Residencies, Alexandria, Va., 1988-91; drama therapist Second Genesis, Bethesda, Md., 1988—; arts access dir. Bethesda (Md.) Acad. Performing Arts, 1988—. Author: Wings To Fly: Bringing Theatre Arts to Students with Disabilities, 1993; screenwriter, co-dir. ednl. video Making Connections, 1994. Mem. Nat. Orgn. for Drama Therapy (registered drama therapist). Home: 1102 Merwood Dr Takoma Park MD 20912 Office: Bethesda Acad Performing Arts 7300 Whittier Blvd Bethesda MD 20817

BAILEY, SUSAN CAROL, commercial banking executive; b. Muskogee, Okla., Apr. 10, 1954; d. William E. and Lula M. (Holloway) Green; m. Wayne M. Bailey, Aug. 6, 1976; 1 child, Nathan W. BS in Fin., So. Ill. U., 1982, MBA, 1983. Tech. asst. ops. Marsh Stencil Machine Co., Belleville, Ill., 1973-85; loan officer Delmar Fin. Co., Belleville, 1985-86; asst. v.p., asst. br. mgr. Fidelity Fed. Savs. and Loan Assn., Fairview Heights, Ill., 1986; asst. v.p., br. mgr. Fidelity Fed. Savs. and Loan Assn., Belleville, 1986-87, v.p., br. mgr., 1987-89, v.p., br. mgr., Metro E. Deposit Acquisition & Fin. Svcs. officer, 1989-90; v.p., comml. loan officer Union Bank Ill., Swansea, 1991—; fin. cons., Caseyville, Ill., 1985-86. Mem., treas. Belleville Welcome Wagon; mem. allocations bd. United Way Greater St. Louis; active leadership program Leadership Ctr. St. Louis, 1993-94, Civic Leader Tour, Scott AFB, 1994; chairperson teleparty St. Clair County Am. Heart Assn., 1995. Mem. St. Louis Fedn. Socs. for Coating Tech. (exec. com. 1980-85, chmn. edn. com. 1983-84), Belleville Bd. Realtors, Edwardsville-Collinsville Bd. Realtors, Women's Coun. Realtors, Homebuilders Assn., Belleville Econ. Progress (amb.), Belleville Postal Coun. (bd. dirs.), Ill. Bankers Assn., So. Ill. Network of Women (alliance rep., pres. 1991—), Fin. Women Internat., Fairview Hts. C. of C. (amb.), Swansea C. of C. (bd. dirs.), Rotary. Home: 710 Belleville Rd Caseyville IL 62232-1142 Office: Union Bank of Ill 4387 N Illinois St Belleville IL 62221-1836

BAILEY-AUDETTE, GEORGIA ANNE, rehabilitation counselor; b. Florence, Ala., Aug. 14, 1948; d. Walter Roy and Mary Frances (Andrews) Bailey; m. William Ryan deGraffenried Jr., June 5, 1971 (div. Jan. 1986); children: Ryan III, Frances; m. Francis Henry Audette, Oct. 2, 1993. BS in Biology, U. Ala., 1970, MA in Rehab. Counseling, 1988. Cert. rehab. counselor; cert. case mgr. Biology tchr. Westlawn Jr. High, Tuscaloosa, Ala., 1970-72; sci. tchr. 7th grade Brookwood Forest Elem., Birmingham, Ala., 1972-75; human physiology tchr. Tuscaloosa (Ala.) Acad., 1976-77; relocation dir. Duckworth Morris Real Estate, 1985-86; advt. sales assoc. WZBQ-102.5 Radio, 1986-87; vocat. rehab. counselor State of Ala., 1989-90; rehab. counselor Gen. Rehab. Svcs., Tampa, Fla., 1990-92; sr. rehab. specialist Comprehensive Rehab. Assocs., Tampa, 1992—. Contbg. columnist Tuscaloosa (Ala.) News, 1979-86. Chmn. heritage week Tuscaloosa (Ala.) Preservation Soc., 1980-81; pres. Jr. League Tuscaloosa, 1982-83; area coun. rep. dist. V, Jr. League Am., N.Y.C., 1983-84. Named Outstanding Civic Vol., Tuscaloosa (Ala.) Preservation Soc., 1982. Mem. Am. Rehab. Counseling Assn., Fla. Assn. Rehab. Profls. in Pvt. Sector.

BAILEY-JONES, CARLA LYNN, nursing administrator; b. Balt., June 4, 1957; d. Carlton L. and Helen P. (Wales) B.; m. Dean C. Jones, Mar. 1988. BS in Nursing, U. Md., Balt., 1979; MS in Health Sci., Towson (Md.) State U., 1987. Nurse clinician I, charge nurse, clin. nurse U. Md. Med. Systems, Balt., 1981-87; maternal transport coord. U. Md. Med. Systems Hosp., Balt., 1979—; rsch. nurse Tokos Med. Corp., Balt., 1988-91; perinatal care coord. U. Md. Med. Systems/Hosp., 1993—; assoc. faculty U. Md. Sch. Nursing; mem. fetal and infant mortality rev. bd. Healthy Start; mem. state commn. Infant Mortality Prevention. Mem. Assn. Women's Health, Obstetric and Neonatal Nurses, Md. Nurse's Assn., Nat. Perinatal Assn., Md. Perinatal Assn.

BAILLIE-DAVID, SONJA KIRSTEEN, controller; b. Lac Megantic, Quebec, Canada, Mar. 26, 1961; came to the U.S., 1964; d. Patrick Eugene and Erika (Bagdonowich) Baillie-David; m. Glenn Frank Skoff, Nov. 12, 1988; 1 child, Elaine Elise Skoff. AA, Joliet Jr. Coll., 1983; BBA, Coll. St. Francis, 1985; MBA in Entrepreneurship, DePaul U., 1992. CPA, Ill. Auditor Peat, Marwick Main, Chgo., 1985-87; auditor Ill. Tool Works, Chgo., 1987-88, fin. analyst, 1988-89; fin. systems project mgr. Ill. Tool Works, Glenview, Ill., 1989-94; controller U.S. Wire-Tie Systems, Woodridge, Ill., 1994—. Mem. Ill. CPA Soc., NAFE, Am. Mgmt. Assn. Roman Catholic. Office: US Wire-Tie Systems 2401 Internationale Pky Woodridge IL 60517-4913

BAIMAN, GAIL, real estate broker; b. Bklyn., June 4, 1938; d. Joseph and Anita (Devon) Yalow; m. James F. Becker, Oct. 1970 (div. 1978); children: Steven, Susan, Barbara. Student Bklyn. Coll., 1955-57. Lic. real estate broker, N.Y., Pa., Fla. Personnel-pub. relations dir. I.M.C., Inc., N.Y.C., 1970-72; pres., broker Gayle Baiman Assocs., Inc., N.Y.C., 1972-74; v.p., broker Tuit Mktg. Corp., Mt. Pocono, Pa., 1974-83; pres., broker Ind. Timeshare Sales, Inc., St. Petersburg, Orlando and Helen, Ga. 1983—. Author: Vacation Timesharing, A Real Estate, 1992. Mem. Am. Resort Developers Assn., Better Bus. Arbitrator Assn., Internat. Resale Brokers Assn. (co-founder), Chmns. League, Better Bus. Bur. Arbitrators. Office: Ind Timeshare Sales Inc 10344 66 St N Pinellas Park FL 34666

BAIN, ELAINE RUGIENIUS, educator; b. Pottsville, Pa., Aug. 17, 1944; d. Adolph Andrew and Helen Eleanor (Bluis) Rugienius; m. Donald Bruce Bain Jr., Dec. 2, 1966; children: Elizabeth Rebecca, Donald Bruce III, Alexander McKay. Cert., Temple U., 1971; BA, Pa. State U., 1966; MA, Ea. Mich. U., 1989; postgrad., Madonna U., 1992-94. Cert. tchr. Pa., Va., Mass., Mich. Tchr. York (Pa.) City Schs., 1966, Alexandria (Va.) City Schs., 1967, Shikellamy Schs., Sunbury, Pa., 1967-68, Groton (Mass.) Sch. Dist., 1968-69, Phila. City Schs., 1969, Plymouth (Mich.) Canton Cmty. Schs., 1990—; adj. instr. Schoolcraft Coll., Livonia, Mich., 1988—. Pres. Plymouth Cmty. Arts Coun., 1988-90; mem. EMU Circle Excellence. Mem. AAUW (edn. found. projects chair), Nat. Coun. Tchrs. English, Mich. Reading Assn., Pa. State Alumni Assn., Theta Phi Alpha, Phi Kappa Phi. Episcopalian. Office: Plymouth Canton Cmyt Schs 454 S Harvey St Plymouth MI 48170

BAIN, KATHY LOUISE, elementary counselor; b. Miami, Aug. 23, 1956; d. Franklin Allen and Mary Jane (Walker) Daniel; m. Stephen Craig Jones, Aug. 25, 1978 (div. May 1990); children: Danielle Marie Jones, Kalyn Dawn Jones, Stephen Boyd Jones; m. M. Dewey Bain, Nov. 22, 1990. BS, David Lipscomb Coll., 1978; MA in Edn., U. Tex., 1992. Cert. elem. sch. counselor; cert. tchr. K-8. Kindergarten tchr. Sumner County Pub. Schs., Hendersonville, Tenn., 1979; 1st grade tchr. Cypress-Fairbanks Ind. Sch. Dist., Houston, 1982-86, 88, kindergarten tchr., 1987-88; kindergarten tchr. Northside Ind. Sch. Dist., San Antonio, 1988-94, elem. counselor, 1994—; team leader Northside Ind. Sch. Dist., 1993-94, C.H.I.L.D. process leader, 1993-94. Vice pres. Rudder Middle Sch. PTA, San Antonio, 1993-94. Mem. Tex. Counseling Assn., South Tex. Counseling Assn., Am. Sch. Counselor Assn., Northside Counseling Assn. Mem. Ch. of Christ. Home: 5719 Quail Crown San Antonio TX 78249-3137 Office: Northside Ind Sch Dist Leon Valley Elem Sch 7111 Huebner San Antonio TX 78240-3199

BAIN, NANCY REMUS, geography educator, ombudsman; b. Mpls., Oct. 9, 1942; d. Joseph Augustus and Audrey Lucille (Rudser) Remus; m. George William Bain, Mar. 15, 1969; children: Daniel J., Emily C., William G. BA in History and Elem. Edn., Coll. St. Catherine, 1964; MA in History, U. Minn., 1967, PhD in Geography, 1973. Tchr. 7th grade St. Raphael's Sch., Crystal, Minn., 1964-67; instr. Coll. St. Catherine, St. Paul, 1967-68; teaching asst. geography dept. U. Minn., Mpls., 1968-69; instr. Minn. State Jr. Coll., Mpls., 1970-71; tchr. Ohio U., Athens, 1971—, head geography dept., 1983-88, ombudsman, 1991—; cons. Appalachian Regional Commn., Washington, 1979, Ohio Valley Regional Devel., Portsmouth, 1980—, Ohio Mid-Ea. Govt. Assn., Cambridge, 1983-88. Contbr. articles to profl. jours. Mem. regional planning commn. Athens Regional Planning Commn., 1976—; mem. bd. zoning appeals City of Athens, 1975-84; coun. mem. Athens City Coun., 1984—. Mem. Assn. Am. Geographers (local adjutant East Lakes Assn. of Assn. Am. Geographers 1989, pres. regional bd. dirs. East Lakes Assn. of Assn. Am. Geographers 1991-93), Ohio Geography Alliance, Univ. Coll. Ombudsman Assn., Athens Mediation Group. Democrat. Roman Catholic. Home: 110 Columbia Ave Athens OH 45701 Office: Ohio U Geography Dept Cuippenger Lab Athens OH 45701

BAINBRIDGE, DONA BARDELLI, international marketing executive; b. Irvington, N.J., Feb. 27, 1953; d. Alfred and Dona Ellen (Self) B.; m. Harry M. Bainbridge, May 23, 1981 (dec.); 1 child, Harry Michael. Certificat de Langue, Sorbonne, U. Paris, 1974; BA, U. Ky., 1975; MA in Internat. Studies, Am. U., 1978; MS in Econ. and Social Planning in Developing Countries , U. London, 1979. Research assoc. Woodrow Wilson Internat. Ctr. for Vis. Scholars, Washington, 1976-77, World Bank, Washington, 1977-79; legis. asst. to Congressman Marc Lincoln Marks, Washington, 1979-80; internat. trade analyst Internat. Trade Adminstrn., U.S. Dept. Commerce, Washington, 1980-82; internat. mgmt. cons. Coopers and Lybrand, 1982-86 ; v.p. Bankers Trust Co., Internat. Pvt. Banking, 1986-88; sr. mktg. dir. internat. services BDO Seidman, N.Y.C., 1988-90; founder, pres. D.H. Bainbridge Assocs., 1990—. Chair person nat. mem. Am. Friends of London Sch. Econs., 1981-83, nat. bd. dirs., 1982-84, 1994—, mem. steering com. women's studies in religion, Harvard Divinity Sch.; chmn. mem. com.; mem. ops. com., bd. dirs. Camp Sloane YMCA. Lakeville, Conn.; endowment com. Women's Studies in Religion program Harvard Divinity Sch.; mem. adv. bd., chmn. White Plains Salvation Army, 1992-93. Mem. NAFE, Soc. for Internat. Devel. D.C. Chpt., Bus. and Profl. Women's Clubs Am. (acad. scholar 1971), Nat. Press Club, Fin. Women's Assn. N.Y., Kiwanis. Democrat. Lutheran.

BAINES, JEAN MARIE, computer developer/analyst; b. Louisville, Oct. 3, 1967; d. James Robert and Carole Anne (Moch) B. BA, Bellarmine Coll., Louisville, 1989; postgrad., U. Louisville, 1994—. Food supr. Ky. Kingdom, Louisville, 1987; intern CSX Tech., Jacksonville, Fla., 1988; info. specialist EnTrade/Tenneco Gas, Louisville, 1989-93; developer/analyst Ventech Sys., Inc., Louisville, 1994—. Youth counselor vol., youth tutor vol. Bellarmine Acad. scholar, 1985-89, service award, 1989.

BAINS, LESLIE ELIZABETH, banker; b. Glen Ridge, N.J., July 28, 1943; d. Pliny Otto and Dorothy Ethel (Keeley) Tawney; m. Harrison Mackellar Bains Jr.; Harrison III, Tawney Elizabeth. BA, Am. U., 1965. Asst. treas. Citicorp, N.Y.C., 1965-73; v.p. Mfrs. Hanover, N.Y.C., 1973-80; v.p., div. exec. Chase Manhattan Bank, N.Y.C., 1980-86, v.p., group exec., 1986-87, sr. v.p. group exec., 1987-91; mng. dir. Citibank, N.Y.C., 1991-93; exec. v.p. Republic Nat. Bank, N.Y.C., 1993—; bd. dirs. Interplast, 1990—, Bankers Lawyers Com., 1983—. Chmn. Ednl. Cable Consortium, Summit, N.J., 1987-91; mem. corp. adv. panel N.J. Coun. of Chs., 1990—; mem. bd. visitors Kogod Sch. Bus., Am. U., 1992—; mem. bd. visitors N.Y. Philharm. Consol. Fund, chmn., 1983-84; trustee Am. U., 1994—; mem Coun. Fgn. Rels., 1991—. Named Achiever of Yr. YWCA, 1985, One of Top 100 Women in Corp. Am., Bus. Month., 1989. Mem. Am. Bankers Assn. (bd. dirs. pvt. banking coun.), Fin. Women Internat. (treas. 1981-83, v.p. 1983-84, pres. 1984-85, vice chmn. Edn. Found. 1980-81), Fin. Women's Assn., Women and Founds./N.Y. Soc. of Security Analysts. Office: Republic Nat Bank 452 5th Ave New York NY 10018-2706

BAIR, LINDA HERMAN, educational consultant; b. Phila., Nov. 13, 1956; d. Walter Hood and Joyce Frances (Nitt) Herman; m. Mark Emerson Bair, Sept. 6, 1981; children: Devon Francis, Brooke Herman. BS, Northwestern U., 1978; MEd, U. Houston, 1984, EdD, 1993. Cert. elem. tchr., K-8, supervision K-12, midmgmt. K-12, supt. K-12. Tchr. Pitts., 1978-81, Houston, 1981-86; prin. elem. sch. Houston Ind. Sch. Dist., 1986-90; cons. Houston, 1991—; adj. prof. U. Houston, 1993—; mem. Odyssey of the Mind State/Regional Bd., Houston, 1987-94. Alumni admission counselor/dir. Northwestern U., Evanston, 1984-94. Mem. ASCD, Tex. Elem. Prins. and Suprs. Assn., Houston Edn. Exch., Phi Delta Kappa. Home: 4146 Swarthmore Houston TX 77005

BAIR, MYRNA LYNN, state senator; b. Huntington, W.Va., Oct. 26, 1940; d. Charles Thomas and Velma Elvera (Schoenlein) North; B.S. in Chemistry, U. Cin., 1962; Ph.D., U. Wis., 1968; m. Thomas Irvin Bair, Mar. 12, 1966; children—Thomas Irvin, Catherine Lynn. Asst. prof. chemistry Beaver Coll., Glenside, Pa., 1966-70; instr. chemistry U. Del., 1974-76, asst. prof. edn., 1977-79; asst. dir. pub. info. Del. Energy Office, Wilmington, 1978-79; mem. Del. Senate, 1981—; vice chair women's network, assembly on states Nat. Conf. of State Legislatures, 1994-95; sr. mgmt. advisor Coll. Urban Affairs and Pub. Policy, dir. women's leadership tng. program, 1989—. Contbr. articles to sci. jours. Bd. dirs. Del. Lung Assn.; trustee Wesley Coll.; mem. Nat. Republican Com., Wilmington Rep. Women's Club. Recipient Freshman award Chem. Rubber Co., 1959; DuPont Co. Teaching award, 1963, Pres.'s award Jr. League, 1988; NSF fellow, 1964-66. Mem. AAUW, Phi Beta Kappa, Iota Sigma Pi, Alpha Lambda Delta. Methodist. Office: Del State Senate State Capital Bldg Dover DE 19901

BAIR, SALLY J., technology coordinator; b. Phila., Sept. 9, 1953; d. C. Wayne and Jean B. (Bohner) B. BS in Music Edn., Mansfield U., 1974; MA in Ednl. Theatre, NYU, 1988; MS in Instrnl. Tech., Bloomsburg (Pa.) U., 1990. Cert. Pa. instructional II sch. specialist. Music tchr. Minersville (Pa.) Area Sch. Dist., 1974-84; music educator Schuylkill Haven (Pa.) Area Sch. Dist., 1984-89; coord. computer edn. Pine Grove (Pa.) Area Sch. Dist., 1989—; computer edn. inservice trainer and presenter in field. Auditor, Sandpoint Festive Conductor Tng., 1985; faculty mem. Pa. Gov.'s Sch. for Teaching, 1991, 92; laserdisc inservice trainer for Blue Mountain Area Sch. Dist., 1991, St. Clair Area Sch. Dist., 1993. Recipient Minersville Rotary Community Svc. award, 1980, Minersville Lions Community Svc. award, 1980, Northwestern U. Summer Music fellowship, 1984, Pa. Gov.'s Sch. for Teaching award for Excellence, 1991, Duquesne U. Teaching Excellence award, 1992, Pine Grove Area Sch. Dist. Cert. of Excellence for Computer Edn., 1992, Merit Networking Seminar scholarship, 1993, Hon. Mention in the ISTE Telecomputing Competition, 1993. Office: Pine Grove Area Sch Dist 103 School St Pine Grove PA 17963-1610

BAIR, SHEILA COLLEEN, commissioner; b. Wichita, Kans., Apr. 3, 1954; d. Albert E. and Clara F. (Brenneman) B.; m. Scott Cooper; 1 child, Preston Carlos. BA in Philosophy, U. Kans., 1975, JD, 1978. Bar: Kans. 1979. Teaching fellow Sch. Law, U. Ark., Fayetteville, 1978-79; atty.-advisor HEW, Kansas City, Mo., 1979-81; legal and policy advisor Office of Senator Bob Dole, Washington, 1981-86; of counsel Kutak, Rock & Campbell, Washington, 1986-87; dir. rsch. Bob Dole for Pres., Kans., 1987-88; legis. counsel N.Y. Stock Exch., Washington, 1988-91; commr. Commodity Futures Trading Commn., Washington, 1991—, acting chmn., 1993. Candidate U.S. Ho. of Reps. from 5th Kans. dist., 1990; mem. bd. govs. Sch. Law, U. Kans., 1990-93; bd. dirs. Women's Campaign Fund, 1991—. Mem. ABA. Home: 3704 Brandywine St NW Washington DC 20016 Office: Commodity Futures Trading Commn 2033 K St NW 8th Fl Washington DC 20581

BAIRD, BONNIE SUE, chiropractor; b. Miilw., Feb. 22, 1960; d. Richard Allen and Gloria Christine (Stevenson) Smithyman; m. Andrew Fielden, Jan. 29, 1983; children: Brandon Alexander, Kelsey Nicole; 1 stepchild, Stacey Kay. BS in Biology, Lewis U., 1983; D of Chiropractic, Parker Coll. Chiropractic, 1987. Chiropractic assoc. Raleigh (N.C.) Neck & Back Clinic, 1988-89, Yowell Chiropractic, Fuquay-Varina, N.C., 1989-91; pvt. practice Fuquay-Varina, N.C., 1991-93; prin. Baird Chiropractic, Fuquay-Varina, N.C., 1993—. Vol. sci. fair Lincoln Hts. Elem. Sch., Fuquay-Varina, 1993-94; fin. and scrapbook com. Credit Profl. Internat., Fuquay-Varina, 1990. Mem. Internat. Chiropractic Assn., N.C. Chiropractic Assn., We Care Chiropractic Assn., Parker Coll. Chiropractic Resource Found. Lutheran. Home: PO Box 1346 Fuquay Varina NC 27526 Office: Baird Chiropractic 1301 E Academy St # B Fuquay Varina NC 27526-2610

BAIRD, DELPHA, state legislator; b. Brigham City, Utah, Dec. 13, 1930; m. Steven Baird; 9 children. BS, U. Utah, 1983. Treas. Holladay Cottonwood Community Coun., 1985—; sec., treas. Archl. Ornamentation Inc., 1985—; mem. Utah State Senate from 9th dist. Mem. Profl. Rep. Women, Utah Women's Legis. Coun. Republican. Mem. LDS Ch. Address: 2574 Kentucky Ave Salt Lake City UT 84117-5465 Office: Senate House State Capitol Salt Lake City UT 84114*

BAIRD, IRENE CEBULA, educational administrator; b. Ware, Mass.; d. Frank M. and Ann Elizabeth (Bigda) Cebula; m. Irwin Lewis Baird, Aug. 30, 1949 (dec. Apr. 1981); children: Lisa M., Nina J., Mara L. AB, Smith Coll., 1945; MA, U. Kans., 1947; DEd, Pa. State U. Harrisburg, 1994. Rsch. assoc. PROBE, Pa. State Harrisburg, Middletown, 1982-88, coord./facilitator Job Link Program, 1988-91, supr./facilitator Adult Basic Edn./Gen. Edn. Devel. program, 1991-92; project dir. Pa. Commn. for Women, Harrisburg, 1992; dir. Women's Enrichment Ctr. Pa. State Harrisburg, 1994—; Spanish instr. U. Kans., U. Mass. Contbr. chpts. to Pa. Vocat. Edn. Mktg. Manual; mem. editorial bd. Alumnae Quar., Smith Coll., 1987-91; contbr. articles to profl. jours.; presenter in field. Mem. task force Adult Literacy and Lifelong Learning, Capital Region 2000, 1991—; mem. exhibits/community edn. coms. Susquehanna Art Mus., 1991—, bd. dirs. 1991—; bd. dirs. Pa. coun. for Future of Women in the Workplace, 1987—; mem. career edn. adv. bd. Harrisburg Sch. Dist., 1986—, mem. community adv. com., 1991-93. Mem. Am. Assn. Adult and Continuing Edn. (selected participant confs. Montreal, Can. 1991, Anaheim, Calif. 1992, Dallas 1993, Nashville 1994), Am. Assn. Tchrs. Spanish and Portuguese, Ctrl. Pa. Assn. Women Execs., Nat. Assn. Women in Edn., Pa. Assn. Adult and Continuing Edn. (one of Outstanding Adult Students in Higher Edn. 1995), Wider Opportunities for Women, Women's Legis. Exch. Home: 115 Rodney Ln Camp Hill PA 17011-1323 Office: Pa State Harrisburg-Eastgate 1010 N 7th St Harrisburg PA 17102-1400

BAIRD, LOURDES G., federal judge; b. 1935. BA with highest honors, UCLA, 1973, JD with honors, 1976. Asst. U.S. atty. U.S. Dist. Ct. (ctrl. dist.) Calif., L.A., 1977-83, U.S. atty., 1990-92; ptnr. Baird & Quadros, 1983-84, Baird, Munger & Myers, 1984-86; judge East L.A. Mcpl. Ct., 1986-87; adj. prof. law Loyola U., L.A., 1986-90; judge L.A. Mcpl. Ct., 1987-88, L.A. Superior Ct., 1988-90; U.S. atty. ctrl. dist. Calif., 1990-92; judge U.S. Dist. Ct. (ctrl. dist.) Calif., L.A., 1992—; faculty civil RICO program Practicing Law Inst., San Francisco, 1984-85, western regional program Nat. Inst. Trial Advocacy, Berkeley, Calif., 1987-88; adj. prof. trial advocacy Loyola U., L.A., 1987-90. Recipient Silver Achievement award for the professions YWCA, 1994; named Woman of Promise, Hispanic Womens' Coun., 1991, Alumnus of Yr., UCLA Sch. Law, 1991. Mem. Mexican-Am. Bar Assn., Calif. Women Lawyers, Hispanic Nat. Bar Assn., UCLA Sch. Law alumni Assn. (pres. 1984). Office: US Dist Ct Ctrl Dist Calif Edward R. Roybal Bldg 255 E Temple St Ste 770 Los Angeles CA 90012-3334*

BAIRD, ZOË, insurance company executive, lawyer; b. Bklyn., June 20, 1952; d. Ralph Louis and Naomi (Allen) B.; m. Paul Gewirtz, June 8, 1986; 1 child, Julian Baird Gewirtz. AB, U. Calif., Berkeley, 1974, JD, 1977. Bar: Washington, 1979, Calif. 1977, Conn. 1989. Law clk. Hon. Albert Wollenberg, San Francisco, 1977-78; atty., advisor Office Legal Counsel U.S. Dept. Justice, Washington, 1979-80; assoc. counsel to the Pres. The White House, Washington, 1980-81; assoc., then ptnr. O'Melveny & Myers, Washington, 1981-86; counsellor, staff exec. GE, Fairfield, Conn., 1986-90; v.p., gen. counsel Aetna Life & Casualty, Hartford, 1990—; bd. dirs. Sci. Pk. Devel. Corp., New Haven, So. New Eng. Telecom. Corp., mem. bd. contbrs. Mem. Am. Lawyer Media, N.Y.C. (bd. contbrs.). Office: Aetna Life & Casualty 151 Farmington Ave Hartford CT 06156-0002*

BAIRSTOW, FRANCES KANEVSKY, labor arbitrator, mediator, educator; b. Racine, Wis., Feb. 19, 1920; d. William and Minnie (DuBow) Kanevsky; m. Irving P. Kaufman, Nov. 14, 1942 (div. 1949); m. David Steele Bairstow, Dec. 17, 1954; children: Dale Owen, David Anthony. Student U. Wis., 1937-42; BS, U. Louisville, 1949; student Oxford U. (Eng.), 1953-54; postgrad. McGill U., Montreal, Que., 1958-59. Rsch. economist U.S. Senate Labor-Mgmt. Subcom., Washington, 1950-51; labor edn. specialist U. P.R., San Juan, 1951-52; chief wage data unit WSB, Washington, 1952-53; labor rsch. economist Canadian Pacific Ry. Co., Montreal, 1956-58; asst. dir. indsl. rels. ctr. McGill U., 1960-66, assoc. dir., 1966-71, dir., 1971-85, lectr., indsl. rels. dept. econs., 1960-72, asst. prof. faculty mgmt., 1972-74, assoc. prof. faculty mgmt., 1974-83, prof., 1983-85; lectr. Stetson Law Sch., Fla. spl. master Fla. Pub. Employees Rels. Commn., 1985—; dep. commr. essential svcs. Province of Que., 1976-81; mediator So. Bell Telephone, 1985—, AT&T and Comm. Workers Am., 1986—; cons. on collective bargaining arbitrator to OECD, Paris, 1979, Orlando Utilities Commn. Orlando Bldg. and Trade Council, 1994—; cons., Nat. Film Bd. of Can., 1965-69; arbitrator Que. Consultative Coun. Panel of Arbitrators, 1968-83, Ministry Labour and Manpower, 1971-83, United Airlines and Assn. Flight Attendants, 1990—, State U. System of Fla., 1990—, Tampa Gen. Health Care, 1994—; Orlando Utilities Commn., Orlando, 1994; mediator Canadian Public Svc. Staff Rels. Bd., 1973-85; contbg. columnist Montreal Star, 1971-85. Chmn. Nat. Inquiry Commn. Wider-Based Collective Bargaining, 1978. Fulbright fellow, 1953-54. Mem. Canadian Indsl. Rels. Rsch. Inst. (exec. bd. 1965-68), Indsl. Rels. Rsch. Assn. Am. (mem. exec. bd. 1965-68, chmn. nominating com. 1977), Nat. Acad. Arbitrators (bd. govs. 1977-80, program chmn. 1982-83, v.p. 1986-88, nat. coord. 1987-90). Home and Office: 1430 Gulf Blvd Apt 507 Clearwater FL 34630-2856

BAISLEY, HARRIET ESTHER, biographical research adviser; b. Bklyn., Jan. 9, 1917; d. William Taylor and Florence (Lindner) B. Student, Campbell Coll., 1950, Duke U., 1952, U. Richmond, 1952-53; LLD (hon.), U. Rome, 1963. Pvt. practice, biographical cons., inventory control Esther's Enterprises, Richmond, Va., 1929-89, owner, mgr., chief exec. officer, 1983—; hwy. inspector State of Va., Richmond, 1961-73. Co-author: The Fly and the Man, 1956, The Word of God, 1960. Named Woman of Yr., 1991. Mem. Am. Mgmt. Assn. Roman Catholic. Home and Office: Esthers Enterprises 210 Hospital St Apt 11G Richmond VA 23219-1128

BAJOIE, DIANA E., state legislator; b. July 8, 1948. Former mem. La. State Ho. Reps. from 91st dist.; mem. La. State Senate. Alt. del. Dem. Nat. Party Conf., 1978. Office: La State Senate State Capitol Baton Rouge LA 70804*

BAK, DIANN LEE, accountant; b. Chgo., Oct. 10, 1949; d. Joseph Stanley and Stella Mary (Waclawek) B. AA in Bus. Adminstrn., Daley Coll., Chgo., 1987; BA in Acctg., DePaul U., Chgo., 1991. With HHS, Chgo., 1967-81, supr., 1981—. Mem. Am. Soc. Women Accts. (chair com. Chgo. chpt. 1990-93), Golden Key Club, Delta Mu Delta, Beta Gamma Sigma, Beta Alpha Psi. Roman Catholic. Office: Social Security Adminstrn 9730 S Western Ave Evergreen Park IL 60642-2814

BAK, SUNNY, photographer; b. N.Y.C., July 25, 1958; d. Chun Suk and Bie Liang (Kwik) B. AB, CCNY, 1976; postgrad., New Sch. for Social Rsch., N.Y.C., 1982-85, UCLA, 1987. Pres. Sunny Bak Photography, N.Y.C., 1976-83; staff photographer The Hamptons Newspaper Mag., Southampton, N.Y., 1978-84; sec., treas. Sunny Bak Studio, Inc., N.Y.C., 1983-87, pres., 1988—; pres. Sunny Bak Pub. Rels., N.Y.C., 1984-85; dir. pub. rels. H.H. Assocs., N.Y.C. and L.A., 1985-87; dir. west coast ops. KCG Prodns., N.Y.C., 1987-88. Photographer: Vamps, Sirens, Temptresses, 1984-85, 32 covers of Womans World mag., 1985-88, Lic. to Ill, 1987, Pupple, 1988, Detail's mag. cover, 1989. Mem. Advt. Photographer's Am., Assn. Asian Pacific Am. Artists, Asian Pacific Women's Network. Democrat. Buddhist.

BAKAS, DEMETRA, physical therapist; b. Danville, Va., Sept. 22, 1954; d. Tom and Elizabeth (Maurakis) B.; m. Teddy Wilchere Worrell, Feb. 18, 1978 (div. Mar. 1987). Student, Va. Polytechic Inst. and State U., 1972-74; BS in Phys. Therapy, Va. Commonwealth U., 1976. Registered phys. therapist. Staff therapist VA Med. Ctr., Salem, Va., 1976-78, 79-80; asst. dir. Smyth County Cmty. Hosp., Marion, Va., 1978-79; pvt. practice phys. therapy Draper, Va., 1980-87; staff therapist Piedmont Phys. Therapy, High Point, N.C., 1988-91; owner Health Promotions, Greensboro, N.C., 1991—; holistic health practitioner, condr. wellness seminars, 1992—. Author: (with others) A Break in the Clouds. Mem. Am. Phys. Therapy Assn., N.C. Phys. Therapy Assn. (v.p.), Ptnrs. of the Ams.-N.C. (Piedmont dist.), Nat. Assn. Profl. Saleswomen. Greek Orthodox. Home: 103 Wendell Ct Danville VA 24540 Office: Health Promotions PO Box 38211 Greensboro NC 27438

BAKELAAR, DONNA, state assembly staff member; b. Long Beach, Calif., July 22, 1945; children from previous marriage: Paul, Mark, Anne; m. Robert J. Bakelaar, Aug. 6, 1994; stepchildren: Jason, Jaime, Joshua. RN, Cmty. Hosp., 1966. Campaign mgr. Congressman Michael Milirakis, Palm Harbor, Fla., 1982, spl. asst., 1983-84; campaign mgr. N.J. Assembly Rep. Majority, Trenton, N.J., 1985; dir. constituent svcs. N.J. Assembly Rep. Office, Trenton, 1986-91; clk. N.J. Gen. Assembly, Trenton, 1992—. Trustee N.J. State Mus., Trenton, 1993—, Hagedorn Geropsychiat. Ctr., Glen Gardner, N.J., 1989—; pres. Friends of the State House, Trenton, 1992—. Recipient Svc. award Art Pride N.J., Inc., 1994. Mem. Am. Soc. Legis.

Clks. and Secs. Greek Orthodox. Office: NJ Gen Assembly State House CN-098 Trenton NJ 08625

BAKEMAN, CAROL ANN, administrative services manager, singer; b. San Francisco, Oct. 27, 1934; d. Lars Hartvig and Gwendolyne Beatrice (Zimmer) Bergh; student UCLA, 1954-62; m. Delbert Clifton Bakeman, May 16, 1959; children: Laurie Ann, Deborah Ann. Singer, Roger Wagner Chorale, 1954-92, Los Angeles Master Chorale, 1964-86, The Wagner Ensemble, 1991—; librarian Hughes Aircraft Co., Culver City, Calif., 1954-61; head econs. library Planning Research Corp., L.A., 1961-63; corporate librarian Econ. Cons., Inc., Los Angeles, 1963-68; head econs. library Daniel, Mann, Johnson & Mendenhall, architects and engrs., L.A., 1969-71, corporate librarian, 1971-77, mgr. info. services, 1978-81, mgr. info. and office services, 1981-83, mgr. adminstrv. services, 1983—; pres., Creative Library Systems, Los Angeles, 1974-83; library cons. ArchiSystems, div. SUMMA Corp., Los Angeles, 1972-81, Property Rehab. Corp., Bell Gardens, Calif., 1974-75, VTN Corp., Irvine, Calif., 1974, William Pereira & Assos., 1975; mem. office systems and bus. edn. adv. bd. Calif. State U. Northridge, 1992—. Mem. Assistance League, So. Calif., 1956-86, mem. nat. auxilaries com. 1968-72, 75-78, mem. nat. by laws com. 1970-75, mem. asso. bd. dirs., 1966-76. Mem. AFTRA, SAG, Am. Guild Musical Artists, Adminstrv. Mgmt. Soc. (v.p. Los Angeles chpt. 1984-86, pres. 1986-88, internat. conf. chmn. 1988-89, internat. bd. dirs. 1988-90, internat. v.p. mgmt. edn. 1990-92), Los Angeles Master Chorale Assn. (bd. dirs. 1978-83), L.A. Bus. Travel Assn. (bd. dir. 1995—), Nat. Bus. Travel Assn. (nat. convention seminar com.).

BAKER, AMANDA SIRMON, academic administrator, nursing educator; b. Daphne, Ala., Apr. 3, 1934; d. Joel Green and Edna Mae (Miller) Sirmon; m. Malcolm Davis Baker, Mar. 30, 1957; children: Leonard Eric, Michael Davis. BSN, U. Ala., Tuscaloosa, 1955; M in Nursing, U. Fla., Gainesville, 1972, PhD, 1974; cert., Bryn Mawr Coll., 1983. Office nurse R.P. Maxon, M.D., Ft. Walton Beach, Fla., 1955-58; pub. health nurse County Health Dept., Clovis, N.Mex., 1963-64; staff nurse, night supr. Pheobe Putney Hosp., Albany, Ga., 1964-67; developer, implementor home svc. nursing program for children and adults with cerebral palsy United Cerebral Palsy, Southwest Ga., 1967-68; instr. in child health, med./surg. and pharmacology Albany (Ga.) Jr. Coll., 1968-69; grad. teaching asst. child health nursing U. Fla., 1972-73, grad. teaching assoc. child health nursing, 1973-74, asst. dean continuing profl. edn. Coll. of Nursing, 1974-76, asst. dean. undergrad. studies, 1976-78, acting dean Coll. of Nursing, 1978-80, asst. dean. undergrad. studies Coll. of Nursing, 1980-81, assoc. dean Coll. of Nursing, 1981-85; dean Sch. of Nursing Troy State U., 1985-89; dean Coll. of Nursing U. South Ala., 1989—; mem. search com. Coll. Medicine, 1990-92, chair search com. VPAA, 1990-91, mem. fin. resources com., 1991-93, chair subcom.; speaker and presenter in field. Contbr. articles to profl. jours. Chair Ala. Nurses Polit. Action Com., 1986-89. Mem. ANA (coun. nurse rschrs., S.E. region accrediting com., charter 1974-78) Nat. League for Nursing (coun. baccalaureate and higher degree edn. 1974—), Ala. State Nurses Assn. (dist. 8 chpt.), Ala. League for Nursing, Soc. for Rsch. in Nursing Edn., Am. Assn. Colls. of Nursing (semi-ann. meetings 1985—, program com. 1990-92, pub. rels. com. 1992-94, govtl. affairs com. 1994—), Ala. Bd. Nursing, So. Coun. on Collegiate Edn. in Nursing, Phi Kappa Phi, Pi Lamda Theta, Sigma Theta Tau. Presbyterian. Office: U South Ala Coll Nursing Springhill Campus Mobile AL 36688

BAKER, ANITA, singer; b. Toledo, Jan. 26, 1958; m. Walter Bridgeforth, Jr., Dec. 24, 1988; 1 child, Walter Baker Bridgeforth. Mem. funk band Chapter 8, Detroit, 1978-80; receptionist Quin & Budajh, Detroit, 1980-82; ind. singer, songwriter, 1982—. Rec. artist: (with Chapter 8) I Just Wanna Be Your Girl, 1980, (solo albums) The Songstress, 1983, Rapture, 1986 (Grammy award for best rhythm and blues vocal performance 1987), Giving You the Best That I Got, 1988 (Grammy awards for best rhythm and blues song, 1988, best rhythm and blues performance, female, single, 1988, best album, 1989), Compositions, 1990 (Grammy award for best rhythm and blues performance, 1990), Rhythm of Love, 1994 (Grammy award nominee for best album 1995, best female vocal 1995, best song 1995); songs include No More Tears, Angel, Caught Up in the Rapture, Sweet Love (Grammy award best rhythm and blues song 1987), Same Ol' Love, You Bring Me Joy, Been So Long, No One in the World. Recipient Grammy award gospel, soul, best performance, duo, group, choir or chorus, 1987, NAACP Image award, best female vocalist and best album of yr. Office: All Baker's Music 804 N Crescent Dr Beverly Hills CA 90210-2918*

BAKER, ANITA DIANE, lawyer; b. Atlanta, Sept. 4, 1955; d. Byron Garnett and Anita (Swanson) B. BA summa cum laude, Oglethorpe U., 1977; JD with distinction, Emory U., 1980. Bar: Ga. 1980. Assoc. Hansell & Post, Atlanta, 1980-88, Kitchens, Kelley, Gaynes, Huprich & Shmerling, 1989-90; asst. gen. counsel NationsBank Corp., 1991—. Mem. ABA (com. on savs. and loan instns., com. on consumer fin. svcs.), Atlanta Bar Assn., Ga. Bar Assn., Atlanta Hist. Soc., Pace Acad. Alumni Assn. (bd. dirs.), Oglethorpe Univ. Alumni Assn. (bd. dirs.), Order of Coif, Phi Alpha Delta, Phi Alpha Theta, Alpha Chi, Omicron Delta Kappa. Office: NationsBank Corp 600 Peachtree St Fl 5 Atlanta GA 30308

BAKER, BETTY LOUISE, retired mathematician, educator; b. Chgo., Oct. 17, 1937; d. Russell James and Lucille Juanita (Timmons) B.; BE, Chgo. State U., 1961, MA, 1964; PhD, Northwestern U., 1971. Tchr. math. Harper High Sch., Chgo., 1961-70; tchr. math. Hubbard High Sch., Chgo., 1970-85, also chmn. dept.; tchr. Bogan High Sch., 1985-94, ret., 1994; part-time instr. Moraine Valley C.C., 1982-83, 84-86. Cultural arts chmn. Hubbard Parents-Tchrs.-Student Assn., 1974-76, 1st v.p., program chmn., 1977-79, 82-84, pres., 1979-81; organist Hope Luth. Ch., 1963—. Univ. fellow, 1969-70; cert. tchr. high sch. and elem. grades 3-8 math., Ill. Mem. Nat. Coun. Tchrs. Math., Ill. Coun. Tchrs. of Math., Math. Assn. Am., Chgo. Tchrs. Union, Nat. Coun. Parents and Tchrs. (life), Sch. Sci. and Math. Assn., Assn. for Supervision and Curriculum Devel., Am. Guild of Organists, Luth. Collegiate Assn., Walther League Hiking Club, Met. Math. Club Chgo., Kappa Mu Epsilon, Rho Sigma Tau, Mu Alpha Theta (sponsor), Kappa Delta Pi, Pi Lambda Theta, Phi Delta Kappa. Contbr. articles to profl. jours. Home: 3214 W 85th St Chicago IL 60652-3727

BAKER, BONNIE ANN, real estate broker; b. Rock Springs, Wyo., Apr. 5, 1946; d. Clarence Heber and Vivian Doan Sargent; m. Joel Cheney Baker, Feb. 7, 1969; children—Michelle Leigh, Joelle Doan. A.A., Western Wyo. Coll., 1971; B.F.A., U. Wyo., 1984. Lic. broker Wyo.; CRS. Mem. public relations staff Janss Corp., Rock Spring, Wyo., 1980-81; salesman Sweetwater Realty, Green River, 1982-85; broker, owner Twin Pines Realty, Green River, 1985—; bd. dirs. Pioneer Nat. Title Co. Trustee, Western Wyo. Coll., 1977-84; mem. Dem. Precinct Com., Green River, 1977-88, 89; pres. Sweetwater County Dem. Women's Club, 1989-90; trustee Castle Rock Hosp. Spl. Dist., 1981-84, City of Green River Tourism Com., 1988-90, Centennial Com., 1989-90, Flaming Gorge Days Com., 1990-91, pres., 1992, co-chmn. Parade. Recipient Wyo. Diana award ESA, 1989. Mem. Sweetwater County Bd. Realtors (chmn. com. 1983—, v.p. 1993, pres. 1994), Green River C. of C. (bd. dirs. 1986-91, pres. 1989-90), Rotary (co-chmn. Mother's day flowers Green River club 1990-91). Avocations: reading, painting, sculpture-lost wax. Home: 184 S 5th West St Green River WY 82935 Office: Twin Pines Realty 489 W Flaming Gorge Way Green River WY 82935-4108

BAKER, BONNIE BARBARA, mental health and school counselor, educator; b. Bklyn., Aug. 22, 1949; d. Irving Charles and Martha (Besner) B.; m. Thomas Andrew Ridgik, Aug. 4, 1990. BAE, U. Fla., 1971, PhD, 1985; MEd, U. N.C., 1972. Lic. mental health counselor, Fla. Sch. counselor Alachua County Schs., Gainesville, Fla., 1972—; mental health counselor Gainesville Counseling and Devel. Ctr., 1985—. Author chpt. to book; editor (booklet) How to Choose a College: A Guide to Students with a Disability. Vol. counselor U. Fla. Student Svcs., 1991—. Recipient Joe Wittmer Leadership award Chi Sigma Iota, 1994. Mem. ACA (mem. ethics com. 1987-88), Am. Sch. Counselor Assn., Am. Mental Health Counselors Assn., Fla. Counseling Assn. (treas. 1979-82, chair govt. rels. 1988-89, Leadership award 1989), Fla. Sch. Counselor Assn. (treas. 1978-80, pres. 1983-84). Home: PO Box 14155 Gainesville FL 32604 Office: Gainesville Counseling & Devel Ctr 2831-F NW 41st St Gainesville FL 32606

BAKER, BRIDGET DOWNEY, newspaper executive; b. Eugene, Oreg., Sept. 14, 1955; d. Edwin Moody and Patricia (Petersen) B.; m. Guy Dominique Wood, June 30, 1977 (div. Oct. 1981); m. Rayburn Keith Kincaid, June 27, 1987; stepchildren: Benjamin, Jacob. BA in English, French and Theatre, Lewis and Clark Coll., 1977; MA in Journalism, U. Oreg., 1985. Circulation dist. supr. The Register-Guard, Eugene, 1978-80, pub. relations coordinator, 1980-83, promotion dir., 1983-86, mktg. dir., 1986-88; corp. pub. rels. dir., 1989—; bd. dirs. Guard Pub. Co., Eugene. Bd. dirs. Wilani Coun. Camp Fire, 1982-88, pres. bd. dirs., 1986-88; bd. dirs. Lane County United Way, 1982-88, community info. com. chairperson, 1982-84; bd. dirs. Eugene Opera, 1988-91, pres. bd. dirs., 1990-91, chair planning com., 1987-88. Recipient 1st pl. advt. award Editor and Pub. Mag., N.Y.C., 1984, also 1st pl. TV promotion, 1st pl. newspaper rsch. award, 1988, Best Mktg. Idea/Campaign award Oreg. Newspaper Pub. Assn., 1984, 85; named Woman of Yr., Lane County Coun. of Orgns., 1994. Mem. Internat. Mktg. Assn. (bd. dirs. Western region 1986-88, 8 1st pl. Best in the West awards 1983-91), Pub. Rels. Soc. Am. (pres.-elect Greater Oreg. chpt. 1994—, Spotlight award 1986), Eugene C. of C. (bd. dirs. 1989-92), U. Oreg. Alumni Assn. (bd. dirs. 1990-93), Downtown Athletic Club, Eugene Yacht Club, Zonta Internat. (pres. Eugene club 1994—). Republican. Office: Guard Pub Co 1065 High St Ste 1 Eugene OR 97401-3254

BAKER, CAROL ANN, English language educator; b. Toledo, Apr. 14, 1946; d. Edward William and Elizabeth Amelia (Minor) Pietrzak; m. Robert Lee Baker, June 19, 1971. BS in Edn., Bowling Green State U., 1968; MEd, U. Toledo, 1977. Tchr. English Mason Consol. Schs., Erie, Mich., 1968-70; tchr. English Rossford (Ohio) Schs., 1970—, yearbook adviser, 1970-86, chair English dept., 1974—, mem. steering com., 1990—. Editor creative arts mag. Cameo, 1987—. Active Elmore (Ohio) Area Citizens Assn., 1992—. Martha Holding Jennings grantee Jennings Found., 1989; Hunt Wesson grantee Rossford Schs., 1993. Mem. NEA, Nat. Coun. Tchrs. English, Ohio Edn. Assn., Rossford Assn. Classroom Tchrs., Alpha Delta Pi.

BAKER, CAROLYN LOUISE, therapist; b. Detroit, Apr. 28, 1959; d. Patrick Walen and Mary Lou (Witte) B. BS, Luth. Bible Inst., Seattle, 1984; MA, Antioch U., 1986. Cert. mental health therapist, child mental health specialist. Mental health therapist St. Francis Cmty. Hosp., Federal Way, Wash., 1986-87; child and family therapist, day treatment program supr. Luther Child Ctr., Everett, Wash., 1987-90; child and family therapist and cons. Highline Mental Health Agy., Seattle, 1990-94; pvt. practice therapist Kent, Wash., 1989—; cons. Seattle South Ctrl. Pub. Sch., 1990—, Highline Sch. Dist., Seattle, 1990—; trainer, presenter Primary Intervention Project, Wash., 1990—. Therapist, vol. Kent City Corrections Dept., 1990—. Mem. ACA, Internat. Assn. Marriage and Family Therapists. Office: 24837 104th Ave SE Ste 200 Kent WA 98031-6800

BAKER, CATHY LORRAINE, computer analyst programmer; b. Lancaster, Pa., Oct. 20, 1953; d. Lester Paul and Jean Graham (Erhart) N. Grad., Va. Computer Coll., 1973; postgrad., Ind. U. Purdue U. Indpls. Tape librarian BC/BS, Indpls., 1974-75, sr. tape librarian, 1975-76, computer operator, 1976-77, sr. computer operator, 1977-78, programmer, 1978-83, programmer analayst, 1983-90, sr. programmer analyst, 1990—. Sec. Bargersville (Ind.) Area Civic Org., 1992, 92, treas., 1993-94.

BAKER, CHARLENE, editor; b. Cleve., Oct. 15, 1948; d. Charles Stephen and Theresa Jenny (Turk) Mato; m. Charles Barkley Baker, Aug. 25, 1979. BA, Mercyhurst Coll., 1970; MA, John Carroll U., 1974. Cert. elem. edn. tchr., Ohio. 4th grade tchr. Euclid (Ohio) Pub. Schs., 1970-74, lang. arts cons., 1974-85; mgr. Associated Mktg. Cons., Cleve., 1985-88; instr. Cleve. State U., 1988-89; mng. editor Collision Repair Industry INSIGHT, Cleve., 1990—; freelance writer in field. Vol. instr. Project Plus, Mentor, Ohio, 1990-93; active NOW, Cleve., 1990—, Naral, 1991—, Nat. Abortion Rights Action League. Mem. Gates Mills Cmty. Club (bd. dirs. 1989), Pi Lambda Theta. Home: PO Box 490 1420 Echo Glen Gates Mills OH 44040 Office: Collision Repair Industry INSIGHT 8491 Mayfield Rd Chesterland OH 44026

BAKER, CORNELIA DRAVES, artist; b. Woodbury, N.J., Mar. 2, 1929; d. Carl Zeno and Cornelia (Powell) Draves.; m. Philip Douglas Baker, July 16, 1955; children: Brinton, Todd, Claudia, Samuel. Student, Ohio Wesleyan U., 1947-50, Goethe U., Frankfurt, Ger., 1950-52. Travel dir. Am. Youth Hostels, Inc., N.Y.C., 1953-57; artist Cornelia Gallery, Kumamoto, Japan, 1990—, L'Atelier Inc. Gallery, Piermont, N.Y., 1994—; gallery dir. Presbyn. Ch., Franklin Lakes, N.J., 1989—. One woman shows include Ramapo Coll., 1986, Shimada Mus., Kumamoto, 1990, Sekaikan Gallery, Tokyo, 1990, Bergen Mus. Art and Sci., 1993, L'Atelier Inc. Gallery, 1994, Ashkal Gallery D'art, Beirut, Lebanon, 1995; represented in permanent collections Bergen Mus. Art and Sci., Paramus, N.J., Beekley Internat. Skiing Fine Art and Graphics. Chair social problems com. Borough of Franklin Lakes Coun., 1973-76. Recipient Best of Show award Ringwood Manor Assn. of the Arts, 1987, Bergen Mus. Art and Sci., 1989, Emeriti award for excellence N.J. Ctr. for Visual Arts, 1989, Excellence cert. Internat. Art Competition, 1988, Women Making History in Arts award Bergen County, N.J., 1993, Crabbie award Art Calendar, 1994. Mem. Nat. Assn. Women Artists (printmaking jury chmn. 1992-94), Salute to Women in the Arts (pres. 1988-90), Altrusa Club of Bergen County, N.J. (pres. 1994-96). Republican. Presbyterian. Home: 293 Greenridge Rd Franklin Lakes NJ 07417-2011

BAKER, COSETTE MARLYN, religion writer, editor; b. Miami, Fla., Sept. 22, 1933; d. Juel Marlyn and Corene Frances (Emery) Baker; BBA, U. Miami, Fla., 1955; MRE, So. Bapt. Theol. Sem., 1959. Dir. childhood edn. First Bapt. Ch., Knoxville, Tenn., 1959-63; minister to children South Main Bapt. Ch., Houston, 1964-73; asst. to minister of edn. Central Bapt. Ch., Miami, Fla., 1973-74; cons. in Sunday Sch. Dept., Bapt. Sunday Sch. Bd., Nashville, 1974-92, children's program editor, 1974-92, children's program design editor, 1985-92, cons. Recipient YWCA award outstanding woman in religious work U. Miami, 1955, cert. achievement award for Bible Study Resource Kit for Children's Worship, 1991.. Mem. Tenn. Assn. for Edn. Young Children, Gamma Alpha Chi. Baptist. Author: God's Outdoors, 1967; writer children's teaching tapes for Broadman Press, 1979-81; writer, on-camera person Bapt. Telecomm. Network, 1984—; editor Children's Leadership, 1985-91, design editor, 1991—; design team chairperson The Sunday Sch. Leader Smaller Ch. Edit.; writer Sunday Sch. Bd. Younger Children's Leadership Tng. Video, 1993, life and work curriculum writer, 1994-95; ret. Home: 100 Longwood Pl Nashville TN 37215-1927

BAKER, DALE ARLENE, psychologist, consultant; b. N.Y.C., Jan. 4, 1946; d. Max Schmerer and Ann (Ramber) Koshar; m. Thomas Eugene Baker, Feb. 13, 1966; children: Paige Alison, Amy Elizabeth. BA, Stephens Coll., 1969; MA, U. Mo., 1981; PhD, Calif. Sch. Profl. Psychology, 1985. Pvt. practice clin. psychologist La Jolla, Calif., 1987—; cons. Sch. Attendance Rev. Bd., San Diego Sch. Dist., 1989—, Univ. Calif. San Diego (Calif.) Career Counseling Office, 1990—. Co-author: Parenting Your Teenager, 1994; lead writer: Caring Connections, 1994. Mem. APA, Calif. Psychol. Assn., San Diego Psychol. Assn. Office: 7946 Ivanhoe Ave Ste 201 La Jolla CA 92037-4517

BAKER, DREAMA GAIL, psychologist; b. Meadow Bridge, W.Va., June 29, 1948; d. Joseph Robert and Gertrude Ethel (Llewellyn) Baker Goddard. Student, Fgn. Lang. League Schs., Jerusalem, Israel, 1969; BS, Salem-Teikyo U., 1970; M in Psychology, Cen. Mich. U., 1973; postgrad., Saybrook Inst., 1992—. Lic. psychologist, W.Va. Psychology intern Bay-Aranac Mental Health Ctr., Bay City, Mich., 1972-73; psychologist Fayette, Monroe, Raleigh, Summers counties Mental Health Clinic, Beckley, W.Va., 1973-74, Beckley Mental Health Ctr., 1974-76, Beckley Appalachian Hosp., 1977-78; psychologist Raleigh Psychiat. Svcs., Beckley, 1978-83, psychologist contractor, 1983—; cons. Beckley Appalachian Regional Hosp., 1978—, chief divsn. psychology, 1986—; cons. Beckley Hosp., 1983—, Wyo. Gen. Hosp., Mullins, 1985-87, Raleigh Gen. Hosp., 1986—, Whelan Med. Clinic, Hinton, 1989-90, Beckley, 1990-91; probable cause hearings co-contractor So. Highlands Cmty. Mental Health Ctr., Itmann, W. Va., 1990—. Contbr. articles to profl. jours. Mem. legis. com. W.Va. Human Resources Assn., 1984-85; mem. adv. bd. Cherry Hill Children's Shelter, 1990-91; mem. human rights adv. com. VOCA, 1992—. Mem. Assn. for Applied Psychophysiology and Biofeedback, W.Va. Psychol. Assn., Biofeedback Soc. Am., W.Va. Human Resources Assn., W.Va. Soc. Autistic Children, Am. Assn. for Mental Retardation (religion div. 1990—), Internat. Platform Assn., People for Ethical Treatment of Animals. Democrat. Home: 271 Hoist Rd Beckley WV 25801 Office: Raleigh Psychiat Svcs Inc PO Box 1025 Mallard Ct Beckley WV 25801

BAKER, EDITH MADEAN, counselor; b. Greeley, Colo., Oct. 7, 1942; d. Richard Luther and Catherine Jane (John) Tatman; m. Richard Dennis Baker, Oct. 24, 1964; children: Kimberly Baker Parker, Gregory. Student, U. No. Colo., 1961; BA, U. Colo., 1964; postgrad., San Jose (Calif.) State U., 1969-70; EdM, Oreg. State U., 1978. Cert. counselor, Oreg. Tchr. Spaulding Sch. Dist., Waukegan, Ill., 1965-67, Alhambra Pvt. Sch., Phoenix, 1968-69; pvt. practice counseling Corvallis, Oreg., 1977-80; counselor Salem (Oreg.) Sch. Dist., 1978-79; testing specialist Corvallis Sch. Dist., 1980, counselor, 1980-88; counselor Springfield (Oreg.) Sch. Dist., 1988—; chair activity curriculum com. Corvallis Sch. Dist., 1984, chair prin. selection com., 1985. Member Symphony Guild, Eugene, Oreg., 1988—, PTA; bd. dirs. Boys and Girls Club, Corvallis, 1984-88, Assn. for Retarded Citizens, Eugene, 1989-90; chair Parent Graduation Celebration, Corvallis, 1985, 88. Mem. NEA, Oreg. Counseling Assn., Oreg. Edn. Assn., Mental Health Assn. of Oreg., Springfield Edn. Assn., Univ. Women's League, Delta Kappa Gamma, Kappa Delta Pi, Delta Delta Delta. Democrat. Home: 3336 Bardell Ave Eugene OR 97401-5801 Office: Thurston Mid Sch 6300 Thurston Rd Springfield OR 97478-7099

BAKER, ELIZABETH CALHOUN, magazine editor; b. Boston; d. John Calhoun and Elizabeth Marshall Evans B. B.A. cum laude, Bryn Mawr Coll.; M.A., Radcliffe Coll. Fulbright scholar Inst. d'Art et d'Archeologie and Ecole du Louvre, Paris; Instr. art history Boston U., Wheaton Coll., Norton, Mass.; assoc. editor Art News, N.Y.C., 1963-65; mng. editor Art News, 1965-73; editor Art in Am. mag., N.Y.C., 1973—; instr. art history Sch. Visual Arts, N.Y.C., 1968-74; freelance art criticism. Recipient Lifetime Achievement award Coll. Art Assn., 1992; Nat. Endowment for Arts grantee, 1972. Office: Art in America Brant Publications 575 Broadway 5th Fl New York NY 10021

BAKER, FAITH MERO, elementary education educator; b. Pitts., May 9, 1941; d. Vincent G. and Georgetta (Rothwell) Mero; m. Gerald A. Baker, Dec. 22, 1968; children: Jeremy D., Kara L. BA, Carlow Coll., Pitts., 1963; MEd, U. Pitts., 1965, postgrad., 1966-68. Cert. elem. and spl. edn. tchr., Pa. Tchr. sci. Pitts. Pub. Schs., 1963-64, tchr. spl. edn., 1968-87, tchr., primary sci. specialist, 1987—; leader instrnl. team Fulton Acad., Pitts., 1988—; facilitator, tchr. Project Wild and project Aquatic Wild, Project Learning Tree, Pitts., 1988—. Leader Girl Scouts U.S.A., Monroeville, Pa., 1979-86; mem. Supts. Roundtable Gateway Schs., Monroeville, Pa., 1987-89. Mem. AAUW, Pitts. Fedn. Tchrs. (bldg. steward 1968—), Pa. Bus. and Profl. Women's Assn. (bd. dirs. dist. 3, 1991—, mem. polit. action com., pres. Monroeville 1987-88, 92-93), U. Pitts. Alumni Assn. (ast v.p. 1987-88, sec. 1989-91), Delta Kappa Gamma, Alpha Delta Kappa (treas. 1992—), Phi Delta Gamma (sec. Kappa chpt. 1986-90, pres. 1982-84, regional coord. 1984-86, nat. v.p. 1992-94, nat. pres. 1994—). Democrat. Roman Catholic. Home: 102 Penn Lear Dr Monroeville PA 15146-4734 Office: Fulton Acad Hampton St Pittsburgh PA 15206

BAKER, G. KAY, state official; b. Lawrence, Kans., Sept. 19, 1945; d. Jess Willard and Madge (Lewis) B. BS, Ark. Tech. U., 1971; MS in Edn., U. Ark., 1975. Lic. bus. edn., vocat. edn., tech. prep. Tchr. jr. high State of Ark., Morrilton, 1971-73, secondary bus. tchr., 1973-76, post-secondary bus. tchr., 1976-83; entrepreneurer Ladies Clothing, Morrilton, 1976-82; tchr. edn. U. Ark., Fayetteville, 1983-85; program supr. State Dept. Edn., Little Rock, 1985—; cons. Tech. Prep., Little Rock, 1990—, Curriculum Devel., Little Rock, 1987—. Author: Arkansas Tech Prep, 1991; editor: Business and Computers, 1990, Business Communications, 1991, Entrepreneurship, 1992. Recipient State Leadership award Gregg Pub. Co., Reno, Nev., 1992. Mem. Am. Vocat. Assn., Nat. Bus. Edn. Assn., So. Bus. Edn. Assn. (chair adminstrn. 1979—), Ark. Vocat. Assn. Democrat. Baptist. Office: 3 Capitol Mall Little Rock AR 72201

BAKER, GERRY LYNNE, public relations executive. BA, Calif. State U., Fullerton. Account mgr. Les Goldberg PR, sr. account mgr., 1990-91; founder, pres. Gerry Lynne Pub. Rels., Huntington Beach, Calif., 1992—. Office: Gerry Lynne Pub Rels 17888 Hawes Ln Huntington Beach CA 92647-7014*

BAKER, GWENDOLYN CALVERT, United Nations official; b. Ann Arbor, Mich., Dec. 31, 1931; m. James Baker; children: JoAnn, Claudia, James Jr. BA, U. Mich., 1964, MA, 1968, PhD, 1972. Tchr. Ann Arbor Pub. Schs., 1964-69; lectr. U. Mich., 1969-70, instr., 1970-72, assoc. prof., 1972-76, dir. affirmative action programs, 1976-78; chief minorities and women's programs Nat. Inst. Edn., Washington, 1978-84; v.p., dean, graduate and children's programs Bank St. Coll. Edn., N.Y.C., 1981-84; nat. exec. dir. YWCA of USA, N.Y.C., 1984-93; pres., CEO U.S. Com. for UNICEF, N.Y.C., 1993—. Office: UNICEF 3 United Nations Plaza New York NY 10017*

BAKER, HARRIET HELENE, business owner, marketing consultant; b. Tuscaloosa, Ala., Aug. 7, 1965; d. Daniel Rex and Peggy Ann (Jones) Holt; m. David Edward Baker, Nov. 30, 1990. BBA, Marymount U., 1987. Mktg. dir. Archtl. Art, San Diego, 1983-92; project cons. Metrum Group, San Diego, 1992—; owner Archtl. Art West, San Diego, 1992—; project cons. various clients, San Diego, 1993—. Mem. pub. issues and advocacy com. Jr. League of San Diego, 1992-93, chair, 1993-94; mem. Big Sister League, San Diego, 1990—, San Diego Mus. Art, 1993—. Mem. Bldg. Industry Assn. San Diego County. Republican.

BAKER, HELEN DOYLE PEIL, realtor; b. Los Angeles, June 26, 1943; d. James Cyril and Jacqueline (White) Doyle; m. Gary Edward Peil, Aug. 5, 1967 (dec. May 6, 1969); children: Andrea Christine, Kevin Doyle; m. Nathaniel W. Baker, Jr., Jan. 1, 1971 (div. July 23, 1983). AA, Santa Monica Coll., 1963; postgrad., U. Wash., 1963-64. Licensed real estate agent. Sales, mgmt. trainee Saks Fifth Ave., Beverly Hills, Calif., 1958-63; flight attendant Am. Airlines, Los Angeles, 1964-67; realtor, assoc. Stapleton Assocs., Honolulu, 1978-80; realtor Dolman Assocs. Inc., Kailua, Hawaii, 1980-87; loan rep. Honolulu Mortgage Co., Kailua, 1986-87; pres., owner, realtor Helen Baker Properties, Inc., Honolulu, 1987-93; v.p. Internat. Property Investment, Inc., Honolulu, 1993-94; owner Property Investment Internat., 1994—; pres. Global Listing Svc. Hawaii Inc., 1990—. Dir. Kailua Community Coun., 1987-91; pres., v.p., sec. Aikahi Community Assn., Kailua, 1980-85; vol. Am. Cancer Soc., Heart Assn. Schs., Kailua, 1971-86. Mem. Nat. Assn. Realtors, Hawaii Assn. Realtors, Honolulu Bd. Realtors, Real Estate Brokerage Council, Realtors Nat. Mktg. Inst., Hist. Hawaii Found., C. of C., Rotary. Office: Property Investment Internat Box 37066 Honolulu HI 96837

BAKER, HELEN MARIE, health services executive; b. Tulsa, Oct. 12, 1946; d. Joseph Donald and Caroline Emma (Nelson) Waldhelm; m. Lewis Edward Browder, 1964 (div. 1966); m. Lawrence Selden Baker, Nov. 23, 1978; children: Lawrence Nelson, Marjorie Lyn. Student, U. Tex., 1965-66. Staff asst. to pres. White House, Washington, 1970-73; v.p. Mgmt., Systems, Sales, Inc., Washington, 1973-74, Inter-Am. Svcs., Inc., Washington and Tex., 1974-83; v.p. Med. Diversified Svcs. Inc., San Antonio, 1983-90, exec. v.p., 1990-92, also bd. dirs., pres., CEO, 1992—. Editor newsletter Physician and Family, 1983-86. Elder St. Andrew Presbyn Ch., San Antonio, 1986-89. Mem. San Antonio Mus. Assn. (sponsor), Club of Sonterra. Republican. Office: Med Diversified Svcs 15600 San Pedro Ave Ste 107 San Antonio TX 78232-3738

BAKER, JENNIFER HOLLAND, accountant; b. Murray, Ky., Jan. 12, 1965; d. Joe Holland and Maxine Holland Sumner; m. Ernie Baker, June 25, 1988; 1 child, Amanda Nicole. BS in Bus., Murray State U., 1987. Cert. mgmt. acct., Ky. Staff acct. York, Neel & Co., CPAs, Madisonville, Ky., 1987-88; chief acct. Ky. Derby Hosiery Co., Inc., Hopkinsville, 1988—. Mem. Inst. Mgmt. Accts. Baptist. Office: Ky Derby Hosiery Co Inc PO Box 550 Hopkinsville KY 42241-0550

BAKER, JOY LYNN, health system consultant, nurse; b. Bonne Terre, Mo., Jan. 15, 1954; d. Leslie Curtis Huber and Lola Mae (Pope) Ruble. BS in

Nursing, Avila Coll., 1976. RN. Staff nurse Kansas City (Mo.) Gen. Hosp., 1976; office nurse Dr.'s Janes and Manley, Overland Park, Kans., 1976-78; operating room nurse Bellaire Gen. Hosp., Houston, 1978-79; scrub nurse Dr. Benton Baker III, Houston, 1979-85; utilization rev. nurse Meml. Care Systems, Houston, 1985-86; mgr. Meml. Care Systems HealthTrack, Houston, 1986-87; v.p. med. utilization review Managed Healthcare, Inc., Houston, 1987-88; cons. healthcare quality assurance, utilization review, 1988—. Designer, developer software program. Pres. Treehouse Homeowners Assn., Houston, 1984-87; bd. dirs. The Guild of St. Joseph Hosp., 1994—. Mem. ANA, Tex. Nurses Assn. (com. mem. continuing edn. approval and recognition program 1986-87), Am. Bd. Quality Assurance and Utilization Rev. (cer. 1985, 1st v.p., bd. dirs. 1988-91), Am. Bd. Quality Assurance Utilization Rev. Physicians (bd. dirs. 1993—, continuing med. edn. com. 1993—). Baptist.

BAKER, KANDRA See INGA, KANDRA JOYCE

BAKER, KATHERINE JUNE, elementary school educator; b. Dallas, Feb. 3, 1932; d. Kirk Moses and Katherine Faye (Turner) Sherrill; m. George William Baker, Jan. 30, 1955; children: Kirk Garner, Kathleen Kay. BS, BA, Tex. Women's U., 1953, MEd, 1979; cert. in religious edn., Meadville Theol. U., 1970; postgrad., North Tex. State U., 1987—; DD (hon.), Am. Fellowship Ch., 1981. Cert. elem. secondary tchr., adminstr., Tex.; lic. min. Kingsway Internat. Ministries, 1991. Mgr. prodn. Woolf Bros., Dallas, 1953-55; display mgr. J.M. Dyer and Co., Corsicana, Tex., 1954; advt. artist Fair Dept. Store, Ft. Worth, 1954-56; artist, instr. Dutch Art Gallery, Dallas, 1960-65; dir. religious edn. 1st Unitarian Ch., Dallas, 1967-69; dir. day care, tchr. Richardson (Tex.) Unitarian Ch., 1971-73; dir. camp Tres Rios YWCA, Glen Rose, Tex., 1975-76; dir. program of extended sch. instrn. Hamilton Park Elem. Sch. Richardson Ind. Sch. Dist., 1975-78, tchr. Dover Elem. Sch., 1979-92, tchr. Jess Harben Elem. Sch., 1979-92; founder ednl., editorial and arts/evang. assn. Submitted Ministries, Richardson, 1992—; dir. Flame Fellowship Internat., 1987—, state rep., 1994—. Contbr. articles to ch. newspaper, 1967-69; exhibited in group show at Tex. Art Assn., 1966; one-woman show Dutch Art Gallery - Northlake Ctr., Dallas, 1965. Advocate day care Unitarian Universalist Women's Fedn., Boston, 1975-76, mem. nominating com., 1976-77. Mem. NEA, ASCD, Nat. Coun. Social Studies, Tex. State Tchrs. Assn. (treas. Richardson chpt. 1984-85), Women's Ctr. Dallas, Sokol Athletic Ctr., Smithsonian Assn., Dallas Mus. Assn., Alpha Chi, Delta Phi Delta (pres. 1952-53), Phi Delta Kappa. Home: 2711 Sherrill Park Dr Richardson TX 75082-3217

BAKER, KATHY WHITTON, actress; b. Midland, Tex., June 8, 1950. Appearences include (theatre) Fool for Love, 1983 (Obie award 1983, Theatre World award 1984), Desire Under the Elms, 1984, Aunt Dan and Lemon, 1986, (films) The Right Stuff, 1983, Street Smart, 1987 (Nat. Soc. Film Critics Best Supporting Actress award 1987), Permanent Record, 1988, A Killing Affair, 1988, Clean and Sober, 1988, Jacknife, 1989, Dad, 1989, Mr. Frost, 1989, Edward Scissorhands, 1990, Article 99, 1992, Jennifer 8, 1992, Mad Dog and Glory, 1993, (TV movies) Nobody's Child, 1986, The Image, 1990, One Special Victory, 1991, (TV series) Picket Fences, 1992— (Emmy award Outstanding Lead Actress in a Drama Series, 1993, Golden Globe award, Best Actress in a TV Drama Series, 1994). Office: ICM Tracey Jacobs 8899 Beverly Blvd Los Angeles CA 90048*

BAKER, LORI ANN, physical therapist; b. Detroit, July 16, 1957; d. Richard Gary and Mary Barbara (Vail) Griffith; m. Joseph Kurtyka, Nov. 22, 1980 (div. Sept. 1984); m. William Randall Baker, June 24, 1989; 1 child, Katherine Elisabeth Baker. BS, U. Mich., 1979; MBA, Kennesaw Coll., 1990. Phys. therapist Lansing Sch. Dist., Mich., 1979-81, Mich. Sch. for Blind, 1980-81, Ingham Med. Ctr., 1980-81; pediatric phys. therapist Toledo Hosp., 1981-84, Childrens Ortho Hosp. and Med. Ctr., Seattle, 1984-85; pediatric clin. specialist Kennestone Hosp., Marietta Ga., 1985-89, supr. acute care therapy, 1989-90; phys. therapist Am. Home Health Care, 1987-91; contract phys. therapist, 1990-91; clin. mgr. Atlanta Rehab. Inst., 1991—. Mem. Am. Phys. Therapy Assn., Neurodevelopmental Treatment Assn. Avocations: stained glass; furniture refinishing, running, biking. Home: 402 Wild Hill Rd Woodstock GA 30188-1972 Office: 1450 S Johnson Ferry Rd Atlanta GA 30319-4316

BAKER, LUCILLE STOEPPLER, sociology and anthropology educator; b. N.Y.C., Aug. 4, 1919; d. Charles W. and Henrietta (Krammer) Stoeppler; m. Walter Hewlett Baker Jr., June 29, 1946 (dec. 1981). BS, Coll. Mt. St. Vincent, 1941; MA in Econs., Fordham U., 1942; PhD, Cornell U., 1969; postgrad., U. Colo., 1967-68. Tchr. social sci. Unquowa Sch., Fairfield, Conn., 1942-46; high sch. adminstr. U.S. Dept. Def., Lajes AFB, Azores Island, 1951-54; vocat. ednl. counselor U.S. Dept. Def., Ramey AFB, P.R., 1956-59; asst. prof. Fla. State U. Ctr., P.R.; lectr. East West Ctr. U. Hawaii, Honolulu, 1964-66; asst. prof., head sociology dept. Wilberforce (Ohio) U., 1966-69; prof. Tompkins-Cortland Community Coll. SUNY, Dryden, 1969—. Trustee Young-Morse Historic Site, Poughkeepsie, N.Y., 1986—, chairperson bicentennial, 1991. NSF fellow U. Boulder, 1966-67; Fordham U. scholar and fellow, 1941-42. Mem. AAUS (program chair 1983-85, pres. 1985-87), Am. Sociol. Assn., Am. Anthrop. Assn., Groton Hist. Assn. (pres. 1994—), Cornell Women's Club (pres. Cortland chpt. 1987-89), Zonta Internat., Delta Kappa Gamma. Office: SUNY Tompkins Cortland CC Dryden NY 13053

BAKER, LYNNE RUDDER, philosophy educator; b. Atlanta, Feb. 14, 1944; d. James Maclin and Virginia (Bennett) Rudder; m. Thomas B. Baker III, Feb. 1, 1969. BA, Vanderbilt U., 1966, MA, 1971, PhD, 1972; student, Johns Hopkins U., 1967-68. Asst. prof. philosophy Mary Baldwin Coll., Staunton, Va., 1972-76; asst. prof. philosophy Middlebury (Vt.) Coll., 1976-79, assoc. prof., 1979-84, prof., 1984-94, acting dean arts and humanities, 1982, chairperson humanities divsn., 1982-85, acting chairperson philosophy, 1986-87; prof. U. Mass., Amherst, 1989—, dir. philosophy grad. program, 1994—; mem. panel to select summer seminars NEH, Washington, 1982, mem. panel to select fellows, 1989-90. Author: A Saving Belief: A Critique of Physicalism, 1988, Explaining Attitudes: A Practical Approach to the Mind, 1995; contbr. scholarly articles to profl. jours. Trustee Vanderbilt U., Nashville, 1969-70, mem. alumni bd. dirs., 1985-89. Mellon fellow, 1974, NEH fellow, 1983-84, Nat. Humanities Ctr. fellow, 1982-83, Woodrow Wilson Internat. Ctr. for Scholars fellow, 1988-89. Mem. Am. Philos. Assn. (program com. 1983, exec. com. 1992—), Soc. for Philosophy and Psychology, Soc. Christian Philosophers (exec. com. 1992—), Soc. Women in Philosophy, Phi Beta Kappa. Democrat. Episcopalian. Office: U Mass Dept Philosophy Amherst MA 01003

BAKER, MARLO, line producer; b. Havana, Apr. 8, 1949; came to the U.S., 1969; d. Alfonso Vicente and Maria D. (Torres) Rivero; m. Joe Don Baker, Dec. 25, 1969 (div. 1980); m. Miguel A. Torres, Mar. 25, 1982 (div.); children: Maria, Michael. Talent coord. NBC, Burbank, Calif., 1979-82; line producer Marcha Films, Madrid, 1987-91, Angel Wings Prodns., L.A., 1992-93; line prodr. music videos Angel Wings Prodns., Ft. Lauderdale, Fla., 1993—; line prodr., music videos and commls. Kree 8 Prodn., Miami, Fla., 1994—. Actress: Sunset Grill, 1992. Nominated for Best Music Video of the Yr., La Mafia "Me Estoy Enamorando", Premio Lo Nuestro Billboard/Univision, 1993, Luis Enrique "La Manana", Premio lo Nuestro/Univision, 1994. Mem. SAG. Home: 1064 NW 123 Ct Miami FL 33182

BAKER, MARY ALICE, communication educator, consultant; b. Stuart, Okla., Sept. 9, 1937; s. James Roy and Emma M. (Bird) B. BS, U. Okla., 1959, MA in Speech, 1966; PhD in Communication, Purdue U., 1983. Speech and debate tchr. SE High Sch., Oklahoma City, 1959-65; instr. Ea. Ill. U., Charleston, 1966-69; assoc. prof. Lamar U., Beaumont, Tex., 1966-75, 78—, dir. forensics, 1969-75, Regents' Merit prof., 1984, pres. faculty senate, 1986-88. Contbr. articles to profl. jours. David Ross fellow, 1977. Mem. Tex. Speech Communication Assn. (regional rep. 1978-88), Speech Communication Assn. Am., Tex. Assn. Coll. Tchrs. (regional v.p. 1985—, pres.-elect 1988-89, state pres. 1989-90), Tex. Forensics Assn. (pres. 1974), Internat. Communication Assn., Zeta Phi Eta, Alpha Delta Pi. Democrat. Episcopalian. Avocations: reading, politics, travel. Office: Lamar U Dept Communication Beaumont TX 77710

BAKER, MARY EVELYN, church librarian, retired academic librarian; b. Columbus, Ohio, May 8, 1912; d. Abram Jackson and Martha Maria (Dailey) Shoemaker; m. Richard Heinley Baker, Sept. 18, 1937 (dec.); children: Richard Shoemaker, David Guy. BA, Ohio State U., 1934; M.S. in Libr. Sci., Western Res. U., Cleve., 1935. Mem. staff libr. Ohio State U., Columbus, 1935-37, 38-44, 1955-74, part-time libr., 1955-66, adminstrv. asst., 1958, serial cataloger, 1958-67, asst. reviser, sr. cataloger, 1967-68, head serial div. catalog dept., 1968-71, head catalog dept., 1971-74; libr. com. First Congl. Ch., Columbus, 1950—, libr. co-chmn., 1962-65, 74-75, libr. chmn., 1976—; past mem. ALA, sec. serials sect., resources and tech. div., 1970-73. Den mother Boy Scouts Am., Columbus, 1953-58; libr. co-chmn. Friendship Village, Dublin, Ohio, 1981—. Mem. Ohioana Libr. Assn. (past chmn. various coms., life mem.), PEO, DAR (Indians com.), Univ. Women's (past pres.), Agrl. Circle (past pres.), Franklin Co-Retired Tchrs. Assn. (life mem.), Ohio Retired Tchrs. Assn. (life mem.), Ohio State Alumni Assn. (life mem.), Ohio State U. Retirees Assn. (bridge chmn. 1984—), Phi Mu. Republican. Home: 6000 Riverside Dr Apt 233A Dublin OH 43017-1494

BAKER, MARY MARGARET, software systems engineer; b. Chgo., Jan. 24, 1945; d. Fred Palmer and Mary Elizabeth (Conley) B. BS in Math., Mundelein Coll., 1966; MS in Math., U. Ill., 1967; MS in Computer Sci., Rensselaer Poly. Inst., 1970. Sr. sci. programmer analyst Pratt & Whitney Aircraft, East HArtford, Conn., 1967-74; computations analyst GE, Evandale, Ohio, 1974-75; mem. tech. staff Bell Tele Labs, Inc., Naperville, Ill., 1975-79; sr. mem. tech. staff GTE Govt. Systems, Mountain View, Calif., 1979—; instr. Cen. TEx. Coll., Misawa AFB, Japan, 1984. Republican. Roman Cathlic. Office: GTE Govt Systems 100 Ferguson Dr Mountain View CA 94039

BAKER, MARY SUSAN, veterinarian; b. Homestead, Fla., June 12, 1957; d. James Arthur and Mary Beth (Kemp) Menor; m. Larry James Baker, June 25, 1982; 1 child, Kristen Louise. DVM, U. Fla., 1985, BS, 1989. Extern Woodford (Ky.) Vet. Clinic, 1984, Newmarket (Eng.) Vet., 1985; assoc. vet. Atlantis (Fla.) Animal Hosp., 1985-89; owner Baker Vet. Clinic, West Palm Beach, Fla., 1990—. Mem. com. Biohazardous Waste Task Force, Palm Beach County, 1991. Recipient scholarship neonatal Study Group, 1984, Mooreman Co., 1981, So. Fla. Fair, 1979. Mem. AMVA, Am. Animal Hosp. Assn., Nat. Assn. Women Bus. Owners (membership com. Palm Beach, Fla. 1990—), Palm Beach Vet. Soc. (pres. 1990-92), Cornell Feline Vet. Assn., Soc. Aquatic Vet. Medicine, Fla. Vet. Medicine Assn. Republican. Roman Catholic. Office: Baker Vet Clinic 2600 Forest Hill Blvd West Palm Beach FL 33406-5931

BAKER, MELISSA ANN, legistative staff aide; b. White Sulphur, W.Va., Dec. 14, 1964; d. Kenneth W. and Shirley A. (Massie) B. BA in Polit. Sci., Marshall U., 1987, MPA, 1989. Grad. asst. Marshall U., Huntington, W.Va., 1987-91; grad. intern W.Va. Legislature, Charleston, 1991, redistricting analyst, 1991—, reapportionment task force. Mem. Pub. System Assocs./Digital Users Group, Greenbrier County Dem. Women's Club. Democrat. Baptist. Home: 8 Stewart Park # 3 Cross Lanes WV 25313 Office: WVa Legislature Legis Svcs E-132 State Capitol Charleston WV 25305

BAKER, PATRICIA MARIE, computer sales executive; b. N.Y., Apr. 26, 1961; d. William Joseph and Patricia Ann (McHugh) B. Student, La Guardia Community Coll., Long Island City, 1979-80, Queensboro Community Coll., Bayside, N.Y., 1985-86. Lic. Real Estate Agt. Real estate agt. A.B.C. Realty Inc., Ozone Park, N.Y., 1979-1981; mktg. rep. Digital Equipment Corp., N.Y., 1981-85; sales rep. Digital Equipment Corp., Tarrytown, N.Y., 1985—. Mem. N.Y. State Realtors Assn., Long Island Bd. Realtors. Republican. Roman. Catholic. Home: 15720 101st St Jamaica NY 11414-3204 Office: Digital Equipment Corp 200 White Plains Rd Tarrytown NY 10591-5805

BAKER, REBECCA LOUISE, musician, music educator, consultant; b. Covina, Calif., Apr. 12, 1951; d. Allan Herman and Hazel Margaret (Maki) Flaten; m. Jerry Wayne Baker, Dec. 22, 1972; children: Jared Wesley, Rachelle LaDawn, Shannon Faith. Grad. high sch., Park River, N.D.; student, Trinity Bible Inst., 1968-69. Sec. Agrl. Stblzn. & Conservation Svc. Office, Park River, N.D., 1969; pianist, singer Paul Clark Singers & Vic Coburn Evangelistic Assn., Portland, Oreg., 1969-72; musician, singer Restoration Ministries Evangelistic Assn., Richland, Wash., 1972-80; musician, pvt. instr. Calvary Temple Ch., Shawnee, Okla., 1980-81; organist, choirmaster St. Francis Episcopal Ch., Tyler, 1984-87; co-founder, owner Psalmist Sch. of Music & Recording Studio, Whitehouse, 1983—; pianist/entertainer Willowbrook Country Club, Tyler, Tex., 1991—; pianist/vocalist Mario's Italian Restaurant, Tyler, 1994—; pianist Garner Ted Armstrong, Tyler, 1986—; pianist, dir. Children's Choir, Calvary Bapt. Ch., Tyler, 1987—; pianist, entertainer Ramada Hotel, Tyler, 1988-90; pianist Whitehouse (Tex.) Sch. Dist. choirs, 1988—; accompanist Tyler Area Children's Chorale, 1988-90, Univ. Interscholastic League; pvt. instr. keyboard and vocal. Composer: Religious songs (12 on albums), 1979; pianist, arranger, producer, recording artist, 6 albums; editor, arranger: Texas Women's Aglow Songbook, 1987; editor Shekinah Glory mag., 1989—; developer improvisational piano course. Performer and speaker for many charitable, civic and religious orgns. in Tex. and throughout U.S. including AAUW, and Kiwanis Clubs; co-founder Psalmist Mins. Internat., 1988—. founder, pres. Christian Music Tchr's. Assn., 1991. Mem. Women's Aglow Fellowship (music dir., speaker, performer at retreats and tng. seminars). Republican. Full Gospel. Home and Office: Psalmist Music & Recording PO Box 961 Whitehouse TX 75791-0961

BAKER, ROSALYN, state legislator; b. El Campo, Tex., Sept. 20, 1946; m. Vaughn Baker. BA, Southwest Tex. State U., 1968; MA, U. Southwestern La., 1969. Lobbyist, asst. dir. Govt. Rels. Nat. Edn. Assn., Washington, 1969-80; owner, retail sporting goods store Maui, Hawaii, 1980-87; legis. aide to Hon. Karen Honita Hawaii Ho. of Reps., Honolulu, 1987, mem., 1989—; majority leader; vice chairwoman transp. com.; mem. fin., labor, pub. employment and intergovtl. rels., and internat. affairs coms.; co-chair rules com. Hawaii State Dem. Conv., 1990. Del.-at-large Dem. Nat. Conv., 1984; mem. exec. com. Maui County Dem. Com., 1986-88; vice chmn. Maui Svc. Area Bd. on Mental Health and Substance Abuse; active Am. Cancer Soc., Work Day Vol., Soroptimist Internat. Democrat. Home: PO Box 10394 Lahaina HI 96761-0394 Office: Hawaii Ho of Reps State Capitol Honolulu HI 96813*

BAKER, ROSE ANN URDIALES, pediatric and mental health nurse; b. Akron, Ohio, July 4, 1947; d. Anthony Ramon and Anita Rita (Martinez) Urdiales; m. Robert Lee Baker, May 25, 1974. Diploma, Akron Gen. Hosp. Sch. Nursing, 1968; BSN, U. Akron, 1972; MSN, Kent State U., 1984. Staff nurse Fallsview Mental Health Ctr., Cuyahoga Falls, Ohio, 1968-71; staff nurse emergency rm. Akron Gen. Med. Ctr., 1971-75; staff nurse pediatrics ICU Children's Med. Ctr., Akron, 1975-76, supr. staff devel., 1976-90, coord. nursing rsch. com., 1988—, chair clin. practice com. continuing nursing edn., 1991—, sr. instr., 1990-94; continuing nursing edn. coord., 1994—; clin. specialist Vis. Nurse Svc., Akron, 1984—; mem. search com. for the dean Kent State U. Sch. Nursing, 1984. Campaign worker Mayoral Race, Akron, 1980; translator Internat. Inst., Akron, 1986—; mem. hispanic health com. Latin Am. Community, Akron, 1990—. Mem. Sigma Theta Tau. Democrat. Roman Catholic. Home: 625 Hickory St Akron OH 44303-2211 Office: Children's Med Ctr Nursing Edn 281 Locust St Akron OH 44302-1813 also: Vis Nurse Svc Summit County 1200 Mcarthur Dr Akron OH 44320-3902

BAKER, S. CHRISTINE, clinical social worker; b. N.Y.C.; d. Arthur Ernest and Sarah Rebecca (Goodale) Crane; children: Barbara Baker Ryan, David C. Jr., Susan Baker Diroma. BA, SUNY, 1978; MSW, Wurzweiler Sch. Social Work, N.Y.C., 1980. Lic. social worker, Conn., N.Y. Clin. social worker family and children div. Greenwich (Conn.) Dept. Social Svcs.; med. social worker Fairfield (Conn.) VNA, Hospice, Cath. Charities, Fairfield; psychiat. social worker Rockland (N.Y.) Psychiat. Ctr.; now pvt. practice various schs. and civic orgn. programs, Stamford and Greenwich, Conn.; cons. in hypnosis, stress mgmt., behavior modification, cognitive restructuring, pastoral counseling, psychoanalysis, family systems, biofeedback.

BAKER, SUSAN MARIE VICTORIA (ERDLEN), writer, performing artist; b. Havertown, Pa., Aug. 30, 1961; d. John Joseph and Dorothy Phyllis (Dispensiere) Erdlen. BA in Liberal Arts/Comm., Rowan State Coll., 1983; postgrad., U. of Arts, Phila. Asst. editor Jersey Woman Mag., Marlton, 1983-85; advt. and editorial asst. Regal Communications, Moorestown, N.J., 1987-88; adminstrv. asst. Adams and Braverman Advt. Inc., Phila., 1989-90, Rosanio, Bailets & Talamo Inc., Cherry Hill, N.J., 1990-92; pub. rels. writer Val Vasil Health Entertainment, Blackwood, N.J., 1986-87; adv. and editl. rep. Phantom Press Publs., New Haven, Conn., 1989—. Art editor Avant mag., 1981; contbr. poetry to various publs.; composer numerous songs. Active animal rights and environ. activities; mem. Newport Cultural Arts Alliance, Newport Film Commn., chmn. spl. events com.; mem. Creative TV of R.I. Recipient 1st pl. award for poetry World of Poetry, 1988. Mem. Phila. Writers Orgn. Home: PO Box 337 Newport RI 02840

BAKER, THERESA ELEANOR, psychotherapist; b. Miami, Fla., Mar. 16, 1959; d. Jack Addison Baker and Janice Marie (Foley) Bessinger; life ptnr. K.V. Bittof. BA in Psychology, U. South Fla., 1990, MA in Counseling, 1993; postgrad., U. No. Colo., 1994—. Crisis counselor Alternative Human Svcs., St. Petersburg, Fla., 1988-90; med. social worker Bayfront Med. Ctr., St. Petersburg, Fla., 1990-93; inpatient counselor Provenant Health Ptnrs., Denver, 1993—; bd. dirs. Abilities, Inc., St. Petersburg, 1992-93; rsch. asst. Mediplex Rehab., Denver, 1993—; crisis vol. Spouse Abuse Ctr., St. Petersburg, 1991-93. Vol. Pinellas Dem. Club, St. Petersburg, 1992; vol. presenter Consider the Consequences, St. Petersburg, 1991-93. Mem. APA (campus rep. 1994—), ACA (grad. student com. 1991-93), Fla. Assn. for Specialists in Group Work (grad. student rep. 1991-93), Fla. Assn. for Adult Aging and Devel. (grad. student rep. 1991-93). Democrat. Home: 9350 Ellen Ct Denver CO 80229-3777

BAKER, TOBI LYNN, county official; b. Cedar Rapids, Iowa, Aug. 15, 1954; d. Roy Edwin and Mary Madelyn (Waddle) Hauser; m. James David Baker, June 7, 1980 (div. July 1989); children: James David II, Ali Marie. BS, Iowa State U., 1976. Probation agt. Dept. of Corrections, Cedar Rapids, 1976-81, Blue Earth County Corrections Dept., Mankato, Minn., 1986—. Adv. bd. Addictions, Recovery Technologies, Mankato, 1994—; instr. Shoplifters Anonymous, Mankato, 1991—; Sunday sch. tchr. Christ the King Luth. Ch., Mankato, 1987, 88, 93; active YMCA, Mothers Against Drunk Driving. Mem. Minn. Assn. County Probation Officers, Minn. Corrections Assn. Democrat. Office: Blue Earth Corrections 710 S Front St Mankato MN 56001-3803

BAKER-ERBISCH, C. B., retired day care director, organizer, communicator; b. Ft. Wayne, Ind.; d. James Edwin Sr. and Susie Mae (Nutter) Doelling; m. Gerald R. Baker, June, 1962 (div. 1966); 1 child, Erin Lee; m. Jeffrey E. Baker, June, 1967 (div. 1972); 1 child, Shannon Rae; m. Gilbert Erbisch, 1985. Student, Internat. Bus. Coll., Ft. Wayne, 1961. Expeditor Wayne Fabricating, Ft. Wayne, 1971; county adminstr. Champaign (Ill.) County Bd., 1974-76; sec. WICD-TV, Champaign, 1976-77; ops. chmn. 40 Plus of Colo., Inc., Denver, 1983, v.p., 1984-85, pres., 1985-86; asst. dir. St. Anne's Extended Day Program, Denver, 1986-88, ret., 1988. Editor The Village Voice newsletter, Savoy, Ill., 1974. Chmn. Winfield Village Swimming Pool Com., Savoy, 1975; dir. Mich. Sugar Festival, 1991. Mem. Am. Bus. Women's Assn.

BAKER KNOLL, CATHERINE, state treasurer; b. Pitts.; d. Nicholas James and Theresa Mary (May) Baker; m. Charles A. Knoll Sr. (dec.); children: Charles A. Jr., Mina B., Albert B., Kim Eric. BS in Edn., Duquesne U., 1952, MS in Edn., 1973. Dir. western Pa. region Safety Adminstrn. Dept. Transp., Pitts., 1971-79; exec. dir. community svc. Dept. of Adminstrn., Allegheny County, Pa., 1980-88; treas. Pa. Treasury Dept., Harrisburg, 1988—; owner, operator pvt. bus. firm, Pitts., 1952-70. Mem. Pa. Dem. State Com., Pa. Fedn. Dem. Women, YMCA Bd., Pitts., Harrisburg, Duquesne U. Alumni Bd., Mom's House, Zontas Inc. Bd. Mem. Nat. Assn. State Treas., Women Execs. in State Gov., Coun. State Gov. (exec. com. ea. region). Roman Catholic. Office: Treasury Dept 129 Fin Bldg Harrisburg PA 17120*

BAKER-LIEVANOS, NINA GILLSON, jewelry store executive; b. Boston, Dec. 19, 1950; d. Rev. John Robert and Patricia (Gillson) Baker; m. Jorge Alberto Lievanos, June 6, 1981; children: Jeremy John Baker, Wendy Mara Baker, Raoul Salvador Baker-Lievanos. Student, Mills Coll., 1969-70; grad. course in diamond grading, Gemology Inst. Am., 1983; student in diamondtology designation, Diamond Coun. Am., 1986—. Cert. store mgr., Jewelers Cert. Coun., Jewelers Am. Artist, tchr. Claremont, Calif., 1973-78; escrow officer Bank of Am., Claremont, 1978-81; retail salesman William Pitt Jewelers, Puente Hills, Montclair, Calif., 1981-83, asst. mgr., 1983; mgr. William Pitt Jewelers, Puente Hills, Santa Maria, Calif., 1983-91, corp. sales trainer, 1988-89; sales and design specialist Merksamer Jewelers, Santa Maria, 1991; mgr. Merksamer Jewelers, San Luis Obispo, Calif., 1991-92, Santa Maria, Calif., 1992-94; diamond specialist cons. Merksamer Jewelers, Santa Maria, 1994—. Artist tapestry hanging Laguna Beach Mus. Art, 1974. Mem. Cen. Coast Pla. Adv. Bd., 1992. Recipient Cert. Merit Art Bank Am., 1968. Mem. NAFE, Internat. Platform Assn., Speaker's Bur., Santa Maria C. of C., Compassion Internat. Republican. Roman Catholic. Office: Merksamer Jewelers 141 Santa Maria Town Ctr Santa Maria CA 93454

BAKER-ROELOFS, MINA MARIE, retired home economics educator; b. Holland, Mich., Mar. 1, 1920; d. Thomas and Fannie (DeBoer) Baker; m. Harold Eugene Roelofs, Aug. 16, 1985; children: Howard, Donald, Ann. BS, Iowa State U., 1942, MS, 1946; postgrad., Ariz. State U., 1965, Ind. State U., 1968, 76. Dietitian Annville (Ky.) Inst., 1942-45; chmn., tchr. home econs. Cen. Coll., Pella, Iowa, 1946-85, ret., 1985; mem. dean's grad. adv. coun. Iowa State U., Ames, 1955-56, coord. coop. plan, 1967-85. Editor: Dandy Dutch Recipes, 1991; co-editor: Pella Collectors Cookbook, 1982, A Taste of the World, 1992. Mem. com. Pell Hist. Soc. Grantee Govt. Cross-Cultural, 1974, NEH, 1980. Mem. AAUW, Am. Home Econ. Assn. (life), Iowa Home Econ. Assn. (pres. 1953-55, sec. 1979-81, Disting. Svc. award 1985), Iowa Elder Hostel Tchr. Ctrl. Coll. Aux., PEO Sisterhood, Women's Social and Literary Club (pres. 1990-92). Republican. Mem. Reformed Ch. Home: 229 Main St Pella IA 50219-2024

BALAKIAN, ANNA, foreign language educator, scholar, critic, writer; b. Constantinople, Turkey, July 14, 1916; came to U.S., 1926; d. Diran and Kohar (Panosian) B.; m. Stepan Nalbantian, Dec. 15, 1945; children: Suzanne, Haig. B.A., Hunter Coll., 1936; M.A., Columbia U., 1938, Ph.D., 1943; L.H.D. (hon.), New Haven U., 1977. Mem. faculty Syracuse U.; prof. French and comparative lit. N.Y. U., 1955—, chmn. comparative lit. dept., 1978-86; vis. prof. City U. N.Y., State U. N.Y., Stony Brook; lectr. in numerous univs., including U. Oxford, Eng., College de France, Paris; producer ednl. radio broadcasts. Author: Literary Origins of Surrealism, 1947 (transl. into Spanish and Portugese), Surrealism: the Road to the Absolute (transl. into Japanese), 1959, 1986, The Symbolist Movement: a critical appraisal, 1967 (transl. into Spanish), Andre Breton: Magus of Surrealism, 1971 (transl. into Spanish), The Fiction of the Poet: from Mallarmé to the Post-Symbolist Mode, 1992; (essays) The Snowflake on the Belfry: Dogma and Disquietude in the Academic Arena, 1994; editor, chief contbr.: The Symbolist Movement in the Literature of European Languages, 1983; editor: André Breton Today, 1989; editor, translator: Eva the Fugitive (Rosamel del Valle), 1990; reviewer Saturday Rev., 1960-73; contbr. numerous articles on 19th and 20th century lit. to French, Am. and English scholarly jours., most recent on the problematics of modernism. Recipient Distinguished Scholar award Hofstra Faculty, 1975; Guggenheim fellow, 1969-70; Nat. Endowment grantee and cons., 1970-79; Am. Council Learned Socs. grantee; Internat. Research Exchange grantee. Mem. Am. Comparative Lit. Assn. (pres. 1977-82), Internat. Comparative Lit. Assn. (v.p. 1982-85), Am. Assn. Tchrs. French (nat. v.p. 1968-71), Modern Lang. Assn., PEN Club, Phi Beta Kappa. Mem. Armenian Apostolic Ch. Home: 16 Linden Ln Old Westbury NY 11568-1610 Office: 19 University Pl New York NY 10003-4501

BALASEKARAN, SAROJA, anesthesiologist; b. India, Feb. 19, 1942; came to U.S., 1977; married; 2 children. MD, Stanley Med. Coll., Madras, India, 1963. Diplomate Am. Bd. Anesthesiology. Intern Stanley Med. Coll., 1964-65; pvt. practice Madras Med. Svc., 1967-77; resident in neurosurgery Boston City Hosp., 1977-78; anesthesia resident Harvard U., 1978-80; staff anesthesiologist Addison Gilbert Hosp., Gloucester, Mass., 1980-81, Winchester

(Mass.) Hosp., 1981-82, Delray Community Hosp., Delray Beach, Fla., 1982-85, St. Paul Med. Ctr., Dallas, 1985—; asst. med. dir. anesthesia St. Paul Med. Ctr., mem. profl. activities com. Mem. Dallas County Med. Soc., Tex. Med. Soc. Home: 5346 W Mockingbird Ln Dallas TX 75209-5606

BALBONI, SUSAN J., artist, educator; b. Raymond, Maine, Feb. 13, 1947; d. Robert and Virginia K. (Balboni) Winslow; m. Jay Tashiro, June, 1976 (div. 1986); children: Vanessa, Suzanne, Rosetta, Ayesha; m. Jonathan Horwitz, Sept., 1994. Student in ceramics, Syracuse U., 1976-80; BA in Art summa cum laude, Kenyon Coll., 1991; MFA, Kent State U., 1993. Instr. Kenyon Coll., Gambier, Ohio, 1980—; art therapist United Way, Cleve., 1993—; instr. Cleve. Inst. Art, 1994—; summer instr. Falmouth (Mass.) Artist's Guild, 1982-86; vis. art lectr. Cleve. Inst. Art, 1994, instr., 1994—; instr. summer scholar program Cleve. Sch. Dist., 1994—; self-employed studio artist, 1980-89; lectr. Cin. Art Acad., Cape Cod Conservatory, Cleve. Inst. Art, Ind. U.; vis. artist Cleve. Sch. Arts, 1994-95, Cleve. Sch. Dist. Summer Scholar Program, 1994-95; presenter numerous seminars. One-woman shows include Carnegie Arts Ctr., Covington, Ky., 1993, Sculpture Ctr., Cleve., 1993, Firelands' Assn. Visual Arts, 1994, C.A.G.E., Cin.; group shows include Everson Mus. Art, Syracuse, N.Y., 1980, Lowe Art Gallery, Syracuse, N.Y., 1981, Hyperborean Gallery, Gambier, Ohio, 1981, Ohio State Fair, 1982, 88, Cooperstown (N.Y.) Art Gallery, 1982, Brea (Calif.) Civic Cultural Ctr. Gallery, 1982, Zanesville (Ohio) Art Ctr., 1982, 87, 88, Signatures Fine Art and Contemporary Craft Gallery, Worthington, Ohio, 1983, Kenyon Coll., 1983, Mansfield (Ohio) Art Ctr., 1984, 85, 86, 88, 89, Ohio U., Athens, 1984, Herndon Ho. Regional Art Gallery, Columbus, Ohio, 1986, Higbee Co., Cleve., 1986, Arromont Sch. Arts and Crafts, Gutlinburg, Tenn., 1986, Of the Heart Gallery, Columbus, 1987, Zanesville Cultural Ctr., 1987, Copeland-Gary Fine Art Gallery, 1988, Worthington Arts Coun., 1988, Widen-Ross Gallery, 1990, Eels Art Gallery, Cleve, 1992, Floyd Court Mus., Albany, 1993, Pa. State U., 1993, U. Akron, Ohio, 1994, Firelands Assn. Visual Arts, Oberlin, Ohio, 1995, Cleve. State U., 1995, Spaces, Cleve., 1995; participant Gt. Lakes Regional Colls. Faculty Travelling Exhibition, 1987-88; represented in permanent collections including Trustcorp Bank, Columbus, Sheffield Corp., India Atlantic, Fla., Sell, Inc., Atlanta; represented in numerous pvt. collections. Vol. instr. Knox county Sch. System, 1982-91. Fellow Vt. Studio Ctr., 1994, Individual Artist fellow Ohio Arts Coun., 1994; recipient Profl. Devel. Assistance award Ohio Arts Coun., 1994, Crafts Nat. Merit award Pa. State U., 1993. Mem. Women's Caucus for Art (editor newsletter 1987-88, v.p. Ohio chpt. 1988-89), Nat. Coun. Edn. Ceramic Arts, Coll. Art Assn., Soc. Layerists in Multi-Media, Nat. Mus. Women in Arts, Amnesty Internat., Artists Against Apartheid, Phi Beta Kappa, Alpha Sigma Lambda. Democrat. Home: 3327 Clarendon St Cleveland OH 44118 Office: Kenyon Coll Gambier OH 43022

BALDASSANO, CORINNE LESLIE, radio executive; b. N.Y.C., May 16, 1950; d. Nicholas and Olga (Phillips) Baldassano. BA cum laude, Queens Coll., CUNY, 1970; MA in Theatre, Hunter Coll., CUNY, 1975; MBA in Fin., NYU, 1986. Program dir., ops. mgr. Sta. KAUM-FM, Houston, 1977-79; dir. programming Sta. WSAI-FM, Cin., 1979-81; dir. programming ABC Contemporary and FM Radio Networks, N.Y.C., 1981-84; regional mgr. affiliate relations United Stations Radio Networks, N.Y.C., 1985-87; dir. ABC Entertainment Radio Network, N.Y.C., 1987-90; v.p. programming ABC Radio Networks, 1990-94; v.p. programming Unistar Radio Networks, L.A., 1994; v.p. programming SW Networks, N.Y.C., 1994—; guest lectr. Wharton Sch. Bus., Phila., 1983, St. John's U., N.Y.C., 1983-84; bd. dirs. Country Radio Broadcasters, Inc., Nashville, 1990—, chmn. agenda com., 1990. Alumni mem. Govs. Com. Scholastic Achievement, N.Y.C., 1984-85. Mem. NYU Bus. Forum (bd. dirs. 1988-91, v.p., treas. 1990-91), Internat. Radio and TV Soc. (planning com., faculty/industry seminar 1986, 87, chmn. Summer Fellowship Program 1988), Nat. Music Found. (N.Y. bd. 1992-93, 94—). Democrat. Roman Catholic. Avocations: travel, theatre, dancing, running, music. Office: SW Networks 1370 6th Ave New York NY 10019

BALDASSARRE, SONIA ELIZABETH, public health nurse; b. Lima, Peru, June 23, 1957; came to U.S., 1983; d. Antero and Blanca (Mateo) Ruiz; divorced; 1 chld, Randall. MSN, San Francisco State U., 1992. RN; cert. pub. health nurse. Night auditor Residence Inn, San Mateo, Calif., 1985-88; nurses aide San Mateo County Gen. Hosp., 1989-91, staff nurse, 1991—.

BALDERRAMA, SYLVIA RAMÍREZ, psychologist, educator; b. Carlsbad, N.Mex., Jan. 12, 1952; d. Andres R. and Luz C. (Ramirez) B.; m. John F. Morley, Aug. 13, 1977; children: Laura de la Luz B. Morley, Lucas Macmillan B. Morley, Nicholas John B. Morley. AB, Harvard U./Radcliffe Coll., 1975; MEd, Boston U., 1977; EdD in Counseling Psychology, Columbia U., 1990. Lic. in psychology, N.Y. Dir. minority recruitment Yale U. Undergrad. Admissions, New Haven, 1977-81; house fellow Vassar Coll., Poughkeepsie, N.Y., 1982-85; psychotherapist Ctr. for Psychol. Svcs., N.Y.C., 1986-87; supr. Columbia U.-Tchrs. Coll., N.Y.C., 1986-87; counselor Cornell U./N.Y. State Sch. Indsl. and Labor Rels., N.Y.C., 1986-87; clin. intern Manhattan Psychiat. Ctr., Ward's Island, N.Y., 1987-88; staff psychologist SUNY, Purchase, 1990-92; dir. psychol. svcs. Vassar Coll., Poughkeepsie, 1992—; instr. Columbia U.-Tchrs. Coll., 1988-90, adj. asst. prof., 1990-92. Charter mem. Arlington Mid. Sch. PTA, Poughkeepsie, 1993. Mem. APA, N.Y. State Psychol. Assn., Hudson Valley Psychol. Assn., Mental Health Assn. Office: Vasser Coll Box 27 124 Raymond Ave Poughkeepsie NY 12601

BALDIZAR, BARBARA J., state senator; b. Chgo., July 29, 1947; m. Robert N. Baldizar; children: Carrie, Brian. Grad., St. Francis Acad., 1969. Sales assoc. Gt. Eastern Properties, Inc., 1984; with code enforcement dept. and mayor's office City of Nashua, N.H., 1985-87; campaign chairwoman Congressman Dick Swett, Southern, N.H., 1990; dist. office dir. Congressman Dick Swett, Nashua, 1991, congl. aide, 1991; polit. dir. N.H. primary Gov. Bill Clinton for Pres., 1991-92; mem. N.H. Ho. of Reps., 1988-92, N.H. Senate, 1993—; vice chairwoman senate jud. com., senate capital budget com.; former chair statewide confn. perinatal chem. addictions com., Nashua legis. del.; chair for N.H. Nat. Women's Legis. Lobby, 1988—. Mem. adv. bd. Rivier Coll., 1988—; bd. dirs. So. N.H. Svcs., 1988—, Nashua Children's Home, 1988—. Recipient Cmty. Svc. award Nat. Assn. Perinatal Rsch., 1993; named One of N.H. Most Powerful, Network Mag., 1994; received 100% rating, N.H. Citizen Action Voting Index, 1994. Democrat. Roman Catholic. Home: 16 Parrish Hill Dr Nashua NH 03063-2717 Office: NH State Senate State House Rm 9 107 N Main St Concord NH 03301

BALDON, CLEO, interior designer; b. Leavenworth, Wash., June 1, 1927; d. Ernest Elsworth and Esther Jane (Hannan) Chute; m. Lewis Smith Baldon, Nov. 20, 1948 (div. July 1961); 1 child, Dirk; m. Ib Jørgen Melchior, Jan. 18, 1964; 1 stepson, Leif Melchior. BS, Woodbury Coll., 1948. Ptnr. Interior Designs Ltd., Los Angeles, 1948-50; freelance illustrator Los Angeles, 1952-54; prin. Cleo Baldon & Assocs., Los Angeles and Venice, Calif., 1954—; ptnr. Galper/Baldon Assocs., Venice, 1970—. Author: Steps and Stairways; contbr. articles to profl. jours.; patentee in field. Recipient City Beautification awards L.A., 1974-77, 80, 83, 85-90, 92, Beverly Hills, 1982, Calif. Landscape Contbr., 1975, 79, Pacifica award Resources Coun., CAlif., 1979. Home: 8228 Marmont Ln West Hollywood CA 90069-1624 Office: Galper/Baldon Assocs 723 Ocean Front Walk Venice CA 90291-3270

BALDRIDGE, BROOKE BAYARD, computer programmer; b. Bridgeport, Conn., May 11, 1963; d. Dickson Bouton and Edith Landell (Dunn) Baldridge; m. Daniel Gregory Pelizza, May 16, 1987 (div. Jan., 1990). BS in Computer Sci., Trinity Coll., Hartford, Conn., 1985. Computer programmer The Travelers Ins. Co., RAleigh, N.C., 1985—. Mem. Raleigh Jaycees (Jaycee of Month 1992, 94, Chmn. of Month 1993, Project award 1994). Republican. Episcopalian. Home and Office: The Travelers Ins Co 7425 Ashbury Ct Raleigh NC 27615

BALDRIGE, LETITIA, writer, management training consultant; b. Miami Beach, Fla.; d. Howard Malcolm and Regina (Connell) B.; m. Robert Hollensteiner; children: Clare, Malcolm. BA, Vassar Coll., 1946; postgrad., U. Geneva, 1946-48; D.H.L. (hon.), Creighton U., 1979, Mt. St. Mary's Coll., 1980, Bryant Coll., 1987, Kenyon Coll., 1990. Personal-social sec. to amb. Am. Embassy, Paris, 1948-51; intelligence officer Washington, 1951-53; asst. to amb. Am. Embassy, Rome, 1953-56; dir. pub. rels. Tiffany & Co., 1956-60; social sec. The White House, 1961-63; pres. Letitia Baldrige Enterprises, Chgo., 1964-69; dir. consumer affairs Burlington Industries, 1969-71; pres. Letitia Baldrige Enterprises, Inc., N.Y.C. and Washington, 1972—; bd. dirs. Outlet Co., Fed. Home Loan Bank Atlanta, Hartmarx Corp. Author: Roman Candle, 1956, Tiffany Table Settings, 1958, Of Diamonds and Diplomats, 1968, Home, 1972, Juggling, 1976, Amy Vanderbilt's Complete Book of Etiquette, 1978, Amy Vanderbilt's Everyday Etiquette, 1979, Entertainers, 1981, Letitia Baldrige's Complete Guide to Executive Manners, 1985, Letitia Baldrige's Complete Guide to a Great Social Life, 1987, Complete Guide to the New Manners for the '90s, 1990, Complete New Guide to the Executive Manners, 1993; (novel) Public Affairs Private Relations, 1990; columnist Copley News Syndicate, New Choices Mag.; contbg. editor Town & Country Mag. Bd. dirs. Woodrow Wilson Found., Inst. Internat. Edn.; mem. adv. bd. Folger Shakespeare Libr., Washington, Mount Vernon Ladies Assn., Washington., Reading is Fundamental. Republican.

BALDWIN, BETTY JO, computer specialist; b. Fresno, Calif., May 28, 1925; d. Charles Monroe and Irma Blanche (Law) Inks; m. Barrett Stone Baldwin Jr.; two daughters. AB, U. Calif., Berkeley, 1945. With NASA Ames Rsch. Ctr., Moffett Field, Calif., 1951-53, math tech. 14' Wind Tunnel, 1954-55, math analyst 14' Wind Tunnel, 1956-63, supr. math analyst Structural Dynamics, 1963-68, supervisory computer programmer Structural Dynamics, 1968-71, computer programmer Theoretical Studies, 1971-82, adminstrv. specialist Astrophys. Experiments, 1982-85, computer specialist, resource mgr. Astrophysics br., 1985—; v.p. B&B Baldwin Farms, Bakersfield, Calif., 1978—. Mem. IEEE, Assn. for Computing Machinery, Am. Geophys. Union, Am. Bus. Womens Assn. (pres., v.p. 1967, one of Top 10 Women of Yr. 1971). Presbyterian. Office: NASA Ames Rsch Ctr Mail Stop 245-6 Moffett Field CA 94035-1000

BALDWIN, CATHY L., occupational health nurse, consultant; b. Ft. Worth, Sept. 28, 1955; d. Jack L. and Alva (Pearce) LeMond; m. Dan L. Baldwin, Aug. 23, 1979; children: Andrew, Matthew, John. BSN, U. Tex., Arlington, 1983; MS, U. LaVerne, 1993. RN, Tex., Calif.; cert. occupational health nurse, occupational health hearing conservationist. Occupational health nurse Motorola, Inc., Ft. Worth, 1985-88, Koch Refinery, Corpus Christi, 1988, Wynn's Climate Systems, Ft. Worth, 1988-90, Kaiser Permanente/So. Calif., Woodland Hills, 1990-94; corp. occupational health nurse Cigna Health Care, Glendale, Calif., 1994—; preceptor UCLA Sch. Occupational Health, 1992—. Author health/wellness articles for employer publs; designer, developer employer occupational health programs. Mentor, speaker Youth Motivation Task Force, Kaiser/Los Angeles County, 1990—. Mem. ANA, Am. Assn. Occupational Health Nurses, So. Calif. Occupational Health Nurses Assn., Kaiser Permanente Women in Mgmt., Kaiser Permanente Regional Occupational Health Coords. (co-chmn. So. Calif. region 1992). Republican. Roman Catholic. Home: 841 Wiladonda Dr La Cañada Flintridge CA 91011 Office: Cigna Occupl Health and Safety 505 N Brand Blvd Glendale CA 91203

BALDWIN, DEANNA LOUISE, dietitian; b. Oklahoma City, Okla., Jan. 14, 1946; d. Jesse Burlin and Celena Mae (Robison) Smith; m. James Stephen Baldwin, Apr. 7, 1989; 1 child, Melissa. BS, Stephen F. Austin, 1985. Dietetic tech. Pasadena (Tex.) Bayshore Hosp., 1969-70; payroll clk. Seismic Computing Corp., Houston, 1971-72; restaurant mgr., mgr. trainer H. Salt Fish n' Chips, Pasadena, 1972-75; asst. food svc. dir. East Tex. Med. Ctr. Hosp., Tyler, 1990-92. Mem. Am. Dietetic Assn.

BALDWIN, DOROTHY LEILA, educator; b. Irvington, N.J., Feb. 28, 1948; d. Daniel Thomas and Lillian Frances (Wainright) B. BA, Kean Coll., Union, N.J., 1969, MA in Edn. and Humanities, 1971; EdD in Adminstrn. and Supervision, Seton Hall U., 1987, cert. reading specialist, 1979, cert. bus. adminstr., 1985. Tchr., reading coord. St. Paul Apostle Sch. Irvington, 1969-74; tchr. Summit (N.J.) Jr. High Sch., 1975-79; social studies coord. K-9, chmn. dept. 7-9 Summit Pub. schs., 1979-87; social studies supr. Livingston (N.J.) Pub. Schs., 1987; prin. Point Road Sch, Little Silver, N.J., 1987-89; dir. gifted edn. K-12 Clifton, N.J., 1989-90; prin. Sch. Two, Clifton, N.J., 1989-90, Deerfield Sch., Mountainside, 1990-92, Eisenhower Sch., Bridgewater-Raritan, N.J., 1992—; adj. prof. Montclair (N.J.) State Coll.; tchr. adult and community schs.; cons. in field; workshop coord. Author books; contbr. articles to profl. jours. PTA scholar, 1965. Mem. ASCD, Nat. Assn. Elem. Sch. Prins., Nat. Coun. Social Studies, Am. Assn. Sch. Adminstrs., N.J. Assn. Elem. Sch. Prins., Somerset County Assn. Elem. Sch. Prins., Phi Delta Kappa, Kappa Delta Pi. Home: 737 River Rd Chatham NJ 07928-1136 Office: Eisenhower Sch Bridgewater NJ 08807

BALDWIN, IRENE S., corporate executive, real estate investor; b. Dodge City, Kans., Sept. 8, 1939; d. Albert A. McMichael and Eleanor L. (Johnson) McMichael McGrath; m. Miles Edward Baldwin, June 30, 1961. BS, Friends U., 1961. Dress designer, Wichita, 1959-61; social worker Sedgwick County, Kans., 1963-65; owner motel chain, Kans., 1965—; comml. and agrl. real estate investor, 1971—; corp. sec.-treas. Baldwin, Inc., Kans., 1970—, fin. advisor, 1970—; pvt. practice fin. cons., Colby, Kans., 1975—; founder, advisor Charitable Found., Kans., 1980—. Fundraiser various charitable orgns., 1982—; pvt. placement of homeless animals, Kans. and Nebr., 1965—. Helped develop 1st artificial front leg for canines, 1985. Avocations: horseback riding, hiking, travel, sewing, drawing. Home and Office: 2320 S Range Ave Colby KS 67701-9056

BALDWIN, JANICE MURPHY, lawyer; b. Bridgeport, Conn., July 16, 1926; d. William Henry and Josephine Gertrude (McKenna) Murphy; m. Robert Edward Baldwin, July 31, 1954; children: Jean Margaret, Robert William, Richard Edward, Nancy Josephine. AB, U. Conn., 1948; MA, Mt. Holyoke Coll., 1950; postgrad. U. Manchester, Eng., 1950-51; MA, Fletcher Sch., Tufts U., 1952; JD, U. Wis., 1971. Bar: Wis. 1971, U.S. Dist. Ct. (we. dist.) Wis. 1971. Staff atty. Legis. Coun., State of Wis., Madison, 1971-74, 75-78, sr. staff atty., 1979-94; pvt. practice, Madison, 1994—; atty. adviser HUD, Washington, 1974-75, 78-79. Mem. AAUW, NOW, LWV, U.S. Women's Polit. Caucus, Legal Assn. for Women, Dane County Bar Assn. (legis. com. 1980-81, long range planning com. 1990—), Wis. Bar Assn. (pres. govt. lawyers divsn. 1985-87, bd. govs. 1985-89, treas. 1987-89, participation of women in the bar com. 1987—, professionalism com. 1990—, bd. bar examiners review 1990—, law-related edn. com. 1992—, govt. lawyers divsn. 1981—), Wis. Women's Network, Wis. Women's Polit. Caucus, U. Wis. Univ. League, Older Women's League (health, legis., marital property, state and local taxation law). Home and Office: 125 Nautilus Dr Madison WI 53705-4329

BALDWIN, LEONA B. (NONI BALDWIN), insurance agent; b. Portland, Jan. 18, 1934; d. Abram Martilla and Ida (Sophia) Heiskari; m. Walter Lee Baldwin, Jan. 26, 1953; children: Cathy Baldwin-Johnson, Keith Baldwin, Julie Templeton, Amy Clifford. Student, Clark Jr. Coll., 1952-53. CLU, Chartered Fin. Cons., Life Underwriter Tng. Fellow. Sec. Bill Pottle, CLU, Anchorage, 1972-75; office mgr. Wilson & Baldwin, Anchorage, 1976-79; life ins. agt. N.Y. Life, Anchorage, 1979—. Mem. Nat. Assn. Life Underwriters (bd. trustees 1993-95), Women Life Underwriters Confedn. (nat. pres. 1987-88, nat. edn. chmn. 1988-90, Nat. Woman of Yr. award 1990), So. Alaska Life Underwriters (pres. 1986-87), Anchorage Estate Planning Coun. (sec. 1991-92, v.p. 1992-93, pres. 1993-94), Am. Bus. Women (pres. Arctic Nugget chpt. 1980-81), Alaska Life Underwriters (pres. 1987-88, nat. committeeman 1990-93, Man of Yr. award 1987). Lutheran. Office: Baldwin Fin Concepts 2525 Blueberry Rd Ste 107 Anchorage AK 99503-2647

BALDWIN, MARYANN POWELL, school counselor, educator; b. Waterbury, Conn., Apr. 22, 1947; d. Harvey A. and Gracemary (Cizek) Stackman; m. Timothy H. Powell, July 26, 1969 (div. June 1983); 1 child, Lisa Anne Powell; m. Dennis A. Baldwin, Nov. 21, 1991. BA in Elem. Edn., Clemson U., 1969, MA in Guidance/Counseling, 1971; PhD in Edn., U. South Fla., 1979. Lic. mental health counselor, Fla. 1st grade tchr. Walhalla (S.C.) Elem. Sch., 1969-70, Ravenel Elem. Sch., Seneca, S.C., 1970-72; guidance counselor Twin Lakes Elem., Tampa, Fla., 1972-80; coll. placement specialist Acad. of Holy Name, Tampa, 1982-84; resource tchr. Plant High Sch., Tampa, 1984-85, guidance counselor, 1985-88; guidance counselor Middleton Jr. High Sch., Tampa, 1988-93, Van Buren Jr. High Sch., Tampa, 1993—; adj. instr. U. South Fla., Tampa, 1977—, Hillsborough C.C., Tampa, 1993—; counselor for migrants Summer Migrant Inst., Tampa, 1993—; pvt. practice therapy, Tampa, 1975—. Co-author: (manual) How to Set Up a Volunteer Tutoring Program, 1990. U. South Fla. Grad. Coun. fellow, 1975, 76; Kappa Kappa Gamma rehab. scholar Clemson U., 1969. Mem. ACA, Fla. Counseling Assn. (conv. sec. 1989), Hillsborough Counseling Assn. (recognition chair 1988-91, mental health liaison chair 1994—), Phi Delta Kappa. Home: 3215 Taragrove Dr Tampa FL 33618 Office: Van Buren Jr High Sch 8715 N 22nd St Tampa FL 33604

BALDWIN, SUSAN OLIN, lawyer; b. Battle Creek, Mich., Sept. 1, 1954; d. Thomas Franklin and Gloria Joan (Skidmore) Olin; m. James Patric Baldwin, Sept. 15, 1979; children: Christopher Mark, David James. BA, Miami U., Ohio, 1976; JD, U. Cin., 1979. Bar: Ohio 1979, Mich. 1984. Assoc. editor Am. Legal Pub. Co., Cin., 1979-80; corp. atty. Hosp. Care Corp., Cin., 1980-84; legal counsel Peak Health Plan, Cin., 1984; assoc. Cook & Goetz, P.C., Bloomfield Hills, Mich., 1984-91; assoc. Pringle & Assocs., P.C., Farmington Hills, Mich., 1991-94; dir. Calhoun County Econ. Devel. Forum, Battle Creek, 1994—. Contbr. articles to profl. jours. Pres. Hunter's Green Homeowner's Assn., Independence, Ky., 1982-83; charter mem. Young Reps., Ashland, Ohio, 1972; chairwoman Safety Town Community Project, Jr. League Battle Creek, 1993—; key communicator, Minges Brook PTA, 1993—, treas., 1994—. Mem. ABA, Nat. Health Lawyers Assn., Am. Acad. Hosp. Attys., State Bar Mich., Am. Businesswomen's Assn. (v.p. 1980-81, editor 1980), Alpha Lambda Delta, Phi Alpha Delta. Club: Birmingham Evening Newcomers (treas. 1986-87, pres. 1988). Office: 164 W Hamilton Ln Battle Creek MI 49015-4030

BALDWIN, VELMA NEVILLE WILSON, personnel consultant; b. Meade, Kans., Aug. 31, 1918; d. Charles Chester and Anna Velma (Neville) Wilson; m. Claude David Baldwin, Jan. 31, 1942 (dec. Nov. 1976). AB, U. Kans., 1940. Placement working students U. Kans., 1940-41; with War Dept., Washington, 1942-45; rsch asst. Dr. A.C. Kinsey, Ind. U., 1946; with Carter Oil Co., Denver, 1948-50; with pers. Bur. Budget, Washington, 1951-55; asst. to dir. pers. Treasury Dept., 1955-59; pers. officer, dir. adminstrn. Office Mgmt. and Budget, 1959-79; cons. in field. Recipient Career Svc. award Nat. Civil Svc. League, 1975. Mem. Am. Soc. Pub. Adminstrn. (past exec. bd.), Soc. Pers. Adminstrn. (exec. bd.), Cosmos Club (Washington), Phi Beta Kappa. Home: 2234 49th St NW Washington DC 20007-1057

BALES, BEVERLY ANN, county official; b. Barnesville, Minn., Jan. 11, 1937; d. Francis Henry and Theresa Catherine (Kieselbach) Hilgers; m. William Dean Bales, May 15, 1970; 1 child, Becky Ann. Student, N.D. State Sch. Sci., 1956-57. Sec. IBM Corp., Des Moines, 1957-58, dispatcher, 1958-68; instr. IBM Corp., White Plains, N.Y., 1968-71; pers. staff asst. IBM Corp., Mpls., 1971-73; bus. owner Diamond Jim's, Nelson, Minn., 1973—; commr. Douglas County, Alexandria, Minn., 1993—. Chair Mid States Com. Health Advisory, Douglas County, 1994; county commr. rep. County Com. on Aging, Douglas, 1993-94; chair Parent Adv. Coun., Carlos and Alexandria, 1979-91; mem. dist. parent adv. couns., 1989, 91, 92; mem. com. Nelson Fun Fest, 1976-85; chair All County Read-A-Thon, Douglas County, 1990; mem. Nat. Bone Marrow Program, 1991—. Recipient Commendation award Gov. of Minn., 1988. Mem. Minn. Citizens Concerned for Life, Nat. Cath. Order Foresters, Lake Carlos Assn., Bus. and Profl. Women, Doulgas County Hist. Soc., Alumni Assn. N.D. State Coll. Sci., VFW Aux. Roman Catholic. Home: 8170 E Lake Carlos NE Carlos MN 56319

BALES, FLOSSIE KATHLEEN, librarian, systems analyst; b. El Dorado, Kans., Sept. 4, 1938; d. Francis Justus and Flossie Mae (Smith) O'Reilly; m. Royal Eugene Bales, Apr. 16, 1960; children: David Scott, Elizabeth Laura. B in Music Edn. magna cum laude, Wichita State U., 1960; MLS, U. Calif., Berkeley, 1968. Tchr. music Larkspur (Calif.)/Corte Madera Sch., 1961-62; libr. clk. Palo Alto (Calif.) Pub. Libr., 1962-67; cataloger Stanford (Calif.) U., 1968; children's libr. Santa Clara County, Los Altos, Calif., 1975; cataloger Santa Clara County Libr., San Jose, Calif., 1976-78; instr. cataloging U. Calif., Berkeley, 1982, 84-85; with user svcs. staff Rsch. Librs. Group, Mt. View, Calif., 1978-80, systems analyst, 1980-89, mgr. online applications, 1989-92, sr. analyst, 1993—. Contbr. articles to profl. jours. Chairperson curriculum com. Los Lomitas Sch., Menlo Park, Calif., 1975-77; bd. dirs. El Camino Youth Symphony, Los Altos, 1983-87, co-pres., 1985-87. Mem. ALA (chairperson cataloging and classification sect. 1991-92, various appts. 1982—), Nat. Info. Standards Orgn. (chairperson standards devel. com. 1990-92). Democrat. Home: 1225 Sherman Ave Menlo Park CA 94025 Office: Rsch Librs Group 1200 Villa St Mountain View CA 94041

BALES, RUBY JONES, special education administrator; b. Fayetteville, Tenn., Aug. 17, 1933; d. Albin O. and Jenny Katherine (Pickett) Jones; m. Emory H. Bales, Jan. 25, 1954; children: N. Katharine (dec.), David Emory, Evelyn Ann, Patrick Lee. BS in Biology, Tenn. Technol. U., 1956; MA in Supervision, Human Rels., George Washington U., 1975; EdD in Curriculum Instrn. and Reading, U. Md., 1984. Cert. tchr. grades 1-6, prin., supr., elem., middle sch. reading tchr. K-12. Tchr. gen. sci., math. Niceville (Fla.) Elem. Sch., 1956-57, Ruckel Jr. H.S., Niceville, 1957-59; tchr. biology, physical sci. Leon H.S., Tallahassee, 1959-60; tchr. 5th grade Potomac Elem. Sch., Dahlgren, Va., 1960-61; tchr. 5th grade Charles County Middle Pub. Sch.s, La Plata, Md., 1965-73, acting adminstrv. asst., 1973-74; program coord. Mitchell Elem. Sch., Charles County, La Plata, 1974-75, adminstrv. asst., 1975-77; prin. Dr. James Craik Elem. Sch., Pomfret, Md., 1977-84, Eva Turner Elem. Sch., Waldorf, Md., 1984-86; instrnl. supr. elem. schs. Charles County Sch. Dist., La Plata, 1986-94. Supt. Charles County Fair Sch. Exhibit, County Fair Bd., 1986-94. NSF scholar Fla. State U., 1958. Mem. ASCD, Internat. Reading Assn., Va. Head Injury Found. Republican. Home: PO Box 373 Dahlgren VA 22448

BALESTER, VIVIAN SHELTON, lawyer; b. Pine Bluff, Ark., Dec. 10, 1931; d. Marvin W. and Mary Lena (Burke) Shelton; m. James Beverly Standerfer, Aug. 1, 1951 (dec. 1952); 1 child, Walter Eric; m. Raymond James Balester, Oct. 19, 1956; children: Carla Maria, Mark Shelton. BA cum laude, Vanderbilt U., 1955; MLS, Case Western Res. U., 1972, JD, 1975. Bar: Ohio 1975, U.S. Dist. Ct. (no. dist.) Ohio 1975. Ind. bibliographic and legal rsch. cons., Cleve., Washington, Nashville, 1959—; head law libr. Squire, Sanders & Dempsey, Cleve., 1975-86; Ohio del. White House Conf. Librs./Information Svcs., 1979; speaker Law Librs. Nat. Conf., 1978, 80, 82; mem. adv. com. on profl. ethics Case Western Res. U., 1982-85. Lay reader St. Alban's Episc. Ch., 1978-90, mem. vestry, 1977-79, 84-86, warden, 1979, 84; mem. coun. Diocese of Ohio, 1980-82, chmn. racial justice com., 1980-86, chmn. nominating com., 1982, del. Nat. Confs. on Faith Pub. Policy, Racism, 1982; dep. gen. Conv. of Episc. Ch. in U.S., 1985; mem. Women's Polit. Caucus, 1978—; founder and co-chmn. Greater Cleve. Ann. Martin Luther King Celebration, 1980-86; convener AIDS Interfaith Coalition of Greater Cleve., 1987—; mem. County Commrs. adv. com. on handicapped, 1980-84; chmn. adolescent health coalition Fedn. Community Planning, 1979-81, mem. health concerns commn., 1981—, vice chairperson, 1986—; regional chmn. alumni edn. Vanderbilt U., 1982-83; mem. community adv. com. Cleve. Orch., 1983—; bd. dirs. Hospice Coun. No. Ohio, 1979-81, vol. atty., 1982-85; bd. dirs. Interch. Coun. Greater Cleve., 1978-84, 86-88, 92, sec. bd. 1993—, AIDS Housing Coun., 1987-94, Health Issues Task Force, 1988-94, SAMM, 1993—; mem. Ohio Com. Nat. Security, 1983; bd. dirs. WomenSpace, 1979-83. Recipient Outstanding Community Svc. award Fedn. Community Planning, 1980, Woman of Profl. Excellence award YWCA, 1983, Cleve. Mayor's award for volunteerism, 1984, Interchurch Council Ecumenical Adv. award 1988, Western Reserve Historical Soc. Community Leader award, 1989; NEH fellow, 1980. Mem. Cleve. Bar Assn. (Merit Svc. award 1979). Democrat. Home and Office: 2460 Edgehill Rd Cleveland OH 44106-2408

BALICK, HELEN SHAFFER, judge; b. Bloomsburg, Pa.; d. Walter W. and Clarissa K. (Bennett) Shaffer; J.D., Dickinson Sch. Law, 1966; m. Bernard Balick, June 29, 1967. Bar: Pa. 1967, Del. 1969. Probate adminstr. Girard Trust Bank, Phila., 1966-68; pvt. practice law, Wilmington, Del., 1969-74; staff atty. Legal Aid Soc. Del., Wilmington, 1969-71; master Family Ct. Del., New Castle County, 1971-74; bankruptcy judge, U.S. magistrate Dist. Del., Wilmington, 1974-80; bankruptcy judge Dist. Del., 1974-94, chief judge, 1994—. guest lectr. Dickinson Sch. Law, 1981-87; lectr. Dickinson Forum, 1982. Pres. bd. trustees Community Legal Aid Soc., Inc., 1972-74; trustee Dickinson Sch. Law; mem. Citizens Adv. Com. Wilmington, 1973-74, Wilmington Bd. Edn., 1974. Named to the Hall of Fame of Del. Women, 1994. Mem. ABA (judicial adminstrn. sect.), Del. Bar Assn., Fed. Bar Assn., Nat. Conf. Bankruptcy Judges (bd. govs. 1986), Nat. Assn. Women Lawyers, Nat.

Conf. Fed. Trial Judges, Del. Alliance Profl. Women (Trailblazer award 1984), Nat. Assn. Women Judges, Wilmington Women in Bus. (bd. dirs. 180-83), Am. Judges Assn., Forum of Exec. Women, Am. Bankruptcy Inst., Dickinson Sch. Law Gen. Alumni Assn. (exec. bd. 1977-80, 87—, v.p. 1981-84, pres. 1984-87, outstanding alumni award 1991), Phi Alpha Delta. Office: US Bankruptcy Ct Marine Midland Plz 824 Market St Wilmington DE 19801

BALIS, JENNIFER LYNN, career planning educator; b. Hamlin, W.Va., Nov. 23, 1946; d. Louis Byron Floyd and Brunilda (Guiterrez) Castillo; 1 child, Theodore Berndt. AA, Del Mar Coll., 1987; BA, U. Tex., 1989; BS, So. Ill. U., 1992. Nursing educator Driscoll Found. Children's Hosp., Corpus Christi, Tex., 1986-88; peer counselor U. Tex., Edinburg, 1989-90; tchr. Mission (Tex.) Ind. Sch. Dist., 1990; instr. San Diego Job Corps, 1992—; cons. Fleet Feet Running Club, San Diego, 1990-91. Chairperson United Way, Corpus Christi, 1988. With USNR, 1984—. Mem. AAUW, Am. Vocat. Assn., Psi Chi (pres. 1989-90). Republican. Roman Catholic. Home: PO Box 390666 San Diego CA 92149-0666 Office: San Diego Job Corps 1325 Iris Ave Imperial Beach CA 91932

BALISH, RUTH REITZ, community health nurse, medical technologist; b. Palmerton, Pa., Oct. 1, 1919; d. Chas. B. and Minnie E. Reitz; m. George F. Balish, Nov. 5, 1949; children: Deidre B. Talarico, Vicki B. DelMonte, Lori S. Hedges. Student, Moravian Coll., 1937-38; diploma in nursing, Grandview Hosp. Sch. Nursing, 1942; BSN, Temple U., 1944; cert., New England Hosp. Women, 1943; diploma in med. tech., Sacred Heart Hosp. Sch., 1945. Chief med. tech. Morris County Chest Clinic, Morris Pl., N.J.; public health nurse City of Summit (N.J.); chief rsch. histologist Merck Co., Rahway, N.J.; pvt. duty nurse Boca Raton, Fla., Clearwater, Fla.; vol. nurse ARC Disaster Shelter, Boca Raton, Fla., Waynesville, N.C., Pinellas County, Fla., Lakeland Fla.; co-owner, med. technologist North Summit Med. Lab., Summit, N.J., 1951-64. Vol. nurse Lakeland Regional Ctr., Morton Plant Hosp., Clearwater Fla.; mem. adv. bd. V.A.V.S. J. Haley Vets. Hosp., Tampa and Bay Pines Vets. Hosp., St. Petersburg, Fla. Mem. Am. Soc. Clin. Pathologists, Am. Chem. Soc., DAR (officer 1961—, bd. dirs. 1991—), Daus. Am. Colonists, Order Eastern Star. Home: 4747 N Rte 33 # 86 Lakeland FL 33805

BALK, MARY DALE, drug prevention specialist; b. Nashville, July 30, 1939; d. Dale Ivan Knox and Mary Lucille (Clower) Cooke; children: Susan Lynne Kradel, Rebecca Lynne Demo, Melissa Lynne Balk. BS in Edn., Miami U., Oxford, Ohio, 1961, MEd, 1967. Cert. addictions prevention profl.; cert. elem. edn. English; cert. specific learning disabilities K-12; cert. guidance counselor. Tchr. Marion (Ind.) High Sch., 1971-73; guidance counselor Justice Jr. High Sch., Marion, 1973-74; tchr. of the emotionally handicapped Red Bug Elem. Sch., Maitland, Fla., 1974-76; English tchr. Teague Middle Sch., Altamonte Springs, Fla., 1976-78, Lake Brantley High Sch., 1988; guidance counselor Lake Mary (Fla.) Elem. Sch., 1978-88; drug prevention specialist Seminole Co. (Fla.) Schs., 1988—; county Red Ribbon chmn. Nat. Red Ribbon Campaign, Seminole County, 1989—; adj. tchr. Seminole C.C.; guest speaker educators convs. Vice chmn. sch. bd. Sweetwater Episcopal Acad., 1985-88; active HRS Community Task Force for Residential Placement for Dep. Children, 1979-80; chmn. Seminole County Red Ribbon Campaign for a Drug-Free Am., 1989—; exec. com. Seminole County Am. Heart Assn. Mem. Winter Park Univ. Club, Fla. Alcohol and Drug Abuse Assn., Fla. Student Assistance Program Network (sec.). Home: 111 Valley Cir Longwood FL 32779-3460 Office: Drug Prevention Office 1401 S Magnolia Ave Sanford FL 32771-3400

BALKAM, JANE JOHNSTON, pediatric nurse practitioner; b. Callicoon, N.Y., Mar. 5, 1950; d. Alfred G. and Esther (Robinson) Johnston; m. Clifford Robert Balkam, Oct. 20, 1979; children: Matthew, Andrew, James, John. BSN, Georgetown U., 1972; MSN, U. Rochester, 1977. RN, D.C., Md.; cert. pediatric nurse practitioner; cert. lactation cons. Internat. Bd. Lactation Cons. Examiners, Inc. Nurse epidemiologist Med. Coll. of Va. Hosp., Richmond, 1973-75; cert. pub. health nurse Sullivan County Pub. Health Nursing Svc., Liberty, N.Y., 1975-76; instr. in nursing Georgetown U. Sch. Nursing, 1977-78; pediatric nurse practitioner Georgetown U. Community Health Plan, 1978-79; asst. prof. nursing The Cath. U. of Am., Washington, 1978-83, Maymount Coll. of Va., Arlington, 1983-84; pediatric nurse practitioner Arlington County Health Dept., 1981-86; program mgr., child and adolescent health program Div. of Family Health Svcs., Montgomery County Health Dept., Rockville, Md., 1985-89; pediatric nurse pracitioner, after hours care unit Kaiser Permanente Health Plan, Landover, Md., 1989—; owner breast pump rental bus., Sanvita Programs Corp. Lactation Franchise; lactation cons., 1991—; PNP, Prince George's County Health Dept., 1987; staff nurse Vis. Nurse Assn. D.C., 1981-83; speaker in field. Contbr. articles to profl. jours. Mem. Commn. on Children and Youth Montgomery County, Md., 1988-89; mem. maternal child health adv. bd. Regional Ctr. for Infants and Young Children, Rockville, Md., 1987; mem. self-assessment examination com. Nat. Bd. of Pediatric Nurse Practitioners and Assocs., 1984-87; chief proctor Washington Ctr., Nat. Bd. of Pediatric Nurse Practitioners and Assocs. Certifying Examination, 1983, 84; vol. nurse Kensington Clinic of Mobile Med. Care, Inc., 1980-82; vol. staff CUA Health Clinic, 1978-81. Fellow Nat. Assn. of Pediatric Nurse Assocs. and Practitioners (cert., sec. Md.-Chesapeake chpt. 1981-83); mem. ANA (cert.), Md. Nurses Assn. (dist. V mem. nominating com. 1981-83, Internat. Lactation Cons. Assn., Lactation Cons. Assn. of Greater Washington, Sigma Theta Tau (recording sec. Tau chpt. 1978-80). Republican. Roman Catholic. Home: 4515 Gladwyne Dr Bethesda MD 20814

BALKCOM, CAROL ANN, insurance agent; b. Newport, R.I., June 20, 1952; d. Robert Terrence and Barbara Ruth (Hilton) Hannaway; m. Richard Roger Balkcom, Oct., 1981; children: Richard Robert, Geoffrey Adam. BA, R.I. Coll., 1974, MA in Teaching, 1981; Cert. Life Underwriter, Am. Coll., 1984, CHFC, 1986. CLU, ChFC. Tchr. Lincoln (R.I.) Jr. High Sch., 1974-78; sales agt. Met. Life Ins. Co., Pawtucket, R.I., 1978-80; mgr., agt. Phoenix Mut. Life Ins. Co., Providence, 1980-94; instr. R.I. Lic. Sch., Providence, 1986-93; dist. mgr. New Eng. Life, New Port Richey, 1994—. Mem. R.I. Life Underwriters (bd. dirs. 1981-84, 90—, 1st v.p. 1983-84). Office: New Eng Life 6313 Adams St New Port Richey FL 34652

BALL, ARDELLA PATRICIA, library science educator; b. Nashville, Dec. 15, 1932; d. Otis Hugh and Mary Ellen (Staples) Boatright; m. Wesley James Ball, Aug. 28, 1957; children: Wesley James, Roderick Lynn, Wesleyn Lynette, Patrick Wayne. AB, Fisk U., 1953; MS in L.S., Atlanta U., 1956; postgrad., St. Louis U.; DSc. in Libr. Sci., Nova U., 1991. Cataloger Ala. A.&M. Coll., Huntsville, 1957-59; sr. cataloger St. Louis U., 1960-65; cataloger Savannah Pub. Libr. (Ga.), 1965-68; cataloger Armstrong State Coll., Savannah, 1968-74, instructional devel. librarian, 1974-77, library media instr., 1977— . Mem. LWV, NAACP, PTA (life), Ga. Library Assn., Southeastern Library Assn., Ga. Library Media Dept; Coastal Ga. Library Assn. Ch. Christ Contbrs. course manuals in library media. Office: Armstrong State Coll 11935 Abercorn Ext Savannah GA 31419-9901

BALL, DORA LOERA, secondary education educator; b. Mexico City, Nov. 22, 1956; came to U.S., 1961; d. G. R. and Anna (Saenz) Loera; m. Larry W. Ball, Sept. 14, 1984; 1 child, Brandon W. BS, North Tex. State U., 1979; MEd, Sul Ross State U., 1984. Tchr. Odessa (Tex.) H.S., 1982—, Permian H.S., Odessa, 1987-93; bilingual subject specialist Ector County Ind. Sch. Dist., 1993—. Mem. Tex. Assn. Bilingual Edn., Tex. Classroom Tchr. Assn., West Tex. Assn. Bilingual Edn., Hispanic Heritage Com. (Excellenc award 1993), Jr. League (prov.), Phi Delta Kappa (v.p. 1993-94).

BALL, EDNA MARION, cardiac rehabilitation nurse educator; b. Sault Ste Marie, Mich., Oct. 22, 1944; d. Stanley Thomas and Clara P. (Lewis) Piteau; m. Richard J. Ball, July 25, 1963; children: Richard Jr., Robin. AS in Nursing, Southwestern Jr. Coll., 1974; BS in Nursing with distinction, U. N. Fla., 1977; postgrad., U. West Fla. RN, Fla.; cert. advanced cardiac life support provider, basic CPR instr. trainer, caridac rehab. nurse therapist, advanced coronary care, exercise specialist. Staff nurse, med./surg. fl., intensive critical care unit Beaches Hosp., Jacksonville Beach, Fla.; weight control for life counselor Bapt. Hosp., Pensacola, Fla., nurse educator, diabetes edn. program, cardiac rehab. and pacer clinic coord.; staff nurse, critical care unit West Fla. Hosp. Coll., Pensacola; clin. instr., adj. faculty mem. Pensacola Jr. Coll. Mem. Am. Assn. Critical Care Nurses (nat. and local chpts.), Pensacola Area Continuing Edn. Resource System, Fla. Assn. Cardiovascular and Pulmonary Rehab., Am. Assn. Cardiovascular and Pulmonary Rehab., Am. Heart Assn. (bd. dirs. local chpt., sec. to bd. dirs. local chpt. 1988-89, Cert. Appreciation 1983, 84), Mended Hearts (exec. bd. local chpt., adv. com., Merit award), Calif. Jr. Coll. Honor Scholarship Soc., Alpha Gamma Sigma (Gamma Pi chpt.).

BALL, JACQUELINE SNYDER, librarian, educator; b. Winston-Salem, N.C., May 4, 1932; d. Henry Edward and Lucy Jane (Lambeth) Snyder; m. James Bryan Ball, Aug. 7, 1960; children: Michaela Anne, Jason Alan. BS in Edn., Appalachian State U., 1955; MS in Libr. and Info. Sci., U. Tenn., 1979; postgrad., Middle Tenn. State U., 1989. Cert. tchr., Tenn. Library media specialist Forsyth County Schs., Winston-Salem, 1955-57, Oak Ridge (Tenn.) Schs., 1957-68, 79-94; with Freeman Comm., Oak Ridge, 1994—; adj. instr. Grad. Sch. Libr. and Information Sci. U. Tenn., 1991—. Host talk show Oak Ridge Today, 1987-89; book reviewer of young adult lit. The Oak Ridger, 1988-89, drama critic, 1992—; TV commentator ednl. news, Oak Ridge, 1992—. Mem. Am. Libr. Assn., Alpha Psi Omega, Beta Phi Mu. Episcopalian. Home: 110 Berwick Dr Oak Ridge TN 37830 Office: Freeman Comm 126 Randolph Rd Oak Ridge TN 37830

BALL, L. JULIA, nurse; b. Halifax, Eng., Mar. 4, 1948; came to U.S., 1966; d. Arthur W. and Laura Barbara (Carter) Greenwood; m. A. Anthony Ball, Dec. 16, 1966; children: Timothy C., Elizabeth C. Diploma in Nursing, Tex. Tech U./Meth. Hosp., Lubbock, 1977; MSN, Med. U. S.C., 1994. RN. Infection control practitioner Athens (Ga.) Regional Med. Ctr., 1986; dir. community edn. and wellness Stephens County Hosp., Toccoa, Ga., 1986-87, nursing staff devel. coord., 1989; dir. spl. projects indsl. medicine Schubert & Salzer, Ingolstadt, Germany, 1981-91; cons. in infection control Tri County Health Care Consortium, Pendleton, S.C. Mem. Pilot Club Internt. (pres.), Sigma Theta Tau. Episcopalian. Home: 150 Wappoo Creek Dr Unit 13 Charleston SC 29412-2140

BALL, PATRICIA ANN, physician; b. Lockport, N.Y., Mar. 30, 1941; d. John Joseph and Katherine Elizabeth (Hoffmaster) B.; m. Robert E. Lee, May 18, 1973; children—Heather, Samantha. B.S., U. Mich., 1963; M.D., Wayne State U., 1969. Diplomate Am. Bd. Internal Medicine, Am. Bd. Hematology, Am. Bd. Med. Oncology. Intern, resident Detroit Gen. Hosp., 1969-71; resident Jackson Meml. Hosp., Miami, Fla., 1971-72; fellow Henry Ford Hosp., Detroit, 1972-74; staff physician VA Hosp., Allen Park, Mich., 1974-77; practice medicine specializing in hematology and oncology, Bloomfield Hills, Mich., 1977—; mem. faculty dept. medicine Wayne State U. Sch. Medicine, Detroit, 1974—. Mem. Founders Soc., Detroit Inst. Arts. Mem. ACP, AMA, Mich. State Med. Soc., Oakland County Med. Soc., Mich. Soc. Hematology and Oncology, Alpha Omega Alpha. Avocations: photography; skiing. Office: 1575 S Woodward Ave Ste 210 Bloomfield Hills MI 48302-0561

BALL, SHARON SMITH, educational research analyst; b. Indpls., Dec. 27, 1942; d. Harold Eugene and Beatrice (Walton) Smith; m. Michael Bar Ball, Nov. 27, 1966 (div. Mar. 1979); 1 child, James Barry Bitzer. BA, U. Indpls., 1966; MA, Western Ill. U., 1968; postgrad., U. N.Mex., 1971—. Instr. English Ill. State U., Normal, 1967-69; tchr. Fremont (Calif.) Unified Schs., 1969-70; tchr. English Am. Sch., The Hague, The Netherlands, 1980-82; tchr. secondary sch. Albuquerque Pub. Schs., 1970-80, 82-86, pub. info. officer, 1986-90, facilities planner, 1990-93; rsch. analyst Legis. Edn. Study Com., Santa Fe, N.Mex., 1993—; presenter in field. Mem. devel. coun. U. N.Mex. Childrens Hosp., 1990-92; chmn. YWCA Women's Leadership Awards Program, Albuquerque, 1991; mem. steering com. Lt. Gov. Campaign, Albuquerque, 1978. Mem. Nat. Sch. Pub. Rels. Assn. (N.Mex. chpt. pres. 1989—, Gold Medallion award 1990), Pub. Rels. Soc. Am. (N.Mex. chpt. sec. 1989—, Silver Anvil award 1991), N.Mex. Press Women, Albuquerque Press Club (dir. 1987-91). Democrat. Home: 761 Camino Floretta NW Albuquerque NM 87107-5713 Office: Legis Edn Study Com State Capitol Santa Fe NM 87501

BALL, VIRGINIA B., investor; b. Jacksonville, Tex., Jan. 1; d. John A. and DeLouise (McClelland) Beall; m. Edmund f. Ball, June 28, 1952; children: Robert, Nancy. Student, Lon Morris Jr. Coll., 1936-37; AB, Baylor U., 1940; grad. student, Tex. Christian U., 1942-43, Ball State U., 1952-54; HHD (hon.), Wabash Coll., 1965; hon. degree, Ball State U., 1976; Hon. degree, Keuka Coll., 1994. V.p. Muncie (Ind.) Airport, Inc., 1992—, B.B.S. Properties, Muncie, 1992—; trustee, chmn. Nat. Wildlife Fed. Endowment, Washington, 1980-93. Bd. dirs. Minnetrista Cultural Found., Muncie Ind. Com. Humanities, 1973-79; mem. adv. bd. Connor Prairie Settlement, Fishers, Ind., Ind. Youth Inst., Indpls., Interlochen (Mich.) Ctr. for Arts, Muncie Children's Mus., Human Genetics and Engring. Lab., Ball State U., Muncie. Recipient Civic award Woman of Influence, Muncie, 1980; Old Main Tower award Baylor U., 1981, Sagamore of Wabash award Gov. of Ind., Indpls., 1984, Baylor Woman of Merit award Omicron Delta Kappa, 1989, Distinction award Ind. Humanities Coun., Indpls., 1990, VIVA award Muncie C. of C., Rotary Club, 1993; named Disting. Alumni, Lon Morris Jr. Coll., 1965. Mem. The Ninety-nines, Explorer's Club, Soc. Woman Geographers, Internat. Woman's Forum, Rotary Club. Republican. Home: 1707 W Riverside Ave Muncie IN 47303 Office: Ball Assocs PO Box 1408 222 S Mulberry St Muncie IL 61857

BALLANFANT, KATHLEEN GAMBER, newspaper executive, public relations company executive; b. Horton, Kans., July 11, 1945; d. Ralph Hayes and Audrey Lavon (Heryford) G.; m. Sid Roberts; children: Andrea, Benjamin. BA, Trinity U., 1967; postgrad. NYU, 1976, Am. Mgmt. Inst., 1977, Belhaven Coll., 1985. Pub. info. dir. Tex. Dept. Community Affairs, Austin, 1972-74; pub. affairs mgr. Cameron Iron Works, Houston, 1975-77, Assoc. Builders and Contractors, Houston, 1982-84; pres. Ballanfant & Assoc., Houston, 1977-82, 84—; pres. Village Life Inc., 1985—; pres., chief exec. officer Village Life Publs.; owner Village Life newspaper, Southwest News newspaper, Houston Observer/Times newspaper, Village Life Printing & Typesetting, South Post Oak newspaper; mem. adv. council on Construction Edn., Tex. So. U., Houston, 1984—; mem. task force on ednl. excellence Houston Ind. Sch. Dist., 1983—; mem. devel. bd. Inter First Fannin Bank, 1986-88; bd. dirs. Ballaire Hosp., Westbury-Southwest Assn. Author: Something Special-You, 1972, Prevailing Wage History in Houston, 1983; editor newspaper Bellaire Texan, 1981-82, Austin Times, 1971. Vice pres. West Univ. Republic Women's Club, Houston, 1984—; fgn. vis. chmn. Internat. Inst. Edn., Houston, 1980—; docent Houston Zoo, 1982. Named Tex. Woman of Achievement Tex. Womans Hosp., 1986; recipient Apollo IX Medal of Honor Gov. Preston Smith, 1970, Child Abuse Prevention award Gov. Dolph Briscoe, 1974, Tex. Community Newspaper Assn. (pres. 1988—, bd. dirs. 1987—). Mem. Bellaire C. of C. (bd. dirs. 1987—, sec., treas. 1988), Rotary. Republican. Presbyterian. Avocations: traveling, racquetball, reading. Office: Village Life Inc 5160 Spruce St Bellaire TX 77401-3309

BALLANTINE, MORLEY COWLES (MRS. ARTHUR ATWOOD BALLANTINE), newspaper editor; b. Des Moines, May 21, 1925; d. John and Elizabeth (Bates) Cowles; m. Arthur Atwood Ballantine, July 26, 1947 (dec. 1975); children—Richard, Elizabeth Ballantine Leavitt, William, Helen Ballantine Healy. A.B., Ft. Lewis Coll., 1975; L.H.D. (hon.), Simpson Coll., Indianola, Iowa, 1980. Pub. Durango (Colo.) Herald, 1952-83, editor, pub., 1975-83, editor, chmn. bd., 1983—; dir. 1st Nat. Bank, Durango, 1976—, Des Moines Register & Tribune, 1977-85, Cowles Media Co., 1982-86. Mem. Colo. Land Use Commn., 1975-81, Supreme Ct. Nominating Commn., 1984-90; mem. Colo. Forum, 1985—, Blueprint for Colo., 1985-92; pres. S.W. Colo. Mental Health Ctr., 1964-65, Four Corners Opera Assn., 1983-86; bd. dirs. Colo. Nat. Hist. Preservation Act, 1968-78; trustee Choate/Rosemary Hall, Wallingford, Conn., 1973-81, Simpson Coll., Indianola, Iowa, 1981—, U. Denver, 1984—, Fountain Valley Sch., Colorado Springs, 1976-89; mem. exec. com. Ft. Lewis Coll. Found., 1991—. Recipient 1st place award for editorial writing Nat. Fedn. Press Women, 1955, Outstanding Alumna award Rosemary Hall, Greenwich, Conn., 1969, Outstanding Journalism award U. Colo. Sch. Journalism, 1967, Distinguished Service award Ft. Lewis Coll., Durango, 1970; named to Colo. Community Journalism Hall of Fame, 1987; named Citizen of Yr. Durango Area Chamber Resort Assn., 1990. Mem. Nat. Soc. Colonial Dames, Colo. Press Assn. (bd. dirs. 1978-79), Colo. AP Assn. (chmn. 1966-67), Federated Women's Club Durango, Mill Reef Club (Antigua, W.I.) (bd. govs. 1985-91). Episcopalian. Address: care Herald PO Drawer A Durango CO 81302

BALLANTYNE, MAREE ANNE CANINE, artist; b. Sydney, NSW, Australia, Oct. 22, 1945; came to U.S., 1946; d. Charles Venice and Yvonne Mavis (McSpeerin) Canine; m. Kent McFarlane Ballantyne, Apr. 22, 1967; children: Christopher Kent, Joel Sokson. AA, Del Mar Coll., 1966; BA in English, U. Tex., 1971; postgrad., U. South Ala., 1974, U. Houston, 1981, Sonoma State U., 1982, 84, 85. Exhibited paintings in Mass., Tex., Ala.; creator logo for Gulf Coast Area Childbirth Edn. Assn., 1972, logo for Calif. Health Resources, 1985; contbr. articles to profl. jours. Charter mem. Gulf Coast Area Childbirth Edn. Assn., Mobile, Ala., 1971-76; mem. Mus. Guild, Corpus Christi, 1978-80, Art Mus., Mobile, 1972-76, Nat. Trust for Hist. Preservation, 1977-80. Recipient Cert. Appreciation, USCG, 1993, Letter of Appreciation USCG, 1993. Mem. Nat. Mus. of Women in the Arts (charter 1987-94), Coast Guard Officers Wives Club. Home: 1920 SW 56th Ave Plantation FL 33317-5938

BALLARD, BARBARA W., state legislator; m. Albert L. Ballard. Rep. dist. 44 State of Kansas, 1993—; adminstr., dir. U. Kans. Democrat. Home: 1532 Alvamar Dr Lawrence KS 66047-1605 Office: U Kans 115 Strong Hall University Of Kansas KS 66045*

BALLARD, BETTY RUTH WESLEY, retired x-ray equipment company executive; b. Birmingham, Ala., Nov. 11, 1924; d. Henry Gaston and Ruth Lorine (Whitfield) Wesley; degree Glenn Tech. Inst., 1942-46; m. Douglas Hayden Ballard, Oct. 24, 1941; 1 son, Douglas Hayden. Mgr., Nbc Restaurant, 1960-68; corp. sec. X-Ray Service and Sales, Inc., 1960-68; pres. Ballard X-Ray Co., Birmingham, Ala., 1968—. Exec. com. Democratic Party; election law commr. State of Ala.; hon. dep. sheriff Shelby County, Ala.; mem. adminstrv. bd. 1st United Methodist Ch., Montevallo, Ala. Mem. LWV, Ala. Soc. Radiol. Technologists, Ala. Hosp. Assn., Inst. Hosp. Auxilians, Ala. Cattlemen's Assn., 20th Spl. Forces Group Aux. Methodist (adminstrv. bd., trustee ch.), The Club Inc. Home: Flying-X-Ranch RR 3 Box 331F Youngsville NC 27596-9510

BALLARD, MARY MELINDA, financial communications and investment banking firm executive; b. Sikeston, Mo., Apr. 21, 1958; d. Claude M. and Mary (Birnbach) B.; m. Emil Pena, Jan. 1, 1989 (div. July 1990); m. Ronald C. Allison, Oct. 1994. BA, Monmouth Coll. 1976, MBA, NYU 1980, postgrad. Columbia U. V.p. corp. comm. United Brands Co., N.Y.C., 1976-79; v.p. mktg. Oscar de la Renta Ltd., 1979-81; pres., chief exec. officer Ficom Internat., Inc., N.Y.C., 1981—; exec. v.p. Ruder Finn Inc., N.Y.C., 1989—; dir., chief exec. officer MBP Interests Inc., 1989—; ptnr. Kamero Ptnrs., 1994—; bd. dirs. Nat. Coun. Real Estate Investment Fiduciaries; cons. to fgn. govts. and major corps. Contbr. articles to profl. jours. Trustee Ballard Family Found., Children's Aid Soc.; exec. mem. Tex. Dem. Roundtable, 1994—. Recipient CLEO Ann. Report award Fin. World, 1984, 86. Mem. Internat. Assn. Bus. Communicators (Golden Quill 1984), Pub. Relations Soc. Am., Urban Land Inst., Nat. Investor Relations Inst. Methodist. Avocations: collecting art, thoroughbred race horses, ranching. Home: PO Box 746 Dripping Springs TX 78620-9720

BALLARD, MELINDA M., public relations executive; b. Houston, Apr. 21, 1951. BA, NYU, 1971, MBA, 1973; PhD, Columbia U., 1975. V.p. comms. United Brands Co., 1975-78; v.p. mktg. and comm. Oscar de la Renta Ltd., 1978-80; pres., CEO Ficom Internat. Inc., 1980-89; pres. Ficom/Ruder Finn, 1989; mng. dir. Investment Resources Internat., Ruder Finn, 1989-92; founder, pres. MBP Interest Inc., Austin, Tex., 1992—. Mem. IABC, Nat. Coun. Real Estate Investment Fiduciaries, Urban Land Assn. Office: MBP Interest Inc 1800 Deerfield Rd Dripping Springs TX 78620*

BALLAS ARMAS, VICTORIA, artist; b. Wilmington, Del., Oct. 9, 1955; d. Peter J. and Janice Ann (Green) Ballas; m. Ricardo Armas, July 9, 1982; children: Alexa Danielle Caudill, Benjamin Armas, Sebastian Armas. BFA, Sch. Visual Arts, N.Y.C., 1983; MA, U. Ala., 1990. Designer Lockwood, Inc., N.Y.C., 1979-83; tchr. Colegio Internat. Caracas, Venezuela, 1983—. One-woman shows 1986, 93. Recipient Premio-Ivan Petrovzsky award Alcaldia de Valencia, Venezuela, 1993. Office: POBA Internat 233 PO Box 02 5255 # 233 Miami FL 33102-5255

BALLENGER, EVA MARIE, librarian; b. Columbus, Ohio, Aug. 20, 1955; d. Albert E. and Frederica M. (Morello) B. BS in Edn., Ohio U., 1985; MLS, Kent State U., 1989. Libr. II State of Ohio, Pickaway Correctional Instn., Orient, 1989-95, Marion Correctional Inst., 1995—; coord. Libr. Svcs. to the Institutionalized, Ohio Libr. Coun., Columbus, 1995. Mem. Ohio Libr. Coun., Order of the Ea. Star. Office: Pickaway Correctional Instn PO Box 209 Orient OH 43146

BALLEW, DORIS EVELYN, accountant, company executive; b. Knox County, Tenn., Sept. 6, 1938; d. James Elmer and Grace Elizabeth (Wright) Dossett; m. George Thomas Reep, Feb. 4, 1955 (div. June 1969); children: Sherrie Lynn Akins, Kimberley Michelle Niles; m. David Woodward Ballew, Oct. 9, 1969 (div. Dec. 1989); 1 child, Melissa Marie. Student, U. P.R., 1957, U. Tenn., 1975-84, Draughon's Coll., 1982, Knoxville Bus. Coll., 1974. CPA, Tenn. Acct. Shoney's Restaurants, Knoxville, Tenn., 1961-64, Tinsley Tire Co., Knoxville, Tenn., 1964-65; chief acct. Kuhlman-Murphy Co., Knoxville, Tenn., 1965-77; v.p., contr., treas. Lawler Wood, Inc. and Wood Properties, Inc., Knoxville, Tenn., 1977—. Mem. Old Smoky Railway Mus. (treas. 1978-83). Mem. Nat. Assn. Accts., Knoxville Jaycettes, AICPA, Tenn. Soc. CPA's, Beta Sigma Phi (pres. 1982-83, 89). Hme: 148 Country Walk Dr Powell TN 37849 Office: 1600 Riverview Tower 900 S Gay St Knoxville TN 37902-1808

BALLING, LOUISE MARY, social worker; b. North Tonawanda, N.Y.; d. Leo and Mary Anna (Achatz) B. BA, D'Youville Coll., 1960; MSW, SUNY, Buffalo, 1970. Cert. social worker, N.Y. Med. social worker Deaconess Hosp. of Buffalo, N.Y., 1972-80; social worker N.Y. State Office of Mental Health, Helmuth, 1981-94, coord. supported case mgmt. team, 1994—; developer high risk pregnancy index and rsch. study. Bd. dirs. Hist. Soc. of Tonawandas, 1985-92; vol. Albright Knox Art Gallery, Buffalo, 1978-91; docent Long Homestead, Tonawanda, 1982—. Mem. English Speaking Union. Home: 57 Park St Springville NY 14141-1116

BALLUS, EMILY JANE, professional soccer league executive, consultant; b. Winston-Salem, N.C., Jan. 23, 1962; d. Gus A. and Jane (Ott) B. BS in Sports Mgmt., Guilford Coll., 1984; MS in Sports Adminstrn., St. Thomas U., Miami, Fla., 1987. Mktg. rep., dir. pub. rels. St. Lauderdale (Fla.) Strikers Profl. Soccer Team, 1987-89; asst. dir. sports info. Fla. Internat. U., Miami, 1989; dir. ops. Miami Sharks Profl. Soccer Team, 1989; asst. gen. mgr. Miami Freedom Pro Soccer Team, 1990-91, gen. mgr., 1991-92; dir. ops. Am. Profl. Soccer League, Washington, 1992—; ops. cons. IFG, Miami, 1990, USA Sports Group, Miami, 1991; event marshall, ofcl. NBC Superstars, Biscayne, Fla., 1986; vol. Budweiser Boat Races, 1986; head boys and girls track coach Berkshire High Sch., Homestead, Fla., 1988. Guardium ad litem Dade County Juvenile Cts., 1986. Mem. Humane Soc. U.S. Mem. Soc. of Friends. Home: 4725 Quiet Woods Ln # B Fairfax VA 22033-5051 Office: Am Profl Soccer League 3702 Pender Dr Ste 210 Fairfax VA 22030

BALLWEBER, HETTIE LOU, archaeologist; b. Pitts., Dec. 27, 1944; d. Nicholas George and Harriett Elizabeth (Tucker) Beresh; m. Walter David Boyce, Aug. 24, 1963 (div. 1984); children: Michael David, Steven Todd; m. William Arterberry Ballweber, Nov. 8, 1986. BA summa cum laude, Calif. U., Pa., 1985; M. Applied Anthropology, U. Md., 1987. Cons. archaeologist Monongahela, Pa., 1980-85; archaeologist archeology div. Md. Geol. Survey, Balt., 1985-86; dir. Md. New Directions, Balt., 1987; cons. Columbia, Md., 1987—; prin. ACS Cons., Columbia, Md., 1987—; bd. dirs. Alternative Directions, Inc., Balt. Author: First People of Maryland, 1985; contbr. articles to profl. jours. State publicity chmn. Pa. Congress Parents and Tchrs., Harrisburg, Pa., 1981-84, regional v.p., 1984. With USN, 1979-87. Fellow Soc. Applied Anthropology; mem. Mon-Yough Archaeol. Soc. (pres. 1983-84), Westmoreland Archaeol. Soc. (v.p. 1982-83), Coun. Md. Archeology (pres. 1990-91), Washington Assn. Profl. Anthropologists, Soc. Hist. Archaeology, Shriners, Order Eastern Star. Home and Office: 3212 Peddicoat Ct Woodstock MD 21163-1132

BALMASEDA, LIZ, columnist; b. Puerto Padre, Cuba, 1959. AA, Miami-Dade (Fla.) C.C., 1979; BS Comm., Fla. Internat. U., 1981. Intern Miami Herald, Fla., 1980, with Spanish lang. publ., 1981, gen. assignment reporter, feature writer, 1987, with Sunday Mag. tropic, 1990, local columnist, 1991; ctrl. Am. bur. chief Newsweek, El Salvador, 1985; field prodr. NBC News, Honduras. Appeared on NBC Today Show, Oprah show. Recipient 2d place Ernie Pyle award Scripps Howard Found, 1984, 3d place feature writing Fla. Soc. Newspaper Editors, 1st prize Guillermo Martinez-Marquez contest Nat. Assn. Hispanic Journalists. 1989, Pulitzer Prize for commentary 1993, 1st prize commentary Fla. Soc. Newspaper editors. Office: The Miami Herald One Herald Plaza Miami FL 33101*

BALOG, IBOLYA, accountant; b. Subotica, Yugoslavia, July 11, 1953; came to U.S., 1969; d. Balint and Adela (Dohocki) B. B.A., Lehigh U., 1975; M.B.A., Temple U., 1980. CPA. Adminstrv. asst. Chain Bike Corp., Allentown, Pa., 1975-77; controller Bicycle Corp. Am., Allentown, 1982-87; acct. Cohen & Rogozinski, CPA's, Allentown, 1987-92; mgr. Parente, Randolph, Orlando, Carey & Assocs., CPA's, 1994—. Bd. dirs. YWCA, Allentown, 1986—, treas. 1993, pres. 1994. Mem. AAUW (treas. 1984 85, Outstanding Woman 1985), Pa. Inst. CPA's, Am. Inst. CPA's, Inst. Mgmt. Accountants, Am. Women's Soc. of CPA's (pres. Lehigh Valley affiliate, 1993-94). Democrat. Home: 1522 1/2 W Chew St Allentown PA 18102-3645 Office: Parente Randolph Orlando Carey & Assocs 1427 Chew St Allentown PA 18102

BALOG, RITA JEAN, librarian; b. Ashtabula, Ohio, Sept. 24, 1930; d. Frederick Carroll and Marguerite Ethel (White) Grady; m. Richard Francis Balog, Oct. 16, 1949; children: Rebecca Kay, Richard Francis Jr., Ronald Frank, Robert Henry. AA, Kent State U., 1977, BA in Gen. Studies, 1978, MLS, 1980. Clk., typist Harbor Pub. Libr., Ashtabula, 1973-75, children's libr., 1975-80; libr., dir. Harbor-Topky Meml. Libr., Ashtabula, 1980—; vol. libr. Thomas Jefferson Elem. Sch., Harbor Spl. Sch., Ashtabula, 1972-75. Sec., mem. Ashtabula Archtl. Restoration and Rev. Bd., 1975—; vol. leader Lake River coun. Girl Scouts U.S., Niles, 1958-73, mem. nominating com., 1989—, bd. dirs., 1991—, child camp dir. Mem. ALA, AAUW, Ohio Libr. Assn., N.E. Ohio Libr. Assn. (regional adv. bd. 1984-86), Coun. Ashtabula County Librs. (pres. 1985-86), Ashtabula Area Mus. and Hist. Soc. (trustee 1992—), Zonta (pres. 1987-89). Democrat. Office: Harbor Topky Meml Libr 1633 Walnut Blvd Ashtabula OH 44004-2814

BALTAROWICH, OKSANA HELENA, radiologist, educator; b. Trenton, N.J., Feb. 11, 1951; d. Roman Joseph and Maria (Krisfalusij) B.; m. George Constantine Hud, Aug. 31, 1980; children: Laryssa, Natalia, Christina Hud. BS in Biology, Wayne State U., 1973, MD, 1976. Diplomate Am. Bd. Radiology. Resident in radiology Mass. Gen. Hosp., Boston, 1977-80; fellow in ultrasound Thomas Jefferson U., Phila., 1980-81, staff radiologist, 1981-88, mem. teaching faculty, 1988—; radiology cons. Am. Med. Imaging Corp., Horsham, Pa., 1988-92, Nat. Imaging Sys., Conshohocken, 1992—; asst. prof. radiology Thomas Jefferson U., 1995—. Contbr. articles to profl. jours. Recipient Young Women's Achievement award Ukrainian Nat. Women's League, 1990. Mem. AMA, Am. Coll. Radiology, Am. Assn. Women Radiology, Am. Inst. Ultrasound Medicine, Radiol. Soc. N.Am., Ukrainian Med. Assn. (treas., v.p., pres. Pa. chpt. 1989—), Greater Delaware Valley Ultrasound Soc. (sec., v.p., pres. 1989-94). Ukranian Catholic.

BALTER, FRANCES SUNSTEIN, civic worker; b. Pitts.; d. Elias and Gertrude (Kingsbacher) Sunstein. Student Sarah Lawrence Coll., 1939-41, New Sch. Social Rsch., 1941-43, Bennington Coll., 1941, 42; cert. Harvard Inst. Arts Adminstrn., 1973; m. James Stone Balter, May 15, 1948; children: Katherine (Mrs. Ross Anthony), Julia Frances, Constance (Mrs. Owen Cantor), Daniel Elias. Adminstrv. asst., assoc. producer Ednl. Television Sta. WQED-TV, Pitts., 1963-67; producer, mng. dir. Freedom Readers, 1964-67; co-founder, incorporator, sec. bd. dirs. Pitts. Coun. for Arts, 1967-70; cultural cons. Mayor's Office, Dir. of Office of Cultural Affairs, Pitts., 1968; initiator Three Rivers Arts Festival 1960; co-dir. Ohio and Miss. River Valley Art Festival, 1961-62; mem. Pa. Coun. on Arts, 1972-78; co-founder Pioneer Crafts Coun. Mill Run Pa., 1972; exec. dir. Poetry On The Buses, 1974—; bd. dirs. Coun. for Arts MIT, 1985-93, Palm Beach Festival, 1987-89. Named Woman of Yr. in Art Post-Gazette, 1969. Mem. Assoc. Councs. on Arts, Nat. Soc. Arts and Letters, Nat. League of Am. PEN Women (Pitts. chpt., assoc. 1990—). Home: 1603 Bayhouse Point Dr Sarasota FL 34231-6774

BALTIMORE, RUTH BETTY, social worker; b. Wilkes-Barre, Pa., Feb. 27, 1926; d. Samuel Jr. and Theresa (Bergsmann (Bloch); m. Martin Joseph Baltimore, Feb. 6, 1949; children: Francie, Sandy. BA in Psychology, Skidmore Coll., 1948; postgrad., U. Scranton, 1965, 70. Sch. social worker Wyoming Valley West Sch. Dist., Kingston, Pa., 1966-89; retired; cons. in field. Co-author: (booklet) Guide for Teachers on Reporting Child Abuse, 1970. Bd. dirs. Youth Svcs. Commn., Wilkes-Barre, Pa., 1986-87, Victims Resource Ctr., Wilkes-Barre, 1990—; bd. dirs. Luz County Adv. Bd. Children and Youth, Wilkes-Barre, 1988—, vice chair, 1991, chair, 1992—. Recipient Connie Coun. Svc. award Nat. Coun. Jewish Women, Wilkes-Barre, 1959. Mem. Valley Tennis and Swim Club (pres.-elect 1994, pres. 1995). Home: 630 Newberry Estate Dallas PA 18612

BALZER, SHARON KAY, physical therapist; b. LaMarque, Tex., Feb. 22, 1956; d. Paul James and Alcie O. (Plowman) B.; m. Clara A. Cohan, Jan. 8, 1991. BS, Tex. A&M, 1978; MS, Tex. Woman's U., 1983. lic. phys. therapist. Pvt. practice Cottonwood, Ariz., 1987—. Mem. Am. Phys. Therapy Assn., Neurodevel. Treatment Assn. Office: PO Box 2012 Sedona AZ 86339-2012

BALZER, WILMA H., retired association executive; b. Newton, Kans., Nov. 21, 1916; d. Jacob Frank and Jennie Alieda (Van Der Smissen) B. BA, Carleton Coll., 1938; MA in Edn. of Deaf, Columbia Tchrs. Coll., 1940; MSW, N.Y. Sch. Social Work, 1950. Tchr. deaf-blind students, dir. deaf-blind dept. N.Y. Inst. Edn. Blind, N.Y.C., 1938-42; mem. recreation staff Jones ctr. Children's Aid Soc., N.Y.C., 1942-43; dir. co-ed teen program west side br. YWCA, N.Y.C., 1943-48; asst. dir. sch. community ctr. N.Y.C. YWCA and N.Y.C. Bd. Edn., 1946-48; dir. teen program East Liberty br. Pitts. YWCA, 1950-51; YWCA dir./ctr. coord. Amsterdam Houses Community Ctr., N.Y.C., 1951-55; asst. dir. group work and recreation N.Y.C. Youth Bd., 1955-60; family case worker Family & Children's Svc., Omaha, 1960-62; met. assoc. exec., dir. downtown br. Houston YWCA, 1962-73; cons. orgn. devel. nat. bd. dirs. YWCA U.S.A., N.Y.C., 1974-82; ret., 1982. Mem. NASW.

BAMBER, LINDA SMITH, accounting educator; b. Columbus, Ohio, Jan. 4, 1954; d. Charles Randall and Martha Jo (Wise) Smith; m. Edward Michael Bamber, Mar. 13, 1981. BS summa cum laude, Wake Forest U. 1976; MBA, Ariz. State U., 1980; PhD, Ohio State U., 1983. Cost acct. RJ Reynolds, Winston-Salem, N.C., 1975-76, gen. acct., 1976-77; tutor, rsch. asst. Ariz. State U., Tempe, 1977-78; teaching asst. Ohio State U., Columbus, 1978-82; asst. prof. U. Fla., Gainesville, 1983-88, assoc. prof., 1988-90; assoc. prof. U. Ga., Athens, 1990—; vis. assoc. prof. Ind. U., Bloomington, 1989-90. Author: Annotated Instructor's Edition of Cost Accounting: A Managerial Emphasis, 1990, 93; assoc. editor: Acctg. Horizon, 1993—; mem. editl. bd. The Acctg. Rev., 1987-89, 93—, Advances in Acctg., 1992—; contbr. articles to profl. jours. Selig fellow U. Ga., 1991; recipient Rsch. Devel. award U. Fla., 1985, Tchg. award Ohio State U. Ga., 1981-94. Mem. Am. Acctg. Assn. (S.E. dir. fin. reporting sect. 1993-94, group leader, panelist New Faculty Consortium 1991-94), Beta Gamma Sigma, Phi Beta Kappa, Phi Kappa Phi. Office: U Ga JM Tull Sch Acctg Athens GA 30602

BAMBERGER, GABRIELLE, public relations executive; b. Berlin, Germany, June 8, 1938; d. Fritz and Kate (Schwabe) B. BA, Oberlin Coll., 1960. Asst. account exec. Philip Lesly Co., N.Y.C., 1961-63, account exec., 1963-68; owner Gabrielle Bamberger Pub. Relations, N.Y.C., 1968—; Editor LBI News Leo Baeck Inst., 1974—, Libr. and Archives News, 1975—. Mem. Am. Women in Radio and TV, Women in Communications, Inc. Home: 215 E 79th St New York NY 10021 Office: 250 W 57th St # 315 New York NY 10107-0001

BAN, CAROL HARRIET, medical technologist; b. N.Y.C., Nov. 23, 1943; d. Leon Israel and Lucile Lena (Wilner) Shachtman; m. Andrew G. Ban, Apr. 27, 1975; children: Jennifer M., Wendy P. BS in Biology and Med. Tech., Am. U., 1966. Cert. med. technologist, Am. Soc. Clin. Pathology. Asst. supr. in hematology O.B. Hunter Meml. Lab., Washington, 1966-69; supr. in serology and urinanalysis Fairfax (Va.) Hosp., 1969-75; staff technologist in hematology Northwestern Meml. Hosp., Chgo., 1975—. Mem. AAAS, Alexander Graham Bell Assn. (area rep. membership sect. 1992—). Home: 609 Bryce Trl Roselle IL 60172-1023

BANACH, ELAINE SUSAN, educational administrator; b. Pittsfield, Mass., Jan. 7, 1964; d. Wayne Henry and Winifred Ruth (Ostrander) Sagendorph; m. Shawn Paul Banach, Nov. 2, 1991. AS in Math. with hons., Columbia-Greene C.C., Hudson, N.Y., 1983; BS in Math., Clarkson U., 1985; postgrad., Union Coll., Schenectady, N.Y., 1986-89, SUNY, Albany, 1993—. Adminstrv. asst. materials mgmt. GE Plastic Bus. Group, Selkirk, N.Y., summer 1984; performance evaluation analyst GE Ordnance Systems Divsn., Pittsfield, Mass., 1985-88; mng. coord. Northeastern Regional Info. Ctr. Albany-Schoharie-Schenectady-Saratoga BOCES, Albany, 1988—. Home: 39 Ridge Rd Ravena NY 12143

BANAS, CHRISTINE LESLIE, lawyer; b. Swindon, Wiltshire, Eng., Oct. 29, 1951; came to U.S. 1957; d. Stanley M. and Helena Ann (Boryn) B.; m. Dale J. Buras, May 1, 1976; children: Eric, Andrea. BA honors program, U. Detroit, 1973; JD, Wayne State U., 1975. Bar: Mich. 1976, U.S. Supreme Ct. 1980. Atty. Hyman & Rice, Southfield, Mich., 1976-77; ptnr. Hyman, Gurwin, Nachman, Friedman & Winkelman, Southfield, 1982-87, Honigman Miller Schwartz and Cohn, Detroit, 1987—; mem. Mich. Housing Coun., Lansing. Contbr. articles to profl. jours. Mem. ABA, State Bar Mich., Fed. Bar Assn., Detroit Bar Assn., Oakland County Bar, Women's Econ. Club, Birmingham Athletic Club. Roman Catholic. Office: Honigman Miller Schwartz & Cohn 2290 1st National Bldg Detroit MI 48226

BANASHEK, MARY-ELLEN, writer, editor; b. Wilkes-Barre, Pa., Dec. 7, 1951; d. Walter Joseph and Irene (Rapchak) Banashek; m. Alan R. Loflin, Sept. 1991. BA, Emira Coll., 1973. Assoc. features editor Mademoiselle mag., N.Y.C., 1973-79; beauty copywriter Harper's Bazaar mag., N.Y.C., 1979-80; beauty and health editor Self mag., N.Y.C., 1980-81; sr. copy writer Avon Products, Inc., N.Y.C., 1982-83; beauty and health editor McCall's mag., N.Y.C., 1983-85; sr. writer Elle mag., N.Y.C., 1986-87; contbg. editor Woman's Day mag., N.Y.C., 1987-90; features editor New Woman Mag., N.Y.C., 1989—. Mem. Phi Beta Kappa. Office: New Woman Mag 215 Lexington Ave New York NY 10016-6023

BANASZYNSKI, JACQUELINE MARIE, newspaper reporter; b. Green Bay, Wis., Apr. 17, 1952; d. Eugene Francis and Ethel Marie (McGillivray) B. BA in Journalism, Marquette U., 1974. Reporter intern Wall St. Jour., Boston, 1973; reporter fellow Indpls. Star, 1974; staff reporter Janesville (Wis.) Gazette, 1974-75, Duluth (Minn.) News Tribune, 1976-78, Eugene (Oreg.) Register-Guard, 1978-80, Mpls. Star and Tribune, 1981-83; became staff reporter St. Paul Pioneer Press Dispatch, 1984; now environment editor The Oregonian, Portland; adj. instr. Coll. of St. Thomas, St. Paul, 1986. Recipient Gene O'Brien Excellence in Journalism award Minn. Press Club, 1985, Disting. Svc. award Gen. News Soc. Profl. Journalists, 1987, Sweepstakes award, 1987, Pulitzer prize, 1988, Dag Hammerskjöld award Physicians Assn. for AIDS Care, 1988, Outstanding Achievement award Melpomene Inst., 1988, Minn. AP award, 1988, Best Sports Event Story award Nat. AP Sports Editors, 1988. Mem. Internat. Newspaper Guild. Office: The Oregonian 1320 SW Broadway Portland OR 97201*

BANCROFT, ANN, polar explorer; b. 1956; d. Dick and Debbie B. Former tchr., coach, wilderness instr. St. Paul, Minn.; mem. Steger Internat. Polar Expedition, 1986 (first woman to reach the North Pole by dogsled); leader Am. Women's Trans-Antartic Expedition, 1993 (first women's team to reach the South Pole on skis). Named Ms. Mag. Woman of Yr., 1987; inductee Girls and Women in Sport Hall of Fame, 1992; recipient Women First award YWCA, 1993. Office: care Rhonda Grider 2110 Laurelwood Dr Thousand Oaks CA 91362*

BANCROFT, ANNE (MRS. MEL BROOKS), actress; b. N.Y.C., Sept. 17, 1931; d. Michael and Mildred (DiNapoli) Italiano; m. Mel Brooks, 1964; 1 son. Broadway stage appearances include Two for the Seesaw, 1957 (Tony award 1957), The Miracle Worker, 1959-60 (Tony award 1960), Devils, 1977, Golda, 1977-78, Duet for One, 1981; stage appearances include Mystery of the Rose Bouquet, 1989; motion pictures include Treasure of the Golden Condor, 1952, Don't Bother to Knock, 1952, Tonight We Sing, 1953, The Kid from Left Field, 1953, Demetrius and the Gladiators, 1954, Gorilla at Large, 1954, The Raid, 1954, A Life in the Balance, 1955, The Brass Ring, 1954, Naked Street, 1955, New York Confidential, 1955, The Last Frontier, 1955, Girl in the Black Stockings, 1957, Restless Breed, 1957, The Pumpkin Eater, 1964, Seven Women, 1966, Slender Thread, 1966, The Graduate, 1967, Young Winston, 1972, The Prisoner of 2nd Avenue, 1975, The Hindenburg, 1975, Lipstick, 1976, Silent Movie, 1976, The Turning Point, 1977, Fatso, 1979, The Elephant Man, 1980, To Be or Not to Be, 1983, Garbo Talks, 1984, Agnes of God, 1985, 'Night, Mother, 1986, 84 Charing Cross Road (Brit. Acad. award 1987), Torch Song Trilogy, 1988, Bert Rigby You're a Fool, 1989, Honeymoon in Vegas, 1992, Love Potion #9, 1992, Point of No Return, 1993, Mr. Jones, 1993, Malice, 1993; TV appearances include Kraft Music Hall, Jesus of Nazareth, 1977, Marco Polo, 1982, Broadway Bound, 1992, Mrs. Cage, PBS, 1992, Oldest Living Confederate Widow Tells All, 1994 (Emmy nomination, Supporting Actress - Miniseries, 1994); dir., writer, star: (TV spl.) Annie-The Woman in the Life of Men, 1970 (Emmy award 1970). Recipient Acad. award for performance in The Miracle Worker, 1962; Best Actress, Cannes Internat. Film Festival for performance in The Pumpkin Eater, 1964. Address: care 20th Century Fox Studios PO Box 900 Beverly Hills CA 90213-0900

BANCROFT, ELIZABETH ABERCROMBIE, publisher, analytical chemist; b. N.Y.C., Mar. 2, 1947; d. John Chandler and Ruth Abercrombie (Robinson) B. AB, Harvard U./Radcliffe Coll., 1979; postgrad. in forensic scis. John Jay Coll. Criminal Justice, 1982. Asst. dir. research Bagley Fordyce Research Labs., N.Y.C., 1979-83, dir. research and publs., Washington office, 1984-86; dir. Nat. Intelligence Book Ctr., 1986—; bd. dirs. Nat. Hist. Intelligence Mus.; pub. Surveillant: Aquisitions and Commentary for Intelligence and Security Professionals. Mem. Assn. Fgn. Intelligence Officers, Naval Intelligence Profls., Nat. Mil. Intelligence Assn., Nat. Hist. Intelligence Mus. (bd. dirs.), Nat. Intelligence Study Ctr., Washington Book Pubs. Assn., Am. Bookseller Assn. Republican. Episcopalian. Clubs: Harvard of N.Y.C., Harvard/Radcliffe of Washington; Chemists of N.Y. Office: Nat Intelligence Book Ctr 2020 Pennsylvania Ave Ste 165 Washington DC 20006

BANDARRA, CHRISTY LEE, real estate agent; b. Bangor, Maine, Dec. 16, 1962; d. James Howard and Diane Alma (Sandstrom) Sahler; m. Brian Edward Bandarra, May 22, 1985; 1 child, Tahler Diane. BS in Computer Sci., U.S. Naval Acad., 1985. Mdse. mgr. Lenscrafters, Cin., 1990-91, sr. acct., 1991-93; asst. gen. mgr. LaSalle Ptnrs. Asset Mgmt., Chgo., 1994—. Lt. USN, 1985-90. Republican. Lutheran. Office: LaSalle Ptnrs Asset Mgmt 200 W Jackson Blvd Ste 2600 Chicago IL 60606

BANDEMER, MAXINE EVANGELINE, religious studies educator, education program coordinator; b. Chgo., July 1, 1916; d. Otto Ferdinand and Hulda Christina (Peterson) Ohlson; m. Irwin Charles, Oct. 18, 1941; children: Karl Irwin, Christine Marie. AA, North Park Coll., 1935. Dir. religious edn., tchr. Plymouth Congl. Ch., Ft. Wayne, Ind., 1954-57; tchr. weekday religious edn. Associated Chs. of Ft. Wayne and Allen County, 1958—, coord., 1991—. Mem. PEO Internat. Soc. (sec. 1976-78, v.p. 1978-80, pres. 1980-82). Home: 2920 Hoagland Ave Fort Wayne IN 46807 Office: Associated Chs 602 E Wayne St Fort Wayne IN 46802

BANE, MARY JO, federal agency administrator; b. Princeville, Ill., Feb. 24, 1942; d. Fred W. and Helen (Callery) B.; m. Kenneth Winston, May 31, 1975. BS in Internat. Rels., Georgetown U., 1963; MAT, Harvard U., 1966, DEd, 1972. Tchr. English U.S. Peace Corps, Liberia, 1963-65; tchr. social studies Arlington (Mass.) Pub. Schs., 1966-67; tchr. English and social studies Brookline (Mass.) Pub. Schs., 1968-71; rsch. assoc. Ctr. Ednl. Policy Rsch. and Huron Inst. Harvard U., Cambridge, Mass., 1971-72, project co-dir. Ctr. Study of Pub. Policy, 1972-75, assoc. prof. edn., lectr. in sociology, 1977-80, assoc. prof. pub. policy, 1981-86, dir. Malcolm Wiener Ctr. for Social Policy, 1987-92, prof. pub. policy, 1986-90, Malcolm Wiener Prof. of Social Policy, 1990-92; lectr. in Sociology U. Mass., Boston, 1972-75; assoc. dir. Ctr. Rsch. on Women, asst. prof. edn., lectr. in sociology Wellesley (Mass.) Coll., 1975-77; dep. asst. sec. for program planning and budget analyst Office Planning and Budget U.S. Dept. Edn., Washington, 1980-81; exec. dep. commr. N.Y. State Dept. Social Svcs., 1984-86, commr., 1992-93; asst. sec. Adminstrn. for Children and Families Dept. Health and Human Svcs., Washington, 1993—; Ida Bean vis. prof. U. Iowa, 1980; chair bd. overseers panel study income dynamics Inst. Rsch. U. Mich., 1982-86; regents lectr. U. Calif., Berkeley, 1987; mem. adv. com. urban poverty NAS, 1986-90, chair com. child devel. rsch. and pub. policy, 1987-90; mem. pres. adv. coun. Columbia U. Tchrs. Coll., N.Y.C., 1988-92; mem. grants adv. coun. Smith Richardson Found., 1989-92; bd. dirs. Manpower Demonstration Rsch. Coun., 1989-92; active William T. Grant Found. Commn. on Work, Family and Citizenship, 1987-88. Author: (with others) Inequality: A Reassessment of the Effects of Family and Schooling in America, 1972, Here to Stay: American Families in the Twentieth Century, 1974, Japanese translation, 1981, Welfare Dependency and Welfare Policy, 1994, (with George Masnick) The Nation's Families 1960-1990, 1980; editor: (with Donald Levine) The Inequality Controversy, 1975, (with Manuel Carballo) The State and the Poor in the 1980s, 1984, (with Kenneth I. Winston) Gender and Public Policy: Cases and Comments, 1993, (with David Ellwood) Welfare Realities: From Rhetoric to Reform, 1994; contbr. articles to profl. jours. Fellow Nat. Acad. Pub. Adminstrn.; mem. Am. Sociol. Assn., Population Assn. Am., Assn. Pub. Policy Analysis and Mgmt. Office: Dept Health and Human Svcs Adminstrn Children and Families 901 D St SW Washington DC 20447

BANGS, CATE (CATHRYN MARGARET BANGS), film production designer, interior designer; b. Tacoma, Mar. 16, 1951; d. Henry Horan and Belva Virginia (Grandstaff) B.; m. Steve Bangs, Nov. 1, 1986. Student, Hammersmith Coll Art and Bldg., London, 1971; BA cum laude, Pitzer Coll., 1973; MFA, NYU, 1978. Owner Flying Pencil Design, Hollywood Hills, Calif., 1981—. Prodn. designer: Lucky Day, 1990, (TV series) My So Called Life, 1994, (TV series and pilot) Fudge-a-Mania, 1994. Bd. dirs. Hollywood Heights Assn., 1985-87, Cahuenga Pass Property Owners Assn.,1990; 1st v.p. Friends of the Highland-Camrose Bungalow Village, 1985—. Recipient Dramalogue Critics award, 1983. Mem. Soc. Motion Picture and TV Art Dirs., Set Designers and Model Makers (cert., exec. bd. 1980—, v.p. 1989-91, pres. 1991—), United Scenic Artists. Democrat. Buddhist. Home: Angel Haven 3180 Oakshire Dr Hollywood CA 90068-1743 Office: 3208 Cahuenga Blvd W # 121 Los Angeles CA 90068-1369

BANIAK, SHEILA MARY, accountant; b. Chgo., Feb. 26, 1953; d. DeLoy N. and Ann (Pasko) Slade; m. Mark A. Baniak, Oct. 7, 1972; 1 child, Heather Ann. Assocs. in Acctg., Oakton Community Coll., 1986; student, Roosevelt U., 1986—; postgrad., North Park Coll., Chgo., 1993—. Cert. enrolled agt. IRS; accredited tax adviser Accreditation Coun. Accountancy and Taxation. Owner, mgr. Baniak and Assocs., Park Ridge, Ill., 1984—; acct. Otto & Snyder, Park Ridge, 1984-87; spl. projects coordinator, supplemental instr. Oakton Community Coll., Des Plaines, Ill., 1986—; acctg. computer instr. Oakton Community Coll., Des Plaines, 1987—; adm. mem. acctg. Oakton C.C., Des Plaines, 1986—, cons., mem. Edn. Found., 1986—; instr. Ray Coll. Design, 1987—, dir. evening sch., 1994, fin. aid officer, Chgo. and Woodfield, 1994; mem. rsch. bd. advisors Am. Biog. Inst., Inc., 1988; tchr. fin. mgmt., retail math., bus. math., bus. computers, strategic retail mgmt. and econs. Author: A Small Business Collection Cycle Primer for Accountants, 1985, The Mathematics of Business, 1989. Ill. CPA Soc. scholar, 1984, Roosevelt U. scholar, 1986, Nat. Assn. Accts. scholar, 1985. Mem. Nat. Assn. Accts. (dir. community responsibility suburban Chgo. chpt. 1986—, speaker 1988, dir. profl. devel. seminars 1988, dir. communications 1989—), Nat. Assn. Tax Practitioners, Nat. Assn. Enrolled Agts., Ill. Soc. Enrolled Agts. (pres.; pres. N.W. Chgo. chpt. 1992, chmn. edn. 1990—). Home: 5718 W Cullom Ave Chicago IL 60634-9999

BANKER, LYNN, professional speaker, author, consultant; b. Holtville, Calif., Oct. 8, 1935; d. Fredrick William and Mary (Stez) Waterman; m. Edward Everett Banker, Sept. 18, 1954 (div. Sept. 1987); children: Bret Howard, Bruce Edward, Bradley Allen; m. Vernon Joseph Ryan, Sept. 19, 1987 (div. Sept. 1994). Office mgr. Design Scis., Inc., El Centro, Calif., 1967-74; office mgr. U. Calif., Irvine, 1979-81, fin. bus. mgr., 1981-85; pres. Lynn Banker & Assoc., Costa Mesa, Calif., 1984—; mem. classification com. U. Calif., 1980-84; pres., v.p. Internat. Tng. in Communications, Huntington Beach, Calif., 1982-84. Author audio tape album, book and single tapes; contbr. articles to profl. jours. Mem. by-laws task force, 1st v.p., bd. dirs. congregation St. Matthews Old Cath. Mission, Huntington Beach, 1988-89. Mem. Nat. Speakers Assn. (bd. dirs. 1986-87, membership chair 1985-87, 1st v.p., program chmn. 1988-89, pres. 1989-90, by-laws com. 1991-92, Bronze Mike 1986, Silver Mike 1987, Gold Mike 1988), Women's Bus. Assn., Connections Club (Cerritos; ethics com. 1986-88), Ind. Cons. Group (L.A.). Republican. Home: 1953 Flamingo Dr Costa Mesa CA 92626-4719 Office: Lynn Banker & Assocs 1953 Flamingo Dr Costa Mesa CA 92626

BANKES, BETTY RUTH, health educator; b. Laureldale, Pa., Mar. 4, 1926; d. Victor Stanley Fritz and Alice Ethel (Boyer) Winnings; m. Robert Leroy Bankes, July 30, 1949; children: Terrylyn, Lori Ann. Diploma, The Reading Hosp. Sch. Nursing, 1947; BA, Albright Coll., 1964; BSN, U. Pa., 1965, MS in Nursing, 1966; MEd, Kutztown U., 1972; cert., Temple U., 1978. RN Pa., Fla. Staff nurse The Reading Hosp. & Med. Ctr., West Reading, Pa., 1944-46; staff nurse, supr. Berks Vis. Nurse Assn., Wyomissing, Pa., 1946-57, dir., 1966-77; educator Villanova (Pa.) U., 1977-79; advisor nursing edn. Pa. State Bd. Nursing, Harrisburg, 1979-92; cons. health care pvt. practice, Reading, Pa., 1992—; pres. Pa. Assembly Home Health Agys., Harrisburg, 1974-77; chair Community Health Nurses Assn., Washington, 1947—. Com. mem. United We Stand, Berks County, 1992—; asst. treas., sec. Temple (Pa.) Fire Co., 1993—; com. mem. United Ch. Christ, Laureldale, Pa., 1993—. Mem. ANA, Pa. Nurses Assn., The Reading Hosp. Alumni Assn. (pres. 1950-53). Home and office: 3408 Stoudts Ferry Bridge Reading PA 19605-1435

BANKS, ANNA DELCEINA, financial planner; b. Newark, Oct. 8, 1952; d. James William and Serena D. (Holland) B. BS, Rutgers U., 1975; grad., U.S. Postal Svcs. Mgmt. Acad., Potomac, Md., 1984; postgrad., NYU, 1988, 90—. Lic. life and health ins. agt., N.J., lic. securities series 6, N.Y., N.J. Clk. U.S. Postal Svc., Newark, 1974-78; acctg/specialist N.Y. Postal Data Ctr., N.Y.C., 1978-83, mgr. women's program, 1983-85, acct., 1985-90; fin. planner PC Tax Prep. Assocs., Newark, 1985—; trainer various personal devel. seminars, 1980-85; workshop leader Basic Fin. Planning, 1990; instr. Am. Assn. Retired Persons, 1991—; instr., promoter Successful Money Mgmt. Seminars, Newark, 1991—; adj. prof. personal fin. Essex County Coll. Sch. Continuing and Community Edn., 1991—; instr. High Sch. Fin. Planning Program, Coll. for Fin. Planning, Denver, 1991—; bus. cons. Jr. Achievement No. N.J., Newark, 1992—. Columnist City News, Newark, 1992—; fin. editor N.J. Perspectus News Mag., Newark, 1990—; fin. columnist Daily Challenge Pubs., N.Y.C., 1994—; contbr. articles to profl. jours. Lay minister Elmwood Presbyn. Ch., East Orange, N.J., 1992—. Named Businessperson of Yr., Future Bus. Leader Am. State Leadership Conf., 1994. Mem. Nat. Assn. Tax Practitioners (nat. bd. dirs. 1993—, corp. sec. 1994—), Nat. Soc. Pub. Accts., Nat. Soc. Notaries, Nat. Tax Practitioners (charter bd. dirs., sec. N.J. chpt. 1987—), Nat. Assn. Negro Bus. and Profl. Bus. Women's Clubs (bd. dirs., treas. N.J. chpt. 1990—), Inst. Cert. Fin. Planners (cert.), Internat. Tng. in Communication Coun. I (pres. 1984-85, 1st place speech contest award 1985). Republican. Office: PC Tax Prep Assocs 78 Pine Grove Ter Newark NJ 07106-1909

BANKS, BETTIE SHEPPARD, psychologist; b. Birmingham, Ala., June 8, 1933; d. Francis Wilkerson and Bettie Pollard (Woodson) Sheppard; B.A., Ga. State U., 1966, M.A., 1968, Ph.D., 1970; m. Frazer Banks, Jr., Mar. 22, 1952; children: Bettie Banks Daley, Lee Frazer III. Clin. asso. Lab. for Psychol. Services, Ga. State U., 1968-70; intern Ga. Mental Health Inst., Atlanta, 1970-71, psychologist, 1971-72, chief psychologist, 1973; pvt. practice, Atlanta, 1972—; adj. assoc. prof. clin. psychology Ga. State U.; adj.

asst. prof. Dept. Psychiatry, Emory U., 1974-83, 94—; mem. peer rev. panel Ga. Med. Care Found., 1980-86, chmn., 1986-88. Diplomate in clin. psychology Am. Bd. Profl. Psychology; Nat. Register Health Svc. Psychology Providers, 1977—. Fellow Ga. Psychol. Assn. (chmn. div. E 1980, program chair ann. meeting 1991, treas. divsn. F 1993-95, co-chair publicity divsn. 1995—); mem. APA, Am. Acad. Psychotherapists (exec. com. 1980-82, sec. 1982-86, 94—, ann. workshop chair 1979, com. ann. Inst. and Conf. 1975, 86, com. ann. workshop 1984), Am. Group Psychotherapy Assn. (clin. mem., co-chair local host com. 1995 Ann. Inst. and Conf.), Atlanta Group Psychotherapy Soc. (bd. exec. com. 1982-83, 91-92), Southeastern Psychol. Assn. Episcopalian. Club: Jr. League. Cons. editor Voices, The Art and Science of Psychotherapy, 1978-84. Office: 595 Wimbledon Rd NE Atlanta GA 30324-4826

BANKS, CHERRY ANN MCGEE, educator; b. Benton Harbor, Mich., Oct. 11, 1945; d. Kelly and Geneva (Smith) McGee; m. James A. Banks, Feb. 15, 1969; children: Angela Marie, Patricia Ann. BS, Mich. State U., 1968; MA, Seattle U., 1977, EdD, 1991. Tchr. Benton Harbor Pub. Sch., 1968; staff assoc. Citizens Edn. Ctr. N.W., Seattle, 1984-85; edn. specialist Seattle Pub. Schs., Seattle, 1985-87; pres. Edn. Material and Svcs. Ctr., Edmonds, Wash., 1987—; asst. prof. edn. U. Wash., Bothell, 1992—; cons. Jackson (Miss.) Pub. Schs., 1988, Seattle Pub. Schs., 1988-90, Little Rock Pub. Schs., 1989, Scott Foreman Pub. Co., Glenview, Ill., 1992—; vis. asst. prof. Seattle U., 1991-92. Co-author: March Toward Freedom, 1978; co-editor: Multicultural Education: Issues and Perspectives, 1989, rev. edit., 1993; assoc. editor Handbook of Rsch. on Multicultural Edn.; contbr. chpts. to books. Mem. Jack and Jill Am., Seattle, 1978-94, First AME Headstart Bd., Seattle, 1981-83; trustee Shoreline C.C., Seattle, 1983—; bd. dirs. King County Campfire, Seattle, 1985-88. Recipient Outstanding Commitment and Leadership of C.C. award Western Region Nat. Coun. on Black Am. Affairs, 1989. Mem. ASCD, Nat. Coun. for Social Studies Programs Com. (vice chairperson Carter G. Woodson Book award com. 1991-92, chair person 1992-93, mem. nominating com.), Am. Rsch. Assn., Phi Delta Kappa (founding, Seattle U. chpt.). Office: U Wash Edn Program 22011 26th Ave SE Bothell WA 98021-4900

BANKS, EVELYN YVONNE, middle school educator; b. Houston, Sept. 7, 1951; d. Fred, Sr. and Mary Killings. BS, U. North Tex., 1974; M degree, Tex. So. U., 1993. Tchr. English, eighth grade North Forest Ind. Sch. Dist., Houston, 1976—. Counselor/coord. N.W. Community Bapt. Ch., 1989-92. Named Secondary Tchr. of Yr., North Forest Ind. Sch. Dist., Houston, 1992. Mem. Greater Houston Area Reading Coun., Tex. State Tchrs. of English, Delta Sigma Theta, Phi Delta Kappa (adv. 1992). Home: 8530 Tilgham Houston TX 77029

BANKS, LAURA NOBLES, association executive, retired school system administrator, consultant; b. Tucson, June 29, 1921; d. James Sr. and Missouri (Johnson) Nobles; m. Jack Leonard Banks, June 6, 1950. BS, U. Ariz., 1943, MA, 1966, EdS, 1970, EdD, 1980. Cert. phys. edn. tchr.; cert. travel agent. Elem. and jr. high sch. tchr. Tucson Pub. Schs., 1943-69; elem. prin. Tucson Unified Sch. Dist., 1969-75, coord. reading programs k-12, 1975-80, asst. supt., 1980-82; pres., owner LNB Enterprises, Tucson, 1982-94; co-owner Jack's Original BBQ, Tucson, 1950-93; agent Group Travel, Inc., Tucson, 1982-85; pub. rels. dir. Meri-Mac Corp., Tucson, 1985-87. Author: (plays) I Am Somebody, 1968, Indian, Chicano and Proud, 1968. Mem. NAACP (golden heritage), City of Hope Commn., 1993, internat. adv. commn., coll. edn. U. Ariz., 1993-95, hon. mem. YWCA Tucson, 1972—. Recipient Disting. Citizen award U. Ariz., 1992, Lifetime Achievement award YWCA 1992, Disting. Educator award Ariz. Alliance Black Sch. Educators, 1992; tree planted in her honor Jewish Nat. Fund, 1993; named to Restaurant Hall of Fame, Ariz. Restaurant Assn., 1994; Paul Harris fellow Rotary. Mem. Tucson Jr. League (cmty. adv. bd. 1990-94), The Links, Inc. (parliamentarian and nat. sec. 1970-76), Tucson Urban League (pres. 1979-81), Resources for Women (bd. dirs. 1984-94), Women At The Top (pres. 1985-94), Soroptomist Internat. (hon.), U. Ariz. Black Alumni (planned giving com. 1992-94), Alpha Kappa Alpha (golden, past local pres.). Democrat. Baptist. Home: 9438 Gray Sage Helotes TX 78023-4137

BANKS, MARGARET AMELIA, law educator, librarian, author, consultant; b. Quebec City, Que., Can., July 3, 1928; d. Thomas Herbert and Bessey (Collins) B. BA, Bishop's U., Lennoxville, Que., 1949; MA, U. Toronto, 1950, PhD, 1953. Archivist Ont. Archives, Toronto, 1953-61; law librarian U. Western Ont., London, 1961-89, assoc. prof. faculty law, 1974-86, prof., 1986-89, prof. emeritus, 1989—. Mem. Can. Assn. Law Libraries, Am. Inst. Parliamentarians, Nat. Assn. Parliamentarians, Osgoode Soc. for Can. Legal History, Arts and Letters Club of Tor. Anglican. Author: Edward Blake, Irish Nationalist, 1957, Using a Law Library, 1971, (with Karen E.H. Foti) 6th edit., 1994, Law at Western, 1959-84, 1984, The Libraries at Western, 1989, Understanding Canada's Constitution, 1991. Home and Office: 231 Windsor Ave Unit 9, London, ON Canada N6C 2A5

BANKS, MARILYN KELLOGG, sculptor; b. Mpls., Sept. 16, 1925; d. Lawrence David and Josephine (Solverson) Kellogg; m. Tyre Edwin Banks, Jr., Nov. 24, 1951 (dec. Jan. 1990); children: Lawrence, Stephen, David, Jane. AA, Pine Manor Jr. Coll., 1947; BFA, Art Inst. Chgo., 1950. Cert. sculptor. pres. Ctrl. La. Art Assn., Alexandria, La., 1965-67; pres., founder Bayou Banks Studio, Alexandria, Amityville, N.Y., 1972; founder, docent Alexandria Mus. Art, 1976, trustee, 1977-90, founder annual fundraiser, 1982, tchr. sculpture, 1982-84, v.p., 1985-87; tchr. sculpture River Oaks Arts & Crafts Ctr., Alexandria, 1986-88, pres., 1989-91; tchr. sculpture Camp Terra Cotta, Landgrove, Vt., 1993-94. Commd. sculpture Episc. Diocese La., 1975, 90, La. State U., 1976, 80, 84, Rapides Regional Med. Ctr., 1989, Pastoral Inst., Columbus, Ga., 1994. Stage mgr. set design-program design Ctrl. La. Community Theatre, 1950-60; founder St. Timothy's Episcopal Ch., Alexandria, 1958; minority founder Future Nurses Orgn., Alexandria, 1965. Recipient Outstanding Svc. award Huey P. Long Meml. Hosp., Pineville, La., 1964. Mem. DAR (loyalty chpt.), Mus. of Modern Art, Walloon Lake Country Club, Green Thumb Garden Club, Town and Country Garden Club (pres.). Republican. Episcopalian. Home: 1720 City Park Blvd Alexandria LA 71301-4600 Office: Bayou Banks Studio 38 Unqua Pl Amityville NY 11701-4231

BANKS, MELANIE ANNE, nutritionist, biochemist, educator; b. McKeesport, Pa., Oct. 27, 1956; d. Raymond Joseph and Emma Dea (Thomas) B. BA in Music, U. Pitts., 1976, BS in Biochemistry, 1977; MS in Chemistry, Duquesne U., 1980; PhD in Nutritional Biochemistry, W.Va. U., 1986. Cert. nutrition specialist. Clin. rsch. technician Children's Hosp., Pitts., 1979-82; rsch. asst. W.Va. U., Morgantown, 1982-86; rsch. assoc. dept. Pathology U. Pitts., Pitts., 1986-87; rsch. assoc. div. respiratory diseases Nat. Inst. of Occupational Safety and Health, Morgantown, 1987-89; rsch. assoc. dept. food sci. and human nutrition U. Fla., Gainesville, 1989-91; instr. div. health sci. Santa Fe C.C., Gainesville, 1989-92; rsch. chemist div. food chem. Am. Bacteriol. and Chem. Rsch. Corp., Gainesville, 1991-92; rsch. chemist lipid nutrition lab. USDA, Beltsville, Md., 1992-94; instr. Biology Prince George's C.C., Largo, Md., 1993-94; asst. prof. biochemistry Lecom, Erie, Pa., 1994—. Vol. entertainer Gainesville area nursing homes, 1989-92; mem. Big Bros./Big Sisters greater Gainesville, 1989-90. Capt. USAR, 1990—. USDA Post-doctoral fellow, 1992, Nat. Rsch. Coun. Post-doctoral fellow, 1986. Mem. Soc. Armed Forces Med. Lab. Scientists, Am. Inst. Nutrition, Assn. Mil. Surgeons of U.S., Sigma Xi. Home: 1203 W 36th St Erie PA 16508 Office: Lecom Erie PA 16509

BANKS, MELBA LUCILLE, minister, chaplain, religious organization executive; b. Asheville, N.C., May 18, 1940; d. Jeter Hezekiah and Rhoda Annie Purdue (White) Riddle; m. David Clyde Burnette, Jan. 21, 1958 (dec.); children: Daniel Lin, Margaret Dawn; m. Ralph Junior Banks, Oct. 23, 1971. BA in Religion, Mars Hill Coll., 1982; MDiv, Southeastern Sem., 1988; D of Ministry, Lexington Theol. Sem., 1994. Pvt. music tchr. Buncombe County, N.C., 1960-68; sec. Christmount Christian Assembly, Black Mountain, N.C., 1969-71, bus. mgr., coord., 1971-77, exec. dir., 1977-94. Vol. chaplain N.C. Dept. Corrections, Black Mountain, Raleigh, 1991—, St. Joseph's Hosp., Asheville, 1986—; pres. Swannanoa Valley Med. Ctr., Black Mountain, 1988-89; chair water safety coun. ARC, Asheville area, 1987; cons. Martin Luther King Corp., Swannanoa, 1994, Black Mountain C. of C., 1986. Recipient Sam Leonard award Kiwanis Club Swannanoa Valley, 1989, Woman of Yr. award Sourwood chpt. Am. Bus. Women's Assn., 1985; Z. Smith Reynolds Found. grantee, 1993, Horizon 2000 Cmty. Based Alternative grantee, 1994. Mem. NAACP, Internat. Assn. Conf. Ctr. Adminstrs., N.C. Correctional Assn. Mem. Disciples of Christ. Home: 228 Pine Grove Rd Black Mountain NC 28711

BANKS, RELA, sculptor; b. Yaroslav, Poland, Oct. 8, 1933; came to U.S., 1947; d. Jacob and Frieda (Weintraub) Heuberg; m. Stanley Frederic Banks, Aug. 9, 1953; children: Andrew Howard, J. Monica, Gary Mitchell. Student, Mus. Modern Art, 1957, Art Students League, N.Y.C. and Woodstock, N.Y., 1958-61, Summit (N.J.) Art Ctr., 1966-75. Chmn. nat. juried exhibit Summit Art Ctr., 1976, mem. adminstrv. com., 1977-79, chmn. standing com. spl. events, trustee; mem. exec. com. Phoenix Gallery, N.Y.C., 1983; chmn. membership com. Stone Sculpture Soc. N.Y., 1980-82. One-woman shows include Robins Art Gallery, South Orange, N.J., 1973, Montclair (N.J.) Coll., 1974, Caldwell (N.J.) Coll., 1974, 83, Summit Art Ctr., 1976, Newark Acad., Livingston, N.J., 1976, Douglas Coll., New Brunswick, N.J., 1978, First Women's Bank, N.Y.C., 1979, Phoenix Gallery, 1979, 81, 83, Morris Mus. Arts and Scis., Morristown, N.J., 1983, Ann Leonard Gallery, Woodstock, 1983, NECCA Mus., Bklyn., Conn., 1985, Schiller-Wapner Galleries, N.Y.C., 1985, 87, Ann Norton Sculpture Galleries, West Palm Beach, Fla., 1987, David Gary Ltd, Millburn, N.J., 1988; exhibited in group shows at Phoenix Gallery, 1979, 83, Morris Mus. Art, 1979, 83, Invitational Woodstock Artists Assn., 1980, 84, Eilaine Benson Gallery, Bridgehampton, N.Y., 1980, Searles Art Ctr., Great Barrington, Mass., 1980, Nabisco Art Gallery, 1981, Summit Art Ctr., 1981, First Womens Bank, 1981, Fairleigh Dickinson U., Madison, N.J., 1983, NYU Grad. Sch. Bus., 1983, AT&T Gallery, Basking Ridge, N.J., 1984, Shering Plough Gallery, N.J., 1984, New Orleans Mus. Art, 1986, Gallery Contemporary Art at U. Colorado Springs, Colo., 1986, Schiller-Wapner Galleries, 1986, Lever House, N.Y.C., 1986, Aldrich Mus. Contemporary Art, Ridgefield, Conn., 1986, Okla. Art Ctr., Oklahoma City, 1987, "After Henry Moore", Emily Lowe Mus., Hofstra U., Hempstead, N.Y., 1988, group exhibition , Poland; represented in permanent collections New Orleans Mus. Art, Everson Mus., Syracuse, N.Y., Morris Mus. Sci. and Art, Okla. Art Ctr., Vassar Coll. Gallery, Poughkeepsie, N.Y., Millburn (N.J.) Pub. Library, Minn. Mus. Art, Mpls., Woodstock Hist. Soc., Fordham U., Lincoln Ctr., N.Y.C., Aldrich Mus. Contemporary Art, Warsaw Mus., Poland, various pvt. and corp. collections. Mem. Woodstock Artists Assn. Office: Rela Banks Studio Mink Hollow Rd Woodstock NY 12498

BANKS, THERESA ANN, elementary education educator; b. Camden, N.J., Apr. 5, 1946; d. Frederick Douglas and Betty Mae (Norman) Clarke; m. James Donald Banks, Feb. 14, 1987; 1 child, Elizabeth Pearl Banks. BS, Cheyney U., 1968. Elem. tchr., grade three Loudenslager Elem. Sch., Paulsboro, N.J., 1968-81, tchr. basic skills, 1981-86; tchr. basic skills Billingsport Elem. Sch., Paulsboro, 1986—; tchr. art activities Enrichment Prog., Paulsboro, 1988—. Chmn. youth program ARC for Paulsboro Sch. System, 1970-80, Sunshine Club/Billingsport Sch., 1990—, Billingsport Sch. Store, 1992—. Honored for 25 yrs. svc. to Paulsboro Sch. Dist., 1993. Mem. NEA, N.J. Edn. Assn., Paulsboro Edn. Assn., Nat. Coun. Tchrs. Math. Baptist. Home: 253 Deptford Ave Woodbury NJ 08096-3508 Office: Billingsport Elem School 5th And Greenwich Ave Paulsboro NJ 08066

BANKS, VIRGINIA ANNE (GINGER BANKS), association executive; b. Dallas, Mar. 19, 1949; d. James Houston and Mary Virginia (Bussey) B. B of Journalism, U. Tex., 1971. Traveling cons. Alpha Omicron Pi Fraternity, Indpls., 1971-73; adminstrv. asst. Alpha Omicron Pi Fraternity, Nashville, 1973-74; pub. info. officer Tex. Dept. of Community Affairs, Austin, 1974-76; asst. dir. of comm. State Bar of Tex., Austin, 1976-78, assoc. editor Tex. Bar Jour., 1977-79, mng. editor Tex. Bar Jour, 1979-91, comm. dir., 1991—, dir. pub. svcs. divsn., 1992—; internat. rush chmn. Alpha Omicron Pi, Nashville, 1976-77, internat. v.p. ops., 1977-81, internat. pres., 1981-85, v.p. found., 1985-90, mem. fraternity devel. com., 1985-89, pres. Pi Kappa Corp., 1991—, mem. Austin Alumnae chpt., 1973—, del. Nat. Panhellenic Conf., 1987-93, chmn. Perry award com., 1992—; com. to devel. relationship statement, Nat. Panhellenic Conf., 1983, del., 1987-93, area advisor coll. Panhellenics com., 1985-88, chmn. liaison com., 1987-88, mem. Project Future collegiate concerns com., 1987-89, field cons. seminar com., 1987, chmn., 1988, resolutions com., 1988, chmn. pub. rels. com., 1991-93, mem. ednl. devel. com., 1991-93. Contbr. articles to mags. Bd. dirs. Lone Star Girl Scout Coun., Austin, 1973-75, Nat. Interfraternity Found., 1986-89, M.L. Roller scholarship com., 1988-89, nominations com., 1988-89; mem. Humane Soc. Austin, 1981—; chmn. mag. adv. com. Ex Students Assn., U. Tex., Austin, 1989—; mem. Tarrytown United Meth. Ch. Recipient presdl. citation State Bar of Tex., 1981, 90, 94, presdl. citation Alpha Omicron Pi, 1988, Rose award Alpha Omicron Pi, 1991. Mem. Am. Soc. Assn. Execs., Assn. Fraternity Advisors, Internat. Assn. Bus. Communicators, Nat. Assn. Bar Execs., Women in Comm., PEO Sisterhood, Pi Kappa (corp. pres. 1991-95), Alpha Omieron Pi (Austin alumnae chpt.). Home: 3108 W Terrace Dr Austin TX 78757-4332 Office: State Bar of Tex PO Box 12487 Austin TX 78711-2487

BANKSTON, BRENDA LEE, accountant, treasurer; b. Louisville, Feb. 14, 1955; m. Lawrence U. Bankston, Jan. 10, 1981; 1 child, Alea Jean. BS in Bus. Adminstrn., U. Louisville, 1993. Acctg. clk. Louisville Cement Co., 1974-85; asst. contr. Cobb Group, Louisville, 1985-88; sec.-treas. Bennington Corp., Louisville, 1988—; sec.-treas. Bus. Devel. Group, Louisville, 1992—. Treas. Met. Children's Mus., Louisville, 1989-90. Mem. Inst. Mgmt. Accts., Nat. Assn. Women Bus. Owners, Beta Gamma Sigma. Democrat. Baptist. Office: Bennington Corp 611 W Main St Louisville KY 40202

BANNAN, KATHRYN E., pharmaceutical government affairs executive; b. Jackson, Mich., Apr. 4, 1960; d. Philip Eugene and Joan Kathleen (Jacob) B. BA in Spanish, Kalamazoo Coll., 1981; MA in Legis. Affairs, George Washington U., 1991. Tchr. Am. Sch. Guatemala, Guatemala City, 1981-84; cons. Arecibo (P.R.) Community Health Care Inc., 1984-85; fed. govt. affairs Assoc. Hoffmann-La Roche, Washington, 1985-92, regional mgr., state govt. affairs, 1992—. Elected mem. Arlington County Rep. Com., Arlington, Va., 1991—; elected del. Va. Rep. Conv., 1992-94, appd. mem. Arlington County Commn. on Status of Women, 1992—; vol. Kyle McSlarrow for Congress, Arlington, 1992, 94. Mem. Washington Area State Rels. Group (bd. dirs. 1992—), Women in Govt. Rels., Arlington Young Reps., Potomac Pachyderms. Roman Catholic. Home: 4623 S 31st Rd A-1 Arlington VA 22202 Office: Hoffmann-La Roche 1300 I St NW Ste 520 West Washington DC 20005

BANNEN, CAROL, information resources manager; b. St. Paul, Oct. 4, 1951; d. Virgil D. and Patricia A. (Kelly) Swanson; m. John T. Bannen, Aug. 16, 1975; children: Ryan, Kelly, Erin. BA, Coll. St. Catherine, St. Paul, 1973. Law libr. Peat Marwick & Mitchell, Mpls., 1972-75; mgr. info. resource ctr. Reinhart, Boerner, Van Dueren, Norris & Rieselbach, Milw., 1975—. Mem. Law Librs. Assn. Wis. (pres. 1987-88), Spl. Librs. Assn. (chmn. ins. and employee benefits div. 1986-87), Libr. Coun. Met. Milw., Am. Assn. Law Librs., Am. Records Mgmt. Assn., Assn. Records Mgrs. and Adminstrs. Office: Reinhart Boerner Van Deuren Norris & Rieselbach 1000 N Water St Ste 2100 Milwaukee WI 53202-0900

BANTA, ANNA ARLENE, counselor; b. Salem, Oreg., Oct. 6, 1933; d. Arthur Arden and Musetta Dell (Naylor) Adams; m. Oren Clifford Banta, Apr. 17, 1950. BS, Eugene Bible Coll., 1986; MA, Western Evang. Sem., 1988. Lic. prof. counselor. Salesperson Luster Craft, Portland, Oreg., 1968-73; pulpit speaker Peninsula Open Bible Ch., Portland, Oreg., 1988-92; min. various retreats, groups and chs., 1979-92; min. Open Bible Std. Ch., Inc., Portland, 1979-92; counselor Peninsula Christian Counseling Ctr., Portland, 1987-92; pvt. practice Eugene, 1992—. Contbr. articles to profl. jours. Vol. counselor William Temple House, Portland, 1987-89. Mem. Am. Counseling Assn., Am. Assn. Christian Counselors, Oreg. Counseling Assn., Christian Assn. Psychol. Studies. Republican. Office: 541 Willamette St Ste 207 Eugene OR 97401-2694

BANTEL, LINDA MAE, art museum director; b. King City, Calif., May 30, 1943; d. Clifford Burnett and Helen Vernelle (Mallicotte) Bantel; m. David Hollenberg, June 15, 1980; 1 child, Matthew Bantel Hollenberg. M.A., NYU, 1973. Research cons. N.Y. Hist. Soc., N.Y.C., 1975-76; guest co-curator Art Mus. of South Tex., Corpus Christi, Tex., 1977-79; research assoc. Met. Mus. Art, N.Y.C., 1978-80; curator, now dir. of mus. Pa. Acad. Fine Arts, Phila., 1980-95. Co-author: (with James Thomas Flexner) The Face of Liberty: Founders of the U.S., 1975; author: The Alice M. Kaplan Collection, 1980; William Rush, American Sculptor, 1982; (with Marcus Burke) Spain and New Spain: Mexican Colonial Arts in Their European Context, 1979; contbr. to American Paintings in the Metropolitan Museum of Art Vol. II: A Catalogue of Works by Artists Born Between 1816-1845, 1985, (with others) Searching Out the Best, 1988, Raphaelle Peale Still Lifes, 1988; contbr. to Antiques mag., 1989. Mem. Coll. Art Assn., Am. Assn. Mus., Assn. Art Mus. Dirs. Home: 703 W Phil-Ellena St Philadelphia PA 19119

BANUELOS, BETTY LOU, rehabilitation nurse; b. Vandergrift, Pa., Nov. 28, 1930; d. Archibald and Bella Irene (George) McKinney; m. Raul, Nov. 1, 1986; children: Patrice, Michael. Diploma, U. Pitts., 1951; cert., Loma Linda U., 1960. RN, Calif.; cert. chem. dependency nurse. Cons. occupational health svcs. Bd. Registered Nurses, 1984—; lectr., cons. in field. Recipient Scholarship U. Pitts. Mem. Dirs. of Nursing, Calif. Assn. Nurses in Substance Abuse. Home and Office: 15 Oak Spring Ln Laguna Beach CA 92656-2980

BAPTIST, SYLVIA EVELYN, data service company executive, consultant; b. Chgo., Feb. 15, 1944; d. Clarence Walter and Evelyn Alphild (Fagerberg) Bonin; m. Jeremy Eduard Baptist, July 21, 1962; children: Sarah, Margaret, Catherine. Student Mich. State U., 1961-62; B.S., Roosevelt U., 1965. Instr. IBM, Chgo., 1965-66, systems engr., Topeka, Kans., 1966-67; tchr. computer sci. Lawrence High Sch., Kans., 1968; pres. Multiple Data Svcs., Leawood, Kans., 1983—; adminstrv. user liaison Kansas City Sch. Dist., 1987-89, sr. adminstrv. user liaison, 1989—; acting telecom. mgr., 1991, project analyst, 1992—; cons. in field. Alumni Disting. scholar Mich. State U., 1961-62, Internat. Ladies' Garment Workers Union scholar Roosevelt U., 1964-65. V.p. Scandinavian Dancers Kansas City, 1987-89. Mem. NAFE, Heart Am. Help Desk Inst. (editor newsletter 1993-94), Internat. Platform Assn., Internat. Netman Users Group (sec. 1993—), Vasa (master ceremonies 1986-87, vice chmn. 1988-89, chmn. 1990-92, 94—, sec. 1992-93, Vasa Star corr. 1993-94), Psi Psi Psi. Avocations: cooking, writing. Office: Multiple Data Svcs 3501 W 92d St Leawood KS 66206

BARAB, PATSY LEE, nutritionist, consultant, realtor; b. Indpls., Sept. 24, 1934; B.S., Mich. State U., 1956, M.A., 1970; m. Richard M. Shulko, Aug. 4, 1973; 1 child, Gregory; m. John D. Barab Jr., April 8, 1995. Asst. prof. Med. Coll. Ga., Augusta, 1972-82; nutrition cons., 1982—; assoc. Meybohm Realty, Inc., Augusta, 1987—. Mem. program com. Gertrude Herbert Art Inst., 1992—; mem. promotion com. Imperial Theater. Mem. Am. Dietetic Assn., Ga. Dietetic Assn., Augusta Dietetic Assn., Am. Home Econ. Assn., Ga. Heart Assn., Ga. Nutrition Coun., Soc. Nutrition Edn., Nutrition Today Soc. (charter), Nutritionists in Nursing Edn. (nat. chmn. 1983-84), AAUP, AAUW, GRI, CRS, Augusta Opera Club, Houndslake Country Club, Racquet Club, Million Dollar Club (life), Omicron Nu, Pi Beta Phi (arrowmont chmn. Augusta Alumnae Club 1992—). Home: 8 South Dorset Ave Ventnor City NJ 08406

BARAD, JILL ELIKANN, toy company executive; b. N.Y.C., May 23, 1951; d. Lawrence Stanley and Corinne (Schuman) Elikann; m. Thomas Kenneth Barad, Jan., 28, 1979; children: Alexander David, Justin Harris. BA English and Psychology, Queens Coll., 1973. Asst. prod. mgr. mktg. Coty Cosmetics, N.Y.C., 1976-77, prod. mgr. mktg., 1977; account exec. Wells Rich Greene Advt. Agy., L.A., 1978-79; product mgr. mktg. Mattel Toys, Inc., L.A., 1981-82, dir. mktg., 1982-83, v.p. mktg., 1983-85, sr. v.p. mktg., 1985-86, sr. v.p. product devel., from 1986, exec. v.p. product design and devel., exec. v.p. mktg. and worldwide product devel., 1988-89; pres. girls and activity toys div. Mattel Toys, Inc. (name now Mattel Inc.), L.A., 1989—; pres., bd. dirs. Mattel USA, El Segundo, Calif., 1990—; pres., COO Mattel, Inc., El Segundo, Calif., 1992—; bd. dirs. Arco Toys, Reebok Internat., Bank of Am. Bd. dirs. Town Hall of Calif.; trustee Queens Coll.; chair exec. adv. bd. Children Affected by AIDS Found. Mem. Am. Film Inst. (charter). Office: Mattel Inc 333 Continental Blvd El Segundo CA 90245-5012

BARAL, LILLIAN, artist, retired educator; b. Perehinsko, Carpathia, Poland; d. Leon and Esther (Ludmer) B. BA, Hunter Coll., 1939, MA in Art, 1969. Lic. fine arts tchr., secondary English tchr., elem. tchr., N.Y. Radio script writer, announcer U.S. Office of War Info., Voice of Am., N.Y.C.; writer, publicity specialist Citizens Com. on Displaced Persons, N.Y.C., Consulate Gen. of Israel, N.Y.C.; publicity specialist Madison Books, Pub. House, N.Y.C., Brandeis U., Waltham, Mass.; pub. rels. dir. Israel Govt. Tourist Office, N.Y.C.; publicity asst. Huntington Hartford Gallery of Modern Art, N.Y.C.; fine arts tchr. Parsons Jr. H.S., Queens, N.Y., 1962-82; painter, sculptor, 1956—; art tour leader 92d St YMHA, 1985, 86. Exhbns. include N.Y. Pub. Libr., Little Gallery, 1966, Whitehouse Gallery, N.Y.C., 1967, Am. House, N.Y.C., 1968, Lord & Taylor, N.Y.C., 1970, Center Art Gallery, N.Y.C., 1971, Marie Pellicone Gallery, N.Y.C., 1979, Womanart Gallery, N.Y.C., 1979, BFM Gallery, N.Y.C., 1980, Bennet Gallery, Fairfield, Conn., 1981, Queens Mus., 1981, New Sch. for Social Rsch., N.Y.C., 1982, Lever House, N.Y.C., 1983, W.C. Post Coll., L.I., N.Y., 1984, Southhampton Coll., L.I., 1984, Queensborough C.C. Art Gallery, N.Y.C., 1985, 86, Yad Vashem Mus., Jerusalem, 1991; represented in numerous pvt. collections; subject newspaper, mag. articles, TV interview. Mem. N.Y. Artists Equity (exec. bd. 1985-86), United Fedn. Tchrs., Portland Mus. Art. Home: 98-50 67th Ave Forest Hills NY 11374 Studio: 30 E 20th St New York NY 10020

BARAN, CHRISTINE, systems analyst; b. Rochester, N.Y., Apr. 21, 1958; d. Wolodymyr and Olga (Zyrak) B. AS, Rochester Inst. Tech., 1978, BS, 1980. Computer programmer Infodata Sys., Rochester, N.Y., 1980-83; sys. analyst Acumenics, Bethesda, Md., 1983-85; staff cons. Martin Marietta, Greenbelt, Md., 1985-88; sys. analyst, computer specialist Smithsonian Inst., Washington, 1988—; cons. USAID, Washington, 1983-86. Mem. NAFE, LWV. Republican. Mem. Ukrainian Catholic. Home: 8607 Chase Glen Cir Fairfax Station VA 22039 Office: Smithsonian Instn Comptr Office 955 L'Enfant Plz Washington DC 20024

BARANAUCKAS, CARLA MAY, journalist; b. Niagara Falls, N.Y., Aug. 9, 1955; d. Charles Francis and Molly Ann (Mullen) B. Student, Allegheny Coll., 1973-75; BA cum laude, St. Olaf Coll., Northfield, Minn., 1977; post-grad., U. N.D., 1982-83. News asst. Mpls. Tribune, 1977-78; reporter Pampa (Tex.) News, 1978; reporter, copy editor Texarkana (Tex.) Gazette, 1978-79, Edwardsville (Ill.) Intelligencer, 1979-81; copy editor Grand Forks (N.D.) Herald, 1981-84, St. Louis Post-Dispatch, 1984-88; sports copy editor The N.Y. Times, 1988-92, mt. copy editor, 1992-94; nat. copy editor, 1994-95, dep. nat. copy chief, 1995—. Participant Coro Found. Women in Leadership, St. Louis, 1987-88, mem. Jr. League of N.Y., 1988—. Recipient English-Speaking Union grantee Internat. Conf. Oxford U., 1993. Mem. NAFE, Nat. Acad. TV Arts and Scis., Nat. Press Club, Internat. Platform Assn., Soc. Profl. Journalists, Assn. for Women in Sports Media (v.p. 1991-92), Investigative Reporters and Editors, Women in Comm., Women in Leadership Alumnae, Coro Alumni, Coro Assocs., English-Speaking Union. Roman Catholic. Home: 124 W 60th St Apt 14J New York NY 10023-7465 Office: The NY Times 229 W 43rd St New York NY 10036-3913

BARANOFSKY, CATHY P., insurance agent; b. Cambridge, Mass., Mar. 17, 1947; d. Richard C. and Catherine M. (Koch) Frank; m. William A. Cook III, Aug. 25, 1973 (dec. July 1985); children: Susan M., Katherine E.; m. John J. Baranofsky, Feb. 20, 1988. BS, Merrimack Coll., 1988. Registered rep. NASD. Phlebotomy coord. Holy Family Hosp., Methuen, Mass., 1980-85; New Eng. sales mgr. Pathology Svcs., Wilmington, Mass., 1989-92; regional dir. Pharm. Mgmt. Svcs., Inc., Tampa, Fla., 1992-93; account rep. Met Life, North Andover, Mass., 1993—. Chair Bd. of Health, Reading, Mass., 1992—. Mem. Bus. and Profl. Women/Reading (pres. 1991—), Mass. Bus. and Profl. Women (mem. chmn. 1994—). Democrat. Roman Catholic. Home: 401 West St Reading MA 01867 Office: Met Life 203 Turnpike St North Andover MA 01845

BARANOWSKI, ANITA KAREN, public relations consultant; b. Baytown, Tex., Jan. 14, 1961; d. Ted August and Shirley Ann (Curry) Rother; m. Robert Baranowski, Oct. 10, 1992. BA in Telecomm., Tex. Tech U., 1982. Reporter Sta. KLBK-TV (CBS), Lubbock, Tex., 1981-82; anchor, reporter

KEND-AM Radio, Lubbock, Tex., 1982-83, Sta. KAMR-TV (NBC), Amarillo, Tex., 1983-84; mktg. mgr. Centel Comm., N.Y.C., 1984-88; pub. rels. mgr. Six Flags Great Adventure, Jackson, N.J., 1988-92; corp. pub. rels. mgr. Hyatt Hotels Corp., Chgo., 1992-93; pub. rels. cons. Crystal Clear Comm., Crystal Lake, Ill., 1993—. Vol. Big Bros./Big Sisters, Amarillo, Tex., 1983-84, Red Bank, N.J., 1991-92, Boy Scouts Am., Ocean County, N.J., 1989-92. Office: Crystal Clear Comm 4703 Strong Rd Crystal Lake IL 60014

BARANSKI, CHRISTINE, actress; b. May 2, 1952; d. Lucien and Virginia (Mazerowski) B.; m. Matthew Cowles, Oct. 15, 1983. BA, Juilliard Sch., 1974. Plays include 'Tis a Pity She's a Whore, The Real Thing (Antoinette Perry award 1984), Cat on a Hot Tin Roof, She Stoops to Conquer, Angel City, Blithe Spirit, Coming Attractions, The Undefeated Rumba Champ, Otherwise Engaged, A Midsummer Night's Dream (Obie award 1983), Rumors (Antoinette Perry award 1989), Nick and Nora, 1991, Lips Together Teeth Apart, 1992; (films) Soup for One, 1981, Lovesick, 1983, Crackers, 1985, 9 1/2 Weeks, 1986, Legal Eagles, 1986, The Pick-up Artist, 1987, Reversal of Fortune, 1990, Life with Mikey, 1993, Addams Family Values, 1993, The War, 1994, The Ref, 1994, (TV series) Cybill, 1995—; (TV movie) To Dance with the White Dog, 1993; (TV appearences) Playing for Time, Murder Ink, All My Children, Big Shots in America, Texas, Another World. *

BARANSKI, JOAN SULLIVAN, publisher; b. Andover, Mass., Apr. 6, 1933; d. Joseph Charles and Ruth G. (McCormack) Sullivan; m. Kenneth E. Baranski, Apr. 20, 1970. B.S., U. Mass., Lowell, 1955. Tchr. Andover Public Schs., 1955-61; assoc. editor sci. and reading sch. dept. Holt, Rinehart and Winston, N.Y.C., 1961-65; promotion coord. sch. dept. Harcourt Brace Jovanovich, N.Y.C., 1965-74; mgr. div. verifiability and testing Harcourt Brace Jovanovich, 1974-75; editor-in-chief Teacher mag., Macmillan Co., Stamford, Conn., 1975-81; editor-in-chief sch. dept. Harper & Row Pubs., N.Y.C., 1981-84; v.p., editor-in-chief Globe Book Co., Simon and Schuster Edn. Group, 1984-88; pub. Joint Coun. Econ. Edn., N.Y.C., 1989-92; pub. Econs. Am., Nat. Coun. on Econ. Edn., N.Y.C., 1992—. Contbg. author: Winston Basic Reading Series, 1963, Little Owl Program, 1964. Home: 250 E 87th St New York NY 10128 Office: 1140 Avenue Of The Americas New York NY 10036-5802

BARASH, YVONNE LINNEA, mental health nurse; b. St. Paul, July 9, 1960; d. Walter Louis and Martha Lorraine (Bruhn) Melnik; m. Mark Barash, June 6, 1981; children: Laura, Eileen. BSN, U. Md., 1982. RN, Md., N.J. Staff nurse Suburban Hosp., Bethesda, Md.

BARB, CYNTHIA MARIE, mathematics educator; b. Akron, Nov. 18, 1962; d. Gene and Mary Barb. BS in Math. magna cum laude, U. Akron, 1985, BS in Statistics, 1985, cert. in Secondary Edn., 1985-86, MS in Math., 1990; postgrad. in curriculum and instrn. math. edn., Kent State U. Secondary Edn. 7-12 Cert. Grad. teaching asst. U. Akron, 1985-86; long term substitute Tallmadge (Ohio) City Schs., 1987-88, Stow (Ohio) City Schs., 1988-89; math. instr. U. Akron, 1989-90, Kent State U. Stark Regional Campus, Canton, Ohio, 1990—. Recipient Grad. Teaching Assistantship Acad. scholarships, U. Akron, 1985-86. Mem. Math. Assn. Am., Nat. Coun. of Tchrs. of Math., Ohio Coun. Tchrs. Math., Phi Sigma Alpha, Alpha Lambda Delta. Office: Kent State U Stark Regional Campus 6000 Frank Ave NW Canton OH 44720-7548

BARBA, ROBERTA ASHBURN, social worker; b. Morgantown, W.Va., June 23, 1931; d. Robert Russell and Mary Belle (Rogers) Ashburn; m. Harry C. Barba, Jan. 28, 1956 (div. June 1963); 1 child, Gregory Robert; m. Robert Franklin Church, May 10, 1972. BSSW, W.Va. U., 1953; postgrad., U. Conn., Hartford, 1953-54; MSSW, NYU, 1957. Diplomate in Am. Bd. Examiners; lic. N.Y., W.Va. Pvt. practice W.Va., 1968—; evaluator P.A.C.E., Star City, W.Va., 1973-74; social worker Family Svc. Assn., Morgantown, W.Va., 1974-75, 85-87; human resources asst., social worker Sundale Rest Home, Morgantown, 1977-79; cons., residential svcs. specialist Coordinating Coun. for Ind. Living, Morgantown, 1983-88; provider W.Va. Dept. Welfare, Human Svcs., Morgantown, 1980-87; social worker maternity svcs. Monongalia County Health Dept., Morgantown, 1985-87; social worker Hospice of Preston County, Kingwood, W.Va., 1988-89; shelter worker, field work instr. Bartlett House W.Va. Sch. Social Work, Morgantown, 1986-90; case mgr. Region VI Area Agy. on Aging, Fairmont, W.Va., 1990-92; case mgr. geriatric program W.Va. U., Morgantown, 1992—. Author: (with others) Working with Terminally Ill, 1990, (short fiction) Kids Know, 1992; freedom writer Amnesty Internat., 1987-90. George Davis Bivens Found. grantee, 1953-54. Mem. NASW (charter mem., cert. diplomate), ACLU, NOW, Acad. Cert. Social Workers, W.Va. Human Resources Assn., W.Va. Child Care Assn., Monongalia County Coun. Social Agys, Phi Beta Kappa. Home: 429 Fairmont Rd Morgantown WV 26505-4244

BARBE, BETTY CATHERINE, financial analyst; b. Chgo., Dec. 24, 1930; d. Norbert Lambert and Helen Weishaar; m. Edward William, Aug. 8, 1953; children: Leonard Walter, Roger Andrew. Student, U. Toledo, 1970, 85. Acct. Gorr Printing, Allstate Ins., Muntz TV, Chgo., 1947-53; hostess Welcome Wagon Internat., Maumee, Ohio, 1965-70; v.p. sec., cost acctg. Craftmaster, Toledo, 1970-72; sec., estimator Grinnell Fire Protection, Toledo, 1972-73; exec. sec., payroll Crow, Inc. Aviation, 1973-77; asst. city clk., payroll City of Perrysburg, 1977-83, tax adminstr., 1983—. Vol. George Bush campaign candidates, 1978—; v.p. bd. Zepf Community Mental Health, Toledo, 1986-87; reader for Sight Ctr.; mem. Women Alive! Coalition, 1987—, Nat. Women's Polit. Caucus, 1987—, MADD, 1987—, YWCA, Perrysburg Arts Coun. Honoree Maumee Valley coun. Girl Scouts U.S., 1990. Mem. Nat. Fedn. Bus. and Profl. Women, Maumee Valley Toastmasters (pres. 1989—, area gov.), Toledo Opera soc., Assn. Two Toledos (sec.), Christ Child Soc., Maumee C. of C. (sec.) Samagama Club., Zonta II (treas.), Rotary (Paul Harris fellow). Republican. Roman Catholic. Home: 724 W Wayne St Maumee OH 43537-1923 Office: City of Perrysburg 201 W Indiana Ave Perrysburg OH 43551-1584

BARBEE, MARY KEENUM, clergywoman; b. North Kansas City, Mo., June 15; d. John Carroll Keenum and Virginia E. Garton Runyon; m. David E. Barbee, Aug. 30, 1956 (div. May 1983); children: Mark, Mike, Midge, Eric. BA, U. No. Colo., 1959; MA, U. N.Mex., 1983; student, So. Meth. U. Cert. assn. exec.; ordained minister United Meth. Ch. Tchr. Roaring Fork Schs., Basalt, Colo., 1962-63; bus. owner The Peppermint Tree, Aspen, Colo., 1963-69; asst. dean students U. N.Mex., Albuquerque, 1978-88; exec. dir. Pi Lambda Theta, Bloomington, Ind., 1988-89, Nat. Interfrat. Found., Indpls., 1989—; minister United Meth. Ch., Trinidad, Colo., 1992—. Mem. Sigma Sigma Sigma (exec. com.). Home: PO Box 788 Aspen CO 81612 Office: PO Box 518 Trinidad CO 81082

BARBER, MARSHA, company executive; b. Peoria, Ill., Dec. 7, 1946; d. Jack R. and Dorothy M. (Zeine) Hursey; m. Thomas L. Barber, June 15, 1968; 1 child, Brett A. BS, So. Ill. U., Carbondale, 1968; postgrad., So. Ill. U., Edwardsville. Ctr. mgr. Exec. Ctrs. Northeast Ohio/Hdqrs. Cos., Columbus; now pres. Plus 1 Exec. Stes, Columbus; instr. elem. edn., Alton, Ill.; regional coun. rep. Ill. Edn. Assn.; mem. So. Ill. U. Edn. Adv. Coun. Mem. Women's Bus. Bd., Columbus, Ohio. Mem. NEA, Columbus Area C. of C. (small bus. adv. coun., exec. com., chair N.W. Area Bus. Coun.), Sports Car Club Am.

BARBER, PATRICIA LOUISE, clinical specialist; b. St. Paul, Jan. 11, 1953; d. James Bernard and Margaret Mary (Neagle) B. BSN, U. Minn., 1975; cert. nurse practitioner, U. Ill., 1978. RN, Colo., Ill., Minn. Staff nurse U. Minn., Mpls., 1974-75; transplant coord. U. Ill., Chgo., 1978-90; nurse practitioner emergency rm. Denver Presbyn., 1990-92; nurse practitioner in-patient svc. cardiovascular Denver Presbyn. St. Luke's Med. Ctr., 1992—; cons. in field, Chgo., 1983—. Editor: Resource Manual for Transplant Coordinators, 1982. Co-chmn. S/A Patient Svcs. Com., 1983-90. Mem. N.Am. Transplant Coords. Orgn. (co-chmn. 1979-90, Honors 1983), Am. Diabetes Assn. (speakers bur. 1982—), Nat. Kidney Found. (bd. dirs. 1983-90). Office: Denver Presbyn St Lukes Med Ctr 1719 E 19th Ave Denver CO 80218-1281

BARBETTA, MARIA ANN, health records administrator, consultant; b. Bristol, Pa., Mar. 20, 1956; d. Eugene Charles and Anna Barbetta. AA, Bucks County Community Coll., 1976; BS, Coll. Allied Health Professions, Temple U., 1978. Dir. med. records Cumberland Regional Health Plan, Vineland, N.J., 1978; dir. med. record dept. St. Mary Hosp., Langhorne, Pa., 1978—; cons. med. records St. Joseph's Home for Aged, Holland, Pa., 1983—; speaker on med. record topics to various orgns., Langhorne, 1983—. Mem. Am. Mgmt. Assn., Nat. Med. Records Imaging Users Group (sec. 1992-93), Am. Health Info. Mgmt. Assn. (contbg. author jour. 1992, 93), Pa. Health Info. Mgmt. Assn. (edn. com. 1985-87, 91-92, project mgr. strategic plan 1987-89, sec. 1990-91, edn. com. 1991-92), RTAS Med. Record Users Group (co-chair 1993-94, 94—), Southeastern Pa. Health Info. Mgmt. Assn. (chmn. membership com. 1987-88, membership com. 1988-89, chmn. program and edn. 1989-90, sec. 1992-93), Medical Record Imaging Users Group (chair 1994—). Avocations: cross-country skiing, volunteer work, reading, traveling. Home: 4707 Grandview Ave Bensalem PA 19020-1011 Office: St Mary Hosp Langhorne-Newtown Rd Langhorne PA 19047

BARBIERI, KIM MARIE, neuroscientist; b. Providence, Aug. 8, 1964; d. Joseph Frank Barbieri and Patricia Ann (Badeau) Patton. Assoc. in Computer Sci. Engring., Control Data Inst., 1984; BS in Biology and Physics, Emmanuel Coll., 1989. Computer cons. Entré Computer Ctr., Boston, 1984-85; physics researcher Hanscom AFB-Geophysics, Bedford, Mass., 1986-87, 88-89; clin. researcher AIDS Beth Israel Hosp., Boston, 1989-90; pres., computer cons. Total Solutions, Boston, 1991—; rsch. neuroscientist Interneuron Pharm. Inc., Lexington, Mass., 1990—, computer cons., 1993—, also bd. dirs. Mem. Nat. Gay and Lesbian Polit. Alliance, Boston. Democrat. Home: 14 Lyne Rd Brighton MA 02135-4018 Office: Interneuron Pharm Inc 128 Spring St Lexington MA 02173-7800

BARBIR, MIRA, lawyer; b. Yugoslavia, Sept. 7, 1964; came to U.S., 1968; BA with honors, U. Chgo., 1986; JD, Northwestern U., 1989. Sr. atty. The First Nat. Bank of Chgo., 1989—. Office: The First Nat Bank of Chgo One First National Plz Chicago IL 60670

BARBO, DOROTHY MARIE, obstetrician-gynecologist, educator; b. River Falls, Wis., May 28, 1932; d. George William and Marie Lillian (Stelsel) B. BA, Asbury Coll., 1954; MD, U. Wis., 1958; DSc (hon.), Asbury Coll., 1981. Diplomate Am. Bd. Ob-Gyn. Resident Luth. Hosp. Milw., 1958-62; instr. Sch. Medicine Marquette U., Milw., 1962-66, asst. prof., 1966-67; assoc. prof. Christian Med. Coll. Punjab U., Ludhiana, India, 1968-72; assoc. prof. Med. Coll. Pa., Phila., 1972-87, prof., 1988-91; prof. U. N.Mex., Albuquerque, 1991—; med. dir. Women's Health Ctr., 1991—; acting dept. chair Christian Med. Coll., Punjab U., 1970; dir. Ctr. for Mature Woman Med. Coll. Pa., 1983-91; examiner Am. Bd. Ob-Gyn, 1984—; bd. dirs. Ludhiana Christian Med. Coll., N.Y.C., Svc. Master Co. Ltd., Downers Grove, Ill., 1982-91. Co-author: Care of Post Menopausal Patient, 1985; editor: Medical Clinics of N.A., vol. 71, 1987; contbr. chpt. to book. Student chpt. sponsor Christian Med. and Dental Soc., Phila., 1973-91, trustee, 1991—; tchr., elder Leverington Presbyn. Ch., Phila., 1988-91; interviewer Reader's Digest Internat. fellowships, Brunswick, Ga., 1982—; bd. dirs. Phila. chpt. Am. Cancer Soc., 1980-86, vol., 1984. Named sr. clin. trainee USPHS, HEW, 1963-65, one of Best Woman Drs. in Am. Harper Bazaar, 1985. Fellow ACS (sec. Phila. chpt. 1990), ACOG, Am. Fertility Soc.; mem. Obstet. Soc. Phila. (pres. 1989-90), Phila. Colposcopy Soc. (pres. 1982-84), Philadelphia County Med. Soc. (com. chmn. 1989-90), Alpha Omega Alpha. Office: U N Mex Dept Ob-Gyn 2211 Lomas Blvd NE Albuquerque NM 87131-5286

BARBOUR, CLAUDE MARIE, minister; b. Brussels, Oct. 2, 1935; came to U.S., 1969; Diploma d'État d'Infirmières, École d'Infirmières, Paris, 1956; diploma d'Études Religieuses, Faculté Libre de Théolog, Paris, 1958; MST, N.Y. Theol. Sem., 1970; DST, Garrett Evang. Theol. Sem., 1973. Ordained to ministry Presbyn. Ch., 1974. Youth counselor Young Women's Christian Assn., Geneva, 1959-61, Edinburgh, 1965-67; missionary Paris Evang. Missionary Soc., So. Africa, 1962-64; deaconess Ch. of Scotland, Edinburgh, 1967-69; from asst. to assoc. pastor First United Presbyn. Ch., Gary, Ind., 1974-80; from asst. to assoc. prof. Cath. Theol. Union, Chgo., 1976-86, prof., 1986—; prof. McCormick Theol. Sem., Chgo., 1990—; founder, dir. Shalom Ministries and Community, Chgo., 1975—; parish assoc. First Presbyn. Ch., Evanston, Ill., 1983—. World Coun. Chs. scholar, Geneva, 1969, United Presbyn. Ch. Commn. on Ecumenical Mission and Rels., N.Y., 1972; recipient Laskey award United Meth. Ch. Womens Div. the Bd. Global Ministries, N.Y., 1972, Civic award Ind. Women's Coun., 1976, Challenge of Peace award Chgo. Ctr. for Peace Studies, 1991. Mem. AAUW, Internat. Assn. for Mission Studies, Nat. Assn. Presbyn. Clergywomen, Am. Soc. Missiology, Assn. Prof. Mission, Midwest Felowship Prof. Mission, Assn. Presbyn. in Cross-Cultural Mission. Home: 1649 E 50th St Apt 21A Chicago IL 60615-6109 Office: Catholic Theological Union 5401 S Cornell Ave Chicago IL 60615 also: McCormick Theol Sem 5555 S Woodlawn Ave Chicago IL 60637

BARCA, KATHLEEN, marketing executive; b. Burbank, Calif., July 26, 1946; d. Frank Allan and Blanch Irene (Griffith) Barnes; m. Gerald Albino Barca, Dec. 8, 1967 (dec. May 1993); children: Patrick Gerald, Stacia Kathleen. Student, Pierce Coll., 1964; B in Bus., Hancock Coll., 1984. Teller Security Pacific Bank, Pasadena, Calif., 1968-69, Bank Am., Santa Maria, Calif., 1972-74; operator Gen. Telephone Co., Santa Maria, Calif., 1974-83, supr. operator, 1983-84; account exec. Sta. KRQK/KLLB Radio, Lompoc, Calif., 1984-85; owner Advt. Unltd., Orcutt, Calif., 1986-88; regional mgr. A.L. Williams Mktg. Co., Los Alamos, Calif., 1988-89; supr. Matol Botanical Internat., 1989-91; account exec. Santa Maria Times, 1989—. Author: numerous local TV and radio commercials, print advt. Activist Citizens Against Dumps in Residential Environments, Polit. Action Com., Orcutt and Santa Maria; chmn. Community Action Com., Santa Maria, Workshop EPA, Calif. Div., Dept. Health Svcs. State of Calif.; vice coord. Toughlove, Santa Maria, 1988-89; parent coord., mem. steering com. ASAP and Friends, 1988-89. Mem. NAFE, Womens Network-Santa Maria, Ctrl. Coast Ad (recipient numerous awards), Santa Maria C. of C. (amb. representing Santa Maria Times 1990-94, asst. chief amb. 1993-94). Democrat. Home: 509 Shaw St Los Alamos CA 93440

BARCLAY, MURIEL A., rehabilitation nurse; b. Acushnet, Mass., Mar. 12, 1947; d. Theodore E. and Muriel A. Bailey; 1 child, James W. Barclay Jr. Diploma, St. Luke's Hosp., 1969; BSN, Worcester State Coll., 1980; MHA, Clark U., U. Mass. Med. Sch., 1987. Cert. ins. rehab. specialist; lic. rehab. counselor, Mass.; cert. case mgr. Charge nurse Cape Cod Hosp., Hyannis, Mass., 1970-77; head nurse Rutland Heights Hosp., Mass., 1977-78; sr. staff nurse, resource nurse U. Mass. Med. Ctr., Worcester, 1978-83; adminstrv. intern Worcester City Hosp., 1985-86; field project cons. Harrington Meml. Hosp., Southbridge, Mass., 1986-87; mktg. mgr. New England Times, Newton, Mass., 1987-88; rehab. specialist Gen. Rehab. Svcs., Waltham, Mass., 1988-93; case mgr. ConServ Co., Swansea, Mass., 1994—. Mem. Ins. Rehab. Nurses New Eng., Assn. Rehab. Nurses. Home: 56 High Ridge Rd Worcester MA 01602-1464

BARCUS, MARY EVELYN, primary school educator; b. Peru, Ind., Apr. 3, 1938; d. Arthur Gibson and Mildred (Neher) Shull; m. Robert Gene Barcus, Aug. 9, 1959; children: Jennifer Sue, Debra Lynn. BS, Manchester Coll., 1960; MA, Ball State U., 1964. Kindergarten tchr. Miami Elem. Sch., Wabash, Ind., 1960-64; elem. tchr. Crooked Creek Sch., Indpls., 1964-72; preschool tchr. Second Presbyn. Preschool, Indpls., 1980-85, Speedway Coop., Indpls., 1985-86; tchr. asst. St. Monica Cath. Sch., Indpls., 1990; preschool tchr., fun club tchr. Arthur Jordan YMCA, Indpls.; preschool tchr. Indpls. (Ind.) Children's Mus., 1979—; docent sch. tours Children's Mus., Indpls., 1987—; interpreter at Indpls. children's mus.; facilitator Systematic Tng. Effective Parenting, Indpls. Writer: (children's songs) Piggback Songs for Infants and Toddlers, 1985, Piggyback Songs in Praise of God, 1986; editor elem. sch. newspaper; producer (with others) weekly show for cable TV. Profl. vol., libr. helper in local sch. systems; office helper North Cen. High Sch.; served on PTOs in various capacities; mem. Crossroads Guild, Parents Day Out of St. Luke's Meth. Ch., mem. ch. bd., Two's Tchr. Early Childhood Ctr.; Sun. sch./vacation ch. sch. tchr.; bd. dirs. Manchester Coll. Parents Assn. Mem. AAUW (charter, sec.), NEA (life), Ind. Assn. Edn. Young Children (state conf. com.), Pi Lambda Theta. Democrat. Mem. Church of Brethren. Home: 2230 Brewster Rd Indianapolis IN 46260-1521

BARDACH, JOAN LUCILE, clinical psychologist; b. Albany, N.Y., Oct. 3, 1919; d. Monroe Lederer and Lucile May (Lowenberg) B. AB, Cornell U., 1940; AM in Psychology, NYU, 1951; PhD in Clin. Psychology, 1957; cert. in psychoanalysis and psychotherapy, NYU, 1970. Supr. clin. psychologist NYU Rusk Inst. Rehab. Medicine, 1959-61; dir. psychol. services Rusk Inst. Rehab. Medicine, 1965-82; research psychologist, mem. faculty N.Y. Med. Coll., 1961-62; clin. prof. rehab. medicine (psychology) NYU, 1976—, supr. postdoctoral program psychoanalysis and psychotherapy, 1978—; pvt. practice clin. psychology and psychoanalysis N.Y.C., 1957—; non-govtl. orgn. rep. to UN Internat. Ctr. Sociol., Penal and Penitentiary Rsch. and Studies, Messina, Italy, 1985—; prin. investigator NIMH, 1976-81; mem. adv. bd. Coalition Sexuality and Disability, Planned Parenthood, 1983-89; cons. in field. Contbr. articles to profl. jours., chpt. to books. Recipient 3 awards for ednl. film, Choices: In Sexuality With Physical Disability, Internat. Film Festivals, Pioneer award for Sexual Attitude Reassessment Workshops The Coalition on Sexuality and Disability, 1989; NIMH fellow Inst. Sex Rsch., U. Ind., 1976. Fellow Am. Orthopsychiat. Assn.; mem. Am. Psychol. Assn., Am. Congress Rehab. Medicine, Sex Info. and Edn. Council U.S., Nat. Register Health Service Providers in Psychology, Eastern Psychol. Assn., N.Y. State Psychol. Assn. Home & Office: 50 E 10th St New York NY 10003-6221

BARDEN, JANICE KINDLER, personnel company executive; b. Cleve.; d. Norman Allen and Bessie G. (Black) Kindler; m. Hal Barden, Nov. 12, 1944 (dec. Jan. 1985) 1 child, Sheryl Andrea. BBA, Miami U., Oxford, Ohio, 1947; M in Indsl. Psychology, Kent State U., 1948. Asst. dir. admissions Fairleigh Dickinson U., Teaneck, N.J., 1950-53; gen. mgr. Pilots Employment Assocs., Teterboro, N.J., 1953-71; founder, pres. Aviation Pers. Internat., New Orleans, 1971—; commr. jury U.S. Dist. Ct. (ea. dist.) La., New Orleans, 1965—; lectr. in field. Chmn. History of Aviation Collection U. Tex., Dallas, 1980—; served on Pres. Com. Rehab. Vietnam POW Pilots; mem. FAA's Blue Ribbon Panel. Recipient Disting. Alumnus award Kent State U., 1986, Cuyahoga Falls H.S., 1988, Doswell award Nat. Bus. Aircraft Assn., 1994. Mem. AAUW, Nat. Bus. Aircraft Assn. (chmn. conf. 1975, 85, 87, 90, 94), Flight Safety Found. (chmn. corp. seminar), Profl. Aircraft Maint. Assn., Bus. and Profl. Women's Club, Kent State Alumni Assn. (bd. dirs. 1976-82), Order of Rainbow (grand coord. 1973-84), Psi Chi. Republican. Episcopalian. Office: Aviation Pers Internat PO Box 6846 New Orleans LA 70174-6846

BAREFOOT, CONSTANCE MAUREEN, special education educator; b. Phila., June 11, 1950; d. Harold John and Berniece Catherine (Quirin) Kaufmann; m. Richard O'Malley, Aug. 17, 1974 (div. 1991); m. Robert Barefoot, July 10, 1993; stepchildren: Sharon, Douglas. BS, Pa. State U., University Park, 1971; Masters equivalency, Pa. State U., King of Prussia, 1974; MEd, U. Houston, 1986. Cert. tchr., Tex., Pa., N.Y.; cert. ednl. diagnostician, Tex. Tchr. spl. edn. George Crothers Meml. Sch., Wallingford, Pa., 1973-78, Chemung County ARC, Elmira, N.Y., 1979-80; resource rm. tchr. Horseheads (N.Y.) Cen. Sch. Dist., 1980-81; tchr. spl. edn. Ft. Bend Ind. Sch. Dist., Sugar Land, Tex., 1981-87; learning support tchr. Sch. Dist. City of York, Pa., 1987—; mem. Lincoln Intermediate Unit # 12 In-Svc. Coun., New Oxford, Pa., 1989—. Mem. NEA, Pa. State Edn. Assn., York City Edn. Assn., Coun. Exceptional Children. Office: William Penn Sr High Sch 101 W College Ave York PA 17403-5497

BAREFOOT, LINDA, pharmaceutical company manager; b. Pensacola, Fla., Jan. 10, 1953; d. Paul and Emma Louise (Barnard) B. AA, Jacksonville (Fla.) C.C., 1973; student, Fla. Atlantic U., 1976; BS summa cum laude, U. North Fla., 1981. Med. staff asst. Shands Tchg. Hosp., U. Fla., Gainesville, 1974-76; med. asst. Edwin A. Sapp, MD, Jacksonville, Fla., 1976-81; hosp. sales specialist Eli Lilly & Co., Jacksonville and Gainesville, Fla., 1981-85, Am. Critical Care, Jacksonville and Gainesville, Fla., 1985-86; hosp. sales rep. specialist DuPont Merck Pharm. Co., Jacksonville and Gainesville, Fla., 1986-90; clin. liaison in clin. devel. and edn. DuPont Merck Pharm. Co., Fla., Ga., N.C., S.C., 1990-92; dist. sales mgr. DuPont Merck Pharm. Co., Knoxville, 1992-94; govt. affairs mgr. DuPont Merck Pharm. Co., Farmington, Conn., 1994—; lobbyist for med. industry; mem. health-care reform coms. Singer in choir Congl. Ch. of Christ. Home and Office: 17 Great Oak Ln Farmington CT 06032

BARENT, BARBARA ANN, elementary education educator; b. Benkelman, Nebr., Dec. 28, 1946; d. Guy Royal and Nellie Melba (Ham) Fries; m. Wayne L. Barent, Apr. 4, 1980; children: DeWayne, Dean, Dan. BA, U. Nebr., 1969; M in Elem. Edn., U. Nebr., Kearney, 1993. Cert. elem., gifted/talented tchr., Nebr. Adult basic edn. tchr. Mid Plains Community Coll., North Platte, Nebr.; tchr. grade 4 Ogallala (Nebr.) pub. schs.; mem. curriculum coord. coun., com. tech. Mem. PTA, Sandhill Reading Coun. Mem. NEA, ASCD, Internat. Reading Assn., Nebr. State Edn. Assn., Ogallala Edn. Assn., Nat. Coun. Social Studies, Nebr. Assn. Gifted. Home: RR 1 Box 257 Ogallala NE 69153-9735

BARFIELD, SARA REBECCA, telecommunications company executive; b. Fayetteville, N.C., Mar. 27, 1949; d. Jennings Lafate and Pauline (Stubbs) B. BA in Polit. Sci., U. N.C., 1972; MBA, So. Ill. U., 1978. Lectr. U. Md., Wiesbaden, Fed. Republic Germany, 1976-78; product mgr. Mobile Chem. Co., Rochester, N.Y., 1978-80; sr. sales rep. Coradian Corp., Syracuse, N.Y., 1980-81; dist. mgr. U.S. Sprint, Boston, 1981-83, Charlotte, N.C., 1983-85; region mktg. mgr. U.S. Sprint, Atlanta, 1985-86, div. mgr., maj. account sales, 1986—; lectr. Powelson Bus. Inst., Syracuse, 1980-81. Vol. Cerebral Palsy Sch., Greensboro, N.C., 1972, Atlanta Humane Soc., 1986-87, St. Joseph's Hosp., Atlanta, 1986-87. Served to capt. U.S. Army, 1973-76. Mem. Women in Telecommunications. Home: 7086 Stonington Dr NE Atlanta GA 30328-1963 Office: 2496 Jett Ferry Rd Atlanta GA 30338-3040

BARG, ROBERTA, artist, gallery owner; b. Stanwood, Iowa, Apr. 30, 1931; d. Henry Carl and Augusta E. (Willert) Portewig; m. Truman John Kadlec, Aug. 12, 1955 (dec. 1965); children: Connie Lea, Kristin Kay. Student, Coe Coll., Cedar Rapids, Iowa, 1949-51. Artist Craemer's, Cedar Rapids, 1951-56; artist/art dir. Ettinger Advt., Cedar Rapids, 1956-60; free-lance artist Cedar Rapids, 1960-70; artist/owner Gallery North, Eagle River, Wis., 1981-85, Barg's Art and Framing, Eagle River, Wis., 1985—. Commd. artist 50th Anniversary Commemorative print-Trees for Tomorrow, 1994; works exhibited in alumni exhbn. Coe Coll., Cedar Rapids, Iowa, 1994; etched glass designer Dahlman Wood Products, Cromwell, Minn. Named Artist of the Yr. Northwoods Wildlife Ctr., Minoqua, Wis., 1989, Ruffed Grouse Soc., 1990, Wis. Wildlife Fedn., 1992. Fellow Sigurd Olson Inst. Lutheran. Home and Office: Barg's Art and Framing 2825 Camp 12 Rd Eagle River WI 54521-9736

BARGER, KAREN SMITH, auditor; b. Elberton, Ga., Sept. 4, 1959; d. Johnny Charles and Beatrice Rosa (Jameson) Slocum; m. Mark Wood Smith, Sept. 1, 1979 (div. Jan. 1985); 1 child, Jonathan Charles Smith; m. Michael Cranfill Barger, Dec. 31, 1992. BBA, U. Ga., 1981. CPA, Ga. Part-time acct. So. Laundry and Dry Cleaners, Swainsboro, Ga., 1984-86; acct. P.O. Youmans, Jr., CPA, Swainsboro, 1985-86, Rayle Tech, Inc., Bogart, Ga., 1986-87, U. Ga. Law Sch. Libr., Athens, 1987; auditor I Internal Auditing divsn. U. Ga., Athens, 1987-92, auditor II, 1992—. Mem. Ga. Soc. CPAs, Golden Key, Phi Kappa Phi, Beta Alpha Psi. Republican. Baptist. Office: Univ Ga Divsn Intrnl Audit 312 Academic Bldg Athens GA 30602

BARGER, ROSEMARY WRIGHT, accountant; b. Troy, N.Y., July 26, 1944; d. S. Kenneth and Lena Florence (Cobb) Wright; m. Edward Albert Bourgeois, Aug. 22, 1964 (dec. Feb. 1973); children: Matthew, Anne; m. Raymond Harold Barger, May 2, 1992. BS, Russell Sage Coll., 1977. CPA, N.Y. Staff acct. Urbach Kahn Werlin, Albany, N.Y., 1977-81; acctg. analyst Cluett Peabody, Troy, 1981-86; dir. budget and cost St. Peter's Hosp., Albany, 1986—. Mem. Inst. Mgmt. Accts., N.Y. State Soc. CPAs, Nat. Assn. Accts. (past pres. Albany chpt. 1988-89). Republican. Roman Catholic.

BARHAM, PATTE (MRS. HARRIS PETER BOYNE), publisher, author, columnist; b. L.A.; d. Frank Barham and Princess Jessica Meskhi Gleboff; student U. So. Calif., U. Ariz.; LittD, Trinity So. Bible Coll.; hon. doctorate, Cambridge, Eng., D Internat. Arts, Sci. and Cable TV. War corr., Korea; syndicated columnist; acting sec. of state, State of Calif., 1980-81; Life mem. AAU, former v.p. pub. rels.; active House Ear Inst.; internat. com. L.A. Philharmonic. Author: Pin up Poems; Rasputin: The Man Behind the Myth,

1977; Peasant to Palace: Rasputin's Cookbook, 1990; Marilyn: The Last Take, 1992. Decorated dame Sovereign Order of Alfred the Great, grand cross, patron of honor; campagnon de la Couronne d'Epines, Ancienne Abbaye-Principaute de San Luigi. Mem. DAR, Outrigger Canoe, Waikiki Yacht (Hawaii); Wilshire Country, Ebell, Balboa Bay; Met. (N.Y.C.); Tokyo Corrs, Delta Gamma. Address: 100 Fremont Pl Los Angeles CA 90005-3867

BARIL, NANCY ANN, gerontological nurse practitioner, consultant; b. Paterson, N.J., May 10, 1952; d. Kenneth Gerald and Jeanette Elenore (Girodet) Keiser; m. Joel Mark Baril, Apr. 15, 1984; children: Jason Kenneth, Jennifer Jean. AA, Gulf Coast Community Coll., 1976; BS in Nursing, Fla. State U., 1978; M in Nursing, UCLA, 1983. Registered pub. health nurse, Calif.; ANA cert. gerontol. nurse practitioner. Charge nurse, nurse preceptor Cedar Sinai Med. Ctr., L.A., 1979-83; RN Nursing Svcs. Incorp., Sherman Oaks, Calif., 1980-83; nurse practitioner Santa Monica Peer Counseling Ctr., Santa Monica, Calif., 1983; nurse cons., gerontol. nurse practioner Summit Health Ltd., Burbank, Calif., 1983-85; nurse cons. Geriatric Assocs., Granada Hills, Calif., 1983-85; nurse cons., gerontol. nurse practitioner Care Enterprises West, Burbank, 1985-86; patient svcs. coord., gerontol. nurse practitioner ARA Living Ctrs., Glendale, Calif., 1986-87; DON, gerontol. nurse practitioner Astoria Convalescent Hosp. Sign of the Dove, Sylmar, Calif., 1988-91; gerontol. nurse practitioner with Dr. Gary Proffett, 1991—. Mem. PTA, Granada Hills, 1985. Mem. ANA, Calif. Coalition of Nurse Practioners, Calif. Nursing Assn., Gerontol. Soc., Sigma Theta Tau (rec. sec. 1983-85). Democrat. Episcopalian. Avocations: reading, crossword puzzles, gardening, jet-skiing. Home: 17831 Tuscan Dr Granada Hills CA 91344 Office: Dr Gary Proffett 10605 Balboa Blvd Ste 200 Granada Hills CA 91344

BARIO, PATRICIA YAROCH, public relations executive; b. Kinde, Mich., Aug. 12, 1932; d. Edmund T. and Marie L. (Meagher) Yaroch; widowed; children: Gianfranco Edmundo and Marco Alessandro. BA in Journalism, Mich. State U., 1954. Reporter The Detroit Free Press, 1954-55; reporter, editor The Detroit News, 1955-61; dir. comm. Senator Philip Hart, Washington, 1963-76; dep. press sec. Pres. Jimmy Carter, Washington, 1977-81; pres., owner Patricia Bario Assocs., Washington, 1981-83; v.p. Burson Marsteller, Washington, 1983-85; pres., owner Patricia Bario Assocs., Washington, 1985—. Recipient Writing award AP, 1952; named Outstanding Citizen, Mich. State U., East Lansing, 1980; winner Silver Anvil Pub. Rels Soc. Am., 1989, 91. Mem. Bus. for Social Responsibility, Bacchus. Democrat. Roman Catholic. Office: 512 11th St SE Washington DC 20003-2830

BARKER, BARBARA, real estate professional; b. Pulaski, Tenn., July 18, 1938; d. Dan and Anna (Butler) Ingram; m. Emmet Barker, Nov. 25, 1960; children: Melanie, Lynn, Harvey, Dan. BS, U. Tenn., 1960. Home economist Knoxville (Tenn.) Utilities Bd.; tchr. Arlington High Sch., Arlington Heights, Ill.; pres. Barbara Barker and Assocs., Brownsville, Tenn., Deerfield (Ill.) Ptnrs.; also owner, mgr. Re/Max Deerfield; broker, assoc. Re/Max Premier Properties, Lake Forest, Ill. Exec. bd., treas. Arden Shore Sch.; elder Presbyn. Ch. Mem. Nat. Assn. Realtors, Ill. Assn. Realtors, Women's Coun. Realtors (pres.-elect 1993-94, exec. bd.), North Shore Bd. Realtors, Tenn. Home Econs. Assn. (v.p.). Home: 1050 Meadowbrook Ln Deerfield IL 60015-3459 Office: 990 S Waukegan Rd Lake Forest IL 60045

BARKER, BARBARA ANN, ophthalmologist; b. Paterson, N.J., Nov. 10, 1943; d. Earle Louis and Dorothy Louise (Williamson) Barker; m. Joel Ira Papernik, July 28, 1972. BA, Conn. Coll., 1965; BS, Yale U., 1967; MA, Rutgers Med. Sch., 1974; MD, Mt. Sinai Sch. Medicine, 1976. Diplomate Am. Bd. Ophthalmology. Intern, Beth Israel Med. Center, 1977; resident Mt. Sinai Sch. Medicine/Beth Israel Med. Center, 1980, fellow in glaucoma, 1980-81, fellow cornea, refractive surgery, 1981-82, now mem. staff; rsch. technician The Rockefeller U., N.Y.C., 1965-66; tchr. Riverdale Country Sch., N.Y.C., 1967-68; rsch. asst. Sloan Kettering Inst., N.Y.C., 1969-72; assoc. clin. prof. Mt. Sinai Sch. Medicine, N.Y.C., 1982—; pvt. practice medicine specializing in ophthalmology, N.Y.C., 1983—; mem. staff N.Y. Eye and Ear Hosp., Cabrini Hosp. Recipient Resident Paper award Beth Israel Med. Center, 1980; Beth Israel Research grantee, 1983; NSF grantee, 1966. Mem. Internat. Soc. Refractive Keratoplasty, AMA, Am. Med. Women's Assn., Women's Med. Soc. N.Y.C., N.Y. County Med. Assn. (mem. com.), Phi Beta Kappa. Home and Office: 11 E 86th St New York NY 10028

BARKER, CELESTE ARLETTE, computer scientist; b. Redding, Calif., Apr. 19, 1947; d. Edwin William Squires and Rachel (Kinkead) Layton; m. Julius Jeep Chernak, Sept. 13, 1970, (div. 1980); children: Sean Matthew, Bret Allen; m. Jackson Lynn Barker, Oct. 8, 1988. BA in Art, San Francisco State U., 1970; AA in Engring. Tech., Coll. Marin, 1980; MBA in Mgmt., Golden Gate U., 1988. Cert. netware engr. Art tchr. San Rafael (Calif.) Schs., 1971-75; owner, photographer Julius Chernak Photography, Novato, Calif., 1970-76; draftsman Donald Foster Drafting, San Rafael, 1975-76; surveyor Parks Dept. State Calif., Inverness, 1976; electric draftsman Pacific Gas & Electric, San Rafael, 1976-78, electric engring. estimator, 1978-79; mktg. rep. Pacific Gas & Electric, Santa Rosa, 1980-85; valuation analyst Pacific Gas & Electric, San Francisco, 1985-86, budget analyst, 1986-88, budget system project mgr., 1988-89; fin. asset mgr. Pacific Gas & Electric, Vallejo, Calif., 1989-90; ops. mgr. San Francisco Mus. Modern Art, 1990-91; cons. CB Cons., Atlanta, 1991-93; computer local area network mgr. Ga. Inst. Tech., Atlanta, 1993-94; systems integrator Bank South, Atlanta, 1994—. Dir. Mariner Green Townhomes Assn., treas. 1987-88. Mem. Network Profls. Assn., Sierra Club. Home: 6261 Indian River Dr Norcross GA 30092

BARKER, CHERYL RAE, occupational health nurse; b. Fayetteville, Ark., June 2, 1958; d. Ronald Louis and Sharlene Vianna (Holland) Sachs; m. James Douglas Knauls, Apr. 4, 1980 (div. Aug. 1986); children: Jamila, Kecia, Tara; m. Donald Phoenix Barker, Nov. 28, 1988; 1 child, Dontrell Phoenix. Degree in nursing, Ark. Valley Tech. Sch., 1987; postgrad., North Ark. C.C. Sec. unit W.O. Boswell Hosp., Sun City, Ariz., 1982-84; LPN St. Edward's Mercy Med. Ctr., Ft. Smith, Ark., 1986-88; LPN, supr. nursing Georges, Springdale, Ark., 1988-89; LPN, coord. worker's compensation Tyson Entree, Fayetteville, Ark., 1989—; instr. CPR, First Aid ARC, Fayetteville, Ark., 1990-94. Active PTA. Mem. Occupational Health Nurse Coun. Baptist. Home: 3003 Skillern Ave Fayetteville AR 72703 Office: Tyson Entree 2615 S School Fayetteville AR 76701

BARKER, EVELYN JANICE, retired elementary education educator; b. Alliance, Ohio, Aug. 17, 1927; d. Harry Elwood and Margaret Marie (Cook) Shuster; m. Lloyd Edward Barker, June 26, 1949; 1 child, Janice Lynn. BA, Mt. Union Coll., 1949; MS in Edn., Westminster Coll., 1952. 7th-9th grade English tchr., 9th grade Biology tchr. New Waterford H.S., Columbiana County, Ohio, 1948-49; 4th, 5th and 6th grade tchr. North Georgetown Sch., Columbiana County, 1949-51; 4th grade tchr. Valley Sch., Columbiana County, Ohio, 1951-52; 4th grade tchr. West Br. Sch. Dist., Beloit, Ohio, 1952-87, sch. bd. mem., 1988-91. Bd. dirs. Sebring br. YMCA, Alliance, 1957-58, Disciples of Christ Ch., 1987-94; vol. Friends of Rodman Libr., Alliance, 1986-94; fashion show chmn. Alliance Sr. Citizen's Ctr., 1992-94; patron Carnation City Players, Alliance, 1993—, Alliance Cmty. Concert, 1993—. Mem. AAUW (Alliance br., charter mem., bd. dirs. 1956-60, 70-94, 2nd v.p. 1957-60, treas. 1969-76, pres. 1981-83, corr. sec. 1985—, 1st v.p. 1993-95), NEA Ret. (life), Ohio Edn. Assn. Ret. (Builder Plaque award 1964), Ohio Ret. Tchrs. Assn. (life), Alliance Area Ret. Tchrs. Assn. (pres. 1990-91), N.Am. Benefit Assn., Alliance Christian Women's Club, Mt. Union Coll. Women's Club, Ch. Women United, Beta Sigma Phi (Girl of Yr. 1958-59, 63-64, Order of Rose 1972, Silver Cir. 1981), Phi Delta Kappa (charter mem., Carnation N.E. Ohio chpt.). Home: 22392 Buck Rd Alliance OH 44601

BARKER, JEANNE WILSON, principal, computer educational consultant; b. Columbus, Ohio, Mar. 10, 1939; d. Robert Sydney and Marjorie Helen (McQuillen) Wilson; m. Larry L. Barker, June 11, 1961 (div. June 1974); children: Theodore Allen, Robert Milford. BS in Edn., Ohio U., 1960, MS, 1963. Cert. edn. specialist, Fla. Music tchr. Newark (Ohio) City Schs., 1960-61; elem. tchr. Logan (Ohio) City Schs., 1962-63, aast. prin. East Elem. Sch., 1963-65; supervising tchr. Ohio U., Logan, 1964-65; dir. R&D Dept. Grant, State of Fla., Tallahassee, 1972-74; pre-sch. tchr. Temple Israel, Tallahassee, 1974-75; elem. tchr. Maclay Sch., Tallahassee, 1975-79, prin., 1980—; dir. Fla. Microcomputer project Fla. State U., Tallahassee, 1983-86, adj. instr., 1988—; computer cons. Jefferson/Wakulla County Schs., 1985—. Contbr. articles to profl. jours.; presenter in field. DeWitt Hooker fellow Fla. Coun. Ind. Schs., Tampa, 1987. Mem. Internat. Reading Assn., Alpha Delta Kappa. Democrat. Methodist. Office: Maclay Sch 3737 N Meridian Rd Tallahassee FL 32312-1199

BARKER, JUDY, foundation executive; b. Burlington, N.C., Feb. 5, 1941; d. Thelma Ferguson; children: Lesa, Lori. Student, Ohio State U., Franklin U.; HHD, Xavier U., 1986. Administrv. asst. Children's Hosp., Columbus, Ohio, 1963-68, Mount Carmel Hosps., Inc., Columbus, 1969-72; administr. Borden Found., Borden, Inc., Columbus, 1973-75, exec. dir., 1975-83, dir. civic affairs, 1977-79, pres., 1983—, v.p. social responsibility, 1979—; Bd. dirs. Ohio State U. Hosps.; mem. Columbus Commn. on Ethics and Values; mem. adv. bd. Ohio State U. Sch. Home Econs.; mem. found. ctr. adv. nat. Nat. Directory Corp. Giving; active N.Y. Contbns. Adv. Group; mem. corp. adv. bd. Philanthropic Adv. Svc.; bd. dirs. Coun. Better Bus. Bur. Found., Greater Columbus Art Coun.; mem. Afro.-Am. adv. bd. Columbus Mus. Art. Bd. dirs. Pub./Pvt. Ventures, Ohio State U. Hosps., Columbus Commn. on Ethics and Values; mem. Sch. Home Econs. adv. bd. Ohio State U.; mem found. ctr. adv. bd. nat. Directory Corporate Giving; active N.Y. Contributions Adv. Group; mem. corp. adv. com. Philanthropic Adv. Svc.; mem., bd. dirs. Coun. Better Bus. Bur. Founds., Greater Columbus Arts Coun.; mem. Afro-Am. adv. bd. Columbus Mus. of Art; bd. dirs Columbus Airport Authority. Recipient award to women achievers YWCA, 1982, 84, 91, named Woman of Yr. YMCA Columbus, Ohio; recipient cmty. svc. award United Negro Coll. Fund, 1981. Office: Borden Inc 180 E Broad St Columbus OH 43215-3707

BARKER, LISA ANN, aerospace engineer; b. Lompoc, Calif., Feb. 1, 1965; d. Robert Andrew and Donna Jean (Eden) B. BS in Aerospace, Purdue U., 1987. Aerospace engr. NASA Marshall Space Flight Ctr., Huntsville, Ala., 1987—. Mem. AIAA.

BARKER, NANCY GRAHAM, healthcare information systems provider; b. Pittsfield, Mass., Mar. 14, 1961; d. Charles James and Marilyn Louise (LaFrance) Graham; m. Richard Brian Barker, Sept. 24, 1994. BA in Bus. Adminstrn., Rhodes Coll., Memphis, 1983. Project leader, sales rep. HBO & Co., San Mateo, Calif., 1983-86; sales dir. Peabody Group, San Francisco, 1986-87, Pacific Pub., Honolulu, 1987-88; acct. exec., sales rep., client svcs. mgr. Gerber Alley, Atlanta, 1988-93; acct. mgr. Cerner Corp., Atlanta, 1993—. Vol. pet therapy Atlanta Humane Soc., 1994—; elder Presbyn. Ch.

BARKER, NANCY LEPARD, university official; b. Owosso, Mich., Jan. 22, 1936; d. Cecil L. and Mary Elizabeth (Stuart) Lepard; m. J. Daniel Cline, June 6, 1956 (div. 1971); m. R. William Barker, Nov. 18, 1972; children—Mary Georgia, Mark Lepard, Richard Earl, Daniel Packard, Melissa Bess, John Charles, Helen Grace, Wiley David, James Glenn. BSc, U. Mich., Ann Arbor, 1957. Spl. edn. instr. Univ. Hosp. U. Mich., Ann Arbor, 1958-61; v.p. Med. Educator, Chgo., 1967-69; asst. to chmn., dir. careers for women Northwood U., Midland, Mich., 1970-77, asst. prof., chmn. dept. fashion mktg. and merchandising, 1972-77, v.p., 1978—; cons. and lectr. in field. Co-author: (children's books) Wendy Well Series, 1970-72; contbr. chpts. to books, articles to profl. jours. Advisor Mich. Child Study Assn., 1972—; chmn. Matrix: Midland Festival, 1978; bd. dirs. Nat. Coun. of Women, 1971—, pres., 1983-85, chmn. centennial com., 1988; bd. dirs. Concerned Citizens for the Arts, Mich., Family and Children's Svcs., Internat. Coun. Women, Paris. Recipient Hon. award Ukrainian Nat. Women's League, 1983, Disting. Woman award Northwood U., 1970, Outstanding Young Woman award Jr. C. of C., 1974; named one of Outstanding Young Women in U.S. and Mich., 1974; nominee (2) Mich. Women's Hall of Fame. Mem. Internat. Coun. Women (bd. dirs. Paris 1991—), The Fashion Group, Internat. Furnishings and Design Assn. (pres. Mich. chpt. 1974-77), Mich. Women's Studies Assn. (founding mem.), Midland Art Coun. (pres. 2 terms, 25th Anniversary award), Internat. Women's Forum, Mich. Women's Forum, Contemporary Rev. Club, Midland County Lawyers' Wives, Zonta, Phi Beta Kappa, Phi Kappa Phi, Alpha Lambda Delta, Phi Lambda Theta, Phi Gamma Nu, Delta Delta Delta. Republican. Episcopalian. Home: 209 Revere St Midland MI 48640-4255 Office: Northwood U Midland MI 48640-2398

BARKER, SARAH EVANS, judge; b. Mishawaka, Ind., June 10, 1943; d. James McCall and Sarah (Yarbrough) Evans; m. Kenneth R. Barker, Nov. 25, 1972. BS, Ind. U., 1965; JD, Am. U., 1969; LLD (hon.) U. Indpls., 1984; Doctor Pub. Svc. (hon.) Butler U., 1987; LLD (hon.) Marian Coll., 1991; LHD U. Evansville, 1993. Bar: Ind., 1969, U.S. Dist. Ct. (so. dist.) Ind., 1970, U.S. Ct. Appeals (7th cir.), 1973, U.S. Supreme Ct., 1978. Legal asst. to senator U.S. Senate, 1969-71, spl. counsel to minority, govt. ops. com., permanent investigations subcom., 1971-72; dir. rsch., scheduling and advance Senator Percy Re-election Campaign, 1972; asst. U.S. atty. So. Dist. Ind., 1972-76, 1st asst. U.S. atty., 1976-77, U.S. atty., 1981-84; judge U.S. Dist. Ct. (so. dist.) Ind., 1984-94, chief judge, 1994—; assoc., then ptnr. Bose, McKinney & Evans, Indpls., 1977-81; mem. long range planning com. Jud. Conf. U.S., 1991—, exec. com., standing com. fed. rules of practice and procedure, dist. judge rep., 1988-91; mem. jud. coun. 7th cir. Ct. Appeals, jud. fellows commn. U.S. Supreme Ct.; bd. advisors, Ind. U., Bloomington and Indpls., Valparaiso Law Sch.; bd. visitors Ind. U. Sch. of Law, Bloomington. Mem. Ind. Hist. Soc., Conner Prairie Bd. Dirs.; bd. dirs. Meth. Hosp. Ind.; bd. govs. Ind. Fiscal Policy Inst. Recipient Peck award Wabash Coll., 1989, Touchstone award Girls Club of Greater Indpls., 1989, Leach Centennial 1st Woman award Valparaiso Law Sch., 1993; named Ind. Woman of Yr., Women in Comm., 1986. Mem. ABA, Ind. Bar Assn., Indpls. Bar Assn. (Antoinette Dakin Leach award 1993), Fed. Judges Assn., Nat. Assn. Former U.S. Attys., Am. Judicature Soc. (bd. dirs.), Lawyers Club, Kiwanis. Republican. Methodist. Office: US Dist Ct 210 US Courthouse 46 E Ohio St Indianapolis IN 46204-1903*

BARKER, SHARON ELIZABETH, university administrator; b. Perth, N.B., Can., July 29, 1949; arrived in U.S.A., 1957; d. Floyd Peterson and Greta Velma (Howlett) B.; 1 child, Adam Barker-Hoyt. BA, U. Maine, 1971, MPA, 1987. Coord. program ops. Penquis Family Planning, Bangor, Maine, 1974-84; staff assoc. women in curriculum program U. Maine, Orono, 1990-91, dir. Women's Resource Ctr., 1991—; cons. Maine Health Info. Ctr., Augusta, 1987-91, Dept. Environ. Protection, Augusta, 1988. Bd. dirs. Greater Bangor (Maine) Rape Crisis Ctr., 1983-85, Mabel Wadsworth Women's Health Ctr., Bangor, 1984-94, former pres., Good Samaritan Agy., Bangor, 1986-92, former pres., Maine Women's Fund, Portland, Maine, 1991—; vice chair Ea. Regional Commn. for Women, Bangor, 1987-89. Mem. Pi Alpha Alpha, Pi Sigma Alpha. Office: U Maine 5728 Fernald Hall Orono ME 04469

BARKER, VIRGINIA LEE, nursing educator. Diploma, Ind. U. Sch. Nursing, 1952, BS, 1955, MS, 1961, EdD, 1969. Dean sch. nursing, prof. Alfred (N.Y.) U.; prof., dean nursing U. Louisville; dean Mary Black Sch. Nursing, prof. U. S.C., Spartanburg; dean profl. studies, prof. nursing SUNY, Plattsburg, 1990—; cons. N.Y. Regents Coll. Nursing Program, 1972-73; project dir. federally funded telenursing project for rural upstate N.Y., 1993—; project dir. for devel. of virtual reality teaching modules for Health Profls., 1994—. Contbr. articles to profl. jours. Mem. ARC. Recipient N.Y. State Nurses Assn. Soc. Disting. Practitioners Grants. Mem. ANA, N.Y. Nurses Assn., Nat. League for Nursing (com. mem.), S.C. League for Nursing, Am. Assn. Higher Edn., AAUW, Ind. U. Sch. Nursing Alumni Assn. (pres.), S.C. Deans and Dirs. Nursing Fedn. (chair), Sigma Theta Tau, Phi Kappa Phi, Kappa Delta Pi.

BARKETT, ROSEMARY, federal judge; b. Ciudad Victoria, Tamaulipas, Mex., Aug. 29, 1939; came to U.S., 1946, naturalized, 1958; BS summa cum laude, Spring Hill Coll., 1967; JD, U. Fla., 1970. Bar: Fla., U.S. Dist. Ct. (so. dist.) Fla., U.S. Ct. Appeals (5th cir.), U.S. Supreme Ct. Pvt. practice West Palm Beach, Fla., 1971-79; judge 15th Jud. Cir. Ct., Palm Beach County, Fla., 1979-84, 4th Dist. Ct. Appeal, West Palm Beach, Fla., 1984-85; assoc. justice Supreme Ct. Fla., Tallahassee, Fla., 1985-92, chief justice, 1992-94; judge U.S. Ct. of Appeals (11th cir.) Fla., Miami, 1994—; mem. faculty U. Nev., Reno, Fla. Jud. Coll. Mem. editorial bd. The Florida Judges Manual. Mem. vis. com. Miami U. Law Sch.; mem. bd. visitors St. Thomas U. Recipient Woman of Achievement award Palm Beach County Commn. on Status of Women, 1985; named to Fla. Women's Hall of Fame, 1986. Fellow Acad. Matrimonial Lawyers; mem. ABA, Fla. Bar Assn. (family law sect., chairperson ct. stats. and workload com. and study commn. on guardianship law, lectr. on matrimonial media and criminal law continuing legal edn.), Palm Beach County Bar Assn., Am. Acad. Matrimonial Lawyers (award 1984), Fla. Assn. Women Lawyers (Palm Beach chpt.), Nat. Assn. Women Judges, Palm Beach Marine Inst. (former chairperson, bd. trustees), Acad. Fla. Trial lawyers (Achievement award 1988), Assn. Trial Lawyers Am. (Achievement award 1986). Office: Rm 1262 99 NE 4th St Miami FL 33132*

BARKIN, ELLEN, actress; b. N.Y.C., Apr. 16, 1955; m. Gabriel Byrne, 1988; 1 son, Jack. Student, CUNY; grad., Hunter Coll. Ind. theatrical, film actress, 1980—. Theatrical prodns. include Shout Across the River, 1980, Killings on the Last Line, 1980, Extremities, 1982; appeared on TV soap Search for Tomorrow; TV films include Kent State, 1981, We're Fighting Back, 1981, Terrible Joe Moran starring James Cagney, 1984, Act of Vengence, 1986, Clinton and Nadine, 1988; film appearances include Diner, 1982, Daniel, 1983, Tender Mercies, 1983, Eddie and the Cruisers, 1983, The Adventures of Buckaroo Banzai, 1984, Harry and Son, 1984, Enormous Changes at the Last Minute, 1985, Down by Law, 1986, Desert Bloom, 1986, The Big Easy, 1987, Siesta, 1987, Made in Heaven, 1987, Sea of Love, 1989, Johnny Handsome, 1989, Switch, 1991, Man Trouble, 1992, Mac, 1993, This Boy's Life, 1993, Into the West, 1993, Bad Company, 1995. Office: 8787 Shoreham Dr Los Angeles CA 90069*

BARKMAN, ANNETTE SHAULIS, real estate management executive; b. Somerset, Pa., Oct. 18, 1948; d. Norman Albert and Janice Lorraine (Robbins) S.; m. Jon A. Barkman, Dec. 1, 1983; children: Caitlin Elizabeth, Meredith Elizabeth. BA, Dickinson Coll., 1969; MA, Indiana U. of Pa., 1975. Psychol. svcs. asso. II Bedford/Somerset Mental Health Clinic, Somerset, 1972-78, Somerset State Hosp., 1978-79; pvt. practice hypnosis cons., Somerset, 1976—; pres. Habitability, Inc., real estate mgmt., Somerset, 1978—; exec. mgr. Gt. N.E. Land & Cattle Co., Somerset, 1980-82; owner, mgr. Somerset Credit and Collection Bur., 1981—; realtor James F. Custer Real Estate, 1980-87; Barkman Realty Inc., 1988—; cons. Somerset County Headstart Program, 1977, 78; mem., bd. dirs. Children's Aid Soc. Somerset, 1986—. Squadron comdr. CAP, Somerset, 1977-78, recipient Meritorious Service award, 1977. Mem. Somerset Welfare League (pres. 1991), Chi Omega. Home: 388 High St Somerset PA 15501-1301 Office: 118 N Center Ave Somerset PA 15501-2027

BARKSDALE, STEPHANIE RUTH, small business owner; b. Danbury, Conn., June 22, 1966; d. Philip Lawrence and Elaine Virginia (Arrigoni) B. BA, U. Maine, Orono, 1988; postgrad., U. Hartford, 1991—. Intern Town of New Milford, Conn., 1987; owner, mgr. Letter Perfect, New Milford, 1988—; project dir. New Milford 2000 Inc., 1989—. Dir., past v.p. United Way, New Milford, 1991—; mem.-at-large Town Coun., New Milford, 1991—. Recipient Recognition award MADD, 1992. Mem. New Milford C. of C. (bd. dirs., past treas. 1990—, Disting. Chamber Mem. of Yr. 1992). Republican. Episcopalian. Home: 21 Frenchmans Rd New Milford CT 06776-4919 Office: Letter Perfect PO Box 1045 34A Main St New Milford CT 06776-2830

BARLEY, BARBARA ANN, accountant; b. Sewickley, Pa., June 19, 1954; d. William Stephen and Maude Adel (Wilt) B. BS in Math., BA in Bus. magna cum laude, Westminster Coll., 1976. CPA, Ohio, Wis. Staff acct. Price Waterhouse & Co., Pitts., 1976-78; internal auditor Federated Dept. Stores, Inc., Cin., 1978-79; gen. ledger mgr. Formica Corp., Cin., 1980-81; staff acct. Bethesda Hosp., Cin., 1981-82; acctg. mgr. Madison Area Assn. for Retarded Citizens Devel. Ctrs. Corp., Madison, Wis., 1982-88; dir. fin. Retardation Facilities Devel. Found., Inc., Madison, Wis., 1988—; treas. Integrated Community Work, Inc., Madison, 1989-90. Treas. Access to Community Services, Inc., 1988—; mem. Environ Def. Fund, 1986—; treas. Peace Project Inc., Madison, 1985—; coms. Wis. Nuclear Weapons Freeze Campaign, Madison, 1985-86, Madison nuclear free zone com., Madison, 1986. Mem. AICPA, ACLU, Wis. Inst. CPAs, Amnesty Internat., Sierra Club, Kappa Mu Epsilon, Omicron Delta Epsilon, Delta Sigma Rho-Tau Kappa Alpha, Omicron Delta Kappa. Unitarian. Home: 186 Dixon St Madison WI 53704-5816 Office: Retardation Facilities Devel Found Inc 2875 Fish Hatchery Rd Madison WI 53713-3120

BARLING, RENEE MEYERS, telecommunications executive; b. N.Y.C., Jan. 10, 1935; d. Abraham and Beatrice (Garb) Meyers; m. Frank Petrillo (div.); children: Marissa Pietschker, Stephanie Petrillo; m. Burton Edward Barling, May 30, 1967; children: Lesley A. Bretz, Bonnie Antonacci. BA, Hunter Coll., 1956; postgrad., Bklyn. Poly. Inst., 1982-83. Project mgr. Equitable Life, N.Y.C., 1978-82, div. mgr., 1982-84, dir. applied rsch., 1984-87; cons. N.Y.C., 1987-89, AGS Info., N.Y.C., 1989-91; mgr. ALLINK Network Mgmt. Co., White Plains, N.Y., 1991—; cons. Schwartz Assn., Mountainside, Calif., 1986—. Mem. IEEE, Soc. for Mgmt. Artificial Intelligence in Fin. Svcs. (advisor to exec. bd. 1986—), Westchester Microcomputer User Group (gov. 1983—), Am. Assn. for Artificial Intelligence. Home: 106 Havilands Ln White Plains NY 10605-3011 Office: AllINK Network Mgmt Co 4 Gannett Dr White Plains NY 10604-3408

BARLOON, BLANCHE EYNON, artist; b. Apr. 22, 1911; d. John Davies and Natalie (Eynon) Davies; m. Marvin Barloon (dec. Sept. 1, 1991); children: Anne, Peter. BS, Sweet Briar Coll., 1933; MS, Case Western Res. U., 1940; cert., Cleve. Inst. Art, 1965. Painter, 1961-94. Exhibited in group shows including Cleve. Mus. of Art, 1961, 63, 66, 67, 71, Nat. Drawing Show, Hartford, Conn., 1970, W.& J. Nat. Painting Show, Washington, Pa., Cleve., 1994 (Jury award).

BARLOTTA, FLORA MARIA, hematologist; b. Newark, Nov. 30, 1936; d. Frank and Lena Flora (Cangemi) B. AB, Coll. St. Elizabeth, 1958; MD, Seton Hall U., 1962. Diplomate Am. Bd. Internal Medicine, Am. Bd. Hematology. Chief hematology Jersey City Med. Ctr., 1968-71; clin. asst. medicine St. Vincent's Hosp., N.Y.C., 1968-74; assoc. attending physician hematology, asst. dir. medicine St. Barnabas Med. Ctr., Livingston, N.J., 1971-77, attending physician, chief hematology sect., 1977—; clin. instr. medicine U. Medicine and Dentistry N.J., Newark. Mem. Am. Soc. Hematology, Am. Soc. Internal Medicine, N.Y. Soc. Study of Blood. Office: Saint Barnabas Med Ctr 94 Old Short Hills Rd Livingston NJ 07039

BARLOW, NADINE GAIL, planetary geoscientist; b. La Jolla, Calif., Nov. 9, 1958; d. Nathan Dale and Marcella Isabel (Menken) B.; m. Michael Ewing Zolensky, Apr. 23, 1989. BS, U. Ariz., 1980, PhD, 1987. Instr., planetarium lectr. Palomar Coll., San Marcos, Calif., 1982; grad. rsch. asst. U. Ariz., Tucson, 1982-87; postdoctoral fellow Lunar and Planetary Inst., Houston, 1987-89; NRC assoc. NASA/Johnson Space Ctr., Houston, 1989-91, vis. scientist, 1991-92, support scientist exploration programs office, 1992; vis. scientist Lunar and Planetary Inst., Houston, 1992—; assoc. prof. U. Houston, Clear Lake, 1991—; co-dir. intern program Lunar and Planetary Inst., 1988-89. Editor (slide set) A Guide to Martian Impact Craters, 1988; assoc. editor Encyclopedia of Earth Sciences; contbr. articles to profl. jours. Named among Outstanding Women and Ethnic Minorities Engaged in Sci. and Engring., Lawrence Livermore Nat. Lab., 1991. Mem. AAUW (pres. Clear Lake chpt. 91-93, program v.p. 93—, v.p. interbr. coun. 90-91, chmn. Tex. task force on women and girls in sci. and math., 91-92, dir. state pub.

policy, 92-94, Tex. Woman of Yr. 1992 , mem. pub. policy com. 1994—, chmn. steering com. Tex. ednl. equity roundtable 91, Tex. task force on edn. equity, 1994—,), Am. Astron. Soc. (pres. officer div. planetary scis. 93—, mem. edn. com. divsn. for planetary scis. 93-96, status of women in astronomy com. 87-90), Am. Geophys. Union, Geol. So. Am., Assn. Women in Sci. (councilor 1994—), Assn. Women Geoscientists. Office: Lunar and Planetary Inst 3600 Bay Area Blvd Houston TX 77058-1113

BARMAN, SUSAN MARIE, physiologist; b. Joliet, Ill., Aug. 28, 1949; d. Vernon Rutherford and Shirley Marie (Shea) B. BS in Biology, Loyola U., Chgo., 1971; PhD in Physiology, Loyola U., 1976. From research assoc. to asst. prof. Mich. State U., East Lansing, 1975-84, assoc. prof., 1984-94, prof., 1994—; sci. cons. NIH, Bethesda, Md., 1981, 83—. Contbr. articles to profl. jours. NIH Heart Lung Blood Inst. grantee. Mem. Soc. for Neuroscience, American Physiological Soc., AAAS. Democrat. Roman Catholic. Office: Mich State U Dept Pharmacology East Lansing MI 48824

BARNARD, ANNETTE WILLIAMSON, elementary school educator; b. Phoenix, Nov. 29, 1948; d. Water Albert and Geraldine Williamson; m. Richard W. Heinrich, Sept. 1969 (div.); 1 child, Jennifer Anne; m. Charles Jay Barnard, June 6, 1981. AA, Mesa C.C., 1979; BA in Spl. Edn., Elem. Edn., Ariz. State U., 1981, postgrad., 1989—. Cert. tchr., Ariz. Tchr. spl. edn. Tempe (Ariz.) Sch. Dist., 1981-83, tchr. Indian community, 1983-84; tchr. elem. sch. Kyrene Sch. Dist., Tempe, 1984-86, 90—; tchr. Chandler (Ariz.) Sch. Dist., 1986-89; chair profl. stds. and cert. com. Ariz. Bd. Edn., Phoenix, 1990-94; chair facilitator Kyrene Legis. Action Community, 1991-94; mentor Kyrene Sch. Dist., 1990—; commencement spkr. Ariz. State U., 1981. Contbg. author: Environmental Education Compendium for Energy Resources, 1991, System of Personnel Development, 1989. Bd. dirs. Ariz. State Rep. Caucus, Phoenix, 1990-94, precinct committeewoman, Tempe, 1990-92. Recipient Profl. Leadership award Kiwanis Club Am., Tempe, 1984; nominee to talent bank Coun. on Women's Edn. Programs U.S. Dept. Edn., 1982; named Tchr. of Yr., local newspaper, 1993. Mem. ASCD, Kyrene Edn. Assn. (chair legis. com. 1990-94), Kappa Delta Pi, Phi Kappa Phi, Phi Theta Kappa, Pi Lambda Theta. Home: 3221 W Jasper Dr Chandler AZ 85226

BARNARD, CATHERINE ELAYNE, psychology educator; b. Battle Creek, Mich., May 12, 1959; d. Dale Emmett and Joyce Ann (Sullivan) Buys; m. William Arthur Barnard, June 20, 1981; children: William Brandon, Ashleigh Sullivan. BS, Western Mich. U., 1984, MA, 1993, postgrad. Lic. profl. counselor. Instr., educator Kellogg C.C., Battle Creek, Mich., 1985-90; tchr. Battle Creek Pub. Schs., 1991-92; psychology instr. Davenport Coll., Battle Creek, 1991—; pvt. practice counselor Battle Creek, 1994—; cons. Davenport Coll., Kalamazoo, 1992—. Mem. ACA, Am. Coll. Pers. Assn., Mich. Assn. for Counseling and Devel., Mich. Coll. Pers. Assn., Am. Psychol. Assn., Am. Sociol. Assn. Home: 85 W Hamilton Ln Battle Creek MI 49015-4025 Office: Davenport Coll 67 Michigan Ave W Battle Creek MI 49017-3630

BARNARD, SANDRA KAY, librarian; b. Redding, Calif., Mar. 8, 1941; d. Hartley Thompson and Edna Catherine (Enos) B. AA, Shasta Coll., Redding, 1963; AB, Calif. State U., Chico, 1966; MS in LS, U. So. Calif., 1973. Media coord. Bass Elem. Sch., Redding, 1977-78; children's libr. Shasta County Libr., Redding, 1979; reference libr. Shasta Info. Ctr., Redding, 1980; docent libr. Redding Mus. of Art and History, 1984-88; reference libr. Calif. State U., Chico, 1988-92; libr. cons. Redding Specialty Hosp., 1991; librarian Redding United Meth. Ch., 1975-79, libr. cons., 1991—. Mem. Shasta County Grand Jury, 1994-95. Mem. ALA, Calif. Libr. Assn., AAUW (yearbook editor Redding br. 1976, reader lit. festival 1985—, leader trailwalker sect. 1992-94), Shasta Ladies Encampment Aux. (chief matriarch 1989-91, dist. dep. grand matriarch 1993-94), Order Ea. Star, Rebekahs (nobel grand 1971, 87, Good Fellowship award 1976), Women of Moose. Republican. Home: 725 Parkview Ave Redding CA 96001-3319

BARNER, ANNABEL MONROE, pastoral counselor; b. Pitts., Nov. 30, 1925; d. Samuel North and Annabel (McKibben) Monroe; m. Charles Ray Barner, Aug. 14, 1948; children: Bruce Monroe, Craig McLean, Leslie Ann. BA, Ohio Wesleyan U., 1947; postgrad., Case Western Res. U., 1974-78; MA, Ashland Theol. Sem., 1979; MDiv (hon.), Pitts. Theol. Sem., 1984; postgrad., Gestalt Inst., 1988, Process Comm. Inst., 1992. Producing dir. WPGH and KDKA radio and TV stas., Pitts., 1943-47; comml. writer, traffic contr. Sta. WRFD and WMRN, Worthington and Marion, Ohio, 1947-50; tutor emotionally disturbed youth Rocky River (Ohio) Bd. Edn., 1967-83; pastoral counselor Rocky River Presbyn. Ch., 1972-82, Samaritan Counseling Ctr., Elyria, Ohio, 1983-88; chaplain Fairview (Ohio) Gen. Hosp., 1980-81; counselor-at-large Greater Cleve. Counseling Svc., Inter Ch. Coun., 1981—; instr. Ohio Wesleyan U., Delaware, 1947-50, teaching fellow, 1948-50; mem. steering com. West Side Extended Care Ctr., Cleve., 1978; field placement counselor emergency svcs. West Side Community Health, Cleve., 1978; psychol. counselor Welsh Home, Westlake, Ohio, 1980-82; pastoral counselor John Knox Presbyn. Ch., North Olmsted, Ohio, 1988—; trainer Kahler Comm., Little Rock, 1991. Author, editor explanations of laws and statutes, State of Miss., 1953-55; author radio scripts and documentaries, 1950; contbr. articles to profl. pubis. Media spokesperson Clergy for Choice, Lorain County, Ohio, 1990—, Friends of the Libr., Rocky River, 1972—; organizer Linden Sch., Lorain, 1988; mem. Open Door West, Cleve., 1990—. Gestalt Inst. scholar, 1985, 86. Mem. NOW, Nat. Trust for Historic Preservation, Am. Assn. Pastoral Counselors, Greenpeace, World Wildlife Fund, Habitat for Humanity, Sierra Club, Cleve. Art Mus., Spring Valley Country Club, Delta Gamma, Theta Alpha Phi. Home: 2694 Goldwood Dr Cleveland OH 44116-3013 Office: John Knox Presbyn Ch 25200 Lorain Rd North Olmsted OH 44070-2092

BARNES, ANNE CRAIG, state legislator; b. Gaston County, N.C., 1932; m. Billy Barnes; children: Billy Jr., Betsy. Mem. N.C. Ho. of Reps., 1982—; chairwoman correction com., 1985-86, vice chairwoman mfg. and labor com., mental health com.; former mem. agr. com., election laws com., health judiciary III com., local govt. I and state pers. com.; former mem. numerous coms. Precinct ofcl. Orange County Dem. Com., 1969-72, mem. exec. com., 1969-76, 1st vice chairwoman, 1972-74, chairwoman, 1974-76; del. N.C. State Dem. Conv., 1970-82, Dem. Nat. Mini Conv., 1974; mem. Orange County Bd. Commn., 1978-81; mem. staff Carter-Mondale Campaign, field rep., 1980. Recipient Legis. award N.C. Sentencing Alternatives Assn., 1989, N.C. Assn. Sch. Ofcl. Pers., 1990, Spl. award N.C. U., 1990, Gwyneth B. Davis award, N.C. Attys. Assn., 1990; named Legislator of Yr., N.C. Parks and Recreation Soc., 1989, N.C. Acad. Trial Lawyers, 1990. Mem. N.C. Inst. Polit. Leaders (bd. dirs.), N.C. Conf. for Social Svc. (bd. dirs.), N.C. Retail Mchts. Assn. (bd. dirs.). Home: 313 Severin St Chapel Hill NC 27516-1512 Office: NC Ho of Reps State Capital Raleigh NC 27611*

BARNES, BELINDA JEANETTE SPAIN, nursing administrator; b. Rome, Ga., Dec. 5; d. Oscar Joe and Eleanor (Camacho) Spain. Diploma, Ga. Bapt. Hosp. Sch. Nursing, Atlanta, 1974; BS in Nursing, Med. Coll. Ga., Augusta, 1976; MS in Nursing, Ga. State U., Atlanta, 1980, postgrad., 1990—. Cert. clin. specialist in med.-surg. nursing, intravenous nurse. Critical care flight nurse Critical Care Medflight, Inc., Atlanta, 1984-88; intravenous therapy coord. DeKalb Gen. Hosp., Atlanta, 1974-81; asst. prof. Mercer U., Atlanta, 1981-87; corp. dir. infusion/high tech. svcs. Kimberly Quality Care, Atlanta, 1988-92; cons. Profl. Learning Systems, 1992—; asst. prof. Clayton State Coll., Morrow, Ga., 1992-94, Ga. Bapt. Coll. Nursing, Atlanta, 1994—. Mem. Intravenous Nurses Soc. (rsch. com.), Am. Nurses Assn., Am. Soc. Parenteral and Enteral Nutrition, Oncology Nurses Soc., Ga. Nurses Assn. Home: 5979 Eton Ct Norcross GA 30071-2030

BARNES, BETTY RAE, counselor; b. Wichita, Kans., June 24, 1932; d. Henry Charles and Vivian Augusta (Lamberth) Archer; m. Orland Eugene Barnes, Mar. 18, 1953; children: Terry Lee, Steven Gregory. BA, Our Lady of the Lake, San Antonio, 1986, MS in Counseling Psychology, 1989. Cert. profl. sec., lic. profl. counselor; lic. marriage and family therapist. Adminstrv. asst. S.W. Rsch. Inst., San Antonio, 1975—; counselor Community Clinic, Inc., San Antonio, 1989—, counseling coord., 1991—; counselor Community Counseling Ctr., Our Lady of the Lake U., San Antonio, 1989-91. Recipient Outstanding Achievement award Sch. Bus. and Pub. Adminstrn., Our Lady of the Lake U., 1984. Mem. Am. Assn. Marriage and Family Therapists, Tex. Counseling Assn., Internat. Assn. for Addictions and Offender Counselors, San Antonio Mus. Assn., Delta Mu Delta. Office: Community Clinic Inc 210 W Olmos Dr San Antonio TX 78212-1956

BARNES, BOBBE MORSE, accounting educator; b. Long Beach, Calif., May 10, 1945; d. Robert Stuart and Nona Irene (Deckert) Morse; m. Thomas G. Barnes III, Sept. 1, 1966 (div. 1980); children: Jeffrey, Eric. AB, U. Rochester, 1968; MPA, U. Tex., 1976. CPA Tex., Colo.; CMA. Acct. Price Waterhouse and Co., Toronto, Can., 1968-70; faculty U. Tex., Austin, 1973-87; editorial v.p. MicroMash, Denver, 1987-91; pres. Editorial Svcs. Inc., Denver, 1991—; faculty U. Colo., Denver, 1989—; faculty Econs. Inst. affiliated U. Colo., Boulder, 1994—; instr. Am. Assoc. Coll. Sch. of Bus. Seminars, Austin, 1986-88. Author: The Shoebox, 1986, The Shoebox Inc., 1987, Study Guide, Managerial Account, 1989, 1990; author (software text) Ethics, 1988; editor in chief Conviser Duffy CPA Review, 1991—; editor: CPA Review Reference, 1990, 91. Cons. Gov. Clements Election Com., Austin, 1982; pres. Heritage High Sch. PTO, Littleton, Colo., 1989-90; participant Leadership Austin, 1987; bd. dirs., coach N.W. YMCA Soccer Coun., Austin, 1985-87. Mem. Inst. Mgmt. Accts. (pres. 1986-87, nat. bd. 1990—, Rocky Mountain coun. pres.-elect 1992-93, pres. 1993-94), Colo. Soc. CPAs (various coms. 1988-92), Tex. Soc. CPAs (various coms. 1986-92), Am. Acctg. Assn., Cherry Creek Lightning Soccer Assn. (treas. 1990-92), Beta Alpha Psi (Outstanding Faculty v.p. 1984, Theta chpt. Acct. of Yr. 1987), Alpha Kappa Psi (Outstanding Prof. 1986). Republican. Episcopalian. Office: Econs Inst 1005 12th St Boulder CO 80302

BARNES, CATHY LEE, special education educator; b. Chattanooga, Mar. 10, 1993; d. William Karl and Nancy Lee (Gerrard) B. BS, U. Tenn., Chattanooga, 1987, MS, 1994. Asst. tchr. Orange Grove Ctr. of Mental Retardation, Chattanooga, 1984-93; community counseling intern Bradley/Cleve. Devel. Ctr., Cleveland, Tenn., 1994—. Vol. Very Spl. Arts Festival, Chattanooga, 1989—, Spl. Olympics, Chattanooga, 1986—. Mem. Mental Health Assn. of Greater Chattanooga. Home: 3314 Idlewild Cir Ste A Chattanooga TN 37411-4135 Office: Bradley/Cleve Devel Ctr 764 Old Chattanooga Pike SW Cleveland TN 37311-8517

BARNES, CONSTANCE INGALLS (MRS. RUSSELL C. BARNES), retired librarian; b. Atchison, Kans., July 30, 1903; d. Sheffield and Lucy (Van Hoesen) Ingalls; B.A., U. Kans., 1925; M.A., U. Mich., 1950, M.A. in L.S., 1955; postgrad. Ecole du Louvre, France, 1960, Vergilian Soc., Cumae, Italy, summer 1963; m. Russell C. Barnes, Oct. 1, 1927; children: Lucie-Jeanne (Mrs. Todd Seymour), John J.I. Librarian, Cranbrook Acad. Art, Bloomfield Hills, Mich., 1955-74, 80-81. Mem. LWV, AAUW, Internat. Arthurian Soc., Alliance Francaise, Founders Soc. Detroit Inst. Arts, Village Woman's Club (Bloomfield Hills), Kappa Alpha Theta. Home: Canterbury-On-The-Lake 5601 Hatchery Rd Waterford MI 48329

BARNES, CORINNE ANN, pediatric nurse, educator; b. Greenock Heights, Pa., July 3, 1928; d. George Julius and Elizabeth Sarah (Smythe) Meerhoff. RN, Allegheny Gen. Hosp., Pitts., 1949; BS in Nursing., U. Pitts., 1960, M of Nuring Edn., 1963, PhD in Nursing, 1974. Pediatric nurse adminstr. Allegheny Gen. Hosp., 1950-58; pediatric nurse specialist Children's Hosp. and U. Pitts., 1966-70; undergrad. tchr. U. Pitts., 1965—, chmn. pediatric dept., 1970-78, program dir. grad. programs in nursing care of children, 1978-92, dir. doctoral program, 1988-92; cons. Editor Maternal-Child Nursing Jour., 1978-94; mem. editorial bd. Jour. Am. Assn. Child Health, 1981-88. Mem. adv. com. Bright Beginnings; pres. Pitts. Women's Tennis Orgn., 1957-88; Recipient Disting. Alumnus award U. Pitts. Sch. Nursing, 1982, 86, Recruitment award Coun. Nurse Researchers, 1982; nursing grantee; named Disting. Dau. of Pa. Gov. of. Pa., 1984. Fellow Am. Acad. Nursing (recipient Kids Need Heroes award 1991); mem. Am. Nurses Assn., Pa. Nurses Assn., Allegheny Gen. Nurses Alumnae (pres. 1952), U. Pitts. Alumnae Assn., Am. Assn. Pub. Health, Assn. Child Care in Health, Soc. Research in Child Devel., Council Nurse Researchers, Pitts. Tennis Assn., Fox Chapel Racquet Club, Univ. Faculty Club, Zonta Internat. (pres. Pitts. chpt. 1989-91, treas. 1985-87), Sigma Theta Tau (pres.-elect 1992-93, 94-95, pres. 1993-94, 95—). Republican. Methodist Episcopalian. Office: 3500 Victoria Hall Sch Nursing Pittsburgh PA 15261

BARNES, CYNTHIA LYNN, lawyer; b. Wilmington, Ohio, Mar. 5, 1954; d. Robert Daisley and Sue Ann (Florence) B.; m. David Chazin, June 14, 1981; children: Lillian, Hannah, Rebecca. BA in Psychology cum laude, Colo. Women's Coll., 1977; JD, U. Denver, 1985. Bar: Colo. 1985, Ill. 1991. Counseling supr. Women in Crisis, Lakewood, Colo., 1979-81; assoc. McKendree Toll & Mares, Denver, 1985-87; legal editor, contract editor Shepard's McGraw Hill, Matthew Bender Inc., Lawyers' Coop., 1987-92; pvt. practice lawyer Cynthia Barnes, Atty. at Law, various locations, Ill./Colo., 1987—; claims analyst discrimination claims U. Ill., Champaign, 1992—; bd. mem. Colo. Coalition Against Domestic Violence, Denver, 1980-81; bd. mem., sec. Champaign (Ill.) County ACLU, 1993—. Editor: New York Wills and Trusts, Revocable Trusts, Handbook of Trial Objections, Federal Information Disclosure, Fraud, Window Dressing and Negligence in Financial Statements, Taxation of Banking Institutions; contbr. chpts. to books and articles to profl. jours. Precinct chair Champaign County Dem. Party, Chgo., 1991—, exec. com., 1993—; Dem. candidate for Champaign County State's Atty., 1992; Dem. candidate for Champaign County Bd., 1994. Mem. NOW (Evergreen chpt. pres. 1977—, Colo. state vice chair 1982), Champaign County Bar Assn. (civil law com. 1992-94), Chgo. Bar Assn. Jewish. Home: 1726 Westhaven Dr Champaign IL 61820-7053 Office: Univ Ill Office Affirmative Action 601 E John St Champaign IL 61820-5711

BARNES, ELIZABETH ANNE, author, retired journalism educator; b. Iron Mountain, Mich., Sept. 18, 1925; d. Eldridge Bachman and Grace Alice (Isley) B. AA, Va. Intermont Coll., 1945; BA, U. N.C., 1947, MA, 1957. Reporter Kingsport (Tenn.) Times-News, 1947-50; adminstrv. asst., pub. rels. dir. Blue-Cross, Kingsport, Tenn., 1950-52; reporter News Leader, Richmond, Va., 1952-56; dir. journalism Stephens Coll., Columbia, Mo., 1957-84, coord. women's studies, 1973-76; vis. journalism prof. Coll. of Santa Fe, 1980-81; journalism tchr. San Felipe and Santa Clara Pueblos, 1980-81. Author: Hand Me Downs, 1985; contbr. articles to profl. jours. Fellow Wurlitzer Found., 1979-80; recipient Gold Key award Coll. Sch. Press Assn., 1975; named outstanding adviser to weekly newspaper in 4-yr. colls. Coll. Media Advisers. Mem. LWV (pub. chmn. 1994—). Democrat. Episcopal. Home: 2 Asta Ter Santa Fe NM 87505

BARNES, EMILY ANN COODY, community health nurse; b. Bleckley County, Ga., Jan. 30, 1928; d. Rufus W. and Beulah Katherine (Simmons) Coody; m. Robert O. Barnes Jr., May 10, 1952 (dec.); children: Cynthia Ann Barnes Hutchins, Robert Woody. Diploma, St. Joseph's Sch. of Nursing, Savannah, Ga., 1951; student, Mid. Ga. Coll., 1957, Ga. Southwestern Coll., 1978. Head nurse Carl Vinson Med. Ctr., Dublin, Ga.; from sr. to lead nurse South Cen. Health Dist., Dublin, ret.; owner Cindy's Place for Ladies Apparel, Cochran, Ga. Home: PO Box 372 Cochran GA 31014-0372

BARNES, GAIL, historic site administrator. Pres. gen. The Alamo, San Antonio, Tex. Office: The Alamo PO Box 2599 San Antonio TX 78299*

BARNES, JHANE ELIZABETH, fashion design company executive, designer; b. Balt., Mar. 4, 1954; d. Richard Amos and Muriel Florence (Chase) B.; m. Howard Ralph Feinberg, Dec. 12, 1981 (div.); m. 2d, Katsuhiko Kawasaki, Feb. 12, 1988. A.S., Fashion Inst. Tech., 1975. Pres., designer Jhane Barnes for ME, N.Y.C., 1976-78, Jhane Barnes Inc., N.Y.C., 1978—. Recipient Coty award Menswear Am. Fashion Critics, 1980, 1984, Contract Textile award Am. Soc. Interior Designers, 1983, 84, Product Design awards Inst. Bus. Designers and Contract Mag., 1983-86, 89, Outstanding Am. Menswear Designer award Woolmark, 1990, Dalmore, 1990; named Most Promising Designer Cutty Sark, 1980, Outstanding Designer, 1982; Outstanding Menswear Designer, Coun. of Fashion Designers Am., 1982, Design Resources Coun., 1989. Office: Jhane Barnes Inc Studio Design 24 W 40th St Fl 14 New York NY 10018-3904

BARNES, JOANNA, author, actress; b. Boston, Nov. 15, 1934; d. John Pindar and Alice Weston (Mutch) B. BA, Smith Coll., 1956. Actress appearing in motion pictures: Auntie Mame, 1958, B.S. I Love You, 1971, Spartacus, 1963, The Parent Trap, 1966, The War Wagon, 1971; TV appearances include What's My Line, The Tonight Show with Johnny Carson, Merv Griffin Show, Trials of O'Brien, Dateline: Hollywood, Murder She Wrote; book reviewer L. A. Times, syndicated columnist Chgo. Tribune, N.Y. News Syndicate, 1963-65; author: Starting from Scratch, 1968, The Deceivers, 1970, Who Is Carla Hart, 1973, Pastora, 1980, Silverwood, 1985. Mem. Phi Beta Kappa.

BARNES, KAREN KAY, lawyer; b. Independence, Iowa, June 22, 1950; s. Walter William and Vashti (Greenlee) Sessler; m. James Alan Barnes, Feb. 12, 1972; children: Timothy Matthew, Christopher Michael. BA, Valparaiso U., 1971; JD, DePaul U., 1978, LLM in Taxation, 1980. Bar: Ill. 1978, U.S. Dist. Ct. (no. dist.) Ill. 1978. Ptnr. McDermott, Will & Emery, Chgo., 1978-88; prin. William M. Mercer, Inc. and predecessor firm, Chgo., 1989-93; staff dir. legal dept. McDonald's Corp., Oak Brook, Ill., 1993—; instr. John Marshall Grad. Sch. Law, Chgo., 1986-87. Contbr. case note to DePaul Law Rev., 1976, note and comment editor DePaul Law Rev., 1976-77, editor Taxation For Lawyers, 1986-88. Mem. ESOP Assn., Chgo. Bar Assn. (chair employee benefits com. 1991-92), Midwest Pension Conf. (name chnged to Midwest Benefits Coun.), WEB (pres. Chgo. chpt. 1986-88, v.p. nat. bd. 1988, pres, 1989-90). Lutheran. Home: 3 S 102 Black Cherry Ln Glen Ellyn IL 60137 Office: McDonald's Corp McDonald's Plz Oak Brook IL 60521

BARNES, LAHNA HARRIS, water treatment company owner; b. New Albany, Ind., May 23, 1947; d. Robert and Catherine (Edwards) H.; m. Michael Barnes, Feb. 15, 1975 (div. 1980); 1 child, Michael. AA, U. Louisville, Louisville, Ky., 1969. Cert. real estate broker, accredited crisis counselor, paralegal. Property mgr. various cos., Jeffersonville, Ind. and Louisville, 1966-76, 78-80, 81-83; sales agt. Century 21, Clarksville, Ind., 1978-83; sales broker Bass & Weisberg Realtors, Jeffersonville, Ind., 1980-81; owner Superior Typing Svc., Jeffersonville, Ind., 1983-89, 91—, Barnes Realty Mgt., Jeffersonville, Ind., 1983-85; corp. sec. Water Energizers Inc., Jeffersonville, Ind., 1983-90; v.p. Water Energizers Inc., Jeffersonville, 1991-92, 94—, co-owner, bd. dirs., 1992—; property mgr. Gardenside Terrace Coop., 1992-93. Author numerous poems; contbr. articles to local newspapers. Active Right to Life, New Albany, 1980—, Realtors Polit. Action Com., 1980-83, NFIB, 1986—, Equal Housing Commn., 1980-83; counselor Ctr. for Lay Ministries, New Albany, Ind., 1972-75; coord. Perot Petition Com. for Clark County, 1992; presdl. elector, Ind., 1992, Clark County, 1992—; vol. ARC. Mem. SCLC (charter mem. So. Ind. chpt., bd. dirs. 1992-94, social justice com. 1992-93, editor The Voice of Freedom newsletter 1992-94). Office: Water Energizers Inc 3008 Middle Rd Jeffersonville IN 47130-5500

BARNES, MAGGIE LUE SHIFFLETT (MRS. LAWRENCE BARNES), nurse; b. nr. Spur, Tex., Mar. 29, 1931; d. Howard Eldridge and Sadie Adilene (Dunlap) Shifflett; m. T.C. Fagan, Jan. 1950 (dec. Feb. 1952); 1 child, Lawayne; m. Lawrence Barnes, Sept. 2, 1960. Student, Cogdell Sch. Nursing, 1959-60, Western Tex. Coll., 1972-76; postgrad. Meth. Hosp. Sch. Nursing, Lubbock, Tex., 1975; BSN, W. Tex. State U., 1977. RN, Tex.; cert. gerontol. nurse, Am. Nurses Credentialing Ctr. Fl. nurse D.M. Cogdell Meml. Hosp., Snyder, Tex., 1960-64, medication nurse, 1964-76, asst. evening supr., 1976-78, charge nurse, after 1978, evening nursing supr., 1980; nursing supr. Scurry, Borden, Mitchel, Fisher, Howard Counties, West Cen. Home Health Agy., Snyder, 1980-83; emergency rm. evening supr. Root-Meml. Hosp., 1983-89; dir. of nurses Snyder Oak Core Ctr., 1989-91, Mountain View Lodge, Big Spring, Tex., 1991-92, Med. Arts. Hosp. Home Health, 1992-93, Metplex Home Health Svcs., Snyder, 1993-94, ret. 1994; part time nurse 1994—; regional coord. home health svcs. Beverly Enterprises, 1983. Den mother Cub Scouts, Boy Scouts Am., Holliday, Tex., 1960-61; mem. PTA, Snyder, Tex., 1960-69; adv. Sr. Citizens Assn.; mem. Tri-Region Health Systems Agy., 1979—; mem. adv. bd. Scurry County Diabetes Assn., 1982—. Mem. Vocat. Nurses Assn. Tex. (mem. bd. 1963-65, div. pres. 1967-69), Emergency Dept. Nursing Assn. Apostolic Faith Ch. (sec., treas. 1956-58). Home: 8239 RR 473 Hermleigh TX 79526-9704

BARNES, MARGARET ANDERSON, business consultant; b. Johnston County, N.C.; m. Benjamin Barnes, Dec. 26, 1959. BS, N.C. Cen. U., 1958; MA, U. Md., 1975; PhD, Columbia Pacific U., 1986. Lic. ins. agt.; ordained Christian elder in World Evangelism, 1992. Math. tchr. Tarboro (N.C.) Sch. System, 1959-61; math. statistician Bur. of Census, Suitland, Md., 1962-67, 69-70, Dist. of Columbia govt., 1967-68; cons. Nat. Insts. of Health, Bethesda, Md., 1970-72, chief of data standards, 1972-73; with exec. clearance office HEW, Rockville, Md., 1973-77; founder, pres. MABarnes Cons. Assoc., Lanham, Md., 1978—; commr. State of Md. Accident Fund, Balt., 1979-89; mem. adv. bd. Universal Bank, Lanham, 1980-83, Interstate Gen. Corp., St. Charles, Md., 1981-83; founder Christian Ministries, 1983—; profiled for First Record: "Women of Achievement in Prince George's County History", 1994. Chairwoman Glenwood Park Civic Assn., Lanham, 1967-80. Democrat. Home: PO Box 586 Lanham Seabrook MD 20703-0586 Office: MABarnes Con Assocs 9470 Annapolis Rd Ste 224 Lanham Seabrook MD 20706-3019

BARNES, PAULETTE WHETSTONE, school system administrator; b. Depew, Okla., Oct. 7, 1942; d. Paul Raymond and Dorothy (Pitts) Whetstone; m. Fredrick Joseph Barnes, Feb. 22, 1964; children: Bradley Mark, Amy Michelle Barnes Harnish. BA, Okla. Coll. for Women, 1964; MS, Emporia State U., 1971. Cert. sch. psychologist, psychometrist, speech pathologist, hearing clinician, elem. and secondary prin., supt., dist. sch. adminstr., Okla., Kans. Speech pathologist Topeka Pub. Schs., 1963-67; tchr. educably mentally handicapped Hutchinson, Kans., 1967-68; speech pathologist Lyons (Kans.) Unified Sch. Dist., 1968-69, Seamon Pub. Schs., Topeka, 1969-70; sch. psychologist Topeka Pub. Schs., 1970-74; coord. spl. edn. Kansas State Dept. Edn., Topeka, 1974-77; coord. 5 County Spl. Edn. Coop., Ardmore, Okla., 1977-78; dir. spl. svcs. Bixby (Okla.) Pub. Schs., 1978-82, 1982-87; asst. supt./prin. Children's Devel. Program, Tulsa County, 1987-88; coord. sec. spl. edn. Tulsa Pub. Schs., 1987-88; dir. edn. Shadow Mountain Inst., Tulsa, 1988-93; supt. Pretty Water Sch. CO-34, Sapulpa, Okla., 1993—; mem. Regional Adv. Bd. for Spl. Needs Children, Tulsa, 1990-93; cons. Child Identification Project of Kans., Topeka, 1977, Okla. State Dept. of Edn., Oklahoma City, 1977-78. Co-author handbook for Okla. State Dept. Edn., 1977-78; contbr. articles to profl. pubis. Mem. Coun. for Exceptional Children (pres. Kans. Fedn. 1976), Okla. Dirs. of Spl. Svcs. (pres. 1981-82, charter mem., Spl. Edn. Adminstr. of Yr. 1986-87), Tulsa Area Dirs. of Spl. Svcs. (pres. 1980-81, sec. 1987-88, area rep. 1990-92), Midwest Regional Dirs. of Spl. Svcs. (chair 1984-85), Coop. Coun. Sch. Adminstrs., Assn. Supervision and Curriculum Devel. Home: 8335 Gary Dr Rt 16 Tulsa OK 74131 Office: Pretty Water Sch CO-34 15223 W 81st St S Sapulpa OK 74066-9804

BARNES, RAMONA, state legislator; b. Pikeville, Tenn., July 7, 1938; d. Ellison Wheeler; m. Larry Barnes, 1960; children: Randall, Michael, Michelle. Attended, Mich. State Coll., Waipahu C.C., Hawaii. Pres. Arctic Rsch. Cons. Internat.; mem. Alaska Ho. of Reps., 1978—; majority leader, spkr. pro tem, 1983-84; minority whip, 1991-92; minority leader, 1992; former chmn. judiciary com.; former mem. numerous coms. Mem. sch. bd. City of Elmendorf, Alaska, 1973-76; mem. adv. sch. bd. City of Anchorage, Alaska, 1975-76, now precinct committeewoman; del. Alaska Rep. State Conv., 1976, 78. Recipient Appreciation award Alaska Peace Ofcl. Assn., 1982, Appreciation cert. Anchorage Cmty. Mental Health Svcs., 1983-85, Am. Outstanding Legislator award Am. Exch. Coun., 1984; named Legislator of Yr., Alaska Sportsmen's Coun. and Nat. Wildlife Fedn., 1980, 81. Mem. Anchorage Rep. Women's Club, Nat. Fedn. Rep. Women, Navy League, Bus. and Profl. Women's Club, Am. Legis. Exch. Coun., Nat. Order Women Legislators. Mem. Ch. of Christ. Home: 2230 Paxson Dr Anchorage AK 99504 also: PO Box 3382 Anchorage AK 99510-0001 Office: Alaska Ho of Reps 3111 C St # 430 Anchorage AK 99503 also: PO Box 103382 Anchorage AK 99510-3382*

BARNES, ROSEMARY LOIS, minister; b. Grand Rapids, Mich., Sept. 17, 1946; d. Floyd Herman and Cora Agnes (Beukema) Herms; m. Louis Herbert Adams, Feb. 22, 1969 (div. Oct. 1976); 1 child, Louis Herbert Jr.; m. Robert Jearold Barnes, Oct. 8, 1976. BA, Calvin Coll., 1968. Ordained to ministry Home Ministry Fellowship, 1980; cert. social worker. Group worker Kent County Juvenile Ct., Grand Rapids, Mich., 1966-68; tchr. Sheldon Elem. Sch., Grand Rapids, 1968-69; social worker Kent Dept. Social Services, Grand Rapids, 1969-75, 75-84; tchr., mission worker Emmanuel House, San Diego, 1975; co-pastor, founder River of Life Ministries, Grand Rapids, 1980—; instr. Gt. Lakes Inst. Bible Studies, Grand Rapids, 1988;

tchr., founder River of Life Sch. Christian Leadership, Grand Rapids, 1981—; v.p. Aglow, Grand Rapids, 1982-83; sec., treas. Western Mich. Full Gospel Ministers Fellowship, Grand Rapids, 1984-85; mem. bd. chaplains Dunes Correctional Facility, Saugatuck, Mich., 1986-91; coord. 1988 Washington for Jesus March, One Nation Under God, Inc.; co-pastor Gun Lake River of Life, 1988; prof. Great Lakes Inst., 1988; county coord. Grand Rapids Full Gospel Ministers Fellowship, 1990-92; co-pastor Defiance, Ohio River of Life, 1992-93. Participant TV show Ask the Pastor, 1993—; dir., producer TV show River Reflections, 1994—; Mich. women's coord. Let The Redeemed of the Lord Say So, 1994; sponsor Grand Rapids cable TV Jewish Jewels, 1995—. Bd. dirs. Alcohol Incentive Ladder, Grand Rapids, 1979. Mem. Women in Leadership. Democrat. Mem. Ind. Charismatic Ch.

BARNES, SANDRA HENLEY, publishing company executive; b. Seymour, Ind., Jan. 15, 1943; d. Ray C. and Barbara (Cockerham) Henley; m. Ronald D. Barnes, Sept. 3, 1961; children: Laura Winkler, Barrett and Garrett (twins). Student, Ind. State U., 1962-63. Asst. sales mgr. Marquis Who's Who, Indpls., 1973-79, sales, svc. mgr., 1979-82, mktg. ops. mgr., 1982-84; mktg. mgr. Marquis Who's Who, Chgo., 1984-86; dir. mktg. Marquis Who's Who, Wilmette, Ill., 1986-87; v.p. mktg. Macmillan Dir. Div., Wilmette, Ill., 1987-88; group v.p. product mgmt. Marquis Who's Who, Wilmette, Ill., 1988-89; pres. Marquis Who's Who, 1989-92; v.p. Reed Reference Pub., New Providence, N.J., 1992—; pub. Marquis Who's Who, New Providence, N.J., 1992—. Republican. Office: Reed Reference Pub 121 Chanlon Rd New Providence NJ 07974

BARNES, SHIRLEY MOORE, psychiatric social worker, genealogist; b. Bedminster, N.J., Jan. 13, 1931; d. George and Marian (Van Nuys) Moore; m. William E. Barnes, Sept. 13, 1952; children: John Leighton, Ellen Leigh, Kimberley Jean. Student, Tusculum Coll., 1948-50; BA, Rutgers U., 1952; MSW, U. Pa., 1954. Lic. clin. social worker, Vt. Caseworker Children's Aid Soc., Phila., 1952-55; psychiat. social worker West Jersey Hosp. and Psychiat. Clinic, Camden, N.J., 1960-61, VA Hosp., Brockton, Mass., 1972; psychiat. social worker Mental Health Svcs. Vt., Springfield, 1973-77, adminstr., coord. aftercare and rehab., 1977-82, psychiat. social worker, supr., 1982—; developer psycho-rehab. for retarded and mentally ill Mental Health Svcs. Vt., Proctorsville, 1980-82, founder Beekman House, 1979. Author: Thomas Edward Currin, Sr., Margaret Jane Cubbon, 1993, The Kindred Venturers, 1994; contbr. articles to various publs. Bd. dirs. J.F. Tatum Sch. PTA, Haddonfield, N.J., 1966-68, High Rock Sch. PTA, Needham, Mass., 1971-72. Recipient 1d place for best all around work in art dept. N.J. Federated Women's Clubs, 1966. Mem. NASW, Acad. Cert. Social Workers, Nat. Geneal. Soc., New Eng. Hist. and Geneal. Soc., Western Pa. Geneal. Soc. Home: 3 Walnut Way Springfield VT 05156 Office: Mental Health Svcs SE Vt 107 Park St Springfield VT 05156

BARNES, VANESSA SUMMERS, state legislator; m. Nicholas T. Barnes. Grad., Mid-Am. Coll. Funeral Svcs. State rep., mem. aged & aging, pub. policy, ethics, vet. affairs & urban affairs coms., chmn. interstate coop. com. Ind. Ho. of Reps., Indpls., 1991—; funeral dir. Summers Funeral Chapel. Named one of Top Ladies of Distinction. Mem. Alpha Kappa Alpha, Alpha Mu Omega. Democrat. Office: Ind Ho of Reps State Capitol Indianapolis IN 46204*

BARNETT, ARLENE MIRIAM, school counselor; b. Phila., Oct. 21, 1938; d. S. Jacob and Bessie (Rabinowitz) Sirinsky; m. William Barnett, June 20, 1960; children: Elise M., Ellen S., Jason M. BS in Edn., Temple U., 1960; MS in Edn, Ctrl. Conn. State U., 1974. Tchr. Bethany (Conn.) Cmty. Sch., 1960-63, U.S. Fed. Pilot Program, Hartford, Conn., 1965; adult counselor Ctrl. Conn. State U., New Britain, 1973-75; dir. testing and group counseling Hartford Coll. for Women, 1974-79; sch. counselor Conn. Regional Vocat. High Schs., Hartford, New Britain and Meriden, Conn., 1979—; tng. cons. Travelers' Ins. Co., Hartford, 1976, Access for Women to Tech., Conn. Tech. Coll., 1976-78; counselor mentor Conn. Vocat. Schs., 1989—; intern supr. Ctrl. Conn. State U. Campaign coord. Newington (Conn.) Dems., 1968; lobbyist Nat. Abortion Rights League, Conn., 1992; mem. women's com. State Senator R. Balducci, Conn., 1993. Mem. Conn. Counseling Assn., Conn. Sch. Counselors Assn.

BARNETT, ERNA JUSTINE, nonprofit organization administrator; b. N.Y.C., Nov. 12, 1945; d. Avrom Barnett and Ella Moewes. BA, U. Colo., 1983. Dir. pub. rels. Seattle Opera Assn., 1964-73; program mgr. Seattle Arts Commn., 1973; gen. coord., CEO Bumbershoot Arts Festival, Seattle, 1973-74; mgr. pub. rels. Centrum Found., Pt. Townsend, Wash., 1974-75; fin. adminstr. Wash. Commn. for Humanities, Seattle, 1986-91; exec. dir. Comty. Ctr. for Performing Arts, Eugene, Oreg., 1991-92; fin. adminstr. Child Care Support Svcs., Portland, Oreg., 1992-93; fin. cons. Oreg. Coun. for Humanities, Portland, 1992—; mktg. cons. Providence Med. Ctr., Portland, 1993—; mgmt. cons. Specialized Housing, Inc., Portland, 1993-94. Contbr. poetry to anthologies, articles to mags. Dir. New City Theater, Seattle, 1991; mem. devel. com. Women's Found. of Oreg., Portland, 1994; grant writer, vol. Friends of Trees, Portland, 1992. Recipient Spl. Achievement award Wash. Press Women, 1972. Mem. Am. Soc. Women Accts. (bd. dirs. 1991), Women in Comms., Inc., Willamette Valley Devel. Officers. Office: PO Box 82606 Portland OR 97282

BARNETT, JAHNAE HARPER, academic administrator; b. Dec. 9, 1946; m. Eddie L. Barnett, Jan. 27, 1968. BSE in Bus., Ark. State U., 1966; M in Bus. Edn., U. Miss., 1967, PhD in Higher Edn. and Student Pers. Svcs., 1972; post doctoral, U. Mo., 1984. Grad. asst. U. Miss., 1966-67; instr. bus. and econs. N.W. Miss. Jr. Coll., Senatobia, 1967-71; spl. cons. planning and evaluation Dept. Edn. State of Mo., Jefferson City, 1972-73; asst. prof. William Woods U., Fulton, Mo., 1973-79, chmn. dept. bus. and econs., 1974-83, coord. adminstrv. and consumer svcs., 1979, assoc. prof., 1979-83, prof., v.p. admissions, retention, and devel., 1983-90, pres., 1990—. Mem. exec. bd. Fulton Area Devel. Corp., Mo. Colls. Fund, chair; 1st vice chair Ind. Colls. and Univs. Mo.; mem. Women's Coll. Coalition; bd. dirs. Great Rivers Coun. Boy Scouts Am.; bd. regents St. Mary's Health Ctr. Home: 1810 Westminster Ave Fulton MO 65251-1068 Office: William Woods Univ Office of President Fulton MO 65251

BARNETT, JANICE ELAINE, critical care nurse; b. Flagstaff, Ariz., Jan. 3, 1951; d. Garland and Evelyn Rose (Benson) Downum; m. Joe Edwin Barnett, Aug. 9, 1972; children: Analie Rose, Daniel Joseph. BA, U. Okla., 1972; BSN summa cum laude, Tex. Woman's U., 1989. Staff nurse in ICU Decatur (Tex.) Community Hosp. Mem. Mortar Board, Phi Beta Kappa, Sigma Theta Tau, Alpha Chi. Home: Rte 1 Box 137 Ponder TX 76259

BARNETT, LINDA KAY SMITH, vocational guidance counselor; b. Booneville, Miss., Nov. 20, 1955; d. John Thomas and Clara Vernell (Brown) Smith; m. William Wayne Barnett, June 26, 1982; 1 child, John William. AA, N.E. Miss. C.C., Booneville, 1975; BS, Miss. State U., 1977, MEd, 1978, EdS, 1982. Vocat. guidance counselor, dist. test coord. Iuka (Miss.) City Schs., 1979-91; vocat. guidance counselor Tishomingo County Schs., Iuka, 1991—. Treas. Iuka High Sch. PTA, 1984-85. Mem. Miss. Sch. Counselors Assn. (state v.p. secondary divsn. 1992-94), N.E. Counseling Assn. (pres. 1989-90, pres.-elect 1987-88, 88-89, sec.-treas. 1982-83), Nat. Bd. for Cert. Counselors (nat. cert. counselor, nat. cert. sch. counselor). Ch. of Christ.

BARNETT, MARIE, real estate executive; b. LaGrange, Ga.; d. George and D. (Moore) B.; m. James Stephens Dick, Dec. 19, 1960 (div.); children: Karen Marie Dick Vidal, Sonya Stephens Dick Tafolla. Student, Fla. State U., 1955, U. Ga., 1956-58, Perry Coll., 1959; grad., Century 21 Internat. Mgmt. Acad., 1988. Lic. Calif. Dept. of Real Estate. Staff Mastrose Devel. Co., Palm Beach, Fla., 1962-65; pres., owner Century 21 Calif. Hills, Orange, Calif., 1973-79; real estate exec. F.M. Tarbell, Orange, Calif., 1979-85; pres., owner Century 21 Assocs., Newport Beach, Calif., 1985-88; real estate exec. Century 21 Inland Pacific, Newport Beach, Calif., 1988—. Pres. Jr. Auxiliary, Pass Christian, Miss., 1965; VIP panel Easter Seals, L.A., 1989; active 552 Club, Cancer Unit Hoag Hosp., Newport Beach, 1989, Cen Pac, Washington, 1989. Mem. Nat. Assn. of Realtors (Grad. Realtors Inst.), Calif. Assn. of Realtors (state dir. 1976, 78-79, realtor-assoc. rels. com., publicity com., co-chmn. Pvt. Property Week, 99 Club), East Orange Bd. of Realtors (chmn. spl. activities 1974-75, chmn. real estate fin. 1976, chmn. realtor-assoc. rels. com. 1977, chmn. Pvt. Property Week 1978, Pres.'s award 1978, chmn. Pvt. Property Week Luncheon 1980-81, communications com. 1980-81, 83, Pvt. Property Week com. 1981), Newport Harbor/Costa Mesa Bd. of Realtors (communications com. 1986—, CANTREE reception 1986, multiple listings com. 1987-88, chmn. Awards and Installation 1987, chmn. Equal Opportunity com. 1988), Corona Del Mar C. of C., Newport Harbor C. of C. Democrat. Office: Century 21 Inland Pacific 2 Corporate Plaza Dr Newport Beach CA 92660-7929

BARNETT, MARILYN, advertising agency executive; b. Detroit; d. Henry and Kate (Boesky) Schiff; BA, Wayne State U., 1953; children: Rhona, Ken. Founder, part-owner, pres. Mars Advt. Co., Southfield, Mich., 1973—. Bd. dirs. Mich. Strategic Fund. Named Outstanding Retail Woman of Yr., Outstanding Retail Mktg. Exec. Mem. AFTRA (dir. 1959-67), SAG, Exec. Women Am., Am. Women in Radio & TV (Top Agy. Mgmt. award, Outstanding Woman of Yr.), Internat. Women Forum, Women's Forum Club, Com. of 200, Women's Econ. Club (Ad Woman of Yr.), Adcraft. Office: MARS Advt 24209 Northwestern Hwy Southfield MI 48075-2551 also: MARS Advt Co 6671 Sunset Blvd Ste 1591 Los Angeles CA 90028

BARNETT, MARY LOUISE, elementary education educator; b. Exeter, Calif., May 1, 1941; d. Raymond Edgar Noble and Nena Lavere (Huckaby) Hope; m. Gary Allen Barnett, Aug. 9, 1969; children: Alice Marie, Virginia Lynn. BA, U. of Pacific, 1963; postgrad., U. Mont., 1979-82, U. Idaho, 1984—. Cert. life elem. tchr., Calif.; standard elem. credential, Idaho; elem. tchr., Mont. Tchr. Colegio Americano de Torrean, Torreon, Coahuila, Mexico, 1962-63, Summer Sch. Primary Grades South San Francisco, 1963-66, Visalia (Calif.) Unified Sch. Dist., 1966-69, Sch. Dist. # 1, Missoula, Mont., 1969-73, Fort Shaw-Simms Sch. Dist., Fort Shaw, Mont., 1976-83, Sch. Dist. #25, Pocatello, Idaho, 1983-93, Greenacres Elem., Pocatello, 1993-94; tchr. 2d grade Bonneville Elem., Pocatello, 1994—. Foster mom Ednl. Found. Fgn. Students, Pocatello, Idaho, 1986-89; vol. Am. Heart Assn., Am. Cancer Soc., Pocatello, 1986-88, Bannock March of Dimes, Pocatello, 1988, Pocatello Laubach Lit. Tutoring, 1989; state v.p. membership, del. to P.W. Australian Mission Study; vice moderator Kendall Presbyn. Women, moderator, 1991—; moderator Kendall P.W. 1990-92. Recipient scholarship Mont. Delta Kappa Gamma Edn. Soc., Great Falls, Mont., 1976, Great Falls AAUW, 1980, Great Falls Scottish Rite, 1981, Five Valleys Reading Assn., Missoula, Mont., 1982. Mem. AAUW (v.p. mem. com. Idaho div. 1990-92), ASCD, NEA, Nat. Coun. Tchrs. English, Internat. Reading Assn., Assn. Childhood Edn. Internat., Laubach Literacy Tutors (sec. 1993—), Bus. and Profl. Women Pocatello (sec. 1993—), Mortar Bd., Alpha Lambda Delta, Delta Kappa Gamma (state fellowship chmn., corr. sec. Pocatello chpt. 1986-88, 2d v.p. 1994—), Moose (musician 1981-82), Order Eastern Star (Musician 1984-85), Gamma Phi Beta (sec. Laubach Tutors 1993—). Democrat. Methodist. Home: 956 Encino St Pocatello ID 83201-2839 Office: Bonneville Elem Sch 320 N 8th Pocatello ID 83201-5504

BARNETT, PATRICIA ANN, public relations professional; b. Culver City, Calif., Jan. 25; d. Howard Taft and Sarah (Ross) B. BJ, U. Tex., 1978. Program specialist Dallas C. of C., 1978-79, comm. specialist, 1979-81; mgr. pub. rels. Trailways Corp., Dallas, 1981-82, dir. pub. rels., 1982-85; sr. account exec. Keller-Crescent Co., Dallas, 1985-87; dir. comm. Office of Pvt. Sector Initiatives The White House, Washington, 1987-89; dir. pub. affairs United Way Am., Alexandria, Va., 1989-91; dir. pub. rels. Daily Advt., Ft. Worth, 1992-94; dir. corp. and found. rels. So. Meth. U., Dallas, 1994—. Mem. Pub. Rels. Soc. Am. (accredited, Silver Anvil award 1985), Women in Comm., Inc. (bd. dirs. Dallas chpt. 1981-82, Matrix 1985), Nat. Press Club, Jr. League Dallas. Republican. Office: So Meth U PO Box 750402 Dallas TX 75275

BARNETTE, MARGE C., marketing director; b. Honolulu, Dec. 15, 1944; d. William Leon Sr. and Margaret Elizabeth Barnette. BA in Acctg., Chaminade U., 1966. Supr. ARA/Slater Food Service, San Francisco, 1966-68; restaurant, catering mgr. Spencecliff Corp., Honolulu, 1968, gen. mgr., 1973-77; clubhouse mgr. Mid-Pacific Country Club, Lanikai, Hawaii, 1977; dir. dining svcs. Tulane U., Dillard U., U. Houston, 1978-79, U. Houston ARA, 1978-79; ops. analyst ARA Svcs., Dallas, 1980; labor rels. mgr. Rockwell Internat. ARA Svcs., L.A., 1981; dist. mgr. ARA Svcs., Phila., 1984-88; pers. dir. ARA Olympic Food Svcs., L.A., 1983-84; ptnr. db Connections-Food Industry Cons., Kirkland, Washington, 1989—; pres., owner MCBA inc., Seattle, 1990-91; mktg. dir. US West Edn. Found., Seattle, 1991—. Roman Catholic. Home: 10278 NE 129th Ln Kirkland WA 98034-2882

BARNEY, CHRISTINE MARIE, public relations executive; b. Yonkers, N.Y., Sept. 25, 1963; d. Alfred John Cuozzo and Barbara Jean (Cambetes) Sarver; m. John Charles Barney (div. Mar. 1992); m. Robert Lewis Bishopric, Apr. 4, 1993; 1 stepchild, Katherine Chloe. BS, Ithaca Coll., 1985. Asst. acct. exec. Burson Marstellar, N.Y.C., 1986-89; acct. exec. Bruce Rubin Assocs., Miami, Fla., 1989-91; group supr. Bruce Rubin Assocs., Miami, 1991-92, exec. v.p., 1992-93; ptnr., pres. Rubin Barney & Birger, Inc. (formerly Bruce Rubin Assocs.), Miami, 1993—. Recipient Mature Media Silver award Nat. Mature Media Awards, 1992, Grand APEX award Awards for Pub. Excellence, 1993. Mem. Pub. Rels. Soc. Am. (accredited, bd. dirs. Miami chpt. 1994, pres. Miami chpt. 1995), Greater Miami C. of C. (vice chairwoman Hispanic bus. mktg. group 1993-94), Leadership Miami. Office: Rubin Barney & Birger Inc 255 Alhambra Circle Ste 500 Coral Gables FL 33134

BARNHART, ELIZABETH ANNE, data processing specialist; b. Daytona Beach, Fla., Oct. 14, 1955; d. David Richards and Elizabeth Frances (Frederick) B. AS in Computer Scis., Daytona Beach C.C., 1975. Cert. data processor; cert. systems profl. Computer programmer Melweb Signs, Daytona Beach, Fla., 1976; supr. data processing Bunnell (Fla.) Gen. Hosp., 1976-77; computer programmer, operator Daytona Budweiser, Port Orange, Fla., 1977-80; data processing mgr. City of Port Orange, 1980—; cons. Volusia-Lake-Flagler Pvt. Industry Corp., Daytona Beach, 1984-86. Mem. Data Processing Mgmt. Assn. (exec. v.p. Halifax Area chpt. 1983-84, pres. 1985, bylaws dir. 1986, awards dir. 1987, several awards). Democrat. Roman Catholic. Office: City of Port Orange 1000 City Center Cir Port Orange FL 32119-4144

BARNHART, JO ANNE B., government official; b. Memphis, Aug. 26, 1950; d. Nelson Alexander and Betty Jane (Fitzpatrick) Bryant; m. David Lee Ross, Feb. 14, 1976 (div. June 1983); m. David Ray Barnhart, May 24, 1986. Student U. Tenn., 1968-70; B.A., U. Del., 1975. Space and time buyer deMartin-Marona & Assocs., Wilmington, Del., 1970-73; adminstrv. asst. Mental Health Assn. Wilmington, 1973-75; dir. SERVE nutrition program Wilmington Sr. Ctr., 1975-77; legis. asst. to Senator William V Roth, Jr., Washington, 1977-81; dep. assoc. commr. Office Family Assistance, HHS, Washington, 1981-83, assoc. commr., 1983-86; Rep. staff dir. U.S. Senate Govt. Affairs Com., 1987-90; asst. sec. family support HHS, Washington, 1990-91, asst. sec. for children and families, 1991-92; staff U.S. Sen. William V. Roth, 1993—. Republican. Methodist.

BARNHILL, CYNTHIA DIANE, accountant; b. Wilmington, N.C., Oct. 15, 1958; d. James Randolph Barnhill and Mildred Butler Nobles. AAS, Cape Fear C.C., Wilmington, N.C., 1979; BS, N.C. Wesleyan Coll., Rocky Mount, 1991; cert. nonprofit mgmt., Duke U., 1994, postgrad., 1994—. Cert. employee benefit specialist. Site supr. New Hanover Summer Feeding Program, Wilmington, 1977; clk. III, nursing svc. New Hanover Regional Hosp., Wilmington, 1979-84; prodn. tech. Amhoist, Wilmington, 1985-86; account rep. V U. N.C. Hosps., Chapel Hill, 1987-88; personnel specialists U.N.C., Chapel Hill, 1988-89; acct. OCCHS, Inc., Carrboro, N.C., 1989—. Vol. N.C. Rep. Party. Mem. Nat. Assn. Accts., Am. Coll. Healthcare Execs., Carolinas Chpt. CEBS, Phi Beta Lambda. Baptist. Office: Orange-Chatham Comp Health 400 Roberson St Carrboro NC 27510

BARNHOUSE, LILLIAN MAY PALMER, retired medical, surgical nurse, researcher, civic worker; b. Canton, Ohio, Sept. 26, 1918; d. Frank Barnard and Jenny Mildred (Leggett) Shear; m. Arnold Barnhouse, June 26, 1940; 1 child, James Wilson. Diploma, Aultman Hosp. Sch. Nursing, Canton, 1939. RN, Ohio, obstetrics specialty. Supr., 1943-44; nurse physician's office Canton, Ohio, 1943-49; ind. critical care nursing local hosps., 1953-68. Instr., blood bank worker ARC, 1940-70; mem. Rep. Nat Com., 1980—; vol. genetic researcher, 1972—; vol. in community. Mem. Ohio Nurses Assn. (past v.p., past chmn. dist. legis. com.), First Families of Ohio, Ladies Oriental Shrine.

BARNHOUSE, RUTH TIFFANY, priest, psychiatrist; b. La Mur, Isere, France; d. Donald Grey Barnhouse and Ruth W. Tiffany; m. Francis C. Edmonds Jr. (div.); children: Francis, Ruth; m. William F. Beuscher (div. 1968); children: Robert, Wiliam, Christopher, Thomas, John. Student, Vassar Coll.; BA, Barnard Coll., Columbia U.; MD, Columbia U., 1950; postgrad., Boston Psychoanalytic Inst., 1966-67, Episcopal Theological Sch., 1969-70; ThM, Weston Coll. Sch. Theology, 1974. Diplomate Am. Bd. Psychiatry and Neurology; ordained priest Episcopal Ch., 1980. Intern Monmouth Meml. Hosp., Long Branch, N.J., 1950-51; resident in psychiatry McLean Hosp., Waverly, Mass., 1953-55, staff psychiatrist, 1958-78; fellow in psychiatry Mass. Gen. Hosp., Boston, 1955-56; pvt. practice, 1956—; prof. psychiatry and pastoral care Perkins Sch. Theology So. Meth. U., Dallas, 1980-89, prof. emerita, 1989—; staff psychiatrist Mass. Mental Health Ctr., 1958-59; clin. asst. Harvard U., 1959-78; vis. lectr. in pastoral theology Weston Coll. Theology, 1973-75; adj. prof. pastoral theology Va. Theol. Sem., 1978-80, Loyola Coll., Columbia, Md., 1978-80; with courtesy staff Sibley Hosp., 1979-80; lectr., workshop leader in field. Author: Identity, 1984, Clergy and the Sexual Revolution, 1987, A Woman's Identity, 1994; asst. editor Anglican Theol. Rev.; co-editor: Male and Female: Christian Approaches to Sexuality; contbr. numerous articles to profl. jours. Pres. Peacemakers, Inc., 1989-90, Isthmus Inst., 1989-91. Recipient Maura award Women's Ctr. of Dallas, 1987. Fellow Am. Psychiat. Assn. (life, vice chmn. com. on religion), Royal Soc. Medicine; mem. AAAS, AAUP, Am. Med. Women's Assn., Am. Acad. Psychoanalysis (sci. assoc.), Am. Acad. Religion, Assn. Women Psychiatrists (pres. 1991-93), Analytical Psychology Assn. Dallas, Conf. Anglican Theologians (past pres.), Dallas Area Women Psychiatrists, Hermetic Acad., Internat. Physicians for Prevention of Nuclear War, Mass. Med. Soc., North Tex. Psychiat. Soc., Physicians for Social Responsibility. Home and Office: 100 B Turtle Creek Village # 350 Dallas TX 75219

BARNICK, HELEN, retired judicial clerk; b. Max, N.D., Mar. 24, 1925; d. John K. and Stacy (Kankovsky) B. BS in Music Edn. cum laude, Minot State Coll., 1954; postgrad., Am. Conservatory of Music, Chgo., 1975-76. With Epton, Bohling & Druth, Chgo., 1968-69; sec. Wildman, Harrold, Allen & Dixon, Chgo., 1969-75; part-time assignments for temporary agy. Chgo., 1975-77; sec. Friedman & Koven, Chgo., 1977-78; with Lawrence, Lawrence, Kamin & Saunders, Chgo., 1978-81; sec. Hinshaw, Culbertson et al., Chgo., 1982; sec. to magistrate judge U.S. Dist. Ct. (we. dist.) Wis., Madison, 1985-91; dep. clk., case adminstr. U.S. Bankruptcy Ct. (we. dist.) Wis., Madison, 1992-94; ret., 1994. Active chancel choir 1st Bapt. Ch., Mpls.; mem. choir Moody Ch., Chgo., dir. sr. high choir; mem. chancel choir 4th Presbyn. Ch., Chgo.; chancel choir Covenant Presbyn. Ch., Madison; dir. chancel choir 1st Bapt. Ch., Minot, N.D.; bd. dirs. Peppertree at Tamarack Owners Assn., Inc., Wisconsin Dells, Wis., sec.-treas.; mem. Festival Choir, Madison. Mem. Christian Bus. and Profl. Women (chmn.), Bus. and Profl. Women Assn., Sigma Sigma Sigma. Home: 7364 Old Sauk Rd Madison WI 53717-1213

BARNS, DORETHA MAE CLAYTON, librarian, organization executive; b. Fairmont, W.Va., Nov. 28, 1917; Sylvester Richard and Della Pearl (Morgan) Clayton; m. William Derrick Barns, Sept. 3, 1947. AB, Fairmont State Coll., 1939; MA, W.Va. U., 1940; BS in L.S., Western Res. U., 1947. Tchr., librarian Wetzel County (W.Va.) Schs., 1940-41; Preston County Schs., 1944-46; teaching fellow dept. English W.Va. U., 1941-43; sec. to dean grad. sch., 1942-44, cataloguer library, 1947-48; dir., Internat. relations chmn. LWV, W.Va., 1969-89, 2d v.p., 1981-83, 87-89; bd. dirs. W.Va. affiliate Coun. of Internat. Programs, 1975-87. Author: An Outline of the West Virginia Merit System, 1957; West Virginia's Interest in Foreign Trade, 1971; International Services Available to West Virginia Businesses, 1980. Mem. Women's Internat. League for Peace and Freedom, Order Ea. Star, Kappa Delta Pi, Nu Alpha Phi. Republican. Mem. Soc. Friends. Home: 512 Beverly Ave Morgantown WV 26505-4920

BARNS, JUSTINE, state legislator; b. Wilkes-Barre, Pa., Feb. 2, 1925; m. Jonathan Barnes, 1943 (dec.); children: Duane, Scott. Mem. Mich. Ho. of Reps., 1983—; chmn. sr. citizens and retirement com.; mem. edn. com., mem. legis. retirement and pub. health com.; vice chmn. govt. ops. and pensions com. Mem. Westland City Charter Commn., 1964-66, v.p. Wayne County, 1981-83; active Westland City Coun., 1966-83, Wayne-Ford Civic League, United Fund Drive. Named Citizen of Yr., Ford Motor Co., 1967, Woman of Yr., City of Westland, 1975, Legislator of Yr., Mich. Assn. Chiefs of Police, 1983, Leader of Yr., YMCA, 1989. Mem. Westland Bus. and Profl. Women, Westland C. of C., Rotary. Democrat. Home: PO Box 85533 Westland MI 48185-0533 also: 34139 Tawas Rd Westland MI 48185 Office: Mich Ho of Reps State Capital Lansing MI 48909*

BARNSTONE, GERTRUDE LISETTE LEVY, sculptor; b. Houston, Sept. 5, 1925; d. Arthur Gustavus and Gisella Ruth (Schwarz) Levy; m. Howard Barnstone (dec.); children: Dora Barber, Lily Wells, George. BA, Rice Univ., 1945. vis. artist North Harris County C.C., 1986, Sam Houston State Univ., Huntsville, 1984. Prin. works include sculptures at numerous galleries including Galveston Art Ctr., 1987, Dallas Women's Caucus for Arts, Dallas, 1987, Art League of Houston, 1988, Blue Collar Gallery, San Antonio, Nieman Marcus (shown nation-wide), 1988-89, Economos Gallery, Santa Fe, 1989, Domus Internat., 1989, Gallery of Functional Art, Santa Monica, 1989, Tex. Fine Arts Assn., 1989, L.A. Art Fair, 1990, Artera Gallery, Houston, 1992, 93, four sculptures for BBC movie, 1992, steel gate Washington Sch., Houston, 1991; represented in collections: Harris County, Tex., Anthony Found., Houston, U.S. Green Stamp Co., Houston, Menil collection, Houston, Como No? Gallery, Santa Fe, Frank McIntosh-Henri Bendel, N.Y.C., Boston, Chgo., Zoo Galleries, L.A., Newbill Collection by the Sea, Seaside, Fla.; patentee in field. State pres. Women's Equity Action League, Tex., 1973-74; pres. Houston Women's Caucus for Art, Houston, 1980-81; bd. trustees Houston Ind. Sch. Dist., 1965-70; bd. dirs. Tex. ACLU, 1986-90; del. Nat. Dem. Conv., N.Y.C., 1976. Named Woman of Yr. in Art, Houston YWCA, 1994. Home and Office: 1401 Harold St Houston TX 77006

BARNUM, MARY ANN MOOK, information management manager; b. Arlington, Va., Apr. 3, 1946; d. Conrad Payne and Barbara Heer (Held) Mook; m. William Douglas Barnum, Aug. 10, 1968. BS in Math., Radford U., 1967. Cert. tchr., Va., N.J., N.Mex. Math. tchr. Prince William County Schs., Woodbridge, Va., 1967-68; mathematician RCA Svc. Co., Andros Island, Bahamas, 1968-70; math. tchr. Cinnaminson (N.J.) Schs., 1970-73, Alamagordo (N.Mex.) Sch. System, 1973-74; data svcs. supr. A.M. Best Co., Oldwick, N.J., 1975-78; assoc. mgr. AT&T Communications, Piscataway, N.J., 1978-86; mgr. AT&T Info. Mgmt. Svcs., Piscataway, N.J., 1986-90, AT&T Bus. Comm. Svcs., Somerset, N.J., 1990-91; mem. tech. staff AT&T Network Systems, Berkeley Heights, N.J., 1991—. Sec. Cherry Hill (N.J.) Jaycettes, 1972-73; trustee Friends of Clarence Dillon Libr., Bedminster, N.J., sec., 1989-90, pres., 1990-92, vol., 1986—; mem. Far Hills Environ. Commn., 1990-92, chmn., 1992-94; mem. Far Hills Planning Bd., 1994—. Mem. IEEE Computer Soc., Am. Soc. Quality Control, DAR, Descendants of Washington's Army at Valley Forge (capt. of the guard 1988-90, dep. adjutant gen. 1990-92, adjutant gen. 1992—), Soc. of the Descendants of the Mayflower, Kappa Delta Pi. Presbyterian. Home: PO Box 893 Lake Rd Far Hills NJ 07931

BAROKAS, JUDY, policy research consultant; b. Phila., Dec. 16, 1947; d. Bernard and Reba (Cohen) Uhr; m. Rifat Barokas, Feb. 21, 1971 (div. Oct. 1990); children: Benjamin, Sara. BA in Sociology, Barnard Coll., 1970; MA in Counseling, Va. Poly. Inst. and State U., 1981, PhD in Ednl. Rsch., 1992. Dir. Alternative Sch. for Jewish Edn., 1981-82; rsch./teaching asst. Va. Poly. Inst. and State U., Falls Church, 1982-85; project dir. Rsch. Mgmt. Corp., Falls Church, 1985-87; sr. assoc. Caliber Assocs., Fairfax, Va., 1987-89; pres. Consulting Rsch. and Info. Svcs., Reston, Va., 1989—; instr. ESL in Guayaquil, Ecuador, Barranquilla, Colombia and Managua, Nicaragua, 1970-78; internat. bus. corr. Bus. Internat., Inc., 1975-76. Contbr. articles to profl. jours. Women's Rsch. Inst. grantee, 1990; recipient Comdrs. medal Greater Mil. Community of Stuttgart, 1988. Mem. Am. Edn. Rsch. Assn. (Disting. Dissertation award Rsch. on Women in Edn. group 1994), Coun. for Exceptional Children, NOW, Washington Evaluation Group, Phi Delta

Kappa, Phi Kappa Phi. Democrat. Jewish. Office: Consulting Rsch & Info Svcs 1616 Wainwright Dr Reston VA 22090

BAROLINI, HELEN, writer, translator, educator; b. Syracuse, N.Y., Nov. 18, 1925; m. Antonio Barolini, Nov. 8, 1950 (dec.); children: Teodolinda, Susanna, Nicoletta. AB magna cum laude, Syracuse U., 1947; MLS, Columbia U., 1959. Lectr. Pace U., Pleasantville, N.Y., 1990—; lectr. Padua, Italy and Westchester C.C., Valhalla, N.Y., 1988; writer-in-residence Quarry Farm, Elmira Coll., 1989; resident scholar Rockefeller Found.'s Bellagio Study Ctr., Lake Como, Italy, 1991. Creative works include Chiaroscuro, 1995, Aldus and His Dream Book, 1991, Festa, 1988, Love in the Middle Ages, 1986, The Dream Book, 1985, Umbertina, 1979; stories in Literary Olympian II, Love Stories by New Women, and numerous jours.; translated 7 books from Italian; scholar-cons., advisor to film Tarantella. Recipient Susan Koppelman award Am. Culture Assn., 1987, Am. Book award 1986, Ams. of Italian Heritage Literary award, 1984, Marina-Velca Journalism prize, Italy, 1970; Nat. Endowment for Arts grantee, 1976; fellow MacDowell Colony, 1974, Yaddo fellow, 1965. Mem. Soc. for Study of Multi-Ethnic Lit. of U.S., PEN Am. Ctr., Nat. Writers Union, Hudson River Writers Assn., Phi Beta Kappa. Home and Office: 3 Ridgedell Ave Hastings Hdsn NY 10706-1409

BARON, CAROLYN, editor, author, publishing executive; b. Detroit, Jan. 25, 1940; d. Gabriel and Viola Cohn; m. Richard W. Baron, Nov. 14, 1975. B.A. in Liberal Arts, U. Mich., 1961. Editor, editorial prodn. dir. Holt, Rinehart & Winston, N.Y.C., 1965-71; mng. editor E.P. Dutton Co., Inc., N.Y.C., 1971-74; exec. editor E.P. Dutton Co., Inc., 1974-75; adminstrv. editor Pocket Books, Simon & Schuster, N.Y.C., 1975-78; v.p., editor-in-chief Pocket Books, Simon & Schuster, 1978-79, Crown Pubs., N.Y.C., 1979-81; v.p., pub. Dell Pub. Co., N.Y.C., 1981-86, pres., pub., 1986—. Office: Dell Pub Co Inc 1540 Broadway New York NY 10036-4039

BARON, LINDA M., psychotherapist, consultant; b. N.Y.C., Feb. 12; d. Jack and Sylvia (Paff) B. BE in Elem. Edn., U. Miami, MEd in Learning Disabilities, 1973, MEd in Counseling Psychology, 1974. Lic. mental health counselor, Fla., marriage and family therapist, Fla.; cert. addictions profl., Fla., mental health counselor, Wash.; nat. cert. counselor; internat. cert. alcohol and drug counselor; cert. master practitioner neuro-linguistic programming. Tchr. elem. sch. Dept. Def. Overseas Sch. System, Japan, The Philippines, Eng.; rehab. counselor Office Vocat. Rehab., Miami, Fla.; acting supr., clin. counselor Metro-Dade Alcohol and Drug Abuse Counselor, Miami, 1978-80, dir. community and media rels., 1980-87; pvt. practice North Miami, Fla., 1980—; adj. prof. psychology St. Thomas U., Miami, 1977-80; cons. Miami Vice and Crime Story TV shows, 1984-91; cons., seminar leader in stress mgmt. and women's issues various orgns., bus., media, 1990—; founder, pres. P.R.I.S.M.-Program Relaxation, Imagery and Stress Mgmt., 1994—. Prodr. Alcohol and Drug Abuse pub. svc. announcement, 1985 (Emmy nomination). Organizing vol. various Dem. candidates, 1971—; vol. ARC, Dade County, Fla., 1992; activist Am. Rights Found. Fla.; founding bd. dirs. Informed Families Dade County, 1981-85; bd. dirs. MADD, 1984-91. Recipient Citation of Appreciation, Am. Bus. Woman's Assn., 1991. Mem. NATAS, Am. Counseling Assn., Am. Assn. Marriage and Family Therapy (clin. mem.), Fla. Alcohol and Drug Abuse Assn., Assn. Advance Ethical Hypnosis, Assn. Applied Psychophysiology and Biofeedback, Assn. Humanistic Psychology. Democrat. Home and Office: 2533 NE 135 St Miami FL 33181

BARON, PATRICIA BURRELL, university director; b. Glen Ridge, N.J., Dec. 16, 1949; d. Leo Duncan and Mollie Amelia (Scard) B.; m. William Robert Baron, June 17, 1972. BA, Allegheny Coll., 1972; MA in Librarianship, U. Denver, 1973; MEd in Ednl. Adminstrn., U. Maine, 1980; EdD in Ednl. Adminstrn., No. Ariz. U., 1987. Reference libr. U. Maine, Orono, 1975, asst. to grad. dean, 1976-80, asst. to acad. v.p., 1980-82; asst. to grad. dean No. Ariz. U., Flagstaff, 1982-87, asst. grad. dean, 1987-93, assoc. grad. dean, dir. grad. admissions, 1993—. Contbr. articles to profl. jours. Active commn. on status of women Ariz. Bd. of Regents, Phoenix, 1989-91. Named Woman of Distinction, Soroptomist Internat., 1993. Mem. Am. Assn. U. Women, Nat. Assn. Women in Edn., Nat. Assn. Grad. Admissions, Univ. Career Women (founder, chair 1991-92), Phi Kappa Phi. Office: No Ariz U PO Box 4125 Flagstaff AZ 86011

BARONDESS, LINDA HIDDEMEN, professional society executive; b. Phila., Aug. 25, 1945; d. William and Audrey (Roan) Hiddemen; m. Jeremiah A. Barondess, Dec. 10, 1982. Dir. med. edn. ACP, Phila., 1978-83; exec. v.p. Am. Geriatrics Soc., N.Y.C., 1983—. Contbr. articles to profl. jours. Mem. Cosmopolitan Club. Office: Am Geriatrics Soc 770 Lexington Ave New York NY 10021-8165

BARONE, ANGELA MARIA, artist; b. Concesio, Brescia, Italy, June 29, 1957; came to U.S., 1983; d. Giuseppe and Adelmina (D'Ercole) B. Laurea cum laude in geol. scis., U. Bologna, Italy, 1981; PhD in Marine Geology, Columbia U., 1989. Cert. in profl. photography, N.Y. Inst. Photography, N.Y.C., 1992; cert. in the fine art of painting and drawing North Ligh Art Sch., Cin., 1993. Collaborative asst. Marine Geology Inst., Bologna, 1981-83, Inst. Geology and Paleontology, Florence, Italy, 1982-83, Sta. de Geodynamique, Villefranche, France, 1982; grad. rsch. asst. Lamont-Doherty Geol. Obs., Palisades, N.Y., 1983-89; postdoctoral rsch. asst. Lamont-Doherty Geol. Obs., Palisades, 1989; postgrad. rschr. Scripps Instn. of Oceanography, La Jolla, Calif., 1990-92; artist San Diego, 1993—. Contbr. articles to profl. jours. Mem. Am. Geophysical Union (co-pres. meeting session 1990), Nat. Mus. Women in the Arts (assoc. mem.). Christian. Home: 7540 Charmant Dr Apt 1222 San Diego CA 92122-5044

BARONE, CAROL PARKER, health facility administrator, infection control practitioner; b. New Orleans, Oct. 8, 1956; d. Floyd Adrian and Freda Virginia (Carroll) Parker; m. Jed Barone, Aug. 14, 1976; children: Joshua Martin, Amber Nicole, Christopher Parker. Diploma, Touro Infirmary, New Orleans, 1979; student, Graceland Coll. Cert. in inpatient obstetrics, advanced fetal monitoring, childbirth education, neonatal resuscitation. Labor and delivery staff nurse Lakeside Hosp., Metairie, La., 1979-83; office charge nurse ob-gyn. office, Metairie, 1981-84; labor and delivery staff nurse, preceptor Humana Hosp. New Orleans, 1984-86, labor and delivery nurse mgr., 1986-91, nursing quality assurance coord., nurse recruiter, 1991-92, dir. quality mgmt., 1992-94, infection control, employee health coord., 1994—; mem. obstetrics task force Humana Corp. Mem. NAACOG, So. Perinatal Aassn., Touro Infirmary Sch. Nursing Alumni Assn. Home: 100 Valerie St New Orleans LA 70123-1824 Office: Lakeland Med Ctr 6000 Bullard Ave New Orleans LA 70128

BARONE, ROSE MARIE PACE, writer, former educator; b. Buffalo, Apr. 26, 1920; d. Dominic and Jennie (Zagara) Pace; m. John Barone, Aug. 23, 1947. BA, U. Buffalo, 1943; MS, U. So. Cal., 1950; cert. advanced study, Fairfield (Conn.) U., 1963. Tchr. Angola (N.Y.) High Sch., 1943-46, Puente (Calif.) High Sch., 1946-47, Jefferson High Sch., Lafayette, Ind., 1947-50; dir. Warren Inst., Bridgeport, Conn., 1951-53; instr. U. Bridgeport, 1953-54; tchr. bus. subjects Bassick High Sch., Bridgeport, 1954-74, Harding High Sch., Bridgeport, 1974-80; instr. Fairfield U., Conn., 1969; freelance writer, 1980—; freelance writer, 1980—; chair State Poetry Festival, 1987. Founder Pet Rescue; chmn. community affairs com Area Coun. Cath. Women, 1988-90, sec., 1990-91, chmn. family affairs com., 1991, v.p., 1992-93; chmn. community affairs Ch. Women United, 1992—. Pace-Barone Minority scholar Fairfield U., Auerbach Found. scholar, 1956; recipient Playwriting prize Conn. Federated Women's Clubs, 1955, 1st prize for poetry, 1985, Short Story award Federated Women Conn., 1987, 88, 90, Citizen award Bridgeport Dental Assn., 1982, State/Town Hero award, 1986, Anniversary medal and marble statuette Fairfield U., Cmty. Care Successful Aging award, 1992, Salute to Women award YWCA, 1993, Woman of Substance award, 1994, craft and flower awards. Mem. NEA, Am. Assn. Ret. People (v.p. 1987-88, pres. 1988-89, 94—, instr. 55 Alive, community affairs chair 1990-94), Owl (sec. 1987-89, pres. 1989-90), AAUW (treas. 1957-58, named gift grant 1989, cultural and poetry chair 1992—, rec. sec., 1992-93, internat. rels. 1993-94), Nat. League Am. PEN Women (Bridgeport historian 1966-84, state historian 1983—, treas. br. 1985-88, state pres. 1986-88, state lit. chair 1988—, br. membership chair 1990, Nat. Historian award 1976, 88), Fairfield Area Poets (founder, pres. 1990—, editor 4 vols. Conn. poets), UN Assn. USA (pres. Bridgeport 1964-66, 68-70, v.p. 1988—, chmn. area UN Days 1960—, pres. Conn. 1971—, state chmn. UNICEF to 1984, area UNICEF Ctr.1984—, state historian 1984—), Conn. Bus. Tchrs., Bridgeport Edn. Assn. (sec. 1966-68), VFW (aux. 1989), Am. Legion (aux. contest chair 1989—, historian 1993—, Aux. Nat. Community Svc. award 1993), Fairfield Philatelic Soc. (sec. 1971-78, founder advisor Philatelic Jrs. 1972-80), Fairfield U. Women's Club (founder, pres. 1950, 74—, v.p. 1973-74), Southport Women's Club (garden dept. sec. 1981-85, chmn. 1985-87), Pi Omega Pi. Home: 1283 Round Hill Rd Fairfield CT 06430-7329

BARONE, SANDRA M., state legislator; b. Providence, Oct. 31, 1946; d. Henry and Esther Siegel Factoroff; m. John Barone Jr., 1973; 1 child, Raechel. BA, R.I. Coll., 1968; postgrad., U. R.I. Vol. Peace Corps, Liberia, 1969-70; realtor T.R. Little Realtors, 1985—; mem. R.I. Ho. of Reps., 1991—; mem. HEW com., 1991—; vice chmn. adoption registry com.; mem. steering com. for healthy families; mem. internship com.; mem. com. to study state scholarships and disability com. Active ACLU, Common Cause, Coalition to Preserve Choice, Barrington Dem. Town Commn. Mem. R.I. Assn. Realtors, R.I. Women's Legis. Caucus, R.I. Women's Polit. Caucus. Democrat. Jewish. Home: 19 Rustwood Dr Barrington RI 02806 Office: RI Ho of Reps State House Providence RI 02903*

BARR, CYNTHIA MARIE, accountant; b. Lancaster, Pa., Sept. 16, 1966; d. Edwin F. and Mary C. (McLaughlin) B. BS, Elizabethtown (Pa.) Coll., 1989. CPA, Pa. Sr. acct. Ross Buehler Falk & Co., Lancaster, Pa., 1989—. Mem. AICPA, Pa. Inst. CPA, Inst. of Mgmt. Accts., Alpha Lambda Delta, Sigma Mu Delta. Roman Catholic. Office: Ross Buehler Falk & Co 1500 Lititz Pike Lancaster PA 17601

BARR, DIXIE, geriatrics nurse; b. Butler, Ohio, Mar. 11, 1934; d. Gerald Edward and Aldine Marie (Barre) Beam; children: Daniel, Dennis, Denise. Lic. practical nurse, Timken-Mercy Hosp., Canton, Ohio, 1971; ADN, Walsh Coll., Canton, 1990. Charge nurse Wyandot County Nursing Home. Home: 855 S Hazel St Apt 4 Upper Sandusky OH 43351

BARR, JO ANN, educational administrator; b. Louisville, Mar. 30, 1940; d. W.B. and Zelma (Burton) Rigdon; m. Robert Barr, Nov. 5, 1960; children: Jennifer Barr Crumbacker, Greg. BS in Elem. Edn., Spalding U., Louisville, 1972, MA in Elem. Edn., 1974, reading specialist cert.; Rank I in Adminstrn., Western Ky. U., 1975. Tchr. Louisville Cath. Schs., 1966-72; dir. parent involvement Bullitt County Schs., Shepherdsville, Ky., 1974-75, reading specialist, 1972-74, 75-76, prin. Nichols Elem. Sch., 1976-83, prin. Cedar Grove Elem. Sch., 1983-91; instructional supr. Bullitt County Bd. Edn., Shepherdsville, Ky., 1991-94; dir. elem. edn., 1994—; presenter in field at local, state and nat. meetings; mem. Ky. Ednl. Leadership Inst., 1984-85. Sunday sch. tchr. lst Bapt. Ch., Shepherdsville; bd. dirs. YMCA, Shepherdsville; com. chmn. Bullitt County chpt. Am. Cancer Soc., 1988; chmn. to establish Bullitt County Arts Coun., 1985; pres. Bullitt County Woman's Club, 1975. Named Ky.'s Nat. Disting. Prin., 1989; named to prins. honor role Ky. PTA, 1985; recipient Outstanding Prin.'s award 4th Dist. PTA, 1984; scholar, Fed. Republic Germany, 1989. Mem. NAESP (nat. fellow 1983), Ky. Assn. Elem. Sch. Prins. (sec. 1978, pres.-elect 1979, pres. 1980, exec. dir. 1985—), Ky. Assn. Sch. Adminstrs. (bd. dirs. 1982-86, Leadership award for elem. prins. 1988), Bullitt County Assn. Sch. Adminstrn. (pres. 1985-86), PTA (life). Democrat. Home: 478 Tollview Dr Shepherdsville KY 40165-6160 Office: Bullitt County Bd Edn Shepherdsville KY 40165

BARR, MARLENE JOY, volunteer; b. Grosse Pointe Farms, Mich., Feb. 25, 1935; d. Max John and Viola Christina (Funke) Bielenberg; m. John Monte Barr, Dec. 17, 1954; children: John Monte Jr., Karl Alexander, Elizabeth Marie. Student, Mex. City Coll., 1955; BA cum laude, Mich. State U., 1956; MA, Ea. Mich. U., 1959. Cert. elem. edn. Tchr. A.G. Erickson Sch., Ypsilanti, Mich., 1956-66; chair 5th grade tchrs., sec. curriculum coun. Ypsilanti Pub. Schs., 1961-66; receptionist Barr, Anhut, and Assoc., P.C., Ann Arbor, Mich., 1989—; vol. Thrift Shop Assn. of Ypsilanti, 1969—; block coord. Ypsilanti Recycling, 1990—. Mem. Fletcher Sch. Adv. Coun., 1980-81, Ann Arbor Power Squadron, 1965—, Emmanuel Luth. Ch. Chancel Choir, 1980—, youth coord., 1983-89, sec. youth standing com., 1983-89, ch. coun., 1986-90; v.p. Thrift Shop Assn. Ypsilanti, 1979-81, pres., 1981-83, scheduling chmn., 1993—; bd. dirs. Ypsilanti Community Choir, 1984—; asst. leader Girl Scouts U.S., 1978-81; sec. troop 290 Boy Scouts Am., 1989—; rm. mother Fletcher Elem. Sch., Ypsilanti, 1982-83. Mem. AAUW (life, chmn. gourmet arts study group 1968—), Ann Arbor Womens City Club, Friends of the Ypsilanti Dist. Libr., Depot Town Assn., Law Wives of Washtenaw County (editor 1970-72), Ladies Literary Club (corr. sec. 1976-78, sec. bd. trustees 1982-86, v.p. 1986-90, pres. 1990-92, treas. bd. trustees 1992—), Chandler Birthday Club (treas. 1990), Alpha Delta Kappa (pres. Beta Zeta chpt. 1965-68, historian 1986-88, pres. Area X Pres. Coun. Mich. ADK chpt. 1966-68), Ypsilanti Hist. Soc. (life), P.E.O. (chaplain 1991-93). Lutheran. Home: 1200 Whittier Rd Ypsilanti MI 48197-2152 Office: Barr Anhut and Assoc PC 210 E Huron St Ste D Ann Arbor MI 48104-1913

BARR, MARYLIN LYTLE, poet, artist; b. Boston, Aug. 11, 1920; d. W. Vernon and Maude S. Lytle; m. Orlando Sydney Barr, Nov. 6, 1942; children: Margaret Hoover, Joyce Manley, Mark Sydney. BA, Beecher Coll., 1942; postgrad., Syracuse U., 1962-63; MA, Bank St. Coll. Edn., N.Y.C., 1967; postgrad., NYU, 1979. Lic. early childhood tchr. N.Y. Interviewer Winchester Repeating Arms, New Haven, 1942-43, work simplification engr., 1943-44; tchr. Glen Ridge Nursery Sch., Hamden, Conn., 1946-47, City of N.Y. Bd. Edn., 1966-85; freelance poet, artist N.Y.C., 1972—; writing workshops Sullivan County Cmty. Coll., Loch Sheldrake, N.Y., 1987-94. Author: Drawn From the Shadows, 1991, Concrete Considerations, 1993; artist exhibiting in Mass. and N.Y. State; contbr. articles to profl. jours. Mem. Alchemy Club, Stone Ridge Poetry Soc., Catskill Reading Soc., Mass. State Poetry Soc., Poetry Soc. N.H., Greater Haverhill Poetry Soc., Catskill Art Soc. (hon. mention 1990), Catskill Caravan, Essex Writers Guild. Episcopalian. Office: Arts Gallery PO Box 75 Grahamsville NY 12740-0075

BARR, SHIRLEY, public relations executive; b. Wilson, Okla., Nov. 24, 1936. BS in Journalism, U. North Tex., 1958. Assoc. editor Conoco, 1958-61; freelance mag. writer Women's Day, Field & Stream, etc., 1962-71; freelance pub. rels. specialist Playcare Ctrs. of Am., 1971-74; dir. spl. events CG, 1974-87; sr. v.p., media rels. group Churchill Group, 1988-91; founder, chmn. Shirley Barr Pub. Rels., Houston, 1991—. Recipient Excalibur awards, 1989-92. Mem. Pub. Rels. Soc. Am. (publicity chmn. Houston chpt. 1982-83). Office: Shirley Barr Pub Rels 5177 Richmond Ave Ste 750 Houston TX 77056*

BARRAGRY, MARY ANN, librarian; b. Chgo., Jan. 13, 1948; d. John James and Dorothy Mae (Cylkowski) B. BS in Chemistry, Mundelein Coll., 1970; MS in Libr. Sci., U. Ill., 1971. Asst. sci. libr. Northwestern U., Evanston, Ill., 1971-76; indexer ADA, Chgo., 1976-78, head indexer, 1978-80; info. analyst Am. Hosp. Supply Corp., Evanston, 1980-85; asst. libr. Wis. Electric Power Co., Milw., 1985-88, libr., 1988—. Pres. Club MSO, Milw. Symphony Orch., 1989-90. Fellow Beta Phi Mu; mem. Spl. Librs. Assn. (pres. Wis. chpt. 1992-93). Office: Wis Electric Power Co 231 W Michigan St Milwaukee WI 53203

BARRANGER, MILLY SLATER, performing arts company executive, writer; b. Birmingham, Ala., Feb. 12, 1937; d. C. C. Slater and Mildred (Hilliard) Hinson; m. G. K. Barranger, 1961 (div. 1984); 1 child, Heather Dalton Barranger Case. BA, U. Montevallo, 1958; MA, Tulane U., 1959, PhD, 1964. Lectr. La. State U., New Orleans, 1964-69; asst. to assoc. prof. Tulane U., New Orleans, 1969-82, chmn. dept. theatre, 1971-82; prof., chmn. dramatic art U. N.C., Chapel Hill, 1982—; producing dir. PlayMakers Repertory Co., Chapel Hill, 1982—; pres. Am. Theatre Assn., 1978-79; disting. vis. assoc. prof. U. Tulsa, 1981; vis. young prof. in humanities U. Tenn., Knoxville, 1981-82; scholar-in-residence Yale Sch. Drama, New Haven, Conn., 1982. Author: Theatre: A Way of Seeing, 1980, 86, 91, 94, Theatre: Past and Present, 1984, Understanding Plays, 1990, 94, Jessica Tandy, 1991, Margaret Webster, 1994; co-editor: Generations: An Introduction to Drama, 1971, Notable Women in the American Theatre, 1989; contbr. articles to profl. jours. Trustee The Paul Green Found., 1982—. Recipient New Orleans Bicentennial award for achievement in the arts, 1976, award for profl. achievement S.W. Theatre Conf., 1978, Pres.'s award U. Montevallo, 1979. Fellow Coll. of Fellows of the Am. Theatre; mem. Nat. Theatre Conf. (pres. 1978-79, bd. dirs. 1991-93), Assn. Theatre in Higher Edn., League Profl. Theatre Women N.Y. Office: U NC CB # 3230 Chapel Hill NC 27599-3230

BARRASSO, DIANE SPESS, molecular biologist; b. Allentown, Pa., Dec. 17, 1959; d. Vincent Edwin and Claire B. (Gillespie) Spess; m. Michael J. Barrasso, Aug. 6, 1983; children: Christopher Michael, Dana Marie. BS in Biology, Lehigh U., 1981, MS in Biology, 1983; PhD in Microbiology, Rutgers U., 1988. Rsch. fellow Waksman Inst., Piscataway, N.J., 1983-88; prin. cons. Barrasso Biotech., Westfield, N.J., 1989—. Mem. Sigma Xi. Office: Barrasso Biotech Cons Assoc 1004 Harding St Westfield NJ 07090-1218

BARRATT, CYNTHIA LOUISE, pharmaceutical company executive; b. El Paso, Tex., Feb. 13, 1953; d. John Edward and Louise Joy (Lacy) B.; m. Nat G. Adkins, Jr., Oct. 5, 1980. BJ, U. Tex., 1975. Buyer Joske's of Tex., San Antonio, 1975-80, Craigs of Tex., Houston, 1981-83; v.p. sales ops. Akorn, Inc., Abita Springs, La., 1980-86; chief exec. officer, chmn. bd. dirs. NGLC Corp., Richmond, Tex., 1983—; pres., bd. dirs. CynaCon/Ocusoft, Richmond, 1986—. Mem. NAFE, Rosenberg/Richmond C. of C., DAR, Ft. Bend County Mus. Assn. Office: OcuSoft Inc PO Box 429 Richmond TX 77406-0429

BARREDO, RITA M., auditor; b. Torrington, Conn., June 24, 1953; d. Avelino and Josephine (DiNoia) B. BA, U. Conn., 1975; BS, Post Coll., 1981; MS in Acctg., U. Hartford, 1984, MBA, 1990. CPA, Conn.; cert. info. sys. auditor. Timekeeper Timex Corp., Waterbury, Conn., 1976-85; auditor Def. Contract Audit Agy., Lexington, Mass., 1985—. Mem. AICPA, Am. Women's Soc. CPAs, Conn. Soc. CPA (continuing profl. edn. com. 1989—), Inst. Mgmt. Accts. (sec. Waterbury chpt. 1994—), Inst. Internal Auditors, Info. Sys. Audit and Control Assn. Home: 130 Dawes Ave Torrington CT 06790 Office: Def Contract Audit Agy 400 Main St East Hartford CT 06108

BARRERA, ELVIRA PUIG, counselor, therapist, educator; b. Alice, Tex., Dec. 11, 1943; d. Carlos Rogers and Delia Rebecca (Puig) B.; 1 child, Dennis Lee Jr. BA, Incarnate Word Coll., 1971; M of Counseling and Guidance, St. Mary's U., San Antonio, 1978; specialist degree in marriage and family therapy, St. Mary's U., 1989. Lic. profl. counselor; lic. marriage & family therapist; lic. chem. dependency counselor. Tchr. Edgewood Ind. Sch. Dist., San Antonio, 1965-74, Dallas Ind. Sch. Dist., 1971-72, Northside Ind. Sch. Dist., San Antonio, 1974; ednl. cons. Region 20-Edn. Service Ctr., San Antonio, 1974-79; career edn. coordinator San Antonio Ind. Sch. Dist., 1979-84, counselor, 1984-91; family coord. C.A.T.C.H. Project, U. Tex. Health Sci. Ctr., Houston and Austin, 1991—; cons. Small Bus. Adminstrn., 1981, U.S. Office Edn., Washington, 1981-82, Tex. Edn. Agy., Austin, 1979-80; cons., writer San Antonio Ind. Sch. Dist. and Tex. Edn. Agy., 1985; cons. to various edn. publs. Chairperson career awareness exploring div. Boy Scouts Am., 1982-87. Named Disting. Alumna, Incarnate Word Coll., 1983; recipient Spurgeon award Boy Scouts Am., 1985, Merit award, 1986, Growth award, 1986. Mem. So. Tex. Pers. and Guidance Assn. (bd. dirs. 1981-82), San Antonio Area Women Deans, Adminstrs. and Counselors Assn. (treas. 1984-86), Austin Assn. for Marriage and Family Therapy, Incarnate Word Coll. Alumni Assn. (mem. adv. bd. 1990—), San Antonio Hash House Harriers (treas. 1990-91), Ctrl. Tex. Counseling Assn., Delta Kappa Gamma (2d v.p. 1982-84, 1st v.p. 1986-88), Chi Sigma Iota. Roman Catholic. Home: 907 Aurora Cir Austin TX 78757-3415 Office: U Tex Edn Annex 3 # 203 Austin TX 78712

BARRERE, JAMIE NEWTON, real estate executive; b. Russellville, Ark., June 7, 1946; d. James Edward Jr. and Martha (Spillers) Newton; m. Clement Adolph Barrere Jr., Aug. 30, 1969; 1 child, John Coleman. BA in Math., U. Ark., 1968. Cert. residential broker. Asst. programmer, analyst Conoco, Ponca City, Okla., 1968-69; programmer, analyst Bonner & Moore Assocs., Houston, 1969-70; tchr. math. Lamar Consol. High Sch., Rosenberg, Tex., 1970-72; assoc. broker Betty James, Realtors, Houston, 1972-78; pres. Barrere & Co., Realtors, Houston, 1978—; mem. adv. bd. Western Bank-Westheimer, Houston, 1986. Active Harris County Heritage Soc., Houston, 1970—, Houston Jr. Forum, 1980—, Am. Heart Found., Houston Zool. Soc.; mem. Mus. Fine Arts, Houston, 1978—; trustee St. Luke's United Meth. Ch.; bd. dirs. Friends of the Sch. of Music, U. Houston, 1992—; life mem. Tex. Real Estate Polit. Action Com. Mem. Nat. Assn. Realtors (mem. Equal Opportunity Com. 1985), Tex. Assn. Realtors (bd. dirs. 1989—, mem. Multiple Listing Svc. com. 1985-90), Houston Assn. Realtors (bd. dirs. 1986-89, 93—, v.p. 1993, mem. and chmn. various coms.), Houston C. of C. (amb. 1986), DAR, U. Ark. Alumnae Assn. (life, v.p. Houston chpt. 1985-88), Delta Delta Delta Alumnae Assn. (various offices), Lakeside Country Club, Petroleum Club, Briar Club, Tanglewood Garden Club (Houston, bd. dirs. 1973-86, 93—). Office: Barrere & Co 5850 San Felipe St Ste 125 Houston TX 77057-3012

BARRETO, CARMEN IVETTE, accountant; b. Arecibo, P.R., Oct. 5, 1967; d. Jose Miguel and Rosario (Velez) B. BBA in Pub. Acctg. cum laude, Pace U., 1989. Asst. acct. KPMG Peat Marwick, N.Y.C., 1989-90, staff acct., 1990-91, 1st yr. sr., 1991-92, 2d yr. sr., 1992-93, supervising sr., 1993; debt compliance analyst Dean Witter, Discover & Co., N.Y.C., 1993—. Mem. NAFE. Office: Dean Witter Discover & Co 2 World Trade Ctr New York NY 10048

BARRETT, BEATRICE HELENE, psychologist; b. Cin., Dec. 8, 1928; d. Oscar Slack and Helen (Kaiper) B.; m. Harold Sheffield Van Buren, Oct. 6, 1966 (div. Oct. 1985). BA, U. Ariz., 1950; MA, U. Ky., 1952; PhD, Purdue U., 1957. Lic. psychologist, Mass. Grad. tchg. asst. in psychology U. Ky., Lexington, 1950-52; psychology asst. Longview State Hosp., Cin., 1951, staff psychologist, 1952; staff psychologist Children's Outpatient and Cons. Svcs. Ind. U. Med. Ctr., Indpls., 1954-57, chief psychologist, 1957-59; instr. psychology Ind. U. Med. Sch., Indpls., 1956-60; rsch. assoc. dept. psychiatry Ind. U. Med. Ctr., Indpls., 1959-60; pvt. practice clin. psychology Indpls., 1957-60; research fellow in psychology Sch. of Medicine Harvard U., Boston, 1960-62; lectr. in spl. edn. Grad. Sch. Edn., Boston U., 1962-63; dir. psychol. rsch. Walter E. Fernald State Sch., Belmont, Mass., 1962-69; dir. behavior prosthesis lab. Walter E. Fernald State Sch., Belmont, 1963-92; chief psychologist, 1969-92; assoc. psychologist Enuice Kennedy Shriver Ctr. for Mental Retardation, Inc., Waltham, Mass., 1982—; instr. Mass. Psychol. Ctr., 1972; lectr. in spl. edn. Lesley Coll. Grad. Sch., 1974-76; adj. assoc. prof. Northeastern U., 1983—; psychology cons. Carter Meml. Hosp., Indpls., 1959-60; mem. exec. com. Boston Behavior Therapy Interest Group, 1973-74. Cons. editor, mem. adv. bds. various profl. jours.; contbr. numerous articles to profl. jours. Mem. Ind. Gov.'s Youth Coun., 1959-61; mem. spl. adv. com. on mental retardation Ind. Dept. Pub. Instrn., 1959-61; mem. task force Mass. Mental Retardation Planning Project, 1965-66; mem. adv. bd. Cambridge Ctr. for Behavioral Studies, 1981-87, 93-94, trustee, 1987-93, 94—, chair devel. com., 1987-89, mem. subcom. on Planned Giving, 1992—, chair nominating com., 1992-93, mem. 1993—, exec. com., 1993, 94—, mem. subcom. on Acad. and Sci. programs, 1992—; mem. com. on dance edn. Spl. Commn. on Performing Arts, 1976-77; mem. art acquisition com. DeCordova Mus., 1978-80, mem. contemporary arts coun., 1985-87; trustee Boston Repertory Ballet, 1977-79; trustee Boston Ballet Co., 1970-76, sec. bd., 1974-75, exec. com., 1974-76. Grantee Nat. Assn. for Retarded Citizens, 1963, NIHM, 1963-76. Fellow APA, Mass. Psychol. Assn., Behavior Therapy and Rsch. Soc. (charter clin.); mem. Assn. for Mentally Ill Children (human rights com. 1979-81), Am. Acad. on Mental Retardation (v.p. 1969-74, at-large exec. com. 1975-77), Ea. Psychol. Assn., Assn. for Advancement Behavior Therapy, Assn. Behavior Analysis (jour. adv. bd. 1983-87, chair task force on right to effective edn. 1986-91, Presdl. Adv. Group on edn. and pub. policy 1994—), Stage Harbor Yacht Club (Chatham, Mass., race com. 1984-86). Home: RFD 5 Box 236A Winter St Lincoln MA 01773

BARRETT, CAROLYN HERNLY, paralegal; b. Geneva, Ill., Jan. 17, 1954; d. Wayne Francis and Genevieve (Moyer) Hernly; m. Bradley Clayton Barrett, June 20, 1976; children: Heather Hernly, Lance Clayton, Colin Courtney. Grad., Moser Bus. Coll., 1975. Legal sec. Rathje, Woodward, Dyer & Burt, Wheaton, Ill., 1975-77; paralegal Chadwell, Kayser, Ruggles, McGee & Hastings, Chgo., 1978-80, Patrick James Perretti, Glen Ellyn, Ill., 1992—. Pres. Forest Glen PTA, Glen Ellyn, 1988-90; mem. Rep. Senatorial Innter Cir., Washington, 1991—, Nat. Trust for Hist. Preservation; chair ways and means com. Glen Ellyn Hist. Soc., 3d v.p., 1992—. Recipient

Medal of Freedom, Rep. Senatorial Inner Cir., 1994. Mem. DAR, Nat. Fedn. Rep. Women, Women in Arts (charter). Presbyterian. Home: 675 N Main Glen Ellyn IL 60137

BARRETT, ELEANOR EDIE, lawyer, mediator; b. N.Y.C., Feb. 20, 1945; d. Leslie Charles and Margie Eloise (Crawford) Edie; m. Alan Kliner, July 31, 1966 (div. 1975). BA in Sociology and French, Dickinson Coll., Carlisle, Pa., 1967; JD cum laude, Whittier Coll., 1978. Bar: Calif. 1978. Caseworker N.Y.C. Dept. Social Svcs., 1968-69; supr., caseworker Los Angeles County Dept. Pub. Social Svcs., L.A., 1969-73, appeals worker, 1973-78; dep. dist. atty. Los Angeles County Dist. Atty.'s Office, L.A., 1978—; mediation co-chair Lawyers for Human Rights, L.A., 1991-93. Co-chair adv. coun. Lesbian/Gay Cmty. Mediation Project, 1993—; mem. City of West Hollywood's Gay and Lesbian Issues Task Force, 1989. Recipient Angel Amidst award City of West Hollywood, 1993. Mem. NOW (legal coord. 1981-83, Hollywood pres. 1984-85, 88-90), L.A. County Bar Assn. (Wiley W. Manual award for pro bono legal svcs. 1992, commendation for vol. legal svcs. 1983, bd. dirs. Dispute Resolution Svcs. 1993—), Women Lawyers of L.A., League of Women Prosecutors. Democrat. Office: Los Angeles County Dist Atty's Office 849 S Broadway Fl 11 Los Angeles CA 90014-3206

BARRETT, ELIZABETH ANN MANHART, nursing educator, psychotherapist, consultant; b. Hume, Ill., July 11, 1934; d. Francis J. and Grace C. (Manhart) Fridy; children: Joseph B., Jeffrey F., Paula G. Brown, Pamela M. Shetler Carpino, Scott D. BS in Nursing summa cum laude, U. Evansville, 1970, MA, 1973, MS in Nursing, 1976; grad. Gestalt Assocs. for Psychotherapy, 1982; PhD in Nursing, NYU, 1983. Instr. nursing U. Evansville, Ind., 1970-73, asst. prof., 1973-76; staff nurse Welborn Bapt. Hosp., Evansville, 1975-76; staff nurse Bellevue Psychiat. Hosp., N.Y.C., 1976-79; clin. tchr. CUNY, 1977-82; asst. prof. Adelphi U., 1979-80; group practice Nurse Healers, 1979-82; pvt. practice psychotherapy, 1980—; nurse researcher Mt. Sinai Med. Ctr., N.Y.C., 1982-86, asst. dir. nursing, 1983-86; assoc. prof. Hunter Coll., N.Y.C., 1986-89, prof., 1994—, dir. grad. studies, 1989-92, coord. Ctr. for Nursing Rsch., 1993—; cons. Internat. Soc. Univ. Nurses. Mem. com. Regional Health Planning Council, Evansville, 1974-77. Fellow Am. Acad. Nursing; mem. Am. Nurses Assn. (cert. psychiat.-mental health, coun. nurse rschrs.), Nat. League Nursing, Ea. Nursing Rsch. Assn. (charter), Soc. Rogerian Scholars (founder, 1st pres. 1988-90), NOW, Phi Kappa Phi, Sigma Theta Tau (Upsilon chpt. pres. 1986-88), Alpha Tau Delta, Sigma Xi. Home: 415 E 85th St Apt 9E New York NY 10028-6358 Office: Hunter Coll 425 E 25th St New York NY 10010-2590

BARRETT, EVELYN CAROL, education educator; b. Ocean Springs, Miss., Feb. 6, 1928; d. Charles Edward and Irene Effie (Hopkins) Engbarth; diploma with honors Jr. Coll., (now Miss. Coast Coll.) Perkinston, Miss., 1945; BS in Commerce with high honors, Miss. So. Coll. (now U. So. Miss.), 1947; MBA in Acctg., La. State U., 1950; also numerous continuing edn. courses, 1950-82; m. Arthur James Barrett, June 10, 1951; children: George Stanley, Ruth Anne, James Sidney, Carolyn Jean. Bookkeeper-sec. Non-Commn. Officers Club, Kessler AFB, Miss., summer 1947; asst., secretarial practice office and div. research, instr. in typing Coll. Commerce, La. State U., 1947-50; instr. Miss. So. Coll., summer 1950; clk.-stenographer dept. physics U. Ill., Urbana, 1951-52; instr. in shorthand Ill. Comml. Coll., 1951-52; tchr. Milford (N.H.) High Sch., 1957-58; tchr. bus. edn. Merrimack (N.H.) High Sch., 1958-90, head dept. bus. edn., 1971-81, ret., 1990; instr. auditing Rivier Coll., 1982; registered rep. R. Danais Investment Co., Manchester, N.H.; account exec. John, Edward & Co., Lebanon, N.H.; ind. beauty cons. Mary Kay Cosmetics, Merrimack; tutor in shorthand, acctg.; cons. acctg. systems. Grad. asst. La. State U., 1947-50. Active Girl Scouts U.S.A., including Cadette leader, 1959-63, sr. troop leader Swiftwater council, 1970-72, adult vol. trainer, 1964-66, troop program cons., 1963-64. Mem. N.H. Bus. Educators Assn. (v.p. 1964-65, pres. 1965-67, rep. to N.H. Vocat. Assn. 1986-87 (sec. 1967-68, treas. 1973-75, historian 1986-87), N.H. Supervisory Union 27 (sec.-treas. 1961-62), NEA, N.H. Edn. Assn., Merrimack Tchrs. Assn. (Disting. Educator award 1980, Excellence in Edn. award 1985, sec. 1984-85), New Eng. Bus. Educators Assn., Am. Vocat. Assn., N.H. Assn. Computer Edn. Statewide, Eastern Bus. Edn. Assn., Nat. Bus. Edn. Assn., AAUW, Delta Zeta, Phi Theta Kappa, Pi Omega Pi, Delta Pi Epsilon, Alpha Delta Kappa (chpt. award of appreciation 1980, historian N.E. region 1981-83, v.p. N.H. Alpha chpt. 1978-79, pres. N.H. Alpha chpt. 1979-82, N.H. State sgt.-at-arms 1982-84, N.H. State treas. 1984-88, State membership chmn. 1988-92, State chaplain 1992-94, N.H. State pres. elect, 1994—), Delta Sigma Epsilon (chpt. corr. sec.). Roman Catholic. Clubs: Gen. Electric Women's, Manchester Coll. Women's, Our Lady of Mercy Ch. Guild, Merrimack Sr. Citizen.

BARRETT, JANE HAYES, lawyer; b. Dayton, Ohio, Dec. 13, 1947; d. Walter J. and Jane H. Barrett. BA, Calif. State U.-Long Beach, 1969; JD, U. So. Calif., 1972. Bar: Calif. 1972, U.S. Dist. Ct. (cen. dist.) Calif. 1972, U.S. Ct. Appeals (9th cir.) 1982, U.S. Supreme Ct. Assoc. Arter, Hadden, Lawler, Felix & Hall, L.A., 1972-79, ptnr., 1979-94, mng. ptnr., 1984-93; ptnr. Preston, Gates & Ellis, 1994—; mng. ptnr. Preston, Gates & Ellis, L.A., 1994—; lectr. bus. law Calif. State U., 1973-75. Mem. adv. bd. Harriet Buhai Legal Aid Ctr., 1991—; pres. Pilgrim Parents Orgn. 1990-91. Named Outstanding Grad. Calif. State U., Long Beach, 1988, Outstanding Alumnae Polit. Sci., 1993. Fellow Am. Bar Found.; mem. ABA (gov. 1980-84, chmn. young lawyers divsn. 1980-81, chair com. on delivery of legal svcs. 1985-89, exec. coun., legal edn. and admissions sects. 1985-89, fin. sec. torts and ins. practice 1982-83, adv. mem. fed. judiciary com. 1994—, sec. Am. Bar Endowment 1984-90, bd. dirs. 1990—, sec. 1993—, bd. fellows young lawyers divsn. 1992—), Calif. State Bar (com. adminstrn. justice, editorial bd. Calif. Lawyers 1981-84), Legion Lex (bd. dirs. 1990-93). Democrat.

BARRETT, JESSICA (DONNA ANN NIPERT), psychotherapist; b. Paterson, N.J., July 25, 1952; d. Donald Alfred and Gloria Emma (Lustica) Nipert; m. John David Barrett, Sept. 9, 1977 (div. June 1982); 1 child, Ashley Elizabeth. BA, UCLA, 1975; MA, Azusa Pacific U., 1981. Lic. marriage, family, child counselor; cert. hypnosis profl. With employee relations Engrs. and Architects Exec. Assn., L.A., 1975-79; practicing psychotherapy Toluca Lake and Burbank, Calif., 1983—; instr., supr. Calif. Family Study Ctr., North Hollywood, Calif., 1986-94; psychotherapist Pasadena (Calif.) Outpatient Eating Disorders Program, 1987-88; cons. Texaco Employee Assistance Program, Studio City, 1985-86, NBC Employee Assistance Program, Burbank, 1986-87, 93—; lectr. various groups, Burbank, San Fernando Valley, 1983-87; spl. therapist Am. Psych-Mgmt. Inc., Preferred Health Care, Value Behavior Health, Vista Health Mgmt., Managed Health Network, MCC/Cigna EAP and Provider; assessment and referral liaison Nat. Resource Cons., San Diego, 1983-93, Employee Support Systems Corp., Orange, Calif., 1985-94, Health and Human Resource Ctr., 1984-92. Mem. Employee Assistance Profls. Assn. (bd. dirs. 1983-86), Am. Assn. Marriage and Family Therapists (clin.), Stepfamily Assn. Am., Calif. Family Study Ct. Alumni Assn. (sec.-treas. 1987-88, v.p. programs 1988-89).

BARRETT, JUDITH ANN, English language educator; b. Pitts., Feb. 23, 1944; m. Edward A. Barrett; children: Matthew, Joel. BA in English, Allegheny Coll., Meadville, Pa., 1966; MA in Anthropology, U. Pitts., 1991. Tchr. Ringgold Sch. Dist., Monongahela, Pa., 1978—, chairperson English dept., 1982—. Author: The Mound-Building Generations, 1991. Mem. Nat. Coun. Tchrs. English, Western Pa. Coun. Tchrs. English. Office: Ringgold Sch Dist 1200 Chess St Monongahela PA 15063-2716

BARRETT, LENORE HARDY, state legislator, mining and investment consultant; b. Newkirk, Okla., June 16, 1934; d. Floyd Jack and Minnie Bell (O'Dell) Hardy; m. Robert Sidney Cloud (div.); m. Robert Michael Barrett, 1964; 1 child, Michael Hardy. BS, Okla. Bapt. U., 1956. Pvt. practice Challis, Idaho; state legislator Ho. of Reps., Boise, Idaho, 1993—. Active Idaho Farm Bureau Political Action Com., 1990-92; dir. Salmon River Electric Coop., Inc., Challis; police commr. Challis City Coun., 1984-89; mem. Assn. Idaho Cities Legis. Com., 2 yrs.; state committeewoman Custer County Rep. Ctrl. Com., Challis, 1982—. Mem. Nat. Inholder's Assn., Idaho Rep. Party, Ctrl. Idaho Mining Assn. (sec.), Custer County Farm Bureau, Grassroots for Multiple Use, Blue Ribbon Coalition, Order of Eastern Star (Grand Organist award Grand Chpt. Idaho 1985-86). Baptist. Home: PO Box 347 143 W Pleasant Challis ID 83226 Office: Idaho Ho of Reps State Captiol Boise ID 83720*

BARRETT, LIDA KITTRELL, mathematics educator; b. Houston, May 21, 1927; d. Pleasant Williams and Maidel (Baker) Kittrell; m. John Herbert Barrett, June 2, 1950 (dec. Jan. 1969); children: John Kittrell, Maidel Horn, Mary Louise. BA, Rice U., 1946; MA, U. Tex., Austin, 1949; PhD, U. Pa., 1954. Instr. math. U. Conn., Waterbury, 1955-56; vis. appointment U. Wis., Madison, 1959-60; lectr. U. Utah, Salt Lake City, 1956-61; assoc. prof. U. Tenn., Knoxville, 1961-70, prof., 1970-80, head math. dept., 1973-80; assoc. provost No. Ill. U., DeKalb, 1980-87; dean, arts and scis. Miss. State U., Mississippi State, 1987-91; sr. assoc. Edn. and Human Resources Directorate NSF, Washington, 1991—; ind. math. cons., Knoxville, Tenn., 1964-80. Contbr. articles on topology and math. edn. to profl. jours. Mem. Math. Assn. Am. (pres. 1989, 90), Am. Math. Soc., Soc. Indsl. and Applied Math., Nat. Coun. Tchrs. Math., Am. Assn. Higher Edn., Phi Kappa Phi, Sigma Xi. Episcopalian. Office: Nat Sci Found 4201 Wilson Blvd Ste 805 Arlington VA 22202

BARRETT, LINDA L., real estate executive; b. Hudson, Mich., Aug. 16, 1948; d. David John and Georgia Elizabeth (Spengler) B.; 1 dau., Toni. Student, U. Mich., 1970-73. Cert. residential brokerage mgr. Sales mgr. Collins Real Estate, Hudson, Mich., 1973-79; owner, broker Homeland Real Estate, Lake Leann, Mich., 1979-82; mgr. broker Mid-Mich. Real Estate, Jackson, Mich., 1982-85; exec. v.p. Michael Saunders & Co., Sarasota, Fla., 1986—; mem. adv. bd. Sotheby's Internat. Mem. Internat. Real Estate Fedn., Nat. Mktg. Inst., NAFE, Nat. Assn. Realtors, Fla. Assn. Realtors, Sarasota C. of C., Bradenton C. of C., Com. of 100, 2000 Notable Am. Women (profl. standards com. women's coun.), Econ. Devel. Coun., CRB, Estates Club. Office: Michael Saunders & Co 1801 Main St Sarasota FL 34236-5969

BARRETT, LOIS YVONNE, minister; b. Enid, Okla., Nov. 9, 1947; d. Hugh Preston and Audrey Lucille (Wilson) B.; m. Thomas Bruce Mierau, June 26, 1977; children: Barbara, Susanna, John. BA, U. Okla., 1969; MDiv, Mennonite Bibl. Sem., 1983; PhD, Union Grad. Sch., 1992. Ordained to Christian ministry, 1985. Assoc. editor The Mennonite, Newton, Kans., 1971-77; editor The House Ch. newsletter, Wichita, Kans., 1978-80, 83-85; instr. Great Plains Sem. Edn. Prog., North Newton, Kans., 1985, 90, 92; co-pastor Mennonite Ch. of the Servant, Wichita, Kans., 1983-92; exec. sec. Commn. Home Ministries Gen. Conf. Mennonite Ch., Newton, 1992—; mem. exec. coun. Inst. Mennonite Studies, Elkhart, Ind., 1983—; mem. ecumenical peace theology working group Mennonite Cen. Com., Akron, Pa., 1988-92; writer Inter-Mennonite Confession of Faith com., 1988—; editorial com. Mennonite Ency. V, 1985-87. Author: The Vision and the Reality, 1983, Building the House Church, 1986, The Way God Fights, 1987, Doing What is Right, 1989. Convener Chs. United for Peacemaking, Wichita, 1986, 88-89, bd. dirs., 1983-90; pres. Midtown Citizens Assn., 1977-78; mem. Citizens Participation Orgn., 1977-80. Recipient Am. Bible Soc. award, 1983. Mem. Am. Acad. Religion, Am. Soc. Ch. History, Phi Beta Kappa. Home: 1508 Fairview St Wichita KS 67203-2634 Office: Gen Conf Mennonite Ch Commn Home Ministries 722 Main Newton KS 67114

BARRETT, LORETTA ANNE, publishing executive; b. Mt. Vernon, N.Y., July 1, 1941; d. Edward Vincent and Irene Marie (Wynne) B. Student, Rosemont (Pa.) Coll., 1958-60; BA cum laude, U. Pa., 1962, MAT, 1965. Editor Doubleday & Co. Anchor Press, N.Y.C., 1965-67; editorial dir. Doubleday & Co. Special Projects, N.Y.C., 1967-72; exec. editor, publisher Anchor Press, Doubleday & Co., N.Y.C., 1972-83; exec. editorial v.p. Doubleday & Co., N.Y.C., 1983-90; pres. Loretta Barrett Books, Lit. Agy., 1990—; bd. dirs. Reading is Fundamental, Washington, 1967—, Through the Flower, Santa Fe, N.Mex., 1986—. Assoc., trustee Coun. Pa. Women U. Pa., 1989; bd. dirs. Athena Inst., Haverford, Pa., 1987—, Grandparenting Found., Lake Placid, N.Y., 1987. Mem. Women in the Media, Assn. of Author's Reps., Inc. Democrat. Roman Catholic. Office: Loretta Barrett Books 101 5th Ave New York NY 10003-1008

BARRETT, LYNN S., public relations executive; b. Dec. 18, 1943. BA, Sullins Coll., 1963. Assoc. dir. network TV/radio Rowland Co., 1967-71, dir. TV, 1977-79, sr. v.p., 1979-85; publicist Mobil Oil Corp., 1971-74; mgr., press. and pub. rels. Sta. WCBS-TV, N.Y.C., 1974-75; dir. comm. CBS Sports, N.Y.C., 1975-77; founder, pres. Primetime Concepts Inc., N.Y.C., 1985—. Mem. adv. coun. Internat. U. of Comm. Mem. NATAS, AWRT. Office: Primetime Concepts Inc 20 West 37th St New York NY 10018*

BARRETT, PAULETTE SINGER, public relations executive; b. Paris, Dec. 20, 1937; came to U.S., 1947; d. Andrew M. and Agatha (Kinsbrunner) Singer; m. Laurence I. Barrett, Mar. 9, 1957 (div. 1983); children: Paul Meyer, David Allen, Adam Singer. BA, NYU, 1957; MS in Journalism, Columbia U., 1958. News dir. Yardney Electric Corp., N.Y.C., 1958-61; freelance writer newspapers and pub. relations orgns., N.Y.C. and Washington, 1961-73; assoc. dir. pub. info. Columbia U., N.Y.C., 1973-77; from account exec. to v.p., then sr. v.p. Edelman Pub. Rels. Worldwide, N.Y.C., 1977-80, sr. v.p. and gen. mgr., 1980, exec. v.p., gen. mgr., 1986-88, exec. v.p., dir. corp. affairs div., 1988-89; exec. v.p. Rowland Co., N.Y.C., 1980-82; exec. dir. communications UJA-Fedn./N.Y., N.Y.C., 1982-86; sr. v.p., mng. dir. Hill and Knowlton, Chgo., 1989-90; pres. Barrett Comm., Chgo., 1990—; bd. dirs. Ballet Chgo. Mem. bus. and mktg. coms. Ill. Arts Alliance Found.; internat. adv. bd. Elmhurst Coll. Holocaust Edn. Project. Mem.. Am. Soc. Health Care Mktg. and Pub. Rels., Women in Charge. Office: Barrett Comms 1555 N Astor St Ste 23 Chicago IL 60610

BARRETTA-KEYSER, JOLIE, professional athletics coach, author; b. Phila., Aug. 17, 1954; d. Philip Francis and Norma Roberta (Podoszek) Barretta; m. Joel D. Keyser; children: Evan Barrett, Kyra Lani. Student, U. Calif., Long Beach, 1972-76, U. Florence, Italy, 1974-75. Tchr. gymnastics Los Angeles City Sch. Dist., 1973-77, judge, 1976-82; coach, choregrapher Kips Gymnastic Club, Long Beach, Calif., 1976-78, So. Calif. Acrobatics Team, Huntington Beach, Calif., 1979-81, UCLA, 1980-82; pres. West Coast Waves Rhythmic Gymnastics, Rolling Hills Estates, Calif., 1980—; mem. coaching staff U.S. Nat. Rhythmic Gymnastics Team, 1983—; coach Centro Olimpico Nazionale Italia, Rome, 1974-76; lectr. dance, phys. edn. Calif. State U., Dominguez Hills, Carson, 1981-92; French lang. mistress of ceremonies rhythmic gymnastics event U.S. Olympic Games, L.A., 1984; invited observer Inst. Phys. Culture, Bejing, 1985, Bulgarian Gymnastics Fedn., Sophia, 1982-90; meet dir. state and regional championships, L.A. County, 1984, '86; internat. lectr. body alignment; pres. Rhythymic Gymnasts Devel. Program, 1984—; developer RIGOR (Rhythmic Gymnastics Outreach) for U.S.A. recreation programs; mem. rhythmic gymnastics adv. com. & bd. Internat. Spl. Olympics, 1990—. Author: Body Alignment, 1985; columnist Internat. Gymnast Mag., 1987-90. Tour leader Acad. Tours Inc. U.S./Bulgaria Friendship Through Sports Am. Tour, N.Y. and Bulgaria, 1987. Recipient recognition plaque U.S. Womens Sports Awards Banquet, 1984-89. Mem. U.S. Rhythmic Gymnastics Coaches Assn. (pres. 1984—), U.S. Gymnastics Fedn. (bd. dirs. 1985—, nat. team coach 1984—, mem. del., coach internat. competitions U.S., Mex., Hungary, Bulgaria, Belgium, Can. 1984—, choreographer age group devel. compulsory div. 1987, staff Olympic Tng. Ctr. 1984—), Inst. Noetic Scis., Internat. Spl. Olympics (adv. bd. rhythmic gymnastics). Republican. Office: West Coast Waves Ste 609 11661 San Vicente Blvd Los Angeles CA 90049

BARRETT-CONNOR, ELIZABETH LOUISE, epidemiologist, educator; b. Evanston, Ill., Apr. 8, 1935; m. James D. Connor. BA, Mt. Holyoke Coll., 1956; MD, Cornell U., 1960. Diplomate Am. Bd. Internal Medicine, Nat. Bd. Med. Examiners. Instr. medicine U. Miami, Fla., 1965-68, asst. prof. medicine, 1968-70; asst. prof. community and family medicine U. Calif., San Diego, 1970-74, assoc. prof. community and family medicine, 1974-81, prof. community and family medicine, 1981—, acting chair dept. community and family medicine, 1981-82, chmn. dept. family and preventative medicine, 1982—; vis. prof. Royal Soc. Medicine, London, 1989; mem. hosp. infection control com. VA Med. Ctr., San Diego, 1971—. Contbr. articles to profl. jours. NIH grantee, 1970-89, 78-80, 91-95, Janssen Pharm., 1976-78, Am. Heart Assn. grantee, 1980-81. Mem. Am. Heart Assn. (chmn. budget com. coun. on epidemiology 1987-88, chmn. coun. on epidemiology 1988-89), Am. Pub. Health Assn. (chmn. epidemiology sect. 1989—), Assn. Tchrs. Preventive Medicine (bd. dirs. 1987—), Inst. Medicine. Office: U Calif # 0628 La Jolla CA 92093

BARRIE, AMY ROBIN, computer company executive, technical writer; b. Glenridge, N.J., Aug. 25, 1960; d. David Burton and Berenice Carol (Bloom) Ellis; m. James Scott Barrie, Nov. 8, 1986; children: Matthew Ellis, Sarah Rowe. BA in Math., U. Vt., 1978. Customer svc. rep. U.S. Trust Co., Boston, 1979-80; sales rep. Neiman-Marcus, Boston, 1980-82; tech. writer Draper Labs., Cambridge, Mass., 1982-84; quality assurance analyst Data Architects, Waltham, Mass., 1984-86; tech. writer Logica Data Architects, Waltham, 1986-90; mgr., tech. writer Logica N.Am., Waltham, 1990-93; documentation mgr. Logica Inc., Lexington, 1993—; tech. writer, cons. Cullinet Software, Westwood, Mass., 1989, Applix Corp., Westborough, Mass., 1988. Mem. Editorial Soc. New Eng. Home: 166 Harrington Ave Concord MA 01742-4025 Office: Logica Inc 32 Hartwell Ave Lexington MA 02173

BARRIE, BARBARA ANN, actress; b. Chgo., May 23, 1931; d. Louis and Frances Rose (Boruszak) Berman; m. Jay Malcolm Harnick, July 23, 1964; children: Jane Caroline Harnick, Aaron Louis Harnick. BFA, U. Tex., 1953. Appeared with N.Y. Shakespeare Festival, 1960, 65, 69, Am. Shakespeare Festival, 1958-59; appeared on Broadway in: Wooden Dish, 1955, Beaux Stratagem, 1959, Company, 1970, Prisoner of Second Ave., 1972, Selling of the President, 1971, California Suite, 1976, The Killdeer, 1974 (Obie award, Drama Desk award 1974), Big and Little Phoenix Theatre, N.Y.C., 1979, Isn't it Romantic, 1984, Fugue, Long Wharf Playhouse, 1986, After-Play, 1995; numerous TV appearances including Barney Miller, Two of a Kind, 1982, Barefoot in the Park, 1982, Double Trouble (series), 1984-85, as Mamie Eisenhower in Backstairs at the White House, Family Ties, 1987, Mr. President, 1987, TV movie The Execution; appeared in films One Potato, Two Potato, 1964 (Cannes Festival Acting award 1964), The Caretakers, 1963, Breaking Away, 1979 (Oscar nomination), Private Benjamin, 1980, Real Men, 1986, The Passage, End of the Line, 1986. Active ERA. Mem. AFTRA, SAG, Actors Equity Assn., Acad. Motion Picture Arts and Scis. Office: care Innovative Artists Talent & Literary Agency 8942 Wilshire Blvd Blvd Ste 300 Los Angeles CA 90025*

BARRIE, JOAN PARKER, elementary education educator; b. L.A., Aug. 25, 1932; d. Joseph Alexander and Madeline Agnes (Smith) Parker. EdB, Seattle U., 1959; MEd, Loyola Marymount, 1973. Cert. elem., secondary tchr., Calif.; cert. reading specialist, lang. devel. specialist. 6th grade tchr. Sisters of Immaculate Heart, Hollywood, Calif., 1953-56; reading specialist Lakewood (Wash.) Schs., 1959-60, Beverly Hills (Calif.) Sch. Dist., 1960-62; 2nd grade tchr., 6th grade reading specialist Inglewood (Calif.) Unified Sch. Dist., 1962-76; owner Everest Cultural Enrichments, L.A., 1975—; various positions Torrance and Redondo, Calif., 1979-82; office mgr. Starbecca Records, Redondo Beach, Calif., 1982-83; 5th and 6th grades tchr. St. Anthonys, El Segundo, Calif., 1984-85; 2nd grade bilingual tchr. Hawthorne (Calif.) Sch. Dist., 1985—. Author, illustrator; Did You See It, Too?, 1982, Tiggy, Primary Academies, 1989, Reading English, 1994, Reading Spanish, 1995; composer, lyricist: Valentine, 1986; composer, librettist: Lovers in the Moon, 1993. Active United We Stand, 1994, Concern America, Redondo Beach, 1994. Mem. NEA, Calif. Tchrs. Assn., Nat. Coun. Social Studies, S.W. Manuscripters, Dramatist Guild, Smithsonian, Ednl. Dealer. Roman Catholic. Office: Everest Cultural Enrichments PO Box 7000-445 Redondo Beach CA 90277

BARRISH, CAROL LAMPERT, psychologist; b. N.Y.C., Oct. 6, 1945; d. J. William and Sally (Bobrick) Lampert; m. Michael Louis Barrish, June 30, 1974; children: Jordan Seth, Jessica Lynne. BA, Queens Coll., 1967; MA, Columbia U., 1972; PhD, NYU, 1993. Cert. psychologist; cert. learning disabilities cons.; lic., cert. spl. edn. tchr.; cert. reading specialist; cert. tchr. Tchr., team leader elem. sch. Englewood (N.J.) Bd. Edn., 1969-72, reading cons., 1973-74; curriculum coord. Adams Town House, N.Y.C., 1974-75; ednl., learning disabilities cons. N.Y.C., 1974—, reading/learning disabilities specialist, 1975—; clin. psychology intern Risk Inst., NYU Hosp., N.Y.C., 1990-91; psychologist Com. for Spl. Edn., Bd. of Edn., N.Y.C., 1992—. Author: (with others) Assessment of Social Skills Problems with Learning Disabled Adolescents, 1993. Mem. APA, N.Y. State Psychol. Assn., Orton Dyslexia Soc., Children and Adults with Attention Deficit Disorder, Kappa Delta Pi. Office: 305 E 86th St New York NY 10028

BARRISKILL, MAUDANNE KIDD, primary school educator; b. Balt., Apr. 2, 1932; d. John Graydon and Maudine (Adams) Kidd; m. Peter Herbert Barriskill, Nov. 30, 1957; children: John, Michael. BA, So. Meth. U., 1954; student early childhood edn., Old Dominion U., 1970; student, Katharine Gibbs Sch., N.Y.C., 1954-55, Juilliard Sch. Music, N.Y.C., 1948-50. Exec. sec., copywriter trainee J. Walter Thompson Advt. Agy., N.Y.C., 1955-59; founder Maude Barry Interior Design, Virginia Beach, 1970-73; founder, dir. The Home Sch., Virginia Beach, 1975—; tchr. Ea. Shore Chapel Presch., Virginia Beach, 1970-75, Montessori Child Devel. Ctr., Virginia Beach. Author children's books and workbooks. Tchr. Sunday sch. Home: 4721 Newgate Ct Virginia Beach VA 23455-4033

BARRON, CLAIRE L., psychologist; b. Kansas City, Mo., Oct. 19, 1951; d. Beach Henry and Jean Elizabeth (Meyers) Tuckness; m. Timothy Kent Barron, Aug. 14, 1982; children: Sarah L., Timothy W. BA in Psychology, Human Devel. and Family Life, U. Kans., 1974, MA in Human Devel. and Family Life, 1976; PhD in Counseling Psychology, U. So. Miss., 1988. Lic. psychologist, Kans., Mo., sch. psychologist, Mo. Dir. summer activities program Kansas City Regional Ctr. Developmentally Delayed, 1974; grad. rsch. asst. U. Kans., Lawrence, 1974-76; mental health specialist children's svcs. Community Mental Health Ctr.-South, Kansas City, 1976-80, program leader early childhood intervention and screening program, 1979-80; pvt. practice Kansas City, 1980-81; grad. asst. dept. counseling psychology U. So. Miss., Hattiesburg, 1981-83; psychology intern Western Mo. Mental Health Ctr., Kansas City, 1983-84, psychologist pre-adolescent unit, 1988-90, intern supr., 1988-90; sch. psychologist Child World Sch., Kansas City, 1984-86, Raytown (Mo.) C-2 Sch. Dist., 1986-88; pvt. practice Prairie Village, Kans., 1990—; prin. rsch. investigator Head Start program U. Kans., 1973-74, grad. rsch. asst. and therapist family tng. program bur. child rsch., 1974-76; grad. instr. U. Kans. Med. Ctr., Kansas City, 1976; teaching asst. dept. counseling psychology U. So. Miss., 1981, 82; cons. Raytown C-2 Sch. Dist., 1985-86, Salvation Army Children's Shelter, Kansas City, 1992, Raytown Sch. Dist., 1992—, Raymore-Peculiar (Mo.) Sch. Dist., 1993—; instr. Avila Coll., Kansas City, 1990; presenter in field. Co-author: (manual) Behavior Management System, 1987. Mem. APA. Office: 3520 W 75th Ste 201 Prairie Village KS 66208

BARRON, PEGGY PENNISI, management consultant; b. Chgo., Jan. 27, 1958; d. Louis Legendre and Jane Harriet (Peters) Pennisi; m. Stan Barron, May 3, 1986; children: Brian Alexander, Christine Deanna. BS with honors, U. Ill., Chgo., 1979. Data processing mgr. Oasis Aviation, Inc., L.A., 1980-87; pres. Millennium Enterprises, Marina Del Rey, Calif., 1987—. Mem. NAFE, Phi Beta Kappa, Phi Kappa Phi. Home and Office: 3008 Yale Ave Marina Dl Rey CA 90292-5539

BARRON, PURIFICACION CAPULONG, nursing administrator and educator; b. Pampanga, The Philippines, Jan. 24, 1932; d. Alfonso E. and Lucia N. (Nabong) Capulong; m. Rodrigo I. Barron, July 7, 1968; 1 child, Joseph Rodney. Diploma, St. Luke's Hosp., Manila, 1951; student, St. Louis U., 1954-55; BSN, Columbia U., 1960; MA, Philippine Women's U., 1966. Sch. nurse Manila City Schs., 1951-54; staff nurse Mt. Sinai Hosp., N.Y. Polyclinic, St. Clare Hosp., St. Luke's Women's Hosp.,, 1954-60; prin., chief nurse, instr. Ortanez Gen. Hosp. and Sch. Nursing, Quezon City, Philippines, 1960-66; chief nurse Am. Hosp. and St. Catherine Hosp., Manila, 1964-65; lectr. Ottawa (Ont.) U. Sch. Nursing, 1966-71; asst. prof. Ind. State U. Sch. Nursing, Terre Haute, 1971-74; DON Holiday Home, Clinton, Ind., 1974-75; pvt. duty nurse, 1975-90; dir. Countryside Health Ctr., Buchanan, Ga., 1991-92; co. nurse SAHA Union Internat., Ga., 1992—; dir. nursing Pine Knoll Nursing, Carrollton, Ga., 1992—; medicare and nursing care plan coord. Meadowbrook Manor of Carrollton, 1994—, dir. nursing, 1994—; instr. Cen. Luzon Sch. Nursing, Martinez Sch. Nursing, The Philippines, Lorrain Sch. Nursing, Pembroke, Ont., Can.; paramed. examiner ins. applicants, 1982-90; nurse Camp McIntosh, summer 1987. Mem. ANA, Philippine Nursing Assn. (life), St. Luke's Hosp. Alumni Assn. (life.). Home: 103 Kristy Ln Carrollton GA 30117-2527

BARRON, ROBERTA, human resources management consultant; b. N.Y.C., May 11, 1940; d. Irv and Roslyn (Engerow) Yellin; m. Harold S.

Barron, Nov. 17, 1963; children: Lawrence Ira, Jean Louise. Student, UCLA, 1960-61; BA, Conn. Coll., 1962; MSIR, Loyola U., Chgo., 1987. Corp. pub. dept. staff Time Inc., N.Y.C., 1962-64; pub. relations cons., 1965-87; cons. Exec. Assets, Chgo., 1987-88, Barron Assocs., Inc., Chgo., 1988—. Mem. ASTD, IAOP, Women's Athletic Club. Office: 180 E Pearson St Chicago IL 60611-2130

BARRON, SUSAN, clinical psychologist; b. Chgo., May 13, 1940; d. Earl and Trixie (Chernoff) B.; m. Eugene Pratt, Jan. 18, 1975 (div. 1983). BBA, CCNY, 1960, MA, 1963; PhD, CUNY, 1973. Lic. psychologist. Intern psychologist Bellevue Psychiat. Hosp., N.Y.C., 1964-65, psychologist, 1966-67; teaching fellow CUNY, 1965-66; staff psychologist Lighthouse, N.Y. Assn. for the Blind, N.Y.C., 1968-71, sr. clin. psychologist, 1971-74; dir. psychol. counseling svcs. Peninsula Ctr. for the Blind, Palo Alto, Calif., 1974-75; cons. psychologist N.Y. State Commn. for Blind and Visually Handicapped, N.Y.C., 1975-78, 86—; dir. psychol. svcs. Thoms Rehab. Hosp., Asheville, N.C., 1978-79; state coord. psychol. svcs. N.Y. State Office Vocat. Rehab., Albany, 1979-85; founder, dir. Family Support Program ICU N.Y. Infirmary-Beekman Downtown Hosp., N.Y.C., 1982-84; cons. clin. psychologist N.Y. Hosp. Cornell U. Med. Ctr., 1987—; pvt. practice, 1987—; behavioral seicnetist diabetes control/complications trial NIH Cornell U. Med. Ctr., N.Y.C., 1987—; cons. clin. psychologist Joslin Ctr. for Diabetes St. Luke's-Roosevelt Hosp. Ctr./Columbia U. Phys. and Surg., N.Y.C., 1994—; consulting clin. psychologist Joslin Ctr. Diabetes, St. Lukes-Roosevelt Hosp. Ctr., U. Hosp. of Columbia U. Coll. of Physicians and Surgeons, N.Y.C., 1994—; mem. Nat. Human Svcs. Adv. Bd.-Retinitis Pigmentosa Found., Balt., 1975-82; cons. Del. State Commn. for Blind, 1975-78, Am. Found. Blind, 1974-82, Calif. Dept. Rehab., 1974-82, Hawaii State Svcs. Blind, 1974-82, Ariz. State Svcs. Blind, 1974-82, Nev. State Svcs. Blind, 1974-82; speaker Nat. Multiple Disabilities Conf., 1982, NAS, 1981; mem. adv. bd. doctoral psychology internship program Rusk Inst. of Rehab. Medicine, NYU Med. Ctr., 1979-84; behavioral scientist Diabetes Control and Complications Trial NIH-Cornell U. Med. Ctr., 1987—. Contbr. articles to profl. jours. Recipient Leadership award Alumni Assn. CCNY, 1960, 62, Rsch. award Retinal Dystrophy Soc., Australia, 1975. Fellow Am. Orthopsychiat. Assn.; mem. APA, AAAS, Calif. State Psychol. Assn., N.Y. Acad. Sci. Office: Joslin Ctr for Diabetes St Lukes-Roosevelt Hosp Ctr 425 W 59th St 9th Fl New York NY 10019

BARROS-SMITH, DEBORAH LYNNE, publishing executive, editor; b. Washington, Jan. 19, 1959; d. Ford Gibson and Carole Lynne Barros; m. Marcellus Drummer Smith III; 1 child, Marcellus Drummer IV. AS, Oakwood Coll., 1980; BA, Temple U., 1983; postgrad., Lansdale Sch. of Bus., 1982-83. News announcer Sta. WOCG, Huntsville, Ala., 1978-79; news announcer, news dir. Sta. WEUP, Huntsville, 1979-80, talk show host, 1992-93; asst. audience coord. Sta. KYW-TV, Phila., 1981-83; freelance writer Phila., 1982-84; writer, prodr. Cable Adnet, Phila., 1983-86; owner Praise Consultants, Spring City, Pa., 1985-89; city editor Speakin Out News, Huntsville, 1990-92; pub., editor The Valley Informer Inc., Huntsville, 1994—. Youth adv. Pottstown, Pa., Phila., Huntsville, 1980—; lobbyist Welfare Rights Orgn., Phila., 1982; active Minority Prevention of AIDS Through Choices and Tng., Huntsville, 1991-93; co-founder North Ala. Youth Congress, Huntsville, 1991—; HIV/AIDS presenter ARC, Huntsville, 1991—; pub. rels. and field worker Heart, Body and Spirit (Health Outreach Project), Huntsville, 1993—; journalism tchr. Girls Inc., Huntsville, 1994; speaker on child abuse, 1994—; mem. Ala. State Bd. Breast and Cervical Cancer Coalition, Montgomery, 1994—; mem. cable access bd. COMPAT, Huntsville, 1994—; mem. bd., media com. Stop The Violence, Eradication Task Force, Huntsville, 1994—; mem. bd. Family Life Ctr., Ala. A&M U., 1995. Recipient Cert. of Appreciation, U.S. Senator John Heinz, 1982, Welfare Rights Orgn., Phila., 1982, U.S. Congressman Bud Cramer, 1993, Madison County Commr. Dr. Prince Preyer, 1993, Best Media award Twenty Disting. Young Men of Huntsville, Ala., 1993; named Citizen of Yr., Omega Psi Phi, 1994; Poynter Inst. Media Studies scholar, 1991. Mem. Nat. Assn. Black Journalists, Nat. Assn. Female Execs., North Ala. African Am. C. of C., Huntsville Press Club (bd. dirs.). Democrat. Seventh-day Adventist. Home: 6314 Creighton Ave NW Huntsville AL 35810 Office: The Valley Informer Inc PO Box 3585 Huntsville AL 35810

BARROW, MARY, public relations executive. Publicist Universal Studios Tour; newswriter, prodr. Sta. KABC-TV, L.A.; publicist Sta. KTLA-TV, L.A., 1975-80; dir. publicity GWB TV divsn., 1980-81; dir. corporate comm. Golden West Broadcasters, 1981-83; founder, owner Barrow/Hoffman PR, Duarte, Calif., 1983—. Office: Barrow Hoffman PR 2998 Hacienda Dr Duarte CA 91010*

BARROW, DAME RUTH NITA, governor general; b. St. Lucy, Barbados, Nov. 15, 1916; d. Reginald Grant and Ruth Alberta (O'Neal) B. RN, Barbados Gen. Hosp., 1940, Port-of-Spain Hosp.; diploma in nursing edn., U. Toronto, 1943, diploma in pub. health, 1945; diploma, Edinburgh U., 1951; BS, Columbia U.; LLD (hon.), U. West Indies, U. Toronto, U. Manitobia, Spellman Coll., York U., Smith Coll., Queen's U. of Can., Adelphi U., 1994; DSc (hon.), Macmaster U.; DHun (hon.), Morris Brown U.; HHD, Mt. St. Vincent; LittD, Wilfrid Laurier U., 1994. Mem. various staff, teaching and adminstrv. posts in nursing and pub. health Barbados and Jamaica, 1940-56; prin. nursing officer Jamaica, 1956-62; nursing advisor Pan Am. Health Orgn., 1967-71; assoc. dir. Christian Med. Commn. World Coun. Chs., Geneva, 1971-75, dir., 1975-80; health cons. WHO, 1981-86; amb. to UN, 1986-90; gov.-gen. Barbados, 1990—; convenor Eminent Persons Group 1st UN Global Conf. on Sustainabe Devel. of Small Island Developing States, 1994. Mem. exec. com. World of YWCA, 1955-67, v.p., 1963-67, pres., 1975-83; pres. Quadrennial Coun., 1975-79, 83, Internat. Coun. for Adult Edn., 1982-90, WCC, 1983-91; participant numerous internat. confs. on population, health and women; chmn. health sect. Forum '80, Copenhagen; convenor UN Forum, Nairobi, Kenya, 1985, Eminent Persons Group, 1st UN Global Conf. Sustainable Devel. Small Island Developing States, 1994; mem. Commonwealth Group Eminent Persons on S.A., 1986; dir. Global Fund for Women, USA, 1986—, L.A. chpt.; bd. dirs. Found. for Internat. Tng. Can., 1986-90; mem. Internat. Adv. Synergos Inst., U.S.A., 1987-88, 89-90; mem. Jury Liberty Medal, 1988-90, steering com. on leadership and devel. Rockefeller Found. Internat., 1992. Recipient Caribbean prize Caribbean Coun. Chs., 1986, Caricom award Commonwealth Caribbean, 1987, Christine Reisman award Internat. Coun. Nurses, 1989, Louise McManua award Columiba U., 1989, award Afro Am. Inst., 1991, Women First award YWCA, 1993, Order of the Caribbean Cmty., 1994; named Dame Grand Cross of the Most Disting. Order of St. Michael and St. George, Dame of St. Andrew in the Order of Barbados. Fellow Royal Coll. Nursing (London); mem. Jamaica Nurses Assn. (founder, pres.), Internat. Peace Acad. (bd. dir. 1986-90). Office: Office of Gov Gen, Bridgetown Barbados

BARROWS, DEBORAH ALLEN, elementary educator; b. Melrose, Mass., July 24, 1937; d. Ralph Allen and Ethelda May Barrows. BS in Edn., Wheelock Coll., 1959; MA in Edn., Tufts U., 1962. Tchr. grade 2 Barnstable (Mass.) Schs., 1959-60, art specialist, 1960-94; ret., 1994; computer instr. continuing edn. Worcester (Mass.) State, 1985-88; cons. Logo Terrapin Probability Book Computer Programs. Contbr. watercolors to Little Nettie & Edna Stories (Nettie O'Toole), 1990; contbr. photos to mags., newspapers and books. Recipient Tchr. award Instr. Mag. Mem. Internat. Soc. for Tech. in Edn., Barnstable Tchrs. Assn., Nat. Art Edn. Assn. (pres. local chpt. 1960, 65, ea. regional rep.), Mass. Tchrs. Assn., Boston Computer Soc., Trout Unltd., Tufts Club. Office: Barnstable Pub Schs 230 South St Hyannis MA 02601

BARRY, BONNIE B., trade association executive; b. Pocatello, Idaho, July 17, 1940; d. Kyle and Lael Corrine (Smith) Bettilyon; 1 child, Robyn Matthies Randall. Student, Mills Coll., 1958-59; BA, U. Utah, 1962; cert., ITCA, 1976. CCIM. Spl. svcs. mgr. Sperry Rand Missile Div., Salt Lake City, 1962-64; mgr. travel dept. Utah Motor Club, Salt Lake City, 1965-67; owner Aggie Travel Svc., Davis, Calif., 1968-77, also bd. dirs.; founding ptnr. SECRET Travel Svc., Maui, Hawaii, 1979—; exec. v.p. Assn. Retail Travel Agts., 1979—; pres., CEO Bettilyon Investment Co., Salt Lake City, 1990—; tng. dir. ednl. work-study programs for mem. travel agys., U.S. and Can.; mem. faculty U. Calif. Extension, Davis, 1974-77. Mem. Nat. Travel Agts. (adv. bd. to Pan Am. World Airways 1973-77), Assn. Retail Travel Agts. (nat. bd. dirs. 1974-78), Giants Travel Coop. (v.p. Western chpt. 1972-74), Am. Assn. Retail Travel Agts., Soroptomists. Republican. Morman. Home: 3 Nail Driver Ct Box 1388 Park City UT 84060 Office: Bettilyon Investment Co 333 S 2d E Salt Lake City UT 84111

BARRY, JANET CECILIA, educator; b. Jersey City, May 12, 1944; d. John Aloysius and Mary Elizabeth (Hart) B.; BA, Paterson State Coll., 1966; MA, Georgian Ct. Coll., 1978. Tchr., Paterson (N.J.) Pub. Sch. No. 12, 1966-68; tchr. Walnut St. Elem. Sch., Toms River (N.J.) Regional Sch. System, 1968-88; supr. instrn. Cedar Grove Elem. Sch., Toms River Regional Sch. System, 1988-90; supr. instrn. North Dover Elem. Sch., 1990-94, Hooper Ave. Elem. Sch., 1995—; supr. instruction Toms River Regional Schs. Mem. Aviation Space Edn. Found. Recipient N.J. Gov.'s Excellence in Teaching award, 1987. Mem. NEA, Nat. Coun. Tchrs. English, Nat. Sci. Tchrs. Assn., N.J. Edn. Assn., Ocean County Edn. Assn., Toms River Edn. Assn., Assn. for Supervision and Curriculum Devel., N.J. Reading Assn., N.J. Assn. for Supervision and Curriculum Devel., Internat. Reading Assn., Ocean County Reading Coun. (rec. sec., 1st v.p., pres.), Georgian Ct. Coll. Grad. Sch. Alumni Assn. (sec.), N.J. Prins. and Suprs. Assn., Challenger Ctr. for Space Edn. Educator's Network, Coun. for Elem. Sci. Internat., Delta Kappa Gamma (chmn. programs, ednl. svcs., communications, Zeta chpt.).

BARRY, JOYCE ALICE, dietitian; b. Chgo., Apr. 27, 1932; d. Walter Stephen and Ethel Myrtle (Paetow) Barry; student Iowa State Coll., 1950-52, Loyala U., 1952-58; B.S., Mundelein Coll., 1955; postgrad. Simmons Coll., 1963-64, U. Ga., 1979, Calif. Western U., 1980—. Prodn. supr. Marshall Field & Co., Chgo., 1955-59; dir. food services Women's Ednl. and Indsl. Union, Boston, 1959-62; dir. food services Wellesley Public Schs., Mass., 1962-70; cons. Stokes Food Services, Newton, Mass., 1960-70; regional dietitian Canteen Corp., Chgo., 1970-83; gen. mgr. bus. devel. Plantation-Sysco, Orlando, Fla., 1983-87; dir. product devel. corp. procurement Mariott Internat. Hdqrs., Washington, 1987—; vis. lectr.; research adv. council Restaurant Bus. Mag.; career adv. council, Am. Dietetics Assn.; treas. Dietitians in Bus. Mem. AAUW, Am. Home Econs. Assn., Internat. Fedn. Home Economists, Home Economists in Bus., Am. Dietetics Assn., Nat. Assn. Female Execs., Dietitians in Bus., Tex.-Mex. Frozen Food Coun., Internat. Food Technologists, Nat. Frozen Food Coun. Republican. Roman Catholic. Club: La Chaine des Rotisseurs. Home: 175 Heron Bay Cir Lake Mary FL 32746-3423 Office: Marriott World Hdqrs 1 Marriott Dr Washington DC 20058-0001

BARRY, LEI, medical equipment manufacturing executive; b. Fitchburg, Mass., May 27, 1941; d. Leo Isaacson and Irene Helen (Melanson) Isaacson Godbout; m. Delbert M. Berry (div.); children: David M., Susan L.; m. Frank H. Mahan III, June 25, 1976; stepchildren: Jodi L., Sarah C., Amy S., Frank H. IV. Grad. high sch., Waltham, Mass. Advt. salesperson, broadcaster various radio and TV stas., N.C. and Tex., 1961-67; New Eng. sales rep. Hollister, Inc., Chgo., 1967-71, Northeastern sales mgr., 1971-76; v.p., ptnr. Mahan Assocs., Blue Bell, Pa., 1976—; pres. Blue Bell Bio-Med., Inc., 1982—. Bd. mgrs. YMCA, Ambler. Mem. Whitpain Twp. Planning Commn., 1986-91; pres., bd. dirs. Interfaith of Ambler; elder Boehm's United Ch. of Christ, 1978—; mem. affordable housing adv. coun. Fed. Home Loan Bank, Pitts. Mem. NAFE, Health Mfrs. Mktg. Coun. (bd. dirs.), Blue Bell Rotary, Wissahickon Valley C. of C. (bd. dirs. 1987-92), Wissahickon Valley Hist. Soc. (past bd. dirs.), Health Industry Reps. Assn. Republican. Avocations: tennis, skiing, gourmet cooking. Office: Blue Bell Bio-Med Inc PO Box 455 Blue Bell PA 19422-0455

BARRY, MARYANNE TRUMP, federal judge; b. N.Y.C., Apr. 5, 1937; d. Fred C. and Mary Trump; m. John J. Barry, Dec. 26, 1982; 1 child, David W. Desmond. BA, Mt. Holyoke Coll., 1958; MA, Columbia U., 1962; JD, Hofstra U., 1974, LLD (hon.); LLD (hon.), Seton Hall U., Caldwell Coll. Bar: N.J. 1974, N.Y. 1975, U.S. Ct. Appeals (3d cir.), U.S. Supreme Ct. Asst. U.S. Atty., 1974-75, dep. chief appeals div., 1976-77, chief appeals div., 1977-82, exec. asst. U.S. Atty., 1981-82, 1st asst., 1981-83; judge U.S. Dist. Ct., N.J., 1983—; chmn. Com. on Criminal Law Jud. Conf. of U.S. Fellow Am. Bar Found.; mem. ABA, N.J. Bar Assn., Am. Judicature Soc. (bd. dirs.), Assn. Fed. Bar State of N.Y. (pres. 1982-83). Office: US Dist Ct PO & Courthouse Bldg Fed Square, PO Box 999 Newark NJ 07101-0999*

BARRY, MIRANDA ROBBINS, television producer, writer; b. N.Y.C., Jan. 18, 1951; d. Philip Semple and Patricia Allen (White) B. AB, Stanford U., 1972; postgrad Columbia Law Sch., N.Y.C., 1978-79. Prodn. rsch. coord. The Best of Families/CTW, N.Y.C., 1975-77; freelance story analyst CBS Inc., N.Y.C., 1976-81; asst. mgr. spl. programs devel. Sta. WNET 13, N.Y.C., 1977-78; exec. coord. Nat. TV Theatre, N.Y.C., 1981-82; story editor Am. Playhouse, N.Y.C., 1982-83, dir. program devel., 1983-87, exec. story cons., 1987; dir. internat. prodn. McNeil/Allyn Films, London, 1987-88; sr. producer (TV series) Ghostwriter CTW, 1990—, supervising producer, 1991-94; instr. TV writing New Sch. Social Rsch., N.Y.C., 1982-83; instr. screen writing Womens Interart Center, N.Y.C., 1981-83; adj. assoc. prof. Columbia U. Sch. Film, 1986-87, prof. 1988, 94—; writer One Life to Live, ABC-TV, N.Y.C., 1994—; co-dir., organizer TV Theater Workshop Sta. KTCA, Mpls., 1983; creator TV series Mom and Dad/Embassy-NBC, 1983. Author: (play) Friends and Relations, 1981, (TV adaptation) A World to Care For, (TV series) MedSchool, 1980, (TV miniseries) Sara and Gerald, 1988) Who Is Max Mouse?, 1993; co-author: Quincy script Blood Ties, 1980, Basil, 1990; (screenplay) Pinkerton's Angel, 1989; scriptwriting resource person Sundance Inst., 1984-86; story editor Eugene O'Neill Nat. Playwright's Conf., 1984—. Rape victim counselor St. Luke's Hosp., N.Y.C., 1979-81; mem. alumnae bull. com. Miss Porter's Sch., 1979-84. McKnight grantee Playwright's Center, Mpls., 1983. Mem. Writers Guild Am.-East, Dramatists Guild, N.Y. Women in Film (sec., bd. dirs. 1984-85, 90-91). Office: ABC-TV 56 W 66th St New York NY 10023

BARRY, NADA DAVIES, retail business owner; b. London, Dec. 2, 1930; d. Ernest Albert J. and Natalie Emma (Rossin) Davies; m. Jacob J. Ebeling-Koning, Aug. 1952 (div. 1962); m. Robert I Barry, 1963 (div. 1976); children: Natasha E.-K. Sigmund, Derek B. Ebeling-Koning, Gwen E.-K. Waddington, Trebor C. Barry. Student, Mills Coll., 1948-50; BA, Barnard Coll., 1952. Owner The Wharf Shop, Sag Harbor, N.Y., 1968—. Bd. dirs. The Hampton Day Sch., Bridgehampton, N.Y., 1966-74; active Noyac Civic Coun., Ladies Village Improvement Soc., Sag Harbor, LWV of The Hamptons. Mem. Sag Harbor C. of C. (bd. dirs.), Barnard Coll. Club. Office: The Wharf Shop PO Box 922 Sag Harbor NY 11963-0025

BARRY, SUSAN BROWN, writer, manufacturer; b. San Antonio, Tex., Sept. 14, 1944; d. Earl A. Jr. and Betty (Galt) Brown; m. Richard Hanley Barry, June 25, 1966 (div. 1973); children: Andrew Earl, Brice Galt. AB, Sweet Briar (Va.) Coll., 1966. Lic. real estate agt. Houston, 1983—; scriptwriter Stas. KUHT-TV, KDOG-TV, KEYT Radio, Houston, 1972-77; originator, adminstr., cons. publ. program Rice U., Houston, 1977-79; liaison book promotion Dell. Publs., Viking Publs., and others, Houston, 1979-85; pres. Savage Designs, Houston, 1985-88; cons. U. Calif., Santa Barbara, 1985; rare book, manuscript catalogue, writer Randall House Rare Books. Producer hospice-related tng. video and articles; book critic Houston Post; designer greeting cards Neiman-Marcus Dept. Stores; writer Bicentennial Play Houston Pub. Schs. (now in Nat. Archives). Founding coord. Reach to Recovery program Am. Cancer Soc.; rep. Choice In Dying, 1994—; mem. adv. bd. HeARTS for AIDS Found., 1992—. Mem. Assn. for Death Edn. and Counseling (chmn. pub. rels. 1992-94), Jr. League (numerous comms. and chairmanships), Asia Soc. (adv. com., fin. chmn. Houston chpt. 1984-85), Austin Coun. on Fgn. Affairs. Republican. Unitarian. Home and Office: PO Box 8741 Horseshoe Bay TX 78657

BARRYMORE, DREW, actress; b. L.A., Feb. 22, 1975; d. John Jr. and Jaid Barrymore. Appearences include (films) Altered States, 1980, E.T.: The Extra-Terrestrial, 1982, Irreconcilable Differences, 1984, Firestarter, 1984, Cat's Eye, 1985, Poison Ivy, 1992, Bad Girls, 1994, Boys on the Side, 1995, Batman Forever, 1995, Mad Love, 1995; (TV episodes) Amazing Stories, 1985, Con Sawyer and Hucklemary Finn, 1985, 2000 Malibu Road, 1992; (host) Hansel and Gretel, 1986; (TV movies) Suddenly Love, 1978, Bogie, 1980, The Screaming Woman, 1986, Babes in Toyland, 1986, Conspiracy of Love, 1987, Beyond Control: The Amy Fisher Story, 1993; (TV spls.) Screen Actors Guild 50th Anniversary, 1984, Night of 100 Stars II, 1985, Happy Birthday, Hollywood, 1987, Disney's 30th Anniversary, 1987. Office: William Morris Agy 151 S El Camino Dr Beverly Hills CA 90212-2704*

BARSOM, VALERIE, state legislator. BA, Clark U., 1982; JD, New Eng. Sch. Law, 1991. Sales asst. KVR Inc., Springfield, Mass., 1982-84; clk. Kamberg, Berman, Gold & West, Springfield, 1984-85; legis. asst. to Hon. Robert Howarth Mass. Ho. of Reps., Boston, 1985-92, mem., 1993—. Republican. Home: 667 Tinkham Rd Wilbraham MA 01095 Office: Mass Ho of Reps State Capitol Boston MA 02133*

BARSY, JANET ZOE, lawyer; b. Chgo., Nov. 5, 1953; d. Herbert and Beverly Jean (Hafermann) B. BSFS, Georgetown U., 1975, JD, 1985. Bar: D.C. Congrl. rels. officer U.S. Arms Control and Disarmament Agy., Washington, 1979-81; assoc. Galland, Kharasch, Morse & Garfinkle, Washington, 1985-86, Akin, Gump, Strauss, Hauer & Feld L.L.P., Washington, 1986-95; atty., adv. U.S. Dept. of Energy, 1995—; cons. Ctr. for Fgn. Policy Devel., Brown U., Providence, R.I., 1981. Co-author: Government Contractor Liability for Design Defects After Boyle, 1990, Drug-Free Workplace Obligations of Defense Contractors, Vol. II, 1989; contbr. articles to profl. jours. Recipient McGuire medal for Outstanding Sr., Sch. of Fgn. Svc., Georgetown U., 1975; awardee travel-study grant for Ea. Europe Circumnavigators Club Found., 1974. Mem. D.C. Bar Assn., ABA, Nat. Contract Mgmt. Assn., Women in Def., Women in Housing and Fin., Phi Beta Kappa. Home: 3302 21st Ave North Arlington VA 22207-3821 Office: Office Asst Gen Counsel for Procurement US Dept Energy GC-61 1000 Independence Ave SW Washington DC 20585

BART, GEORGIANA CRAY, artist, educator; b. Wilkes-Barre, Pa., Oct. 30, 1948; d. William Getamyne and Jean Marie (Milisaukas) Cray; m. Michael Douglas Bart, Dec. 2, 1972; children: Jean Michelle, Marjorie Alison, Michael Douglas William Jr. BA in Fine Arts and Art Edn., Wilkes Coll., 1970; MEd in Art Edn., U. Pitts., 1972; pvt. studies in painting. Tchr. art Wyoming Valley West Sch. Dist., Kingston, Pa., 1971-72; substitute tchr., adult art instr. Pub. Sch. Price Georges County, Md., 1972-76; instr. early childhood edn. dept., tchr. adult art Luzerne County C.C., Nanticoke, Pa., 1976-78; tchr. elem. art Wyoming Valley Montessori Sch., Kingston, 1991-92; subsitute tchr. Wyoming Sem. Lower Sch., Forty Fort, Pa., 1984-94; represented by Laura Craig Galleries, Scranton, Pa., A Little Gallery, Mont Alto, Pa., Bixler Gallery, Stroudsburg, Pa.; mem. Art Jury, Wilkes-Barre, 1977-78. One-woman shows include Sheehy Student Ctr., Kings Coll., Wilkes-Barre, 1993, Hanover Bank, West Pittston, Pa., 1993, Am. Savings Bank, Hazelton, Pa., 1994, Doshi Ctr. Contemporary Art, 1995; exhibited in group and juried shows at Wyoming Valley Art League galleries and off-site exhbns., 1989— (2nd pl. painting award 1990, Purchase award 1991, Grumbacher gold medallion 1993, 2d pl. pastel 1994, 3d pl. painting 1994), Lackawanna Arts Coun., Scranton, Pa., 1989, 90, 91, 92, 93 (2nd pl. painting award 1992, 2nd pl. graphics award 1993), 36th Annual Nat. Juried Exhib. of Mamaroneck Artists Guild Westbeth Gallery, N.Y.C., 1994, Nat. Arts Club, N.Y.C., 1994, 95 (Catharine Lorillard Wolf Pres.'s award 1994, Still Life Painting award 1994), several others; represented in permanent pvt. and pub. collections. Set designer pvt. sch. theatrical prodn., Forty Fort, 1993; vol. Am. Heart Assn., 1992-93, Am. Cancer Soc., 1992-93; mem. area Rep. com., Wilkes-BArre, 1983-85. Recipient 1st pl. painting award Moscow County Fair, 1990, 92, 3rd pl. painting award, 1991, 1st pl. painting award, 1992, 3rd pl. drawing award, 1993, Purchase award Hazleton (Pa.) Art League, 1991, 2nd pl. graphics award Wilkes-Barre Fine Arts Fiesta, 1993, honorable mention award Contemporary Gallery, Marywood Coll., Scranton, 1993. Mem. Wyoming Valley Art League, Artists for Art of AFA Gallery, MacDonald Art Gallery, Sordoni Art Gallery, Cider Painters Am., Contemporary Arts Corridor, Doshi Ctr. for Contemporary Art, Pa. Plein Air Soc., Art Assn. Harrisburg. Roman Catholic. Home: 123 Brader Dr Wilkes-Barre PA 18705

BART, POLLY TURNER, commercial real estate developer; b. Peterborough, N.H., Feb. 28, 1944; d. Benjamin Franklin and Catherine (James) B.; m. Harry Nelson Pharr II, Oct. 27, 1969 (div. May 1972); 1 child, Greta Rose Bart. BA, Radcliffe Coll., 1965; M in City Planning, U. Calif., Berkeley, 1974, PhD, 1979. Cons. city planning Marshall Kaplan, Gans, & Kahn, San Francisco, 1967; city planner County of Napa, Calif., 1968-69; asst. instr. U. Tex., Austin, 1971-72; cons. Dept. HUD, Washington, 1979-81; asst. prof. U. Md., College Park, 1981-84; real estate salesperson Coldwell Banker Comml. Real Estate Services, Balt., 1984-87; pres. Investment Properties Brokerage, Inc., Balt., 1988—; faculty Johns Hopkins U., Berman Real Estate Inst., 1993—; bd. dirs. assoc. Columbia Forum, Md., 1981-85; contbr. Nat. Urban Policy Report to Congress, 1980. Fellow Radcliffe Coll., 1962-64, Danforth Found., 1975-79, Ford Found., 1981. Mem. Comml. Real Estate Women (co-founder). Home: 629 S Hanover St Baltimore MD 21230-3841 Office: Investment Properties Brokerage Inc 629 S Hanover St Baltimore MD 21230-3841

BARTEE, ROBERTA P., nursing educator; b. Gulfport, Miss., Oct. 16, 1945; d. Vaughn Eugene and Blanche Marie (Phillips) Purvis; m. James H. Bartee, Sept. 4, 1971. Diploma, Charity Hosp. Sch. Nursing, 1966; BS, Northwestern State U., 1968; MS, U. Colo., 1971; postgrad., U. Hawaii, 1981-82. RN, La. Acting head nurse surg. unit Charity Hosp. New Orleans; asst. prof. La. State U. Med. Ctr., New Orleans, U. Hawaii, Honolulu, Linfield Coll., Portland, Oreg.; coord. staff devel. Tulane Hosp., New Orleans. Mem. ANA, AACN, ASTD, Nat. League Nursing, New Orleans Dist. Nurses Assn. (bd. dirs.), Am. Soc. Health Care Edn. and Tng., Nat. Nursing Staff Devel. Orgn., Sigma Theta Tau. Home: 7015 Longvue Dr Mandeville LA 70448-7043

BARTEL, PATRICIA RHODEN, masters fine art educator; b. Toledo, July 29, 1950; d. Alfred Edward and Virginia June (Bramwelo) Rhoden; m. Gary L. Bartels, Nov. 17, 1973; children: Lance R., Christopher L. B, Toledo U., 1971; MA, Bowling Green U., 1976, MFA, 1977. Tchr. art Liberty Ctr. (Ohio) Pub. Sch., 1974-81, Brown County Pub. Sch., Nashville, Ind., 1983-93. One-woman shows include Ft. Wayne Mus., Tweed Mus., Toledo Mus. Art Collectors Corner, group shows include San Guiseppi Coll. St. Joseph, Craftsman Gallery; represented in permanent collection Ft. Wayne Mus. Wallbridge Sinclair grantee Toledo Mus. Art, 1972, Art Interest grantee, 1973; Kent Blossom Summer Arts scholar, 1973; Eli Lily Creative fellow, 1992; NEH grantee, 1994. Mem. Psi Iota Xi. Home: 2510 S State Rd 135 Nashville IN 47448 Office: Brown County Jr High Sch School House Ln Nashville IN 47448

BARTELMAY, JANE See CAMP, JANE

BARTELS, BETTY J., nurse; b. Cin., Mar. 7, 1925; d. William Charles and Irene Agnes (McLean) Roth; m. Donald Arthur Bartels Sr.; children: Donald A. Jr., Virginia, Frederick, Bernadette. Nursing diploma RN, Good Samaritan Hosp., 1946; postgrad. libr. sci., Barry Coll., 1966-70. RN Sun Ray Health Resort, Miami, Fla., 1949-51; vol. libr. St. James Cath. Sch., Miami, 1966-70; RN North Shore Med. Ctr., Miami, 1970-72; charge RN Villa Maria Rehab. Ctr., Miami, 1972-76; pvt. duty RN Miami, 1976-80; staff RN North Shore Med. Ctr., Miami, 1979-91; vol. Villa Maria Rehab. Ctr., Miami, 1990—. Vol. Bon Secours Hosp./Villa Maria Nursing Ctr., 1990—. 2d lt. USAR, 1948-51. Mem. Third Order of St. Dominic (pres., prioress 1976-79, 92—). Democrat. Roman Catholic.

BARTELS, SUSAN HERDMAN, art educator, artist; b. Yonkers, N.Y., May 29, 1941; d. Raymond Charles and Ellen (Saunders) Herdman; m. John C. Barker, June 12, 1965 (div. July 1984); children: Jennifer, Carrie, John; m. Robert John Bartels, Apr. 7, 1990. BFA, Alfred U., 1963; MA, U. Iowa, 1965. Art educator Muscatine (Iowa) Pub. Schs., 1965-66, Iowa City Pub. Schs., 1966-67, Regina High Sch., Iowa City, 1967-68; artist, owner Custom Stained Glass, Bettendorf, Iowa, 1979-84, Native Images, Bettendorf, Iowa, 1992—; art educator Lincoln and Hoover Schs., Davenport, Iowa, 1985—. Group shows include Drake U., Des Moines, 1984, U. Iowa, Iowa City, 1987, 91, Davenport Mus. Art, 1987, Quad City Arts Coun., Rock Island, Ill., 1987, Whispering Winds Gallery, Iowa City, 1991, Quincy (Ill.) Art Ctr., 1992, Walton Art Ctr., Fayetteville, Ark., 1992, 93, Alias Gallery, Atlanta, 1992, Ga. Tech., Atlanta, 1992, Colorado Springs (Colo.) Art Gallery, 1992, 93, Mus. Contemporary Art, Chgo., 1992, Davenport (Iowa) Mus. Art, 1992, Mus. Anthropology U. Calif., Chico, 1992, Red Mesa Art Gallery, Gallup, N.Mex., 1992, Putnam County Arts Coun., Mahopac, N.Y., 1992, Near Northwest Arts Coun., Chgo., 1993, North Platte Valley Art Guild, Scottsbluff, Nebr., 1993, Gallery Space, Iowa, 1993, Chautaugua Art Assn. Galleries, 1993, Greater Harrisburg (Pa.) Arts Coun., 1993, 94, Fla. Soc.

Fine Arts, Miami, Fla., 1993, Columbia Arts Ctr., Vancouver, Wash., 1993, Eiteljorg Mus. Am. Indian and Western Art, Indpls., 1994, Maude Kerns Art Center, Eugene, Oreg., 1994, Soc. Contemporary Photography, Kansas City, 1994, Mus. Northwest Colo., Craig, 1994, Fuller Mus. Art, Brockton, Mass., 1994; permanent collections include Am. Indian Art Ctr., Chgo., Mus. Anthropology U. Calif., Chico., Deere and Co., Moline, Ill, Eiteljorg Mus. Native Am. & Western Art, EverColor Corp., El Dorado Hills, Calif. Mem. Nat. Mus. Am. Indian, Nat. Mus. Women in Arts; tchr. liaison Davenport Indian Parent Adv. Com., 1991—. Recipient Best of Show award Quad City Arts Coun., 1987, Best of Photography Ann. Photographers Forum Mag., 1993, others. Mem. NEA, Art Educators Iowa, Iowa Alliance for Arts Edn., Iowa State Edn. Assn., Nat. Art Edn. Assn., Quad City League of Native Ams. Home: 3303 Oxford Dr Bettendorf IA 52722

BARTELSTONE, RONA SUE, gerontologist; b. Bklyn., Jan. 10, 1951; d. Herbert and Hazel (Mittman) Canarick; m. Alan Joel Markowitz. BS in Social Welfare, SUNY, Buffalo, 1972; MSW, Ind. U., 1974. Licensed Clin. Social Worker, Fla. Diplomate of Social Work. Social worker YM-YWHA of Greater N.Y., 1974-75; dist. supr. N.Y.C. Housing Authority, Bklyn., 1975-77; field instr. Barry U. Sch. Social Work, 1980-81; project dir. United Family & Children's Svcs., 1977-81; faculty Miami Dade Community Coll., 1981-82; adult educator Sch. Bd. Dade County, 1981-82; med. social worker Mederi Home Health Agy., 1979-82; mem. adj. faculty Nova U., 1986-88; pvt. practice Rona Bartelstone Assocs., Inc., Ft. Lauderdale, Fla., 1981—; cons. and trainer in field. Contbr. articles to various mags. Bd. dirs. Jewish Vocat. Svcs., Miami, 1985-92; mem. funding panel Area Agy. on Aging, Miami, 1985-89; Active Freinds of the Family Counseling Svcs., Miami, 1983-88; adv. bd., chair internship subcom., Lynn U., 1993—; exec. bd. Fla. Geriatric Care Mgrs., 1993—; chair tng. com., 2d v.p. Alzheimer's Assn., Miami, 1994; co-chair Nat. Acad. Cert. Care Mgrs., 1994—. Recipient Dade County Citizen of the Yr. award, 1982, NASW Social Worker of the Yr. award, 1982-83, Trail Blazer award, 1984, Up & Comers award in health care Price Waterhouse and So. Fla. Bus. Jour., 1990. Mem. NASW (treas. 1987-89), Gerontology Soc. Am., Am. Soc. on Aging, Nat. Coun. on Aging, Assn. Profl. Geriatric Care Mgrs. (pres. 1988-94, chmn. credential com. 1993—), Nat. Acad. Cert. Care Mgrs. (co-chmn. 1994—), Fla. Geriatric Care Mgrs. Assn. (exec. bd. 1993—). Democrat. Jewish. Home: 2365 N 37th Ave Hollywood FL 33021-3645 Office: 2699 Stirling Rd Ste 304C Fort Lauderdale FL 33312-6546

BARTH, KATRINE, advertising agency executive; b. N.Y.C., Mar. 27, 1947; d. Frank and Gertrude (Flamm) B.; 1 child, Ariana. Certificat d'Etudes Politiques, Institut d'Etudes Politiques, Paris, 1967; BA, Sarah Lawrence Coll., Bronxville, N.Y., 1968; MA, Brandeis U., 1969, PhD, 1970. Prof. advanced degree program Goddard Coll., Plainfield, Vt., 1972-74; asst. account exec. Frank Barth Advt., Inc., N.Y.C., 1976-77, account exec., 1977-79, gen. mgr., 1979-81, creative dir., exec. v.p., 1981-84, pres., 1984—; COO Richard James Specialty Chems. Corp., 1993—. Pres.: (documentary films) The Link Between Us, (Cine Bronze award 1980), Parade (Cine Gold award 1986). Jewish. Office: Frank Barth Inc Richard James Specialty Chem Co 33 W Main St Elmsford NY 10523

BARTHELS, KATHY ANN, marriage and family therapist; b. Oshkosh, Wis., Dec. 19, 1961; d. Bobby Edward and Shirley Jane (Selenka) B. BS in Psychology, U. Wis., Oshkosh, 1989, MS Edn., 1991; grad., Family Therapy Tng. Inst., Milw., 1994. Nat. cert. counselor. Nursing asst. Evergreen Manor, Oshkosh, 1982-86; program asst. autistic schizophrenics Residential Care for Developmentally Disabled, Oshkosh, 1988; juvenile delinquency counselor Tellurian Cmty. Group Home, Oshkosh, 1990-91; sole proprietor, therapist Perspectives, Cudahy, Wis., 1993—. Recipient Scholarships Mental Health Assn. Winnebago County, 1990, AAUW, 1990-91. Mem. Assn. Counseling and Devel., Internat. Assn. Marriage and Family Therapy, Assn. Women in Psychology, Am. Assn. Marriage and Family Therapy. New Age. Office: Perspectives 3620 E Layton Ave Ste # 14 Cudahy WI 53110

BARTHOLD, CLEMENTINE B., judge; b. Odessa, Russia, Jan. 11, 1921; came to U.S., 1925; d. Joseph Anton and Magdalene (Richter) Schwan; m. Edward Brendel Barthold, July 5, 1941 (dec.); children: Judith Anne Barthold DeSimone, John Edward. Student Aberdeen Bus. Coll., 1940; BGS, Ind. U. Southeast, 1978; JD, Ind. U.-Indpls., 1980. Bar: Ind. 1980, U.S. Dist. Ct. (so. dist.) Ind., 1980. Sec. and asst. to mgr. Clark County C. of C. (Ind.), 1959-60; chief probation officer Clark Circuit Ct. and Superior Cts., Jeffersonville, 1960-72; rsch. cons. Pub. Action Correctional Effort, Clark and Floyd Counties, 1972-75; instl. parole officer Ind. Women's Prison, Indpls., 1975-80; atty. State of Ind., 1980-83; judge Clark Superior Ct. No. 1, Jeffersonville, 1983—. Active in developing and implementing juvenile delinquency prevention and alternative programs, group counseling for juvenile delinquents and restitution programs. Recipient Good Govt. award Jeffersonville Jaycees, 1966, Good Citizenship award, 1967; Wonder Woman award, 1984, Robert J. Kinsey award, 1986, Sagamore of Wabash award, 1986, Outstanding Community Svc. award Social Concerns League, Jeffersonville, 1966, Disting. Svc. award, Outstanding Contbn. to Field of Correction award, Women of Achievement award, Jeff BPW Appreciation award, Juvenile Justice award, Disting. Contemporary Women in History award, Disting. Leadership award, Women of Achievement award 1982-83, Appreciation award VIPO, 1983, Children and Youth Recognition award 1984, Gov's Exemplary award, 1985, 88, 89, 92, Commitment to Youth award 1987, Warren W. Martin award, 1973, 87, Outstanding Child Advocacy in Ind. award, 1987, Community Svc. award, 1988, Orgnl. Renewal award, 1988, Parents Without Ptnrs. award, 1989, Ind. Youth Investment award, 1992, Excellence in Pub. Info. & Edn. award, 1992. Mem. ABA, Ind. Bar Assn., Clark County Bar Assn., Ind. Correctional Assn. (pres. 1971, Disting. Service award 1967, 85), Ind. Judges Assn., Nat. and Ind. Juvenile and Family Ct. Judges (bd. dirs.), Ind. Juvenile Justice Task Force, Am. Judges Assn., NAACP, Jefferson Hosp. Governing Bd., Ind. U. Alumni Assn., Howard Steamboat Mus., LWV, Bus. and Profl. Women's Club, Ladies Elks Aux. Democrat. Roman Catholic. Home: 948 E 7th St Jeffersonville IN 47130-4106 Office: Clark Superior Ct No 1 500 E Court Ave Jeffersonville IN 47130-4028

BARTHOLOMEW, ANITA, freelance writer; b. Bay Shore, N.Y., Jan. 14, 1949; d. Guido and Elizabeth (Ornato) Del Giudice m. Frank J. Tomaino, Oct. 5, 1968 (div.); 1 child, Alexander G. Tomaino. Student, SUNY, Purchase, 1981-83, Sch. Visual Arts, N.Y.C., 1984. Copywriter Ventura Assocs., N.Y.C., 1982-83, Equity Advt., N.Y.C., 1983-84, Pace Advt., N.Y.C., 1984-85; prin. Bartholomew & Co., Tarrytown, N.Y., 1985—; dir. mktg. Chacma Inc., N.Y.C., 1991-92; sr acct. supr. Tech. Solutions Inc., 1992-93; freelance copywriter Donnelley Mktg., Holt, Rinehart/CBS Pub., SAS Airlines, The Luce Corp., Westchester Women's News, IBM, RAM Mobile Data, numerous others. Contbr. articles to Woman's Day mag., Omni mag., Computer Pictures mag., YM mag., Longevity mag., many others. Mem. Am. Soc. Psychical rsch., Pub. Rels. Soc. Am., People for Ethical Treatment of Animals, Nat. Assn. Sci. Writers, Mensa.

BARTLE, ANNETTE GRUBER (MRS. THOMAS R. BARTLE), artist, writer, photographer; Came to U.S., 1940; d. Henry and Maria (Harczyk) Gruber; m. Thomas R. Bartle, Dec. 5, 1957 (dec. 1964); 1 child, Eve Marie. Bacheliere, Sorbonne, Paris, 1940; BA, Elmira Coll., N.Y., 1943; student, Ecole des Beaux Arts, Paris, 1940, Art Student League (scholar 1949), 1947-50. One-woman shows include: Midtown Galleries, N.Y.C., 1957, 60, 63, 66, Feingarten, Chgo., 1957, Wickersham Gallery, 1970; exhibited in group shows: AAAL, 1963, Detroit Art Inst., 1958, 62, 65, 67, Pa. Acad., 1959, 60, 66, Butler Art Inst., 1960, 64, 65, Cin. Art Mus., 1960, 62, 67; represented in permanent collections: Am. Internat. Underwriters, Union Carbide, Conn. Mut. Life, Mural Port Authority Heliport, N.Y. Worlds Fair; author: African Enchantment, 1980; contbr. articles and photographs to mags., newspapers, jours. including: N.Y. Times, Christian Sci. Monitor, Phila. Inquirer, L.A. Times, Palm Beach Life, Travel Weekly, Diversion, American Way, Senior World, Good Housekeeping since 1991, numerous others. Trustee Morris Animal Found.; active various community drives. Pan Am. Travelling fellow, 1950; recipient citation for outstanding achievements 90th U.S. Congress, 1968. Mem. Am. Fedn. Arts, Artists Equity, Travel Journalists Guild Ltd., Women's Nat. Republican Club. Address: 231 E 76th St New York NY 10021

BARTLETT, DEBORAH ANN, financial management consultant; b. Aberdeen, Md., Aug. 4, 1953; d. James L. and Theresa A. (Leskowits) Taylor; m. Michael J. Bartlett, July 23, 1986. Cert. investment mgmt. analyst, U. Pa., 1992. Adminstrv. asst. Merrill Lynch, Everett, Wash., 1981-84, fin. cons., 1984-92, sales mgr., 1992—. Contbr. articles to bus. jours. Donor, patron Everett Cmty. Theater. Mem. Nat. ESOP Assn., Investment Mgmt. Cons. Assn., Nat. Ctr. for Employee Ownership, Chmn.'s Club Merrill Lynch. Office: Merrill Lynch 2707 Colby Ave Ste 1401 Everett WA 98201

BARTLETT, DIANE SUE, clinical mental health counselor; b. Laconia, N.H., Dec. 6, 1947; d. Fred Elmer and Dorothy Pearl (Wakefield) Davis; m. Josiah Henry Bartlett, Aug. 23, 1980; 1 child by previous marriage, Fred Louis Hacker; 1 step child, Juliet. AA, Plymouth State Coll., 1982; B in Gen. Studies summa cum laude, U. N.H. Sch. for Lifelong Learning, 1984; MEd., Plymouth State Coll., 1988. Cert. clin. mental health counselor. Police communications specialist Div. Motor Vehicles, Concord, N.H., 1970-76, br. office mgr., 1976-83, coordinator motor vehicles registrations, 1983-84; tax collector City of Dover, N.H., 1984; intern Lakes Region Mental Health Div., Laconia, N.H., 1985; counselor Latchkey Pastoral Counseling, Laconia, 1984-87; family therapist, Children's Best Interest, Laconia, 1988—; mental health counselor Carroll County Mental Health Svcs., Wolfeboro, N.H., 1988—. Mem. Town of Moultonboro Sch. Feasibility Study Commn., 1978; adminstrv. bd. mem., chmn. pastor-parish relations com. United Meth. Ch., Moultonboro, N.H., 1983—, N.H. annual conf., 1986-88, participant N.H. Ann. Conf. on Status and Role of Women, Concord, 1985—. N.H. Charitable Found. grantee, 1985. Avocations: skiing, swimming, reading, writing. Home: PO Box 14 Moultonborough NH 03254-0014

BARTLETT, ELIZABETH EASTON, interior designer; b. Cleve., Apr. 1, 1937; d. Walter James Easton and Elizabeth (Scott) Easton Sullivan; m. Peter B. Bartlett, Nov. 24, 1956 (div. Sept. 1987); children: Elizabeth Kimberley Bartlett Kernan, Christopher, Katherine. Student, Skidmore Coll., 1959. Model Cluett, Peabody & Co., N.Y.C., 1958-65; pvt. practice N.Y.C., 1978—; buyer, bd. dirs. Boutique de Noël, N.Y.C., 1976-87. Trustee, vice chmn. St. Barnabas Hosp., Bronx, N.Y., 1978—; v.p. N.Y. Soc. for Prevention of Cruelty to Children, N.Y.C., 1979; trustee, bd. dirs. Youth Counseling League, N.Y.C., 1974. Mem. Rolling Rock Club. Episcopalian. Home and Office: 30 E 72nd St New York NY 10021-4248

BARTLETT, ELIZABETH (ROBERTA), editor, writer; b. N.Y., July 20, 1911; d. Lewis Winters and Charlotte (Rose) Field; m. Paul A. Bartlett, Apr., 19, 1943. BS, Tchr. Coll., 1941; postgrad., Columbia U., 1941-43. Instr. Speech & Theatre Dept., Dallas, 1946-49; dir. Creative Writers Assn., New Sch. for Social Research, N.Y., 1955; asst. prof. San Jose State Univ., 1959-60; assoc. prof. Univ. Calif., 1960-64; poetry editor ETC Review of Gen. Semantics, San Francisco, 1963-76; lect. San Diego State Univ., 1979-81; lectr. English dept. U. San Diego, 1982; poetry editor Crosscurrents, 1983-88; editor, dir. internat. anthology Literary Olympians, 1992. Author: 17 books of poetry including Poems of Yes and No, 1952, It Takes Practice Not to Die, 1964, Selected Poems, 1970, Address in Time, 1979, Memory is No Stranger, 1981, Around the Clock, 1989; invented the 12-tone poem. PEN fellow, 1983, 85, McDowell, Yaddo, Montalvo, Dorland, Ragdale, Huntington-Hartford Found. grantee, 1959—. Mem. Poetry Soc. Am., Internat. Soc. Gen. Semantics, Internat. Women Writers Guild, PEN, Authors Guild. Home: 2875 Cowley Way Apt 1302 San Diego CA 92110-1014

BARTLETT, ELIZABETH SUSAN, audio-visual specialist; b. Bloomington, Ind., Sept. 11, 1927; d. Cecil Vernon and Nell (Helfrich) Bartlett; m. Frederick E. Sherman, July 8, 1955 (div. 1978). Student, Ind. U., 1946-48. Traffic-continuity dir. WTTS-Radio, Bloomington, Ind., 1947-48; program dir. WTTV-TV, Indpls., 1949-59; creative dir. Venus Advt. Agy., Indpls., 1960-68; prodn. mgr. Nat. TV News, Detroit, 1968-71; owner, producer Susan Sherman Prodns., Greenwich, Conn., 1971-73; audiovisual officer NSF, Washington, 1973—; lectr. in field. Concept writer/producer film: The Observatories, 1981, Brain, Books, Curiosity, 1992; producer: Science: Woman's Work; 1982, Keyhole of Eternity, 1975, What About Tomorrow?, 1978, The American Island, 1970, The New Engineers, 1986, Discover Science, 1988, A Brain, Books and a Curiosity, 1992, others. Recipient Silver award Internat. Film and TV Festival of N.Y., 1970, 74, Gold medal Nat. Ednl. Film Festival, 1982, 89, Chris Bronze plaque Columbus Film Festival, 1982, Bronze award Internat. Film & TV Festival of N.Y., 1982, Gold award 1976, Gold Camera award U.S. Indsl. Film Festival, 1982, Silver Cindy award, Info. Film Producers Assn., 1982, award for creative excellence U.S. Indsl. Film Festival, 1975, Techfilm Festival award, 1979, 80, 88, Gold award Houston Internat. Film Festival, 1987, Art Direction Mag. Creativity award, 1988; named Outstanding Woman for Contbn. in Arts, Federally Employed Women, 1984. Mem. Am. Women in Radio and TV (chpt. pres. 1953-56, 69-70), Washington Film and Video Coun. (pres. 1978-79), Coun. on Internat. Non-Theatrical Events (adv. bd., Golden Eagle award 1970, 74, 76-79, 82, 87), Women in Film and Video. Home: 809 S Columbus St Alexandria VA 22314-4206 Office: NSF Audiovisual 4201 Wilson Blvd Arlington VA 22230

BARTLETT, SHIRLEY ANNE, accountant; b. Gladwin, Mich., Mar. 28, 1933; d. Dewey J. and Ruth Elizabeth (Wright) Frye; m. Charles Duane Bartlett, Aug. 16, 1952 (div. Sept. 1982); children: Jeanne, Michelle, John, Yvonne. Student, Mich. State U., 1952-53, Rutgers U., 1972-74. Auditor State of Mich., Lansing, 1951-66; cost acct. Templar Co., South River, N.J., 1968-75; staff acct. Franco Mfg. Co., Metuchen, N.J., 1975-78; controller Thomas Creative Apparel, New London, Ohio, 1978-80; mgr. gen. acctg. Ideal Electric Co., Mansfield, Ohio, 1980-85; staff acct. Logangate Homes, Inc., Girard, Ohio, 1985-88; pvt. practice acctg. Youngstown, 1985—; acct. Universal Devel. Enterprises, Liberty Twp., Ohio, 1987-88; v.p. Lang Industries, Inc., Youngstown, 1984-93. Author: (play) Our Bicentennial-A Celebration, 1976. Soloist various orchestras, Mich., Va.; mem. Human Relations Commn., Franklin Township, 1971-77, Friends of Am. Art; treas. Heritage Found., New Brunswick, N.J., 1973-74, New London Proceeds Corp., 1979-83; commr. Huron Park Commn., Ohio, 1979-83; elected Dem. com. mem., N.J., Ohio, 1970-82; mem. planning com. Youngstown State U. Tax Insts., 1990—, presenter, 1990—. Mem. NOW (treas. Youngstown chpt. 1986—), Am. Soc. Women Accts. (bd. dirs. 1986-88, v.p. 1988-89, pres. 1989-91), NAFE, Bus. and Profl. Women (v.p. 1980—), Am. Soc. Notaries, Women's Jour. Network, Citizen's League of Greater Youngstown, Internat. Platform Assn., Friends of Am. Art, Youngstown Opera Guild. Democrat. Unitarian. Club: Franklin JFK (treas. 1970-72, v.p. 1973-78), Chataqua Literary, Scientific Circle (pres. 1979—). Home and Office: Bartlett Acctg Svcs 18 Norwick Dr Liberty Township OH 44505

BARTLETT, SUE, state legislator; b. Billings, Mont., July 4, 1947; m. Gene Fenderson. BA, Wash. U. Clk., recorder Lewis and Clark County, 1983-91; asst. sec. Mont. Senate, 1991-92, mem.; tech. writer. Democrat. Home: 416 N Beattie St Helena MT 59601-3701*

BARTLEY, MARY LOU RUF, school administrator; b. Orange, N.J., Feb. 10, 1940; d. Julius and Florence (Holland) Ruf; 1 child, Marcia Lyn. AB, Upsala Coll., 1961; MA, Seton Hall U., 1965; EdD, Rutgers U., 1976. Dir. testing, lang. arts coordinator East Orange (N.J.) Sch. Dist., 1968-72; prin. Deane-Porter Sch., Rumson, N.J., 1972-73; supt. Rumson (N.J.) Sch. Dist., 1973-78, River Dell Regional Sch. Dist., Oradell, N.J., 1978—; instr. Upsala Coll., 1967-72, Georgian Ct. Coll., Lakewood, N.J., 1977-78. Fellow Rutgers U., 1971-72; Fulbright Found. grantee, 1966-67. Mem. Am. Assn. Sch. Adminstrs., N.J. Assn. Sch. Adminstrs., N.J. Council Edn. (com. chmn. 1982—), N.J. Tchr. Edn. Roundtable (state pres. 1985-86), Bergen County Sch. Adminstrs. Assn. (pres. 1991-92), Northeast Coalition Ednl. Leaders, River Edge Rotary, Gamma Sigma Sigma, Phi Delta Kappa. Roman Catholic. Home: 506 Linwood Ave Ridgewood NJ 07450-3556 Office: River Dell Regional Schs Adminstrv Offices Pyle St Oradell NJ 07649

BARTLING, PHYLLIS MCGINNESS, oil company executive; b. Chillicothe, Ohio, Jan. 3, 1927; d. Francis A. McGinness and Gladys A. (Henkelman) Bane; m. Theodore Charles Bartling, Aug. 2, 1946; children—Pamela, Theodore, Eric C. Student, Ohio State U., 1944-47. Bookkeeper, Bartling & Assocs., Bartling Oil Co., Houston 1974-80; sec.-treas., dir. both cos., 1980—. Co-chmn. ticket sales Tulsa Opera, 1956-61; bd. dirs. Tex. Speech and Hearing Ctr., Houston, 1967-70. Republican. Episcopalian. Avocations: gardening, bicycling, cooking, golf. Home and Office: 11 Inwood Oaks Houston TX 77024-6803

BARTNOFF, JUDITH, judge; b. Boston, Apr. 14, 1949; d. Shepard and Irene F. (Tennenbaum) B.; m. Eugene F. Sofer, Sept. 10, 1978; 1 child, Nelson Bartnoff Sofer. B.A. magna cum laude, Radcliffe Coll., 1971; J.D. (Harlan Fiske Stone scholar), Columbia U., 1974; LL.M., Georgetown U., 1975. Bar: D.C. 1975, U.S. Dist. Ct. D.C. 1975, U.S. Ct. Appeals (D.C. cir.) 1980, U.S. Ct. Appeals (fed. cir.) 1985, U.S. Ct. Appeals (11th cir.) 1988, U.S. Ct. Appeals (3d cir.) 1989, U.S. Claims Ct. 1991. Fellow Inst. Pub. Interest Representation, Georgetown Law Ctr., Washington, 1974-75; staff atty. Council Pub. Interest Law, Washington, 1975-77; spl. asst. to asst. atty. gen. criminal div. Dept. Justice, Washington, 1977-78; assoc. dep. atty. gen. Dept. Justice, 1978-80; spl. asst. U.S. atty. D.C., 1980-81, asst. U.S. atty., 1982-85; assoc. firm Patton, Boggs & Blow, 1985-87, ptnr., 1988-94; assoc. ind. counsel, 1993-94; assoc. judge Superior Ct. of D.C., Washington, 1994—; mediator U.S. Dist. Ct. D.C., 1991-94; mem. com. on pro se litigation U.S Dist. Ct., 1991-94. Fellow Am. Bar Found.; mem. Am. Judicature Soc. Office: 500 Indiana Ave NW Washington DC 20001

BARTO, DEBORAH ANN, physician; b. West Chester, Pa., July 27, 1948; d. Charles Guy and Jeannette Victoria (Golder) B. BA, Oberlin Coll., 1970; MD, Hahnemann U., 1974. Dir. med. oncology Evergreen Hosp., Kirkland, Wash., 1980-85, head oncology quality assurance, 1992—; med. dir. Cmty. Home Health Care Hospice, Seattle, 1981-84. Mem. Evergreen Women's Physicians. Democrat. Buddhist. Office: Evergreen Profl Plz Ste E-60 12911 120th Ave NE Kirkland WA 98034-3027

BARTOL, ANGELA, banker; b. Garfield Twp., Mich., Dec. 18, 1923; d. Anton and Antonia (Zgonc) Laurich; m. Frank J. Bartol June 24, 1944 (dec. 1986); children: Marcia A. Bartol Heath, Jon R. Student, Cloverland Community Coll., Escanaba, Mich., 1942, Mich. State U., 1970. Clk. U.S. Postal Svc., Trenary, Mich., 1941-42; book-keeper Alger County Creamery, Treanary, Mich., 1942-45; with Trenary State Bank, 1949—; asst. v.p. ops. 1st Nat. Bank & Trust Co., Marquette, Mich., 1991—, sr. teller, 1993; ins. agt., asst. sec.-treas. Trenary Agy. Inc., 1970-88. Sec. Limestone Twp. Sch. Dist., Traunik, Mich., 1948-73; treas. altar soc. St. Rita's Ch., eucharistic minister choir. Mem. Trenary Lioness Club. Democrat. Roman Catholic. Home: HC R1 Box 58 Traunik MI 49890 Office: MFC 1st Nat Bank 101 W Washington St Marquette MI 49855

BARTOLETTI, LAURA ANN, painting contractor, social worker; b. Virginia, Minn., May 31, 1963; d. Everett Pacifico and Claire Ruth (Carlson) B. BASW, Coll. of St. Catherine's, St. Paul, 1985. Residential care counselor Wilder Found., St. Paul, 1985-90; asst. coord. J.E.C. Miller, Inc., Bloomington, Minn., 1991-92; contractor Liquid Wallpaper of Minn., St. Paul, 1994—. Editor newsletter Women in the Trades, 1994. Mem. St. Paul Assn. Responsible Landlords, 1993. Mem. NOW, NASW, Minn. Women in the Trades.

BARTOLO, DONNA M., hospital administrator, nurse; b. Springfield, Ill., Mar. 21, 1941; d. Elmer Ralph Bartolomucci and Zoe (Rose) Cavatorta. Diploma in nursing, St. John's Sch. Nursing, Springfield, Ill., 1962; BS, Milliken U., 1976; MS, Sangamon State U., 1978. Pediatric nurse Springfield Clin., 1962-64, physician's asst., 1972-74; gynecol. nurse Watson Clin., Lakeland, Fla., 1964-66; cons. state sch. nurses Office of Edn. State of Ill., Springfield, 1974-78; assoc. dir. operating rm. svcs. Cedars-Sinai Med. Ctr., L.A., 1978-82, co-dir. div. nursing, 1981-82; surg. nurse Emory U. Hosp., Atlanta, 1966-70, asst. dir. nursing, surg. svcs., 1982-94; DON surg. svcs., 1994—; asst. prof. Nell Hodgson Woodruff Sch. Nursing Emory U. Mem. editorial bd. Perioperative Nursing Quarterly; contbr. articles to nursing jours. Mem. Org. Nurse Execs., Ga. Assn. Nurse Exec. (pres. elect, pres. 1992), Assn. Operating Rm. Nurses, Sigma Theta Tau (sec. 1990—). Home: 1328 Mill Glen Dr Dunwoody GA 30338-2720

BARTOLO, MARLENE BETH, lawyer; b. McPherson, Kans., Jan. 10, 1963; d. Harold Marvin and Opal Janice (Jantz) Hanson; m. Kevin J. Bartolo, May 7, 1994. BS in Mktg., Psychology and Bus. Adminstrn. summa cum laude, Kansas Newman Coll., 1985; JD magna cum laude, U. Notre Dame, 1989. Bar: Calif., Kans., N.Y., D.C., Conn. 1995. From assoc. to sr. atty. PepsiCo, Inc., Somers, N.Y., 1989—. Office: PepsiCo Inc 1 Pepsi Way Somers NY 10589

BARTON, ANN ELIZABETH, financial executive; b. Long Lake, Mich., Sept. 8, 1923; d. John and Inez Mabel (Morse) Seaton; m. H. Kenneth Barton, Apr. 3, 1948; children: Michael, John, Nancy. Student Mt. San Antonio Coll., 1969-71, Adrian Coll., 1943, Citrus Coll., 1967, Golden Gate U., 1976, Coll. Fin. Planning, 1980-82. CFP. Tax cons., real estate broker, Claremont, Calif., 1967-72, Newport Beach, Calif., 1972-74; v.p., officer Putney, Barton, Assocs., Inc., Walnut Creek, Calif., 1975-94. Mem. Internat. Assn. Fin. Planners (registered investment advisor), Calif. Soc. Enrolled Agts., Nat. Assn. Enrolled Agts., Nat. Soc. Public Accts., Inst. CFP. Office: Putney Barton Assocs Inc 1243 Alpine Rd Ste 219 Walnut Creek CA 94596-4431

BARTON, DIANE, physician; b. Queens, N.Y., Apr. 29, 1959; d. Howard Edwin and Naomi Muriel (Steinberg) B. BS in Nutrition, Cornell U., 1980; MD, Temple U., 1984. Diplomate Am. Bd. Internal Medicine, Am. Bd. Geriatric Medicine. Intern in internal medicine Pa. Hosp., 1984-85; resident in phys. medicine and rehab. Temple U., 1985-86; resident in internal medicine U. of Medicine and Dentistry of N.J., Camden, 1986-88, chief med. resident, 1988-89; lectr. Am. Heart Assn. Recipient Dorothea Glass Rehab. award, 1984, Top Physician award Phila. Mag., 1994. Mem. ACP, Soc. Gen. Medicine, Am. Med. Women's Assn., Am. Heart Assn. (speakers bur.), Nat. Cancer Inst. (speakers bur.), Cornell U. Ambs. Network, N.Am. Assn. for Study of Obesity, Alpha Omega Alpha. Office: Cooper Hosp 3 Cooper Plz Ste 220 Camden NJ 08103

BARTON, JACQUELINE K., chemistry educator; b. N.Y.C., May 7, 1952; d. William and Claudine (Gutchen) Kapelman; m. Peter Brendan Dervan, Mar. 3, 1990. AB summa cum laude, Columbia U., 1974, PhD, 1978; postdoctoral, Yale U., 1979-80. Asst. prof. Hunter Coll, N.Y.C., 1980-82; asst. prof. Columbia U., N.Y.C., 1983-85, assoc. prof., 1985-86, prof. chemistry and biology, 1986-89; prof. Calif. Inst. Tech., Pasadena, 1989—; vis. rsch. assoc. dept. biophysics Bell Labs., 1979; mem. chemistry adv. com. NSF, 1985-88; mem. metallobiochemistry study sect. NIH, 1986-90, chmn., 1988-90; bd. dirs. Dow Chem. Co., Cortech. NSF predoctoral fellow, 1975-78, NIH postdoctoral fellow, 1979-80, Alfred P. Sloan fellow, 1984, MacArthur Found. fellow, 1991—; Camille and Henry Dreyfus Tchr. scholar, 1986-91; recipient Harold Lamport award N.Y. Acad. Scis., 1984, Alan T. Waterman award NSF, 1985, Fresenius award Phi Lambda Upsilon, 1986, Eli Lilly Biochemistry award, 1987, Pure Chemistry award Am. Chem. Soc., 1988, Sci. and Tech. award Mayor of N.Y., 1990, Baekeland medal Am. Chem. Soc., 1991, Garven medal Am. Chem. Soc., 1992, Am. Acad. Arts and Scis. medal 1991. Office: Calif Inst Tech Divsn Chemistry 127 # 72 Pasadena CA 91125

BARTON, JANICE SWEENY, chemistry educator; b. Trenton, N.J., Mar. 22, 1939; d. Laurence U. and Lillian Mae (Fletcher) S.; m. Keith M. Barton, Dec. 20, 1967. BS, Butler U., 1962; PhD, Fla. State U., 1970. Postdoctoral fellow Johns Hopkins U., Balt., 1970-72; asst. prof. chemistry East Tex. State U., Commerce, 1972-78, Tex. Woman's U., Denton, 1978-81; assoc. prof. Washburn U., Topeka, 1982-88, prof., 1988—, chair chemistry dept., 1992—; mem. undergrad. faculty enhancement panel NSF, Washington, 1990; mem. NSF instr. lab. improvement panel, 1992. Contbr. articles to profl. jours. Active Household Hazardous Waste Collection, Topeka, 1991, Solid Waste Task Force, Shawnee County, Kans., 1990; mem. vol. com. YWCA, Topeka, 1984-87. Rsch. grantee Petroleum Rsch. Fund, Topeka, 1984-86, NIH, Topeka, 1985-88; instrument grantee NSF, Topeka, 1986. Mem. Am. Chem. Soc. (sec. Dallas-Ft. Worth sect. 1981-82), Kans. Acad. Sci. (pres.-elect 1991, pres. 1992), Biophys. Soc., Sigma Xi (pres. TWU club 1980-81), Iota Sigma Pi (mem.-at-large coord. 1987—). Home: 3401 SW Oak Pky Topeka KS 66614-3218 Office: Washburn U Dept Chemistry Topeka KS 66621

BARTON, JUDITH MARIE, lawyer, lobbyist; b. Grosse Pointe, Mich., Feb. 19, 1953; d. Joseph J. and Shirley (Fisher) B.; m. A. Scott MacGuidwin, Sept. 19, 1980; children: Stephen Fisher, Richard Joseph, Elizabeth Ashley, James Scott. BA, U. Mich., 1975; JD, Thomas M. Cooley Sch. Law, 1979. Bar: Mich. 1981, U.S. Dist. Ct. (we. and ea. dists.) Mich. 1982. Mgr. bus. and circulation Football News/Basketball Weekly, Grosse Pointe, 1975-77; legis. asst. Mich. Ho. of Reps., Lansing, 1977-80, legal specialist, 1980-81; staff dir. Mich. State Senate, Lansing, 1981-83; pvt. practice Lansing, 1983-93; majority gen. coun. Mich. House of Reps., 1993—, chief policy and legal counsel, 1994—; lobbyist Mich. Rental Housing Assn., 1989-93. Bd. dirs. Common Cause, Lansing, 1983-89, state chairperson, Mich., 1987-89; bd. dirs. Landlords of Mid-Mich., Lansing, 1985-89. Mem. ABA, Mich. Bar Assn., Ingham County Bar Assn., Women's Law Assn., Pub. Action Com., Capitol Area Women's Network (bd. dirs. 1983-84), Civitan Internat., Pi Beta Phi. Republican. Roman Catholic. Home: 4317 Manitou Dr Okemos MI 48864-2715

BARTON, KATHLEEN MARIE, electronics educator, computer technician; b. Milford, Mass., Jan. 26, 1951; d. Americo Bartone and Margaret Marie O'Rourke. BA, Elms Coll., 1973; MEd, Westfield State Coll., 1993. Field svc. technician Xerox Corp., Hartford, Conn., 1979-85; instr. electronics Mass. Career Devel. Inst., Springfield, Mass., 1985-88, Putnam Vocat. Tech. High Sch., Springfield, 1988-94, Westfield (Mass.) Vocat. Tech. H.S., 1995—; cons. in field Bergwall Prodns., N.Y.C., 1990-93. Author scripts for video series Power Supplies Explained, 1992, Semicondrs. Explained, 1993. Mem. Mass. Tchrs.' Assn., Springfield Edn. Assn. (bargaining team 1993-94), Mass. Vocat. Assn., Electronics Industries Assn. Home: 34 Williston Ave Easthampton MA 01027-2219 Office: Westfield Vocal Tech High Sch 33 Smith Ave Westfield MA 01085

BARTON, PAULINE, writer; b. Hollister, Mo., Apr. 13, 1923; d. Clinton Ben and Rosa Victoria (Kaneaster) Layton; m. Benjamin Lee Barton, Dec. 22, 1945; children Ben Lee, John Paul. BS in Edn., S.W. Mo. State U., 1960; MS in Edn., Drury Coll., 1967. Wartime assembly line GM, Anderson, Ind., 1942-44; tchr. Hollister (Mo.) Schs., 1945-46, 49-51, 56-59; bus. tchr. Branson (Mo.) Schs., 1959-77, adult edn., 1981-83, home bound educator, 1983-84; freelance writer Mo., 1984—; Chmn. Taney County Bus. Tchrs., 1960-61, Southwest Mo. Bus. Tchrs., 1976-77; historian, White River Valley Hist. Soc., Mo., 1987-90, sec., treas., 1994—. contbr. articles to profl. jours., books. Leader Boy Scouts of Am., Branson, Mo., 1954-62; counselor Am. Field Service Exchange student, Branson, Mo., 1972-80; Bd. and aide Christian Action Ministry, Branson, Mo., 1986–. mem. AAUW, Ozark Writer's League, Tri-Lakes Community theatre, LWV, Am. Cancer Soc., Women of the Ch., Am. Legion Aux., VFW Aux. Republican. Presbyterian. Home: 1159 Bee Creek Rd Branson MO 65616-9120

BARTOW, DIANE GRACE, marketing and sales executive; b. Maspeth, N.Y., Apr. 20, 1948; d. Alfred Otto and Charlotte Florence (Bronnenkant) Bruggeman; m. Eugene A. Bartow, Aug. 29, 1992; children: Jason, Trudi. AAS, Queensborough Community Coll., 1967; BS, Nova U., 1979. Jr. acct. Exxon, N.Y.C., 1967-69; acct. BRM Assos., N.Y.C., 1969, Texaco, N.Y.C., 1969-74; supr. Eutectic, Flushing, N.Y., 1974-76; regional industry dir. Am. Express, N.Y.C., 1976-83; v.p. Eastern Exclusives, Boston, 1983-85; pres. The Mktg. Dept., 1985-86, sr. v.p., gen. mgr. Rogers Merchandising Inc., 1986-92; exec. v.p., COO Bartow Ins. Agy., Inc., 1992—. Author tng. manual, Travel newsletter, 1982, Ins. Update, 1992. Active Murray Hill Community, 1982, 7 E. 35th Coop, 1983. Recipient VISTA award Am. Express, 1983. Mem. Am. Soc. Travel Agts (tour relations com. 1983), Am. Hotel and Motel Assn., Am. Film Assn., Am. Mgmt. Assn., Sigma Mu Omega (pres. Bayside, N.Y. 1966-67). Home: 7 E 35th St New York NY 10016-3810

BARTSCHE, KATHRYN MARY, elementary education eduator; b. Trenton, N.J., Apr. 2, 1963; d. Philip J. and Pauline M. (Berescik) Kecmer; m. Emil Alvin Bartsche, Apr. 23, 1988. BS, U. Del., 1985. Tchr. art Bayonne Bd. Edn., 1985-89, Marlboro (N.J.) Bd. Edn., 1989—; art coord. Summer Arts, Marlboro, 1993. Bayonne Bd. Edn. grantee, 1989. Mem. Nat. Art Edn. Assn., N.J. Assn. Art Edn., N.J. Edn. Assn. Republican. Roman Catholic. Home: 1511 River Ave Pt Pleasant NJ 08742-4313 Office: Robertsville Elem Sch Menzel Ln Morganville NJ 07751

BARTUCCI, JANET EVELYN, marketing communications executive; b. Flushing, N.Y., Jan. 14, 1952; d. Louis Joseph and Evelyn Doris (Montleon) B.; m. Reuben Samuel, Oct. 18, 1981; children: Alexandra Elizabeth, David Lawrence. AAS in Communications, Fashion Inst. Tech., N.Y.C., 1972. Asst. account exec. Saul Krieg, N.Y.C., 1972-74; publicity mgr. Grosset & Dunlap, N.Y.C., 1974-76; account exec. Burson Marsteller, N.Y.C., 1976-79; v.p. Myers CommuniCounsel, N.Y.C., 1979-85; pres. Bartucci-Samuel, Inc., N.Y.C., 1985-91; sr. v.p., dir. consumer products M Booth & Assocs., N.Y., 1991—. Mem. Women in Communications, Am. Inst. Wine and Food, James Beard Found. Office: M Booth & Assocs Inc 470 Park Ave S New York NY 10016

BARUCH, MONICA LOBO-FILHO, psychological counselor; b. Rio de Janeiro, Jan. 11, 1954; d. Max and Margot (Hollander) Lobo-Filho; m. Robert Karl Baruch, Dec. 30, 1973 (div. May 1985). BA in Psychology, U. Rochester, 1975; MA in Counseling Edn., U. Mo., Kansas City, 1978. Cert. Nat. Bd. Cert. Counselors. Tchr. curriculum devel. St. Patrick's Sch., Rio de Janeiro, 1974-76; tchr., soccer coach Pembroke Country Day Sch., Kansas City, Mo., 1977-78; tchr., trainer Berlitz Sch. Langs., Kansas City and Washington, 1976-79; counselor, cons. Youth Understanding, Washington, 1979-81; pvt. practice, 1981—; academic faculty counselor Georgetown U., Washington, 1982-90. Co-author: Weight Control: A Guide for Counselors and Therapists, 1987. Named one of Outstanding Young Women in Am., 1981. Mem. ACA, Am. Mental Health Counselors Assn., Multiple Personality Study Group, Md. Mental Health Counselors Assn. (program chmn. 1989, exec. bd. 1993), Md. Assn. Counseling and Devel. (ethics com. 1990).

BARVILLE, REBECCA PENELOPE, elementary school educator; b. Tulare, Calif., Nov. 7, 1936; m. David Leopold Barville, June 8, 1958; children: Mark, Becky, Curtis. BA, Simpson Coll., San Francisco, 1958; MA summa cum laude, Fresno State U., 1974. Cert. reading specialist, edn. adminstr., elem. tchr., Calif. Social worker Tulare County Welfare Dept., Porterville, Calif., 1961-63, San Bernadino Welfare, Ontario, Calif., 1963-65; tchr., reading specialist Pleasant View Sch., Porterville, 1969—; instr. Porterville Coll., 1993. Pres. PTA, Lindsay, Calif., 1966-67. Fellow Delta Kappa Gamma; mem. AAUW (bd. dirs. 1974-83), Calif. Reading Assn. (sec. 1974), Pleasant View Educators Assn. (past pres., sec. 1985—). Republican. Presbyterian. Club: P.E.O. (v.p. 1986-87).

BARZOLOSKI-O'CONNOR, BARBARA ANN, surgical nurse; b. Eglin AFB, Fla., Oct. 22, 1965; d. Lawrence Leonard and Sylvia Susan (Chrzan) Barzoloski; m. John Moreland O'Connor Jr., June 1, 1991. AA in Nursing, Prince Georges Community Coll., Largo, Md., 1986; BSN, U. Md., Catonsville, 1987; MSN, U. Md., 1993. RN, Md., D.C. Nurse Providence Hosp., Washington, 1986—, nurse, unit educator, 1992—. Mem. Sigma Theta Tau, Phi Kappa Phi. Home: 551 State Route 32 Sykesville MD 21784-5640 Office: Providence Hosp 1150 Varnum St NE Washington DC 20017-2180

BASA, ENIKÖ MOLNÁR, librarian; b. Huszt, Hungary, Sept. 7, 1939; came to the U.S., 1950; d. Julius Valentine and Terézia (Fejér) Molnár; m. Péter Basa, Nov. 19, 1966. BA, Trinity Coll., 1962; MA, U. N.C., 1965, PhD, 1972. Instr. U. Md., College Park, 1965-69; asst. prof. Dunbarton Coll., Washington, 1970-72; lectr. Am. U., Washington, 1972-75, Hood Coll., Frederick, Md., 1975-76; editor, libr. Libr. of Congress, Washington, 1977—. Author: Sandor Petöfi, 1980; editor: Twayne World Authors, 1974—, Hungarian Literature, 1993; translator: (play) Screenplay from Örkény, 1983; assoc. editor The Comparatist, 1976-82, editorial bd., 1992—; jour. rev. editor: Hungarian Studies Newsletter, 1975-82; guest editor: Rev. Nat. Lits., 1992; contbr. chpts. to books and articles and book revs. to profl. jours. Mem. MLA (Hungarian sect. chair 1980, 90), So. Comparative Lit. Assn. (founding v.p. 1977-79, 89—, sec.-treas. 1985-89, pres. 1992-94), Am. Hungarian Educators Assn. (pres. 1974-80, 88-92, exec. dir. 1980-88, 92—), Internat. Assn. Hungarian Studies, Libr. Congress Profl. Assn. (v.p. 1991). Home: 707 Snider Ln Silver Spring MD 20905-4165 Office: Serial Record Libr Congress Washington DC 20540

BASDEN, BARBARA HOLZ, psychology educator; b. Coeur d'Alene, Idaho, Feb. 10, 1940; d. Albert R. and Carol (Utter) Holz; m.David R. Basden, May 25, 1962; children: Leslie H., Derin E. BA, Coll. Idaho, 1962; PhD, U. Calif., Santa Barbara, 1969. Asst. prof. psychology Calif. State U., Fresno, 1973-78, assoc. prof. psychology, 1978-82, prof. psychology, 1983—. Author: (study guide) Psychology, 1984, 2d edit., 1987, 3d edit., 1991, Directed Forgetting Memory and Aging, Retrival Inhibition, 1987-94; contbr. articles to profl. jours. Fellow Am. Psychol. Soc.; mem. APA, Psychonomic Soc., Western Psychol. Assn. Office: Calif State U Dept Psychology 5310 N Campus Dr Fresno CA 93740-0011

BASDEN, CAMERON, ballet mistress, dancer; b. Dallas. Scholarship student, The Joffrey Ballet Sch., 1976-77. Dancer Dallas Ballet, 1975-76, Joffrey II Dancers, N.Y.C., 1977-79; dancer The Joffrey Ballet, N.Y.C., 1979—, asst. ballet mistress, ballet mistress, 1993—. Office: The Joffrey Ballet 130 W 56th St New York NY 10019-3818*

BASHAM, DEBRA ANN, archivist; b. Hattiesburg, Miss., Mar. 18, 1960; d. John Crosby and Barbara May (Dunn) B.; m. Ernest Richard Fauss, Apr. 26, 1986; children; Ernest James Fauss, John Richard Fauss. BA in History, Millsaps Coll., 1982; MA in History, U. Del., 1984. Archivist W.Va. State Archives, Charleston, 1984—. Mem. MARAC (state rep.), Soc. Am. Archives Conf. Democrat. Methodist. Office: Culture & History Div W Va State Archives 1900 Kanawha Blvd E Charleston WV 25305-0300

BASHAM-TOOKER, JANET BROOKS, geropsychologist, educator; b. Hampton, Va., Sept. 27, 1919; d. Thomas Westmore and Cora Evelyn Brooks; m. Linwood Cecil Basham (div. 1968); m. Frederick Fitch Tooker. BA cum laude, U. N.C., Greensboro, 1948; ABD in Psychology, Calif. State U., L.A., 1981; MA in Human Devel., Pacific Oaks Coll., 1984. Tchr., Calif. Grad. asst. psychology Duke U., Durham, N.C., 1948-49; tchr. Albuquerque City Schs., 1950-51; tchr. L.A. City Schs., 1953-54, counselor, 1981; lectr. L.A., 1988—; docent Las Angelitas del Pueblo, L.A., 1971-74; active project with autistic children, through Pepperdine Univ., UCLA Neuropsychiatric Inst., L.A., 1974. Author numerous poems. Mem. planning com., women's conf. Commn. on Status of Women, Pasadena, Calif., 1982-85, sr. com. Task Force on Aging, San Marino, Calif., 1986-89, United Way, Arcadia, Calif., 1984-88, Symphony Guild, Fayetteville, 1990; adv. mem. San Gabriel Presbytery Commn. on Aging, 1984-88; mem. grad. studies subcom. Calif. State U., L.A., 1975-78; v.p. San Marino Aux. Meth. Hosp., Arcadia, Calif., 1985-86; docent Duarte Hist. Soc., Calif., 1986-89; moderator sr. adults 1st United Presbyn. Ch., Fayetteville, 1990; facilitator fin. info. program for women AARP, Fayetteville, 1990; vol. in gerontology Fayetteville (Ark.) City Hosp., 1991, Health Care Unit, Butterfield Trail Village, Fayetteville, 1993; adv. com. Single Parent Scholarship Fund, Fayetteville, 1992. Recipient Margaret Noffsinger award Va. Intermont Coll., 1937. Mem. AAUW, Am. Soc. Aging, Mental Health Assn., Older Women's League, Flaming Hills Garden Club, League of Woman Voters, Phi Beta Kappa, Phi Theta Kappa. Republican. Presbyterian.

BASHORE, IRENE SARAS, research institute administrator; b. San Jose, Calif.; d. John and Eva (Lionudakis) Saras; m. Vincent Bashore (div.); 1 child, Juliet Ann. BA, Pepperdine U., 1950; MA, Calif. State U., Fullerton, 1977. Founder, exec. dir. Inst. for Dramatic Rsch., Fullerton, Calif., 1967—.

BASIA (BASIA TRZETRZELEWSKA), musician, vocalist; b. Jaworzno, Poland; d. Stanislaw and Kazia Trzetrzelewska. Formed pop group Perfect, 1979; with Matt Bianco on album Who's Side Are You On?, 1985; soloist, 1987—. Albums include (with Matt Bianco) Which Side Are You On?, 1985, (solo) Time and Tide, 1987, London Warsaw New York, 1989, Brave New Hope, 1991, The Sweetest Illusion, 1994; appeared on-stage in Basia on Broadway, 1994. Office: CBS Records Inc 51 W 52nd St New York NY 10019-6101*

BASILETTI, JANICE RITA, artist, educator; b. Royal Oak, Mich., July 12, 1960; d. John Cesar and Naomi Wilhelmena (Warmanen) B.; m. Faan-Hoan Liu, May 19, 1984; 1 child: Tamara Nicole. AA, Coll. DuPage, Glen Ellyn, Ill., 1981; BFA, U. Ill., 1983; MFA, San Jose State U., 1991. Art instr., coord. Little City Found., Palatine, Ill., 1983-84; silk screen printer A-1 Printers, Addison, Ill., 1984; design cons. Jantra Decor, Naperville, Ill., 1984-86; lighting cons. Riverside Lighting, Santa Cruz, Calif., 1986-88; drawing asst. instr. Cabrillo Coll., Santa Cruz, Calif., 1989; drawing, ceramic instr. Santa Clara (Calif.) U., 1990; drawing instr. San Jose (Calif.) State U., 1991; profl. artist Santa Cruz, 1991-94, Hollis, N.H., 1994—. Author: Leisure Activities for the Young and Mentally Handicapped, 1984; exhbns. include San Jose Inst. Contemporary Art, 1989, 90, 91, 92, 93, 94, San Jose State U., 1989, 90, 91, Downtown Gallery San Jose Art League, 1989, 91, Santa Cruz Civic Auditorium, 1993, Santa Cruz County Govt. Ctr., 1993, Second Story Gallery, Seattle, 1993, Park West Gallery, Cocoanut Grove, Santa Cruz, 1993, Creative Arts Ctr., Sunnyvale, 1994, Pub. TV KTEH, San Jose, 1994; collections include KVIE, PC Resources, Ill., Quest Tech., Ill., numerous pvt. collections. Mem. San. Jose Inst. Contemporary Art, Coll. Art Assn., San Jose Mus. Art, Beaver Brook Assn., Phi Theta Kappa. Roman Catholic.

BASINGER, KAREN LYNN, renal dietitian; b. Mechanicsville, Md., July 4, 1955; d. Leonard Marcus and Mary Jane (Harding) Brookbank; m. Joseph Andrew Basinger, Nov. 17, 1984; 1 child, James Marcus. BS, U. Md., 1977; MS, Hood Coll., 1987. Lic. nutritionist. Libr. technician Bowie (Md.) State Coll., 1973-79; instr. St. Mary's County Adult Edn., Leonardtown, Md., 1979-80; home economist Zamoiski Co., Balt., 1977-83; nutritionist/WIC coord. South County Health Plan, Prince Frederick, Md., 1979-80; nutritionist Walter Reed Army Med. Ctr., Washington, 1980-82; renal dietitian Mid Atlantic/BMA, Camp Springs, Md., 1982-87, Kidney Care Ctr., Landover, Md., 1987—; instr. dietary intern program Andrews AFB, 1988-91; lectr. in field. Mem. profl. adv. bd. Nat. Kidney Found./NCA, 1989-94; chair coun. on renal nutrition Nat. Kidney Found., 1993-94, program chair, 1990-92. Recipient Spl. Recognition Nat. Kidney Found./NCA, 1990, 92, Recognized Renal Dietitian/NCA, 1991, 94. Mem. Am. Nutritionists Assn., Am. Home Econs. Assn., Md. Home Econs. Assn. (bylaws chair 1982-94), Am. Dietetic Assn., Washington Metro. Coun. on Renal Nutrition (chair 1986-91, nutrition symposium chair 1989), U. Md. Alumni Assn. Democrat. Lutheran. Office: Kidney Care Ctr 1300 Mercantile Ln Ste 194 Landover MD 20785-5339

BASINGER, KIM, actress; b. Athens, Ga., Dec. 8, 1953; d. Don Basinger; m. Ron Britton, 1980 (div. Feb. 1990); m. Alec Baldwin, August 19, 1993. Student, Neighborhood Playhouse, N.Y.C. Model Eileen Ford Agy., N.Y.C., 1972-77; ind. actress, 1977—. Starring role (TV series) Dog and Cat, 1977; TV films include Katie-Portrait of a Centerfold, 1978, The Ghost of Flight 401, 1978, Killjoy, 1981, (TV miniseries) From Here to Eternity, 1979; (feature films) Hard Country, 1981, Mother Lode, 1982, Never Say Never Again, 1983, The Man Who Loved Women, 1983, The Natural, 1984, Fool for Love, 1985, 9 1/2 Weeks, 1986, No Mercy, 1986, Blind Date, 1987, Nadine, 1987, My Stepmother is an Alien, 1988, Batman, 1989, The Marrying Man, 1991, Final Analysis, 1992, Cool World, 1992, The Real McCoy, 1993, The Getaway, 1994, Ready to Wear (Prêt-à-Porter), 1994. Office: Creative Artists Agy Inc care Michael Menchel 9830 Wilshire Blvd Beverly Hills CA 90212-1825*

BASKIN, ROBERTA, television correspondent; b. Atlanta, Jan. 16, 1952; d. Alan Baskin and Suzanne Pallister; m. James Albert Trengrove, Sept. 19, 1987; children: Chelsea, Vanessa. Student, Elmira Coll., 1969-70. Dir. Consumer Affairs Office, Syracuse, N.Y., 1974-77; consumer reporter Sta. WMAQ-TV, Chgo., 1977-79; investigative reporter Sta. WLS-TV, Chgo., 1979-84; consumer editor Sta. WJLA-TV, Washington, 1984-91; corr. CBS News, Washington, N.Y.C., 1992—; bd. mem. Fund for Investigative Journalism, Washington, 1992-94. Telethon host Sta. WETA-TV, Washington, 1987-94. Recipient Peabody awards U. Ga., 1982, 86, Edward R. Murrow award Radio-TV News Dirs. Assn., 1983, 90, duPont-Columbia awards Columbia U. Sch. of Journalism, 1987, 90, Ohio State awards. Mem. NATAS (16 local Emmy awards Chgo., Washington chpts.), Am. Fedn. TV and Radio Artists (bd. dirs. 1993-94). Office: CBS News Washington Bureau 2020 M St NW Washington DC 20036

BASS, ELIZABETH RUTH, editor; b. N.Y.C., July 12, 1951; m. Joseph R. Masci; 1 child, Jonathan Samuel. BA in English with honors, Cornell U., 1972. Reporter Hornell Evening Tribune, 1972-76, L.I. Press, 1972-76; rschr., editor Mass. Fair Share, 1975-80; copy editor, dep. nat. editor, dep. fgn. editor Newsday, 1980-90, sci. and health editor, 1990—. Mem. Phi Beta Kappa. Office: Newsday Inc 235 Pinelawn Rd Melville NY 11747-4226

BASS, HEIDI LORAYNE, utility administrator; b. Akron, Ohio, Dec. 30, 1964; d. R. Lamar and Janet Patricia (Key) B. ABA, Occidental Coll., 1987; MBA, U. LaVerne, 1994. Spl. rsch. asst. pers. City of L.A., 1987, mgmt. asst., 1987-93, utility mgmt. analyst, 1993—. Office: LA Dept Water and Power 9450 San Fernando Rd Sun Valley CA 91352-1420

BASS, LINDA JEAN, rehabilitation nurse; b. Holyoke, Mass., Aug. 9, 1946; d. Murray and Isabel (Mahler) Epstein; m. Eugene L. Bass, June 16, 1968; 1 child, Elena Lisa. BA in Sociology cum laude, U. Mass., 1968; MEd, Salisbury (Md.) State Coll., 1977; PhD in Adult Edn., Columbia Pacific U., 1985; BSN, Coll. Notre Dame of Md., 1991. Cert. ins. rehab. specialist; cert. nursing adminstr. Psychiat. social worker Northampton (Mass.) State Hosp., 1968-69; substitute tchr. Bd. of Edn., Salisbury, 1969; staff nurse Deer's Head Hosp. Ctr., Salisbury, 1973-78, insvc. edn. coord., 1978-87; dir. nursing River Walk Manor, Salisbury, 1987-88; rehab. specialist Comprehensive Rehab. Assocs., Balt., 1988—; CPR instr./trainer Am. Heart Assn., Salisbury, 1981-90; EMT, Md., 1987-93. Chair county health planning com. Health Planning Coun. of Md., 1985-87. Recipient Freedoms Found. award for editorial writing, 1963. Mem. Sigma Theta Tau. Office: PO Box 123 Fruitland MD 21826-0123

BASS, LINDA SUE, economic development specialist; b. Roanoke, Va., Apr. 7, 1949; d. Jack Kenneth Payne and Dorothy Louise (Brewer) Vocker; m. Michael Robert Lake, May 7, 1972 (div. Feb. 1975); m. Joseph Carl Bass, Jr., May 22, 1982 (div. Aug. 1992); 1 child, Mary Catherine. BS in Math., Va. Poly. Inst. and State U., 1971, MBA, 1983. Statistician Equal Employment Opportunity Commn., Washington, 1971-72; programmer, analyst Singer Bus. Machines, San Leandro, Calif., 1972-74; med. researcher Western Health Systems, Rapid City, S.D., 1974; systems analyst State of Alaska, Juneau, 1974, Datacare, Inc., Roanoke, Va., 1975-82; v.p. systems and programming, co-owner Precision Med. Data, Roanoke, 1983-88; econ. devel. specialist City of Roanoke, 1988—. Bd. dirs., treas. Bethany Hall, Roanoke, 1985-89. Named Woman of Yr., Shenandoah chpt. Am. Bus. Women's Assn., 1985. Mem. Va. Econ. Devel. Assn. Episcopalian. Office: City of Roanoake Dept Econ Devel, Mcpl Bldg 215 Church Ave SW Rm 357 Roanoke VA 24011

BASS, LYNDA D., medical/surgical nurse, educator; b. Suffolk, Va.; d. H.M. and Katie Lea Bass. BSN, N.C. Agrl. and Tech. State U., Greensboro, 1968; MS in Nursing, Cath. U. Am., 1974; Gen. Surgery Clin. Specialist, George Washington U. Hosp., Washington. Clin. instr. Suburban Hosp., Bethesda, Md.; edn./tng. quality assurance coord. Howard U. Hosp., Washington; clin. educator Providence Hosp., Washington. Capt. U.S. Army, 1968-71, Vietnam. Mem. Chi Eta Phi.

BASS, MARIAN, police captain; b. West Palm Beach, Fla., Sept. 26, 1935; d. Ray and Ossie (Thompson) B.; 1 child, Dennis Michael Schultz. AAS, Erie C.C., 1963; BS, Buffalo State U., 1971; MA, SUNY, Albany, 1972; MS, SUNY, Buffalo, 1979. Cert. police instr., juvenile delinquency specialist. Police officer Buffalo Police Dept., 1960-68, desk lt., 1968-72, lt., 1972-78, capt., 1978-93, dir. crime prevention bur., 1980-87, comdr. precinct # 10, 1989-93, ret., 1993; project dir. Youth Alcohol Diversion Program; adj. prof. criminal justice dept. Erie C.C. City Campus, 1980-87; tutor and evaluator of prior coll. level learning and life experience Empire State Coll., Buffalo; sr. contbg. editor Blue Line; lectr., trainer E.C. Cen. Police Svcs. Tng. Acad., Erie C.C. South; faculty Empire State Coll.; bd. dirs. Judges and Police Conf. Western N.Y., 1994. Contbr. articles to profl. jours. Sr. arbitration specialsit Better Bus. Bur. of Western N.Y.; bd. dirs. Niagara Frontier Assn. for Sickle Cell Disease, 1989, Community Action Orgn., 1993, BUSC Alumni Assn., 1989, Red Cross, 1983; chair Affirmative Action Com., ECC, 1980; mem. task force on rape and sexual assault, Erie County, task force on discipline/weapons/drugs Buffalo Sch. System, task force on substance abuse control in pub. and parochial schs., Erie County; bd. dirs. Community Action Orgn., 1993. Recipient Sr. Arbitration Specialist award Better Bus. Bur. Western N.Y., 1990, Outstanding Achievement award, 1992, Arbitrator of Yr. award, 1993, Leadership award Afro-Am. Police Assn. of Buffalo, 1990, Woman of Yr. award Spl. Police Benevolent Assn. of Buffalo, 1991, Leadership award YWCA, 1991, Profl. Achievemnt award Cecil Brown Dem. Club, 1992. Mem. Internat. Assn. of Women Police, Am. Bus. Women's Assn. (frontier chpt.), LWV, Judges and Police Confs. of Western N.Y., N.Y. State Police Juvenile Officers Assn., Afro-Am. Police Assn., Buffalo State U. Coll. Alumni Assn. (criminal justice chpt.), Criminal Justice Chpt. Alumni Assn., Nat. Assn. of Blacks in Criminal Justice, Police Benevolent Assn. Home: 44 Campus Dr W Amherst NY 14226-2532

BASS, MARTHA POSTLETHWAITE, high school principal; b. Wichita, Kans., Dec. 6, 1942; d. John Emmett and Norma Louise (Lanning) Postlethwaite; m. Elmer Lee Bass, July 22, 1981; step children: Sheryl, Terry. BA in Edn., U. N.Mex., 1964, MA, 1966. Endl. lic. adminstr., supt., English tchr., drama speech tchr., counselor. Asst. dean women, instr. Hanover (Ind.) Coll., 1966-68; asst. dean women U. N.Mex., Alburquerque, 1968-69; elem. counselor Alburquerque Pub. Schs., 1969-74, guidance coord., 1974-77, high sch. asst. prin., 1977-87; high sch. prin. Del Norte High Sch. Alburquerque Pub. Schs., 1987—; bd. dirs. Albuquerque Child Guidance Ctr.; pres., cons. Acad. Ednl. Leadership, Alburquerque, 1986-90. Title VII Fed. grantee Child Encouragement Project, Alburquerque, 1977; named Woman on the Move YWCA, Alburquerque, 1990. Mem. Nat. Assn. Secondary Sch. Prins., Albuquerque Assn. Secondary Sch. Prins. (past. bd. mem., treas., 1986-87), Rotary Club of Albuquerque (RYLA chair, 1990—). Office: Del Norte High Sch 5323 Montgomery Blvd NE Albuquerque NM 87109-1300

BASS, MELISSA BETH ROBNETT, administrative executive; b. Columbia, Mo., July 14, 1958; d. James Overton Robnett II and Linda Ann (Levy) Bennett. Student, U. Mo., 1979; AS, Columbia Coll., 1984; cert. profl. sec., Inst. for Certifying Secs., 1983. Sec. to pres. Local 50 AFL-CIO, St. Louis, 1978-79; sec. to dean U. Mo., Columbia, 1979-80, med. sec., 1980-82; sec. to dir. Columbia Coll., 1982-84; administrv. assoc. Christian Ch., Columbia, 1984-93; co-owner Muttley's Restaurant & Pub., 1993—; cons. B and R Assocs., Columbia, 1980—, pres. 1982-84, chmn. bd., 1984-86. Columnist Clergy Jour., 1991-92. Rec. sec. Arts Resources Coun., Columbia, 1986-90; election judge Boone County Elections Office, Columbia, 1976—. Mem. Profl. Secs. Internat. (pres. 1989-90), Disciples Secs. Assn., Am. Mgmt. Assn., ABWA, NAFE, Women's Network, VFW (pres. ladies aux. 1981-83). Democrat. Jewish. Home: 121 Holly Park Vlg Columbia MO 65202-2048 Office: B&R Assocs 306 Hirth Ave Columbia MO 65203

BASS, SHIRLEY ANN, lawyer; b. Brockton, Mass., Mar. 1, 1938; d. Ernest Francis and Clarissa May (Atwood) Marcotte; children: Thomas, Robert, John. Cert. Katharine Gibbs Sch., 1958; student San Diego State U., 1963-64; BA, Portland State U., 1975; JD, Lewis and Clark Law Sch., 1979. Bar: Oreg. 1980. With Cyr, Moe & Benner, P.C., 1980-88; pvt. practice, Portland, Oreg., 1988—. Bd. dirs. Oreg. Fair Plan, 1982-87, Oreg. Women Lawyers, 1990-92, Holladay Park Hosp. Found., 1992-94; vol. lawyer Sr. Law Project, 1985—; mem. planned giving com. Loaves and Fishes, Inc., 1987—, vice chair bd. dirs., chair devel. com., mem. planned giving com. Recipient Estate Planning award Am. Jurisprudence, 1979. Mem. Oreg. Bar (editorial bd., legis. com. estate planning sect.), ABA (estate and gift tax com. taxation sect.), Multnomah Bar Assn., Washington County Bar Assn., Estate Planning Council Portland, P.E.O., Phi Alpha Delta. Office: 415 Riviera Plz 1618 SW 1st Ave Portland OR 97201

BASSETT, ANGELA, actress; b. N.Y.C., Aug. 16, 1958. Appeared in (plays) Colored People's Time, 1982, The Mystery Plays, 1984-85, The Painful Adventures of Pericles, Prince of Tyre, 1986-87, Joe Turner's Come and Gone, 1986-87, (Broadway) Ma Rainey's Black Bottom, (Broadway) Joe Turner's Come and Gone, 1988, King Henry IV Part I, 1987; (TV movies) Line of Fire: The Morris Dees Story, 1991, The Jacksons: An American Dream, 1992; (films) F/X, 1986, Kindergarten Cop, 1990, Boyz N the Hood,

1991, City of Hope, 1991, Innocent Blood, 1992, Malcolm X, 1992, Passion Fish, 1992, What's Love Got to Do with It, 1993 (Acad. award nominee for best actress 1993, Golden Globe award best actress in a musical or comedy 1994), Strange Days, 1995. Office: care Krost/Chapin 9911 W. Pico Blvd Penthouse I Los Angeles CA 90035*

BASSETT, BARBARA WIES, editor, publisher; b. Dec. 5, 1939; m. Norman W. Bassett. BA, U. Conn., 1961; student, New Sch. for Social Rsch., 1961-62. Product devel. Fearn Soya, Melrose Park, Ill., 1973-75; product devel. Modern Products, Milw., 1973-75; editor, pub. Bestways Mag., Carson City, Nev., 1977-89; pub. The Healthy Gourmet Newsletter, 1989-91, Fine Wine-Good Food Newsletter, 1991—; publicity dir. Nev. Artists Assn., 1994-95; owner Gualala (Calif.) Galleries, 1989-90; owner, operator cooking sch. Greensboro N.C. 1969-73. Author: Natural Cooking, 1968, Wok and Tempura, 1969, Japanese Home Cooking, 1970, The Wok, 1971, Super Soy, 1973, The Healthy Gourmet, 1981, International Healthy Gourmet, 1982; one-woman show paintings Dolphin Gallery, Gualala, Calif., 1990, River Gallery, Reno, 1994; 2-women show 1992, Dolphin Gallery, Calif., 1994, solo exhbn. Nev. Artists Assn. Gallery, 1993, 95. Mem. Inst. Food Technologists, Pastel Soc. of the West Coast, Inst. Am. Culinary Profls.

BASSETT, CAROL ANN, magazine, video, and radio documentary writer, producer; b. Langley AFB, Va., Mar. 2, 1953; d. William Brainard and Genevieve (Rivaldo) B. BA summa cum laude in Humanities, Ariz. State U., 1977; MA in Journalism, U. Ariz., 1982. Freelance writer Tucson, 1980—; pntr. Desert West News, Tucson, 1985-90; Contbr. numerous articles to nat. and internat. mags. including N.Y. Times. Contbr. numerous articles to nat. and internat. mags. and newspapers. Recipient 2d Place Gen. Reporting award Ariz. Press Club, 1987, Gold medal for best environ. documentary Houston Enternat. Film Festival, 1990; co-recipient Alfred I. duPont Columbia award, 1984-85, First Place award Investigative Reporting, 1986, 1st Place Polit. Reporting, 1989, First Amendment Journalism award, 1986; grantee Fund for Investigative Journalism, 1985, 87, Corp. for Pub. Broadcasting, 1988, Oxfam Am., 1991.

BASSETT, TINA, communications executive; b. Detroit; m. Leland Kinsey Bassett; children: Joshua, Robert. Student, U. Mich., 1974, 76-78, 81, Wayne State U., 1979-80. Advt. dir. Greenfield's Restaurant, Mich. and Ohio, 1972-73; dir. advt. and pub. relations Kresco, Inc., Detroit, 1973-74; pub's. rep. The Detroiter mag., 1974-75; pub. relations dir. Detroit Bicentennial Commn., 1975-77; prin. Leland K. Bassett & Assocs., Detroit, 1976-86; intermediate job devel. specialist Detroit Council of the Arts, 1977; project dir. Detroit image campaign Dept. Pub. Info., City of Detroit, 1975, spl. events dir., 1978; dep. dir. Dept. Pub. Info. City of Detroit, 1978-83, dir., 1983-86; pres., prin. Bassett & Bassett, Inc., Detroit, 1986—. Publicity chmn. Under the Stars IV, V, VI, VII, VIII, IX and X, Benefit Balls, Detroit Inst. of Arts Founders Soc., 1983-88, Detroit Inst. of Arts Founders Centennial Ball, 1985, publicity chmn. Mich. Opera Theater, Opera Ball, 1987; program lectr. Wayne County Close-Up Program, 1984; mem. ctrl. planning com. Am. Assn. Mus.; mem. Founders Soc., Detroit Inst. Arts, 1988—; mem., publicity chair Grand Prix Ball, 1989; co-chair, producer Mus. Ball Ctr. for Performing Arts. Named Outstanding Woman in Agy. Top Mgmt., Detroit chpt. Am. Women in Radio and TV, 1989. Mem. AIA (hon., pub. dir. 1990-91, Richard Upjohn fellowship 1991), Detroit Hist. Soc., Music Hall Assn., Pub. Rels. Soc. Am. (Advt. Woman of Yr. 1989), Woman's Advt. Club Detroit. Home: 30751 Cedar Creek Dr Farmington Hl MI 48336-4989 Office: Bassett & Bassett Inc 672 Woodbridge St Detroit MI 48226-4302

BASSI, TERESA ANN, human services executive; b. Johnston, Pa., Apr. 28, 1956; d. Leo Joseph and Shirley Anne (Williams) B. B.A., Seton Hill Coll., 1979; M.A., Indiana U. Pa., 1985. Resident adviser Seton Hill Coll., Greensburg, Pa., 1978-79, dorm coordinator, 1979-81; residential program worker Life Mgmt. Assocs., Greensburg, Pa., 1979-80, residential supr., 1980-82, dir. residential services, 1982-85, adminstrv. officer, 1985—; pvt. counseling, 1985—, adminstrv. officer, 1985-86, cons. therapist, 1986—; facilitator drug and alcohol service, 1985—. Lector, Holy Trinity Ch., Ligonier, Pa., 1984—. Mem. Am. Assn. Counselors, Am. Assn. Mental Deficiency, Nat. Assn. Pvt. Residential Facilities Dirs., Health and Welfare Council, Westmoreland Assn. Vol. Adminstrs. Democrat. Roman Catholic. Avocations: Reading; birding; sports; woodworking. Home: RR 1 Box 216A Latrobe PA 15650-9507 Office: Three Rivers Youth 2039 Termon Ave Pittsburgh PA 15212-1700

BASSMAN, LYNETTE EVE, psychologist; b. Norwalk, Conn., June 9, 1959; d. Eugene Benjamin and Betty (Hirsh) Herman; m. Larry Fredrick Bassman, Aug. 13, 1989. BA, Brandeis U., 1981; MEd, Columbia U., 1984; PhD, NYU, 1990. Lic. psychologist. Psychology intern Kings County Hosp. Ctr., Bklyn., 1989-90; staff psychotherapist Nat. Neighborhood Counseling Ctr., Bklyn., 1990-93; cons. Westchester Psychomatrix, Cross River, N.Y., 1993—; pvt. practice N.Y.C., 1992—; tchr. NYU, N.Y.C., 1985, 90, Manhattan Coll., Riverdale, N.Y., 1985; mentor for psychology majors The Coll. of New Rochelle, Bronx, N.Y., 1991; tchr. Audrey Cohen Coll., N.Y.C., 1992—; adj. asst. instr. dept. psychiatry Coll. of Medicine, SUNY Health Sci. Ctr., Bklyn., 1989-90; psychotherapist Whitman Inst. for Counseling and Psychotherapy, Bklyn., 1985-89, Queens Coll. Summer Pre-Freshman Basic Skills program, 1986-88; asst. residence dir. Barnard Coll., N.Y.C., 1983-84. Editor The Whole Mind Catalogue: Options in Mental Health Care; contbr. articles to profl. jours. Mem. Natural Resources Def. Couns., World Wildlife Fund, Co-op Am. Mem. APA. Office: Ste 6B 31 W 11th St New York NY 10011-8619

BASSO, KATHLEEN ALYSSA, lawyer; b. Allenhurst, N.J., Jan. 29, 1964; d. Michael Joseph and Marianne (Neapolitan) B. Student, U. Manchester, 1984-85; BS, Tulane U., 1986; JD, Boston Coll., 1989. Assoc. Parker, Chapin, Flattau & Klimpl, N.Y.C., 1989-93; corp. counsel Automatic Data Processing, Inc., 1993—. Vol. Presdl. Election Campaign, Boston, 1988, Vols. of Legal Svcs., Inc., N.Y.C., 1991, Lawyers for Arts, N.Y.C., 1994. Mem. Beta Gamma Sigma. Democrat. Roman Catholic. Home: 125 W 85th St # 2R New York NY 10024-4415 Office: Automatic Data Processing Inc Fin Info Svcs Inc Legal Dept 2 Journal Square Plz Jersey City NJ 07306

BASS-RUBENSTEIN, DEBORAH SUE, social worker, educator, consultant; b. Springfield, Ill., Jan. 21, 1951; d. Ralph and Dorothy Bernice (Feuer) Bass; m. Jeffrey Rubenstein, Oct. 12, 1975; children: Jonathan, Benjamin. BA, MSW, U. Ill., 1973. Social worker Dept. Human Resources, Washington, 1974-75; analyst Asst. Sec. for Planning and Evaluation, Washington, 1975-76, Adminstrn. for Pub. Svcs., Washington, 1976-79, Health Care Financing Adminstrn., Washington, 1979; sr. analyst OHDS, Washington, 1979-83, 84-87, Adminstrn. on Aging, Washington, 1983-84; dir. Office Human Devel. Svcs., Exec. Secretariat, HHS, Washington, 1987-90; cons. and pres. Deborah Bass Assocs., Manassas, Va., 1990—; assoc. faculty Johns Hopkins Sch. Continuing Studies, 1993; sec. U.S. com. Internat. Coun. on Social Welfare, Washington, 1991-93, bd. dirs., 1987-90; convenor Fed. Social Workers Consortium, Washington, 1986-90; participant Dartmouth-Hitchcock Med. Ctr. Project on Family Support, 1993. Author: Caring Families, 1990, Helping Vulnerable Youths, 1992; contbr. Ency. Social Work, 1995. Co-pres. Coles Sch. PTO, Manassas, 1987-88; bd. dirs. Mid-County Coalition, Prince William County, Va., 1986. James scholar U. Ill., 1969-73. Mem. NASW (program com. 1988-90). Home and Office: 7092 Kings Arms Dr Manassas VA 22111-3237

BAST, KAREN RUTH, sales representative; b. Galveston, Tex., Mar. 9, 1964. BS in Home Econs., Tex. Tech U., 1985. Cert. secondary sch. tchr., Tex. Sales support/tng. Xerox, San Antonio, 1986-89; pharm. sales rep. Abbott Labs., Corpus Christi, Tex., 1989-90; acct. exec. Abbott Labs., Abilene, Tex., 1990-91; nat. sales trainer Abbott Labs., Chgo., 1991-92; pharm. sales rep. Abbott Labs., Ft. Worth, 1992—; field trainer, product and mktg. cons. Abbot Labs., Ft. Worth, Chgo., 1992—. Mem. Delta Delta Delta (chair collegiate rels. 1988, rush com. 1994—), Pharm. Rep. Assn. (Tarrant County). Republican. Methodist. Home and Office: 4801 Misty Ridge Dr Fort Worth TX 76137

BASTARDI, MARILYN PATRICIA, printing executive; b. Newark, Mar. 17, 1945; d. Anthony Frank and Janet Louise (Richliano) Petrozzino; m. Anthony Vincent Bastardi, June 24, 1967; children—Noelle, Anthony III, Matthew, Christian. B.A. in English, Caldwell Coll., 1966. Cert. elem. tchr., N.J. Tchr. Wayne Bd. Edn., N.J., 1966-68, supplemental tchr. learning disabilities, 1975-77; pres. Presto Printing Ctr., Parsippany, N.J., 1980—. Pres. Gateway No. N.J., 1978-80; mem. gifted edn. com. Hanover Twp. Bd. Edn., N.J., 1980; bd. dir. Delbarton Sch. Mother's Guild, 1994—. Named Rookie of Yr., Sir Speedy Franchises, 1981. Mem. Middle Atlantic Sir Speedy Owners Assn., AAUW (chmn. scholarship com. 1982), Caldwell Coll. Alumni Assn. (exec. com. 1985-93, sec. 1988-89, v.p. 1989-93), Delta Epsilon Sigma. Republican. Roman Catholic. Avocation: gourmet cooking. Home: 14 Wexford Dr Mendham NJ 07945-2008 Office: Sir Speedy Printing 1543 Route 46 Parsippany NJ 07054

BASTIANELLO, SANDRA CREWS, therapist; b. Winston-Salem, N.C., Aug. 29, 1950; d. Howard Clarence and Rachel Gray (Gentry) Crews; m. Arthur George Bastianello, Aug. 4, 1973; children: Laura Michelle, Cynthia Marie. BA, U. N.C., 1972; MS, Old Dominion U., 1982; postgrad., Ga. State U., 1991-94. Cert. P-5 tchr. Tchr. Surry County Schs., Dobson, N.C., 1972-73, Chatham County Schs., Pittsboro, N.C., 1973-75, High Meadows Sch., Roswell, Ga., 1982-92; cons. Marietta, Ga., 1992-93; ednl. therapist Counseling and Assessment Ctr., Marietta, 1993-94; therapist Dr. Spencer Gelernter & Assocs., Marietta, 1994—; tchr. in-svc. facilitator High Meadows Sch., Roswell, 1983-92. Evaluator: (tchr.'s guide) Free the Horses: A Self-Esteem Adventure, 1990. Grad. tuition grantee Sch. of Grad. Study, Old Dominion U., Norfolk, Va., 1980. Mem. Am. Counseling Assn., Play Therapy Assn. (vol. internat. conf. 1993), Am. Sch. Counselor Assn., Assn. for Specialists in Group Work, Assn. for Humanistic Edn. and Devel., Chi Sigma Iota (steering com. 1993-94). Democrat. Home: 4280 Post Oak Tritt Rd Marietta GA 30062-5700 Office: Spencer Gelernter & Assocs Paper Mill Village/Bldg 21B 690 Village Trace Marietta GA 30067-4069

BASTO, LA DONNA JOAN, business administrator; b. Mpls., July 22, 1933; d. Mayland and Irene (Bennett) Bussart; m. Ronald Martin Basto, June 5, 1952; children: Patricia Ann, Richard Martin, Judith Renee. Bookkeeper various cos., Wichita, Kans., 1964-74; office mgr. William F. Hurst Co., Inc., Wichita, 1974-92, v.p., 1993—. Trustee AMS Found, 1993-95. Mem. Adminstrv. Mgmt. Soc. (bus. expo chmn. 1984-86, exec. v.p. 1985-86, pres. 1986-87, pres.-elect 1992-93, internat. dir. 1989-91, internat. v.p. area/chpt. ops. 1991—, asst. area dir. 1987-89, bd. dirs. AMS found. 1983-85, trustee AMS found. 1993-94, chmn. strategic planning com. 1987—, mem. nominating com. 1988—, mem. internat. membership com. 1988-89, Achievement award 1985, Cert. of Appreciation 1986, Disting. Svc. award 1993). Republican. Presbyterian. Office: Wm F Hurst Co Inc PO Box 771069 Wichita KS 67277-1069

BASULTO, TANYA LEE CARROLL, chemicals professional; b. Lima, Ohio, Sept. 30, 1959; d. Randall Thomas Carroll and Patricia Jane (Thomas) Shelor; divorced; 1 child, Randall Patrick. Asst. mgr. Mings Wholesale, Key West, Fla., 1986-90; ops. mgr. ion supply chem. dept. I/N Tek / I/N Kote, New Carlisle, Ind., 1990—; ISO 9000 auditor I/N Kote, hazardous waste incident comdr., confined space entry trainer, mem. womens com., active cultural diversity issue work. With USN, 1979-83. Recipient numerous tech. certs. Inland Steel and Nippon Steel, 1990—, Arus Andritz Ruthner, 1992, Nippon Steel, 1992. Democrat. Home: 52156 Hickory Rd Granger IN 46530

BATCH, MARY LOU, guidance counselor, educator; b. McKeesport, Pa.. BS in Edn., Cen. State U., Wilberforce, Ohio, 1970; MS, Syracuse U., 1971; PhD in Counselor Edn., U. Pitts., 1982. Cert. in spl. and elem. edn., Ohio; cert. in elem. and mid. sch. edn., secondary guidance, Va.; cert. in NK-4 elem. edn., 4-8 mid. edn., edn. of mentally retarded, Va. Various edn. and counseling positions Va. schs., military and other insts., 1965-72; tchr. adult edn. Big Bend C.C., Germany. Am. Coll. System Overseas, 1973-75; counselor, coord. U. Pitts., 1976-79; asst. prof. spl. edn. Ind. U. of Pa., 1979-85; testing specialist C.C. of Allegheny County, Braddock Ctr., Pa., 1985-86; guidance counselor Henrico High Sch., Henrico County Schs., Richmond, Va., 1987-91, John Rolfe Middle Sch., Richomd, 1991—; edn. specialist U.S. Govt. in Germany, 1974-75; cons., workshop conductor, in Pa., N.J., Va. at ednl. facilities, civic orgns. and with parent groups, 1978—; mem. So. States Evaluation Team, Manassas Va., 1988; mem. peer advisor steering com. and student peer advisor supr. Henrico High Sch., 1987-90; extended del. position Citizen Ambassador Program of People to People Internat. to Soviet Union and Hungary, Am. Sch. Counselor Assn., 1991, U.S./China Joint Conf. on Edn., 1992. Bd. dirs. Richmond Residential Svcs., 1989—, sec., 1990-91, chmn. program and planning com., 1991-92, vice chmn., 1992—; group facilitator Henrico County Ct. Alternative; mem. Henrico County Edn. 2000 Commn., mem. action team; active in Head Start movement and teen parenting counseling; mem. Statewide Mid. Sch. Coun., 1994—; mem. tech. pres. steering com. Henrico County Pub. Schs., 1994—; active Nat. Multiple Sclerosis Soc., inductee leadership cir., 1995; mem. steering com. Tech Prep Henrico County, Richmond, Va., 1994-95; mid. sch. state rep. coun. mem., 1995. Inductee, Nat. Leadership Circle. Mem. LWV, ASCD, Am. Fedn. Tchrs., Nat. Coun. of Negro Women, Va. Personnel and Guidance Assn., Va. Sch. Counselors Assn., Richmond Personnel and Guidance Assn., Henrico County Guidance Assn. (pres. 1989-91), Va. Assn. Multicultural Devel., Greater Richomnd Involved Parents, Nat. Coun. for Self Esteem, Nat. Coun. Sr. Citizens, Alpha Kappa Mu, Zeta Phi Beta. Home: 5022 W Seminary Ave Richmond VA 23227-3408 Office: John Rolfe Mid Sch 6901 Messer Rd Richmond VA 23231-5507

BATCHELDER, ALICE M., federal judge; b. 1944; m. William G. Batchelder III; children: William G. IV, Elisabeth. BA, Ohio Wesleyan U., 1964; JD, Akron U., 1971; LLM, U. Va., 1988. Tchr. Plain Local Sch. Dist., Franklin County, Ohio, 1965-66, Jones Jr. High Sch., 1966-67, Buckeye High Sch., Medina County, 1967-68; assoc. Williams & Batchelder, Medina, Ohio, 1971-83; judge U.S. Bankruptcy Ct., Ohio, 1983-85, U.S. Dist. Ct. (no. dist.) Ohio, Cleve., 1985-91, U.S. Ct. of Appeals (6th cir.), Cleveland, 1991—. Mem. ABA, Fed. Judge's Assn., Medina City Bar Assn. Office: 807 E Washington St Ste 200 Medina OH 44256

BATCHELDER, ANNE STUART, former publisher, political party official; b. Lake Forest, Ill., Jan. 11, 1920; d. Robert Douglas and Harriet (McClure) Stuart; m. Clifton Brooks Batchelder, May 26, 1945; children: Edward, Anne Stuart, Mary Clifton, Lucia Brooks. Student Lake Forest Coll., 1941-43. Clubmobile driver ARC, Eng., Belgium, France, Holland and Germany, 1943-45; pub., editor Douglas County Gazette, 1970-75, 79-90; bd. dirs. Firstier Bank Omaha; dir., treas. U.S. Checkbook Com. Mem. Rep. Cen. Com. Nebr., 1955-62, 70-83, vice chmn. Central Com., 1959-64, chmn., 1975-79, mem. fin. com., 1957-64; chmn. women's sect. Douglas County Rep. Finance Com., 1955, vice chmn. com., 1958-60; v.p. Omaha Woman's Rep. Club, 1957-58, pres., 1959-60; alt. del. Nat. Conv., 1956, 72, del., 1980, 84, 88; mem. Rep. Nat. Com. for Nebr., 1964-70; asst. chmn. Douglas County Rep. Central Com., 1971-74; 1st v.p. Nebr. Fedn. Rep. Women, 1971-72, pres., 1972-74; chmn. Nebr. Rep. Com., 1975-79; chmn. fundraising com. Nat. Fedn. Rep. Women, 1981-93, vice chmn., 1994—; mem. Nebr. State Bldg. Commn., 1979-83; Rep. candidate for lt. gov., 1974. Sr. v.p. Nebr. Founders Day, 1958; bd. dirs. YWCA, 1983-89, Omaha Libr. Found., 1987—; past trustee Brownell Hall, Vis. Nurse Assn., Omaha Libr. Found., Brownell Talbot Sch. Found.; trustee Hastings Coll., Nebr. Meth. Hosp. Found.; past pres. Nebr. chpt. Freedoms Found. at Valley Forge; chmn. fin. George Bush for Pres., Nebr., 1987-88; apptd. Kennedy Ctr. Performing Arts, 1989, 94, Pres.' Adv. Com. on the Arts, 1990—; mem. Nebr. Rep. State Fin. Com., 1990, Nat. Fin. Com. Bush-Quayle, 1992. Elected to Nebr. Rep. Hall of Fame, 1984. Mayflower Soc., Colonial Dames, P.E.O., Nat. League Pen Women Omaha Country, Omaha. Presbyterian (trustee). Home: 6875 State St Omaha NE 68152-1633

BATEMAN, IRIS HENDRIX, merchandise coordinator; b. Greer, S.C., Oct. 6, 1940; d. Walter Lee and Rosa Bell (Quinn) Hendrix; m. Robert B. Bateman, May 20, 1961. Diploma in bus., Doughn's Bus. Coll., 1959; cert. in bus., Greenville Tech., 1961. Sec. Springs Industries, Lyman, S.C., 1958-90, from sec. to merch. coord., 1990—. Bapt. Women's dir. Greer Bapt. Assn. Named Woman of Yr., Am. Bus. Woman, 1980, Heritage World, 1981. Mem. NAFE, Am. Bus. Women's Assn. (sec. inner circle 1975, v.p. 1976), Nat. Notary Assn., Greer Jaycettes (sec. 1970, pres. 1971). Home: 9 Cottage Ln Taylors SC 29687-9255 Office: Springs Industries Pacific St Lyman SC 29365-1707

BATEMAN, SHARON LOUISE, public relations executive; b. St. Louis, Oct. 18, 1949; d. Frank Hamilton and Charlotte Elizabeth (Hogan) B. Student, Drury Coll., 1967-69; BJ, U. Mo., 1971. Asst. dir. pub. relations Cardinal Glennon Hosp. for Children, St. Louis, 1971-76; staff asst. pub. relations Ozark Air Lines, St. Louis, 1976-80; mgr. corp. relations Kellwood Co., St. Louis, 1980-83; mgr. corp. communications May Dept. Stores Co., St. Louis, 1983-86, dir. corp. communications, 1986—. Recipient Best Regional Airline Employee Publ. award Editor's Assn. Am. Transp. Assn., 1978. Mem. Internat. Assn. Bus. Communications (pres. St. Louis chpt. 1977), Pub. Rels. Soc. Am. (sec. St. Louis chpt. 1983, bd. dirs. 1988-90, v.p. 1991). Republican. Office: May Dept Stores Co 611 Olive St Saint Louis MO 63101-1721

BATES, BEVERLY JO-ANNE, artist, educator; b. Pitts., Jan. 29, 1938; d. Joseph Whitfield and Thelma Alease (McMullen) Loftin; divorced; children: Roy F. Jr., Brian Whitfield, Stephen Jeffrey. BS in Art Edn., W.Va. State Coll., 1959; MEd in Art Edn., U. Pitts., 1973, postgrad., 1985-88; postgrad., Temple U., 1963-64, RISD, 1984. Art tchr. Pitts. Pub. Sch. System, 1959, 70-75, print tchr. Brashear High Sch., 1975-78, coord. art dept., printmaking tchr. Pitts. High Sch., 1970—; art tchr. N.J. Pub. Schs., Camden, N.J., 1961; print instr. Selma Burke Art Ctr., Pitts., 1971, Pitts. Arts and Crafts Ctr., 1972; panel mem. visual arts Pa. Coun. on Arts, Harrisburg, 1979—; com. mem. Links Inc. Nat. Art Com., Washington, 1992—; mem. adv. bd. Manchester Craftsman's Guild, Pitts., 1985—, Visions, 1990—. Author: (catalogues) Black American Art, 1977 (Meade award 1977), 1978 (W. Pa. Prize 1978); one-person shows include Westmoreland Mus., 1991, Visual Arts Gallery, C.C. of Allegheny County, 1991, Kipp Gallery, Indiana U. Pa., 1991, Westminster Coll. Art Gallery, 1991, others; exhibited in group shows at Pitts. Ctr. for Arts, 1982, 83, 84, 85, 87, 88, 90, 91, 92, Carnegie Mus., 1982, 86, 90, 92, S.G. Galleries, 1992, LaTeste, France, 1992, U. Pitts. Kimbo Gallery, 1990, 91, 92, Carson St. Gallery, 1991, others. Bd. trustees Pitts. Ctr. for Arts, 1989—; bd. dirs. Soc. Contemporary, Pitts., 1990—, Soc. Arts and Crafts. Honors fellow R.I. Sch., Providence, 1984; recipient Frick Fellowship award Pitts. Bd. Edn., 1975, Outstanding Art Edn. award Pitts. Bd. Edn., 1984, Youth Arts award Pa. Art Edn. Assn., Pitts., 1988, Outstanding Art Edn. award Pratt Inst., Bklyn., 1989, Jurors award Pitts. Print Group, 1991, Images show U. Pitts., 1992. Mem. The Links Inc. (bd. mem. nat. arts com.), Nat. Art Edn. Assn., Pa. Art Edn. Assn., Pa. Coun. on Arts (past panel mem.), Pitts. Print Group (past bd. mem.), Associated Artists Pitts. (past bd. mem.), Nat. Conf. Artists, Pa. Alliance for Art Edn. (bd. mem.). Home: 6922 Meade St Pittsburgh PA 15208 Office: Pitts High Sch 925 Brushton Ave Pittsburgh PA 15208

BATES, JANET LOUISE, association executive; b. Fort Wayne, Ind., Dec. 2, 1940; d. Kenneth John and Helen Louise (Green) Rupp; m. Robert Bates, June 30, 1972 (div. Mar. 1983); children: David, Denise, Molly Procise. Student, Ball State U., 1959-61; BS in Bus., St. Mary of the Wood (Ind.) Coll., 1987. Cert. fund raising exec. Exec. dir. Martin Luther King Sch., Fort Wayne, 1975-79; asst. exec. dir. YWCA of Fort Wayne, 1979-90; dir. devel. Villages of Ind., Indpls., 1990-91; exec. dir. YWCA of Indpls., 1991-94; mgr. of programs, resource devel. United Way of Ctrl. Ind., 1995—; bd. dirs. Ind. Sports Corp. Bd. dirs. Friends of Women's Study, Indpls., 1992—. Grantee Leadership Fort Wayne, 1987; named Outstanding Vol. AIDS Task Force, 1990, Coalition of Youth Svcs., Fort Wayne, 1990. Mem. Nat. Soc. Fund Raising Execs. (bd. dirs. Ind. chpt. 1990—), Rotary, Stanley K. Lacy Alumni. Democrat.

BATES, KATHY, actress; b. Memphis, June 28, 1948. BFA, So. Meth. U., 1969. Film appearances include Taking Off, 1971, Straight Time, Come Back to the Five and Dime, Jimmy Dean, Jimmy Dean, Summer Heat, Arthur 2: On the Rocks, Signs of Life, High Stakes, Men Don't Leave, Dick Tracy, White Palace, Misery (Acad. award for Best Actress 1990, Golden Globe award), At Play in the Fields of the Lord, 1991, The Road to Mecca, Prelude to a Kiss, Fried Green Tomatoes (Golden Globe nomination, BAFTA nomination), Used People, A Home of Our Own, North, Curse of the Starving Class, Dolores Claiborne, 1994; stage appearances include Vanities, 1976, Semmelweiss, Crimes of the Heart, The Art of Dining, Goodbye Fidel, 1980, Chocolate Cake and Final Placement, 1981, 5th of July, Come Back to the 5 & Dime, Jimmy Dean, Jimmy Dean, 'night, Mother, 1983 (Tony nomination, Outer Critics Circle award), Two Masters: The Rain of Terror, 1985, Curse of the Starving Class, Frankie and Johnny in the Clair de Lune (OBIE award 1988), The Road to Mecca; TV appearances include (series) The Love Boat, St. Elsewhere, Cagney & Lacey, L.A. Law, China Beach, (miniseries) Murder Ordained, (movies of the week) Johnny Bull, No Place Like Home, Roe vs. Wade, Hostages, The Stand; dir. Talking With, PBS Great Performances. Office: Susan Smith & Assocs 121 N San Vicente Blvd Beverly Hills CA 90211

BATES, LINDA MARIE, quality control technologist; b. Boston, Oct. 27, 1962; d. Robert J. and Marie E. (Dowd) B. BS, Boston Coll., 1984; MS, Framingham (Mass.) State U., 1993. Rsch. asst. Tufts U., Boston, 1985-86; cell culturist Damon Biotech, Needham Heights, Mass., 1986-88; sr. rsch. lab. assoc. Advanced Instruments, Norwood, Mass., 1988-92; sr. quality control technologist Serono Labs., Randolph, Mass., 1994—. Mem. Inst. Food Tech., Phi Beta Kappa, Alpha Sigma Nu. Roman Catholic.

BATES, LURA WHEELER, trade association executive; b. Inboden, Ark., Aug. 28, 1932; d. Carl Clifton and Hester Ray (Pace) Wheeler; m. Allen Carl Bates, Sept. 12, 1954; 1 child, Carla Allene. BSBA, U. Ark., 1954. Cert. constrn. assoc. Sec.-bookkeeper, then officer mgr. Assoc. Gen. Contractors Miss., Inc., Jackson, 1958-77, dir. adminstrv. svcs., 1977—, asst. exec. dir., 1980—; owner, Ditty Bag Supply Co., 1987—; adminstr. Miss. Constrn. Found., 1977—; sec. AIA-Assoc. Gen. Contractors Liaisonship Coms., 1977—; sec. Carpenters Joint Apprenticeship Coms., Jackson and Vicksburg, 1977—. Sec. Marshall Elem. Sch. PTA, Jackson, 1962-64, v.p., 1965; sec.-treas. Inter-Club Coun. Jackson, 1963-64; tchr. adult Sunday sch. dept. Hillcrest Bapt. Ch., Jackson, 1975-82; dir. Bapt. Women WMU, 1987—, sec., 1992—; tchr. adult Sunday sch. dept. 1st Bapt. Ch., Crystal Springs, Miss., 1989—; mem. exec. com. Jackson Christian Bus. and Profl. Women's Coun., 1976-80, sec., 1978-79, pres., 1979-80. Named Outstanding Woman in Constrn. Miss., 1962-63, Outstanding Mem. Nat. Assn. Women in Constrn. Fellow Internat. Platform Assn.; mem. AAUW, NAFE, Nat. Assn. Women in Constrn. (life, chpt. pres. 1963-64, 76-77, 92-93, nat. v.p. 1965-66, 77-78, nat. dir. Region 5, 1967-68, nat. sec. 1970-71, 71-72, pres. 1980-81, coord. cert. constrn. assoc. program 1973-78, 83-84 guardian-contr. Edn. Found. 1981-82, chmn. nat. bylaws com. 1982-83, 85-88, nat. parliamentarian 1983-92), Nat. Assn. Parliamentarians, U. Ark. Alumni Assn. (life, pres. ctrl. Miss. chpt. 1992-93, 93-94), Delta Delta Delta. Editor NAWIC Image, 1968-69, Procedures Manual, 1965-66, Public Relations Handbook, 1967-68, Profl. Edn. Guide, 1972-73, Guidelines & Procedures Handbook, 1987-88; author digests in field. Home: 1007 Lee Ave Crystal Springs MS 39059-2546 Office: 2093 Lakeland Dr Jackson MS 39216-5010

BATES, MARGARET HELENA, special education educator; b. Irvington, N.J., Jan. 27, 1943; d. Marcel Bogstahl and Helena Christina (Yarosczynsky) Bogstahl; divorced; children: Robert Crew, Diane Carlyle. BA, Coll. Steubenville, 1966; MS, St. Cloud State U., 1982. Cert. Eng. tchr., spl. edn. tchr., emotionally/behaviorally disturbed and learning disabilities tchr., Minn. Tchr. Ind. Sch. Dist. # 742, St. Cloud, 1976—. Adv. bd. Minn. Acad. Excellence Found., St. Paul., 1993-94; state coun. chair Minn. Edn. Assn., 1993—; co-chair. St. Cloud Edn. Assn., 1979-84; sec. Audubon Soc., 1992—; historian Stearns County Theatrical Co., 1992, 93, 94; bd. dirs. The New Tradition Theatre Co., 1988-89. Recipient grant Bremer Found., 1991, Moose Club, 1988, 89. Mem. Delta Kappa Gamma. Home: 825 17th Ave S Saint Cloud MN 56301-5234 Office: Area Learning Ctr 809 12th St N Saint Cloud MN 56303-2847

BATES, PATRICIA STAMPER, accountant; b. Baton Rouge, Feb. 13, 1947; d. Ernest Rudolphus and Avis (Patton) Stamper; m. James Rogers, Aug. 11, 1968 (div. 1974); 1 child, Brian James; m. Ronald Dean Bates, Feb. 27, 1976. BS in Math and English Edn., La. State U., 1968, M in Supervision with honors, 1978; postgrad., Texas A & I, 1982-83, Lamar U., 1992—. CPA, La., Tex.; cert. tchr. La., Tex., Va. Tchr. East Baton Rouge Schs.,

1968-70, East Baton Rouge and Bishop (Tex.) Ind. Sch. Dist., 1977-81; personnel mgr. La. Dept. Fire and Police Civil Service, Baton Rouge, 1971-76; acct. Womack and Womack, CPAs, Kingsville, Tex., 1982, W. Wayne Rasmussen, CPA, Inc., Corpus Christi, Tex., 1982-83; chief acct., pres. dir. Mueller Engrng. and Exploration, Inc., Corpus Christi, 1983-84; dir. acctg. Conoco, Inc., Westlake, La., 1984-89; coord. refining cost, downstream tng. coord. Conoco, Inc., Ponca City, Okla., 1989-91; coord. refining cost RMTA Acctg., 1989-91; sr. acctg. specialist DuPont Sabine River Works, Orange, Tex., 1991—; co-chair women's info. network Conoco Inc., 1990-91, cultural diversity task force, 1989-91, tng. subcom., 1989-91. Mem. Tex. Soc. CPAs, Southwest La. C. of C., La. State U. Alumni Group, St. Joseph's Acad. Alumni Group. Clubs: Hickory Ridge Garden (Baton Rouge) (sec. 1978-79); Continental (Westlake). Office: DuPont Sabine River Works Fm1006 Bldg 720-116 Orange TX 77630

BATES STOKLOSA, EVELYNNE (EVE BATES STOKLOSA), educational consultant, educator; b. Camden, N.J., Mar. 13, 1946; d. Linwood T. and Eve Mary (Widzenas) Bates; m. Leslie E. Stoklosa, Apr. 15, 1968; children: Phillip J., Kristine L. BS in Home Econs. Edn., Buffalo State U. Coll., 1968, MS in Home Econs. Edn., 1971, Cert. Advanced Studies, 1994. Cert. sch. dist. adminstr. Tchr. Parkside Elem. Sch., Kenmore, N.Y., 1968-69, Kenmore West High Sch., 1968-71, 73-75, Kenmore Jr. High Sch., 1977-80, Ken-Ton Continuing Edn., Kenmore, 1980-87, Kenmore Mid. Sch., 1981—; owner, pres. EBS Decors, Tonawanda, N.Y., 1986-87; edn. cons. Villa Maria Coll., Buffalo, N.Y., 1980—, adv. bd. interior design dept., 1980—; facilitator student of the month award program Kenmore Mid. Sch., 1982—, active mem. sch. planning team, 1984—, facilitator design team, 1990-93; participant Buffalo Summit, 1994. Editor parent informational pamphlet, 1992, faculty informational newsletter, 1992-94. Erle County Nutrition Assn. grantee. Mem. AAUW (bd. dirs. 1992-94), ASCD, Am. Vocat. Assn., Am. Fedn. Tchrs., N.Y. State Home Econs. Tchrs. Assn. (Tchr. of Yr. 1992-93, Most Outstanding Leadership and Creativity award 1987), N.Y. State United Tchrs., Western N.Y. Women in Adminstrn., Kenmore Tchrs. Assn. (bldg. rep.), Phi Delta Kappa, Phi Upsilon Omicron. Home: 165 Greentree Rd Buffalo NY 14150 Office: Kenmore-Town of Tonawanda 1500 Colvin Blvd Kenmore NY 14223-1118

BATEY, SHARYN REBECCA, clinical research scientist; b. Nashville, Apr. 19, 1946; d. Robert Thomas and Sue (Alred) B. BS in Pharmacy, U. Tenn., 1969, D of Pharmacy, 1975; MS in Pub. Health, U. S.C., 1984. Registered pharmacist, Tenn. Hosp. pharmacist Vanderbilt Hosp., Nashville, 1969-71, VA Hosp., Beckley, W.Va., 1971-72, Gainesville, Fla., 1972-73, Battle Creek, Mich., 1973-74; hosp. pharmacy resident VA Hosp., Memphis, 1974-76; psychopharmacy resident Menninger Found., Topeka, 1976-77; clin. pharmacist William S. Hall Psychiat. Inst., Columbia, S.C., 1977-82; asst. prof. U. S.C. Coll. Pharmacy, Columbia, 1977-83, asst. prof. Sch. Medicine, 1981-83, assoc. prof. Coll. Pharmacy and Sch. Medicine, 1983-89; prof., 1989; chief clin. pharmacy services and ednl. programs William S. Hall Psychiat. Inst., Columbia, 1982-89; clin. rsch. scientist Burroughs Wellcome Co., Research Triangle Park, N.C., 1989—; clin. drug research/drug devel. fellow U. N.C. and Burroughs Wellcome, Research Triangle Park, N.C., 1983-84; pharmacist cons. NIMH, Bethesda, Md., 1983-84, Health Care Fin. Adminstrn., Balt., 1985-89. Author audio visual programs Psychotropic Medication Education Program for Adults, Adolescents and Children, 1978, 84, 88, 89; contbr. articles on psychopharmacology to profl. jours. Recipient Significant Achievement award Am. Psychiat. Assn., 1980, Sci. Exhibit award Am. Psychiat. Assn., 1981. Mem. Am. Coll. Clin. Pharmacy, Am. Soc. Hosp. Pharmacists (chmn. edn. and tng. working group of psychopharmacy spl. interest group 1983-85, chmn. elect 1985-86, chmn. 1986-87, past chmn. 1987-88, project leader psycopharmacy specialty recognition petition 1986-89, psychopharmacy fellow selection com. 1986-88, chmn. psychopharmacy spl. practice group 1989), S.C. Dementia Registry (pres. user policy coun. 1989). Avocations: travel, reading. Home: 4824 Highgate Dr Durham NC 27713-9417 Office: Burroughs Wellcome Co Research Triangle Park NC 27709

BATORSKI, JUDITH ANN, art association administrator; b. Eden, N.Y., Oct. 8, 1949; d. John Michael and Ethel (Owens) B.; m. Michael J. Rocco (div. Oct. 1980); 1 child, Flora. Student retail mgmt., Colo. Springs Coll. Bus., 1981; AS in Fine Arts, Suffolk Community Coll., 1983; BA, SUNY, Stonybrook, 1985, MA, 1987; postgrad., Columbia Coll. Chgo. Film Sch., 1985. Caretaker, asst. mgr. Farmer's Shared Home, Danbury, N.H., 1979-80; cert. educator Assn. for Childbirth at Home, Internat., L.A., 1980; accts. payable clk. Pikes Peak Community Coll., Colorado Springs, Colo., 1981-82; office mgr. Three Village Meals-on-Wheels, Stonybrook, 1984; grad. sec. art dept. SUNY, 1986-87, art gallery intern Fine Arts Ctr., 1987; dir. ops., dir. master classes and free concerts Islip Arts Coun., East Islip, N.Y., 1987-89; cons. N.Y. State Coun. on the Arts, N.Y.C., 1989—; participant Arts in Bus. Mgmt. seminar Citibank/ABC, N.Y.C., 1987, cmty. leaders luncheon Fox Channel 5, N.Y.C., 1987; asst. to dir. Newsday's L.I. Summer Arts Festival Cmty. Affairs Dept., 1989, Suffolk County Motion Picture and TV Commn., Hauppauge, N.Y., 1988, 89, 90—, Summer Film Festival, 1988-90; cons. N.Y. State Coun. Arts, 1989-90, cons., 1990-91; interior decorator Trans-Designs, 1992; ind. contractor KM-Matol Corp, Que., Can., 1993; intern Nat. Inst. Inner Healing, Rich in Mercy Inst. Photographs included in Photography Forum's Coll. Photography Ann., 1985. Campaign dir. Food for Poland, Colorado Springs, 1982; organizer Granite State Alliance, Portsmouth, N.H., 1979, Safe 'n' Sound anti-nuclear campaign, Shoreham, N.Y., 1979; grad. rep. Sch. Continuing Edn. SUNY Stonybrook, judicial com. on acad. standing, SUNY Stonybrook, 1986-87; vol. Vietnam Vets. Theatre Ensemble, 1988, New Community Cinema, Huntington, N.Y., 1988; active exec. com. Dowling Coll. Spring Tribute Concert, Oakdale, N.Y., 1989; asst. to dir. Newsday Community Rels. Dept. L.I. Arts 89, 1989; founding mem. com. corr. L.I. Green Party, Brookhaven Twp., 1990—; participant Life in the Spirit seminar Cath. Charismatic Renewal, N.Y., 1992; tchr. Our Lady of Mt. Carmel Ch., N.Y., 1991—; active Pastoral Coun., 1992—. Mem. Internat. Platform Soc., Contemporary Hispanic Artists of L.I. (advisor to bd. dirs. Ctrl. Islip 1988-89). Roman Catholic. Home: 40-74 W 4th St Patchogue NY 11772

BATSHAW, MARILYN SEIDNER, educational administrator; b. East Orange, N.J., Aug. 19, 1946; d. Gerald and Sylvia (Weinstein) Seidner; 1 child, Andrew Curt. BA, Newark State Coll., Union, N.J., 1968; MA, Kean Coll., Union, 1972, 0prin. cert., 1984. Cert. hearing aid dispenser, audiologist, elem. and deaf and hearing impaired tchr., supr., prin., N.J. Tchr. of deaf N.J. Dept. Edn., Trenton, 1972-74; audiologist N.J. Dept. Edn., Trenton, N.J., 1974-82; cons. in spl. edn. N.J. Dept. Edn., Trenton, 1982-86; prin., dir. edn. Lakeview Sch., Cerebral Palsy Assn. Middlesex County, Edison, N.J., 1986-94; prin. ARC Essex Sch., Maplewood, N.J., 1994—. Officer Parents for Deaf Awareness. Mem. ASCD, N.J. ASCD, Ednl. Audiology Assn., Am. Speech-Lang. and Hearing Assn. (cert. clin. competence in audiology), A.G. Bell Assn., Am. Auditory Soc., Am. Acad. Audiology, N.J. Speech-Lang. and Hearing Assn., Coun. Exceptional Children, N.J. Coun. Exceptional Children, Nat. Assn. Edn. Young Children. Home: 166 Westgate Dr Edison NJ 08820-1158 Office: ARC Essex Sch 1812 Springfield Ave Maplewood NJ 07040

BATT, ALYSE SCHWARTZ, programmer, analyst; b. Bronx, N.Y., Aug. 8, 1960; d. Irwin Aaron and Beryl (Leff) Schwartz; m. David Charles Batt, Feb. 14, 1993. AAS, SUNY, Farmingdale, 1980; BBA, Hofstra U., 1987; postgrad., Long Island U., 1993—. Programmer trainee State Ins. Fund, N.Y.C., 1980; programmer analyst cons. Bradford Nat. Corp., N.Y.C., 1981-83; programmer E.F. Hutton, N.Y.C., 1983; programmer analyst Chase Manhattan Bank, N.Y.C., 1983-87; sr. systems analyst Met. Life Ins. Co., N.Y.C., 1987-89; sr. programmer analyst Orion Pictures Corp., N.Y.C., 1989-91, Chase Manhattan Bank, New Hyde Park, N.Y., 1991—. Mem. Bayshore Skating Club, Commack Skating Club, Massapequa Road Runners Club, N.Y. Road Runners Club, Plainview-Old Bethpage Road Runners Club. Republican. Jewish. Home: 153 Massachusetts Ave Massapequa NY 11758-4111

BATTANI, NANCY LEE, rehabilitation nurse; b. Romeo, Mich., Mar. 23, 1934; d. George F. Jersey; m. Paul F. Battani, June 2, 1956; 1 child, Mary Ann. Diploma, Deaconess Hosp. Sch. Nursing, 1955; BSN, Wayne State U., 1983; MS, Cen. Mich. U., 1989. Supr. Oakland Gen. Hosp., Madison Hgts., Mich., 1964-72; dir. nursing Cambridge Nursing Ctr., Madison Hgts., Mich., 1975-76; asst. dir. nursing Rehab. Inst., Detroit, 1976-88, Orchard Hills Nursing Ctr., Pontiac, Mich., 1989—; bd. dirs. Detroit Med. Ctr. Adv. Bd., 1985-88. Contbr. articles to profl. jours. Mem. Guardian Angels Alter Soc., Clawson, Mich., 1966—; instr. ARC, Detroit, 1978—; mem. Am. Legion Aux., Detroit, 1980—. Recipient Svc. award ARC, 1983, honoree Nat. Disting. Svc. Registry; named Golden Key scholar Wayne State U., 1983. Mem. Assn. Rehab. Nurses (cert.), Congress Rehab. Medicine, Mich. League for Nursing, Wayne State U. Alumni Assn., Women of Wayne State U., Wayne State U. Alumni Coll. Nursing, Sigma Theta Tau.

BATTIN, PATRICIA MEYER, librarian; b. Gettysburg, Pa., June 2, 1929; d. Emanuel Albert and Josephine (Lehman) Meyer; m. William Thomas Battin, June 16, 1951 (div. 1975); children—Laura, Joanna, Thomas. B.A., Swarthmore Coll., 1951; M.S. in Libr. Sci., Syracuse U., 1967. Asst. libr. SUNY-Binghamton, 1967-69, asst. dir. for reader svcs., 1969-74; dir. libr. svcs. Columbia U., N.Y.C., 1974-78, v.p., univ. libr., 1978-87; interim pres. Research Libraries Group, Palo Alto, Calif., 1982, also dir., 1974-87; pres. Commn. on Preservation and Access, Washington, 1987—; trustee Coun. on Library Resources, Washington, EDUCOM, Princeton, N.Y., 1982-88, Lehigh U., 1989—. Contbr. articles to profl. jours. Mem. ALA, Assn. Rsch. Librs. (trustee 1982-85), Phi Beta Kappa, Beta Phi Mu. Club: Grolier (N.Y.C). Office: Commn on Preservation & Access Ste 313 1785 Massachusetts Ave NW Washington DC 20036

BATTLE, KATHLEEN DEANNA, soprano; b. Portsmouth, Ohio, Aug. 13, 1948; d. Grady and Ollie (Layne) B. MusB, U. Cin., 1970, MusM, 1971, D of Performing Arts (hon.), 1983; D of Performing Arts (hon.), Westminster Choir Coll., Ohio U.; D of Music (hon.), Xavier U., 1989; DHL, Amherst Coll., 1990. Appeared with Met. Opera, San Francisco Opera, Chgo. Opera, Salzburg Festival, N.Y. Philharm., Boston Symphony, Phila. Orch., Chgo. Symphony, Berlin Philharm., Vienna Staatsoper, Paris Opera, Royal Opera/Covent Garden, others; roles include Semele, Cleopatra in Julius Caesar, Pamina in Magic Flute, Susanna in Marriage of Figaro, Zerlina in Don Giovanni, Blonde in Abduction from the Seraglio, Rosina in Barber of Seville, Adina in Elixir of Love, Norina in Don Pasquale, Sophie in Der Rosenkavalier, Zerbinetta in Ariadne auf Naxos, Zdenka in Arabella; recordings include At Carnegie Hall, Bel Canto, A Christmas Celebration, Great American Spirituals, Pleasures of Their Company, Salzburg Recital, (with Placido Domingo) Live in Tokyo, (with Wynton Marsalis) Baroque Duet, (with Itzhak Perlman) The Bach Album. Recipient Grammy awards, 1987, 88. Mem. Delta Omicron. Methodist. Office: care Columbia Artists Mgmt Inc 165 W 57th St New York NY 10019-2201*

BATTLE, LUCY TROXELL (MRS. J. A. BATTLE), retired middle school dean; b. Bridgeport, Ala., June 28, 1916; d. John Price and Emily Florence (Williams) Troxell; student U. Ala., Montevallo, 1934-35; B.S. Fla. So. Coll., 1951; postgrad. U. Fla., 1954, Fla. State U., 1963, Oxford (Eng.) U., 1979, 80, 81; M.A., U. South Fla., 1970; m. Jean Allen Battle, Aug. 25, 1940; 1 dau., Helen Carol. Asst. postmaster, Bridgeport, Ala., 1936-40; asst. dir. personnel office Sebring (Fla.) AFB, 1942-44; tchr. Cleveland Court Sch., Lakeland, Fla., also Forest Hill Sch., Carrollwood Sch., Tampa, Fla., 1949-64; dean of girls Greco Jr. High Sch., Tampa, 1964-68. Bd. dirs. Tampa Oral Sch. for Deaf. Recipient Outstanding Service award Fla. So. Coll. Woman's Club, 1942. Mem. NEA, Am. Childhood Edn. Internat., AAUW, Delta Kappa Gamma, Kappa Delta Pi, Phi Mu. Methodist. Club: Carrollwood Village Golf and Tennis. Author: (with J.A. Battle) The New Idea in Education, 1968. Home and Office: 11011 Carrollwood Dr Tampa FL 33618-3905

BATTLES, MARJORIE H., state legislator; b. Ipswich, Mass., Apr. 30, 1952; m. Robert Battles; 3 children. Attended, Hesser Coll., 1988, U. N.H., 1991. Mem. N.H. Ho. of Reps., 1993—. Vol. Swasey Sch., 1990—; active Friends of Libr., 1988-90. Mem. Bus. and Profl. Women. Republican. Office: NH Ho of Reps State Capitol Concord NH 03301*

BATTLES, ROXY EDITH, novelist, consultant, educator; b. Spokane, Wash., Mar. 29, 1921; d. Rosco Jirah and Lucile Zilpha (Jacques) Baker; m. Willis Ralph Dawe Battles, May 2, 1941; children: Margaret Battles Holmes, Ralph, Lara. AA, Bakersfield (Calif.) Coll., 1940; BA, Calif. State U., Long Beach, 1959; MA, Pepperdine U., 1976. Cert. tchr. English, adult basic edn. and elem. edn., Calif. Free-lance writer 50 nat. and regional mags., 1940—; tchr. elem. Torrance (Calif.) Unified Schs., 1959-85; tchr. adult edn. Pepperdine U., Torrance, 1969-79, 88-89; free-lance children's author, 1966—; mystery novelist Pinnacle Publs., N.Y.C., 1980; with Tex. A&M U., 1988; author-in-residence Young Authors Festival, Am. Sch. Madrid, 1991; lectr. in field. Author: Over the Rickety Fence, 1967, The Terrible Trick of Treat, 1970, 501 Balloons Sail East, 1971, The Terrible Terrier, 1972, One to Teeter-Totter, 1973, 2d edit., 1975, Eddie Couldn't Find the Elephants, 1974, reprints, 1982, 84, 88, What Does the Rooster Say, Yoshio?, 1978, The Secret of Castle Drai, 1980, The Witch on Room 6, 1987, 3d edit., 1989 (nominee Garden State, Nene, and Hoosier awards), The Chemistry of Whispering Caves, 1988, The Nurse of Whispering Caves, 1994. Active So. Calif. Coun. on Lit. for Children and Young People, 1973-80, 87—. Recipient Commendation UN, 1979; Hoosier award nominee, 1990; Garden State award nominee, 1990, Nene award nominee, 1992, 93. Mem. S.W. Manuscripters (founder), Surfwriters. Home: 560 S Helberta Ave Redondo Beach CA 90277-4353

BATTS, DEBORAH A., judge; b. Phila., Apr. 13, 1947; d. James Alexander Emmanuel, Jr. and Ruth Violet (Silas) Batts; 2 children. BA, Radcliffe Coll., 1969; JD, Harvard U., 1972. Summer atty. Foley, Hoag & Eliot, Boston, Mass., 1970, Kaye, Scholer, Fierman, Hays & Handler, N.Y.C., 1971; law clerk to Hon. Lawrence W. Pierce U.S. Dist. Ct. (so. dist.) N.Y., N.Y.C., 1972-73; assoc. atty. Cravath, Swaine & Moore, N.Y.C., 1973-79; asst. U.S. atty. criminal divsn. U.S. Dist. Ct. (so. dist.) N.Y., N.Y.C., 1979-84; assoc. prof. law Fordham U., 1984-94, adj. prof. law, 1994—; spl. assoc. counsel dept. investigation N.Y.C., 1990-91; commr. law revision com. State of N.Y., 1990-94; judge U.S. Dist. Ct. (so. dist.) N.Y., N.Y.C., 1994—; mem. sch. com. Cathedral Sch., N.Y.C., 1990—; mem. faculty Corp. Counsel Trial Advocacy Program, 1988—. Contbr. articles to legal jours. Trustee Spence Sch., 1987—. Mem. ABA, NASD (bd. arbitrators 1986—), Second Cir. Fed. Bar Coun., Assn. Bar. City N.Y. (lesbians and gay men in the profession 1991—), Lesbian and Gay Law Assn. Greater N.Y., Met. Black Bar Assn. Office: US Courthouse 40 Centre St Foley Sq Rm 2904 New York NY 10007*

BATY, PEGGY JUNE, college administrator, dean, consultant; b. San Diego, Apr. 2, 1956; d. Thomas Russell and Margaret June (Czykoski) Cox; m. Bruce W. Baty, Mar. 22, 1980. BS, Mid. Tenn. State U., 1980; PhD, U. Tenn., 1985. Chmn. dept. aviation Ga. State U., Atlanta, 1985-86; dir. Ctr. Excellence for Aviation and Space Edn., Embry-Riddle Aero. U., Daytona Beach, Fla., 1986-88; dean acad. support Embry-Riddle Aero. U., Prescott, Ariz., 1988-90; assoc. v.p., acad. dean Parks Coll. St. Louis U., Cakokia, Ill., 1990—; mem. cons. staff Nat. Congress on Aviation and Space Edn., Maxwell, Ala., 1986—; dir., founder Nat. Women in Aviation Conf., St. Louis, 1990—. Contbg. author: Emergency Management Handbook, 1991; contbr. articles on avication edn., women in aviation and air disasters to profl. jours. Recipient nat. championship award for excellence in aviation edn. FAA, 1989. Mem. Univ. Aviation Assn. (trustee 1988-91, pres. 1992-93), Exptl. Aircraft Assn. (bd. dirs. found., chpt. pres. 1988-90), Coun. Aviation Accreditation, Rotary. Home: One Seminole Dr Columbia IL 62236 Office: Parks Coll of St Louis U Cahokia IL 62206

BAU, ANNETTE MARION, national financial advisor, marketing consultant; b. Sturgis, S.D., Oct. 28, 1963; d. Virgil and Kathleen A. (Cassidy) B.; 1 child, Paige A. Bau Laniewski. BS, Ariz. State U., 1988; student, Ariz. Investment Sch., 1989. CFP. Assoc. Northwestern Mutual Life Ins., Phoenix, 1987-88; agt. Phoenix Mutual Life Ins., Phoenix, 1988-90; co-owner, co-founder, fin. cons. Associated Resource Cons., Phoenix, 1990—; cons. Maricopa County C.C., Phoenix, 1990—; fin. planning chair Ariz. State Fin. Planning, 1993, 94; co-chair fin. planning, relocation referral Mesa Tempe Chandler Co., 1993; spkr. in field; spkr. Women's Coun. Realtors Scottsdale, Luxury Home Tour Group, Ariz. Field Svc. Mgrs., Jewish Cmty. Ctr., Newday; frequent author, lectr. nationally to real estate groups and profls. Speaker, mem. Newday, Tempe, 1990. Mem. Nat. Assn. Life Underwriters, Coll. for Fin. Planning, Ariz. State U., Women's Coun. Realtors (fin. planning chmn. Ariz. state 1993, 94), Phoenix Women's Coun. Realtors (planning chair, 1993), Golden Key Nat. Honor Soc. (life).

BAUCUM, JANET MARTIN, critical care nursing educator; b. Seminary, Miss., Apr. 17, 1937; d. Will A. and Annie Maebell (Lowery) Davis; m. Johnnie Martin, Feb. 21, 1959 (dec. Nov. 1982); children: John Milton Martin, Melody Jane Martin; m. Hilton Baucum, Mar. 24, 1989. Diploma, Meth. Hosp., Hattiesburg, Miss., 1964; BSN, William Carey Coll., Hattiesburg, 1978; MS, U. So. Miss., Hattiesburg, 1979, EdD in Adult Edn., 1982. ACLS, PALS. Staff nurse Forrest Gen. Hosp., Hattiesburg, 1966-67, 69-77; office nurse Hattiesburg, 1967-69; staff devel. Meth. Hosp., Hattiesburg, 1979-81; instr. nursing Pearl River Community Coll., Poplarville, Miss., 1981-82; sophomore coord. U. Southwestern La., Lafayette, 1982-83; DON Conva Best, Hattiesburg, 1983-86; staff nurse Northshore Regional Med. Ctr., Slidell, La., 1985-86; staff nurse Forrest Gen. Hosp., Hattiesburg, 1986-88, rsch. chair, coord. organ/tissue donation for transplantation program and critical care edn., 1988—; instr. nursing U. So. Miss., Hattiesburg, 1992. Group leader United Way, Hattiesburg, 1990. Mem. AACN, So. Nursing Rsch. Soc., Sigma Theta Tau. Republican. Methodist. Home: 2911 Williamsburg Rd Hattiesburg MS 39402 Office: Forrest Gen Hosp PO Box 16389 Hwy 49 South Hattiesburg MS 39404-6389

BAUER, BARBARA ANN, marketing consultant; b. Fairfield, Ohio, Dec. 4, 1944; d. Charles P. and Grace J. (Peteka) B.; m. Joseph J. Strojinowski. AA, So. Sem. Jr. Coll., Buena Vista, Va., 1964; BA, Am. U., 1966. Pub. relations, advt. specialist Sta. WOR-AM-FM-TV, N.Y.C., 1966-67; pub. relations mgr. Continental Corp., N.Y.C., 1967-68; dir. corp. communications Am. Internat. Group, N.Y.C., 1968-80; dir. mktg. mgmt. infos. CIGNA Corp., Phila., N.Y.C., 1980-83; asst. v.p. Citicorp Credit Services Inc., N.Y.C., 1983-87; v.p., dir. mktg. Skandia Am. Group, N.Y.C., 1987-88, v.p. corp. communications, 1988-89; pres. Bauer Mktg. and Communications, Roslyn Heights, N.Y., 1989—. Lifetime mem. Girl Scouts U.S. Mem. Pub. Relations Soc. Am. (accredited, counselors' acad.), Women Execs. Pub. Relations (dir. 1986—), Assn. Ind. Reins. Cons., Assn. Profl Ins. Women (chair pub. rels., advisor bd. dirs.).

BAUER, BARBARA GAE, literary executive; b. Bklyn., Sept. 1, 1948; d. James Vincent and Gaetanina Antoinette (Palumbo) Mangano; m. Clinton Bonaventure Bauer, 1975 (div. 1994); children: Guy, Lucy. BA, Hunter Coll., 1970; MA, St. John's U., 1971, PhD, 1979. Pres., founder Barbara Bauer Lit. Agy., Matawan, N.J., 1984—. Democrat. Roman Catholic. Office: Barbara Bauer Lit Agy 179 Washington Ave Matawan NJ 07747-2944

BAUER, CARLA ANN, secondary school counselor; b. Coatesville, Pa., Feb. 6, 1963; d. Carl W. and Rosemary E. (Overbaugh) Cook. Student, U. Barcelona, Spain, 1984; BA in Psychology, Spanish & Polit. Sci. cum laude, Millersville U., 1986, MEd in Counseling, 1990. Cert. secondary guidance counselor, Pa.; nat. cert. counselor. Crisis intervention specialist Lancaster (Pa.) Guidance Ctr., 1986-87, mental health/retardation counselor, 1987; psychiat. asst. Philhaven Hosp., Mt. Gretna, Pa., 1987-88, residential counselor, 1988-89; bilingual counselor Sch. Dist. of Lancaster, 1989-90; high sch. counselor Hershey (Pa.) High Sch., 1990-93; jr. high sch. counselor Ea. York Jr./Sr. High Sch., Wrightsville, Pa., 1993—; grad. asst. Career Planning and Placement Ctr., Millersville U., 1989-90. Mem. NEA, Pa. Sch. Edn. Assn., Pa. Sch. Counselor Assn. Democrat. Office: Ea York Sch Dist Cool Creek Rd PO Box 2002 Wrightsville PA 17368

BAUER, CYNTHIA JEAN, school district administrator; b. Tyler, Tex., June 10, 1937; d. Owen Alfred and Leola Alma (Kuhn) Scrogin; m. J.W. Bauer, June 9, 1962; 1 child, Zane Randell. BS in Edn., Tex. Luth. Coll., 1959. Tchr. Fredericksburg (Tex.) Ind. Sch. Dist., 1959-65, 67-69; bus. mgr. Llano (Tex.) Sch. Dist., 1970—. Mem. Tex. Assn. Sch. Bus. Ofcls. Republican. Lutheran. Home: HC10-Box 92 Llano TX 78643 Office: 1402 Oatman Llano TX 78643

BAUER, DONNA MAREE HEIDKE, educator, realtor; b. Algona, Iowa, Sept. 29, 1932; d. Howard William and Vera Maree (Webster) Heidke; children: Maree Lisa Wederquist, Sara Beth Bartleson; m. Edward Frank Bauer, Sept. 29, 1972 (div. Aug. 1979). BS, Iowa State U., 1954; MA, Colo. U., 1969. Sci. tchr. Cheyenne Mt. Schs., Colorado Springs, Colo., 1962-63, German tchr., 1963-93; realtor Broadmoor Agy., Colorado Springs, Colo.; com. for German lang. exam. Ednl. Testing Svcs., Princeton, N.J., 1980-85; cons. in German The Coll. Bd. for Colo./Wyo., Denver, 1975-87. Author: Starting an Advanced Placement Program, 1976. Precinct leader Dem. Party El Paso County, Colorado Springs, 1965-70, 72-76, 80-84, 88-92; commr. Colorado Springs Planning Com., 1994—. Fulbright scholar, 1967, 81. Mem. NEA, Colo. Edn. Assn., Cheyenne Mountain Edn. Assn., Am. Assn. Tchrs. German, Am. Coun. Teaching Fgn. Langs., Colo. Congess Fgn. Lang. Tchrs. Home: 1614 Ridgeway Ave Colorado Springs CO 80906-3036

BAUER, ELAINE LOUISE, ballet dancer; b. Indpls., July 18, 1949; d. Thomas Bryant and Elenita Mae (Bodwell) B.; m. D. David Brown, June 5, 1971. BA in Dance magna cum laude, Butler U., 1971, DFA (hon.), 1989. Registered fine arts crafts person. Mem. corps. de Ballet Boston Ballet Co., 1971; soloist Boston Ballet Co., Boston, 1972, principal ballerina, 1974-89; ret., 1989; ballet mistress Boston Ballet Co., 1990—; artistic dir. Boston Ballet Sch's. Children's Summer Workshop, 1986-90. Starred (with Rudolf Nureyev in) N.Y.C. debut of La Sylphide., 1980. Com. mem. Task Force on Future of Butler U. Fine Arts Coll., Indpls., 1986; co-organizer Glasnost Dance Medicine Conf., 1990; mem. bd. visitors Walnut Hill Sch. Fine Arts, 1991—. Recipient Alumni Achievement award, Butler U., 1987, Eliot Norton award for lifetime achievement in dance Boston Theater Dist. Orgn., 1990; named to North Cen. High Sch. Alumni Hall of Fame, 1991. Office: Boston Ballet 19 Clarendon St Boston MA 02116

BAUER, ELIZABETH KELLEY (MRS. FREDERICK WILLIAM BAUER), consulting energy economist; b. Berkeley, Calif., Aug. 7, 1920; d. Leslie Constant and Elizabeth Jeanette (Worley) Kelley; A.B., U. Calif. at Berkeley, 1941, M.A., 1943; Ph.D. (fellow), Columbia U., 1947; m. Frederick William Bauer, July 5, 1944; children: Elizabeth Katherine Bauer Keenan, Frederick Nicholas. Instr. U.S. history and studies Barnard Coll., N.Y.C., 1944-45; lectr. history U. Calif. at Berkeley, 1949-50, 56-57; rsch. asst. Giannini Found., 1946-49, asst. rsch. agrl. economist, 1957-60; exec. sec. Internat. Conf. on Agrl. and Coop. Credit, U. Calif. at Berkeley, 1952-53, exec. sec. South Asia Project, 1955-56; registrar Holy Names Coll., Oakland, Calif., 1971-72; rsch. assoc. Brookings Instn. and Nat. Acad. Pub. Adminstrn., Washington, 1973; fgn. affairs officer Internat. Energy Affairs, Fed. Energy Adminstrn. Washington, 1974-77; fgn. affairs officer Office of Current Reporting, Internat. Affairs, Dept. Energy, Washington, 1977-81; dir. policy analysis and evaluation Nat. Coal Assn., Washington, 1981-83. Mem. Calif. Com. to Revise the Tchrs. Credential, 1961; trustee Grad. Theol. Union, Berkeley, 1972-74; bd. dirs. St. Paul's Towers and Episcopal Homes Found, Oakland, 1971-72. Recipient Superior Achievement award Dept. Energy, 1980; U. Calif. Alumni citation, 1983, 93. Mem. AAUW (Calif. chmn. for higher edn. 1960-62), Prytanean Honor Soc., AAAS, P.E.O., Mortar Bd., Phi Beta Kappa, Pi Lambda Theta, Sigma Kappa Alpha, Phi Alpha Theta, Pi Sigma Alpha. Democrat. Episcopalian. Author: Commentaries on the Constitution, 1790-1860, 1952; (with Murray R. Benedict) Farm Surpluses: U.S Burden or World Asset?, 1960; (with Florence Noyce Wertz) The Graduate Theological Union, 1970. Co-author, editor: The Role of Foreign Governments in the Energy Industries, 1977. Home: 708 Montclair Dr Santa Rosa CA 95409-2822

BAUER, JEAN MARIE, accountant; b. Morristown, N.J., Sept. 10, 1958; d. Earl F. and Patricia A. (O'Brien) W.; m. Ronald F. Bauer, Sr. AA in Acctg., County Coll. of Morris, 1978; BSBA, Coll. of St. Elizabeth, Convent Station, N.J., 1986. Sec. to payroll supr. Monroe Calculator, Morris Plains, N.J., 1979-80; clk. typist Stewart Title, Morris Plains, 1980-81; with BASF Corp., Parsippany, N.J., 1981—, credit rep. chems. div., 1986-88; sr. property acct. chems. div. BASF Corp., Clifton, N.J., 1988—. Co-leader folk group Sacred Heart Ch. of Dover, N.J., 1981, adult leader youth group, 1982, eucharistic minister, 1986-93; eucharistic minister, vol., religious edn. chr. St. Jude Ch., Budd Lake, N.J., 1993; spl. dep. registrar boro Mountain Lakes, N.J., 1976. Named one of Outstanding Young Women in Am., U.S. Jaycees, 1985. Mem. Cath. Daughters Am. (treas. Dover chpt. 1987-89, regent 1989-91). Republican. Home: 18 Indian Ln Hackettstown NJ 07840

Office: BASF Corp Property Acctg 3000 Continental Dr N Mount Olive NJ 07828-1234

BAUER, JUDY MARIE, minister; b. South Bend, Ind., Aug. 24, 1947; d. Ernest Camiel and Marjorie Ann (Williams) Derho; m. Gary Dwane Bauer, Apr. 28, 1966; children: Christine Ann, Steven Dwane. Ordained to ministry Christian Ch., 1979. Sec. adminstrv. asst. Bethel Christian Ctr., Riverside, Calif., 1975-79; founder, pres. Kingdom Advancement Ministry, San Diego, 1979—, trainer, mgr. cons., Tex., Ariz., Calif., Oreg., Washington, Ala., Okla., Idaho and Republic of South Africa, Guam, Egypt, The Philippines, Australia, Can., Mozambique, Malarwie, Mex., Zimbabwe, Guatemala, Israel, Scotland, Ireland, Japan, Eng.; Zambia, Botheswana, Holland, 1979—; pres. Witty Outerwear Distbrs. Internat., Inc., 1993—; founder, co-pastor Bernardo Christian Ctr., San Diego, 1981-91; evangelism dir. Bethel Christian Ctr., 1978-81, undershepherd minister, 1975-79, adult tchr., 1973-81; pres., founder Bethel Christian Ctr. of Rancho Bernardo, Calif., 1991—; condr. leadership tng. clinics, internat. speaker, lectr. in field. Author syllabus, booklet, tng. material packets. Pres., founder Bethel Christian Ctr. of Rancho Bernardo, 1991—, Bernardo Christian Ctr., San Diego, 1981-91. Mem. Internat. Conv. Faith Ministries, Inc. (area bd. dirs. 1983-88).

BAUER, MARION DANE, writer; b. Oglesby, Ill., Nov. 20, 1938; d. Chester and Elsie (Hempstead) Dane; m. Ronald C. Bauer, June 25, 1959 (div. Dec. 1988); children: Peter Dane, Elisabeth Alison. AA, LaSalle-Peru-Oglesby Jr. Coll., 1958; student, U. Mo., 1958-59; BA in Lang. Arts, U. Okla., 1961, postgrad., 1961-62. Author: Shelter from the Wind, 1976 (Notable Children's Book ALA, 1976), Foster Child (Golden Kite Honor Book award Soc. Children's Book Writers 1977), Tangled Butterfly, 1980, Rain of Fire, 1983 (Tchrs.' Choices award Nat. Coun. Tchrs. of English 1984, Revs. Choice award ALA Booklist 1983, Children's Book award Jane Addams Peace Assn. 1984), Like Mother, Like Daughter, 1985, On My Honor, 1986 (Newbery Honor Book 1987, Notable Children's Book ALA 1986, Best Books of 1986 Sch. Libr. Jour., Editors' Choice Booklist 1986, Pub.'s Weekly Choice The Yr.'s Best Books 1986, Flicker Tale Children's Book award, N.D., 1989, Golden Archer award, Wis. 1989, William Allen White Children's Book award, Kans., 1989, BBY, IRA selection for Janusc Korczak Lit. Competition Poland 1990), Touch the Moon, 1987, A Dream of Queens and Castles, 1990; (drama) God's Tears: A Woman's Journey, Face to Face, 1991 (Children's Book of Distinction, Hungry Mind Review, 1992), What's Your Story? A Young Person's Guide to Writing Fiction, 1992 (Notable Children's Book ALA 1992), Ghost Eye, 1992, A Taste of Smoke, 1993, A Question of Trust, 1994; editor: Am I Blue? Coming Out from the Silence, 1994, When I Go Camping With Grandma, 1995, A Writer's Story, From Life to Fiction, 1995; contbr. articles, short stories to mags. and books in field. Mem. Authors Guild, Authors League Am., Soc. Children's Book Writers and Illustrators. Democrat. Home: 8861 Basswood Rd Eden Prairie MN 55344-7407 Office: Clarion 215 Park Ave S New York NY 10003-1603

BAUER, PATRICIA ANN, secondary education educator; b. Kent, Ohio, July 21, 1937; m. Richard G. Bauer, July 26, 1958; children: Richard, Gregg, Keith. BS, Bowling Green State U., 1959; MEd, Kent State U., 1965. Tchr. sci. Kent (Ohio) Pub. Schs., 1959-64; instr. anatomy Kent State U., 1972-80; tchr. biol., sci. Ellet H.S., Akron, Ohio, 1979—; adv. Sci. Olympiad Team, Akron, Environ. Soc., Akron. Recipient Margaret Brigham award ARC Portage County, Outstanding Tchr. award Parent Tchr. Student Assn., 1994. Mem. AAUW (past pres., various offices), Nat. Assn. Biol. Tchrs., Sci. Edn. Coun. Ohio (bd. dirs. Dist. IV 1992—), Nat. Sci. Tchrs. Assn., Akron Edn. Assn. (rep. 1988-90). Office: Ellet HS 309 Woolf Ave Akron OH 44312-1629

BAUER, RUTH WARFIELD, elementary education educator; b. Bristol, Conn., Mar. 11, 1936; d. Charles Henry and Ruby (Martin) Warfield; m. June 22, 1958; children: Hans H. Bauer Jr., Paul M., Betsy. BA, Bates Coll., 1957; MS, Yeshiva U., 1958; cert. advanced study, Conn. Wesleyan U., 1978; PhD, U. Conn., 1988. Tchr. elem. and spl. edn. South Providence Elem. Sch., 1958-61; pvt. tutor, substitute tchr. Cheshire, Conn., 1961-68; dir. music 1st Congl. Ch., Cheshire, 1965-70, interim dir. music, 1979; tchr. elem. Chapman Sch., Cheshire, 1968-71; Highland Sch., Cheshire, 1971-81; tchr. elem. and English Dodd Jr. High Sch., Cheshire, 1981-91; edn. cons., 1991—; adj. prof. L.I. U. Rockland, 1991—, academic adv., 1993—; mem. Town of Cheshire Mid. Sch. Com., 1987—; tchr. trainer Beginner Educator Support and Tng., Conn. State Dept. Edn., 1988—. Presenter Nat. Conv. Madeleine L'Engle, Washingtonk 1982; site visitor, rev. panelist, select panelist Blue Ribbon Schs. Program U.S. Dept. Edn., 1989—. Mem. NEA, Nat. Coun. Tchrs. of English, Conn. Edn. Assn., Edn. Assn. of Cheshire, Phi Delta Kappa, Delta Kappa Gamma (1st v.p.). Home and Office: 62 West Rd South Salem NY 10590-2600

BAUGH, LYNDA LOUISE, real estate company executive; b. Riverside, Calif., Apr. 15, 1962; d. Perry Dean and Sandra Louise (Macek) B. Student, Belmont Coll., 1980, Phillips Bus. Coll., 1981-82. Owner, pres. Reel Time Recording Co., Houston and Nashville, 1982-84; pvt. practice acctg. Nashville, 1985; real estate agt. About Town, Inc., Nashville, 1986-87, Faxon Homes, Nashville, 1987-89; real estate sales & mktg. Phillips Builders Inc, Nashville, 1989—. Fund raiser Bullshooters, Nashville, 1986—; pres. beautification Percy Priest Woods Homeowners, Nashville, 1987—. Mem. NAFE, Nashville Bd. Realtors (comm. community svcs. 1988). Roman Catholic. Home: PO Box 201 Brentwood TN 37024-0201

BAUGHMAN, JENNIFER JANE, automotive executive; b. Youngstown, Ohio, Dec. 14, 1967; d. Gail William and Mary Linda (McCoy) B. B. Bus./ Mgmt., Temple U., 1990, MBA, 1994. Tng. mgr. environ. scis. Marriott Corp., Phila., 1990-94; zone mgr. Ford Motor Co., Detroit, 1994—. Mem. NAFE, Temple Owl Club, Pi Sigma Epsilon. Presbyterian. Home: 5040 Heather Dr Dearborn MI 48126

BAUGHMAN, KATHY, public relations executive; b. Chgo., Feb. 18, 1949. BS, U. Ill., 1971. Freelance pub. rels. specialist, 1971-73; prin. LB & Assocs. PR, Chgo., 1974-78; founder, pres. Haddon, Lynch, Baughman, Chgo., 1978—. Office: Haddon Lynch Baughman 875 N Michigan Chicago IL 60611*

BAUGHMAN, LEONORA KNOBLOCK, lawyer; b. Bad Axe, Mich., Mar. 21, 1956; d. Lewie L. and Jannette A. (Krajenka) K.; m. Jene W. Baughman, Dec. 5, 1981; children: Wesley J. and Adrianne J. Student, Cen. Mich. U., 1973-75; AB, U. Mich., 1977; JD, U. Notre Dame, 1981. Bar: Mich 1981, U.S. Dist. Ct. (ea. dist.) Mich. 1982. Assoc. Foster, Swift, Collins & Coey, P.C., Lansing, Mich., 1981-86; staff atty. Chrysler Fin. Corp., Troy, Mich., 1987—. Mem. ABA, Mich. Bar Assn., Nat. Assn. Women Lawyers, Am. Bankruptcy Inst., State Bar Mich. (chair bus. law sect., speaker 4th ann. comml. law seminar). Office: Chrysler Financial Corp 27777 Franklin Rd Southfield MI 48034-2337

BAUGHMAN, LOUISE SLOAN, community health nurse in gerontology; b. Walhalla, S.C., Mar. 13, 1932; d. John Thomas and Janie Elizabeth (Moss) Sloan; m. William F. Baughman Sr.; children: Melanie, Cheryl, Frank Jr., Michelle. Grad., Anderson Meml. Hosp., 1953. RN, S.C.; cert. gerontology, EKG technician. Office nurse lab., x-ray therapeutic treatments, 1953-55; pvt. duty nurse Nurse's Profl. Registry, 1956-67; sch. nurse Social Svcs., 1967-68; pvt. practice, 1968-80; supr. Lowman Home, 1981-89; coord. health svcs. Lexington County (S.C.) Recreation and Aging Commn., 1989—; supr. home care program, care mgmt., outreach, referral, counseling, community edn., and Alzheimer's edn. Lexington County. Contbr. Homemaker-Home Health Aide Training Curriculum, 1990 edit. Mem. Am. Soc. Aging, S.C. Fedns. Older Ams., S.C. Gerontol. Soc. Baptist. Home: 225 Mcleod Rd Chapin SC 29036-8598

BAUKNECHT, BARBARA BELLE, educator; b. Gleason, Wis., Apr. 21, 1933; d. William John and Jessie Marie (Fox) Beyer; m. Ross Eugene Bauknecht, Aug. 11, 1956; children: JoDee Ann Moran, Shelley Marie Courter, Wanda Jean Pace, Todd Randall. Tchr. cert., Lincoln County Normal, Merrill, Wis., 1953; BS, U. Wis., Stevens Point, 1964, M, 1974. Lic. tchr. grades 1-8, reading tchr. K-12, reading specialist K-12. Tchr. grades 5 and 6 Crandon, Wis., 1953-57; tchr. grades 7 and 8 Elcho, Wis., 1957-59; pub. libr. Three Lakes, Wis., 1963-66; tchr. Title 1, reading tchr. Three

Lakes, 1966-74, tchr., reading specialist, 1974—; tchr., founder Story Hour - Presch. Program, Three Lakes and Sugar Camp, Wis., 1964—; reading coord. Three Lakes and Sugar Camp, 1978—; tchr. grades 4, 5, 6, 7, 8 Sch. Dist., Crandon and Elcho, Wis., 1957-59; mem., chmn. Read Com. Three Lakes Dist., 1978—. Co-founder Ecumenical Vaction Bible Sch., 1978—; chmn. bd. Ed U. Demmer Meml. Libr., Three Lakes, 1989—; Sunday sch. supt. Union Congl. Ch., Three Lakes, 1977—, moderator, 1988—; local organizer, leader Campfire Girls, 1970-75. Recipient Ind. Celebrate Lit. award Headwaters Reading Coun., Rhinelander, Wis. 1990; Kohl Scholarship/Fellowship CESA Dist. Winner, 1992. Congregationalist. Mem. Ch. of Christ. Home: 6653 Schoenfeldt Rd Three Lakes WI 54562-9703 Office: Sch Dist Three Lakes PO Box 280 Three Lakes WI 54562-0280

BAUL, MARY ANN, correctional counselor; b. Chgo., Nov. 28, 1958; d. Robert Louis and Shirley Mary Ann (Jones) B. BA in Sociology/Criminology, Spelman Coll., 1980; MA in Criminal Justice Adminstrn., Atlanta U., 1986. Cert. pers. cons., counselor. Intern Gov.'s Intern Program, Atlanta, 1984-85; alcohol/drug counselor New Start Drug Program, Atlanta, 1985-86; legal asst. Hyatt Legal Svcs., Atlanta, 1986-90; pers. cons. Charlie Brown's Legal Resources, Atlanta, 1987-88; night counselor Salvation Army Youth Lodge, Atlanta, 1990-93; correctional counselor Ga. Dept. of Corrections, Savannah, 1993—; vol. Ga. Dept. of Corrections, Atlanta, 1985—. Dem. pollster, Atlanta, 1993. Fellow NAFE (cert.), NAACP, Spelman Coll. Alumnae. Democrat. Roman Catholic. Home: 1238 Comer St Savannah GA 31401 Office: Ga Dept of Corrections 1303 E President St Savannah GA 31404

BAUM, CYNTHIA GAIL, psychologist, educator, association administrator; b. Balt., July 27, 1957; d. Paul Arthur and Marjorie Joan (Hinkle) B.; m. Steven Joseph Choquette, Aug. 10, 1985; 1 child, Emily Michelle. BS, Denison U., 1978; MS, U. Ga., 1980, PhD, 1982. Lic. psychologist, Md., Va., D.C. Intern Med. U.S.C., Charleston, 1980-81; asst. prof. psychology Va. Polytechnic Inst. and State U., Blacksburg, 1982-86, dir. undergrad. psychology program, 1985-86; asst. prof. Cath. U. Am., Washington, 1986-89; dir. spl. projects APA, Washington, 1989, dir. edn. programs, 1990-92, asst. exec. dir. for edn., 1993-94; dean Am. Sch. Profl. Psychiatry, Arlington, Va., 1994—; cons. Hollins Coll., Roanoke, Va., 1983-86, Counseling Assocs. S.W. Va., 1986, Gaithersburg (Md.) Guidance and Evaluation Svcs., 1989-94; adj. assoc. prof. Cath. U., Washington, 1990-94; invited spkr. Georgetown U. Hosp., Washington, 1990; spkr., vol. Summit Mall Elem. Sch., Gaithersburg, 1989-90. Author: (with others) Handbook of Child Psychopathology, 1989; producer: (videotape) Career Encounters in Psychology, 1991; editor: Graduate Study in Psychology, 1990-94; contbr. articles to profl. jours. Grantee Nat. Inst. Drug Abuse, 1992, Johnson Found., 1991, Profl. Exam. Svc., 1993, Phi Beta Kappa, Phi Kappa Phi; named alumni scholar Denison U., 1993. Mem APA (co-chair task force on scholarly work 1992), Assn. for the Advancement of Behavior Therapy (coord. conv. edn. 1993—), Am. Assn. for Higher Edn., Southeastern Psychol. Assn., Sigma Xi. Home: 16923 Horn Point Dr Gaithersburg MD 20878-2085 Office: ASPP 1400 Wilson Blvd # 110 Arlington VA 22209

BAUM, ELEANOR, electrical engineering educator, academic administrator; b. Poland, Feb. 10, 1940; came to U.S., 1942; d. Sol and Anna (Berkman) Kushel; m. Paul Martin Baum, Sept. 2, 1962; children: Elizabeth, Jennifer. B.S.E.E., CUNY, 1959; M.E.E., Poly Inst N.Y., 1961, Ph.D., 1964; DS (hon.), Union Coll., 1993, Notre Dame, 1995. Engr. Sperry Gyrosoope Co., N.Y.C., 1960-61; instr. Poly. Inst. N.Y., N.Y.C., 1961-64; asst. prof. elec. engring. Pratt Inst., N.Y.C., 1964-67, assoc. prof., 1967-71, prof., chmn. dept. elec. engring., 1971-84, dean Sch. Engring., 1984-87; dean Sch. Engring., Cooper Union for Advancement Sci. and Art, N.Y.C., 1987—; exec. dir. Cooper Union Rsch. Found., N.Y.C., 1987—; cons. engring. to various corps.; accreditation visitor Accreditation Bd. Engring. and Tech., 1983—, bd. dirs., 1992—; organizer career confs. for careers in engring., careers for women, N.Y.C., 1970—; chair bd. examiners Grad. Record Exam., 1984-90; bd. dirs. Alleghany Powers Systems, U.S. Trust Co., Aunet, Inc.; commr. Engring. Workforce Commn., 1990—; mem. engring. adv. bd. NSF, 1989-94; mem. adv. bd. Duke U., Rice U., U.S. Mcht. Marine Acad., 1992—. Contbr. tech. articles and articles on engring. careers and edn. to profl. jours. Recipient Disting. Alumnus award Poly. Inst. N.Y., 1986, Alumni Achievement award CCNY, 1986, Emily Warren Roebling award Womens' Hall of Fame, 1988, Achievement award Mich. State U., 1992, Outstanding Woman Scientist award, 1992 Assn. Women Sci. (Fellow IEEE (Steinmetz award 1987), Soc. Women Engrs. (Upward Mobility award 1990); mem. Am. Soc. Engring. Edn. (bd. dirs. 1989—, v.p. 1992-93, pres.-elect 1994—, various nat. task forces), Nat. Engring. Deans Coun. (bd. dirs. 1987—, chair 1990-93), N.Y. Met. Deans Assn. (1985-90), N.Y. Acad. Scis. (bd. govs. 1994—), Order of Engr. (bd. govs. 1985-92, competitiveness policy coun. subcom. critical techs. 1992—, nat. rsch. coun. bd. energy edn. 1991—), Eta Kappa Nu, Tau Beta Pi. Office: Cooper Union Advancement Sci & Art Office of Dean 51 Astor Pl New York NY 10003-7139

BAUM, INGEBORG RUTH, librarian; b. Berlin, Sept. 20; d. Ella Koch; Oberlyceum (scholar), Kassel, Germany, 1926-33; postgrad. Georgetown U., 1963-70; m. Albert Baum, Feb. 16, 1938 (div. 1960); children—Harro Siegward, Helma Sigrun (Mrs. George Meadows). Came to U.S., 1951, naturalized, 1957. Export corr. Bitter-Polar, Germany, 1933-35, Henschel Locs., Germany, 1936; exec. sec. Fieseler Airplane Mfrs., Germany, 1936-38; interpreter, sec. UNRRA, Germany, 1946-48; payroll supr., civilian dept. U.S. Army, Wetzlar PX, Germany, 1948-51; asst. librarian Supreme Council, Ancient and Accepted Scottish Rite, Washington, 1951-70, librarian and museums curator, 1970—; appraiser rare books and documents; v.p. Merical Elec. Contractors, Inc., Forestville, Md., 1974-83. Mem. Am. Soc. Appraisers, Calligraphers Guild. Mem. Ch. Jesus Christ of Latter-day Saints. Free-lance contbr. to Pabelverlag, Rastatt, Germany, Harle, Ofcl. Publs., Inc., others. Home: 2480 16th St NW Apt 416 Washington DC 20009-6702 Office: 1733 16th St NW Washington DC 20009-3199

BAUM, LIN(DA), artist; b. Ann Arbor, Mich., July 20, 1950. BFA, U. Mich., 1971; postgrad. Wayne State U., 1978-79. Painting instr. Downriver Painting Class, Trenton, Mich., 1982-85; drawing instr. Wayne State U., Southgate, Mich., 1986; art instr. for terminally ill youth Discovery: Arts with Youth in Therapy, 1988-89; design assoc. Visual Svcs., Inc., Livonia, Mich., 1985-90; art instr. Schoolcraft Coll., 1990-91, 95—, Holy Cross Ctr.-Boysville, Boysville, Detroit, 1991; art cons. Howard Beach Sr. Ctr., Bklyn., 1992—; artist cons. N.Y.C. Housing Authority, 1994—; painting and drawing instr. Livonia Pub. Schs., 1983-88; guest lectr. U. Windsor (Ont., Can.), 1991, Mich. Art Edn. Assn., 1990, Sch. Art Inst. Chgo., 1989, No. Mich. U., Marquette, 1989. Solo exhbns. include Scarab Club, Detroit, 1984, 85, 88, 90, Galleria Casa de Unidad, Detroit, 1986, Cunniff Originals Gallery, Lake Orion, Mich., 1986, Swords into Plowshares Peace Gallery, Detroit, 1987, Stubnitz Gallery, Adrian Coll., Mich., 1990, Detroit Coun. for Arts City Arts Gallery, 1991; other exhbns. include Art Ctr., Mount Clemens, 1984, 85, Detroit Artists Mkt., 1984, 85, 86, Comerica Gallery, Detroit, 1984, Detroit Focus Gallery, 1985, Artsource Gallery, Flint, Mich., 1985, Renaissance Ctr., Detroit, 1985, Galerie Jaques, Ann Arbor, Mich., 1987, Pointe Z Gallery, Paris, 1987, Scarab Club, 1988, 90, Englander's, Birmingham, 1988, Galvez Art Studio, 1989, Sherry Washington Gallery, Detroit, 1989, Lawrence Street Gallery Invitational, 1991. Mem. Women's Internat. League for Peace and Freedom, 1992—, Mich. Coalition for Human Rights, 1986—, UN-NGO Com. on So. Africa, 1991—; lay assoc. Sisters of St. Dominic, Racine, Wis., 1993—.

BAUM, PHYLLIS GARDNER, travel management consultant; b. Ashtabula, Ohio, Dec. 13, 1930; d. Charles Edward Schneider and Stella Elizabeth (Schaefer) Gardner; m. Kenneth Walter Baum, Oct. 21, 1948 (div. July 1971); children: Deidre Adair, Cynthia Gail; m. Dennis Carl Marquardt, Sept. 22, 1979 (dec. 1991). Grad. high sch., Cleve. Am. Soc. Travel Agents. Travel cons. Fredo Travel Svc., Ashland, Ohio, 1960-66; sales mgr. Travelmart, Willoughby, Ohio, 1966-68; br. mgr. Travelmart, Mentor, Ohio, 1966-68, Diners Fugazy Travel, Sun City, Ariz., 1968-69; travel cons. Jarrett's Travel Svc., Phoenix, 1969-72; sr. cons. Loyal Travel, Phoenix, 1972-74; co-mgr. Palm Carr Travel, Sun City, 1974-77; tour ops. mgr. ASL Travel, Phoenix, 1978-79; owner, mgr. Travel Temporaries, Glendale, Ariz., 1979—; cons. and lectr. in field. Adv. bd. mem. Small Bus. Devel. Ctr., Phoenix, 1986—. Mem. Pacific Asia Travel Assn. Ariz. (bd. dirs. 1986—), Ariz.

Women in Travel, NAFE, Altrusa. Republican. Home and Office: Travel Temporaries 10249 N 45th Ave Glendale AZ 85302-1901

BAUM, SELMA, customer relations consultant; b. Bklyn., Jan. 15, 1924; d. Samuel and Tillie (Bayer) Goldman; m. Milton W. Baum, Jan. 19, 1947; children: Victor C., Cynthia Baum-Baicker. Student, NYU New Sch. for Social Rsch. Communications mgr. Sobel & Goldman, Inc., N.Y.C., 1941-48; pub. rels. cons., 1948-65; comparison shopper Gimbels, Valley Stream, N.Y., 1965-67, mgr. comparison shopping office N.Y. div., N.Y.C., 1967-75, dir. consumer affairs East div., 1975-84; dir. corp. customer rels. Saks Fifth Ave., N.Y.C., 1984-89; cons. customer rels., Palm Beach, Fla., 1989—; lectr., writer in field. Arbitrator Met. N.Y. Better Bus. Bur. Mem. NAFE, Am. Mgmt. Assn. (industry panelist), N.Y. & N.J. Retail Mchts. Coun. (v.p.), Women in Communication (award N.Y. chpt. 1984), Nat. Retail Mchts. Assn. (consumer affairs com.), Fashion Group, Am. Coun. on Consumer Interests, Soc. Consumer Affairs Profls. in Bus. (chpt. pres. 1981-82, nat. dir. 1983-86, bd. dir. Found. 1985-89; nat. treas., fin. chmn., v.p. 1986-87, award N.Y. chpt. 1983), Greater N.Y. WINS (regional affairs com.), Detroit Mktg. Assn. (customer rels. coun. 1987-88). Home and Office: Ste 715 3460 S Ocean Blvd Palm Beach FL 33480

BAUM, SHARON NAOMI, assistant principal; b. L.A., Mar. 2, 1953; d. Orville Ollie and Virginia Isabelle (Bruhn) Baugh; m. John Henry Baum, June 25, 1977. BS in Edn., Oreg. Coll. Edn., 1975; MS in Counseling, Western Oreg. State Coll., 1985. Lic. sch. counselor, Oreg. Phys. edn. tchr. Carlton (Oreg.) Elem. Sch., 1975-77; phys. edn. tchr., coach San Pasqual H.S., Winterhaven, Calif., 1977-79; fitness dir., mgr. Albany (Oreg.) Athletic Club, 1980-81; phys. edn. tchr. Harney County Sch. Dist., Burns, Oreg., 1981-83, dist. counselor, 1983-85; sch. counselor Sweet Home (Oreg.) Sch. Dist., 1985-87, Silverton (Oreg.) Sch. Dist., 1987-94; asst. prin. Lebanon (Oreg.) Sch. Dist., 1994—. Mem. NEA, Am. Counseling Assn. (Govt. Rels. award 1989, Disting. Svc. award 1989-90), Am. Sch. Counselor Assn. (bd. dirs., pub. rels. com. 1994—, govt. rels. com. 1990-93), Oreg. Sch. Counselor Assn. (pres., bd. dirs. 1991-94, Promising, Innovative, and Practices award award 1987, govt. rels. com. 1987-90), Oreg. Counseling Assn. (bd. dirs., pres. 1993-96). Democrat. Baptist. Home: 954 Ratcliff Dr SE Salem OR 97302-3241

BAUM, WILLOW ANN, public relations executive; b. Ft. Campbell, Ky., Nov. 22, 1966; d. Arnold Reinhold and Patricia Ann (Caffrey) B. BS in Screenwriting, Syracuse U., 1988. Asst. acct. exec. Fleishman-Millard, Inc., N.Y.C., 1988-90, acct. exec., 1990-92; sr. acct. exec. Porter/Novelli Inc., N.Y.C., 1992-94, acct. supr., 1994—. Home: 33 Greenwich Ave Apt 3C New York NY 10014 Office: Porter/Novelli 237 Madison Ave New York NY 10022

BAUMAN, BARBARA ANN, nurse; b. Detroit, Apr. 17, 1949; d. Martin Carl and Patricia Brush (Chope) B. BSN, U. N.C., 1971; MS, Boston U., 1978; MPA, Harvard U., 1989. RN, Mass. Clin. nurse specialist Carney Hosp., Dorchester, Mass., 1978-80; nurse specialist Beth Israel Hosp., Boston, 1980-83, nurse mgr., 1983-88; staff specialist Mass. Gen. Hosp., Boston, 1989—. Office: Mass Gen Hosp Fruit St Boston MA 02114

BAUMAN, SHARON ANN, computer systems administrator; b. Rochester, N.Y.; d. Sy and Irene (Branch) B. BA, SUNY, Binghamton, 1969. Cert. 3Com 3Wizard. Adminstrv. sec. to dean Grad. Sch. Edn. Syracuse (N.Y.) U., 1969-71; adminstrv. sec. to libr. Ind State U., Terre Haute, 1971-73; adminstrv. asst. to dean dept. neurosurgery Med. Coll. Ohio, Toledo, 1973-75; adminstrv. asst. to v.p. Nat. Ctr. Resource Recovery, Inc., Washington, 1975-78; legis. asst. U.S. Senate Com. on Appropriations, Washington, 1979-83; legis. asst. U.S. Senate Com. on Banking, Housing and Urban Affairs, Washington, 1983-87, dir. info. sys., 1987—; pres., founder Senate Microcomputer Users' Group, Washington, 1988—, vice chair, then chair Capitol Hill Women's Polit. Caucus, Washington, 1980-82; mem. presdl. adv. com. Am. Numis. Assn., 1993—. Mem. U.S. Senate Systems Adminstrs. Group. Office: US Senate Banking Com 1st And C St NE Washington DC 20510

BAUMANN, CAROL EDLER, political science educator; b. Plymouth, Wis., Aug. 11, 1932; d. Clarence Henry and Beulah Hanetta (Weinhold) E.; m. Richard Joseph Baumann, Feb. 28, 1957; children: Dawn Carol, Wendy Katherine. BA in Internat. Rels., U. Wis., 1954; PhD in Internat. Rels. London Sch. Econs./Polit. Sci., 1957. Chmn. Internat. Rels. Major, Milw., 1962-79; dep. asst. sec. Bur. of Intelligence and Rsch./Dept. of State, Washington, 1979-81; prof. U. Wis., Milw., 1972—, dir. internat. studies and programs, 1982-88; dir. Inst. of World Affairs, Milw., 1964—. Author: Program Planning About World Affairs, 1991, The Diplomatic Kidnappings, 1973; editor: Europe in NATO: Deterrence, Defense, and Arms Control, 1987, Western Europe: What Path to Integration?, 1967. Active Gov.'s Commn. on the UN, 1964-79, 82-89; dem. candidate 9th Congl. Dist., 1968; mem. World Affairs Coun. of Milw., 1964-75. Named Marshall scholar, 1954-57; recipient Pub. Svc. Achievement award Common Cause in Wis. 1991. Mem. Atlantic Coun. of the U.S. (edn. com., bd. dirs.), China Coun. of the Asia Soc., Coun. on Fgn. Rels., Fgn. Policy Assn. (bd. dirs. 1990—, editl. adv. com. 1977-79, 82-88), Nat. Coun. World Affairs Orgns. (pres. 1977-79, bd. dirs. 1992—), UN Assn. of USA (Bd. dirs. 1977-79, 82-89), Soc. for Citizen Edn. in World Affairs (pres. 1977-79), Com. on Atlantic Studies, Internat. Studies Assn., Phi Kappa Phi, Phi Beta Kappa. Democrat. Lutheran. Home: W 6248 Lake Ellen Dr Cascade WI 53011 Office: Inst of World Affairs Garland Hall 202A Milwaukee WI 53201

BAUMANN, PATRICIA LYNN, occupational health nurse, ambulatory care nurse, consultant; b. Carbondale, Pa., Jan. 30, 1962; d. John Frederick and Catherine Anne Hunt; div.; children: Donnell Patricia and Taryn Frances Thorne. BSN, Wilkes Coll., 1987. Staff nurse, pulmonary and float Mercy Hosp., Scranton, Pa., 1987-88; asst. mgr. CMC Found., Scranton, 1988-89; mgr. CMCI Community Med. Ctr. Found., Scranton, 1989-90; dir. profl. svcs. Above All Home Health and Hospice, Taylor, Pa., 1991-93; surveyor, cons. Primary Care and Home Health divsn, Pa. Dept. Health, 1993—; instr. DEPMED Power Distbn. 34th Gen. Hosp., Ashley, Pa. 1st lt. USAR, Desert Shield/Desert Storm Saudi Arabia, 1990-91. Mem. Res. Officers Assn., Rotary (charter, v.p. 1994—).

BAUMBACH, ALICE THOMPSON, educator, b. North Shore Community Coll., 1975; BS in Elem. Edn., U. Colo, 1978; postgrad. in edn., Lesley Coll., 1988. Paraprofl. Boulder Valley Sch. Dist., 1978-79; tchr. Denver Pub. Schs., 1979—. Mem. sch. bldg. and sch. improvement accountabilty coms. Kaiser Family Tchr. Orgn. Recipient Outstanding Citizenship award State of Mass., scholar. Mem. Denver Classrm. Tchr. Assn. Home: 2610 S Gaylord St Denver CO 80210-6048

BAUMEL, JOAN PATRICIA FRENCH, educator, writer, lecturer; b. Winona, Minn., Mar. 12, 1930; d. William Oswald and Gertrude Marie (Fitzgerald) French; m. Herbert Baumel, July 11, 1971. Student, l'Ecole du Louvre, France, 1950-51; student with high honors, Inst. Phonétique Sorbonne, Paris, 1950-51; BA magna cum laude, Douglass Coll.; 1952; postgrad., U. Detroit, 1952-55, Case Western Reserve U., 1960, U. Akron, 1962, U. Notre Dame, 1963, Manhattanville Coll., 1971; MA in French, Rutgers U., 1965; PhD in Modern Langs., Fordham U., 1985. Tchr. French lang. and culture, elem. and coll. levels various schs. including Mother House of Religious of the Sacred Heart, Kenwood, Albany, N.Y., Ohio, Mich., 1955-66; tchr. French White Plains (N.Y.) Pub. High Sch., 1966-86; curricula creator Akron (Ohio) Pub. Schs., 1962-63; co-dir. Baumel Assocs., Yonkers, N.Y., 1984—; Concerts and Lectures with Herbert Baumel 1991—; Words and Music Programs with Herbert Baumel, 1991—, Waverly Heights, Gladwyne, Pa., 1993, Workmen's Circle Lodge, Sylvan Lake, N.Y., 1994; lectr. French lang. and culture Yonkers (N.Y.) Pub. Libr., 1992, Greenburgh (N.Y.) Pub. Libr., 1992, anti-semitism CUNY Grad. Ctr., B'nai B'rith Internat. Mus., Washington, 1st Unitarian Soc., Westchester, N.Y., Rockland (NY.) Ctr. for Holocaust Studies, Unitarian Ch. of All Souls, N.Y.C., Temple Beth Israel, Port Washington, N.Y., Holocaust Resource Ctr. and Archives, Queensborough C.C., CUNY, 1991, Women's Am. ORT, Midchester Jewish Ctr., Yonkers, 1992, Ctrl. Queens YM & YWCA, N.Y.C., 1992. Author: Paul Claudel and the Jews: A Study in Ambivalence, 1985; lectr. topics include French Anti-Semitism; The Gallic Road to the Concentration Camp; Klaus Barbie and the Children of Izieu, numerous others;

numerous concerts and lectures with Herbert Baumel, including Words and Music program, 1991—. Mem. adv. bd. Mark Brent Dolinsky Meml. Found. Recipient Woodrow Wilson fellowship, 1958-59. Mem. Am. Assn. Tchrs. French, Nat. Writers Union, White Plains Tchrs. Assn., Am. Coun. Tchg. Fgn. Langs., N.Y. State Assn. Fgn. Lang. Tchrs., French Inst./Alliance Francaise, Alliance Francaise Westchester, Phi Beta Kappa. Home and Office: Baumel Assocs 86 Rosedale Rd Yonkers NY 10710-3033

BAUMGARDNER, BARBARA ANN, publishing consultant; b. Harrisburg, Pa., Nov. 8, 1937; d. Otto Lockhart Borke and Margaretta Mildred (Feigley) Borke Traugh; m. E. Wayne Baumgardner, July 12, 1958; children: Brian Wayne, Bruce Edward. AB, Gettysburg (Pa.) Coll., 1959; MLA, Western Md. Coll., 1976, MEd, 1982. Cert. secondary tchr., Md. Sales promoter Scott, Foresman & Co., Chgo., 1959-60; tchr. Carroll County Pub. Schs., Westminster, Md., 1964-84; cons. McDougall, Littell & Co., Evanston, Ill., 1984-91; adj. prof. Western Md. Coll., Westminster, 1975. Mem. Savannah Symphony Women's Guild. Mem. AAUW, Women's Assn. Hilton Head, Hilton Head Art League, Mensa, Fed. Garden Clubs of Md., Phi Mu. Republican. Presbyterian. Home: 9 Man O War Hilton Head Island SC 29928-5248 also: 6635 Silver Lake Dr Park City UT 84060

BAUMGARTEN, DIANA VIRGINIA, geriatrics nurse; b. Bklyn., May 24, 1943; d. Francis and Leah (Cuoghi) DeMarco; married; children: Elizabeth Salonia, Matthew, Edward. AS, Broward C.C., 1991. RN, Fla. Pediats. staff nurse North Broward Med. Ctr., Pompano Beach, Fla., 1991; staff nurse Tamarac (Fla.) Convalescent Ctr., 1992; nursing supr. Tamarac (Fla.) Convalescent Ctr., Ft. Lauderdale, Fla., 1992-93; corp. nurse cons. HBA Health Mgmt. Corp., Ft. Lauderdale, Fla., 1993-94; acting DON Broward Convalescent Home, Ft. Lauderdale, 1994; acting asst. DON Springtree Walk Nursing Ctr., Sunrise, Fla., 1994; resident assessment coord., infection control officer Broward Convalescent Home, Ft. Lauderdale, 1994-95; asst. DON Hillhaven Convalescent Ctr. of Delray Beach, 1995—. Mem. ANA, Fla. Nurses' Assn., Phi Theta Kappa. Home: 11417 Little Bear Dr Boca Raton FL 33428

BAUMGARTEN, SHIRLEY MAY, medical/surgical nurse; b. Watervliet, Mich., May 12, 1935; d. Oliver Spencer Turner and Eleaner (Emma) Heisler; m. Richard August Baumgarten, Mar. 16, 1957; children: Kathryn Ann, Richard Oliver, Jean Marie. Cert., Chgo. Pub., 1957; student, Oakton Community Coll., Des Plaines, Ill., 1988. Nurse Chgo. Pub. Sch., 1954-55; staff nurse med.-surg. Ill. Cen. Hosp., Chgo., 1955-57, Ressurection Hosp., Chgo., 1963-69; ind. nurse home care Des Plaines, Ill., 1974-88; nurse home care A-Abiding Home Care, Park Ridge, Ill., 1989—; nurse organizer Adult Day Care, Des Plaines, 1992—. Vol. Rainbow Hospice, Inc., Des Plaines, 1982-92. Recipient Humanitarian and Theodore A. Krause Sr. Grup Meml. award, 1991, 93. Methodist. Home: 856 Woodlawn Ave Des Plaines IL 60016-3234 Office: A Abiding Home Care 133 E Northwest Hwy Park Ridge IL 60068

BAUMGARTNER, EILEEN MARY, government official; b. St. Cloud, Minn.; d. Florian H. and Kathleen (Keefe) B.B.A., Coll. St. Catherine, St. Paul, 1964; M.P.A., U. Minn., Mpls., 1970. Tchr., U.S. Peace Corps, Ethiopia, 1964-66; researcher N.Y. Med. Coll., N.Y.C., 1967-68, Minn. State Planning Agy., St. Paul, 1970-73; legis. analyst tax com. Minn. Ho. of Reps., St. Paul, 1973-78; legis. dir. to Congressman Sabo, U.S. Ho. of Reps., Washington, 1979-90, adminstrv. asst., 1991-93; chief staff Ho. Budget Com., 1993-94, minority staff dir. Ho. Budget Com., 1995—. Mem. Am. Soc. Pub. Adminstrn. Democrat. Roman Catholic. Office: 222 O'Neil House Office Bldg Washington DC 20515

BAUMRIND, ROSALYN MURIEL GREENWALD, psychologist; b. N.Y.C., Aug. 3; d. Samuel Howard and Rose (Halpern) Greenwald; m. Seymour Harvey Baumrind, Dec. 31, 1950 (div. 1969); children: Martin Mark, Lydia, Sandra. BA magna cum laude, Bklyn. Coll., 1950, MA, 1954; PhD, Adelphi U., 1967. Cert. clin. psychologist, N.Y. High sch. tchr. N.Y.C. Bd. Edn., 1950-62, Hebrew Inst. L.I., 1957-62; psychologist, phys. medicine and rehab. Elmhurst Gen. Hosp., Queens, N.Y., 1964; asst. psychologist VA Hosp. Ft. Hamilton, Bklyn., 1965-67; asst. prof. sch. edn. Bklyn. Coll., CUNY, 1967-85; pvt. practice N.Y.C., 1967—; cons. in field. Contbr. articles to profl. pubs.; author TV tapes. Recipient award NIMH, 1963-65. Mem. Am. Acad Psychotherapists (exec. coun. 1984-90), Am. Psychol. Assn., Am. Group Psychol. Assn., Phi Beta Kappa. Home and Office: 141 E 37th St New York NY 10016-3117

BAUMSLAG, NAOMI, pediatrician; b. Republic of South Africa, July 19, 1936; d. Kalman and Braine (Ginsburg) B.; children: Victor, Barry, Ruth. MD, U. Witwatersrand, 1958; MPH, Johns Hopkins U., 1976. Intern, resident Baragwanath Hosp., Johannesburg, South Africa, 1959-62; dir. office internat. health nutrition divsn. Dept. Health and Human Svcs., Rockville, Md., 1979-84; pres. Womens Internat. Pub. Health Network, Bethesda, Md., 1987—; clin. prof. pediatrics Georgetown U. Med. Sch., Washington, 1987—. Author: A Women's Guide to Vaginal Yeast Infection, 1992, Mother and Child Health, 1994, Milk Money and Madness: The Battle for the Breast, 1995. Mem. adv. bd. La Leche League, Dearborn, Mich., World Alliance Breastfeeding Assns., Penang, Malaysia, 1994. Recipient Alumna award for Outstanding Alumnae Johns Hopkins Sch. Hygiene and Pub. Health, 1976. Mem. Am. Pub. Health Assn. (mem. governing coun. 1993-95), Nat. Coun. Internatl Health (mem. governing bd. 1990), UNICEF Nutrition Working Group. Home: 7100 Oak Forest Ln Bethesda MD 20817 Office: Womens Internat Pub Health 7100 Oak Forest Ln Bethesda MD 20817

BAUNER, RUTH ELIZABETH, library administrator, reference librarian; b. Quincy, Ill.; d. John Carl and M. Irene (Nutt) B. BS in Edn., Western Ill. U., 1950; MS, U. Ill., 1956; postgrad., So. Ill. U., 1974, PhD, 1978. Asst. res. libr. Western Ill. U., Macomb, 1950; tchr., libr. Sandwich (Ill.) Twp. High Sch., 1950-54; circulation dept. asst. U. Ill. Libr., Urbana, 1955; asst. edn. libr. So. Ill. U., Carbondale, 1956-63, acting edn. lbir., 1963-64, edn. and psychology libr., 1965—, assoc. prof. curriculum and instrn. dept., 1971—; dir. Grad. Residence Ctr. Librs., So. Ill. U., 1973-79; cons. in field; subject matter expert Learning Resourceds Svc. Interactive Video, Carbondale, 1990-91, also scriptwriter. Co-author: The Teacher's Library, 1966; contbr. articles to profl. jours. Pres. alumni constituency bd. Coll. Edn., Carbondale, 1988-89; bd. dirs. So. Ill. U. chpt. UN, 1985-86; mem. Carbondale Bd. Ethics, 1989—. Recipient Luck Has Nothing To Do With It award Onyx Press, 1993. Mem. ALA, AAUP (v.p. So. Ill. U. chpt. 1972-73), AAUW (univ. rep. Carbondale br. 1988-89), Assn. Coll. and Rsch. Librs. (chmn. edn. and behavioral scis. sect. 1976-77, Most Active Mem. award 1968-93), Ill. Libr. Assn., Phi Delta Kappa, Phi Kappa Phi, Delta Kappa Gamma. Office: So Ill U Faner Hall 2427 Carbondale IL 62901-4522

BAUR, ISOLDE NACKE, translator, freelance writer, public speaker; b. Dresden, Saxonia, Fed. Republic Germany, May 27, 1923; came to U.S., 1954; d. Otto Ernst and Anna Louise (Liebscher) Nacke; m. Karl Baur, Oct. 23, 1943 (dec. Oct. 1963); children: Ulrich, Marieluise Baur-Kailing. Student, Draughton's Bus. Coll., Dallas, 1964, U. Tex., Arlington, 1974. Milliner Cohn Co., Dresden, Fed. Republic Germany, 1937-39; drill press operator Zeiss-Ikon Corp., Dresden, 1939-41; engring. aid Messerschmitt Aircraft Corp., Augsburg, Fed. Republic Germany, 1941-43; blue print collaborator Ling-Temco-Vought Aerospace Corp., Dallas, 1963-64; office clk. Barnes Group Inc., Grand Prairie, Tex., 1964-69; freelance translator, writer, pub. speaker, 1969-71; manpower analyst Xerox Corp., Dallas and Ft. Worth, 1971-76; owner Baur Translation Svc., 1972—. Contbr. articles to jours. Mem. coun. German Day in Tex. Coun., Dallas, 1964—, awards chmn., 1978-88, hon. chmn., 1981; bd. dirs. Dallas Goethe Ctr., 1964-74, 2d v.p., membership chmn., 1970-72, 1st v.p./program chmn., 1973-75; sec. Unitarian Universalist Ch. Arlington, 1968-70; vol. guardian Tarrant County, Ft. Worth, 1988—; co-leader Girl Scouts Am., 1955-63. Mem. Soaring Soc. Am., Am. Translators Assn. (exec. com. conv. 1981), Texa Soaring Assn. (hon. life, treas. 1964-66, sec. 1976-78, editor Spirals newsletter 1978-80), Acad. Flying Club U. Tech./Stuttgart (hon. sr.), German-Am. C. of C. Office: Baur Translation Svc 5802 Earle St Arlington TX 76016-1115

BAURES, MARY MARGARET, psychotherapist, author; b. St. Petersburg, Fla., Sept. 13, 1947; d. Robert A. and Ruth S. Baures; divorced. BS, U. Fla., 1969; MA, Boston U., 1976, EdM, 1984; Cert. Advanced Grad. Study in Human Devel., Harvard U., 1986; D in Clin. Psychology, Antioch New Eng., 1994. Instr. Emerson Coll., Boston, 1981-86; counselor Beverly (Mass.) Hosp., 1984-86; emergency svc. clinician Ctr. for Mental Health, Waltham, Mass., 1987-91; psychotherapist Seacoast Counseling, Danvers, Mass., 1989—, Human Resource Inst., Brookline, Mass., 1993—; mem. faculty psychology adult degree program Vt. Coll., 1989—; neuropsychology intern Northshore Children's Hosp., Salem, Mass., 1990-91; founder, dir. Boycott Anorexic Mktg., 1993—. Author: Undaunted Spirits-Portraits of Recovery, 1994. Office: Seacoast Counseling 85 Constitution Ln Danvers MA 01923-3627

BAUTISTA, CAROL STONEY, electric power industry administrator; b. South El Monte, Calif., Nov. 3, 1949; d. Floyd Oakland and Madge V. (Roberts) Stoney; m. Ben Benito Makahanohano Bautista; children: Patty Kawohikukapulani, Oakland N. Kaululaau. AA, Rio Hondo Coll., 1969; BA, Calif. State U., 1977. Cert. ESL and adult edn. tchr., Calif. Various positions So. Calif. Edison Co., Rosemead, 1972-88, project administr., 1988—; seminar chairperson Women and Minority Bus. Enterprises, Rosemead; adv. L.A. County Office of Emergency Mgmt., assistance to fire victims. Author feminist poetry and short stories; contbr. articles to profl. jours.; cartoonist and letterer newspapers and mags. Activist United Farmworkers Union, 1960's, 70's; local organizer Neighborhood Watch Program, 1982—; guest AM L.A. TV Program, 1988—, Channel 7 News, 1988—; instr. Coalition for Literacy, 1987; counselor Amnesty; instr. ESL Program, 1987; bd. dirs., mgr. Bobby Sox Softball, 1979-85; bd. dirs. Hui O'Hana Waialua, 1984—, Team USA Women's Softball, 1985; chair reunion com. Rosemead High Sch. Class 1967, 1986—. Recipient Women in Leadership award Calif. State Senate, Cmty. Svc. award Vietnam Vets. Vols., Mgmt. awards YWCA of L.A.. Mem. NAFE, NOW, Women's History Project, Edison Roundtable (steering com., com. chair). Democrat. Home: 2296 S Oldridge Dr Hacienda Hgts CA 91745-5637 Office: So Calif Edison Co PO Box 800 Rosemead CA 91770-0800

BAUTISTA-MYERS, LILIAN, writer, editor; b. San Diego; d. Jose Delos Angeles and Juanita (Perez) Bautista; m. Jimmy Clarence Brinkley, June 6, 1959 (div. 1964) 2 children; m. Donald Allen Myers, Oct. 28, 1966 (div. 1990); children: Sherri Lynn, Johnny Martin, David Allen. BA in English, Calif. State U., Northridge, 1970; MS in Edn., SUNY, Albany, 1972; EdD in Ednl. Adminstrn., Okla. State U., 1980. Adminstrv. officer, writer Capitol Hill Educator, Albany, 1972-73; asst. to dir., tech. editor/writer, coordinator grant and contract activities, contracts and grants mgmt. officer Okla. State U., 1973-79; co-owner/writer The Last Word, writing and graphic arts, Omaha, 1979-81; freelance writer, copywriter, editor, 1972—; speaker, fundraiser; coordinator grants mgmt. and devel. Met. Tech. C.C., Omaha, 1981-83; devel. officer Cath. Dept. Edn., Archdiocese of Omaha, 1984-85; exec. dir. Cooperating Hampton Rds. Orgns. for Minorities in Engring. CHROME, Inc., Norfolk, Va., 1985-90; dir. Ctr. Indsl. Engring. Tech., Conn. State U., 1990-91; dir. grants and contracts Coll. Edn. U. South Fla., Tampa, 1992—. Author, editor in field. Democrat. Home: 15401 Plantation Oaks Dr Tampa FL 33647-2116

BAUTZ, LAURA PATRICIA, astronomer; b. Washington, Sept. 3, 1940; d. Charles Kothe and Laura (Stauverman) B. BA in Physics, Vanderbilt U., 1961; PhD in Astronomy, U. Wis., Madison, 1967. From instr. to assoc. prof. astronomy Northwestern U., Evanston, Ill., 1965-75; program dir. astronomy sect. NSF, Washington, 1972-73, sr. staff assoc. NSF, 1975-79, dep. dir. physics divsn., 1979-81, dir. astronomy divsn., 1982-90; vis. researcher Lawrence Berkeley Lab., 1990-92, dep. dir. physics divsn. NSF, 1992-93, internat. programs divsn., 1994—. Fellow AAAS; mem. Internat. Astron. Union, Am. Phys. Soc., Phi Beta Kappa. Home: 1325 18th St NW Apt 506 Washington DC 20036-6510 Office: 4201 Wilson Blvd Arlington VA 22230-0001

BAVLNKA, CAROL ANN, association administrator, counselor; b. Berwyn, Ill., June 21, 1946; d. Max John and Margaret Joann (Rose) Kadner; m. George William Bavlnka Sr. (dec. Aug. 25, 1988), Nov. 30, 1974; 1 child, Scott Richard. BA, Rosary Coll., 1967; postgrad., Concordia Tchr.'s Coll., 1968-69. Cert. tchr., Ill., N.Y. German tchr. St. Benedict High Sch., Chgo., 1969-72; file clk. Glenn Ingram & Co., Chgo., 1973-74; sub. tchr. Cairo/Durham (N.Y.) Sch. Dist., 1981-83; tchr. Catskill (N.Y.) High Sch., 1983-86, Windham (N.Y.)-Ashland-Jewitt, 1986-87; program coord. Schoharie (N.Y.) ARC, 1987-90; mgr. Bethesda Luth. Home, Montgomery, Ill., 1990-91; supr. AAA-Chgo. Motor Club, Naperville, Ill., 1991—. Election judge, Naperville, 1992-93. Democrat. Roman Catholic. Home: 267 Gregory St Apt 5 Aurora IL 60504

BAXTER, BETTY CARPENTER, educational administrator; b. Sherman, Tex., 1937; d. Granville E. and Elizabeth (Caston) Carpenter; m. Cash Baxter; children: Stephen Barrington, Catherine Elaine. AA in Music, Christian Coll., Columbia, Mo., 1957; MusB in Voice and Piano, So. Meth. U., Dallas, 1959; MA in Early Childhood Edn., Tchrs. Coll., Columbia, 1972, MEd, 1979, EdD, 1988. Tchr. Riverside Ch. Day Sch., N.Y.C., 1966-71; headmistress Episcopal Sch., N.Y.C., 1972-87, headmistress emeritus, 1987—; founding head Presbyn. Sch., Houston, 1988-94. Author: The Relationship of Early Tested Intelligence on the WPPSI to Later Tested Aptitude on the SAT. Mem. ASCD, Nat. Assn. Episcopal Schs. (former gov. bd., editor Network publ.), Nat. Assn. Elem. Sch. Prins., Ind. Schs. Assn. Admissions Greater N.Y. (former exec. bd.), Nat. Assn. for Edn. of Young Children, Houston Area Assn. for Edn. of Young Children, Houston Area Assn. Ind. Schs., Houston Area Assn. Edn. Young Children, Nat. Assn. Elem. Sch. Prins., Assn. Supervision and Curriculum Devel., Kappa Delta Pi, Delta Kappa Gamma. Republican. Presbyterian. Office: 316 W 79th St New York NY 10024

BAXTER, CARLA LOUISE CHANEY, insurance product specialist; b. Indpls., Nov. 4, 1955; d. Carlton S. and Jennie B. (Yates) Chaney; m. Andrew Louis Baxter, Sept. 20, 1980; 1 child, Andranise Louise. BA in Mktg., Ball State U., 1979. Lic. realtor, Ind.; CPCU (bd. dirs., instr. Ind. chpt.); cert. profl. ins. woman; assoc. risk mgmt.; assoc. mgmt. Zoning technician Dept. Met. Devel., Indpls., 1975; dir. mktg. Urban Tng. and Devel. Systems Inc., Indpls., 1979-80; casualty underwriter Wausau Ins. Cos., Indpls., 1980-84; sr. casualty underwriter CNA Ins. Cos., Indpls., 1984-85; nat. accounts underwriter Nationwide Ins. Cos., Columbus, Ohio, 1985-87; sr. casualty underwriter Home Ins. Co., Indpls., 1987-90; product specialist Am. States Ins. Cos., 1990-94, field sales mgr., 1994—; instr. Profl. Ins. Agts. of Ind. Speaker various chs. and civic groups; dir. choir Trinity Ch., Indpls., 1983—; mem. Consortium African-Am. Christian Women. Statonian scholar, 1975-76; N.G. Gilbert scholar Ball State U., 1978. Mem. Cert. Profl. Ins. Women, Indpls. Assn. Ins. Women, Indpls. Underwriters Assn., Ins. Inst. Am. (cert.), Urban League, Alpha Kappa Alpha (Career Day group leader 1984, scholar 1974-75, 75-76). Baptist. Avocations: roller skating, aerobics, singing. Office: Am States Ins Co 500 N Meridian St Indianapolis IN 46204-1275

BAXTER, CATHERINE ELAINE, securities broker; b. N.Y.C., Jan. 2, 1964; d. Comer Cash and Betty Nan (Carpenter) B. BA, Duke U., 1986, MBA, 1987. Assoc. Morgan Stanley & Co., Inc., N.Y.C., 1987—; alumni coun. mem. Fuqua Sch. Bus., Durham, N.C.; alumni bd. dirs. Nightingale Bamford Sch., N.Y.C., mem. alumnae bd. Hockaday Sch., Dallas. Sec., bd. dirs. Burden Ctr. for Aging, N.Y.C., 1991—; active Jr. League, N.Y.C., 1982—. Mem. NAFE, Am. Women's Econ. Devel. Assn. Republican. Presbyterian. Office: Morgan Stanley & Co Inc 1251 Avenue of Americas New York NY 10020-1104

BAXTER, CINDI CHOATE, librarian; b. Nashville, Tenn., Mar. 21, 1958; d. Ralph Edsil and Patty Gail (Kennemur) Choate; m. Michael Wayne Baxter, June 20, 1976; 1 child, Barry Michael. Assoc. degree, Columbia State C.C., 1979; Bachelor's degree, U. North Ala., 1981. Social worker Dept. Human Svcs., Hohenwald, Tenn., 1981-82; libr. asst. Blue Grass Regional Libr., Columbia, Tenn., 1982; tchr. Lewis County Mid. Sch., Hohenwald, 1982-85; libr. Lewis County High Sch., Hohenwald, 1985—; sponsor Future Tchrs. of Am., Hohenwald, 1991—. Mem. Profl. Educators Tenn., Tenn. Libr. Assn., Am. Quilters Soc.

BAXTER, DUBY YVONNE, government official; b. El Campo, Tex., July 21, 1953; d. Ray Eugene and Hazel Evelyn (Roades) Allenson; m. Loran Richard Baxter, April 7, 1979. Student, Alvin Jr. Coll., 1971, Tex. Tech U., 1972; cert. legal sec., Alaska Bus. Coll., 1974; student, Alaska Pacific U., 1981, Anchorage Community Coll., 1981-85, U. Santa Clara, 1982-83; BBA in Mgmt. cum laude, U. Alaska, Anchorage, 1985. Sr. office assoc., legal sec. Municipality of Anchorage, 1975-78; exec. sec. Security Nat. Bank, Anchorage, 1978-80, Alaska Renewable Resources Corp., Anchorage, 1980-82; pers. mgmt. specialist Dept. of Army, Ft. Richardson, Alaska, 1986-87; pers. mgmt. specialist, position classification specialist 10th Mtn. Div. (Light) Civilian Pers. Office, Ft. Drum, N.Y., 1987-89; pers. mgmt. specialist Civilian Pers. Office Alaska Dist. U.S. Army C.E., Anchorage, 1989-90; position classification specialist Civilian Pers. Office, 6th Inf. Divsn. (Light)-USA Garrison, Ft. Richardson, Alaska, 1990-91; position mgmt. and classification specialist 11th AF Cen. Civilian Personnel Office, Elmendorf AFB, Alaska, 1991-93; position classification specialist U.S. Army C.E., Anchorage, 1994—; small bus. owner, 1994—; by-laws com. mem. spl. emphasis program Fed. Women's Program, Ft. Richardson, 1986-87; instr. Prevention of Sexual Harassment, Ft. Richardson, 1986-87. Contbr. Alaska Repertoire Theater, Anchorage, 1982-87; leader Awana Christian Youth Orgn., Anchorage, 1985-87; ch. treas. Watertown (N.Y.) Bible Brethren Ch., 1988-89; mission bd. mem. Anchorage Grace Brethren Ch., 1991-92. Mem. NAFE, Classification and Compensation Soc., Missions Bd., U. Alaska Alumni Assn., Bernese Mountain Dog Club, Safari Club Internat., N.Am. Hunting Club, Concerned Women for Am. Office: USACE CENPA-HR PO Box 898 Anchorage AK 99510-0898

BAXTER, MEREDITH, actress; b. Los Angeles, June 21, 1947; d. Tom and Whitney (Blake) Baxter; m. David Birney, Apr. 10, 1974 (div. 1989); children: Ted, Eva, Kate, Peter and Mollie (twins). Student, Interlochen Arts Acad., Mich. Actress (films) including Ben, 1972, Stand Up and Be Counted, 1972, Bittersweet Love, 1976, All the President's Men, 1976, The November Plan, 1976, (TV movies) The Cat Creature, 1973, The Stranger Who Looks Like Me, 1974, The Imposter, 1975, The Night That Panicked America, 1975, Target Risk, 1975, Little Women, 1978, The Family Man, 1979, Beulah Land, 1980, The Two Lives of Carol Letner, 1981, Take Your Best Shot, 1982, Family Ties Vacation, 1985, The Rape of Richard Beck, 1985, Kate's Secret, 1986, The Long Journey Home, 1987, Winnie, 1988, She Knows Too Much, 1989, Jezebel's Kiss, 1990, The Kissing Place, 1990, Burning Bridges, 1990, A Bump in the Night, 1991, A Mother's Justice, 1991, A Woman Scorned: The Betty Broderick Story, 1992, The Betty Broderick Story: Part 2, 1992, (also exec. prodr.) Darkness Before Dawn, 1993, My Breast, 1994, One More Mountain, 1994, For the Love of Aaron, 1994; (plays) Guys and Dolls, Talley's Folley, Butterflies are Free, Varieties; star (TV series) Bridget Loves Bernie, 1972-73, Family, 1976-80, Family Ties, 1982-89; (TV spls.) Vanities, 1981, Missing...Have You Seen This Person?, 1985, Diabetes Update, 1986, Other Mothers, 1993, TV's Funniest Families, 1994; other TV appearances include The Interns, Police Woman, Medical Story, City of Angels, McMillan and Wife, The Streets of San Francisco. Mem. Am. Diabetes Assn. Office: care William Morris Agency 151 El Camino Beverly Hills CA 90212*

BAXTER, MILLIE MCLEAN, business owner, educator; b. Denver, Mar. 14, 1926; d. Stanley Allan and Jessie (Brown) McL.; m. Glenn A. Hettler, Dec. 28, 1949 (div. Mar. 1969); children: Douglass Kent, Linda Horn, Joni Birdsall; m. Jack Stanley Baxter, Feb. 4, 1977; children: David, Fred. Grad., Dickenson Bus. Sch., 1944; student, U. Colo., 1944-46; grad., McConnell Modeling Sch., 1946, Jones Real Estate Coll., 1971. With sales and mktg. The Arnold Corp., Denver, 1973-84; broker, mgr. Evergreen (Colo.) Properties, 1984-87; broker, owner Century 21 Evergreen Real Estate, 1987-92; ind. mgr. Real Estate Tng. Ctr., Evergreen, 1987-91; personal life history tchr. Sr. Resource Ctr., Evergreen, 1992—; distbr. Bay Formula D Products, Evergreen, 1993—; vol. computer instr. for srs., 1991—. Author: How to Write Your Life History for a Family Legacy, 1994. Mem. Denver Bd. Realtors (Salesperson of Yr. 1978), Denver Brokers Council, Evergreen Bd. Realtors, Jefferson County Bd. Realtors, Sales and Mktg. Council (Salesperson of Yr. 1979, Golden Medallion award 1978, 79, 80, 81, 82, 83). Republican. Office: Bax Products Inc PO Box 733 Evergreen CO 80439

BAYARD, SUSAN SHAPIRO, educator, small business owner; b. Boston, Dec. 26, 1942; d. Morris Arnold and Hester Muriel (Blatt) Shapiro; m. Edward Quint Bayard, Jan. 4, 1969; children: Jeffrey David, Lucy Quint. BA, Syracuse U., 1964; MA, U. Calif., Berkeley, 1966; Cert. Advanced Grad. Study, Boston U., 1984. Rsch. chemist Harvard Med. Sch., Boston, 1966; asst. scientist Polaroid Corp., Cambridge, Mass., 1966-67; instr. Boston U., 1968-70, Wheelock Coll., Boston, 1978-81; chmn. sci. dept. Tower Sch., Marblehead, Mass., 1981-85; dir., owner Bayard Learning Ctr., Marblehead, 1985—; vis. lectr. Salem State Coll., 1994—; ednl. cons./workshop facilitator Swampscott (Mass.) Pub. Schs., Lynn (Mass.) Pub. Schs., Salem (Mass.) State Coll., 1986-91; instr./cons. N.E. Consortium, North Andover, Mass., 1986—. Mem. Town Mtg., Swampscott, 1988—, Supt. Screening Com., Swampscott, 1987, Mass. Ednl. TV Prog. Selection Com., 1979-87, Sch. Improvement Coun., Swampscott, 1988-89, Curriculum Evaluation Com., Swampscott, 1978-80. Grantee NSF, Syracuse U., 1962, 64; named Outstanding Woman Grad. Student, Boston U. Women's Guild, 1977. Mem. Nat. Sci. Tchrs.'s Assn., Pi Lambda Theta. Jewish. Office: Bayard Learning Ctr PO Box 604 Swampscott MA 01907

BAYLES, MARJORIE LOUISE, nurse; b. Winchester, Ky., June 3, 1943; d. Bernie Lee Burns Jr. and Mary Katherine Parker Richardson; m. Othal Ray Watts (div. 1970); children: Anthony Ray, Alan Eugene, Teressa Kaye, Darin Scott, James Clay; m. Michael Dale Bayles (dec. 1990). Diploma in Nursing, Fanshawe Coll. Sch. Nursing, London, Ont., 1983. Staff/charge nurse palliative care and rehab. medicine St. Mary's Hosp., London, 1983-84; staff nurse Paramed Health Care, London, 1983-85; orthopaedic/gynecologic staff nurse Univ. Hosp. at U. Western Ont., London, 1984-85; charge nurse for hosp./emergency rm. dept. Lake Butler Hosp. and Hand Surgery Ctr., Lake Butler, Fla., 1985-87; charge nurse spinal cord injury unit/orthopaedics Univ. Hosp., Jacksonville, Fla., 1987-88; staff nurse and temp. charge Shands Teaching Hosp., Gainesville, Fla., 1986-88; charge nurse emergency Tallahassee Meml. Hosp., 1988-92, charge nurse/coord. pediatric emergency, 1992—; staff devel. coord. Arbors at Tallahassee, 1994—. Mem. ANA, Trauma Nurse Corps. Baptist. Home: 1755 Brookside Blvd Tallahassee FL 32301-6769 Office: Arbors at Tallahassee 1560 Phillips Rd Tallahassee FL 32301

BAYNARD, MILDRED MOYER (MRS. ROBERT S. BAYNARD), civic worker, corporate executive; b. Lincoln, Nebr., May 10, 1902; d. Charles Calvin and Flora (Harter) Moyer; m. Robert S. Baynard, May 24, 1927; 1 child, Lester B. Student, Sullins Coll., 1921, U. So. Calif., 1922; BA, U. Nebr., 1925. Tchr. pub. schs., Lincoln, 1926-27, Crescent City, Fla., 1925-26; sec. Venice Land Co., Inc., 1949-69; sec. Fla. Bridge Co., 1960-68; ptnr. Ind. Parking, 1965-72; v.p. Venice-Nokomis Bank, Venice, Fla., 1947-62, bd. dirs., 1947-62; pres. Venice Land Co., 1969-72. Mem. editorial adv. bd. Florida Lives. Mem. Fla. State Dist. Welfare Bd., 1948-52; pres. bd. dirs. YWCA, 1953-56; Fla. chmn. Nat. Soc. Prevention Blindness, 1957-60, bd. dirs., 1960-67, v.p., 1963-66; nat. v.p., pres. Fla. affiliate Nat. Soc. to Prevent Blindness, 1958-64, v.p., 1967-68, also mem. Fla. exec. com., hon. life mem., hon. bd. dirs., exec. com. Fla. affiliate, 1983-85; bd. dir. Ctr. for Blind, 1956; pres. Suncoast div. Arthritis Found. Inc., 1966-67; pres. North Ward PTA, 1938; mem. Heritage Found., Rep. Nat. Com., The Conservative Caucus, Inc., Nat. Rep. Senatorial Com., sec. St. Petersburg (Fla.) Woman's Club, 1945-46; mem. St. Margaret's Guild, St. Thomas Episcopal Ch., St. Petersburg; trustee St. Petersburg Jr. Coll. Devel. Found., Inc., 1984-94; Dem. precinct committeewoman, 1936. Recipient Outstanding Citizen's award Pinellas County Commn., 1964, Cable award, 1964, Shield award, 1973, Sarah Schwab Deutsch award, 1978, Women of Yr. award St. Peterburg Panhellenic, 1987. Mem. St. Petersburg Hist. Soc., Mus. Fine Arts, Fla. Suncoast Opera Guild (sustaining 1989), All Childrens Hosp. Guild, U. Neb. Alumni Assn., Nat. Taxpayers Union, DAR., St. Petersburg Bar Aux., Delta Gamma (province officer 1950-56, conv. chmn. 1964, house corp. 1969-70, hon. fellow found. 1974), Sorosis Club, Yacht Club of St. Petersburg, Panhellenic, Women's Club, Interlock (sec. 1942-44), Venice Nokomis Woman's (life), Women of Rotary (pres. Venice chpt. 1962), Women of Rotary (St. Petersburg). Home: 627 Brightwaters Blvd NE Saint Petersburg FL 33704-3715

BAYNE, KATHRYN ANN LOUISE, veterinarian; b. Santa Monica, Calif., Feb. 4, 1959; d. Richard Harry and Loretta Mary (Kennedy) B.; m. Mark Cofer Haines, May 19, 1990. BS cum laude, Calif. State Poly. U., 1979; MS, Wash. State U., 1982, PhD, 1986, DVM, 1987. Vet. behaviorist NIH, Bethesda, Md., 1987-94; assoc. dir for accreditation (inactive res.) Am. Assn. for the Accreditation of Lab. Animal Care, Rockville, Md., 1994—; cons. in field. Inventor in field; author publs. in field. Comdr. USPHS. Mem. Am. Vet. Med. Assn., Animal Behavior Soc., Commd. Officers Assn., Res. Officers Assn., Am. Soc. Lab. Animal Practitioners. Office: AAACAC Ste 1211 11300 Rockville Pike Rockville MD 20852-3035

BAZIN, NANCY TOPPING, English language educator; b. Pitts., Nov. 5, 1934; d. Frank Williamson Topping and Helen Luther Arnold Wilson; m. Maurice Jacques Bazin, Dec. 21, 1958 (div. 1978); children: Michel Francois, Christine Nicole; m. Robert Eliot Reardon, Jan. 4, 1992. BA, Ohio Wesleyan U., 1956; MA, Middlebury Grad. Sch. French, 1958; PhD, Stanford U., 1969; postgrad., Inst. Higher Edn. Adminstrn., 1977. Asst. prof. English Rutgers U., New Brunswick, N.J., 1970-77; dir. women's studies U. Pitts., 1977-78; assoc. prof. English and women's studies Old Dominion U., Norfolk, Va., 1978-84, dir. women's studies, 1978-85, chair dept. English, 1985-89, prof. English and women's studies, 1984—; manuscript reader for various publs.; exch. faculty lectr. U. Rabat, Morocco; vis. scholar Inst. for Advanced Studies, Ind. U., Bloomington, 1994. Author: Virginia Woolf and the Androgynous Vision, 1973; co-editor: Conversations with Nadine Gordimer, 1990; contbr. articles to various jours., essays to books in field. Recipient Outstanding Faculty award State Coun. for Higher Edn. in Va., 1994; Ball Bros. Rsch. Found. fellow, 1994; Resident fellowship Va. Ctr. for the Humanities, 1995. Mem. MLA (v.p. women's caucus 1978-81), South Atlantic MLA, Nat. Women Studies Assn., African Lit. Assn., Nat. Coun. Tchrs. English, Phi Beta Kappa, Phi Kappa Phi, Sigma Tau Delta, Kappa Delta Pi (mortar bd.). Democrat. Home: 4005 Gosnold Ave Norfolk VA 23508-2917 Office: Old Dominion U Dept English Norfolk VA 23529-0078

BEACH, DOROTHY RIGDON, university counselor, educator; b. Bklyn., Sept. 24, 1933; d. Lynn Shafer and Mary Estelle (Marine) Rigdon; m. Eugene Hamilton Beach, Oct. 9, 1967; children: Daryl S. Mattson, Dana L. Emery. BA, U. S. Fla., 1970, MA, 1972; EdD, Nova U., 1975. Lic. mental health counselor. Univ. counselor, asst. prof. U. South Fla., Tampa, 1972-93, dir., responsible conduct of rsch. projects, 1993—. Author: Two For the Money, 1981. Bd. dirs., pres. Ctr. for Women, Tampa, 1979-80; bd. dirs. The Children's Home, Inc., Tampa, 1979-81. Mem. The Athena Soc. (pres. 1978-79), Campus Episcopal Ministry (trustee 1991-92). Home: 814 Lutz Lake Fern Rd W Lutz FL 33549-5027 Office: Fowler Ave Tampa FL 33620

BEACH, LINDA MARIE, total quality management professional; b. Washington, May 5, 1949; d. Robert L. and Agnes I. (O'Brien) B.; m. Robert L. Riley; 1 child, Grace. AAS in Bus. and Mktg. cum laude, No. Va. Community Coll., 1973; BA cum laude, Luther Rice Coll., 1975; MBPA, Southeastern U., 1977; DBA, Pacific Western U., 1988. Computer systems adminstr. Def. Mapping Agy., Brookmont, Md., 1967-80; mgr. methods and procedures Bur. Nat. Affairs, Inc., Washington, 1980-82; quality and reliability engr. Gen. Electric, Arlington, Va., 1982; sr. product assurance engr. Fairchild Industries, Germantown, Md., 1982-84, CIT-ALCATEL, Reston, Va., 1984-86; software product assurance mgr. Contel, Fairfax, Va., 1986-87; group leader quality engring. Software Productivity Consortium, Reston, 1987-89; dir. quality assurance NYMA, Inc., Greenbelt, Md., 1989—; product mgr. P4, Inc., Sterling, Va., 1989-92; instr. Learning Tress Internat., Vienna, Va., 1988-92; assoc. prof. No. Va. C.C., Sterling, 1984-89. Contbg. editor Info. Mgmt., 1983-85. Mem. IEEE, Am. Soc. for Quality Control, Assn. for Computing Machinery, Internat. Test and Evaluation. Home: 1704 Plane Tree Way Bowie MD 20721-3019 Office: NYMA Inc 7501 Greenway Center Dr Greenbelt MD 20770-3514

BEACH, MILDRED A., state legislator; b. Wolfeboro, Mar. 2, 1924. Degree, U. N.H. Mem. Air Resources Coun., 1979-92, vice chair 1984-90; mem. Wolfeboro Bd. of Adjustment, 1980-92, vice chair 1984-90; pres. N.H. Travel Coun., 1986-88; dir. N.H. Hospitality Assn., 1987-90; Laconia adv. mem. N.H. Vocat. Tech. Coll., 1986-90; mem. N.H. Joint Promotion Program Matching Grants, 1985-92. Home: PO Box 696 Wolfeboro NH 03894-0696 Office: NH Ho of Reps State Capitol Concord NH 03301*

BEADERSTADT, ANDREA ANGLIN, journalism educator; b. Detroit, Feb. 11, 1949; d. Hartley Raymond and Margaret Mary (Ward) Anglin; m. John Henry Beaderstadt, Dec. 22, 1977; children: Matthew Geoffrey, Christopher Erik. BA in Journalism magna cum laude, Wayne State U., 1970; MA in Print Communications, Am. U., Washington, 1971. Legis. asst. Rep. Martha W. Griffiths, Mich., 1971-74; legis. specialist LWV, Washington, 1974-75; legis. asst. Rep. James V. Stanton, Ohio, 1976-77; instr. Ferris State Coll., Big Rapids, Mich., 1977-78; dir. Small World, Inc., Kodiak, Alaska, 1980-81; personnel asst. USCG, Kodiak, 1981-82; copy editor The Anchorage Times, 1982-83; asst. prof. St. Michael's Coll., Winooski, Vt., 1983-89; with English dept. SUNY, Plattsburgh, 1989—; reporter The Alaska Fisherman mag., Juneau, 1980; del. Ctr. for Study Can., Northeast and Mid. Atlantic Conf. Can. Studies. Bd. dirs. Vt. Woman, 1988-90. Research fellow St. Michael's Coll. Ctr. for Advancement of Pvt. Higher Edn., Japan, 1987. Mem. Nat. Fedn. Press Women, Nat. Newspaper Assn., Am. Coun. Que. Studies, New Eng. Press Assn. (writing coach), New Eng. Newspaper Assn., Vt. Press Assn. (sec. 1984-89), Women in Communication. Lutheran. Home: RR 2 Box 153E Alburg VT 05440 Office: SUNY English Dept Valley Hall 216 Champlain Dr Plattsburgh NY 12901-6055

BEAL, DONNA LEE, association executive; b. Ticonderoga, N.Y., Aug. 22, 1952; d. Donald Lee and Beverley Ann (Burlow) McIntyre; m. Allan Grant Beal, July 15, 1972; children: Andrew, Alison. Assoc., Pierce Coll. for Women, 1972. Office mgr. Med.-Family Practice, Hamilton, N.Y., 1972-74, Gen. Dentistry, Westport, N.Y., 1978-84; sec. The Adirondack Coun., Elizabethtown, N.Y., 1984-85, adminstrv. asst., 1985-86, adminstr., 1986-89, acting co-dir., 1989, adminstr., dir. membership, CFO, 1990-94; adminstr. Ecologically Sustainable Devel., Inc., Elizabethtown, 1994—; treas. Environ. Fedn. N.Y., Albany, 1991-94, vice chair Adirondack Centennial Com., Paul Smiths, N.Y., 1990-92; project dir. Conf. Mng. Growth and Devel. in Unique, Natural Settings, Elizabethtown, 1990. Vice chmn. Essex County Sch. Bds. Assn., 1986; bd. dirs. Depot Theatre, Westport, 1988-94, Champlain Health Concerns, Mineville, N.Y., 1980; mem. bd. edn. Westport Ctrl. Sch., 1982-86; mem. pastoral rels. com. Westport Federated Ch., 1990-91. Republican. Office: Ecologically Sustaining Devel Inc PO Box 848 2 Church St Elizabethtown NY 12932

BEAL, ILENE, bank executive. BA, Wellesley Coll., 1967. Mgmt. trainee Nat. Shawmut Bank, Boston, 1967-71; from asst. sec. to exec. v.p. BayBanks, Inc., Boston, 1972—; successively asst. v.p., v.p., sr. v.p. BayBanks, Inc., now exec. v.p., sec., clk. Office: BayBanks Inc 175 Federal St Boston MA 02110-2210

BEAL, JUDITH MAGNUSON, counselor; b. Lancaster, Ohio, Jan. 5, 1941; d. Paul LeBlonde and Mary Mildred (Englander) Magnuson; m. Ronald M. Beal, June 6, 1962; children: Kimberly C., Deron M. BS, Ohio State U., 1963; MEd, Ohio U., 1978. Lic. profl. clin. counselor, Ohio; cert. clin. mental health counselor Nat. Acad. Mental Health Counselors; nat. cert. coun. Nat. Bd. Cert. Counselors Inc. Outpatient therapist and coord. clin. svcs. Fairfield Family Counseling Ctr., Lancaster, 1978-93; clin. counselor Lancaster, 1982—. Bd. dirs., com. chmn. Lancaster-Fairfield Community Hosp., Lancaster, 1986-92 pres.-elect Ctr. for Visually Impaired, Lancaster, 1992—; nominating com. and elder, First Presbyn. Ch., Lancaster, 1992—. Mem. Ohio Mental Health Counseling Assn. (v.p., chmn. confs. 1989, pres. 1990, Outstanding Mental Health Counselor award 1992), Am. Counseling Assn., Am. Mental Health Counselors Assn., Ohio State Alumni Assn. (sec. 1984), Ohio Counseling Assn. (chair ethics com. 1992-93). Office: 1611 Tiki Ln Lancaster OH 43130-8729

BEAL, SARAH ALLEN, art gallery administrator, artist; b. Huntington, W.Va., July 26, 1959; d. Lander Lowell and Sue (Beckwith) B.; m. Larry A. Oyster, Dec. 1988 (div. Nov. 1993); 1 child, Chris. Student, Marshall U., 1980; BA, Marietta Coll., 1982. Tchr. art St. Joseph High Sch., Huntington, 1983-84; sales rep., head poster div. Posner Gallery, Milw., 1984-86; art reach coord. Huntington Mus. Art, 1987-88, dir. exhbn. 280 honors fellowship program, 1988-90, instr. painting, 1988-89; owner, dir., instr. painting Young People's Art Studio, Huntington, 1991—; owner, co-mgr. Beal Gallery, Huntington, 1993—; lectr. Huntington High Sch., 1989, Ft. Gay (W.Va.) Mid. Sch., 1989, Buffalo High Sch., Kenova, W.Va., 1990, Barboursville (W.Va.) Mid. Sch., 1993. Exhibited in group shows W.Va. U. Mountainlair Gallery, Morgantown, 1988, Ohio U. So. Br. Collins Ctr., Ironton, 1989, Cultural Ctr., Charleston, W.Va., 1989, Paramount Art Ctr., Ashland, Ky., 1991, Roanoke Coll. Soyer Gallery, Salem, Va., 1991, Studio 602, Charleston, 1992, Gallery 41, New Boston, Ohio, 1993; represented in permanent collection VA Chaplain Sch., Hampton, Va. Mem. Huntington Main Street. Chosen to participate in New Masters Program, Huntington Mus. Art, 1988, 89, 90. Home: 3049 Wallace Cir Huntington WV 25705-1624 Office: 919 4th Ave Huntington WV 25701-1408

BEAL, WINONA ROARK, retired church administrator; b. Birchwood, Tenn., Aug. 11, 1924; d. Thomas Jefferson and Minnie Belle (Price) Roark; m. Charles Hugh Beal, Aug. 6, 1949; children: Jeremy Lawrence, Eric David. BS in Bus. Adminstrn., Tenn. Tech. U., 1948; postgrad., So. Bapt. Theol. Sem., 1950-54, U. Louisville, 1951-53, Manatee Community Coll., 1958-60. Tchr. Washington (Ga.) High Sch., 1948-50; asst. to treas. So. Bapt. Theol. Sem., Louisville, Ky., 1951-54; asst. to bus. mgr. Agnes Scott Coll., Decatur, Ga., 1968-71; religious edn. dir. Bay Haven Bapt. Ch., Sarasota, Fla., 1976-84, office program dir., 1985-89; ret., 1989; spiritual guide, dir. Bay Haven Elem. Sch., Sarasota, 1965-68; mem. Sapphire Stores-Indian Beach Assn., Sarasota, 1985-94, State Bd. Missions, Fla. Bapt. Conv., 1993-95, mem. program com., 1993-94. Mem. S.W. Fla. Bapt. Assn. (exec. com. 1976-89, dir. Vacation Bible Sch. 1976-89, student work 1976-80), S.W. Manatee Assn. (pres. of Metochai), Pastors Wives of S.W. Fla. Assn. (pres. 1972, 80, 84-89), Fla. Pastors' Wives Conf. (v.p. 1975, program chair 1979, sec.-treas. 1983, conf. historian 1983). Democrat. Home: 638 Beverly Dr Sarasota FL 34234-2706

BEALE, BETTY (MRS. GEORGE K. GRAEBER), columnist; b. Washington; d. William Lewis and Edna (Sims) B.; m. George Kenneth Graeber, Feb. 15, 1969. A.B., Smith Coll. Columnist, Washington Post, 1937-40; reporter and columnist Washington Evening Star, 1945-81; weekly columnist North Am. Syndicate (formerly Field Newspaper Syndicate), 1953-89; ret., 1989; lectr. in field. Author: Power at Play: A Memoir of Parties, Politicians and The Presidents in My Bedroom, 1993. Recipient Freedom Found. award, 1969, named Woman of Distinction, 1987. Address: 2926 Garfield St NW Washington DC 20008-3536

BEALE, GEORGIA ROBISON, historian; b. Chgo., Mar. 14, 1905; d. Henry Barton and Dora Belle (Sledd) Robison; m. Howard Kennedy Beale, Jan. 2, 1942; children: Howard Kennedy, Henry Barton Robison, Thomas Wight. AB, U. Chgo., 1926, AM, 1928; PhD, Columbia U., 1938; student Sorbonne and Coll. de France, 1930-34. Reader in history U. Chgo., 1927-29; lectr. Barnard Coll., 1937-38; instr. Bklyn. Coll., 1937-39; asst. prof. Hollins (Va.) Coll., 1939-41, Wellesley Coll., 1941-42, Castleton (Vt.) State Coll., 1968-70; vis. assoc. prof. U. Ky., Lexington, 1970-72; professorial lectr. George Washington U., 1983-84. Author: Revelliere-lépeaux, Citizen Director, 1938, 72, Academies to Institut, 1973, Bosc and the Exequatur, 1978; contbg. author Historical Dictionary of the French Revolution, 1985; also articles. Mem. Madison (Wis.) Civic Music Assn. and Madison Symphony Orch. League, 1958—; hon. trustee Culver-Stockton Coll., 1974—. Univ. fellow Columbia U., 1929-30. Mem. AAUW (European fellow 1930-31), Am., So. hist. assns., Soc. French Hist. Studies, Western Soc. French History (hon. mem. exec. council), Am., Brit. socs. 18th century studies, Phi Beta Kappa, Pi Lambda Theta, Phi Alpha Theta, Pi Kappa Delta. Clubs: Reid Hall (Paris); Brit. Univ. Women's (London). Office: The Ridge Orford NH 03777 also: 2816 Columbia Rd Madison WI 53705-2259 also: 110 D St SE Washington DC 20003-1821

BEALE, JOAN RAILEY, psychotherapist; b. Franklin, Va., July 23, 1951; d. Richard Edward and Hazel Joyner (Bradshaw) Railey; m. John Milton Beale, Nov. 26, 1976 (div. Sept. 1991); 1 child, Juliette Faircloth. BA, U. N.C., 1973; MEd in Emotional Distubrance, U. Va., 1976; MEd in Agy. Counseling, Coll. William and Mary, 1992. Grad. student U. Va., Charlottesville, 1974-76; instrnl. supr. Idlewood Schs., Franklin, Va., 1976-78; psychoednl. therapist Franklin Pub. Schs., 1978-79; counselor James Camp, YMCA, Franklin, 1979-80; youth community advisor Episcopal Diocese So. Va., Norfolk, 1980-87; coord. outreach svcs., crisis counselor YWCA of South Hampton Roads, Norfolk, 1988-91; pride in parenting facilitator Child Abuse Prevention Svcs., Norfolk, 1990-92; coord. sexual assault svcs. CONTACT Peninsula, Inc., Newport News, Va., 1992—; freelance liturgical clown and counselor, 1985-89. Bd. dirs. Va. Against Domestic Violence, Richmond, 1989-91, Va. Aligned Against Sexual Assault, 1993—; mem. Hampton Roads Com. for Prevention Chil Abuse, Norfolk, 1989—, Child Sexual Abuse Task Force, Newport News, 1993—. Mem. ACA, NOW, Am. Profl. Soc. Child Abuse, Found. for Shamanic Studies. Democrat. Home: 307 Bay Tree Beach Rd Seaford VA 23696-2673 Office: CONTACT Peninsula Inc 6901 Huntington Ave Newport News VA 23607

BEALL, INGRID LILLEHEI, lawyer; b. Cedar Falls, Iowa, June 18, 1926; d. Ingebrigt Larsen and Olive (Allison) Lillehei; m. George Brooke Beall, Dec. 21, 1951 (div. 1971). A.B., U. Chgo., 1945, M.A., 1948, J.D., 1956. Bar: Ill. 1956. Assoc. firm McDermott, Will & Emery, Chgo., 1956-58, Baker & McKenzie, Chgo., 1958-61; ptnr. Baker & McKenzie, Chgo., Brussels and Paris, 1961—. Mem. ABA, Ill. Bar Assn., Chgo. Bar Assn. Home: 175 E Delaware Pl Chicago IL 60611-1756 Office: Baker & McKenzie 1 Prudential Plz 130 W Randolph Dr Chicago IL 60601

BEALL, JOANNA MAY, painter; b. Chgo., Aug. 17, 1935; d. Lester Thomas and Dorothy Welles (Miller) B.; student Yale U. Sch. Fine Arts, 1953-57, Art Inst. Chgo., 1957; m. H.C. Westermann, Mar. 31, 1959. One-man shows include: Great Bldg. Crack-Up Gallery, N.Y.C., 1973, James Corcoran Gallery, Los Angeles, 1974, Gallery Rebecca Cooper, Washington, 1975; group shows: Allan Frumkin, Chgo., 1960, 61, Whitney Mus., N.Y.C., 1973, Art Inst. Chgo., 1976, Univ. Galleries, Los Angeles, 1979, Xavier Fourcade, N.Y.C., 1980, 85; vis. artist U. Colo., Boulder, 1979, 84. Mem. Artists Equity Assn., Visual Artists and Galleries Assn. Article The World of Joanna Beall (Melinda Wortz) appeared in Art Week mag., 1974. Home: PO Box 5028 Brookfield CT 06804-5028

BEALL, JULIANNE, librarian; b. Portland, Oreg., July 16, 1946; d. Marsh Flagg and Ruth Gildersleeve (Large) B.; m. William Tobin Amatruda, Jan. 6, 1979. BA, Lewis & Clark Coll., 1967; PhD in English Lit., UCLA, 1974, MLS, 1977. Decimal classification specialist Libr. of Congress, Washington, 1977-86, asst. editor Dewey decimal classification, 1986—. Prin. author: DDC 004-006 Data Processing and Computer Science, 1985; asst. editor: Dewey Decimal Classification, 20th edit., 1989, Abridged Dewey Decimal Classification, 12th edit., 1990. UCLA fellow, 1967-70. Mem. ALA, Spl. Librs. Assn., Internat. Fedn. Libr. Assns. and Instns. (affiliate), Beta Phi Mu. Home: 9506 St Andrews Way Silver Spring MD 20901-3259 Office: Libr of Congress Decimal Classification Div Washington DC 20540-4330

BEALL, PAMELA HONN, psychological consultant; b. Mattoon, Ill., Mar. 24, 1955; d. Kenneth Franklin and Dorothy Marie (Linder) Honn; m. Thomas Allen Beall IV, June 23, 1985; children: Christopher Allen, Brittany Alane. BS in Psychology, Evangel Coll., Springfield, Mo., 1976; MS in Edn., Ea. Ill. U., Charleston, 1979. Nat. cert. counselor. Community care coord. East Ctrl. Ill. Area Agy. on Aging, Bloomington, 1979-80; outpatient therapist Iroquois Mental Health Ctr., Watseka, Ill., 1981-86, 90-91, cons., part-time outpatient therapist, 1987-89, 91-93; program psychologist Paxaton (Ill.) Community Hosp., 1986-87; coord. good beginnings program Ctr. for Children's Svcs., Danville, Ill., 1987-88; psychol. cons., Milford, Ill., 1993—; instr. psychology Kankakee (Ill.) C.C., 1981-84, 89, Danville Area C.C., 1983-86; cons. evaluator Dept. Rehab. Svcs., Danville, 1981-85; mem. exec. bd. Tgn. and Edn. Coordinating Com., Champaign, Ill., 1985-93. Tchr. religion Milford Christian Ch., 1992-93, soloist, mem. mus. team, 1993; vol. reading programs sch. sys., Milford. Mem. ACA, Ill. Assn. Mental Health Counselors, Evangel Coll. Alumni Assn. Home: RR 3 Box 52D Milford IL 60953

BEALS, ANN TALCOTT, author, publisher; b. Louisville, Aug. 24, 1927; d. Harry Summrell and Julia Jeannette (Talcott) Smith; m. Robert Louis Beals, June 11, 1949 (div. Nov. 1986); children: Charles Louis, John Robert. Student, Washington U., 1945-48. Christian Sci. practitioner Christian Sci. Ch., Sharon, Mass., 1968-74; pub., founder Bookmark, Pasadena, Santa Clarita, Calif., 1980—. Author: (booklet) Animal Magnetism, 1974, (book) Crisis in Christian Science Church, 1979, others. Office: Bookmark PO Box 801143 Santa Clarita CA 91380-1143

BEALS, NANCY FARWELL, state legislator; b. El Paso, July 21, 1938; d. Fred Whitcomb and Katharine Doane (Pier) Farwell; m. Richard William Beals, June 30, 1962; children: Katharine, Robert, Susannah. BA in Polit. Sci., Bryn Mawr Coll., 1960; MA in Teaching, Harvard U., 1961. Gropu leader Exptl. Internat. Living, Putney, Vt.; jr. high sch. tchr. Wincehster (Mass.) Pub. Schs., 1961-62; high sch. tchr. Hamden (Conn.) Pub. Schs., 1962-64; state rep. Conn. Gen. Assembly, Hartford, 1993—. Mem. various local and regional offices PTA, Chgo. and Hamden, 1970-83; local pres., state bd. dirs. LWV, Conn., 1979-82; mem., sec., chmn. Hamden Bd. Edn., 1983-92. Recipient Citizenship award for Conn. Philip Morris Corp., 1992, Hamden Notable award Friends of Hamden Libr., 1986; named Legislator of Yr. Conn. Libr. Assn., 1994. Democrat.

BEAM, JOANNA MCKEE, lawyer; b. Palo Alto, Calif., Mar. 3, 1948; d. A. Walter and Mary Kathryn (Helmers) B.; m. Peter Van Arsdale, June 30, 1990. BA, U. Wis., 1970; JD, Santa Clara U., 1974. Bar: Calif. 1975, U.S. Dist. Ct. (no. dist.) Calif. 1975. Atty. Katz, Cole & Beam, San Jose, Calif., 1974-76, Office of State Wide Health Planning & Devel., Sacramento, 1977-80; dep. atty. gen. Dept. Justice, State of Calif., Sacramento, 1980-83; univ. counsel U. Calif., Oakland, 1983—; negotiator Office of Gov., Sacramento, 1983. Fund raiser Breast Cancer Rsch. Fund U. Calif., San Francisco, 1993—. Mem. State Bar Calif., Am. Academy and Hosp. Attys. Office: U Calif Office Gen Counsel 300 Lakeside Dr 7th Fl Oakland CA 94612

BEAMAN, MARGARINE GAYNELL, scrap metal broker; b. Feb. 26; d. Margaret Lena Geisweidt; m. Robert W. Beaman; children: Richard Beaman, Ronald Beaman, Lorene Barrera, Jessica Barrera, Vincent Thompson. Student, U. Houston, U. Mich. Pres. Beaman Metal Co., Inc., Austin, 1972—; pres. Beaman Acctg. and Cons., Austin, 1975—. Bd. dirs., pres. Ctrl. East Austin Community Orgn.; bd. dirs. Austin Resource for Ind. Living, City of Austin/Travis County Pvt. Industry Coun.; vol. Juveniles in Jail, Women Prisoners, Old Bakery; vol. tax preparer VITA, TCE; founder project for ind. living for blind; fund raiser Austin Crime Stoppers; Brailled and installed 1st ATM Braille Instrns. in U.S.; chair task force on equity and displaced homemakers Austin C.C., chair equity and non-traditional task force; mem. Tex. Adv. Com. gender equity and non-traditional jobs. Recipient Gov.'s Vol. of Yr. award, 1982, Mayor's Meritorious award, 1982, Svc. awards Sertoma Club, N.Y. Am. Coun. of Blind, Nat. Community Schs. award, Citizen Leadership award Freedom Found. at Valley Forge, 1986, Migel Medal award Am. Found. for Blind N.Y.C., 1992; inducted into Tex. Assn. Pvt. Colls. Hall of Fame, Austin Women's Hall of Fame; named Outstanding Blind Worker of Tex., 1982, Most Worthy Citizen of Austin, 1989, Austin's Most Worthy Citizen, 1989; numerous other awards. Mem. Tex. Fedn. Bus. and Profl. Women's Clubs, Exec. Women Internat. (past state pres.), Zonta Internat., Cert. Consumer Credit Execs., Nat. Assn. Fin. Aid Adminstrs., Austin C. of C., Austin Women's C. of C., Gen. Fedn. Women's Club, Pvt. Industry Coun., Am. Coun. of Blind. Home: 1406 Wilshire Blvd Austin TX 78722-1129 Office: 3409 E 5th St Austin TX 78702-4911

BEAMER, BETSY DAVIS, state official; b. Charleston, W.Va., Feb. 6, 1959; d. Donald Dallas and Laura (Steward) Davis; m. James William Beamer; Aug. 1, 1992. BA in Journalism, Radford U., 1981. News reporter Va. Leader, Pearlsburg, 1980-81, News Gazette, Lexington, Va., 1982; program coord. Muscular Dystrophy Assn., Roanoke, Va., 1983; fin. dir. Stafford for Congress, Pearlsburg, 1984, Chichester for Lt. Gov., Richmond, 1985, Nat. Rep. Congress Commn., Washington, 1985, Epperson for Congress, Winston-Salem, N.C., 1986-90, Rep. Party Va., Richmond, 1990-92; sec. of commonwealth State of Va., Richmond, 1992—. Mem. Nat. Assn. Secs. State, Herrico GOP Women. Republican. Baptist. Home: 1503 Old Compton Rd Richmond VA 23233 Office: Old Finance Bldg Capitol Sq Richmond VA 23219

BEAMER, PHYLLIS LOUISE, financial planner; b. Hamilton, Ohio, Oct. 4, 1941; d. Arch Miller and Esther Pearl (Stewart) Fraley; m. Gary L. Beamer, Aug. 25, 1961; children: Steven Gary, David Arch. BA, Otterbein Coll., 1963; cert., Coll. Fin. Planning, 1988. Cert. fin. planner. Tchr. French and English Hamilton City Schs., 1963-64; tchr. English Sabattus (Maine) Pub. Schs., 1964-65; tchr. French and English Butler County Schs., Hamilton, 1965-66; tchr. French Florence (Ala.) City Schs., 1973-78; ins. sales person Fidelity Union, Dallas, 1978-81, Horace Mann Ins., Springfield, Ill., 1981-86; fin. planner Stegall Harrison, Columbus, Miss., 1986-88; cert. fin. planner Fin. Concepts, Columbus, 1988—. Bd. dirs., sec. Habitat for Humanity, Columbus, 1992—; bd. dirs. C. of C., Columbus, 1992—. Recipient Emma K. Elzy award First United Meth. Ch., 1993. Mem. AAUW (pres. 1988-90, Woman of Achievement award 1992), Internat. Assn. Fin. Planners, Internat. Bd. Cert. Fin. Planners. Office: Financial Concepts 1121 Second Ave N Columbus MS 39701

BEAMER, YVONNE MARIE, psychotherapist, counselor; b. Cumberland, Md., Jan. 6, 1947; d. William Walter and Ruthella Louise (Smith) Barr; m. Charles Wesley Beamer, Jan. 5, 1974; children: Marie Lynn, Ann Christine. BA, W. Va. U., 1969. Cert. alcoholism counselor, Ohio; nat. cert. alcoholism counselor. Tchr. English and lang. arts Ft. Ashby (W. Va.) High Sch., 1969-70; field advisor, field dir. Shawnee G.S. Coun., Cumberland, Md., 1970-73; job counselor Md. Correctional Tng. Ctr., Hagerstown, Md., 1973-74; home tchr. Frederick (Md.) County Bd. of Edn., 1984-86; addictions counselor Frederick County Substance Abuse Program, 1986-88; intake admissions counselor Laurelwood Hosp., Willoughby, Ohio, 1988-92; intake/admissions counselor Glenbeigh Hosp., 1992; addictions counselor Cmty. Action Against Addiction, 1993—. Ch. organist All Souls Episc. Ch., Balt., 1976-82, St. James Episc. Ch., Mt. Airy, Md. 1982-88; choir mem. Grace Episc. Ch., Willoughby, 1988—. Mem. Buckeye Squares, Phi Beta Kappa, Sigma Phi Omega. Home: 26700 Loganberry Dr Apt E307 Richmond Heights OH 44143 Office: Cmty Action Against Addiction 5209 Euclid Ave Cleveland OH 44103

BEAMGUARD, ELIZABETH PARKS, librarian; b. Fayetteville, Tenn.; d. Joel Dodson and Emma Wenifred (Puckett) Parks; m. Elbert Strode Beamguard; 1 child, Elizabeth Beamguard Swanson. AB in Journalism, U. Tenn., 1931; BS in Library Sci., Emory U., 1944; postgrad., U. Chattanooga; DHL (hon.), Livingston U., 1981. Librarian Hamilton County Sch. System, Chattanooga, 1940-44, Huntsville (Ala.) Madison County Library, 1944-55, U. Ala., Huntsville, 1953-54; field rep. Ala. Pub. Library Service, Montgomery, 1955-60; instr. U. Ala. Library Sch., Tuscaloosa, 1962-66; dir. Ala. Pub. Library Service, Montgomery, 1960-76; library cons. Montgomery, 1975—; chmn. sr. univ. adv. bd. continuing edn. div. Auburn U., Montgomery, 1984—; library cons. Battelle Columbus Labs., Columbus, Ohio, 1975. Contbr.: (poetry) Southern Style, 1984, Contemporaries from Tennessee; contbr. articles to profl. publs. Bd. mem. Friends of Ala. Archives, Montgomery, 1987—, Coun. on Aging, Montgomery, 1985; mem. So. State Work Conf. Adult Edn., 1976—; pres. Zonta Internat., Montgomery chpt., 1975-76; mem. exec. bd. Montgomery Area on Aging., 1986—. Recipient Citation for Service, U.S. Congress, Washington, 1967, Ala. State Legis., Montgomery, 1967. Mem. ALA (John Cotton Dana award 1971), Ala. Libr. Assn. (Exceptional Svc. award 1976), AAUW (pres. Montgomery br. chpt. 1975-79), Nat. Assn. Adult Edn., S.E. Libr. Assn. Home: 3373 Dartmouth Cir Montgomery AL 36111-1501 Office: Auburn U Sr Univ Adv Bd Div Continuing Edn Montgomery AL 36193

BEAN, PAMELA B., state legislator; b. Rutland, Vt., Apr. 25, 1942; m. Linwood H. Jr.; 3 children. Mem. Lebanon City Coun.; mayor City of Lebanon. mem. Lebanon Planning Bd.; mem. bd. dirs. Lebanon Indsl. Assn., Valley Health Care Coalition. Home: HC 64 Box 54 Lebanon NH 03766-9805 Office: NH State Senate State Capital Concord NH 03301*

BEANE, JUDITH MAE, psychologist; b. Durham, N.C., Mar. 28, 1944; d. Joseph William Sr. and Antoinette Gwathmey (Dew) Sr. BA, Campbell U., 1967; MRE, Golden Gate Bapt. Theol. Sem., Mill Valley, Calif., 1972; PhD, Profl. Sch. of Psychology, San Francisco, 1988. Lic. psychologist, Calif. Home missionary So. Bapt. Home Mission Bd., Atlanta, 1967-69; loan officer Coop Credit Union, Corte Madera, Calif., 1969-70; emergency svcs. specialist Community Action Marin, San Rafael, 1976-78; program coord. Marin Treatment Ctr., San Rafael, Calif., 1980-85; church sec. St. Paul's Episcopal Church, San Rafael, 1979-81; psychol. intern Raleigh Hills Hops., Redwood City, Calif., 1984; psychol. asst. Lic. Psychologisis, San Anselmo, Calif., 1985-92; bd. dirs. The Open Door Ministries, Inc., Sausalito, Calif., 1971—; psychologist Mill Valley, Calif., 1992-93; cons. Ross (Calif.) Hosp., 1991. Guest speaker for Turn on Marin, San Rafael, Calif., 1985. Recipient award Marin County People Speaking, 1985. Mem. Am. Psychol. Assn. (assoc.), Calif. State Psychol. Assn., Marin County Psychol. Assn., Am. Counseling Assn. Baptist. Home: PO Box 172 Lancaster VA 22503-0172

BEARCE, JEANA DALE, artist, educator; b. St. Louis; d. Clarence Russell and Maria Emily Dale; m. Lawrence F. Rakovan, June 7, 1969; children: Barbara Emily, Luke, Francesca. B.F.A., Washington U., St. Louis, 1951; M.A., N.Mex. Highlands U., 1954. Vis. artist, various lectureships India, Pakistan, 1961-62, 93; founder art dept. U. Maine, Portland, 1965, chmn. and dept. rep., 1965-70, asst. prof. art, 1967-70; assoc. prof. U. Maine, 1970-81, prof., 1982—; Reflections South India sabbatical, 1992-93. Exhibited one-woman shows, Portland Mus. Art, Maine, 1958, U. Maine, Orono, 1958, 65, 69, 77, 80, Madras Govt. Mus., India, 1962, Gallery 65, Paris, 1964, Bristol Mus. Art, R.I., 1965, Center Gallery, N.Y.C., 1974, Benbow Gallery, Newport, R.I., 1979, Ctr. for the Arts, Chocolate Ch., Bath, Maine, 1988, USM Gallery, 1991, Main Gallery U. So. Maine, 1991, others, group show, Boston Mus. Art, Library of Congress, Phila. Print Club, Springfield Mus., Mo., Birmingham Mus. Art, Ala., others; represented permanent collection, St. Louis Art Mus., U.S. Edn. Found. in India, New Delhi, U. Maine, Orono and Portland, Bklyn. Mus. Art, Cornell U. Mus. Art, Calif. Coll. Arts and Crafts, Sarasota Art Assn., Fla., Bowdoin Coll., Brunswick, Maine; executed murals, N.Mex. Highlands U., Bowdoin Longfellow-Hawthorn Library, Brunswick, sculpture reliefs, St. Bartholomew, Cape Elizabeth, Maine, St. Charles Ch. Brunswick; retrospective, Maine Ctr. for the Arts, 1988. Mem. artist's com. Maine Art Gallery, 1957-75, 80-87; mem. Maine com. Skowhegan Sch. Painting and Sculpture, 1972—. Recipient various awards; recipient Fannie Cook award People's Competition, 1958, 59; sabbaticals to India: Return to India-Creative Paintings and Printmaking, 1987, South India-Painting and Printmaking, 1993. Mem. Bowdoin Coll. Mus. Assocs. Home: 327 Maine St Brunswick ME 04011-3310 Office: U So Maine College Ave Gorham ME 04038-1004

BEARD, ANN SOUTHARD, government official, travel company executive, art framing company executive; b. Denver, Jan. 13, 1948; d. William Harvey and Cora Alice Cornelia (Caldwell) Southard; m. Terrill Leon Beard, Dec. 20, 1970 (div. Oct. 1980); 1 son, Jeffery Leon; m. Rainer G. Froehlich, Feb. 12, 1988 (div. 1992). BA, Willamette U., 1970; postgrad U. Calif.-San Diego, 1981-82. Exec. asst. Kidder Peabody & Co., San Francisco, 1970-72; adminstrv. aide Arthur Anderson & Co., Portland, Oreg., 1972-73; owner, mgr. Beard's Frame Shoppes, Inc., Portland, 1973-80; dir. mktg. Multnomah County Fair, Portland, 1979; owner, CEO Ann Beard Spl. Events, San Diego, 1980-82; pres. Frame Affair, Inc., San Diego, 1982-86, Jack Oil Co., Inc., Greeley, 1982—; co-owner, v.p. Froehlich Internat. Travel, La Jolla, Calif., 1987-92; chief of protocol Mayor Susan Golding's Office, City of San Diego, 1993—; v.p. 146 Co., Inc., Greeley, pres., 1970-88; lectr., cons. SBA, San Diego, 1980-85. Mem. Civic Light Opera, Old Globe Theatre; bd. dirs. San Diego Master Chorale, 1981-92; mem. state bd. Miss Calif. Pageant/Miss Am., 1982-87; mem. citizens adv. bd. Drug Abuse Task Force/Crime Prevention Task Force, San Diego, 1983-87; campaign coord. Bill Mitchell for City Coun., 1985; candidate for Congress; staff aide to dep. mayor, 1987; mem. Lead San Diego Alumni, 1988, Scripps Hosp. Aux., 1992—, Internat. Visitors Coun., 1993—, San Diego County Commn. on the Status of Women, 1993—; mem. Internat. Affairs Bd., San Diego, 1993—; bd. dirs. La Jolla Rep. Women Fedn., 1992—. Mem. Am. Mktg. Assn., World Affairs Coun., San Diego C. of C., Save Our Heritage Orgn., Charter 100 San Diego, San Diego 1988 Alumna Willamette U., 1909 Univ. Club (bd. dirs. 1992—), Univ. Club San Diego (mktg., devel. and social dir. 1987-88), Delta Gamma. Office: 6671 S La Jolla Scenic Dr La Jolla CA 92037-5735

BEARD, CAROL ELAINE, art educator; b. Boston, May 26, 1945; d. William John and Madolyn Ruth (Johnson) Beard; children: John C. Zajac, Matthew D. Zajac. BSE, Mass. Coll. Art, 1967; student, U. Mass., Dartmouth, 1986, Stonehill Coll., Stoughton, Mass., 1989. Cert. art tchr., art supr., Mass. Art tchr. Framingham (Mass.) Sch. Dept., 1967-71; art dir. Norfolk (Mass.) Recreation Dept., 1974-83; instr. art Franklin (Mass.) High Sch. Adult Edn., 1986-87; dir. art Norfolk Sch. Dept., 1980—, student coun. advisor, 1993—; freelance artist graphic designs for various town bds. and orgns, 1967—; collaborator Step-Outside: Cmty.-Based Art Edn., 1994. Author: (poetry) Fallen Requiem, 1964; designer soft sculptures. Mem. Norfolk Ins. Com., 1989—, Norfolk Sch. Com., 1990—; chair Collective Bargaining Com., Norfolk, 1988—; invited exch. tchr. Wash. Ambassadorship Program, 1994. Mem. ASCD, NEA, Mass. Tchrs. Assn., Norfolk Tchrs. Assn. (pres. 1988—, Tchr. of Yr. 1992), Nat. Art Edn. Assn., Mass. Art Edn. Assn., Norfolk County Tchrs. Assn. Home: 26 Farrington St Franklin MA 02038 Office: Centennial Sch 70 Boardman St Norfolk MA 02056

BEARD, LILLIAN B. MCLEAN, physician, consultant; b. N.Y.; d. John Wilson and Woodie (Durden) McLean; m. Delawrence Beard, Aug. 20, 1967. BS, Howard U., 1965, DM, 1970. Diplomate Nat. Bd. Med. Examiners, Am. Bd. Pediatrics. Pvt. practice pediatrics Lillian M. Beard, Washington, D.C., 1973—; assoc. prof. pediatrics George Washington U., 1983—; asst. prof. community medicine Howard U., 1983—; contbg. editor Good Housekeeping Mag., N.Y., 1989—; health adv. WUSA-TV, Washington, 1993—; communications cons. to industry including: Carnation Nutritional Products, Quaker Oats; mem. bd. dirs. Nat. Women's Econ. Alliance, 1993—, Children's Hosp., 1993—. Recipient Disting. Leadership award Nat. Assn. Equal Oportunity in Higher Edn., 1993, Disting. Svc. award Nat. Med. Assn., 1990, Hall of Fame in Medicine award, 1994. Mem. NMA, AAP (physician recognition awards 1993—). Home: 10517 Alloway Dr Potomac MD 20854 Office: 5505 5th St NW Washington DC 20011-6513

BEARDMORE, DOROTHY, state education administrator; b. Chgo.; m. William Beardmore; 2 children. BA, Cornell U. Cert. due process spl. edn. hearing officer Mich. Dept. Edn. Mem. Bd. Edn. Rcohester Community Schs., 1967-75, Bd. Edn. Oakland Schs., Oakland County Intermediate Sch. Dist., 1974-84; treas., v.p., sec. State Bd. Edn., Lansing, Mich., 1984-90, pres., 1990-92, treas., 1992—; mem. profl. devel. adv. coms. State Bd., Dept. Edn., Mich. Legis., Mich. Assn. Sch. Bds.; chair study Nat. Assn. State Bds. Edn., 1988, bd. dirs. representing 12 midwestern states, chair by-laws com.; apptd. by gov. Midwestern Higher Edn. Com.; at-large del. Southeast Mich. Coun. Govts. Mem. rsch. divsn. United Community Svcs. Met. Detroit; dir. Rep. Women's Forum. Recipient Disting. Svc. award Mich. Assn. Career Edn., 1989, Svc. award Phi Delta Kappa, 1989, Can Doer award Sci. and Tech. Quest Honor Roll, 1991; Paul Harris fellow Rotary Internat., 1989. Mem. Delta Kappa Gamma (hon.). Office: Edn Bd PO Box 30008 Lansing MI 48909-7508

BEARE, MURIEL ANITA NIKKI, public relations executive, author; b. Detroit, Mar. 7, 1928; d. Elbert Stanley and Dorothy Margaret (Welch) Brink; m. Richard Austin Beare, June 15, 1946; 1 child, Sandra Lee. AA, Miami Dade Community Coll., 1974; BA, Skidmore Coll., 1979. Writer, Key West Citizen (Fla.), 1959, Miami News (Fla.), 1967; field dir. Fla. Project HOPE, 1967-68, southeastern area dir., 1968-69; asst. v.p. pub. relations I/D Assocs., Inc., Miami, 1969-70; pres. Nikki Beare & Assocs., Miami, 1971—; v.p. South Fla. office Cherenson, Carroll & Holzer, Livingston, N.J., 1973; sr. v.p. D.J. Edelman, Inc., 1981-83; moderator, producer Women's Powerline, Sta. WIOD, Miami, 1972-77; co-owner South Miami Travel Service, South Miami, 1976-78; pres. Gov.'s Sq. Travel, Inc., Tallahassee, 1979-85, Travel Is Fun, Miami, 1985-90; bd. dirs, corp. sec. Imperial Bank. Author: Pirates, Pineapples and People: Tales and Legends of the Florida Keys, 1961; From Turtle Soup to Coconuts, 1964; Bottle Bonanza, A Handbook for Antique Bottle Collectors, 1965; producer cable TV program Traveler's Digest, 1986-92. Chmn. adv. bd. Met. Dade County Library, 1964; active Greater Miami Host Com.; former chair Met. Dade County Com. Status Women, 1971-76, City of Miami Commn. Status Women, 1985-92; active Met. Gen. Land Use Master Planning Com., 1973-74; Gov.'s Com. Employment Handicapped, 1970-72; chmn. Met. Dade Fair Housing and Employment Appeals Bd., 1975-78; active Miami YWCA's; chmn. Handicapped and Elderly subcom. Met. Dade Transit Devel. Com.; mem. Fla. Ins. Commn. Task Force, 1975, Dade County Democratic Exec. com., 1972-76, South Fla. Health Planning Council, 1972-74; founding mem. Nat. Women's Polit. Caucus, 1971—; v.p. Herstory, 1971—; candidate Fla. Senate, 1974, Fla. Ho. of Reps., 1976; past pres. adv. bd. Inst. for Women, Fla. Internat. U.; pres. Fla. Feminist Credit Union, 1975-78; bd. dirs. Community Health Inst. South Dade County, 1975-77; mem. Jobs for Miami, 1980-88; chmn. Fla. Gov.'s Small Bus. Adv. Council, 1981-83, Greater Miami Tourism Coalition, 1983-85; del. White House Conf. on Small Bus., 1980, 86; chmn. publicity com. Asta World Congress, 1989; co-chmn. FIU Sch. Journalism and Mass Communications Adv. Bd. Recipient Silver Image award Pub. Relations Assn., 1967-68. Mem. AAUW, LWV, NOW, Hist. Assn. So. Fla., Friends of Everglades, Women's C. of C. So. Fla., Am. Soc. Travel Agts., Women in Communications, Nat. Assn. Women Bus. Owners, Pub. Rels. Soc. Am., Fla. Pub. Rels. Soc., Women's Inst. for Freedom of the Press, Antique Bottle Collectors Assn. Fla., Caribbean Tourism Orgn., YWCA, Miami Internat. Press Club, Manatee Bay Club, South by Southeast Women In Travel. Democrat. Office: Nikki Beare & Assocs Inc 14301 SW 87th Ave Miami FL 33176

BEARE-ROGERS, JOYCE LOUISE, former research executive; b. nr. Pickering, Ont., Can., Sept. 8, 1927; d. Frederick John and Sarah May (Michell) Beare; m. Charles Graham Rogers, Dec. 30, 1961; 1 child, Anne Catherine. BA, U. Toronto, Ont., 1951, MA, 1952; PhD, Carleton U., Ottawa, Ont., 1966; DSc (hon.), U. Man., Winnipeg, Can., 1985, U. Guelph, Ont., Can., 1993. Rsch. assoc. U. Toronto, 1952-54; instr. Vassar Coll., Poughkeepsie, N.Y., 1954-56; chemist Food, Drug Directorate (name now Health Protect Br.), Ottawa, 1956-65, rsch. scientist, 1965-75; rsch. mgr. Bur. Nutritional Scis., Ottawa, 1975-91; rsch. mgr. Bur. Nutritional Scis., Ottawa, 1975-91; adj. prof. U. Ottawa, 1980-92; cons. Food and Agrl. Orgn. UN, 1992-94. Editor: Methods for Nutritional Assessment of Fats, 1985, Fat Requirement for Development and Health, 1988; contbr. articles on dietary fats to profl. jours. Decorated Order of Can.; recipient Queen's Jubilee medal Govt. of Can., 1977, Medaille Chevreul award Inst. Corps Gras, 1984, Crompton award McGill U., 1986, Normann medal German Assn. for Fat Rsch., 1987, Commemorative medal for 125th Anniversary of Fedn. of Can., 1992. Fellow Royal Soc. Can., Am. Inst. Nutrition; mem. Am. Oil Chemists Soc. (pres. 1985-86), Internat. Soc. Fat Rsch. (pres. 1991-92), Can. Soc. for Nutrition Scis. (pres. 1984-85, Bordon award 1971, McHenry award 1993), Can. Biochem. Soc. Home: 41 Okanagan Dr, Nepean, ON Canada K2H 7E9

BEARMAN, TONI CARBO, information scientist; b. Middletown, Conn., Nov. 14, 1942; d. Anthony Joseph and Theresa (Bauer) Carbo; m. David A. Bearman, Nov. 14, 1970; 1 dau., Amanda Carole. AB, Brown U., 1969; MS, Drexel U., 1973, PhD, 1977. Bibliog. asst. Am. Math. Soc., Math. Revs., 1962-63; supr. Brown U. Phys. Scis. Library, Providence, R.I., 1963-66, 67-71; subject specialist U. Wash. Engring. Library, Seattle, 1966-67; teaching and research asst. Drexel U., 1971-74; exec. dir. Nat. Fedn. Abstracting and Indexing Services, Phila., 1974-79; cons. for strategic planning and new product devel. Instn. Elec. Engrs., London, 1979-80; exec. dir. U.S. Nat. Commn. on Libraries and Info. Sci., Washington, 1980-86; dean Sch. Library and Info. Sci. U. Pitts., 1986—; mem. adv. com. U.S. Dept. Commerce, Patent and Trademark Office, 1987-90; trustee Engring. Info., Inc., 1985-87; Lazerow lectr. U. Ind., 1984; Schwing lectr. La. State U., 1988; lectr. No. Ohio Am. Soc. Info. Sci./Spl. Librs. Assn., 1990, Beta Phi Mu., Phila., 1992; mem. U.S. Adv. Coun. Nat. Info. Infrastructure, 1994—; mem. U.S. del. G-7 Info. Soc. Conf. Co-editor Internat. Info. and Libr. Rev., 1989-92, editor, 1993—; contbr. articles to profl. jours., mem. editorial bds. profl. jours. Bd. dirs. Greater Pitts. Literacy Coun.; mem. presdl. adv. com. Carnegie Mellon U. Libr. Recipient Disting. Alumni award Drexel U. Coll. Info. Studies, 1984, 100 Most Disting. Alumni award, 1992, 100th Anniversary medal Drexel U., 1992. Fellow AAAS (chmn. sect. T 1992-93), Inst. Info. Scientists, Spl. Librs. Assn.; mem. ALA (coun. 1988-92), Am. Soc. for Info. Sci. (chmn. planning and nominations com. 1990-91, chmn. networking com., chmn. 50th ann. conf., pres. 1989-90, Watson Davis award 1983), Pa. Libr. Assn. (adv. bd. Pa. Gov.'s Conf. on libr. and info. svcs.), Nat. Info. Standards Orgn. (bd. dirs. 1987-90), Spl. Librs. Assn. (rsch. com. 1987-92, internat. rels. com., 1991—), Internat. Fedn. for Info. and Documentation (vice chair U.S. nat. com. 1990—, chair info. policy com. 1991—, chair global infrastructure and superhwys. taskforce 1993—), Assn. for Libr. and Info. Sci. Edn., Laurel Initiative (bd. dirs.). Home: 1309 N Sheridan Ave Pittsburgh PA 15206-1759 Office: U Pitts Sch Libr & Info Sci 135 N Bellefield Ave Pittsburgh PA 15260

BEARWALD, JEAN HAYNES, company executive; b. San Francisco, Aug. 31, 1924; d. Joseph Robert and Edna Haynes (Goudey) Bearwald; m. William Henry Sherburn, Apr. 12, 1969 (dec. 1970); 1 child by previous marriage, David Richard Cross. BA, Stephens Coll., Columbia, Mo., 1945. Adminstrv. asst. Bearwald & Assocs., Sacramento, 1966-78; acct. Truck Parts Co., Sand City, Calif., 1979-80; pres., chief exec. officer Bearwald and Assocs., Fresno, Calif., 1980-89, Las Vegas, N.Mex., 1989-91; owner Jean Bearwald & Assocs., Santa Fe, 1991—; program dir. hosp. and institution State of Calif. Ann. Conf., Carmel, 1980-82. Chmn. Sunset Serenade Gala, Santa Fe Opera Guild, 1993-94. Republican. Episcopalian. Home and Office: 941 Calle Mejia # 1604 Santa Fe NM 87501

BEARY, SHIRLEY LORRAINE, retired music educator; b. New Albany, Kans., Feb. 4, 1928; d. Howard Warren and Bertha Adelia (Wilcox) Fogelsanger; children: Stephanie Beary Johnson, Susan Beary Maloney. BA, Andrews U., 1949; MusM, U. Redlands, 1967; D Mus. Arts, Southwestern Bapt. Theol. Sem., 1977. Tchr. music Nevada, Iowa, 1949-50; prof. music Southwestern Adventist Coll., Keene, Tex., 1959-84, lectr. Christian ethics, 1978-84; prof. music Oakwood Coll., Huntsville, Ala., 1984-94; ret., 1994; ch. organist Seventh-day Adventist Ch., Kalamazoo, 1951-59, Keene, 1959-80, min. music, 1980-82. Mem. bd. advisors Am. Biog. Inst., Raleigh, N.C. Mem. Coll. Music Soc., Am. Hymn Soc., Internat. Adventist Music Assn. Democrat. Home: 2615 Oak Valley Dr Yreka CA 96097

BEASLEY, DIANA LEE, social studies educator; b. Akron, Ohio, Aug. 9, 1952; d. Walter and Margaret (Webb) Sims; 1 child, Leon. BS, Cent. State U., 1973; MA, Howard U., 1983; doctoral cand. U. Md., 1991-. Cert. tchr. Md. Tchr. Prince Georges (Md.) County Pub. Schs., 1975-89; coord. social studies Largo (Md.) High Sch., 1989-91; coord. program Potomac High Sch. Acad. Law and Pub. Policy, Oxon Hill, Md., 1991-; adv. bd. Ctr. for Rsch. and Devel. in Law Related Edn., Wake Forest U., 1992—; tchr. cons. Houghton Mifflen Pub. Co., 1989; chair Potomac High Sch. Multicultural Com., 1993-94; instr. African Am. history and culture staff devel. course Prince Georges County Pub. Schs., 1994. Co-author: Study Guide for Nile Valley Contributions to Civilization, 1994. Nat. Endowment for the Humanities fellow, 1988, 89. Mem. Nat. Coun. Socail Studies (chair 1989-), Minority Involvement Com., Nat. Alliance Black Sch. Educators (sec. 1991-92), Largo High Parent Tchr Assn., Phi Alpha Theta. Democrat. Methodist. Home: 666 Harry S Truman Dr Upper Marlboro MD 20772-2069

BEASLEY, LINDA RUTH HAWKINSON, food scientist, biologist; b. Aurora, Ill., Sept. 5, 1961; d. Richard Hawkinson and Jeanette Irene (Hawkinson) Barker; m. Boyd Calvin Beasley, Feb. 6, 1994. BS in Biology, U. Ill., 1983, MS in Food Sci., 1993. Quality control supr. Milk Specialties, Inc., Dundee and Huntley, Ill., 1986-89; quality assurance specialist, auditor Slim Fast Foods Co., N.Y.C., 1989-92; sr. quality assurance auditor Chiquita Brands Internat., Cin., 1992-94; insp. USDA, 1994—. Mem. Inst. Food Tech., Am. Soc. Quality Control. Home: 1558 SW Bayshore Blvd Port Saint Lucie FL 34983-2966

BEASLEY, MARY CATHERINE, home economics educator, administrator, researcher; b. Portersville, Ala., Nov. 29, 1922; d. Albert Otis and Beulah Green (Killian) Reed; m. Percy Wells Beasley, Dec. 15, 1956 (dec. Dec. 1958). BS in Home Econs., Bob Jones U., 1944; MS, Pa. State U., State College, 1954, EdD, 1968. Tchr. Geraldine and Collinsville (Ala.) High Sch., 1944-45; vocat. home econs. tchr. Glencoe (Ala.) High Sch., 1945-48, Washington County High Sch., Chatom, Ala., 1948-51; home econs. tchr. Homewood Jr. High Sch., Birmingham, Ala., 1958-60; asst. supr. and subject matter specialist Ala. Dept. Edn., Montgomery, 1951-57; asst. prof. Samford U., Birmingham, 1960-62; instr. U. Ala., Tuscaloosa, 1951, asst. prof. then assoc. prof., 1962-68, dir. continuing edn. in home econs., 1968-84, prof., 1984-88, prof. emeritus consumer sci. Coll. Human Ecology, 1988—. Author: (with others) Human Ecological Studies, 1986. Pres. Joint Legis. Coun. of Ala., Tuscaloosa, 1973-75; dir. On Your Own Program, 1970-80. Recipient Creative Programming award Nat. U. Extension Assn., 1979. Mem. Am. Home Econs. Assn. (chmn. rehab. com. 1973, 75, leader 1986), Southeastern Coun. on Family Rels. (pres. 1982-84, Disting. Svc. award 1988), Ala. Home Econs. Assn. (pres. 1961-63, leader 1985), Ala. Coun. on Family Rels. (pres. 1981-83, Disting. Svc. award 1987), Altrusa Club of Tuscaloosa, Inc. (pres. 1988-89, exec. bd. Ft. Payne/DeKalb 1989-93), Alpha Delta Kappa (treas. Tuscaloosa chpt. 1973-75), Phi Upsilon Omicron, Kappa Omicron Nu. Republican. Baptist. Home: RR 3 Box 201 Collinsville AL 35961-9171

BEASLEY, MAURINE HOFFMAN, journalism educator, historian; b. Sedalia, Mo., Jan. 28, 1936; d. Dimmitt Heard and Maurine (Hieronymous) Hoffman; m. William C. McLaughlin, May 20, 1966 (div. 1969); m. Henry R. Beasley, Dec. 24, 1970; 1 child, Susan Sook. BJ, BA in History, U. Mo., 1958; MS in Journalism, Columbia U., 1963; PhD in Am. Civilization, George Washington U., 1974; Cert. in Brit. History, U. Edinburgh, Scotland, 1964. Edn. editor Kansas City (Mo.) Star, 1959-62; staff writer Washington Post, 1963-73; asst. prof. journalism U. Md., College Park, 1975-80, assoc. prof., 1980-86, prof. 1987—. Author: Eleanor Roosevelt and the Media: A Public Quest for Self-Fulfillment, 1987; (with others) Women in Media, 1977, The New Majority, 1988, Taking Their Place! Documentary History of Women and Journalism, 1993 (One of Outstanding Acad. Books, Choice 1994); editor: (with others) Voices of Change: Southern Pulitzer Winners, 1978, One Third of a Nation (hon. mention Washington Monthly Book Award 1982), 1981; editor: White House Press Conferences of Eleanor Roosevelt, 1983; mem. adv. bd. Am. Journalism, 1983—, Jour. of Mass Media Ethics, Mass Com. Rev., Electronic Jour. Comm.; corr. editor Journalism History, 1995—; contbr. articles to acad. jours. Violinist, Montgomery Coll. Symphony Orch., 1975—; pres., Little Falls Swimming Club, Inc., 1988-89. Gannett Teaching Fellowships Program fellow, 1977; Pulitzer traveling fellow Columbia U., 1963; Eleanor Roosevelt studies grantee Eleanor Roosevelt Inst., 1979-80; named one of nation's outstanding tchrs. of writing and editing Modern Media Inst. and Am. Soc. Newspaper Editors, 1981, most outstanding woman U. Md., Coll. Park Pres. Commn. on Women's Affairs, 1993. Mem. Assn. Edn. in Journalism and Mass Communications (commn. on status of women 1994, exec. com. 1990-91, 94-95, standing com. on profl. freedom and responsibility 1985, vice chair 1987-89, chair 1990-91, sec. history div. 1986-87, vice-head 1987-88, head 1988-89, pres. elect 1992, pres. 1993-94, leader People-to-People delegation to China and Hong Kong 1994, Outstanding Contbn. to Journalism Edn. award 1994), Am. Journalism Historians Assn. (pres.-elect 1988-89, pres. 1989-90), Am. News Women's Club (bd. govs. 1986-87), Women in Communications (bd. dirs. Washington chpt. 1985-87), Nat. Fedn. Press Women, Soc. Profl. Journalists (chair nat. hist. site com. 1986-87, bd. dirs. Washington chpt. 1988-90, pres. Washington chpt. 1990-91, dir. region 2 and mem. nat. bd. 1991-92), Internat. Assn. Mass Comm. Rsch., Internat. Comm. Assn., Phi Beta Kappa, Omicron Delta Kappa. Democrat. Unitarian. Home: 4920 Flint Dr Bethesda MD 20816-1746 Office: U Md Coll Journalism College Park MD 20742

BEASLEY, MAXINE HUGHES, office manager; b. LaCamp, La., Mar. 23, 1930; d. John Ezra and Vergie Lee (Kemp) Hughes; m. Steve Marion Beasley, Apr. 15, 1950 (dec. 1987); children: Patricia Naomi, Steve Michael, David Randall. Grad., Elliotts Bus. Sch., Beaumont, Tex., 1949; student, Lamar U., 1950. Teller Am. Nat. Bank, Beaumont, 1949-50, Calcasieu Marine Nat. Bank Br., DeQuincy, La., 1950-61; asst. mgr. Lakeside Nat. Bank, Sulphur, La., 1961-68; advt. dir. Southwest Daily News, Sulphur, 1968-88; office mgr. McMillin Hearing Aid Svc., Lake Charles, La., 1988—. Future Farmers of Am. Sulphur chpt. mother, 1969-73; pres. Sulphur High Sch. Band Boosters, 1969-72, 4-H and Rodeo Band Boosters, 1967-73. Mem. Am. Bus. Womens Assn. (pres., woman of yr. 1984). Democrat. Pentocostal. Home: 2317 Beasley Rd Sulphur LA 70663

BEASON, ROSE ANN MCDANIEL, school board official, educator; b. Marion, N.C., Dec. 11, 1939; d. William Boyd and Gertrude (McMahan) McD.; m. Robert Glenn Beason, May 26, 1963 (div. 1985); children: Lori L., Mark R. BS in English, Social Studies, Appalachian State U., 1961, MA in Reading, English, 1963; Ednl. Specialist, U. Fla., 1975. Cert. 1A specialist in English, Social Studies, Reading, Adminstrn. and Supervision. Tchr. English Fairfax (Va.) High Sch., 1961-62; tchr. English and reading Duncan Fletcher Jr. Sr. High Schs., Jacksonville, Fla., 1963-66, chmn. English dept., 1968-71; tchr. adult edn. Fla. Jr. Coll., Jacksonville, 1963-66; tchr. English and drama William T. Sampson High Sch., Guantanamo Bay, Cuba, 1966-67; elem. sch. reading resource tchr. U.S. Navy, Guantanamo Bay, 1967-68; tchr. English and reading, dept. chmn. Sandalwood Jr. Sr. High Sch., Jacksonville, 1971-72; teaching specialist Duval County Sch. System, Jacksonville, 1972-79; Edn. Consol. and Improvement Act Chpt. 1 supr. Duval County Sch. Bd., Jacksonville, 1979-89, dir. fed. compensatory edn., 1989—; part-time instr. Jacksonville U., 1977-80; presenter fall statewide technical assistance meeting, Hollywood, Fla., 1986, Miami, Fla., 1989, div. of pub. schs. conf. Fla. Dept. Edn., Tampa, 1983, team mem., com. mem. 1983—; mem. state and local Right to Read task forces. Recipient EVE award Fla. Times-Union, 1985. Mem. AAUW, Internat. Reading Assn. (state coord., presenter 34th ann. conv. 1989), Fla. Reading Assn. (bd. dirs. IRA state coord. 1990—, chair scholarships and awards com. 1989-90, dist. dir. 1986-89, author Image brochure, organizer leadership conf., presenter 1982), Duval County Reading Coun. (bd. dirs. 1980—), Kappa Delta Pi (pres. 1989-90, corres. sec. 1988-89), Delta Kappa Gamma (Beta Rho chpt.). Home: 217 Oceanwood Dr Neptune Beach FL 32266-3800 Office: Duval County Sch Bd 1701 Prudential Dr Jacksonville FL 32207-8182

BEATO, KAREN ELIZABETH, banker; b. Alameda, Calif., Nov. 26, 1964; d. Melvyn Clark and Nancy Joyce (McDaniel) Nutter; m. Keith Lawrence Beato, Apr. 23, 1988; children: Lauren Nicole, Elizabeth Ann. BS, Azusa Pacific U., 1986; MBA, San Francisco State U., 1991. Sr. MIS analyst Bank of America, Concord, Calif., 1987-88, sr. ops. mgr., 1989, project cons., 1990-91, mgr. quality assurance testing, 1991—. Mem. Bay Area Quality Assurance. Republican. Christian. Office: Bank of Am 2001 Clayton Rd # 6900 Concord CA 94520-2401

BEATON, SARAH THÉRÈSE, federal agency administrator; b. N.Y.C., Jan. 10, 1966; d. William Patrick and Kathleen Ann (Cashman) B. BS in Bus. and Econs., Coll. New Rochelle, 1987; student, Univ. Coll., Dublin, 1985-86. With dept. internat. econ. and social affairs UN, 1987; grants specialist U.S. Dept. Edn., Washington, 1990-93, program officer internat. studies br. ctr. internat. edn., 1993—. Organizer Women's Book Club, Washington, 1990—; vol. St. Augustine's Cath. Ch., Washington, 1992—. Democrat. Home: 2604 N 9th St Arlington VA 22201

BEATRÍZ, DULCE, artist; b. La Habana, Cuba, Mar. 17, 1931; came to U.S. 1960, naturalized 1970; d. José Mariá and Dulce Amelia (Moreno de Ayala) Hernández; m. Leonardo Beatríz, Mar. 30, 1959. Grad. Tchr.'s Coll., Havana, 1949; M.A. in Music, Conservatory Peyrellade, Havana, 1953; M.F.A., San Alejandro, Havana, 1955. First tech. dir. Cuban dept. fine arts, prof. drawing and painting, mem. judging bd. City Hall, Havana, 1956-59. Exhibited in 61 one-woman shows, more than 150 group shows; represented in permanent collections in N.Am., Central Am., S.Am., Europe. Recipient Hall of Fame Internat. award for painting and sculpture Hispanic Internat. Research Inst., New York, 1971, Internat. award Honor Al Merito, 1974, Royal Order of Isabel La Católica decoration for painting and sculpture, Spain, 1983, Gold Keys, Dade County, Fla., 1983; travel prize San Alejandro, Havana, 1956, Gold medal Havana City Hall, 1956, commendation City of Miami, 1970; Lincoln-Marti nat. award Dept. HEW, 1971; named Eminent Alumna, Conservatory Peyrellade, Havana, 1953; hon. ambassador, Dade County, Fla., 1977. Fellow Royal Soc. Arts, London, 1977; mem.

Hispania Nostra, Spain, 1978, Círculo de Cultura Panamericana, 1978. Republican. Roman Catholic.

BEATTIE, ANN, author; b. Washington, Sept. 8, 1947; d. James and Charlotte (Crosby) B.; m. Lincoln Perry. B.A., Am. U., 1969; M.A., U. Conn., 1970; L.H.D. (hon.), Am. U., 1983. Vis. asst. prof. U. Va., Charlottesville, 1976-77, vis. writer, 1980; Briggs Copeland lectr. English Harvard U., Cambridge, Mass., 1977. Author: Chilly Scenes of Winter, 1976, Distortions, 1976, Secrets and Suprises, 1979, Falling In Place, 1980, Jacklighting, 1981, The Burning House, 1982, Love Always, 1985, Where You'll Find Me, 1986, (art criticism) Alex Katz, 1987, Picturing Will, 1990, (story collection) What Was Mine, 1991. Recipient Disting. Alumnae award Am. U., 1980, award in lit. Am. Acad. and Inst. Arts and Letters, 1980; Guggenheim fellow, 1977. Mem. Am. Acad. and Inst. of Arts and Letters, 1992, PEN, Authors Guild. Office: care Janklow and Nesbit 598 Madison Ave New York NY 10022*

BEATTIE, MARY JARVIS, public relations executive; b. Potosi, Mo., Aug. 31; d. Eugene William and Hallie (Elliott) Jarvis; m. Orville Carl Beattie, June 5; children: Barbara Beattie Liljegren, David Carl, Phyllis Gertrude. Student, Northwestern U., 1982-84; BS, Nat. Coll. Edn., 1985; MS, Northwestern U., 1988. Profl. vol. Chgo. area, 1960-94; v.p., pub. rels. Benjamin-Beattie Arts, Chgo., 1980—; commr. Lake County (Ill.) Bd., 1992—. Editor (pub. rels. handbook) Lamb's Farm Winter Market, 1980; (handbook guide) If You Can Read, You Can Win, 1980; (booklets) Tiffany Stained Glass Windows, 1988, Grateful Review, Happy Pastor, 1994. Dir., founder Brain Rsch. Found., Chgo., 1953-95; founder Women's Coun. Brain Rsch. Found., Chgo., 1963-95, Child/Serve Svc. League, Chgo., 1952-95; mem. women's bd. Ravinia Festival Chgo. Symphony Orch., 1974-95; mem. sustaining fellow program com. Art Inst. Chgo., 1988-95; jr. dir. Ill. Gen. Fedn. Women's Clubs, 1958-60; mem. exec. com. pub. rels. Lake County Rep. Party, Libertyville, Ill., 1980-95; township chair, committeeman Shields Township Rep. Party, Lake Forest-Lake Bluff, Ill., 1980-95; pres. Lake Forest-Lake Bluff Women's Rep. Club, 1988-90; bd. dirs. LWV, Lake Forest-Lake Bluff, 1974-95; deacon First Presbyn. Ch. of Lake Forest. Recipient Lake County Grass Roots Worker award Lake County Rep. Party, 1983, Vol. Svc. award Brain Rsch. Found. Women's Coun., 1989, Creativity award Brain Rsch. Found. Women's Coun., 1993. Mem. Northwestern U. Club Chgo. Presbyterian. Home: 145 N Sheridan Rd Lake Forest IL 60045 Office: Benjamin-Beattie Fine Arts Ltd 1000 N Lake Shore Dr Chicago IL 60611

BEATTY, CONNY DAVINROY, lawyer; b. Belleville, Ill., July 28, 1959; d. William Thomas and Kay (Schuck) Davinroy; m. Daniel Patrick Beatty, Aug. 23, 1986; children: Robert Daniel, Alexandria Marie. BA, Monmouth Coll., 1981; JD, St. Louis U., 1987, MBA, 1987. Bar: Mo. 1987, U.S. Dist. Ct. (ea. dist.) 1987, Ill. 1988, U.S. Dist. Ct. (so. dist.) 1988. Assoc. Thompson & Mitchell, St. Louis, 1987—. Recipient Disting. Young Alumni award Monmouth Coll., 1995. Mem. ABA, Mo. Bar Assn., Ill. Bar Assn., Bar Assn. Met. St. Louis, Healthcare Fin. Mgmt. Assn. (advanced mem.), Millstadt Community Band, Pi Beta Phi. Home: 11 Coronation Dr Millstadt IL 62260-1809 Office: Thompson & Mitchell Ste 3400 One Mercantile Ctr Saint Louis MO 63101

BEATTY, FRANCES, civic worker; b. Chgo., Apr. 17, 1940; d. Pasquale and Rose (Brunetti) Calomeni; m. Robert Alfred Beatty, Aug. 24, 1963; children: Bradford, Roxanna. BA, Northwestern U., 1961; MA, U. Chgo., 1967. Tchr. math. Proviso West High Sch., Hillside, Ill., 1961-66. Active Oak Brook Dist. 53 Sch. Bd., 1979-85; womens bd. mem. Field Mus. Natural History, Chgo., 1985—; mem. founders coun., 1988—, treas. womens bd., 1991-93; governing bd. Chgo. Symphony, 1985-92; trustee Chgo. Symphony Orch., 1992—; womens bd. Ravinia Festival, Highland Park, Ill., 1987—, Northwestern U., Evanston, Ill., 1988—; bd. dirs. Northwestern U. Libr., 1992—; governinc coun. Wellness House, Hinsdale, Ill., 1994—. Mem. Womens Athletic Club Chgo. (3d v.p. 1985-87, 1st v.p. 1992-94, pres. 1994—), The Womens Bd. U. Chgo., Alumnae Northwestern U., John Evans Club.

BEATTY, LINDA L., state legislator; b. Boone, Iowa, Sept. 13, 1942; d. Kenneth L. and Ruth Plant Jackson; m. Jerry K. Beatty, 1968; children: Elizabeth, Theodore. BA, U. No. Iowa, 1964. Mem. Iowa Ho. of Reps. Former Warren County Dem. chair; active Trinity United Presbyn. Ch. Mem. AAUW. Home: 1100 E Girard Ave Indianola IA 50125-1541 Office: Iowa Ho of Reps State Capitol Des Moines IA 50319*

BEAUBIEN, ANNE KATHLEEN, librarian; b. Detroit, Sept. 15, 1947; d. Richard Parker and Edith Mildred Beaubien. Student, Western Mich. U., 1965-67; BA, Mich. State U., 1969; AM in Libr. Sci., U. Mich., 1970. Reference libr., bibliographic instr. U. Mich. Libr., Ann Arbor, 1971-80, dir. MITS, 1980-85, head coop. access svcs., 1985—. Author: (booklet) Psychology Bibliography, 1980; co-author: Learning the Library, 1982; contbr. articles to profl. jours., editor, conf. proc., 1987. Pres. Ann Arbor Ski Club, 1978-79; mem. vestry St. Clare's Episcopal Ch., Ann Arbor, 1986-89. Recipient Woman of Yr. award Ann Arbor Bus. and Profl. Women's Club, 1982, Disting. Alumnus award Sch. Info. and Libr. Studies, U. Mich., 1987. Mem. ALA, Assn. Coll. and Rsch. Librs. (pres. 1991-92). Office: U Mich Libr 106 Hatcher Grad Libr Ann Arbor MI 48109

BEAUDET, PATRICIA SUZANNE, photography editor; b. Chgo., Aug. 6, 1951; d. André Marcel and Helen Gertrude (Joiner) B. Assoc. photography editor Playboy Enterprises Inc., Chgo., 1970—. Contbg. photographer Rolling Stone Illustrated History of Rock and Roll, 1992; rschr., photo editor: The Playboy Book: Forty Years, 1994. Democrat. Roman Catholic. Home: PO Box 31351 Chicago IL 60631

BEAUDOIN, CAROL ANN, psychologist; b. Lowell, Mass., Mar. 30, 1949; d. Adrien P. and Rita J. (LeBlanc) B.; B.A. with honors, U. Fla., 1971; M.Ed. in Counseling, Boston U., 1973, Ed.D. in Counseling Psychology, 1979. Psychiat. aide U. Fla.-Shands Teaching Hosp., Gainesville, 1970-71; trainee VA Hosp., Gainesville, 1971-72; attendant Boston State Hosp., 1972, intern, 1973; intern Univ. Hosp., also Counseling Center, Northeastern U., Boston, 1973-74, Dorchester Mental Health Center, also Carney Hosp., 1974-75; staff psychologist Human Resource Inst., Boston, 1974-80, treatment team leader, 1975-80; pvt. practice psychology, Brookline, Mass., 1980—. Mem. Am. Psychol. Assn. Office: 1101 Beacon St Brookline MA 02146-5502

BEAUDRY, MARY CAROLYN, archaeology educator, consultant; b. Great Lakes, Ill., Nov. 25, 1950; d. Eugene James and Mary Mason (Barkaloo) B. BA, William and Mary Coll., 1973; MA, Brown U., 1975, PhD, 1980. Asst. prof. archaeology Boston U., 1980-90, assoc. prof. archaeology, 1990—; acting dir. preservation studies program Boston U., 1991. Editor: Documentary Archaeology in New World, 1988; co-editor: The Art and Mystery of Historical Archaeology, 1992; contbr. articles to profl. jours. Bd. dirs. Hist. Soc. Old Newbury, Mass., 1993. NEH grantee, 1992; fellow Brown U., 1973-75, NEH, Winterthur Mus., 1994—. Fellow Coun. for N.E. Hist. Archaeology (bd. dirs. 1985-93, editor jour. 1986); mem. Soc. Hist. Archaeology (pres. 1989), Am. Anthropol. Assn., Soc. Indsl. Archeology. Home: Ste 4 2 Morgan Ave Newbury MA 01951 Office: Boston Univ Dept Archaeology 675 Commonwealth Ave Boston MA 02215-1406

BEAUMONT, DOROTHY JEAN, medical/surgical nurse; b. Jamaica, W.I., Apr. 12, 1948; came to U.S., 1967; d. Vernon Obadiah and Elizabeth Abrozina (Jones) Burke; m. Pezlie George Beaumont, May 2, 1970; children: Pierre, Oscar. BSN, SUNY Downstate Med. Ctr., Bklyn., 1987. RN, N.Y.; cert. med.-surg. Staff nurse med.-surg. unit Bklyn. Hosp., 1987—. Mem. N.Y. State Nurses Assn. Baptist. Home: 225-10 113th Ave Queens Village NY 11429

BEAUMONT, MONA, artist; b. Paris; d. Jacques Hippolyte and Elsie M. (Didisheim) Marx. m. William G. Beaumont; children: Garrett, Kevin. Postgrad., Harvard U., Fogg Mus., Cambridge, Mass. One-woman shows include Galeria Proteo, Mexico City, Gumps Gallery, San Francisco, Palace of Legion of Honor, San Francisco, L'Armitiere Gallery, Rouen, France, Hoover Gallery, San Francisco, San Francisco Mus. Modern Art, Galeria Van der Voort, San Francisco, William Sawyer Gallery, San Francisco, Palo Alto (Calif.) Cultural Ctr., Galerie Alexandre Monnet, Brussels, Honolulu Acad. Arts; group shows include San Francisco Mus. Modern Art, San Francisco Art Inst., DeYoung Meml. Mus., San Francisco, Grey Found. Tour of Asia, Bell Telephone Invitational, Chgo., Richmond Art Ctr., L.A. County Mus. Art, Galerie Zodiaque, Geneva, Galerie Le Manoir, La Chaux de Fonds, Switzerland, William Sawyer Meml. Exhibit, San Francisco, others; represented in permanent collections Oakland (Calif.) Mus. Art, City and County of San Francisco, Hoover Found., San Francisco, Grey Found., Washington, Bulart Found., San Francisco; also numerous pvt. collections. Mem. Soc. for Encouragement of Contemporary Art, Bay Area Graphic Art Coun., San Francisco Art Inst., San Francisco Mus. Modern Art, Capp Street Project, others. Recipient ann. painting award Jack London Square, 2 ann. awards San Francisco Women Artists, One-man Show award San Francisco Art Festival; purchase award Grey Found., San Francisco Women Artists (2), San Francisco Art Festival; included in Printworld Internat., Internat. Art Diary, Am. Artists, N.Y. Art Rev., Calif. Art Rev., Art in San Francisco Bay Area. Address: 1087 Upper Happy Valley Rd Lafayette CA 94549-2805

BEAUPAIN, ELAINE SHAPIRO, psychiatric social worker; b. Boston, Nov. 1, 1949; d. Abraham and Anna Marilyn (Gass) S.; m. Dean A. Beaupain, Feb. 14, 1987; 1 child, Andrew. BA, McGill U., Montreal, Que., 1971, MSW, 1974. Ind. clin. social worker, Mass.; cert. social worker, Maine; cert. social worker with ind. practice lic., Maine; lic. ind. clin. social worker, Mass. Psychiat. social worker Bangor (Maine) Mental Health Inst., 1974-75; outpatient therapist The Counseling Ctr., Bangor, 1975-76, The Counseling Ctr., Millinocket, Maine, 1979-86; asst. core group leader adolescent unit Jackson Brook Inst., Portland, Maine, 1986-87; area dir. Community Health and Counseling Svcs., 1981-86; pvt. practice social work, 1987—, psychotherapy with individuals, couples and families Millinocket and Bangor, 1987—. Mem. AAUW, Nat. Assn. Social Workers, Acad. Cert. Social Workers (diplomate 1992). Republican. Office: 122 Pine St Bangor ME 04401-5216

BEAUPRE, ELAINE MARCIA KENOW, chamber of commerce executive; b. Faribault, Minn., Oct. 28, 1942; d. Sylvester John and Marcella Marie (Karp) D.; m. Richard Thomas Kenow, Jan. 25, 1964 (dec.); children: Cheryl Marie, William Richard; m. James Francis Beaupre, Jan. 2, 1988. Student high sch., Bethlehem Acad., 1960. Med. sec. Dr. Paul Bauer, Faribault, Minn., 1956-60; med. asst. Drs. Ersfeld, McGroarty, Shelander, St. Paul, 1960-64; bookkeeper, office mgr. Town & Country Inc., Faribault, 1964-66; sales person Fabric Store, Faribault, Karp's Shoe Store, Faribault, 1968-79; asst. mgr. Nelson's Super Valu Deli, Minn., 1979-84; mgr. pub. rels. Faribault C. of C., 1984-85, exec. asst., 1985-86, exec. dir., 1986—; cons. Faribault Festivals Inc., 1984—; mem. adv. bd. Sales & Mktg. Tech. Inst., Faribault, 1986—, adv. bd. Small Bus. Devel. Ctr. Faribault, 1986—, planning com. Minn. C. of C. Execs.; mem. adv. bd. S.E. Minn. Pvt. Industry Coun., 1991—. Bd. dirs. Fairbault Regional Ctr. Cmty. Support Employment Adv. Bd., 1987, River Bend Inst. for Art, Faribault, 1988; mem. adv. bd., disaster com. Rice County Child Care, Citizens Liaison Coun. for Corrections Facility, Faribault; mem. adv. bd. Downtown Devel. Com.; mem. adv. com. Hist. Soc. for Alexander Faribault on hist. register; dir. tourism Bur. Faribault, div. Faribault C. of C. Mem. Mid. Am. Chamber Exec. Exch. Club (pub. rels. sec.), S.E. Minn. Exec. Chamber Assn. (pres. 1994, treas. 1995). Democrat. Roman Catholic. Home: 1500 Wellington Cres Faribault MN 55021-6731 Office: Faribault C of C 530 Wilson Ave Faribault MN 55021-0434

BEAUREGARD, LUCILLE EILEEN, banking officer; b. Danbury, Conn., June 22, 1963; d. James Frances Jr. and Lucille Doris (Elwell) Mann; m. Kenneth Richard Beauregard, Sept. 4, 1993. Grad. h.s., San Diego, 1981. Br. mgr. Far West Savs., San Marcos, Calif., 1982-92; customer svc. specialist North County Bank, Escondido, Calif., 1992-93; ops. asst. UnionBank, San Marcos, 1993—. Ambassador City of San Marcos, 1989-93. Roman Catholic. Office: Union Bank 669 S Rancho Santa Fe Rd San Marcos CA 92069

BEAUSOLEIL, DORIS MAE, federal agency administrator, housing specialist; b. Chelmsford, Mass., Jan. 9, 1932; d. Joseph Honorius and Beatrice Pearl (Smith) B.; student State Tchrs. Coll., Lowell, Mass., 1949-51; BA in Sociology and Psychology, Goddard Coll., Plainfield, Vt., 1954; MA in Human Relations, N.Y.U., 1957; postgrad. CUNY, N.Y.C., 1988—. With div. human rights N.Y. State, N.Y.C., 1960-69, housing dir., 1966-68; housing cons. Nat. Com. Against Discrimination in Housing, N.Y.C., 1969-70; housing cons. Edwin Gould Found., N.Y.C., 1970-71; human resources cons. interfaith housing strategy com., housing cons. Fedn. Prot. Welfare Agencies, Inc., N.Y.C., 1971-72; self-employed housing cons., 1972-74; equal opportunity compliance specialist N.Y./N.J. HUD, N.Y.C., 1975—, Fed. women's program coordinator, 1975-79; br. chief Title VI Sect. 109 Compliance div. fair housing and equal opportunity Region II, HUD, N.Y.C., 1979-84; founding mem. N.Y. State HUD Com.; adv. panel Housing Mag., 1979; cons., examiner N.Y. State Civil Svc. Commn., 1970-93. Mem. Nat. Assn. Human Rights Workers (Outstanding Service award 1974), Citizens Housing and Planning Coun., Nat. Assn. Housing and Devel. Ofcls., Goddard Coll. Alumni Assn. (sec. 1988-90), Rep. Bus. Women's Club (pres. 1985-88, bd. dirs. 1989-91). Republican. Unitarian. Home: 392 Central Park W New York NY 10025-5860 Office: 26 Federal Plz Rm 3532 New York NY 10278

BEBKO-JONES, LINDA, state legislator. Student, Erie Bus. Acad., 1964-65. Legal sec. Silin, Eckert & Burke, Erie, Pa., 1964-66; office mgr., legal sec. Atty. Joseph Knowacki, Erie, 1975-83; adminstrv. asst. Hon. A. Buzz Andrezeski Pa. Senate, Erie, 1984-89; dir. Women Against Sexual Harassment, Erie, 1989-92; caseworker Community House for Women, Erie, 1990-92; caseworker Hon. Harris Wofford U.S. Senate, Erie, 1991-92; mem. Pa. Ho. Reps., Harrisburg, 1993—, sec. mil. and vets. affairs, mem. health and welfare com., state govt. com., aging and youth com., task force on violence as health concern, mem. firefighters caucus, freshman non-partisan caucus, Northwest caucus, substance abuse caucus, tax reform caucusm women's caucus; one on one reporter Presque Isle Mag., 1991-92; mem. adv. bd. Soldiers and Sailors Home; resident asst. Edmund Thomas Detention Hall; Erie County coord. Children's Lobby Kid Pix Program; apptd. to Pa. Commn. for Women; coord. Pa. Children's Legis. Conf./Coun. State Govts.; del. East Side Fedn. Mem. Dem. Exec. Com. Erie County, Dem. Women's Coun. Erie County; trainer in-svc. tng. program Mcpl. Police Officer's Edn. and Tng. Commn. Recipient Erie Woman of Yr. award, 1994. Mem. Am. Bus. Women's Assn., Slovsk Nat. Club (life). Home: 460 E 26th St Erie PA 16504-2802 Office: Pa Ho of Reps PO Box 72 Harrisburg PA 17108-0072*

BEBOUT, TARA L., insurance company executive; b. Battle Creek, Mich., Oct. 10, 1963; grandaghter of James and Pauline Bebout and Gus and Mildred Nescheff; m. Jack T. Akers III. Student, U. Akron. Purchasing mgr. Waste Heat Techs. Inc., Wadsworth, Ohio, 1983-86; with ins. sales and mortgage brokering SBL Inc., Akron, Ohio, 1986-88; owner Akers Ins. Agy., Wadsworth, 1988—. Mem. Wadsworth Area C. of C. Republican. Home: 3275 Rohrer Rd Wadsworth OH 44281 Office: Akers Agy Inc 130 Main St Wadsworth OH 44284

BECCHETTI, RITA J. HAEDEL, health facility education coordinator; b. Phila., Dec. 13, 1946; d. Peter P. and Alfreda Haedel; children: Meredith, Chris. Diploma nursing, Thomas Jefferson U., 1967; BA magna cum laude, Jersey City State Coll.; MHS, Washington U. RN, Mo.; cert. in nursing staff devel. and continuing edn., ANCC. Charge/asst. head nurse Neurologic Inst. Columbia Presbyn. Med. Ctr., N.Y.C.; instr. Mid-West Inst., St. Louis; educator community/corp. health VNA Corp. Health, St. Louis; community health specialist Normandy Osteopathic Hosp., St. Louis; coord. staff devel. Shriner's Hosp., St. Louis. Bd. dirs., chmn. edn. com. Mo. chpt. Nat. Neurofibromatosis Found. Mem. Am. Soc. Health Edn. Tng., Nat. Assn. Orthopedic Nurses (mem. edn. com., alt. del., Ednl. scholar 1991, Fall Inst. grantee 1993), Nat. Nursing Staff Devel. Orgn. (charter), Greater St. Louis Soc. Health Educators (bd. dirs., pres. 1995), Mo. Assn. Healthcare Educators (bd. dirs. dist. V rep., chmn. mem. com., mentor program coord.), Alumna Assn. Thomas Jefferson U., Soc. Pediatric Nurses (founding mem. St. Louis chpt., program com.), Kappa Delta Pi. Home: 12 Briarbrook Trl Saint Louis MO 63131-3947 Office: 2001 S Lindbergh Blvd Saint Louis MO 63131

BECCIO, LINDA HUNTINGTON, psychotherapist; b. Cleve., Jan. 9, 1934; d. Alton Raeburn and Lois Kathryn (Rheingans) Huntington; divorced; children: William M. Beccio, Susan M. Beccio Cormio, Catherine A. Beccio Mathews. BA in Edn., U. Mich., 1956; MEd, Bridgewater State U., 1985; EdD, U. San Francisco, 1993. Tchr. San Francisco, 1956-58; group coord., counselor Family Svc. Agy., Burlingame, Calif., 1986-89; pvt. practice psychotherapy San Mateo, Calif., 1989—. Vol. various civic orgns., 1966—. Mem. APA, Calif. State Psychol. Assn., N. Calif. Group Psychol. Soc., Calif. Assn. Marriage and Family Therapists, Am. Assn. Behavior Therapists. Office: 30 S El Camino Real San Mateo CA 94401

BECCUE, DIANA LYNN, marketing executive, consultant; b. Denver, Sept. 1, 1955; d. Charles Henry and Helen Eileen (Warner) Beccue. BS in Home Econs., Colo. State U., 1977. Cert. home economist. Food technologist Keebler Corp. Mfg. Tech. Center, Denver, 1977-78; consumer cons. Colo. Beef Promotion Bd., Denver, 1979-82; mgr. membership promotion Am. Waterworks Assn., Denver, 1982; acct. supr. pub. relations Sam Lusky Assocs. Inc., Denver, 1982-83; pres. Beccue-Brown & Assocs., 1983-88; exec. v.p., Triangle Mktg. Enterprises, 1988-92; pres. C.C.D. and Co., 1992—. Office: CCD and Co PO Box 1358 Loveland CO 80539-1358

BECHERER, DEBORAH ZORN, banker; b. Youngstown, Ohio, Feb. 9, 1958; d. Robert L. and Joan M. (Wilkos) Zorn; m. William B. Becherer Jr., May 22, 1983. BS in Bus. Edn. magna cum laude, Youngstown State U., 1980; MBA, Coll. of William and Mary, 1983; cert., Grad. Sch. Banking, Madison, Wis., 1989. Trainee advanced mgmt. Bank One of Ea. Ohio, Youngstown, 1983-84, officer comml. loans, 1984-86, asst. v.p., 1986—. Mem. allocation com. United Way Planning, Youngstown, 1984-86; pres. Lake to River coun. Girl Scouts U.S., 1987-91; liaison bd. dirs. Mahoning County Red Cross, Youngstown, Cen. Christian Day Care Ctr., Youngstown. Mem. NAFE, Am. Inst. Banking, Jr. League of Youngstown, Alumni Assn. Coll. of Wm. and Mary, Delta Zeta Alumni Assn. Republican. Methodist. Home: 7099 Oak Dr Youngstown OH 44514-3763 Office: Bank One of Ea Ohio 6 Federal Plz W Youngstown OH 44503-1410

BECHTEL, SHERRELL JEAN, psychotherapist; b. Birmingham, Ala., Sept. 23, 1961; d. Lewis Eugene and Sarah Rozelle (Sherrell) B. BS in Social Work, U. Ala., Birmingham, 1989; MSW, U. Ala., Tuscaloosa, 1990. Cert. addiction specialist. Vol. counselor Planned Parenthood, Birmingham, 1986-88; intern Bradford Adult Chem. Dependency, Birmingham, 1989; rsch. staff asst. U. Ala., Tuscaloosa, 1989-90; intern counselor Bradford Adolescent Chem. Dependency, Birmingham, 1990; primary counselor The Crossroads, Chattanooga, 1990-92; owner S. J. Bechtel LCSW, CAS, Chattanooga, 1991—; rschr. Ala. Commn. Youth, Montgomery, 1989-90; trainer Legal and Jud. Aspects Child Welfare, Decatur, Ala., 1989; presenter Ala. Victim Compensation, Mobile, 1990; speaker Limestone Correctional Facility, Huntsville, 1990; lectr. Grad. Sch. Social Wk., Tuscaloosa, 1990, U. Tenn., Chattanooga. Subcom. mem. Atty. Gen. Alliance Against Drug Abuse, Birmingham, 1989; speaker Victims of Crime and Leniency, Tuscaloosa, 1990; planning com. Holistic Health Retreat, Birmingham, 1988; mem. Tenn. Coun. on Children and Youth-Legis./Policy. Mem. NASW (pres. student orgn. 1986-89), Tenn. Alcohol Drug Assn., Jewish Community Ctr., Phi Kappa Phi. Office: 7405 Shallowford Rd Ste 280 Chattanooga TN 37421

BECHTHOLD, ALISA RAE, financial planner; b. Carrington, N.D., Sept. 1, 1964; d. Kurby Ray and Elaine May (Tininenko) B. BS in Molecular Biology, Calif. State U., Sacramento, 1989; MIBA in Strategic Mgmt., U.S. Internat. U., San Diego, 1994. Profl. rep. Merck, Sharp & Dohme, San Luis Obispo, Calif., 1989-91; profl. med. rep. Syntex Labs., San Diego, 1991-94; registered rep. Cigna Fin. Advisors, Atlanta, 1994—. Vol. family aide Homestart, Inc., San Diego, 1992-93. Mem. Atlanta Women in Bus., Nat. Assn. Female Execs. Office: Cigna Fin Advisors Inc 1800 Parkway Pl Ste 900 Marietta GA 30067

BECK, ARIADNE PLUMIS, psychologist, psychotherapist, management consultant; b. Orange, N.J., Jan. 24, 1933; d. George Nicholas and Panagiota Beatrice (Drevas) Plumis; m. Robert Nason Beck, Feb. 16, 1958. AAS, Fashion Inst. Tech., N.Y.C., 1952; BS, Cornell U., 1954; MA, U. Chgo., 1969. Lic. clin. psychologist, Ill. Teaching asst., rsch. asst. U. Chgo., 1955-60; staff counselor Counseling and Psychotherapy Rsch. Ctr., U. Chgo., 1959-66; dir. instruction in programs of counseling the disadvantaged Extension div., U. Chgo., 1960-71; dir. Counseling Ctr., Ill. Inst. Tech., Chgo., 1971-77; pvt. practice Oak Brook, Ill., 1972—; mgmt. cons. SAGE Cons., 1987—; coord. Chgo. Group Devel. Rsch. Team, Indian Head Park, 1980—; lectr., workshop leader various mental health, edn. and bus. instns., 1961—. Contbr. chpts. to books; contbr. articles to profl. jours. Inspired Ariadne P. Beck scholarship Ill. Sch. Profl. Psychology, Chgo., 1989. Mem. APA, ACA, Am. Group Psychotherapy Assn. (chmn. rsch. com. 1986-88), Soc. for Psychotherapy Rsch., Ill. Group Psychotherapy Assn. (pres. 1977, Disting. Svc. award 1986, Ariadne P. Beck scholarship named in her honor 1994). Home and Office: 6357 Blackhawk Trl La Grange IL 60525-4315 Office: 1010 Jorie Blvd Ste 356 Oak Brook IL 60521

BECK, AUDREY, computer consultant; b. Mpls., July 23, 1954; d. John George and Shirley Hope (Dahley) Neis. Student, Hennepin County Vo-Tech. Coll. Software engr. CPT Corp., Mpls., 1978-85, Datamyte Corp., Minnetonka, Minn., 1985; sr. system support rep. Moore Data Mgmt. Services, Mpls., 1985-92; computer contractor, Mpls., 1980—. Avocations: programming, electronics, horses, carpentry. Home and Office: 5601 Judy Ln Minneapolis MN 55430-2925

BECK, DOROTHY FAHS, social researcher; b. N.Y.C.; d. Charles Harvey and Sophia (Lyon) Fahs; m. Hubert Park Beck, Aug. 20, 1930 (dec. Jan. 1989); 1 child, Brenda E.F. AB, U. N.C., 1928; MA, U. Chgo., 1932; PhD (Gilder fellow), Columbia U., 1944, postdoctoral study, 1955-56. Am.-German Student Exch. fellow, Fed. Republic Germany, 1928-29. Dir. econ. rsch. ADA, 1929-32; social worker Emergency Relief Adminstrn. N.J., 1933-34, statistician, 1934-35; statistician U.S. Office Edn., 1935-36; assoc. social economist U.S. Cen. Statis. Bd., 1936-38; rsch. supr., author Am. Coll. Dentists, 1940-42; statistician Am. Heart Assn., 1947-53, Cornell U. Med. Coll., 1951-53; asst. prof. biostats. Am. U. Beirut, 1954; dir. rsch. Family Svc. Am., N.Y.C., 1956-81, dir. study counselor attitudes and feelings, 1982-87, evaluation rsch. cons., 1982-87. Co-founder, Fahs-Beck Fund for Rsch. and Experimentation; donor-adviser The N.Y. Community Trust, 1986—. Fellow Am. Sociol. Assn.; mem. Acad. Cert. Social Workers, Am. Assn. Marriage and Family Therapy (affiliate), Nat. Coun. Family Rels., Groves Conf., Am. Statis. Assn., Nat. Assn. Social Workers, Soc. Study Social Problems, Am. Pub. Health Assn., Phi Beta Kappa. Unitarian-Universalist. Author: Patterns in Use of Family Agency Service, 1962, Marriage and the Family Under Challenge, 1976, New Treatment Modalities, 1978, Counselor Characteristics: How They Affect Outcomes, 1988; co-author: Costs of Dental Care Under Specific Clinical Conditions, 1943, Myocardial Infarction, 1954, Clients' Progress within Five Interviews, 1970, How to Conduct a Client Follow-Up Study, 1974, 2d enlarged edit., 1980, Progress on Family Problems, 1973. Home: Apt 50 Crosslands Kennett Square PA 19348

BECK, ELLEN, public relations executive; b. N.Y.C., May 22, 1961. BA, Am. U., 1984. Dir. sta. rels. PubSat, 1985-86; v.p. Britt-Vasarely and Assocs., 1986-87; sr. account exec. Fleishman-Hillard, 1987-90; account exec. Richardson, Myers and Donofri, 1990, Porter/Novelli, 1990-92; founder, pres. Beck Comm., Ellicott City, Md., 1992—. Office: Beck Comms 9542 Westwood Dr Ellicott City MD 21042*

BECK, J. GAYLE, psychologist, educator; b. Richmond, Ind., Dec. 12, 1956; d. Robert Warren and Sallie Gayle Beck. AB, Brown U., 1979; PhD, SUNY, Albany, 1984. Lic. psychologist, N.Y., Tex. Asst. prof. psychology U. Houston, 1984-90, assoc. prof. psychology, 1990-93; assoc. prof. psychology SUNY, Buffalo, 1993—; cons. in field. Author: (with others) Patterns of Sexual Arousal: Psychophysiological Processes and Clinical Applications, 1988, Handbook of Clinical Behavior Therapy, 2d. edit., 1992, Handbook of Sexual Dysfunctions, 1993, Innovations in Clinical Practice, vol. 12, 1993, Adult Behavior Therapy Casebook, 1994, others; mem.

editorial bd. Jour. Anxiety Disorders, Archives Sexual Behavior, Behavior Therapy; cons. editor Annals of Behavioral Medicine; reviewer jours.; contbr. articles to profl. jours. Presdl. fellow SUNY, 1979-82; grantee U. Houston, 1984-86, NIH, 1985-86, Am. Heart Assn., 1986-90, Tex. Higher Edn. Coordinating Bd., 1989-94. Fellow APA (sec. divsn. 38, 1990-93 program reviewer 1989—); mem. AAAS, Tex. Psychol. Assn. (chair behavior therapy com. 1987-89), Houston Psychol. Assn. (continuing edn. com. 1987), Houston Behavior Therapy Assn. (treas. 1985-86), Assn. for Advancement Behavior Therapy (publs. com. 1988-91, coord. workshop 1991-94), Internat. Acad. Sex. Rsch., Soc. Psychophysiol. Rsch., Soc. Sex Therapy and Rsch. Office: SUNY Dept Psychology 230 Parkdale Ave Buffalo NY 14213-1429

BECK, JOAN WAGNER, journalist; b. Clinton, Iowa, Sept. 5, 1923; d. Roscoe Charles and Mildred (Noel) Wagner; m. Ernest William Beck, Sept. 9, 1945; children—Christopher, Melinda. B.J. cum laude, Northwestern U., 1945, M.S. in Journalism, 1947. Radio script writer O.W.I. Voice of Am., 1945-46; copy writer Marshall Field & Co., 1947-50; feature writer Chgo. Tribune, 1950-61, writer syndicated column about young people, 1956-61, syndicated column about children, 1961-72, editor daily features sect., 1972-75, mem. editorial bd., 1975-92; syndicated editorial page columnist, 1974—. Author: How to Raise a Brighter Child, 1967, (with Dr. Virginia Apgar) Is My Baby All Right?, 1973, Effective Parenting, 1976, Best Beginnings, 1983. Hon. chmn. Mother's March of Met. Chgo. chpt. Nat. Found. March of Dimes, 1970-75; trustee Ill. Children's Home and Aid Soc., 1971-92, life trustee, 1992—; mem. Women's Bd. Northwestern U. Coun. of 100, 1993—. Recipient AP award for best newspaper feature series award Ill., 1964, best feature, 1966, best columns, 1983, 84, Alumni Merit award Northwestern U., 1965, Alumnae award, 1977, Nat. award of Achievement Alpha Chi Omega, 1966, 1st pl. award Penny-U. Mo., 1973, Lisagor award dor editorials, 1982, 88, 91, and commentary, 1994, UPI Ill. award for editorial writing, 1984, commentary award Am. Soc. Newspaper Editors, 1994; named to Chgo. Journalism Hall of Fame, 1994. Mem. Chgo. Network, Chgo. Headline Club, Theta Sigma Phi, Alpha Chi Omega. Methodist. Office: Chgo Tribune PO Box 25340 435 N Michigan Ave Chicago IL 60611-4001

BECK, JUDY ANNA, educational administrator, association executive; b. Washington, Sept. 21, 1949; d. Paul Edward and Lillieanna (Powell) B.; life ptnr. Allida M. Black. BA, W.Va. Wesleyan Coll., 1971; postgrad., Duke U., 1971-72; MA in Human Resource Mgmt., Marymount U., 1992. Coordinating editor Duke U., 1979-83; adminstrv. coord., affirmative action officer Arapahoe County Task Force on Alcohol Problems, Denver, 1984; program asst. Community Cash Flow Fund, Denver, 1984-85; coord. women's work force network Wider Opportunities for Women, Inc., Washington, 1985-88, asst. dir. special projects/products, nat. programs divsn., 1988-90; assoc. dir. mgmt. Clearinghouse on Teaching and Tchr. Edn., Ednl. Resources Info. Ctr., Washington, 1990—; tng. sessions and presentations in field. Contbr. articles to profl. jours. Pres., bd. dirs. YWCA of Durham, 1979-81; nat. bd. mem. YWCA of U.S.A., 1982-88, 88-94, chmn. Program Devel. Com., Pub. Policy Com., mem. Nominating Com. Home: 5429 N 24th St Arlington VA 22205

BECK, LOIS GRANT, anthropologist, educator; b. Bogota, Colombia, Nov. 5, 1944; d. Martin Lawrence and Dorothy (Sweet) Grant; m. Henry Huang; 1 dau., Julia. BA, Portland State U., 1967; MA, U. Chgo., 1969, PhD, 1977. Asst. prof. Amherst (Mass.) Coll., 1973-76, Univ. Utah, Salt Lake City, 1976-80; from asst. to assoc. prof. Washington U., St. Louis, 1980-92, prof., 1992—. Author: Qashqa'i of Iran, 1986, Nomad, 1991; co-editor Women in the Muslim World, 1978. Grantee Social Scis. Rsch. Coun., 1990, NEH, 1990-92. Mem. Middle East Studies Assn. (bd. dirs. 1981-84), Soc. Iranian Studies (exec. sec. 1979-82, edit. bd. 1982-91). Office: Washington U Dept Anthropology 1 Brookings Dr Saint Louis MO 63130-4899

BECK, MARY CLARE, librarian; b. Chgo., Mar. 31, 1941; d. Thomas Milton and Elizabeth (Tuomy) B. BA in History, U. Chgo., 1963; MLS, U. Denver, 1966; MA in Social Studies, Ea. Mich. U., 1976, postgrad., 1977. Reference libr. Fordham U., Bronx, 1966-70; govt. documents libr. Ea. Mich. U., Ypsilanti, 1970—. Author: 1980 Census Resources, a Directory for Washtenaw County Data Users, 1980; editor: Know Your County: a Handbook of Washtenaw County Government, 1984; contbr. articles to profl. jours. Mem. ALA (var. coms.), Mich. Acad. Scis. Arts and Letters (var. offices), League of Woman Voters. Office: Ea Mich Univ University Library Ypsilanti MI 48197

BECK, NANCY MANN MCCONNICO (MRS. EARL C. BECK, JR.), civic worker; b. Memphis, Aug. 31, 1933; d. John Davis and Pauline (Hilton) McConnico; m. Dean Carlton DuBois, Aug. 19, 1950 (div. Nov. 1963); children: Denise Hilton, Dean Carlton; m. Earl Crafton Beck, Jr.; 1 son, John McConnico Harrington. Grad., So. Sem. and Jr. Coll., 1949. Asst. buyer sportswear John Gerber Co., Memphis, 1949-50; fashion coordinator J. Hilton McConnico, Designer, Paris, 1963-65; buyer, mgr. Bridal Salon Goldsmiths, Memphis, 1965-72, buyer, mgr. French Room, 1970-72. Press relations Hunter Lane for mayor, 1967; v.p. West Memphis Fine Arts CTR., 1977-79; v.p. Ct. Sq. Properties; chmn. Crittenden County-Memphis, regional chmn. Mid-South Billy Graham Crusade, May 1978; chmn. Children's Art Day, Memphis, 1976-78, Memphis Symphony Ball, 1981; chmn. Crittenden County Jim Guy Tucker for U.S. Senate; bd. dirs. Crittenden Fine Arts Center, 1979-82, Memphis Orchestral Soc., 1981-86, Memphis Arts Council; bd. dirs. Am. Symphony Orch. League, 1985-88, v.p., conf. chmn. vol. council, 1974-75; bd. dirs. Memphis Symphony League, 1977-78, chmn. Symphony Ball, 1981; dir. devel. St. George's Day Sch., Germantown, Tenn., 1987—, pres., 1980-81, chmn. of ball 1981; trustee So. Sem. Coll., Buena Vista, Va., 1982—; chmn. Maestro Vincent De Frank Tribute Com., 1984-85; bd. dirs. Ark. Gov.'s Mansion Assn., 1986-88; mem. Memphis Bd. Edn. Tchr. Initiative Grants Com., 1987—; mem. devel. com. 1st Tenn. Young Artist Competition, 1988. Recipient Nat. Ednl. award for Children's Arts Day, 1978, Tenn.-Ark.-Miss. Girl Scout Council award, 1986-87, Memphis Hebe award, 1986. Mem. Episc. Churchwomen (pres. 1983-85), Josephine Circle (pres. 1963-64), Memphis Woman's Exchange. Episcopalian. 0 Club: Town and Country Garden (pres. 1975-77). also: 1855 New Riverdale Rd Germantown TN 38138-2603 Office: RR 1 Box 50 Hughes AR 72348-9801

BECK, ROSALIE A., art educator; b. Madison, Wis., Oct. 19, 1954; d. Eugene Aloysius and Mary Magdeline (Weitzel) B. BS, U. Wis., 1978; MFA, U. Wis., Milw., 1986. Teaching asst. U. Wis., Milw., 1983-85, lectr. figure drawing, 1984-86; asst. prof. drawing U. Wis., Parkside, 1986-87; instr. painting and drawing Coll. St. Rose, Albany, N.Y., 1988-90; instr. drawing and design Sage Jr. Coll. of Albany, 1988—, instr. drawing, 1994—; juror N.Y. State Scholastic Art Awards, Albany, 1992; guest critic Albany Artist League, 1992—. One woman shows include Utica Coll. of Syracuse U., 1993, Greene County Coun. on Arts, 1994. N.Y. State Arts Found. grantee Rensselaer County Coun. on Arts, 1994. Mem. Coll. Art Assn. Home: 2 W Erie St Albany NY 12208

BECK, VICKEY MAI, counselor; b. Leavenworth, Kans., Feb. 3, 1938; d. Frank Killian Beck and Vina Louise (Mennesson) Beck Coffin. BS in Edn., Emporia State U., 1959; MEd, Wichita State U., 1966; cert. edn. specialist, Pitts. State U., 1991. Cert. elem. and secondary counselor, Kans. Tchr. phys. edn. Haysville (Kans.) Sch. Dist., 1959-60, Unified Sch. Dist. 259, Wichita, Kans., 1960-74; tchr. phys. edn. and psychology Unified Sch. Dist. 479, Colony and Kincaid, Kans., 1976-90; elem. counselor Unified Sch. Dist. 257, Iola, Kans., 1990—. Mem. ACA, NEA, Am. Sch. Counselor Assn., Kans. Edn. Assn., Kans. Counseling Assn. (sec. 1994—), Kans. Sch. Counselor Assn. (sec.-treas. 1992-94), S.E. Kans. Counseling Assn. (treas. 1993—). Home: 1006 S Broadway Ave La Harpe KS 66751 Office: Lincoln Elem Sch 700 N Jefferson St Iola KS 66749-2219

BECKEMEYER, NANCY SCOTT, landscape architect; b. Atlanta, Apr. 1, 1953; d. Delmont Emil and Frances Rentz (Howell) B. B in Landscape Architecture, U. Ga., 1977. Registered landscape architect, Ga. Owner So. Landscape Designs, Hattiesburg, Miss., 1977-81; instr. DeKalb Coll., Atlanta, 1990, 91; pres. Autumn Ridge Inc. Landscape Architecture & Constrn. Firm, Atlanta, 1981—; instr. Clayton State Coll., Morrow, Ga., 1981—, Kennesaw (Ga.) Coll., 1985—, Sutton Community Sch., Atlanta, 1986—; instr. Landscape Architecture Uniform Nat. Exam. Rev., 1990, 91, 92, 93, 94. Past pres. appointed to Cen. Atlanta Progress Adv. Coun. Named Outstanding Young Woman of Am., 1981, 83; recipient Award of Merit Sch. Environ. Design, 1977. Mem. Am. Soc. Landscape Architects (awards program chmn. 1985, sec. Ga. chpt. 1986, pres. 1990, nat. nominating com. 1991—), Am. Bus. Women's Assn. (pres. So. Miss. chpt., Woman of Yr. 1981), U. Ga. Alumni Assn. (sch. environ. design, steering com. 1983-86, pres. 1992-94, 1st Quar. Club, SEDAA pres. 1993-94).

BECKENHAUPT, PATRICIA MARY, hospital administrator; b. Bklyn., July 26, 1948; d. Edgar Newell and Mary Agnes (Eichner) Cordle; m. Kenenth R. Beckenhaupt, July 16, 1994; children from previous marriage: Laura Anne, Kathleen Mary, Raymond Francis. Diploma, Mary Immaculate Hosp., 1968; BS, Charter Oak Coll., 1985; MS, Ea. Conn. State U., 1987; MPH, U. Conn., 1994. Oper. staff nurse Mary Immaculate Hosp., Jamaica, N.Y., 1968-74; childbirth educator No. Shore Hosp., Manhasset, N.Y., 1975-78; coord. nursing ARC, Nassau County, N.Y., 1975-78; coord. parent edn. Hartford (Conn.) Hosp., 1979-85; adminstrv. dir. mktg. and community svcs. Johnson Meml. Hosp., Stafford Springs, Conn., 1987—; coord. CanSurmount Am. Cancer Soc., Manchester, Conn., 1989-91, bd. dirs.; adj. prof. Springfield (Mass.) Coll., 1991. Producer: (documentary) Psychodrama, 1990. Panelist Springfield Coll., 1991. Recipient Lifesaver award Am. Cancer Soc., Quality of Life award, 1991, Mgmt. Inst. award Springfield Coll., 1991, Edward B. Kovar Meml. Lecture award New Eng. Pub. Health Assn., 1992; grantee Conn. Dept. Labor, North Ctrl. Area Agy. on Aging, 1991-94. Mem. Am. Assn. Occupational Health Nurses. Home: 19 Pinecrest Rd West Willington CT 06279-2216 Office: Johnson Meml Hosp 201 Chestnut Hill Rd Stafford Springs CT 06076

BECKER, ANNE MARGARET, neonatal nurse; b. San Rafael, Calif., Sept. 4, 1953; d. Robert E. and Helen (Grondorf) Spitzer; m. Michael Becker, Nov. 21, 1973; children: Miriam, Davina. Diploma, St. Luke's Sch. Nursing, San Francisco, 1974; AS, San Francisco Community Coll., 1974; BS, U. Calif., San Francisco, 1984, MS, 1986. RN, Calif.; cert. high-risk perinatal nurse ANCC. Staff nurse II Children's Hosp. Med. Ctr., Oakland, Calif., 1974-86; outreach educator Children's Hosp., San Francisco, 1986; staff nurse Med. Personnel Pool, San Francisco, 1986-87; staff nurse II-IV Stanford (Calif.) U. Hosp., 1987-91; staff nurse IV Lucile Salter Packard Children's Hosp., Stanford, Palo Alto, Calif., 1991—, acting clin. nurse specialist, 1993—. Mem. editorial bd. Neonatal Network jour., Petaluma, Calif., 1987—; peer reviewer Jour. Am. Acad. Nurse Practitioners, Pitts., 1990-92; author (poetry) Waiting, 1989. Vol. Quention Kopp for State Senator Campaign, South San Francisco, 1990; pres. local chpt. PTA, South San Francisco, 1987. Mem. ANA (exec. com. coun. on maternal-child nursing 1993-94, exec. com. mem. coun. for acute care nursing practice 1994-95), ANCC (perinatal nurse test devel. com. 1989-92, bd. on cert. for maternal-child nursing 1989-91), Calif. Nurses Assn. (chair nursing practice commn. 1991-93, commr. 1991-94, co-founder, vice chair coun. on children and families 1991-94), Nat. Assn. Neonatal Nurses, U. Calif. San Francisco Nursing Alumni Assn. (editorial cons. grad. nursing students 1991-92). Republican. Episcopalian. Home: 612 Stonegate Dr South San Francisco CA 94080-1564

BECKER, BETSY See ASWAD, BETSY

BECKER, BETTIE GERALDINE, artist; b. Peoria, Ill., Sept. 22, 1918; d. Harry Seymour and Magdalene Matilda (Hiller) B.; m. Lionel William Wathall, Nov. 10, 1945; children: Heather Lynn (dec.), Jeffrey Lee. BFA cum laude, U. Ill., Urbana, 1940; postgrad. Art Inst. Chgo., 1942-45, Art Student's League, 1946, Ill. Inst. tech., 1948. Dept. artist Liberty Mut. Ins. Co., Chgo., 1941-43; with Palenskie-Young Studio, 1943-46; free lance illustrator N.Y. Times, Chgo. Tribune, Saturday Rev. Lit., 1948-50; co-owner, operator Pangaea Gallery/Studio, Fish Creek, Wis.; pvt. tutor, tchr. studio classes. Exhibited one-man show Crossroads Gallery, Art Inst. Chgo., 1973; exhibited group shows including Critics' Choice show Art Rental Sales Gallery Art Inst. Chgo., 1972, Evanston-North Shore exhbns., 1964, 65, Chgo. Soc. Artists, 1967, 71, Union League, 1967, 72, Women in Art, Appleton (Wis.) Gallery Art, Milw. Art Mus., 1986, Neville Pub. Mus., Green Bay, Wis., 1987, Valperine Gallery, Madison, Wis. 1989, 92, Wis. Arts Gallery, Allouez, 1990, 94, North Cen. Coll., Naperville, Ill., 1991, Neville Mus., Green Bay, Wis., 1990, 91, Art Works Gallery, Green Bay, 1992, 94, Tria II Gallery, Fish Creek, Wis., Oesterle Gallery, N. Ctrl. Coll., Naperville, 1993, Neville Mus., Green Bay, 1993-94, Rabbi Joseph L. Baron Mus., Milw., 1994, Beacon St. Gallery, Chgo., 1995; represented in permanent collection Witte Meml. Mus., San Antonio, Miller Art Ctr., Stugeon Bay, Wis., Neville Mus., Green Bay, Wis.; executed mural (with F. Wiater) Talbot Lab. U. Ill., Urbana, 1940; contbr. articles and illustrations to mags. and newspapers. Active Campfire Girls, Chgo., 1968, 70; art chmn., mem. exec. bd. local PTA, 1959-60; active various art festivals, 1967—. Mem. Chgo. Soc. Artists (rec. sec. 1968-77), Wis. Arts Coun., N.E. Wis. Arts Coun. (bd. dir.), Alumni Assn. Art Inst. Chgo., Door County Art League, Wis. Women in the Arts, Soc. Exptl. Artists. Republican. Mem. Unity Ch. Home: 46 E Pine St Sturgeon Bay WI 54235-2726

BECKER, COLLEEN MARIE, counselor; b. Kansas City, Mo., Sept. 30, 1954; d. Robert Leo and Constance Marie (Warner) Gilday; m. L.F. Becker, Aug. 24, 1974 (div. Feb. 1993); children: Paul Austin, John Barrett, Amy Lyn; m. D.L. Fischer, Aug. 24, 1993. B Music Therapy, U. Mo., 1977, EdS, 1990; MS in Counseling/Psychology, Northwest Mo. State U., 1984. Lic. profl. counselor; bd. cert.-registered music therapist. Dir. music therapy dept. St. Joseph (Mo.) State Hosp., 1978-85; psychologist Woodson Children's Psychiat. Hosp., St. Joseph, 1985-88; psychologist-in-tng. Clin. Counseling and Cons. Svcs., St. Joseph, 1985-90; counselor Cath. Charities, St. Joseph, 1985-87; psychologist St. Joseph State Hosp., 1989-91; substance abuse counselor, family therapist St. Joseph Youth Recovery Ctr., 1991-92, Renaissance West-Women's Place, Kansas City, Mo., 1992-93; profl. counselor St. Joseph, 1993—; adv. bd. Job Corps, St. Joseph, 1994-95. Mem. Hist. Mus. Hill Neighborhood Assn., St. Joseph, 1994-95, Nat. Trust for Hist. Preservation. Mem. Mo. Assn. for Home-Based Svcs., Am. Assn. Marriage and Family Therapy (assoc.), Am. Counseling Assn., Assn. Specialists in Group Work, Internat. Assn. Marriage and Family Therapy, North Am. Assn. for Master's in Psychology, Mo. Counseling Assn., Mo. Mental Health Counselors Assn., U. Mo.- Kansas City Alumni Assn. Office: 416 S 12th St Saint Joseph MO 64501

BECKER, DOROTHY ANNE, social worker; b. Rochester, N.Y.; d. John Edward and Harriet Lorraine (Legler) Becker. MEd, Boston Coll., 1976; MSW, Marywood Coll., 1983. Cert. social worker, alcoholism counselor, N.Y.; lic. clin. social worker Assn. Cert. Social Workers; diplomate Am. Bd. Marriage and Family Therapy. Assoc. dir. Family Support Program, Elmira, N.Y., 1976-80; clin. social worker Broome County Alcoholism Ctr., Binghamton, N.Y., 1980-86, Tidewater Psychiatric Inst., Virginia Beach, Va., 1986-88, Ctr. Psychiatrists, Virginia Beach, Va., 1988, Ctr. for Personal Recovery, Virginia Beach, Va., 1988—. Fellow NASW, Am. Assn. Marriage and Family Therapy. Office: Ctr for Personal Recovery 168 Business Park Dr # 101 Virginia Beach VA 23462-6532

BECKER, GAIL ROSELYN, museum director; b. Long Branch, N.J., Oct. 22, 1942; d. Joseph and Adele (Michelsohn) B. BA, Vassar Coll., 1964. Exhibit project officer U.S. Info. Agy., Washington, 1967-87, chief devel. and prodn. exhibits, 1987-91; exec. dir. Louisville Sci. Ctr. (formerly Mus. History and Sci.), 1991—; mem. adv. com. Ky. Ctr. Health Edn., Louisville, 1991—; mem. adv. com. Rauch Planetarium, Louisville, 1991—; bd. dirs. Louisville Advanced Tech. Coun., 1993—, Muhammad Ali Mus. and Internat. Ctr., 1994—. Active tourism adv. coun. Louisville Conv. & Visitors Bur. Recipient Presdl. Design awards Nat. Endowment for the Arts, Washington, 1984, 88, 92, Special Achievement award U.S. Info. Agy., Washington, 1988. Mem. Am. Assn. Mus. (bd. dirs. 1994—), Am. Assn. Advancement Slavic Studies, Louisville Com. Fgn. Rels. (bd. dirs.), Assn. Sci.-Tech. Ctrs. (bd. dirs. 1992—), Leadership Louisville, Vassar Coll. Alumnae Assn., Ky. Sci. & Tech. Coun. (bd. dirs. 1993—), Rotary. Office: Louisville Sci Ctr 727 W Main St Louisville KY 40202

BECKER, JOANN ELIZABETH, insurance company executive; b. Chester, Pa., Oct. 29, 1948; d. James Thomas and Elizabeth Theresa (Barnett) Clark; m. David Norbert Becker, June 7, 1969. BA, Washington U., St. Louis, 1970, MA, 1971. Tchr. Kirkwood (Mo.) Sch. Dist., 1971-73; devel. and sr. devel. analyst Lincoln Nat. Life Ins. Co., Ft. Wayne, Ind., 1973-77, systems programming specialist, 1977-79, sr. project mgr., 1979-81, asst. v.p., 1981-85, 2d v.p., 1985-88, v.p., 1988-91; pres., CEO The Richard Leahy Corp., Ft. Wayne, 1991-93; pres. Lincoln Nat. Corp. Equity Sales Corp, Ft. Wayne, 1993-94; v.p. portfolio mgmt. group Lincoln Nat. Investment Mgmt. Co., Ft. Wayne, 1994—. Contbr. articles to profl. jours. Bd. dirs. Ind. Humanities Coun., Indpls., 1991—, treas., mem. exec. com., 1994—. Named Women of Achievement, YWCA, Ft. Wayne, 1986, Sagamore of Wabash, Gov. State of Ind., 1990. Mem. Master Life Mgmt. Inst. Soc. Ft. Wayne (CLU, pres. 1983-84, designation with honor 1980), Life Ins. Mktg. Rsch. Assn. (Leadership Inst. fellowship designation, mem. exec. devel. com. 1993-94, mem. fin. svcs. com. 1993-94), Am. Mgmt. Assn., Ft. Wayne C. of C. (mem., chmn. audit-fin. com. 1989—, mem. legis. coun. 1995—).

BECKER, JUDITH IRIS, educator; b. Mobile, Ala., Feb. 21, 1941; d. James and Belle (Lupin) Gutel; m. Stanley Charles Becker, Dec. 27, 1964; children: Marci Gail Becker Blumenfeld, Joel Howard, David Alan. BS in Edn., U. Ala., Tuscaloosa, 1963; MEd, U. Mo., St. Louis, 1991. Cert. bus. edn., 7-12 social studies, K-12 art tchr., Mo. Tchr. typing and social studies N.E. Houston Sch. Dist., 1963-65; substitute tchr. Ladue, Parkway and Pattonville sch. dists., St. Louis, 1988-90; tchr. art Pattonville Sch. Dist., 1990-91, Ft. Zumwalt Sch. Dist., O'Fallon, Mo., 1991—; bd. dirs. Frame Factory Ltd., Maryland Heights, Mo. Contbg. author: Using Recyclables Grades K-1, 1991, Grades 2-3, 1991; contbg. artist: The Sagarin Review, Vol. 3, 1993. Mem. NEA, Mo. Edn. Assn., Pattonville Edn. Assn., Ft. Zumwalt Edn. Assn., Nat. Art Edn. Assn., Mo. Art Edn. Assn., Greater St. Louis Artists Assn. (past sec.). Jewish.

BECKER, JULIETTE, psychologist, marriage and family therapist; b. L.A., Sept. 22, 1938; d. Louis Joseph and Elissa Cecelia (Bevacqua) Cevola; m. Richard Charles Sprenger, Aug. 13, 1960 (div. Dec. 1984); children: Lisa Anne, Stephen Louis, Gina Marie, Paul Joseph, Gretchen Lynette; m. Vance Benjiman Becker, Nov. 7, 1986. BA in Psychology, Calif. State U., Fullerton, 1983; M in Marriage and Family Therapy, U.S. Internat. U., 1985; PhD in Clin. Psychology, William Lyon U., 1988. Therapist Villa Park (Calif.) Psychol. Svcs., 1985-88, psychologist, 1988—. Mem. APA, Am. Assn. Marriage, Family and Child Therapists, Calif. Assn. Marriage, Family and Child Therapists. Office: Villa Park Psychol Svcs 17871 Santiago Blvd Ste 206 Orange CA 92667-4131

BECKER, KAREN ANN, program director; b. Willoughby, Ohio, Apr. 9, 1963; d. William Herbert and Janet Mae (Wilkins) B. BA in English and Speech, Allegheny Coll., 1985, MEd, 1986; postgrad., Baldwin-Wallace Coll., 1987-88; PhD, Ohio State U., 1993. Cert. tchr. English and speech provisional, Ohio. Student asst. Allegheny Coll., Meadville, Pa., 1981-85; high sch. tchr. North Royalton (Ohio) City Schs., 1985-87, substitute tchr., 1987-88; instr., researcher Townsend Learning Ctr., Chagrin Falls, Ohio, 1987-90; cognitive interventionist Excellence in Learning, Upper Arlington, Ohio, 1990; rsch. asst. Nat. Assn. Secondary Sch. Prins., Va., 1990; grad. teaching assoc. Ohio State U., Columbus, 1988-93; adj. faculty Columbus State C.C., 1989-94, Capital U., 1994—, Franklin U., 1994—; instr. and cons. Learning 20/20 and Kids in Coll., 1993-94, village acad. learning unlimited Internat. Sch. Inc., 1994. Rsch. author: Word Atlas, 1988. Mem. ASCD, Phi Kappa Phi. Home: 208 W Como Ave Columbus OH 43202-1039 Office: 72 Woodlands Ave Columbus OH 43203

BECKER, MAGDALENE NEUENSCHWANDER, educator; b. Beaverdam, Ohio, Sept. 5, 1915; d. Walter and Viola Etta (Gratz) Neuenschwander; m. Homer Gerald Becker, Aug. 18, 1935; 1 child, Rachel Etta. BA, Westminster Coll., New Wilmington, Pa., 1954, MEd in Guidance and Counseling, 1971; postgrad. in English, U. Pitts., 1962-65. Cert. tchr. Tchr. pub. speaking New Castle (Pa.) Sr. High Sch., 1954-61; tchr. advanced English Butler (Pa.) Area Sr. High Sch., 1961-77; with Learning Ctr. Sheldon Jackson Coll., Sitka, Alaska, 1977-79; cataloger, reference librarian Lees Coll., Jackson, Ky., 1979-83; coordinator conf. ctr. Cook Christian Tng. Sch., Tempe, Ariz., 1983-85; tutor Armstrong-Ind. County Intermediate Unit, Indiana, Pa., 1985-92; tutor ESL Lakeland, Fla., 1992—; evaluator Mid-Atlantic Sch. Examiners, 1966; examiner Nat. Coun. Tchrs. of English, 1964-76. Author 11 computer discs of GED programs, 1987-88. Tchr. Sunday Sch., Presbyn. Ch., 1940—, deacon, elder, 1985—, vice moderator women's gathering, 1993—; bd. dirs. Group Homes, Indiana, 1986-89; vol. in nursing home, 1985—; sec. Lake Hunter Fellowship. Mem. NEA, Pa. State Edn. Assn., Indiana County Edn. Assn., AAUW (pres. Indiana br. 1988-90, exec. v.p. 1986-88). Republican. Home: 16 Lake Hunter Dr Apt A303 Lakeland FL 33803-1280

BECKER, MARY LOUISE, political scientist; b. St. Louis; d. W. R. and Evelyn (Thompson) Becker; divorced; children: James, John. BS, Washington U., St. Louis, 1949, MA, 1951; PhD, Radcliffe Coll., 1957; postgrad., U. Karachi (Pakistan), 1953-54. Intelligence rsch. analyst Dept. State, Washington, 1957-59; internat. rels. officer AID, Washington, 1959-64, community rels. officer, 1964-66, sci. rsch. officer, 1966-71, UN rels. officer, 1971-91; pres. Internat. Devel. Enterprises, Washington, 1992—; adviser U.S. dels. 19th, 21st, 23d, 24th, 26th, 28th, 30th, 32d, 34th Governing Coun. sessions UN Devel. Program; adv. U.S. del. 3d prep. com. meeting World Conf. UN Decade for Women; adviser U.S. dels. UNICEF exec. bd. sessions, 1987-91; lectr. internat. rels. civic orgns., student groups, 1954—; mem. U.S. Com. for UN Fund for Women. Author: Muhammed Iqbal, 1965; contbg. editor: Concise Ency. of Middle East, 1973; contbr. articles to govt. publs. Mem. adv. bd. chmn. internat. student placement Washington Citizenship Seminar, Nat. YMCA-YWCA, Washington, 1961-71. Blewett fellow Washington U., 1951, Resident fellow Radcliffe Coll., 1952-56; Fulbright scholar U. Karachi, 1953-54. Mem. AAUW, Am. Polit. Sci. Assn., Soc. Internat. Devel., Assn. Asian Studies, Asia Soc., Middle East Inst., UN Assn. (bd. dirs. Nat. Capital area 1991—), South Asian Muslim Studies Assn. (v.p. 1992—), Mo. Soc. Washington (sec. 1959-60), Mortar Bd., Chimes, Internat. Club, Harvard Club (Washington), Alpha Lambda Delta, Beta Gamma Sigma, Eta Mu Phi, Pi Sigma Alpha. Presbyterian. Office: North Bldg Ste 700 601 Pennsylvania Ave NW Washington DC 20004

BECKER, SANDRA JANE, computer educator; b. Decatur, Ill., Sept. 28, 1955; d. Omer Kenneth and Donna Pauline (Jones) B.; m. John H. Slater, June 18, 1983 (div. Oct. 1991). BBA, Nat. U., 1982; M in Elem. Edn., Ea. Mich. U., 1990. Cert. elem. tchr., Mich., N.Y. Legal sec., office mgr. San Diego lawyer's Guild, San Diego, 1981-85; instr. computer Saudi Arabian Internat. Sch., Riyadh, 1986-90; instr. computers, coord. Ann Arbor (Mich.) Pub. Schs., 1991-92; mktg. and sales adminstr. UniCoil, Inc., Livonia, Mich., 1992-94; instr. computers, sales New Horizons, Atlanta, 1994—; ednl. tech. specialist Kennesaw State Coll., 1994—. Contbr. articles to mags. Sgt. USMC, 1976-80, Res., 1981-83. Home: 4901 Tree Corners Pkwy Norcross GA 30092

BECKER, SUSAN KAPLAN, management consultant, educator; b. Newark, Jan. 4, 1948; d. Charles and Janet Kaplan; m. William Paul Becker, 1969 (div. 1977). BA in English cum laude, with distinction, U. Pa., 1968, MA, 1969, PhD, 1973, MBA in Fin., 1979. Instr. English Bryn Mawr (Pa.) Coll., 1972-74; assoc. editor U. Pa., Phila., 1975, asst. dir., lectr. urban studies, 1975-77; fin. analyst Phila. Nat. Bank, 1979-82; asst. v.p. Chem. Bank, N.Y.C., 1982-84; v.p. Bankers Trust Co., N.Y.C., 1984-85; prin. Becker Cons., N.Y.C., 1985—; adj. assoc. prof. mgmt. comm. Stern Sch. Bus. N.Y.U., 1990—; cons./evaluator Pa. Humanities Council, Phila., 1977-78; mem. editorial bd. Mgmt. Comm. Quar., 1993—. Author: How to Develop Profitable Financial Products for the Institutional Marketplace, 1988; contbr. articles and revs. to profl. jours. Vol., N.Y. Cares, 1989—. U. Pa. fellow, 1968-72; E.I. DuPont de Nemours fellow, 1979, N.Y. Regents Coll. Teaching fellow, 1968-70. Mem. Am. Mktg. assn. (leadership coun. N.Y. chpt. 1988-91, EFFIE judge 1990-92), Internat. Comm. Assn. (reviewer tech. and comm. divsn. 1991), Fin. Women's Assn. N.Y. Democrat. Office: 155 E 29th St New York NY 10016-8173

BECKER, SUSAN MARY, English language educator; b. Oshkosh, Wis., May 10, 1938; d. Robert C. and Alicia J. (Webster) Schwandt; m. Bruce R. Becker, June 6, 1964; children: Robert Bruce, Jillian Elizabeth. Student, U. Edinburgh, Scotland, 1958-59; AB, Rockford Coll., 1960; MS, U. Wis., 1963. Assoc. prof. English Ill. Ctrl. Coll., East Peoria, 1968—; editor Assembly on Expanded Perspectives, Nat. Coun. Tchrs. English, Urbana, Ill., 1992—; advisor Phi Theta Kappa, Peoria, Ill., 1992—; resume cons. to various students, Peoria, 1988—. Co-author: Presence of Mind, 1994, (bull.) Assn.

for Bus. Comms., 1988; author: (booklet) Beyond the Cognitive, 1993. Bd. dirs. Ctr. for Performing Arts, East Peoria, 1990—, Artist in Residence, Ill. Ctr. Coll., 1992—. Recipient Meritorious Svc. award Mcpl. Clks. Assn., 1990, Horizon award Phi Theta Kappa, 1993. Mem. AAUW (various offices 1965—), Delta Kappa Gamma (chair 1990—). Office: Ill Ctrl Coll One College Dr East Peoria IL 61635

BECKER, TERESA ANN, neonatal nurse practitioner; b. Bangor, Maine, Apr. 22, 1957; d. George Robert and Marlene Ellen (Mueller) B. BSN, East Tenn. State U., 1980; cert. nurse practitioner, Georgetown U., 1988; post-grad., U. Tenn. RN, Tenn.; cert. regional instr. neonatal resuscitation, pediatric advanced life support instr. Charge nurse newborn Johnson City (Tenn.) Med. Ctr., 1980-82, staff nurse SCN, 1982-84, staff nurse NICU, 1984-85, charge nurse NICU, 1985-88, neonatal nurse practitioner, 1989—; regional instr. neonatal resuscitation AAP, Johnson City, 1989—; instr. PALS Am. Heart Assn., Johnson City, 1991—. Bd. dirs. March of Dimes, Johnson City, 1992—; chmn. Health Profl. Adv. Com., 1992-93. Mem. AWHONN, Perinatal-Neonatal Assn., Nat. Assn. Neonatal Nurses, Sigma Theta Tau. Roman Catholic. Home: 4117 Aztec Dr Johnson City TN 37604-1144 Office: Johnson City Med Ctr 400 N State Of Franklin Rd Johnson City TN 37604-6035

BECKER, VANETA G., state representative; b. Alton, Ill., Oct. 7, 1949; m. Andrew C. Guarino. Attended, U. Evansville. Rep. dist. 75 State of Ind., 1981-91, rep. dist. 78, 1991—, ranking minority leader, 1991—; mem. pub. health & cities & towns coms.; mem. asst. minority caucus State of Ind.; realtor Don Cox & Assoc.; mem. bd. dirs. Albion Fellows Bacon Ctr., Patchwork Cent. Recipient Legis. Excellence award United Mine Workers, 1989; named Legislator of the Yr. Ind. Primary Health Care Assn., 1990. Mem. Nat. Assn. Realtors, Ind. Primary Health Care Assn., Evansville Zool. Soc., A Network of Evansville Women, Leadership Evansville, Crisis Prevention Nursery. Republican. Methodist. Home: 420 E Buena Vista Rd Evansville IN 47711-2720 Office: Ind Ho of Reps State Capitol Indianapolis IN 46204*

BECKERER, CAROLE ANN, gerontology nurse; b. Pittsfield, Mass., Aug. 16, 1945; d. Stanley L. and Helen Esther (Howes) Calkins; m. Frank S. Beckerer, Aug. 27, 1966; children: Wendy, Tara, F. Sean. Student, Hartford (Conn.) Hosp. Sch., 1966, St. Joseph's Coll., Windham, Maine. Cert. IV therapy instr. In-svc. coord. Golden Hill Health Care Ctr., Milford, Conn.; dir. of nurses New Fairview Health Care Ctr., New Haven, DON. Mem. Alzheimers Suport Group. Mem. Consortium of Health Care In-Svc. Dirs., Parents of Children with Learning Disabilities. Home: 199 Gulf St Milford CT 06460-4818

BECKER-ROUKAS, HELANE RENÉE, securities analyst, financial executive; b. N.Y.C., May 7, 1957; m. Arnold and Ella Florence (Feldman) Becker; m. George Paul Roukas, Sept. 6, 1980; children: Samuel Matthew, Hannah Beth. BA, Montclair State Coll., 1979; MBA in Fin., NYU, 1984. Options coord. Donaldson Lufkin & Jenrette, N.Y.C., 1979-81; mktg. coord. E.F. Hutton & Co., N.Y.C., 1981-82; securities analyst Prudential-Bache Securities, N.Y.C., 1982-86; v.p., analyst Drexel Burnham Lambert, N.Y.C., 1986-87; mng. dir., analyst Lehman Bros., N.Y.C., 1987-94; v.p., analyst Smith Barney, N.Y.C., 1995—; speaker various airline industry confs. and panels. Columnist Corp. Travel Mag., 1990. Named to Internat. Investor All-Am. Rsch. Team, 1985-94. Mem. Soc. Airline Analysts, Profl. Women in Bus., Wings Club. Club: Wings (N.Y.C.). Office: Smith Barney Am Express Tower 200 Vesey St New York NY 10285-1400

BECKERT, NATALIE A., artist, educator; b. Jamaica, N.Y., May 3, 1937; d. Martin Arthur and Kathryn Elizabeth (Quinn) Myerson; m. James T. Beckert, June 25, 1960; children: Suzanne, Joseph, Jason, Juliane. BA in English, CUNY, 1959; postgrad., West Conn. State U., 1972-77; MFA in Painting, Drawing, Printmaking, Winthrop U., 1990. Tchr., instr. Ctrl. Piedmont C.C., Charlotte, N.C., 1990-94, Winthrop U., Rock Hill, S.C., 1993-94; dir., mgr. Spirit Sq. Print Studio, Charlotte. Solo shows include Mooresville (N.C.) Art League, 1991, Wilkesboro (N.C.) Gallery, 1991, Christa Faut Gallery, Davidson, N.C., 1993, WSOC-TV Lobby, Charlotte, 1994, Pope Gallery, Charlotte, 1994, Union Bldg., Davidson Coll., 1994; represented in collections at Wachovia Bank, Winston-Salem, N.C., 1977, Winthrop U., Rock Hill, S.C., 1989, Nationsbank, High Point, N.C., 1991, others. Judge, registrar Mecklenburg County, N.C., 1988-90; speaker Ctrl. Piedmont C.C., Charlotte, 1990-94; bd. dirs., sec. Friends of Art at Queens Coll., Charlotte, 1990-94. Mem. Phi Kappa Phi.

BECKET, JOHANNA NINA, special education educator; b. Bronx, N.Y., Dec. 14, 1949; d. Vincent Angelo and Jenny (Filippino) Vecchione; children from previous marriage: Jenny, Victoria; m. Lee Hatton, Nov. 8, 1991. BA, Adelphi U., 1964, MA, 1968; MS, Barry U., 1981. Art tchr. Syosset (N.Y.) Pub. Schs., 1964-74; art therapist Jackson Meml. Hosp., Miami, 1978-81; brain mapping technician St. Francis Hosp., Miami, 1981-83, head nuerometrics dept., 1981-83; tchr. severely emotionally disturbed Dade County Pub. Schs./Miami Sunset Sr. High, 1983—, dept. head, spl. edn., 1988—; psychotherapist Christian Counseling Ctr, Meml. Med. Ctr. East Tex., 1992-93, Four Corners Mental Health-Green River High Sch., 1992-93. Editor Counselor Assn. newspaper, 1980-81. Co-chmn. Very Spl. Arts, 1988. Recipient Found. for Excellence grant, Miami, 1988, Citicorp Success Fund grant, 1988; named region VI finalist, Tchr. of the Yr., Dade County Pub. Schs., 1991-92. Mem. Coun. Exceptional Edn., United Tchrs. Dade. Democrat. Roman Catholic. Home: 455 W Ferron Creek Dr Ferron UT 84523 Address: PO Box 1263 Castle Dale UT 84513

BECKETT, KATHLEEN ANNE, insurance agent; b. Wilmington, Del., July 29, 1954; d. William R. and Jean R. (Kyle) Davis; m. Richard Lyle Beckett, July 9, 1983. AAS, Del. Tech. Coll., Wilmington, 1977; A in Risk Mgmt., Am. Inst., Malvern, Pa., 1987. CPCU. Rsch. analyst Rollins Burdick Hunter, Chgo., 1980-83; mtkg. analyst Rollins Burdick Hunter, L.A., 1983-85; underwriter Bolton & Co., Pasadena, Calif., 1985-87; sr. account coord. Fred S. James & Co., L.A., 1987-88; account exec. Sedgwick, Ft. Myers, Fla., 1988-93; customer svc. rep. Poe & Brown, Inc., Ft. Myers, Fla., 1993—; adminstr. Ins. Ednl. Alliance, Ft. Myers, 1991—. Mem. Libertarian Party of Lee County, Bokeelia, Fla., 1991—; mem., tutor Literacy Vols. of Lee County, Ft. Myers, 1992—. Mem. Nat. Assn. Ins. Women (Individual Ednl. Achievement award 1991, Ins. Woman of Yr. Fla. State Coun. 1992, Kay Cooper Scholarship award 1994), Soc. CPCUs (dir. 1994—, edn. chmn. 1994—), Fla. Assn. Ind. Agts. (state catastrophe com. 1993—), Ins. Women of S.W. Fla. (pres., dir., pres.-elect 1988—, Ins. Woman of Yr. 1990), Lee County Assn. Ind. Ins. Agts. (v.p. 1989—). Office: Poe & Brown Inc 4210 Metro Pky Ste 300 Fort Myers FL 33916-9409

BECKEY, CARRIE LYNNE PIAZZA, software consultant; b. Johnstown, Pa., Sept. 11, 1961; d. Frank D. and Rita H. Piazza; m. Christopher T. A. Beckey, May 11, 1991. BS in Math/Computer Sci., Pa. State U., 1983; postgrad., Johns Hopkins U., 1986-87. Programmer Computer Entry Systems Corp., Silver Spring, Md., 1984-86; programmer analyst Computer Entry Systems Corp., Silver Spring, 1986-88; software engr. Roadnet Techs., UPS, Timonium, Md., 1988-92; software cons. RDA Cons. Ltd., Timonium, 1992—. Mem. NAFE, Soc. Women Engrs.

BECKLAKE, MARGARET RIGSBY, physician, educator; b. London, May 27, 1922; d. James Thomas and Dorothy Mabel (Mills) B.; m. Maurice McGregor, Mar. 20, 1949; children: James, Margaret. MBBCh, U. Witwatersrand, 1944, MD, 1951, MD (hon.), 1974. Lectr. U. Witwatersrand, 1950-57; asst. prof. exptl. medicine McGill U., 1961-65, prof., 1967—, prof. epidemiology and medicine, 1973—; career investigator Med. Rsch. Coun. Can., 1968-93. Contbr. articles to med. jours. Named hon. prof., U. Witwatersrand, 1984-85. Fellow Royal Coll. Physicians, Royal Soc. (Can.); mem. Am. Thoracic Soc., Can. Thoracic Soc., Am. Physiol. Soc. Home: 532 Pine Ave W, Montreal, PQ Canada H2W 1S6 Office: McGill U, Dept of Epidemiology & Biostats, 1110 Pine Ave W, Montreal, PQ Canada H3A 1A3

BECKLEY, JEANINE SUSAN, nuclear medicine technologist; b. Rome, N.Y., Jan. 31, 1964; d. Jerry Slater and Glada Ruth (Kingsbury) B. AA, Prince George's C.C., Largo, Md., 1989. Cert. nuclear medicine technologist. Nuclear medicine technologist Nuclear Cardiology Lab., Silver Spring, Md., 1989-93; chief nuclear medicine technologist So. Md. Nuclear Cardiology, Clinton, 1993—; mem. rsch. apprentice program Naval Rsch. Lab., Washington, 1982; student rep. med. isotope tech. program Prince George's C.C., 1987-89. Acad. scholar Findlay (Ohio) U., 1982, music scholar, 1982, senatorial scholar Prince George's C.C., 1987-89. Mem. Soc. Nuclear Medicine, Am. Soc. Nuclear Cardiology (assoc.), Am. Soc. Radiologic Technologists. Republican. Methodist. Office: So Md Nuclear Cardiology 9131 Piscataway Rd # 305 Clinton MD 20735

BECKMAN, JUDITH KALB, financial counselor and planner, educator, writer; b. Bklyn., June 27, 1940; d. Harry and Frances (Cohen) Kalb; m. Richard Martin Beckman, Dec. 16, 1961; children: Barry Andrew, David Mark. BA, Hofstra U., 1962; MA, Adelphi U., 1984. Cert. fin. planner; registered investment adviser, stockbroker. English tchr. Long Beach High Sch., 1962-65; Promotion coordination pub. rels. Mandel Sch. for Med. Assts., Hempstead, N.Y., 1973-74; exec. dir. Nassau Easter Seals, Albertson, N.Y., 1974-76; dir. pub. info. Long Beach Meml. Hosp., Albertson, N.Y., 1976-77; account rep. First Investors, Hicksville, N.Y., 1977-78; sales asst., then account exec. Josephthal & Co. Inc., Great Neck, N.Y., 1978-81; v.p., cert. fin. planner Arthur Gould Inc., Great Neck, N.Y., 1981-88; pres. Fin. Solutions (affiliated with Seco West Ltd., Goldner Siegfried Assocs. Inc.), Westbury, N.Y., 1988—; adj. instr. Adelphi U., Garden City N.Y., 1981-83, Molloy Coll., Rockville Ctr., N.Y., 1982-84; lectr. SUNY-Farmingdale, 1984-85; creater, presenter seminars, workshops on fin., investing, 1981—. Fin. columnist The Women's Record, 1985-93; writer quar. newspaper The Reporter, 1987. Coord. meat boycott, L.I., 1973; mentor SUNY Old Westbury, 1989—; co-founder, chair L.I. del. High Profile Men and Women, Colonie Hill, Hauppauque, N.Y., 1985; treas. L.I. Alzheimer's Found., 1989-93, trustee, 1993-95; apptd. to Nassau County Women's Adv. Coun. by County Exec., 1990; chief adv. coun. Ctr. for Family Resources. Recipient citation for leadership Town of Hempstead, N.Y., 1986, 89, L.I. Press Club award, 1987, 92, Mentor award SBA, 1989, Fin. Svcs. award SBA, 1991, L.I. Assn. Fin. Svc. Advocate award, 1991, Woman of Distinction in Bus. award Women on the Job, 1989, Bus. Leadership citation Nassau County, N.Y., 1989, Supr. award Town of Hempstead, 1989. Mem. Nat. Assn. Women Bus. Owners L.I. (bd. dirs. 1987-89), Women's Econ. Developers of L.I. (bd. dirs. 1985-92), Internat. Assn. Fin. Planners, Inst. Cert. Fin. Planners, L.I. Ctr. Bus. and Profl. Women (pres. 1984-86, pres.'s award 1992), Nat. Assn. Life Underwriters, Kiwanis (bd. dirs. 1994—, chair fund raising 1994—). Republican. Jewish. Home: 2084 Beverly Way Merrick NY 11566-5418 Office: Fin Solutions Fin Planning Office 2084 Beverly Way Merrick NY 11566-5418 also: 400 Post Ave Ste 200 Westbury NY 11590

BECKMAN, RUBY DOWNING, accountant; b. Fayetteville, N.C., July 7, 1940; d. Thadeus Dean and Billie Cornelia (Clark) Downing; m. Donald Raymond Beckman, Dec. 26, 1959; 1 child, Steven Donald. AAS in Acctg., Rock Valley Coll., Rockford, Ill., 1984; BS in Bus., Rockford (Ill.) Coll., Rockford, Ill., 1991. Cost acct. Alton Box Bd. Co., Alton, Ill., 1963-67; office mgr. Fin. Surveys, Inc., Denver, 1967-68; mgr. acctg. APV Rockford (Ill.), Inc., 1978—. Mme. Inst. Mgmt. Accts., Phi Theta Kappa. Home: 2229 Rexford Dr Rockford IL 61109-2323 Office: APV Rockford Inc 1303 Samuelson Rd Rockford IL 61109-3645

BECKMANN, MICHELE LILLIAN, secretary; b. Bklyn., Feb. 15, 1957; d. Anton and Alice Naomi (Williams) Prudich; m. Robert Westcott Beckmann, Apr. 18, 1981; children: Andrew Isaac, Walter Ian (twins). BA, Ea. Wash. U., 1978. Cert. profl. sec. Lead sec. New Way Homes, Spokane, 1980-81; libr. asst. Spokane Pub. Librs., 1981-82; office asst. Spokane County Assesor's Office, 1982; data processing clk. Aztech-Comstock, Spokane, 1983-84; finishing opr. Hollister-Stier Labs., Spokane, 1984; pvt. sec. Danial Kallestad, CLU, ChFC, Spokane, 1985; office asst. Wash. State U., Pullman, 1986-87, sec. III, 1987-89, project sec., 1989-92; owner Bhunkey Bros. Ink, Colfax, 1992—. Mem. Pullman Fair Housing Commn., 1989—, vice chmn., 1989-90; mem. local coun. Camp Fire, Inc., 1989-90; precinct officer Whitman County Dems., Colfax, Wash., 1988-90. Recipient WO-HE-LO Medallion Camp Fire Ind., 1975; cert. appreciation Pullman Fair Housing Commn., 1989, 91. Democrat. Home and Office: 1702 N Riverside Ln Colfax WA 99111-9755

BECKMANN, ROBERTA JEAN, counselor; b. Quinter, Kans., Oct. 8, 1944; d. Lester Carl and Velda Mae (Roberts) Albin; m. Paul L. Beckmann, Oct. 25, 1969; children: Jon Paul, Jason Andrew. RN, Wesley Sch. Nursing, Wichita, Kans., 1967; BA in Psychology, Kans. Newman, Wichita, Kans., 1970; MEd in Counseling, Wichita State U., 1984. Missionary nurse Ch. of the Brethern, Castaner, P.R., 1967-68; charge nurse-surg. unit Wesley Med. Ctr., Wichita, Kans., 1968; nursing instr. Wesley Sch. of Nursing, 1968-73; bereavement coord. Hospice of Wichita, 1984-85; kids cancer coord., counselor Victory In the Valley, Wichita, 1990-94; counselor/pvt. practice Wichita, 1985-94; family therapist Asbury United Meth. Ch., Wichita, 1992—; cons. for children in grief chs. and schs., Wichita, 1984—, presenter seminars, 1984—; support group facilitator grief and cancer groups, Wichita, 1984—. Author: (manual) I'm Glad to Be Me, 1986, (book) Children Who Grieve, 1990, (workbook) It's Okay to Feel, 1991. Active spl. gov.'- commn. on children and families, 1989; ct. apptd. spl. advocate for abused/neglected children Roots and Wings, Wichita, 1987-94, bd. dirs. 1988-93; vol. counselor United Meth. Urban Ministries, Wichita, 1986-87. Mem. Am. Counseling Assn., Assn. for Play Therapy, Christian Assn. for Psychol. Studies. Methodist. Home: 1724 Amarado St Wichita KS 67212-1230

BECKNELL, PATRICIA ANN, service company owner; b. Spartanburg, S.C., May 6, 1950; d. Joseph Lloyd and Annie (Wofford) B. Student, U.S.C., 1969-70; BS in Bus. Mgmt., Limestone Coll., 1978-81. Market research asst. Spartan Mill Sales, Spartanburg, 1970-73; bookkeeper, auditor Realtec Inc., Sapphire, N.C., 1973-76; computer coordinator Internat. Minerals and Chemical, Spartanburg, 1976-84; mgr. Tropical Design Inc., Lyman, S.C., 1984-88, pres., 1988-93; also bd. dirs. Tropical Design BHM, Birmingham, Ala., 1988-93, Tropical Design USA, Lyman, 1988-93; owner At Your Service, Tryon, N.C., 1993—. Mem. Am. Bus. Women's Assn. (pres. 1983-84, v.p. 1982-83, rec. sec. 1981-82, Woman of the Yr. 1983), Inst. Bus. Designers (membership chair 1990), Upper State Apt. Assn., Constrn. Specifiers Inst. (sec. 1991—), Profl. Bus. Women's Golf Network (pres.). Episcopalian. Office: At Your Service 7315 Jennings St Spartanburg SC 29303

BECK-OWEN, JENNIFER LOUISE, mental retardation administrator; b. Toledo, May 20, 1961; d. Arnold William and Norma Jean (DuPuis) Beck; m. Shawn T. Wilde, Aug. 17, 1990 (div. Mar. 1994); m. Mark Alan Owen, Apr. 29, 1994; children: Jeremy Beck, Robert Owen, Angela Owen. AAS, U. Toledo, 1984, BS, 1989. Lic. social worker, Ohio. Activities asst. West Ctr., Toledo, 1984; group supr. Sunshine Children's Home, Maumee, Ohio, 1984-85; mental health profl. Mercy Hosp., Toledo, 1985-86; apts. day coord. West Ctr., Toledo, 1986-87, apts. supr., 1987-90; cmty. svcs. dir. Josina Lott Found., Toledo, 1990-92; program coord. Anne Grady Ctr., Holland, Ohio, 1992-94, supr. supported living, 1994—. Home: 1814 Princeton Dr Toledo OH 43614 Office: Anne Grady Ctr 1525 Eber Rd Holland OH 43528

BECKS, CHERRY MARION, nurse; b. Windsor, N.C., Jan. 24, 1941; d. Stephen McCrah and Pearle (Bunche) Cherry; m. Godfrey Gerald Becks, Apr. 5, 1957 (div. Sept. 1977); 1 child, Cheryl Denise. AA in Nursing, Contra Costa Coll., San Pablo, Calif., 1972; BSN, St. Mary Coll., Moraga, Calif., 1979. RN, Calif.; CNOR. Nurse Brookside Hosp., San Pablo, 1973—, staff educator oper. room, 1990—. Mem. Assn. Oper. Room Nurses, Calif. Nurses Assn. Democrat. Roman Catholic. Home: 193 Cardinal Way Hercules CA 94547

BECKWITH, BARBARA JEAN, journalist; b. Chgo., Dec. 11, 1948; d. Charles Barnes and Elizabeth Ann (Nolan) B. BA in Journalism, Marquette U., 1970. News editor Lake Geneva (Wis.) Regional News, 1972-74; asst. editor St. Anthony Messenger, Cin., 1974-82, mng. editor, 1982—; mem. U.S. Cath. Conf. Communications Com., 1990-92. Mem. Cath. Press Assn. (bd. dirs. 1986—, v.p. 1988-90, pres. 1990-92, best interview 1982, best photo story 1985), Women in Communications, Cin. Editors Assn., Fedn. Ch. Press Assns. of Internat. Cath. Union of the Press (3d v.p. 1989-92, pres. 1992—). Office: St Anthony Messenger 1615 Republic St Cincinnati OH 45210-1298

BECKWITH, CLAUDIA JOY, family nurse practitioner; b. Passaic, N.J., Feb. 9, 1955; d. Aaron and Jane Beckwith; m. William Ferguson, Nov. 23, 1984; children: Taylor Allen, Caitlin Alana. BA, Grinnell Coll., 1977; MSN, Pace U., 1984. RN; registered family nurse practitioner. Family nurse practitioner Maternal Child Wellness Program Clinic, Grinnell, Iowa, 1989—, Ctrl. Iowa Family Planning, Marshalltown, 1989—, Grinnell Med. Assocs., 1989—; speaker on health care topics, 1984—. Mem. Am. Assn. Nurse Practitioners, Iowa Assn. Nurse Practitioners (bd. dirs.), Nat. Assn. Pediat. Nurse Assocs. & Practitioners, Sigma Theta Tau. Democrat. Jewish.

BECKWITH, FAYE LORRAINE, real estate broker; b. Fulton, N.Y., Nov. 15, 1946; d. Riley W. and Leona Cooper Scott; m. Jack Myron Beckwith, Nov. 25, 1964; children: Jack Steven, Noelle A. Beckwith Salmonsen, Scott Charles. Student, SUNY, Oswego, 1964. Cert. Grad. Realtor Inst.; cert. residential specialist. Saleswoman Freedom Real Estate, Fulton, 1985-87, broker, 1987, owner, broker, 1987—; owner, mgr. Christmas tree farm. Chmn. bd. trustees Hannibal (N.Y.) United Meth. Ch., 1991—; treas Hannibal Rep. Com., 1980-93. Named 4-H Leader of Yr., Oswego County 4-H, Mexico, N.Y., 1984. Mem. Nat. Assn. Realtors, N.Y. State Assn. Realtors (bd. dirs. 1992—, honor soc. 1990-93), N.Y. State Soc. Real Estate Appraisers, Oswego County Bd. Realtors (sec. 1991-92, pres. 1993—, Realtor of Yr. award 1993), Residential Sales Coun., Women's Coun. Realtors. Republican. Home: RD 1 Box 238 Hannibal NY 13074 Office: Freedom Real Estate 604 S 4th St Rt 481 Fulton NY 13069

BECKWITH, SANDRA SHANK, lawyer, judge; b. Norfolk, Va., Dec. 4, 1943; d. Charles Langdale and Loraine (Sterneberg) Shank; m. James Beckwith, Mar. 31, 1965 (div. June 1978); m. Thomas R. Ammann, Mar. 3, 1979. BA, U. Cin., 1965, JD, 1968. Bar: Ohio 1969, Ind. 1976, Fla. 1979, U.S. Dist. Ct. (so. dist.) Ohio 1971, U.S. Dist. Ct. Ind. 1976, U.S. Supreme Ct. 1977. Sole practice, Harrison, Ohio, 1969-77, 79-81; judge Hamilton County Mcpl. Ct., Cin., 1977-79, 81-86; judge Ct. Common Pleas, Hamilton County Div. Domestic Rels., 1987-89; assoc. Graydon, Head and Ritchey, 1989-91; judge U.S. Dist. Ct. (so. dist.) Ohio, 1992—; mem. Ohio Chief Justice's Code of Profl. Responsibility Commn., 1984, Ohio Gov.'s Com. on Prison Crowding, 1984-90. Methodist. Office: 85 Marconi Blvd Rm 302 Columbus OH 43215

BEDDOW-SPEARS, DEBORAH SUSAN, marketing professional; b. Phila., Dec. 28, 1952; d. James Adam and Dolores Gladys (Humes) Fernz; m. Dale A. Beddow, Nov. 27, 1971 (div. Dec. 1980); 1 child, Matthew D.; m. Larry R. Spears, Apr. 23, 1994. BA Gen. Studies, Wichita State U., 1984, AA in Legal Assistance, 1984. Aircraft assembly Cessna Aircraft Co., Wichita, Kans., 1974-76; expeditor Boeing, Wichita, 1980-81; data control analyst Learjet Corp., Wichita, 1981-82; buyer Boeing, Wichita, 1986-87, Boeing Electronics, Irving, Tex., 1987; sr. buyer Gen. Dynamics Corp., Ft. Worth, 1987-90; salesperson Models & Tools, Troy, Mich., 1990—. Pres. High Sch. Band Parents Orgn., Tulsa, 1992-94; chmn. Reading is Fundamental, Wichita, 1982-85. Office: Models & Tools 1880 E Maple Rd Troy MI 48083

BEDELIA, BONNIE, actress; b. N.Y.C., Mar. 25, 1948; d. Philip and Marian (Wagner) Culkin; m. Kenneth Luber, Apr. 15, 1969; children: Yuri, Jonah. Student, Hunter Coll., N.Y.C.; studied with Uta Hager, Herbert Berghof studios; studied with Lee Strasberg, Actors Studio. Stage appearances include The Glass Menagerie, 1970, The Sea Gull, 1970, As You Like It, 1970, Midsummer Night's Dream, 1970; Broadway appearances include Isle of Children, 1960, Enter Laughing, 1963, The Playroom, 1965, Happily Never After, 1966, My Sweet Charlie, 1967 (Theatre World award 1967); film appearances include Gypsy Moths, 1969, They Shoot Horses, Don't They?, 1969, Lovers and Other Strangers, 1970, Rosalie, 1972, Between Friends, 1973, The Big Fix, 1978, Heart Like a Wheel, 1983, Death of an Angel, 1986, The Boy Who Could Fly, 1986, Violets are Blue, 1986, The Stranger, 1987, Die Hard, 1988, Prince of Pennsylvania, 1988, Fat Man & Little Boy, 1989, Presumed Innocent, 1990, Die Hard II, 1990, Needful Things, 1993, Speechless, 1994; TV series Love of Live, 1961-67, The New Land, 1974, mini-series Salem's Lot, 1979; TV films Then Came Bronson, 1969, Sandcastles, 1972, Hawkins on Murder, 1973, A Message to My Daughter, 1973, A Time for Love, 1973, Heatwave, 1974, A Question of Love, 1978, Walking Through the Fire, 1979, Fighting Back, 1980, Million Dollar Infield, 1982, Memorial Day, 1983, The Lady from Yesterday, 1985, Alex, The Life of a Child, 1986, When the Time Comes, 1987, Somebody Has to Shoot the Picture, 1990, Switched At Birth, 1991, A Mother's Right: The Elizabeth Morgan Story, 1993, The Fire Next Time, 1993, Fallen Angels (The Quiet Room), 1993 (Emmy nomination, Guest Actress - Drama, 1994). Recipient Golden Globe award, 1983. Office: 1021 Georgina Ave Santa Monica CA 90402*

BEDENBAUGH, ANGELA LEA OWEN, chemistry educator, researcher; b. Seguin, Tex., Oct. 6, 1939; d. Wintford Henry and Nelia Melanie (Fischer) Owen; m. John Holcombe Bedenbaugh, Dec. 27, 1961; 1 child, Melanie Celeste. BS cum laude, U. Tex., 1961; PhD in Organic Chemistry, U. S.C., 1967. Geol. mapping asst. Roland Blumberg Assocs., Seguin, summer 1958, 59; chemistry lab. instr. U. Tex., Austin, 1960-61; rsch. assoc. chemistry U. So. Miss., Hattiesburg, 1966-80, rsch. assoc. prof. chemistry, 1980—. Author: (with John H. Bedenbaugh) Handbook for High School Chemistry Teachers, 1985, (with John H. Bedenbaugh) Teaching First Year Chemistry, 1988, 3d rev. edition, 1990. Mem. adminstrv. bd. Parkway Heights United Meth. Ch., 1974-75, womens unit leader, 1973-75, womens unit treas., 1977, Wesleyan Svc. Guild v.p., 1970, Sunday Sch. tchr., 1973-74; bd. dirs. Forrest Stone Area Opportunity Inc., 1970-72, bd. dirs. exec. com., 1972, mem. com. to rewrite personnel policies and procedures, 1971, mem. Headstart monitoring com., 1971-72, mem. personnel screening com., 1971; mem. Nat. Women's Polict. Caucus, 1976—; mem. Toastmasters Internat., 1986—. Prin. investigator rsch. grant U.S. Dept. Energy, U. So. Miss., 1980; co-prin. investigator rsch. grant NSF, U. So. Miss., 1985, adminstrv. dir. rsch. grant, 1988-92, 93—. Mem. NSTA (mem. nat. resource rev. panel for rev. of instrnl. materials), Am. Chem. Soc. (chairperson 1984-85, program chairperson 1983-84, Chemist of Yr. 1991), Miss. Sci. Tchrs. Assn. (Disting. Sci. Tchr. award 1994, exec. bd. 1994—), Delta Kappa Gamma (pres. Miss. state br. 1989-91, chairperson internat. rsch. com. 1980-82, chairperson internat. computer share fair at internat. conv. 1994), Sigma Xi (charter, sec.-treas. 1967-69, treas. 1970, pres. 1973-74, program chairperson 1972-73). Democrat. Methodist. Home: 63 Suggs Rd Hattiesburg MS 39402-9642 Office: Univ So Miss PO Box 8466 Hattiesburg MS 39406-8466

BEDFORD, AMY ALDRICH, public relations executive, corporation secretary; b. Pendleton, Oreg., July 13, 1912; d. Edwin Burton and Elsie (Conklin) Aldrich; m. J.M. Bedford (wid.); 1 child, Jacqueline Bedford Brown. BS, Oreg. State U., 1933. Mgr. comml. dept. East Oregonian, Pendleton, 1950-75, mgr. pub. rels., 1975—; corp. sec. East Oregonian Pub. Co., Pendleton, 1950—. Bd. dirs. Oreg. Status of Women Com., 1972-75, Oreg. Law Enforcement Commn., 1975-82, Arts Coun. Pendleton. Recipient Pendleton First Citizen award C. of C., 1962, Gov.'s award for the Arts, 1988. Mem. Women in Communications, Oreg. Press Women, AAUW (pres. 1956-58, grantee 1965), LWV, Pendleton River Parkway Found., World Affairs Coun. Oreg., Altrusa. Home: PO Box 1456 Pendleton OR 97801-0360 Office: East Oregonian Pub Co PO Box 1089 Pendleton OR 97801-1089

BEDFORD, VICTORIA HILKEVITCH, psychology educator; b. Chgo., Jan. 31; d. Aaron and Rhea (Rubisoff) Hilkevitch; m. Eric Doulgas Bedford, Apr. 16, 1977; children: Sibyl Ruth, Iris Cornelia. BA cum laude, Brandeis u., 1966; MEd, Boston U., 1974; PhD, Rutgers U., 1986. Asst. prof. psychology U. Indpls., 1990—; vis. asst. prof. Ind. U., Bloomington, 1987; vis. scholar U. Stockholm and U. Uppsala, 1988. Editor: Handbook of Aging and the Family, 1995; editor spl issue jour. Am. Behavioral Scientist, 1989; contbr. articles to profl. jours. HEW fellow, 1968-69, NIH fellow, 1988-90; faculty grantee U. Indpls., 1992. Mem. APA, Internat. Soc. for Study Pers. Relationships, Internat. Network Pers. Relationships, Gerontol. Soc. Am., Midwest Coun. Social Rsch. on Aging (coun. 1994—), Soc. for Rsch. Child Devel. Home: 1701 Circle Dr Bloomington IN 47401-6027

BEDICS, LYNN FAY, nurse; b. Scranton, Pa., May 13, 1947; d. Gerald Joseph and Esther Naomi (Sachse) O'Malley; m. Francis J. Bedics, Jr., Mar. 11, 1989. Grad., St. Luke's Hosp. Sch. Nursing, N.Y.C., 1968; BSN cum laude, Cedar Crest Coll., 1982. RN, Pa.; cert. comty. health nurse and med. surg. nurse ANA Credentiality Ctr. Staff nurse emergency room Allentown Gen. Hosp., 1971; part-time charge nurse Phila. VA Hosp., 1971-72; critical care nurse St. John's Hosp., Tulsa, 1972-74; ICU nurse Allentown Osteo. Hosp., 1975-79; staff nurse VA Outpatient Clinic, Allentown, 1979-86; head nurse Dept. Vets. Affairs, Outpatient Clinic, Allentown, 1986—; instr.-trainer CPR, Am. Heart Assn., Allentown, 1980-89. Mem. coord. com. Combined Fed. Campaign, Lehigh Valley, Pa., 1984-86; bd. dirs. YWCA, Allentown, 1986-88, Korea-Vietnam Meml. Inc., Lehigh Valley, 1987—, sec., 1991-94. 1st lt. Nurse Corps, U.S. Army, 1967-70, Vietnam. Decorated Bronze Star medal; recipient excellence in Nursing award Dept. Vets. Affairs, 1989, VA Adminstr.'s Hands and Heart award Dept. Vets. Affairs Med. Ctr., Wilkes-Barre, Pa., 1989, Legion of Honor award Chapel of Four Chaplains, 1994. Mem. Assn. for Ambulatory Care Providers Ea. Pa. (v.p. 1987-89, pres. 1989-90, bd. dirs., chairperson edn. com. 1994—), United Women Vets. Pa. VFW, Sigma Theta Tau, Beta Sigma Phi (internat. honr.). Republican. Home: 1118 N 27th St Allentown PA 18104-2904 Office: Dept Vets Affairs Outpatient Clinic 2937 Hamilton Blvd Allentown PA 18103-2819

BEDINGER, ELIZABETH ANNE, investment broker; b. Orlando, Fla., Oct. 8, 1962; d. Robert Hudgins Bedinger and Elizabeth Anne (Radcliff) Patterson; m. Demetrious Stamtis Stroubakis, Feb. 4, 1992 (div. July 1993). BS in Fin., Va. Tech., 1985. Cert. master in graphonalysis. Closing asst. AmeriBank, Virginia Beach, Va., 1986; investment broker Marion Bass Securities, Virginia Beach, 1986-87, A.G. Edwards & Sons, Orlando, Fla., 1987—; owner handwriting analysis bus. Script Insyte. Founding mem. United We Stand, Mobile, Ala., 1992. Mem. Internat. Graphoanalyst Soc. (presenter grad. address 1993), Fla. chpt. Graphonalyst Soc., Nat. Assn. Women Bus. Owners. Presbyterian. Office: AG Edwards and Sons 815 N Magnolia Ave Orlando FL 32803-3810

BEDNARZ, SHIRLEY DIANE, publishing company executive; b. Wis. Rapids, Wis., Sept. 15, 1946; d. Stewart Fausch and Marge (Lyons) Peterson; m. Timothy F. Bednarz, Aug. 14, 1989. B in Edn., U. Wis., Stevens Point, 1974, M in Profl. Devel. magna cum laude, 1981; PhD in Bus. Adminstrn., Pacific Western U., 1994. Tchr. Wis. Rapids Pub. Schs., 1974-90; CEO Bednarz Bus. Strategies, Stevens Point, Wis., 1990—; pres., owner Menagerie Pet Ctr., Wis. Rapids, 1977-90. Mem. NAFE, Nat. Assn. Univ. Women. Home and Office: Bednarz Bus Strategies 2025 Main St Stevens Point WI 54481

BEDORE, CARRIE A. RAYMOND, lawyer; b. Madison, Wis., Nov. 22, 1959; d. Lou August and Janet Evelyn Raymond; m. James Michael Bedore, Oct. 7, 1989; 1 child, Benjamin Raymond. BA, U. Wis., 1982; JD, U. Minn., 1985. Atty. Reinhart, Boerner, Van Deuren, Norris & Rieselbach, Milw., 1985-87, Firstar Corp., Milw., 1987—. Mem. Wis. State Bar, Milw. Bar Assn., Assn. Women Lawyers (pres. 1987-92), Profl. Dimensions. Office: Firstar Corp 777 E Wisconsin Ave Milwaukee WI 53202

BEDRICK, BERNICE, retired science educator, consultant; b. Jersey City, Sept. 29, 1916; d. Abraham Lewis and Esther (Cowan) Grodjesk; m. Emanuel Arthur Bedrick, Dec. 25, 1938 (dec. 1967); children: Allen Paul, Jane Bedrick Abels; m. Samuel Milberger, Sept. 23, 1984 (dec. 1984); stepchildren: Susan Milberger Rafael, Stanford. BS, U. Md., 1938; MA, NYU, 1952. Cert. tchr., N.J. Tchr. Linden (N.J.) Pub. Sch. System, 1950-69, supr. sci. curriculum, 1969-79, sch. prin., 1979-87; ret., 1987. Co-author: A Universe to Explore, 1969; developer program of safety and survival N.J. Dept. Edn., 1975. Founder, mem., bd. dirs. Temple Mekor Chayim, Linden; pres. bd. trustees Linden Pub. Libr., 1989-90, v.p., 1991; pres. Friends of Linden Libr., 1987-92, 95—. Recipient Cmty. Vol. Svc. award B'Nai B'Rith, 1993. Mem. NEA (life), N.J. Edn. Assn. (life), Am. Fedn. Sch. Adminstrs. (chpt. pres. 1984-86), Linden Edn. Found. (bd. dirs.), N.Y. Acad. Scis., N.J. Prins. and Suprs. Assn., N.J. Sci. Tchrs. Assn., Nat. Sci. Tchrs. Assn., Alumni Assn. U. Md. (life), N.J. PTA (life), Hadassah (life), Linden Ceramics Club (sec. 1991-92), Nat. Coun. Jewish Women (life), Alpha Lambda Delta, Phi kappa Phi. Home: 2016 Orchard Ter Linden NJ 07036-3719

BEDSOLE, ANN SMITH, state senator; b. Selma, Ala., Jan. 7, 1930; d. Malcolm White and Sybil (Huey) Smith; m. Massey Palmer Bedsole, 1958; children: Mary Martin Bedsole Riser, John Henry Martin, Loraine Bedsole Demmas. Student, U. Ala., 1948, U. Denver, 1955-56; LLD (hon.), Mobile Coll., 1984, Huntingdon Coll., 1985. Mem. Ala. Rep. Exec. Com., 1966-74; del. seconded nomination Nixon for Pres. Rep. Nat. Conv., 1972; Rep. Presdl. Elector, 1972; Ala. state rep., 1978-82; Ala. state senator, 1982-94, chair com. on agr., conservation and forestry, mem. coms. on edn., health, judiciary, mem. joint interim com. on mcpl. govt., mem. com. arts, tourism and cultural resources; mem. Nat. Conf. State Legislatures. Trustee Huntington Coll., Spring Hill Coll.; founder, bd. dirs. Ala. Sch. Math. and Sci.; mem. Jr. League of Mobile; bd. dirs. Vol. Mobile, Inc.; mem. steering com. Mobile United. Recipient M.O. Beale Scroll of Merit award Mobile Press Register, 1971-72, award for outstanding contbn. to forestry in Ala. Soc. Am. Foresters, 1986, Legislative Conservationist of Yr. award Ala. Wildlife Fedn., 1987; named 1st Lady of Mobile, 1972, Mobilian of Yr., 1993; inducted into Women's Acad. of Honor, 1987. Methodist. Office: Ala Senate State Capitol Montgomery AL 36130*

BEDSWORTH, O. DIANE, retail executive; b. Detroit, Nov. 30, 1942; d. William H. and Olive Emily (Ludwig) Goodson; m. Gary J. Bedsworth, Apr. 4, 1964 (div. Feb. 1983); children: Jay William, Pamela Diane. Student, Mich. State U., 1961-64. Interior designer Dayton-Hudson Corp., Mpls., 1973-85; pres. Bedsworth Design Internat., Blackhawk, Calif., 1985—; owner Bedsworth Style, Danville, Calif., 1989—; cons. San Souci Hotel, Taipei, Taiwan, 1980—, Hotel Group, Inc., 1982-83, Corp. Homes, Damman, Saudi Arabia, residential homes, Hawaii, Calif., Ariz., 1986—. Mktg. dir. Sta. KTCA-TV Pub. Auction, Mpls., 1979-83, chairwoman, 1983, 84. Mem. Am. Soc. Interior Designers (profl.), Blackhawk Country Club. Republican. Episcopalian. Office: Bedsworth Style 661-B San Ramon Valley Blvd Danville CA 94526

BEEBE, CAROL ANN, school system administrator, principal; b. Niagara Falls, N.Y., Aug. 9, 1948; d. Bernard A. and Helen Marie (Kitchen) Blake; m. Philip J. Beebe, Aug. 21, 1982. AAS, Trocaire Coll., 1968; BE, Medaille Coll., 1970; MEd, Niagara U., 1972. Cert. adminstr. Elem. tchr., then sch. dist. supr., sch. dist. adminstr. Niagara Wheatfield Ctrl. Sch. Dist., Sanborn, N.Y., 1970—, summer sch. prin. K-12, 1981-91; head tchr. Colonial Village Sch. Colonial Village Sch., Sanborn, N.Y., 1977-80, acting prin., 1986, computer tchr., 1986-92, asst. prin., 1986-92, prin., 1992—; presenter in field. Amb. United Way for Niagara County, 1992; mem. com. Oppenheim Zoological Soc. of Niagara County, 1970—. Recipient Hilda Maehling Fellowship award NEA, 1974, Russell M. Look Educator of Yr. award Alcoholism Coun. of Niagara County, 1994. Mem. Sch. Adminstrs. Assn. N.Y. State, Niagra Wheatfield Adminstrs. Assn., Coun. Exceptional Children, Delta Kappa Gamma. Democrat. Roman Catholic. Home: 1 Main St Apt 3 Youngstown NY 14174 Office: Niagara Wheatfield Ctrl Sch Dist 2794 Saunders Sett Rd Sanborn NY 14132

BEEBE, CORA PRIFOLD, government official; b. San Francisco, Nov. 3, 1937; d. George and Beatrice (Ehni) Prifold; m. Ronald Beebe, Jan., 1959 (div.). Student, Hollins Coll., Va., 1955-57, Am. U., 1957-58; BA, U. Mich., 1959, MA, 1961; LHD (hon.), Southeastern U., 1993. Adminstrv. asst. Am. Polit. Sci. Assn., 1962-64; research assoc. Inst. Comparative Studies of Polit. Systems, Washington, 1963-65; program planning and evaluation specialist U.S. Office Edn., Washington, 1965-68, planning coordinator, 1968-73, dir. planning and budget div., 1973-80; prin. dep. asst. sec. for elem. and sec. edn. Dept. Edn., Washington, 1980-81; asst. sec. adminstrn. U.S. Treasury Dept., Washington, 1981-84; dir. office of policy, budget and program mgmt. OSWER, EPA, Washington, 1984-86; dir. office of planning, budget and evaluation Dept. Commerce, Washington, 1986-87; commerce & justice br. chief Office of Mgmt. and Budget, 1987-94, advisor to assoc. dir. gen. govt. and fin., 1994; dir. adminstrn. Office of Thrift Supervision, Washington, 1994—. Mem. women's com. Washington Performing Arts Soc., 1983-87. Recipient HEW Superior Svc. award, Presdl. Rank award, 1989; Inst. World Affairs fellow, 1956, Am. Edn. Abroad fellow, 1960. Mem. Exec. Women in Govt. Program and Budget Analysis. Home: 303 N St SW Washington DC 20024-2903 Office: Office Thrift Supervision 1700 G St NW Washington DC 20552

BEEBE, MARGUERITE J., auction company executive; b. Seattle, Wash., Sept. 14, 1939; d. Arthur Stephen and Esther Helena (Anderson) Hutchins; children: Tedd, Brad, Denise. Student, Seattle Vocat. Sch., 1959. Cert. comml. aviator. Aviation ground sch. and link trainer instr. MAGS, Seattle; investment ptnr., office mgr. Gulf Shore Auction Co., Sarasota, Fla. Mem. Wash. State Women Pilots Assn., 49ers Women's Pilot Assn., Federated Women's Club, Yacht Club, League of Voters, Beta Sigma Phi (Award of Honor and Excellence, Girl of Yr.). Home: 4366 Bldg C Independence Ct Sarasota FL 34234

BEEBE, NAOMI MARIE, financial consultant, accountant; b. Schenectady, N.Y.; m. William Lloyd Beebe, Nov. 5, 1983. AA in Bus. Adminstrn., Schenectady C.C., 1979; postgrad., Union Coll., 1983, U. Phoenix, San Jose, Calif., 1989-90. Lic. tax preparer, Calif. Sr. cost acctg. clk., cost specialist, labor analyst GE, Schenectady, N.Y., 1973-83; acct. Accts. Inc., 1986-89; owner, fin. cons. Real-Time Consulting, Bookkeeping & Tax Svc., Santa Clara, Calif., 1989—; del. to Fin. Mgmt. and Auditing Delegation to Russia People to People Internat.; authorized reseller, software cons. State of the Art (Mas90) Accounting Software, 1994—. Creator: (software enhancement) Financial Analysis, 1983 (Merit award 1983). Ch. youth advisor Fisher United Meth. Ch., Schenectady, 1983; treas. Sunnyvale (Calif.) Homeowners Assn., 1990. Mem. Nat. Soc. Pub. Accts., Inst. Mgmt. Accts., Calif. Assn. Ind. Accts. (chpt. pres. 1991-92), Inland Soc. Tax Cons. (sec. 1993—). Office: Real-Time Consulting # 103 1556 Halford Ave Santa Clara CA 95051

BEEBE, SANDRA E., artist, writer, former educator; b. March AFB, Calif., Nov. 10, 1934; d. Eugene H. and Margaret (Fox) B.; m. Donald C. Thompson. AB in English and Speech, UCLA, 1956; MA in Secondary Edn., Calif. State U., Long Beach, 1957. Tchr. English, Garden Grove (Calif.) High Sch., 1957-93, attendance supr., 1976-83; watercolor artist, 1964—. Contbr. articles to English Jour., chpts. to books; exhbns. include AWS, NWS, Okla. Watercolor Soc., Watercolor West, San Diego Internat., La. Watercolor Soc., San Diego Art Inst., Knickerbocker Artists N.Y., Montana WCS, Midwest Watercolor Soc., Butler Inst. Am. Art, Youngstown, Ohio, Kings Art Ctr., Audubon Artists N.Y.; cover artist Exploring Painting, 1990, title page Understanding Watercolor, American Artist, 1991. Named one of the Top Ten Watercolorists The Artists Mag., 1994. Mem. Am. Watercolor Soc., Nat. Watercolor Soc., Midwest Watercolor Soc., Watercolor West, Nat. Arts Club, Knickerbocker Artists N.Y., Audubon Artists N.Y., West Coast Watercolor Soc., Rocky Mountain Nat. Watermedia Honor Soc., Jr. League Long Beach, Kappa Kappa Gamma. Republican. Home: 7241 Marina Pacifica Dr S Long Beach CA 90803-6153 Studio: B-Q Gallery 3920 E 4th St Long Beach CA 90814 also: 239 Mira Mar Ave Long Beach CA 90803

BEEL, LORRAINE KUHN, tutor; b. Bklyn., July 9, 1921; d. Harold Edmond and Regina Hermenia (Doscher) Kuhn; m. Samuel Lee Painter, July 11, 1942 (dec. July 1961); children: Karen Melfi, Patricia Murphy, Pamela Brown, Thomas Painter, Susan Peterson, Laurie Pace; m. Lawrence Samuel Ronald, Apr. 19, 1968 (dec. 1980);. BS, Cornell U., 1942; MA, U. N.Mex., 1957. Cert. tchr. of handicapped, Calif., elem. tchr., Calif., N.Mex. Asst. supr. Daysch., tchr. home econs. Norwood (Ohio) Schs., 1942-44; elem. tchr. Dep. Schs. Overseas, Linz, Austria, 1949-50; supr. kindergarten day nursery Sandia Base, Albuquerque, 1955-56, Albuquerque Pub. Schs., 1959-61; tchr. pre-kindergarten Monzano Day Sch., Albuquerque, 1962-63; elem. tchr., spl. edn. tchr. Palo Alto (Calif.) Unified Schs., 1963-82; tutor pvt. and pub. schs., Albuquerque, 1982—. Fellow Albuquerque Assn. Ednl. Retirees (v.p. 1994—), Delta Kappa Gamma (v.p. 70s, scholarship 1974), Alpha Delta Kappa (v.p. 1977-78, pres. 1978-79), Pi Lambda Theta (v.p. 1958, 1985, regional treas. 1992-94).

BEER, ALICE STEWART (MRS. JACK ENGEMAN), musician, educator; b. Redwood Falls, Minn., Sept. 29, 1912; d. Robert and Isabel (Montgomery) Stewart; m. Jack Engeman, Dec. 14, 1974; children by previous marriage: W. Robert, Jane K. Beer Mosher, Elizabeth S. Beer-Shilling. MusB, Northwestern U., 1934, MusM, 1952; postgrad., Johns Hopkins U., 1954, 60, Mexico City Coll., 1956, U. Md., 1957. Tchr. pub. schs., Lawton, Mich., 1934-39, Battle Creek, Mich., 1949-51; tchr. Balt. Pub. Schs., 1951-53, supr. music, 1953-77; tchr. summer sessions various colls. and univs., 1957-85; adj. faculty Peabody Inst., John's Hopkins U., Balt., 1981-85; cons. Alliance for Arts in Edn., Balt. County Pub. Schs., 1982-90, cons. curriculum, 1984-91. Author: Teaching Suggestions, Birchard Music Series II and III, 1962, Teaching Music: What, How and Why, 1973, Teaching Music to the Exceptional Child: A Handbook for Mainstreaming, 1980, Teaching Music, 1982, Patriotic Color Sound Filmstrips/Videos, 1967-69; mem. editorial bd. Maryland Music Educator Jour., 1990—; contbr. articles to profl. jours. Mem. bd. lady mgrs. Balt. Street Clinic, 1986—; ordained elder Townson Presbyn. Ch. Recipient Director's Recognition award for commitment to music edn. and extraordinary contbn. to art of teaching, 1986; inductee Md. Music Educators Hall of Fame, 1989. Mem. AAUW (mem. Towson br.), Nat. Conf. Music Educators, Md. Music Educators Assn., Pres.'s Club Cir. U. Md., Officers and Faculty Club of U.S. Naval Acad., Pres.'s Club Circle, Phi Beta. Republican. Home: 615 Chestnut Ave # 1401 Baltimore MD 21204-3745

BEER, CLARA LOUISE JOHNSON, retired electronics executive; b. Bisbee, Ariz., Jan. 14, 1918; d. Franklin Fayette and Marie (Sturm) Johnson; m. Philip James McElmurry, May 15, 1937 (div. July 1944); children—Leonard Franklin, Philip James Jr.; m. William Sigvard Beer, July 15, 1945 (dec. Aug. 31, 1977); 1 son, Douglas Lee; m. Kenneth Christy Huntwork, May 1, 1982. Student, Merritt Bus. Sch., Oakland, Calif., 1935, Bus. Instrn. Sch., Palo Alto, Calif., 1955. Sec., artist M.R. Fisher Studios, Oakland, 1936-40; piano, organ instr. Anna May Studios, Palo Alto, 1948-50; pvt. piano, organ instr. Palo Alto, 1949-56; sec. Stanford Electronics Labs., Stanford U., 1955-58; corporate sec. and exec. sec. to chmn. bd. Watkins-Johnson Co., Palo Alto, 1958-88; dir., sec. Watkins-Johnson Internat., 1968-88, Watkins-Johnson Ltd., 1971-88, Watkins-Johnson Assocs., 1977-88. Mem. Nat. Secs. Assn., Christian Bus. and Profl. Women's Coun. (sec. 1966-67, adviser 1968). Home: 24157 Hillview Rd Los Altos CA 94024-5222

BEER, ESTHER RAE, elementary education educator; b. Chgo., Feb. 16, 1949; d. Jack and Fay Beer. BS in Edn., No. Ill. U., 1971, MS in Edn., 1975. Cert. elem. tchr., cert. adminstr. 3d-4th grade tchr. Sch. Dist. 146, Oak Forest, Ill., 1971-78, 5th-6th grade tchr., 1978-88, 6th grade tchr., 1988—; gifted instr. Sch. Dist. 146, Oak Forest, 1980-89, gifted coord., 1989-92; speaker ADAPT, Oak Forest, 1992; tchr. Lewis U., Bolingbrook, Ill., 1988. Recipient Golden Apple award Golden Apple Found., 1988. Fellow Golden Apple Acad.; mem. Ill. Coun. for Gifted, Phi Delta Kappa. Office: Fierke Edn Ctr 6535 W Victoria Dr Oak Forest IL 60452

BEERBOWER, CYNTHIA GIBSON, lawyer; b. Dayton, Ohio, June 25, 1949; d. Charles Augustus and Sarah (Rittenhouse) Gibson; m. John Edwin Beerbower, Aug. 28, 1971; children: John Eliot, Sarah Rittenhouse. BA, Mt. Holyoke Coll., 1971; JD, Boston U., 1974; LLB, Cambridge U., Eng., 1976. Bar: N.Y. 1975. Assoc., Cadwalader, Wickersham & Taft, N.Y.C., 1975-76; assoc. Simpson, Thacher & Bartlett, N.Y.C., 1977-81, ptnr., 1981-93; internat. tax counsel U.S. Dept. Treasury, Washington, 1993-94, dep. asst. sec. tax policy, 1994—. Mem. ABA, Assn. Bar City N.Y., N.Y. State Bar Assn. (com. co-chmn. 1987-93). Presbyterian. Home: 3330 N St NW Washington DC 20007-2807 Office: US Dept Treasury 1500 Pennsylvania Ave NW Washington DC 20220

BEERING, DONNA BOYER, pilot; b. Roanoke Rapids, N.C., Oct. 15, 1964; d. Donald Eugene and Janet Lois (Beck) Boyer; m. David Randall Beering, Dec. 22, 1990. B in Applied Sci., Purdue U., 1986. Flight instr. Purdue U., West Lafayette, Ind., 1985-86; flight inst., charter pilot Lafayette Aviation, West Lafayette, Ind., 1986-88; pilot Jetstream Internat. Airlines, Dayton, Ohio, 1988-89, United Airlines, Chgo., 1989—. Spokesperson for career and higher edn. United, Chgo. Mem. Nat. Space Soc., Planetary Soc., Internat. Soc. Women Airlines Pilots, Ninety-nines.

BEERMANN, JUDITH ANA, broadcast executive, real estate broker; b. Falls City, Nebr., May 19, 1945; d. August and Minnie (Ohlenschlen) Biermann; m. William A. Beermann, Feb. 13, 1977 (dec. Jan. 1, 1990); childreN: Kristine Kay, Angeline Kay. Student Art, Kans. State U.; BA in Electroincs (hon.), Moana Coll., Honolulu, 1993. Owner, CEO KDI Radio, Honolulu, 1962—. Bd. dirs. Honolulu Hosp., 1994—. Named Woamn of Yr., Honolulu, 1993-94. Mem. NAFE, Soc. Bus. and Profl. Women (chmn. of bd., Honolulu 1990-94). Republican. Lutheran. Home: PO Box 4240 Honolulu HI 96817 Office: 1500 Pine St Omaha NE 68108-3525

BEERS, CHARLOTTE LENORE, advertising agency executive; b. Beaumont, Tex., July 26, 1935; d. Glen and Frances (Bolt) Rice; m. Donald C. Beers, 1971; 1 dau., Lisa. B.S. in Math. and Physics, Baylor U., Waco, Tex., 1958. Group product mgr. Uncle Ben's Inc., 1959-69; sr. v.p., dir. client services J. Walter Thompson, 1969-79; chief operating officer Tatham-Laird & Kudner, Chgo., from 1979, mng. ptnr., chmn. and chief exec officer; vice chmn. RSCG Group Roux Seguela, Cayzac & Goudard, France; chmn., CEO Ogilvy & Mather Worldwide, N.Y.C., Ogilvy Group Inc., N.Y.C. Named Nat. Advt. Woman of Yr. Am. Advt. Fedn., 1975. Mem. Am. Assn. Advt. Agencies (chmn. from 1987), Women's Advt. Club Chgo., Chgo. Network. Republican. Episcopalian. Office: Ogilvy Group Inc/Ogilvy & Mather Worldwide Inc 309 W 49th St #12 New York NY 10019

BEETS, HUGHLA FAE, retired secondary school educator; b. Eustace, Tex., Aug. 1, 1929; d. Hubert Edgar and Beatrice (Roark) Bonsal; m. Anneel Randolph Beets, Sept. 14, 1946. BA, North Tex. State U., 1958, MA, 1960; postgrad., U. Mass., 1967. Cert. tchr., Tex. Tchr. Seagoville (Tex.) Ind. Sch. Dist., 1958-65, Dallas Ind. Sch. Dist., 1965-70; owner, mgr. Mabank (Tex.) Ins. Agy., 1970-77, Beets Interiors, Mabank, 1970—; ptnr., mgr. Cedar Creek Title Co., Mabank, 1977-80; tchr. govt. and econs. Athens (Tex.) Ind. Sch. Dist., 1981-91; cons. U.S. Office Edn., Washington, 1968-69; mem. devel. com. Edn. Profl. Devel. Act Tex. Edn. Agy., 1969. Cons. edn. com. Goals for Dallas, 1969; vice chairperson Kaufman (Tex.) County Improvement Council, 1975. Chmn. beautification com. Keep Tex. Beautiful, Mabank, 1990-91; grant adminstr. Avanti Cmty. Theater, 1993-95, bd. dirs., 1993—, pres., 1990-92; co-chair United Way campaign, 1991-92, dir. Henderson County, 1992—; mem. Planning and Zoning Commn., City of Mabank, 1992—; sec. Indsl. Found., 1971-75. Recipient Outstanding Ex-Student award Trinity Valley C.C., Athens, 1974; Cert. of Recognition, Internat. Thespian Soc., 1994. Mem. NEA, Athens Edn. Assn. (pres. 1982-83), Tex. State Tchrs. Assn. (pres.-elect dist. X 1970), Tex. Classroom Tchrs. Assn. (state bd. dirs. 1969-70), Classroom Tchrs. Dallas (pres. 1968-69), Mabank C. of C. (bd. dirs. 1978-80, 91-92, Citizen of Yr. 1977). Democrat. Methodist. Home: 112 N Canton St PO Box 318 Mabank TX 75147

BEEZLEY, LINDA D., state legislator, lab supervisor. Spl. projects coord. Samaritan Health Sys., Phoenix, 1982-84, supr. adminstrv. support, compensation and benefits, 1984-91, spl. projects coord. human resources, 1991—; state rep. Ariz. Legis. Dist. 20, 1991—; mem. govt. ops., health com., human svcs. com. Legis. Dist. 20, 1991—; mem. Phoenix (Ariz.) Arts Commn., 1989, co-chair planning com. edn. and the arts, 1990, nomination com., 1991, advocacy com., 1991-93. Exec. com. mem. Boy Scouts Am., 1976-86, cub scouts leader, 1976-84, Webelos leader, 1978-84; team mother, mgr. Catalina/Barcelona Little League, 1976-86; T-ball and soccer coach YMCA, 1976-80; active Alhambra Dist. Liaison Com., 1986—; campaign worker and coord. United Way Campaign, 1982-90; governing bd. mem. Alhambra Elem. Sch.Dist. No. 68, 1986—, governing bd. pres., 1989. Recipient Art Edn. Advocacy award Ariz. Art Edn. Assn., 1990, award of merit Ariz. Sch. Pub. Rels. Assn., 1990, award of excellence Ariz. Sch. Pub. Rels. Assn., 1990, All Ariz. Bd. award for Excellence in Boardmanship Ariz. Sch. Bds. Assn., 1993. Mem. Ariz. Sch. Bds. Assn. (sec. 1989-90, founder, dir. mini-grants program 1989—, pres. 1990-91). Address: Ho of Reps 1700 W Washington St Phoenix AZ 85007-2812

BEGGS, SYBLE MARIE, program coordinator; b. Oklahoma City, Aug. 24, 1953; d. Frank V. and Rosetta Pairlee (Floyd) Kirby; m. Ernie Dale Beggs, Oct. 1, 1985; children: Wanda, Dawn. Diploma, Kiamichi VoTech, McAlester, Okla., 1978; BSN, East Cen. U., Ada, Okla., 1989. Staff nurse in critical care McAlester Regional Hosp., nurse mgr. Rehab. unit, adminstr., dir. skilled nursing facility, program coord., concurrent case mgmt.-utilization rev. Home: 416 E Osage Ave Mcalester OK 74501-6453

BEGLEY, EVELYN MARIA, sign language interpreter; b. N.Y.C., July 7, 1953; d. Peter Francis and Theresa Rose Begley. BA in English, L.I. Univ., 1977; MA in Spl. Edn. with Splty. in Deaf Edn., Columbia U., 1983. Cert. in transliteration, sign. lang. interpreter. Interpreter N.Y. Soc. for the Deaf, N.Y.C., 1975-83, 86—; tchr. deaf St. Francis De Sales Sch., Bklyn., 1983-86. Contbr. to book Insider's Baseball, 1983. Home and Office: 625 E 14th St New York NY 10009

BEHAR, DIANE SUSAN, marketing and public relations professional, freelance writer, consultant; b. N.Y.C., May 17, 1952; d. Solomon and Frieda Behar. Spanish language cert., La Universidad Internacional, 1969; BA, Cornell U., 1974; MBA, U. Pa., 1983. Legis. analyst Com. on the Budget U.S. Ho. of Reps., Washington, 1975-77, legis. asst. and speechwriter Office of Congressman Oberstar, 1977-81; account exec. Doyle Dane Bernbach Advt., N.Y.C., 1983-85; dir. of pub. affairs and speechwriter Mayor's Office of Bus. Devel., N.Y.C., 1985-88; dir. of mktg. Mayor's Offfice of Bus. Devel., N.Y.C., 1988-91; sr. mktg. analyst Dep. Mayor's Office for Econ. Policy and Mktg., N.Y.C., 1991—; mktg. cons. Work Late/Eat Right Gourmet Food Delivery Svcs., N.Y.C., 1985-87; lectr. in field. Contbr. articles to profl. jours. Mem. coun., fundraiser Fresh Air Fund, 1987—; bd. dirs., fundraiser Pentacle Danceworks, 1984—; v.p. bd. dirs. Children's Orch. Soc., 1990—. Morgenthau fellow, 1981-83, Dupont fellow, 1981-83, fellow Nat. Endowment for Arts, 1983. Mem. NAFE, Am. Mgmt. Assn., Am. Mktg. Assn., Women Execs. in Pub. Rels. (bd. dirs.), Global Bus. Assn N.Y., Musicians Soc. N.Y., Cornell Club. Home: 201 E 69th St New York NY 10021-5470 Office: NYC Office of Econ Policy & Mktg 110 William St New York NY 10038-3901

BEHBEHANIAN, MAHIN FAZELI, surgeon; b. Kermanshah region, Iran; d M Jaafar and Ozra (A.) B.; m. Abolfath H. Fazeli, Sept, 4, 1969; children: Pouneh, Pontea. BS, Wilmington (Ohio) Coll., 1961; MD, Med. Coll. of Pa., Phila., 1965; general surgeon, Lankenan Hosp., Phila., 1970. Diplomate Am. Bd. Surgery, 1981. Chief surgery, pres. med. staff Imperial Ct. Hosp., Teheran, Iran, 1971-79; gen. surgery Riddle Meml. Hosp., Media, Pa., 1980—; pvt. practice Chester, Media, Phila., Pa., 1984—; Mem. operating room com. Riddle Meml. Hosp., Media, 1988—, also Emergency room com., utilization com. Editor-in-chief Behkoosh Jour. of Medicine, Teheran, 1976-79. Recipient Gilson Colby Engel award, 1966. Fellow Am. Coll. Surgeons; mem. AMA, Am. Women Surgical Soc., Pa. Med. Soc., Del. County Med. Soc. Office: Riddle Meml Health Care Ctr 1088 W Baltimore Pike Media PA 19063-5140

BEHLAR, PATRICIA ANN, political science educator; b. New Orleans, Jan. 16, 1939; d. James Edward and Maude Albertine (Davis) B. BA, U. New Orleans, 1966; MA, La. State U., 1968, PhD, 1974. Instr. Northwestern State U. of La., Natchitoches, 1971-72; instr. Pan Am. U., Edinburg, Tex., 1974-76; asst. prof. Pan Am. U., Edinburg, 1976-77, U. Ark., Pine Bluff, 1977-84; asst. prof. Pittsburg (Kans.) State U., 1986-92, assoc. prof., 1992—; mem. U. Ark. Pine Bluff Winthrop Rockefeller lectures steering com., 1980-82; referee Ark. Polit. Sci. Jour., 1983-84; alt., edit. com. Univ. Press of Kans., 1991-93; mem., edit. com. Univ. Press of Kans., 1993—; book rev. editor, The Midwest Quarterly, 1994—. Audio reader for the blind, Pittsburg, 1992. Recipient La. State U. fellowship, 1970-71. Mem. Am. Polit. Sci. Assn., Sou. Polit. Sci. Assn., Kans. Polit. Sci. Assn., Southwestern Social Sci. Assn., Phi Kappa Phi. Democrat. Roman Catholic. Home: 508 Hobson Dr Pittsburg KS 66762-6315 Office: Dept Social Sci Pittsburg State U Pittsburg KS 66762

BEHLER, DIANA IPSEN, Germanic language and literature educator; b. N.Y.C.; d. Walter F. and Marie M. (Kroger) Ipsen; m. Ernst Behler, Nov. 24, 1967; children: Sophia, Caroline. B.A., U. Wash., 1965, M.A., 1966, Ph.D., 1970. Asst. prof. Germanics Germanics U. Wash., Seattle, 1971-74; assoc. prof. Germanics and comparative lit. U. Wash., Seattle, 1974-81, prof., 1981—; chmn. dept Germanics U. Wash., 1978-88, 1990. Author: The

Theory of the Novel in Early German Romanticism, 1978; translations: Hegel, Jacobi, Fickle; contbr. articles to profl. jours. Younger Humanist fellow NEH, 1972-73. Mem. Am. Assn. Tchrs. German, N.Am. Nietzsche Soc. Home: 5525 NE Penrith Rd Seattle WA 98105-2844 Office: U Wash Dept Germanics Denny 343 DH-30 Seattle WA 98195

BEHLMAR, CINDY LEE, business manager, consultant; b. Smyrna, Tenn., July 4, 1959; d. James Wallace and Barbara Ann (Behlmar) Gribble. BBA, Coll. William and Mary, 1981; postgrad., Old Dominion U., 1992—. Adminstrv. extern Hampton (Va.) Gen. Hosp., 1981-82; mktg. rep., then supr. mktg. svcs. PruCare of Richmond, Va., 1983-85; exec. dir. PhysicianCare, Inc., Newport News, Va., 1986-89; provider rels. cons. Va. Health Network, Richmond, 1989-91; ind. cons. Tidewater Health Care, Virginia Beach, Va., 1991-92; chief ops. officer Tidewater Phys. Therapy, Inc., Newport News, 1993—; sec., bd. dirs. Greater Peninsula Area Med.-Bus. Coalition, Newport News, 1987-89; symposium faculty mem. Am. Hosp. Assn., Orlando, Fla., 1987, Washington, 1988. Mem. ch. coun. St. Mark Luth. Ch., Yorktown, Va., 1988-91. Fin. Exec. Inst. scholar, 1993. Mem. Inst. Mgmt. Accts., Peninsula Toastmasters. Home: 103 Jean Pl Yorktown VA 23693 Office: Tidewater Phys Therapy Inc Bldg C Ste 203 732 Thimble Shoals Blvd Newport News VA 23606

BEHN, ANITA J., education specialist; b. Batavia, N.Y., June 27, 1938; d. Abraham Chaim and Rose (Barsuk) Davidovitz; m. Melvyn Lawrence Behn, Sept. 5, 1960; children: Michael Irwin, Philip Scott, Sharon Faith. BA, Syracuse U., 1959; MA, SUNY, Albany, 1974. Lic. tchr. social studies. Social svcs. case worker Erie County Dept. Social Svcs., Buffalo, N.Y., 1959-60; tech. editor GE, Syracuse, N.Y., 1960-61; tchr. Hebrew Acad. of the Capital Dist. Pub. Schs., Albany, 1974-76; coord. svcs. Edn. Bur., N.Y. State Mus., N.Y. State Edn. Dept., Albany, 1976-88; edn. specialist N.Y. State Edn. Dept., Albany, 1988—; bd. dirs. Schenectady (N.Y.) Headstart, Parenting Edn. Network, Albany; mem. Mus. Educators Assn., Washington, 1987-91. Columnist: Albany Times-Union, 1976-92; contbr. articles to profl. jours. active Temple Israel, 1969-89, bd. edn. PTA bd. 1972-82; leader Girl Scouts Am., Guilderland, N.Y., 1972-74; various bd. positions including assoc. dir., asst. dir. Capital Dist. N.Y. State PTA, 1972-82; pub. rels. chair McKownville (N.Y.) Improvement Assn., 1979-81; poll watcher, vote observer Albany (N.Y.) LWV, 1988—; active Congregation Agudat Achim, 1990—, bd. mem., 1991-92. Mem. AAUW (v.p. 1991-92), N.Y. State Alliance for the Arts, Capital Dist. Assn. for Edn. Young Children, Pi Sigma Alpha, Phi Kappa Phi, Phi Delta Kappa. Democrat. Jewish. Office: Rm 367 NY State Edn Dept Albany NY 12234

BEHNKE, MARYLOU, neonatologist, educator; b. Orlando, Fla., Sept. 1, 1950; d. Ernest Edmund and Elizabeth (Kolb) B. BS in Chemistry, U. Fla., 1972, MD, 1976. Diplomate Am. Bd. Pediatrics, Am. Bd. Neonatology-Perinatology. Intern dept. pediatrics Coll. Medicine, U. Fla., Gainesville, 1976-77, resident, 1977-79, chief resident, 1979-80, fellow in neonatology, 1981-83, asst. prof., 1979-81, 83-89, assoc. prof., 1989—; adj. asst. prof. Coll. Nursing, Gainesville, 1988-89, adj. assoc. prof., 1989—, mem. senate-at-large, 1984-89, mem. grad. studies faculty, 1988—; med. dir. neonatology ICU Shands Hosp., Gainesville, 1983-89, neonatal developmental follow-up program, 1989—; presenter at nat. and internat. meetings, 1981—; ad hoc mem. spl. rev. com. on human devel. rsch. NIH, 1991—, chair, 1993, 94. Mem. editl. bd. Death Studies, 1983-94; contbr. articles to med. jours., chpts. to books. Grantee NIH, 1984-87, 91—, Nat. Inst. on Drug Abuse, 1991—, Ctr. for Substance abuse Treatment, 1993—. Fellow Am. Acad. Pediatrics; mem. Fla. Med. Assn., Alachua County Med. Soc., Nat. Perinatal Assn., So. Soc. for Pediatric Rsch., Fla. Soc. Neonatal Perinatologists. Republican. Mem. Ch. of Christ. Home: 426 SW 40th St Gainesville FL 32607-2749 Office: J Hillis Miller Health Ctr Dept Pediatrics Box 100296 Gainesville FL 32610

BEHRENS, BARBARA BLAUTH, healthcare administrator; b. Bklyn., Apr. 20, 1937; d. Robert James and Theresa (Enriquez) Blauth; m. Herbert Harry Behrens, Mar. 21, 1959 (div. July 1986); children: Christopher Charles, Catherine Ann. RN grad., Bellevue Sch. Nursing, N.y.C., 1957; BA with distinction, U. of Redlands, 1976, MA in Mgmt. Human Resources with distinction, 1979. RN, Hawaii, Calif., N.Y.; cert. advanced cardiac life support, basic cardiac life support instr./trainer, cert. emergency nurse, mobile intensive care nurse. Staff nurse med.-surg. and critical care depts. U. Calif., Moffett Hosp., San Francisco; with Bellevue Hosp., N.Y.C.; relief nurse all units Stanford (Calif.) Univ. Hosp., 1962-69, staff nurse IV, acting insvc. instr., 1972-76, ednl. coord., 1976-78, clin. nursing coord., 1978-82, asst. dir. dept. emergency svcs., 1982-86; dir. critical care and emergency svcs. Queen's Med. Ctr., Honolulu, 1986-89; exec. dir. Queen's Heart Inst., 1989—; mem. affiliate faculty U. Redlands. Mem. ACCA, Am. Coll. Cardiovascular Adminstrs. (state dir. Hawaii chpt.), Am. Acad. Med. Adminstrs. (state dir. Hawaii chpt.), Am. Heart Assn. (Hawaii ACLS faculty, bd. dirs. exec. com. Hawaii affiliate), Am. Orgn. Nurse Execs. (chair nominating com., legis. com.), Emergency Nurses Assn. Home: 1030 Aoloa Pl # 304A Kailua HI 96734 Office: Queens Med Ctr Heart Inst 1301 Punchbowl St Honolulu HI 96813

BEHRENS, BEREL LYN, physician, academic administrator; b. New South Wales, Australia, 1940. MB, BS, Sydney (Australia) U., 1964. Cert. pediatrics, allergy and immunology. Pediatric pulmonary intern Royal Prince Alfred Hosp., Australia, 1964; resident Loma Linda (Calif.) U. Med. Ctr., 1966-68; with Henrietta Egleston Hosp. for Children, Atlanta, 1968-69, T.C. Thompson Children's Hosp., Chattanooga, 1969-70; instr. pediatrics Loma Linda U., 1970-72, with dept. pediatrics, 1972—, dean Sch. Medicine, 1986-91, pres., 1990—. Office: Loma Linda U Office of the President Loma Linda CA 92350

BEHRENS, DIANE R., nursing educator; b. East Orange, N.J., Dec. 9, 1941; d. Samuel N. and Sylvia Irene (Lucas) Rankin; m. Otto Karl Behrens, Jr., Dec. 22, 1962; children: Connie, Cheryl, Karl, Carrie. BSN, Columbia U., 1964; MA in Nursing, Ball State U., 1984; MSEd, Ind. U., 1991. Cert. oncology nurse, med. surg. nurse, clin. specialist in med.-surg. nursing, CPR instr. Paramed. examiner Prudential Ins. Co., Merrillville, Ind., 1979-81; instr. pharmacology Valparaiso (Ind.) U., 1983; staff nurse St. Joseph Hosp., Ft. Wayne, Ind., 1978-81, relief nurse, nutritional support team, 1981; instr., assoc. prof. Luth. Coll. Health Professions, Ft. Wayne, 1981-93; asst. prof. St. Francis Coll., Ft. Wayne, 1993—. Mem. ANA (cert.), Ind. State Nurses Assn., Oncology Nursing Soc. (Three Rivers chpt.), Ind. Mental Health Assn., Sigma Theta Tau, Kappa Delta Phi. Home: 1685 W 600 N Columbia City IN 46725-9531 Office: St Francis Coll Dept Nursing 2701 Spring St Fort Wayne IN 46808

BEHRMANN, JOAN METZNER, newspaper editor; b. N.Y.C.; d. Jerome and Jeannette (Silberman) Metzner; m. Larry Jinks, Oct. 2, 1960 (div. 1970); children: Laura Beth, Daniel Carlton; m. Nicolas Lee Behrmann, Dec. 21, 1972. BA, Queens Coll., 1956; MS, Columbia U., 1958. Reporter Miami (Fla.) Herald, 1960-63; asst. prof. Miami-Dade Community Coll., 1968-72; lifestyle editor Middlesex News, Framingham, Mass., 1973-75; assoc. prof. Boston U., 1975-78; Sunday editor The Saratogian, Saratoga Springs, N.Y., 1978-80; mng. editor, city editor Westchester-Rockland Newspapers, White Plains, N.Y., 1980-82; page one editor USA Today, Arlington, Va., 1982-84, entertainment editor, 1984-87; exec. editor The Desert Sun, Palm Springs, Calif., 1987—. Co-author: Questioning Media Ethics, 1978. Founding mem. Every Woman's Coun., Glens Falls, N.Y., 1978-80; rec. sec. Palm Springs Opera Guild, 1990-91; bd. dirs. Coll. of Desert Found., 1992—. Mem. AP Mng. Editors Assn. (com. chmn. 1989-90, 91-95, bd. dirs. 1991—), Am. Soc. Newspaper Editors, Women in Comm. Home: 785 N High Rd Palm Springs CA 92262-4322 Office: The Desert Sun PO Box 2734 750 N Gene Autry Trl Palm Springs CA 92262-5464

BEIGHLE, JENNIFER MARIE, sales executive; b. Detroit, Aug. 26, 1962; d. Richard Wallace and Grace Emelene (Darby) B.; m. David Franklin Long, Sept. 4, 1983 (div. Apr. 1991); m. Philip George Loprinzi, Dec. 24, 1994. BS in Bus., U. Colo., 1988. Mem. pharm. sales staff Eli Lilly Pharm., Indpls., 1988-91; mem. med. sales staff Lifescan/Johnson & Johnson, Milpitas, Calif., 1991—. Vol. Am. Diabetes Assn., Gt. Falls, Mont., 1991-94, bd. dirs., 1992-93; ski instr. for disabled Eagle Ski, Bozeman, Mont., 1991-93. Mem. Toastmasters Internat.

BEIGHT, JANICE MARIE, interior designer; b. Toledo, Oct. 9, 1947; d. Clyde Harding and Ida Belle (Ragland) McCluskey; children: Stephen C., Scott J. BA in Interior Design, Chgo. U., 1974. Pres. Interiors by Janice, Poland, Ohio, 1974—; fin. planner Primerica Fin. Svcs.; real estate investor. Contbr. poems to Women of West Minster, 1980, Angels and Friends Cookbook, 1980, 91. Mem. NAFE, Internat. Platform Assn., Angels of Easter Seal, Am. Lung Assn., Am. Cancer Soc. Republican. Mem. Ch. of Christ.

BEIL, KAREN MAGNUSON, editor, writer, educator; b. Boston, Feb. 15, 1950; d. Victor Berger and Dorothy (Hall) Magnuson; m. James A. Beil, Feb. 24, 1973; children: Kimberly Erika, Kirsten Annika. Student, Upsala Coll., 1967-68; BA cum laude, Syracuse U., 1971. Reporter City News Bur. of Chgo., 1971-72; research editor N.Y. State Dept. Environ. Conservation, Albany, 1973-75, asst. editor, 1975-76, editor, 1976-78, assoc. dir. info. services The Conservationist Mag., N.Y. State Environ. Notice Bull., 1978-81; freelance editor and writer, 1981—; cons. in field. Author: Grandma According to Me, 1992; contbr. articles to profl. jours. Mem. Nat. Audubon Soc., Soc. Children's Book Writers and Illustrators.

BEINECKE, CANDACE KRUGMAN, lawyer; b. Paterson, N.J., Nov. 26, 1946; d. Martin and Sylvia (Altshuler) Krugman; m. Frederick W. Beinecke II, Oct. 2, 1976; children: Jacob Sperry, Benjamin Barrett. BA, NYU, 1967; JD, Rutgers U., 1970. Bar: N.Y. 1971. Assoc., then ptnr. Hughes, Hubbard & Reed, N.Y.C., 1970—; lectr., chmn. Practising Law Inst., N.Y.C. Bd. dirs. Merce Cunningham Found., N.Y.C., Jacob's Pillow Dance Festival, Lee, Mass., Trinity Episcopal Sch. Corp., N.Y.C. Mem. ABA, Assn. Bar City of N.Y., River Club, Women's Forum. Office: 998 Fifth Ave New York NY 10004-1412

BEIRNE, DANIELLE ULULANI, state legislator; m. David Haili Keawe; 4 children. AA, Windward C.C., 1988; BA, U. Hawaii, 1988, postgrad., 1988-92. Rep. dist. 46 State of Hawaii; with Outrigger Hotels; mem. bd. dirs. Hui Na'auao; v.p. Kahana 'Ohana Unity Coun. Mem. Ko'olauloa Hawaiian Civic Club (v.p.), Ka'a'awa, Kahana, Punaiu'u, Hauula, Laie, Kahalu'u & Ko'olauloa Cmty. Assns. Democrat. Home: PO Box 653 Kaneohe HI 96744-0653 Office: Hawaii House Reps State House Honolulu HI 96813*

BEIRNE, SHERYL MARTHA, conference coordinator, educator; b. N.Y.C., July 17, 1949; d. Sherman and Phyllis Caroline (Wolff) Schochet; m. Owen Ross Beirne, Aug. 23, 1970; children: Samuel, Deborah. AB, U. Calif., Berkeley, 1969; MAT, Boston Coll., 1970. Secondary sch. tchr. San Francisco and various cities, Mass., 1969-73; benefits asst. Kaiser Industries, Oakland, Calif., 1971-72; adminstrv. positions U. Calif. San Francisco, UCLA, 1973-77; dir. personnel/payroll svcs. Harbor Regional Ctr., Carson, Calif., 1977-79; conf. coord. Shoreline C.C., Seattle, 1991-94; mem. local arrangements com. U.S. Secretariat for World Conf., San Francisco Conf. for Women, Conf. UN Decade for Women, San Francisco; tchr. Temple B'nai Torah, Mercer Island, Wash., 1992—. Pers. counselor Women Organized for Employment, 1979-80; comty. adv. King County Pub. Hosp. Dist., Kirkland, Wash., 1988-90; art and history docent San Francisco Mus. Modern Art, Calif. Hist. Soc., 1979-85; meeting planner AAUW, San Francisco and Seattle, 1983, 91. Recipient Rosalie M. Stern award U. Calif. Berkeley Alumni Assn., 1983. Mem. AAUW, PTA.

BEITZ, ALEXANDRA GRIGG, political activist; b. Cin., Oct. 15, 1960; d. Kenneth Andrew and Betty Ann (Carpenter) Grigg; m. Charles Arthur Beitz III, Oct. 17, 1987; 1 child, Madeleine Grigg Beitz. BA, Vassar Coll., 1982; MBA, Wake Forest U., 1985. Asst. buyer Bloomingdale's, N.Y.C., 1982-83; dept. mgr. Bloomingdale's, Stamford, Conn., 1983; intern Ciba-Geigy Corp., Greensboro, N.C., 1984; retail sales promotion mgr. Hanes Hosiery, N.Y.C., 1985-86; market rep. May Co., N.Y.C., 1986-87; freelance polit. cons. Winston-Salem, N.C., 1990—. Vol. Planned Parenthood, Winston-Salem, N.C., 1988—, Southeastern Ctr. for Contemporary Art, Winston-Salem, 1992—, exec. bd. dirs. Friends, 1993, v.p.-pres. elect, 1994; vol. Am. Cancer Soc., Winston-Salem, 1992-94; bd. dirs. Planned Parenthood of the Triad, Winston-Salem, 1995—.

BEKELMAN, JUDITH WELLES, public affairs executive; b. N.Y.C., Jan. 15, 1946; d. John and Millicent (Richman) Welles; m. Alan M. Bekelman, June 26, 1966 (div. Sept. 1994); children: David B., Justin E. BA, Vassar Coll., 1963. Speechwriter, editor U.S. Dept. Interior, Washington, 1965-66; asst. to dir. VISTA, Washington, 1967-70; speechwriter to sec. HHS, Washington, 1971-76, mgr. pub. affairs, 1977-86; dir. comm. and pub. affairs Pension Benefit Guaranty Corp., Washington, 1987—. Commr. County Health Planning Commn., Md., 1968-88. Recipient 1st place ann. report competition Fin. World, 1991, 92. Mem. Nat. Assn. Govt. Communicators (Gold Screen award 1992, award of Excellence 1994). Office: Pension Benefit Guaranty Corp 1200 K St NW Washington DC 20005-4026

BEKER, GISELA U., artist; b. 1932, Zoppot, Ger.; came to U.S., 1956. Student The Kunst-Institut, Rostock, E.Ger.; pupil of Rudolf Kroll. Solo shows include Bodley Gallery, N.Y., 1973, Women's Bldg., Los Angeles, 1973, Mus. Art, Huntsville, Ala., 1974, Tower Gallery, Southampton, N.Y., 1974, Arts and Sci. Ctr., Baton Rouge, 1975, Wilkes Coll., Pa., 1975, Tower Gallery, 1975, NYU, 1976, Everson Mus., Syracuse, 1976, Tower Gallery, 1976, Wilkes Coll., 1976, G. Sander Fine Art, Daytona Beach, Fla., 1985, Mus. Modern Art, Warsaw, Poland, 1989, Deland (Fla.) Mus. Art, 1989; represented in permanent collections of Chrysler Mus., Norfolk, Va., New Orleans Mus. Art, Aldrich Mus., Ridgefield, Conn., Fine Art Ctr., Nashville, Okla. Art Ctr., Oklahoma City, Everson Mus., Syracuse, Palm Spring Mus., Calif., Long Beach Mus., Calif., Mus. Art, Huntsville, Ala., Arts and Sci. Ctr., Baton Rouge, Phoenix Art Mus., Mus. Art, Lodz, Poland, others; exhibited in group shows at Jersey City Mus., 1973, Nat. Acad. N.Y., 1973, State Capitol Mus., Olympia, Wash., 1973, Fairleigh Dickenson U., 1973, U. Portland, 1974, Central Wyo. Mus. Art, Casper, Northeastern Okla. A&M Coll., 1974, Rosenberg Library, Galveston, Tex., 1974, Mus. Modern Art, Paris, 1974, 20th Salon de Thouars, France, 1974, Marathon Mus., Warsau, Wis., 1974, Hoyt Inst. Fine Arts, Pa., 1974, Spring Arbor coll., Mich., 1975, LaSalle Coll. Union, Phila., 1975, Pensacola Art Ctr., Fla., 1975, Art Ctr., Richmond, Ind., 1975, Jesse Beser Mus., Alpena, Mich., 1976, Bronx Mus. Art, 1976, Charles and Emma Frye Mus., Seattle, 1976, Watkins Inst., Nashville, 1976, Louisville Sch. Art, 1977, Cayuga Mus. History and Art, Auburn, N.Y., 1977, Tower Gallery, 1977, others. Contbr. articles to profl. jours.

BEKEY, SHIRLEY WHITE, psychotherapist; b. L.A.; d. Lawrence Francis and Alice (King) White; m. George Albert Bekey, June 10, 1951; children: Ronald S., Michelle E. BA in Psychology, Occidental Coll., 1949; MSW in Psychiat. Social Work, UCLA, 1954; PhD in Edn. Psychology, U. So. Calif., 1980. Lic. social worker, Calif.; cert. pupil-personnel credential, 1957, parent-child edn. credential, 1972. Caseworker outpatient svcs. Calif. State Dept. Mental Health, Montebello; caseworker Lowman Sch. for Handicapped, L.A. Unified Sch. Dist., North Hollywood, Calif., 1971-72; psychotherapist Hofmann Psychiat. Clinic, Glendale (Calif.) Adventist Hosp., 1973-75; pvt. practice psychotherapy Encino, Calif., 1980—; mem. staff Van Nuys (Calif.) Hosp.; spkr. nat. radio, TV expert on children's emotional problems. Mem. World Affairs Coun., L.A., 1960—. Fellow Soc. for Clin. Social Work; mem. NASW, APA, Am. Ednl. Rsch. Assn., Nat. Assn. Gifted Children, Assn. Ednl. Therapists, So. Calif. Soc. Clin. Hypnosis, Assn. for Transpersonal Psychology, Nat. Assn. Poetry Therapy, Analytical Psychology Club L.A. Democrat. Office: 18075 Ventura Blvd Encino CA 91316

BELANGER, DIAN RAE OLSON, historian; b. Virginia, Minn., Nov. 22, 1941; d. Raymond Wilford and Esther Ellen (Silta) Olson; m. Brian C. Belanger, June 16, 1962. BS in History summa cum laude, U. Minn., Duluth, 1962; MA in Am. Studies, George Washington U., 1982. Tchr. history Poly. Sch., Pasadena, Calif., 1962-67; docent Smithsonian Inst., Washington, 1973-83; historian Nat. Mus. Am. History, Smithsonian Instn., Washington, 1983-84; sr. historian, dir. comms. History Assocs., Inc., Rockville, Md., 1984—. Author: Managing American Wildlife, 1988 (Wildlife Soc. Book award 1990); contbr. articles to profl. jours. Mem. selection com. Md. Women's Hall of Fame, Annapolis, 1985-89, chair, 1988-89; mem. Montgomery County Commn. on the Humanities, Rockville, 1988-92, vice chair, 1990. Mem. AAUW (Middle Atlantic regional dir. 1989-93, bd. dirs. Legal Advocacy Fund 1991-93, exec. com. 1989-90, state pres. 1985-88, Project Renew grantee 1980-81), Soc. for History in the Fed. Govt., Nat. Coun. on Pub. History, Am. Studies Assn., Orgn. Am. Historians. Unitarian. Office: History Assocs Inc 5 Choke Cherry Rd Rockville MD 20850-4004

BELCHER, JULIANNA, lawyer; b. Ft. Lauderdale, Fla., Nov. 5, 1963; d. Frederic Hoberg and Bette Lynn (Stewart) Burrall; m. John Michael Belcher, Sept. 8, 1991. BA in English, U. Fla., 1984; MBA in Finance, Fla. State U., 1988, JD, 1991. Bar: Ga., Fla. Assoc. atty. Tinkler & Groff, Decatur, Ga., 1992-93; atty.-at-law pvt. practice, Marietta, Ga., 1993; so. mgr. and counsel Nat. Automatic Merchandising Assn., Marietta, 1993—. Office: Nat Automatic Merchandising Assn 1640 Powers Ferry Rd Bldg 24 # 250 Marietta GA 30067

BELCHER, LA JEUNE, automotive parts company executive; b. Chgo., Nov. 16, 1960; d. Lewis Albert and Dorthy (Brandon) B. BA, Northwestern U., 1982; postgrad., Am. Inst. of Banking, 1983-84. Notary pub.; securities lic.; ins. lic., Ill. Securities processor Am. Nat. Bank, Chgo., 1983, divisional asst., 1983-84; mgmt. trainee Toyota Motor Distbrs., Carol Stream, Ill., 1984-85, dist. parts mgr., 1985-90, sr. customer rels. adminstr., 1990—; fin. rep. Waddell and Reed, 1992; rep. to Japan-U.S. Toyota Dealer Meeting, Tokyo, 1985. Mem. alumni admissions coun. Northwestern U., Evanston, Ill.; bd. dirs. Boys and Girls Club. Mem. NAFE, NAACP, Northwestern Club Chgo., Toastmasters (edn. v.p. 1988, 91-92, advt. v.p. 1989, pres. 1990-93), Delta Sigma Theta. Home: 1212 S Michigan Ave Chicago IL 60605-2416 Office: Toyota Motor Distbrs 2350 Sequoia Dr Aurora IL 60506-6211

BELCHER-REDEBAUGH-LEVI, CAROLINE LOUISE, nursing home administrator, registered nurse; b. Dixon, Ill., May 23, 1910; d. Charles R. and May Caroline (Barnes) Kreger; m. Richard E. Belcher, Nov. 24, 1934 (dec. 1964); children: Richard Charles (dec.), Mary; m. Charles H. Redebaugh, Dec. 3, 1966 (dec. 1979); m. Paul Levi, July 20, 1985 (dec. Sept. 1993). R.N., Katherine Shaw Bethea Sch. Nursing, 1930. Nurse, various hosps., 1930-49; administr. Orchard Glen Nursing Home, Dixon, Ill., 1949-76; coordinator Sr. Action Ctr., Springfield, Ill., 1977-87; charter mem. Ill. Nursing Home Adminstrs. Licensure Bd., 1970-76; mem. Sauk Valley Community Coll. Found., Dixon, Ill., 1988, adv. com. for sr. programs, 1988, chmn. ball com., 1989-90, Co Coun. on Aging, 1988, various adv. coms. advocating for srs. Contbr. articles to profl. jours. Mem. nat. adv. com., del. White House Conf. on Aging, 1961-81; v.p. Ill. Joint Council to Improve Health Care for Aged, 1953, pres., 1954; chair Sec. State George Ryan Adv. Com. Health Maintenance, 1991; charter mem. bd. dirs. Lee County Vol. Care Ctr., 1994, Free Health Clinic. Mem. Capitol City Rep. Women (v.p. 1983-90), Lee County Rep. Women, State Council on Aging, Am. Coll. Nursing Home Adminstrs. (charter, edn. com., pres.), Am. Nursing Home Assn. (v.p. 1953), Ill. Nurses Assn. (bd. dirs.), Ill. Nursing Home Adminstrs (charter), Sr. Illinoisian's Hall of Fame (charter). Home: 1420 Eustace Dr Dixon IL 61021-1742

BELCHER-WILLIAMS, PATRICIA ANN, small business consultant, education official; b. Fresno, Calif., Jan. 17, 1951; d. Clevie Belcher and Erma LaVerne (Brown) Houff; divorced; children: Carrie Williams-Reed, Arthur, Danny, Pamala. Student, Trade Technical Coll., 1976-78; BS in Pub. Adminstrn., Calif. State U., Carson, 1987; postgrad., U. LaVerne (Calif.), 1991—. Adminstrv. mktg. Constrn. Control Svcs. Corp., L.A., 1983-84; co-dir. Women's Econ. Agenda Project, Oakland, Calif., 1983-85; legal technician, legal assistance ctr. U.S. Dept. of Navy, Long Beach, Calif., 1987-88; bus. cons. Small Bus. Cons. Svcs., Antelope Valley, Calif., 1989—; founder, exec. dir. Antelope Valley Community Human Rels. Com., 1989—. Mem. Sen. Watson's Task Force on the Feminization of Poverty, L.A., Sacramento, 1984; mem. adv. bd. Pres. Bush's Am. 2000 Literacy Project, Lancaster, Calif., 1991. Mem. AAUW, Am. Soc. Pub. Adminstrs., Dressage Riders of the Antelope Valley. Office: Antelope Valley Cmty Human Rels Com PO Box 1783 Lancaster CA 93539-1783

BELDEN, URSULA, set designer; b. Weimar, Fed. Rep. Germany, Sept. 27, 1947; came to U.S., 1949; d. Ernest J. and Edith G. (Pütter) Mugdan; 1 child, Willow Allegra. MA, U. Mich., 1972; MFA in Design, Yale U., 1976. Designer (plays) include Broadway, Off-Broadway and internat., Lay of the Land, 1994, Edith Stein, 1994, Night of the Iguana, Cleve., (Peggy Elekiel award U.S. Inst. Theatre Tech. 1993), Trinity, 1991, Waitin' in the Wings, 1990, Spare Parts, 1989, A Murder of Crows, 1988 (Peggy Elekiel award U.S. Inst. Theatre Tech. 1989), Pieces of Glass, 1987, Quilters, 1984, Weekend, 1983, Living Quarters, 1983, I Can't Keep Running in Place, 1981, Amadeus, 1980, 82, A Dream Play, 1980 (Villager award for outstanding scene design 1981), Dark Ages, 1980, Shortages, 1979, Where Memories are Magic and Dreams Invented, 1978, Galileo, 1979, At Her Age, 1979, The Importance of Being Ernest, 1979, The Eastern Opera Theatre, 1977, Patience, The Mikado, 1977. Ricipient Peggy Ezekiel Scene Design award U.S. Inst. of Theatre Tech., 1989, 93, Prague Quadrenial, 1994. Mem. United Scenic Artists (local 829). Office: 84 Prospect Ave Flushing NY 11363-1340

BELENCHIA, ELIZABETH SHAFFER, international industrial realtor, environmental marketing consultant; b. Fort Wayne, Ind., July 19, 1944; d. George P. and Mildred M. (Rawles) Shaffer; m. James F. Carroll, July 24, 1965 (div. May 1985); children: David, Kristin, Stephen, Brian; m. Thomas Alexander Belenchia, Dec. 30, 1989. RN, The Toledo Hosp. Sch. Nursing, 1964. Head nurse The Toledo Hosp., 1964-65; head nurse St. Vincent Hosp., 1965-70, cons., 1970-72; realtor Grogan Co., 1972-73, Gallinger Realtors, Syracuse, N.Y., 1973-74; sales mgr. Still-Newton Realtors, Spartanburg, S.C., 1975-76; pres. Belenchia Mktg., Spartanburg, 1993—, Internat. Environ. Inc., Spartanburg, 1990—, Carroll Properties Corp., Spartanburg, 1976—; chmn. pub. rels. Spartanburg Bd. Realtors, 1978-80, Washington legis. liaison, 1980-81; mem. bd. dirs. S.C. Assn. Realtors, 1979-82; pres. MLS, Spartanburg, 1980-81. developer indsl. project UDAG Grants, 1982-84, teen ctr. from grants, 1982— (presdl. citation 1985); implementer internat. youth camp S.C. Assn. Lions INternat., 1988—. leadership S.C. U. S.C., 1984-85; leadership Spartanburg C. of C., 1980-81; state chmn. Lions Internat. Youth Exchange, 1994. Recipient Leadership Spartanburg Alumnae of the Yr. award Spartanburg C. of C., 1982, Pres's. award West S.C. Internat. Trade Assn., 1990; Parenting Program award United Way, 1993-94, Flagstar Corp., 1994. Mem. Internat. Realtor Fedn., Soc. Indsl. & Office Realtors, People to People (amb. China), Lions Internat. (state youth exec. chmn., asst. chmn. 1989-94, internat. pres. 1990). Democrat. Roman Catholic. Home: 1340 Pinecrest Rd Spartanburg SC 29302 Office: Carroll Properties Corp 1151 Cedar Crest Rd Spartanburg SC 29301

BELETZ, ELAINE ETHEL, nurse, educator; b. N.Y.C., Jan. 5, 1944; d. Harry and Rose (Friedman) B. RN, Mt. Sinai Hosp., N.Y.C., 1968; BS in Nursing, Fairleigh Dickinson U., 1970; MA, NYU, 1974; MEd, Columbia U., 1978, EdD, 1979. Staff nurse ICU Mt. Sinai Hosp., 1968-70, asst. head nurse, 1970; adminstrv. supervisory relief nurse, 1973-74, 77-78; clin. instr. Roosevelt Hosp. Sch. Nursing, N.Y.C., 1970-73; nurse gerontologist St. Luke's Hosp. Ctr., N.Y.C., 1974; asst. dir. nursing Bklyn. Hosp., N.Y.C., 1975-77; asst. prof. nursing Hunter Coll., CUNY, 1978-81; v.p. nursing Mt. Sinai Hosp., Med. Ctr., Chgo., 1982-83; assoc. prof. nursing Villanova (Pa.) U., 1983—; lectr.; cons. nursing adminstrn., labor relations in health care; mem. task force on block grants. Ill. Dept. Health. Contbr. articles to profl. jours. Bd. dirs. Hadassah Nurses Coun., Phila., 1993-94; pres.-elect, 1994—. Recipient Disting. Achievement award Columbia U. Nursing Edn. Alumni Assn., 1989. Fellow Am. Acad. Nursing; bd. dirs. Phila. chpt. Hadassah Nurses Coun.; mem. Am. Nurses Assn. (bd. dirs. 1982-87, mem. polit. action com. 1982-86), N.Y. State Nurses Assn. (treas. 1977-78, pres.-elect 1978-79, pres. 1979-81, bd. trustees, cert. of appreciation 1981, hon. recognition award 1987), Pa. Nurses Assn. (nominating com. 1985-86, chair polit. action com. 1990-92), N.Y. Counties Registered Nurses Assn. (nominating com. 1973, dir. 1975-78, Amanda Silvers award 1981), Shershower Benevolent Assn., Nursing Edn. Alumni Assn. (Leadership award 1989), Sigma Theta Tau, Phi Kappa Phi. Jewish. Office: Villanova U Grad Program Nursing Health Care Adminstrn Coll Nursing Villanova PA 19085

BELFI, KENDRA LEE JENSEN, physician; b. N.Y.C.; d. Harlan E. and Naomi Louise (Geiger) Jensen; m. Victor Allen Belfi, June 7, 1969; children: Christopher, Peter, Katherine. BA, Rice U., 1968; MD, U. Tex., 1972.

Diplomate Am. Bd. Internal Medicine, Am. Bd. Geriatrics. Intern Dallas VA Hosp., 1972-73; resident U. Tex. Southwestern Health Scis. Ctr., Dallas, 1973-75; physician The Ft. Worth Clinic, 1976—; med. dir. Trinity Ter. Retirement Ctr., Ft. Worth, 1983, Lakewood Village Retirement Ctr., Ft. Worth, 1983—; co-med. dir. James L. West Spl. Care Ctr., Ft. Worth, 1993—; mem. long term task force Tex. Health and Human Svcs. Commn., Austin, 1993-94; mem. adv. com. for nursing facility affairs Tex. Dept. Human Svcs., Austin, 1992—. Fellow ACP; mem. Tex. Med. Dirs. Assn. (pres. 1991-93), Tex. Med. Assn. (mem. long term care com. 1993—), Tex. Soc. Internal Medicine (bd. dirs. 1989-92), Tex. Geriatric Soc. (bd. dirs. 1993—). Office: Ft Worth Clinic 1221 W Lancaster Ave Fort Worth TX 76102-4511

BELFORT, ANNE ELLEN, computer industry manager; b. N.Y.C., Apr. 6, 1954; d. Alan Michael and Anne Dorothy Belfort. Student, Georgetown U., 1972, U. Pa., 1975; BA, Hollins Coll., 1975; MS in Mgmt., Purdue U., 1976. Mgmt. services industry specialist, Info. Services Bus. div. GE, Rockville, Md., 1978-79; assoc. mktg. rep., Data Processing div. IBM Corp., Chgo., 1979-80, mktg. rep., Data Processing div., 1980-81, account mktg. rep., Nat. Accounts div., 1982-85; adv. instr., Southwest Mktg. div. IBM Corp., Irving, Tex., 1985—. Editor corp. news mag. The Bottom Line, 1978. Bd. dirs. Vanderbilt U. Model UN Econ. and Social Council, 1974; rep. Hollins (Va.) Coll. Student Govt., 1972-75; sec. gen. Hollins Coll. Model UN, 1975; mem. Purdue U. Pres.'s Council, 1977—, Purdue U./Krannert Sch. Dean's Adv. Council, 1985—, Purdue U./Krannert Grad. Sch. Alumnae Bd., 1980-82. Named One of Outstanding Young Women of Am., 1979; recipient Leadership award YWCA, Chgo., 1980, Voltaire medal Ecole Champlain, Paris, 1970. Mem. Assn. MBA Execs., AAAS. Republican. Club: Alliance Française.

BELIFORD, CYNTHIA ANN, secondary education educator; b. Omaha, Feb. 11, 1952; d. William Lloyd and Ida Corine (Beliford) Washngton. BS in Edn., U. Nebr., 1974, MA in Counseling Psychology, 1990. Educator Lincoln (Nebr.) Pub. Schs., 1974—; supr. FBG Custodial Svcs., Lincoln, 1988-89; health care worker Max W. Taylor Family, Lincoln, 1990—; com. mem. Lincoln Pub. Schs., 1990—, multicultural adv. com. for supt. equity leadership team, 1989—. Co-author/editor: Flyer - Diversity is Our Strength, 1992, framework for multicultural ednl. program, 1993-94; coord. Arnold Elem. Sch. Culture Fair, 1989-93. Mem. Dem. Party, Lincoln. Named Outstanding Educator Lincoln Jour./Star Newspaper, Lincoln, 1991; recipient Ednl. scholarship Nat. Coun. Negro Women, Lincoln, 1970. Mem. NAACP, Lincoln Edn. Assn., Nebr. State Edn. Assn., NEA. Office: Hartley Sch/Lincoln Pub Sch 730 N 33rd St Lincoln NE 68503-3298

BELISSARY, GAIL BOUKNIGHT, nurse; b. Columbia, S.C., Nov. 22, 1938; d. Junior Rozelle and Ruth (Wise) Bouknight; m. James Charles Belissary, Aug. 11, 1959 (dec.); children: Karen, John, Gary, Christine. Student, Francis Marion Coll., 1971-72; ASN, Florence-Darlington Tech., 1974; BSN, U. S.C., 1984. Staff nurse, head nurse McLeod Regional Med. Ctr., Florence, S.C., 1974-78; staff nurse, charge nurse Florence Dialysis Ctr., 1978-79; charge nurse Darlington (S.C.) Hosp., 1979-80; supr. dept. mental retardation Pee Dee Ctr., Florence, 1980-83; mgr. cen. processing McLeod Regional Med. Ctr., 1983-87; adminstr. Florence Vis. Nurses Svc. Inc., 1987-89; staff nurse Wilson Clinic & Hosp., Darlington, 1989-92; pres., adminstr. Home Health Inc., Florence, 1992-93; staff/charge nurse ICU Wilson Clinic and Hosp., Darlington, S.C., 1993-94; care plan coord. Oakhaven Nursing Home, Darlington, S.C., 1994—; mem. adv. bd. Florence Vis. Nurses Svc., Inc., 1987-89; mem. numerous coms. McLeod Regional Med. Ctr., 1983-84; instr. Pe Dee Health Edn. Ctr., 1989-93; bd. dirs. Home Health, Inc.; cons. Health Care Products, Inc., Florence, 1990; cons. Home Health Nursing, 1992. Vol., mem. MADD, Florence, 1990-91; vol. ACS, AHA, AARC, NSAC, Florence; mem. Friends of Mus., Florence, 1991-92, Handgun Control, Inc., 1994—. Mem. ANA, NAFE, Med. U. S.C. Nursing Alumni Assn., Sigma Theta Tau. Democrat. Greek Orthodox. Office: Oakhaven Nursing Home 123 Oak St Darlington SC 29532

BELISSARY, KAREN, interior designer; b. Columbia, S.C., May 20, 1959; d. James Charles and Linda Gail (Bouknight) B. BFA in Design, N.Y. Sch. Interior Design, 1989; grad., Nat. Ctr. Paralegal Studies, Atlanta, 1991. Pvt. practice interior design, Florence, S.C., 1989—; dir. Pee Dee region Am. Intercultural Exch., Florence, 1989—. Sec. Soc. for Autistic Children, Florence, 1983; v.p. Florence County Dem. Com., 1985; group leader Friends Florence Mus., 1986; bd. dirs. Heart Fund, Florence, 1987, Internat. Women's Club Florence, 1988-89, Florence Area Arts Coun., 1986-87; mem. Friends of Libr., Florence. Named Outstanding Mem., Soc. for Autistic Children, 1983; grantee Young Adult League, 1987. Mem. NOW, Am. Soc. Interior Designers, Amnesty Internat., Greenpeace, Cosmopitan Book Club (pres.), The Door (pres.), Colonial Heights Garden Club. Greek Orthodox. Home: 3719 Gentry Dr Florence SC 29501-7717 Office: Am Intercultural Exch 804 Loop Rd # 2D Florence SC 29501

BELKE, GENEVIEVE ORTAGGIO, accountant, tax preparer; b. Chgo., Oct. 13, 1923; d. Samuel and Rella Irene (Grappy) Ortaggio; m. Arnold Harold Belke, Sept. 29, 1956; children: Denise A., John A. Degree in acctg., Gov.'s State U., 1985. Contr. Boodell, Sears, etal, Chgo., 1957-68, Allied Leasing Co., Inc., Northfield, Ill., 1968-73, R.J. MacDonald Internat., Inc., Elk Grove Village, 1979-80; real estate agt. Arlington Heights, Ill., 1973-80; asst. contr. CBS Mus. Instruments Inc., Deerfield, Ill., 1980-82; pres. No. Ind. Bus. Svcs., Inc., Elkhart, Ind., 1984—. Life mem. Inst. Mgmt. Acctg. (emeritus, chpt. pres. 1979-80, nat. com. 1980-83). Office: No Ind Bus Svcs Inc PO Box 4825 Elkhart IN 46514-0825

BELKIN, JANET EHRENREICH, lawyer; b. N.Y.C., Feb. 17, 1938; d. Irving and Pauline (Hamburger) Ehrenreich; m. Myron D. Belkin, June 29, 1958; children: Lisa Belkin Gelb, Gary, Kira. AB, Vassar Coll., 1958; PhD, St. John's U., 1975; JD, Hofstra U., 1978; LLM, NYU, 1983. Bar: N.Y. 1979, U.S. Dist. Ct. (so. dist.) N.Y. 1979. Vice pres., counsel Equitable Life Assurance Soc., N.Y.C., 1978-91; with Coll. of Ins., N.Y.C., 1991-92; exec. dir. Ctr. Internat. Ins. Studies Coll. of Ins., 1992—; cons. Reg. of Fin. Svcs.; exec. dir. Ctr. Internat. Ins. Studies. Mem. ABA (coun. mem. adminstrv. law sect. 1985-88, chair sect. 1994-95). Home: 3014 Hewlett Ave S Merrick NY 11566-5313 Office: Coll of Ins 101 Murray St New York NY 10007-2132

BELKOV, MEREDITH ANN, landmark administrator; b. Chgo., Sept. 26, 1939; d. Louis and Sylvia (Charak) B. Student, U. Md. Recreation dir. Dept. Pks. and Recreation, Washington, 1960-69; outdoor recreation specialist Nat. Pk. Svc., Washington, 1971-73; chief disvn. recreation Golden Gate Nat. Recreation Area, San Francisco, 1973-75; chief interpretation and visitor svcs. Nat. Visitor Ctr., Washington, 1975-78, Dept. Interior Mgmt., Washington, 1978-79; supt. Chickamauga (Ga.) and Chattanooga (Tenn.) Nat. Mil. Park, 1979-87, Jean Lafitte Nat. Hist. Pk. and Preserve, New Orleans, 1987-90, Statue of Liberty, Ellis Island, N.Y.C., 1990—; bd. dirs. N.Y. Conv. and Visitors Bur., Greater New Orleans Tourist and Conv. Commn., Inc., New Orleans Jazz and Heritage Found. V.p. Chattanooga Symphony and Opera, U. Tenn. Roundtable, Chattanooga Audubon Soc. Fellow NCCJ; recipient Freedom Found. award. Mem. Nat. Pk. and Recreation Assn., Hist. Soc., Mus. Coun. N.Y. Jewish. Office: Statue of Liberty Nat Monument Liberty Island New York NY 10004*

BELL, ANGELA HODGES, accountant, educator; b. Columbus, Miss., June 19, 1959; d. W.E. and Jane Hodges; m. John H. Bell, July 11, 1976; 1 child, Andrew Johnathan. AA, U. Hawaii, 1979; BA, Jacksonville State U., 1981, MBA, 1982; DBA, Miss. State U., 1990. CPA; cert. mgmt. acct.; cert. internal auditor. Prof. acctg. Jacksonville (Ala.) State U., 1982—. Mem. Inst. Mgmt. Accts. (dir. Coosa Valley chpt. 1987-94, Nicholson award 1991). Office: Jacksonville State U Dept Acctg Jacksonville AL 36265

BELL, CORINNE REED, psychologist; b. Holly Springs, Miss., July 6, 1943; d. Robert Norris and Laura Kathleen (Robinson) Reed; m. John B. Jarratt; children: Jeffrey Kenneth, Jennifer Bell Monroe. BA with highest honors, U. Tenn., 1976, MA, 1978, PhD, 1985. Lic. psychologist, Tenn. Rsch. asst. Lakeshore Mental Health Inst., Knoxville, 1976; instr. psychology dept. Roane State C.C., Harriman, Tenn., 1978; cons., sch. psychologist dept. spl. edn. U. Tenn., Knoxville, 1979-80; pvt. practice psychology Knoxville, 1979—; founder, psychologist, ptnr. Clin. & Sch. Assocs., Knoxville, 1985—; cons. social svcs. Dept. Human Svcs., Tenn., 1985—. Contbr. articles to profl. jours. Mem. adv. bd. John Tarleton Children's Home, Knoxville, 1987-93; bd. dirs. Sexual Assault Crisis Ctr., Knoxville, 1987-94; mem., cons. Knox County Child Abuse Rev. Team, Knoxville, 1982—; adv. bd. Florence Crittendon Agy., 1994—; vol. Knox County Mental Health Assn. and Interfaith Health Clinic. Acad. scholar U. Tenn., 1974; rsch. grantee Knox County Children's Found., 1979. Mem. APA, Tenn. Psychol. Assn. (pub. rels. chair 1992-94), Knoxville Area Psychol. Assn. (treas. 1986-88, pub. rels. chair 1989-90, pres. 1990-91), Unified Psychology Coalition (co-founder, legis. chair/spokesperson 1989-92), Tenn. Assn. Sch. Psychologists, Mortar Bd., Phi Kappa Phi, Phi Beta Kappa. Episcopalian. Office: Clin and Sch Assocs 5912 Toole Dr Ste B Knoxville TN 37919-4172

BELL, DELORIS WILEY, physician; b. Solomon, Kans., Sept. 30, 1942; d. Harry A. and Mildren H. (Watt) Wiley; children—Leslie and John. B.A., Kans. Wesleyan U., 1964; M.D., U. Kans., 1968. Diplomate Am. Bd. Ophthalmology. Intern St. Luke's Hosp., Kansas City, Mo., 1968-69; resident U. Kans. Med. Ctr., Kansas City, 1969-72; practice medicine specializing in ophthalmology, Overland Park, Kans., 1973—. Mem. AMA, Kans. Med. Soc. (pres. sect. ophthalmology 1985-86, speaker of the house 94-95), Am. Acad. Ophthalmology (counciller 1988-93, chair state govtl. affairs 93, 94), Kans. Soc. Ophthalmology (pres. 1985-86), Kansas City Soc. Ophthalmology and Otolaryngology (sec. 1984—, pres.-elect 1988, pres. 1989). Avocations: photography; travel. Office: 7000 W 121st St #100 Shawnee Mission KS 66209-2010

BELL, DENISE LOUISE, newspaper editor, photographer; b. Washington, Nov. 27, 1967; d. Richard Keith Bell and Kay Lorraine (Sutherland) Reynolds. Student, Inst. Adventiste du Salare, Collonges, France, 1988; BA in French, Loma Linda U., 1990. Yearbook editor Loma Linda U., La Sierra, Calif., 1989-90; desk technician Loma Linda U., Loma Linda, Calif., 1990-92; staff writer Inland Empire Cmty. Newspapers, Colton, Calif., 1990-91; city editor Inland Empire Cmty. Newspapers, San Bernardino, Calif., 1991-94; asst. circ. supr. Del Webb Meml. Libr. Loma Linda (Calif.) U., 1994—. Asst. leader Girl Scouts U.S., Walla Walla, Wash., 1986; co-leader Girl Scouts Switzerland, Geneva, 1987, Girl Scouts U.S., Loma Linda, 1988-93. Mem. Toastmasters (club pres.). Home: 25421 Cole St Apt U Loma Linda CA 92354-3112

BELL, DOROTHY ANN COMFORT, rehabilitation nurse; b. Harrisburg, Pa., Sept. 11, 1958; d. Nathaniel Lawrence and Edwina Marie (Cox) Comfort; m. Lance Meade Bell, Aug. 19, 1989. Diploma, Richmond Meml Hosp Sch Nursing, Richmond, Va., 1979. Staff nurse Richmond Meml. Hosp., 1979, Johnston-Willis Hosp., Richmond, 1979-81, Sheltering Arms Rehab. Hosp., Richmond, 1981-85; staff nurse Univ. Hosp. Rehab. Ctr., Elizabethtown, Pa., 1985-87, 3-11 relief supr., 1987-88, 3-11 supr., 1989; rehab. counselor, cons. LRC Rehab. Consultants, Inc., Paoli, Pa., 1990-93; pediatric rehab. nurse Milton S. Hershey Med. Ctr., Hershey, Pa., 1993—; rehab. cons. LRC Rehab. Cons., Inc., Paoli, 1990-93. Mem. Hershey Cmty. Chorus, 1990—, publicity chmn. 1992, bd. dirs., 1994—; recorder membership com. 1st United Meth. Ch., Hershey, 1992—. Mem. Assn. Rehab. Nurses (cert. rehab. RN, bd. dirs. Ctrl. Pa. chpt. 1994—), ARC (cert. 1979). Home: 344 Maple Ave Hershey PA 17033-1738 Office: Milton S Hershey Med Ctr PO Box 850 Hershey PA 17033

BELL, FRANCES LOUISE, medical technologist; b. Milton, Pa., Apr. 28, 1926; d. George Earl and Kathryn Robbins (Fairchild) Reichard; m. Edwin Lewis Bell II, Dec. 27, 1950; children: Ernest Michael, Stephen Thomas, Eric Leslie. BS in Biology cum laude, Bucknell U., 1948; MT, Geisinger Meml. Hosp., 1949. Registered med. technologist. Med. technologist Burlington County Hosp., Mt. Holly, N.J., 1949-50, Robert Packer Hosp., Sayre, Pa., 1950, Carle Hosp./Clinic, Urbana, Ill., 1951-52, St. Joseph Hosp., Reading, Pa., 1972-83. Vol. Crime Watch, City Hall, Reading, 1985-90, Am. Heart Assn., Reading, 1956—, March of Dimes, Reading, 1956-72, Am. Cancer Soc., Reading, 1956-71, Multiple Sclerosis, Reading, 1956-72, Reading Musical Found., 1985-90, Hist. Soc. Berks County; corr. sec. women's aux., 1986-90; fin. sec. women's aux. Albright Coll., 1988—; hospitality co-chmn. women's com. Reading Symphony Orch., 1985-90, co-editor yearbook women's com., 1990-92, editor yearbook women's com., 1992—; chmn. hospitality Reading-Berks Pub. Librs., 1988-91; mem. Friends Reading Mus., Berks County Conservancy. Mem. AAUW (assoc. editor bull. 1961-63, cultural interests rep. 1967-68), Woman's Club of Reading (treas. 1986-88, fin. sec. 1991—), United Meth. Women, World Affairs Coun. Berks County, Libr. Soc. Albright Coll., Phi Beta Kappa. Republican. Methodist. Home: 1454 Oak Ln Reading PA 19604-1865

BELL, JEANNE VINER, public relations counselor; b. Los Angeles, Feb. 27, 1923; d. Herman and Mary (Kaufman) Spitzel; m. Melvin A. Viner, Feb. 1, 1942 (dec.); children: Michael, Karen Viner Fawcett; m. 2d, J. Raymond Bell, Dec. 15, 1974 (dec.). Student UCLA, Am. U., George Washington U. Prin. Jeanne Viner Spl. Services, Washington, 1958-61; prin. Jeanne Viner Assocs., Washington, 1961-82; pub. rels. counselor, 1982—; bd. dirs. Independence Fed. Bank, Washington, Independence Fed. Fin. Corp., Washington. Contbr. articles to profl. jours. Presdl. appointee to adv. council SBA, 1983—, Pres.'s Com. on People with Disabilities, 1982—; bd. dirs. Arthritis Found. of Met. D.C., 1982—; mayoral appointee to D.C. Adv. Com. on Resources and Budget, 1981-90, D.C. Pvt. Industries Council, 1983—. Recipient Outstanding Leadership and Achievement award State Bus. and Profl. Women's Clubs, Washington, 1981. Fellow Pub. Rels. Soc. Am.; mem. Capital Press Women (pres. 1980-82, Woman of Achievement 1982, Communicator of Achievement 1983), Am. News Women's Club (bd. govs. 1969-70, pres. 1988-90). Club: Nat. Press (Washington). Address: 3506 Winfield Ln NW Washington DC 20007-2344 also: 9460 Hidden Valley Pl Beverly Hills CA 90210-1310

BELL, JUANITA L., state legislator; b. Youngstown, Ohio, Feb. 26, 1923; m. Silas Joseph; 2 children. Degree, Wilberforce U., U. N.H. sec. Rockingham County Democrats, 1980-86, vice chmn. 1985-88, Portsmouth City Democrats, 1972, Dem. State Com., 1982—. Mem. NEA (N.H. mem. bd. dirs. 1976-88), NAACP, LWV, New England Assn. Black Educators (pres. 1975—), Assn. Portsmouth Tchrs. (bldg. rep., cmty. rels. chmn. 1975-88), New Hope Baptist Ch. Home: 26 Taft Rd Portsmouth NH 03801-5758 NH State Senate: State Capitol Concord NH 03301*

BELL, JUDY KAY, disaster survival planning company executive; b. Burbank, Calif., July 8, 1947; d. Robert Francis and Geraldine (Wutschel) Ball; m. George L. Sellers, Aug. 24, 1969 (div. 1975); 1 child, Thomas R.; m. Kenneth G. Bell, Apr. 16, 1988. BA in English, Calif. State U., Northridge, 1967; MBA in Mgmt., Golden Gate U., 1980. Cert. emergency planner Nat. Coordinating Coun. Emergency Mgmt. Div. mgr. Pacific Bell, various cities, Calif., 1965-88; pres. Disaster Survival Planning, Inc., Port Hueneme, Calif., 1988—; spkr. bus. and govt. seminars. Author: Disaster Survival Planning: A Practical Guide for Businesses, 1991; contbr. articles to profl. jours. Mem. Am. Soc. Profl. Emergency Planners, Bus. and Industry Coun. for Emergency Planning and Preparedness (bd. dirs. 1991-92, treas. 1991-92), So. Calif. Emergency Svc. Assn. Republican. Home and Office: Disaster Survival Planning Inc 669 Pacific Cove Dr Port Hueneme CA 93041-2171

BELL, KAREN GROEZINGER, accountant, consultant; b. Columbus, Ohio, Aug. 29, 1942; d. Walter William and Clara Elizabeth (Bohlander) Groezinger; m. Forest Edward Bell II, May 24, 1969; children: Forest Edward III, Penelope Elizabeth. BA in Journalism, Ohio State U., 1963, MA in Journalism, 1964; MS in Acctg., George Mason U., 1994. CPA, Va.; CMA. From sales assoc. to mgr. store J.C. Penney Co., Inc., various locations, 1957-91; sr. acct. Keller Bruner & Co., P.C., Alexandria, Va., 1994—. Treas. Elder Crafters of Alexandria, 1994, dir., 1987—; v.p., dir. Anne Arundel County Pub. Schs. Mktg. Found., Annapolis, Md., 1988—. Mem. Inst. Mgmt. Accts., Alpha Chi Omega. Home: 6289 Dunaway Ct Mc Lean VA 22101

BELL, LORI JO, psychiatric nurse, HIV/AIDS education specialist; b. Pitts., Dec. 16, 1960; d. John Spencer and Nancy Carol (Schleicher) B. ADN, C.C. Allegheny Co., Pitts., 1987; BS in Psychology, U. Pitts., 1984; postgrad. cmty. counseling, Dusquesne U., 1993—; Duquesne U. Cert. in adult psychiat./mental health nursing, cert. crisis intervention, cert. pre/post HIV counseling. Primary counselor Mon Yough Mental Health/Mental Retardation, McKeesport, Pa., 1984; residential advisor Chartiers Mental Health/Mental Retardation, Bridgeville, Pa.; primary counselor C.C. Allegheny County, Bridgeville, Pa., 1985-87; psychiat. nurse in acute/admissions bldg. Eastern State Hosp., Williamsburg, Va., 1987; postgrad. St. Francis Med. Ctr., Pitts., 1987-91; cmty. AIDS educator; microbiology tutor Duquesne U., 1994. Contbr. articles to profl. jours. Mem. ACA, Pa. Counseling Assn., Chi Sigma Iota. Home: 337 Shadowlawn Ave Mount Lebanon PA 15216

BELL, MARILYNN MARIA, academic supervisor; b. Wellsville, Mo., July 9, 1956; d. Harold Glenn Bell and Lois Imogene (Brunner) B.; m. Marvin John Pennell, Aug. 18, 1978 (div. June 1985); children: Jessica Maria, Jonathan David. BS in Vocat. Edn., U. Mo., 1978, student, 1993—. Cert. secondary tchr., Mo. Tchr. Am. history St. Clair (Mo.) R-13 Schs., 1979-80; comml. loan sec. Tex. Commerce Bank, N.A., Houston, 1980-82; tchr. biology and Am. history Laquey (Mo.) R-5 Schs., 1982-83, tchr. elem., 1983-84; comml. loan sec. Boone County Nat. Bank, Columbia, Mo., 1984-86; home econs. tchr. Jefferson Jr. High, Columbia, 1986-87; owner, dir., tchr. Marilynn's Day Care, Columbia, 1987-92; supr. adult cmty. continuing edn., customized tng. coord, adult basic edn. dir. Mexico (Mo.) Area Vocat.-Tech. Sch., 1992—; owner Needles 'n Thread Alterations, Columbia, 1984-86; adult edn. tchr. Columbia Pub. Schs., 1987-92. Copyright poems The Works of Boady, 1991, More Works of Boady, 1993. Mem. Mo. Assn. Adult Continuing and Cmty. Edn. (treas. 1994-96), Mo. Vocat. Assn., Mo. Tchrs. Assn., Mo. Child Care Providers Assn. (coord. 1989-91, workshop and conf. coord. 1989-91), Mexico Pers. Mgrs. Assn., Kiwanis, Altrussa Club. Office: Mexico Area Vocat Tech Sch 905 N Wade Mexico MO 65265

BELL, MARY E. BENITEAU, accountant; b. San Antonio, Dec. 20, 1937; d. Thomas Alfred and Mary Elizabeth (McMurrain) Beniteau; BBA, Baylor U., 1959; MBA, U. Tex., 1960; m. William Woodward Bell, May 31, 1969; children: Susan Elizabeth, Carol Ann. Teaching asst. U. Tex., Austin, 1959-60; prin. Deloitte & Touche CPAs, Dallas, 1960-69; county auditor Brown County, Tex., 1972-78; pvt. practice acctg., Brownwood, Tex., 1969—; acct. Brownwood Regional Hosp. Women's Aux., 1969—. Mem. bus. and audit com. Bapt. Gen. Conv. Tex., 1985-90, vice chmn., 1987-88, chmn., 1988-89; bd. dirs., sec. Brownwood Civic Improvement Found., Inc., 1991—, pres., 1993-95. Named Outstanding 4-H Leader, Dist. 8, Tex., 1992, Outstanding Woman Over 35, Brownwood Jaycees, 1986, Outstanding Com. Chmn., Dallas chpt. CPA's, 1968-69; CPA, Tex. Mem. Brownwood C. of C. (dir. 1979-82, sec.-treas. 1981-82), Tex. Soc. CPA's (dir. 1979-82, chair rels. with AICPA com. 1988-89, trustee found. 1981-89, sec.-treas. 1982-84, pres. 1984-86, Kenneth W. Hurst fellow 1990, quality rev. com. 1993—, CPA's helping Schs. Com., 1994—), AICPA's, Nat. Soc. Daughters of Am. Revolution (Mary Garland chpt.), Abilene Chpt. CPA's (dir. 1984-85, 87-88, CPA of Yr. 1984-85), Brownwood Com. CPA's (pres. 1987-88), Pi Beta Phi, Baylor U. Alumni Assn. (dir. 1979-82). Baptist. Clubs: Brownwood Woman's (pres. 1980-81), Rotary Ann of Brownwood (pres. 1983-84. Home: PO Box 1564 Brownwood TX 76804-1564 Office: 109 N Fisk Ave Brownwood TX 76801-8207

BELL, M(ARY) KATHLEEN, retired government official, civic leader; b. Washington, July 7, 1922; d. Daniel W. and Sadie (Killeen) B. AB, Smith Coll., 1943, MA (hon.), 1959. With Dept. of State, Washington, 1944-73; fgn. affairs officer Office Internat. Econ. and Social Affairs Bur. Internat. Orgn. Affairs, Washington, 1950-56, officer in charge, 1964-66, chief div. instnl. devel. and coordination, 1966-71, dir. system coordinations staff, 1971-73, cons., 1973-75, retired, 1975; asst. to exec. sec. U.S. del. San Francisco Conf. UN, 1945; mem. staff UNESCO, London, 1945-46; asst. to U.S. rep. to 2nd, 3rd, 4th, 5th sessions Econ. and Social Coun., 1946-47; advisor to U.S. rep. Econ. and Social Council, 1948-70; alt. rep. Econ. and Social Coun., N.Y.C. and Geneva, 1971-73; U.S. mem. on com. on non-govt. orgns. Econ. and Social Coun., 1955-65, U.S. mem. interim com. program meetings, 1950-67, chmn. interim com. program meetings, 1952-54; adviser to U.S. del. prep. commn. Internat. Atomic Energy Agy., Vienna, 1957; advisor to U.S. del. Internat. Atomic Energy Agy., 1957-61; adviser to U.S. del. 1st Assembly Inter-govtl. Maritime Consultative Orgn., London, 1959; advisor U.S. Rep. to Coun., London, 1959; del. ad hoc com. rules procedures 1st Assembly Inter-govtl. Maritime Comsultative Orgn., London, 1960; adviser to U.S. del. 16th Gen. Assembly of UN, N.Y.C., 1961; mem. spl. com. on coordination 16th Gen. Assembly of UN, 1964; advisor to U.S. rep. Tech. Assistance Com., 1964; advisor U.S. del. 9th, 10th and spl. session governing council UN Devel. Program, N.Y.C. and Geneva, 1970; dep. U.S. rep. to governing council UN Devel. Program, Geneva, 1973; alt. U.S. rep. Joint Meeting Adminstrv. Com. Coordination and Spl. Com. Coordination, N.Y.C., 1971-72; alt. U.S. rep. 1st session Rev. and Appraisal Com., N.Y.C. and Geneva, 1972; trustee Washington Theol. Consortium, also v.p. bd., chmn. bd., 1972-79; trustee Smith Coll., 1976-82, chmn. bd., 1979-82; mem. Carnegie Coun. Ethics and Internat. Affairs, 1983-89; bd. dirs. Chs. Ctr. for Theology and Pub. Policy, 1985—, v.p., 1987—; mem. exec. com. Assn. Theol. Schs., 1984-88; bd. dirs. Capitol Area div. UN Assn., 1986-89, UN Assn. Am., 1988-90. Recipient Outstanding Svc. award Dept. of State, 1959; decorated Lady Comdr. with star, Order of Holy Sepulchre. Home: 3816 Gramercy St NW Washington DC 20016-4226 also: 1043 Hillsboro Mile Hillsboro Bch FL 33062-2108

BELL, MAXINE TOOLSON, state legislator, librarian; b. Logan, Utah, Aug. 6, 1931; d. John Max and Norma (Watson) Toolson; m. H. Jack Bell, Oct. 26, 1949; children: Randy J. (dec.), Jeff M., Scott Alan (dec.). Assocs. in Libr. Sci., Coll. So. Idaho; CSI, Idaho State U., 1975. Librarian Sch. Dist. 261, Jerome, Idaho, 1975-88; mem. Idaho Ho. of Reps., 1988-. Bd. dirs. Idaho Farm Bur., 1976-77; rep. western states Am. Farm Bur. Women, 1990-93, vice chmn., 1993—; vice chmn. Am. Farm Bur., 1992—; mem. Jerome County Rep. PRecinct Com., 1980-88. Home: 194 S 300 E Jerome ID 83338-6532

BELL, MILDRED BAILEY, lawyer, educator; b. Sanford, Fla., June 28, 1928; d. William F. and Frances E. (Williford) Bailey; m. J. Thomas Bell, Jr., Sept. 18, 1948 (div.); children: Tom, Elizabeth, Ansley. AB, U. Ga., 1950, JD cum laude, 1969; LLM in Taxation, N.Y. U., 1977. Bar: Ga. 1969. Law clk. U.S. Dist. Ct. No. Dist. Ga., 1969-70; prof. law Mercer U., Macon, Ga., 1970-94, prof. emeritus, 1994—; mem. Ga. Com. Constl. Revision, 1978-79; bd. dirs. Arrowhead Travel, Inc. Bd. editors Ga. State Bar Jour., 1974-76; contbr. articles to profl. jours., chpts. in books. Mem. ABA, Ga. Bar Assn., Phi Beta Kappa, Phi Kappa Phi. Republican. Episcopalian. Home: 516 High Point North Rd Macon GA 31210-4802 Office: Mercer U Sch Law Georgia Ave Macon GA 31207

BELL, PATRICIA SLAY, accountant; b. Memphis, Apr. 12, 1942. BS in Bus. Adminstrn. magna cum laude, U. Tenn., 1986. CMA. Acctg. mgr. Provident Life & Accident Ins. Co., Chattanooga, Tenn., 1986-89, mgr. individual svcs., 1989-92, dir. adminstrv. svcs., 1992-93, dir. fin. adminstrn., 1993-94. Co-dir. Heart Assn., Chattanooga, 1990—. Mem. Inst. Mgmt. Accts. (bd. dirs. 1976—), Life Office Mgmt. Assn. Office: Provident Life & Accident Ins Co 1 Fountain Sq Chattanooga TN 37402

BELL, PEGGY DEANE HALL, credit bureau executive; b. Hartsville, Tenn., Apr. 27, 1919; d. M. Burnly and Prudie (Stubblefield) Hall; m. Charlie Berkeley Bell, June 23, 1943 (dec. May 1962); children: C. Berkeley Jr., William Hall, Hayden Darragh, Prudence. LLB, Cumberland U., 1941. Bar: Tenn. 1946. Owner Credit Bureau Greenville, Tenn., 1948—. Mem. Greenville Bar Assn., Assn. Credit Bureau. Democrat. Episcopalian. Avocations: sewing, dancing, grandmothering. Office: Credit Bureau Greenville 214 Susong Ln Greenville TN 37743

BELL, REGINA JEAN, communications company executive; b. Lebanon, Mo.; d. Stephen S. and Ida M. (Reaves) B. B.A., Draughens U., 1948; postgrad., Butler U., 1958, Ind.-Purdue U., Indpls., 1968. Prodn. mgr. Howe Mfg. Co., Inc., Indpls., 1958-64; v.p. budgetary control Howe Engring. Co., Inc., Indpls., 1964-67; mgr. material control Nat. Aluminum Div., Indpls., 1968-84; formerly owner Brown County Letter Shop, Nashville, Ind.; now ops. supr. Sprint Svcs. United Telecom, Indpls. Mem. Indpls. Real Estate Assn.

BELL, ROBERTA ALYSOUN, neuropsychologist; b. Monticello, Ark., Aug. 17, 1957; d. William Robert and Shirley Jean (McElroy) B. BA, Hendrix Coll., 1977; MA, U. Ark., 1981, PhD, 1985. Lic. psychologist, La.

Psychology intern La. State U. Med. Sch., New Orleans, 1982; clin./rsch. assoc. La. State Med. Sch., New Orleans, 1984-85, instr. neurology, 1985-87, clin. asst. prof., 1992—; psychometrist N.W. Ark. Psychol. Group, Fayetteville, Ark., 1983-84; neuropsychologist F. Edward Hebert Hosp., New Orleans, 1987-88, Sun Creek Ranch, Folsom, L.A., 1988; program coord. Healthsouth Rehab. Ctr., Harahan, La., 1987-91, dir. neuropsychology, 1988-91; pres., neuropsychologist Neuropsychology Assoc., Inc., Metairie, La., 1991—; cons. La. Rehab. Inst., New Orleans, 1991-93; mem. med. staff Med. Ctr. La., New Orleans, 1991-93, Touro Infirmary, New Orleans, 1992-93; mem. tech. assistance com. La. Head Injury Task Force, 1990-93. Copy editor jour. Rehab. in Rev., 1993; editor newsletter La. Head Injury Found.: Looking Ahead, 1993. Mem. APA, Internat. Neuropsychol. Soc., La. Psychol. Assn., New Orleans Neuropsychol. Soc. (charter), New Orleans Young Leadership Coun. Democrat. Office: Neuropsychology Assocs Inc Ste 700 3929 Veterans Memorial Blvd Metairie LA 70002-5616

BELL, SAMANTHA SMITH, entrepreneur; b. Conway, Ark., Aug. 8, 1950; d. Lionel and Lois Smith; m. James T. Bell, Sept. 30, 1977; children: Lynn, Eric, Erin, Matt, Maegan. BBA, U. Ctrl. Ark., 1972. Office mgr. Shaw Realty & Ins. Co., 1972-74; exec. sec. Dept. Fin., 1974; in real estate mgmt., 1975, personal real estate mgmt., 1977-83; loan portfolio analyst numerous savs. and loan instns., 1983-91; founder, owner, pres. Positive Action Learning Systems, Inc., 1992—; acct. Cajun Wharf, 1976-77; seminar presenter and speaker in field. Patentee for potty tng. children with disappearing images; author publs.; composer, writer poetry, children's stories and songs; various radio interviews. Pres. and v.p. Atlanta Found., 1980-83; active Cancer Crusade, Easter Seals, March of Dimes, others, 1983; bd. dirs. Florence Crittenden Home, 1982-84; active in various orgns. of the banking industry and orgns. for housing fgn. students and bus. people, 1983-93; citizen amb. People's Rep. China, 1994. Named to Outstanding Young Women of Am., 1983; recipient Outstanding Exec. award, 1984. Home: 80 Robinwood Dr Little Rock AR 72207

BELL, SHARON KAYE, small business owner; b. Lincoln, Nebr., Sept. 14, 1943; d. Edwin B. and Evelyn F. (Young) Czachurski; m. James P. Kittrell (div. Sept. 1974); children: Nathan James, Nona Kaye; m. Joseph S. Bell, June 5, 1976; stepchildren: Eugene, Patricia, Bobbie, Linda. Continuing edn./active tax preparer/interviewer assoc., H&R Block, Laguna Hills, 1987—. Various positions mgmt., bookkeeping, 1961-71; bookkeeper Internat. Harvester, Chesapeake, Va., 1971-73, Cheat'AH Engring., Santa Ana, Calif., 1973-74, Fre Del Engring., Santa Ana, Calif., 1974-75; bookkeeper/mgr. Tek Sheet Metal Co., Santa Ana, Calif., 1975-79; owner, bookkeeper Bell's Bookkeeping, Huntington Beach, Calif., 1979-86, Fountain Valley, Calif., 1986—, Laguna Hills, Calif., 1986—; tax preparer H.R. Block, 1989—. Mem. Inst. Mgmt. Accts. (bd. dirs. 1985-86, sec. 1986-87, v.p. 1987-90, dir. manuscripts 1990-91), Nat. Notary Assn., NAFE, Wives of Submarine Vets. World War II (v.p. L.A. chpt. 1986-87, treas. 1990-92), Nat. Soc. Pub. Accts., Internat. Platform Assn. Republican. Office: Bells Bookkeeping PO Box 2713 Laguna Hills CA 92654-2713

BELL, SUSAN JANE, nurse; b. Columbus, Ohio, July 24, 1946; d. Donald Richard Bell and Martha Jane (McDowell) Nichols; m. Robert Earlin Ward, Oct. 24, 1964 (div. 1984); children: Duane Allen Ward, Melissa Jane Ward, Bryan Thomas Ward. Degree in nursing, Columbus Sch. Practical Nursing, 1986; ADRN, Columbus State C.C., 1989; student, Franklin U., 1993—. RN, Ohio; cert. CPR; notary pub., Ohio. Nurse's asst. Riverside Meth. Hosp., Columbus, 1970-80, Norworth Convalescent Ctr., Columbus, 1980-86; lic. practical nurse, charge nurse Heartland Thurber Care Ctr., Columbus, 1986-89; staff nurse Am. Nursing Care, Columbus, 1989—; medicare home visitation, staffing and pvt. duty nurse Telemed, Columbus, 1989—; asst. head nurse Northland Terr., Columbus, 1989; supr. Elmington Manor, Columbus, 1989; staff nurse cardiac step down unit Grant Hosp., Columbus, 1989-92; nurse med. ICU, CCU and pediatric ICU, 1992-93; charge nurse critical/skilled unit First Community Village Health Care Ctr., Columbus, 1992-93; pres. Bell Mktg. Distbrs., pvt. duty ALS ventilator patients Med. Pers. Poole; regional claims rep. Fed. Resources Group. Notary pub.; Rev. Am. Fellowship Ch. Mem. NAFE, Libr. of Congress, Internat. Clergy Assn., Nat. Audubon Soc., Waken Ctr. Assocs.

BELL/JACKSON, MARIANNE JEANNE, elementary education educator; b. Chgo., Feb. 13, 1944; d. David Vincent and Jeanne Elizabeth Bell; m. Michael Ross Jackson, Aug. 12, 1989; m. Roscoe Edward Mitchell; 1 child, Atala-Nicole; m. Jerry Alan Levy. B Art History, U. Chgo., 1967; M Elem. Edn., U. Wis., Platteville, 1985. Lic. tchr. 1st - 8th grades. Sec. The Filter People, Chgo., 1960-66; office mgr. U. Chgo. Maroon, 1966-68; asst. program dir. Emerson & Taylor House Community Ctrs., Chgo., 1968-71; child advocate Lawndale Day Care Ctr., Chgo., 1971-73; potter, owner Burnt Earth Pottery, Hollandale, Wis., 1973-85; tchr. Madison (Wis.) Met. Sch. Dist., 1985—; cons. Ednl. Devel. Ctr., Newton, Mass., 1991-92; Search for Extra Terrestrial Intelligence pilot program tchr., 1993-94; resource agt. Am. Astronomy Soc., 1994—. Author: Model for a 4th Grade Curriculum, 1990, (with Larry Johns) Proposal for Construction of an Effigy Mound, 1990, (with Atala-Nicole Mitchell) The Great Green Dog, 1995, Coloran-Draw Number 1; contbt. to Poetry Out of Wisconsin, 1982; inventor ColoranDraw Books, 1995. Recipient 1st pl. for pottery, 1st pl. for hand painted ceramics Cambridge (Wis.) Art Fair, 1979; named to Golden Apple Club Madison Met. Sch. Dist., 1993. Mem. Madison Tchrs., Inc., Wis. Earth Sci. Tchrs., Greenpeace, Amnesty Internat., Alliance for Animals, People for Ethical Treatment of Animals. Lutheran Buddhist. Home: 6251 Portage Rd De Forest WI 53532-2900 Office: Madison Met Sch Dist Lake View Elem 1802 Tennyson Ln Madison WI 53704-2323

BELLAMY, CAROL, federal agency administrator; b. Plainfield, N.J., 1942. BA with honors, Gettysburg Coll., 1963; JD, NYU. Asst. commr. Dept. Mental Health and Mental Health Retardation Svc., N.Y.C.; with Peace Corps., Guatemala, Ctrl. Am.; assoc. Cravath, Swaine & Moore, N.Y.C.; mem. N.Y. State Senate; managing dir. Morgan Stanley & Co., N.Y.C.; dir. Peace Corps., Washington, 1993—. Office: Peace Corps 1990 K St NW Rm 8114 Washington DC 20526-0002*

BELLANTONI, MAUREEN BLANCHFIELD, manufacturing executive; b. Warren, Pa., Mar. 18, 1949; d. John Joseph and Patricia Anne (Southard) Blanchfield; m. Michael Charles Bellantoni, Aug. 12, 1972; children: Mark Christopher, Melissa Catherine. BS in Fin., U. Bridgeport, 1976; MBA, U. Conn., Stamford, 1979. Fin. analyst Dictaphone Corp., Rye, N.Y., 1970-73, Gen. Telephone & Electronics, Stamford, 1973-74, Smith Kline Ultrasonic Products, now Branson, Danbury, Conn., 1974-77; fin. mgr. Gen. Foods, White Plains, N.Y., 1977-80; contr. Branson Ultrasonics Corp. div. Emerson Electric, Danbury, Conn., 1980-88; v.p. fin. Branson Ultrasonics Corp. div. Emerson Electric, Danbury, 1988-90; v.p. fin., CFO Automatic Switch Co. divsn. Emerson Electric, Florham Park, N.J., 1990-93, PYA/Monarch, Inc. divsn. Sara Lee Corp., Greenville, S.C., 1993-94; v.p. fin. CFO Meat Group Sara Lee Corp., Cordova, Tenn., 1994—. Mem. bd. The Franciscan Sisters of Poor Found. at S.C. Mem. Fin. Execs. Inst., S.C. C. of C., Danbury C. of C. (leadership program 1989), Beta Gamma Sigma. Office: 3407 Lake Pointe Cove Memphis TN 38125

BELLER, JOAN ROTHSCHILD, marketing consultant; b. Balt., May 9, 1932; d. Morton Kahn and Bertha Berney (Sondheim) Rothschild; m. Robert Winter Beller, July 10, 1955; children: Susan Beller Hughes, Harry Robert. BA, Wellesley Coll., 1954; MA in Teaching, Manhattanville Coll., 1974; MA, Columbia, 1986. Biochemist Huntington Meml. Lab., Mass. Gen. Hosp., Boston, 1954-55, SUNY Downstate Med. Ctr., Bklyn., 1955-57, Einstein Coll. of Medicine, Bronx, N.Y., 1957; computer programmer Princeton (N.J.) U., 1964-66; elem. sch. tchr. Greenburgh Ctrl. Sch. Dist., Hartsdale, N.Y., 1972-75, resource rm. tchr., 1975-89; ptnr. Mktg. Answers Cons., Ardsley, N.Y., 1989—. Vol. Westchester Children's Assn., White Plains, N.Y., 1968-70. Mem. Soc. Competitive Intelligence Profls., Westchester Bus. Network, Coun. Am. Survey Rsch. Orgns., Nat. Coun. Tchrs. Math., Internat. Reading Assn., Internat. Soc. Tech. in Edn., Wellesley in Westchester, Kappa Delta Pi. Office: Mktg Answers Cons Inc 73 Bramblebrook Rd Ardsley NY 10502-2233

BELLER, LUANNE EVELYN, accountant; b. Ft. Dodge, Iowa, Feb. 5, 1950; d. Gerald L. and Evelyn E. (Liston) Heyl; m. Stephen M. Beller, June 28, 1970; children: Clancy D., Corby L. BA, Oreg. State U., 1977; MBA, Rochester Inst. Tech., 1981. CPA, Ill. Plant acct. DuBois Plastic Products, Avon, N.Y., 1977-79; coll. acct. SUNY, Geneseo, 1979-81; gen. acctg. supr. M&M/Mars, Inc., Cleveland, Tenn., 1981-83, Hackettstown, N.J., 1983-84; sales rep. M&M/Mars, Inc., Jacksonville, Ill., 1984-86, terr. sales supr., 1986-88; gen. acctg. coord. Kal Kan Foods, Inc., Columbus, Ohio, 1988-90, fin. info. coord., 1990-92, gen. acctg. specialist, 1992—. Vol. Girl Scouts Am., Jacksonville, 1985-88, Bexley, Ohio, 1988-94; mem. edn. com., mem. sound control com. Bexley United Meth. Ch., 1989—. Mem. Phi Kappa Phi, Beta Gamma Sigma, Beta Alpha Psi. Democrat.

BELLES, ANITA LOUISE, health care researcher; b. San Angelo, Tex., Aug. 30, 1948; d. Curtis Lee and Margaret Louise (Perry) B.; m. John Arvel Willey, July 13, 1969 (div. Aug. 1978); children: Suzan Heather, Kenneth Alan. BA, U. Tex., 1972; MS in Health Care Adminstrn., Trinity U., 1984. Registered EMT; cert. CPR instr., emergency med. technician tchr., La. Regional emergency med. service tng. coordinator Bur. Emergency Med. Service, Lake Charles, La., 1978-79; exec. dir. Southwest La. Emergency Med. Service Council, Lake Charles, 1979-83; project coordinator Tulane U. Med. Sch., New Orleans, 1982-83; dir. La. Bur. of Emergency Med. Service, Baton Rouge, 1982; pres. Computype, Inc., San Antonio, 1983-86, Emergency Med. and Safety Assocs., La. and Tex., 1982—; dir. family planning Bexar County Hosp. Dist., Tex., 1987; mgmt. engr. Inpatient Support Applications, 1987-88; instr. grad. sch. health care adminstrn. S.W. Tex. State U. Editor A.L.E.R.T., 1980-83, San Antonio Executive News, 1987—, Family Living, 1987-88; feature writer Bright Scrawl, 1985-86; contbr. numerous articles on emergency med. services to profl. jours. Bd. dirs. Thousand Oaks Homeowner's Assn., sec., treas., 1985; active Trinity U. Health Care Alumni Assn., Jr. League San Antonio, The Parenting Ctr., Baton Rouge, 1982-83, Jr. League Lake Charles, 1982, Campfire Council Pub. Relations Com., Lake Charles, 1982; newsletter editor Community Food Co-Op, Newsletter Editor, 1979; vol. Lake Charles Mental Health Ctr., 1974. Recipient Outstanding Service award La. Assn Registered Emergency Med. Technicians, 1983, Southwest La. Assn. Emergency Med. Technicians, 1983; named Community Leader KPLC TV, Lake Charles, 1981, regional winner Assn U. Programs in Health Adminstrn., HHS Sec's. Competitions for Innovations in Health, 1982. Mem. Nat. Assn. Emergency Med. Technicians., Tex. Assn. Emergency Med. Technicians, Am. Coll. Health Care Execs., Am. Assn. Automotive Medicine, Southwest La. Assn. Emergency Med. Technicians (founding mem., v.p. 1979-80, CPR com. chmn. 1980-81, pub. relations com. chmn. 1981-82, bd. dirs. 1980-82), Am. Mgmt. Assn., Nat. Soc. Emergency Med. Service Adminstrs., Nat. Coalition Emergency Med. Services, Am. Composition Assn. Methodist.

BELLES, CHRISTINE FUGIEL, office administration educator; b. Hamtramck, Mich., Sept. 6, 1945; d. Ted and Theresa (Ellman) Fugiel; m. Duane Allen Belles, Aug. 10, 1973; children: Douglas, Michael. BA, Mich. State U., 1967, MA, 1970. Clk. Warren Schs. Credit Union, Centerline, Mich., 1963; sec. to dean of students Mich. State U., East Lansing, 1964-67, Consumers Power Co., East Detroit, 1964-65; key punch oper. Fisher Body div. GMC, Warren, Mich., 1966, sec., 1967, 69; legal sec. Rollins, Genser and White, Detroit, 1974; tchr. Lakeview High Sch., St. Clair Shores, Mich., 1967-73; prof. office adminstrn. Macomb Community Coll., Warren, 1973—, cert. profl. sec., 1974—; exam. proctor Profl. Secs. Internat., 1983-89. Recipient Excellence in Teaching award, 1993. Mem. Nat. Assn. Desktop Pubs., Nat. Bus. Edn. Assn., Delta Pi Epsilon, Pi Omega Pi. Office: Macomb Community Coll 14500 E 12 Mile Rd Warren MI 48093-3896

BELLEVILLE, JANET RONICE, investment executive, association executive; b. Youngstown, Ohio, Aug. 16, 1943; d. Russell Joseph and Sarah Alice (Trickett) Cox; m. Elmer L. Belleville, Jan. 30, 1965; children: Kelley S. Belleville Clark, Mark Lloyd, Douglas Eric. Student, Youngstown State U., 1963-65. Cert. fin. planner. Svc. rep. Ohio Bell, Youngstown, 1962-66, from svc. rep. to mgr., 1974-83; sales mgr. AT&T, Youngstown, 1983-85; stockbroker, v.p. Butler Wick & Co. Inc., Youngstown, 1986—. Divsn. leader United Way, Youngstown, 1989-91; mem. nominating com. Girl Scouts U.S.A., Youngstown, 1993—; participant Leadership Youngstown, 1993; bd. dirs., treas. YWCA, Youngstown, 1989-93, pres. bd. dirs., 1993—. Mem. NAFE, Inst. CFPs (N.E. Ohio chpt.). Office: Butler Wick & Co Inc 700 City Centre One Youngstown OH 44503

BELLM, JOAN, civic worker; b. Alton, Ill., June 20, 1934; d. Harvey Jacob and Alma Lorene (Roberts) Goldsby; m. Earl David Bellm, Oct. 1, 1955; children: David, Lori, Michael. Editor Best of IDEA newsletter, 1991—. Organist, dir. jr. choir St. Mary's Cath. Ch., 1958-78; mem. adv. bd. Carlinville (Ill.) Area Hosp., 1981-86; trustee Blackburn Coll., Carlinville, 1983-86; bd. dirs. Cath. Children's Home, Diocese of Springfield, Ill., 1986—; founder, bd. dirs., state networker Ill. Drug Edn. Alliance, 1982-86, pres., 1987-89; bd. dirs., nat. networker Nat. Fedn. Parents for Drug-Free Youth, Washington, 1984-86; mem. Ill. Gov.'s Adv. Coun. on Alcoholism and Substance Abuse, 1989-93; founder Drug Watch Internat., 1991, Internat. Drug Strategy Inst., 1993, invited participant Internat. Private Sector Conf. on Drugs, Seville, 1993, advisor U.N. Internat. Drug Ctrl. Program, 1994 ; numerous others. Recipient letter of endorsement Pres. of U.S., 1981, citation of recognition Ill. Dept., Am. Legion, 1981, Meritorious Svc. award, 1982, award Ill. Drug Edn. Alliance award, 1984, Southwestern Ill. Law Enforcement Commn., 1984, Carlinville Sch. Bd., 1985, Outstanding Svc. award Nat. Fedn. Parents, 1986, award Ill. Alcohol and Drug Dependence Assn., 1986, Optimist Internat., 1987, Ill. Drug Edn. Alliance, 1988, Outstanding Citizen award Blackburn U., 1989, Citizen of Yr. award, Carlinville, 1990. Home: PO Box 227 Carlinville IL 62626-1544

BELLO, SHERE CAPPARELLA, personal care industry consultant; b. Norristown, Pa., Sept. 4, 1956; d. Anthony Carmen and Patsy Ann (Robbins) Capparella. BA in Langs., Rosemont (Pa.) Coll., 1978; postgrad. in mktg., Ursinus Coll., 1986-91; student, Institut Internat. D'Enseignement de la Langue Française, France, 1992, Escuela de Idiomas, Spain, 1992; MEd in Multicultural Edn., Eastern Coll., 1993. Cert. in French/Spanish. Salesperson Spectrum Communications Corp., Norristown, 1977-79, sales and mktg. mgr., 1986-87; asst. sales and adminstrv. asst. Tettex Instruments, Inc., Fairview Village, Pa., 1979-83; owner, instr. Shere's World of Dance and Fine Arts, Jeffersonville, Pa., 1982-88; multilingual exec. sec. Syntex Dental Products, Inc., Valley Forge, 1984-86; v.p. Captrium Devel. Corp., Exton, Pa., 1987-89; sales cons. Mary Kay Cosmetics, 1988—; sales mgr. Spectrum Communications, 1989-92; tchr. fgn. langs. Middletown (Pa.) Area Sch. Dist., 1992-94; free-lance model, 1977—; v.p. La Bella Modeling Agy., Collegeville, Pa., 1979-82; choreographer and dance instr. La Bella Sch. Performance, Collegeville, 1979-82. Judge state and nat. pageants Miss Am. Scholarship, Jr. Miss. Nat. Teen and Pre-Teen, All-Am. Talent, Ofcl. Little Miss Am., Little Miss Diamond, Talent Olympics, Talent Unltd., 1979—; producer, choreographer Miss Montgomery County Pageant, Plymouth Meeting, Pa., 1985; co-producer, choreographer Miss Del. Valley Pageant, Horsham, Pa., 1983-84; confraternity Christian Doctrine kindergarten tchr. Visitation Parish, 1987-88. Recipient award Internat. Leaders in Achievement, 1989, Community Leaders of Am., 1989. Mem. NAFE, NEA, Am. Coun. Tchrs. Fgn. Langs., Am. Assn. Tchrs. French, Pa. State MLA, Pa. State Edn. Assn., Christian Children's Fund, Am. Assn. Tchrs. Spanish, Kappa Delta Pi, Phi Kappa Delta. Roman Catholic. Home: 4700 Cumberland St Harrisburg PA 17111

BELLOCK, PATRICIA RIGNEY, county government official; b. Chgo., Oct. 14, 1946; d. John Dungan and Dorothy (Comiskey) Rigney; m. Charles Joseph Bellock, Nov. 8, 1969; children: Colleen, Dorothy. BA, St. Norbert Coll., 1968. With customer rels. 3M Corp., Chgo., 1968-69; tchr. jr. h.s. Milw. and Fairbanks, Alaska, 1970-72; v.p. sports corps. Dor-Mor-Pat Corp., River Forest, Ill., 1976-84; mem. DuPage County (Ill.) Bd. from Dist. #3, 1992—; sec. Hinsdale Investment Group, 1990-91. Precinct committeeman Downers Grove Rep. Twp. Orgn., Ill., 1981-87; mem. sch. bd. St. Isaac Jogues Sch., Hinsdale, Ill., 1989-91; bd. dirs. Hinsdale Cmty. House, 1987-89, U. Ill. Gerontology Rsch., 1988-91, Hinsdale Youth Ctr., 1987-90, DuPage County Bd. of Health, Wheaton, 1990—, Care and Counseling Ctr., Downers Grove, 1977—, pres., 1986-89. Recipient Health Dept. award State of Ill., 1992. Roman Catholic. Home: 138 E 6th St Hinsdale IL 60521 Office: Office County Board DuPage County Ctr 421 N County Farm Rd Wheaton IL 60187

BELLO-REUSS, ELSA NOEMI, physician, educator; b. Buenos Aires, Argentina, May 1, 1939; came to U.S., 1972; naturalized, 1989; d. Jose F. and Julia M. (Hiriart) Bello; B.S., U. Chile, 1957, M.D., 1964; m. Luis Reuss, Apr. 15, 1965; children: Luis F., Alejandro E. Intern J.J. Aguirre Hosp., Chile, 1963-64; intern, then resident in internal medicine U. Chile, Santiago, 1964-66; pvt. practice medicine specializing in nephrology Santiago, 1967-72; prof. pathophysiology Sch. Nutrition U. Chile, 1970-72; Internat. NIH fellow U. N.C., Chapel Hill, 1972-74; vis. asst. prof. physiology U. N.C., Chapel Hill, 1974-75; Louis Welt fellow U. N.C.-Duke U. Med. Ctr., 1975-76; mem. faculty Jewish Hosp. St. Louis, 1976-83, asst. prof. medicine, physiology and biophysics Washington U. Sch. Medicine, St. Louis, 1976-86, assoc. prof. physiology dept. cell biology and physiology, 1986; assoc. prof. medicine U. Tex. Med. Br., Galveston, 1986-94, prof. dept. internal medicine and dept. phys. and biophys. medicine, 1994—; mem. reviewers res. study sect. NIH, 1991—; chair Women's Coun. Internat. Medicine U. Tex. Med. Bd. chpt., 1993—. Author: (with others) The Kidney and Body Fluids in Health and Disease, 1983; contbr. articles on nephrology and epithelial electrophysiology to med. and physiology jours. Mem. Internat., Am. Socs. Nephrology, Royal Soc. Medicine, Nat. Kidney Found. of S.E. Tex. (med. adv. bd., chairperson med. adv. bd., bd. dirs.), Coun. of Women in Nephrology, Tex. Med. Assn., Am. Fedn. Clin. Rsch., Am. Soc. Renal Biochemistry and Metabolism, Internat. Soc. Renal Nutrition and Metabolism, Am. Physiology Soc., Am. Heart Assn., Kidney Coun., Soc. Gen. Physiologists, Math. Assn. Am., Gt. Houston and Gulf Coast Nephrology Assn., NIH Gen. Medicine B Study Sect. (mem. 1987-91), Reserve reviewer 1991—, VA grant reviewer, Sigma Xi. Office: U Tex Med Br Dept Medicine Nephrology OJS 4 200 Galveston TX 77555-0562

BELLOS, SOFIA, librarian; b. Lynwood, Calif., Sept. 2, 1964; d. Paul and Elba Iris B.; m. G. Borneman, July 5, 1986 (div. May, 1991). BA in Liberal Studies, Azusa (Calif.) Pacific U., 1985, Ryan multiple subject credential, 1985; MLS, UCLA, 1989. Substitute tchr. Thousand Oak (Calif.) Sch. Dist., 1986-87; libr. asst. Ventura (Calif.) County Libr. System, 1986-87; libr. intern Thousand Oaks Libr., 1988; student libr. L.A. Pub. Libr., 1989; adult reference libr. Oxnard (Calif.) Pub. Libr., 1989—; mem. Calif. state libr. coun., 1991-92. Contbr. (newspaper column) Oxnard Press Courier, 1989-93; Funk & Wagnall's New Encyclopedia, 1993. Recipient Minority scholarship Calif. State Libr., 1987-89. Mem. Refomra (vice chair Santa Barbara chpt. 1990-91, chair 1991-92), Calif. Libr. Assn. (awards and scholarship com. 1993—). Republican. Office: Oxnard Pub Libr 251 S A St Oxnard CA 93030-5750

BELMONTÉ, KATHRYN (KIKI BELMONTÉ), adult special education educator; b. Tallahassee. BA, Fla. A&M U.; m. Joseph Belmonté; children: Angela, Cynthia; MEd, Fla. Atlantic U. Tchr., Palm Beach County Schs., West Palm Beach, Fla., workshop mgr. adult spl. edn., 1985—, arts amb., adult edn., health coord., 1985-86, chair self-study, exceptional student edn., 1986-87; owner KiKi's Creative Assembly for Native Am. Arts & Crafts; developer Helping Hands Classroom Sheltered Workshop for Mentally Handicapped Adults, 1988—. Author: Black, Brown and Amber, 1979, Comes a Riderless Horse, 1983, reading home tutoring system Tutor Your Child, 1983; compiler, editor Where to Find Thrift Treasures, 1988, Where to Buy Antiques in Palm Beach County, 1989. Dir. Kambi Youth Theatre, West Palm Beach, 1979-82, Creative Arts Workshop, Cities in Schs., 1985; organizer, dir. SRO Players Dramatics Club for Handicapped Adults; tech. dir. Performing Arts Summer Sch., Palm Beach Gardens, Fla., 1983-84, 85; workshop originator lecturer Seminole Indian History 1992, Mobile Art Craft Show 1993; active Palm Beach County Cultural Coun., Lake Worth Art League, Palm Beach County Art in Pub. Places Com., 1991-92, Nat. Mus. Am. Indian. Recipient 1st place award Cleveland Creative Arts, Tenn., 1981, Walter Bogle award Creative Arts Guild, 1983; grantee Palm Beach County Edn. Found., 1987, Community Found. Palm Beach and Martin Counties. Mem. NEA, South Fla. Poetry Assn., Nat. Writers Club (hon. mention 1983), Fla. Freelance Writers Assn. (1st pl. awards 1984, 85, 3rd pl. 1990, honorable mention 1991), Classroom Tchrs. Assn., N. Palm Beach C. of C., Poets of Palm Beaches, South Fla. Poetry Inst., Norton Gallery Art, Armory Sch. Arts, Fla. Humanities Coun., St. Labre Indian Sch., Arrow Club. Avocations: drawing, painting, collecting Native Am. art, photography. Home: 312 Baker Dr West Palm Beach FL 33409-3806

BELOBRAIDICH, SHARON LYNN GOUL, elementary education educator; b. Detroit, Oct. 21, 1940; d. William A. and Lillian Mae (Atkinson) Goul; m. Frank Glen Belobraidich, Mar. 24, 1962 (dec. May 1987); children: Caryn Lyn, Ellyn Elizabeth. BA, Mich. State U., 1962; MA, Ea. Mich. U., 1968. Tchr. Waverly Schs., Lansing, Mich., 1962-63, Plymouth (Mich.) - Canton Schs., 1963—; bldg. rep. Plymouth Canton Edn. Assn., 1963-94, sec., 1974-90, v.p., 1990—; del. to rep. assembly NEA, Mich. Edn. Assn., 1990—. Experienced Tchr. fellow U.S. Govt., 1967-68. Mem. AAUW, Mich. Diabetes Assn. (bd. dirs. 1971-87), Alpha Delta Kappa (sec. 1968-70, pres. 1972-74, 76-78). Home: 12498 Pine Crest Dr Plymouth MI 48170

BELOVANOFF, OLGA, retired health care facility administrator; b. Buchanan, Sask., Can., July 1, 1932; d. Frederick Alexander and Dora (Konkin) B. Grad. high sch., Kamsack, Sask., Can. From clk. to adminstrv. officer Sask. Health Dept. Cancer Clinic, Saskatoon, 1951-78; bus. mgr. Sask. Cancer Found. Saskatoon Clinic, 1979-90. Dir. Sask. Br. Can. Tenpin Fedn., Inc. Home: 420 3d Ave N, Saskatoon, SK Canada S7K 2J3

BELSKY, KATHLEEN MARILYN, public relations executive; b. Phila., Feb. 7, 1949; d. Albert and Jean Masurat; m. Glenn Stuart Belsky, May 26, 1979; 1 child, Steven. BS, Phila. Coll. Textiles and Scis., 1985, MBA, 1988. Ednl. cons. Bell of Pa., Phila., 1975-77, coordinator handicapped services, 1978-83, mgr. direct mktg., 1983-86, staff mktg. mgr., 1986-87; staff mgr. revenue mgmt./product line mgmt. BellAtlantic, Phila., 1987-88, staff mgr. regional promotional advt. coordination and tracking, 1988-89; product mgr. Product Line Mgmt., 1989; dir. ext. affairs Bell Atlantic, 1989—; dir. Nevil Trust-Girard Bank Telephone Device for the Deaf Project, Phila., 1977-79; adj. faculty Bucks County C.C., 1989—; bd. dirs. Del Vly Indsl. Devel. Authority, Del Vly Philharmonic Orch. Bd. dirs. Pa. Soc. for Advancement the Deaf, Phila., 1985-87, Hero Scholarship Fund Bucks County; officer United Way, Bucks County, 1990—; pres. Bucks County Opportunity Coun., 1993, Greater Willow Grove C. of C., 1993-94, Citizens Crime Commn. Bucks County, 1990-91; adv. bd. mem. Upper Southampton Natural Resources, 1989-91, bus. edn. Hatboro-Horsham Sch. Dist., Bristol Twp. Sch. Dist., Pennridge Sch. Dist.; mem. econ. adjustment com. Naval Air Warfare Ctr., 1993—. Recipient Outstanding Community Svc. award Del. Valley Region Telecom. for the Deaf, 1986, Vol. Leadership award United Way of Bucks County, 1991, Continuing Edn. Student of Yr. award, 1985, Community Svc. award Greater Willow Grove C. of C., 1992, Bus. Assoc. of Yr. award Positive Horizons chpt. Am. Bus. Women's Assn., 1992, Patricia Clatch Meml. award Ctrl. Bucks C. of C., 1993. Mem. Pub. Rels. Soc. Am., Acad. Mgmt., Ctrl. Montgomery County C. of C. (bd. dirs. 1994—), Lower Bucks C. of C. (pres. 1994—). Republican. Home: 1220 Cushmore Rd Southampton PA 18966-4141 Office: Bell Atlantic PO Box 68 Southampton PA 18966-0068

BELSTERLING, JEAN INNES, retired librarian; b. Phila., Feb. 2, 1928; d. George McNeely Belsterling and Mary Thornton (Innes) Bowman. Grad., Bryn Mawr Hosp. Sch. Nursing, 1948; BA, U. Pa., 1974; MS, Drexel U., 1976. RN, Pa. Nurse Bryn Mawr (Pa.) Hosp., 1948-51; commd. ensign USN, 1951, advanced through grades to lt. comdr., 1961; ret., 1971; med. libr. West Jersey Health System, Voorhees, N.J., 1976-90, ret., 1990; coord. S.W. N.J. Libr. Consortium, 1985-90. Deacon Trinity Presbyn. Ch., Cherry Hill, N.J., 1976-79, trustee, elder, 1984-87. Home: 214 Shady Ln Marlton NJ 08053-2716

BELT, AUDREY E(VON), social worker, consultant; b. New Orleans, June 23, 1948. BS in Social Work and Psychology, Grambling State U., 1970; MSW in Adminstrn. and Policy, U. Mich., 1972. Adult probation officer City/County San Francisco Hall of Justice, 1973-74; child welfare worker dept. social svcs. City/County San Francisco, 1974-79; rsch. and planning specialist City of Ann Arbor (Mich.) Model Cities Interdisciplinary Agy; cons. San Francisco; cons. in field. Grambling State U. scholar, 1966-70, U. Mich. scholar, 1971-72. Mem. ABA, NASW (edn. task force), Am. Orthopsychiat. Assn., Am. Humane Soc., Child Welfare League Am., N.Y. Acad. Scis., Smithsonian Rsch. Instn., Alpha Kappa Delta. Democrat.

Roman Catholic. Home and Office: 610 Polk St PO Box 424288 San Francisco CA 94142-4288

BELT, JEAN RAINER, art gallery owner; b. Selma, Ala., Sept. 12, 1942; d. Sterling Price and Saidee (Crook) Rainer; m. Kemplin C. Belt, Aug. 31, 1963; children: Keven Curtis, Kelly. BS in Math., U. Ala., 1964. Founder, ptnr. Corp. Art Source, Montgomery, Ala., 1983-92, owner, 1992—; owner CAS Gallery & Frames, Montgomery, Ala., 1994; juror Jubilee Galleria Art Show, Montgomery, 1987, Riofest, Harlingen, Tex., 1989-90, BCA on My Own Time, Montgomery, 1990; guest lectr. Riofest, 1990; dir. Armory Gallery Arts Coun. Montgomery, 1989-91; advisor Montgomery Bus. Com. Arts, 1990-94 (Bus. in Arts award 1989); curator Armory Gallery, Montgomery, 1989. Bd. dirs Arts Coun. Montgomery, 1980-94, pres., 1985-87, 92-93; mem. adv. bd. Montgomery Symphony Assn., 1993—; pres. Jr. League Montgomery, 1984, treas., 1981; Stephen min. 1st United Meth. Ch., Montgomery, 1992-94. Named. Vol. Action Ctr. Vol. of Yr. award, 1989. Mem. Nat. Assn. Corp. Art Mgrs., Montgomery C. of C., U. Ala. Alumni Assn. Office: Corp Art Source 2960-F Zelda Rd Montgomery AL 36106

BELTAIRE, BEVERLY ANN, public relations executive; b. Detroit, Aug. 21, 1926; d. Charles H. and Henrietta (Lucker) Strauss; m. Mark A. Beltaire, Nov. 7, 1947; children: Mark IV, Jeffrey, Barbara, Suzanne. Student, Highland Community Coll., Highland Park, Mich., 1944-45, Wayne State U., 1946-47; HHD (hon.), Siena Heights Coll., 1990. Writer Detroit Free Press, 1945-47; pub. The Skyline mag., Detroit, 1947-55; v.p. Gille Beltaire, Inc., Detroit, 1956-59; women's editor Sta. WXYZ-TV, Detroit, 1956-59; pres. Beltaire, Vincent & Hull, Detroit, 1959-61; pres. and chief exec. officer PR Assocs., Inc., Detroit, 1961—; bd. dirs. Fed. Res. Bank Chgo., Detroit., Standard Fed. Bank. Mem. Pvt. Industry Coun., Gov.'s Commn. Future for Higher Edn.; sec. Mich. Bus. Ptnrship., Detroit Com. of 200; chmn. Leadership Detroit; bd. govs. Greater Mich. Found., Lansing; bd. dirs. Econ. Alliance for Mich., Met. Detroit Conv. and Visitors Bur., Detroit Econ. Growth Corp. Named Advt. Woman of the Yr., Women's Ad Club, 1978, Mich. Woman of the Yr., Am. Lung Assn. Southeastern Mich., 1985; recipient Nat. Clarion award Women in Communications, Inc., 1978, Disting. Community Svc. award Anti-Defamation League B'nai B'rith, 1990, Humanitarian of the Yr. award March of Dimes, 1991, Silver awards (4) Pub. Rels. Soc. of Am., 1972, 83, 88, 92. Mem. Pub. Rels. Soc. Am. (Silver Anvil award 1972, 83, 88, 92), Women in Communications, Inc. (Headliner award 1982), Greater Detroit C. of C. (chmn. bd. dirs. 1982-83), Adcraft Detroit Club, Econ. Detroit Club (exec. bd. dirs.), Detroit Club, Renaissance Club, Hunt Club. Office: Pub Rels Assocs Inc 418 Ford Bldg 615 Griswold Ste 418 Detroit MI 48226

BELTON, SHARON SAYLES, mayor; m. Steve Belton; 3 children. Student, Macalester Coll. Asst. dir. Minn. Program for Victims of Sexual Assault; parole officer Minn. Dept. Corrections; mayor City of Mpls., 1994—. Pres. Nat. Coalition Against Sexual Assault; co-founder, pres. Harriet Tubman Shelter for Battered Women; mem. Mpls. City Coun. 8th Ward, 1983-93, pres. 1989-93; bd. dirs. Bush Found., Macalester Coll., Children's Theater, Neighborhood Revitalization Policy Bd., United Way, Greater Mpls. Food Bank, Affordable Housing Coalition, Youth Coord. Bd., Turning Point, Affordable Day Care Coalition, Mpls. Initiative Against Racism, Met. Task Force on Devel. Disabilities, econ. devel. strategy steering com. Mpls. C. of C. Office: Office of the Mayor Rm 331 City Hall 350 S Fifth St Minneapolis MN 55415-1393

BELTON, SUSAN JANE, artist; b. Chgo., Apr. 14, 1951; d. Albert Lee and Edith Jane (Magee) Rogers; m. David Joseph Belton, June 4, 1973; children: Elizabeth Jane, Samuel James. Grad., Sch. Mus. Fine Arts, 1979; BA, Colby Coll., 1973. Placement officer Sch. Mus. Fine Arts, Boston, 1980-86, assoc. faculty, 1982—. One-woman shows include Thoma Segal Gallery, Boston, 1982, 85, Arden Gallery, Boston, 1995; group shows include Mus. Fine Arts, Boston, 1983, Hayden Gallery, Cambridge, MAss., 1983, Artspace, New HAven, COnn., 1990, Provincetown (Mass.) Art Mus., 1992. Clarissa Bartlett fellow, 1983, Painting fellow, 1981. Mem. Womens Caucus Art. Home: 32 Plowgate Rd Chestnut Hill MA 02167-3723 Studio: 46 Waltham St # 401A Boston MA 02118-2106

BELTZNER, GAIL ANN, music educator; b. Palmerton, Pa., July 20, 1950; d. Conon Nelson and Lorraine Ann (Carey) Beltzner. BS in Music Edn. summa cum laude, West Chester State U., 1972; postgrad., Kean State Coll., 1972, Temple U., 1972, Westminster Choir Coll., 1972, Lehigh U., 1972. Tchr. music Drexel Hill Jr. High Sch., 1972-73; music specialist Allentown (Pa.) Sch. Dist., 1973—; tchr. Corps Sch. and Cmty. Devel. Lab., 1978-80, Corps Cmty. Resource Festival, 1979-81, Corps Cultural Fair, 1980, 81. Mem. aux. Allentown Art Mus., aux. Allentown Hosp.; mem. womans com. Allentown Symphony; bd. dirs. Allentown Area Ecumenical Food Bank. Decorated Dame Comdr., Ordre Souverain et Militaire de la Milice du St. Sepulcre; recipient Cert. of Appreciation, Lehigh Valley Sertoma Club; Excellence in the Classroom grantee Rider-Pool Found., 1988, 91-92. Mem. AAUW, NAFE, ASCD, Am. String Tchrs. Assn., Pa.-Del. String Tchrs. Assn., Internat. Platform Assn., Allentown Edn. Assn., Music Educators Nat. Conf., Pa. Music Educators Assn., Am. Orff-Schulwerk Assn., Soc. Gen. Music, Am. Assn. Music Therapy, Internat. Soc. Music Edn., Assn. for Tech. in Music Instrn., Choristers Guild, Lenni Lenape Hist. Soc., Lehigh Valley Arts Coun., Midi Users Group, Allentown Symphony Assn., Allentown 2d Civilian Police Acad., Nat. Sch. Orch. Assn. Republican. Lutheran. Home: PO Box 4427 Allentown PA 18105-4427

BELZER, ELLEN J., negotiations and communications consultant; b. Kansas City, Mo., May 22, 1951; d. Meyer Simmon and Fay (Weinstein) B. Student, U. Okla., 1969-70, U. Ibero-Americana, Mexico City, 1971; BA, Northwestern U., 1973; MPA, U. Mo., Kansas City, 1976. Rsch. asst. dept. polit. sci. Northwestern U., Evanston, Ill., 1970-73; adminstrv. asst. Ctrs. for Regional Progress Midwest Rsch. Inst., Kansas City, 1974; various positions to dir. socioecons. div. Am. Acad. Family Physicians, Kansas City, 1974-86; pres. Belzer Seminars and Cons., Kansas City, 1986-92; prin. Belzer Broderick & Assocs., Kansas City, 1993-94; pres. Belzer Seminars and Consulting, Kansas City, 1994—; instr. communication Avila Coll., Kansas City, 1987-92, dept. continuing edn. U. Kans., Lawrence, 1989-92; speaker on negotiation strategies, conflict resolution techniques, communication skills, 1986—; mediator for hosps., physician groups, state health depts., community health ctrs., others. Contbr. articles to profl. publs., also monographs. Campaign vol. for local candidate, Kansas City, 1970, 82. Democrat. Home: 21 W Bannister Rd Kansas City MO 64114-4009 Office: 7140 Wornall Rd Ste 203 Kansas City MO 64114

BEMIS, MARY FERGUSON, magazine editor; b. N.Y.C., Dec. 28, 1961; d. Edmund Augustus and Anne Adoian (Nalbandian) B. BFA in Writing, Johnson State Coll., 1983. Co-editor, co-pub. Ave. Literary Rev. Ave. Publs. Inc., Burlington, Vt., 1983-85; editor Unique Hair and Beauty Mag., 1994; editor Lady's Circle Mag. Lopez Publs., N.Y.C., 1987-94, editor, project mgr. 1001 Christmas Ideas, 1989-94; freelance editor, writer Mus. Sci., Boston, 1991-93. Co-editor: The Green Mountain Rev., 1982-83, Nature Through Her Eyes; Art and Literature by Women, 1994, Journey Into the Wilderness, 1994. Mem. Women in Comm., Inc. Democrat. Mem. Unitarian Ch. Home and Office: 117 E 11th St New York NY 10003-5336

BEMIS, SUSAN MARIE, real estate developer, consultant; b. San Rafael, Calif., Aug. 2, 1950; d. Leon Elmers and Martha Ann (McLean) B. Student, U. Calif., Irvine, 1978-80. Adminstrv. asst. Gfeller Devel., Irvine, 1978-80; project mgr. State Wide Developers, Los Alamitos, Calif., 1980-83, Tarnutzer Cos., Newport Beach, Pa., 1984-89; sr. project mgr., asst. v.p. Wells Fargo Bank, L.A., 1990—. Adv. com. Girls Inc. Mem. Home Builders Coun. Republican. Roman Catholic. Office: Wells Fargo Bank 2970 Harbor Blvd Ste 201 Costa Mesa CA 92626-3994

BEMKER, MARY, counselor; b. Louisville, Ky., Feb. 18, 1958; d. Norbert James and Hattie (Hagan) Boemker; divorced, 1979; 1 child, Victoria Leigh. BS, Spalding U., Ind. U.; MS, Ind. U.; Specialist Degree in Counseling Psych., Spalding U.; MSN, U. Ala. Cert. tchr., Ind., Ky., sch. psychologist, Ind., counselor and ednl. tester, Ky.; registered nurse, Ky., Ind.; cert. family life edn., CD nurse, CD mgr. Ednl. psychologist Ky. Bapt. Hosp., Louisville, 1976-77; substance abuse counselor River Region, Louisville, 1977-78; nurse cons. Changing Patterns, Inc., Louisville, 1981-84; academic counselor, lectr. Ind. U. Sch. Nursing, New Albany, 1985-88; ednl. prevention intervention coord., rsch. coord. youth/family activity, cons. Choice, Inc., Louisville, 1988—; counselr substance abuse Morton Ctr.; advisor in field. Contbr. articles to profl. jours. Panel mem. Gatorade Sports Medicine; mem. Ky. Women's Substance Abuse Network. Named to Honorable Order of Ky. Colonels. Mem. Ky. Women's Substance Abuse Network, Am. Assn. Counseling and Devel., Am. Assn. Profl. Hypnotherapists, Ky. Nurses Assn. (mem. coun.), Am. Assn. Social Psychiatry, Internat. Coun. Nurses, Assn. for Humanistic Orthopsychiatry, Gatorade Panel Sports Medicine, Nat. Wildlife Fedn., Sierra Club, Sigma Theta Tau, Kappa Delta Phi, Pi Lambda Theta. Roman Catholic. Home: 1209 Curlew Ave Louisville KY 40213-1209

BENACH, SHARON ANN, physician assistant; b. New Orleans, Aug. 28, 1944; d. Wilbur G. and Freda Helen (Klaas) Cherry; m. Richard Benach, Dec. 6, 1969 (div. Oct. 1976); children: Craig, Rachel. Degree, St. Louis U., 1978. Physician asst. VA Hosp., St. Louis, 1982-84, Maricopa County Health Svcs., Phoenix, 1984—. Served with USPHS, 1978-82. Recipient Outstanding Performance award HHS. Mem. Maricopa Faculty Assn. (div. internal medicine), Mensa. Jewish. Home: 5726 N 10th St No 5 Phoenix AZ 85014-2273

BENAIM-DEMAN, MIREYA, psychologist; b. Caracas, Venezuela; came to U.S., 1990; d. Carlos and Rayita (Napadensky) Benaim-Pinto; m. Michael DeMan, 1990. B in Psychology cum laude, U. Católica, Caracas, 1976; M in Psychology, U. Simón Bolívar, Caracas, 1981, M in Philosophy, 1982, M in Counseling and Human Devel., 1985; M in Clin. Psychology, Hosp. Militar, Caracas, 1986; postgrad., Union Inst., Cin., 1990—. Instr. psychology U. Católica, 1976-77, 80-84; asst. prof. dept. sci. and tech. of behavior U. Simón Bolívar, 1986-89, asst. prof. teaching coord., 1990, aggregate prof. dept. sci. and tech. of behavior, 1990—; clin. psychologist and counselor Unidad Clínica Esmeralda, Caracas, 1988-90; lectr. various univs. and conferences in Venezuela, U.S. and Europe. Author: Psychosomatic Disorders, Towards an Integrative Approach, 1986; contbr. articles to profl. jours. Mem. AAAS, AAUW, APA (assoc.; mem. divsns. counseling psychology, theoretical and philos. psychology, religious issues, clin. neuropsychology), European Assn. Rsch. and Devel. Higher Edn., Venezuelan Assn. Psychosomatic Med., Venezuelan Coll. Psychologists, Venezuelan Fedn. Transactional Analysis, Venezuelan Assn. Advancement Sci., Venezuelan Assn. Students Affairs, Venezuelan Assn. Ednl. Rsch., Assn. R&D Higher Edn., Inst. Advancement Health, N.Y. Acad. Scis. Home: PO Box 22269 Juneau AK 99802-2269 also: Altamira, Apartado Postal 68215, Caracas 1062-A, Venezuela

BENAVIDEZ, CELINA GARCIA, state legislator; b. Denver, Feb. 6, 1954; d. Robert Lee and Alice (Crespin) Garcia. BS in Bus., Pub. Adminstrn., U. Alberquerque, Denver, 1978. Civil rights investigator Colo. Civil Rights Divsn., Denver, 1979-80; program adminstr. human resources Colo. Dept. Transp., Denver, 1980-92; mem. Colo. Ho. Reps., 1992—. Bd. dirs. Auraria Community Ctr., Denver, 1986, chair 1988-89. Recipient Vol. of Yr. award Women In Community Svc., 1988, Colo. Social Worker award 1992. Mem. NOW, Vol. Women in Community Svc., Mexican-Am. Policy Inst. (bd. dirs., chair women's causes), Jane Jefferson Hispanic League. Democrat. Roman Catholic. Home: 2825 W 34th Ave Denver CO 80211 Office: State Capitol State Capitol Bldg Denver CO 80203*

BENBERRY, CUESTA RAY, historian; b. Cin., Sept. 8, 1923; d. Walter and Marie (Jones) Ray; m. George Lynn Benberry, Mar. 25, 1951; 1 child, George Valdez Benberry. BA, Stowe Tchrs. Coll., St. Louis, 1945; postgrad., St. Louis U., 1954-56; Cert. Library Sci., Harris-Stowe Coll., St. Louis, 1968; MEd, U. Mo., St. Louis, 1974. Reading specialist St. Louis pub. schs., 1945-85; ind. scholar and lectr. quilt history St. Louis, 1969—; cons. Calif. Afro-Am. Mus., L.A., 1985, Ferrero Films, San Francisco, 1985-86, Williams Coll. Mus. Art, Williamstown, Mass., 1988-89, Met. Mus. Art, N.Y.C., 1990; curated quilt exhbn. St. Louis Art Mus., 1992-93. Author: Always There: The African-American Presence in American Quilts, 1991; co-author: A Patchwork of Pieces: An Anthology of Early Quilt Stories, 1845-1940, 1993; rsch. editor Nimble Needle mag., 1972-76, Nat. African-Am. Craft Exhibition and Symposium, Wilberforce U., Ohio, 1992—; contbr. articles to profl. jours. Established African-Am. Quilt Archive, Vaughn Cultural Ctr., Urban League, St. Louis, 1984; bd. dirs. African-Am. Arts and Crafts Conf., Wilberforce U., 1992—. Named to Quilters Hall of Fame, Continental Quilting Congress, Vienna, Va., 1983; First Place in the Arts, African Meth. Episcopal Ch., Tucson, 1989, award for Leadership in the Arts, YWCA, St. Louis, 1989, for contbn. to arts, Sigma Gamma Rho, St. Louis, 1981. Mem. Am. Quilt Study Group (bd. dirs. 1983-86), Elder Craftsmen of N.Y.C. (adv. com. 1990—), Nat. Quilting Assn., Quilters Guild London, Afro-Am. Hist. Genealogical Soc. AME Ch. Home and Office: 5150 Terry Ave Saint Louis MO 63115-1051

BENCINI, SARA HALTIWANGER, concert pianist; b. Winston Salem, N.C., Sept. 2, 1926; d. Robert Sydney and Janie Love (Couch) Haltiwanger; m. Robert Emery Bencini, June 26, 1954; children: Robert Emery, III, Constance Bencini Waller, John McGregor. Mus. B., Salem Coll., 1947; postgrad. grad. Juilliard Sch. Music, 1948-50; M.A., Smith Coll., 1951; D In Mus. Arts, U. N.C., Greensboro, 1989. Head piano dept. Mary Burnham Sch. for Girls, Northampton, Mass., 1949-51; pianist, composer dance and drama dept. Smith Coll., 1951-52; head music dept. Walnut Hill Sch. for Girls, Natick, Mass., 1952-54; pvt. piano tchr., High Point, N.C., 1954-66; concert pianist appearing in Am. and Europe, 1948—; duo-piano performances with PBS-TV, Columbia, S.C., 1967, Winston Salem Symphony, N.C., 1964-68, Ea. Mus. Festival, Greensboro, N.C., 1969. Democrat. Presbyterian.

BENDER, BETTY ANN, Salvation Army officer, personnel administrator; b. Sioux Falls, S.D., Oct. 31, 1947; d. Leo Simon and Violet Ann (Dyce) B. Officer's commn., Salvation Army Sch. Officers' Tng., 1968. Program asst. Salvation Army Booth Meml. Home and Hosp., Chgo., 1968-71, Grand Rapids, Mich., 1971-74; asst. adminstr. Salvation Army Booth Meml. Home and Hosp., Detroit, 1974-76; adminstr. Salvation Army Booth Meml. Home and Hosp., Omaha, 1976-79; asst. dean students Salvation Army Sch. for Officers' Tng., Chgo., 1979-84, dean of students, 1986-88; divisional youth sec., Western Mich.-No. Ind. divsn. Salvation Army, Grand Rapids, 1984-86; officer, dir. employee svcs. dept., ctrl. territory hdqrs. Salvation Army, Des Plaines, Ill., 1988—. Office: Salvation Army 10 W Algonquin Rd Des Plaines IL 60016-6006

BENDER, BETTY BARBEE, food service professional; b. Lexington, Ky., Apr. 29, 1932; d. Richard Carroll and Sarah Elizabeth (Rodes) Barbee; m. David H. Bender, Dec. 14, 1957; children: Bruce, Carroll. BA in Home Econs., Mont. State U., 1954; MS in Food Service Mgmt., Miami U., Oxford, Ohio, 1980. Adminstrv. dietitan Mass. Gen. Hosp., Boston, 1955-56; asst. chief dietitan Meth. Hosp., Indpls., 1957-61; chief dietitan Community Hosp., Indpls., 1961-63; supervising dietitian Chgo. Area ARA, 1963-67; asst. food service supr. Dayton (Ohio) Bd. Edn., 1969, mgr. food service, 1969—; cons. Nat. Frozen Food Assn., Washington, 1983, Crescent Metal Products Co., Cleve., 1985. Contbr. articles to profl. jours. Recipient 26th Ann. Foodsvc. Facilities Design award Instrs. Mag. for Commissary Design, 1972, Silver and Gold Plate awards Internat. Foodsvc. Mfrs. Assn., 1985, Pres.'s award Ohio Sch. Food Svc. Assn., 1987, FAME Golden Star award, 1992; recognized for outstanding contbns. to child nutrition program Ohio Ho. of Reps., 1972, 84. Mem. Am. Sch. Food Svc. Assn. (nat. pres. 1983, chmn. 1978-80, maj. city sect.), Ohio Sch. Food Svc. (pres. 1977), Dayton Sch. Adminstr. Assn., Dayton Sch. Mgmt. Assn. (pres. 1993-94), Am. Dietetic Assn. (cert., chair dietary practice group 1990-91, award for Excellence in Mgmt. Practice 1992, Food Svc. Dir. Yr. 1994), Ohio Dietetic Assn., Dayton Dietetic Assn., Soc. Nutrition Edn. (panel 1983). Democrat. Home: 7217 Tarryton Rd Dayton OH 45459-3450 Office: Dayton Bd Edn Food Svc Dept 125 Heid Ave Dayton OH 45404-1217

BENDER, BETTY WION, librarian; b. Mt. Ayer, Iowa, Feb. 26, 1925; d. John F. and Sadie A. (Guess) Wion; m. Robert F. Bender, Aug. 24, 1946. B.S., N.Tex. State U., Denton, 1946; M.A., U. Denver, 1957. Asst. cataloger N. Tex. State U. Library, 1946-49; from cataloger to head acquisitions So. Meth. U., Dallas, 1949-56; reference asst. Ind. State Library, Indpls., 1951-52; librarian Ark. State Coll., 1958-59, Eastern Wash. Hist. Soc., Spokane, 1960-67; reference librarian, then head circulation dept. Spokane (Wash.) Public Library, 1968-73, library dir., 1973-88; vis. instr. U. Denver, summers 1957-60, 63, fall 1959; instr. Whitworth Coll., Spokane, 1962-64; mem. Gov. Wash. Regional Conf. Libraries, 1968, Wash. Statewide Library Devel. Council, 1970-71. Bd. dirs. N.W. Regional Found., 1973-75, Inland Empire Goodwill Industries, 1975-77, Wash. State Library Commn., 1979-87, Future Spokane, 1983-88, vice chmn., 1986-87, pres., 1987-88. Recipient YWCA Outstanding Achievement award in Govt., 1985. Mem. ALA (mem. library adminstrn. and mgmt. assn. com. on orgn. 1982-83, chmn. nominating com. 1983-85, v.p./pres.-elect. 1985-86, pres. 1986-87), Pacific N.W. Library Assn. (chmn. circulation div. 1972-75, conv. chmn. 1977), Wash. Library Assn. (v.p./pres.-elect 1975-77, pres. 1977-78), AAUW (pres. Spokane br. 1969-71, rec. sec. Wash. br. 1971-73, fellowship named in honor 1972), Spokane and Inland Empire Librarians (dir. 1967-68), Am. Soc. Pub. Adminstrn. Republican. Lutheran. Club: Zonta (pres. Spokane chpt. 1976-77, dist. conf. treas. 1972). Home: E221 Rockwood Blvd # 504 Spokane WA 99202

BENDER, FLO-ANN, insurance company executive; b. Cygnet, Ohio, June 8, 1941; d. Ralph and Mary Ellen (Wichner) Rayle; m. Harold Jonathan Bowersox, Dec. 30, 1961 (div. Feb. 1983); children: Launa Maureen, Stephanie Ann; m. Mark Stephen Bender, Mar. 20, 1987. BS in Edn., Bowling Green (Ohio) State U., 1962. Cert. securities rep. Owner, operator Flo Ann Sch. Dance, North Baltimore, Ohio, 1956-62; libr. asst. Bowling Green State U., 1960-62; tchr. Lincoln Elem. Sch., Bergenfield, N.J., 1962-63, Millard (Mo.) Sch., 1964-65; state case account rep. State Dept. Welfare, Kirksville, Mo., 1965-69; office mgr. Harold J. Bowersox, DO, Hanover, Pa., 1974-81, H & R Block, Gettysburg, Pa., 1981-82, Marshall A. Angotti, DDS, Hanover, 1982-84; fin. account rep. Prudential, York, Pa., 1984-88, Met. Life Ins. Co., York, 1988—; seminar ptnr. fin. dept. Met. Life, York, 1993. Dancing tchr. ballet and individual style dancing, 1957-62; creator second grade social studies program, 1962-63. Bd. mem. Vis. Nurses Assn., Hanover, Pa., 1972-75, YWCA, Hanover, 1970-73, Hanover Hosp. Aux., 1973-76; tchr. St. Marks Luth. Ch., Hanover, 1970-81. Fellow Life Underwriters Tng. Coun. (Outstanding Achievement award 1993); mem. AAUW, Nat. Assn. Life Underwriters, York Assn. Life Underwriters (chairperson 1990-93, bd. mem. 1990-93, Doers award 1992), Pa. Assn. Life Underwriters, AHIA, Order of Eastern Star, Md. Yacht Club (cheer officer 1993-94). Republican. Home: 3892 Stony Brook Dr York PA 17402-2741 Office: Met Life 3214 E Market St York PA 17402-2506

BENDER, GAIL PAPERMASTER, oncologist; b. Mpls., May 21, 1947. BA in History, Cornell U., 1969; MA in Edn., Stanford U., 1970; MD, U. Minn., 1975. Diplomate Nat. Bd. Med. Examiners, Am. Bd. Internal Medicine; bd. cert. in med. oncology. Assoc. editor, project dir. CTB/McGraw-Hill, Monterey, Calif., 1970-72; resident internal medicine U. Minn. Affiliated Hosps., Mpls., 1975-77; resident internal medicine Ohio State U. Hosps., Columbus, 1977-78, postdoctoral fellow hematology/oncology, 1978-80; staff physician internal medicine, med. oncology VA Hosp., Mpls., 1981-82; med. oncologist pvt. practice Gail P. Bender, M.D., P.A., St. Louis Park, Minn., 1982—; rsch. affiliateions with Nat. Cancer Inst., 1981—, Ea. Coop. Oncology Group, 1981—, West Met. Mpls. Cmty. Clin. Oncology Program, 1983—, Adria Labs., 1986—, Surg. Adjuvant Breast and Bowel Project, 1989—, Va. Piper Cancer Inst., 1991—; bd. dirs. Meth. Hosp. Found., Mpls., 1984-94, Medica, Mpls., 1987-94, Minn. Med. Found., Mpls., 1990—, HealthSystem Minnesota, Mpls., 1993—. Contbr. articles to profl. jours. Mem. cancer com. Meth. Hosp.; exec. com. mem. West Metro Ind. Physicians Assn.; quality assurance and utilization rev. com. CareVan Med. Systems; sci. tech. rev. com. Minn. Soc. Clin. Oncology. Recipient AAUW Fellowship award, 1975, Twin West C. of C. Woman of Achievement award, 1988. Mem. West Metro Ind. Physicians Assn., Hennepin County Med. Soc., Minn. Med. Assn., Am. Soc. Clin. Oncology, Minn. Soc. Clin. Oncology. Office: Gail P Bender MD PA 6490 Excelsior Blvd Ste W-106 Saint Louis Park MN 55426

BENDER, JANET PINES, artist; b. Chgo., June 14, 1934; d. Nathan and Hana (Leff) Pines; m. Irwin Robert Bender, Feb. 25, 1966. BS, U. Wis., 1955; MA, Northwestern U., 1956; postgrad., U. Ill./Loyola U., Chgo., 1955-56, Tyler Sch. Fine Arts, Phila., 1957. Paintings exhibited in one-woman shows including One Ill. Ctr., Chgo., 1979, 87, Olive Hyde Gallery, Fremont, Calif., 1980, 81, N.A.M.E. Gallery, Chgo., 1982, W.A.R.M. Gallery, Mpls., 1984, A.R.C. Gallery, Chgo., 1985, 87, 89, 94, R.H. Love Galleries, Chgo., 1989, 92, Soho 20 Gallery, N.Y.C., 1990, Galerie Thea Fischer-Reinhardt, West Berlin, Germany, 1990, R.H. Love Contemporary Gallery, Chgo., 1992; group exhbns. include Rockford (Ill.) Art Mus., 1994, U. Wis. Art Gallery, Madison, Amos Enos Gallery, N.Y.C., 1993, Tonali Gallery, Mex. City, 1992, Renaissance Soc., Chgo., 1986, Ill. State Mus., 1983, 72nd Newport (R.I.) Nat. Exhibition, 1983, Chauttaqua Nat. Exhibition, 1981, Zolla Leiberman Gallery, Chgo., 1980; permanent collections include Young & Rubicam, Chgo., Brown-Forman Corp., Louisville, Nugent Wenckus Corp., Chgo., Louis Zahn Drug Co., Melrose Park, Ill., Fuller Commercial Brokerage Co., Chgo., Dynamark Inc., Chgo., Aabott Distbn., Miami, Art Beasley Inc., San Diego, Siegel, Denberg, Vanasco, Shivkovsky, Moses and Shoenstadt, Chgo., Altschuler, Melvoin & Glassner, Chgo., Shafer, Meltzer & Lewis Assoc., Wilmette, Ill., Schiff, Hardin & Waite, Chgo. Bd. dirs. A.R.C. Gallery, Chgo., 1984—; juror IAFA Awards, 1993. Recipient Ill. Arts Coun. Project Completion grants, 1979, 81-82, Visual Arts Fellowship grant Ill. Arts Coun., 1983; fellow Northwestern U., 1955-56. Mem. NAFE, Women's Caucus for Art, Mus. Contemporary Art, Art Inst. Chgo., Chgo. Artist Coalition, Ill. Arts Alliance, Mus. Modern Art (N.Y.), Met. Mus. Art (N.Y.), Coll. Art Assn., Peace Mus., Ill. State Gallery, Com. for Artist Rights (organizing com., 1988), Pi Lambda. Studio: 2001 N Elston Ave Chicago IL 60614

BENDER, LINDA ARLENE, trust company executive; b. Ft. Wayne, Ind., Sept. 4, 1951; d. Edward Walter and Lois C.L. (Bender) Dinkel; m. Dale Alan, June 10, 1971; children: Jennifer, Emily, Andrew. Student, U. Hawaii, 1969-73; BA in Sociology, Ind. U., Ft. Wayne, 1975; postgrad., St. Francis Coll., 1994—. Media dir. HPN, Inc., Ft. Wayne, 1981-84; media mgr. North Am. Van Lines, Ft. Wayne, 1984-88, mgr. advt. and pub. rels., 1988-92; mgr. mktg. NBD Bank, Ft. Wayne, 1992—; bd. dirs. Ft. Wayne Advt. Assn. Editor: Ft. Wayne Ad Assn., 1984-85. actress Ft. Wayne Civic Theater, 1988—, Purdue-Ind. Theatre. Mem. Ft. Wayne Advt. Assn. Home: 8826 Village Grove Dr Fort Wayne IN 46804-2645 Office: NBD Bank 1 Summit Sq PO Box 2345 Fort Wayne IN 46801-2845

BENDER, SUSAN ARLYCE, secondary school educator; b. Seattle, Apr. 12, 1962; d. Alvin F. and Betty H. B. BS in Edn., Jackson State U., 1984; postgrad., Miss. Coll., 1986—. Cert. tchr., Miss. Tchr. Northwest Rankin Sch., Brandon, Miss., 1984-92, Jim Hill High Sch., Jackson, Miss., 1992—. Co-author: Mississippi State Science Curriculum, 1994. Nominee Presdl. award for Math. and Sci., 1994. Mem. NSTA, Miss. Acad. Sci., Nat. Sci. Tchrs. Assn., Miss. Mus. Natural Sci., Miss. Sci. Tchrs. Assn. (legis. rep. 1989-91, sec. 1991, pres. 1993—), Ctrl. Miss. H.S. Chemistry Tchrs. Assn. (pres. 1994—). Home: PO Box 855 Brandon MS 39043-0855 Office: Jim Hill High Sch 2185 Fortune St Jackson MS 39204-2387

BENDER, VIRGINIA BEST, computer science educator; b. Rockford, Ill., Feb. 10, 1945; d. Oscar Sheldon and Genevieve (Windle) Best; m. Robert Keith Bender, July 19, 1969; children: Victoria Ruth, Christopher Keith. BS in Chemistry, Math., No. Ill. U., 1967; postgrad., U. of Ill. Coll. of Med., 1967-69; MBA, Loyola U., Chgo., 1973. Cert. computer profl. Sr. systems rep. Burroughs Corp., Chgo., 1969-73; systems analyst Marshall Field & Co., Chgo., 1973-74; project leader Fed. Home Loan Bank, Chgo., 1974-76; sr. systems analyst United Air Lines, Elk Grove Village, Ill., 1976-78; supr. Kemper Group, Long Grove, Ill., 1978-82; prof., coord. William Rainey Harper Coll., Palatine, Ill., 1982—; speaker Midwest Computer Conf., DeKalb, Ill., 1988, moderator, 1991; exch. prof. Maricopa Community Colls., Mesa, Ariz., 1990, rsch. sabbatical, 1993. Nation chief YMCA mother-dau. group Indian Maidens, Des Plaines, 1982-83. Named Tchr. of the Month Burroughs Corp., Chgo, 1972. Mem. Inst. Certification Computer Profls. (life), Ill. Assn. of Date Processing Instrs., No. Ill. Computer Soc., Bay Area Multimedia Coll. Consortium, No. Ill. Alumni Assn. (life). Methodist. Home: 411 W Hackberry Dr Arlington Heights IL 60004-1938 Office: William Rainey Harper Coll 1200 W Algonquin Rd Palatine IL 60067-7398

BENDERSON, IDA OLSEN, social services administrator; b. Shedrin, Russia, Dec. 6, 1903; came to U.S., 1905; d. Philip and Sarah (Caplan) Olsen; m. Jacob Benderson, Sept. 12, 1933 (dec. Jan. 1992); children: Eric Stuart, Bruce Ronald. Degree in libr. sci., Syracuse U., 1923. Asst. libr. Syracuse (N.Y.) U. Libr., 1923-28, head readers dept., 1928-42; dir. adult activities Syracuse Jewish Community Ctr., 1964-71, exec. dir., 1971-80; mem. adv. coun. Onondaga County Pub. Libr., Syracuse, 1977—. Contbr. articles to profl. jours. Vice chair Onondaga County Dem. Com., Syracuse, 1956-66; mem. N.Y. State Dem. Exec. Coun. Women's Divsn., N.Y.C., 1960-68; del. Dem. Nat. Conv., Atlantic City, N.J., 1964; pres. Women's Dem. Club, Onondaga County, 1983-84; commr., chair Syracuse Housing Authority, 1972—; mem. Gov.'s Adv. Com. Aging, Albany, N.Y., 1974—; founding mem., 1st chair Met. Commn. Aging, Syracuse and Onondaga County, 1974—; bd. trustees Women's Exec. Coun. N.Y. State Fair, Syracuse, 1976—. Mem. Found. N.Y. State Nurses Assn. (v.p. 1992—). Jewish. Home: 301 Hurlburt Rd Syracuse NY 13224-1822

BENDICKSON, SANDRA CHRISTINE, preschool educator; b. Blue Earth, Minn., Jan. 29, 1952; d. Charles Junior and Harriet Ruth (Arndt) Besendorf; m. Ross Dee Bendickson, June 19, 1976; children: David Douglas, Peter Daniel. AA, U. Minn., Waseca, 1976; BS, Mankato State U., 1979. Parent educator Mankato (Minn.) Schs., 1979-81; sub. presch. tchr. Learning Co., Lake City, Minn., 1981-85; parent educator Sch. Dist. 813, Lake City, Minn., 1985—, presch. program coord., 1985—; mental health cons. Wabasha (Minn.) Citizens Action Coun., 1984-85. Pres. First Luth. Ch. Women, 1987-93; sec. First Luth. Ch. Coun., 1988-90. Sgt. U.S. Army, 1970-73, USAR, 1973-88, USAF, 1988—. Mem. Am. Legion. Office: Sch Dist 813 300 S Garden St Lake City MN 55041-1664

BENDIG, JUDITH JOAN, information systems specialist, computer company executive; b. Erie, Pa., Oct. 28, 1955; d. Richard W. and Rhea Agnes (Hain) B. B.S. in Music Edn. magna cum laude, Edinboro State Coll., 1977. Tech. cons. Inco, Inc., Washington, 1982; sr. systems analyst Devel. Sci. Services, Inc., Washington, 1982-85; dir. computer systems ADEENA Corp., Arlington, Va., 1985-86; prin. systems cons., integration mgr. WANG Labs., Inc., Bethesda, Md., 1986—; v.p. F&B Computer Assocs., Bethesda, Md., 1985—. Mem. Arlington Community Band, 1986—. Served to comdr. USNR, 1978—, with USN, 1978-82. Mem. NAFE, Assn. Computing Machinery, IEEE (assoc.), Naval Res. Assn. Republican. Roman Catholic. Home: 2783 Stone Hollow Dr Vienna VA 22180-7073

BENDIX, LINDA ANN, librarian; b. Racine, Wis., Dec. 15, 1951; d. Kenneth Frank and Virginia Lois (Krueger) Abrahamson; m. Gary Louis Bendix, Aug. 11, 1973; 1 child, Alison Abra. BA, U. Wis., Kenosha, 1973; MLS, U. Wis., Madison, 1976, MA, 1979. Head libr. Lakeland Coll., Sheboygan, Wis., 1976-81; reference libr. Manitowoc (Wis.) Pub. Libr., 1986-88, head tech. svcs., 1988-92, head reference svcs., 1992-94; head info. and adult svcs., 1994—. Mem. ALA, Wis. Libr. Assn., Manitowoc-Calumet Libr. Assn. Office: Manitowoc Pub Library 808 Hamilton St Manitowoc WI 54220-5326

BEN-DOR, GISÈLE, conductor; b. Montevideo, Uruguay; married; 2 children. Student, Acad. of Music, Tel Aviv, Yale Sch. of Music. Music dir. Annapolis Symphony, Md., Pro Arte Chamber Orchestra of Boston, Mass.; condr. Santa Barbara Symphony, Calif.; resident condr. Houston Symphony, Tex.; guest condr. Dayton Philharmonic, Ohio, 1994. Office: Santa Barbara Symphony Orch Arlington Theatre 1900 State St Ste G Santa Barbara CA 93101*

BENEDICT, LINDA SHERK, insurance company executive; b. Hartford, Conn., Jan. 25, 1945; d. Robert William and Marjorie Joan (Drysdale) Sherk; m. Geoffrey Clinton Benedict, Sept. 13, 1969 (div. 1981). AB in Social Psychology magna cum laude, Harvard U., 1967; MBA in Fin., U. Conn., 1980; postgrad., Harvard Bus. Sch., 1991. CLU, 1981. Analyst market rsch. Polaroid Corp., Cambridge, Mass., 1967-70, Transaction Tech., Cambridge, 1970-72; mgr. market rsch. Ocean Spray Cranberries, Hanson, Mass., 1972-76; with Conn. Gen. Life, Bloomfield, 1976-86, regional v.p. claims, 1983-86; with Blue Cross Blue Shield of Md., Balt., 1986-93, v.p., gen. mgr. individual market divsn., 1986-92; chair Sterling Health Svcs., Inc., 1988-93, v.p. consumer svcs. medicare and individual market, 1992, sr. v.p. ins. bus., 1992-93; v.p., gen. mgr. sr. markets Trigon Blue Cross Blue Shield, Roanoke, Va., 1994—. Chmn. Blue Cross United Way campaign, Balt., 1987; bd. dirs. Columbia Freestate Health Sys., Balt., 1987-93; bd. dirs.; mem. fin. and exec. coms., treas., 1st v.p., chmn. fin. com. Meals on Wheels, 1987-94; active Lit. Vols., Hartford, 1985-86, bd. dirs., 1984-86; participant The Leadership Greater Balt. Com., 1990. NSF grantee, 1966-67; Disting. scholar Wall St. Jour. U. Conn., 1980. Mem. Am. Mgmt. Assn., C. of C. Bloomfield (pres. 1977-79). Home: 5936 Saddleridge Rd Roanoke VA 24018

BENEDICT, MARGARET ROSE (PEGGY BENEDICT), English language and speech educator; b. Sheridan, Wyo., Jan. 4, 1948; d. Francis William and Carlotta Hamilton (Whitney) B.; m. Robert Morrell Dorsey, June 26, 1994. BA, U. No. Colo., 1970; Masters, U. Colo., 1978. Master cert. tchr., Colo. Comms. specialist Union Oil of Calif., L.A., 1970-72; tchr. English and drama Pacific Palisades (Calif.) Sch., 1972-74; tchr. English John Dewy Jr. H.S., Thornton, Colo., 1974-75, Highland H.S., Thornton, 1975-79; tchr. speech/debate, asst. coach speech team Cherry Creek H.S., Englewood, Colo., 1980—, head coach debate team and forensics team, 1992-94. Sec., bd. dirs. Nat. Abortion Rights Action League, 1991-95. Head coach state champion debate team, Colo., 1982—; asst. forensics coach nat. champion team, 1992. Mem. NOW, NEA, Nat. Coun. Tchrs. English, Nat. Forensics League (One Diamond Coach award 1993), Colo. Edn. Assn. (state rep. 1972—), Colo. Lang. Arts Soc., Mapleton Edn. Assn. (pres. 1974-76), Cherry Creek Tchrs. Assn. (faculty rep. 1979—), Phi Delta Kappa. Democrat. Episcopalian. Home: 730 Humboldt St Denver CO 80218 Office: Cherry Creek Schs 9300 E Union Ave Englewood CO 80111

BENEDICT, MARY-ANNE, nursing educator; b. Cambridge, Mass., Apr. 14, 1944; d. Preston E. and Mary Rose (Murphy) Woodward; m. Charles A. Benedict, Sept. 20, 1969; children: Annmarie, Helene, Laura. BS in Nursing, Boston Coll. Sch. Nursing, 1967; postgrad., Salem State Coll. Cert. orthopedic nurse. Instr. Sch. Nursing New Eng. Bapt. Hosp., Boston, 1969-79, edn. specialist, 1979—. Lt. (j.g.) USN, 1966-69. Mem. Nat. Assn. Orthopedic Nurses, Sigma Theta Tau (Alpha Chi chpt.). Home: 84 Rockland Pl Newton MA 02164-1234

BENEDICT, THERESA MARIE, mathematics educator; b. East Rutherford, N.J., Feb. 6, 1939; d. Michael and Rosaria Trivigno; m. William F. Benedict, Oct. 3, 1964' children: Gerard Michael, Willliam Francis. BS in Edn., Seton Hall U., 1978; MA in Adminstrn., Jersey City State Coll., 1989. Math tchr. Wayne (N.J.) Hills High Sch., 1978-79, Ramsey (N.J.) High Sch., 1980, Lakeland Regional High Sch., Wanaque, N.J., 1980—; advisor Vol. in Edn., Passaic County, N.J., 1986-89, Student Asst. Team, Lakeland High Sch., Wanaque, N.J., 1990—; coord. student/tchr. lunch program for at-risk students, 1991—. Leader 4-H Clubs, Wayne, N.J., 1975-88; advisor Parish Ch. Coun., Wayne, N.J., 1989—. Mem. Assn. Math. Tchrs. N.J., Nat. Tchrs. of Math., ASCD. Roman Catholic. Home: 45 Brandywine Rd Wayne NJ 07470

BENEFIEL, DIANE MARIE, obstetrics, home health nurse supervisor, educator; b. Albuquerque, June 15, 1957; d. Bryant Michael and Barbara (Thomason) Curry; m. Randy Benefiel, June 1, 1979; children: Darin Michelle, Bryant Randal. BSN, Point Loma Coll., 1979; MSN, Calif. State U. Dominguez Hill, Carson, 1993. RN, Calif.; cert. pub. health nurse; cert. BCLS instr. Am. Heart Assn.; cert. neonatal resuscitation hosp. based instr. Am. Heart Assn. Charge and staff RN St. Francis Hosp., Tulsa, 1979-80; staff RN Boswell Meml. Hosp., Sun City, Ariz., 1980-82, Sharp Meml. Hosp., San Diego, 1982-83; charge RN diabetic edn. Coll. Pk. Hosp., San Diego, 1982-84; edn. dir., staff RN Santa Paula (Calif.) Meml. Hosp., 1984-89; staff RN Antelope Valley Hosp. Meml. Ctr., Lancaster, Calif., 1989-90; clin. instr. Antelope Valley Community Coll., Lancaster, 1990—; staff RN Visiting Nurse's Assn., Lancaster, 1990-94; supr. Antelope Valley Home Care, 1994—. Mem. NAACOG, Phi Kappa Phi. Nazarene. Home: 2810 W Avenue L8 Lancaster CA 93536-3339

BENENSON, ESTHER SIEV (MRS. WILLIAM BENENSON), nursing home administrator, gerontologist; b. Jerusalem, Aug. 16, 1925 (parents Am. citizens); d. Joshua and Anna (Sanders) Siev; A.A.S., Queens Coll., 1957; B.S., Hunter Coll., 1972, M.S., 1974; M.Ed., Tchrs. Coll., Columbia U., 1976, Ed.D. in Gerontology, 1981; m. William Benenson, Sept. 15, 1957; children—Michael J., Sharon G., Amy L., Blanche S. Exec. dir. Flushing (N.Y.) Manor Nursing Home, 1959—, Flushing Manor Care Center, 1974—. Registered nurse; lic. X-ray technician; adj. asso. prof. C.W. Post Coll., L.I. U., 1972-77, also mem. adv. bd., dept. health care and public adminstrn.; mem. Bd. Examiners Licensing Nursing Home Adminstrs. N.Y. State, 1970-74; adv. council N.Y. State Health Planning Commn., 1974; bd. dirs. Health Systems Agy. of N.Y.C., 1994, 1st v.p. Queensboro Council Social Welfare. Fellow Am. Coll. Health Care Adminstrs., Am. Acad. Med. Adminstrs., Royal Soc. Health; mem. Soc. Public Health Educators, Gerontol. Soc., N.Y. State Nursing Home Assn. Am. Public Health Assn.

BENES, SUSAN CARLETON, neuro-ophthalmologist; b. Cleve., Jan. 2, 1948; d. Edward Fulton and Rita Elyse (True) Carleton; m. James David Benes, Dec. 27, 1969; children—Jennifer, David, Olivia. B.S., U. Mich., 1970, cert. tchr., 1969; M.D., Med. Coll. Pa., 1975. Diplomate Am. Bd. Ophthalmology. Resident in internal medicine Lankenau Hosp., Phila., 1975-76; resident in ophthalmology Wills Eye Hosp., Phila., 1976-79, fellow in neuro-ophthalmology, 1979-80, staff physician Wills Eye and Grad. Hosp., 1980-81; lectr. in neuro-ophthalmology Kenyatta U., Nairobi, Kenya, 1980; asst. prof. neuro-ophthalmology Ohio State U., Columbus, 1981-86, assoc. prof., 1987—; cons., Quito, Ecuador, 1985, Dept. Energy in Marshall Islands, South Pacific, 1987; cons. surgeon blindness and malnutrition survey, Honduras, 1992; advisor to undergrads. Ohio State U., 1984-86. Contbr. chpts. to books, articles to profl. jours. Bd. govs. First Community Ch.; leader Camp Fire Girls, Columbus, 1983-88. Recipient Wakian Service award Camp Fire, Inc., 1986; grantee NIH, 1984-87, 87-94. Fellow Am. Acad. Ophthalmology; mem. AMA, Ohio State Med. Assn., Franklin County Med. Soc., Alpha Omega Alpha, Kappa Kappa Gamma.

BENES DANIELS, LAURA, utilities administrator; b. Milw., Sept. 4, 1958; d. Raymond Joseph and Carol Rae (Mecikalski) Mrowinski; m. Robert Gary Benes, Apr. 24, 1984 (div. 1991); children: Lane Benes, Blair Benes; m. Michael Robert Daniels, May 22, 1993; 1 child, Lauren Daniels. BS, U. Wis., Platteville, 1980. Cert. labor/mgmt. rels. Loss control rep. U.S. Ins. Group, Edince, Minn., 1980-82; tech. rep. Home Ins. Co., Brookfield, Wis., 1982-84; safety specialist Milw. Water Works, 1984-86, water distbn. asst. mgr., 1986-90, water distbn. mgr., 1990—. Mem. NAFE, Am. Water Works Assn. (com. chair 1984—), Am. Pub. Works Assn., Wis. Assn. Equal Opportunity. Office: Milw Water Works 841 N Broadway Milwaukee WI 53202

BENGEL, BERYL KENNEY, retired elementary education educator; b. Brooksville, Ky., Oct. 18, 1911; d. Lewis Wadsworth and Nicie Elizabeth (Kirk) Kenney; m. Joseph Nichlas Bengel, Aug. 15, 1942. BA, U. Ky., 1941; MS, U. So. Calif., 1954. Tchr. art, sci. Bracken County Schs., Brooksville, 1935-43; tchr. art, linguistics Lynwood (Calif.) Unified Sch. Dist., 1946-76. Moderator of deacons Oceanside, Calif. Presbyn. Ch., 1990-92, elder, 1995—; 1st v.p. Oceanside Dem. Club, 1991-92; pres. Stars of Palomar, 1987-89, Oceanside chpt. AARP, 1992-94, San Luis Rey Sr. Ctr., 1985-87, 94-95. Winner 3 top awards for watercolor painting Oceanside Festival of Arts, state, nat. convs. Gen. Fedn. Woman's Clubs. Mem. NEA, AAUW (pres. Huntington Park chpt. 1959-60), Calif. Tchrs. Assn. (life), PTA (life), Calif. Red. Tchrs. Assn., Woman's Club of Carlsbad (pres. 1982-84, Woman of Yr. 1984), North County Art Assn., Calrsbad Oceanside Art Assn., San Diguito Art League, Parliamentary Law Club, Palomar Orchid Soc., Cymbidium Soc. Am., Am. Orchid Soc., Epsilon Sigma Omicron, Delta Kappa Gamma (pres. chpt. 1862-67, 86-88). Democrat. Presbyterian. Home: 2730 MacDonald St Oceanside CA 92054

BENHAM, PRISCILLA CARLA, religion educator, college president; b. Berkeley, Calif., Jan. 30, 1950; d. Carl Thomas and Bebe (Harrison) Patten; m. Donald W. Benham, Mar. 30, 1986; 1 child, Charmaine P. Benham. BS summa cum laude, Patten Coll., 1969; BA in Psychology, Coll. Holy Names, 1971; MA in New Testament with honors, Wheaton Coll., 1972; PhD in New Testament, Drew U., 1976. Prof. New Testament Patten Coll., Oakland, Calif., 1975—, pres., 1983—; v.p. Christian Evang. Chs. Am., Oakland, 1989—; co-pastor Christian Cathedral, Oakland, 1964—; co-founder Christian Cathedral Chorale, Oakland, 1975—; tree planting participant David Ben Gurion Forest, Israel, 1975. Co-author: Before the Times, 1989, The World of the Early Church, 1991; mem. editorial bd. Pentecostal Theology; contbr. articles to profl. jours. Violinist Redwood Symphony. Mem. AAUP, Am. Assn. Higher Edn., Am. Assn. Pres. Ind. Colls. and Univs. (bd. dirs.), Am. Coun. Edn., Assn. Ind. Calif. Colls. and Univs., Soc. Bibl. Lit., Am. Acad. Religion, Bar-Ilan Assn. of the Greater Bay Area, Western Coll. Assn. Pres. Small Ind. Colls., Regional Assn. East Bay Colls. and Univs. (mem. at-large exec. com.), Oakland C. of C., Nat. Assn. Intercollegiate Athletics, Rotary of Oakland, Phi Delta Kappa. Office: Patten Coll 2433 Coolidge Ave Oakland CA 94601

BENICA, SHERRY L., pediatric critical care nurse; b. Phila.; d. Harry W. and Katherine P. (Coulter) Waples; m. Arthur G. Benica, Mar. 26, 1983. Diploma, Chestnut Hill Hosp., Phila., 1974; BS in Biology, Chestnut Hill Coll., Phila., 1976; BSN, U. Pa., 1981, MSN, 1987. Cert. critical care nurse. Staff nurse, head nurse, ednl. nurse specialist Children's Hosp. of Phila., 1976-91; head nurse pediatric and neonatal critical care Robert Wood Johnson U. Hosp., New Brunswick, N.J., 1989-92; dir. critical care nursing svcs. Children's Nat. Med. Ctr., Washington, 1992—; lectr. in field. Contbr. articles to profl. jours. Mem. AACN, SCCM, Am. Orgn. Nurse Execs., Sigma Theta Tau.

BENING, ANNETTE, actress; b. Topeka, May 29, 1958; m. Steven White (div.); m. Warren Beatty, 1992; children: Kathlyn Bening Beatty,Benjamin Beatty. Student, Mesa Coll.; theatre degree, San Francisco State U.; studied at, Am. Conservatory Theatre. Films include The Great Outdoors, 1988, Valmont, 1989, The Grifters, 1990 (Acad. award nomination best supporting actress 1990), Postcards from the Edge, 1990, Guilty by Suspicion, 1991, Regarding Henry, 1991, Bugsy, 1991, Love Affair, 1994; stage appearances Coastal Disturbances, 1986, (Tony award nomination 1986, Clarence Derwin award 1987, Theatre World award 1987), Spoils of War, 1988; TV movies Manhunt for Claude Dallas, 1986, Hostage, 1988. Office: care CAA 9830 Wilshire Blvd Beverly Hills CA 90212

BENJAMIN, ADELAIDE WISDOM, community volunteer and activist; b. New Orleans, Aug. 23, 1932; d. William Bell and Mary (Freeman) Wisdom; m. Edward Bernard Benjamin Jr., May 11, 1957; children: Edward Wisdom, Mary Dabney, Ann Leith, Stuart Minor. Student, Hollins Coll., 1950-52; BA in English, Newcomb Coll., 1954; JD, Tulane U., 1956; student, Loyola U., New Orleans, 1980-81; grad. extension program Sewanee Theol. Sch., U. South, 1982. Assoc. Wisdom, Stone, Pigman and Benjamin, New Orleans, 1956-58; tchr. ext. courses Tulane U., 1984—; postgrad.; speaker, panelist on school issues various local and nat. groups. Mem. Tulane Law Rev., 1954-56. Pres. bd. New Orleans Symphony, 1984-89; trustee, Mary Freeman Wisdom Charitable Found., sec., 1987-92, pres., 1990-94, treas., 1994—; pres. E&A Charitable Found., New Orleans, 1983—; bd. dirs. Nat. Symphony Orch., Washington, 1992—, RosaMary Charitable Found., New Orleans, 1978—, Loyola Univ., New Orleans, 1989—, La. Mus. Found. Bd., New Orleans, 1989—, exec. com., 1991—, Children's Hosp., New Orleans, 1976-79, Southeast La. Girl Scouts Coun., New Orleans, 1989—, Louise S. McGehee Sch., New Orleans, 1990—, v.p., 1991—, La. Nature and Sci. Ctr., New Orleans, 1992—, Newcomb Children's Ctr., New Orleans, 1991-94, New Orleans Mus. Art Fellows Forum, 1991—; mem. adv. bd. dept. psychiatry LSU Med. Ctr., 1992—; active Trinity Episc. Ch., New Orleans, sec. parish coun., 1973-75, sec. vestry, 1975-79, leader Trinity Quartet, 1979-84; local YWCA, 1967-75, 76-79, sec. bd. dirs., 1967-68, 1st v.p., 1968-69; trustee Metairie Park Country Day Sch., 1971-79, sec., 1976-79, pres. PTA, 1975-76; mem. Loving Cup selection com. New Orleans Times Picayune, 1985, Bur. Govtl. Rsch.; adv. bd. Pub. Radio Sta. WWNO, 1980—; bd. dirs Parenting Ctr., 1981—, chmn. by-laws com., 1983-84, chmn. pers. com., 1982-83; adv. bd Tulane Summer Lyric Theatre, Tulane U., 1972—, pres. adv. bd., 1977-79. Recipient Weiss Brotherhood award Nat. Conf. Christians and Jews, 1986, Outstanding Philanthropist, Nat. Soc. Fundraising Execs., 1986, Volunteer Activist Award, St. Elizabeth Guild, 1986, Jr. League Sustainer award, 1987, Disting. Alumna award McGehee Sch., 1987, George Washington Honor Medal for Individual Achievement, Freedom Found. at Valley Forge, 1988, Living and Giving award Juvenile Diabetes Found. 1991, Outstanding Citizen New Orleans award La. Colonials, 1994, Jacques Yenni award Outstanding Community Svc. Sch. Bus. Adminstrn. Loyola Univ., 1994, Integritas Vita award for outstanding cmty. svc. Loyola U., 1994; named Goodwill Ambassador for Louisiana Gov.'s Commn. Internat. Trade, Industry and Tourism, 1987, Sweet Art, Contemporary Arts Ctr., 1988, Significant Role Model, Young Leadership Coun., 1988, Woman of Distinction S.E. La. Girl Scout Coun., 1992. Mem. ABA, LWV, La. Bar Assn., New Orleans Bar Assn., Jr. League New Orleans (exec. com. 1971-72, bd. dirs. 1967-72), Ind. Women's Orgn., Com. 21, Am. Symphony Orch. League, Quarante Club (2d v.p. 1978-79), Sybarites Club, Debutante Club, Le Debut des Jeunes Filles Club, New Orleans Town Gardners (pres. 1979-80), Thomas Wolfe Soc. (life mem.). Home: 1837 Palmer Ave New Orleans LA 70118-6215

BENJAMIN, ANN-ELDEENE ISOBEL, psychiatric nurse, educator; b. Detroit, Mar. 18, 1921; d. Charles Ludwig and Ruby Eldeene (Brokaw) Bruckner; m. Arthur Gregory Walsh, Oct. 1941; children: Gregory, Margaret Mary Kools, Patricia Marshall; m. Frank Anson, June 25, 1965; m. Austin Charles Benjamin, May 2, 1981. ASN, Edison C.C., Port Charlotte, Fla.; BS, Edgecliff Coll., 1963; MEd, Xavier U., 1965. RN, Fla.; cert. tchr., Ohio. Dist. health coord., dir. guidance dept. Williamsburg (Ohio) Local Schs., 1966-81; staff nurse Englewood (Fla.) Community Hosp.; RN, supr. 1st shift Charlotte Community Mental Health, Port Charlotte, Fla.; staff nurse, educator, quality mgmt. Able Care Home Health, Englewood. Mem. Ohio Edn. Assn. (life). Home: 8237 Archie St Grove City FL 34224 Office: Able Care Home Health 549 S Indiana Ave Englewood FL 34223

BENJAMIN, ELLEN JANE, public policy analyst; b. Boston, Mar. 11, 1950; d. Alan K. and Peggy Ann (Biel) B. BA in Social Svc. Adminstrn. and Policy, Park Coll., 1976; postgrad., U. N.H., 1980, Portland State U., 1991—. Rsch. asst. to dir. planning and rsch. State Office Mo. Dept. Social Svcs., Jefferson City, Mo., 1974-75; com. asst. Maine Legis. Com. Health and Instl. Svcs., Augusta, Maine, 1976-77; planning and rsch. asst. York County Employment and Tng. Agy., Biddeford, Maine, 1978-79; rsch. assoc. small bus. devel. program Whittemore Sch. Bus. and Econs., U. N.H., Durham, 1980; legis. rsch. asst. Office Legis. Svcs. Rsch. Divsn., Concord, N.H., 1981; legis. analyst joint com. rev. agys. and programs, sunset com. Gen. Ct. N.H., 1981-82; senate rsch. analyst Pres. of the N.H. Senate, Concord, 1983; dist. coord. U.S. Senator Ernest Hollings 1984 Presdl. Primary, Dover, N.H., 1984; sr. policy analyst com. on human resources Ea. Regional Conf., Coun. of State Govt., N.Y.C., 1984-86; dir. policy New Eng. Coun., Inc., Boston, 1987; pub. policy analyst Portland, Oreg., 1988-94, San Diego, 1994—. Mem. NAFE.

BENJAMIN, GINA G., screenwriter, producer, author; b. Trenton, N.J., Mar. 22, 1959; d. Syd and Isabella Benjamin. BA, Rollins Coll. V.p., creative mgr. Winner Communications Corp., 1985-88. Producer, writer (documentary series) All The Best; producer, co-writer (suspense drama) Ripcord--The D.B. Cooper Mystery, 1991, All the Best, 1991—, (documentary film) The Castle; producer (action advencure film) Ace--The Bill Lancaster Story; author: A Chute in the Dark: The Making of the Motion Picture Ripcord, (with Gene Cetrone) Ripcord--The D.B. Cooper Mystery, Fade to Black: Sudden Death and Dissolution in Hollywood, 1992, Hollywood Wedding Album, 1992; assoc. editor The Valley Voice; con. Mem. Assn. Ind. Video and Film Makers, Am. Film Inst., Nat. Audubon Soc., N.Y. Sci. Acad., Internat. Women's Writing Guild, Producer's Club. Democrat. Office: Panda Pictures Corp 20507 Dag Hammarskjold New York NY 10017-2201

BENJAMIN, JANICE YUKON, small business owner; b. Kansas City, Mo., Aug. 12, 1951; d. Stanley and Frances (Weneck) Yukon; m. Bert Lyon Benjamin, June 14, 1975; children: Brett David, Blair Yukon. AS, Bradford Coll., 1971; BA, Newcomb Coll., 1973; MA, U. Mo., 1978. Tchr. secondary, dept. chmn. Shawnee Mission (Kans.) Sch. Dist., 1973-80; career counselor Career Mgmt. Ctr., Kansas City, 1980-82, pres., owner, 1982—; ptnr. Career Mgmt. Press, Kansas City, 1983—, The MBL Human Resources Cons. Group, 1989-91. Contbr. articles to profl. jours.; co-author career planning book. Bd. dirs. community jr. League, Kansas City, 1988-89, v.p. 1989-90, pres.-elect 1990-91, pres. 1991-92; bd. dirs. Menorah Med. Ctr. Aux., Kansas City, 1984— (auditor 1990-92, v.p. 1994—), Women's Found. Greater Kansas City, 1991—, chmn. bd. devel., 1993—; bd. dirs. Kansas City Friends of Alvin Ailey, 1992-94, co-chmn. planning com. adv. bd., 1994—; bd. dirs. Cen. Exch., Kansas City, 1988-90; mem. adv. bd. women's coun. U. Mo., Kansas City, 1988-89; initiator, sponsor Kansas City Youth Vol. Svc. awards United Way, 1989-90, adv. com. Heart of Am., 1994—; mem. Promise Project Steering Com., Kansas City Consensus, 1994—, co-chmn. Youth Declaration. Recipient Miss T.E.E.N. Encouraging Excellence award, 1990; named One of 25 Up and Comers award Jr. Achievement of Mid. Am., 1994. Mem. ASTD, Heart of Am. Relocation Coun. (bd. dirs.), K.C. Employment Mgrs. Assn. Republican. Jewish. Office: Career Mgmt Ctr 8301 State Line Rd # 202 Kansas City MO 64114-2019

BENJAMIN, SHEILA PAULETTA, secondary education educator; b. Sept. 28, 1948. AA, Montreat-Anderson Coll., 1966; BA in History, Belhaven Coll., 1968; MEd in History, U. Tampa, 1979. Cert. gifted, social studies and bible tchr. Tchr. Eisenhower Jr. H.S., Gibsonton, Fla., 1980-93; now tchr. internat. baccalaureate Internat. Baccalaureate Hillsborough H.S., Tampa, Fla.; clinician tchr. Suncoast Area Tchr. Tng. Honors Program; supervising tchr. Fla. Beginning Tchr. Program; dir. workshops in field. Aviation educator USAF-CAP. Recipient Photography awards Fla. Strawberry Festival and Hillsborough County Fair; Latin Am. Studies grantee NEH, 1983, African Studies 1985; Fulbright scholar Egypt, 1986, Honduras, 1993. Mem. ASCD, DAR, Nat. Space Soc., Nat. Coun. Soc. Studies, World Aerospace Edn. Orgn. (U.S. del., Amman, Jordan), Gulf Coast Archeol. Soc., Fla. Alliance for Geography, Fla. Aerospace Edn. Assn. (bd. dirs.), Fla. Anthrop. Soc. (bd. dirs., Appreciation award, Preservation award), Men of Menendez (Historic Fla. Militia Inc.), Mid. East Educators Network, Hillsborough Classroom Tchr. Assn. (NEA), Hillsborough County/Fla. Social Studies Coun., Young Astronauts, Bibl. Archeol. Soc., Challenger Ctr. Found. (founding sponsor), Fulbright Alumni Assn., Sun-N-Fun EAA, Phi Delta Kappa. Home: 605 Fieldstone Dr Brandon FL 33511-7936 Office: Hillsborough High Sch 5000 Central Ave Tampa FL 33603

BENJAMIN, SUSAN HARRIS, counselor; b. Balt., Oct. 14, 1944; d. Harry Sherman and Dorothy Lee (Cohee) Harris; m. Raymond McAllister, Nov. 28, 1968 (div.); m. James Philip Benjamin, Jan. 30, 1983; children: Kyle Harris, Tess Margaret. AA in Retailing, Richmond (Va.) Profl. Inst., 1965; BA in Applied Psychology, Southwestern Coll., Sante Fe, 1993, postgrad. in Art Therapy, 1993—. Asst. buyer Woodward and Lothrop, Washington, 1965-67, Derry and Toms, London, 1967; buyer Lane Bryant, N.Y.C., 1968-71, Honeybee, N.Y.C., 1972-73; office mgr./bookkeeper Coleman Assocs., Hoboken, N.J., 1973-80; owner Custom Bookkeeping Svc., 1980-93; parent-aide vol. Child Abuse Prevention, Parent Assistance Ctr., 1988-91; case mgr. Parent Asst. Ctr., Sante Fe, 1991-93, dir. parent-aide program, 1993—. Recipient award Point of Light Found., 1992. Mem. Mothers Against Drunk Drivers. Democrat. Zen Buddhist. Office: Parent Assistance Ctr 185 Airport Rd Santa Fe NM 87505-2802

BENLON, LISA L., state legislator; b. July 9, 1953; m. Randel; 2 children. Student, Johnson County C.C. Councilman City of Shawnee, 1988-91; rep. dist. 17 State of Kans., 1991—; mgr. acctg. office. Home: 7303 Earnshaw St Shawnee KS 66216-3505 Office: Kans Ho of Reps State Capitol Topeka KS 66612*

BENNER, MARY WRIGHT, marketing professional; b. Chgo., Aug. 4, 1956; d. Robert V.L. and Sara Helen (Beeler) W.; m. Thomas G. Benner, Aug. 8, 1987; children: Sara Eleanor, Robert Fox. BA, Conn. Coll., 1979; MBA, Columbia U., 1983. Rsch. assoc. Acad. for Contemporary Problems, Washington, 1979-81; rating specialist Standard & Poor's, N.Y.C., 1983-84; asst. adminstr. Twp. of Princeton, N.J., 1984-86; v.p. Fin. Guaranty Ins. Co., N.Y.C., 1986—. Mem. Pub. Works Forum (bd. dirs. 1986-88), Assn. for Govtl. Leasing and Fin. (bd. dirs. 1991—, treas. 1994—). Methodist.

Home: 33 Sommer Ave Maplewood NJ 07040-3127 Office: Fin Guaranty Ins Co 115 Broadway New York NY 10006

BENNETT, ANNA DELL, minister, religion educator, retired elementary school educator; b. Cobb Hill, Ky., Jan. 11, 1935; d. James Edison Shoemaker and Chrystal (Abney) Shoemaker-Hurst; m. Stanley Bennett, Oct. 7, 1950 (dec. Jan. 1987); children: Eddie Wayne, James Lloyd, Kathryn Melissa. BS, U. Dayton, 1966; MS in Elem. Classroom Teaching, Wright State U., 1974, M in Gifted Teaching, 1980; Assoc. Bibl., Centerville Bible Coll., 1985, degree in theology, 1987. Lic. minister, Ohio; ordained minister Open Bible Standard Chs., 1992. Tchr. West Carrollton (Ohio) Bd. Edn., 1966-86; dir. Christian edn., Way of the Cross Ch., Dayton, Ohio, 1989—; founder, adminstr. Noah's Ark Pre-Sch., 1994; adj. prof. Mt. St. Joseph Coll., Cin., 1981-85. Recipient plaque Mt. St. Joseph Coll., Cin., 1985. Republican. Home: 1916 Hickory Ridge Dr Beavercreek OH 45432 Office: Open Bible Way of the Cross Ch 612 Beatrice Dr Dayton OH 45404-1411

BENNETT, BERNICE E., association executive, healthcare administrator; b. New Orleans, Aug. 4, 1948; d. Philip Kemp and Bernice Mitchell Alexander; m. Glen Carlson Bennett, Nov. 26, 1969; children: Dwight Alexander, Denise Lynn. BS, Grambling State U., 1969; MPH, U. Mich., 1973. Cert. health edn. specialist. Tchr. Denver Pub. Sch. System, 1969-71; coord. patient edn. West Balt. Health Care Corp., 1973-74; instr. Johns Hopkins U., Balt., 1974-77; project dir. Community Coun. Greater Dallas, 1977-79; agy. mgr. Dallas Area Agy. on Aging, 1979-82; dir. patient svcs. and discharge planning Parkland Meml. Hosp., Dallas, 1982-87; dir. health promotion and wellness Group Health Assn., Washington, 1987-93; dir. spl. projects Nat. Assn. Pub. Hosps., Washington, 1993—; partnership coord. Am. Internat. Health Alliance, Washington, 1993—. Participant Leadership Plano, 1987; pres. Briggs Chaney Mid. Sch., Silver Spring, Md., 1991-93; mem. del. coun. Nat. Coun. on Aged, Washington, 1992—; pres. bd. dirs. YWCA Nat. Capitol Area, Washington, 1994. Mem. APHA, Alpha Kappa Alpha. Office: Nat Assn Pub Hosps 1212 New York Ave Ste 800 Washington DC 20335

BENNETT, BETH ANN, accountant; b. Berwyn, Ill., Aug. 10, 1950; d. Tom R. and Margaret E. (Culton) Kollmeyer; m. Apr. 11, 1970 (dec. Apr. 5, 1985); children: Lori, Marcus, Lisa. AAS in Acctg., Danville Area C.C., 1989; BS in Acctg., St. Mary of the Woods, 1995. Sec. NCR, Danville, Ill., 1968-73, United Meth. Ch., Covington, Ind., 1985-87; acct. Manning Acctg., Veedersburg, Ind., 1987—. Auditing com. United Meth. Ch., Covington, 1992—, Sun. sch. tchr., 1982-90. Recipient scholarship Am. Soc. Women Accts., 1992. Mem. Inst. Mgmt. Accts. Home: 1017 Orchard Dr Covington IN 47932

BENNETT, BETH HANEY, caseworker; b. Calhoun, Ga., Dec. 21, 1949; d. Jack Carter and Ruby Elizabeth (Drummond) Haney; m. Harry Jolley Bennett, July 9, 1971 (div. Jan. 9, 1985); 1 child, Chet Austin. BA in Social Work, West Ga. Coll., 1971; postgrad., U. Ga., 1994—. Exec. dir. Voluntary Action Ctr., Calhoun, Ga., 1971-75; career ednl. counselor Calhoun (Ga.) High Sch., 1979-81; sales exec. Haney Jewelry Co., Calhoun, 1981-83; cons., career educator Dalton (Ga.) Coll., 1983-85; social worker N.W. Psychoeducational Program, Rome, Ga., 1985-88; social svc. specialist I Whitfield City Dept. of Family and Children Svcs., Dalton, 1988-91, caseworker, supr., 1991—. Mem. Cursillos (Episcopal), 1991—. Grantee Ga. County Welfare Bd. Assn., 1993. Mem. AAUW, Ga. County Welfare Assn., NOW, Kiwanis. Democrat. Episcopalian. Home: 3087 Hurricane Rd Rocky Face GA 30740 Office: Whitfield County Dept Family/Children Svcs 1142 Chattanooga Rd PO Box 1203 Dalton GA 30722-1203

BENNETT, BOBBIE JEAN, state official; b. Gwinnett County, Ga., July 13, 1940; d. William Claude and Clara Maude (Nichols) Holcome; BBA magna cum laude, Ga. State U., 1973; 1 child, Terri Lynne. With Ga. State Merit System, Atlanta, 1960—, sr. acct., 1967, asst. div. dir., 1968-70, fiscal officer, 1970-74, div. dir., 1975-78, asst. dep. commr., 1978—, asst. commr., 1985—, dep. commr., 1992, commr. 1992. Mem. Ga. Fiscal Mgmt. Coun., Ga. Coun. Pers. Adminstrn., Employers Coun. Flexible Compensation (bd. dirs.), Nat. Assn. Deferred Compensation Adminstrs. (sec., past pres.), Nat. Assn. State Personnel Execs. (mem. exec. bd.), Ga. Govt. Benefit Assn., Atlanta Govt. Benefit Assn., Atlanta Health Care Alliance, State and Local Govt. Benefit Assn. (past pres.), Internat. Personnel Mgmt. Assn. (pres. Atlanta chpt.), Internat. Found. on Employee Benefits (com. mem.), Beta Gamma Sigma, Phi Kappa Phi, Beta Alpha Psi. Democrat. Home: 2072 Malabar Dr NE Atlanta GA 30345-1624 Office: State Merit System 200 Piedmont Ave SE Atlanta GA 30334-9000

BENNETT, CAROL(INE) ELISE, reporter, actress; b. New Orleans, Dec. 27, 1938; d. Gerald Clifford Graham and Edna Doris (Toennies) Kerr; m. Ralph Decker Bennett Jr., Feb. 27, 1966; children: Ralph Decker III, Katherine Elise. BA, U. B.C., Vancouver, Can., 1960; BLS, McGill U., Montreal, Que., Can., 1962. Libr. various locations, 1962-76; reporter TV/radio Washington-Ala. News Reports, Washington, 1981—. Appeared on stage Girl in My Soup, 1978; in film Prime Risk, 1984; host weekly TV program Modern Maturity, 1986-88. Vol. reader Recording for the Blind, Washington, 1985—. Mem. SAG, AFTRA, Actor's Equity, Soc. Profl. Journalists. Home: 115 Southwood Ave Silver Spring MD 20901-1918

BENNETT, CAROLYN, government agency administrator; b. St. Louis, Sept. 5, 1943; d. Haywood Parker and Hettie (Jackson) Pease; m. Franklin Lewis Bennett, Aug. 28, 1965; children: Franklin Christopher, Nicole Denise. BA, Ind. U./Purdue U., Indpls., 1982; MS, Ind. U., Indpls., 1986. Lic. practical nurse, Ind. Practical nurse Meth. Hosp., Indpls., 1965-66; clk. U.S. Postal Svc., Indpls., 1966-78, tng. technician, 1978-84, assoc. tng. and devel. specialist, 1984-86, EEO counselor, investigator, 1986-88, supr. tnr., 1988-90, mgr. tng., 1990-93, employee assistance program coord., 1993—; counselor Human Svc. Assoc., Inc., Indpls., 1986-94; pvt. practice, 1994—. Sec. Black Presbyn. Caucus, Indpls., 1993. Inducted into Nat. Disting. Svc. Registry for Counseling and Devel. Mem. ACA, Delta Sigma Theta. Democrat. Office: Human Svc Assocs Inc 6100 N Keystone Ave # 528 Indianapolis IN 46220

BENNETT, CATHERINE JUNE, data processing manager, educator, consultant; b. Augusta, Ga., June 19, 1950; d. Robert Stogner and Catherine Sue (Jordan) Robinson; m. Danny Marvin Bennett, Sept. 5, 1971; children: Timothy Jordan, Robert Daniel. BS in Stats., U. Ga., 1971, MA in Bus., 1973. Programmer William M. Shenkel & Assocs., Athens, Ga., 1971-73; systems analyst U. Ga., Athens, 1973-76; product cons. ISA/SUNGARD, Atlanta, 1976-78, project leader, 1978-80, mgr. product support, 1980-85, hotline mgr., sr. fin. specialist, 1986-88; mem. edn. staff Investment Client Support, 1988-90, mgr. investment reporting, 1990-91, mgr. reporting, 1991-93, mgr. devel., 1993—. Den leader pack # 419 Cub Scouts, 1989-90, treas., 1990-95; head official Duluth Thunderbolts, 1994; mem. Duluth coun. Gwinnett County (Ga.) Swim League. Avocations: bridge, swimming, travel. Home: 3604 N Berkeley Lake Rd Duluth GA 30136 Office: ISA/SUNGARD 500 Northridge Rd Atlanta GA 30350-3315

BENNETT, CHRISTINE LORA, English language educator; b. Summit, N.J., July 25, 1948; d. Carl Emil and Helen Katherine (Rajoppi) Gerber; m. James Martin Bennett, Nov. 25, 1971; children: Stephan, Karin, John-David. BA, Fairleigh Dickinson U., 1970; MA, Kean Coll., 1989; postgrad., U. Md., 1975, U. Heidelberg, Fed. Republic Germany, 1975. Tchr. Elliott St. Sch., Newark, 1970-71, Lake Parsippany (N.J.) Sch., 1971-74; art specialist Big Bend Community Coll., Mannheim, Fed. Republic of Germany, 1975-76; instr. English as a Second Lang. Inlingua Sch. Langs., Summit, N.J., 1980-81, Summit Sch. System, 1986-89, Summit Community Sch., 1989—; adj. faculty Union County Coll., Cranford, N.J., 1989—. Vice chair Young Reps., Summit, 1966-70; mem. Union County Environ. Health Adv. Com., Westfield, N.J., 1971-73. Mem. N.J. Tchrs. English to Speakers of Other Langs.-Bilingual Educators, Inc., Phi Kappa Phi, Kappa Delta Pi. Republican. Presbyterian.

BENNETT, CONNIE SUE, food products executive, real estate investor; b. Richland Center, Wis., Oct. 4, 1955; d. Robert Eugene And Lillian Theresa (Crusan) Cottrill; m. James A. Bennett III, Oct. 22, 1977 (div. Jan. 1989). Grad. high sch., Ithaca, Wis. Owner, chef A Taste Of Heaven Restaurant, Anchorage, 1978-80, Saucy Sisters Catering, Anchorage, 1980-86; pres. Good Taste Inc., Anchorage, 1986—, Sable Properties, 1990—, Flamingo Properties, 1989—. Mem. adv. bd. Hugh O'Brian Found., 1987-89. Named Small Bus. Person of Yr. State of Alaska, 1987, U.S. Western Region, 1987. Mem. Internat. Assn. Cooking Profl., Am. Inst. Wine and Food, James Beard Found., Inflight Food Svc. Assn. Office: PO Box 202530 Anchorage AK 99520-2530

BENNETT, DEBIE ANN, English language educator; b. Salem, Oreg., May 15, 1950; d. Wilburn Orion and Corinne Marie (Passarella) B.; m. Robert Joseph Matuszak, July 22, 1972 (div. June 1982); 1 child, Daniel Robert; m. Bobby S. Grzywacz, Aug. 6, 1988. BA, No. Ill. U., 1972; MA, Miami U., Oxford, Ohio, 1974. Cert. secondary English tchr. Tchr. English Manitou Springs (Colo.) H.S., 1974—; instr./presenter Ednl. Kinesiology, Colo., 1992—. Contbr. poetry to profl. jours. Mem. NEA, ASCD, Colo. Lang. Arts Soc., Pikes Peak Edn. Assn. Home: PO Box 4317 Woodland Park CO 80866-4317 Office: Manitou Springs H S 401 El Monte Pl Manitou Springs CO 80829-2502

BENNETT, DEBRA PEARL, interior designer; b. Atlanta, Aug. 28, 1957; d. William Walter and Dorothy (Sabb) B. BA in Art History, Swarthmore Coll., 1979; BA in Interior Design Magna Cum Laude, Mt. Vernon Coll., 1989. cert. NCIDQ, 1994. Asst. fashion coord. Raleigh Stores Corp., Washington, 1979-80; sec., traffic mgr. Kal & Salan Advt., Bethesda, Md., 1980-84; office mgr. Nat. Safety Coun., Washington, 1984; legal sec. Patton, Boggs & Blow, Washington, 1984-89; jr. designer Bennett-Hattan Design, Washington, 1988-89; intern Copeland, Kreiger Assocs., Washington, 1989; interior designer Rita St. Clair Assocs., Balt., 1989-92; designer, pres. DB Interiors, Balt., 1992-94; sr. designer Victor Shargai & Assocs, Washington, 1994—; cons. Austin Kuester, Inc., Alexandria, Va., 1993-94, Janet Schirn Design Group, Chgo., 1993, Ch. Svcs. Restoration Contractors, Inc., Balt.; instr. Mt. Vernon Coll., Washington, 1993; lectr. Howard Univ., Washington, 1994. Co-designer (interiors) Bonnie View Country Club, 1993, Nat. Symphony Orch. Decorator's Showhouse, 1993, Balt. Washington, Internat. Airport Food Cts., 1994. Mem. Balt. Urban League, 1990-91, Swarthmore Coll. Alumni Gospel Choir, 1994—; pres. Lafayette Sq. II Coun., Balt., 1993. Mem. Am. Soc. Interior Designers (program com. 1991-92), Orgn. Black Designers. Office: Victor Shargai & Assocs 2158 Wisconsin Ave NW Washington DC 20007

BENNETT, DORINE LEE, health information management educator; b. Madison, S.D., Sept. 8, 1957; d. Raymond and Lavonne Laura (Stoneback) Williams; m. Daniel Lee Bennett, Feb. 19, 1977; children: Teresa Marie (dec.), Lee Daniel. AA, Dakota State Coll., 1978; BS, Dakota State U., 1989. Registered record adminstr.; accredited record technician. Office mgr. Community Health Program, Madison, S.D., 1978-87; med. records mgr. Nebr. Vet.'s Home, Grand Island, Nebr., 1987; faculty Dakota State U., Madison, 1987—; cons. to healthcare facilties, 1978—; workshop presenter in field. Contbr. articles to profl. jours. Mem. AAUW (sec. 1989-93), Am. Health Info. Mgmt. Assn., S.D. Health Info. Mgmt. Assn., Delta Kappa Gamma (sec. 1994—). Office: Dakota State Univ Coll Bus/Info Systems Madison SD 57042

BENNETT, EDITH LILLIAN, lay church worker, radio personality; b. Livermore, Ky., June 21, 1931; d. Dorsey Slade and Isa Carey (Taylor) B. AS, Owensboro (Ky.) Bus. Coll., 1950; student, Mid Continent Bible Coll., Owensboro, Ky., 1991—. Various positions including sec., office mgr., writer-dir. Sta. WOMI, Owensboro, 1950—; fin. sec. Third Bapt. Ch., Owensboro, 1981—. Radio personality 4-VOC, Haiti, WOMI Radio weekly; author, compiler, editor numerous publs. on Livermore history, genealogy and slavery. Sunday sch. tchr. Third Bapt. Ch. Named to Honorable Order of Ky. Colonels, 1969, Someone Spl., Owensboro, 1984. Mem. Owensboro Choral Soc. (co-chmn., presenter MESSIAH benefits 1940—), DAR (local and state officer 1989—). Home: PO Box 6060 725 Scherm Rd 5C Owensboro KY 42302-6060 Office: Third Bapt Ch 527 Allen St Owensboro KY 42303-3438

BENNETT, ELSIE MARGARET, music school administrator; b. Detroit, Mar. 30, 1919; d. Sy and Ida (Carp) Blum; m. Morton Bennett, June 20, 1937 (dec.); children—Ronald, Kenneth. Cert., Ganapal Conservatory Detroit, 1941; B.Mus. in Theory, Wayne State U., 1945; M.A. in Music Edn., Columbia U., 1946; postgrad. Columbia U., Manhattan Sch. Music. Music studio mgr., tchr. Bennett Music Sch., Bklyn., 1946—, dir. 1946—; music arranger, 1946—; tchr. Schiff Sch. Music, 1972-80, owner, 1972—; tchr. Robotti Accordion Acad. and Pkwy. Music Sch., 1945-46; owner Margolies Sch. Music, Acad. of Music Sch.; editor Accordion World Mag., 1945-56; works include: Easy Solos for Accordion, 1946; Bass Solo Primer, 1948; Hebrew and Jewish Songs and Dances for Accordion, 1959, Vol. 1, 1951, Vol. 2, 1953; Hanon for Accordion, 1953; Accordion Music in the Home, 1953; Folk Melodies for Accordion, 1954; Five Finger Melodies for Accordion, 1954; First Steps in Scaleland for Accordion, 1956; First Steps in Chordland for Accordion, Vol. 1, 1961, Vol. II, 1961. Mem. Bklyn. Community Council. Mem. Am. Accordionists Assn. (governing bd., pres. 1973-74, plaque, 1962, service to governing bd. award 1942-60, Silver Cup 1974-75), Bklyn. Music Tchrs. Guild (dir., past sec.),, Accordion Tchrs. Guild, L.I. Music Tchrs. Assn.

BENNETT, HARRIET COOK, social worker, educator; b. Telfair County, Ga., Aug. 3, 1945; d. Harry A. and Amy H. Cook; B.A., LaGrange (Ga.) Coll., 1967; M.S.W., U. Ga., Athens, 1969; postgrad. Tulane U., 1970; m. Fredrick E. Bennett, Jr., June 6, 1971; children—Amy, Andrew. Med. social reviewer state rev. team, Dept. Family and Children Services, Atlanta, 1969-71; social worker/instr. U. Mo. Med. Center, Columbia, 1971-73; social worker Easter Seal Rehab. Center, Tampa, Fla., 1978-79, Children's Home Society Fla., St. Petersburg, 1984—; dir. LaPetite Acad., Tampa, 1980, tchr. kindergarten, 1981-84; vol. cons. Desenzano, Italy, 1976-78. Vol. fundraiser Nat. Kidney Found., Arthritis Found. Lic. clin. social worker. Mem. Northdale Civic Assn., Nat. Assn. Social Workers, Acad. Cert. Social Workers, Hillsborough County PTA. Methodist. Home: 16006 Honeysuckle Pl Tampa FL 33624-1723

BENNETT, JACQUELINE BEEKMAN, school psychologist; b. Santa Paula, Calif., Sept. 4, 1946; d. Jack Edward and Margaret Blanche (MacPherson) Beekman.; m. Thomas LeRoy Bennett Jr., Aug. 5, 1972; children: Shannon, Brian, Laurie. BA, U. Calif., Davis, 1968; MS, Colo. State U., 1975, PhD, 1984. Histologist Sch. Veterinary Medicine, Davis, 1969-71; sch. psychologist Poudre Sch. Dist. R-1, Ft. Collins, Colo., 1983—. Mem. augment panel Colo. State Grievance Bd., 1988—; nominating chmn. United Presbyn. Women, Timnath, Colo., 1982, pres., 1986; mem. Women and the Ch. com. Boulder Presbytery, Colo., 1985-86; elder Timnath Presbyn. Ch., 1985—. Mem. Colo. Soc. Sch. Psychologists (cert.), Nat. Assn. Sch. Psychologists (cert.), NEA, Am. Psychol. Assn., Ft. Collins Parents of Twins (pres. 1977-78), Sigma Xi, Phi Kappa Phi. Democrat. Club: Squaredusters (Ft. Collins) (v.p. 1977-78). Home: 213 Camino Real Fort Collins CO 80524-8907 Office: Poudre Sch Dist R-1 2407 La Porte Ave Fort Collins CO 80521-2211

BENNETT, JANICE E., insurance executive; b. St. Charles, Ill., Feb. 21, 1961; d. James L. and LaDonne J. (Rhymer) Gibbons; m. Eric L. Bennett, Dec. 12, 1986; children: Rebecca, Sarah, Nicholas. B degree cum laude, Ind. State U., 1986; cert. in gen. ins., Ins. Inst. Am., 1991. Math. tchr. Marshall (Ill.) H.S., 1986-87; customer svc. rep. Forrest Sherer, Inc., Terre Haute, Ind., 1987-89, unit leader, insurance producer's asst., 1989—. Youth leader Y Group St. Stephen's Episcopal Ch., Terre Haute, 1993—, soprano, soloist ch. choir, 1984—. Mem. Ins. Profls. Wabash Valley (pres. 1993-94), Nat. Assn. Ins. Women (sec. local chpt. 1989-90, pres.-elect 1992-93; awards chair Ind. State Coun. 1994-95). Office: Forrest Sherer Inc PO Box 900 24 N 6th St Terre Haute IN 47808-0900

BENNETT, JESSIE F., lawyer; b. Bridgeport, Conn., Mar. 2, 1958; d. Cornelius T. and Jessie F. (Sutcliffe) B.; m. Ronald J. Canuel, Nov. 3, 1990. BS in Fin. with honors, Fairfield U., 1980; JD magna cum laude, U. Bridgeport, 1986. Bar: Conn., 1986; U.S. Dist. Ct. Conn., 1987, U.S. Dist. Ct. (so. and ea. dists.) N.Y. 1989, U.S. Ct. Appeals (2d cir.) 1989, D.C. Ct. of Appeals, 1989, U.S. Supreme Ct., 1989. Jud. clk. U.S. Dist. Ct., New Haven, 1986; atty. Cohen & Wolf, Danbury, Conn., 1987-88, Davidson & Naylor, Norwalk, Conn., 1988-92, State of Conn., 1992—. Mem. ABA, Conn. Bar Assn., Danbury Bar Assn., Greater Bridgeport Bar Assn., Assn. Trial Lawyers Am., Conn. Trial Lawyers Assn., Westport Bar Assn., D.C. Bar Assn., Stamford Regional Bar Assn., Waterbury Bar Assn., Phi Delta Phi, Phi Alpha Delta (Am. Jurisprudence award in Remedies and Family Law, Kristin Ann Carveth Meml. Scholastic award). Roman Catholic. Home: 16 Hitching Post Ln Trumbull CT 06611

BENNETT, LOIS, real estate broker; b. N.Y.C., Dec. 23, 1933; d. Richard and Fern (Steinberg) B.; m. Barry Silverstein, June 8, 1958 (div. May 1978); children: Mark Shale, Susan Beth, Thomas Benjamin. BA, Smith Coll., 1955. Cert. residential specialist, broker/salesman, Fla. Counselor Women's Health Ctr., Sarasota, Fla., 1977-78; investment counselor, stockbroker Pvt. Bourse Inc., Sarasota, 1978-79; realtor-assoc. Harrison Properties, Inc., Sarasota, 1984-86; broker/salesman Mt. Vernon Realty Co., Inc., Sarasota, 1986-91; broker-salesman Re/Max Properties, Sarasota, 1991—. Bd. dirs. Planned Parenthood SW Fla., Sarasota, 1978-84, fundraising chmn., 1982-84; bd. dirs. Family Counseling Ctr., Sarasota, 1978-81, 90, Sarasota County Arts Coun.; mem. exec. com., bd. dirs. Fla. Studio Theatre, Sarasota, 1981-87; bd. dirs. Fla. West Coast Symphony, Sarasota, 1982-88; chmn. spl. events 1st ann. Sarasota French Film Festival, 1989, co-chmn. spl. events, 1990; bd. dirs. Asolo Performing Arts Ctr., Sarasota, 1990—; bd. dirs. Sarasota French Film Festival, 1989-94; mem. film commn. Com. of 100, 1989-92; chmn. Sarasota County Arts Day, 1994—. Mem. Women's Coun. Realtors, Realtors Inst. (grad.), Re/Max 100% Club, Sarasota C. of C. Office: RE/MAX Properties 1950 Landings Blvd Sarasota FL 34231

BENNETT, LYNNE DEE, writer; b. Seattle, Feb. 28, 1953; d. Hale Burroughs and Marge Ruth (Perkins) B.; m. Mark Robert Clark, Apr. 23, 1983; 1 child, Jessica Bennett Clark. BA, U. Nev., 1974; MBA, U. Calif., Berkeley, 1987. Contracts mgr. U.S. Govt., Washington, Italy, Singapore, 1975-85; freelance writer Pleasant Hill, Calif., 1987—. Contbr. articles on bus. and lifestyle subjects to numerous mags. Mem. AAUW (chair communications local br. 1989-90, treas. 1990—), Mensa.

BENNETT, M. DEE, state legislator; b. Little Rock, Ark., Aug. 20, 1935. Rep. dist. 59 State of Ark., 1993—; cons. Greater Friendship, Inc. Democrat. Office: Ark State Reps State Capitol Little Rock AR 72201*

BENNETT, MARGARET AIROLA, lawyer; b. San Francisco, July 20, 1950; d. Virgil Raymond and Caroline (Maccoun) Airola; m. Eugene Le Brun Bennett, Mar. 1, 1980; children: Scott, Brad, Elizabeth. AB cum laude, U. Calif., Berkeley, 1972; JD, U. San Francisco and Loyola U., 1976. Bar: Ill.1976, U.S. Dist. Ct. (no. dist.) Ill. 1977, U.S. Ct. Appeals (7th cir.) 1983. Intern Cook County State's Atty.'s Office, Chgo., 1975-76; assoc. Dunlap, Thompson & Boyd, Ltd., Libertyville, Ill., 1977-79; ptnr. Bennett & Bennett, Ltd., Oak Brook, Ill., 1980—; atty. rep. McDonald's Corp., Oak Brook, 1982—, County of DuPage, Wheaton, Ill., 1990—. Counsel fo DuPage Ill. Fair and Exposition Authority, County of DuPage, 1991—, co-chmn. next generation com.; mem. devel. coun. Good Samaritan Hosp., 1988-92. Mem. DuPage County Bar Assn. (chmn. real estate law com., Cert. of Appreciation 1989), Ill. State Bar Assn. (cert. of Appreciation 1990), Womens Bar Assn. DuPage County, Evang. Health Found. (bd. sponsors 1988-92). Republican. Roman Catholic. Home: 11 Lochinvar Ln Oak Brook IL 60521 Office: Bennett and Bennett Ltd 1301 W 22d St Ste 815 Oak Brook IL 60521

BENNETT, MARTHA M., quality assurance professional; b. Richmond, Va., Dec. 29, 1951; d. Maurice Anthony Miller and Esther Anne Bray; m. Dean Allan Barlow, May 1, 1982. BS, U. Tenn., 1972. Cert. regulatory affairs profl. Investigator FDA, Nashville, 1972-76; sr. compliance officer FDA, Rockville, Md., 1976-82, sr. policy analyst, 1982-85; pres. Bennett and Co., Clarksville, Md., 1985—. Author: (cookbook) Friends to Friends, 1989, 90; (techbook) Practical Guide to Validation, 1994. Mem. Regulatory Affairs Profl. Soc. (v.p. programs 1989-91, cert. regulatory affairs profl.), Parenteral Drug Assn., Internat. Soc. Pharm. Engrs., Soc. Quality Assurance. Office: Bennett and Co 13560 Brighton Dam Rd Clarksville MD 21029

BENNETT, MARY See THOMPSON, DIDI CASTLE

BENNETT, MONA BLEIBERG, psychiatrist, clinical services director; b. Newark, Aug. 22, 1941; d. Jacob and Claire (Barban) Bleiberg; m. Michael Isaiah Bennett, Apr. 11, 1975; children: Rebecca Leah, Sarah Bleiberg. BA, U. Chgo., 1959-63; MD, Harvard U., 1967. Diplomate Am. Bd. Psychiatry. Resident in medicine Beth Israel Hosp., Boston, 1967-69; resident in psychiatry Mass. Mental Health Ctr., Boston, 1969-71, resident in child psychiatry, 1971-73, psychiatrist, 1973-84, dir. outpatient and emergency svcs., 1978-84; dir. mental health Brookside Park Family Life Ctr., Boston, 1973-78; dep. commr. Mass. Dept. Mental Health, Boston, 1984-91; adminstr. McLean Hosp., Belmont, Mass., 1991—; dir. office clin. svcs. dept. psychiatry Harvard Med. Sch., Belmont, 1991—; asst. prof. Harvard Med. Sch., Boston, 1993—; assoc. prof. U. Mass. Med. Sch., Worcester, 1986-93. Fellow Am. Psychiat. Assn.; mem. Am. Coll. Psychiatrists, Acad. Child and Adolescent Psychiatry, Phi Beta Kappa, Alpha Omega Alpha. Jewish. Office: McLean Hosp 115 Mill St Belmont MA 02178

BENNETT, NANCY ELAINE, office manager; b. Kittanning, Pa., July 29, 1941; d. Dale Russell and Grace Bernice (Miller) McKelvey; m. Perry Henry Bennett, Nov. 14, 1968. Diploma, Grace Martin Sec., Pitts., 1960. Mut. funds dept. Pitts. Nat. Bank, 1960-65; receptionist, bookkeeper West Penn Power Co., Kittanning, Pa., 1965-73; bookkeeper Sumco Mfg. Co., Akron, Ohio, 1973-77, Pitts Tire & Retreading, Akron, 1977-79; teller Valley Nat. Bank, Kittanning, 1979-81; front desk clk. Port LaBelle Inn, LaBelle, Fla., 1988-90; bookkeeper Port LaBelle Conv. Store, 1991; office mgr. A & B Harvesting, Inc., LaBelle, 1983—; part-time staff mem. Seminole Gaming Palace, Immokalee, Fla., 1994—. Vol. Charlotte County chpt. LaBelle br. ARC, 1990—. Mem. VFW Aux., DAV Aux., Mil. Order Cooties Aux., Am. Bus. Women's Assn. (vol. blood drive for Edison Regional Blood Ctr., Fort Myers).

BENNETT, NINA BIELBY, financial planner, analyst; b. Deland, Fla., Aug. 17, 1960; m. David Bennett, Oct. 14, 1991. BSBA, U. Fla., 1982, MBA, 1984; MA, Washington U., St. Louis, 1988. Internat. fin. analyst Monsanto Co., St. Louis, 1984-87, internal auditor, 1987-89; sr. fin. analyst MCI Telecom., Washington, 1989-90; sr. fin. analyst Augat, Inc., Boston, 1990-91, mgr. fin. planning & analysis, 1991—.

BENNETT, OLGA SALOWICH, civic worker, graphic arts researcher, consultant; b. Detroit, June 30, 1925; d. Nicholas Stefanovich and Maria Elarionovna (Mikuliak) Salowich; m. Robert William Bennett, Dec. 20, 1947; 1 child, Susan Roberta. Student, U. Mich., 1943-45, Parsons Sch. Design, 1948, U. Md., Nagoya, Japan, 1959; BA, NYU, 1975. Graphic artist Silver & Co., N.Y.C., 1948-50; editor, pub. Bull., organizer radio series LWV, Pitts., 1950-55; instr. Nanzan U., Nagoya, 1959; aide, cons. to U.S. hon. consul, Safi, Casablanca, Morocco, 1962-65; chmn. internat. affairs LWV, Montclair, N.J., 1966-73; conf. coord. UN Assn., Madison, N.J., 1974; weekly broadcaster LWV, San Juan, P.R., 1979-81; lectr. color theory Cunard, Ltd., London, Miami, Fla., 1985-88; bd. dirs., docent Ctr. Fine Arts, Miami, 1990-92; docent Bass Mus. Art, Miami Beach, Fla., 1990-92, Vizcaya Mus. Art, Miami, 1983—; cons. on corp. overseas placement. Author artist brochures, ednl. pamphlets; translator Russian-Am. Conf., Miami, 1990. Mem. panel theater award com. New Theater, Miami, 1991. Mem. AAUW, LWV (bd. dirs.), UN Assn. (bd. dirs.) NYU Alumni Assn., New Sch. Alumni Assn., Fgn. Policy Assn., Great Decisions Program. Democrat. Russian Orthodox. Home: Kings Creek S Apt A1-402 7727 SW 86 St Miami FL 33143-7283

BENNETT, PEGGY ELIZABETH, librarian, library director, educator; b. Columbus, Ga., Aug. 22, 1935; d. William Osborne and Ola Lee (McMahan) B. BA in Chemistry, So. Coll., 1956; cert. med. technologist, Glendale Sch. Med. Tech., Glendale, 1957; MS in Libr. Sci., Fla. State U., 1971. Med. technologist Glendale (Calif.) Hosp., 1957-59, Columbus (Ga.) Med. Ctr., 1960-61; sec. Seventh-Day Adventists Ch. Orgns., various, 1961-67; med. technologists Warm Springs (Ga.) Found., 1967-69, Thrash Labs.,

Columbus, Ga., 1969-70; libr. So. Coll. Seventh-Day Adventist, Collegedale, Tenn., 1971—; dir. librs. So. Coll. of Seventh-Day Adventist, Collegedale, 1986—; presenter in field, 1979-87; developer Processing Ctr. for Southeastern Adventist Sch. Librs., 1981; cons. Adventist Network of Gen. Ednl. Librs., Collegedale, 1981—, Girl's Preparatory Sch., Chattanooga, 1984-85. Author: Library Pathfinder for MIT, 1972; contbr. articles to profl. jours. Mem. ALA, Assn. of Seventh-Day Adventists Librs. (v.p. 1981-82, pres. 1982-83), Southeastern Libr. Assn., Chattanooga Area Libr. Assn., Solinet Lambda Users' Group (exec. com. 1984, steering com.), Beta Phi Mu. Seventh Day Adventist. Home: 4640 Pierson Dr Collegedale TN 37315 Office: So Coll of SDA Industrial Dr Collegedale TN 37315

BENNETT, SHIRLEY ANN, maintenance executive, business technologist educator; b. Buffalo, Nov. 5, 1952; d. Edward Stoklosa and Florence (Ulanowski) Valin; m. Jeffrey Michael Bennett, July 3, 1975; children: Tara, Shauna, Shira, Brett, Eric. BS in Edn., SUNY Coll. at Buffalo, Buffalo, 1974; MBA, SUNY, Buffalo, 1982. Cert. tchr., N.Y. Tchr. Niagara Falls (N.Y.) Bd. Edn., 1974-75, Kensington Bus. Inst., Buffalo, 1976-80; lectr. SUNY, Buffalo, 1980—; v.p. Bennett Janitorial Svc., Williamsville, N.Y., 1976—. Active Jewish Ctr. of Greater Buffalo, Amherst, 1983—, Girl Scouts U.S., Buffalo, 1985—. Mem. Epsilon Delta Epsilon, Iota Lambda Sigma (Alpha Lambda chpt.). Home: 76 Alran Dr Williamsville NY 14221-1409 Office: SUNY at Buffalo EOC 465 Washington Buffalo NY 14203

BENNETT, SUSAN GAIL, English language educator; b. Cin., Dec. 1, 1946; d. Raymond Sidney and Helen Rae (Markell) B.; m. Patrick Sullivan Hurley, July 17, 1977; children: Karinna Bennett Hurley, Alexandra Bennett Hurley. BS, Ohio State U., 1968; MA, U. Calif., Berkeley, 1971, PhD, 1978. Cert. secondary tchr., C.C. tchr., Calif. Lang. arts tchr. Sierra Vista Jr. High Sch., La Puente, Calif., 1968-70; supr. student tchrs. U. Calif., Berkeley, 1976-78; asst. prof. U. Tex., Austin, 1978-85, assoc. prof., 1987-87; prof. Humboldt State U., Arcata, Calif., 1987—; bd. dirs. Redwood Writing Project, Arcata; site dir. Nat. Writing Project, Calif. Writing Project; presenter in field. Fellow Phi Delta Kappa, Pi Lambda Theta; mem. NOW, Nat. Coun. Tchrs. of English. Jewish.

BENNETT, TOMMIE JEANETTE, business owner; b. Palatka, Fla., Nov. 11, 1946; d. Hershel and Laudis (Hogsed) Nelson; m. Wayne Ramonn Bennett, Dec. 24, 1965; children: John Wayne, Kimberly Kay. Clerk typist St. Johns Chevrolet, Palatka, 1964-66; tchr. Peniel Acad., Palatka, 1979; owner Wayne R. Bennett Ferneries, Palatka, 1985—; office mgr. John W. Stone Inc., Palatka, 1983—. Republican. Office: John W Stone Inc P O Box 74 Hastings FL 32145

BENNETT, VERNA GREEN, employee relations executive; b. Memphis, Oct. 4, 1942; d. Agee and Philistine Louvenia (Jackson) Green; m. John Paul Bennett, Sept. 24, 1966 (div. Dec. 3, 1978). BS in Bus. Edn., Knoxville Coll., 1965. Tchr. Stevens Lee High Sch., Asheville, N.C., 1965-66; adminstr. external affairs Youth in Action, Bklyn., 1966-67; adminstr. cmty. rels., pub. rels. Pepsi Cola Co., N.Y.C., 1967-70; staff asst., coll. rels. coord., hdqrs. recruiter Mobil Corp., N.Y.C., 1970-80; western region recruiter Mobil Corp., L.A., 1980-87; EEO rels. mgr. Mobil Corp., Fairfax, Va., 1987—; mem. corp. adv. bd. Nat. Assn. Minority Engr. Adminstrs., Chgo., 1980-94, Am. Indian Sci. and Engring., Boulder, 1990-94, NAACP ACTSO, Balt., 1989-94; motivational spkr., lectr. in field. Mem. New Dominion chpt. Nat. Coalition of 100 Black Women, 1992-94, chmn. chpt. devel. com., nat. bd. dirs., 1993-94; commr. Nat. Com. Working Women, Washington, 1990-94; chmn. bd. Coun. on Career Devel. of Minorities, Dallas, 1986—; mem. No. Va. Urban League, Alexandria, 1990-94;. Recipient Donald H. McGannon award Nat. Urban League, N.Y.C., 1992, Delta Sigma Theta Youth award, 1992, Presdl. Achievement and Nat. Amigo of Yr., SERJOBS for Progress, Dallas, 1988, 89, 90, 94. Mem. Bus. and Profl. Women (corp. adv. resource devel. mem. 1992-94). Democrat. Presbyterian. Home: Apt 1425 1600 N Oak St Arlington VA 22209 Office: Mobil Corp Ste 2C917 2335 Gallows Rd Fairfax VA 22037

BENNETTS, DEBRA L., public relations executive; b. Bronx, N.Y., Dec. 2, 1951. BA in English, U. Conn., 1973; MBA, NYU, 1982. Reporter, editor Glen News Pub., 1973-74, Brooks Newspapers, 1974-78; comm. specialist Richardson-Vicks, 1978-80, mgr. comm., 1980-85, asst. dir. comm., 1985-86, dir. comm., 1986-92; founder, prin. Strategic Comm., 1992—. Recipient Bronze Quill award Conn. IABC, 1983, 84, 85, Nicholson award Nat. Assn. Investors, 1985, Bell Ringer award Publicity Club of New Eng., 1990. Mem. WICI (v.p. membership 1980-82, pres. 1982-83, chmn. long range planning com. Fairfield County chpt. 1983-84), Pub. Rels. Soc. Am. Office: Strategic Comms 4 Toilsome Ave Norwalk CT 06851*

BENNICH, AGATHE LOUISE, art educator, artist; b. Stockholm, Sweden, Aug. 1, 1939; came to U.S., 1962; d. Lars G. and Ebba S. (Hederstierna) B.; m. Jean R. McLean, Feb. 2, 1963 (div. 1967); m. Tron J. Bykle, May 11, 1972; 1 child, Odin Tronson Bykle. BFA, San Francisco Art Inst., 1969, MFA, 1972. Mem. faculty San Francisco City Coll., 1972-74, 76-78, 81—, Lone Mountain Coll., San Francisco, 1973, Coll. Marin, Kentfield, 1974, U. Hawaii Manoa Campus, Oahu, 1979; mem. jury various art shows. One-woman shows include City Lights Books, 1968, U. Calif., 1971, Nanny Goat Hill Gallery, San Francisco, 1974, Berthold Brecht Ctr. Opening, 1975, French-Am. Bilingual Sch., 1984, J.F. Kennedy U., Orinda, Calif., 1994, others; exhibited in group shows at Sassoferrato, Italy, 1961, Richmond Art Ctr., 1971-72, San Francisco Art Inst., 1971, 81, 85, 86, 87, 88, Coll. Marin, 1973, 90, Internat. Mus. Erotic Art, 1973-74, Civic Ctr., San Francisco, 1981, Am. Indian Film Festival, 1981, Bridge Gallery, 1982, South of Market Cultural Ctr., 1982, 94, San Francisco Arts Festival, 1985, Natalini Galleries, Chgo., 1986, 87, 88, Artists Soc. Internat., San Francisco, 1987, City Art Gallery, 1987, San Francisco City Coll., 88, Imago Gallery, 1989, Knecht, Haley, Lawrence & Smith Law Offices, San Francisco, 1991, Art Store Gallery, San Francisco, 1994, Kennedy Gallery, San Francisco, 1994-95, others; writer, illustrator several children's books; contbr. illustrations to This Is Women's Work, 1973; contbr. 12 Womens Calendar, 1993. Mem. Tchrs. Union (2121 local). Office: San Francisco City Coll Art Dept 50 Phelan Ave San Francisco CA 94112

BENO-CLARK, CANDICE LYNN, chemical company executive; b. New Brunswick, N.J., Mar. 25, 1951; d. Andrew Jule and Claire May (Blanchard) Beno; m. John W. Clark, Sr., Dec. 8, 1990. BA magna cum laude, U. Conn., 1973, MS in Biochemistry, 1974, postgrad., 1974-75. Grad. asst. U. Conn., 1973-75; lab. technician Linde div. Union Carbide Corp., Keasbey, N.J., 1976-78, sr. lab. technician Linde div., 1978-79; regional tech. supr. Linde div. Union Carbide Corp., South Plainfield, N.J., 1979; asst. staff engr. Linde div. Union Carbide Corp., Springfield, N.J., 1979-82, staff engr. Linde div., 1982-84; tech. bus. cons. Linde div. Union Carbide Corp., Danbury, Conn., 1984-85; staff engr. Linde div. Union Carbide Corp., Somerset, N.J., 1985-87; mgr. Linde div. Union Carbide Corp., Springfield, 1987-89; mgr. Linde div. Union Carbide Indsl. Gases, Inc., Danbury, Conn., 1989-91, internat. mgr., 1991—; internat. mgr. Praxair, Inc., Danbury; supr. Landmark Edn., Edison, N.J., 1984-87; guest seminar leader, 1985—, course mgr., 1984-86. Mem. Am. Soc. Quality Control, Compressed Gas Assn. (chmn. 1984-91, vice chmn. 1982-88, Svc. award 1991), Semicondr. Equipment and Material Inst. (co-chmn. 1987-91, editor jour. 1982-88, Outstanding Svc. award 1884-89, Leadership award 1988, Mortar Board, Phi Beta Kappa, Phi Kappa Phi. Democrat. Home: 405 Newark Ave Point Pleasant Beach NJ 08742-4143 Office: Praxair Inc 39 Old Ridgebury Rd M-1524 Danbury CT 06810

BENOIT, NANCY LOUISE, state legislator, educator; b. New Haven, Conn., Jan. 25, 1944; d. James Michael and Florence Louise (Bray) Wynne; m. Raymond George Benoit, Aug. 8, 1970; children: Michael, Patrick. BA, Albertus Magnus Coll., 1965; MEd, Wayne State U., 1969. Tchr. St. Vincent de Paul High Sch., Detroit, 1965-69; community organizer Social Progress Action Corp., Woonsocket, R.I., 1969-71; dir. Little Shares Day Care Ctr., Woonsocket, 1971-73; edn. coordinator Northwest Head Start, North Providence, R.I., 1978-84; mem. R.I. Ho. of Reps., 1985—, chair joint legis. commn. on child care, 1985—, mem. adult edn. commn., 1985-88, mem. health, edn. and welfare com., 1986-88, mem. fin. com., 1989-92; dep. majority whip, 1991-92; chair permanent legis. oversight commn. Dept. for Children, Youth and Families; chair House com. on Health, Edn. and Welfare, 1993—. Bd. dirs. Woonsocket Head Start and Day Care, R.I. affiliate Literacy Vols. of Am., 1985-88; commr. Blackstone River Valley Nat. Corridor Commn.; bd. mgrs. Woonsocket Family and Child Care Svcs., 1973-87; v.p., bd. dirs. Health Svcs., Inc., Woonsocket, 1974—; founder Women for Women, 1983—; vol. coord. Vols. in Action, Providence, 1984-86; grant coord. C.C. R.I., Lincoln, 1986-87. Named one of Outstanding Young Women in Am., Woonsocket and E.I. Jaycees, 1980, Legislator of Yr. United Way of Southeastern New England; recipient Francesco Cannistra Svc. award Health Svcs., Inc., 1986, Outstanding Svc. award R.I. Day Care Dirs. Assn., 1986. Mem. Common Cause, Sierra Club, Audubon Soc. Democrat. Roman Catholic. Office: RI Gen Assembly Providence RI 02903

BENSEL, CAROLYN KIRKBRIDE, psychologist; b. Orange, N.J., Sept. 21, 1941; d. William Everitt and Margaret Mary (McGlynn) B.; A.B. with honors in Psychology, Chestnut Hill Coll., 1963; M.S., U. Mass., 1964, Ph.D. (Univ. fellow), 1967. Teaching asst. U. Mass., Amherst, 1963-64, research asst., 1964-66; human factors psychologist Grumman Aerospace Corp., Bethpage, N.Y., 1967-71; chief human factors group U.S. Army Natick (Mass.) Research, Devel. and Engring. Ctr., 1971—. Lic. psychologist, Mass. Fellow Human Factors Soc., APA; mem. Ergonomics Soc., Soc. Engring. Psychologists, Internat. Ergonomics Assn., AAAS, Sigma Xi. Editor: Proc. 23d Ann. Meeting of Human Factors Soc., 1979. Office: Sci & Advanced Tech Directorate Army Natick Research Devel Engring Ctr Kansas St Natick MA 01760

BENSEN, ANNETTE WOLF, graphic art company executive; b. Bklyn., Aug. 7, 1938; d. Isidor and Sylvia Wolf; m. Gene Bensen, Oct. 14, 1979. AAS, N.Y.C. C.C., 1958; postgrad., Pratt Inst., 1974-75, Sch. Visual Arts, N.Y.C. With Wagner-Ellsberg, Inc., N.Y.C., 1958-62; art dir. Island Pen Mfg. Inc., Stacie Pen, Curtis Rand Industries, Inc., N.Y.C., 1962-68; with G.S. Lithographers, Inc., N.Y.C., 1968-70; ptnr., pres. Rembrandt's Mother, Inc., N.Y.C., 1970-72; co-owner, pres. Film Comp., Inc., N.Y.C., 1972-75; mgr. Expertype, N.Y.C., 1975-90, Expertype & The Graphic Word Co., N.Y.C., 1990-92; sr. v.p. Expertype divsn. JCH Group Ltd., N.Y.C., 1992-93; v.p. Metro Comms. Group Inc., N.Y.C., 1993—; adj. lectr. N.Y.C. C.C., 1971-75; adv. commn. dept. graphic arts & advt. tech., N.Y.C. Tech. Coll./CUNY, 1994—. Pres. Edn. Found. for Graphic Arts, Inc., 1994—. Mem. N.Y. Postscript Users Group, N.Y. Mac Users Group, Advt. Women N.Y., Assn. Graphic Arts (chair edn. com.), Sales Assn. Graphic Arts (chair edn. com.), Sales Assn. Graphic Arts, Women in Prodn., Inc., Aircraft Owners and Pilots Assn. (bd. dirs. ob bldg.), Club Printing Women N.Y. (pres.). Office: Metro Comm Group 33 W 34th St New York NY 10001

BENSEN, PAMELA PARKE, emergency medicine physician, educator; b. Plainfield, N.J., Dec. 27, 1944; m. C. (Kork) Bensen III; children: Jeannie McKay, C. (Neil) W. Bensen IV. Student, Northwestern U., 1964; BS in Biology and Chemistry, Upsala Coll., 1966; MD, Med. Coll. Pa. Diplomate Am. Bd. Emergency Medicine; cert. ACLS, BLS, Advanced Trauma Life Support, Advanced Pedit. Trauma Life Support. Intern in emergency medicine Med. Coll. Pa., resident in emergency medicine; mem. emergency medicine staff St. Mary's Gen. Hosp.-St. Mary's Regional Med. Ctr., Lewiston, Maine, 1973—, chief emergency svcs., 1974-78, dir. Ctrl. Maine Vocat. Inst. Paramedic Tng. Program, 1978-79; dir. emergency svcs. St. Mary's Gen. Hosp.-St. Mary's Regional Med. Ctr., Lewsiton, Maine, 1982-87; mem. staff Bath (Maine) Meml. Hosp., 1986—, dir. emergency svcs., 1989-90; mem. staff Miles Meml. Hosp., Damariscotta, Maine, 1989—, dir. emergency svcs., 1989-91; mem. staff St. Andrews Hosp., Boothbay Harbor, Maine, 1990-93, dir. emergency svcs., 1990-91; adj. asst. prof. clin. medicine Dartmouth Med. Sch., Hanover, N.H., 1990—; mem. med. adv. com. Region I Medicare, Maine Medicaid, Maine Blue Shield; instr. ACLS, ATLS, Pediat. Advanced Life Support, EMT to schs., gen. public, medical pers.; med. dir. New Eng. Med. Svcs., 1987—; co-founder Dictate, Inc., 1987—, pres., 1991—, med. advisor, 1922—; mem. med. adv. bd. Virutal Physician, 1994—; spkr. TV, radio, confs., programs, assemblies in field; med. advisor Lost Valley Ski Patrol, 1974-79; bd. dirs. Androscoggin Valley Red Cross, 1975; co-dir. Lewiston-Auburn Rape Crisis Intervention Team, 1977-79; dir. Alert Ambulance, Lewiston, Maine, 1978-79; bd. dirs. Tri-County Regional EMS Coun., med. control com., edn. standards and evaluation com.; mem. physician adv. bd. Maine EMS Med. Dir., 1982-85; mem. Nat. Bd. Med. Examiners, 1986-87; mem. So. Maine Med. Control Com., 1988-92, EMS Coun., 1990-92, v.p. 1990-92; EMS dir. Regional Meml. Hosp., 1988-90; mem. Mid Coast Maine Med. Control Com., 1989-91; chair Coastal Edn. and Evaluation Com., 1989-90; pres. Maine Emergency Physicians, P.A., 1979-82, 83-89, sec., 1989—; pres., CEO Emergency Medicine Assocs., 1985—; med. advisor Poland Rescue, 1973-88; part-time Ctrl. Maine Med. Ctr., Lewiston, Kennebec Valley Med. Ctr., Augusta, Maine, Sebasticook Valley Hosp., Pittsfield, Maine, Stephens Meml. Hosp., Norway, Maine, Waldo County Hosp., Belfast, Maine; instr. various paramedic courses, 1973—. Editor Maine Emergency Physicians Interim Comm., 1979-84, 88-93; mem. editl. bd. Maine EMS Jour., 1990-93, ED Mgmt., 1989—; co-editor Women in Emergency Medicine, 1986-89. Recipient Disting. Alumnae award Upsala Coll., 1985, Cmty. Svc. award Am. Woman's Med. Assn., 1991, Appreciation award Bath/Brunswick EMS, 1992; grantee Emergency Medicine Found., 1993. Fellow Am. Coll. Emergency Physicians (grad. edn. com. resident rep. 1971-73, continuing med. edn. com. 1973-79, ACEP-Chubb malpractice ins. claims rev. bd. N.E. sect. 1973-75, pub. rels. com. 1981-82, spkrs. bur. 1983, bd. nominating com. 1988-89, profl. liability com. 1988-90, medico-legal com. 1990-92, ED design resources list 1992—, liaison to Physician Insurers Assn. Am. 1992-94, emergency medicine practice com. 1994—, councilor State of Maine 1973-82, 89-92, coun. awards com. 1990, coun. steering com. 1978-80, chair coun. nominating com. 1979-81, pres. Maine chpt. 1974-79, nat. bd. dirs.-numerous coms., sects., Coun. Meritorious Svc. award 1989, editor newsletter 1989-92); mem. AMA, Am. Coll. Physician Execs., Maine Med. Assn., Med. Transcription Svc. Owners, Med. Transcription Industry Alliance (bd. dirs. 1993—). Office: RFD 1 Box 750 Oxford ME 04270

BENSHOOF, JANET L., lawyer, association executive; b. Detroit Lakes, Minn., May 10, 1947; m. Richard Klein; children: David, Eli. BA summa cum laude, U. Minn., 1969; JD, Harvard U., 1972. Dir. law reform South Bklyn. Legal Svcs., 1972-77; dir. reproductive freedom project ACLU, N.Y.C., 1977-92; founder, pres. Ctr. Reproductive Law & Policy, N.Y.C., 1992—; guest lectr. Yale U., Columbia U., Rutgers U., Case Western Reserve U. Contbr. articles to profl. jours. Recipient Margaret Sanger award, 1986, Christopher Tietze Humanitarian award Nat. Abortion Fedn., 1988, Gloria Steinem award Ms. Found. Women, N.Y.C., 1989, 10 for 10 award Ctr. Population Optiums, 1990; named one of 100 Most Influential Lawyers in Am. Nat. Law Jour., 1991, 94; MacArthur Found. Fellowship grantee, 1992—. Mem. ABA, Am. Pub. Health Assn., N.Y.C. Bar Assn. Office: Ctr Reproductive Law & Policy 120 Wall St New York NY 10005

BENSMAN-ROWE, CHERYL, soprano, voice educator; b. Wyandotte, Mich., July 28, 1955; d. Lawrence Solomon and Barbara Janet (Rose) Bensman; m. Paul Youmans Rowe, July 5, 1987; children: Alison Hannah Rowe, Julia Meadows Rowe. Diploma, Interlochen Arts Acad., 1973; MusB, Boston U., 1977, MusM, 1979. Asst. prof. voice Vanderbilt U., Nashville, 1993—; assoc. prof. voice Mid. Tenn. State U. Soloist Steve Reich and Musicians, N.Y.C., 1981—, Waverly Consort, N.Y.C., 1981-83, Western Wind Vocal Ensemble, 1986-92, N.Y. Philharmonic, N.Y.C., 1982, Israel Philharmonic, Tel Aviv, 1987, Chgo. Symphony, 1982; debut Carnegie Hall, N.Y.C., 1989; recordings include Hidden Voices, 1990, Tehillem, 1980, The Christmas Story, 1980. Banff (Can.) Ctr. for the Arts fellow, 1986, Aspen (Colo.) Music Festival fellow, 1977, 79, 85; Berkshire Music Ctr. scholar, 1981. Mem. AFTRA, Nat. Assn. Tchrs. of Singing. Democrat. Jewish. Home: 3409 Springbrook Dr Nashville TN 37204 Office: Vanderbilt U 2400 Blakemore Nashville TN 37212

BENSON, BARBARA ELLEN, state agency administrator; b. Rockford, Ill., June 5, 1943; d. Olander Anton and Eleanor Margaret (Lydon) B. BA, Beloit Coll., 1965; MA, Ind. U., 1969, PhD, 1976. Editor Eleutherian Mills-Hagley Found., Wilmington, Del., 1973-80; dir. libr. Hist. Soc. Del., Wilmington, 1980-90, exec. dir., 1990—. Author: Logs and Lumber, 1989, (with Michael Biggs) Wilmington: the City and Beyond, 1990; contbr. articles to jours., chpts. to books. Vice chair Del. Humanities Forum, 1987-92, chair, 1992-94; bd. dirs. Sister Cities, Wilmington, 1985-89 (ofcl. visitor to Kalmar, Sweden, 1985), State Records Commn. Del., 1987—; rev. bd. Del. Hist. Preservation, 1990—; bd. dirs. Hist. Red Clay Valley, 1994—. Mem. Nat. Soc. of Fund Raising Execs., Am. Assn. of Mus., Am. Assn. State and Local History (state awards chmn. 1987—), Mid Atlantic Regional Archivists (bd. dirs. 1983-87). Office: Hist Soc Delaware 505 N Market St Wilmington DE 19801-3091

BENSON, BERNICE LAVINA, elementary education educator; b. Wolford, N.D., Sept. 30; d. Therman George and Annie Catherine (Hittle) Ritzman; m. Benjamin Melvin Benson, June 11, 1941 (dec.); 1 child, Beverly Ann. Student, Jamestown Coll.; BS in Edn., No. State Coll., 1964, MA equivalent. Cert. elem. tchr., S.D. Tchr. 1st-6th grade Southam (N.D.) Sch. System, 1935-41; tchr. 1st grade Pierre (S.D.) Sch. System, 1953-84; tchr. Title I Fed. Devel. Reading Program, Pierre, 1984-87; tchr.-tutor Title IV Fed. Tutorials for Native Americans, Pierre; supr. student tchrs. No. State Coll., Pierre. Past officer, past mem. various state coms. Delta Kappa Gamma; charter mem. Capital U., Pierre; sponsor Discovery Ctr., Pierre; mem. YMCA, Pierre; spl. events worker VFW Aux., Pierre; mem. Fine ARts Coun., Pierre; actress Never Too Late, Pierre Players Drama Assn.; mem. planning com. for new bldg., mem. meml. com. Luth. Meml. Ch. Mem. NEA (state exec. uni-serve com.), Pierre Edn. Assn., S.D. Edn. Assn., Pierre Tchrs. Assn. (pres.), Internat. Reading Assn., Assn. for Childhood Edn., AAUW, DAR (past offices), PEO (past pres., all offices), Annie D. Tallent Club. Home: 324 Mary Ln Pierre SD 57501-2213

BENSON, BETTY G., state legislator; b. Pioneer, Tenn., Mar. 29, 1943; M. Jim A. Benson; children: Timothy, James, Krisila. BS, U. Idaho, 1987, MS, 1994. Senator Idaho State Senate, Boise, 1990-92. Mem. Gamma Theta Upsilon, Sigma Xi. Democrat. Home: 2305 Wallen Rd Moscow ID 83843

BENSON, BETTY JONES, school system administrator; b. Barrow County, Ga., Jan. 11, 1928; d. George C. and Bertha (Mobley) Jones; m. George T. Benson; children: George Steven, Elizabeth Gayle, James Claud, Robert Benjamin. BS in Edn., N. Ga. U., Dahlonega, 1958; MEd in Curriculum and Supervision, U. Ga., Athens, 1968, edn. specialist in Curriculum and Supervision, 1970. Tchr. Forsyth County (Ga.) Bd. Edn., Cumming, 1956-66, curriculum dir., 1966—; asst. supt. for instrn. Forsyth County Schs., 1981—. Active Alpine Ctr. for Disturbed Children; chmn. Ga. Lake Lanier Island Authority; mem. North Ga. Coll. Edn. Adv. Com., Ga. Textbook Com.; adv. Boy Scouts; Sunday sch. tchr. 1st Baptist Ch. Cumming; active Forsyth County Substance Abuse Commn., Forsyth County Drug Task Force, Forsyth County Vision 20/20 Com., Forsyth County Drug Commn., Forsyth County Interagency Council for Children and Youth, local coord. council Family and Children Svcs., Blue Ridge Cir. Ct.-Cherokee/Forsyth County Domestic Violence Task Force. Mem. NEA, Ga. Assn. Educators (bd. dir.), Nat. Assn. Supervision and Curriculum Devel., Ga. Assn. Supervision and Curriculum Devel. (pres.), Assn. Childhood Edn. Internat., Bus. and Profl. Women's Club, Internat. Platform Assn., Ga. Future Tchrs. Adv. Assn. (pres.), Profl. Assn. Ga. Educators, Ga. Assn. Ednl. Leaders (dir.), HeadStart Dirs. Assn., Forsyth County Hist. Soc., Sawnee Mountain Community Ctr. Assn., Ga. Cumming/Forsyth County C. of C. (mem. edn. com.), Mountain Local Coord. Coun. Home: 1235 Dahlonega Hwy Cumming GA 30130-4525 Office: 101 School St Cumming GA 30130-2427

BENSON, DEBRA ANN, television executive; b. Huntsville, Ala., Oct. 14, 1953; d. Vernon and Betty Lou (Taylor) B. Student, Jacksonville State U., 1971-73; BS in Mktg., U. Ala., 1986. Blind aide Jacksonville (Ala.) State U., 1971-73; sec., Recreation Dept. City of Madison, Ala., 1974-77; sales fin. rep. First Nat. Bank, Huntsville, Ala., 1977-81; asst. program dir. Sta. WAAY-TV, Huntsville, Ala., 1981-84, promotion mgr., 1984-88, program dir., 1988—. Newsletter editor: Tommy Battle for City Coun., Huntsville, 1985. Mem. Stop Child Abuse Now (SCAN), Huntsville, 1989-90; bd. dirs. Crime Stoppers, Huntsville, 1985-90; campaign mgr. Betty Benson for Tax Collector, Huntsville, 1984. Recipient Addy Muscle Shoals Ad Club, Florence, Ala., 1985, Greater Huntsville Ad Club, 1986-87. Mem. Nat. Assn. TV Programming Execs., Nat. Fedn. Press Women, Broadcast Promotions and Mktg. Execs., Ala. Press Women, Viewers for Quality TV. Home: 106 Suffolk Dr Madison AL 35758-8549 Office: Sta WAAY-TV 1000 Monte Sano Blvd SE Huntsville AL 35801-6137

BENSON, ELIZABETH POLK, Pre-Columbian art specialist; b. Washington, May 13, 1924; d. Theodore Booton and Rebecca Dean (Albin) B. BA, Wellesley Coll., 1945; MA, Cath. U. Am., 1956. Mus. aide, curator Nat. Gallery of Art, Washington, 1946-60; curator Pre-Columbian Collection, Dumbarton Oaks, Washington, 1962-79, dir. Ctr. for Pre-Columbian Studies, 1971-79; rsch. assoc. Inst. Andean Studies, Berkeley, Calif., 1980—; lectr. Cath. U. Am., Washington, 1968, 69; adj. prof. Columbia U., N.Y.C., 1973; sr. lectr. U. Tex., Austin, 1985; Andrew S. Keck disting. vis. prof. Am. U., Washington, 1987; cons. Montreal Mus. Fine Arts, 1980-84, 90-92, Princeton U. Art Mus., 1980, 82, 87; mem. adv. bd. Latin Am. Indian Lits. Jour., Pitts., 1989—. Author: The Maya World, 1967, 72, 77, The Mochica, 1972; co-author: Museums of the Andes, 1981, Atlas of Ancient America, 1986. Mem. Soc. Woman Geographers, The Lit. Soc., Latin Am. Indian Lits. Assn. (v.p. 1989—). Home and Office: 8314 Seven Locks Rd Bethesda MD 20817

BENSON, JOAN ELLEN, dietetics educator, researcher; b. San Francisco, Aug. 26, 1954; d. Lloyd F. and Joan A. (Sullivan) B.; m. Dwight T. Hibdon, July 13, 1977. BS with honors, U. Calif., Berkeley, 1977, registered dietician, 1978; MS, U. Utah, 1987. Cert. dietitian, Utah. Clin. dietitian Contra Costa County Med. Svcs., Martinez, Calif., 1978-85; nutrition cons. Cardiovascular Genetics, Salt Lake City, 1987-90; adj. instr. dietectics U. Utah, Salt Lake City, 1987—, rsch. assoc. Sch. Medicine, 1991—; nutrition cons. Ctr. for Sports Medicine, St. Francis Hosp., San Francisco, 1984-87; vis. rsch. assoc. Inst. Rsch., Eidgenössische Sportschule, Magglingen, Switzerland, spring 1987; nutrition cons. Optifast progrAm LDS Hosp., Salt Lake City, 1978-90; book reviewer Benjamin Cummings Pub. Co., Redwood City, Calif., 1989—, Mosby-Yearbook Pubs., St. Louis, 1990-91. Author: Coaches Guide to Nutrition, 1990; contbr. articles to profl. publs., chpts. to books; creator 15 part TV series Sci. Founds. of Human Nutrition, KULC, 1995. Com. chmn. Am. Heart Assn., Salt Lake City, 1991-92. Calif. State scholar, 1975-77, Phoebe Hearst scholar, 1975-77; Spikes biomed. rsch. grantee U. Utah, 1986. Mem. Am. Dietetic Assn., Utah Dietetic Assn., Sports and Cardiovascular Nutritionists (state rep. 1990-91), Nat. Off-Road Biking Assn. (Utah Vet Mountain bike champion 1990, 92), Phi Kappa Phi. Democrat. Roman Catholic. Home: 4716 Silver Meadows Dr Park City UT 84060-5939 Office: U Utah Family-Preventive Medicine 50 N Medical Dr Salt Lk Cy UT 84132-0001

BENSON, LAURA F., banker; b. Butte, Mont., Feb. 15, 1950; d. Fred Melvin and Margaret May (Franks) Benson. BBA, Idaho State U., 1972; postgrad., Pacific Coast Banking Sch., 1983-85. Mgmt. trainee 1st Security Bank Idaho, Boise, 1972-73; ops. officer 1st Security Bank Idaho, Payette, 1973-74, Boise, 1974-77; systems analyst 1st Security Co., Salt Lake City, 1977-78; ops. officer, asst. v.p. 1st Security Bank Utah, Salt Lake City, 1978-82, tng. officer, asst. v.p., 1982-85, bus. devel officer, v.p., 1985-89, pvt. banking officer, v.p., 1989—; chair 12th Ann. Women and Bus. Conf., Salt Lake City, 1987. Author: Pathfinder, 1988, Yesterday's Girl Scout Today's Successful Woman, 1989. Treas., bd. dirs. Utah coun. Girl Scouts U.S.A., 1988-90; bd. dirs. Cath. Cmty. Svcs. Utah, Salt Lake Ballet Guild. Named Woman of Yr. Woman's Info. Network, Salt Lake City, 1986, Woman to Watch Network Publs., Salt Lake City, 1987. Office: 1st Security Bank Utah PO Box 30007 79 S Main St Salt Lake City UT 84111-1921

BENSON, LOIS, state legislator; b. Milford, Del., Mar. 13, 1947; d. Francis Holden and Louise Holiday H.; m. Robert Scott Benson, 1969; children: Anna Holiday, Megan Elizabeth. BA, Emory U., 1969. Tchr. Edina H.S., Minn., 1969-70, Camp Lejeune H.S., N.C., 1970-71; pres. Holden Interiors, Inc., 1979—; councilwoman City of Pensacola, Fla., 1987-90; mem. state selection com. Vietnam Wall S, 1991; chairwoman City-County Coord. Com., 1991-92; rep. dist. 22 State of Fla., 1992—. Named Bus. Leader of the Yr. News Jour. & C. of C., 1988. Mem. Pensacola Cultural Ctr. (memb. bd. dirs. 1988—), Vietnam Wall S Found. (sec. 1990—), Lear House Project (chmn. 1991—), Drug Free Workforce (co-chair & founding ptnr. 1981-92), Hotel San Carlos Restoration Com. (chmn. 1992), Phi Beta Kappa. Republican. Methodist. Office: Fla House of Reps State Capitol Tallahassee FL 32301*

BENSON, LUCY PETERS WILSON, political and diplomatic consultant; b. N.Y.C., Aug. 25, 1927; d. Willard Oliver and Helen (Peters) Wilson; m. Bruce Buzzell Benson, Mar. 30, 1950 (dec. Mar. 1990). B.A., Smith Coll., 1949, M.A., 1955; L.H.D. (hon.), Wheaton Coll., Norton, Mass., 1965; LL.D. (hon.), U. Mass., 1969; L.H.D. (hon.), Bucknell U., 1972; LL.D. (hon.), U. Md., 1972; L.H.D. (hon.), Carleton Coll., 1973; LL.D. (hon.), Amherst Coll., 1974, Clark U., 1975; H.H.D., Springfield Coll., 1981; L.H.D. (hon.), Bates Coll., 1982. Mem. jr. exec. tng. program Bloomingdale's, N.Y.C., 1949-50; asst. dir. pub. rels. Smith Coll., 1950-53; rsch. asst. dept. Am. studies Amherst Coll., 1956-57; pres. Amherst LWV, Mass., 1957-61; pres. Mass. LWV, 1961-65, nat. pres., 1968-74; mem. Gov.'s cabinet and sec. human svcs. Commonwealth of Mass., 1975; mem. spl. commn. on adminstrv. rev. U.S. Ho. of Reps., Washington, 1976-77; under sec. State Security Assistance, Sci. and Tech. U.S. Dept. State, Washington, 1977-80; cons. U.S. Dept. State and SRI Internat., Washington, 1980-81; pres. Benson and Assocs., Amherst and Washington, 1981—; vice chmn. Citizen Network for Fgn. Affairs; trustee N.E. Utilities, 1971-74, 76-77; bd. dirs. Continental Group, Inc., Dreyfus Fund, Dreyfus Liquid Assets, Dreyfus Asset Allocation Fund, Dreyfus 401K Fund, Dreyfus Third Century Fund, Inc., Grumman Corp., Comms. Satellite Corp., Gen. Reins. Corp., Dreyfus Worldwide Dollar Money Market Fund, Inc., Logistics Mgmt. Inst. Mem. steering com. Urban Coalition, 1968, exec. com., 1970-75, 80-84, co-chmn., 1973-75; mem. Gov. Mass. Spl. Com. Rev. Sunday Closing Laws, 1961; mem. spl. commn. Mass. Legislature to Study Budgetary Powers of Trustees U. Mass., 1961-62; mem. Gov. Mass. Com. Rev. Salaries State Employees, 1963, Mass. Adv. Bd. Higher Ednl. Policy, 1962-65, Mass. Bd. Edn. Adv. Com. Racial Imbalance and Edn., 1964-65, Mass. adv. com. U.S. Commn. Civil Rights, 1964-73; vice chmn. Mass. Adv. Council Edn., 1965-68; mem. Mass. Com. Children and Youth Com. to Study Report by U.S. Children's Bur., Mass. Youth Svc. Div., 1967; mem. pub. adv. com. U.S. Trade Policy, 1968; mem. vis. com. John F. Kennedy Sch. Govt.; mem. Trilateral Commn., Coun. Fgn. Rels. Mem. town meeting, Amherst, 1957-74, finance com., 1960-66; trustee Edn. Devel. Center, Newton, Mass., 1967-72, Nat. Urban League, 1974-77, Smith Coll., 1975-80, Brookings Instn., 1974-77, Alfred P. Sloan Found., 1975-77, 81—, Bur. Social Sci. Rsch., Inc., 1985-87; bd. dirs. Catalyst, 1972-90, Internat. Exec. Svc. Corps, Atlantic Coun. of U.S., 1988—, vice chmn., 1993—; former bd. govs. Am. Nat. Red Cross, Common Cause, Women's Action Alliance; bd. govs. Internat. Ctr. on Election Law and Adminstrn., 1985-87; trustee Lafayette Coll., 1985—, vice chmn., 1990—. Recipient Achievement award Bur. Govt. Research, U. Mass., 1963; Distinguished Service award Boston Coll., 1965; Smith Coll. medal, 1969; Distinguished Civil Leadership award Tufts U., 1965; Distinguished Service award Northfield Mount Hermon Sch., 1976; Radcliffe fellow Radcliffe Inst., 1965-66, 66-67. Mem. NAACP, ACLU, Nat. Acad. Pub. Adminstrn., UN Assn., Urban League, Assn. Am. Indian Affairs, East African Wildlife Soc., Jersey Wildlife Preservation Trust Channel Islands, Internat. Inst. Strategic Studies. Home and Office: 46 Sunset Ave Amherst MA 01002-2097

BENSON, S. PATRICIA, artist, educator; b. Phila., July 27, 1941; d. Thomas Edward and Sarah Adelaide (Shute) McMahon; children: Sarah Letitia Benson, Erin Aurora Peck. BFA, Mich. State U., 1963; MFA, Fla. State U., 1967. Textile artist Brewster Finishing, N.Y.C., 1963-64; instr. of art Fla. State U., Tallahassee, 1967-69; asst. prof. art Sonoma (Calif.) State Coll., 1970-71; printmaking instr. San Francisco Art Inst., 1971-75, Portland Sch. of Art, 1978-80; art instr. U. So. Maine, Gorham, 1976-80, 1988—; & U. Maine, Augusta, 1993—; art cons. grades 7-12, Waterboro (Maine) Sch. Dist. # 57., 1988—. Represented in numerous permanent collections at La. State U., SUNY-Albany, Mobile Art Mus., Fla. State U., South Ga. Coll., Tallahassee Jr. Coll., State of N.Y., U. of Pacific, Okla. Art Ctr., U. Dallas, Hawaii Acad. Art, Calif. Palace of Legion of Honor, Achenbach Found., U. N.D., Anchorage (Alaksa) Fine Art Mus., Cin. Mus. Art, U. Minn. Tweed Mus., Indpls. Mus. Art, Famsworth Mus., Rockport, Maine, 1st Nat. Bank of Boston, New Eng. Coll., Einstein Coll., Bklyn. Mus., Internat. Comm. Agy.; one person shows incl. Bi National Cultural Inst., Santiago, Chile, La Paz, Bolivia, Lima, Peru, Bogota, Columbia, Mexico City, Mexico, Caracus, Venezuela, Jacksonville Mus. Art, Attleboro Mus. Art., San Francisco Mus. Art., Fendrick Gallery, Washington, and others. Mem. Part Time Faculty Assn. for U. Maine System (pres. of union). Democrat. Home and Studio: Box 340 Alfred ME 04002

BENSON, SANDRA JEAN, media specialist; b. Winona, Minn., Apr. 13, 1949; d. Artha B.O. and Virginia H. (McNamer) Thompson. BS, U. Wis., River Falls, 1975, MAT in Elem. Edn., 1982. Libr. Cen. High Sch., Paddock Lake, Wis., 1974-76; media specialist Hudson (Wis.) Pub. Schs., 1976—; instr. U. Wis., River Falls, 1991-92; cons. tech. several ednl. and bus. orgns., River Falls, 1990—. Mem. ALA, Wis. Ednl. Media Assn., Soc. Sch. Librs. Internat., Assn. for Ednl. Communications and Tech. (div. sch. media specialist). Office: Hudson Mid Sch 1300 Carmichael Rd Hudson WI 54016

BENSON, SANDRA SEXTON, program manager; b. Appalachia, Va., Aug. 19, 1943; d. Charles Taze Russell and Margaret Doris (Cornett) Sexton; m. Charles Richard Benson. BS, Rollins Coll., 1971; MBA, Stetson U., 1974; Sr. Exec. Fellow, Harvard U., 1992; postgrad., U. Va., 1993. Statistician Bendix Corp., Kennedy Space Center, Fla., 1967-71, sr. engr., 1971-77; bus. mgr. Bendix Corp., Marshall Space Flt. Ctr., Ala., 1978-81; ops. rsch. analyst U.S. Army, Huntsville, Ala., 1981-86, supr. indsl. engr., 1986-88, systems analysis mgr., 1988-90, program mgr., 1990—; instr. Brevard C.C., Cocoa, Fla., 1975-77. Mem. Friends of the Symphony, Huntsville, Mus. of Art Assn., Huntsville, U. Ala. Hunstville Athletic Assn. Mem. AAUW, Nat. Contracts Mgmt. Assn., Ops. Rsch. Soc. of Am., Nat. Mgmt. Assn. (chpt. v.p. 1975-77, bd. dirs. 1971-77), Am. Soc. Mil. Comptrollers, Soc. Cost Estimating/Analysis, Def. Systems Mgmt. Coll. Alumni Assn., Harvard Alumni Assn.

BENSON, SARA ELIZABETH, real estate broker, real estate appraiser; b. Columbia, S.C., Nov. 29, 1960; d. Herbert Lankford Benson and Anna Marian (Stanley) Tucker; m. Donald Edward O'Connor, Apr. 29, 1984 (div. Oct. 1993); m. Donald Joseph DeBat, Aug. 20, 1994; children; from previous marriage: D. Edward, Herbert L. Benson IV. Student, U. S.C., 1977, Am. Conservatory Music, Chgo., 1978-81. Lic. real estate broker, Ill., S.C.; designated cert. real estate brokerage mgr.; approved ind. fee appraiser; cert. real estate appraiser, Ill. V.p. O'Connor & Assocs., Chgo., 1982-92; pres., owner Buyer's Resource Metro Properties, Chgo., 1990—; owner Sara Benson Cons., Inc., Chgo., 1992—; fee appraiser FHA, HUD, Chgo., 1986—; speaker, author in field. Mem. NAFE, Nat. Assn. Realtors, Assn. Fed. Appraisers, Real Estate Buyer's Agt. Coun., Ill. Assn. Realtors, Chgo. Assn. Realtors (chair profl. standards com.), North Shore Bd. Realtors, Real Estate Brokerage Mgrs. Coun., MLS No. Ill., Nat. Assn. Ind. Fee Appraisers, Bus. Execs. Assn. Chgo. Office: Buyer's Resource Met Prop 1708 N Wells St Chicago IL 60614-5806

BENSON, SHARON JOAN, mathematics educator; b. Glendale, Calif., Aug. 23, 1964; d. Paul John and Arleen Camille (Green) B. BS in Math., Calif. Poly. State U., 1987; MST in Math., U. N.H., 1992. Cert. single subject clear math., Calif. Tchr. math. Victor Valley Union High Sch. Dist., Victorville, Calif., 1988—; part-time instr. Victor Valley C.C., Victorville, 1993—. Mem. Nat. Coun. Tchrs. Math., Calif. Math. Coun., Oreg. Coun. Tchrs. of Math., Assn. Women in Math. Republican. Roman Catholic. Office: Victor Valley High Sch 16500 Mojave Dr Victorville CA 92392

BENSON, SHARON STOVALL, primary school educator; b. Clovis, N.Mex., Apr. 18, 1946; d. Travis and Anna Gene (Crump) Stovall; m. Merle John Benson, Aug. 21, 1966; children: Brenda Kay, Linda Carol. BS, U. N.Mex., 1968, MA, 1980. Cert. tchr., N.Mex. Kindergarten aide Albuquerque Pub. Schs., 1976-78; tchr. LaMesa Little Sch., Albuquerque, 1987-88, Congl. Presch., Albuquerque, 1991—; parent rep. South Atlantic Regional Resource Ctr., Plantation, Fla., 1986-87; sec. bd. Albuquerque Spl. Presch., 1975. Trained evaluator Assn. Retarded Citizens, Albuquerque, 1988—. Mem. Parents Reaching Out, Assn. Retarded Citizens, N.Mex. Assn. Edn. Young Children, Pi Lambda Theta. Methodist. Home: 7409 Carriveau NE Albuquerque NM 87110

BENSON-MONTAGUE, BARBARA JEAN, secondary school educator; b. Winfield, Kans., Feb. 5, 1938; d. Roy George and Edna Beatrice (Myers) David; m. James Frederick Benson, Feb. 27, 1960 (div. Mar. 6, 1986); children: Julie L., Amy J.; m. H.F. Montague, Mar. 21, 1992. BS in Home Econs. Edn., Kans. State U., 1960, MS in Occupational and Vocat. Edn., 1978; postgrad., Ottawa (Kans.) U., 1988-91, Pittsburg (Kans.) State U., 1980-87. Cert. tchr., Kans. Tchr. home econs. Shawnee Mission (Kans.) Sch. Dist., 1960—; personal wardrobe cons. in fashion Jones Store Co., Overland Park, Kans., 1986—; educator/facilitator substance abuse groups Shawnee Mission Schs., 1989; presenter seminars in field. Mem. NEA, AAUW. Home: 10733 W 116th St Overland Park KS 66210-3812

BENT, JAN BRIGHAM, college official; b. Berkeley, Calif., June 25, 1939; d. Carroll Walter and Elizabeth Anne (Anderson) B.; m. John Walter Strohbehn (div. 1977); children: Jo Anne, Kris, Carolyn; m. Charles Colby Bent. Student, San Diego State Coll., 1957; MA, Dartmouth Coll., Hanover, N.H., 1982. Retail mgr. Omer's and Bob's, Hanover, N.H., 1970-74; co-chair, coach Ford Sayre Racing Team, Hanover, N.H., 1973-74; tennis coach Dartmouth Coll., Hanover, N.H., 1973-75, Hanover (N.H.) High Sch., 1973-75; conf. coordinator Dartmouth Coll. The Amos Tuck Sch. Bus. Administrn., Hanover, N.H., 1973-76; rsch. coord. dept. edn. Dartmouth Coll., N.H., 1976-78; dir. Champion-Tuck awards minority and bus. exec. seminar and Amos Tuck sch. Dartmouth Coll., 1978-86; exec. dir. Dartmouth Inst. Dartmouth Coll., Hanover, 1986-94, assoc. dir. Office Alumni Rels., 1994—; lectr., presenter Nat. Minority Supplier Devel. Coun., Detroit, 1984; cons. Nat. Bus. Coun., Detroit, 1984, Nat. Bus. League, Atlanta, 1985, Mt. Holyoke Coll., South Hadley, Mass. Co-author, editor: Aspirations and Attitudes of Rural High School Students: A Report of the Options Project, 1977; author: Approximate Shorelines for Lakes Hitchcock and Upham, 1982. Ski instr. Ford Sayre Alpine Racing Program, 1963-76, co-chair, treas., 1973-77, publicity chair LWV, Hanover, 1964-67. Office: Dartmouth Coll Office Alumni Rels 6068 Blunt Ctr Hanover NH 03755-3590

BENTLEY, DORIS BROUSSARD, retired educator, consultant; b. Loreauville, La., July 8, 1919; d. Jean Edmond and Martha Anna (Camos) Broussard; m. George F. Bentley, July 7, 1945 (dec. Mar. 1953); children: George F. Jr., Edmond B., Suzanne M., Richard C., William C. BS, La. State U., 1938, MEd, 1956, PhD, 1971. Adminstrv. sec. McNeese State U., Lake Charles, La., 1939-43; sec., clk. U.S. Army, New Orleans, La., 1943-44; tchr. Iberia Parish Schs., New Iberia, La., 1953-59; prof. U. S.W. La., Lafayette, 1959-86; cons., vol. Lafayette, 1986—. Treas. Bayou Coun. Girl Scouts USA, Lafayette, 1985—; region II, alt. regional mgr., coord. women Bus. Ownership Svc. Corps of Retired Execs., Lafayette, 1987—; mem. Mcpl. Civil Svc. Bd., Lafayette, 1985-94. Mem. NEA, AAUW (state pres. 1980-82), La. Retired Tchrs. Assn., Cath. Daughters of Am.

BENTLEY, JEANETTE SPRAGUE, public relations executive; b. Escondido, Calif., Apr. 2, 1959; d. Durham Daniel and Jeannette Lalani (Thomas) Sprague, m. Scott Alan Bentley, Oct. 18, 1986. AA, San Diego Mesa Jr. Coll., 19982; BA, San Diego State Coll., 1988. Asst. promotions Sta. KGB-FM Radio, San Diego, 1984-86; dir. program, cons. Say NO to Drugs Inc., San Diego, 1987—; dir. br. Leukemia Soc. Am., San Diego, 1986-88; sole proprietor Sprague-Bentley and Assocs., San Diego, 1987—. Mem. Nat. Assn. Female Execs., Pub. Relations soc., Meeting Planners Internat., San Diego Mus. Art, Young Connoisseurs, Arthritis Found., P.S. We Care (founder), San Diego Alumni Assn. (mem. Hall of Champions). Republican. Office: Sprague-Bently and Assocs 701 "B" St # 1300 San Diego CA 92101

BENTON, MICHELLE MARIE, accountant; b. Thief River Falls, Minn., June 21, 1963; d. Martin Edward Jr. and Louise Marie (Knutson) Solseng; m. Timothy Scott Benton, June 18, 1983. BS in Acctg., St. Cloud State U., 1985. CPA, Minn. Supr. Charles Bailly & Co., Mpls., 1985-90; ptnr. Anderson, Poissant, Kays & Co., Thief River Falls, 1990—; adv. mem. acctg. N.W. Tech. Coll., Thief River Falls, 1991—; bd. dirs. N.W. Regional Enterprise Fund, Thief River Falls. Bd. dirs., treas. Northland Cmty. Hospice, Thief River Falls, 1993—. Recipient Outstanding Performance award Dale Carnegie Tng., 1993. Mem. AAUW (treas.), AICPA, Minn. Soc. Cert. Pub. Accts., Women's Network, Rotary Club (program com.), Thief River Falls C. of C. (amb. 1991—). Lutheran. Office: Anderson Poissant Kays & Co PO Box 637 116 3rd St W Thief Rvr Fls MN 56701-1915

BENTON-BORGHI, BEATRICE HOPE, educational consultant, author; b. San Antonio, Nov. 7, 1946; d. Donald Francis and Beatrice Hope (Peche) Benton; BA in Chemistry, North Adams State Coll., 1968; MEd, Boston U., 1972; m. Peter T. Borghi, Aug. 12, 1980; children: Kathryn Benton Borghi, Sarah Benton Borghi. Tchr. chemistry Cathedral High Sch., Springfield, Mass., 1968-69; tchr. sci. and history Munich (W.Ger.) Am. High Sch., 1969-70; tchr. English, Tokyo, Japan, 1970-71; tchr. chemistry and sci. Marlborough (Mass.) High Sch., 1971-80; project dir., adminstr. ESEA, Marlborough Pub. Schs., 1976-77; project dir., proposal writer Title III, Title IX, U.S. Dept. Edn., 1975-76, 76-77; evaluation team New Eng. Assn. Schs. and Colls., 1974, 78; mem. regional dept. edn. com., 1977-78; ednl. cons., lectr., 1978—. Author: Project ABC (Access By Computer), 1991, Alternative Funding/Recycling Project, 1991, Down the Aisle, 1995, Best Friends, 1995, Open Minds, 1995. Energy conservation rep. Marlborough's Overall Econ. Devel. Com., 1976; chmn. Marlborough's Energy Conservation Task Force, 1975; dir. Walk for Mankind, 1972; sec. Group Action for Marlborough Environment, 1975-76; bd. dirs. Girls Club, Marlborough, 1979; pres. Sisters, Inc., 1979-83. Mem. AAUW, Council for Exceptional Children, Nat. Women's Health Network. Home and Office: 2449 Edington Rd Columbus OH 43221-3047

BENZIES, BONNIE JEANNE, clinical and industrial psychologist; b. Chgo., May 3, 1943; d. Roy Benzies and Margaret Lucille (Hernly) Benzies-Sorensen. BS, MacMurray Coll., 1965; MS, Ill. Inst. Tech., 1971, PhD, 1980. Lic. psychologist, Ill. Statistician, psychologist State of Ill., Chgo., 1966-73; psychologist State of Ill., Manteno, 1976-82; psychologist adminstr. State of Ill., Elgin, 1988—; psychologist Ingalls Meml. Hosp., Harvey, Ill., 1982-84, Cook County Juvenile Ct., Chgo., 1987-88; pvt. practice Chgo., Hanover Park, Palatine, Ill., 1984—; cons., trainer PREVENTION PLUS of Palatine, 1994—; grad. tchg. asst. Ill. Inst. Tech., Chgo., 1973-74; mem. staff Hoffman Estates Med. Ctr., Woodland Hosp., Hoffman Estates. Co-author psychol. test: Time Questionnaire, 1979. Mem. Nat. Task Force on Depressive Disorders, 1991—; mem. Statewide Subcom. on Mentally Ill Substance Abuser, 1991-93. MacMurray scholar, 1961-65, Am. Legion scholar, 1963-64; recipient Achievement award in addictions counseling Loop Coll., 1986. Mem. APA, Chgo. Assn. for Psychoanalytic Psychology, Employee Assistance Profls. Assn., Christian Assn. Psychol. Studies, Internat. Critical Incident Stress Found., Inc., Palatine C. of C. Home and Office: PREVENTION PLUS of Palatine 1531 E Anderson Dr Palatine IL 60067-4101

BERA, REGINA HELEN, nursing administrator; b. Bayonne, N.J., July 1, 1938; d. Charles John Hagan and Helen Theresa (Regan) Hewitt; m. Walter Stanley Bera, May 3, 1957; children: Catherine, Jeanette, Ronald, Stacie, Colleen, Melanie. AS in Nursing, NYU, 1983; cert. in gerontology, Kean Coll., 1990. From lic. practical nurse to RN Bayonne (N.J.) Hosp., 1976-87; dir. nursing svcs., asst. dir. Sr. Health Ctr., Bayonne (N.J.) Hosp., 1987—. Mem. Nat. Gerontology, Nat. League Nursing, Acad. Honor and Profl. Soc. Sigma Phi Omega, Marine Corps. League Aux. Democrat. Roman Catholic. Office: Sr Health Ctr Bayonne Hosp 115 W 42nd St Bayonne NJ 07002-2035

BERARDINI, JACQUELINE HERNANDEZ, lawyer; b. Pueblo, Colo., Sept. 16, 1949; d. Basilio Hernandez and Lorenza (Huerta) Zamarripa; stepfather John E. Zamarripa; m. Jose A. Soliz, Aug. 1971 (div. 1980); 1 child, Christopher A.; m. Brian J. Berardini, Oct. 17, 1981; 1 child, Michael J. BA in Psychology, U. Colo., 1971; MA in Counseling, U. No. Colo., 1973; JD, U. Denver, 1980. Bar: Colo. 1980, U.S. Dist. Ct. Colo. 1980, U.S. Ct. Appeals (10th cir.) 1990, U.S. Supreme Ct. 1991. Sr. rehab. counselor divsn. rehab. Colo. Dept. Social Svcs., 1974-77; assoc. Jeffrey A. Springer, P.C. law firm, 1980-85; dep. atty. gen. Office of Colo. Atty. Gen., 1985-91; asst. to dir., dir. multi-media focal group Office of Environment, Colo. Dept. of Health, Denver, 1991—; apptd. to superfund rev. subcom. Nat. Adv. Com. on Environ. and Policy and Tech., EPA; apptd. to subcom. on transport and opening of waste isolation pilot plant Western Govs.' Assn.; mem. subcom. on federal facilities compliance Nat. Govs.' Assn.; apptd. Pueblo Army Depot Chem. Demilitarization Citizen Rev. Com.; alt. mem. high-level radioactive waste com. Western Interstate Energy Bd.; presenter in field. Contbr. articles to profl. jours. Trustee Thorne Ecol. Inst. Mem. Colo. Bar Assn., Denver Bar Assn., Colo. Hispanic Bar Assn., Colo. Hispanic League. Office: Colo Dept Health OE-B2 4300 Cherry Creek Dr S Denver CO 90222-1530

BERCOVITCH, HANNA MARGARETA, editor; b. Chgo., Il., Sept. 5, 1934; d. Sven Victor and Elizabeth (Rubin) Malmquist; m. Sacvan Bercovitch, July 29, 1956 (div. Mar. 1987); 1 son, Eytan. Student, St. Thomas More Coll., 1960, Sir George Williams Coll., Montreal, 1960-61. Acquisition librarian Honnold Library, Claremont, Calif., 1961-62, acting rare book librarian, 1962-63, spl. project staff, 1963-64; asst. editing Partisan Rev., Rutgers U. Congress Monthly, N.Y.C., 1974-75, 78-80; free lance research assoc. Columbia U., N.Y.C., 1965-80; sr. editor Library of Am. Literary Classics, N.Y.C., 1980-86, editor-in-chief, 1986—; guest curator Melville Whitman Exhibit, N.Y. Pub. Libr., 1982. Environ. commr. City of Leonia, N.J., 1971-73. Mem. Grolier Club (N.Y.C.). Office: Libr Am Lit Classics US 14 E 60th St New York NY 10022-1006

BEREGI, LISA ANN, pharmacist; b. New Brunswick, N.J., Mar. 8, 1964; d. Charles Richard and Donna Jean (Scott) B. Student, Wofford Coll., 1982-84; PharmD, Mercer U., 1988. Staff pharmacist Johnson City (Tenn.) Med. Ctr. Hosp., 1988-90, surgery pharmacy coord., 1990—; mem. adj. faculty, preceptor Mercer U., Atlanta, 1993—. Mem. Am. Soc. Hosp. Pharmacists, Tenn. Pharmacist Assn., Tenn. Operating Rm. Pharamcy Satellite Assn., N.E. Tenn. Pharmacist Assn., Kappa Epsilon (v.p. 1993—). Roman Catholic. Home: 321 Brookwood Dr Bristol TN 37620-2810 Office: Johnson City Med Ctr Hosp Pharmacy Svcs 400 State of Franklin Johnson City TN 37604

BERENS, BETTY KATHRYN MCADAM, community program administrator; b. Wheeling, W.Va., Dec. 17, 1927; d. Will and Elizabeth Margaret (Wickham) McAdam; m. Alan Robert Berens, June 18, 1949; children: Robert Seton, Kathryn Elizabeth. BA cum laude, We. Res. U., 1949; postgrad., Kent State U., 1967. Vol. various cities, Ohio, 1963-88; founder We. Res. Human Svcs., Akron, Ohio, 1975-84; cons. Hudson (Ohio) Local Schs., Addison County, Vt., 1968-88, coord. community/sch. vol. program (VIP); pres. aux. bd. Porter Med. Ctr., Middlebury, Vt., 1990-92; vol. Hawthornden State Hosp., Cleve., 1963-65; vol. probation officer Mcpl. Ct., Cuyahoga Falls, Ohio, 1973-74; comms. chmn. Elderly Svcs. Inc., Middlebury, 1990—; bd. dirs. Porter Med. Ctr., 1990-92; community sch. vol. cons. Ohio Dept. Edn., Columbus, 1984-88. Bd. dirs. Internat. Inst., Akron, 1983-88, pres., 1986-87; mem. Summit County Bd. Edn., Akron, 1977-88, pres., 1981, 86; chmn. Hudson Cares, 1974-76; comm. chair Addison County United Way, 1990—. Recipient Community Svc. award Hudson Jaycees, 1984, Commendation for Outstanding Svc. in Edn. Pres. Ronald Reagan, 1988. Mem. Phi Delta Kappa (Leader in Edn. 1977, 88). Home: RR 2 Box 3510 Middlebury VT 05753-8904

BERENSTAIN, JANICE, author, illustrator; b. Phila., July 26, 1923; d. Alfred J. and Marian (Beck) Grant; m. Stanley Berenstain, Apr. 13, 1946; children: Leo, Michael. Student, Phila. Coll. Art, 1941-45. Works exhibited in Met. Mus. Art, N.Y.C.; works represented at U. Kans., Kans. State U.; author, illustrator (with Stanley Berenstain): The Berenstain's Baby Book, 1951, Sister, 1952, Tax-Wise, 1952, Marital Blitz, 1954, Baby Makes Four, 1956, Lover Boy, 1958, It's All In The Family, 1958, Bedside Lover Boy, 1960, And Beat Him When He Sneezes, 1960, Call Me Mrs., 1961, It's Still In The Family, 1961, Office Lover Boy, 1962, The Facts of Life For Grown-Ups, 1963, Flipsville-Squaresville, 1965, Mr. Dirty vs. Mr. Clean, 1967, You Could Diet Laughing, 1969, Be Good or I'll Bet You, 1970, Education Impossible, 1970, Never Trust Anyone Over 13, 1970, How To Teach Your Children About Sex Without Making A Complete Fool Of Yourself, 1970, How To Teach Your Children About God Without Actually Scaring Them Out Of Their Wits, 1971, Are Parents For Real?, 1972, What Your Parents Never Told You About Being a Mom or Dad, 1995; author, illustrator (with Stanley Berenstain) children's series Berenstain Bears; writer TV teleplays include The Berenstain Bears' Christmas Tree, 1979, The Berenstain Bears Meet Bigpaw, 1980, The Berenstain Bears' Easter Surprise, 1981, The Berenstain Bears' Comic Valentine, 1983, The Berenstain Bears' Play Ball, 1983, The Berenstain Bers' CBS Show, 1986-87. Recipient Sch. Bell award NEA, 1960, Best Book award Am. Inst. Graphic Arts, 1970, Silver award Internat. Film and TV Festival, 1980, 82, 87, Young Readers' award Mich. Coun. Tchrs. English, 1981, Children's Classic award Internat. Reading Assn., 1982, 83, 84, 87, Buckeye award Ohio State Libr. Assn., 82, 85, Ariz. Children's Book award nominee, 1985, Ariz. Young Reader's award, 1985, Ludington award, 1989; named various books Best Book U. Chgo. Ctr. for Children's Books, 1972, 74, Brit. Book Ctr. Honor Book, 1968, Honor Book Phila. Libr. Children's Reading Round Table, 1972, 73, 74, 76, 80, 82, 83, 84, 85, 87, 88, 89, 91, 93, Children's Book of Yr. by Child Study Assn., 1977, 82. Office: Sterling Lord 1 Madison Ave New York NY 10010-3603*

BEREZIN, TANYA, artistic director, actress; b. Phila., Mar. 25, 1941; d. Maurice and Bettye (Shifrin) Berezin; m. Robert Leeming Thirkield, June 29, 1969 (div. June 1977); children: Lila Joy, Jonathon Schuyler; m. Mark Beers Wilson, Oct. 18, 1987. Student, Boston U., 1959-63. Co-founder Circle Repertory Co., N.Y.C., 1969, artistic dir., 1986—. Appeared in (TV shows) St. Elsewhere, 1984, Law and Order, 1992, 93, 94, (play) Angels Fall, 1983, Moundbuilders, 1975 (Obie award), (film) Awakenings, 1993; producer Prelude to a Kiss, Destiny of Me, Three Hotels. Office: Circle Repertory Co 632 Broadway 6th Fl New York NY 10012

BERFIELD, SUE ANN, city commissioner, legal assistant; b. Fremont, Ohio, Nov. 20, 1940; d. William J. and Mary L. (Fetter) Mautz; m. James L. Berfield, Dec. 29, 1962; children: Kimberly, Kristine. Student, Ill. State Normal U., 1959. Bd. dirs. Jolley Trolley Corp., Clearwater, Fla., Clearwater Marine Sci. Ctr.; chairperson Pinellas Planning Coun., Clearwater. Mem. bd. Performing Arts Ctr., Clearwater; commr. City of Clearwater, vice chairperson Cmty. Redevel. Agy.; vice mayor City of Clearwater, 1991-92; Rep. precinct committeewoman, Clearwater; mem. Pinellas County Rep. Exec. Com. Mem. Leadership Pinellas, Clearwater Cmty. Womens' Club,. Baptist. Home: 1466 Flora Rd Clearwater FL 34615 Office: City of Clearwater 112 S Osceola Clearwater FL 34616

BERG, EVELYNNE MARIE, geography educator; b. Chgo.; d. Clarence Martin and Mildred (Strnad) B.; BS with honors, U. Ill., 1954; MA, Northwestern U., 1959. Geography editor Am. Peoples Ency., Chgo., 1955-57; social studies tchr. Hammond (Ind.) Tech.-Vocat. High Sch., 1958-59; geography tchr. Carl Schurz High Sch., Chgo., 1960-66; faculty geography Morton Coll., Cicero, Ill., 1966—. Asst. leader Cicero coun. Girl Scouts U.S.A., 1951-53; Fulbright scholar, Brazil, 1964; NSF scholar, 1963, 65, 71-72; NDEA fellow, 1968-69; fellow Faculty Inst. S. and S.E. Asia, 1980; NEH scholar DePaul U., 1984; recipient award Ill. Geog. Soc., 1977. Fellow Nat. Coun. Geog. Edn. (state coord. 1973-74, exec. bd. 1973-77); mem. Nat., Ill. (sec.-treas. 1968-69, sec. 1969-70, v.p. 1970-71, pres. 1971-72), Am. Overseas Educators (sec. Ill. chpt. 1974-76, v.p. chpt. 1977-78), AAUW (Chgo. br. rec. sec. 1963-65), Assn. Am. Geographers, Ill., Acad. Sci., AAAS (scholar 1973-74), Ill. Coun. Social Studies, Geol. Soc. Am. (membership chair Morton Coll. chpt.), Ill. C.C. Faculty Assn. (v.p. membership and del. affairs 1982-84), Des Plaines Valley Geol. Soc., Fulbright Assn., Sierra Club, Sigma Xi, Gamma Theta Upsilon, Delta Kappa Gamma (pres. Gamma Omicron chpt. 1988-90, parliamentarian 1990-94, membership chair 1992-94, nominations chair. 1994—), Des Plaines Valley Geological Soc. Clubs: Order Eastern Star, Bus. and Profl. Women's (acting pres. 1980-81, parliamentarian 1989-90). Contbr. to profl. jours. Home: 3924 N Pioneer Ave Chicago IL 60634-2050 Office: Morton Coll 3801 S Central Ave Cicero IL 60650-4306

BERG, LILLIAN DOUGLAS, chemistry educator; b. Birmingham, Ala., July 9, 1925; d. Gilbert Franklin and Mary Rachel (Griffin) Douglas; m. Joseph Wilbur Berg, June 26, 1950; children: Anne Berg Jenkins, Joseph Wilbur III, Frederick Douglas. BS in Chemistry, Birmingham So. Coll., 1946; MS in Chemistry, Emory U., 1948. Instr. chemistry Armstrong Jr. Coll., Savannah, Ga., 1948-50; rsch. asst. chemistry Pa. State U., University Park, 1950-54; instr. chemistry U. Utah, Salt Lake City, 1955-56; prof. chemistry No. Va. C.C., Annandale, 1974—. Mem. Am. Chem. Soc., Am. Women in Sci., Mortar Bd. Soc., Iota Sigma Pi, Sigma Delta Epsilon, Phi Beta Kappa. Home: 3319 Dauphine Dr Falls Church VA 22042-3724 Office: No Va CC 8333 Little River Tpke Annandale VA 22003-3796

BERG, LORINE MCCOMIS, retired guidance counselor; b. Ashland, Ky., Mar. 28, 1919; d. Oliver Botner and Emma Elizabeth (Eastham) McComis; m. Leslie Thomas Berg, Apr. 27, 1946; children: James Michael, Leslie Jane. BA in Edn., U. Ky., 1965; MA, Xavier U., 1969. Tchr. A.D. Owens Elem. Sch., Newport, Ky., 1963-64, 6th dist. Elementary Schs., Covington, Ky., 1965-69; guidance counselor Twenhofel Jr. H.S., Independence, Ky., 1969-78, Scott H.S., Taylor Mill, Ky., 1978-84. Bd. dirs. Mental Health Assn., Covington, Ky, 1970-76, v.p., 1973 (valuable svc. award 1973); mem. Lakeside Christian Ch., Ft. Mitchell, Ky. Named to Honorable Order of Ky. Colonels, Hon. Admissions Counselor U.S. Naval Acad.; cited by USN Recruiting Command for Valuable Assistance to USN, 1981. Mem. Am. Assn. of Univ. Women, Covington Art Club, Retired Tchrs. Assn., Kappa Delta Pi, Delta Kappa Gamma, Phi Delta Kappa. Democrat. Home: 11 Idaho Ave Covington KY 41017-2925

BERG, SISTER MARIE MAJELLA, university chancellor; b. Bklyn., July 7, 1916; d. Peter Gustav and Mary Josephine (McAuliff) B. BA, Marymount Coll., 1938; MA, Fordham U., 1948; DHL (hon.), Georgetown U., 1970, Marymount Manhattan Coll., 1983. Registrar Marymount Sch., N.Y.C., 1943-48; prof. classics, registrar Marymount Coll., N.Y.C., 1949-57; registrar Marymount Coll. of Va., Arlington, 1957-58, Marymount Coll., Tarrytown, N.Y., 1958-60; pres. Marymount U., Arlington, Va., 1960-93, chancellor, 1993—; pres. Consortium for Continuing Higher Edn. in Va., 1987-88; mem. com. Consortium of Univs. in Washington Met. Area, 1987-93, chmn., 1992-93. Contbr. five biographies to One Hundred Great Thinkers, 1965; editor Otherwords column of N.Va. Sun newspaper, Arlington. Bd. dirs. Internat. Hospice, 1984—, HOPE, 1983—, SOAR, 1993—, 10th Dist. Congl. Award Coun., No. Va.; vice chmn. bd. Va. Found. Ind. Colls., 1992-93; cmty. advisor Jr. League No. Va., 1992—; mem. Friends of TACTS, 1994—. Recipient commendation Va. Gen. Assembly, Richmond, 1990, 93, Elizabeth Ann Seton award, 1991, Arlington Notable Women award Arlington Commn. on Status of Women, 1992, Voice and Vision award Arlington Cmty. TV Channel 33, 1993, Pro Ecclesia et Pontifice medal Holy See, 1993; elected to Va. Women's Hall of Fame, 1992; named Washingtonian of Yr., Washingtonian mag., 1990. Roman Catholic. Home and Office: Marymount U Office of Chancellor 2807 N Glebe Rd Arlington VA 22207-4224

BERG, MARY JAYLENE, pharmacy educator, researcher; b. Fargo, N.D., Nov. 7, 1950; d. Ordean Kenneth and Anna Margaret (Skramstad) B. BS in Pharmacy, N.D. State U., 1974; PharmD, U. Ky., 1978. Lic. pharmacist, N.D., Ky., Iowa. Fellow in pharmacokinetics Millard Fillmore Hosp./SUNY, Buffalo, 1978-79; asst. prof. U. Iowa, Iowa City, 1980-85, assoc. prof., 1985—; with dept. clin. rsch., clin. pharmacology/pharmacokinetics F. Hoffmann-La Roche, Ltd., Basel, Switzerland, 1992; mem. adv. com. rsch. on women's health NIH, 1995—. Reviewer Cin. Pharmacy, 1984—, Epilepsia, 1987—; editor: Internat. Leadership Symposium, The Role of Women in Pharmacy, 1990, Pharmacy World Congress '91: Women-A Force in Pharmacy Symposium, 1992; contbr. articles to Drug Intelligence & Clin. Pharmacy, New Eng. Jour. of Medicine, Jour. Forensic Scis., Therapeutic Drug Monitoring, Epilepsia. Advisor Kappa Epislon, Iowa City, 1980—; pres. Mortar Bd. Alumnae, Iowa City, 1986-88. NIH grantee, 1984, Nat. Insts. on Drug Abuse grantee, 1986; recipient Career Achievement award Kappa Epsilon, 1985. Mem. Am. Assn. Pharm. Scientists, Am. Soc. Hosp. Phrmacists (chair spl. interest group of clin. pharmacokinetics 1987-89), Am. Epilepsy Soc., Am. Pharm. Assn., Internat. Forum for Women in Pharmacy (U.S. contact), Fedn. Internat. Pharmaceutique (del. World Health Assembly 1992), Leadership Internat., Women in Pharmacy (bd. dirs. 1991—), Sigma Xi, Rho Chi, Kappa Epsilon, Phi Beta Delta. Lutheran. Office: U Iowa Coll of Pharmacy Iowa City IA 52242

BERGÉ, CAROL, author; b. N.Y.C., 1928; d. Albert and Molly Peppis; m. Jack Bergé, June 1955; 1 child, Peter. Asst. to pres. Pendray Public Relations, N.Y.C., 1955; disting. prof. lit. Thomas Jefferson Coll., Allendale, Mich., 1975-76; instr. adult degree program Goddard Coll. at Asilomar, 1976; tchr. fiction and poetry U. Calif. Extension Program, Berkeley, 1976-77; assoc. prof. U. So. Miss., Hattiesburg, 1977-78; vis. prof. Honors Ctr. and English dept. U. N.Mex., 1978-79, 87; vis. lectr. Wright State U., 1979, SUNY, Albany, 1980-81; tchr. Poets and Writers, Poets in the Schs. (N.Y. State Council on Arts), 1970-72, Poets in the Schs. (Conn. Commn. Arts); proprietor Blue Gate Gallery of Art and Antiques, 1988-95. Author: (fiction) The Unfolding, 1969, A Couple Called Moebius, 1972, Acts of Love: An American Novel, 1973 (N.Y. State Coun. on Arts CAPS award 1974), Timepieces, 1977, The Doppler Effect, 1979, Fierce Metronome, 1981, Secrets, Gossip and Slander, 1984, Zebras, or, Contour Lines, 1991; (poetry) The Vulnerable Island, 1964, Poems Made of Skin, 1968, The Chambers, 1969, Circles, as in the Eye, 1969, An American Romance, 1969, From a Soft Angle: Poems About Women, 1972, The Unexpected, 1976, Rituals and Gargoyles, 1976, A Song, A Chant, 1978, Alba Genesis, 1979, Alba Nemesis, 1979; editor: Center Mag., 1970-84, pub. 1991—; editor Miss. Rev., 1977-78, Subterraneans, 1975-76, Paper Branches, 1987, History Book: The NYC Coffeehouse Poets of the 1960's, 1994; contbg. editor Woodstock Rev., 1977-81, Shearsman mag., 1980-82, S.W. Profile, 1981; editor, pub. CENTER Press, 1991-93; pub. Medicine Journeys (Carl Ginsburg), Coastal Lives (Miriam Sagan), 1991; co-pub. Zebras (Carol Berge). Nat. Endowment Arts fellow, 1979-80. Mem. Authors' League, Poets and Writers, MacDowell Fellows Assn., Nat. Press Women. Home: 562 Onate Pl Santa Fe NM 87501

BERGEN, CANDICE, actress, writer, photojournalist; b. Beverly Hills, Calif., May 9, 1946; d. Edgar and Frances (Westerman) B.; m. Louis Malle, Sept. 27, 1980; 1 dau., Chloe. Ed., U. Pa. Model during coll. Films include The Group, The Sand Pebbles, The Day the Fish Came Out, Live for Life, The Magus, Soldier Blue, Getting Straight, The Hunting Party, Carnal Knowledge, T.R. Baskin, The Adventurers, 11 Harrowhouse, Bite the Bullet, The Wind and the Lion, The Domino Principle, The End of the World in Our Usual Bed in a Night Full of Rain, Oliver's Story, Starting Over, Rich and Famous, Gandhi, 1982, Stick, 1985; TV series: Murphy Brown, 1988— (Emmy award, Leading Actress in a Comedy Series, 1988-89, 89-90, 91-92, 93-94); TV films Arthur the King, 1985, Murder by Reason of Insanity, 1985, Mayflower Madam, 1987; TV miniseries Hollywood Wives, 1985, Trying Times, Moving Day; author Knockwood; photojournalist credits include articles for Life, Playboy; dramatist: (play) The Freezer (included in Best Short Plays of 1968). Recipient Emmy awards for lead actress in a comedy series, 1989, 90, 92, 94.

BERGEN, DONNA CATHERINE, neurologist; b. Crawfordshire, Ind., Mar. 17, 1945; d. Donald Walter and Phyllis (Noland) B.; m. Thomas Arthur Madden, May 28, 1978. BA, Vassar Coll., 1967; MD, U. Ill., Chgo., 1971. Diplomate Am. Bd. Neurology and Psychiatry. Intern in internal medicine Evanston (Ill.) Hosp., 1971-72; resident in neurology Rush-Presby.-St. Luke's Med. Ctr., Chgo., 1972-75, asst. attending neurologist, 1975-82, assoc. attending neurologist, 1983-89, sr. attending neurologist, 1989—, dir. Electroencephalography Lab., 1975-88; asst. prof. dept. neurol. scis. Rush Med. Coll., 1975-82, assoc. prof. neurol. scis., 1982—, asst. chmn. dept. neurol. scis.; cons. neurologist Cook County Hosp., 1992—; mem. staff Rush North Shore Hosp., Chgo., 1993—; hon. clin. asst. electroencephalography Nat. Hosp. for Nervous Diseases, London, 1974, hon. clin. asst. Evoked Potential Lab., 1981; cons. for neurology St. Basil's Clinic, Chgo., 1989—; mem. profl. adv. bd. Epilepsy Svcs. Northwestern Ill., 1986—, Epilepsy Svcs. of Greater Chgo., 1993—; cons., lectr. in field; organizer, moderator, presenter seminars in field; examiner Am. Bd. Qualification in Electroencephalography, 1982, 88. Reviewer Neurology, 1987-93, Archives of Neurology, 1988-91, Electroencephalography and Clin. Neurophysiology, 1987-92, Epilepsia, 1990-93, Jour. AMA, 1989-93; contbr. articles, abstracts, revs., chpts. to profl. pubs. Grantee Lorex Pharms., 1986-87, Burroughs Wellcome Co., 1988-90, McNeil Pharm. Co., 1988-90, 89-92, Epilepsy Found. Am., 1988-89, Parke Davis, 1989-93, Wallace, 1989-91, 90-92, Marion Merrell Dow, 1990-92, 91, Cyberonics, 1990-92, Abbott Labs., 1991—, Dainippon Pharm. Co., 1993—. Fellow Am. Acad. Neurology, Am. EEG Soc., Royal Soc. Medicine; mem. Am. Epilepsy Soc., Am. Acad. Neurology, Chgo. Neurol. Soc. (pres. 1992-93), Ea. EEG Soc., Chgo. Neurol. Soc. (sec.-treas. 1989-90, v.p. 1991-92), Soc. for Clin. Autonomic Disorders, World Fedn. Neurology (founding mem., rsch. group on orgn. and delivery of neurol. svcs. 1990—), Alpha Omega Alpha. Office: Rush Med Coll 1725 W Harrison St Chicago IL 60612-3828

BERGEN, POLLY, actress; b. Knoxville, Tenn.; d. William and Lucy (Lawhorn) Burgin; m. Freddie Fields, Feb. 13, 1956 (div. 1976); children: Kathy, Pamela, Peter. Pres. Polly Bergen Cosmetics, Polly Bergen Jewelry, Polly Bergen Shoes. Author: Fashion and Charm, 1960, Polly's Principles, 1974, I'd Love To, But What'll I Wear, 1977; author, producer for TV: Leave of Absence, 1994; Broadway plays include Champagne Complex, John Murray Andersons' Almanac, First Impression, Plaza Suite, Love Letters; films include Cape Fear, Move Over Darling, Kisses for My President, At War with the Army, The Stooge, That's My Boy, The Caretakers, A Guide for the Married Man, Making Mr. Right, Cry-Baby, 1990, Dr. Jekyll and Ms. Hyde, When We Were Colored, 1994; performed in one woman shows in Las Vegas and Reno, Nev.; albums: Bergen Sings Morgan, The Party's Over, All Alone By the Telephone, Polly and Her Pop, The Four Seasons of Love, Annie Get Your Gun and Do Re Mi, My Heart Sings, Act One Sing Too; numerous TV appearances including star of The Polly Bergen Show, NBC-TV; other TV appearances include The Helen Morgan Story, 1957 (Emmy award as best actress), To Tell the Truth, Death Cruise, Murder on Flight 502, How to Pick Up Girls!, Born Beautiful; (co-star) TV series Baby Talk; miniseries include The Winds of War (Emmy nomination), 79 Park Ave, War and Remembrance, 1988 (Emmy nomination); starring in TV series Baby Talk, 1991-92; writer, prodr. NBC movie Leave of Absence, 1994. Bd. dirs. Martha Graham Dance Center; hon. canister campaign chairperson Cancer Care, Inc., Nat. Cancer Found.; founder Nat. Bus. Coun. for ERA; mem. Planned Prenthood Fedn., Am. Bd. Advocates; nat. adv. com. NARAL, Hollywood Women's Polit. Com.; bd. dirs. Calif. Abortion Rights Action League, Show Coalition. Recipient Fame award Top Ten in TV, 1957-58, Troupers award Sterling Publs., 1957, Editors and Critics award Radio and TV Daily, 1958, Outstanding Working Woman award Downtown St. Louis, Inc., Golden Plate award Am. Acad. Achievement, 1969, Outstanding Mother's award Nat. Mothers' Day Com., 1984, Best Achievement in New Jewelry Design, 1986, Cancer Care award, 1989, Woman of Achievement award LWV, 1990, Extraordinary Achievement award Nat. Women's Law Ctr., 1991; Polly Bergen Cardio-Pulmonary Rsch. Lab., Children's Rsch. Inst. and Hosp., Denver dedicated, 1970. Mem. AFTRA, AGVA, SAG, Actors Equity, AGVA, AFTRA, Show Coalition (bd. dirs.), Soc. Singers (bd. dirs.), Calif. Abortion Rights Action League (bd. dirs., Freedom of Choice award 1992). Office: care Jan McCormack 11342 Dona Lisa Dr Studio City CA 91604-4315

BERGEN, VIRGINIA LOUISE, principal, language arts educator; b. St. Louis, Apr. 5, 1945; d. Roland Daniel Paton and Gladys (Crawford) Gibson; m. Robert Elwood Bergen, July 11, 1964; children: Robert Brandon, Jennifer Lynn. BA, So. Ill. U., 1971, MS, 1973, EdS, 1975; Ednl. Adminstrn. Cert., U. Oreg., 1981. Cert. K-12 Ed. Ad., K-9 tchr., K-12 spl. edn., speech corr., reading specialist, Colo., Oreg., Ill, Mo., N.Mex. Speech therapist Dist. #175, Belleville, Ill., 1971-73; K-12 clin. tchr. Collinsville (Ill.) Unit #10, 1973-74, jr. high sch. LD tchr., 1974-78; edn. resource cons. Douglas Edn. Svc. Dist., Roseburg, Oreg., 1978-80; child devel. specialist Roseburg Dist. #4, 1980-82; asst. prin. Mesa County Valley Dist. #51, Grand Junction, Colo., 1982-85, prin., 1985—; vis. lectr. So. Ill. U., 1976-78; instr. Met. State Coll., Denver, 1989-91; lectr. Mesa State Coll., Grand Junction, 1991-92; in-svc. provider Mesa County Valley Sch. Dist. #51, 1982—; founding mem. governance bd. Basil T. Knight Staff Devel. Ctr., Dist. #51, Grand Junction, 1986-89. Mem. Colo. Assn. Sch. Execs., Phi Delta Kappa. Office: Fruitvale Elem Sch 585 30 Rd Grand Junction CO 81504-5658

BERGER, ANITA HAZEL, psychotherapist, adult educator; b. N.Y.C., Mar. 27, 1930; d. Harry William and Sadye (Lauzar) Fink; m. Ramon Francis Berger, May 6, 1951; children: Elizabeth Harrie, Gideon Samuel. BA cum laude, Bklyn. Coll., 1951; MSW, U. Pa., 1953; postgrad., Columbia U., NYU. Cert. social worker, N.Y. Psychotherapist Jewish Community Svcs. L.I., N.Y.C., 1953-57; psychotherapist, field work instr. Jewish Family Svc., N.Y.C., 1957-60; supr. lower Manhattan social svc. dept., dir. student unit N.Y.C. Housing Authority, 1972-74; asst. prof. SUNY Grad. Sch. Social Work, Buffalo, 1974-75; psychotherapist Ch. Mission of Hope Family Svc., Erie County Mental Health Svcs., Buffalo, 1975-77; pvt. practice Providence, 1978—; instr. Brown Learning Community Brown U., 1988-92; cons. orgnl. leadership Quest for Excellence, Providence, 1992—; cons. in field. Coord. Community Ctf. Art Show, N.Y.C., 1964-71; rep. community planning bd. 2 Congressman Koch's, N.Y.C., 1968-71; mem. adv. com. to bd. dirs. Mental Health Clinic, Buffalo, 1976-77; bd. dirs., chmn. tng. and edn. com., trainer Vols. in Action, Providence, 1979-85; mem. R.I. adv. com. U.S. Commn. on Civil Rights, 1981-85; rep. R.I. Coalition Against Bigotry, 1982-85; mem. allocations and budget com. United Way Southeastern New Eng., Providence, 1981-84; mem. R.I. Gov.'s Adv. Commn. on Women, 1982-85. Recipient Woman of Yr. award Providence Bus. and Profl. Women's Orgn., 1984. Fellow N.Y. State Soc. Clin. Social Work Psychotherapists; mem. Nat. Assn. Social Workers, R.I. Group Psychotherapy Assn. (pres. 1988-89), Alpha Kappa Delta. Jewish. Office: 155 Laurel Ave Providence RI 02906

BERGER, BARBARA PAULL, social worker; b. St. Louis, June 18, 1955; d. Ted and Florence Ann (Vines) Paull; m. Allan Berger, Dec. 27, 1980; children: Melissa Dawn, Tammi Alyse, Jessica Lauren. BS, U. Tex., 1977; MSSW, U. Wis., 1978. Lic./cert. social worker, Tex., Miss., Ky.; bd. cert. diplomate Am. Bd. Examiners Clin. Social Work. Clin. social worker Child and Family Svcs., Buffalo, 1980-81, United Cerebral Palsy Assn., St. Louis, 1982-83; clin. social worker/coord. Jewish Family Life Edn. Jewish Family Svc., Dallas, 1984-85, 88-90; instr. Miss. Delta C. C., Greenville, 1991; child and adolescent therapist United Behavioral Systems, Louisville, 1993-94; therapist Inpsych, Louisville, 1994—. Mem. NASW, Acad. Cert. Social Workers, Am. Assn. Marriage and Family Therapy, Phi Kappa Phi, Pi Lambda Theta, Omicron Nu. Home: 2719 Avenue of the Woods Louisville KY 40241

BERGER, DENISE A., chemical engineer; b. Syracuse, N.Y., July 14, 1961. BSChemE, Tex. A&M U., 1983. Lic. engr. in tng., Tex. Rsch. engr. Sperry Sun, Houston, 1983-85; process control engr. TXE/EMC Controls, Houston, 1985-86, Champion Paper, Sheldon, Tex., 1986-88; process control engr. W.R. Grace, Deer Park, Tex., 1988-90, sr. process control engr., 1990-91; process control group leader Hampshire Chem. Corp., Deer Park, 1992—. Mem. Am. Inst. Chem. Engrng., Instrument Soc. Am., Indsl. Computing Soc. Office: Hampshire Chem Corp 739 Battleground Rd Deer Park TX 77536

BERGER, DIANNE GWYNNE, educator; b. N.Y.C., Mar. 10, 1950; d. Harold and Mary Bell (Mott) Gwynne; m. Robert Milton Berger, Aug. 25, 1974; children: Matthew Robert Gwynne, Daniel Alan Gwynne. BS, Cornell U., 1971; MS, Drexel U., 1974; PhD, U. Pa., 1992. Cert. sex educator, home. econs. and family life educator, Pa. Tchr. home econs., sexuality edn. Wallingford-Swarthmore Sch. Dist., 1972—; cons., Swarthmore, 1986—, Elwyn Insts., Media, Pa., 1989-91, Phila. Task Force on Sex Edn., 1991-93. Cons. Trinity Coop. Day Nursery, Swarthmore, 1980-93, Renaissance Edn. Assn., Valley Forge, Pa., 1987—, A Better Chance, Inc., Swarthmore, 1990-91. Grantee Impact, Inc., 1990. Mem. NEA, Am. Home Econs. Assn., Soc. for Sci. Study of Sex, Nat. Coun. on Family Rels., Am. Assn. Sex Educators, Counselors and Therapists. Home: 304 Dickinson Ave Swarthmore PA 19081-2001

BERGER, ELLEN LOUISE, management consultant; b. Cedar Rapids, Iowa, May 16, 1960; d. John Norman and Viola Mae (Trautmann) B. BA, Wesleyan U., 1982; MBA, Stanford U., 1988. Environ. planner Gilbert Assocs., Reading, Pa., 1982-83; assoc. ICF Inc., Washington, 1984-86; cons. Boston Consulting Group, N.Y.C., 1987-90; cons., Washington and San Francisco, 1990—. Vol. Plenty, Dominica, W.I., 1988; fundraiser Zest, Washington, 1992. Mem. Stanford U. Grad. Sch. Bus. Alumni Assn., Potomac Boat Club.

BERGER, MARCI REISS, public information executive; b. Passaic, N.J., May 20, 1965; d. Sidney Holder and Anester (Feld) Reiss; m. Eric Hamilton Berger, May 24, 1992. BA in History, Cornell U., 1987; MA, Rutgers U., 1992, postgrad., 1993—. Legis. asst. Congressman Sam Gejdenson Ho. of Reps., Washington, 1987-89, legis. asst. Congressman Ron Machtley, 1990; legis. asst. N.J. Hosp. Assn., Princeton, 1991-92, mgr. state govt. rels., 1992-94; dir. pub. info. Planned Parenthood of Greater No. N.J., Morristown, 1994—; Past mem. bd. dirs. Planned Parenthood Middlesex County, New Brunswick, N.J., 1992-94; past mem. childcare allocation com. United Way of Ctrl. Jersey, Milltown, N.J., 1993-94; bd. dirs. Metuchen (N.J.) LWV, 1993—; mem. Cornell U. Alumni Ambs., Ctrl. N.J.,1991—. Mem. Nat. Women's Polit. Caucus. Home: 239 C Amboy Ave Metuchen NJ 08840 Office: Planned Parenthood 196 Speedwell Ave Morristown NJ 07960

BERGER, MIRIAM ROSKIN, creative arts therapy director, educator, therapist; b. N.Y.C., Dec. 9, 1934; d. Israel and Florence (Frankel) Roskin; m. Meir Berger, July 16, 1967 (div. June 1981); children: Jonathan Israel. Student, Barnard Coll., 1952-53; BA, Bard Coll., 1956; postgrad., CCNY, 1956-58, NYU, 1981—; ArtsD, 1995. Alumni dir. Bard Coll., Annandale-on-Hudson, N.Y., 1958-59; dance therapist Manhattan Psychiatric Ctr., N.Y.C., 1959-60; performer, educator Jean Erdman Theater of Dance, N.Y.C., 1959-62; dir. adult program Hebrew Arts Sch., N.Y.C., 1964-68; faculty Dance Notation Bur., N.Y.C., 1974-75, 77; asst. prof. dance therapy program NYU, 1975—, acting dir. dance therapy program, 1991, dir. dance edn. program, 1993—; dir. creative arts therapies Bronx Psychiatric Ctr., N.Y.C., 1970-90; leader internat. workshops on dance/movement therapy, Gt. Britain, France, Sweden, Brazil, Italy, Yugoslavia, Germany, Holland, Russia; mem. editl. bd. The Arts in Psychotherapy. Producer off-Broadway The Coach with the Six Insides, 1962-63; author, producer Non-Verbal Group Process, 1978; co-editor Am. Jour. Dance Therapy, 1991-94; led dance therapy session Senate hearing on Aging, 1992; contbr. articles to profl. jours. Bd. dirs. Theater Open Eye, 1978-82, v.p. bd. trustees, 1982-89, pres., 1989-94. Recipient NYU scholarship, 1981, Best Paper award Med Art World congress on Arts and Medicine, 1992. Mem. Am. Dance Therapy Assn. (founder, bd. dirs. 1967-76, v.p. 1974-76, credential com. 1976, 82, keynote spkr. nat. conf. 1991, v.p. 1992, pres. 1994, keynote speaker Internat. Congress on Dance Therapy 1994), Acad. Registered Dance Therapists, Am. Orthopsychiat. Assn. Home: 2 Horizon Rd Fort Lee NJ 07024-6525 Office: NYU 35 W 4th St New York NY 10012-1172

BERGER, PATRICIA WILSON, retired librarian; b. Washington, May 1, 1926; d. Thomas Decatur Wood and Nina Hughes; m. George Hamilton Combs Berger, May 20, 1970. BA, George Washington U., 1965; MSLS, Cath. U. Am., 1974. Asst. librarian, ops. rsch. office Johns Hopkins U., Chevy Chase, Md., 1949-51; asst. ops. rsch. analyst Johns Hopkins U., 1951-54; head librarian CEIR, Washington, 1954-55; chief, tech. info. and library services Human Relations Area Files, Yale U., 1955-57; tech. info. officer, chief librarian Inst. for Def. Analyses, Washington, Arlington, Va., 1957-67; dir. tech. info. and security programs Lambda Corp., Arlington, 1967-71; chief librarian U.S. Commn. on Govt. Procurement, Washington, 1971-72; head gen. reference br., later dep. chief librarian U.S. Patent and Trademark Office, Arlington, 1972-76; chief library div. U.S. Nat. Bur. Standards, Gaithersburg, Md., 1976-78; dir. info. resources and services U.S. EPA, Washington, 1978-79; chief library and info. services U.S. Nat. Bur. Standards, 1979-83, chief info. resources and services, 1983-91; dir. Office Info. Svcs. Nat. Inst. Standards and Tech., 1990-92; ret., 1992; cons. libr., info. and security matters, 1965—; del. White House Conf. on Librs. and Info. Svc., 1979; bd. dirs. Universal Serial and Book Exch., 1983-84; chmn. Nat. Info. Standard Orgn., Am. Nat. Standard Inst., 1981-83, elected Nat. Info. Standard Orgn. fellow, 1989. Mem. editl. bd. Sci. and Tech. Librs., 1979-92; contbr. articles to profl. jours. Appointed by Govs. of Va. to State Library Bd., 1986-90, 90-95, vice chair, 1992-93, chair, 1993-94; bd. dirs. Va. Commn. for Reenactment of Battle First Bull Run, 1960-61; bd. dirs. Freedom to Read Found., 1988-90, 92-94; appointed U.S. Postmaster Gen's. Commn. Lit., 1990-92. Recipient Internat. Women's Yr. award Dept. Commerce, 1976, Bronze medal, 1980, Silver medal, 1984, Outstanding Adminstrv. Mgr. award, 1985, H.W. Wilson Pub. Co. award, 1980, Disting. Svc. award U. Richmond Librs., 1989, Cert. of Recognition, Gov. State of Va., 1989, Resolution of Esteem, Va. State Libr. Bd., 1988, award Coun. Libr. and Media Technicians, 1989; named Outstanding Alumnus in Libr. and Info. Sci., Cath. U. Am., 1988. Mem AAAS (elected assn. fellow 1992), Spl. Librs. Assn. (exec. bd. Washington chpt. 1970-71, pres. Washington chpt. 1977, elected assn. fellow 1987), ALA (coun. 1984-88, exec. bd. 1986-90, v.p./pres.-elect 1988-89, pres. 1989-90, immediate past pres. 1990-91), Va. Libr. Assn., D.C. Libr. Assn., Fed. Librs. Roundtable (pres. 1982-83, Achievement award 1985), Cosmos Club, Chi Omega, Beta Phi Mu. Democrat. Episcopalian. Home: 105 Queen St Alexandria VA 22314-2610

BERGER, PEARL, library director; b. N.Y.C., Nov. 30, 1943; d. Baruch Mayer and Tova (Brandwein) Rabinowitz; m. David Berger, June 14, 1965; children: Miriam Esther, Yitzhak, Gedalyah Aaron. B in Religious Edn., Yeshiva U.; BA, Bklyn. Coll., 1965; MLS, Columbia U., 1974. Diploma tchr. Hebrew. Tchr. Hebrew & Jewish studies Yeshiva of Crown Heights, Bklyn., 1963-65; asst. libr. YIVO Inst. Jewish Rsch., N.Y.C., 1976-80; head tech. svcs. Librs. Yeshiva U., N.Y.C., 1980-81, head libr. Pollack Libr., 1981-83, head libr. main ctr. librs., 1983-85, dean librs., 1985—; v.p. Coun. Archives & Rsch. Librs. in Jewish Studies, 1984-86, pres. 1986-89. Assoc. editor: Jour. Judaica Librarianship, 1983; contbr. articles to profl. jours.; compiler catalog Guide to Yiddish Classics on Microfiche, 1980. Recipient Benjamin Gottesman Libr. Chair Yeshiva U. Me. Am. Libr. Assn., Metro. Ref. Rsch. Libr. Agency (trustee), Assn. Jewish Librs. (rsch., spl. librs. divsn., v.p. 1982-84, pres. 1984-86), Beta Phi Mu. Office: Yeshiva U Dean of Libraries 500 W 185th St New York NY 10033-3201

BERGER, RENEE AVA, management consultant. BA in English summa cum laude, SUNY, Buffalo, 1969, MA in Humanities/Planning, 1974; postgrad. in pub. adminstrn., George Washington U., 1977-80. Pres. TEAMWORKS, San Francisco, Washington, 1985—; adj. prof. George Washington U., 1978-80; vis. prof. Griffith U., Australia, 1983; edn. and tng. cons. Buffalo Psychiat. Ctr., Gowanda Psychiat. Ctr., 1974-77; sr. rsch. assoc. Com. for Econ. Devel., Washington, 1978-81; dir. partnerships White House Task Force on Pvt. Sector Initiatives, 1982; cons. Aspen Inst., German Marshall Fund, Orgn. for Econ. Coop. and Devel., Paris, 1983-85. Co-author: Public-Private Partnership in American Cities: Seven Case Studies, 1982, Public-Private Partnership: An Opportunity for Urban Communities, 1981, Profiles of Excellence: Achieving Success in the Non-Profit Sector, 1991; contbr. numerous articles to profl. jours. Office: TEAMWORKS 9 Van Buren San Francisco CA 94131 also: Teamworks 1001 Connecticut Ave NW Washington DC 20036-5504

BERGER, THELMA LEE, counselor, psychotherapist; b. New Bedford, Mass., Nov. 14, 1931; d. Abram Joseph and Bertha (Alpert) Cohen; m. Harvey R. Berger, July 11, 1954. BS in Edn., Fitchburg State Coll., 1953; MEd, Northeastern U., 1972; EdD, La. State U., 1975. Cert. counseling psychologist. Tchr. pub. schs. Somerset, Mass., 1953-54, Nahant, Mass., 1955-59, Marblehead, Mass., 1959-87; nat. svc. officer Jewish War Vets., Boston, 1985-94, Providence, 1991-94; cons. Fed. Assisted Sch. Programs, Salem, Mass., 1960-74; counselor, therapist Counseling and Testing Svc. of North Shore, Revere, Mass., 1975-80; adj. prof. Salem State Coll., 1976; cons. spl. needs pub. schs., Revere, 1987-89. Nat. dir. Wavette program Jr. Naval Cadets Am., 1968—; pres. Greater Lynn (Mass.) Mental Health and Retardation Area Bd., 1967-68; mem. governance bd. Greater Lynn Cmty. Mental Health Ctr., 1972-90; life patron Jewish War Vets. U.S., 1975—; life benefactor, sec.-treas. Am. Women in Torah, Lynn, 1987—, nat. bd. dirs., 1993—, life; sec.-treas. Congregation Chevra Tehillim, Lynn, 1990—; mem. Lynn Coun. for children, 1967-72; life mem. Orgn. Vols. for Israel and Torah; mem. alumni coun. Fitchburg State Coll. Mem. AAUW (life), DAV Aux. (life), Am. Legion Aux. (life; pres. 1962-63, Essex County historian 1964, Essex County sec. 1965), Jewish Rehab. Ctr. of North Shore Aux. (life), Daus. of the Nile, Order of the Amaranth, Ladies Oriental Shrine of N.Am., Order Eastern Star (trustee 1994—). Republican.

BERGER, VIVIAN OLIVIA, lawyer, educator; b. N.Y.C., July 22, 1944; d. Jacob and Rita (Both) Berger; m. Curtis Jay Berger, June 17, 1973. BA, Harvard U., 1966; JD, Columbia U., 1973. Bar: N.Y. 1974, U.S. Dist. Ct. (so. and ea. dist.) N.Y. 1974, U.S. Ct. Appeals (2d cir.) 1974, U.S. Supreme Ct. 1979, U.S. Dist. Ct. (no. dist.) N.Y. 1980, U.S. Ct. Appeals (10th cir.) 1986. Law clk. to judge U.S. Ct. Appeals (2d cir.), N.Y.C., 1973-74; asst. prof. law Columbia U., N.Y.C., 1975-77, assoc. prof. law, 1977-80, prof. law, 1983—; vice dean Columbia U., 1989-93, Nash prof. law, 1993—; asst. dist. atty. N.Y. County, N.Y.C., 1977-83; of counsel Hoffinger Friedland Dobrish Bernfeld & Stern, P.C., N.Y.C., 1994—; mem. adv. comm. 1st dept. N.Y. Appellate Div., N.Y.C., 1984—; asst. counsel Legal Def. Fund NAACP, N.Y.C., 1986—. Contbr. articles to profl. jours. Vol. mediator Queens Mediation Ctr., 1985-85; arbitrator small claims N.Y.C. Civil Ct., 1986—;

nat. bd. dirs. ACLU, N.Y.C., 1980—, gen. counsel, 1986—; bd. dirs. First Dept. Assigned Counsel Corp., 1991—, So. Ctr. for Human Rights, 1990—. Mem. ABA, Assn. of Bar of City of N.Y. (civil rights com. 1979-82, criminal cts. com. 1983-86, 91-94, criminal advocacy com. 1986-89, coun. on criminal justice 1991—, spl. com. on capital representation 1994—, coun. on jud. adminstrn. 1989-91), N.Y. Women's Bar Assn., N.Y. State Dist. Atty.'s Assn., Am. Law Inst., N.Y. Lawyers Against the Death Penalty. Office: Columbia Law Sch 435 W 116th St New York NY 10027-7201 also Office: Dobrish Bernfeld & Stern 110 E 59th St New York NY 10022*

BERGER-KRAEMER, NANCY, speech and language pathologist, artist; b. N.Y.C., Aug. 15, 1941; d. George G. and Ruth (Kirsch) Berger; m. Aaron Kraemer, July 10, 1966; children: Lea, Steven. BA, Adelphi U., 1963; MS in Edn., Queens Coll., 1968; cert. clin. competency in speech pathology. Lic. and cert. speech and lang. pathologist, N.Y., N.J.; permanent cert. speech and hearing for handicapped, N.Y. Speech therapist Dist. # 24 Sch. Sys., Valley Stream, L.I., 1962-64; dir. speech and lang., hearing/speech pathologist Port Chester Sch. Dist., Rye, N.Y., 1965-66; speech and lang. pathologist Roselle Park (N.J.) Sch. Sys., 1966-67, Willis Sch. for Educationally Handicapped, Plainfield, N.J., 1967-68, St. Barnabas Med. Ctr., West Orange, N.J., 1971-73; pvt. practice Maplewood, N.J., 1968—; lectr., spkr., spl. edn. cons. in field. Numerous one-woman shows in N.J., N.Y., N.Y.C.; group exhbns. include N.J. Ctr. Visual Arts, Summit, N.J., City Without Walls, Newark, Bergen Mus., Jersey City Mus., Trenton City Mus., N.J. State Mus., Montclair Art Mus., Noyes Mus., Phoenix Gallery, Veridian Gallery, Pindar Gallery, Gallerie Ambiente, Germany, William Carlos Williams Ctr. for Arts, San Diego Art Inst., Stedman Art Gallery, New Brunswick, N.J., Fordham U.-Lowenstein Libr., N.Y.C., SUNY Gallery, Stony Brook, N.Y., Johnson & Johnson, Cali Assocs., Bellemead Devel. Corp., AT&T, Nabisco Brands, Beneficial Ins. Co., Prudential Ins. Co., Pleiades Gallery, N.Y.C., Art Ctr. Northern N.J., Art Assn. Harrisburg, Stamford Art Assn., Princeton (N.J.) Art Assn., Bucknell U. Ctr. Gallery, others. Mem. Am. Speech Lang. Hearing Assn., Auditory Verbal Internat. (charter, lectr. 1975—), Alexander Graham Bell Assn., N.J. Speech and Hearing Assn.

BERGESON, MARIAN, state legislator; m. Garth Bergeson; children: Nancy, Garth Jr., Julie, James. Student UCLA; BA in Edn. Brigham Young U.; postgrad. UCLA. Pres., regional dir. Calif. Sch. Bds. Assn.; officer, dir. Orange County Sch. Bds. Assn.; mem. Newport Beach City Sch. Dist. Bd. Edn., 1964-65; mem. Newport-Mesa Unified Sch. Dist. Bd. Edn., 1965-77; mem. Calif. Assembly, 1978-82, Calif. Senate, 1984—. Past mem. Orange County Juvenile Justice Commn., Riles-Younger Task Force for Prevention of Crime and Violence in the Schs., Com. for Revision State Edn. Code, Joint Com. on Revision Penal Code; mem. Calif. YMCA Model Legislature/Ct.; mem. bd. advisors Calif. Elected Women's Assn. Edn. and Research; bd. dirs. Sta. KBIG Adv. Bd.; mem. govt. relations com. Orange County Arts Alliance. Recipient Marian Bergeson Community Services award Orange County Sch. Bds. Assn., 1975; Anchor award Newport Harbor C. of C., women's div., 1967; Community Services award AAUW, 1976; Disting. Women's award Irvine Soroptimists, 1981; Disting. Service award Brigham Young U., 1980-81; Woman of Achievement award Newport Harbor Zonta Club, 1981; Silver Medallion, YWCA, 1983; Pub. Service award Calif. Speech-Lang.-Hearing Assn., 1983; named Outstanding Pub. Ofcl., Orange County chpt. Am. Soc. Pub. Adminstrn., 1983, Woman of Yr., Anti Defamation League B'nai B'rith, 1987, So. Dist. Legislator of Yr., Calif. Assn. for Health., 1987. Address: State Senate 3063 State Capital Sacramento CA 95814 also: State Senate Offices PO Box 3151 Newport Beach CA 92659-0775*

BERGGREN, BONNIE LEE, education educator; b. L'Anse, Mich., June 2, 1940; d. Alvin Carl and Erma Leola (Wandell) Lydman; m. Grant Lorns Berggren, Jr., Aug. 22, 1959; children: Grant Victor, Rex Alvin, Konnie Kay. BA, U. Hawaii, 1961; MA, Ea. Mich. U., 1988; M Ednl. Adminstrn., No. Mich. U., 1991. Tchr. home econs. Baraga (Mich.) Twp. Schs., 1960-61, L'Anse Twp. Schs., 1963-65, Spencerport (N.Y.) Cen. Schs., 1979-84; presch. tchr. NCA Sch., Community Action Agy., Hermansville, Mich., 1971-73; circulation supr. Spring Arbor (Mich.) Coll. Libr., 1985-87; adj. prof., supr. student tchrs. No. Mich. U., Marquette, 1989—; co-owner, co-mgr. Menominee (Mich.) Floral; tchr. trainer Negaunee (Mich.) Pub. Schs., 1988-90; workshop leader Republic (Mich.)-Michigamme Schs., 1989-90; mem. evaluation team Marquette Pub. Schs., 1991; mem. tchr. edn. adv. coun. No. Mich. U., 1991—, mem. Hoppes award com., 1990-92, mem. pers. com., 1992. Illustrator: Grandmother Wandell's Rainbow Book of Poems, 1977. Mem. libr. bd. Republic-Michigamme Schs., 1988-91; speaker Christian Women's Club, Ironwood, Marquette, 1989-90; bd. regents Liberty U., 1990-91. Recipient Excellence in Edn. award No. Mich. U., 1990. Fellow Roberts Wesleyan Coll.; mem. AAUP, AAUW, DAV Aux. (life, Mich. historian 1975), Univ. Women No. Mich. U., Ea. Mich. U. Alumni Assn., Concerned Women Am., Phi Kappa Phi, Phi Delta Kappa. Baptist. Home: 2713 14th Ave Menominee MI 49858 Office: No Mich U Marquette MI 49855

BERGIN, DIANA BEATRICE, sales executive; b. Augusta, Ga., July 30, 1956; d. Louis Herbert and Gisela Hedwig (Masuth) Bergin. BS, Radford (Va.) U., 1978. Asst. office mgr. Surrey & Morse, Washington, 1979-86; corp. svcs. mgr. Comsat Corp., Washington, 1986-89; product mgr. Comsat Mobile Communications, Washington, 1989-91, sales mgr., 1991—. Mem. Propeller Club (Washington chpt.). Home: 678 Gateway Dr SE # 906 Leesburg VA 22075

BERGIN-MELLEM, DOROTHY, optometrist, educator; b. College Place, Wash., June 28, 1923; d. Richard A. and Maude E. (Leadsworth) B.; m. Claude J. Mellem (dec.); children: Carl Jerome, Richard Gary, Lisa Gay. BS, L.A. Coll. Optometry, 1945, OD, 1952; MS in Edn., U. So. Calif., 1975. Clin. Optometrist L.A. County Gen. Hosp., 1945-47; asst. prof. L.A. Coll. Optometry, 1948-49, dir. clinics, 1949-52; assoc. prof. So. Calif. Coll. Optometry, Fullerton, 1962-75, prof., 1975-82, prof. emeritus, 1982—; optometrist pvt. practice, La Habra, Calif., 1976-93; vis. clinician U. Calif., Berkeley, 1969; mem. editorial coun. Archives Am. Acad. Optometry, 1971-73; faculty advisor So. Calif. Coll. Optometry, 1976, 78, 79. Author, editor: Handbook for Teachers of Optometry, 1978; contbr. articles to profl. jours. Com. chair La Hambra C. of C., 1976-79; bd. dirs. Help for Brain Injured Children, La Hambra, 1976-79; judge speakers contest Lions CLub, 1979. Mem. AAUW. Home: 1120 Beechwood Dr Brea CA 92621-2302

BERG-JOHNSON, KAREN ANN, photographer, art educator; b. Mpls., Sept. 25, 1959; d. Wallace Edgar and Sylvia June (Schyman) Berg; m. Jay Timothy Johnson, May 20, 1983; 1 child, Christina Berg Johnson. BFA, U. Minn., 1981, MFA, 1984. Instr., chair photography dept. Art Ctr. of Minn., Crystal Bay, 1982-84; teaching asst. studio art dept. U. Minn., Mpls., 1983; instr. of art Bethel Coll., St. Paul, 1984-87, asst. prof., 1988-92, assoc. prof., 1992—, chairperson art dept., 1994—; juror mus. workers show Katherine Nash Gallery, U. Minn., 1989, chair adv. com., 1981-83. One woman show include Honors Gallery, U. Minn., 1981, Art Ctr. of Minn., Crystal Bay, 1983, Katherine Nash Gallery, 1983, Jewish Community Ctr., Mpls., 1984; exhibited in group shows at Studio Arts Gallery U. Minn., Mpls., 1980, 84, Katherine Nash Gallery, 1981, 88, Coffman Gallery 1, 1982-83, U. Art Mus., 1987, NA Gallery, Northfield, Minn., 1983, Art Ctr. of Minn., Crystal Bay, 1984, Daedalus Gallery, Mpls., 1984, 310 Arts Gallery, Mpls., 1984, Wall St. Gallery, St. Paul, 1984, B Square One Gallery, Mpls., 1984, Eugene Johnson Gallery of Art Bethel Coll., St. Paul, 1984-87, Minn. State Fair, St. Paul, 1986, Mpls. Inst. of Arts, 1986, Sioux City (Iowa) Art Ctr., 1987, Pinder Gallery, N.Y.C., 1987, Foundry Gallery Washington, 1987, San Diego Art Inst., 1987, Mpls. Coll. Arts and Design Gallery, 1988, Mid Hudson Arts and Sci. Ctr., Poughkeepsie, N.Y., 1988, N.J. Ctr. for Visual Arts, Summitt, 1989, Forum Gallery, Mpls., 1989, Miami Expo '89, Fla., 1989, Cen. Mo. State U. Art Ctr. Gallery, Warrensburg, 1990, Jewish Community Ctr. of Houston, 1990, W.A.R.M. Gallery, Mpls., 1990, Phipps Ctr. for Arts, Hudson, Wis., 1990, Laguna Gloria Art Mus., Austin, Tex., 1991, Barrett House Galleries, Poughkeepsie, N.Y., 1991, ARC Gallery, Chgo., 1991, Pleiades Gallery, N.Y.C., 1991, Univ. Gallery U. Del., 1992, Downey Mus. Art, Calif., 1992, Mus. Without Walls, Internat., Bemus Point, N.Y., 1993, New England Fine Art Inst., Boston, 1993, The Phipps Ctr. for Arts, Hudson, Wis., 1993; numerous others. U. Minn. grantee, 1981-83; recipient Juror's award Leedy Voulkos Art Ctr., 1991, Artist's Choice award Phipps Ctr. for Arts, 1990, Juror's award N.J. Ctr. for Visual Arts, 1989, NA Gallery, 1983, Purchase award Univ. Art Mus., 1987. Mem. Soc. for Photographic Edn. Home: 3688 Woodland Trl Saint Paul MN 55123-2406 Office: Bethel Coll Art Dept 3900 Bethel Dr Saint Paul MN 55112-6902

BERGKOETTER, MILIA BETH, psychotherapist; b. Danville, Ill., Dec. 22, 1954; d. Russell Hurley and Ethel Kathryn (Starkey) Hance; m. Abbas Hosseini, Jan. 7, 1976 (div. 1990); children: Sheila Adrienne, Ali-Shawn; m. Vernon Lee Bergkoetter, Aug. 11, 1990; stepchildren: West Lee, Luke Robert. AA, DACC, 1975; BSW, So. Ill. U., Edwardsville, 1977; MFCC, MS, Calif. State U., Fullerton, 1987. Outreach counselor Vis. Nurses and Family Svcs., Alton, Ill., 1977-78; social work designee St. Edna Convalescent Ctr., Santa Ana, Calif., 1978-79; activity counselor Petit Amis Care Home, Garden Grove, Calif., 1978-79; med. social worker Carle Hosp., Urbana, Ill., 1979-81; psychotherapist HopeHouse Inc., Anaheim, Calif., 1986-88, United Samaritans Med. Ctr., Danville, 1988-91; pvt. practice psychotherapy Danville, 1991—; inst. DACC continuing edn., Danville, 1993. Mem. ACA, Women's Exec. Club, Internat. Assn. of Marriage, Family and Child Counselors. Home: 2211 Smith Danville IL 61832 Office: Family Counseling 1022 N Vermillon Danville IL 61832

BERGLIN, LINDA, state senator; b. Oakland, Calif., Oct. 19, 1944; d. Freeman and Norma (Lund) Waterman; m. Glenn Sampson; 1 child, Maria. BFA, Mpls. Coll. Art and Design. Mem. Minn. Ho. of Reps., St. Paul, 1972-80; mem. Minn. Senate, St. Paul, 1980—, chmn. Health and Human Svcs. Com.; mem. senate judiciary com., family svcs. com., tax and tax laws com., others; mem. various legis. commns. including Econ. Status of Women, Healthcare Oversight Commn.; U.S. rep. U.S.-Japan Legis. Exch. Program; seminar participant health care reform U.S.-Sweden, also Austria, 1981; studied health care reform Great Britain, 1992; rep. Nat. Coun. State Legislatures Women's Network Del., Korea, 1989. Bd. dirs. Freedom House, Better Jobs for Women, founding mem., CornerHouse, Whittier Alliance, founding, St. Stephen's Guild Hall, Orgnl. Industrialization Ctrs., Children's Theater; mem. scattered site housing com. Powderhorn Cmty. Coun., Food and Land Resource Ctr., Joint Urban Mission Project, Phillips Neighborhood Improvement Assn., numerous others; trustee Inst. Arts. Recipient Pub. Citizen of Yr. award Nat. Assn. Social Workers, 1980, Nursing Home Residents Adv. Coun. award, 1983, NAACP Cert. Appreciation, 1984, Common Space Mutual Housing award, 1984, Award of Excelence Minn. Dept. Human Svcs., 1986, Leadership award Mpls. Conv. Ctr. Greater Mpls. C. of C., 1986, Children's Champion award Children's Defense Fund, 1987, March of Dimes award, 1988, Child Health Care citation Am. Acad. Pediatrics and Children's Defense Fund, 1988, Health Span Coalition award, 1989, Outstanding Achievement award Med. Alley, 1989, Minn. Psychol. Assn. award, 1990, Disting. Svc. award Minn. Assn. Edn. Young Children, 1991, Cert. of Merit Minn. Women's Consortium, 1992, Minn. Assn. Cmty. Mental Health Programs, Inc., 1993, Pub. Svc. award Planned Parenthood Minn., 1993, others; named Outstanding Woman of Yr. YWCA, 1980, Legislator of Yr. ARC, 1989, Pub. Official of Yr. Minn. Homes for the Aging, 1991, many other honors. Mem. Dem.-Farmer-Labor Party. Office: Minn Senate State Capital Saint Paul MN 55155*

BERGMAN, ANNE NEWBERRY, foundation administrator, civic activist; b. Weatherford, Tex., Mar. 12, 1925; d. William Douglas and Mary (Hunter) Newberry; m. Robert David Bergman, Aug. 17, 1947; children: Elizabeth Anne Bozzell, John David, William Robert. BA, Trinity U., San Antonio, 1945; postgrad., UCLA, 1946-47. Councilperson City Weatherford (Tex.), 1986-91, mayor pro tem, 1990-91; pres. Weatherford Libr. Found., 1989—; mem. Heritage Gallery Com., Weatherford Pub. Libr. (Mary Martin Collection), 1993—; bd. dirs. Manna Store House, Inc., 1990—. Founder Hist. Home Tour, Weatherford, 1972; co-chair Spring Festival Bd., 1976; co-chair Weatherford Planning and Zoning Commn., 1980-85; fund raising chair Weatherford Libr. Found., 1985-86; chair Tex. State Rev. Com. Cmty. Devel. Block Grants, 1987-91; pres. Tex. Fedn. Rep. Women (Outstanding Rep. Woman 1981), 1975-77; regional coord. George Bush for Pres., 1980, 88; co-chair Congl. Dist. 12, Bush-Quayle, 1992, Tex. Women Support Pres., 1983-84; del. 1988 Nat. Rep. Conv. Mem. Tex. Women's Alliance (charter), Parker County Rep. Women, DAR (Weatherford chpt.), Weatherford C. of C. (Outstanding Citizen of the Yr. 1988), Friends Weatherford Pub. Libr. (life, charter pres. 1959-61, pres. 1973-74). Episcopalian. Home: 609 W Josephine St Weatherford TX 76086-4055

BERGMAN, CLAIRE ALICE, violist; b. N.Y.C., Sept. 9, 1954; d. Samuel and Shirley (Friedman) B.; m. Kouichi Hori, Sept. 2, 1985. MusB, Manhattan Sch. Music, 1975, MusM, 1977. Violist Steve Reich Ensemble, N.Y.C., 1979-82; violist, quartet-in-residence Amacorda String Quartet, Am. String Tchrs.' Assn., Glassboro, N.J., 1982-84; violist Concertina String Quartet, N.Y.C., 1983-84, De Salo Chamber Artists, N.Y.C., 1983-87, Martha Graham Dance Co., N.Y.C., 1983-87; prin. violist Into the Woods-Martin Beck Theatre, N.Y.C., 1988-89, Dance Theatre of Harlem, N.Y.C., 1985-87; violist N.Y.C. Opera, 1980—, N.Y. Pops, N.Y.C., 1985—. Editor-in-chief: (lit. mag.) Ken, 1970-71; violist: (record) Steve Reich: Music for a Large Ensemble, 1980; contbr. by-line and book revs. Allegro, 1984-92. Mem. steering com. Assn. for Union Democracy Women's Project, N.Y.C., 1988-91; chair local 802 Women's Caucus, N.Y.C., 1983—; v.p. bd. dirs. 854 W. 181 Corp., N.Y.C., 1991-94. Mem. NOW, LWV, Am. Fedn. Musicians (local 802, trial bd. clk. 1986-89), Am. Viola Soc., N.Y. Viola Soc.

BERGMAN, DIANE E., health care executive; b. Pitts., Mar. 16, 1957. BS in Health Planning and Adminstrn., Pa. State U., 1979; MS in Bus. Adminstrn., Robert Morris Coll., 1983. Dir. health maintenance orgn. Ctrl. Med. Health Svcs., Pitts., 1979-83; v.p. adminstrn. and ops. Ctrl. Med. Health Plan, Pitts., 1983-87; ops. officer Capital Dist. Physicians' Healthcare Network, Albany, N.Y., 1991-92; dir. internal ops. Ind. Health/Capital Dist. Physicians' Health Plan, Albany, N.Y., 1987-92, exec. dir., 1992—. Active ARC. Mem. NAFE, Am. Fin. Assn., Am. Coll. Healthcare Execs. (affiliate), Albany-Colonie Regional C. of C. (bd. dirs.). Home: 17 Duchess Path Clifton Park NY 12065 Office: Capital Dist Physicians' Health Plan One Columbia Circle Albany NY 12203

BERGMAN, ELLEN MARIE, state legislator; b. Lincoln, Nebr., Mar. 19, 1942; d. Ralph Celestine and Barbara Ellen (McGinley) Roach; m. Paul Albert Berman, Nov. 9, 1963; children: Barry, Patrick, Bradley, Christopher. Grad. parochial high sch., Beatrice, Nebr. Hairdresser various shops, Lincoln, 1961-65; checker Henry's Market, Scottsbluff, Nebr., 1974-76; sales clk. J.C. Penney Co., Miles City, Mont., 1977-81; prosthesis technician Home Health Spltys., Miles City, 1990—; mem. Mont. Ho. of Reps., Helena, 1992-93. Reporter Family Issues Forum, Miles City, 1988—; vol. local nursing home and retirement home; vol. reach to recovery Am. Cancer Soc. Republican. Mem. Assembly of God. Home: 1019 S Strevell Ave Miles City MT 59301-4917*

BERGMAN, NANCY PALM, real estate investment company executive; b. McKeesport, Pa., Dec. 3, 1938; d. Walter Vaughn and Nellie (Sullivan) Leech; 1 child, Tiffany Palm Taylor. Student, Mt. San Antonio Coll., 1970, UCLA, 1989-93. Corporate sec. U.S. Filter Corp., Newport Beach, Calif., 1965—; pres. Jaguar Research Corp., Los Angeles and Atlanta, 1971—; owner Environ. Designs, Los Angeles, 1976—; pres. Prosher Corp., Los Angeles., 1978-83; now pres., dir. Futura Investments, Beverly Hills; chief exec. officer Rescor, Inc. Author: Resident Managers Handbook. Home: 8 Fincher Way Rancho Mirage CA 92270-3036 Office: 144 S Beverly Dr Ste 500 Beverly Hills CA 90212-3023

BERGMAN, TERRIE, psychic consultant; b. Phila., Mar. 4, 1942; d. Harry Bernard and Berthe Rose (Simons) Goldberg; m. Clifford Coulston, May 4, 1960 (div. 1967); 1 child, Lori Coulston; m. Joel David Bergman, Dec. 22, 1979. B Metaphys. Sci., D Metaphys. Counseling, U. Metaphysics, 1994. Ordained to metaphys. ministry, 1994. Indsl. trainer, vocat. evaluator, mktg. mgr. Atlantic County Opportunity Ctr. for Handicapped, Atlantic City, N.J., 1971-74; job developer, vocat. evaluator, counselor Narcotics Addicts Rehab. Orgn., Atlantic City, 1974-75; psychic cons. Atlantic City & Las Vegas, 1973—; seminar facilitator on death and dying Las Vegas, 1990—; 1st, 2d, and 3d degree Reiki healer, Atlantic City and Las Vegas, 1984—. Appeared on TV programs, including People Are Talking, Hour Mag., others, 1974—; contbr. articles to mags. and newspapers. Vol. Nathan Adelson Hospice, 1989-94. Named 1 of 83 People to Watch, Atlantic City Mag., 1983; recipient Dynamics of Leadership cert. of achievement Human Factors, Inc., 1981, 82, 86. Mem. Network of Exec. Women in Hospitality. Home and Office: 208 Desert View Las Vegas NV 89107

BERGSTROM, BETTY HOWARD, consulting executive; b. Chgo., Mar. 15, 1931; d. Seward Haise and Agnes Eleanor (Uek) Guinter; BS in Speech, Northwestern U., 1952, postgrad., 1983; postgrad U. Nev., Reno, 1974; m. Robert William Bergstrom, Apr. 21, 1979; children: Bryan Scott, Cheryl Lee, Jeffrey Alan, Mark Robert, Philip Alan. Dir. sales promotion and pub. relations WLS-AM, Chgo., 1952-56; account exec. E.H. Brown Advt. Agy., Chgo., 1956-59; v.p. Richard Crabb Assocs., Chgo., 1959-61; pres., owner Howard Assocs., Calif. and Chgo., 1961-76; v.p. Chgo. Hort. Soc., 1976-90; pres. Bergstrom Assocs., Chgo., Carefree, Ariz., 1990—. Del., Ill. Constl. Conv., 1969-70, mem. com. legis. reform, 1973-74, cts. and justice com., 1971-74; apptd. mem. Ill. Hist. Library Bd., 1970, Ill. Bd. Edn., 1971-74. AAUW fellowship grant named in her honor; recipient Communicator of Yr. award Women in Communication, 1983. Mem. Nat. Soc. Fund Raising Execs. (cert. fund raising executive, bd. dirs. 1983-92, sec. 1986, v.p. 1990-92, nat. bd. dirs., 1990-92, Pres's. award, 1988), Fortnightly Club (bd. dirs. 1994—), Am. Assn. of Museums, Am. Assn. Bot. Garden and Arboreta, Garden Writers Am., AAUW, Northwestern U. Alumni, U. So. Calif. Alumni Assn., LWV. Mem. editorial bd. Garden mag. Glenview Community Ch., 1977-89, Fourth Presbyn. Ch., 1990—, trustee, 1994—; editor Garden Talk, 1976-86; contbr. articles on fund devel., horticulture, edn. advt. and agr. to profl. jours.; editor Ill. AAUW Jour., 1966-67. Office: 401 E Ontario St Apt 3509 Chicago IL 60611-4442 also: PO Box 5253 100 Easy St Carefree AZ 85377

BERGSTROM, LESLIE LOCKHART, communications company executive; b. Norwich, Conn., Dec. 5, 1930; d. George Bartley and Lucille Alice (Zimmerman) Lockhart; m. James Catherall Bergstrom, Sept. 12, 1952; children: Kim Karen, Kirk Eric. BA in English magna cum laude, Colo. Coll., 1952. Owner, pres. Talk of the Town, Colorado Springs, Colo., 1978—; freelance tour guide, Colorado Springs, 1979—; instr. Elderhostel Program, 1988—. Author: Trips on Twos, 1978, Trips on Wheels, 1985, Scenic San Diego, 1987. Docent Colorado Springs Fine Arts Ctr., 1964—, Cheyenne Mountain Zoo, 1970-91, Bear Creek Nature Ctr., 1977-90; orientation chmn. ARC, 1953-90; instr. water safety Pikes Peak YMCA, 1960-90; mem. TakeCare Mem. Health Partnership Coun. Mem. AAUW, Women's Ednl. Soc., Internat. Platform Assn., Colorado Springs Conv. and Visitors Bur. (tourism liaison com.), Colorado Springs Meeting Planners Assn., Phi Beta Kappa, Kappa Kappa Gamma. Republican. Episcopalian.

BERIO, BLANCA, educational editor; b. San Juan, P.R., Aug. 26, 1950; d. Gaspar and Blanca (Morales) B.; m. Martin Martino, Nov. 11, 1972; children: Blanca Iris, Martin, Bibiana. BA, U. P.R., 1968, M, 1972; EdD, U. P.R., 1994, 1995. Prof. Guadalajara (Mex.) Autonomus U., 1973-76; tchr. Spanish Colegio Rosabell, Guaynabo, P.R., 1979-80, Colegio de La Salle, Bayamón, P.R., 1980-88; prof. edn. U. Sacred Heart, Santurce, P.R., 1984-91; ednl. editor Editorial Norma, Cataño, 1991-92; chief editor Editorial Rio Ingenio, 1992—; cons. Lear Aid, Rio Piedras, P.R., 1990-94. Author: De 13 a 19, 1969, El Paso, 1971, Tapatea, 1987, 2d edit., 1994, Bibliografia de literatura puertorriqueña paraniños, 1994; editor bull. Algo Nuevo, 1990, (software) Nos comunicamos; contbr. articles to profl. jours. Recipient Excelsa Benjamina Assn. Autores Puertorriqueños San Juan, 1971. Mem. Internat. Reading Assn., Assn. Grads. U. P.R., Alpha Delta Kappa. Roman Catholic. Home: Rio Hondo 2 Calle Rio Ingenio AH 14 Bayamon PR 00961 Office: Rio Ingenio Bayamon PR 00961

BERISTAIN, VICTORIA HELEN, artist; b. Greensburg, Pa., Jan. 25, 1940; d. Stephen and Helen Margaret Muka; m. Charles Dan Beristain, Dec. 30, 1960; children: Melissa Ann, Suzanne Elizabeth Beristain Martin. Student, U. Pitts., 1957-59, Elmira Coll., 1964, U. Hartford, 1975, Wesleyan U., 1978. vol. art tchr. to children; pvt. art tchr., West Hartford, Conn., 1980-93. One-woman shows include YWCA, Elmira, N.Y., 1961, Arnon Art Mus., Elmira, 1962, Chemung Canal Bank, Elmira, 1964, Mechanics Sav. Bank, 1977, Wesleyan U., 1978, Ethel Walker Sch., 1979, West Hartford Pub. Libr., 1985, Town and Country Club of Hartford, 1987; group exhbns. include Assn. of Am. Artists-Old State House, 1980, Bethel Temple, 1982, Wadsworth Atheneum, 1979, New Britain Mus. Am. Art, 1976, 78, John Slade Ely House, 1976, Conn. Commn. on the Arts Exhbns., Legis. Bldg., Hartford, 1987, Capitol Bldg., Hartford, 1991, 93; numerous pub. and pvt. collections. Bd. dirs. Arrot-Ogden Mus., Elmira, N.Y., 1964-66, YWCA, Elmira, 1965, Jr. League, Elmira, 1966. Mem. NOW (alumnae mem.), Conn. Commn. on Arts, Nat. Mus. Women in Arts. Democrat. Roman Catholic. Home and Studio: 15 Sulgrave Rd West Hartford CT 06107-3346

BERK, KERRY MACCARTNEY, telecommunications industry executive; b. Mt. Holly, N.J., Jan. 25, 1953; d. William H. and Marilyn (Raisner) Mac Cartney; m. Michael Alan Berk, Jan. 3, 1981; children: Kelly Lynn, Karen Ann. BA summa cum laude, Gettysburg Coll., 1975; MS with honors, Drexel U., 1981. Mgmt. asst. pub. rels. dept. Bell of Pa./Bell Atlantic, Phila., 1975-76, account exec. mktg. dept., 1976-78, promotions mgr. mktg. dept., 1978-79, assessor and assessment ctr. leader pers. dept., 1979-80, staff mgr. strategic planning/witness support, 1980-84, staff mgr. sales delivery and regulatory dept., 1984-85, project mgr. tng. and devel., 1985-86, mng. editor employee communications, 1986-87, dir. employee communications, 1987—; cons. pub. rels.; leader seminars and workshops. Officer bd. fellows Gettysburg (Pa.) Coll., 1979-83, bd. trustees, 1984-88, chair student affairs com., 1987-88; exec. bd. PTA Lynnewood Sch. Named Outstanding Young Leader, Gettysburg Coll., 1979, one of mems. Outstanding Com. of Yr., Phila. Jaycees, 1980, VIP, RVRHS, 1994. Mem. NAFE, Internat. Assn. Bus. Communicators (cert., accrediteed bus. communicator), Pub. Rels. Soc. Am., Nat. Assn. for Edn. of Young Children, Phi Beta Kappa. Office: Bell of Pa One Parkway 9C Philadelphia PA 19102

BERK, NICOLE SUSAN, diamond dealer; b. N.Y.C., Nov. 3, 1950; d. Henri and Greta Etty (Querido) Polak; m. Paul David Berk, Apr. 6, 1991. BA, NYU, 1972. Prodn. asst. Doubleday & Co., N.Y.C., 1972-75; indsl. diamond dealer Henri Polak Diamond Corp., N.Y.C., 1975—; buyer at Diamond Trading Co., 1976—. Reader Lighthouse for the Blind, N.Y.C., 1984-88; vol. St. Luke's/Roosevelt Hosp., N.Y.C., 1987-88. Recipient Diamonds Today award N.W. Ayers for DeBeers, 1983. Mem. Diamond Trade Assn. N.Y. Home: 1212 5th Ave Apt 13D New York NY 10029 Office: Henri Polak Diamond Corp 22 W 48th St New York NY 10036

BERKA, MARIANNE GUTHRIE, health and physical education educator; b. Queens, N.Y., Dec. 25, 1944; d. Frank Joseph and Mary (DePaul) Guthrie; m. Jerry George Berka, June 1, 1968; children: Katie, Keri. BS, Ithaca Coll., 1966, MS, 1968; EdD, NYU, 1990. High sch. tchr. Northport High Sch., 1966-67; full prof. health, phys. edn. and recreation Nassau Community Coll., Garden City, N.Y., 1968—. Mem. AAHPERD, AAHPER, Assn. Women Phys. Educators N.Y. State (chpt. chmn. 1973-74, chpt. treas. 1980-84), N.Y. State Assn. Health, Phys. Edn. and Recreation (J.B. Nash scholarship com. 1983—), Am. Assn. Sex Educators, Counselors and Therapists (cert. sex educator), Am. Coll. Sports Medicine. Roman Catholic. Home: 90 Bay Way Ave Brightwaters NY 11718-2008 Office: Nassau Community Coll P226 HPER Garden City NY 11530

BERKBIGLER, MARSHA LEE, political organization executive; b. Flint, Mich., May 2, 1950; d. Herbert Ules and Rosy Vernell (Grimes) Cornelison; m. Gary Robert Koontz, June 22, 1968 (div. Nov. 1976); children: Deron Robert, Alicia Michelle; m. James Herbert Berkbigler, Dec. 16, 1977. A. in Bus., Reno Bus. Coll., 1979. Hosp. coordinating sec. LaHabra Community Hosp., Calif., 1973-76; sec., office mgr. Sierra Med. Assocs., Reno, 1976-78; claims rep. Equifax, Reno, 1978-79; legal asst. Freeport Export Co., Reno, 1979-85; dir. govt. rels. Freeport-McMoRan Gold Co., Reno, 1985-89; pres. Legis. Cons., Reno, 1989—; cons. Nev. Wilderness Minerals Exploration Coalition, Denver, 1985. Named one of 88 people to watch in 1988, Reno Mag., 1988. Mem. Nev. Rep. Woman's Caucus, Reno, 1986, 94; apptd. Reno Commn. Status of Women, 1985. Mem. Nev. Mining Assn., Nev. Landman's Assn., Assn. Exec. Females, Nev. Coun. Econ. Edn. (exec. com.), Reno Sparks C. of C. (bd. dirs., v.p. community affairs), Coalition for Quality Lifestyle, Concerned Nevadans for Practical Wilderness, Health Reform

Coalition. Avocations: skiing, golf, travel. Office: 3660 Baker Ln Reno NV 89509

BERKE, AMY TURNER, health science association administrator; b. Cleve., Oct. 27, 1942; d. Elliott L. and Evelyn (Silverman) Glicksberg; m. Donald Alan Turner, Dec. 16, 1962 (div. 1979); children: Matthew, Kelli; m. Joseph Jerold Berke, June 21, 1981; children: Richard, Rachel, Jason. Student, Ohio State U., 1960-63; BS, Wayne State U., 1965, MA, 1966. Tchr. Waterford (Mich.) Sch. System, 1965-67; v.p. Apt. Referral Service, Oak Park, Mich., 1970-73; instr. Detroit Coll. Bus., Dearborn, Mich., 1975-79; exec. dir. Detroit Neurosurgical Found., 1979—; bd. dirs. Internat. Mus. Surgical Scis. Bd. dirs. Friends Belle Isle Detroit, Internat. Mus. Surg. Scis.; mem. citizens adv. Wayne County Juvenile Ct. Detroit, 1988, Met. Detroit Health Edn. Coun., New Detroit Summer Youth Assistance Com.; sec. bd. dirs. Tribute Fund Detroit; chmn. Recreational Adv. Commn., 1988. Mem. Coun. Mich. Founds. Host Com., Project Pride Detroit C. of C., Wayne State U. Alumni Club, Ohio State U. Alumni Club. Office: Detroit Neurosurg Found 8900 E Jefferson Ste 1117 Detroit MI 48214-2961

BERKE, ANITA DIAMANT, literary agent; b. N.Y.C., Jan. 15; d. Sidney J. and Lea (Lyons) Diamant; m. Harold Berke, Dec. 22, 1945 (dec. 1972); 1 child, Allyson. B.S., NYU. Mem. editorial bd. Forum Mag., N.Y.C., McCalls Mag.; reporter Macy Newspapers; literary agt., pres. Anita Diamant Lit. Agy., N.Y.C.; adj. prof. L.I.U. Contbr. articles to profl. jours. Mem. Women in Communications, Inc. (past pres. N.Y. chpt.), Nat. Assn. Newspaper Women, Soc. Author's Reps. Club: Overseas Press (pres. 1981-86). Home: 16 Fanton Hill Rd Weston CT 06883-2420 Office: 310 Madison Ave New York NY 10017

BERKELEY, BETTY LIFE, educator; b. St. Louis, May 25, 1924; d. James Alfred and Anna Laura (Voltmer) Life; m. Marvin Harold Berkeley, Feb. 7, 1947; children—Kathryn Elizabeth, Barbara Ellen, Brian Harrison, Janet Lynn. A.B., Harris Tchrs. Coll., 1947; M.A. in Ednl. Adminstrn., Washington U., St. Louis, 1951; Ph.D., U. North Tex., 1980. Tchr. St. Louis pub. schs., 1946-48, Clayton pub. schs., Mo., 1948-49, Lamplighter Pvt. Sch., Dallas, 1964-67; program devel. specialist Richland Coll., Dallas, 1980-84, instr., 1981—; adj. prof. U. North Tex., Denton, 1981—, cons. Sch. Community Services Ctr. for Studies on Aging, 1981—; pres. Retirement Planning Services, Dallas, 1984—. Contbr. articles to profl. jours. Named Outstanding Alumna Coll. of Edn. U. of North Tex., 1992. Mem. Dallas Commn. on Status of Women, 1975-79; bd. dirs. Dallas Municipal Library, 1979-83, Sr. Citizen Greater Dallas, 1986-92, Council on Adult Ministry Lovers Lane United Meth. Ch., 1982; charter mem. bd. dirs., life mem. Friends of U. North Tex. Libr.; mem. Pres.'s Coun. U. North Tex., mem. vol. mgmt. edn. task force, 1978-82. Mem. AAUW (pres. 1973-75; Outstanding Woman of Tex. 1981). Club: Women's Council of Dallas County (v.p. 1977-79). Avocations: travel, cooking, gardening, needlework. Home and Office: 13958 Hughes Ln Dallas TX 75240-3510

BERKEY, JUDITH OSTERHOUDT, computer science consultant; b. Kingston, N.Y., Jan. 15, 1943; d. Edmund Francis and Margaret Elizabeth (Lachmann) Osterhoudt; m. Walter Harry Berkey, June 26, 1965; children: Edmund Osterhoudt, Judson Lawrence. BS, Syracuse U., 1964; MS, George Mason U., 1986, PhD, 1990. Programmer IBM Corp., Endicott, N.Y., 1964-67; systems engineer IBM Corp., Charleston, S.C., 1967-68; lectr. George Mason U., Fairfax, Va., 1987-90; pvt. practice Manassas, Va., 1990—; systems analyst EG&G Analytical Svcs. Ctr., Inc., Manassas, 1991—; lectr. George Washington U., 1992; cons. Booz-Allen & Hamilton, 1993-94. Contbr. articles to profl. jours. Recipient Woman of Yr. award Manassas Jour. Messenger, 1978, Keep Am. Beautiful award, 1979. Mem. IEEE, AAUW (div. bd. 1982-83), Assn. of Computing Machinery. Home and Office: 1307 Sawbridge Way Reston VA 22094-1323

BERKHEMER-CREDAIRE, BETSY, public relations executive; b. Washington, Jan. 31, 1947; d. Robert Walter and Claire (Myers) Berkhemer; m. Criston Credaire, Mar. 23, 1985. B.S. in History, UCLA, 1968. Reporter Ventura (Calif.) Star Free Press, 1965-68; editor Gardena (Calif.) Valley News, 1968-70; writer Sta. KTTV Metromedia News, Los Angeles, 1970-71; publicist Disney Studios, NBC, Burbank, Calif., 1971-73; pres., owner Berkhemer & Kline Inc., Pub. Rels., Los Angeles, 1973-88; pres. Berkhemer, Kline, Golin, Harris Communications, 1988-93, exec. v.p. western region bus. devel., 1993—. Chmn. bd. dirs. March of Dimes So. Calif., Alliance Bus. for Childcare Devel., L.A. Edn. Ptnrship. Mem. UCLA Alumni Assn. (chmn. bd. dirs.). Office: Berkhemer Kline Golin/Harris One Bunker Hill 601 W 5th St Fl 4 Los Angeles CA 90071-2004*

BERKLEY, EMILY CAROLAN, lawyer; b. Richmond, Va., Mar. 2, 1950; d. Charles Garvice and Edna Gray (Berkley) Broom; m. Richard E. Bird, Sept. 6, 1969 (div. Mar. 1988); children: Jessica A. Bird, Martel J. Bird. Student, Coll. of William and Mary, 1968-70; BS in Psychology cum laude, Tufts U., 1972; JD magna cum laude, Temple U., 1977. Ptnr. Ballard, Spahr, Andrews & Ingersoll, Phila., 1977—; panelist Pa. Bar Inst. Seminar, 1992, Practicing Law Inst. Seminar, 1993, 94, 95. Mem. long range planning com. Performing Arts for Tredyffrin-Easttown Sch. Dist., Berwyn, Pa., 1989, chair subcom. on creativity, futures com., 1990; Ballard, Spahr, Andrews & Ingersoll chair United Way, 1989-91; bd. dirs. Devon-Strafford Little League, 1992—. Fellow Am. Bar Found.; mem. ABA (com. on legal opinions, uniform comml. code com., comml. fin. svcs. com., vice chmn. interest and usury subcom. 1989-93, panelist satellite seminar fundamentals of asset based financing 1990, instr. Ctrl. and Ea. European law initiative 1993, internat. law sect.), Am. Coll. Comml. Fin. Lawyers (bd. regents 1993—), Pa. Bar Assn. (steering com., legal options drafting group, real estate opinion project), Phila. Bar Assn. Office: Ballard Spahr Andrews et al 51st Fl 1735 Market St Philadelphia PA 19103

BERKLEY, ERMA VAN METER, retired librarian; b. Thayer, Kans., Nov. 18, 1922; d. George William and Elizabeth (Hamill) Van Meter; m. Donald William Berkley, May 28, 1944 (dec. 1980); children: Ann Elizabeth, James Donald. BA in Bus. Edn. magna cum laude, Western Wash. U., 1964; MLS, U. Wash., 1973. Cert. profl. libr., 1976. Sec., bookkeeper Blue Ribbon Growers, Inc., Yakima, Wash., 1941-44; aircraft communicator CAA, Kodiak, Alaska, 1944-47; libr., sec., tchr. Crescent Consol. Sch., Joyce, Wash., 1965-66; asst. libr., reference libr. Port Angeles (Wash.) High Sch., 1966-68, secretarial tchr., 1968-75, head libr., 1975-86; ret., 1986; bd. dirs. exec. com. Wash. Libr. Network, 1979-81; N.W. rep.-at-large Washington Libr. Media Assn., 1983-84; del. Gov.'s Conf. on Libr. and Info. Svcs., Olympia, 1979; sec. Western Wash. Bus. Edn. Assn., 1973-74. Mem. AAUW (treas. 1966-67, pres. 1982-84, v.p. 1988-90), PEO, Nat. Ret. Tchrs. Assn., Am. Philatelic Soc., Phi Theta Kappa, Beta Phi Mu.

BERKLEY, MARY CORNER, neurologist; b. Balt., Apr. 6, 1926; d. Henry Evans and Eleanor (Diggs) Corner; m. Kelly McKenzie Berkley, Sept. 3, 1955 (dec. Oct. 1984); children: Henry Evans, Robert Bruce; m. Warren Frederick Gorman, May 31, 1986. AB, Bryn Mawr Coll., 1946; MD, Johns Hopkins U., 1950. Diplomate Am. Bd. Psychiatry and Neurology. Intern, resident Cin. Gen. Hosp., 1950-52; resident in medicine Strong Meml. Hosp., Rochester, N.Y., 1952-53, fellow in neurology, 1953-56; pvt. practice Rochester, 1956-58, Janesville, Wis., 1958-60; resident in neurology U. Mich. Med. Ctr., Ann Arbor, 1960-64; sr. instr. Hahnemann Med. Coll., Phila., 1965-68; pvt. practice neurology Gallipolis, Ohio, 1968-70, Mt. Vernon, Ill., 1970-76; staff neurologist VA Med. Ctr., Phoenix, 1976-95, ret., 1995. Fellow Am. Acad. Neurology; mem. Alpha Omega Alpha.

BERKLEY-CARTER, DEBORAH LYNNE HALL, counselor; b. Halifax, Va., June 14, 1952; d. Robert Lee and Madeline (Foster) Hall; m. Karl Edward Carter, Aug. 9, 1989; children: Jason Ryan Berkley, William Justin Berkley. BS, Longwood Coll., 1973; MS, Va. Poly. Inst. and State U., 1979; MEd, Lynchburg (Va.) Coll., 1988; Ed. S., Coll. William and Mary, 1994, doctoral candidate, 1994. Lic. profl. counselor. Tchr. Nottoway (Va.) County Pub. Schs., 1975-77; co-owner, dir. The Children's Dept., Lynchburg, 1980-86; co-owner Foods With a Flair, Lynchburg, 1979-86; tchr. Amherst (Va.) County, 1985-86; tchr., counselor Campbell County Pub. Schs., 1986-91; counselor Williamsburg-James City County Pub. Schs., Williamsburg, Va., 1991-93, New Vistas Sch., Lynchburg, 1993—; The Rivermont Sch., Lynchburg, Va., 1994; pvt. practice Deborah Berkley-Carter and Assocs., Lynchburg, 1993—. Mem. ACA, Lynchburg Counseling Assn., Va. Counseling Assn., Mental Health Assn., Kappa Omicron Phi, Kappa Delta. Office: 2486 Rivermont Ave Lynchburg VA 24503-1546

BERKMAN, CLAIRE FLEET, psychologist; b. New Orleans, Dec. 5, 1942; d. Joel and Margaret Grace (Fishler) Fleet; m. Arnold Stephen Berkman, Apr. 27, 1975; children: Janna Samantha, Micah Seth Siegel. BA, Boston U., 1964; EdM, Harvard U., 1966; EdD, Boston U., 1970. Asst. prof. Counseling Ctr., Mich. State U., East Lansing, 1971-75, assoc. prof., 1975-78, assoc. prof. dept. psychiatry, 1975-82, clin. assoc. prof., 1986-87; pvt. clin. practice, 1975—; cons. Cath. Family Social Service, Lansing, 1979-83; mem. adv. bd. Cir. Ct. Family Counseling Program, 1982-88. V.p. Kehillat Israel Synagogue, 1975-76, pres. 1992-94; bd. dirs. Jewish Welfare Fedn., Lansing, 1974-75, 84-87; mem. children's task force State Bar Mich., 1993—. NDEA fellow, 1968-70. Mem. Am. Psychol. Assn., Mich. Psychol. Assn., Mich. Soc. Forensic Psychologists. Office: 4084 Okemos Rd Okemos MI 48864-3258

BERKMAN, LILLIAN, foundation executive, corporation executive, art collector; b. N.Y.C.. B.A. summa cum laude, NYU, 1942, M.A. summa cum laude, 1943, H.H.D. (hon.), 1976. Dir. pub. relations J.I. Case Co., 1957-60; pres. Gen. Alarm Corp., N.Y.C., 1965—; corp. dir., head advt. and pub. relations Am. Tractor Corp., 1948-56; dir. Allied Stores Corp., 1974-86, Mich. Nat. Corp., 1977-86, Mich. Nat. Bank, Detroit, 1977-87, Mich. Nat. Investment Corp., 1978-87, MNC-Western Leasing, 1980-87, Capital Corp., 1980—; pres. Rojtman Found., Inc., 1967—; cultural advisor Coca Cola Co., 1978—; bd. dirs. Sterling Nat. Bank N.Y., Sterling Nat. Corp., Sterling Bancorp.; v.p., asst. to chmn. for corp. planning and devel. Associated Comm. Corp., 1988-94, vice chmn., 1990-94; v.p., asst. to chmn. long range planning Associated Group, Inc., 1995—. Fellow in perpetuity Met. Mus. Art, N.Y.C., 1964—; donor Rojtman Medieval Sculpture Gallery, 1964, trustee medieval art com., 1974—; mem. exec. council Inst. Fine Arts, N.Y. U., 1972—; trustee Am. Wing, 1976—, Poly. Inst. N.Y., 1977—; nat. adv. coun. St. Petersburg (Fla.) Mus. Fine Arts, 1990—; fellow Pierpont Morgan Library, 1969—, Frick Mus., N.Y., 1980—, Nat. Council San Francisco Museums, 1985—; bd. dirs. United Cerebral Palsy Research and Ednl. Found., Inc., 1973—, Inner City Scholarship Fund, 1980—, Salvation Army, 1986—; mem. Met. Opera Nat. Council, 1973—; overseer U. Pa. Mus., 1982—; dir. Latin Am. Arts Council, 1988—; chmn. Theban expdn. to Valley of the Kings, Egypt, 1977—; cultural advisor to Costa Rica, 1978—; chmn., bd. dirs. Associated American Artists, Inc., 1983—. Recipient Highest Honor award Nat. Indsl. Advertisers Assn., 1956, Pere Marquette award Marquette U., 1966, Philippine Golden Heart Presdl. award for cultural interchange, 1976, Kairos award Marquette U., 1992. Mem. Nat. Assn. Corp. Dirs., Economic Club of N.Y., Lotos Club, Univ. Club of N.Y., Phi Beta Kappa Assocs. (bd. dirs., v.p. Middle Atlantic dist.). Home: 22 E 64th St New York NY 10021-7212

BERKOVITS, MARIANNE (MARI BIRO), educator, sculptor, painter; b. Cluj, Romania, July 19, 1948; came to U.S., 1965; d. Josef and Agnes (Csato) Marmarosch; m. Alexander Schlesinger, 1972 (div. 1979; 1 child, Julian; m. Tibor Berkovits, Sept. 23, 1982; children: Michael, Diana. BFA with honors, Pratt Inst., 1972; postgrad., CUNY, 1972, 89. Tchr. English, Yeshiva Ohel Moshe, Bklyn., 1978-79, Yeshiva R'tzahd, Bklyn., 1979-81, Dist. 15 and 20 Bd. Edn., Bklyn., 1990-92; tchr. art Yeshiva Shalshelet, Bklyn., 1992—. Group exhbns. include Hansen Gallery, Soho, N.Y., 1975, Salmagundi Club, N.Y.C., 1990, Sunset Arts exhbn., Bklyn., 1992, 93, Bklyn. Waterfront Artists Coalition, 1992, 93, 94; works in permanent collections of Librarie Francaise, Rockefeller Ctr., N.Y.C., collection of Morris Jaffe, collection of Philip Morse. Mem. Bklyn. Waterfront Artists Coalition, Nat. Assn. Women Artists, Orgn. Ind. Artists, Art Initiatives, Artists Talk on Art. Home: 834 44th St Brooklyn NY 11220-1609

BERKOWITZ, LYNN B., artist, educator; b. Flushing, N.Y., Feb. 6, 1953; d. Samuel S. Berkowitz and Shirley (Steinberg) Goodman; m. Robert Wedge. Student, Phila. Coll. of Art, 1971-74; BFA, Kutztown U., 1982; MFA, Temple U., 1989. Gallery dir. Luckenbach Mill Gallery, Historic Bethlehem (Pa.), Inc., 1989-91; lectr. II Marywood Coll., Scranton, Pa., 1992—; cons. Touchstone Theatre, Bethlehem, Pa., 1992—, Open Space Gallery, Allentown, 1993—, Mayfair, Allentown, Pa., 1993-94; lectr. in field. Curator various art exhbns., 1991, 94, 95, 96; work shown nationally and internationally. Mem. craft adv. panel Pa. Coun. on Arts, Harrisburg, Pa., 1990-93. AAUW scholar, 1981; recipient Sharing the Arts purchase award N.J. Coun. on Arts, 1989. Mem. Am. Craft Coun., Coll. Arts Assn., Mid Atlantic Fiber Assn., New Arts Program, Surface Design Assn., Textile Soc. N.Y. Home: PO Box 121 Slatedale PA 18079 Office: Marywood Coll Visual Arts Ctr 2300 Adams Ave Scranton PA 18509

BERLAGE, GAI INGHAM, sociologist, educator; b. Washington, Feb. 9, 1943; d. Paul Bowen and Grace (Artz) Ingham; m. Jan Coxe Berlage, Aug. 7, 1965; children: Jan Ingham, Cari Coxe. BA, Smith Coll., 1965; MA, So. Meth. U., 1968; PhD, NYU, 1979. Tchr. math. Piner Jr. High Sch., Sherman, Tex., 1968-69; asst. prof. sociology Iona Coll., New Rochelle, N.Y., 1971-83, assoc. prof., 1983-88, chmn. dept., 1981-90, prof., 1988—; coord. urban studies program, 1984-90, gerontology program, 1984-90; treas. The N.Am. Soc. for Sociology of Sports, 1992-93. Author: Experience with Sociology: Social Issues in American Society, 1983, Understanding Social Issues: Sociological Fact Finding, 1987, 3d edit., 1993, Women in Baseball: The Forgotten History, 1994; mem. editl. bd. Jour. Sport and Social Issues, 1990-94; contbr. articles to profl. jours. Commr. Wilton Commn. on Aging and Social Svcs., 1980-88, chmn., 1982-88; co-chmn. Wilton Task Force on Youth Coun., 1988; chmn. Wilton Task Force Com. for Outreach Program, 1981-82, Wilton Task Force on Day Care, 1983-88; mem. Wilton Task Force for Pub. Health Nursing Assn., 1981-82, Wilton Sport Coun., 1985-88; bd. dirs. Wilton Meals on Wheels, 1983-88; fellow N.Am. Faculty Network of Northeastern Univs. Ctr. for Study of Sport in Soc. Recipient Best Profl. Paper award Third Annual Cooperstown Symposium on Baseball and the Am. Cultre; named to Iona Coll. Women of Achievement, 1993. Mem. Am. Sociol. Assn., N.Am. Soc. Sociology of Sport, Internat. Com. on Sociology of Sport, Wilton Assn. for Gifted Edn. (pres. 1980-81), N.Am. Soc. for Sport History, Soc. for Am. Baseball Rsch., Women's Sport Found. Office: Iona Coll Dept Sociology New Rochelle NY 10801

BERLAND, KAREN INA, psychologist; b. N.Y.C., Nov. 14, 1947; d. Max and Lillian (Graf) B. BA in Psychology, SUNY, Buffalo, 1969; MEd in Ednl. Psychology, U. Ill., 1971; D. Psychology, U. Denver, 1984. Cert. sch. psychologist, clin. psychologist. Sch. psychologist City Sch. Dist. Rochester (N.Y.), 1971-73, Denver Pub. Sch., 1973—; psychology intern Vets. Hosp., West Haven, Conn., 1983-84; psychologist Aurora (Colo.) Community Mental Health Ctr., 1985-92; expert witness Denver County Ct. Mem. APA, Colo. Soc. Sch. Psychologists (pres. 1986-87, Leadership award 1987), Colo. Psychol. Assn. (fin. com., treas.), Colo. Women's Psychologists, Nat. Assn. Sch. Psychologists (Western Regional dir. and Colo. rep. 1976-83), Assn. for Advancement of Behavior Therapy, Mensa. Democrat. Jewish. Home: 1171 Forest St Denver CO 80220-4450

BERLET, NANCY WEIR, cultural organization administrator; b. Niskayuna, N.Y., June 8, 1949; d. John Declan and Phyllis Marie (Colls) Weir; m. Bruce Edward Berlet, Apr. 19, 1975; 1 child, Brooke Elizabeth Grace. BA in Elem. Edn., St. Joseph Coll., 1971. Tchr. Corpus Christi Schs., Wethersfield, Conn., 1971-75; sportswriter (1st woman sportswriter hired) The Hartford Courant, Hartford, Conn., 1974-79; cons. Moses Assocs., West Hartford, Conn., 1986-87; freelance writer Glastonbury, Conn., 1980—; exec. dir. Historical Soc. of Glastonbury, 1987—; mem. bd. dirs. Conn. League Hist. Socs., 1993—, v.p., 1994—. Author: Historical Soc. of Glastonbury Newsletter, 1987—. Bd. dirs. Jr. League of Hartford, 1988-89, editor newsletter, 1984-86; mem. rep. Greater Hartford Assn. Hist. Houses and Mus., 1987—, v.p., 1989-91, pres., 1991—; mem. steering com. Glastonbury's Tercentenary Clelbration, 1987-93. Home: 202 Carriage Dr Glastonbury CT 06033-3232 Office: Hist Soc Glastonbury PO Box 46 Glastonbury CT 06033-0046

BERLIN, BEATRICE WINN, visual artist, printmaker; b. Phila., May 27, 1922; d. Benjamin and Pauline (Neubauer) Winn; m. Herbert Edward Berlin, Oct. 21, 1945; m. 2d., Warren Joseph Sturmer, Aug. 21, 1971; children—Arlene (dec.), Janice. Student Moore Coll. Art, Phila., Phila. Coll. Art; student Samuel Maitin, Hitoshi Nakazato, Kenjilo Nanao. Lectr. Phila. Print Club, Phila., 1964-68; instr. Intaglio techniques Long Beach Island Ctr. Arts and Sci., N.J., 1970; freelance artist, Pa., 1963-76, Calif., 1976—; represented in pub. collections including Phila. Mus. Art., Bklyn. Art. Mus., N.Y. Public Library, Phila. Main Library, De Cordova Mus., Mass., U. So. Calif., N.J. State Mus., Temple U., Phila., U. Pa., Phila., Lebanon Valley Coll., Pa., Ocean City Cultural Ctr., N.J., San Francisco Art Mus., Achenback Coll. Recipient Phila. Water Color Club drawing prize, 1976, 82, Ocean City (N.J.) Boardwalk best in show prize, 1973. Lebanon Valley (Pa.) Coll. purchase prize, 1973, Hazelton (Pa.) Art League purchase prize, 1972, Cheltenham (Pa.) Art Ctr. Nat. Print Exhbn. first prize, 1970. Mem. Calif. Soc. Printmakers, Artists Equity Assn.

BERLIN, DORIS ADA, psychiatrist; b. Newark, May 23, 1919; d. Samuel and Fanny (Lippman) B.; m. Saul R. Kelson; children: Joel, Tamar. BS in Pharmacy, Columbia U., 1940; MD, Med. Coll. Va., 1948; MPH in Community Mental Health, U. Mich., 1966. Cert. Am. Bd. Psychiatry and Neurology; lic. psychiatrist N.Y., Va., Ohio, Mich., Tex., Calif. Intern Beth Israel Hosp., N.Y.C., 1948-49; resident in psychiatry Bellevue Hosp., N.Y.C., 1949-52; pvt. practice N.Y.C., 1952-57, Toledo, 1957-66, Fishkill and Poughkeepsie, N.Y., 1984—; clin. asst. in psychiatry NYU Coll. Medicine, 1952-57; asst. in psychiatry U. Hosp., N.Y., 1952-53; clin. asst. vis. neuropsychiatrist Bellevue Hosp., N.Y., 1954-57; lectr. mental health Sch. Pub. Health U. Mich., 1966-68; dir. profl. edn. Toledo State Hosp., 1969-70; clin. assoc. prof. N.Y. Sch. Psychiatry, 1970-81; dir. residency program Hudson River Psychiat. Ctr., Poughkeepsie, 1970-83, others. Mem. citizen's adv. bd. Lucas County (Ohio) Welfare Dept., 1963-67, chair, 1965-66; bd. dirs. Jewish Family Svc., Toledo, 1969-70; mem. policy coun., rehab. com. Toledo Area Program on Drug Abuse, 1970; bd. dirs. Dutchess County Assn. for Sr. Citizens, 1993—. Grantee NEH, 1979. Fellow Am. Psychiat. Assn. (cert. qualified psychiat. adminstr., chair editorial bd. Hospital and Community Psychiatric Jour., 1979-80, task force on community mental health ctrs. 1983-88, com. on advertisers and exhibitors 1989-92, vice chair lifers caucus 1990-91, chair lifers orgn. 1992—), Am. Coll. Psychiatrist (Laughlin fellowship com. 1976-79); mem. Am. Acad. Psychoanalysis (com. on psychoanalysis and community mental health 1967-68), Dutchess County Med. Soc. (psychiatrists' rep. to coun. 1985—, treas. 1987). Home and Office: 66 Mitchell Ave Poughkeepsie NY 12603-3423

BERLIN, KATHRYN E., retired public health nurse; b. Pemberville, Ohio, Nov. 5, 1937; d. Jurdin Deforest and Janet Mary (Hathaway) Smith; m. Albert James Rubel, (div. Sept. 1972); children: Douglas James, Jeffrey Dean, Cynthia Sue, Craig Alan; m. James Vernon Berlin, July 1984. Diploma, Flower Hosp. Sch. Nursing, 1959. RN, Ohio. Head nurse, emergency rm. Flower Hosp., Toledo, 1959-62; occupational health nurse Brush Wellman-Berrylium, Elmore, Ohio, 1962-65; nurse, emergency rm., ICU, recovery rom. Wood County Hosp., Bowling Green, Ohio, 1967-68; office nurse Drs. H.W. Mannhard and R.J. Wherry, Bowling Green, 1968-73; occupational health nurse H.J. Heinz Co., Bowling Green, 1972-73; pub. health nurse Wood County Health Dept., Bowling Green, 1973-79; occupational health nurse Chrysler Machining, Perrysburg, Ohio, 1977-80; occupational nurse Hunt Wesson Foods, Perrysburg, 1979; charge nurse St. Charles Hosp., Toledo, 1979-80; pub. health nurse, nurse surveyer Ohio Dept. Health, Toledo, 1980-91; cert. reviewer Health Facilities in NWDO, 1980-91. Sunday sch. tchr., organist, officer United Meth. Ch., 1950-70; sr. 1st class Girl Scouts U.S. Mem. AARP, ANA, Ohio Nurses Assn., Wood County Dist. Nurses Assn. (treas. 1960), Toledo Zool. Soc., Flower Hosp. Alumni Assn. Home: Kitty Hawk Estates Rte # 8 Box 226-F Live Oak FL 32060

BERLIN, LISA CAROLE, volunteer, educator; b. Ridgewood, N.J., Jan. 9, 1969; d. Norman M. and Anne (Hauptman) B. BA in English and History, Rutgers Coll., 1991. Health advocate Rutgers Coll., New Brunswick, N.J., 1990-91; coord. vols., edn. coord., health educator AIDS Resource Found. for Children, Newark, 1992-93; vol. and speakers bur. mem. Hyacinth Found., New Brunswick, 1990-91; edn. com. vol. N.J. Women and AIDS Network, New Brunswick, 1992—. Mem. Phi Beta Kappa. Home: PO Box 1405 Somerset NJ 08875

BERLINER, BARBARA, librarian, consultant; b. Bklyn., July 14, 1947; d. Robert and Mildred M. (Sklar) Morris; 1 child, Stefanie Lauren. BA in Anthropology, NYU, 1969; MLS, Columbia U., 1970. Libr. N.Y. Pub. Libr., N.Y.C., 1970-81, sr. libr., telephone reference, 1981-86, supervising libr., telephone reference, 1986-92, head libr., Mid-Manhattan sci. and bus., 1992-93, coord. corp. svcs., 1993—; cons. John Wright, N.Y.C., 1991; bibliographer Collier's Encyclopedia. Author: The Book of Answers, 1990. Mem. ALA, Spl. Librs. Assn., N.Y. Libr. Assn., Planetary Soc. Home: 74 W Columbia Ave Palisades Park NJ 07650 Office: N Y Pub Libr Corp Svcs 5th Ave and 42d St New York NY 10018

BERLINER, RUTH SHIRLEY, real estate company executive; b. N.Y.C., June 20, 1928; d. Irving William and Florence (Tomback) Blum; m. Arthur Ivan Berliner, Sept. 23, 1948; children: Daniel Scott, Michael Robert, Eric Lance. BA, Empire State Coll., Westbury, N.Y., 1974; diploma, Wilsey Sch. Interior Design, Hempstead, N.Y., 1975; MBA, Adelphi U., 1980. Lic. real estate broker, N.Y. Sec. to dir. librs. NYU, N.Y.C., 1948-50; sec. Paragon Mut. Syndicates Inc., N.Y.C., 1958-72; v.p. Paragon Mut. Investors Svcs., N.Y.C., 1972-78; pres. Ruth S. Berliner, Inc., N.Y.C., 1978-94; pres. Irmed Corp., 1983-94; cons. E. 59th St. Assocs., N.Y.C., 1962-70, Amrep Corp., N.Y.C., 1968-75, FKBA Assocs., N.Y.C., 1974-78; mem. stores com. Real Estate Bd. N.Y., 1984-94. Vice pres. NYU Dental Sch. Parents Assn., 1974-76; bd. dirs. Hadassah, Hewlett, N.Y., 1978-87; advisor Citizens for Charter Change, N.Y.C., 1987—. Mem. Nat. Assn. Realtors, Real Estate Bd. N.Y. (store com. 1984-95, econ. devel. com. 1994), Inwood Club. Office: 450 7th Ave Rm 2309 New York NY 10001

BERLINSKY, ELLEN BETH, psychologist; b. Providence, Sept. 3, 1953; d. Everett and Sandra Marilyn (Pliner) B.; B.A. magna cum laude, Syracuse U., 1975; M.A., Columbia U., 1976; Ph.D., U. R.I., 1981; m. Gary L. Schine, Mar. 19, 1978; children: Adam Ross Berlinsky-Schine, Laura Jane Berlinsky-Schine. Lic. psychologist, Mass. Clin. psychologist No. R.I. Community Mental Health, Woonsocket, 1979-81; psychologist Counseling and Family Services, Taunton, Mass., 1981; clin. psychologist, asst. prof. U. Mass. Med. Ctr., Worcester, 1981-90; clin. psychologist Human Resource Inst., Norton, Mass., 1981-89; clin. psychologist Bridgewater (Mass.) Psychol. Assocs., 1985-88; cons. Applied Media Group, Providence, 1981-87; pvt. practice, Middleboro, Ma., 1989-94, Taunton, Mass., 1995—. Writer, narrator: (videotape) Getting Ready to Learn. Mem. Am. Psychol. Assn., Mass. Psychol. Assn., Phi Beta Kappa, Phi Kappa Phi. Author: (with Henry Biller) Parental Death and Psychological Development, 1982, (with Gary Schine) If the President Had Cancer, 1993. Home: 39 Brenton Ave Providence RI 02906-2414

BERLOWE, PHYLLIS HARRIETTE, public relations counselor; b. N.Y.C.; d. Louis and Rose (Jachez) Berlowe. Student, Hunter Coll., 1950-52. Account exec. Ted Sills & Co., N.Y.C., 1959-63, Harshe-Rotman & Druck, N.Y.C., 1963-65; exec. v.p. Edward Gottlieb & Assocs, N.Y.C., 1965-78; v.p. Hill & Knowlton, Inc., N.Y.C., 1972-79; v.p., group supr. Doremus & Co., N.Y.C., 1980-83, Marketshare div. Doremus & Co., N.Y.C., 1983-86; pres. The Berlowe Group, N.Y.C., 1986—. Mem. Pub. Relations Soc. Am. (citations 1976-78, 80-83, Silver Anvil 1977), Counselors Acad. (chmn. 1981), Women Execs. in Pub. Relations (pres. 1982), World Future Soc. Clubs: Marco Polo, Publicity Club of N.Y. (Disting. Service award 1960-62). Office: The Berlowe Group 201 W 77th St New York NY 10024-6606

BERMAN, BARBARA, educational consultant; b. N.Y.C., Oct. 15, 1938; d. Nathan and Regina (Pasternak) Kopp; children: Adrienne, David. BS, Bklyn. Coll., 1959, MS, 1961; adminstrv./supervision cert., Coll. S.I., 1971; EdD, Rutgers U., 1981. Tchr. N.Y.C. Pub. Schs., 1959-70; project coord., dir. fed. projects Rutgers U., New Brunswick, N.J., 1976-80; math. cons. B & F Ednl. Cons., Inc., S.I., N.Y., 1978—; dir. fed. math. project Ednl. Support Systems, Inc., S.I., 1981—; adminstrv. dir. Foresight Sch., S.I., 1985—; dir. Great Beginnings Infant and Toddler Ctr., 1989—. Co-author: (books) Fractions and Decimals for Junior High School: A Model Integrating Process and Content Skills, 1980, Metric Mini-Course, 1981, Mathematics: Getting in Touch, Books I and II, 1985, Color Tiles, 1986, Mathematics

Through Measurement, 1983, Mathematics Institute for the Elementary School Teacher, 1980, Math Corners: Probability, 1993; revs. for N.Y. State Math. Tchrs. Jour., Arithmetic Tchr.; contbr. articles to profl. jours. Mem. Nat. Coun. Tchrs. Math., Nat. Staff Devel. Coun., N.Y. Acad. Scis., Nat. Coun. Suprs. Math., Mensa, Kappa Delta Pi. Home: 512 Valleyview Pl Staten Island NY 10314-5535 Office: Ednl Support Systems Inc 446 Travis Ave Staten Island NY 10314-6149

BERMAN, CAROL SIEGEL, artist; b. Cleve., June 4, 1932; d. Maurice Myron and Florence (Blatt) Siegel; m. Sidney A. Berman, July 20, 1956; children: Steven Eric, Adrian Jennifer. Student, New Orleans Acad. Art, 1949-50, Tulane U., 1951, Thomas Nelson Coll., 1969-70. Studio owner, portrait artist Reston, Va., 1970—; tech. illustrator, No. Va., 1974-84; represented by Herndon (Va.) Old Town Gallery, 1986-87, Reston Art Gallery, 1988, Greater Reston Art Ctr., 1987—. One woman shows include Herndon Old Town Gallery, 1986, 87, Greater Reston Art Ctr., 1988; group exhibitions at Greater Reston Art Ctr., 1987, 88, 89, Foundry Gallery, 1989. Recipient 1st Place Drawing award Va. Fine Arts Festival, 1987, Best in Show award Jewish Coun. on Aging, 1992. Mem. League of Reston Artists (Best in Show award 1983, 1st Place mixed media award 1994). Democrat. Jewish.

BERMAN, ELEANORE, artist; b. N.Y.C., Sept. 2, 1928; d. Isidor and Elsie (Goldstein) Berman; children: Deborah Nicholas, Jan Nicholas, Anthony Nicholas, David Lazarof. BA, UCLA, 1950. One-woman shows include: Kirk De Gooyer Gallery, L.A., 1982, Kouros Gallery, N.Y.C., 1982, L.A. City Hall, 1984, Gallery Xt, Brussels, 1985, New Eng. Ctr. for Contemporary Art, Mass., 1985, Mcpl. Gallery, Kampen, The Netherlands, 1986, Mcpl. Gallery, Amstelveen, The Netherlands, 1986, Rose Cafe, Venice, Calif., 1988, Lisa Kurts Gallery, Memphis, 1989, Boritzer/Gray Gallery, Santa Monica, Calif., 1991; exhibited in group shows: LAART, N.Y.C., 1986, U. Hawaii, Hilo, 1986, Elaine Starkman Gallery, N.Y.C., 1982, L.A. County Mus. Art, 1981, Boston Ctr. for the Arts, 1981, Wesleyan Coll., Conn., 1980, Newport (R.I.) Harbor Mus., 1977, Nat. Acad. Western Art Traveling Exhbn., 1988, L.A.-U.K. Print Connection, 1989, Bonnie Fridholm Gallery, Asheville, N.C., 1989; represented in permanent collections: L.A. County Mus. Art, Bklyn. Mus., Milw. Art Ctr., Grunwald Graphic Art Ctr., UCLA, others. Mem. Nat. Assn. of Women Artists, So. Calif. Women's Caucus for the Arts, L.A. Printmaking Assn., Nat. Watercolor Soc., Artists Equity Assn. (adv. bd. 1980-84).

BERMAN, ETHEL WARGOTZ, artist, educator; b. N.Y.C.; d. Louis Israel and Eva (Wajnglas) Wargotz; m. Harold Berman; children: Mary Jane, Lucy Berman-Edelman. BS, CCNY; MS, Syracuse U. Spl. educator N.Y.C. Pub. Schs.; French tchr. Norwich (N.Y.) High Sch.; spl. edn. tchr. Sherburne (N.Y.) BOCES. Active Chenango County Voters For Choice, Planned Parenthood, Norwich, Am. Cancer Soc. Reach to Recovery, YMCA, Norwich. Mem. Norwich Fine Arts Guild (bd. dirs.), Home Ext. Norwich, Monday Evening Musical Club, Smithsonian Instn., Nat. Woman's Mus. Art (charter). Home: 27 Sunset Dr Norwich NY 13815

BERMAN, JOANNA, dancer; b. San Rafael, Calif.. Studies with Maria Vegh, Marin Ballet Sch.; student, San Francisco Ballet Sch. Apprentice San Francisco Ballet, 1984, joined Corps de Ballet, 1984-87, soloist, 1987-88, prin. dancer, 1988—; Teacher, Acad. of Ballet, San Francisco, 1993; teacher, Pacific Regional Ballet Festival, Modesto, Calif., 1993; teacher, San Francisco Ballet Sch., 1992; teacher, Marin Ballet Sch., 1992; performed with the Royal Ballet, Tokyo, 1989; featured artist, New World Festival of Arts, Miami, 1981. Dancer in numerous ballets including The Sleeping Beauty, Swan Lake, Con Brio, Handel-A Celebration, Giuliani: Variations on a Theme, Bizet Pas de Deux, Concerto in d: Poulenc, The Wanderer Fantasy, The Sons of Horus, Rodeo, Nutcracker, Harvest Moon, Le Corsaire, Hearts, Connotations, Narcisse, Hamlet and Ophelia pas de deux, Tchaikovsky pas de deux, Symphony in C, Ballo della Regina, Rubies, Tarantella, A Midsummer Night's Dream, New Sleep, Forgotten Land, The Concert, In The Night, Opus 19: The Dreamer, Divertissement d'Auber, La Sylphide, Two Plus Two, Haffner Symphony, Le Quattro Stagioni, Who Cares?, Job, Seeing Stars, Connotations, Narcisse, Hamlet and Opelia, Pas de Deux, Le Corsaire Pas de Deux, Hearts, Company B, La Pavane Rouge, Filling Station, Airs de Ballet; appeared in television broadcasts Jinx, 1984, Cinderella, 1985. Semi-finalist for Am. team Internat. Ballet Competition, Moscow, 1981. Office: San Francisco Ballet 455 Franklin St San Francisco CA 94102-4471*

BERMAN, LAURA, freelance writer; b. Detroit, Dec. 8, 1953; d. Seymour Donald and Rose (Mendelson) B.; m. Christopher M.F. Norris, Feb. 24, 1985. AB, U. Mich., 1975. Writer, reporter Detroit Free Press, 1976-86; columnist The Detroit News, 1986-93; freelance writer, 1994—.

BERMAN, LORI BETH, lawyer; b. N.Y.C., June 27, 1958; d. George Gilbert and Sara Ann (Abrams) B.; m. Jeffrey Ganeles, Nov. 26, 1983; children: Caryn Elissa, Steven Aaron. BA magna cum laude, Tufts U., 1980; JD, George Washington U., 1983. Assoc. Margolies, Edelstein & Scherlis, Phila., 1983-84, White and Williams, Phila., 1984-87, Brownstein Zeidman & Schomer, Washington, 1987-89; v.p. legal & compliance Pointe Savs. Bank, Boca Raton, Fla., 1990—. Mem., Jour. Internat. Law and Econs. Mem. exec. coun. United Jewish Appeal Fedn., Washington, 1987-89, Boca Raton, 1990—, Leadership Boca, 1992. Mem. ABA, D.C. Bar Assn., Fla. Bar Assn., Boca Raton C. of C. Democrat. Jewish.

BERMAN, MIRA, advertising agency executive; b. Danzig, June 1, 1928; d. Max and Riva (Gutman) B.; m. Richard D. Freedman, Jan. 23, 1972. Student, Profl. Children's Sch., Berkshire Music Sch. and Festival, Juilliard Sch. Music, David Mannes Coll. Music, NYU, Columbia U. Chief copywriter Girl Scouts U.S.A., 1948-50; sr. copywriter Bamberger's, 1950-52; advt. dir., head women fashions Bond Stores, 1952-55; copy dir. Robert Hall, 1955-56; advt. copy dir. Gimbel's, N.Y.C., 1956-57; dir. pub. rels., fashion Snellenburg's, 1957-59; sr. v.p. pub. rels. and advt. Lavenson Bur. Advt., 1959-66; pres. Allerton, Berman & Dean, 1966-76; chairperson, chief exec. officer Gemini Images, Inc., 1976-86; pres. The Bradford Group, 1986—; mem. faculty master's degree program in tourism and travel adminstrn. New Sch. for Social Research, N.Y.C.; Co-chmn. 1st ann. Internat. Symposium Travel and Tourism, Am. Mgmt. Assn.; co-chmn. 1st ann. Marketing Through Retailers Symposium, 1966-67, staff lectr., 1967-70; condr. Modern Bank Practices Seminars; Am. Assn. Advt. Agencies rep. to Nat. Advt. Rev. Bd. Author: Marketing Through Retailers, 1967, also Spanish and Japanese edits; Travel editor: Woman's Life Mag. Exec. dir. Am. Friends of Ezrath Nashim Hosp., Jerusalem Geriatric and Mental Health Ctr., 1986-91, The Africa Travel Assn., 1990—, Assembly of Nat. Tourist Office Reps., 1991—, Nat. Coun. of Women U.S.A., 1988-90, Am. Israel Opera Found., 1986-89; dir. devel. PROMESA Found., Inc. Recipient Israel Ministry Tourism award; Fashion Gold medal; Carl V. Cesery award Tile Contractors Assn. Am.; silver award; bronze award; AMITA Sister award; winner Gold medal Internat. Film and TV Festival N.Y., Grand award. Mem. Am. Advt. Fedn. (named one of Ten Top Women in Advt.), Fin. Publicist Assn. Am., The Fashion Group, Pub. Rels. Soc. Am. (bd. govs.), Phila. Pub. Rels. Assn., Am. Soc. Travel Agts., Soc. Advancement Travel for Handicapped (dir. travellers with disabilities awareness week), International Tourism Assn., Nat. Coun. Women., Women Execs. Internat. (exec. dir.). Home: 116 Central Park S New York NY 10019-1529 Office: 347 5th Ave Ste 610 New York NY 10016-5010

BERMAN, MONA S., actress, playwright, theatrical director and producer; b. Jersey City; d. Edward and Mary (Auster) Solomon; m. Carroll Z. Berman; children—Marcie S. Berman Ries, Laura Jane. B.A., Beaver Coll., postgrad. Columbia U., M.F.A., Boston U. Tchr. English, drama Jersey City High Schs.; actress indsl., stage, TV, Valley Players, Holyoke, Mass., The Millbrook Playhouse, Mill Hall, Pa., 1991; owner, dir. The Theatre Sch. and Producing Co., Maplewood, N.J.; chmn. drama edn. YM-YWHA of Met. N.J. Cons., Clark Ctr. for Performing Arts, N.Y.C., 1965-66; instr. South Orange, Maplewood Adult Sch., 1967; artistic dir. Children's Theatre Co. Inc., Maplewood, 1968-70; cons. The Whole Theater Co.; dir. pub. relations Co. 3 by 2. Playwright: Hello Joe, That Ring in the Center, The Big Show, Interim, Who Can Belong?, Sudden Changes, Without Malice, Interim 2; producer, dir. A Night of Stars; guest theatre reviewer El Paso Herald Post, 1980-82. Active Boston United Fund, 1955-59, chmn. Boston residential area, 1957; bd. dirs. Greater Boston Girl Scouts Am., 1956-58, Tufts Med. Faculty Wives, 1956-58. Mem. Am. Theater Assn., Playwrights Unit 42d St. Theater Ctr. N.Y.C., Dramatists Guild, Actors Equity Assn., Waterfront Ensemble N.J. Address: 454 Prospect Ave # 176 West Orange NJ 07052-4103

BERMAN, MURIEL MALLIN, civic worker; b. Pitts.; d. Samuel and Dora (Coopersman) Mallin; m. Philip I. Berman, Oct. 23, 1942; children: Nancy, Nina, Steven. Student, U. Pitts., 1943, Carnegie Tech. U., 1944-45; BS, Pa. State Coll. Optometry, 1948; postgrad., U. Pitts., 1950, Muhlenberg Coll., 1954, Cedar Crest Coll., 1953; DFA (hon.), Cedar Crest Coll., 1972; hon. degree, Hebrew U., Israel, 1982; DHL (hon.), Ursinus Coll., 1987, Lehigh U., 1991. Lic. Pa., N.J. Practice optometry Pitts.; sec.-treas., dir. Philip and Muriel Berman Found.; underwriting mem. Lloyd's of London, 1974-87; lectr. on travels, art, UN activities, women's status and affairs. Producer: weekly TV show College Speak-Out, 1967—; producer, moderator: TV show Guest Spot. Active in UNICEF, 1959—, ofcl. non-govtl. orgns., 1964, 74; U.S. State Dept. del. UN Internat. Women's Yr. Conf., Mexico City, 1975; mem. State Dept. Arts and Humanities Com. Nat. Commn. on Observance of Women's Yr., 1975; adv. com. U.S. Ctr. for Internat. Womens Yr., Washington; founder, donor Carnegie-Berman Coll. Art Slide Library Exchange; mem. Aspen (Colo.) Inst. Humanistic Studies, 1965, Tokyo, 1966; chmn. exhibits Great Valley council Girl Scouts U.S.A., 1966; adminstrv. head, chmn. various events Allentown Bicentennial, 1962; vice-chmn. Women for Pa. Bicentennial, 1976; co-chmn. Lehigh County Bicentennial Bell-Trek, 1976; patron Art in Embassies Program, Washington, 1965—; chmn. Lehigh Valley Ednl. TV, 1966—; program chmn. Fgn. Policy Assn. Lehigh County, 1965-67; treas. ann. ball Allentown Symphony, 1955—; mem. art adv. com. Dieruff High Sch., Allentown, 1966—; co-chmn. art. com. Episcopal Diocese Centennial Celebration, 1971; mem. Pa. Council on Status of Women, 1968-73; reappointed Pa. Gov.'s Commn. on Women, 1984; chmn. numerous art shows; mem. Art Collectors Club Am., Am. Fedn. Art, Friends of Whitney Mus., Mus. Modern Art, Mus. Primitive Art, Jewish Mus., Kemmerer Mus., Bethlehem, Pa., Univ. Mus., Phila., Archives of Am. Art, Met. Opera Guild, others; ofcl. del. Dem. Nat. Conv., 1972, 76, mem. Democratic Platform Com., 1972; mem. Pa. Humanities Coun., 1979—; bd. dirs. Heart Assn. Pa., Allentown Art Mus. Aux., Phila. Chamber Symphony, Baum Art Sch., Lehigh County Cultural Ctr., Heart Assn. Pa., Baum Art Sch., Young Audiences, Israel Mus., Hadassah Womens Orgn.; bd. govs. Pa. State System of Higher Edn., 1986—; trustee Kutztown State Coll., 1960-66, vice-chmn. bd., 1965; trustee, sec. bd. Lehigh Community Coll.; mem. nat. bd. UN-U.S.A., 1977—; trustee Pa. Council on Arts, Pa. Ballet, Smithsonian Art Council, Bonds for Israel, Hadassah (nat. bd. with portfolio), Am. Friends Hebrew U., 1984; bd. regents Internat. Ctr. for Univ. Teaching of Jewish Civilization, Israel, 1982—; fine arts chmn. Women's Club; mem. com. on Prints, Drawings, & Photography Pa. Mus. Art, 1984; hon. chmn. Bucks County Coillectors Art Show. Named Woman of Valor State of Israel, 1965; recipient Centenial Yr. hon. citation Wilson Coll., 1969; Henrietta Szold award Allentown chpt. Hadassah; Outstanding Woman award Allentown YWCA, 1973; George Washington Honor medal Freedoms Found. at Valley Forge, 1985; Hazlett award Outstanding Service to Arts Pa.; Outstanding Citizen award Boy Scouts Am., 1982, Myrtle Wreath award Pa. Region Hadassah, Mt. Scopus award State of Israel Bonds, 1984, Woman of Yr. award Am. Friends Hebrew U., Phila., 1984, others; hon. fellow Hebrew U., 1975; Centennial citation Wilson Coll., 1969. Mem. LWV, YWCA, Hist. Soc. Lehigh County, Lehigh Art Alliance, Phila. Art Alliance, UN We Believe, Am. Fedn. of Art., Pa. Hist. Soc. (life), Jewish Publ. Soc. Am. (former pres., chmn. bd. 1984), Disting. Daughters of Pa. Jewish. Club: Wellesley. Address: Ste 203 1150 S Cedar Crest Blvd Allentown PA 18103

BERMAN, PATRICIA KARATSIS, arts specialist; b. San Francisco, Oct. 2, 1953; d. George Emanuel and Hermoine Linda (Foster) Karatsis; m. William Issachar Berman, May 15, 1979; children: Ian, Melissa, Benjamin. BS, Duke U., 1975; MA, NYU, 1977. Dir. Vorpal Gallery, N.Y.C., 1976-83; visual arts coord. East End Arts Coun., Riverhead, N.Y., 1983-89, program dir., 1989-94, exec. dir., 1994—; cons. N.Y. State Coun. on Arts, N.Y.C., 1985—, Suffolk Assn. Jewish Schs., Huntington, N.Y., 1985; adj. lectr. dept. anthropology Bklyn. Coll., 1976-77, Drew U., 1977; adj. tech. asst. Dept. of Instrn. Suffolk County C.C., 1992-93. Contbr. articles to East End Arts News; host cable arts show, 1986-87. Trustee Commack Jewish Ctr., N.Y., 1984-86. Home: 22 Daisy Ln Commack NY 11725-4106 Office: East End Arts Coun 133 E Main St Riverhead NY 11901-2455

BERMAN, PHYLLIS MIRIAM, microbiologist, researcher; b. Boston, Dec. 26, 1951; d. Irving and Mildred (Reitman) Berman; m. Larry Steven Rivais, June 21, 1981; 1 child, Elaina Justine. BS in Pub. Health, U. Mass., 1973, MS in Microbiology, 1981. Lab technician dept. plant pathology U. Mass., Amherst, 1973-76, rsch. asst., 1976-79, sr. tech. asst., 1979-81, rsch. assoc., adminstrv. asst., 1981—. Contbr. articles to profl. jours., chpt. to book. Active Mass. Soc. Prevention of Cruelty to Animals, Hist. Deerfield (Mass.) Soc., Ctr. Marine Conservation, Washington, World Wildlife Fund, Washington. Mem. Am. Soc. Microbiology, Am. Phytopathol. Soc. (northeastern divsn.), Internat. Soc. Plant Molecular Biology, Internat. Soc. Plant-Microbe Interactions, Pioneer Valley Computer Users Group. Office: U Mass Dept Plant Pathology Amherst MA 01003

BERMAN, SANDRA RITA, retired personnel director; b. Washington, June 21, 1938; d. Max and Ethel (Gerber) Fulton; m. Malcolm C. Berman, Mar. 3, 1957; children: Steven, Gary, Richard. Student, Towson U., Villa Julie Coll. Lic. real estate agt., Md. Dir. pers. Fairfax Savs. Assn., Balt., 1983-94, ret., 1994. Former den mother, organizer Boy Scouts Am.; past pres. Mothers Club, Homewood Sch., former pres. Ft. Garrison Elem. Sch. PTA; 1st v.p. Beth El Sisterhood, Balt., 1982-84, pres., 1984-86; del. Women's League for Conservative Judaism, Balt., 1984; trustee Beth El Congregation, 1984—, also chmn. various coms.; bd. dirs. Md. Bd. Barber Examiners, 1987-94. Mem. Hadassah (life), Order Ea. Star. Democrat.

BERMAN-HAMMER, SUSAN, public relations executive; b. Buffalo, Sept. 12, 1950; d. Leonard and Judith H. (Goldenberg) Berman; m. Tony Hammer, Aug. 17, 1975; 1 child, Erik Jason. BA, Northwestern U., 1972, MS in Journalism, 1975. Pub. info. asst. Sta. WBBM-TV, Chgo., 1972; news asst. exec. trailer Dem. Nat. Conv. ABC-TV News, Miami, Fla., 1972; writer Chgo. Conv. and Visitors Bur., 1973-75; Washington corr. Sta. WYEN, Des Plaines, Ill., 1975; sr. v.p. Herbert H. Rozoff Assocs., Inc., Chgo., 1976-82; pres., owner Susan L. Berman Assocs., Inc., Deerfield, Ill., 1982—; v.p. corp. communications Sheldon Good & Co., Chgo., 1988-89; chairperson Chgo. Communications/10, a consortium in field, 1982-83. Asst. regional dir. Nat. Movement for Student Vote, Chgo., 1972; bd. dirs. Chgo. Women in Broadcasting, 1972-76, Younger Set Jewish Fedn., Dallas, 1985-87; founder, chair steering com. Safe Home Program North Shore Sch. Dists. 112 & 109, 1994—; Sherwood Sch. PTO, Highland Park, Ill., 1990—; liaison North Shore Sch. Dist. 112 and CIC Legis. com. Highland Park, 1994—; mem. young women's exec. bd., v.p. community devel., co-chair Trendsetter luncheon, co-chair Insights com., nominating com. Shalom Chgo. com., mem. campaign cabinet Jewish United Fund Chgo., 1991—; bd. dirs. nat. women's com. North Shore chpt. Brandeis U., 1991-93; exec. bd., v.p. programming and membership, nominating com. Tamarisk chpt. ORT, Deerfield, Ill., 1990—; chair comm. com. North Shore Congregation Israel, Glencoe, Ill., 1993-94; spokesperson and co-leader Parents Against Proposed Annexation of Deerfield subdivsns. from North Shore Sch. Dist. 112 into Deerfield Sch. Dist. 109, 1993-94. Mem. Nat. Assn. Real Estate Editors, Chgo. Soc. Clubs, Multiplex, Northwestern U. Club Chgo., Alpha Lambda Delta. Office: 9 Tamarisk Deerfield IL 60015

BERN, LYNDA KAPLAN, women's health, pediatric nurse; b. N.Y.C., Apr. 17, 1960; d. Melvin and Marilyn Kaplan; m. Jay Bern, June 1986. BSN, SUNY, Binghamton, 1981. RN, N.Y., MD., D.C., N.J. Clin. nurse Gt. Neck (N.Y.) Pediatrics, 1981-82, North Shore Ob-Gyn, Bayside, N.Y., 1982-84; clin. ladder level three nurse North Shore U. Hosp., Manhasset, N.Y., 1981-88; breast feeding cons., instr. childbirth preparation Shady Grove Adventist Hosp., Rockville, Md., 1989-90, 91-92; relief nurse Md. Profl. Staffing Svc., Bethesda, Md., 1989-92; staff nurse St. Peter's Med. Ctr., New Brunswick, N.J., 1993—; instr. maternal-child series St. Peters Med. Ctr., 1994—; mem. nursing hon. com. SUNY, mem. hosp. stds. of care com. nursing adv. com., quality assurance team; mem. peer rev. com., preceptor Adelphia Sr. Nursing Students. Vol. March of Dimes Health Screening Fair. Nursing scholar Good Citizenship League.

BERN, PAULA, columnist; b. Pitts., July 27, 1934; m. Joseph Bern, Dec. 21, 1954; children: Bruce, Caryn, Marshall, Samuel, Rona. BA, Pa. State U., 1956; MA, U. Pitts., 1978, PhD, 1980. Editor-in-chief Jaffe Pub. Co., Los Angeles, 1958-63; on-air producer Sta. WQED-TV, Pitts., 1963-65; dir. univ. relations and devel. Robert Morris Coll., Pitts. and Coraopolis, 1965-69, Point Park Coll., Pitts., 1969-72; pres. Bern Assocs., Inc., 1972—; CEO The Exec. TV Workshop, Pitts., 1987—; tchr. sr. exec. seminars Grad. Sch. Urban and Pub. Affairs, Carnegie Mellon U., 1985-90; contbg. editor New Women mag., 1988—; columnist Scripps Howard News Svc., Washington, 1994—. Author: Point Park College: A History, 1980; How to Work for a Woman Boss (Even if You'd Rather Not), 1987, Keep Your Feet Off the Desk, 1994. Trustee Pitts. Ballet Theatre, Inc., 1973—; bd. dirs. Council for Internat. Visitors, 1975-91, Exec. Women's Council, 1980—; mem. adv. council Internat. Poetry Forum, 1979—, Pa. Commn. for Women, Nat. Commn. for Women. Recipient Am. Coun. on Edn. award, 1982. Mem. Women in Communications, Pub. Relations Soc. Am., Delta Sigma Rho, Phi Beta Kappa. Office: Scripps Howard News Svc 1090 Vermont Ave NW Washington DC 20005

BERNARD, ARLENE TERESA, respiratory therapist; b. Wichita, Kans., Aug. 10, 1961; d. Francis Gordon and Judith Ramona (Keasler) Reville; m. Jack Alan Bernard, May 2, 1992; 1 child, Jack Alan Jr. BS in Respiratory Therapy, Med. Coll. Ga., 1991. Registered respiratory therapist. Staff respiratory therapist Univ. Hosp., Augusta, Ga., 1980-84; dir. cardiopulmonary svcs. Meml. Hosp. Washington County, Sandersville, Ga., 1984-87; staff respiratory therapist Augusta Regional Med. Ctr., 1987—; cons. for cardiopulmonary dir. Meml. Hosp. Washington County, 1987; clin. instr. Med. Coll. Ga., Augusta, 1987-89. Mem. Am. Assn. Respiratory Care, Ga. Soc. Respiratory Care. Republican. Roman Catholic. Office: Augusta Regional Med Ctr Respiratory Care 3651 Wheeler Rd Augusta GA 30907

BERNARD, CATHY S., management corporation executive; b. Bronx, N.Y., Nov. 13, 1949; d Burton and Norma (Ebb) B. BBA, George Washington U., 1971, M of Pub. Adminstrn., 1978; MA, U. Miami, 1972. Cert. property mgr. Staff asst. HEW, Washington, 1970-74; evaluation specialist OEO, Washington, 1974; tchr. St. Patrick's Acad., Washington, 1975; asst. prof. No. Va. Community Coll., Woodbridge, 1976; staff dir. Dem. Nat. Conv., N.Y.C., 1976; pres., chief exec. officer CSB Assocs. Mgmt. Corp., Riverdale, Md., 1977—; mem. Housing Opportunities Commn., Kensington, Md., 1979-93, chmn., 1988, vice chair, 1980, 87, chair pro tem, 1986, chair housing honor roll, 1985-88, ModeratePriced Dwelling Unit commn.; mem. exec. coun. Inst. Real Estate Mgmt., Washington, 1982—, cert. property mgr. Mem. adv. coun. Suburban Hosp., Bethesda, Md., 1984-89; bd. dirs. Ivymount Sch. for Handicapped, Potoman, Md., 1987—; treas. Jewish Coun. on Aging, 1988; treas., bd. dirs. Jewish Found. for Group Homes, Rockville, Md., 1989-91; trustee Roundhouse Theater, 1992—, treas., 1994; bd. trustees Temple Emanuel, Kensington, Md.; candidate Md. State Legislature, 1986; pres. Cmty. Housing Res. Bd., 1985. Recipient Hughes award for property mgmt., 1980, Jewish Coun. award, 1989. Mem. Montgomery County C. of C. (bd. dirs., v.p. housing com. 1981-82), Apt. and Office Bldg. Assn. (bd. dirs., chmn. affordable housing com. 1990—). Office: CSB Assocs Mgmt Corp PO Box 647 Riverdale MD 20738

BERNARD, JAMI, film critic, author; b. N.Y.C., Aug. 10, 1956; d. Sam and Gloria (Weiss) B. BA, Columbia U., 1978. Film critic N.Y. Post, N.Y.C., 1986-94, N.Y. Daily News, N.Y.C., 1994—; chmn. N.Y. Film Critics Circle, 1991; asst. entertainment editor N.Y. Post, 1985-87, editor, reporter, columnist, 1978-94. Author: First Films: Illustrious, Obscure and Embarrasing Movie Debuts, 1993, Total Exposure: The Movie Buff's Guide to Celebrity Nude Scenes, 1995, Biography of Quentin Tarantino, 1995; freelance author on entertainment issues; frequent guest on nat. TV and radio shows; judge various film festivals. Nominee Pulitzer prize, 1991. *

BERNARD, MARY-ELAINE CASH, educational administrator, artist; b. Stamford, Conn., Jan. 29, 1947; d. John Harrison and Mary Casimir (Daly) Cash; m. Lewis Brent Bernard, Feb. 20, 1971 (div. Apr. 1987); children: John Lewis, Edward Brent, Julie Elizabeth. BA in Art, Coll. of New Rochelle, 1968; postgrad., U. Tenn., 1983, 85, 87, 89, S.W. Craft Ctr., San Antonio, 1987, 88, Idyllwild Sch. Music and Art, Calif., 1986. Cert. K-12 tchr. art, N.Y., Conn., La.; cert. tchr. talented-visual arts, La. Art cons. Stamford (Conn.) Pub. Schs., 1968-69; art therapist Tex. Inst. for Rehab. and Rsch., Houston, 1969-71; tchr. secondary art Mt. Carmell High Sch., New Iberia, La., 1972-73, New Iberia Mid. Sch., 1986-87; art cons. to gifted Iberia Parish Schs., New Iberia, 1980; tchr. mid. sch. art Episcopal Sch. Acadiana, Cade, La., 1987-91; asst. coord., tchr. visual arts talented art program St. Tammany Schs., Covington, La., 1991—; instr. art in edn. Acadiana Arts Coun., Lafayette, La., 1989-91; instr. art summer enrichment U. S.W. La., Lafayette, 1989-91; instr. pottery St. Tammany Art Assn., Covington, 1993—. Exhibited in numerous groups including Baton Rouge Gallery, 1988, Arrow Mont Sch. Arts & Crafts, Gatlinburg, Tenn., 1988, 94, 2nd Internat. Ceramics Competition, Japan, 1989, Masur Mus. Art, Monroe, La., 1990, 91, 93, La. Crafts Coun. Gallery, 1989, 90, Coll. of New Rochelle, N.Y., 1990, 94, Lafayette Art Gallery, 1990, Galleria Mesa, Mesa, Ariz., 1990, Ga. State U., Atlanta, 1989, River Oaks Sq. Arts & Crafts Ctr., Alexandria, La., 1991, Quinlan Arts Ctr., Gainesivlle, Ga., 1991, Louise Janin Gallery, Covington, La., 1991, 92, 94, Maxtrix Gallery, Sacramento, 1992, Nicholls State U., Thibodeaux, La., 1992, St. Tammany Art Assn., Covington, 1993, 14th Biennale Internat. de Ceramique D'art, Vallauris, France, 1994, others. Chmn. cultural arts North Lewis Street Elem. Sch. PTA, New Iberia, 1980; den mother Cub Scouts Am., New Iberia, 1982-83; bd. dirs. Moving South Dance Co., Lafayette, 1989-90. Recipient hon. mention 2d Internat. Ceramic Competition, 1989; purchase award River Oaks Arts and Crafts Ctr., Alexandria, La., 1990, spl. juror's award, 1991; purchase award Masur Mus. Art, 1990, spl. juror's award Galeria Mesa, Ariz., 1990, honorarium Matrix Gallery, Sacramento, 1992. Mem. Am. Crafts Coun., St. Tammany Art Assn., New Orleans Mus. Art, Contemporayr Art Ctr. New Orleans. Office: St Tammany Schs Harrison Curriculum Ctr 706 W 28th Ave Covington LA 70433-1466

BERNARD, THELMA RENE, property management professional; b. Phila.; d. Michael John and Louise Thelma (Hoffman) Campione; m. Gene Bernard (div.). Sec. Penn. Mut. Life Ins. Co., Phila., Suffolk Franklin Savs. Bank, Boston, Holmes and Narver, Inc., Las Vegas; constrn. site office mgr. Miles R. Nay, Inc., Las Vegas; adminstrv. asst to pres. N.W.S. Constrn. Corp., Inc., Las Vegas, 1982-86, corp. sec., 1982-86; gen. mgr., corp. sec. D.A.P., Inc. property mgmt. com, Las Vegas, pres., 1991—. Author: Blue Marsh, 1972, Winds of Wakefield, 1972, Moonshadow Mansion, 1973, 2d edit., 1976, Spanish transl., 1974, German transl., 1977; contbr. articles to Doll Reader, Internat. Doll World, other mags.; past editor Cactus Courier; editor, pub. The Hoyer Enthusiastic Ladies Mail Assn., 1980-90, Friendly Tymes, 1991—; writer song lyrics. Mem. Nat. League Am. Pen Women (v.p. Red Rock Canyon br. 1986-88), Original Paper Doll Artists Guild, Am. Rose Soc., Heritage Rose Soc., Bookmark Collector Club. Office: PO Box 14002 Las Vegas NV 89114-4002

BERNARD, VIOLA WERTHEIM, psychiatrist; b. N.Y.C., Feb. 22, 1907; d. Jacob and Emma (Stern) Wertheim; m. T.C. Bernard, Aug. 1, 1934 (div. June 1938). BS, NYU, 1933; MD, cornell U., 1936. Diplomate Am. Bd. Psychiatry and Neurology. Intern Jersey City Med. Ctr., 1937-38; resident in psychiatry Grasslands Hosp., Valhalla, N.Y., 1938-39, N.Y. State Psychiat. Inst. and Hosp., 1939-40; mem. staff Harlem Bur. Child Guidance N.Y. Bd. Edn., 1940-42; practice medicine specializing in psychiatry and psychoanalysis N.Y.C., 1940—; assoc. in psychiatry Columbia, 1948-55; asst. clin. prof., 1955-57, assoc. clin. prof., 1957-61, clin. prof., 1961-72; founder, dir. div. community and social psychiatry, dept. psychiatry Sch. Pub. Health and Adminstrv. Medicine, 1956-69; attending psychiatrist Presbyn. Hosp., 1963-72; cons. psychiat. svcs., 1972-82; tng. analyst Columbia Psychoanalytic Ctr., 1946—; faculty N.Y. Sch. Social Work, Columbia, 1947-58; psychiat. cons. Ethical Culture Schs., 1947-56; rsch. cons. Bank St. Coll. Edn., 1950-61; chief psychiat. cons. Louise Wise Svcs., 1942-81; sr. psychiat. cons. 1981—; chair, mental health sect. Citizens Com. for Childrenof N.Y., Inc., 1945-65, charter mem., 1945-71; mem. N.Y. State Dept. of Health, Bd. for Profl. Med. Conduct, 1975-77; sci. program cons. to chief mental health study ctr., div. mental health svc. programs, NIMH, 1978-79. Co-editor: Urban Challenges to Psychiatry, 1969, Crises of Family Disorganization, 1971; contbr. chpt. to Am. Handbook of Psychiatry, 1974; contbr. articles to profl. jours. Co-chair, com. psychiat. svcs. for children City of N.Y. Dept. of Hosps., 1961-63; mem. N.Y.C. Mayor's Com. on Cts., 1956-57; spl. cons. to tng. com. NIMH, USPHS, 1950-54; mem. State of N.Y. Com. for Children, 1971; bd. dirs. Wiltwyck Sch. for Boys, 1942-69, chair com. on treatment program, 1950-69. Fellow Am. Coll. Psychoanalysts, Am. Pub. Health Assn., Am. Psychiat. Assn. (life, v.p. 1971-72, chair commn. on childhood and adolescence, 1973-76, coun. on children, adolescents and their families, 1976-77, cons., com. on psychol. effects of nuclear arms devel., 1987-88, mem. counc. on nat. affairs, 1983-87, cons. 1988-93), Am. Orthopsychiat. Assn., Am. Psychoanalytic Assn. (life, chair com. community psychiatry, 1968-77, cons. 1988-93), N.Y. Acad. Medicine; mem. AMA, AAAS, N.Y. State Med. Soc., N.Y. County Med. Soc., Am. Acad. Child Psychiatry, Group for Advancement of Psychiatry (life, mem. com. social issues, dir. 1961-63, 73-77, com. on psychiatry and politics, 1977-80, com. on preventive psychiatry, 1981-94), N.Y. Coun. on Child Psychiatry, N.Y. Acad. Scis., World Fedn. Mental Health. Home and Office: 930 Fifth Ave New York NY 10021-2651

BERNAY, BETTI, artist; b. 1926; d. David Michael and Anna Gaynia (Bernay) Woolin; m. J. Bernard Goldfarb, Apr. 19, 1947; children: Manette Deitsch, Karen Lynn. Grad. costume design, Pratt Inst., 1946; student, Nat. Acad. Design, N.Y.C., 1947-49, Art Students League, N.Y.C., 1950-51. Exhibited one man shows at Galerie Raymond Duncan, Paris, France, Salas Municipales, San Sebastian, Spain, Circulo de Bellas Artes, Madrid, Spain, Bacardi Gallery, Miami, Fla., Columbia (S.C.) Mus., Columbus (Ga.) Mus., Galerie Andre Weil, Paris, Galerie Hermitage, Monte Carlo, Monaco, Casino de San Remo, Italy, Galerie de Arte de la Caja de Ahorros de Ronda, Malaga, Spain, Centro Artistico, Granada, Spain, Circulo de la Amistad, Cordoba, Spain, Studio H Gallery, N.Y.C., Walter Wallace Gallery, Palm Beach, Fla., Mus. Bellas Artes, Malaga, Harbor House Gallery, Crystal House Gallery, Internat. Gallery, Jordan Marsh, Fontainebleau Gallery, Miami Beach, Carriage House Gallery, Galerie 99, Pageant Gallery, Carriage House, Miami Beach, Rosenbaum Galleries, Palm Beach; exhibited group shows at Painters and Sculptors Soc., Jersey City Mus., Salon de Invierno, Mus. Malaga, Salon des Beaux Arts, Cannes, France, Guggenheim Gallery, Nat. Acad. Gallery, Salmagundi Club, Lever House, Lord & Taylor Art Gallery, Nat. Arts Gallery, Knickerbocker Artists, N.Y.C., Salon des Artistes Independants, Salon des Artistes Francais, Salon Populiste, Paris, Salon de Otono, Nat. Assn. Painters and Sculptors Spain, Madrid, Phipps Gallery, Palm Beach, Artists Equity, Hollywood (Fla.) Mus., Gault Gallery Cheltenham, Phila., Springfield (Mass.) Mus., Met. Mus. and Art Center, Miami, Fla., Planet Ocean Mus., Charter Club, Trade Fair Ams., Guggenheim Gallery, N.Y.C.; represented in permanent collections including Jockey Club Art Gallery, Miami, Mus. Malaga, Circulo de la Amistad, I.O.S. Found., Geneva, Switzerland, others. Bd. dirs. Men's Opera Guild; mem. adv. bd. Jackson Meml. Hosp. Project Newborn; mem. women's com. Bascom Palmer Eye Inst.; mem. working com. Greater Miami Heart Assn., Am. Heart Assn., Am. Cancer Soc., Alzheimer Grand Notable, 2d Generation Miami Heart Inst., Sunrisers Mentally Retarded, Orchid Ball Com., Newborn Neonatal Intensive Care Unit, U. Miami, Jackson Meml. Hosp. Recipient medal City N.Y., medal Sch. Art Leagues, N.Y.C., Prix de Paris Raymond Duncan, 1958, others. Mem. Nat. Assn. Painters and Sculptors Spain, Nat. Assn. Women Artists, Société des Artistes Français, Société des Artistes Independants, Fedn. Francais des Sociétés d'Art Graphique et Plastique, Artists Equity, Am. Artists Profl. League, Am. Fedn. Art, Nat. Soc. Lit. and Arts, Met. Mus. and Arts Center Miami, Pres.'s Club U. Miami. Clubs: Palm Bay, Jockey, Turnberry, Club of Clubs Internat. Address: 10155 Collins Ave Apt 1705 Bal Harbour FL 33154-1629

BERNE, KATRINA HARRIET, psychologist; b. N.Y.C., Mar. 14, 1947; d. Arthur A. and Claire M. (Beck) B.; m. Bary R. Bertiger, June 23, 1968 (div. 1983); children: Karen, Jeffrey; m. Eldon L. Husted, Jan. 17, 1986. AB in Art Edn., Douglass Coll., 1968; MA in Fine Arts, Montclair State Coll., 1972; M in Counseling Psychology, Ariz. State U., 1979; PhD in Clin. Psychology, Union Inst., 1989. Lic. psychologist, Ariz. Art tchr. N.J. Pub. Schs., Parsippany, 1968-69, Boonton, 1969-73; freelance artist Scottsdale, Ariz., 1973-76; instr. Mesa (Ariz.) C.C., 1979-87, Ariz. State U., Tempe, 1987-89; clin. psychologist Berne & Assocs., Mesa, 1979—. Author: Chronic Fatigue Immune Dysfunction with 1/3 the Seriousness, 1989, Running on Empty: Chronic Fatigue Immune Dysfunction Syndrome, 1992; author, prodr. (audiotapes) Chronic Fatigue Syndrome, 1991, Chronic Fatigue Syndrome for Those Who Care, 1993, Neurocognitive Aspects of Chronic Fatigue Syndrome, 1995, Chronic Fatigue Syndrome and Self Esteem, 1995. Exec. bd. mem. Chronic Fatigue Syndrome Assn. Ariz., Phoenix, 1990—. Mem. ACA, Chronic Fatigue Immune Dysfunction Syndrome Assn. Am. (physicians honor roll 1991—), Am. Assn. Chronic Fatigue Syndrome, Chronic Fatigue Syndrome Assn. Ariz. (mem. exec. bd., mem. med. adv. bd.). Office: Berne & Assocs Ste F 761 E University Mesa AZ 85203

BERNER, JUDITH, mental health nurse; b. Tamaqua, Pa., June 19, 1938; d. Ralph Edgar and Ethel Mary (Williams) B. Diploma in nursing, Temple U. Hosp., 1959; AS, Coll. of Ganado, 1975, MS in Community Health, D of Med. Adminstrn. (hon.); BA, Stephens Coll., 1977; MEd, U. Ariz., 1980; LD (hon.), U. Iceland. RN, Ariz., N.Mex., Pa. Nursing adminstr. Project HOPE Internat. Office & Hosp. Ship, Washington, 1970-72; assoc. adminstr. Navajo Nation Health Found., Ganado, Ariz., 1972-79; clin. instr. psychiat. nursing Mo. So. State Coll., Joplin, 1986; nurse/therapist Presbyn. Kaseman Hosp., Albuquerque, 1986-93; emergency svcs. clinician for mental health svcs. Presbyn. Healthcare Systems, also Hts. Psychiat. Hosp., Albuquerque, 1994—. Mem. ANA (cert. in psychiat. and mental health nursing), AACD, Internat. Acad. Behavioral Medicine, Counseling and Psychotherapy, Inc.

BERNFIELD, LYNNE, psychotherapist; b. N.Y.C., Mar. 16, 1943; d. Meyer and Lilian Claire (Pastel) B.; m. Arthur Dawson Richards, June 16, 1982. BA, Hofstra U., 1964; MA, Asuza Pacific U., 1981. Lic. marriage, family, and child therapist, Calif. Founder, dir. Writers & Artists Inst., L.A., 1984—. Author: When You Can You Will, 1993. Mem. ASCAP, Calif. Assn. Marriage and Family Therapists, Am. Assn. Marriage and Family Therapists.

BERNHAGEN, LILLIAN FLICKINGER, school health consultant; b. Cleve., Oct. 1, 1916; d. Norman Henry and Bertha May (Rogers) Flickinger; m. Ralph John Bernhagen, Sept. 2, 1940; children: Ralph, Janet Elizabeth Darling, Penelope Anne Braat. Student, Ohio Wesleyan U., 1934-37; B.S., R.N., Ohio State U., 1940, M.A., 1958; postgrad., LaVerne Coll., 1972-73. Cert. health edn. specialist. Asst. dir. Kiwanis Health Camp for Underprivileged Children, Steubenville, Ohio, summer 1940; asst. dir. nurses Jefferson Davis Hosp., Houston, 1940-41; ARC instr. Ohio State U., 1943, 63, elem. edn. lectr., 1970; dir. health services Worthington (Ohio) City Schs., 1951-76; health edn. instr. Ohio State U., 1976-77; spl. cons. venereal disease and sex edn. Ohio Dept. Health, 1976-82; sch. health cons., 1976—; vice chmn. medicine/edn. com. on sch. and coll. health AMA, 1976-78, chmn., 1978-80. Author: Sex Education: Understanding Growth and Social Development, 1968, What A Miracle You Are-Boys, 1968, 3d rev. edit., 1986, What A Miracle You Are-Girls, 1968, 3d rev. edit., 1986, Toward a Reverence for Life, 1971, Personality, Sexuality and Stereotyping, 1974, (with others) Growth Patterns and Sex Education: A Suggested Curriculum Guide K-12, 1967; contbr. articles to profl. jours., mags. Bd. dirs. Hearing and Speech Ctr. of Columbus and Franklin County, 1954-57, sec., 1957; mem. nat. adv. com. Nat. Ctr. for Health Edn., 1978-82; sec.-tres. Ohio Wesleyan U. Class of 38, 1968-78, 83-88; bd. dirs. V.D. Hotline Columbus and Franklin County, 1974-87, bd. expansion chmn., 1978-85, pres., 1985-86; mem. profl. adv. com. Ptnrs. Home Health Inc., 1991—; mem. Worthington Hist. Soc., Doll Docent, 1982—; mem King Ave. United Meth. Ch., 1938—; mem. choir, 1950—, pres., 1961-63, pastor/parish rels. com., 1985-88, bd. trustees, 1989-92, adminstrv. coun., 1992—, edn. commn., 1982-85, nominations and pers., 1992-94; treas. Franklin County Women's Golf Tournament, 1992. Recipient Centennial award Ohio State U., 1970, Outstanding Alumna award Ohio State U. Sch. Nursing, 1964, Disting. Service award Mich. Sch. Nurses Assn., 1972, hon. mention La Sertoma Internat. Woman of Yr., 1972. Fellow Am. Sch. Health Assn. (v.p. 1974, pres. 1976, governing coun. 1973-88, chmn. health guidance in sex edn. com. 1963-67, 71-77, chmn. sr. adv. coun. 1983-89, Disting. Service award 1969, Howe award 1979, cert. of merit, 1985, mem. awards com. 1986-89, mem. hist. com. 1989—), Am. Pub. Health Assn. (chmn. com. on urban health problems 1972); mem. NEA (life, ret.), Assn. for Advancement of Health Edn., Sex Edn. and Info. Coun. of U.S., Worthington Edn. Assn. (v.p. 1961-62, Tchr. of Year 1972-73), Cen. Ohio Tchrs. Assn. (chmn. sch. health svcs. sect. 1963), Ohio State U. Women's Golf Assn. (chmn. 1973, parliamentarian 1988—), Ohio Wesleyan U. Alumni Assn. (chmn. alumni recognition com. 1994-95, bd. dirs. 1989—, chmn. bylaws revision com., mem. orgn. com.), Columbus Women's Dist. Golf Assn. (treas. 1985, sec. 1987, v.p. 1989, pres. 1990, adv. bd. 1991—), Columbus Computer Soc., Chi Omega (pres. Columbus Alumnae chpt. 1947-49, fin. adv. Ohio Wesleyan U. 1964-76, Outstanding Alumna of Yr. Ohio State U. 1986), Pi Lambda Theta (citation award 1971, mem. program com. 1986-89, chmn. by laws revision com. 1990—, parliamentarian), Sigma Theta Tau, Phi Delta Kappa. Clubs: Monnett, Worthington Women's. Home and Office: 5916 Linworth Rd Worthington OH 43085-3357

BERNHARD, SANDRA, actress, comedienne, singer; b. Flint, Mich., June 6, 1955; d. Jerome and Jeanette B. Stand-up comedienne nightclubs, Beverly Hills, Calif., 1974-78; films include Cheech and Chong's Nice Dreams, 1981, The King of Comedy, 1983 (Nat. Soc. Film Critics award), Sesame Street Presents: Follow That Bird, 1985, Track 29, 1988, Without You I'm Nothing, 1990, Hudson Hawk, 1991, Truth or Dare, 1991, Inside Monkey Zetterland, 1993; also appears in Heavy Petting, 1988, Perfect, 1985, The Whoopee Boys, 1986, Casual Sex?, 1988; stage appearances (solo) Without You I'm Nothing, 1988, Giving Till It Hurts, 1992; TV appearances (host) Living in America, 1990; regular guest The Richard Pryor Show, Late Night with David Letterman; TV series Roseanne; albums (co-author 8 songs) I'm Your Woman, 1985, Without You I'm Nothing, 1989; books include Confessions of a Pretty Lady, 1988, Love Love and Love, 1993. Office: care Michael Green Gallin Morey Assocs 8730 Sunset Blvd Penthouse West Los Angeles CA 90069*

BERNHARD JACKSON, GABRIELE JOHANNA, English literature educator; b. Berlin, Nov. 17, 1934; came to U.S., 1939; d. Ernest George Bernhard and Ruth Friederike (Friedlander) Engel; m. Thomas Herbert Jackson, Dec. 16, 1961; children: Olivia Kate, Emily Anne. BA, Bard Coll., 1955; postgrad., Oxford U., 1955-56; MA, Yale U., 1958, PhD, 1961. Instr. English Yale U., New Haven, 1961-63; asst. prof. English Wellesley (Mass.) Coll., 1963-68; assoc. prof. English Temple U., Phila., 1968-70, prof., 1970—, interim dean Grad. Sch., 1977-80; vis. assoc. prof., prof. U. Pa., Phila., 1968, summers 1970, 81, 82, 85, 87, 90; vis. prof. Bryn Mawr (Pa.) Coll., 1990; rsch. fellow Am. Coun. Learned Socs., Eng., 1971-72; dir. summer seminar for coll. tchrs. NEH, Temple U., 1985; dir. affirmative action program grad. students HEW, Temple U. Grad. Sch., 1978-80. Author: Vision and Judgment in Ben Jonson's Drama, 1968, Ben Jonson's Every Man in His Humor, 1969; editorial bd. Assays; contbr. articles to profl. jours., chpts. to books. Recipient Fulbright Scholarship, U.S. Govt., Eng., 1955-56. Mem. Renaissance Soc. Am., Shakespeare Assn. Am., Soc. Study Early Modern Women, 16th Century Studies Conf., N.E. Modern Lang. Assn. Office: Temple U Dept English Philadelphia PA 19122

BERNHARDSON, IVY SCHUTZ, lawyer; b. Fargo, N.D., Aug. 22, 1951; d. James Newell and Phyllis Harriet (Iverson) Schutz; m. Mark Elvin Bernhardson, Sept. 1, 1973; children: Andrew Schutz, Jenna Clare. BA, Gustavus Adolphus Coll., 1973; JD, U. Minn., 1978. Bar: Minn. 1978, U.S. Dist. Ct. Minn. 1978. Staff atty. Gen. Mills Inc., Mpls., 1978-83, asst. sec. to bd. dirs., 1982—, assoc. counsel, 1983-85, sr. assoc. counsel, 1985—, v.p., 1988—. Trustee Gustavus Adolphus Coll., 1989—, vice chair bd. dirs., 1992—; trustee Fairview Southdale Hosp., 1993—; dir. Minn. Citizens Coun. on Crime and Justice. Mem. ABA, Minn. Bar Assn., Hennepin County Bar Assn., Am. Soc. Corp. Secs. Lutheran. Office: Gen Mills Inc 1 General Mills Blvd Minneapolis MN 55426-1347

BERNHARDT, MIMI MAY, addictions counselor; b. Wellesley, Mass., Jan. 24, 1957; d. Wilfred Lee and Mary Frances (Domermuth) Brooke; m. Victor David Bernhardt, Oct. 19, 1984 (div. Dec., 1988); 1 child, Rachel Angela. AA, Aims C.C., Greeley, Colo., 1993; student, U. Northern Colo., 1993—. Cert. addictions counselor (sr.), Colo. Owner, supr. J&M Builders, Denver, 1978-81; mgr. Freebies Restaurant, Fort Collins, Colo., 1981-85; dir. of admissions New Beginnings, Fort Collins, 1988-90; owner, dir. Addiction Recovery Ctr., Greeley, 1990—; mem. U. Northern Colo. Drug Prevention Team. Vol. TEAM Fort Collins, 1992-93. Office: Addiction Recovery Ctr 800 8th Ave Ste 200 Greeley CO 80631-1100

BERNIER, CAROL ANN, investor; b. Lawrence, Mass., Dec. 24, 1941; d. Valmore W. and Emma F. (Custeau) Patient; m. Emery Bernier, Sept. 9, 1961; children: Philip, David, Richard. Mortgage loan advisor Essex Broadway Savs. Bank, Lawrence, 1960-63; owner, mgr. Bernier Studio, stained glass, Andover, Mass., 1962-65, Bernier Studio, stained glass restoration, Wentworth, N.H., 1975-84; owner, mgr., buyer Bernier Studio, craft and antique shop, Wentworth, 1965-84, Boutique Feminine Fashions, Wentworth, 1974-84; owner, buyer The Boutique Bridals, Laconia, N.H., 1981-85; owner Heritage Apts., Plymouth, Campton, Rumney, N.H., 1977-84; investor Hilton Head Island, S.C., 1985—; polit. columnist Hilton Head Monthly, 1990—. Pres. Baker River Valley Assn., N.H., 1974-76, Resident Home Owners' Coalition, Hilton Head Island, 1988-91; candidate for town coun., Hilton Head Island, 1987. Mem. Profl. Women Hilton Head Island (treas. 1988-90), Women's Assn. (chmn. bookmarkers 1987-90). Home: 18 Saint Johns Pl Hilton Head Island SC 29928-4938

BERNSON, MARCELLA S., psychiatrist; b. N.Y.C., Aug. 24, 1952; d. Maxwell Isaac and Priscilla Edith (Zuckerman) Bernson; m. Richard A. Sherman, Apr. 3, 1974; children: Eric Z., Gregory I. BA in Biology summa cum laude, Hofstra U., 1973; MD, Albert Einstein Coll. Medicine, 1976. Diplomate Am. Bd. Psychiatry and Neurology. Resident in psychiatry Bronx (N.Y.) Mcpl. Hosp. Ctr., 1976-79; assoc. dir. med. student edn. in psychiatry U. Medicine and Dentistry of N.J.-N.J. Med. Sch., Newark, 1979-81; pvt. practice psychiatry Westfield, N.J., 1981-86; cons. psychiatrist Healthwise EAP, Elizabeth, N.J., 1985-86; med. chief adult ambulatory svcs. dept. psychiatry Elizabeth Gen. Med. Ctr., 1986-87, asst. dir. dept. psychiatry, 1987-88; dir. tng. psychiat. svc. VA Med. Ctr., E. Orange, N.J., 1988-89; med. dir. partial care Occupl. Ctr. Union County, Roselle, N.J., 1989-92; cons. psychiatrist Union County Ednl. Svcs. Commn., Westfield, 1992—; instr. U. Medicine and Dentistry of N.J.-N.J. Med. Sch., Newark, 1979-81, asst. prof. clin. psychiatry, 1988-89; staff psychiatrist Elizabeth Gen. Med. Ctr., 1985-88, 92—. Mem. Am. Psychiat. Assn., N.J. Psychiat. Assn. (tri-county chpt., Union County rep. 1989-90), Assn. Women Psychiatrists. Office: Elizabeth Gen Med Ctr Dept Psychiatry 655 E Jersey St Elizabeth NJ 07206

BERNSTEIN, CARYL SALOMON, lawyer; b. N.Y.C., Dec. 22, 1933; d. Gustav and Rosalind (Aron) Salomon; m. William D. Terry, June 12, 1955 (div. 1967); children: Ellen Deborah, Mark David; m. Robert L. Cole, Jr., Oct. 25, 1970 (div. 1975); m. George K. Bernstein, June 17, 1979. B.A. with honors, Cornell U., 1955; J.D., Georgetown U., 1967. Bar: D.C. 1968, U.S. Dist. Ct. D.C. 1968, U.S. Ct. Appeals (D.C. cir.) 1968, U.S. Supreme Ct. 1971. Atty. Covington & Burling, Washington, 1967-73; staff atty. Overseas Pvt. Investment Corp., Washington, 1973-74, asst. gen. counsel, 1974-77, v.p. for ins., 1977-81; sr. v.p., gen. counsel, sec. Fed. Nat. Mortgage Assn., Washington, 1981-82, exec. v.p., gen. counsel, sec., 1982-93; sr. counsel Shaw, Pittman, Potts & Trowbridge, Washington, 1993—. Contbr. articles to profl. jours., chpt. to book; mem. bd. editors Georgetown Law Jour., 1966-67; mem. editorial adv. bd. Housing and Devel. Reporter, 1986-87; mem. bd. dirs. Nat. Housing Conf., 1983-93, 94—. bd. dirs. Citizens Bank Md., 1989-92, 94—, Nat. Housing Conf., 1983-93, 94—, Marine Spill Response Corp., Nat. Symphony Orch. Assn. N.Y. Regents scholar, 1951-55. Mem. ABA, Fed. Bar Assn. D.C. Bar Assn., Am. LAw Inst., Adminstrv. Conf. U.S. Office: Shaw Pittman Potts & Trowbridge 2300 N St NW Washington DC 20037

BERNSTEIN, PATRICIA ROBIN, podiatrist; b. Jacksonville, Fla., Sept. 20, 1956; d. Sol and Artelia (Moorman) B. Student, Jacksonville U., 1974-75; BA in Biology, Hofstra U., 1978; MS in Med. Biology, L.I. U., 1988; DPM, Pa. Coll. Podiatric Medicine, 1993. Cert. chemistry supr., N.Y., med. technologist in chemistry, hematology, microbiology, blood bank, and urinalysis. Fla., supr. for chemistry, hematology and microbiology, Fla. Med. technologist St. Clare's Hosp. & Health Ctr., N.Y.C., 1982-89; med. technologist Meml. Sloan-Kettering-Cancer Ctr., N.Y.C., 1984-89; lab. rep. pub. relations com. St. Clare's Hosp. & Health Ctr., N.Y.C., 1983-84; chairperson for Nat. Med. Lab. week, 1984; chemistry chairperson Nat. Med. Lab. week Meml. Sloan Kettering Cancer Ctr., N.Y.C., 1988. Mem. NAFE, Am. Soc. Clin. Pathologists (assoc.), Am. Soc. for Microbiology, Am. Assn. Women Podiatrists, Pa. Podiatric Med. Students Assn., Iota Sigma Pi. Home: 5117 Spring Glen Rd Jacksonville FL 32207

BERNSTEIN, PHYLISS LOUISE, psychologist; b. Balt., Nov. 27, 1940; d. Samuel Wilfred and Helen Dorothy (Gerson) Wilke; m. Robert Bernstein, June 7, 1964; children: Steve, Susan, David. BA in Psychology summa cum laude, Avila Coll., 1980, MS in Psychology summa cum laude, 1981; PhD in Couseling Psychology with high honors, U. Mo., Kansas City, 1986. Lic. psychologist, Mo. Psychotherapist Community Counseling Ctr., Kansas City, Mo., 1983-85; assoc. psychologist Counseling and Human Devel. Svcs., Kansas City, Mo., 1985-86; ptnr., psychologist Counseling Psychologists and Assocs., Kansas City, Mo., 1987—; staff priviliges Bapt. Med. Ctr., Menorah Med. Ctr.; dir. Jewish Vocat. Svcs., Kansas City, 1988-91, U. Mo. Edn. Dept., Kansas City, 1991—, Jewish Family and Children Svcs., 1992—. Contbr. articles to profl. jours. Life mem. Nat. Coun. Jewish Women. Kansas City; vol. Children's Pl. Day Care Ctr. for Abused Children, Kansas City. Mem. APA, Nat. Register Health Svc. Providers in Psychology, Greater Kansas City Psychol. Assn., Phi Kappa Phi, Pi Lambda Theta, Psi Chi. Office: Counseling Psychologists 4901 Main St Ste 302 Kansas City MO 64112-2674

BERNSTEIN, SHIRLEY JOAN, artist, educator; b. Phila., Nov. 29, 1943; d. William Bernstein and Hattie (Rothschild) Rauch. BFA with honors, U. of the Arts, Phila., 1965; MFA with honors, Ind. U., 1967. Assoc. faculty Kokomo (Ind.) ext. Ind. U., 1965-66; teaching asst. Ind. U., Bloomington, 1966-67; instr. Knoxville (Tenn.) Coll., 1967-68; teaching/tech. asst. Cooper Union Sch. Art, N.Y.C., 1970-73; instr. Kean Coll. N.J., Union, 1973-75; tchr. The Printmaking Workshop, N.Y.C., 1976; asst. prof. Ea. Conn. State U., Willimantic, 1989-90, 91-92; part-time faculty Beaver Coll., Glenside, Pa., summers 1976, 77, U. of Arts, Phila., 1976-78, Fashion Inst. of Tech., N.Y.C., 1981-82, Three Rivers Cmty.-Tech. Coll., Norwich, Conn., 1993—, Quinebaug Valley Cmty. Tech. Coll., Danielson, Conn., 1993—; lectr., juror and workshop leader in field, various galleries and univs. One woman shows include Ind. U. Mus., Bloomington, 1967, Dogwood Arts Festival, Knoxville, 1968, Bergen St., Ustler Gallery, Bklyn., 1984, St. Marks Gallery, Bklyn., 1985, Putnam Arts Coun., Mahopac, N.Y., 1987, Pastels, Northstar Restaurant, Northampton, Mass., 1988, Pump House Gallery, Hartford, 1994; exhibited in group shows at 58th Conn. Acad. Fine Arts, Wadsworth Atheneum, Hartford, Conn., 1968, Western Mich. U., Kalamazoo, 1968, Cooper Union Sch. Art, N.Y.C., 1971, Women's Interart Ctr., N.Y.C., 1972, Seaport Mus., N.Y.C., 1972, Kean Coll. N.J., Union, 1973, 74, A.I.R. Gallery, Soho, N.Y., 1973, Studio 81, Jersey City, 1974, New Eng. Ctr. Continuing Edn., Durham, N.H., 1975, Hansen Gallery, Soho, 1975, 76, The Printmaking Workshop, N.Y.C., 1976, Lehman Coll., Bronx, 1976, Bard Coll., N.Y.C., 1976, Carrier Clinic, Bellemead, N.J., 1976, Va. Commonwealth U., 1977, CUNY, 1978, Hibbs Gallery, N.Y.C., 1980, Frank Marino Gallery, Soho, 1982, 22 Wooster St. Gallery, Soho, 1983, A.I.F. Gallery, Portchester, N.Y., 1985, Mark Humphrey Ltd., South Hampton, N.Y., 1986, Women's Resource Ctr., Mahopac, N.Y., 1988, Akus Gallery, Willimantic, Conn., 1989, 90, Charter Oak Gallery, Hartford, Conn., 1989, Muscarelle Mus., Williamsburg, Va., 1990, Slater Meml. Mus., Norwich, Conn., 1991, 92, 94, Greater Mansfield Coun. Arts, Conn., 1991, Gallery Atelier, Phila., 1991, 92, Pen and Brush Gallery, N.Y.C., 1991, Montserrat Gallery, N.Y.C., 1992, Bradley Internat. Airport, Winsor Locks, 1993, New Eng. Art Exposition, Woburn, Mass., 1993, Canton Artists' Guild, Canton Green, Conn., 1994, Fairfield (Conn.) U., 1994, others; represented in pub. collections Chase Manhattan Bank, N.Y.C., 1st Pa. Bank, Phila., Henri Bendel, Genesco, N.Y.C., Ind. Univ. Mus., Bloomington, Neiman Marcus, Chgo., Phila. Savs. Fund Soc., Union Carbide Corp., N.Y.C., The Printmaking Workshop, N.Y.C.; represented in pvt. collections in U.S., France, Spain, Eng. and B.C. Del. Citizen Ambassador Program of art edn. to Egypt, Israel and Turkey (part of People to People Internat.), 1994. Recipient Cert. Excellence, Montserrat Gallery, N.Y.C., 1992, summer painting scholar U. R.I., 1964, printmaking scholar U. of the Arts, 1961-65, Ind. U., 1965-67. Mem. Nat. Mus. Women in Arts, Printmaking Network of So. New Eng., Coll. Art Assn., Women's Caucus for Art (founding mem. N.Y.C. chpt. 1979—). Home: PO Box #2 Hampton CT 06247-0002

BERNSTEIN, SUSAN GERDA, artist, musician; b. Frankfurt-on-the-Main, Germany; came to U.S., 1939; d. Maurice L. and Elizabeth (Barach) Gillman; m. Arnold S. Bernstein, Aug. 25, 1957 (dec. Nov. 1987); children: James D., Marjorie Bernstein Fried. Cert., Whitney Sch. Art, New Haven, Conn., 1950; student, U. Conn., 1952-54; Degree, Stone Bus. Coll., New Haven, Conn., 1956. Pvt. sec. to Rabbi Nelson Congregation Rodeph Sholom, 1958-63; sec. to dean arts and humanities U. Bridgeport, Conn., 1980-85; artist Technion, 1991, Paine Webber, Smith Barney Shearson Lehman, Peoples Bank, 1994-95, various profl. offices and residences, 1995; tchr. fine arts Jewish Cmty. Ctr., Bridgeport and Fairfield, Conn., 1985, FFLD Woods Jr. High. Illustrator: Cookbook "Epes t'su Essen", 1961, Jewish Home for the Elderly Women's Aux. Cookbook, 1994; pianist Hapassah-Donor Stage Show, Fairfield, 1974, Sta. WFAC-TV, 1993; concerts include Cellist, 1994; exhibited work at group shows including Silvermine Art Show, 1980; tchr. art classes, 1994. Pres. PTA, Stratfield Sch., Fairfield, 1972-73, Fairfield Woods Jr. H.S., 1973-74, 1974-75; treas. bd. edn. Fairfield Coun., 1976-77; chmn. fund raiser Auction and Book Fair, Fairfield, 1980; pianist Jewish Home for Elderly, Fairfield, 1993, Congregation Rodelph Sholom-Sisterhood, Bridgeport, 1970. Recipient 1st prize mixed media New Canaan Art Show, 1977. Mem. Nat. Coun. Jewish Women (chmn. 1994), Judeo-Christian Women's Assn., United Jewish Coun., B'nai Brith. Home: 160 Fairfield Woods Rd Apt 21 Fairfield CT 06432-3340

BERNSTEIN-SIEGEL, DEBRA LYNN, marketing administrator, dance educator; b. Chgo., Nov. 3, 1951; d. Joseph W. and Emily (Jurs) Bernstein; m. Barry G. Siegel, Sept. 9, 1979; children: Aaron, Samuel. BFA, Ohio State U., 1973, MA, 1976. Dance therapist Barclay Hosp., Chgo., 1979-83; owner Comprehensive Movement, Birmingham, Mich., 1983-87, Vitality Mag., Birmingham, 1987-91; instr. Marygrove Coll., Detroit, 1990—; mktg. rep. Albaum, Mairoana & Assocs., Royal Oak, Mich., 1992—. Author: Comprehensive Movement, 1986. Bd. trustees Temple Beth El, Birmingham, 1991—; active Jewish Welfare Fedn., Birmingham, 1989—. Mem. Adcraft Club of Detroit.

BERO, MARY, artist; b. Two Rivers, Wis., Mar. 2, 1949; d. Donald Joseph and Mary Elizabeth (O'Grady) B.; m. Dennis Paul Nechvatal, Jan. 17, 1970. BS, Stout State U., 1971. Self-employed artist Madison, Wis., 1986—; lectr. Smithsonian Instn., Washington, 1993. Solo exhbns. include Octagon Gallery, Evanston, Ill., 1981, Triton Mus., Santa Clara, Calif., 1981, Mich. Tech. U., 1981, Mobilia, 1982, Kohler Arts Ctr., Sheboygan, Wis., 1985, Hand Workshop, Richmond, Va., 1989, Objects Gallery, Chgo., 1991, 92, The Farrell Collection, Washington, 1993, Ann Nathan Gallery, 1994; numerous group exhbns. Individual artist grantee Wis. Arts Bd., 1994, devel. grantee 1991-92; fellow NEA, 1986, 92, Arts Midwest NEA Regl. Visual Arts, 1985. Office: 2002 Atwood # 215 Madison WI 53704

BERON, GAIL LASKEY, real estate analyst, consultant, appraiser; b. Detroit, Nov. 13, 1943; d. Charles Jack Laskey and Florence B. (Rosenthal) Eisenberg; divorced; children: Monty Charles, Bryan David. Cert. real estate analyst, Mich. Chief/staff appraiser Ft. Wayne Mortgage Co., Birmingham, Mich., 1973-75; pvt. practice fee appraiser S.C., Iowa, Mich., 1976-80; pres. The Beron Co., Southfield, Mich., 1980—; cons. ptnr. Real Estate Counseling Group Conn., Storrs, 1983—, Real Estate Counseling Group Am., prin., 1984—; lectr. real estate confs. Recipient M. William Donnally award Mortgage Bankers Assn. Am., 1975. Mem. Appraisal Inst. (nat. faculty 1991—), Soc. Real Estate Appraisers (bd. dirs. Detroit chpt. 1980-82, nat. faculty 1983-91), Am. Inst. Real Estate Appraisers (bd. dirs. Detroit chpt. 1982-86, nat. faculty 1984-91), Nat. Assn. Realtors, Detroit Bd. Realtors, Southfield Bd. Realtors, Women Brokers Assn. (treas. Southfield chpt. 1981-83), Young Mortgage Bankers (bd. dirs. 1974-75), B'nai B'rith. Home: 7008 Bridge Way West Bloomfield MI 48322-3527 Office: Beron Co 17228 Westhampton Rd Southfield MI 48075-4351

BEROTTE-FRANCIS, MIRIAM, human resources professional; b. Bklyn., June 1, 1961; d. Leonce C. and Nadia (Giordani) Berotte; m. Carl E. Francis,

Jan. 19, 1985; 1 child, Alexandra. BS, Cornell U., 1983. Pers. rep. Republic Nat. Bank N.Y., N.Y.C., 1983-85; compensation analyst 1st Boston Corp., N.Y.C., 1985-87; adminstr. human resources Archdiocese N.Y., N.Y.C., 1987-90; asst. v.p. human resources Easter Seal Soc. N.J., East Brunswick, 1990—. Mem. Soc. for Human Resource Mgmt., Human Resources Coalition, Alpha Kappa Alpha. Office: Easter Seal Soc NJ PO Box 1076 1 Kimberly Rd East Brunswick NJ 08816

BERRESFORD, SUSAN VAIL, philanthropic foundation executive; b. N.Y.C., Jan. 8, 1943; d. Richard Case and Katherine Vail (Marsters) Berresford Hurd; m. David F. Stein (div.); 1 son, Jeremy Vail Stein. Student, Vassar Coll., 1961-63; B.A. cum laude in Am. History, Radcliffe Coll., 1965. Vol. UN Vol. Services, N.Y.C., summer 1962; sec. to Theodore H. White, summer 1964; program officer Neighborhood Youth Corps, N.Y.C., 1965-67; program specialist Manpower Career Devel. Agy., N.Y.C., 1967; human resources adminstrn. specialist Manpower Career Devel. Agy., 1968; freelance cons., writer Europe and U.S., 1968-70; program officer nat. affairs div. Ford Found., N.Y.C., 1970-80; program officer in charge Ford Found., 1980-81, v.p., 1981—. Home: 211 Central Park W New York NY 10028 Office: Ford Found 320 E 43rd St New York NY 10017

BERRETH, MICHELLE RENÉE, medical/surgical nurse; b. Mass., Feb. 15, 1961; m. Tim Berreth, Nov. 13, 1982; 1 child, Dustin. Diploma, St. Luke's Sch. Nursing, Sioux City, Ia., 1982. Cert. ACLS, NALS, RN intravenous. Staff nurse ICU Marion Health Ctr., Sioux City, 1985; staff nurse CCU McKennan Hosp., Sioux Falls, S.D., 1983-85; I.V. therapy supr., staff nurse Hawarden (Iowa) Community Hosp., 1985—. Mem. Intravenous Nursing Soc. (past pres. Siouxland chpt., dist. leader Nat. Coun. Edn. 1994—). Office: Hawarden Community Hosp 1111 11th St Hawarden IA 51023-1999

BERRIGAN, HELEN GINGER, judge; b. 1948. BA, U. Wis., 1969; MA, Am. U., 1971; JD, La. State U., 1977. Staff rschr. Senator Harold E. Hughes, 1971-72; legis. aide Senator Joseph E. Biden, 1972-73; asst. to mayor City of Fayette, Miss., 1973-74; law clk. La. Dept. Corrections, 1975-77; staff atty. Gov. Pardon, Parole and Rehab. Commn., 1977-78; prin. Gravel Brady & Berrigan, New Orleans, 1978-94, Berrigan, Litchfield, Schonekas, Mann & Clement, New Orleans, 1984-94; judge U.S. Dist. Ct. (ea. dist.) La., New Orleans, 1994—; active La. Sentencing Commn., 1987. Active Com. of 21, 1989, pres., 1990-92, ACLU of La., 1989—, v.p., 1993—, Forum for Equality, 1990—, chmn., 1993—, Amistad Rsch. Ctr. Tulane U., 1990—. Mem. La. State Bar Assn. (mem. fed. 5th cir. 1986—), La. Assn. Criminal Def. Lawyers, New Orleans Assn. Women Attys. Office: US Dist Ct 500 Camp St Rm 556 New Orleans LA 70130*

BERRY, ANN THACKREY, journalist; b. Manhattan, Kans., July 11, 1930; d. Russell Ira and Emily Ethel (Sheppeard) Thackrey; m. Hardy D. Berry, Jan. 27, 1950; children: Russell Stuart, Elizabeth Lee, John Newell. BS in Journalism, Kans. State U., 1951; postgrad., Mont. State U., 1958-59; MS in Pub. Affairs, N.C. State U., 1973. Reporter, editor Manhattan Tribune-News, 1949-52; copy editor Raleigh (N.C.) Times, 1966-67, consumer reporter, 1972-74, editorial writer, columnist, 1974-89; editorial writer The News & Observer, Raleigh, 1989—. Co-chair Raleigh Pre-Sch., 1964-65. Recipient 1st Pl. Editorial Writing award N.C. Press Assn., 1983, 87, 91, 3d Pl. Editorial Writing award, 1986, 92, 3d Pl. Columns award, 1987. Democrat. Episcopalian. Office: News & Observer 215 S Mcdowell St Raleigh NC 27601-1331

BERRY, BEVERLY A., real estate investment executive; b. Wayne County, Ohio, Aug. 3, 1939; d. Arleigh Lester and Mabel Bell (Weltmer) Cooper; m. David P. Berry, June 9, 1957; children: Wesley, Tamala, Stephanie. Student, Akron U., 1976-78. Cert. real estate broker, residential specialist, Ohio. Sec., asst. underwriter Westfield Ins. Cos., Westfield Center, Ohio, 1957-69; office mgr., sec. of bd. Johnson Mfg. Co., West Salem, Ohio, 1972-76; prin. acct. Johnson Mfg. Co., West Salem, 1974-76; real estate agt. Gerspacher Realty, Lodi, Ohio, 1976-79, Rickel Realty, Lodi, 1979-82; pres., owner Bev Berry Ins. Agy., Inc., Lodi, 1982-90, Bev Berry Realty, Inc., Auction Co., Lodi, 1982—; mem. of Bus. Option Adv. Com. at Wayne Gen. and Tech. Coll., U. Akron, 1989-90. Mem. Nat. Assn. Real Estate Appraisers, Profl. Ins. Agt. Assn., Women's Coun. Realtors, Realtors Polit. Action Com. (life), Medina County Bd. Realtors (sec. 1986-87, bd. dirs. 1982-86, sec., trustee 1991, Broker of Yr. 1986, Sales Achievement award 1981, Realtor of Yr. 1991), Wayne County Bd. Realtors, Ashland County Bd. Realtors, Lodi C. of C., Medina C. of C., Ruritan. Lutheran. Office: PO Box 131 Lodi OH 44254-0131

BERRY, CAROL A., insurance executive; b. Walla Walla, Wash., Sept. 8, 1950; d. Alan R. and Elizabeth A. (Davenport) B. BA, Wash. State U., 1972. Asst. mgr. L.A. reg. claims CIGNA, Santa Monica, Calif.; reg. adminstr. Equicor, Sherman Oaks, Calif.; dir. system for managed care Blue Cross of Calif., Woodland Hills, Calif.; dir. field account svcs. Managed Health Network, L.A.; dir. VertiHealth Adminstrv. Svcs., Burbank, Calif.; lectr. in field. Mem. Pres.'s Commn. on Status of Women. Mem. NAFE, Assn. Info. Mgrs. Healthcare Industry, Wash. State U. Alumni Assn. Home: 6155 Lockhurst Dr Woodland Hills CA 91367 Home: 6155 Lockhurst Dr Woodland Hills CA 91367

BERRY, CHARLENE HELEN, librarian, musician; b. Highland Pk., Mich., Jan. 4, 1947; d. Harold Terry and Mattie Lou (Colvin) B. BSE, Wayne U., 1964-68, MA, 1969-70, MLS, 1971-74; postgrad., Howard Sch. Broadcast Arts, 1992. Ordained music minister. Libr. asst. Wayne State U., Detroit, 1970-74; libr. serials cataloger SUNY, Stony Brook, 1975-79; cataloger Madonna U., Livonia, Mich., 1980—; organist various area chs., Detroit, 1981—, 1st Ch. of Christ, Wyandotte, Mich., 1986—; music min. Gospel Light House Ministries, Detroit, 1991—; scholar, performer, tchr. hammer dulcimer, 1988—; libr. cons. Superior Twp. (Mich.) Libr. Bd., 1989-91; host Charlene Berry's Dulcimer World, Sta. WCAR, Garden City, Mich.. Composer: Dulcimer Delights, 1991, marches, waltzes, free compositions and solo symphony, 1993, Dulcimer Praise, 1993, Fruits of the Spirit, 1993; solo recs.: Traditional Dulcimer, 1989, Christmas Dulcimer, 1989, Sacred Dulcimer, 1990, Dulcimer Fun, 1991, Dulcimer Americana, 1994, Dulcimer Praise, 1993, Fruits of the Spirit, 1993; (video) Hammering the Hammer Dulcimer, 1994. Pres. Libr. Staff Assn., SUNY, 1978-79; ch. libr. Ch. Bds. Coms., Long Island, Detroit, 1975—; bd. dirs. Livonia Symphony Soc.; performing artist Mich. Touring Arts Agy., 1994-96. Recipient Performance award Silver Springs Dulciner Soc., 1988, 89, 90, Interat. Order of Merit, ASCAP; named Internat. Woman of Yr., 1992-93, Most Admired Woman of Decade. Fellow Internat. Biographical Assn. (life). Am. Biographical Inst. (Woman of Yr. 1993); mem. AAUW, ALA, NAFE, Am. Biographical Rsch. Assn. (hon. dep. gov.), Bus. and Profl. Women, Am. Soc. of Notaries, Am. Fedn. Musicians, Am. Guild Organists (bd. dirs. 1985-88), Plymouth C. of C., Luth. Ch. Musicians Guild, Order Ea. Star, Kappa Delta Pi. Home and Office: Dulcimer Evente 49614 Oak Lot 67 Plymouth MI 48170

BERRY, CORNELIA TATE, service executive, consultant; b. Rock Hill, S.C., Mar. 28, 1944; d. Rodney Norris and Annie Mary (Cole) Putnam; divorced; children: William Edward, Mary Elizabeth, Barbara Ann. Student, Martinsville (Va.) C.C., 1972-73, Va. Commonwealth U., 1973-75; BS in Pharmacy, Med. Coll. Va., 1978. Lic. pharmacist Va., Colo., S.C. Pharmacist Drug Fair, Richmond, Va., 1978-81; staff pharmacist Laurens (S.C.) Dist. Hosp., 1981-84, dir. pharmacy, 1984—; mem. panel Delta Mktg. Dynamics, Jamesville, N.Y., 1982-91; cons. pharmacist Bailey Nursing Home, Clinton, S.C., 1984-92; dir. pharmacy Laurens County Health Care Sys., 1984—. Mem. Laurens County Arts Coun., 1987—; bd. dirs. Good Shepherd Clinic Laurens, 1994—. Mem. Am. Soc. Hosp. Pharmacists, S.C. Pharm. Assn., Student Pharm. Assn. (pres. 1977-78), Kappa Epsilon. Republican. Baptist. Home: Pineland Shores Cross Hill SC 29332 Office: Laurens County Hosp PO Box 976 Clinton SC 29325-0976

BERRY, GAYNOR M., health facility administrator; b. Whiston, Eng., Aug. 11, 1957; d. John and Kathleen (Chee) B.; m. Bradley K. Thesman, May 1, 1982 (div. Mar. 1990); children: Kevin Edward, Steven Andrew. BS in Dietitics, CPSU, 1979; BS in Health Svcs. Adminstrn., Calif. State U., 1985. Dir. food svcs. Long Term Care, Inc., Glendale, Calif., 1979-80; food svc. specialist Monterey (Calif.) Peninsula Unified Sch. Dist., 1980-82; owner Care Van Med. Transp., Glendale, 1982-88; mgr. contracts Huntington Meml. Hosp., Pasadena, Calif., 1988-91; contract specialist Kaiser Permanente, Pasadena, 1991-92; asst. dir. managed care St. Joseph Med. Ctr., Burbank, Calif., 1992, dir. managed care, 1992—. Mem. Group Health Assn. Am., Healthcare Forum, Women in Health Adminstrn. Democrat. Office: St Joseph Med Ctr 501 S Buena Vista Ave Burbank CA 91505

BERRY, HALLE, actress; b. Cleve., Aug. 14, 1968; d. Jerome and Judith (Hawkins) B.; m. David Christopher Justice, Jan. 1, 1993. Appeared in films Jungle Fever, 1991, The Last Boy Scout, 1991, Strictly Business, 1991, Boomerang, 1992 (Image award nominee 1992), Fatherhood, 1993, The Program, 1993, The Flintstones, 1994, Losing Isaiah, 1995; TV mini-series Queen, 1992, Solomon & Sheba, 1995; TV series include Living Dolls, 1989, Knots Landing, 1992; also appeared in episodes of Amen, A Different World, They Came From Outer Space. Named Miss Teen All-Am., 1985, Miss U.S.A., 1987. Office: William Morris Agy 151 El Camino Beverly Hills CA 90212*

BERRY, JACQUELINE KAY, health administrator; b. Anadarko, Okla., Sept. 16, 1942; d. L.T. Moore and Christeene L. (Barbee) Blythe; 1 child, Nina Christine. BA in Polit. Sci., U. Hawaii, 1976, MA in Polit. Sci., 1978, MPH, 1979. Coord. Dept. Labor/Teenage Unemployment, Honolulu, 1979-81; coord. youth employment KEY Project, Kaneahe, Hawaii, 1981-83; dir. Nat. Health Screening, Honolulu, 1983-85; adminstr. Hansen disease program Dept. of Health, Honolulu, 1985-86, adminstr. Office Family Planning, 1986-89, planner devel. disabilities, 1989-90; dir. vol. svcs. Hospice Hawaii, Honolulu, 1990-92; exec. dir. Exodus, Inc., Novato, Calif., 1992-93, Hospice of Humboldt, Eureka, Calif., 1993—. Bd. mem. Child & Family Svc., Honolulu, KEY Project, Kaneohe; mem. AIDS Task Force. Pub. health trainee USPHS, Honolulu, 1979. Mem. AAUW, Soc. Pub. Health Educators (past pres.), Phi Beta Kappa. Office: Hospice of Humboldt 2010 Myrtle Ave Eureka CA 95501-3322

BERRY, JANIS MARIE, lawyer; b. Everett, Mass., Dec. 20, 1949; d. Joseph and Dorothy I. (Barbato) Sordillo; m. Richard G. Berry, Dec. 27, 1970; children: Alexis, Ashley, Lindsey. BA magna cum laude, Boston U., 1971, JD cum laude, 1974. Bar: Mass. 1974, U.S. Dist. Ct. Mass. 1975, U.S. Ct. Appeals (1st cir.), 1980, U.S. Supreme Ct. 1982. Law clk. Mass. Supreme Jud. Ct., Boston, 1974-75; assoc. Bingham, Dana & Gould, Boston, 1975-80; asst. U.S. atty. Boston, 1980-81; spl. atty. dept. justice N.E. Organized Crime Strike Force, Boston, 1981-84; chief atty. dept. justice N.E. Organized Crime Drug Task Force, Boston, 1986-94; ptnr. Ropes & Gray, Boston, 1986-94, Berry Ottenberg & Dunkless, Boston, 1995—, Berry, Ottenberg & Dunkless, Boston, 1995—; instr. Harvard Law Sch., 1983-86, Inst. Trial Advocacy, Boston, 1984-87; lectr. Dept. Justice Advocacy Inst., 1986; mem. Mass. Bd. of Bar Overseers, 1989-93; chair merit selection panel U.S. Magistrate, 1989, Mass. Jud. Nominating Coun., 1991-92. Author: Defending Corporations Public Contracts Jour., (with others) Federal Criminal Practice, 1987. Bd. dirs. Mass. Com. for Pub. Counsel Svcs., Boston, 1986-91; v.p. Boston Inn of Ct., 1990-91; trustee Atlanticare Hosp., 1990—. Spl. Commendation award Dept. of Justice, Washington, 1983. Fellow Mass. Bar Found.; mem. ABA, Mass. Bar Assn., Boston Bar Assn., Am. Law Inst., Women's Bar Assn., Boston Inn of Ct. (v.p. 1990-91), Phi Beta Kappa. Office: Berry Ottenberg & Dunkless 260 Franklin St Boston MA 02110

BERRY, JONI INGRAM, hospice pharmacist, educator; b. Charlotte, N.C., June 6, 1953; d. James Clifford and Patricia Ann (Ebener) Ingram; m. William Rosser Berry, May 29, 1976; children: Erin Blair, Rachel Anne, James Rosser. BS in Pharmacy, U. N.C., 1976, MS in Pharmacy, 1979. Lic. pharmacist, N.C. Resident in pharmacy Sch. Pharmacy, U. N.C., Chapel Hill, 1977-79, adj. asst. prof., 1985—; pharmacist Durham County Gen. Hosp., Durham, N.C., 1977-79; coord. clin. pharm. Wake Med. Ctr., Raleigh, N.C., 1979-80; co-dir. pharmacy edn. Wake Area Health Edn. Ctr., Raleigh, 1980-85; pharmacist cons. Hospice of Wake County, Raleigh, 1980—. Mem. editorial adv. bd. Hospice Jour., 1985-91, Jour. Pharm. Care in Pain and Symptom Mgmt., 1992—; reviewer Am. Jour. Hospice Care, 1986—; contbr. articles to profl. jours. Troop leader Girl Scouts U.S.A., Raleigh, 1987—, trainer, 1989-91, mgr. svc. unit, 1990-94; Sunday sch. tchr. St. Phillips Luth. Ch., Raleigh, 1990-92, 94-95. Recipient Silver Pinecone award Girl Scouts U.S., 1991, Golden Rule award J.C. Penney Co., 1991. Mem. Am. Pharm. Assn. (hospice pharmacist steering com. 1990—), Am. Soc. Hosp. Pharmacists, Nat. Hospice Assn., Am. Pain Soc., N.C. Pharm. Assn. (Don Blanton award 1985, mem. continuing edn. com. 1986-87, com. chairperson 1981-84), N.C. Soc. Hosp. Pharmacists (bd. dirs. 1984-86, program com. 1988-91), Wake County Pharm. Assn. (sec. 1982-85), Rho Chi. Democrat. Office: Hospice Wake County 4513 Creedmoor Rd Fl 4 Raleigh NC 27612-3815

BERRY, LAURIE ANN, critical care nurse; b. Duluth, Minn., Dec. 13, 1954; d. Robert Reginald and Claire Olivia (Hood) Johnson. RN, St. Luke's Hosp., Duluth, Minn., 1976. Gen. staff nurse med./neurosurgery Mercy San Juan Hosp., Citrus Hts., Calif., 1979-80; gen. staff nurse MSICU St. Luke's Hosp., Duluth, 1980-84; gen. staff nurse SICU St. Francis Hosp., Tulsa, 1984-85; gen. staff nurse bone marrow transplant U. Minn., Mpls., 1985—. Mem. Minn. Nurses Assn.

BERRY, MARY FRANCES, history and law educator; b. Nashville, Feb. 17, 1938; d. George Ford and Frances Southall (Wiggins) B. B.A., Howard U., 1961, M.A., 1962; Ph.D., U. Mich., 1966, J.D., 1970; hon. degree, Cen. Mich. U., Howard U., U. Akron, 1977, Benedict Coll., U. Md., Grambling State U., 1979, Bethune-Cookman Coll., Clark Coll., Del. State Coll., 1980, Oberlin Coll., Langston U., 1983, Marian Coll., Haverfod Coll., 1984, Colby Coll., CUNY, 1986, DePaul U., 1987. Bar: D.C. 1972. Asst. prof. history Central Mich. U., Mt. Pleasant, 1966-68; asst. prof. Eastern Mich. U., Ypsilanti, 1968-69; assoc. prof. Eastern Mich. U., 1969-70, U. Md., College Park, 1969-76; acting dir. Afro-Am. studies, 1970-72, dir., 1972-74, acting chmn. div. behavioral and social scis., 1973-74, provost div. behavioral and social scis., 1973-76; prof. history, prof. law U Colo. at Boulder, 1976-80, chancellor, 1976-77; prof. history and law Howard U., Washington, 1980—; Geraldine R. Segal prof. Am. Social Thought U. Pa., 1987—; asst. sec. for edn. HEW, Washington, 1977-80; mem. U.S. Commn. on Civil Rights, 1980—, now chmn.; adj. assoc. prof. U. Mich., 1970-71; mem. com. visitors U. Mich. Law Sch., 1976-80; mem. nat. adv. panel on minority concerns Coll. Bd., 1980-84; mem. adv. bd. Feminist Press, 1980—; mem. research adv. com. Joint Ctr. for Polit. Studies, 1981—; mem. editorial adv. com. Marcus Garvey Papers, 1981—; mem. adv. bd. Inst. for Higher Edn. Law and Governance, U. Houston, 1983—; Geraldine R. Segal prof. of am. social thought U. Pa., 1987—. Author: Black Resistance/White Law, 1971, Military Necessity and Civil Rights Policy, 1977, Stability, Security and Continuity, Mr. Justice Burton and Decision-Making in the Supreme Court, 1945-58, 1978, (with John Blassingame) Long Memory: The Black Experience in America, 1982; Why ERA Failed, 1986; asso. editor Jour. Negro History, 1974-78; contbr. articles, revs. to profl. jours. Bd. dirs. ARC, Washington, 1980—; trustee Tuskegee U., 1980—; mem. adv. bd. Project '87, 1978—; mem. council UN U., 1986—. Recipient Athena (disting. alumni) award U. Mich., 1977, Roy Wilkins Civil Rights award NAACP, 1983, Image award, 1983, Allard Lowenstein award, 1984, President's award Congl. Black Caucus Found., 1985, Woman of Yr. award Nat. Capital Area YWCA, 1985, Hubert H. Humphrey Civil Rights award Leadership Conf. on Civil Rights, 1986, Rosa Parks award SCLC, Black Achievement award Ebony Mag., Woman of Yr. award Ms. Mag., 1986. Mem. ABA, Nat. Bar Assn., D.C. Bar Assn., Nat. Acad. Public Adminstrn., Orgn. Am. Historians (exec. bd. 1974-77), Assn. Study of Afro-Am. Life and History (exec. bd. 1973-76), Am. Hist. Assn. (v.p. for profession 1980-83), Am. Soc. Legal History, Coalition 100 Black Women (hon.), Delta Sigma Theta (hon.). Office: Commn on Civil Rights Office of Chmn 624 9th St NW Washington DC 20425*

BERRY, NANCY REID, mental health therapist and consultant; b. Wyandotte, Mich., Sept. 5, 1942; d. Hugh C. Reid and Louise M. Walsh; m. R. Thomas Berry; children: Chad Thomas, Jennifer Marie. BS in Edn., Ind. State U., 1964, MS in Edn., 1969; MS in Counseling and Human Svcs., Ind. U., South Bend, 1993. Lic. profl. counselor, Mich.; cert. clin. social worker, Ind., cert. social worker, Ind.; lic. tchr., Ind. Tchr. City of Mishawaka (Ind.) Pub. Schs., 1964-86; part-time English tchr. South Bend Sch. Corp., 1987-94; writing instr. Ind. U., South Bend, 1991—; therapist/cons. Mishawaka, 1993—; counselor Argos (Ind.) Cmty. Schs., 1994—; parent cons./speaker Concord High Sch., Elkhart, Ind., 1994; cons. stress mgmt. Internat. Assn. Bus. Communicators, Ft. Wayne, Ind., 1993; lectr. in field; condr. workshops in field. Author: Billy and the Land of Better-Believe-It, 1994; contbr. articles to profl. jours. Cmty. advocate Housing for Homless Teen Mothers, South Bend, 1993; bd. dirs. Christian Bus. and Profl. Women, South Bend, 1986-88. Grantee South Bend Sch. Corp., 1987, Jr. League, South Bend, 1988; Alpha Omicron Pi scholar, 1962, Delta Kappa Gamma scholar, 1991. Mem. ACA, Am. Mental Health Counselors Assn., Ind. Sch. Counselor's Assn., Ind. Counseling Assn., Univ. Club of Notre Dame, Delta Kappa Gamma (project Starwalk chmn. 1992-93). Republican. Home: 746 E 18th St Mishawaka IN 46544

BERRY, NORMA JEAN, social worker; b. Charleston, W.Va., Jan. 7, 1946; d. Carl E. and Dora Lee (Hamm) Inman; m. Julian, July 5, 1974, (div. 1980); m. Vincent L. Swadis, Sept. 12, 1985. BS, Morris Harvey Coll., 1967; MSW, W.Va. U., 1975. Social Worker. Social worker Fla. State Dept. of Welfare, Crestview, 1968-69; asst. adminstr. Hilltop Home for the Elderly, Charleston, 1970-71; social worker W.Va. Dept. of Welfare, Charleston, 1971-74; social worker VA Hosp., Huntington, W.Va., 1974-82, Temple, Tex., 1982-1990; psychotherapist Minirth-Meier, Tunnell & Wilson Psychiat. Clinic, Belton, Tex., 1990-91; social worker Vets. Affairs Med. Ctr., Temple, Tex., 1991—; cons. VA Hosp., Temple, 1974-82; real estate agt. Bruzzese Realty Co., Huntington, 1980-81; salesperson Mary Kay Cosmetics, Temple, 1983-84. Recipient Outstanding Svc. award DAV, 1981. Mem. NASW. Republican. Home: 8920 Trailridge Dr Temple TX 76502-5210 Office: Olin E Teague Vets Ctr Temple TX 76504

BERRY, PHYLLIS GOODMAN, public relations executive; b. N.Y.C., Sept. 7, 1946; d. Bernard Jacob and Claire (Rosenberg) Goodman; m. Narendar Gopal Berry, Nov. 22, 1992. BS, Cornell U., 1967. Ext. home economist Nassau County Ext. Svc., Mineola, N.Y., 1967-68; editl. asst. Funk & Wagnalls, N.Y.C., 1968-69; sr. v.p. Glick & Lorwin, Inc., N.Y.C., 1969-80, Sci. and Medicine, N.Y.C., 1980-82; v.p. Hill and Knowlton, Inc., N.Y.C., 1982-85; assoc. v.p. comm. and pub. affairs St. Luke's-Roosevelt Hosp. Ctr., N.Y.C., 1985-92; owner Goodman Berry Pub. Rels., Albuquerque, 1993-95; sr. v.p. corp. comm. Sun Healthcare Group, Inc., Albuquerque, 1995—; mem. com. pub. affairs Greater N.Y. Hosp. Assn., 1988-92. Mem. Am. Soc. Health Care Mktg. and Pub. Rels. (treas. N.Mex. chpt. 1993-94), Pub. Rels. Soc. Am. (v.p. N.Mex. chpt. 1994, pres.-elect N.Mex. chpt. 1995), Healthcare Pub. Rels. and Mktg. Soc. Greater N.Y. (pres. 1990-91), Westside C. of C. N.Y.C. (bd. dirs. 1986-92), Pi Lambda Theta. Office: Sun Healthcare Group Inc 5131 Masthead NE Albuquerque NM 87109

BERRY, ROBERTA MILDRED, civic worker; b. Medinah, Ill., Feb. 27, 1926; d. Judson Stewart and Anna Doretha (Neddermeyer) Lawrence; m. Moses Berry, June 29, 1948; children—Scott, Mark. B.Mus., Cornell Coll., 1948. Choir dir. Presbyterian, Methodist Chs., Cedar Rapids, Iowa, 1949-71; tchr. assoc. Cedar Rapids Community Schs., 1963-73; bd. dirs. Pioneer Village, Cedar Rapids, 1982-83; dir. Linn Community Food Bank, Cedar Rapids, 1983—; pres. Chs. United, Cedar Rapids, 1984-85, v.p. Iowa state bd., 1994—; orginator Grade Sch. Picture Lady Program, Cedar Rapids, 1968-69; pres. Seminole Valley Farm, Cedar Rapids, 1980-81; v.p. Ch. Women United, Cedar Rapids, 1985-86, also bd. dirs., editor newsletter for Iowa State. Bd. dirs. YWCA, Cedar Rapids, 1970-72, Cedar Rapids Symphony Guild, 1983-88, Iowa Rails to Trails, Cedar Rapids, 1983-88; pres. Methwick Manor Aux., Cedar Rapids, 1985; sec. Council on Aging, Cedar Rapids, 1984-85; rep. Civic Newcomers, 1986-93; pres. Cedar Rapids Area Peace Network Guide; pres. Brucemore Hist. Home, 1982—. Mem. UN Assn. (Iowa state bd. 1993—). Clubs: Beethoven (pres. 1964-65), College (pres. 1965-66), PEO (pres. 1982-83), Demolay Mothers Aux (pres. 1974-75), Postal Workers Aux (pres. 1974-75) (Cedar Rapids). Avocations: oil painting, needlework, tennis, biking. Home: 1118 Maplewood Dr NE Cedar Rapids IA 52402-4710

BERT, CAROL LOIS, educational aide; b. Bakersfield, Calif., Oct. 15, 1938; d. Edwin Vernon and Shirley Helen (Craig) Phelps; m. John Davison Bert, Sept. 26, 1964; children: Mary Ellen, John Edwin, Craig Eric, Douglas Ethan. BS in Nursing, U. Colo., 1960. Med. surg. nurse U.S. Army, Washington, 1960-62, Ascom City, Korea, 1962-63, San Antonio, 1963, Albuquerque, 1964-65; ednl. asst. Jefferson County Schs., Arvada, Colo., 1979—. Sec. Parent, Tchr., Student Assn. Arvada West High Sch., 1987-88. Club: Colo. Quilting Coun. (1st v.p. 1988, 89, inducted into Hall of Fame, 1992). Avocations: reading, quilting, camping, fishing, tennis. Home: 5844 Oak St Arvada CO 80004-4739 Office: Allendale Elem Sch 5900 Oak St Arvada CO 80004-4741

BERT, CLARA VIRGINIA, home economics educator, administrator; b. Quincy, Fla., Jan. 29, 1929; d. Harold C. and Ella J. (McDavid) B. BS, Fla. State U., 1950, MS, 1963, PhD, 1967. Cert. tchr., Fla.; cert. home economist; cert. pub. mgr. Tchr. Union County High Sch., Lake Butler, Fla., 1950-53, Havana High Sch., Fla., 1953-65; cons. rsch. and devel. Fla. Dept. Edn., Tallahassee, 1967-75, sect. dir. rsch. and devel., 1975-85, program dir. home econs. edn., 1985—; cons. Nat. Ctr. Rsch. in Vocat. Edn., Ohio State U., 1978; field reader U.S. Dept. Edn., 1974-75. Author, editor booklets. U.S. Office Edn. grantee, 1976, 77, 78; named Disting. Alumna, Coll. Human Scis., Fla. State U., 1994. Mem. Am. Home Econs. Assn. (state treas. 1969-71), Am. Vocat. Assn., Fla. Vocat. Assn., Fla. Vocat. Home Econs., Fla. Home Econs., Am. Vocat. Edn. Rsch. Assn. (nat. treas. 1970-71), Nat. Coun. Family Rels., Am. Ednl. Rsch. Assn., Fla. State U. Alumni Assn. (bd. dirs. home econs. sect.), Havana Golf and Country Club, Kappa Delta Pi, Omicron Nu (chpt. pres. 1965-66), Delta Kappa Gamma (pres. 1974-76), Sigma Kappa (pres. corp. bd. 1985-91), Phi Delta Kappa. Office: Fla Dept Edn FEC Tallahassee FL 32399

BERTEA, HYLA HOLMES, real estate investor; b. L.A., June 14, 1940; d. George Dawson Holmes and Beth (Bay) Maher; m. Richard Bertea, Mar. 15, 1964; children: Baret Bertea Walker, Alex, Blake, Bay. BS, U. So. Calif., 1962. Tchr. L.A. City Schs., 1962-65; realtor Dalebout Assn., Newport Beach, Calif., 1988-90, Grubb & Ellis, Newport Beach, 1990—; bd. dirs. Pacific Enterprises, L.A.; founding presiding ptnr. Women's Investments., Co-commr. gymnastics L.A. Olympic Organizing Com., 1981-84; bd. dirs., co-chair U. So. Calif. Planning and Devel., Orange County; trustee Lewis and Clark Coll., Portland, Oreg.; commr. Calif. Horse Racing Bd. Recipient City of L.A. Commendation award U.S. Olympics, 1984. Republican. Presbyterian. Office: 23 Corporate Plaza Newport Beach CA 92660-5900

BERTEL, SHARON FAITH, dietitian; b. N.Y.C., Dec. 9, 1949; d. Alfred and Genessa (Kapen) B.; m. Carl P. Nicholson, Nov. 15, 1987; children: (twins) Kayla, Meredith. BA, Ithaca Coll., 1971; MA, Tufts U., 1975; postgrad., Simmons Coll., 1977-79; MEd, Boston U., 1986. Registered dietitian. Dietetic intern Beth Israel Hosp., Boston, 1979-80; clin. dietitian St. Elizabeth's Med. Ctr., Brighton, Mass., 1980-89, chief clin. dietitian, 1990—; clin. assoc. prof. Sargent Coll. of Allied Health Professions/Boston U., 1991—. Scholarship Tufts U., 1971-72. Mem. Am. Dietetic Assn., Mass. Dietetic Assn., Am. Soc. of Parenteral and Enteral Nutrition (ctrl. New Eng. chpt.). Office: St Elizabeths Med Ctr 736 Cambridge St Brighton MA 02135

BERTELLE, JEANNE T., publishing company executive, human resources director; b. Bklyn., Oct. 14, 1947; d. John A. and Florence (Bellitti) B.; m. Silvio Rosato. BA in English, Bklyn. Coll., 1968; postgrad. in Drama, Hunter Coll., 1975-77. Pers. adminstr. Chem. Bank, N.Y.C., 1968-70; employment interviewer L.I. Coll. Hosp., Bklyn., 1970-71; sr. job analyst health svcs. mobility study, Rsch. Found. CUNY, N.Y.C., 1971-76; pers. mgr. Doubleday & Co., N.Y.C., 1976-88; dir. human resources McGraw-Hill Inc., N.Y.C., 1988—; com. mem. Direct Mail Assn., N.Y.C., 1984; cons., editor Health Svcs. Mobility Study, N.Y.C., 1976-77. N.Y. State Regents scholar, 1964-68. Mem. Am. Soc. Pers. Adminstrs., Assn. Am. Pubs. (chair industry salary survey 1987—). Roman Catholic. Club: Scott House (Bklyn.) (v.p.). Home: 1104 Hunters Run Dobbs Ferry NY 10522-3404 Office: McGraw-Hill Inc 1221 Ave Of The Americas New York NY 10020-1001

BERTENSHAW, BOBBI CHERRELLE, producer; b. Bklyn., Oct. 22, 1961; d. Eli and Marcia Janet (Forman) Slachofsky; m. William H. Bertenshaw III, Dec. 16, 1984. Diploma, Nat. Broadcast Sch., Phila., 1982, Health

Maintenance Inst., Flushing, N.Y., 1985. Radio, TV producer Coun. of Chs., N.Y.C., 1981-84, Radio and TV Roundup Prodns., N.Y.C., 1982—; producer WOR Radio, N.Y.C., 1982—; dir. communications Delfon Rec. Soc., 1987—; chief exec. officer Radio & TV Roundup Prodns., 1991—; programming cons. N.J. NetworkPublic TV, 1992—; communications dir. Delfon Recording Soc., 1987—; producer-dir. Stat. WOR Radio N.Y., 1983—; co-producer People Working for People, Sta. WWOR TV N.Y. and Cable TV Network of N.J., 1988—. Recipient Cape TV award Cable TV Network N.J., 1987, N.J. State Fair awards, 1990, 91, 92, 93, 94; named Miss Lima Bean Nat. Lima Bean Assn., 1986-87. Mem. Women in Communications, Internat. Platform Assn., Am. Symphony Orch. League, N.J. Coun. of Chs. (dept. communications 1983—), Feathered Fanciers Soc. (sec. 1992—), Nat. Lima Bean Assn. (co-chmn. 1988—). Home: 427 Sunset Blvd Cape May NJ 08204-4110 Office: Delfon Rec Soc 305 3rd Ave W Newark NJ 07107-2301

BERTHOLD-ROSEN, BONNIE MADELINE, realtor, consultant; b. Sellersville, Pa., Nov. 23, 1950; d. Willard Miller and Anna Agnes (Dugard) Berthold; m. Robert G. Rosen. BS in Elem. Edn. cum laude, Kutztown State U., Pa., 1972; MS in Edn. with disting. recognition, Temple U., 1975; Prin.'s cert., U. Pa., 1978. Elem. sch. tchr. Reading Sch. Dist., Pa., 1972-79, summer sch. instr., 1972-79, workshop presenter, 1972-79, curriculum developer, 1974-79, adminstv. inter, 1977-79; owner, adminstr. Wooly Bear Day Care Sch., Lansdale, Pa., 1979-94; asst. prof. Montgomery County C.C., Blue Bell, Pa., 1985—; realtor RE/MAX Ctrl. Inc., Lansdale, 1994—; substitute tchr. No. Penn Sch. Dist., 1995—. cons. in field; presenter coll. and community workshops. Contbr. articles to mags. Bd. dir. No. Penn Boy's and Girl's Club. Recipient Outstanding Tchrs. Am. award Bd. of Advisors, 1975; named Tchr. of Yr. Reading/Berks County C. of C., 1976; George B. Hancher scholar Kutztown State U., 1971. Mem. Montgomery/Bucks Assn. for Edn. of Young Children (pres. 1982-84, bd. dirs. 1993—), Nat. Assn. for Edn. of Young Children, Pa. Assn. for Edn. of Young Children, Pa. Assn. Child Care Adminstrs., Small Bus. Coun. (presenter), Del. Valley Child Care Council (sec.), North Penn C. of C. (small bus. coun.). Republican. Lutheran. Avocations: piano, water sports, reading, constructing and designing learning materials. Home: 106 Holly Dr Lansdale PA 19446-1617 Office: RE/MAX Ctrl Inc 1110 N Broad St Lansdale PA 19446-1182

BERTINI, JUDITH EMERLINE, government agency administrator; b. Phila., Feb. 25, 1944; d. John C. and Mildred A. Emerline; m. Francis A. Bertini. BA, Syracuse U., 1966; MA, U. Cin., 1967; MLS, Cath. U., 1977; postgrad., George Washington U., 1987, Harvard U., 1990. Archivist asst. Fed. Records Ctr. Nat. Archives, Washington, 1968; intelligence rsch. specialist CIA, Washington, 1968-71, Dept. Army, Washington, 1971-73; intelligence rsch. specialist dangerous drugs unit, Asian heroin unit, spl. analysis unit, estimates unit, organized crime unit Drug Enforcement Adminstrn., Washington, 1975-81, supervisory intelligence rsch. specialist, organized crime and terrorism unit, operational intelligence sect., 1981-84, supervisory intelligence rsch. specialist, operational intelligence sect., 1984-89, assoc. dep., asst. adminstr. for intelligence, 1989-92, dept. asst. adminstr. intelligence divsn. Office of Intelligence Liaison and Policy, 1992—. Office: Drug Enforcement Adminstrn Washington DC 20537

BERTINO, SHEILA ELAINE, college relations and marketing director; b. Erin, Tenn., Sept. 1, 1949; d. Claude Preston and Dorothea Marie (Roberts) Brooks; m. James J. Bertino Sr., Oct. 18, 1980; 1 child, Matthew Brooks. BS, U. Tenn., 1970, MS, 1975; postgrad., Union Coll., 1976-77; cert., Fla. Atlantic U., 1986. Cert. elem., secondary sch. tchr. Tenn., Ky. Secondary edn. tchr. Knox County Schs., Knoxville, Tenn., 1971-77; extension agt. County of Fayette, Lexington, Ky., 1978-79; state program specialist U. Ky., Lexington, 1979-80; info. svcs. specialist Seattle City Light, 1981-83; pub. info. officer Palm Beach County Govt., West Palm Beach, Fla., 1984-87; dir. coll. rels. Palm Beach C.C., Lake Worth, Fla., 1987—. Campaign coord. United Way, Seattle, 1982, West Palm Beach, 1985, Lake Worth, 1987; mem. com. Airport 88, West Palm Beach, 1985-88. Recipient Model Program award Tenn. PTA, 1976. Mem. Nat. Coun. Mktg. and Pub. Rels. (state bd. dirs. 1989, dist. II bd. dirs.), Fla. Assn. Cmty. Colls., Kappa Omicron Nu, Alpha Delta Pi. Republican. Methodist. Office: Palm Beach CC 4200 Congress Ave Lake Worth FL 33461-4705

BERTRAM, JEAN DESALES, writer; b. Burlington, Iowa, Sept. 28; d. Val Randall and Ruth Cecilia Bertram; 1 child, Larkin Montgomery Bertram-Cox. BA, U. N.C., Greensboro, 1942; MA, U. Minn., 1951; PhD, Stanford U., 1963. Reporter Greensboro News Record, 1942-43; founder dept. pub. rels. Burlington Industries, Greensboro, 1943-49; asst. to dean edn. U. N.C., Greensboro, 1949-50; instr. U. Minn., Mpls., 1950-51; dir. radio performance Mpls. Vocat. High Sch., 1951-52; dir. Children's Theatre Touring Co., Jr. League Mpls., 1951-52; prof. theatre arts San Francisco State U., 1952-88; cons. Wadsworth Pub. Co., Belmont, Calif., 1966; dir. Readers' Repertory, San Francisco State U., 1967-72; dir. Jean De Sales Bertram Players, San Francisco, 1971-74; founder, developer storytelling program San Francisco State U., 1971-88; cons. Scott-Foresman, Chgo., 1983; senator acad. senate San Francisco State U., 1983-84, dir. com. for lectures, arts and spl. programs, 1985-87; tax preparer, 1994. Author: (textbooks) The Oral Experience of Literature, 1967, The Actor Speaks, 4 edits., 1981-87, Tell Me a Story!, 5 edits., 1982-88; author, dir. pageant Finding Your Own Adventure, 1955; prodr., dir., adapter, editor: (religious plays) A Symphonetic Easter Drama, 1954, The Awakening, 1954, The Vision of Isaiah, 1970, The Cherry Tree, 1971; author, dir.: (play) American Cameos, 1976; author: (poem) Cosmorama, 1971; actress one-woman show numerous women from Shakespeare's plays, 1971-88; contbr. articles to profl. jours. Stanford-Wilson fellow Stanford U., 1962-63. Mem. Found. Bibl. Rsch., Phi Beta Kappa (sec. Omicron of Calif. chpt. 1977-79, 83-88, pres. 1979-81, v.p. 1981-83, ofcl. del. Triennial coun. 1979, 82).

BERTRAM, MANYA M., lawyer; b. Denver; d. Samuel and Ruby (Feiner) Boran; m. Barry Bertram, June 19, 1938; children: H. Neal, Carel. JD magna cum laude, Southwestern U., 1962. Ptnr. Most and Bertram, L.A., 1963-83; of counsel Levin, Ballin, Plotkin, Zimring & Goffin, North Hollywood, Calif., 1983-92, Janice Fogg, 1993—. Former trustee Southwestern U. Sch. Law Alumni; former bd. advisors Whittier Coll. of Law, L.A., Beverly Coll. Law; former commr. Calif. Commn. on Aging, Sacramento, 1977-82; bd. dirs. Jewish Family Svc., L.A. Mem. ABA, Calif. State Bar Assn., L.A. County Bar Assn., Federacion Internac. de Abagados, Iota Tau Tau, B'nai B'rith (life mem.), Hadassah (life mem.). Office: 12650 Riverside Dr North Hollywood CA 91607-3421

BERTRAM, PHYLLIS ANN, lawyer, communications executive; b. Long Beach, Calif., July 30, 1954; d. William J. and Ruth A. Bertram; AA, Long Beach City Coll., 1975, BS in Acctg., U. So. Calif., 1977; MBA, Calif. State U., Long Beach, 1978; JD, Western State U., 1982. Bar: Calif. 1982, U.S. Ct. Appeals (9th cir.), U.S. Dist. Ct. Instr., lifeguard City of Long Beach, Calif., 1972-78; sports ofcl. swimming, softball, volleyball, and basketball, 1972—; asst. commr. Met. Conf. Community and Jr. Colls., Long Beach, 1978-84; instr. seamanship, fire sci. and bus. adminstrn. Long Beach City Coll., 1977—; mgmt. cons., 1978—; mgr. Pacific Bell, 1983—, Spl. Access Tariffs, Interconnection/Collocation Tariffs, Individual Case Basis Tariffs; guest lectr. sports officiating camps and tng. sessions. Instr. CPR, water safety, small craft, first aid ARC, 1972—; mem. Rep. Nat. Com. Recipient resolutions Calif. Senate and Assembly, Long Beach City Council; numerous service awards ARC; Ednl. research grantee, City of Long Beach, 1972. Mem. U. So. Calif. Alumni Assn., U. So. Calif. Commerce Assocs., Assn. of MBA Execs., Bay Area Career Women, Inc. (corp. sec., bd. dirs.), So. Calif. Volleyball Ofcls. Assn., Nat. Assn. Sports Ofcls., So. Calif. Basketball Ofcls. Assn., Women's Basketball Ofcls. Assn., Women's Swim Ofcls. Assn. (pres.), So. Calif. Softball Umpires Assn., State Bar Calif., ABA, Fed. Bar Assn. Los Angeles, Internat. Platform Assn., Town Hall Calif., Commonwealth Club of Calif., Los Angeles County Bar Assn., Calif. State U. at Long Beach Alumni Assn., U. So. Calif. Alumni Assn., Delta Theta Phi. Republican. Club: Seal Beach Yacht. Office: 140 New Montgomery Ste 2503 San Francisco CA 94105

BERTRAND, ANNABEL HODGES, civic worker, artist, calligrapher; b. Birmingham, Ala., Jan. 4, 1915; d. Thomas Edmund and Mae (Crawford) Hodges; m. John Raney Bertrand, Oct. 23, 1942; children: John Thomas, Diana Bertrand Williams, Karen Bertrand Wilson, J'May Bertrand Rivara. BS, Tex. Woman's U., 1935, MA, 1936; postgrad., Columbia U., 1938. Tchr. White Deer (Tex.) Consol. Sch., 1936-37, Tyler (Tex.) Pub. Sch. System, 1938-39; instr. Sam Houston State U., Huntsville, Tex., 1939-42; interim tchr. Portsmouth (N.H.) Pub. Sch., 1943. Bd. dirs. Rome Area Coun. for the Arts, 1980—, Ga. Coun. for Arts and Humanities, Atlanta, 1979-83, Mental Health Assn. Floyd County, Rome, Ga., 1980—; active High Mus. Art, Atlanta, 1979—, Rome Symphony Guild, 1980—, Friends of Rome/Floyd County Libr., 1985—, Christian Personhood Book Discussion Group of First United Meth. Ch., 1980—. Mem. AAUW, United Meth. Women, Rome Music Lovers Club, Sigma Alpha Iota (patroness). Republican. Home: 18 Rosewood Rd Rome GA 30165-4269

BERTRAND, CARLINNA LEJEUNE, controller; b. Crowley, La., Dec. 9, 1963; d. James Allen and Barbara Ann (Bollich) LeJeune; m. Stacy Bertrand, Oct. 11, 1986; children: Christian Michael, Jordan Michael, Jill Claire. BSBA, U. Southwestern La., 1985. CPA, La. Staff acct. Broussard, Poche, Lewis & Breaux, Crowley, 1986-91; corp. contr. John N. John Trucklines, Crowley, 1991—. Mem. AAUW, AICPA, Soc. La. CPAs, Am. Trucking Assn. (nat. acctg. and fin. coun. 1992—). Roman Catholic. Home: 256 Edgewood Dr Crowley LA 70526-6721 Office: John N John Trucklines 1213 W Highway 90 Crowley LA 70526

BERTRAND, JOAN LESLIE, human resource director; b. Worcester, Mass., Mar. 12, 1956; d. Edward Paul and Mae Loretta (Wilhelmi) Metirier; m. Bruce Kenneth Bertrand, June 24, 1984; children: Jeffrey Edward, Sarah Elizabeth. BA, Anna Maria Coll., Paxton, Mass., 1978, MBA, 1982. Gen. mgr. Singing Hills, Inc., Worcester, 1982-84; human resource and ops. mgr. Joseph Horne Co., Pitts., 1984-88; dir. human resources AdCare Hosp., Worcester, 1988-92, Santa Marta Hosp., East L.A., 1992-93, St. Francis Med. ctr., Lynwood, Calif., 1993—. Bd. dirs. Salisbury Singers, Inc., Worcester, 1991-92. Mem. Am. Soc. Hosp. Human Resource Assn., Calif. Hosp. Human Resource Assn., Mass. Hosp. Human Resource Assn. (program com. 1992), Daughters of Charity (western region, human resource task force 1994). Roman Catholic. Office: St Francis Med Ctr 3630 E Imperial Hwy Lynwood CA 90262

BERUBE, GEORGETTE B., State senator 16th dist., Maine, 1985—. Democrat. Office: Maine State Senate State Capitol Augusta ME 04333 also: 195 Webster St Lewiston ME 04240*

BERUBE, MARGERY STANWOOD, publishing executive; b. Middleborough, Mass., Nov. 18, 1943; d. John Peter and Dorothy Cole (Stanwood) Wholan; m. Edgar Roger Berube, Sept. 12, 1967. BA in English, Wilkes Coll., 1965. Creative and prodn. mgr., dir. editorial ops. Med. div. Houghton Mifflin Co., Boston, 1978-81, dir. editorial ops. Reference div., 1982-85, v.p., dir. editorial ops. Trade and Reference div., 1986-87, v.p., dir. editorial art prodn. and mfg. services, 1987-91, v.p., dir. lexical pub., prodn. and mfg. svcs., 1991—. Mem. Bookbuilders (bd. dirs. 1976-80). Office: Hougton Mifflin Co 222 Berkeley St Boston MA 02116-3764

BERWICK, MARY CREGAR, retired information specialist, consultant; b. Camden, N.J., July 13, 1922; d. Percy Mitchell and Edna Elizabeth (Shafer) Cregar; m. Leonard Berwick, Dec. 20, 1948 (dec. July 1980); children: Philip C., Robert C., Elizabeth C., Barbara B. Wright. AB, Wilson Coll., 1943; MA, Bryn Mawr Coll., 1945; PhD, U. Pa., 1949. Assoc. dept. pathology U. Pa. Med. Sch., Phila., 1948-55; lectr. Bryn Mawr (Pa.) Coll., 1950-52; dir. tutoring svc. Widener U., Chester, Pa., 1969-71; info. specialist biomed. libr. U. Pa., Phila., 1971-92; cons. dept. pathology U. Pa. Med. Ctr., Phila., 1992-94. Mem. AAUW (pres. Ea. Delaware County 1966-68, 81-83, Woman of the Yr. Pa. divsn. 1983, 85), MLA (Phila. region).

BERZAK, ARLYNE LEVINSON, gerontologist, educator; b. Jersey City, N.J., Mar. 19, 1936; d. Joseph George and Esther (Cohen) Levinson; divorced; children: Jeri Fried Cohen, Caren Fried Pomerantz; m. William Berzak, Sept. 6, 1992. BA, William Paterson Coll., 1968, MEd in Counseling, 1990. Cert. secondary sch. tchr. English, Fine Arts, N.J. Tchr. English Saddle Brook (N.J.) High Sch., 1968-71; pres., mgr. Creative Catering, Clifton, N.J., 1972-84; dir. Federation Apts., Paterson, N.J., 1984-89; exec. dir. Classic Residence by Hyatt, Teaneck, N.J., 1989-94, sr. exec. dir., 1994—; adj. prof. William Paterson Coll., Paterson, N.J., 1990—. Facilitator N.J. Gov.'s Task Force on Housing, 1991-92, 2d Gov.'s Task Force, 1994; active Com. to Develop Curriculum in Gerontology, 1991, Com. to Develop Sr. Living Options Info. Bergen County Coun. on Aging, 1992-94; mem. Teaneck Affordable Housing Com., 1992. Mem. NAFE, B'nai B'rith Women (past pres., mem. South Bergen chpt. 1958-59), Hadassah (life mem.), William Paterson Coll. Alumni Assn., Kappa Delta Pi, Pi Lambda Theta. Office: Classic Residence by Hyatt 655 Pomander Walk Teaneck NJ 07666

BERZINS, ERNA MARIJA, physician; b. Latvia, Nov. 27, 1914; d. Arturs and Anna (Steckenbergs) Meilands; came to U.S., 1951, naturalized, 1956; M.D., Latvian State U., 1940; m. Verners Berzins, Aug. 24, 1935; children—Valdis, Andis. Mem. pediatric faculty Latvian State U., 1940-44; intern Good Samaritan Hosp., Dayton, Ohio, 1951-52; resident in pediatrics Children's Hosp. of Mich., Detroit, 1953-55; practice medicine specialising in pediatrics, Detroit, 1956-60; with ARC, Cleve., 1961-63; physician pediatric outpatient dept. Cleve. Met. Gen. Hosp., 1963-84; asst. prof. emeritus Case-Western Res. U., Cleve., 1985. Mem. AMA, Ohio Med. Assn., Acad. Medicine, No. Ohio Pediatric Soc., Am. Women's Med. Assn., Am. Med. Polit. Action Com. Lutheran. Address: 5460 Friar Cir Cleveland OH 44126-3011

BESCH, BERNICE KATHLEEN, civic volunteer; b. Palmyra, Nebr., Aug. 4, 1924; d. William James and Anna Wilhelmina (Lemmermann) Heather; m. Wayne Leslie Besch, Sept. 11, 1948 (dec. 1986); children: Roger Wayne, Steven Charles, Clark Alan, William Leslie. Cert. in stenography, Lincoln (Nebr.) Sch. Commerce, 1943. Stenographer Allied Dry Forces of Nebr., Lincoln, 1943-45; sec. Calif. Temperance Fedn., San Francisco, 1945; stenographer in Purchasing Dept. U. Nebr., Lincoln, 1946-47, sec. Mech. Engring. Dept., 1947-48. Den mother Cub Scouts of Am. Dodge City, Kans. 1958-59; bd. dirs. and founding mem. Family YMCA, Dodge City, treas., 1966-69, co-chmn. Fund Drives, 65-70; sec. and bd. dirs. United Nat. Assn. USA Chpt. 100, Lincoln, 1979-82; former pres. United Presbyn. Women, First Presbyn. Ch., Dodge City, Kansas, 1968-70, ch. sch. tchr., 1960-65, deacon, 1965-68, elder, 1969-71, leader of Women's Cir., 1966-68; former ch. sch. supr. Fourth Presbyn. Ch., Lincoln, 1973-79; mem. search com., 1974-75, chmn. Diamond Jubilee Com., 1982-83, elder, 1991—; sec. United Presbyn. Women, Lincoln, 1989-93, pres. 1981-83, former coordinator Mission Interpretation, 1976-78; mem. Homestead Presbytery, co-chmn. peacemaking strategy team, 1983-89, Hunger Action Enabler, 1992—; mem. Soc. Justice and Peacemaking Com., 1989—, Homestead Presbyn. Hunger Action Enabler, 1992—, Presbyn. adv. for Mid. East, Cen. Am., Reverse Arms Race, 1983-92, Hunger, 1992—, peace and hunger coord. Homestead Presbyn. Women, 1989-93; charter mem. Better World Soc., 1988. Recipient Svc. award Family YMCA, Dodge City, 1968, Cert. of Appreciation, 4th Presbyn. Ch., Lincoln, 1983; named Dedicated Svc. (with husband) 47th Troop Carrier Squadron/313 Troop Carrier Group, 1981. Mem. Lincoln Amateur Radio Club, UNA/USA chpt. 100, Greenpeace, Nat. Wildlife Fedn., Union of Concerned Scientists, Nature Conservancy, Nat. Pks. and Conservation Assn. Democrat.

BESCOS, JONI, legal secretary, consultant; b. Monterey Park, Calif., Aug. 22, 1936; d. John Patrick and Shirley Jane (Rich) Meyers; m. Frank Perona Bescos, Aug. 18, 1962 (div. Sep. 1986); children: Glenn, Donald, Jeanine. MA in Music Edn., Calif. State U., 1985. Cert. profl. legal sec. Legal sec. Miller, Hiersche, Martens & Hayward, Dallas, 1987-89; exec. asst. Wyndham Hotels and Resorts, Dallas, 1989-90; legal sec. Strasburger & Price, Dallas, 1990—; musical cons. Sweet Adelines Internat., Tulsa, 1963—; owner J.B. Music, Inc., Dallas, 1981—. Author: How to Arrange Barbership Harmony, 1970, 2d Edition, 1988. Mem. Am. Soc. Composers, Authors and Pubs., Dallas Assn. Legal Secs. (treas. 1991-92, 94—), Sweet Adelines Internat. (bd. dirs. 1966-72, pres. The Coronet Club 1993—, Internat. Champion Coronet Club award 1984). Republican. Office: Strasburger & Price 901 Main St Ste 4500 Dallas TX 75202-3755

BESHUR, JACQUELINE E., animal training consultant; b. Portland, Oreg., May 8, 1948; d. Charles Daniel and Mildred (Domreis) Beshears. BA, UCLA, 1970; MBA, Claremont Grad. Sch., 1980; postgrad., City U., Seattle, 1989-90. Dir. and founder L.A. Ctr. for Photog. Studies, 1972-75; precious gem distbr. Douglas Group Holdings, Australia, 1976-78; small bus. owner Janitorial/Home Maintenance, Seattle, 1981-90; cons. BeSure Tng., Carnation, Wash. Author: Good Intentions Are Not Good Enough, 1992. Mem. Wash. Pot-bellied Pig Assn. (sec. 1992), Nature Conservancy, Wash. Wilderness Coalition, Issaquah Alps Club, Bridges for Peace. Republican. Fundamentalist. Office: BeSure Tng PO Box 225 Carnation WA 98014-0225

BEST, ALYNDA KAY, emergency physicians service administrator; b. Amarillo, Tex., June 20, 1947; d. William Otho and Ruby Jewel (Hamby) Mauldin; m. Paul Wesley Best, Mar. 31, 1978; children: Brett Allison, Trevor William. BA, Tex. Tech. U., 1969; MBA, U. Tex. of Perian Basin, Odessa, 1983. Asst. bus. mgr. Med. Arts Clinic, Lubbock, Tex., 1969-72; fin. supr. Tex. Dept. Human Resources, Lubbock, 1972-79; pvt. practice bus. dir. Odessa, 1979-87; corp. mgr. Midland (Tex.) Emergency Physicians, 1987—. Co-author: (pamphlet) Midland Municipal Water Supply, 1992. Treas. LWV, Odessa/Midland, 1980-82, chmn. nat. res. Midland 1990-93; treas. Hospice of Odessa, 1983-85, Santa Rita PTA, Midland, 1990-92; dir. outreach First Christian Ch., Midland, 1991-93; mem. yearbook com. Midland/Odessa Symphony, 1994; leader Girl Scouts/Boy Scouts, 1986-94; active Midland Cmty. Theatre. Mem. AAUW, Am. Med. Soc., Midland Med. Assn. (excursion coord. 1994-95), Tex. Med. Assn. Aux. (state dist. rep.).

BEST, SHARON LOUISE PECKHAM, college administrator; b. Elmira, N.Y., Aug. 4, 1940; d. Paul Arthur and Beatrice L. (Hunter) Peckham; m. Willard C. Best, Sept. 3, 1961; children: Meryl Elizabeth, Kevin Hunter. BA cum laude, William Smith Coll., 1977. Acting dir. alumnae relations William Smith Coll., Geneva, N.Y., 1976-77; assoc. dir. devel. Hobart & William Smith Colls., Geneva, 1977, dir. devel., 1978-81, exec. dir. devel., 1981-87, v.p. for devel., 1988—; cons. Nazareth Coll., Rochester, N.Y., 1985. Active Ontario County (N.Y.) rep. com., 1968-78, Geneva Hist. Soc., 1975-80; active Geneva Concerts, Inc., 1965—, bd. dirs. 1974-82, pres., 1976-78. Recipient Coun. on Advancement and Support of Edn. award capital fundraising USX Found., 1988. Mem. Coun. for Advancement and Support Edn. (bd. trustees Mid-Atlantic Dist. II 1987-89, Gold Medal-Decade Improvement in Fund Raising 1987, Circle of Excellence in Ednl. Fund Raising award 1994), Nat. Soc. Fund Raising Execs., LWV, Phi Beta Kappa, Phi Sigma Iota. Presbyterian. Club: Geneva Country. Home: 859 S Main St Geneva NY 14456-3205 Office: Hobart & William Smith Colls Geneva NY 14456-3397

BEST, SUSAN MARIE, artist, educator; b. Peoria, Ill., July 4, 1949; d. Robert H. and Shirley (Critchlow) Coyle; m. David G. Best, Sept. 12, 1970 (div. May 1987); children: Timothy, Molly, Abby, George. BPhar, U. Ill., Chgo., 1972; MA in Fine Arts, Ill. State U., Normal, 1988, MFA, 1991. Grad. pharmacist S&C Drugs, Peoria, 1972, Indian Hosp., Pine Ridge, S.D., 1974-76; instr. art Ill. State U., Normal, 1988-91, Bradley U., Peoria, 1992-93, Ill. Ctrl. Coll., Peoria, 1991-93; artist, 1970—; gallery artist Struve Gallery, Chgo., 1991-93. Bd. dirs. St. Thomas Sch., Peoria, 1980-83, Amateur Mus. Club, Peoria, 1982-84; bd. dirs. Peoria Art Guild, 1994—. Recipient various awards for art; Ill. State U. fellow, 1988-91. Mem. AAUP, NOW, Artists Coalition of Ctrl. Ill. (treas.), Chgo. Artists Coalition, Lakeview Art Mus., Sun Found. Democrat. Studio: 934 S 2d St Chillicothe IL 61523

BESTEHORN, UTE WILTRUD, retired librarian; b. Cologne, Germany, Nov. 6, 1930; came to U.S., 1930; d. Henry Hugo and Wiltrud Lucie (Vincentz) B. BA, U. Cin., 1954, BEd, 1955, MEd, 1958; MS in Library Sci., Western Res. U. (now Case-Western Res. U.), 1961. Tchr. Cutter Jr. High Sch., Cin., 1955-57; tchr., supr. libr. Felicity (Ohio) Franklin Sr. High Sch., 1959-60; with libr. sci. dept. Pub. Libr. Cin. and Hamilton County, 1961-78, with libr. info. desk, 1978-91; ret., 1991; textbook selection com., Felicity-Franklin Sr. High Sch., 1959-60; supr. Health Alcove Sci. Dept. and annual health lectures, Cin. Pub. Library, 1972-77. Book reviewer Library Jour., 1972-77; author and inventor Rainbow 40 marble game, 1971, Condominium game, 1976; patentee indexed packaging and stacking device, 1973, mobile packaging and stacking device, 1974. Mem. Clifton Town Meeting, 1988—; mem. Bookfest 90 com. Pub. Libr. Cin. and Hamilton County. Recipient Cert. of Merit and Appreciation Pub. Library of Cin., 1986. Mem. Cin. Chpt. Spl. Libraries Assn. (archivist 1963-64, 65-70, editor Queen City Gazette bull. 1964-69), Pub. Library Staff Assn. (exec. bd., activities com. 1965, welfare com. 1966, recipient Golden Book 25 yr. service pin, 1986), Friends of the Library, Greater Cin. Calligraphers Guild (reviewer New Letters pub. 1986-88), Delta Phi Alpha (nat. German hon. 1951). Republican. Mem. United Ch. of Christ. Home: 3330 Morrison Ave Cincinnati OH 45220-1440

BETANZOS, AMALIA V., social services administrator; b. N.Y.C., July 23, 1928; d. Severino Migues and Margarita (Hassel) Carcasin; m. Odon Betanzos, Mar. 21, 1953; 1 child, Manuel. BA, NYU, 1950, postgrad. Administrv. coord. Summer in the City Program, N.Y.C., 1966-68; chief exec. officer, administr. P.R. Community Devel. Project, N.Y.C., 1968-70; spl. asst. to Mayor for housing, neighborhood affairs, social svcs. N.Y.C., 1970; deputy administr., commr. Housing & Devel. Administrn. of City of N.Y., 1970-72; exec. sec. to Mayor of N.Y.C., 1972; commr. youth svcs., exec. dir. youth bd. Human Resources Administrn.-Youth Svcs. Agency, N.Y.C., 1972-73; commr. N.Y.C. Housing Authority, 1973-78; pres., chief exec. officer Wildcat Svc. Corp., N.Y.C., 1978—; lectr. Lehman Coll., Bronx, N.Y., 1960-70; mem.-at-large N.Y.C. Bd. Edn. Tchrs. Retirement Bd., 1988-90; mem. N.Y.C. Bd. Edn., 1987-90; bd. dirs. Nat. P.R. Coalition, Inc., Washington. Edit. adv. com. El Diario/La Prensa. Trustee Cath. Charities, N.Y.C., St. Barnabas Hosp., P.R. Community Found., Fund for the City of N.Y., Pub. Edn. Assn.; mem. N.Y.C. Outward Bound Ctr., Alcoholism Coun. Greater N.Y., The Children's Fund, Citizens Union of the City of N.Y., Women's Forum, Inc., Citizens Commn. on AIDS, Charter Revision Commn. '82-'83, '87-'89, N.Y.C. Private Industry Coun., Com. Integrity in Govt., N.Y.C. Loft Bd., numerous others; bd. dirs. Bklyn. Navy Yard, Community Service Soc., Correctional Soc. N.Y., N.Y. Urban League, Vera Inst. Justice, Drug Abuse Coun., P.R. Community Devel. Project, St. Lukes Hosp., Fortune Soc.; chairperson Nat. P.R. Coalition, Inc., Social Devel. Commn. Archdiocese of N.Y., N.Y.C. Rent Guidelines Bd.; pres. Manhattan Valley Spanish Civic Assn., Nat. Assn. P.R. Civil Rights, N.Y.S. Industries for Handicapped; ptnr. N.Y.C. Partnership; sec. bd. overseers Ctr. New Social Rsch.; steering com. Nat. Urban Coalition; mem. adv. bd. Cath. Interracial Coun. of N.Y., Inc., Bureau Community Edn., Consumer Protection N.Y. Bar Assn.; mem. Mayor's adv. com. Police Mgmt. & Personnel Policy; mem. many other adv. bds., coms., couns. Recipient Pub. Edn. award Pub. Edn. Assn., 1990, Golden Palm award INTAR, 1990, Las Casas award NE Pastora Coun., 1982; named Woman of the Yr. Nat. Coun. P.R. Women, 993. Democrat. Roman Catholic. Home: 125 Queen St Staten Island NY 10314-5350 Office: Wildcat Service Corporation 161 Hudson St New York NY 10013-2101

BETHEL, DIANA GONZALEZ, publishing executive; b. Havana, Cuba, Mar. 28, 1937; came to the U.S., 1960; widowed; one child. Student, Cuban-Am. Inst., Havana, 1958, U. Miami. Gen. mgr. WRHC Radio; chief researcher Latin Am. Report, Washington; exec. asst. to pub. affairs officer U.S. Info. Agy., Miami; exec. asst. to press attache-pub. affairs officer Am. Embassy, Havana; pres., pub. Aboard Publs., Coral Gables, Fla., 1976—. Mem. Citizen Adv. Coun. on Status of Women, 1969-76; apptd. to Dade County Health Task Force; active Nat. Adv. Com. for Re-election of Pres. Mem. Ponce Assn., Coral Gables C. of C., Nat. Press Club, Internat. Advt. Assn., Coral Gables Country Club. Office: North South Net Inc 100 Almeria Ave Ste 220 Coral Gables FL 33134-6027

BETHEL, PAULETTE MARTINEZ, military officer; b. New Orleans, Sept. 24, 1952; d. Ernest and Mary Ann (Ferdinand) Carrie; m. Charles Ruffin Burchell, Mar. 3, 1973 (div. 1980); m. Ralph Bethel, Mar. 18, 1984; children: Ralph Alvin, Wendy Taiwai, Kimberly Yvonne, Marc Alexander. BS, La. State U., Baton Rouge, 1977; MPA, U. of The Philippines, 1986. Commd. 2d lt. USAF, 1980, advanced through grades to Maj.; chief combat ops. support flight USAF, Lackland AFB, Tex., 1993—; mem. Lackland AFB Speaker's Bur. Mentor for teenage girls at high risk for pregnancy with Dayton (Ohio) City Pub. Sch. Sys., 1986-90, Edgewood Ind. Sch. Dist., San Antonio, 1991-92. Mem. NAFE, Women's Officer's Assn., Soc. of Logistics Engrs., Alpha Kappa Alpha. Home: 11810 Radcliff Ct San Antonio TX 78253-5951

BETHKE, PATRICIA ANN, accountant; b. Ft. Benning, Ga., Feb. 5, 1964; d. James Monroe Jr. and Carol Ann (Cardillo) Nichols; m. James David Bethke, July 28, 1990. BBA, North Ga. Coll., 1986. CPA, Tex. Sr. auditor I Hosp. Corp. Am., Nashville, 1986-90; regional asst. contr. St. Mary of the Plains Hosp., Lubbock, Tex., 1990-91; asst. contr., materiels mgr. South Park Med. Ctr., Lubbock, 1991-94; sr. acct. Austin (Tex.) Diagnostic Med. Ctr., 1995—. Home: 12810 Steeple Chase Dr Austin TX 78729-7360

BETHUNE, IVY, actress; b. Sevastopol, Russia, June 1, 1918; d. Irving and Sonia (Sobol) Vigder; m. William Bethune, Mar. 7, 1939 (dec. 1950); 1 child, Zina; m. Stuart Gage Lancaster, Dec. 28, 1971. BA, Bklyn. Coll., 1940. Pvt. dramatic coach, Hollywood, Calif., 1964-92. Actress (TV) as Miss Tuttle in Father Murphy, 1980-82, Abigail in General Hosp., 1982-83; guest star in Barney Miller, 1980, Chips, 1982, Star Trek: The Nex Generation, 1986, (Films) Wrong Is Right, 1986, Back to the Future, 1987, (plays) Rhinoceros, 1960, Prisoner of 2nd Ave, 1975, all the Way Home, 1987, Cemetary Club, 1990. Activist Last Chance for Animals, L.A., 1985, Actors and Others for Animals, L.A., 1985. Recipient Robby award for part of Mrs. Van Daan in Diary of Anne Frank, Data Boy Mag., 1980, Drama Logue awards, 1982, 91. Mem. Actors Equity Assn., Screen Actors Guild, Am. fedn. TV and Radio Artists.

BETHUNE, ZINA, actress, dancer, singer, choreographer; b. N.Y., Feb. 17, 1950; d. William Charles and Ivy (Vigder) B.; m. Sean Feeley, Dec. 27, 1975. Grad. high sch., N.Y.C. Artistic dir., choreographer, performer Bethune Theatredanse, L.A., 1980—. Actress TV soap opera The Guiding Light, 1956, TV series The Nurses, 1964-67, film Who's That Knocking at My Door, 1969, Nutcracker: Money, Madness, Murder, 1987; dancer Broadway show Most Happy Fella, Nutcracker, N.Y.C., 1957, N.Y.C. Ballet, 1965-69, Royal Danish Symphony, Arhus, Denmark, 1979; singer, actress (stage) Carnival, Chgo., 1967; dancer, singer (stage) Sweet Charity, 1969-70; choreographer (stage) The Trials of Saint Joan, 1986, Mind's Eye-Year 2031, 1988; dance, choreograher (stage, video) The Rose, 1987; dir., choreographer (video) Cradle of Fire, 1988; dir., choreographer (stage) Cradle of Fire, 1993; head sound technician, assoc. prodr. Paradigm Film, N.Y.C.; spl. invitation to teach and perform by the govt. of China; spl. invitation to dance at the White House, 1989; starring role (Broadway show) Grand Hotel-The Musical, 1991. Dance tchr. for disabled children Dance Outreach, L.A., 1983—. Recipient 2 citation awards Mayor of N.Y.C., 1965-69, 2 proclamation awards and an award of commendation from each Mayor of L.A., 1985-94, Cece Robinson's Humanitarian award L.A., 1986, Cmty. Svc. award Gov.'s Com. for Employment of Handicapped, Media Access award, awards of commendation from Pres. Reagan, Pres. Bush, Pres. Clinton. Mem. SAG, AFTRA, Actors Equity Assn. Democrat. Office: Bethune Theatredanse 8033 W Sunset Blvd Ste 221 Los Angeles CA 90046-2427

BETLACH, MARY CAROLYN, biochemist, molecular biologist; b. Madison, Wis., June 12, 1945; d. William Thompson Stafford and Carolyn Jesse Gillette McCormick; m. Charles J. Betlach, Nov. 14, 1970 (div. 1978); children: John F., Melanie Carolyn. Student, U. Wis., 1963-68; PhD, U. Calif., San Francisco, 1992. Staff rsch. assoc. dept. pathology and biochemistry U. Wis., Madison, 1967-69; staff rsch. assoc. dept. biol. scis. U. Calif., Santa Barbara, 1969-70; staff rsch. assoc. dept. pediatrics U. Calif., San Francisco, 1970-72, staff rsch. assoc. dept. microbiology/biochemistry, 1972-83, rsch. specialist dept. biochemistry, 1983-93; sr. scientist Parnassus Pharms., Alameda, Calif., 1993—; adj. asst. prof. dept. pharm. chemistry, U. Calif., San Francisco, 1993—; mem. various grant rev. panels. Contbr. chpts. to books, articles to Gene, Microbiology, Nucleic Acids Rsch., Biochemistry, Jour. Bacteriology, others. Mem. AAAS, Biophys. Soc., Am. Soc. for Microbiology.

BETTERIDGE, FRANCES CARPENTER, retired lawyer, mediator; b. Rutherford, N.J., Aug. 25, 1921; d. James Dunton and Emily (Atkinson) Carpenter; m. Albert Edwin Betteridge, Feb. 5, 1949 (div. 1975); children: Anne, Albert Edwin, James, Peter. A.B., Mt. Holyoke Coll., 1942; J.D., N.Y. Law Sch., 1978. Bar: Conn. 1979, Ariz. 1982. Technician in charge blood banks Roosevelt Hosp., N.Y.C. and Mountainside Hosp., Montclair, N.J., 1943-49; substitute tchr. Greenwich High Sch. (Conn.), 1978-79; intern and asst. to labor contracts office Town of Greenwich, 1979-80; vol. referee Pima County Juvenile Ct., Tucson, 1981-85, judge Pro Tempore Pima County Justice Cts., 1988-91; sole practice immigration law, Tucson, 1982-87; commr. Juvenile Ct., Pima County Superior Ct., Tucson, 1985-87; hearing officer Small Claims Ct., Pima County Justice Cts., Tucson, 1982; mediator Family Crisis Svc., Tucson, 1982-85. Pres. High Sch. PTA, Greenwich, 1970, PTA Council, 1971; mem. Greenwich Bd. Edn., 1971-76, sec., 1973-76; com. chmn. LWV Tucson, 1981, bd. dirs., 1984-85; bd. dirs., sec. Let The Sun Shine Inc., Tucson, 1981—; vol. referee Pima County Superior Ct., 1981-85; lectr. Tucson Mus. Art, 1994—; part time program dir. Elderhostel, Oaxaca, Mex., 1995. Mem. ABA, Conn. Bar Assn., Ariz. Bar Assn., Pima County Bar Assn., Ariz. Women Lawyers Assn., Point o'Woods Club. Republican. Congregationalist. Avocation: imports folk art from Oaxaca, Mex. Home and Office: 5320 N Campbell Ave Tucson AZ 85718-4908

BETTIKOFER, ROSEMARY ELIZABETH, computer scientist; b. Pitts., Feb. 21, 1947; d. William W. and Elizabeth M. (Hanus) Rupert; m. John E. Bettikofer, Jan. 22, 1971 (div. Jan. 1981); children: Gina M., Teresa M. Student, U. Vienna, Austria, 1963-64; cert., Goethe Inst., Brannenberg-Degerndorf, Germany, 1964; BA in English, Hiram Coll., 1965; AS, Pa. State U., New Kensington, 1985. Reservationist United Airlines, Rocky River, Ohio, 1969-70; counselor Children's Aid Soc., Cleve., 1970-71, Childrens Home Denver, 1971-72; reservationist, agt. Aspen Airways, Denver, 1972; mgr. Children's Nursery, Bamberg, Germany, 1971-73; instr. Pa. State U., 1984-85; programmer Bell Labs., Holmdel, N.J., 1985-88; tech. saleswoman Bell Labs., Lincroft, N.J., 1988-91, project mgr., 1991—; mem. tng. coun. AT&T Easy Link Svcs., Lincroft, 1992—. Counselor, bd. dirs. Displaced Homemakers, New Kensington, 1984-85; counselor Ft. Monmouth Youth Group, Eatontown, N.J., 1986—; v.p., sec., pres. Ft. Monmouth Swim Team, 1986—; elder, deacon Presbyn. Ch. at Sherwsbury, N.J., 1988—. Mem. AT&T Facilitators Orgn. (quality improvement facilitator 1985-87). Republican. Home: 105 Alameda Ct Shrewsbury NJ 07702 Office: AT&T LZ 1C 216 307 Middletown-Lincroft Rd Lincroft NJ 07738-1526

BETTIN, JANENE EDNA, real estate broker; b. Schaller, Iowa, Nov. 11, 1943; d. Robert A. and Edna (Harris) Bath; m. Thomas L. Bettin, June 20, 1964; 1 child, Christopher. Student U. No. Iowa, 1961; BS, Tex. A&I U., 1965. Grad. Realtors Inst.; cert. residential specialist, residential brokerage mgr. Tchr. high sch., Corpus Christi, Tex., 1965-70; tchr. Village Acad., Mt. Lebanon, Pa., 1973-76; broker, assoc. Re/Max Metro Properties, Inc., Denver, 1977-86; broker, br. mgr. Perry & Butler, Littleton, Colo., 1986-89; broker Van Schaack Residential Realty, Inc., 1989; broker, owner Prime Properties, Englewood, Colo., 1989-94, Moore & Co., Denver, 1994—. Chmn. Blood Bank, South Suburban Bd. Realtors, 1980, chmn. Schs. Com., 1980; pres. South Suburban Bd. Realtors, 1985-86. Bd. dirs., officer Bristol Cove Homeowners Assn., Littleton, Colo., 1983; officer, treas. Arapahoe Youth League-Warriors, 1981. Mem. Realtors Nat. Mktg. Inst., Womens Coun. Realtors (pres. 1982-83), Colo. Assn. Realtors (instr. 1981—, dir. 1984, v.p. 1987), Cert. Residential Specialists (pres. Colo. chpt. 1984, nat. instr. 1985-86), Cert. Residential Brokerage Mgrs. (instr. 1986-92), Omega Tau Rho. Republican. Methodist. Club: Mt. Lebanon Newcomers (pres. 1973-74). Home: 7540 S Cove Cir Littleton CO 80122-3332

BETTINGER, JUDITH PEDERSEN, soprano, voice educator; b. Omaha; d. Paul David and Lilly Pedersen; m. Wilmer Clark Bettinger; 1 child, Christine. Diploma, London Opera Centre, 1968; BA magna cum laude, St. Olaf Coll., 1970; MusM with honors, Ind. U., 1972; student, Acad. Vocal Arts, Phila., 1984-85; studied with Dalton Baldwin, Giorgio Tozzi, Gary Magby, R. Grooters, S. Lee, V. MacWatters, N. Howlett, D. Hoiness. Artistic dir., founder Brandywine Opera Connection; artist in residence arts in edn. program Del. Divsn. of Arts, 1992-96; pvt. instr. voice, Wilmington, Del., 1980—; instr. music Del. Tech. and C.C., Dover, 1977-78, Salem C.C., Penn Grove, N.J., 1978-79; mem. mgmt. Am. Performing Artists, Ltd. Prin. singer operas including A Masked Ball, 1972, Myshkin, 1975 (Peabody award), Sleeping Beauty, 1977, Little Red Riding Hood, 1984, Albert Herring, 1985, La Boheme, 1985, The Telephone, 1990; operettas include The Mikado, 1974, HMS Pinafore, 1978, The Gondoliers, 1987, Pirates of Penzance, 1991, also others; musicals include Oklahoma 1973, Fiddler on the Roof, 1974, Kismet, 1975, Kiss Me Kate, 1976, also others; numerous art song recitals and recs. Winner Am. Opera Auditions, 1984. Mem. Nat. Assn. Tchrs. of Singing, Music Tchrs. Nat. Assn. (cert.), Del. State Music Tchrs. Assn. (cert.), Skating Club of Wilmington (historian 1980-90). Democrat. Lutheran. Home: 1007 Jeffrey Rd Wilmington DE 19810-3007

BETTS, BARBARA STOKE, artist, educator; b. Arlington, Mass., Apr. 19, 1924; d. Stuart and Barbara Lillian (Johnstone) Stoke; m. James William Betts, July 28, 1951; 1 child, Barbara Susan (dec.). BA, Mt. Holyoke Coll., 1946; MA, Columbia U., 1948. Cert. tchr., N.Y., Calif., Hawaii. Art tchr. Walton (N.Y.) Union Schs., 1947-48, Presidio Hill Sch., San Francisco, 1949-51; free-lance artist San Francisco, 1951; art tchr. Honolulu Acad. Arts, summer 1952, 59, 63, 85, spring 61, 64; libr. aide art rm. Libr. of Hawaii, Honolulu, 1959; art tchr. Hanahauoli Sch., Honolulu, 1961-62, Hawaii State Dept. Edn., Honolulu, 1958-59, 64-84; owner Ho'olaule'a Designs, Honolulu, 1973—. Illustrator: Cathedral Cooks, 1964, In Due Season, 1986; exhibited in Hawaii Pavilion Expo '90, Osaka, Japan, State Found. of Culture and Arts, group shows since 1964. Mem. Hawaii Watercolor Soc. (newsletter editor 1986-90), Nat. League Am. Pen Women (art chmn. 1990-92, sec. 1992-94), Honolulu Printmakers (dir. 1986, 87), Assn. Hawaii Artists, Honolulu Printmaking Workshop. Republican. Episcopalian. Home: 1520 Ward Ave Apt 203 Honolulu HI 96822-3550

BETTS, DIANNE CONNALLY, economist; b. Tyler, Tex., Sept. 23, 1948; d. William Isaac and Martine (Underwood) Connally; m. Floyd Galloway Betts Jr., Feb. 14, 1973. BA in History, So. Meth. U., 1976, MA in History, 1978; MA in Econ., U. Chgo., 1986; PhD in Econ., U. Tex., 1991. Affiliated scholar Inst. for Rsch. on Women and Gender/Stanford U., 1993—; mem. women studies coun. So. Meth. U., 1993-94, Fulbright campus interviewing com. mem. 1992-93, pub. rels. and devel. liaison dept. econ., 1990-92, faculty mentor U. honors first year mentoring program,adj. asst. prof. dept. econ. and history So. Meth. U., 1992—, vis. asst. prof. 1990-92, faculty, Oxford, summer 1991-93, adj. instr. dept. history, 1989-90, adj. instr. dept. econ., 1985-89, teaching asst. dept. history, spring 1980; lectr. dept. polit. economy U. Tex., Dallas, summer 1988. Author: Crisis on the Rio Grande: Poverty, Unemployment, and Economic Development on the Texas-Mexico Border, 1994, Historical Perspecitves on the American Economy: Selected Readings, 1995; contbr. articles to profl. jours. Rsch. Planning grant NSF, 1992; recipient Marguereta Deschner Teaching award, 1991; Humanities and Scis. Merit scholar, 1978. Mem. Am. Econ. Assn., Am. History Assn., Econ. History Assn., Cliometric Soc., Social Sci. History Assn., N.Am. Conf. on British Studies, Nat. Coun. for Rsch. on Women (affiliate), Omicron Delta Epsilon, Phi Alpha Theta. Home: 6267 Revere Pl Dallas TX 75214 Office: Smith Barney 500 N Akard # 3900 Dallas TX 75201

BETTS, NORA LINDEN, kennel owner; b. Toledo, July 31, 1961; d. Bryan Jesse and Patricia Lynn (Sullivan) Wilkerson; m. Jeffrey Allen Betts, Mar. 15, 1985. Student, Davis Bus. Coll., 1980-81, 81-83, Cornell U., 1991. Cert. small animal dietitian/nutritionist, cert. animal behaviorist/psychologist. Kennel supr. Karnik Inn of Toledo, Holland, Ohio, 1989-90; vet. technician Trilby Animal Hosp., Toledo, 1989-90; kennel mgr. Pampered Pet Petel, Erie, Mich., 1983-89, kennel owner, 1990—. Contbr. articles to profl. newsletters. Speaker in field Bedford Pub. Schs., Lambertville, Mich., 1989, 90, 91, 92, Monroe (Mich.) County Libr. System, 1992; active Nat. Audubon Soc., 1993—, Defenders of Wildlife, 1991—, World Wildlife Fund, 1992—, Maumee Valley Save-A-Pet, 1992—. Mem. ASPCA, Nat. Humane Edn. Assn., People for the Ethical Treatment of Animals, Am. Boarding Kennels Assn. (cert. kennel technician, cons. 1990—), Nat. Fedn. Ind. Bus., Nat. Dog Groomers Assn., Toledo Vet. Med. Assn., Humane Soc. Monroe. Methodist. Office: Pampered Pet Petel 7190 Dixie Hwy Erie MI 48133-9660

BETZER, SUSAN ELIZABETH BEERS, family physician, geriatrician; b. Evanston, Ill., Aug. 24, 1943; d. Thomas Moulding and Mary Ella (Waidner) Beers; m. Peter Robin Betzer, June 18, 1965; children: Sarah Elizabeth, Katherine Hannah. AB in Biol. Scis. magna cum, Mount Holyoke Coll., 1965; PhD in Oceanography, U. R.I., 1972; MD, U. Miami, 1978. Diplomate Am. Bd. Family Practice, Am. Bd. Geriatrics. Rsch. assoc. dept. marine sci. U. South Fla., St. Petersburg, 1973-74, rsch. scholar, scientist, 1975-76; resident in family practice Bayfront Med. Ctr., St. Petersburg, 1978-81; pvt. practice St. Petersburg, 1982—; clin. asst. prof. dept. family medicine U. South Fla., Tampa, 1982—; consulting physician Fed. Employee Health Clinic, Honolulu, 1981-82. Contbr. articles to profl. jours. Mem. sch. adv. com. 16th St. Mid. Sch., St. Petersburg, 1993—; bd. dirs. Fla. Orch., Tampa, 1983-86, 88—, pres., 1985-86, mem. exec. com., 1988—, founder, chair audience devel. com., St. Petersburg, 1990-94; bd. dirs. Suncoast Ctr. Cmty. Mental Health, St. Petersburg, 1992-93; trustee Bayfront Med. Ctr., Bayfront Health Svcs., 1992—, vice chair, 1993—. Recipient Golden Baton award St. Petersburg Fla. Orch. Guild, 1994; named Woman of Distinction, Suncoast coun. Girl Scouts U.S., 1994. Mem. Am. Acad. Family Physicians (Mead Johnson award 1980), Am. Med. Women's Assn., Fla. Acad. Family Physicians, Mount Holyoke Alumnae Assn. (vol. fund raiser, mem. alumnae honors rsch. com. 1988-91), Phi Beta Kappa. Home: 1830 7th St N Saint Petersburg FL 33704 Office: 461 7th Ave S Saint Petersburg FL 33701

BEU, MARJORIE JANET, music director; b. Elgin, Ill., Nov. 22, 1921; d. Herman Henry and Hattie Belle (Beverly) B. MusB, Am. Conservatory Music, 1949; B Musical Ed, 1949, M in Musical Ed., 1953; advanced cert. No. Ill. U., 1969; DEd, U. Sarasota, 1979. Music tchr. Sch. Dist. 21, Wheeling, Ill., 1961-64; music and fine arts coord., 1964-68, asst. supt. instrn., 1968-79; min. of music United Meth. Ch., Sun City Center, Fla., 1980—; dir. Sun City Ctr. Kings Point Community Chorus, 1984-89; pres. Council Study and Devel. Ednl. Resources, 1971-79. Pres., Wheeling Community Concerts Assn.; dir. Community Chorus; pres. Sun City Center Concert Series. Mem. NEA, Am. Guild Organists and Choir Dirs., Music Educators Nat. Conf., Assn. Supervision and Curriculum Devel., Ill. Edn. Assn., Ill. Council Gifted, No. Ill. Assn. Ednl. Research, Evaluation and Devel. (pres.), Mu Phi Epsilon, Phi Delta Kappa (sec. N.W. Suburban Cook County chpt.), Kappa Delta Pi (pres. also counselor alumni com.). Home: 610 Ft Duquesna Dr Sun City Ctr FL 33573-5156

BEUERLEIN, SHEILA DAVIS, marketing professional; b. Great Falls, Mont., Aug. 10, 1962; d. Mark Keith Davis and Mary Lynn (Steele) McSkimming; m. David Lewis Beuerlein, Nov. 5, 1988. BS in Aerospace Engring., Tex. A & M U., 1985; MBA, U. Tex., Austin, 1993. Engr. Gen. Dynamics, Ft. Worth, 1985-88, sr. engr., 1988-91; product dir. Johnson & Johnson Med., Inc., Arlington, Tex., 1993—; adv. bd. mem. AIAA, Ft. Worth, 1987-90. Co-author: Aerospace Design Engineers Guide, 1987; contbg. author: (conf. procs.) Soc. Women Engrs., 1987. Vol. Ft. Worth (Tex.) Children's Med. Ctr., 1990-91. Winner Deloitte & Touche Consulting Challenge, Deloitte & Touche Mgmt. Consulting, Dallas, 1992. Mem. Innovation Mgmt. Assn. (v.p. 1992-93). Roman Catholic. Office: Johnson & Johnson Med Inc PO Box 90130 Arlington TX 76004-3130

BEUGEN, JOAN BETH, communications company executive; b. Chgo., Mar. 9, 1943; d. Leslie and Janet (Glick) Caplan; B.S. in Speech, Northwestern U., 1965; m. Sheldon Howard Beugen, July 16, 1967. Founder, prin., pres. The Creative Establishment, Inc., Chgo., N.Y.C., San Francisco and Los Angeles, 1969-87, founder, pres. Cresta Communications Inc., Chgo. 1988—; speaker on entrepreneurship for women. Del., White House Conf. on Small Bus., 1979; vice-chmn. Ill. Del. to White House Conf., 1979; trustee Mt. Sinai Hosp. Med. Ctr.; bd. dirs. Chgo. Network; bd. dirs. Chgoland Enterprise Ctr. Recipient YWCA Leadership award, 1985; named Entrepreneur of Yr., Women in Bus. Mem. Nat. Assn. Women Bus. Owners (pres. Chgo. chpt. 1979), Ill. Women's Agenda, Chgo. Assn. Commerce and Industry, Midwest Soc. Profl. Cons., Chgo. Audio-Visual Producers Assn., Chgo. Film Council, Women in Film, Com. of 200, Nat. Women's Forum, Overseas Edn. Fund Women in Bus. Com. Contbr. articles in field to profl. jours. Office: The Cresta Group 1050 N State St # 2 Chicago IL 60610

BEVAN, RUTH ELIZABETH, systems programmer; b. Ebbw Vale, Gt. Britian; d. Roy and Eunice (Francis) B. BS in Computer Sci./Physics, Norfolk State U., 1985; MS in Theoretical Physics, Coll. of William and Mary, 1987. Engr. Sharebase, Inc., Los Gatos, Calif., 1987-89; sr. engr. Tandem Computers, Cupertino, Calif., 1989-91, Ford Motor Co., Dearborn, Mich., 1991-93; engr. Warner Lambert/Parke Davis, Ann Arbor, Mich., 1993—; career devel. com. Parke Davis, Ann Arbor, 1993—; cons. Labsoft, Inc., London, Ont., Can., 1982-85, bd. dirs. Mem. NOW, NAFE, Sierra Club, Sigma Tau Delta (English scholarship 1985), Alpha Kappa Mu, Beta Kappa Chi. Home: 515 W Liberty Ann Arbor MI 48103 Office: Parke Davis Rsch 2800 Plymouth Rd Ann Arbor MI 48105

BEVERLEY, CORDIA LUVONNE, gastroenterologist; b. Jamaica, W.I., Oct. 19, 1950; d. Hurdley Aston and Joyce Ruby (Baker) B.; B.A., Hunter Coll., 1971; M.D., N.Y. U., 1975. Diplomate Am. Bd. Gastroenterology, Am. Bd. Internal Medicine. Intern, Columbia U., Harlem Hosp. Center, N.Y.C., 1975-76, resident in medicine, 1976-78; clin. fellow div. gastroenterology N.Y. Hosp./Cornell U. Med. Coll., N.Y.C., 1979-82; asst. physician Rockefeller U. Hosp., N.Y.C., 1978-81. Nat. Inst. Alcohol Abuse and Alcoholism postdoctoral fellow, 1980-82. Mem. Women's Med. Assn. N.Y.C. Office: 1085 Park Ave New York NY 10128-1180

BEVERLY, BETTY MOORE, counselor; b. Clarksville, Va., Oct. 4, 1939; d. Junius Chappell and Edna (Burton) Moore; m. Aubrey S. DesPortes, Aug. 31, 1962 (div. Oct. 1973); children: Aubrey S. DesPortes Jr., Betty Layne DesPortes; m. Elton R. Beverly, Apr. 7, 1975; 1 stepchild, Roberta B. Eddy. BA in Psychology, U. S.C., 1962; MS in Rehab. Counseling, Va. Commonwealth U., 1987. Lic. counselor, Va.; cert. substance abuse counselor. Order libr. U. S.C., Columbia, 1962-63; tchr. spl. edn. Chesterfield (Va.) Pub. Schs., 1973-75; coord. outpatient treatment HCA Poplar Springs Hosp., Petersburg, Va., 1988-90; pvt. practice Chesterfield, Va., 1990—. Author: History of Buckhead, 1976. mem. Chesterfield Cmty. Svc. Bd., 1988-93, chmn., 1990-92; mem. state coun. Mental Health Planning Coun., Richmond, Va., 1989-94; mem. Chesterfield Comprehensive Svcs. Policy and Mgmt. Team, 1994—; mem. Chesterfield County Cmty. Mobilization. Pathfinder scholar U.S. Govt., 1986. Mem. ACA, Mental Health Assn. Va., Chesterfield Mental Retardation Assn., Chester Garden Club (past pres.), Chester Rotary Club Internat. Republican. Methodist. Home: PO Box 967 4740 Crossgate Rd Chester VA 23831 Office: 10111 Krause Rd Ste 202 Chesterfield VA 23832

BEVIS, JUDITH ANNE, psychologist; b. Phila., Oct. 15, 1954; d. George and Eleanor (Mlodzikowski) B.; m. May 10, 1987. AB, Princeton U., 1976; MA, Boston U., 1982, PhD, 1986. Lic. psychologist, Mass. Staff psychologist Eliot Community Mental Health Ctr., Concord, Mass., 1985-87; assoc. clin. dir. Danvers State Hosp., Hathorne, Mass., 1987-89; asst. attending child psychologist McLean Hosp., Belmont, Mass., 1988-90; cons. psychologist Mass. Disability Determination Svcs., Boston, 1989—; pvt. practice Marblehead, 1989—; group practice The Neuropsychology Svc., Beverly, Mass., 1994—. Mem. APA. Office: One Widger Rd Marblehead MA 01945

BEYER, CHARLOTTE BISHOP, investment management marketing executive; b. N.Y.C., Oct. 16, 1947; d. Edward Morton and Charlotte Reid (Handy) Beyer; BA, Hunter Coll., 1969; m. Warren P. Weitman, Jr., July 28, 1967; children: Catherine Scott, Michael Benjamin. With Bankers Trust Co., N.Y.C., 1970-81, v.p. trust svcs. and securities ops., 1979-81; v.p. prin. client svc. and mktg. Wood Struthers and Winthrop Mgmt. Corp. subs. Donaldson Lufkin and Jenrette, N.Y.C., 1985-89, sr. v.p., 1987-89; v.p. Lazard Freres Asset Mgmt., N.Y.C., 1989-90; founder, cons., researcher Charlotte Beyer Assocs., 1990—; founder Inst. Pvt. Investors Rsch. and Ednl. Forum, 1992. Trustee Westover Sch., Middlebury, Conn., 1987-93. Episcopalian. Office: Charlotte Beyer Assocs Inc 469 Morris Ave Summit NJ 07901-1568

BEYER, CONSTANCE LUCILLE, marketing professional; b. Ridgewood, N.J., Oct. 4, 1952; d. Daniel A. and Beryl A. (Metz) B.; m. M.P.D. King, May 24, 1975 (div. Dec. 1983); m. Michael A. Sprayberry, Jan. 31, 1993; 1 child, Skyler Anne. BA cum laude, U. Vt., 1975. Account rep. So. Pacific Comms. (now Sprint), Arlington, Va., 1977-79; dist. sales mgr. Cable and Wireless, Vienna, Va., 1979-80, product mgr., 1980, regional sales mgr., 1981, div. sales mgr., 1981-83, dir. mktg., 1983-86, v.p. mktg., 1986—. Elected town lister Town of Duxbury, Vt., 1976; del. Rep. Party, Vt., 1976. Office: Cable and Wireless 1819 Gallows Rd Vienna VA 22182

BEYER, KAREN HAYNES, social worker; b. Cleve. BA, Ohio State U., 1965; MSW, Loyola U., Chgo., 1969; postgrad. Family Inst., Northwestern U., 1979; MPA, Roosevelt U., 1992. Lic. clin. social worker Ill. With Cuyahoga County Div. Child Welfare, Cleve., 1965, Dallas County Child Welfare Unit, Dallas, 1966; with Luth. Social Svcs. Ill., Chgo., 1967-73; pvt. practice psychotherapy, family mediation, Schaumburg, Ill., 1975-93; therapist Family Svcs. Assn. Greater Elgin (Ill.), 1973-77, dir. profl. svcs., 1977-83; dir. HHS Village of Hoffman Estates, Ill., 1983-93; exec. dir. Larkin Ctr., Elgin, Ill., 1993—. Mem. NASW, Am. Assn. Marriage and Family Therapy. Unitarian. Office: Larkin Ctr 1212 Larkin Ave Elgin IL 60123

BEYER, SUZANNE, advertising agency executive; b. N.Y.C., Dec. 28, 1928; d. Harry and Jennie Hillman; student Nassau Community Coll., 1963-65; grad. Conservatory of Musical Art, N.Y.C., 1947; m. Isadore Beyer, Oct. 19, 1947; children—Pamela Claire, Hillary Jay. Singer, tchr. piano, N.Y.C., 1947-66; asst. to v.p. media dir. Robert E. Wilson, Advt., N.Y.C., 1967-72; media planner, media buyer Frank J. Corbett div. BBDO Internat., N.Y.C., 1972-77; media planner, media buyer Lavey/Wolff/Swift div. BBDO Advt., N.Y.C., 1977-80, sr. media planner, 1980-83, media supr., 1983-94; media supr. Lyons, Lavey, Nichel, Swift, N.Y.C., 1995—; soprano Opera Assn. Nassau, 1976—; soprano United Choral Soc., Woodmere, L.I., 1970—, Armand Sodero Chorale, Baldwin, L.I., 1980-86, Rockville Centre Choral Soc, 1986—. Mem. Pharm. Advt. Council, L.I. Advt. Club, Healthcare Bus. Women's Assn. Home: 66 Fonda Rd Rockville Centre NY 11570-2751 Office: 488 Madison Ave New York NY 10022-5702

BEYERLE, SUSAN LYNN, finance director; b. Akron, Ohio, Apr. 1, 1959; d. Jay Eben and Sandra Ann (Dahlinger) B. BS in Fin., Pa. State U., 1981. Auditor Eastman Kodak Co., Rochester, N.Y., 1981-85, fin. analyst film mfg., 1985-86, fin. analyst clin. slide mfg., 1986-87, fin. analyst health scis. divsn., 1987-90, sr. auditor-U.K., 1990-91, fin. analyst European, African, Mid. Ea. divsn., 1991-94, worldwide fin. dir. image utilization consumer imaging, 1994—. Active Welcome Wagon, Fairport, N.Y., 1994. Mem. Pa. State U.-Rochester Alumni Club, Kappa Alpha Theta Alumnae Club (treas., pres. 1986-90). Home: 3 Woodbury Way Fairport NY 14450 Office: Eastman Kodak Co 343 State St Rochester NY 14650

BEYER-MEARS, ANNETTE, physiologist; b. Madison, Wis., May 26, 1941; d. Karl and Annette (Weiss) Beyer. B.A., Vassar Coll., 1963; M.S., Fairleigh Dickinson U., 1973; Ph.D., Coll. Medicine and Dentistry N.J., 1977. NIH fellow Cornell U. Med. Sch., 1963-65; instr. physiology Springside Sch., Phila., 1967-71; teaching asst. dept. physiology Coll. Medicine & Dentistry N.J., N.J. Med. Sch., 1974-77, NIH fellow dept. ophthalmology, 1978-80; asst. prof. dept. ophthalmology U. Medicine and Dentistry N.J., N.J. Med. Sch., Newark, 1979-85, asst. prof. dept. physiology, 1980-85, assoc. prof. dept. physiology, 1986—, assoc. prof. dept. ophthalmology, 1986—; cons. Alcon Labs. Contbr. articles in field of diabetic lens and kidney therapy to profl. jours. Chmn. admissions No. N.J., Vassar Coll., 1974-79; mem. minister search com. St. Bartholomew Episcopal Ch., N.J., 1978, fund-raising chmn., 1978, 79; del. Episc. Diocesian Conv., 1977, 78; long range planning com. Christ Ch., Ridgewood, N.J., 1985-87. Recipient NIH Nat. Rsch. Svc. award, 1978-80, Found. CMDNJ Rsch. award, 1980; grantee Juvenile Diabetes Found., 1985-87, NIH, NEI grantee, 1980—, Pfizer, Inc. grantee, 1985-89, 93—. Mem. Am. Physiol. Soc., N.Y. Acad. Scis., Soc. for Neurosci., Am. Soc. Pharmacology and Exptl. Therapeutics, Assn. for Rsch. Vision & Ophthalmology, Internat. Soc. for Eye Research, AAAS, The Royal Soc. Medicine, Internat. Diabetes Found., Am. Diabetes Assn., Aircraft Owners and Pilots Assn., Sigma Xi. Office: NJ Med Sch Dept Physiology 185 S Orange Ave Newark NJ 07103-2714

BEYERSDORF, MARGUERITE MULLOY, elementary education educator; b. Terry, Mont., Apr. 20, 1922; d. John William and Laura Agnes (Mahar) Mulloy; m. Curtis Alexander Beyersdorf, 1946; 1 child, Mary Jo Wright. Kindergarten-Primary Cert., Coll. St. Catherine, St. Paul, 1942; PhB, Marquette U., 1945; postgrad., Gonzaga U., Spokane, Wash., 1957-62, Ea. Wash. State U., 1977-79. Tchr. grade 3 Sacred Heart Sch., Oelwein, Iowa, 1942-43; tchr. grades 1 and 2 Jr. Mil. Acad., Chgo., 1943-44; tchr. history, English Fairfield (Wash.) High Sch., 1945-46; substitute tchr. Riverside High Sch., 1957; tchr. Mead (Wash.) Sch. Dist., 1958-75; owner/mgr. First Ave. Parking Lot, Spokane, Wash., 1957—. Vol. Spokane N.W. Communities Found., 1982—; active United Way Spokane, 1950, ARC, Am. Cancer Soc., Multiple Sclerosis Soc., others; vol. coord. Dominican Outreach Found. to Domicile Single Parent Families; canteen vol. Spokane Blood Bank, 1981—; vol. Miryam's House of Transition, 1989—. Recipient Vol. of Yr. Golden Rule award J.C. Penney Co., 1993; grantee NSF, Whitworth Coll., 1967. Mem. NEA, APGA, AAUW (bd. dirs. Spokane br., chmn. scholarship com.), Wash. Edn. Assn.-Retired (del. rep. assembly, mem. comm. com 1993—, chmn. comm. commn. 1993—), Mead Edn. Assn. (sec., exec. bd., former bldg. rep., mem. curriculum com.).

BHATT, KIRAN, physician, educator; b. Poona, India, Feb. 13, 1951; d. Ved Prakash and Pushpa Vati (Kapila) Pathak; m. Ganesh Bhatt, Feb. 9, 1974 (div. Dec. 1988); 1 child, Biren Deo. MB, BS, Christian Med. Coll., Ludmiana, India, 1974; MD, U. Wash., 1975, MS, 1979. Diplomate Am. Bd. Phys. Med. and Rehab. Attending physician, asst. clin. prof. rehab. medicine U. Calif., Irvine, 1980-82; physician Northwest Permanente PC, Portland, 1982-84; fellow in spinal cord injury Milw. VA Med. Ctr., 1985-87; chief rehab. med. svc. Muskogee (Okla.) VA Med. Ctr., 1987-88; physician Neuro-Ortho Assocs., L.A., 1990-93; med. dir. Family Health Care, Long Beach, Calif., 1993; physician spinal cord injury svc. Palo Alto (Calif.) VA Med. Ctr., 1994—; asst. clin. prof. neurology Oregon Health Scis. U., 1982-84; asst. prof. rehab. medicine Med. Coll. Wis., Milw., 1985-87; adj. asst. prof. medicine Tulsa Med. Coll., 1987-88; physician Long Beach VA Med. Ctr., 1979-80. Active PTA, Anaheim, Calif., 1990-94. Fellow Am. Acad. Phys. Medicine and Rehab. (life); Am. Assn. Electrodiagnostic Medicine (assoc., hist. com. 1987-88). Office: Palo Alto VA Med Ctr 3801 Miranda Ave Palo Alto CA 94304

BHATTI, NEELOO, environmental scientist; b. New Delhi, Jan. 30, 1955; arrived in Can., 1958, came to U.S., 1982; d. Daljeet Singh and Abnash (Singh) B.; m. James Joseph McAndrew, Sept. 14, 1985. MES, Yale U., 1984, PhD, 1988. Rsch. asst. McGill U., Montreal, Que., Can., 1976-78; teaching asst. Yale U., New Haven, 1983; rsch. intern Cary Arboretum, Millbrook, N.Y., 1983; postdoctoral fellow Argonne (Ill.) Nat. Lab., 1989-90, energy and environ. scientist, 1990—; environ. effects specialist, cons. World Bank, Washington, 1989—. Author: Dispelling the North American Acid Rain Clouds, 1988, Responding to Threat of Global Warming: Options for Asia and Pacific, 1989, Acid Rain in Asia, 1992. F.C.A.C. scholar Govt. Que., 1983-87; Yale U. fellow, New Haven, 1984-88. Mem. Am. Chem. Soc., Am Soc. Foresters, Sigma Xi. Home: 15425 Purley Ct Lockport IL 60441 Office: Argonne Nat Lab 9700 Cass Ave Argonne IL 60439

BIANCARDI, LINDA ANN, therapeutic recreation director; b. Stamford, Conn., Apr. 18, 1962; d. Patsy Joseph and Nadjezhda (Rataj) B. BA in Psychology, Fairfield U., 1984. Cert. in therapeutic recreation, Conn. Recreation therapist Waveny Care Ctr., New Canaan, Conn., 1985-90; therapeutic recreation specialist Fairfield Manor, Norwalk, Conn., 1991; therapeutic recreation dir. Mediplex of Danbury, Conn., 1991—; vol. coord. Mediplex of Danbury, 1992—. Parish coun. sec. St. Mary's Holy Assumption Russian Orthodox Ch., Stamford, 1991—, choir dir., 1994—. Mem. Conn. Assn. Therapeutic Recreation Dirs. (sec. region 1 1988). Home: PO Box 4325 Stamford CT 06907

BIANCHI-BIGELOW, CHERYL ANN, mental health facility director; b. Rochester, N.Y., July 1, 1957; d. Samuel Gene and Marlene Ann (Conte) Bianchi; m. Howard Francis Bigelow, Oct. 30, 1984; 1 child, Alexa Anne. BA in Sociology, SUNY, Cortland, 1979; MSW, Syracuse U., 1984. Cert. social worker, mental health and gerontology profl. Psychiat. social worker, psychotherapist, intern Hillside Children's Ctr., Rochester, 1982-83; psychiat. social worker Veteran's Hosp., Canadagula, N.Y., 1983-84; from clin. coord. to assoc. dir. DePaul Mental Health Svcs., Rochester, 1984-88, dir., 1987-92; chief exec. officer, pres. The Bread Harbor, Inc., Chatham, Mass., 1991—. Recipient Best Bus. Display of Christmas Spirit award Chatham Yule Bowl, 1993, Award of Excellence, Best Chefs of Cape Cod, 1994. Mem. NAFE, NASW, NASE, Chatham Merchants Assn., Chatham C. of C., U. Club Rochester, Women's Network, Phi Beta Kappa. Home: 56 Augustine St Rochester NY 14613-1425 Office: The Bread Harbor Inc Chatham MA 02633

BIBBS, LONA CAROL, educational program administrator; b. Chgo., Jan. 6, 1948; d. Willie P. and Canara (Graham) Cooley; m. Guy L Bibbs, Sept. 6, 1970; children: Lona Demetria, Guy Lee III. BA, Bradley U., 1970; MS, Northeastern U., 1975; postgrad., Loyola U., Chgo. Children's dir. Carver Community Ctr., Peoria, Ill., 1968-70, med. ctr. supr., 1970-72; tchr. Chgo. Bd. Edn., 1972-75, guidance counselor, 1975-85, sr. counselor, chmn. guidance dept., 1985-89; asst. dir. summer transition program Northeastern Ill. U., 1989—; facilitator Bur. of Vocat. and Technol., Chgo., 1985—, program chmn. Dist. 31 Coll. Fair, Chgo. 1986-87; counselor articulation bd. DePaul U. Coach NAACP ACT-So Program, Chgo., 1986—, Midwest Community Council. Chgo., 1988; mem. individualized student career plan task force Ill. State Bd. Edn.; mem. The Nat. Disting. Svc. Registry. Recipient Outstanding Vocat. Articulation Facilitator Chgo. Bd. of Ed. Bur. of Vocat. and Technol. Edn. Awds. Chair Ill. Sch. Counselors Assn., Connections 2000 award Ill. State Bd. Edn. Mem. ACA, ASCD, AAUW, NAFE, Aux. to Chgo. Dental Soc., Caux Ill. Assn. Counseling and Devel., Sec. Sch. Counselors Coun. (pres. 1987), Nat. Coun. Negro Women, Nat. Hook-up of Black Women Inc. (v.p.), Loyola U. Leadership and Policy Studies Assn. (sec.), Nat. Bd. Cert. Counselors, Inst. for Athletes in Edn., Dental Wives of Chgo. (pres.), Am. Vocational Assn., Ill. Vocational Assn., Ill. Assn. Supervision & Curriculum Devel. Democrat.

BIBBY, REGINA NANETTE, manufacturing company executive; b. Jacksonville, Fla., Sept. 20, 1960; d. Allan Harvey and Dorothy Jeanette (Munster) B.; 1 child, Christal Shanti Bibby. BS, Brenau Coll., Gainesville, Ga. Customer svc. staff Tandem Computer Co., Marietta, Ga., 1982-83; office mgr. Am. Indsl. Design, Atlanta, 1983-84; dir. Kato Spring of Ga. Inc., Duluth, 1984—. Co-membership chair Nat. Congress of Parents and Tchrs., Ga. Dist. 13, 1990—; local sch. adv. com., 1993, 94. Mem. Am. Prodn. and Inventory Control Soc., Am. Mgmt. Assn., Gwinnette Safety Profl. Assn., Atlanta C. of C., Gwinnett C. of C. Republican. Roman Catholic. Office: Kato Spring of Ga Inc 2590 Breckinridge Blvd Duluth GA 30136-4982

BIBLE, FRANCES LILLIAN, mezzo-soprano, educator; b. Sackets Harbor, N.Y.; d. Arthur and Lillian (Cooke) B. Student, Juilliard Sch. Music, 1939-47. Artist-in-residence Shepherd Sch. of Music Rice U., Houston, 1975-91. Appeared throughout U.S., Australia, Europe including Vienna Staatsoper, Karlsruhe Staatsoper, Dublin Opera Co., N.Y.C. Opera, NBC-TV Opera, San Francisco Opera, Glyndebourne Opera, San Antonio Opera Festival, New Orleans Opera, Houston Grand Opera, Miami Opera, Dallas Opera; appeared in concert with major symphonies. Mem. Am. Guild Mus. Artists (past 3d v.p., bd. dirs. 1989-91), Sigma Alpha Iota (hon.), Beta Sigma Pi (hon.). Republican. Episcopalian. Home: 2377 Thata Way Hemet CA 92544-7009

BIBLIOWICZ, JESSICA M., financial analyst; b. 1960. Formerly with assesment mgmt. divsn. Shearson Lehman Bros.; past dir. sales and mktg. Prudential Mutual Funds; now exec. v.p., overseer mutual funds Smith Barney, N.Y.C. Office: Smith Barney Inc 1345 Ave of the Americas New York NY 10105*

BICK, KATHERINE LIVINGSTONE, scientist, international liaison consultant; b. Charlottetown, Can., May 3, 1932; came to U.S., 1954; d. Spurgeon Arthur and Flora Hazel (Murray) Livingstone; m. James Harry Bick, Aug. 20, 1955 (div.); children: James A., Charles L. (dec.); m. Ernst Freese, 1986 (dec. 1990). BS with honors, Acadia U., Can., 1951, MS, 1952; PhD, Brown U., 1957; DSc (hon.), Acadia U., 1990. Research pathologist UCLA Med. Sch., 1959-61; asst. prof. Calif. State U., Northridge, 1961-66; lab. instr. Georgetown U., Washington, 1970-72, asst. prof., 1972-76; dep. dir. neurol. disorder program Nat. Inst. Neurol. and Communicative Disorders and Stroke, NIH, Bethesda, Md., 1976-81, acting dep. dir., 1981-83, dep. dir., 1983-87; dep. dir. extramural research Office of Dir. NIH, 1987-90; sci. liaison Centro Studio Multicentrico Internazionale Sulla Demenza, Washington, 1990—; cons. Nat. Rsch. Coun., Italy, 1991—, The Charles A. Dana Found., N.Y.C., 1993—. Editor: Alzheimer's Disease: Senile Dementia and Related Disorders, 1978, Neurosecretion and Brain Peptides, Implications for Brain Functions and Neurol. Disease, 1981, The Early Story of Alzheimer's Disease, 1987, Alzheimer Disease, 1994; contbr. articles to profl. jours. Pres. Woman's Club, McLean, Va., 1968-69; bd. dirs. Fairfax County (Va.) YWCA, 1979-80; pres. Emerson Unitarian Ch., 1964-66; mem. Bethesda Pl. Cmty. Coun., 1992—, pres., 1993-94. Recipient Can. NRC award Acadia U., 1951-52, NIH Dir.'s award, 1978, Spl. Achievement award NIH, 1981, 83, Superior Svc. award USPHS, 1986, Presdl. Rank award meritorious sr. exec., 1989; Universal Match Found. fellow Brown U., 1956-57, Fed. Exec. Inst. Leadership fellow, 1980. Fellow AAAS; mem. Am. Neurol. Assn., Am. Acad. Neurology, Assn. for Rsch. in Nervous and Mental Disease, Internat. Brain Rsch. Orgn., World Fedn. Neurology Rsch. Group on Dementias (exec. sec. Am. region 1984-86, chmn. 1986-93), Soc. for Neuroscience. Office: Centro SMID USA 7300 Greentree Rd Bethesda MD 20817-1552

BICKEL, CHRISTINE KAY, medical/surgical nurse; b. Williamsport, Pa., Oct. 27, 1959; d. George Tyson and Joyce Irene (Alexander) B. Cert. in nursing, Williamsport Area Community Coll., 1978. LPN, Pa. Nurse Williamsport Hosp. and Med. Ctr., 1978—. Democrat. Home: RR 4 Box 375 Williamsport PA 17701 Office: Williamsport Hosp and Med Ctr 777 Rural Ave Williamsport PA 17701

BICKERSTAFF, MINA MARCH CLARK, university administrator; b. Crowley, Tex., Sept. 27, 1936; d. Winifred Perry and Clara Mae (Jarrett) Clark; m. Billy Frank Bickerstaff, June 12, 1954 (div. 1960); children: Billy Mark, Mina Gayle Bickerstaff Basaldu. AA, Tarrant County Jr. Coll., 1982; BBA, Dallas Bapt. U., 1991. Dir. pers. svcs. Southwestern Bapt. Theol. Sem., Ft. Worth, 1976—. Mem. Coll. and Univ. Pers. Assn., Seminary Woman's Club (past treas.), Alpha Chi. Baptist. Office: Southwestern Bapt Theol Sem PO Box 22000 Fort Worth TX 76122

BICKFORD, GAIL HOLMGREN, publishing executive; b. N.Y.C., Feb. 14, 1930; d. R. John and Emilie Mary Antonia Doyle (Pope) Holmgren; m. Arthur Fillmore Bickford, Dec. 16, 1951 (div. Jan. 1980); children: Geoffrey, Alison. BA, Wellesley (Mass.) Coll., 1951; MA, U. Pa., 1956, PhD, 1972. Asst. instr. U. Pa., Phila., 1953-58; prof. Cape Cod Community Coll., Hyannis, Mass., 1965-68; owner, operator Freedom (N.H.) Press Assocs., 1979—; lectr. to Freedom, Ossipee (N.H.) and Brownfield (Maine) Hist. Socs., 1991; editor, designer, pub. A Potpourri of Pleasantries, 1992—; owner Emilie's Treasure Box. Author: Here Is Freedom, 1975, Freedom Crossroads, 1989; editor: Reminiscences of the French War, 1988, Tales of Effingham, 1988; columnist Carroll County Ind., 1988-89, 91—; designer, layout artist, and typesetter The Good News, Conway, N.H.; pub. A Potpourri of Pleasantries, 1993, A Village Pastor Looks Back, 1993; contbr. articles to various mags. Mem. com. Dennis (Mass.) Sch., 1966-76; trustee Freedom Pub. Libr., 1985-91; sec. Old Home Week Assn., 1988—; rec. sec. Freedom Conservation Commn., 1987-89; sec. Friends of the Libr., 1991-94; exec. bd., chmn. pubs. com., Freedom Hist. Soc., 1991—, wrtier, editor Quicksilver Times, 1992—; moderator Freedom Water Precinct, 1994—; mem. task force on community econ. devel. sponsored by Lakes Region Charitable Found. and Ford Found. Democrat. Office: Freedom Press Assocs 88 Maple St Freedom NH 03836-0088

BICKFORD, JEWELLE WOOTEN, investment banker; b. Evanston, Ill., Dec. 12, 1941; d. James A. Wooten and Phyllis (Taber) Kades; m. Nathaniel J. Bickford, Feb. 1, 1962; children: Laura C., Emily A. BA, Sarah Lawrence Coll., 1977. Trustee, chair com. on gen. programs and issues Community Svc. Soc., N.Y.C., 1973-77; dir. community bd. assistance unit Office of the Mayor, N.Y.C., 1977-80; v.p. Citibank, N.A., N.Y.C., 1980-84; v.p. Dillon, Read & Co., Inc., N.Y.C., 1984-85, sr. v.p., 1985-88; pres. Trepp, Bickford Fin. Svcs. Inc., 1988-90, Bickford & Ptnrs., Inc., N.Y.C., 1991-94, Bickford Capital Advisors, L.P., 1991-94; mng. dir. Rothschild, Inc., N.Y.C., 1994—; mem. adv. bd. First Womens Bank, 1975-78. Trustee South St. Seaport Theater, chmn. bd., 1978-83; trustee Coro Found., 1982-89; mem. Citizens Com. for Children; bd. dirs. Phoenix House Found.; trustee, v.p. bd. trustees Fountain House; mem. bus. com. Met. Mus. Art. Mem. Fin. Women's Assn., Women's Forum (bd. dirs.). Democrat. Episcopalian. Club: River (N.Y.C.). Home: 969 5th Ave New York NY 10021 Office: Rothschild Inc 1251 Ave of Americas New York NY 10020

BIDDLE, ISABEL RICHARDS COTTO, nurse; b. Ceiba, P.R., Nov. 29, 1940; d. Flor Richards Jiminez and Maria Cotto Rivera; m. Marshall Biddle, Jr., June 10, 1967; children: Jackeline, Ellen, Marshall H. Grad., Sch. Nursing, Fajardo, P.R., 1966; student, Norfolk State U., 1992-94, Tidewater C.C., 1994—. LPN. Nurse Fajardo Hosp., 1966-69, Luquillo (P.R.) Hosp., 1966-67, Justiniano Clinic, 1967-69, USPHS, Norfolk, Va., 1978-81, Medictr. of Am. Nursing Home, Norfolk, 1976-78, Naval Hosp., Portsmouth, Va., 1982-87, VA Hosp., Hamoton, Va., 1987-89, Sentara Nursing Home, Portsmouth, 1990-91, Kimberly Quality Care, Norfolk, 1991—. Recipient numerous awards and certs. Democrat. Methodist. Home: PO Box 3371 Portsmouth VA 23701-0371

BIEGEL, EILEEN MAE, hospital executive; b. Eau Claire, Wis., Nov. 13, 1937; d. Ewald Frederic and Emma Antonia (Conrad) Weggen; student Dist. One Tech. Inst., 1974, also part time, corr. student U. Wis., Madison; grad. mgmt. seminars; student Upper Iowa U., 1984—; m. James O. Biegel, Oct. 6, 1956; children: Jeffrey Alan, John William. Exec. sec. to pres. Broadcaster Services, Inc., Eau Claire, Wis., 1969-74; exec. sec. to exec. v.p. Am. Nat. Bank, Eau Claire, 1975-77; exec. asst. to pres. Luther Hosp., Eau Claire, 1977—, asst. corporate sec., 1984—; mem. exec. staff, 1985—; asst. corp. sec. Luther Health Care Corp., 1984—; mem. secretarial adv. council Dist. One Tech. Sch. 1975—; corp. sec. Northwest Health Ventures, 1988-92, bd. dirs. State pres. Future Homemakers Am., 1955; mem. governance com. Wis. Hosp. Assn. Cert. profl. sec., 1980; sec. bd. dirs. Chestnut Properties. Mem. Eau Claire Womens Network (founder, mem. steering com.), Profl. Secs. Internat. (chmn. goals and priorities com., pres. Eau Claire chpt. 1982-83), Wis. Hosp. Assn. (gov. com.). Home: 4707 Tower Dr Eau Claire WI 54703-8717 Office: 310 Chestnut St Eau Claire WI 54703-5230

BIEHLE, KAREN JEAN, pharmacist; b. Festus, Mo., July 18, 1959; d. Warren Day and Wilma Georgenia (Hedrick) Hargus; m. Scott Joseph Biehle, Aug. 22, 1981; children: Lauren Rachel, Heather Michelle. Student of pre-pharmacy, U. Mo., Columbia, Mo., 1977-79; BS in Pharmacy, U. Mo., Kans. City, Mo., 1982. Reg. Pharmicist. Pharmacy res. U. Iowa Hosp. & Clinics, Iowa City, Iowa, 1982-83; pharmacist Jewish Hosp. of St. Louis, St. Louis, 1983-86; pharmacy mgr. Foster Infusion Care, St. Louis, 1986-88; staff pharmacist Cardinal Glennon Children's Hosp., St. Louis, 1988-90; pres. Lauren's Specialty Foods, Inc., St. Louis, 1988-89; pharmacy mgr. Curaflex Health Svcs., St. Louis, 1989-91; asst. dir. Cobb Hosp. and Med. Ctr., Austell, Ga., 1991-94; asst. dir. pharmacy Publix Supermarkets, Marietta, Ga., 1994—; preceptor St. Louis Coll. Pharmacy, 1984-91, U. Ga. Sch. Pharmacy, 1992. Vol. March of Dimes Walk-a-thon, 1985-90. Recipient Roche Pharmacy Communications Award, Roche Pharmaceuticals, Kans. City, 1982, I Dare You Award, 4-H Club, Nevada, Mo., 1976. Mem. Am. Soc. Hosp. Pharmacists, Kappa Epsilon, Alpha Delta Pi (St. Louis Alumnae pres. 1989-90). Republican. Baptist. Home: 2431 Westport Cir Marietta GA 30064-5707

BIELEFELDT, CATHERINE C., sales executive; b. Bellwood, Ill.; d. William Anton and Linda (Buchert) B. MusB in Piano Performance, Chgo. Conservatory Coll.; student El Conservatorio de Mex., Mexico City; postgrad. Northwestern U., CBS Sch. Mgmt., 1980. Dept. mgr. Fair Store, Oak Park, Ill., 1950-62; piano sales cons. Lyon & Healy Co., Oak Park and Oak Brook, Ill., 1963-77; dir. Steinway Hall, dir. nat. sales tng. Steinway & Sons, Long Island City, N.Y., 1978-82; v.p. sales, pub. rels. and advt. Hendricks Music Co., Downers Grove, Ill., 1983—; sales seminar instr. Jordan-Kitt's Music, Wells Music, Washington and Denver, 1983-85, Lauzon Music, Ottawa, Can., 1986—, Meridian Music, Indpls., 1989. Author: The Wonders of the Piano, The Anatomy of the Instrument, 1984, rev. edit., 1992; editor The Keynote Newsletter; contbr. articles to profl. jours. Mem. Evanston Music Club, Sigma Alpha Iota (past pres. alumnae chpt., recipient numerous awards). Republican. Lutheran. Home: 190 S Wood Dale Rd Apt 1101 Wood Dale IL 60191-2246 Office: Hendricks Music 421 Maple Ave Downers Grove IL 60515-3806

BIELKE, PATRICIA ANNE, psychologist; b. Bay Shore, N.Y., May 11, 1949; d. Lawrence Curtis and Marcella Elizabeth (Maize) Widdoes; m. Stephen Roy Bielke, July 10, 1971; children: Eric, Christine. BA, Carleton Coll., 1971; PhD, U. Minn., 1979. Lic. psychologist, Wis. Rsch. asst. Nat. Inst. Mental Health, Washington, 1972-74; sch. psychologist Roseville Pub. Schs., St. Paul, 1978-79; psychologist Southeastern Wis. Med. and Social Svcs., Milw., 1979-93; staff psychologist Elmbrook Meml. Hosp., 1986—; pvt. practice Brookfield, Wis., 1991—; Lic. psychologist, Wis.; cert. marriage & family therapist. Bd. dirs. LWV, Brookfield, 1984-88, Elmbrook Sch. Bd., 1989—. Mem. APA, Am. Assn. Marriage and Family Therapists. Home: 17455 Bedford Dr Brookfield WI 53045-1301 Office: 17000 W North Ave Brookfield WI 53005-4423

BIEN, SUE ELLEN, medical technologist; b. Belleville, Ill., Jan. 5, 1950; d. Gordon Dwight and Rita Olinda (Schmidt) Bien; children: Kelli Susan, Matthew George. BS in Med. Tech., So. Ill. U., 1986. Registered med. technologist. Med. technologist Washington U., St. Louis, 1987-89, Meml. Hosp., Belleville, Ill., 1989-92, Deacones Hosp., St. Louis, 1992-93, Barnes-Jewish-Christian Hosp., St. Louis, 1992—. Mem. NAFE, Am. Bus. Women's Assn., Noble Bachelors, Am. Soc. Clin. Pathologists (assoc.). Roman Catholic. Home: 60 Hollandia Belleville IL 62221-1300 Office: Barnes Hosp 1 Barnes Hospital Plaza Saint Louis MO 63110

BIERY, EVELYN HUDSON, lawyer; b. Lawton, Okla., Oct. 12, 1946; d. William Ray and Nellie Iris (Nunley) Hudson. BA in English and Latin summa cum laude, Abilene (Tex.) Christian U., 1968; JD, So. Meth. U., 1973. Bar: Tex. 1973, U.S. Dist. Ct. (we. dist.) Tex. 1975, U.S. Dist. Ct. (so. dist.) Tex. 1977, U.S. Dist. Ct. (no. dist.) Tex. 1979, U.S. Ct. Appeals (5th cir.) 1979, U.S. Ct. Appeals (11th cir.) 1981, U.S. Supreme Ct. 1981. Atty. Law Offices of Bruce Waitz, San Antonio, 1973-76; mem. LeLaurin & Adams, P.C., San Antonio, 1976-81; ptnr., head bankruptcy, reorganization and creditors' rights sect. Fulbright & Jaworksi, 1981—; speaker on creditors' rights, bankruptcy and reorganization law at numerous seminars; lectr. Southwestern Grad. Sch. Banking, Dallas, 1980, La. State U. Sch. Banking, 1994; presiding officer, U. Tex. Sch. of Law Bankruptcy Conf., 1976, 94, State Bar Tex. Creditors' Rights Inst., 1985, State Bar Tex. Advanced Bus. Bankruptcy Law Inst., 1985, State Bar Tex. Inst. on Advising Officers, Dirs. and Ptnrs. in Troubled Bus., 1987, State Bar Tex. Advanced Creditors Rights Inst., 1988; pres. San Antonio Young Lawyers Assn., 1979-80; mem. bankruptcy adv. com. fifth cir. jud. coun., 1979-80; vice-chmn. bankruptcy com. Comml. Law League Am., 1981-83; mem. exec. bd. So. Meth. U. Sch. Law, 1983-91. Editor: Texas Collections Manual, 1978, Creditor's Rights in Texas, 2d edit., 1981; author: (with others) Collier Bankruptcy Practice Guide, 1993. Del. to U.S./Republic of China joint session on trade, investment and econ. law , Beijing, 1987; designated mem. Bankruptcy Judge Merit Screening Com. State of Tex. by Tex. State Bar Pres., 1979-82; patron McNay Mus., San Antonio; rsch. ptnr. Mind Sci. Found., San Antonio; diplomat World Affairs Coun., San Antonio. Recipient Outstanding Young Lawyer award San Antonio Young Lawyers Assn., 1979. Fellow Soc. of Internat. Bus. Fellow, Am. Coll. Bankruptcy Attys., Tex. Bar Found. (life), San Antonio Bar Found.; mem. Tex. Bar Assn. (chair bankruptcy com. 1982-83, chair corp., banking and bus. law sect. 1989-90), Tex. Assn. Bank Counsel (bd. dirs. 1988-90), San Antonio Young Lawyers Assn. (pres. 1979-80), Plaza Club San Antonio (bd. dirs. 1982—), Zonta (Chair Z club com. 1989-90), Order of Coif. Office: Fulbright & Jaworski 300 Convent St Ste 2200 San Antonio TX 78205-3792

BIESEL, DIANE JANE, librarian; b. N.Y.C., Feb. 15, 1934; d. Douglas and Runa (Patterson) Stevens; m. Donald W. de Cordova, June 24, 1956 (div. July 1971); m. David Barrie Biesel, Sept. 25, 1982. BS, Trenton State Coll., 1956; MLS, Rutgers U., 1969; MA in Edn., Seton Hall U., 1974, cert. in supervision, 1976. Tchr., librarian Arlington (Va.)) Bd. Edn., 1956-58; media specialist elem. schs., librs. River Edge (N.J.) Bd. Edn., 1958-91; lectr., instr. children's lit. Alphonsus Coll., Woodcliff Lake, N.J., 1969-72; field svc. cons. N.J. Dept. Edn., 1969-71; cons. New Books Preview Baker and Taylor Co., 1972-76; adj. prof. Seton Hall U., 1978-79; mem. award com. Rutgers U. Grad. Sch. Libr. Svc., 1978-79; series editor Scarecrow Press, Metuchen, N.J., 1992—. Editor: School Library Media Series. Mem. com. academically gifted River Edge Bd. Edn., 1977-83, study skills com., 1988-90, affirmative action com., 1988-90, River Dell Librs. Coop., 1988-91; mem. choir All St.'s Ch., Bergenfield, 1971—, lay reader, 1973—, vestrywoman, 1980-83, del. Diocesan Conv., 1978—; active Affirmative Action, 1988-90; mem. ecumenical commn. Dioceses Newark, 1992. Mem. ALA, Am. Assn. Sch. Librarians (mem. com. instrnl. media 1971-76, affiliate assembly by-laws com. 1977-78, program com. 1992-93, rep. kid diversity programming com. 1993—, ABC Clio award com. 1994—, legis. com. 1994—), Ednl. Media Assn. N.J. (state chmn. recruitment 1968-69, state chmn. hospitality 1972-73, state chmn. county liaison 1973-74, co-pres. 1977-78), Bergen County Sch. Librs. Assn. (pres. 1966-68), River Edge Tchrs. Assn. (pres. 1964-66), Assn. Ednl. Communications Tech. (nat. nominating com. 1978-79, council 1978-79, steering com. 1979-80, evaluation com. 1979, co-chmn. liaison com. with Am. Assn. Sch. Librarians 1979-83, nat. nominating com. 1980-82, awards com. 1981-89), Sch. Media Specialists (program com. 1982-84, bd. dirs. region II 1983-84, pres. 1986, mem. task force on librs. and info. sci., White House, writing com., co-author: Information Power, 1988), Nat. Button Soc., N.J. Button Soc., Bergen Button Buffs (founding grandmother 1993). Home: 315 Schraalenburgh Rd Haworth NJ 07641-1200

BIESS, BARBARA DZIEDZIC, communications executive; b. Detroit, Mar. 26, 1963; d. Joseph Roman and Emma Lucy (Lewinski) Dziedzic; m. Robert Donald Biess, Oct. 8, 1988. AB with distinction, U. Mich., 1985, BSA with distinction, 1985. Mktg. asst. Park West Galleries, Inc., Southfield, Mich., 1985; market researcher Gen. Motors Corp., Warren, Mich., 1985; staff cons. KPMG Peat Marwick, Detroit, 1986-87, assoc. cons., 1987-87, dir. communications, 1987-90; mgr. communications and mem. svcs. Mich. Assn. CPAs, Farmington Hills, 1990-92; mgr. mktg. svcs. Harley Ellington Pierce Yee Assocs., Inc., Southfield, Mich., 1992—. Mem. Internat. Assn. Bus. Communicators (pres. Detroit chpt., v.p. membership, bd. dirs., mem. mission statement com., mem. profl. devel. com., mem. job referral svc.), Internat. Freedom Festival (past vice-chmn., mem. exec. com.), Soc. Mktg. Profl. Svcs. (mem. mktg. awards com., cert. mktg. profl.), Engring. Soc. Detroit (mem. publs. com.), U. Mich. Alumni Assn. Roman Catholic. Office: Harley Ellington Pierce Yee Assocs Inc 26913 Northwestern Hwy Ste 200 Southfield MI 48034-3476

BIGELOW, MARTHA MITCHELL, retired historian; b. Talladega Springs, Ala., Sept. 19, 1921; divorced; children: Martha Frances, Carolyn Letitia. B.A., Montevallo U., 1943; M.A. (tuition fellow, Julius Rosenwald scholar 1943-44, Cleo Hearson scholar, summer 1944, Ency. Brit. fellow 1944-45), U. Chgo., 1944, Ph.D., 1946. Assoc. prof. history Miss. Coll., Clinton, 1946-48, Memphis State U., 1948-49; Assoc. prof. history U. Miss., 1949-50; assoc. curator manuscripts Mich. Hist. Collections, U. Mich., Ann Arbor, 1954-57; prof. history Miss. Coll., 1957-71, chmn. dept. history and polit. sci., 1964-71; dir. Bur. of History, Mich. Dept. State, 1971-90; sec. Mich. Hist. Commn., Mich. Dept. State, state historic preservation officer, 1971-90; coord. for Mich., Nat. Hist. Publs. and Recs. Commn., 1974-90. Contbr. articles profl. publns. Mem. Am. Assn. State and Local History (v.p. 1979-80, pres. 1980-81, fellow summers 1958, 59), Orgn. Am. Historians, Nat. Assn. State Archives and Recs. Assn., So. Hist. Assn., Mich. Hist. Soc., Miss. Hist. Soc. Home: 201 N Jefferson St Clinton MS 39056-4237

BIGELOW, PAGE ELIZABETH, public policy professional; b. Louisville, Feb. 9, 1948; d. William Simpson and Page Elizabeth (Smith) B. BA, Wells Coll., 1970; postgrad., NYU, 1971-72, Gen. Theol. Sem., 1971-72. Rsch. asst., libr. Nat. Mcpl. League, N.Y.C., 1970-75, rsch. dir. ethics govt. project, 1975-80, dir. representation project, 1981-84; sr. assoc. Nat. Civic

League (formerly Nat. Mcpl. League), N.Y.C., 1983-87; staff cons. state-city commn. on integrity in govt. N.Y., N.Y.C., 1986-87; mem. sr. staff Inst. Pub. Adminstrn., N.Y.C., 1987—. Author: Lobbying Laws in the States: A Comparative Study, 1980, From Norms of Rules, Regulating the Outside Interests of Public Officials, 1989, Annotated Bibliography on Citizenship and Ethics, 2d edit., 1993, Money, Politics and the Public Trust: Gifts, Illegal Gratuities, Bribery, Extortion and Campaign Contributions, 1995; editor: Forms of Local Representation, 1982. Mem. citizens adv. panel to joint legis. com. on revision and simplification of tax code, N.Y., 1982-86; del. Ednl. Priorities Panel, N.Y.C., 1984-94; mem. Citywide Sch. Bd. Elections Com., N.Y.C., 1985—. Mem. Coun. on Govtl. Ethics Laws, Jr. League N.Y.C. (corp. sec. 1986-88, 90, Honored Vol. 1990). Episcopalian. Office: Inst Pub Adminstrn 55 W 44th St New York NY 10036-6609

BIGGERS, PATRICIA A., social services administrator; b. Winchester, Ind., Nov. 25, 1948; d. Natividad and Christina Mena (Ramos) Gonzales; m. Gerald M. Biggers, Jr., April 22, 1972. BA, Northern Ill. U., 1970—. Mgr. Social Security Adminstrn., Balt., Chgo., Kansas City, 1975-91; regional dir., program and integrity reviews Social Security Adminstrn., Boston, 1991—; policy bd. mem. Boston Fed. Exec. Bd., 1993—. Office: Social Security Adminstrn Program & Integrity Reviews 10 Causeway St Boston MA 02222

BIGGERS, PAULA BOWERS, medical, surgical nurse; b. Allendale, S.C., July 10, 1956; d. Paul Ford and Jessie (King) Bowers; m. William Alan Biggers Jr., Jan. 19, 1987. Student, U. S.C., 1974-75; A in Dental Assisting, Midlands Tech. Coll., 1975-76; BS in Nursing, U. S.C., 1979-82. RN, Tex., S.C.; cert. med.-surg. nurse, nephrology nurse. Asst. head nurse Richland Meml. Hosp., Columbia, S.C., 1982-84; asst. head nurse Dorn Vets. Hosp., Columbia, S.C., 1984-91; unit mgr. weekends Hermann Hosp., Houston, 1992-94, unit mgr., 1994—; mem. procedure com. Dorn Vets. Hosp., Columbia, 1989-91, nurse quality control, 1990-91; preceptor hemodialysis unit Dorn Vets. Hosp., Columbia, 1989-91; instr. cardio-pulmonary resuscitation ARC, Columbia, 1985-91; CPR instr., Houston, 1991—, unit guideline com., 1991—. Contbr. articles to profl. jours. Blood pressure screening ARC, Columbia, 1985-91. Mem. AACCN (mid-state chpt., pub. rels. 1989-90, pres. elect 1990-91, pres. 1991-92), Sigma Theta Tau (Alpha XI chpt. 1991). Republican. Baptist. Home: 10826 Herald Square Dr Houston TX 77099-1817 Office: Hermann Hosp 6411 Fannin St Houston TX 77030

BIGGERT, JUDITH BORG, lawyer, state representative; b. Chgo., Aug. 15, 1937; d. Alvin Andrew and Marjorie Virginia (Mailler) Borg; m. Rody Patterson Biggert, Sept. 21, 1963; children: Courtney Ray, Alison Mailler, Rody Patterson, Adrienne Taylor. B.A., Stanford U., 1959; J.D., Northwestern U., 1963. Bar: Ill. 1963. Law clk. to presiding justice U.S. Ct. Appeals (7th cir.), Chgo., 1963-64; sole practice, Hinsdale, Ill., 1964—; rep. Ill. Gen. Assembly, 1993—; minority spokesperson 81st Dist. Judiciary I Com., 1993-94. Mem. bd. editors Law Rev., Northwestern U. Sch. Law, 1961-63. Pres., bd. dirs. Hinsdale Twp. High Sch. Dist. 86 Bd. Edn., 1983-85, 78-85; pres. Jr. League Chgo., 1976-78, treas., bd. bd. mgrs., 1966—; chmn. Hinsdale Antiques Show, 1980; pres. Oak Sch. PTA, Hinsdale, 1976-78; pres.-treas. Chgo. jr. bd. Travelers Aid Soc., 1965-70; Sunday sch. tchr. Grace Episcopal Ch., Hinsdale, 1978-80, 82-85; chair, treas., 2d v.p., bd. dirs. Vis. Nurses Assn. Chgo., 1978. Recipient Servian award Jr. aux. U. Chgo. Cancer Research Found. Mem. ABA, Ill. Bar Assn., Du Page Assn. Women Lawyers, Coalition Women Legislators. Republican. Home: 6301 S Cass Ave Westmont IL 60559

BIGGS, ANTOINETTE BAILEY, real estate broker; b. Rhinebeck, N.Y., May 24, 1936; d. Donald Cheney and Felicita Mercedes (Rivera) Bailey; m. Robert Laney Bush, June 5, 1955 (div. Mar. 1971); children: Denise Lee McLeod, Lisa Anne Mooney, Amy Suzanne Curry, Patrick Laney Bush; m. Hubbard Kavanaugh Biggs, June 27, 1973. AA with honors, Polk Community Coll, Winter Haven, Fla., 1992; BA in Interpersonal Comm. cum laude, U. Ctrl. Fla., 1994. Cert. real estate brokerage mgr., real estate specialist. Legal sec. Fagan & Crouch, Attys., Gainesville, Fla., 1953-61; real estate salesperson Huskey Realty, Realtors, Maitland, Fla., 1968-70, Roberts & Gilman, Realtors, Maitland, 1970-73; real estate broker Hubbard K. Biggs, Realtor, Lake Wales, Fla., 1973-74; pres. Biggs Appraisal & Realty, Inc., Lake Wales, 1974-93, Biggs & Biggs, Inc., Lake Wales, 1974—; pres. Lake Wales Bd. of Realtors, 1983, 84, also multiple chairmanships; edn. chmn. Winter Haven Bd. of Realtors, 1974, 81. Mem. real estate adv. com. Polk Community Coll., 1980—. Recipient Excellence in Ed. awards Winter Haven Bd. Realtors, 1974, 75, 76, 77, 81, 82, Realtor of Yr. award, 1984. Mem. DAR, Nat. Assn. Realtors, Lake Wales Bd. Realtors, Women's Coun. Realtors (v.p. 1980-81), Winter Haven Bd. Realtors, Phi Theta Kappa, Phi Kappa Phi, Golden Key Nat. Honor Soc. (pres. U. Ctrl. Fla. chpt. 1993-94). Republican. Roman Catholic. Home: 241 Volusia Dr Winter Haven FL 33884 Office: Biggs & Biggs Inc Realtors 132 W Central Ave Lake Wales FL 33853-4071

BIGGS, MARY, librarian, English language educator; b. N.Y.C., Feb. 8, 1944; d. Magnus C. and Ruth (Murray) Gleason; m. Robert Mancuso, Dec. 15, 1963 (div. 1977); children: Nicholas, Nathan; m. Victor C. Biggs, July, 1978. BA, SUNY, Albany, 1972; MA, SUNY, Buffalo, 1976, MLS, 1977; PhD, U. Chgo., 1986. Humanities libr. U. Evansville, Ind., 1977-79; editorial asst. U. Chgo. Press, 1979-81; instr. U. Chgo., 1982-83, asst. prof., 1984-87; chair info. svcs. Bowling Green (Ohio) state U., 1983-84; asst. prof. Columbia U., N.Y.C., 1987-89; dir. librs. Mercy Coll., Westchester County, N.Y., 1989-92; dean of libr., prof. English Trenton (N.J.) State Coll., 1992—; adv. bd. Columbia U. Press, 1991—. Author: A Gift That Cannot be Refused: The Writing and Publishing of Contemporary American Poetry, 1990; editor: Publishers and Librarians, 1984, Library Quarterly; co-editor: Editor's Choice II, 1987, Men and Women: Together and Alone, 1988; editorial bd. Beta Phi Mu monograph series, 1989-92, Libr. Quar., 1990—; contbr. chpts. to books, articles to profl. publs. Mem. ALA (com. mem.), Assn. Libr. and Info. Sci. Edn. (com. mem.), N.J. Acad. Libr. Network (bd. dirs. 1992—), Beta Phi Mu (dir.-at-large 1989-92, pres. 1993-95). Home: 46 Green Ln Ewing NJ 08638 Office: Trenton State Coll Hillwood Lks Trenton NJ 08650

BIGGS-WILLIAMS, EVELYN ANN, librarian; b. Atmore, Ala., Sept. 27, 1950; d. John Henry and Mary Evelyn (Smith) Biggs; m. Michael Robin Williams, June 14, 1986. BS, U. South Ala., 1971; MLS, Fla. State U., 1972. Libr. Escambia Acad., Atmore, Ala., 1972-73, Jefferson Davis Community Coll., Brewton, Ala., 1973—. Am. host Am. Host Family Sponsor, 1975-76, 78, 80, 93; coord. Telethon Pledge Ctr., Muscular Dystrophy Assn., Escambia County, Ala., 1988-92. Named to Ala. Libr. Hall of Fame, 1992; recipient Leadership Devel. for Women Project award Ala. Coll. System, 1988-89, Award of Exceptional Svc. Libr. and Media Profls. Workshop, Mobile, Ala., 1989. Mem. NEA, ALA, Assn. for Ednl. Comm. and Tech., Ala. Instrnl. Media Assn., Ala. Libr. Assn., Friends of Ala. Librs., Nature Conservancy (Ala. chpt.), CC.C. Assn. for Instrn. and Tech., Nat. Coun. for Learning Resources, FacioScapuloHumeral Soc. Methodist. Office: Jefferson Davis Coll Leigh Libr 220 Alco Dr Brewton AL 36426-2716

BIGHAM, CECILIA BETH, communications executive, marketing professional; b. Harrisburg, Ark., May 13, 1956; d. Jimmy and Patsy Jean (Collins) B.; m. Jeffrey Stephen Yallope, Aug. 31, 1993. BA, U. Ark., 1978. Editor, staff writer Holiday Inns, Memphis, 1981-84; project analyst Hi-Net Comm., Inc., Memphis, 1984-85; sr. comm. specialist, editor mgmt. newsletter, sr. exec. mgmt. meeting prodr. Fed. Express Corp., Memphis, 1985—; freelance video prodr., talent scout Vin Di Bona Prodns., Inc., L.A., 1991-92; cons., joint founding mem. Milpara Computer Sys. Corp., Memphis, 1993—, also bd. dirs.; resumé freelance writer Memphis, 1987—. Vol. Memphis-in-May, 1984-89; vol. fundraiser Am. Cancer Soc., 1990—. Recipient Cert. of Appreciation, Am. Cancer Soc., 1990, 91, Memphis-in-May, 1993. Mem. NAFE, Louis Rukeyser's Wall St. Club, Phi Kappa Phi. Republican. Methodist.

BIGLAND-RITCHIE, BRENDA RACHEL, physiologist, neurophysiology researcher, educator; b. Jordans, Eng., Sept. 23, 1927; came to U.S., 1958; d. Ranulf Aggs and Dorothy Eva (Shaw) Bigland; m. J. Murdoch Ritchie, July 28, 1951; children: Alasdair John, Anne Jocelyn. BSc, U. Coll., London, 1949, PhD, 1968; DSc, London U., 1987. Med. rsch. coun. fellow U. Coll., London, 1949-51, asst. prof. physiology, 1951-53; rsch. instr. Albert Einstein Coll. Medicine, Bronx, N.Y., 1963-66; physiology lectr. Hunter Coll., Bronx, N.Y., 1966-67; asst. prof. biology Marymount Coll., Tarrytown, N.Y., 1967-70; prof. biology and rehab. scis. Quinnipiac Coll., Hamden, Conn., 1973-94; fellow John B. Pierce Lab., New Haven, Conn., 1985-94; prof. pediatrics, lectr neurology Yale U. Sch. Medicine, New Haven, Conn., 1994—; adj. prof. pediatrics Sch. Medicine, Yale U., 1988-94; nat. and internat. lectr.; mem. organizing com. Internat. Union Physiological Scis. Commn. for Human and Exercise Physiology, Helsinki, 1990, Glasgow, 1993. Author 17 book chpts.; contbr. more than 50 articles to profl. jours. Fellow Alexander von Humboldt Found., 1991, NIH, 1976-94, Multiple Sclerosis Found., Muscular Dystrophy Found., 1978-84, among others. Fellow Am. Coll. Sports Medicine; mem. Soc. for Neurosci., Brit. Physiol. Soc., Am. Physiol. Soc., Internat. Union of Physiol. Socs. Office: Yale U Sch Medicine Dept Pediatrics 874 Howard Ave New Haven CT 06519

BIHARY, JOYCE, federal judge; b. Detroit, Oct. 24, 1950; d. Paul and Edith (Uden) B.; m. Jonathan W. Lowe, Aug. 22, 1976; children: Jane, Alexis, James Byron. BA, Wellesley Coll., 1972; JD, U. Mich., 1975. Bar: Ga. 1975. Atty. Alston, Miller & Gaines, 1975-77; atty. Rogers & Hardin, 1977-79, ptnr., 1979-87; bankruptcy judge U.S. Dist. Ct., Atlanta, 1987—. Mem. ABA, Ga. Assn. Women Lawyers, Atlanta Bar Assn., Bar Coun. No. Dist. Ga., 11th Cir. Hist. Soc., Joseph Henry Lumpkin Am. Inn of Ct., Southeastern Bankruptcy Law Inst. Office: US Dist Ct US Courthouse 75 Spring St SW Atlanta GA 30303-3309*

BILANIUK, LARISSA TETIANA, neuroradiologist, educator; b. Ukraine, July 15, 1941; came to U.S., 1951; d. Yaroslav and Myroslava (Hryculak) Zubal; m. Oleksa-Myron Bilaniuk, Nov. 14, 1964; children: Larissa Indira, Laada Myroslava. BA, Wayne State U., 1961, MD, 1965. Diplomate Am. Bd. Radiology. Resident in radiology Hosp. of U. Pa., Phila., 1966-70; fellow Fondation Ophtalmologique, Paris, 1972; assoc. in radiology U. Pa. Sch. Medicine, Phila., 1973-74, asst. prof., 1974-79, assoc. prof., 1979-82, prof., 1982—; with Children's Hosp. of Phila., 1992—; reviewer grants rsch. NIH, Washington, 1983-86; St. Göran lectr. Karolinska Inst., Stockholm, 1984; vis. prof. Grosshadern Clinics, U. Munich, 1988; invited lectr. USSR, 1976, 90, People's Republic of China, 1977, France, 1980, 82, 89, 94, Japan, 1984, 90, Sweden, 1984, 92, Eng., 1985, The Netherlands, 1985, Italy, 1986, 87, 90, 92, Fed. Republic of Germany, 1987, 89, 92, Chile, 1993. Co-editor 3 radiology books; contbr. over 200 articles on radiology to med. jours. and chpts. to books. Rsch. fellow Cancer Rsch. Ctr., Heidelberg, Fed. Republic Germany, 1967-68. Fellow Am. Coll. Radiology; mem. Radiol. Soc. N.Am., Am. Soc. Neuroradiology, European Soc. Neuroradiology, Soc. for Pediatric Radiology, Soc. Magnetic Resonance in Medicine, Ukrainian Med. Assn. N.Am., Sigma Xi. Ukrainian Catholic. Office: Childrens Hosp of Phila 324 S 34th St Philadelphia PA 19104-4345

BILES, MARILYN MARTA, painter; b. Wilmington, Del., Oct. 3, 1935; d. Albert Humbert and Anne Marie (DeRogatis) Marta; m. George Ronald Bower, June 30, 1956 (div. May 1970); children: Michele Bower Alvarado, Nancy Bower Guthrie, Randall William. Student Moore Coll. Art, 1953-54, St. Mary's Coll., 1959-61, Mus. Fine Arts, Houston, 1972-74. Art tchr. Contemporary Arts Mus., Houston, 1969-73, 80-81; head art dept. pre-primary div. Duchesne Acad., Houston, 1970-72; project coord. Nan Fisher, Inc., Houston, 1983-84; one-woman shows include Brown & Scurlock Galleries, Beaumont, Tex., 1st Nat. City Bank, Houston, 1980, Christ Ch. Cathedral, 1981-82, Toni Jones Gallery, 1981, U. Houston, 1982, Station Gallery, Greenville, Del., 1984, Boyar Norton & Blair, 1986, Martha Turner Properties, 1986, Cancerfighters of Houston, 1991, R.S.V.P. Collection, Miami, Fla., 1993, Chateaux Piada, Bordeaux, France, 1993, Musée de la Commanderie d'Unet, Bordeaux, 1993, Tex. A&M U. Coll. Medicine, 1994; group shows include: U. Houston, 1977, 79, Nat. Cape Coral Exhbn., Fla., 1979, Toni Jones Gallery, 1979, Assistance League of Houston, 1979, 80, Golden Crescent Gallery, Houston, 1984, Conrad Gallery, Galveston, Tex. 1991, Pima Coll. Tucson, La Sorbonne, Paris, 1992, Musée de la Commanderie d'Unet, Bordeaux, 1992, Spirit Echoes Gallery Invitational, Austin Tex., 1992, 2nd anniversary show, 1994, Hotel de Ville, Paris, 1993, Wirtz Gallery, Miami, Fla., 1993, New England Fine Arts Inst., Boston, 1993, Spirit Echoes Gallery, Austin, Tex., 1994; coord., designer art programs Spring Branch Schs., Houston, 1968-70. Bd. dirs. Spring Branch YWCA, Houston, 1973-74; docent Harris County Heritage Soc., Houston, 1970-72; mem. bd., v.p. Arcs Found., Inc., Houston, 1983; bd. dirs., gala chmn. Houston Grand Opera Guild, 1983-84, governing bd. assn., 1984-85, co-chmn. gala, 1985; founder, pres. Mus. Med. Sci. Assn., Houston, 1986-87; mem. com. Can-Do-It Charity Fundraiser, Peter W. Guenther Art History Scholarship Fund at U. Houston. Mem. Artists Equity (dir. Houston chpt. 1980), Art League Houston, Tex. Fine Arts Assn., Univ. Club Houston, Houston Racquet Club, World Trade Club (v.p. women's assn. 1974-75). Republican. Episcopalian. Home: 9337 Katy Fwy Ste 171 Houston TX 77024-1515

BILGER, SUSAN ROXSTROM, program manager; b. L.A., Dec. 27, 1963; d. Harry Francis and Marion Rose (Caspary) Roxstrom; m. John Floyd Bilger, July 23, 1988. BSCS, Santa Clara U., 1985, MSCSE, 1989, MBA, 1993. Software engr. GTE, Mountain View, Calif., 1985-89, software mgr., 1989-92; program test mgr. GTE, Mountain View, 1992-94, dep. program mgr., 1994—. Mem. Beta Gamma Sigma, Pi Mu Epsilon. Republican. Roman Catholic. Home: 1425 Calle Alegre San Jose CA 95120-4401

BILL, KAREN S., actress; b. Annapolis, Md., Feb. 22, 1951; d. Charles A. and Orel M. (Heinly) B. BS cum laude, Millersville U., 1973; MEd, Kutztown U., 1976. Tchr. Ephrata (Pa.) Area Sch. Dist., 1973-85; ednl. cons. Scribner Educational Pubs. div. Macmillan Pubs., Delran, N.J., 1985-87; telemation and news coord. Sta. WGAL-TV, Lancaster, Pa., 1986-87; actress in indsl. and ednl. tng. videos, 1984—. Appeared in plays including For The Love of Ike, Jacques Brel Is..., Carousel, Joseph and the Amazing Technicolor Dreamcoat, Gypsy, The King and I, Annie, Here's Love, Cabaret, Stop the World! and Roar of the Greasepaint, The Play, Our Town, Sweet Charity, The Philadelphia Story; films include Silence At Bethany, The Whole Truth; TV appearances in commls., news, voice-overs; radio includes commels. and voice-overs. Mem. Theater Assn. Pa.

BILLAU, ROBIN LOUISE, engineering and consulting executive; b. Denver, Sept. 19, 1951; d. Emerson Roy and Catherine Louise (Brewster) Billau; m. Edward E. Adams. BA, Western State Coll., 1973; MS, Colo. State U., 1977. Cert. indsl. hygienist. Life sci., indsl. hygienist Mont. Energy Devel. & Rsch. Inst., Butte, 1977-79; indsl. hygiene supr. Mountain States Energy, Butte, 1979-81; asst. prof. Mont. Coll. Mineral Sci. Tech., Butte, 1981-83; indsl. hygiene supr. EG & G Idaho, Idaho Falls, 1983-85, unit mgr., 1985-87, group mgr., 1987-88, sr. tech. adv., 1988-90; cons. environ. mgmt., indsl. hygiene RLB Cons., Inc., Houghton, Mich., 1990-92; mgr. Jason Assocs. Corp., Idaho Falls, Idaho, 1992—. Mem. Am. Indsl. Hygiene Assns., Am. Bd. Indsl. Hygiene Idaho Am. Indstl. Democrat. Home: 174 Quinn Creek Rd Bozeman MT 59715 Office: Jason Assocs Corp 591 Park Ave Ste 202 Idaho Falls ID 83402

BILLER, GERALDINE POLLACK, curator; b. Milw., Apr. 4, 1933; d. Sidney Samuel and Frieda (Eisenberg) Pollack; m. Joel Wilson Biller, May 1, 1955; children: Sydney Ellen, Andrew John, Charles Benjamin. BS, Northwestern U., 1955; MA, U. Wis., 1991. Tchr. art Va. Sch. System, 1955-56, Internat. Sch., The Hague, The Netherlands, 1959-62; adminstr. internat. rels. program Georgetown U., Washington, 1973-75; freelance graphic designer Washington, Milw., 1978-86; art historian, curator Milw. Art Mus., 1988—. Mem. Wis. State Dem. Adminstrv. Com., 1992-93; v.p. women's divsn. cmty. planning com. Milw. Jewish Fedn., 1986-90; pres. bd. dirs. Jewish Family Svcs., Milw., 1991-94. Home: 4716 N Wilshire Rd Milwaukee WI 53211-1262

BILLER, PAMELA MANNO, real estate agent; b. Balt., Sept. 22, 1954; d. Frank Angelo and Rose Elizabeth (Confrancesco) Manno; m. Michael Pritzter, Aug. 30 1975 (div. Aug. 1979); m. Michael Jay Biller, Se. 16, 1979; children: Aaron Robert, Melissa Lauren. AA, Catonsville Community Coll., 1974. Settlement officier Real Estate Title Co., Balt., 1974-77; media buyer W.B. Doner and Co. Advt., Balt., 1977-79, account exec., 1979-81, broadcast bus. mgr., 1981-83; pres., owner Little Stars Ltd., Owings Mills, Md., 1987—; with real estate sales Hannah Tabor, Inc., Balt., 1983—; bd. dirs. Child Study Assn. Md., Balt. Mem. Million Dollar Assn. Md. (Bronze Statue 1984, gold pin 1987, life), Greater Balt. Bd. Realtors.

BILLETER, ANNE MARGARET, librarian; b. Sanford, Fla., Apr. 11, 1946; d. Jack J. and Barbara (Whipple) B.; m. Robert Luis Hoolko, Nov. 25, 1972; 1 child, Steven John. BA, Rutgers U., 1968; MLS, U. N.C., 1969; PhD, U. Ill., 1979. Youth svcs. libr. Rockingham County Libr., Eden, N.C., 1969-71; rsch. assoc. Libr. Rsch. Ctr. U. Ill., Urbana, 1972-74; vis. lectr. Sch. Libr. Sci. U. So. Calif., L.A., 1975-77; children's libr. Glendale (Calif.) Pub. Libr., 1976-78; ref. libr., lectr. So. Oreg. State Coll., Ashland, 1980; head ref. svcs. Josephine County Libr., Grants Pass, Oreg., 1981-85; adult svcs. coord. Jackson County Libr., Medford, Oreg., 1985—. Compiler: Directory of Southern Oregon Libraries, 1980. Trustee Josephine County Hist. Soc., Grants Pass, 1981-88, So. Oreg. Hist. Soc., Medford, 1992—. Fellow U. N.C., 1969. Mem. ALA (com. chair), So. Oreg. Libr. Fedn., Oreg. Libr. Assn. (v.p., pres.-elect 1993-94, pres. 1994-95), Beta Phi Mu, Phi Kappa Phi. Home: 4999 Griffin Creek Rd Medford OR 97501 Office: Jackson County Libr Svcs 413 W Main St Medford OR 97501

BILLETER, MARIANNE, pharmacy educator; b. Durham, N.C., Feb. 28, 1963; d. Ralph Leonard and Nancy Jane (Chambers) B. BS in Pharmacy, Purdue U., 1986, D in Pharmacy, 1987. Pharmacy Commd. Officer Student Tng. and Extern Program, USPHS-FDA, Rockville, Md., 1983; radiopharmacy Commd. Officer Student Tng. and Extern Program, USPHS-FDA, Bethesda, Md., 1984; pharmacy Indian Health Svc. Commd. Officer Student Tng. and Extern Program, USPHS, Tahlequah, Okla., 1985; pharmacist Beaumont Hosp., Royal Oak, Mich., 1986; pharmacy resident U. Ky., Lexington, 1987-89, fellow in infectious diseases, 1989-90; asst. prof. Xavier Univ. of L.A., New Orleans, 1990—; relief pharmacist Ochsner Med. Instns., New Orleans, 1991—; cons. Abbott Labs., Abbott Park, Ill., 1991—. Contbr. chpts. to books and articles to profl. jours. With Operation Smile, La. Chpt., 1992—. Mem. Am. Assn. Colls. Pharmacy, Am. Coll. Clin. Pharmacy, Am. Soc. Hosp. Pharmacists, La. Soc. Hosp. Pharmacists, Soc. Infectious Diseases Pharmacists (bd. dirs), Am. Soc. Microbiology. Office: Xavier Coll Pharmacy 7325 Palmetto St New Orleans LA 70125

BILLINGS, CHERYL SUSAN, controller; b. Hanford, Calif., Sept. 28, 1948; d. Charles E. and Betty J. (Hurt) Ruff; m. John S. Billings, Oct. 16, 1982. BS, San Jose State U., 1986. CPA, Calif.; CMA. Contr. A. B. Dick Co., Calif., 1977-83; sr. auditor Price Waterhouse, San Jose, Calif., 1986-89; gen. acctg. mgr. Cisco Sys., Menlo Park, Calif., 1990-92; corporate contr. Silicon Valley Rsch., Mountain View, Calif., 1992—. Mem. Inst. Mgmt. Accts. (nat. v.p. 1991-92), Inst. Cert. Mgmt. Accts. (regent 1992-94), Am. Women's Soc. CPAs (chpt. pres. 1992-93), Alpine Hills Tennis (bd. dirs., treas. 1993—). Office: Silicon Valley Rsch 300 Ferguson Dr # 300 Mountain View CA 94043

BILLINGS, JUDITH A., state education official. Supt. public instrn. State of Washington, 1988—. Office: Public Instruction Dept PO Box 47200 Olympia WA 98504-7200

BILLINGS, PATRICIA ANN COLLINS, nurse practitioner; b. San Diego, Jan. 31, 1946; d. Normon Clyde and Mary Asunda (Fantoni) Collins; m. George M. Whitehead, June 12, 1966 (div. Mar. 1975); children: Garrett Grafton Rayne, Sharna Raynel, Adrianna Megan, Autumn Leigh; m. Russell F. Billings II, Aug. 19, 1989. BS in Nursing, Loma Linda (Calif.) U., 1967, MPH, 1971; cert. Pediatric Nurse Practitioner, U. Calif, San Diego, 1979. RN, Calif., Idaho; cert. nurse practitioner, Idaho, Calif. Pub. health nurse San Bernadino County, Calif., 1967-72, San Diego County, 1974; sch. nurse, pediatric nurse practitioner Vista (Calif.) Unified Sch. Dist., 1974-85; pediatric nurse practitioner Sharp Rees-Stealy Med. Group, San Diego, 1985-94; pediatric nurse practitioners Pediatric Ctr., Twin Falls, Idaho, 1994—. Contbg. editor Pediatric Nursing, 1994—. Mem. Pres.'s Council, San Diego, 1984-85. Recipient USPHS scholarship, 1971. Fellow Nat. Assn. Pediatric Nurse Practitioners (cert. chmn. 1987-93); mem. Am. Acad. Pediats. (mem. Idaho chpt.), San Diego Assn. Pediatric Nurse Practitioners (legis. chair 1993-94, editor pedits. nursing assessment 1995—, 1993 Pediatric Nurse Practitioner of Yr.). Republican. Office: Pediatric Ctr 388 Martin St Twin Falls ID 83301

BILLINGS, PATRICIA ANNE, human resources executive; b. N.Y.C., Feb. 21, 1943; d. George James and Anne Marie (Murray) B.; 1 child, Daniel. BS in Edn. cum laude, Seton Hall U., 1971; MA in Am. Studies, Fairfield U., 1976. Cert. elem. and secondary tchr., N.Y., N.J., Conn. Various teaching positions Conn., N.Y., 1962-78; tng. specialist Morgan Guaranty Trust Co., N.Y.C., 1979-81; asst. treas. Bankers Trust Co., N.Y.C., 1981-83, asst. v.p., 1983-84; mgr. tng. Emergy & Purolator Worldwide, Wilton, Conn., 1984-89; v.p. Chase Manhattan Bank, 1989-92, AT&T, 1992—; bd. dirs. Long Ridge Sch., Stamford, Conn., 1986-94; cons. in field. Mem. ASTD. Democrat. Roman Catholic.

BILLINGSLEY, JUDITH ANN SEAVEY, oncological nurse; b. Manchester, Conn., Aug. 4, 1947; d. John Frank and Carol Jean (Wood) Seavey; m. Michael Billingsley, June 7, 1969; children: Tamara Lynn, Tara Lynn. Diploma, Hartford Hosp. Sch. Nursing, 1968; student, Coll. of Albemarle, 1985-86, No. Va. Community Coll., 1990; grad. with honors, George Mason U., 1992. Staff nurse ICU Manchester Meml. Hosp., 1968-69; staff nurse recovery room Burlingame (Calif.) Hosp. and Med. Ctr., 1972-73; staff nurse St. Joseph's Hosp., Atlanta, 1987-89; clin. nurse Alexandria (Va.) Hosp., 1989-91; admissions nurse Hospice of No. Va., 1991-92; neuro-oncology clin. rsch. nurse Winship Cancer Ctr. Emory U. Sch. Medicine, Atlanta, 1992—. Mem. Sigma Theta Tau, Golden Key Nat. Honor Soc., Alpha Chi. Home: 1273 Gray Squirrel Xing Marietta GA 30062-6275

BILLINGSLEY, NANCY JANE, small business owner; b. Beverly, Mass., Mar. 3, 1956; d. Edward Charles and Jane Veronica (Holak) O'Connell; m. Barnaby Fitzgerald Billingsley, Feb. 13, 1993. AA, North Shore C.C., Beverly, Mass., 1976; BA, Ea. Nazarene Coll., 1994. Customer svc. specialist Eigner and Mazonson Ins., Lynn, Mass., 1981-84; new bus. underwriter Electric Ins., Lynn, 1984-85; supr. underwriters Gen. Accident, Peabody, Mass., 1985-89; pres. O'Connell Cleaning, Magnolia, Mass., 1990—. Republican. Roman Catholic. Home and Office: 9 Norman Ave Magnolia MA 01930

BILLITER, FREDA DELOROUS, elementary education educator; b. McAndrews, Ky., Oct. 15, 1937; d. David Wilson and Evelyn May (Puckett) Kendrick; m. William Jefferson Billiter, Sept. 12, 1954; 1 child, Cynthia Delorous. BS in Edn., Ohio U., 1969, MEd, 1987. Cert. elem. tchr., media specialist, reading specialist. Departmental tchr. Ironton (Ohio) City Schs., 1965-66, 3d grade tchr., 1966-67; 2d grade tchr. Portsmouth (Ohio) City Schs., 1969—. Coord. sec. Scioto County Hist. Soc., Portsmouth, 1980-82; choir mem. Shawnee State U. and Cmty. Choir, Portsmouth, 1973—, Wesley United Meth. Ch. Chancel Choir, Portsmouth, 1985—, Portsmouth Cmty. Chorale, 1993—; mem. Scioto County Hist. Soc. and Nat. Trust. Martha Holden Jennings scholar Ohio U., 1988-89; recipient Cert. of Participation, Portsmouth Area Arts Coun., 1990. Mem. NEA, AAUW, Ohio Edn. Assn., Internat. Reading Assn., S.E. Ohio Coun. Tchrs. English, Scioto County Mus. and Cultural Ctr., Ohio Hist. Soc., Order Ea. Star, Phi Delta Kappa (awards chmn. 1990-91), Delta Kappa Gamma (1st v.p. 1990-92, pres. 1992-94), Ohio Bus. and Profl. Women, Kappa Delta Pi (svc. award 1986). Republican. Home: 2890 Circle Dr Portsmouth OH 45662-2445 Office: Wilson Elem Sch 613 Campbell Ave Portsmouth OH 45662-4468

BILLS, BERYL BOBINETTE, marketing professional; b. Chgo., Mar. 25, 1943; d. Charles Kenneth and Lydia (Rockenbach) Bobinette; m. David Baird Bills; children: Colin, Corey. BA, DePauw U., 1965; MBA, Northwestern U., 1970. Research chemist Quaker Oats Co., Barrington, Ill., 1965-69; analyst The Gillette Co., Chgo., Ill., 1970-74; sr. analyst Abbott Labs., N. Chgo., Ill., 1974-75; mktg. cons. Glenview, Ill., 1975—. Mem: AAUW, Qualitative Rsch. Cons. Inc.

BILSKI, VICTORIA CARRIER, writer; b. Suffern, N.Y., Sept. 29, 1956; d. Peter and Miriam (Munger) B.; m. Matthew Charles Sussman, Sept. 20, 1985; 2 children. BA, SUNY, Oswego, 1979; postgrad., Wesleyan U., Middletown, Conn. Writer prose. Contbr. short stories to Kenyon Rev., Blak Warrior Rev., 13th Moon, The Literary Cafe.

BILYEW, ANN MARGARET, health care consultant; b. Groton, Conn., Apr. 24, 1966; d. Charles Herbert and Annie Francis (Marchese) B. BS with highest distinction, U. Kans., 1990; MBA, Harvard U., 1994. Acct. exec. Barkley & Evergreen, Shawnee Mission, Kans., 1989-91; internal cons. Swope Pky. Health Ctr., Kansas City, Mo., 1991-92; assoc. APM, Inc., N.Y.C., 1994—. Bd. dirs. Human Rights Project, Kansas City, Mo., 1990-93; tutor Wilson Middle Sch., Boston, 1992-94; coord. Congrl. dist. Human Rights Campaign Fund, Boston, 1994. Recipient Prism Pub. Rels. Soc. Am., 1991; scholar Am. Bus. Women's Assn., 1992, Harvard U., 1992. Mem. NOW (editor/sr. v.p. Kansas City chpt, 1990-92), Harvard Club (N.Y.C.), Phi Kappa Phi. Democrat. Office: APM Inc New York NY 10019

BILZ, LAURIE S., medical/surgical nurse; b. Hackensack, N.J., Nov. 27, 1951; d. Richard F. and Lila (Russell) B. AAS, Bergen Community Coll., Paramus, N.J., 1972; BSN, Dominican Coll., 1990; cert. British health care system, Wroxton Coll., Eng., 1990; MSN, Seton Hall U., 1992; MPA, L.I. U., 1994. RN, N.J.; cert. med.-surg. nurse; cert. clin. specialist in med.-surg. nursing. RN Pascack Valley Hosp., Westwood, N.J.; clin. nursing instr. Bergen C.C., 1993—. Mem. ANA, N.J. Nurse's Assn., NLN. Home: 509 Bergen Ave Westwood NJ 07675-5244

BINDER, MADELINE DOTTI, counselor; b. Chgo., Oct. 7, 1942; d. Martin and Anne (Sweet) Binder; children: Mark Nathan, Marla Susan. BEd, Nat. Coll. Edn., 1964, MS, 1972, MS in Human Svcs.-Counseling, 1993. Tchr., Rochester Schs. (Minn.), 1963-64, Orange County Schs., Orlando, Fla., 1967-68; reading cons. Palatine Schs. (Ill.), 1972-73; instr. Parent Effective Tng., Wilmette, Ill., 1974-76, tchr. Effectiveness Tng., 1974-76; pres. Profls. Diversified, Wilmette, Ill., 1976-89; remedial and enrichment reading tchr. Waukegan (Ill.) Pub. Schs., 1986; pres. Lifeline, 1989-90; mgmt. cons. World Wide Diamonds Assn., Schaumburg, Ill., 1979-89, Artistic Color, Dallas, 1983-87; Pearl direct distbr. Amway Corp., Ada, Mich., 1976-94; exec. distbr. NU Skin, 1992; distbr. Starlight Internat., 1994—. Author: Organic Gardening, 1975, The Go-Getters Planner, 1986, Singles Guide to Disneyland, 1995. Leader, Camp Fire Girls, Evanston, Ill., 1963, 75. Recipient Ednl. Scholarship, Nat. Coll. Edn., 1971. Mem. Phi Delta Kappa, Alpha Delta Omega. Jewish.

BINDER, MILDRED KATHERINE, retired county public welfare agency executive; b. York, Pa., Jan. 5, 1918; d. Jemie Irving and Emma Jane (Billet) Binder. BA magna cum laude in Sociology, Hood Coll., 1940. Sec., mgr. Stock's Appliances, York, 1940-42; caseworker York County Bd. Assistance, Pa. Dept. Public Welfare, 1942-49, 1953-58, supr., 1949-53, 1958-59, exec. dir., 1959-83. Past mem. exec. com. York County Employment and Tng. Com.; past mem. dept. task forces state Social Service Delivery to Client Info. System, also mem. state ops. rev. bd.; past mem. bd. York County Council Alcoholism, 1959-62, Community Progress Council, 1965-67; co-chmn. Community Dialogue Com., 1968-69; mem. bd. Pre-Paid Health York, Inc., 1979; mem. human services planning coalition United Way, 1978-83, chmn. council agy. execs., 1967-71, 1976-78; past mem. consumer adv. councils Gen. Telephone, Met. Edison; bd. dirs. Literacy Council of York County, 1985-86; mem. York County Human Services Adv. Com., 1983-87; mem. York County Area Agy. on Aging Adv. Com., 1989—. Named Boss of Yr., Am. Bus. Women, 1973; named in commendations Pa. gov., Pa. Ho. of Reps. Mem. Am. Public Welfare Assn., AAUW (bd. dirs. York br. 1984—), York County Hist. Soc. (bd. dirs. 1989—), York Transp. Club (bd. dirs. 1987-91), Coll. Club York (bd. dirs. 1994—), Hood Coll. Club (pres. 1993—). Home: 1611 W Market St York PA 17404-5416

BINGAMAN, ANNE K., lawyer; b. Jerome, Ariz., July 3, 1943; d. William Emil and Anne Ellen (Baker) Kovacovich; m. Jeff F. Bingaman, Sept. 14, 1968; 1 child, John. BA in History, Stanford U., 1965; gen. course cert. with honors, London Sch. of Econs., England, 1964-65; LLB, Stanford U., 1968. Bar: Calif. 1969, N.Mex. 1969, Ariz. 1969, U.S. Dist. Ct. D.C. 1983. Atty. Brown & Bain, Phoenix, 1968-69, N.Mex. Bur. Revenue, Santa Fe, 1969-70, Modrall, Sperling, Roehl, Harris & Sisk, Albuquerque, 1970, N.Mex. Atty. Gen.'s Office, Santa Fe, 1970-72; asst. prof. to assoc. prof. U. N.Mex. Sch. Law, Santa Fe, 1972-76; founding ptnr. Bingaman & Davenport, Santa Fe, 1977-82; ptnr. Brown, Bain & Bingaman, Santa Fe and Washington, 1982-84, Onek, Klein & Farr, Washington, 1984-85, Powell, Goldstein, Frazer & Murphy, Washington, 1985-93. Contbr. articles to profl. jours. Mem. exec. com. Stanford Law Sch. Bd. Visitors, 1978-80, 88-90; mem. for N.Mex. of 10th Cir. Jud. Nominating Panel, 1977-80. Ford Found. fellow 1975; recipient Nat. Vol. award Stanford Assocs., 1989. Fellow Am. Bar Found.; mem. ABA, N.Mex. Bar (founder, vice-chair antitrust sect. 1982-85, chair com. to rewrite comm. property & other state laws to conform to ERA), Am. Law Inst. Democrat. Episcopalian. Office: US Dept Justice Antitrust Div 10th & Constitution Ave NW Washington DC 20530

BINGHAM, BARBARA GILMOUR, public relations executive; b. Wayne, N.J., Jan. 10, 1957; d. William Rutherford and Louise Randolph (See) B.; m. Michael Joseph Kalavik, May 23, 1987; children: Gavin, Alejna Natasha. BA, Lafayette Coll., Easton, Pa., 1979. Sales rep. Lexington-Andrews, Boulder, Colo., 1979-80; communications asst. UGI Corp., Valley Forge, Pa., 1980-82; writer, editor UGI Corp., 1982-83; pub. relations mgr. Avant-Garde Computing, Mt. Laurel, N.J., 1983-85; account supr. Myers CommuniCounsel, N.Y.C., 1985-87, Creamer Dickson Basford, N.Y.C., 1987-88; v.p. Creamer Dickson Basford, 1988-90; v.p. acct. dir. Creamer Dickson Basford, N.Y.C., 1990-91; v.p. Fleishman-Hillard, N.Y.C., 1991-92; prin. Bingham Comms., Pompton Plains, N.J., 1992—. Adv., Lafayette Coll. Publs., Easton, Pa., 1983-89. Cons., publicist Packanack Community Ch., Wayne, N.J., 1987-88; bd. dirs., publicist Packanack Coop. Nursery Sch., 1994—; bd. dirs. Newsletter Pompton Plains Nursery Sch., 1994—. Recipient PRSA Silver Anvil award, Ace for Excellence in Client Svc. award, Top Banana award for Strategic Creativity. Mem. Internat. Asns. Bus. Communicators, Pub. Rels. Soc. Am. (Silver anvil, other awards). Home and Office: 36 Prospect Ave Pompton Plains NJ 07444-1335

BINGHAM, JINSIE SCOTT, broadcast company executive; b. Greencastle, Ind., Dec. 28, 1935; d. Roscoe Gibson and Alpha Edith (Robinson) Scott; m. Frank William Wokoun, Jr. (dec.); children: Douglas Scott, Richard Frank; m. Richard Innes Bingham, June 24, 1964. Student, DePauw U., Greencastle, 1952-53, Northwestern U., 1953, Coe Coll., 1953-54. Exec. sec. Ind. Young Dems., 1958-60; receptionist Ind. House of Reps., Indpls., 1959; saleslady Avon Products, Greencastle, 1961-64; sales mgr. Sta. WJNZ (formerly WXTA), Greencastle, 1969-77, owner, pres., gen. mgr., 1977-94; owner Radio Greencastle, 1997—; former ptnr. Sta. WVTL, Monticello, Ill., Sta. KBIB, Monette, Ark.; speaker DePauw U. Communications Seminar, 1981, 85; vis. lectr., 1986—. Com. chair Legis. Awareness Seminar, 1978-86; co-chair Greencastle Gaelic Festival, 1983-84; charter mem. Greencastle 2001, 1985—, Greencastle Civic League, 1984—, Greencastle Merchant's Assn., 1983—, Community Resources Council, 1982—; charter mem., corp. sec. Main Street Greencastle, 1983-87, v.p., 1987-88, pres., 1989-90, chmn., 1990-91; charter mem., bd. dirs. Greencastle Vol. Fire Dept., 1986, Greencastle Devel. Ctr., 1988-89, Greencastle Community Child Care Ctr., 1983—, Putnam County United Way, 1992—; mem. Greencastle Zoning Bd. Appeals, 1984—, v.p., 1985-88, pres., 1988—; announcer Putnam County Fair Parade, 1977—; community host Hoosier Hospitality Days, 1981-84; active Putnam County Com. for Econ. Strength, 1979-83; mem. Gov.'s Commn. for Drug Free Ind., 1992—, Putnam County Visions, 1992—, Greencastle Jaycees, 1981 (named Outstanding Citizen), Putnam County Found., 1992—; v.p. Putnam County Hist. Assn.; founding chmn. Greencastle Cmty. Schs. Scholarship Fund Drive, 1995—. Named Outstanding Citizen by Jaycees, 1981. Mem. Putnam County Bd. Realtors, Am. Women in Radio and TV (pres. Ind. chpt. 1979-82), Indpls. Network Women in Bus. (charter), Women in Communications, Inc. (bd. dirs. 1983-84, MATRIX co-chair 1984, Frances Wright award, 1993), Am. Legion Aux., Nat. Assn. Broadcasters, Broadcast Pioneers, Ind. Broadcasters Assn. (v.p. FM 1982), Greencastle Bus. and Profl. Women's Club (pres. 1976-77, 79-80, Woman of Yr. 1994), Indpls. Ad Club, Women's Press Club Ind., Indpls. Press Club, Nat. Fedn. Press Women, Ind. Dem. Editorial Assn. (sec. 1987, v.p. 1988, pres. 1990), Ind. C. of C., Greencastle C. of C. (bd. dirs. 1979-83, pres. 1982), VFW (pres. ladies aux. 1966-68), Ind. Geneal. Soc., Milestone Car Soc., Packard Club Ind., Ind. Soc. Pioneers, Daus. of 1812 (pres. Tippecanoe chpt. 1981, state v.p. 1982), DAR, Daughters of the Union, Soc. Descendants of Valley Forge, Rotary (bd. dirs., pres. 1994-95), Delta Theta Tau, Sigma Delta Chi, Soc. Profl. Journalist. Mem. Christian Ch. (Disciples of Christ). Club: Windy Hill Country. Lodges: Order Eastern Star, Internat. Order Job's Daus. (life), Women of Moose.

BINGHAM, JUNE, writer, playwright; b. White Plains, N.Y., June 20, 1919; d. Max J.H. and Mabel (Limburg) Rossbach; m. Jonathan B. Bingham, Sept. 20, 1939 (dec. July 1986); children: Sherry B. Downes, Micki B. Esselstyn, Timothy, Claudia B. Meyers; m. Robert B. Birge, Mar. 28, 1987; 1 stepchild, Robert R. Student, Vassar Coll., 1936-38; BA, Barnard Coll., 1940. Writer, editor U.S. Treasury, Washington, 1943-45; editorial asst. Washington Post, 1945-46; writer Tarrytown (N.Y.) Daily News, 1946. Author: Do Cows have Neuroses?, Do Babies Have Worries?, Do Teenagers have Wisdom?, Courage to Change: An Introduction to Life and Thought of Reinhold Niebuhr, 1961, paperback, 1992, U Thant: The Search for Peace, 1970, (play) Triangles, 1986, You and the I.C.U., 1990, (with others) The Inside Story: Psychiatry and Everyday Life, 1953, The Pursuit of Health, 1985, (musical) Squanto and Love, 1992, Young Roosevelts, 1993; contbr. articles to nat. mags., newspapers and profl. jours. Bd. dirs. Barnard Coll., 1970-76, African-Am. Inst., N.Y.C., 1973-90, Riverdale Mental Health Assn., 1983—, Woodrow Wilson Found., Princeton, N.J., 1959-64, 83-89, Lehman Coll. Found., 1983-90, Ittleson Ctr. for Childhood Rsch., 1958-90; founder T.L.C.; trained liaison comforter Vol. Program of Presbyn. Hosp., N.Y.C. Named Alumna of the Yr., Rosemary Hall, 1976. Mem. Authors Guild (nominating com. 1987-90), Dramatists Guild, PEN, Cosmopolitan Club. Democrat. Home: 5000 Independence Ave Bronx NY 10471-2804

BINGHAM, MAXINE M., public relations executive; b. San Francisco. BA, U. Calif., Berkeley, 1975, MA, 1981. Pres. Maxtec Comm., 1988-92; founder, pres., CEO Agora Mktg. Internat. Inc., Santa Clara, Calif., 1992—. Active Jewish High Tech Cmty. Recipient PRfect award, 1991. Mem. Bus. Mktg. Assn. (judge ProComm Awards 1991, bd. dirs. Silicon Valley chpt. 1993—), Commonwealth Club of Calif. (program chair 1992—). Office: Agora Mktg Internat Inc 4655 Old Ironsides Dr Ste 250 Santa Clara CA 95054*

BINGHAM, URSULA WOLCOTT GRISWOLD, retired association executive; b. Greenwich, Conn., June 28, 1908; d. William Edward Schenck and Evelyn (Sloane) Griswold; m. Woodbridge Bingham, June 28, 1928 (dec. May 1986); children: Anne, Clarissa, Evelyn, Marian. Grad. high sch., Middleburg, Va. Bd. dirs. U. Calif. chpt. YWCA, Berkeley, 1940-80; nat. bd. dirs. YWCA U.S.A., N.Y.C., 1955-61. Author: A Lady's Life: New England, Berkeley, China, 1983. Active USO, San Francisco, 1944-70; bd. dirs. Pacific Sch. Religion, Berkeley, 1944-81.

BINION, LINDA DIANE, systems technologies researcher; b. Birmingham, Ala., Apr. 21, 1948; d. James Marvin and Sara Meredith (Moore) Binion; m. Norman Willard Holman, June 20, 1981 (div. 1983); m. Paul Anthony DeLorenzo, Aug. 16, 1986. Student, U. Ala.-Tuscaloosa, 1966-67, U. Ala.-Birmingham; BS in Computer Info. Mgmt., Southwest U., 1992. Data base adminstr. Carraway Methodist Med. Ctr., Birmingham, Ala., 1970-78; mgr. systems and program Brookwood Health Services Inc., Birmingham, 1979-80; sr. v.p. Innovative Systems Inc., Birmingham, 1980-83; pres. Amitec Inc., Birmingham, 1983-85; dir. research-info. systems technologies Ala. Metal Industries Corp., Birmingham, 1986; pres. AMICO Research Corp., 1986-90; mgr. IEF EBSCO Industries, 1990-95; dir. customer svc. Salcris Sys., Birmingham, 1995—; cons. in field. Designer: (software system) Innovative Healthcare Support System, 1980. Guest speaker U. Ala. Sch. Community Allied Health Services, 1986, numerous others. Mem. C. of C. (Birmingham), Mensa, Assn. Systems Mgmt. (past pres.), Internat. Platform Assn. Democrat. Am. Baptist. Office: Salcris Sys 800 Concourse Pky Birmingham AL 35244

BINKLEY, YILDIZ BARLAS, library director; b. Istanbul, Turkey, Nov. 16, 1943; came to the U.S., 1967; d. Riza and Belkis (Balin) Barlas; m. Donald Hugh Binkley, Dec. 28, 1942. BLS, U. Ankara, Turkey, 1966; MLS, Vanderbilt U., 1971; EdD, Tenn. State U., 1944. Libr. Tenn. Mcpl. League, Nashville, 1970-71; REF, ACQ, SER libr., asst. dir. Tenn. State U., Nashville, 1971-89, dir. librs. MCS, 1989—. Recipient grant Nat. Sec. Ag., Nashville, 1992-94. Mem. Tenn. Libr. Assn. (chairperson membership com. 1984, chairperson nominations com., 1986, Southeastern Libr. Assn. Office: Tenn State Univ 3500 John A Merritt Blvd Nashville TN 37209-1561*

BINKS, REBECCA ANNE, communications executive; b. Oak Park, Ill., July 23, 1955; d. Donald Melvin and Elizabeth June (Lobdell) B.; m. Cary Emmett Donham, June 22, 1980; 1 child, Samuel Joseph Donham. Student, Goodman Sch. Drama, Chgo., 1973-76; BA in Liberal Arts, Columbia Coll., Chgo., 1983; MS in Mktg., Roosevelt U., 1993. Freelance lighting designer, theater tech. Chgo., N.Y.C., 1975-80; retail mgr. Coffee and Tea Exch., Chgo., 1981-84; sales assoc. K&S Photographics, Chgo., 1984-87; supr. client services AGS&R Communications, Chgo., 1987-88; mgr. Meeting Express Systems, Chgo., 1988-90; pres. Binks & Assocs. Inc., Chgo., 1990—; mem. faculty mktg. comm. dept. Columbia Coll., Chgo., 1992—; tchr. travel photography, Chgo., 1987. Designer: (cookbook) Kitchen Angst, 1993; exhibited in group and one-woman shows. Mem. internal communications com. Girl Scouts, Chgo., 1989-91. Mem. NAFE, Chgo. Coun. on Fgn. Rels., Am. Mktg. Assn., Internat. Assn. Bus. Communications.

BINNEY, CAROLINE THORN, ballet dancer, choreographer; b. Newport, R.I., Sept. 4; d. Horace and Constance (Sturtevant) B. Ballerina N.Y. Dance Ensemble, N.Y.C., 1972-75, Internat. Dance Ensemble, 1974—, N.Y.C. Opera, 1977—; tarantella dancer Mamma Leone's Ristorante, N.Y.C., 1978-85; dancer, singer Tomov Yugoslav Dance Ensemble, 1982-84; dir., choreographer, dancer N.Y. Folk Ballet, N.Y.C., 1983—; dancer Met. Opera Co., N.Y.C., 1986—; choreographer, dancer Opera Classics of N.J., Hackensack, 1987-88; singer Double Image Theater Chorus, Interracial Fellowship Chorus. Dancer numerous cos. including Am. Ballet Theater, London Festival Ballet, Stuttgart Ballet, The Royal Ballet, Le Ballet de L'Opera de Paris, La Scala Opera Ballet, The Little Dancing Co., Russian Kirov Ballet, Manhattant Opera Theatre, Monteverdi Opera Co., (dance prodns.) Romeo and Juliet, Isadora, Carmen, Swan Lake, La Traviata, Turnadot, Gypsies, Petrouchka, Firebird, Le Corsaire, Sleeping Beauty, Napoli, Le Cid, (opera prodns.) Louise, Andrea Chénier, Der Freischütz, Attila, La Bohème, Carmen, Le Cid, Manon, Faust, Lakmé, Giulio Cesare, Le Coq d'Or, Lucia di Lammermoor, Madama Butterfly, Manon, Pilléas et Mélisande, Don Carlo, I Puritani, La Bohème, Aïda, Salome, La Traviata, Turandot; also appearing as Bin Bin the Clown. Mem. Am. Guild Mus. Artists, AFTRA. Republican. Episcopalian. Home: 314 W 58th St Apt 3B New York NY 10019-1811

BINNIE, NANCY CATHERINE, nurse, educator; b. Sioux Falls, S.D., Jan. 28, 1937; d. Edward Grant and Jessie May (Martini) Larkin; m. Charles H. Binnie. Diploma, St. Joseph's Hosp. Sch. Nursing, Phoenix, 1965; BS in Nursing, Ariz. State U., 1970, MA, 1974. Intensive care charge nurse Scottsdale (Ariz.) Meml. Hosp., 1968-70, coordinator critical care, 1970-71; coordinator critical care John C. Lincoln Hosp., Phoenix, 1971-73; prof. nursing GateWay Community Coll., Phoenix, 1974—; coord. part-time evening nursing programs Gateway Community Coll., 1984—, interim dir. nursing, 1989, 91. Mem. Orgn. Advancement of Assoc. Degree Nursing. Office: Gateway C C 104 N 40th St Phoenix AZ 85034-1704

BINNS, LINDY ANNE, sports event administrator; b. Joplin, Mo., June 17, 1958; d. Robert Eugene and DeAnne Rae (Ball) B. BS in Phys. Edn., Mo. So. State Coll., 1980; MS in Phys. Edn. Adminstrn., Emporia State U., 1982. Head softball coach Crowder Coll., Neosho, Mo., 1980; head volley ball, basketball, mens and womens tennis, phys. edn. Neosho C.C., Chanute, Kans., 1982-84; mktg. and sales coord. Nat. Assn. Intercollegiate Athletes, Kansas City, Mo., 1984-86, assoc. dir. championship events, 1986-93; sports planning mgr. Atlanta Com. for Olympic Games, 1993—; mem. festival com. U.S. Olympic Com., Colorado Springs, Colo., 1989-92. Mem. Ga. Womens Intersport Network, Women's Sports Found. (chair coaches adv. roundtable 1988-89, Pres. award 1994), Grand Lake Sailing Club, Devil's Backbone Ski Club. Home: 3212 G Post Woods Dr NW Atlanta GA 30339 Office: Atlanta Com for Olympic Games 250 Williams St Atlanta GA 30303

BINSFELD, CONNIE BERUBE, lieutenant governor; b. Munising, Mich., Apr. 18, 1924; d. Omer J. and Elsie (Constance) Berube; B.S., Siena Heights Coll., 1945, D.H.L. (hon.), 1977; postgrad. Wayne State U., 1966-67; m. John E. Binsfeld, July 19, 1947; children—John T., Gregory, Susan, Paul, Michael. County commr., Leelanau County, Mich., 1970-74; mem. Mich. Ho. of Reps., 1974-82, asst. rep. leader, 1979-81; del. Nat. Conv., 1980, 88, 92; mem. Mich. Senate, 1982-90, asst. rep. leader, 1979, 81; lt. gov. State of Mich., 1990—. Mem. adv. bd. Nat. Park System. Named Mich. Mother of Year, Mich. Mothers Com., 1977; Northwestern Mich. Coll. fellow. Mem. Nat. Council State Legislators, LWV, Siena Heights Coll. Alumnae Assn. Republican. Roman Catholic. Home: RR 2 Maple City MI 49664-9802 Office: Office of Lt Gov State Capitol Bldg Lansing MI 48909*

BINTLIFF, BARBARA ANN, law librarian, educator; b. Houston, Jan. 14, 1953; d. Donald Richard and Frances Arlene (Appling) Hay; m. Byron A. Boville, Aug. 20, 1977 (div. 1992); children: Bradley, Bruce. BA, Cen. Wash. U., 1975; JD, U. Wash., 1978, MLL, 1979. Bar: Wash. 1979, U.S. Dist. Ct. (ea. dist.) Wash. 1980, Colo. 1983, U.S. Dist. Ct. Colo. 1983. Libr. Gaddis and Fox, Seattle, 1978-79; reference libr. U. Denver Law Sch., 1979-84; assoc. libr., sr. instr. Sch. Law U. Colo., Boulder, 1984-88, assoc. prof., libr. dir., 1989—; legal cons. Nat. Ctr. Atmospheric Rsch., Environ. and Societal Impacts Group, Boulder, 1980. Editor: A Representative Sample of Tenure Documents for Law Librarians, 1988, 2nd edit., 1994, Chapter Presidents' Handbook, 1989, Representatives Handbook, 1990; mem. editorial bd. Legal Reference Svcs. Quarterly, Perspectives: Teaching Legal Research and Writing; contbr. articles to profl. jours. Mem. Am. Assn. Law Librs., Colo. Bar Assn., Colo. Assn. Law Librs. (pres. 1982), Southwestern Assn. Law Librs. (pres. 1987-88, 91-92). Episcopalian. Office: U Colo Law Libr Campus Box 402 Boulder CO 80309

BIOW, LISA, computer consultant, author; b. Manhasset, N.Y., Aug. 6, 1955; d. Edward Jacob and Gloria (Stevenson) B.; life ptnr. Deborah Alice Craig. BA with honors, NYU, 1988. Adminstrv. dir. Nat. Lawyers Guild, N.Y.C., 1982-86; computer cons. Oakland, Calif., 1986—. Author: Quattro Pro Made Easy, 1988, dBase IV: Secrets, Solutions & Shortcuts, 1989, Quattro Pro 2 Made Easy, 1990, Quattro Pro 3 Made Easy, 1991, Quattro Pro 4 Made Easy, 1992, Quattro Pro 5 Made Easy, 1993, HELP! Paradox for Windows, 1993, How to Use Your Computer, 1993. Mem. Assn. Database Developers, Digital Queers. Office: 5737 Thornhill Dr Ste 207 Oakland CA 94611

BIR, MICHELLE MARIE, sales executive; b. Canandaigua, N.Y., June 29, 1965; d. Thomas A. and Carol A. (Genecco) B. BS in Econs., Wells Coll., 1987. Merchandiser Bratt-Foster, Syracuse, N.Y., 1988-89; sales exec. 110 Winner Eastman-Kodak Co., Cape Girardeau, Mo., 1989—. Mem., starter Make-A-Wish Found., Cape Girardeau, 1989. Mem. Am. Women's Econ. Devel. Assn. Democrat. Roman Catholic. Office: Eastman Kodak Co Ste 300 510 Maryville College Dr Saint Louis MO 63141-5801

BIRCH, GRACE MORGAN, library administrator, educator; b. N.Y.C., June 3, 1925; d. Milton Melville and Adeline Ellsdale (Springer) Morgan; m. Kenneth Francis Birch, Oct. 26, 1947; children: Shari R., Timothy F. B.A., U. Bridgeport, 1963; M.L.S., Pratt Inst., 1968. With Bridgeport Pub. Library, Conn., 1949-66; asst. town librarian Fairfield Pub. Library, Conn., 1966-69; dir. Trumbull Library System, Conn., 1969—; lectr. Housatonic Community Coll., Bridgeport, 1970—; lectr. self-motivation, 1989—. Judge, Barnum Festival Soc. Bridgeport, 1971-73; mem. Trumbull Multi-Arts Com., Trumbul Prevention Coun. Mem. ALA, New Eng. Library Assn., Conn. Library Assn. (pres. 1972), Southwestern Conn. Library Council (pres. 1975-77), Fairfield Library Adminstrs. Group (pres. 1976-77). Democrat. Episcopalian. Avocations: sketching, dancing, traveling. Home: 175 Brooklawn Ave Bridgeport CT 06604-2011 Office: The Trumbull Libr 33 Quality St Trumbull CT 06611-3140

BIRCHENOUGH, KAREN BROWN, management consultant; b. Santa Ana, Calif., July 7, 1942; d. Wendell Maurice Brown and Jacqueline Ann (Morgan) Voris; m. Robert Anderson, Feb. 24, 1960 (div. Nov. 1962); children: T. Eileen Boeckholt, Tory Annette Cramer; m. Robert J. Birchenough Jr., Feb. 12, 1972 (dec. Nov. 1982); children: Robert J. III, James R. III. Grad. high sch., Red Bluff, Calif. Credit supr. Gensler-Lee Diamonds, Oakland, Calif., 1962-68; acct. U.S. Army, Frankfurt, Fed. Republic Germany, 1968-71, Omni Mobile Homes, Athens, Tenn., 1972-73; farm mgr. B-K Ranch, Pulaski, Tenn., 1972-75; school bus driver Giles County Schs., Pulaski, 1973-75; agt. Patterson Real Estate, Houma, La., 1979-82; owner K&V Investments, Inc., Houston, 1983—, The Brief-Case Success Motivation Inst., Houston, 1987—; instr. San Jacinto Jr. Coll. Cen. Campus, Houston, 1988—; conductor seminars Houston YWCA, 1988; owner Future Innovations; asst. dir. pub. affairs for LDS Ch. Journalist, news writer Brooks (Tex.) Citizen, 1988—; illustrator books The Garden, 1986, Single Man's Survival Kit, 1988. Mem. Texans for Civil Justice, Houston, 1987-88; chair Spring Forest/Dunmoor versus Friendswood, 1988. Mem. Clear Lake City C. of C., Toastmasters, Rotary (dist. youth exch. officer). Republican. Office: The Brief-Case 15922 Spring Forest Dr Houston TX 77059-3811

BIRD, LINDA W., realtor; b. Millington, Tenn., Mar. 19, 1952; d. Lawrence F. and Sara Teresa (Kori) Watermolen; m. Dennis Keith Bird, July 29, 1978; children: Kristin Ann, Lauren Elizabeth. BS, Fla. State U., 1974; MEd, Fla. Atlantic U., 1976. Broward County 4H coord. Fla. Cooperative Ext. Svc. U. Fla., Gainesville, 1974-76; sales rep. mgmt. tng. program Proctor and Gamble Distbg. Co., Cin., 1976; with mktg. mgmt. faculty Broward Community Coll., Ft. Lauderdale, Fla., 1978; pub. rels. coord. Port Everglades Authority, Ft. Lauderdale, 1978-80; flight attendant in charge Delta Air Lines, Miami, Fla., 1980-85; pres. Bird Realty, Inc., Ft. Lauderdale, 1984—. Pres. Kids in Distress Aux., 1986-87, Child Care Connection Aux., 1989-90; bd. dirs. Lakes Estates Homeowner Assn., 1982-93; chair Our House Jr. League Greater Ft. Lauderdale, Inc., 1994-95; mem. panel TV show 30 Below, 1972; troop coord. Girls Scouts USA, Pine Crest Sch. Fla. Jr. Coll. Presdl. scholar, Fla. Home Ext. scholar; named one of ten Women of Yr. Thousand Plus Club Am. Cancer Soc., 1986-87. Mem. Fort Lauderdale Panhellenic Assn. (tres. 1978), Delta Delta Delta (pres. 1988-90), Omicron Nu. Democrat. Methodist. Home: 2790 NE 57th Ct Fort Lauderdale FL 33308-2724 Office: Bird Realty Inc 2790 NE 57 Ct Fort Lauderdale FL 33308

BIRD, MARY LOVAS, computer systems engineer, consultant; b. Cleve., Aug. 9, 1945; d. Frank John and Ann Elizabeth (Noonan) Lovas; m. David Paul Bird, July 5, 1969; children: Ellen, Sarah. BA in Math., Coll. Mt. St. Joseph, Cin., 1967; postgrad., U. Md., 1987—. Systems engr. IBM Corp., Cleve. and Washington, 1967-70; dir. litigation systems U.S. Railway Assn., Washington, 1976-82; prin. systems engr. PRC, Inc., McLean, Va., 1983-92; dir. systems integration I-NET, Inc., Bethesda, Md., 1992-95, TRI-COR Industries, Inc., Landover, Md., 1995—; presenter Fed. Computer Conf., Washington, 1980, Fed. Imaging Conf., Washington, 1993. Contbr. articles, photographs to profl. jours. Troop leader Girl Scouts U.S., Washington, 1980-87; PANDA vol. Parents Anonymous, Prince George's City, 1993—. Recipient 1st Pl. award Ohio Coll. Newspaper Assn., 1967. Mem. Assn. Info. and Image Mgmt. Office: TRI-COR Industries Inc 8181 Professional Pl Ste 201 Landover MD 20785

BIRD, SHARLENE, clinical psychologist; b. N.Y.C., Sept. 3, 1957; d. Rubin and Dina Bird. BA in Psychology & Hispanic Studies, Vassar Coll., 1979; MA in Applied Psychology, Adelphi U., 1986; MA in Human Resources Mgmt., New Sch. for Social Rsch., N.Y.C., 1987; PsyD in Clin. Psychology, Yeshiva U., 1992. Lic. psychologist, N.Y. Clin. extern St. Mary's Children & Family Svcs., Syosset, N.Y., 1980-81; behavior modifier Flower Hosp./Terence Cardinal Cooke, N.Y.C., 1981-82; clin. psychology extern Met. Ctr. for Mental Health, N.Y.C., 1986-87; clin. psychology intern NYU Med. Ctr./Bellevue Hosp., N.Y.C., 1989-90; postdoctoral fellow in human sexuality N.Y. Hosp./Cornell Med. Ctr., 1990-92; family therapist Roberto Clemente Family Guidance Ctr., N.Y.C., 1991-93; healthcare planning analyst Inst. for Family & Community Care, N.Y.C., 1993—; supr. NYU Med. Ctr./Bellevue Hosp., N.Y.C., 1992—; tng. cons. Inst. for Family & Cmty. Care, N.Y.C., 1993; weekly permanent radio guest host Siempre a Tu Lado, Sta. WADO 1280-AM, 1992—. Chair bd. dirs. Mothers of Childrens with AIDS, N.Y.C., 1991-93. Mem. APA, N.Y. State Psychol. Assn., Am. Orthopsychiat. Assn., Assn. Hispanic Mental Health Profls., Am. Assn. Sex Educators, Counselors & Therapists, Am. Group Psychotherapy Assn.,

Assn. for Advancement of Behavior Therapy, Sigma Delta Phi. Office: 112 W 56th St Ste 15-5 Rm C New York NY 10019-3834

BIRD-PORTO, PATRICIA ANNE, personnel director; b. N.Y.C., June 16, 1952; d. Jacques Robert and Muriel (Cooper) Bird; m. Joseph Porto, May 5, 1984; 1 child, Jennifer Ashley. BA, U. So. Calif., 1975; cert. in legal assistantship, U. Calif., Irvine, 1987. Cert. in transp. demand mgmt. Orange County Transit Dist., 1988. Mgr. Bullock's Westwood, West L.A., 1976-78; mgr. ops. Lane Bryant, L.A., 1978-79; supr. employment, dir. personnel May Co. Dept. Stores, 1979-81; adminstr. personnel, dir. benefits Zoetrope Studios, Hollywood, Calif., 1981-82; personnel and ops. analyst Auntie Barbara's, Beverly Hills, Calif., 1982-86; dir. personnel Baylylop, Santa Ana, Calif., 1986-88; pres. Creative Pers. Assocs., 1986-91; owner Flowerman Corona, Del Mar, Calif., 1985—. Bd. dirs. Planned Parenthood; co-chair Pro-Wilson Orange County. Mem. Personnel Indsl. Relations Assn. Home: 7 Stardust Irvine CA 92715-3769 Office: PO Box 9663 Newport Beach CA 92658-9663

BIRDSALL, LAUREEN ANNE, city assessor; b. Paw Paw, Mich., Aug. 10, 1960; d. Ralph E. and Betty H. (Deforrest) B. Cert. Level 4 Assessor, Mich. Appraiser City of Kalamazoo, 1982-85, Kalamazoo County Equalization, Kalamazoo, 1985-86; twp. assessor Comstock Twp., Mich., 1986-89, Redford Twp., Mich., 1989-91; dir. equalization Genessee County, Flint, Mich., 1991-92; city assessor City of Grand Rapids, Mich., 1992—; guest speaker, facilitator, moderator in field. Mem. Mich. Assessors Assn., Kent County Assessors Assn., Internat. Assn. Assessing Officers. Office: City of Grand Rapids 300 Monroe Ave NW Grand Rapids MI 49503-2206

BIRDSEY, ANNA CAMPAS, civil engineer, architect; b. Balt., Nov. 21, 1949; d. William and Katy (Hondros) Campas; m. Tom D. Birdsey, June 3, 1973; children: Thomas William, Scott Stratton. BArch, Rensselaer Polytech. Inst., 1972; BSCE, Union Coll., 1977. Registered profl. engr., architect, N.Y. Staff architect-engr. GE Co., Schenectady, N.Y., 1972-73; architectural designer Fay Evans, P.C., Troy, N.Y., 1974-75, Golub Corp., Schenectady, 1975-77, Einhorn, Yaffee, Prescott, P.C., Albany, N.Y., 1979-80; jr. engr. N.Y. State Office Gen. Svc., Design and Constrn. Group, Albany, 1980-82, asst. bldg. structural engr., 1982-87, sr. bldg. structural engr., 1987—; bd. dirs. Montessori Sch. of Albany, 1990-92. Mem. Bethlehem Music Assn. (treas.), Rensselaer Alumni Assn. (class corr. alumni news). Home: 41 Darroch Rd Delmar NY 12054-3916

BIRDSONG, ALTA MARIE, volunteer; b. Ft. Worth, July 18, 1934; d. Alton Roy and Artie Marguerite (Bentley) Flowers; m. Kenneth Layne Birdsong, Oct. 18, 1958; children: Suzanne Denise, Jeffrey Layne. BBA in Acctg. magna cum laude, U. North Tex., 1955. Cost engr. Tex. Instruments, Inc., Dallas, 1955-62; self-employed part-time acct. Atlanta, 1972—. Mem. DeKalb County Community Rels. Com., 1981-93, chair, 1984-87; mem. Atlanta Regional Com. Adv. Group, 1981-88, Met. Atlanta United Way, 1985—; chair child care sub-com. Children At Risk Area of Need; chair Sch. Age Child Care Coun., 1987-90; mem. DeKalb County Task Force on Personal Care Homes, DeKalb County Task Force on Domestic Violence; mem. steering com. for bond referendum DeKalb Bd. Edn.; mem. Vision 2020 Governance Stakeholders ARC, 1994-95. Recipient John H. Collier award for Camp Fire, 1991, Luther Halsey Gulick award for Camp Fire, 1993, Frederic E. Ruccius award for Camp Fire, 1993, Mortar Bd. Alumni Achievement award, 1991, Woman of Yr. award Atlanta Alumnae Panhellenic, 1983, Women Who Have Made a Difference award DeKalb YWCA, 1985. Mem. AAUW (div. pres. 1987-89, pres. elect 1987-89, mem. v.p. 1984-86, recording sec. 1982-84, nom. com. 1993—), Ednl. Info. and Referral Svc. Inc. (chmn. 1983-84, treas. 1981-83, 87-90, sec. 1986-87), Atlanta Coun. Camp Fire (pres. 1992-94, v.p. 1990-92, region fin. officer 1989-90, region nominating com. chair 1991-92), Atlanta Alumnae Panhellenic (pres. 1978-79, v.p. 1977-78), Freedoms Found. at Valley Forge (Atlanta chpt. pres. 1991-92, v.p. 1990-91, v.p. publicity 1988-89, treas. 1985-87, sec. 1983-85, ea.-so. region adv. 1994—), Nat. Women's Conf., Delta Gamma Alumnae (Atlanta chpt. 1st v.p. 1985-87, treas. 1972-74, Oxford award 1992). Home: 5241 Manhasset Cv Atlanta GA 30338-3413

BIRMAN, JOAN S., mathematician, educator; b. N.Y.C., May 30, 1927; d. George and Lilian (Siegel) Lyttle; m. Joseph Leon Birman, Feb. 22, 1950; children—Kenneth, Deborah, David. Student, Swarthmore Coll., 1944-46; BA, Barnard Coll., 1948; MA in Physics, Columbia U., 1950; PhD in Math., NYU, 1968. Systems analyst Gen. Precision Equipment, 1950-53, W. L. Maxson Corp., 1953-55; staff mem. Tech. Rsch. Group, 1955-60; asst. prof. math. Stevens Inst., N.Y.C., 1968-71; assoc. prof. math. Stevens Inst. Tech., 1972-73; prof. math. Barnard Coll., N.Y.C., 1973—, chmn. dept. math., 1973-87, 89-91; vis. asst. prof. Princeton (N.J.) U., 1971-72; assoc. prof. U. Paris Sud, fall 1980, U. Paris VII, fall 1987; Lady Davis vis. prof. Technion, spring 1981; vis. prof. Hebrew U. Jerusalem, 1988, Inst. Advanced Study, spring 1988; rev. com. Fulbright Scholars, 1983-86; conf. bd. Math. Scis. Rev. Panel, 1984-85; topology panel Internat. Cong. Mathematicians, 1990; mem. U.S. Nat. Com. for Math., 1991-94; conf. organizer; internat. invited lectr. in field various univs., rsch. ctrs. and profl. confs. Author, editor chpts. to books; mem. editorial bd. Math. Rsch. Letters, 1993—, Topology and its Applications, 1993—; contbr. numerous rsch. articles, revs. to profl. jours. Sloan Found. fellow, 1974-76, Sr. Sci. Faculty fellow, Great Britain, spring 1981, Japan Soc. Promotion of Sci. fellow, Sept. 1980, Guggenheim fellow, 1994-95; NSF summer rsch. grantee, 1973—, U.S.-Israel Binational Sci. Found. grantee, 1990-93, Inst. Sci. Exch. grantee, Torino, Italy, summer 1986, Institut des Hautes Etudes Scientifiques grantee, Bures-sur-Yvette, France, summer 1991. Mem. Am. Math. Soc. (nominating com. 1989-91, mem.-at-large 1978-80, 90-93, human rights com. 1989-91, exec. com. 1992-96, long range planning com. 1993-95, chair 1994-95), N.Y. Acad. Scis. (women in sci. com. 1983-84). Home: 100 Wellington Rd New Rochelle NY 10804-3708 Office: Columbia U Dept of Math New York NY 10027

BIRMINGHAM, LINDA ROBIN, environmental engineer; b. Boston, June 2, 1958; m. Harry James Birmingham, June 4, 1988; 1 child, Branden. BS, U. R.I., 1980; MS, Northeastern U., 1990. Chemist ERT, Concord, Mass., 1982-83, Metcalf & Eddy, Boston, 1983-86; environ. engr. City of Peabody, Mass., 1988—. Mem. Am. Water Works Assn., New Eng. Water Works Assn., Pub. Works Assn.

BIRNBAUM, S. ELIZABETH, lawyer; b. Ft. Belvoir, Va., Jan. 20, 1958; d. Myron Lionel and Emma Jane (Steiner) Birnbaum. AB, Brown U., 1979; JD, Harvard U., 1984. Bar: Colo. 1984, D.C. 1985, U.S. Dist. Ct. D.C. 1987, U.S. Ct. Appeals (D.C. cir.) 1988, U.S. Ct. Appeals (10th cir.) 1988, U.S. Ct. Appeals (4th cir.) 1990, U.S. Supreme Ct. 1990. Clk. to Justice Dubofsky Supreme Ct. Colo., Denver, 1984-85; assoc. Dickstein, Shapiro & Morin, Washington, 1985-87; counsel to water resources program Nat. Wildlife Fedn., Washington, 1987-91; counsel com. resources U.S. Ho. Reps., Washington, 1991—. Editor-in-chief Harvard Environ. Law Rev., 1984. Mem. Am. Water Resources Assn., D.C. Bar (steering com., sect. environment, energy and natural resource law). Office: 1329 Longworth House Office Bldg Washington DC 20515

BIRNE, CINDY FRANK, business owner; b. Chgo., Nov. 13, 1956; d. Gordon D. and Paula (Feldman) Frank; m. Robert E. Birne, June 27, 1981. BA, Ohio State U., 1979. Creative coord. Point-Communications div. Tracy-Locke Advt., Dallas, 1983; asst. to Tex Schramm, pres. of Dallas Cowboys, 1984, sales and advt. rep., tour dir. Dallas Cowboys, 1985—; sports mktg., comml. endorsements agt. Talent Sports Internat., Dallas; founding mem., exec. dir. QB, Inc.-The Internat. Assn. Profl. Quarterbacks; rep. various high profile athletes; affiliated cons., pub. rels. mgmt. promotion mktg. Burson Marsteller Sports Ptnrs. Internat., Dallas; dir. pub. rels., mktg. Dupree/Miller Literary, Inc.; founder, owner Sinthia Prodns., Dallas, 1993—. Active Ohio campaign Ronald Reagan for Pres., 1980-81; vol. Cystic Fibrosis Found.; event coord. Legends Sports Promotions, Tex. Shoot-Out Classic for Troy Aikman Found.-Juvenile Diabetes Children's Miracle Network, 1993-94; assoc. Thomas Cook Travel Million Dollar Shoot-Out-ARC, 1993; ann. fundraiser Ann. Nat. Coun. for Jewish Women; bd. dirs. Golden Acres Nursing Home for Jewish Aged, Dallas, 1993; assoc. Legends Sports Promotions.

BIRNKRANT, JEANNE ANN, artist, actress, social worker; b. N.Y.C.; d. William Benjamen and Dorothy Leona (Solow) B. BA, Barnard Coll.; MSW, Columbia U.; postgrad., New Sch. Social Research, 1968-70, Arts Students League, 1970-75, Berghoff Acting Studios, 1975-80, 88-89. Chief psychiat. social worker N.Y. Psychoanalytic Inst., 1970-76; children's psychotherapist Bellevue Hosp., N.Y.C., 1976-78; psychotherapist, dir. social work Met. Hosp., N.Y.C., 1978-84; actress various cos.; chief psychiatric social worker N.Y.C. Madison Ave. Med. Ctr., 1991—; dir. Park Ave Psychotherapy Ctr., N.Y.C., 1988-89; psychotherapist Creedmore Psychiat. Ctr., Queens, N.Y. Prin. sculpture works include (bronze) Strident Man (1st prize South Park Artist Group, N.Y.C. 1984), Winged Bird Fantasy (1st prize Nantucket Contemporary Gallery, Mass., 1985), Screaming Motherland and Child (1st prize 1989), Nat. Contemporary Juries Art Show, 1989, Fifth Ave Contemporary Gallery, N.Y.C., 1989, Whyte Gallery Sculpture Show, N.Y.C., 1992; appeared in movies Turk 182, Cotton Club, Nuts, Radio Days, Ghostbusters, Ghostbusters II, Go Beverly, Round Midnight, Prizzi's Honor, Fatal Attraction, Last Exit to Brooklyn, See No Evil, Hear No Evil, Mortal Thoughts, 1990, Frankie and Johnnie, 1991, Boomerang, 1992, The Concierge, 1992, Batman Returns, 1992, Malcom X, 1993, City Hall, 1994, Smoke, 1994, Dead Presidents, 1994; theater includes On Golden Pond, 1991; appeared in TV shows Superman Anniversary Spl., 1988, Dreamstreet, Coach, 1994, The Cosby Mysteries, 1995, N.Y. Undercover, 1995. County Com. woman Village Ind. Dems., N.Y.C.; patron Mus. Modern Art. Nat. Mental Health fellow, Jewish Guild for Blind fellow. Mem. Screen Actors Guild, Actors Equity Assn., Nat. Assn Social Workers (cert.), AFTRA. Home and Office: PO Box 20953 New York NY 10023-1497

BIRO, MARI See BERKOVITS, MARIANNE

BIRON, CHRISTINE ANNE, medical science educator, researcher; b. Woonsocket, R.I., Aug. 8, 1951; d. R. Bernard and Theresa Priscilla (Sauvageau) B. BS, U. Mass., 1973; PhD, U. N.C., 1980. Rsch. technician U. Mass., Amherst, 1973-75; grad. researcher U. N.C., Chapel Hill, 1975-80; postdoctoral fellow Scripps Clinic and Rsch., La Jolla, Calif., 1980; fellow U. Mass. Med. Sch., Worcester, 1981-82, instr., 1983, asst. prof., 1984-87; vis. scientist Karolinska Inst., Stockholm, 1984; asst. prof. Brown U., Providence, R.I., 1988-90, assoc. prof., 1990—; mem. AIDS and related rsch. study sect. 3 NIH, 1991-93; mem. exptl. immunology study sect. NIH, 1993—. Assoc. editor Jour. Immunology, 1990-94; bd. editors Proceedings of Soc. for Exptl. Biology and Medicine, 1993—; contbr. articles, revs. to sci. jours. Leukemia Soc. Am. fellow, 1981, Spl. fellow, 1983, scholar, 1987; grantee NIH, 1985—; rsch. grantee MacArthur Found., 1991—. Mem. AAAS, Am. Assn. Immunologists (co-chmn. symposium 1990, 94), Am. Soc. Virology, Sigma Xi. Office: Brown U Biomed Ctr Box G-B618 Providence RI 02912

BIRSTEIN, ANN, writer, educator; b. N.Y.C., May 27, 1927; d. Bernard and Clara (Gordon) B.; m. Alfred Kazin, June 26, 1952 (div. 1982); 1 child, Cathrael. BA, Queens Coll., 1948. Lectr. The New Sch. Queens Coll., N.Y.C., 1953-54; writer-in-residence CCNY, 1960; lectr. The Writers Workshop, Iowa City, 1966, 72; lectr. Sch. Gen. Studies Columbia U., N.Y.C., 1985-87; dir., founder Writers on Writing Barnard Coll., N.Y.C., 1988—; adj. prof. English Hofstra U., Long Island, 1980, Barnard Coll., N.Y.C., 1981-93; film critic Vogue mag. Author: Star of Glass, 1950, The Troublemaker, 1955, The Sweet Birds of Gorham, 1966, Summer Situations, 1972, Dickie's List, 1973, American Children, 1980, The Rabbi on Forty-Seventh Street, 1982, The Last of the True Believers, 1988; co-editor: The Works of Anne Frank; past contbg. editor Inside mag.; contbr. to Book World, Confrontation, Connoisseur, Geo, Inside, Mademoiselle, McCall's, N.Y. Times Book Rev., The New Yorker, The Reporter, Vogue, Washington Post, among others. Grantee Nat. Endowment of the Arts, 1983; Fulbright fellow, 1951-52. Mem. PEN, Authors Guild, Phi Beta Kappa (hon.). Democrat. Jewish.

BISAGA-CHATTINGER, APRIL DARLENE, marketing executive, health facility administrator; b. Wisconsin Rapids, Wis., Apr. 8, 1950; d. Lawrence C. and Arlene Ella (Hause) Lee; m. Emil Mark Bisaga, July 1, 1972 (dec. 1984); children: Richard L. Bisaga, April L. Bisaga; m. Paul Francis Chattinger, June 29, 1985. RN, Deaconess Hosp., Milw., 1971; BS in Nursing, Govs. State U., University Park, Ill., 1981; postgrad., Keller Grad. Sch. Mgmt., Chgo., 1985—. Charge nurse Milw. Children's Hosp., 1972-73; charge nurse critical care St. James Hosp. Med. Ctr., Chicago Heights, Ill., 1972-75, trauma coordinator, 1975-78, dir. emergency health edn., 1978-84, dir. ednl. services, 1984-86, dir. mktg. and emergency health edn., 1986—; cons. Zabo Industries, Oak Brook, Ill., 1984, Ford Motor Co., Chicago Heights, 1986. Bd. dirs. Am. Cancer Soc., Cook County, Ill., 1986—. Recipient Award of Excellence Nat. Registry Emergency Med. Technicians, 1981. Mem. Am. Mktg. Assn., Am. Bus. Women Club, Altrusa Women's Club (sec. 1986—). Roman Catholic. Office: South Suburban Hosp 17800 S Kedzie Ave Hazel Crest IL 60429

BISCHEL, MARGARET DEMERITT, physician, managed care consultant; b. Moorhead, N.D., Nov. 8, 1933; d. Connie Magnus Nystrom and Harriett Grace (Petersen) Zorner; m. Raymon DeMeritt, 1953 (div. 1958); 1 child, Gregory Raymon; m. John Bischel, 1961 (div. 1964); m. Kenneth Dean Serkes, June 7, 1974. BS, U. Oreg., Eugene, 1962; MD, U. Oreg., Portland, 1965. Diplomate Am. Bd. Internal Medicine, Nat. Bd. Med. Examiners. Resident, straight med. intern Los Angeles County/U. So. Calif. Med. Ctr., 1965-68, NIH fellow nephrology, 1968-70, asst. prof. renal medicine, 1970-74; asst. prof., instr. medicine U. So. Calif., 1968-74; instr. nephrology East L.A. City Coll., 1971-74; dir. med. edn. Luth. Gen. Hosp., Park Ridge, Ill., 1974-78, dir. nephrology sect., 1977-80, pres. med. staff, 1974-88; founding mem., med. dir., dir. med. svcs. Luth. Health Plan, Park Ridge, 1983-87; clin. assoc. prof. medicine Abraham Lincoln Sch. Medicine U. Ill., 1975-80; sr. cons. Parkside Assocs., Inc., Park Ridge, 1986-88; pvt. practice Chgo., 1974-88; physician Buenaventura Med. Clinic, Ventura, Calif., 1989—, med. dir., 1992—; prin. Apollo Managed Care Cons., Santa Barbara, Calif., 1988—; trustee Luth. Health Care System, Park Ridge, 1986-90, Unified Med. Group Assn., Seal Beach, Calif., 1993-94; hon. lifetime staff mem. Luth. Gen. Hosp., Park Ridge; mem. formulary com. HealthNet, 1992-94, med. adv. com. TakeCare, 1993-94, quality assurance com. PacifiCare, 1993-94; mem. doctor's adv. network AMA, 1994—. Mem. editorial adv. bd. PHO Report, PHO Update, Capitation Mgmt. Report; contbr. articles to profl. jours., chpts. to books. Fellow Am. Coll. Physicians (Calif. Gov.'s advisor 1993—); mem. Am. Coll. Physicians Execs., Am. Coll. Med. Quality, Nat. Assn. Physician Hosp. Orgns., Nat. Assn. Managed Care Physicians, Sigma Xi. Office: Apollo Consulting Group 860 Ladera Ln Santa Barbara CA 93108

BISCHOF, MARY ANNA, pharmacist; b. Bethpage, N.Y., Feb. 6, 1963; d. Aloysius J. and Anna P. (Dionisio) B. AA, U. Ctrl. Fla., 1984; BS in Pharmacy, U. Fla., 1987. Registered pharmacist, Fla. Pharmacist Eckerd Drugs, Palm Beach Gardens, Fla., 1987—, pharmacy mgr., 1989—; pharmacy intern instr. Coll. Pharmacy, U. Fla., Palm Beach Gardens, 1990—; pharmacy preceptor, Fla. Bd. Pharmacy, Palm Beach Gardens, 1990—. Mem. Am. Pharm. Assn., Nat. Cath. Pharm. Guild, U. Fla. Pharmacy Alumni Assn., fla. Pharmacy Assn., Palm Beach County Pharmacy Assn., Alpha Chi Omega Frat. Republican. Roman Catholic.

BISCHOFF, JOYCE ARLENE, information systems consultant, lecturer; b. Chgo., Apr. 1, 1938; d. Carl Henry and Gertrude Alma (Lohn) Winterberg; m. Kenneth B. Bischoff, June 6, 1959; children: Kathryn Ann, James Eric. BS in Math., Ill. Inst. Tech., 1959; cert. computer tech., U. Del., 1979. Programmer, analyst Inst. of Gas Tech., Chgo., 1959-60, U. Ghent, Belgium, 1960-61; database adminstr. Med. Ctr. Del., Wilmington, 1979-84; sr. database analyst ICI Ams., Wilmington, 1984-87; sr. cons. CSC Ptnrs., Malvern, Pa., 1987-90; pres. Bischoff Cons., Inc., Hockessin, Del., 1990—; chairperson, founder Del. Valley DB2-SQL/DS Users Group, Phila., 1986-90; task force leader DB2 performance task force Guide Internat., Chgo., 1987-90; speaker, mem. conf. planning com. Internat. DB2 Users Group. Author: (with others) Handbook of Data Management, 1993; contbr. articles to profl. jours. Recipient McGrath award Del. Valley DB2-SQL/DS Users Group, 1990, Quality award Guide Internat., 1989. Mem. Internat. Platform Assn., N.Y. Acad. Scis., Assn. for Computing Machinery (Del. Valley chpt. pres. 1986-87, program chair 1985-86), Data Processing Mgmt. Assn. (Wilmington chpt.), Network of Women in Computer Tech., Sigma Kappa (pres. 1958-59). Home and Office: Bischoff Cons Inc 1007 Benge Rd Hockessin DE 19707-9242

BISCHOFF, MARILYN BRETT, social worker; b. Mt. Vernon, N.Y., Apr. 16, 1930; d. Arthur Cushman and Mary Kathryn (Clark) Brett; m. Walter A. Bischoff, Mar. 25, 1961; children: Holly, Robert. BA magna cum laude, CCNY, 1959; MSW, Columbia U., 1961; D in Social Work, Boston Coll., 1985. Diplomate Clin. Social Work. Clin. social worker Providence Child Guidance Clinic, 1961-65, 69-73; pvt. practice clin. social worker Providence, Attleboro, Mass., 1965—; instr. Providence Coll., 1988-89; speaker in field. Active Attleboro (Mass.) Area Mental Health Assn., 1975—. Columba Univ. fellow, N.Y.C., 1959-60; Nat. Inst. Mental Health fellow, 1960-61. Mem. NASW (sec./treas. S.E. Mass. chpt. 1967-68, mem. speaker's bur. R.I. chpt. 1987), Acad. Cert. Social Workers, R.I. Group Psychotherapy Soc. (membership com. 1985—), Am. Group Psychotherapy Assn., Northeastern Soc. Group Psychotherapy, Columbia U. Alumni Assn., Phi Beta Kappa. Club: Attleboro Ski. Home: 10 Norfolk Row Attleboro MA 02703-1629 Office: 10 Norfolk Row Attleboro MA 02703-1629

BISCHOFF, SUSAN ANN, newspaper editor; b. Indpls., July 31, 1951; d. Thomas Anthony and Betty Jean (Coons) B.; m. Jim B. Barlow, June 20, 1975; 1 child, Samantha Lynn. BA, Ind. U., 1973. Rschr.-reporter Congl. Quar., Washington, 1973-74; city desk reporter Houston Chronicle, 1974-75, bus. reporter, 1975-79, asst. bus. editor, 1979-84, bus. editor, 1984-86, asst. mng. editor, 1986—; Houston corr. Kiplinger, Tex. Letter, Washington, 1980-85. Bd. dirs. Houston Chronicle Employees Fed. Credit Union, 1980-87, House Mus. Natural Scis.; mem. exec. com. U.S. Olympic Festival VII, Houston, 1985-86; mem. exec. com. Gulf Coast March of Dimes Birth Defects Found.; mem. class policy Leadership Houston, 1992-94; founding bd. dirs. Greater Houston Women's Found.; mem. exec. com., chmn. mktg. com. Gulf Coast affiliate United Way. Named Outstanding Woman in Houston Journalism YWCA, 1989, Fabulous Femme Greater Houston Women's Found., 1994. Mem. Soc. Profl. Journalists, Soc. Newspaper Design, Am. Assn. Sunday and Feature Editors (dir.), Tex. Club, Press Club of Houston Ednl. Found. (founding bd. dirs.). Home: 6407 Schuler St Houston TX 77007-2064 Office: Houston Chronicle 801 Texas St Houston TX 77002-2996

BISHIRJIAN, KATHRYN ANN, dietitian; b. Fairmont, W.Va., Feb. 18, 1928; d. Luigi and Elizabeth C. (LaCova) Oliverio; m. Charles H. Bishirjian, Oct. 8, 1955; 1 child, Charles A. Bishirjian. BS in Home Econs., Fairmont State Coll., 1949; AB in Retailing/Edn., Fairmont (W.Va.) State Coll., 1949; MS, Duquesne U., 1974. Registered dietitian, nutrition specialist I; tchr. cert. Home economist WVa. Extension Svc., Elkins, W.Va., 1949-52; adminstrv. dietitian various hosps., Pitts., 1953-59; food svc. dir. Allegheny Valley Schs., Springdale, Pa., 1966-71; food mgmt. prof. Westmoreland C.C., Pitts., 1972-76; cons. dietitian Pitts., 1976—; bur. chief Allegheny County Dept. Aging, Pitts., 1976—; instr. C.C., Pitts., 1988—; cons. weight control/older adults, Pitts., 1978—;. Author: VIC Nutrition is FUN, 1984. Adv. coun. Carnegie Sci. Ctr., Pitts., 1993. Mem. Am. Dietic Assn. (del. 1984-90, Svc. award 1987-90, Gerontol. Nutritionist Practice Group), Gerontol. Nutritionist (chmn. 1992-93, Svc. award 1993), Nat. Assn. of Nutrition and Aging Programs, Nat. Assn. of Meal Programs (tech. assistance com. 1992-93), Pa. Dietetic Assn. (Keystone award, Outstanding Dietitian award), Pa. Dietetic Assn., Am. Sch. Food Svc. Assn., Keystone Sch. Food Svc. Assn., Pa. Restaurant Assn., Nat. Tchrs. Assn., Pa. Tchrs. Assn., Nat. Meals Assn., Nutrition Coun. of Pa. Democrat. Roman Catholic. Home: 1707 Williamsburg Pl Pittsburgh PA 15235-4949 Office: Allegheny County Dept of Aging 441 Smithfield St Pittsburgh PA 15222-2219

BISHOP, AMELIA MORTON, freelance writer; b. Dallas, Dec. 31, 1920; d. Walter Pierce and Alice (Stanton) Morton; m. J. Ivyloy Bishop, Dec. 18, 1955; children: Dan, Judith. BA, U. Tex., El Paso, 1942; MRE, Southwestern Bapt. Theol. Sem., Ft. Worth, 1953. Reporter Hollywood (Calif.) Citizen-News, 1942-43; in advt. and pub. rels. New Orleans, 1943-48; Tex. state young people's sec. Woman's Missionary Union, Dallas, 1953-56; tchr. Plainview (Tex.) High Sch., 1963-80; instr. Wayland Bapt. U., Plainview, 1957-60, 81-83; freelance writer, 1960—; state v.p. Woman's Missionary Union of Tex., Dallas, 1980-84, state pres., 1984-88, nat. v.p., 1984-88. Author, photographer: The Gift and the Giver, 1984, The Flame and the Candle, 1987; contbr. numerous articles to publs. Recipient Tex. Bapt. Elder Statesman award Bapt. Gen. Conv. Tex., 1989. Democrat. Home: PO Box 163523 Austin TX 78716-3523

BISHOP, BARBARA N., librarian, archivist; b. Louisville; d. Bernard Ross and Mayme Nell (Thompson) Higgason; children: Anthony Taylor, Christopher Allen, Sarah Jean. AAS, U. Louisville, 1981, BA, 1981, MA, 1988; MSLS, U. Ky., 1989. Project archivist City of Louisville Archives, 1984; archivist Cabbage Patch Settlement House, Louisville, 1984-85; asst. archivist Ind. U. S.E., New Albany, 1986-88, ref. and archives librarian, 1988-90; dir. libr. svcs.Montgomery Libr. Campbellsville (Ky.) Coll., 1990-91; Glasgow Campus libr. Western Ky. U., 1991—; cons. in field. Author: Oakdale: An Early Twentieth Century Suburb, 1989; author booklet: Love and Hope Throughout the Years: The Cabbage Patch Settlement House, 1985. Pres. Oakdale Neighborhood Assn., Louisville, 1988-89, bd. dirs., 1984-86; mem. 4th & Central Task Force, Louisville, 1986-88, Operation South Louisville, 1986-88. Ky. Humanities Council grantee, 1985-86; Ind. U. Pres. Council on Social Scis. Pub. grantee, 1988. Mem. Soc. Am. Archivists, Ky. Coun. on Archives, Assn. Records Mgrs. and Adminstrs., Ancient Ky. Hist. Assn., ALA, Ky. Libr. Assn. Office: Western Kentucky Univ Glasgow Regional Campus 213 Liberty St Glasgow KY 42141

BISHOP, C. DIANE, state agency administrator, educator; b. Elmhurst, Ill., Nov. 23, 1943; d. Louis William and Constance Oleta (Mears) B. BS in Maths., U. Ariz., 1965, MS in Maths., MEd in Secondary Edn., 1972. Lic. secondary educator. Tchr. math. Tucson Unified Sch. Dist., 1966-86, mem. curriculum council, 1985-86, mem. maths. curriculum task teams, 1983-86; state supt. of pub. instrn. State of Ariz., 1987—; mem. assoc. faculty Pima C.C., Tucson, 1974-84; adj. lectr. U. Ariz., 1983, 85; mem. math. scis. edn. bd. NRC, 1987-90, mem. new standards project governing bd., 1991—; dir. adv. bd. sci. and engring. ednl. panel, NSF; mem. adv. bd. for arts edn. Nat. Endowment for Arts. Active Ariz. State Bd. Edn., 1984—, chmn. quality edn. commn., 1986-87, chmn. tchr. crt. subcom., 1984—, mem. outcomes based edn. adv. com., 1986-87, liaison bd. dirs. essential skills subcom., 1985-87, gifted edn. com. liaison, 1985—; mem. Ariz. State Bd. Regents, 1987—, mem. com. on preparing for U. Ariz., 1983, mem. high sch. task force, 1984-85; mem. bd. Ariz. State Community Coll., 1987—; mem. Ariz. Joint Legis. Com. on Revenues and Expenditures, 1989, Ariz. Joint Legis. Com. on Goals for Ednl. Excellence, 1987-89, Gov.'s Task Force on Ednl. Reform, 1991, Ariz. Bd. Regents Commn. on Higher Edn., 1992. Woodrow Wilson fellow Princeton U., summer 1984; recipient Presdl. Award for Excellence in Teaching of Maths., 1983, Ariz. Citation of Merit, 1984, Maths. Teaching award Nat. Sci. Research Soc., 1984, Distinction in Edn. award Flinn Found., 1986; named Maths. Tchr. of Yr. Ariz. Council of Engring. and Sci. Assns., 1984. Mem. AAUW, NEA, Nat. Coun. Tchrs. Math., Coun. Chief State Sch. Officers, Women Execs. in State Govt. (bd. dirs. 1993), Ariz. Assn. Tchrs. Math., Women Maths. Edn., Math. Assn. Am., Ednl. Commn. of the States (steering com.), Nat. Endowment Arts (adv. bd. for arts edn.), Nat. Forum Excellence Edn., Nat. Honors Workshop, Phi Delta Kappa. Democrat. Episcopalian. Office: Ariz Dept Edn 1535 W Jefferson St Phoenix AZ 85007-3209

BISHOP, CAROLYN BENKERT, public relations counselor; b. Monroe, Wis., Aug. 28, 1939; d. Arthur C. and Delphine (Heston) Benkert; m. Lloyd F. Bishop, June 15, 1963. BS, U. Wis., 1961; grad., Tobe-Coburn Sch., N.Y.C., 1962. Merchandising editor Co-Ed Mag., N.Y.C., 1962-63; advt. copywriter Woodward & Lothrop, Washington, 1963-65; home furnishings editor Co-Ed Mag., N.Y.C., 1965-68; editor Budget Decorating Mag., N.Y.C., 1968-69; home furnishings editor Family Cir. Mag., N.Y.C., 1969-75; v.p., pub., editorial dir. Scholastic, Inc., N.Y.C., 1975-80; owner Mesa Store Home Furnishings Co., Aspen, Colo., 1980-83; dir. pub. rels. Snowmass Resort Assn., Snowmass Village, Colo., 1983-86; pres. Bishop & Bishop Mktg. Communications, Aspen, 1986—; mem. media rels. com. Colo. Tourism Bd., Denver, 1987-90. Author: 25 Decorating Ideas Under $100, 1969; editor: Family Circle Special Home Decorating Guide, 1973. Bd. dirs. Aspen Camp Sch. for the Deaf, 1987-90. Recipient Dallas Market Editorial award Dallas Market Ctr., 1973, Dorothy Dawe award Chgo. Furniture Market, 1973, Guardian of Freedom award, Anti-Defamation League Appeal, 1974. Mem. Rocky Mountain Pub. Rels. Group (chmn. 1991-93), Pub. Rels. Soc. Am. (accredited, small firms co-chair counselors acad. 1992-93), Aspen Writers' Found. (bd. dirs. 1991-93), Tobe-Coburn Alumni Assn., U. Wis. Alumni Assn. Democrat. Office: Bishop & Bishop Mktg Comms PO Box 300 1511-13th Ave Monroe WI 53566

BISHOP, CLAIRE DEARMENT, engineering librarian; b. Youngstown, Ohio, Oct. 12, 1937; d. Eugene Howard and Ruth (Bright) DeA.; m. Carl R. Meinstereifel, 1956 (div. 1964); children: Paul, Dawn; m. Olin Jerry Dewberry, Jr., 1974 (div. 1979); m. J. Bruce Bishop, May 6, 1992. B.S., Clarion State U., 1967; M.L.S., Ga. State U., 1977. Cert. libr. media specialist, Ga. Libr. Henry County, Stockbridge, Ga., 1967-69; head libr. Russell High Sch., East Point, Ga., 1969-84; engring. libr. Rockwell Internat., Duluth, Ga., 1984-88; rep. GIDEP, Corona, Calif., 1984-88; libr. Raytheon Co., 1990, MSD, Bristol, Tenn., 1988-90; owner rubber stamp store Claire's Collectables, St. Augustine. Author newsletter: Blueline. Mem. Mensa. Democrat. Avocations: computers, writing, information broker. Home: 238 Ravenswood Dr Saint Augustine FL 32084

BISHOP, ELIZABETH SHREVE, psychologist; b. Ann Arbor, Mich., Nov. 18, 1951; d. William Warner Jr. and Mary Fairfax (Shreve) B. AB, U. Mich., 1972; MA, Ohio State U., 1973, PhD, 1976. Lic. psychologist, Mich. Psychologist Franklin County Program for the Mentally Retarded, Columbus, Ohio, 1974, WC Mental Health, Willmar, Minn., 1977-83; chief psychologist Battle Creek (Mich.) Child Guidance Ctr., 1981; dir. psychometrics Meridian Profl. Psychol. Cons., East Lansing, Mich., 1983-92; pres. Arbor Psychol. Cons., Ann Arbor, 1991—. Troop leader Girl Scouts U.S.A., Minn., Mich., Ohio, 1971-87; v.p. Willmar LWV, 1989-81. Assoc. Univ. London Inst. Edn., 1976. Fellow Am. Orthopsychiat. Assn.; mem. LWV, AAUW, Am. Psychol. Assn., Mich. Psychol. Assn., Coun. for Exceptional Children (local pres. 1977-78), Internat. Coun. Psychologists, Internat. Sch. Psychology Assn. Home: 1612 Morton Ave Ann Arbor MI 48104-4441 Office: Arbor Psychol Cons 1565 Eastover Pl Ann Arbor MI 48104

BISHOP, ETHEL MAE See GULLETTE, ETHEL MAE BISHOP

BISHOP, KATHRYN ELIZABETH, film company executive, writer; b. Seattle, July 7, 1945; d. Wesley Thomas Bishop and Muriel (Robert) Leisher; divorced; 1 child, Zachary. BA, Wartburg Coll., 1966. Voice over talent Chgo. Bd. Edn. Radio Network, 1960-62; prodn. asst. Sta. CBS-TV, WBBM-TV, Chgo., 1961-63; disk jockey, engr., writer Sta. KWAR-FM, Waverly, Iowa, 1964-65; assoc. producer Bing Crosby Prodns. Inc., Chgo., 1966-69; producer Sedelmaier Films, Chgo., 1969-73; v.p., head prodn. Wakeford/Orloff Inc., L.A., 1977-78; producer Katy Bishop Prodns. Inc., L.A., 1973—; founder, owner Stiles-Bishop Prodns. Inc., L.A., 1974—; exec. producer The Colman Group Inc., L.A., 1982-87; co-founder, co-owner Rapport Films, Inc., Hollywood, Calif., 1987-92. Co-author: (screenplay) Millionaire's Club; screenwriter: Cinnamon Bear. Mem. TV Acad. Arts and Scis., Dirs. Guild Am. Office: Stiles-Bishop Prodns Inc 12652 Killion St North Hollywood CA 91607

BISHOP, LEAH MARGARET, lawyer; b. N.Y.C., Nov. 2, 1954; d. Franklin Gerald and Evelyn (Fremed) B.; m. Gary M. Yale, Aug. 10, 1975; children: Elizabeth Yale, Rebecca Yale. BA, Brandeis U., 1975; JD, Columbia U., 1979. Bar: N.Y. 1980, U.S. Dist. Ct. (ea. dist., so. dist.) N.Y. 1980, Calif. 1981, U.S. Dist. Ct. (cen. dist.) Calif. 1981. Law clk. to judge U.S. Dist. Ct. (so. dist.), N.Y., 1979-80; assoc. O'Melveny & Myers, L.A., 1980-87, ptnr., 1987—. Fellow Am. Coll. Trusts and Estates Coun. Democrat. Jewish. Office: O'Melveny & Myers Ste 700 1999 Ave of the Stars Los Angeles CA 90067

BISHOP, LINDA DILENE, lawyer, small business owner; b. La Grange, Ill., Dec. 21, 1961; d. James William and Margaret Ann (Howell) B. BA, U. Colo., 1985, JD, 1987. Bar: Colo., 1988, Ill., 1989, Fla., 1990, Fed. Ct. (no. dist. Ill.) 1992, (cen. dist. Ill.) 1994; cert. travel cons.; cert. real estate broker. Dep. dist. atty. Colorado Springs (Colo.) Dist. Atty., 1987-89, Jefferson County Dist. Atty., Golden, Colo., 1989-91; owner, pres. Bishop and Bishop, Oak Brook, Ill., 1991—, Great Lakes Installation Co., Oak Brook, 1991—, Bishop Travel Ctr., Oak Brook, 1992—; analyst draft codes for ea. Europe Ctrl. & East European Law Initiative, Washington, 1993. Mem. Colo. Bar Assn., Ill. Bar Assn., Assn. Retail Travel Agents, Pacific Assn. Travel Agents, Internal Forum Travel and Tourism. Republican. Home: 18 E 8th St Hinsdale IL 60521 Office: Bishop and Bishop 1111 W 22d St C-40 Oak Brook IL 60521

BISHOP, LOUISE WILLIAMS, state legislator; b. Cairo, Ga., June 27, 1933; d. Elijah and Sarah (Hines) Williams; m. James Alburn Bishop (div.); children: Todd James, Tabb Jody, Tamika Joy, James Alburn Jr. B in Communications and Radio Broadcasting, Am. Found. Dramatic Arts. Ordained min. Baptist Evangelist Ch., 1978. With Sta. WHAT; program host Sta. WDAS; mem. Pa. Ho. of Reps., Harrisburg, 1988—. Recipient numerous awards including Richard Allen award African Meth. Episc.Ch., Community Svc. award Missionary Baptist Pastors Conf., Outstanding Citizen award Phila. Mayor's Coun. on Youth Opportunity. Mem. Pa. Legis. Black Caucus (sec.), NAACP, Nat. Assn. Women Legislators, Nat. Polit. Congress Black Women, Nat. Assn. Women's Clergy, Bapt. Min.'s Conf., Afro-Am. Hist. and Cultural Mus. Democrat. Home: 2460 N 59th St Philadelphia PA 19131-1208 Office: Pa Ho of Reps State Capitol Harrisburg PA 17120*

BISHOP, MARY LOU, artist; b. Tulsa, Jan. 6, 1929; d. George W. and Frances Pearl (Hendrix) Nesmith; m. Thomas Ray Bishop, Sept. 1, 1951; children: Thomas R. II, Frances Joann Bishop Faber. Student, Columbia U., 1948; BA, U. Houston, 1949, MEd, 1951; student, U. Wash., 1954; postgrad., U. Houston, 1983-84; pvt. studies with, James Jennings, Opal Walls, Ruth Pershing Uhler, Lowell Collins. Cert. tchr., Tex. Fine artist, painter specializing in portraits, 1951—, freelance artist, 1975—, pvt. tchr. pastels and oils; condr. portrait seminars Tidwell Art Ctr., Houston. Exhibited in one-woman shows in Washington, Ala., Tex.; group shows at Bellevue Arts Fair, Washington; represented in permanent collections at 1st Bapt. Ch., Houston, Unitarian Ch., Huntsville, Ala., also corp. and pvt. collections in U.S. and Europe; executed murals for Unitarian Ch., Huntsville. Recipient scholarship Houston Mus. Fine Art, 1939-50, numerous awards for art. Mem. AAUW, Houston Soc. Illustrators, Profl. Picture Framer's Assn., Phi Kappa Phi, Phi Theta Kappa, Kappa Delta Pi. Unitarian. Home: 2202 Viking Dr Houston TX 77018

BISHOP, PATRICIA HOOVER, reading specialist; b. Hanover, Pa., July 28, 1935; d. Aaron Jones and Edith (Leichliter) Hoover; m. William Alexander Bishop, June 29, 1957; children: Tamilyn Sue, Philip Alan. BS, Maryville Coll., 1957; cert. reading specialist, Pa. State U., 1978. Elem. tchr. Ridgway (Pa.) Area Sch. Dist., 1957-60; tchr. reading Clearfield (Pa.) Area Sch. Dist., 1970-80, coord. reading and fed. programs, 1981—; mem. Keystone State Reading Coun., 1970—, Internat. Reading Assn., 1965—. Mem., past officer Mid-State Literacy Coun., State College, Pa., 1983-89; mem. Cen. Pa. Dist. Libr. Bd., 1985—, pres. 1993; bd. dirs. Joseph and Elizabeth Shaw Pub. Libr., 1984—, elder Presbyn. Ch. Mem. AAUW (pres. 1970-72, v.p. program 1991-93, Woman of the Yr. 1972), Pa. Assn. Fed. Program Coords. Republican. Home: 220 Charles Rd Clearfield PA 16830-1019

BISHOP, RUTH ANN, coloratura soprano, voice educator; b. Homewood, Ill., Feb. 21, 1942; d. George Bernard and Grace Mildred (Hoke) Riddle; m. John Allen Reinhardt, June 9, 1962 (div. 1975); children: Laura, Jonathon; m. Merrill Edward Bishop, Aug. 16, 1975; stepchildren: Mark, Lynn. BS in Music Edn., U. Ill., 1962; M of Music in Voice, Cath. U. Am., 1972; postgrad., U. Md., 1975. Music tchr. Prince Georges County (Md.) Schs., 1963-71, Yamaha Music Co., College Park, Md., 1971-73; voice tchr. Prince Georges Community Coll., Largo, Md., 1972-75, U. Md., College Park, 1975; profl. lectr. voice Chgo. Mus. Coll. Roosevelt U., 1977-82; tchr. voice McHenry County Coll., Crystal Lake, Ill., 1978—, Elgin (Ill.) Community Coll., 1981—; pvt. voice tchr. Crystal Lake, 1975—; dir. music Epworth United Meth. Ch., Elgin, 1984-86, Cherub choir 1st Congl. Ch., Crystal Lake, 1986-88; mem. Camerata Singers, Lake Forest, 1988; performer, vocal dir. Woodstock (Ill.) Mus. Theatre Co., 1983—; soprano soloist Internat. Band Festival, Besana Brianza, Italy, 1993. soprano soloist, Oratorio- The Psalms of David, 1986, opera, The Light of the Eye, 1985-86, Children's Day at the Opera, Washington, 1972, U.S. Navy Band, The White House, 1969; soloist with Crystal Lake Community Choir and Band, 1987—, First Congl. Ch., 1975—, others. Ill. State scholar, 1959. Mem. Nat. Assn. Tchrs. Singing (chpt. rec. sec. 1984-86), Arts Chorale of Elgin Choral Union, Sigma Alpha Iota, Pi Kappa Lambda, Kappa Delta. Republican. United Ch. of Christ. Home: 951 Cambridge Ln Crystal Lake IL 60014-7608 Office: Elgin Community Coll Dept Music 1700 Spartan Dr Elgin IL 60123-7193

BISHOP, SALLY, artist, educator. Student, Worcester Art Mus. Sch.; MFA, U. Mass., 1981. Mem. faculty Worcester (Mass.) Art Mus., 1982—; tchr. drawing & painting workshop Worcester Art Mus. Summer Art Inst. Exhibited in one-person show Arden Gallery, Boston. Home: 40 Westwood Dr Worcester MA 01609

BISHOP, THEDA YVETTE, state official; b. Huntington, W.Va., May 4, 1928; d. Theodore Roosevelt and Mamie Elizabeth (Poindexter) J.; m. William Bishop, June 13, 1949 (dec. May 1986); 1 child, Sharon Leah. BA, Storer Coll., Harpers Ferry, W.Va., 1949; MSW, Wayne State U., 1971, PhD, 1981; student, NYU, 1975, 81. Tchr., head English divsn. Mound Bayou (Miss.) High Sch., 1949-50; supr. spl. projects U.S. Army, Centerline and Detroit, Mich., 1950-55; police woman Detroit Police Dept., 1955-63; probation officer Wayne County, City of Detroit, 1963-73, supr. recorder's ct. women's drug unit, 1973-74, dir. recorder's ct. drug divsn., 1974-75, dep. dir. recorder's ct. probation, 1976-78, dir. recorder's ct. probation, 1979-81; dep. dir. probation svcs. Dept. of Corrections, State of Mich., Detroit, 1981-85, dep. regional adminstr., 1985—; adj. asst. prof. Wayne State U. Coll. Edn., 1982—; cons. in field. Contbr. articles to profl. jours. Mem. Mich. Credentialling Bd. of Addictions Profls., 1985-87; mem. crime task force City of Detroit, 1987-89, mem. strategic planning com., 1987; mem. criminal justice task force City Coun., Detroit, 1987; adv. bd. Family Approach to Crime and Treatment, 1991. Recipient United Negro Coll. Fund award, 1980, Martin Luther King award, 1992. Mem. NAACP, Am. Corrections Assn., Nat. Assn. Black Orgn., Nat. Treatment Alternative to St. Crime Assn., Nat. Assn. Black Social Workers, Nat. Assn. Black Law Enforcement Execs., Mich. Correctional Assn., Mich. Assn. Social Workers, Mich. Assn. Ret. Sch. Pers. Detroit Assn. Program Dirs., Detroit Compact, Detroit Assn. Black Orgn., Detroit Assn. Black Social Workers, W.Va. State Alumni Assn., Wayne State U. Alumni, Women of Wayne State U. Assn. Episcopalian. Home: 5975 Springwater Ln West Bloomfield MI 48322

BISHOP, VIRGINIA WAKEMAN, retired librarian and humanities educator; b. Portland, Oreg., Dec. 28, 1927; d. Andrew Virgil and Letha Evangeline (Ward) Wakeman; m. Clarence Edmund Bishop, Aug. 23, 1953; children: Jean Marie Bishop Johnson, Marilyn Joyce. BA, Bapt. Missionary Tng. Sch., Chgo., 1949, Linfield Coll., McMinnville, Oreg., 1952; MEd, Linfield Coll., McMinnville, Oreg., 1953; MA in Librarianship, U. Wash., 1968. Ch. worker Univ. Bapt. Ch., Seattle, 1954-56, 59-61, pre-sch. tchr. parent coop presch., 1965-66; libr. N.W. Coll., Kirkland, Wash., 1968-69; undergrad. libr. U. Wash., Seattle, 1970; libr., instr. Seattle Cen. Community Coll., 1970-91. Leader Totem Coun. Girl Scouts U.S., 1962-65; pres. Wedgwood Sch. PTA, Seattle, 1964-65; chairperson 46th Dist. Dem. Orgn., Seattle, 1972-73; candidate Wash. State Legis., Seattle, 1974, 80; bd. dirs. U. Bapt. Children's Ctr., 1989—, chairperson, 1990-95; vol. Ptnrs. in Pub. Edn., 1992—. Recipient Golden Acorn award Wedgwood Elem. Sch., 1966. Mem. LWV of Seattle (2d v.p. 1994—), U. Wash. Grad. Sch. Libr. and Info. Sci. Alumni Assn. (1st v.p. 1986-87, pres. 1987-88). Baptist. Home: 3032 NE 87th St Seattle WA 98115-3529

BISHOP, WANDA CAROLINE, geriatrics nurse, medical/surgical nurse; b. Newark, July 18, 1937; d. Paul and Karolina (Werynska) Serafin; children: Carol Jean, Steven Michael; m. Eric J. Bishop, July 6, 1981. BSN, U. Cen. Okla., 1983, MEd in Gerontology, 1989. Cert. med. surg. nurse, gerontol. nurse. Med. office mgr. Henry J. Pearce, M.D., Edmond, Okla., 1969-81; staff nurse VA Med. Ctr., Oklahoma City, 1983-86; owner, adminstr. HomeCare Nursing Svcs., Inc., Edmond, 1985-89; dir. nursing Okla. Christian Home, Edmond, 1993—. Bd. dirs. Edmond Advs. for the elderly, Edmond, 1989. Mem. ANA (coun. gerontol. nursing), Okla. Nurses Assn. (legis. com. 1992), Okla. Alliance on Aging, Cen. State U. Alumni Assn., Alphi Chi, Sigma Phi Omega. Home: 108 Woodbridge Cir Edmond OK 73003 Office: Okla Christian Home Edmond OK 73034

BISHOPRIC, SUSAN, public relations executive; b. N.Y.C., June 3, 1946. AAS, Fashion Inst. Tech., 1965; student, N.Y. Sch. Interior Design, New Sch. Social Rsch. Exec.-in-tng. Bloomingdales, Abraham & Strauss; merchandise coord. Seventeen mag.; publicity dir. Germaine Monteil Cosmetiques; account exec. Rowland Co., 1968-69, account supr., 1969-73, v.p., 1973-75, sr. v.p., creative dir., 1975-78, exec. v.p., 1979-81; pub. rels. dir. Susan Gilbert & Co., 1984-86; head pub. rels. divsn. Beber Silverstein & Ptnrs., 1986-89; founder, pres. Bishopric Agy., Coral Gables, Fla., 1989—. Office: Bishopric Agy 400 Viscaya Ave Coral Gables FL 33134*

BISKIN, JILL BERTA, artist, scenic artist for opera, theater and film; b. San Antonio, Apr. 6, 1953; d. Harvey Chester and Bayla (Sheinberg) B. BFA in Painting, R.I. Sch. Design, 1975; student, Studio Nerina Simi, Florence, Italy, 1976-77, Studio and Forum Stage Design, N.Y.C., 1979-81, NAD, N.Y.C., 1985. Scenic artist selected Broadway and other theaters, ballet, feature films, N.Y.C., 1980-85; scenic artist Met. Opera Co., N.Y.C., 1985—; instr. scene painting Studio of Scene Painting, N.Y.C., 1988-90; designer, muralist various residences and showrooms, N.Y.C., 1981-88; vis. artist Am. Acad., Rome, 1994. Exhibited in solo shows at McNay Art Mus., San Antonio, 1986, Kurts Bingham Gallery, Memphis, 1992, Parchman Stremmel Galleries, San Antonio, 1995; group shows include Maggio Toscano, Prato, Italy, 1979, Ydessa Gallery, Toronto, 1981, Artists' Choice Mus., N.Y.C., 1985, Ruth Siegel Gallery, N.Y.C., 1987, 88, Read Stremmel Gallery, San Antonio, 1988, 89, Carrington/Gallagher, San Antonio, 1992, Stiebel Modern, N.Y.C., 1992, Jansen Perez Inc., San Antonio, 1993, Parchman Stremmel Gallery, San Antonio, 1994, K&E Gallery, N.Y.C., 1994, Blue Hill Cultural Ctr., Pearl River, N.Y., 1995; represented in numerous collections, N.Y., L.A., Balt., others. Grantee in painting E.T. Greenshields Found., Rome and Florence, 1978-79; Child Meml. Found. grantee, Rome, 1979. Mem. United Scenic Artists. Home: 160 W 73d St New York NY 10023

BISKO, ROSLYN JEAN, secondary education educator; b. Spangler, Pa., Apr. 21, 1948; d. Ross Joseph and Adeline Dorothy (Shutty) Formeck; widowed; children: Kimberly Anne, Nicole Lynn. BA, U. Pitts., 1969; M in Elem. Edn., St. Francis Coll., 1978. Social worker Youth and Need Svcs., Youngstown, Ohio, 1971-72; elem. edn. tchr. No. Cambria Cath. Sch., Barnesboro, Pa., 1976-79; mid. sch. tchr. No. Cambria Sch. Dist., Barnesboro, Pa., 1980—; dir. Pius Reading Club, No. Cambria Cath. Schs., Barnesboro, 1978-80; mem. math. com. No. Cambria Sch., Barnesboro, 1986—, sente com., 1990-92, staff devel. com., reconstruction com., 1993—. Mem. PTA, Barnesboro. Mem. NEA, Pa. State Edn. Assn., No. Cambria Edn. Assn. Democrat. Roman Catholic. Home: 308 Susquehanna St Barnesboro PA 15714 Office: No Cambria Mid Sch 600 Joseph St Barnesboro PA 15714

BISSELL, BETTY DICKSON, retired stockbroker; b. Salina, Kans., Sept. 9, 1932; d. Henry Shields and Alta May Dickson; m. Buford Lyle Bissell, Jr., Nov. 1, 1952; 1 child, Bradford Dickson. Student, U. Kans., 1949-52; cert. fin. planner, Coll. Fin. Planning, 1976. With Dean Witter Reynolds Inc., Menlo Park, Calif., 1975—, asst. br. mgr., 1978-82, asso. v.p. investments, 1980-82, 1st v.p. investments, 1982-86, sr. v.p. investments, 1986-94; ret., 1994; cons. in field. Pres. Jr. League San Jose (Calif.), 1963-64. Mem. Internat. Assn. Fin. Planners, Internat. Bd. Cert. Fin. Planners, Peninsula Stock and Bond Club, Pi Beta Phi, Commonwealth Club Calif., Summit League Club (Saratoga-Los Gatos), Jr. League Club (San Jose, Calif.). Republican. Episcopalian. Office: 1010 El Camino Real Ste 200 Menlo Park CA 94025-4306

BISSET CARPENTER, SUZANNE See FOX, SELENA MARIE

BISSETT, BARBARA ANNE, steel distribution company executive; b. Cleve., Sept. 27, 1950; d. George Jr. and Helen (Kirkwood) B.; m. Kerry Mark Kitchen, Oct. 6, 1979; children: Mark Jeffrey, Lauren Brooke. BFA, U. Denver, 1974. Inside sales rep. Bissett Steel Co., Cleve., 1977-78, inside sales mgr., 1978-80, v.p., 1980-88, pres., 1988—; mentor strategic planning course Greater Cleve. Growth Assn., 1987—. Bd. dirs. Greater Cleve. Growth Assn., 1994—; trustee Enterprise Devel., Inc., 1994—. Mem. Am. Soc. Metals, Steel Svc. Ctr. Inst. (v.p. programming young leadership forum 1989, pres. 1991-93, bd. dirs. No. ohio chpt., v.p. 1994), Coun. Smaller Enterprises (leadership coun. 1989—, bd. dirs. 1990—), Assn. Women in Metals Indusries, Steel Svc. Ctr. Inst. (pres. N. Ohio chpt. 1995—), Cleve. Yacht Club, Women's City Club. Republican. Presbyterian. Home: 1994 Coes Post Run Cleveland OH 44145-2059 Office: 9005 Bank St Cleveland OH 44125-3400

BISSON, MICHELLE, reporter, playwright; b. N.Y.C., Oct. 20, 1956; d. Russell Howard and Hedy (Zelmanovits) Engle; m. Maurice Charles Bisson, Nov. 25, 1982. BA with honors, CUNY, 1978; MS with distinction, Northwestern U., Chgo., 1993. Prodn. asst. Am. Lung Assn., N.Y.C., 1980-81; asst. editor Dermatology News, N.Y.C., 1984-85; editor Jour. Pediatric Orthopaedics, Seattle, 1987-92; reporter Bellingham (Wash.) Herald, 1993—; co-chair network of editors and writers U. Wash., Seattle, 1991-92. Author (plays) Mrs. Rothman, 1988 (Arts Commn. grant 1988, Playwrights' Festival honors 1988), Prisons, 1990; book reviewer The Seattle Times, 1986-93, KIRO-AM radio, Seattle, 1990-92. Recipient Mack award CUNY, 1978, Blethen award Seattle Times, 1994. Mem. Kappa Tau Alpha. Office: Bellingham Herald 1155 N State St Bellingham WA 98227

BITLER, CATHY FITZPATRICK, economic development and public affairs executive; b. Ft. Benning, Ga., Apr. 24, 1958; d. Benjamin Elbert and Barbara (Hayman) Fitzpatrick; m. David Levi Bitler, Sept. 11, 1982; 1 child, Sarah Kathryn. BS in Communications, Ohio U., 1980. Reporter Sta. WHOK Inc., Lancaster, Ohio, 1980-83; dir. news Sta. WHOK Inc., Lancaster, 1983-88, dir. promotions, 1985-88; econ. devel. asst. South Cen. Power, Lancaster, 1988—. Author: Fairfield Monthly, 1984. Pres. United Cerebral palsy Lancaster, 1986-89; mem. adv. com. Southeastern Correctional Inst., 1983-87; mem. adv. bd. Fairfield County Youth, 1985-87, Spl. Wish Found., 1986-88; mem. nat. alumni bd. Ohio U. Mem. Ohio Assn. Press (bd. dirs. 1984-85, best regularly scheduled news award 1986), Ohio Associated Press, Circleville Pickaway C. of C. (bd. dirs. 1993—), Lancaster Fairfield County C. of C. (bd. dirs. 1995—), Unity Singers, Ohio U. Alumni Assn. (nat. bd. dirs., Disting. Svc. award 1989), Lancaster Women's Club. Republican. Home: 566 Lynwood Ln Lancaster OH 43130-8739 Office: South Cen Power PO Box 250 Lancaster OH 43130-0250

BITNER, JERRI LYNNE, information systems professional; b. York, Pa., May 11, 1951; d. Ernest Maclellan and Gertrude Pauline (Beck) B. BS, Pa. State U., 1974. Procurement agt. Def. Indsl. Supply Ctr., Phila., 1975-77; contracts specialist Navy Ships Parts Control Ctr., Mechanicsburg, 1977-81; procurement analyst, then supr. Navy Fleet Material Support Office, Ctrl. Design Agy., 1981-87, dir. procurement systems div., 1987-94, dir. APADE/C2/Reengineering divsn., 1994—. Methodist. Avocations: skiing, tennis, golf, camping. Office: USN Fleet Material Support Office PO Box 2010 Mechanicsburg PA 17055-0792

BITTEL, MURIEL HELENE, managing editor; b. N.Y.C., Mar. 22; d. Ernest Henry and Helen Minnie (Seibel) Albers; m. Robert Gifford Walcutt, June 15, 1946; children—Lynn Lowell Walcutt, Mark James Walcutt, Judith Anne Walcutt; m. Lester Robert Bittel, May 8, 1973. B.A., Douglass Coll. Feature writer Daily Home News, New Brunswick, N.J.; editor Fawcett Pubs., N.Y.C., 1940-46; pub. relations dir. Electrovox/Walco Inc., East Orange, N.J., 1946-62; mng. editor Acad. Hall Pubs., Bridgewater, Va., 1974—. Mng. editor: Ency. Profl. Mgmt., 1978; Handbook Profl. Mgrs., 1985. Home: 106 Breezewood Ter Bridgewater VA 22812-1433

BITTENCE, MARY M., lawyer; b. Houghton, Mich., Jan. 1, 1952. BA summa cum laude, Cleve. State U., 1976, JD summa cum laude, 1982. Bar: Ohio 1982. Ptnr. Baker & Hostetler, Cleve. Bus. editor: Cleveland State Law Review, 1981-82. Mem. ABA, Ohio State Bar Assn., Cleve. Bar Assn. Office: Baker & Hostetler 3200 Nat City Ctr 1900 E 9th St Cleveland OH 44114-3485*

BITTERMAN, MARY GAYLE FOLEY, broadcasting executive; b. San Jose, Calif., May 29, 1944; d. John Dennis and Zoe (Hames) Foley; m. Morton Edward Bitterman, June 26, 1967; 1 child Sarah Fleming. BA, Santa Clara U., 1966; MA, Bryn Mawr Coll., 1969, PhD, 1971. Exec. dir. Hawaii Pub. Broadcasting, Honolulu, 1974-79; dir. Voice of Am., Washington, 1980-81, Dept. Commerce, Honolulu, 1981-83, E.-W. Ctr. Inst. Culture and Comm., Honolulu, 1984-88; cons. pvt. practice, Honolulu, 1989-93; pres., CEO KQED, Inc., San Francisco, 1993—; Bd. dirs. Bank of Hawaii, Honolulu, 1984—, Internat. Ctr. Comm., San Diego, Calif., 1992—; vice chmn. TIDE 2000, Tokyo, 1984-93. Producer: (film) China Visit, 1978; contbr. numerous articles on internat. telecomms. to various pubs. Bd. dirs. United Way, Honolulu, 1986-93; chmn. Kuakini Health System, Honolulu, 1991-94. Recipient Candle of Understanding award Bonneville (Utah) Internat. Corp., 1985; named hon. mem. Nat. Fedn. Press Women, 1986. Fellow Nat. Acad. Pub. Info.; mem. Pacific Forum, CSIS (bd. govs.), Bay Area Coun. (bd. dirs.), World Affairs Coun. (bd. dirs.). Office: KQED Inc 2601 Mariposa St San Francisco CA 94110-1400

BITTLE, POLLY A., nephrology nurse, researcher; b. Orlando, Fla., Jan. 15, 1963; d. James T. and Maybell (Wendel) B. ADN, Valencia Community Coll., Orlando, 1984, AA, 1986; BSN, U. South Fla., 1987. Cert. in CPR, emergency cardiac care. Clin. rsch. coord. nephrology, hypertension, cardiothoracic surgery U. South Fla. Coll. Medicine, Tampa, 1987—; interim dir. nursing U. S. Fla. Dialysis Ctr., Tampa, 1994—. Contbr. articles to profl. jours. Mem. Am. Heart Assn., Am. Nephrology Nurses Assn., Fla. Nurses Assn., Sigma Theta Tau, Phi Theta Kappa. Home: 4402 Bradley Ave Orlando FL 32839-1419

BITTNER, BARBARA JANE, management consultant; b. Pitts., July 27, 1947; d. Sylvan F. and Dolores Eileen (Mikulski) B.; m. William R. Haushalter, Sept. 1, 1979; children: Laura B., Vanessa B. BS in Hotels, Restaurants and Instns., Pa. State U., 1969; MBA in Fin., U. Pitts., 1979. Mgmt. trainee Army and Air Force Exch. Svc., Plattsburgh, N.Y., 1969-71; food and beverage mgr. San Jeronimo Hotel, San Juan, P.R., 1971-74, Elangeni Hotel, Durban, Republic South Africa, 1974-75, Princess Hotels, Acapulco, Mex., 1975-76; conf. dir. U. Pitts., 1976-78; fin. analyst J&L Steel Corp., Pitts., 1979-83; pres. Profl. Cons. Assocs., Pitts., 1983—. Vol. instr. PHA, Pitts., 1990-91; sec. Alpha Parent Assn., Pitts., 1991. Mem. Nat. Assn. Women Bus. Owners, Pa. Hotel and Restaurant Soc., Western Pa. Restaurant Assn. (assoc.), Legatus. Office: Profl Cons Assocs 7078 Bennington Woods Dr Pittsburgh PA 15237

BITTNER, MARY LOUISE, public administrator; b. Pitts., Nov. 21, 1946; d. Bernard Lawrence and Pauline Louise (Kozusko) Pack; children: George Richard Hill, Leonard Michael Hill; m. Keith John Bittner; children: Keith Joseph, Daniel James, Christopher Lee. AA in Acctg., C.C. Allegheny County, Monroeville, Pa., 1978; BS in Natural Scis., U. Pitts., 1990, MPA, 1993. Systems mgr., operator Municipality of Monroeville, 1985-88; mgr. shared fin. Steel Valley Coun. Govts., Homestead, Pa., 1988-90; dir. fin., tax collector City of Clairton, Pa., 1990-92; dir. fin. Borough of Wilkinsburg, Pa., 1992; interim mgr. Borough of West Mifflin, Pa., 1993-94. Co-editor mag. Afterimage, 1977-79; contbr. articles to mags. Mem. disciplinary subcom. strategic planning com. Penn Hills Sch. Dist.; recorder, facilitator Pitts. Urban Zoning Code Project. Recipient Disting. Budget Presentation award, 1991, 92. Mem. Am. Soc. Pub. Adminstrn. (budgeting and fin. mgmt. sec., exec. coun. Pitts. chpt.), Govt. Fin. Officers Assn. (chair state conf. planning com., pres. S.W. Pa. chpt.), Internat. City and County Mgmt. Assn., Grad. Sch. Pub. and Internat. Affairs Alumni Assn., Phi Theta Kappa. Home: 323 Idlewood Rd Pittsburgh PA 15235-3818

BIVENS, CONSTANCE ANN, elementary school educator; b. Madison, Ind., June 26, 1938; d. Nelson and Virginia (Cole) B. BS, George Peabody Coll. for Tchrs., now Vanderbilt U., 1960, MA, 1966; EdD, Nova U., Ft. Lauderdale, Fla., 1982. Cert. educator. Tchr. Broward County Schs., Ft.

Lauderdale, Fla., 1960-61, 65—, Jefferson County Schs., Louisville, Ky., 1961-62, Ft. Knox (Ky.) Schs., 1962-64, Madison (Ind.) Consol. Schs., 1964-65; chmn. K-Adult Coun., Nova Schs., Ft. Lauderdale, 1976-78; cons. 1978-80. Author: Boots, Butterflies, and Dragons, 1982. Mem. Hollywood Hills United Meth. Ch., 1966—, mem. adminstrv. bd. Sing in Chancel Choir, pres. Sunday Sch. class, 1991-94, Walk to Emmaus, 1990, 91-92; active Children's Cancer Caring Ctr. Inc., Broward County chpt., 1986—, Hollywood Hist. Soc., Zool. Soc. Fla., Nat. Audubon Soc. Mem. AAUW, ASCD, NEA, Fla. Reading Assn., Hist. Madison, Inc., Jefferson County Hist. Soc., Internat. Order King's Daus. and Sons, Irish Cultural Inst., Delta Kappa Gamma (internat. expansion com. 1986-88, chmn. internat. program of work com. 1988-90, internat. rep. World Confedn. Orgns. of Teaching profession 1989, chmn. S.E. regional conf. 1991, internat. nominations com. 1992—, chmn. 1994—, 1st v.p. Mu state 1993—, Sara Ferguson Achievement award 1990). Republican. Methodist. Home: 5516 Arthur St Hollywood FL 33021-4608 Office: Nova Blanche Forman Elem Sch 3521 Davie Rd Fort Lauderdale FL 33314-1604

BIVINS, SUSAN STEINBACH, systems engineer; b. Chgo., June 5, 1941; d. Joseph Bernard and Eleanor Celeste (Mathes) S.; BS, Northwestern U., 1963; postgrad. U. Colo., 1964, U. Ill., 1965, UCLA, 1971; m. James Herbert Bivins, June 7, 1980. With IBM, 1967-94, support mgr. East, White Plains, N.Y., 1977-78, systems support mgr., western region, L.A., 1978-81, br. market support mgr., 1981-84, mgr. IBM ops. and support L.A. Summer Olympics, 1984; mgr. IBM office supporting devel. FAA air traffic control system for 1990's, 1984-88, mgr. complex systems mktg., 1988-89, acct. devel. mgr. aerospace engrng. and mfg., 1989-91, mgr. cons. and outsourcing indsl. sector trading area, 1991-92, cons. orgn. task forces, 1992-93; project exec. IBM Integrated Sys. Solutions Corp., 1993-94; delivery exec. BDM Tech., Inc., 1995—; pres. Jastech, 1986—. Vol. tchr. computer sci. Calif. Mentally Gifted Minor Programs; vol. L.A. Youth Motivation Task Force; dir. pub. rels. Lake of the Ozarks Jazz Festival, 1993-95; bd. dirs. Greater Lake Area Arts Coun., 1993-95. Mem. Systems Engrng. Symposium, Pi Lambda Theta. Developed program to retrieve data via terminal and direct it to any appropriate hardcopy device, 1973. Office: BDM Tech Inc 1999 Broadway Ste 2000 Denver CO 80202

BIVONA, VIRGINIA SIENA, graphic products manufacturing company executive; b. Cleve., May 16, 1931; d. Vincent James Sr. and Virginia Catherine (Johnson) Siena; divorced; children: Mark, Lawrence, Stephanie, Matthew, Elizabeth. Student, Western Res. U., 1950-53. Advt. dir. Am. Direct Mail Mktg., Dallas, 1981-78; pres. Tex. Grid Systems, Inc., Richardson, 1982-93; gen. mgr. Tex. Grid Systems (div. Visu-Com Inc.), Balt., 1993—. Author: Notes from a Chameleon, 1984, Dirty Dining, A Cookbook for Lovers, 1991, For My Daughters, A History of Women that History Forgot, 1994. Vol. Hist. Preservation League, Dallas, 1987—. Mem. Noetic Sci. Inst., Dallas Ft. Worth Writers Workshop, Nat. Mus. Women in Arts, Philosophers Forum, Internat. Platform Assn. Home and Office: 12920 Audelia Rd Apt 254 Dallas TX 75243

BIXENSTINE, KIM FENTON, lawyer; b. Providence, Feb. 26, 1958; d. Barry Jay Fenton and Gail Louise (Traverse) Weinstein; m. Barton Aaron Bixenstine, June 25, 1983; children: Paul Jay, Nathan Alexis. BA, Middlebury Coll., 1979; JD, U. Chgo., 1982. Bar: Ohio 1982, U.S. Dist. Ct. (no. and so. dists.) Ohio 1983, U.S. Ct. Appeals (6th cir.) 1983. Law clk. to presiding judge U.S. Dist. Ct. (so. dist.) Ohio, Cin., 1982-83; assoc. Jones, Day, Reavis & Pogue, Cleve., 1983-90, ptnr., 1991—. Bd. dirs. Planned Parenthood Greater Cleve., 1991—, sec. 1992-93, v.p. 1994—. Mem. Ohio Bar Assn. (bd. govs. litigation sect.), Ohio Women's Bar Assn. (chair legis. com., 1994—), Cleve. Bar Assn. (bd. dirs. 1993—, chair standing com. on lawyer professionalism 1994—, minority outreach com. 1993—, chair commn. on women in the law 1992-93). Office: Jones Day Reavis & Pogue N Point 901 Lakeside Ave Cleveland OH 44114

BIXLER, MARGARET TRIPLETT, former manufacturing executive; b. Bluffton, Ohio, Sept. 15, 1917; d. Ray Leon and Etta Mabel (Lantz) Triplett; m. Roland M. Bixler, July 1, 1939; children: Katharine, David. AB, U. Mich., 1939; MA, U. New Haven, 1982. Sec. of bd. J-B-T Instruments, Inc., New Haven, 1940-76, chmn. of bd., 1976-91; ret., 1992. Author: Winds of Freedom, 1991.

BIZIC, MILANA, librarian. BS in Elem. Edn., U. Pitts., 1962, MEd in Elem. Edn., 1967, postgrad., 1969-70, 81. Tchr. first and second grades, libr. coord. Quaker Valley Sch. Dist., Sewickley and Osborne, Edgeworth,, Sewickely and Osborne, Pa., 1962-70; substitute tchr., 1970-78; tchr. fourth grade Edgeworth Elem., Sewickley, 1978-81; tchr. gifted students, grades one to six Edgeworth Elem., Sewickeley, 1981-92; libr./multi-media specialist Edgeworth Elem., 1992—; tchr. Pa. State U./Beaver Campus, 1982—; cons. Pa. Dept. Edn., Harriburg, 1992-93, USA Today, 1992, U.S. Dept. Energy, 1992, Serbian Unity Congress, Yugoslavia, 1991, U. Pitts., 1991, U.S. Patent Office, Washington, 1990, Invent America!, Washington, 1987-89, others; mem. spl. Pa. Delegation Cultural Edn. Exch. of 30 educators to Omiya, Japan, 1993; moderator and facilitator Project HOPE, 1992; speaker in field. Contbr. articles to profl. jours., ethnic and numismatic newspapers. Sponsor Whistle Stop Bus Tour for children, 1992; v.p. trustees, Indian Arts Assn. of Pitts., 1976-89, Sewickley Valley Hist. Soc., 1976-85; co-chmn. Sewickley Bridge Celebration Com., 1981; chmn. Leet Twp. Bicentennial Commn., 1976; guest speaker numerous church and civic orgns. Recipient numerous awards including selection to spl. Pa. Delegation Cultural Edn. Exch. of 30 Educators to Omiya, Japan, 1993; scholar U.S. Dept. Energy, 1992; grantee Soc. for Analytical Chemists Pitts., Spectroscopy Soc. Pitts., 1992; grand prize co-winner First Johnny Appleseed Nat. Awards Contest, 1990, first-place winner Apple Computer Clubs Nat. Merit competition, 1985, 86, 87, 90; state winner Pa. Commn. for Women, 1990, Thanks to Tchrs. award Group W Broadcasting, 1990. Office: Media AV Svcs Libr Edgeworth Elem Sch 200 Meadow Lane Edgeworth Sewickley PA 15143-1105

BIZUB, JOHANNA CATHERINE, library director; b. Denville, N.J., Apr. 13, 1957; d. Stephen Bernard and Elizabeth Mary (Grizzle) B.; m. Scott Jeffrey Smith, 1992. BS in Criminal Justice, U. Dayton, 1979; MLS, Rutgers U., 1984. Law libr. Morris County Law Libr., 1981-83, Clapp & Eisenberg, Newark, 1984-86; dir. libr. Sills Cummis, 1986-94; libr. dir. Montville (N.J.) Twp. Pub. Libr., N.J., 1994—. Mem. ALA, ABA, Assn. Legal Adminstrs., N.J. Law Librs. Assn. (treas. 1987-89, v.p. pres.-elect 1989-90, pres. 1990-91, past pres. 1991-92), Am. Assn. Law Librs. (pvt. law librs. SIS, vice chair/chair-elect 1992-93, chair 1993-94, past chair 1994-95), N.J. Libr. Assn., Spl. Libr. Assn. N.J. (treas. 1990-92), Law Libr. Assn. Greater N.Y., Am. Legion Aux. (treas. Rockden unit 175 1983-93). Democrat. Roman Catholic. Home: 11 Elm St Rockaway NJ 07866-3108 Office: Montville Twp Pub Libr 90 Horsneck Rd Montville NJ 07045-9626

BJORKLUND, JANET VINSEN, speech pathologist; b. Seattle, July 31, 1947; d. Vernon Edward and Virginia Lea (Rogers) B.; m. Dan Robert Young, Dec. 04, 1971; children: Emery Allen, Alanna Vinsen, Marisa Rogers. Student, U. Vienna, Austria, 1966-67; BA, Pacific U., 1969; student, U. Wash., 1970-71; MA, San Francisco State U., 1977. Cert. clin. speech pathologist, audiologist. Speech pathologist, audiological cons. USN Hosp., Rota, Spain, 1972-75; traineeship in audiology VA Hosp., San Francisco, 1976; speech pathologist San Lorenzo (Calif.) Unified Schs., 1975-77, 78-81; dir. speech pathology St. Lukes Speech and Hearing Clinic, San Francisco, 1977-78; audiologist X.O. Barrios, M.D., San Francisco, 1977-81; cons. Visually Impaired Infant Program, Seattle, 1981-82; speech pathologist Everett (Wash.) Schs., 1982-93; supr. pediat. programs speech pathology Group Health Coop. of Puget Sound, Seattle, 1994—; cons. Madison House, Kirkland, Wash., 1983-88, NW Devel. Therapists, Everett, 1985-87, Providence Hosp. Childrens Ctr., Everett, 1985-93, Pacific Hearing and Speech, 1988-93. Author: (with others) Screening for Bilingual Preschoolers, 1977, (TV script), Clinical Services in San Francisco, 1978, Developing Better Communication Skills, 1982. Coord. presch. Christian edn. Kirkland Congl. Ch., 1983-85; organizer Residents Against Speeding Drivers, Madison Park, Seattle, 1985-87; chmn. staff devel. com. Everett Schs., 1988-89; rep. Barrier Resolution Project, 1989-89; mem. Strategic Planning Com., 1989-93. Mem. Am. Speech-Lang. and Hearing Assn., Wash. Speech and Hearing Assn. (regional rep. 1985-86, chair licensure task force 1986-88, rep. Birth to Six Project 1988-91, pres.-elect 1992, pres. 1993, past. pres. 1994), Phi Lambda Omicron (pres. Pacific U. chpt. 1968). Congregationalist. Office: Group Health Speech/Lang Learning Svcs 125 16th Ave Seattle WA 98112-5260

BJORNSON, MARIA, theatrical designer. Theatrical designer London, 1971—. Designer (mus.) over one hundred prodns. including: The Phantom of the Opera (Antoinette Perry awards for best scenic design and best costume design 1988, Drama Desk award for Best Set and Costume 1988), Follies (Drama Mag. Designer of Yr.), Aspects of Love (Drama Mag. Designer of Yr.), (operas) Janacek Cycle (Prague Silver medal design), Cosi Fan Tutte, Mahagonny, Figaro, Carmen, Valkyrie, Toussaint L'Ouverture, Donnerstag Aus Licht, Tales of Hoffmann, Rosenkavalier (theatre) Blue Angel, Measure for Measure, Lulu, Camille, A Midsummer's Night Dream, Hamlet, The Tempest, Hedda Gabler, Katya Kasanova, 1994, Sleeping Beauty, 1994. recipient Designer's Designer Great Britain Observer Mag., 1989.

BLACHEK, JUDITH A., technical editor; b. Montrose, Pa., July 23, 1958; d. John Arthur and Rose Mary (Mangieri) B.; m. Michael John Kolesar, Sept. 22, 1980 (div. Aug. 1984); m. John Thomas Paolillo, May 20, 1989; children: Gina Rose, Thomas John. BA, Marywood Coll., 1976-80. Writer U. Ky., Lexington, 1980-81; proofreader Singer Inc., Binghamton, N.Y., 1982-84; tech. editor Digital Equipment Corp., Nashua, N.H., 1984—. Vol., editor newsletter Nat. Scoliosis Found., Belmont, 1986-89. Mem. NOW (state pres., v.p., treas. 1985—, pres. v.p. Nashua chpt. 1985—), YWCA (named Disting. Woman Leader Nashua chpt. 1992), Scoliosis Support Group N.H. (state pres. 1985-89). Democrat. Office: Digital Equipment Corp 2KO1-2/F2 110 Spit Brook Rd Nashua NH 03062

BLACHMAN, ROCHEL SARA, lawyer, business executive; b. Borås, Sweden, Oct. 8, 1952; came to U.S., 1954; d. Berek (Ben) and Ester (Altman) Blachman. BA, UCLA, 1974; JD, U. Calif., Berkeley, 1977. Atty. Wyman, Bautzer, Rothman, Kuchel, L.A., 1977-81; sr. v.p. bus. affairs Orion Pictures Corp., L.A., 1982-93, Paramount Pictures Corp., Hollywood, Calif., 1993—. Office: Paramount Pictures Corp 5555 Melrose Ave Hollywood CA 90038

BLACK, AGNES MARIE, criminal investigator; b. Jamaica, N.Y., Aug. 5, 1962; d. Robert Gain and Agnes Marie (McKenna) B. BA in History and Govt. Politics, St. John's Univ., 1984. Investigative asst. Immigration and Naturalization Svc., N.Y.C., 1991-92, criminal investigator, spl. agt., 1992—. 2d lt. U.S. Army, 1984-87. Mem. Am. Fedn. Govt. Employees (shop steward local 917 1993—), Phi Alpha Theta. Republican. Roman Catholic. Home: 318 Woodlake Manor Dr Lakewood NJ 08701 Office: Immigration and Naturalization 26 Federal Plz New York NY 10278

BLACK, ALICE ANN, neonatal and pediatrics nurse educator; b. Paris, Tex., Mar. 2, 1955; d. James M. and Jimmie Lorayne (Reeves) Black; m. James Everett Ghiron, Sept. 1983 (div. 1985); 1 child, Chad Darek; m. Enoch Callaway Brabant, May 23, 1987; 1 child, Kristen Leigh. ADN, Paris Jr. Coll., 1975; BSN, U. Tex., Arlington, 1980; MSN, U. San Francisco, 1990. Clin. nurse McCuistion Regional Med. Ctr., Paris, 1975-77, Children's Med. Ctr., Dallas, 1977-82, U. Calif., San Francisco, 1982-90; neonatal/pediatric educator coord. Community Hosp., Santa Rosa, Calif., 1990—; affiliated faculty Am. Heart Assn. PALS, Santa Rosa, 1992. Mem. Drug Alcohol Abuse Coun., Santa Rosa, 1990—. Mem. Nat. Assn. Neonatal Nurses, Sigma Theta Tau. Democrat. Methodist. Home: 5952 Yerba Buena Rd Santa Rosa CA 95409-3960 Office: Community Hosp 3325 Chanate Rd Santa Rosa CA 95404-1797

BLACK, BARBARA ARONSTEIN, legal history educator; b. Bklyn., May 6, 1933; d. Robert and Minnie (Polenberg) A.; m. Charles L. Black, Jr., Apr. 11, 1954; children—Gavin B., David A., Robin E. BA, Bklyn. Coll., 1953; LLB, Columbia U., 1955; MPhil, Yale U., 1970, PhD, 1975; LLD (hon.), N.Y. Law Sch., 1986, Marymount Manhattan Coll., 1986, Vt. Law Sch., 1987, Coll. of New Rochelle, 1987, Smith Coll., 1988, Bklyn. Coll., 1988, York U., Toronto, Can., 1990, Georgetown U., 1991. Assoc. in law Columbia U. Law Sch., N.Y.C., 1955-56; lectr. history Yale U., New Haven, 1974-76, asst. prof. history, 1976-79, assoc. prof. law, 1979-84; George Welwood Murray prof. legal history Columbia U. Law Sch., N.Y.C., 1984—, dean faculty of law, 1986-91. Editor Columbia Law Rev., 1953-55. Active N.Y. State Ethics Commn. Recipient Fed. Bar Assn. prize Columbia Law Sch., 1955. Mem. Am. Soc. Legal History (pres. 1986-90), Am. Acad. Arts and Scis., Am. Philos. Soc., Mass. Hist. Soc., Supreme Ct. Hist. Soc., Selden Soc., Century Assn., N.Y. State Ethics Commn. Office: Columbia U Sch Law 435 W 116th St New York NY 10027-7201

BLACK, BARBARA CROWDER, educator, consultant; b. Woodbine, Iowa, Feb. 11, 1922; d. John Hershel and Elsie May (Jenkins) Crowder; m. (Estel) Eugene Black, Sept. 1, 1944; 1 child, (Estel) Eugene Jr. (dec. 1993). AB, N.Mex. Western U., 1946; teaching credential, UCLA, 1964; cert. in reading, math., Calif. State U., 1969, 72; postgrad., Sacramento State U., 1977-89. Cert. tchr., Calif. Tchr. Chavez County Schs., Roswell, N.Mex., 1942-44; tchr. ESL 6th St. Elem. Sch., Silver City, N. Mex., 1946-47; girls athletic coach Silver City Jr. High Sch., Silver City, N. Mex., 1946-47; tchr. Lovington (N.Mex.) Pub. Schs., 1950-51, Long Beach (Calif.) Unified Sch. Dist., 1951-58, Santa Maria (Calif.) Elem. Sch. Dist., 1958-59; tchr. spl. edn. Bellflower (Calif.) Unified Sch. Dist., 1959-67; instr. Sacramento Unified Sch. Dist., 1968-79; co-owner, v.p. El Paso Southwestern R.R. Ednl. Consultants, Sacramento, 1985—; demonstration tchr. Long Beach Unified Sch. Dist., 1952-59; master tchr. to student tchrs. Calif. State U., Long Beach, 1954-59, Sacramento, 1972-73; supr. tchr. aides Sacramento Unified Sch. Dist., 1969-79; co-editor revision of math. testing materials, 1977; English instr. Jian Ping Mid. Sch., Shanghai, China, 1992; pvt. tutor computers, math., and reading elem. sch. children, 1994—. Co-author tchr. manuals in sci. and arithmetic, tchrs. guide for social studies; cons., editor pub. of Barking at Shadows, 1994. Elder Westminster Presbyn. Ch., Sacramento, 1973—; docent Calif. State R.R. Mus., Sacramento, 1980—; vol. Jed Smith Sch. Computer Class, Sacramento, 1989, Habitat for Humanity, 1994. Grantee Sacramento County Office Edn., 1969, Calif. Dept. Edn., 1972-73; recipient cert. spl. commendation Calif. Dept. Parks, 1988. Mem. NAFE, ASCD, Calif. Tchrs. Assn., Calif. Ret. Tchrs. Assn., Sacramento State Parks Docent Assn. (membership chair 1981-87, Outstanding Svc. award 1983, 86, 87, 89). Office: El Paso Southwestern R R Capitol Towers Ste 14M 1500 7th St Sacramento CA 95814-5439

BLACK, BEVERLY HOLSTUN, psychiatric social worker; b. Thomaston, Ga., Sept. 27, 1942; d. Gordon Robinson and Louise (Hooten) Holstun; m. Frank Anderson Black, Dec. 27, 1963 (div. 1988); children: Sereina Louise, Margot Elisabeth; m. Michael Summers Lynch, Dec. 31, 1992. BA in English, U. Denver, 1963; MSW, U. S.C., 1979. Diplomate in social work. Tchr. Sumter County, S.C., 1975-77; clin. social worker Santee-Wateree Mental Health Ctr., Sumter, S.C., 1979-81; psychiat. social worker Ctr. for Personal and Family Growth, Valdosta, Ga., 1981-83; dir. Anxiety Disorders Ctr., Round House Psychiat. Ctr., Alexandria, Va., 1983—; speaker, lectr. on anxiety disorders, 1985—. Editor, expert videos for United Way, 1986, 87; appearances on TV as expert on anxiety disorders. Mem. adv. bd. No. Va. Women's Ctr., Vienna, 1985—; advisor 1st Family Support Ctr. in Air Force, Moody AFB, Valdosta, 1982, YMCA Women's Shelter, Sumter, 1980; mem. adv. bd. CIA, Washington. Mem. AAUW, Nat. Assn. Social Workers. Republican. Baptist. Home: 6313 Mori St Mc Lean VA 22101-3153 Office: Round House Sq Psychiat Ctr 1444 Duke St Alexandria VA 22314-3485

BLACK, CATHLEEN PRUNTY, newspaper executive; b. Chgo., Apr. 26, 1944; d. James Hamilton and Margaret (Harrington) B. BA, Trinity Coll., 1966. Advt. sales rep. Holiday mag., N.Y.C., 1966-69, Travel & Leisure mag., N.Y.C., 1969-70, New York mag., 1970-72; advt. dir. Ms. mag., 1972-75, assoc. pub., 1975-77; assoc. pub. New York mag., 1977-79, pub., 1979-83; pres. USA Today, 1983, pub., 1984-91; exec. v.p. mktg. Gannett Co., Inc., from 1985, also bd. dirs.; pres., CEO Newspaper Assn. Am., Reston, Va., 1992—. Home: 2915 Woodland Dr NW Washington DC 20008-3542 Office: Newspaper Assn Am 11600 Sunrise Valley Dr Reston VA 22091-1412

BLACK, DENISE LOUISE, secondary school educator; b. Ft. Sill, Okla., Apr. 16, 1950; d. Nelson Arthur and Virginia Mary (Smith) Taber; AA, C.C. of Allegheny County, Boyce campus, 1970; BS, Slippery Rock State Coll., 1972; MA, Eastern Mich. U., 1978; m. Robert Paul Black, Aug. 12, 1972; children: Paula Ann, Jennifer Lea. Adult edn. tchr. ecology and physiology Huron Valley Schs., Milford, Mich., 1973-74; tchr. gen. biology and earth sci. Howell (Mich.) Public Schs., 1974-75; adult edn. tchr. life sci. Holly (Mich.) Area Schs., 1978-80, Hartland (Mich.) Consol. Schs., 1978-86; tchr. biology Walled Lake (Mich.) Consol. Schs., 1988—, Hartland (Mich.) Consolidates Schs., 1990—. Coach, Milford Youth Athletic Assn., 1973-85; leader 4-H Club; sec. Huron Valley Horse Com.; youth advisor Mich. State Rabbit Breeders Assn. Cert. guidance and counselor. Mem. Nat. Assn. Biology Tchrs., Mich. Assn. Biology Tchrs., Mich. Adult Curriculum Connection (bd. dirs.), Mich. Sci. Tchrs. Assn., Beta Beta Beta, Phi Kappa Phi, Phi Theta Kappa. Methodist. Home: 2576 Shady Ln Milford MI 48381-1438

BLACK, DOROTHY ANNE, retired anesthesiologist; b. Jersey City, Oct. 13, 1929; d. Gustav Anton and Louise Kathryn (Bell) Hufnagel; divorced. BA, Rutgers U., 1957; MA, Columbia U., 1959; MD, Harvard U., 1965. Asst. prof., attending anesthesiologist Columbia-Presbyn. Med. Ctr., N.Y.C., 1966-93; ret., 1993. Home: 37 W 12th St New York NY 10011

BLACK, EILEEN MARY, elementary school educator; b. Bklyn., Sept. 20, 1944; d. Marvin Mize and Anne Joan (Salvia) B. Student, Grossmont Coll., El Cajon, Calif., 1964; BA, San Diego State U., 1967; postgrad., U. Calif., San Diego, Syracuse U. Cert. tchr., Calif. Tchr. La Mesa (Calif.)-Spring Valley Sch. Dist., 1967—. NDEA grantee Syracuse U., 1968; recipient 25 Yrs. Svc. award La Mesa-Spring Valley Sch. Dist., 1992. Mem. Calif. Tchrs. Assn., Calif. Young Reps. Roman Catholic. Home: 9320 Earl St Apt 15 La Mesa CA 91942-3846 Office: Northmont Elem Sch 9405 Gregory St La Mesa CA 91942-3811

BLACK, FRANCES PATTERSON, library administrator; b. Huntsville, Ala., July 27, 1949; d. Fred C. and Mary Jane (Baird) Patterson; m. Larry David Black, Aug. 29, 1970; 1 child, Amy Susan. BA, U. Ala., 1971, MLS, 1972. Dir. Fairhope (Ala.) Pub. Library, 1972-77; rsch. asst. State Libr. Ohio, Columbus, Ohio, 1977-78; head tech. and extension svcs. Southwest Pub. Librs. (formerly Grove City Pub. Libr.), Grove City, Ohio, 1978-86; asst. dir. pub. svcs. Southwest Pub. Librs., Grove City, Ohio, 1986-88, dir., 1988—; mem. libr. adv. bd. Orient (Ohio) Correctional Instn., 1988-91; mem. adult basic edn. adv. bd. Southwestern City Schs., 1991-94. Mem. planning Grove City Arts in the Alley, 1988—; bd. dirs. OHIONET, 1991, pres., 1992-95. Mem. ALA, AAUW, Pub. Libr. Assn., Libr. Adminstrn. and Mgmt. Assn., Ohio Libr. Coun. (mem. legis. network 1987—, Blue Ribbon commn. for Ohio Pub. Libr. Info. Network 1994-95), Grove City Area C. of C., Westland Area Bus. Assn. Office: SW Pub Librs 3359 Park St Grove City OH 43123-2699

BLACK, KANDIA PATRICIA, English language educator; b. Clarion, Pa., May 15, 1956; d. Edward LaRue and Patricia Ivan (Brown) B. BS in Comm., Bloomsburg U., 1978; MEd, Bowie State U., 1984. Cert. tchr. Mktg. profl. Circus World, Orlando, Fla., 1979; tchr. No. Mid. Sch., Owings, Md., 1979-92; tchr. English No. High Sch., Owings, 1992—; dir. No. High Spring Mus., 1993—, No. Mid. Spring Mus., 1980-93; asst. varsity volleyball coach No. High, 1990—; coach No. High Swim Team, 1992—. Mem. bicentennial com. Constitution, Calvert County, Cornelia DeLange Found., Collinsville, Conn. Recipient Agnes Meyer Tchg. award, 1994. Mem. U.S. Masters Swim Program, U.S. Volleyball Assn., Calvert Marine Soc., Delta Kappa Gamma. Republican. Home: 4420 Camp Kaufmann Rd Huntingtown MD 20639-9351 Office: No High Sch 2950 Chaneyville Rd Owings MD 20736-9665

BLACK, LYNDA SUE, educator, education consultant, artist; b. Waverly, Iowa, Feb. 23, 1948; d. Duane Elwyn and Burneile Grace (Miller) Wylam; m. Douglas J. Black, July 17, 1971 (div.); 1 child, Christopher John. BA in Art Edn., U. No. Iowa, 1970; MA in Art Edn., U. Iowa, 1987. Cert. permanent profl. tchr., Iowa. Tchr. elem. art Cedar Rapids (Iowa) Cmty. Schs., 1970-71, 76—; dir. creative dramatics Erskine Sch., Cedar Rapids, 1977-93. Contbr. articles to ednl. jours.; set designer symphony children's concerts, 1992—; author, dir. 2 children's plays, 1983, 85. Mem. ASCD, Nat. Art Edn. Assn. (state del., presenter 1988-91, nat. elem. dir. 1993—), Art Educators Iowa (leadership trainer and cons. 1986—, past v.p., elem. rep., pres. 1987-91, state bd. dirs.). Home: 1922 9th St SW Cedar Rapids IA 52404-5507 Office: Cedar Rapids Cmty Schs 346 2nd Ave SW Cedar Rapids IA 52404-2045

BLACK, MARTHA FODASKI, English education educator, writer; b. Milford, Mich.; d. Ralph McKinley and Allie Marie (Cockrell) Haller; m. Sergei Wilde, 1953 (div. 1956; m. Robert B. Fodaski, 1960 (div. 1968); children: Steven Wilde, Corinna Stewart, David Fodaski, Danielle Black. BA, Wayne State U., 1951; MA, U. Wisc., 1952, PhD, 1962. Assoc. prof. Madison U., Harrisonburg, Va., 1957-62; prof. English Bklyn. Coll. CUNY, 1962—; lectr. Scarsdale (N.Y.) Adult Sch., 1968-74, assoc. dir. humanities divsn. (Overseas) Inst. for Irish Studies, Dublin, 1974-78, program head Irish Studies, Bklyn., 1978—. Author: George Barker, 1969, Shaw and Joyce: The Last Work in Stolentelling, 1995; contbr. articles to profl. jours. Ford Found. fellow 1956, 57, Mary Adams and 5 other fellowships, U. Wisc., 1952-57. Mem. MLA, James Joyce Found., Golden Key Honor Soc. (hon.), Alpha Sigma Lambda (hon.). Home: 656 E 26 St Brooklyn NY 11210 Office: Bklyn Coll English Dept 2308 Boylan Hall Brooklyn NY 11210

BLACK, MAUREEN, realty company executive; b. Manchester, Eng., Feb. 4, 1937; came to U.S., 1957, naturalized, 1962; d. William Henry and Kathleen Mary (Cleaver) Jackson; grad. Felt and Tarrant Comptometer Sch., Eng., 1953; student Alamogordo br. N.Mex. State U., 1959-60, 62-63; m. Charles J. Dugan, Nov. 1979; 1 dau., Karen Elizabeth Black. Office mgr., personnel dir. J.C. Penney Co., Alamogordo, 1958-66; exec. sec. to project mgr. Re-entry System div. Gen. Electric Co., Holloman AFB, 1967-68; soc. editor, columnist Alamogordo Daily News, 1968-73; regional corr. El Paso (Tex.) Times, 1968-75; free lance writer and photographer; script writer Film Unit 505, Alamogordo, 1971; realtor asso. Shyne Realty, Alamogordo, 1975-77, West Source Realtors, 1977-80; owner, broker Hyde Park West Realty Co., 1980—. Pres., Alamogordo Music Theatre, 1971-72. Mem. planning com. tourism, recreation, convs. Gov. of N.Mex., 1965; mem. N.Mex. State Film Commn., 1973-74; life mem. Aux. of Zia Sch. for Handicapped Children, pres. Aux., 1975-76, 80-82; mem. Zia Sch. Bd., 1988-89, v.p., 1991-92; pres. Zia Found., 1988-89, 91-92, v.p. Zia Found. 1994—. Recipient service award Nat. Found., March of Dimes, 1971; Americanism medal DAR, 1972; named Career Woman of Yr., Alamogordo chpt. Am. Bus. Women's Assn., 1971. Mem. Alamogordo C. of C. (chmn. convs. and motion picture com. 1965—), Nat. Assn. Realtors, Realtors Assn. N.Mex., Internat. Realtors Assn. Alamogordo Bd. Realtors (chmn. public relations com., v.p. 1981-82, pres. 1983-84), N.Mex. Opera Guild. Home: 1206 Desert Eve Dr Alamogordo NM 88310-5503 Office: PO Box 2021 Alamogordo NM 88311-2021

BLACK, NAOMI RUTH, writer, editor; b. Springfield, Mass., Oct. 19, 1957; d. Henry Arnold and Zelda Edith (Hodosh) B.; m. John Ian Bralower, July 22, 1990; 1 child Thomas Hart Bralower. BA in Anthropology, Beloit Coll., 1979; student, Radcliffe Pub. Procedures. Project coordinator, editor Woodward-Clyde Cons., San Francisco, 1978-80; asst. editor, travel editor William Morrow Co., N.Y.C., 1980-83; mng. editor Quarto Mktg. Ltd., N.Y.C., 1983-85; freelance writer N.Y.C., 1985—; assoc. editor Colors mag., N.Y.C., 1991, sr. editor, 1992-93. Author: Seashore Entertaining, 1987, Dude Ranches of the American West, 1988, Ten Terrific Parties, 1990, (as N.R. Gordon) Seashells, 1990, The Ghost Town Storyteller, 1992; co-author: The American Mail-Order Gourmet, 1986, East Coast Bed and Breakfast Guide, 1989, The New England Companion, 1990; editor Appie News, N.Y.C., 1992; contbr. articles to profl. jours. Bd. dirs. Writers and Pubs. Alliance for Nuclear Disarmament, N.Y.C., 1987-88. Mem. Appalachian Mountain Club (Appie News editor 1992).

BLACK, PAGE MORTON, civic worker; b. Chgo.; d. Alexander and Rose Morton; m. William Black, Mar. 27, 1962. Student, Chgo. Mus. Coll. Singer, pianist, Pierre Hotel, N.Y.C., Warwick Hotel, One Fifth Ave. Sherry Netherland Hotel; singer radio show and comml. Chock Full o' Nuts Corp.; rec. artist Atlantic Records, Den Records; co-founder Page and William

Black Post-Grad. Sch. Medicine, Mt. Sinai Med. Sch., 1965—; chmn., mem. exec. bd. Parkinsons' Disease Found., Columbia U. Med. Ctr. (mem. adv. coun.); mem. nat. vis. coun. Columbia U. Health Scis. Faculties; hon. chmn. Chock Full O' Nuts Corp., 1983-90; founding mem. ASPCA. Recipient Ann. award Parkinsons' Disease Found., 1987, Police Athletic League, 1992, Mahattan Mag. award, 1992. Home: Premium Pt New Rochelle NY 10801

BLACK, PATRICIA JEAN, medical technologist; b. Milw., Oct. 22, 1954; d. Dale B. and Geraldine L. (Milligan) Heywood; m. Robert S. Black, Oct. 14, 1978. BS, Millikin U., 1978; degree in med. tech., St. Mary's Hosp., 1978. Med. technologist Mercy Hosp., Urbana, Ill., 1978-85; biol. lab. technician No. Regional Rsch. Ctr., USDA Agrl. Rsch. Svc., Peoria, Ill., 1985-88; lab. mgr. Chapman Cancer Ctr., Joplin, Mo., 1989—. Patentee in field. Mem. AAUW, Am. Soc. Clin. Pathologists (cert., assoc.), Clin. Lab. Mgmt. Assn., Zeta Tau Alpha (scholar chmn. 1976, house mgr. 1977), Sigma Zeta.

BLACK, REBECCA JANE, counselor; b. Richmond, Ind., Nov. 3, 1956; d. Louis Melville and Oda Grace (Sheets) Black. BA, Purdue U., 1979, MS, 1980, PhD, 1990. Lic. profl. counselor. Counselor Ga. Southwestern Coll., Americus, 1980-83; residence hall dir. Ball State U., Muncie, Ind., 1983-85; counselor Ind. Vocat. Tech. Coll., Lafayette, 1986-88; counselor/cons. PerPro Devel., Mt. Pleasant, 1991-94; asst. prof. counseling ctr. Cen. Mich. U., Mt. Pleasant, 1988-93, assoc. prof. counseling ctr., 1993-94; cons. Nat. Evaluation Systems, Amherst, Mass., 1990-94. Mem. ACA, Am. Coll. Personnel Assn., Am. Coll. Counseling Assn., Assn. for Counseling & Supervision (outstanding grad. student 1987). Home: 302 S Elizabeth Mount Pleasant MI 48858 Office: Counseling Ctr Foust Hall Cen Mich U Mt. Pleasant MI 48859

BLACK, RITA ANN, communications executive; b. Newark, Sept. 2, 1950; d. Henry and Mary (Solomon) Black; m. David Joseph Franus, Dec. 30, 1973. B.A. in English, U. Rochester, 1972; M.S. in Journalism, Columbia U., 1975. Accredited bus. communicator. Sr. editor Book Prodn. Industry, mag., New Canaan, Conn., 1972-74, 75-76; mgr. publs. AAUP, N.Y.C., 1976-78; sr. communication specialist Ciba-Geigy Corp., Ardsley, N.Y., 1978-80, mgr. internal communication, 1980-84; exec. speechwriter IBM Corp., Armonk, N.Y., 1984-86, sr. info. rep., 1986-88; program adminstr. U.S. media rels., 1988-90; program mgr. corp. media rels., 1990-91; sr. program adminstr. corp. image advt., 1991-92; nat. mktg. mgr. Deloitte & Touche LLP, Wilton, Conn., 1993—. Mem. Pub. Relations Soc. Am., Internat. Assn. Bus. Communicators (dir. 1982-84, Gold Quill 1983, 84, Dist. I award of excellence 1982), Phi Beta Kappa. Office: Deloitte & Touche LLP 10 Westport Rd Wilton CT 06897-4522

BLACK, ROSALIE JEAN, human resources manager; b. Dunsmuir, Calif., Dec. 29, 1938; d. Allen B. Henry and Margaret R. Albonico Luther Lea (stepfather); m. James H. Black, June 12, 1956 (div. 1965); 1 child, Kimberly Elaine. AA equivalent, Foothill and Ohlone, 1964-74. Ops. planner/adminstr. Lockheed Missiles & Space Co., Inc., Sunnyvale, Calif., 1958-81; dir. human resources Dialog Info. Svcs., Inc., Palo Alto, Calif., 1981—; instr. Supervisory program, 1982-84; mem. Lockheed Univ. Rels. and Mgmt. Adv. Couns., Calabassas, Calif., 1982-88; lectr., guest panel mem.; mem. adv. counsel U. Santa Clara U. Devel. Ctr. Recipient Cert. Human Resources Inst., 1982, Achievement award in English, Bank of Am., 1956. Mem. Soc. Human Resources Mgmt., No. Calif. Human Resources Coun. (mem. orgn. planning com. 1967-68), Calif. Scholarship Fedn. (life), Bay Area Human Resources Forum. Democrat. Lutheran. Home: 1400 Fallen Leaf Ln Los Altos CA 94024-5809 Office: Dialog Info Svcs Inc 3460 Hillview Ave Palo Alto CA 94304-1338

BLACK, SHAWN MORGADO, dancer; b. Tuscaloosa, Ala., Sept. 29, 1964; d. Hank Scott Jr. and Olivia Jane (Matthews) B.; m. Jeffrey R. Bornemann, July 7, 1988. Grad., Ala. Sch. Fine Arts, 1982. Prin. dancer Alabama Ballet, Birmingham, 1981-83; dancer Atlanta Ballet, 1983-84; mem. corps de ballet Am. Ballet Theatre, N.Y.C., 1984-91, soloist, 1991—; dancer Twyla Tharpe Dance Co., N.Y.C., 1993—. Performances with ABT include La Bayadere, Bruch Violin Concerto No. 1, Fall River Legend, The Rite of Spring, Rodeo, The Sleeping Beauty, Swan Lake, Symphonic Variations. Democrat. Lutheran. Office: Am Ballet Theatre 890 Broadway New York NY 10003-1211*

BLACK, SHIRLEY TEMPLE (MRS. CHARLES A. BLACK), former ambassador, former actress; b. Santa Monica, Calif., Apr. 23, 1928; d. George Francis and Gertrude Temple; m. John Agar, Jr., Sept. 19, 1945 (div. 1949); 1 dau., Linda Susan; m. Charles A. Black, Dec. 16, 1950; children: Charles Alden, Lori Alden. Ed. under pvt. tutelage; grad., Westlake Sch. Girls, 1945. Rep. to 24th Gen. Assembly UN, N.Y.C., 1969-70; amb. to Ghana Accra, 1974-76; chief of protocol White House, Washington, 1976-77; amb. to Czechoslovakia Prague, 1989-92; mem. U.S. Delegation on African Refugee Problems, Geneva, 1981; mem. public adv. com. UN Conf. on Law of the Sea; dep. chmn. U.S. del. UN Conf. on Human Environment, Stockholm, 1970-72; spl. asst. to chmn. Pres.'s Council on Environ. Quality, 1972-74; del. treaty on environment USSR-USA Joint Commn., Moscow, 1972; mem. U.S. Commn. for UNESCO, 1973—. Began film career at age 3 1/2; first full-length film was Stand Up and Cheer; other films included Little Miss Marker, Baby Take a Bow, Bright Eyes, Our Little Girl, The Little Colonel, Curly Top, The Littlest Rebel, Captain January, Poor Little Rich Girl, Dimples, Stowaway, Wee Willie Winkie, Heidi, Rebecca of Sunnybrook Farm, Little Miss Broadway, Just Around the Corner, The Little Princess, Susannah of the Mounties, The Blue Bird, Kathleen, Miss Annie Rooney, Since You Went Away, Kiss and Tell, 1945, That Hagen Girl, War Party, The Bachelor and the Bobby-Soxer, Honeymoon, 1947; narrator, actress: TV series Shirley Temple Storybook, NBC, 1958, Shirley Temple Show, NBC, 1960; author: Child Star: An Autobiography, 1988. Dir. Bank of Calif.; dir. Fireman's Fund Ins. Co., BANCAL Tri-State Corp., Del Monte Corp.; Mem. Calif. Adv. Hosp. Council, 1969, San Francisco Health Facilities Planning Assn., 1965-69; Republican candidate for U.S. Ho. of Reps. from Calif., 1967; bd. dirs. Nat. Wildlife Fedn., Nat. Multiple Sclerosis Soc., UN Assn. U.S.A.; bd. dirs. exec. com. Internat. Fedn. Multiple Sclerosis Socs. Appointed col. on staff of Gov. Ross of Idaho, 1935; commd. col. Hawaiian N.G.; hon. col. 108th Rgt. N.G. Ill.; dame Order Knights Malta, Paris, 1968; recipient Ceres medal FAO, Rome, 1975, numerous other state decorations. Mem. World Affairs Council No. Calif. (dir.), Council Fgn. Relations, Nat. Com. for U.S./China Relations. Club: Commonwealth of Calif. *

BLACK, SUSAN, public relations executive; b. N.Y.C., Feb. 24, 1953; d. Owen Joseph and Joan Anne (Gorman) B.; m. John Berard, May 23, 1992; 1 child, Alexander Black Mitchell. BA, Conn. Coll., 1974. Asst. editor Continental Ins., N.Y.C., 1975-76; pub. affairs officer Citibank, N.Y.C., 1976-78; mgr. Gen. Signal, Stamford, Conn., 1978-81; account exec., v.p., sr. v.p. Hill and Knowlton, N.Y.C., 1981-91; prin. Dilenschneider Group Inc., N.Y.C., 1991—. Office: Dilenschneider Group Inc 200 Park Ave 26th Fl New York NY 10166-0005

BLACK, SUSAN HARRELL, federal judge; b. Valdosta, Ga., Oct. 20, 1943; d. William H. and Ruth Elizabeth (Phillips) Harrell; m. Louis Eckert Black, Dec. 28, 1966. BA, Fla. State U., 1965; JD, U. Fla., 1967; LLM, U. Va., 1984. Bar: Fla. 1967. Atty. U.S. Army Corps of Engrs., Jacksonville, Fla., 1968-69; asst. state atty. Gen. Counsel's Office, Jacksonville, 1969-72; judge County Ct. of Duval County, Fla., 1973-75; judge 4th Jud. Cir. Ct. of Fla., 1975-79; judge U.S. Dist. Ct. (mid. dist.) Fla., Jacksonville, 1979-90, chief judge, 1990-92; judge U.S. Ct. Appeals (11th cir.) Fla., Jacksonville, 1992—; faculty Fed. Jud. Ctr.; mem. U.S. Judicial Conf. Com. on Judicial Improvements; bd. trustees Am. Inns. Ct. Found. Trustee emeritus Law Sch. U. Fla.; past pres. Chester Bedell Inn of Ct. Mem. Am. Bar Assn., Fla. Bar Assn., Jacksonville Bar Assn. Episcopalian. Office: US Dist Ct PO Box 53135 Jacksonville FL 32201-3135*

BLACK, SUZANNE ALEXANDRA, clinical psychologist, researcher; b. N.Y.C., May 6, 1958; d. Lawrence E. and Aline R. (Amsellem) B. BA in Psychology, Clark U., 1980; MA in Gen. Psychology, Yeshiva U., 1984, PsyD in Clin. Psychology, 1987; cert. in psychoanalytical psychotherapy, Inst. Contemporary Psychoanalysis, 1992-93. Lic. psychologist, Calif., 1989. Rsch. assoc. Inst. for Study of Exceptional Children Roosevelt Hosp. Ctr., 1980-82; rsch. cons. Sch. Pub. Health Columbia U., N.Y.C., 1982-83; clin. psychology extern Albert Einstein Coll. of Medicine Bronx Psychiat. Ctr., 1983-84; clin. psychology extern Jewish Bd. Family and Children's Svcs., N.Y.C., 1984-85; clin. psychology, neuropsychol. extern NYU Med. Ctr./Bellevue Hosp., N.Y.C., 1985-86; pre-doctoral clin. psychology/neuropsychology intern Rusk Inst. Rehabilitation NYU Med. Ctr., N.Y.C., 1986-87; post-doctoral clin. psychology fellow in psychiat. emergency room and adult in-patient psychiatry Harbor/UCLA Med. Ctr., Torrance, 1987-89; inpatient and outpatient pvt. practice clin. psychology and neuropsychology Torrance, 1989-93; rsch. assoc. depts. neurology and psychiatry Harbor/UCLA Med. Ctr., 1987-93; dir. clin. svc. Adult Inpatient Psychiat. unit Suncrest Hosp. of South Bay, Torrance, Calif., 1992; inpatient and outpatient pvt. practice in psychology pvt. practice, San Francisco & Kentfield, Calif., 1993—; co-founder, co-therapist Marin Group Psychotherapy Assocs.; vice chair, divsn. of Psychology Main Gen. Hosp., 1994—; mem. group pvt. practice Behavioral Medicine Assocs., Marin County, 1993—; clin. asst. prof. psychology Fuller Grad. Sch. Psychology, Pasadena, Calif., 1987-88; clin. supr. psychiat. residents and psychology externs Harbor/UCLA Med. Ctr., 1987-89; lectr. in field; crisis specialist psychiat. emergency svc. Marin County Dept. Health and Human Svcs. Exec. producer teen talk show TeenVision TV, Viacom Cable TV, Main Channel 31, 1994. Vol. cert. in disaster mental health Bay Area chpt. ARC. NIMH grantee, 1986-87. Mem. APA, Calif. Psychol. Assn., Marin County Psychol. Assn., (chair ethics com.), San Francisco Psychol. Assn., Mental Health Assn. of Marin (bd. dirs., co-pres.). Office: Ste 100-5 1030 Sir Francis Drake Blvd Kentfield CA 94904 also: 3354 Sacramento Sr Ste C San Francisco CA 94118

BLACK, VIRGINIA MORROW, writer; b. Glassport, Pa., July 1, 1926; d. Bernard James and Anna Bernice (Ashton) Morrow; m. Anthony R. Black, July 23, 1949; children: Stephanie Ann, Robert Joseph, Mary Kay, Bernard Morrow. BA, Seton Hill Coll., 1948; postgrad., U. Pitts., 1949, Ind. U., South Bend, 1965. Cert. tchr., Ind. Tchr. Pierre Navarre Sch., South Bend, 1952-53, John Adams High Sch., South Bend, 1966-68, St. Joseph High Sch., South Bend, Ind., 1968-70, Marian High Sch., Mishawaka, 1972-78, Washington High Sch., South Bend, 1978-85. Author: Tackling Notre Dame, 1986; author: (plays) Dilemma with Emma, 1989, Bed-Time Story, 1989, Dust to Dust, 1990, While Stands the Colosseum, 1990; contbr. articles to Christian and tchr. mags. Pres. St. Joseph County Right to Life, South Bend, 1982-83; vol. St. Vincent de Paul Soc., South Bend, 1980—; precinct committeeman Rep. Party, 1980-91; active Emmaus Group for Mentally Handicapped, South Bend, 1988—; Repl Congl. candidate 3d Dist. Ind., 1974. Named Guardian of Yr. Logan Sch., South Bend, 1990. Mem. Assn. Ind. Retired Tchrs. Republican. Roman Catholic. Home: 53546 Elmhurst St South Bend IN 46637

BLACKBURN, A. KIMBERLIN, artist; b. Honolulu, Jan. 21, 1954; d. George Hughes and Patricia Louise (Peacock) B.; m. James Etsuzo Nishida, Dec. 19, 1992. BA, Livingston Coll., 1975; MFA, Rutgers U., 1980. Mgr., silversmith From the Hands of Man, Metuchen, N.J., 1975-78; instr. textile design Livingston Coll., Piscataway, N.J., 1975-79, instr. photography, 1979-80; co-adj. photography lab., lectr. Douglass Coll. Rutgers U., New Brunswick, N.J., 1981; artist-in-residence gifted and talented program Plainfield (N.J.) Schs., 1986-87; co-owner, designer LightBeams, crystal jewelry, N.J., Hawaii, 1989-90; designer, owner Talkstory Designs, Hawaii, 1988-93; trustee, mem. exhbn. com. Tweed Arts Group, Plainfield, 1982, v.p., 1983-84; freelance advisor N.J. State Coun. on Arts, 1985-87; juror Watchung (N.J.) Arts Festival, 1976-77, Douglass Coll. Folk Arts Festival, 1977-79; curator Tweed Gallery, 1985-94, co-curator, 1983, 84, also others. One-woman shows include The Art Loft, Honolulu, 1986, Stones Gallery, Lihue, Hawaii, 1986, Ten Park Place, Montclair, N.J., 1988, Contemporary Mus., Honolulu, 1993; 2-person shows include Bakkus Gallery, Honolulu, 1990, Stones Gallery, 1990, A Pacific Café, Kapaa, Hawaii, 1993; 3- and 4-person shows include City Without Walls Gallery, Newark, 1979, Royal Culture Art Gallery, Honolulu, 1986, The Art Shop, Lihue, 1988—; exhibited in numerous group shows, 1976—, including Calif. Inst. Art, Valencia, 1979, Monmouth (N.J.) Mus., 1983, Hunterton Art Ctr., N.J., 1985, Kauai Mus., Lihue, Honolulu, 1988, 90, 91, Honolulu Acad. Arts, 1989, 90, 92, Acad. Art Ctr., Honolulu, 1994; represented by ArtLoft, Honolulu, Oahu, Hawaii, also others. Mem. Kauai Soc. Artists (pres., coord. exhbns. 1988-94). Home and Studio: 6510 Puupilo Rd PO Box 181 Kapaa HI 96746

BLACKBURN, SHARON LOVELACE, federal judge; b. 1950. BA, U. Ala., 1973; JD, Samford U., 1977. Law clk. to Hon. Robert Varner U.S. Dist. Ct. Ala., 1977-78; staff atty. Birmingham Area Legal Svcs., 1979; asst. U.S. atty. U.S. Atty's. Office, 1979-91; judge U.S. Dist. Ct. (no. dist.) Ala., Birmingham, 1991—. Mem. Birmingham Bar Assn. Office: Hugo L Black US Courthouse 1729 5th Ave NRm 730 Birmingham AL 35203*

BLACKBURN, VICKIE CARLEE, vocational rehabilitation counselor; b. Hazard, Ky., Jan. 11, 1951; d. Moscoe James and Wynona Rose (Hawkins) B.; divorced; 1 child, Kelly Carlee Turner. BA, U. Ky., 1974, MA, 1976, Rank I in Learning Behavior Disorders, 1978. Tchr. spl. edn. Fayette County, Lexington, Ky., 1976-84; legal cons. Office of Exceptional Children, Frankfort, Ky., 1984-85; accreditation counselor Office of Exceptional Children, Frakfurt, Ky., 1985-89; cons. Vocat. Rehab., Lexington, 1989—. Vol. Greater Lexington Conv. and Visitor's Bureau, 1989—, Lexington Host Com., 1989—; mem. fund raising com. Am. Cancer Soc., 1989-91, Leukemia Soc., 1990-91, Lexington Children's Mus., 1991-92; bd. dirs. Lexington Child Abuse Coun., 1992—, chmn. fundraiser, 1992-93; bd. dirs. Ctrl. Ky. Women's Ctr., 1993—, chmn. fundraiser, 1993-94; mem. pub. rels. bd. DISMAS Charities, Inc. 1992—; mem. publicity com. United Way Blue Grass Spl. Events, 1994; mem. domestic prevention com. Lexington Fayette Co. Gov., 1994; mem. Lexington Jr. League, 1994. Mem. Nat. Rehab. Assn., S.E. Region Nat. Rehab. Assn. (exhibitor com., publicity com., decoration com.), Ky. Rehab. Assn. (co-chair exhibitor com. 1993), Greater Lexington C. of C. (apple laison, ambassador program, athletic/bus. coun., mktg., promotion and advt. com., participant study on ctrl. adminstrn. Fayette County Bd. of Edn.). Office: Ky Workforce Devel Cabinet Vocat Rehab 627 W 4th St Lexington KY 40508

BLACK-DENNIS, KATHY JO, state agency administrator, educator, training consultant; b. Pewee Valley, Ky., Aug. 17, 1954; d. Harold and Mary Jo Black; m. Gary Lynn Dennis, May 24, 1980; 1 child, Kathryn Taylor Dennis. BS in Law Enforcement, Ea. Ky. U., 1976; MS in Corrections Adminstrn., Xavier U., 1980. Correctional officer Ky. Dept. Corrections, Burlington, 1976-77; classification and treatment officer Ky. Dept. Corrections, La Grange, 1977-80, classification and treatment supr., 1980-83; br. mgr.-planning Ky. Dept. Corrections, Frankfort, 1989—; corrections specialist Nat. Inst. Corrections, Boulder, Colo., 1985-87; facility dir. Dismas Charities, Louisville, 1988; mem. adj. faculty U. Louisville, 1988—; cons. Child Support Enforcement Project Ea. Ky. U., 1989. Assoc. bd. dirs. Actors Theatre of Louisville, 1992-94; active Friends of Oldham County Mus., La Grange, 1994—; appointed to personal steering com. Gov. of Ky., 1994. Named Ky. Colonel, Gov. of Ky., 1976. Mem. NAFE, Am. Correctional Assn. (del. assembly 1992-94), So. States Correctional Assn., Acad. Criminal Justice Scis., Alpha Phi Sigma (hon.), Chi Omega (pres. 1982-84), Ky. Coun. Crime and Delinquency (pres. 1992-94). Democrat. Methodist. Office: Ky Dept Corrections 500 State Office Bldg Frankfort KY 40601

BLACKER, HARRIET, public relations executive; b. N.Y.C., July 23, 1940; d. Louis and Rebecca (Siegel) B.; m. Roland Algrant, Aug. 6, 1970 (div. Jan. 1981); m. Matthew E. Harlib, Aug. 25, 1988. B.A., U. Mich., 1962. Exec. dir. publicity Random House, N.Y.C., 1974-79; East Coast v.p. Pickwick Maslansky Koenigsberg, N.Y.C., 1980-81; v.p. pub. relations Putnam Pub. Group, N.Y.C, 1981-85; pres. Harriet Blacker, Inc., N.Y.C., 1986-90; ptnr. Blacker Hunter Pub. Rels. Inc., N.Y.C., 1990-93; pres. Blacker Communications, N.Y.C., 1993—. Mem. Publishers Publicity Assn. (sec. 1973-75, treas. 1982-83, pres. 1983-85), Women's Media Group.

BLACKHAM, ANN ROSEMARY (MRS. J. W. BLACKHAM), realtor; b. N.Y.C., June 16, 1927; d. Frederick Alfred and Letitia L. (Stolfe) DeCain; m. James W. Blackham Jr., Aug. 18, 1951; children: Ann C., James W. III. AB, Ohio Dominican Coll., 1949; postgrad., Ohio State U., 1950. Mgr. br. store Filene & Sons, Winchester, 1950-52; broker Porter Co. Real Estate, Winchester, 1961-66; sales mgr. James T. Trefrey, Inc., Winchester, 1966-68; pres., founder Ann Blackham & Co. Inc., Realtors, Winchester, Mass., 1968—. Mem. bd. econ. advisors to Gov., 1969-74; participant White House Conf. on Internat. Cooperation, 1965; mem. Presdl. Task Force on Women's Rights and Responsibilities, 1969; mem. exec. coun. Mass. Civil Def., 1965-69; chmn. Gov.'s Commn. on Status of Women, 1971-75; regional dir. Interstate Assn. Commn. on Status of Women, 1971-74; mem. Gov. Task Force on Mass. Economy, 1972; mem. Gov.'s Jud. Selection Com., 1972, Mass. Emergency Fin. Bd., 1974-75; mem. bd. registration Real Estate Brokers & Salesman Commonwealth of Mass., 1991-94, chmn. 1994—; corporator, trustee Charlestown Savs. Bank, 1974-84; corporator Winchester Hosp., 1983—; mem. Winchester 350th Anniversary Commn.; mem. design rev. commn. Town of Winchester; bd. dirs. Phoenix Found., Bay State Health Care, Mass. Taxpayers Found., Speech and Hearing Found., Baystate Health Mgmt.; mem. regional selection panel White House Fellows, 1973-74; mem. com. on women in svc. U.S. Dept. Def., 1977-80; 2d v.p. Doric Dames, 1971-74, bd. dirs., 1974—; dep. chmn. Mass. Rep. State Com., 1965-66; sec. Mass. Rep. State Conv., 1970, del., 1960, 62, 64, 66, 70, 72, 74, 78, 90; state vice chmn. Mass. Rep. Fin. Com., 1970; alt. del.-at-large Rep. Nat. Conv., 1968, 72, del., 1984; pres. Scholarship Found., 1976-78, Mass. Fedn. Women's Clubs. Recipient Pub. Svc. award Commonwealth of Mass., 1978, Merit award Rep. Party, 1969, Pub. Affairs award Mass. Fedn. Women's Clubs, 1975; named Civic Leader of Yr., Mass. Broadcasters, 1962. Mem. Greater Boston Real Estate Bd. (bd. dirs.), Eastern Middlesex Bd. Realtors (life mem. multi million dollar club), Mass. Assn. Real Estate Bds. (bd. dirs.), Nat. Assn. Real Estate Bd. (women's coun.). Brokers Inst., Coun. Realtors (pres. 1983-84), Winchester C. of C. (bd. dirs.), Greater Boston C. of C., Nat. Assn. Women Bus. Owners, ENKA Soc., Rotary Internat., Capitol Hill Club, Ponte Vedra Club, Winchester Boat Club, Winchester Country Club, Wychemere Harbor Club, Womens City Boston Club, Winton Club (sec., bd. dir.). Home: 60 Swan Rd Winchester MA 01890-3747 Office: Ann Blackham & Co Inc 9 Thompson St Winchester MA 01890-2999

BLACKMAN, GHITA WAUCHETA, natural energy consultant; b. Chgo., Feb. 19, 1932; d. William Harveston Joseph and Zelda (Booth) Harris; m. David Edward Blackman, June 7, 1953 (div. Oct. 1976); children—Anasa, Anthony, Cynthia, Tracy. Student NYU, 1949-50, U. Dayton, 1952-53. Various secretarial positions U.S. Air Force, Dayton, Ohio, then Am. Humanist Assn., Yellow Springs, Ohio, 1950-64; sec. Antioch Coll., Yellow Springs, 1964-66, Fels Research Inst., Yellow Springs, 1966-70; cons. direct sales Fashion Two Twenty, Dayton, 1966-72; mem. sales staff Prophet & Friends Inc., New Britain, Conn., 1972-76; customer relations clk. Conn. Natural Gas Corp., Hartford, 1976-80, natural energy cons., 1980—. Mem. Dayton Jr. Philharm. Orch., 1947-53, second violin Springfield Symphony, Ohio, 1956-64; v.p. Conn. Capitol Area chpt. Older Women's League, Hartford, 1985-87; sec. Spiritual Assembly of the Baha'is of West Hartford, Conn., 1977-78; corr. sec. Spiritual Assembly of the Baha'is of Hartford, 1982—. Mem. Nat. Assn. Female Execs., Nat. Assn. Profl. Saleswomen. Avocation: music. Home: 31 Woodland St Hartford CT 06105-4335 Office: Conn Natural Gas Corp 100 Columbus Blvd Hartford CT 06103-2805

BLACKMAN, HELEN JANE, ophthalmologist; b. Indpls., Dec. 17, 1944; d. Robert C. and Helen M. B.; m. John H. Lossing, July 17, 1976; children: Robert, Rebecca. AA with honors, Columbia Coll., 1964; AB in Med. Scis., Ind. U., 1965, MD, 1969. Intern Kaiser Found. Hosp., San Francisco, 1969-70; resident U. Wis. Sch. Medicine Dept. Ophthalmology, Madison, 1970-73; ophthalmologist pvt. practice, Washington, 1978—; clin. dir. Georgetown U. Hosp., Washington, 1980, researcher, 1979-83; dir. Uveitis Svc. Washington Hosp. Ctr., 1978-85, cons., 1988—; chmn. dept. ophthalmology Sibley Meml. Hosp., Washington, 1992—; cons. Nat. Eye Inst., NIH, Bethesda, Md., 1979-85. Contbr. articles to profl. jours. Mem. med. recs. com. Georgetown U. Hosp., 1982-83; mem. credentials com. Sibley Hosp., 1982-84; mem. pharmacy formulary com. Washington Hosp. Ctr., 1984-86. Francis I. Proctor Found. Eye Rsch. fellow, San Francisco, 1974-76, NIH Staff fellow, 1976-78; recipient Teaching award Dept. Ophthalmology Washington Nat. Eye Ctr., 1984. Mem. Am. Acad. Ophthalmology (mem. basic sci. com. 1992—), Am. Uveitis Soc., Am. Med. Women's Assn., D.C. Med. Soc. (membership com. 1979-81), Assn. Proctor Fellows, Contact Lens Assn. Ophthalmologists. Office: 3301 NMex Ave NW Washington DC 20016

BLACKMAN, JANA COHEN, lawyer; b. Miami Beach, Fla., Aug. 30, 1962; d. Stanley Leon and Sonia (Auerbach) Cohen; m. Philip Martin Blackman, Feb. 11, 1990; 1 child, Nicole Leah. BA, Northwestern U., 1984; JD, U. Chgo., 1987. Assoc. Kirkland & Ellis, Chgo., 1987-90; gen. counsel Thresholds, Chgo., 1990—; low income housing developer Thresholds, 1990—. Dir. Nonprofit Fin. Ctr., Chgo., 1992—. Mem. Ill. Bar Assn., Chgo. Bar Assn. Democrat. Jewish. Home and Office: The Thresholds 552 W Brompton Ave #1-5 Chicago IL 60657

BLACKMAN, JEANNE A., lobbyist; b. Decatur, Ill., Sept. 23, 1943; d. Robert Russell and Elizabeth Irene (DeWolfe) Shulke; m. Gary L. Blackman, Apr. 16, 1963 (div. Aug. 1983); children: Jeffrey Lynn, Stephanie Sue. BS Elem. Edn., Ind. U., 1965; MS in Edn. Adminstrn., Eastern Ill. U., 1979. Cert. tchr. and administr.; lic. real estate salesperson. Elem. tchr. Taylorville (Ill.) Community Sch. Dist., 1965-86; real estate salesperson Craggs-Adams Realtors, Taylorville, 1985-87; adminstrv. asst. to chief of staff Ill. Dept. of Aging, Springfield, 1986-87, consumer adv., 1987-89; lobbyist Ill. Guardianship and Advocacy Commn., Springfield, 1989—; pres. Taylorville Edn. Assn., 1983-85; mem. adv. council Gov.'s Rehab., Springfield, 1987—. Co-founder, treas. Ill. Vol. Optometry Svcs. to Humanity, Taylorville, 1976—; pres. Capitol City Rep. Women's Club, 1988—; pres. Women in Mgmt., 1989—, bd. dirs., 1990; fundraiser, chairperson Ill. Women's Polit. Caucus, Springfield, 1985—; pres. Am. Field Svc. Student Exch. Program, Taylorville, 1985-87; bd. dirs. LWV Springfield chpt., 1984—; pres. bd. dirs. Mental Health Ctrs. Ctrl. Ill., 1994—; trustee Lincolnland C.C., 1989, vice chair 1992-93, chmn. 93-94; pres. Ill. C.C. Trustees Assn., 1992; mem. Mayor's Commn. Internat. Visitors. Mem. AAUW (edn. chairperson Taylorville chpt. 1985—), DAR, Sister Cities Assn. Springfield, Ill. Women in Govt. (bd. dirs. 1988—, v.p. 1990—), Women's Legis. Network, Ill. Fedn. Rep. Women (v.p., bd. dirs. 1988—, ways and means com. 1987—, world affairs coun. 1990—), Greater Springfield C. of C., Rotary, Delta Delta Delta. Presbyterian. Home: 19 Washington Pl Springfield IL 62702-4634 Office: Ill Guardianship and Adv Commn 421 E Capitol Ave Springfield IL 62701-1737

BLACKMAN, LINDA LOUISE, educational administrator; b. Harrisburg, Ill., Jan. 20, 1952; d. Virgil Howard and Amy Louise (Lewis) B. BS, So. Ill. U., 1974, MS, 1975, PhD, 1978, postdoctoral, 1984-86. Cert. secondary tchr.; cert. elem. and secondary sch. adminstr. Manpower planner I, jr. compliance auditor Dept. Commerce and Cmty. Affairs, Springfield, Ill., 1979-81; labor market facilitator Five County Regional Vocat., Tamms, Ill., 1981; career guidance facilitator Region 14 Career Guidance Ctr., Cairo, Ill., 1981-82; tng. instr., assessment specialist Region 12 Career Guidance Ctr., Anna, Ill., 1982, career guidance dir., 1982-83; dir. career devel. and counseling Southeastern Ill. Coll., Harrisburg, 1983-86; ednl. cons. Ill. State U., Normal, 1986; supt. schs. Galatia (Ill.) Cmty. Unit # 1 Sch. Dist., 1986-88; asst. regional supt. schs. Gallatin-Hardin-Pope-Saline Schs., Harrisburg, Ill., 1988-94, regional supt. schs., 1994—; presenter workshops. Contbr. articles to profl. jours. Organizer Alexander-Pulaski Counties Pals, 1979; mem. adv. bd. Egyptian Health Dept. Youth Svcs., Eldorado, Ill., 1988-93; chair IN-TOUCH drug and alcohol abuse prevention edn. program Regional Planning Group Gallatin-Hardin-Pope-Saline Counties, 1988—. Named Outstanding Young Women of Am., 1979; grantee Alexander, Johns, Massac, Pulaski, Union Counties, 1983, Ill. State Bd. Edn., 1983-85, Ill. Dept. Energy and Natural Resources, 1987. Mem. Am. Assn. Sch. Adminstrs., Ill. Assn. Regional Supts. Schs., Ill. Women Adminstrs., Inc., Ill. Bus. and Profl. Women's Assn., Nat. Assn. Secondary Sch. Prins., DAR, Phi Delta Kappa, Iota Lambda Sigma, Delta Kappa Gamma. Democrat. Baptist. Home: 1326 S Granger St Harrisburg IL 62946-3195 Office: Regional Office Edn 112 N Gum St Harrisburg IL 62946-1547

BLACKSTOCK, VIRGINIA LEE LOWMAN (MRS. LEROY BLACKSTOCK), civic worker; b. Bixby, Okla., July 2, 1917; d. Joseph Arthur and Winifred (Lundy) Lowman; student Tulsa Coll. Bus., 1935-37; m. Leroy Blackstock, Dec. 29, 1939; children—Vincent Craig, Priscilla Gay (Mrs. Richard S. Kurz), Burch Lee, Lore Anne (Mrs. Dwight Mitchell), Trena Jan (Mrs. Frank Dale). Legal sec. law firm, Tulsa, 1937-41. Chmn. program Internat. Students in Tulsa, 1955-65; mem. Tulsa Council Camp Fire Girls,

1963-66; mem. youth com. Tulsa Philharmonic Soc., 1969-70; now mem. women's assn.; pres. Eliot Elementary P.T.A., 1961-62, Edison High Sch. P.T.A., 1971-72; mem. Tulsa Opera Guild. Co-chmn. Democratic precinct No. 132, 1960-67. Mem. Tulsa County Bar Aux. (pres. 1954-55, sec. 1962-63, chaplain 1966-67). Baptist. Clubs: Petroleum. Home: 7213 S Atlanta St Tulsa OK 74136-5508

BLACKSTON, SHIRLEY FRANCES, human resources manager; b. Fayetteville, Ark., Aug. 21, 1937; d. Gordon Elliott and Willie Ilah (Todd) Mhoon; m. Norman Elmer Powers, June 4, 1955 (div. 1964); children: Deborah Powers, Rebecca Powers, Martin Powers; m. Jim E. Blackston, Aug. 17, 1968. Student, U. Ark., 1975-76, 82-83. Cert. profl. human resources mgr. Indsl. nurse Shakespear of Ark., Fayetteville, 1965-70, pers. mgr., 1970-82; human resources mgr. Am. Air Filter Internat., Fayetteville, 1982—. Mem. pvt. industry coun. Jos Tng. Partnership Act, N.W. Ark., 1984; chair Washington County (Ark.) Civil Svc. Commn., 1986-87; bd. dirs. United Way Fayetteville, chair campaign dr.; bd. dirs. Abilities Unltd., United Cmty. Svcs., NOARK Pers. Assn., past pres.; mem. adv. bd. east and west campus Fayetteville High Sch., N.W. Ark. Vocat. Tech. Sch. Mem. Altrusa Internat., Fayetteville C. of C. (bd. dirs. 1985-86, treas. bd. dirs. 1994, now vice chair). Office: Snyder Gen/Am Air Filter Co 2355 Armstrong Fayetteville AR 72701

BLACKSTONE, PATRICIA CLARK, bank officer, psychotherapist; b. Louisville, June 30, 1952; d. Robert Phillips and Jeanne Orr (Rice) Clark; m. Patrick H. Thorpe, June 8, 1974 (div. March 1981); m. William M. Blackstone II, Nov. 2, 1985. BA, Indiana U., 1974; MEd, U. North Tex., 1990. Cert. counselor. Mgr. Citizens Fidelity Bank & Trust Co., Louisville, 1974-77; pers. mgr. Am. Gen. Corp., Houston, 1977-81; asst. v.p. human resources MCorp (name now BANK ONE), Dallas, 1983-87, 90; v.p. adminstrn. Tex.-PCS Industries, Inc., Dallas, 1987-89; mgr. employment and tng. First Nat. Bank Pa., Erie, Pa., 1990-92; asst. v.p., mgr. Bank One, Akron, Ohio, 1992—; cons. First Am. Bankshares, Washington, 1987, Interstate Battery Co. Am., Dallas, 1987, Guaranty Fed. Savs. Bank, Dallas, 1989, BANK ONE, Tex., 1990, Lake Erie Presbytery, Erie, Pa.; cert. instr. Main Event Mgmt. Corp., Sacramento, 1977-81. Author: Code of Ethics and Harassment-Free Workplace Guide, 1993; co-author: (with William M. Blackstone II) Preparing for Christian Marriage, 1987. Ruling elder edn. Preston Hollow Presbyn. Ch., Dallas, 1987-90, First Presbyn. Ch. Covenant, Erie, Pa., 1992—; mem. Dallas Mus. Art, 1985-87, The 500, Inc., Dallas, 1986, First Presbyn. Ch. Covenant, 1990—, Akron Symphony Guild, 1994—, Jr. League of Akron; mem. Vol. Ctr., Akron, 1993—. Fellow Life Mgmt. Inst.; mem. ACA, ASTD (bd. dirs. Erie Tri-State chpt.), Soc. Human Resources Mgmt. (designated Sr. Profl. in Human Resources 1990), Am. Inst. Banking (bd. dirs. Erie/Crawford chpt.). Democrat. Presbyterian. Office: Bank One Akron NA 50 S Main St Akron OH 44308

BLACKSTONE, VICKY LEE, computer processing company executive; b. Marietta, Ga., Feb. 5, 1958; d. James O. and Ruth (Kight) B.; m. David Thomas Tillander, Oct. 5, 1991. Student, Clemson U., 1976-78. Owner Add Pizzazz, Greenville, S.C., 1982-88; loan specialist Atlanta, 1990-92; prin. Blackstone Computer Processing, Atlanta, 1992—. J.E. Sirrine Found. scholar, 1976-77.

BLACKWELL, JACQUELINE PFLUGHOEFT, school district administrator; b. Milw., Oct. 31, 1936; d. Arthur Karl and Lucille Henrietta (Kraft) Pflughoeft; m. Clifton Blackwell, Aug. 6, 1955; children: Arthur, Clifton, Jeanne, Corwyn. Student, Mount Senario Coll., Ladysmith, Wis., 1966; BA, San Jose State U., 1969, MA, 1972, MS, 1989; postgrad., Pacific Grad. Sch. Psychology, Palo Alto, Calif., 1986—. Lic. sch. psychologist, Calif., U.S. Tchr. San Jose Unified Sch. Dist., 1970-83, psychologist, 1983-86, dir. spl. edn. and psychol. schs., 1986-90, prin., 1990-94, dir. student svcs., 1994—. Author: District Student Behavior Handbook, District Special Education Guidebook. With WAC-U.S. Army, 1954-55. Mem. Am. Psychol. Assn., Calif. Psychol. Assn., San Jose Tchrs. Assn. (bd. dirs. 1979-83). Office: San Jose Unified Sch Dist 1605 Park Ave San Jose CA 95126-2196

BLACKWOOD, LOIS ANNE, elementary education educator; b. Denver, Sept. 18, 1949; d. Randolph William and Eloise Anne (Green) Burchett; m. Clark Burnett Blackwood, June 26, 1971; children: Anna Colleen, Courtney Brooke. BA, Pacific U., 1971. Tchr. Forest Grove (Oreg.) Pub. Schs., 1971-72, Clarksville (Tenn.) Pub. Schs., 1972-73, Dept. of Defense Schs., Frankfurt, Germany, 1973-76; tchr. St. Vrain Valley Schs., Longmont, Colo., 1977—, presenter insvcs. and symposia, 1977-93, also tchr. of tchrs.; cons. Brush Pub. Schs., 1985; presenter U. No. Colo. Symposium, 1987, Greater San Diego Math. Conf., 1992—, rural math. connections project U. Colo., 1992, 93, So. sect. Calif. Coun. Math. Tchrs., 1993, 94. Recipient sustained superior svc. award U.S. Army, Frankfurt, 1975, outstanding performance award, 1976; Presdl. award for excellence in math. tchg. State of Colo., 1991, 94, Outstanding Elem. Math. Tchr. award Colo. Coun. Tchrs. Math., 1993; named Outstanding Tchr. of Yr., Longmont Area C. of C., 1992. Mem. NEA, Colo. Edn. Assn., St. Vrain Valley Tchrs. Assn. Republican. Home: 1175 Winslow Cir Longmont CO 80501-5225 Office: Ctrl Elem Sch 1020 4th Ave Longmont CO 80501-5356

BLADE, MELINDA KIM, educator, researcher, archaeologist; b. San Diego, Jan. 12, 1952; d. George A. and Arline A. M. (MacLeod) B. BA, U. San Diego, 1974, MA in Teaching, 1975, MA, 1975, EdD, 1986. Cert. secondary tchr., Calif.; cert. community coll. instr., Calif.; registered profl. historian, Calif. Instr. Coronado Unified Sch. Dist., Calif., 1975-76; head coach women's basketball U. San Diego, 1976-78; instr. Acad. of Our Lady of Peace, San Diego, 1976—, chmn. social studies dept., 1983—, counselor, 1984-92, co-dir. student activities, 1984-87, coord. advanced placement program, 1986—, dir. athletics, 1990; mem. archaeol. excavation team U. San Diego, 1975—, hist. researcher, 1975—; lectr., 1981—. Author hist. reports and research papers. Editor U. San Diego pubs. Vol. Am. Diabetes Assn., San Diego, 1975—; coord. McDonald's Diabetes Bike-a-thon, San Diego, 1977, 78; bd. dirs. U. San Diego Sch. Edn. Mem. Nat. Council Social Studies, Calif. Council Social Studies, Soc. Bibl. Archeology, Assn. Supervision and Curriculum Devel., Assn. Scientists and Scholars Internat. for Shroud of Turin, Medieval Acad. Am., Medieval Assn. Pacific, Am. Hist. Assn., Western Assn. Women Historians, Renaissance Soc. Am., San Diego Hist. Soc., Phi Alpha Theta (sec.-treas. 1975-77), Phi Delta Kappa. Office: Acad Our Lady of Peace 4860 Oregon St San Diego CA 92116-1340

BLADES, CAROL BRADY, public relations executive; b. Providence, R.I., Dec. 10, 1947; d. James Joseph and Alice Mary (Hartigan) Brady; children: Matthew Blades, Elizabeth Blades. Student, Trinity Coll., 1965-67, George Washington U., 1967-68; BA in Journalism, NYU, 1969. Exec. v.p. The Softness Group, Inc., N.Y.C., 1979-87, pres., 1987-93, pres., CEO, 1993—. Mem. Women Execs. in Pub. Rels. (bd. dirs. 1990-93, v.p. 1993—). Roman Catholic. Office: The Softness Group Inc 381 Park Ave S New York NY 10016

BLADES, JANE M., educator; b. Jersey City, Dec. 1, 1953; d. Nunzio Thomas and Evelyn Rose (Spizzirro) Savino; m. Brian Hilton Blades, Sept. 20, 1980; children: Adam Hilton, Erik Thomas. BA, Kean Coll., 1983. Cert. handicapped tchr., N.J. Staff asst. AT&T, Parsippany, N.J., 1979-81; spl. edn. tchr. Perth Amboy Pub. Schs., N.J., 1984; mgmt. cons. J. Anthony and Assocs., Inc., Hillsborough, N.J., 1986, project mgr., 1987; cons. Datanomics, Inc., Piscataway, N.J., 1987-88; tchr. of the handicapped Edison (N.J.) Twp. Bd. Edn., 1988—; cons. in field. Mem. NEA, N.J. Edn. Assn., Edison Tchrs. Assn. Republican. Presbyterian. Home: 27 Hill Ave Somerset NJ 08873-3322

BLAESS, DONNA ADELE, psychotherapist, counselor, educator; b. Detroit, Dec. 17, 1948; d. Marvin Julius and Mildred Catherine (Konka) B. BA, U. Tampa, Fla., 1970; MA, U. of South Fla., 1972; PhD, U. Iowa, 1976. Rsch. evaluator Boston U., 1976-77; project dir. Contract Rsch. Corp., Belmont, Mass., 1977-79; adj. prof. Peabody Coll. of Vanderbilt U., Oxford, 1980-81; clin. staff mem. Assocs. for Human Resources, Concord, Mass., 1982-84; program dir., asst. prof. St. Thomas U., Miami, Fla., 1985-91; assoc. prof. Barry U., Miami Shores, Fla., 1991-92; psychotherapist Ctr. for Family Learning, Ft. Lauderdale, Fla., 1986-88; pvt. practice psychotherapy, Miami, 1988-92, Ft. Lauderdale, 1992—; gov.'s appointee Fla. Dept. Profl. Regulation, 1991-92, expert witness, 1991—, chair probable cause panel, 1993—; adj. prof. Nova Southeastern U., 1992—; clin. cons. Children's Diagnostic and Treatment Ctr., Ft. Lauderdale, 1992-94. Edn. cons. homeless program New Horizons Mental Health Ctr., Miami, 1988; mem. adv. com. Parent to Parent, Miami, 1988-89; mem. bd. clin. social work Marriage and Family Therapy, and Mental Health Counseling, 1990-91. Mem. APA, AACD (media rev. bd. 1986-89), Am. Mental Health Counselors Assn., Fla. Mental Health Counselors Assn. (sec. 1988-89, treas. 1989-90, chmn. governance com. 1992-93). Home: West Lake Village 1155 Weeping Willow Way Hollywood FL 33019

BLAIN, CHARLOTTE MARIE, physician; b. Meadeville, Pa., July 18, 1941; d. Frank Andrew and Valerie Marie (Serafin) B.; student Coll. St. Francis, 1958-60, DePaul U., 1960-61; M.D., U. Ill., 1965; m. John G. Hamby, June 12, 1971 (dec. May 1976); 1 son, Charles J. Hamby. Intern, resident U. Ill. Hosps., Chgo., 1967-70; practice medicine specializing in internal medicine, Elmhurst, Ill., 1969—; instr. medicine U. Ill. Hosp., 1969-70; asst. prof. medicine Loyola U., 1970-71; mem. staff Elmhurst Meml. Hosp., 1970—; clin. asst. prof. Chgo. Med. Sch., 1978—. U. Ill. fellow in infectious diseases, 1968-69. Bd. dirs. Classical Symphony. Diplomate Am. Bd. Family Practice, Am. Bd. Internal Medicine. Fellow A.C.P., Am. Acad. Family Practice; mem. AMA, Am. Med. Women's Assn., Am. Soc. Internal Medicine, Am. Fedn. Clin. Research, Am. Profl. Practice Assn., AAAS, Royal Soc. Medicine, DuPage Med. Soc. Roman Catholic. Club: Univ. (Chgo.). Contbr. articles and chpts. to med. jours. and texts. Home: 320 Cottage Hill Ave Elmhurst IL 60126-3302 Office: 135 Cottage Hill Ave Elmhurst IL 60126-3330

BLAINE, DOROTHEA CONSTANCE RAGETTÉ, lawyer; b. N.Y.C., Sept. 23, 1930; d. Robert Raymond and Dorothea Ottilie Ragetté; BA, Barnard Coll., 1952; MA, Calif. State U., 1968; EdD, UCLA, 1978; JD, Western State U., 1981; postgrad. in taxation Golden Gate U. Bar: Calif. 1982, U.S. Dist. Ct. (ea., so. and cen. dists.) Calif., 1982. Mem. tech. staff Planning Rsch. Corp., L.A., 1964-67; assoc. scientist Holy Cross Hosp., Mission Hills, Calif., 1967-70; career devel. officer and affirmative action officer County of Orange, Santa Ana, Calif., 1970-74, sr. adminstrv. analyst, budget and program coord., 1974-78; spl. projects asst. CAO/Spl. Programs Office, 1978-80, sr. adminstrv. analyst, 1980-83; pvt. practice, 1982—; instr. Am. Coll. Law, Brea, Calif., 1987; judge pro tem Orange County Mcpl. Ct., 1988—. Bd. dirs. Deerfield Community Assn., 1975-78, Orange YMCA, 1975-77. Mem. ABA, ACLU, Trial Lawyers Am., Calif. Trial Lawyers Assn., Orange County Trial Lawyers Assn., Calif. Women Lawyers, Nat. Women's Polit. Caucus, Calif. Bar Assn., Orange County Bar Assn. (Orange County del. to Calif. State Bar Conv. 1985-94, bd. dirs. Orange County lawyers referral svc. 1988-92), Delta Theta Phi, Phi Delta Kappa. Office: 3 Imperial Promenade 4th fl Santa Ana CA 92707-5901

BLAINE, GLORIA BECKWITH, volunteer; b. Mpls., Nov. 21, 1924; d. Ralph Monroe and Edna Cathryn (Christenson) Beckwith; m. Charles Gillespie Blaine, Dec. 16, 1944 (div. 1985); children: Cathryn Blaine Muzzy, Susan Blaine Nesbitt, Charles Gillespie Jr. Student, Smith Coll., 1942-45. Mem. jr. bd. Buffalo Gen. Hosp., 1953-61, pres. jr. bd., 1958, patient rep., 1981—, chmn. patient rep. program, 1985-91. Bd. dirs. Psychiat. Clin. for Children and Adolescents, Buffalo, 1952-58, 67-73, United Way, Buffalo and Erie County, 1960-66, Planned Parenthood, Buffalo and Erie County, 1962-68; trustee Buffalo Sem., 1967-73; bd. dirs. United Way of Buffalo and Erie County, 1960-66, chmn. women's div., 1961; mem. Buffalo Fine Arts Acad., Buffalo Philharm Soc., Buffalo Zool. Soc., Buffalo Women for Downtown. Mem. Garret Club. Republican. Episcopalian. Home: 751 W Ferry St Buffalo NY 14222-1646

BLAIR, ANGELA, mental health nurse; b. Bklyn., Dec. 21, 1967; d. Charles Abhue and Dorothy Lee (Parrot) B. BSN, Syracuse U., 1989. RN, N.Y. RN, staff nurse Met. Hosp., N.Y.C., 1989-91, head nurse, 1991—; various coms. Met. Hosp., N.Y.C., 1991—. Mem. Am. Psychiat. Nurses Assn., N.Y. State Nurses Assn., Black Nurses Assn. Democrat. Baptist.

BLAIR, BONNIE, professional speedskater, former Olympic athlete; b. Cornwall, N.Y., Mar. 18, 1964; d. Charlie and Eleanor B. Student, Mont. Tech. Univ. Gold medalist, 500m Speedskating Calgary Olympic Games, 1988; Gold medalist, 500m Speedskating Albertville Olympic Games, 1992, Gold medalist, 1000m Speedskating, 1992; Gold medalist, 500m Speedskating Lillehammer Olympic Games, 1994, Gold medalist, 1000m Speedskating, 1994; pro tour speedskater, 1994—. Office: Advantage Internat Mgmt Inc 1025 Thomas Jefferson St NW Washington DC 20007-5201*

BLAIR, KATHIE LYNN, social services worker; b. Oakland, Calif., Sept. 29, 1951; d. Robert Leon Webb and Patricia Jean (Taylor) Peterson; m. Terry Wayne Blair, Dec. 29, 1970 (div. 1972); 1 child, Anthony Wayne. Eligibility worker Dept. Social Services, San Jose, Calif., 1974-76; adult and family services worker State of Oreg., Portland, 1977-90; guest speaker welfare advocacy groups, Portland, 1987. Translator: Diary of Fannie Burkhart, 1991; contbr. articles to profl. jours. Mem. Nat. Geog. Soc., A Brotherhood Against Totalitarian Enactments, Oreg. State Pub. Interest Rsch. Group, Clan Chattan Assn., Portland Highland Games Assn., Harley Owners Group, Ladies of Harley. Democrat.

BLAIR, LAUREL MANENTI, public relations executive; b. Chgo., Oct. 3, 1950; d. Charles William and Selma Marie (Knief) Brantman; m. Thomas Lee Blair, Jan. 11, 1986. BJ, U. Mo., 1971; M in Journalism, Northwestern U., 1976. Account exec. The Lynne Farnol Group, Inc., N.Y.C., 1971-73; pres. The Laurel Manenti Group, Inc., Chgo., 1973-78; v.p., dir. spl. programs Burson-Marsteller, Inc., Chgo., 1978-83; pres. The Communications Group, Inc., Chgo., 1983-85; dir. pub. rels. and consumer products Alberto-Culver Co., Melrose Park, Ill., 1985—. Co-chmn. Bruno Bartoletti Event Lyric Opera, Chgo., 1981; coord. publicity 50th Anniversary Mus. Sci. and Industry, Chgo., 1980; bd. dirs. Friends of Prentice Hosp., Chgo. Mem. Carlton Club. Office: Wheatley Blair Inc 325 W Huron St Chicago IL 60610

BLAIR, MARIE LENORE, educator; b. Maramec, Okla., Jan. 9, 1931; d. Virgil Clement and Ella Catherine (Leen) Strode; m. Freeman Joe Blair, Aug. 26, 1950; children: Elizabeth Ann Blair Crump, Roger Joe. BS, Okla. A&M Coll., 1956; MS, Okla. State U., 1961, postgrad., 1965-68. Reading specialist Pub. Schs. Stillwater (Okla.), 1966-88. Past bd. dirs. Okla. Reading Council. Mem. Internat., Okla., Cimarron (past pres.) reading assns., NEA, Okla. Edn. Assn., Stillwater Edn. Assn., Kappa Kappa Iota. Democrat. Mem. Disciples of Christ. Lodges: Demoley Mothers, Rainbow Mothers, Lahoma, White Shrine Jerusalem (past worthy high priestess). Order White Shrine Jerusalem (past supreme queen's attendant), Internat. Order of Rainbow for Girls (Okla. exec. com.), Order Eastern Star (past grand Martha, past grand rep. of Nebr. in Okla.). Home: RR 1 Maramec OK 74045-9801

BLAIR, PATRICIA MCCULLARS, occupational health nurse; b. Anniston, Ala., Apr. 2, 1959; d. Edwar Harlon and Bobbie Jean (Sanders) McC.; children: Shannon Eliga, Joshua Michael. Student, Gadsden State Jr. Coll., 1980-81; LPN, Harry M. Ayers Tech. Coll., 1979. Floor nurse Stringfellow Meml. Hosp., Anniston, Ala., 1979-82; office nurse Irwin Army Hosp., Ft. Riley, Kans., 1982-83; floor nurse N.E. Ala. Regional Med. Ctr., Anniston, 1983-84; office nurse Pratt Med. Ctr., Fredericksburg, Va., 1984; indsl. nurse Tyson Foods, Inc., Heflin, Ala., 1987-91; med. svcs. adminstr. Maplehurst, Inc., Carrollton, Ga., 1991—. Baptist. Office: Maplehurst Inc 62 Adamson Industrial Blvd Carrollton GA 30117-9370

BLAIR, PATRICIA WOHLGEMUTH, economics writer; b. N.Y.C., Nov. 30, 1929; m. James P. Blair, Aug. 13, 1964; children: David A., Matthew W. BA with honors, Wellesley Coll., 1950; MA, Haverford Coll., 1952. Officer U.S. Agy. Internat. Devel., New Delhi, 1953-55, 63-64; editor Carnegie Endowment for Internat. Peace, N.Y.C., 1956-63, Devel. Digest, Nat. Planning Assn., Washington, 1965-68; staff assoc. Commn. on Internat. Devel., World Bank, Washington, 1969-70; ind. cons., writer, editor, 1970—. Editor: Health Needs of the World's Poor Women, 1980; contbr. articles to profl. publs. Mem. adv. com. Unitarian-Universalist Holdeen India Fund, Washington, 1984—; bd. dirs. Equity Policy Ctr., Washington, 1980-85. Mem. Soc. Internat. Devel. (internat. governing coun. 1975-79), Assn. Women in Devel., Asia Soc., UN Assn. Home and Office: 1411 30th St NW Washington DC 20007-3141

BLAIR, ROBIN ELISE FARBMAN, financial and management consultant, accountant; b. Detroit, Jan. 22, 1951; d. Aaron A. and Marie A. (Prager) Farbman. B.A., Mich. State U., 1974; postgrad. Wayne State U., 1976, Pace U., 1985, New Sch. for Social Rsch., 1992-93. Drama critic Lansing State Jour., Mich., 1974; asst. editor Gale Research Co., Detroit, 1974-77; copy chief Ballantine Books, Random House, N.Y.C., 1977-79; fin. mgr. and adminstr. Ark Restaurants Corp., N.Y.C., 1980-83; owner, pres. Robin Blair Acctg. Services, N.Y.C., 1984—. Mem. Nat. Assn. Female Execs., N.Y. SBA. Democrat. Unitarian. Avocations: writing; piano. Address: 59 W 76th St New York NY 10023

BLAIR, RUTH REBA, government official; b. New Orleans, Aug. 21, 1934; d. Joseph Aloysius and Ruth (Labostrie) Porter; m. William Jennings Blair, Sept. 22, 1961; children: Joseph Vernon, Constance Eileen. AS in Bus. Adminstrn., Loyola U., New Orleans, 1980; BA in English, U. New Orleans, 1984; masters cert. in govt. contracting, George Washington U., 1992. Cert. assoc. contracts mgr.; cert. mem. fed. acquisition corps. Various positions Michoud Assembly Facility, New Orleans, 1964-84; contract specialist NASA, Marshall Space Flight Ctr, Ala., 1985-86; contracting officer USCG, New Orleans, 1986-87; contract adminstr. (supercomputers) Naval Rsch. Lab., Stennis Space Ctr., Miss., 1987—. author, adminstr. Primary Oceanographic Prediction System contract for Navy's Large Scale Computer Supercomputer System. Mem. ABA (assoc., sects. pub. contracts law, bus. law, govt. and pub. sector lawyers div.), AAUW, Federally Employed Women. Home: 5815 Franklin Ave New Orleans LA 70122-6405 Office: Naval Rsch Lab S Contracts Office Code 3250/RPB Stennis Space Center MS 39529

BLAIR, RUTH VIRGINIA VAN NESS, writer; b. St. Michael, Alaska, June 9, 1912; d. Elmer Eugene and Eula Willie (McIntosh) Van Ness; m. Glenn Myers Blair, June 27, 1934; children: Glen Myers, Sally Virginia Coleman. Diploma, Seattle Pacific Coll., 1932; voice studies, Seattle, 1930-34, N.Y.C., 1937-38. Tchr. Everett (Wash.) Pub. Schs., 1932-34, Champaign, Ill., 1952-61; presenter Writing for Children workshops U. S. Fla. at St. Petersburg, Fla. So. Coll., writers' confs. Author: (children's books) Puddle Duck, 1966, A Bear Hibernates, Why Can't I?, 1972, Willa Willa, The Wishful Witch, 1972, Mary's Monster (Jr. Lit. Guild Selection), 1975; contbr. poetry to Voices Internat., Lyric, Classical Outlook, The Pen Women; contbr. stories, articles to Athene Mag., Mus. Jour., Christian Living, Amelia, Cricket, Young World Plays, Ranger Rick, Good Old Days, St. Petersburg Times; contbr. Ency. Britannica, 1974, chpt. poetry textbook, 1983; editor Symphony Guild Tchrs. Guide, 1974. Soloist Champaign-Urbana (Ill.) chs., 1938-61; edn. chmn. Symphony Guild, Champaign-Urbna, 1970-74. Mem. Nat. League Am. Pen Women (pres. Clearwater chpt. 1980-82), Chgo. Children's Reading Round Table, Clearwater (Fla.) Friends Library, Fla. State Poetry Assn., Nat. Soc. Children's Book Writers. Club: Univ. (Urbana). Home and Office: 51 Island Way Clearwater FL 34630-2262

BLAIR, SANDRA SIMKO, librarian; b. Dearborn, Mich., Feb. 7, 1940; d. Bela John and Barbara Margaret (Komaromi) Simko; m. Howard Douglas Blair, May 19, 1962; 1 child, Susan Diane. Student, Northwestern Mich. Coll., 1959-60; BS in Edn., Wayne State U., 1965, MSLS, 1970. Cert. permanent tchr., libr.'s profl. cert., Mich. Sch. libr. Cherry Hill High Sch., Inkster, Mich., 1965-67, Southgate (Mich.) High Sch., 1968-69; pub. libr. Huron-New Boston (Mich.) Pub. Libr., 1975-80; gen. edn. devel. testing assoc. Huron Sch. Dist., New Boston, 1978-88; pub. libr. Canton (Mich.) Pub. Libr., 1985—; chairperson young adult svcs. com. Wayne-Oakland Libr. Fedn., 1991-92. Vol. Huron Civic Theatre, New Boston, 1982-86. Mem. Mich. Libr. Assn. Roman Catholic. Home: 19595 Merriman Rd Romulus MI 48174-9490 Office: Canton Pub Libr 1200 S Canton Center Rd Canton MI 48188-1608

BLAIR, VIRGINIA ANN, public relations executive; b. Kansas City, Mo., Dec. 20, 1925; d. Paul Lowe and Lou Etta (Cooley) Smith; m. James Leon Grant, Sept. 3, 1943 (dec. July 1944); m. Warden Tannahill Blair, Jr., Nov. 7, 1947; children: Janet, Warden Tannahill, III. BS in Speech, Northwestern U., 1948. Free-lance writer, Chgo., 1959-69; writer, editor Smith, Bucklin & Assocs., Inc., Chgo., 1969-72, account mgr., 1972-79, account supr., 1979-80, dir. pub. relations, 1980-85; pres. GB Pub. Rels., 1985—; judge U.S. Indsl. Film Festival, 1974, 75; instr. Writer's Workshop, Evanston, Ill., 1978; dir. Northwestern U. Library Council, 1978-91, dir. alumnae bd., 1986—, John Evans Club bd., 1990—. Emmy nominee Nat. Acad. TV Arts & Scis., 1963; recipient Service award Northwestern U., 1978, Creative Excellence award U.S. Indsl. Film Festival, 1976, Gold Leaf merit cert. Family Circle mag. and Food Council Am., 1977. Mem. Pub. Rels. Soc. Am. (counselors acad.), Am. Advt. Fedn. (lt. gov. Ill. 6th dist.), Women's Advt. Club Chgo. (pres.), Publicity Club Chgo., Nat. Acad. TV Arts & Scis., John Evans Club (bd. dirs.), Woman's Club Evanston (pres.), Zeta Phi Eta (Svc. award 1978, 93), Alpha Gamma Delta, Philanthropic and Ednl. Orgn. Ill. (PEO chpt. pres.). Author dramas (produced on CBS): Jeanne D'Arc: The Trial, 1961; Cordon of Fear, 1961; Reflection, 1961; If I Should Die, 1963; 3-act children's play: Children of Courage, 1967. Home and Office: 463 Highcrest Dr Wilmette IL 60091-2357

BLAIR, WAYNE (MRS. DONALD S. BLAIR), association administrator. Pres. gen. Nat. Soc., Daughters of the Am. Revolution, D.C. Office: Daughters of the Am Revolution 1776 D St NW Washington DC 20006-5392*

BLAIR-LARSEN, SUSAN MARGARET, educator; b. Plainfield, N.J., May 28, 1950; d. Adam Craig and Edith Elizabeth Blair; m. Bruce Osborn Larsen, July 15, 1989. BS, Castleton (Vt.) State Coll., 1972; MS, U. Scranton, Pa., 1974; EdD, U. Pa., 1984. Tchr. Palisades Sch. Dist., Kintnersville, Pa., 1973-75; reading specialist Lakewood (N.J.) Sch. Dist., 1975-84; prof. U. Minn., Morris, 1984-85, Rutgers U., Newark, 1985-88, Trenton (N.J.) State Coll., 1988—. Author: An Integrative Approach to Language Instruction, 1993; co-author: Joining the Forces to Guide the New Teacher, 1993. Mem. Mantoloking and Bay Head (N.J.) Women's Rep. Club. Mem. Internat. Reading Assn., Ea. Ednl. Rsch. Assn., Phi Delta Kappa (10 Yr. award 1990), Pi Lambda Theta. Roman Catholic.

BLAIS, MARIE-CLAIRE, novelist, poet, playwright; b. Quebec, Oct. 5, 1939; d. Fernando Blais and Veronique Nolin. Student, Laval (Que.) U., Harvard U. Author: A Season in the Life of Emmanuel, Manuscripts of Pauline Archange, St. Lawrence Blues, Deaf to the City, Mad Shadows, Tete Blanche, The Woolf, David Sterne. Mem. Writers Union Can., Union des Écrivains, Union des Auteurs Dramatiques, Pen Club, Compagnon de l'Order du Can., Royal Soc., Acad. Royale de la Belgique. Home: 448 Chemin Sims, Kingsbury, PQ Canada J0B 1X0

BLAKE, BENNIE RUTH, nurse; b. Houston, Oct. 22, 1946; d. Ben and Celestine (Martin) Brantley; m. Robert Louis Blake, Sept. 1968 (div. 1975). BSN, Alverno Coll., 1982; MS in Ednl. Leadership, Troy State U., 1993. Cert. BLS, ACLS. Commd. 2d lt. U.S. Army, 1982, advanced through grades to capt., 1985; charge and staff nurse Jefferson Davis Hosp., Houston, 1971-75; oper. rm. technician USN, 1975-82; charge and staff nurse Northwest Gen. Hosp., Milw., 1980-82; staff nurse USA MEDDAC, Ft. Eustis, Va., Ft. Knox, Ky., 1982-86, 97th Gen. Hosp., Frankfurt, Germany, 1987-89; surp., head nurse USAAMC, Ft. Rucker, Ala., 1989-90; head nurse USA MedElement-Joint Task Force, Honduras, 1991, 121 Evacuation Hosp., Seoul, 1991-92; head nurse cysto/urology Houston VA Med. Ctr., 1993—; edn. coord. U.S. Army, 1983-92, infection coord., 1991; instr. continuing edn. drug awareness, 1989, aseptic technique, 1990, perioperating nursing, 1990. Organizer teens group Teens Effective Tng., Daleville, Ala., 1990; officer-in-charge Camayagua (Honduras) Orphanage, 1991; mem. health com. NAACP, Houston, 1993—. Maj. USAR, 1994—. Decorated Army Achievement, Navy Meritorious, Navy Good Conduct. Mem. Assn. Oper. Rm. Nurses (parliamentarian 1988), Order Ea. Star (mem.-at-large). Methodist. Home: 10926 Cheeves Dr Houston TX 77016-2434

BLAKE, CATHERINE C., judge; b. Boston, July 27, 1950; d. John Ballard and Jean Place (Adams) B.; m. Frank Eisenberg, June 22, 1974; 3 children. BA magna cum laude, Radcliffe Coll., 1972; JD cum laude, Harvard Law Sch., 1975. Bar: Mass. 1975, Md. Ct. Appeals 1977, U.S. Ct. Appeals (4th cir.) 1977, U.S. Dist. Ct. Md. 1977, D.C. 1979. Assoc. Palmer &

Dodge, Boston, 1975-77; asst. U.S. atty. Dist. of Md., Baltimore, 1977-83, first asst. U.S. atty., 1983-85, 86-87; U.S. atty. (court-appointed) Baltimore, 1985-86; judge U.S. Dist. Ct. Md., Baltimore, 1987—. Mem. Fed. Bar Assn., Md. Bar Assn., Nat. Assn. of Women Judges, Fed. Magistrate Judges' Assn. Office: US Courthouse 101 W Lombard St Rm 110 Baltimore MD 21201*

BLAKE, DARLENE EVELYN, political worker, consultant, educator, author; b. Rockford, Iowa, Feb. 26, 1947; d. Forest Kenneth and Violet Evelyn (Fisher) Kuhlemeier; m. Joel Franklin Blake, May 1, 1975 (dec. Jan. 1989); 1 child, Alexander Joel. AA, North Iowa Area Community Coll., Mason City, 1967; BS, Mankato (Minn.) State Coll., 1969; MS, Mankato (Minn.) State U., 1975. Cert. profl. tchr., Iowa; registered art therapist. Tchr. Bishop Whipple Sch., Faribault, Minn., 1970-72; art therapist C.B. Wilson Ctr., Faribault, 1972-76, Sedgwick County Dept. Mental Health, Wichita, Kans., 1976-79; cons. Batten, Batten, Hudson & Swab, Des Moines, 1979-81; pres. J.F. Blake Co., Inc., Des Moines, 1984—; polit. cons. to Alexander Haig for Pres., 1987-88; mgmt. tng. specialist Comms. Data Svcs., Inc., Des Moines, 1988-90, exec. mgr. customer svc. spl. interest fulfillment div., 1990-92; mem. nat. adv. bd. Alexander Haig for Pres., 1987-88; cert. cons. assoc. Drake, Beam, Morin, Inc., Des Moines, 1993—. Exhibited in one-woman show at local libr., 1970. Mem. U.S. Selective Svc. Bd. 26 and 27, Polk County, Iowa, 1981—; sustaining mem. Rep. Nat. Com.; Rep. cand. Polk County Treas., Des Moines, 1982; chmn. Polk County Rep. Party, 1985-88; commr. Des Moines Commn. Human Rights and Job Discrimination, 1984-89; mem. Martin Luther King Scholarship Com., 1986-88; mem. Iowa State Bd. Psychology Examiners, 1983-90; mem. 5th Dist. Jud. Nominating Commn., 1990—. Mem. Am. Art Therapy Assn., Iowa Art Therapy Assn. (pres. elect 1984-85, founder), Internat. Platform Speakers Assn., Toastmasters, Des Moines Garden Club (pres. 1984-85), Polk County Rep. Women (pres. elect 1983-85). Lutheran. Home and Office: 3815 SW 30th St Des Moines IA 50321-2050

BLAKE, ELIZABETH, pediatric nurse practitioner; b. Mpls., Oct. 14, 1951; m. Steven Blake. ADN with honors, Normandale Community Coll., Bloomington, Minn., 1985; BSN with distinction, U. Minn., 1987; MA in Nursing, Coll. of St. Catherine, St. Paul, 1994. Cert. pediatric nurse practitioner. Sch. nurse, pediatric nurse practitioner Minn. Dept. Health, Mpls., 1992—; vol. rural clinic Ecuador, 1992—. Author publs. in child health. Vol. at rural clinic, Ecuador, 1991. Mem. Sigma Theta Tau, Phi Kappa Phi.

BLAKE, JANE SALLEY, publishing, public relations, and management consultant; b. Tallahassee, Fla., Sept. 3, 1937; d. George Lawrence Salley and Eleanor (King) Hookham; m. Arthur Copeland Blake Jr., Sept. 5, 1959 (div. 1991); children: A. Copeland III, Tarrant Salley. BA in Fine Arts, Fla. State U., 1958. Exec. sec. Hist. Homes Found., Louisville, 1975-76; chair Ky. Heritage Weekend U.S. Bicentennial Celebration, Louisville, 1976; founder, pres., chmn. Arts Forum, Inc., Louisville, 1978-84; pres. Blake Publs., Inc., Louisville, 1983-86; pres., prin. The Center mag., Inc., Louisville, 1986—, J.S. Blake Communications Group, Louisville, 1986—. V.p. Art Ctr. Assn., Louisville, 1967-72; bd. dirs., publicity chair Children's Theatre, 1968; v.p., bd. dirs. Crusade vs. Crime, 1972-74; bd. dirs. Farmington Hist. Home, 1973-75, 77-80, actor/singer Actors' Theatre, Lunchtime Theatre, 1974; mem. theatre a la carte troupe, 1976-77; founder, chmn. Potpourri of the Arts, 1979-83; mem. pub. rels. com. Jefferson County Police, 1987-88. Recipient Gov.'s Arts award for media excellence, 1989. Mem. Pub. Rels. Soc. Am. (Landmark of Excellence award 1988, 89), Advt. Club Louisville (13 Louie awards for publs. 1981-84), Entrepreneur Soc. (mem. exec. com., bd. dirs. 1989-91, Above and Beyong the Call of Duty award 1990), Soc. Profl. Journalists, Women's Club Louisville, Women's Alliance. Democrat. Office: The Center Mag Inc JS Blake Comm Group PO Box 22312 Louisville KY 40252

BLAKE, JEANNETTE BELISLE, psychotherapist; b. Manchester, N.H., Aug. 1, 1920; d. Emile Henry and Mathilda Cecelia (Martin) Belisle; m. Roland Oscar Royer, Sept. 6, 1937 (div. 1948); 1 child, Dorothy Marie Royer Lyman; m. Albert Willard Blake Sr., Aug. 11, 1979. Cons. Al Blake Advt. Cons., Manchester, N.H., 1959-68; pvt. practice Manchester, 1968—; founder, dir. N.H. Metaphys. Establishment, Manchester, 1976—; presenter workshops in field. Recipient medal N.H. Metaphysicians, 1978; cert. Greater Manchester Mental Health Ctr., 1985, 86. Mem. N.H. Assn. for Counseling and Devel., N.H. Assn. of Family Counselors, Am. Assn. of Mental Health Counselors (N.H. br.), Therapeutic Touch Healing (Manchester chpt.), Soc. for Psychic Rsch. of N.H. and Mass. (adv. bd.). Roman Catholic. Home and Office: 131 Russell St Manchester NH 03104-3769

BLAKE, JOAN JOHNSTON WALLMAN, playwright, lyricist; b. Nashville, May 14, 1930; d. Graham Walpole Johnston and Emilie (Wright) Roberts; m. John Christian Wallman, May 13, 1950 (div. 1960); children: Joan, Tia, Chris, Chellie, Parker, Peter; m. Octave Blake, Jan. 28, 1962 (dec. Jan. 1969). Student, Finch Jr. Coll., N.Y.C., 1948-49, Concordia U., Montreal, Que., Can., 1973-76. Author, host radio sta. WEEB, Southern Pines, N.C., 1949-50; editorial asst. Polar Oceans Conf., 1974; co-founder, co-owner Double Hook Book Shop, Montreal, 1974—; freelance journalist, broadcaster; dir. LePiggerie Theatre, Que., 1964-67; founder Amanda Theater, 1990; lectr. on Can. studies for the Humanities, N.Y., Vt., N.H., 1982; regional liaison dir. N.C. Playwright's Ctr., 1994. Co-author: (musical) Amanda and Atwater Square, 1985, Amanda and the Northern Lights, 1990, Christobal and the Dancing Masks, 1991; co-author: Tia Wallman (music) Max Dunbar, Bad Lady, 1993, The Night of the Thousand Volunteers, 1992; author, hostess (documentary) Vermont PBS, 1983. Mem. U.S. Trotting Assn., 1962-72. Recipient award of Merit Assn. for Can. Studies, 1988. Mem. Can. Booksellers Assn., Playwright/Lyricist Dramatist Guild. Home: 260 Saint Andrews Dr Pinehurst NC 28374-9506

BLAKE, LAURA, architect; b. Berkeley, Calif., Dec. 26, 1959; d. Igor Robert and Elizabeth (Denton) B. BA in Art History, Brown U., 1982; MArch, UCLA, 1985. Architect The Ratcliff Architects, Berkeley, 1986-90, IDG Architects, Oakland, Calif., 1990-92, ELS Architects, Berkeley, 1992—. Organizer charity ball Spinsters San Francisco, 1988, sec., 1988-89, mem. adv. bd., 1989-92; mem. San Francisco Jr. League. Recipient Alpha Rho Chi bronze medal, 1985. Mem. AIA. Republican. Episcopalian. Office: ELS Architects 2040 Addison St Berkeley CA 94704-1104

BLAKE, ROBIN VALERIE ROBSON, paralegal; b. Boston, June 21, 1950; d. Paul Britton and Jeanne Athalie (Northridge) Robson; m. Richard Edward Blake, June 7, 1980 (div.); children: Jonathan Northridge Blake, Britton Richard Blake. BA, Stonehill Coll., 1972; Paralegal Cert., Northeastern U., 1992. Personnel adminstr. Honeywell, Inc., Wellesley, Mass., 1976-82; paralegal/office mgr. Marc S. Alpert, Boston, 1985—. Past pres. Home-Sch. Assn., Plymouth, Mass., 1991-92; ct. advocate South Shore Women's Ctr., Plymouth, 1993; Sunday Sch. tchr. St. John's Ch., Sandwich, Mass., 1988-94, nominating com., 1993-94. Named Parent of Yr. Edn. Assn. Plymouth County, 1991. Mem. NAFE, Mass. Paralegal Assn. Episcopalian. Office: Marc S Alpert PC 50 Stanford St Boston MA 02114

BLAKE, TRUDI ODELLA, odemaker; b. Itaaca, Mich., Apr. 21, 1921; d. Leo Charles Lepley and Grace Cornelia (Street) Lepley-Reed; m. George Blake; children: Russell, Kevin, Lorene, Suzanne, Philip. Student, Detroit Sch. of Bus., 1941, Hollywood Sch. of Comedy Writing, 1966. Former writer local and nat. TV stas.; former writer for Phyllis Diller. Author: (odes) Forever Grand and Glorious, Ode to Soapy, a Huckleberry Friend, Ode to the Tigers, Dear Hearts and Republican People, A Voyage That's Socko, to Spain and Morocco, Over the Rainbow to Liberal, We The People - 200, Ode to a Bunch of Swells, From Sauks to Saginaw, A Ode to Michigan, To Conquer Tomorrow, Michigan City Ode, A Miracle in Our Midst; contbr. odes to various bus. Recipient Cert. of Special Tribute State of Mich., 1988. Mem. Nat. Speakers Assn. (named Official Odemaker 1984), Oakland County Writers Assn. Home and Office: PO Box 2842 Farmington MI 48333-2842

BLAKELEY, LINDA, writer, producer, psychotherapist; b. Bklyn., July 26, 1941; d. Charles and Blanche (Josephson) Berkow; m. Dec. 17, 1961 (div. 1983); children: Stacey, Scott. BA, UCLA, 1964; MA, Calif. State U., Northridge, 1977; PhD, Calif. Grad. Inst., 1985. Founder, dir. Parents Sharing Custody, Beverly Hills, Calif., 1984-87; pvt. practice specializing in treatment of eating disorders Beverly Hills, 1984—; trainer Calif. Assn. Marriage and Family Therapists, 1988, 89; producer, host Positive Self Images interview/talk show. Author: ABC's of Stress Management, 1989, Do It with Love-Positive Parenting After Divorce, 1988, Success Strategies, 1992, Audio Tape. Mem. adv. bd. Nat. Coun. Alcoholism and Drug Abuse, 1991-92. Mem. Calif. Psychol. Assn. (state bd. dirs. media com. 1989-92, chair-elect media divsn.), Calif. Assn. Marriage and Family Therapists (chmn. ethics com. L.A. chpt.), Beverly Hills C. of C. (pres. women's network 1989-90, chmn. health care com. 1989), Women in Film, Nat. Assn. Anorexia, Bulimia Assn. Disorders. Office: 420 S Beverly Dr Ste 100 Beverly Hills CA 90212-4410

BLAKELY, CAROLYN FRAZIER, university dean; b. Mangolia, Ark., Feb. 13, 1936; d. James D. and Mary E. (Brewer) Frazier; m. Neal Nathanial Blakely, June 7, 1959; children: Karen Joy, Earl Kevin. BA in English, Ark. AM&N Coll., 1957; MA in English, Atlanta U., 1964; PhD, Okla. State U., 1984. Tchr. various schs., Magnolia, 1957-62; asst. prof. English Grambling (La.) State U., 1963-66; asst. prof. English U. Ark., Pine Bluff, 1968-86, asst. to chancellor, 1986-90, interim vice chancellor academic affairs, 1990-91, interim chancellor, 1991, dean honors coll., 1992—; instr. writing lab Okla. State U., 1978-79. Contbr. articles to profl. jours. Bd. dirs. Delta Cultural Ctr., Helena, Ark., 1986—, Knox Nelson State Literacy Bd., Little Rock, 1985—, United Way Arts & Scis. Ctr., Pine Bluff, 1986—, vice chmn.; Worthen's Women's Adv., 1986—; past pres. Sister Cities, Pine Bluff; sec. Ark. Inst. Bd., Ark. Humanities Coun. Mem. Nat. Coun. Tchrs. English, Southern Regional Honors Coun. (pres. 1991-2), Nat. Collegiate Honor Soc., Leadership Pine Bluff (pres. 1989-90), Sigma Tau Delta Nat. English Honor Soc., Alpha Kappa Alpha Sorority (pres. 1985-86). Democrat. Baptist. Home: 1101 W 23rd Ave Pine Bluff AR 71603-4201 Office: U of Ark Honors Coll 1200 University Dr Pine Bluff AR 71601-2799

BLAKELY, MARY LOUISE, elementary educator; b. Kalamazoo, Apr. 10, 1950; d. Ray and Elizabeth (Hathaway) Deur; m. John Robert Blakely, June 12, 1971 (div. 1983); children: Chad, David, Kara. BS in Edn., Ctrl. Mich. U., 1971; MA in Reading, Western Mich. U., 1986. Tchr. Mattawan (Mich.) Consolidated Schs., 1983—; CEO Azuray Corp., Portage, Mich., 1989—, Azuray Learning, Inc.; hypnotherapist Ednl. Multi-sensory Ctr., Portage, 1993—. Author (audio tapes) Rap Pak series, 1989, Star Brights series, 1993. Facilitator, master hypnotherapist Attitudinal Healing Found., Kalamazoo, 1993. Mem. NEA, Inst. of Noetic Scis., Nat. Assn. Exec. Women, Mich. Edn. Assn., Internat. Assn. Counselors & Therapists, Assn. of Holistic Healing Ctrs. Home: 7803 Pickering St Portage MI 49002 Office: Azuray Corp PO Box 1748 Portage MI 49081-1748

BLAKELY, REGINA HOPPER, lawyer; b. Albuquerque, Apr. 21, 1959; d. Bobby Gene and Lois Marie (Oels) H.; m. Mark Kevin Blakely, Aug. 3, 1985. BA in Polit. Sci., U. Ark., 1981, JD, 1985. Bar: Ark. 1985, U.S. Dist. Ct. (ea. and we. dists.) Ark. 1986, U.S. Ct. Appeals (8th cir.) 1986. Entertainer Dept. of Def., Washington, 1983-84, Miss Ark. Miss Am. Pageant, Atlantic City, 1983-84; assoc. Arnold, Grobmyer and Haley, Little Rock, 1983-87; reporter Sta. KTHV-TV, Little Rock, 1987; new reporter, anchor Sta. KATV-TV, Little Rock, 1987-91; corr. CBS News, N.Y.C., 1991-92, CBS News/Newspath, Washington, 1992—. Fundraiser Easter Seals, Little Rock, 1988; mistress of ceremonies Miss Ark. Pageant, Hot Springs, 1984—. Recipient Emmy award, 1992. Mem. ABA (securities com. 1985-92), Ark. Bar Assn. (securities com. 1985-92), Ark. Assn. Securities Dealers (exec. sec. 1985-92), Zeta Tau Alpha. Methodist. Office: CBS News 2020 M St NW Washington DC 20036

BLAKEMAN, CAROL ANN, medical and surgical nursing educator; b. Jacksonville, Fla., Aug. 17, 1954; d. John Raymond and Marion Alice (Lasher) B.; m. Key Miller Sargent, Mar. 22, 1984. AA, Fla. Jr. Coll., Jacksonville, 1974; BSN, U. South Fla., 1976; MSN, U. Fla., 1989. Cert. advanced RN practitioner, Fla. Staff and head nurse Bapt. Med. Ctr., Jacksonville, 1976-84; staff nurse Winter Haven (Fla.) Hosp., 1984-88; instr., assoc. prof. Cen. Fla. C.C., Ocala, 1988—; on-call endoscopy nurse, Jacksonville, 1982-83; instr. Polk C.C., Winter Haven, Fla., 1987; cons. Student Nurses Assn., Ctrl. Fla. C.C., Ocala, 1989—, BCLS instr., 1988-91; judge competition Health Occupation Students Am., Orlando and Ocala, 1989, 90, 92, 94, 95; health examiner Nat. Youth Sports Program, Orlando, 1987. Mem. ANA, Fla. Nurses Assn., Dist. III Nurses Assn. (treas. 1993, pres. 1994), Fla. Nursing Students Assn., Sigma Theta Tau, Phi Theta Kappa. Democrat. Roman Catholic. Home: 2405 SE 17th Cir Ocala FL 34471-8300

BLALOCK, SHERRILL, investment advisor; b. Newport News, Va., June 9, 1945; d. David Graham and Martha Lee (Bennett) B.; m. Jonathan L. Smith, Oct. 27, 1985; 1 child, Graham C.G. BA, Smith Coll., 1967. Chartered fin. analyst. Investment broker Legg Mason & Co., Washington, 1968-77, Blyth Eastman Dillon, Washington, 1977-80; portfolio mgr., mng. dir. Mitchell Hutchins, N.Y.C., 1980-88; gen. ptnr., portfolio mgr. Weiss Peck & Greer, N.Y.C., 1988-95, Delphi Asset Mgmt., N.Y.C., 1995—. Mem. investment com. Diocese of N.Y. of Episcopal Ch., 1992—. Mem. Washington Soc. Investment Analysts, Inst. Chartered Fin. Analysts. Office: Delphi Asset Mgmt 20th Fl 485 Madison Ave New York City NY 10022

BLANCHARD, COLLEEN DIANA, association administrator; b. Madison, S.D., May 7, 1945; d. Dale Roland Coates and Clair B. (Frewaldt) Kubik; m. Rodney James Blanchard, Mar. 9, 1966 (div. Apr. 1985); children: Brent Alan, Darin Layne. BS, Dakota State Coll., 1968; postgrad., N.E. Mo. State U., 1972, Pers. Dynamics Inst., 1973, Laverne U., 1973-74. Cert. tchr., Iowa. Tchr. Laverne (Calif.) U., 1973-74, Oskaloosa (Iowa) Community Schs., 1968-85; owner C. J.'s Hallmark Shop, Oskaloosa, 1985-89; south cen. states dist. mgr. Jerry Elsner Co., N.Y.C., 1989-91; mgr., spl. regional trainer Nat. Fedn. Ind. Bus., Omaha, 1991; presenter at seminars and workshops in field, Oskaloosa, 1973-75. Diplomat Oskaloosa C. of C., 1986-89; project dir. Community Devel. Found., Oskaloosa, 1984; vol. United Community Svcs., Oskaloosa, 1980-85; campaign worker Rep. Party, Oskaloosa. U.S. Dept. Edn. grantee, 1976; recipient Outstanding Educator award Oskaloosa Edn. Assn., 1974, Summit award, 1994. Mem. Pres.'s Club. Roman Catholic. Home: 11905 Wakeley Plz # 5 Omaha NE 68154-2431

BLANCHET, MADELEINE, research executive; b. Quebec, Apr. 26, 1934; d. Romeo and Lucie (Samson) B.; m. Pierre Cazalis, Aug. 11, 1974; children: Vincent, Catherine. AB, Coll. des Ursulines, Que., 1952; MD, Laval U., Que., 1957; pub. health cert., U. Montreal, 1961; MS in Pub. Health, Harvard U., 1967. Med. diplomate. Dir. Hochelaga Health Unit, Montreal, 1963-66; cons. Commn. of Inquiry on Health, Montreal, 1970-71; coord. Nutrition Can. Survey, Ottawa, 1971-72; chief of studies on health status Dept. Social Affairs, Que., 1973-79; pres. Coun. of Social Affairs, Que., 1980-91; v.p. rsch. Forum for Employment, Levis, Que., 1992—; v.p. Olo Found. for Poor Mothers, Sherbrooke, Que., 1992—; cons. Fedn. of Local Health Ctrs., Montreal, 1992. Editor: Health Goals, 1984; contbr. articles to profl. jours. Recipient annual prize Can. Inst., Que., 1980, prize for the promotion of women Womens!, Montreal, 1980, Ordre du Que., Govt. of Que., 1992. Fellow Royal Soc. Can. Home: 1264 Chenin du Moulin, Saint-Nicolas, PQ Canada GOS 2ZO

BLANCHETTE, JEANNE ELLENE MAXANT, artist, educator, performer; b. Chgo., Sept. 25, 1944; d. William H. and L. Barbara (Martin) Maxant; m. Yasuo Shimizu, Apr. 28, 1969 (div. 1973); m. William B. Blanchet, Aug. 21, 1981 (dec. May 1993). BA summa cum laude, Northwestern U., 1966; MFA, Tokyo U., 1971; MA, Ariz. State U., 1978; postgrad., Ill. State U., 1979-80; PhD, Greenwich U., 1991. Instr. Tsuda U., Kodaira, Japan, 1970-71; free-lance visual, performing artist various cities, U.S., 1973—; artist in residence YMCA of the Rockies, Estes Park, Colo., 1976-81 summers; prof. fine arts Rio Salado Coll., Surprise, Ariz., 1976-91; lectr. Ariz. State U. West, Sun City, 1985-93; lectr., evaluator several arts couns. including Ariz. Humanities Coun., 1993; Prescott Melodrama ragtime pianist, 1993, 94; artist with Performing Arts for Youth, 1994—. Selected for regional, state, nat. juried art shows, 1975—, mus. and gallery one-woman shows of computer art, 1988—; author: Original Songs and Verse of the Old (And New) West, 1987, A Song in My Heart, 1988, Reflections, 1989, The Mummy Story, 1990; contbr. articles to newspapers, profl. jours. Founding mem. Del Webb Hosp. Woodrow Wilson fellow, 1966; ADA B.C. Welsh scholar, 1980; recipient numerous art, music awards, 1970—, major computer art awards in regional, nat., and internat. shows, 1990—. Mem. Nat. League Am. Pen Women (sec. chpt. 1987, v.p. 1988, pres. 1990-92), Ariz. Press Women (numerous awards in original graphics and writing 1980s, 90s), Nat. Fedn. Press Women, Northwestern U.'s John Evans Club, Henry W. Rogers Soc., P.E.O., Phi Beta Kappa. Home and Office: 411 Lakewood Cir # C-907 Colorado Springs CO 80910

BLANCO, LAURA, film, television, theatrical and recording industry producer; b. Havana, Cuba, July 3, 1956; came to U.S., 1960; d. Lauro and Marina (Mardones) B.; m. Robert F. Shainheit, June 30, 1988. Asst. box office treas., press agt. Zev Bufman Entertainment, Inc., Orlando, St. Petersburg, Fla., 1978-83; press agt. Kool Jazz Festival and Heritage Fair, Orlando, 1982; producer La. World Exposition Inc., New Orleans, 1983-84, Festival Ventures, Inc., Miami, Fla., 1985-86; producer/dir. hispanic events Festival Prodns., Inc., N.Y.C., 1986-87; pres. Blanco Shainheit Prodns., Blanco Shainheit Music, N.Y.C., 1988—; ptnr. unanimo, 1992—; ASCAP Pop Songwriters' Workshop, 1992. Prodr. short film The Summer of My Dreams, 1994. Bd. dirs. Artists Community Fed. Credit Union, 1988-90. Mem. ASCAP, Am. Latin Music Assn. Democrat. Jewish.

BLAND, JILL ANN, county official; b. Kalamazoo, Mich., Apr. 4, 1962; d. Paul Richard and Joan Isabelle (LaLiberte) Hartman; m. Victor Lewis Bland, Nov. 28, 1987; 1 child, Meghan Ashley. B in Bus. Adminstrn., We. Mich. U., 1984. Coord. bus. assistance Van Buren County, Paw Paw, Mich., 1985-87, coord. econ. devel., 1987-89, dir. community devel., 1989—. Bd. dirs. S.W. Mich. Tourist Coun., Benton Harbor, Mich., 1989-94, Action West, Battle Creek, 1989—, pres., 1992-93, v.p., 1993-94, sec. 1994—. Mem. Mich. Soc. Planning Ofcls., Kalamazoo Lawyers Aux., Rotary (charter), Theta Theta. Republican. Methodist. Office: Van Buren County 212 Paw Paw St Paw Paw MI 49079

BLANK, JOAN GILL, journalist, illustrator; b. Buffalo, Apr. 3, 1928; d. Ralph C. and Miriam A. Epstein; m. Harvey Blank, Sept. 14, 1975; children: Robin, Susan, Prudence. AB, Sarah Lawrence Coll., 1949. Editor, art dir. Investment Sales Monthly, Coral Gables, Fla., 1964-68, Fla. Commentary, Hollywood, 1973-75, Communique, Miami, Fla., 1974-75; editor, designer Born of The Sun, 1975-76; freelance writer, 1950—; cons. in field, 1963—; pres. Grapetree Prodns., Inc., 1981—. Author: Give Your Whole Self, 1981; author, illustrator: Laugh Lines, 1982; contbr. articles & photo-features to mags. and newspapers. Mem. Nat. Press Club, Phi Theta Kappa, Chi Delta Phi. Democrat. Address: 600 Grapetree Dr Apt 10cn Key Biscayne FL 33149-2704

BLANKE, GAIL ANN, communications executive; b. Cleve., Jan. 20, 1941; d. Warren J. and Isabelle (Voigt) B.; m. Franklin James Cusick, Feb. 22, 1969; children—Katharine Jennings, Abigail Jennings. A.B., Sweet Briar Coll., 1963. Mgr., Lifetime Sports Found., Washington, 1965-66, CBS, N.Y.C., 1966-69; v.p. Allen & Dorwood Advt., N.Y.C., 1969-72; v.p. communications Avon Products, Inc., N.Y.C., 1972-91, sr. v.p. corp. affairs and communications, 1991—. Mem. YWCA's Acad. Women Achievers, 1984; bd. dirs. Child Care Action Campaign. Recipient Gold Key award PR News, 1987. Mem. Am. Women in Radio and TV (bd. dirs. 1971), Internat. Assn. Bus. Communicators, Assn. Nat. Advertisers (bd. dirs. 1989), Women's Forum of N.Y., Soc. of Mayflower Descendants, Met. Club, Lawrence Beach Club, Rockaway Hunt Club, The Doubles Club. Office: Avon Products Inc 9 W 57th St New York NY 10019-2600

BLANKENSHIP, BARBARA STRICKLIN, dean of students, academic administrator; b. Arkadelphia, Ark., June 17, 1945; d. Maurice and Maurine (Allison) Stricklin; m. T. Larry Blankenship, Feb. 13, 1970; children: Michele, Amy. BS in Edn., Henderson State U., 1967; MS in Edn., U. Ark., Fayetteville, 1969; EdD, U. Miss., 1983. Jr. high math. tchr. Green Cove Springs, Fla., summer 1969, Woodrow Wilson Jr. High, Pine Bluff, Ark., 1967-68; grad. asst. counseling U. Ark., Fayetteville, 1968-69; union and program dir. sororities Miss. State U., Starkville, 1969-76, asst. dean student life, 1976-83; dist. dir. pub. rels. Hinds C.C., Raymond, Miss., 1983-85, dist. dean of students, 1985—. Contbr. articles to profl. jours. Trainer Miss. Atty. Gen.'s Drug Task Force, Jackson, 1989-92; tchr., dir. Sunday sch. and Bible study Raymond Bapt. Ch., 1984—. Mem. So. Assn. Coll. Student Affairs (com. task force chair for community colls. 1975—), So. Assn. Colls. and Schs. (mem. steering com.), Nat. Assn. Student Pers. Adminstrs., Pilot Club Internat. (pres. and numerous offices 1975-80), Kappa Delta Pi, Alpha Xi Delta, Omicron Delta Kappa, Mortar Board, Phi Theta Kappa. Democrat. Baptist. Office: Hind C C Box 1276 Raymond MS 39154

BLANKENSHIP, CHERYL KAY, health care administrator, educator; b. Fargo, N.D., July 12, 1946; d. Carl Albert and Ruth Pauline (Pribbernow) Freeberg; m. Charles P. Berry, Dec. 18, 1965 (div. 1973); 1 child, Craig; m. Dennis Michael Blankenship, May 14, 1977; children: Michael, Ross. BA, Gustavus Adolphus Coll., 1966; BS in Med. Record Adminstrn., Coll. St. Mary, 1974; MS in Health Care Adminstrn., U. Nebr., 1977. Tchr. Fargo Pub. Sch. System, 1966-70; asst. prof. U. Nebr. Med. Ctr., Omaha, 1974-77; instr. Metro Community Coll., Omaha, 1975-77; adminstr. Baylor Med. Ctr., Dallas, 1977-81; instr. Tex. Women's U., Dallas and Denton, 1980-81; adminstr. Texarkana (Ark.) Kidney Disease and Hypertension Ctr., Inc., 1984—, also bd. dirs.; instr., advisor Texarkana Community Coll., 1986—; cons. Omaha Home for Girls, 1974-76. Participant panel TV program Youth Wants to Know, 1987; dir., author instructional film A Medical Secretary, 1976; contbr. articles to profl. jours. Chpt. sec. Am. Diabetes Assn., Texarkana, 1986—, pres., 1987&; mem. exec. bd. Bowie-Miller County Med. Aux., Texarkana, 1986—; chpt. exec. com. Nat. Kidney Found., 1985—; mem. Women for Arts., 1985—, Mother-to-Mother Group, 1983. Recipient Fishel Askanase award Askanase Family, 1962. Mem. Nat. Renal Adminstrs Assn. (govt. affairs com. 1988), Am. Med. Record Assn., NEA (faculty del. 1969), Nat. Dialysis Assn. (bd. dirs. Washington hdqtrs. 1986—). Roman Catholic. Home: 6205 Stoneridge Dr Texarkana TX 75503-1118 Office: Texarkana Kidney Disease Hypertension 422 Beech St Texarkana AR 75502-5310

BLAS, ANGELA S., computer information systems educator; b. Bklyn., Nov. 9, 1943; d. Michael J. and Margaret Louise (McDermott) Saraniero; m. Joe Michael Blas, Aug. 13, 1966; children: Michelle Carole, Cynthia Teresa. BA in Math., U. Miami, Fla., 1965, MEd, 1968; cert. data processing, SUNY, Farmingdale, 1986. Math. tchr. Palmetto Jr. H.S.; mgmt. analyst Human Resouces Devel., Sacramento, Estee Lauder Inc., Melville, N.Y.; assoc. prof. data processing SUNY, Farmingdale, N.Y., dir. assessment, now assoc. prof. computer info. sys.; tchr. continuing edn. Rocky Point (N.Y.) H.S. Mem. Am. Assn. Higher Edn., Ctr. Application Psychol. Type, Profl. and Orgnl. Devel. Network in Higher Edn. Home: 4 Pickwick Ct Stony Brook NY 11790 Office: SUNY Farmingdale Whitman Hall Farmingdale NY 11735

BLASER, LAURA LEE, small business owner; b. Cleve., July 12, 1966; d. Earl Lee, Jr. and Elaine Blaser. BSBA in Acctg., U. S.C., 1989. Sec.-treas. So.Electronic Mfg. Co., Inc., Lexington, S.C., 1989-94; owner, photographer The Sports Sect., Columbia, S.C., 1994—; mgr. gen. acctg. Colonial Life & Accident Ins. Co., Columbia, S.C., 1994—; cons. in field. Mem. at-large Inst. Mgmt. Accts., Am. Mgmt. Assn. Office: The Sports Section PO Box 25164 Columbia SC 29224

BLATNIK, THAIS FRANCES, state legislator; b. Treveskyn, Pa., Nov. 20, 1919; d. Thomas William and Thais (Larkin) O'Donnell; m. Albert M. Blatnik, 1952; children: Floyd Schuler, David Schuler, Judy Schuler (Mrs. Luff). BA, West Liberty State Coll. Former del. W.Va. State; mem. W.Va. State Senate from dist 1. Del. Dem. Nat. Conv. Mem. YWCA, Wheeling Housing Authority, Diocese of Wheeling-Charleston Cath. Community Svc., Ohio County Wildlife League. Democrat. Office: WVa State Senate State Capital Charleston WV 25305*

BLATTNER, MEERA MCCUAIG, computer science educator; b. Chgo., Aug. 14, 1930; d. William D. McCuaig and Nina (Spertus) Klevs; m. Minao Kamegai, June 22 1985; children: Douglas, Robert, William. BA, U. Chgo., 1952; MS, U. So. Calif., 1966; PhD, UCLA, 1973 . Rsch. fellow in computer sci. Harvard U., 1973-74; asst. prof. Rice U., 1974-80; assoc. prof. applied sci. U. Calif. at Davis, Livermore, 1980-91, prof. applied sci., 1991—; adj. prof. U. Tex., Houston, 1977—; vis. prof. U. Paris, 1980; program dir. theoretical computer sci. NSF, Washington, 1979-80. Co-editor: (with R. Dannenberg) Multimedia Interface Design, 1992. NSF grantee, 1977-81, 93—. Mem. Soc. Women Engrs., Assn. Computing Machinery, IEEE Computer Soc. Contbr. articles to profl. jours. Office: U Calif Davis/Livermore Dept Applied Sci Livermore CA 94550

BLATZ, KATHLEEN ANN, state legislator; B.A. summa cum laude, U. Notre Dame, 1976; M.S.W., U. Minn., 1978; J.D. cum laude, U. Minn., 1984. Psychiat. social worker, 1979-81; mem. Minn. Ho. of Reps., St. Paul, 1978—, chmn. crime and family law, fin. instns. and ins. coms.; mem. Legis. Commn. to Rev. Adminstrv. Rules, Council on Econ. Status of Women. Mem. LWV, Minn. Mental Health Assn., Phi Beta Kappa. Independent Republican. Office: Minn State Senate State Capital Saint Paul MN 55155*

BLATZ, LINDA JEANNE, marketing professional; b. N.Y.C., Dec. 8, 1950; d. William Edmund and Jeanne Grace (Hyman) B. BS, U. Md., 1972. Mgr. sales Milliken & Co., N.Y.C., 1972-81; retail market mgr. Greenwood Mills Mktg. Co., N.Y.C., 1981-89; dist. mgr. Steelcase Inc., N.Y.C., 1989-94, tng. cons., 1994—. Contbr. articles to profl. jours. Mem. N.Y.C. Ballet Guild, PEO; mem. jr. com. N.Y.C. Ballet; v.p. membership, bd. mgrs. exec. com. N.Y. Jr. League (Outstanding Vol. award 1991-92). Recipient Outstanding Vol. of the Yr. award N.Y. Jr. League, 1992. Mem. AAUW, Nat. Assn. Uniform Mfrs. and Distbrs., U. Md. Alumni Assn., Am. Woman's Econ. Devel. Corp., East River Rowing Club, Sandbar Beach Club (membership bd.), Alpha Gamma Delta. Congregationalist. Home: 2 Tudor City Pl New York NY 10017-6800 Office: 510 Fifth Ave New York NY 10036-7507

BLAUSEY, JEANNE MARTHA, accountant, financial systems analyst; b. Toledo, Ohio, Aug. 21, 1958; d. Richard Herman and Dorothy Lucille (Flury) B. A in Bus. Tech. summa cum laude, Tiffin U., 1978; BA summa cum laude, Siena Heights Coll., 1983; MA, George Washington U., 1990. Acct. The Prestolite Co., Toledo, 1978-83, SCA Svcs., Inc., Boston, 1983-84; enlisted USN, 1984, advanced through grades to lt., 1991; data processor USN, Norfolk, Va., 1984-89; systems analyst Electronic Data Systems, Detroit, 1990; plant acct. Prestolite Electric, Inc., Dearborn Heights, Mich., 1990; fin. systems analyst U.S. Navy, Bethesda, Md., 1991-94; cons. acctg. software Solomon Software, Findlay, Ohio, 1994—; adj. prof. acctg. Univ. Md., College Park, 1991-92. Mem. Inst. Mgmt. Accts., Am. Legion. Republican. Roman Catholic.

BLAXALL, MARTHA OSSOFF, economist; b. Haverhill, Mass., Feb. 2, 1942; d. Michael M. and Eve Joan (Kladky) Ossoff; BA, Wellesley Coll., 1963; PhD, Fletcher Sch., Tufts U., 1971; m. John Blaxall, May 15, 1970 (div. 1989); children: Jenifer, Johanna. Economist, Abt Assocs. Inc., Cambridge, Mass., 1965-68; budget examiner Office Mgmt. and Budget, 1969-72; sr. profl. asso. Inst. Medicine, Nat. Acad. Scis., 1972-76; dir. rsch. Health Care Fin. Adminstrn., U.S. Dept. Health and Human Svcs., 1976-79; dir. Office Utilization and Devel., Nat. Marine Fisheries Svc., Dept. Commerce, 1979-82; assoc. prof. dept. community and family medicine Georgetown U. Med. Sch., 1982; pres. BBH Corp., 1982-87; prin. Chase, Brown & Blaxall, Inc., 1983-87; v.p. ICF Inc., Washington, 1987-89; Hill and Knowlton Econs. Group, Washington, 1990-91; dir. agribusiness trade and investment group, Devel. Alternatives Inc., Bethesda, Md., 1991-93, dir. mktg. devel. group, 1993—, bd. dirs., 1994—; treas. Fedn. Orgns. Profl. Women, 1974-76, 83-84, exec. coun., 1982; active Inst. Women Policy Studies, 1993—. Trustee Sheridan Sch., Washington, 1978-86, Coun. for Excellence in Govt., 1991—, Washington-Moscow Exchange, 1991-92, bd. dirs., 1990-93, Children's Health and Environ. Ctr.; active Inst. Women's Policy Studies, 1993—. NDEA fellow, 1964-65. Mem. Am. Econ. Assn., Nat. Economists Club (v.p. 1990-91). Co-editor: Women in the Workplace: The Implications of Occupational Segregation, 1976. Home: 3516 Winfield Ln NW Washington DC 20007-2344

BLAYDES, STEPHANIE ANNE, congressional aide; b. East Lansing, Mich., Aug. 6, 1963; d. David Fairchild and Sophia (Boyatzies) B. BA in Philosophy, Gettysburg Coll., 1985. Staff asst. to Majority Whip Tom Foley U.S. House Reps., Washington, 1986-87, staff asst. to Majority Whip Tony Coelho, 1987-89, spl. asst. to Hon. Robert E. Wise Jr., 1989-93, mem. svcs. advisor House info. sys., 1993-94; sr. health program analyst Dept. Def., Washington, 1995—. Vol. Bob Wise for Congress, Washington, 1989-93; mem. host com. Kids Count dinner Stewart B. McKinney House, Washington, 1993—; vol. cons. Doug Castle for U.S. Senate, Washington, 1994. Mem. W.Va. Soc. of Washington (program chairperson bd. govs. 1994-95). Democrat. Greek Orthodox. Home: 1403 Sharps Point Rd Cottage 4 Annapolis MD 21401 Office: Dept Def 1B657 The Pentagon Washington DC 20301

BLAZEK-WHITE, DORIS, lawyer; b. Easton, Md., Nov. 17, 1943; d. George W. and Nola M. (Buterbaugh) Defibaugh; children: Christine T., Judson M.; m. Thacher W. White. BA, Goucher Coll., 1965; JD, Georgetown U., 1968. Bar: D.C. 1969, Virgin Islands 1969, U.S. Ct. Appeals (3d cir.) 1969, U.S. Ct. Appeals (D.C. cir.) 1971, Md. 1979. Gen. practice with Judge Warren H. Young, U.S. Virgin Islands, 1968-70; assoc. Covington & Burling, Washington, 1970-76, ptnr., 1976—. Mem. Am. Coll. Trust and Estate Counsel. Office: Covington & Burling PO Box 7566 1201 Pennsylvania Ave NW Washington DC 20044

BLAZINA, CHRISITNE PALISI, museum manager; b. Bronx, N.Y., Dec. 23, 1938; d. Anthony Mario and Rose (Pontrandolfi) Palisi; m. V. John Blazina, Dec. 3, 1966; children: Jennifer Ann, David Robert. BA in English, Wilmington Coll., 1960; BA in Edn., San Francisco State Coll., 1964; MAT in Mus. Edn., George Washington U., 1991. Tchr. Prince Georges Pub. Schs., Lanham, Md., 1964-66, Garden City (N.Y.) Pub. Schs., 1966-67, Menlo-Atherton Pub Schs., Menlo Park, Calif., 1967-68; mgr. College Park (Md.) Airport Mus., 1991-95; sec. Field of Firsts Bd. Coll. Park Aviation Mus. Polit. officer Montgomery Med. Soc. Aux., 1974-75; bd. dirs. Quilters Hall of Fame; docent Corcoran Gallery Art, Washington, 1980-89; mem. adv. bd. Hyattsville br. OASIS. Mem. Am. Assn. Museums, Mus. Edn. Roundtable.

BLAZINA, JANICE FAY, transfusion medicine physician; b. Youngstown, Ohio, Apr. 20, 1953; d. Joseph and Cordelia Evelyn (Mitchell) B. BS, Youngstown State U., 1975; MD, Ohio State U., 1978. Diplomate Am. Bd. Pathology. Resident in anat. and clin. pathology U. Ala. Med. Ctr., Birmingham, 1978-82; assoc. pathologist various hosps., Bryan, Tex., 1982-83, High Plains Bapt. Hosp., Amarillo, Tex., 1983-84; fellow in blood banking Baylor U. Med. Ctr., Dallas, 1984-85; asst. prof. dept. pathology Ohio State U., Columbus, 1985—, asst. prof. Sch. Allied Med. Professions, 1987—; asst. dir. transfusion svc. Ohio State U. Hosp., 1985-89, assoc. dir., 1989-90, dir., 1990—, med. dir. histocompatibility, paternity, apheresis, and phlebotomy svcs., 1987—, div. med. tech., 1987—; asst. med. dir. Carter Blood Ctr., Ft. Worth, 1993—. Contbr. articles to profl. publs. Grantee: Bremer Found., 1987. Mem. AMA, Am. Soc. Apheresis, Am. Soc. Histocompatibility and Immunogenetics, Am. Assn. Blood Banks (insp. 1987—), Am. Med. Womens Assn., Ohio Assn. Blood Banks (trustee 1990-93, sec. 1992-93), Ohio Acad. Sci., Grad. Women Sci., Assn. Women Sci. Cen. Ohio (v.p. 1989-90, pres. 1990-91). Mem. Church of Christ. Office: Carter Blood Ctr 1263 W Rosedale Fort Worth TX 76104-2899

BLECK, PHYLLIS CLAIRE, surgeon, musician; b. Oak Park, Ill., Mar. 10, 1936; d. William Fred and Mildred A. (Jones) B. BS, U. Ill., 1958; MM, Northwestern U., 1968; DMA, U. So. Calif., 1970; postgrad., Autonoma U., Guadalajara, Mex., 1973-76; MD, Rush Med. Coll., 1979; MS in Surgery, U. Ill., 1983. Diplomate Am. Bd. Surgery, Am. Bd. Thoracic Surgery. Prin. trumpet Fla. Symphony Orch., 1960-66, Orch. Sinfonica Nat. de Peru, 1965; instr. Thornton Jr. Coll., 1966-68; lectr. U. So. Calif., 1969-73; asst. prof. Whittier Coll., 1973; intern Rush Presbyn. St. Luke's Med. Ctr., Chgo., 1979-80, resident, asst. in gen. surgery, 1980-82, instr. gen. surgery, 1982-84; resident in cardiothoracic surgery U. Medicine and Dentistry N.J., 1984-87; pvt. practice medicine specializing in cardiothoracic surgery, Aurora, Ill., 1987—. Editor: Mozart Divertimento for Winds; research on vascular ischemia. Fellow ACS, Am. Coll. Chest Physicians, Ill. Thoracic Surg. Soc., Ill. Surg. Soc.; mem. AAAS, Soc. Thoracic Surgeons, Kappa Delta Pi, Pi Kappa Lambda, Sigma Alpha Iota. Office: 1315 N Highland Ave Aurora IL 60506-1400

BLECK, VIRGINIA ELEANORE, illustrator; b. Waukegan, Ill., Dec. 22, 1929; d. George William and Eugenia (Van Honder) Pavlik; m. Thomas Frank Bleck, June 16, 1951; children: Thomas G., James H., Catherine Bleck-Muschler, Marilynn Bleck-Cobbs, Robert F., Susan M. Bleck-Gibbs, Linda Bleck-Mai, John W., Charles D. U. Ill. Art Inst. Chgo., 1947-50, Student, 1947-50. Free lance artist Waukegan, 1950-86; artist Merrill-Chase Galleries, Chgo., 1972-77, Hallmark Cards Inc., Kansas City, Mo., 1977—; owner, operator Bleck Tree Farms, Waukegan, Green Oaks and Grayslake, Ill., 1972—. Republican. Roman Catholic. Home and Office: 10330 W Yorkhouse Rd Waukegan IL 60087-2402

BLECKER, NAOMI PERLE, credit manager; b. N.Y.C., Mar. 3, 1956; d. Sidney and Zelda (Pologe) B. Student, CUNY, 1973-77. Credit mgr. new accounts Gimbel's Dept. Store, N.Y.C., 1975-78; credit mgr. Eue/Screen Gems div. Columbia Pictures Corp., N.Y.C., 1977-82; credit mgr. Trans Am. Video, Svcs. AME, Inc., N.Y.C., 1982-92; credit mgr. Editel divsn. of Unitel Video, N.Y.C., 1992—. Mem. Nat. Assn. Credit Mgmt. (chmn. motion picture and t.v. group 1982—), Nat. Assn. Female Execs., Am. Jewish Congress. Democrat. Home: Briarwood 14130 Pershing Cres Jamaica NY 11435-1952

BLEIER, CAROL STEIN, writer, researcher; b. N.Y., Jan. 31, 1942; d. Shelley and Ruth (Brown) Stein; m. Michael Bleier, Oct. 9, 1966; children: Thomas, Lisa, Mark. BA in English Lit., Syracuse U., 1963; MLS, U. Pitts, 1986. Pub. info. specialist IRS, Washington, 1964-68; columnist Springfield (Va.) Ind., 1977-78; mktg. cons. Greater Pitts. Mus. Coun., 1986-88; pub. rels. dir. Greater Pitts. Literacy Coun., 1988-89; writer, 1985—. Author: (periodicals) Wilson Libr. Bulletin, 1985, 87, 88; co-author: (corp. history book) The Ketchum Spirit: A History of Ketchum Communications Inc., 1992; contrib. (ency.) Encyclopedia of Library History, 1994. Mem. ALA, Beta Phi Mu. Democrat. Jewish. Home: 214 Lynn Haven Dr Pittsburgh PA 15228

BLEIL, JANICE MARIE, knowledge-transfer technologist; b. Lansing, Mich., May 27, 1947; d. Carl Edward and Vera Marie Bleil; m. James Warren Corcoran, Apr. 1, 1972. BA, Mich. State U., 1969; MA, Stanford U., 1976, PhD, 1980. V.p., CEO User Tng. Corp., Los Gatos, Calif., 1980-86; pres. User Tng. & Svcs. Group, Palo Alto, Calif., 1986-90; pres., CEO Qtrain Corp., Palo Alto, 1991—; also bd. dirs. Missaticum, Inc., Palo Alto. Office: Qtrain Corp 125 University Ave Ste 145 Palo Alto CA 94301-1630

BLESCH, KATHY SUZANN, small business owner; b. Evansville, Ind., Dec. 14, 1951; d. Robert Lee McBride and E. Jean (Oliver) Schumacher; m. Larry J. Blesch, Aug. 17, 1974; children: Nicholas R., Spencer A., Clayton W. Grad. Grad. Realtors Inst., Ind. U., 1979; cert. residential specialist, Nat. Assn. Realtors, 1980. Waitress, hostess Skyway & Pete's, Evansville, Ind., 1971-73; operator, asst. mgr. Stecklers T.A.S., Evansville, 1969-71; salesperson, broker Midwest Realty, Evansville, 1973-78; broker, owner Blesch Realty, Evansville, 1978-80; broker, salesperson Brand Realty, Evansville, 1980-83; owner, operator Nick Nackery Pl., Evansville, 1985—. Bd. dirs. Hope of Evansville, 1976-79. Mem. Nat. Costumers Assn. Home and Office: 201 E Virginia St Evansville IN 47711-5529

BLESSEN, KAREN ALYCE, free-lance illustrator, designer; b. Columbus, Nebr.. BFA, U. Nebr., 1973. Freelance illustrator, 1973-86; designer Dallas Morning News, 1986-89, freelance illustrator, designer, 1989—; owner, illustrator Karen Blessen Illustration, Dallas, 1989—. Rep. Tex. in Absolut Statehood series, Absolut; illustrator: Be An Angel, 1994. Recipient Pulitzer prize for explanatory journalism, 1989; awards from N.Y. Art Dirs. Club, Soc. Newspaper Design, Dallas Press Club; commd. by Absolut to represnet Tex. in Absolut Statehood series. Office: Karen Blessen Illustration 6327 Vickery Blvd Dallas TX 75214-3348

BLESSING, CAROLE ANNE, human resources manager; b. Phila., Nov. 27, 1945; d. Walter Francis and Margaret Jane (Hindman) Thompson; m. Robert Bochenko, Nov. 22, 1980 (div. May 1983); m. William Blessing, May 26, 1991. BA, Temple U., Phila., 1978. Cert. occupational health and safety, Temple U., Villanova U. asst. safety supr. Phila. Coke Co. Inc., Phila., 1969-71, safety supr., 1971-73, dir. personnel and safety, 1973-78; div. mgr. safety and security Kelsey Hayes Co., Phila., 1978-86, mgr. human resource, Heintz Corp., 1986-91; mgr. employee rels. Jefferson Smurfit-CCA, Phila., 1991—; exec. v.p., dir. Powell Envirn., Inc., 1988—; pres., chmn. Data Research, Inc., Phila., 1983—; dir. Affiliated Med., Phila., 1983—; lectr. Drexel U., 1983-84; cons in field Contbr. articles to profl. jours. Chmn. first aid and safety programs ARC, Phila., 1974-76. Recipient safety achievement awards Phila. Safety Council. Mem. AAUW, NAFE, Am. Soc. Safety Engrs. (treas. Phila. chpt. 1978-79, 80), Nat. Safety Mgmt. Soc., Am. Soc. Personnel Adminstrs., Nat. Fire Protection Assn., Ind. Relations Assn. Phila., Am. Mgmt. Assn. Republican. Home: 1 Maple Dr White Marsh PA 19428

BLETHEN, NANCY E., public relations executive; b. Schenectady, N.Y., Nov. 11, 1940. BA, Tufts U.; MEd, Rutgers U. Legis. aide N.J. Assembly, 1976-79; sr. account exec. Coleman, 1980-85; v.p. Coleman & Pellet, 1985-89; pres. The Blethen Group, 1989-92; founder, pres. Blethen & Youdovin, Inc., Montclair, N.J., 1992—. Mem. Pub. Rels. Soc. Am. (mem. counselors acad.). Office: Blethen & Youdovin Inc 144 Summit Ave Montclair NJ 07043*

BLETHEN, SANDRA LEE, pediatric endocrinologist; b. San Mateo, Calif., May 16, 1942; d. Howard Albion and Laura Katherine (Wolf) B.; m. Fred I. Chasalow, Nov. 26, 1966. SB in Biochemistry, U. Chgo., 1961; PhD in Biochemistry, U. Calif., Berkeley, 1965; MD, Yeshiva U., 1975. Diplomate Am. Bd. Pediatrics. Fellow biochemistry Brandeis U., Waltham, Mass., 1965-68; instr. biochemistry U. Calif., San Diego, 1968-69; asst. prof. San Francisco State U., 1969-71; resident in pediatrics Columbia Presbyn. Med. Ctr., N.Y.C., 1975-77; fellow pediatric endocrinology U. N.C., Chapel Hill, 1977-79; asst. prof. pediatrics Washington U., St. Louis, 1979-84; assoc. prof. pediatrics SUNY, Stony Brook, 1985—; assoc. attending pediatrician L.I. Jewish Med. Ctr., New Hyde Park, N.Y., 1984-90; attending pediatrician Univ. Hosp., Stony Brook, 1991—; cons. Genentech, Inc., South San Francisco, Calif., 1985—, Diagnostic Systems Labs., Webster, Tex., 1989—. Mem. editorial bd. Steroids, 1990—; contbr. 61 articles to profl. jours. Predoctoral fellow NSF, 1961-63, Postdoctoral fellow USPHS, 1965-67. Mem. Am. Pediatric Soc. (program com. 1994), Endocrine Soc., Lawson Wilkens Pediatric Endocrine Soc. (membership chair 1994—), Soc. for Pediatric Rsch., Phi Beta Kappa, Alpha Omega Alpha. Office: SUNY Stony Brook Dept Pediatrics Stony Brook NY 11794-8111

BLEVINS, BARBARA JEAN, social services executive director; b. Canton, Ohio, Oct. 18, 1949; d. Paul R. Eilhousen and Mary Evelyn (Paterson) Harold; m. Robert Maurice Eisenbrei, Sept. 4, 1971 (div. Oct. 3, 1992); children: Matthew Eliot, Jonathan Edward; m. Jeffery Dean Blevins, Nov. 21, 1993. BASW, Kent State U., 1971; MA, Walsh Coll., 1988. Chem. dependency therapist Massillon (Ohio) Community Hosp., 1987; therapist, exec. dir. Domestic Violence Project, Inc., Canton, 1988—; presenter in field. Com. mem. ADAPT, Canton, 1993; adv. bd. jobs com. Quest, Canton, 1993; mem. United Way Execs., 1992; mem. Community Corrections Bd., Stark County, 1993, Stark County Domestic Violence Task Force, 1993. Mem. Chi Sigma Iota (exec. bd. 1989-91, 94—). Presbyterian. Home: 5305 Schuller Dr NE Canton OH 44705 Office: Domestic Violence Project PO Box 9432 Canton OH 44711-9432

BLEVINS, DONNA CATON, writer; b. Naha City, Okinawa, Japan, Jan. 13, 1965; came to U.S., 1967; d. Donald Herbert Jr. and Setsuko (Ukuda) Caton; m. Gary Lee Blevins, Feb. 29, 1992. BA in English, Ga. State U., 1991. Prin. dancer Ruth Mitchell Dance Co., Atlanta, 1976-83; paper distbr. U.S. A. Today newspaper, Roswell, Ga., 1983-84, Atlanta Jour./Constitution, 1986-88; optical technician Dr. John W. Hollier, O.D., Roswell, 1983-85; aerobics instr. Am. Fitness Ctr., 1984-86; waitress Kobe Steaks, Atlanta, 1988; air import specialist Nippon Express U.S.A., Inc., Atlanta, 1988-92; writer's asst., editor Laurie Lee Dovey, Alpharetta, Ga., 1992-93; freelance writer, photographer Roswell and Plano, Tex., 1993—; cons., Atlanta, 1993—. Contbr. articles to mags. and newspapers. Pell grantee, 1984-85. Mem. Nat. Orgn. Outdoor Women, Dog Writers Assn. Am., Cat Writers Assn.

BLEVINS, KERRIANNE M., educational administrator, association executive; b. Mpls., Aug. 18, 1963; d. Robert L. and Virginia N. Blevins; m. Michael J. Walstrom, Apr. 22, 1989. BA, U. Minn., 1987. Bus. mgr. Ctr. Sch. Inc., Mpls., 1989-92, program dir., 1993—; exec. dir. Minn. Women Lawyer, Mpls., 1992-93; adv. U. Minn., Mpls., 1986—. Editor Community Newspaper, 1993—. Nat. bd. mem. YWCA of U.S.A., N.Y.C., 1988—; del. Minn. Dem. Farmer Labor Com., Mpls., 1991—; mem. steering com. Neighborhood Revitalization Program.

BLEVINS, PATRICIA M., state legislator. Mem. Del. State Sen. Office: 209 Linden Ave Wilmington DE 19805-2515 Office: Del State Senate State Capital Bldg Dover DE 19901*

BLEY, CARLA BORG, jazz composer; b. Oakland, Calif., May 11, 1938; d. Emil Carl and Arlene (Anderson) Borg; m. Paul Bley, Jan. 27, 1959 (div. Sept. 1967); m. Michael Mantler, Sept. 29, 1967 (div. 1992); 1 dau., Karen. Student public schs., Oakland. mem. adv. bd. Jazz Composers Orch. Assn. Freelance jazz composer, 1956—, pianist, Jazz Composers Orch., N.Y.C., 1964—, European concert tours, Jazz Realities, 1965-66; founder, WATT, 1973—, toured Europe with Jack Bruce Band, 1975; leader, Carla Bley Band, touring, U.S. and Europe, 1977—; composed, recorded: A Genuine Tong Funeral, 1967, (with Charlie Haden) Liberation Music Orch., 1969; opera Escalator Over the Hill, 1970-71 (Oscar du Disque de Jazz 1973), Tropic Appetites, 1973; composed: chamber orch. 3/4, 1974-75; film score Mortelle Randonnée, 1983; recorded: Dinner Music, 1976, The Carla Bley Band: European Tour, 1977, Musique Mecanique, 1979, (with Nick Mason) Fictitious Sports, 1980, Social Studies, 1980, Carla Bley Live!, 1981, Heavy Heart, 1984, I Hate to Sing, 1985, Night Glo, 1985, Sextet, 1987, Duets, 1988, Fleur Carnivore, 1989, The Very Big Carla Bley Band, 1991, Go Together, 1993, Big Band Theory, 1993, Songs With Legs, 1995. Named winner internat. jazz critics poll Down Beat mag., 1966, 71, 72, 78, 79, 80, 83, 84; Best Composer of Yr., Down Beat Readers' Poll, 1984, composer/arranger of yr., 1985-92; Guggenheim fellow, 1972; Cultural Coun. Found. grantee, 1971, 79; Nat. Endowment for the Arts grantee, 1973; named Best in Field Jazz Times critics poll, 1990, Best Arranger, Downbeat Critics Poll, 1993, 94; recipient Prix Jazz Moderne from Academie du Jazz for The Very Big Carla Bley Band album, 1992. Office: care Ted Kurland Assocs 173 Brighton Ave Allston MA 02134-2003

BLIEBERG, HELENE ANDREA, communications executive; b. N.Y.C., Aug. 13, 1955; d. Seymour and Esther (Kaplan) B. BA in Broadcast Mktg., English, SUNY, Buffalo, 1977; postgrad., Polytechnic of Cen. London, 1977. Account exec. The Softness Group, Inc., N.Y.C., 1977-78; dir. pub. relations The Grossinger (N.Y.) Hotel, 1978-79, mgr. sales, 1979-80, dir. mktg., 1980-82; mgr. press. info. CBS Radio Networks, N.Y.C., 1982-83; mgr. sales devel. and promotion CBS Nat. Sales, N.Y.C., 1983-84; dir. media rels. CBS Radio div. CBS Inc., N.Y.C., 1984-89, dir. communications, 1989-94, v.p. communications, 1994—. Mem. Internat. Radio and TV Soc., Internat. Assn. Bus. Communicators, Pub. Relations Soc. of America, Promotion and Mktg. Execs. in the Elec. Media (mem. bd. dirs.). Office: CBS Inc 51 W 52nd St New York NY 10019-6119

BLINDER, JANET, art dealer; b. L.A., Sept. 21, 1953; d. Joseph and Margaret (Nadel) Weiss; m. Martin S. Blinder, Dec. 10, 1983. Founder Nationwide Baby Shops, Santa Monica, Calif., 1976-82; adminstr. Martin Lawrence Ltd. Editions, Van Nuys, Calif., 1982-90; art dealer L.A., 1990—. Mem. benefit com. AIDS Project L.A., 1988, prin. sponsor ann. fundraiser, 1990; mem. benefit com. Art Against AIDS, L.A., 1989; patron, sponsor Maryvale Orphanage, Rosemead, Calif., 1984—. Recipient Commendation for Philanthropic Efforts City of L.A. Mayor Tom Bradley, 1988. Mem. Mus. Modern Art, Whitney Mus. Am. Art, Guggenheim Mus., Palm Springs Mus. Art, Mus. of Contemporary Art (founder).

BLINSTRUBAS, SANDRA JOYCE, satellite communications company executive; b. Waterbury, Conn., Feb. 28, 1957; d. Edmund John and Joyce (Knapp) B.; m. Charles Kenneth Schumann III, Aug. 26, 1989; 1 child, Alexander Charles. BS, U. Conn., 1979; MF, Yale U., 1982. Environ. analyst State of Conn., Hartford, 1982-84; project mgr. Wolfe & Assocs., Anchorage, 1984-86; pres. Sateo Inc., Anchorage, 1987—; fin. mgr. AmRusscom, Anchorage, 1992—; bd. dirs. Pacific Rim Telecom., Anchorage, Asian Am. Telecom, Anchorage, Farcom Inc., Anchorage, Washington Fitness Corp., Seattle. Home: PO Box 93250 Anchorage AK 99509 Office: Sateo Inc 1153 E 72d Ave Anchorage AK 99518

BLISS, JOY V., writer; b. Grand Forks, N.D., July 7, 1942; d. Harald Nesset and Edna Adeline (Ellingson) B.; m. Gay Leon Dybwad, Feb. 14, 1990. BS, Jamestown Coll., 1963; BS in Medicine, U. N.D., 1965; MD, U. Nebr., Omaha, 1968; JD, U. Mo., Kansas City, 1989. Bar: Mo. 1989; diplomate Am. Bd. Anesthesiologists. Pvt. practice Kansas City and Excelsior Springs, Mo., 1968-73; resident in anesthesiology Kans. U. Med. Ctr., Kansas City, 1973-75; anesthesiologist Olathe (Kans.) Med. Ctr., 1975-86; freelance author Albuquerque, 1990—; chmn. bylaws com. Olathe Cmty. Hosp., 1980-86. Co-author: Annotated Bibliography: World's Columbian Exposition, Chicago 1893, 1992. Vol. Hospice/Home Health Care, Albuquerque, 1991—, Rio Grande Nature Ctr., Albuquerque, 1993—; active United Meth. Women, 1992—. Recipient Yearning for Learning award Jamestown Coll., 1994. Mem. PEO.

BLISS, NONIE JANET, librarian; b. Royal Oak, Mich., Dec. 26, 1955; d. Robert Russell and Janet Lenore (MacLeod) B. BS in Social Scis., Ctrl. Mich. U., 1979; MLS, N.C. Ctrl. U., 1988; PhD in Libr. Sci., Tex. Woman's U., 1991. Rsch. libr. N.C. Ctrl. U., Durham, 1988-89; asst. libr. Sch. Libr. and Info. Sci., Tex. Woman's U., Denton, 1990-91; info. systems libr. Shotwell & Carr, Inc., Dallas, 1991-92; cons., electronic pub. editor Silver Platter Info., Dallas, 1993-94; dir. Children's/Adolescents AIDS Mastery Northern Lights Alternatives, Dallas, 1994—; bd. dirs. Northern Lights Alternatives, Dallas. Abstract editor: Play, Learn and Grow, 1992; contbr. articles to profl. jours. Bd. dirs. Nexus, Dallas, 1994—; vol. Dallas Sch. Librs., 1992—, Nat. Child's Rights Assn., Dallas, 1989—, Literacy Program, Tex., 1991—; civic vol. Wake County Women's Prison, N.C., 1989, Denton County Jail, 1990-91. Mem. ALA, NOW, Am. Soc. Info. Sci., Soc. Tech. Comm., Spl. Libr. Assn., Assn. Libr. and Info. Sci. Educators, Beta Phi Mu. Office: Northern Lights Alternatives PO Box 59685 Dallas TX 75229

BLISSITT, PATRICIA ANN, nurse; b. Knoxville, Tenn., Sept. 23, 1953; d. Dewitt Talmadge and Imogene (Bailey) B. BSN with high honors, U. Tenn., 1976, MSN, 1985. RN; cert. neurosci. nurse; cert. in case mgmt.; cert. critical care nursing. Staff nurse neurosci. unit City of Memphis Hosp., 1976-78, head nurse neurosci. unit, 1978-79; physician's asst. Dr. John D. Wilson, Columbus, Miss., 1979-81; staff nurse med.-surg.-trauma intensive care unit U. Tenn. Meml. Hosp., Knoxville, 1982-83; staff nurse neurosci. intensive care unit Bapt. Meml. Hosp., Memphis, 1985-86, clin. nurse specialist neurosci., 1986-94, trauma coord., 1991-93, neuro case mgr., 1993-94; staff nurse neurosurgical ICU Harborview Med. Ctr., Seattle, 1994—; nurse cons. neurosci. VA Hosp., Memphis, 1986; mem. adv. com. Tenn. Bd. Nursing Practice. Author: (with others) Critical Care Nursing in Clinics of North America, 1990, Jour. Neurosci. Nursing, 1986, 92; contbr. articles to sci. jour.; mem. editl. cons. bd. Focus on Critical Care, 1990-92. Mem. ANA (coun. med.-surg. nurses, coun. clin. nurse specialist), Am. Assn. Neurosci. Nurses (cert. neuroscience nurse, pres. local chpt. 1989-90, treas. local chpt. 1987-89, nat. lectr., resource devel. com., continuing edn./ann. scientific program com., program/seminar chair local chpt. 1990-93, nurse practice com., chair patient edn. project 1991-92, program/seminar com., program/seminar chair mid-South chpt. 1990-93, chair nat. resource devel. com. 1992-94), Am. Assn. Spinal Cord Injury Nurses, AACN (life, cert. critical care nurse, lectr., CCRN corp. exem. devel. com. 1989-92, NTI speaker 1992, editorial cons. bd. 1990-92, pres.-elect greater Memphis area chpt. 1989-90, pres. 1990-91, immediate past pres., chair nat. critical care awareness week 1990-93, Greater Memphis Area chpt. life mem., 1993—, chpt. cons. region II 1991-93, chpt of yr. com. chair 1992-94), Tenn. Nurses Assn. (com. on practice 1992-93), Tenn. Nursing Congress (pres. 1990-94).

Methodist. Avocation: music. Home: The Decatur Apts # 405 1105 Spring St Seattle WA 98104

BLITT, RITA LEA, artist; b. Kansas City, Mo., Sept. 7, 1931; d. Herman Stanley and Dorothy Edith (Sofnas) Copaken; m. Irwin Joseph Blitt, Apr. 18, 1951; 1 child, Chela Connie. Student, U. Ill., 1948-50; BA, Kansas City U., 1952; postgrad., Kansas City Art Inst., 1952-54. Freelance painter, sculptor Leawood, Kans., 1958—. One-woman exhbns. include Unitarian Gallery, Kansas City, Mo., 1965, Spectrum Gallery, N.Y.C., 1969, Angerer Gallery, Kansas City, Mo., 1974, Battle Creek (Mich.) Civic Art Ctr., 1975, Harkness Gallery, N.Y.C., 1977, Martin Schweig Gallery, St. Louis, 1977, Gargoyle Gallery, Aspen, Colo., 1978, Tumbling Waters Mus., Montgomery, Ala., 1978, St. Louis U., 1980, Leedy-Voulkos Gallery, Kansas City, Mo., 1987, Joy Horwich Gallery, Chgo., 1987, Goldman Gallery, Haifa, Israel, 1989, Bet Shmuel, Jerusalem, 1989, Goldman Kraft Gallery, Chgo., 1990, Singapore Nat. Mus., 1991, Albrecht-Kemper Mus., St. Joseph, Mo., 1991, Aspen (Colo.) Inst., 1992, Mackey Gallery, Denver, 1992, U. Ill., Urbana, 1994, Kennedy Mus.-U. Ohio, Athens, 1994; group exhbns. include Kansas City (Mo.) Mus., 1959, Ringling Mus., Sarasota, Fla., 1967, Springfield (Mo.) Mus., 1967, Joslyn Mus., Omaha, 1972, Doug Drake Gallery, Kansas City, 1975, Conry Gallery, Kansas City, Mo., 1976, Cyvia Gallery, New Haven, 1977, Gargoyle Gallery, Aspen, Colo., 1979, Putney Gallery, Aspen, 1979, Carrefour Gallery, N.Y.C., 1979, Elaine Benson Gallery, Bridgehampton, N.Y., 1980, Tall Grass Fine Arts Gallery, Kansas City, Mo., 1980, 81, Art and Design Gallery, N.Y.C., 1982, Winter Manhattan (Kans.), Streker, Gallery, 1983, Joanne Lyons Gallery, Aspen, 1984, Banaker Gallery, San Francisco, 1987, 88, Andrea Ross Gallery, Santa Monica, Calif., 1990, LA 90, L.A., 1990, Eva Cohon, Chgo., 1995, Kennedy Mus., Athens, Ohio, 1995, many others; permanent collections include Albrecht-Kemper Mus., St. Joseph, Mo., JFK Libr., Cambridge, Mass., Kennedy Mus., Nat. Mus. Singapore, Skirball Mus., L.A., Spertus Mus., Chgo., Kansas City (Mo.) Children's Mus., and other numerous pvt. and pub. collections; sculptures in numerous pub. places. Mem. Soc. Fellow The Nelson Gallery Found., The Aspen Inst.; bd. dirs. Trio Found.; mem. The Stop Violence Coalition. Mem. Internat. Sculpture Ctr., Kansas City Artists Coalition. Office: 8900 State Line #333 Leawood KS 66206

BLITZ, PEGGY SANDERFUR, corporate travel management company official; b. Pitts., Apr. 12, 1940; d. Charles I. and Rebecca Polk (McBride) Wallace; m. Clark L. Blitz, Aug. 25, 1962 (div. Apr. 1974); children: Danette L., Jonathan D. BS, Ball State U., 1962; postgrad., No. Ill. U., 1976-77. Cert. speech therapist, spl. edn. tchr. Tchr. mentally retarded Anderson (Ind.) Pub. Schs., 1962-64; speech therapist Elgin (Ill.) Pub. Schs., 1964-66; pvt. practice speech therapy Elgin, 1966-68; tchr. mentally retarded Easter Seal Rehab. Ctr., Elgin, 1968-77; account exec. Whitehall Hotel, Chgo., 1977-79; regional mgr. IVI Travel Inc., Milw., 1979-85; sr. v.p. IVI Travel Inc., Dallas, 1985-88; pres. Travelmasters, Inc., Chgo., 1988-91; staff devel. Kemper Securities, Inc., Chgo., 1991-92; pres. Travel Mgmt. Cons., St. John, V.I., 1991—; property mgr. Short-Term Vacation Rentals, 1992—. Presbyterian. Home and Office: PO Box 8333 Cruz Bay VI 00831

BLITZ-WEISZ, SALLY, speech pathologist; b. Buffalo, Nov. 9, 1954; d. Isaac and Paula (Goldstein) Blitz; m. Andrew Weisz, Dec. 16, 1984; 1 child, Naomi Ariel Weisz. BA in Speech Pathology, Audiology, SUNY, Buffalo, 1976, MA in Speech Pathology, 1978; MS Sch Counseling, pupil pers credential, U. LaVerne, 1991. Lic. speech/lang. pathologist, Calif. Speech, lang. pathologist Lang. Devel. Program, Tonawanda, N.Y., 1978-82, Bailey and Drown Assocs., La Habra, Calif., 1982-83; speech, lang. specialist, cons. Pasadena (Calif.) Unified Schs., 1983—. Active Anti-Defamation League, San Fernando Valley, 1985-86; mem. 2d Generation Holocaust Survivors, Los Angeles, 1986—. Recipient Excellence in Studies award Temple Shaarey Zedek, Buffalo, 1968. Mem. Am. Speech-Lang.-Hearing Assn. Democrat. Club: Jewish Young Adults. Lodge: B'nai Brith. Home: 11671 Amigo Ave Northridge CA 91326-1849 Office: Pasadena Unified Sch Dist 351 S Hudson Ave Pasadena CA 91101-3599

BLIZNAKOV, MILKA TCHERNEVA, architect; b. Varna, Bulgaria, Sept. 20, 1927; came to U.S., 1961, naturalized, 1966; d. Ivan Dimitrov and Maria Kesarova (Khorozova) Tchernev; m. Emile G. Bliznakov, Oct. 23, 1954 (div. Apr., 1974). Architect-engr. diploma, State Tech. U., Sofia, 1951; Ph.D., Engring.-Structural Inst., Sofia, 1959; Ph.D. in Architecture, Columbia U., 1971. Sr. researcher Ministry Heavy Industry, Sofia, 1950-53; pvt. practice architecture Sofia, 1954-59; assoc. architect Noel Combrisson, Paris, 1959-61; designer Perkins & Will Partnership, White Plains, N.Y., 1963-67; project architect Lathrop Douglass, N.Y.C., 1967-71; assoc. prof. architecture and planning Sch. Architecture, U. Tex., Austin, 1972-74; prof. Coll. Architecture, Va. Poly. Inst. and State U., Blacksburg, 1974—; prin. Blacksburg, 1975—; bd. dirs. founder Internat. Archives Women in Architecture, Va. Poly. Inst. and State U. The Parthena award, 1994. Prin. works include Speedwell Ave. Urban Renewal, Morristown, N.J., 1967-69, Wilmington (Del.) Urban Renewal, 1968-70, Springfield (Ill.) Ctrl. Area Devel., 1969-71, Arlington County (Va.) Redevel., 1975-77, New Perspectives on Russian and Soviet Artistic Culture, 1994; author: (with others) Utopia e Modernitá, 1989, Reshaping Russian Architecture, 1990, Russian Housing in the Modern Age, 1993, Nietzsche and Soviet Culture, 1994. William Kinne scholar, summer 1970, vis. scholar Inst. Advanced Russian Studies, The Wilson Ctr. of Smithsonian Instn., 1988; NEA grantee, 1973-74, Am. Beautiful Found. grantee, 1973, Internat. Rsch. and Exch. Bd. grantee, 1984-93; Fulbright Hays rsch. fellow, 1983-84, 91; recipient Parthend award, 1994. Mem. Internat. Archive Women in Architecture (founder, chair bd. dirs.), Am. Assn. Tchrs. Slavic and East European Langs., Soc. Archtl. Historians, Nat. Trust Hist. Preservation, Am. Assn. Advancement of Slavic Studies, Assn. Collegiate Schs. of Planning, Inst. Modern Russian Culture (chairperson architecture, co-founder, dir.), Assn. Collegiate Schs. of Architecture. Home: 2813 Tall Oaks Dr Blacksburg VA 24060-8109 Office: Coll Architecture Va Poly Inst And State Blacksburg VA 24061

BLIZZARD, LINDA KAY, software engineer; b. Anthony, Kans., Sept. 21, 1946; d. Roger Milton and Meribe Jane (Fawkes) B. BA, U. Okla., 1968; MA, U. Chgo., 1970; women in sci. cert., U. Tex., 1981. Program specialist Tex. Dept. Human Svcs., Austin, 1970-81; software design engr. Texas Instruments, Lewisville, Tex., 1982-84; sr. software engr. UTL Corp., Dallas, 1984-85; software engr. Sci. Comms., Garland, Tex., 1985-88; software engr. III DSC Comms., Plano, Tex., 1988-91; sr. software engr. E-Sys., Inc., Garland, 1991—. Founder, mem. Dallas (Tex.) Women Against Rape, 1973-75, pres., 1975-76. Mem. Zeta Tau Alpha. Democrat. Roman Catholic. Home: 2820 Creekwood Dr North Grapevine TX 76051 Office: Emass E-Systems 1200 S Jupiter Rd Garland TX 75042

BLOCH, ANDREA LYNN, physical therapist; b. Cleve., Nov. 25, 1952; d. Sanford and Nadalane Lee (Benchell) B. BA in Zoology, Miami U., Oxford, Ohio, 1974; MA in Allied Health Scis., Kent State U., 1975; Cert. in Phys. Therapy, Ohio State U., 1977. Lic. phys. therapist, Ohio; bd. cert. orthopedic clin. specialist. Asst. dir. phys. therapy The Mt. Sinai Med. Ctr., Cleve., 1977-86; dir. rehab. therapy svcs. Marymount Hosp., Garfield Heights, Ohio, 1986-88; pres., owner Bloch Phys. Therapy, Inc., University Heights, Ohio, 1988—; speaker Arthritis Found., speaker in field. Editor newsletter Cleve. Phys. Therapy Orthopedic Study Group, 1989-91; contbr. articles to profl. jours. Chmn. essay-poster contest University Heights Meml. Day Parade, 1985-91; mem. coun.-at-large City of University Heights. Mem. NAFE, AAHPERD, Am. Phys. Therapy Assn. (pvt. practice sect., orthopedic sect., reimbursement chmn. N.E. dist. Ohio 1992—), Am. Back Soc., Am. Soc. Profl. and Exec. Women, Ohio Phys. Therapy (bd. dirs. 1994—), Delta Zeta Cleve. Eastside Alumnae (program chmn. 1985-87, ways and means 1987-88, v.p. 1988-90, pres. 1990-92), Delta Zeta (province alumnae dir. V-N 1991-94, DZ Oustanding Province V Alumna award 1992), Eta Sigma Gamma. Office: 2195 Warrensville Center Rd Univ Hts OH 44118-3155

BLOCH, BARBARA JOYCE, writer, editor; b. N.Y.C., May 26, 1925; d. Emil William and Dorothy (Lowengrund) B.; m. Joseph B. Sanders, Aug. 3, 1944 (div. 1961); children: Elizabeth Sanders, Ellen Janice Benjamin; m. Theodore S. Benjamin, Sept. 20, 1964. Student, NYU, 1943-45, New Sch. Social Rsch., 1966. Office mgr. Writers War Bd., N.Y.C., 1943-45, Westchester Dem. Com., White Plains, N.Y., 1955-56; mgr. Westchester Symphony Orch., 1957-62; mng. editor Cooking Ency., Rutledge Books, N.Y.C., 1970-71; pres. Internat. Cookbook Services, White Plains, 1978—; columnist House Beautiful, 1984-87; cookbook editor Benjamin Co., 1990—; cons. in field; tchr. cooking classes White Plains, 1975-80; lectr. in field. Author: Anyone Can Quilt, 1975; Meat Board Meat Book, 1977; If It Doesn't Pan Out, 1981; Garnishing Made Easy, 1983, Microwave Party Cooking, 1988, A Little Jewish Cookbook, 1989, A Little New England Cookbook, 1990, A Little Southern Cookbook, 1990, A Little New York Cookbook, 1990; editor/author: All Beef Cookbook, 1973; In Glass Naturally, 1974; Fresh Ideas with Mushrooms, 1977; Holly Farms Complete Chicken Cookbook, 1984; Gulden's Cookbook, 1985, A Centennial Celebration of Recipes from Solo, 1988, Salute to the Great American Chefs, 1988, TCBY and More, 1989, GoldStar Micro-Convection Cookbook, 1991, Healthy Cooking with Amway Queen Cookware, 1993, McCormich/Schilling's New Spice Cookbook, 1994; Am. adapter The Cuisine of Olympe, 1983, Baking Easy and Elegant, 1984, series of 3 English cookbook mags., 1984-87, Best of Cold Foods, 1985, Cakes and Pastries, 1985, series of 12 Creative Cuisine books, 1985, The Art of Cooking, 1986, The Art of Baking, 1987, Perfect Pasta, 1992, Rocky Food, 1994; editor contbr. various books; contbr. articles to profl. jours. Nat. bd. dirs. Emcampment for Citizenship, N.Y.C., 1966-72; bd. dirs. YWCA Central Westchester, 1965-71, Westchester Ethical Humanist Soc., 1968—; exec. com., pres. Internat. Student Exchange of White Plains, 1955-70; bd. dirs. Westchester Chamber Music Soc., 1986—. Jewish. Home and Office: Internat Cookbook Svcs 21 Dupont Ave White Plains NY 10605-3537

BLOCH, JULIA CHANG, bank executive, former government official; b. Chefoo, Peoples Republic of China, Mar. 2, 1942; came to U.S., 1951, naturalized, 1962; d. Fu-yun and Eva (Yeh) Chang; m. Stuart Marshall Bloch, Dec. 21, 1968. BA, U. Calif., Berkeley, 1964; MA, Harvard U., 1967, postgrad. in mgmt., 1987; DHL (hon.), Northeastern U., Boston, 1986. Vol. Peace Corps, Sabah, Malaysia, 1964-66, tng. officer East Asia and Pacific region, Washington, 1967-68, evaluation officer, 1968-70; mem. minority staff U.S. Senate Select Com. on Nutrition and Human Needs, Washington, 1971-76, chief minority counsel, 1976-77; dep. dir. Office of African Affairs, U.S. Internat. Communications Agy., Washington, 1977-80; fellow Inst. Politics, Harvard U., Cambridge, Mass., 1980-81; asst. adminstr. Bur. for Food for Peace and Voluntary Assistance, AID, Washington, 1981-87, asst. administr. Bur. for Asia and Near East, 1987-88; assoc. U.S.-Japan Rels. Program, Ctr. for Internat. Affairs, Harvard U., Cambridge, Mass., 1988-89; ambassador to Kingdom of Nepal, 1989-93; group exec., v.p. Bank Am., San Francisco, 1993—; dir. Am. West Airlines, 1994—; U.S. Senate rep. World Conf. on Internat. Women's Yr., Mex., 1975; advisor U.S. Del. to Food and Agr. Orgn. Conf., Rome, 1975; rep. Am. Council Young Polit. Leaders, Peoples Republic China, 1977; charter mem. Sr. Exec. Service, 1979; head U.S. del. Biennial Session World Food Programme, Rome, 1981-86, Devel. Assistance Com. Meeting on Non-Govtl. Orgns., Paris, 1985, Intergovtl. Group on Indonesia, The Hague, The Netherlands, 1987, World Bank Consultative Group Meeting, Paris, 1987, mem. exec. women in govt., 1988-93, mem. coun. fgn. rels., 1991—; mem. com. to visit art mus. Harvard U., 1989—; mem. U.S. Nat. Com. for Pacific Econ. Cooperation, 1984—; mem. adv. bd. Women's Campaign Fund, 1976-78, trustee, bus. leadership circle, 1994—; exec. bd. mem. Internat. Ctr. for Research on Women, 1974-81; mem. presdl. adv. coun. Peace Corps, 1988-89; mem. Am. Himalayan Found. Bd., 1994, Am. Refugee Com. Bd., 1993—. Author: A U.S.-Japan Aid Alliance, 1991; co-author: Chinese Home Cooking, 1986; mem. Nat. Presdl. Debate Forum, 1987-92; mem. nat. adv. council Experiment in Internat. Living, 1981-83; commr. Asian Art Mus., San Francisco, 1994. Recipient Hubert Humphrey award for internat. service, 1979, Humanitarian Service award AID, 1987, Leader for Peace award Peace Corps, 1987, Asian Am. Leadership award, 1989; named Outstanding Woman of Color, Nat. Inst. for Women of Color, 1982, Woman of Distinction, Nat. Conf. for Coll. Women Student Leaders and Women of Achievement, 1987, Woman of Yr. Orgn. Chinese Am. Women, 1987, Disting. Pub. Svc. award Nat. Assn. Profl. Asian Pacific Am. Women, 1989; Ford Found. Study fellow for internat. devel. Harvard U., 1966, Paul Harris award Rotary, 1992, Award of Honor Narcotic Enforcement Assn., 1992. Mem. Orgn. Chinese Am. Women (founder, chair 1977—, bd. dirs., Woman of Yr. 1987), Asia Soc. (pres. coun. 1989, trustee 1994), Prytannean Honor Soc., Coun. Fgn. Rels., Mortar Bd. Republican. Avocations: ceramics, gourmet cooking, collecting art. Office: Bank Am Corp Rels 8139 555 California St Ste 4730 San Francisco CA 94104-1712

BLOCK, FRANCINE ELLEN, educational consultant; b. Barre, Vt., Apr. 10, 1947; d. Joseph and Anna (Moisoff) Rome; m. Alan Joseph Block, July 27, 1969; children: Justin Andrew, Darren Stuart. BS, U. Vt., 1969, MAT, 1972. Tchr. Burlington High (Vt.) Sch., 1969-72; dir. career and coll. resource ctr. Westborough (Mass.) High Sch., 1979-84; ednl. cons., chief exec. officer Am. Coll. Admissions Cons., Richboro, Pa., 1984—; alumni admissions rep. U. Vt., Burlington, 1978—; co-founder No-Name Conf., FRanklin and Marshall Coll., 1992—. Regional officer Assn. Jr. League Internat, N.Y.C., 1987-88; bd. dirs., officer Jr. League, Worcester, Mass., 1980-86, Princeton, N.J., 1989-90; chmn. allocations United Way Bucks County, 1990—; co-chmn. Bucks County Women's History Week Award, 1990—. Mem. AAUW (bd. dirs. 1989—), Am. Coll. Counseling Assn., Am. Sch. Counselors Assn., Am. Bus. Women's Assn., Nat. Assn. Coll. Admissions Counselors, Nat. Assn. Fgn. Student Affairs, New Eng. Assn. Coll. Admissions Counselors, Pa. Assn. Secondary Schs. and Coll. Admissions Counselors (admissions practices com., profl. devel. com.), N.Y. Assn. Coll. Admissions Counselors, N.J. Assn. Coll. Admissions Counselors, Bucks County C. of C. (chmn. perc com. 1994—), Hadassah Internat. (bd. dirs. Newtown chpt. 1990-93, v.p. Hosp. Guild chpt. 1990-94, pres., 1994—, supt. sch. adv. panel 1991—). Office: Am Coll Admissions Cons PO Box 701 Richboro PA 18954-0701

BLOCK, JANET LEVEN (MRS. JOSEPH E. ROSEN), public relations consultant; b. Chgo.; d. Benjamin J. and Rosebud (Goldsmith) Leven; student Brenau Coll. for Women, Gainesville, Ga., Northwestern U.; m. Albert William Block, Sept. 27, 1947 (div.); m. Joseph E. Rosen, Dec. 5, 1985; children: Mitchell Block, Stephanie Block McEwen. Reporter, Chgo. Am. Newspaper, 1939-40; catalog advt. Alden's Chgo. Mail Order Co., N.Y.C., Chgo., 1940-42; stylist and public relations dir. Fashion Advt. Co., N.Y.C., 1942-44; asst. account exec., stylist Buchanan & Co., Advt. Agy., N.Y.C., 1944-46; advt. agy account exec. Abbott Kimball Co., Chgo., 1946-47; free-lance merchandising and public relations rep., Cin., 1960-64; v.p. public relations, spl. events Lazarus (previously Shillito's), Cin., 1964-87; cons. pub. relations and advt. Cin., 1987—. Bd. dirs. Children's Heart Assn., 1975—; bd. dirs. Friends of Hamilton County Parks, 1979-80, treas., 1982; vice chair adv. bd. Hoxworth Blood Ctr., 1986-88; bd. dirs. ARC, 1984-86, Salvation Army, 1983-85, Friends of U. Cin. Conservatory of Music, 1994—, Great Rivers council Girl Scouts U.S.A., 1980-83, Family Service, 1985-88; Cin. Commn. on the Arts, Cin. Ballet 1985-91; mem. licensing com. Cin. Bicentennial Com., 1985-87; trustee Wood Hudson Cancer Rsch. Lab., 1988—; mem. adv. bd. Sch. Nursing U. Cin., 1992—. Recipient Silver Medal award Advertisers' Club Cin., 1976; named YWCA Career Woman of Achievement, 1982, Woman of Yr. Cin. Enquirer, 1991. Mem. Fashion Group Cin. (past regional dir.), Downtown Council (promotion chmn. 1975-76, 80-81), Public Relations Soc. Am. (dir. 1974-75, sec. 1976, treas. 1977), TV Soc. Am., Bus. and Profl. Women's Club, Advt. Club. Cin. (dir. 1967-87, v.p. 1972, Advt. Woman of Yr. 1972, mem. Speakers Bur. 1973—, pres. 1973-74, AAF Silver medal 1976), Women in Communications. Home: 2324 Madison Rd # 1107 Cincinnati OH 45208

BLOCK, RUTH, retired insurance company executive; b. N.Y.C., Nov. 7, 1930; d. Albert and Celia (Shapiro) Smolensky; BA, Adelphi U., 1952; m. Norman Block, April 5, 1952. With Equitable Life Assurance Soc. of U.S., 1952-87, v.p., planning officer, 1973-77, sr. v.p. in charge individual life ins. bus., 1977-80, exec. v.p. individual ins. bus.'s, 1980-87, duties expanded to include group life and health bus.'s, chief ins. officer, 1984-87; chmn., chief exec. officer Equitable Variable Life Ins. Co., 1980-84; bd. dirs. Amoco Corp., Ecolab Inc., (40) ACM Mut. Funds; trustee Life Underwriter Tng. Coun., 1983-85; vis. exec. Mobil Co. U. Iowa, 1978. Bd. dirs. Stamford (Conn.) YWCA, 1977-80, Donaldson, Lufkin & Jenrette, 1983-86, Avon Products, 1985-91, St Lukes Community Svcs., 1991—; nat. chmn. Equitable United Way, 1978. Recipient Disting. Alumni award Adelphi U. Sch. of Bus., 1979, Catalyst award 1983, WEAL award, 1983, N.Y.C. YMCA award. Mem. Nat. Assn. Securities Dealers (gov. at large 1982-84), Com. of 200, Womens Econ. Round Table, Rsch. Bd.(emeritus), Bus. Execs for Nat. Security, Women's Forum N.Y. and Conn. Office: PO Box 4653 Stamford CT 06907-0653

BLOCK, RUTH ANNE, artist; b. Tampa, Dec. 11, 1947; d. Saul Arnold and Elaine (Steiner) Kantro; m. Richard G. Smith, Feb. 14, 1983 (div. Apr. 1991); 1 child, Jaimie Block-Smith; m. Richard F. Overgaard, Apr. 3, 1994. BA in Art Edn., Mich. State U., 1969, MA in Guidance and Counseling, 1972; postgrad., Instituto Allende, San Miguel de Allende, Mex., 1978-79. Art therapist Ingham County Juvenile Detention Home, Lansing, Mich., 1968-69; freelance artist, instr. Mich., Fla., Calif., N.Mex., 1969—; counselor, therapist Mental Health Ctr. Polk County, Lakeland, Fla., 1972-74, St. George Homes, Inc., Berkeley, Calif., 1976-77; propr. Artists Interactive Video, Berkeley and Albuquerque, 1988—; art instr. Berkeley Adult Sch., 1985-89, Studio One Art Ctr., Oakland, Calif., 1989-93, Art Masters Acad., Albuquerque, 1993—; exhibiting artist, art instr. N.Mex. Art League, Albuquerque, 1994—; co-dir., co-producer Artists Interactive Video, Albuquerque, 1988—; art cons., Mich., Fla., Calif., N.Mex., Mexico, 1969—; dir., coord. Fire Art Project, Oakland and Berkeley, 1992; guest panelist Nat. Summer of Svc. Program, San Francisco, 1993; coord., chmn. Ad Hoc Com. Proposal for Cmty. Arts Ctr., Berkeley, 1988; artist in residence Arts in Residence Program, Berkeley Pub. Schs., 1989-93; counselor, supr. Nat. Music Camp, Interlochen, Mich., summer 1984. Artist, illustrator: The Hidden Valley, 1977; author: (video series) Life Drawing Video Workshops, 1988-91; one-woman shows include Pergola Gallery, San Miguel, Mex., 1979, Christensen Heller Lowe, Berkeley, 1991, 92, Studio 11, Oakland, 1992, 93,, Atahaulpa Gallery, Albuquerque, 1994; exhibited in group shows at Pro Arts Open Studios and Gallery, 1990-93, N.Mex. Art League, 1993-94, Magnifico, 1994; represented in permanent collections at Radical Things Gallery, Corrales, N.Mex.; pvt. collections. Recipient 1st Place award Richmond Art Ctr., 1983, Nomination Oakland Bus. Arts award Oakland C. of C., 1993; named one of 10 Best Tchrs. on Tape The Artist's Mag., N.Y.C., 1993. Mem. N.Mex. Art League (in house ednl. chairperson 1994). Office: Artist Interactive Video Ste 1-210 2400 Rio Grande NW Albuquerque NM 87104

BLODGETT, ELSIE GRACE, association executive; b. Eldorado Springs, Mo., Aug. 2, 1921; d. Charles Ishmal and Naoma Florence (Worthington) Robison; m. Charles Davis Blodgett, Nov. 8, 1940; children: Carolyn Doyel, Charleen Bier, Lyndon Blodgett, Daryl (dec.). Student Warrensburg (Mo.) State Tchrs. Coll., 1939-40; BA, Fresno (Calif.) State Coll., 1953. Tchr. schs. in Mo. and Calif., 1940-42, 47-72; owner, mgr. rental units, 1965—; exec. dir. San Joaquin County (Calif.) Rental Property Assn., Stockton, 1970-81; prin. Delta Rental Property Owners and Assocs., 1981-82; propr. Crystal Springs Health World, Inc., Stockton, 1980-86; bd. dirs. Stockton Better Bus. Bur. Active local PTA, Girl Scouts U.S., Boy Scouts Am.; bd. dirs. Stockton Goodwill Industries; active Vols. in Police Svc., 1993. Named (with husband) Mr. and Mrs. Apt. Owner of San Joaquin County, 1977. Mem. Nat. Apt. Assn. (state treas. women's div. 1977-79), Calif. Ret. Tchrs. Assn. Republican. Methodist. Lodge: Stockton Zonta. Home and Office: 2285 W Mendocino Ave Stockton CA 95204-4005

BLOEMER, ROSEMARY CELESTE, bookkeeper; b. St. Louis, Jan. 26, 1930; d. Edward J. and Leslie F. (McCreary) Walsh; m. Edward H. Bloemer, Sept. 4, 1948; children: Stephen, Diane, Janet. Cert. in court reporting, Bayside Coll., San Francisco, 1948; student, U. Mo., St. Louis, 1949-51, 83. Teller Roosevelt Savs. & Loan, 1967; income tax sec. Boatmen's Nat. Bank, St. Louis, 1968-73; sec. psychology dept. Washington U., St. Louis, 1978; beverages contr. Chase-Park Plaza Hotel, St. Louis, 1977-81; owner Bloemer Tax Svc., St. Louis, 1975—; legal sec. Lickhalter Law Office, St. Louis, 1970-88, Law Office of James K. Steitz, St. Louis, 1981-83; bookkeeper, tax advisor Mo. Hwy. Patrol Assn., Inc., St. Louis, 1981-83; bookkeeper, tax acct. Mo. State Hwy. Patrol Civilian Employees Assn., St. Louis, 1983-92; acct. Clarion Hotel, St. Louis, 1986, Bel-Air Hilton Inn, St. Louis, 1984-85; consignment std. stock machine screws, contr. accounts receivable Consol. Aluminum Co., 1973-75; sec. to 5 fin. specialists Cmty. Devel. Agy., St. Louis, 1980-81; tax preparer H&R Block, 1991-95; mem. team of reporters Price Waterhouse, 1990-94. Arbitrator, shopper, speaker Better Bus. Bur. St. Louis, 1980—; sec. to pres. Bd. Higher Edn., Christian Ch., 1975-77; vol. in choir Shrine of St. Joseph, St. Louis. Mem. Nat. Soc. Tax Profls., Nat. Assn. Tax Practitioners, Am. Soc. Notaries; Internat. Platform Assn. Roman Catholic. Home and Office: 1435 Trampe Ave Saint Louis MO 63138-2541

BLOEMINK, BARBARA JOAN, museum director and curator; b. N.Y.C., Apr. 18, 1953; d. Robert F. and Doris (Lazlo) Heins; m. Harry Bloemink, Nov. 8, 1985 (div. 1988). BA with honors, Stanford U., 1975; MA, Inst. Fine Arts, 1981; MPhil, Yale U., 1983, PhD, 1993. Intern Met. Mus. Art, N.Y.C., 1975; cataloguer Sotheby's, N.Y.C., 1976-79; dir. 19th century paintings dept. Sotheby's, L.A., 1979-81; v.p. fine arts Phillips Son & Neale, N.Y.C., 1986-88; acct. exec. Ogilvy & Mather, N.Y.C., 1982-84; dir., chief curator Hudson River Mus., Yonkers, N.Y., 1988-90; coord. pub. art City of Raleigh (N.C.) Arts Commn., 1991; guest curator Katonah Mus., Mint. Mus., 1992-94; dir., Willima T. Kemper curator Kemper Mus. Contemporary Art & Design, Kansas City, Mo., 1994—. Yale U. Paul Mellon fellow, 1992-93, Rose Herrick fellow, 1982-83, Nat. Mus. Art fellow, 1981-82. Mem. Am. Mus. Assn., Coll. Art Assn., Art Table. Office: Kemper Mus Contemporary Art 4420 Warwick Blvd Kansas City MO 64111

BLOME, DOROTHY CARTER, pediatrics nurse; b. Dallas, Aug. 16, 1943; d. Paul Gilbert and Dorothy Mae (Lamb) Carter; div.; children: Craig A., Glenn C. BS, Tex. Woman's U., 1965; MN, Emory U., 1968; postgrad. pediatric nurse practitioner, U. Tex., Arlington, 1994. RN, CPNP, advanced nurse practitioner, Tex. Staff nurse pediatrics Parkland Meml. Hosp., Dallas, 1965, Bapt. Hosp., Pensacola, Fla., 1965; staff nurse Egleston Children's Hosp., Atlanta, 1966-67; staff nurse neonatal ICU Baylor Med. Ctr., Dallas, 1977; staff nurse, then head nurse pediatrics Richardson (Tex.) Med. Ctr., 1977-82; mem. faculty pediatric nursing Tex. Woman's U., Denton, 1982-88; clin. nurse specialist Children's Med. Ctr., Dallas, 1988—. Contbg. author: Nursing Care of Infants and Children, 1991. Mem. ANA, Tex. Nurses Assn. (Gt. 100 Nurse award 1992), Sigma Theta Tau. Office: Childrens Med Ctr 1935 Motor St Dallas TX 75235-7794

BLOMQUIST, CECILE LA CHANCE, quality assurance professional, technologist; b. Asheboro, N.C., May 20, 1956; d. Edward F. and Gayle La Chance; m. Paul R. Blomquist, Sept. 25, 1983; children: Erik, Stefan. BS in Zoology, U. Mass., 1978. Toxicology technologist Internat. Clin. Labs., Randolph, Mass., 1979-83; asst. scientist quality control Baxter-Travenol Diagnostics, Cambridge, Mass., 1983-86; quality control chemist Serano Diagnostics, Norwell, Mass., 1986-87; assoc. rsch. scientist tech. support group GENE-TRAK Systems, Framingham, Mass., 1987-88; sr. assoc. rsch. scientist basic rsch. GENE-TRAK Systems, Framingham, 1989-91, sr. assoc. rsch. low end reproducibility, 1991-93, sr. quality assurance assoc., 1993—. Mem. Am. Soc. Quality Control. Home: 588 Poplar St Roslindale MA 02131-4937

BLOMQUIST-STANBERY, RUTH ELLEN, computer company executive, production administrator, educational consultant; b. Chgo., Feb. 12, 1949; d. Roy Theodore Sr. and Ruth Theresa (Johnson) Blomquist; m. Donald Loran Stanbery, Aug. 16, 1985; children: Elyn Nicole Blomquist, Dena Terese Blomquist, Lukas Brock Theodor Stanbery. BA, Elmhurst (Ill.) Coll., 1979; MA, No. Ill. U.; postgrad., Nat. Coll. Edn., Evanston, Ill. Sec., real estate and comml. mortgage First Nat. Bank of Chgo., 1972-73; substitute tchr. DuPage County (Ill.) Schs., 1979-82; tchr., adminstr. DuPage Alt. Elem. Sch., Downers Grove, Ill., 1979-82; with Jewel Foods, Lombard, Ill., 1982-83; office and factory worker Frank's Office Svcs., St. Charles, Ill., 1984-85; in sales and distbn. Homes Mag., Downers Grove, 1987-88; youth counselor Job Tng. Partnership Act, Ogle County, Rochelle, Ill., 1990; in prodn. Del Monte Corp., DeKalb, Ill., 1985-91; on-line prodn. coord. and facilitator The Suter Co., Sycamore, Ill., 1991-93; CEO, owner Stanbery Computer Svcs., Rochelle, Ill., 1994—. Contbr. articles to profl. jours. Mem. AAUW, ASCD, Ill. Edn. Assn., Nat. Coun. Tchrs. English, Order Ea. Star, Job's Daus., Phi Delta Kappa, Omicron Delta Kappa, Kappa Delta Epsilon. Congregationalist. Home: Box 55 Malta IL 60150 Office: Stanbery Computer Svcs 508 N 2d St PO Box 546 Rochelle IL 61068

BLOMSTROM, SUSAN M., computer technician, consultant; b. Middleton, Conn., Dec. 7, 1956; d. Glenn Wilfred and Dessa Mae (Tiedeken) Preuhs; m. Charles Scott Blomstrom, July 18, 1981; 1 child, Tracy

Lynn. AAS in Micro Computer Support Tech., Red Wing (Minn.) Winona Tech., 1993. Prodn. control specialist Josten's Inc., Red Wing, Minn., 1978-84; owner, operator Lazy Acre's Daycare, Maiden Rock, Wis., 1984-89; mgr. Quick Step II, Maiden Rock, 1989-92; cons., educator, hardware and software technician Custom Computer, Maiden Rock, 1991—; computer technician Computers & Stuff, Red Wing, 1993-95. Group leader 4-H, Maiden Rock, 1979-87; sec. summerfest Maiden Rock Community Club, 1990—; sec. Red WingTech. Coll., 1992-93. Recipient scholarship Mpls. Found., 1993. Mem. Bus. Persons of Am. Methodist. Home: W3444 Hwy 35 Maiden Rock WI 59750 Office: W3444 Hwy 35 Maiden Rock WI 54750

BLONDER, BARBARA IRENE, biologist; b. Framingham, Mass., Mar. 24, 1961; d. Fred Daniel and Margery Sharon (Pulda) B.; m. David Arthur Haynes, May 9, 1993. BA in Zoology, U. N.H., 1981; MS in Marine Biology, Fla. Tech., 1985. Marine sci. tchr., divemaster Internat. Field Studies, Andros, Bahamas, 1982-83; biologist Bionetics Corp., Kennedy Space Ctr., Fla., 1985-86; fishery biologist Nat. Marine Fisheries Svc., Panama City, Fla., 1986; biol. sci. II Fla. Dept. Natural Scis., Marathon, Fla., 1986-89; environ. specialist II Fla. Dept. Natural Scis., Apopka, Fla., 1989-91; land steward The Nature Conservancy, Kill Devil Hills, N.C., 1991—. Vol. firefighter Town of Kill Devil Hills, N.C., 1991-93. Office: The Nature Conservancy 701 W Ocean Acres Dr Kill Devil Hills NC 27948

BLONDIN, JOAN, nephrologist educator; b. Beaumont, Tex., Nov. 28, 1936; d. Joseph Albert and Ona Mae (Williamson) B. BS, La. Tech U., 1959; MNS, Cornell U., 1961; MD, La. State U., 1969. Diplomate Am. Bd. Internal Medicine. Instr. U. Ala., Tuscaloosa, 1961-62; rsch. assoc. Cornell U., Ithaca, N.Y., 1962-63; asst. specialist La. State U., Baton Rouge, 1963-65; intern Barnes Hosp., St. Louis, 1969-70, resident, 1970-72; postdoctoral fellow Washington U., St. Louis, 1972-74, asst. prof., 1974-78; ptnr. Nephrology Cons., Monroe, La., 1978—; assoc. prof. La. State U., Shreveport, 1978-89; adj. prof. human ecology La. Tech. U., 1988; active staff St. Francis Med. Ctr., 1978—, North Monroe Community Hosp., 1984—, Glenwood Regional Med. Ctr., 1978, 92—. Contbr. articles to profl. jours. Bd. dirs. Central Bank; bd. trustees Nat. Kidney Found. of La., 1988—; mem. La. Bd. Regents, 1989—; med. dir. North La. Dialysis Ctr., 1992—. Fellow La. Cancer Society, 1966, NIH, 1968. Mem. AAAS, ACP, Internat. Soc. Nephrology, Am. Soc. Internal Medicine, Am. Soc. Nephrology, Am. Soc. Tropical Medicine and Hygiene, Am. Soc. Parenteral and Enteral Nutrition, Am. Heart Assn. (Coun. on Hypertension), Renal Physicians Assn. (bd. dirs., fin. com. 1991—), N.Y. Acad. Scis., La. State Med. Soc. (del. 1988—), Alpha Omega Alpha, Phi Kappa Phi, Sigma Xi, Omicron Nu. Republican. Episcopalian. Home: 301 Country Club Rd Monroe LA 71201-2562 Office: Nephrology Cons 711 Wood St Monroe LA 71201-7549

BLOODWORTH-REED, BRENDA JOY, school guidance counselor; b. Ardmore, Okla., Jan. 15, 1953; d. Bill J. and Jewell Edna (Black) B.; m. Robert L. Reed, Oct. 29, 1994. BS, Southeastern Okla. State U., 1974; M in Counseling, East Ctrl. U., 1985. Cert. tchr., counselor. Tchr. Graham (Okla.) Pub. Schs., 1974-77, Dougherty (Okla.) Mountain Sch., 1977-78, Fox (Okla.) Schs., 1978-89; counselor Lone Grove (Okla.) Schs., 1989—; counselor Youth Am., Inc., Oklahoma City, 1983-86; drug edn. coord. Lone Grove Schs., 1989—. Mem. Carter County Crises Intervention Team, Ardmore, Okla., 1989—, mem. adv. bd. So. Okla. Children's Shelter; mem. Carter County Child Abuse Prevention Task Force. Mem. Okla. Alliance Against Drugs, Okla. Fedn. of Tchrs. and Parents, Compassionate Friends. Democrat. Office: Lone Grove Schs PO Box 1330 Lone Grove OK 73443-1330

BLOODWORTH-THOMASON, LINDA, television producer, writer; b. Poplar Bluff, Mo., 1948; m. Harry Thomason. BA in English, U. Mo. Former mem. advt. staff Wall St. Jour., L.A.; former reporter L.A. Daily Jour.; former instr. English lit. Jordan High Sch., Watts, Calif.; co-founder Mozark Prodns. Work includes: TV writer M*A*S*H (2 Emmy award nominations), One Day at a Time, Rhoda, Filthy Rich, Killing All the Right People (Emmy award nomination 1988, Funders for AIDS award); creator, exec. prodr. Lime Street, 1985; creator, writer, producer, co-exec. producer Designing Women, 1986-91 (Nancy Susan Reynolds award Sexual Responsibility in the Media Ctr. for Population Options, Humanitarian award Funders Concerned About AIDS, Gift of Laughter award Nat. Multiple Sclerosis Soc., Angel award Best TV Comedy, Nat. Commn. Working Women award, Viewers For Quality TV award for Best Quality Comedy, Electronic Media's Critic's Choice award, Genii award Am. Women in Radio and TV, numerous People's Choice awards, numerous Emmy nominations); creator, exec. producer, producer Evening Shade, 1990-94 (Electronic Media's Critic's Choice award, Writer's Guild award nomination 1992); exec. prodr., writer Hearts Afire, 1992—; writer, creator, exec. prodr. Woman of the House, 1995—. Named One of Am.'s 50 Most Powerful Women Ladies Home Jour., 1990; recipient Outstanding Communicator award L.A. Advt. Women's Orgn., 1992; honoree Women's Legal Def. Fund, 1992. Office: Mozark Prodns CBS/MTM Studios 4024 Radford Ave Studio City CA 91604 Office: Richland Wunsch Hohman Agency 9220 Sunset Blvd Ste 311 Los Angeles CA 90069*

BLOOM, CINDY J., interior designer; b. Queens, N.Y., Sept. 28, 1963; d. H. Otto and Grace A. Richheimer; m. Scott M. Bloom, Oct. 23, 1993. BFA, Syracuse U., 1985. Asst. visual merchandising mgr. Bonwit Teller, Manhasset, N.Y., 1985-86; designer/project mgr. EF Hutton, N.Y.C., 1986-87, Shearson Lehman Hutton, N.Y.C., 1987-90; cons. NYNEX Properties Co., N.Y.C., 1990-91; project dir. Empire Office Equipment, N.Y.C., 1991—. Vol. Humane Soc. N.Y. Home: 301 E 79th St Apt 5C New York NY 10021 Office: Empire Office Equipment 21 Murray St New York NY 10007

BLOOM, JAN HETTIE, psychologist; b. Pitts., Nov. 30, 1952; d. Jack M. and Joanne A. Bloom. BA, Tufts U., 1974; EdM, Harvard U., 1975; PhD, U. Minn., 1982. Lic. psychologist, Mass. Predoctoral intern Children's Hosp., Boston, 1981-82, postdoctoral intern, 1982-83; asst. prof. Tufts U., Medford, Mass., 1983-84; postdoctoral intern Phila. Child Guidance Clinic, 1984-85; staff psychologist Human Rels. Svcs., Wellesley, Mass., 1985-90; pvt. practice Newton, Mass., 1990—; lectr. Boston Coll., 1982; cons. to schs., hosps. and physicians, Newton, Wellesley, Weston, Mass., 1990—. Contbr. papers to profl. confs. Active social action coms. for family and children's causes, Mass. NIMH fellow, 1978-81; recipient U. Minn. spl. grant, 1980, fellowship, 1980-81. Mem. APA, Mass. Psychol. Assn., Soc. Rsch. on Child Devel., Nat. Assn. Sch. Psychologists, Phi Beta Kappa, Phi Delta Kappa. Office: 53 Langley Rd Newton Centre MA 02100

BLOOM, KATHRYN RUTH, public relations executive; d. Morris and Frances Sondra (Siegel) B. BA, Douglass Coll.; MA, U. Toronto, Can. Dir. spl. projects United Jewish Appeal, N.Y.C., 1973-78; mgr. pub. affairs Bristol-Myers-Squibb Co., N.Y.C., 1978-86; mgr. pub. rels. pharm. and nutritional Bristol-Myers Squibb Co., N.Y.C., 1986-90, dir. pharm. and rsch. communications, 1990-91; dir. communications Biogen, Inc., Boston, 1992—. Mem. N.Y.C. com. Women's Campaign Fund, 1984-91; v.p., bd. dirs. N.Am. Conf. on Ethiopian Jewry, N.Y.C., 1985—. Mem. Women Execs. in Pub. Relations, Phi Beta Kappa. Office: Biogen Inc 14 Cambridge Ctr Cambridge MA 02142-1481

BLOOM, LINDA SUSAN, art historian; b. Phila., Aug. 6, 1958; d. Irving Isadore and René (Perlmutter) Weiner; m. Brad Lane Bloom, Aug. 30, 1981; 1 child, Leah Aliza. BFA, Ohio State U., 1980, B Art Edn., 1980; MA in Art Edn., U. Cin., 1984; MA in Art History, U. Ill., 1995. Cert. tchr., Ohio; lic. real estate salesperson, Calif. Art educator Cin. Pub. Schs., 1980-84; educator Hebrew Union Coll. Skirball, Cin., 1983-84; founder, chair Koret Judaica Gallery, Palo Alto, Calif., 1984-87; mus. asst. World Heritage Mus., Champaign, Ill., 1988-89; grad. teaching asst. U. Ill., Champaign, 1989-92; family educator Sinai Temple, Champaign, 1993-95; educator children's program Parkland Coll., Champaign, 1989; advisor art/acquisitions com. Sinai Temple, Champaign, 1987-95. Worker Meals-on-Wheels, Champaign-Urbana; bd. mem. Women's Health Ctr., Champaign-Urbana, 1987-88; v.p., bd. Sisterhood Sinai, Champaign-Urbana, 1993-94. Recipient Leadership award Jewish Fedn./Jewish Cmty. Ctr., Palo Alto, 1987, Derber Svc. award Hadassah, Champaign-Urbana, 1993, nat. leadership award Hadassah, 1993. Mem. Am. Assn. Museums, Midwest Art Hist. Soc., Ohio Art Edn. Assn. (v.p. bd. Cin. chpt. 1980-84), Hadassah (v.p. bd. Champaign-Urbana chpt. 1984-94), Phi Delta Kappa. Jewish. Home: 1811 Bridgestone Dr Champaign IL 61821 Office: Cong B'nai Israel 3600 Riverside Blvd Sacramento CA 95818

BLOOM, LISA ELLEN, art history and women's studies educator, critic; b. Bklyn., Aug. 20, 1958; d. Elliott and Flora B. BA, Trinity Coll., Hartford, Conn., 1980; MFA, Rochester (N.Y.) Inst. Tech., 1984; PhD, U. Calif., Santa Cruz, 1990. Lectr., art history bd. U. Calif., Santa Cruz, 1989-91; lectr. art history dept. U. Calif., Irvine, 1991-92; lectr. liberal studies dept. R.I. Sch. Design, 1993; vis. asst. prof. art dept. Stanford U., 1993—; editl. asst. Afterimage Visual Studies Workshop, Rochester, 1983-84. Author: Gender on Ice: American Ideologies of Polar Expeditions, 1993. Mellon postdoctoral fellow Stanford U., 1993—, Brown U. postdoctoral fellow, 1992-93. Mem. MLA, Am. Studies Assn., Coll. Art Assn., Soc. Cinema Studies, Soc. Photographic Edn. Office: Art Dept Stanford U Stanford CA 94305

BLOOM, NAOMI LEE, management consultant; b. Springfield, Mass., Sept. 24, 1945; d. Jack Samuel and Bertha Elizabeth (Zlokower) B.; m. Ronald G. Wallace, June 30, 1972. BA in English Lit., U. Pa., 1967; MBA, Boston U., 1972. Mgr. info. systems Am. Inst. for Rsch., Palo Alto, Calif., 1975-77; sr. prin. Am. Mgmt. Systems, Arlington, Va., 1977-86; mng. ptnr. Bloom & Wallace, Fairfax, Va., 1987—; cons. various orgns. including ALCOA, Hewlett-Packard, Met. Life, PeopleSoft, Oracle, others; presenter in field. Author: Human Resource Management and Information Technology: Achieving a Strategic Partnership, 1992; contbr. articles to profl. jours. Mem. Assn. Human Resource Profls. Jewish. Office: Bloom & Wallace 8302 Professional Hill Dr Fairfax VA 22031-4611

BLOOMGARDEN, KATHY FINN, public relations executive; b. N.Y.C., June 9, 1949; d. David and Laura (Zeisler) Finn; m. Zachary Bloomgarden; children: Rachel, Keith, Matthew. BA, Brown U., 1970; MA, Columbia U., PhD. Pres. Rsch. & Forecasts, N.Y.C., Ruder-Finn, Inc., N.Y.C., 1988—. Bd. dirs. CARE, Women's Forum, N.Y. Arthritis Found. Mem. Pub. Rels. Soc. Am., Nat. Investor Rels. Inst., Swedish-Am. C. of C. Jewish. Home: 1084 North Ave New Rochelle NY 10804-3618 Office: Ruder Finn 301 E 57th St New York NY 10022-2905

BLOUNT, JOANNA F., administrator; b. New Orleans, Dec. 8, 1953; d. John Henry and Rita Catherine (Winstein) Fousse. AA in Social Sci., Matanuska-Susitna Coll.; BS in Psychology, U. Alaska, 1988; Ma in Counseling/Ednl. Psychology, Slippery Rock U., 1990. Lic. prof. clin. counselor; nat. cert. counselor. Energy asst. eligibility technician State of Alaska, Wasilla, 1984-87; admissions specialist/dir. career placement/adminstrv. asst. Matanuska-Susitna Coll., Palmer, Alaska, 1984-89; counselor, test adminstr. Slippery Rock (Pa.) U. Acad. Support Svcs., 1990; dir. counseling, testing & advising Clovis (N.Mex.) C.C., 1990—; ind. test adminstr. Wonderlic Personnel, Clovis, 1992—; mem. N.Mex. ACT Coun., Albuquerque, 1991—; test adminstr. ASE and ACT-PEP, Iowa City, Iowa, 1990—; rep. Nat. SEcondary Edn. Program, Washington, 1993—. Writer, editor: (student handbook) Who, What, When, Where, 1993. Fund raiser Alliance for Mentally Ill, Portales, N.Mex., 1992-93; vol. Salvation Army, Alaska, 1984-88, Cath. Social Svcs., Alaska, 1984-88. Recipient Rising Star award Nat. Asns. Student Pers. Adminstrs., 1992. Mem. Am. Counseling Assn., Am. Coll. Counseling Assn. (nat. media com. 1992—), NAt. Assn. Orientation Dirs. Office: Clovis Community Coll 417 Schepps Blvd Clovis NM 88101

BLUE, ANITA FAE, nurse; b. Webster City, Ia., Apr. 15, 1967; d. Veryl D. and Linda (Sollie) B. BSN, Morningside Coll., Sioux City, Iowa, 1989. RN, S.D.; cert. BCLS. Intern Meth. Hosp., Rochester, Minn., 1988; critical care unit nurse Marian Health Ctr., Sioux City, Iowa, 1989; mental health nurse St. Lukes Regional Med. Ctr., Sioux City, Iowa, 1991; charge nurse children, adolescent and adult psychiat. units Charter Hosp. of Sioux Falls, S.D., 1992—; mem. nursing practice coun., 1992, charting by exception com., 1992; presenter insvc. concerning IV therapy to staff RN's on mental health unit, 1992.

BLUE, CATHERINE ANNE, lawyer; b. Boston, Feb. 17, 1957; d. James Daniel and Angela Devina (Savini) Mahoney; m. Donald Sherwood Blue, Oct. 4, 1980; children: Mairead Catherine, Edward Pierce. BA, Stonehill Coll., North Easton, Mass., 1977; JD, Coll. William and Mary, 1980. Bar: Pa. 1980. Atty., Aluminum Co. Am., Pitts., 1980-83, Pa. Dept. Revenue, Harrisburg, 1983-85, State Workmen's Ins. Fund, Pitts., 1985-87, Met. Pitts. Pub. Broadcasting (name now QED Communications Inc.), 1987-91, gen. counsel, 1991—. Mem. Pa. Bar Assn., Allegheny County Bar Assn. Democrat. Home: 118 Washington St Pittsburgh PA 15218-1352 Office: QED Communications Inc 4802 5th Ave Pittsburgh PA 15213-2956

BLUE, KATHY JO, elementary school educator; b. Martinsburg, W.Va., Nov. 13, 1955; d. Daniel Walker and Agnes Rosalie (Hull) Tabler; m. John Kyner Blue, July 12, 1981; 1 child, Sarah Virginia. AS in Nursing, Shepherd Coll., Shepherdstown, W.Va., 1976; BA in Elem. Edn., Shepherd Coll., Sheperdstown, W.Va., 1979; MA, W.Va. U., 1988; reading authorization, 1988. Cert. profl. elem. tchr., tchr. gifted edn. 1-6, reading, W.Va. Nurse City Hosp., Inc., Martinsburg, 1976-78; substitute tchr. Jefferson and Berkeley counties, Charles Town, Martinsburg, 1979-80; elem. tchr. Morgan County Schs., Berkeley Springs, W.Va., 1980-81; substitute tchr. Jefferson County Schs., Charles Town, 1981-86, Chpt. I tchr. reading, 1986—; tutor, Shenandoah Junction, W.Va., 1989—. Recipient Regional Edn. Svc. Agy. Exemplary Teaching Technique in Lang. award, 1994; grantee W.Va. Edn. Fund, 1988, 89, 95. Mem. NEA, Internat. Reading Coun., W.Va. Reading Coun., Jefferson County Reading Assn., W.Va. Edn. Assn., Jefferson County Edn. Assn., Blue Ridge Elem. PTO, T.A. Lowery PTO, Order Ea. Star (worthy matron Shepherdstown 1983-84, 88-89), Alpha Delta Kappa. Republican. Methodist. Home: PO Box 112 Shenandoah Junction WV 25442-0112 Office: Blue Ridge Elem Sch RR 2 Box 362 Harpers Ferry WV 25425-9423

BLUE, ROSE, writer, educator; b. N.Y.C.; d. Irving and Frieda (Rosenberg) Bluestone. BA, Bklyn. Coll.; postgrad. Bank St. Coll. Edn., 1967. Tchr., N.Y.C. Public Schs., 1967—; writing cons. Bklyn. Coll. Sch. Edn., 1981-83. Author: A Quiet Place, 1969; Black, Black Beautiful Black, 1969, How Many Blocks Is The World, 1970, Bed-Stuy Beat, 1970, I Am Here (Yo Estoy Aqui), 1971, A Month of Sundays, 1972, Grandma Didn't Wave Back, 1972 (teleplay 1983), Nikki 108, 1973, We are Chicano, 1973, The Preacher's Kid, 1975, Seven Years from Home, 1976, The Yo Yo Kid, 1976, The Thirteenth Year, 1977, Cold Rain on the Water, 1979, My Mother The Witch, 1981 (teleplay 1984), Everybody's Evy, 1985, Heart to Heart, 1986, Goodbye Forever Tree, 1987, The Secret Papers of Camp Get Around, 1988, Barbara Bush First Lady, 1990, Colin Powell Straight To The Top, 1991, Barbara Jordan-Politician, 1992, Defending Our Country, 1993, Working Together Against Hate Groups, 1993, People of Peace, 1994; lyricist: Drama of Love, 1964, Let's Face It, 1961, Give Me a Break, 1962, My Heartstrings Keep Me Tied To You, 1963, Homecoming Party, 1966. Contbg. editor: Teacher mag., Day Care mag. Mem. Authors Guild Am., Authors League Am., PEN, Mensa, Profl. Women's Caucus, Broadcast Music, Inc. Home and Office: 1320 51st St Brooklyn NY 11219-3552

BLUESTEIN, JUDITH ANN, rabbi, educator, diversified industry executive; b. Cin., Apr. 2, 1948; d. Paul Harold and Joan Ruth (Straus) Bluestein; BA, U. Pa., 1969; postgrad. Am. Sch. Classical Studies, Athens, Greece, 1968, Vergilian Soc., 1970, 76, 77, 78, Hebrew Union Coll., Jewish Inst. Religion, Jerusalem, 1971, 1979-80, Am. Acad. in Rome, 1975; MA in Religion, Case Western Res. U., 1973, MA in Latin, 1973; MEd, Xavier U., 1984; MA in Hebrew Letters, Hebrew Union Coll.-Jewish Inst. Religion, Cin., 1983; MPhil Hebrew Union Coll., 1989. Ordained rabbi, 1984. Sec., Paul H. Bluestein & Co., Cin., 1964—; v.p. Panel Machine Co., 1966—, Blujay Corp., 1966—, Ermet Products Corp., 1966—; ptnr. Companhia Engenheiros Indsl. Bluestein do Brasil, Cin., 1971—; tchr. Latin, Cin. Public Schs., 1973-79; rabbi Temple Israel, Marion, Ohio, 1980-84, Temple Sholom, Galesburg, Ill., 1985-86, B'nai Israel Congregation, Hattiesburg, Miss., 1990-94, Ames (Iowa) Jewish Congregation, 1994—; campus min. U. So. Miss., 1990-94; co-chmn. Interfaith Plea for Soviet Jews, 1986; lectr. Hebrew Union Coll.-Jewish Inst. Religion, 1986-89; vis. lectr., Jewish chaplain Denison U., 1987-88; vis. lectr. Ind. U., Bloomington, 1989-90; lectr. Hebrew Union Coll., 1994, Xavier U., 1994; instr. Iowa State U., Des Moines, 1995; bd. dirs. Cin. Council for Soviet Jews, 1982-84, 85-89, sec. 1985-87. Fellow Case Western Reserve U., 1970-73, Hebrew Union Coll.-Jewish Inst. Religion, 1985-90; Revson fellow Jewish Theol Sem. Am., 1984-85; Hausmon Meml. fellow Hebrew Union Coll. Jewish Inst. Religion, 1985-86; Isadore and Goldie Millstone fellow Hebrew Union Coll., 1986-87, 94-95, Julia and Leo Forchheimer fellow, 1987-89., Mrs. Henry Morganthau fellow Hebrew Union Coll., 1989-90. Mem. Archeol. Inst. Am., Assn. Jewish Studies, Am. Acad. Religion, Classical Assn. Middle West and South (v.p. Ohio 1976-79), Central Conf. Am. Rabbis, Am. Classical League, Ohio Classical Conf. (council 1976-79), Vergilian Soc., Soc. Bibl. Lit., Cin. Assn. Tchrs. Classics (pres. 1976-78), Am. Philol. Assn., Hattiesburg Interfaith Alliance, Nat. Assn. Profs. of Hebrew, Midwest Jewish Studies Assn., Rotary (bd. dirs. 1992-93). Home: 4201 Victory Pky Apt 212 Cincinnati OH 45229

BLUESTEIN, KAREN ARLENE, computer book publisher; b. Bronx, N.Y., July 9, 1964; d. Maurice and Maris (Werner) B. AB, Smith Coll., 1986; MBA, Ind. Wesleyan U., 1993. Systems analyst, microcomputer tng. dir. Ind. Dept. Adminstrn., Indpls., 1986-88; tech. editor Que Corp., Indpls., 1988-89, acquisitions editor, 1989-90, pub. mgr., 1990, assoc. pub., 1990-91; assoc. pub. Hayden Books, Indpls., 1991-92; dir. pub. Prentice Hall Computer Pub., Indpls., 1992-94; pub. IDG Books Worldwide, Indpls., 1994—; creative cons. Author calendar; editor, product dir. various books. Home: 9856 River Oak Ln Fishers IN 46038 Office: IDG Book Worldwide 7260 Shadeland Sta Indianapolis IN 46256

BLUESTEIN, VENUS WELLER, retired psychology educator; b. Milw., July 16, 1933; d. Richard T. and Hazel (Beard) Weller; m. Marvin Bluestein, Mar. 7, 1954. BS, U. Cin., 1956, MEd, 1959, EdD, 1966. Diplomate Am. Bd. Examiners in Profl. Psychology. Psychologist-in-tng. Longview State Hosp., Cin., 1956-58; sch. psychologist Cin. Pub. Schs., 1958-65; asst. prof. psychology U. Cin., 1965-70, assoc. prof., 1970-79, prof., 1979-93, prof. emerita, 1993—, dir. undergrad. studies, 1991-93, dir. undergrad. advising, 1991-93, dir. sch. psychology program, 1965-70, co-dir. sch. psychology program, 1970-75; cons. child psychologist. Sec., U.S. exec. com. rsch. Children's Internat. Summer Villages, 1964-68; chmn. Ohio Interuniv. Coun. Sch. Psychology, 1967-68. Editor Ohio Psychologist, 1961-68, co-editor, 1972-79; contbr. articles to profl. publs. Vol. Hamilton County parks, 1979—, various ednl. programs Cin. Zoo, 1983—. Recipient George B. Barbour award, 1985. Fellow Am. Acad. Sch. Psychology; mem. AAUP, APA, Ohio Psychol. Assn. (citation 1972, Disting. Svc. award 1968), Cin. Psychol. Assn. (sec. 1961-62), Sch. Psychologists Ohio, Forum for Death Edn. and Counseling, Kappa Delta Pi, Sigma Delta Pi, Psi Chi (award for outstanding mentor 1985, award for outstanding contbns. to undergrad. psychology students 1994). Office: U Cin Dept Psychology ML 376 Cincinnati OH 45221

BLUHM, BARBARA JEAN, communications agency executive; b. Chgo., Mar. 5, 1925; d. Maurice L. and Clara (Miller) B. Student Coll. William and Mary, 1943-45; B.S., U. Wis., 1947. Exec. tng. program Carson Pirie Scott & Co., Chgo., 1947-52; home economist Lever Bros. Co., Chgo., 1952-57; field rep. The Merchandising Group, Chgo., 1957-62; v.p. The Merchandising Group, N.Y.C., 1962-82, pres., 1982-87, chmn., 1987-90. Publicity chmn. James Lenox Ho. Assn., N.Y.C., 1980-90; vol. Ringling Mus., Venice Hosp., Venice Little Theatre; mem. Coll. Club of Venice, Friends of the Venice Art League, Venice Symphony. Republican. Presbyterian. Home: 1470 Colony Pl Venice FL 34292

BLUITT, KAREN, technical manager, software engineer; b. N.Y.C., Oct. 25, 1957; d. James Bertrand and Beatrice (Kaufman) B.; m. Kenneth Mark Curry, Nov. 24, 1979 (div. Dec. 1991). BS, Fordham U., 1979; MBA, Calif. State Poly. U., 1982; postgrad., George Mason U. Software engr. Hughes Aircraft Co., Fullerton, Calif., 1979-81; microprocessor engr. Beckman Instruments Co., Fullerton, 1981-82, Singer Co., Glendale, Calif., 1982-83; sr. software engr. Sanders Assoc., Nashua, N.H., 1983-85; software project mgr. GTE Corp., Billerica, Mass., 1985-86; sr. software engr. Wang Labs, Lowell, Mass., 1986-87; project task leader Vanguard Rsch., Lexington, Mass., 1987-88; program mgr. Applied Rsch. & Engring., Bedford, Mass., 1989-91; program mgr. Sparta, McLean, Va., 1992-93; prin. software engr. Sci. Applications Internat., Arlington, Va., 1993-94; tech. mgr. CACI, Arlington, 1994—. 1st lt. USAR, 1979-88. Scholar Gov. N.Y. Scholarship Com., 1975-79; Beta Gamma Sigma scholar, 1978—. Mem. IEEE, AAUW, Am. Brokers Network, Assn. Computing Machinery, Data Processing Mgmt. Assn., Soc. Women Engrs. Office: CACI 1100 N Glebe Rd Arlington VA 22203

BLUM, BARBARA DAVIS, banker; b. Hutchinson, Kans.; d. Roy C. and Jo (McKinnon) Davis; children: Devin, Hunter, Ragan, Davis. Student, U. Kans.; BA, Fla. State U., MSW, 1959. Mem. faculty Pediatric Psychiatry Clinic, U. Kans. Med. Center, Lawrence; acting adminstr. Suffolk County (N.Y.) Mental Health Clinic, Huntington, L.I.; founder, partner Mid-Suffolk Center for Psychotherapy, Hauppage, L.I., N.Y.; v.p. Restaurant Associates of Ga., Inc., Atlanta; dep. adminstr. U.S. EPA, Washington, 1977-81; mem. Pres.'s Interagy. Coordinating Council; chmn., pres., CEO Abagail Adams Nat. Bancorp; chairperson U.S./Japan Environ. Agreement, 1977; head 1st U.S. Environ. Del. to Peoples' Republic of China, 1978; chmn. Environ. Policy Inst., 1981-84; sr. adviser UN Environment Program; bd. dirs. Washington Bd. Trade; vice chair Ctr. for Policy Alternatives; trustee Fed. City Coun.; mem. nat. adv. coun. U.S. Small Bus. Adminstrn., 1994. Chmn. D.C. Econ. Devel. Fin. Corp.; founder, chmn. Leadership Washington, Nat. Adv. Commn. Resource Conservation and Recovery; del. UN Mid Decade Conf. on Women, 1980; bd. dirs., pres. UN U. for Peace Found.; mem. adv. bd. UN Audio-Visual Trust; bd. dirs. Kaiser Permanente Mid Atlantic; dep. dir. Carter-Mondale U.S. presdl. campaign, 1976; dep. dir. Carter/Mondale Transition Team, Washington, 1976-77; panelist Clinton-Gore Econ. Conf., Little Rock, Ark. Decorated comdr.'s cross Order of Merit W. Ger.; recipient Disting. Service award Federally Employed Women, 1978, Spl. Conservation award Nat. Wildlife Fedn., 1976, Orgn. of Yr. award Ga. Wildlife Fedn., 1974, Disting. Service award Americans for Indian Opportunity, 1978. Mem. Washington Women's Network (dir., founder). Democrat. Club: Cosmos.

BLUM, BARBARA MEDDOCK, association executive; b. Oil City, Pa., Nov. 8, 1938; d. Marvin Lee and Hazel Genevieve (Jackson) Meddock; m. Stuart Hollander Blum, Sept. 21, 1963. BA in Psychology, Allegheny Coll., 1960. Psychometrist, researcher Hofstra U., Hempstead, N.Y., 1960-62; adminstrv. asst., editor The Asia Soc., N.Y.C., 1962-66, exec. asst., 1966-72, adminstrv. officer, 1972-85, dir. adminstrn., 1985-88, ret. 1988.

BLUM, DEBORAH, reporter. Sr. writer The Sacramento (Calif.) Bee; sci. writer in residence U. Wis., Madison, 1993. Author: The Monkey Wars, 1994. Recipient Pulitzer Prize for beat reporting, 1992. Mem. Nat. Assn. Sci. Writers (bd. dirs.), Sigma Xi. Office: Sacramento Bee PO Box 15779 Sacramento CA 95852-0779

BLUM, DOROTHY J. SCRIVNER, counselor, educator; b. McCook, Nebr., Nov. 8, 1929; d. Forrest J. and Eugenia A. (Krause) Scrivner; m. Richard G. Blum, July 25, 1970. AB, Midland Coll., 1951; MM, U. Nebr., 1958; EdD, U. Va., 1975. Tchr. Thomas County Pub. Sch., Colby, Kans., 1954-56, Washington Sch. Dist., Phoenix, 1956-59, Claremont (Calif.) Unified, 1959-61; counselor La Cañada (Calif.) Unified, 1961-66; supr. Pasadena (Calif.) Unified, 1966-68; asst. prin. Bonita HIgh, La Verne, Calif., 1968-70; tchr. Fairfax (Va.) County Pub., 1970-73; asst. prof. Western Md. Coll., Westminster, 1975-78; guidance dir. Marshall High, Falls Church, Va., 1978-88; coord. guidance Fairfax (Va.) County Pub., 1988—; adj. prof. U. Va., Charlottesville, 1975, Falls Church, 1978-83, 93, Va. Tech., Falls Church, 1983-86, 93; cons. overseas schs., Costa Rica, 1991, Mexico, 1992, Guatemala, 1993, El Salvador, 1994. Editor: Group Counseling for Secondary Schools, 1990. Mem. ACA, Va. Counselor Assn. (pres.-elect 1993, Va. Counselor of Yr. 1988), No. Va. Counselor Assn. (pres. 1983-84), Va. Sch. Counselors Assn. (pres. 1985-86), Va. Assn. Counselor Educators (pres. 1991-92), Va. Assn. Specialists (pres. 1984-85). Lutheran. Home: 7412 Calico Ct Springfield VA 22153-1302 Office: Fairfax County Pub Schs 2831 Graham Rd Falls Church VA 22042-1635

BLUM, SARAH LEE, nurse psychotherapist; b. Atlantic City, N.J., Dec. 5, 1939; d. David and Diana (Fedner) B.; m. Joseph J. McGoran, Aug. 24, 1970 (div. 1986); children: Lorna Hope Marie, Sean-David Justin. BSN,

Seattle U., 1971; M in Nursing, U. Wash., 1976. Cert. clin. specialist. Nurse Atlantic City Hosp., 1960-62, Kaiser Found. Hosp., L.A., 1963-66; instr. nursing North Idaho Coll., Coeur D'Alene, 1972-74; pvt. practice Federal Way, Wash., 1977-85, Auburn, Wash., 1985—; nurse psychotherapist Christian Counselling Svc., Tacoma, 1977-83; cons. in field.; presenter workshops. Contbr. articles to profl. jours. Creator Healing Day, 1985. Capt. Nurse Corps, U.S. Army, 1966-71, Vietnam. Fellow Am. Orthopsychiatric Assn.; mem. ANA, Nat. Nursing Hon. Soc., Internat. Transactional Analysis Assn., Inst. Developmental Edn. and Psychotherapy (bd. dirs. 1989-93, chair profl. membership com. 1991-94), Vietnam Veterans of Am. (bd. dirs. 1983-85, 1st woman mem.). Home and Office: 303 O St NE Auburn WA 98002-4645

BLUM, SHARON DUKETTE, state official; b. N.Y.C., Nov. 18, 1946; d. William Henry and Gwendolyn Althea (Clower) Dukette; m. John J. Blum, July 25, 1970; 1 child, Jennifer. BA, St. John's U., Jamaica, N.Y., 1968; MA, St. John's U. Dir. Colony South Bklyn. Houses, Inc., Bklyn.; dir. adminstrn. Willoughby House Settlement, Inc., Bklyn.; dir. child care food program and health and safety svcs. Human Resources Adminstrn., N.Y.C.; project planner, sr. mgr. Mayor's Office of Ops., N.Y.C. Mem. N.Y.C. Managerial Employees Assn., Corp. Women's Network, NAFE, NAACP. Home: 3950 Paulding Ave Bronx NY 10466-4704

BLUMBERG, BARBARA SALMANSON (MRS. ARNOLD G. BLUMBERG), housing consultant, retired state housing official; b. Bklyn., Oct. 2, 1927; d. Sam and Mollie (Greenberg) Salmanson; m. Arnold G. Blumberg, June 19, 1949 (dec. June 1989); children: Florence Ellen Schwartz, Martin Jay, Emily Anne. BA, De Pauw U., 1948; postgrad., New Sch. for Social Rsch., N.Y.C. Mem. pub. rels. dept. Nate Fein & Co., N.Y.C., 1948-51; freelance pub. rels. cons., 1960—; councilwoman North Hempstead, N.Y., 1975-82; adviser to energy com. N.Y. State Assembly, N.Y.C., 1982-84; dir. spl. needs housing Divsn. Housing and Cmty. Renewal, State of N.Y., 1984-89, ret., 1989; mem. bd. visitors Pilgrim State Hosp. Pres. UN Assn. Great Neck, N.Y., 1967-69, chmn. China Study Workshop, 1966-67; pres. Shalom chpt. Hadassah, 1955-57; exec. v.p. Lakeville P.T.A., Great Neck, 1963-65; exec. v.p. Great Neck S. Jr. High Sch., 1965-66; co-chmn. Great Neck UNICEF, 1968-70, mem. speakers bur., 1971—; v.p. Herricks Community Life Ctr., 1976-77, B'nai B'rith, Lake Success, N.Y.; coord., 6th Congl. Dist., N.Y. McGovern for Pres.; bd. dirs. New Dem. Coalition of Nassau, Am. Jewish Congress, Am. Jewish Com., Day Care Coun. of Nassau County, Citizen's Sch. Com., Great Neck; mem. Reform Dem. Assn. Great Neck; mem. platform com. Nassau Dem. Com.; del. Dem. Nat. Conv., 1992; mem. adv. com. to speaker N.Y. State Assembly; mem. resource coun., housing devel. co. Community Advocates; mem. North Hempstead Housing Authority; trustee L.I. Power Authority. Recipient award Anti-Defamation League, New Hyde Park, N.Y., 1975, Alumni award DePauw U., 1977, Hadassah New Life award, 1980, Women's Pole of Honor, North Hempstead, 1994. Mem. N.Y. Alumni Club DePauw U. (trustee), North Shore Archeol. Assn. (chmn. study group), Women in Comm., Intenrat. Platform Assn., L.I. Women's Network (co-convenor), Interfaith Nutrition Network (bd. dirs.), Community Advocates (bd. dirs.), Mental Health Assn. of Nassau County (bd. dirs.), North Shore NAACP, Alpha Lambda Delta. Home: 12 Birch Hill Rd Great Neck NY 11020-1309

BLUMBERG, JUNE BETH, artist; b. Abington, Pa., May 14, 1959; d. Frederick Blumberg and Elin (Brunswick) Binder. A of Gen. Studies, Montgomery Community Coll., 1985; BFA, Moore Coll. of Art, Phila., 1991. Stats. clk. Crime Prevention Assn., Phila., 1980-81; workshop tchr. Jefferson Hosp. Evening Program, Phila., 1986-87; art asst. Mildred Greenberg, Phila., 1988-89; vis. artist Moore Coll. of Art & Design, Phila., 1990; admission rep. Franklin Inst., Phila., 1990-92; rsch. scientist, artist Phila., 1979—. Exhibits painting nationally through Highwire Gallery, Phila.; contbr. rsch. to profl. jours. Tutor Homeless Shelter, 1986. Recipient scholarship, 1983-85, Spl. Merit award Pen and Brush Club, 1990. Mem. NAFE, World Affairs Coun., Pastel Soc. West Coast, Oil Pastel Assn., High Wire Gallery. Democrat. Address: PO Box 148 Bala Cynwyd PA 19004

BLUME, ADRIANNE, aerospace company manager; b. Galveston, Tex., Oct. 23, 1965; d. Adrian Curtis and Barbara Ann (Layne) B. BS, Tex. A&M U., 1988; MBA, U. Houston, 1994. Project mgr. Johnson Space Ctr., Rockwell Space Ops. Co., Houston, 1988—. Mem. Nat. Mgmt. Assn. Methodist. Home: 16203 Rill Ln Houston TX 77062-5030

BLUME, BARBARA ANN, compensation specialist; b. Red Bank, N.J., July 16, 1961; d. Arthur Charles and Margaret Ann (Patterson) Scott; m. Ronald Lee Blume II, Apr. 13, 1985. BSME, W.Va. U., 1983; MS in Mgmt. and Adminstrn. Sci., U. Tex., Dallas, 1987. Cert. compensation specialist. Mech. design engr. Tex. Instruments, Lewisville, 1984-86, supr. assembly line, 1986-87, team facilitator, 1988-89; compensation specialist Tex. Instruments, Dallas, 1989—. Mem. Am. Compensation Assn. Home: 1700 Fernwood Dr Plano TX 75075-7343 Office: Tex Instruments PO Box 65530 Dallas TX 75265

BLUME, GEORGIANA JEAN, insurance agent; b. Phoenix, Feb. 13, 1931; d. George Joseph and Violet A. (Anderson) Bates-Monger; m. Anthony Paul Scrivano, Feb. 23, 1951 (dec. Sept. 7, 1962); children: Catherine Lee Scrivano, Susan Jean Henley; m. Winfried Karl Blume, Aug. 2, 1975. Student, Phoenix Coll., 1969-70. Cert. profl. ins. woman. Owner, agt. Blume-Lamm Ins. Agy., Glendale, Ariz., 1979-89; owner, agt., ptnr. ACU Fin. Svcs. Inc., Phoenix, 1989-93; ind. contractor Insurors Network Ltd., Phoenix, 1993—. Named Outstanding Chmn. of Yr., Sun States Profl. Inst. Assn., 1987, Ins. Profl., 1992, Ins. Womanof Yr., Kachina West Ins. Women, 1990. Mem. Sun States Profl. Ins. Agts. (sec. treas., v.p. 1981-93), Kachina West Ins. Women (bd. dirs., treas., v.p. 1981-92), Blue Goose (com. chmn. 1993—), Epsilon Sigma Alpha. Republican. Lutheran.

BLUME, JUDY SUSSMAN, author; b. Elizabeth, N.J., Feb. 12, 1938; d. Rudolph and Esther (Rosenfeld) Sussman; m. John M. Blume, Aug. 15, 1959 (div. Jan. 1975); children: Randy Lee, Lawrence Andrew; m. George Cooper, June 6, 1987; 1 stepchild, Amanda. B.A. in Edn., NYU, 1960; LHD (hon.), Kean Coll., 1987. Author: (fiction) including The One in the Middle is the Green Kangaroo, 1969, Iggie's House, 1970, Are You There God? It's Me, Margaret (selected as outstanding children's book 1970), Freckle Juice, 1971, Then Again, Maybe I Won't, 1971, It's Not the End of the World, 1972, Tales of a 4th Grade Nothing, 1972, Otherwise Known as Sheila the Great, 1972, Deenie, 1973, Blubber, 1974, Forever, 1975, Tales of a Fourth Grade Nothing, 1976, Starring Sally J. Freedman as Herself, 1977, Superfudge, 1980, Tiger Eyes, 1981, The Pain and the Great One, 1984, Just As Long As We're Together, 1987, Fudge-A-Mania, 1990, Here's to You, Rachel Robinson, 1993, others; (adult novels) Wifey, 1977, Smart Women, 1984; (other writings) The Judy Blume Diary, 1981, Letters to Judy: What Kids Wish They Could Tell You, 1986, The Judy Blume Memory Book, 1988; exec. producer (25 min. film) Otherwise Known As Sheila The Great, Barr Films, 1988. Founder, trustee The Kids Fund, 1981. Recipient Carl Sandburg Freedom to Read award Chgo. Pub. Library, 1984, the Civil Liberties award ACLU, 1986, John Rock award Ctr. for Population Options, 1986; numerous Children's Choice awards, U.S.A., Europe, Australia. Mem. PEN, Authors Guild, Nat. Coalition Against Censorship, Soc. Children's Book Writers (bd. dirs.). Jewish. Office: care Harold Ober Assocs 425 Madison Ave New York NY 10017-1110

BLUMENFELD, SUE DEBORAH, lawyer; b. N.Y.C., Nov. 5, 1952; d. Abraham H. and Judith (Solomon) B.; m. William Charles Rapp, Jan. 1, 1982; children: Adam, Nicholas, David. BA, SUNY, 1974; JD, Rutgers U., Camden, N.J., 1977. Bar: N.J. 1977, D.C. 1981, U.S. Dist Ct. N.J. 1977, U.S. Dist. Ct. D.C. 1981, U.S. Superior Ct. D.C. 1981, U.S. Ct. Appeals (D.C. cir.) 1984. Atty. Bur. Competition FTC, Washington, 1977-79, spl. asst. to chief Common Carrier Bur., 1979-81; assoc. Pierson, Ball & Dowd, Washington, 1981-83; assoc. Willkie, Farr & Gallagher, Washington, 1983-86, ptnr., 1986—. Office: Willkie Farr & Gallagher 1155 21st St NW Ste 600 Washington DC 20036-3384

BLUMENFIELD, BARBARA SUE, town administrator; b. Milw., Apr. 27, 1951; d. Irving and Jennie (Seltzer) Blumenfield. BS, U. Wis., 1973, MS, 1978, postgrad., 1985—. Cert. realtor, Wis. Aldermanic adminstrv. asst. Common Coun. City of Milw., 1973-74; field rep. Congressman Henry S. Reuss, Milw., 1974-80; housing specialist Northwest Action Coun., Milw., 1980-81; assoc. dir.. Wis. State of Israel Bonds, Milw., 1981-83; sr. legis. analyst Common Coun. City of Milw., 1983-92; exec. & legis. liaison Racine (Wis.) County, 1992-94; town adminstr. Town of Caledonia (Wis.), 1994—; ind. cons. in field, Milw., 1985-86; ind. real estate broker, Milw., 1986—. Mem. Women's Am. Orgn. Rehab. Through Tng., Wis. Bd. Realtors, U. Wis. Alumni Assn., Hadassah. Jewish. Office: Town of Caledonia 6922 Nicholson Rd Caledonia WI 53108

BLUMENTHAL, JEANNETTE I., operations research analyst; b. Olean, N.Y., Aug. 6, 1951; d. Louis James and Esther P. (Chavin) B. BS, SUNY Coll. at Buffalo, 1973, MS, 1976; AAS, Thomas Nelson C.C., Newport News, Va., 1984. Grad. teaching asst. SUNY, Buffalo, 1974-76; ops. rsch. intern U.S. Army, Ft. Monroe, Va., 1981, 85-86, ops. rsch. analyst, 1986-88; ops. rsch. analyst U.S. Army, Ft. Benjamin Harrison, Ind., 1988-93, Ft. Lee, Va., 1993—. 1st lt. USAF, 1976-80. Army Ops. Rsch. fellow, 1992. Mem. Am. Mensa Ltd. (local exec. com. 1986-88, spl. interest group coord. 1988-94, newsletter editor 1991-94).

BLUMENTHAL, SUSAN JANE, physician; b. N.Y.C., June 29, 1952; d. Stanley Robert and Eloyse Shirlee (Levine) B.; m. Edward John Markey, June 26, 1988. BA, Reed Coll., 1971; MD, U. Tenn., 1976; MPA, Harvard U., 1982. Diplomate Am. Bd. Psychiatry and Neurology. Intern. Stanford U. Sch. of Medicine, 1976-77, residency and fellowship, 1977-80; fellow NIMH, 1980-81, assoc. dir. Psychiatry Tng. Rev., head suicide rsch. unit and coord. of project depression, 1982-85, chief behavioral medicine program, 1985-93; clin. asst. prof. Tufts Med. Ctr., 1981-82; clin. asst. prof. psychiatry George Washington Sch. Medicine, 1982-86; clin. assoc. prof. psychiatry Georgetown Sch. Med., 1986-91; clin. prof. psychiatry Georgetown Sch. Medicine, Washington, 1991—; chief behavioral medicine Rsch. Br., NIMH, 1993-94; chair NIH Coordinating Com. on Health and Behavior, 1992-94; co-chair NIH Reunion Task Force, 1992-94; dep. asst. sec. health, asst. surgeon gen. HHS, 1994—, chair fed. coordinating com. breast cancer, fed. coordinating com. women's health and the environ., co-chair nat. breast cancer action plan, coordinating com. women's health issues PHS. Editor: Suicide Over the Life Cycle, 1989, Premenstrual Syndrome, 1985; mem. editorial bds. Jour. of Women's Health, Depression; advice columnist First Mag.; contbr. articles to sci. jours. Mem. Nat. Commn. on Sleep Disorders Rsch., workgroup on mental health Pres.' Task Force on Health Care Reform. Capt. USPHS, 1992—. Decorated Outstanding Svc. medal, Commendation medal, Meritorious Svc. medal USPHS. Mem. AMA, Nat. Women's Health Resource Ctr. (bd. dirs.), Am. Psychiat. Assn. (cons. Joint Coun. on Pub. Affairs), Am. Coll. Psychiatrists, Group for Advancement of Psychiatry, Am. Med. Women's Assn. (past chair com. on publicity and pub. rels.), Congl. Club, Internat. Club, Soc. Advancement Women's Health Rsch. (bd. dirs., v.p., scientific dir.), Am. Suicide Found. (bd. dirs. Washington divsn., pres.), Starlight Found. (chmn. sci. adv. bd.). Office: HHS 200 Independence Ave SW Rm 730 B Washington DC 20201

BLUMKIN, LINDA RUTH, lawyer; b. N.Y.C., Aug. 25, 1944; d. Louis and Edith (Fortus) Blumkin. A.B. cum laude, Barnard Coll., 1964; LL.B. cum laude, Harvard U., 1967, LL.M., 1973. Bar: N.Y. 1968, U.S. dist. ct. (so. dist.) N.Y. 1969, U.S. Ct. Apls. (2nd cir.) 1969, U.S. Supreme Ct. 1982. Assoc. Fried, Frank, Harris, Shriver & Jacobson, N.Y.C., 1967-71, ptnr., 1979—; lectr. Boston U., 1971, asst. prof. mgmt., 1972-73; assoc. Breed, Abbott & Morgan, N.Y.C., 1973-77; asst. dir. Bur. Competition FTC, 1977-79. Mem. ABA, N.Y.C. Bar Assn. Office: Fried Frank Harris Shriver & Jacobson 1 New York Pla 24th Fl New York NY 10004-1980

BLUMROSEN, RUTH GERBER, lawyer, educator, arbitrator; b. N.Y.C., Mar. 7, 1927; d. Lipman Samuel and Dorothy (Finklebrand) Gerber; m. Alfred William Blumrosen, July 3, 1952; children: Steven Marshall, Alexander B. BA in Econs., U. Mich., 1947, JD, 1953. Bar: Mich. 1953, U.S. Supreme Ct. 1967, U.S. Ct. Appeals (3d cir.). pvt. practice law, Detroit, 1953-55; cons. civil rights litigation, 1958-65; acting chief advice and analyses, acting dir. compliance EEOC, Washington, 1965; asst. dean Howard U., Washington, 1965-67; consul to chmn. EEOC, 1979-80; expert EEO HHS, Washington, 1980-81; assoc. prof. Grad. Sch. Mgmt., Rutgers U., Newark, 1972-87; resident scholar Rockefeller Found., Bellagio, Italy, 1995. Adviser, N.J. Commn. on Sex Discrimination in the Statutes, 1983—; commr. N.J. Gov.'s Study Commn. on Discrimination in Pub. Works Procurement and Constrn. Contracts, 1990-93. Fulbright scholar So. Africa, 1993. Mem. ABA, Fed. Bar Assn., Indsl. Rels. Rsch. Assn., Nat. Com. Pay Equity. Author: (with A. Blumrosen) Layoff or Worksharing: The Civil Rights Act of 1964 in the Recession of 1975; The Duty to Plan for Fair Employment Revisited: Worksharing in Hard Times, 1975; Wage Discrimination, Job Segregation and Title VII of Civil Rights Act of 1964, 1979; Wage Discrimination and Job Segregation: The Survival of a Theory, 1980; An Analysis of Wage Discrimination in N.J. State Service, 1983; Work-sharing, STC and Affirmative Action in Shorttime Compensation: A Formula for Work-sharing; Remedies for Wage Discrimination., 1987. Home: 54 Riverside Dr New York NY 10024

BLUMSTEIN, RENEÈ J., research and statistical consultant; b. Bklyn., Apr. 1, 1957; d. Robert and Rosalie (Burak) B. BA, Queens Coll., N.Y., 1978; MA, Columbia U., 1980, MEd, 1982, MPhil, 1984, PhD, 1986. Rsch. psychologist CCNY, 1980-85; rsch. cons. AT&T, N.Y.C., 1986; rsch. analyst Citibank, N.Y.C., 1986-87, rsch. and statis. cons., 1987—; rsch. and statis. cons. Informed Decision Svcs., Inc., N.Y.C., N.J.; adj. prof. rsch. methods CUNY, 1990—. Scholar Columbia U., 1981. Mem. Am. Psychol. Assn., Nat. Assn. Women Bus. Owners, Am. Edn. Rsch. Assn. Home and Office: 55 W 95th St Apt 93 New York NY 10025-8509

BLUM-VEGLIA, CHERYL ANN, accountant; b. Elizabeth, N.J., Jan. 5, 1966; d. Kenneth Peter and Mary Jo (Faccone) B. BA in Acctg. and Fin., Muhlenberg Coll., 1988. CPA, Pa. Auditor Deloitte & Touche, Parsippany, N.J., 1988-91; internal auditor N.J. Hwy. Authority, Woodbridge, 1991—. vol. Inst. for Children with Cancer and Blood Disorders. Mem. N.J. Soc. CPA's. Pa. Inst. CPAs, Muhlenberg Coll. Alumni Amb. Assn. Roman Catholic.

BLUNCK, KLAIRE DARLENE, nurse; b. Oconomowoc, Wis., May 3, 1954; d. Wynn F. and Frances Lavern (Bartlein) Kemnitz; m. William Randel Blunck, Aug. 11, 1973; children: Jacob William, Joseph Randel. AD, Milw. Area Tech. Coll., 1974; BSN, Carroll Coll., 1992. Cert. CPR, neonatal resusitation and pitocin adminstrn., lactation educator UCLA, inpatient obstet. nurse (Nat. Cert. Corp. for Ob-Gyn and Neonatal Specialities). Staff nurse Meml. Hosp., Oconomowoc, head quality improvement ob-gyn. unit. Laureate Group scholar.

BLUTH, B. J. (ELIZABETH JEAN CATHERINE BLUTH), sociologist, educator; b. Phila., Dec. 5, 1934; d. Robert Thomas and Catherine Cecelia (Boxman) Gowl; m. Thomas Del Bluth, Aug. 20, 1960 (dec. Aug. 6, 1980); children: Robert Thomas, Richard Del. B.A. in Sociology (Washington semster fellow), Bucknell U., 1953; M.A., Fordham U., 1960; Ph.D., UCLA, 1970. Teaching fellow in methods of social research Fordham U., 1957-58; reading instr. St. Margaret's High Sch., Tappahannock, Va., 1958-59; instr. history, civics and English, Rosary High Sch., San Diego, 1959-60; successively instr., asst. prof. sociology Immaculate Heart Coll., Los Angeles, 1960-65; prof. sociology Calif. State U., Northridge, 1965-87; grantee NASA Ames Research Ctr., Moffett Field, Calif., 1982-83; grantee space sta. program NASA, Washington, 1983-87; aerospace technologist system engring. div. space sta. program office NASA, Reston, Va., 1987-90, spl. asst. to dep. program dir. space sta. freedom program and ops., 1990-94; spl. tech. asst. to dir. Edn. Div. NASA, Washington, 1994—; cons. Immaculate Heart Community, L.A., 1967-69; engring. rsch. NASA Space Sta. design Boeing Aerospace Co., 1982-83; mem. Presdl. Citizens Adv. com. on Space, Coun. Nat. Space Policy, Nat. Tech. Com. on Soc. & Tech., UN teamon relevance os space activities to econ. and social devel.; professor emeritus Calif. State U., 1987—; computational scis. and informatics inst. dir.'s search com. George Mason U., 1992-93. Editor: (with others) Search for Identity Reader, vol. I and II, 1973, (with S.R. McNeal) Update on Space, vol. I, 1961, Parson's General Theory of Action, 1982, Space Station Habitability Report, 1983, Soviet Space Station Analog, 1983, Space Station Human Productivity Study NASA, 1986, Russian Mir Space Station Analog, 1993; contbr. articles to profl. jours. Recipient Alpha Omega faculty awards, 1966, 74, disting. teaching award Calif. State U., Northridge, 1968, NASA superior accomplishment award, 1990, NASA performance awards 1991-93; Inst. Advancement in Teaching and Learning fellow, Calif. State U., 1974. Fellow Am. Astronautical Soc.; mem. AIAA (chpt. award for outstanding program 1980), Am. Sociol. Assn., L5 Soc., Brit. Interplanetary Soc., Inst. Social Sci. Study of Space (acad. adv. bd.), Space Studies Inst., Human Factors Soc., Internat. Acad. Astronautics (com. on space econs. and benefits), Phi Beta Kappa. Republican. Office: NASA Code FE Edn Div 300 East St SW Washington DC 20546

BLYTH, ANN MARIE, secondary education educator; b. Sharon, Pa., June 18, 1949; d. Chester Stanley and Mary Clara (Romian) Kacerski; m. Lynn Allan Blyth, June 26, 1976 (dec. June 1983); 1 stepchild, Breton Alan Blyth; 1 child, Amanda Lynn. BS in Edn., Kent (Ohio) State U., 1971; postgrad., Loyola U., New Orleans, 1973-74; MS in Teaching, John Carroll U., 1978. Cert. comprehensive sci., maths. and physics tchr., Ohio. Jr. high math. tchr. New Philadelphia ((Ohio) Bd. of Edn., 1971-72; high sch. sci. and math. tchr. Hubbard (Ohio) Exempted Village Bd. of Edn., 1972-76, Painesville (Ohio) City Local Bd. Edn., 1976—; instr. math. Morton Salt, Painesville, 1979-80; part-time faculty Lake Erie Coll., 1992. Mem. Adv. Bd. Western Res. br. Am. Lung Assn. of Ohio, Painesville, 1986-89, sec, 1988-89, Northeastern br., Youngstown, Ohio, 1989—; judge state level Nat. Pre-teen and Pre-Teen Petite Pageants. Martha Holden Jennings Found. scholar, 1984-85; named Tchr. of the Yr., Harvey High Sch. Key Club, 1981-82. Mem. NEA, Ohio Edn. Assn., Northeastern Ohio Edn. Assn., Painesville City Tchrs. Assn., Am. Assn. Physics Tchrs., Nat. Sci. Tchrs. Assn., Cleve. Regional Coun. of Sci. Tchrs., Sci. Edn. Coun. of Ohio. Democrat. Episcopalian. Home: 8545 Willow Ln Chardon OH 44024-9231 Office: Thomas W Harvey High Sch 167 W Washington St Painesville OH 44077-3328

BLYTH, MYRNA GREENSTEIN, publishing executive, editor, author; b. N.Y.C., Mar. 22, 1939; d. Benjamin and Betty (Austin) Greenstein; m. Jeffrey Blyth, Nov. 25, 1962; children: Jonathan, Graham. B.A., Bennington (Vt.) Coll., 1960. Sr. editor Datebook mag., N.Y.C., 1960-62, Ingenue mag., N.Y.C., 1963-68; book editor Family Health mag., 1968-71; book and fiction editor, then assoc. editor Family Circle mag., N.Y.C., 1972-78; exec. editor Family Circle mag., 1978-81; editor-in-chief Ladies' Home Jour., 1981—, pub. dir., sr. v.p., 1987—; freelance writer, contbr. mags. Author: (novels) Cousin Suzanne, 1975, For Better and For Worse, 1978; contbr. articles to New Yorker mag., New York mag., Redbook mag., Cosmopolitan mag., Reader's Digest. Bd. dirs. Child Care Action Campaign, N.Y.C., 1989—; mem. nat. adv. bd. Susan G. Komen Breast Cancer Found.; active The Communitarians, Nat. Commn. on Am. Jewish Women. Mem. Am. Soc. Mag. Editors (exec. com. 1989—), N.Y. Women in Comm., Inc. (Amb. of Excellence), Women's Media Group, Authors League, Overseas Press Club (bd. govs.). Office: Ladies' Home Jour 100 Park Ave New York NY 10017-5516

BOAL, LYNDALL ELIZABETH, social worker; b. London, England, Feb. 19, 1936; came to U.S., 1953; d. George Woodall and Mary Barbara (Pearce) Cadbury; m. R. Bradlee Boal Aug. 29, 1959 (div. Sept. 1983); children: Jennifer, Peter. BA (hon.), Swarthmore (Pa.) Coll., 1957; MS, Simmons Coll. Sch. Social Work, Boston, 1959. Cert. sch. social worker, N.Y.; lic. social worker, Mass. Social worker Beth Israel Hosp., Boston, 1959-60, Mt. Sinai Hosp., N.Y.C., 1960-61, Meml. Sloan-Kettering Hosp, N.Y.C., 1961-63; cons. Dist. Nursing Svc., Mt. Kisco, N.Y., 1964-65; exec. dir. Planned Parenthood, Mt. Kisco, N.Y., 1965-68; dir. social worker No. Westchester Hosp., Mt. Kisco, N.Y., 1968-78; social worker Fox lane High Sch., Bedford Schs, 1978-81; chmn. com. on handicapped Bedford (N.Y.) Schs., 1981-86; social worker Chappaqua (N.Y.) Sch., 1988—; instr. Fordham U. Sch. Social Svcs., 1994—; bd. dirs. No. Westchester Guidance Ctr., Mt. Kisco; pres. Soc. Hosp. Social Work Dirs., Westchester, N.Y., 1976-78. Chmn. Narcotics Guidance Coun., Bedford, 1972-75; No. Westchester Coun. Equality pres., Bedford, 1984-86; bd. dirs. Sherrill House, Boston, 1986-88; Dem. Committeeman, Bedford, 1983-86. Mem. NASW (sec. N.Y. state chpt. 1993—, chair state pers. com. 1993-94, pres. Westchester divsn. 1969-71, 91-92, Merit Svc. award Westchester divsn. 1993), Am. Orthopsychiat. Assn., N.Y. State Sch. Social Workers Assn., Kappa Delta Pi. Democrat. Mem. Soc. of Friends. Home: 508 Millwood Rd Mount Kisco NY 10549 Office: Chappaqua Schs Chappaqua NY 10514

BOAL, MARCIA ANNE RILEY, clinical social worker, administrator; b. Carthage, Mo., Sept. 29, 1944; d. William Joseph and Thelma P. (Simpson) Riley; m. David W. Boal, Aug. 12, 1967; children: Adam J. W., Aaron D. Boal. BA, U. Kans., 1966, MSW, 1981. Lic. clin. social worker. Child therapist Gillis Home for Children, Kansas City, Mo., 1981; social worker Leavenworth (Kans.) County Spl. Edn. Cooperative, 1981-84; sch. social worker, dir. health and social svcs. Kans. State Sch. for the Blind, Kansas City, Kans., 1984—; pvt. practice adoption counseling and workshops, 1981—; field instr. Sch. of Social Welfare, Kans. U., 1986—. Author: Surviving Kids, 1983, Teaching Social Skills to Blind and Visually Impaired Children, 1987. Nat. networking chmn. Jr. League Kansas City, 1977-81; bd. dirs. Wyandotte House Ind, 1973-81, Kans. Action For Children, Topeka, 1981, Gov.'s Commn. on Parent Edn., Topeka, 1984—, Lake of the Forest, 1994— (sec.). Named Kans. Sch. Social Worker of Yr., 1989. Mem. Council Exceptional Children, Nat. Assn. Social Workers, Kans. Assn. Sch. Social Workers, Am. Orthopsychiat. Assn., Kans. Conf. Social Welfare, R.P. Found., Phi Kappa Phi. Home: Lake Of The Frst Bonner Springs KS 66012 Office: Kans State Sch for Blind Handicapped 1100 State Ave Kansas City KS 66102-4411

BOARMAN, MARJORIE RUTH, manufacturing company executive, consultant; b. Lakeland, Fla., Apr. 14, 1953; d. Hugh Francis and Nancy Addair (McCracken) Roberts; m. Edward F. Moore, June 28, 1975 (div. 1986); children: Kulani Anne, Brittany Elizabeth; m. James Louis Boarman, Feb. 5, 1987; 1 child, Joshua; stepchildren: Steven, Christina, Paulette. BS in Edn., Fla. State U., 1975; MEd, U. Hawaii/Manoa, 1978. Cert. tchr., Fla., Mo. Substitute tchr. KCCA Preschs., Honolulu, 1975; tchr. Hickam Day Care Ctr., Hickam AFB, Hawaii, 1975-77; tchr., sales rep. Grolier Interstate Inc., Honolulu, 1977; tchr. Kiddie Kollege Presch., Hickam AFB, 1977-79, Our Lady of Sorrows Schs., St. Louis, 1979-80; program dir. Clayton (Mo.) YWCA, 1981-82; cons. Parent Talk Svcs., Phoenix, 1983-85; tchr. Polk County Schs., Polk City, Fla., 1986-89; co-owner Boarman Built Inc., Green Ridge, Mo., 1989—. Co-creator: Bon Voyage board game, 1992. Leader, coord. Camp Fire Boys and Girls, Lakeland, 1988—; bd. dirs. Boswell PTA, Auburndale, 1991-92. Mem. NAFE, Assn. Craft and Creative Industries, Auburndale C. of C. (bd. dirs. 1991-92), Green Ridge C. of C. (bd. dirs. 1994—), Sedalia BPW (2d v.p. membership chmn. 1993—), Kappa Delta Pi. Republican. Pentacostal. Home and Office: Boarman Built Inc PO Box 145 Green Ridge MO 65332

BOATWRIGHT, CHARLOTTE JEANNE, hospital marketing and public relations executive; b. Chattanooga, Dec. 12, 1937; d. Clifton Gentry and Veltina Novella (Braden) Blevins; m. Robert W. Boatwright; children: Lynn Kay, Janis Ann, Karen Jean, Mary Ruth, Melody Susan, April Celeste. Diploma, Erlanger Sch. Nursing, Chattanooga, 1963; BS, U. Tenn., Chattanooga, 1976, MEd, 1981; PhD, Columbia Pacific U., San Rafael, Calif., 1987. RN, Tenn. Surgeon's asst. William Robert Fowler, M.D., Chattanooga, 1963-64; instr. med.-surg. nursing Baroness Erlanger Hosp. Sch. Nursing, 1964-67, instr. fundamentals nursing, 1971-74, chmn. dept. mental health-psychiat. nursing, 1977-81; staff nurse Meml. Hosp., Chattanooga, 1967-68, nursing supr., 1968-70; dir. inservice edn. Hutcheson Med. Ctr., Ft. Oglethorpe, Ga., 1970-71; youth work cons. Sewanee Dist. Episcopal Chs., Chattanooga, 1975-76; dir. spl. projects North Park Hosp., Chattanooga, 1984-87, dir. mktg. and pub. rels., 1987—; freelance writer;. mem. dept. youth work Episcopal Diocese Tenn., 1975-77; condr. adult ch. sch. groups St. Martin's Episcopal Ch., Chattanooga; vice chmn. Brynewood Park Community Assn., 1985, 86. Mem. Am. Coll. Healthcare Execs. (nominee), Tenn. Hosp. Assn., Tenn. Soc. for Hosp. Mktg. and Pub. Rels., Chattanooga C. of C., U. Tenn. Alumnae Assn., Columbia Pacific U. Alumnae Assn., Chi Sigma Iota. Republican.

BOAZ, DONIELLA CHAVES, psychotherapist, consultant; b. Grand Junction, Colo., Apr. 8, 1934; d. Leon T. and Marian (Fonder) Hutton; m. Richard Boas, Apr. 7, 1956 (div. 1983); children: Roxanne, Annika, Becca; m. Jack J. Chaves, Mar. 11, 1995. Cert. pastoral ministry Seattle U., 1978;

cert. clin. pastoral edn. Va. Mason Hosp., 1979; BA, Antioch West, 1980; postgrad. Lan Ting Inst. cross-cultural studies PROC, 1986, 92, 94, C.G. Jung Inst., Zurich, 1986, 87, 89. Cert. neuro-linguistic programmer, 1991. Owner Donalee's Studio of Dance, Kirkland, Wash., 1952-63; adminstrv. asst. Ch. of Redeemer, Kenmore, Wash., 1974-76; counselor Eastside Mental Health, Bothell, Wash., 1976-79; psychotherapist, Seattle, 1979—; owner, cons. Optimum Options, Seattle, 1979—; founder DISCOVERIES Seminars, various other govt., bus., non-profit orgns., nat. and internat. trainer, cons.; mem. adj. faculty Seattle U., Northwest Coll. Holistic Studies and Huston Sch. Theology, 1980-87; mem. Wash. State Dept. Health Adv. Com. for Cert. Mental Health Counselors, 1994—. Author: Embrace Your Child-Self: Change Your Life, 1993. V.p. Episcopal Ch. standing com. on stewardship, 1979-81; active in local politics., 1968-80; mem. Clin. Pastoral Edn. Mem. Seattle Counselors Assn. (pres.). Avocations: philosophy, carpentry, bridge, entertaining, traveling. Office: Lane's End Pub Co Grosvenor House 500 Wall St Apt 309 Seattle WA 98121-1534

BOBENHOUSE, NELLIE RUTH, insurance company executive; b. Spickard, Mo., May 3, 1936; d. Joseph Howard and Nellie Elizabeth (Tuttle) Yates; m. Lewis L. Griffin, Apr. 22, 1956 (div. Jan. 1964); 1 child, Elizabeth Anne Griffin Schafer; m. Robert A. Bobenhouse, Aug. 28, 1965. Student, St. Joseph (Mo.) Jr. Coll., 1955, Grandview Coll., 1980. Sec. News-Press & Gazette, St. Joseph, 1954-56; sec., bookkeeper Wilson's Locker & Ins., Spickard, Mo., 1956-60, Oyler's Locker, Spickard, 1960-64; sec. Equitable of Iowa Agy., Des Moines, 1964-68, agy. office supr., 1968—. City clk. City of Spickard, 1959-60; support group leader, co-founder Chronic Fatigue Syndrome Soc., Des Moines, 1988—; bd. dirs. Iowa Chronic Fatigue Syndrome/CFIDS Assn., Cedar Rapids, 1991; mem. Des Moines Women's Club, 1994—, Urbandale Garden Club, 1994—. Fellow Life Mgmt. Inst.; mem. Ins. Women Des Moines (com. chmn. 1975), P. Buckley Moss Soc., Beta Sigma Phi (sec.-treas. 1958-60, Woman of Yr. 1959). Republican. Disciple of Christ. Home: 905 59th St West Des Moines IA 50266-7516 Office: Equitable of Iowa Agy Hub Towers Ste 1300 Des Moines IA 50309

BOBERG, DOROTHY KURTH, author; b. Lincoln, Nebr., Mar. 17, 1930; d. Herman R. and Regina E. Kurth; m. John Elliott Boberg, Sept. 17, 1951; 1 child, Mark Craig. BA, U. Nebr., 1951; postgrad., Calif. State U., Northridge, 1959-62, U. So. Calif., 1981. Libr. Nebr. Legis. Coun., Lincoln, 1952; child welfare worker L.A. County, 1953-57, 67-68; rsch. assoc. Nuclear Facilities/Radiation Monitoring in Calif. Another Mother for Peace, Beverly Hills, Calif., 1975; exec. v.p. So. Calif. divsn. UN Assn., L.A., 1977-78. Author: Evolution and Reason Beyond Darwin, 1993; editor Nebraska Blue Book. Resolutions chair L.A. County Dem. Cen. Com.; chair UN Internat. Solar Exhibition, L.A., 1978, Mayor's Lifeline Com., Earthquake Prediction Task Force; pres. Northridge Civic Assn., 1971-73. Recipient Achievement award Nebr. Sec. State, 1993, Admiral, Nebr. Navy/Gov. State Nebr., 1993. Mem. AAAS, Soc. Study Evolution, AAUW (pres. San Fernando Valley Br. 1966-67), Phi Beta Kappa, Psi Chi, Alpha Kappa Delta. Home: 10912 Nestle Ave Northridge CA 91326

BOBERG, JANET ANN, police officer, educator; b. Eau Claire, Wis., May 13, 1960; d. John Richard and Yvonne Charolette (Nelson) B.; m. Jeffrey Alan Johnson, Oct. 20, 1984 (div. Aug. 1985). BA in Sociology, Ariz. State U., 1986, postgrad., 1994—. Cert. detention officer, Ariz. Police asst. Ariz. State U. Police, Tempe, 1980-81; surg. nurse asst. Scottsdale (Ariz.) Meml. Hosp., 1981-84; detention officer Maricopa County Sheriffs Office, Phoenix, 1985-88; police recruit Peoria (Ariz.) Police Dept., 1988, police/field tng. officer, 1988—; part-time instr. Glendale (Ariz.) C.C., 1993—; Drug Abuse Resistance Edn./Gang Resistance Edn. and Tng. officer Peoria Police Dept., 1992—; instr. various police-related acads., 1990—. Mem. U.S. Police Ski Team, Boulder, Colo., 1990. Recipient Acad. Excellence award Phoenix Regional Police Acad., 1988. Mem. Peoria Police Officers Assn., Nat. D.A.R.E. Officer's Assn., Ariz. D.A.R.E. Officer's Assn., Peoria Unidos, Kiwanis (Peoria breakfast club). Republican. Home: PO Box 2483 Peoria AZ 85380 Office: Peoria Police Dept 8343 W Monroe St Peoria AZ 85345

BOBET, MADELINE B., paralegal; b. N.Y.C., June 5, 1951; d. Mariano and Helen (Santiago) Rodriguez Bobet; m. Raul Suarez (div. Mar. 1983); children: Raul III, Paul, David, Candi-Marie; m. Michael Anthony Perez, June 11, 1993. Student in prelaw, Bklyn. Coll., 1985. Exec. sec. Holex Office Systems Inc., Bklyn., 1980-85; paralegal trust and estate divsn. Lent & Abrams, N.Y.C., 1985-87; paralegal def. litigation Jacobowitz, Garfinkel & Lesman, N.Y.C., 1987—. Pres. Community League, N.Y.C., 1986—; exec. com. Case Mgmt. for Retarded Children, Wassaic, N.Y., 1993—. Mem. N.Y. State Assn. Retarded Children (bd. govs. 1986—), Internat. Order Rainbows (chmn. adv. bd. 1991—), Order Ea. Star (historian 1991—), Regina Pacis Choir (soprano). Democrat. Roman Catholic. Home: 1357 65th St Brooklyn NY 11219

BOBO, BECKY PARKS, computer science teacher; b. Ft. Worth, Tex., Nov. 24, 1963; d. Bernard Weldon and Bobbie Dell (Streater) Parks; m. Benny Carl Bobo, Feb. 5, 1983; children: Brandon Robert, Bryce Taylor. BS, Tarleton State U., 1986; Teaching Cert., Tex. Women's U., 1989. Cert. tchr. phys. edn., bus. edn. and computer sci., Tex. Tchr./coach Chico (Tex.) Ind. Sch. Dist., 1989-90; tchr. Slidell (Tex.) Ind. Sch. Dist., 1990—. Mem. Profl. Bus. Women's Assn., Phy. Edn. Majors and Minors Assn. (grad. rep. 1988-93), Interscholastic Press League. Baptist. Home: 821 Minuteman Blue Mound TX 76131 Office: Slidell ISD PO Box 69 Slidell TX 76267

BOBO, GENEVIEVE TOWNSEND, marriage and family therapist; b. Bronx, N.Y., Jan. 19, 1932; d. George Arthur Lawrence and Jennie (Fisher) Townsend; m. Laurence Thorne Brockway, Sept. 1, 1950 (div. Sept. 1969); children: Loren David, Kari Ellen, Morgan Scott, Jennifer Brockway; m. Murno Clyde Bobo, Nov. 8, 1970. BA in English, Calif. State U., Fullerton, 1969, MS in Spl. Edn., 1975; MS in Marriage Family Counseling, Sierra U., Santa Monica, Calif., 1983; PhD in Counseling Psychology, Newport U., 1982. Tchr. English Fullerton Union H.S. Dist., 1969-74, adminstrn. designee, tchr. pregnant minors, 1974-75, dept. chairperson, spl. edn. tchr., 1975-90, learning disabilities tchr., 1990-94; therapist Fullerton, 1994—; counselor, trainer New Hope Telephone Crystal Cathedral, Garden Grove, Calif., 1975-85, Friends Against Suicide, 1980-85, counselor Prison Ministry, 1983-87; advisor Key Club Sonora H.S., La Habra, Calif., 1993-94. Author: (with Murno C. Bobo) Divergence I: Something Different in Reading, 1972, Divergence II: Something Different in Writing, 1975; co-author: No Place To Go: Male Survivors of Abuse. Youth leader Cub Scouts and Campfire Girls, Fountain Valley, Calif., 1960-65; co-facilitator Battered Men's Group Yorba Hills Hosp. Mental Health Group, 1994; cons., program vol. Orange County Ct.'s Kids' Turn, 1994—. Mem. Christian Counselors Assn., Calif. Assn. Marriage and Family Therapists, Kiwanis Internat. (youth sponsor 1992—). Democrat. Home: 15791 Las Flores St Westminster CA 92683 Office: Brief Term Tehrapy Ctr 1031 Rosecrans # 212A Fullerton CA 92635

BOBRUFF, CAROLE MARKS, radio show producer, personality; b. N.Y.C., Nov. 11, 1935; d. Morris Frank and Harriet (Lehman) Marks; m. Jerome Bobruff, June 20, 1954 (div. 1986); children: Ellen, Neal, Paul, Mark. Student, Quinnipac Coll., 1954-55, U. N.C., 1955-56; AS, U. New Haven, 1981; BS in Human Services, N.H. Coll., 1982. Founder, dir. Tyndall Air Force Daycare Ctr., Panama City, Fla., 1957-60; med. asst. Digestive Disease Assocs., New London, Conn., 1974-82; program coord. Pre-Trial Release Program, Norwich, New London, Conn., 1982-84; case mgr., counselor residential criminal justice program Cochegan House, Montville, Conn., 1984-85; exec. dir. Ret. Sr. Vol. Program So. New London County, 1984-91; producer, host radio program Senior Focus Sta. WSUB, Groton, Conn., 1991—; treas. Dir. Vols. in Agys., New London, 1986—, Conn. RSVP Dirs., 1987; bd. dirs. Cochegan House, Widowed Persons Service, Waterford, Conn. Editor: Senior Citizens Guide to Discounts and Services, 1988; editor, author: RSVP Newsletter, 1984—; columnist: The Day, 1987. Pres. women's aux. New London County Med. Assn., 1986-87; bd. dirs. League Women Voters, New London, HOSPICE, New London, Am. Cancer Soc. New London County. Recipient Proclamation Community award Town of Waterford, 1989, Community Service award The Connection, Inc., 1987. Mem. Women's Network New London County, Children and Family Services, Pub. Relations Network, Nat. Assn. Female Execs., Brandeis U. Jewish. Home: 223 Flanders Rd Unit 10 Niantic CT 06357-1223

BOCCELLI, JANET MARY, general contractor, restaurant owner; b. Stoneham, Mass., July 11, 1956; d. Robert Francis and Nancy Beryl (Decker) Walsh; m. Joseph Anthony Boccelli, May 16, 1980; children: Joseph II, Steven J., Lauren A. Grad. high sch., Cambridge, Mass. Cert. real estate salesperson. Archtl. design sec. Architects Collaborative, Cambridge, 1975-80; gen. contractor A.F.J. Inc., Wakefield, Mass., 1980-93; owner, gen. contractor HER Constrn., Inc., Plymouth, Mass., 1993—; bd. dirs., owner Cranberries Restaurant/Entertainment Complex (formerly known as Indian River Inn), Plymouth, Mass., 1993—. Democrat. Roman Catholic. Home: 55 Buckskin Path Plymouth MA 02360

BOCCHICCHIO, LUCILLE M., management consultant. BS in Math. with honors, U. R.I., 1961. Engr., computer analyst Sikorsky div. United Tech., Stratford, Conn., 1961-64; systems programmer, analyst Unisys Corp., N.Y.C., 1964-65; sr. cons. Advanced Computer Techniques, N.Y.C., 1965-69; dir. tng. Levin-Townsend Service Corp., N.Y.C., 1969-70; mgmt. cons. L.M. Bocchicchio, Ltd., N.Y.C., 1970-91; pres. LMB Enterprises, N.Y.C., 1991—. Author: Our Child's Medical History, 1982; contbr. articles to profl. jours.

BOCCHINO, FRANCES LUCIA, oil company official; b. Bronx, N.Y., July 5, 1944; d. Pasquale and Mary Ruth (Lacerenza) B. Grad. high sch., Bklyn., 1962. Various positions Texaco Inc., N.Y.C., 1965-86; sr. analyst exec. dept. Texaco Inc., Harrison, N.Y., 1987-90, transfer agt., 1990—. Active Whitestone (N.Y.) Taxpayers Assn. Mem. Corp. Transfer Agts. Assn. Republican. Roman Catholic. Home: 15-15 150th St Whitestone NY 11357 Office: Texaco Inc 2000 Westchester Ave White Plains NY 10604-3613

BOCCHINO, LINDA ELIZABETH, jewelry store executive, registered nurse; b. Lynn, Mass., Sept. 28, 1948; d. Anthony Hamilton and Ruth J. (Moran) Dyczus; m. Anthony Bocchino. Student, Fitchburg (Mass.) State Coll., 1967; RN diploma, Burbank Hosp., 1969; grad. gemologist, Gemological Inst. Am., Santa Monica, Calif., 1989. RN, Mass.; cert. gemologist appraiser. Surg. nurse Beverly (Mass.) Hosp., 1970-71; charge nurse Louise Caroline Nursing Home, Saugus, Mass., 1971-72; supr. nursing Saugus Hosp., 1972-78; with sales dept. Germain Monteil Cosmetics, Peabody, Mass., 1978; pres. Martoni Jewelers, Peabody, Mass., 1978—; tchr. adult edn. dept. North Shore Community Coll., Beverly, Mass. Author poem published in 1989 New American Anthology (Golden Poet award 1988). Named Top 100 Women in Bus., Boston Woman mag., 1988; recipient Silver Poet award, 1989. Mem. Gemological Inst. Am. (Alumni Mem. award 1988, 89, Outstanding Mem. award 1991), Gemolological Inst. Am. Alumni Assn. (pres. New England chpt. 1990-92), Am. Gem Soc. (registered jeweler), Internat. Soc. Appraisers (designated), Boston Jewelers Club, Mass.-R.I. Jewelers Assn. (bd. dirs. 1988-92), Order Ea. Star. Office: Martoni Jewelers Inc 215 Newbury St Peabody MA 01960-2499

BOCCIA, JUDY ELAINE, home health agency executive, consultant; b. San Diego, Aug. 29, 1955; d. Robert Garrett and Jerry Athalee (Carruth) Stacy; m. John Michael Boccia, July 29, 1977; 1 child, Jennifer Lynn. BSN, Calif. State U., San Diego, 1978. RN, Calif.; lic. pub. health nurse, Calif. Staff nurse Univ. Hosp., U. Calif., San Diego, 1978-80, 81-82, Moffitt Hosp., San Francisco, 1980-81, Humana Huntington, Huntington Beach, Calif., 1982-84; intravenous and hospice vis. nurse Town & Country Nursing, Garden Grove, Calif., 1984-85; vis. nurse Vis. Nurse Assn., Orange, Calif., 1985-86; v.p. Doctors and Nurse Med. Mgmt., Newport Beach, Calif., 1986-89; dir. nursing HMSS, So. Calif., 1989-90; pres. Premier Care, Irvine, 1990-91; exec. v.p. Homecare Nursing, Inc., Lake Forest, Calif., 1991—; cons., Calif., 1987—, Homelife Nursing, Inc., Lake Forest, 1992—; pres. Frontlines Nursing, Inc., Homelife Nursing/Staffbuilders, Lake Forest, 1995; educator AIDS; presenter in field. Mem. Oncology Nursing Soc., Intravenous Nurse Soc. Democrat. Methodist. Home: 28232 Festivo Mission Viejo CA 92692-2617 Office: Homelife Nursing Inc 23832 Rockfield Blvd Ste 280 Lake Forest CA 92630-2820

BOCK, CAROLYN ANN, author, consultant, trainer; b. New Bavaria, Ohio, Jan. 25, 1942; d. Wilfred Ignatius and Marcella Mary (Birkemeier) Gerschutz; m. Donald Charles Bock, Sept. 7, 1974; 1 son, Jonathon Edward. Student Notre Dame Coll., 1960-62, 87, John Carroll U., 1962-66. With sales and promotions dept. Schaffer Diversified Corp. and other cos., Cleve., 1962-74; columnist, writer West Life Newspaper, Westlake, Ohio, 1980-83, Westlaker Times, Lorain, Ohio, 1983-84; owner Dynamic Living Assocs., Westlake, 1986—. Feature writer, bus., arts, families, health. Author: Authors, Artists and Auras, 1988, Gerschutz family history, 1989. Co-founder, trustee Community Action Team, Westlake, 1980-85, Westlake Arts Council, 1984—, co-founder, 1983-84, pres., 1984-85; chmn. Morning Seminar, Rocky River, Ohio, 1981-85; pres. Westlake PTA Council, 1980-82, Parkside Jr. High PTA, Westlake, 1983-84; active Boy Scouts, Cub Scouts, Westlake, 1977-82; mem. Clague Playhouse, Westlake, 1983—, Westlake Hist. Soc., 1985—. Recipient Outstanding Service award Westlake Cub Scouts, 1980; hon. life mem. Ohio PTA, 1982; Ohio Arts Council grantee, 1984, 85 . Mem. Am. Entrepreneurs Assn., Westlake C. of C., Soc. Profl. Journalists, Acad. Profl. Cons. and Adminstrns. Republican. Unitarian Universalist. Avocations: traveling, reading, cooking. Home and Office: 23553 Belmont Dr Cleveland OH 44145-2797

BOCK, JOANNE, art history educator; b. New Haven, Aug. 29, 1940; d. W. Lawrence and Anne (Mauro) B. BA in Art, Coll. New Rochelle, 1962; MA in History of Edn., Cath. U. Am., 1968; MA in Am. Folklore, SUNY, Oneonta, 1970; PhD in Am. Culture, U. Mich., 1986, postgrad., 1994. Docent Yale U. Art Gallery, New Haven, 1968; photo archivist Amon Carter Mus. Western Art, Ft. Worth, 1960-70; bicentennial project coord. Nat. Portrait Gallery Smithsonian Instn., Washington, 1971-72, mus. specialist Mus. History and Tech., 1972-73; rsch. asst. Bentley Libr., Mich. Hist. Coll., Ann Arbor, 1974; cultural developer Mich. Ethnic Studies Ctr., Detroit, 1974; lectr. in humanities Wayne State U., Detroit, 1986; profl. tutor Washtenaw C.C., Ann Arbor, 1987-88; asst. prof. art history Kendall Coll. Art, Grand Rapids, Mich., 1988-90, Ft. Lewis Coll., Durango, Colo., 1991—. Author: Pop Wiener: Naive Painter, 1970; contbr. articles to profl. jours. Grantee Scriven Found., 1968-69, Andrew W. Mellon Found., 1974, NEH, 1973-74, Am. Culture Program, 1974-75, 75, 80, 81, Romanian Assn., 1975-77, IREX, 1978, 79, 80-81, Rackham Grad. Sch., 1980, 82-83, others. Mem. Am. Studies Assn., Coll. Art Assn., Immigration History Soc., Civa. Roman Catholic. Home: 901 Florida Rd Apt 11 Durango CO 81301-4768 Office: Ft Lewis Coll Art Dept 107 Fa Durango CO 81301

BOCK, LINDA C., public relations executive. BA, U. Utah; MS, Syracuse U. With Provandie & Chirurg Inc.; dir. comm. The Travelers, 1980-81, dir. older americans program, 1981-82, dir./pub. rels., 1982-85; v.p. corp. comms. Home Life Ins. Co., 1985-91; v.p. comm. Mutual of N.Y., 1991—. Mem. Pub. Rels. Soc. Am. Office: Mutual of NY 1740 Broadway New York NY 10019*

BOCKIAN, DONNA MARIE, data processing executive; b. N.Y.C., June 4, 1946; d. Forrest Mager and Mary C. (Lovelace) Hastings; m. James Bernard Bockian, Sept. 16, 1984; children: Vivian Shifra, Adrian Adena, Lillian Tova. BA in Psychology, Vassar Coll., 1968; diploma in systems analysis NYU, 1978. Computer programmer RCA, N.Y.C., 1968-71; systems analyst United Artists Corp., N.Y.C., 1971-78; project leader Bradford Nat. Corp., N.Y.C., 1978-81; project mgr. Mfrs. Hanover Trust, N.Y.C., 1981-83; project mgr. Chem. Bank, N.Y.C., 1983-86; mgr. fin. systems Salomon Bros., N.Y.C., 1986-87; v.p. James B. Bockian and Assocs., 1987-93; mgr. systems quality assurance GAB Bus. Svcs., Inc., Parsippany, N.J., 1989-91; mgr. bus. systems GAB Bus. Svcs., Inc., Parsippany, N.J., 1991-93; mgr. cons. ADIA Info. Techs., Inc., Piscataway, N.J., 1994—. Mem. Assn. Women in Computing (exec. com. 1982-83), Data Administrn. Mgmt. Assn. N.J., Vassar Club. Avocation: photography. Home: 26 Farmhouse Ln Morristown NJ 07960-3019

BOCKSTEIN, MINDY AVA, legislative administrator; b. Bklyn., Feb. 9, 1960; d. Hyman and Belle (Rubin) B. BA magna cum laude, U. Miami, 1980; postgrad., Bklyn. Coll., 1990. Legal clk., researcher Hillsborough County Atty., Tampa, Fla., 1978; tchr. Judaic studies Beth Torah Congregation, North Miami Beach, Fla., 1979-80; tchr. gen. elem. studies East Midwood Jewish Ctr., 1980-84; tchr. Judaic studies Madison Jewish Ctr., Bklyn., 1980-84; sr. legis. asst. to assemblyman Dan Feldman N.Y. State Assembly, Albany, 1985-90, legis. dir. to assemblyman Dan Feldman, 1990—; press sec. Bklyn. Dist. Atty. Campaign, summer, 1989; bd. dirs. Midwood Devel. Corp. Art dir. yearbook for East Midwood Jewish Ctr., 1981-82; author: (brochure) Your Rights When the PVB is Wrong, 1987, 93. Bd. dirs. Nottingham Civic Assn., Bklyn., 1991—; vol. Jewish Assn. for Svcs. for the Aged Sr. Alliance Ctr., Bklyn., 1989—; organizer Bklyn. chpt. MADD, Bklyn. Phone Friend; organizer, cons. Marine Park/Nottingham Recyclers, 1989-93; active Dem. Women of Legislature, Nat. Women's Polit. Caucus, Giraffe Project; vol. polit. campaigns for state and city elected offices, Bklyn., 1987-93; youth leader Young Judea, Fla., 1977-79; mem. Nat. Com. on Effective Crime Policy, 1995. Recipient Disting. Svc. award Jewish War Vets., 1991; presdl. scholar U. Tampa, 1976-78, acad. merit scholar U. Miami, 1978-80, Judaic studies scholar U. Miami, 1979-80; named to Outstanding Young Women of Am., 1985. Mem. Am. Polit. Sci. Assn., Pub. Adminstrn. Assn., Golden Key Nat. Honor Soc., Nat. Coll. Register, Phi Kappa Phi, Phi Sigma Alpha, Delta Theta Mu. Office: NY State Assembly Rm 526lob Albany NY 12248

BOCKWITZ, CYNTHIA LEE, psychotherapist, counselor, psychology and women's studies educator; b. Hallock, Minn., Apr. 11, 1954; d. Rodney Lee and Jeanette Yvonne (Vilen) B. AA in Arts and Scis., Richland Coll., 1983; BA in Psychology, U. Tex., Dallas, 1985; MA in Counseling Psychology, Tex. Woman's U., 1992. Lic. profl. counselor, Ga. Pers. adminstr. Automatic Data Processing, Miami, Fla., 1974-77; office mgr. G.A. Dexter Co., Atlanta, 1977-79; human resources mgr. No. Telecom, Atlanta and Dallas, 1979-84; mental health worker Timberlawn Psychiat. Hosp., Dallas, 1984-85; acct. NEC Am., Dallas, 1986-87; asst. program dir. Arbor Creek Hosp., Sherman, Tex., 1989; lic. profl. counselor Trinity Counseling Ctr., Carrollton, Tex., 1989-93, Atlanta, 1993—; adj. instr. psychology Tex. Woman's U., Denton, 1988-92; instr. psychology DeKalb Coll., Atlanta, 1993—; cons. The Resource Ctr., Atlanta, 1993-94, Laurel Heights Hosp., 1994—; mem. exec. com. Women Clinicians Network, Atlanta, 1994, 95. Mem. Olympic Vol. Force, Habitat for Humanity. Mem. ACLU, NOW (fin. contbr.), APA (assoc.), Am. Assn. for Marriage and Family Therapy (assoc.), Assn. for Women in Psychology, Ga. Mental Health Counselors Assn., Ga. Marriage and Family Therapy Assn. (legis. com. 1993-94), Ga. Psychol. Assn., Phi Kappa Phi, Psi Chi. Democrat. Home: 711 Tuxworth Circle Decatur GA 30033 Office: Laurel Heights Hosp 934 Briarcliff Rd Atlanta GA 30306

BODA, VERONICA CONSTANCE, lawyer; b. Phila., Oct. 8, 1952; d. Louis Paul and Helen Ann (Zwigaitis) B. AB, Wilson Coll., 1974; JD, Vermont Law Sch., 1978; LLM in Taxation, Villanova U., 1989. Staff atty. Cape-Atlantic Legal Services, Atlantic City, 1978-79; sole practice Phila., 1980—; tchr. Am. Inst. for Paralegal Studies, Phila., 1982-86; instr. bus. adminstrn. program Pa. State U., Media, Pa., 1987-88; ins. agt. Prudential Ins. Co., Wayne, Pa., 1985-86; ins. broker V C Boda & Co., Phila., 1986—. Author: (with others) Newberg on Class Actions, 1985; editor Women Lawyers Jour., 1993—; contbr. articles to profl. jours. Bd. dirs. Emergency Aid of Pa. Found., 1994—, Colonial Phila. Hist. Soc., 1983, pres., 1984-89; asst. treas. Independence Hall Assn., 1989—. Mem. Nat. Assn. Women Lawyers (treas., pres.), Phila. Bar Assn. (chair com. real estate sect. 1984-86). Democrat. Roman Catholic.

BODDEWYN, MARILYN STIEFEL, recruiting firm executive; b. N.Y.C., Dec. 17, 1946; d. David and Reba (Lane) Stiefel; m. Jean J. Boddewyn, Dec. 27, 1979. BBA, CUNY, Baruch, 1980. Pres. Bodner, Inc., N.Y.C., 1984—. Office: Bodner Inc 372 Fifth Ave # 91C New York NY 10018-8106

BODE, BARBARA, foundation executive; b. Evanston, Ill.; d. Carl and Margaret Emilie (Lutze) B. B.A. magna cum laude, U. Md., MA; scholar, Ludwig-Maximillians-Universitat, Munich; English Speaking Union scholar, U. London; Bundesrepublik scholar, Goethe Institut, Lubeck, W. Ger.; postgrad. NDEA fellow, UCLA. Woodrow Wilson teaching fellow N.C. Central U., Durham; pres. Children's Found., Washington, 1970-86, Council on Founds., 1986-89; v.p. Coun. Better Bus. Bur., 1990—; exec. dir. Coun. Bettter Bus. Bur. Found., 1990—. Bd. dirs. Children's Found., Rainboe TV Works, Nat. Com. for Responsive Philanthropy, Disability Rights, Edn. and Def. Fund Partnership, Women's Campaign Fund, 1984-88; mem. Women of Washington, 1992—, Leadership Washington, 1993-94. Woodrow Wilson Nat. Found. fellow, 1963-64. Mem. Women of Washington, Women and Founds. Corp. Philanthropy. Episcopalian. Home: 1661 Crescent Pl NW Washington DC 20009-4074 Office: Coun of BBB 4200 Wilson Blvd Arlington VA 22203

BODE, SUSAN, set decorator. Films include: Heartburn, 1986, Wall Street, 1987, The Secret of My Success, 1987, The Glass Menagerie, 1987, The Believers, 1987, Big, 1988, Fletch Lives, 1989, Crimes and Misdemeanors, 1989, New York Stories (Oedipus Wrecks), 1989, Quick Change, 1990, Alice, 1990, The Hard Way, 1991, Husbands and Wives, 1992, Used People, 1992, Manhattan Murder Mystery, 1993, Don't Drink the Water, 1994 (TV Movie), Bullets Over Broadway, 1994 (Acad. award nom., Best Art Direction), Wolf, 1994. Office: IATSE Local 876 11365 Ventura Blvd #315 Studio City CA 91604*

BODI, SONIA ELLEN, academic librarian; b. Chgo., June 24, 1940; d. Franz Frithiof and Elsa (Noren) Bergquist; m. Peter Phillip Bodi, July 30, 1966; 1 child, Eric Christopher; stepchildren: Glenn Peter, John Jeffrey. Student, U. Edinburgh (Scotland), 1960-61; BA, Augustana Coll., Rock Island, Ill., 1962; MA Libr. Sci., Rosary Coll., 1977; MA, Northwestern U., 1986. English and history tchr. Gemini Jr. High Sch., Niles, Ill., 1962-64, Nagoya (Japan) Internat. Sch., 1964-65; English tchr. Old Orchard Jr. High Sch., Skokie, Ill., 1965-67; reference libr. Wilmette (Ill.) Pub. Library, 1976-79, Kendall Coll., Evanston, Ill., 1979-81; head reference and instructional libr. North Park Coll., Chgo., 1981—, asst. prof. bibliography, 1985-87, assoc. prof. bibliography, 1988—, chair divsn. humanities, 1988—, prof. bibliography, 1992—. Contbr. articles to profl. jours. Pres. PTA, Lincolnwood, Ill., 1977-79; mem. Bd. Edn., Lincolnwood, 1980-91, sec., 1981-84, pres., 1984-87; mem. 1st Presbyn. Ch. of Evanston, elder, 1989—. Mem. Ill. Libr. Assn., ALA, Am. Assn. Coll. & Rsch. Librs., Lincolnwood Friends of the Libr., Beta Phi Mu. Democrat. Home: 6710 N Trumbull Ave Lincolnwood IL 60645-3740 Office: North Park Coll 3225 W Foster Ave Chicago IL 60625-4895

BODIE, CAROL HOOVER, computer services professional; b. Orangeburg, S.C., Sept. 18, 1957; d. Richard and Lucy Virginia (Bolton) Hoover; m. Thomas Odom Bodie, Jr., May 20, 1978; children: Chadwick, Matthew. BS in Mgmt. Sci., U. S.C., 1980, MBA, 1984. Rsch. analyst S.C. Electric & Gas Co., Columbia, 1978-83, programmer analyst, 1983-89; systems analyst Dupont, Aiken, S.C., 1989; systems analyst Westinghouse Corp., Aiken, 1989-90, mgr., 1990—; basketball ofcl. O'Dell Weeks Parks & Recreation, 1991—. Mem. Nat. Help Desk Inst., Nat. Fedn. Interscholastic Ofcls. assn. (basketball ofcl. 1992—), Civitans (sec. 1981-82). Baptist. Home: 167 Cheltenham Dr Aiken SC 29803-6633 Office: Westinghouse Savannah River 1993 S Centennial Ave Aiken SC 19803

BODIS, SUZANNE JUNE, small business owner, community activist; b. Milw., June 1, 1947; d. Richard Cleveland and Edith Dorothy (Ullstrup) Burdick; m. Raymond Eugene Bodis, Dec. 20, 1969; children: Carroll Lyn, Christina Lyn. BA in Social Studies, Carroll Coll., Waukesha, Wis., 1969; postgrad., Denver Paralegal Inst., 1985. Tchr. Hamilton High Sch., Sussex, Wis., 1969-73; curatorial asst. Hist. Denver Inc., 1980-84; closing coord. Van Schaack & Co., Denver, 1985-88; office adminstr. St. Paul Presbyn. Ch., Aurora, Colo., 1989-93, Calvary Presbyn. Ch., 1994—; pres. Bodis Group Inc., Aurora, 1988—. Bd. dirs. Aurora Hist. Commn., 1985-93, Spirit of Aurora, 1989—; mem. exec. com. Capital Choices Com., Aurora, 1992-93; charter mem., pres. Aurora Mus. Found., 1989-94; mem. Arapahoe County Cultural Coun., 1995—. Named Vol. of Week, Aurora Sentinel, 1992. Mem. AAUW (life; br. pres. 1988-90, state pres. 1994-96, named honor award Edn. Found. 1992). Republican. Presbyterian.

BODKIN, RUBY PATE, corporate executive, real estate broker, educator; b. Frostproof, Fla., Mar. 11, 1926; d. James Henry and Lucy Beatrice (Latham) P.; m. Lawrence Edward Bodkin Sr., Jan. 15, 1949; children: Karen Bodkin Snead, Cinda, Lawrence Jr. BA, Fla. State U., 1948; MA, U. Fla., 1972. Lic. real estate broker. Banker Barnett Bank, Avon Park, Fla., 1943-44, Lewis State Bank, Tallahassee, 1944-49; ins. underwriter Hunt Ins.

Agy., Tallahassee, 1949-51; tchr. Duval County Sch. Bd., Jacksonville, Fla., 1952-77; pvt. practice realty Jacksonville, 1976—; tchr. Nassau County Sch. Bd., Jacksonville, 1978-83; sec., treas., v.p. Bodkin Corp., R&D/Inventions, Jacksonville, 1983—; assoc. Brooke Shields Innovative Designer Products, Inc., Kendall Park, N.J., 1988—. Mem. Jacksonville Symphony Guild, 1985—, Southside Jr. Woman's Club, Jacksonville, 1957—, Garden Club Jacksonville, 1976—; bd. dirs. (fin. dir.) Riverside Woman's Club of Jacksonville, 1991-92. Recipient 25 Yr. Service award Duval County Sch. Bd., 1976, Tchr. of Yr. award Bryceville Sch., 1981. Mem. Ponte Vedra Inn and Club, San Jose Country Club. Home: 1149 Molokai Rd Jacksonville FL 32216-3273 Office: Bodkin Jewelers & Appraisers PO Box 16482 Jacksonville FL 32245-6482

BOECKE-GONZALEZ, JANET ERNA, nurse; b. N.Y.C., July 22, 1950; d. Ernest H. and Ilse (Engel) Boecke; m. James R. Gonzales, Mar. 12, 1983 (div.); children: James E., Jeffrey R. BSN, Hunter Coll.-Bellevue Sch., 1972; MA, NYU, 1977; student, Adelphi U., 1977. RN, N.Y., N.J.; cert. in perinatal nursing; cert. childbirth educator. Perinatal nurse clinician St. Charles Hosp., Port Jefferson, N.Y., 1977-79; perinatal clin. specialist Univ. Hosp., Stony Brook, N.Y., 1979-81; neonatal nurse instr. North Shore Univ. Hosp., Manhasset, N.Y., 1981-82; perinatal clin. specialist Winthrop Univ. Hosp., Mineola, N.Y., 1982-83; dir. maternal-child nursing Robert Wood Johnson U. Hosp., New Brunswick, N.J., 1983-86; maternal-child health instr. Christ Hosp., Jersey City, 1986-89; nursing instr. Edn. PRN, Franklin Lakes, N.J., 1986—; pvt. practice childbirth educator Old Bridge, N.J., 1986—; asst. prof. Adelphi U. Sch. Nursing, Garden City, N.Y., 1981-83. Lectr., vol. Arthritis Found., Iselin, N.J., 1992-93. Mem. ANA, Perinatal Assn. N.J. (trustee 1986-90), Assn. Women's Health, Obstet. and Neonatal Nurses. Home: 239 Community Cir Old Bridge NJ 08857

BOECKL, CHRISTINE MARIA, art history educator; b. Vienna, Austria, July 24, 1933; came to U.S., 1956; d. Josef and Margarethe (Adler) Pfundner; m. Leopold B. Boeckl, July 17, 1956 (div. 1990); children: Michael, Leopold, Maria. BA in Art History, U. Vienna, 1956; MA in Art History, U. Md., 1984, PhD in Art History, 1990. Asst. prof. U. Mont., Bozeman, 1988-89, Colo. Coll., Colorado Springs, 1990-91; assoc. prof. U. Nebr., Kearney, 1991—. Contbr. articles to profl. jours. Senator Faculty Senate, U. Nebr., 1992—. Dissertation fellow U. Md., 1989-90; Travel grantee U. Nebr., 1992, Rsch. Svc. Coun. grantee, 1993-94. Mem. Rocky Mountain Medieval Renaissance Soc., Coll. Art Assn., Alumni Assn. U. Md. Home: 5010 Keokuk St Bethesda MD 20816 Office: U Nebr Fine Arts Bldg #317 Kearney NE 68849

BOEDECKER, ANNE LOUISE, psychologist, business owner; b. Poughkeepsie, N.Y., Jan. 20, 1951; d. Ray F. and Elizabeth (Hutchinson) B.; m. Terrence P. Kimper, Aug. 19, 1979; 1 child, Wendy. Student, Dartmouth Coll., 1971-72; BA, Vassar Coll., 1973; MS, Pa. State U., 1975, PhD, 1978. Lic. psychologist, N.H. Adj. prof. Pa. State U., College Park, 1977-78; intern U. Tex. Counseling Ctr., Austin, 1978-80; staff psychologist Cen. N.H. Community Mental Health Svcs., 1980-81; prof. Grad. Sch. Antioch Coll., Keene, N.H., 1981-83; counselor, cons. Rundlett Jr. High Sch., Concord, N.H., 1983-85; adj. prof. New Eng. Coll., Henniker, N.H., 1985-86, Notre Dame Coll., Manchester, N.H., 1986-87; pvt. practice Concord, 1981—; exec. dir. Wellspring Ctr. for Human Devel., Concord, 1987—; mem. adv. coun. counseling program Notre Dame, Manchester, 1985-88; cons. Rape & Domestic Violence Crisis Ctr., Concord, 1986-88; mem. psychiatry dept. Concord Hosp., 1989—. Editor: Women Therapists Resource Directory New Hampshire Psychol. Orgn., 1986; contbr. articles to profl. jours. Founder, sec. Coalition Against Sexual Exploitation, Concord, 1987-89; mem. Bow (N.H.) PTA, 1989—. Rufus Choate scholar Dartmouth Coll., 1972. Fellow N.H. Psychol. Assn. (chair women and minorities com. 1986-89, editor Networker 1991—, sec. 1992—); mem. APA. Home: 4 One Stack Dr Bow NH 03304-4707 Office: Wellspring Ctr Human Devel 6A Hills Ave Concord NH 03301-4053

BOEHM, TONI GEORGENE, seminary dean; b. New Kensington, Pa., Dec. 28, 1946; d. Sylvio Chipoletti and Eula Gene (Smittle) Fox; m. Raymond Stawinski, Dec. 11, 1965 (div. Sept. 1978); 1 child, Michelle Stawinski Ivy; m. Jay Thomas Boehm, Apr. 28, 1983; children: Jonathon, Kimberly, Allison Cole, Amanda. Diploma, Allegheny Valley Sch. Nursing, Natrona Heights, Pa., 1967; family nurse practitioner cert., U. Kans., 1976; BA in Edn., Ottawa (Kans.) U., 1978; MSN, U. Mo., Kansas City, 1981; grad., Unity Sch. of Christianity, Unity Village, Mo., 1989. Cert. occupational health nurse; ordained to ministry Assn. of Unity Chs. Nurse Allegheny Valley Hosp., Natrona Heights, 1967-74; head nurse, dir. nursing Truman Med. Ctr., Kansas City, Mo., 1974-78; mgr. med. Hallmark Card Inc., Kansas City, Mo., 1978-85; sr. staff specialist ANA, Kansas City, Mo., 1985-87; dean of adminstrn. Unity Sch. Christianity, 1987—; freelance speaker and writer for ministry and teaching. Mem. nat. steering com. for fundraising Unity Sch. of Christianity; mem. women's coun. U. Mo. Recipient scholarships. Mem. ANA, NCCJ, Mo. Nurses Assn. (bd. dirs. 1975-85), U. Mo. Sch. Nursing Alumni Assn., Assn. Unity Chs. (urban curriculum com. 1987—, ministerial edn. com. 1987—, field licensing com. 1990). Republican. Home: 430 N Winnebago Dr Lk Winnebago MO 64034-9321 Office: Unity Sch Christianity Usrs Unity Village MO 64065

BOEHMER, RAQUEL DAVENPORT, television producer, newsletter editor; b. Bklyn., Feb. 24, 1938; d. John Joralemon Davenport and Fanny (Barberis) Allison; m. Peter Joseph Boehmer; children: Kristian Ludwig, Louisa, Timothy Joralemon. BA, Wells Coll., 1959. Radio producer Maine Pub. Broadcasting Network, Bangor, 1977—; developer, editor consumer newsletter Seafood Soundings, Monhegan, Maine, 1986-92; columnist, copy editor newsletter New Monhegan Press, Monhegan, Maine, 1989—; speaker Seafare, L.A., 1986; keynote speaker Beyond Wells Day, Wells Coll., Aurora, N.Y., 1988; dir. Monhegan Artists' Residency Corp., 1995. Writer, producer (radio commentary) Whole Foods for All People, 1977—; producer, host (TV cooking program) Different Kettle of Fish, 1984; author: A Foraging Vacation, 1982, Raquel's Maine Guide to New England Seafoods, 1988, Raquel's Maine Guide to Northeast Winter Vegetables. Writer legislation, Maine legis., 1985, 87, 91; treas. Monhegan Plantation, 1970-72, chair bicentennial com., 1976; chair Monhegan Sch. Bd., 1973-74; co-chair Monhegan Solid Waste Com., 1988—. Recipient Pub. Svc. award Maine Nutrition Coun., Alumnae award Wells Coll., 1992; named Gt. New Eng. Cook, Yankee mag., 1986. Mem. Women's Fisheries Network (bd. dirs. N.E. chpt. 1992-94, sec. to nat. bd. dirs. 1994—, v.p. N.E. chpt.), Colonial Dames Am., Women's Strike for Peace, Yankee Exch. Home and Office: Lobster Cove Rd Monhegan ME 04852-0365

BOEHNE, PATRICIA JEANNE, foreign languages educator, department chair; b. Paris, Feb. 4, 1940; (parents Am. citizens); d. Jean Atlee and Mary Anna (McFarland) Graffis; m. Edward George Boehne, Jan. 24, 1960; children: Lisa Elena, Edward Mark. BA, Ind. U., 1961, MA, 1962, PhD, 1969. Cert. tchr. Spanish and French. Teaching asst. Ind. U., Bloomington, Ind., 1961-62, 65-66; high sch. Spanish tchr. Martinsville (Ind.) H.S., Martinsville, Ind., 1962-63; instr. French and Spanish Bradley U., Peoria, Ill., 1963-65; asst. prof. Spanish Franklin and Marshall Coll., Lancaster, Pa., 1968-70; assoc. prof. French, Spanish, Russian Ea. Coll., St. Davids, Pa., 1970-78; prof. romance langs. Ea. Coll., 1978—, chairperson romance langs., 1975—; humanist evaluator for pub. com. Humanities in Pa., 1978—; chairperson orgnl. mgmt. Eastern Coll., 1988—, chairperson faculty devel., 1989—, acad. study abroad chairperson and other coms.; bd. dirs. Basic Needs Internat., 1987—; chairperson conf. Les Pays Africains Francophones, 1988; strategic planning chairperson on global awareness, 1988, strategic planning acad. com., 1988-89; task force to internat. acad. program. Author: Dream and Fantasy in 14th and 15th Century Catalan Prose, 1975, An Introduction to Catalan Literature, 1977, J.V. Foix, 1980, The Renaissance Catalan Novel, 1989; contbr. articles to profl. jours. Vestry mem., alt. deanery del., lic. lay reader, chalice bearer and other positions Ch. of the Good Samaritan, Paoli, Pa.; chair Diocese of Pa. Hispanic Ministry Com., 1978-81, 88-89; Dem. committeeperson Easttown Twp. Pa. 7th precinct, 1974-80; Dem. candidate for twp. supr., 1975, 77; chair Easttown Dem. Com., 1975-79; del. candidate Birch Bayh-Dem. Nat. Conv., 1979. Recipient NDEA Title IV and VI fellowships, 1963, 65-68; Mellon fellowship Vatican Microfilm Libr., 1982, Am. Philos. Soc. fellowship, 1982, NEH grant, 1983, Del. Valley Faculty Exchange fellowship U. Pa., 1984, Lindback award for outstanding teaching, 1988. Mem. Modern Language Assn. (exec. com. Catalan-Provencal discussion group 1977-80, 90-92), Am. Assn. Tchrs. Spanish and Portuguese, World Affairs Coun. Greater Valley Forge (bd. mem. 1990—, pres. 1991-92, v.p. 1992-93), N.Am. Catalan Soc. (bd. mem. 1978-85, sec. 1982—, v.p. 1990-93, pres. 1993—), Phi Sigma Iota (chpt. founder, Iota Pi advisor), Sigma Delta Pi, Kappa Delta Pi. Democrat. Episcopal. Office: Eastern Coll 10 Fairview Dr Saint Davids PA 19087-3696

BOEHNING, AGNES FRIEDA, health facility administrator, critical care nurse; b. Hoyleton, Ill., Mar. 8, 1941; d. Paul and Gertrude (Koelling) Krueger; m. Richard Carl Boehning; children: Edith, Jonathan, Victoria, Christine. ADN, Kaskasia Coll., 1973; BSN, St. Louis U., 1981; postgrad., Webster U., 1982-85; MSN, Community Health, So. Ill. U., 1990; grad., Air Command & Staff Coll., 1993. Cert. ACLS; cert. adult nurse practitioner, Ill. Staff nurse ICU and critical care unit Good Samaritan Hosp., Mt. Vernon, Ill., 1973-74; staff nurse ICU and critical care unit, CPR instr., relif supr. St. Mary's Hosp., Centralia, Ill., 1974-89; dir. health svcs. Hoyleton Youth and Family Svcs., 1982-91; staff nurse ICU and critical care unit Deaconess Hosp., St. Louis, 1989-91; instrn. nursing program Ill. East Community Coll., Olney, 1990-91; adminstr. Washington County Health Dept., Nashville, 1991-93; asst. chief nurse 13th Contingency Hosp., Scott AFB, Ill. Lt. col. USAFR, 1981—, Desert Shield/Storm. Named Citizen of Yr. Hoyleton Jaycee Women, 1983. Mem. ANA, APHA, VFW, Assn. Pub. Health Adminstrs., Assn. Pub. Health Nurses, Ill. Nurses Assn. (bd. dirs.), Washington County Rotary (project dir.), Bus. and Profl. Women, Res. Officers Assn., Aerospace Assn. (membership com. Washington chpt. 1980—), Sigma Theta Tau. Republican. Lutheran. Home: 161 W Locust St Hoyleton IL 62803-2043

BOEKHOUDT-CANNON, GLORIA LYDIA, business education educator; b. Portsmouth, Va., Jan. 18, 1939; d. William and Clara (Virgil) Boekhoudt; m. George Edward Cannon, Dec. 27, 1959. AB in Sociology/Psychology, Calif. State U., San Diego, 1977; MA in Spl. Edn./Learning Disabilities, Calif. State U., Sacramento, 1981; EdD in Orgn. and Leadership of Higher Edn. and Curriculum and Instrn., U. San Francisco, 1989. Instr. bus. edn. Midway Adult Sch. extension San Diego City Coll., San Diego, 1974-78, San Diego City Coll., 1974-78, Sacramento City Coll., 1979—. Author: Fundamentals of Business English, 1986. Mem. Women in Community Colls., Phi Delta Kappa. Democrat. Jewish. Office: Sacramento City Coll Dept Bus 3835 Freeport Blvd Sacramento CA 95822-1386

BOELENS, PATRICIA ANN, accountant, registered nurse; b. Grinnell, Iowa, May 21, 1943; d. Harold Willis and Mary Louise (Phipps) Andes; m. William Carl Laubengayer, Aug. 15, 1963; children: Karl E., Kevin E.; m. Francis Raymond Boelens, Sept. 19, 1992; stepchildren: Kristina M., Kirk M. Diploma in nursing, St. Lukes Hosp., Cedar Rapids, Iowa, 1965; BSN, Coe Coll., 1976; AAS in Acctg. Tech., Kirkwood C.C., Cedar Rapids, 1987. Staff nurse Cedar Rapids, 1974-77; dir. nursing North Brook Manor Care Ctr., Cedar Rapids, 1977-78; staff nurse Linn County Pub. HEalth, Cedar Rapids, 1979-81; staff acct. Jean E. Kruse, CPA, Cedar Rapids, 1987-88; office mgr. Gordon Mollman, PA, Cedar Rapids, 1988-89; staff acct. Cindy Davis & Assocs., Moline, Ill., 1990-93, Watts & Assocs., Moline, Ill., 1993-94; AAA Iowa, Bettendorf, 1994—; spkr. continuing edn. workshops for various orgns., 1977-79; Iowa Nurses Assn. rep. Iowa Health Sys. Agy., Iowa City, 1979-83. Chair vol. adv. com. Linn County Coun. on Aging, Cedar Rapids, 1978-81. Nominee Nurse of Yr., Jour. Gerontol. Nursing, 1978. Mem. ANA (Iowa del. 1982), Iowa Nurses Assn. (continuing edn. rev. panel 1976-78, 3d v.p. 1978-80), Inst. Mgmt. Accts. (treas. Illowa chpt. 1992-94), Nat. Assn. Tax Practitioners, Kiwanis (com. chair Moline chpt. 1991-94), Phi Theta Kappa, Sigma Theta Tau. Home: 2915 56th St Ct Moline IL 61265 Office: AAA Iowa 2900 AAA Ct Bettendorf IA 52722

BOER, PATRICIA MULCAHY, academic counselor, administrator; b. Quantico, Va., Feb. 4, 1938; d. Francis Patrick and Elizabeth (Bertrand) M.; m. Westinus Boer II, June 18, 1961 (div. Jan., 1978); children: Kathryn Elizabeth, Karol Southwick, Virginia Remington. BA, U. San Diego, 1959; MS, Ind. State U., 1978. Cert. career counselor. Tchr. Coronado (Calif.) Unified Schs., 1960-61, Byrum Sch., Greenwich, Conn., 1961-62, Meadowbrook Elem. Sch., Norfolk, Va., 1963-64, Brunswick (Ga.) Pub. Sch.; ind. contractor, instr. effective tng. Solano, Calif., 1973-76; supr. Ind. U.-Purdue U. at Indpls., 1978-80, dir. Continuing Edn. Ctr. Women, 1980-86, dir. Office of Women's Rsch. and Resource, 1986-94; counselor, owner Career Counseling Svcs., Indpls., 1989-90, dir., owner, 1994—; assoc. dir. women's studies Sch. of Liberal Arts Ind. U./Purdue U., Indpls., 1990—; bd. dirs. Catalyst Nat. Career Resource, N.Y.C. Author, producer, host TV Series, 1980-81, Women Forming Partnerships, 1986. Bd. dirs. Selective Svc. Commn., Ind. 1984—. Recipient Community Involvement award for Vietnam, Nat. Univ. Continuing Edn. Assn., 1986-87, Women and Work Conf. '94 for Outstanding Leadership in Support of Women and Work. Mem. Am. Assn. Counseling Devel., Nat. Women's Studies Assn., Network of Women in Bus., Women's Rotary Indpls., Exec. Club, Coronado Jr. Women's Club, Am. Fedn. Women's Clubs, Officer's Wives Club. Democrat. Roman Catholic. Office: Career Counseling Svcs 8060 Knue Rd Ste 115 Indianapolis IN 46250-1938

BOESE, SANDRA JEAN, publishing executive; b. Ely, Minn., July 31, 1940; d. John Frank and Millie Jean (Prebeg) Simonick; m. Lee Robert Boese Sr., June 15, 1963; children: Lee Robert Jr., Joy Karin. BA in Speech and Elem. Edn., Marquette U., 1962. Elem. tchr., 1962-67; pub., editor Classroom Connections, Inc., Merced and Sacramento, 1988—, also chmn. bd.; pres. Calif. State Bd. Edn., Sacramento, 1984-86. Trustee Merced City Sch. Dist., 1975-83; commr. Calif. Post-Secondary Edn. Commn., Sacramento, 1983; bd. dirs. Far-West Lab., San Francisco, 1984, The Achievement Coun., San Francisco, 1985. Recipient Commendation of Exempary Svc. award Calif. State Senate, 1983, Cert. of Appreciation, Calif. State Dept. Edn., 1983; named Woman of Distinction Soroptimist Internat., 1987. Mem. AAUW (Woman of Distintion 1986), Calif. Sch. Bds. Assn. (bd. dirs. del. assembly, 1978-81, chmn. conf. 1979-80, founder chmn. polit. action com. 1982-83, Outstanding Svc. award 1982, Spl. Recognition 1986), Merced City C. of C. (pres. 1985-86, Athena award 1988), Nat. Assn. State Bds. Edn. (bd. dirs. 1984-86), Assn. Marquette U. Women (Mary Neville Bielefeld award 1986). Republican. Roman Catholic. Office: Classroom Connections Inc 2824 Park Ave Ste C Merced CA 95348-3375

BOETTCHER, JANET L., water resources company executive; b. Santa Barbara, Calif., May 30, 1943; d. Martin Henry and Gladys Aleda (Van Daam) Lee; m. Don Schrock, Dec. 24, 1967 (div. 1974); children: Debra Alden, Dani Michelle Birch.; m. Fred W. Boettcher, Feb. 23, 1978. BS in Mgmt., Linfield Coll., 1982; MPA, Lewis & Clark Coll., 1989. Office mgr. Lorrette Larson Comml. Design co., Mill Valley, Calif., 1963-68, R.J. deRecat Co. Internat., San Rafael, Calif., 1968-76; asst. mgr. Hutchinson Indsl. Corp., San Rafael, Calif., 1976-77; bus. mgr. E.C. Ernst Engr./U.S. Steel, Virginia, Minn., 1977-78; gen. mgr. Tumalo Water Dist., Bend, Oreg., 1978-83; asst. mgr. Water and Energy Resource Svcs., Salem, Oreg., 1983—. Contbr. articles to profl. jours. Mem. adv. com. YWCA, Salem, 1991-92. Named one of Top Ten Nat. Bus. Women Am. Bus. Women Assn., 1988, Top Four Tribute to Women YWCA, 1992. Mem. AAUW, Nat. Water Resources Assn. (bd. dirs. 1989-91, Pres.'s award 1989, 91), Oreg. Water Resources Congress (bd. dirs. 1979-83), Women Entrepreneurs Oreg. (state bd. dirs., pres., v.p. 1987-90, membership chair 1991-92, Woman of Yr. 1991), Nat. Women's Polit. Caucus (Washington and Salem, Oreg. chpts.), Reps. for Choice (Washington). Republican. Lutheran. Home: 5393 Vitae Springs Rd S Salem OR 97306-9707 Office: Water & Energy Resources 727 Center St NE Ste 107 Salem OR 97301-3800

BOETTCHER, NORBE BIROSEL, chemist; b. Manila, June 6, 1932; d. Dionisio Martinez and Filomena (Cuaresma) Birosel; m. Robert Arnold Boettcher, June 6, 1961; 1 child, Heidi Noriko. BS in Chemistry, Philippine Women's U., 1953; postgrad., U. Iowa, 1955-57. Chemist, rsch. and devel. Lawry's Foods, Inc., L.A., 1957-61; chemist, quality control, rsch. and devel. Sunsweet Products, San Jose, Calif., 1964-68; teaching asst., rsch. chemist Coe Coll., Cedar Rapids, Iowa, 1969-77; chemist, rsch. and devel. Penford Products Co., Cedar Rapids, 1977-92, analytical chemist customer lab. svc., 1992—. Mem. Brucemore, Inc., Cedar Rapids, Met. Opera Guild, N.Y.C. Mem. AAAS, AAUW, Cedar Rapids Art Mus., Philippine-Am. Club (social chmn. 1987-89, pres. Linn County, Iowa 1989-91, bd. dirs. 1992—), Iowa Poetry Assn., Internat. Soc. Poets. Republican. Roman Catholic. Home: 348 7th St Marion IA 52302-3325 Office: Penford Products Co 1st St SW Cedar Rapids IA 52406

BOGAN, ELIZABETH CHAPIN, economist, educator; b. Morristown, N.J., Aug. 22, 1944; d. Daryl Muscott and Tirzah (Walker) Chapin; m. Thomas Rockwood Bogan, June 5, 1965; children: Nathaniel Rockwood, Andrew Allerton. AB, Wellesley Coll., 1966; MA, U. N.H., 1967; PhD, Columbia U., 1971. Mem. faculty Fairleigh Dickinson U., Madison, N.J., 1971-92, prof. econs., 1982-92; chmn. merit scholarship com. Farleigh Dickinson U., Madison, N.J., 1981-82, chmn. dept. econs. and fin., 1981-84, 87-91, reviewer univ. press; mem. faculty Princeton (N.J.) U., mem. faculty, sr. lectr. in econs., 1992—; vis. prof. Princeton U., 1991. Reviewer: Fin. Analyst Jour.; author articles and macroecons. text. Recipient Outstanding Tchr. award Fairleigh Dickinson U., 1979, 86, 87; NSF fellow, Pres'. fellow, Earhart fellow Columbia U., 1968-71. Mem. AAUP, Am. Econ. Assn., Ea. Econ. Assn., Atlantic Econ. Assn. Congregationalist. Clubs: Wellesley, Beacon Hill. Home: 41 Windermere Ter Short Hills NJ 07078-2254 Office: Princeton U 109 Fisher Hall Princeton NJ 08544

BOGAN, MARY FLAIR, stockbroker; b. Providence, July 9, 1948; d. Ralph A.L. and Mary (Dyer) B.; B.A., Vassar Coll., 1969. Actress, Trinity Sq. Repertory Co., R.I., Gretna Playhouse, Pa., Skylight Comic Opera, Milw., Cin. Playhouse, Playmakers' Repertory, N.C.; mem. nat. co. No Sex, Please, We're British; also TV commls., 1970-77; account exec. E.F. Hutton & Co., Inc., Providence, 1977-86; account v.p. Paine Webber, 1986—; econ. reporter Sta. WPRI-TV, 1982-85, Sta. WJAR-TV, 1987—. Treas. Red Bridge Council Rep. Women; chmn. new mems. com. R.I. Fedn. Rep. Women. Recipient Century Club award, 1980, 81, 82, 83, 85; Blue Chip Sales award, 1983, 85, Pacesetter Sales Award, 1986-90. Named. Woman of the Yr. Profl. Bus. and Rep. Women's Assn. Mem. Women's Assn., Barker Players, Univ. Club, Brown Faculty, Barker Players. Home: 18 Cooke St Providence RI 02906-2023 Office: Paine Webber 900 Citizens Plz Providence RI 02903

BOGAN-RIDLEY, KIMBERLY RENEÉ, security specialist; b. Chgo., May 12, 1969; d. Fred and June (Powell) Jones; m. Rickey Ridley, Sept. 25, 1993. BA in Liberal Arts and Criminal Justice, U. Ill., Chgo., 1993. Sales clk. Zayre, Chgo., 1987-89; custodian U.S. Main Post Office, Chgo., 1988-89; clk. Popper & Wisniewski Law Offices, Chgo., 1989-91; phys. security specialist GSA, Fed. Protective Svc., Chgo., 1991—. Recipient Patriotic Svc. award U.S. Dept. Treasury, 1993. Mem. NAFE. Roman Catholic. Home: 9751 S Sangamon St Chicago IL 60643-1547

BOGARD, CAROLE CHRISTINE, lyric soprano; b. Cin.; d. Harold and Helen Christina (Whittlesey) Geistweit; m. Charles Paine Fisher, Dec. 30, 1966; children: Christine, Pamela. Student, San Francisco State U. Debuts include: Despina in Cosi fan Tutte (Mozart), San Francisco, 1965, Poppea in Coronation of Poppea (Monteverdi), Netherlands Opera, 1971; other appearances include, Boston Opera, N.E.T., orchs. Boston, Madrid, Minn., Phila., Pitts., San Francisco, summer festivals, Mostly Mozart, N.Y., Tanglewood, Carmel, Aston Magna, Gt. Barrington, Mass., appeared in concerts throughout Europe and with Smithsonian Chamber Players, 1976—; recorded numerous albums including 1st rec. of songs of John Duke for his 80th birthday, 1979, recital of Groupe des Six; premiered songs of Dominic Argento in, Holland, 1978, songs of Richard Cumming (in collaboration with Donald Gramm); regular participant rec. and scholarly projects, Smithsonian Instn.; judge regional auditions, Boston; tchr., with emphasis on technique as taught in last Century. Mem. Sigma Alpha Iota. Home: 161 Belknap Rd Framingham MA 01701-3803

BOGARD, MIMI LYNETTE, educational library media specialist; b. Canton, Ohio, Mar. 20, 1949; d. Charles Jay and Ada Marguerite (Kildow) B. AB summa cum laude, Ohio U., 1971; MEd, Kent State U., 1978. Cert. tchr. grades 7-12, English and ednl. media, Ohio. Tchr. English Sandy Valley Local Schs., Magnolia, Ohio, 1971-82, libr. media specialist, 1982—; appointed mem. Ohio Lang. Arts Tchr. Leader Network, Columbus, 1988-90; mem. tchr. exch. com. Edn. Enhancement Partnership, Canton, 1992—. Manuscript referee (jour.) Ohio Media Spectrum, 1989—. Jennings scholar Martha Holden Jennings Found., 1981-82. Mem. Ohio Ednl. Libr. Media Assn. (regional dir. 1990-91), Phi Delta Kappa (sec. McKinley chpt. 1991-93, Educator of Yr. 1990), Phi Beta Kappa. Office: Sandy Valley Local Schs 5362 State Route 183 Magnolia OH 44643-9613

BOGARDUS, NANCIE BERWICK, health facility administrator; b. Roseburg, Oreg., Nov. 4, 1952; d. James E. and Mary E. (Keller) Berwick; m. John Harker Bogardus; children: Bradley Harker, Brian Keller. BS in Community Health, Oreg. State U., 1974. Office mgr. L.C. Robertson, M.D., Lakeview, Oreg., 1977-93; dir. Lake County Commn. on Children & Families, Lakeview, Oreg., 1993-94; adminstr. XL Home Health & Hospice, Lakeview, Oreg., 1993—. Fundraiser Oreg. Health Scis. Univ., 1991—; legis. chair hosp. aux. Lake Dist. Hosp., 1992, 93, trustee, 1992; bd. dirs. Cascades East Area Health, 1990—, Sunshine Children Ctr., Lakeview, 1983-87; mem. Rural Health Coord. Coun., 1989-93. Recipient Statewide Vol. Leadership award Oreg. Primary Care Assn., 1993, Lake County Jr. First Citizen award Lake County C. of C., 1992, Outstanding Contbn. to Health award Oreg. Nursing Assn., 1992. Mem. AAUW, Elkettes.

BOGART, CAROL LYNN, small business owner; b. Lakewood, Ohio, Mar. 9, 1949; d. Lloyd William and Evelyn Mary (Overmyer) B.; 1 child, Michael Lloyd. BLS, Bowling Green State U., 1973. Reporter, anchor WNEP-TV, Scranton, Pa., 1975-76; reporter WXIA-TV, Atlanta, 1976-79; reporter, fill-in morning anchor Sta. WLS-TV, Chgo., 1979-82; anchor, reporter KMGH-TV, Denver, 1982-89; media cons., video producer, voice-over and on-camera talent Bogart Inc., Denver, 1989-93, Cleve., 1994—; guest speaker various schs. and univs., Denver, 1982-93. Actress with J.F. Talent, Denver, 1989-93, with David & Lee, Cleve., 1994—. Mem. Greater Cleve. Growth Assn., Coun. of Small Enterprises; pet therapy vol. Mem. AFTRA, SAG, Nat. Assn. Broadcast Engrs. and Techs. Presbyterian.

BOGART, GRACE ELIZABETH, information scientist; b. Bolton, Mass., June 10, 1923; d. Francis Gould and Grace Effie (Smith) Mentzer; m. Lindsay Boyd, Aug. 6, 1944 (dec.); children: David Gordon, Bethanne, Sandra Lindsay; m. Victor Brociner, Nov. 13, 1971 (dec.); m. Stanley C. Bogart, Aug. 7, 1977 (dec.). BS, U. Mass., 1945; M.S., Simmons Coll., 1975 . Librarian, Lincoln Lab. Library, MIT, Lexington, 1959-77; dir. info. services Roberts Info. Service, Inc., Fairfax, Va., 1977-78; pres. Bogart-Brociner Assocs., Bolton, Mass., 1978-89; ret.; rep. to adv. bd. Nat. Transls. Center, John Crerar Library, Chgo., 1975-86. Mem. Spl. Libraries Assn. (chmn. spl. com. translation problems 1973-76), Am. Soc. Info. Sci. (local arrangements chmn. nat. conf. Boston 1975, publicity chmn. nat. conf. 1980, mem. nat. conf. com. 1983, chmn. Nat. Conf. Boston arrangements 1987), Compiler; A Guide to Scientific and Technical Journals in Translation, 1972; How to Obtain a Translation, 1976. Home and Office: 295 Main St Bolton MA 01740-1104

BOGART, JUDITH SAUNDERS, public relations executive; b. Batesville, Ind., Nov. 16, 1936; d. David Rodman and Anne Eva (Kohles) Saunders; m. William Robert Bogart, Oct. 22, 1971. BA, Baldwin-Wallace Coll., 1958. Dir. pub. relations Greater Cin. Girl Scout Council, 1958-61, Nation's Capital Girl Scout Council, Washington, 1963-65; Gt. Rivers Girl Scout Council Cin., 1965-68; account rep. Edn. Funds Inc., Providence, 1967-68; dir. community relations Cin. Human Relations Commn., 1968-76; community relations cons. Cin., 1976-77; v.p. pub. relations Jewish Hosp. Cin., 1977-85; exec. v.p. Diversified Communicatons Inc., Cin., 1985-88; pres. Judith Bogart Assocs., Cin., 1989-91; dir. pub. rels. Sive/Young & Rubicam, Cin., 1991—. Pres. Gt. Rivers coun. Girl Scouts U.S.A., 1984-87, bd. dirs., 1987—; bd. dirs. Nat. Coun. Internat. Visitors, Washington, 1988—, chmn., 1991-93; trustee Cin. Internat. Visitors Ctr., 1981-87; co-chmn. pub. rels. Greater Cin. Bicentennial, 1985-88; mem. planning bd. United Way, Cin., 1987—; mem. community rels. bd. Xavier U., Cin., 1983—, chmn., 1991—. Named Career Woman of Achievement, YWCA, 1983. Fellow Accredited in Pub. Rels., Pub. Rels. Soc. Am. (nat. pres. 1983, pres. Cin. chpt. 1976, Outstanding Mem. 1977); mem. Women in Communications Inc. (nat. headliner 1982, nat. pub. rels com., Outstanding Woman in Communications 1976), N.Am. Pub. Rels. Coun. (pres. 1989). Office: Sive/Young & Rubicam 36 E 7th St Apt 2500 Cincinnati OH 45202-4462

BOGART, WANDA LEE, interior designer; b. Ashville, N.C., Feb. 26, 1939; d. Bob West and Virginia Elizbeth (Worley) McLemore-Snyder; m. Sterling X. Bogart, Feb. 12, 1962; children: Kevin Sterling, Kathleen Elizabeth. BA, San Jose (Calif.) State U., 1961. Cert. interior designer. Tchr. Redondo Beach (Calif.) Sch. Dist., 1962-65; free-lance interior designer Ladera, Calif., 1970-75; designer MG Interior Design, Orange, Calif., 1975-80; prin., pres. Wanda Bogart Interior Design Inc., Orange, 1980—. Contbr. articles to profl. jours. Named one of Top 20 Interior Designers in So. Calif. Ranch and Coast Mag., 1987. Mem. Internat. Interior Design Assn. (profl. mem., cert.), Am. Soc. Interior Design (cert.), Orange C. of C. Office: Wanda Bogart Interior Design Inc 1440 E Chapman Ave Orange CA 92666-2229

BOGDAN, CAROLYN LOUETTA, financial specialist; b. Wilkes-Barre, Pa., Apr. 15, 1941; d. Walter Cecil and Ethna Louetta (Kendig) Carpenter; m. James Thomas Bogdan, May 5, 1961; 1 child, Thomas James. Grad. high sch., Kingston, Pa. Head bookkeeper Forty Ft. (Pa.) State Bank, 1959-63, U.S. Nat. Bank, Long Beach, Calif., 1963-65; office mgr. United Parts Exchange, Long Beach, 1976-81; contract adminstr. Johnson Controls, Inc., Rancho Dominguez, Calif., 1981-88, credit coord., 1989—; co-owner, acct. Bogdan Elec. R & D, Lakewood, Calif., 1981—. Mem. Radio Amateur Civil Emergency Svc., Los Angeles County Sheriff Dept., 1974—, records keeper, 1988-93, radio comms. officer, 1994—. Mem. NAFE, Nat. Notary Assn., Am. Inst. Profl. Bookkeepers, Tournament of Roses Radio Amateurs (pin chmn. 1975—), Calif. State Sheriff's Assn. (assoc.). Republican. Home: 3713 Capetown St Lakewood CA 90712-1437 Office: Johnson Controls Inc 19118 S Reyes Ave Compton CA 90221-5898

BOGEN, BEVERLY WINSTON, artist; b. Jersey City; d. Louis and Gale (Beyer) Winston; m. Morton Arthur Bogen; children: Wendy Alison, Shelley Denise. BA, Syracuse U., 1942; postgrad., Traphagen Sch. of Fashion, N.Y.C., 1942-43, Adelphi Coll., Nassau, L.I., N.Y., 1956, Pratt Graphic Ctr., 1967. Fashion illustrator freelance Dept. Stores, Advt. Agencies, N.Y.C., 1943-80; asst. advt. mgr. Kirby Block Inc., N.Y.C., 1943-44; advt. mgr. Selber Bros., Shreveport, La., 1944-45, Bar Mart, N.Y.C., 1945-53; art dir. Wise Stores, N.Y.C., 1953-62; art gallery dir. Yellow House Gallery, Huntington, N.Y., 1964-69; faculty mem. Parsons Sch. of Design, N.Y.C., 1979-94. Exhibited in numerous solo and group exhbns. including Fine Arts Mus. of L.I., C.W. Post Coll., Hall of Congress, Washington, Nat. Acad. Galleries, N.Y.C., Nassau Mus. Fine Art, Roslyn, N.Y., Stephen Haller Gallery, N.Y.C., Charles Mann Gallery, N.Y.C.; represented in over 500 pvt. and corp. collections including Bank of Va., Washington, Esquire Mag., N.Y.C., Roger Ailes Assn., N.Y.C., Ms. Reynolds, Former Dean Parsons Sch. of Design. Recipient Spl. award in Sculpture, Nassau County Mus. Fine Arts, 1988. Mem. Artists Equity of N.Y. Democrat. Home: 19 Kay St Jericho NY 11753-2649

BOGGIO, MIRIAM ALTAGRACIA, lawyer; b. N.Y.C., July 28, 1952; d. Marco Antonio and Estella (Tejeda) B.; m. Michael Dandry, Jan. 4, 1981; children: Andrew P. Boggio-Dandry, Edward M. Boggio-Dandry, Gregory A. Boggio-Dandry. B.A. in Political Science, CUNY-Queens Coll., 1973; J.D., St. John's U., 1976; A.A. in Fashion Design, Fashion Inst. Tech., 1984. Bar: N.Y. 1977, Fla. 1977, U.S. Dist. Ct. (ea. and so. dists.) N.Y. 1978, U.S. Tax Ct. 1982, U.S. Supreme Ct. 1982. Assoc. Schwartzman Weinstock Garelik & Mann P.C., N.Y.C., 1977-84; counsel N.Y. Assembly Judiciary Com., Albany, 1977-84; dep. supt. N.Y. State Ins. Dept., N.Y.C., 1984—. Named to Dean's list, Queen's Coll., 1970-73; SEEK scholar, 1973; recipient SEEK honors, 1973. Mem. Fla. Bar Assn., Phi Beta Kappa. Democrat. Roman Catholic. Office: NY State Ins Dept 160 W Broadway New York NY 10013

BOGGS, CORINNE CLAIBORNE (LINDY BOGGS), former congresswoman; b. Brunswick Plantation, La., Mar. 13, 1916; d. Roland Philoman and Martha Corinne (Morrison) Claiborne; m. Thomas Hale Boggs, Jan. 22, 1938 (dec.); children: Barbara Boggs Sigmund (dec.), Thomas Hale Jr., Corinne Boggs Roberts, William Robertson (dec.). BA, Sophie Newcomb Coll., Tulane U., 1935, LLD (hon.); LittD, U. St. Thomas; DPub Svc. (hon.), Trinity Coll., Washington, 1975; hon. degree, St. Mary of Woods; LLD, Loyola U., Notre Dame U., Wesleyan U., Cath. U. Law Sch., Xavier U., St. Mary's Coll., St. Thomas Aquinas Coll., Univ. New Orleans, Our Lady of Holly Cross Coll., Notre Dame Sem., Coll. of St. Elizabeth. Tchr. history and English St. James Parish, La., 1936-37; elected to 93d Congress to fill vacancy caused by death of husband, 1973; re-elected to 94th-101st Congresses from 2d La. Dist., 1973-91; ret., 1991; mem. appropriations com. majority mem. from Ho. of Reps., Am. Revolution Bicentennial Adminstrn. Bd., chmn. Commn. Ho. of Reps. Bicentenary; mem. campaign com. Dem. Nat. Com., 1974; first chairwoman Dem. Nat. Conv., 1976; mem. Com. on Bicentennial of U.S. Constn. Pres., Dem. Congl. Wives Forum, 1954, Womans Nat. Democratic Club, 1958-59, Congl. Club, 1971-72; co-chmn. Inaugural Balls for Presidents John F. Kennedy, 1961, Lyndon Johnson, 1965; mem. Nat. Hist. Publs. and Records Com.; bd. dirs. La. Council for Music and Performing Arts; hon. bd. dirs. Met. New Orleans chpt. Nat. Found. March of Dimes; bd. advisers. CLOSE-UP and Presdl. Classroom; regent emeritus Smithsonian Instn.; mem. president's council Tulane U. Recipient Weiss Meml. award NCCJ, 1974; Nat. Oak award La. Assn. Ind. Colls. and Univs., Disting. Service medal Saint Mary's Dominican Coll., 1976, Humanitarian award AMVETS Nat. Aux., Torch of Liberty award B'nai B'rith, 1976, Gala IV award Birmingham So. U., 1976, Eleanor Roosevelt Humanitarian award, 1977, E. Roosevelt Centennial award, 1984, 1st woman recipient Disting. Alumna award Tulane U., 1986; 1st woman recipient VFW Congl. award, 1986; bldg., rm. in U.S. Capitol bldg. and dam named in her honor. Mem. Nat. Soc. Colonial Dames, LWV, Internat. Fedn. Cath. Alumni, Internat. Women's Forum. Mailing Address: 6823 St Charles Ave New Orleans LA 70118

BOGGS, WILLENE GRAYTHEN, abstractor, oil and gas broker, consultant; b. Vancouver, Wash., Mar. 10, 1939; d. William Louis and Zorah (Williams) Graythen; m. Ray Buck Glasgow, Feb. 8, 1964 (div. June 1969); m. Harry Maurice Boggs, May 23, 1993. BA in History, Centenary Coll., 1975; postgrad., La. State Law Sch., 1984, S.E. La. U., 1989. Tchr., educator St. Tam Parish Sch. Bd., Lacombe, La., 1964-65; abstractor St. Tam Parish Legal News, Covington, La., 1965-66, Kansas City Title Ins. Co., New Orleans, 1966-69, Lawyers Title Ins. Corp., New Orleans, 1975-77, Frawley, Wogan, Miller & Co., New Orleans, 1977-79; owner, mgr. Idea House and Sweet Home Antiques, Metairie, La., 1973-76; owner, mgr., abstractor, oil and gas broker Willene Glasgow & Assocs., Metairie, 1969-73; owner, mgr., abstractor Willene Glasgow & Assocs., Covington, La., 1979-93; pres. WCV Mgmt., Inc., Nashville, 1993—. Author: Decoupage and Related Crafts, 1972. Bd. dirs. Air, Water and Earth Inst., Covington, 1989; bd. dirs., pres. Pontchartrain Area Recycling Coun., Inc., Covington, 1989, 90, 91, 92, 93; mem. Citizens Adv. Com. on Solid Waste, 1988, 89, 90, 91, 92; coord. Pontchartrain Area Recycling Conv., 1988; fund raiser March of Dimes, Am. Cancer Soc., Arthritis Found., others, 1986—. Named hon. sec. state State of La., 1987. Mem. Petroleum Landman's Assn., Covington C. of C. (legis. chmn. 1988—, Mem. of Yr. award 1988), AAUW (conf. chmn. 1988-89, 92-93, chmn. Ednl. Found. 1989-91, Mem. of Yr. award Covington-Mandeville br. 1989, v.p. membership 1991-93). Home and Office: 251 Cumberland Cir Nashville TN 37214 also: PO Box 140877 Nashville TN 37214

BOGGUS, SHARI LYNN, data processing executive; b. Dalton, Ga., May 25, 1963; d. Hubert Henry Boggus and Deanna Louise (Kincaid) Pankey; m. Gary W. Whittenburrg, Oct. 22, 1983 (div. July 1988). AA, Cumberland Coll., 1983. Mgr. front desk Fairfield Glade Resort, Crossville, Tenn., 1983-84; mgr. data processing Alpha Equipment Co., Crossville, 1984—; asst. to chief of staff for Sen. Jim Sasser U.S. Senate, Washington, 1990. Democrat. Baptist. Home: 216 Bent Tree Dr Crossville TN 38555 Office: Alpha Equipment Co PO Box 3609 Crossville TN 38557-3609

BOGGUSS, SUZY, country music singer, songwriter; b. Aledo, Ill., Dec. 30, 1956; m. Doug Crider, Nov. 1986. Art degree, Ill. State U. Headliner at Dollywood, Nashville, 1985-88; opening act for Willie Nelson, Alabama, Oak Ridge Boys, Clint Black; albums: Somewhere Between, 1989, Moment of Truth, 1990, Aces, 1991, (co-prodr.) Voices in the Wind, 1992, Something Up My Sleeve, 1993, Greatest Hits, 1994, (with Chet Atkins) Simpatico, 1994. Named Best New Female Vocalist by Acad. Country Music, 1988; recipient Grammy nomination best country duet (with Lee Greenwood) Hopelessly Yours, Horizon award Country Music Assn., 1992. Office: Gurley & Co. 1101 17th Ave S Nashville TN 37212*

BOGHOSIAN, PAULA DER, computer business consultant; b. Watervliet, N.Y., Nov. 11, 1933; d. Harry and Osgi (Piligian) der B. BS magna cum laude, Syracuse U., 1964, MS, 1967; postgrad., SUNY, Oswego, 1972, SUNY, Albany, 1974. Cert. profl. sec., 1974. Asst. prof. Cazenovia (N.Y.) Coll., 1964-73; instr. Bd. of Coop., Syracuse, N.Y., 1973-76, dir. bus. careers, 1976-92; cons. computer bus., prin. Syracuse, 1984—. Zonta scholar, 1964; Jessie Smith Noyes grantee Syracuse U., 1965. Mem. Assn. Info. Systems Profl. (com. chmn.), Bus. Tchrs. Assn. of N.Y. State, Adminstrv. Mgmt. Soc., Eastern Bus. Tchrs. Assn., Assn. for Supervision and Curriculum Devel., Assn. of Am. Jr. Colls., Assn. of Am. U. Profs., Nat. Assn. for Armenian Studies and Rsch. Harvard U., Internat. Tng. Communications (v.p. 1985-86), Delta Pi Epsilon, Beta Gamma Sigma, Phi Kappa Phi, Pi Lambda Theta, Sigma Lamda Delta. Republican. Mem. Armenian Apostolic. Home: 3181 Bellevue Ave Apt B6 Syracuse NY 13219-3156

BOGLE, JOEANN ROSE, florist; b. St. Louis County, Mo., July 27, 1934; d. Albert Ray and Lillian Ann (Wilson) Weston; m. J.W. Bogle, Oct. 31, 1956; children: Jerome Alan, Janice Kim Bogle Bohr. Cert. in practical nursing, Lincoln Inst., Chgo., 1954; student, Pope Pius Early Childhood Inst, 1984; cert. in flower arranging, Lifetime Career Schs., 1988. Office mgr. Monumental Life Ins. Co., St. Louis, 1952-57; co-owner, flower arranger Only Yours-Silk Wedding Flowers, St. Louis, 1985—. Active Hazelwood Schs. PTA, 1963-75; den leader, pack leader St. Louis area Boy Scouts Am., 1965-69; cons., sec., troop leader St. Louis area Girl Scouts U.S., 1967-80; dir. concession stands Hazelwood Khoury League, 1966-71; coord., tchr. Our Lady of Mercy Ch., Hazelwood, 1966—, dir. ch. flowers, 1984—; active Archdiocesan Deanery Councillor Coun., St. Louis, 1981—; active support dogs for handicapped, Humane Soc., St. Louis, 1979—. Mem. MADD, K.C. Ladies Aux., Our Lady of Mercy Women's Coun. Home: 946 Chula Dr Hazelwood MO 63042-1207

BOGORAD, BARBARA ELLEN, psychologist; b. N.Y.C.; d. Albert Lyon and Miriam Ida (Serlin) B. BA, CUNY, 1969; MS, Rutgers U., 1972, Yeshiva U., 1981; PsyD, Yeshiva U., 1983. Lic. psychologist, N.Y.; diplomate Am. Bd. Profl. Psychol., 1992. Psychotherapist South Shore Ctr. Psychotherapy, Merrick, N.Y., 1978-82; psychology intern Birch Ctr. Exceptional Children, Queens, N.Y., 1980-81; clinical intern Long Island Jewish Hosp., Glen Oaks, N.Y., 1981-82; clin. intern South Oaks Hosp., Amityville, N.Y., 1982-83; staff psychologist St. John's Episc. Hosp., Far Rockaway, N.Y., 1984-86, St. Charles Hosp., Port Jeff, N.Y., 1987-88; pvt. practice Amityville, 1985-94; staff psychologist South Oaks Hosp., Amityville, 1988-94, dir. sexual abuse recovery program, 1991-94; pvt. practice Massapequa, N.Y., 1994—; speaker in field; radio and TV appearances 1990—. Vol. crisis relief worker Nassau and Suffolk counties, N.Y., 1990—. Mem. APA, Ea. Psychol. Assn., N.Y. State Psychol. Assn., Nassau County Psychol. Assn., Suffolk County Psychol. Assn., Am. Assn. Psychiat. Svcs. Children., Psychologists in Hosp. Practice, Am. Profl. Soc. Abuse of Children, Nat. Assn. Childcare Resource and Referral Agys. (aux.). Office: 627 Broadway Massapequa NY 11758-5031

BOGSTAHL, DEBORAH MARCELLE, market research consultant; b. Irvington, N.J., June 5, 1950; d. Marcel and Helena Christina (de Jaroszynsky) Bogstahl; m. Richard Neil Press, Mar. 20, 1976; children: Alexandra Boman, Michelle Boman. BA in English Edn., Trenton State Coll., 1972. Cert. tchr., N.J. Project dir. U.S. Testing Co., Hoboken, N.J., 1973-75; project dir. J. Walter Thompson Co., N.Y.C., 1975-77; rsch. account exec. Dancer Fitzgerald Sample, N.Y.C., 1977-80; group rsch. mgr. Bristol-Myers Co., N.Y.C., 1980-87; dir. rsch. Med. Econs. Co., Inc., Oradell, N.J., 1987-90; market rsch. mgr. The Mennen Co., 1991-92, L&F Products, Montvale, N.J., 1992—; Contbr. poetry to anthology. Mem. Am. Mktg. Assn., Pharm. Adv. Coun., Healthcare Bus. Women's Assn. Democrat. Roman Catholic. Avocations: sailing, reading, writing, music.

BOHANNON, SARAH VIRGINIA, personnel operations technician; b. Roanoke, Va., Mar. 1, 1947; d. Laurence Stimis and Sarah Elizabeth (Smith) B. AA in Bus. Adminstrn. Mgmt., Nat. Bus. Coll., 1983. Pers. appointment clk. IRS, Richmond, Va., 1983-84; pers. ops. technician Commonwealth of Va., Richmond, 1985—. Mem. NAFE, Am. Biog. Inst. (life, dep. gov. 1991, hon. mem. rsch. bd. advisors 1991, mem. women's inner circle of achievement 1991), Va. Pub. Health Assn. Home: 2220 Clarke St Richmond VA 23228-5938 Office: Commonwealth of Va Richmond VA 23219-2110

BOHANON, KATHLEEN SUE, neonatologist, educator; b. Mpls., 1951. BA summa cum laude, U. Minn., 1973, MD, 1977. Diplomate Am. Bd. Pediats., Am. Bd. Neonatal-Perinatal Medicine. Commd. 2d lt. USAF, 1973; advanced through grades to col. Case Western Res. U., 1995; resident in pediats. Case Western Res. U., Cleve., 1977-80; gen. pediatrician USAF, 1980-85; fellow in neonatology Wilford Hall Med. Ctr., San Antonio, 1985-87; neonatologist, dir. NICU USAF Med. Ctr., Wright-Patterson AFB, Ohio, 1987—; asst. clin. prof. pediats. U. N.D. Sch. Medicine, Grand Forks, 1981-82, Wright State U. Sch. Medicine, Dayton, Ohio, 1987—, Uniformed Svc. U. Health Scis., Washington, 1988—; mem. com. Infant Bio-Ethics Com., Dayton, 1990—. Mem. Am. Acad. Pediats. Office: 74th MDOS/SGOC 5030 Pearson Rd Dayton OH 45433

BOHLE, SUE, public relations executive; b. Austin, Minn., June 23, 1943; d. Harold Raymond and Mary Theresa (Swanson) Hastings; m. John Bernard Bohle, June 22, 1974; children: Jason John, Christine K. BS in Journalism, Northwestern U., 1965, MS in Journalism, 1969. Tchr. pub. high schs Englewood, Colo., 1965-68; account exec. Burson-Marsteller Pub. Relations, Los Angeles, 1969-73; v.p., mgr. pub. relations J. Walter Thompson Co., Los Angeles, 1973-79; founder, pres. The Bohle Company, L.A., 1979—; former exec. v.p. Ketchum/Bohle Pub. Relations, Los Angeles; free-lance writer, instr. communications Calif. State U. at Fullerton, 1972-73; instr. writing Los Angeles City Coll., 1975-76; lectr. U. So. Calif., 1979—. Contbr. articles to profl. jours. Dir. pub. rels. L.A. Jr. Ballet, 1971-72; pres. Panhellenic Advisers Coun., UCLA, 1972-73; mem. adv. bd. L.A. Valley Coll., 1974-75, Coll. Communications Pepperdine U., 1981-85, Sch. Journalism U. So. Calif., 1987—, Calif. State U., Long Beach, 1988-93; bd. visitors Medill Sch. Journalism Northwestern U., 1984—. Recipient Alumni Svc. award Northwestern U., 1995; Univ. scholar, 1961-64, Panhellenic scholar, 1964-65. Fellow Pub. Rels. Soc. Am. (bd. dirs. L.A. chpt. 1981-90, v.p. 1983, pres. 1989, del. nat. assembly 1980, co-chmn. long-range strategic com. 1990, president's adv. coun. 1991, exec. com. Counselors Acad. 1984-86, sec.-treas. 1990, chmn.-elect 1991, chmn. 1992, sec. Coll. Fellows 1993, chmn.-elect 1994, chmn. 1995); mem. Pub. Rels. Orgn. Internat. (founding U.S.), Women in Commn., Shi-ai, Delta Zeta (editor The Lamb 1966-68, Woman of Yr. award 1993), Kappa Alpha Tau. Office: 1999 Ave of Stars Ste 550 Los Angeles CA 90067

BOHLKEN, DEBORAH KAY, data processing executive, lobbyist; b. Anchorage, Nov. 16, 1952; d. Darrell Richard and Gertrude Ann (Merkel) B. BA, U. Ark., 1975, MSW, 1977. Specialist community devel. State of Ark., Little Rock, 1976-77, supr. community area, 1977-78, mgr. evaluation and data processing, 1978-80; corp. analyst Systematics, Inc., Little Rock, 1980-83, mgr. corp. planning and rsch., 1983-85, group mgr. planning, rsch., Washington Congl. liasion, 1985-89, 91—, corp. mgr. legis. and regulatory, legal dept., 1990-91; mktg., planning and devel. mgr. Systematics, Inc., 1992—; mgr. legis. and regulatory govt. svcs. Systematics Info. Svcs., Inc., Little Rock, 1992—, v.p. govt. affairs and risk mgmt., 1994—. Contbr. articles and papers to profl. publs. Bd. dirs. Cen. Ark. Radiation Therapy Inst. Hotline, Little Rock, 1980-82, Cancer Soc., Little Rock, 1986-89; state chair Cansurmount, Little Rock, 1985-89. Nat. Juvenile Justice Law Enforcement Adminstrn. explimary data processing grantee, 1976-78. Mem. NAFE, Nat. Assn. Bank Svcs., Fin. Mgrs. Assn., Am. Mgmt. Assn. Methodist. Office: Systematics Inc 4001 N Rodney Parham Rd Little Rock AR 72212-2448

BOHN, CHARLOTTE GALITZ, real estate executive; b. Chgo., Aug. 7, 1930; d. Chester Charles and Sarah Madelyn (McCarthy) B; m. Robert Allan Galitz, Nov. 25, 1955; children: Charles Robert, Thomas Allan, Madelyn Clare, (div. Sept. 1965). Student, Northwestern U., 1955, City Coll., Chgo., 1989. Lic. real estate salesperson, N.C. Lab. tech. Kraft Foods Rsch. Lab., Glenview, Ill., 1950-56; researcher data processing control Kemper Ins. Co., Chgo., 1967-70; jr. acct. Tractor Supply Co., Chgo., 1970-75; real estate salesman MGM Realty Co., Chgo., 1975-81, 85-88, Prime Realty, 1989—; broker Bohn Real Estate Agy, Raleigh, N.C., 1981-85; founder, pres. Pvt. Rsch., Chgo., 1985—; researcher zoning map City of Raleigh, 1980-81; bd. dirs. Off-Campus Writers Workshop. Contbr. various rsch. projects and sci. proposals. Vol. Chgo. Boy's Club; treas. churchwomen of St. Mary's, Crystal Lake, Ill.; vol. Lifeguard Easter Seal Soc.-Multiple Sclerosis, Raleigh, 1983-84, PTA, 1967-77; bd. dirs. Off-Campus Writer's Workshop; chair grammar sch. 50th reunion, 1994. Recipient Adviser Emblem of Merit award Jr. Achievement, 1955. Mem. AAAS, Smithsonian Inst. (assoc.), Nat. Trust Hist. Preservation, Raleigh C. of C., Jaycee Aux. (restaurant mgr.), Chgo. N. Side Realty Bd., Nat. Geog. Soc., Wilson Ctr. Assn., Mensa (nominating), Am. Assn. Ret. Persons, Irish Am. Heritage Ctr., Libr. Congress (assoc. charter). Episcopalian. Home: 6126 W Roscoe St Chicago IL 60634-4145 Office: Private Rsch 6126 W Roscoe St Chicago IL 60634-4145

BOHN, MARTHA LEE, political consultant; b. New Rochelle, N.Y., July 14, 1962; d. Alfred Christian and Nancy Devlin (Schrum) B. BA, Hampshire Coll., 1984. From cafe and dining rm. mgr. to asst. food & beverage mgr. Claremont Resort Hotel, Oakland, Calif., 1984-87; phone bank coord. Dukakis for Pres., White Plains, N.Y., 1988; congressional caseworker Congressman Eliot Engel, Yonkers, N.Y., 1989. chmn. Pelham Town Dem. Com., 1991-94; dir. ops. Westchester County Dem. Com., White Plains, 1990-91; dep. campaign mgr. Mrazek for U.S. Senate, N.Y.C., 1991-92; campaign mgr. Spano for County Clk., White Plains, 1989, Lowey for Congress, White Plains, 1992, Spano for County Exec., White Plains, 1993, Lynn for Congress, Mt. Kisco, N.Y., 1994; youth activities advisor Huguenot Meml. Ch., Pelham, N.Y., 1992-94. Home and Office: Bohn Consulting 151 6th St Pelham NY 10803-1323

BOHNE, JEANETTE KATHRYN, mathematics and science educator; b. Quincy, Ill., June 7, 1936; d. Anton Henry and Hilda Wilhelminia (Ohnemus) B. BA, Ursuline Coll., Louisville, 1961; MA, St. Louis U., 1962. Cert. math. and chemistry tchr., N.D., Ill., Mo. Math. tchr. Ryan High Sch., Minot, N.D., 1962-66, Althoff Cath. High Sch., Belleville, Ill., 1966-72, St. Francis Borgia High Sch., Washington, Mo., 1974-77; math. tchr. St. Louis Pub. Schs., 1977—, head dept. math., 1977-85; speaker in field. Treas. Welcome Wagon Club, Washington, 1974-76; pres. Bus. and Profl. Women's Club, Washington, 1978-79; active Animal Protective Assn., Zoo Friends of St. Louis Zoo, S.W. Garden Neighborhood Assn., S.W. Garden Neighborhood Assn. Mobile Patrol. Mem. AAUW, NEA, Mo. State Tchrs. Assn., St. Louis Tchrs. Union, Nat. Coun. Tchrs. Math., Math. Assn. Am., Math. Educators Group St. Louis, Mo. Coun. Tchrs. Math., St. Louis Sci. Ctr., Urban Math. Collaborative St. Louis. Home: PO Box 2252 Saint Louis MO 63109-0252 Office: St Louis Pub Schs 911 Locust St Saint Louis MO 63101-1401

BOHNEN, MOLLYN VILLAREAL, nurse educator; b. Balete, Aklan, Philippines, Nov. 1, 1941; came to the U.S., 1964; d. Wenceslao Macahilig Villareal and Amparo Feliciano Fulgencio; m. Robert Frank Bohnen, June 20, 1965; children: Sharon Kay, Scott Owen David, Paul Alan. BSN, U. Philippines, 1962; MSN, U. Utah, 1971; EdD, U. San Francisco, 1984. Staff nurse U. Philippines Med. Ctr., Manila, 1962-64, St. Lukes Hosp., N.Y.C., 1964-65, Greystone Park Hosp., Morristown, N.J., 1965, Buffalo (N.Y.) Children's Hosp., 1965-66; vol. staff nurse Peace Corps, Cebu City, Philippines, 1966-68; asst. prof. Calif. State U., Sacramento, 1973-76, 82-84, lectr., 1979-82, assoc. prof., 1984-87, prof., 1987—; instr. Am. River Coll., Sacramento, 1977-78; medico-legal cons. Calif. law firms, 1975—; internat. nursing edn. cons. B/B Creation, Rancho Cordova, Calif., 1988—. Contbr. articles to profl. jours. Recipient Golden Medallion award U. Philippines, 1994. Mem. Calif. Nurses Assn. (commr. nursing edn. region 8 1991-94, treas. 1982-84, Outstanding Svc. awards 1984, 86, Agnes Dix award for profl. excellence region 8 1992), Golden Key, Sigma Theta Tau (treas. Zeta Eta chpt. 1982-84, Rsch. award 1984), Phi Delta Kappa. Democrat. Roman Catholic. Home: 1441 Wild Plum Ct Klamath Falls OR 97601-1983 Office: Calif State U 6000 J St Sacramento CA 95819-6069

BOHNET, BETH ANN, psychologist; b. Mpls., Jan. 19, 1940; d. Herbert Leslie and Ruth Marie (Heig) B.; m. John Edward Kocourek, Aug. 29, 1959 (div. Feb. 1972); children: Tracy Lynn Kocourek Schmille, Jill Elizabeth Kocourek Balogh, Amy Ruth Kocourek Byrn; m. Stephen Earle Glass, Apr. 8, 1972 (div. Feb. 1985). BS in Elem. Edn., U. Kans., 1970, B of Gen. Studies, 1976, MS in Counseling, 1978, PhD in Counseling Psychology, 1985. Lic. psychologist, Maine. Psychology intern Counseling Ctr., U. Maine, Orono, 1982-83; grad. asst., stat. cons. U. Kans., Lawrence, 1984; counselor Adult Life Resource Ctr., U. Kans., Lawrence, 1984-85; clin. supr., psychologist Augusta (Maine) Mental Health Inst., 1985-87; psychologist Counseling Ctr., U. Maine, Orono, 1987-88; cons. Augusta Mental Health Inst., 1988-90; instr. Husson Coll., Bangor, Maine, 1991; pvt. practice Bangor, Maine, 1987—. Vestry clk. St. John's Ch., Bangor, 1992-94; pres. bd. dirs. Douglas County Hist. Soc., Lawrence, 1978-84; chair, sec., bd. dirs. Lawrence Arts Commn., 1978-84; pres., sec. Lawrence Art Guild, 1970-84; lay leader First Meth. Ch., Lawrence, 1981-84. Mem. APA, Maine Psychol. Assn. (sec./treas. 1987-89, pres. 1990-94), Bangor Area Psychol. Soc. Office: Beth Bohnet PhD 67 Pine St Bangor ME 04401

BOICE, MARGARET ROCKWELL (PEGGY BOICE), charitable organization executive; b. Boise, Idaho, June 27, 1947; d. Edward Henry and Mary Catherine (Bussey) B.; m. Gregory Morgan Jones, June 27, 1969 (div. 1974). BA, Baylor U., 1969; MSSW, U. Tex., Arlington, 1975, MA in Urban Studies, 1978. Lic. master social worker/advanced practitioner, Tex. Office asst. various doctors' offices, Houston, 1963-65; caseworker Meth. Children's Home, Waco, Tex., 1969-70, Florence Crittenton Home, Houston, 1970-71; pub. welfare worker Tex. Dept. Pub. Welfare, Denton, 1972-73; asst. HUD, Dallas, 1974-75; sr. planner Gov.'s Budget and Planning Office, State of Ga., Atlanta, 1975-77; coord. human resources Tex. Office State and Fed. Rels., Washington, 1977-79; sr. assoc., cons. Asst. Group for Human Resource Devel., Silver Spring, Md., 1979-80; dir. pub. policy United Way Tex., Austin, 1980—, convenor, organizer child care working group, 1986-93; mem. govt. rels. adv. com. United Way Am., Alexandria, Va., 1984-85; mem. fed. budget adv. com. Tex. Health and Human Svcs. Coordinating Coun., Austin, 1985-86, convenor, organizer state needs assessment com., 1988-90; mem. Tex. Legis. Subcom. on Child Care, 1989-91; mem. rate setting adv. com. Tex. Dept. Aging., 1990-91; mem. child care rate reimbursement methodologies steering com. Tex. Dept. Human Svcs., 1990-92; mem. project steering com. Gov.'s State Head Start Collaboration, 1990-92; mem. adv. com. Tex. Employment Commn. Child Care Clearinghouse, 1987-92. Author: Public Policy Handbook, 1990, 2d edit., 94; editor: (Booklets) Child Care in Texas, 1988. Organizer Baylor and Waco Vol. Orgn., 1968-69, Interagy. Human Svcs. Coun., Denton, 1972-73, CARE Coalition, child abuse prevention, Austin, 1983-87; organizer, mem. Tex. Mental Health Code Rewrite Com., 1983-85. Recipient cert. of Appreciation Coalition Mental and Devel. Disabilities, 1983, State of Tex., 1984-90, Tex. Maternal and Child Health Coalition, 1985, TEC Child Care Clearinghouse, 1991, Tex. Legis. Subcom. on Child Care, 1991, State Friend of Extension award Epsilon Sigma Phi, 1992, Cert. of Recognition for work on Tex. Head Start Collaboration Project, Tex. Gov. Ann Richards, 1993, Commendation, Tex. Child Care Working Group, 1993. Mem. Tex. Assn. for Edn. Young Children, Austin Assn. for Edn. Young Children (Jeannette Watson Pub. Policy award 1991). Office: United Way Tex 505 E Huntland Dr Ste 455 Austin TX 78752-3714

BOIMAN, DONNA RAE, artist, art academy executive; b. Columbus, Ohio, Jan. 13, 1946; d. George Brandle and Donna Rae (Rockwell) Hall; m. David Charles Boiman, Dec. 8, 1973 (div. Aug. 1990). BS in Pharmacy, Ohio State U., 1969; student, Columbus Coll. Art & Design, 1979-83. Registered pharmacist, Ohio. Pharmacist, mgr. various retail stores, Cleve., 1970-73, Columbus, 1973-77; owner L'Artiste, Reynoldsburg, Ohio, 1977-81; pres. Cen. Ohio Art Acad., Reynoldsburg, 1981-90, Art Acad. Ctrl. Ohio, Reynoldsburg, 1990—; owner Big Red Designs, Reynoldsburg, 1989—; pub. rels. mgr. Freedom Farm Equestrian Ctr., Pataskala, Ohio, 1991—; cons. to Mayor City of Reynoldsburg, 1986-87; ptnr. Broken Horse, Inc. Represented in permanent collections including Collector's Gallery Columbus Mus. Art, Gallery 200, Columbus Art Exch., The Huntington

Collection, Dean Witter Reynolds Collection, Zanesville Art Ctr., Mt. Carmel East Hosp., Columbus, Corp. 2005, Radisson Hotels, Mich. and Ohio, Fifth 3d Bank, Bexley, Ohio, On Line Computer Libr., Dublin, Ohio; author: Anatomy Made Easy: Draw, Color and Learn, Anatomy and Structure: A Guide for Young Artists, 1988. Recipient John Lennon Meml. Award for the Arts, Internat. Art Challenge com., 1987. Mem. Pa. Soc. Watercolorists, Nat. Soc. Layerists in Multimedia, Columbus Art League, Cen. Ohio Watercolor Soc. (pres. 1983-84), Am. Quarter Horse Assn., Ohio Quarter Horse Assn., Allied Artists of Am. (assoc.), Licking County Art Assn., Nat. Wildlife Fedn., Ohio State U. Alumni Assn., Ohio State U. Pharmacy Alumni Assn. (charter), Mid-Ohio Dressage Assn., U.S. Dressage Fedn., Ohio Arabian Horse Assn., Internat. Arabian Horse Assn., Arabian Sport Assn., Inc. Office: Art Acad of Cen Ohio 7297 E Main St Reynoldsburg OH 43068-2105

BOISE, AUDREY LORRAINE, educator; b. Hackensack, N.J., Feb. 12, 1933; d. Paul George and Lillian Rose (Goedecker) B. BA, Wellesley (Mass.) Coll., 1955; MA, Fairleigh Dickinson U., 1977. Cert. tchr. K-8, learning disabilities, supervision. Tchr. Township of Berkeley Heights (N.J.), 1958-67; learning cons. Borough of New Providence (N.J.), 1978-82, 1986—, Scotch Plains/Fanwood (N.J.), 1984-86; instr. Fairleigh Dickinson U., Madison, N.J., 1983, 1975-76; several other short-term teaching positions; supr. student tchrs., 1975-78; lectr. on fgn. countries and U.S. History, N.J., 1967—; travel agt. (part-time) 1972—. Mem. Rep. Nat. Com. Campaign Coun., Nat. Rep. Senatorial Com., Washington, Rep. Presdl. Task Force, Washington, Rep. Presdl. Legion of Merit, N.J. State Rep. Com., Trenton, Nat. Fedn. Rep. Women, Washington. Mem. NEA, AAUW, N.J. Assn. Learning Cons., Assn. for Children with Learning Disabilities, N.J. Edn. Assn., Internat. Platform Assn., Fortnightly Club, Hist. Soc. Summit. Methodist. Office: New Providence Bd Edn Dept Spl Svcs 340 Center Ave New Providence NJ 07974

BOK, SISSELA, philosopher, writer; b. Stockholm, Dec. 2, 1934; d. Gunnar and Alva (Reimer) Myrdal; m. Derek Bok, May 7, 1955; children—Hilary, Victoria, Tomas. BA, George Washington U., 1957, MA, 1958, LHD (hon.), 1986; PhD, Harvard U., 1970; LLD (hon.), Mt. Holyoke Coll., 1985; LHD (hon.), Clark U., 1988, U. Mass., 1991, Georgetown U., 1992. Lectr. Simmons Coll., Boston, 1971-72; lectr. Harvard-MIT Div. Health Scis. and Tech., Cambridge, 1975-82, Harvard U., Cambridge, 1982-84; assoc. prof. philosophy Brandeis U., Waltham, Mass., 1985-89, prof. philosophy, 1989-92; fellow Ctr. for Advanced Study, Stanford, Calif., 1991-92; Disting. fellow Harvard Ctr. Population and Devel. Studies, Cambridge, Mass., 1993—; mem. ethics adv. bd. HEW, 1977-80; bd. dirs. Population Coun., 1971-77. Author: Lying: Moral Choice in Public and Private Life, 1978 (Melcher award, George Orwell award), Secrets: On the Ethics of Concealment and Revelation, 1982, Alva: Ett kvinnoliv, 1987, A Strategy for Peace, 1989, Alva Myrdal: A Daughter's Memoir, 1991 (Melcher award); mem. editor bd. Ethics, 1980-85, Criminal Justice Ethics, 1980—, Contention, 1990—, Common Knowledge, 1991—. Bd. dirs. Inst. for Philosophy and Religion, Boston U.; mem. Pulitzer Prize Bd., 1989—. Recipient Abram L. Sachar Silver medallion Brandeis U., 1985, Radcliffe Coll. Grad. Soc. medal, 1993. Fellow Hastings Ctr. (dir. 1976-84, 94—); mem. Am. Philos. Assn.

BOLAND, CHRISTINE LYNN, social worker; b. Muscatine, Iowa, May 16, 1964; d. David Randall and Barbara Ann (Dunbar) B. AA, Muscatine C.C., 1985; BA, U. Iowa, 1988; MSW, Boston U., 1992. Cert. social worker. Nurse's aide Hershey Convalescent Home, Muscatine, 1983; cert. nurse's aide Bethesda Care Ctr., Muscatine, 1984-86; residential counselor System's Unlimited, Iowa City, 1986-88; cert. nurse's aide Med. Personnel Pool, Portsmouth, N.H., 1989; residential counselor Cmty. Housing for Adult Independence-Jewish Family and Children's Svcs., Brighton, Mass., 1990-92; social work grad. intern Newton, Wellesley, Weston Com., Auburndale, Mass., 1990-91, Boston U. Hosp., 1991-92; psychiatric social worker St. Lawrence Psychiatric Ctr., Plattsburgh, N.Y., 1992—. Mem. co-coord. accessibility com. for nat. anti-racism conf. Women Against Racism Com., Iowa City, 1988-89; active Humane Soc. U.S., 1994—, The Nature Conservancy, Smithsonian Assocs. Mem. NOW, Nat. Assn. Social Workers, Pub. Employees Fedn. AFL-CIO, Amnesty Internat. Democrat. Home: 182 Bear Swamp Rd Peru NY 12972

BOLAND, LOIS WALKER, retired mathematician and computer systems analyst; b. Newton Center, Mass., Sept. 14, 1919; d. Charles Nelson and Nell Flora (Kruse) Walker; m. Ralph Montrose Boland, June 2, 1943; children: Charles Montrose, William Ralph (dec.), Ann Helen Boland Garner, Mark Alan Boland (dec.). BS, Stetson U., 1940; grad. fellow U. Ala., 1940-41; postgrad. U. Fla., 1948, 51-52, U. Mich., 1958, 65, U. Colo., 1966, 68, Air Force Computer Sch., Keesler AFB, Biloxi, Miss., 1974. Physics tchr., Lakeland Fla. High Sch., 1941-42; chemist, IM&CC, Mulberry, Fla., 1942-43; elec. engrng. draftsman Tampa Ship Corp., Fla., 1943-46; math. tchr. Plant High Sch., Tampa, 1947-50; mathematician/computers, data reduction div. Patrick AFB, Fla., 1951-54; mathematician, computer supr. data reduction div. White Sands Missile Range, N.Mex., 1954-63; ops. research analyst Peterson AFB, Colo. Springs, Colo., 1963-78, ret., 1978. Author: AUPRE Computer Program Manual, 1963, 77; Askania Photheodolite Computer Manual, 1956; editor Q-Point mag., 1966. Elected mem. Democratic exec. com. Volusia County, Fla., 1984-89. Pioneer mathematician Pioneer Group White Sands Missile Range, 1985; math. fellow U. Ala., 1940-41. Mem. Math. Assn. Am. (emeritus), AAUW (pres. DeLand chpt. 1984-86), Mensa, Am. Contract Bridge League. Clubs: Halifax, Lake Beresford Yacht. Avocations: writing; pianist; travel; duplicate bridge; swimming. Home: PO Box 215 Cassadaga FL 32706-0215

BOLAND, PATRICIA ANN, museum director; b. Rochester, N.Y., Aug. 24, 1935; d. James Patrick and Florence Elva (Miller) Neary; m. Gerald Patrick Boland, June 30, 1956 (wid. June 1989); children: Patrick, Matthew, Daniel, Timothy, Sheila, Catherine. Student, Nazareth Coll., Rochester, N.Y., 1952-54. Tchr. St. Michael's Sch., Rochester, 1954-56, St. Peter and Paul Sch., Rochester, 1956-57; edn. dir. Ontario County Hist. Soc., Canandaigua, N.Y., 1972-81; city coun. mem. City of Canandaigua, 1975-79, mayor, 1979-85; owner Gourmet Deli, Canandaigua, 1983-84; dir. Granger Homestead Soc., Canandaigua, 1989—; bd. dirs. Canandaigua Nat. Bank; lectr. Irish history and culture. Author articles on various aspects of Irish history and culture. Mem. Canandaigua Dem. Com., 1975—, Ontario County Dem. Com., 1975—; elected to Ontario County Bd. Suprs., 1991-93; bd. dirs. Bristol Valley Playhouse, Naples, N.Y., 1980-87, Neighbor-to-Neighbor, Canandaigua, 1985—. Recipient William Mitchell award Canandaigua C. of C., 1989, Main St. award N.Y. State, HUD award, 1984. Office: Granger Homestead Soc 295 N Main St Canandaigua NY 14424-1289

BOLDOSSER, NANCY SHILAY, communications company financial executive; b. N.Y.C., June 5, 1957; d. Nicholas and Olga (Chanevich) S.; m. Randy Richard Boldosser, June 13, 1981; children: Katherine Ann, Christina Dawn. BS in Acctg., Lehigh U., 1979, MBA, 1979. CPA, Pa. Staff auditor Price Waterhouse, N.Y.C., 1979-80, sr. tax acct., 1981; sr. tax acct. Deloitte Haskins & Sells, Allentown, Pa., 1981-82; mfg. acct. AT&T, Allentown, 1982-83; resident audit head AT&T, Reading, Pa., 1984-86; staff mgr. results and reporting data systems group AT&T, Morristown, N.J., 1986-87, contr. svcs. product line data systems group, 1987-88; product mgr. AT&T Network Systems, Warren, N.J., 1988—. Mem. AICPA, Inst. Internal Auditors. Republican. Episcopalian. Office: AT&T Rm 2N-Q04 184 Liberty Corner Rd Warren NJ 07059

BOLDUC, JEANNE-MARIE, dental hygienist; b. Laconia, N.H., Feb. 14, 1957; d. Maurice Frank and Rita Janice (Robert) B.; m. Stefan Warner Mattlage, Feb. 16, 1980 (div. 1985); 1 child, Amy Justin Mattlage. Diploma in dental assisting, Western Wis. Tech. Inst., 1981; AS, N.H. Tech. Inst., Concord, N.H., 1994. Registered dental hygienist; cert. orthodontic asst., dental asst. Dental asst. Midwest Dental Care, S.C., La Crosse, Wis., 1981-82, Dr. Leo B. SanBacon, Laconia, N.H., 1984-93; dental hygienist Dr. Rodney E. Burdette, Concord, N.H., 1994, Dr. Stephen Rosenberg, Concord, 1994—; mem. dental asst. adv. panel Johnson & Johnson Med., Inc., 1991—; table clinic presenter 32nd ann. N.E. Regional SADHA Conf., Paramus, N.J., 1994; presenter in field. Particpant Gilford (N.H.) H.S. Career Orientation Program, 1991-93. Mem. Am. Dental Assts. Assn., Am. Dental Hygienists Assn., N.H. Dental Hygienists Assn., N.H. Dental Assts. Assn., Phi Theta Kappa. Office: Rodney E. Burdette DDS 199 Loudon Rd Concord NH 03301

BOLENE, MARGARET ROSALIE STEELE, bacteriologist, civic worker; b. Kingfisher, Okla., July 11, 1923; d. Clarence R. and Harriet (White) Steele; student Oreg. State U., 1943-44; B.S., U. Okla., 1946; m. Robert V. Bolene, Feb. 6, 1948; children: Judith Kay, John Eric, Sally Sue, Janice Lynn, Daniel William. Technician bacteriology dept. Okla. Dept. Health, Oklahoma City, 1946-48; asst. bacteriologist Henry Ford Hosp., Detroit, 1948-49; bacteriol. cons., also asst. bus. mgr. Ponca Gynecology and Obstetrics, Inc., 1956-92, retired. Organizing dir. Bi-Racial Council, 1963; lay adviser Home Nursing Service, 1967-68; mem. exec. bd. PTA, 1956-71; active various community drives; sponsor Am. Field Service; patron Ponca Playhouse; bloodmobile vol. ARC; vol. Helpline. Republican precinct organizer, 1960. Mem. AAUW (treas. 1964-66), DAR (sec.-treas. 1961-67, 1st vice regent 1972-73, chpt. treas. 1974-84, chpt. chaplain 1991, state schs. chmn. 1990-94), Kay-Noble County Med. Aux. (treas. 1957-58, 66-67), Ponca City Art Assn., Pioneer Hist. Soc., Okla. Heritage Assn., Okla. Hist. Soc., Daus. Founders and Patriots (state pres. 1980-84, registrar 1993—), Nat. Huguenot Soc., Hereditary Order First Families Mass. Daus. Am. Colonists (chpt. regent 1982-84, state flag chmn. 1990-92), Magna Charta Dames (treas. Okla. chpt. 1984), Order Colonial Physicians and Chirurgiens (life), Ancient and Honorable Arty. Co. Women Descs. Okla. Ct. (treas. 1983-84, registrar 1986—), Dames of Ct. of Honor, Colonial Dames of 17th Century, Daus. of Colonial Wars, Colonial Daus. 17th Century, U. Okla. Assn. (life), Lambda Tau, Phi Sigma, Alpha Lambda Delta. Presbyterian (elder 1983-86). Clubs: Ponca City Country, Ponca City Music, Red Rose Garden (pres. 1983-84, treas. 1993—), Twentieth Century (rec. sec. 1992-94). Home: 2116 Juanito Ave Ponca City OK 74604-3813

BOLES, LENORE UTAL, nurse psychotherapist, educator; b. N.Y.C., July 3, 1929; d. Joseph Leo and Dorothy (Grosby) Utal; m. Morton Schloss, Dec. 17, 1955 (div. May 1961); 1 child, Howard Alan Schloss; m. Sam Boles, May 24, 1962; children: Anne Leslie, Laurence Utal. Diploma in nursing, Beth Israel Hosp. Sch. Nursing, 1951; BSN, Columbia U., 1964; MSN, U. Conn., 1977. Lic. clin. specialist in adult psychiatry/mental health nursing. Staff nurse Beth Israel Hosp., N.Y.C., 1951, Kingsbridge VA Hosp., Bronx, N.Y., 1951-55; night supr. Gracie Square Hosp., N.Y.C., 1959-60; head nurse Elmhurst City Hosp., Queens, N.Y., 1960-62; nursing instr. Norwalk (Conn.) Hosp., 1966-74; asst. prof. U. Bridgeport, Conn., 1976-78; nurse psychotherapist Nurse Counseling Group, Norwalk, 1979—; nursing faculty Western Conn. State U., Danbury, 1978-80; adj. asst. prof. Sacred Heart U., Bridgeport, Conn., 1983-89; adj. faculty Western Conn. State U., Danbury, 1994; nurse cons. Bradley Meml. Hosp., Southington, Conn., 1982, Lea Manor Nursing Home, Norwalk, 1982, St. Vincent's Hosp., Bridgeport, 1982-92; staff devel. nurse Silver Hill Hosp., New Canaan, Conn., 1980-86, 94—; cons. in field, 1980—. Author: (book chpt.) Nursing Diagnoses for Psychiatric Nursing Practice, 1994. V.p. Sisterhood Beth El, Norwalk, 1969-71; bd. dirs. religious sch. Congregation Beth-el, Norwalk, 1971-75, 79-80, rec. sec., be. trustees, 1975-77, v.p. congregation, 1977-80, bd. trustees, 1980-83. Named Speaker of Yr., Am. Cancer Soc., 1976. Mem. ANA, Northeastern Nursing Diagnosis Assn. (chair N.E. region conf. 1985, chair planning com. 1984-85, chair nominating com. 1989-91), N.Am. Nursing Diagnosis Assn., Coun. Psychiat./Mental Health Clin. Specialists, Conn. Nurses Assn. (Del. to convs. 1977—, legis. com. dist. 3 1984-86, nominating com. 1988-90, Florence Wald award 1984, Conn. Nursing Diagnosis Conf. Group 1980-87), Conn. Soc. Nurse Psychotherapists (founding mem.). Democrat. Jewish. Home: 173 E Rocks Rd Norwalk CT 06851 Office: Nurse Counseling Group 150 East Ave Norwalk CT 06851

BOLEY, DONNA JEAN, state legislator; b. Bens Run, W.Va., Dec. 9, 1935; d. Glen A. and Grace (Jones) Northcraft; m. Jack Edward Boley, 1956; children: Kari Lynn, Brian Lee. Student, W.Va. U., Parkersburg. Assoc. chair State Rep. Exec. Com., 1970-75; chmn. Pleasant County Rep. Exec. Com., 1978—; mem. W.Va. Senate, 1986—; chmn. Rep. Platform. Com., W.Va.; 1st woman minority leader State Senate, 1991, 92. Mem. Nat. Rep. Platform Com. from W.Va., Houston, 1992; exec. com. Nat. Rep. Com., 1992. Mem. St. Marys Women's Club (pres. 1972-74, 80-81). Republican. Methodist.

BOLEY BOLAFFIO, RITA, artist; b. Trieste, Italy, June 7, 1898; d. Angelo Luzzatto and Olga Senigaglia; came to U.S., 1939, naturalized, 1944; diploma with Joseph Hoffmann, Kunstgewerbe Schule, Vienna, Austria; diploma violin Music Conservatory, Vienna; student of F. Ondricek; m. Orville F. Boley; children: Lucius R., Bruno A. Fashion, textile and interior designer Wiener Werkstatte, Vienna and Milan, Italy; contbr. Harper's Bazaar; murals and displays for Saks Fifth Ave, Bergorf Goodman, Lord & Taylor and throughout U.S., maj. exhbns. collage and assemblage include Mus. of Art, Columbia, S.C., Am. House, N.Y.C., J.L. Hudson Gallery, Detroit, Pen and Brush Club, N.Y.C., Richard Kollmar's Gallery, N.Y.C., Guild Hall Mus., East Hampton, N.Y., James Pendleton Gallery, N.Y.C. Washington Art Assn. Conn., Galerie St. Etienne, N.Y.C., Hudson River Mus., Yonkers, N.Y., Lamborghini Gallery, N.Y.C., 1990; represented in pvt. collections, also represented in European and Am. publs. Recipient Premio Ciglione della Malpensa award for equitation, 1936, Poetry prize Premio di Sorrento, 1965. Mem. arts group ARC, 1942-44. Mem. Composer, Author and Artists Am. Studio: 310 W 106th St New York NY 10025

BOLGER, VIRGINIA JOAN, nursing administrator; b. N.Y.C.; d. Vincent and Lillian (Stryker) Cerrato; m. Lawrence Bolger; children: Wayne, Debra, Susan, Robert. AAS in Nursing, Suffolk County C.C., 1973; BSN, L.I. U., 1975, MPS in Health Care Adminstrn., 1977. Head nurse Patchogue (N.Y.) Nursing Ctr., Ross Nursing Home, Brentwood, N.Y.; dir. nursing and healthcare Little Flower Childrens Svcs., Wading River, N.Y.; com. mem. spl. edn. Little Flower Sch. Dist. Past chairperson Health Care Coords. Diocese of N.Y. Named to Dean's List Suffolk Community Coll. Mem. Profl. Nursing Assn. Suffolk County. Home: 109 Carroll Ave Ronkonkoma NY 11779-4232 Office: Little Flower Children's Svc North Wading River Rd Wading River NY 11792

BOLING, JEWELL, retired government official; b. Randleman, N.C., Sept. 26, 1907; d. John Emmitt and Carrie (Ballard) B. Student, Women's Coll., U. N.C., 1926, Am. U., 1942, 51-52. Interviewer N.C. Employment Service, Winston-Salem, Asheboro, 1937-41; occupational analyst U.S. Dept. Labor, Washington, 1943-57, placement officer, 1957-58, employment service adviser, 1959-61, occupational analyst, 1962, employment service specialist counseling and testing, 1963-69, manpower devel. specialist, 1969-74, ret., 1974. Author: Counselor's Handbook, 1967; Counselor's Desk Aid, Eighteen Basic Vocational Directions, 1967; Handbook for New Careerists in Employment Security, 1971; contbr. articles to profl. publs. Recipient Meritorious Achievement award U.S. Dept. Labor, 1972. Mem. AAAS, ACA, ASCD, AAUW, Am. Rehab. Counseling Assn. (archivist 1964-68), Nat. Capital Astronomers (editor Star Dust 1949-58), Nat. Career Devel. Assn., Internat. Platform Assn., N.Y. Acad. Scis., Assn. Measurement in Counseling and Devel., Assn. Humanistic Psychology, Planetary Soc., Smithsonians, Sierra Club, Nature Conservancy, Audubon Naturalist Soc., Wilderness Soc. Address: 5071 US Hwy 220 Bus N Randleman NC 27317-7655

BOLING, JUDY ATWOOD, civic worker; b. Madras, India, June 19, 1921 (parents Am. citizens); d. Carroll Eugene and Marion Frances (Ayrer) Atwood; m. Jack Leroy Boling, Apr. 8, 1941 (dec. July 1988); children: Joseph Edward, Jean Ann, James Michael, John Charles. AA, San Antonio Jr. Coll., 1940; student Rogue Community Coll., Grants Pass, Oreg., 1978-79, So. Oreg. State Coll., Ashland, 1982—. Contbr. articles to profl. jours. First aid instr. ARC, various locations, 1940-65, chmn. vols., Calif., 1961-62, Eng., 1964-65; den mother cub scouts Boy Scouts Am., Monterey, Calif., 1951-52; active Girl Scouts U.S., 1953—, coun. pres., Winema (Oreg.) Coun., 1971-73, 79-82, historian, 1990—, del. to nat. coun., 1966, 72, 81, cons. for nat. pubs., 1971, 79; Sunday sch. tchr. Base Chapel, Pyote, Tex., 1949-51, choir dir., 1951; Sunday sch. adminstr. Base Chapel, Morocco, 1954-55; Sunday sch. tchr. Hermon Free Meth. Ch., L.A., 1956-57; active United Way campaign, 1967-84, Childrens Festival, 1974-88; former liaison with local people in Japanese-Am., Franco-Am., Anglo-Am. orgns.; mem., patron Rogue Craftsmen Bd., Grants Pass, 1972-85, sec., 1972-78, v.p., 1978-85; bd. dirs. Rogue Valley Opera Assn., 1978-85, sponsor/mem., 1978—; bd. dirs. Community Concert, 1979-88, 92—, mem. Grants Pass Friends of the Symphony, 1989— (bd. dirs. 1992—); vol. RSVP, 1982—; historian Josephine County Rep. Women, 1982-86, treas., 1986-94, sec., 1995—; elected Rep. precinct committeeperson, 1991—; sustaining mem. Sta. KSYS pub. TV; mem. Sta. KSOR pub. radio; frequent pub. speaker. Recipient Thanks badge Girl Scouts U.S., 1957, 60, 73, Girl Scouts Japan, 1959, U.K. Girl Guides, 1982; others; cert. of appreciation USAF, 1959, City of Hagi, City of Fukuoka (Japan), Gov. of Fukuoka Prefecture; 2 citations Internat. Book Project; Oreg. Vol. award Sen. Packwood, 1983; Community Woman of Year award Bus. and Profl. Women, 1984. Mem. Josephine County Hist. Soc. (bd. dirs. 1991—), So. Oreg. Resources Alliance, Am. Host Found., Friends of Libr., Grants Pass Art Mus., Knife and Fork Club (bd. dirs. 1994—). Address: 3016 Jumpoff Joe Creek Rd Grants Pass OR 97526-8778

BOLING, MARY JO, accountant; b. Evansville, Ind., Aug. 10, 1955; d. Walter J. and Frances (Eastwood) Schmuck; m. Larry G. Duncan, Dec. 21, 1973 (div. Jan. 1987); m. Mark A. Boling, Aug. 3, 1990. AA, U. Ky., 1980; BA, U. Evansville, 1991. Acct. Big Rivers Elec., Henderson, Ky., 1980—. Mem. Inst. Mgmt. Accts. Baptist. Home: 290 Ray Melton Rd Dixon KY 42409-9515 Office: Big Rivers Elec 201 3rd St Henderson KY 42420-2979

BOLINGER, JANICE EARLENE, mental health services professional; b. Martinsville, Ind., Mar. 3, 1948; d. Isaac Earle and Sallie Annice (Goss) Powell; m. Donal Louis Bolinger, Jan. 23, 1970; children: Donal Jason, Jamie Alan. BS, Ind. State U., 1970, MS, 1971. High sch. tchr. Martinsville Sch. Dist., 1971-83; ins. underwriter Farm Bur. Ins., Indpls., 1988-90, Golden Rule Ins., Lawrenceville, Ill., 1990-91; sec. Comprehensive Community Mental Health Ctr., Vincennes, Ind., 1991-94; admissions officer South Ctrl. Cmty. Mental Health, Bloomington, Ind., 1994—; adv. bd. home econ. dept. Martinsville H.S., 1978-83, student club sponsor, 1971-74, 80-83, dir. Bldg. Trades Corp., 1978-83; active Ind. State Textbook Adoption Com., 1977-78. Dept. supt. Morgan County Fair Assn., Martinsville, 1976, 78-80; den leader Cub Scouts, Martinsville, 1984-85, pack com. mem., 1984-86, Miami dist. cub scout tng. team for adult leaders, Ind., 1985-86, instr., advisor merit badges, 1986-90. Named one of 10 Outstanding Young Women of Am., 1983, Homemaker of Month, Morgan County Ext. Homemakers, 1986, Ind. DAR Outstanding Jr. and East Ctrl. Divsn. winner, 1983. Mem. DAR (state chmn. 1980—, nat. vice-chmn. 1989—, Ind. state rec. sec. 1991-94, state historian 1994—, local chpt. officer 1978—, regent 1984-86, 88-90), Daughters the Union (Ind. state dir. 1986-88), U.S. Daughters 1812 (Ind. state chmn. 1982-84), Daughters the Am. Colonists, Colonial Dames the XVIIth Century, Continental Soc. Daughters Indian Wars, Soc. Ind. Pioneers, Children the Am. Revolution (Ind. sr. state 2d v.p. 1990-92, 1st v.p. 1992—, sr. soc. pres., officer 1980—, Ind. sr. state chmn. 1982-84), Morgan County Musical Soc. (soloist). Church of Christ. Home: 399 Valley Dr Martinsville IN 46151

BOLITHO, LOUISE GREER, educational administrator, consultant; b. Wenatchee, Wasn., Aug. 13, 1927; d. Lon Glenn and Edna Gertrude (Dunlap) Greer; m. Douglas Stuart, June 17, 1950 (div. Dec. 1975); children: Rebecca Louise, Brian Douglas. BA, Wash. State U., 1949. With Stanford (Calif.) U., 1967-91, adminstrv. asst. physics labs., 1974-77, mgr. ctr. for research in internat. studies, 1977-84, law sch. fin. and adminstrv. services dir., 1984-86; computer cons., Palo Alto, Calif., 1984—; acting mgr. Inst. for Internat. Studies, 1987-88, fin. analyst, 1988-91. Mem. Peninsula vols., Menlo Park, Calif., 1986-94; budget com. chmn., bd. dirs. Mid-Peninsula Support Network, Mountain View, Calif., 1984-86; chairperson active older adults com. YMCA; pres. 410 Sheridan Ave. Homeowners Assn., 1989-93, treas., 1993—. Mem. AAUW (bd. dirs. 1987-88). Home and Office: 410 Sheridan Ave Apt 445 Palo Alto CA 94306-2020

BOLLAG, WENDY BOLLINGER, medical educator; b. Pitts., May 17, 1962; d. Joseph Martin and Carolyn (Cope) Bollinger; m. Roni Jaakow Bollag, June 7, 1986; 1 child, Katherine Amanda. BS, Pa. State U., 1984; MS, Yale U., 1987, MPhil, 1987, PhD, 1990. Coord., lectr. physiology course Yale Physician Assoc. Program, New Haven, 1987-90, Norwalk Hosp./Yale Physician Assoc. Surg. Residency Program, New Haven, 1987-90; postdoctoral rsch. assoc. Hoffmann-La Roche, Nutley, N.J., 1991-92; asst. prof. biology Seton Hall U., South Orange, N.J., 1992-93; assoc. prof. medicine Med. Coll. Ga., Augusta, 1993—. Contbr. articles to profl. jours., chpt. to book. NSF predoctoral fellow, 1984-87. Mem. Soc. Investigative Dermatology, Am. Soc. Cell Biology, Sigma Xi. Office: Med Coll Ga 1120 15th St Augusta GA 30912-3175

BOLLHEIMER, (CECILIA) DENISE, marketing professional, finance executive; b. Memphis, Sept. 8, 1950; d. Parker Cecil Jr. and Kathleen Alice (Reinhart) Henderson; m. Philip Anthony Bollheimer Jr., June 10, 1972. Student, Rhodes Coll., 1968-69; BBA in Mktg., Memphis State U., 1972, MBA in Fin., 1979; cert. in Banking, Rutgers U., 1983; cert. in Trust Ops., So. Trust Sch., 1984. Research analyst, mgr. Union Planters Corp., Memphis, 1973-75, asst. to mktg. dir., 1975-76, asst. v.p., 1976-77, v.p. mktg. div., 1977-83; sr. v.p. trust group Union Planters Nat. Bank, Memphis, 1983-84; sr. v.p. fin. mgmt. group Union Planters Corp., Memphis, 1984-86; dir. advt., promotions, mktg. communications Meth. Health Systems, Memphis, 1986-87, dir. mktg., 1987-88; v.p. mktg. and planning UT Med. Group, Inc., Memphis, 1988—; dir. mktg. U. Tenn. Med. Ctr., 1989—; instr. health care fin. Memphis State U., 1988-90. Mem. planned giving coun. Rhodes Coll., Memphis, 1985-86, alumni fund-raising com. 1987; mem. Leadership Memphis, 1985—, class rep., 1985-93; chmn. world championship barbecue cooking contest Memphis in May Internat. Festival, 1986-88, mktg. steering com., 1990, speakers bur., 1991-93; chmn. advt. com. entertainment com. Am. Heart Assn., Memphis, 1986, 87, advt. and communications com., Memphis, 1990—; bd. dirs. Commitment Memphis, 1984-87, pres., 1987; bd. dirs. Memphis Lit. Coun., 1986-90, chmn. bd., 1989-90, Lupus Found. Am., Memphis, 1987-88; mem. fin. com., bd. dirs. Memphis/Shelby County chpt. ARC, 1990—; group leader YWCA Capital Campaign, Memphis, 1990; bd. trustees Hemophilia Found., Memphis, 1990—; bd. dirs. U. Memphis Soc., Inc., 1995—. Mem. Med. Group Mgmt. Assn., Am. Inst. Banking (Banker of Yr. Memphis region 1981), Kiwanis (sec. bd. dirs. Kiwanis Charities 1988-90, 92—, membership com. 1990—, program com. 1993—, bd. dirs. 1994—), Beta Gamma Sigma, Alpha Omicron Pi. Home: 628 N Trezevant St Memphis TN 38112-1721 Office: UT Med Group Inc 66 N Pauline St Memphis TN 38105-5102

BOLLING, GAIL WILDMAN, cardiovascular clinical research coordinator, educator; b. N.Y.C., Sept. 22, 1948; d. Richard David and Dolores Allison (Wildman) Wildman; m. Lloyd Alfred Bolling, Oct. 10, 1970; children: Rachel, Karri, Cameron. Grad., St. Josephs Hosp. Sch. Nursing, Yonkers, N.Y., 1969; ADN, Montgomery Coll., Takoma Park, Md., 1982; BSN, Am. U., 1987; postgrad., U. Md., Balt. RN, Md.; CCRN; cert. BLS provider, cons.; legal nurse cons. Staff supr. Asbury Meth. Village-Herman Wilson Health Care Ctr., Gaithersburg, Md., 1978-83; ICU charge nurse, staff nurse, preceptor Shady Grove Adventist Hosp., Rockville, Md., 1983—; clin. instr. Montgomery Coll., 1988—; founder, exec. dir. Nursing Cons., Inc., Rockville, 1990—; asst. dir. Cardiovascular Fitness Inc., Rockville, 1988-92; vol. aeromed. flight nurse Mercy Med. Airlift, Manassas, Va., 1991—; bd. chmn. med. and cmty. programs Am. Heart Assn.; clin. mgr. Montgomery Grove Health Ctr., Johns Hopkins Med. Svcs. Corp., 1992-93. Contbr. articles to profl. jours. Chair Am. Heart Assn., Rockville, Md., 1992. Health Svcs. Cost Rev. Commn. grantee, 1985; Charlotte Newcomb scholar St. Joseph's Sch. Practical Nursing; recipient cert. outstanding performance Shady Grove Adventist Hosp. Mem. ANA, AACN, NAFE, Md. Nurses Assn., Black Nurses Assn., Nat. League for Nursing, Am. Assn. Legal Nurse Cons. (bd. dirs., sec. Greater Balt. Area chpt.), Nat. Coun. for Negro Women, Nat. Nurses in Bus. Assn., Am. Assn. Black Women Entrepreneurs Corp., Sigma Theta Tau. Home: 24029 Bush Hill Rd Gaithersburg MD 20882-3903

BOLLINGER, PAMELA BEEMER, health facilities administrator; b. Chgo., Apr. 7, 1947; d. Eldred Harlan and Shirley Pearl (Olsen) Beemer; m. Gary Allen Bollinger, Aug. 23, 1969. BS, Millikin U., 1969. Med. technologist Rush-Presbyt. St. Luke's Med. Ctr., Chgo., 1969-70, exec. technologist, 1975-77; hematology supr. Meml. Hosp. DuPage County, Elmhurst, Ill., 1970-75; chief med. technologist U. Tex.-M.D. Anderson Hosp., Houston, 1977-88; lab. dir. Northeast Med. Ctr. Hosp., Humble, Tex., 1988—; cons. Technicon Instruments Corp., Tarrytown, N.Y., 1984-88, Coulter Electronics, Inc., Hialeah, Fla., 1978-83. Contbg. author: Clinical

Laboratory Annual, 1984, Phlebotomy Handbook, 1984, Clinical Hematology: Principles, Procedures, Correlations, 1988. Vol. Ponderosa Forest Civic Assn., Houston, 1985, Muscular Dystrophy Assn., Houston, 1980-81. Mem. Am. Soc. Clin. Pathology (cert.), Am. Soc. Med. Tech. (Joseph J. Kleiner meml. award 1985), Tex. Soc. Med. Tech. Home: 5037 Albany Plano TX 75293 Office: Corning Nichols Inst 1212 Coit Rd Plano TX 75075

BOLLMAN, DEBORAH ANN, health therapist; b. Buffalo, N.Y., Feb. 7, 1954; d. Russell John and Norma Doris (Zucchiatti) Cordova; m. Jerry Ingle, Feb. 7, 1976 (div. Aug. 1989); 1 child, John. AAS in Human Svcs. and Social Scis., Erie C.C., Buffalo, 1980; BSW, Buffalo State U., 1982; MSW, SUNY, Buffalo, 1986. Cert. social worker; cert. hypnotherapist. Workshop coord. and teen counselor Amherst Youth Ctr., 1980-81; fin. aid counselor Displaced Homemaker Ctr. of Western N.Y., 1982-85; intern Cantalician Ctr. for Learning, 1985-86; counselor, hypnotherapist Counseling and Hypnosis, Inc., Buffalo, 1989—. Home and Office: Counseling and Hypnosis Inc 3769 Teachers Ln Ste 7 Buffalo NY 14127

BOLOTIN, LORA M., business owner, electronics executive; b. Dallas; d. Joseph and Bertha Marshall; m. M. L. Bolotin, June 21, 1953; children: Linda Susan, Scott Evan, Kent Carter. BA in Edn., Roosevelt U., 1952; postgrad., UCLA, 1980, Calif. State U., Northridge, 1988. Cert. tchr., Ill. Tchr. Chgo. Bd. Edn., 1952-55; v.p. Bolotin Assocs., Inc., Woodland Hills, Calif., 1973-83, pres., 1984—. Art Inst. of Chgo. scholar, 1946; recipient 2 Sterling Silver Art medals, Am. Legion, 1946, 47. Home: 16663 Calneva Dr Encino CA 91436-4167 Office: Bolotin Assocs Inc 21241 Ventura Blvd Ste 268 Woodland Hills CA 91364-2187

BOLSON, ADELE BRADY, accountant; b. N.J., Mar. 1, 1952; d. Jack Emerson and Audrey (Johnson) Brady; m. Edward Louis Bolson, Aug. 3, 1978; 1 child, Jennifer Ruth. BA in Bus. Adminstrn., U. Puget Sound, 1975. CPA. Fin. sec. U. Puget Sound, Tacoma, Wash., 1972-75; acctg. mgr. Math. Scis. Northwest, Bellevue, Wash., 1975-77; acctg. supr. Paccar, Renton, Wash., 1977-79; controller Everett (Wash.) Herald, 1979; sole shareholder Adele Brady Bolson, CPA PS, Bellevue, 1979—; mem. bd. dirs. Wash. Acad. Perf. Arts, Redmond, 1992-95, treas. 1993-94. mem. Bellevue C. of C., 1980—. Mem. Am. Inst. CPA's (mem. of coun. 1994—), Wash. Soc. of CPA's (pres. elect bd. dirs. 1994-95), Inst. Mgmt. Accts. Office: Adele Brady Bolson CPA PS 10655 NE 4th St Ste 502 Bellevue WA 98004

BOLSTER, JACQUELINE NEBEN (MRS. JOHN A. BOLSTER), communications consultant; b. Woodhaven, N.Y.; d. Ernest William Benedict and Emily Claire (Guck) Neben; student Pratt Inst., Columbia U.; m. John A. Bolster, May 8, 1954. Promotion mgr. Photoplay mag., 1949-53; merchandising mgr. McCall's, N.Y.C., 1953-64; dir. promotion and merchandising Harper's Bazaar, N.Y.C., 1964-71; dir. advt. and promotion Elizabeth Arden Salons, N.Y.C., 1971-76; dir. creative services Elizabeth Arden, Inc., 1976-78, dir. communications Elizabeth Arden Salons, 1978-87, communication cons., 1987—. Recipient Art Director's award 1961, 66. Mem. Fashion Group, Fashion Execs. Roundtable, Inner Circle, Advt. Women N.Y. (life), Women's Nat. Rep. Club (life). Episcopalian. Home and Office: 8531 88th St Woodhaven NY 11421-1308 also: Halsey Neck Ln Southampton NY 11968

BOLT, EUNICE MILDRED DEVRIES, artist; b. Clifton, N.J., Oct. 31, 1926; d. Lambert H. and Cora (Martin) DeVries; m. Maurice L. Bolt (dec. Nov. 1989); children: Macyn Bolt, Tamsen Bolt Clark, Valerie Bolt Wegner. Grad., Pratt Inst. Art & Design, Bklyn., 1949; BA, Calvin Coll., 1952; MA, Western Mich. U., 1973. Book illustration Fideler Pubs., Grand Rapids, Mich., 1952-53, Zondervan Pub. Co., Grand Rapids, Mich., 1953-56; prof. Calvin Coll., Grand Rapids, Mich., 1962-67, Grand Rapids Community Coll., 1968-91; represented by Bergsma Gallery, Grand Rapids, Rental/Sales Gallery of Grand Rapids Art Mus.; internat. art study tours coord. and guide, 1978—; lectr. art history, 1991—, presenter watercolor workshops, 1991—. Exhibited in group shows at Grand Rapids Art Mus., Kalamazoo Inst. Art, U. Mich. Schlusser Gallery, Pitts. Ctr. for the Arts, Westmoreland Mus. Art, Detroit Inst. Art. Home and Studio: 2421 Breton Rd SE Grand Rapids MI 49546-5627

BOLT, MARY KEMPER, school librarian; b. Ashland, Ky., Apr. 12, 1948; d. Hubert Ghent and Ruth (Lensing) K.; m. Donald Bolt, May 20, 1972 (div. June 1980); children: D. Grant Bolt, Mayme Ghent Bolt. BS, Morehead State U., 1970, Rk. II, 1976, Rk. I, 1993. Libr. Cannonsburg Elem., Ashland, 1971, Nichols County Elem., Carlisle, Ky., 1971-72, Prichard Elem., Grayson, Ky., 1972-91, E Carter Jr. H.S., Grayson, Ky., 1991-94, E Carter Mid. Sch., Grayson, 1994—; mem. adv. bd. Carter County Schs., Grayson, 1992—, preview bd. Ky. Edn. Television, Lexington, 1992—. Active read-a-thron March of Dimes, Ashland. Mem. NEA, Ky. Sch. Media Assn., Ky. Libr. Assn., Ea. Ky. Edn. Assn. Democrat. Presbyterian. Home: 214 Kemper Ln Grayson KY 41143

BOLTON, (MARGARET) ELIZABETH, artist, poet; b. Cranston, R.I., Sept. 7, 1919; d. James Ewart and Pamela (White) Hill; m. Archer Leroy Bolton Jr., Nov. 29, 1941; children: Wendy, Daria, Pamela, James. Student, Colby Sawyer Coll., 1936-39. Sec. Dr. Augustus Thorndike, Boston, 1939-41; sec. rehab. orgn. Mass. Gen. Hosp., Boston, 1950-51; sec. Nat. Acad. Scis., Washington, 1957-60, Mitre Corp. Electronics, Burlington, Mass., 1961-62; exec. sec. Manpower, Burlington, 1961-69; sec. RCA, Burlington, 1962-63; substitute tchr. art pub. high schs., various cities, Mass., 1970-81. Exhibited in various group shows (1st prize 1979, 80); poetry pub. in New Voices, 1981, Golden Treasury of Great Poems, 1989, Vol. II, 1989, Summer Treasury of Poems of American, 1992, Fall Treasury of Poems of American, 1992. Mem. Friends of the Libr., 1986—. Recipient 2d prize Newburyport Art Assn., 1977, 1st prize Nashua Art Assn., 1986, Award of Merit Certs. (2) World of Poetry, 1988, Golden Poet award, 1989, Golden Poet award World of Poetry, 1992. Mem. Haverhill Art Assn., Seacoast Art Assn. Mem. Christian Ch. Home: 12 Glen Dr Hampstead NH 03841-2242

BOLTON, JULIA GOODEN, hospital administrator; b. Wilmington, Del., Nov. 11, 1940; d. Merrill Harvey and Mary Rose (Amoroso) Gooden; m. Roger Edwin Bolton, June 27, 1964; children: Christopher Andrew, Jonathan Hughes. RN with honors, Johns Hopkins Hosp., Balt., 1961; BSN with honors, Case Western Res. U., Cleve., 1964; postgrad., Boston U., 1964-65; MS with honors, Russell Sage Coll., 1986. Lic. nurse, Vt. Staff nurse operating rm., clin. instr. Johns Hopkins Hosp., Balt., 1961-62; instr. practical nursing, acting coord. med. programs Charles H. McCann Vocat. Sch., North Adams, Mass., 1966, clin. instr. manpower devel. tng. act program, 1968, clin. instr. med., surg. and pediatric nursing, 1972-73; staff orientation and tour program for children North Adams Regional Hosp., 1973-74; health edn. cons. Williamstown (Mass.) Pub. Schs., 1978-81, Pine Cobble Sch., 1978-81; clin. cons. patient care stds. project North Adams Regional Hosp., 1985-86; dir. staff edn. and quality assurance Southwestern Vt. Med. Ctr., Bennington, 1986-87, asst. v.p. nursing, 1988, v.p. nursing, 1988-92, interim pres., 1991, sr. v.p., 1992—; mem. client adv. com. Sodexho Corp., 1992; mem. bd. dirs. United Way of Bennington County, 1995. Adv. com. Putnam Meml. Sch. Practical Nursing, 1989-94; profl. adv. com. Bennington Home Health Agy., 1988; alt. del. Diocesan Conv. No. Berkshire Deanery, Episcopal Ch., 1987; dir. Vt. div., Bennington County unit, Am. Cancer Soc., 1986-88; mem. Williamstown Betterment Study Com., 1985; adv. com. to plan for declining enrollments Mt. Greylock Reg. High Sch., 1985; bd. dirs. exec. com. Vt. Nursing Initiative Implementation Grant, Pew Charitable Trust Grant, 1992; vestry St. John's Episcopal Ch., Williamstown, 1992; active many other civic and charitable orgns. in past. Recipient Hannah Karp award as outstanding student, Russell Sage Coll., 1985, traineeship, 1983-85, others. Mem. Am. Coll. Healthcare Execs., Am. Orgn. Nurse Execs., Nat. Forum Women Health Care Leaders, Nat. League for Nursing, Vt. Orgn. Nurse Execs. (pres.-elect 1994, co-pres. 1995), New Eng. Healthcare Assembly (evaluation com. 1994), Rotary, Phi Kappa Phi, Sigma Theta Tau.

BOLTON, MARTHA O., writer; b. Searcy, Ark., Sept. 1, 1951; d. Lonnie Leon and Eunice Dolores Ferren; m. Russell Norman Bolton, Apr. 17, 1970; children: Russell Norman II, Matthew David, Anthony Shane. Grad. high sch., Reseda, Calif. Freelance writer for various comedians, 1975-86; newspaper columnist Simi Valley Enterprise, Simi, Calif., 1979-87; staff writer Bob Hope, 1986—. Author: A Funny Thing Happened to Me on My Way Through the Bible, 1985, A View from the Pew, 1986, What's Growing Under Your Bed?, 1986, Tangled in the Tinsel, 1987, So, How'd I Get to be in Charge of the Program?, 1988, Humorous Monologues, 1989, Let My People Laugh, 1989, If Mr. Clean Calls Tell Him I'm Not In, 1989, Journey to the Center of the Stage, 1990, If You Can't Stand the Smoke, Get Out of My Kitchen, 1990, Home, Home on the Stage, 1991, TV Jokes and Riddles, 1991, These Truths Were Made For Walking, 1992, When the Meatloaf Explodes It's Done, 1993, Childhood Is A Stage, 1993, Honey, It's Time to Weed the Carpets Again, 1994, Walk A Mile in His Truths, 1994, The Cafeteria Lady on the Loose, 1994, On The Loose, 1994, If the Pasta Wiggles, Don't Eat It, 1995. Pres. Vista Elem. Sch. PTA, Simi, 1980-81. Recipient Emmy award nomination for outstanding achievement in music and lyrics NATAS, 1988, Internat. Angel award, 1990, 91. Mem. Nat. League of Am. Pen Women (br. pres. 1984-86, Woman of Achievement award Simi Valley br. 1984), Writers Guild Am. West (award nomination 1994), ASCAP, Soc. Children's Book Writers, Acad. T.V. Arts and Scis. Office: PO Box 1212 Simi Valley CA 93062-1212

BOLTON, PATRICIA J. M., accountant; b. Utica, N.Y., Dec. 8, 1967; d. Robert Gerard and Regina Jane (Gouse) B. BS in Acctg., SUNY, Albany, 1990. Auditor Ernst & Young, Albany, N.Y., 1990-91; dir. finance and pers. AIDS Coun. NENY, Albany, 1991—. Democrat. Office: AIDS Coun NENY 88 4th Ave Albany NY 12202-1922

BOLTZ, MARLYS PETERSON, nurse administrator; b. Blomford, Minn., Nov. 25, 1936; d. John B. and Gladys L. (Peterson) Peterson; m. Thomas J. Boltz, May 29, 1958; children; Gregg Alan, Brett Allison. Diploma, Swedish Hosp. Sch. Nursing, Mpls., 1957; BSN, Calif. State U., Sacramento, 1978; M Health Systems Leadership, U. San Francisco, 1986. RN, Calif. Staff nurse ICU VA Med. Ctr., Martinez, Calif., 1970-78, head nurse med. svc., 1978-79, head nurse ICU, 1979-84, nursing supr., 1984—; head nurse VA No. Calif. System of Clinics, Martinez, 1992—. Mem. AACN (cert., pres. Contra Costa chpt. 1991—). Republican. Baptist. Home: 663 Odin Dr Pleasant Hill CA 94523 Office: 150 Muir Rd Martinez CA 94523

BOLTZ, MARY ANN, aerospace materials company executive, travel agency executive; b. Far Rockaway, N.Y., Jan. 12, 1923; d. Thomas and Theresa (Domanico) Caparelli; m. William Emmett Boltz; children: Valerie Ann Boltz Austin, Beverly Theresa, Cynthia Marie Boltz O'Rourke. Grad. high sch., Lawrence, N.Y., 1941. Publicist CBS, N.Y.C., 1943-48; mgr. Coast-Line Internat. Distbrs. Ltd., Lindenhurst, N.Y., 1961-80, v.p., 1980-86, pres., 1987-90, CEO, 1990—; chief exec. officer Air Ship 'N Shore Travel, Woodmere, N.Y. and Marco Island, Fla., 1978—; pres. Bangor Realty, 1975. Formerly radio and TV editor local publs., writer Gotham Guide mag. Sec. Inwood Civic & Businessmen's Assn., 1952-64, pres., 1964-66, chmn. bd., 1967-68; pres. Lawrence Pub. Schs. System PTA, 1956-58; pres., life mem. Cen. Coun. PTA, 1958-60; founder Inwood Civic Scholarship Fund, 1964; v.p. Econ. Opportunity Coun., Inwood; mem. fundraising bd. yearly ball St. Joachim Ch., Cedarhurst, N.Y.; gift chmn. L.I. Bd. Boys Town of Italy; bd. dirs. Marco Island Cancer Fund Dr.; dir., promoter Marco Island Philharmonic Symphony; dir. polit. campaign William Sieffert, Oceanside, N.Y.; chmn. 30 yr. reunion Class of 41, 1971, 50 yr. reunion, 1991; asst. chmn. 50 yr. reunion Class of 42, 1991; fundraiser Stecker and Horowitz Sch. Music Dinner Com., 1978, Am. Bus. Women's Assn., Long Island charter chptr., Rockville Centre, N.Y., 1990-92, United fund, Red Feather Ball, 1992. Recipient awards Nassau Herald Newspaper, Cedarhurst, Inwood Civic Assn., PTA Life Membership award, 25 Yr. Silver Medallion Boys Town of Italy. Mem. Am. Bus. Women's Assn. (L.I. charter chpt.), Nissoquogue Golf Club, Sun 'N Surf Beach Club, Island Country Club (Marco Island, Fla.), Desert Mountain Country Club. Republican. Roman Catholic. Home: 149 Hempstead Ave Rockville Centre NY 11570-2904 Office: Coast-Line Internat Distbrs 274 Bangor St Lindenhurst NY 11757-3697

BOMBA, MARGARET ANN, lawyer; b. Bklyn., July 1, 1947; d. Fred S. and Mary (Alban) Bomba; B.S., St. Francis Coll., 1975; postgrad. Columbia U., 1977; J.D., Bklyn. Law Sch., 1982; m. John N. Pizzuto, May 27, 1978. Sec., adminstrv. asst. Fieldcrest Mills, Inc., N.Y.C., 1966-71, product mgr. textiles for the home 1973-84; pvt. practice, N.Y.C., 1984—; sales and product mgmt. Wamsutta Mills Inc., N.Y.C., 1972-73; prof. law Parsons Sch. Design, 1985—; arbitrator N.Y. Stock Exchange, 1987—; pvt. practice, N.Y.C., Newark, 1984—; mem. faculty Practising Law Inst., 1993—; mem. faculty mental hygiene law N.Y. State Office Ct. Adminstrn., 1993—. Mem. N.Y. County Lawyers Assn. (trade regulation com. 1985, real property com. 1986), ABA, Assn. Bar City of N.Y., Assn. Trial Lawyers Am., N.Y. State Bar Assn. (elder law sect., ethics and practice com. 1991—, mem. exec. com. elder law sect. 1994—, chair fraud and abuse com. 1994—, mem. faculty continuing legal edn. divsn. 1994—). Office: 14 Wall St New York NY 10005-2101 also: 430 Springfield Ave Berkeley Heights NJ 07922

BOMBECK, ERMA LOUISE (MRS. WILLIAM BOMBECK), author, columnist; b. Dayton, Ohio, Feb. 21, 1927; d. Cassius Edwin Fiste and Erma (Fiste) Harris; m. William Lawrence Bombeck, Aug. 13, 1949; children: Betsy, Andrew, Matthew. BA, U. Dayton, 1949; holder 16 hon. degrees. Columnist Newsday Syndicate, 1965-70, Pubs.-Hall Syndicate (now N.Am. Syndicate), 1970-85, Los Angeles Times Syndicate, 1985-88, Universal Press Syndicate, Kansas City, Mo., 1988—; contbg. editor: Good Housekeeping mag., 1969-74. Author: At Wit's End, 1967, Just Wait Till You Have Children of Your Own, 1971, I Lost Everything In The Post-Natal Depression, 1974, The Grass Is Always Greener Over The Septic Tank, 1976, If Life is a Bowl of Cherries, What Am I Doing in the Pits?, 1978, Aunt Erma's Cope Book, 1979, Motherhood: The Second Oldest Profession, 1983, Family: The Ties That Bind... and Gag!, 1987, I Want To Grow Hair, I Want To Grow Up, I Want To Go To Boise, 1989, When You Look Like Your Passport Photo, It's Time To Go Home, 1991, A Marriage Made in Heaven... or Too Tired for an Affair, 1993. Mem. Am. Acad. Humor Columnists, Theta Sigma Phi (Headliner award 1969). Office: Universal Press Syndicate 4900 Main St Kansas City MO 64112-2644

BOMCHILL, FERN CHERYL, lawyer; b. Chgo., Feb. 25, 1948. BA, U. Mich., 1969; JD, U. Chgo., 1972. Bar: Ill. 1972, U.S. Dist. Ct. (no. dist.) Ill. 1972, U.S. Ct. Appeals (7th cir.) 1986. Ptnr. Mayer, Brown & Platt, Chgo. Mem. ABA, Fed. Bar Assn. (bd. dirs. Chgo. chpt.), Chgo. Coun. Lawyers, Law Club Chgo., Legal Club Chgo., The Menomonee Club for Boys and Girls (bd. dirs., pres. 1993-94). Office: Mayer Brown & Platt 190 S La Salle St Chicago IL 60603-3410

BONAZZI, ELAINE CLAIRE, mezzo-soprano; b. Endicott, N.Y.; d. John Dante and Zina (Rossi) B.; m. Jerome Ashe Carrington, Sept. 21, 1963; 1 step-son, Christopher. B.M. (George Eastman scholar), Eastman Sch. Music. Artist-in-residence SUNY, Stonybrook; forme mem. faculty Peabody Conservatory, SUNY, Stony Brook; vis. prof. Eastman Sch. Music, Rochester, N.Y., 1979. Debuts, Santa Fe Opera, 1958, Opera Soc. Washington, 1960, N.Y.C. Opera, 1965, Opera Internacional, Mexico City, Mexico, 1966, Mini-Met, 1973, Europe, West Berlin Festival opera, 1961, Spoleto (Italy) Festival, 1974, Castel Franco Festival Venetian Music, Venice, Italy, 1975, Berlin Bach Festival, 1976, Netherlands Opera, 1978, Minn. Opera, 1985, Artpark Festival, 1987, Opera Theater of St. Louis, 1988, New Orleans Opera, 1988, Paris, 1979, Spoleto-Charleston Festival, 1981, Edmonton Opera Can., 1990, New Orleans Opera, 1990, Winnipeg Opera, 1993; frequent Libr. of Congress concerts; title role in Pique Dance, Washington Opera, Rostropovich conducting, 1989, in Vanessa, Opera Theatre of St. Louis, 1988, Carlson's Midnight Angel, Opera Theatre of St. Louis, 1993; currently leading roles with N.Y.C. Opera; soloist, with most major Am. orchs., Canadian Broadcasting Corp., NET Opera Theatre, NBC, ABC, CBS TV networks, recs. on, Candide, Columbia, Vanguard, CRI, Folkways, Vox, Grenadilla, Pro Arte and Nonesuch Records; over 40 world premiers of major works by leading composers with major orchs. and opera cos. Named 1 of 6 honored alumni 50th Anniversary Year, Eastman Sch. Music, 1971, Trustees Council U. Rochester, 1976; formerly William Matheus Sullivan grantee. Mem. Mu Phi Epsilon. Home: 650 West End Ave New York NY 10025-7355 Office: care Trawick Artists 1926 Broadway New York NY 10023

BONCHER, MARY, talent agent; b. Green Bay, Wis., Jan. 19, 1946; d. Anthony Peter and Bernice Mary (Lannoye) Williams; m. Joseph Phillip Boncher, Jan. 7, 1967; children: Yvette, Noelle. Diploma, Rosemary Bischoff Sch. Modeling, Milw., 1965. Dir. Mary Boncher Model Agy. & Sch. Ltd., Bloomington and St. Charles, Ill., 1970-80, Mary Boncher Model Agy. Ltd., St. Charles, 1980-84, Mary Boncher Model Mgmt. Ltd., Chgo., 1985-91; ptnr. ARIA Model & Talent Mgmt. Ltd., Chgo., 1992—; fashion reporter TV and radio Men's Fashion Assn., N.Y.C., 1975-80, Eleanor Lambert's Am. Designer, N.Y. Fashion Press, N.Y.C., 1975-80; fashion corr. Green Bay Daily News, 1975-76. Lector Cath. mass, 1983-90, 92—. Mem. Am. Security Coun. (nat. adv. bd.) Ams. for Responsible TV and Radio, Nat. Assn. Women Bus. Owners, Internat. Platform Assn. Republican. Roman Catholic. Office: ARIA Model & Talent Mgmt Ltd 1017 W Washington St Ste 2A Chicago IL 60607

BOND, JOAN, elementary school educator; b. Americus, Ga., Dec. 24, 1945; d. Doyle Holden and Frances (Brown) B. BS in Elem. Edn., U. Ga., 1975, MEd, 1979, EdS, 1982. Clk. emergency room St. Mary's Hosp., Athens, Ga., 1963-64; receptionist, asst. Office Dr. Shu-Yun T. Tsao, Athens, 1964-66; tchr. remedial reading Danielsville (Ga.) Elem. Sch., 1975-76, primary tchr., 1975—. Tchr., dir. presch. Hull (Ga.) Bapt. Ch., 1970-84, asst. tchr. adult class, 1985—; mem. honor roll com. Danielsville Elem. Sch. PTO, 1990-92. Mem. Profl. Assn. Ga. Educators. Democrat. Home: 48 Glen Carrie Rd Hull GA 30646-9778 Office: Danielsville Elem Sch PO Box 67 Danielsville GA 30633-0067

BOND, MEG ALISON, psychology educator; b. LaJolla, Calif., May 8, 1952; m. William Madsen; children: Arlyn, Erik. BA in Psychology with distinction and honors, Stanford U., 1974; MA in Clin. Psychology, U. Oregon, 1976, PhD in Clin., Community Psychology, 1983. Clin. intern Health Scis. Ctr. U. Colo., Denver, 1981-82; clin. extern Family Systems Program Inst. Juvenile Rsch., Chgo., 1984-85; trainee U.S. Pub. Health Svc. Dept. Psychology, U. Oreg., 1974-76, instr., 1976, grad. teaching fellow, 1978-80; instr. psychology clinic U. Oreg., 1979-81; rsch. assoc. Inst. Study Devel. Disabilities U. Ill., Chgo., 1982-83, adj. asst. prof. Dept. Psychology, 1984-88, asst. dir. mgmt. orgn. devel. program Inst. Study Devel Disabilities, 1983-88; family therapist, cons. Ctr. Family Studies & Ctr. for Group and Orgnl. Studies Northeast Psychiatric Assocs., Nashua, N.H., 1988-89; asst. prof. mgmt. studies & human svcs. Lesley Coll., Cambridge, Mass., 1988-89; coord. Ctr. for Family, Work and Com. U. Mass., Lowell, 1990-93, asst. prof. Dept. Psychology, 1989-93, assoc. prof., 1993—; editorial bd. mem. Am. Jour. Community Psychology, 1993—. Editorial bd. Am. Jour. Community Psychology, 1993—; reviewer various jours.; contbr. chpts. to books, articles to profl. jours. Mem. APA, Soc. Com. Rsch. and Action (nat. sec. 1992—, nat. mem. at large, 1988-91, convention chair 1991, chair com. on women 1983-87), Assn. Women in Psychology, Assn. Women in Psychology (Boston area). Office: Dept Psychology U Mass Lowell MA 01854

BOND, VICTORIA ELLEN, conductor, composer; b. L.A., May 6, 1945; d. Philip and Jane (Courtl) B.; m. Stephan Peskin, Jan. 27, 1974. B Mus. Arts, U. So. Calif., Los Angeles, 1968; M Mus. Arts, Juilliard Sch. Music, 1975, D Mus. Arts, 1977; DFA (hon.), Washington and Lee U., 1992. Condr., composer; mem. N.Y. State Coun. Arts Music Panel, 1987-90; bd. dirs. Am. Music Ctr., 1987—, N.Y. Women Composers, 1992—. Guest condr. Cabrillo Music Festival, Calif., 1974, White Mountains Music Festival, N.H., 1975, Aspen (Colo.) Music Festival, 1976, Shenandoah Music Festival, W.Va., 1977, Colo. Philharm., 1978, Houston Symphony, 1979, 86, Buffalo Philharm., 1979, Pitts. Symphony, 1980, N.W. Chamber Orch., Seattle, 1980, Anchorage Symphony, 1980, 82, Ark. Symphony, 1981, Hudson Valley Philharm., N.Y., 1981, Newton Symphony, Boston, 1982, Hartford Symphony, 1982, RTE Symphony, Dublin, Ireland, 1983, Albany Symphony Orch., 1984-85, Houston Symphony Orch., 1986, Richmond Symphony Orch., 1987, Williamsburg Symphony Orch., Greenville Symphony Orch., Des Moines Symphony Orch., Utah Symphony Orch., Cape Cod Symphony Orch., Tallahassee Symphony Orch., Va. Symphony Orch, 1988-90, Shanghai Symphony, 1993, 94; music dir. New Amsterdam Symphony Orch., N.Y.C., 1978-80, Pitts. Youth Symphony Orch., 1978-80, Empire State Youth Orch., 1982-86, Southeastern Music Ctr., 1983-84, Bel Canto Opera, 1983-86, Roanoke (Va.) Symphony Orch., 1986-95; artistic dir. Bel Canto Opera Co., 1986-88, Opera Roanoke, 1989-95; Exxon/Arts Endowment condr., Pitts. Symphony, 1978-80; recs. include Twentieth Century Cello, Two American Contemporaries, The Frog Prince, An American Collage; commd. by Pa. Ballet, 1978, Jacob's Pillow Dance Festival, 1979, Am. Ballet Theater, 1981, Empire State Inst. Performing Arts, 1983, 84, Stage One, Louisville, 1986, Ga. State U., 1986, L'Ensemble, 1990, Renaissance City Winds, 1990, Audubon String Quartet, 1990, Women's Philharm., San Francisco, 1993, Va. Explore Park and The Shanghai Symphony, 1994, D Day Found., 1994, Linda Plaut, 1994, The Billings (Mont.) Symphony, The Elgin (Ill.) Symphony. Mem. Am. Music Ctr. Recipient Victor Herbert award 1977, Perry F. Kendig award, 1988, ASCAP Composition award 1973—; Nat. Inst. for Music Theater grantee in opera conducting N.Y.C. Opera, 1985, Martha Baird Rockefeller grantee, 1978-79, Meet-The-Composer grantee in Composition, 1973—; Juilliard scholar, 1972-77; Juilliard fellow, 1975-77, Aspen Music Festival fellow, 1973-76; named Exxon/Arts Endowment Conductor, 1978-80, Woman of Yr. in Va., 1990, 91; featured on NBC Today show, 1990, profiled in C.S. Monitor, 1987, Wall Street Jour., 1987, other mags. and shows. Mem. ASCAP (recipient awards 1975—), Am. Symphony Orch. League, Am. Fedn. Musicians, N.Y. Women Composers, Mu Phi Epsilon. Office: Am Internat Artists 515 E 89th St Ste 6B New York NY 10128

BOND, WILMA MCCRARY, secondary school educator; b. Madison, Tenn., Sept. 17, 1938; d. Keller Brit and M. Lee (Reid) McCrary; m. Thomas Jefferson Bond Jr., Mar. 14, 1959; children: Thomas Jefferson III, Julia Anne. BS, Vanderbilt U., 1959; MA, Va. Tech. U., 1974. Cert. bus. edn. tchr., social studies, tchr., adminstrn., Va., Tenn., Ky., Fla., N.Mex. Sec. trust dept. 1st Tenn. Bank, Chattanooga, 1959-60; tchr. Hamilton County Pub. Schs., Chattanooga, 1960-61; exec. sec. to sr. ptnr. Witt, Gaither et al, Attys., Chattanooga, 1961-62; sec. Irvine Ins. Agy., Chattanooga, 1962; tchr. Hamilton County Pub. Schs., Chattanooga, 1962-63, Jefferson County Pub. Schs., Louisville, 1963-64, Fairfax County (Va.) Pub. Schs., 1967-69, Bernalillo County Pub. Schs., Albuquerque, 1969-72, Fairfax County Pub. Schs., 1972—; docent Smithsonian Instn. Mus. Am. History, Washington, 1977-82, 92—. Author (pamphlets) A Word to the Wives, 1967, Buenos Dias Amigos, 1970. Pres. Friends of Libr., Titusville, Fla., 1964-65. Mem. Nat. Order of Blue and Gray (founder, comdr. gen. 1990—), Dame Commandeur Sovereign Mil. Order Temple of Jerusalem (counselor 1994-95), Daus. of Union Vets., Daus. of Loyal Legion of U.S., Ladies of Grand Army of Republic, Sons of Union Vets. Aux. Home: PO Box 1301 Vienna VA 22183

BONDAR, ROBERTA LYNN, Canadian astronaut; b. Sault Sainte Marie, Ont., Can., Dec. 4, 1945. BS in Zoology and Agr., U. Guelph, 1968; MS in Exptl. Pathology, U. Western Ont., 1971; PhD in Neurobiology, U. Toronto, 1974; MD, McMaster U., 1977; D.Hum.L. (hon.), Mt. St. Vincent U., 1990; DSc (hon.), Mt. Allison U., 1989, U. Guelph, 1990, Lakehead U., 1991, Laurentian U., 1991, McMaster U., 1992, U. Toronto, 1992, McGill U., 1992, York U., 1992, Royal Roads Military Coll., 1993, Meml. U., 1993, Laval U., 1993, Carleton U., 1993; LLD (hon.), U. Regina, 1992, U. Calgary, 1992; DU (hon.), U. Otawa, 1992; DSL (hon.), U. Toronto, 1993. Postdoctorate fellow Nat. Rsch. Coun. Can., 1974; intern Toronto Gen. Hosp., 1977-78; resident U. Western Ont., 1978-80; neuro-ophthalmology fellow Tufts's New England Med. Ctr., Boston, 1981, Toronto Western Hosp., 1981-82; asst. prof. medicine, dir. Multiple Sclerosis Clinic McMaster U., 1982-84; asst. prof. dept. medicine divsn. neurology Ottawa Gen. Hosp., Ont., 1985-88; Canadian astronaut Govt. of Can., Ottawa, 1983-92, chairwoman Canadian Lifescis. Subcom. for Space Sta., 1985; payload specialist candidate 1st Internat. Microgravity Lab. Shuttle Flight, 1989-90, prime payload specialist, 1990-92; disting. prof. Ryerson Poly. Inst., 1992-93; rsch. asst. Dept. Fisheries and Forestry, 1963-68; coach archery team, lectr. phys. edn. U. Guelph, 1966-67, histology tech. dept. zoology, 1967-68; teaching asst. U. Toronto, 1970-74; lectr. dept. nursing U. Ottawa, 1985-88; chmn. Can. life scis. com. for space sta. Nat. Rsch. Coun. Can., 1985-89; life scis. rep. Can. Adv. Coun. on Sci. Utilization Space Sta., 1986-88; lectr. dept. nat. def. flight surgeon course Biomed. Aspects Space Flight, 1986-92; civil aviation med. examiner Health and Welfare, Can., 1986-93; mem. sci. adv. panel Premier's Coun. on Sci. and Tech., 1988-89; mem. sci.

staff Sunnybrook Med. Ctr., 1988-93; rsch. fellow Playfair Inst. Oculomotor Lab. Toronto Western Hosp., 1989; bd. trustees Nat. Mus. Sci. and Tech., 1990-93; bd. regents Can. Mobile Athlete and Sport Hosp., 1992-93; mem. pub. adv. com. State of Environment Reporting, 1992-93; mem. adv. bd. Order of Can., 1993; sr. advisor Royal Commn. on Edn., Ont., 1993; adj. prof. dept. biology U. N.Mex., Albuquerque, 1991-93, vis. rsch. scholar dept. neurology, 1993-94; vis. disting. fellow Faculty Health Scis. McMaster U., 1993-94; vis. rsch. scholar Univs. Space Rsch. Assn. Johnson Space Ctr., Houston, 1993-94; lectr. in field. Recipient Career Scientist award Ont. Ministry Health, 1982, Vanier award Jaycess of Can., 1985, William A. Vanderburgh Sr. Travel award, 1976, Presdl. Citation of Honor, Ala. Agrl. and Mech. U., 1990, Paul Harris Recognition award Rotary Club Ancaster, 1992, Space medal NASA, 1992, Merit award U. Western Ont. Alumni, 1992, La Personalité de l'Année, La Presse, 1992, Medaille de L'Excellence, L'Assn. des. Médecins de Langue Française du Can., 1992, Pres.'s award Coll. Physicians and Surgeons Ont., 1992, Alumnus of Yr. award U. Western Ont., 1992, Can. 125 medal, 1992, Kurt Hahn award Outward Bound, 1993, Woman of Distinction award YWCA, 1993, Outstanding Can. award Armenian Cmty. Ctr. Toronto, 1993, Alumnus of Yr. award U. Guelph, 1993; fellow U. Western Ont., 1971, Ont. Ministry Health, 1981, Ryerson Poly. Inst., 1990; Nat. Rsch. Coun. Canada scholar, 1971-74; officer Order of Can., 1992, Order of Ont., 1993; inductee Hamilton Gallery Distinction, 1993; first Canadian woman to travel in space. Fellow Royal Coll. Physicians and Surgeons Can.; mem. Am. Acad. Neurology (Presdl. citation 1992), Am. Soc. Gravitational and Space Biology, Canadian Neurol. Soc., Canadian Aeros. and Space Inst., Canadian Soc. Aerospace Medicine (William R. Franks award 1990), Can. Soc. Aviation Medicine (treas. 1983-84, sec. 1984-85), Can. Med. Protective Assn., Can. Assn. Sports Medicine, Fedn. Med. Women in Can., Albuquerque Aerostat Ascension Assn., Coll. Physicians and Surgeons Ont., Flying Ninety-Nines Internat. Women Pilots Assn., Canadian Stroke Soc., Aerospace Med. Assn. (Hubertus Strughold award Space Medicine Br. 1992), Royal Astron. Soc. Can., The Lung Assn. (exec. coun.), Assn. Space Explorers, Canadian Fedn. Univ. Women (hon.), Zonta (hon.). Office: 1200 Main St W, Hamilton, ON Canada L8N 3Z5*

BONDINELL, STEPHANIE, counselor, former educational administrator; b. Passaic, N.J., Nov. 22, 1948; d. Peter Jr. and Gloria Lucille (Burden) Honcharuk; m. Paul Swanstrom Bondinell, July 31, 1971; 1 child, Paul Emil. BA, William Paterson Coll., 1970; MEd, Stetson U., 1983. Cert. elem. educator, Fla.; guidance counselor grades K-12, Fla. Tchr. Bloomingdale (N.J.) Bd. Edn., 1971-80; edn. dir. Fla. United Meth. Children's Home, Enterprise, 1982-89; guidance counselor Volusia County Sch. Bd., Deltona, Fla., 1989—. Sec. adv. com. Deltona Jr. High Sch., 1984-88; sec. Deltona Jr. PTA, 1982; vice-chmn. adv. com. Deltona Mid. Sch., 1988, chmn., 1989-91, chmn., 1991-92; mem. secondary sch. task force Volusia County Sch. Bd., 1986—; mem. Volusia County Rep. Exec. Com., Rep. Presdl. Task Force; mem. state adv. bd. Fla. Future Educators Am., 1991-92. Acad. scholar Becton, Dickinson & Co., N.J., 1966; N.J. State scholar, 1966-70; named girls state rep. Am. Legion, N.J., 1966; recipient Vol. Svc. award Volusia County Sch. Bd., Deland, 1985; named Teacher of Yr. Deltona Lakes, 1991, 95. Mem. Am. Assn. for Counseling and Devel., Assn. for Curriculum Devel., Coun. for Exceptional Children, Div. for Learning Disabilities, Fla. Pers. and Guidance Assn., N.J. Edn. Assn., Internat. Platform Assn., Deltona Civic Assn., Deltona Rep. Club (v.p. 1991), 4 Townes Federated Rep. Women's Club (sec., v.p.). Home: 1810 W Cooper Dr Deltona FL 32725-3623 Office: Volusia County Sch Bd 2022 Adelia Blvd Deltona FL 32725-3976

BONDS-WHITE, FRANCES ELIZABETH, psychologist, consultant; b. Docena, Ala., Nov. 29, 1939; d. Erskine Webster and Lois Elizabeth (Graham) Bonds. BA in English Lit. with honors, Birmingham So. Coll., 1960; MEd, Temple U., 1973, D of Edn., 1987. Lic. psychologist, Pa.; cert. teaching and supervising transactional analyst. Clin. asst. prof. psychology in psychiatry Sch. Medicine U. Pa.; sr. group psychotherapy cons. Phila. Child Guidance Clinic; owner, dir. Counseling and Consultation Assocs.; pvt. practice Phila. and West Chester, Pa.; adj. clin. asst. prof. Inst. for Grad. Clin. Psychology, Widener U., Chester, Pa.; presenter sci. programs and confs. Delaware Valley Group Psychotherapy Soc., Ea. Group Psychotherapy Soc., French Inst. Transactional Analysis, Paris, European Soc. Transactional Analysis, Scuola Superiore di Analisi Transazionela, Rome, Latin Am. Assn. for Transactional Analysis, others; cons. Austrian Soc. for Group Dynamics and Group Therapy, Vienna, Bad Boll Inst., Tromm, Germany, Evangelishe Acad., Bad Boll, Germany, U. Vienna Inst. for Depth Psychology and Group Psychotherapy, Widener U., Antioch U., Temple U., Villanova U., St. Christopher's Hosp. for Children, Phila., Friend's Hosp., Phila., Sch. Dist. of Phila., Berean Inst., Volt Corp., Washington, C & I Construction Divsn. Bechtel Corp., and various other organizations. Contbr. articles to profl. jours. Fellow Am. Group Psychotherapy Assn. (tng. com. 1987-90, affiliate assembly 1990, co-chair women in group psychotherapy spl. interest group 1992, presenter); mem. APA (psychotherapy divns., psychology of women divsn., psychoanalysis divsn., group psychotherapy divsn., nominating com. 1993, presenter), U.S. Transactional Analysis Assn., Internat. Transactional Analysis Assn. (editorial bd. 1984-88, co-chair tng. standards com. 1988-91, v.p. cert. and tng. 1992-96, presenter) Internat. Assn. for Group Psychotherapy (conf. com. 1995, 98, presenter), Group Analytic Soc., Delaware Valley Group Psychotherapy Soc (exec. bd. 1988, pres. elect 1990, pres. 1992, presenter). Office: Counseling and Cons Assocs 1713 Pine St Philadelphia PA 19103-6701

BONDURANT, JENNIFER LEE, management consultant; b. Berkeley, Calif., May 17, 1964; d. Lee Roy and Nancy (Napier) B. BS in Acctg., U. Utah, 1986. Sr. acct. Deloitte Touche, Boise, Idaho, 1987-89; internal cons. Fidelity Investments, Boston, 1989—. Mem. vol. group United Way, 1992—. Mem. Am. Mgmt. Assn., Marblehead Arts Assn., Kappa Kappa Gamma (bd. dirs. 1989—). Office: Fidelity Investments 82 Devonshire Boston MA 02109

BONDY, COLEEN DENISE, journalist; b. Burlingame, Calif., Nov. 16, 1966; d. Kenneth Bruce and Gayle Elizabeth (Enochs) B.; m. Jeffrey Andrew McMahon, Nov. 7, 1992. Student, UCLA, 1984-86; BS in Journalism, Calif. Poly. State U., 1989. Staff writer Merced (Calif.) Sun Star, 1989-90, Ctrl. Coast Sun Bull., Morro Bay, Calif., 1991-93, San Luis Obispo (Calif.) County New Times, 1993—; contbg. writer Dive Tng. Mag., Boynton Beach, Fla., 1992—. Recipient 1st place for beginners Calif. Channel Islands Underwater Photographic Soc., 1988, 1st place for investigative reporting Calif. Newspaper Pubs. Assn., 1992, 1st place in pub. svc., 1992. Office: San Luis Obispo Co New Time 197 Santa Rosa St San Luis Obispo CA 93405-2431

BONE, JANET WITMEYER (JAN BONE), author; b. Shamokin, Pa., Dec. 19, 1930; d. Paul Eugene and Kathryn (Bender) Witmeyer; BA, Cornell U., 1951; MBA, Roosevelt U., 1987; m. David P. Bone, Oct. 27, 1951; children: Jonathan, Christopher, Robert, Daniel. Newspaper and trade mag. writer, freelance writer, 1962—; sr. writer spl. advt. sects. Chgo. Tribune, 1986—; writer newsletter Rand McNally, 1988-90; writer articles Nat. Safety Coun., 1989—; tchr. creative writing adult edn. Sch. Dist. 211, Palatine, Ill., 1974-92; instr. English composition Roosevelt U., 1992—. Co-author: Understanding the Film, 4th edit., 1990; author: Opportunities in Film Production, 2d edit., 1990, Opportunities in Cable Television, 1983, 2d edit., 1992, Opportunities in Telecommunications, 1984, rev. edit., 1989, Opportunities in Computer-Aided Design and Computer-Aided Manufacturing (CAD/CAM), 1986, 2nd edit. 1993, Opportunities in Robotics, 1987, 2nd rev. edit., 1993, Opportunities in Laser Technology, 1988, Opportunities in Plastics Careers, 1991. Trustee William Rainey Harper Community Coll., Palatine, 1977-85, sec. bd. trustees, 1979-85. Recipient Chgo. Working Newsman's award, 1968, Sch. Bell award Ill. Edn. Assn., 1968, Am. Polit. Sci. Assn. award disting. reporting pub. affairs, 1970. Mem. Ind. Writers of Chgo. (bd. dirs. IWOCCORP 1991—, publicity chair, 1994), Nat. Coun. Tchrs. of English (internat. consortium chair, publicity and mktg. com. 1994), Phi Theta Kappa, Alpha Omicron Pi. Address: 353 N Morris Dr Palatine IL 60067

BONEY, NORMA MARIE DAVIS, elementary school educator; b. San Antonio, Aug. 13, 1950; d. Odie E. Jr. and Nadine (Jefferson) Davis; m. Marcus Boney, Sept. 26; 1 child, Marcus Boney II. BS, Prairie View A&M U., 1972, MEd, 1974. Cert. tchr. home econs., elem. edn., guidance and counseling, phys. edn.; cert. mid-mgmt. adminstr., Tex. Tchr. various subjects, including phys. edn. Shadydale Elem., Houston, 1973—, counselor, 1994—; elem. phys. edn. cons. North Forest Ind. Sch. Dist., Houston, 1990-91. Author: (dist. curriculum guides) Science, 1988, Physical Education, 1985—, Art, 1987-91, APEX, 1989-90, Health 1990—. Prog. chmn. Shadydale PTA, Houston; site coord. Mayor's Summer Fun Youth Prog., Houston, 1977; sr. counselor Young Men's Christian Assn., San Antonio, 1985, 87. Named Tchr. of Yr., Shadydale Elem., Houston, 1986-87, 89-90, Elem. Tchr. of Yr., North Forest Ind. Sch. Dist., 1989-90, Outstanding Educator, 1990-91, Outstanding Coach, Shadydale Elem. and PTA, 1990-91. Mem. AFT, AAHPERD, NEA, Tex. State Tchrs. Assn., Greater Houston Reading Coun., Tex. Edn. Agy. (mem. Tex. state book com., site-based decision-making com. 1992—, prin.'s adv. bd. 1992—, Meritorious award 1986), Tex. Counseling Assn., Am. Softball Assn., Tex. Assn. Health, Phys. Edn., Recreation and Dance, Houston Area Alliance Black Sch. Educators. Methodist. Home: 6315 Westover St Houston TX 77087-6545

BONFANTE, LARISSA, classics educator; b. Naples, Italy; came to U.S., 1939, naturalized, 1951; d. Giuliano and Vittoria (Dompé) B.; m. Leo Ferrero Raditsa, May 2, 1973; 1 child, Sebastian; 1 child, by previous marriage, Alexandra Bonfante-Warren. Student, Radcliffe Coll., 1950, U. Rome, 1951; B.A., Barnard Coll., 1954; M.A., U. Cin., 1957; Ph.D., Columbia U., 1966. Mem. faculty NYU, 1963—, prof., 1978—, chmn. dept. classics, 1978-84, 87-90; cons. in field. Author: Etruscan Dress, 1975, Reading the Past, Etruscan, 1990, (with Giuliano Bonfante) Out of Etruria, 1981, The Etruscan Language, 1983 (transl. into Italian 1985); editor: Etruscan Life and Afterlife: Handbook of Etruscan Studies, 1986 (with Francesco Roncalli) Antichità dall'Umbria a New York, 1991, (with Judith Sebesta, ed.) The World of Roman Dress, 1993; translator: Chronology of the Ancient World (E.J. Bickerman), 1986, The Plays of Hrotswitha of Gandersheim, 1979; also articles. Mem. Archaeol. Inst. Am. (gov. bd. 1982-88), Istituto di Studi Etruschi (fgn.), German Archaeol. Inst. (corres. mem.). Office: Classics Dept 25 Waverly Pl New York NY 10003-6759

BONFIELD, BARBARA GOLDSTEIN, municipal agency administrator; b. Lincoln, Ala., Jan. 12, 1937; d. Samuel Jacob and Margaret (Embry) Goldstein; m. Robert Lawrence Bonfield, Feb. 26, 1959; children: Barney, Susan. BA, Ala. Coll., 1958; MSW, U. Ala., 1976. Lic. cert. social worker. Social worker Jefferson County Dept. Pub. Welfare, Birmingham, Ala., 1958-59; child welfare worker Children's Aid Soc., Birmingham, 1960-71; human resources officer Jefferson County Commn., Birmingham, 1976-77, dir. agea agy. on aging, 1977—. Recipient Community Svc. award B'nai B'rith Women, Birmingham, 1983, Social Worker of Yr. award Ala. Conf. Social Work, 1993, State of Ala. Sr. Citizen Hall of Fame award 1993. Fellow Gerontol. Soc. Am.; mem. NASW (Social Worker of Yr. Birmingham chpt. 1978), Ala. Gerontol. Soc. (Profl. of Yr. 1986), Nat. Assn. Area Agys. on Aging, Southeastern Assn. Area Agys. on Aging (sec., bd. dirs. 1981), Acad. Cert. Social Workers. Democrat. Jewish. Home: 233 Beech Cir Birmingham AL 35213-2021 Office: 2601 Highland Ave S Birmingham AL 35205-1700

BONGHI, SHERRI LYNN, marketing professional; b. Bryn Mawr, Pa., Oct. 19, 1960; d. Leonard Joseph Sr. and Dorothy Joan (Emery) B. BS in Acctg., Villanova U., 1984. Mgr. Liberace & DeLiberty Law Office, Broomall, Pa., 1978-80; office mgr. Busch & Schramm Law Office, Bala Cynwyd, Pa., 1980-83; ops. mgr. Shihadeh Carpets, Ardmore, Pa., 1983-89, Phila. Music. Found., 1989-91; pres., owner Star Farm Music, Havertown, 1991—; cons. Beale Cons., Bala Cynwyd, 1992—; bd. dirs. Delaware Valley Music Poll Awards, Phila.; bd. dirs. Video Producer 1993 Awards, coproducer, 1993, 94. Leader Girl Scouts USA, Havertown, 1978-82. Mem. Antique Automobile Club Am., Optimists (leader 1st female 1982-84). Republican. Office: Star Farm Music PO Box 1544 Havertown PA 19083-0335

BONHAM-YEAMAN, DORIA, lawyer, educator; b. Los Angeles, June 10, 1932; d. Carl Herschel and Edna Mae (Jones) Bonham; widowed; children: Carl Q., Doria Valerie-Constance. BA, U. Tenn., 1953, JD, 1957, MA, 1958; EdS in Computer Edn., Barry U., 1984. Instr. bus. law Palm Beach Jr. Coll., Lake Worth, Fla., 1960-69; instr. legal environment Fla. Atlantic U., Boca Raton, 1969-73; lectr. bus. law Fla. Internat. U., North Miami, 1973-83, assoc. prof. bus. law, 1983—. Editor: Anglo-Am. Law Conf., 1980; Developing Global Corporate Strategies, 1981; editorial bd. Attys. Computer Report, 1984-85, Jour. Legal Studies Edn., 1985—. Contbr. articles to profl. jours. Bd. dirs. Palm Beach County Assn. for Deaf Children, 1960-63; mem. Fla. Commn. on Status of Women, Tallahassee, 1969-70; mem. Broward County Democratic Exec. Com., 1982—; pres. Dem. Women's Club Broward County, 1981; mem. Marine Coun. of Greater Miami, 1978—, Svc. award, 1979. Recipient Faculty Devel. award Fla. Internat. U., Miami, 1980; grantee Notre Dame Law Sch., London, summer 1980. Mem. AAUW (pres. Palm Beach county chpt. 1965-66), U.S. Coun. for Internat. Bus., No. Dade C. of C., Acad. Legal Studies in Bus., Alpha Chi Omega (alumnae club pres. 1968-71), Tau Kappa Alpha. Episcopalian. Office: Fla Internat U North Miami FL 33181

BONI, MIKI, artist; b. Bklyn., Nov. 10, 1938. BA, U. Guanajuato, 1974; divorced; children: Andrew, Viki. Dir. advt. and pub. relations Kebo, Inc., Natick, Mass., 1965-74; tchr. painting and drawing U. Guanajuato (Mex.), 1974-76; exec. dir. Kreativ Assos., Watertown, Mass., 1976-82; prin. Miki Boni Assocs., 1982-86; editor, designer publ. Interface Found., Watertown, 1987-89, program dir., 1989-91; founder, propr. Silk Road, 1991. Exhbn. Russian-Am. Cultural Ctr., Boston. Recipient spl. painting award Lincoln Center, 1978. Mem. Nat. Assn. Neurolinguistic Programming (master practitioner), Women Art Profls. (co-founder, v.p.).

BONIFER, SHERYL L., congressional aide; b. Alexandria, Va., Sept. 22, 1955; d. Robert R. and Marjorie A. (Davis) Price; m. Arthur J. Bonifer, Jr., Oct. 16, 1976 (div. 1992); children: Melissa, Justin. Various positions U.S. Ho. of Reps., Washington, 1975-79; asst. to pres. Bailey/Deardourff & Assocs., McLean, Va., 1980; office mgr. Office of Rep. Stan Parris, Washington, 1981-85; assoc. staff, legis. dir. Office of Rep. James H. Quillen, Washington, 1985-92; with minority counsel, subcom. on legis. process Com. on Rules, Ho. of Reps., Washington, 1993—. Republican. Office: Rules Subcom on Legis Process 101 Cannon House Office Bldg Washington DC 20515

BONINO, FERNANDA, art dealer; b. Torino, Italy, Jan. 5, 1927; came to U.S., 1963; d. Francesco Pogliani and Marina Collino; m. Alfredo Bonino, July 29, 1925 (dec. Jan. 1981). M in Art, U. Italy, Torino, 1942. Dir. Galeria Bonino Ltd., N.Y.C., 1963-90, dir., pres., 1981—. Mem. Art Dealers Assn. Am. Office: Galeria Bonino Ltd 48 Great Jones St New York NY 10012-1133

BONK, SHARON CATHERINE, librarian; b. North Tonawanda, N.Y., Nov. 28, 1943; d. Joseph J. and Ann (Danylow) B. BS in Edn., SUNY, Geneseo, 1965; MA in Am. Studies, U. Minn., 1969, MA in Libr. Sci., 1969. High sch. libr. Sch. Dist. 3, Huntington, N.Y., 1965-67; social scis. selector Northeastern U. Librs., Boston, 1969-81, head, periodicals dept., 1978-82; head acquisitions dept. SUNY Albany Librs., Albany, 1978-83; asst. dir. tech. svcs. SUNY Librs., Albany, 1984-88, interim dir., 1988-89, asst. dir. rsch. svcs., 1989-90; asst. direct user svcs. Albany, 1990-93; dir. Queens Coll. Librs. CUNY, 1993—. Contbr. articles to profl. jours.; author chpts. in monographs; assoc. editor Serials Rev. Trustee Sand Lake (N.Y.) Town Libr., 1987-89. Recipient Fulbright Fellowship, 1989, Chancellor's Award for Excellence in Librarianship, SUNY, 1986, Lambert Scholarship, Blackwells Coll. of Libr. Wales, U.K., 1981. Mem. Assn. for Libr. Collections and Tech. Svcs./ALA (bd. dirs. 1989-92), Beta Phi Mu. Office: Rosenthal Library Queens Coll Kisseha Blvd Flushing NY 11367

BONNEAU, SARAH K., state legislator; b. Keene, N.H., Oct. 1, 1951; m. Robert A. Bonneau; 2 children. Attended, Beloit Coll., 1970, U. N.C., 1973; BA, Keene State Coll., 1982; MST, Antioch/New Eng., 1984. Mem. N.H. Ho. of Reps.; mem. resources com., recreation com., devel. com. Chair Westmoreland Sch. Bd., 1987-91, mem. budget com., 1988-91; trustee New Eng. Coalition Nuclear Pollution, 1982-91. Democrat. Home: Poocham Rd Westmoreland NH 03467 Office: NH Ho of Reps State Capitol Concord NH 03301*

BONNELL, PAMELA GAY, library administrator; b. Monterey, Calif., Feb. 2, 1948; d. Dewey L. and Marlyce I. (Hansen) Scoggins; m. Chrisman E. Bonnell, Mar. 2, 1974 (div. 1983); m. Verneil S. Henerson, June 18, 1966 (div. 1971), 1 child, V. Samuel III; m. Hugh R. McElroy, Nov. 10, 1990. BA, Cameron U., Lawton, Okla., 1972; MLS, U. Okla., 1972-73. Libr. Met. Libr. System, Oklahoma City, 1974-75, Office of the City Mgr., Dallas, 1977-80; dir. audience devel. Dallas Symphony Orch., 1980-81; libr. Dallas Morning News, 1981-83; libr. mgr. Plano (Tex.) Pub. Libr. System, 1983-91; dir. libr. svcs. Waco-McLennan County Libr. System, Waco, Tex., 1992—. Author: Fund Raising for Small Libraries, 1983; contbr. chpt. to book, articles to profl. jours. Gala chmn. Easter Seal Soc., Dallas, 1988; bd dirs. Women's Shelter, Plano, Tex., 1991; pres. Townbluff Homeowners Assn., Plano, 1984-90; trustee Dallas Symphony Orch., 1981. Recipient SIRS Intellectual Freedom award Tex. Libr. Assn., 1990. Mem. ALA (councilor-at-large 1990-94, pres. Intellectual Freedom Round Table 1993-94, Shirley Olofson Meml. award 1974, Cert. of Spl. Thanks 1986, John Phillip Immroth award 1990), Ctrl. Tex. Women's Alliance (bd. dirs. 1992—), Leadership Waco Alumni Assn., Rotary, Jr. League. Home: 4713 Nocona Dr Plano TX 75024 Office: Waco-McLennan County Libr Sys 1717 Austin Ave Waco TX 76701

BONNER, BESTER DAVIS, school system administrator; b. Mobile, Ala., June 9, 1938; d. Samuel Matthew and Alma (Davis) Davis; m. Wardell Bonner, Nov. 28, 1964; children: Shawn Patrick, Matthew Wardell. BS, Ala. State Coll., 1959; MS in Library Sci., Syracuse U., 1966; PhD, U. Ala., 1982. Cert. tchr. Librarian Westside High Sch., Talladega, Ala., 1959-64; librarian, tchr. lit. Lane Elem. Sch., Birmingham, Ala., 1964-65; head librarian Jacksonville (Ala.) Elem. Lab. Sch., 1965-70; asst. prof. library media Ala. A&M U., Huntsville, 1970-74; adminstv. asst. to pres. Miles Coll., Birmingham, 1974-78, chmn. div. edn., 1978-85; specialist media Montgomery County Pub. Schs., Md., 1987-88; dir. libr. and media svcs. div. curriculum and ednl. tech. Dist. of Columbia Pub. Schs., 1988—; forum leader Nat. Issues Forum, Domestic Policy Assn. U. Ala., Birmingham, 1983-84; mem. Libr. Svcs. Construction Act Adv. Com. Contbr. writer The Developing Black Family, 1975. Chmn. ethics commn. St. Ala., Montgomery 1977-81; radiothorn site coordinator United Negro Coll. Fund, Birmingham 1981. Mem. ALA, Ala. Instructional Media Assn. (pres. dist. II 1971-72), Assn. Women Deans and Adminstrs., Com. 100, D.C. Assn. Sch. Librs., D.C. Libr. Com., Am. Assn. Sch. Librs., Nat. Assn. State Ednl. Profls. Democrat. Methodist.

BONNER, MARY CHRISTINE, secondary education educator, school system administrator; b. Phila., Dec. 12, 1934; d. Joseph Fanelli and Christine Mary (Ferri) Gabage; m. John Joseph Bonner, Sept. 11, 1954; children: Lynne M. Appino, Brian Patrick. BA in English, Gwynedd-Mercy Coll., 1973; MA in English, Villanova U., 1976. Cert. English tchr., Pa., Hawaii. Instr. evening divsn. Gwynedd Mercy Coll.; elem. sch. tchr. St. Cath., St. John B., Bucks County, 1956-59, 68-73; English tchr. St. Hubert High Sch., Phila., 1973-74, A.B. Wood Girls High Sch., Warminster, Pa., 1974-81; chmn. English dept. Bishop Egan High Sch., Fairless Hills, Pa., 1981-88; dean of activities A.B. Wood High Sch., Warminster, 1988—, asst. prin. for student affairs, 1994—; mem. English curriculum com. for diocese of Phila. (Pa.), Secondary Sch. System, Archdiocese of Phila., 1980-88; lectr. in English sch. cont. studies La Salle U., 1981—; presenter in field. Mem. Lambda Iota Tau Internat. (v.p. 1973-74, pres. 1980-81), Delta Kappa Gamma Internat. Office: AB Wood High Sch 655 York Rd Warminster PA 18974-2001

BONNER, SHIRLEY HARROLD, business communications educator; b. Pitts., July 22, 1929; d. William DeWitt Jr. and Erma Dorothy (Ruppert) Harrold; m. Joseph A. Bonner, Apr. 21, 1956; children: Margaret Leslie, Joseph Edward. BS in Edn., U. Pitts., 1951, MEd, 1971, PhD, 1981. With Gulf Oil Corp., Pitts.; tchr. Three Rivers Bus. Sch., Pitts., Antwerp (Belgium) Internat. Sch., Duff's Bus. Sch., Pitts., C.C. of Allegheny County, Pitts., Learning Ctr. Chatham Coll., 1994—. Author: Margaret of Austria, Governess of the Low Countries, 1507-1530, 2 vols.; contbr. articles to The Balance Sheet. Past bd. dirs. Am. Protestant Ch. of Antwerp. Mem. AAUW (pres. DuBois area br. 1967-69), Assn. for Bus. Communication, World Affairs Coun Pitts. (consul), Delta Zeta. Republican. Home: 403 Denniston Ave Pittsburgh PA 15206-4411

BONNEVIE, KELLY MARIE, lawyer; b. Portland, Maine, June 13, 1965; d. George Joseph Jr. and Margaret Ann (Curran) B. BA cum laude, Dartmouth Coll., 1987; JD, Northeastern U., 1992. Bar: Mass. 1992. Devel. project intern Overseas Devel. Network, Delhi, India, 1987-88; paralegal Thornton & Early, Boston, 1988-89; law clk. to the justices Mass. Superior Ct., Boston, 1992-93; assoc. Beth S. Herr & Assocs., Cambridge, Mass., 1993—; mentor Northeastern U. Sch. Law Alumni Mentoring Program, Boston, 1993—. Vol. Mass. Com. for Children and Youth, Boston, 1985, Rosie's Place Homeless Shelter, Boston, 1988-90, AIDS Action Com., Boston, 1993—. Recipient Edison prize in govt. Dartmouth Coll., 1986, Richardson fellowship Dartmouth Coll., 1987. Mem. Women's Bar Assn. Office: Beth S Herr & Assocs 330 Broadway Cambridge MA 02139-1894

BONO, CHARLENE CECILIA, elementary school educator; b. New Orleans, Mar. 19, 1949; d. Charles Eugene and Cecilia Hattie (Poche') B. BA in Elem. Edn., Nicholls State U., 1967-71; summer student, Nicholls State/La. Tech., Rome, 1971, U. N.O., Austria, 1976, St. Mary's Dominican, Europe, 1983. Tchr. Jefferson Parish Sch. Bd., Metairie, La., 1972—; chairperson Instl. Cm. Sch. Effectiveness Team, Metairie, 1988-90; coop. tchr. U. New Orleans, 1993-94. Career Edn. grantee Jefferson Parish, Metairie, 1986; named Tchr. of Yr. Bridgedale Elem., Metairie, 1989, Supr. Tchr. U. New Orleans, 1993-94. Mem. Internat. Reading Assn. Democrat. Roman Catholic.

BONOSARO, CAROL ALESSANDRA, professional association executive, former government official; b. New Brunswick, N.J., Feb. 16, 1940; d. Rudolph William and Elizabeth Ann (Betsko) B.; m. Donald D. Kummerfeld, Sept. 8, 1962 (div. Jan. 1970); m. Athanasios Chalkiopoulos, Nov. 21, 1976 (separated Dec. 1990); 1 dau., Melissa. B.A., Cornell U., 1961; postgrad., George Washington U., 1961-62. Analytical statistician Office Mgmt. and Budget, Exec. Office of Pres., Washington, 1961-66; asst. dir. fed. programs div. U.S. Commn. on Civil Rights, Washington, 1966-68; dir. Office Fed. Programs U.S. Commn. on Civil Rights, 1968-69, dir. tech. assistance div., 1969-71, spl. asst. to staff dir., 1972, dir. women's rights program, 1972-79, asst. staff dir. for program planning and evaluation, 1979-80, asst. staff dir. congressional and public affairs, 1980-86; pres. Sr. Execs. Assn., Washington, 1986—. Vice chmn. Nat. Com. on Asian Wives of U.S. Servicemen, 1975-85; pres. Catholics for a Free Choice, 1980-83. Mem. Exec. Women in Govt., Sr. Exec. Assn. (dir. 1981-86, chmn. bd. dirs. 1983-86). Democrat. Home: 5504 Jordan Rd Bethesda MD 20816 Office: Sr Execs Assn PO Box 7610 Washington DC 20044-7610

BONSACK, KAREN NANCY, physical therapist; b. Easton, Pa., Aug. 3, 1959; d. James Paul and RoseMary (Hatem) B. BS in Life Scis., Lynchburg Coll., 1981; BS in Phys. Therapy, U. Md., 1985. Phys. therapist Children's Hosp., Balt., 1985-87, Orthopedic and Hand Rehab., Dundalk, Md., 1987-88; owner, phys. therapist Bonsack Phys. Therapy and Sports Rehab., Aberdeen, Md., 1988—. Mem. Harford County C. of C. Home: 3341 Deepwell Ct Abingdon MD 21009-1046

BONSACK, ROSE MARY HATEM, state legislator, physician; b. Havre de Grace, Md., Oct. 24, 1933; d. Joseph Thomas and Nasma (Joseph) Hatem; m. James P. Bonsack, Aug. 24, 1957; children: Jeanette, Karen, Thomas, David, James J. BS in Chemistry cum laude, Washington Coll., 1955; MD, Med. Coll. Pa., 1960. Intern Easton (Pa.) Hosp., 1961; physician outpatient clinic Kirk Army Hosp., Aberdeen Proving Ground, Md., 1962-74; chief outpatient clinic Kirk Army Hosp., Aberdeen Proving Group, Md., 1968-72, chief dept. hosp. clinics, 1972-74; contract physician Harford County Dept. Health, Md., 1975-78; utilization rev. officer Harford Meml. Hosp., Havre de Grace, 1981-82; pvt. practice Aberdeen, Md., 1981—; mem. Md. Gen. Assembly, vice chmn., chmn. Harford County del.; coord. clinics Hypertensive Coun. Md., 1977-81; reviewer quality assurance for nursing homes in Harford County, Md. Licensing Div., 1977-81; utilization rev. officer Harford Meml. Hosp., Havre de Grace, 1981-82; med. dir. Ashley Alcoholic Rehab., Havre de Grace, 1983-84; mem. Bd. Med. Examiners Md.; mem., exec. sec. Commn. on Med. Discipline, 1985-88. V.p. St. Joan of Arc Home-Sch. Assn., 1968, pres., 1969, mem., 1968-85; v.p. No. Md. Heart Assn., 1969, pres., 1970, bd. dirs. 1973; bd. dirs. Mann House, Bel Air, Md., 1973-82, Harford County Cancer Soc., 1973-86; mem. John Carroll Home-Sch. Assn., 1974—, 1st v.p., 1975, pres., 1975; bd. dirs. John Carroll High Sch., 1975—, pres. bd. dirs., 1980-86; mem. Harford County Dem. Ctrl. Com., 1987-90; mem. chief exec.'s coun. Harford C.C., 1990. Recipient Outstanding Contbn. to Md. Traffic Safety citation State of Md., 1969, Cert. of Merit for svc. Md. Cancer Soc., 1977, Women Helping Women award Soroptomists Harford and Cecil Counties, 1983-84. Mem. Am. Acad. Family Physicians, Med. Chirurgical Faculty Md., Hartford County Med. Soc. (sec. 1967, pres. 1968, v.p. 1978, 87, Outstanding Community Svc. citation 1979), Md. Acad. Family Physicians (v.p. 1987, pres. 1988). Office: Md Gen Assembly 118 W Bel Air Ave Aberdeen MD 21001

BOOHER, ALICE ANN, lawyer; b. Indpls., Oct. 6, 1941; d. Norman Rogers and Olga (Bonke) B. BA in Polit. Sci., Butler U., 1963; LLB, Ind. U., 1966, JD, 1967. Bar: Ind. 1966, U.S. Dist. Ct. (so. dist.) Ind. 1966, U.S. Tax Ct. 1970, U.S. Ct. Customs and Patent Appeals 1969, U.S. Ct. Mil. Appeals 1969, U.S. Ct. Appeals (D.C. cir.) 1969, U.S. Supreme Ct. 1969; cert. tchr., Ind. Rsch. asst., law clk. Supreme and Appellate Cts. Ind., Indpls., 1966; legal intern, atty., staff legal advisor Dept. State, Washington, 1966-69; staff legal adviser Bd. Vets. Appeals, Washington, 1969-78, sr. atty., 1978—, counsel, 1991—; former counselor D.C. Penal Facilities and Shelters. Author: The Nuclear Test Ban Treaty and the Third Party Non-Nuclear States, also children's books; contbr. articles to various publs., chpts. to Whiteman Digest of International Law; exhibited crafts, needlepoint in juried artisan fairs. Bd. dirs. numerous community groups, including D.C. Women's Commn. for Crime Prevention, 1980-81; pres., legal adviser VA employees Assn. Recipient various awards; named Ky. Col., 1988. Mem. DAV Aux., VFW Aux., LWV, Women's Bar Assn. D.C., D.C. Sexual Assault Coalition (chmn. legal com.), Butler U. Alumni Assn., Nat. Mus. Women in Arts, Bus. and Profl. Women (pres. D.C. 1980-81, nat. UN fellow 1974, nat. bd. dirs. 1980-82, 87—, Woman of Yr. award D.C. 1975, Marquerite Rawalt award D.C. 1986), USO, Women Officers Profl. Assns., Navy League U.S.A., Am. Legion Aux., Vietnam Vets. Am., Nat. Task Force on Women of the Mil. and Women Vets (chmn. 1986-90), Salute to Am. Women Mil. POWs.

BOOHER, PATRICIA GAIL, clinical research specialist; b. Gary, Ind., June 18, 1957; d. Ivan Paul and Naomi Lucille (Coffin) B. BA, Purdue U., 1987. Emergency rm. clk. AMI-Culver Union Hosp., Crawfordsville, Ind., 1974-87, outpatient admitting supr., 1984-85; project mgr., interview core mgr. Regenstreif Inst., Indpls., 1987-89; rsch. coord. dept. nuclear medicine Ind. U. Hosp., Indpls., 1990-93, clin. rsch. specialist hematology/oncology, 1993—. Contbr. articles to profl. jours. Active Big Sisters of Ctrl. Ind., Indpls., 1988—. Episcopalian. Home: 3209 Summerfield Dr Indianapolis IN 46214-1869 Office: Ind U Hosp Dept Medicine Div Hematology/ Oncology 550 University Blvd # 2240 Indianapolis IN 46202-5149

BOOKER, BETTY MAE, writer; b. Allentown, Pa., Nov. 26, 1948; d. Harold George and Bessie (Bealer-Miller) Bartholomew; m. Samuel Efford Booker III, June 27, 1970; children, Liesel Tamarah, Dacey Justin, Jaeson Bartholomew. BA in English, Millersville State Coll., 1970. Contbr. poetry to jours. and lit. mags. including Plainsong, America, The Christian Century, Poetry Now. Home: 27826 Island Dr Salisbury MD 21801-8507

BOOKER, NANA LAUREL, public relations executive; b. Waco, Tex., Aug. 5, 1946; d. Karl and Helen Dorothy (Keene) B. BA, Baylor U., 1968; MA, U. Fla., 1970; MBA, Pepperdine U., 1980. Accredited by Pub. Relations Soc. Am. Asst. prof. communications U. New Orleans, 1970-74, 1977-78; pub. relations cons. New Orleans, 1974-78; dir. pub. relations Touro Infirmary, New Orleans, 1976-78; dir. communications Lifemark Corp., Houston, 1978-81; pres. Communications Alliance, Houston, 1981-82, Nana Booker & Assocs., Houston, 1984-90, Nana Booker & Assocs. (name now Booker/Hancock & Assocs.), Houston, 1991—; dir. internat. relations, communications mayor's office City of Houston, 1982-84. Co-author: Introduction to Theatrical Arts, 1972. Mem. South Tex. Dist. Export Coun., Houston, 1988-92; press aide campaign K. Whitmire for Mayor, Houston, 1982; mem. exec. adv. bd. coll. bus. adminstrn. Houston U., 1990—; bd. dirs. Escape Ctr., 1990-93, YWCA, Houston, 1991-92. Mem. Internat. Pub. Rels. Assn., Pub. Rels. Soc. Am. (accredited; Excalibur award 1988, chair internat. sect. 1993—), Houston World Trade Assn. (bd. dirs. 1986—), Houston-Shenzhen Sister City Assn. (bd. dirs. 1987-94), Swiss-Am. C. of C. (bd. dirs. 1987-90), River Oaks Breakfast Club.

BOOKS, ROBERTA PAULA, real estate finance executive; b. Boston, Apr. 4, 1943; d. Leonard and Mary (Karsh) Books; m. Jay S. Negin, May 20, 1973; children: Martha Alice Books Negin, Samuel Benjamin Books Negin. AB in Math., Bryn Mawr Coll., 1964, AM in Physics, 1969; MBA, Harvard U., 1971; postgrad., NYU, 1966. Account mktg. rep. IBM, N.Y.C., 1966-69; v.p. Morgan Stanley, N.Y.C., 1971-81; spl. asst. to the comptroller Office of the Comptroller of the Currency, Washington, 1977-79; mng. dir. Prudential Ins. Co. Am., Newark, 1982-86; v.p., co-head real estate capital markets Salomon Bros., N.Y.C., 1986-90; v.p. Citicorp Real Estate, N.Y.C., 1991-94; mng. dir. Chem. Bank, N.Y.C., 1994—. Author pamphlet. Chair fin. com. The Thurnauer Sch. Music, Tenafly, N.J., 1989—; mem. media literacy com., Morrow Soc. bd. Elisabeth Morrow Sch., Englewood, N.J., 1993—; mem. maj. gifts com. Bryn Mawr (Pa.) Coll., 1991—. Mem. Real Estate Bd. N.Y., Fin. Women's Assn. N.Y. Office: Chem Bank 380 Madison Ave New York NY 10017-2513

BOONE, ALICIA KAY LANIER, marketing communications consultant, writer; b. Ft. Worth, Sept. 3, 1941; d. John David and Reba Louise (Smith) Lanier; m. William T. Boone, July 22, 1967 (div. June 1988); children: Katherine, Suzanne, Lisa, Norma, Matthew. Student, Abilene (Tex.) Christian U., 1959-60, North Tex. State U., 1960-64; BA in Sociology cum laude, U. Tex., Dallas, 1993. Reporter Daily Oklahoman/Oklahoma City Times, 1964-66; feature writer Houston Post, 1967; info. rep. Okla. Dept. Inst., Social and Rehab. Services, Oklahoma City, 1967-73; dir. pub. info. United Way Mecklenburg-Union, Charlotte, N.C., 1974-76; account mgr., sr. writer Epley Assocs./Pub. Relations, Charlotte, 1977-78; account mgr. Yarbrough Co./Advt., Pub. Relations, Dallas, 1979-82; owner Boone & Assoc./Pub. Relations and Advt., Richardson, Tex., 1982-88; v.p. Yarbrough Co./Advt., Dallas, 1988-90; owner The Creative Solution, Dallas, 1990—; bd. dirs Hope Cottage, 1993—; pub. Adoption Triad Forum, 1993—. Author, editor History of Child Welfare In Oklahoma, 1976. Mem. SBA (region VI adv. coun. 1990—), Pub. Rels. Soc. Am., Assn. Women Entrepreneurs of Dallas (pres. 1987-88), Richardson C. of C. (editor newsletter 1986-87), Dallas Women in Bus. (Advt. of Yr. 1988), Small Bus. Congress in Dallas (co-chair 1988).

BOONE, BRENDA SUE, small business owner; b. Rupert, W.Va., Dec. 26, 1952; d. James and Gearldine Mae (Terry) Davis; m. Larry Lane Boone, Aug. 31, 1971; children: Gregory, Tanjala, Mindalyn. Supr. Decor & More, Summersville, W.Va., 1983-93; mgr. Richwood (W.Va.) Body Shop; owner Satin-n-Lace Boutique, Richwood, 1993—; co-owner Richwood Body Shop. Vol. Dept. Human Svc., 1991, Greenbrier Food Pantry, Quinwood, W.Va., 1984, Toys for Tots, Rupert, 1980-85, Sch. Projects, Rainelle-Quinwood, 1970-92. Named Mother of Yr., 1978, Working Woman for a Day, 1991. Office: Satin-n-Lace 15 1/2 E Main St Richwood WV 26261

BOONE, CELIA TRIMBLE, lawyer; b. Clovis, N.Mex., Mar. 3, 1953; d. George Harold and Barbara Ruth (Foster) T.; m. Billy W. Boone, Apr. 21, 1990. BS, Ea. N.Mex. U., 1976, MA, 1977; JD, St. Mary's U., San Antonio, 1982. Bar: Tex. 1982, U.S. Dist. Ct. (no. dist.) Tex. 1983, U.S. Ct. Appeals (5th cir.) 1985, U.S. Supreme Ct. 1986. Instr. English, Eastern N.Mex. U., Portales, 1977-78; editor Curry County Times, Clovis, 1978-79; assoc. Schulz & Robertson, Abilene, Tex., 1982-85, Scarborough, Black, Tarpley & Scarborough, 1985-87; ptnr. Scarborough, Black, Tarpley & Trimble, Abilene, Tex., 1988-90, Scarborough, Black, Tarpley & Boone, 1990-94, of counsel Scarborough, Tarpley, Boone & Fouts, 1994—; instr. legal rsch. and writing St. Mary's Sch. Law, 1981-82. Legal adv. to bd. dirs. Abilene Kennel Club, 1983-85; mem. landmarks commn. City of Abilene, 1989-90. Recipient Outstanding Young Lawyer of Abilene, 1988. Mem. ABA, State Bar Tex. (mem. disciplinary rev. com. 1989-93), Am. Trial Lawyers Assn., Tex. Trial Lawyers Assn., Tex. Criminal Def. Lawyers Assn., Tex. Acad. Family Law Specialists, Tex. Bd. Legal Specialization (cert. 1987), Abilene Bar Assn. (bd. dirs. 1985-86, 87-88, sec./treas. 1985-86), Abilene Young Lawyers Assn. (bd. dirs. 1985-86, 87-89, treas. 1985-86, pres.-elect 1987-88, pres. 1988-89), NOW, ACLU, Phi Alpha Delta. Democrat. Avocations: needlework, gardening. Office: Scarborough Black Tarpley & Boone 104 Pine St Abilene TX 79601-5926

BOONE, DOROTHY MAE, county official; b. Gordon, Nebr., May 29, 1919; d. C.H. and Ethel Mae (Lewis) Perkins; m. M.H. Boone Oct. 2, 1943 (dec. Sept. 1954). AA, Iowa Western Community Coll., Council Bluffs, 1977; grad., Am. Legion Officers Sch., Indpls., 1973. Notary pub., Iowa. Nat. VA accredited svc. rep. Office Gen. Counsel, Washington, 1976—; exec. sec., adminstrv. asst., adminstrv. sec. Pottawattamie County Veterans' Affairs Commn., Council Bluffs, Iowa; dir. Veteran Affairs Commn., Pottawattamie County, 1987-92; profl. svc. officer DAV, 1989—; mem. local bd. SSS, Washington, 1980—; mem., chair Harrison, Shelby and Pottowattomie counties SSS, 1981—. Recipient cert. appreciation Kiwanis, 1985, VA Nat. Svc. Officers award, 1960, SSS, 1991, commendation DAV, 1987, County Svc. award Nat. VA, 1986, 92, Woman of Yr. award Am. Biol. Inst., 1993. Home: 1320 N 21st St Council Bluffs IA 51501-0909

BOONE, KATHRYN LEA, counselor; b. Crocker, Mo., Feb. 7, 1949; d. Kenneth Paul and Marjorie Merle (Anderson) Bandy; m. William Thomas Boone, May 24, 1969; children: Jennifer, Andrew, Ryan. BA in Elem. Edn., S.W. Bapt. U., 1971; MS in Guidance and Counseling, S.W. Mo. State U., 1988. Lic. profl. counselor, Mo. Tchr. kindergarten Miller (Mo.) Pub. Sch., 1971; tchr. Friendship Circle Presch., West Plains, Mo., 1978-79, Nixa (Mo.) Elem. Sch., 1982-85, Aurora (Mo.) Elem. Sch., 1985-87; grad. asst. Learning Diagnostic Clinic, So. Mo. State U., Springfield, 1987-88; elem. sch. counselor Springfield Pub. Schs., 1988-90; family therapist, play therapist Human Potential Counseling, Springfield, 1988—. Named one of Outstanding Young Women of Am., 1980. Mem. ACA, Internat. Assn. Marriage and Family Counselors, Am. Assn. Christian Counselors, Assn. for Play Therapy (registerd play therapist and supr.), Mo. Assn. for Play Therapy (pres. 1993—). Office: Human Potential Counsl Foun 1722 S Glenstone Ave Ste X Springfield MO 65804-1516

BOONE, SUZANNE VAGLIA, financial planning manager; b. Bradford, Pa., Mar. 5, 1962; d. Roger Hazen and Marilyn Ann (Hohn) Vaglia; m. Otho Newman Boone, Aug. 14, 1993. BBA in Fin., U. Cin., 1985; MBA in Mktg., Loyola Coll., 1993. Contr.'s adminstr. Westinghouse, Balt., 1985-88; fin. planning mgr. Ohmeda, Columbia, Md., 1988—. Mem. Am. Mktg. Assn. (treas. 1993-94), Loyola Alumni Assn. Office: Ohmeda 9065 Guilford Rd Columbia MD 21046-1836

BOONSHAFT, HOPE JUDITH, public relations executive; b. Phila., May 3, 1949; d. Barry and Lorelei Gail (Rienzi) B. BA, Pa. State U., 1972; postgrad. Del. Law Sch., Kellogg Inst. Mgmt. Tng. Program writer Youth Edn., N.Y.C., 1972; legal aide to judge, Phila., 1973; dir. spl. projects Guiffre Med. Center, Phila., 1975; Arlen Specter senatorial campaign fin. dir., Phila., 1975; fin. dir. Jimmy Carter Presdl. Campaign, Atlanta, 1976; nat. fin. dir. Dem. Nat. Com., 1977-78; dir. devel. World Jewish Congress, N.Y.C., 1978; dir. devel. Yeshiva U., L.A., 1979; dir. communications Nat. Easter Seal Soc., Chgo., 1979-83; chief exec. officer Boonshaft-Lewis & Savitch Pub. Rels. and Govt. Affairs, L.A., 1983-93; sr. v.p. Edelman Worldwide, 1993; spl. adv. community rels. The White House, 1977-80; guest lectr. U. Ill., 1982, May Co.'s Calif. Women in Bus. Bd. dirs. L.A. Arts Coun., Hollywood Heritage Coun., Show Coalition, Jewish TV Network. Named 1 of 6 Non Stop Achievers, GermaineMonteil. Mem. Nat. Soc. Fundraisers, Am. Inst. Wine and Food (bd. dirs.), Am. Jewish Com. (exec. com.), Nat. Conf. Christians & Jews (bd. dirs.), Show Coalition, Jewish TV Network (bd. dirs.), Women's Nat. Dem. Club, Alpha Chi Omega. Home: 13168 Boca De Canon Ln Los Angeles CA 90049 Office: Edelman Worldwide 5670 Wilshire Blvd Ste 1500 Los Angeles CA 90036-5615

BOORKMAN, JO ANNE, librarian; b. San Jose, Calif., July 21, 1947; d. Charles John and Ruth Ellen (Reuss) B. BA, Scripps Coll., 1969; MS, U. Ill., 1971. Bibl. search analyst biomed. library UCLA, 1971-73, reference librarian Darling biomed. library, 1973-77; head pub. svcs. health scis. library U. N.C., Chapel Hill, 1977-80, head collections devel. health scis. library, 1980-84; head pub. svcs. Carlson health scis. library U. Calif., Davis, 1985-86, acting asst. univ. librarian health scis., 1986-87, head Carlson library, 1988—. NSF fellow, 1969-70. Mem. ALA, Spl. Librs. Assn., Med. Libr. Assn. (bd. dirs. 1988-91), No. Calif. and Nev. Med. Libr. Group (pres. 1988-89), Mid-Atlantic chpt. Med. Libr. Assn. (pres. 1983-84), P.E.O. Office: U Calif Carlson Health Scis Libr Davis CA 95616-5291

BOORSTEIN, BEVERLY WEINGER, judge; b. Chgo., Apr. 25, 1941; d. Morris Aaron and Bess (Meisel) Weinger; m. Sidney L. Boorstein, July 3, 1962; children: Robin Anne, Michelle Loren. BA, Brandeis U., 1961; JD, Boston U., 1964. Bar: Mass. 1964, U.S. Dist. Ct. Mass. 1967. Assoc. Siskind & Siskind, Boston, 1965-70; sole practice, Boston, 1971-79; ptnr. Beverly Weinger Boorstein, P.C., Boston, 1980-92; assoc. justice Middlesex County Probate and Family Ct., 1992—; commr. Jud. Conduct Comm.; treas. Mental Health Legal Advisors Com. Mem. Bd. of Bar Overseers (bd. dirs.), Mass. Bar Assn., Middlesex County Bar Assn., Mass. Assn. Women Lawyers (adv. bd.), Boston Bar Assn. Contbr. articles to legal publs.

BOOTH, BARBARA RIBMAN, civic worker; b. N.Y.C., May 2, 1928; d. Benjamin C. and Ceclia (Lowe) Ribman; m. Mitchell B. Booth, July 13, 1952; 1 child, Brian S. AA, Centenary Jr. Coll., Hackettstown, N.Y., 1948; BA, Barnard Coll., 1950. Pres. women's alliance, chmn., Christmas fair 1st Congl. Ch. of City of N.Y., 1959-63; mem. vol. com. Sheltering Arms Children's Svc., N.Y.C.; vol., coord. high sch. visits, pres. aux. N.Y. Hosp., 1989-91; trustee Florence K. Griswold Meml. Fund. Com., All Souls Unitarian Ch., N.Y.C.; bd. dir. women's div. Jefferson Dem. Club. N.Y.C.; committeewoman N.Y. County Dem. Com.; bd. govs., v.p. N.Y. Fruit and Flower Mission, Inc.; del. city conv., chmn. East Manhattan br. LWV. Home: 75 E End Ave New York NY 10028

BOOTH, BONNIE NELSON, compensation benefits consultant; b. Lynn, Mass., Aug. 28, 1942; d. Vincent Carl and Merchelle Romaine (Eastman) Nelson. Student, Mary Washington Coll., 1960-61, Columbia U., 1965, Carnegie-Mellon U., 1962, 78-80; EdM in Adminstrn., Planning and Social Policy, Harvard U., 1979. Exec. sec. Kenyon and Eckhardt, Inc., N.Y.C., 1964-65; exec. sec., asst. to assoc. dir. Am. Press. Inst., Columbia U., N.Y.C., 1965; prin. sec. to chief housing sect. UN Hdqrs., N.Y.C., N.Y.C., 1965-68; adminstrv. asst. sec. UN Mission, Magadiscio, Somalia, 1968, Tripoli, Libya, 1968-69; research asst. Stockholm Sch. Econs., 1970; adminstrv. sec. to dep. dir. UN Conf. Trade and Devel./GATT, Geneva, 1970; adminstrv. asst. Harvard U., 1970-74, personnel officer dept. psychology and social relations, 1974-75; adminstrv. asst. Dravo Corp., Pitts., 1975-76; assoc. dir. admissions Chatham Coll., Pitts., 1976-77, acting dir. admissions, 1977-78; mgmt. devel. trainer and adminstr. Westinghouse Credit Corp., Pitts., 1981-86, human resources adminstr., 1986-89, human resources cons., 1989-91, pension cons., 1991—. Dem. committeewoman 7th Ward, Pitts., 1980—, vice chmn., 1990-93, chmn., 1993-94; del. Shadyside Action Coalition, 1988—, sec., 1991-92, pres., 1992—; mgmt. vol. cons. Pitts. Fund for Arts Edn., 1994. Recipient Hon. diploma for outstanding performance Internat. Seminar on Rural Housing and Community Facilities, Venezuelan Govt., 1967, Outstanding Quality Circle Facilitator award Westinghouse Electric Corp., 1985. Mem. ASTD, Internat. Assn. Quality Cirs. (pres. Pitts. chpt. 1985-90), Am. Soc. Exec. Women, Rotary. Episcopalian. Home: 5825 5th Ave Pittsburgh PA 15232-2749 Office: Westinghouse Electric Corp Gateway 3d Fl 11 Stanwix St Pittsburgh PA 15222-1312

BOOTH, ELIZABETH MARIE, corporate account executive; b. N.Y.C., Oct. 29, 1944; d. James Charles Hudson Booth and Elsa-Marie (Opp) Koehler; m. Edward J. Michel, Aug. 10, 1963 (div. 1987); children: Bartlett, Barrett, Edward, David. BA, Barnard Coll., 1965; MS, CCNY, 1966; MBA, Western Conn. State U., 1986. Dir. devel. Wyckham Rise, Washington, Conn., 1982; tchr. Norwalk (Conn.) Pub. Schs., 1985-87; exec. community banker Conn. Bank & Trust, Greenwich, 1987-88; asst. mgr. Union Trust Co., Stamford, Conn., 1988-89; account mgr. Xerox Corp., Stamford, 1990—. Cons., bd. dirs. Alton Bay (N.H.) Bible Conf., 1983-90. NSF scholar, 1960. Mem. NAFE, Am. Mus. Natural History, New Canaan Nature Ctr., Smithsonian Assocs., Fairfield Network Female Execs., Barnard Bus. and Profl. Women, Barnard Coll. Club N.Y. (bd. dirs.). Republican.

BOOTH, JANE SCHUELE, real estate broker, executive; b. Cleve.; d. Norman Andrew and Frances Ruth (Hankey) Schuele; m. George Warren Booth, Dec. 6, 1968. AA, Stephens Coll., 1946; student, U. Mo., 1946-47. Lic. real estate broker, Fla. Assoc. J.M. Mathes Inc., N.Y.C., 1947-48; dept. supr. Lord and Taylor, Scarsdale, N.Y., 1948-50; art coord. J. Walter Thompson, Inc., N.Y.C., 1953-58; art buyer SSC&B Inc. Advt., N.Y.C., 1959-80; pres. Jane Schuele Booth Realty, Ocala, Fla., 1982—. Mem. Fla. Thoroughbred Fillies, Ocala, 1980—; charter mem., trustee Royal Dames for Cancer Rsch., Inc., Ocala, 1986—; treas. Ladies Aux. Fla. H.C.H. Inc., Ocala, 1986-90; bd. visitors Fla. Horsemen's Children's Home, Inc., 1983-90. Mem. Ocala/Marion County C. of C., Equine Coun., Fla. Assn. Realtors, Nat. Assn. Realtors, Estates Club. Home: 1771 SW 55th Street Rd Ocala FL 34474-5933 Office: PO Box 5538 Ocala FL 34478-5538

BOOTH, JODY SHELTON, executive director; b. Norton, Kans., Aug. 4, 1944; d. James Pratt and Rita Merle (Thompson) Shelton; m. Michael Gerard Booth, Feb. 11, 1984. BA, Ottawa U., 1967; MEd, Emporia State U., 1977; EdD, Kans. U., 1991. Tchr. Belvoir Elem. Sch., Topeka, 1967-68, Ctrl. Elem. Sch., Olathe, Kans., 1968-77; prin. Westview Elem. Sch., Olathe, Kans., 1977-80, Tomahawk Elem. Sch., Olathe, Kans., 1980-88; exec. dir. human resources Olathe Dist. Schs., 1988—; cons. Master Tchr., Manhattan, Kans., 1981-86; adj. prof. Emporia (Kans.) State U., 1990—; chair North Ctrl. Edn. Team, 1984; mem. adv. coun. Sch. Edn., Kans. U., Lawrence, 1992—; mem. com. Five Yr. Tech. Plan, Olathe, 1991—. Contbr. articles to profl. jours. Recipient Outstanding Jayne award Jaycees, 1972, Outstanding Young Woman Kans., 1980. Mem. NAESP (Nat. Disting. Prin. award 1987-88), AASPA (affiliate), Kans. Career Devel. and Placement Assn., Kans. Assn. Elem. Sch. Prins. (pres., Nat. Disting. Prin. award 1987-88, Olathe C. of C., United Sch. Admisntrs. (bd. dirs.), Optimist. Home: 11546 Brentwood Olathe KS 66061 Office: Olathe Dist Schs 1005 Pitt St Olathe KS 66061

BOOTH, MARGARET A(NN), communications company executive; b. N.Y.C., Dec. 25, 1946; d. Herbert and Alice (Traum) B.; m. Marvin E. Schechter, Jan. 22, 1984. BS, U. Wis., 1968. Editl. asst. Bantam Books, N.Y.C., 1968-70; publicity asst. Ruder & Finn Inc., N.Y.C., 1970-71, dir. radio and TV, 1971-76, v.p., 1974-76; pres. Pub. Interest Pub. Rels., N.Y.C., 1976—, M. Booth & Assocs., Inc., N.Y.C., 1983—. Author: Promoting Issues and Ideas, 1987; contbr. articles to profl. jours. Bd. dirs. Task Force on Permanancy Planning for Foster Children, 1994. Recipient YWCA Salute to Women Achievers, City of N.Y., 1985. Mem. Pub. Rels. Soc. Am., Women in Comm. (Matrix award for Pub. Rels. 1987), Women Execs. in Pub. Rels. Office: M Booth & Assocs Inc 470 Park Ave S # 10N New York NY 10016-6819

BOOTH, ROSEMARY, management educator; b. New Rochelle, N.Y., Mar. 23, 1941; d. Robert Roche and Margaret Mary (Hogan) B. BA, Marquette U., 1962; MBA, Iona Coll., 1971; PhD, U. Ky., 1991. Sec. IBM, White Plains, N.Y., 1965-69; word processing mgr. IBM, N.Y.C., 1969-71; communications profl. IBM, Franklin Lakes, N.J., 1971-79; info. mgr. IBM, Lexington, Ky., 1979-89; IBM faculty loan Midway Coll., Lexington, Ky., 1988-89; asst. prof. U. N.C., Charlotte, 1991—; instr. United Way Leadership Devel. Program, Lexington, 1985-87. Bd. dirs. YWCA, Lexington, 1981-87, Vol. Ctr. Blue Grass, Lexington, 1986-90; adv. bd. Charlotte Vol. Ctr., 1994—. Mem. Acad. Mgmt., Speech Comm. Assn., Assn. Bus. Comm. Home: 9503 Marsena Ct Charlotte NC 28213-3760 Office: U NC Dept Mgmt Charlotte NC 28223

BOOTHE, GRACE MCDONOUGH, artist; b. Bklyn., May 18, 1937; d. Anthony and Anna (Downs) Molitor; m. John J. McDonough (dec.); children: John, Glenn, Kevin, Maureen, Diane, Patrick, Timothy, Sean. Student, SUNY, 1975-77, Palomar Coll., 1982-86, U. Am., Aix-en-Provence, France, 1986-87, Atelier-du-Sufranier, Antibes, France, 1986-90. Exhibited in group shows at Combined Orgn. for Visual Arts, San Diego, Carlsbad Oceanside Art League, San Diego, Fallbrook Art Assn., San Diego, Escondido Art Assn., San Diego, Rancho Bernardo, San Diego; and pvt. and pub. collections. Recipient Homage de la Ville de Mention, France, 1987, and other awards. Mem. La Jolla Art Assn., Navy League U.S., Naval Res. Assn. (past sec.). Home and Studio: 17538 Caminito Balata San Diego CA 92128-1855

BOOZ, GRETCHEN ARLENE, marketing executive; b. Boone, Iowa, Nov. 24, 1933; d. David Gerald and Katherine Bevridge (Hardie) Berg; m. Donald Rollett Booz, Sept. 3, 1960; children: Kendra Sue (dec.), Joseph David, Katherine Sue. AA, Graceland Coll., 1955. Med. asst. Robert A. Hayne M.D., Des Moines, 1955-61; mktg. services mgr. Herald Pub. House, Independence, Mo., 1975—. Author: (book) Kendra, 1979. Mem. Citizens Adv. Bd., Blue Springs, Mo., 1979-91, Mayor's Christmas Concert Com., Independence, 1987-91; bd. dirs. Comprehensive Mental Health, 1981-83, Child Placement Svcs., Independence, 1987-94, Hope House, Inc., Independence, 1987-91, Ctr. for Profl. Devel. and Life-long Learning, Inc., 1995—; trustee Graceland Coll., Lamoni, Iowa, 1984—. Mem. Leadership Edn. Action Devel. (L.E.A.D.), Independence C. of C. (diplomat, Outstanding Mem. award 1981). Republican. Mem. Reorganized Ch. Jesus Christ Latter Day Saints. Home: 1200 Crestview Dr Blue Springs MO 64014-2312 Office: Herald Pub House 3225 S Noland Rd Independence MO 64055-1317

BOOZER, BRENDA LYNN, mezzo-soprano; b. Atlanta, Jan. 25, 1948; d. Jack Stewart and Ruth Malcolm (Tate) B.; m. Robert Keith, Apr. 1973 (div. 1989); 1 child, Alexander. BA, Fla. State U., 1970; postgrad., Juilliard Sch. Music. Appearances include Met. Opera, Theatre Musical Paris, Covent Garden, Stadtische Buhnen Frankfurt, Netherlands Opera, Gran Teatro de Santiago Chile, Teatro Communale of Florence, Lyric Opera Chgo., Houston Grand Opera, Santa Fe Opera, San Francisco Spring Opera, Phila. Orch., L.A. Philharm., Nat. Symphony, St. Louis Symphony, Seattle Symphony, others; recs. include Falstaff (nominated for Grammy for Best Opera Recording 1993). Home: 765 Bedford Rd Tarrytown NY 10591-1203

BORAWSKI, KATHLEEN, meteorologist, radio broadcaster; b. Sharon, Pa., Aug. 20, 1956; d. Thomas Daniel and Marie C. (Kopnicky) B.; m. Richard K. Heller. BS in Meteorology, Pa. State U., 1978. Meteorologist Weather Forecast Inc. of Ohio, Cleve., 1979-82; meteorologist, expert sr. forecaster Accu-Weather, Inc., State College, Pa., 1982—; mentor for forecasters in tng. Accu-Weather, Inc., 1993. Mem. Am. Meteorol. Soc., NOW, ACLU, Greenpeace. Democrat. Roman Catholic. Home: 800 Stratford Dr Apt 33 State College PA 16801-4331 Office: Accu-Weather Inc 619 W College Ave State College PA 16801-3733

BORCHERS, KAREN LILY, child welfare administrator; b. Detroit, Apr. 4, 1940; d. Albert Oscar and Lily Louise (Denzler) B. BA in Psychology and Sociology, Mich. State U., 1961; AM in Social Svc. Adminstrn., U. Chgo., 1964; MS in Spl. Edn. Adminstrn., No. Ill. U., 1976; EdD in Early Childhood Edn./Adminstrn., Nova U., 1982. Cert. social worker. Child welfare worker Ill. Dept. Children & Family Svcs., Rockford, 1962-65; sch. social worker Komarek Schs., N. Riverside, Ill., 1965-67; exec. dir. Seguin Sch., Berwyn, Ill., 1967-72, Seguin Tng. Ctr., Cicero, Ill., 1967-72; adminstr. Orchard Hill, Madison, Wis., 1972-76; exec. dir. Children's Home Soc. Fla., West Palm Beach, 1976—; pres. Pathways to Growth, Inc., West Palm Beach, 1986—. Pres., founder Masterworks Chorus of the Palm Beaches, West Palm Beach, 1978—, Teen Musical Theatre, Inc., West Palm Beach, 1984—, Internat. Children's Chorus of the Palm Beaches, West Palm Beach, 1988-90; pres. Palm Beach Regional Achievement Ctr., West Palm Beach, 1979-84. Recipient Excellence in Health and Social Svcs. award Palm Beach County Commn., 1979. Mem. NASW, Civitan, Mensa. Home: 11984 Suellen Cir Wellington FL 33414 Office: Childrens Home Soc Fla 3600 Broadway West Palm Beach FL 33407

BORDA, DEBORAH, symphony orchestra executive; b. N.Y.C., July 15, 1949; d. William and Helene (Malloy) B. BA, Bennington Coll., 1971; postgrad., Royal Coll. Music, London, 1972-73. Program dir. Mass. Coun. Arts and Humanities, Boston, 1974-76; mgr. Boston Musica Viva, Boston,

1976-77; gen. mgr. Handel and Haydn Soc., Boston, 1977-79, San Francisco Symphony, 1979-86; pres. St. Paul Chamber Orch., 1986-88; exec. dir. Detroit Symphony Orch., 1988-90; pres. Minn. Orch., Mpls., 1990-91; exec. dir. N.Y. Philharm., N.Y.C., 1991—. Office: NY Philharm Avery Fisher Hall 10 Lincoln Ctr Plaza New York NY 10023-6973

BORDALLO, MADELEINE MARY (MRS. RICARDO JEROME BORDALLO), lieutenant governor of Guam, wife of former governor of Guam; b. Graceville, Minn., May 31, 1933; d. Christian Peter and Mary Evelyn (Roth) Zeien; m. Ricardo Jerome Bordallo, June 20, 1953; 1 dau., Deborah Josephine. Student, St Mary's Coll., South Bend, Ind., 1952; A.A., St. Katherines Coll., St. Paul, 1953; A.A. hon. degree for community service, U. Guam, 1968. Presented in voice recital Guam Acad. Music, Agana., 1951, 62; mem. Civic Opera Co., St. Paul, 1952-53; mem. staff KUAM Radio-TV sta., Agana, 1954-63; freelance writer local newspaper, fashion show commentator, coordinator, civic leader, 1963, nat. Dem. committeewoman for Guam, 1964-94, 1st lady of Guam, 1974-78, 81-85; senator 16th Guam Legislature, 1981-82, 19th Guam Legislature, 1987-88, 20th Guam Legislature, 1989-90, 21st Guam Legislature, 1991-92, 22nd Guam Legislature, 1993-94; Dem. Party candidate for Gov. of Guam, 1990, Lt. Gov. of Guam, 1994; Lt. Gov. of Guam, 1995—; del. Nat. Dem. Conv., 1964, 68, 72, 76, 80, 84, 88-92, pres. Women's Dem. Party Guam, 1967-69; rep. Presdl. Inauguration, Washington, 1965, 77, 85; del. Dem. Western States Conf., Reno, 1965, L.A., 1967, Phoenix, 1968, conf. sec., 1967-69; del. Dem. Women's Campaign Conf., Wash., 1965, Dem. Inauguration, 1992. Pres. Guam Women's Club, 1958-59; del Gen. Fedn. Women's Clubs Convs., Miami Beach, Fla., 1961, New Orleans, 1965, Boston, 1968; v.p. Fedn. Asian Women's Assn., 1964-67, pres., 1967-69; pres. Guam Symphony Soc., 1967-73, del. convs., Manila, Philippines, 1959, Taipei, Formosa, 1960, Hong Kong, 1963, Guam, 1964, Japan, 1968, Taipei, 1973; chmn. Guam Christmas Seal Drive, 1961; bd. dirs. Guam chpt. ARC, 1963, sec., 1963-67; pres. Marianas Assn. For Retarded Children, 1968-69, 73-74, 84—; bd. dirs. Guam Theatre Guild, Am. Cancer Soc.; mem. Guam Meml. Hosp. Vols. Assn., 1966—, v.p., 1966-67, pres., 1970-71; chmn. Hosp. Charity Ball, 1966; pres. Women for Service, 1974—, Beauty World Guam Ltd., 1981—, First Lady's Beautification Task Force of Guam, 1983—; pres. Palace Restoration Assn., 1983—; nominee Dem. party for Gov. of Guam, 1990. Mem. Internat. Platform Assn., Guam Rehab. Assn. (assoc.), Guam Lytico and Bodig Assn. (pres. 1983—), Spanish Club of Guam, Inetnon Famalaoan Club (pres. 1983-86), Guam Coun. of Women's Club (pres. 1993—). Home: PO Box 1458 Agana GU 96910-1458 Office: PO Box 2950 Agana GU 96910

BORDELEAU, JO ANN, city official; b. Paris, Mo., Aug. 6, 1938; d. Edward Franklin Jr. and Elsie Lee (Robbins) Wood; m. Gerald Fraser Bordeleau, July 18, 1961; children: George Edward, Terry Ray. Assoc. in Bus. Adminstrn., St. Louis Community Coll., 1981; BSBA summa cum laude, U. Mo., St. Louis, 1985. Acctg. clk. A P Green Firebrick, Mexico, Mo., 1955-56; office mgr. MFA Cen. Coop., Paris, 1956-59, Fenix & Scisson, Inc., Tulsa, 1959-62; payroll clk. Signal Gas & Oil, San Jose, Calif., 1962-64; bookkeeper City of Ferguson, Mo., 1966-78; data processing & acctg. mgr. City of Ferguson, 1978-83, fin. mgr., 1983-86, dir. fin., 1986—. Bd. dirs. Mo. Mcpl. League, 1994—. Mem. Mcpl. Fin. Officers and Treas. Assn. (bd. dirs. St. Louis 1982-92, pres. 1984-85, state bd. dirs. 1983—, v.p. 1988-90, pres. 1990-91), Mo. Mcpl. League (bd. dirs. 1994—), Govt. Fin. Officers Assn. (cert. of achievement for fin. reporting 1985-94), Mcpl. Treas. Assn., Assn. Govtl. Accts., Ferguson Sta. Bus. Assn. Office: City of Ferguson 110 Church St Saint Louis MO 63135-2411

BORDELON, BARBARA JO, lawyer; b. Orange, Tex., May 6, 1948; d. Percy J. and Dorothy R. (White) B.; m. Phillip L. Fry (div.). BA in Govt., U. Tex., 1970, JD, 1973. Bar: Tex. 1974, Pa. 1990. Staff atty. Gen. Land Office, Austin, 1973-77; landman Chevron USA, New Orleans, 1977-80; sr. landman Transco Exploration, Houston, 1980-88; gen. counsel The Eastern Group, Inc., Washington, 1987—. Mem. ABA, Fed. Energy Bar Assn., Tex. Bar Assn., Pa. Bar Assn. Democrat. Roman Catholic. Home: 609 S Saint Asaph Alexandria VA 22314 Office: The Eastern Group Inc 2900 Eisenhower Ave Ste 300 Alexandria VA 22314

BORDEN, SANDRA MCCLISTER, day care center administrator, dancer; b. Trenton, Oct. 18, 1946; d. Harry Arthur and Ruth West McClister; m. Robert Stetson Borden, Mar. 23, 1968; children: Robert Freeman, Randolph McClister, David Buckley, Christian Delano. BA, Eastern Nazarene Coll., Quincy, Mass., 1968; MA, Nova U., 1986. Tchr. kindergarten Doves Nest Day Care Ctr., Rockland, Mass., 1979-84, owner, adminstr., 1979—; owner, adminstr. Dove's Nest Day Care Ctr., Weymouth, Mass., 1980-82, Abington, Mass., 1980-83; owner, editor Barter & Trade Jour., Rockland, 1980-83; owner Dove's Nest Family Day Care System, Rockland, 1984—; co-owner Carriage House Day Care Ctr., Brockton, Mass., 1986-92, Commonwealth Child Care Cons., 1987—, Bevell Assocs., Stoughton, Mass., 1987-90, Beginning Roots Day Care Ctr., Stoughton, 1987-93; pres. Ednl. Videos of New Eng., 1990—; owner Angels Consignment Shop, Rockland, Mass.; ptnr. Tender Loving Child Care Inc., 1988-89; dancer Foggs Dancers, Boston, 1980—; dir. Country Dance Soc., Boston, 1982—, v.p., 1986—, dancer, 1984-85, pres., 1988; co-founder, dancer Rapscallion Rapper Sword Team, 1985—. Foster mother for Helping Hands monkey, Boston U. Sch. Medicine; bd. dirs. LWV, Rockland, 1972-73. Mem. Nat. Assn. Young Children, Royal Scottish Dance Soc., Country Dance Soc. , Rose Galliard N.W. Clog Team, 1989—), NAFE, Assn. for Childhood Edn. Internat., Women Aglow Club (sec., bd. dirs.), New Eng. Folk Festival Assn. Boston. Baptist. Home: 1040 Plymouth St Abington MA 02351-2617

BORDERS, CAROL LEE, primary school educator; b. Peoria, Ill.; d. Boyce Bradshaw and Alice Edna Victoria (Peterson) B. BS, Bradley U., 1958; MS, Ill. State U., 1967. Tchr. Lee Sch., Peoria, 1958-68, Kellar West, Peoria, 1968-80, Lindbergh Sch., Peoria, 1980-86, Kellar Cen. Primary Sch., Peoria, 1986—; bd. dirs. Peoria County Extension Svc.-Youth Coun., 1991—; steward Nature Conservancy, 1992. Bd. dirs., pres. botany sect. Peoria Acad. Scis., 1983—. Grantee Ill. Math and Sci. Acad., Kellar Sch., 1991, First of Am. Bank, 1994, Ill. Math & Sci. Acad.; scholar Alpha Delta Kappa. Mem. AAUW (1st v.p., sec.), Ill. Native Plant Soc. (treas. 1988-90), Lincoln Soc., Peoria County Old Settlers (bd. dirs. 1966-91), Phi Delta Kappa, Alpha Delta Kappa (pres., altruistic chmn. 1988—, scholar 1992), Sigma Kappa (2d v.p. alumni 1987-88). Presbyterian. Home: 2328 W Sherman Ave Peoria IL 61604-5458

BORDERS, JEAN HAILE, accountant, educator; b. Aug. 15, 1945; m. Lucian C. Borders, Nov. 15, 1964; 1 child, Mira Jane. BS summa cum laude, U. Tenn.; postgrad., Mid. Tenn. State U. CPA, Tenn. Tchr. Vol. C.C., Gallatin, Tenn.; CPA Jean H. Borders, CPA, Gallatin, Tenn. Recipient John Lewis award Nat. Acctg. Assn., 1975. Mem. AICPA, Tenn. Soc. CPAs, Gallatin C. of C., Bus. and Profl. Women's Club, U. Tenn. Alumni Assn., Gallatin Coll. Women's Study Club, Kiwanis, Beta Sigma. Baptist. Office: Jean H Borders CPA PO Box 415 Gallatin TN 37066

BORDERS, L. DIANNE, counselor, educator, researcher; b. Gaffney, S.C., Apr. 7, 1950; d. Hugh L. and Dorothy M. (Smith) B.; 1 child, Jacob Nestor. BA, U. N.C., Greensboro, 1972; MEd, Wake Forest U., 1979; PhD, U. Fla., 1984. Lic. profl. counselor; nat. cert. counselor. English tchr. High Point (N.C.) Ctrl. High Sch., 1972-77; counselor Lifespan Ctr. for Women Salem Coll., Winston-Salem, N.C., 1979-81; asst. prof. counselor edn. Oakland U., Rochester, Mich., 1984-87; asst. prof., then assoc. prof. counselor edn. U. N.C., Greensboro, 1987—. Author: Handbook of Counseling Supervision, 1987 (Excellence in Publ. in Counselor Edn. and Supr. award 1989); co-author: Evaluation of School Counseling Programs, 1992; rsch. editor Jour. Counseling and Devel., 1993—; author chpts. to books; contbr. articles to profl. jours. Vol. local, state and nat. adoption orgns., 1991—. Recipient Profl. Writing and Rsch. award N.C. Assn. Counseling and Devel., 1991. Mem. ACA (chair ethics com.). Office: U NC Greensboro 228 Curry Bldg Greensboro NC 27412-5001

BORELLA, MARY DOROTHY, volunteer; b. Detroit, May 21, 1919; d. Gustave Adam Luka and Mary Amanda Suta; m. Arthur A. Borella, Aug. 11, 1942; children: Patricia, Arthur Jr., Peter, Joanna, Edwin, Eugenie, Richard. AB in Basic Scis., Wayne State U., 1939; postgrad., Bob Jones U., 1939-40. Various positions U.S. Postal Svc., Detroit, 1965-83; receptionist, typist ARC Office Vols., Detroit, 1985-91. Active ARC, Detroit, 1985—, Founders Soc. of Detroit Inst. Art, 1985-91, Girl Scouts U.S.A., Detroit; trustee Rep. Presdl. Task Force, Washington, 1989-91. Mem. Internat. Cultural Inst., Smithsonian Instn., Toastmasters Internat. Roman Catholic. Home: 11750 Wilshire Dr Detroit MI 48213-1619 Office: American Red Cross 100 Mack Ave Detroit MI 48201-2416

BOREN, LYNDA SUE, small business owner, educator; b. Leesville, La., Apr. 1, 1941; d. Leonard and Doris (Ford) Schoenberger; m. James Lewis Boren, Sept. 1, 1961; 1 child, Lynda Carolyn. BA, U. New Orleans, 1971, MA, 1973; PhD, Tulane U., 1979. Prof. Northwestern State U., Natchitoches, La., 1987-89; tchr. gifted children Leesville (La.) H.S., 1992—; propr. Colony Country House, New Llano, La., 1992—; vis. prof. Newcomb Coll., Tulane U., New Orleans, 1979-83, U. Erlangen-Nuremburg, Germany, 1991-82, Middlebury (Vt.) Coll., 1983-84, Ga. Inst. Tech., Atlanta, 1985-87, Srinakharinwirot U., Bangkok, 1989-90; mem. planning com. 1st Kate Chopin Internat. Conf., Natchitoches, La., 1987-89; Fulbright lectr. USIA and Bd. Fgn. Scholars, 1981-82, 89-90. Author: Eurydice Reclaimed: Language, Gender and Voice in Henry James, 1989; co-editor, author: Kate Chopin Reconsidered, 1992; contbr. numerous articles to profl. jours. Founding mem. John F. Kennedy Libr. Recipient awards for watercolors; Mellon fellow Tulane U., 1977-78; NEH seminar fellow Princeton U., 1986. Mem. MLA, AAUW, DAR, IPA, Fulbright Alumni Assn., Women in the Arts, Art Guild, Audubon Soc. Democrat. Home: RR 1 Box 1 New Llano LA 71461 Address: PO Box 395 Leesville LA 71496-0395

BORETZ, NAOMI MESSINGER, artist, educator; b. Bklyn., June 9, 1935; d. Joseph and Sarah (Lesser) Messinger; m. Benjamin A. Boretz, Sept. 1, 1954; 1 child, Avron Albert. BA, Bklyn. Coll., 1957; MFA, CUNY, 1971; MA, Rutgers U., 1976; postgrad., Art Students League N.Y. Assoc. prof. fine arts, dir. arts program Wilson Coll., Chambersburg, Pa., 1985—. Exhbns. include Westminster Arts Coun. Arts Ctr., London, 1971, Hudson River Mus., N.Y.C., 1975, Carnegie-Mellon Art Gallery, Pitts., 1989, Condeso-Lawler Gallery, N.Y.C., 1987, The Nelson Atkins Mus. of Art, St. Louis, 1994, others; represented in pub. collections Met. Mus. Art, N.Y.C., Solomon R. Guggenheim Mus., N.Y.C., Brit. Mus., London, Nat. Mus. Am. Art, Washington, Yale U. Art Gallery, Joslyn Art Mus., Omaha, Walker Art Ctr., Mpls., Miami U. Art Mus., Oxford, Ohio; contbr. to arts publs. Artist-fellow Va. Ctr. Creative Arts, 1973, 86, Ossabaw Found., 1975, Tyrone Guthrie Arts Ctr., Ireland, 1987, Writers-Artists Guild Can., 1988; grantee N.J. State Coun. on Arts, 1985-86. Home: 15 Southern Way Princeton NJ 08540-5318 Office: Wilson Coll Chambersburg PA 17201

BORG, RUTH I., mental health nurse, long-term medical nurse; b. Chgo., Mar. 29, 1934; d. Axel Gunner and Charlotte (Benston) B. Diploma, West Suburban Sch. Nursing, 1956; tchr.'s degree, Chgo. Conservatory, 1958; BSN, Alverno Coll., 1981. Staff nurse Boath Meml. Hosp., Chgo.; head nurse psychiatry, head nurse long-term medicine VA North Chgo. Med. Ctr.; staff nurse, night supr. intermediate care VA Clement Zabiocki Med. Ctr., Milw.; pool nurse Milw. County Mental Health Complex. Contbr. 2 articles to profl. jours. Mem. ANA.

BORGEN, NANCY JEAN, credit corporation manager; b. La Crosse, Wis., May 3, 1939; d. Myron Rossmore and Valera Georgia (Plikuhn) Thoreson; m. Jon Ralph Borgen, Dec. 31, 1957 (div. Feb. 1986); children: Lori, Amy, Michael, Jon Patrick, Christoffer, Bradley. Student, St. Olaf Coll., 1957-58. Cert. collector, instr. in credit and collections. Asst. night credit mgr. Brandeis Dept. Store, Omaha, 1976-77, sales assoc., 1977-78; owner Clothes Encounter, La Crosse, Wis., 1979-83; v.p., gen. mgr. Credit Bur Datainc, La Crosse, 1983—. Fund raiser Gundersn Med. Found., La Crosse, 1991; tchr. Univ. Wis. Bus. Outreach, La Crosse, 1993-94; account exec. United Way, La Crosse, 1992-94, vice chair adv. bd. consumer credit counseling svc., La. Crosse, 1993—; mem. Cmty. Attitudes Task Force, La Crosse, 1994—. Mem. Am. Collectors Assn. (nat. bd. dirs., 1993—, Redcoat Club 1989, Beacon award 1994), Wis. Collectors Assn. (bd. dirs. 1984-94, nat. legis. dir. 1993-94, pres. 1991-92), Optimists (chair program com. 1993-94), Avant, La Crosse C. of C. Republican. Lutheran. Home: N1954 Hickory Ln La Crosse WI 54601-7111

BORGES, WANDA, lawyer; b. Bronx, N.Y., Aug. 29, 1950; d. Jaime Nemesio Borges and Ada C. (Pujadas) Borges Mady. Bar: N.Y. 1979, U.S. Dist. Ct. N.Y. 1979, U.S. Supreme Ct. 1984. Legal sec. firm Jules Teitelbaum, N.Y.C., 1972, law clk., 1972-79, assoc., 1979-82; assoc. Teitelbaum & Gamberg P.C., N.Y.C., 1982-84; ptnr. Jules Teitelbaum P.C., N.Y.C., 1985—; lectr. Am. Mgmt. Assn., 1982—, Nat. Assn. Credit Mgmt., N.J., 1983—; adj. prof. Seton Coll., Yonkers, N.Y., 1986—. Recipient Human Valor award, 1985. Mem. ABA, Fed. Bar Council, N.Y. State Bar Assn., Bankruptcy Lawyers Bar Assn., Mercy Coll. Alumni Assn. (v.p., dir.). Roman Catholic. Club: Fairfield County Chorale; U.S. Power Squadron. Home: 1096 Main St Stamford CT 06902-4330 Office: 98 Cuttermill Rd Great Neck NY 11021-3006

BORGGREN, JANET RUTH, communications professional; b. Chgo., Nov. 16, 1958; d. Robert Richard and Grace Elaine Borggren. BA in English and Math., Augustana Coll., 1980; MA in English, U. Chgo., 1981. Cert. in prodn. and inventory mgmt. Math. tchr. Eisenhower High Sch., Blue Island, Ill., 1981-82, Bloom High Sch., Chicago Heights, Ill., 1982-84; tech. writer Andersen Cons., Chgo., 1984-90, documentation mgr., 1990-93, user interface and usability architect, 1993—. Bd. mgrs. Covenant Children's Home, Princeton, Ill., 1993-94; vol. Lakeview Homeless Shelter, Chgo., 1988-93, Bottomless Closet, Chgo., 1990-94. Mem. Soc. Tech. Comm. (sr., Disting. Tech. Comm. award 1994), Usability Profls. Assn., Assn. Computing Machinery. Office: Andersen Cons 100 S Wacker Dr Chicago IL 60606

BORGMANN, NORMA LEE, superintendent; b. Belleville, Ill., Sept. 9, 1948; d. William Henry and Loraine Anna (Wolff) B. BA, Greenville Coll., 1970, BS, 1973; MS in Edn., So. Ill. U., 1979, specialist degree in edn. adminstrn., 1994. Cert. adminstr., tchr., Ill. Tchr. elem. edn. Patoka (Ill.) Community Unit # 100, 1971-90, tchr. jr. high sch., adminstrv. asst., 1990-91, tchr. jr. high sch., prin., 1991-92, prin. K-12, 1992-94, supt., 1994—. Author: (cookbook) Our Family Favorites, 1987; compiler: (cookbook) Cookin' with DuBois Center Auxiliary, 1983. Recipient Human Svcs. award Ill. Edn. Assn., 1984. Mem. Ill. Assn. Sch. Adminstrs., Am. Camping Assn., Ill. Women Adminstrs., Patoka Cmty. Edn. Assn. (sec.-treas. 1977-79, v.p. 1979-81, pres. 1981-83), Beta Sigma Phi (v.p., preceptor Delta chpt. 1992-93, 4 Mem. of Yr. awards, pres. preceptor Delta chpt. 1993-94). Mem. United Ch. of Christ. Home: 502 E Bond Patoka IL 62875-0024 Office: Patoka Community Unit # 100 1220 Kinoka Rd Patoka IL 62875

BORHI, CAROL, data processing executive; b. N.Y.C., Oct. 23, 1949; d. Carl and Elsie Elizabeth (Varady) Chaky; m. Nicholas Anthony Borhi, Sept. 23, 1972; children: Christy Nicole, Nicholas James. Assoc. in Applied Sci., Manhattan Community Coll., 1970; student, Hunter Coll., 1967-68, 70-71. Programmer asst. N.Y. Telephone, N.Y.C., 1970-73, programmer, 1974-76, programmer analyst, 1976-83; staff analyst Nynex Svc. Co., N.Y.C., 1984-87; systems analyst Nynex Corp., N.Y.C., 1987; assoc. dir. Nynex Corp., White Plains, N.Y., 1987-90; staff dir. Nynex Corp., White Plains, 1987-91, White Plains, N.Y., 1991—; pres. Personal Touch Computing, N.Y.C., 1981-86. Mem. Telephone Pioneers Am. (charter), Creative Investors Am. Republican. Roman Catholic. Club: Sacred Heart. Office: Nynex Corp 1111 Westchester Ave White Plains NY 10604-3509

BORLAND, CAROL LOUISE, chemist; b. Marion, Ohio, July 1, 1958; d. John A. and Helen L. (Ruhl) B. BA in Chemistry, BA in Biology, Malone Coll., 1980. Chemist Wadsworth/Alert Labs., Canton, Ohio, 1980-85, GC-MS mgr., 1985-86; chemist quality control Roxane Labs., Columbus, Ohio, 1987-88; chemist II Westreco, Inc., Marysville, Ohio, 1988-92, devel. technologist, 1992—. Sec. Camp Union, Byhalia, Ohio, 1991-94. Mem. Am. Chem. Soc., Inst. Food Technologists. Office: Westreco Inc Marysville OH 43040

BORMASTER, LISA CURTIS, publisher; b. Greeley, Colo., Mar. 21, 1960; d. Arnold Raymond and Karen Denise (Wetig) Napoleon. BSBA summa cum laude, Ariz. State U., 1983. Assoc. account exec. DBG&H Mktg., Advt., Phoenix, 1983-84; advt. rep. Ind. Newspapers, Inc., Phoenix, 1984-85, advt. mgr., 1985-86, mktg. dir., 1986-88, publ., gen. mgr., 1988-90, dir. sales and mktg., 1990-91; display advt. mgr. Ariz. Bus. Gazette, Phoenix, 1991-92; dir. advt. Washington Bus. Jur., 1992-94; pub. Austin (Tex.) Bus. Jour., 1995—; mem. Bd. of Trade. Bd. dirs. BBB, 1991-92, Austin Quality Coun. Mem. Phoenix Advt. Club (bd. dirs. 1988-92, pres. 1991-92), Scottsdale C. of C., Paradise Valley C. of C. (bd. dirs. 1989-90). Republican. Office: Austin Bus Jour Ste B224 1301 S Capital of Texas Hwy Austin TX 78746

BORN, EMILY MARIE, editor, association executive; b. Lawton, Okla., Oct. 2, 1959; d. George Arthur and Sumiko (Nagamine) B. BS, Ball State U., 1981. Cert. rural electric communicator Nat. Rural Electric Coop. Assn. Feature writer The News-Sentinel, Fort Wayne, Ind., 1981-83; wire editor The Noblesville (Ind.) Daily Ledger, 1983; staff writer Ind. Statewide Assn. Rural Electric Coops., Indpls., 1983-84, mng. editor, 1984-85, editor, 1985—. Author: Power to the People, 1985. Mem. Coop. Communicators Assn. (Michael Graznak award 1990), Internat. Assn. Bus. Communicators (award of excellence dist. 7 1985), Elec. Women's Round Table Inc. (Power award 1994), Electric Inst. Ind., Rural Electric Statewide Editors Assn. Office: Ind Statewide Assn RECs 720 N High School Rd Indianapolis IN 46214-3756

BORN, ETHEL WOLFE, church worker; b. Kasson, W.Va., Jan. 6, 1924; d. Otto Guy and Nancy Grace (Nestor) Wolfe; m. Harry Edward Born, Apr. 4, 1944 (dec. Aug. 1992); children: Rosemary Ellen (dec.), Barbara Anne Born Craig. Student, Ecumenical Inst., Geneva, 1983; BA, Mary Baldwin Coll., 1991. Author: A Tangled Web--A Search for Answers to the Question of Palestine, 1989, By My Spirit, Methodist Protestant Women in Mission, 1879-1939, 1990; contbr. articles to religious publs. Va. pres. United Meth. Women, 1972-76; bd. dirs. United Meth. Gen. Bd. Global Ministries, N.Y.C., 1976-84, v.p. women's div., 1980-84, v.p. com. on relief, 1980-84, Mid. East cons. women's div., 1984-88; chmn. N.Am. Coordinating Com. for Non-govtl. Orgns. on Question of Palestine, 1986-87, chmn. UN Symposium, N.Y.C., 1986, 87; pres. N.Am. area, asst. world treas. World Fedn. Meth. Women, 1986-91, archivist, 1992—; mem. United Meth. Gen. Comm. Christian Unity and Inter-Religious Concerns, N.Y.C., 1988—. Mem. Nat. League Am. Pen Women. Home: 3789 Knollridge Rd Salem VA 24153-1938

BORNE, BONITA H., ballet dancer, assistant artistic director; b. L.A., July 2, 1953; d Hal and Rose Frances (Ducoff) B. Student, Le Lycée Francais, L.A., Sch. Am. Ballet, 1969-70. Dancer N.Y.C. Ballet Co., 1970-80; soloist Zurich (Switzerland) Ballet, 1980-82; dancer William Carter Dance Ensemble, N.Y.C., 1982-84; asst. dir. Zurich Ballet, 1985; teacher Carol Sumner's Amer. Ballet Acad., Stamford, Conn., 1984; ballet mistress, asst. artistic dir. San Francisco Ballet Co., 1985—; Asst. dir., Dance Dept. of the Chautauqua Inst. of the Arts. Repertoire includes roles in Chaconne, Interplay, Emeralds, A Midsummer Night's Dream, Coppelia, Apollo; staged numerous Balanchine works including Rubies, Tarantella, Tchaikovsky Pas de Deux, Symphony in C, Ballo della Regina, The Four Temperaments, Valse-Fantasie, Minkus Pas de Trois, Pas de Dix, Raymonda variations; staged William Forsythe's In the Middle, Somewhat Elevated for the ballet of British Columbia, Vancouver. Jewish. Office: San Francisco Ballet 455 Franklin St San Francisco CA 94102-4471*

BORNEMAN, ALICE GREGORY, educator; b. Wilkes-Barre, Pa., June 15, 1940; d. Dwight Lewis and Margaret Elizabeth (Wolfe) Gregory; m. Edward Leo Borneman, Dec. 29, 1962; children: Margaret Ann, Linda Marie, Edward Gregory, Clayton Gregory. BS in Edn., Rider Coll., Lawrenceville, N.J., 1962; MA in Edn., Rider Coll., 1989. Bus. edn. tchr. Woodstown (N.J.) High Sch., 1962-64, Interboro High Sch., Glenolden, Pa., 1966-67, Parkland High Sch., El Paso, Tex., 1967-69, Lower Cape May (N.J.) High Sch., 1972-73; bus. edn. tchr. Wildwood (N.J.) High Sch., 1979—, chmn. dept. computer and bus., 1990—; adj. prof. Atlantic Community Coll., 1990—. Exec. bd. mem. N.J. Bus. Edn. Assn., 1994-96; sec. Wildwood Civic Club, 1983-88; adv. coun. Cape May County Vocat. Sch., 1989—; mem. mastectomy support group Burdette Tomlin Meml. Hosp.; vol. Reach for Recovery; co-facilitator cancer support group Burdette-Tomlin Meml. Hosp. Recipient Walter A. Brower award for devotion to excellence in field of bus. edn., Rider Coll., 1989, Career Achievement award Wildwood Bd. Edn., 1994. Mem. AAUW, Delta Pi Epsilon, Delta Kappa Gamma. Republican. Roman Catholic. Home: 8504 Seaview Ave Wildwood NJ 08260-3544 Office: Wildwood High Sch 4300 Pacific Ave Wildwood NJ 08260-4689

BORNINO-GLUSAC, ANNA MARIA, mathematics educator; b. Naples, Italy, Apr. 2, 1946; came to U.S., 1946; d. Bruno and Anna Maria (De Simone) B.; m. Howard Keith Wolff, July 29, 1966 (div. 1971); 1 child, Francesca Yvonne Wolff; m. Ronald G. Glusac, Sept. 4, 1993. BA in Chemistry, Calif. State U., Dominguez Hills, 1968, MA in Edn. Adminstrv. Svcs., 1986. Cert. standard secondary tchr., Calif., preliminary adminstrv., Calif., Spanish lang. fluency, Calif. Tchr. math. L.A. Unified Sch. Dist., 1968—, dept. chair, 1982-84, 90—. Editor: Accreditation Report, 1983. Mem. Math. Assn. Am., United Tchrs. L.A. Democrat. Roman Catholic. Office: Narbonne High Sch 24300 Western Ave Harbor City CA 90710-1799

BORNSTEIN, RITA, academic administrator; b. N.Y.C., Jan. 2, 1936; d. Carl and Florence (Gates) Kropf; children: Rachel, Mark, Per; m. Harland G. Bloland. BA in English, Fla. Atlantic U., 1970, MA in English, 1971; PhD in Ednl. Leadership and Instrn., U. Miami, 1975. Tchr., adminstr. Dade County Pub. Schs. (Fla.), 1971-75; adminstr. dept. edn. U. Miami, Coral Gables, 1975-81, adminstr. divsn. of devel., 1981-85, v.p., 1985-90; pres. Rollins Coll., Winter Park, Fla., 1990—; dir. Barnett Bank Ctrl. Fla., Barnett Banks, Inc. Author: Freedom or Order: Must We Choose?, 1976; Title IX Compliance and Sex Equity: Definitions, Distinctions, Costs and Benefits, 1981; contbr. articles to profl. jours. Mem. Am. Coun. on Edn. (mem. com. leadership devel. 1991-93, bd. dirs. 1995—), Nat. Assn. Ind. Colls. and Univs. (bd. dirs. 1992-95, chair govt. rels. com. 1994-95), Fla. Coun. of 100. Office: Rollins Coll Office of Pres 1000 Holt Ave-2711 Winter Park FL 32789-4499

BOROWSKI, JENNIFER LUCILE, corporate administrator; b. Jersey City, Oct. 23, 1934; d. Peter Anthony and Ludwika (Zapolska) B. BS, St. Peter's Coll., 1968; postgrad., Pace Coll., 1976-77. Mgr. benefits Amerada Petroleum Corp., N.Y.C., 1951-66, Mt. Sinai Hosp., N.Y.C., 1966-67; mgr. payroll and payroll taxes Haskins & Sells, N.Y.C., 1967-74; mgr. payroll and payroll tax Cushman & Wakefield, Inc., N.Y.C., 1975-89. Mem. Am. Payroll Assn. (bd. dirs. 1979-81, cert.), Am. Mgmt. Assn., Am. Soc. Payroll Mgrs., Internat. Platform Assn. (hon.), Am. Soc. Profl. Exec. Women, NAFE. Home: 36 Front St North Arlington NJ 07031-5822

BORSOS, ERIKA, medical-surgical and cardiac care nurse; b. Bakonycsernye, Hungary, May 8, 1952; d. John and Elizabeth (Nyevrikel) B. ADN, Thornton Community Coll., 1974, AS, 1979; BSN cum laude, U. S. Fla., 1984. RN Fla., Ind., Ill.;cert. BLS, ACLS Am. Heart Assn. Staff nurse, relief charge nurse Ingalls Meml. Hosp., Harvey, Ill., 1974-79; staff nurse, team leader Sarasota (Fla.) Meml. Hosp., 1979-84; staff nurse/clin. nurse I/cardiac cath. recovery/preceptor Venice (Fla.) Hosp., 1985—. Editor, writer Cardiac Courier. Vol. pub. edn. Am. Cancer Soc., Sarasota Fla., 1983-90. Ill. State scholar, 1970. Mem. AACCN, NLN (advocacy), Inst. Noetic Sci., Venice Hosp. Found., Folk Dance Coun., Sigma Theta Tau, Phi Theta Kappa (scholar). Home: 7416 Bounty Dr Sarasota FL 34231-7920

BORST-MANNING, DIANE GAIL, management consultant; b. Rochester, N.Y., Nov. 5, 1937; d. Howard Louis and Emily Kathleen (Crew) Borst; m. Steven Manning, Sept. 11, 1979 (dec. May 1991); m. Norman Edward Berg, Apr. 4, 1992. B.A. cum laude, Wagner Coll., 1959; M.B.A., N.Y.U., 1966. Planner N.Y.U. Med. Ctr., N.Y.C., 1962-76, assoc. dir. planning, 1976-78, dir. mgmt. services, 1978-80; dir. human resources Mt. Sinai Med. Ctr., N.Y.C., 1980-85, dir. planning, 1985-86; sr. v.p. The Manning Orgn., Inc., 1986—; pres. Diane Borst Manning Assocs., Inc., 1986—; instr. dept. health care mgmt. CUNY, 1982-92; adj. faculty Orange County Community Coll., 1986-88, Sarah lawrence Coll., New Sch. Social Research, 1986-92, St. Joseph's Coll., 1992—. Editor: Managing Non-Profit Organizations, 1979. Author: (cassette) Managers and Secretaries—How to Achieve Teamwork, 1980. Chairperson grants Port Jervis Council for Arts; mem. Health Systems Agy. Bd., N.Y.C., 1976-79; trustee Helene Fuld Sch. Nursing, N.Y.C., 1989—; mem. planning com. of bd. Mercy Community Hosp., Port Jervis, N.Y.; mem. adv. bd. Inst. Bus. Industry & Govt. Orange County Community Coll. Fulbright fellow, 1959. Mem. N.Y. Personnel Mgmt. Assn. (bd. dirs. 1974-76), Greater N.Y. Hosp. Assn., Am. Compensation Assn., Bur. Nat. Affairs (personnel policy forum 1983-84), Am. Assn. Hosp. Planners, Assn. Am. Med. Colls. Group on Instrl. Planning. Club: City (N.Y.) Avocations: gardening; auto mechanics; carpentry, real estate. Office: 40 W 55th St Ste 9D New York NY 10019-5316

BORUCKI, LYNDA SUE, economic and financial consultant; b. Milw., Aug. 2, 1958; d. Quentin J. and Joan T. Borucki. BA in Math. and Econ., U. Wis., 1980; MS Managerial Econs. and Decision Scis., Northwestern U., 1984, postgrad., 1985-90. Rsch. asst. Christensen & Assocs., Madison, Wis., 1980-83; lectr. Northwestern U., Evanston, Ill., 1986-90; assoc. Putnam, Hayes & Bartlett, Cambridge, Mass., 1990-92, The Brattle Group, Cambridge, 1992—; fellow Northwestern U., 1983-87. Vilas scholar, 1976-77. Mem. NOW, Am. Econ. Assn., Crucible, Phi Beta Kappa, Phi Kappa Phi, Sigma Epsilon Sigma, Omicron Delta Epsilon. Office: Brattle/IRI 50 Church St Cambridge MA 02138

BORUT, JOSEPHINE, insurance executive; b. Bridgeport, Conn., Aug. 3, 1942; d. Frank and Catherine (Russo) Occhipinti; m. Arthur Lee Borut, Nov. 22, 1963; 1 child, Adam Seth. BS in Art, Hofstra U., 1964, MA in Humanities, 1971; cert. in mgmt., Adelphi U., 1984. Cert. art tchr., N.Y.; cert. mtgs. profl. Art tchr. Cen. Islip (N.Y.) Elem., 1964-65; coord. art dept. Mineola (N.Y.) Jr. High, 1965-70; art tchr., coord. Brandeis Sch., Lawrence, N.Y., 1979-81; mgr. community rels. Empire Blue Cross/Blue Shield, N.Y.C., 1984-85, mgr. conf. planning, 1985—; freelance artist, East Meadow, 1978-79; lectr. meeting planning. Contbr. articles to profl. jours. Recipient hon. mention L.I. Art Tchrs. Assn. Art Show,1966, 3d pl. art show Hofstra U., 1966, 2d pl. East Meadow Pub. Libr. Juried Art Show, 1979; Inst. II scholar, 1991, Profl. Edn. Conf. scholar, 1990. Mem. NAFE, NOW, Am. Soc. Assn. Execs., Meeting Planners Internat. Greater N.Y. (bd. dirs., com. chmn., pres. 1992-93, Meeting Planner of Yr. 1991), Am. Soc. Profl. and Exec. Women, Ins. Conf. Planners. Home: 1823 Kent St Westbury NY 11590-5305 Office: Empire Blue Cross/Blue Shield 622 3d Ave New York NY 10017

BORYSEWICZ, MARY LOUISE, editor; b. Chgo.; d. Thomas J. and Mabel E. (Zeien) O'Farrell m. Daniel S. Borysewicz, June 11, 1955; children: Mary Adele, Stephen Francis, Paul Barnabas. BA, Mundelein Coll., 1970; postgrad. in English lit., U. Ill, 1970-71; grad. exec. program, U. Chgo., 1982. Editor sci. publs. AMA, Chgo., 1971-73; exec. mng. editor Am. Jour. Ophthalmology, Chgo., 1973—; asst. sec., treas Ophthalmic Pub. Co., 1985—; guest lectr. U. Chgo. Med. Sch., 1979, Harvard U. Med. Sch., 1978, Northwestern U. Med. Sch., 1979, Am. Acad. Ophthalmology, 1976, 81. Editor: Ophthalmology Principles and Concepts, 7th edit., 1992; contbr. articles to sci. publs. Active vol. svcs. Art Inst. Chgo. Mem. Am. Soc. Profl. and Exec. Women, Coun. Biol. Editors (bd. dirs. 1988-91, mem. fin. com. 1985-88, mem. teller com. 1992—). Office: 77 W Wacker Dr Chicago IL 60601

BORYSOW, ALEKSANDRA, physicist, educator; b. Warsaw, Poland, Aug. 9, 1955; d. Kazimierz Jan and Halina Stefania (Dreszer) Jankowska; m. Jacek Ireneusz Borysow, Feb. 5, 1976 (div. Nov. 1994); 1 child, Michael. BSc, MS, U. Warsaw, 1979; PhD, U. Tex., 1985. Rsch. assoc. Inst. for Nuc. Rsch., Warsaw, Poland; rschr., instr. U. Warsaw, 1979-82; rsch. assoc. U. Tex., Austin, 1982-85, postdoctoral rsch. assoc., 1985-87; rsch. assoc. Joint Inst. for Lab. Astro., Boulder, Colo., 1987-89; asst. prof. Mich. Tech. U., Houghton, 1989-94, assoc. prof., 1994—. Contbr. numerous articles to profl. jours. Grantee NATO Collaborative Rsch. Grants, 1989, 94, rsch. planning grantee NSF, 1990, rsch. grantee NASA Divsn. Planetary Atmospheres, 1992, 93, 94. Mem. Am. Phys. Soc., Am. Astro. Soc. (divsn. planetary scis.), Planetary Soc. Office: Mich Tech U 1400 Townsend Dr Houghton MI 49931

BORZI, PHYLLIS C., counsel; b. Port Jefferson, N.Y., Aug. 10, 1946; d. Phillip L. and Marie R. (Mirabelli) B. BA, Ladycliff Coll., 1968; MA, Syracuse U., 1969; JD, Cath. U., 1978. Bar: D.C. 1978. Tchr. high sch. English, 1969-75; rsch. asst. pension consulting firm, 1975-77; assoc. Hogan & Hartson, 1978-79; majority legis. assoc. Ho. Pension Task Force, 1979-81; counsel pensions and employee benefits Subcom. Labor-Mgmt. Rels. Ho. Com. Edn. and Labor, 1981—. Editor-in-chief Cath. U. Law Rev. Mem. ABA, Bar Assn. of D.C., D.C. Bar Assn., Women's Bar Assn., Women Employee Benefits (past pres.). Office: Subcom on Labor Mgmt Relations 112 Cannon House Office Bldg Washington DC 20515*

BOSCH, DONNA, home health nurse administrator; b. Emmons County, N.D., Sept. 26, 1945; d. Peter and Rose (Ternes) Silbernagel; m. Frank Bosch, June 5, 1965; children: Lynette, Darrin, Wade. BSN, Mary Coll., 1967; MSN, U. Mary, Bismarck, N.D., 1988. RN, N.D.; cert. in community health, 1986, 91. Instr. Mary Coll., Bismarck; EPS coord. Bismarck Burleigh Nursing Svc., home health nurse; home care coord., exec. dir. Home Med. Resources, Bismarck. N.D. Nurses Assn. grantee. Mem. ANA, N.D. Pub. Health Assn., Cath. Daus. Am., Sigma Theta Tau. Home: 4885 Wildrose Cr Bismarck ND 58501

BOSCOE, CLAUDIA FRANCES, office machine company executive; b. Chgo., Aug. 3, 1948; d. Leland Orville and Marie (Swakow) Stromquist; m. John J. Boscoe, Apr. 17, 1983. Paralegal cert., Pa. State U., 1992. Cert. flight attendant. Sec. The Selz Orgn., Chgo., 1966-68; flight attendant Republic Air Lines, Mpls., 1969-84; pres. Concepts Unltd., Inc., Chester Heights, Pa., 1988—. Co-chair Libr. Fundraising Campaign, Concord Twp., 1987-88; chair Dedication Com. Twp. and Libr. Bldgs., Concord Twp., 1989; bd. dirs. Fox Valley Community Assn., Glen Mills, Pa., 1985-86, pres., 1987; bd. dirs. Delaware County S.P.C.A., 1991; minority insp. Dem. Party Deleware County, Concord Twp., 1989; legal vol. Domestic Abuse Project Del. County, 1993—. Mem. 2d Edit. Cub (pres. 1988-89), Welcome Wagon Club (pres. 1986-87). Roman Catholic.

BOSEKER, BARBARA JEAN, educator; b. Milw., Dec. 2, 1944; d. Edward Herbert and Alice Margaret (Maas) B.; student U. Nigeria, Nsukka, 1966; BS (hon.) in Secondary Edn. (Elks Nat. and State Youth scholar), U. Wis., Milw., 1968; MA in Anthropology (Ford Found. fellow 1968-69, NDEA fellow 1970-71), U. Wis., Madison, 1971, PhD in Edn. (NDEA fellow), 1978; m. Dale Leslie Sutcliffe, Aug. 8, 1975. Chemistry lab. technician Allen-Bradley Corp., Milw., 1963; coordinator Neighborhood Youth Corps, Madison, 1970; program devel. specialist Tchr. Corps, Madison, 1976-77; asst. prof. edn. Occidental Coll., 1978-80, Moorhead State U., 1980-86, assoc. prof., 1986-90, prof., 1990—; cons. Inst. Latin Am. Studies, U. Tex., Austin, 1980. Grant writer Fargo-Moorhead (N.D.) Indian Center, 1980; evaluator Indian edn. grant Fargo Pub. Schs., 1985-90. Cert. intermediate and secondary English tchr., Wis. Mem. NEA, Minn. Edn. Assn., Nat. Women's Studies Assn., Mortar Bd., Phi Kappa Phi, Pi Lambda Theta, Kappa Delta Pi, Sigma Tau Delta, Sigma Epsilon Sigma. Democrat. Christian Scientist. Contbr. articles to profl. jours. Home: 809 19th Ave S Fargo ND 58103-4926 Office: Moorhead State U Moorhead MN 56563

BOSHIER, MAUREEN LOUISE, health facilities administrator; b. Elizabeth, N.J., Oct. 1, 1946; d. John Henry and Mary Hanora (McGarry) B.; m. Robert Hall Rea, May 23, 1987. BSN, Coll. Misericordia, Dallas, Pa., 1968; MS in Psychiat. Nursing, U. Colo., 1973; MBA, U. Phoenix, 1987. Clin. specialist psychiat. nursing Denver Gen. Hosp., 1973-74; dir. rehab. services N.Mex. Cancer Control, Albuquerque, 1976-80; exec. dir. N.Mex. State Bd. Nursing, Albuquerque, 1980-84; exec. v.p. N.Mex. Hosp. Assn., Albuquerque, 1984-88; adminstr. surg. services, sr. nursing adminstr. U. N.Mex. Hosp., Albuquerque, 1988-94; CEO, pres. N.Mex. Hosps. and Health Systems Assn., Albuquerque, 1995—; dir. Profl. Seminar Cons., Inc., Albuquerque, 1982—; v.p. exec. bd. N.Mex. Health Resources, Albuquerque, 1981—, pres., 1989; vice chmn., bd. dirs. Hosp. Home Health Care, Albuquerque, 1978—; dir. Acad. Seminars, Inc., 1982—. Contbr. articles to profl. jours. Sec. N.Mex. Ballet Co., Albuquerque, 1982-87; vice chmn. Gov.'s Task Force on Nursing Issues, Albuquerque, 1982-88; adv. bd. Sub-area Coun. Health Systems, Albuquerque, 1980-84. Capt. U.S. Army, 1967-71. Recipient Woman on the Move award YWCA, 1992, Wharton Sch. of Bus. fellowship for health care execs., 1993. Mem. Am. Orgn. Nurse Execs. (vice chmn. legis. advocacy com. 1992-94, chmn. 1993-94), N.Mex. Orgn. Nurse Execs. (treas. 1988-89, pres. 1990), N.Mex. League for Nursing, N.Mex. Nurses Assn. (Nurse Adminstr. award 1984), Rotary, Albuquerque C. of C. (quality of life com. 1994—), Sigma Theta Tau (pres.-elect 1994, pres. 1995—, Mentor award Gamma Sigma chpt. 1994). Democrat. Home: 214 Tornasol Ln NE Albuquerque NM 87113-1213 : NM

BOSLEY, KAREN LEE, English and journalism educator; b. Beech Grove, Ind., Sept. 23, 1942; d. Lowell Holmes and Kathryn Gertrude (Drake) Foley; AB in Lang. Arts summa cum laude, U. Indpls., 1965; MA in English, Northwestern U., 1967; MA in Journalism, Ball State U., 1984; postgrad. (Newspaper Fund fellow), U. Mo., 1973, Ohio U., 1977; m. Norman Keith Bosley, Dec. 21, 1964; children: Mark Harold, Rachael Kathryn, Keith Lowell, Sidney Clark. Copy editor, reporter Indpls. News, 1963-65; English tchr., yearbook adviser Beech Grove (Ind.) Jr. High Sch., 1965-66; English tchr. So. Regional High Sch., Manahawkin, N.J., 1967-68; prof. humanities, journalism and English, student newspaper adviser Ocean County Coll., Toms River, N.J., 1971—; part time reporter Daily Times-Observer, Toms River, 1972-77, part-time copy editor, 1993. Trustee Long Beach Island Hist. Assn., Friends of Island Library, 1975-79; pres. Long Beach I. PTA; chmn. Long Beach Twp. Dem. Mcpl. Com., 1971-78; Dem. committeeman Long Beach Twp. Dist. 2, 1971-78, 85—; mem. Long Beach Twp. Recreation Commn., 1972-77, chmn., 1972-75; bd. dirs. Ocean County Red Cross, 1972-78, Ocean County Family Planning, Inc., 1972-78, Student Press Law Ctr., 1989—; chmn. Cub Scout pack 32, Ocean County Council Boy Scouts Am.; founder, bd. dirs. Long Beach I. Hist. Assn., Island Democrats, Inc.; adminstrv. bd. First United Meth. Ch. Beach Haven Terrace (N.J.). Mem. AAUW (pres., dir. Barnegat Light Area br.), NEA, N.J. Edn. Assn., Ocean County Edn. Assn., Faculty Assn. Ocean County Coll. (v.p. 1984-85), Coll. Media Advisers, Inc. (disting. newspaper adviser for U.S. 2-yr. colls. 1978, dir., sec.), Assn. Edn. in Journalism and Mass Communications, Community Coll. Journalism Assn. (dir., v.p.), Soc. Profl. Journalists, Sigma Delta Chi. Contbr. article to publ. in field. Home: 9 E Old Whaling Ln Long Beach Township NJ 08008-2930 Office: Ocean CC PO Box 2001 College Dr Toms River NJ 08754-2001

BOSSCAWEN, SUSAN, banking executive; b. Rockville Center, N.Y., Feb. 13, 1956; d. William Henry and Beatrice Marie (Shunk) Koelbel. BSBA, Coll. St. Rose, 1978; MBA, U. Miami, Fla., 1988; postgrad., Harvard U., 1994. Fin. analyst Southeast Bank, Miami, 1978-80; ops. support Pan Am. Bank, Miami, 1980-82; v.p. support svcs. Am. Savs. & Loan, Miami, 1982-87; v.p. mgmt. svcs. NCNB, Charlotte, N.C., 1987-89; sr. v.p. NationsBanc Svc. Co., Inc., Dallas, 1989—. Mem. adv. bd. All Our Children, Dallas, 1993. Mem. NAFE, NOW, Treasury Mgmt. Assn. Republican. Roman Catholic.

BOSTED, DOROTHY STACK, public relations executive; b. Newark, Apr. 6, 1953; d. Richard Joseph and Dorothy Marie (Irvin) S.; m. Kenneth James Bosted, Aug. 22, 1976; 1 child, Danielle Whitney. Student, Lyndon State Coll., 1971-73; BA, NYU, 1975. Reporter The Daily Advance, Succasunna, N.J., 1974-75; producer, tech. intern Manhattan Cable TV, N.Y.C., 1975; editorial asst. Calif. Sch. Employees Assn., San Jose, 1975-76; news dir., anchor UA-Columbia Cablevision, Oakland, N.J., 1977-79; dir. pub. relations Overlook Hosp., Summit, N.J., 1981-84; pres. Dorothy Bosted Pub. Relations, Harding Twp., N.J., 1984-86; dir. pub. relations, communications Middlesex County Coll., Edison, N.J., 1986-88; mgr. corp. communications Hoechst Celanese Corp., Bridgewater, N.J., 1988-89; ptnr. Bosted-Burton Assocs., Coral Springs, Fla., 1986—; cons. Coral Springs, 1986—. Co-author: Writing with Impact, 1986; contbr. articles to N.Y. Times, various mags. Seminar leader Kinnelon (N.J.) Enrichment Program, 1978; trustee Middlesex County Coll. Found., Edison, 1986-88; bd. dirs. Middlesex County Coll. Alumni Assn., 1986-88. Recipient News Program ACE award Nat. Cable TV Assn., 1979, Spectrum of Talent merit award Internat. Assn. Bus. Communicators, 1982, Percy award N.J. Hosp. Mktg. and Pub. Relations Assn., 1982, 84, Tribute to Women and Industry award YWCA, Ridgewood, N.J., 1979; Mennen Co. scholar, 1971, Neighborhood House scholar, 1971, KP scholar, 1971. Mem. Tribute to Women and Indsutry Mgmt. Forum (v.p. pub. rels. Ridgewood chpt. 1986-87, bd. dirs. cen. N.J. chpt. 1989-91), Pub. Rels. Soc. Am. (editor N.J. chpt. newsletter 1987-89, bd. dirs. N.J. chpt. 1989-91). Home: 8738 NW 19th Dr Coral Springs FL 33071-6155

BOSTEK-BRADY, EVA MARIA, veterinarian; b. Passaic, N.J., June 21, 1961; d. Charles and Stella (Stepien) Bostek; m. Thomas Michael Brady Jr., May 23, 1992. BS with distinction, Cornell U., 1983; DVM summa cum laude, Ohio State U., 1987. Lic. N.J., N.Y., Mass., N.H., Vt., Pa. Veterinarian Anchor Animal Hosp., North Dartmouth, Mass., 1987-89, Madison (N.J.) Vet. Hosp., 1989—; cons. vet. The Seeing Eye, Inc., Morristown, N.J., 1989-91, St. Hubert's Giralda, Madison, N.J., 1989—; vet. coll. tutor Ohio State U., Columbus, 1985; coll. teaching asst. Cornell U., Ithaca, N.Y., 1981-83. Team capt. Ohio State U. Fund Raising Campaign, Mass., 1989; mem. exec. com. student chpt. Am. Vet. Med. Assn., Columbus, 1983-87; fin. aid com. grad. profl. coun., Columbus, 1983-85. Scholarship Am. Soc. of Animal Sci., 1983; named Presdl. Scholars finalist U.S. Office Edn., 1979. Mem. Am. Vet. Med. Assn., Am. Animal Hosp. Assn., Met. N.J. Vet. Med. Assn., Ohio State Vet. Medicine Alumni Assn., Cornell Agrl. and Life Scis. Alumni Assn., Cornell Clubs, Phi Kappa Phi, Phi Zeta, Omega Tau Sigma (class rep. 1983-86). Democrat. Roman Catholic. Home: 17 Old Army Rd Bernardsville NJ 07924-1808 Office: Madison Vet Hosp 262 Main St Madison NJ 07940-2210

BOSTIC, JACQUELINE WHITING, management consultant, retired postmaster, association executive; b. Houston, Jan. 3, 1938; d. Samuel and Martha (Countee) Whiting; m. Joseph W. Bostic, July 15, 1960 (dec. 1991); children: Shelby Lance, Ursula Jimmison, Kirksten Sinclair, Jacqueline F. Student, Fisk U., Hofstra Coll.; BA in Psychology, Tex. So. U., Houston. Libr. asst. N.Y. Pub. Libr., 1958-59; edn. specialist U.S. Postal Svc., 1967-74, investigator so. region, 1974-86; officer-in-charge U.S. Postal Svc., Highlands, Tex., 1980; postmaster U.S. Postal Svc., Porter, Tex., 1986-92; officer-in-charge U.S. Postal Svc., Pearland, Tex., 1988; comms. mgr. U.S. Postal Svc., 1990; pres. Mgmt.-Orgn. Cons., 1992—; substitute tchr. Houston Ind. Sch. Dist., 1968-70; chmn., bd. dirs. Houston Postal Credit Union, 1990-92; lectr. mgmt. seminars., 1968—. Editor Intercom, Jack & Jill Am. Found. Nat. v.p. Jack & Jill Am., Inc., 1982-86; bd. dirs. Jack & Jill Am. Found.; nat. bd. dirs. YWCA of U.S.A., 1987-94, vol. mgmt. trainer, 1981—; pres. and chmn. bd. dirs. Houston Met. YWCA, 1982-86; active A-PLUS, UNCF, Telethon Gala; trustee Antioch Missionary Bapt. Ch., YWCA Retirement Fund; commnr. Clean Houston Commn.; legis. rep. Tex. Postal Workers. Recipient Black Houstonians Making History award, 1986, Dist. Achievement award Nat. Coun. Negro Women, Civic award Houston chpt. YWCA, Outstanding Svc. award United Negro Coll. Fund; named Vol. of Yr., Houston chpt. YWCA, Outstanding Vol., United Way/YWCA, Outstanding Jiller, Jack & Jill Am., Inc.; named to Pres.'s Cir., Houston C. of C. Mem. AFL-CIO (pres. Clerk Craft, Am. Postal Workers Union 1980-82, mem. ctrl. labor coun., bd. dirs. Tex. chpt.), NAACP, HMAC (bd. dirs.), NAFE, Nat. League Postmasters, Nat. Assn. Postmasters, Am. Bus. and Profl. Women, Network, United Negro Coll. Fund (Outstanding Svc. award), Rotary, Booker T. Washington Alumni Assn., Fisk Univ. Alumni Club, East Montgomery County C. of C., Delta Sigma Theta (bd. dirs., pres. Houston met. chpt. 1982-86, v.p. Delta Edn. and Charitable Found. 1992—). Home: 4410 Roseneath Dr Houston TX 77021-1617

BOSTON, BETTY LEE, investment broker, financial planner; b. Agana, Guam, Dec. 21, 1935; d. Homer Laurence and Bessie Margarete (Leech) Litzenberg; m. Filibert Roth Boston, Aug. 12, 1956; children: William Litzenberg, Beth Boston Tedesco, Brent Litzenberg. BA, U. Mich., 1958. Cert. Fin. Planner. Stockbroker I.M. Simon & Co., Murray, Ky., 1976-78, Ist of Mich. Corp., Murray, 1978-86; investment broker J.J.B. Hilliard, W.L. Lyons, Inc., Murray, 1986—; instr. adult edn. investment classes Murray State U., 1977—; investment commentator Sta. WKMS, Murray, 1987—. Investment columnist Purchase Area Bus. Jour., 1989-90. Chmn. Inter-Faith Coalition Congregations, Ann Arbor, 1971-73; pres. Need Line Ch. and Community Ministry, Murray, 1981-83; mem. Murray regional bd. Ky. Coun. on Econ. Edn., 1987—. Mem. AAUW (treas. Murray br. 1982-87, pres. Murray br. 1991—), Murray Bus. and Profl. Women (pres. 1988-90, Woman of Yr. award 1988), Rotary (sec. Murray chpt. 1990—). Methodist. Home: 917 N 16th St Murray KY 42071 Office: JJB Hilliard WL Lyons Inc 414 Main St Murray KY 42071

BOSTON, BILLIE, costume designer; b. Oklahoma City, Sept. 22, 1939; d. William Barrett and Margaret Emeline (Townsend) Long; m. William Clayton Boston, Jr., Jan. 20, 1962; children: Kathryn Gray, William Clayton III. BFA, U. Okla., 1961, MFA, 1962. Asst. to designer Karinski of N.Y., N.Y.C., 1966-67; prof. Oklahoma City U., 1987—; rep. Arts Coun., Oklahoma City, 1987-90, Arts Festival, Oklahoma City, 1972-80; dir. ETC Theater, Oklahoma City SW Coll., 1979-83; actress Lyric Theatre, Oklahoma City, 1979-81. Exhibited in group shows at Taos, N.Mex., Santa Fe; represented in permanent collection in Dallas, Taos, Santa Fe, Tulsa, N.Y.C., LaJolla; costume designer Ballet Okla., Oklahoma City, 1979-84, Agnes DeMillie's Rodeo Ballet Okla., 1982, Royal Ballet Flanders, 1983, Pitts. Ballet, 1983, BBC's Childrens Prodn., 1984, 86, Lyric Theatre, Oklahoma City, 1987—, Red Oak Music Theatre, Lakewood, N.J., 1988, Winter Olympics, 1988, Miss Am. Pagent, 1988, for JoAnne Worley in Hello Dolly, San Francisco Opera Circus, 1991, Jupiter (Fla.) Theatre, 1991—, Mame prodn. Conn. Broadway Theatre, 1991-92, Mobile (Ala.) Light Opera, 1992. Rep. Speakers Bur. Oklahoma City for Ballet, 1979-85; judge State Hist. Speech Tournament, Oklahoma City, 1985-87; chmn. State of Okla. Conf. on Tchr./Student Relationships, Oklahoma City, 1981. Recipient Gov.'s Achievement award, 1988, Lady in the News award, 1987. Mem. Alpha Chi Omega (house corp. bd. 1986-90). Methodist. Home: 1701 Camdenway Oklahoma City OK 73116

BOSTON, LEONA, organization executive; b. Joliet, Ill., Aug. 4, 1914; d. Dorie Philip and Margaret (Mitchell) B. Student LaSalle Extension U., 1936-37, 1946, U. Chgo., 1944-45. Tchr., Nat. Stenotype Sch., Chgo., 1937; stenotypist Rotary Internat., Evanston, Ill., 1937-44, sec. to comptroller, 1944-50, head personnel dept., 1950-65, exec. asst. to gen. sec., 1965-77; mem. exec. com. North Shore Festival of Faith, Northfield, Ill., 1978. Bd. dirs. YWCA, Evanston, 1961-63. Mem. Bus. Profl. Women's Club Evanston, 1965-80, chmn. fin. com., 1977-78. Evangelical (fin. sec. Bible Ch., Winnetka 1965-68, treas. 1979-80). Club: Zonta (Evanston, v.p., chmn. program com. 1969-70, pres. 1970-71, mem. membership com. 1976-78, 93-94, chmn. membership com. 1976-78, historian 1979-84, mem. past pres.' com. 1972—, mem. fin. com. 1985-89, 93—, chmn. fin. com. 1987-89, 94—, chmn. club history and archives com. 1989-91, parliamentarian 1991-92, mem. internat. rels. com. 1993-94). Home and Office: 350 W Schaumburg Rd Schaumburg IL 60194-3450 also: 2025 San Marcos Dr SE Winter Haven FL 33880-6632

BOSTON, MARCIA ANN, elementary school educator; b. Akron, Ohio, Jan. 19, 1938; d. Mark Emmett and Mary Elizabeth (McMuldren) Henery; m. Roger Eugene Boston, Aug. 18, 1963; children: Mark Eugene, Craig Henery. BA, Grand Canyon U., 1960. Cert. elem. tchr., Ariz. Tchr. Glendale (Ariz.) Dist., 1960-64; sub. tchr. Itazuke (Japan) Air Base Sch., fall 1964, Washoe County, Reno, Nev., 1965-66, Albany (Oreg.) Sch. Dist., 1968-69; sub. tchr. Wash. Dist., Phoenix, 1970-71, tchr., 1972—. Recipient St. Cecilia award for choir, 1990. Mem. NEA, ASCD, Ariz. Edn. Assn., Washington Dist. Edn. Assn., S.W. Marine Educators Assn., Order Ea. Star (organist Sunnyslope chpt. 47, 1962, 77, 78, 79, 81, 82), Glendale Mothers Club (pres. 1981), Order of Demolay (state pres. 1983-84), Delta Kappa Gamma. Republican. Episcopalian. Office: Orangewood Sch 7337 N 19th Ave Phoenix AZ 85021-7998

BOSWELL, NATHALIE SPENCE, speech pathologist; b. Cleve., May 9, 1924; d. Harrison Morton and Nathalie Muriel (Clem) Spence; student Skidmore Coll, 1941-42; MusB in Edn., Northwestern U., 1945; MA, Western Res. U., 1961; m. June 15, 1946; children: Louis Keith, Donna Spence, Deborah Anne. Speech therapist Highland View Hosp., Cleve., 1961-64; speech pathologist Cleve. VA Hosp., 1964-87 ; chmn. Equal Employment Opportunity Counselors, 1969-74, Fed. Women Speakers Bur., 1968-87, Fed. Career Info. Program, 1970-72, Fed. Coll. Rels. Coun., 1970-74, Fed. Exec. Bd., 1972-73; adj. instr. Case Western Res. U., 1982-87; mem. adv. coun. sch. electromedicine scis., City U. Los Angeles, 1985; mem. adv. bd. Nat. Inst. Electromedicine Info., 1985; trustee, cons. Donna Spence Boswell Massther, 1992—. Mem. Cleve. Orch. Chorus, 1969-82; vol. Seamen's Svc., 1976—; patron Police Athletic League; mem. Citizen Adv. Com on Solid Waste, Cleveland Heights Ohio, 1989-94. Endowed Tuba Chair, Cleve. Orch., 1983. Recipient Performance award Equal Employment Opportunities, 1973; Quality Increase award, 1980; others; lic. speech pathologist, Ohio. Mem. Am. Speech and Hearing Assn. (cert. clin. competence), Ohio Speech and Hearing Assn., Aphasiology Assn. Ohio, Chi Omega Alumni Assn., Musical Arts Assn., Western Res. Hist. Soc., Cleve. Mus. Natural History (vol. 1988—), Cleve. Mus. Art, Smithsonian Assos., Nat. Wildlife Fedn., Audubon Soc., Nat. Trust Hist. Preservation, Am. Heritage Soc. Mem. Ch. Reorganized Latter-Day Saints. Author: Guidelines for EEO Counselors in their Training Program, 1973; prin. author: Laryngectomy-Orientation for Patients and Families, 1981; contbr., asst. editor: Am. Jour. Electromedicine, 1984. Home: 2946 Berkshire Rd Cleveland OH 44118-2444

BOSWELL, WINTHROP PALMER, writer; b. Bklyn., Dec. 17, 1922; d. Carleton Humphries and Winthrop (Bushnell) Palmer; BA, Smith Coll., 1943; postgrad. U. S.C., 1956-58; MA, San Francisco State Coll., 1969; m. James Orr Boswell, Oct. 26, 1946; children: James Lowell, Rosalind Palmer, John Winthrop. Rsch. asst. G-2 Spl. Br., U.S. Army, 1943-46; rsch. asst. Hoover Instn., Stanford, Calif., 1976; docent Filoli, 1979-80; books include The Roots of Irish Monasticism, 1970; Irish Wizards in the Woods of Ethiopia, 1971; The Snake in the Grove, 1972; The Killing of the Snake King in Abyssinia, 1973; Hisperica Famina or The Garden of God, 1974; Bruce and the Question of Geomancy at Axum: The Evidence from the Norman Bayeux Tapestry, 1986, Abyssinian Elements in the Life of Saint Patrick, 1991. Mem. Soc. History of Discoveries, Peninsula Country Club (San Mateo, Calif.), Francisca Club (San Francisco).

BOSWELL-SCHLERETH, CINDA, elementary school counselor, educator; b. Spokane, Wash., Feb. 18, 1949; d. Oscar Wayne and Helen Muriel (Smith) Boswell; m. Robert Louis Schlereth, July 31, 1976 (div. Aug. 16, 1991); 1 child, Meigan Kristin. BA, Wash. State U., 1976, Ctrl. Wash. State U., 1981; MEd, City Univ., Seattle, 1993. Elem. tchr. Orondo (Wash.) Sch. Dist., 1982-84, Wenatchee (Wash.) Sch. Dist., 1984-90; elem. K-2 migrant tchr. North Franklin Sch. Dist., Connell, Wash., 1991; elem. tchr. Manson (Wash.) Sch. Dist., 1991-92, North Franklin Sch. Dist., Connell, Wash., 1992-93; elem. counselor Kennewick (Wash.) Sch. Dist., 1993—. Mem. AAUW, Am. Counselor Assn., Wash. State Am. Counselor Assn., Nat. Assn. for Edn. of Young Children, North Ctrl. Wash. Quilt Guild (sec.), Tri-City Quilt Guild, Omicron Nu. Democrat. Episcopalian. Home: # F 136 2455 George Washington Way Richland WA 99352

BOSWORTH, VICTORIA LYNN, credit manager; b. Midwest City, Okla., July 13, 1961; d. Foster Louis and Martha Kathryn (Dies) B.; m. Grady Paul Havens, Apr. 12, 1980 (div. Dec. 1984); m. Edward Dennie Toiley Jr., June 1, 1990; 1 child, Garrett Edward-Bosworth. BA in Psychology, U. Tex., 1990. Acct. exec., sales exec. Barclays Bank, PLC, Dallas, 1980-84, regional sales mgr., 1984-85; EFT-cons. Transfirst-Moneymaker, Dallas, 1985-87; dir. mktg. & sales MTech, Dallas, 1987-88; bus. planning mgr., acct. mgr., product mgr., debit card bus. mgr. EDS, Plano, Tex., 1988—. Home: 18044 Benchmark Dr Dallas TX 75252 Office: EDS 5400 Legacy Dr MS B1-2F-D9 Plano TX 75024

BOTHA, BEVERLY ANN, counselor; b. Yonkers, N.Y., Nov. 7, 1927; d. John George and Gertrude (Bordollo) Hill; m. Darlow Graham Botha, June 18, 1950; children: Darlow Graham Jr., Colin Graham. BA in Psychology, Boston U., 1949; MS in Psychology, Rutgers U., 1951; MS in Counseling, Wright State U., 1984. Social worker Children's Home, Elizabeth, N.J., 1950-51; exec. trainee Bamberger's, Newark, N.J., 1950-52; social worker Family Svcs., Elmira, N.Y., 1953, Balt. County Welfare Bd., Towson, Md., 1953-57; tchr. Roosevelt Rds., Fajardo, P.R., 1958-60, FLA Extension, San Juan, P.R., 1958-60; editor Allyn & Bacon, Boston, 1960; counselor B.V. Counseling Svcs., Boston, 1961; various to tchr. Sawyer Bus. Sch., Dayton, Ohio, 1980-83, Sylvan, Cedar Rapids, Iowa, 1992—; instructor Arthur Murray Dance, Newark, 1952-53. Vol. Cedar Rapids Mus. Docent, pub. schs., others; bd. dirs. LWV, Dayton, 1977-84, pres. and bd. dirs., Cedar Rapids, 1985-90; sch. vol. (award recipient) in reading, 1991-94; literacy tutor, 1991-94; mem. Friends of Libr., 1991-94, Follies, 1991, 93, 94. Recipient Gov.'s award Des Moines, Iowa, 1989. Mem. AAUW, UNA,

LWV, Writers League. Home: 2600 Skywalker Dr Apt 2049 Houston TX 77058-1508

BOTHWELL, CHUNG THI NGUYEN, resource manager; b. Saigon, Vietnam, Nov. 19, 1949; came to U.S., 1969, naturalized, 1978; d. Tang Van and Nghi Thi (Tran) Nguyen; BBA, U. Miami (Fla.), 1974, MBA, 1980; m. Anthony Peirson Xavier Bothwell, Dec. 22, 1973; children: Anthony Peirson Xavier II, Thomas Theodore Nguyen. Budget analyst Fla. Power & Light Co., Miami, 1973-78; asst. to assoc. dean grad. program Sch. Nursing, U. Wis., Madison, 1978-79; mgr. budgets and costs Central Life Assurance Co., Madison, 1980-83; sr. budget analyst Lawrence Livermore Nat. Lab., Calif., 1983-84, prin. acct., 1984-85, asst. to ops. mgr., laser isotope separation program, 1985-86, asst. ops. mgr. free electron laser optical sci. and tech. program, 1986-87, resource mgr. laser advanced applications program, 1987—. Project chmn. Madison chpt. ARC, 1978-79; human services commr. City of Madison, 1982-83; mem. City of Livermore Social Concerns Com., 1984-85, chairperson, 1985-86; mem. Alameda County Human Relations Commn., 1985-, sec., 1989—. Internat. student scholar, 1973. Mem. Nat. Assn. Accts. (bd. dirs., newsletter editor 1984-85, assoc. dir. hospitality 1985-86, dir. community responsibility 1986-87, pres. 1989—, S. Alden Pendleton award 1987, Pub. Rels. award 1988), Am. Acad. Mgmt., AAUW (corp. relations chairperson 1984-85, membership v.p. 1985-86). Republican. Roman Catholic. Home: 682 Oriole Ave Livermore CA 94550-2654 Office: Lawrence Livermore Nat Lab PO Box 5508 Livermore CA 94551-5508

BOTHWELL, DORR, artist; b. San Francisco, May 3, 1902; d. John Stuart and Florence Isabel (Hodgson) B. Student, Calif. Sch. Fine Arts, Rudolph Schaeffer Sch. Design, U. Oreg. Painter Tau, Manu'a, Am. Samoa, 1928-29, France, 1930-31, 49-51, 89, Eng., 1960-61, 89, West Africa and North Africa, 1966-67, Indonesia, 1974, People's Republic China, 1982, Japan, 1985, Mex., 1987; instr. Calif. Sch. Fine Arts, San Francisco, 1945-58, San Francisco Art Inst., 1959-60, Rudolph Schaeffer Sch. Design, 1960-61, Mendocino (Calif.) Art Ctr., 1962—, San Francisco Art Inst., 1961; instr. Sonoma State Coll., summer 1964, U. Calif., Mendocino Art Ctr., 1965-71, 90; faculty Ansel Adams Yosemite Workshop, 1964-77, Victor (Colo.) Sch., 1979. Exhibitor, West Coast exhbns., 1927—, 3d biennial São Paulo, Brazil, Pitts. Internat., 1952, 55, Art: U.S.A., 1958, Bklyn. Mus., 1976, Mendocino (Calif.) Art Ctr., 1992; one-man shows include De Young Meml. Mus., San Francisco, 1957, 63; retrospective exhbn. Bay Window Gallery, Mendocino, 1985, Spl. Anniversary exhbn. 1986-87, Tobey Moss Gallery, L.A., 1989, 91, 93, Bothwell Studio, Mendocino, Calif., 1989, Mendocino Art Ctr., 1992, Gallery Mendocino, 1994; works in permanent collection, San Diego Gallery Fine Art, Crocker Gallery, Sacramento, San Francisco Mus. Art, Whitney Mus. Am. Art, Bklyn. Mus., Mus. Modern Art, Fogg Mus., Met. Museum, Victoria and Albert Museum, London, Brit. Mus., London, Bibliothèque Nationale, Paris, France, Worcester (Mass.) Art Mus., Cleve. Mus. Art, Boston Mus. Art, Oakland (Calif.) Mus., DeYoung Mus., San Francisco; author: Notan: The Principle of Dark-Light Design, 1968, 2d edit., 1976, Danish edit., 1977, 3d edit., 1991. Recipient 1st prize, 4th ann. exhbn. San Francisco Soc. Women Artists, 1929; Pres.'s purchase prize, 1941; Leisser-Farnham award 7th ann. exhbn. San Diego Art Guild, 1932; hon. mention 7th ann. exhbn. So. Calif. Artists, 1933; spl. prize 9th ann. exhbn., 1937; Artists Fund prize ann. exhbn. drawings and prints San Francisco Art Assn., 1943; hon. mention 2d spring ann. Calif. Palace Legion of Honor, San Francisco, 1947; purchase prize 2d nat. print ann. Bklyn. Mus., 1948; 1st prize 9th ann. Nat. Serigraph Soc., N.Y.C., 1948. Home: 925 N Plaza Rd SP93 Apache Junction AZ 85220 Office: Tobey Moss Gallery 7321 Beverly Blvd Los Angeles CA 90036

BOTKIN, KAREN R., librarian; b. N.Y.C.; d. Sam and Shirley (Rosen) B. BA, William Paterson Coll., 1977; MS, Columbia U., 1978. Cert. librarian, N.Y., N.J. Music acquisitions librarian Hebrew U., Jerusalem, 1979; research librarian N.J. State Library, Trenton, N.J., 1979; research, cataloger Nat. Broadcasting Co., N.Y.C., 1980-87; mgr. info. services Creamer Dickson Basford, N.Y.C., 1987-88; head tech. svcs. Paul, Weiss, Rifkind, Wharton & Garrison Libr., N.Y.C., 1988-94; asst. dir. Bloomfield (N.J.) Pub. Libr., 1994—. Mem. Am. Assn. Law Librs., Spl. Librs. Assn. (chmn. elect. N.Y. chpt. comm. div. 1987-88, chmn. 1988-89, editor Chpt. News 1989-91, 93-94, chmn. profl. devel./mentoring 1991-93), Theatre Libr. Assn., Music Libr. Assn. (rep. Spl. Libr. Assn. 1987, 92-93), Assn. Recorded Sound Collections, N.Y. Law Librs. Tech. Svcs. Roundtable (founder, chair 1990-91, sec. 1993-94), N.J. Libr. Assn., N.Y. Internet Users' Group. Office: Bloomfield Pub Libr 90 Broad St Bloomfield NJ 07003

BOTNICK, BRIGITTE MUEHLE, capriculturist; b. Berlin, Germany, Apr. 2, 1956; came to U.S., 1976; d. Hans and Gerda (Masslow) Muehle; m. Ralph C. Botnick, May 17, 1981 (div. Nov. 1987). BS in Animal Sci., U. Conn., 1985. Owner, mgr. Windchild Farm, Stafford Springs, Conn., 1981—; cons. goat project Latvia, Land O'Lakes Internat. Devel., Mpls., 1993. Contbr. articles to profl. jours. Mem. Am. Dairy Goat Assn., Cat Writers Assn., Gamma Sigma Delta. Office: Windchild Farm PO Box 134 Stafford Springs CT 06076-0134

BOTOE, CARLOTTA See CARLCANO, CARLOTTA MIGUELINA

BOTTEL, HELEN ALFEA, columnist, writer; b. Beaumont, Calif.; d. Alpheus Russell and Mary Ellen (Alexander) Brigden; m. Robert E. Bottel; children: Robert Dennis, Rodger M., R. Kathryn Bottel Bernhardt, Suzanne V. Bottel Peppers. A.A., Riverside Coll. Calif.; student, Oreg. State U., 1958-59, So. Oreg. Coll., 1959. Writer, editor Illinois Valley News, Cave Junction, Oreg., 1950-56; writer Grants Pass (Oreg.) Courier, Portland Oregonian, Medford (Oreg.) Mail Tribune, 1952-58; daily columnist Helen Help Us King Features Syndicate, N.Y.C., 1958-83; mem. adv. bd. Internat. Affairs Inst., N.Y.C. and Tokyo, 1986—; freelance mag. writer, author, lectr., 1956—. Author: To Teens with Love, 1969, Helen Help Us, 1970, Parents Survival Kit, 1979; contbg. editor, columnist Real World mag., 1978-84; weekly columnist Yomiuri Shimbun, Tokyo, 1982-90; thrice weekly columnist Sacramento Union, 1986-88; newspaper and mag. columnist Look Who's Aging (with dau. Kathy Bernhardt), 1992—; contbr. nonfiction to books and nat. mags. Staff mem. ACT Handicapped Children Games, Sacramento, 1986—; bd. dirs. Illinois Valley Med. Center, 1958-62, Childrens Center, Sacramento, 1969, Family Support Programs, Sacramento, 1991—; mem. Grants Pass br. Oreg. Juvenile Adv. Com., 1960-62, Students League Against Narcotics Temptation, 1968-70; charter patron Cosumnes River Coll., Sacramento, 1972—; mem. nat. adv. bd. Nat. Anorexic Aid Soc., 1977—; mem. Nat. Spina Bifida Assn.; scholarship com. judge Exec. Women Internat., 1985. Recipient Women's Svc. Cup Riverside Coll., citation for aid to U.S. servicemen in Vietnam Gov. Ga., 1967, Disting. Merit citation NCCJ, 1970, 1st place award for books Calif. Press Women, 1970, Sacramento Regional Arts Coun. Lit. Achievement award, 1974, Alumna of Yr. award Riverside Coll., 1987, Gold and Silver medals Calif. Sr. Games (tennis), 1990-91. Mem. Am. Soc. Journalists and Authors, Internat. Affairs Inst. Presbyterian. Clubs: Calif. Writers, Southgate Tennis. Home: 2060 56th Ave Sacramento CA 95822-4112

BOTTENBERG, JOYCE HARVEY, social services executive; b. Melrose, Mass., June 29, 1945; d. Robert Willis and Amy Sheppard (Wood) Harvey; 1 child, Joanne Harvey; m. Norman G. Bottenberg, 1985. BA, U. Mass., 1967, diploma grad. journalism program, 1969; diploma, Simmons Coll. Grad. Sch. Mgmt., 1984. Lic. social worker, Mass. Sr. tech. writer Itek Corp., Lexington, Mass., 1967-70; dir. pub. info. Walla Walla (Wash.) Community Coll., 1970; profl. interviewer McGraw Hill Research, N.Y.C., 1971-73; coordinator pub. relations James B. Rendle Assocs., Malden, Mass., 1973-76; exec. dir. ARC, Melrose, Mass., 1976-80, regional mgr., 1980-84; regional mgr. ARC, Lynn, Mass., 1984-85; tech. writer Municipality of Met. Seattle, 1985-86; exec. dir. Epilepsy Assn. Western Wash., Seattle, 1986-87; dir. devel. ARC, Seattle, 1988—, mgr. svc. ctr., 1994—. Chmn. adv. bd. Mass. Dept. Pub. Welfare Community Service Area; mem. Melrose Mayor's Energy Commn.; civic adv. bd. Met. Bank and Trust; instr. 1st aid, CPR, ARC; merit badge counselor Boy Scouts Am. New Eng. Newspaper fellow, 1969; Cert. of merit ARC, 1981. Mem. AAUW, DAR, NAFE, Nat. Conf. Social Welfare, Soc. Mayflower Descendents, Soc. Tech. Communications, Nat. Ski Patrol System (sr. patroller), Northwest Devel. Officers Assn., Washington Planned Giving Coun., Alpha Phi Gamma. Episcopalian. Lodge: Zonta. Home: 2205 197th Ave SE Issaquah WA 98027-9644 Office: 1900 25th Ave S Seattle WA 98144-4708

BOTTOMLEY, SANDRA JOHNSON, editor; b. West Covina, Calif., June 6, 1966; d. Burl Franklin and Marilyn Anne (Paar) Johnson; m. John William Bottomley, Feb. 3, 1991. BA in Eng., Math/Computer Sci., Rhodes Coll., 1988. Editor computer books TAB Books, divsn. McGraw-Hill, Blue Ridge Summit, Pa., 1988-90, sr. editor, 1990-91, mng. editor, 1991-92, devel. editor, 1990-93; acquisitions editor Stevens Pub., Washington, 1993-94; cons. Gargoyle Renaissance, Waynesboro, Pa., 1990—. Co-author: Lotus 1-2-3 for Macintosh Simplified, 1991. Elder Hawley Meml. Ch., Blue Ridge Summit, 1989-92; tutor Franklin County Literacy Coun., Chambersburg, Pa., 1990. Mem. NAFE, Nat. Press Club, Bookbuilders of Washington, Pub Mktg. Assn., Am. Booksellers Assn. Presbyterian. Home: 315 Cleveland Ave 2d Flr Waynesboro PA 17268

BOTTOMLEY, SYLVIA STAKLE, hematologist, educator, researcher; b. Riga, Latvia, Mar. 9, 1934; came to U.S., 1950; d. John Waldemar and Leontine (Miluns) Stakle; m. Richard Harold Bottomley, June 5, 1958; children: Astrid Elizabeth Morrison, Ian Philip. BS, Okla. State U., 1954; MD, U. Okla., 1958. Diplomate Am. Bd. Internal Medicine, Am. Bd. Hematology. Intern U. Utah/County Gen. Hosp., Salt Lake City, 1958-59; resident U. Okla. Health Sci. Ctr., Oklahoma City, 1959-61, fellow in hematology, 1961-65; instr. in medicine U. Okla. Coll. of Medicine, Oklahoma City, 1964-67, asst. prof. medicine, 1967-71, assoc. prof. medicine, 1971-75, prof. medicine, 1975—, adj. assoc. prof. pathology, 1973—; dir. spl. hematology lab. VA Hosp., Oklahoma City, 1969—; clin. investigator VA, Oklahoma City, 1965-69, VA program specialist in hematology, Washington, 1977-80; women liaison officer AAMC, Washington, 1979-83; sabbatical in hematology rsch. Harvard Med. Sch., Boston, 1983-84; cons. field reader FDA Office of Orphan Products Devel., Washington, 1988—; bd. dirs. Iron Overload Diseases Assn., West Palm Beach, Fla., 1992—; mem. various ad hoc coms. NIH, Washington. Contbr. articles to profl. jours., chpts. to books. Named Physician of Yr. in Academia, U. Okla. Coll. Med. Alumni Assn., 1987; Rsch. grantee VA, NIH. Mem. ACP, Am. Fedn. Clin. Rsch., Am. Soc. Hematology, Ctrl. Soc. Clin. Rsch., So. Soc. Clin. Investigation, Alpha Omega Alpha, Sigma Xi (pres. local chpt. 1975). Republican. Lutheran. Office: VA Med Ctr Hematology/Oncology Sect (111J) 921 NE 13th St Oklahoma City OK 73104

BOTTOMS, BARBARA ANN, nurse; b. Ozark, Ala., Sept. 8, 1948; d. Homer Eugene and Etta (Simmons) B. Assoc. degree in nursing, Wallace St. Community Coll., Napierfield, Ala., 1974; BS in Nursing, Auburn U., Montgomery, Ala., 1981. RN, Tex., Fla.; cert. med.-surg.,ANCC. Nurses aide Ozark (Ala.) Nursing Home, 1967-68, nurses aide Flowers Hosp., Dothan, Ala., 1969-74, charge nurse, 1974-76, evening supr., 1976; staff nurse, charge Enterprise Hosp., Ala., 1976; charge nurse Baptist Med. Ctr., Montgomery, 1976-77, head nurse, 1977-78; staff nurse med. surg. unit U. Med. Ctr., Montgomery, 1978; staff nurse VA Adminstrn. Med. Ctr., Montgomery, 1978-86; staff nurse neurosurgery unit Tampa (Fla.) Gen. Hosp., 1986, SE Ala. Med. Ctr., Dothan, 1986-88, Flowers Hosp., 1988-89; nurse level III neurosurgery Meth. Hosp., Houston, 1989—, coord. patient care, 1994—, mem. nursing standards com., 1993—, vice chair, 1994, mem. blood dr. com., 1993, 94, mem. nursing standards and procedures, 1995. Mem. Am. Assn. Neurosci. Nurses, Sigma Theta Tau (sec. Kappa Omega chpt. 1984-85, Zeta Pi chpt.). Avocations: reading, crocheting, knitting, watching sports, collecting mugs and models. Home and Office: 6239 Lymbar Dr Houston TX 77096-4620 Office: Meth Hosp 6565 Fannin St Houston TX 77030-2707

BOTTONE, JOANN, health services executive; b. Bklyn., June 20, 1943; d. Anthony and Claire (Bisesti) B.; m. William Recevuto, Feb. 12, 1989; children: Matthew, Sandra. RN, Kings County Hosp. Ctr., Bklyn., 1963; BS, St. Francis Coll., Bklyn., 1980; MPA, Russell Sage Coll., Albany, N.Y., 1986; PhD in Pub. Adminstrn., Kensington U., Calif., 1995. From staff nurse, head nurse, quality assurance coord. Victory Meml. Hosp., Bklyn., 1961-81; instr. infection control Community Hosp. Bklyn., 1981-82; dir. quality assurance Profl. Stds. Rev. Orgn., Bklyn., 1982-85; adminstr. Community Svc. Dept., Greater N.Y. Blood Program, N.Y.C., 1985-88; coord. HIV program and epidemiology edn. program Health Sci. Ctr. SUNY, Bklyn., 1988—; tchr. SUNY Coll. Health Related Professions. Contbr. articles to profl. jours.

BOTWAY, JACLYN COOPER, antique dealer, consultant; b. St. Louis, Sept. 14, 1935; d. Sterling Ellis and Thelma Adeline (Kinder) Cooper; m. Clifford Alan Botway, July 29, 1950; children: Cooper Alan, Jill Robyn-Sterling. BA, MA, U. Ga., 1947; MSW, N.Y. Sch. Social Work, 1950. Med. social worker Met. Hosp., N.Y.C., 1950-55; owner, mgr. Jaclyn J. Inc. (doing bus. as Rainbarrel), Salt Point, N.Y., 1980—; pres., dir. Hist. Hudson Valley Antiquity, Clinton Corners, N.Y., 1980—; dir. Dutchess County Hist. Roads, Poughkeepsie, N.Y., 1985—. Author: Finding Art Treasures at Home, 1979, Auctions Mania, 1980, Money in the Attic, 1985, The Ancients Collectively, 1986. Mem. Clinton Hist. Road Commn.; founder Clinton Hist. Soc., 1989; v.p. New Rochelle (N.Y.) League for Svc., 1955-81; vol. Internat. Garden Club, Pelham, N.Y., 1955—; sec. Women's Manor Club, Pelham, 1955-57; v.p. Little Guild of St. Francis for Animals, Key West, Fla., 1982—; founder Art and Hist. Soc., Key West, 1982, Martello Mus., Key West, 1982, Tennessee Williams Arts Ctr. and Theatre, Key West, 1982—. Named Rep. Woman of Dutchess County, Nat. Rep. Com., 1963. Mem. Oldest House Mus., Mus. Modern Art, Mus. Natural History, Clinton Hist. Soc., Phi Beta Kappa. Home: 460 Beechmont Dr New Rochelle NY 10804-4613 Office: Rainbarrel No 2 Salt Point Turnpike Salt Point NY 12514

BOUCHER, JEANNETTE MILLS, volunteer; b. Providence, Sept. 30, 1938; d. Ernest Merle and Laura Baker (Paine) Mills; m. Franklin Guy Rutan, 1962 (dec. 1968); children: Peter Adams, David Bradford; m. Raymond E. Boucher, Sept. 11, 1978. BA in Piano, Tulane U., 1960; student, Sorbonne, Paris, 1958-59. Officer Confrérie de la Chaîne des Rôtisseurs, Bailliage des Etats-Unis, 1993—, pres. Naples chpt., 1990-93; bd. dirs. Naples Coun. on World Affairs, 1988-91, Naples Philharm., 1985-91; pres. Plainfield (N.J.) Symphony Aux., Plainfield Music Club. Mem. Mayflower Soc. (life), Jamestowne Soc. (life), First Families Miss., LWV (dir. Collier County chpt. 1991-93, pres. 1985-88). Office: La Chaine des Rotisseurs PO Box 413005# 308 Naples FL 33941-3005

BOUDETTE, ROBIN DENISE, psychologist; b. Clinton, Ind., May 7, 1961; d. John Boudette and Mary (McGuire) Saraco. BS, Lynchburg Coll., 1983; PhD, Calif. Sch. Profl. Psychology, Berkeley, 1989. Dual diagnosis coord. Belmont Hills, Belmont, Calif., 1988-90; program dir. Redwoods Hosp., Santa Rosa, Calif., 1990-93; clin. dir. Carrier Found., Belle Mead, N.J., 1993—; leader for assault prevention and empowerment workshops for women. Mem. APA, Redwoods Psychol. Assn. Office: Carrier Found PO Box 147 Belle Mead NJ 08502-0147

BOUDREAUX, GLORIA MARIE, nurse, educator; b. Lafayette, La., May 2, 1935; d. Simon Zepherin and Orta Marie (Pierret) B. Diploma, Charity Hosp. Sch. Nursing, 1962; BA maxima cum laude, St. Edward's U., 1974; MS in Psychiatric-Mental Health Nursing, Tex. Women's U., 1976. Head surg., med. nurse Lafayette (La.) Charity Hosp., 1962-65; commd. 1st lt. U.S. Army, 1965; advanced through grades to col. Nurse Corps, U.S. Army, 1983; psychiat. staff nurse VA Hosp., New Orleans, 1968-72; psychiatric nurse U.S. Army Nurse Corps, San Francisco and Augusta, Ga., 1966-67; instr. Tex. Woman's Univ. Sch. of Nursing, Houston, 1976-80; clin. specialist VA Med. Ctr., Houston, 1980-87; psychiat. nursing coord. Spring Shadows Glen, Houston, 1987-88; instr. assoc. degree nursing program Houston Community Coll., 1988-91; asst. prof. nursing La. State U., Eunice, 1992—; clin. specialist, cons. in psychiat.-mental health nursing. Recipient Nat. Def. Svc. medal, 1968, Army Res. Component medal, 1972, Armed Forces Res. medal, 1977 (10-yr. device 1988), Army Commendation medal, 1978, Army Meritorious Svc. medal, 1990, Presdl. Sports award, 1989, 90, 91. Mem. Am. Psychiatric Nurses Assn., Am. Orthopsychiatric Assn., Soc. for Edn. amd Rsch. in Psychiatric-Mental Health Nursing, Res. Officers Assn. (chpt. pres. 1981-83), Assn. Mil. Surgeons of U.S., ANA (cert. in psychiat. mental health nursing), Vietnam Vets. Assn., Sigma Theta Tau. Home: 307 Meadow Ln Lafayette LA 70506

BOUEY, ORA JAMES, nursing educator; b. Alamonte Springs, Fla., Nov. 23, 1931; d. Condor E. and Mary (James) Merritt; m. David L. Bouey, July 23, 1952; children: Daizzee Donaae Bouey-Noland, David L. II. Nursing diploma North Country Community Hosp., Glen Cove, N.Y., 1956; A.A.S., Suffolk Community Coll., 1969; M.A., NYU, 1977, postgrad. 1978—. Charge emergency dept. Meadowbrook Hosp., East Meadow, N.Y., 1956-72; staff critical care Huntington (N.Y.) Hosp., 1957-80; instr. Bd. Coop. Ednl. Services, Dix Hills, N.Y., 1970-72; instr. SUNY-Stony Brook, 1972-77, asst. prof., 1977-82, assoc. prof., 1982—, chmn. dept. adult health nursing, 1982-89, dir. profl. resources devel., dir. acad. advancement, 1989—, asst. dean acad. advancement, 1993—; cons. in field. Contbg. author: Guide to Patient Evaluation, CGFNS Examination Review. Recipient Congl. award for meritorious service, 1980; Chancellors award SUNY, 1981, N.Y. State Black Faculty Staff award, 1982; Disting. Alumni award SUNY-Stony Brook, 1983. Bd. dirs. Youth Devel. Assn., Youth Devel. Ctr., Pederson Krag Ctr., 100 Black Women Inc., R.S.V.P. Suffolk County, Planned Parenthood Suffolk County. Mem. NAS, NAACP, UUP (N.Y. State legis. com., NYSUT laison FNHP), Am. Assn. Black Women in Higher Edn., Am. Assn. Critical Nurses, Am. Nurses Assn., N.Y. Acad. Sci., N.Y. State Nurses Assn., N.Y. State Conf. Aging, Am. Assn. Higher Edn., AAUP, AAUW, Assn. Black Nursing Faculty, Nat. League Nurses, Suffolk County Mental Health Assn., Chi Eta Phi, Sigma Theta Tau, Alpha Kappa Alpha. Presbyterian. Home: 158 Manor Rd Huntington NY 11743-5733 Office: SUNY-Stony Brook Health Scis Ctr 204 Stony Rm 233 Level 2 Stony Brook NY 11794-8240

BOUGHAN, TAMMY LYNN, legislative aide; b. Middletown, Ohio. BS in Indsl. Design, Ohio State U., 1988. Legislative aide Senator Barry Levey, Middletown. Home: 609 N Marshall Rd Middletown OH 45042-3831

BOUGHTON, LILIAN ELIZABETH, secondary education educator, retired; b. Cumberland, Md., May 15, 1913; d. Orble Brooks and Christine (McAlpine) B. Student, Potomac State Coll., 1930-32; BA, Western Md. Coll., 1934; MA, Columbia U., 1938. Tchr. English Pennsylvania Ave. Jr. High Sch., Cumberland, Md., 1934-36, Ft. Hill High Sch., Cumberland, 1936-73; sch. evaluation team mem. Md. State Sch. System for N.E. Evaluation Team, Baltimore City, 1940s; chairperson bylaws com. Md. State Tchrs. Assn., Balt., 1950s; conv. com. mem. Md. Retired Tchrs. Assn. Conv., Ocean City, 1983. Elder, circle leader Presbyn. Ch. Recipient cert. March of Dimes, 1983, plaque, 1984. Mem. AAUW (pres. 1975-77, 83-86, activities chair 1985—, publicity com., name honored 1983-84, 2 plaques Cumberland br. 1993), Allegany County Ret. Tchrs. Assn. (pres. 1982-83, newsletter editor 1983-94, publicity com.), Hist. Soc. (life, curator 1980, vol. 1985—), Women's Civic Club (edn. chair 1992—).

BOULDEN, JUDITH ANN, federal judge; b. Salt Lake City, Dec. 28, 1948; d. Douglas Lester and Emma Ruth (Robertson) Boulden; m. Alan Walter Barnes, Nov. 7, 1982; 1 child, Dorian Lisa. BA, U. Utah, 1971, JD, 1974. Bar: Utah 1974, U.S. Dist. Ct. Utah 1974. Law clk. to A. Sherman Christenson U.S. Cts., Salt Lake City, 1974; assoc. Roe & Fowler, Salt Lake City, 1975-81, McKay Burton Thurman & Coudie, Salt Lake City, 1982-83; Chpt. 7 trustee U.S. Trustee, Salt Lake City, 1976-82, Standing Chpt. 12 trustee, 1987-88, Standing Chpt. 13 trustee, 1988-89; sr. ptnr. Boulden & Gillman, Salt Lake City, 1983-88; U.S. Bankruptcy judge U.S. Cts., Salt Lake City, 1988—. Mem. Utah Bar Assn. *

BOULDING, ELISE MARIE, sociologist, educator; b. Oslo, Norway, July 6, 1920; came to U.S., 1923, naturalized, 1929; d. Joseph and Birgit (Johnsen) Biorn-Hansen; m. Kenneth Boulding; Aug. 31, 1941; children: John Russell, Mark David, Christine Ann, Philip Daniel, William Frederic. B.A., Douglass Coll., 1940; M.S., Iowa State Coll., 1949; Ph.D., U. Mich., 1969. Research asso. Survey Research Inst., U. Mich., 1957-58, Mental Health Research Inst., 1959-60; research devel. sec. Center for Research on Conflict Resolution, 1960-63; prof. sociology, project dir. Inst. Behavioral Sci., U. Colo., Boulder, 1967-78; Montgomery vis. prof. Dartmouth Coll., 1978-79, chmn. dept. sociology, 1979-85; prof. emerita, 1985; sec. gen. Internat. Peace Rsch. Assoc., 1989-91; mem. program adv. council Human and Social Devel. Program, UN Univ., 1977-80; mem. governing council, 1980-86. Author: (with others) Handbook of International Data on Women, 1976, Bibliography on World Conflict and Peace, 1979, Social System of Planet Earth, 1980, Women and the Social Costs of Economic Development, 1981; author: The Underside of History: A View of Women Through Time, 1975, rev. edit. 1992, Women in Twentieth Century World, 1977, Children's Rights and the Wheel of Life, 1979, Building a Global Civic Culture: Education for an Interdependent World, 1988, 90, One Small Plot of Heaven, 1990, (with Kenneth Boulding) The Future: Images and Processes, 1994; editor: Peace Culture and Society: Translational Research and Dialogue with Clovis Brigagao and Kevin Clements (eds.), 1990, New Agendas for Peace Research: Conflict and Security Reexamined (ed.), 1992; Building Peace in the Middle East: Challenges for States and Civil Society, (ed.), 1993. Internat. chair Womens Internat. League for Peace and Freedom, 1967-70; mem. Exploratory Project on Conditions for Peace, 1984-90; mem. U.S. Commn. for UNESCO, 1978-84; mem. UNESCO Peace Prize jury, 1980-87; chair bd. Boulder Cmty. Parenting Ctr., 1988-92; bd. dirs. Am. Friends Svc. Com., 1990-94. Recipient Disting. Achievement award Douglass Coll., 1973, Ted Lentz Peace prize, 1977, Nat. Woman of Conscience award, 1980, Athena award, 1983, Nat. Women's Forum award, 1985, Inst. of Def., Disarmament, Peace and Democracy award, 1990—; named to Rutgers Hall of Disting. Alumni, 1994; Danforth fellow, 1965-67. Mem. Am. Sociol. Assn. (Jessie Bernard award 1982, Peace and War sect. award 1994), Internat. Sociol. Assn., Internat. Peace Rsch. Assn. (newsletter editor 1983-87), World Future Studies Fedn., Internat. Studies Assn., World Future Soc., Colo. Women's Forum, U. Mich. Alumni Assn. (Athena award 1983). Quaker. Home: 624 Pearl St Apt 206 Boulder CO 80302-5072

BOULIER, VANESSA, manufacturing executive; b. Fort Fairfield, Maine, Oct. 9, 1953; d. Charles Joseph Jr. and Marilyn Kimball (Lewis) B. AAS, Waterbury State Tech. Coll., 1973; BS, Bryant Coll., 1975; MBA, U. New Haven, 1983. Customer svc. supr., inventory control supr. Burndy Corp., Norwalk, Conn., 1975-82; inventory control mgr. Tuttle and Bailey Inc., New Britain, Conn., 1982-84; material svcs. mgr. ABB Electro-Mechanics, New Britain, 1984—. Mem. Am. Prodn. and Inventory Control Soc. (cert.). Republican. Roman Catholic. Home: 224 Perch Rock Trl Winsted CT 06098-1961 Office: ABB Electro-Mechanics 150 John Downey Dr New Britain CT 06051-2904

BOULTINGHOUSE, (DANNIE) CAROL, business development specialist; b. Dallas, Sept. 11, 1954; d. Daniel Calvin and Mary Bennette (Temple) Wilkinson; m. Steven Ed Boultinghouse, Feb. 21, 1981 (div. June 1986); 1 child, Brian Steven. AD in Liberal Arts, Eastfield C.C., Mesquite, Tex., 1975; student, Abilene Christian Coll., Garland, Tex., 1976-77. Various secretarial positions Dallas, 1974-80; sec. CIGNA Internat., Dallas, 1980-83, underwriting asst., 1983-85, assoc. underwriter, 1985-87, account rep., 1987-92, bus. devel. specialist, 1992—. Mem. Marine Corps League Aux. Roman Catholic. Home: 3039 Sharpview Ln Dallas TX 75228-6084 Office: CIGNA Internat 600 Las Colinas Blvd E Ste 900 Irving TX 75039-5633

BOULTINGHOUSE, MARION CRAIG BETTINGER, editor; b. New Albany, Ind., Oct. 7, 1930; d. Losson Edward and Marion Craig (Klarer) Bettinger; m. Ray Allen Boultinghouse, Jan. 1, 1973. Student, Hanover Coll., 1948-50; BS, Fla. So. Coll., 1952; M.Ed., U. Louisville, 1960. Tchr. pub. schs. Lakeland, Fla., 1952, New Albany, 1953-55, 58-60, New Haven, 1955-58; editor Am. Edn. Publs., Middletown, Conn., 1960-63, Holt, Rinehart & Winston, N.Y.C., 1963-64, 69-72, Macmillan, Inc., N.Y.C., 1964-69, 72-75; editorial dir., v.p. sch. div. Macmillan, Inc., 1975-79; pres. Boultinghouse & Boultinghouse Inc.; pub. consultants Boultinghouse & Boultinghouse Inc., N.Y.C., 1976—. Author: Follow Me, Everybody, 1968. Office: 153 E 30th St New York NY 10016-7340

BOUNDAS, LOUISE GOOCH, editor; b. Yazoo City, Miss.; d. James Clifford and Anne (Butler) Gooch; m. George Basil Boundas, Sept. 29, 1966. BA, U. N.C., 1959; MS, Yeshiva U., N.Y.C., 1969. Mng. editor Electro-Tech. mag., N.Y.C., 1962-68, Pub. Affairs Com, Inc., N.Y.C., 1970-72; mng. editor Stereo Rev. mag., N.Y.C., 1972-86, editor in chief, 1987—; editorial dir. Car Stereo Rev., Sound and Image, Stereo Rev. Spl. Publs., N.Y.C., 1987-92; v.p. Hachette Filipacchi mags., 1991—. Named to YWCA Acad. Women Achievers. Mem. Am. Soc. Mag. Editors, Overseas Press Club. Office: Stereo Review 1633 Broadway New York NY 10019-6708

BOUNDS, NANCY, modeling and talent company executive; b. Rodney, Ark.; d. William Thomas and Mary Jane (Fields) Southard; m. Robert S. Bounds, 1960 (div. 1965); 1 child, Ronnie Jean; m. Mark Curtis Sconce, Nov. 28, 1972. Exec. dir. Internat. Fashion/Modeling Assn., N.Y.C., 1978; founding pres. Internat. Talent and Model Schs. Assn., N.Y.C., 1979-80; pres. Nancy Bounds Internat., Omaha, 1959—. Contbr. articles to profl. jours. Producer TV Heart Fund Auction, 1965; dir., choreographer fashion show N.Y. fashion editors, 1989, Czechoslovakian Model Search, Prague, 1991. Chairperson Douglas/Sarpy County Heart Assn., Omaha, 1966, 73-74. Recipient Nat. Tchr.'s award MiLady Pub. Co., 1965, Outstanding Service award Mayor of Omaha, 1984, Uta Halee Girls Village, 1983-87, March of Dimes service award, 1977, 84, Toys for Tots service award, 1986, Muscular Dystrophy citation of merit, 1982; named Best of Omaha, 1988-92, Woman of Distinction YWCA, 1992, 93, 94; Nancy Bounds Day proclaimed by City of Omaha, 1994. Avocations: reading, painting, travel, golf, tournament bridge. Home and Office: 4803 Davenport St Omaha NE 68132-3108

BOUNDS, SARAH ETHELINE, historian; b. Huntsville, Ala., Nov. 5, 1942; d. Leo Deltis and Alice Etheline (Boone) Bounds; AB, Birmingham-So. Coll., 1963; MA, U. Ala., Tuscaloosa, 1965, Ed.S. in History, 1971, PhD, 1977. Tchr. social studies Huntsville City Schs., 1963, 65-66, 71-74; residence hall adv., dir. univ. housing U. Ala., Tuscaloosa, 1963-65, 68-71; instr. history N.E. State Jr. Coll., Rainsville, Ala., 1966-68; instr. history U. Ala., Huntsville, 1975, 78-80, 85—, dir. Weeden House Mus., 1981-83; asst. prof. edn., supr. student tchrs. U. North Ala., Florence, 1978. Mem. AAUW, Assn. Tchrs. Educators, Nat. Council Tchrs. Social Studies, NEA, Ala. Hist. Assn., Ala. Assn. Historians, Ala. Assn. Tchrs. Educators, Huntsville Hist. Soc., Historic Huntsville Found., Alpha Delta Kappa (state pres. Ala. 1990-92, regional sec. 1991-93, internat. mem. com. 1993—), Kappa Delta Pi, Phi Alpha Theta. Methodist. Club: Huntsville Pilot (pres. 1990-91, club builder 1991-93). Home: 1100 Bob Wallace Ave SE Huntsville AL 35801-2807

BOUNDS-SEEMANS, PAMELLA J., artist; b. Milton, Del., Nov. 5, 1948; d. James Wilson Bounds and Marguerite Edna (Rickards) Bounds Carey; m. Jeffrey Wayne Seemans, Mar. 20, 1984; children: Misty Autumn, Sterling Hunter, Jordan Windsor. BA, N.Mex. Highlands U., 1971, MA, 1972. Tchr. elem. art Indian River Sch. Dist., Frankford, Del., 1973-79; lectr. U. Md., 1981, U. Del., 1986, Del. Tech. and C.C., 1988, 75th Del. Womens Day Conf. at U. Del. Exhibited in group shows including Rehoboth (Del.) Art League, 1980, 89, 90, 92, 93, Tideline Gallery, Rehoboth Beach, Del., 1980—, Greenville, Del., 1993, Wicomico Art League, 1980, Del. Tech. and C.C., Georgetown, 1981, U. Md., 1981, Meth. Ch. Gallery, Milford, Del., 1981, Bluestreak Gallery, Wilmington, Del., 1989—, Blue Streak Art Gallery, Wilmington, 1993, Jamison Gallery, Santa Fe, 1993—, 75th Del. Womens Day Conf. at U. Del.; represented in permanent collections Sussex County Courthouse, also numerous pvt. collections. Donator art work to charitable orgns., Beebe Hosp. Found., Am. Diabetes Found., Girls, Inc. of Del., Del. Music Sch., Del. Assn. Battered Women, Children's Beach Ho.; mem. Del. Arts Coun., 1983, Sussex County Arts Coun., Friends of Milton Libr. Recipient award for outstanding body of work Torpedo Factory, Alexandria, Va., 1982; fellow State of Del. Divsn. of the Arts, 1995. Mem. Nat. Mus. of Women in the Arts, Del. Art Mus., Rehoboth Art League (2d prize 1981, Tunnel 2d place award for most outstanding work in exhibit 1990, Popular Vote award 1992, 1st place award 1993), Del. Ctr. for Contemporary Arts, Del. Ctr. for Creative Arts, Newark Arts Alliance, Del. Nature Soc., Mothers Multiple Births (v.p. 1987), Wicomo Art League (hon. mention 1981). Episcopalian. Home and Studio: 1203 Greenbank Rd Wilmington DE 19808-5842

BOUR, PAMELA JEAN, human resources administrator; b. Pitts., Mar. 31, 1959; d. Donald James and Regina Elizabeth B. BA in Social Work, Shippensburg (Pa.) U., 1981; MSW, U. Pitts., 1986; postgrad., Point Park Coll., Pitts., 1993—. Caseworker Allegheny County Children and Youth Svcs., Pitts., 1983-85; case mgmt. dir. No./S.W. Mental Health/Mental Retardation, Pitts., 1987-89; ct. liaison supr. Allegheny County Mental Health/Mental Retardation, Pitts., 1985-87, 89-92; discharge tracking supr. Renaissance Ctr., Pitts., 1992—. Vol. Com. to Elect Michelle Madoff, Pitts., 1989, Com. to Elect Jeanne Clark, Pitts., 1987, Com. to Elect Byrd Brown, Pitts., 1988. Recipient Allegheny County Commrs. award for excellence in county govt., 1991, Common Ground award Shippensburg C. of C., 1980. Mem. AAUW, NOW (program chair 1987-88, membership chair 1988-89), Am. Chem. Soc. (student). Democrat. Home: 911 Braddock Rd Pittsburgh PA 15221

BOURDEAUX, NORMA SANDERS, state legislator; b. Birmingham, Ala., June 10, 1930; d. Hanson Earle and Ethelyn Lou (Milton) Sanders; m. Thomas DeVane Bourdeaux Jr., Oct. 11, 1952; children: Lisa B. Percy, Marian B. Barksdale, Ellen D., Thomas D. III. AA, Stephen's Coll., 1950; BA, U. Ala., 1952. Cert. picture framer. Tchr. art Meridian (Miss.) Separate Sch. Dist., 1961-63, 71-73; instr. art U. So. Miss., Meridian, 1966-72; owner Bourdeaux Frame & Gallery, Meridan, 1981-92; mem. Miss. House Reps., Jackson, 1992—. Chmn. Govs. Commn. for Children & Youth, Jackson, 1982-88, Govs. Adv. Human & Health Svcs., Jackson, 1984-88; bd. dirs. Hilltop House for Boys, Meridian, 1980—, Greater Meridian C. of C., 1980-85. Democrat. Epsicopalian. Home: PO Box 3686 Meridian MS 39303-3686 Office: Miss Ho of Reps State Capitol Jackson MS 39201

BOURGAIZE, LINDA HARPER, educational administrator; b. Tacoma, Wash., May 1, 1947; d. Donald William and Helen (Harper) Bourgaize; 1 child, Matthew Harris. BA, San Jose State U., 1971, MS, 1973. Psychologist Whisman Sch. Dist., Mountain View, Calif., 1972; psychologist, coord., dir. pupil pers. svcs. Mt. Pleasant Sch. Dist., San Jose, 1972-81; dir. San Benito/Santa Cruz Counties Spl. Edn. Local Plan Area, Aptos, Calif., 1981-91; pvt. ednl. cons. La Selva Beach, Calif., 1991—; dir. Washington Twp. spl. edn. local plan area, dir. spl. svcs. Fremont (Calif.) Unified Sch. Dist., 1993—; cons. Calif. Dept. Edn., Sacramento, 1977—, cons., lobbyist, 1994—; pvt. practice psychology and edn. cons., Calif., 1975—. Mem. steering com. Coalition for Adequate Funding for Disabled Children, Sacramento, 1987-93; chair Spl. Edn. Coalition, 1991-93. Mem. ASCD, LWV, PEO, Coun. Exceptional Children, Calif. Spl. Edn. Local Plan Area Adminstrs. (chmn. 1989-90, legis. chairperson 1990—), Assn. Calif. Sch. Adminstrs., Phi Delta Kappa. Democrat. Home: 27 Altivo Ave La Selva Beach CA 95076

BOURGEOIS, LOUISE, sculptor; b. Paris, 1911; came to U.S., 1938, naturalized, 1953; Student, Sorbonne U., 1932-35; baccalaureate, Ecole des Beaux Arts, 1936-38; postgrad., Ecole du Louvre, 1936-37, Acad. Grande Chaumiere; D.F.A. (hon.), Yale U., 1977, Calif. Coll. Arts and Crafts, 1988, Moore Coll. Art, Mass. Coll. Art, 1983, Md. Art Inst., 1984, The New Sch., 1987. Instr. Md. Art Inst., Balt., 1984, New Sch. Social Rsch., N.Y.C., 1987. One-woman shows include Norlyst Gallery, 1947, Peridot Gallery, 1949, 50, 53, Allan Frumkin Gallery, Chgo., 1953, White Art Mus., Cornell U., Ithaca, N.Y., 1959, Stable Gallery, 1964, Rose Fried Gallery, 1963, 112 Greene St., N.Y.C., 1974, Xavier Fourcade Gallery, N.Y.C., 1978-80, Max Hutchinson Gallery, N.Y.C., 1980, Renaissance Soc., 1981, Mus. Modern Art, N.Y.C., 1982, retrospective Contemporary Art Mus., Houston, 1983, Daniel Weinberg Gallery, L.A., 1984, Robert Miller Gallery, 1982, 84, 87-89, 91, Serpentine Gallery, London, 1985, Maeght-Lelong, Zurich, 1985, Paris, 1985, Taft Mus., Cin., 1987-89 (travelled to The Art Mus. at Fla. Internat. U., Miami, Fla., Laguna Gloria Art Mus., Austin, Tex., Gallery of Art, Washington U., St. Louis, Henry Art Gallery, Seattle, Everson Mus. Art, Syracuse, N.Y.), Mus. Overholland, Amsterdam, The Netherlands, 1988, Dia Art Found., Bridgehampton, N.Y., retrospective Frankfurter Kunstverein, Frankfurt, Fed. Republic Germany, 1989 (travelled to Städtische Galerie im Lenbachhaus, Munich, 1990, Riverside Studios, London, 1990, Musée d'Art Contemporain, Lyon, 1990, Fondacion Tapies, Barcelona, Spain, Kunstmuseum, Berne, Switzerland, Kröller-Müller Mus., Otterlo, The Netherlands), Linda Cathcart Gallery, Santa Monica, Calif., 1990, Barbara Gross Gallerie, Munich, 1990, Karsten Schubert, London, 1990, Galerie Krinzinger, Vienna, 1990, Karsten Greve Gallery, Cologne, 1990, Ginny Williams Gallery, 1990, Monika Spruthe Galerie, Cologne, 1990, Robert Miller Gallery 1986, 1987, 1988, 1989, 1991, Galerie Lelong, Zurich, 1991; solo exhbns. include Parrish Art Mus., Southampton, N.Y., Ydessa Hendeles Found., Toronto, 1991, 92, Milwaukee Art Mus., 1992, The Fabric Workshop, Phila., Galerie Karsten Greve, Paris, Linda Cathcart Gallery, Santa Monica, Calif., Second Floor, Reykjavik, Iceland; exhibited in numerous group shows, U.S., Europe; represented in permanent collections Mus. Modern Art, N.Y.C., Whitney Mus., Met. Mus. Art, Hirshorn Mus., Musée Nat. D'Art Moderne, Paris, R.I. Sch. Design, NYU, Albright-Knox Art Gallery, Buffalo, Australian Nat. Gallery, Canberra, Musée d'Art Moderne, Paris, Mus. Fine Arts, Houston, Guggenheim Mus., N.Y.C., Kunstmus. Bern, Kunstmus. Lucerne, Albertina, Vienna, Mus. Modern Art, Vienna, Walker Art Ctr., Mpls., Storm King Art Ctr., Mountainville, N.Y. Recipient Outstanding Achievement award Women's Caucus, 1980, Pres.'s Fellow award R.I. Sch. Design, 1984, Skowhegan medal sculpture Skowhegan (Maine) Sch. Painting, and Sculpture, Gold medal of honor Nat. Arts Club, 1987, Creative Arts Medal award Brandeis U., 1989, Grand Prix Nat. de Sculpture French Ministry of Culture, 1991; recipient Lifetime Achievement award Coll. Art Assn., 1989, Internat. Sculpture Ctr., 1991; named Officer of Arts and Letters French Ministry of Culture, 1984. Fellow Am. Acad. Arts and Scis.; mem. Am. Acad. and Inst. Arts and Letters, Sculptors Guild, Am. Abstract Artists, Coll. Art Assn. (Disting. Artist award for lifetime achievement 1989). Office: care Robert Miller Gallery 347 W 20th St New York NY 10011-1908*

BOURJAILY, MARY JO, advertising executive; b. Detroit, Sept. 1, 1953; d. Tirigi and Lorraine (Lindberg) Galli; m. Randal Alan, Oct. 16, 1981; children: Richard Joseph, Ryan Patrick. BA in Journalism, Mich. State U., 1974, MA in Advt., 1976. Reporter, editor South Haven (Mich.) Daily Tribune, 1974; news anchor Sta. WEYI-TV, Flint, Mich., 1975-76, Sta. WILX-TV, Lansing, Mich., 1976-78; pub. rels. rep. Ford Motor Co., Dearborn, Mich., 1978-79; mgr. corp. comm. United Techs., Dearborn, 1980-81; mgr. pub. rels. Manning Selvage & Lee, Bloomfield Hills, Mich., 1981-86; mng. dir. pub. rels. DMB&B, Bloomfield Hills, 1986-93, sr. v.p., acct. dir. fin. svcs. and products, 1993—. Mem. Advt. Club of Detroit, Detroit Athletic Club, Women's Econ. Club of Detroit. Roman Catholic. Office: Darcy Masuis Benton & Bowles PR 74 W Long Lake Rd PO Box 811 Bloomfield Hills MI 48303

BOURNE, CAROL ELIZABETH MULLIGAN, biology educator, phycologist; b. Rochester, N.Y., May 4, 1948; d. William Thomas and Ruth Townsend (Stevens) Mulligan; m. Godfrey Roderick Bourne, Dec. 21, 1968. BA in Botany/Bacteriology, Ohio Wesleyan U., 1970; MS in Botany, Miami University, Oxford, Ohio, 1978; PhD in Natural Resources, U. Mich., 1992. Lab. asst. Ohio Wesleyan U., Delaware, 1968-70; biol. lab. tech. USDA-Forest Svc., Delaware, 1970-73; grad. rsch. asst. botany dept. Miami U., Oxford, 1973-75; electron microscopist coll. medicine U. Cin., 1975-76; rsch. asst. sch. pub. health U. Mich., Ann Arbor, 1978-80, rsch. assoc. coll. medicine, 1981-83, grad. rsch. asst. sch. natural resources, 1983-86, grad. teaching asst. dept. biology, 1987; postdoctoral scientist U. Fla., Ft. Lauderdale, 1990-92; adj. instr. ecology Fla. Atlantic U. Coll. Liberal Arts, Davie, 1992-93; adj. asst. prof. dept. biology U. Mo., St. Louis, 1994—; adj. asst. prof. biology U. Mo.-St. Louis. Contbr. articles to scholarly jours. Grantee NSF, 1987-89. Mem. Am. Inst. Biolog. Scis., Am. Soc. Plant Taxonomists, Phycological Soc. Am., Internat. Soc. for Diatom Rsch., Internat. Soc. for Plant Molecular Biology, Brit. Phycological Soc., Soc. for Study of Evolution. Office: U Mo at St Louis Dept Biology 8001 Natural Bridge Rd Saint Louis MO 63121

BOURNE, ELIZABETH, public service representative; b. Chgo., Oct. 28, 1965; d. Mission Clabron and Dessie Mae (Franklin) B. BS, Drake U., 1987. Sec. Drake U., Des Moines, 1986-87; feature writer The Communicator, Des Moines, 1986-87; pub. svc. rep. Chgo. Tribune, 1989—; copywriter Advt. class, Des Moines, 1986. Contbr. articles to profl. jours. Mem. People United to Save Humanity, Chgo., 1988. Mem. Am. Mktg. Assn., NAFE. Democrat. Baptist. Home: 10837 S Green St Chicago IL 60643-3805 Office: Chgo Tribune PO Box 25340 Chicago IL 60625-0340

BOURRET, MARJORIE ANN, educational advocate, consultant; b. Denver, Sept. 9, 1925; d. Walter Brewster and Grace Helen (Thompson) Leaf; m. Raymond Roland Bourret, May 28, 1955; children: Robert B., Ronald P. BSEE, BS in Engring. Physics, U. Colo., 1947. Cons. for child advocacy and interagy. coordination San Benito-Santa Cruz Spl. Edn. Local Plan Agy., Aptos, Calif., 1991; project coord. for Linkup to Learning Valley Resource Ctr., Ben Lomond, Calif., 1992—. Contbg. author: Board/Superintendent Roles, Responsibilities and relationships, 1980; prin. author: Citizens Guide to Scotts Valley, 1984; also articles. Trustee, pres. Scotts Valley (Calif.) Union Sch. Dist., 1970-81; mem., chmn. policy devel. com. San Benito-Santa Cruz Spl. Edn. Coordinating Agy., 1980-81; cons. on code sect. 7579, 1990; Calif. Adv. Commn. on Spl. Edn., Sacramento, 1984-89, chmn. legis. com., 1984, chmn. policy rev. com., 1987-89; mem. chmn. Hazardous Materials Adv. Commn., Santa Cruz, 1984-87; organizer, bd. dirs. Friends Long Marine Lab., U. Calif., Santa Cruz, 1979-84; bd. dirs. Group Home Soc., Santa Cruz, 1984-86, others.*. Recipient Disting. Engring. Alumna award Coll. Engring. & Applied Sci. U. Colo., 1994. Mem. Nat. Sch. Bds. Assn. (fed. rels. network 1977-81), Calif. Sch. Bds. Assn. (bd. dirs., com. chmn. 1977-81, mem. del. assembly 1974-81), LWV (pres. Santa Cruz County chpt. 1967-69). Home: 1160 Whispering Pines Dr Scotts Valley CA 95066-4627

BOUTELLE, JANE CRONIN, fitness consultant; b. Arlington, Mass., Nov. 3, 1926; s. William Francis and Sara (Gillis) Cronin; m. G. William Boutelle, 1953 (dec. 1973); children—Jeanne E., William R., James G. B.S., Boston U., 1948; M.A., Columbia U., 1953. Cert. tchr., Mass. Tchr. dance and health edn. Newton High Sch., Mass., 1948-51, Scarsdale High Sch., N.Y., 1951-55, Marymount Coll., Tarrytown, N.Y., 1955-58, Manhattanville Coll., Purchase, N.Y., 1958-59; pres., fitness cons. The Boutelle Method, Inc., Greenwich, Conn., 1973—. Author: Lifetime Fitness for Women, 1978. Contbr. articles to mags. Pres Westchester Dance Council, Westchester County, N.Y., 1956-57; mem. Nat. Alumni Bd. Boston U., 1981— (chmn. 40th reunion); mem. woman's com. Lighthouse, Westchester County, N.Y., 1983. Recipient Bravo award Greenwich YWCA, 1978. Mem. AAUW (chmn. edn. 1963-68), Soroptimists Internat. (chmn. scholarship com.), Greenwich Woman's Club Gardeners (chmn. scholarship com.) Assn. Women in Phys. Edn. (chmn. 1954-55), Greenwich Assn. Pub. Schs. (chmn. 1968-73). Home: Huckleberry Ln Greenwich CT 06831 Office: The Boutelle Method Inc Huckleberry Ln Greenwich CT 06831

BOVA, LINDA CAROL, consulting company executive, editor; b. Pomona, Calif., July 25, 1947; d. Robert Bruce and Wanda Georgine (Wellman) Middough; m. Stephen R. Bova, Jan. 20, 1968 (div. May 1981); children: Karen E., Lori L. Student, El Camino Coll., Gardena, Calif., 1965-66. Sec. TRW, Inc., Manhattan Beach, Calif., 1967-68, USAF NCO Clubs, Mildenhall, Eng., 1968-70; adminstrv. asst. Prudential-Bache Securities, N.Y.C., 1970-73, Tex. Instruments, Inc., Dallas, 1980-83; asst. to pres. Acclivus Corp., Dallas, 1983-85, mgr. design and prodn., 1985-88, mgr. ops., 1988-89, v.p. ops., 1989—; cons. Digital Equipment Corp., Boston, 1984-89. Editor: (books and videotapes) BASE for Sales Performance, 1984, Acclivus Sales Negotiation, 1985, The New BASE for Sales Excellence, 1989, Major Account Planning and Strategy, 1993, Building on the BASE (award for best new tng. products Human Resource Exec.), 1993. Organizer Meals on Wheels, Denton, Tex., 1977; leader youth group United Meth. Ch., Denton, 1984-87; sponsor Trinity Youth Players, Denton, 1986-90; editor, pub. Denton Bible Ch., 1993—. Mem. ASTD, Instructional Systems Assn., Nat. Soc. for Performance and Instrn., Soc. for Applied Learning Tech., Soc. for Accelerative Learning and Teaching, Internat. Listening Assn. Republican. Home: 2001 Stonegate Dr Denton TX 76205-8259 Office: Acclivus Corp 14500 Midway Rd Dallas TX 75244-3109

BOVITZ, CAROLE JONES, psychotherapist; b. Tulsa, July 9, 1936; d. John Wesley Jones and Vada L. (Dailey) Friesen; m. Richard Stanley Bovitz, May 28, 1959; children: J. Scott, Jennifer Jean. BA in Psychology, Calif. State U., Northridge, 1969; MA in Psychology, Pepperdine U., 1982. Lic. marriage, family, child therapist; cert. employee assistance profl. Ptnr. Personnel Research Assocs., Chatsworth, Calif., 1979-82; pres. Carole Bovitz & Assocs., Huntington Beach and Torrance, Calif., 1982-88; provider rels. mgr. Personal Performance Consultants Inc., Irvine, Calif., 1988-92; pvt. practice Long Beach and Cerritos, Calif., 1992—; dir. presenting services Am. Bus. Concepts, Torrance, 1986-87; seminar cons., trainer Children's Hosp., Orange, Calif., 1986-87; cons. mgmt. seminars C. of C., Riviera Village Assocs., Redondo Beach, Calif., 1988. Pres. Calif. Legis. Roundtable, Sacramento, 1985-86; trustee governing bd. Sch. Dist., Goleta, Calif., 1976; bd. dirs. Calif. Ednl. Congress, Sacramento, 1984-86, Calif. Coalition Fair Sch. Fin., 1984-86. Mem. AAUW (vol. community leadership trainer 1985-88, state pres. 1984-86, state rep. to nat. bd. dirs. 1978-82, state dir. leadership 1988-89, pres. Orange County interbr. council pres.'s 1987-88, Calif. state fellowship endowment named in her honor 1986 in perpetuity, research grant named in her honor 1986 in perpetuity, gift honoree local chpts. 1976, 86, 94), Calif. Assn. Marriage and Family Therapists. Democrat. Office: 11558 South St Ste 47 Cerritos CA 90703

BOWDEN, ANN, bibliographer, educator; b. East Orange, N.J., Feb. 7, 1924; d. William and Anna Elisabeth (Herrstrom) Haddon; m. Edwin Turner Bowden, June 12, 1948; children: Elisabeth Bowden Ward, Susan Turner, Edwin Eric; m. William Burton Todd, Nov. 23, 1969. BA, Radcliffe Coll., 1948; MS in Library Services, Columbia U., 1951; PhD, U. Tex., 1975. Cataloger, reference asst. Yale U., 1948-53; manuscript cataloger, rare book librarian, librarian Humanities Research Ctr., librarian Acad. Ctr., U. Tex., Austin, 1958-63, lectr., sr. lectr. Grad. Sch. Library and Info. Sci., 1964-85, 88-89; coordinator adult services Austin Pub. Library, 1963-67, asst. dir., 1967-71, dep. dir., 1971-77, assoc. dir., 1977-86; bd. dirs. Tex. Info. Exchange, Houston, 1977-78; bd. dirs. AMIGOS Bibliog. Council, Dallas, 1978-82, chmn. bd., 1980-81, trustee emeritus, 1986—; chmn. AMIGOS '85 Plan, 1984-86; scholar in residence Rockefeller Found. Villa Serbelloni, Bellagio, Italy, 1986, Ransom Ctr. scholar U. Tex., Austin, 1990—; Zachariah Polson fellow Libr. Co. of Phila., 1990. Author (with W.B. Todd) Tauchnitz International Editions in English, 1988; editor: T.E. Lawrence Fifty Letters: 1921-1935, 1962; Maps and Atlases, 1978; assoc. editor Papers of the Bibliographical Soc. Am., 1967-82; contbr. articles to profl. jours. Served as cpl. USMC Women's Res., 1944-46. Mem. ALA (council 1975-79), Assn. Coll. and Research Libraries (chmn. rare book and manuscript sect. 1975-76), Tex. Library Assn. (chmn. publs. com. 1965-71), Bibliog. Soc. Am., Phi Kappa Phi, Kappa Tau Alpha. Club: Grolier (N.Y.C.).

BOWDEN, CINDY A., appraisal company executive, artist; b. Seminole, Okla., May 7, 1950; d. Hugh Allan and LaJoyee Sue (Harber) McBride; m. Barry Dean Bowden, Mar. 31, 1969 (dec. July 1993); children: Christian Reneé Bowden Evans, Justin Harber. Student, NW Okla. State U., 1968-69, Redlands, 1970. Sec. Auto Damage Appraisals, Enid, Okla., 1985-90; owner Bowden Ins. Agy., Hennessey, Okla., 1985-90; owner, cons., tchr. Brush and Shutter Art, Hennessey, 1985-88; owner, v.p. Heartland Appraisal Svc., Inc., Hennessey, 1986-93, owner, pres., 1993—, also chmn. bd.; owner Ars Longa, Vita Brevis, Hennessey, 1972—, cons., tchr., 1986-94. Exhbns. Okla. Gov.'s Gallery State Arts Coun., Okla. City, 1990, New Eng. Fine Arts Inst., Boston, 1992. Mem. Enid Art Assn., Lioness Club. Republican. Home and Office: 103 Holly Dr Rt # 3 Hennessey OK 73742

BOWDEN, GLENDA EDWARDS, secondary education eduator; b. Mineral Falls, Tex., Dec. 14, 1949; d. William Artra Jr. and Wilma June (McClish) Edwards; m. James Bruce Bowden, July 31, 1970; children: Alyssa Denise, Serena Noelle. BS, Tarleton State U., 1971; MS, Baylor U., 1973; postgrad. in Edn., Abilene Christian U., 1994—. Tchr. Math and Sci. Wylie High Sch., Abilene, 1994—. Named Tchr. of Yr. Kiwanis, Abilene, 1993. Mem. Assn. Bus. Women, Assn. Tex. Profl. Educators, Abilene Edn. Assn.

BOWDEN, SALLY ANN, choreographer, teacher, dancer; b. Dallas, Feb. 27, 1943; d. Cloyd MacAnally and Sally Estelle. Student, Boston U., 1960-62. Mem. Paul Sanasardo Dance Co., N.Y.C., 1963-67; pvt. tchr., choreographer N.Y.C., 1968-70; faculty Merce Cunningham Dance Studio, N.Y.C., 1971-76; faculty, co-dir. Constrn. Co. Dance Studio, N.Y.C., 1972-77; choreographer Constrn. Co. Theater/Dance Assocs., N.Y.C., 1972—; artist-in-residence U. Wis., Madison, fall, 1975, N.C. Sch. of Arts, winter, 1978, U. Minn., Duluth, 1979, 1981-82, Kenyon (Ohio) Coll., fall 1980. Choreographer: Three Dances, 1969, Sally Bowden Dances and Talks at the New School, 1972, The Ice Palace, 1973, White River Junction, 1975, The Wonderful World of Modern Dance or The Amazing Story of the Plie, (1976) Wheat, 1976-77, Kite, 1978, Voyages, 1978, Morningdance, 1979, Crescent, 1980, Diverted Suite, 1983, Baby Dance, 1984. Recipient Creative Artists Public Service award for choreography, 1976-77; Nat. Endowment for the Arts Choreography fellow, 1975. Office: Theater/Dance Assocs 41 E 1st St New York NY 10003-9307

BOWEN, BARBARA LYNN, computer company executive; b. Toledo, May 19, 1945; d. John Thomas and Grace Elizabeth (Spaulding) B. AB, Oberlin Coll., 1967; M.S., So. Conn. U., 1968; PhD, Cornell U., 1972. Asst. prof. Queens Coll., Flushing, N.Y., 1979-81; mgr. mktg. support-tng. Logo Computer Systems, Inc., N.Y.C., 1981-83; dir. Apple Edn. Found., Apple Computer, Inc., Cupertino, Calif., 1983-84; program dir. edn. affairs Apple Computer, Inc., Cupertino, 1984-86, mgr. external rsch., 1986—; mem. Nat. Task Force on Ednl. Tech., 1984-86; bd. advisers N.E. Regional Exch. Teleconf. Project, Bolton, N.H., 1984-85, Nat. Ctr. on Computer Equity, N.Y.C., 1985-88. Author: Apple Logo Training Manual, 1983. Mem. editorial bd. Nat. Rural Spl. Edn. quar., 1986-88, Edn. & Computing Jour., 1988—. Bd. dirs. Ctr. for Econ. Conversion, Mountain View, Calif., 1985, 86, pres. bd. dirs., 1986. Mem. Am. Mgmt. Assn., Bus. Execs. for Nat. Security, Pres.'s Coun. Cornell Women, Computer Profls. Social Responsibility, Leadership Am. Home: 1018 Taylor St Port Townsend WA 98368-5435 Office: Apple Computer Inc 20525 Mariani Ave # 763C Cupertino CA 95014

BOWEN, CLOTILDE DENT, retired army officer, psychiatrist; b. Chgo., Mar. 20, 1923; d. William Marion Dent and Clotilde (Tynes) D.; m. William N. Bowen, Dec. 29, 1945 (dec.). B.A., Ohio State U., 1943, M.D., 1947. Intern, Harlem Hosp., N.Y.C., 1947-48; resident and fellow in pulmonary diseases, Triboro Hosp., Jamaica, L.I., N.Y., 1948-50; resident in psychiatry VA Hosp., Albany, N.Y., 1959-62; pvt. practice, N.Y.C. 1950-55; chief pulmonary disease clinic, N.Y.C. 1950-55; asst. chief pulmonary disease svc., Valley Forge Army Hosp., Pa., 1956-59; chief psychiatry VA Hosp., Roseburg, Oreg., 1962-66, acting chief of staff, 1964-66; asst. chief neurology and psychiatry Tripler Gen. Hosp., Hawaii, 1966-68; psychiatr. cons. and dir. Rev. Br., Office Civil Health and Med. Program, Uniform Svcs., 1968-70; commd. capt. U.S. Army, 1955, advanced through ranks to col., 1968; neuropsychiat. cons. U.S. Army Vietnam, 1970-71; chief dept. psychiatry Fitzsimons Army Med. Ctr., 1971-74; chief dept. psychiatry. Tripler Army Med. Ctr., 1974-75; comdr. Hawley Army Clinic, Ft. Benjamin, Harrison, Ind., 1977-78, chief dept. primary care and community medicine, 1978-83, chief psychiat. consultation svc., Fitzsimons Army Med. Ctr., 1983-85; chief psychiatry svc. med./regional office ctr. VA, Cheyenne, Wyo., 1987-90; staff psychiatrist Denver VA Satellite Clinic, Colorado Springs, Colo., 1990—; surveyor, Joint Commn. on Accreditation Healthcare Orgns., 1985-92; assoc. prof. psychiatry U. Colo. Med. Center, Denver, 1970-83. Decorated Legion of Merit, several other medals. Fellow Am. Psychiat. Assn. (life), Acad. Psychosomatic Medicine; mem. AMA, Nat. Med. Assn., Menninger Found. (charter). Home: 1020 Tari Dr Colorado Springs CO 80921-2257

BOWEN, DEBRA LYNN, lawyer, state legislator; b. Rockford, Ill., Oct. 27, 1955; d. Robert Calvin and Marcia Ann (Crittenden) Bowen. B.A., Mich. State U., 1976; Rotary Internat. fellow Internat. Christian U., Tokyo, 1975; J.D., U. Va., 1979. Bar: Ill. 1979, Calif. 1983. Assoc., Winston & Strawn, Chgo., 1979-82, Washington, 1985-86, Hughes Hubbard & Reed, Los Angeles, 1982-84; sole practice, Los Angeles, 1984—; mem. Calif. State Assembly, 1992—; gen. counsel, State Employee's Retirement System Ill., Springfield, 1980-82; adj. prof. Watterson Coll. Sch. Paralegal Studies, 1985. Exec. editor Va. Jour. Internat. Law, 1977-78; contbr. articles to profl. jours. Mem. mental health law com. Chgo. Council Lawyers, 1980-82. Wigmore scholar Northwestern U. Sch. Law, Chgo., 1976; . Mem. ABA, Los Angeles County Bar Assn., Calif. Bar Assn. (exec. com. pub. law sect. 1990—), Phi Kappa Phi. Office: Dist Office 18411 Crenshaw Blvd Ste 280 Torrance CA 90504-5043*

BOWEN, JEAN, music librarian, consultant; b. Albany, N.Y., Mar. 23, 1927; d. John W. and Grace Lester (Quier) B.; m. Henry F. Bloch, June 26, 1962; 1 child, Pamela A. Bloch. AB, Smith Coll., 1948, AM, 1956; MS, Columbia U., 1957. Curator Rodgers & Hammerstein Archives of Recorded Sound, N.Y.C., 1962-67; asst. chief music divsn. N.Y. Pub. Libr., N.Y.C., 1967-85, chief music divsn., 1985—; cons. Rockefeller Bros. Fund., N.Y.C., 1963, 67, N.Y. Philharm., N.Y.C., 1984, Schubert Archives, N.Y.C., 1982; mem. faculty Rare Book Sch. Columbia U., N.Y.C., 1984, 87, 91; bd. dirs.

Am. Music Ctr., N.Y.C., Composers Recs. Inc., N.Y.C., Amphion Found., N.Y.C. Contbr. articles to High Fidelity, Opera News, Am. Record Guide, Saturday Rev., MLA Notes, New Grove Dictionary of Am. Music. Mem. Music Libr. Assn. Office: NY Pub Libr Music Divsn 40 Lincoln Ctr Plz New York NY 10023-7498

BOWEN, KATHRYN ANN, pediatrician, educator; b. Spokane, Wash., June 2, 1953; d. Francis John Bowen and Rosalind (Adams) Fogleman. BA, U. Colo., 1975; MD, St. Louis U., 1979. Diplomate Am. Bd. Pediatrics. Instr. pediatrics St. Louis U., 1982-84, asst. prof. pediatrics, 1984-89; asst. prof. pediatrics U. Ariz., Tucson, 1989—; with EMS Coun., Tucson, 1994—. Fellow Am. Acad. Pediatrics (chmn. Ariz. chpt. child abuse com. 1994); mem. Am. Profl. Soc. Abuse Children, Pima County Pediatric Soc. Office: U Ariz Dept Pediatrics 1501 N Campbell Blvd Tucson AZ 85724

BOWEN, MARCIA KAY, customs house broker; b. Bradford, Pa., July 20, 1957; d. George W. Allen Jr. and Katherine (Jema) Allen; m. Glenn Edward Rollins, June 26, 1975 (div. 1979); m. Michael James Bowen, Dec. 27, 1983; children: James Derek, Kodie Ann. Student Houston Community Coll., 1978-81, Am. Mgmt. Assn., 1984-85. Lic. customs house broker. Asst. mgr. W.R. Zanes & Co. of La., Inc., Houston, 1975-76; sec. Westchester Corp., Houston, 1973-75; import br. mgr. Schenkers Internat., Inc., Houston, 1976-85; br. mgr. F.W. Myers & Co., Inc., El Paso, 1985-88, regional mgr., 1989-91; v.p. Southwest region The Myers Group (US) Inc., 1992—. Mem. NAFE, Houston Customs House Brokers Assn. (sec. 1977-79, mem. U.S. customs com. 1979-83), El Paso Customs House Brokers Assn. (v.p. 1994), Houston Freight Forwarders Assn., El Paso Fgn. Trade Zone Assn., Soc. Global Trade Execs., El Paso/Juarez Transp. and Distbn. Assn., Inc., El Paso Custon Brokers Assn. (v.p. 1994). Roman Catholic. Office: The Myers Group (US) Inc 34 Spur Dr El Paso TX 79906

BOWER, BARBARA JEAN, nurse; b. Akron, Ohio, Aug. 25, 1942; d. William Howard and Maxine (Goodykoontz) Sturm; m. Howard Bower, Aug. 25, 1961 (dec. 1989); children: Nancy, Janet; m. Richard Chavez, Dec. 24, 1993. BA, Elmhurst Coll., 1974, postgrad., 1987—; diploma, Evang. Sch. Nursing, 1970; PhD, U. Chgo., 1993. RN. Supr. nursing Med. Ctr.; nurse critical care Loyola U., Maywood, Ill., 1970-78, Med. Staffing Services, Oak Park, Ill., 1978-84; pres. Heart Care Unltd., Bridgeview, Ill., 1982—; one of first ind. nurse contractors in Ill. Creator ednl. programs for cardiac patients, families, 1971—. Mem. AAUW, Am. Nurses Assn., Am. Assn. Critical Care Nurses, Am. Heart Assn., Elmhurst Coll. Alumni Assn. Mem. Christ Ch. Home: 3203 York Rd Oak Brook IL 60521 Office: Heart Care Unltd PC PO Box 2027 Oak Lawn IL 60455-6027

BOWER, CATHERINE DOWNES, communications and public relations executive; b. Balt., Dec. 29, 1947; m. Réjean Pierre Proulx, Apr. 28, 1990. BA, Kent State U., 1969. Editor East Ohio Gas Co., Cleve., 1971-74; editor Personnel Administrator mag., Berea, Ohio, 1974-79, dir. communications, 1979-84; v.p. communications, pub. Am. Soc. Pers. Adminstrn. (name Soc. Human Resource Mgmt.), Alexandria, 1984-86; v.p. communications and pub. relations Am. Soc. Pers. Adminstrn. (name Soc. Human Resource Mgmt.), Alexandria, Va., 1986-91; sr. ptnr. Tecker Cons., Trenton, N.J., 1991—; pres. Cate Bower Communications, Alexandria and West River, Md., 1991—; project dir. Work in the 21st Century, 1984. Editor: Work Life Visions, 1987. Pres. Oak Cluster Community Council, Alexandria, 1985-89. Fellow Am. Soc. Assn. Execs. (cert., vice chmn. comms. sect. coun. 1986-87, chmn. 1987-88, com. sect. 1984-89, planning com. 1989-91, bd. dirs. Found. 1989-93, Best Pub. Pub. Rels. Program award 1984); mem. Internat. Assn. Bus. Communicators (pres. Cleve. chpt. 1974), Greater Washington Soc. Assn. Execs. (chair visibility task force 1994-95). Office: Cate Bower Comms 5109 Holly Dr West River MD 20778

BOWER, CINDY LOU, property management and resort hotel company executive; b. Scottsbluff, Nebr., Apr. 6, 1957; d. Raymond Eugene and Kathleen Coila (Roberts) B. B.S. in Psychology, U. Wyo., 1980. Profl. basketball player Washington Metros, 1979; asst. to mng. dir. Western Services Corp., Silver Springs, Md., 1980-82; v.p., gen. mgr. Key Resort Mgmt., Crested Butte, Colo., 1982—. Mnr. Crested Butte Soccer Team, 1982—; capt. Crested Butte Softball, 1982—; mem. Crested Butte/Mount Crested Butte Adv. Bd., 1983—. Named to Women's Collegiate All-Am. Basketball Team, region VII Nat. Scouting Assn. and Women Pro Basketball League, 1979. Mem. Nat. Assn. Female Execs., Denver/Colo. Conv. Bur., Colo. Soc. Assn. Execs., Am. Hotel/Motel Assn., Colo./Wyo. Hotel/Motel Assn., Crested Butte/Mount Crested Butte C. of C., Gunnison County C. of C., Crested Butte Bus. and Profl. Women's Club (v.p.). Republican. Lutheran. Home: 508 North Ave E Missoula MT 59801-6004 Office: Key Resort Mgmt 21 Emmons Rd Mount Crstd Btte CO 81225

BOWER, DORIS J., education educator; b. Jackson, Minn., Feb. 28, 1938; d. Edward Joseph and Ethel (Madsen) Doyscher; m. Forrest G. Wahl, Sept. 9, 1966 (div. 1977); children: John-Charles Wahl, Andrew Wahl; m. James Philip Bower, June 30, 1979; 1 child, Joshua Bower. BS, Mankato State U., 1962, MS, 1975; EdS, St. Thomas U., 1986; postgrad., U. Wash., 1987. Cert. tchr. and adminstr. K-12, Wash. Mktg. dir. Videodiscovery, Seattle, 1987-90; dir. A+ Learning Ctr., Bellevue, Wash., 1990—; cons. Northwest Regional Ednl. Labs, Lake Washington Schs. and Control Data Corp., Seattle, Mpls.; mem. planning coms. in field; adj. faculty Seattle Pacific U. Mem. Bellevue Champer, 1993. Recipient Apple's Tchr. Tng. Scholarship, Murray Scholarship, Best Microcomputer Software of Yr. award. Mem. ASCD, Edn. Data Systems, Reading Coun., Edn. Technology Assn. Mem. Unity Ch. Office: A+ Learning Ctr 13401 Bel Red Rd Bellevue WA 98005-2322

BOWER, FAY LOUISE, academic administrator, nursing educator; b. San Francisco, Sept. 10, 1929; d. James Joseph and Emily Clare (Andrews) Saitta; BS with honors, San Jose State Coll., 1965; MSN, U. Calif., 1966, DNSc, 1978; children: R. David, Carol Bower Tomei, Dennis James, Thomas John. Office nurse Dr. William Grannis, Palo Alto, Calif., 1950-55; staff nurse Stanford Hosp., 1964-72; asst. prof. San Jose State U., 1966-70, assoc. prof., 1970-74, prof., 1974-82, coord. grad. program in nursing, 1977-78, chairperson dept. nursing, 1978-82; dean U. San Francisco, 1982-89, v.p. acad. affairs, 1988-89, dir. univ. planning and instl. rsch., 1989-91, pres. Clarkson Coll., 1991—; speaker; cons. univs.; vis. prof. Harding Coll., 1977, U. Miss., 1976; lectr. U. Calif., San Francisco, 1975. Cert. pub. health nurse, sch. nurse, Calif. Fellow Am. Acad. Nursing; mem. Calif. Nurses Assn., Nurses Assn. Coll. Ob-Gyn, Calif. Tchrs. Assn., Pub. Health Assn. Calif., Nat. League Nursing (bd. dirs.), Calif. League for Nursing (pres.), Western Gerontol. Assn., Sigma Theta Tau (internat. pres. 1993—), Jesuit Deans in Nursing (chair). Democrat. Roman Catholic. Club: Commonwealth (San Francisco). Author: (with Em O. Bevis) Fundamentals of Nursing Practice: Concepts, Roles and Functions, 1978; (with Margaret Jacobson) Community Health Nursing, 1978; The Process of Planning Nursing Care, 3d edit., 1982; Theoretical Foundations of Nursing I, II, and III, 1972; editor: Normal Development of Body Image, 1977; Distortions in Body Image in Illness and Disability, 1977; Foundations of Pharmacologic Therapy, 1977; Nursing Assessment, 1977. Home: 1114 S 113th Plz Omaha NE 68144-1870 Office: Clarkson Coll Office of Pres 101 S 42nd St Omaha NE 68131-2739

BOWER, JEAN RAMSAY, court administrator, lawyer; b. N.Y.C., Nov. 25, 1935; d. Claude Barnett and Myrtle Marie (Scott) Ramsay; m. Ward Swift Just, Jan. 31, 1957 (div. 1966); children: Jennifer Ramsay, Julia Barnett; m. Robert Turrell Bower, June 12, 1971 (dec. June 1990). A.B., Vassar Coll., 1957; J.D., Georgetown U., 1970. Bar: D.C. 1970. Exec. dir. D.C. Dem. Cen. Com., Washington, 1969-71; pvt. practice, Washington, 1971-78; dir. Counsel for Child Abuse and Neglect Office, D.C. Superior Ct., 1978-94. Mem. Mayor's Com. on Child Abuse and Neglect, 1973—, vice chmn., 1975-79; mem. Family Div. Rules Adv. Com., 1977-94; pres., bd. dirs. C.B. Ramsay Found., 1984—. Active D.C. Child Fatality Rev. Com., 1992—. Named Washingtonian of the Yr. Washing. Mag., 1978; recipient Beahice Rosenberg award D.C. Bar, 1994. Mem. Women's Bar Assn. (bd. dirs. 1993—, found. 1986-91, Woman Lawyer of Yr. 1986), D.C. Bar Assn. (election bd. 1994—, Beatrice Rosenberg award, 1994), Women's Bar Assn. Found (bd. dirs. 1986-91).

BOWERS, BEGE K., English educator; b. Nashville, Tenn., Aug. 19, 1949; d. John and Yvonne (Howell) B. BA in English cum laude, Vanderbilt U., 1971; student, U. Mich., 1985; MACT, U. Tenn., 1973, PhD, 1984. Asst. loan officer Ctr. for Fin. Aid and Placement, Baylor U., Waco, Tex., 1975-76; editorial asst. Wassily Leontief, NYU, N.Y.C., 1976-78; instr. bus. English Florence-Darlington Tech. Coll., Florence, S.C., 1979-80; tchr. English and French St. John's High Sch., Darlington, S.C., 1980-82; teaching asst. dept English U. Tenn., Knoxville, 1982-84; asst. prof. English Youngstown (Ohio) State U., 1984-88, assoc. prof., 1988-92, prof., 1992—, composition coord. dept. English, 1985-94, acting chmn. dept., 1989, asst. to dean Coll. Arts and Scis., 1992-93; part-time freelance editor MLA, N.Y.C., 1978-80; cons. Project Arete, Youngstown and Mahoning County Pub. Schs., 1984-87, Youngstown Pub. Schs., 1986, 87-88, 90-91, Macmillan Pub. Co., 1986, Trumbull (Ohio) County Schs., 1988. Co-editor: CEA Critic, CEA Forum 1988—, (with Barbara Brothers) Reading and Writing Women's Lives: A Study of the Novel of Manners, 1991, (with Chuck Nelson) Internships in Technical Communication, 1991; editorial bd. South Atlantic Review, 1987-89; editor: of more than 40 pamphlets, 7 children's books, and 1 videoscript. Recipient John C. Hodges award U. Tenn., 1973; Alumni Found. Rsch. fellow U. Tenn., 1978, Dissertation fellow U. Tenn., 1983, Davis Editorial fellow U. Tenn., 1984; Grad. Rsch. Coun. grantee Youngstown State U.; named Disting. Grad. Faculty Youngstown State U., 1988—. Mem. MLA, Coll. English Assn. (exec. bd.), Coll. English Assn. Ohio, Nat. Coun. Tchrs. English, Conf. on Coll. Composition and Comm., New Chaucer Soc. (asst. bibliographer 1986—), Assn. Tchrs. Tech. Writing, Soc. for Tech. Commn., No. Ohio Soc. for Tech. Commn., Gould Soc. (faculty com. pres. 1991-93), Phi Beta Kappa, Phi Kappa Phi (pres. 1991-92, sec. 1994—). Office: Youngstown State U Dept English Youngstown OH 44555

BOWERS, DONNA JEAN, office administrator; b. Trinidad, Colo., Apr. 7, 1946; d. Walter Lee and Evalyn Margaret (Gagliardi) Degurse; m. John R. Hurley, Sept. 28, 1963 (div. Sept. 1974); children: John D., Marc L., Justin R. AAS, Trinidad State Jr. Coll., 1966. Key punch operator Dept. Revenue, State of Colo., Denver, 1969-71; asst. libr. Lower Arkansas Valley Regional Libr., Las Animas, Colo., 1971-81; head bookkeeper Machine Supply Co. Inc., Garden City, Kans., 1981—; office mgr. Tatro Plumbing Co. Inc., Garden City, 1990—. Office: Tatro Plumbing Co Inc 3997 W Jones Ave Garden City KS 67846-8741

BOWERS, DOROTHY C., state legislator; married; 4 children. Mem. N.H. State Senate; mem. children, youth and juvenile justice com. Del. 2 state convs., Constl. Conv., 1984; mem. Hills. County and State Rep. Commn., N.H. Higher Edn. and Health Facilities Authority; state co-chair N.H. Women for Reagan-Bush, 1984; pres. Greater Manchester Rep. Women's Club; mem. Bedford Budget Com.; bd. dirs. Am. Cancer Soc.; pres., charter mem. PTA. Mem. Settlement Assn. N.H. (bd. dirs. 1985—), Bedford Women's Club (former pres.), Garden Club (sec.). Home: 17 Heritage Dr Bedford NH 03110-6014 Office: NH State Senate State Capital Concord NH 03301*

BOWERS, PATRICIA ELEANOR FRITZ, economist; b. N.Y.C., Mar. 21, 1928; d. Eduard and Eleanor (Ring) Fritz. Student scholar, Goucher Coll., 1946-48; B.A., Cornell U., 1950; M.A., NYU, 1953, Ph.D., 1965. Statis. asst. Fed. Res. Bank N.Y., N.Y.C., 1950-53; lectr. Upsala Coll., East Orange, N.J., 1953-59; researcher Fortune mag., N.Y.C., 1959-60; teaching fellow NYU, N.Y.C., 1960-62, instr., 1962-64; mem. faculty Bklyn. Coll., CUNY, 1964—, prof. econs., 1974—. Author: Private Choice and Public Welfare, 1974. Sec. Friends of the Johnson Mus., Cornell U., 1989—. Mem. Am. Econ. Assn., Econometric Soc., N.Y. Acad. Scis., Fgn. Policy Assn., Women's Econ. Round Table, Met. Econ. Assn. (sec. 1963-68, pres. 1974-75), Am. Statis. Assn. (univs. chmn. ann. forecasting confs. 1970-71, 71-72), Cornell Club N.Y., Kappa Alpha Theta. Home: 145 E 16th St New York NY 10003-3405 Office: CUNY Bklyn Coll Dept Econs Brooklyn NY 11210

BOWERS, PATRICIA NEWSOME, communications executive; b. Baton Rouge, June 21, 1944; d. Carl Allen and Sue Mayre (Powell) Newsome; m. Robert Lloyd Bowers Jr., Aug. 19, 1967 (div. Nov. 1979); children: Paige Ivy, Katherine Elizabeth. BJ, La. State U., 1967. Sr. writer, editor Litton Industries, Pascagoula, Miss., 1978-80; sr. presentations supr. Martin Marietta Aerospace, Orlando, Fla., 1980-81; mgr. presentations Martin Marietta Aerospace, Balt., 1981-85, mgr. pub. rels., 1985-90; dir. pub. rels. and corp. comm. Contraves USA, Pitts., 1990-92; sr. mgr. sector communications Harris Electronic Systems sector Harris Corp., Melbourne, Fla., 1992—. Coach Parkville Recreation Council, Balt., 1985-87; bd. dirs. Salvation Army, Human Resources Devel. Agy. Balt. County, Brevard Symphony Youth Orch.; adv. bd. Nat. Aquarium in Balt.; active Brevard Leadership. Mem. Pub. Rels. Soc. Am. (bd. dirs. Chesapeake conf. 1987, Silver Anvil Judge, 1991, 92), Nat. Press Club, Navy League (bd. dirs. Balt. council 1986-87), Balt. County C. of C. (leadership program 1986-87), Pitts. Press Club. Republican. Episcopalian. Office: Harris Corp PO Box 37 Melbourne FL 32902-0037

BOWERS, RUTH MORENO, communications executive; b. McKeesport, Pa., Dec. 13, 1960; d. George Frank and Ruth Arlene (Jeffrey) M.l m. Raymond Hills, Oct. 10, 1981 (div. Dec. 10, 1985); m. Ronald Lee Bowers, Jan. 16, 1987; 1 child: Zakry Charles George. Student, Seton Hill Coll., 1978-79; student in Computer Ops., Computer Tech., 1980; BS in Info. Sys., Strayer Coll., 1994. Network technician, network specialist Electronic Data Systems, Dallas, 1980-86; communications analyst, mgr. projects CBIS Fed., Inc., Fairfax, Va., 1986—. Author: (short story) Other World, 1993. Mem. NOW, Planetary Soc. Democrat. Home: Rt 1 Box 136 M Boyce VA 22620 Office: 12750 Fair Lakes Cir Fairfax VA 22033

BOWERS, ZELLA ZANE, real estate broker; b. Liberal, Kans., May 24, 1929; d. Rex and Esther (Neff) Powelson; m. James Clarence Bowers, Aug. 12, 1949; (div. 1977); 1 child: Dara Zane. BA, Colo. Coll., 1951. Cert. real estate brokerage mgr. Sec. Bowers Ins. Agy., Colorado Springs, Colo., 1955-59, Cen. Colo. Claims Svc., Colorado Springs, 1959-63; pres. Premium Budgeting Co., Colorado Springs, 1962-67; pres., owner Monument Valley Realty, Inc., Colorado Springs, 1981-89; mng. broker The Buick Co. Buyer's Market; broker Haley Realty, Inc., Colorado Springs, 1990—; pres. Realtor Svcs. Corp., 1989. Hon. trustee The Palmer Found., Colorado Springs, 1980—, pres., 1983-84; trustee Pikes Peak United Way, 1988-91; pres. Vis. Nurse Assn., Colorado Springs, 1966-67, 74; dir. Colo. League Nurses, Denver, 1968; steering com. The Kennedy Ctr. Imagination Celebration, Colorado Springs, 1989-93, chmn., 1990-92; sec. Care & Share, Colorado Springs, 1984; chmn. McAllister House Mus., Colorado Springs, 1973-74; docent chmn. Colorado Springs Fine Arts Ctr., 1969-70; mem. historic preservation bd. City of Colorado Springs, 1989-94, chmn. 1989-92, mem. Compreshnsive Plan Task Force City of Colo., 1990-91; charter rev. commn. City of Colorado Springs, 1991-92; pres. Friends of the Libr., 1971-72; pres. Woman's Ednl. Soc. Colo. Coll., 1974-77; civil adminstrv. staff asst. Air Def. Filter Ctr., 1956-57, ground observer, 1956, others. Recipient Women's Trade Fair Recognition award, 1987. Mem. Nat. Assn. Realtors, Colo. Assn. Realtors (dir. 1987-91, v.p. S.E. dist. 1992, trustee edn. found. 1988-92, dir. housing opportunity found. 1991-93, Disting. Svc. award 1991, Polit. Svc. award 1992), Colorado Springs Bd. Realtors (pres. 1987-88, named Realtor of Yr. 1989), Pikes Peak Assn. Realtors, Children of the Am. Revolution (pres. 1956-57), Gamma Phi Beta. Avocations: genealogy, travel. Home: 128 W Rockrinnon Blvd # 104 Colorado Springs CO 80919-1876 Office: Haley Realty Inc 109 E Fontanero St Colorado Springs CO 80907-7494

BOWES, ROSEMARY TOFALO, psychologist, consultant; b. Boston, Nov. 14, 1948; d. Francis and Margaret (Kaim) Tofalo; m. David Bigelow Bowes, Oct. 29, 1988. BA, U. Md., 1970; MS, Howard U., 1972, PhD, 1975. Lic. psychologist, D.C., Md. Tng. fellow NIMH, Rockville, Md., 1971; pvt. practice Coachiing to Clarity, Washington; prin. mental health cons. Job Corps, U.S. Dept. Labor, Washington; mem. med. staff Columbia Hosp. for Women, Washington, Psychiat. Inst. Washington; mem. faculty Nat. Women's Health Resource Ctr., Washington. Bd. dirs. Westbridge Condominium Assn.; mem. Chapel Guild, Columbia Hosp. for Women. Mem. APA, Md. Psychol. Assn., N.Am. Menopause Soc., Women of Washington, City Tavern Club, Psi Chi. Home: The Oaks Keedysville MD 21756 Office: 2300 M St NW Washington DC 20037-1434

BOWIE, JOANNE WALKER (JONI BOWIE), state legislator; b. Terre Haute, Ind., June 18, 1937; d. Philip and Iona Brown Walker; children: Michelle Elizabeth Bowie Gray, Amy Jo. BS, W.Va. U., 1960, MS, 1962. Former comm. specialist USDA; mem. N.C. Ho. of Reps., 1988—, vice-chmn pub. transp. and human resources coms., mem. various coms.; mem. Rail Passenger Svc. Task Force Com., 1991. Past mem. adminstrv. com. Nat. League Municipalities; city councilwoman Greens City Coun., 1977-88; pres. Guilford County Med. Aux., 1982; mem. State Bd. C.C., 1985; past mem. Guilford County Conv. and Visitors Bd.; active Mar. of Dimes, Symphony Guild, Greensboro Preservation Soc. Mem. Greensboro C. of C., Guilford County Rep. Womens Club, Rep. Women's Club. Roman Catholic. Home: 106 Nut Bush Rd E Greensboro NC 27410-5518 Office: NC State Senate State Capitol Raleigh NC 27611*

BOWKER, CYNTHIA ANN, competitive information specialist; b. Battle Creek, Mich., Jan. 29, 1948; d. Kenneth Calvin and Marjorie Marie (Stoll) Brillhart. BBA, Western Mich. U., 1970. Cert. libr. sci., U.S. Govt. Libr. U.S. Fish & Wildlife Svc., Ann Arbor, Mich., 1974-87; info. specialist Domino's Pizza, Inc., Ann Arbor, 1987-88, dir. competitive analysis, 1988-92; mgr. collection development Nat. Ctr. Mfg. Scis., Ann Arbor, 1992-94, Greater Yellowstone Coalition, Bozeman, Mont., 1995—; mem. rsch. com. CREST/NPD, Chgo., 1989-92. Mem. Greater Ann Arbor Quilt Guild (program v.p.). Office: Greater Yellowstone Coalition 13 S Wilson Bozeman MT 59715

BOWLBY, LINDA ARLENE, secondary school educator; b. Martins Ferry, Ohio, Sept. 12, 1947; d. Theodore Roosevelt and Jessie Edith (Berry) Nicholls; m. James Keith Bowlby, July 18, 1970. BS in Home Econs., Ohio State U., 1969; MS in Applied Human Ecology, Bowling Green State U., 1991, MA in Guidance and Counseling, 1991. Lic. social worker. Consumer homemaking tchr. Wynford High Sch., Bucyrus, Ohio, 1969-91, Wynford Satellite, Pioneer Joint Vocat. Sch., Shelby, Ohio, 1991—; seamstress Korral Kreations, Sycamore, Ohio, 1994—. Co-author: The Sidesaddle Legacy, 1994; author: (booklets) 4-H Manual for Sidesaddles, 2d rev. edit., 1993, Sidesaddles, 1986; editor All Aside newsletter, 1980-89. Leader Girl Scouts U.S., Mansfield/Nevada, Ohio, 1955-72. Mem. Edn. Assn. of Pioneer, Am. Vocat. Assn., Ohio Vocat. Assn., World Sidesaddle Fedn., Inc. (pres., founder 1980—, Mem. of Yr. 1987, 93), Internat. Side Saddle Orgn. (Hall of Fame), Am. Quarter Horse Assn., Ohio Quarter Horse Assn., No. Ohio Quarter Horse Assn., N.W. Ohio Future Homemakers of Am. (dir., founder mem.), Wynford Edn. Assn. (sec.-treas. 1981-91), Wynford Future Homemakers of Am. (advisor), Wynford Chess Club (advisor). Home: 5619 State Rt 19 Bucyrus OH 44820

BOWLER, MARIANNE BIANCA, judge; b. Boston, Feb. 15, 1947; d. Richard A. and Ann C. (Daly) B. BA, Regis Coll., 1967; JD cum laude, Suffolk U., 1976, LLD, 1994. Bar: Mass. 1978. Rsch. asst. Harvard Med. Sch., Boston, 1967-69; med. editor Mass. Dept. of Pub. Health, Boston, 1969-76; law clk. Mass. Superior Ct., Boston, 1976-77, dep. chief law clk., 1977-78; asst. dist. atty. Middlesex Dist. Atty.'s Office, Cambridge, Mass., 1978; asst. U.S. atty. U.S. Dept. of Justice, Boston, 1978-90, exec. asst. U.S. atty., 1988-89, sr. litigation counsel, 1989-90; U.S. magistrate judge U.S. Dist. Ct. Mass., Boston, 1990—; chmn. bd. trustees New England Bapt. Hosp., Boston, 1990—. Mng. editor This Week in Pub. Health, 1969-75. Trustee Suffolk U., Boston, 1994—. Mem. Jr. League Boston, Suffolk Law Sch. Alumni Assn. (pres. 1979-80), Vincent Club. Democrat. Roman Catholic. Home: Brookline MA 02146 Office: US Dist Ct 908 McCormack Post Office Boston MA 02109*

BOWLER, MARY E., lawyer; b. White Plains, N.Y., Aug. 24, 1956; d. Garrett Francis and Constance Marie (Stiles) B.; m. Kenneth Alan Jones, Jun. 28, 1986; children: Matthew Garrett Jones, Daniel Adam Jones. BS, Cornell U., 1978; JD, Boston U., 1981. Lawyer E.I. du Pont de Nemours & Co., Wilmington, Del., 1981-85; counsel E.I. du Pont de Nemours & Co., Wilmington, 1985-91, sr. counsel, 1991—. Mng. editor Am. Jour. of Law and Medicine, 1980-81. Leader Girl Scouts of USA, Wilmington, 1982—; auction fin. chair Emmanuel Homeless Dining Room, Wilmington, 1984—; bd. dir. Jr. League of Wilmington, 1986—. Mem. Del. Bar Assn., Mass. Bar Assn., Cornell Alimni Assn. (Class 78 pres. 1988—). Roman Catholic. Home: 718 Hertford Rd Wilmington DE 19803 Office: Du Pont De Nemours & Co 1007 Market St Wilmington DE 19898

BOWLER, SHIRLEY, state legislator; b. New Orleans, Oct. 2, 1949; d. Louis L. and Rose Clare (Mandina) Duvigneaud; m. Michael Joseph Bowler, June 11, 1971; children: Kathleen, Michael, Mary. BA, U. New Orleans, 1971. English tchr. Jefferson Parish Schs., Gretna, La., 1971-77; video producer D.H. Holmes Co., Ltd., New Orleans, 1980-87; alumnae coord. St. Mary's Dominican High, New Orleans, 1989-92; state legislator La. Dist. 78, Harahan, La., 1992—; mem. textbook adoption and curriculum devel. coms. Jefferson Parish Schs. Dir. awards for (indsl. video) The Sensormatic System, 1985; dir./writer (indsl. video) Benefits News, 1986; dir./writer-editor (indsl. video) Fashion Trends, 1986. Mem. Rep. Women's Club of Jefferson, 1991. Mem. Dominican High Alumnae Assn., Nat. Assn. Desktop Pubs., Harahan Rotary Club (bd. mem 1993). Republican. Roman Catholic. Office: Legis Office 1321 Hickory Ave Harahan LA 70123

BOWLES, CAROLYN ANN, physician; b. Washington, May 6, 1947; d. Cabell Bryan Bowles and Gerdis Linnia (Lind) Doyle; m. Craig S. Roth, Apr. 29, 1981; children: Matthew Easter Bowles-Roth, Caitlin Linnia Bowles-Roth. BS, Simmons Coll., 1969; MD, Boston U., 1977. Diplomate Am. Bd. Internal Medicine. Asst. prof. medicine, staff cons. Mayo Clinic, Rochester, Minn., 1984-92; rheumatologist Health Ptnrs., Inc., Mpls., 1992—. Fellow ACP, Am. Coll. Rheumatology. Mem. Unitarian Universalist Ch. Office: Group Health/Health Ptnrs 205 Wabasha Ave S Saint Paul MN 55107

BOWLES, LIZA K., construction executive. Pres. NAHB Rsch. Ctr., Upper Marlboro, Md. Office: NAHB Rsch Ctr 400 Prince Georges Blvd Upper Marlboro MD 20772-8731

BOWLING, JOYCE BLANKENCHIP, critical care nurse; b. White Deer, Tex., Nov. 17, 1932; d. Roy Lee and Myrtle Dove (Milhoan) Blankenchip; m. J.C. Bowling, July 24, 1952. Diploma, Northwest Tex. Sch. Nursing, 1953; AS, Amarillo Coll., 1953; BSN, West Tex. State U., 1983. RN, Tex.; cert. med.-surg. nursing, gerontology, nursing adminstrn. AACN; cert. emergency nurse. Staff nurse emergency rm. Parkland Hosp., Dallas, 1960-62; staff nurse Meth. Hosp., Dallas, 1962-68; staff nurse medicine, then head nurse CCU St. Paul Hosp., Dallas, 1969-73; charge nurse, supr. Southwestern Dialysis Ctr., Dallas, 1973-74; dir. nurses Caruth Rehab. Inst., Dallas, 1974-75; staff nurse VA Med. Ctr., Dallas, 1976-79; staff nurse VA Med. Ctr., Amarillo, Tex., 1979-85, head nurse surg. unit, 1985-88, clin. coord., 1988—. Mem. AACN (cert.), Emergency Nurses Assn. (cert.), Tex. Nurses Assn., Am. Heart Assn., Nat. Kidney Found., Am. Cancer Soc., Sigma Theta Tau. Home: RR 1 Box 556a-10 Amarillo TX 79121-9754 Office: VA Med Ctr 6010 W Amarillo Blvd Amarillo TX 79106-1924

BOWMAN, CYNTHIA ANN, state education official; b. Newark, May 7, 1959; d. James Robert and Anita R. (Petorella) B. BS, Trenton State Coll., 1981, MEd, 1982. Tchr. mktg. edn. Keansburg (N.J.) Bd. Edn., 1982-85, Middlesex County Vocat. Sch., Piscataway, N.J., 1985-86, Sayreville (N.J.) Bd. Edn., 1986-89; edn. planner N.J. Dept. Edn., Trenton, 1989-92, edn. devel. program specialist, 1992—; program mgr. Supermarket Career Tng. Programs, 1993. Vol. N.J. Spl. Olympics, Robbinsville, 1992—. Recipient Exemplary Program award, 1993. Mem. N.J. Mktg. Edn. Assn. (pres. 1983-89, sec., v.p., Ctrl. Region Tchr. of Yr. 1986, 87). Office: NJ Dept Edn CN 500 Trenton NJ 08625

BOWMAN, DOROTHY LOUISE, artist; b. Hollywood, Calif., Jan. 20, 1927; d. Bruce L. and Dorothy L. (Kalkman) B; m. Howard Hugh Bradford, Dec. 30, 1949 (div. 1965); children: Brock, Cyndra, Tal Scott, Heather, Delia, Callia. Student, Chouinard Art Inst., Calif., 1945-48, Jepson Art Inst., L.A., 1948-49; BA, Webster U., 1979. Serigrapher, printmaker, painter: represented in permanent collections: Immaculate Heart Coll., L.A. County Mus., Bklyn. Mus., Long Beach Mus., Crocker Art Gallery, Mus. Modern Art, Phila., Mus. Fine Arts, San Jose State Coll., De Cordova and Danna Mus., Boston Pub. Libr., Boston Mus. Fine Arts, N.Y. Pub. Libr., Rochester Meml. Gallery, U. Wis., U. Hawaii, U. Ill., U. Kans., Santa Barbara Mus., Achenbach Found. Legion of Honor, Mus. Modern Art,

Monterey, Calif., Libr. Congress, Calif. State Libr. Archives, Arquivos Historicos De Arte Contemporanea Museu De Arte Moderna, San Paulo, Brazil, Ch. of Latter Day Saints History Mus., Salt Lake City; twice juried internat. show 27 countries, 1987. Address: 824 Lyndon St Apt C Monterey CA 93940-1976

BOWMAN, DOROTHY MARIE, librarian; b. North Tazewell, Va., May 20, 1937; d. Roy and Thelma Vivian Ann (Shrader) Brewster; m. John LeRoy Bowman, Dec. 28, 1957; children: Annette Toner, Kathleen Rader, Alice Newell. BS in Edn., Radford (Va.) Coll., 1958; MLS, Cath. U. Am., 1989. Tchr., librarian Virginia Beach (Va.) Pub. Schs., 1958-59; tchr. Norfolk (Va.) City Schs., 1959-60; librarian Albemarle Pulp & Paper Mfg. Co., Richmond, Va., 1961-64; tchr. Henrico (Va.) Pub. Schs., 1966-67, asst. librarian, 1967-70; librarian Chickahominy Acad., Henrico County, 1972-73, Nasemond-Suffolk (Va.) Acad., 1975—. Pres. Highland Springs (Va.) United Meth. Women, 1973-74; residential campaign chmn. Am. Cancer Soc., Richmond, 1972-73; co-chair evaluation steering com. Nansemond-Suffolk Acad., 1984-85, chair tech. task force, 1992, mem. assessment policy com., 1991cons. self study com., 1992—; co-chair Main St. United Meth. Ch. Coun. on Ministries, Suffolk, 1983-85. Mem. AAUW (br. treas. 1983-87), Va. Library Assn., Sans Souci Lit. Club (pres. Suffolk chpt. 1985-87), Highland Springs Jr. Woman's Club (pres. 1970-71), Delta Kappa Gamma (chpt. pres. 1986-88). Republican. Home: 100 Ayers Creek Ln Suffolk VA 23434-7508 Office: Nansemond Suffolk Acad 3373 Pruden Blvd Suffolk VA 23434-7235

BOWMAN, GERALDINE DAVIS, gifted/talented education educator, inn owner; b. Columbus, Ohio, May 8, 1938; d. Thomas Llewellyn and Elvarie Loraine (Jacobs) Davis; m. Alan Dale Henderson, Aug. 30, 1959 (div. Oct. 1966); 1 child, Anthony Joseph Henderson; m. Samuel S. Bowman, Aug. 25, 1980. BS in Art Edn., Ind. U., 1961, MS in Art Edn., 1971; postgrad. cert. in Gifted Edn., Miami U., U. Rio Grande, 1994. Lic. K-12 Art, K-12 Gifted, Ohio. Tchr. 4th grade Mt. Vernon (Ind.) Sch. Corp., 1961-62, tchr. 6th grade, 1962-63, jr. h.s. tchr. art, 1965-67; h.s. tchr. art Eville-Vanderburgh Sch. Corp., Evansville, Ind., 1967-80; elem. tchr. art Jackson (Ohio) City Schs., 1982-86, tchr. gifted/talented, 1986—; owner Bowman House bed and breakfast, Jackson, 1992—; advisor, coach h.s. acad. team, 1992—; coach sci. olympiad team, 1990—. One person show mixed media Gallery, New Harmony, Ind.; jewlery designer (purchase award 1971). Cantor, soloist Holy Trinity Ch., 1990-94; vocalist choral socs., 1960—; sponsor, dir. Tri Hi Y for H.S. girls, 1989-93; sec. Humane Soc., Jackson, 1990-92; mem. Democrats for Lloyd, Evansville, Ind., 1975. Mellon fellow Berea Coll., 1990, Martha Holden Jennings fellow, 1985, Miami U. Geology scholar, 1990, Jennings Found.-Ohio U. sci. and math. scholar 1989. Mem. Ind. Art Edn. Assn. (life, v.p.), Ohio Assn. Gifted Children, Nat. Assn. Gifted Children, So. Hills Art Coun. (v.p. 1989-94), Jackson Women's League. Democrat. Roman Catholic. Home: 92 E South St Jackson OH 45640 Office: Jackson City Schs 379 E South St Jackson OH 45640

BOWMAN, HAZEL LOIS, retired English language educator; b. Plant City, Fla., Feb. 18, 1917; d. Joseph Monroe and Annie (Thoman) B.; AB, Fla. State Coll. for Women, 1937; MA, U. Fla., 1948; postgrad. U. Md., 1961-65. Tchr., Lakeview High Sch., Winter Garden, Fla., 1939-40, Eagle Lake Sch., Fla., 1940-41; welfare visitor Fla. Welfare Bd., 1941-42; specialist U.S. Army Signal Corps, Arlington Hall, Va., 1942-43; recreation worker, asst. procurement officer ARC, CBI Theater, 1943-46; lab. technician Am. Cyanamid Corp., Brewster, Fla., 1946-47; instr., asst. prof. gen. extension div. U. Fla., Fla. State U., 1948-51; free-lance writer, editor, indexer, N.Y., Fla., 1951-55; staff writer Tampa (Fla.) Morning Tribune, 1956; staff writer, telegraph editor Winter Haven (Fla.) News-Chief, 1956-57; registrar/admissions officer U. Tampa, 1957-59; coll. counselor, Atlantic states, 1959-60; registrar/freshman adviser Towson State Tchrs. Coll., Balt., 1960-62; dir. student personnel, guidance, admissions Harford Jr. Coll., Bel Air, Md., 1962-64; instr. York (Pa.) Coll., 1965-66, asst. prof. English, journalism, 1966-69; tchr. S.W. Jr. High Sch., Lakeland, Fla., 1969-70; tchr. learning disabled Vanguard Sch., Lake Wales, Fla., 1970-82; libr. asst. Polk County Hist. and Geneal. Libr., Bartow, Fla., 1986-91. Editor Tampa Altrusan, 1958-60, Polk County Hist. Calendar, 1986-90. Mem. AAUW, NOW, Nat. Geneal. Soc., Mortar Bd., Polk County Hist. Assn. (Gov. Lawton Chiles commn. appointee, editor Newsletter 1990-94), Alpha Chi Alpha, Chi Delta Phi. Home: 511 NE 9th Ave Mulberry FL 33860-2620

BOWMAN, KATHLEEN GILL, academic administrator. BS English & Spanish, U. of Minn., 1964, MA English Edn., 1967, PhD English Edn., 1977. Rsch. assoc. Legis. Adv. Coun. on the Econ. Status of Women, St. Paul, MN, 1976-77; asst. dir. of grad. studies, asst prof. of edn. Reed Coll., Portland, OR, 1977-79; exec. asst. to the pres., dir. of spl. programs Reed Coll., 1979-82; assoc. dir., program officer Fred Meyer Charitable Trust, Portland, OR, 1982-84; assoc. v.p. for rsch. U. of Oreg., Eugene, OR, 1985-89; vice-provost for internat. affairs U. of Oreg., 1989-94; pres. Randolph-Macon Woman's Coll., Lynchburg, VA, 1994—. Fulbright Sr. Scholar award, Japan & Korea, 1993. Office: Randolph-Macon Womans Coll Office of the Pres 2500 Rivermont Ave Lynchburg VA 24503-8139*

BOWMAN, LINDA KAY, clinical psychologist; b. La Grange, Ill., Dec. 2, 1958; d. Dwight Gordon and Marian Ruth (Small) B. BS in Human Devel. with highest honors, U. Calif., Davis, 1980; MS in Counseling and Mental Health, Calif. State U., Hayward, 1984; PhD in Clin. Psychology, Calif. Sch. Profl. Psychology, Fresno, 1990. Lic. clin. psychologist, Wash.; cert. sch. counselor, Calif. Houseparent, teaching asst. Arbutus Youth Assn.-Summit Ranch, San Jose, Calif., 1981-82; counselor Community Counselling Ctr. Calif. State U., 1983, instr. edn. psychology dept., 1984; intern counselor Ohlone Coll., Fremont, Calif., 1983-84; adminstrv. asst. neurobiology dept. Stanford (Calif.) U., 1984-85; child and family therapist Margaree Mason Ctr. for Domestic Violence, Fresno, Calif., 1985-87; psychol. trainee CSPP Psychol. Svc. Ctr., 1986; psychology intern Devereux Found., Santa Barbara, Calif., 1987-88, CPC Vista del Mar Psychiat. Hosp., Ventura, 1988-89; psychologist III and IV, Rainier Sch., Buckley, Wash., 1990-92; psychologist V, Western State Hosp., Tacoma, 1992—; pvt. practice psychology, Tacoma, 1991—. Contbr. to profl. publs. Recipient Community Svc. award Fresno County United Way, Outstanding Performance citation human devel. dept. U. Calif.; adopted Tlinget Indian. Mem. APA, Wash. State Psychol. Assn., Christian Assn. for Psychol. Studies, Wash. Adults with Learning Disabilities Group, U. Calif.-Davis Alumni Assn., Phi Kappa Phi (life), Omicron Nu (life). Presbyterian. Office: Western State Hosp 8805 Steilacoom Blvd SW Tacoma WA 98498-4771

BOWMAN, MARJORIE ANN, physician, academic administrator; b. Grove City, Pa., Aug. 18, 1953; d. Ross David and Freda Louise (Smith) Williamson; m. Robert Choplin; one child, Bridget Williamson Foley. BS, Pa. State U., 1974; MD, Jefferson Med. Coll., 1976; MPA, U. So. Calif., L.A., 1983. Intern, then resident in family practice Duke U., Durham, N.C., 1976-79; med officer USPHS, Hyattsville, Md., 1979-82; clin. instr. uniformed svcs. U. of the Health Scis., Bethesda, Md., 1980-83; dir. family practice residency Sch. Medicine Georgetown U., Washington, 1983-86; prof., chair dept. family and community medicine Wake Forest U., Winston-Salem, N.C., 1986—; Author: Stress and Women Physicians, 1985; contbr. articles to profl. jours. Fellow Am. Acad. Family Physicians; mem. AMA, Soc. Tchrs. Family Medicine (bd. dirs. 1984-88, bd. dirs. Found. 1984—, v.p.1988-91, pres. 1991-92), Am. Pub. Health Assn. Republican. Unitarian. Office: Bowman Gray Sch Medicine Family & Cmty Medicine Medical Center Blvd Winston Salem NC 27157-1084

BOWMAN, NAOMA SUSANN, elementary school educator; b. Dublan, Mex., Feb. 17, 1951; d. Samuel Keith and Mary Naoma (Haynie) B. BS in Elem. Edn., Brigham Young U., 1984. Cert. tchr., Utah. Tchr. Escuela Manuel Dublan, 1972-81; tchr. Spanish adult edn. program Mission Tng. Ctr., Provo, Utah, 1981-84, teacher trainer, 1984-85; tchr. Spanish immersion Meadow Elem. Sch., Lehi, Utah, 1985-89, Northridge Elem. Sch., Orem, Utah, 1989—; asst. dir. Spanish immersion curriculum com. Alpine Sch. Dist., American Fork, Utah, 1986-89, new-tchr. orienter, 1987-92, chair Spanish Immersion Conf., 1989-91, dir. Spanish immersion summer camp, 1991—, rep. Orem Cluster, 1991—, peer evaluator, 1991—, mem. prin. screening com., 1989-90; tchr. summer migrant program, Nebo Sch. Dist., 1992, 93. Grantee Utah Humanities Coun., 1992, City of Orem, 1992. Fellow NEA, ASCD, Alpine Edn. Assn., Utah Edn. Assn., Utah Educators of Tchrs. Assn., Utah Fgn. Lang. Assn. (sec. 1988-90), Utah Fgn. Lang. in Elem. Assn. (pres. 1987-88, Tchr. of Yr. 1989), Phi Delta Kappa. Republican. Mormon. Office: Northridge Elem Sch 1660 N 50 E Orem UT 84057-2145

BOWMAN, PATRICIA LYNN, lawyer; b. Mpls., July 5, 1956; d. Robert Lee and Delores Helen (Roberts) B. BA in History with distinction, Stanford U., 1978; JD cum laude, Harvard U., 1981. Assoc. Perkins Coie, Seattle, 1981-84, Foster, Pepper & Shefelman, Seattle, 1984-89; v.p., assoc. counsel Washington Mut. Bank, Seattle, 1989—. Bd. dirs., vice chair Common Ground, Seattle, 1987-93; bd. dirs. Elderhealth Northwest, Seattle, 1994—. Mem. ABA, Wash. State Bar Assn., Seattle-King County Bar Assn., Seattle Mortgage Bankers Assn. (mem. legal com.), Phi Beta Kappa. Office: Washington Mut Bank 1201 3rd Ave Seattle WA 98101

BOWMAN-DALTON, BURDENE KATHRYN, elementary education educator, computer consultant; b. Magnolia, Ohio, July 13, 1937; d. Ernest Mowles and Mary Kathryn (Long) Bowman; BME, Capital U., 1959; MA in Edn., Akron U., 1967, postgrad. 1976-87; m. Louis W. Dalton, Mar. 13, 1979. Profl. vocalist, various clubs in the East, 1959-60; music tchr. East Liverpool (Ohio) City Schs., 1959-62; music tchr. Revere Local Schs., Akron, Ohio, 1962-75, elem. tchr., 1975-80, elem. team leader/computer cons., 1979-85, tchr. middle sch. math., gift-talented, computer literacy, 1981-92, dist. computer specialist, 1987—, dist. statis. for standardize local testing, 1987-91, dist. tech. coord., 1993—; local and regional dir., Olympics of the Mind, also World Problem Captain for computer problem, 1984-86; cons., workshop presenter State of Ohio, 1987-91, dist. test coord., 1991—. Mem. Citizen Com., Akron, 1975-76; profl. rep. Bath Assn. to Help, 1978-80; mem. Revere Levy Com. 1986, Revere Bond Issue Com., 1991; audit com. BATH, 1977-79; vol. chmn. Antique Car Show, Akron, 1972-81; dist. advisor MidWest Talent Search, 1987-93; dist. statistician of standardized rech. test results. Martha Holden Jennings Found. grantee, 1977-78; Title IV ESEA grantee, 1977-81. Mem. Assn. for Devel. of Computer-Based Instructional Systems(dir. 1992—), Ednl. Mgmt. Info. System (coord. for Revere Schs. 1992—), Assn. Supervision and Curriculum Devel., Phi Beta. Republican. Lutheran. Home: 353 Retreat Dr Akron OH 44333-1623 Office: 3195 Spring Valley Rd Bath OH 44210-0339

BOWMAN-RANDALL, GAYLE DARLENE, equal employment specialist, writer; b. Tallahassee, Mar. 5, 1964; d. Ollie Monroe and Gaynelle Annette (Sharpe) Bowman; m. David Keith Randall, Feb. 14, 1992; 1 child, Sterling Noelle. BS in Mktg., Hampton U., 1986. Admissions counselor Hampton U., 1984-87; equal employment specialist U.S. Dept. Def., Warren, Mich., 1987—; owner Diversified Writing and Bus. Svcs., Oak Park, Mich., 1989—. Author poetry. Mem. NAFE, Internat. Women's Writing Guild, Nat. Writers Assn., Alpha Kappa Alpha. Democrat. Presbyterian.

BOWNE, SHIRLEE PEARSON, credit union executive, real estate executive; b. High Shoals Twp., N.C., Mar. 11, 1936; d. Lloyd E. Pearson and Parnell (James) Garland; divorced; 1 child, Gregory Charles. Grad. high sch., Gaffney, S.C. Various secretarial positions, 1955-64; sales repr., pres. Real Estate Marketers, Inc., Tallahassee, FL, 1964-80; chief exec. officer Shirlee Bowne Mktg. & Devel. Inc., Tallahassee, 1980-91; vice chmn. Nat. Credit Union Adminstrn., Washington, 1991—; Consult. in field. Treas. Rep. Party Fla., 1988-91. Episcopalian.

BOWSER, ANITA OLGA, state legislator, education educator; b. Canton, Ohio, Aug. 18, 1920; d. Nicholas B. Alby and Emile Stobbe. AB, Kent State U., 1945; LLB, William McKinley U., 1949; MS, Purdue U., 1967; MA, U. Notre Dame, 1972, PhD, 1976. Instr. Kent (Ohio) State U., 1945-46; prof. Purdue U. North Cen. Campus, Michigan City, Ind., 1950—; mem. Ind. Ho. Reps., 1980-92, Ind. State Sen., 1992—. Mem. Delta Kappa Gamma. Home: 1912 E Coolspring Ave Michigan City IN 46360-6406 Office: Ind State Senate State Capitol Indianapolis IN 46204*

BOWSER, GENEVA BEATRICE, secondary school educator, principal; b. Hackensack, N.J., June 20, 1936; d. John Thomas and Earline (Briggs) Schultz; m. Lloyd Thomas Bowser, Dec. 20, 1959; children: Lydell Dana, Lloyd Thomas Jr., Lester Kenneth. BS in Nursing, Johns Hopkins U., 1973; MS in Adminstrn., Supervision, Morgan State U., 1981, EdD, 1989. Staff nurse N.Y. Hosp., Cornell Med. Ctr., N.Y.C., 1957-59, U.S. Pub. Health Hosp., Balt., 1962-67; dir. nursing Community Health Ctr., Balt., 1967-73; tchr. Balt. City Pub. Schs., 1973-82, dept. chair, 1982-89, dept. head, 1989-94, asst. prin. secondary edn., 1994—. Health educator New Shiloh Bapt. Ch., Balt.; mem. Morgan Park Improvement Assn., Project Awareness (Am. Cancer Soc.). Recipient Gov.'s Citation State of Md., 1982, Cert. Merit, Md. Coun. on Vocat. Edn., 1989; nominated Tchr. of Yr., Balt. City Schs., 1989. Mem. ASCD, Vocat. Indsl. Club, Md. Vocat. Assn. Chi Eta Phi, Phi Delta Kappa, Chi Eta Phi. Home: 2404 College Ave Baltimore MD 21214-2426 Office: Balt City Pub Schs 100 N Calhoun St Baltimore MD 21229

BOWYER, JOAN ELIZABETH, medical technologist, realtor; b. Ellensburg, Wash., July 11, 1944; d. Chester Joseph and Rita Geneva (Newell) Howarth; 1 child, Suzanne Elise. BA, Ft. Wright Coll. of Holy Names, 1966; grad., Real Estate Sch. Oreg., 1982. Lic. med. technologist. Med. technologist Lab. of Clin. Medicine, Seattle, 1967-69, Sacred Heart Gen. Hosp., Eugene, Oreg., 1969-73, 74-76, McKenzie Willamette Hosp., Springfield, Oreg., 1976-77, Mid-Columbia Hosp., The Dalles, Oreg., 1977-82; realtor Red Carpet/Rick Hall Realty, Hillsboro, Oreg., 1982-85, Century 21 Columbia Realty, Portland, 1985—; med. technologist ARC, Portland, 1982-89, Corning Nicholas Inst. formerly Physicians Med. Lab., 1989-95, East Moreland Hosp., 1995—. Co-editor: The Dalles Gen. Hosp. Newspaper, 1980-82. Pres. Wasco County Edn. Service Dist. Parents Group, The Dalles, 1978-82; founder, pres. Mid-Columbia Parents of Deaf, 1978-82; parental spokesperson Spl. Edn. Adv. Com., Salem, Oreg., 1980-82; activist parent for deaf/hearing impaired, 1977—. Mem. Med. Technologists of Am. Soc. Pathologists, Nat. Assn. Realtors, NAFE, Century 21 Investment Soc., Million Dollar Club. Democrat. Avocations: photography, dancing, hiking, travel. Home: 704 SE 38th Ave Portland OR 97214-3206 Office: Century 21 Columbia 2208 SE 182nd Ave Portland OR 97233-5608

BOWYER, SHIRLEY CAROLINE SMITH, accountant; b. Greenville, Ala., Nov. 3, 1949; d. Newton B. Smith and Alma Caroline (Kummel) Smith; m. Patrick E. Bowyer, May 1, 1981 (div. July 1983). Student, Faulkner Jr. Coll., Bay Minette, Ala., 1968-70; BA in Acctg., Fin. and Mgmt., U. West Fla., 1972. Payroll adminstr. Cook Constrn. Co., Inc., Jackson, Miss., 1972-73; acctg. supr. Starco Corp., Jackson, 1973-74; acct., credit mgr. Equipment, Inc., Jackson, 1974-76; field office mgr., asst. to project engr. Algernon Blair, Inc., Montgomery, Ala., 1976-78; instr. bus. subjects Phillips Coll., Jackson, Miss., 1977; acct., office mgr. Chandler Ford Sales, Inc., DeQueen, Ark., 1978-80; field office mgr. Zellner Constrn. Co., Inc., Memphis, 1980-81; mgr. Das A. Borden & Co., Muscle Shoals, Ala., 1981-82; asst. adminstr., credit mgr. S.F. Parker & Co., P.C., CPA's, Foley, Ala., 1982-86; acct. City of Gulf Shores, Ala., 1986-92, acctg. mgr., 1992—. Mem. South Baldwin Hosp. Aux., Foley, 1990. Recipient Cert. of Commendation, City of Gulf Shores, 1989. Mem. Govt. Fin. Officers Assn. Ala., Ala. Assn. Pub. Accts., Am. Soc. Women Accts. Methodist. Home: Mimosa Pl 106 S Beech St Foley AL 36535

BOXER, BARBARA, senator; b. Bklyn., Nov. 11, 1940; d. Ira and Sophie (Silvershein) Levy; m. Stewart Boxer, 1962; children: Doug, Nicole. BA economics, Bklyn. Coll., 1962. Stockbroker, econ. rschr. N.Y. Securities Firm, N.Y.C., 1962-65; journalist, assoc. editor Pacific Sun, 1972-74; congl. aide to rep. 5th Congl. Dist. San Francisco, 1974-76; mem. Marin County Bd. Suprs., San Rafael, Calif., 1976-82; mem. 98th-102d Congresses from 6th Calif. dist., mem. armed services com., select com. children, youth and families; majority whip at large, co-chair Mil. Reform Caucus, chair subcom. on govt. activities and transp. of house govt. ops. com., 1990—, U.S. Senator from Calif., 1993—. Pres. Marin County Bd. Suprs., 1980-81; mem. Bay Area Air Quality Mgmt. Bd., San Francisco, 1977-82, pres., 1979-81; bd. dirs. Golden Gate Bridge Hwy. and Transport Dist., San Francisco, 1978-82; founding mem. Marin Nat. Women's Polit. Caucus; pres. Dem. New Mems. Caucus, 1983. Recipient Open Govt. award Common Cause, 1980, Rep. of Yr. award Nat. Multiple Sclerosis Soc., 1990, Margaret Sanger award Planned Parenthood, 1990, Women of Achievement award Anti-defamation League, 1990. Jewish. Office: US Senate 112 Hart Senate Office Bldg. Washington DC 20510-0505

BOXWILL, HELEN ANN, secondary education educator; b. Washington, Feb. 28, 1946; d. Melvin E. and Ann (Magnotta) Dorenbaum; children: Hope, David, Andre. BA, Dickinson Coll., Carlisle, Pa., 1967; MA, New Sch. Social Rsch., 1976; MS in Adminstrn. and Supervision, Coll. New Rochelle, 1995, MS in Adminstrn. and Supervision, Cert. in Staff Devel., 1995. Lic. reading specialist, elem. tchr., English tchr., sch. adminstr., N.Y. Caseworker City of N.Y., 1967-71; dir. Harriet Tubman Day Care Ctr., Bklyn., 1971-73; family counselor Family Inst. for More Effective Living, Westbury, N.Y., 1976-80; elem. tchr. Carousel Day Sch., Hicksville, N.Y., 1980-82, Pub. Sch. 160 Elem. Sch., Queens, N.Y., 1982-83; reading specialist Soterios Ellenos Parochial Sch., Bklyn., 1983-84, Hempstead (N.Y.) Pub. Schs., 1984-90; tchr. SAT The Sch. for Student Achievement, Jericho, N.Y., 1991-93; reading specialist L.I. U., Greenvale, N.Y., 1984-93; reading tchr. Robert Moses Mid. Sch., North Babylon, N.Y., 1990-93, North Babylon (N.Y.) High Sch., 1993—; advisor Sch. Improvement Planning Com., Hempstead, N.Y., 1987-89; mem. Dist. Planning Com., 1993—, Curriculum Adv. Com., 1993—; advisor/advisee com., staff devel. com., lang. arts com., site based mgmt. com. North Babylon Sch. Dist., 1991—; tchr., trainer Nassau Tract Tchrs. Ctr., 1985-89, North Babylon Schs., 1991—, Hempstead Schs., 1985-90, insvc. courses Owl Tchrs. Ctr., 1991, 93—. Contbr. articles to profl. jours. Advisor Youth of Distinction, Huntington, N.Y., 1991-92; leader Girl Scouts Am., Westbury, 1978. Grantee City of N.Y. Children's Aid Soc., Tract Ctr., Owl Ctr. Mem. ASCD, Internat. Reading Assn., Nat. Coun. Tchrs. English, Orton Dyslexia Soc., Nassau Reading Coun. Home: 44 Foxwood Dr E Huntington Station NY 11746

BOYAJIAN, CAROLE L., graphic designer, interior designer; b. Fresno, Calif., Jan. 6, 1948; d. Armon K. and Louise (Josephine) B.;. BFA cum laude, The Art Ctr. Coll. Design, L.A., 1969. Typographical liaison Doyle Dane Bernbach Advt., N.Y.C., 1969-70; prin. The Enchanted Nook Co., Pasadena, Calif., 1972-78; cons., pvt. practice pub. relations developer Ajijic, Jalisco, Mex., 1978-80; sales assoc. Forbes Monselle Inc., Los Angeles, 1980-84; prin. Carol Boyajian & Assocs., Beverly Hills, Calif., 1980—; co-owner ZERO Gallery, L.A., 1968-69; owner's rep./interior designer Robert Evans Co.; interior designer Internat. Mgmt. and Pub. Rels. div. of The Gordy Co., medical offices of Dr. Zion Yu and George Harrison; with West Coast Industries, Inc. Cons. Los Angeles Theater Ctr., 1985. Recipient Cert. Merit, Nat. Fedn. Music Tchrs., Fresno, Calif., 1965. Mem. AIA (profl. affiliate Los Angeles chpt.), Am. Soc. Interior Designers (cert.), Nat. Fedn. Music, Network Exec. Women in Hospitality. Republican. Home: 365 W Alameda Ave Apt 308 Burbank CA 91506-3340 Office: PO Box 663 Beverly Hills CA 90213-0663

BOYATT, JESSICA ALLYN, photographer; b. Washington, Apr. 12, 1964; d. Thomas David and Mary Penelope (Freedman) B. BA, Brown U., 1986; MA, Ohio U., 1992. Dir. internat. ops. Oakland Group, Boston, 1989-90; dir. visual comm. Insights, Boston, 1992-94, creative dir., 1994—; pvt. practice photography Boston, 1992—. Photographer: (photo essays) Blacks in Appalachia, 1990 (Leica Student of Yr. 1991), Children at Risk, 1991 (2d pl. documentary Coll. Photographer of Yr. 1992); photographer, designer, editor: Congregations Making A Difference, 1993. Recipient Fellowship in Photography, New England Found. for the Arts, Cambridge, 1993; represented in permanent collection Nat. Mus. of Women in the Arts, Washington, 1993. Mem. NOW, Nat. Press Photographers Assn. Home: 228 Chestnut St Cambridge MA 02139-4621 Office: Insights 11 Beacon St Ste 915 Boston MA 02108-3001

BOYCE, ANDREA ZYGMUNT, nurse; b. Miami, Fla., Sept. 17, 1956; d. Joseph A. and Eleanor F. (Haduck) Zygmunt; m. Brian W. Boyce, Apr. 27, 1985. BS in Nursing, Our Lady of Angels Coll., 1978. RN, Pa., Calif., Utah; cert. ACLS, BCLS, NRP, PALS. Staff nurse, then asst. head nurse pediatric intensive care St. Christopher's Hosp. Children, Phila., 1978-84; head nurse neonatal ICU, pediatrics Osteo. Med. Ctr., Phila., 1985-88, staff nurse pediatrics, emergency rm., 1988-90; staff nurse emergency rm. Doctors Hosp. of Montclair, 1990; mobile intensive care nurse emergency dept. Ontario (Calif.) Community Hosp., 1992-94; staff nurse pediatric intensive care Primary Childrens Med. Ctr., Salt Lake City, 1994—. Home: 1888 E Foxmoor Pl Sandy UT 84092-5211

BOYCE, EMILY STEWART, retired library and information science educator; b. Raleigh, N.C., Aug. 18, 1933; d. Harry and May (Fallon) B. BS, East Carolina U., 1955, MA, 1961; MS in Library Sci., U. N.C., 1968; postgrad., Cath. U. Am., 1977. Librarian Tileston Jr. High Sch., Wilmington, N.C., 1955-57; children's librarian Wilmington Pub. Library, 1957-58; asst. librarian Joyner Library East Carolina U., Greenville, N.C., 1959-61, librarian III, 1962-63; ednl. supr. II ednl. media div. N.C. State Dept. Pub. Instrn., Raleigh, 1961-62; assoc. prof. dept. library and info. scis. East Carolina U., Raleigh, 1964-76, prof., 1976-92, chmn. dept., 1982-89; retired, 1992; cons. So. Assn. Colls. and Schs., Raleigh, 1975—. Mem. Pitt County Hist. Preservation Soc., Greenville, Pitt County Mental Health Assn. Mem. ALA, AAUW, N.C. Library Assn., Southeastern Library Assn., Assn. Library and Info. Sci. Educators, Spl. Libraries Assn., LWV, NOW. Democrat. Home: 99 Moody Cove Rd Weaverville NC 28787

BOYCE, KAY ELLEN, school counselor; b. Clarksburg, West Va., Apr. 29, 1959; d. Carlton Dale and Patricia Ann (Williams) B. BA in Edn., Fairmont State Coll., 1980; MA in Counseling, West Va. U., 1985. Libr. dir. Taylor County Pub. Libr., Grofton, W.Va., 1981-85; counselor Valley View Elem. Sch., Martinsburg, W.Va., 1985-89, Lovettsville, Waterford and Lucketts (Va.) Elem. Schs., 1989-91, Algonkian Elem. Sch., Sterling, Va., 1991—; counselor pvt. practice Hamilton, Va. 1992, Reston Va., 1993—; radio guest, Washington, 1993. Facilitator Sisters (teen group), Sterling, Va., 1993. Democrat. Methodist. Office: Algonkian Elem Sch 20196 Carter Ct Sterling VA 20165

BOYCE, MELODIE STARITA, researcher; b. Bklyn., Sept. 4, 1958; d. Alwin M. and Delcena M. (Parris) B. BA, Bklyn. Coll., N.Y., 1979; MA, U. of Conn., Storrs, 1981; EdD, SUNY, Albany, 1992. Ednl. coord. Adelphi Inst., Bklyn.; dir. Sutton Bus. Sch., N.Y.; instr. English NYU, N.Y.C.; instr. ESL L.I. U.; instr. comm. Bklyn. Coll.; rschr. SUNY, Albany, sr. dir. spl. projects; presenter, speaker in field. Active N.Y. Missions Soc. Recipient Bernard McDonald award for rsch. in philanthropy Assn. of Black Found. Exec.'s. Mem. Nat. Alliance of Black Sch. Educators, Nat. Assn. of Black Women in Higher Edn., 100 Black Women, Am. Assn. of Higher Edn. (doctoral student of yr. award), Alpha Kappa Alpha.

BOYD, BARBARA H., state legislator; m. Robert Boyd, Jr.; 1 child, Janine. BS in Edn., St. Paul's Coll., Va. Former tchr. Cleve. Pub. Schs.; mem. coun. City of Cleveland Heights, Ohio, 1983-91, vice mayor, 1991, former mayor; current mem. dist. 9 Ohio Ho. Reps., Columbus. Former vol. coord. Cuyahoga County Juvenile Ct.; Dem. vice chair Cuyahoga County; past pres. Black Woman's Polit. Action Com.; former mem. youth violence com. Task Force on Violent Crimes; African-Am. adv. com. Notre Dame Coll. Ohio; ARTS Ednl. Theatre Co.; formerly active Monticello Field Supporters; active St. Andrew's Episc. Ch., Cleveland Heights. Mem. LWV (Cleveland Heights-University Heights chpt.), Cleveland Heights Dems., East Cleveland Dem. Club, Kiwanis, Delta Sigma Theta. Home: 3418 Washington Blvd Cleveland OH 44118 Office: Ohio Ho Reps 77 S High St Columbus OH 43215-6108

BOYD, BETTY, government official; b. Tulsa, Dec. 9, 1924; d. Theodore Wood and Victoria Marie (Fairchild) Carman; m. William Wray Boyd, Aug. 31, 1943; children: Beverlie J. Boyd Bryant, Barry Wray Boyd. Student, U. Tulsa, 1941-42, 45-46, Iowa State U., 1942-43. Broadcaster, pub. svc. dir. KOTV-Channel 6, Tulsa, 1955-65; broadcaster, pub. rels. dir. KTUL-TV-Channel 8, Tulsa, 1965-80; dir. pub. rels.-mktg. Tulsa County Area Vo-Tech. Dist., Tulsa, 1980-91; mem. Okla. Ho. of Reps., Dist. 23, Tulsa, 1991—. Author: Travelchatter: My Green Country, 1980, If I Could Sing I'd be Dangerous, 1983; contbr. articles to profl. jours. Bd. dirs. Tulsa Gridiron Trust, 1988—, Goodwill Ind. of Tulsa, 1985—, Osteopathic Found. of Tulsa Reg. Med. Ctr., 1989—; adv. bd. Okla. Alcohol & Drug Abuse Prevention and Life Skills Edn. Recipient Golden Mike for Pub. Svc., Am. Women in Radio & TV, 1970, Brotherhood award Nat. Conf. Christians & Jews, 1969.

Mem. Am. Vocat. Assn. (Svc. award 1990), Nat. Coun. State Legislatures (edn. com.), So. Legis. Conf., Tulsa Coalition of Older People, Women in the Svcs. (def. adv. com.), Tulsa Press Club (bd. dirs. 1984—). Democrat. Baptist. Home: 11039 E 26th Pl Tulsa OK 74129-7519 Office: Okla House of Reps State Capital Oklahoma City OK 73105*

BOYD, DEBORAH ANN, pediatrician; b. Urbana, Ohio, Jan. 30, 1955; d. John A. Sr. and Juanita Jean (Routt) B. BA cum laude, Wittenberg U., 1977; MD, U. Cin., 1982. Diplomate Am. Bd. Pediatrics, Nat. Bd. Med. Examiners. Intern Children's Hosp. Med. Ctr., Cin., 1982-83, pediatric resident, 1982-85; pediatrician Nat. Health Svc. Corps, Springfield, Ohio, 1985-89, Community Hosp. Health Care Ctr., Springfield, 1989—; mem. Continuing med. edn. com. Mercy Med. Ctr., Springfield, 1989—, infection control com., 1987—. Adv. com. Miami Valley Child Devl. Ctr., Springfield, 1985—, New Parents as Tchrs., 1986—. Democratic. Home: 2310 N Limestone St Apt 118 Springfield OH 45503-1144 Office: Community Hosp Health Care 144 W Pleasant St Springfield OH 45506-2206

BOYD, EMILIE LOU, elementary school educator, consultant; b. Millvale, Pa., July 14, 1935; d. Ralph William and Melba Margaret (Cochran) Popp; m. Thomas Boyd, Aug. 25, 1957 (div. Feb. 1969); children: Michael Thomas, Elizabeth Michelle Boyd Spalding. BS, Pa. State U., 1957; MEd, U. Tex., 1959; postgrad., Am. U., 1973. Cert. elem., spl. reading tchr., prin., supr. spl. edn., Tex., Va. Tchr., reading specialist El Paso (Tex.) Pub. Schs., 1958-69; asst. prin., prin. Fairfax (Va.) Pub. Schs., 1970-71, 75-76, specialist learning disabilities, 1973-75; dir. Summer Learning Disabilities Inst., Fairfax, 1971-76; bd. dirs. Staff Devel. Inst., Fairfax, 1975-76; developer Intensive readiness Staff Devel. Inst., 1981-84; counselor elem. sch., 1984-89; learning disabilities specialist Marshall Rd. Sch., 1989—; speaker on remedial reading and tech. Va. Tech. Conv., 1994. Author: (film) Learning Disabilities Childhood Resources. Mem. Nat. Assn. Mini Enthusiasts (editor newsletter 1986—), Fairfax Miniature Enthusiasts (editor newsletter 1986—), Pi Lambda Theta, Delta Gamma Delta, Pi Delta Gamma, Phi Delta Kappa. Roman Catholic.

BOYD, JANE GAIL, educator; b. Bentonville, Ark., Oct. 26, 1960; d. James Carson and Frances Grace (Gammon) B. BS in Edn., U. Ark., 1984; postgrad., East Tex. State U., 1985. Tchr. drama, speech Ark. High Sch., Texarkana, 1984-88; dir. debate and forensics Grapevine (Tex.) High Sch., 1988—; coach championship team Univ. Interscholastic League Cross-Exam. Debate, 1993-94. Chair Task Force Communication, Grapevine, 1993-94, polit. action com. NEA, Texarkana, 1987-88. Named Ark. Young Speech Tchr. of Yr., 1985; Barton scholar Nat. Debate Coaches Assn., 1992. Mem. Nat. Debate Coaches Assn., Tex. Forensic Assn., Nat. Forensic League (Diamond coach, dist. chmn. 1992-94, dist. com. 1990-92). Democrat. Presbyterian.

BOYD, JULIA GREER, library director; b. Petersburg, Tenn., July 2, 1925; d. Jacob Claude and Verna (Allen) Greer; m. Alvin Whitten Boyd, Apr. 25, 1959. BS, U. Tenn., 1950; MA, Peabody Coll., 1954. Libr. Obion County Libr., Union City, Tenn., 1945-48; bookmobile libr. Reelfoot Regional Libr., Martin, Tenn., 1951-56; dir. Upper Cumberland Regional Libr., Cookeville, Tenn., 1956—. Mem. ALA, AAUW (v.p. Tenn. div. 1985-86, pres. Cookeville br. 1981-83), Southeastern Libr. Assn. (chair planning and devel. com. 1990—), Tenn. Libr. Assn. (sec. 1956-57, treas. 1983-84, pres. 1987-88), Inner Wheel Club (pres. 1989-90). Presbyterian. Office: Upper Cumberland Reg Libr 208 Minnear St Cookeville TN 38501-3914

BOYD, JULIA MARGARET (MRS. SHELTON B. BOYD), lay church worker; b. Newton Grove, N.C., Mar. 7, 1921; d. Isaiah and Mary Lela (Blackman) Tart; m. Shelton Bickett Boyd, Feb. 21, 1944; children: Mary (Mrs. Edward Southerland III), Deborah (Mrs. John Wayne Pearson). BS, East Carolina U., 1942. V.p. WSCS, Lillington (N.C.) U. Meth. Ch., 1948-49; pres. Woman's Soc. Christian Svc., Mt. Olive, N.C., 1951-55, 59-61; sec. various coms. WSCS, 1st United Meth. Ch., Mt. Olive, N.C., from 1950, mem., sec. adminstrv. bd. and coun. ministries, from 1955, mem. local work area on edn., 1960-82, chmn., 1971-75, chmn. spiritual growth, 1971-75, mem. fin. com., 1985-87, 90-94; counselor United Meth. Youth Fellowship, 1960-67; adult del. Nat. Convocation Meth. Youth, 1964; pres. Goldsboro dist. United Meth. Women, 1955-59; mem. N.C. Conf. Bd. Edn., 1964-72; mem. N.C. Coun. on Youth Ministries, 1964-82, chmn., 1972-76; mem. adult staff youth, sr. high mins., 1972-82; mem. N.C. Conf. Coun. on Ministries, 1972-82; mem. Goldsboro dist. Coun. on Ministries, 1970—, sec., 1971—; also coord. youth ministries Goldsboro dist., 1964-82; del. SEJ Youth Conf., Arlington, Va., 1976, SEJ Leadership Devel. Workshop, Lake Junaluska, 1977; lay rep. Goldsboro dist. Conf. Coun. on Ministries, 1982-92, ann. conf. United Meth. Ch., 1985, 87, 90, dist. trustee, 1993—; rep. N.C. Christian Advocate, 1985—; bd. dirs. Meth. Home for Children, 1993—; mem., sec. dist. adv. com. Fremont Youth Home, 1988—. Editor Meth. Messenger, 1965-68. Pres. PTA, Mt. Olive, 1955-56, Mt. Olive High Sch. and So. Wayne High Sch. Band Patron's Club, 1964-66; leader Girl Scouts U.S.A., 1956-57; active Community Chest. Named Lay Person of Yr. N.C. Conf. United Meth. Ch., 1979, (with husband) Outstanding Sr. Citizens of Mt. Olive, 1990; recipient cert. appreciation United Meth. Youth Fellowship, 1980, 83. Mem. Women's Aux. of N.C. Pharm. Assn. (corr. sec. 1976-77, rec. sec. 1977-78, 2d v.p. 1978-79, 1st v.p. 1979-80, pres. 1980-81, mem. nominating com. 1988—, mins. com. 1988-89, hospitality com. 1989), United Meth. Women (mem. hist. com. Goldsboro dist. 1984, chairperson 1989, 94, v.p. local chpt. 1988-89), So. Wayne Country Club. Home: 400 W Main St Mount Olive NC 28365-2018

BOYD, LAURA WOOLDRIDGE, state legislator; b. Charlottesville, Va., June 5, 1949; d. Oscar Bailey Wooldridge and Martha Jane (Clarke) Jordan; m. Harry Sterling Boyd, July 31, 1979 (div. Apr. 1984); m. Joseph David Rambo, May 1, 1986; children: Susan Rebecca, Brooke Caitlin. BA in German, Duke U., 1970; MS in Huamnistic Edn., Marywood Coll., 1978; PhD in Counseling Psychology, Internat. Coll., 1982. Nat. cert. clin. mental health counselor. Pvt. practice Doylestown, Pa., 1975-78; project dir. Ct. Appointed Advocate Program for Cleve. County, 1984-85; owner, adminstr. The Family Ctr., Norman, Okla., 1978—; mem. Okla. Ho. Reps., Oklahoma City, 1992—; adj. faculty Mary Coll., Scranton, 1976-79. Reviewer Jour. on Traumatic Stress, 1990—, Trasactional Analysis Jour., 1984—; contbr. articles to profl. jours. Mem. Cleve. County Citizen's Adv. Bd.; bd. dirs. Alternative Support Edn. Progra; asst. coach Optimist League Girls Basketball; chair Norman Pub. Sch. Crisis Intervention Team; mem. St. John's Episcopal Ch.; parent vol. McKinley Elem. Sch. and Whittier Middle Sch.; kettle ringer Salvation Army; solicitor United Way; frequent leader Norman Regional Hosp. Breast Cancer Support Group; affiliate staff Norman Regional Hosp.; adv. com. Moore-Norman Vo-Tech Options Program. Mem. ACA, Am. Assn. for Marriage and Family Therapy (supr., chairperson profl. practice com. 1990-92), Am. Psychol. Assn. (Okla. state liaison to divsn. 43 family psychology 1987-90), Internat. Transactional Analysis Assn., Assn. of Family and Conciliation Cts., Profl. Assn. of Custody Evaluations (diplomate), Nat. Coun. on Family Rels., Okla. Psychol. Assn., Acad. Family Mediators (sr.), Am. Assn. Family Counselors and Mediators, Inc. (cert. supr.), Okla. Assn. for Marriage and Family Therapy, Norman Bus. Assn., Norman C. of C., Rotary Clubs Internat. Democrat. Episcopalian. Office: Okla Ho of Reps State Capitol Oklahoma City OK 73105

BOYD, LEONA POTTER, retired social worker; b. Creekside, Pa., Aug. 31, 1907; d. Joseph M. and Belle (McHenry) Johnston. Grad. Ind. (Pa.) State Normal Sch., 1927, student Las Vegas Normal U., N.Mex., 1933, Carnegie Inst. Tech. Sch. Social Work, 1945, U. Pitts. Sch. Social Work, 1956-57; m. Edgar D. Potter, July 16, 1932 (div.); m. Harold Lee Boyd, Oct. 1972. Tchr. Creekside (Pa.) Pub. Schs., 1927-30, Papago Indian Reservation, Sells, Ariz., 1931-33; caseworker, supr. Indiana County (Pa.) Bd. Assistance, 1934-54, exec. dir., 1954-68, ret. Bd. dirs. Indiana County Tourist Promotion, hon. life mem.; former bd. dirs. Indiana County United Fund, Salvation Army, Indiana County Guidance Ctr., Armstrong-Indiana Mental Health Bd.; cons. assoc. Community Rsch. Assocs., Inc.; mem. Counseling Ctr. Aux., Lake Havasu City, Ariz., 1978-80; former mem. Western Welcome Club, Lake Havasu City, Sierra Vista Hosp. Aux., Truth or Consequences, N.Mex. Recipient Jr. C. of C. Disting. Svc. award, Indiana, Pa., 1966, Bus. and Profl. Women's Club award, Indiana, 1965. Mem. Am. Assn. Ret. Persons, Daus. Am. Colonists, Sierra County Hist. Soc., Common Cause (Washington), Nat. Parks and Conservation Assn. Lutheran. Home: 444 S Higley Rd Apt 219 Mesa AZ 85206-2186

BOYD, VICTORIA LOUISE, data communications director; b. Osceola, Iowa, Sept. 5, 1951; d. Keith Eugene and Shirley Louise (Bishop) Kent; m. Ronald Gene Boyd, June 3, 1972; children: Aaron William, Ryan Eugene. BS in Math., Iowa State U., 1972; postgrad., U. Minn., 1992. Various engr. positions US West/Ops., Des Moines, 1972-77, 77-83; dir. engring. US West/Network Ops., Des Moines, 1983-88; dir. svc. US West/Large Bus. Markets, Mpls., 1988-91; dir. ops. US West.Advanced Communication Svcs., Mpls., 1991-93; dir. bus. devel. & implementation Time Warner Comm., Englewood, Colo., 1994; dir-operations US West Interprise Networking Svcs., Mpls., 1994—. Bd. dirs. Groves Acad., St. Louis Park, Minn., 1994—; bd. trustees Valley Com. Presbyn. Ch., Golden Valley, Minn., 1994—, chari stewardship, 1994—. Mem. Am. Soc. Quality, Nat. Communications Forum, Soc. Women Engrs., Alpha Lambda Delta. Office: US West 150 South 5th St Ste 3200 Minneapolis MN 55402

BOYD-BROWN, LENA ERNESTINE, history educator, education consultant; b. New Orleans, July 3, 1937; d. Eugene A. and Rosemary (Lewis) Boyd. BA, Xavier U., 1958; MA, Howard U., 1960; EdD, Rutgers U., 1979. History instr. So. U., New Orleans, 1960-61; tchr. Washington Pub. Schs., 1961-62; history instr. So. U., Baton Rouge, 1962-63; residence counselor N.C. Cen. U., Durham, 1963-64; counselor, instr. Howard U., Washington, 1964-65; asst. prof. history Grambling (La.) State U., 1965-68, Tuskegee (Ala.) U., 1968-70; assoc. examiner history Ednl. Testing Svc., Princeton, N.J., 1970-79; assoc. prof. history, edn. Dillard U., New Orleans, 1979-88; dir. testing, assoc. prof. history Hampton (Va.) U., 1988-89, assoc. prof. history, dept. history chairperson, 1989-91; assoc. prof. history div. social and polit. sci. Tex. A&M U., Prarie View, 1991—; testing cons. Lincoln (Pa.) U., 1974, So. U., Baton Rouge, 1979, New Orleans, 1986-89, Hampton U., 1988. Contbg. author, editor profl. jours. Martin L. King Jr. fellow, Rutgers U., 1977-78; fellow Howard U., 1958-60, Carnegie-Mellon U., Pitts., 1966-67. Mem. Assn. for Study Negro Life and History, Nat. Coalition of 100 Black Women (New Orleans chpt.), Orgn. Am. Historians, AKA Sorority (Alpha Beta Omega chpt.), So. Hist. Soc., Southwestern Soc. Sci. Assn., Phi Alpha Theta, Phi Delta Kappa, Kappa Delta Pi. Office: Prairie View A & M Univ Div Social And Sci Prairie View TX 77446

BOYER, DIANE WALTZEK, interior designer; b. Chgo., Dec. 25, 1945; d. William John and Anne (Socha) Waltzek; m. Gerald Rodney Boyer, Sept. 10, 1966 (div. 1995); children: Amanda Kristin, Stephanie Ann. BFA in Graphic Design, U. Ill., 1969; MS in Packaging Design, Pratt Inst., 1973; cert. interior design, N.Y. Sch. Interior Design, 1979. Cert. interior designer. Grpahic designer Johannes Regn Inc., N.Y.C.; interior designer Ellen Standish Interiors, Parsippany, N.J.; chmn. fine and performing arts dept. Montclair (N.J.) Kimberly Acad.; pres., interior designer Boyer-Cooper Interiors Ltd., Midland Park, N.J., 1991-95; owner, prin. designer Diane Boyer Designers, Montclair, 1979—. Design work in nat. and local publs. and books. Mem. Am. Soc. Interior Designers (v.p. 1989-91, pres. 1991-92, past pres. 1992-93, Presdl. Citation award 1989, Medalist award 1993). Democrat. Unitarian.

BOYER, ELIZABETH SARAH, accountant; b. Reading, Pa., Aug. 8, 1927; d. Harvey Elmer and Edna Marie (Adams) Dice; m. Howard James Boyer, June 10, 1950 (div. Mar. 1973); children: Sharon E. Blankenship, Carol A. Santee, Janet M. Comberiate. Cert., U. Pa., 1948, Pace Inst., 1985. Pers./payroll clerk Am. Casualty Co. (name now CNA), Reading, 1950-52; acctg. clerk CNA Ins., Reading, 1956-63; full charge bookkeeper United Community Svcs. of Berks County, Reading, 1963-64; full charge acct. Garrison Ins. Agy., Reading, 1964-66; full charge bookkeeper Brown Engring. Co., Reading, 1966-72, Kurtz, Dowd, & Nuss, Inc., Reading, 1972-73; prodn. control/acctg. clerk Talbott Knitting Mills, Reading, 1973-74; jr. acct. C. Malcom Smith & Co., Reading, 1974; full charge bookkeeper Local Indsl. Fork Trucks, Inc., Bernville, Pa., 1975-76; asst. to controller, pers. coord. Manson-Billard, Inc., Reading, 1977-85; notary pub., Berks County, Wyomissing, Pa., 1990-94. Author: (poetry) Our Proud Symbol, 1990 (honorable mention 1990), Someone Cares You Know Who, 1991 (honorable mention 1991). Leader Camp Fire Girls, Reading, 1962-72, head leader's assn., 1961-67; Hospice vol. Cmty. Gen. Hosp., Reading, 1993—. Mem. Inst. Mgmt. Accts. (past bd. dirs., sec., treas. and v.p., award 1980-81, 82-83), Berks County Geneal. Soc., Northmont Fellowship Assn. (pres. aux. 1987-93), Cath. Woman's Club Berks County (pres. 1984-86). Home: 819 Church St Reading PA 19601-2219

BOYER, KAYE KITTLE, association management executive; b. Peoria, Ill., July 5, 1942; d. Keith Howard and Evelyn Pearl (Benson) K.; m. Jon Frederick, March 20, 1965; children: Tristan Donna, Kristine Monique. Student, Merrill Palmer Inst., Detroit, 1964; BS in Home Economics, The Pa. State U., University Park, 1964; MA in Sociology, Rutgers State U., New Brunswick, 1967. Cert. Assn. Exec., Cert. Home Economist. Creative researcher Nat. Inst. Drycleaning, Silver Spring, Md., 1963; extension home economist Md. Cooperative Extension Service, Westminster, 1964-65; coord. human resources N.J. Cooperative Extension Service, New Brunswick, 1966-67; instr. Douglass Coll., Rutgers U., New Brunswick, 1967-70; coord., instr. pilot project Urban Coalition of Met. Wilmington Inc., Wilmington, Delaware, 1972; asst. to chmn. 4-H Youth Devel. Dept., Cook Coll., 1973-74; feasibility study dir. Ocean County Coll., Toms River, N.J., 1975; exec. dir. N.J. Home Economics Assn., Manalapan, 1975-86; pres. Boyer Mgmt. Svcs., Manalapan, N.J. and Earleville, Md., 1984—; mgr. Costume Soc. Am. Earleville, Md., 1984—; cons. Plumpton Park Zool. Gardens Rising Sun, 1988-89, bd. dirs., 1990-92; cons. N.J. White House Conf., Trenton, 1980; bd. dirs. N.J. Soc. Assn. Execs., Belle Mead, 1985-86, Md. Soc. Assn. Execs., Balt., 1989-90, sec., 1990-92, v.p., 1992-93, pres.-elect, 1993-94, pres., 1994—. Editor Exchs. Newsletter; resource dir., N.J. Programs and Svcs. Related to Adolescent Pregnancy. Adv. com. Dept. Community Edn. Rutgers, New Brunswick, 1979-84; vol. Soroptimists Internat. of Elkton, Md., 1987—; player U.S. Pub. Links Amateur. Mem. AAUW (N.J. div. v.p. for program devel. 1984-86), Am. Home Econs. Assn. (Ruth O'Brien Project grantee), Md. Home Econs. Assn., Com. Libr. of Cecilton (pres., bd. dirs. 1986-92), Am. Assn. Family and Consumer Scis., Am. Soc. Assn. Execs., Assn. Advance Am. Com., Kappa Omicron Nu (v.p. fin. 1992-93). Democrat. Home: PO Box 73 55 Edgewater Dr Earleville MD 21919

BOYER, LAURA MERCEDES, librarian; b. Madison, Ind., Aug. 3, 1934; d. Clyde C. and Dorcas H. (Willyard) Boyer. A.B., George Washington U., 1956; A.M., U. Denver, 1959; M.L.S., George Peabody U., 1961. Pub. sch. tchr., Kankakee, Ill., 1957-58; asst. circulation librarian U. Kans., Lawrence, 1961-63; asst. reference librarian U. of Pacific Library, Stockton, Calif., 1963-65, head reference dept., 1965-84, coordinator reference services, 1984-86; reference librarian Calif. State U.-Stanislaus, Turlock, 1987-90, ref. coord., 1990—. Author: The Older Generation of Southeast Asian Refugees: An Annoteted Bibliography, 1991; compiler of Play Anthologies Union List, 1976; contbr. articles to profl. jours. Mem. Am. Soc. Info. Sci., ALA, Calif. Library Assn., AAUP, Nat. Assn. for Edn. and Advancement of Cambodian, Laotian and Vietnamese Ams., DAR, Daughters of Am. Colonists, Phi Beta Kappa, Kappa Delta Pi, Beta Phi Mu. Republican. Episcopalian. Home: 825 Muir Rd Modesto CA 95350-6052

BOYER, LILLIAN BUCKLEY, artist, educator; b. Paterson, N.J., Mar. 1, 1916; d. George and Adele (Roomy) Buckley; m. Floyd E. Boyer, Jr., Sept. 7, 1935; 1 child, Karen Boyer Lloyd. BA in Art Edn., U. Ky., 1975. Field interviewer Survey Rsch. Ctr., U. Mich., 1963-68; 20 regional one-woman shows; instr. art U. Ky., Lexington; Ky. reporter for Sunshine Artists mag., 1976-85. Crusade chmn. Am. Cancer Soc., Anaheim, Calif., 1958, Orange County, Calif., 1959; active, hon. life mem. PTA, 1950-62; mem. Lexington Arts & Cultural Coun., Ky. Citizens for the Arts, Friends of Ky. Ednl. TV, JB. Speed Art Mus., Headley Whitney Mus., Friends of Lexington Pub. Libr.; pres., dir., life mem. Lexington Art League, 1976-80, 82-83, 84-86. Recipient 56 awards for print-making, painting and sculpture. Mem. U. Ky. Alumni Assn., Living Arts and Sci. Ctr., Friends of U.K. Art Mus., Nat. Mus. Women in Arts. Methodist. Address: 969 Holly Springs Dr Lexington KY 40504-3119

BOYER, SUSAN ELAINE, psychotherapist, consultant, speaker; b. Detroit Lakes, Minn., Aug. 1, 1948; d. Chauncey Alcott and Lucille Mildred (Aull) B.; 1 child, Belden George Sadler. BA, U. Minn., 1972, postgrad., 1986-87; MS in Counseling Psychology, Chaminade U. of Honolulu, 1990. Lic. profl. counselor. Case aide Ottertail County Welfare, Fergus Falls, Minn., 1973-74; social worker/sr. social worker Hennepin County, Mpls., 1974-85; house dir. Sigma Delta Tau, Mpls., 1978-79, Delta Gamma, Mpls., 1979-81; pvt. practice counselor Mpls., 1986-87; psychiat. social worker State of Hawaii, Honolulu, 1988; substitute tchr. State of Hawaii, Oahu, 1989-90; home studies specialist Contract-Cath. Svcs., Honolulu, 1989; group facilitator Parents United, Honolulu, 1990-92; clin. social worker/cmty. liaison Salvation Army, Honolulu, 1990-91; clin. social worker Teen Intervention Program, Honolulu, 1991-92; counselor pvt. practice Honolulu, 1987-92, Denver, 1992—; counselor, cons. AT&T-NSD, Denver, 1992—; group facilitator Adoptees in Search, Denver, 1993—; speaker in field of adoptive triad, search, and reunion, adult children of alcoholics, reparenting inner child, co-dependency, 1986—. Frear and Leemosynary scholar Chaminade U. of Honolulu, 1988, C.T.C. Ching Meml. scholar, 1989. Mem. Employee Assistance Program Assn., Colo. Mental Health Counselors Assn., Concerned United Birth Parents, Adoptees in Search-Facilitator-Support Group (bd. dirs. 1993—). Office: PO Box 101981 Denver CO 80250

BOYERS, MARGARITA ANNE (PEGGY BOYERS), editor, periodical, writer, translator; b. San Tome, Anzuategui, Venezuela, Aug. 16, 1952; d. John Joseph O'Higgins and Maria Josefa Lluriá de O'Higgins; m. Robert Boyers, Dec. 16, 1975; children: Lowell, Zachary, Gabriel. BA, Skidmore Coll., 1975. Exec. editor Salmagundi Mag. Skidmore Coll., 1975—. Co-editor The Bennington Review, 1978-83. Mem. PEN. Democrat. Office: Salmagundi Skidmore College Saratoga Springs NY 12866

BOYETT, JOAN REYNOLDS, arts administrator; b. L.A., May 2, 1936; d. Clifton Faris Reynolds and Jean Margaret (Howard) Hauck; m. Harry William Boyett, Oct. 5, 1956; children: Keven William, Suzanne Marie Boyett Liebherr. Student, Occidental Coll., 1954-55, Pasadena Playhouse, 1955-57. Mgr. youth activities L.A. Philharmonic Orch., 1970-79; dir., founder Music Ctr. Edn. Divsn. Music Ctr., L.A. County, 1979—; v.p. for edn. Music Ctr. L.A. County, 1988—; cons. NEA, Washington; chmn. arts edn. task force Calif. Arts Coun., Sacramento, 1993—; arts edn. mem. Nat. Working Group, Washington, 1992—. Active various coms. and task forces, L.A., Sacramento. Named Woman of Yr. L.A. Times, 1976; recipient Labor's award of honor County Fedn. Labor, L.A., 1984, Susan B. Anthony award Bus. and Profl. Women, 1986, Gov.'s award Calif. Arts Coun. and Gov., 1989. Mem. Calif. Art Edn. Assn. (Behind the Scenes award 1985), Calif. Dance Educators Assn. (Svc. award 1985), Calif. Ednl. Theatres Assn. (Outstanding Contbn. award 1990). Republican. Presbyterian. Home: PO Box 1805 Studio City CA 91614 Office: The Music Ctr 135 N Grand Ave Los Angeles CA 90012

BOYKIN, CATHERINE MARIE, health care administrator; b. Phila., Dec. 25, 1944; d. William Lee (dec.) and Marie Eleanor (Hewson) B.; m. Walter Miller Morris Jr., Sept. 3, 1977; 1 child, William Martin Boykin-Morris. BSN, Villanova U., 1966; cert. PNP, U. Conn., 1973. Cert. PNP, Vt. Pub. health nurse U.S. Peace Corps, Osorno, Chile, 1967-68; coronary care specialist Queen of the Angels Hosp., L.A., 1969-70; pub. health nurse Orthopaedic Hosp., L.A., 1970-72; PNP N.E. Kingdom Mental Health Svcs., Newport, Vt., 1973-75, The Child Health Ctr., St. Johnsbury, Vt., 1975-81; pvt. practice nurse practitioner New Directions in Health, St. Johnsbury, 1981-84; PNP The Burke Schs., Burke Hollow, Vt., 1983-84; dir. health Lyndon Inst., Lyndon Center, Vt., 1984—; chair Vt. Joint Practice Com.: Vt. State Nurses Assn., Vt. State Med. Soc., 1981-83; coord. Drug-Free Schs., Lyndon Inst., Lyndon Center, 1984—; bd. mem. Heart Healthy Vermonter Adv. Bd., St. Johnsbury, 1985-90; pediatric rep. Vt. State Bd. Nursing Nurse Practitioner Adv. Com., 1985—. Vice chairperson Caledonia County Dem. Com., St. Johnsbury, 1990—; Justice of the Peace, Lyndonville, 1990—; chairperson Lyndon Town Dem. Com., Lyndonville, 1991—. Recipient Founding Assoc. award Club de Abstemios Nuevo Amanecer, Osorno, 1968. Mem. ANA, Vt. State Nurses Assn. (chairperson coun. of nursing practice 1975-77), Coun. Nurses in Advanced Practice, Vt. State Sch. Nurses Assn., Vt. Pediatric Nurse Practitioners (treas. 1987-89, co-chair 1990—), Vt. Nurse Practitioners Inc., Am. Sch. Health Assn., Nat. Assn. Sch. Nurses, Nat. Family Life Edn. Network. Roman Catholic. Home: RR 2 Lyndonville VT 05851-9802 Office: Lyndon Institute Lyndon Center VT 05850

BOYKIN, NANCY MERRITT, academic administrator; b. Washington, Mar. 20; d. Matthew and Mary Gertrude (White) Merritt; m. Ulysses Wilhelm Boykin, Apr. 17, 1965 (dec. 1987); 1 child by previous marriage, Taunya Lovell Banks. BS, D.C. Tchrs. Coll.; MA, Howard U., MSW, 1965; PhD, U. Mich., 1976. Employee rels. counselor Office Chief of Fin., U.S. Army, Washington; adminstrv. asst. to Civilian Aide to Sec. of Def., Washington; policewoman Met. Police Dept., Washington; social worker Dept. Pub. Welfare, Washington; adminstrv. asst. to dir. Active Community Teams, Inc., Detroit, 1965-66; dir. continuing edn. for girls program Detroit Pub. Schs., 1966-87; edn. cons. and community outreach coord. New Health Ctr., Livonia, Mich., 1988-90; cons U.S. Dept. Edn., 1982; presdl. appointee Nat. Adv. Coun. on Extension and Continuing Edn., 1973-80. Contbr. articles to profl. jours. Mem. Mich. Bd. Examiners of Social Workers, 1978-83; mem. Mich. Rep. Com., 1975-80, 83—; presdl. appointee to nat. adv. bd. Community Coll. of Air Force, 1984—; gov.'s appointee Mich. Youth Adv. Com., 1984-87, Commn. on Svcs. to Aging, 1992; sec. 1st Rep. Dist., 1973-77; mem. Nat. Black Republicans., 1972—. Named Educator of Yr., Nat. Black Women's Polit. Leadership Caucus, 1981, Hon. Lt. Col. Aide De Camp in Ala. Militia, Gov. Wallace, 1986; recipient Disting. Contbn. plaque Pres.'s Nat. Adv. Com., 1973-80, Spirit of Detroit award, 1979, Meritorious Svc. plaque, Air Force Bd. Vis., 1986, Superior Svc. to USAF Enlisted Pers. plaque, Air Force Bd. Vis., 1986, Nat. Kool Achiever's award in Edn. Brown and Williams Tobacco Co., 1987, Outstanding Contbns. to Community award Assn. Black Judges Mich., 1988-90, Community Svc. award YWCA, 1992, plaque for Svc. on Bd. Dirs., Lula Belle Stewart Ctr., Inc., 1994, Pioneer award Frederick Douglas Soc., 1994, others; The Nancy Boykin Continuing Edn. Ctr. named in her honor Detroit Pub. Sch. Bd., 1993; honored by Spl. Legis. Tribute for advocacy of comprehensive edn. for student parents, State of Mich., 1993. Mem. Profl. Women's Network, Nat. Assn. Supervision and Curriculum Devel., Detroit Orgn. of Sch. Adminstrs., Nat. Assn. Black Sch. Educators, Detroit Assn. Univ. Mich. Women, Sch. Edn. Alumni Assn. Wayne State U. (bd. govs.), U. Mich. Alumnae Assn., Mich. Assn. Concerned with Sch. Age Parents (founding mem., past pres., Recognition award, 1986, Outstanding Svc. award 1993), Phi Delta Kappa, Eta Phi Beta (Outstanding Profl. Woman award 1992), Alpha Kappa Alpha. Home and Office: 17224 Fairfield St Detroit MI 48221-3084

BOYKIN, REBECCA ELLEN, marketing professional; b. Balt., Feb. 26, 1955; d. William Augustine III and Nancy Joan (Bickelhaupt) B.; m. Robert Chester Schwaner, Jr., Sept. 23, 1983 (div. 1994); children: Victoria Lee Claiborne, Robert Chester III. AA in Nursing, Wesley Coll., 1975; BA in History, Loyola Coll., 1981; postgrad., U. of South, Sewanee, Tenn., 1992—. RN. Operating room nurse Med. Coll. Va., Richmond, 1975-76; acting head nurse Children's Hosp. Inc., Balt., 1976-81; clin. nurse shock trauma Md. Inst. Emergency Med. Svcs. Systems, Balt., 1981-83; rsch. coord. S. Gregory Smith, M.D., Wilmington, Del., 1984-87; clin. coord. Owensville Med. Ctr., West River, Md., 1989-91; mktg. rep., asst. mgr. Md. Magnetic Imaging, Frederick, 1992—. Leader human sexuality workshop Episcopal Ch., Thurmont, Md., 1993. Bd. dirs. Pvt. Industry Coun. of Frederick County (chair client svcs. com.). Maj. Md. Army NG, Parkville, 1977—. Recipient res. medal Md. Army Nat. Guard, 1987, army achievement medal, 1988, oak leaf cluster, 1989, army svc. ribbon, 1980. Mem. Nat. Officers Assn., Nat. Soc. Colonial Dames in Md. (co-chair hospitality com.), Frederick Profl. Women's Network, Frederick County C. of C. (chair activities team mem. com., 1993—). Republican. Home: 15 Mountain Rd Thurmont MD 21788-1821 Office: Md Magnetic Imaging 900 Toll House Ave Frederick MD 21701-4547

BOYKIN, RUTH, dentist; b. Madison, Wis., May 15, 1952; d. William Baynard S. and Matilda Ann (Sweet) B.; m. John R. Conaway, Oct. 1, 1982 (div. Oct. 1987). BS in Zoology, Clemson U., 1974, MS in Zoology, 1979; DMD, MUSC, 1986. Grad. teaching asst. Clemson (S.C.) U., 1974-76; Ga. supr. Millikin Mills, LaGrange, S.C., 1976-77; 2d grade tchr. Robert E. Lee Acad., Bishopville, S.C., 1978; exec. legal sec. Curtis, Morris & Safford,

N.Y.C., 1979-82; pvt. practice Greenville, S.C., 1989—. Mem. Palmetto Toastmasters (sec.1991, treas. 1992). Home: 53 Maple Ln Travelers Rest SC 29690-2008 Office: Family Dentistry 1140 N Pleasantburg Dr Ste D Greenville SC 29607-1223

BOYLE, ANTONIA BARNES, audio producer, writer; b. Detroit, May 21, 1939; d. James Merriam and Florence (Maiullo) B.; 1 child, Caitlin Merriam. BS in Speech, Northwestern U., 1962. Staff announcer WEFM-FM, Chgo., 1975-78; pres. Boyle Communications, Chgo., 1978-85; exec. producer Nightingale-Conant Corp., Chgo., 1985-90, Cassette Prodns. Unltd., Irwindale, Calif., 1990-92; pres. Antonia Boyle & Co., 1992—. Author: The Optimal You, 1990, Taping Yourself Seriously, 1991; co-author: (with Jay Gordon) Good Food Today, Great Kids Tomorrow, 1994 (with Scott McKain) Just Say Yes, 1994. Chmn., bd. dirs. Horizons for the Blind, Chgo., 1984. Mem. Am. Fedn. Radio, TV Artists, Com.100 Northwestern U., NU Club, San Francisco. Home: 2526 39th Ave San Francisco CA 94116-2751 Office: Antonia Boyle & Co 236 W Portal Ave San Francisco CA 94127-1423

BOYLE, BARBARA JANE, insurance company executive; b. Shenandoah, Iowa, Mar. 1, 1936; d. Thomas Henry and Hazel Ingred (Gell) Hill; m. Richard F. Smith, Jan. 6, 1990; children: Jill, Chris Richardson. BA, Iowa State Tchrs. Coll., Cedar Falls, 1960. Tchr. elem. United Community Schs., Boone, Iowa, 1975-79; mgr. dist. sales World Book Ency., St. Paul, 1980-83; ins. agt. Allstate Ins. Co., St. Paul, 1983-84; mgr. market sales Allstate Ins. Co., Eden Prairie, Minn., 1985-88, market mgr. ind. agts., 1989-94, mgr. agy., 1995—. Fellow Life Underwriting Tng. Coun.; mem. Nat. Assn. Life Underwriters, Minn. Ind. Agt. Assn. Methodist.

BOYLE, BARBARA PRINCELAU, retired intelligence officer; b. Oakland, Calif., Sept. 21, 1923; d. Paul and Mary Emilie (Rueger) Princelau; m. John Joseph Boyle, Oct. 21, 1950 (dec.). BA, U. Calif., Berkeley, 1948. Intelligence officer CIA, Langley, Va., 1954-82. Bd. dirs. The Thrift Shop, Washington, 1988-92; mem. Women's Bd. Columbia Hosp. for Women Med. Ctr., Washington, 1986—, mem. exec. com., 1989-91; mem. com. Washington Antiques Show, 1989—; active Rep. Womens Fed. Forum, Washington. Recipient Cert. of Distinction CIA, 1982. Mem. Ctrl. Intelligence Retiree Assn., Assn. Former Intelligence Officers (bd. dirs. 1993—), Sulgrave Club, U. Calif. Berkeley Alumni Club of Washington (rec. sec. 1976-77, v.p. 1984-86), Sigma Kappa (v.p. No. Va. alumnae 1992-95, devel. com. Sigma Kappa Found., Inc. 1993—). Episcopalian. Home: 5101 River Rd Bethesda MD 20816-1512

BOYLE, CAROLYN MOORE, public relations executive, marketing communications manager; b. Los Angeles, Jan. 29, 1937; d. Cory Orlando Moore and Violet (Brennan) Baldock; m. Robert J. Ruppelt, Oct. 8, 1954 (div. Aug. 1964); children: Cory Robert, Traci Lynn; m. Jerry Ray Boyle, June 1, 1970 (div. 1975). AA, Orange Coast Coll., 1966; BA, Calif. State U., Fullerton, 1970; student, U. Calif., Irvine, 1970-71. Program coordinator Newport Beach (Calif.) Cablevision, 1968-70; dir. pub. relations Fish Communications Co., Newport Beach, 1970-74; mktg. rep. Dow Pharm. div. Dow Chem. Co., Orange County, Calif., 1974-77, Las Vegas, Nev., 1980-81; mgr. product publicity Dow Agrl. Products div. Dow Chem. Co., Midland, Mich., 1977-80; mgr. mktg. communications Dowell Fluid Services Region div. Dow Chem. Co. Houston, 1981-84; adminstr. mktg. communications Swedlow, Inc., Garden Grove, Calif., 1984-85; cons. mktg. communications, 1985-86; mgr. mktg. communications Am. Convertors div. Am. Hosp. Supply, 1986-87; mgr. sales support Surgidev Corp., Santa Barbara, Calif., 1987-88; owner Barrel House, Victorville, Calif., 1988-91, Saratoga Fences, Las Vegas, 1991; pub. info. officer nuclear waste divsn. Clark County Comprehensive Planning, Las Vegas, 1992—; guest lectr. Calif. State U., Long Beach, 1970; seminar coordinator U. Calif., Irvine, 1972; mem. Western White House Press Corps, 1972; pub. relations cons. BASF Wyandotte, Phila., 1981-82. Author: Agricultural Public Relations/Publicity, 1981; editor Big Mean AG Machine (internal mag.), 1977; contbr. numerous articles to trade publs.; contbg. editor Dowell Mktg. Newsletter, 1983; creator, designer Novahistine DMX Trial Size nat. mktg. program, 1977. Com. mem. Dow Employees for Polit. Action, Midland, 1978-80; bd. dirs. Dowell Employees for Polit. Action Com., Houston, 1983-84. World Campus Afloat scholar, U. Seven Seas, 1966-67; recipient PROTOS award, 1985. Mem. Pub. Relations Soc. Am. (cert.), Soc. Petroleum Engrs., Internat. Assn. Bus. Communicators. Episcopalian. Recipient first rights to televise President Nixon in Western White House. Office: 6340 Lanning Ln Las Vegas NV 89108

BOYLE, MARCIA JANE, financial planner; b. Easton, Pa., Mar. 21, 1953; d. John Francis and Marie Elizabeth (McLaughlin) B.; m. David Alan Bryan, May 14, 1993. BS, U. Dayton, 1974, BSEE, 1977; MSE in Sys. Engring., U. Pa., 1982; postgrad., N.Y.U., 1990. CFP. Scientific programmer Tech. Inc., Dayton, Ohio, 1974-76; sr. engr. RCA, Camden, N.J., 1978-82; staff engr. IBM, Danbury, Conn., 1982-85; sr. engr. TIE Inc., Shelton, Conn., 1985-87; supr. mem. tech. staff NYNEX, White Plains, N.Y., 1987-89; fin. advisor Am. Express Fin. Advisors, Inc., Danbury, Conn., 1989—. Mem. Danbury Area Women's Network (pres. 1991-92). Office: Am Express Fin Advisors 57 North St Ste 403 Danbury CT 06810-5629

BOYLE, MARYLOU OLSEN, nursing administrator; b. Butte, Mont., Aug. 8, 1937; d. Paul Bogvang and Rose Patricia Olsen; m. John Anthony Boyle, July 8, 1978. Diploma, Sacred Heart Sch. Nursing, Spokane, Wash., 1958; BSN, U. Wash., 1969, M. Nursing, 1971; MS in Counseling Psychology, Pepperdine U., Quantico, Va., 1978. Dir. perioperative nursing Alexandria (Va.) Hosp., 1982-87; dir. surg. svcs. Arroyo Grande (Calif.) Community Hosp., 1987-89; DON Cottage Care Ctr., Santa Barbara, Calif., 1989-90, Marian Extended Care Ctr., Santa Maria, Calif., 1990-91; crisis intervention specialist, psychiat. assessment team Vista Del Mar Hosp., 1992—. Religious edn. tchr. confirmation II, coord., counselor weigh down program St. Mary's Assumption Ch. Mem. Assn. Oper. Rm. Nurses (past pres. Coastal Valley chpt., mem. No. Va. chpt.), Naval Res. Assn. (life), Assn. Mil. Surgeons U.S., Ret. Officers Assn., Marine Corps Assn., U. Wash. Alumni Assn. Office: CPC Vista del Mar Hosp 801 Seneca St Ventura CA 93001

BOYLE, NANCY REYNOLDS, home health agency administrator; b. Rochester, N.H., Dec. 11, 1932; d. Robert Hodgkins and Helen Lee (Estey) Reynolds; R.N., New Eng. Baptist Hosp. Sch. Nursing, 1953; B.A., New Eng. Coll., 1977; m. John Emmanuel Boyle, Dec. 29, 1956. Pvt. duty nurse, Boston, 1953; neurosurg. nurse Lahey Clinic, Boston, 1953-56; staff nurse various hosps., N.H., Ky., 1956-58; staff nurse Dover Dist. Nursing Assn., 1959-62, supervising nurse, 1962-70, exec. dir., 1970-85; exec. dir. Squamscott Home Health, Inc., 1985—; dir. Strafford Hospice Care, 1982-89; mem. mgmt. team Wentworth-Douglass Hosp., 1994—; dir. S.E. Bank for Savs.; bd. dirs. Great Bay Bankshares, Inc., Constitution Trust Co. Home nursing instr. Dover Girl Scouts and Campfire Girls, 1960-70; dir. N.H. Soap Box Derby, 1962-72; mem. City Adv. Com. on Urban Renewal, 1964-70, chmn., 1967; dir. Dover United Way, 1962-74; dir. Dover 350th Anniversary Celebration, 1973; dir. Dover Tomorrow, Inc., 1975-82, mem. adv. com. Dover Adult Edn., 1962-76; bd. dirs. Strafford County unit Am. Cancer Soc., 1980-88, ABC of Dover, 1970—, Cocheco Chpt. ADA, 1985-89; mem. Gov.'s Adv. Com. Cancer and Chronic Diseases, 1985—; mem. Diaconate Bd., 1991-95. Mem. Nat. Assn. Home Care, Nat., N.H. (dir. 1981-83) leagues for nursing, Am. Public Health Assn., Mass. Diploma Nurses Assn., Community Health Care Assn. N.H. (dir. 1981-85), Bus. and Profl. Women's Club (past pres.), Dover Rotary. Club: Dover Quota (sec. 1977-78). Republican. Congregationalist. Home: 4 Bellamy Rd Dover NH 03820-4302 Office: 89 Old Rochester Rd Dover NH 03820

BOYLE, PATRICIA JEAN, judge; b. Detroit, Mar. 31, 1937. Student, U. Mich., 1955-57; B.A., Wayne State U., 1963, J.D., 1963. Bar: Mich. Practice law with Kenneth Davies, Detroit, 1963; law clk. to U.S. Dist. judge, 1963-64; asst. U.S. atty., Detroit, 1964-68; asst. pros. atty. Wayne County; dir. research, tng. and appeals Wayne County, Detroit, 1969-74; Recorders Ct. judge City of Detroit, 1976-78; U.S. dist. judge Eastern Dist. Mich., Detroit, 1978-83; assoc. justice Mich. Supreme Ct., Detroit, 1983—. Active Women's Rape Crisis Task Force, Vols. of Am. Named Feminist of Year Detroit chpt. NOW, 1978; recipient Outstanding Achievement award Pros. Attys. Assn. Mich., 1978, Spirit of Detroit award Detroit City Council, 1978, Mich. Women's Hall of Fame award, 1986. Mem. Women Lawyers Assn. Mich., Fed. Bar Assn., Mich. Bar Assn., Detroit Bar Assn., Wayne State U. Law Alumni Assn. (Disting. Alumni award 1979). Office: Mich Supreme Ct PO Box 30052 2d Fl Law Bldg Lansing MI 48909*

BOYLE, RENÉE KENT, cultural organization executive, translator, editor; b. Cairo, July 4, 1926; came to U.S., 1946; d. Maurice Colin and Victoria Smith; m. John E. Whiteford Boyle, Feb. 2, 1950; children: Vanessa Whiteford Wayne, Christopher, Andrea Heller, Mara Holloway. Diploma, St. Clare's Coll., Heliopolis, Egypt, 1944; postgrad., Rice U., 1947-48, Santa Monica Coll., 1950-51. Dep. dir. Am. Friends of Mid. East, Tehran, Iran, 1959-62, Les Amis Americains du Maghreb, Tunis, Tunisia, 1962-64; v.p. Fgn. Services Research Inst., Washington, 1964—; v.p. Whiteford Internat. Enterprise, Villars sur Ollon, Switzerland, 1967-74; vice dir. Essentialist Philosophical Soc., 1992—; pres. Wheat/Forders Press. Editor: Primers for the Age of Inner Space series, Beyond the Present Prospect, 1978, The Indra Web, 1982, Graffiti on the Wall of Time, 1982, Of the Same Root: Heaven, Earth & I, 1990, The Way of the Essentialist: Contra Sartre's Existentialism. Mem. Dem. Nat. Com., Washington, 1982—. Mem. Acad. Ind. Scholars (exec. dir.), Ams. for Dem. Action, People for Ethical Treatment of Animals, Sierra Club. Unitarian. Avocation: cordon bleu cooking. Home: 2718 Unicorn Ln NW Washington DC 20015-2234 Office: Fgn Svcs Rsch Inst PO Box 6317 Washington DC 20015-0317

BOYLE, SUSAN JEAN HIGLE, elementary school educator; b. Tarrytown, N.Y., June 15, 1956; d. George Edward and Barbara Jean (Deverill) Higle. BA in Psychology, Elem. Edn., Ladycliff Coll., 1978; MS in Learning Disabilities, Fordham U., 1980; EdS in Ednl. Leadership, Stetson U., 1988. Cert. tchr., Fla. Tchr. St. Ursula Sch., Mt. Vernon, N.Y., 1978-81, Blue Lake Elem. Sch., DeLand, Fla., 1982-86, Deltona (Fla.) Lakes Elem., 1986-88, Discovery Elem. Sch., Deltona, 1988-89, Tomoka Elem. Sch., Ormond Beach, Fla., 1989-90, Ormond Beach Mid. Sch., 1990—; mem. discipline task force, Volusia County Schs., 1989, health task force, 1989. Eucharistic minister St. Brendan Ch. TOPS grantee, 1985, 86. Mem. Phi Delta Kappa, Daytona Beach Hummel Collectors Club. Office: Ormond Beach Mid Sch 151 Domicilio Ave Ormond Beach FL 32174-3918

BOYLES, CAROL ANN PATTERSON, career development educator; b. Waverly, N.Y., Aug. 26, 1932; d. Paul Bryan and Ruth Marion (Wilbur) Patterson; widowed 1981; 1 child, Scott Patterson. BA, Keuka Coll., 1953; MEd, U. Fla., 1957. Cert. tchr., Fla. Admissions officer Keuka Coll., Keuka Park, N.Y., 1953-56; residence counselor Fla. State U., Tallahassee, 1957-59; dir. guidance and counseling, assoc. dean student affairs Cen. Fla. Community Coll., Ocala, 1959-67; asst. dean student activities, orgns., asst. dean women Fla. State U., Tallahassee, 1967-69; dir. guidance Fla. Community Coll., Jacksonville, 1970-72; dir. coop. edn., placement U. North Fla., Jacksonville, 1972-83; dir. Career Devel. Ctr. U. North Fla., 1983-88, dir. Ctr. Exptl. Learning/Testing, 1988—; chmn. Career Expo, Jacksonville, 1977-91; chmn., mem. interuniv. sys. com. on career devel., 1972—; cons. coop. edn. programs; field reader U.S. Dept. Edn. Chmn. bd. dirs. Southside Christian Counseling Ctr., 1992-94, mem. 1988-94. Mem. ASTD, So. Coll. Placement Assn. (v.p. 1972—), Fla. Coop. Placement Assn. (pres. 1976-77, John Brownlee Leadership award 1991), Coop. Edn. Assn., Nat. Soc. Exptl. Edn., Jacksonville C. of C. (workforce preparation bd. bus. sch. partnership com. State of Fla. Coll.-legel Acad. Skills Test adv. com. 1994—), Keuka Coll. Alumni Assn., Kappa Delta Pi. Baptist. Home: 7804 Catawba Dr Jacksonville FL 32217-3642 Office: Univ N Fla 4567 St Johns Bluff Rd S Jacksonville FL 32224-6606

BOYNTON, NANCY HOGAN, electronics company executive; b. Meriden, Conn., Oct. 19, 1933; d. Edmund Peter and Althine Victoria (Wilbur) Hogan; m. Richard Studley Boynton, June 28, 1958; children: Anne, John, Thomas, Polly Jane. BA in English and Am. Lit., Brown U., 1955; cert., Hickox Sec. Sch., Cambridge, Mass., 1955; cert. in advanced German lit., Wesleyan U., 1956. Asst. adv. mgr. Yale U. Press, New Haven, 1956-58; adminstrv. asst. zoology dept. Yale U., New Haven, 1959-60; v.p., corp. sec. Space Electronics Inc., Berlin, Conn., 1961—. Author: (poetry) Traveling the River, 1984. Mem. AAUW (v.p. 1967-69). Methodist. Home: 30 Fowler Ln Middlefield CT 06455 Office: Space Electronics Inc 81 Fuller Way Berlin CT 06037

BOYRIVEN, MARIETTE HARTLEY See HARTLEY, MARIETTE

BOYSEN, MELICENT PEARL, finance company executive; b. Houston, Dec. 1, 1943; d. William Thomas and Mildred Pearl (Walker) Richardson; m. Stephen M. Boysen, Sept. 10, 1961 (dec. 1973); children: Marshella, Stephanie, Stephen. Student, Cen. Mo. State, 1973-75. Owner, pres. Boysen Enterprises, Kansas City, Mo., 1973—, Boysen Agri-Services, Kansas City, 1984—; fin. cons., underwriter New Eng. Life Ins. Co., Kansas City, 1978-81; cons. San Luis Rey (Calif.) Tribal Water Authority, Wind River (Wyo.) Reservation, Cheyenne River (S.D.) Sioux, Iroquois Nations (N.Y.), 1983—; founding bd. dirs. , pres. Am. Indian Youth Orgn., Visible Horizons, 1987—. Founding bd. dirs. Rose Brooks Ctr. Battered Women, Kansas City, 1979—, treas., 1979-81; exec. dir. The Flame Spirit Run; citationist 1993 Pres. Vol. Action Awards Program. Recipient Women of Conscience award Panel Am. Women of Greater Kansas City. Mem. Internat. Fin. Planners Assn., Internat. Agri-Bus. Assn., DAR, Kans. C. of C. and Industry, Kansas City C. of C. Republican. Methodist. Office: Boysen & Assocs PO Box 9104 Shawnee Mission KS 66201-1704

BOZA, CLARA BRIZEIDA, marketing and communications executive; b. Havana, Cuba, Apr. 18, 1952; came to U.S., 1957; d. Eduardo Otmaro and Hubedia Marta (Garcia) B. BA in English summa cum laude, Barry Coll., 1973, MA in Communication Media, 1988. Legal asst. supr. Steel Hector & Davis, Miami, Fla., 1978-80; program adminstr. Dade County Council Arts & Scis., Miami, 1980-82; dir. program devel. Nat. Found. for Advancement in Arts, Miami, 1982-85; exec. dir. Bus. Vols. for Arts/Miami, 1985-86; dir. mktg. Steel Hector & Davis, Miami, 1986—; S.E. regional cons. Arts and Bus. Coun., N.Y.C., 1986-88; panelist So. Arts Fedn., Atlanta, 1983-84, Fla. Arts Coun., 1983-84, 86-87; panelist and spkr. various local, state, and nat. orgns. and assns. Recipient ednl. scholarship Barry Coll., Miami, 1969-73, Fla. Bd. Regents, 1969-73. Mem. ABA (commn. on advt., 1994—), Nat. LAw Firm Mktg. Assn. (bd. dirs. 1993, 94), Am. Mktg. Assn. (bd. dirs. Miami chpt. 1992—), Fla. Bar (standing com. on advt. 1993—). Office: c/o Steel Hector & Davis 4000 First Union Fin Ctr 200 S Biscayne Blvd Miami FL 33131-2310

BOZONE, BILLIE RAE, librarian, consultant; b. Norphlet, Ark., Oct. 7, 1935; d. Guy Samuel and Vera (Jones) B. B.S. in Library Sci, Miss. State Coll. for Women, 1957; M.A., George Peabody Coll. for Tchrs., 1958. Asst. ref. librarian Miss. State U., State College, 1958-61, serials librarian, 1961-63; asst. ref. librarian U. Ill. at Urbana, 1963-65; asst. librarian New Eng. Mut. Life Ins. Co., Boston, 1965-67; sr. ref. librarian U. Mass., Amherst, 1967-68; head circulation dept. Smith Coll., Northampton, Mass., 1968-69; asst. librarian Smith Coll., 1969-71, coll. librarian, 1971-91; libr. cons., 1991—; bd. dirs. Hampshire Inter-library Center, Amherst, 1971-91; mem. exec. com. NELINET, 1977-79; chmn. Five Coll. Librarians Council, 1980-82, 90-91. Mem. ALA, Assn. Coll. and Research Libraries, Alpha Beta Alpha, Alpha Psi Omega. Home: 164 Red Gate Ln Amherst MA 01002-1845

BRAASCH, BARBARA LYNN, banker; b. Santa Monica, Calif., Apr. 14, 1958; d. C. Duane and René Barbara (Siegel) B. Student, Golden Gate U., 1989-91. Asst. v.p., sr. fin. analyst Wells Fargo Bank, San Francisco, 1976-94, asst. v.p., mgr., 1994—; mentor Jr. Achievement, L.A., 1980-83. 1st class scout Girl Scouts Am., 1976, leader, asst. leader, 1976-79, 84-87; vol. Open Hand, San Francisco, 1991-92, San Francisco AIDS Found., various women's groups, 1989—. Democrat. Jewish. Office: Wells Fargo Bank 525 Market St Fl 18 San Francisco CA 94105-2708

BRABEC, ROSEMARY JEAN, retail executive; b. St. Paul, Apr. 5, 1951; d. Peter Michael and Mary Jane (Nigro) Jacovitch; m. Loren W. Brabec, Sept. 16, 1972; children: Brenda Marie, Daniel Joseph. BS in Elem. Edn., St. Cloud State U., 1973. Tchr. Ind. Sch. Dist. 314, Braham, Minn., 1975-78; owner, mgr. Rosemary's Quilts and Baskets, Braham, 1988—; dir. Community Edn. Adv. Coun., Braham, 1978—, chmn., 1992—. Designer quilt block representing Minn. div. AAUW for display at Internat. Fedn. Univ. Women conv., Calif. Chmn. P.I.C.K. Immunization Clinic, Braham, 1978-85; vol. driver coord. Home Delivered Meals, Braham, 1984—; vol. coord. Com. to Build Robert Leathers Playground, Braham, 1985. Mem. AAUW (Minn. sec. 1985-87, v.p. 1987-89), Minn. Quilters, Braham Civic and Commerce Assn. Office: Rosemarys Quilts and Baskets 103 W Central Dr Braham MN 55006-0329

BRABSTON, MARY ELIZABETH, management educator; b. Birmingham, Ala., July 2, 1948; d. Donald C. Sr. and Mary Jane (Coolman) B. BA, Vanderbilt U., 1969; cert., Ala. Trust Sch., 1976; MBA, U. Ala., Birmingham, 1990; PhD, Fla. State U., 1994. From mgmt. trainee to asst. trust officer 1st Ala. Bank, Birmingham, 1970-77; asst. campaign mgr. for George McMillan Birmingham, 1978, 82-86; exec. asst. to lt. gov. State of Ala., Birmingham, 1979-83; adminstrv. systems dir. devel. office U. Ala., Birmingham, 1987-90; teaching assoc. Fla. State U., Tallahassee, Fla., 1990-93; asst. prof. U. Tenn., Chattanooga, 1993—. commr. Ala. Film Commn., 1976-83; mem. Nat. Conf. State Legislatures Arts and States Com., Denver, 1979-83, vice chairperson, 1982-83; treas. Birmingham Internat. Ednl. Film Festival, 1976-81, Birmingham Festival Theatre, 1979-80, sec. bd. dirs. 1988-90; bd. dirs. Ala. Epilepsy Council, Birmingham, 1975-77, Ala. Sch. Fine Arts, 1982-87, Found. for Pastoral Counseling, Birmingham, 1985-86; bd. dirs., exec. com. Birmingham Cultural and Heritage Found., 1988-90, bd. dirs., 1988-90; campaign treas. for George McMillan, 1973-86, for David Herring, 1974-83; deacon Northminster Presbyn. Ch. Named Outstanding Young Career Woman, Met. Bus. and Profl. Women, 1976. Mem. Birmingham Jaycees (hon. 1976, Outstanding Young Women in Am. 1978, 79, 80, 81, 82, 83), Doctoral Bus. Students Assn. (treas. 1991-92). Democrat. Club: Birmingham Vanderbilt (pres. 1979). Home: 1727 Starboard Dr Hixson TN 37343

BRACCO, GLORIA JEAN, elementary education educator; b. Modesto, Calif., Dec. 20, 1946; d. Charlie and Ida Lena (Morandi) B.; m. Ed Rusca, July 11, 1992. AA, Modesto Jr. Coll., 1967; BA, Chico State Coll., 1970. Cert. elem. edn. tchr. Tchr. first grade Cardozo Elem. Sch., Riverbank, Calif., 1970-73; tchr. first and second grade Rio Altura Sch., Riverbank, 1973-90; tchr. first grade Calif. Ave. Sch., Riverbank, 1990—; speaker Elem. Sch. Sci. Assn., Modesto and Vallejo, Calif., 1983-84; cons. steering com. for outdoor edn. curriculum, Modesto, 1980-82, Mi Wok adv. com., Modesto, 1981-82; presentor Poetry Anthology, Modesto, 1981-82. Co-editor: (periodical) Scenes, 1980-82; contbg. tchr. Frank Schaffer's School Days mag., 1994, 95. Patron Modesto Performing Arts, 1989; assoc. Modesto Symphony, 1991—; mem. Yosemite (Calif.) Assn., 1986—. Recipient Cert. of Recognition, Assemblyman C. Perrino, Sacramento, 1980. Mem. AAUW (gift honoree for ednl. found. 1986, pres. 1982-83), Stanislaus Reading Coun. (sec. 1985-87), Parent/Tchr. Club (treas. 1992-93, VIP award 1993), Stanislaus County Commn. for Women (Outstanding Woman award 1994), Modesto Ski Club (pres. 1984-85, Wagoner trophy 1986), Delta Kappa Gamma. Avocations: tennis, skiing, travel, bicycling, gardening.

BRACCO, LORRAINE, actress; b. Bklyn., 1955; m. Harvey Keitel (div.); m. Edward James Olmos, Jan. 28, 1994; children: Margaux, Stella. Studied, Actors Studio; studied with Stella Adler, Ernie Martin, John Strasberg. model in Europe. Films include The Pick-Up Artist, 1987, Someone to Watch Over Me, 1987, Sing, 1989, The Dream Team, 1989, Goodfellas, 1990 (Acad. award nominee for best supporting actress 1990), Talent for the Game, 1991, Switch, 1991, Medicine Man, 1992, Radio Flyer, 1992, Traces of Red, 1992, (Showtime movie) Scam, 1993, Being Human, 1994, Even Cowgirls Get the Blues, 1994, The Basketball Diaries, 1995; off-Broadway play Goose and Tom-Tom. Office: 110 Hudson St Apt 9A New York NY 10013-2352*

BRACEY, ANN ELIZABETH, municipal official; b. Oklahoma City, Nov. 5, 1942; d. Ray Shuffle and Emma Ruth (Reid) Barger; m. James Lea Bracey, June 13, 1964; 1 child, James McLeod. BA, Tex. Christian U., 1966; MLS, U. North Tex., 1972. From libr. asst. to pub. svc. coord. Ft. Worth Pub. Libr., 1971-88, floater libr., 1971-76, mgr. Riverside br., 1976-81, mgr. Wedgwood br., 1981-85, mgr. Ridglea br., 1985, mat. coord., 1985-86, pub. svc. coord., 1986-88; mgmt. intern City of Ft. Worth, 1988-89, employee benefits ombudsman, 1989—; cons. Ft. Worth Acad., 1985-88, The Oakridge Sch., Ft. Worth, 1985-87. Editor: Employee Handbook-City of Ft. Worth, 1990. Bd. dirs. Ft. Worth Acad., 1989-93, Alzheimers Assn. Tarrant County, 1991—, chair, 93 Memory Walk, co-chair 94 Memory Walk, v.p. 1994, pub. policy co-chmn., 1995; active Forum Ft. Worth; vol. Arts Coun. Ft. Worth, Shakespear in the Park, Ft. Worth. Mem. AAUW (named gift honoree 1983-84, Outstanding Woman Tarrant County br. 1984), Tex. Libr. Assn. (life, conf. co-chair 1987, 91, editor Selection Policy Manual 1984, co-chair local arran. 1991), Woman's Club Ft. Worth (dept. chmn.). Democrat. Presbyterian. Office: City of Ft Worth Risk Mgmt 1000 Throckmorton St Fort Worth TX 76102

BRACKEN, KATHLEEN ANN, nurse; b. Chgo., Mar. 14, 1947; d. Thomas James and Catherine Anastasia (Cowal) B.; RN, CNA, Little Company of Mary Hosp., Evergreen Park, Ill., 1968; BSN, Lewis U., 1984, MBA, 1989. Mem. staff Little Company of Mary Hosp., Evergreen Park, 1968-69, 71-73, supr. ICUs, 1976-79, dir. ICUs, 1979-91; v.p. patient care svcs. South Chgo. Community Hosp., 1991-93; staff nurse coronary care unit Little Co. of Mary Hosp., Torrence, Calif., 1969-70; staff nurse Chgo. Lying-In Clinic, U. Chgo., 1970-71; nurse mgr. VA Westside Med. Ctr., Chgo., 1994—; bd. dirs., chmn. nursing cardiovascular com. South Cook Heart Assn., 1977-83, recipient Meritorious Service award, 1979, 81, 82, 83, 84, 85, 86. Mem. NAFE, Council on Nursing Adminstrn., Chgo. Heart Assn., Assn. Critical Care Nurses (pres. Southside Chgo. Area chpt. 1983-84, rec. sec. 1984-85), Am. Heart Assn. (cardiovascular nursing council), Ill. Orgn. Nursing Execs., Chgo. Healthcare Exec. Forum, Delta Epsilon Sigma, Sigma Theta Tau. Home: 10321 S Campbell Ave Chicago IL 60655-1016 Office: VA Westside Med Ctr 820 S Damen Ave Chicago IL 60612

BRACKEN, PEG, author; b. Filer, Idaho, Feb. 25, 1918; d. John Lewis and Ruth (McQuesten) B.; m. John Hamilton Ohman, June 15, 1991; 1 child from previous marriage, Johanna Kathleen Edwards. A.B., Antioch Coll., 1940. Author: The I Hate to Cook Book, 1960, The I Hate to Housekeep Book, 1962, I Try to Behave Myself, 1963, Peg Bracken's Appendix to The I Hate to Cook Book, 1966, I Didn't Come Here to Argue, 1969, But I Wouldn't Have Missed It for the World, 1973, The I Hate to Cook Almanack - A Book of Days, 1976, A Window Over the Sink, 1981, The Complete I Hate to Cookbook, 1986.

BRACKIN, PHYLLIS JEAN, recruiting professional; b. Aliquippa, Pa., Oct. 5, 1946; d. Matthew Edward and Trula Estelle (Venable) Plonka; children: Keith, Kevin. Student, Georgetown U., 1966, U. S. Fla., 1981. Librarian Def. Intelligence Agy., Washington, 1966-70, Aerospace Corp., Los Angeles, 1975-78; personnel mgr. Badger Engrs. Inc., Tampa, Fla., 1979-85; dir. career devel. PTC Inst., Tampa, 1985-86; dir. mktg. & pub. rels. RADS Radiography Svc.ice Inc., Clearwater, Fla., 1986—. Author: Personal Skills Development, How to Hire Eagles, 1988, Recruitment Services: A Viable Option, 1988, How to Get a Job and Keep It, 1990, Are We Having Fun Yet?, Celebrate Your Profession, 1992, Are You Hiring Ziggers or Zaggers?, Celebrate You!, 1994. Mem. NAFE, ASTD, Fla. Soc. Pers. Cons., Am. Healthcare Radiology Adminstrs. Republican. Roman Catholic. Home: 8207 Olivewood Pl Tampa FL 33615

BRADBURY, BETTY MARIE, history and music educator; b. Madison, Ind., Mar. 5, 1933; d. Lawrence Allen and Elsie Margret (Spivey) Bladen; m. Robert Lesley Bradbury, Aug. 23, 1952; children: Robert A., Jonathan R., Randall E., Daryl R., Robert II. Diploma, Sherwood Music Sch., 1966; Assoc. in Gen. Studies, Ind. U., Kokomo, 1989, B Gen. Studies, 1990, postgrad. Cert. tchr., adminstr. Tchr. Malta (Ohio) Christian Sch., 1971-73, Beaver Valley Wesleyan, Vanport, Pa., 1973-77; pvt. piano tchr. Madison, Ind., 1977-80; tchr. Bible Wesleyan Acad., Crab Orchard, W.Va., 1980-82, Beckley (W.Va.) Pentecostal Acad., 1983-84; tchr., prin. Bible Wesleyan Acad., Crab Orchard, 1984-87; tchr. Union Bible Acad., Westfield, Ind., 1989-90, prin., 1990-92; prof. Union Bible Coll., Westfield, 1992—; seminar leader-tchr. Evang. Bible Mission, Haiti, 1993; mem. exec. com. Union Bible Coll., Westfield, 1990-92. Author: The Walls Talk, 1993. Jr. ch. leader Pilgrim Holiness Ch., Indpls., 1993-94; sec.-treas. Pilgrim Holiness Ch.,

Muncie, Ind., 1969-71; den mother Cub Scouts, Middletown, Ind., 1966-69; missionary pres. Bible Wesleyan Ch., Crab Orchard, 1984-86. Mem. Alpha Chi. Republican. Home: Union Bible Coll Box 2A Westfield IN 46074

BRADBURY, KATHLEEN CHARLOTTE, librarian; b. Ft. Worth, June 19, 1949; d. Leonard Stanley George and Maureen (Davidson) Hart. BA, Tex. Woman's U., 1971, MLS, 1972. With Ft. Worth Pub. Libr., 1972—, br. mgr. Meadowbrook br., 1985-88, head of media dept., 1990—. Mem. AAUW (Ft. Worth chpt. v.p. 1982-84, cultural chmn. 1987, treas. 1992-93), LWV, ALA, Nat. Parks and Conservation Assn., Tex. Libr. Assn. (chair dist. 7 1982-83, chmn. continuing edn. div. 1990-91), North Tex. Irish Cultural Assn., Friends of Ft. Worth Pub. Libr., Librs. of Tarrant County (vice chair 1990-91, chair 1991-92), Ft. Worth Sister Cities Orgn., Internat. Friends Orgn., Nature Conservancy, Sierra Club, Beta Phi Mu chpt. Beta Lambda (chair 1985-86). Home: 701 Timberview Ct N Fort Worth TX 76112-1715

BRADDOCK, NONNIE CLARKE, religious organization administrator; b. Rye, N.Y.; d. Peter Benedict and Nora Bridget (Devins) Clarke; m. Eugene Stephen Braddock, Sept. 7, 1962; children: Stephen E., Brian B., Glenn C. Adminstr. Beaver Farm Retreat and Conf. Ctr., Yorktown Heights, N.Y.; deputy city clk. City of Rye, N.Y.; founder, pres. Celebrations; dir. Security Enforcement Bur.; part-time therapist; with Marriage Encounter movement, co-founder, chmn. bd., team leader No. Westchester-Putnam (N.Y.) Interfaith Marriage Encounter, 1981-87. Vol. Boy Scouts Am., numerous polit. orgns. and cmty. groups, 1970—; chair Warmth for Christmas clothing drive, N.Y.C. shelters; facilitator mil. family support group; organizer food collections for needy, Heart to Heart, coord. Angel Fund; organizer, sponsor Weekly Cable TV program featuring peace, 1991; bd. dirs. Homeless Shelter; adv. com. Comty. Mem. Interfaith Clergy Coun., Rite Christian Initiation for Adults, Right to Life, North Am. Retreat Dirs. Assn., Pax Christi Metro, Westchester Assn. Vol. Adminstrs., Feminists for Life, Fedn. Christian Ministries. Office: Beaver Farm Retreat Ctr Underhill Ave Yorktown Heights NY 10598

BRADE, COLLEEN ANNE SWIERCZNSKI, educational development professional; b. Albion, N.Y., July 28, 1964; d. Stanley Theodore and Mary Geraldine (Palmer) Swierczynski; m. Ricky Lee Brade, Oct. 12, 1991. BS in Mktg., Canisius Coll., 1986; postgrad., St. Bonaventure U., 1990-92. Mktg. asst. Office Automation, Inc., Williamsville, N.Y., 1986-87; asst. dir. devel. rsch. St. Bonaventure (N.Y.) U., 1987-88, dir. devel. rsch., 1988-92; dir. devel. Notre Dame High Sch., Batavia, N.Y., 1992—; mem. devel. com. N.Y. State Spl. Olympics, Albany, 1992—. Mem. Am. Prospect Rsch. Assn. (v.p., sec. Upstate N.Y. chpt. 1990-91, program dir. 1992-93). Democrat. Roman Catholic. Home: 120 Harvester Ave Batavia NY 14020-3345 Office: Notre Dame High Sch 73 Union St Batavia NY 14020-1399

BRADEN, BETTY JANE, legal association administrator; b. Sheboygan, Wis., Feb. 5, 1943; d. Otto Frank and Betty Donna (Beers) Huettner; children: Jennifer Tindall, Rebecca Leigh; m. Berwyn Bartow Braden, Nov. 5, 1983. BS, U. Wis., 1965. Cert. elem. tchr., Wis. Tchr. Madison (Wis.) Met. Sch. Dist., 1965-70, 71-72, sub. tchr., 1972-75; adminstrv. asst. ATS-CLE State Bar Wis., Madison, 1978, adminstrv. asst. Advanced Tng. Seminars-Continuing Legal Edn., 1979, coordinator, 1980, adminstr. coordinator, 1980-84, adminstrv. dir., 1984-87, dir. adminstrn., bar svcs., membership, 1987—; mem. rels. and pub. svcs. dir. Legal Edn., 1992—; speaker Bar Leadership Inst. of ABA. Mem. Meeting Planners Internat. (sec. Wis. chpt. 1981-82, pres. 1982-83); Adminstrv. Mgmt. Soc., Am. Mgmt. Assn., Am. Soc. for Personnel Adminstrn., Am. Soc. of Assn. Execs., Wis. Soc. of Assn. Execs., LWV, Nat. Assn. Bar Execs. Home: 52 Golf Course Rd Madison WI 53704-1423 Office: State Bar of Wis 402 W Wilson St Madison WI 53703-3614

BRADEN, DEBORAH BOATMAN, school system health director; b. San Diego, Oct. 26, 1950; d. Alvin Fulton and Esther Ruth (Gartner) Boatman; m. Michael Wayne Braden, Dec. 27, 1971; children: John Eric, Suzanne Michelle, William Michael, Daniel Edward. BS, Tex. Woman's U., 1972, MS, 1982. RN, Tex. Staff nurse Granville C. Morton, Dallas, 1972; staff nurse pediatrics St. Paul Hosp., Dallas, 1972-73, East Town Osteo. Hosp., Dallas, 1973-75; rsch. nurse ob.-gyn. U. Tex. Health Sci. Ctr., Dallas, 1975-77; clin. nurse specialist Meth. Med. Ctr., Dallas, 1981-86; dir. maternal child health HCA Med. Ctr. Plano, Tex., 1986-88; sch. nurse Mesquite (Tex.) Ind. Sch. Dist., 1988-93, dir. health svcs., 1993—. Mem. Tex. Assn. Sch. Nursing (region X conf. dir. 1992), Dallas Area Sch. Health Assn. (treas. 1991-93). Republican. Roman Catholic. Office: Mesquite Ind Sch Dist Health Svcs Dept 405 E Davis St Mesquite TX 75149

BRADFORD, BARBARA REED, lawyer; b. Cleve., June 13, 1948; d. William Cochran and Martha Lucile (Horn) B.; m. Warren Neil Davis, Oct. 9, 1976 (div. 1989); m. S. Jack Odell, Dec. 12, 1991. BA, Pitzer Coll., 1970; JD, Georgetown U., 1975, MBA, 1985. Bar: N.Y. 1976, D.C. 1976. Staff asst. Sen. Edward M. Kennedy, Washington, 1970-71; assoc. Breed, Abbott & Morgan, N.Y.C., 1975-76, Verner, Liipfert Law Firm, Washington, 1976-78; atty. AID, Washington, 1978-83; atty., regional dir. Trade and Devel. Agy., U.S. Dept. State, Washington, 1986—; pres. Georgetown Export Trading, Inc., Washington, 1984-86. Bd. dirs. Jr. League, Washington, 1977-78. Mem. D.C. Bar Assn., Bar of State of N.Y., Potomac Hunt Club. Democrat.

BRADFORD, BARBARA TAYLOR, writer, journalist, novelist; b. Leeds, Eng.; came to U.S., 1964; d. Winston and Freda (Walker) Taylor; m. Robert Bradford, Dec. 24, 1963. Student pvt. schs., Eng.; LittD (hon.), Leeds U., London, 1990. Women's editor Yorkshire (Eng.) Evening Post, 1951-53, reporter, 1949-51; editor Woman's Own, 1953-54; columnist London Evening News, 1955-57; exec. editor London Am., 1959-62; editor Nat. Design Center Mag., 1965-69; syndicated columnist Newsday Spls., L.I., 1968-70; nat. syndicated columnist Chgo. Tribune-N.Y. (News Syndicate), N.Y.C., 1970-75, Los Angeles Times Syndicate, 1975-81. Author: Complete Ency. Homemaking Ideas, 1968, A Garland of Children's Verse, 1968, How to be the Perfect Wife, 1969, Easy Steps to Successful Decorating, 1971, Decorating Ideas for Casual Living, 1977, How to Solve Your Decorating Problems, 1976, Making Space Grow, 1979, Luxury Designs for Apartment Living, 1981; (novels) A Woman of Substance, 1979, Voice of the Heart, 1983, Hold the Dream, 1985, screen adaptation, 1986, Act of Will, 1986, To Be the Best, 1988, The Women in His Life, 1990, Remember, 1991, Angel, 1993, Everything to Gain, 1994. Recipient Dorothy Dawe award Am. Furniture Mart, 1970, 71, Matrix award N.Y. Women in Communications, 1985. Mem. Authors Guild, Nat. Soc. Interior Designers (Distinguished Editorial award 1969, Nat. Press award 1971), Authors Guild Am. (coun. mem. 1989—), Am. Soc. Interior Designers. Office: 450 Park Ave New York NY 10022-2605

BRADFORD, CAROL SCHLOSNAGLE, communications executive; b. Carlisle, Pa., Dec. 23, 1950; d. Eugene Stanley and Ethel Mae (Smeltzer) S.; B.A. in English Lit., Hood Coll., 1972; MBA, U. Wash., 1988. Photojournalist, feature writer Carlisle Evening Sentinel, Carlisle, 1968-71, Frederick (Md.) News-Post, 1971-72; v.p. public rels. Cole & Weber, Inc., Seattle, 1974-82; v.p. communications Group Health Coop., Seattle, 1982-901 mng. dir. Ogilvy & Mather Pub. Rels., Kuala Lumpur, Maylaysia, 1990—. Publicity dir., fund raiser Am. Expdn. to K2, Pakistan, 1978; v.p. bd. dirs. Pike Market Community Clinic; mem. recruitment and pub. rels. coms. Leadership Tomorrow; bd. dirs. Nat. Coop. Bus. Found. Mem. Seattle Advt. Fedn., Public Rels. Soc. Am. (Wash. State chpt. award of Merit, 1978), Am. Hosp. Assn., Mktg. Communicators Exec. Internat. Republican. Presbyterian. Clubs: Washington Athletic, Seattle Press, Seattle. City publicity and travel writer and photographer for consumer and trade mags., newspapers. Home: 107 Jalan Ara, Bangsar Barv, 59100 Kuala Lumpur Malaysia Office: Ogilvy & Mather Wisma MCIS, Jalan Barat, Petaling Jaya, Selangor Malaysia

BRADFORD, CHRISTINA, newspaper editor; b. Dec. 23, 1942; d. J. Robert and Lesley (Jones) Merrill; m. Alan Bradford, Sept. 24, 1966 (div. 1973). AA, Stephens Coll., Columbia, Mo., 1962; BS in Journalism, U. Mo.-Columbia, 1964. Asst. city editor Detroit Free Press, 1975-80; asst. mng. editor Democrat and Chronicle, Rochester, N.Y., 1980-82, mng. editor, 1982-86; mng. editor/news Detroit News, 1986-89, mng. editor, 1989—. Mem. AP Mng. Editors, Am. Soc. Newspaper Editors, Detroit Athletic Club. Home: 208 Main Sail Ct Detroit MI 48207-5008 Office: Detroit News 615 W Lafayette Blvd Detroit MI 48226-3124*

BRADFORD, GAIL IDONA, secondary school educator; b. Mobile, Ala., Sept. 12, 1947; d. Estes Paul and Doris (Roe) B.; m. Benjamin C. Lann, Jr., May 28, 1971 (div. May 1986). AA, Clarke Meml. Coll., Newton, Miss., 1967; BS, Miss. Coll., 1969; MA, La. Tech U., 1973; postgrad., Western Ky. U., 1979-82, 88-92. Cert. tchr., sch. adminstr., counselor, home economist. Vocat. counselor Mobile Rehab., 1970-71; tchr. kindergarten Lincoln Parish Schs., Ruston, La., 1971-73; state staff coord. Head Start, U. South Ala., Mobile, 1973-74; dep. dir. Jefferson County Com. for Econ. Opportunity, Birmingham, Ala., 1975-76; instr. vocat. edn. Lawson State C.C., Birmingham, 1977; mental health technician Commonwealth of Ky., Louisville, 1978-79; exec. dir. Tchr. Corps, Western Ky. U., Bowling Green, 1979-82; tchr. spl. edn. Jefferson County Pub. Schs., Louisville, 1982-88, tchr. vocat. home econs., 1988—; cons., condr. workshops various pub. programs, Ala., Ky., 1973—; tchr. workshops Ky. Tech. Coll., Jefferson State U., Louisville, 1989—; mem. com. practitioners Commonwealth of Ky. Workforce Cabinet, 1990—. Bd. dirs. Ministries United South Cen. Ky., Louisville, 1989—; active various Rep. campaigns, La., Ky., 1971-86; mem. nat. adv. bd. Safe Places, 1991—; mem. campaign staff Rep. John Buchanan of Ala., 1975-77; dir. counselors Hugh O'Brian Youth Found., 1989-91, state chmn., 1991—. Recipient Tchr. award Louisville Commmunity Found., 1986, Leadership Edn. award Bellarmine Coll., Louisville, 1987; named Ky. col. Commonwealth of Ky., 1988. Mem. Ky. Vocat. Home Econs. Tchrs. (pres. region 6, 1990-91), Ky. Home Econs. Assn. (chmn. adult, secondary and elem. edn. 1988—), Am. Vocat. Assn., Coun. for Exceptional Children, Am. Insts. Parliamentarians, Thomas Jefferson Parliamentarians (treas. 1986), Toastmasters (area gov. dist. 11, 1986-87, Able Toastmaster award 1984), Golden Key, Kappa Delta Pi. Methodist. Home: 3113 Osprey Rd Louisville KY 40213-1226

BRADFORD, JANE TURNER, librarian; b. Indpls., July 10, 1946; d. Roy Orlando and Ruthann (Vandivier) Turner; m. Bruce Carlton Bradford, Sept. 1, 1968 (div. 1985); 1 child, Amanda Elizabeth. BA, Stetson U., 1968; MA, Pa. State U., 1970; MS, U. Ill., 1987. Instr. Stetson U., De Land, Fla., 1976-85, asst. prof., ref. libr., 1987-92, assoc. prof., 1992—. Co-author: (libr. handbook) A Guide to Rsearh, rev. edit. 1993. Pres. ParentCraft, De Land, 1979-81; mem. intellectual freedom com. Fla. Libr. Assn., 1988-90, chair publs. com., 1992-93. Libr. Exchange-Moscow, Stetson U., 1992, China, 1988. Mem. ALA, AAUW (univ. liaison 1987—), Am. Assn. of Coll. and Rsch. Librs., Nat. Coun. Tchrs. English, Fla. English Assn., Fla. Libr. Assn., Assn. of Coll. and Rsch. Librs. Fla. (univ. liaison 1987—), Beta Phi Mu, Sigma Tau Delta. Office: Stetson Univ PO Box 8418 421 N Woodland Blvd De Land FL 32720

BRADFORD, LOUISE MATHILDE, social worker; b. Alexandria, La., Aug. 3, 1925; d. Henry Aaron and Ruby (Pearson) Bradford; B.S., La. Poly. Inst., 1945; cert. in social work La. State U., 1949; M.S., Columbia U., 1953; postgrad. Tulane U., 1962, 64, La. State U., 1967; cert. U. Pa., 1966. Diplomate Am. Bd. Clin. Social Work. With La. Dept. Public Welfare, Alexandria, 1945-78, welfare caseworker, 1950-53, children's caseworker, 1957-59, child welfare cons., 1959-73, social services cons., 1973-78, state cons. day care, 1963-66; dir. social services St. Mary's Tng. Sch., Alexandria, La., 1978—; del. Nat. Day Care Conf., Washington, 1964; mem. early childhood edn. com. So. States Work Conf., Daytona Beach, Fla., 1968; mem. La. adv. com. 1970 White House Conf. on Children, also del.; mem. So. region planning com. Child Welfare League Am., 1970-73; mem. profl. adv. com. Cenla chpt. Parents Without Partners, 1970—; adj. asst. prof. sociology La. Coll., Pineville, 1969-85, lectr. Kindergarten workshop, 1970-72; mem. La. 4-C Day Care Licensing Rev. Com., Central La. 4-C Steering Com.; social services cons. La. Spl. Edn. Ctr., Alexandria, 1980-86; del. Internat. Conf. on Social Welfare, Nairobi, 1974, Jerusalem, 1978, Hong Kong, 1980, Brighton, 1982, Montreal, 1984. Recipient Social Worker of Yr. award Alexandria br. NASW La. Conf. Social Welfare, 1984, Hilda C. Simon award, 1987, George Freeman award, 1987. Bd. dirs. Cenla Community Action Com., Alexandria, 1966-68. Mem. NASW, Acad. Cert. Social Workers, La. Bd. Cert. Social Worker, So. La. Assns. Children under Six, La. Conf. Social Welfare (George Freeman award 1987), Internat. Council on Social Welfare, Am. Pub. Welfare Assn. (S.W. region planning com. 1965), Am. Assn. on Mental Retardation (La. social work chair 1989-94), DAR, Central La. Pre-Sch. Assn. (dir. 1967-70), Rapides Golf and Country Club. Methodist (kindergarten bd. 1967-87, ofcl. bd. 1974-75, 77-81, 83-85). Home: 5807 Joyce St Alexandria LA 71302-2510 Office: PO Box 7768 Alexandria LA 71306-0768

BRADFORD, PAMELA SUE, real estate appraiser, broker; b. Denver, Jan. 15, 1963; d. William David and Jeanette E. (Call) B. Lic. real estate appraiser, real estate broker, tax preparer. Coord. profl. devel. STK, Louisville, Colo., 1983-87; property mgr. Omni Group, Denver, 1987-90; pvt. practice tax preparation Denver, 1990-93, real estate appraiser, broker, mgr., cons., 1993—; appraiser Bd. Real Estate Appraiser; realtor/broker Bd. Realtors. Mrem. Appraisal Inst. (sr. real estate appraiser).

BRADFORD, SUSAN ANNE, reporter; b. Pasadena, Calif., Dec. 2, 1969; d. Wesley Gene and Nancy Cornelia (Dixon) B. Student, Coll. Cevenol, Le Chambon Sur Lignon, France, 1985, St. Andrews U., Scotland, 1989-90; BA in English, U. Calif., Irvine, 1992. Editor-in-chief Gandalf's Gazette, Irvine, Calif., 1987-88; news editor New Univ., Irvine, Calif., 1987-88; intern Sta. CBS-TV News, L.A., 1989; host, exec. producer Witness the News TV show, Irvine, 1990-92; prodn. asst. PBS Red Car Film Project, L.A., 1992-93; intern in news writing Sta. KNX News, L.A., 1993; reporter City News Svc., L.A., 1994—. Author poems; contbr. articles to profl. jours. Bd. dirs. HWPC Scholarship Found., Hollywood, Calif., 1992-93. Recipient Writing awards Palos Verdes Nat. Bank, 1987, AFL-CIO, 1987, 3d Pl. award Nat. Fedn. Press Women, 1992. Mem. Calif. Press Women (pub. rels. chair 1991-92), Hollywood Women's Press Club (bd. dirs. 1989-94), Irvine Women's Crew (founder, pres.). Mem. United Ch. of Christ. Office: City News Svc 6255 Sunset Blvd Ste 1905 Los Angeles CA 90028 also: PO Box 7000-245 Rolling Hills Estates CA 90275

BRADFORD, VALERIE JEANNE, clinical social worker; b. Lincoln, Nebr., Feb. 13, 1950; d. Michael Joseph and Barbara Findley (Bickel) Truby; m. David Allen Baker, 1966 (div. 1974); children: Victoria Jeanne Baker, David Keith Baker. BA in Psychology with honors, Calif. State U., Fullerton, 1987; MSW, U. So. Calif., 1989; postgrad., Calif. Sch. Profl. Psychology. Lic. clin. social worker; cert. alcohol and drug abuse counselor, cert. hypnotherapist. Therapist Starting Point, Costa Mesa, Calif., summer 1988; assessor and treatment planner Brea Hosp. Neuropsychiat. Ctr., 1989; therapist Counseling Inst. of Orange County, 1989-90, Fullerton (Calif.) Assocs. for Counseling and Psychotherapy, 1990-93; clin. social worker, alcohol and drug abuse counselor Orange County Health Care Agy., Anaheim, Calif., 1989-92; pvt. practice Anaheim Hills (Calif.) Psychotherapy, 1992-94, Fullerton, Calif., 1994—. Mem. NASW, Am. Psychol. Assn. (student mem.), Calif. Psychol. Assn. (student mem.), Nat. Assn. of Cert. Alcohol and Drug Abuse Counselors (Calif. bd.), Phi Kappa Phi. Home: 250 W Central Ave # 215 Brea CA 92621

BRADLEY, KIM ALEXANDRA, sales and marketing specialist; b. Glen Cove, N.Y., Aug. 27, 1955; d. Harold William and Helen Doris (Rosenthal) Shepard; m. Gary Morgan Bradley, Oct. 2, 1982; children: Hunter Morgan, Parker Davis, Preston Carter. BS, U. Ill., 1977. Media estimator Lee King & Ptnrs., Chgo., 1977-78; asst. buyer Grey North Advt., Chgo., 1978; broadcast negotiator J. Walter Thompson, Chgo., 1978-80; acct. exec. Katz Communications, Inc., Chgo., 1980-84, sales mgr., 1984-88, v.p. sales mgr., 1988-93; prin., pres. The Encore Group, Inc., Chgo., 1993; pres., owner Bradley Mktg. Group, Lake Forest, Ill., 1993—. Mem. mktg. com. Child Abuse Prevention Svcs.; alliance mem. Art Inst. of Chgo.; vol. Infant Welfare Soc. Mem. Inst. Mgmt. Cons., Am. Mktg. Assn., Broadcast Advt. Club (bd. dirs., v.p., exec. v.p., pres., chair for Child Abuse Prevention Svcs. charity com.). Home: 30 Barnswallow Ln Lake Forest IL 60045-2984

BRADLEY, LAURIE MICHELE, child's therapist; b. Atlanta, June 28, 1963; d. Burton Herbert and Joyce (Ray) Bradley. BA in Psychology, U. West Fla., 1992; MA in Counseling, Troy State U., Pensacola, Fla., 1994. Substitute tchr. DeKalb County Schs., Atlanta, 1987-89; drug awareness counselor Charter Peachford Hosp., Atlanta, 1987-89; children's therapist The Avalon Ctr. of Bapt. Health Care, Inc., Milton, Fla., 1992—. Office: The Avalon Ctr Bapt Health Care Inc 6024 Spikes Way Milton FL 32572

BRADLEY, LISA, artistic director, ballet master, educator; b. Elizabeth, N.J., Oct. 12, 1941; d. Robert Michael and Florence Grace (Tryon) Wilsey; m. Michael Uthoff, Mar. 5, 1966; 1 child, Michelle. Degree in bus. adminstrn., Sawyer Sch. Bus., 1982; dance tng., 1959-80. Ballerina Joffrey Ballet, N.Y.C., 1960-78, artistic staff, 1978—; ballerina First Chamber Dance Co., Hartford Ballet Co., 1970-76; co-dir. Hartford Ballet, 1972-76; dance tchr., coach profl. dancers in N.Y.C. Schs. and throughout U.S.; adminstr. Worldwide Marriage Encounter, 1982, Our Lady of Sorrows Ch., 1983-86; mem. cultural exch. program, Dept. State, 1960-70. Author: Meditations on the Writings of St. Bernard, 1991. Vol. No. Lights, N.J. and N.Y., 1992-93; vol. program Milw. Gen. Hosp., Turtle Bay Dance Therapy Program. Named Conn. Woman of Yr., 1976; Fulbright scholar, 1980. Mem. DAR (civic activities 1961). Roman Catholic. Office: Joffrey Ballet 130 W 56th St New York NY 10019-3818

BRADLEY, LISA M., artist; b. Columbus, Ohio, Dec. 15, 1951; d. Phillip Raymond Bradley and Jean Lichtenstein. BA, Boston U., 1973. Assoc. dir. Pace Primitive, N.Y.C., 1977-84, dir., 1984—. One-woman shows include Boston City Hall, 1973, Harvard U., Cambridge, Mass., 1976, Boston Ctr. for the Arts, 1977, Ludlow Hyland Gallery, N.Y.C., 1978, 79, Bette Stoler Gallery, N.Y.C., 1979, Major-Saxbe Gallery, Urbana, Ohio, 1986, Phillip Dash Gallery, N.Y.C., 1987, Donahue Gallery, N.Y.C., 1989, Ratner Gallery, Chgo., 1991, Donahue Gallery, 1993; exhibited in group shows Essex Inst., Salem, Mass., 1972, Cambridge Art Assn., 1972, 73, New Bertha Schaeffer Gallery, N.Y.C., 1975, Gallery 200, Columbus, 1975, Galeria Rosanna, Boston, 1976, Baak Gallery, Cambridge, 1977, 78, Betty Parsons Gallery, N.Y.C., 1978, 79, 80, 81, Bette Stoler Gallery, N.Y.C., 1979, 80, 81, 1st Women's Bank, N.Y.C., 1981, Fay Gold Gallery, Atlanta, 1982, Deicas Art, La Jolla, Calif., 1982, Elayne Marquis Gallery, San Francisco, 1982, Soker-Kaseman Gallery, San Francisco, 1983, Phillipe Guimiot Gallery, Brussels, 1983, Kouros Gallery, N.Y.C., Leonardo Di Mauro Gallery, N.Y.C., 1985, Chronocide Gallery, 1986, Mokotoff Gallery, 1986, Jan Baum Gallery, L.A., 1986, Phillip Dash Gallery, N.Y.C., 1986, Lavrov Gallery, Paris, 1987, Sensibilites Contemporaines, Cie Moderne & Contemporaine, Paris, 1991, Musee de Nationale de Dakar, Senegal, 1992, E.M. Donahue Gallery, N.Y.C., 1993, Solway Gallery, Cin., 1993; pub., The Art of Seeing, Fisher & Telanski, "The Spiritual in Art", 1993. Jewish. Home: 356 W 20th St Apt 3B New York NY 10011-3385 Office: Pace Primitive 32 E 57th St New York NY 10022-2513

BRADLEY, MARILYN LOUISE, primary school educator; b. Denver, Sept. 21, 1947; d. Max Ford and Genevieve Louise (Van Buren) Williams; m. Larry Ray Bradley, May 5, 1979; 1 child, Scott William. AS, Boise Coll., 1968; BS in Home Econs. Edn., U. Idaho, 1971. Cert. standard elem., secondary tchr. vocat. home econ., gen. sci., art grades 1-8, 7-12, Idaho. Substitute tchr. Boise, Meridian, Idaho, 1971-76; graphic designer Design & Lithography Co., Boise, 1972-73; electronics assembler Hewlett Packard Co., Boise, 1974-83; art therapist Roger's Counseling Ctr., Clarkston, Wash., 1987; edn. tchr. NezPerce Tribal Head Start, Lapwai, Orofino, Kamiah, Idaho, 1987-90; substitute tchr., aide, instr. numerous local sch. dists., 1987—. Mem. Idaho Parents Unltd. Inc., Order of the Eastern Star. Baptist. Home: 609 Park Ave Lewiston ID 83501-4612

BRADLEY, MARILYNNE GAIL, advertising executive, advertising educator; b. Rockford, Ill., Apr. 12, 1938; d. Sherwin S. and Lillian (Leopold) Gersten; m. Charles S. Bradley, Dec. 28, 1959; children: Suzanne, Scott. BFA, Washington U., 1960; MAT, Webster U., St. Louis, 1975; MFA, Syracuse U., 1981; postgrad., St. Louis Tchrs. Acad., 1990. With Essayons Studio, St. Louis, 1968-69; tchr. Webster Groves High Sch., St. Louis, 1970—; instr. Webster Coll., St. Louis, 1973-82, U. Mo., 1980—, St. Louis U., St. Louis, 1978—, Washington U., St. Louis, 1984-87; sec. Mo. Art Edn., State of Mo., 1986-87; mem. Tchrs. Acad. 1990-92. Author, illustrator: Arpens and Acres, 1976, Packets on Parade, 1980; illustrator: St. Louis Silhouettes, 1977; editor: (videos) 12 Water Color Lessons, 1987, Techniques of American Watercolor, 1990, The Santa Fe Trail Series, 1993, Over Gauguin's Shoulder, 1994, Aboriginal Art Techniques, 1994. Bd. govs. Webster Groves (Mo.) Hist. Soc., 1965-72, 94—; mem. St. Louis Philharmonic Soc., 1956-72. Named Tchr. of Yr., 1987. Mem. So. Watercolor Soc. (sec. 1978-80), St. Louis Woman Artists, St. Louis Artist Guild (sec. 1985-86, pres. 1989-92, Disting. Woman 1987), Monday Club (chmn. 1979-83).

BRADLEY, MARTHA ELLEN, accounts payable administrator; b. L.A., Apr. 23, 1963; d. Ralph Leo and Alice Arlene (Wion) Leffler; m. Dennis Dale Bradley, May 20, 1984; 1 child, Robert Leo. BSBA in Acctg., Mo. Western State Coll., 1985. Account payable clk. Boehringer Ingelheim A.H.I., St. Joseph, Mo., 1986-90, account payable coord., 1991—; dir. St. Joseph Pony-Express I.M.A. newsletter, 1993-94. Home: 403 S Beech Savannah MO 64485

BRADLEY, SISTER MYRA JAMES, health science facility executive; b. Cin., Feb. 1, 1924; d. John Joseph and Mary (McMannus) B. BS in Edn., Atheneum Ohio, 1950; BS in Nursing, Mt. St. Joseph Hosp., 1954; MHA, St. Louis U., 1959; LHD (hon.), Coll. Mt. St. Joseph, Cin., 1993; HHD (hon.), Xavier U., 1993. RN, Ohio. Mem. faculty U. Dayton, Ohio, 1955-57, Good Samaritan Hosp., Dayton, 1955-57; asst. adminstr. St. Mary-Corwin Hosp., Pueblo, Colo., 1960; adminstr. St. Joseph Hosp., Mt. Clemens, Mich., 1960-65; pres., chief exec. officer Penrose Hosp., Colorado Springs, Colo., 1965-90, Penrose-St. Francis Cath. Healthcare, Colorado Springs, Colo., 1987-91; pres., CEO Good Samaritan Hosp., Cin., 1991—. Recipient Bus. Citizen of Yr. award Colo. Springs C. of C., 1990, Disting. Svc. award U. Colo., 1983, Civic Princeps award Regis Coll., Colorado Springs, 1984, Elizabeth Ann Seton nursing award for excellence dept. nursing Penrose Hosp. and Penrose Community Hosp., 1987, Sword of Hope Am. Cancer Soc., 1988; named woman of Distinction Soroptimist Internat., 1988. Mem. Cath. Hosp. Assn., Am. Hosp. Assn., Colo. Hosp. Assn. (trustee), Nat. Coun. Community Hosps. (trustee), Am. Coll. Hosp. Adminstrs., Healthcare Forum (trustee), Downtown Rotary Club. Office: Good Samaritan Hosp 375 Dixmyth Ave Cincinnati OH 45220-2489

BRADLEY, PAULA E., state legislator; b. New Haven, Conn., Oct. 11, 1924; married; 3 children. BA, Hiram Coll., 1945; postgrad., Middlebury Coll., 1946, Hartford Seminary, 1983-84. Ret. rsch. assoc. univ. devel. Yale U.; mem. N.H. Ho. of Reps.; mem. econ. devel. com. Coos County del.-at-large N.H. State Dem. Com., 1992—; treas. Randolph Dem. Party, 1992—; mem. 19th Ward Dem. Com., New Haven, 1976-85; bd. dirs. Caucus Conn. Dems., 1977-80; mem. Randolph Home Dem., 1988—; mem. Ch. of Redeemer, New Haven. Mem. AAUW (Androscoggin br. 1990—), Randolph Mountain Club (bd. dirs. 1986-91, 92—, treas. 1989-91). Office: NH Ho of Reps State Capitol Concord NH 03301*

BRADLEY, WANDA LOUISE, librarian; b. Havre de Grace, Md., June 6, 1953; d. William Smith and Josephine Viola (Miller) B. BA, U. Md., 1975; MSLS, Atlanta U., 1976; postgrad., Cath. U.; MPA (scholar), U. Balt., 1986. Libr. Harford County Pub. Libr., Bel Air, Md., 1976, Harford County Bd. Edn., Bel Air, Md., 1977-81, Nat. Grad. U., Arlington, Va., 1982, Md. State Dept. Edn., Balt., 1982-83, U.S. Dept. Labor, Washington, 1984, Balt. Gas and Electric Co., 1984-85, Morgan State U., Balt., 1985, Coppin State Coll., Balt., 1985-86, Montgomery County Pub. Sch. System, Rockville, Md., 1985-86, Community Coll., Balt., 1987-88; grant adminstr. Howard County Pub. Libr., 1988; libr., media specialist Balt. City Pub. Sch. System, 1992—; acad. advisor George Mason U., Fairfax, Va., 1981-82. Dept. Edn. fellow, 1983-84; U. Balt. Merit scholar, 1984, Atlanta U. scholar, 1976, U. Md. scholar, 1971; Howard County Pub. Libr. grantee, 1988. Mem. ALA, ASIS, Md. Libr. Assn., Spl. Librs. Assn., Med. Libr. Assn. Methodist. Office: Balt City Pub Sch Sys Greenspring Mid Sch Greenspring Ave Baltimore MD 21231

BRADNA, JOANNE JUSTICE, manufacturer's representative; b. Evergreen Park, Ill., May 1, 1952; d. John George and Virginia Dorothy (Breault) Justice; m. William Charles Bradna, Aug. 20, 1972; children: Trevor William,

Cameron Jon. Student, North Cen. Coll., Naperville, Ill., 1970-72; BS, Northwestern U., 1974; MS, U. Ill., Chgo., 1981. Med. technologist Northwestern U. Med. Sch., Chgo., 1974-76, Good Samaritan Hosp., Downers Grove, Ill., 1977-78; instr. med. lab. scis. U. Ill., Chgo., 1976-81, asst. prof., 1984-89, clin. coord., 1984-89, admissions coord., 1988-89; tech. sales rep. Analytab Products, Plainview, N.Y., 1981-84; owner, mgr. Rochelle Sci., mfr.'s reps. lab. equipment and supplies, Oak Brook, Ill., 1989—; ednl. cons. Hinsdale (Ill.) Hosp., 1979-80; mem. adv. com. Moraine Valley C.C., Palos Hills, Ill., 1982-92. Contbr. articles and abstracts to profl. jours. V.p. St. Isaac Jogues Home Sch. Assn., 1990-91, pres., 1991-92; mem. youth commn. St. Isaac Jogues Ch., Hinsdale, 1986-90, mem. edn. commn., 1988-92; bd. dirs. Care and Counseling Ctr., Downers Grove, Ill., 1993—, treas., 1994—; treas. Hinsdale Jr. Women's Club, 1983-85, 88-89, pres., 1985-86; 3rd v.p. 5th dist. Ill. Fedn. Women's Clubs, 1986-88, treas., 1988-90; mem. alumni bd. U. Ill. Coll. Associated Health Professions, 1992—, v.p. alumni bd., 1993—. Recipient Lifetime Svc. award 5th/6th Dist. Jr. Orgn., 1990, Heart of Gold citation United Way, 1994. Mem. Am. Soc. Clin. Pathologists, Am. Soc. Med. Tech. (Cert. Appreciation, 1977), Chgo. Soc. Med. Tech. (bd. dirs. 1977-80, cert. recognition, 1978-80), Am. Soc. Microbiology, Ill. Soc. Microbiology (sec. 1981-83, bd. dirs. 1985-87, 1992-94, nominations com. 1987-89, tellers com. 1994—, Tanner Shaughnessy Merit award 1992), Ill. Med. Technologists Assn. (cert. recognition 1978, 79), South Cen. Assn. Clin. Microbiology, Ill. Fedn. Women's Club (3d v.p. 5th dist. 1986-88, treas. 1988-90, life time svc. award 1990), Hinsdale Jr. Woman's Club (outstanding mem. 1981, 82, treas. 1983-85, 88-89, pres. 1985-86). Roman Catholic. Office: Rochelle Sci PO Box 3274 Hinsdale IL 60522-3274

BRADSHAW, CAROLYN FRANCES CURTIS, special education educator; b. Alvin, Tex., June 12, 1945; d. Olin Varner and Edith Cordelia (Dodge) Curtis; m. Billy Dan Bradshaw, June 20, 1970. AA, Wharton (Tex.) Jr. Coll., 1965; BS, Sam Houston U., 1967, MS, 1968. Cert. tchr. elem., mentally retarded, visually handicapped. Spl. edn. tchr. Palacios (Tex.) Ind. Schs. Dist., 1968—, tchr., coord., 1970-72, program leader, 1972—. Head coach Spl. Olympics, Tex., 1975—; bd. dirs. Matagorda Svcs., Inc. Sheltered Workshop, Tex., 1983-93; sec., bd. dirs. Bd. of Palacios Libr., Inc., 1978—. Named Handicapped Profl. of Yr. Pilot Club, 1987, Spirit Spl. Olymics award Area III Spl. Olympics, 1990, Outstanding Tchr. of Yr. Palacious C. of C., 1984. Mem. Tex. State Tchrs. Assn., Assn. Tex. Profl. Educators (v.p. 1981), Coun. for Exceptional Children (treas., sec., 1978, 88), Matagorda County Assn. for Retarded Citizens (sec. 1979), Delta Kappa Gamma (v.p. 1990-92). Baptist. Office: Ctrl Elem 1001 5th St Palacios TX 77465

BRADSHAW, LILLIAN MOORE, retired library director; b. Hagerstown, Md., Jan. 10, 1915; d. Harry M. and Mabel E. (Kretzer) Moore; m. William Theodore Bradshaw, May 19, 1946. BA, Western Md. Coll., 1937, DLitt (hon.), 1987; BLS, Drexel U., 1938, LittD (hon.), 1978; LHD (hon.), So. Meth. U., 1990—. Asst. adult circulation dept. Utica (N.Y.) Pub. Libr., 1938-41, asst. head, 1941-43; adult libr. Enoch Pratt Free Libr., Balt., 1943-44; asst. coord. work with young adults Enoch Pratt Free Libr., 1944-46; br. libr. Dallas Pub. Libr., 1946-47, readers adviser, 1947-52, head dept. circulation, 1952- 55, coord. work with adults, 1955-58, asst. dir., 1958-62, dir., 1962-84; asst. mgr. City of Dallas, 1984-85; mem. adv. group on librs. Libr. of Congress, 1976-77. Mem. bd. publs. So. Meth. U., 1970-78; mem. curriculum com. Leadership Dallas, 1978-79, mem. adv. com., 1978-82; mem. Tex. Gov.'s Commn. on Status of Women, 1970-72, Tex. Com. for Humanities, 1980-84, Nat. Reading Coun., Washington, 1970-73; pres. Tex. Humanities Alliance, 1986-88, bd. dirs., 1988-92; mem. Urban Design Adv. Coun., Dallas, 1987-92; conferee, asst. task force leader Goals for Dallas, 1966-69, vice chmn. achievement com. for continuing edn., 1971, chmn., 1972, chmn. citizen info. and participation com., 1976-77, trustee, 1977-78, sec., 1977, treas., 1979-83, exec. com., 1977-84; hon. chair Literacy Vols. Am., Dallas, 1987-90; mem. Com. to Plan the Future Goals for Dallas, 1973-74; mem. Dallas County Hist. Found., 1987-93, treas., 1990-93; mem. adv. bd. Tex. Library Systems Act, 1974-77; del. White House Conf. on Library and Info. Services; mem. ad hoc com. for planning and monitoring White House Conf. follow-up activities, 1980; bd. dirs. Hoblitzelle Found., 1971—, Univ. Med. Ctr., 1984-87, Friends of Fair Pk., 1989—; trustee Lamplighter Sch., 1974-81, Friends of Dallas Pub. Library, 1984—, pres., 1994—, Dallas Ballet, 1986-88, Dallas Arboretum and Bot. Garden, 1986-88, Employees' Retirement Fund, City of Dallas, 1989-91, mcpl. adv. bd. Dallas Pub. Libr., 1991-93. Named Tex. Libr. of Year, 1961; recipient Disting. Alumnus award Drexel U. Libr. Sch., 1970; Titche's Arete award for epitome of excellence in chosen field, 1970; Public Adminstr. of Yr. award, 1981; Excellence in Community Svc. award Dallas Hist. Soc., 1981; citation of honor Dallas chpt. AIA, 1982; Lillian Moore Bradshaw chair in libr. and info. studies established in her honor Tex. Woman's U. Mem. ALA (v.p. adult svcs. div. 1966-67, pres. adult svcs. div. 1967, 68, coun. 1968-69, pres. 1970-71, endowment trustee 1984-88, Honor Roll, Freedom to Read Found. 1993), Tex. Libr. Assn. (pres. 1964-65, chmn. pub. librs. div. 1955-56, chmn. awards com. 1973-74, 79-80, Disting. Svc. award 1975), Tex. Soc. Architects (hon. 1982), Dallas Hist. Soc. (trustee 1984-87), Zonta (pres. Dallas I 1976-77, Svc. award 1981, Dallas Humanitarian award 1991). Club: Zonta (pres. Dallas I 1976-77, Svc. award 1981, Dallas Humanitarian award 1991). Home: 6318 E Lovers Ln Dallas TX 75214-2016

BRADY, ADELAIDE BURKS, public relations agency executive, giftware catalog executive; b. N.Y.C., June 27, 1926; d. Earl Victor and Audrey (Calvert) Burks; B.S., Boston U., 1946; m. James Francis Brady, Jr., June 22, 1946 (div. 1953); 1 son, James Francis. Exec. v.p. Media Enterprises, 1952-55; dir. group relations Save the Children Fedn., N.Y.C., 1955-59; dir. pub. affairs div. Girl Scouts U.S.A., N.Y.C., 1959-69; pres. Communication Internat., Inc., Washington, 1969-73, Burks Brady Communications, N.Y.C., 1972—, Adelaide's Angel Shopper Catalog Inc., Wilton, Conn., 1976— ; exec. v.p. Arts in the Parks Inc., Washington, 1971—; bd. dirs. Lenox Hill Hosp., N.Y.C.; past bd. dirs. Achievement Rewards for Coll. Scientists Found.; pres. Animal Lovers Inc. Mem. Nat. Womens Rep. Club., N.Y.C. Recipient Silver Reel award for film The Children of Now, Save the Children Fedn.; decorated cmmdr. Order St. John of Jerusalem (Eng.), 1974. Mem. Nat. Assn. Women Bus. Owners, Public Relations Soc. Am., AAUW, NEA, Am. Women in Radio and TV, Nat. Ednl. Broadcasters Assn., Am. Soc. Profl. and Exec. Women, Women Execs. in Public Relations, N.Y. Press Women, Nat. Fedn. Press Women (state pres.), Women's Econ. Roundtable, Nat. Assn. Profl. Women, Nat. Assn. Female Execs., DAR. Episcopalian. Club: Capitol Hill (Washington), Yacht and Country Club (Fla.), MDW Officers (Wash.). Home: 312 Harvest Commons Westport CT 06880 also: Yacht Country Club 3664 SE Fairway E Stuart FL 34997 Office: 785 Park Ave New York NY 10021-3552

BRADY, CAROL DOWNS, accountant, city council member; b. York, Pa., Apr. 13, 1957; d. James Douglas and Beatrice Blanche (Bortz) Downs; m. David Chauncey Brady, Jan. 27, 1979. BS, York Coll. of Pa., 1979. CPA, Pa. Office mgr., acct. Ski Liberty, Fairfield, Pa., 1979-81; office mgr., contr. Cor-Box, Inc., York, 1981-83; contr. AAA So. Pa., York, 1983-88; supr. Philip R. Friedman & Assocs., York, 1988-92; dir. fin. York County C. of C., York, 1992—; cons. Office of Minority Bus. Devel., York, 1992—. Mem. York City Planning Commn., 1992—; mem. York City Coun., 1994—. Mem. AICPA, Pa. Inst. CPAs, NOW (pres. York chpt. 1980-81), Optimists (lt. gov. 1991-92). Democrat. Lutheran. Home: 249 W Philadelphia St York PA 17404 Office: York County C of C One Market Way East York PA 17401

BRADY, JEAN STEIN, librarian; b. Concord, Mass., Nov. 4, 1930; d. Walfred and Mary Selina (Jussila) Stein; m. Maurice Goodrich Klein, Feb. 22, 1957 (div. 1982); 1 child, Audrey Elaine; m. Lawrence Kevin Brady, Oct. 15, 1988. BS, Simmons Coll., 1952; cert. d'Etudes, U. Grenoble, France, 1954; MA, Northwestern U., 1957. Cert. pub. libr., N.Y. Sr. libr. N.Y. Pub. Libr., 1952-53, 57-60; cataloger Columbia U., N.Y.C., 1954-55; reference asst. Northwestern U., Evanston, Ill., 1955-57; cataloger U. W.Va., Morgantown, 1960-61; book reviewer ALA, Chgo., 1961-63; sr. cataloger Cleve. Pub. Libr., 1964-70; sr. catalog libr. Yale U. Libr., New Haven, Conn., 1970-92; cataloger Columbia U., N.Y.C., 1993—. Revision asst. Bibliographical Guide to Romance Langs. and Lits., 1956-57; reviewer: Booklist and Subscription Books Bulletin, 1961-63. Mem. ALA, New Eng. Libr. Assn. Democrat. Episcopalian.

BRADY, KIMBERLY ANN, editorial director; b. Omaha, Sept. 22, 1956; d. John Henry and Margaret Florence (Swatek) Robinson; m. Charles J. Brady Jr., June 19, 1976; 1 child, Jonathan Charles Brady. Student, Corcoran Sch. Art, Washington, 1974-75, George Mason U., 1974-76, Christopher Newport Coll., Newport News, Va., 1976-79. Editor-in-chief student newspaper Christopher Newport Coll., 1977-79; photojournalist Gloucester-Matthews Gazette-Jour., Gloucester, Va., 1979-80; mng. editor Journal of Analytical Toxicology Preston Publs., Niles, Ill., 1980-81; mng. editor Darkroom Techniques and Creative Camera Preston Publs., 1981-84; art dir., prodn. mgr. Profl. Photographers of Am., DesPlaines, Ill., 1984-86; sr. editor Professional Photographer Profl. Photographers of Am., 1990-91; editor-in-chief PHOTO Electronic Imaging Profl. Photographers of Am., DesPlaines, Atlanta, 1991-94; editorial dir. Atlanta, 1994—; editorial cons., photographer, graphic artist Chgo., 1986-90; instr. Winona Internat. Sch. of Profl. Photography, Mt. Prospect, Ill., 1987; judge photography competitions, Chgo., 1981-84, electronic imaging competition, L.A., 1993. Exec. dir. Lake Shore Sr. Svc. Ctr., Chgo., 1988-93; vol. Adult Literacy Program, Chgo., 1988; coord. Mayor Harold Washington campaign, Chgo., 1983. Recipient Va. Press Assn. Journalism award, 1979, Christopher Newport Coll. Journalism award, 1977-78. Mem. Profl. Photographers of Am. Office: Profl Photographers of Am 57 Forsyth St NW Ste 1600 Atlanta GA 30303-2206

BRADY, LISA MARIA, marketing engineer; b. N.Y.C., Feb. 3, 1964; d. Thomas Joseph and Marietta Sue (D'Adolf) B. BSEE, Bucknell U., 1985. Applications engr. AT&T Microelectronics, Allentown, Pa., 1985-87, product mktg. engr., 1987-90, product mktg. mgr., 1990-91, sr. product mktg. engr., 1991—. Home: 14 Lincoln Pl Whitehall PA 18052

BRADY, M. JANE, state official; b. Wilmington, Del., Jan. 11, 1951; m. Michael Neal. BA, Univ. of Del., 1973; JD, Vilanova Univ. Dep. atty. gen. Wilmington and Kent County; chief prosecutor Sussex County, 1987-90; solo law practice, 1990-94; atty. gen. State of Del., 1995—. Office: Office of Attorney General Carvel State Office Bldg PO Box 1401 Dover DE 19903*

BRADY, MARY ROLFES, music educator; b. St. Louis, Nov. 26, 1933; d. William Henry and Helen Dorothy (Slavick) Rolfes; m. Donald Sheridan Brady, Aug. 29, 1953; children: Joseph William, Mark David, Douglas Sheridan, John Rolfes, Todd Christopher. Student, Stanford U., 1951-54, UCLA, 1967, U. So. Calif., 1972-73; pvt. studies with, Roxanna Byers, Dorothy Desmond, and Rudolph Ganz. Pvt. practice tchr. piano L.A., 1955—; TV and radio performer; pres. Jr. Philharmonic Com. L.A., 1975-76; legis. coord., bd. dirs. Philharmonic Affiliates, L.A., 1978-80. Life mem. Good Samaritan Hosp., St. Vincent Med. Ctr., L.A., The Amazing Blue Ribbon, 1979—; bd. dirs. Hollygrove-L.A. Orphans Home, Inc.; trustee St. Francis Med. Ctr., 1984-88. Mem. Am. Coll. Musicians Club, Stanford Women's Club (past bd. dirs., pres. L.A. chpt. 1977—), The Muses, Springs Country Club.

BRADY, MARY SUE, pediatric dietitian, educator; b. Sedalia, Mo., Mar. 29, 1945; d. H. Wesley and K. Virginia (McGaw) Steele; m. Paul L. Brady, Sept. 2, 1967; 1 child, Chad W. BA, Marian Coll., Indpls., 1968; MS, Ind. U., Indpls., 1970, DMSc, 1987. Registered dietitian. Pediatric dietitian J.W. Riley Hosp. Children, Ind. U. Sch. Medicine, Indpls., 1970-75, acting dir. pediatric nutrition, 1975-78, 80-82, neonatal dietitian, 1978-80, dir. pediatric nutrition, 1982—; asst. prof. Ind. U. Sch. Medicine, Indpls., 1975-88, assoc. prof., 1988—. Contbr. articles to Jour. of Am. Dietetic Assn., Pediatric Pulmonology, Jour. of Pediatrics. Recipient Glenn W. Irwin, Jr., M.D. Experience Excellence Recognition award Ind. U.-Purdue U., Indpls., 1994. Mem. Am. Dietetic Assn. (mem. jour. bd. 1988-94, sec. pediat. nutrition practice group 1989-91, Outstanding Mem. of Yr. 1994, Excellence in Practice of Clin. Nutrition award 1991), Sigma Xi. Office: JW Riley Hosp for Children 702 Barnhill Dr Rm 1010 Indianapolis IN 46202-5200

BRADY, OUIDA JANE, accountant; b. Greensboro, N.C., Aug. 23, 1948; d. Harold Wade and Mary Jane (Anderson) Jones; m. Michael Gregg Bennett, Aug. 21, 1970 (div. June 1984); m. James Edward Brady, June 18, 1986; children: James Edward, Jr., Brian Christopher. BS in Acctg., Elon Coll., 1976. Head teller NCNB, Burlington, N.C., 1966-75; acctg. supr. Custom Industries, Greensboro, 1975-78; sr. acct. Carolina Steel Corp., Greensboro, 1978—; pres. Steel Credit Union, Greensboro, 1982-84. Advisor Jr. Achievement, Greensboro, 1980-82. Mem. Inst. Mgmt. Accts. (dir. 1992-94). Republican. Baptist. Home: 3017 Royalton Dr Greensboro NC 27406 Office: Carolina Steel Svc Ctr Inc 1451 S Elm-Eugene St Greensboro NC 27406

BRADY, SHERRY SLUDER, guidance counselor; b. Campbellsville, Ky., Oct. 11, 1951. BA, Campbellsville Coll., 1977; MA, Western Ky. U., 1980, Rank I in Edn., 1982. Cert. tchr., secondary guidance, secondary adminstrn., prin. and supr. endorsement, Ky. Tchr. English and psychology Casey County High Sch., Liberty, Ky., 1977-85, guidance counselor, 1986—; instr. psychology Somerset (Ky.) C.C., 1989, liaison acad. counselor, 1989—. Mem. Mid-Cumberland Counselor Assn. (sec.-treas. 1986-88), Ky. Assn. Sch. Adminstrs., Ky. Counselor Assn., Ky. Sch. Counselor Assn., Ky. Assn. Secondary and Coll. Admissions Counselors. Baptist. Home: 104 Dandelion Dr Campbellsville KY 42718-3349 Office: Casey County High Sch RR 4 Liberty KY 42539-9804

BRADY, VIOLA CATT, lawyer, psychologist; b. Bremen, Ind., June 28, 1946; d. Clarence Earnald and Mary Jane (MacDonald) Rouch; m. Patrick Brady, Dec. 24, 1976; childrten: Bruce, Colleen, David. BA, Ind. U., 1968; MA, Denver U., 1972, PhD, 1973; JD, Ind. U., 1979. Asst. prof. Lycoming Coll., Williamsport, Pa., 1973-76; atty. Lincoln Nat. Life Ins., Fort Wayne, Ind., 1979-81, Helsell Fetterman Martin Todd Hokansen, Seattle, 1981-84; sr. atty. The Boeing Co., Seattle, 1984—. Contbr. article to profl. jour. cons. Adoption Advocates, Seattle, 1992-94. Rsch. grantee Nat. Inst. Mental Health, 1971-73. Mem. Wash. State Bar Assn., Ind. State Bar Assn. Office: Boeing Company 2.25 Bldg 3d Flr 7755 E Marginal Way S Seattle WA 98124

BRADY-BORLAND, KAREN, reporter; b. Buffalo, Mar. 13, 1940; d. Charles A. and Mary Eileen (Larson) B.; m. Gregg Robinson Borland, Sept. 6, 1969 (div. July 1985); children: Caitlin Luise, Kristin Robinson, Leila Nell. BA in English, Daemen Coll., 1961; MS in Journalism, Columbia U., 1962. Summer reporter Buffalo News, 1961, reporter, 1965-68, columnist, 1968-81; editor Prentice-Hall, Inc., Englewood, N.J., 1962-65; press officer for Rep. Max McCarthy U.S. Ho. Reps., Washington, 1967. Recipient numerous awards Buffalo Newspaper Guild, 1960-79, N.Y. State award for Major Dailies Mag. Writing AP, 1982, numerous community awards. Office: Buffalo News 1 News Plz Buffalo NY 14203-2930

BRAEMAN, KATHRYN MOEN, lawyer; b. Chgo., May 21, 1940; d. Raymond C. and Beaulah B. (Barger) M.; div.; children: Elizabeth, David. BA, Northwestern U., 1962; MA, U. Kans., 1968; JD, U. Nebr., 1975. Bar: D.C. 1975, Md. 1985, U.S. Ct. Appeals 1980. Tchr. English Pine Hill Sch., Sherburn, Mass., 1962, Highline (Wash.) H.S., 1962-65; ednl. TV specialist Great Plains Nat. Inst. TV, Lincoln, Nebr., 1968-69; instr. legal edn. U.S. Office/Pers. Mgmt., Washington, 1975-78; dep. dir. office info. law and policy U.S. Dept. Justice, Washington, 1978-83; exec. dir. Women's Law Fund, Cleve., 1983-84; legal asst. U.S. Senate, Washington, 1984-85; gen. counsel Def. Investigative Svc., Washington, 1985-87; trial atty. def. office hearings and appeals Dept. Def., Arlington, Va., 1987—. Editor: From Yellow Pats to Computers, 1987, 90; co-editor: (newsletter) Heartbeat, 1990-94. Bd. dirs. UN Assn. Nat. Area Coun., Washington, 1993-94; chair heart com. Joseph Priestly Dist. Unitarian Universalist, Wilmington, Del., 1991-94. Mem. ABA (coun. mem. 1982-85, chair membership com. 1988-91, chair women and min. of outreach 1991-94). Office: DOHA Dept Def PO Box 3656 4015 Wilson Blvd Ste 300 Arlington VA 22203-1954

BRAHAM, DELPHINE DORIS, government accountant; b. L'Anse, Mich., Mar. 16, 1946; d. Richard Andrew and Viola Mary (Niemi) Aho; m. John Emerson Braham, Sept. 23, 1967 (div. Dec. 1987); children: Tammy, Debra, John Jr. BS summa cum laude, Drury Coll., 1983; M in Mgmt., Webster U., St. Louis, 1986. Bookkeeper, Community Mental Health Ctr., Marquette, Mich., 1966-68; credit clk. Remington Rand, Marietta, Ohio, 1971-72; acctg. technician St. Joseph's Hosp., Parkersburg, W.Va., 1972-74; material mgr. U.S. Army, Ft. Leonard Wood, Mo., 1982-86, accountant, 1986-92; acct. Dept. Defense Indpls., 1992—; instr., adj. faculty Columbia Coll., 1987-92, Park Coll., 1988-92. Leader Girls Scouts U.S., Williamstown, W.Va., 1972-74, Hanau, Germany, 1977-79. Mem. AAUW (treas. Waynesville br. 1986-90), NAFE, Assn. Govt. Accts., Am. Soc. Mil. Comptrs., Waynesville Bus. and Profl. Women's Orgn. Home: 8820 Pendleton Pike # 542 Lawrence IN 46226

BRAINARD, JAYNE DAWSON (MRS. ERNEST SCOTT BRAINARD), civic worker; b. Amarillo, Tex., Nov. 1; d. Bill Cross and Evelyn (McLane) Dawson; m. Ernest Scott Brainard, Nov. 26, 1950; children: Sydney Jane, Bill Dawson. AB, Oklahoma City U., 1950. Sec.-treas. E.S. Brainard Inc., from 1980, now v.p. pers. and mktg.; v.p. J. Thornton Cattle Co., 1981—. Guardian Camp Fire Assn., 1960-65; vol. N.W. Tex. Hosp. Aux., 1960-63; state chmn. Am. Heritage, DAR, 1963-67, regent chpt., 1966-67, parliamentarian chpt., 1975-79, state historian, state chmn. marshalls, 1967-70, 73-76, mem. state organizing com., 1967-70, nat. vice chmn. marshalls, 1969-79, state rec. sec., 1970-73, editor cookbook, 1972, nat. vice chmn. motion picture com., 1971-73, mem. nat. bd. mgmt., nat. chmn. state regent's dinner, 1980-81, mem. Nat. Officers Club, 1979—, Nat. Chmn.'s Assn., 1981—, mem. Tex. speakers staff, 1972-76, 76-79, Tex. vice-regent, 1976-79, pres. nat. vice-regents club 1977-78, vice chmn. state fin. com., 1976-79, Tex. DAR Gen. Conf. chmn., 1975, 78, state chmn. state regents project, 1973-76, area rep. nat. speakers staff, 1977-80, 82-83, editor Tex. Roster, 1976, mem. state by law com., 1973-76, pres. chpt. regents Club, 1973-74, pres. vice-regents club, 1977-78, Tex. state regent, 1979-82, pres. Tex. DAR State Officers Club, 1980-81, state parliamentarian, 1982-85; state bylaws chmn., 1991—; organizing pres. Children Am. Revolution, 1963-65, state chmn. mag. sustaining fund; organizing regent Daus. Am. Colonies, 1972, chmn., 1974-76; bd. dirs. Tamassee DAR Sch., Kate Duncan Smith Sch.; pub. relations Amarillo Little Theater, 1965-69, pres., 1968-69, dir., 1966-69; bd. mem., program com. chmn. Amarillo Camp Fire Council, 1965-67, 75—, vice chmn. council, 1976—, pres., 1977-78; chmn. Camp Fire Leaders Assn., 1964-65, bd. dirs., 1974-79, pres. Amarillo council, 1977-78; br. pres. AAUW, 1963-65, pub. relations, 1965-67, world affairs rep., 1965-67; sec.-treas. group League Dem. Women, 1964; pres. Panhandle Geol. Soc. Aux., 1959, Starlighters Dance Club, 1963-64; pres. Speaking of Living Study Club, 1962-63, sec., 1973-74, parliamentarian, 1976-77, pres., 1977-78; pres. Rep. Woman's Club, 1968, 73, v.p., 1972; steering com. Nat. Libr. Week, 1966, 67, 68, Amarillo Chischom Trail Centennial, 1967; vol. St. Anthony's Hosp. Aux., parliamentarian, 1991-92, bylaws chmn., 1991—, pres. 1993, 94, 2nd v.p., 1995; mem. Revitalize Amarillo Com., 1972, Amarillo Heart Bd., 1972-73, Historic Markers Task Force; mem. St. Anthony's Hosp. Found. Bd., 1994—. Recipient Martha Washington award and medal of appreciation SAR. Mem. Internat. Platform Assn., U.D.C. (rep. to Amarillo Geneal. Adv. Bd. 1973-74, 75-76, 76-77, pres. Amarillo Geneal. Adv. Bd. 1982-84), Nat. Assn. Parliamentarians (profl., registered parliamentarian, chmn. dist. 6, conf. 1990, pres. Hazel Crowley unit 1980-81, unit v.p. 1986-87, Palo Duro unit, 1988—, Yearbook 1987-88, Parlimentarian of Yr. award 1987, 90, pres. 1990-91), Tex. State Assn. Parliamentarians (rec. sec. 1988-89, 2d v.p. 1989-90, 1st v.p. 1990-92, state chmn. edn. 1989-90, chmn. ext. 1990-92, chmn. long range planning com. 1990-91, state pres. 1991-92, nominating chmn. 1994—), United Daus. 1812 (organizing regent, state chmn. 1984-86), Daus. Colonial Wars, Nat. Soc. So. Dames (nat. protocol chmn. 1984-85), Godparents Club (sec.-treas. 1991-92), Lone Star Ballet (bd. dirs. 1989—, parliamentarian 1989-91, sec. 1991-92, pres.-elect 1993, chmn. devel. commn. 1993—, pres. 1994—), Bravo! Amarillo Opera (bd. dirs. 1991—, parliamentarian, 1991-94, corr. sec. 1993—), Ladies Golf Assn. (partnership chmn. 1994), Amarillo Country Club (reporter 1988-89, treas. 1990-91, v.p. 1992, pres. 1993, parliamentarian 1993, 94), Jr. Travel Study Club (pres. 1991-92). Mem. Christian Ch. (bd. parliament 1965-66). Home: 2119 S Lipscomb St Amarillo TX 79109-2236 Office: PO Box 1101 Amarillo TX 79105-1101

BRAISTED, MADELINE CHARLOTTE, financial planner; b. Jamaica, N.Y., Nov. 23, 1936; d. Melvin Vincent and Charlotte Marie (Klos) B. AAS, Nassau C.C., 1968; BA, Hofstra U., 1973, MA, 1975, grad. Command and General Staff Coll., 1985, Coll. for Fin. Planning, 1991. CFP. Enlisted, U.S. Marine Corps., Cherry Point, N.C., 1954-57; reservations agt. Airline Industry, N.Y.C., 1957-64; reservations controller Auto Lease Industry, N.Y.C., 1964-66; nuclear medicine technician Queens Gen. Hosp., Jamaica, N.Y., 1969-70; lab. mgr. CUNY, 1970-80; commd. capt. U.S. Army Res., 1977-80, advanced through grades to major, 1984; cons. Energy Etcetera, Flushing, N.Y., 1979-85; capt. U.S. Army Res., Fort Totten, N.Y., 1975-80; USA Health Profl. Support Agy., Office Surgeon Gen. Washington, 1980-92. Author, pub. Energy Etcetera catalog, 1981-85; artist On Shore painting (hon. mention 1974). Merit badge counselor Boy Scouts Am., Queens County, N.Y., 1980-83; active mem. PTA, Jamaica, 1980-84. Decorated Legion of Merit, Army Commendation medal with one oak leaf, Army Achievement medal with one oak leaf cluster; named Community Leader and Noteworthy Am., Hist. Preservation of Am., 1976. Mem. NAFE, APHA, Am. Acad. Med. Adminstrs., Internat. Assn. Fin. Planners, Assn. Mil. Surgeons of U.S., Res. Officers Assn., Soc. Nuclear Medicine. Roman Catholic. Avocations: painting; sculpture. Office: 1983 Marcus Ave Ste 260 Lake Success NY 11042

BRAITERMAN, THEA GILDA, economics educator, state legislator; b. Balt., Md., Sept. 11, 1927; d. Isaac E. and Clara (Fink) Bloom; m. Marvin Braiterman, Mar. 21, 1948; children: Kenneth, Marta, David. BS, Johns Hopkins U., 1949; MA, U. Md., 1966; PhD, Union Inst., 1977. Assoc. prof. econs. Balt. Coll. of Commerce, 1966-73; prof. econs. New England Coll., Henniker, N.H., 1973—; mem. N.H. Ho. of Reps., 1988—; cons. on retirement, 1988—. Author: Workbook on Economic Theory, 1966; contbr. articles to profl. jours. Sec., bd. govs. United Way of Merrimack County, Concord, N.H., 1984—; v.p., bd. govs. Community Svcs. Coun., Concord, 1980-84. Recipient Jane Addams Grant, Jane Addams Peace Assn., 1976-77, Gilmore Grant, New England Coll., 1988—. Mem. Am. Econ. Assn., Ea. Econ. Assn. Home: PO Box 686 Henniker NH 03242-0686 Office: New England Coll Henniker NH 03242

BRAITMAN, MARY BETH, lawyer; b. Indpls., Sept. 23, 1950; d. Virgil William and Albina Mary Haag; m. Robert Braitman, June 2, 1973; 1 child, David. BS, Ind. U., 1971; JD, Ind. U., Indpls., 1981. Bar: Ind. 1981, U.S. Dist. Ct. (so. dist.) Ind. 1981. Agt., employee benefit specialist IRS, Indpls., 1974-81; assoc. Ice Miller Donadio & Ryan, Indpls., 1981-87, ptnr., 1987—. Mem. Ind. Pension Conf., Network of Profls. Working in Employee Benefits, Ind. Mcpl. Lawyers Assn. Office: Ice Miller Donadio & Ryan One American Sq Indianapolis IN 46282-0002

BRAJDIC, MARGIE KATHERINE BADROV, brokerage house executive; b. Chgo., Jan. 31, 1966; d. Ivan and Nevenka (Buskain) Badrov; m. Jerko Brajdic, Sept. 21, 1991. BA in Econs., U. Chgo., 1987, MBA, 1988. Internat. equity analyst Merrill Lynch Capital Markets, N.Y.C., 1988-89; jr. options trader Rayner and Stonington, N.Y.C., 1989-90; asst. dir. derivatives rsch. Am. Stock Exch., N.Y.C., 1990-94; asst. v.p. equity derivatives Lehman Bros., Inc., N.Y.C., 1994—. Mus. dir. Kardinal Stepinac, Croatian Tamburitzans, N.Y.C., 1990—. Mem. Croatian New Yorker Bus. Club, U. Chgo. Grad. Sch. Bus. Club (sponsor, interviewer admissions N.Y.C. chpt. 1990—). Home: 6 Alexander Dr Syosset NY 11791 Office: Lehman Bros Inc 3 World Financial Ctr 6th Fl New York NY 10285

BRAKE, KRISTI LOUISE, editor; b. Sonoma, Calif., Jan. 27, 1964; d. Donald Harold Hinchman and Marjorie Mae (Oaks) Youngdahl; m. John Douglas Brake, Apr. 30, 1994. BA in Journalism, Calif. State U., Chico, 1987. Entertainment editor The Orion, Chico, 1986; editor Kaleidoscope Mag., Chico, 1987; assoc. editor Videomaker Mag., Chico, 1987-88; news editor Camarillo (Calif.) Daily News, 1988-89; assoc. editor Radio and Records, L.A., 1989-92, Nashville, 1994—; editor Blast! Magazine, Nashville, 1992-93; assoc. editor Nashville Parent Mag., 1993. Editor Kaleidoscope Mag., 1987 (Best spl. sect. 1988). Copy editing scholarship The Dow Jones Newspaper Fund, 1987. Office: Radio and Records 1106 16th Ave S Nashville TN 37212-2310

BRALEY, KIM BARBARA, administrative assistant; b. Rutland, Vt., Dec. 10, 1955; d. Wesley Arthur and Barbara Bates (Spaulding) B. AA in Bus., Florence-Darlington Tech. Coll, 1986; BS, Coker Coll., 1994. Adminstrv.

asst. Florence-Darlington (S.C.) Tech. Coll., 1988—. Home: 203 Mechanicsville Hwy Darlington SC 29540-8306

BRAM, ELIZABETH, artist, author; b. N.Y.C., Dec. 5, 1948; d. Joseph and Jean (Rhys) B. Student, Silvermine Coll. Art, New Canaan, Conn., 1969-71. One-woman shows include Judith Wolov Gallery, Boston, 1992, Ctr. Psychological Studies, Albany, Calif., 1993, Quay Gallery, Sudbury, Eng., 1994, Aberdeen (Scotland) Arts Ctr., 1994, Minot Art Gallery, N.D., Orca Gallery, Vidalia, Ga., 1994, Daylight Gallery, London, Eng., 1995; 2 person show Eden Ct. Theatre Art Gallery, Inverness, Scotland, 1993, Cuneen Hackett Cultural Ctr., N.Y., 1993; exhibited in group shows, 1992—; author: The Door in the Tree, 1977, A Dinosaur Is Too Big, 1977, The Man on the Unicycle, 1978, I Don't Want To Go to School, 1978, One Day I Closed My Eyes and the World Disappeared, 1979, There Is Someone Standing on My Head, 1979, Saturday Morning Lasts Forever, 1980, Woodruff and the Clocks, 1980. Travel grantee East End Arts Coun., 1993. Home and Studio: 4 Prospect St Baldwin NY 11510-3204

BRAM, ISABELLE MARY RICKEY MCDONOUGH (MRS. JOHN BRAM), civic worker; b. Oskaloosa, Ia., Apr. 4; d. Lindsey Vinton and Heddy (Lundee) Rickey; B.A. in Govt., George Washington U., 1947, postgrad., 1947-49; m. Dayle C. McDonough, Jan. 20, 1949; m. 2d, John G. Bram, Nov. 24, 1980. Dep. tax assessor and collector Aransas Pass Ind. Sch. Dist., 1939-41; sec. to city atty., Aransas Pass, Tex., 1939-41; info. specialist U.S. Dept. State, Washington, 1942-48. Treas. Mo. Fedn. Women's Clubs, Inc., 1964-66, 2d v.p., 1966-68, 1st v.p., 1968-70, pres., 1970-72; bd. dirs. Gen. Fedn. Women's Clubs. Mem. steering com. Citizens Com. for Conservation; mem. exec. com. Missourians for Clean Water. Pres., DeKalb County Women's Democratic Club, 1964. Bd. dirs. DeKalb County Pub. Library, pres., 1966; bd. dirs. Mo. Girls Town Found.; dir. DeKalb County Little Theater Inc. Mem. AAUW, Nat. League Am. Pen Women, DeKalb County Hist. Soc., Internat. Platform Assn., Law Soc. U. Mo., Jefferson Club of U. Mo., Zeta Tau Alpha, Phi Delta Delta, Phi Delta Gamma. Democrat. Episcopalian. Mem. Order Eastern Star. Clubs: Tri Arts, Shakespeare, Wimodausis, Gavel, Ledgers, Jefferson. Editor: Mo. Clubwoman mag. Home: Sloan and Cherry Sts PO Box 156 Maysville MO 64469-0156

BRAMAN, HEATHER RUTH, technical writer, editor, consultant, antiques dealer; b. Wilmington, Ohio, Apr. 27, 1934; d. William Barnett and Violet Ruth (Davis) Hansford; m. Barr Oliver Braman, June 29, 1957 (div.); children: Sean Robert, Heather Paige. BA, Hiram Coll., 1956; postgrad., Sinclair Community Coll., Dayton, Ohio, 1977-85, Wright State U., Dayton, 1986. Pers. clk. USAF, Wright-Patterson AFB, Ohio, 1956, specifications editor, 1956-57, publs. editor, writer, 1957-63; vol. Children's Med. Ctr., 1963-67, Dayton Pubs. Schs., 1969-87; tchr. Gloria Dei Montessori Sch., Dayton, 1973-77; asst. mgr., acctg. mgr., mgr. tennis club USAF, Wright-Patterson AFB, Ohio, 1977-81; tech. writer Miclin Inc., Alpha, Ohio, 1982, Indsl. Design Concepts, Dayton, 1982-83; tech. writer, cons. Belcan Corp., Cin., 1984—; owner Chimney Sweep Antiques Shoppe, Arcanum, Ohio, 1991—; real estate investor. Founder, bd. dirs. Trotwood (Ohio) Women's Open Tennis Tournament, 1976-81; mem. Harrison Twp. Parks Bd., 1980-82; ballpersons coord. Dayton Pro Tennis Classic, 1977-80; pres. Dayton Tennis Commn., 1978-80; mem. parents exec. com. Hiram (Ohio) Coll., 1985—; ct.-appointed Spl. Advocate/Guardian Ad Litem (CASA GAL), 1988—; tutor English as a second lang. citizenship classes, 1991—. Mem. NOW, NAACP, Dayton Pub. Schs. Orgns., Dayton Tennis Umpires Assn., Mothers Against Drunk Drivers., AARP, WWF, HALT, Sigil of Phi Sigma. Democrat. Mem. Soc. Friends. Home: 320 Elm Hill Dr Dayton OH 45415-2943 Office: Belcan Corp 10200 Anderson Way Cincinnati OH 45242-4700

BRAME, MARILLYN A., hypnotherapist; b. Indpls., Sept. 17, 1928; d. David Schwalb and Hilda (Riley) Curtin; 1 child, Gary Mansour. Student, Meinzinger Art Sch., Detroit, 1946-47, U. N.Mex., 1963, Orlando (Fla.) Jr. Coll., 1964-65, El Camino Coll., Torrance, Calif., 1974-75; PhD in Hypnotherapy, Am. Inst. Hypnotherapy, 1989. Cert. and registered hypnotherapist. Color cons. Pitts. Plate Glass Co., Albuquerque, 1951-52; owner Signs by Marillyn, Albuquerque, 1952-53; design draftsman Sandia Corp., Albuquerque, 1953-56; designer The Martin Co., Orlando, 1957-65; pres. The Arts, Winter Park, Fla., 1964-66; supr. tech. publs. Gen. Instrument Corp., Hawthorne, Calif., 1967-76; pres. Camart Design, Westminster, Calif., 1977-86, Visual Arts, El Toro, Calif., 1978—; mgr. tech. publs. Archive Corp., Costa Mesa, Calif., 1986-90; adj. instr. Orange Coast Coll., Costa Mesa, 1985-90; hypnotherapist, Lake Forest, 1986—; bd. dirs. Orange County chpt. Am. Bd. Hypnotherapy. Author: Lemon and Lime Scented Herbs, 1994, (textbook) Folkdancing is for Everybody, 1974; inventor, designer dance notation sys. MS Method. Mem. bd. govs. Lake Forest II Showboaters Theater Group, 1985-88, 90-95. Mem. Soc. Tech. Communication (v.p. programs, 1987, newsletter editor 1986-87, newsletter prodn. editor 1985-86).

BRAMLETT, SHIRLEY MARIE WILHELM, interior decorator, artist; b. Scottsboro, Ala., June 14, 1945; d. Robert David and Alta (Reeves) Wilhelm; m. Paul Kent Bramlett, June 5, 1966; children: Paul Kent II (dec.), Robert Preston. BS, David Lipscomb U., 1966; postgrad., U. Miss., 1966-68; pvt. study art, 1976—. Decorator The Anchorage House, Oxford, Miss., 1966-67, Interiors by Shirley, Tupelo, Miss., 1971-80; tchr. Oxford City Schs., 1967-69; decorator, buyer Donald Furniture, Tupelo, 1969-71; owner, importer Bramblewood Interiors & Antiques, Belden, Miss., 1976-80; owner, decorator, artist The Cottage on Caldwell, Inc., Nashville, 1980—. Represented in art galleries Gallery Fine Art, Destin, Fla., Lyzon Gallery, Nashville, Magic Memories, Franklin, Tenn., elegant Creations Gallery, Brentwood, Tenn.; introduced and presented House of Parliament, Luxembourg; commd. for watercolor print fortnightly Musicale of Miss., 1991-92; European representation by Internet Internat. Bd. dirs. Found. for Christian Edn., 1988—, Ea. European Missions, Vienna, Austria, 1986— (commd. for watercolor print used in internat. fundraising); del. Miss. Dem. caucus, 1970; fundraiser Agape Artist, 1991. Named Woman of Decade, David Lipscomb Coll., 1986, one of Outstanding Young Women of Am., 1979; selected Centennial Artist, David Lipscomb U., Nashville, 1991, one of ten Master Tenn. Artists, Lyzon Gallery, Nashville, 1991. Mem. Nat. Mus. Women in Arts, Tenn. Watercolor Soc., Nat. Soc. Tole and Decorative Painters, Green Hills Garden Club (cover artist for nat. conv. garden clubs 1985), Assoc. Ladies Lipscomb (bd. dirs. 1991-92). Mem. Ch. of Christ. Home: 930 Caldwell Ln Nashville TN 37204-4016

BRAMMER, BARBARA RHUDENE, retired secondary education educator; b. Dawson, Tex., Aug. 20, 1936; d. William Alpheus and Eunice (Priddy) Hargis; m. Jerry Lane Brammer, Apr. 15, 1960; children: Cathy DeLane Brammer Francis, David Wayne Brammer, Karen Ann Brammer Shelfer. BS in Secondary Edn., U. North Tex., 1958. Cert. math tchr., Tex. Tchr., coach N.W. Ind. Sch. Dist., Justin, Tex., 1957-62; tchr. math. N.W. High Sch., Justin, Tex., 1970-93, dept. head, 1984-93; tchr., coach Decatur (Tex.) Ind. Sch. Dist., 1966-68; substitute tchr. math. dept. N.W. High Sch., Justin, Tex., 1993—; coach Acad. Decathlon Team, World Book Ency., 1986-90; advisor Merrill Pub. Co., 1989-91. Recipient Tchr. award Tandy Computers & Tex. Christian U., 1989; named One of 300 Outstanding Tex. Tchrs., Ex-Students Assn./U. Tex., Austin, 1989, One of 36 Outstanding Alumnus, Sch. Edn. U. North Tex., 1990; coach of State Champion Acad. Decathlon team. Mem. NEA, Tex. State Tchrs. Assn. (life), Tex. Ret. Tchrs. Assn., Tex. Math. Tchrs., Rhome Womens Club (pres. 1981-82). Mem. Ch. of Christ. Home: Rt 1 Box 130 Rhome TX 76078

BRAMSON, BERENICE LOUISE, soprano, teacher; b. Omaha, Nebr., May 29, 1929; d. Harry Lazarus and Irene (Schiffer) Sommer.; m. Alan Lewis Bramson, Sept. 10, 10, 1950; children: Barbara E. Bramson Dodge, Steven S. Grad. high sch., Omaha, Nebr. Co-dir. The Center for Music in Westchester, Westchester, N.Y., 1980—; founder, dir. The Sch. for Singers, Katonah, N.Y., 1981—; guest instr. Skidmore Coll., SUNY Binghamton, Cornell U. Opera appearances: Vancouver Opera Assn., N.Y. Grand Opera, Bklyn. Opera Soc.; soloist with: Denver Symphony, Buffalo Philharmonic, Wichita Symphony, Amarillo Symphony, Caramoor Festival Orchestra, Goldman Band, New Orchestra of Westchester, Chappaqua (N.Y.) Orchestra and others; solo appearances Weill Hall at Carnegie Hall, Merkin Hall, Alice Tully Hall, Town Hall, N.Y.C. and others; premiered music of American composers; recordings: Gemini Hall "Women's Work", 1975 and others. Home: 24 Hillside Ave Katonah NY 10536-2012

BRAMWELL, MARVEL LYNNETTE, nurse; b. Durango, Colo., Aug. 13, 1947; d. Floyd Lewis and Virginia Jenny (Amyx) B. Diploma in lic. practical nursing, Durango Sch. Practical Nursing, 1968; AD in Nursing, Mt. Hood Community Coll., 1972; BS in Nursing, BS in Gen. Studies cum laude, So. Oreg. State Coll., 1980; cert. edn. grad. sch. social work, U. Utah, 1987, cert. counselor alcohol, drug abuse, 1988, MSW, 1992; M in Social Work, 1992. RN, Utah, Oreg., Ind.; cert. social worker, Utah, Ind. Staff nurse Monument Valley (Utah) Seventh Day Adventist Mission Hosp., 1973-74, La Plata Community Hosp., 1974-75; health coordinator Tri County Head Start Program, 1974-75; nurse therapist, team leader Portland Adventist Med. Ctr., 1975-78; staff nurse Indian Health Service Hosp., 1980-81; coordinator village health services North Slope Borough Health and Social Service Agy., 1981-83; nurse, supr. aides Bonneville Health Care Agy., 1984-85; staff nurse Latter Day Saints Adolescent Psychiat. Unit, 1985-86; coordinator adolescent nursing CPC Olympus View Hosp., 1986-87, 91; charge and staff nurse adult psychiatry U. Utah, 1987-88; nurse MSW Community Nursing Svc., Salt Lake City, 1989-90; with Community Nursing Svc. and Hosp., Clearfield, Utah, 1993—; med. social worker Meth. Home Health, Indpls., 1994—; assisted with design and constrn. 6 high tech. health clinics in Ala. Arctic, 1982-83; psychiat. nurse specialist Community Nursing Svc. Contbr. articles to profl. jours. Active Mothers Against Drunk Driving, Program U. Alaska Rural Edn., 1981-83. Recipient Cert. Appreciation Barrow (Alaska) Lion's Club, 1983, U.S. Census Bur., Colo., 1970. Mem. NOW, Nat. Assn. Social Workers, Assn. Women Sci. Home: 925 N Alabama Indianapolis IN 46202

BRANCALEONE, LAURIE ANN, social worker; b. Mineola, N.Y., Oct. 9, 1963; d. Peter and Kathleen (Marsala) B. B Social Worker, Adelphi U., 1985, MSW, 1986. Cert. clin. social worker. Caseworker III, Nassau County Dept. Social Svcs., Mineola, 1986-88; med. social worker Mercy Med. Ctr., Rockville Centre, N.Y., 1988—; pvt. practice in psychotherapy Garden City, N.Y., 1992—; cons. counselor St. Vincent De Paul Parish Outreach, Elmont, N.Y., 1985—. Bd. dirs. West Nassau Mental Health, Franklin Sq., N.Y., 1988. Mem. NASW, Acad. Cert. Social Workers. Roman Catholic. Home: 497 Tulip Ave Floral Park NY 11001-3205

BRANCH, BRENDA SUE, library director; b. Buffalo, Apr. 27, 1947. BS in Edn., SUNY, Cortland, 1969; MLS, SUNY, Buffalo, 1972, postgrad., 1972; postgrad., S.W. Tex. State U., 1973-74, Stephen F. Austin State U., 1975-76; MPA, S.W. Tex. State U., 1985. Tchr. Kenmore Ind. Sch. Dist., 1969-70; asst. health scis. libr. SUNY, Buffalo, 1971-73; br. mgr. Austin Pub. Libr., 1973-75; acquisitions libr. Tex. Ea. U., 1975; humanities libr. Stephen F. Austin State U., 1975-76; dist. libr. coord. Longview Ind. Sch. Dist., 1976-77; program devel. coord. Austin Pub. Libr., 1977-80, supr. br. svcs., 1980-86, assoc. dir. pub. svcs., 1986-91, dir., 1991—; project mgr. reduction-in-force project City of Austin, 1988, co-chair customer svc. task force, coord. creativity program, 1990; mem. long range planning com. svcs. spl. populations Tex. State Libr., 1992. Active Travis County Continuing Edn. Adv. Bd., Austin, 1981—, Tex. Mcpl. League, Mayor's Coalition Workplace Literacy, 1990—, Literacy and Fundamental Edn. Speaker's Bur., 1991—, Leadership Austin, 1991—, chair kids program, 1993; tutor, trainer Travis County Adult Literacy Coun., 1986-89; chair City of Austin Workplace Literacy Task Force, 1989—; mem. speaker's bur. United Way, 1990—; mem. MPA adv. coun. S.W. Tex. State U., 1993—; bd. dirs. Big Bros./Big Sisters, 1986-90, chair pub. rels. com., 1986-90, fundraiser, 1986-90, com. co-chair, 1986-90. Recipient Outstanding Achievement for Govt. Svc. award YWCA, 1991. Mem. ALA, Tex. Libr. Assn. (treas. dist. V 1976-77, mem. continuing edn. com. 1978-79, mem. membership com. 1986-89, mem. ann. conf. placement ctr. 1989—, mem. literacy com. 1990—, chair 1990-93, mem. resource sharing com. 1990—, mem. ad hoc property com. 1992, mem. minority recruitment com. 1992-93, co-chair legis. day 1992-93, chair elect pub. libr. divsn. 1994—), Austin Soc. Pub. Adminstrn. (chair membership com. 1984-89, newsletter editor 1984-89), Toastmasters (v.p., pres., newsletter editor). Office: Austin Public Library PO Box 2287 800 Guadalupe St Austin TX 78768-2287

BRANCH, MICHELLE EVE, daycare provider; b. Michigan City, Ind., June 26, 1964; d. George Donald and Jane Alice (Moldenhauer) McRae; divorced; children: Madison Marie, Autumn Rose. B of Arts and Scis., Western Mich. U., 1986. Bridal cons. Wedding Belles, Stevensville, Mich., 1987-88; sales person Carter Lumber, Bridgman, Mich., 1988-89; lab technician Great Lakes Food Testing, St. Joseph, Mich., 1989; tchrs. aide Bridgman Pub. Schs., 1989-92; ind. daycare provider Bridgman, 1993—; mem. sch. improvement com. Bridgman Pub. Schs., 1992. Mem. Alpha Lambda Delta. Republican. Evangelistic Lutheran. Home and Office: 11429 Baldwin Rd Bridgman MI 49106

BRANDEISKY, KATHLEEN SEXTON, social worker, consultant; b. Evergreen Park, Ill., Jan. 23, 1961; d. Stephen Richard Sexton and Margaret Louise (Nemann) Schreibeis; m. Howard Paul Brandeisky, Sept. 6, 1987; children: Kara Veronica, Paul Stephen. BS in Social Welfare, Ohio State U., 1983; MA, U. Chgo., 1985. Cert. social worker, N.Y. Med. social worker Westchester County Med. Ctr., Valhalla, N.Y., 1985-87; psychiat. social worker St. Vincents Hosp., Harrison, N.Y., 1987-89, supervising psychiat. social worker, 1989-91; pvt. practice Mt. Kisco, N.Y., 1992-94, The Therapy Ctr., Mt. Kisco, 1994—; coord., cons. Mt. Kisco Drug & Alcohol Abuse Prevention Coun., 1989—. Mem. NASW (qualified clin. social worker), Nat. Register Clin. Social Workers. Home: 31 Manchester Dr Mount Kisco NY 10549 Office: The Therapy Ctr 241 Lexington Ave Mount Kisco NY 10549

BRANDENBURG, ANNABEL JUNE, small business owner; b. Beaver Dam, Wis., June 6, 1936; d. Charles George and Sylvia Agnes (Woolery) Marthaler; m. Orville F. Brandenburg (dec. July 1986); children: Cindy, Russel, Krystal, Charles, Sujen. Owner, truck driver Brandenburg Trucking, Beaver Dam, 1964-89; owner Sew & So Shop, 1990—, Annabel's Bridals, 1991—. Lutheran. Home: 300 Sarah Ln Beaver Dam WI 53916-2744

BRANDES, MARGOT, humanities educator; b. Zweibruecken, Germany, Dec. 9, 1930; came to U.S., 1939; d. Eleazar and Martha (Uhlfelder) Bernstein; m. Joseph Brandes, Aug. 16, 1953; children: Cheryl, Lynn Marcia, Susan Michele, Aviva Joy. BS, NYU, 1954; MS, City Coll. N.Y., 1957. Cert. tchr. grades K-8, N.Y., N.J. Instr., curriculum coord. Ramaz Acad., N.Y.C., 1955-56; instr. N.Y.C. Bd. Edn., 1956-58; instr., head tchr. Fair Lawn (N.J.) Jewish Ctr., 1959-89; instr. secular dept. Yavneh Acad., Paramus, N.J., 1968-80, Moriah Acad., Englewood, N.J., 1977-81; instr. ESL Ctr. Acad. Support William Paterson Coll., Wayne, N.J., 1981; lectr., instr. humanities dept. Bergen C.C., Paramus, 1981—; lectr. Columbia U., N.Y.C., summers 1982, 83; cons. Ednl. Testing Svc., Princeton, N.J., 1990—; evaluator, ednl. programmer N.J. Com. for Humanities, New Brunswick, 1994; book reviewer Prentice Hall; lectr. for acad. and scholarly svc. orgns. Author: (workbook) 'Round the Jewish Year, 1970, 'Round the Jewish Year Sequel, 1974; sculptures exhibited in various instns. Mem. regional bd., chair Hebrew Hadassah, Fair Lawn, 1985—; Yale U. archival rsch. assoc. Ramapo (N.J.) Coll., 1991—; creator coffee house for youth Fair Lawn Jewish Community Coun., 1975-78; mem. N.J. State Planning Commn., 1986—, Face Lift Community Improvement Com., End Violence Now, 1991—, N.E. Regional Conf. English, 1989—. Recipient Scholastic Press award Scholastic Mag., 1978, Original Teaching Aids award Calif. Tchrs. Assn., 1979, State Resolution award Senate, 1988; Melton Rsch. grantee Jewish Theol. Sem., 1986; Brith Abraham fellow NYU, 1954. Mem. Jewish Fedn. North Jersey (bd. trustees, coord. 1979—). Office: Bergen CC 400 Paramus Rd Paramus NJ 07652

BRANDES-BOWEN, ILA ANN, entrepreneur; b. Charlotte, Apr. 3, 1954; d. Roddy Arthur and Marguerite (Johnson) Brandes; m. Timothy Ray Bowen, July 1, 1984; 1 child, Timothy Brandes. B.A., U. N.C., Greensboro, 1977. Asst. supr. quality control Ball Corp., Asheville, N.C., 1977-79, indsl. engr., Muncie, Ind., 1979-80, methods and standards engr., 1980-82, materials handling engr., 1982-85, customer service engr., 1983-85; cons. Porsche Market Group, Rockaway, N.J., 1985-86; owner, pres. IAM, Asheville, N.C., 1985-87; owner PIP, Statesville, N.C., 1986—, TAOF, Inc., Statesville, 1989—; addressed 1984 Internat. Exposition Food Processors (speech pub.). Counselor Young Life, Greensboro, 1972-77, Jr. Achievement, Muncie, 1979-81; bd. dirs. Muncie Symphony Membership Dr., 1981, Corp. Challenge, Muncie, 1981-83, United Way Fund Dr., Muncie, 1982-83, Downtown Statesville Devel Corp., 1988-91, officer, 1989-91, Fox Creek Farms, Inc., Troutsdale, Va., 1989—. Republican. Presbyterian.

BRANDON, GLORIA JEAN, data processing; b. Red Bank, N.J., Dec. 7, 1949; d. John Eric and Mable Juanita (Bolton) B. BA in Elem. Edn., Va. Union U., 1972; postgrad., Va. Commonwealth U., 1973-74, U. Poaz, Ctrl. Am., 1986. Cert. elem. tchr., Va. Elem. tchr. Richmond (Va.) Pub. Schs., 1973-74, Red Bank Pub. Schs., 1974-75; asst. adminstr. Companion Care Health Svcs., Richmond, 1975-87; composition computer operator Richmond Newspapers, Inc., 1987—; spl. corr. Media Gen., Inc., Richmond, 1990—; hostess So. Govs. Assn./African Heads of State Summit, Richmond, 1993, Va. Corps of Vols., Nat. Bapt. Congress, U.S.A., Richmond, 1994. Hostess Gov. Exec. Mansion, Richmond, 1990—; dept. rep. United Way, Richmond, 1990—; poetry reader Morning Star Bapt. Ch., Cuba, Ala., 1986, Greater Mt. Herman Ch., Meridian, Miss., 1986. Columbia Sem. scholar, 1986. Mem. Nat. Black Media Coalition, Am. Bus. Womens Assn. (chpt. editor 1986-90, inter coun. mem., pub. rels. chair 1988-90, membership chair 1986-89, bulletin chair 1986-90, poetry reading 1985-90, Woman of Yr. 1989). Episcopalian. Office: Richmond Newspapers Inc 333 E Grace St Richmond VA 23293-1000

BRANDON, HOWELL FRANCES SWEENEY, elementary education educator; b. Nashville, June 23, 1916; m. Charles Morris Brandon; children: Stacia Ruth, Carl Morris. BS, Middle Tenn. State U., 1939; MA, Peabody Coll., Nashville, 1959. Tchr. elem. sch. Nashville City Schs. Author (children's books) Rosie the Rockhound, 1963, Lonnie and the Flicker Family, 1967, A Treasury of Witchcraft and Devilry, 1975, The Day the Woods Went Crazy, 1990. Exec. sec. ARC, Rutherford County, Tenn., 1969-71; pres. Ch. Women United, Murfreesboro, Tenn.; ecol. activist, 1978-94. Home: 5152 Rucker Christiana Rd Christiana TN 37037

BRANDON, KATHRYN ELIZABETH BECK, pediatrician; b. Salt Lake City, Sept. 10, 1916; d. Clarence M. and Hazel A. (Cutler) Beck; MD, U. Chgo., 1941; BA, U. Utah, 1937; MPH, U. Calif., Berkeley, 1957; children: John William, Kathleen Brandon McEnulty, Karen (dec.). Intern, Grace Hosp., Detroit, 1941-42; resident Children's Hosp. Med. Center No. Calif., Oakland, 1953-55, Children's Hosp., L.A., 1951-53; pvt. practice, La Crescentia, Calif., 1946-51, Salt Lake City, 1960-65, 86—; med. dir. Salt Lake City public schs., 1957-60; dir. Ogden City-Weber County (Utah) Health Dept., 1965-67; pediatrician Fitzsimmons Army Hosp., 1967-68; coll. health physician U. Colo., Boulder, 1968-71; student health physician U. Utah, Salt Lake City, 1971-81; occupational health physician Hill AFB, Utah, 1981-85; child health physician Salt Lake City-County Health Dept., 1971-82; cons. in field; clin. asst. U. Utah Coll. Medicine, Salt Lake City, 1958-64; clin. asst. pediatrics U. Colo. Coll. Medicine, Denver, 1958-72; active staff emeritus Primary Children's Hosp., LDS Hosp., and Cottonwood Hosp., 1960-67. Diplomate Am. Bd. Pediatrics. Fellow Am. Pediatric Acad., Am. Pub. Health Assn., Am. Sch. Health Assn.; mem. Utah Coll. Health Assn. (pres. 1978-80), Pacific Coast Coll. Health Assn., AMA, Utah Med. Assn., Salt Lake County Med. Soc., Utah Public Health Assn. (sec.-treas. 1960-66), Intermountain Pediatric Soc. Home and Office: PO Box 58482 Salt Lake City UT 84158-0482

BRANDON, LYNNE S., human services administrator, consultant; b. N.Y.C., Dec. 30, 1948; d. Stanley Brandon and Meryl Elise (Kann) Daw. BS in Animal Sci. cum laude, U. N.H., 1970; PhD in Women's Studies, The Union Inst., 1979. Assoc. program dir. New England Hosp. Assembly, Durham, N.H., 1974-78; asst. to pres. McIntosh Coll., Dover, N.H., 1979-80; contr. The Center House, Inc., Boston, 1980-84; fiscal mgr. Women, Inc., Dorchester, Mass., 1984-86; ind. cons. in fin. mgmt. Boston, 1986-94; exec. dir. Social Justice for Women, Inc., Boston, 1993—; adj. faculty Antioch New England Grad. Sch., Keene, N.H., 1981, U. Mass, Boston, 1993, Tufts U., Medford, Mass., 1994; pres. Capricorn Software, Inc., Somerville, Mass., 1988-93. Co-prodr. (theatre/multi media) They Fought Back: Jewish Resistance to the Holocaust, 1981. Mem. fin. com. Bromfield St. Ednl. Found., Boston, 1989-90; chair fin. com. Haymarket Peoples Fund, Boston, Mass., 1989—, bd. dirs., 1992—. Mem. N.H. Assn. for Mental Health (bd. dirs. 1976-80), Inst. Mgmt. Accts., Boston Computer Soc., Phi Kappa Phi, Sigma Xi. Democrat. Jewish. Office: Social Justice for Women Inc 108 Lincoln St Boston MA 02111

BRANDT, ANN SUE, psychologist; b. N.Y.C., Oct. 19, 1950; d. Jacob Lampel and Janet (Kaplan) B. BA, U. Maine, 1973; PhD, Tex. Woman's U., 1979. Lic. psychologist, Fla. Asst. prof. Ind. State U., Evansville, 1979-81; account exec., industry cons. AT&T, Ft. Lauderdale, Fla., 1981-85; mgmt. cons. Touche Ross & Co., Miami, 1985-87; clin. psychologist Anne Goff & Assocs., Plantation, Fla., 1987—; exec. dir. Sept. Svcs. of Fla., Coral Springs, 1987-90; v.p. The Curtiss Group, Inc., Ft. Lauderdale, 1990—; dir., assoc. prof. Inst. for the Study of Aging, Nova U., Ft. Lauderdale, 1987-92; dir. sr. svcs. Jewish Family Svc. of Broward County, 1992—; bd. dirs. Broward Meals on Wheels, Ft. Lauderdale, mem. adv. com. Ctr. on Aging and Devel. Disabilities, U. Miami. V.p., bd. dirs. Svc. Agy. for Sr. Citizens. Recipient funding grant, Retirement Rsch. Found., 1988-90; named Outstanding Young Woman in America, 1979; finalist Up and Coming awards Broward County, 1990. Mem. Am. Psychol. Assn., Gerontol. Soc. Am., Am. Assn. Marriage and Family Therapy (clin. mem.), Fla. Psychol. Assn., Broward Women in Network. Democrat. Jewish. Home: 7560 Plantation Rd Fort Lauderdale FL 33317-1054 Office: Jewish Family Svc of Broward 8358 W Oakland Park Blvd Fort Lauderdale FL 33351

BRANDT, ELAINE SUZANNE, artist; b. Cleve., Jan. 5, 1942; d. Joseph and Sylvia (Opper) B.; m. Kevin Keith Clifton, June 10, 1964 (dec. Feb. 1974). BFA in Drawing, Ariz. State U., 1994. Designer apparel Robert Sloan Sportswear, N.Y.C., 1964-68; designer Ginori, N.Y.C., 1968-70, Kimberly Knits, N.Y.C., 1970-72; designer sportswear Sequel I, N.Y.C., 1972-75, Geoffrey Beene, N.Y.C., 1975-79; designer Kasper for Joan Leslie, N.Y.C., 1979-81, Villager, N.Y.C., 1981-84, J.G. Hook Inc., N.Y.C., 1984-89. Illustrator (fashion) Vogue mag., 1968-71, J. Walter Thompson Agy., 1968. Home and office: 11011 N 92nd St Unit 1106 Scottsdale AZ 85260-6141

BRANDT, GRACE BORGENICHT, art dealer; b. N.Y.C., Jan. 25, 1915; d. Samuel Lazarus and Jeanette (Salny) Lubell; m. J. Borgenicht, Jan. 20, 1938; children: Jan Schwartz, Berta Kerr, Lois Borgenicht; m. Warren Brandt, Dec. 27, 1960. MA, Columbia U., 1937. Dir., owner Grace Borgenicht Gallery, Inc., N.Y.C., 1951—; adviser Tupperware Art Found. Scholarship, Bus. Meets the ArtYoung Pres.'s Orgn. One-woman shows include Laurel Gallery, N.Y.C., 1947, 48, 50, Philbrooks Mus., Tulsa, 1948, Everhart Mus., Scranton, Pa., 1948; exhibited in group shows at Nat. Assn. Women Artists, 1948, 49, L'Association Nationale des Femmes Artistes Americaines, 1949, Internat. Watercolor Exhbn., 1949, 53, 55, 59, Contemporary Am. Painting, 1951, N.Y. Soc. Women Artists, 1953, Whitney Mus. ann. exhbn., 1954, Aquarelles Contemporaines aux Etats-Unis, France, 1954, Martha Jackson Gallery, N.Y.C., 1955; represented in permanent collections Philbrook Mus., Everhart Mus. Mem. Nat. Assn. Women Artists (first prize watercolor 1949), Art Dealers Assn. Am., N.Y. Soc. Women Artists, N.Y.C. Artists Club. Office: Grace Borgenicht Gallery 724 Fifth Ave New York NY 10019-4106

BRANDT, IRENE HILDEGARD, educator; b. Meriden, Conn., June 6, 1942; d. Walter M. and Hildegard E. Brandt. BS, Ctrl. Conn. State U., 1964, cert. 6th yr. degree, 1989, MS, 1969, postgrad., 1989. Cert. 7-12 math. tchr., K-12 adminstrn. and supervision, intermediate supervision, Conn. Tchr. math. Jefferson Jr. H.S., Meriden, 1964-67, Platt H.S., Meriden, 1967—. Active Summit Club, Meriden, 1972—. Yearbook dedicated to her Platt H.S., 1971, named outstanding tchr. by srs., 1990. Mem. ASCD, Nat. Coun. Tchrs. Math., New Eng. Math. Tchrs. Assn., Assn. Tchrs. Math. in Conn. (conv. presider 1990-93), Am. Fedn. Tchrs., Conn. Fedn. Tchrs., Meriden Fedn. Tchrs. (sec. 1982-90). Home: 70 Genest St Meriden CT 06450-4538

BRANDT, KATHY A., public relations executive, secondary school educator; b. Chgo., June 2, 1942; d. Leo J. and Helen J. (Briskin) Weisel; m. John M. Brandt, Nov. 28, 1967; children: Debra, Lee. BA, U. Iowa, 1963;

MA, Fairfield U., 1975. Cert. secondary sch. tchr. Tchr. Golden Valley Jr. H.S., San Bernardino, Calif., 1963-64, Lake Forest (Ill.) H.S., 1964-68, Stamford (Conn.) H.S., 1968-72; pres. Brandt Assocs., Inc., Westport, Conn., 1984—. Vol. tchr., aide, mem. curriculum com. Westport Schs., 1976-83; editor newsletter Kings Hwy. Sch. PTA, Westport, 1984; mem. parent's com. Pine Manor Coll., Chestnut Hill, Mass., 1994—. Mem. LWV, N.Am. Ski Journalists Assn. Home and Office: Brandt Assocs Inc 29 Washington Ave Westport CT 06880

BRANIGAN, HELEN MARIE, educational administrator; b. Albany, N.Y., Sept. 24, 1944; d. James J. and Helen (Weaver) B. BS in Bus. Edn., Coll. St. Rose, Albany, 1967, MA in English, 1972; postgrad., SUNY, Albany, 1973-81. Tchr., chair dept. bus. edn. S. Colonie Sch. Dist., Albany, 1968-81; assoc. Bur. Bus. Edn. N.Y. State Edn. Dept., Albany, 1981-87; assoc. Bur. Occupational Edn. Program Devel., Albany, 1987-91, Bur. Occupational Edn. Innovation and Quality, Albany, 1991-93, Cen./So. Regional Field Svcs., Albany, 1993—; mem. adv. coun. SUNY, Cobbleskill, 1985-94; bd. trustees St. Catherine's Found., 1993—; sr. cons. Internat. Cr. for Leadership in Edn., Schenectady, N.Y., 1991—. Editor McGraw-Hill Book Co., Glencoe Pub., 1986—; contbr. articles to profl. jours. Lay vol. Archdiocese of Anchorage, 1967-68; mem. N.Y. State Staff Devel. Coun. Mem. ASCD, Am. Vocat. Assn., Nat. Assn. State Suprs. Bus. Edn., Bus. Tchrs. Assn. N.Y. State, Ea. Bus. Edn. Assn., Nat. Bus. Edn. Assn., Delta Pi Epsilon. Roman Catholic. Home: 540 New Scotland Ave Albany NY 12208-2318 Office: NY State Edn Edn EBA Rm 461 Albany NY 12234

BRANNICK, ELLEN MARIE, management consultant; b. Rochester, Minn., Aug. 10, 1934; d. Daniel Ryther and Grace Ellen (Mills) Markham; m. Thomas L. Brannick,. BS in Health, Phys. Edn., MacMurray Coll., 1956, MS, 1959. Elem. phys. edn. Ritenour Consol. Sch. Dist., Overland, Mo., 1958-61; head tchr., summer dir. Civic League Day Nursery, Rochester, 1961-64; recreation therapist Rochester State Hosp., 1964-68; rehab. dir. Rochester State Hosp., 1968-70; rehab. therapist Napa State Hosp., Calif., 1971; indsl. therapy con. Napa State Hosp., 1971-73, community liaison rep., 1973—. Mem. Friends Napa County Library, 1977, Napa County Humane Soc., 1978. Mem. Calif. Alliance for Mentally Ill, Napa Valley AIDS Project, Napa County Hist. Soc. Democrat. Office: Napa State Hosp 2100 Napa Vallejo Hwy Napa CA 94558-6293

BRANNON, TAMMY REBECCA, systems analyst; b. Florala, Ala., Jan. 7, 1965; d. John Henry and Reba Elizabeth (Mitchell) Pelham; divorced; 1 child, Chelsea Nicole. BS in Systems Sci., U. West Fla., 1986; MBA, Augusta Coll., 1992. Programmer, analyst GTD Computer Systems, Birmingham, Ala., 1987-88, Med. Coll. Ga., Augusta, 1988-91; EDI project mgr. Greenfield Inds., Augusta, 1991—.

BRANNON, TREVA LEE (WOOD), insurance company executive; b. Burleson, Tex., Oct. 6, 1932; d. William Albert and Virginia May (Garner) Wood; m. Lone J. Brannon, Aug. 3, 1951 (dec. Apr. 1989); 1 child, Ralph Eugene. Grad. high sch., Godley, Tex. Acctg. clk. Internat. Svcs. Life Ins. Co., Ft. Worth, 1950-63; sec. John Hancock Life Ins. Co., Ft. Worth, 1963-64; asst. v.p. Olympic Life Ins. Co., Ft. Worth, 1964-70; v.p. Transport Life Ins. Co., Ft. Worth, 1970—. Mem. Soc. Ins. Licensing Adminstrs. Home: 349 Heirloom Fort Worth TX 76134-3950 Office: Transport Life Ins Co 714 Main St Fort Worth TX 76102

BRANNON-PEPPAS, LISA, chemical engineer, researcher; b. Houston, Sept. 19, 1962; d. James Graham and Patricia Ann (Hightower) Brannon; m. Nicholas A. Peppas, Aug. 10, 1988. BS, Rice U., 1984; MS, Purdue U., 1986, PhD, 1988. Sr. formulations chemist Eli Lilly & Co., Indpls., 1988-91; pres., founder Biogel Tech., Indpls., 1991—. Author, editor: Absorbent Polymer Technology, 1990; contbg. editor Polymer News, 1989—; contbr. articles to profl. jours. Vol. Indpls. Mus. Art, 1990—, Humane Soc. Indpls., 1990—, Indpls. Zoo, 1994—. Recipient Harold B. Lamport award Biomed. Engring. Soc., 1989. Mem. AIChE (exec. bd. programming coun., dir. materials divsn., chmn. subcom. biomaterials divsn. 1990-93, dir.-at-large food, pharm. and bioengring. divsn. 1992-94, 2nd vice chair materials divsn. 1994-95), Am. Chem. Soc. (membership com. 1990—), Controlled Release Soc. (internat. planning com. 1991, bd. govs. 1992—), Jr. League Indpls. (bd. dirs. 1992-94). Office: Biogel Tech PO Box 681513 Indianapolis IN 46278

BRANSCOMB, ANNE WELLS, communications consultant; b. Statesboro, Ga., Nov. 22, 1928; d. Guy Herbert and Ruby Mae (Hammond) Wells; m. Lewis McAdory Branscomb, Oct. 13, 1951; children: Harvie Hammond, Katharine Capers. BA, Ga. Coll., 1949, U. N.C., 1949; postgrad., London Sch. Econs., 1950; MA, Harvard U., 1951; JD with honors, George Washington, 1962. Bar: D.C. 1962, Colo. 1963, N.Y. 1973, U.S. Supreme Ct. 1972. Rsch. assoc. Pierson, Ball and Dowd, Washington, 1962; law clk. to presiding judge U.S. Dist. Ct., Denver, 1962-63; assoc. Williams & Zook, 1963-66; pvt. practice Boulder, 1966-69; assoc. Arnold and Porter, Washington, 1969-72; communications counsel Teleprompter Corp., N.Y.C., 1973; v.p. Kalba-Bowen Assocs. Inc., communication cons., Cambridge, Mass., 1974-77, chmn. bd., 1977-80, sr. assoc. dir., 1980-82; pres. The Raven Group, Concord, Mass., 1986—; trustee Pacific Telecomm. Coun., 1981-83, 86-93; mem. tech. adv. bd. Dept. Commerce, 1977-81; vis. scholar Yale U. Law, 1981-82; mem. program on info. resources policy Harvard U., 1986—; chmn. program com. Legal Symposium Telecom '87, Internat. Telecomm. Union, 1986-87; bd. dirs. Pub. Interest Radio, 1986-88; adj. prof. internat. law Tufts U., 1987-89; sr. scholar-in-resident Annenberg Sch. Comm. Pub. Policy Ctr. U. Pa., 1994-95. Author: Who Owns Information?, 1994; mem. editl. bd. Info. Soc.; editor: Toward a Law of Global Communications Network; contbg. editor Jour. Comm., 1980-90; contbr. articles to profl. jours. Bd. dirs. Nat. Pub. Radio, 1975-78; vice chmn. Colo. Dem. State Ctrl. Com., 1967-69; del. mem. permanent orgn. com. Dem. Nat. Conv., 1968; trustee, exec. com. Rensselaer Poly. Inst., 1980-89; trustee Telluride Inst., 1994—. Recipient Alumni Achievement award Ga. Coll., 1980; Rotary Found. fellowship, 1950-51; Inaugural fellow Freedom Forum Media Studies Ctr., Columbia U., 1985. Mem. ABA (nat. conf. lawyers and scientists ABA/AAAS 1985-91, chmn. communications com. sci. and tech. sect. 1980-82, chmn. communications law div. 1982-84, mem. coun. and tech. sect. 1981-85), Am. Polit. Sci. Assn., Internat. Inst. Communication, Internat Intercommunications Union (legal symposium organizer 1983, chmn. program com. 1987), Soc. Preservation of First Wives and First Husbands (pres.), Order of Coif, Valkyries, Phi Beta Kappa, Alpha Psi Omega, Pi Gamma Mu.

BRANSFIELD, JOAN, principal. Prin. Sch. St. Mary, Lake Forest, Ill. Recipient Elem. Sch. Recognition award U.S. Dept. Edn., 1989-90. Office: Sch of St Mary 185 E Ill Rd Lake Forest IL 60045

BRANSFIELD, LYNNE KIRKHAM, special education educator; b. N.Y.C., Aug. 11, 1949; d. Donald Francis and Ruth Marie (Hirtreiter) Kirkham; m. Robert Carroll Bransfield, Nov. 11, 1982; children: Douglas Ryan, Craighton Robert, Courtney Lynne. BS in Edn., Seton Hall U., 1971; MEd, Trenton State Tchrs. Coll., 1975; postgrad., U. San Francisco, 1978. Cert. elem. edn. educator, tchr. of handicapped. Urban edn. asst. S.H.U.-South Eighth St. Sch., Newark, 1968-70; tchr. of handicapped North Jersey Tng. Inst., Totowa, 1971-72; tchr. of handicapped Children's Psychiat. Ctr., Eatontown, N.J., 1972-78, tchr./coord. grad. studies, 1974-78; with partial hospitalization program Children's Psychiat. Ctr.- Marlboro State Hosp., Red Bank, N.J., 1976; coord. residential svcs. High Point Ctr., Morganville, N.J., 1978; currently with Therapeutic Cmty. Homes, Children's Behavioral Healthcare, Morganville, N.J.; co-facilitator Riverview Hosp., 1983. Co-dir. day camp for handicapped YMCA, Red Bank, 1976; commr. Boy Scouts of Am., Ocean Township, N.J., 1977; mem. juvenile conf. com. Monmouth County Probation Dept., Middletown, N.J., 1980; cons., participant Mrs. Barbara Bush-Project Literacy, 1998-90; coord. Children in Olympics pub. info. campaign; ednl./legal cons. Hyacinth House, New Brunswick, N.J. Mem. Nat. Assn. Pvt. Schs. for Exceptional Children, Seton Hall Univ. Alumni (chmn. 1991), Kappa Delta Pi. Republican. Home: 4 Jockey Hollow Ct Holmdel NJ 07733

BRANSON, KAREN MARIE, nurse; b. Phila., Aug. 22, 1956; d. Floyd Ralph and Regina (Marter) Banbury; m. John Joseph Branson III, Oct. 23, 1977 (div. 1991); children: John Joseph IV, Katherine Marie; m. Steven Wayne Berry, July 4, 1992. BSN, San Diego State U., 1991. RN, Calif.; EMT, Japan, BCLS EMT; cert. ACLS provider, BLS instr., Post Anesthesia Care Unit. Unit asst. Cooper Med. Ctr., Camden, N.J., 1975-76; pvt. duty nurse aide Nursing Staff, Annapolis, Md., 1977; ward clerk Community Hosp., Chula Vista, Calif., 1979-80; unit asst. Bay Gen. Hosp. ICA, Chulavista, 1985-86; med. asst. Dr. D. Burrows, ob.-gyn., San Diego, 1988-89; RN Scripps, Chula Vista, 1990; ensign nurse corp. Naval Hosp. Camp Pendleton, Oceanside, Calif., 1990-91, Naval Hosp. Camp. Pendleton, Oceanside, 1991-93; clin. cons. 21 Area Br. Med. Clinic, 1993—; mem. edn. and tng. com. Camp Pendleton, 1991—, mem. ward rm. social com., nurse corp. social com., 1991-92, chmn. social com., 1993-94, nurse corp. strategic task force, 1993-94; troop nurse Adult Girl Scout Troop #5053, 1991—; mem. command infection control com Naval Hosp. Camp Pendleton, 1994; interium clinic supr. 21 Area Br. Med. Clinic, 1994. Interviewer Navy Relief Soc., Pensacola, Fla. 1977-79; pres./sec. Helicopter Sq. 8/HS-10, San Diego, 1979-86; fundraiser Atsugi Wives Club, Japan, 1986-88; vol. ARC, Japan, 1986-88. Lt. (j.g.) USN, 1993. Decorated Meritorious Svc. medal; recipient Cert. Appreciation award Dept. Def. Schs., 1987, ARC, Japan, 1987, Alfred award Navy League U.S. Newport County Coun., 1991. Mem. Calif. Nurses Assn., Navy Nurse Corps Social Com, Wardroom Com., Sigma Theta Tau Internat. Republican. Home: 523 Chantel Ct Chula Vista CA 91910-7438 Office: Naval Hosp Camp Pendleton Oceanside CA 92055

BRANSON, MARY LOU, family therapist, military agency administrator; b. Tulsa, June 11, 1932; d. Clarence Leo and Peg (McDonald) Jester; m. Robert K. Branson, Sept. 8, 1956 (div. Dec. 1976); children: Malinda, Scott, Craig. BA, Okla. State U., 1956; MS, Tex. Woman's U., 1981, PhD, 1984. Cert. marriage and family therapist. Claims rep. Social Security Adminstrn., Ohio, La., N.Mex., 1957-63; reconsideration specialist State of Fla. Disability Determinations, Tallahassee, 1975-79; intern Office Families, Washington, 1982; sr. regional employee assistance program counselor Control Data Corp., Dallas, 1983-85; dir. Family Svc. Ctr., Naval Support Activity, Naples, Italy, 1985-87, dep. dir., 1994—; dir. Family Svc. Ctr., Naval Support Activity, Holy Loch, Scotland, 1987-89; dir., dep. dir. Family Svc. Ctr., Naval Support Activity, Dallas, 1989-94; mem. com. single parent families Nat. Council Family Relations, Mpls., 1984-85, co-op edn. bd. Tex. Woman's U., Denton, 1985-86. Author, editor: (book) Tallahassee Coloring Book, 1972. Dir. Cerebral Palsy Nursery Sch., Baton Rouge, 1961; bd. dirs. Diablo Valley Montessori Sch., Lafayette, Calif., 1966; pres. La. State U. Faculty Wives, Baton Rouge, 1962. U. Tulsa scholar, 1950, Tex. Woman's U. scholar, 1980-84; recipient Operation Desert Storm/Desert Shield Spl. Recognition. Mem. Am. Assn. Marriage and Family Therapy (clin.), Nat. Coun. on Family Rels., Internat. Family Therapy Assn., Clan Donald Assn., Kappa Alpha Theta Alumni Club (v.p. 1973). Office: Family Svc Ctr Naples Italy PSC 810 Box 53 FPO AE 09619

BRANSTEAD, ELIZABETH GRACE, workforce management consultant, writer; b. Oakland, Calif., June 26, 1940; d. Robert Beeson and Louise Amelia (Crafts) B.; m. Ralph Wayne Moir, June 8, 1963 (div. Apr. 1991); children: Sara Louise Moir Larasua, Steven Hershey Moir, Christina Elizabeth Moir Harjehausen. BA in English, U. Calif., Berkeley, 1962; MA in English, Boston U., 1963; MA in Edn., Counseling, San Jose State U., 1978. Instr. Boston U., 1963-67, Chabot Valley Coll., Livermore, Calif., 1969-74; cons. Livermore, 1975-78; trainer Lawrence Livermore Nat. Lab., 1978-85, tng. & OD mgr., 1985-89; mgmt. coord. Office of Pres., U. Calif., Oakland, 1989-91; pres. The Branstead Group, Pleasanton, Calif., 1990—; chair Calif. Career Conf., San Jose, 1994. Author: From Downsizing to Recovery, 1994. Pres. Tri Valley Human Resource Assn., Pleasanton, 1994; bd. dirs. Valley Vol. Ctr., Pleasanton, 1986-88, 90-92. Outplacement Inst. fellow, 1994. Mem. Internat. Assn. Career Mgmt. Profls. (bd. dirs. 1990—, editor newsletter Highlighter 1990—). Democrat. Office: Branstead Group 7270 Valleyview Ct Pleasanton CA 94588

BRANTLEY, MARY DAVID, epidemiologist, medical technologist; b. Macon, Ga., Dec. 27, 1951; d. David Hiram and Mary Edwina (Nims) Hogan; m. Walter LaMon Brantley, Aug. 27, 1971 (div. July 1979); children: Leigha Carmen and Kimberly Lauren (twins). BS, Mercer U., 1973; MPH, Emory U., 1989. Registered med. technologist with specialist cert. in immunology. Med. technologist Douglas Gen. Hosp., Douglasville, Ga., 1974-77, Ga. Bapt. Hosp., Atlanta, 1977-78, West Paces Hosp., Atlanta, 1978-79, Cobb Med. Ctr., Austell, Ga., 1979-81, Emory U. Hosp., Atlanta, 1981-87; rsch. specialist III Emory U. Sch. Medicine, Atlanta, 1987-90; project dir. spl. projects Ga. Dept. Human Resources, Atlanta, 1990-91; data mgr. DeKalb County Bd. Health, Decatur, Ga., 1992; project mgr. perinatal epidemiology Ga. Dept. Human Resources, Atlanta, 1992—; cons. Ga. Assn. for Primary Health Care, Atlanta, 1991-92, March of Dimes, Atlanta, Georgians for Children, Atlanta. Layout editor newsletter Ga. Epidemiology Report, 1990—. Recipient Sellars-McCroan award Ga. Dept. Human Resources/Ga. Pub. Health Assn., 1992. Mem. APHA, Am. Soc. Clin. Pathologists, Ga. Pub. Health Assn. Episcopalian. Office: Ga Dept Human Resources Perinatal Epidemiology 2 Peachtree St NW Atlanta GA 30303

BRASEL, JO ANNE, physician; b. Salem, Ill., Feb. 15, 1934; d. Gerald Nolan and Ruby Rachel (Rich) B. BA, U. Colo., 1956; MD, U. Colo., 1959. Diplomate Am. Bd. Pediatrics, Am. Bd. Pediatric-Endocrinology. Pediatric intern, resident Cornell U. Med. Coll.-N.Y. Hosp., N.Y.C., 1959-62; pediatric endocrine fellow Johns Hopkins U. Sch. Medicine, Balt., 1962-65, asst. prof. pediatrics, 1965-68; asst. prof. then assoc. prof. pediatrics Cornell U. Med. Coll., N.Y.C., 1969-72; assoc. prof. then prof. pediatrics Columbia U. Coll. Physicians and Surgeons, N.Y.C., 1972-79, asst. dir. Inst. Human Nutrition, 1972-79; prof. pediatrics Harbor-UCLA Med. Ctr., UCLA Sch. Medicine, 1979—, program dir. Gen. Clin. Research Ctr., 1979-93, prof. medicine, 1980—; mem. adv. com. FDA, Rockville, Md., 1971-75; mem. nutrition study sect. NIH, Bethesda, Md., 1974-78; mem. select panel for promotion of child health HEW, Washington, 1979-80; mem. life scis. D adv. screening com. Fulbright-Hays program, Washington, 1981-84, digestive disease and nutrition grant review group NIADDK, 1985-89, U.S. Govt. Task Force on Women, Minorities and the Handicapped in Sci. and Tech., 1987-89. Recipient Rsch. Career Devel. award NIH, 1973-77, Irma T. Hirschl Trust Career Sci. award, 1974-79, Sr. Fulbright Sabbatical Rsch. award, 1980. Mem. Soc. Pediatric Rsch. (sec.-treas. 1973-77, pres.-elect 1977-78, pres. 1978-79), Am. Fed. Clin. Rsch., Endocrine Soc., Am. Soc. Clin. Nutrition, Am. Inst. Nutrition, Western Assn. Physicians, Lawson Wilkins Pediatric Endocrine Soc. (bd. dirs., mem. bd. 1972-74, pres.-elect 1991-92, pres. 1992-93), Am. Pediatric Soc., Assn. Program Dirs. for Gen. Clin. Rsch. Ctrs. (pres. 1982-83), N.Am. Assn. for Study Obesity, Western Soc. Pediatric Research, Phi Beta Kappa, Alpha Omega Alpha. Office: Harbor-UCLA Med Ctr PO Box 446 1000 W Carson St Torrance CA 90509-2910

BRASH, SALLY MILLER, theater educator, playwright; b. Donora, Pa., Jan. 18, 1911; d. Mose and Rachel Leah (Kwass) Miller; m. J. Eugene, June 27, 1934 (dec. 1966); 1 child, Edward. BA, Chatam Coll., 1932; cert. in TV, U. Pa., 1949. Asst. prof. Harcum Jr. Coll., Bryn Mawr, Pa., 1969—; dramatic dir. Children's Theatre, Phila., Stevens Sch., Phila., K.I. Temple, Phila., Forest Acres Camp, Fryeburg, Maine, Plays for Living, Phila., Penn Charter, Phila.; cons., presenter workshops Nat. Headstart, 1965-69, 87—; tchr. in creative drama various elem. and preschs. Author: Teaching Children Through Drama, 1988, (plays) If Books Could Talk, 1944, Five Tested Plays, 1944, Hanukah Pickets, 1945, The Magic Book Shop, 1946; dir. Plays For Living. Advisor Allen's Lane Art Ctr., Phila., Plays for Living, Family Svc. Home: 440 W Sedgwick St # 123D Philadelphia PA 19119-3045 Office: Harcum Jr Coll Bryn Mawr PA 19010 also: 3940 E Timrod St # 166 Tucson AZ 85711

BRASHEAR, DIANE LEE, marital and sex therapist; b. Parkersburg, W.Va., July 21, 1933; d. Ralph Elijah and Dorothea Esther (McDade) Blake; m. Richard Evers Brashear, Aug. 31, 1956; children: Allison, Meredith Kay. BS in Social Adminstrn., Ohio State U., 1955, MSW, 1957; PhD, Purdue U., 1971. Diplomate Am. Bd. Sexology. Chief social worker Ind. Sch. for Blind, Indpls., 1965-68; asst. prof. social work Ind. U., Indpls., 1970-72; dir. Brashear Ctr., Inc., Indpls., 1972-84; news reporter marriage & family coun. Sta. WTHR-TV, Indpls., 1980—; assoc. prof. ob-gyn. Ind. U. Sch. Medicine, Indpls., 1984—; vis. prof. Purdue U., West Lafayette, Ind., 1971-72; bd. dirs. Alan Guttmacher Inst., National, 1985-93. Author: Social Worker as Sex Educator, 1977; editor Indpls. Mo., 1975-91; contbr. articles, book chpts. and video tapes. Pres. Planned Parenthood Greater Indpls., 1985-87; bd. dirs. Planned Parenthood Fedn. Am., 1983-88, 1991-93; vice chmn. Greater Indpls. Progress Community, 1989-92, United Way, Indpls, 1989—; pres. Community Svc. Coun., Indpls., 1989-91. Recipient Pauline Selby award, Big Sisters Greater Indpls., 1986, Leadership award YWCA, Ind., 1986, Disting. Svc. award Planned Parenthood Cen. Ind., 1991. Mem. Am. Assn. Marriage & Family, Am. Coll. Ob/Gyn, Am. Soc. Psychosomatic Ob/Gyn, Soc. Scientific Study Sex, Soc. Sex Therapy & Rsch. Office: Ind U 550 University Blvd #5202 Indianapolis IN 46202-5203

BRASSELL, ROSELYN STRAUSS, lawyer; b. Shreveport, La., Feb. 19, 1930; d. Herman Carl and Etelka (McMullan) Strauss. BA, La. State U., 1949; JD, UCLA, 1962. Bar: Calif. 1963. Atty. CBS, Los Angeles, 1962-68, sr. atty., 1968-76, asst. gen. atty., 1976-83, broadcast counsel, 1983-91; pvt. practice law L.A., 1991—; instr. TV Prodn. Bus. and Legal Aspects, UCLA Extension, 1992. Co-writer: Life After Death for the California Celebrity, 1985; bd. editors U. Calif. Law Rev., 1960-62. Named Angel of Distinction Los Angeles Cen. City Assn., 1975. Mem. Calif. Bar Assn., L.A. County Bar Assn. (exec. com. 1970—, sect. chmn. 1980-81), Beverly Hills Bar Assn., L.A. Copyright Soc. (treas. 1977-78, sec. 1978-79, pres. 1981-82), Am. Women in Radio and TV (nat. dir.-at-large 1971-73, nat. pub. affairs chmn. 1977-78, Merit award So. Calif. chpt. 1989), NATAS, Women in Film, Orange County World Affairs Coun., U. Calif. Law Alumni Assn. (dir. 1971-74), Order of Coif, Alpha Xi Delta, Phi Alpha Delta. Republican. Home: 33331 Gelidium Cir Monarch Beach CA 92629-4451 Office: 645 Wilcox Ave Ste 1-D Los Angeles CA 90004-1121

BRASSFIELD, PATRICIA ANN, psychologist; b. Lebanon, Oreg., Apr. 22; d. John James and Mabel Dolores (Scott) Smith; children: Byron Scott, Robert Kent, Lisa Michelle Best. Student, U. Oreg.; BS, Oreg. State U.; MEd, U. Hawaii, 1974; PhD, U.S. Internat. U., 1980. Lic. psychologist, Hawaii, Ariz.; cert. substance abuse counselor, Hawaii, cert. hypnotherapist, marriage, family and child counselor, Calif., nat. cert. addiction counselor II. Family counselor Psychiat. Svcs., Honolulu, 1974-78, San Diego Ctr. for Psychotherapy, 1979-82; unit team mgr. Oahu Community Corrections, Honolulu, 1982-83; sch. counselor Kalaheo & Moanalua High Schs., Oahu, Hawaii, 1983-85; dir. Waipahu (Hawaii) Community Counseling Ctr., 1985-87; forensic psychologist criminal ct. Hawaii Dept. Health, Honolulu, 1987-91; sch. psychologist San Diego City Schs., 1981-82; family counselor Fairlight, Inc., Honolulu, 1983-84; clin. psychologist, pvt. practice, Oahu and Maui, Hawaii, 1982—; cons. United Airlines, Honolulu, 1989—, Sex Abuse Intervention, Wailuku, Maui, 1990—, Family Ct., Wailuku, 1990—. Contbr. articles to profl. jours. Mem. APA, Nat. Assn. Drug and Alcohol Counselors, Mensa. Office: 99-209 Moanalua Rd Ste 314 Aiea HI 96701-4042 also Office: Ste 225 1063 E Main Maui HI 96793

BRASWELL, JACKIE TERRY, medical, surgical nurse; b. Raleigh, N.C., Oct. 15, 1961; d. Charles Thurman and Laura (Russell) Terry; 1 child, Matthew Russell Braswell. BSN, U. N.C., 1983. Cert. ACLS, med.-surgical nursing. Staff nurse orthopedics/neurology unit Wake County Med. Ctr., Raleigh, staff nurse cardiac telemetry step-down unit; asst. head nurse orthopedics unit Raleigh Community Hosp., staff nurse telemetry unit; charge nurse vent unit IHS, Raleigh, 1993—. Mem. AACN, ANA, N.C. Nurses Assn.

BRASWELL, JANET LYNN, graphic designer; b. Bay City, Tex., June 16, 1965; d. James Lonnie Sr. and Cora Louise (Morgan) Jackson; m. James Anderson Braswell Jr., Apr. 5, 1984. A in Visual Comm., Art Inst. Houston, 1986. Graphic designer Houston Ind. Sch. Dist., 1986-89, Avon Behren, San Antonio, 1989, Am. Cancer Soc., Austin, Tex., 1989—; creative dir. JB Prodns., Austin, 1994; graphic designer Lucila Dance Prodns., Austin, 1991-93, One Am. Massage, Austin, 1993, Chain Malle Fashions, Austin, 1992-93. Editor Austin Bellydance Assn. newsletter, 1992-93. Home: 1702 Ferguson Ln Austin TX 78754 Office: Am Cancer Soc 2433 Ridgepoint Dr A Austin TX 78754

BRATCHER, CARLA ELIZABETH, obstetrician-gynecologist; b. Wichita, Kans., Sept. 18, 1942; d. Carl E. and Armilda Elizabeth (Salmans) Dillon; m. Carl E. Bratcher III, Apr. 9, 1983. Student, U. Wash., 1960-62; BS, U. Fla., 1966; MD, U. Pa., 1979. Diplomate Am. Bd. Ob-Gyn. Rsch. technician Nat. Cancer Inst.-NIH, Bethesda, Md., 1967-73, Wistar Inst., Phila., 1973-75; ob-gyn intern Madigan Army Med. Ctr., Tacoma, 1979-80, resident in ob-gyn, 1980-83; chief ambulatory care svc. ob-gyn. 2d Gen. Hosp., Landstuhl, Fed. Republic Germany, 1984-87; pvt. practice, Grand Prairie, Tex., 1988-89; pvt. practice ob/gyn. Redmond, Oreg., 1990—; vol. instr. dept. ob-gyn Dallas-Ft. Worth Med. Ctr., 1988-89. Maj. M.C., U.S. Army, 1979-87. Fellow Am. Coll. Obstetricians and Gynecologists; mem. AMA, AAUW, Oreg. Med. Assn., Am. Med. Women's Assn. Democrat. Office: Redmond Ob/Gyn 1228 NW Canal Blvd Redmond OR 97756-1335

BRATHWAITE, HARRIET LOUISA, nursing educator; b. Rye, N.Y., Aug. 28, 1931; d. James Pierce and Mattie (Collins) Bowling; m. Leroy L. Brathwwaite, Feb. 18, 1950; 1 child, Helene Ann Brathwaite Ward. AAS in Nursing, Bklyn. Coll., 1959; BSN, L.I. U., 1965; postgrad., Tchrs. Coll. of Columbia U., 1965-68; MSN, Adelphia U., 1973. Staff nurse Kings County Hosp., Bklyn., 1959; head nurse City Hosp. at Elmhurst, Queens, N.Y., 1959-62; instr. Kings County Hosp. Sch. Nursing, 1963-65, Downstate Med. Ctr. Sch. Nursing, 1965-69; nurse community mental health South Beach Psychiat. Ctr., 1969-73; cons. psychiat. nursing service HEW and N.Y. State Health Dept., Albany, 1973-74; chief of service Creedmoor Psychiat. Ctr., Queens Village, N.Y., 1974-87; asst. prof. nursing L.I. U., 1987-92. Co-leader Allied Dems., Jamaica, N.Y., 1959-62; bd. dirs. South Queens Dems., Howard Beach, N.Y.; mem. adv. bd. Transitional Services, Queens, 1983-85. Mem. AAUW, NAACP, ANA, Nat. Black Nurses Assn. (chmn. legis. com. Queens chpt. 1981—, Cert. of Appreciation 1989), N.Y. State Nurses Assn. (dist. 14, coun. on legis. 1990—, trustee Polit. Action Com. 1991—, 25 Yr. Membership award 1986, Legis. award 1988, Ruth W. Harper award for Disting. Svc. 1991), 100 Black Women of L.I., Knickerbocker Club (chmn. fin. and scholarship com.), Chi Eta Phi, Kappa Eta. Home: PO Box 1841 10 Cuffee Dr Sag Harbor NY 11963-0064

BRATHWAITE, MELLISSA ANNETTE, radio announcer, producer; b. Bklyn., Aug. 2, 1961; d. Erskine and Virginia (Higgins) B. BBA, Howard U., 1985, postgrad., 1991—. Mgmt. asst. Sta. WHMM-TV, 1980-82; mgmt. asst., assoc. producer Sta. WHUR, Washington, 1982-85; mgmt. asst. Sta. WHMM-TV, 1980-82, Sta. WBLS/WLIB, N.Y.C., 1983, Sta. NBC/WKYS, Washington, 1985; announcer, engr. Sta. WOL, Washington, 1985; mktg. rep. Diaspora Records, Washington, 1985-86; music dir., announcer, engr. Sta. WYCB, Washington, 1985-87; promotions rep. A&M/Word Records, Washington, 1986-87; producer, announcer, engr. Sta. WOL, 1987—; asst. community affairs dir. Sta. WHUR-FM, Washington, 1990—; bd. engr. Sta. WAVA-Radio, 1992—; radio monitor Video Monitoring Services, Washington, 1986. Author, publisher: Sunshine: A Collection of Poetry, 1985. Counselor Cath. Charities, Washington, 1986; counselor/recruiter Nat. Council on Negro Women, Washington, 1986; adv. bd. mem. SPECTRUM: Cobra Assocs., 1984; coord. Just Say No To Drugs program YMCA, vol. Big Sister Growin'Up program, intergeneration program; vocal minister, eucharistic minister St. Augustine Gospel Choir; mem. N.Y. Mission Soc., Black Women in Ministry, 1991-92; aerobic instr. Roman Catholic.

BRATTAIN, ARLENE JANE CLARK, interior designer; b. Phila., July 27, 1938; d. Franklin Corning Clark and Nora May Robertson; children: Kathy, Kurt, Karen, David. Cert. in interior design, N.Y. Sch. Interior Design, 1975; BS, U. Minn., 1986. Exec. United Way, Mpls., 1980; interior designer AB Interiors, Minnetonka, Minn., 1982—; pvt. practice color analyst, Minnetonka, 1984—; cons. showroom Rollin B. Child Tile, Plymouth, Minn., 1985; interior designer Room & Bd. Stores, Minnetonka, 1985-86. Designer Window Fashions mag., 1988—, Am. Soc. Interior Designers Showcase Home, 1987, Showcase Home for March of Dimes, 1988, Showcase Vignette, 1989. Trainer dist. Camp Fire Girls, Minnetonka, 1967-78; trainer, leader Boy Scouts Am., Mpls., 1967-80; pres. PTA, Minnetonka, 1970; pres. Music Boosters, Minnetonka, 1976-84. Recipient Silver Fawn award Boy Scouts Am., 1973. Mem. Am. Soc. Interior Designers (profl.), Internat. Furnishings and Design Assn. (exec. 1988—), Nat. Trust for Hist. Preservation, Mensa.

BRATTON, IDA FRANK, mathematics educator; b. Glasgow, Ky., Aug. 31, 1933; d. Edmund Bates and Robbie Davis (Hume) Button; m. Robert Franklin Bratton, June 20, 1954; 1 son, Timothy Andrew. B.A., Western Ky.

U., 1959, M.A., 1962. Cert. secondary tchr., Ky. Tchr. math. and sci. Gottschalk Jr. High Sch., Louisville, 1959-65; tchr. math. Iroquois High Sch., Louisville, 1965-79; tchr. Waggener High Sch., Louisville, 1979—, chair math. dept. co-chair sch. based decision making coun. Waggener High Sch. Mem. NEA, Ky. Edn. Assn., Jefferson County Tchrs. Assn., AAUW. Democrat. Methodist. Avocations: travel, needle crafts. Home: 304 Paddington Ct Louisville KY 40222-5541 Office: Waggener High Sch 330 S Hubbards Ln Louisville KY 40207-4099

BRAUER, GWENDOLYN GAIL, real estate agent; b. Middletown, Ohio; d. Robert J. and Mary M. (Kurry) Flynn; m. William H. Brauer Jr., Oct. 4, 1986; 1 child, John. CFP. Sales assoc. Better Homes Realty, Fairfax County, Va., 1976-81, Town & Country Properties, Fairfax County, 1981-84, ReMax Xecutex Real Estate, Fairfax County, 1984—. Mem. Nat. Assn. Realtors (cert. residential specialist, Million Dollar Sales Club 1980—), Employee Relocation Coun. (cert. relocation profl.), Internat. Bd. CFPs, No. Va. Assn. Realtors (Top Producers Club 1985—), Va. Assn. Realtors, Remax 100 Club (Hall of Fame 1994—). Home: 12021 Popes Head Rd Fairfax VA 22030-5828 Office: ReMax Xecutex Real Estate 2911 Hunter Mill Rd Ste 101 Oakton VA 22124

BRAULT, G(AYLE) LORAIN, healthcare executive; b. Chgo., Jan. 3, 1944; d. Theodore Frank and Victoria Jean (Pribyl) Hahn; m. Donald R. Brault, Apr. 29, 1971; 1 child, Kevin David. AA, Long Beach City Coll., 1963; BS, Calif. State U.-Long Beach, 1973, MS, 1977. RN, Calif. Dir. nursing Canyon Gen. Hosp., Anaheim, Calif., 1973-76; dir. faculty critical care masters degree program Calif. State U., Long Beach, 1976-79; regional dir. nursing and support svcs. Western region Am. Med. Internat., Anaheim, Calif., 1979-83; v.p. Hosp. Home Care Corp. Am., Santa Ana, Calif., 1983-85; pres. Hosp. Home Health Care Agy. Calif., Torrance, 1986-92; v.p. Hosp. Coun. So. Calif., L.A., 1993—; invited lectr. China Nurses Assn., 1983; cons. AMI, Inc., Saudi Arabia, 1983; advisor dept. grad. nursing Calif. State U., L.A., 1988, advisor Nursing Inst., 1990-91; guest lectr. dept. pub. health UCLA, 1986-87; assoc. clin. prof. U. So. Calif., 1988-93; advisor RN Times, Nurseweek, 1988—. Contbr. articles to profl. jours., chpts. to books. Commr. HHS, Washington, 1988. HEW advanced nurse tng. grantee, 1978. Mem. Women in Health Adminstrn. (sec. 1989, v.p. 1990), Nat. Assn. Home Care, Am. Orgn. Nursing Execs., Calif. Assn. Health Svcs. at Home (task force chmn. 1988, bd. dirs. 1988-93, chmn. bd. dirs. 1990-93), Calif. League Nursing (bd. sec. 1983, program chmn. 1981-82), Am. Coll. Health Care Execs., ASAE, AONE, Phi Kappa Phi. Republican. Methodist. Home: 1032 E Andrews Dr Long Beach CA 90807-2406

BRAUN, EUNICE HOCKSPEIER, author, religious order executive, lecturer; b. Alta Vista, Iowa; d. George Phillip and Lydia (Reinhart) Hockspeier; student Gates Coll., 1932-34, Coe Coll., 1937-39, Northwestern U., 1944-47; m. Leonard James Braun, May 29, 1937. Freelance writer for mags., newspapers, 1947-52; bus. mgr. Baha'i Publishing Trust, Wilmette, Ill., 1952-55, mng. dir., 1955-71; internat. news editor Baha'i News, 1952-70; tchr. Baha'i schs., Alaska, Can., Europe and U.S., 1958—; lectr. Baha'i Faith in U.S., Central Am., Europe, Africa, Asia, 1953—; cons. Baha'i Pub. Trust, New Delhi, India, 1972; mem. aux. bd. Continental Bd. Counselors, Baha'i Faith in the Ams., 1972-86. Mem. Nat. League Am. Pen Women, Baha'i Faith, Iota Sigma Epsilon. Author: Know Your Baha'i Literature, 1959; The Dawn of World Peace, 1963; Baha'u'llah: His Call to the Nations, 1967; From Strength to Strength, Half Century of the Formative Age of the Baha'i Faith, 1978; A Crown of Beauty, 1982; The March of the Institutions, 1984; A Reader's Guide: The Development of Baha'i Literature in English, 1986; From Vision to Victory, 1993; contbr. essays to Baha'i World, Internat. Record. Home: 1025 Forestview Ln Glenview IL 60025-4433

BRAUN, LILIAN JACKSON, writer. Editor Detroit Free Press, until 1978. Author: The Cat Who Could Read Backwards, 1966, The Cat Who Ate Danish Modern, 1968, The Cat Who Turned On And Off, 1968, The Cat Who Saw Red, 1986, The Cat Who Played Brahms, 1987, The Cat Who Played Post Office, 1987, The Cat Who Knew Shakespeare, 1988, The Cat Who Sniffed Glue, 1988, The Cat Who Had Fourteen Tales, 1988, The Cat Who Went Underground, 1989, The Cat Who Talked to Ghosts, 1990, The Cat Who Lived High, 1990, The Cat Who Knew A Cardinal, 1991, The Cat Who Wasn't There, 1992, The Cat Who Moved A Mountain, 1992, The Cat Who Went Into The Closet, 1993, The Cat Who Came to Breakfast, 1994, The Cat Who Blew the Whistle, 1995. Office: Blanche C Gregory Inc 2 Tudor Pl New York NY 10017*

BRAUN, MARY LUCILE DEKLE (LUCY BRAUN), therapist, consultant, counselor; b. Tampa, Fla.; d. Guthrie J. and Lucile (Culpepper) Dekle; children: John Ryan, Matthew Joseph, Jeffrey William, Douglas Edwin. AB, Brenau Coll.; MA, U. Cen. Fla.; EdD, U. Fla. Cert. ins. rehab. specialist; lic. mental health counselor; lic. marriage and family therapist. Coord. Orange County Child Abuse Prevention, Orlando, Fla., 1983-88; cons. Displaced Homemaker Program, Orlando, 1989—, DCS, Oviedo, Fla., 1990-92; adj. prof. U. Ctrl. Fla., Orlando, 1989—; clin. dir. Response, Sexual Abuse Treatment Program, 1993—; mem. adv. bd. Fla. Hosp. Women's Ctr., Orlando, 1989—; bd. dirs. Parent Resource Ctr., Orlando, Children with Attention Deficit Disorders, Orlando, 1989—. Author: Someone Heard, 1987, Humor Us Soup, 1989; contbg. author: Death from Child Abuse, 1986. Sustaining mem. Jr. League of Orlando and Winter Park, Fla., 1989—. Program recipient Community Svc. award Walt Disney World, 1987. Mem. ACA, Fla. Counseling Assn., Nat. Bd. Cir. Counselors, Phi Kappa Phi, Kappa Delta Pi, Chi Sigma Iota.

BRAUN, VIRGINIA VICKERS, publications professional; b. Little Falls, N.Y., Nov. 22, 1947; d. Harry Dan and Frances (Steele) Vickers; m. Eric R. Braun, Mar. 26, 1971; children: Eric Daniel, Alexander Crockett. BA in English, St. Lawrence U., 1969; MJ, U. Mont., 1984. Features editor The Lebanon (Tenn.) Democrat, 1974-78; editorial asst. U.S. Forest Svc., Missoula, Mont., 1978-80; news writer U. Mont., Missoula, 1981-83, publs. editor, 1983-89, publs. mgr., 1989—. Editor mags. including The Montanan, 1983-90, Vision, 1984-90. Recipient 1st place Lifestyles, Tenn. Press Assn., 1976, 77, 78, 2d place, 1975, 3d place U. Network Pub., 1984, 1st place Coun. for Advancement and Support of Edn., 1987. Mem. Missoula C. of C. (bd. dirs. conv. and visitors bur. 1989-92), Missoula Bus. Women's Network. Home: 4425 Duncan Dr Missoula MT 59802-3301 Office: U Mont 321 Brantly Hall 317 Brantly Hall Missoula MT 59812

BRAUNSTEIN, DIANE KAREN, state agency administrator; b. Bklyn., Feb. 20, 1956; d. Elliott Bernard and Barbara (Stadin) B. Grad. in polit. sci., Kenyon Coll., 1977. Constituent aide Congressman Bill Green, N.Y.C., 1978; legis. aide Congressman Bill Green, Washington, 1979-80; social ins. planning specialist Social Security Adminstrn., Balt., 1981-84; staff asst. soc. security subcom. U.S. House Ways and Means Com., Washington, 1983; legis. analyst Office of Asst. Sec. for Legislation HHS, Washington, 1984-86, 88-89, acting dep. asst. sec. for human svc. legislation Office of Asst. Sec. Legislature, 1990; Congl. affairs advisor Social Security Adminstrn., Washington, 1987-88; dep. staff dir. U.S. Senate Com. on Aging, Washington, 1990-91; dir. rsch. and policy devel. White House Conf. on Aging, Washington, 1981-92; dir. Mich. Office of Svcs. to Aging, Lansing, 1993—; mem. steering com. Inst. Gerantology, Wayne State U., Detroit, 1993—. Contbr. articles to profl. jours. With goodwill exchange mission Konrad Adenhaver Found., B'nai Brith, Germany, 1994. Mem. AARP (hon.), Nat. Acad. Social Ins. Office: Office of Svcs to the Aging PO Box 30036 Lansing MI 48909

BRAVO, ROSE MARIE, retail executive; b. N.Y.C., Jan. 13, 1951; d. Biagio and Anna (Bazzano) LaPila; m. Charles Emil Bravo, June 13, 1971 (div. 1977); m. William Selkirk Jackey, Oct. 9, 1983. B.A. in English, Fordham U., 1971. Exec. trainee, dept. mgr. A&S, Bklyn., 1971-74; assoc. buyer Macy's, N.Y.C., 1974-75, buyer, 1975-79, councilor, 1979-80, adminstr., 1980-84, group v.p., 1984-85, sr. v.p. 1985-88; chmn., chief exec. officer, I. Magnin, San Francisco, 1988-92; pres., dir. merchandising Saks & Co., Inc., N.Y.C., 1992—. Chmn. retail com. March of Dimes Birth Defects Found., 1980-81. Office: Saks & Co Inc 12 E 49th St 19th Fl New York NY 10017*

BRAWER, CATHERINE COLEMAN, foundation executive, public affairs director, museum curator; b. N.Y.C., Feb. 19, 1943; d. Joseph A. and Beatrice R. Coleman; m. Robert A. Brawer, Sept. 7, 1962; children: Christopher Paul, Nicholas Andrew. BA, Sarah Lawrence Coll., 1964; MA in Art History, NYU, 1966. Publicity coord. Evehjem Mus. Art, Madison, Wis., 1970-75, curator Liebman Collection, 1974-75; mktg. mgr. Maidenform, Inc., N.Y.C., 1975-78; ind. curator N.Y.C., 1978; v.p. Ida and William Rosenthal Found., N.Y.C., 1981-90, pres., 1990—; dir. pub. affairs Maidenform Inc., N.Y.C., 1990—; curator Maidenform Mus.; dir. Maidenform, Inc., N.Y.C., 1970—; trustee Katonah (N.Y.) Mus. Art, 1982—, Ind. Curators, Inc., N.Y.C., 1989—, Inst. Fine Arts, NYU, 1993—. Author: (catalogues) The Auspicious Dragon in Chinese Decorative Arts, 1978, Many Trails: Indians of the Lower Hudson Valley, 1983, Trade Winds: The Lure of the China Trade, 1985; (book) Making Their Mark: Women Artist Move into the Mainstream 1970-85, 1989, Chinese Export Porcelain from the Liebman Porcelain Collection, 1992. Mem. Am. Ceramic Circle N.Y., Regional Assn. Grantmakers (mem. com. 1990-91), Art Table N.Y.

BRAWLEY, MARGARET WACKER, communications executive; b. Washington, Dec. 12, 1951; d. Warren Ernest Clyde and Ann Romeyn (MacMillan) W.; m. Richard Warren Brawley, Feb. 26, 1994. BA, Carnegie Mellon U., 1974. Promotion specialist Millipore Corp., Bedford, Mass., 1974-77, dir. comm. Lab. Products div., 1981-82, corporate comm. mgr., 1982-88, human resources project mgr., 1989-93, sr. acct. mgr. bioscience divsn., 1993-94, mgr. tech. publs. and life sci. promotion lab., health care products divsn., 1994—; dir. advt. IVAC div. Eli Lilly Co., San Diego, 1977-79, dist. sales mgr., L.A., 1979-80; bus. unit mgr. Sage div. Orion Rsch., Cambridge, Mass., 1980-81; counselor to handicapped individuals in bus. Mem. Boston Computer Soc. Democrat. Episcopalian. Avocations: painting, sewing. Home: The Brook House Atrium 99 Pond Ave Unit 322D Brookline MA 02146-7129 Office: Millipore Corp 80 Ashby Rd Bedford MA 01730-2271

BRAXTON, TONI, popular musician. Albums include Toni Braxton, 1993; contbr. Boomerang soundtrack, 1992. Recipient Grammy award Best Female R&B Vocal, 1994, 95. Office: Arista Records care of LaFace 6 W 57th St New York NY 10019*

BRAY, CAROLYN SCOTT, educational administrator; b. Childress, Tex., May 19, 1938; d. Alonzo Lee and Frankie Lucile (Wood) Scott; m. John Graham Bray, Jr., Aug. 24, 1957 (div. May 1980); children: Caron Lynn, Kimberly Anne, David William. BS, Baylor U., 1960; MEd, Hardin-Simmons U., 1981; PhD, U. North Tex., 1985. Registered med. technologist. Rsch. asst. Fairleigh-Dickinson Rsch. Ctr., Hardin-Simmons U., Abilene, Tex., 1979; adj. prof. bus. communication Hardin-Simmons U., 1981-84; dir. career placement, 1979-82, assoc. dean students, 1982-85; assoc. dir. career planning and placement U. North Tex., Denton, 1985—, adj. prof. higher edn. adminstrn., mem. Mentor program; cons. univs. Organizer, mem. Abilene Women's Network, 1982-85; mem. Abilene Art Mus., 1975-86, Abilene Philharm. Assn., 1969-79; mem. scholarship com. U. North Tex. League for Profl. Women, v.p. 1988-89; mem. com. Honors Day U. North Tex., 1991-95; mem. pers. com. First Bapt. Ch., 1992-95; bd. dirs. Irving Christian Counseling, Inc., chmn. persl. com. and nom. com.; active Edn. Focus Group for Denton I.S.D.. Mem. Assn. Sch., Coll. and Univ. Staffing (bd. dirs. 1989-94, chair. mem. com. 1988-90, conf. planning com. 1988-90, treas. 1994-95), S.W. Placement Assn. (vice chair ops. 1992, 93, chair ann. conf. registration, 1991, 92, membership com. 1993—), Tex. MBA Consortium (treas. 1993-95, co-chmn. 1995—), Tex. Assn. Sch., Coll. and Univ. Staffing (v.p. 1986-87, pres. 1987-88), Coll. Placement Coun., North Cen. Tex. Assn. Sch. Pers. Adminstrs. and Univ. Placement Pers. (pres. 1987-88, sec. 1988—), Tex. Assn. Coll. and Univ. Student Pers. Adminstrs., Denton C. of C. (pub. rels. com., chair new mem. orientation), Dallas Human Resources Mgmt. Assn., Leadership Denton (co-dir. curriculum 1988-89, chair membership selection com. 1990, 93, 94, steering com. 1990, 93, 94, program com. chmn. alumni assn. 1991-92), Friend of the Symphony, Denton Cultural Arts Assn., U. North Tex. Alumni Assn. (bd. dirs. 1990-93), Pi Lambda Theta, Kappa Kappa Gamma (chpt. advisor, chmn. adv. bd. Zeta Sigma chpt. 1987-93). Republican. Avocations: skiing, tennis, golf, reading. Office: U North Tex PO Box 13378 Denton TX 76203-6378

BRAY, JOAN, state legislator; b. Sept. 16, 1945; m. Carl Hoagland; 1 child, Noel, Kolby. BA, Southwestern U.; MEd, U. Mass. Former tchr., sch. counselor, former dist. dir. for Congresswoman Joan Kelly Horn; mem. Mo. Ho. of Reps. Bd. dirs. Univ. City Residential Svc. Mem. PTO, Nat. Womens Polit. Caucus. Democrat. Home: 7120 Washington Ave Saint Louis MO 63130 Office: Mo Ho of Reps State Capitol Jefferson City MO 65101*

BRAY, NANCY A., oceanographic administrator. Dir., Scripps Inst. of Oceanography U. of Calif. San Diego, La Jolla, Calif. Office: Univ of Calif San Diego Scripps Inst Of Oceano La Jolla CA 92093*

BRAY, SHARON ANN, management company executive; b. Long Beach, Calif., June 12, 1944; d. George Knight and Oweta Izeda (Little) B.; m. Larry Dwane Collins, Jan. 29, 1967 (dec. July 1981); children: Elinor F., Claire J. BA in Sociology, San Jose (Calif.) State U., 1967; MEd, Mt. St. Vincent U., Halifax, Nova Scotia, 1981; EdD in Applied Psychology, U. Toronto, Can., 1986. Cert. tchr., Calif. Tchr. San Jose, Ottawa and Halifax Schs., 1967-80; psychologist Halifax County Sch. Bd., 1980-83; instr. St. Mary's U., Halifax, 1981-83; pvt. cons. Toronto, 1985-86; sr. cons. Stevenson, Kellogg, Ernst & Whinney, Toronto, 1985-86; dir. profl. svcs. Right Assocs., Toronto and Cupertino, Calif., 1988-90; v.p., dir. profl. svcs. Lee Hecht Harrison, San Jose, Calif., 1990-91, sr. v.p., gen. mgr., 1991—, regional sr. v.p., 1994—; disting. vis. lectr. Calif. Polytech. U., San Luis Obispo, 1987; keynote speaker Calif. Career Devel. Conf., Calif., 1992. Author: This Way to Canada, 1978; contbr. articles to profl. jours. Bd. dirs. Young Peoples' Theatre, Toronto, Ont., 1988-90, TheatreWorks, Palo Alto, Calif., 1990-92, Project Hired, Sunnyvale, Calif., 1992—. Mem. Am. Assn. Counseling and Devel., Calif. Career Devel. Assn., No. Calif. Human Resources Coun., Soc. for Human Resources Mgmt. Democrat. Methodist. Office: Lee Hecht Harrison 1740 Technology Dr # 400 San Jose CA 95110-1315

BRAYMAN, JEANNIE SUE, English educator; b. Omaha, Mar. 20, 1949; d. Guy M. and Lela R. (Russell) Blakey; m. John M. Brayman, Nov. 28, 1969 (dec. July 1990). BA summa cum laude, U. Nebr., 1971; MA in English, Creighton U., 1973. Lifetime teaching cert., Nebr., Iowa. Tchr. Plattsmouth (Nebr.) Community Schs., 1973-76, Metro Tech. C.C., Omaha, 1976-78, Creighton Prep. Sch., Omaha, 1978—; various offices Met. English Lang. Arts Assn., Omaha, 1977-87; speaker in field. Contbr. articles to profl. jours. Recipient grant for summer study Nebr. Writing Project, 1978, grant Nat. Endowment for Humanities, 1991; named Outstanding Young Educator, Omaha Jaycees, 1981, Nebr. Jaycees, 1982. Mem. Nat. Coun. Tchrs. English, Nebr. Coun. Tchrs. English, Nebr. Assn. for the Gifted. Office: Creighton Preparatory Sch 7400 Western Ave Omaha NE 68114-1833

BRAZA, MARY KATHRYN, lawyer; b. Toledo, Aug. 15, 1956; d. Paul Albert and Mary Elizabeth (Pfeiffer) Mullenhoff; m. James Edward Braza, Oct. 9, 1982; children: Laura Jeanne, Carolyn Ann. AB, Cornell U., 1978, JD, 1981. Bar: Tex., 1981, Wis., 1982. Assoc. Fulbright & Jaworski, Houston, 1981-82; ptnr. Foley & Lardner, Milw., 1982—; instr. Nat. Inst. Trial Advocacy, Chgo., 1989-92; vis. lectr. U. Wis. Law Sch., Madison, 1992—. Mem. Wis. Task Force on Injury Prevention for Children, Madison, 1989-90; bd. dirs. Arts in Motion, Milw., 1990—. Mem. ABA, Wis. Bar Assn., Bar Assn. for Seventh Cir. Ct. Appeals, Am. Intellectual Property Law Assn. Office: Foley & Lardner 777 E Wisconsin Ave Milwaukee WI 53202-5302

BRAZEAL, AURELIA E., ambassador; b. Chgo., Nov. 24, 1943. BS, Spelman Coll., 1965; M of Internat. Affairs, Columbia U., 1967; postgrad., Harvard U., 1972. With Foreign Svc., 1968; consular and econ. officer U.S. Embassy, Buenos Aires, 1969-71; econ. reports officer Econ. Bureau U.S. State Dept., 1971-72, watch and line officer Office of Secretariat, 1973-74, desk officer Uruguay, Paraguay, 1974-77, dir. dept. econs. Office Japan Affairs, 1982-84; review officer Office of Secretariat U.S. Dept. Treasury, 1977-79; econ. officer Tokyo, 1979-82; mem. sr. seminar, 1986-87; min. and counselor econ. affairs U.S. Embassy, Tokyo, 1987-90; amb. to Micronesia, 1990-93; nominated U.S. amb. to Kenya, 1993—. Office: Am Embassy Kenya, Moi/Haile Selassie Ave POB 30137, Nairobi Kenya*

BRAZEAL, DONNA SMITH, psychologist; b. Greenville, S.C., Feb. 10, 1947; d. G.W. Hovey and Ollie Occena (Crane) Smith; m. Charles Lee Brazeal, June 27, 1970 (div. May 1980). BA, Clemson U., 1971, MEd, 1975; postgrad., Western Carolina U., 1974, Furman U., Greenville, 1977; PhD, Columbia Pacific U., 1994. Lic. sch. psychologist, S.C., N.C. Instr., head med. record dept. Greenville Tech. Coll., 1971-73; chief psychologist Greenville County Schs., 1975-80, Union County Schs., Monroe, N.C., 1980—; pvt. practice psychology Monroe and Charlotte, N.C., 1986—; mem. learning disabilities com. Greenville County Schs., 1978-79; co-founder, bd. dirs. Ctr. for Spiritual Awareness of N.C., Monroe, 1982—. Co-author, co-editor: School Psychologist, 1980. Child find program coordinator Union County, 1980-85; mem. various coms. Assn. for Retarded Citizens, Monroe; mem. interagy. council Piedmont Mental Health, Monroe, 1983—. Catawba Bus. Women scholar, 1965; N.C. Dept. Pub. Instrn. Pre-Sch. Incentive grantee, 1984. Mem. Nat. Assn. Sch. Psychologists, N.C. Assn. Sch. Psychologist (mem. pub. relations com. 1984-85), Animal Protection Inst. Am., Greenpeace, Union County Humane Soc., River Hills Community Ch. (mem. adult edn. com. 1985-86), Delta. Libertarian. Unitarian. Home: PO Box 240173 Charlotte NC 28224-0173

BRAZELL, LINDA SUE, nursing administrator, educator; b. Chgo., Oct. 8, 1949; d. Monav Donithan Patton; children: Quest Nelson, Quint Nelson, Jacob, Joseph. AA, BSN, So. Ill. U., Edwardsville, 1990. RN, Ill. Staff practical nurse Fairview Nursing Home, Rosiclare, Ill., 1974-86, dir. nursing, 1984-86; night supr. Hardin County Gen. Hosp., Rosiclare, 1986-92; dir. nursing Ferrell Hosp., Inc., Eldorado, Ill., 1992—; instr. first aid, CNA program, clin. lic. practical nurse instr. Southeastern Ill. Coll., Harrisburg, 1990—. Home: 370 Wolf Creek Rd Eldorado IL 62930-3525 Office: Ferrell Hosp Inc 1201 Pine St Eldorado IL 62930-1634

BRAZIER, MARY MARGARET, psychology educator, researcher; b. New Orleans, Feb. 4, 1956; d. Robert Whiting and Margaret Long (Mc Waters) B. BA, Loyola U., New Orleans, 1977; MS, Tulane U., 1985, PhD, 1986. Assoc. prof. Loyola U., 1986—. NSF grantee, 1987. Mem. APA, Am. Psychol. Soc., Southeastern Psychol. Assn., Midwestern Psychol. Assn., Ea. Psychol. Assn., Southwestern Psychol. Assn. (coun. 1988—), So. Soc. Philosophy and Psychology (exec. coun. 1989-92). Roman Catholic. Office: Loyola U Dept Psychology 6363 Saint Charles Ave New Orleans LA 70118-6143

BRDLIK, CAROLA EMILIE, accountant; b. Wuerzburg, Germany, Mar. 11, 1930; came to U.S., 1952; d. Ludwig Leonard and Hildegard Maria (Leipold) Baumeister; m. Joseph A. Brdlik; children: Margaret Louise, Charles Joseph. BA, Oberrealschule Bamberg, Fed. Republic Germany, 1948; MA, Bavarian Interpreter Coll., Fed. Republic Germany, 1949; Cert., Internat. Accts. Soc., Chgo., 1955. Interpreter, exec. sec. NCWC Amberg, Schweinfurt, Ludwigsburg and Munich, Fed. Republic Germany, 1949-52; exec. sec. Red Ball Van Lines, Jamaica, N.Y., 1952; interpreter Griffin Rutgers Inc., N.Y.C., 1952-53; office mgr., exec. sec. Rehab. Ctr. Summit Co., Inc., Akron, 1953-56; pvt. practice acctg. Cuyahoga Falls, Ohio, 1956-61, Uniontown, Ohio, 1961-81; sec., treas. Omaca, Inc., Uniontown and Deerfield Beach (Fla.), 1981-86; pres. Omaca, Inc., Uniontown and Jupiter, 1986—; sec.-treas. Shipe Landscaping, Inc., Greensburg, Ohio, 1968-92, Sattler Machine Products, Copley, Ohio, 1981-88; asst. treas. Mar-Lynn Lake Park, Inc., Streetsboro, Ohio, 1969—. Bd. dirs., trustee Czechoslovak Refugees, Cleve. and Cin., 1968. Mem. Nat. Soc. Tax Profls. (cert. accredited taxation and accountancy), Nat. Soc. Pub. Accts., Nat. Assn. Tax Preparer's, Nat. Assn. Enrolled Agts., Fla. Soc. Enrolled Agts., Fla. Soc. Acctg. and Tax Profls. Roman Catholic.

BREAKSTONE, KAY LOUISE, public relations executive; b. Allentown, Pa., Sept. 9, 1936; d. Morris H. and Mabel (Gruber) Senderowitz; B.S., N.Y. U., 1967; m. Jules L. Breakstone, Dec. 3, 1960; children—Enid, Jessica. With N.Y. Conf. Bd., 1967-69, Bache, Halsey Stuart, N.Y.C., 1969-70; securities analyst Dean Witter, N.Y.C., 1970-71; vice-pres. Burson Marsteller, Inc., N.Y.C., 1971-79; dir. investor relations Kennecott Corp., Stamford, Conn., 1979-81; sr. v.p. Burson-Marsteller, 1981-87, exec. v.p., 1987-92; pres., CEO Ludgate Comm., N.Y.C., 1993—. Mem. Nat. Investor Relations Inst. (pres. 1980-81). Office: Ludgate Comm 747 3rd Ave New York NY 10017-2803

BREAKWELL, SUSAN LYNN, nursing director; b. Pa., 1954. Diploma in nursing, Wesley-Passavant Sch. Nursing, Chgo., 1975; BSN, Loyola U., 1979; MS in Community Health Nursing, No. Ill. U., 1985. Staff nurse U. Ill. Hosp., Chgo., 1975-77; staff nurse float pool Weiss Meml. Hosp., Chgo., 1977-78; staff nurse Med. Pers. Pool, Evanston, Ill., 1981-82; staff nurse, dir. nursing Chgo. Home Health Svcs., Chgo., 1978—; asst. No. Ill. U., DeKalb, 1982; instr. nursing dept. continuing edn. William Rainey Harper Coll., Palatine, Ill., 1985-86; clin. faculty sch. nursing, community and mental health dept. Loyola U., Chgo., 1990—. Patentee med. equipment devel. Mem. APHA, Ill. Continuity of Care, Inst. Medicine, Midwest Assn. Nursing Informatice, Sigma Theta Tau. Office: Chgo Home Heatlh Svcs 1229 N North Branch St # 102 Chicago IL 60622-2411

BREARLEY, CANDICE, fashion designer; b. Trenton, N.J., Jan. 2, 1944; d. Joseph William and Lillian (Mieler) Szalay; m. Purvis Brearley, Sept. 2, 1965. BFA, Mus. Sch., Phila., 1965, MFA, 1968; BFA, Parsons Sch. Design, 1975, New Sch. Social Rsch., 1975. Freelance portrait artist Trenton, 1965-72; asst. designer Malcolm Starr, N.Y.C., 1974-75; designer Originala, N.Y.C., 1975-77, Vignette, N.Y.C., 1977-78; pres., designer Candice Brearley, Inc., Trenton, 1978—; pres. Wickford Corp. of N.J., Trenton, 1986—; bd. dirs. Beta Con Corp., Lawrenceville, N.J. One-woman shows Nat. State Bank, N.J., 1971; exhibited in group show at N.J. State Mus., Trenton, 1970. Recipient award Lane Bryant Design Competition, 1974. Fellow Phila. Mus. Art, Met. Mus. Art, Princeton U. Mus., N.J. State Mus. Roman Catholic. Office: Candice Brearley Inc 128 Buckingham Ave Trenton NJ 08618-3314

BRECHA, SONIA ASTRID, accounting educator; b. Barre, Vt., Oct. 14, 1933; d. Evert Olof and Martha Elfriede (Junge) Nylen; m. Harry Charles Brecha, Nov. 28, 1959 (dec. June 1990); children: Robert Joseph, David Andrew, Diane Marie. BS in Commerce, Ohio U., 1956; MS in Acctg., Kent State U., 1974, DBA, 1983. CPA, Ohio. Acctg. clk. Glidden Co., Cleve., 1956-59; part time instr. acctg. Lorain County C.C., Elyria, Ohio, 1969-72; teaching fellow acctg. Kent (Ohio) State U., 1973-75, temporary instr. acctg., 1975-76; instr. acctg. Wright State U., Dayton, Ohio, 1976-79, asst. prof., 1979—, chair dept accountancy, 1993—. Mem. ARC, Dayton, 1992—. Mem. AICPA, Am. Acctg. Assn., Inst. Mgmt. Accts. Episcopalian. Office: Wright State U Dept Accountancy 3640 Col Glenn Hwy Dayton OH 45435

BRECHT, SALLY ANN, quality assurance executive; b. Trenton, N.J., Aug. 5, 1951; d. Charles L. and Helen (Orfeo) B. BBA, Coll. William & Mary in Va., 1973; MBA, Rider Coll., 1981. Cert. quality engr., quality auditor. Electronic data processing auditor McGraw Hill, Inc., Hightstown, N.J., 1976-79, State of N.J., Mercerville, 1979-80, NL Industries, Hightstown, 1980-84; systems tech. planning specialist Ednl. Testing Svc., Princeton, N.J., 1984-85, acting div. dir. application devel., 1985-87, mgr. computer standards and security, 1987-88, asst. dir. office corp. quality assurance, quality engr., 1988—. Contbr. articles to popular publs. Office: Ednl Testing Svc Rosedale Rd Princeton NJ 08540-6702

BRECKEL, ALVINA HEFELI, librarian; b. Chgo., Dec. 6, 1948; d. William Christ and Liselotte (Herrmann) Hefeli; m. Theodore A. Breckel, Feb. 10, 1973. BFA cum laude, Bradley U., 1970; MALS, Rosary Coll., River Forest, Ill., 1973. Cert. art tchr., media libr., Ill. Tchr. art Chgo. Pub. Schs., 1971-84; libr. Oakton Community Coll., Des Plaines, Ill., 1988—. Editor News & Notes, 1988-89. Rep. election judge New Trier Twp., Ill., 1988; com. mem. Villagers for a Safe Winnetka, 1989; mem. women's bd. Howard Area Community Ctr., 1990—; chmn. Fuller Lane Cir., Winnetka, 1991-92, 94—; mem. Midwestern Antiques Club, 1993—. Mem. AAUW (bd. dirs. New Trier chpt. 1989-90), Sandwich (Mass.) Hist. Soc., Winnetka Hist. Soc., Art Inst. Chgo. (life), Nat. Greentown Glass Assn., Internat. Platform Assn., Nat. Early Am. Glass Club (life, founding mem. James H. Rose chpt., chpt. sec. 1992—), Greater Chgo. Area Glass Collectors Club, Pi Lambda Theta (life, art editor chpt. Notes 1977-84), Delta Zeta (v.p. Chgo. North Shore chpt. 1987-90). Home: 185 Fuller Ln Winnetka IL 60093-4212 Office: Oakton CC 1600 E Golf Rd Des Plaines IL 60016

BRECKENRIDGE, BETTY GAYLE, management development consultant; b. Austin, Tex., Dec. 8, 1945. BA, Baylor U., 1966; MA, So. Meth. U, 1984. Cons. AT&T Human Resources Assessment, 1993—, Bellsouth Corp. Mgmt. Skills Assessment, 1990—. Office: 332 W Fairmount Ave State College PA 16801-4604

BRECKENRIDGE, REBECCA K., nurse consultant; b. Greenville, Miss., May 13, 1946; d. Louis Hardie and Frances Mildred (Wiggs) Kent; m. George E. Breckenridge, Jan. 7, 1966; children: Louis Kent, Benjamin Ellis. AA, Miss. Delta Jr. Coll., 1966. Cert. nursing adminstrn. RN supr. Calhoun County Hosp., Bruce, Miss.; dir. nurses, asst. adminstr. Yalousha County Nursing Home, Water Valley, Miss., pub. health nurse; ind. nurse cons. North Miss. Med. Sonographers, Water Valley; office nurse DCIM, Las Vegas. Named Mother of Yr., 1984; recipient recognition Medicaid Commn. and Health Care Commn. Mem. ANA, NRA (life), Miss. Nurses Assn., Nev. Nurses Assn., Am. Cancer Soc., Am. Assn. Office Nurses. Home: 8155 W Charleston # 56 Las Vegas NV 89117

BREDEKAMP, CAROLINE MARGARET ANN, gifted/talented education educator; b. Maquoketa, Iowa, July 12, 1966; d. Emil and Margaret Alwine (Wildfang) B. AA in Early Childhood, Mt. St. Clare Coll., 1986; BA in Elem. Edn., Early Childhood Edn., U. No. Iowa, 1988, MA in Elem. Edn., Gifted/Talented Edn., 1993. Cert. tchr., Iowa. Sub. tchr. Andrew (Iowa) Community Schs., 1988-90, East Ctrl. Community Schs., Miles, Iowa, 1988-89, Maquoketa Community Schs., 1988-91, Preston (Iowa) Community Schs., 1988-91; 4th and 5th grade tchr. AEA7 Agy., Cedar Falls, Iowa, 1991-92; tchr., adv., protector staff Prairie House, Maquoketa, 1990-91; K-12 coord. talented and gifted programs Ctrl. Community Schs. of Clinton County, DeWitt, Welton, and Grand Mound, Iowa, 1993—; tutor Vocat. Rehab. U. No. Iowa, Cedar Falls, 1992-93, Ctr. for Urban Edn., 1992. Vol./treas. The Worker House, Waterloo, Iowa, 1992-93. Smith-Arey scholar U. No. Iowa, 1987-88; recipient Rsch. award Iowa Talented and Gifted Assn., 1994. Mem. NEA, Iowa State Edn. Assn., Omicron Delta Kappa, Kappa Delta Pi. Democrat. Lutheran. Home: 115-1/2 S 2d Apt 3 Maquoketa IA 52060 Office: Ctrl Community Schs PO Box 240 DeWitt IA 52742

BREED, HELEN ILLICK, ichthyologist, educator; b. New Cumberland, Pa., Mar. 12, 1925; d. Joseph Simon and Della May (Brotzman) Illick; m. Henry Eltinge Breed, Jr., Nov. 23, 1957; children: Henry E., Joseph I., Brenda E. BS, Syracuse U., 1947, MS, 1949; PhD, Cornell U., 1953. Tchr. sci. Lyons (N.Y.) Cen. High Sch., 1949-50; instr. zoology and physiology Akron (Ohio) U., 1953-54; postdoctoral Ford Found. fellow, instr. physiology Vassar Coll., Poughkeepsie, N.Y., 1954-55; asst. prof. biology Russell Sage Coll., Troy, N.Y., 1955-57; asst. dir. systematic biology NSF, Washington, 1957; assoc. prof. conservation Cornell U., Ithaca, N.Y., 1957-61; rsch. assoc. biology Rensselaer Poly. Inst., Troy, 1964-68; environ. cons. Eltick Rsch. Corp., Troy, 1971-90; environ. advisor, cons. Women's Environ. and Devel. Orgn., N.Y.C., 1991—; internat. environ. liaison and coord. N.Y. State Summit and Agenda's 21 Program, Albany, 1992—; ichthyology cons. Ichthyological Assocs., Lake George Project, Troy, 1969, Ithaca, 1971-80, Lima, Peru, 1973-73; internat. environ. liaison and coord. N.Y. State Summit and Agenda's 21 Program, Albany, 1992—. Contbr. articles to profl. jours. Capital dist. mem. Syracuse U. campaign for excellence, Troy, 1988-90. Nat. Wildlife Fedn. fellow, 1950, Sports Fishing Inst. fellow, 1951-53, Am. Scandinavian Found. fellow, Trondheim, Norway, 1959-60. Mem. AAAS, Am. Soc. Zoologists, Soc. Systematic Zoology, Am. Soc. Ichthyologists and Herpetologists, Am. Fisheries Soc., Brunswick Hist. Soc. Republican. Lutheran. Home and Office: RD 3 PO Box 245B Troy NY 12182-0360

BREEN, JANICE DEYOUNG, health services executive, community health nurse; b. Paterson, N.J., Apr. 15, 1947; d. Corneilius and Catherine (Van Ostenbridge) DeYoung; m. Robert Neal Breen, Aug. 1, 1969; children: Gregory Neal, Karen Elizabeth. BSN, William Paterson Coll., Wayne, N.J., 1970; MEd, Rutgers U., 1976; MSN, U. Pa., 1986. Cert. clin. specialist in community health nursing. Insvc. edn. instr. Community Meml. Hosp., Toms River, N.J.; instr. nursing Ocean County Coll., Toms River, program. coord. for allied health; dir. cmty. svcs. St. Francis Med. Ctr., Trenton, N.J.; pres., CEO West Essex Cmty. Health Svcs., Verona, N.J. Mem. ANA, N.J. State Nurses Assn., Sigma Theta Tau.

BREEN, KAREN BLOCK, library consultant; b. New Orleans, La., Apr. 7, 1943; d. Charles David and Helen Kathryn (Carroll) Block; m. Curtis James Linberg, Mar. 17, 1963 (div. July 1965); 1 child, Kira; m. Patrick Francis Breen, Oct. 9, 1971. BA, U. Mass., 1968; MLS, La. State U., 1970. Children's libr. Queens (N.Y.) Borough Pub. Libr., 1970-75, asst. head children's divsn., 1975-81, head ctrl. libr. children's divsn., 1981-85, coord. children's svcs., 1985-90; cons. Libr. Power Project, N.Y.C., 1990—; owner, bookseller Tiny Tales Bookstore, Bellmore, N.Y., 1992—. Author: Index to Collective Biographies for Young Readers, 1988. Mem. ALA (chair notable children's books 1991-93, mem. Caldecott com. 1989, 90, mem. Newbery com. 1981, mem. Batchelder award com. 1987), Women's Nat. Book Assn. (officer of bd. 1979—), Am. Booksellers Assn., U.S. Bd. on Books for Youth, Assn. Booksellers for Children, Libr. Pub. Rels. Coun. (bd. dirs. 1981-83). Democrat. Office: Library Power 232 Madison Ave Ste 1409 New York NY 10016

BREEN, KATHERINE ANNE, speech and language pathologist; b. Chgo., Oct. 31, 1948; d. Robert Stephen and Gertrude Catherine (Bader) Breen; B.S., Northwestern U., 1970; M.A. (U.S. Rehab. Services trainee), U. Mo., Columbia, 1971. Speech/lang. pathologist Fulton (Mo.) pub. schs., 1971-73; co-dir. Easter Seal Speech Clinic, Jefferson City, Mo., summers 1972, 73; speech/lang. pathologist Shawnee Mission (Kans.) pub. schs., 1973—; staff St. Joseph's Hosp., Kansas City, Mo., 1978-81, Midwest Rehab. Ctr., Kansas City, 1985; pvt. practice speech therapy; cons. East Central Mo. Mental Health Center; guest lectr. Fontbonne Coll., St. Louis. Clin. certification in speech pathology. Mem. Am., Kans. speech and hearing assns., NEA, Mo. State Tchrs. Assn., Kansas City Alumni Assn. of Northwestern U. (dir. alumni admissions council, Outstanding Leadership award for work on alumni admissions council 1981, Svc. award, 1991), Friends of Art Nelson/Atkins Art Gallery and Museum (vol.), Nat. Trust Hist. Preservation, Kansas City Hist. Found., Zeta Phi Eta. Methodist. Home: 6865 W 51st Ter Apt 1C Shawnee Mission KS 66202-1576 Office: 7235 Antioch Shawnee Mission KS 66204

BREGGIN, JANIS ANN, lawyer; b. Rochester, N.Y., Mar. 5, 1955; d. Arnold H. and Eleanor (Wingo) B.; children: Rachel Tyler, Cadiz Safira, Theo Socrates, Thomas Robert. BA, U. Denver, 1976, JD, 1980. Bar: Colo. 1980, U.S. Ct. Appeals (10th cir.) 1980. Assoc. Sherman & Howard, Denver, 1980-82, Jeffrey M. Nobel & Assocs., Denver, 1982-84; assoc. in house counsel Bill L. Walters Cos., Englewood, Colo., 1984-85; assoc. Deutsch & Sheldon, Englewood, 1985-87; ptnr. Breggin & Assocs. P.C., Denver, 1987—. Mem. Denver Women's Commn., 1990-93, chmn. 1991-92. Mem. ABA, Colo. Bar Assn., Denver Bar Assn., Colo. Women's Bar Assn. Office: Breggin & Assocs PC 1999 Broadway #2605 Denver CO 80202

BREIDENBACH, CHERIE ELIZABETH, lawyer, accountant; b. Aberdeen, S.D., Aug. 20, 1952; d. Neil Allen and Portia Elizabeth (Bradner) Johnson; m. Steven Theodore Breidenbach, Aug. 9, 1975. BS, U. S.D., 1975, JD, 1979. Bar: S.D. 1979, Calif. 1981; CPA, Calif. Sole practice La Jolla, Calif., 1982-84; assoc., acct. Sussman & Siegel, San Diego, 1984-86; ptnr. Fout, Breidenbach & Chin, San Diego, 1986-88, Rose, Munns & Fout, Coronado, Calif., 1988-90, Rose, Munns, Breidenbach & Fout, Coronado, 1990-91, Rose, Munns, Fout, Breidenbach & Chin, 1992—. Mem. Calif. Bar Assn., Phi Delta Phi. Republican. Methodist.

BREITENWISCHER, ANN LOUISE, information specialist, librarian, educator; b. Ann Arbor, Mich., Jan. 18, 1942; d. LeRoy O. and E. Louise (Krauss) B. BS, Ea. Mich. U., 1965; MA, U. Mich., 1969; postgrad., Western Mich. U., 1976, 81. Algebra and geometry tchr. Eaton Rapids (Mich.) Pub. Schs., 1965-66; math., geography and bus. tchr. Hartland (Mich.) Consolidated Schs., 1966-67; asst. prof. Ferris State U., Big Rapids, Mich., 1969-81, assoc. prof., 1981-91, prof., edn. liaison, 1991—; mem. adv. bd. Mecosta-Osceola Alternative Sch., Big Rapids, 1987—; vice chair u. ednl.planning com. Ferris State U., 1978-81, mem. outcomes assessment coun., 1992—. Contbr. articles to profl. jours.; columnist AAUW Mich. leader, 1983-85. Mem. NEA (local sec. 1976-78), AAUW (Mich. policy rev. com. 1983-85, Big Rapids br. chair Ednl. Found./Booksale com. 1980-91, Mich. bd. dirs. 1981-85, Big Rapids br. pres. 1985-89, Named Gift recipient 1983), Bus. and Profl. Women/USA (Mecosta County Woman of Yr. 1987, local orgn. pres.-elect 1988-89), Med. Libr. Assn., Mich. Acad. Sci., Arts and Letters (sect. chair 1984-85), Mich. Libr. Assn. (roundtable sec.-treas. 1987-88), Phi Delta Kappa (chpt. pres. 1983-84, 92-94, rsch. rep. 1994—). Office: Ferris State U Libr 1201 S State St Big Rapids MI 49307-2251

BREITMEYER, JO ANNE, sales and marketing executive; b. Ann Arbor, Mich., Mar. 25, 1947; d. Philip and Joan Clista (Thomas) B. Student, U. Tex., 1965-66, Boston U., 1966-67, U. Md., 1967-68; AA, BA, Canada Coll., Redwood City, Calif., 1970. Mktg. sec. Fairchild Camera & Instrument Co., Mountain View, Calif., 1969-70; sec. to v.p. Optimum Systems, Inc., Palo Alto, Calif., 1970-72; sec. to pres. Advanced Memory Systems, Sunnyvale, Calif., 1972-74; asst. to pres. Ness Time, Inc., Mountain View, 1974-75; art dir. Collage, Inc., Mountain View, 1975-76; owner, mgr. Briteday, Inc., Mountain View, 1976-87; with mktg. communications dept. PANAGEA, Cupertino, Calif., 1987-89; with Hewlett Packard Co., Palo Alto, 1989; mgr. adminstrn. Micro Integration Corp., San Jose, Calif., 1989-92; cons. Breitmeyer & Assocs., Mountain View, Calif., 1992-93; v.p. sales and mktg. Aries Trading Co. Ltd., Cupertino, Calif., 1993—. Bd. dirs. Peninsula Little Club, Palo Alto, 1981-87, pub. rels. com., 1984-87; bd. dirs. Peninsula Children's Ctr., Palo Alto, 1984-87, printing chmn. charter aux., 1984—; sec. Cypress Point Homeowners Assn., Mountain View, 1978-80, treas., 1988; mem. Arthritis Found., 1970—, mem. No. calif. chpt. adv. bd., devel. com., printing chmn., nominating com., telethon chmn., 1990-93, v.p. fund devel. South Bay br., 1991—; active Menlo Circus Club Charity Horse Show, 1983-89, Festival of Trees, 1984—; sec. Veterans Meml. Campaign, San Jose/Santa Clara Valley; mem. Japanese Am. Campaign Com., Japanese Nat. Historical Mus.; vol. JACL. Recipient Disting. Svc. award No. Calif. Arthritis Found. South Bay Br., 1993. Mem. Bus. Profl. Advt. Assn., Peninsula Mktg. Assn., Mountain View Women in Bus. (steering com. 1986-87), Am. Electronics Assn., Environ. and Occupational Health Com., Tech. Employment Coop. Silicon Valley, Am. Biog. Inst. (rsch. bd. advisors), Apres Ski Club (publs. com., Outstanding Svc. award), Far West Skiing Assn. (Outstanding Publ. award), Alpha Omicron Pi (chpt. advisor 1988—, pres. Palo Alto Alumnae Chpt. 1992-94, region X advisor inst., 1992—, del. 1992 Leadership conf., Alumnae svc. award 1992, cert. of honor, 1988, 92, del. internat. conv. 1987, 89, 93, Rose award 1993, Outstanding Chpt. Pres., 1993, Outstanding Pub./Newsletter award 1993, mem. regional pubs. com.). Home: 209 Horizon Ave Mountain View CA 94043-4718

BREKKE, JANET FLINT, lawyer; b. Doland, S.D., Jan. 29, 1956; d. Arnet Harry and Marjorie Mina (Ames) Flint; m. Jeffrey Dean Brekke, Aug. 11, 1979; children: Morgan, Logan, Rheann. BA, U. S.D., 1978, JD, 1981. Bar: S.D. 1981. Dep. states atty. Minnehaha County States Atty. Office, Sioux Falls, S.D., 1981-85; asst. city atty. City of Sioux Falls, 1986-89, chief asst. city atty., 1989-95, city atty., 1995—. Mem. Nat. Womens Polit. Caucus, Minnehaha County, 1993; pres. bd. Family Svcs., Inc., Sioux Falls, 1993; adv. bd. mem. Jr. League of Sioux Falls, 1994. Mem. S.D. Trial Lawyers Assn., S.D. Bar Assn. (chair labor law com. 1991-94), Lions (2d v.p. Sioux Falls club 1993). Methodist. Office: City Attys Office 224 W 9th St Sioux Falls SD 57102-0596

BREMER, CELESTE F., judge; b. 1953. BA, St. Ambrose Coll., 1974; JD, Univ. of Iowa Coll. of Law, 1977. Asst. county atty. Scott County, 1977-79; asst. atty. gen. Area Prosecutors Div., Iowa, 1979; with Carlin, Liebbe, Pitton & Bremer, 1979-81, Rabin, Liebbe, Shinkle & Bremer, 1981-82; with legal dept. Deere and Co., 1982-84; corp. counsel Economy Forms Corp., 1985-88; magistrate judge U.S. Dist. Ct. (Iowa no. dist.), 8th circuit, Des Moines, 1985—; instr. Drake Univ. Coll. of Law, 1985-90. Mem. Nat. Assn. of Women Judges, Polk County Bar Assn., Iowa State Bar Assn. (bd. of govs., 1987-90), Am. Bar Assn., Coun. of U.S. Magistrates, Iowa Judges Assn., Am. Judicatore Soc., Polk County Women Attys., Nat. Fed. Magistrate Judges Assn., Iowa Supreme Ct. Coun. on Judicial Selection (chmn., 1986-90), Iowa Orgn. of Women Attys. Office: US Courthouse 123 East Walnut St Rm 429 Des Moines IA 50309*

BREMER, FRANCES WINFIELD, non-profit agency director; b. St. Paul, May 25, 1942; d. William Hood and Alice (Turner) Winfield; m. L. Paul Bremer III, June 11, 1966; children: L. Paul IV, Leila Ames. BA, Conn. Coll., 1964. Cert. tch. English to fgn. speakers. Tchr. Am. Sch., Kabul, Afghanistan, 1966-68, Limbe Convent Sch., Malawi, Africa, 1968-70; founder, pres. Washington Area Refugee Com., 1974-76; dir. Fgn. Student Svc. Coun., Washington, 1976—; docent Folger Shakespeare Libr., Washington, 1971-73; play therapist Childrens Hosp., Washington, 1980-83; organizer Frances Bremer Prize for the Best Essay on Am. Lit., The Hague, Netherlands, 1985. Co-author: Coping With His Success, 1984, Niet Zeuren, 1987. Exec. dir. Fgn. Student Svc. Coun. Republican. Roman Catholic.

BREMMER, SHERYL LYNN, secondary school educator, writer; b. Portland, Oreg., Apr. 3, 1949; d. Jack Phillip and Nelda Lee Bremmer. BA in History and Polit. Sci., Calif. State U., Fullerton, 1971, MS in Edn. and Sch. Adminstrn., 1979, MA in History, 1988. Cert. tchr., Calif. Hostess Disneyland, Anaheim, Calif., 1969-73; tchr. Covina (Calif.) Valley United Sch. Dist., 1973—; chair history dept. Northview H.S., Covina, 1986—. Judge bicentennial competition Constnl. Rights Found., 1987. Mem. Delta Zeta, Phi Alpha Theta. Democrat. Office: Northview HS 1016 W Cypress St Covina CA 91722

BREMSER, ELIZABETH JEAN, educator, consultant; b. Kansas City, Kans., Nov. 28, 1958; d. Lawrence William and Edith Augusta (Ridder) B.; m. Joel Donald Wallerstedt, Oct. 12, 1984 (div. Aug. 1989). BA, Knox Coll., 1980; MA, U. Mo., 1990. Asst. dir. jr. yr. abroad Knox Coll., Galesburg, Ill., 1980-82; French instr. Brookside Day Sch., Kansas City, Mo., 1984-87, Kansas City (Mo.) Acad., 1985-90; adj. prof. French, Longview C.C., Lee's Summit, Mo., 1990—; French lang. cons. Marion Merrell Dow, Kansas City, 1993, Wilcox Electric, Inc., Kansas City, 1994—; translator Merchant/Ivory Films, Kansas City, 1990, patent atty., Kansas City, 1989; mem. talent search staff H&R Block, Kansas City, 1991. Mem., sponsor Homeless Elimination Project (HELP), Kansas City, 1990. Mem. Fgn. Lang. Assn. Mo. (Phi Mu (pres. Pan-Hellenic Assn. 1977-78). Home: 210 W 67th Ter Kansas City MO 64113-2468

BRENKEN, HANNE MARIE, artist; b. Duisburg, Germany, July 6, 1923; arrived in U.S., 1977; d. Hermann and Luise (Werth) Tigler; m. Hans Brenken, Mar. 28, 1942 (div. 1985); children: Karin Brenken Schneider-Henn, Berndt; m. Ricardo Wiesenberg, May 16, 1986. Grad., Landschulheim, Holzminden, Germany, 1941; studied in pvt. art schs., Munich and Bonn, Germany. One-person shows include Contra Kreis Gallery, Bonn, Germany, 1958, Galerie Junge Kunst, Fulda, Germany, 1959, Universa-Galerie, Nurenberg, Germany, 1960, Galleria Monte Napoleone, Milan, Italy, 1961, Galerie Niedlich, Stuttgart, Germany, 1961, 63, Galerie am Jakobsbrunnen, Stuttgart, 1964, 67, Kunst und Kunstverein Mus., Pforzheim, Germany, 1969, Kunstverein Mus., Munich, 1972, Galerie Dorothea Leonhart, Munich, 1974, I.C.L. Gallery, East Hampton, N.Y., 1980, Anne Reid Gallery, Princeton, N.J., 1981, Adagio Gallery, Bridgehampton, N.Y., 1982, 84, Queens Mus., N.Y., 1983, Ericson Gallery, N.Y.C., 1984, 85, Benton Gallery, Southampton, N.Y., 1986, Vered Gallery, East Hampton, N.Y., 1988, Gallery Rodeo, Lake Arrowhead, Calif., Taos, N.Mex., Beverly Hills, Calif., 1990, Brian Logan Art Space, Washington, 1991, The Gallery, Leesburg, Va., 1992, Amerika Haus, Frankfurt, Germany, 1993, Ganser Haus, Wasserburg, Germany, 1993, Ann Norton Sculpture Gardens, West Palm Beach, Fla., 1993, Jean Chisholm Gallery, West Palm Beach, 1994, Okuda Internat. Gallery, Washington, 1995; group shows include Duisburg (Germany) Mus., 1959, Baden-Baden Mus., Germany, 1961, 62, Haus der Kunst, Munich, 1963, 64, 69, 70, 71, 72, 73, Kunstgebäude, Stuttgart, 1963, 71, Acad. Fine Arts, Berlin, 1964, 73, Forum Stadtpark, Graz, Austria, 1965, Folkwang Mus., Essen, Germany, 1965, Munich City Mus., 1967, Karlsruhe (Germany) Kunstverein, 1967, Galerie Heseler, Munich, 1968, Hannover (Germany) Mus., 1969, Modern Art Mus., Munich, 1969, Bonn Mus., 1970, Kunstkreis Gallery, Wasserburg, Germany, 1972, 73, Kunstverein Mus., Rosenheim, Germany, 1972, Mainz Mus., 1974, Kunstverein Mus., Frankfurt, Germany, 1977, Guild Hall Mus., East Hampton, N.Y., 1979, 80, 81, 82, 83, Parrish Art Mus., Southampton, N.Y., 1979, 80, 81, Elaine Benson Gallery, Bridgehampton, N.Y., 1980, 81, Kunstverein Mus., Munich, 1982, Ericson Gallery, 1984, Vered Gallery, East Hampton, 1985, 86, 87, 89, Franz Bader Gallery, Washington, 1989, Ganser Haus, Wasserburg, 1992; permanent collections include Solomon R. Guggenheim Mus., N.Y.C., The Queens (N.Y.) Mus., Phoenix Art Mus., Guild Hall Mus., various mus. in Europe; author: (book) Firlefranz, 1969. Studio: PO Box 3405 Warrenton VA 22186

BRENNAN, DONNA LESLEY, public relations company executive; b. Washington, Mar. 13, 1945; d. Don Arthur and Louise (Tucker) B.; m. Salil Gutt, Jan. 14, 1985. BA, Denison U., 1967. Tchr. Souderton Area High Sch., Pa., 1967-69; mgr. media rels. Ins. Co. N.Am., Phila., 1969-72; dir. press rels. Colonial Penn Group, Phila., 1972-75, 1975-81, dir. communications, 1981-83; v.p. corp. communications Norstar Bancorp, Albany, N.Y., 1983-85; v.p. communications Meritor Fin. Group, Phila., 1986-87; prin. Donna Brennan Assocs., 1988—. Mem. Pub. Rels. Soc. Am. (pres. Phila. chpt. 1988), Phila. Women's Network (founder, bd. dirs.), Women's Assn. for Women's Alternatives (vice chmn., bd. dirs.), Forum of Exec. Women (pres. 1992-93).

BRENNAN, EILEEN HUGHES, nurse; b. Atlanta, Sept. 26, 1951; m. David Lee Altizer, May 11, 1974 (div. Dec. 1978); m. Scott Curtis Brennan, Feb. 6, 1982; 1 child, Bonnie Joy. Student, North Ga. Coll., 1969-70; diploma, Ga. Bapt. Sch. Nursing, 1973; student, Tift Coll., 1970-73, Ga. State U., 1980-85, SUNY, Albany, 1986-91, Brenau Univ., 1994—. Cert. nurse operating room, registered nurse. Orthopedic charge nurse Grady Meml. Hosp., Atlanta, 1974; operating room nurse DePaul Hosp., Norfolk, Va., 1974-76; nurse orthopedics Cabell Huntington (W.Va.) Hosp., 1976; surg. charge nurse VA Hosp., Huntington, 1976-77; mem. operating room open heart team VA Hosp., Deatur, Ga., 1986-88, 89-91; orthopedic nurse specialist Peachtree Orthopedic Clinic, Atlanta, 1982; operating room charge nurse Drs. Meml. Hosp., Atlanta, 1982-85, chmn. operating room policy and procedures, 1982-84, 94—; vascular rsch. coord. #141 Co-operative Study-a-Multi-Ctr. VA Study, Decatur, Ga., 1988-89, #362, 1991-93; acting temporary chair Narcotic Inventory Com., 1994—. Developed multi-media slide presentation for the Perioperative Patient as well as a pamphlet for preop teaching purposes, 1979, rev. 1985; editor: urology pamphlet, 1986, Open Heart Instrumentation, 1987; wrote and presented slide teaching program for coop. study (a multi-ctr. Dept. of Vet.'s Affairs study). Vol. ARC, Atlanta, 1970-94, Am. Heart Assn., Atlanta, 1987-88, Atlanta Lung Assn., 1985-88, Am. Lung Assn., Atlanta, 1988-91, North Fulton County Community Charities including Thanksgiving Lunch, Brown Bag Community Food Bank, Clothes Closet, Homestretch, Battered Women's Shelter, Adopt a Christmas Family, 1991—. Recipient Cert., United Fund Campaign, Atlanta, 1981, Spl. Incentive award VA Med. Ctr., Decatur, Ga., 1981, Performance award Nurse Profl. Standards Bd., Decatur, 1987, Achievement award, 1987. Mem. Assn. Operating Room Nurses (co-chmn. Project Alpha 1986-87). Episcopalian. Home: 9250 Brumbelow Crossing Way Alpharetta GA 30202-6168

BRENNAN, JEAN MARIE, nurse; b. Reading, Pa., Nov. 11, 1955; d. Christofer Joseph and Frances Virginia (Mateich) B.; 1 child, Melissa Elizabeth Mohn. LPN, Pa. Maternity nurse Reading (Pa.) Hosp., 1978-81, staff nurse, 1983—; staff nurse Warren (Pa.) Gen. Hosp., 1981-83. With U.S. Army, 1986-92. Decorated Army Achievement medal. Home: RR 2 Box 76A Morgantown PA 19543-9739

BRENNAN, JOAN STEVENSON, federal judge; b. Detroit, Feb. 21, 1933; d. James and Betty (Holland) Stevenson; m. Lane P. Brennan, June 26, 1954 (div. 1970); children: Suzanne, Steven, Clayton, Elizabeth, Catherine. BA, Skidmore Coll., 1954; JD, Santa Clara U., 1973. Bar: Calif. Dep. dist. atty. Dist. Attys. Office, Santa Clara, Calif., 1974-78; legal counsel U.S. Leasing Internat., San Francisco, 1978-79; asst. U.S. atty. U.S. Dist. Ct. (no. dist.) Calif., San Francisco, 1980-82, U.S. Magistrate judge, 1982—. Mem. Nat. Assn. Women Judges, Nat. Assn. Magistrate Judges. Democrat. Office: US Dist Ct PO Box 36054 16700 Valley View Ave Ste 300 La Mirada CA 90638-5841*

BRENNAN, JUDITH WIATER, business owner; b. Reading, Pa.; d. Edward Joseph and Eleanor Helen Wiater; m. James Edward Brennan Jr., 1967; children: James III, Theresa, Maureen, Susan. Student, U. Calif., Davis, 1964-67; cert., U. Calif., Irvine, 1992; grad., Dale Carnegie Course, 1981. Dir. pub. rels. Pacific Coast Quarter Horse Racing Assn., Inc., Los Alamitos, Calif., 1974-86; pres. Brennan Screen Printing, Inc., Santa Fe Springs, Calif., 1986—; mem. Los Angeles County Econ. Efficiency Com., L.A., 1992-94; mem. policy bd. Pvt. Industry Coun., Cerritos, Calif., 1992-94; rep. Joint Powers Ins. Authority, La Palma, Calif., 1992-94; trustee S.E. Area Animal Control, 1994—. Editor: Pacific Coast Quarter Horse Racing Assn. Newsletter, 1974-86; monthly columnist Pacific Coast Jour.; contbr. feature stories to jours. and mags. Mem. City Parks and Recreation Commn., Norwalk, Calif., 1989, City Planning Commn., Norwalk, 1989-92; mem. City Coun., Norwalk, 1992—, mayor pro tem, 1994—; trustee Southeast Area Animal Control Authority, 1994—; del. Norwalk/L.A. County Sheriff, 1992—; eucharistic min. St. John of God Ch., 1982-90, mem. women's coun., pres., 1974-86. Mem. Santa Fe Springs C. of C., Norwalk C. of C., Whittier C. of C. Republican. Roman Catholic. Office: Brennan Screen Printing Inc 13677 Bora Dr Santa Fe Springs CA 90670-5005

BRENNAN, LINDA STOKESBURY, designer, artist; b. Lansing, Mich., Nov. 11, 1948; d. Elwood L. and Louise (Olinger) Stokesbury; m. Thomas M. Brennan, May 12, 1990; children: Bryan James, Amy Lynn. BA in Arts, Mich. State U., 1990. Designer Lansing (Mich.) C.C., 1980-81, MEA, East Lansing, 1984-93; owner ABBI Creative Design Studio, Lansing, 1990—. Author: Artist Success Kit, 1991. Mem. Lansing Art Gallery, 1974—; mem. Capitol Area Women's Network, Lansing, 1992—. Mem. NAFE, Lansing Art Guild (v.p. 1990, pres. 1994), Lansing Ad Club (bd. dirs. 1992—), Nat. Watercolor Assn., Mich. Pub. Rels. Assn. (bd. dirs. 1994—). Office: ABBI Creative Design PO Box 80321 Lansing MI 48908-0321

BRENNAN, MARY M., state legislator; b. Valparaiso, Fla., May 17, 1954; d. Robert Vincent and Margaret Mary (Saville) B. Student, U. South Fla., 1973; BS, U. Fla., 1976; postgrad., U. South Fla., 1987. Journalist St. Petersburg (Fla.) Times, 1977-79; editor Pinellas Park (Fla.) Post, 1979-80; pub. Pinellas Park (Fla.) Press, 1980-82; legis. aide State Rep. Patricia Bailey, Pinellas Park, 1982-84; editor Pinellas Park (Fla.) News, 1984-86; pub. info. officer City of Pinellas Park, Fla., 1986-90; mem. Fla. Ho. of Reps., Pinellas Park, 1990—. Bd. mem. Girls Inc. of Mid-Pinellas, Pinellas Park, 1979—; mem. pub. rels. Girls Club of Pinellas Park, Fla., 1982. Recipient Community Svc. to Children award Pinellas Emergency Mental Health Svc., 1992. Mem. Fla. Govt. Communicators, Pinellas Park Hist. Soc., Soroptimist Internat. Pinellas Park (Svc. award 1983, Women Helping Women award 1991), Greater Pinellas Park C. of C. (bd. mem. 1981-86, 90-92, Svc. award 1981, Outstanding Community Svc. award 1983). Democrat. Roman Catholic. Office: Fla House Reps 6251 44th St Ste 7 Tallahassee FL 32301*

BRENNAN, MARYANN, banking corporation executive; b. Passaic, N.J., Aug. 3, 1946; d. Reuben John and Marie Katherine (Lamos) MacBride; m. Donald Jerome Brennan, Dec. 4, 1981. BA in Psychology, Columbia U., 1971; MBA in Fin., St. John's U., 1990. Cert. quality analyst. Psychiatric therapist Albert Einstein Coll. Medicine, Bronx, N.Y., 1973-80; mgr. billing Citibank, N.A., N.Y.C., 1980-84; portfolio asst. Skandia Am. Group, N.Y.C., 1982-84; account mgr. Stein Roe & Farnham, N.Y.C., 1984; v.p. quality mgmt. Chem. Banking Corp., N.Y.C., 1984—. Contbr. articles to profl. publs. Sr. examiner, trainer N.Y. State Gov.'s Excelsior award, 1993-95. Recipient Best-of-Best award Quality Assurance Inst., 1990; scholar Columbia U., 1970-71. Mem. TOMC Fin. Svcs. Coun. (chair conf. bd. 1995), Am. Soc. for Quality Control, Am. Productivity and Quality Ctr. (mem. banking forum 1994—), Banking Adminstrn. Inst. (mem. cash mgmt. quality forum 1991—), Quality Productivity and Mgmt. Assn. (program dir. Met. N.Y. Coun. 1993-94, chmn. 1993-96, v.p. elect, editor newsletter 1991-92, bd. dirs. 1993-96), Coalition Quality Orgns. Greater N.Y. (founder, chmn. 1993—). Office: Chemical Banking Corp 55 Water St Rm 541 New York NY 10041-0001

BRENNAN, MAUREEN A., lawyer; b. Morristown, N.J., Aug. 7, 1949. BA magna cum laude with honors, Bryn Mawr Coll., 1971; JD cum laude, Boston Coll., 1977. Bar: Pa. 1977, Ohio 1989, U.S. Dist. Ct. (ea. dist.)

Pa. 1978. Atty. U.S. EPA, Phila., Washington, 1977-80; asst. dist. atty. Phila. Trial, Appellate Divsns., 1980-84; in-house environ. counsel TRW Inc., 1985-87; adj. prof. Case Western U. Law Sch., 1990-91; ptnr. Baker & Hostetler, Cleve., 1990—. Trustee Clean-Land Ohio, 1990—; mem. Cleve. Tree Commn., 1991, 92, 93, co-chair, 1993-94. Recipient Bronze Medal for Achievement, U.S. EPA, 1980. Mem. ABA (mem. environ. law com.), Pa. Bar Assn. (mem. environ. law com.), Ohio State Bar Assn. (mem. environ. law com.), Cleve. Bar Assn. (chmn. wetlands com., mem. environ. law com. Office: Baker & Hostetler 3200 Nat City Ct 1900 E 9th St Cleveland OH 44114-3485

BRENNAN, NORMA JEAN, professional society publications director; b. Helena, Mont., Apr. 16, 1939; d. Harland Sanford Herrin and Elizabeth (Wardlaw) Brumfield; m. Anthony E. Brennan, Dec. 4, 1964 (div. Mar. 1986); children: Christopher E., Kimberly A. BA, U. Pacific, 1960. Editorial asst. Am. Rocket Soc., N.Y.C., 1961-62, asst. mng. editor, 1962-65; mng. editor AIAA, N.Y.C., 1978-80; publs. divsn. dir. AIAA, N.Y.C., Washington, 1980—. Mem. Young Republicans, Stockton, Calif., 1958-60; vol. Mt. Sinai Hosp., N.Y.C., 1962-64. Mem. AIAA (sr., Space Shuttle Flag award), Soc. for Scholarly Pub. (chair edn. com.), Coun. Biology Editors, Assn. Am. Pubs., European Assn. Sci. Editors, Coun. Engring. and Sci. Soc. Execs., N.Am. Serials Interest Group, Washington Women's Info. Network. Home: 11551 Links Dr Reston VA 22090-4820 Office: AIAA 370 L'Enfant Promenade SW Washington DC 20024-2518

BRENNAN, PATRICIA BONNIE MARY, reference librarian, educator; b. Morristown, N.J., Feb. 24, 1953; d. John Pershing and Dorothy Margaret (O'Brien) B.; m. Joel Stephen Silverberg, Aug. 16, 1981; 1 child, Sarah Mae Brennan Silverberg. AB in Music, Brown U., 1975; MS in Libr. Scis., Columbia U., 1976. Rsch. asst. Joint Ctr. for Urban Studies Harvard U./MIT, Cambridge, Mass., 1976-77; music libr. rsch. divsn. Boston Pub. Libr., 1977-83; asst. prof., reference libr. James P. Adams Libr. R.I. Coll., Providence, 1983-90, asst. prof., head of reference James P. Adams Libr., 1990—; chair HELIN-RefPAC Com., Providence, 1991—; mem. NELINET-Reference Tech. Adv. Com., Newton, Mass., 1991-94. Editor: Directory of N.E. Music Libraries and Collections, 1989; contbr. revs. and articles to profl. jours. Vol. Keep Providence Beautiful, 1985—, Fox Point Citizens Assn., 1992—; bd. dirs. Providence Singers, 1993—; charter mem. Nat. Mus. for Women in the Arts, 1986—. Mem. ALA, Music Libr. Assn. (chair stats. com. 1988-91, chair pub. com. New Eng. chpt. 1987-92, vice chair, chair New Eng. chpt. 1990-93). Democrat. Jewish. Office: R I Coll James P Adams Libr Providence RI 02908

BRENNEMAN, GAYNE, physician; b. Pitts., Feb. 18, 1952; d. Richard H. and MaryLou (Black) B; m. Robert D. Slay, Oct. 14, 1975; children: Tyner, Cara-Rayne. BA, U. Calif., Santa Barbara, 1973; MD, U. Tex., San Antonio, 1981. Intern in internal medicine U. Tex. Health Sci. Ctr., San Antonio, 1981-82, resident in anesthesiology, 1982-84; staff anesthesiologist San Antonio, 1984-89; fellow in cardiac anesthesiology U. Ala., Birmingham, 1986-87; staff anesthesiologist Kaiser Hosp., San Diego, 1992—; asst. clin. faculty U. Calif., San Diego, 1993—. Mem. Am. Soc. Anesthesiology, Soc. Cardiovascular Anesthesiology. Republican. Mem. Mennonite Ch. Home: 703C Castile Ct Richmond VA 23233-6002

BRENNER, AMY REBECCA, podiatrist; b. N.Y.C., Dec. 31, 1958; d. Frank and Betty (Gitelman) B.; m. Peter Louis Klinge Jr., June 28, 1985. BS, Ithaca Coll., 1980; MA, Columbia U., 1982; D of Podiatric Medicine, N.Y. Coll. Podiatric Medicine, 1988. Cert. athletic trainer; health edn. instr., N.Y. State. Fellow Rusk Inst. Rehab. Medicine, N.Y.C., 1978; podiatrist, athletic trainer Athletic Events, N.Y., 1976—; physiology intern Chase Manhattan Cardiovascular Fitness Lab., N.Y.C., 1981; asst. athletic trainer Barnard Coll., N.Y.C., 1980-81; surg. resident Liberty Med. Ctr., Inc., Balt., 1989; staff podiatrist N.Y. Med. Group P.C., N.Y.C. and Westchester County, 1990—; pvt. practice podiatry N.Y.C. and Westchester County, 1990—; staff podiatrist DOCS office, Westchester County, 1992-93; European cons., Paris, 1993; test site adminstrs. com. Nat. Athletic Trainers Assn. Bd. Certification, Greenville, N.C., 1990—. Contbr. articles to profl. jours including Jour. Am. Podiatric Med. Assn. V.p. Bd. Dirs. Vernon Woods Apts., Inc., Mount Vernon, N.Y., 1990—; lectr. Am. Podiatric Med. Assn. Region VIII Meeting, Bethesda, Md., 1989, Liberty Med. Ctr., Inc., Balt., 1989. Mem. Am. Podiatric Med. Assn., Nat. Athletic Trainers Assn., Am. Coll. Sports Medicine, Am. Assn. for Women Podiatrists, Am. Alliance Health, Phys. Edn., Recreation and Dance. Home and Office: 154 Pearsall Dr Apt 4E Mount Vernon NY 10552-3905

BRENNER, ANNE MANON, pediatrician, allergist; b. Jacksonville, Fla., Oct. 21, 1944. BA, Tex. Tech. U., 1966; MD, U. Tex., 1971. Diplomate Am. Bd. Allergy and Immunology, Am. Bd. Pediatrics. Intern in family practice John Sealy Hosp. U. Tex., Galveston, 1971-72, resident in pediatrics, 1972-74; pediatric practice Galveston, 1974-77; fellow in immunology and respiratory medicine Nat. Asthma Ctr., Denver, 1977-80; sr. staff physician Nat. Jewish Ctr., Denver, 1981—; assoc. prof. pediatrics U. Colo. Health Scis. Ctr., Denver. Contbr. articles to profl. jours. Mem. Am. Acad. Pediatrics, Am. Acad. Allergy and Immunology. Roman Catholic. Office: Nat Jewish Ctr Immunology and Respiratory Medicine 1400 Jackson St Denver CO 80206

BRENNER, BETTY, bead sculptor, librarian; b. Luck, Wolyn, Poland; came to U.S., 1937; d. Nathanial and Sonia (Ariker) Gitelman; children: Jay Marlow, Matthew Adam, Amy Rebecca, Diane Rachel. BA in English, U. Pitts., 1950; MS in Radio, TV, Syracuse U., 1951; MLS in Libr. and Info. Sci., St. John's U., 1975. Chief copy writer Station Promotions, Inc., N.Y.C., 1952-53; scriptwriter, supr. 3-Dimensional Films, Inc., N.Y.C., 1953-54; writer pub. rels. N.Y.C. Housing Authority, 1954-55; originator bead-wire sculpture Brenner Studio, Hollis Hills, N.Y., 1968—; reference libr. Queensborough C.C., Queens, N.Y., 1981-82; head serials libr. N.Y.C. Tech. Coll., CUNY, Bklyn., 1982—, asst. prof., 1985-91, assoc. prof., 1992—; lectr., cons. bead-wire sculpture, N.Y.C., 1971—; researcher-collector menus N.Y.C. Tech. Coll. Libr., Bklyn., 1982—. Writer 1st TV and radio campaign on personal permanent voter registration in state of N.Y. LWV, 1957; pres., mem. bd. dirs. Parents Assn. in Pub. Sch., Queens, 1969-77; publicity chmn. Friends of the Queens Mus., 1974-76. Recipient 1st prize Man on Moon bead sculpture Queens Village Centennial, 1971; fellow Syracuse U., 1951; Profl. Staff Congress-CUNY grantee to document bead-wire sculpture, France, 1994-95. Mem. Artists-Craftsmen of N.Y. (exhibitor group shows), Ctr. for Study of Beadwork (exhibitor). Home: 81-14 218 St Hollis Hills NY 11427 Office: NYC Tech Coll 300 Jay St Brooklyn NY 11201-2902

BRENNER, ERMA, author; b. N.Y.C., Dec. 1, 1911; d. Robert and Amy (Schoenbrunn) Brandt; m. Charles Brenner, Sept. 8, 1935; children: Elsa Brenner Cohen, Lucy (Mrs. Barrie Biven). Student, Harvard, 1931-34; studied with, Eduard Steuermann, 1954-61. Dir., owner Camp Sherbo, Bridgeton, Maine, 1933-40; tchr. nursery sch. Children's Ctr., Roxbury, Mass., 1942-44, Colonial Heights Nursery Sch., Yonkers, N.Y., 1946-48; owner, developer Scenichrome, 1946-48; mem. staff White Plains (N.Y.) Day Care Ctr., 1976-77; coordinator play ctr. dept. child psychiatry, mem. staff therapeutic nursery Albert Einstein Med. Coll., 1977—; cons. to staff children's day hosp. N.Y. Hosp. Westchester Div., 1980-81; creator, dir. Small House Program for emotionally disturbed children N.Y. Hosp., Cornell Med. Ctr., Westchester divsn., Rockland State Children's Psychiat. Hosp., Queens Children's Psychiat. Hosp.; cons. Parent Child Ctr., N.Y. Psychoanalytic Inst., N.Y.C., 1993—, Therapeutic Nursery, 1994. Author: A New Baby! A New Life!, 1973, repub. as When Baby Comes Home, (with others) The Vulnerable Child, vol. 2, 1994. Recipient Christophers award, 1973. Home: 30 Rugby Ln Scarsdale NY 10583-2114 Office: 35 E 85th St New York NY 10028

BRENNER, ESTHER HANNAH, elementary school educator; b. N.Y.C., Apr. 12, 1940; d. Israel Eli and Elsie (Lipschitz) B. BEd, U. Miami, 1963. Cert. tchr., Fla. Elem. tchr. Dade County Bd. Pub. Edn., Miami, Fla., 1963—. Unit chmn. Jackson Meml. Hosp., Miami, 1963-73; instr. trainer first aid and CPR, Greater Miami chpt. ARC, 1987—, chmn. safety svcs. Homestead br., 1989-92, chmn. nursing and health programs S.W. br., youth chmn., 1988-90, disaster shelter mgr.; adult trainer South Fla. coun. Girl Scouts U.S.A., 1987—; pres. PTA, 1986-88. Recipient Sarah Cullipher award, 1992, Woman of Yr. award Am. Cancer Soc., 1990—, Clara Barton Honor award, 1985, Ayme Carroll Meml. award, 1988, Health and Safety award ARC, 1989, 1st Aid/CPR Instr. of Yr., 1990, Appreciation Plaque, Advocate for Victims, 1985, Plaque of Appreciation, PTA, 1989. Mem. NSTA, Fla. Assn. Sci. Tchrs., Dade County Sci. Tchrs. Assn. (Sci. Tchr. of Yr.), Advocates for Victims (plaque of appreciation 1987), Gamma Sigma Sigma (past historian, sec., v.p., pres. Gerater Miami chpt., bd. dirs. so. region 1975-79, nat. pub. rels. dir. 1979-83, Woman of Yr. 1973, Outstanding Alumnae award 1977, Disting. Svc. award 1987). Democrat. Jewish. Home: 12310 SW 111th S Canal Street Miami FL 33186-4826 Office: Richmond Elem Sch 16929 SW 104th Ave Miami FL 33157-4299

BRENNER, ESTHER LERNER, fundraiser; b. Washington, July 27, 1931; d. Mayer and Ethel Sarah (Kawarsky) Lerner; children: Mayer Alan, Saul Daniel, Matthew Hy. BA with distinction, George Washington U., 1953; MBA, U. Judaism, L.A., 1987. Speech therapist Alexandria area schs. for handicapped, Va., 1952-54; speech therapist, pvt. practice L.A., 1954-62; tchr. L.A. area pvt. schs., 1962-72; exec. dir., lobbyist Mfrs. Assn., L.A., 1980-82; exec. dir. Citizens for Constl. Rights, Beverly Hills, Calif., 1982-86; regional coord. U.S. Holocaust Meml. Council, Washington, 1986-89; pres. L.A. Hebrew High Sch., 1987-89; dir. devel. Aviva Ctr., L.A., 1992—; bd. dirs. Bur. Jewish Edn., L.A. Pres. Beverly-Angeles Homeowners Assn., 1978-87, bd. chair, 1992-95; sec., bd. dirs. Westside Civic Fedn., L.A., 1978-89; bd. dirs. Meals on Wheels, Beverly Hills, Friends of Beverly Hills Pub. Libr.; bd. dirs., v.p. 1939 Club. Mem. Nat. Soc. Fund Raising Execs., Soc. of Calligraphers, So. Calif. Council of Jewish Communal Service, Phi Beta Kappa. Home: 1264 Beverly Green Dr Beverly Hills CA 90212-4106

BRENNER, JANET MAYBIN WALKER, lawyer; b. Arkansas City, Kans.; d. D. Arthur and Maybin (Gardner) Walker; children: Margaret Maybin Burns, Theodore Kimball Jonas, Amanda Nash Freeman; m. Edgar H. Brenner, Aug. 4, 1979. AB, U. So. Calif.; JD, George Washington U., 1978. Bar: D.C. 1978; U.S. Dist. Ct. (D.C.). Sole practice law, Washington, 1979—. Mem. women's com. Corcoran Gallery Art, Washington, 1969—, Pres.'s Cir., Planned Parenthood D.C., 1990—, Found. for Preservation of Historic Georgetown. Mem. D.C. Bar Assn., Women's Bar of D.C., Women's Legal Def. Fund, Sulgrave Club (Washington). Home: 3325 R St NW Washington DC 20007-2310 also: Shadow Ridge Farm Washington VA 22747

BRENNER, LINDA, artist, educator; b. Phila.; d. Milton Aaron and Esther (Wein) B. BFA, RISD, 1962; postgrad., Tyler Sch. Fine Arts, 1962-63. Instr. dept. architecture Spring Garden Coll., Phila., 1983-90; instr. drawing and sculpture Pa. Acad. of Fine Arts, Phila., 1988—, chmn. sculpture dept., 1992—; guest lectr. C.C. Phila., 1992, Ecole des Beaux Arts, Paris, 1992. Artist, fabricator archtl. models of Nat. Gallery of Art, 1982, Louis I. Kahn In the Realm of Architecture, 1990-91, Ea. State Penitentiary, 1994. Mem. Internat. Sculpture Ctr., Nat. Trust for Historic Preservation. Home: 2117 Spruce St Philadelphia PA 19103 Office: Pa Acad Fine Arts 118 N Broad St Philadelphia PA 19102

BRENNER, PAUL HILARY, marketing professional; b. Northampton, Eng., Mar. 11, 1964; came to U.S., 1988; m. George Brenner, June 10, 1989. BSc with honors, U. Warwick, Eng., 1985; MBA, Columbia U., 1990. Sales adminstr. Mercedes-Benz U.K. Ltd., Milton Keynes, Eng., 1985-88; asst. mktg. mgr. Alpo Pet Foods, Allentown, Pa., 1991-92; assoc. mktg. mgr. Nabisco Foods Inc., East Hanover, N.J., 1993, mktg. mgr., 1993—.

BRENNER, RENA CLAUDY, communications executive; b. Camden, N.J.; d. John Lawler and Louretta (Du Fresene) Morgan; m. Edgar W. Claudy (div. 1968); 1 child, Renee; m. Millard Brenner, Nov. 6, 1971 (dec. 1975); children: Sally, Malcolm, Hugh. Student, U. Pa., 1978, U. Mich., 1983. Reporter Tribune-Telegram, Salt Lake City, 1943-45, Times Chronicle, Jenkintown, Pa., 1950-55; free-lance writer Enfield, Pa., 1955-60; pub. relations dir., advt. mgr. Gen. Atronics/Magnavox, Phila., 1960-70; mgr. corp. pub. relations ITE-Imperial, Phila., 1970-73, dir. corp. comm., 1973-76; dir. corp. comm. Parker-Hannifin Corp., Cleve., 1976-83, v.p. corp. comm., 1983-85; pres. Brenner Assocs., Clearwater, Fla., 1986—. Recipient Creative Direction award Phila. Club Advt. Women, 1970, Clarion award Women in Communications, 1982, Gold Key award Pub. Relations News, 1984. Mem. Bus. Profl. Advt. Assn. (life), Pub. Relations Soc. Am. (life), Nat. Investors Relations Inst.. Office: Brenner Assocs 1501 Gulf Blvd Apt 607 Clearwater FL 34630-2903

BRENT, REBECCA KEMP, volunteer, calligrapher and textile artist; b. Columbus, Ga., Sept. 18, 1959; d. John Richard and Patricia Louise (Jackson) Kemp; m. James Burkhart Brent, Jan. 11, 1985; children: Patricia Marie, Jonathan Lawrence. BS summa cum laude, U. Ala., Tuscaloosa, 1979; PhD, U. Tenn., 1983. Pattern and design cons. Texsel, Inc., West Point, Ga., 1979; asst. to assoc. dean Coll. Home Econs. U. Tenn., Knoxville, 1981, grad. teaching asst. dept. textiles, merchandising and design, 1979-82; designer, cons. Frey Assocs., Knoxville, 1982; operator Alteration Svc., Knoxville, 1982-83; product devel. and design Vol. Apparel, Inc., Knoxville, 1983-87. Contbr. articles to local newspapers. Instr. Children's Mus. of Oak Ridge, 1987; lay reader St. Francis' Ch., Norris, Tenn., 1993—; bd. dirs. YWCA Oak Ridge, 1989—, pres., 1993-94, instr., 1988—. Named to Group Study Exchg. Pakistan by Rotary Internat., 1992.

BRENT, RUTH STUMPE, design educator, researcher, educator; b. Washington, Mo., Sept. 11, 1951; d. Clarence Frank and Dorothy May (Horstick) Stumpe; m. Edward Everett Brent, Jr., May 14, 1972; children: Jessica Elizabeth, Jonathan Edward. BS cum laude, U. Mo., 1972; MA, U. Minn., 1974, PhD, 1978. Cert. of qualification Nat. Coun. Interior Design. Postdoctoral fellow in socio-clin. geriatrics NIMH, 1978-79; asst. prof. U. Mo., Columbia, 1981-86, assoc. prof. design, 1986-92, prof., 1992—, acting dept. chair, 1984-85, chair environ. design dept., 1985—; project dir. Adminstrn. on Aging Grant, 1979-81; v.p. Idea Works, Inc., Columbia, 1981—. Co-author (computer software) Home-Safe-Home, 1989; contbr. articles to profl. jours. Active Mayor's Task Force, Columbia Low-Income Housing, 1984-85; mem. Main St. adv. coun. dept. econ. devel. State of Mo., 1989-90; regional chairperson dists. 84 and 85 United Way, Columbia, 1989, 90; mem. adv. bd. Pub. Housing Authority, Columbia, 1984-85; chairperson North Cen. Region-54 Agrl. Expt. Sta. Rsch., 1989-91; mem. Columbia Regional Home Health and Hospice Adv. Bd., Columbia Regional Hosp., 1993—. Grantee Adminstrn. on Aging, 1979-81, VA, 1981, Am. Home Econs. Assn., 1981-82, 2 Joel Polsky Found. Interior Design Rsch. grantee, 1986, 87; recipient Fulbright award Chinese History and Culture, 1988, exch. faculty award Prince of Sonkla U., Thailand, 1990, Chonnam U., Korea, 1992; Fulbright fellow to Morocco and Tunisia, 1993. Mem. Am. Home Econs. Assn. (chmn. art/design sect. 1984-87, New Achievers award 1987), Am. Assn. Housing Educators, Am. Soc. Interior Designers (allied mem., chmn. position papers com. 1988—, Presdl. Citation 1990), Interior Design Educators Coun., Nat. Coun. for Interior Design (cert.), Environ. Design Rsch. Assn., Gerontol. Assn., Mo. Fulbright Alumni Assn. (membership chmn. 1989-90, v.p. 1990-92, pres. 1992-94), U. Club Inc. (pres. 1991-92, bd. dirs., sec. 1993-94, U. Mo. faculty alumni award 1992), Gamma Sigma Delta (pres. 1992-93), Omicron Nu, Phi Upsilon Omicron. Home: 100 W Briarwood Ln Columbia MO 65203-1678 Office: U Mo 137 Stanley Hall Columbia MO 65211

BRENTON, MARIANNE WEBBER, state legislator, technical librarian; b. Freeport, Maine, Feb. 25, 1933; d. Milton and Leah (Hamilton) W.; m. Richard P. Brenton, Mar. 4, 1955; children: Anne, Joan, Peter. BA in Biology, Bates Coll., 1955. Sci. tchr. Southboro (Mass.) High Sch., 1956-57; tech. libr. Trans-Sonics Inc., Burlington, Mass., 1957-59, MKS Instruments, Andover, Mass., 1978-90; state rep. Mass. Ho. of Reps., Boston, 1991—. Trustee Tewksbury (Mass.) State Hosp., 1967-83; mem. Burlington Sch. Com., 1972-81, also past chmn. Republican. Home: 16 Nelson Rd Burlington MA 01803 Office: Rm 443 State House Boston MA 02133

BRESLIN, EVALYNNE L. W., retired psychiatric nurse; b. Richmond, Ohio, July 7, 1931; d. Evan P. and Ada Augusta (Huscroft) Wood-Robertson; m. Donald Joseph Breslin, Jan. 30, 1954; children: Lisa Karen, Mark Nathaniel (dec.), Paul Andrew Scott. Diploma, Cleve. Met. Gen. Hosp., 1952; student, Case Western Res. U., Akron U.; HHD (hon.), London Inst. of Applied Rsch., 1973. Lic. RN, Ohio, Mass; RN, Ohio, Mass. Head nurse Cleve. Met. Gen. Hosp., Cleve. State Receiving Hosp.; cons. mental illness and addictions Mass.; ret. Bd. dirs. Triple Trouble; retired vol. monitor state hosp. facilities Alliance for Mentally Ill.; vol. nursing/psychiat. work with abandonded teenagers. Mem. ANA, NLN, Mass. Nurses Assn. (coun. on mental health Boston).

BRESLOW, MARILYN GANON, portfolio manager; b. Cleve., Apr. 23, 1944; d. Joseph M. and Edith (Rubin) Ganon; m. Jan L. Breslow, June 27, 1965; children: Noah J., Nicholas M. BA, Barnard Coll., 1965; MBA, Harvard U., 1970. Market rsch. analyst Polaroid Corp., Cambridge, Mass., 1965-68, project cons., 1973-78, bldg. W-4 mgr., 1978-80, dir. mktg. svcs., 1980-83; cons. Peat, Marwick, Mitchell & Co., Washington, 1970-71; assoc. ICF, Inc., Washington, 1971-73; cons. Brookline, Mass., 1983-84; v.p. Dillon, Read & Co., Inc., N.Y.C., 1984-90; gen. ptnr. Concord Ptnrs., 1984-90; portfolio mgr., analyst W.P. Stewart & Co., Inc., N.Y.C., 1990—; also bd. dirs. W. P. Stewart & Co., Inc., N.Y.C.; bd. dirs. Alteon, Inc., Northvale, N.J. Mem. N.Y. Soc. Security Analysts, IEEE. Home: 10 Horseguard Ln Scarsdale NY 10583-2311

BRESLOW, TINA, public relations executive; b. Phila., Feb. 18, 1946; d. Harry and Doris (Stein) Horowitz; m. Alan Breslow, Aug. 28, 1965 (div. 1970); children: Peter, Jennifer, Brett. Office mgr. Temple U. Ctr. City, Phila., 1976-79; publicist Temple U. Theater, Phila., 1979-81; mgr. pub. rels. Hershey Phila. Hotel, 1981-83; dir. pub. rels. Franklin Plaza Hotel, Phila., 1983-84; account mgr. Sommers Rosen, Inc., Phila., 1984-85; prin. Tina Breslow Pub. Relations, Phila., 1985—; pub. rels. cons. Dock St. Beer, Phila., 1986-87, Sheraton Soc. Hill Hotel, Phila., 1985-86. Chmn. pub. rels. com. Phila. Convention and Vis. Bur., 1985; pub. rels. cons. Phila. City Planning Commn., 1988, Phila. Commn. on AIDS, 1988. Recipient Super Communicator award Women in Communication, 1984, Best New Bus. Intro. award Phila. Better Bus. Bur., 1986, Community Svs. award Hotel Sales and Mktg. Assoc. Internat., 1988, Golden Bell award, 1988, Breakfast for Champions and Olymic Fundraiser The Alexander Hotel's, 1988. Mem. Phila. Pub. Rels. Assn., Pub. Rels. Soc. Am. Jewish. Office: Tina Breslow Pub Rels 2042 Rittenhouse Sq Philadelphia PA 19103-5621

BRESNAHAN, JUDY FUSSELL, accountant; b. Savannah, Ga., Aug. 24, 1942; d. Robert Lewis and Mildred (Brewton) Fussell; m. Roy D. Mixon, Mar. 9, 1966 (div. Feb. 1985); children: Cynthia Gayle Mixon Dubberly, Eric David Mixon; m. Lawrence A. Bresnahan, Apr. 26, 1986. BBA, U. No. Fla., 1977; postgrad., Jacksonville U., 1985. Bookkeeper Fla. Nat. Bank, Fernandina Beach, 1962-64; ins. clk. Humphreys Meml. Hosp., Fernandina Beach, 1964-65; payroll clk. J.C. Penneys, Lawton, Okla., 1966; inventory clk. Terminal Paper Bag, Yulee, Fla., 1967; lab. clk. ITT Rayonier Inc., Fernandina Beach, 1968-72, acctg. clk., 1972-74, cost acct., 1974-78, mgr. budgets and forecast, 1978-80, mgr. acctg. and asst. controller, 1980-85; controller Allied Colloids, Inc., Suffolk, Va., 1985—; part-time instr. Fla. Jr. Coll., Fernandina Beach, 1979; asst. sec. Allied Colloids, Inc., Suffolk, Va., 1992—. Mem. Inst. Mgmt. Accts. (v.p. adminstrn. 1991), Kiwanis (sec./treas. Kiwanis Found., Suffolk 1991-93, mem. coms. 1991—, v.p. Suffolk chpt.), Springfield Homeowners Assn. (treas. 1992—). Office: Allied Colloids Inc 2301 Wilroy Rd Suffolk VA 23434

BRETSCH, MARY LUCILLE, school librarian; b. Urbana, Ill., May 27, 1946; d. Lowell Francis and Lucille Rosetta (House) Belcher; m. Michael Bonnell, July 31, 1968 (div. Aug. 1971); 1 child, Melinda Anne; m. Darwin O. Bretsch, Apr. 14, 1979; 1 child, Joanna Lynn; stepchildren: Ryan Daniel, Kathleen Rae. BA in Latin, Monmouth Coll., 1968; MLS, U. Ill., 1975. Cert. tchr., supr. Sch. libr. West Jr. H.S., Kankakee, Ill., 1969-72, Belleville (Ill.) West H.S., 1972-89, Belleville East H.S., 1989—. asst. organist St. Paul United Ch. of Christ, Belleville, 1981—. Mem. AAUW (2d v.p. 1990), Ill. Sch. Libr. Media Assn., Riverwind Storytellers, Beta Phi Mu. Home: 3322 W A St Belleville IL 62223-6212

BRETT, JAN CHURCHILL, illustrator, author; b. Hingham, Mass., Dec. 1, 1949; d. George and Jean (Thaxter) B.; m. Daniel Bowler, Feb. 27, 1970 (div. 1979); 1 child, Lia; m. Joseph Hearne, Aug. 18, 1980. Student, Colby Jr. Coll., 1968-69, Boston Mus. Fine Arts Sch., 1970. Author, illustrator: Fritz and the Beautiful Horses, 1981 (Parent's Choice award Parents' Choice Found., 1981), Good Luck Sneakers, 1981, Annie and the Wild Animals, 1985, The First Dog, 1988, Beauty and the Beast, 1989, The Wild Christmas Reindeer, 1990, The Twelve Days of Christmas, 1990, The Mitten, 1990, Goldilocks and the Three Bears, 1990, The Owl and the Pussycat, 1991, Berlioz the Bear, 1991, The Trouble with Trolls, 1992, Christmas Trolls, 1993, Town Mouse, Country Mouse, 1994; illustrator: Woodland Crossings, 1978, Inside A Sand Castle and Other Secrets, 1979, The Secret Clocks Time Senses of Living Things, 1979, St. Patrick's Day in the Morning, 1980 (Parent's Choice award Parents' Choice Found. 1981), Young Melvin and Bulger, 1981, In the Castle of the Cats, 1981, Some Birds Have Funny Names, 1981 (Amb. Honor award English Speaking Union U.S. 1983), I Can Fly, 1981, Prayer, 1983, The Valentine Bears, 1983, Some Plants Have Funny Names, 1983, Where Are All the Kittens, 1984, Old Devil Is Waiting, 1985, The Mother's Day Mice, 1985, Scary, Scary Halloween, 1986, Noelle of the Nutcracker, 1986, The Enchanted Book, 1987, Happy Birthday, Dear Duck, 1988. Overseer Boston Symphony Orchestra; trustee Thayer Acad., Braintree, Mass. Mem. Nat. Soc. Colonial Dames Am. Office: 132 Pleasant St Norwell MA 02061-2523

BRETZ, KELLY JEAN, actuary; b. Wadena, Minn., Oct. 30, 1962; d. Edmund Leroy and Glenyce Clara (Andrie) B. BA in Math., Moorhead State U., 1984. Asst. actuary Northwestern Nat. Life Ins. Co., Mpls., 1984-92; assoc. actuary TMG Life Ins. Co., Fargo, N.D., 1993-94, MSI Life Ins. Co., Arden Hills, Minn., 1994, MidAm. Mut. Life Ins. Co., Roseville, Minn., 1994—; grader Soc. Actuaries' Exam 220, 1992, 93. Contbr. articles to co. jours. Organizer blood drive Mpls. Blood Bank, 1992; meal deliverer Meals on Wheels, Fargo, 1993; meal server Sharing and Caring Hands, Mpls., 1992. Fellow Soc. Actuaries (mem. fin. and investment mgmt. practice edn. com.); mem. Am. Acad. Actuaries, Twin Cities Actuarial Club, Whitewater Investment Club, Life Ins. Mktg. and Rsch. Assn. (fin. mktg. and svcs. com. 1993). Office: MidAm Mut Life Ins Co 1801 W County Rd B Roseville MN 55113

BREUER, NANCY LOIS, management consultant; b. Paterson, N.J., Oct. 20, 1947; d. Edward Jr. and Lois Mary Breuer; m. S. Scott Bartchy, Nov. 19, 1988. BA cum laude, Middlebury (Vt.) Coll., 1969; MA, Fuller Theol. Sem., Pasadena, Calif., 1983. Instr. English Monument Mt. Regional High Sch., Great Barrington, Mass., 1969-72, South Burlington (Vt.) High Sch., 1972-77; writer Regal Books, Glendale, Calif., 1977-79; asst. dir. extended edn. Fuller Theol. Sem., Pasadena, 1979-84; dir. contract edn. ARC, L.A., 1984-89, dir. HIV/AIDS edn., 1989-91; cons., writer Breuer Cons., L.A., 1991—; course designer, facilitator trainer Hollywood Supports, 1992—. Author: A Guide to Self Care for HIV Infection, 1991, AIDS in the Workplace: Facilitator's Manual, 1993, (with others) AIDS in the Workplace, 1994; editor jour. Pacific Ctr., 1991-94; contbr. articles to profl. jours. Mem. exec. com. Am. Lung Assn., L.A., 1984-87; commr. L.A. County AIDS Commn., 1989-91; chair AIDS in the workplace com. United Way, L.A., 1988—. Recipient Med. Category award for video U.S. Indsl. Film & Video Festival, 1992, Pro award Publicity Club L.A., 1993. Mem. ASTD, Am. Mgmt. Assn., Nat. Leadership Coalition on AIDS. Home: 2260 N Cahuenga Blvd Apt 207 Los Angeles CA 90068-2799 Office: Breuer Cons 2260 N Cahuenga Blvd Apt 207 Los Angeles CA 90068-2799

BREUNIG, KATHY LYNN, secondary school counselor; b. Kansas City, Mo., Jan. 18, 1955; d. Geroge Lawrence and Velma Kathaleen Maxwell; m. Vincent Eugene Breunig, May 2, 1980 (div. 1990); 1 child, Amber. BS in Edn., Ctrl. Mo. State U., 1976, MS in Edn., 1979; MS in Counseling Psychology, Our Lady of the Lake Coll., 1992. Lic. profl. counselor, marriage and family therapist, Tex. Spl. edn. tchr. Thomas Ultican Elem. Sch., Blue Springs, Mo., 1976-83; self contained classroom spl. edn. tchr. Sycamore Mid. Sch., Kokomo, Ind., 1983-84; tchr. of ednl. mentally retarded Kokomo High Sch., 1984-86; tchr. of learning disabled Houser Mid. Sch., Conroe, Tex., 1986-87; tchr. of spl. edn. Omar Bradley Mid. Sch., San Antonio, 1990-91, tchr. self contained classroom, 1990-91; student-tchr.-asst. network specialist Madison High Sch., San Antonio, 1991-92; guidance counselor Roosevelt High Sch., San Antonio, 1992—. Active local PTO, 1976—. Mem. ACA. Democrat. Presbyterian. Home: 753 Summerwood

Dr New Braunfels TX 78130-3626 Office: Roosevelt High Sch 5110 Walzem Rd San Antonio TX 78218-2194

BREVIK, JUDITH ELAINE MCNEIL, nurse; b. Panama City, Fla., Nov. 14, 1947; d. L.C. and Elaine Anna (Wendt) McNeil; m. Charles R. Brevik, Sept. 21, 1968; children: Eric, Raymond, Bethany. RN, Touro Infirmary Sch. Nursing, New Orleans, 1968; student, Chapman Coll., Gulf Coast Community Coll.; BSN, Minot State U. Cert. operating room nurse. Head nurse operating rm. Valley Community Hosp., Santa Maria, Calif.; operating rm. edn. coord. Trinity Med. Ctr., Minot, N.D.; oper. rm. clin. educator Mem. Hosp. of So. Okla., 1994—. Active numerous community orgns. Mem. Assn. Oper. Rm. Nurses (del. nat. congress 1993), N.D. Nurses Assn. (state continuing edn. com., dist. del. to state nurses conv. 1992, 93, alternate del., 1994, chair task force for mandatory continuing edn., chair dist. bylaws com., dist. bd. dirs., pres.-elect. dist. 2, 1993-94, state govt. rels. com. 1992-94, rsch. coun. and congress on edn. and profl. practice), Okla. Nurses Assn.. Home: 421 Railhead Loop Ardmore OK 73401

BREWER, ANNE ALEXANDER, physician; b. Kansas City, Mo., Mar. 16, 1949; d. Chester Leland and Martha Alexander Brewer; m. James Kowalski, Sept. 4, 1976; children: Rebecca, Matthew. AB, Brown U., 1971; MDiv, Episc. Divinity Sch., Cambridge, Mass., 1979; MD, U. Vt., 1979. Diplomate Am. Bd. Family Practice, Am. Bd. Geriatrics. Instr. U. Conn. Affiliated Hosp., Hartford, 1982-83; emergency room physician Manchester (Conn.) Hosp., 1983-85; pvt. practice Manchester, 1985-87, East Hartford, Conn., 1987-90, Hartford, Conn., 1990-94, Stamford, Conn., 1994—; med. dir. CorpCare Occupl. Med. Ctr., Manchester, 1987-93; med. advisor Town of Manchester, 1987—, Manchester Bd. of Edn., 1988—. Mem. Am. Acad. Family Physicians, Hartford County Med. Assn. (Cmty. Svc. award 1993), Fairfield County Med. Assn. Office: 1275 Summer St Stamford CT 06905

BREWER, CHERYL ANN, obstetrics-gynecology educator; b. New Rochelle, N.Y., Oct. 31, 1959; d. John Paul and Marie Elizabeth (Royance) B. BS, Miss. U. for Women, 1981; MD, Ind. U., Indpls., 1985. Resident in ob-gyn. SUNY Health Scis. Ctr., Syracuse, 1985-89, asst. prof. ob-gyn., 1989-91; asst. prof. dept. ob-gyn. Ind. U., Indpls., 1991-92; fellow in gynecologic oncology U. Calif., Irvine, 1992—. Fellow Am. Coll. Ob-Gyn. Home: 17632 Jordan Ave Apt 40B Irvine CA 92715-2976 Office: U Calif Med Ctr 101 The City Dr Irvine CA 92715

BREWER, CYNTHIA MARGARET, personnel executive; b. Bangor, Maine, Mar. 24, 1959; d. Alex James and Margaret Ann (Palmer) B. BS, U. Maine, 1981, MBA, 1987. Sr. human resource cert. Part-time office asst. ADCO Surg. Supply Co., Bangor, 1976-81; budget analyst Bangor Hydro-Electric Co., 1981-87, rate engr., 1987-88; pers. asst. Bangor Dydro-Electric Co., 1988-92, asst. dir. pers., 1992—. Account exec., fund distrn. com. United Way, Bangor, 1989—; human resource com. YMCA, 1991-94; bd. dirs. Bangor Hydro Fed. Credit Union, 1990-94; pers. com. Literacy Vols., 1994; bus. adv. coun. Projects with Industry, 1991-94. Mem. ASTD, Human Resource Assn. of Ea. Maine (chair), Phi Kappa Phi, Beta Gamma Sigma. Home: 393 Mount Hope Ave Bangor ME 04401-4210

BREWER, JANET LESTER, legal assistant; b. Van, Tex., Feb. 28, 1935; d. Grady Washington and Melba Theo (Johnson) Lester; m. Alvis Don Brewer, Aug. 15, 1933; children: Larry Don, Jana Lynn. Student, Lee Coll., Baytown, Tex. Legal sec. Reid, Strickland & Gillette, Baytown, 1953-57, 58-64; title ins. sec. Bay Title Co., Baytown, 1966-69; sec. to engring. divsn. Diamond Shramrock, Deer Park, Tex., 1969-71; legal sec. Glenn Vickery, Baytown, 1971-74; title examiner Bay Title Co., Baytown, 1974-75; legal asst. Don Smith, Atty., Baytown, 1975-82, Glenn Vickery & Assocs., Baytown, 1982—. Named Legal Sec. of Yr., Baytown Legal Secs. Assn., 1977-78. Mem. State Bar Assn. Tex. (legal assts. divsn.), Beta Sigma Phi (Preceptor Gamma chpt., rec. sec. 1995). Democrat. Baptist. Home: 2902 Ronson Ln Baytown TX 77521-9219 Office: Glenn Vickery & Assocs 1300 Rollingbrook St Ste 601 Baytown TX 77521-3846

BREWER, JANICE KAY, state legislator, property and investment firm executive; b. Hollywood, Calif., Sept. 26, 1944; d. Perry Wilford and Edna Clarice (Bakken) Drinkwine; m. John Leon Brewer, Jan. 1, 1963; children: Ronald Richard, John Samuel, Michael Wilford. Med. asst. cert. Valley Coll., Burbank, Calif., 1963, practical radiol. technician cert., 1963; D in Humanities (hon.) L.A. Chiropractic Coll., 1970. Pres., Brewer Property & Investments, Glendale, Ariz., 1970—; mem. Ariz. Ho. of Reps., Phoenix, 1983-86, Ariz. Senate, 1987—, majority whip, 1993—. State committeeman, Rep. Party, Phoenix, 1970, 1983; legis. liaison Ponderosa Rep. Women, Phoenix, 1980; bd. dirs. Motion Picture & TV Commn. Active NOW. Recipient Freedom award Vets. of Ariz., 1994; named Woman of Yr., Chiropractic Assn. Ariz., 1983, Legislator of Yr., Behaviour Health Assn. Ariz., 1991, NRA, 1992. Mem. Nat. Fedn. Rep. Women, Am. Legis. Exch. Coun. Lutheran. Home: 6835 W Union Hills Dr Glendale AZ 85308-8058 Office: Ariz State Senate State Capitol Phoenix AZ 85007*

BREWER, KARA PRATT, planned giving director; b. Reno, Nev., Oct. 29, 1930; d. Kenneth and Kara (Lucas) Pratt; m. David P. Brewer, Sept. 10, 1949; children: Margaret, Martin, Kenneth, Paul, Elena, Clare, Sam, Matthew. Student, Smith Coll., 1948-49; BA, U. of the Pacific, 1969, MA, 1972, ArtsD, 1976. Asst. editor Pacific Historian U. of the Pacific, Stockton, Calif., 1971, instr., 1971-75, writer-in-residence, 1976, dir. alumni and parent program, 1977-91, dir. planned giving, 1991—; conf. chair Irish Studies meeting, Western Regional Am. Conf., 1991. Author: Pioneer or Perish: A History of the University of the Pacific, 1977. Bd. dirs. St. Mary's Interfaith Dining Room, 1983—. Fellow Danforth Found., 1969-73. Mem. Am. Com. for Irish Studies, CASE (ann. conf. chair Dist. VII 1983, ann. conf. co-chair 1982), Pope John XXIII Found. (bd. dirs. 1970—), Phi Kappa Phi. Democrat. Roman Catholic. Home: 94 W Knoles Way Stockton CA 95204-3112 Office: U of the Pacific Planned Giving # 2 Burns Twr Stockton CA 95211

BREWER, KAREN, librarian; b. Janesville, Wis., Apr. 29, 1943; d. Gordon A. and Charlotte (Warren) Schultz; m. Eugene N. Brewer, June 22, 1963. BA, U. Wis., 1965, MA, 1966; PhD, Case Western Res. U., 1983. Libr. Middleton Med. Libr. U. Wis., Madison, 1966-67; libr. Med. Libr. U. Tenn., Memphis, 1968-69; libr. Cleve. Health Sci. Libr. Case Western Res. U., Cleve., 1970-76; dir. libr. Coll. Medicine Northeastern Ohio U., Rootstown, 1976-88; dir. libr. Med. Ctr. NYU, 1988—. Mem. editorial bd. Ann. Stats. Acad. Health Sci. Librs., 1986-91. Fellow N.Y. Acad. Medicine; mem. Assn. Acad. Health Sci. Librs. (sec.-treas. 1986-89, pres.-elect 1994, pres. 1995), Med. Libr. Assn. (bd. dirs. 1991-94), Acad. Health Info. Profls. (disting. mem.), Am. Med. Informatics Assn. Office: NYU Med Ctr Libr 550 1st Ave New York NY 10016-6402

BREWER, SHERYL ANNE, social worker, dental hygienist; b. Orlando, Fla., Jan. 9, 1946; d. Allen Frank Jr. and Nell Marian (Thompson) B. BS in Dental Hygiene, Tex. Woman's U., 1973; MSSW, U. Tex., Arlington, 1982; postgrad., Tex. Woman's U., 1991. Cert. social worker, Acad. Cert. Social Workers; lic. master social worker; lic. marriage and family therapists; lic. and cert. chem. dependency specialist; registered dental hygienist. Dental hygienist Dr. J.A. Hardgrave, Crowley, Tex., 1976-89, Dr. Jack Martin, 1992—; exec. asst. Dr. R.J. Shaeffer, Ft. Worth, 1980-92; instr. social work various univs., 1980—; instr. Tarrant County Jr. Coll., Ft. Worth, 1985—; pvt. practice Ft. Worth, Arlington, 1987—; cons. Women's Ctr. Tarrant County, 1981-89, Rubicon, Ft. Worth, 1985-90; lectr. Nat. Orgn. for Victim Assistance, Washington, 1985—. Mem. Tarrant Coun. Alcoholism and Drug Abuse, Women of All Saints, Ctr. for the Prevention of Sexual and Domestic Violence; counselor Women's Ctr. of Tarrant County, 1981-87. Mem. NASW, APHA, Am. Assn. World Health, Am. Soc. Clin. Hypnosis, Am. Dental Hygienist Assn., Nat. Orgn. Victim Assistance, Fla. Dental Hygienist Assn., Tex. Dental Hygienist Assn., Tarrant County Psychol. Assn., Nat. Assn. Coun. for Children, Eta Sigma Gamma. Episcopalian. Office: 6500 West Freeway Ste 701 Fort Worth TX 76116 also: 6702 W Poly Webb Arlington TX 76016 Mailing Address: PO Box 100582 Fort Worth TX 76185

BREWSTER, ELIZABETH WINIFRED, English language educator, poet, novelist; b. Chipman, N.B., Can., Aug. 26, 1922; d. Frederick John and Ethel May (Day) Brewster. B.A., U. N.B., 1946; M.A., Radcliffe U., 1947; B.L.S., U. Toronto, Ont., Can., 1953; Ph.D., Ind. U., 1962; D.Litt., U. N.B., 1982. Cataloger Carleton U., Ottawa, Ont., 1953-57; cataloger Ind. U. Library, Bloomington, 1957-58, N.B. Legis. Library, 1965-68, U. Alta. Library, Edmonton, Can., 1968-70; mem. English dept. Victoria U., B.C., 1960-61; reference libr. Mt. Allison U. Libr., Sackville, N.B., 1961-65; vis. asst. prof. English U. Alta., 1970-71; mem. faculty U. Sask., Saskatoon, Can., 1972—, asst. prof. English, 1972-75, assoc. prof., 1975-80, prof., 1980-90, prof. emeritus, 1990—. Author: East Coast, 1951, Lilloot, 1954, Roads, 1957, Passage of Summer, 1969, Sunrise North, 1972, In Search of Eros, 1974, Sometimes I Think of Moving, 1977, The Way Home, 1982, The Sisters, 1974, It's Easy to Fall on the Ice, 1977, Digging In, 1982, Junction, 1982, A House Full of Women, 1983, Selected Poems 1944-84, 2 vols., 1985, Visitations, 1987, Entertaining Angels, 1988, Spring Again, 1990, The Invention of Truth, 1991, Wheel of Change, 1993. Recipient E.J. Pratt award for poetry U. Toronto, 1953, Pres. medal for poetry U. Western Ont., 1980, Lit. award Can. Broadcasting Corp., 1991. Mem. League Can. Poets, Writers' Union Can., Assn. Can. Univ. Tchrs. English. Office: U Saskatchewan, Dept English, Saskatoon, SK Canada S7N 0W0

BREWSTER, LINDA JEAN, family nurse practitioner; b. Portland, Maine, Nov. 6, 1956; d. Thomas Stuart and Patricia Noreen (Dixon) Warden; m. James Ernest Brewster, Aug. 20, 1977; children: Ryan James, Seth Thomas. BS summa cum laude, U. So. Maine, 1987, MS, 1992; FNP, U. N.H., 1995. Cert. nurse clinician, cert. family nurse prctitioner; cert. ACLS. Staff nurse II Maine Med. Ctr., Portland, 1987-89, clin. level nurse III, 1989-91, case mgr., 1990-91, asst. head nurse, 1991-94; ICU and emergency rm. nurse So. Maine Med. Ctr., 1994—; intravenous nurse clinician Homedco, Lewiston, Maine, 1994—; instr. nursing So. Maine Tech. Coll., South Portland, 1994—; site investigator Multisite Study Harvard Med. Sch., 1993-94; co-investigator Maine Med. Ctr., 1993. Author: Section Review Book for RNC Certification Examination, 1994; developer in field. Bd. dirs. Am. Heart Assn., 1989-93, programs chair, 1991-93. Mem. ANA, Maine State Nurses Assn., Sigma Theta Tau (Kappa Zeta chpt.). Methodist. Home: 27 Old Gray Rd Cumberland Center ME 04021

BREWSTER, OLIVE NESBITT, retired librarian; b. San Antonio, July 19, 1924; d. Charles Henry and Olive Agatha (Nesbitt) B.; B.A., Our Lady of Lake Coll., 1945, B.S. in L.S., 1946. Asst. librarian aeromed. library U.S. Air Force Sch. Aviation Medicine, Randolph AFB, Tex., 1946-60, chief cataloger aeromed. library Sch. Aerospace Medicine, Brooks AFB, Tex., 1960-83, chief tech. processing, 1983-88; ret., 1988. Mem. ALA, Am. Soc. Indexers, Mensa. Anglican. Home: 1906 Schley Ave San Antonio TX 78210-4332

BREWSTER, REBECCA LYNN, city official; b. Sherman, Tex., Dec. 17, 1957; d. Okey D. and Patsy A. (Collins) Lucas; m. Mark Brewster, Mar. 24, 1979; children: Tristan, Brandon. BS in Elem. Edn., Angelo State U., 1979; MA in Pub. Adminstrn., Sul Ross State U., 1991. Cert. mcpl. clk.; registered profl. mcpl. clk., Tex. assessor/collector; cert. tchr., Tex.; BLS instr., CPR instr. City sec./chief adminstrv. officer Town of Van Horn, Tex., 1979—. Vol. dir. Rainbow Express Day Care Ctr., Van Horn, 1991—, pres., 1987—; adv. bd. YWCA Child Care Mgmt. Svcs., El Paso, Tex., 1992—; mem. govt. application rev. & comment com. Rio Grande Coun. Govts., El Paso, 1987—; mem. Regional Solid Waste Adv. Com., El Paso, 1989—, Regional Recycling Com., El Paso, 1992—. Mem. Tex. Mcpl. Clks. Assn. (pres., sec., treas. west Tex. chpt., Lila Fern Martin scholarship 1990), Tex. Mcpl. League (regional sec. 1989-90, legis. policy com. 1986), Internat. Inst. Mcpl. Clks., Tex. City Mgrs. Assn., Govt. Fin. Officers Assn. of Tex., Tex. Assn. Assessing Officers, Tex. Assn. Mcpl. Tax Adminstrs. (sec./treas. 1994-95), Tex. Treas.' Assn., others. Office: Town of Van Horn PO Box 517 Van Horn TX 79855-0517

BREWSTER-WALKER, SANDRA JOANN, public relations executive, publishing executive, genealogist, historian, consultant; b. Copiaque, N.Y., June 16, 1942; d. Willis Hodges and F. Wilda (Scurlock) Brewster; m. Stuart M. Walker (div. 1984); children: Jeffrey, Carlton, Cassandra. Cert., Island Drafting Sch., 1965; BA, Dowling Coll., 1972; MA, SUNY, New Paltz, 1978. Acting asst. dir. Urban Ctr., Vassar Coll., Poughkeepsie, N.Y., 1972-74; tchr. Middletown Jr. High Sch., N.Y., 1974-78; elec. mfg. engr. Perkin-Elmer Corp., Norwalk, Conn., 1978-84; pub., editor Ram's Horn Pub. Co., Stamford, Conn., 1983-84; software mgr. Pergamon Press, Inc., Elmsford, N.Y., 1985-86; pres., owner The Brewster Group, Inc., Stamford, 1986—; dep. dir. pub. affairs (apptd. by Pres. Clinton) USDA, Washington, 1993—. Pub., editor Conneticut Update, 1984; editor: Augustus M. Hodges Project, 1978-86, Fairfield County Black Biograph. Index Project, 1980—; contbr. to Westchester Women mag., 1985. Mem. Town of Walkill Bicentennial Com., 1976, Bicentennial Com., Middletown Pub. Schs., 1976; mem. Circleville Pub. Sch. PTA, 1975-77, v.p., 1977-78; instr. genealogy Greater Orange YMCA, Middletown, N.Y., 1975, 77, mem. planning bd., 1976; vice chmn. to corp. campaign advisor United Negro Coll. Fund, Lower Fairfield, Conn., 1980-81; mem. John Anderson for Pres. Com., 1980; exec. dir. Conn. Legis. Black Caucus, Hartford, 1981-82; aide to State Senator J.C. Daniels, 1981-82; founder, bd. dir. Bridgeport Black History Project, 1982-83; adv. com. Conn. Democrats, 1984; inaugural com. Mayor Serrani, Stamford, 1984-85; coord. Lower Fairfield County Mondale/Ferraro Campaign, 1984; state coord. Com. to Elect Jesse Jackson Pres., 1984; Stamford coord., 1988—; mem. Conn. chpt. Coalition of 100 Black Women, 1980-81, Nat. Project Vote, 1984, adv. com. black women's exhibit L.I. and Bklyn. Hist. Soc.; vol. Alberta Jagoes for Mayor campaign, Milford, Conn., 1982, Christine M. Niedermeier for Congress Com., 1984; mem. steering com. Margaret Morton for Congress, 1987; candidate state rep. 145th dist., 1988; advance team and convention operation Clinton for President '92, Clinton/Gore '92. Named Woman of Month, Conn. Women's Mag., 1983, Working Woman of Month, Essence mag., 1983. Mem. NAFE, NOW, Coalition of 100 Black Women (Lower Fairfield chpt. 1986, 89-90), Nat. Abortion Rights Action League, Rainbow Coalition (computer cons.), National Club, Advance Team Clinton/Gore. Office: OC 14th & Independence Ave Washington DC 20006

BRIAN, PATRICIA ANN, social services administrator; b. Sioux Falls, S.D.; d. Lawrence Alexander and Ethelyn Lucille (Milaney) Dumas; children: Robert Milling III, Courtney Dumas. BS, Northwestern U., 1959; postgrad., So. Ill. U., 1982. Cert. instr. human potential, parent effectiveness tng., rational behavior theory. Tchr. Belleville (Ill.) Pub. Schs., 1963-76; instr., project dir., dir. spl. svcs. ctr. Belleville Area Coll., 1977—; cons. Ill. Bd. Edn., 1978—, Ill. C.C. Bd., 1985—; presenter seminars. Author, editor: (resource books) Help for Addictive Diseases, 1988, Out of the Darkness: Arresting Rape, 1988, Survival Study Skills, 1989, Values Clarification, 1979, Attitudes and Communications, 1986. Bd. dirs. So. Ill. Network for Women, Parents in Action, Living Independently Now Ctr., Care and Counseling Social Svcs., Metro East, Ill., 1991—, Pregnant Teen Svcs.; mem. mayoral steering com. Belleville's 175th Birthday, 1989, co-chmn. Celebration Ball, 1989. Recipient Bright Idea award Ill. Coun. C.C. Adminstrs., 1994. Mem. Nat. Assn. Vocat. Edn. Spl. Needs Pers., Ill. Assn. Vocat. Edn. Spl. Needs Pers. (pres. 1994, Person of Yr. 199), Ill. Vocat. Assn. (bd. dirs. 1993-94, Outstanding Programming in Cmty. and Coll. Alcohol Awareness award 1988). Office: Belleville Area Coll 2500 Carlyle Rd Belleville IL 62221-5899

BRIANT, MARYJANE, newspaper editor; b. Cape May Court House, N.J., Dec. 29, 1951; d. William Lincoln and Jane Hutchison (Bicking) B.; 1 child, Erica Nicole. BS in Journalism, Boston U., 1974. Reporter The Cape May County Times, North Wildwood, N.J., 1975; reporter The Gazette-Leader, North Wildwood, 1976, city editor, 1977, mng. editor, 1978-79; copy editor The Press of Atlantic City, Pleasantville, N.J., 1979; asst. city editor The Press, Pleasantville, 1984-87; news editor The Press of Atlantic City, Pleasantville, 1987-90; asst. mng. editor The Gazette-Leader, North Wildwood, 1990-91; mng. editor The Press of Atlantic City, Pleasantville, N.J., 1992—. Bd. dirs. Boys and Girls Club Atlantic City, 1992—. Mem. N.J. Press Assn., Atlantic City Press Club (presenter Headliners Awards 1993-94). Office: The Press of Atlantic City Devins Ln Pleasantville NJ 08232

BRICCETTI, JOAN THERESE, symphony manager, arts management consultant; b. Mt. Kisco, N.Y., Sept. 29, 1948; d. Thomas Bernard and Joan (Filardi) B. AB in Am. History, Bryn Mawr Coll., 1970. Adminstrv. asst., program guide editor Sta. WIAN-FM, Indpls., 1970-72; adminstrv. asst. T. Briccetti, condr., Indpls., 1970-72; dir. pub. rels. The Richmond (Va.) Symphony, 1972-73, mgr., 1973-80; mgr. St. Louis Symphony Orch., 1980-84, gen. mgr., 1984-86, chief oper. officer, 1986-92; ind. cons. for arts Arts & Edn., 1993—; cons., panelist Arts Couns. Ohio, Va., Ky. Active orch. and planning sects., music programs Nat. Endowment fot the Arts, 1974-78, chmn. orch. panel, 1975-78, cons., evaluator, panelist, 1974—, mem. first challenge grant rev. panel, 1977, co-chmn. recording panel, 1983-84; mem. grant rev. panel Va. Commn. for the Arts, 1976-78; adv. bd. Eastern Music Festival, 1977-83, Richmond Friends Opera, 1979-80; adv. coun. Va. Alliance for Arts Edn., 1978, Federated Arts Coun. Richmond, 1979-80; steering com. BRAVO Arts, 1978-79 (gov.'s award); cons. Tenn. Arts Commn., 1979-80; bd. dirs. Theatre IV, Richmond, 1974-80, Am. Music Ctr, N.Y.C., 1980-84, St. Louis Forum, 1983—, New City Sch., St. Louis, 1987—, Metro Theatre Co., 1994—; mem. challenge grant evaluation panel Ky. Arts Commn., 1983; participant Leadership St. Louis, 1983-84, bd. dirs., 1987-89; commr. subdistrict Mo. History Mus., 1987—, sec., 1993; speaker, panelist, cons. numerous arts orgns. Mem. Am. Symphony Orch. League (chmn. orch. library info. svc. adv. com., recruiter, mem. final interview com., advisor mgmt. fellowship program), Regional Orch. Mgrs. Assn. (v.p. 1976, policy com. 1977-79), Women's Forum Mo.

BRICKER, BETSY JEANNETTE, genetic engineer; b. L.A., Jan. 14, 1953; d. James S. and Maryann T. Bricker; m. Clark F. Ford, Dec. 29, 1976 (div. Jan. 1993); children: Rose H., Robin A. BA cum laude, UCLA, 1975; PhD, U. Iowa, 1982. Rsch. microbiologist Nat. Animal Disease Ctr., Ames, Iowa, 1985—; speaker and presenter in field. Contbr. chpts. to books and rsch. papers to profl. jours. Postdoctoral fellow U. Va. Dept. Microbiology, Charlottesville, 1982-85; Postgoctoral Tng. grantee NIH, 1982-85. Mem. AAAS, Am. Soc. Microbiology, Sigma Delta Epsilon. Office: NADC PO Box 70 Ames IA 50010-0070

BRICKER, VICTORIA REIFLER, anthropology educator; b. Hong Kong, June 15, 1940; came to U.S., 1947, naturalized, 1953; d. Erwin and Henrietta (Brown) Reifler; m. Harvey Miller Bricker, Dec. 27, 1964. A.B., Stanford U., 1962; A.M., Harvard U., 1963, Ph.D., 1968. Vis. lectr. anthropology Tulane U., 1969-70, asst. prof., 1970-73, assoc. prof., 1973-78, prof., 1978—, chmn. dept. anthropology, 1988-91. Author: Ritual Humor in Highland Chiapas, 1973, The Indian Christ, The Indian King: The Historical Substrate of Maya Myth and Ritual, 1981 (Howard Francis Cline meml. prize Conf. Latin Am. History), A Grammar of Mayan Hieroglyphs, 1986; book rev. editor: Am. Anthropologist, 1971-73; editor: Am. Ethnologist, 1973-76; gen. editor: Supplement to Handbook of Middle American Indians, 1977—. Guggenheim fellow, 1982; Wenner-Gren Found. Anthropol. Rsch. grantee, 1971; Social Sci. Rsch. Coun.l grantee, 1972; NEH grantee, 1990. Fellow Am. Anthrop. Assn. (exec. bd. 1980-83); mem. NAS, Am. Soc. Ethnohistory (exec. bd. 1977-797), Linguistic Soc. Am., Seminario de Cultura Maya, Societe des Americanistes, Am. Acad. Scis. Office: Tulane Univ Dept Anthropology New Orleans LA 70118

BRICKERT, TINA SUE, nursing educator; b. Greencastle, Ind., Feb. 8, 1965; d. Jack Edward Lee and Rosella (Sheese) Taylor; m. Clayton L. Brickert, June 23, 1984; 1 child, Charles Riley. Cert. IVTC, ICTC, 1984; Assoc. in Nursing, Marian Coll., 1986, BSN summa cum laude, 1988; MSN in Perinatology, Ind. U., 1991; student nurse-midwife, 1994—. Lic. practical nurse. Staff nurse Brownsburg (Ind.) Family Med. Ctr., 1985-88, Morgan County Meml. Hosp., Martinsville, Ind., 1988—; instr. Marian Coll., Indpls., 1989-90, academic advisor, 1990-91; instr. U. Indpls., 1991-92; clin. nurse specialist St. Francis Hosp. Ctr., Indpls., 1991-92; instr. U. Indpls., 1992—. Mem. Assn. Women's Health, Obstet. and Neonatal Nursing, Ind. State Nursing Assn., Marian Coll. Hon. Soc. of Nursing (v.p. 1990-94), Am. Coll. Nurse-Midwives, Sigma Theta Tau. Baptist. Office: U Indpls 1400 E Hanna Ave Indianapolis IN 46227

BRICKMAN, RAVELLE, public relations writer and consultant; b. N.Y.C., Aug. 26, 1936; d. Arthur M. and Eva S. (Kaplan) Silberman; m. Anthony Brickman, Mar. 4, 1962 (div. Sept. 1979); children: Joshua Mark, David Meyer; m. Michael J. Bonner, Nov. 25, 1993. BA, Smith Coll., 1958. Writer, editor various book and mag. pubs., N.Y.C. and London, 1958-71; editor Aphra, N.Y.C., 1971-73; various pub. relations positions YMCA Greater N.Y., N.Y.C., 1973-76, dir. mktg. services, 1976-79; account exec. Zachary & Front Pub. Relations, N.Y.C., 1979-81; account supr., v.p., sr. v.p., creative dir. Richard Weiner, Inc., N.Y.C., 1981-86; pres. The Brickman Group, Mktg. and Pub. Rels., N.Y.C., 1986-93; writer, cons. in pub. rels. pvt. practice, N.Y.C., 1993—; writer, cons. NYNEX, Nat. Sci. Found., N.J. Inst. of Tech., City of N.Y. Mem. Pub. Rels. Soc. Am. (bd. dirs. 1981-84, Silver Anvil award 1984, Big Apple awards 1988), Counselors Acad., Women Execs. in Pub. Rels. (bd. dirs. 1989-90), Publicity Club N.Y. (bd. dirs. 1986-87, v.p., treas. 1986-88, 1st v.p. 1992-93, pres. 1993—), City Club N.Y., Smith Coll. Alumnae Assn. (chmn. 1998 reunion). Democrat. Jewish.

BRIDGE, MARGARET CRAWFORD, assistant dean; b. Newark, Dec. 27, 1947; d. Bernard Keating and Beatrice (Corn) Crawford; children: David A., Allison J., Michele L. BA, U. Rochester, 1970; JD, Seton Hall U., 1982. Asst. sec. Standard Tool & Mfg. Co., Lyndhurst, N.J., 1977-85, v.p., corp. counsel, 1985-88; pvt. practice Montclair, N.J., 1982-85, 88-91; dir. corp. & found. rels. Seton Hall U., South Orange, N.J., 1991-93; asst. dean, dir. devel. Rutgers U. Law Sch., Newark, 1993—. Trustee, sec. Keating Crawford Found., Verona, N.J., 1975—; trustee, bd. pres. Montclair Kimberley Acad., 1986-95. Mem. N.J. State Bar Assn. Office: Rutgers U Law Sch 15 Washington St Newark NJ 07102

BRIDGEFORD, LORI MARIE, medical esthetician; b. Grand Forks, N.D., Oct. 18, 1958; d. Patrick Lloyd and Eleanore Mary (Mack) B. AA, Moorhead State U., 1979; BA, Loyola Marymount U., 1989; MA, Pepperdine U., 1992. Med. esthetician Torrance, Calif., 1985—; psychol. educator Acadia Counseling Assocs., Hermosa Beach, 1993. Med. news editor: Advanced Dermatolgic News, 1993—; contbg. editor: Les Nouvelles Esthetiques, 1992; author: Dermatology Nursing jour., 1990; contbr. articles to profl. jours. Educator So. Bay Adult Edn., L.A., 1993; tchr. aide/asst. Salvation Army presch., L.A., 1993. Mem. Calif. Assn. of Marriage, Family Therapists (intern), Am. Psychol. Assn. of Calif., So. Bay Family Violence Coun., Am. Counseling Assn., Alliance of Med. Estheticians (co-founder), NOW, Assn. of Women in Psychology, Psi Chi. Home: 2214 Manhattan Beach Blvd "B" Redondo Beach CA 90278 Office: Coast Dermatology 4201 Torrance Blvd # 390 Torrance CA 90503

BRIDGES, BERYL CLARKE, marketing executive; b. N.Y.C., Oct. 27, 1941; d. David and Edith (Foster) Clarke; m. R. Shaw Bridges, Sept. 2, 1962 (div. May 1985); children: Robert Shaw Jr., Margaret Clarke, John Morrison; m. Robert A. McMillan, July 25, 1992. BA in English, Philosophy, Wheaton Coll., 1963. Acct. exec. McMoran-Redington Pub. Rels., Greenwich, Conn., 1975-77; mgr. sales promotion Lindenmeyr Graphic Resource Ctr., Greenwich, 1977-79; corp. mgr. promotions Lindenmeyr Paper Corp., Greenwich, 1979-81; mgr. southeastern region Paper Sources Internat. subs. Lindenmeyr Paper Corp., 1981-83, v.p. mktg., 1983-84; pres. Zanders USA, Inc. (subs. Internat. Paper Co.), Wayne, N.J., 1984—; cons. and lectr. in field. V.p. Greenwich Hist. Soc., 1974-77; mem. Jr. League, Greenwich, 1971-78. Mem. Am. Inst. Graphic Arts. Republican. Unitarian. Home: 18 Lake Dr Boonton NJ 07005-1047 Office: 100 Demarest Dr Wayne NJ 07470-6743

BRIDGES, JUDY CANTRELL, gifted and talented education educator; b. Dallas, Feb. 17, 1947; d. William and Jewel Alexandria (Autrey) C.; m. Gary L. Bridges, Aug. 17, 1969; children: John Drewry, Judith Alexandria. BA, Tex. Tech. U., 1969; gifted/talented endorsement, Sul Ross State U., Alpine, Tex., 1992, MEd, 1993; cert. in mid-mgmt., Sul Ross State U., 1994. Lic. secondary edn. math. and English. Tchr. New Deal (Tex.) Ind. Sch. Dist., 1969-70, Indpls. Pub. Schs., 1970, USDESEA, Zweibruecken, Germany, 1971-73, Lubbock (Tex.) Ind. Sch. Dist., 1973-76; tchr. Ector County Ind. Sch. Dist., Odessa, Tex., 1976-85, 87-90, tchr. gifted spl. edn., 1990-92, gifted/talented coord., 1992—; acct. Walter Smith CPA, Odessa, 1977-82; real estate appraiser Appraisal Assocs., Odessa, 1985-87; vis. lectr. Sul Ross State U., Odessa, 1994; mem. gifted/talented adv. com. Region 18 Edn. Svc. Ctr., Midland, Tex., 1993-94. Author: (poem) Paradigm Shifts in the West Texas Sand, 1991. Treas. Campaign to Elect County Judge, Odessa, 1991; mem. bd. Permian High Sch. Football Booster Club, 1993; advisor, officer Jr. League of Odessa, Inc., 1980—, treas./treas. elect, 1986-88. Recipient Dept.

of Def. Commendation, U.S. Dependent Edn. System, Zweibruecken, 1973, Cert. of Appreciation-Stop of Felony Odessa Police Dept., 1992. Mem. ASCD, NEA, Tex. State Tchrs. Assn. (treas. Ector County unit 1991-92), Tex. Assn. Gifted and Talented, Am. Creativity Assn., Nat. Coun. Tchrs. Math. Baptist. Home: 4243 Lynbrook Ave Odessa TX 79762 Office: Ector County Ind Sch Dist PO Box 3912 Odessa TX 79760-3912

BRIDGES, SHEILA MARGARET, art educator; b. Buffalo, Feb. 27, 1943; d. Connell A. and Ursula (Desmond) Cavanaugh; m. Bruce Bridges, June 15, 1968; 1 child, Patrick James. BS, SUNY, Buffalo, 1964. Tchr. Buffalo Sch. System, 1964-65; home svc. rep. N.Y. State Elec. & Gas, Lancaster, 1965-69; tchr. North Olmsted (Ohio) Schs., 1970-72; real estate sales, broker Homefinders, Chgo., 1972-73, Ruhl &Ruhl, Davenport, Ohio, 1974-76; art dir. Montessori Chateau, Slidell, La., 1981-84, Good Shepherd Episc. Day Sch., Kingwood, Tex., 1985—; tchr. art after sch. program Humble Ind. Sch. Dist., Kingwood, Tex., 1989—; judge art masterpiece reflections Humble Ind. Sch. Dist., 1989-94; C.D.A. advisor Phillips U., Okla., 1994—. Vol. March of Dimes, Houston, 1990-92, St. Martha's Food Kitchen, Houston, 1992—. Recipient Creative Tchr. award Crayola, 1989. Mem. AAUW (sec. 1989-90, edn. found. chair 1991, v.p. 1981-83), St. MArtha's Women's Club. Republican. Home: 2802 Rustic Woods Dr Kingwood TX 77345-1390

BRIDGEWATER, NORA JANE, medical/surgical nurse; b. Rodgers, Tex., Feb. 27, 1924; d. Wiley Levi and Phoebajane (Owens) Shelgren; m. Joe Garland Bridgewater, Aug. 7, 1940; children: Garland, Janie William Clayton, Richard, Allen, Paula, Shewanna, Russell. AA in Psychology, Bakersfield Coll., 1970, BSN, 1978. Med. nurse Kern Med. Hosp., Bakersfield, Calif., 1964-68, Mercy Hosp., Bakersfield, 1969-78, Sherrif's Dept., Laredo, Calif., 1978-87; nurse Sheriff Facility, Bakersfield, 1986-87. Sgt. U.S. Army Nurses Corps, 1938-40. Mem. Calif. Nursing Assn. Democrat. Baptist. Home: 1110 Tulare St Apt C Bakersfield CA 93305

BRIDWELL, BEVERLY ANN, business finance officer; b. Vardaman, Miss., Jan. 5, 1938; d. Curtis Hartwell and Pearl (Spratlin) Hardin; m. Billy Gene Hardin, Sr., Mar. 24, 1962 (dec. Apr. 1964); 1 child, Billy Gene Jr.; m. Ernest D. Bridwell, May 30, 1977. AA, Wood Jr. Coll., Mathiston, Miss., 1956. Clk. Indsl. Supply Co., Memphis, Tenn., 1957-64; bookkeeper Calhoun County Schs., Pittsboro, Miss., 1964-78; bus. fin. mgr. Pontotoc (Miss.) County Schs., 1978—; bus. fin. mgr. Cert. Ednl. Office Employee, Pontotoc, 1978—. Nursery coord. West Heights Bapt. Ch., Pontotoc, 1993. Home: RR 6 Box 371 Pontotoc MS 38863-9252 Office: Pontotoc County Schs 285 Highway 15 S Pontotoc MS 38863-3527

BRIDWELL, DARLA RENEÉ, accountant; b. Greenville, S.C., May 28, 1963; d. Robert Joseph and Barbara Ann (Jones) B. AS summa cum laude, Rutledge Coll., Greenville, 1983. Accounts receivable clk. M&S Chems., Greenville, 1983-84; data entry clk. Belk Simpson Co., Greenville, 1986-87, acctg. assoc., 1987-89, sr. acct., 1989—. Co. coord. United Way Greenville County, 1989. Scholar Rutledge Coll., 1981, Profl. Secs. Internat., 1981. Mem. NAFE, Nat. Honor Soc. Democrat. Baptist. Home: 8333 Whitesburg Way SE Apt 26 Huntsville AL 35802-3474 Office: Belk Simpson Group Office 14 S Main St Greenville SC 29601

BRIEGER, TANYA GAIL, sales executive; b. Jackson, Miss., Oct. 21, 1959; d. Simon Alan and Wanda Gail (Davis) B. AAS, Hinds Jr. Coll., Raymond, Miss., 1979; BS, Belhaven Coll., Jackson, 1985; MBA, Millsaps Coll., Jackson, 1993. Svc. rep. Bell South, Jackson, 1979-84, telemktg. account rep., 1984-87, sr. account exec., 1987—. Corp. sponsorship chair Miss. Hearts Against AIDS, Jackson, 1993, 94; AIDS awareness chair Telephone Pioneers, Jackson, 1994—. Mem. MBA Assn. of Miss., Kappa Kappa Gamma. Methodist. Home: 274 Planters Grove Ridgeland MS 39157 Office: Bell South PO Box 811 Rm 47SLMC 175 E Capitol Jackson MS 39201

BRIELOFF, PHOEBE ANNE, development director; b. Flushing, N.Y., Sept. 20, 1963; d. Harry Traulsen and Doris Beverly Forrest; m. Lawrence Mark Brieloff, July 25, 1987. Student, Ohio U. Exec. asst. CCR Video, N.Y.C., 1983-84; mgr. scheduling and client svcs. Movielab Video, N.Y.C., 1984-87; dir. corporate/found. support Dooley Found.-Intermed, N.Y.C., 1988-91, dir. devel., 1993—; devel. assoc. OHSU Found., Portland, Oreg., 1991-93; fund raising cons., N.Y.C., Oreg., 1993—. Mem. devel. com. Am. Advt. Mus., Portland, 1994. Mem. NAFE, Nat. Soc. Fund Raising Execs. Office: Dooley Found-Intermed Rm 225 7276 SW Beaverton Hillsdale Hwy Portland OR 97225

BRIER, EVELYN CAROLINE, retired investment company executive, business consultant; b. Plentywood, Mont., Mar. 1, 1932; d. Idwal and Evelyn Nettie (Kellar) Jones; m. Richard R. Merritt, Nov. 27, 1970 (dec. 1988); children by previous marriage: Patricia Ann Brier, Edward David Brier. Grad. high sch., Seattle. Various secretarial and adminstrv. positions in mortgage loan, constrn., importing/exporting Seattle, 1948-59; adminstrv. asst. to sr. officer Seattle World's Fair, 1959-62; adminstrv. asst. to sr. legal officer Western Internat. Hotels, Seattle, 1962-68; asst. corp. sec. Western Internat. Hotels, 1968-72; corp. sec. New Eng. Fish Co., Seattle, 1972-79; owner/cons. Corporate Cons. Services., 1980-88; v.p., corp. sec. Matthew G. Norton Co., 1982-94. Mem. speakers bur. Seattle/King County Conv. and Visitors com., 1975, bd. dirs., 1975-81; trustee Seattle Ctr. Found., pres., 1983-85; chmn. adminstrv. bd. Haller Lake United Meth. Ch., 1983-86, 90—; pres. Seattle Ctr. Found., 1990-91, bd. dirs., 1981-94. Mem. Am. Soc. Corp. Secs. (regional group pres. 1974-75, nat. v.p. 1975-76, nat. dir. 1976-79). Methodist. Home: 507 N 169th St Seattle WA 98133-5212

BRIGEOIS, EVELYNE BRIGITTE, artist, publisher; b. Troyes, Aube, France, Feb. 18, 1946; came to U.S., 1984.; Student, B.E.P.C., Aix-en-Othe, France, 1951. Trilingual exec. sec., Eng., France, Germany, Spain, 1965-79; owner, mgr. Brigeois Pub., Vallejo, Calif., 1987—. One woman shows include Lawrence Gallery, Portland, Oreg., 1984, Scott Gallery, Orinda, Calif., 1985, Leslie Levy Gallery, Scottsdale, Ariz., 1986, 89, Charleston Heights Art Ctr., Las Vegas, Nev., 1987, Horvath Gallery, Sacramento, 1993 ; exhibited in group shows Transco Gallery, Houston, 1988, numerous others; represented by Leslie Levy Gallery, Scottsdale, Ariz., Blue Heron Gallery, Yountville, Calif., Studio 42, Los Gatos, Calif. Recipient numerous awards, including Robert Wiegand Meml. award La. Watercolor Soc., 1985, award Detroit Inst. Arts Drawing and Print Club, 1985, award of honor Birmingham Mus. Art, 1986, lst place award Assoc. Artists Southport, N.C., 1986. Mem. Nat. Watercolor Soc. (Helen Wurdeman award 1985), Ala. Watercolor Soc.

BRIGGS, ADA JANE, emergency nurse; b. Lakin, Kans., July 20, 1942; d. Stephen Dale and Thelma L. (Rider) Frazee; m. Joe F. Briggs, Nov. 20, 1978; children: Mike, Dana, Dale. ADN, Dodge City Community Coll., Dodge City, Kans., 1985; BSN magna cum laude, Ft. Hays State U., 1990. Cert. ACLS, CEN, PALS Am. Heart Assn., trauma nurse core course provider. Staff nurse St. Catherine Hosp., Garden City, Kans., 1985-86, charge nurse, 1986-93; staff nurse Western Plains Regional Hosp., 1994—. Mem. Emergency Nurses Assn. (cert.). Home: PO Box 41 Cimarron KS 67835-0041

BRIGGS, CYNTHIA ANNE, educational administrator, clinical psychologist; b. Berea, Ohio, Nov. 9, 1950; d. William Benajah and Lorraine (Hood) B.; m. Thomas Joseph O'Brien, Nov. 28, 1986; children: Julia Maureen, William Thomas. B Music Edn., U. Kans., 1973; MusM, U. Miami, 1976; D. Psychology, Hahnemann U., 1988. Lic. psychology, Mo.; bd. cert. music therapist. Music therapist Parsons (Kans.) State Hosp., 1973-74; grad. asst. U. Miami, Coral Gables, Fla., 1974-76; asst. prof., dir. Hahnemann U., Phila., 1976-85, asst. prof., 1985-91; psychology resident Assocs. in Psychol. and Human Resources, Phila., 1988-91; clin. dir. Child Ctr. of Our Lady, St. Louis, 1991—. Contbr. chpts. to books in field. Mem. Am. Assn. Music Therapy (pres. 1987-89), Nat. Coalition Arts Therapies Assns. (chair 1991-93). Democrat. Office: Child Ctr of Our Lady 7900 Natural Bridge Saint Louis MO 63121

BRIGGS, JANET MARIE LOUISE, nurse practitioner; b. Pitts., June 11, 1951. Cert. family med. nurse practitioner. Staff nurse neonatal ICU Univ. Hosps. Cleve., 1972-73; staff nurse gen pediatrics Mt. Sinai Hosp. Cleve., 1973-76; head nurse health svc. Mt. Sinai Med. Ctr., Cleve., 1976-82; grad. rsch. asst. Case Western Res. U., Cleve., 1983-84; dir. nursing Ashtabula County Health Dept., Jefferson, Ohio, 1984-85; staff nurse, dir. nursing insvc., coord., clin. nurse specialist, coord. infection control Meml. Hosp. Geneva, Ohio, 1985-87; nurse practitioner, unit mgr. Parkside Health Mgmt. Corp., Toledo, 1986-87; nurse practitioner ambulatory surgery. Met. Gen. Hosp., Cleve., 1987; nurse practitioner domiciliary homeless program VA Med. Ctr., Cleve., 1987-91, clin. nurse specialist, nurse practioner AIDS team, 1991—; project dir., chmn. Child and Family Health Svc. Grant, Ashtabula County, Ohio, 1984-85; cons. case mgmt. head injuries subcom. Gov.'s Task Force, Ohio, 1988; nurse practitioner Free Clinic, Cleve., 1988—; mem. ethics com. VA Med. Ctr., 1989—; adj. clin. faculty Kent. State U., 1993—; investigator multiple clinically based AIDS rsch. projects. Lectr., group leader Hitchcock House, Cleve., 1981-83. Grantee Fed. Facility Based HIV/AIDS Edn. Demonstration, 1991, Fed. Facility HIV/AIDS Edn. Rsch., 1992, 93, Dept. of Vet. Affairs. Mem. APHA, Sigma Theta Tau. Roman Catholic.

BRIGGS, JOANNE MARIE, public relations specialist; b. Framingham, Mass., July 26, 1949; d. Joseph James and Lorraine Rita (Peloquin) Pavia; m. John Henry Briggs, Sept. 21, 1988 (div. Apr. 1992). BA in English, Framingham State Coll., 1972. Pub. rels. specialist, employee comms. supr. Prime Computer, Inc., Natick, Mass., 1978-83; pub. rels. specialist, employee comms. mgr. Apolla Computer, Inc., Chelmsford, Mass., 1983-87; asst. mgr. corp. comms. MITRE Corp., Bedford, Mass., 1987-90; employee comms. specialist Bull Info. Systems, Billerica, Mass., 1992; dir. resident svcs. The Gables, Winchester, Mass., 1992—. Mem. Social Activities Dirs. in Ind. Living Socs. Roman Catholic. Home: 136 Central Bl Hudson MA 01749

BRIGGS, SHARON LOUISE, secondary education educator; b. Long Beach, Calif., June 11, 1945; d. Kenneth Leroy and Ruby Louise (White) Cook; m. James Willard Briggs, Mar. 25, 1967 (div. 1994); children: Scott Willard, Alisa Michele. BA, U. Md., 1972; Cert. for Tchrs. of Deaf, Cambridge U., 1978; MA, Am. U., 1989, postgrad., 1994. Tchr. Sapporo Sch. of Langs., Sapporo, Hokkaido, Hokkaido, Japan, 1969-70; tchr. GED St. Louis High Sch. Extension, Okinawa, Japan, 1973; tchr. Fairfax (Va.) County Pub. Schs., 1979-80, team facilitator, English tchr., 1985—; tchr. Seoul Fgn. Sch., 1980-81, Sifundzani Sch., Mbabane, Swaziland, Africa, 1982-84; ptnr. Sound Reading Assocs., Clifton, Va., 1990—; founder Sifundzani Libr., Swaziland, Africa, 1982-84; presenter ASCD, San Antonio, 1990, NCTE, Washington D.C., 1992, Nat. Reading Styles Inst., Chgo., Atlanta, 1990-92, Va. Remediation Conf., Richmond, Va., 1990. Co-author: (handbook and cassette package) How to Rescue At-Risk Students, 1990 (NEA award 1991); chpt. co-author: How to Record Books for Maximum Reading Gains, 1989; contbg. author: New Teachers Handbook, 1988, NMSA Visions of Teaching and Learning, 1990. Grantee in Edn. Washington Post, 1988, program grantee Impact II, 1988; recipient acad. scholarship Am. U., Washington, 1991-93. Mem. Va. Edn. Assn. (instrn. and profl. devel. com.), ASCD (presenter), Nat. Mid. Sch. Assn., Internat. Reading Assn., Nat. Coun. Tchrs. of English, Phi Kappa Phi. Home: 5924 Veranda Dr Springfield VA 22152-1416

BRIGGUM, SUE MARIE, corporate executive; b. Harrisburg, Pa., Apr. 8, 1950; d. John Gehring and Blanche Faye (Hess) B.; m. Martin Rose, Jan. 6, 1984; 1 child, Lauren. BA, U. Pitts., 1972; MA, U. Wis., 1973, PhD, 1979; JD, Harvard U., 1980. Bar: D.C. 1980. Lectr. U. Wis., Madison, 1973-77; assoc. Wald, Harkrader & Ross, Washington, 1980-86, Piper & Marbury, Washington, 1986-87; dir. govt. affairs WMX Techs., Inc., Washington, 1987—. Co-author: Concordance to Almayer's Folly, 1980, Hazardous Waste Regulation Handbook, 1983, rev. edit 1985; co-editor: Modernism in Literature, 1976. Office: WMX Technologies Inc 1155 Connecticut Ave NW Washington DC 20036-4306

BRIGHAM, JUDITH ANN, deputy city clerk; b. Garnett, Kans., Sept. 19, 1958; d. Thomas Dean and Darlene Kathleen (Hastert) Thompson; m. Ronald David Gull, June 23, 1977 (div. Apr. 1986); children: Kaci Danielle, Kari Marie; m. Michael Thomas Brigham, 1986. AS in Bus. Adminstrn., Allen County C.C., Iola, Kans., 1991. Cert. mcpl. clk. Customer clk. City of Iola, 1979-81, billing clk., 1981-91, dep. city clk., 1991—; com. mem. City of Iola Self Ins., 1991—, City of Iola Employee Benefits, 1991—. Treas. Jefferson Sch. PTA, Iola, 1989-91, pres., 1991-92, v.p., 1992-93; v.p. Iola Band Boosters, 1994—; bd. dirs. Iola Girls Softball League, 1993—. Mem. City Clks. and Mcpl. Fin. Officers, Internat. City Clks. & Mcpl. Fin. Officers. Republican. Roman Catholic. Home: 411 S Cottonwood Iola KS 66749 Office: City of Iola PO Box 308 2 W Jackson Iola KS 66749

BRIGHAM, THERESE ANN, sales executive; b. Plymouth, Mass., June 25, 1965; d. Joseph R. and Catherine Ann (Benea) B. BA, U. N.H., 1987. Cert. for instrn. alpine skiing for developmentally delayed Profl. Ski Instructors Assn. Am., Nat. Handicapped Sports. Customer svc. rep. Costar Corp., Cambridge, Mass., 1988-89; tech. sales rep. Binax, Inc., Portland, Maine, 1989-94; adaptive specialist Seafax, Inc., Portland, 1994—. Vol. pedi playroom Maine Med. Ctr., Portland, 1991—; campaign coord. Binax Inc. for United Way of Greater Portland, 1992, 93. Mem. NOW, Nat. Handicapped Sports (vol. ski instr. 1991—), U. N.H. So. Maine Alumni Assn.

BRIGHT, PATRICE RENEE, personnel administrator; b. Mobile, Ala., Dec. 7, 1961; d. W. Ray and Evelyn A. (Howell) Stanley; m. Stacey A. Bright, Apr. 20, 1985; children: Jared Nathaniel, Parker Benjamin. AS in Office Adminstrn., Clayton State Coll., 1983; BBA in Mgmt., Ga. State U., 1986. Pers. asst. Altus Mortgage, Atlanta, 1985-87; employment specialist, bank officer 1st Am. Bank, Atlanta, 1987-89; pers. officer Clayton County Bd. Commrs., Jonesboro, Ga., 1989-93; pers. dir. Clayton County Bd. Commrs., Jonesboro, 1993—. Mem. placement com. MAGNET Program, C.L. Harper H.S., Atlanta, 1987-89; blood donor coord. ARC, Atlanta, 1989—. Mem. Internat. Pers. Mgmt. Assn. (mem. Atlanta chpt.), Ga. Local Govt. Pers. Assn. (bd. dirs. 1991). Office: Clayton County Bd Commrs 112 Smith St 1st Fl Jonesboro GA 30236

BRIGHTON, RUTH LOUISE, lay worker, educator; b. Harrisburg, Pa., Apr. 18, 1931; d. Paul Gerhard and Ruth Genevieve (Lee) Krentz; m. Carl T. Brighton, July 27, 1954; children: David, Susan, Andrew, Joel. BA, Valparaiso U., 1953; MS in Math., U. Wis., 1955. Cert. tchr. Tchr. Sunday sch., adult Bible class Christ Meml. Luth. Ch., Malvern, Penn., 1969—; coord. adult edn., Ea. dist. Luth. Ch.-Mo. Synod, Buffalo, 1986-89, bd. dirs., 1988-90; bd. dirs. Concordia Pub. House, St. Louis. Teaching fellow in math. U. Wis., 1953. Home: 14 Flintshire Rd Malvern PA 19355-1108

BRILES, JUDITH, writer, speaker, consultant; b. Pasadena, Calif., Feb. 20, 1946; d. James and Mary Tuthill; MBA, Pepperdine U., 1980; PhD Nova U., 1990; children: Shelley, Sheryl, Frank (dec.), William (dec.). Brokers asst. Bateman, Eichler, Hill, Richards, Torrance, Calif., 1969-72; account exec. E. F. Hutton, Palo Alto, Calif., 1972-78; pres. Judith Briles & Co., Palo Alto, 1978-85, Briles & Assocs., Palo Alto, 1980-86; ptnr. The Briles Group, Inc., 1987—; instr. Menlo Coll., 1986-87, Skyline Coll., 1981-86; instr. U. Calif.-Berkeley Sch. Continuing Edn., U. Calif.-Santa Cruz Sch. Continuing Edn., U. Hawaii; mem. adv. coun. Miss Am. Pageant, 1989—, No-nonsense Panty Hose, 1989—, Colo. Women's News, 1993—. Pres., v.p., sec., bd. dirs. Foothill-DeAnza Coll. Found., Los Altos Hills, Calif., 1979-90, bd. dirs. Col. Nurses Task Force, Col. League Nursing; mem. adv. bd. Flint Ctr., Cupertino, Calif. Mem. NAFE (adv. bd. bus. woman's mag. 1981-86), Peninsula Profl. Women's Network, Nat. Speaker's Assn. (bd. dirs.). Republican. Club: Commonwealth. Author: The Woman's Guide to Financial Savvy, 1981; Money Phases, 1984, Woman to Woman: From Sabotage to Support, 1987, Dollars and Sense of Divorce, 1988, Faith and Savvy Too!, 1988, When God Says No, 1990, The Confidence Factor, 1990, Money Guide, 1991, The Workplace: Questions Women Ask, 1992, Financial Savvy for Women, 1992, The Briles Report on Women in Healthcare, 1994, Money Sense, 1995, Gender Traps, 1995.

BRILEY, NOREEN GALVIN, nurse, educator; b. New Haven, Dec. 9, 1943; d. John Joseph and Helen Jane (Doherty) Galvin; m. Philip L. Briley, Aug. 27, 1966; children: Eileen M., Paula T., Beth A. Diploma in Nursing, Hosp. St. Raphael Sch. Nursing, 1964; BSN, Cath. U. Am., 1967, MSN, 1979. Staff nurse Greater S.E. Community Hosp., Washington, 1970-72, asst. head nurse, 1972-75; nurse assoc. Guy W. Gargour, M.D., Bethesda, Md., 1975-76; lectr. Prince George's Community Coll., Largo, Md., 1975-78; asst. dir. nursing So. Md. Hosp. Ctr., Clinton, 1977-82, dir. planning, 1982-85; nursing adminstr. Parkwood Hosp., Clinton, 1985-86; staff nurse Phsycians Meml. Hosp., La Plata, Md., 1986-88; assoc. prof. Charles County Community Coll., La Plata, 1988—; nurse cons. Nancy C. Taber, Ft. Washington, Md., 1983-85. Pres. Brandywine (Md.) Dem. Club, 1979, 88, Brandywine Heights Citizens Assn., 1980—; vice chmn. So. Md. Health Systems Agy., Clinton, 1985-90. St. Raphaels Hosp. scholar, 1964. Mem. ANA, AAUW, Acad. of Med.-Surg. Nursing, Orgn. for the Advancement Assoc. Degree Nursing, Md. Nurses Assn. (bd. dirs. 1989—), Lioness (3d v.p. Brandywine chpt. 1985-86, pres. 1994-95), Sigma Theta Tau. Roman Catholic. Home: 8600 Timothy Rd Brandywine MD 20613-7622 Office: Charles County Coll PO Box 910 La Plata MD 20646-0910

BRILL, SUZANNE MARGARET, insurance agent; b. Milw., May 22, 1953; d. Kenneth Eugene and Mary L. (Gilday) B.; m. Thomas James Curtis, Aug. 21, 1982; children: Bailey, Kennedy, Callan. Cert in dental hygiene, Marquette U., 1977, BA in dental hygiene, 1979. Cert. in dental hygiene. Dental hygienist Dr. Jeff C. Becherer, Wauwatosa, Wis., 1974-82, Dr. Dan Holzhauer, Milw., 1979-81; agt., office mgr. John R. Mueller, Milw., 1984—. Mem. NOW. Home: 1505 Longwood Ave Elm Grove WI 53122-1956 Office: John R Mueller 111 E Kilbourn Ave Milwaukee WI 53202-6611

BRILL, YVONNE CLAEYS, engineer, consultant; b. St. Norbert, Manitoba, Canada, Dec. 30, 1924; d. August and Julienne (Carette) Claeys; m. William Franklin Brill, Dec. 15, 1951; children: Naomi, Matthew, Joseph. BS, U. Manitoba, Canada, 1945; MS, U. So. Calif., 1951. Mathematician Douglas Aircraft, Santa Monica, Calif., 1945-46; research analyst Rand Corp., Santa Monica, 1946-49; group leader Marquardt Corp., Van Nuys, Calif., 1949-52; staff engr. UTC Research, East Hartford, Conn., 1952-55; project engr. Wright Aeronautical, Wood Ridge, N.J., 1955-58; mgr. propulsion systems RCA AstroElectronics, Princeton, N.J., 1966-81, staff engr., 1983-86; mgr. solid rocket motor NASA Hdqrs., Washington, 1981-83; with space engring segment Internat. Maritime Satellite Orgn., London, 1986-91; cons. Brill Assocs., Skillman, N.J., 1991—; mem. USAF Sci. Adv. Bd., Washington, 1982-83, Nat. Acad. Engring. Internat. Affairs Adv. Com., 1991-92, program adv. com., 1992-94; apptd. mem. aerospace safety adv. panel NASA, 1994—. Contbr. articles to sci. jours.; patentee in field. Bd. dirs. Princeton YWCA, 1981-82. Recipient Engr. of Yr. award Cen. Jersey Engring. Councils, 1979, Diamond Superwoman award Harpers Bazaar/DeBeers Corp., 1980, Marvin C. Demlar award AIAA, 1983. Fellow AIAA, Soc. Women Engrs. (dir. student affairs 1979-80, 83-84, treas. 1980-81, Engring. Achievement award 1986, Resnik Challenger medal 1993); mem. NAE, Internat. Astronautical Acad. (academician, edn. com. 1983-85), Sigma Xi, Tau Beta Pi. Republican. Home and Office: 914 Route 518 Skillman NJ 08558-2616

BRILLIANT, BARBARA, television host, producer, consultant; b. Montreal, Que., Canada, Sept. 24, 1935; d. Saul and Esther (Saltzman) Lecker; m. Erwin Brilliant, June 29, 1958; children: Bradley, Todd, Michelle. Student, McGill Tchrs. Coll., 1953, McGill Conservatory of Music; AA, Sir George Williams U., Montreal, 1955; BA in Psychology summa cum laude, Boston Coll., 1975. Tchr. Protestant Sch. Bd., Montreal, 1953-58, dir. drama sch., 1957-58; artist-in-residence City of Boston, 1978-83; TV host, producer Sta. WBZ-TV, Boston, 1979-90; freelance news producer AARP News Network, 1989—; freelance writer, composer, lyricist; columnist A&E Picks, "Dear Barbara," advice for people 40 plus; advisor Radcliff Coll., Cambridge, Mass., 1985—; pres. SpeechWorks; media and pub. speaking coach and trainer. Actress Montreal area, 1957-58, Boston area, 1985—; artistic dir. City of Boston, 1985—; vocalist, mus. dir. Two on the Aisle, Newton, Mass., 1985—; contbg. writer Vitality Mag., Boston Woman Mag., N.H. Senior Times, among others; composer songs (with Charles Segal) You're Not Alone, Time to Care, Talk to Me, many others; columnist: "Tell It to Barbara" in the Jewish Advocate, 1992—, Senior Times, Arts & Entertainment, A&E Picks; producer, cost-host nat. cable TV show "Barbara & Bill". Advisor Cultural Affairs Commn., Newton, Mass., 1980-82, Nat. Com. to Study and Resolve Problems of Older Ams., Boston, 1984—; mem. adv. bd. Radcliffe Coll. Women; spokesperson Alzheimers Disease and Related Disorders aslsn., Boston, 1985—; mem. White House Conf. on Aging, Washington, 1981; mem. Time Capsule Harvard Schlessinger Libr., Cambridge, Mass., 1980; advisor to Mass. Sec. Elder Affairs, 1992-93. Recipient Cert. of Recognition City of Boston, 1979, Media award Am. Assn. Retired Persons, 1980, Lifestyle Achievement award WW Group Internat., Boston, 1987, Sandoz Gerentol. Found. awards, 1989, 91; Nat. Press Found., fellow, Washington, 1987; named to Hon. Order Ky. Cols., 1987, One of Boston's 100 Most Interesting Women, Boston Woman Mag., 1988, Gov. Michael Dukakis proclamation service in media to elderly, 1989; Mayor Raymond Flynn declared Barbara Brilliant Day, Sept. 24, 1989; Awareness of Aging tree planted in her honor Newton City Hall. Mem. Screen Actors Guild, Am. Fedn. TV and Radio Artists. Office: Brilliant Communications PO Box 310 Newton MA 02161-0004

BRILLIANT, ELEANOR LURIA, social work educator; b. Bklyn., Nov. 25, 1930; d. Joseph and Leah (Cohen) Luria; m. Richard Brilliant, June 24, 1951; children: Stephanie, Livia, Franca, Myron. BA, Smith Coll., Northampton, Mass., 1952; MS, Bryn Mawr (Pa.) Coll., 1969; DSW, Columbia U., 1974. Asst. in prodn. course Harvard Bus. Sch., Cambridge, Mass., 1952-54; instr. Bryn Mawr Coll., 1969-71; adminstr., dir. Lower East Side Family Union, N.Y.C., 1974-75; dir. planning/evaluation United Way of Westchester, White Plains, N.Y., 1975-78, assoc. exec. dir., 1978-80; asst. prof. Columbia U., N.Y.C., 1980-84, assoc. prof., 1984-85; assoc. prof. social work Rugers U., New Brunswick, N.J., 1986—; dir. BSW program Rutgers U., Livingston Coll., New Brunswick, 1987-89; cons. United Way of Westchester, White Plains, 1980, Family Info. and Referral Svc. Teams, Inc., White Plains, 1980-83, 87. Author: The Urban Development Corporation: Private Interests and Public Authority, 1975, The United Way: Dilemmas of Organized Charity, 1990. Mem. Westchester County Homeless Crisis Action Group, 1985-86, chair long range planning com. 1986; mem. Westchester Commn. on the Homeless, 1986-87; bd. mem. Hudson Valley Health Systems Agy., 1978-86; bd. mem. Nat. Ctr. for Social Policy and Practice, 1986-88; mem. ho. of dels. Coun. Social Work Edn., 1987-89. U.S. Fulbright grantee, 1972-73, NIMH grantee 1968-69; fellow Douglass Coll., Rutgers U., 1992—. Mem. NASW (rep. to del. assembly 1987, 90, nat. treas. 1989-91), Nat. Network for Social Work Mgrs., Assn. for Rsch. on Non-Profit Orgns., and Vol. Action, Nat. Coun. for Rsch. on Women, Assn. for Cmty. Orgn. and Social Adminstrn. Home: 10 Wayside Ln Scarsdale NY 10583-2908 Office: Rutgers U Sch Social Work 536 George St New Brunswick NJ 08903-5058

BRIN, PAMELA YALE, art dealer, mirror and glass designer; b. Mpls., Apr. 11, 1927; d. George Brooks and Florence Jacobs; m. Dec. 5, 1948; children: Barbara Brin Beal, Nancy Brin Polski. BA, U. Minn., 1948. Owner Mirror Mirror, Mpls., 1972—, Poster for Gt. Walls, 1972—. Mem. Humphry Inst. Mem. Nat. Home Fashion League, Poster Soc. Am., Nat. Women's League of Conservative Judaism, Nat. Coun. Jewish Women.

BRIN, RUTH FIRESTONE, writer, educator; b. St. Paul, May 5, 1921; d. Milton Phillip and Irma (Cain) Firestone; m. Howard Brin, Aug. 6, 1941 (dec. June 1988); children: Judith, Aaron, David, Deborah. BA, Vassar Coll., 1941; MA, U. Minn., 1972; PhD (hon.), Reconstructionist Rabbinical, Wyncote, Pa., 1986. Lectr. Macalester Coll., St. Paul, 1974-84; librettist Hadassah, N.Y.C., Ashworth Pub., Phila. Author: Harvest: Collected Poems and Prayers, 1986, (poetry and liturgy) A Time to Search, 1959, Interpretation for the Weekly Torah Reading, 1965, A Rag of Love, 1965, A Hush of Midnight, 1969, Kol Nidre Service, 1971, (for children) Butterflies Are Beautiful, 1976, David and Goliath, 1977, Contributions of Women: Social Reform, 1977, Shabbat Catalogue, 1978, Wildflowers, 1983, (libretto) Kristallnacht, 1988; founder and editor Identity Mag., 1966-73; book reviewer Mpls. Star Tribune, 1968—. Grantee Nat. Jewish Fedn., 1977. Mem. Book Critics Cir., Phi Beta Kappa. Home: 2950 Dean Pky Apt 1703 Minneapolis MN 55416-4428

BRINCKMEYER, LYNN MAY, music educator; b. Kingfisher, Okla., Feb. 14, 1952; d. Allen Dietrich Brinckmeyer and Ida May (Cross) Kemper; m. William Stanley Pierce, Dec. 7, 1968 (div. 1983); children: Lanette Dawn Pierce, William Dale Pierce. BS in Elem. Edn. summa cum laude, Ea.

N.Mex. U., 1983, MME in Elem. Mus. Edn.; 1986; PhD in Music Edn., U. Kans., 1993. Cert. tchr., N.Mex. Grad. tchg. asst. Ea. N.Mex. U., 1985-86, U. Kans., Lawrence, 1987-88; music specialist Sacred Heart Sch., Clovis, N.Mex., 1986-87, Dora (N.Mex.) Pub. Schs., 1986-87, Alamogordo (N.Mex.) Pub. Schs., 1986-87; pvt. voice tchr., 1986—; asst. prof. music Ea. Wash. U., Cheney, 1992—; mem. adj. faculty Ea. N.Mex. U., 1987; vis. instr. music dept. Idaho State U., 1990-92; presenter workshops in music. Profl. vocalist: N.Mex. State U. Orch., 1987, 88, Coll. Light Opera Co., Falmouth, Mass., 1987, Ea. N.Mex. Jazz Ensemble, Portales, 1987, St. Patrick's Cathedral, N.Y.C., 1988, Masterworks Choir, N.Y.C., 1988, Idaho State U., 1991, 1st Meth. Ch., Pocatello, Idaho, 1990-92, Spokane Symphony Chorale, 1992—; performed in various theatre roles; contbr. articles to profl. jours. Recipient Diva award Coll. Light Opera Co., 1986. Mem. Am. Choral Dirs. Assn., Internat. Soc. Music Edn., Nat. Assn. Tchrs. Singing, Wash. Music Educators Nat. Conf., Coll. Music Soc., Music Educators Nat. Conf. (chairperson higher edn. divsn. N.W. divsn. planning sessions com. 1993—), Inland Empire Orff Assn., Phi Kappa Lambda, Phi Delta Kappa, Phi Kappa Phi. Republican. Methodist. Home: E 6121 6th Ave # K117 Spokane WA 99212 Office: Ea Wash U MS-100 Cheney WA 99004

BRINE, DOLORES RANDOLPH, chemist; b. Marion, N.C., Nov. 26, 1945; d. Carl Lee and Addie (Ritter) Randolph; m. George Atkins Brine, Aug. 3l, 1968. BS, Duke U., 1968. Rsch. chemist Research Triangle Inst., Research Triangle Park, N.C., 1968—. Contbr. articles to profl. jours., chpts. to books. Mem. Am. Chem. Soc. Episcopalian. Home: 6505 Hunters Ln Durham NC 27713-9738

BRINK, MARION ALICE, employee assistance professional; b. Boston, Feb. 15, 1928; d. Martin Bernhard and Astrid Marie (Bjaastad) Windedal; m. A. Rudie Shobaken, Feb. 5, 1947 (div. 1963); children: Richard Michael, Ron Eric; m. James A Brink, Jan. 29, 1977. Student, Cambridge Jr. Coll., 1945-47, Framingham State Coll., 1967, Boston U., 1967-69; BA, U. N.H., 1983; M in Theol. Studies, Harvard U., 1987. From lab tech. to chemist Liberty Mut. Rsch., Hopkinton, Mass., 1963-77; asst. to mgr. Rec. Sec. Office Harvard U., 1977-79; sec. Sloan Sch. MIT, 1980-82; owner tech. typing svc. New Castle, N.H., 1982-84; counseling intern Green Pastures Counseling Ctr., Dover, N.H., 1984-85; alcohol educator Freedom From Chem. Dependency Found., Inc., Needham, Mass., 1985-87; dir. devel., editor News Bulletin Freedom From Chem. Dependency Found., Inc., Needham, 1987-88; ptnr. Palmerbrink, Charlestown, Mass., 1989-90; founder MB Assocs., Charlestown, 1991—. Counselor Women's Resource Ctr., Portsmouth, 1980; treas., bd. dirs., mem. canteen com. Friends of Erich Lindemann Mental Health Ctr. Mem. Older Women's League, Community Assn. Serving Alcoholics, Employee Assistance Profls. Assn., Am. Acad. of Health Care Providers in the Addictive Disorders, Ctr. for Process Studies. Democrat. Unitarian. Home: 35 Monument Ave Charlestown MA 02129-3323

BRINKEMA, LEONIE MILHOMME, federal judge; b. Teaneck, N.J., June 26, 1944; d. Alexander Juste and Modeste Leonie (Macksoud) Milhomme; m. John Robert Brinkema, Dec. 22, 1966; children: Robert Aaron, Eugenie Alexandra. BA with honors, Douglass Coll., 1966; MLS, Rutgers U., 1970; JD with honors, Cornell U., 1976. Bar: D.C. 1976, Va. 1978. Trial atty. U.S. Dept. Justice, Washington, 1976-77, 1983-84; asst. U.S. atty. U.S. Atty's Office Ea. Va., Alexandria, 1977-83; prin. Leonie M. Brinkema Atty., Alexandria, 1984-85; U.S. magistrate judge U.S. Dist. Ct. (ea. dist.) Va., Alexandria, 1985-93, U.S. dist. judge, 1993—; legal lectr. Va. State Bar Professionalism Faculty, 1990-92, No. Va. Criminal Justice Acad., 1984-85; guest lectr. Alexandria Bar Assn., Alexandria Women Attys. Assn., Va. Women Attys. Assn., U.S. Dept. Justice Advocacy Inst., Va. Law Found. Active Fairfax Choral Soc., Alban Chorale. Woodrow Wilson grad. fellow, 1966, Danforth Found. grad. fellow, 1966. Mem. ABA, Va. State Bar, D.C. Bar, Nat. Assn. Women Judges, Va. Women Attys. Assn., George Mason Inn of Ct. (master), Phi Beta Kappa. Office: US Dist Ct 200 S Washington St Alexandria VA 22314

BRINKLEY, CHRISTIE, model; b. L.A., Feb. 2, 1953; d. Don and Marge B.; m. Jean François Allaux, 1974 (div. 1981); m. Billy Joel, 1985 (div.); 1 child, Alexa Ray; m. Ricky Taubman, 1994. Attended, U. Calif., Los Angeles, U. Calif., Northridge, La Grande Chaumiere. Model Elite Model Mgmt. modeled for over 200 mag. covers incl. Sports Illustrated's annual swimsuit issue, 1979, 80, 81, product promotions incl. Cover Girl makeup, Revlon cosmetics, Clairol hair care items, Chanel No. 19 perfume, Mastercard, Kinney Shoes, Anheuser-Busch beer; pub. Christie Brinkley's Outdoor Beauty and Fitness Book, 1983; cameo appearance (film) National Lampoon's Vacation, 1983, (video) Billy Joel's "Uptown Girl"; designed album cover Billy Joel's "River of Dreams"; introduced line of dolls (with Beverly Johnson) The Real Model Collection Matchbox Toys; past host Living in the 90's with Christie Brinkley CNN. Office: Ford Models Inc 344 E 59th St New York NY 10022-1570 also: Christie Brinkley Inc c/o Golfland Rennert & Feldman 6 E 43d St 22d Flr New York NY 10017*

BRINKLEY, PHYLLIS, speaker, program artist; b. Madison, Wis., May 28, 1926; d. Reynale R. and Florence (Jarvis) Crosby; BA in Speech and English, U. Wis., 1948, postgrad. in speech and oral interpretation of lit., 1949; m. William Malry, Jr., Aug. 5, 1949. Speaker, program artist, 1956—; current programs include First Ladies of Our Land, Women of Worth, Portrait of the Lincolns, A Walk With Mr. Lincoln, Mary and Abraham, Stained Glass: Gift of Light; radio artist Focus on Books, Sta. WHA, 1967-72; tchr. speech, 1951-56; interpretative reader, 1950-58. Vol. hosp. aux.; public affairs chmn. Madison Civics Club; pres. Madison Women's Mcpl. Golf League, 1959; chmn. Little Sisters of Sisters of St. Benedict, 1968-69; pres. Evang. Luth. Ch. Am. Women, Sun Prairie, Wis., 1986-87; tchr. Bible Norway Grove Meml. Luth. Ch., DeForest, Wis., 1990-94; tutor literacy students, 1991—. Recipient award of excellence Wis. Fedn. Women's Clubs; named hon. cannoneer St. Louis Civil War Roundtable. Mem. Am. Assn. Univ. Women (chmn. antiques group 1991-93), Internat. Platform Assn., Nat. League Am. Pen Women, Phi Beta. Author: Abraham Lincoln and His Wife, Mary: Two Human Beings, 1975; The Lincolns: Targets for Controversy, 1986. Home: 6115 Imperial Dr Waunakee WI 53597-9686

BRINKMAN, FRANCES BLANCHE, electrical engineer; b. Casper, Wyo., Oct. 10, 1962; d. Thomas Alva and Rose Madelynne (Anselmi) Lockhart; m. Matthew James Brinkman, Mar. 8, 1986; children: Wyatt Thomas, Heath Michael. BSEE, U. Wyo., 1986. Registered profl. engr., Oreg. Electronics engr. USAF, Hills AFB, Utah, 1986-87; elec. engr. U.S. Army Corps of Engrs., Tucson, 1987-88; electrical engr. U.S. Army Corps of Engrs., Waltham, Mass., 1988-91; elec. engr. U.S. Army Corps of Engrs., Portland, Oreg., 1991—. Mem. IEEE (local pres. 1993, v.p. 1994).

BRINKMAN, JOYCE ELAINE, state legislator; b. Louisville, Oct. 4, 1944; d. Jess Weber and Marie (French) Hopewell; children: Shane, Muffett. BA in History, Hanover Coll. Lic. real estate agt., Ind. Engrossing and enrolling clk. Ind. State Senate, Indpls., 1973, legis. asst., 1974-75; mem. Ind. Ho. Reps, Indpls., 1985—; committeewoman Pike Twp., Indpls., 1973-76; field representative Rep. Nat. Com., Indpls., 1976; mem. City-County Council, Indpls., 1976-83; realtor F.C. Tucker, Indpls., 1979—; exec. dir. Near North Devel. Corp., Indpls., 1983-85. Named Female Young Rep. of Yr. Ind. Young Reps., 1974. Mem. Marion County Council Rep. Women (v.p. 1974-76, pres. 1976-88), Hendricks County Rep. Women's Club, Nat. Bd. Realtors, Metro Indpls. Bd. Realtors. Methodist. Home: 5276 Deer Creek Dr Indianapolis IN 46254-3557*

BRINKMAN, KATHLEEN M., lawyer; b. Cincinnati, Feb. 7, 1943; d. Joseph Sixtus and Rosaleen Esther (D'Arcy) Voss; m. George Brinkman, Aug. 27, 1966; 1 child, Jennifer K. BA, Edgecliff, 1964; JD, U. Cin., 1975. Bar: Ohio 1975, U.S. Dist. Ct. (so. dist.) Ohio 1975, U.S. Dist. Ct. (ea. dist.) Ky. 1979, U.S. Ct. Appeals (6th cir.) 1979. Atty. Cin. Gas & Electric Co., 1975-80; asst. U.S. atty. for so. dist. Ohio U.S. Dept. Justice, Cin., 1980—, dep. dir. criminal div. Asset Forfeiture Office, 1990-91, sr. litigation counsel, 1994—. Contbr. (book) Proving Fed. Crimes, 1981. Mem. ABA, Ohio Bar Assn., Cin. Bar Assn., Fed. Bar Assn. Office: US Atty So Dist Ohio 220 Potter Stewart US Courthouse 100 E 5th St Cincinnati OH 45202-3905

BRINKMEYER, LOUISE, metallurgical engineer; b. St. Louis, May 7, 1954; d. Milton Harold and Mariam (Lamb) B. BS in Metallurgical Engr-

ing., Carnegie Mellon U., 1976; MS in Metallurgical Engring., U. Pitts., 1979; PhD in Chem. & Materials Engring, U. Auckland, 1991. Rsch. engr. ALCOA, Pitts., 1976-77; tech. sales rep. Union Carbide, Pitts., 1979-80; assoc. rsch. engr. U.S. Steel, Monroeville, Pa., 1980-83; chief metallurgist Goodyear, Luxembourg, 1983-84; sr. engr. Westinghouse, Monroeville, 1984-87; mgr. quality assurance Weirton (W.Va.) Steel, 1992—; mem. adv. bd. Carnegie Mellon Ctr. Iron and Steel Making Rsch., Pitts., 1992—. Contbr. articles to tech. jours. Judge Pa. Jr. Acad. Senate, Pitts., 1984—; Carnegie Mellon Engring. Competition, Pitts., 1994. Postdoctoral fellow Carnegie Mellon U., Pitts., 1991-92. Mem. AIME, Am. Iron and Steel Inst. (com. on casting 1992—, chairperson 1995). Office: Weirton Steel Corp 400 Three Springs Dr Weirton WV 26062

BRINKMEYER, MARY FOSS, school system administrator; b. Cin., Sept. 28, 1949; d. Edward Henry and Amelia Louise (Hamberg) Foss; m. Joseph Edward Brinkmeyer, July 1, 1972; children: Lauren, Joseph Edward III. AB, Trinity Coll., 1971; MEd, Xavier U., 1972, postgrad. in Ednl. Administrn., 1989-91. Cert. sch. supt. Ohio. Tchr. Children's World, Schaumburg, Ill., 1972-74; directress Summit Country Day Sch., Cin., 1974-78, asst. to headmaster 1989—, chmn. ednl. orgn. study, 1992-93; mem. prin.'s ctr. Harvard Grad. Sch. Edn. Fellow Inst. Devel. Ednl. Activities (Disting. Edn. award 1992, chmn. strategic planning com., chmn. educating for character program); mem. ASCD, Am. Montessori Soc., Jr. League Cin., NAFE, Nat. Inst. Bus. Mgmt., ASCDX, Nat. Ctr. for Effective Schs. R&D, Ctr. for Advancement Ethics and Character. Roman Catholic. Office: Summit Country Day Sch 2161 Grandin Rd Cincinnati OH 45208

BRIONES, ELLEN MARGARET, legal assistant, researcher; b. Boston, June 17, 1962; d. Michael and Shirley Ann (Lasch) Menaker; m. Jon Eric Briones, June 22, 1985; children: Demetris Alexander, Nikkita Alisha. BA in English Lit., U. Oreg., 1985, JD, 1991. Loan processor Home Fed. Savs., Eugene, Oreg., 1985-86; rsch. asst. Grad. Sch. U. Oreg., Eugene, 1987 summer; vault and sr. teller West One BancCorp, Eugene, 1988; law clk., rsch. asst. various attys. Eugene, 1990-94; student rep. BARBRI, Eugene, 1991-92; vol. coord. L. Holland's Lane County Dist. Ct. Jud. campaign, 1992-93; legal asst. Sahlstrom & Dogdale, Eugene, 1994, Buck, Hogshire & Tereskerz, Charlottesville, Va., 1994—; part time telefund coord. U. Oreg. Found., Eugene, 1981-85; conf. planner sch. law U. Oreg., 1992-93. Mem. ABA, Oreg. Women Lawyers Asn., Lane County Women Lawyers Assn., Alpha Lambda Delta, Phi Eta Sigma. Home: 2675 Meriwether Dr Charlottesville VA 22901

BRISCO, MARGARET, obstetrician-gynecologist, educator; b. Trieste, Italy; b. Anna Loncarica; children—Ralph C. Stefanelli, Anna Maria Stefanelli. MD, U. Padova (Italy), 1956. Intern, Martland Med. Center, Newark, 1956-57, resident in ob-gyn, 1957-60; practice medicine specializing in ob-gyn, Belleville, N.J., 1961—; dir. ob-gyn Clara Maas Hosp., Belleville, 1978—; mem. staff Mountainside Hosp., Montclair, N.J. Active NOW. Mem. AMA, Am. Med. Women's Assn., Med. Soc. N.J. Author: Woman Doctor and Her Patients, 1975, Childbirth a Unique Experience, 1988. Office: 36 Newark Ave Belleville NJ 07109

BRISCO, VALERIE, track and field athlete; b. Greenwood, Miss., July 6, 1960; d. Arguster and Guitherea Brisco; m. Alvin Hooks (div.); 1 child, Alvin. Student, Calif. State U., Northridge. Track competitions include Assn. for Intercollegiate Athletics for Women, 1979, Athletic Congress Nat. Championships, 1984, Olympic Games, Los Angeles, 1984, UCLA Invitational, 1985, Bruce Jenner Meet, San Jose, Calif., 1984, European Track Circuit, 1984, 85, Millrose Games, 1985, Times-Herald Invitational, 1985, Olympic Games, 1988. Co-chairperson Minnie Riperton Cancer Week, 1986-90. Recipient 3 Gold medals 1984 Olympics, Los Angeles, Silver medal 1988 Olympics, Seoul, Republic of Korea; Outstanding Mother's award Nat. Mother's Day Com., 1986; ranked #1 in U.S. in 400 meters, Track and Field News, 1986, #2 in U.S. in 200 meters, Track and Field News, 1986, #3 in U.S. in 100 meters, Track and Field News, 1986, #4 in U.S. in 200 meters, Track and Field News, 1988, #2 in U.S. in 400 meters, Track and Field News, 1988, #6 in world in 400 meters, Track and Field News, 1988. Office: World Class Athletes PO Box 21053 Long Beach CA 90801-4053*

BRISCOE, ANNE M., retired scientist, educator; b. N.Y.C., Dec. 1, 1918; M.A., Vassar Coll., 1945; Ph.D. (Sterling jr. fellow, USPHS fellow), Yale U., 1949; m. William A. Briscoe, Aug. 20, 1955 (dec. Dec. 1985); m. Theodore H. Heinly Sr., Jan. 21, 1989. From research asso. to asst. prof. Cornell U. Med. Coll., 1950-56; faculty Columbia U. Coll. Physicians and Surgeons, N.Y.C., 1956—, prof. emeritus, 1987, spl. lectr., 1987-89; lectr. Harlem Hosp. Center Sch. Nursing, 1968-77; adj. asst. prof. Hunter Coll., 1951-64, 73-75. Mem. N.Y.C. Commn. on Status of Women, 1979—, vice chairperson, 1982-93; non-govtl. orgn. del. to UN; mem. adv. council Inst. Nuclear Power Ops., 1979-84. Recipient Yale medal, 1986, Susan B. Anthony award, 1989. Fellow Am. Inst. Chemists (sec. N.Y. chpt. 1981-83), N.Y. Acad. Scis. (chairperson women in sci. com. 1978-92, bd. govs. 1981); mem. AAAS (mem. council 1982-85), Am. Chem. Soc., Am. Soc. Clin. Nutrition, Am. Fedn. Clin. Research, Harvey Soc., Fedn. Orgns. for Profl. Women (treas. 1978-80), Assn. Women in Sci. Ednl. Founds. (pres. 1978-82), Assn. Women in Sci. (editor newsletter 1971-74, nat. pres. 1974-76), Assn. Yale Alumni (assembly rep. 1978—, bd. govs. 1982-85), Yale Grad. Sch. Alumni Assn. (pres. 1981-86). Contbr. articles to profl. jours. Home: 15 Quarry Hill Rd East Hampton CT 06424 Address (winter): 2116 Sea Crescent Ruskin FL 33570

BRISCOE, BARBARA JUNE, nurse; b. Newark, Ohio, Nov. 20, 1938; d. Eugene Harvey Cooper and Eileen (Pierce) Roche; m. Robert William Briscoe, Feb. 4, 1961 (div. Feb. 1973); children: Michael Edward, Kimberly Anne. BSN, Ohio State U., 1960; MA in Psychology, Calif. Grad. Inst., 1981; M of Nursing, UCLA, 1992. Cert. nurse adminstr.; cert. clin. nurse specialist-adult psychiat. mental health. Sr. psychiatric nurse Fairview State Hosp., Costa Mesa, Calif., 1960-64; instr. Orange Coast Jr. Coll., Costa Mesa, Calif., 1964-65; head nurse, adminstrv. nurse II U. Calif. Med. Ctr., Orange, 1965-82, assoc. dir. nursing, 1982-85, clin. nurse specialist, 1985—; clin. faculty dept. psychiat. human behavior U. Calif. Irvine; part-time nursing faculty Cerretos Jr. Coll. Author: (chpt.) Contemporary Strategies in Nursing, 1986. Group leader Vital Options, L.A., 1990. Mem. Sigma Theta Tau. Presbyterian. Home: 20025 Baywood Ct Yorba Linda CA 92686-6761 Office: U Calif Med Ctr 101 The City Dr S Orange CA 92668-3201

BRISCOE, CHARLOTTE MARIE, compensation manager; b. N.Y.C. BA cum laude, CUNY, 1975, MBA, 1985. Cert. compensation professional. Compensation asst. Kennecott Copper Corp., N.Y.C., 1977-78; pers. asst. Philipp Bros., N.Y.C., 1979-80; compensation asst. Revlon, Inc., N.Y.C., 1983-84; wage and salary analyst St. Luke's-Roosevelt Hosp. Ctr., N.Y.C., 1984-86; assoc. mgr. compensation and records St. Vincent's Hosp. & Med. Ctr., N.Y.C., 1986-89; compensation mgr. Cushman & Wakefield, Inc., N.Y.C., 1989—. Mem. Am. Compensation Assn., N.Y. Compensation Assn. (bd. dirs., asst. treas. 1992-94), Soc. for Human Resource Mgmt. (Metro chpt.).

BRISCOE, MARIAN DENISE, real estate agent, lyricist; b. Balt., Sept. 15, 1958; d. Donald and Bernice (Cofield) Cox; m. James McA. Briscoe, Nov. 2, 1979; children: Crystal Joy and Jennelle Denise. Student music, Morgan State U., 1977; cert. hotel mgmt., C.C.B., Balt., 1979. Therapeutic tech. Union Meml. Hosp., Balt., 1978-80; auditor Holiday Inn, Balt., 1979-81; lyricist J.J. Prodns., Balt., 1981—; realtor Homecoming Realty, Balt., 1991—. Mem. Nat. Assn. Realtors, Greater Balt. Bd. Realtors. Democrat. Home: 1214 N Calhoun St Baltimore MD 21217 Office: Homecoming Realty 4134 Edmondson Ave Baltimore MD 21229

BRISSETTE, MARTHA BLEVINS, lawyer; b. Salisbury, Md., Apr. 30, 1959; d. Reuben Wesley and Miriam Rebecca (Walters) Blevins; m. Henry Joseph Brissette III, May 24, 1980. BA, U. Richmond, 1981, JD, 1983. Bar: Va. 1983, U.S. Supreme Ct. 1987. Law clk. Supreme Ct. Va., Richmond, 1983-84; atty. Dept. Justice, Washington, 1984-88; staff atty. Office of the Exec. Sec. Supreme Ct. Va., Richmond, 1988; asst. atty. gen. Office of the Atty. Gen. of Va., Richmond, 1989-92; atty. regulatory coun. Lawyers Title Ins. Corp., Richmond, 1992—. Mem. Va. Bar Assn., Phi Beta Kappa. Democrat. Roman Catholic. Home: 8221 Brookfield Rd

Richmond VA 23227 Office: Lawyers Title Ins Corp Nat Hdqs 6630 W Broad St Richmond VA 23230

BRISTAH, PAMELA JEAN, librarian; b. Highland Park, Mich., May 13, 1956; d. James Werner and Emily Ann (Josif) B.; m. David Dukehart Wright, July 20, 1984. MusB, Westminster Choir Coll., 1978; MLS, Columbia U., 1985. Cataloger Manhattan Sch. Music, N.Y.C., 1985-88, head libr., 1988—. Mem. Music Libr. Assn. Office: Manhattan Sch Music 120 Claremont Ave New York NY 10027-4698

BRISTER, BARBARA ANN, association executive; b. Cotton Valley, La., Jan. 23, 1948; d. Herman Austin Elkins and Marie (Merritt) Hayes; m. Terry Charles DelaVega; children: David Kip DelaVega, Mark Brandon DelaVega; m. Wentz Frederick Brister, May 3, 1985. Head teller La. Savings & Loan, Alexandria, 1974-80; asst. sec.- treas. Home Fed. Savings & Loan, Shreveport, La., 1981-85; dir. Natchitoches La. Arthritis Found., Shreveport, 1990-92; exec. dir. YWCA of Alexandria-Pineville, Alexandria, La., 1992—. V.p. bd. dirs. YWCA, 1986-90; coord. MADD, Alexandria, 1986—; vol. Caddo-Bossier Coun. Self-Esteem, Shreveport, 1992-94; v.p. Mayor's Commn. for Women, 1988-90; vol. coord. Vols. of Am., Alexandria, 1989; fin. advisor United Way, Alexandria, 1989; bd. dirs. Cenla Chem. Dependency Coun., Alexandria, 1989. Named Belle of Shreveport, Western Electric, 1968; recipient Bus. Devel. award Shreveport Banks, 1989, People Who Care award Telephone Pioneers, 1991. Mem. Pub. Rels. Assn. La., Alexandria C. of C. (leadership tng. 1994). Home: 4027 Huntwick Blvd Alexandria LA 71301 Office: YWCA of Alexandria-Pineville 5912 James St Alexandria LA 71301

BRISTOL, LOUISE FITZGERALD, nurse; b. Moorestown, N.J., Mar. 24, 1935; d. Edward William and Katherine (D'Arcy) Fitzgerald; children: John Edward, Eric Charles. RN, W. Jersey Hosp., 1956; BSN, U. Pa., 1975; MS, U. Del., 1985; postmasters cert. in nursing adminstrn., Villanova U., 1987. RN, N.J. Nurse West Jersey Hosp., Camden, N.J., 1956-57, Mount Holly (N.J.) Hosp., 1957-59, Good Samaritin Hosp., Syracuse, N.Y., 1959-61, Syracuse VA Med. Ctr., 1961-64; med. staff nurse Phila. VA Med. Ctr., 1967-80, staff nurse ICU, 1969-70, surg. staff nurse ICU, 1970-73, night coord., 1973-80; nurse Wilmington (Del.) VA Med. Ctr., 1984-86; headnurse/supr. Coatesville (PA.) VA Med. Ctr., 1986-89; geriatric gerontol. clin. nurse specialist VA Med. Ctr., Coatesville, Pa., 1989—; bd. dirs. NOVA Nat. Com. Mem. Nurses of VA (bd. dirs., chair chpts. com.), ANA (gerontology coun.), Kansas City ANA (cert.), Brandywine Valley Assn. Roman Catholic. Office: Coatesville Vet Adminstn Med Ctr Coatesville PA 19320

BRISTOW, ANN, librarian; b. Chgo., Jan. 11, 1940; d. Benjamin Thompson and Martha Ann (Wall) B.; divorced; children: Ana Teresa Beltran, Patricia Maria Beltran. AB, U. Mich., 1961, AM, 1964, MLS, 1972. Asst. reference libr. Ind. U. Librs., Bloomington, 1975-77, personnel libr., 1977-79, head reference libr., 1979—, acting assoc. dean for pub. svcs., 1988-89. Contbr. articles to profl. jours. Mem. AAUP, MLA, ALA. Democrat. Home: 620 S Woodlawn Ave Bloomington IN 47401-4934 Office: Ind U Librs Bloomington IN 47405

BRITA, SUSAN, legislative staff director. Past employers include Gen. Svcs. Adminstrn., Dept. Treas., Ho. Govt. Ops. Com.; staff dir. subcom. pub. bldgs. and grounds Ho. Com. on Pub. Works and Transp., 1992—. Office: Subcom on Pub Bldg & Grounds B-376 Rayburn House Office Bldg Washington DC 20515*

BRITT, ANGELIA GAIL, freelance designer; b. Troy, N.C., Dec. 24, 1955; d. Howard Delbert and Loretta Gay (Blake) B. BS, East Carolina U., 1978. Staff designer, dir. Burlington Furniture, Lexington, N.C., 1978-83; staff designer Rowe Furniture, Salem, Va., 1983-86; pres., owner AB Designs, High Point, N.C., 1986—; pres. Innovations By Design, High Point, 1993—. Illustrator: Lower Limb Amputations: A Guide to Rehabilitation, 1986. Bd. dirs., sec. The Hearing Clinic, High Point, 1990—. Mem. Sertoma (Gem award High Point 1992, Sertoman of Yr. award 1993). Home and Office: AB Designs 150 Asbill Ave High Point NC 27265-1907

BRITT, MAISHA DORRAH, protective services official; b. S.C.; d. Charles Joseph Britt and Versena (Kennedy) Dorrah; m. W. Benjamin Williams, Dec. 14, 1963 (div. June 1976); children: Terri Rochelle, Trina Michelle. AS, BS, Phila Coll. Textiles and Sci.; MA, Antioch U., Phila., 1986. Cert. in Electronic Surveillance. Physician's asst. Dr. Leonard B. Segal, Phila., 1973-76; police officer Phila. Police Dept., 1976-79; sgt. county detective Phila. Dist. Atty's. Office, 1979-90; spl. agt. Bur. Consumer Protection Office of Atty. Gen., Phila., 1990-91; orgn. devel. cons., v.p. Applied Resource Mgmt., Inc., 1991—; cert. family devel. specialist Norristown Family Ctr., 1994—; founder, dir. Creative Awareness Workshop, Phila., 1978—. Sec. bd. Horizon House, Phila., 1992—; vol. Women Against Abuse, Phila., 1983—; youth adv. New Gethsemane Bapt. Ch., Phila., 1978—; mem. bd. trustees Ctr. for Literacy, 1990—, vice chmn. Recipient award of Appreciation Dobbins High Sch. Alumni Assn., 1991, Woman of Yr. citation Pa. Fedn. Bus. and Profl. Women's Clubs Inc. Mem. Am. Soc. for Indsl. Security, County Detectives Assn. Pa. (exec. bd. 1990—), Fraternal Order of Police, Internat. Police Assn., Internat. Assn. Women Police, Nat. Women's Hall of Fame, Nat. Assn. Chiefs of Police, Bus. and Profl. Women's Club, Internat. Platform Assn. Republican. Address: PO Box 1381 Dover DE 19901

BRITTAIN, NANCY HAMMOND, accountant; b. Athens, Pa., Oct. 29, 1954; d. Charles Avery Hammond and Leona May (Rolls) Mc Creary; m. Edward M. Brittain, Sept. 6, 1975. AS in Bus. Elmira Coll., 1989, BS in Acctg. summa cum laude, 1994. Legal sec. Friedlander, Friedlander, Reizes, Joch & Littman, P.C., Waverly, N.Y., 1973-84; corp. acct., office mgr. Foundry div. Ajax X-Ray, Inc. Sayre, Pa., 1984—. Mem. Athens Borough Zoning Bd., 1991—. Mem. Inst. Mgmt. Accts., Alpha Sigma Lambda (mem. exec. com. Beta Tau chpt., various offices 1988—). Republican. Methodist. Home: 614 Church St Athens PA 18810-1806 Office: Ajax X-Ray Inc Foundry Divsn 150 Bradford St Sayre PA 18840

BRITTIN, MARIE ELEANOR, communication, psychology educator, speech and hearing science educator; b. Wichita, Kans.; d. F. E. and A. M. Brittin. BS, Northwestern U.; MA, U. Iowa; PhD, Northwestern U. Lic. speech pathologist Ohio, Wash. Instr. U. Wis., Madison, 1950-53; coord. comm. disorders Tacoma Pub. Schs., 1956-64; dir. speech and hearing Coll. Edn. Ohio State U., Columbus, 1964-73, assoc. prof. speech and hearing sci., 1973-89; cons. Kent (Wash.) Pub. Schs., 1991; chair Chauncey D. Leake award for excellence in pharmacology, 1991-92; elected mem. compensation and benefits com. Ohio State U., 1985-89; adj. faculty comm. U. Wash., 1994—; pvt. cons. in field. Editor: Ohio Jour. Speech and Hearing, 1984-85. Pres., com. chair Zonta Internat., Tacoma, Columbus. Fellow Am. Speech-Lang.-Hearing Assn. (legis. coun. 1989, 90, 91, site visitor 1982-84, Ace award 1986); mem. APA, Internat. Assn. Logopedics and Phoniatrics (presenter), AAAS, Nat. Aphasia Assn., PEO, Christian Med. and Dental Soc., Ohio State U. Faculty Women's Club (pres. 1966-67), Pi Lambda Theta (pub. adv. bd. 1983-85), Delta Kappa Gamma (pres. Alpha Tau cmpt. 1964). Home: 1220 7th Ave SW Puyallup WA 98371-6759 Office: Ohio State U Speech and Hearing Sci 1070 Carmack Rd Columbus OH 43210-1002

BRITTON, DEANNA LYNN, librarian; b. Ravenna, Ohio; d. James Harding and Dorothy Sue (West) Roberts; m. Oscar Walter Britton. BS in English, SUNY, Brockport, 1976; MLS in Libr. and Info. Sci., U. Tenn., 1981. Tchr. Polo (Ill.) Sch. Dist. 222, 1976-79; info. analyst Oak Ridge (Tenn.) Nat. Lab., Dept. of Energy, 1980-81; edn. bibliographer U. Ga. Librs., Athens, 1982-87, head ednl. resources dept., 1987-91, head social scis. dept., 1991—; profl. devel. comm. Libr. Resources, U. Ga., 1985-86. Contbr. articles to profl. jours. Mem. Spl. Librs. Assn. (asst. editor Bulletin 1989-90, editor 1990-93, chair long-range planning 1989-90, chair pub. rels. 1990-93, sec./treas. 1993—). Office: U Ga Librs Main Libr Social Scis Athens GA 30602

BRITTON, KIM BARNETT, medical/surgical nurse; b. Lubbock, Tex., July 5, 1957; d. Dennison Jones and Carmaleta (Campbell) Barnett; m. Patrick Carl Britton, May 19, 1979; children: Brian Andru, Julie Denise. BSN, West Tex. State U., 1979. RN, Tex. Staff nurse oper. rm. Good Shepherd Med. Ctr., Longview, Tex., 1979-84, staff devel. nurse, coord. health sch., 1984-87, med.-surg. staff nurse, 1989-91. Pub. affairs chmn. Jr. League Longview, 1994, edn. chair. Republican. Baptist.

BRITZ, DIANE EDWARD, investment company executive; b. York, Pa., June 15, 1952; d. Everett Frank and Billie Jacqueline (Sherrill) B.; m. Marcello Lotti, Sept. 9, 1978 (dec. Apr. 1990); children: Ariane Elizabeth, Samantha Alexis. BA, Duke U., 1974; MBA, Columbia U., 1982. Asst. mgr. Columbia Artists, N.Y.C., 1974-76; gen. mgr. Eastern Music Festival, Greensboro, N.C., 1977-78; v.p. Britz Cobin, N.Y.C., 1979-82; pres. Pan Oceanic Mgmt., Inc., N.Y.C., 1983-90; chmn. Pan Oceanic Mgmt., Inc., 1990—; also bd. dirs. Pan Oceanic Mgmt., Inc., N.Y.C.; pres. Pan Oceanic Advisors, Ltd., N.Y.C., 1988-94; chmn. Pan Oceanic Mgmt. Ltd., N.Y.C., 1994—; also bd. dirs Pan Oceanic Advisors, Ltd., N.Y.C.; bd. dirs. Qualitech, Inc., 1990-91. Bd. advisors Turtle Bay Music Sch.; bd. dirs., treas. The 1148 Corp. Mem. Fin. Women's Assn. (bd. dirs.), Caramoor Ctr. for Music and Arts, Inc. (bd. dirs., steering com. capital campaign), Columbia Bus. Sch. Club of N.Y., Doubles Club. Quaker. Office: 1148 5th Ave # 14B New York NY 10128-0807

BROADBENT, AMALIA SAYO CASTILLO, graphic arts designer; b. Manila, May 28, 1956; came to U.S., 1980, naturalized, 1985; d. Conrado Camilo and Eugenia de Guzman (Sayo) Castillo; m. Barrie Noel Broadbent, Mar. 14, 1981; children: Charles Noel Castillo, Chandra Noel Castillo. BFA, U. Santo Tomas, 1978; postgrad. Acad. Art Coll., San Francisco, Alliance Francaise, Manila, Karilagan Finishing Sch., Manila, Manila Computer Ctr.; BA, Maryknoll Coll., 1972. Designer market research Unicorp Export Inc., Makati, Manila, 1975-77; asst. advt. mgr. Dale Trading Corp., Makati, 1977-78; artist, designer, pub. relations Resort Hotels Corp., Makati, 1978-81; prodn. artist CYB/Young & Rubicam, San Francisco, 1981-82; freelance art dir. Ogilvy & Mather Direct, San Francisco, 1986; artist, designer, owner A.C. Broadbent Graphics, San Francisco, 1982—; faculty graphic design & advt. depts. Acad. Art Coll., San Francisco. Works include: Daing na Isda, 1975, (Christmas coloring) Pepsi-Cola, 1964 (Distinctive Merit cert.), (children's books) UNESCO, 1973 (cert.). Pres. Pax Romana, Coll. of Architecture and Fine Arts, U. Santo Tomas, 1976-78, chmn. cultural sect., 1975; v.p. Atelier Cultural Soc., U. Santo Tomas, 1975-76; mem. Makati Dance Troupe, 1973-74. Recipient Merit cert., Inst. Religion, 1977. Mem. NAFE, Alliance Francaise de San Francisco, Internat. Platform Assn., San Francisco Bus. & Profl. Women's Prayer Group. Roman Catholic.

BROADFOOT, ELMA J., mayor; b. Chgo.; m. Fred Broadfoot; children: Stefanie L., Stacie A. BA in English, Sacred Heart. Mayor City of Wichita, Kans., 1993—; corp. comm. dir. Pioneer Balloon Co.; v.p. advancement Kansas Newman Coll.; exec. dir. Wichita Festivals, Inc.; reporter/writer Wichita Eagle and Beacon. Bd. dirs. Sci. Ctr., Botanica, Conv. and Visitors Bur.; mem. exec. com. Exploited and Missing Children's Unit. Mem. Kans. Mayors Assn. (pres.), Assn. Legis. Action of Rural Mayors, Local Elected Ofcls., Pvt. Industry Coun. Office: Office of the Mayor/City Coun 455 N Main St Wichita KS 67202-1603

BROADWAY, NANCY RUTH, landscape design and construction company executive, consultant, model and actress; b. Memphis, Dec. 20, 1946; d. Charlie Sidney and Patsy Ruth (Meadows) Adkins. BS in Biology and Sociology cum laude, Memphis State U., 1969; postgrad., Tulane U., 1969-70; MS in Horticulture, U. Calif.-Davis, 1976. Lic. landscape contractor, Calif. Claims adjuster Mass. Mut. Ins., San Francisco, 1972-73; community garden coord. City of Davis, Calif., 1976; seed propagation supr. Bordier's Wholesale Nursery, Santa Ana, Calif., 1976-78; owner, founder Calif. Landscape Co., 1978-88, Design & Mgmt. Consultare, 1988—. Actress: Visions of Murder, 1993, Eyes of Terror, 1994. NDEA fellow Tulane U., 1969-70. Fellow Am. Hort. Soc.; mem. Nat. Assn. Gen. Contractors, Calif. Native Plant Soc., Stockton C. of C. Democrat. Home and Office: 220 Atlantic Ave Unit 112 Santa Cruz CA 95062-3800

BROCK, DEE SALA, television executive, educator, writer, consultant; b. Covington, Okla., June 7, 1930; d. Lester Edward and Vera Mae (Bowers) Sala; m. Robert Wesley Brock, June 8, 1952 (div. 1979); children: Baron Sala, Bishop Chapman, Bevin Bowers. BA, U. North Tex., 1950, MA, 1956, PhD, 1985. Tchr. high sch. Dallas Ind. Sch. Dist., 1952-66; mem. faculty, adminstr. Dallas County Community Coll. Dist., 1966-74, telecourse writer, producer, adminstr., 1974-75, dir. mktg. info., 1975-80; dir., v.p. PBS, Washington, 1980-89; sr. v.p. edn. PBS, Alexandria, Va., 1989-90; pres. Dee Brock & Assocs., Plano, Tex., 1991—; bd. dirs. Pub. Svc. Satellite Consortium, U.S. Basics; mem. adv. bd. Learning Link, 1987-90, Telcon Industry, 1990-91; chair exec. coun. U. of the World, 1989-91; mem. adv. coun. Triangle Coalition, 1989-91. Author: Writing for a Reason: Study Guide, 1974 (with Jeriel Howard) Writing for a Reason, 1978, (with Laura Derr) The World of F. Scott Fitzgerald, 1980; mem. editorial bd. Am. Jour. Distance Edn., 1987-90; producer (internat. teleconf.) Out of the Red, 1991; producer, writer (TV series and workbook) Communicating in English in the Healthcare Workplace, 1994; speaker in field; contbr. articles in field; co-patentee video indexing system. Trustee Coun. for Adult and Experiential Learning, 1989—; bd. dirs. Coalition for the Advancement of Citizenship, 1988-90, active Met. Police Chief's Boys and Girls Club, Washington, PTA, Dallas. Reynolds Econ. fellow U. N.C., 1966; Literacy award N. Tex. Reading Coun., 1980, Nat. Person of Yr. award Nat. Coun. on Community and Continuing Edn., 1985, Award for Excellence in TV Programming NEA, 1986; recipient Outstanding Career Achievement award ITC Am. Assn. Community and Jr. Colls., 1990. Mem. NEH (nat. bd. cons. 1980-85), U.S. Distance Learning Assn. (bd. dirs. 1989-91, mem. adv. bd. 1989), So. Assn. Colls. and Schs. (mem. Project 1990 task force 1984-86), Nat. Assn. Ednl. Broadcasters (steering com. 1979-81), Assn. Ednl. Communications Technology, Nat. Coun. Tchrs. English (pres. S.W. regional coun. 1972-74). Methodist. Home and Office: 3533 Piedmont Dr Plano TX 75075-6254

BROCK, EUNICE LEE MILLER, realtor; b. Memphis, Mar. 17, 1930; d. Glendon Lee and Kellner (Carter) Miller; children: Clifton Michael, Douglas Martin, Melinda Kellner. BS, Miss. Univ. for Women, 1951; MS, U. N.C., 1964. Cert. residential specialist. Writer I. P. Callison, San Diego, 1952-54; real estate broker Mel Rashkis & Assocs. Inc., Chapel Hill, N.C., 1963-81; real estate prin. Little, Bryan, Worth, Lucas & Brock Inc., Chapel Hill, 1981-86, Eunice Brock & Assocs., Chapel Hill, 1989—; gen. ptnr. The Fountains, 1989-91; cons. Cameron Glen, Chapel Hill, 1985-90, West Franklin Preservation Ptnr., Chapel Hill, 1986—, West Rosemary Ptnrs., 1989-92. Real estate columnist Chapel Hill Newspaper, 1980—; contbr. articles to profl. jours. Chmn. Recreation Commn., Chapel Hill, 1974, Chapel Hill Appearance Commn., 1978, Pub. Pvt. Ptnr., 1986—, Downtown Commn., 1987—; v.p. YMCA, Chapel Hill, 1984; publicity chairperson Town of Chapel Hill Bicentennial, 1993-94; bd. visitors U. N.C. Libr. Sch., 1993—. Mem. Nat. Assn. Realtors, Realtors Nat. Mktg. Inst., Chapel Hill Bd. Realtors (v.p. 1980). Democrat. Presbyterian. Office: Eunice Brock & Assocs 311 W Rosemary St Chapel Hill NC 27516-2514

BROCKA, M. SUZANNE, controller; b. Moline, Ill., May 25, 1960; d. Paul Edmund and Therese Clemence (Fleischman) St. Ledger; m. Bruce Brocka, Mar. 17, 1984; children: Melinda Athena, Bennett Paul. BA in Acctg., St. Ambrose U., Davenport, Iowa, 1981; postgrad., Teikyo-Marycrest U., Davenport, Iowa, 1984-86. CPA, Ill. Acct. Iowa-Ill. Gas and Elec. Co., Davenport, 1981-86; acctg. supr. Frank E. Basil/Gen. Dynamics, Rock Island, Ill., 1986-87, mgr. fin., 1988-90, mgr. fin./contracts, 1990-91; controller City of Davenport, 1991—; cons. Frank E. Basil Inc., Washington, 1990-91, Rocky Mountain Metals Inc., Raton, N.Mex., 1994—. Author: Quality Management, 1992. Bd. dirs. Scott County Historic Preservation Soc., Davenport, 1985-88. Mem. Am. Mgmt. Assn., Fin. Mgmt. Assn., Am. Econ. Assn., Govt. Fin. Officers Assn., Alpha Chi. Home: 1005 Mississippi Ave Davenport IA 52803-3938 Office: City of Davenport 226 W 4th St Davenport IA 52801-1398

BROCKET, JUDITH ANN, mathematics educator; b. Muscatine, Iowa, Feb. 3, 1942; d. Kenneth McKay and Dorothy Pearl (Stewart) Uebe; m. Raymond Gene Brocket, July 28, 1963; 1 son, Jamie. AA, Muscatine Jr. Coll., 1962; BA, Parsons Coll., 1965; grad., Children's Inst. of Lit., 1987. Cert. tchr., Iowa. Swim instr. for handicapped ARC, Burlington, IA, 1965; 3d grade tchr. Burlington Community Sch. Dist., 1965-68, 5th grade tchr., 1970-80, chpt. I math. tchr., 1980—; 4th grade tchr. West Burlington (Iowa) Community Sch. Dist., 1968-70; presenter in field; mem. North Cen. Accreditation Com., 1984-87; mem. Lit. Mag. Com., 1988—. Contbr. articles to profl. publs.; author math. workbooks, curriculum guide. Pres. Burlington PTA, 1981-82, treas., 1988-89; mem., spokesperson Burlington Sch. Dist. Adv. Com., 1980—; mem. Burlington Parent Adv. Com., 1980—. Recipient cert. of merit U.S. Dept. Edn., 1987; Fed. Govt. grantee, 1983, 84. Mem. NEA, Iowa State Edn. Assn., Burlington Edn. Assn., Burlington Art Guild. Democrat. Lutheran. Home: 13084 115th St Burlington IA 52601

BROCKMEYER, ANN HARTMANN, financial planner; b. Detroit, Mar. 5, 1941; d. Robert Allan and Eunice Elizabeth (Seitz) Wilson; m. James Cline Hartmann, July 18, 1970 (dec.); m. Richard W. Brockmeyer, Oct. 1, 1994. BA, Montclair State Coll., 1962; MBA in Fin., Rutgers U., 1974. CLU; chartered fin. cons. Tchr. Bloomfield (N.J.) Bd. Edn., 1962-63; adminstr. Girl Scouts USA, Pa., Mich., 1963-72, YWCA of Am., N.J., Ohio, 1972-77; dir. fin. and field personnel Sycor, Inc., Ann Arbor, Mich., 1977-79; sr. cons. Health Systems Group, Ann Arbor, 1979-80; fin. planner Hartmann & Assocs., Toledo, 1980—; adj. faculty U. Toledo, 1983-87, Lourdes Coll., Sylvania, Ohio, 1987—; faculty Cigna Nat. Edn. Events, 1984—; speaker in field. Editor: (newletter) Money Talks, 1982—. Pres. Maumee Valley Girl Scout Coun., Toledo, 1990—,; 1st. v.p. Girls Clubs of Am., N.Y.C., 1985-87; nat. aquatic sch. staff instr., trainer ARC, Mich., Pa., 1974-80. Named Hines award Honoree Nat. Bd. Child Welfare, 1986. Mem. Internat. Assn. Fin. Planners, Am. Arbitration Assn. (comml. panel), Am. Soc. CLU/ChFC (pres. Toledo chpt. 1988-90, nat. bd. 1993—), Zonta Club Toledo (bd. dirs. 1987-88), Toledo Assn. Life Underwriters (v.p. 1991-94, pres. elect 1994), Toledo Estate Planning Coun. (bd. dirs. 1992—). Republican. Methodist. Office: Hartmann & Assocs 6635 W Central Ave Toledo OH 43617-1029

BROCKWAY, LAURIE SUE, editor, journalist; b. N.Y.C., Dec. 18, 1956; d. Lee L. and Shirley Ruth Brockway; 1 child, Alexander Kent Garrett. AA Laguardia Community Coll., 1978; student, Hunter Coll. CUNY, 1978-81. Features editor, crime reporter The Bklyn. Paper, 1978-81; editor-in-chief The Iniator, N.Y.C., 1982-83; pub., editor The Transformer, N.Y.C., 1983-84; co-producer, writer The Brockway Good News Report, N.Y.C., 1984-85; N.Y. bur. chief Women's News, N.Y.C., 1983-85, mng. editor, 1990, Manhattan corr., 1985—; account supr., Brockway Assocs., Inc., N.Y.C., 1985-88; free lance editor, writer, 1988—; editor/owner, syndicated writer Star Reporter News Svc. 1989-94; editor in chief Playgirl Mag., N.Y.C., 1994—. co-producer, writer, host, news anchor/writer, moderator This Is the New Age, The One Show, Whole Life Expo. Author: Seductions, 1991, Women at Work, 1993, The Doctor is In, 1994; med. correspondent Life in Medicine mag., 1992-94; contbr. articles to mags., newspapers. Recipient LaGuardia Meml. award, 1978, Laguardia Student Coun. scholar, 1978, Expository Writing award, LaGuardia English Dept., 1978.

BRODAY, JEAN ALBANO, art dealer; b. Canton, Ohio, Jan. 12, 1943; d. Milton R. and Marcella (Silver) Maitin; m. Dennis V. Albano, Feb. 6, 1965 (div. Sept. 1990); children: Julie, Douglass; m. Albert Jay Broday, Apr. 21, 1991. BA, Scripps Coll., 1965. Pres., owner Jean Albano Gallery, Chgo., 1985—; docent Mus. Contemporary Art, Chgo., 1981—. Pres. Congregation Beth Or, Deerfield, Ill., 1979-82; bd. dirs. N.S.A. Mus. contemporary Art, Chgo., 1988—, concertante di Chgo., 1992—. Jewish. Office: Jean Albano Gallery 311 W Superior St Chicago IL 60610-3537

BRODE, CAROL RIGHI, art educator; b. Pitts., Dec. 9, 1952; d. Earl Thomas and Grace Louise (Snyder) Righi; m. Kenneth M. Brode, Nov. 11, 1972; children: Samuel, Adam, Benjamin, Noah. BA magna cum laude, Ind. U. of Pa., 1979. Cert. tchr. of art, Pa. Instr. art Arts in the Park, Pitts., 1981-85; instr. workshops in art The Ellis Sch., Pitts., 1986-91; instr. children's programs The Carnegie Mus. of Art, Pitts., 1981-93; gallery dir. Harlan Gallery, Seton Hill Coll., Greensburg, Pa., 1987—; instr. Seton Hill Coll., Greensburg, Pa., 1987—. Exhibited in group shows including Carnegie Mus. of Art; curator Image Song exhbn., 1994. Grantee Mid-Atlantic Arts Found., N.Y.C., 1993, 94; recipient Harlan Gallery grant Pa. Coun. on the Arts, 1993. Mem. Associated Artists of Pitts., Coll. Art Assn. Home: RR 1 Box 219 Jeannette PA 15644-9734 Office: Seton Hill Coll Seton Hill Dr Greensburg PA 15601-1599

BRODER, PATRICIA JANIS, art historian, writer; b. N.Y.C., Nov. 22, 1935; d. Milton W. and Rheba (Mantell) Janis; m. Stanley H. Broder, Jan. 22, 1959; children: Clifford James, Peter Howard, Helen Anna. Student, Smith Coll., 1953-54; B.A., Barnard Coll., Columbia U., 1957; postgrad., Rutgers U., 1962-64; DHL (hon.), St. Lawrence U., 1993. Stock brokerage trainee A.M. Kidder & Co., N.Y.C., 1958; registered rep. Thomson & McKinnon, N.Y.C., 1959-61; ind. registered investment advisor, 1962-64; art cons.; art investment advisor. Writer on art history; books include Bronzes of the American West (Best Art Book award Nat. Acad. Western Art, 1975), Great Paintings of the Old American West, American Indian Painting and Sculpture, Taos: A Painter's Dream (Western Heritage Wrangler award for best art book Nat. Cowboy Hall of Fame and Western Heritage Ctr., 1980, Art Book award Border Regional Libr. Assn., 1981), Hopi Painting: The World of the Hopis, Dean Cornwell: Dean of Illustrators, The American West: The Modern Vision (New award 1984, Trustees award Cowboy Hall of Fame 1984), Shadows on Glass: The Indian World of Ben Wittick, 1990. Recipient Herbert Adams Meml. medal for svc. to Am. sculpture Nat. Sculpture Soc., 1975, Western Heritage Wranglers award for best article on Am. west Nat. Cowboy Hall of Fame and Western Heritage Ctr., 1975, Trustees Gold medal for outstanding contbn. to the west Nat. Acad. Western Art, 1984. Mem. Western History Assn., AAUW. Home: 488 Long Hill Dr Short Hills NJ 07078-1227

BRODERICK, MARSHA, interior designer, general contractor; b. Alameda, Calif., Oct. 15; d. Edwin and Lois Ione (Mockel) Mullin; m. Don Plehn, May 24, 1975; children: Tracy, Veronica. Student, San Diego City Coll., 1961-64, San Diego State Coll., 1961-64. Lic. gen. contractor, Calif. Sec., city mgr. San Diego, 1966-69; pres. Pink Ladies Design and Constrn., Calabasas, Calif., 1971—; lectr. to contractors and educators. Contbr. articles on constrn. and design to profl. jours.; appeared on numerous TV and cable shows. Mem. adv. commn. Equity Re-entry program L.A. Trade Tech. Coll., 1987-88; chair Women's Implementation Century Freeway Adv. Bd., L.A., 1990; state commr. Senator Roberti's Small Bus. Adv. Commn.; v.p. disabled access divsn. L.A. City Commn., Dept. Bldg. and Safety; mem. Senate Select Com. on Northridge Earthquake. Recipient People Who Make a Difference award USA Today, 1985, Golden Nike award Bus. and Profl. Women's Club, 1986, Woman of Achievement award YWCA/YMCA, 1987, Commendations L.A. City Coun., Mayor Tom Bradley, Cal Trans - Century Fwy., others. Mem. Internat. Soc. Interior Design (chair San Fernando Valley 1984-88, pres. 1988-90, 1st pl. comml. divsn. 1992, 1st pl. residential divsn. 1993), Am. Soc. Interior Designers (cert. profl. interior designer). Office: Pink Ladies Design & Constrn Co 23501 Park Sorrento # 218 Calabasas CA 91302

BRODERS, JANET G., food technologist; b. Sacramento, Apr. 12, 1964; d. John Charles and Gay Louise (Giuliani) Ritner; m. Roland Broders, Apr. 20, 1991. BS in Food Sci., Calif. Poly. State U., 1986. Sanitation cons. Rose Svcs., San Francisco, 1987-88; lab. technician Nestle Beverage, Union City, Calif., 1988-90; quality assurance mgr. J.B.R. Gourmet Foods Inc., San Leandro, Calif., 1990—. Mem. Inst. Food Technologists, Kappa Delta (Golden Gate chpt.). Home: 35 Leonard Ct Alameda CA 94502-7941 Office: JBR Inc Gourmet Foods 1933 Davis St Ste 180 San Leandro CA 94577

BRODHEAD, SHEILA ANN, psychologist; b. Morristown, N.J., Mar. 20, 1956. BA in Music Edn., Fairleigh Dickinson U., 1978; D in Psychology, Rutgers U., 1991; postgrad., Inst. for Psychoanalysis and, Psychotherapy of N.J., 1991—. Pvt. practice Morris County, N.J., 1991—; mem. adj. faculty Fairleigh Dickinson U., Madison, N.Y., 1992—. Recipient Garden State fellowship, 1986-89. Mem. APA, N.J. Psychol. Assn., Morris County Psychol. Assn. (program chairperson 1993—), N.J. Assn. Women Therapists.

BRODIAN, LAURA, broadcasting and illustration studio executive, professional illustrator; b. Newark, Oct. 16, 1947; d. Sol and Jean Dolores (Posner) B.; m. Frank Kelly Freas, June 30, 1988. BA, Kean Coll., 1972; M in Music Edn., Ind. U., 1974, D in Mus. Edn., 1982. Lic. radio and TV operator. Tchr. various schs., N.J., 1967-72; assoc. instr. Ind. U., Bloomington, 1973-74; edn. dir. Ind. Arts Commn., Indpls., 1975-76; announcer, engr. Sta. WFIU-FM, Bloomington, 1979-80; announcer, producer Sta. KQED-FM, San Francisco, 1982-87; exec. producer, announcer Sta. KUSC-FM, L.A., 1987-88; exec. dir. fin., mktg., pub. rels. Kelly Freas Studios, 1988—. Host (syndicated classical music show) Music Through the Night, 1988, classical music in-flight program Delta Airlines, 1989—, illustrator, 1990—. Toastmaster, Bay Con'94 SciFi Convention, San Jose, Calif., 1994; artist guest of honor LepreCon 21, Sci. Fiction Convention, 1995. Recipient Chesley award for best sci. fiction mag. cover Assn. Sci. Fiction and Fantasy Artists, 1990. Mem. Nat. Assn. broadcast Employees and Technicians, Assn. Sci. Fiction and Fantacy Artists (we. regional dir.), Bay Area English Regency Soc. (founder), Southern Calif. Early Music Soc. (past pres.), Customer's Guild West (dir. at large).

BRODKIN, ADELE RUTH MEYER, psychologist; b. N.Y.C., July 8, 1934; d. Abraham J. and Helen (Honig) Meyer; m. Roger Harrison Brodkin, Jan. 26, 1957; children: Elizabeth Anne, Edward Stuart. BA, Sarah Lawrence Coll., 1956; MA, Columbia U., 1959; PhD, Rutgers U., 1977. Lic. psychologist, N.J. Sch. psychologist pub. schs., River Edge, Norwood, 1961-66, Morristown, Chatham, N.J., 1967-73; cons. psychologist United Hosp. Newark, 1973; assoc. dir. Infant Child Devel. Ctr. St. Barnabas Med. Ctr., Livingston, N.J., 1977-79; clin. asst. prof. dept. psychiatry U. Medicine and Dentistry N.J., Newark, 1979-90, clin. assoc. prof., 1990—; vis. scholar Hasting (N.Y.) Ctr. for Life Scis., 1979; mem. Essex County Mental Health Adv. Bd., Essex County, N.J., 1985-87; cons. Scholastic, Inc., 1988—; clin. assoc. prof. psychiatry UMDNJ-N.J. Med. Sch., 1990—. Author: Between Teacher and Parent, Supporting Young Children As They Grow, 1994, (with A.T. Jersild and E. Alina Lazar) The Meaning of Psychotherapy in the Teacher's Life and Work, 1962; author, prodr. (video documentary) Competing Commitments, 1984 (best ednl. videotape award N.J. Cable); co-author, prodr. Passage to Physicianhood, 1985, The Insidious Epidemic, 1986; columnist Between Tchr. and Parent, Pre-K Today mag., 1988-93, child devel. columnist, 1991-92; columnist You and Today's Child, Instr. mag., 1990-92, Parent, Teacher and Child, Instr. mag., 1993—, Kids in Crisis, Instr. mag., 1993—; columnist Adolescent Devel., Mid. Yrs. mag., 1990—; columnist Between Tchr. and Parent, Early Childhood Today mag., 1993—;. Grantee Gannett Found., Community Found. for N.J., Carter-Wallace, Inc., Schering Corp.; Adelaide M. Ayer fellow Columbia U., 1962-63, NIMH fellow, 1962, Louis Bevier fellow Rutgers U., 1976-77. Fellow Am. Orthopsychiat. Assn.; mem. Am. Psychol. Assn., N.J. Psychol. Assn. (Psychol. Recognition 1982, 86, 90), Am. Sociol. Assn., N.Y. Acad. Scis. Home and Office: 2 Trevino Ct Florham Park NJ 07932

BRODSKY, CAROLE FERGUSON, psychologist; b. N.Y.C., June 20, 1944; d. Robert Schuyler and Helene (Berlin) Ferguson; m. Paul David Brodsky, Dec. 23, 1972; children: Suzanne, Lauren. AB, Mount Holyoke Coll., 1966; MA, NYU, 1969. Cert. sch. psychologist. Sch. psychologist N.Y.C. (N.Y.) Bd. Edn., 1969-73, Sachem Sch. Dist., Holbrook, N.Y., 1973-74, 88—, Shoreham (N.Y.) Sch. Dist., 1976-77, United Cerebral Palsy, Commack, N.Y., 1983-88. Mem. APA, N.Y. State Psychol. Assn., Suffolk County Psychol. Assn. Office: Sachem Sch Dist 245 Union Ave Holbrook NY 11741-1800

BRODSKY, SYLVIA ARLENE, psychologist, consultant; b. Phila., May 20, 1924; m. Ben Brodsky, Sept. 18, 1949; children: Allen, Sandra Hope, Marla Beth. BA, Temple U., 1945, MED, 1949; cert. in family therapy, Family Inst. Phila., 1974. Lic. psychologist, Pa., sch. psychologist, Pa., guidance counselor, Pa. Dir. social svs. Jewish Fedn. Camden (N.J.) County, 1945-47; dir. early childhood edn. Germantown Jewish Ctr., Phila., 1947-49; family therapist Paley Day Care Ctr., Phila., 1972-75; cons. Bensalem (Pa.) Sch. Dist., 1976-78; family therapist Therapeutic Ctr. Fox Chase, Phila., 1978-82; pvt. practice Phila., 1982—; cons. Abington Psychol. Assocs., Jenkintown, Pa., 1988—; mem. Montgomery County Mental Health Com., Norristown, Pa., 1983—; bd. dirs. Carbon, Monroe, Pike Drug and Alcohol Commn., Stroudsburg, Pa., 1989—; Aldersgate Youth Svc. Bur., Willow Grove, Pa., 1991—. 1st v.p. York Rd. Coun., Abington, 1962-72; chair Anti Defamation League B'nai Brith Women, Phila., 1969-71, March of Dimes, Cheltenham Twp., Pa., 1970; bd. dirs. YMCA, Abington, 1978-81. Recipient Achievement award March of Dimes, Cheltenham Twp., Pa., 1970, Disting. Svc. award S.E. Mental Health Assn., Phila., 1989, cert. appreciation Ea. State Sch. and Hosp., Trevose, Pa., 1989. Mem. AACD, Family Inst. Phila., Am. Psychol. Assn., Montgomery Women's Network (chair 1985-87), Environ. Edn. Ctr. (chair vols. 1989—). Office: 8200 Fenton Rd Laverock PA 19038-7144

BRODY, ANITA BLUMSTEIN, judge; b. N.Y.C., May 25, 1935; d. David Theodore and Rita (Sondheim) Blumstein; m. Jerome I. Brody, Oct. 25, 1959; children—Lisa, Marion, Timothy. AB, Wellesley Coll., 1955; JD, Columbia U., 1958. Bar: N.Y. 1959, Fla. 1960, Pa. 1972. With Office Atty. Gen., State N.Y., 1958-59; dep. asst. atty. gen. State N.Y., 1959; sole practice, Ardmore, Pa., 1972-79; ptnr. Brody, Brown & Hepburn, Ardmore, 1979-81; judge Pa. Ct. Common Pleas 38th Jud. Dist., Norristown, 1981-92; judge U.S. Dist. Ct. (ea. dist.) Pa., Phila., 1992—; lectr. in law U. Pa., Phila., 1978-79. Mem. ABA, Am. Judicature Soc., Nat. Assn. Women Judges, Pa. Bar Assn., Montgomery Bar Assn. (bd. dirs. 1979-81), Temple Am. Inn of Ct. (pres. 1994-95). Republican. Jewish. Office: 3825 Us Courthouse Philadelphia PA 19106

BRODY, JACQUELINE, editor; b. Utica, N.Y., Jan. 23, 1932; d. Jack and Mary (Childress) Galloway; m. Eugene D. Brody, Apr. 5, 1959; children: Jessica, Leslie. A.B., Vassar Coll., 1953; postgrad., London Sch. Econs., 1953-56. Assoc. editor Crowell Collier Macmillan, N.Y.C., 1963-67; writer Coun. Fgn. Rels., N.Y.C., 1968-69; mng. editor Print Collector's Newsletter, N.Y.C., 1971-72, editor, 1972—. Office: 119 E 79th St New York NY 10021-0339

BRODY, JANE ELLEN, journalist; b. Bklyn., May 19, 1941; d. Sidney and Lillian (Kellner) B.; m. Richard Engquist, Oct. 2, 1966; children: Lee Erik and Lorin Michael Engquist (twins). B.S., N.Y. State Coll. Agr., Cornell U., 1962; M.S. in Journalism, U. Wis., 1963; HHD (hon.), Princeton U., 1987; LHD (hon.), Hamline U., 1993. Reporter Mpls. Tribune, 1963-65; sci. writer, personal health columnist N.Y. Times, N.Y.C., 1965—; mem. adv. council N.Y. State Coll. Agr., Cornell U., 1971-77. Author: (with Richard Engquist) Secrets of Good Health, 1970, (with Arthur Holleb) You Can Fight Cancer and Win, 1977, Jane Brody's Nutrition Book, 1981, Jane Brody's The New York Times Guide to Personal Health, 1982, Jane Brody's Good Food Book, 1985, Jane Brody's Good Food Gourmet, 1990, (with Richard Flaste) Jane Brody's Good Seafood Book, 1994. Recipient numerous writing awards, including; Howard Blakeslee award Am. Heart Assn., 1971; Sci. Writers' award ADA, 1978; J.C. Penney-U. Mo. Journalism award, 1978; Lifeline award Am. Health Found., 1978. Jewish. Office: NY Times 229 W 43nd St New York NY 10036

BRODZINSKI, HILARY LEWIS, sales executive; b. Bath, Eng., June 21, 1956; came to U.S., 1981; d. Graham James and May (Meredith) Lewis; divorced; children: Lily Irene, Claudia Marie. Cert. in edn., Oxford U., 1978; BA in edn. magna cum laude, Webster U., 1982. Cert. tchr., Mo. Tchr. pre-sch. Gateway Nursery Sch., Oxford, Eng., 1978-81; curriculum specialist in math/sci. Childgrove Sch., St. Louis, 1981-86; mktg. dir. reading program The Learning Ctr., St. Louis, 1986-88; sales exec. domestic and internat., team mgr. Bankers Tng. and Consulting Co., divsn. Westcott Comm., St. Louis, 1988—; dir. summer camps Childgrove Sch., 1984, 85, dir. extended day program, 1983-84. Mem. Anglican Ch. Home: 1222 Oak Borough Ballwin MO 63021

BROENING, ELISE HEDWIG, writer; b. Bronx, N.Y., Feb. 10, 1941; d. Herman Berhardt and Lillian Marie (Kraft) B. BS in English, NYU, 1962, MA in Ednl. Psychology, 1969; postgrad., NYU Reading Inst., 1968-69, SUNY, Binghamton, 1963-91, Cornell U., Ithaca Coll., P.R., Cin. U. Tchr. English Jr. High Sch. # 104, N.Y.C., 1961-62, Union Endicott (N.Y.) Cen., 1962-63; tchr. English and Reading Johnson City (N.Y.) Schs., 1963-87; freelance writer San Diego, 1987—. Contbr. articles to profl. jours. Mem. Met. Opera Guild, San Diego Opera Guild, Tri-Cities Opera Guild, NYU Alumni Assn., Kappa Delta Pi. Home and Office: 606 3rd Ave Apt 201 San Diego CA 92101-6838

BROERING, NAOMI CORDERO, librarian; b. N.Y.C., Nov. 24, 1939; d. Julius and Emily (Perez) Cordero; B.A., Calif. State U., 1961, M.A. in history, 1963; postgrad. UCLA, 1964, M.L.S. in Library Sci., 1966, postgrad. (NIH fellow), 1967; postgrad. Sch. of Law, U. West Los Angeles, 1970; m. Arthur J. Broering, 1971 (dec. 1992). Acquisitions and reference librarian U. So. Calif., 1967-68; chief librarian Children's Hosp., Los Angeles, 1968-71; asst. librarian Walter Reed Gen. Hosp., Washington, 1972; chief reader services, grant officer VA, Washington, 1972-75; assoc. libr. Med. Ctr., Georgetown U., Washington, 1975-78, libr., 1978—; Med. Ctr. libr. Dahlgren Meml. Library, dir. Biomed. Info. Resources Ctr., 1983—, P.I. Georgetown, Integrated Acad. Info. Mgmt. System, 1986—; mem. adj. faculty Cath. U. Editor: Bull. Med. Libr. Assn. Fellow Am. Coll. Med. Informatics, Med. Libr. Assn. (dir. 1979-82); mem. ALA, Am. Med. Informatics Assn., Am. Soc. Info. Sci., AAAS, Assn. Acad. Health Sci. Library Dirs., Spl. Library Assn., Acad. Health Info. Profls. (disting. mem.). Author, editor: High Performance Medical Libraries, 1993; contbr. articles to profl. jours. Office: Georgetown U Med Ctr Libr 3900 Reservoir Rd NW Washington DC 20007-2187

BROERS, KIMBERLY ANN, editor, writer; b. Dayton, Ohio, Sept. 20, 1956; d. Deryl Dean and Valerie Carol (Devine) B. Cert., Univ. Bordeaux, France, 1977; BA in Writing and French summa cum laude, William Jewell Coll., 1978. Editor, proofer Johnson City Community Coll., Overland Park, Kans., 1978-79; sr. staff writer Women in Bus. mag., Kansas City, Mo., 1979-81; freelance writer, editor Kansas City, 1981-94; editor nat. mag. VFW Aux., Kansas City, 1984-94; copywriter Tappan Design, Shawnee Mission, Kans., 1989-94. Author, editor: Celebrate 75 Years, 1989; contbr. numerous articles to mags. Judge nat. publs. VFW, 1987-93. Mem. Women in Comms., Inc. (newsletter editor 1987-88, roster editor 1988-92), Nat. Soc. for Protection of Animals (newsletter editor 1989-94). Home: 2549 Charlotte St Kansas City MO 64108-2735 Office: VFW Aux 406 W 34th St Kansas City MO 64111-2736

BROGAN-WERNTZ, BONNIE BAILEY, police officer, municipal agency administrator; b. Pine Grove Mills, Pa., Mar. 28, 1941; d. Gilbert Chester and Rosalie Evelyn (Reed) Bailey; m. Donald M. Brogan, Aug. 12, 1960 (div. Oct. 1971); children: Donna Lynn Gregory, Rodney Marshall Brogan; m. Robert R. Werntz, Aug. 28, 1982 (dec. June 7, 1992). A in Criminal Justice, Ind. U., 1976, BS, 1981. Cert. instr. law enforcement tng., Ind. Stenographer South Bend (Ind.) Police Dept., 1970-73, police officer, 1973—, cpl. accident investigation, 1975-80, detective sgt., investigator sex crimes, 1980-85, field tng. officer adminstr., shift comdr. lt., 1985-88, dir. tng., lt., 1988-92; investigative supr., lt., 1992—; bd. dirs. Women's Com. on Sex Offenses, South Bend; vol., trainer rape crisis Sex Offense Services, South Bend, 1980-87; recorder, treas. Child Sexual Abuse Consortium, South Bend, 1982-85; mem. Giarretto Task Force/Family and Children Ctr., Mishawaka, Inc., 1985. Iniator ordinance St. Joseph County Funds for Examinations and Victims of Sex Crimes, 1983. Bd. dirs. Parents Anonymous, South Bend, 1982, Women's Shelter for Battered Women, South Bend, 1985, South Bend Credit Union Supervisory Commn., 1983; mem. Children and Adolescent Adv. Council, South Bend, 1984. Recipient Joseph J. Newman award Protective Bd./Council for Retarded St. Joseph County, 1982, Child Abuse Investigator award The Breakfast Exchange Club, 1982, award for Exceptional Quality in Investigative Child Abuse/Neglect, Child Protective Services of St. Joseph County Dept. Pub. Welfare, 1983, Outstanding Service award Women's Com. on Sex Offenses, 1983, Outstanding Officer of Yr. award, St. Joseph County Council of Clubs, 1985, Police Officer of Yr. award, Ind. Council Fraternal Vets. and Social Scis., 1985, Outstanding Achievement award YWCA Tribute to Women, 1986. Mem. Internat. Assn. of Women Police (Hon. Mention Officer of Yr. 1985), Fraternal Order of Police. Democrat. Home: 1709 Altgeld St South Bend IN 46614-1601 Office: South Bend Police Dept 701 W Sample St South Bend IN 46601-2890

BROGLIATTI, BARBARA SPENCER, television and motion picture executive; b. L.A., Jan. 8, 1946; d. Robert and Lottie (Goldstein) Spencer; m. Raymond Haley Brogliatti, Sept. 19, 1970. BA in Social Scis. and English, UCLA, 1968. Asst. press info. dept. CBS TV, L.A., 1968-69, sr. publicist, 1969-74; dir. publicity Tandem Prodns. and T.A.T. Comm. (Embassy Comm.), L.A., 1974-77, corp. v.p., 1977-82, sr. v.p. worldwide publicity, promotion and advt. Embassy Comm., L.A., 1982-85; sr. v.p. worldwide corp. comm. Lorimar Telepictures Corp., Culver City, Calif., 1985-89; pres., chmn. Brogliatti Co., Burbank, Calif., 1989-90; sr. v.p. worldwide TV publicity, promotion and advt. Lorimar TV, 1991-92; sr. v.p. worldwide TV publicity, promotion and pub. rels. Warner Bros. Inc., Burbank, 1992—. Mem. bd. govs. TV Acad., L.A., 1984-86; bd. dirs. KIDSNET, Washington, 1987—, Nat. Acad. Cable Programming, 1992-94; vice chmn. awards com. TV Acad.; mem. Hollywood Women's Polit. Com., 1992-93. Recipient Gold medallion Broadcast Promotion and Mktg. Execs., 1984. Mem. Am. Diabetes Assn. (bd. dirs. L.A. chpt. 1992-93), Am. Cinema Found. (mem. bd. dirs. 1994—), Dirs. Guild Am., Publicists Guild, Acad. TV Arts and Scis. (vice chmn. awards com.). Office: Warner Bros Studios 4000 Warner Blvd Ste 1057 Burbank CA 91552

BROMBERG, CATHERINE SHAHAN, state agency administrator; b. Bethesda, Md., Aug. 13, 1963; d. Richard Michael and Ann (Pennell) Shahan; m. Hillel Bromberg, June 26, 1988; 1 child, Caleb Milian. BS in Broadcasting Film, Boston U., 1985. Reporter, editor UPI, Boston, 1985-88; pub. edn. dir. State Ethics Commn., Boston, 1988-93; comm. dir. Mass. Dept. Revenue, Boston, 1993-95; roundtable coord. Coun. Govtl. Ethics Laws, 1993-94, mem., 1991-94. Author: (ednl. booklet) A Practical Guide to the Conflict of Interest and Financial Disclosure Laws, 1993; editor (newsletter) Taxpayer Adv. Bulletin, 1993—; editor, contbg. writer (newsletter) Dance Umbrella, 1992—. Pres. Minyan Shaleym Synagogue, Brookline, Mass., 1991-94; mem. steering com. Mandala Internat. Folk Dance Ensemble, Cambridge, Mass., 1991—; mem., singer Balkan music band Zdravets, Cambridge, 1992—; vol. Pro Arte Chamber Music Ensemble, Cambridge, 1993-94. Mem. Pub. Rels. Soc. Am. Office: Mass Dept of Revenue 100 Cambridge St Rm 806 Boston MA 02204

BROMLEY, THERESA ANN, psychologist; b. Phila., Dec. 9, 1962; d. Paul J. and Violet M. (Maines) B. MS in Psychology, Villanova U., 1986; PhD in Clin./Sch. Psychology, Hofstra U., 1993. Cert. sch. psychologist. group facilitator AIDS Ctr. of Queens County, Rego Park, N.Y., 1992—; cons. Bd. Edn., Bklyn., 1992—. Mem. APA. Republican. Roman Catholic. Home: 1 Cornell Dr Great Neck NY 11020-1101 Office: United Cerebral Palsy of Queens 82-25 164th St Jamaica NY 11432

BRONSKI, BETTY JEAN, health care consultant; b. Chgo., Mar. 21, 1952; d. Joseph Jacob and Helen Margaret (Hruby) B. BS, Marquette U., Milw., 1974, MS, 1975; MS, Cardinal Stritch Coll., Milw., 1987. Speech pathologist Sch. Dist. BrownDeer, 1974-79; project analyst Eaton Corp., Milw., 1979-82; mktg. rsch. dir. SSM- Mgmt. Services, Milw., 1982-86; adminstr. asst. SSM-Ministry Corp., Milw., 1986-87; dir. planning & devel. St. Mary's Hill Hosp., Milw., 1987-89; pres. Carefinders, Inc., 1989—. Vol. Greater Milw. Area Spl. Olympics, 1979-82; Alzheimer's Assn. S.E. Wis., 1992-93; bd. dirs. St. Clare Mgmt., 1992—. Roman Catholic. Home: 5150 N Berkeley Blvd Milwaukee WI 53217-5503 Office: Carefinders Inc PO Box 17900 # 146 Milwaukee WI 53217-0900

BRONSKI, DONNA MARIE, lawyer; b. Detroit, Jan. 21, 1959; d. Eugene W. and Mary K. (Schultz) B.; m. John A. Wagner. BS, Ariz. State U., 1981; JD, U. Calif., Davis, 1984. Bar: Ariz. 1987. Assoc. Martinez & Curtis, P.C., Phoenix, 1987—. Mem. Maricopa County Bar Assn. (chair hunger com. 1993—). Office: Martinez & Curtis PC 2712 N 7th St Phoenix AZ 85006-1090

BRONZINA, ISABEL AZUCENA, lawyer; b. Ituzaingo, Argentina, Sept. 28, 1948; came to U.S., 1969; d. Juan Angel Sergio and Azucena Martina (Etchepare) B.; m. Douglas Craig Williams, Oct. 30, 1970 (div. Oct. 1977); children: Wendy Alison, Adriana Day. BS Psychology, Sociology magna cum laude, U. Utah, 1979, JD, 1983. Bar: N.Mex. 1983. Med. social worker Latter-day Saints Hosp., Salt Lake City, 1970; outreach worker Salt Lake County, Salt Lake City, 1979-81; law clk. Utah Legal Svcs., Salt Lake City, 1981-83; staff atty. No. N.Mex. Legal Svcs., Santa Fe, 1983-84; asst. city atty. City of Alamogordo, N.Mex., 1984-85; asst. dist. atty. Dist. Atty.'s Office, Alamogordo, 1985, dep. dist. atty., 1986-89; gen. atty. Office of Dist. Counsel, INS, L.A., 1989-94; U.S. immigration judge Dept. of Justice, Ariz., 1994—. Chicano Scholarship com. scholar, 1980. Mem. ABA, N.Mex. Bar Assn., Phi Beta Kappa, Phi Kappa Phi. Democrat. Roman Catholic. Office: Office of Immigration Judge Ste 366 1705 E Hanna Eloy AZ 85231

BROOK, JUDITH SUZANNE, psychiatry and psychology educator; b. N.Y.C., Dec. 31, 1939; d. Robert and Helen E. (Zimmerman) Muser; m. David W. Brook, Dec. 15, 1962; children: Adam, Jonathan. BA, CUNY, 1961; MA in Psychology, Columbia U., 1962, EdD in Devel. and Ednl. Psychology, 1967. Lic. psychologist, N.Y. Asst. prof. psychology Queens Coll., CUNY, Flushing, 1967-69; rsch. assoc. Columbia U., N.Y.C., 1969-77, sr. rsch. assoc., 1977-80; assoc. prof. psychiatry Mt. Sinai Sch. Medicine, N.Y.C., 1980-90, adj. prof., 1990—; prof. N.Y. Med. Coll., Valhalla, N.Y., 1990—; rsch. scientist devel. Nat. Inst. on Drug Abuse, 1982-90, rsch. scientist, 1992—, ad hoc reviewer, 1989—; ad hoc reviewer NIMH, NSF. Author: The Psychology of Adolescence, 1978; contbr. articles to profl. jours. Recipient 1st ann. Dean's Disting. award N.Y. Med. Coll., 1992; grantee Nat. Inst. on Drug Abuse, 1979—. Mem. APA, Am. Psychol. Soc. (liaison officer 1989—), Assn. for Med. Edn. and Rsch. in Substance Abuse, N.Y. State Psychol. Assn. Office: NY Med Coll Psychiat Inst Valhalla NY 10595 also: 4 E 89th St New York NY 10128

BROOK, SUSAN G., state agency administrator, horse farmer; b. N.Y.C., Dec. 7, 1949; d. Alvin Ira and Sally (Behar) Greenberg. BA, Northwestern U., 1971; MA in Child Devel. and Pub. Adminstrn., Mich. State U., 1975. Community rep. Office Child Devel. HEW, Chgo., 1971-72; program asst. office of pres. OEO, Chgo., 1972-73; exec. coord. Mich. 4-C Coun. Mich. Dept. Mgmt. and Budget, Lansing, 1973-80; adminstr. office interagy. transp. coordination Mich. Dept. Transp., Lansing, 1980-83; adminstr. freight svcs. and safety Bur. Urban and Pub. Transp., Mich. Dept. Transp., Lansing, 1983—; chairperson legis. com. Mich. Coun. Family Rels., Lansing, 1976-77; mem. coalition on children and youth, Lansing, 1976-80; co-chairperson Mich. White House Conf. on Families, Lansing, 1979-80, gov's liaison Internat. Yr of the Child, Lansing, 1978-79; guest lectr. Mich. State U., East Lansing, 1976, Davenport Coll., 1985; inst. Lansing Community Coll., 1978; mem. curriculum devel. adv. com. Lansing community coll., 1979-80. Advisor neighborhood health clinic, Chgo., 1969; youth group advisor Shaare Tikvah Congregation, Chgo., 1967-71; campaign treas. city council candidate, East Lansing, Mich., 1981. Mem. ASPCA, Am. Morgan Horse Assn., Am. Donkey and Mule Soc., Nat. Assn. Edn. Young Children, Nat. Assn. State Dirs. Child Devel., Nat. Conf. State Ry. Ofcls., Am. Horse Shows Assn., Mich. Horse Show Assn., Mich. Justin Morgan Horse Assn., Mich. Morgan Horse Breeders Futurity, Mich. Assn. Edn. Young Children (hon.), Mich. Farm Bur., Capital Area Humane Soc., Calif. Marine Mammal Ctr., Gt. Lakes Miniature Horse Club, Ingham County Farm Bur., Soc. Women in Transp., Women in State Govt., Animal Protection Inst., Am. Miniature Horse Assn., Australian Shepherd Club Am., Hadassah. Office: Mich Dept Transp 425 W Ottawa St Lansing MI 48933-1516

BROOKE, VIVIAN M., state legislator; b. N.Y.C., Feb. 6, 1943; m. Joseph Brooke; 4 children. Attended, U. South Fla.; BA, Carroll Coll. Mem. Mont. Ho. of Reps.; office mgr. Mont. Com. Humanities. Democrat. Home: 1610 Madeline Ave Missoula MT 59801-5806 Office: Mt State Senate State Capitol Helena MT 59620-0001*

BROOKER, LENA EPPS, human services administrator; b. Lumberton, N.C., Oct. 13, 1941; d. Frank Howard and Grace Evelyn (Smith) Epps; m. James Dennis Brooker, July 30, 1966; children: Lora, Lindsey. AB, Meredith Coll., Raleigh, N.C., 1962. Cert. elem. sch. tchr., N.C. Elem. sch. tchr., Charlotte, Robeson County, N.C., Winchester, Va., Chevy Chase, Md., Raleigh, 1962-75; coord. human svcs. program N.C. Commn. Indian Affairs, Raleigh, 1975-78; planner, adminstr. human svcs. program N.C. Dept. Natural Resources and Community Devel., Raleigh, 1978-86; diversity mgt. dir. The Women's Ctr., Raleigh, 1990—; developer model program U.S. Dept. Labor, Raleigh, 1976; presenter Pres.'s Commn. on Status of Women, Raleigh, 1979; facilitator Internat. Yr. of Woman, Winston-Salem, N.C., 1977; speaker on status of Am. Indians to univs., schs., chs. and orgns., 1975—. Contbg. writer The Carolina Call. Chaplain, entertainment chmn. Dem. Women Wake County, Raleigh, 1989-91; mem. task force on native Am. ministry N.C. Conf. United Meth. Ch., chmn. ethnic minority local ch. concerns com., 1988-91, mem. bd. evangelism, 1986-91, audit com. coun. fin. and adminstrn, 1990-91, coun. ministries, 1992-94, mem. bishops task force on staff and structure, 1993-95; mem. Wake County Mammography Task Force, 1990-93; mem. cultural diversity com. Wake County Arts Coun., 1990; bd. dirs. Internat. Festival Raleigh, 1990-91, Triangle OIC, 1991-93, N.C. Civil Liberties Union, 1992-94; mem. steering com. for Yr. of Native Am., N.C. Mus. Natural History, 1986; mem. City of Raleigh Human Resources & Human Rels. Commn., 1990-93; pres. bd. dirs. Women's Fund of N.C., 1993—; bd. advisors Heritage Arts Found., 1993, N.Am. Health Edn. Fund, 1994;. Grantee N.C. Arts Coun., Duke-Semans Fine Arts Found., 1986; recipient Personal Advocacy for Women in N.C. Carpathian award N.C. Equity, 1993. Mem. N.C. Natural Scis. Soc. (bd. dirs. 1987-90), Triangle Native Am. Soc. (past coord. spl. projects), Meredith Coll. Alumne Assn. (bd. dirs. 1994-95). Home: 2110 Fairview Rd Raleigh NC 27608 Office: The Women's Ctr 128 E Hargett St Raleigh NC 27601

BROOKER, SUSAN GAY, employment consultant; b. Washington, Sept. 4, 1949; d. Robert Morris and Mildred Ruby (Parler) B. BA, St. Mary's Coll., St. Mary's City, Md., 1971. News editor WPGC Radio, Lanham, Md., 1971; mgr. trainee Household Fin. Corp., Silver Spring, Md., 1972; career counselor Place-All, Bethesda, Md., 1972-73; exec. v.p. New Places, Inc./Get-A-Job, Washington, 1973-89; employment cons., owner, pres. SGB Consultants, Reston, Va., 1989—; mem. Emploibank, Washington, 1978-79/. Outreach vestry chair Grace Episcopal Ch., 1992-94; conservation chairperson Silver Spring Woman's Club, 1993-94. Recipient Cert. Appreciation U.S. Fish and Wildlife Assn., 1985. Mem. Pell-Capital Pers. Svc. Asssn. (cert.), St. Mary's Coll. (Md.) Alumni Assn. (bd. dirs. 1987-91). Democrat. Home and Office: 2209 Coppersmith Sq Reston VA 22091-2305

BROOKS, ANDRÉE AELION, journalist, educator, author; b. London, Feb. 2, 1937; d. Leon Luis and Lillian (Abrahamson) Aelion; m. Ronald J. Brooks, Aug. 16, 1959 (div. Aug. 1986); children: Allyson, James. Journalism cert., N.W. London Poly., 1958. Reporter Hampstead News, London, 1954-58; story editor Photoplay mag., N.Y.C., 1958-60; N.Y. corr. Australian Broadcasting Co., N.Y.C., 1961-68; editor Elstree, Eng., 1973-74; columnist N.Y. Times, N.Y.C., 1978—; free-lance journalist, 1978—; adj. prof. journalism Fairfield U., Conn., 1983-87; assoc. fellow Yale U., 1989—; founder and pres. Women's Campaign Sch. Yale U., 1993—. Author: Children of Fast Track Parents, 1989 (Best Non-fiction Book award 1990). Mem. exec. bd. Am. Jewish Com., 1987-91; trustee Temple Israel, Westport, Conn., 1991—. Recipient numerous awards including 1st place for news writing Conn. Press Women, 1980, 83, 85, 86, Outstanding Achievement award Nat. Fedn. Press Women, 1981, 1st place award Fairfield County chpt. Women in Comms., 1982, 83, 86, 87, 92, 2d place award in mag. writing Nat. Assn. Home Bldrs., 1983, Spl. Svc. award Conn. chpt. Am. Planning Assn., 1983, 1st place award for mag. writing Nat. Fedn. Press Women, 1983; named one of Am. Women of Achievement Am. Jewish Com., 1989. Mem. Conn. Press Women (chmn. nominating com. 1983-86), Women in Communications (contest co-chmn. 1983-84). Home: 15 Hitchcock Rd Westport CT 06880-2630

BROOKS, ANITA HELEN, public relations executive; b. N.Y.C.; d. Arthur and Bertha (Stewart) Sayle; m. Arnold Brooks, July 1, 1954 (div.). BA, Hunter Coll., 1950; MA, Columbia U., 1952, MLS, 1954. Tchr. Latin Hunter Coll. High Sch., N.Y.C., 1955; publicity rep. WOR Radio, N.Y.C., 1955; writer King Features Syndicate, N.Y.C., 1955-59; pub. relations writer NBC-TV, N.Y.C., 1956; dir. pub. relations N.Y. State Mental Health Fund Campaign, 1956, WMCA Radio, N.Y.C., 1957; account exec. various pub. rels. agys., N.Y.C., 1957-65; pres. Anita Helen Brooks assocs., Pub. Relations, N.Y.C., 1965—; lit. agt. Anita Brooks Lit. Agt., N.Y.C., 1956—. Writer radio-TV shows. Vice chair Sinatra for Meml. Sloan-Kettering Cancer Hosp. Benefit; mem. patronesscom. Harkness Ballet Found., benefit com. Mannes Coll. of Music, N.Y.C. Decorated Dame Comdr. Knights of Malta; named hon. citizen Venezuela. Mem. Am. Women in Radio and TV, Pub. Rels. Soc. Am., Internat. Radio and TV Soc., Publs. Publicity Assn., Assn. Motion Picture Advertisers, Mystery Writers Am., Columbia U. Alumni Assn., Sisters in Crime Soc., Smithsonian Assocs., N.Y. Press Club, Eta Sigma Phi, Latin/Greek Honor Soc. Office: Anita Helen Brooks Assocs 155 E 55th St New York NY 10022-4038

BROOKS, CARLA JO, financial services regulatory advisor; b. Cedar Rapids, Iowa, July 9, 1956; d. Carleton Paul and Gladys Jane (Benning) Groszkruger; m. Thomas Robert Brooks, Sept. 28, 1979; children: Chera MoRae, Erica Love, Heather Joyzelle, Victoria JoLee. BA, Coe Coll., 1978; MS, U. Tex., Dallas, 1983. Fin. analyst Fed. Res. Bank of Dallas, 1978-83, mgr., 1983-85; sr. mgr. KPMG Peat Marwick LLP, Dallas, 1985—; instr. FRS Bd. Govs., Washington, 1985-87; instr. Southwestern Grad. Sch. Banking, Dallas. Republican. Methodist. Club: P.E.O. (Richardson, Tex.). Office: KPMG Peat Marwick LLP 200 Crescent Ct Ste 300 Dallas TX 75201-1885

BROOKS, CHER (SHARON BROOKS), federal agency administrator; b. Dec. 2, 1947; d. Robert E. and Shirley (Kunkel) B. BA, U. Calif., Berkeley, 1970, JD, 1974. Bar: N.C. 1975, D.C. 1978. Counsel N.C. State Govt., 1974-77; with Dem. Nat. Com., 1977-78; assoc. chief counsel FAA, 1978-81; counsel Com. Mcht. Marine and Fisheries, 1981-92; chief counsel Subcom. Mcht. Marine, 1993; dir. Office External Affairs Maritime Adminstrn., Dept. Transp., Washington, 1993—. Author: Status of Women in North Carolina, 1975, Before and After the ERA, 1975. Mem. Phi Beta Kappa. Office: Maritime Adminstrn Dept of Transp 400 7th St SW Rm 7206A Washington DC 20590*

BROOKS, DIANA D., auction house executive; b. Glen Cove, N.Y., 1950; m. Michael C. Brooks; 2 children. Student Miss Porter's Sch., Farmington, Conn., 1965-68, Smith Coll., 1968-69; AB in Am. Studies, Yale U., 1972. Lending officer nat. banking group Citibank, N.A., N.Y.C., 1973-79; with Sotheby's North & South Am., N.Y.C., 1979—, sr. v.p., chief fin. & adminstrv. officer, 1982-84, exec. v.p., 1984-85, chief oper. officer, 1985-87, pres., 1987-90, pres. & chief exec. officer, 1990—, also bd. dirs.; bd. dirs. Sotheby's Holdings, Inc., pres., CEO, 1994. Trustee Yale U., Allen-Stevenson Sch., Deerfield Acad.; pres. coun. assocs. Frick Art Reference Libr. Office: Sotheby's Inc 1334 York Ave New York NY 10021-4806

BROOKS, DONNA STAPLES, state legislator; b. June 9, 1946; m. Richard Brooks; 3 children. BS, W. Ga. Mem. Ga. Ho. of Reps., 1992—; mem. reapportionment com., state planning com., cmty. affairs com., transp. com., ins. agent. Republican. Methodist. Home: PO Box 2037 Newnan GA 30264 Office: Ga House of Reps 412 Legis Office Bldg Atlanta GA 30334*

BROOKS, FREIDA DEAN, fiscal officer, controller; b. Gadsden, Ala., Apr. 18, 1956; d. Adgie B. McNair and Wanda Dean (Whisenant) White; m. Billy Joe Brooks, Nov. 25, 1987; Dana M. Paris. Associates degree, Gadsden State C.C., 1975; BS, U. Ala., Birmingham, 1977; MBA, Jacksonville State U., 1988. Cert. mgmt. acct. Office mgr. Havatampa, Gadsden, 1977; acct. Culp Iron & Metal Co., Gadsden, 1978-80; cost acct. Lee Brass Co., Anniston, Ala., 1981-89; cost acct. supr. Southwire Copper Divsn., Corrollton, Ga., 1989-92; controller SPS Mech. Co., Inc., Anniston, Ala., 1993; fiscal officer Children's Svcs., Inc., Anniston, 1994—; cons., controller Jones Mfg. Co., Inc., Birmingham, 1994. Tchr. Sunday Sch. Coldwater Bapt. Ch., Oxford, Ala., 1988—, dir. decipleship tng., 1993—. Mem. Inst. Cert. Mgmt. Accts., Inst. Mgmt. Accts. (Coosa Valley chpt.). Home: Rt 2 Box 207 Heflin AL 36264 Office: Children's Svcs Inc PO Box 962 Anniston AL 36202

BROOKS, GLADYS SINCLAIR, public affairs consultant; b. Mpls.; d. John Franklin and Gladys (Phillips) Sinclair; m. Wright W. Brooks, Apr. 17, 1941; children: Diane Brooks Montgomery, John, Pamela (Mrs. Jean Marc Perraud). Student U. Geneva, Switzerland, 1935; BA, U. Minn., 1936; LLD, Hamline U., 1966. Dir. Farmer's and Mechanics Bank, 1973-82; mem. Met. Council, 1975-83; lectr. world affairs, 1939—; mem. Mpls. City Council, 1967-73; mem. Met. Airports Commn., 1971-74; pres. World Affairs Ctr. U. Minn., 1976-83; instr. continuing edn. for women U. Minn.; lectr. on world tour as Am. specialist U.S. Dept. State, 1959-60; pres. Brooks/Ridder & Assocs., 1983-94. Mem. Mpls. Charter Commn., 1948-51; pres. YWCA, Mpls., 1953-57, 62-65, mem. nat. bd., 1959-71, del. world meeting, Denmark; pres. Minn. Internat. Ctr., 1953-63; chmn. Minn. Women's Com. for Civil Rights, 1961-64; mem. U.S. Com. for UNICEF, 1959-68; mem. Gov.'s Adv. Com. Children and Youth, 1953-58, Minn. Adv. Com. Employment and Security, 1948-50; Midwest adv. com. Inst. Internat. Edn.; mem. nat. com. White House Conf. Children and Youth, 1960; chmn. Gov.'s Human Rights Commn., 1961-65; dir. Citizens Com. Delinquency and Crime, 1969-93; chmn. Mpls. Adv. Com. on Tourism, 1976-82, Ctr. Women in Govt., 1987-92; chmn. adv. com. Office World Trade, 1988-92; vice chmn. Nat. Community Partnerships Seminars, 1977-82; mem. Midwest Selection Panel, White House Fellows, 1981. Del. Rep. Nat. Conv., 1952; state chmn. Citizens for Eisenhower, 1956; founder, pres. Rep. Workshop; co-chmn. Mpls. Bicentennial Commn., 1974-76; pres. Internat. Center for Fgn. Students; dir. Minn. Alumni Assn.; trustee United Theol. Sem., YWCA, Met. State U.; bd. dirs. Hamline U., Midwest China Ctr., Walker Health Services; mem. pres.'s adv. council St. Catherine's Coll.; trustee Hamline U., Met. State U. Recipient Centennial Women of Minn. award Hamline U., 1954, Woman of Distinction award AAUW, Mpls. 1956, Outstanding Achievement award U. Minn., 1962, Woman of Yr. award YWCA, 1973, Brotherhood award NCCJ, 1975, State Bar award for community leadership, 1976, Service to Freedom award Minn. State Bar Assn., 1976, Community Leadership award YWCA, 1981, Svc. Beyond Self award Rotary, 1990. Mem. World Affairs Council (pres. 1942-44), Minn. LWV (dir. 1940-45), Mpls. Council Ch. Women (pres. 1946-48), Nat. Council of Chs. (mem. gen. bd., v.p. 1961-69), Minn. Council of Chs. (1st woman pres. 1961-64, Christian service award 1967), Mpls. Council of Chs. (v.p. 1946-48), United Ch. Women (bd. mgrs.), Minn. UN Assn. (dir.), Nat. League Cities (human resources steering com. 1972-73), Am. Acad. Polit. Sci., Mpls. C. of C., Minn. Women's Polit. Caucus, Minn. Women's Econ. Roundtable, AAUW, Women's Symphony Assn., Delta Kappa Gamma (hon.). Presbyn. Clubs: Horizon 100, Women's. Home: 5056 Garfield Ave Minneapolis MN 55419-1253

BROOKS, GWENDOLYN, writer, poet; b. Topeka, June 7, 1917; d. David Anderson and Keziah Corinne (Wims) B.; m. Henry L. Blakely, Sept. 17, 1939; children: Henry L., Nora. Grad., Wilson Jr. Coll., Chgo., 1936; L.H.D., Columbia Coll., 1964. Instr. poetry Columbia Coll., Chgo., Northeastern Ill. State Coll., Chgo.; mem. Ill. Arts Council; cons. in poetry Library of Congress, 1985-86; Jefferson lectr., 1994. Author: (poetry) A Street in Bronzeville, 1945, Annie Allen, 1949, Maud Martha; (novel) Bronzeville Boys and Girls, 1953; (for children) The Bean Eaters, 1956; poetry, 1960, Selected Poems, 1963, In the Mecca, 1968, Riot, 1969, Family Pictures, 1970, Aloneness, 1971, To Disembark, 1981; (autobiography) Report From Part One, 1972, The Tiger Who Wore White Gloves, 1974, Beckonings, 1975, Primer for Blacks, 1980, Young Poets' Primer, 1981, Very Young Poets, 1983, The Near-Johannesburg Boy, 1986, Blacks, 1987, Gottschalk and the Grande Tarantelle, 1988, Winnie, 1988, Children Coming Home, 1991. Named one of 10 Women of Yr., Mademoiselle mag., 1945; recipient Creative Writing award Am. Acad. Arts and Letters, 1946; Guggenheim fellow, 1946, 47; recipient Pulitzer prize, 1950, Anisfield-Wolf award, 1969, Essence award, 1988, Frost medal Poetry Soc. Am., 1989; named Poet Laureate of Ill., 1968; recipient Lifetime Achievement award Nat. Endowment for the Arts, 1989; inducted into Nat. Women's Hall of Fame, 1988; Gwendolyn Brooks Chair in Black Literature and Creative Writing established in her honor, Chgo. State U., 1990, The Gwendolyn Brooks Ctr., 1992, Aiken-Taylor award, 1992, Jefferson lectr. award NEH, 1994, Nat. Book Found. medal for lifetime achievement, 1994. Mem. Soc. Midland Authors. Home: 5530 S South Shore Dr Apt 2A Chicago IL 60637-1904

BROOKS, HELENE MARGARET, editor-in-chief; b. Jersey City, Apr. 1, 1942; d. Sinclair Duncan and Helen Margaret (McDermott) B.; m. Joseph F. Olivieri, Dec. 10, 1987 (dec. July 1991). BA, C.W. Post Coll., 1977; MBA, Dowling Coll., 1992. Asst. editor McCall's mag., N.Y.C., 1969-72, assoc. editor, 1972-75, editor features and travel, 1975-83; managing editor 50 Plus mag. Whitney Commn., N.Y.C., 1983; exec. editor 50 Plus mag. Whitney Comm., N.Y.C., 1983-87; editor in chief Network mag./Airlines Travel Agt. Network, N.Y.C., 1987—; editorial cons. Am. Hairdressing Industry , N.Y.C. 1983. Mem. Am. Soc. Mag. Editors, Delta Mu Delta, Phi

Eta. Democrat. Presbyterian. Home: 84 Trellis Ln Wantagh NY 11793-1939 Office: Internat Airlines Travel 300 Garden City Plz Ste 342 Garden City NY 11530-3331

BROOKS, LEMITA, army officer; b. Leesburg, Ga., Oct. 30, 1953; d. Thomas and Adella (Arnold) B.; 1 child, Rico Alexander Brooks. AA, U. Md., Aschaffenburg, Germany, 1991; BS, Wayland Bapt. U., Anchorage, 1993. Enlisted U.S. Army, 1977, advanced through grades to sgt., 1980; pers. sgt. 178th Pers. Svc. Co., Aschaffenburg, 1989-90, Saudi Arabia, 1990-91; chief pers. info. br. 203rd Pers. Svc. Co., Ft. Richardson, Alaska, 1992—. Decorated Army Commendation medal (4), Kuwaiti Liberation medal. Mem. NAFE, Adj. Gen. Regtl. Assn. Democrat. Mem. Ch. Christian Science. Home: 18710 N Lowrie Loop Eagle River AK 99577-8609

BROOKS, LILLIAN HAZEL ASHTON, adult education educator; b. Grand Rapids, Mich., May 27, 1921; d. Walter Brian and Lillian Church; m. Frederick Morris Drilling, 1942 (div. Apr. 1972); children: Frederick Walter, Stephen Charles, Lawrence Alan, Lynn Anne; m. Richard Moreton Ashton, Aug. 25, 1973 (dec.); m. Ralph J. Brooks, May 21, 1994. Student, Grand Rapids Jr. Coll., 1939-41, Wayne State U., 1941-42, Grand Rapids Art Inst., 1945-49, UCLA, 1964-69, Loyola Marymount Coll., Westchester, Calif., 1970-73. Life teaching credential, Calif. Decorator John Widdicomb Furniture Co., 1945-49; tchr. art Inglewood (Calif.) Sch. Dist., 1965-73; tchr. adult edn. art Downey (Calif.) Unified Sch. Dist., 1973-95; lectr. Downey Art League, 1990-92, Whittier (Calif.) Art Assn., 1991, h.s. and mid. sch. lectr., 1994-95; judge Childrens' Art Exhibit, Downey, 1992; participant Getty Found. at San Francisco, 1993, Getty Found. seminar at Cranbrook, 1992, Cin. U. 1992, El Segundo, 1994; mem. state accreditation com. Inglewood and Downey United Sch. Dists., 1966-70, 75-80, 85—. One woman shows include El Segundo Mcpl. Libr., 1965, Pico Rivera Art Gallery, 1978; exhibited in group shows at Fairlane Show, Dearborn, Mich., 1959, Jane Lessing Art Gallery, 1966, Westchester Mcpl. Libr., 1971, Inglewood City Hall, 1973, Aegina Sch., Greece, 1973, Downey Art Mus., 1992; represented in permanent collection at U. Mich. Former mem. Mich. Cultural Com.; art commr. City of Dearborn, Mich., 1954-59; former pres. Dearborn Art Inst., Pacific Art Guild; bd. dirs. Downer Art Mus.; pres. Downey Art League, 1991-92, 93-94, Exhibition Ch., 1995. Recipient Cmty. Svc. award for Outstanding Svc. Downey Rotary, 1994; named Tchr. of Yr., Masons, Downey, 1986. Mem. Calif. Coun. on Art Edn. (parliamentarian Downey 1990-92, Calco Excellence in Tchg. award 1991, various certs.). Home: 9318 Fostoria St Downey CA 90241-4020

BROOKS, LORRAINE ELIZABETH, educator; b. Port Chester, N.Y., Mar. 10, 1936; d. William Henry Sr. and Marion Elizabeth (Harrell) B. BS in Music Edn., SUNY, Potsdam, 1958; M of Performance, Manhattan Sch. Music, 1970. Dir. Camp Spruce-Mountain Lakes, North Salem, N.Y., 1964-73; youth adviser St. Peter's Episcopal Ch., Port Chester, N.Y., 1964-65, St. Andrew's-St. Peter's Ch., Yonkers, N.Y., 1970-73; v.p. South Yonkers Youth Council, 1970-76; assoc. Sisters Charity of N.Y., Scarsdale, 1978—; eucharistic minister, lector Our Lady of Victory Ch., Mt. Vernon, N.Y., 1981-93, echucharistic ministry lector, youth dir., 1988—; Roman Cath. chaplain White Plains (N.Y.) Med. Ctr., 1981—; cons. Quincy Tenants Assn., Mt. Vernon, 1986—. Soloist Greenhave Correctional Facility retreat, N.Y., 1994; recital St. Mary's Ch. Outreach Program, 1994. Vestrywoman St. Andrew's Episc. Ch., Yonkers, 1971-75; contralto soloist St. Peter's Episc. Ch., Port Chester, 1959-69, Cape Cod Roman Cath. Charismatic Conf., 1993; mem. Collegiate Chorale, N.Y.C., 1958-68; svc. team mem. Charismatic Cmty., Scarsdale, 1975-91; v.p. Willwood Tenant Assn., Mt. Vernon, 1981-82, pres., 1982-84; vol. speaker N.Y. Regional Transplant Program, 1992—; active Montefiore Med. Ctr. TRIO, 1991—, presenter kidney transplant program, 1995; active Teen/Twenty Encounter Christ, 1990—; lector, eucharistic min. St. Mary's Roman Cath. Ch., 1993—, facilitator RENEW program, 1994—. Mem. Westchester County Sch. Music Assn. (exec. bd.), Scarsdale Tchrs. Assn. (exec. bd.), Music Educators Nat. Conf. Democrat. Roman Catholic. Office: Scarsdale Pub Schs Mamaroneck Rd Scarsdale NY 10583-5008

BROOKS, PATRICIA SCOTT, principal; b. St. Louis, July 19, 1949; d. John Edward and Doris Louise (Webb) Scott; m. John Robert Brooks, May 22, 1986; 1 child, Ollie. BS, W.Va. State Coll., 1971; MA, Marshall U., 1974; adminstrv. cert., Ind. U., 1990. Cert. tchr., Ind. Tchr. spl. edn. Huntington (W.Va.) State Hosp., 1971; tchr. elem. edn. Kanawha County Sch., Charleston, W.Va., 1971-78; tchr. elem. edn. Washington Twp., Indpls., 1979-82, tchr. mid. sch., 1982-90, adminstrv. intern, 1989-90, asst. coord., 1990, 92, asst. prin., 1990-93; prin. Pike Twp., Indpls., 1993—; chair Devel. of Curriculum Com., Indpls., 1988; participant Ind. U. Tchr. as a Decision Maker Program, Bloomington, 1989; mem. Gifted and Talented Screening Com., Indpls., 1991—. Active Urban League, Indpls., 1990—. Recipient Tchr. Spotlight award Topics Newspaper, 1983; named one of 100 Outstanding Black Women in State of Ind., Nat. Coun. Negro Women, 1990; Danforth fellow Ind. U., 1989. Mem. ASCD, Nat. Coun. Social Studies, Ind. Assn. for Gifted, Ind. Assn. for Elem. and Mid. Sch. Prins., Phi Delta Kappa, Delta Sigma Theta. Methodist. Home: 2711 Pomona Ct Indianapolis IN 46268-1248

BROOKS, SHARON LYNN, dentist, educator; b. Detroit, Oct. 19, 1944; d. Edward Haggit Doubleday and Ila Annabelle (Bobier) Kitamura; m. David Howard Brooks, Aug. 29, 1965. ABEd, U. Mich., 1965, DDS, 1973, MS, 1976, 84, 89. Diplomate Am. Bd. Oral and Maxillofacial Radiology, Am. Bd. Oral Medicine. Pvt. practice Ann Arbor, 1973-76; clin. instr. dentistry U. Mich., Ann Arbor, 1973-76, asst. prof., 1976-80, assoc. prof., 1980-86, prof., 1986—; assoc. prof. radiology Sch. Medicine U. Mich., 1992—; chair oral radiology sect., 1993-94; vis. prof. U. Rochester (N.Y.), 1991.; cons. VA Med. Ctr., Ann Arbor, 1981—, Allen Park, 1983—; nat. bd. test constructor dental hygiene Joint Commn. Nat. Dental Examinations, Chgo., 1986-91. Contbr. articles to profl. jours. Rep. U. Mich. Senate Assembly, Ann Arbor, 1981-84, 87-91; bd. dirs. Ann Arbor YWCA, 1985-88; mem. Senate Assembly Com. on U. Affairs, 1989-90. Mem. ADA, Mich. Dental Assn., Washtenaw Dist. Dental Soc. (pres. 1990-91), Orgn. Tchrs. Oral Diagnosis (pres. 1988-89), Am. Assn. Dental Schs. (chair oral diagnosis sect. 1991-92, oral radiologist sect. 1993-94), Internat. Assn. Dental Rsch., Am. Bd. Oral Medicine (bd. dirs. 1990—), Am. Acad. Oral and Maxillofacial Radiology (bd. dirs. continuing edn. 1985-88), Internat. Assn. Oral Maxillofacial Radiology, Health Physics Soc. Office: U Mich Sch Dentistry Dept Oral Med Pathology Surgery Ann Arbor MI 48109-1078

BROOKS, SUSAN M., mayor; b. N.Y.C., Mar. 8, 1950; d. Edward P. Mittermeier and Loretta Marie (Geiger) Van Tassel; m. James C. Brooks, Aug. 24, 1974; children: Aaron, Meredith. AA, Nassau C.C., 1970; BS, SUNY, Buffalo, 1972; MA, Columbia U., 1973. Cert. tchr. K-12 spl. edn., art. Unit leader orthopedically and learning disabled N.Y.C. Pub. Schs., 1973-76; adminstrv. intern learning disabled, chair high sch. dept. Arlington (Va.) Pub. Schs., 1976-85; home/hosp. instr. learning and emotionally handicapped L.A. County Schs., 1985-87; dir. pub. rels. Palos Verdes Art Ctr., 1987-89; pres. Brooks Comms., 1988—; mayor City of Ranchos Palos Verdes, Calif., 1993, councilwoman, 1991—; exec. bd. dirs. Calif. Contract Cities Assn., chair by-laws com.; mem. Regional Coun. So. Calif. Assn. Govts., vice chair N.Am. Free Trade Agreement com. Bd. dirs. Rolling Hills Little League, 1990-91; v.p., co-founder East Peninsula Edn. Coun., 1986; vol., cons. various Rep. campaigns; bd. dirs. LWV, 1987; del. Rancho Palos Verde Coun. Homeowners Assn., 1986-89; pres. Mira Catalina Homeowners Assn., 1988-91. Mem. NAFE, Calif. Elected Women's Assn. for Edn. and Rsch., Palos Verde C. of C. Roman Catholic. Home: 3419 Corinna Dr Palos Verdes Peninsula CA 90274-6213 Office: City of Rancho Palos Verdes 30940 Hawthorne Blvd Palos Verdes Peninsula CA 90274-5391

BROOKS, TERESA ANN, dietitian; b. Moline, Ill., May 21, 1966; d. Thomas Lee and Sharon Kay (Bandy) B. Student, Queens Coll., Glasgow, Scotland, 1986-87; BS in Dietetics, Iowa State U., 1990, BS in Consumer Food Sci., 1990. Registered dietitian. Book author Ames, Iowa, 1989-90; dietitian Canterbury Skilled Nursing Facility, Palos Verdes, Calif., 1991; dietitial Harbors-UCLA Hosp., Torrance, Calif., 1991; cons. nutritionist Fishman & Assocs., Pasadena, Calif., 1991-92; health edn. dietitian FHP (Health Maintenance Orgn.), Downey, Calif., 1991-93; health club nutritionist Spectrum Health Club, Aguora Hills, Calif., 1993; adminstrv. dietition Cedars-Sinai Med. Ctr., L.A., 1993—; cons. quality food auditor RQA, Chicago, IL, 1993—. Author: Cooking Made Simple, 1989. Advisor Diabetes Support Group, San Gabriel Valley, Calif., 1992; advising dir. Children's Diabetes Summer Camp, Big Bear, Calif., 1992. Mem. Am. Dietetics Assn., Calif. Dietetic Coun. (hostess com. 1992), Calif. Dietetic Assn., Phi Upsilon Omicron. Office: Cedars Sinai Med Ctr 8700 Beverly Blvd Los Angeles CA 90048

BROOKS-KORN, LYNNE VIVIAN, artist; b. Detroit, July 6, 1951; d. Loren Edward and Edith Zona (Gaub) Brooks; m. Howard Allen Korn, Apr. 17, 1977. BFA magna cum laude, U. Mich., 1973, MFA, 1976. Teaching fellow U. Mich. Sch. Art, Ann Arbor, 1976; vis. lectr. various history of art depts.; over 150 solo and group shows since 1992. Numerous one-woman shows, including Grants Pass (Oreg.) Mus. Art, 1993, Red River Valley Mus., Vernon, Tex., 1993, Coll. Ea. Utah, 1994, Aberdeen Arts Ctr. (Scotland), 1995, Carlsbad Mus. (N.Mex.), 1995; exhibited in numerous group shows, 1968—, including Foster City (Calif.) Mus. Gallery, 1993, San Bernardino County Mus., Redlands, Calif., 1993, Ohio State U., 1994, Bryn Mawr Coll. (Pa.), 1995; represented in permanent collections San Bernardino County Mus., Longwell Mus., Downey Mus. Art, Red River Valley Mus., Yosemite Mus., The British Mus., Bryn Mawr Coll., also others; work reviewed in numerous publs.; various commns. Recipient numerous awards for art, including Internat. Art Competition, 1987, 88, 89, Nepenthe Mundi Soc., Wichita, Kans., 1989, Haggin Mus., Stockton, Calif., 1990, Menlo Park Civic Ctr., 1991, San Bernardino County Mus., 1992, Sweetwater County Art Guild, 1993, East Tex. State U., 1993, Breckenridge Fine Arts Ctr., 1993, Lake Worth Art League, Inc., 1993, 94, Amador County Arts Coun., 1993, Coastal Ctr. for Arts, St. Simons Island, Ga., 1993, Soc. We. Artists Signature Mem., 1994, Ea. Washington WC Soc., 1994; Rackham grantee U. Mich., 1975. Mem. Coll. Art Assn. Democrat. Home and Studio: 700 Loma Vista Ter Pacifica CA 94044

BROOME, CLAIRE VERONICA, epidemiologist, researcher; b. Tunbridge Wells, Kent, England, Aug. 24, 1949; came to U.S., 1951; d. Kenneth R. and Heather C. (Platt) B.; m. John F. Head, Apr. 2, 1988; children: Gabriel K., Steven G. BA, Harvard U., 1970, MD, 1975. Diplomate Am. Bd. Internal Medicine. Dep. chief spl. pathogens br. Ctrs. for Disease Control, Atlanta, 1979-80, chief meningitis, spl. pathogens br., 1981-90, assoc. dir. sci., 1991-94, acting dir., nat. ctr. injury prevention and control, 1992-93, dep. dir., 1994—; cons. vaccine devel. AID, 1988—, WHO, NIH, various univs.; mem. steering com. on encapsulated bacterial vaccines, WHO, Geneva, 1989-91, chmn., 1992—; mem. adv. com. on vaccines FDA, Washington, 1990-94. Contbr. numerous articles to profl. jours. Recipient M. C. Rockefeller fellowship, 1970-71, Meritorious Svc. medal USPHS, 1986, rsch. grants NIH, FDA, Dept. of State. Fellow Infectious Diseases Soc. Am. (Bristol-Myers Squibb award 1993); mem. ACP, Am. Epidemiologic Soc., Am. Soc. Microbiology, Common Cause, Phi Beta Kappa, Alpha Omega Alpha. Office: Ctrs for Disease Control # D14 Atlanta GA 30333

BROQUE, SUZANNE, law librarian; b. Paris, Mar. 16, 1948; came to the U.S., 1958; d. Simon and Rose (Bartman) Borenstein; m. Samuel Broque, May 2, 1970; children: Alexander, Danielle. BA, CCNY, 1970; MLS, CUNY, 1973. Intern Bronx (N.Y.) Botan. Gardens Libr., 1972-73; libr. in charge Boyce Thompson Inst. for Plant Rsch., Yonkers, N.Y., 1973-78; libr. Aetna Life & Casualty Law Libr., Hartford, Conn., 1982-83; law libr. CIGNA Corp., Hartford, 1983—. Reach to recovery vol. Am. Cancer Soc., Hartford, 1985-93, Can Surmount vol., founding mem., 1989-93. Recipient Quality of Life award for rehab. Am. Cancer Soc., 1992. Mem. Am. Assn. Law Librs., So. New England Law Librs. Assn. (bd. dirs. 1992—), Spl. Librs. Assn., So. New England Law Librs. Assn. (bd. dirs., treas.). Democrat. Jewish. Office: CIGNA Corp Law Libr W26L Hartford CT 06152

BROSNAN, CAROL RAPHAEL SARAH, arts administrator, musician; b. Paterson, N.J., July 19, 1931; d. Basil Roger Warnock and Mary Ellen Carroll (McDonald) B. Student, George Washington U., Washington, 1956-61, U. Va., 1975, U. Oxford (Eng.), 1975; BA in History, George Washington U., 1981, postgrad., 1983-87; studied with Iris Brussels and Helen Yakobson, 1983-87. Adminstrv. clk. Dept. of Army, Def., Pentagon, Office of asst. chief of staff intelligence, Washington, 1955-58; clk. fgn. sci. info. program NSF, Washington, 1958-60, adminstrv. clk., 1960-65, adminstrv. fellowship clk. grad. fellowship program, 1965-72; staff asst. to Jane Alexander, chmn. Nat. Endowment for the Arts, Washington, 1972—; music tchr. piano, Paterson, N.J., 1945-53; piano recitalist U.S., Heidelberg, W. Ger. Served with WAC, 1953-55. Recipient Young People's Concerts award, 1945. Hon. fellow Harry S. Truman Libr. Inst. Nat. and Internat. Affairs, 1975. Fellow Intercontinental Biog. Assn.; mem. Am. Assn. for Advancement Slavic Studies, Am. Hist. Assn., Am. Philol. Assn., Acad. Polit. Sci. (contbg.), Am. Classical League, Friends of Bodleian Libr. (Oxford U.), Luther Rice Soc. of George Washington U. (life), Phi Alpha Theta. Home: 6030 Sunset Ridge Ct Centreville VA 22020-3051 Office: Nat Endowment for Arts 1100 Pennsylvania Ave NW Washington DC 20506-0001

BROSZ, MARGARET HEADLEY, pediatrics nurse; b. Dover, N.J., Dec. 31, 1951; d. Charles E. and Carolyn (Cobb) H.; m. Walter J. Brosz, May 28, 1978. Student, Douglass Coll., New Brunswick, N.J., 1970-72; BS in Nursing, Cornell U., 1974; MS, Boston Coll., Chestnut Hill, Mass., 1978. Cert. trainer medication adminstrs. Nurse Vis. Nurse Assn. Boston, 1974-76; pediatric nurse practitioner Wrentham (Mass.) State Sch., Boston Children's Hosp., 1978-80; staff nurse pediatrics ICU Thomas Jefferson U. Hosp., Phila., 1980-81; employee health clinician Children's Hosp. Phila., 1981-83; unit nurse, campus relief nurse The Woods Svcs., Langhorne, Pa., 1983—. Mem. Devel. Disabilities Nurses Assn.

BROTHERS, JOYCE DIANE, television personality, psychologist; b. N.Y.C.; d. Morris K. and Estelle (Rapoport) Bauer; m. Milton Brothers, July 4, 1949; 1 child, Lisa Robin. BS, Cornell U., 1947; MA, Columbia U., 1950, PhD, 1953; LHD (hon.), Franklin Pierce Coll., Gettysburg Coll. Asst. in psychology Columbia U., N.Y.C., 1948-52; instr. psychology Hunter Coll., N.Y.C., 1948-52; ind. psychologist, writer, 1952—. Co-host: TV program Sports Showcase, 1956; appearances: TV program Dr. Joyce Brothers, 1958-63, Consult Dr. Brothers, 1960-66, Ask Dr. Brothers, 1965-75; hostess (TV syndication) Living Easy with Dr. Joyce Brothers, 1972-75; columnist TV syndication, N.Am. Newspaper Alliance, 1961-71, Bell-McClure Syndicate, 1963-71, King Features Syndicate, 1972—, Good Housekeeping mag., 1962—; appearances Sta. WNBC, 1966-70; radio program Emphasis, 1966-75, Monitor, 1967-75, Sta. WMCA, 1970-73, ABC Reports, 1966-67, NBC Radio Network Newsline, 1975—; news analyst radio program, Metro Media-TV, 1975-76, news corr., TVN, Inc., 1975-76, Sta. KABC-TV, 1977-82, Sta. WABC-TV, 1980-82, , 86-88, Sta. WLS-TV, 1980-82, NIWS Syndicated News Service, 1982-84, The Dr. Joyce Brothers Program, The Disney Channel, 1985, Sta. KCBS-TV News, 1987—; spl. feature writer Hearst papers, UPI; current affairs spl. corr. Fox TV Syndication, 1990—; author: Ten Days to a Successful Memory, 1959, Woman, 1961, The Brothers System for Liberated Love and Marriage, 1975, How to Get Whatever You Want Out of Life, 1978, What Every Woman Should Know About Men, 1982, What Every Woman Ought to Know About Love and Marriage, 1988, The Successful Woman, 1989, Widowed, 1990, Positive Plus: The Practical Plan to Liking Yourself Better, 1994. Co-chmn. sports com. Lighthouse for Blind; door-to-door chmn. Fedn. Jewish Philanthropies, N.Y.C.; mem. fund raising com. Olympic Fund; mem. People-to-People Program. Winner $64,000 Question TV Program, 1956, $64,000 Challenge, 1957; recipient Mennen Baby Found. award, 1959, Newhouse Newspaper award, 1959, Am. Acad. Achievement award, Am. Parkinson Disease Assn. award, 1971, Sigma Delta Chi Deadline award, 1971, Pres.'s Cabinet award U. Detroit, 1975, Woman of Achievement award Women's City Club Cleve., 1981, award Calif. Home Econs. Assn., 1981, award Distributive Edn. Clubs Am., 1981, Golden Gavel Excellence in Communication award Toastmasters, 1982, Pub. Service award Ridgewood Women's Club, 1987, Women Who Make a Difference award, Sen. Bill Bradley, 1990, Great Am. award Bards of Bohemia, 1993, Diamond award, 1994. Mem. Sigma Xi. Office: NBC Westwood One Radio Network 1700 Broadway New York NY 10019-5905

BROTHERTON, MAUREEN SALTZER, newspaper executive; b. Winchester, Mass., Mar. 21, 1959; d. William Charles Saltzer and Janet Ann (Quigley) Child; m. O. Lee Brotherton, June 27, 1981 (div. 1984). BS in Journalism summa cum laude, Boston U., 1981; postgrad., Northeastern U., Boston, 1984, U. Calif., Riverside, 1994. Freelance corr. Concord (N.H.) Monitor, 1981-82; advt. sales rep. N.H. Times, Concord, 1981-82, circulation mgr., 1982-83; circulation and promotion mgr. Century Publs. Inc., Winchester, Mass., 1983-84, asst. gen. mgr., 1984-85; ad dir., ops. mgr. Provincetown (Mass.) Adv., 1985-86; gen. mgr. Healdsburg (Calif.) Tribune, Lesher Communications, 1986-87, Valley Times, Lesher Communications, Pleasanton, Calif., 1987-90; corp. oper. bd. dirs. Lesher Communications Inc., Walnut Creek, Calif.; pub., v.p. Victor Valley Daily Press div. Freedom Newspapers, Victorville, Calif., 1990—. Bd. dirs. Desert Cmtys. United Way, campaign chmn., 1992, v.p., 1993, pres., 1994; bd. dirs. Victor Valley Cmty. Svcs. Coun., pres., 1993; hotline listener First Call for Help; treas. High Desert Regional Eco. Devel. Authority; bd. dirs. Victor Valley Coll. Found. Recipient Woman of Achievement award Bus. and Profl. Women, San Orco, 1991, Golden Nike award, 1991, 94, Hall of Fame-Bus. award for State of Calif., 1992, Humanitarian award Desert Comtys., United Way, 1991; named Citizen of Yr., Boy Scouts Am. Serrano Dist., 1994. Mem. Am. Newspaper Pubs. Assn., Calif. Newspaper Pubs. Assn. (1st v.p. so. unit 1993, pres. 1994, state bd. dirs. 1994—, 2d pl. excellence award 1989), Internat. Newspaper Mktg. Assn., Internat. Newspaper Advt. and Mktg. Execs. Assn. (best TV comml. award 1992), Apple Valley C. of C., Victorville C. of C. (leadership com., fundraising com.), Rotary. Democrat. Home: 20672 Sholic Rd Apple Valley CA 92308-6367 Office: Victor Valley Daily Press PO Box 1389 Victorville CA 92393-1389

BROTMAN, BARBARA LOUISE, columnist, writer; b. N.Y.C., Feb. 23, 1956; d. Oscar J. and Ruth (Branchor) Brotman; m. Chuck Berman, Aug. 28, 1983; children: Robin, Nina. BA, Queens Coll., 1978. Writer, columnist Chgo. Tribune, 1978—. Recipient Ill. Newspapers Column Writing award UPI, 1984, Peter Lisagor award Sigma Delta Chi, 1984. Office: Chgo Tribune Co 435 N Michigan Ave Chicago IL 60611-4001

BROTMAN, PHYLLIS BLOCK, advertising and public relations executive; b. Balt., Mar. 23, 1934; d. Sol George Block and Delma (Herman) Brotman; student Balt. Jr. Coll., U. Va., Mary Washington Coll.; m. Don N. Brotman, Aug. 16, 1953; children: Solomon G., Barbara Brotman Kaylor. Assoc., Channel 13 TV, 1953-55; free-lance pub. relations, 1960-66; coordinator pub. relations Md. Council Ednl. TV, 1965-66; pres. Image Dynamics, Inc., Balt., 1966—; lectr., cons. Md. Gen. Assembly Legis. Info. Program, 1968-70. Panelist TV, radio; columnist Balt. Bus. Jour. Coord. spl. events Balt. Jr. Coll., 1965; state chmn. U.S. Olympics Com. Mid-Atlantic Region, 1989-92; chmn. mem. com. Greater Balt. Com., 1985-87, mem. econ. devel. coun., 1990-91; adv. bd. mem. Nat. Aquarium Balt., 1988—; bd. dirs. Nat. Adv. Review Bd., 1988-89; mem. Balt. Pub. Rels. Coun.; bd. dirs. Balt. Symphony Orch., 1989—, mem. mktg. com. 75th anniversary season, 1991; chmn. adv. bd. Children and Youth Trust Fund, 1989—; bd. dirs. Internat. Visitors Ctr., co-chair mktg. com., 1990—; founding mem. Chamber Symphony of San Francisco, 1984, bd. dirs. 1984-91; mem. pub. rels. com. U. Md. System, 1988—, mem. pres. adv. coun., 1988—; mem. 20th anniversary conf. com. Internat. Urban Fellows Program Johns Hopkins Inst. Policy Studies, 1989-90; mem. community resources bd. Jr. League Balt., 1982-87; bd. dirs. New Directions for Women, 1979, 1987-90, Stella Maris Hospice Oper. Corp., 1985-87, Jewish Family and Children's Soc., 1980-83; mem. communications United Way Ctrl. Md., 1981-83; mem. mktg., pub. rels. com. Balt. Mus. Art, 1982-84, hon. com. Joshua Johnson Coun. and Endowment Fund, 1988; mem. U. Md. Endowments Com., 1978-79; nat. commr. B'nai B'rith Youth Commn.; bd. electors Balt. Hebrew Congregation, pres. parents' assn., mem. religious sch. com., bd. congregation; bd. dir. Nat. Coun. Jewish Women, life mem. award; former bd. dirs. Assoc. Placement and Guidance Bur., Levindale Home and Infirmary Ladies Auxiliary, Sinai Hosp. Auxiliary, Nat. Jewish Welfare Fund; chmn. Balt. County Econ. Devel. Commn., 1987-91; appointed commn., 1980; appointed Mayor's Commn. Telecommunications, 1987-90; appointed State of Md. Legis. Compensation Commn., 1979-82, 83-86, 87-90, 91—; appointed Mayor's Com. Internat. Bus., 1988-90; appointed Balt. County Bd. Edn. Study Com.; appointed vice chmn. Nat. UN Day Com., 1978-81; appointed Mayor Balt. Bus. Delegation for Balt. Conv. Ctr., 1979; bd. trustees Loyola Coll. Balt., 198--86, 87-93, treas., 1981, 82-83; bd. adv. Towson State U., 1989—, bd. vis., mem. adv. coun. Sch. Bus. & Econs., 1983-85; Found. bd. dirs. Mary Washington Coll., 1985-87, 88-92, speaker jr. class ring ceremony, 1981; mem. exec. com. Inst. Politics and Govt. Coll. Continuing Edn. U. So. Calif.; commencement speaker U. Ky. Coll. Dentistry, 1982. Recipient Cert. of Achievement Young Women's Leadership Coun., Cert. Appreciation for Svc. to Md. Gen. Assembly by Md. Senate, Cert. Achievement in Profession Md. Ho. Dels., Cert. Achievement in Profession Legis. Info. Program Pub. Rels. Soc. Am. Maryland Chpt., Cert. Appreciation Pub. Svc. Md. Area Residences Youth, Pub. Rels. award Great Chesapeake Balloon Race Pub. Rels. Soc. Am. Md. Chpt., Leadership award nat. svc. to profession Internat. Orgn. Women Execs., 1980, Dedicated Svc. award Jewish Family and Children, 1983, Pres. Citation private sector initiatives, 1985, Guardian of Menorah Internat. award B'nai B'rith, 1986, Silver Anvil award Pub. Rels. Soc. Am., 1988; named One Balt. Most Powerful Women Balt. Mag., One Balt. Outstanding Women Mgrs. WMAR-TV, U. Balt., 1983, Woman of Yr. Arlene Rosenbloom Wyman Guild/Univ. Md. Cancer Ctr., 1984, Women of Yr. B'nai B'rith Internat., 1985, Media Advocate of Yr. for Md. U.S. Small Bus. Adminstrn., 1985, Most Admired Company Balt. Mag., 1987, 88, 89, Entrepreneur of Yr. Balt. County Econ. Devel., 1990, Woman of Yr. project Avon Products, Inc., 1990, Save-A-Heart Humanitarian of Yr., 1991, Woman of Yr. B'nai Ben of Balt., 1994. Mem. Am. Assn. Adv. Agencies (chmn. mid-Atlantic region 1981-82, gov. eastern region 1982, 83, 84, chmn. eastern region 1986-87, bd. dirs. 1982-87, gov. rels. com. 1982-87), Ctr. Club Balt. (bd. dirs. 1983—, communications chmn. 1983—), Md. C. of C. (v.p. membership 1991—, v.p. leadership Md. bd. govs. 1992-93, v.p. ctrl. dist. 1985-91, legis. conf. chmn. 1990, exec. com. 1986—, bd. dirs. 1984—), Am. Assn. Political Cons. (pres. 1976-80, bd. dirs. 1974-76, 1980—), Pub. Rels. Soc. Am. Md. Chpt. (nat. chmns. rountable 1987-88, co-chmn. nat. conf., 1980, v.p. Md. chpt. 1968, lifetime achievement award 1993), Am. Adv. Fedn. (co-chair pub. rels. com. 1986-88, nat. govt. rels. coun. 1982—, chmn. legis. com. 1981), Meeting Planners Internat. (co-chmn. pub. rels. 1978-80, task force election by-laws 1979), Adv. Assn. Balt. (bd. dirs. 1974-76), Md.-DC-Del. Press Assn. (co-chmn. assocs. sect. 1982-83), Am. TraumaSoc. (nat. bd. dirs. 1981-87, Md. bd. dirs. 1982-89), Beta Gamma Sigma, Alpha Sigma Nu. Avocations: tennis, flying (cert. aviation solo flight single engine aircraft), wine competitions(tasting, selecting). Home: 8105 Mcdonogh Rd Baltimore MD 21208-1005 Office: Image Dynamics Inc 1101 N Calvert St Baltimore MD 21202-3801

BROTT, BARBARA JO, gifted and talented education educator; b. Chgo., May 29, 1947; d. Walter David Berry and Joann Berry Manka; m. T. Michael Brott, Feb. 23, 1981. BA, U. Ill., 1968, MEd, 1981. Cert. tchr., libr. sci.-media specialist, Ill. Tchr. Sch. Dist. 230, Orland Park, Ill., 1968-69, Sch. Dist. 135, Orland Park, 1969—; cons. edn. of gifted, talented various sch. dists., 1985—. Monthly columnist Jour. Journies, Writing! mag. Bd. dirs. Andrew Scholarship Found., Orland Park, Ill., 1989—; bd. dirs. Children's Rsch. Found., Western Springs, Ill., 1991—. Mem. S. Suburban Reading Coun., Orland Coun. Edn. (officer). Office: Sch Dist 135 8851 151st St Orland Park IL 60462-3450

BROUGHTON, HAZEL CALLEN, rehabilitation counselor, consultant; b. Avant, Okla., Feb. 13, 1920; d. Melvin Harvey and Dorothy Lee (Avant) C.; m. Seldon Broughton, Jan. 15, 1944 (div. Oct. 1978); children: Nancy, Richard, Carol. AA, Del Mar Coll., Corpus Christi, Tex., 1975; BA magna cum laude in Comm.-Sociology, Tex. A&I State U., 1976, MA in Comm., 1976. Cert. rehab. counselor, vocat. expert, Tex. Ind. field interviewer, Corpus Christi, 1965-70; owner, mgr. Broughton Market Rsch. Field Svc., Corpus Christi, 1970-79; pers. cons. Barron Pers., Houston, 1980-83; mgr. Heakin Market Rsch., Houston, 1983-84; job readiness trainer and counselor Tex. Rehab. Commn., Houston, 1984—, impartial hearings officer, 1990—; Tex. del. Nat. Rehab. Govtl. Affairs Seminar, Washington, 1990-91. Mem. Women's Polit. Caucus, Corpus Christi, 1973-78; pres. Women's Equity Action League, Corpus Christi, 1976. Mem. Tex. Rehab. Assn. (pres. job placement div. 1988-89, bd. dirs. 1990-92, Bottom Line award 1989), Teal Run Investment Club (founder, pres. 1994—), Phi Theta Kappa.

BROUN, ELIZABETH, art historian, museum administrator; b. Kansas City, Mo., Dec. 15, 1946; d. Augustine Hughes and Roberta Catherine (Hayden) Gibson; m. Ronald Broun, June 5, 1968; 1 dau., Katherine. B.A., U. Kans., 1968, Ph.D., 1976; cert. advanced study, U. Bordeaux, France, 1967. Curator prints and drawings Spencer Mus. Art, Lawrence, Kans.,

1976-83; asst. prof. U. Kans., Lawrence, 1978-83; asst. dir. chief curator Nat. Mus. Am. Art, Washington, 1983-88; acting dir., 1988-89; dir. Nat. Mus. Am. Art, Washington, 1989—. Author: exhbn. catalogues Prints of Zorn, 1979, Prints and Drawings of Pat Steir, 1983, Patrick Ireland; Drawings 1965-85, 1986, Albert Pinkham Ryder, 1989; co-author: Benton's Bentons, 1980, Engravings of Marcantonio Raimondi, 1981. Woodrow Wilson fellow, 1968-69; Ford. Found. fellow, 1970-72. Mem. Phi Beta Kappa. Office: Nat Mus Am Art 8th & G Sts NW Washington DC 20560

BROUSSARD, CAROL MADELINE, writer, literary consulting agent, photographer; b. Albany, Calif.; d. Roy E. Avila and Adele (Belfils) Cazet; m. Marvin E. Broussard; children: Valerie Madeline, Sean Hunter Rutledge. Student, West Hill Coll., Coalinga, Calif., Coll. Sequoias, Visalia, Calif., Inst. Metaphysics, La Brea, Calif. Former pub. and investigative journalist; pub. TV Watch, Tyler, Tex., 1969-74; resource sec. John C. Fremont Sch., Corcoran, Calif., 1974-77; editor Coalinga (Calif.) Record, 1978-81; pub., prodn. mgr. Kern Valley Chronicle, Lake Isabella, Calif., 1981-84; freelance writer, 1990—; featured TV show Writing Procedures, 1992; instr. home pub. Calif. State U., Fresno, 1992, 95; instr. photography Clovis (Calif.) Adult Edn., 1993—, instr. ethnic watercolors, 1993-94, instr. investigative journalism. 1994, instr. freelance journalism, 1995; tchr. photog. lab. Clovis Teen Summer Sch., 1992-94. Author poetry; composer lyrics for Cajun Hoedown Man Century, summer 1990, theme song Karma for Cinnimin Skin, Lance Mungia film, 1994. Vol., Literacy Progra for WIN/WIN, Fresno Unified Sch. Dist., 1992. Recipient Photo-Journalist award Calif. Newspaper Assn., 1983, Best Feature Photo award Calif. Justice System, 1984, World of Child Photo award Fresno City and County Offices, 1980, Poetic Achievement award Amherst Soc., 1990, award of merit World of Poetry, 1990, Golden Poet award, 1990, 91, Iliad Literary award, 1990, Poetry Editor's Choice award, 1992-93; spotlight interview Writers' Journal, 1992. Mem. Writers Internat. Network (speaker 1991, 92, coord. Vols. Conf. awards 1991). Republican. Office: A&A Literary Agy PO Box 25866 Fresno CA 93729-5866

BROUSSEAU, CATHERINE F., school health services director; b. Lowell, Mass., Oct. 24, 1942; d. Martin J. and Beatrice M. (Moynihan) Dalton; m. Richard C.J. Brousseau, Sept. 6, 1965; 1 child, Margaret E. Diploma, St. Josephs Hosp., Lowell, 1963; BA, New Eng. Coll., Henniker, N.H., 1977, MS, 1982. Cert. AIDS facilitator. Emergency rm. charge nurse St. Josephs Hosp.; pub. health nurse City of Lowell, school health svcs. program dir. Author articles and manual. Mem. Mass. Pub. Health Assn., Mass. Sch. Nurses Assn., Am. Sch. Health Assn., Nat. Sch. Nurses Assn., Sigma Theta Tau. Home: 467 Arlington St Dracut MA 01826-5228

BROWAR, LISA M., librarian; b. N.Y.C., Jan. 22, 1951; d. Elliott Andrew and Shirley (Kahn) B. B in English Lit., Ind. U., 1973, MLS, 1977; M in English Lit., U. Kans., 1976. Asst. curator Beinecke Libr. Yale U., New Haven, Conn., 1979-81, archivist Sterling Meml. Libr., 1981-82; curator spl. collections Vassar Coll. Libr., Poughkeepsie, N.Y., 1982-87; asst. dir. rare books and manuscripts N.Y. Pub. Libr., N.Y.C., 1987—. Mem. ALA, Assn. Coll. and Rsch. Librs. (sec. rare books and manuscripts sect. 1987-89, chair, 1994-95), Am. Printing History Assn., Soc. Am. Archivists, Bibliog. Soc. Am. Democrat. Office: NY Public Lib Rare Book & Manuscript Divsn 5th Ave & 42nd St New York NY 10018

BROWES, PAULINE, Canadian legislator; b. Harwood, Ont., Can., May 7, 1938; d. Robert Earle and Clara (Sandercock) Drope; m. George Harold Browes, Sept. 2, 1961; children: Tammy, Janet, Jeffrey. Student, Toronto Tchrs. Coll., York U., McLaughlin Coll. Mem. for cen. Scarborough Can. Ho. of Commons, 1984-93; min. of state (environment) Can. Ho. Commons, 1991-93, min. of state (employment and immigration), min. Indian affairs and Northern Devel., 1993. Chmn. Scarborough Bd. Health, 1979-84. Mem. Progressive Conservative Party. Anglican. Club: Albany of Toronto, U. Women's Club, Scarborough Golf and Country Club. Address: 16 Colteswood Pl, Scarborough, ON Canada M1G 3P7

BROWN, ALICE MARY, pharmacist; b. Kalamazoo, Mich., Jan. 2, 1947; d. Clarence Walter and Era Rice; m. Jack R. Brown, Apr. 14, 1971; children: Jennifer, Heather, Alice. BS in Pharmacy, Wayne State U., 1969; PharmD, U. Mich., 1971. Intern pharmacist Dearborn (Mich.) Pharmacy, 1966-69; staff pharmacist Lynn Hosp., Allen Park, Mich., 1968-71, Mt. Carmel Hosp., Detroit, 1969-71; staff/relief pharmacist Granger Nitz Pharmacy (later changed to Mey Pharmacy), Saginaw, Mich., 1972-74, 76-82, 1986-89; cons. pharmacist Caro (Mich.) Regional Ctr., 1974-76; relief pharmacist Meijer Pharmacy, Saginaw, 1982-83; clin. researcher, vascular technician Dr. Jack Brown, Saginaw, 1984—; relief pharmacist Arbor Drug (formerly Mey Pharmacy and Granger Nitz Pharmacy), Saginaw, 1990—; lectr. drug abuse prevention Wayne State U., Detroit, 1967-69; program producer WUCM-TV, Delta Coll., 1976-79, resident pharmacist, 1978; co-developer Poisoned Peter Puppet Show, 1979; cons. Citizens for Substance Abuse Svcs., Lansing, Mich., 1981-82; developer poison prevention tray liner. Contbr. articles to profl. jours. Homeroom mother Liskow Elem. and Shields Elem., Saginaw, 1980-86; co-troop leader Brownies, Saginaw, 1981. Grantee U./ Mich., 1983-84, KPR-L'eggs, 1989, ThorLo Hosiery Inc., 1991. Fellow Am. Farriers Assn., Mich. Pharmacists Assn. (com. mem., Pub. Svc. award 1980, Hall of Honor recognition 1992), Saginaw County Pharmacists Assn. (com. mem., past v.p., pres., and exec. bd. mem., Achievement award 1980, Pres. award 1985), Applied Pharmacy Practice. Office: 7974 Gratiot Rd Saginaw MI 48609-5026

BROWN, ANN CATHERINE, investment company executive; b. St. Louis, Aug. 12, 1935; d. George Hay and Catherine Doratha (Smith) B. B.A., Northwestern U., 1956; M.B.A., U. Mich., 1958. Copywriter Fred Gardner Advt. Co., N.Y.C., 1959-61, Batten, Barton, Durstine & Osborn, N.Y.C., 1961-63, Ogilvy & Mather Co., N.Y.C., 1963-64; copy group head Benton & Bowles Co., N.Y.C., 1964-66; pvt. investor, 1966-69; with Baker, Weeks & Co., Inc., N.Y.C., 1969-76; v.p. Baker, Weeks & Co., Inc., 1973-76; exec. v.p., dir. Melhado, Flynn & Assocs., Inc., N.Y.C., 1976-83; chmn., investment exec. A.C. Brown & Assocs. Inc., 1983—. Columnist Forbes mag., 1976-90. Home: PO Box 30098 Sea Island GA 31561-0098

BROWN, ANNE MARIE, marketing executive; b. Washington, Oct. 28, 1966; d. Beverley and Margaret Brown. BA in Math., Vanderbilt U., 1988; MBA in Mktg., U. N.C., 1992. Tng. and devel. specialist Intel Corp., Santa Clara, Calif., 1988-90; sr. field support analyst Janssen Pharmaceutica, Johnson & Johnson, Titusville, N.J., 1992-93, sr. market rsch. analyst, 1993—. Tchr. Jr. Achievement, Princeton, N.J., 1993. Office: Janssen Pharmaceutica 1125 Trenton Harbourton Rd Titusville NJ 08560-1504

BROWN, ARLENE PATRICIA THERESA (RÉNI), artist; b. Elizabeth, N.J., Jan. 3, 1953; d. William J. and Adelaide Elizabeth (Von Krasa) B.; student Union Coll., 1971. BA, Kean Coll., 1980. Owner, pres. Reni Co., Roselle Park, N.J., 1979—; pvt. tchr. art, Glass and Mirror Abrasive Etching , air brush artist designer, metal and wood engraving, Roselle Park, 1979—; owner Twinks Trademark and Associated Characters. Exhibited in The Children's Mus., Ind.; patentee in field. Recipient 3d Place award Custom Car and Van Show, Meadowlands, N.J., 1981, 2d place award Custom Car and Van Show, Asbury Park, N.J., 1982. Mem. Graphic Artists Guild, Artists' Equity Assn., Summit Art Assn., Princeton Art Assn.,, Am. Women's Econ. Devel. Assn., Found. Christian Living, Positive Thinkers Club, N.J. Art Dirs. Club, Westfield Art Assn., Alumni Assn. Kean Coll. Mailing Address: PO Box 186 Roselle Park NJ 07204

BROWN, BARBARA BERISH, lawyer; b. Washington, June 26, 1946; d. Alfred Edward and Sylvia (Kaufman) B.; m. Robert F. Berish, Mar. 26, 1988; 1 child, Jared. BA, Radcliffe-Harvard, 1968; JD, Yale U., 1971. Law clk. to Hon. J. Joseph Smith U.S. Ct. Appeals, Phila., 1971-72; staff atty. Defender Assn. Phila., 1972-74; atty. Women's Law Project, Phila., 1974-76; assoc. Litvin, Blumberg, Matuson & Young, Phila., 1976-80; ptnr. Pepper Hamilton & Scheetz, Washington, 1980-84; mng. ptnr. Paul Hastings Janofsky & Walker, Washington, 1984-92; ptnr. Paul Hastings Janofsky & Walker, 1993—. Co-author: Personnel Director's Legal Guide, 1984, 2d rev. edit., 1990; bd. editors Individual Employment Rights jour., 1992. Mem. ABA (chair program divsn., EEO com. Labor and Employment Law sect.). Office: Paul Hastings Janofsky & Walker 10th Fl 1299 Pennsylvania Ave NW Fl 10 Washington DC 20004-2400

BROWN, BARBARA ELLEN, guidance counselor; b. St. Louis, July 19, 1939; d. George Raymond and Ann Ruth (Koebbe) Berry; m. Stanislaw Ostrowski, Nov. 27, 1961 (div. Aug. 1973); children: Kirk Stan, Shaugh Eric, Laura Andreé; m. Theodore E. Brown, Jan. 1, 1983. BS, St. Louis U., 1961; MA, U. Fla., 1990, EdS, 1990. Cert. counselor, Fla. Math. and sci. tchr. Pinnelas County Schs., Tarpon Springs, Fla., 1978-79; remedial reading tchr. East Las Vegas Schs., 1979-80; math. and English tchr. Tucumcari (N.Mex.) Schs., 1980-82; math. chairperson Nueces County Schs., Corpus Christi, Tex., 1982-86; math. tchr. Clay County Schs., Orange Park, Fla., 1986-87; grad. asst. U. Fla., Gainesville, 1989-90; sch. guidance counselor Bradford County Schs., Starke, Fla., 1990-92; guidance counselor Gilchrist County Schs., Bell, Fla., 1992-93; behavioral specialist Apalachee Ctr. for Human Svcs., Crawfordville, 1993—; co-chairperson on math. book selection Nueces County Schs., Corpus Christi, 1983, chairperson, 1984; presenter word processing program Tex. Computer Edn., McAllen, 1986. Co-Author: Algebra I Curriculum Guide, 1983, Basic Math I Curriculum Guide, 1985, Corpus Christi School Districts Basic Math, 1983; co-author (with others) Joe Wittmore's: Managing Your School Counseling Program, 1992. Office worker Right-to-Life, Gainesville, 1990-93; educator Our Lady Queen of Peace, Gainesville, 1991-93; mem. choir St. Elizabeth Ann Seton, Crawfordville, 1993—; lectr. Our Lady of Loretta, Flour Bluff, 1983-86, Our Lady Queen of Peace, 1991-93, St. Elizabeth Ann Seton, 1993—. Recipient Outstanding Svc. to Student Housing, U. Fla., 1989, Outstanding Contbn. award Ministry of Persons with Disabilities, 1988, Ongoing Support award Red Cloud Indian Sch., 1986—, Appreciation award as religious educator, Our Lady of Loretta, 1983-86. Mem. ACA, Am. Sch. Counselor Assn., Nat. Coun. Tchrs. Math. (presider conv. 1984), Chi Sigma Iota (sec. 1988-89, mem. adv. bd. 1990-92). Roman Catholic. Home: RR 1 Box 3380 Panacea FL 32346 Office: Apalachee Ctr for Human Svc PO Box 773 6 High St Crawfordsville FL 32327

BROWN, BARBARA JONES, health care administrator; b. Tuscaloosa, Ala., Sept. 12, 1950; d. John Thomas and Kathryn Irene (Clifton) Jones; m. Randy Lee Brown, Mar. 26, 1971 (div. 1979); 1 child, Randy Lee II. BSN, U. Ala., 1978; MSN, U. Fla., 1984. Staff nurse VA Med. Ctr., Tuscaloosa, 1978-82, Murfreesboro, Tenn., 1982; asst. dir. nursing Grant Ctr. Hosp., Citra, Fla., 1984-87; dir. nursing Harbour Shores Hosp., Ft. Pierce, Fla., 1987-88, Sonora Desert Hosp., Tucson, Ariz., 1988-90; dir. clin. svcs. Woodland Hills Hosp., West Monroe, La., 1990-92, Bibb Med. Ctr., Centreville, Ala., 1992—; cons. Innovative Healthcare, 1990-92. Mem. Sigma Theta Tau. Home: 3008 Green Grove Cir NE Tuscaloosa AL 35404-2110 Office: Bibb Med Ctr 164 Pierson Ave Centreville AL 35042-1199

BROWN, BENITA TILLMAN, school district social worker; b. Sanford, Fla., Oct. 31, 1952; d. Angus and Marie (Hadley) Tillman; 1 child, Ericka Terrell Tillman. AA, Seminole C.C., Sanford, 1972; BA, U. Ctrl. Fla., Orlando, 1975; MSW, Barry U., Miami, 1978. Cert. tchr., Fla.; cert. sch. social worker. Coord. pre-admission svcs. Fla. Tech. U. (now U. Ctrl. Fla.), Orlando, 1975-76; social svcs. supr. James E. Scott Community Assn., Miami, 1978-79; asst. exec. dir. YWCA, Miami, 1979-82; exec. dir. YWCA, Washington, Pa., 1982-84; guidance counselor Lee County Sch. Bd., Lehigh Acres, Fla., 1984-85; sch. social worker Lee County Sch. Bd., Ft. Myers, Fla., 1985-87; sch. social worker Volusia County Sch. Bd., Deland, Fla., 1987-93, program specialist, 1993-94; pre-K sch. social worker Volusia County Sch. Dist., 1994—. Mem. steering com. Haitian Refugee Ctr., Miami, 1980-82; mem. Juvenile Justice and Delinquency Task Force, State of Fla., 1976-82. Named to Outstanding Young Women of Am., 1981. Mem. Fla. Assn. Sch. Social Workers (state conf. chair 1989, v.p., sec. 1990-92), Delta Sigma Theta (Alumni chpt., pres. 1990-91). Home: 709 S Brooks Ave Deland FL 32720-6611 Office: PO Box 2118 Deland FL 32721-2118

BROWN, BETTY COFFEE, dean, finance educator; b. Louisville, Apr. 4, 1942; d. William Rodger and Ella Mae (Garbutt) Coffee; m. John J. Brown, Jan. 27, 1967; children: Susan, Sara, Sandra. BSc in Acctg., U. Louisville, 1973, MBA, 1978; PhD in Bus., Va. Tech., 1985. CPA, cert. mgmt. acct., cert. internal auditor. Assoc. prof. accountancy coll. bus. and pub. adminstrn. U. Louisville, 1984—, assoc. dean, 1993—. Editor (jour.) The Woman CPA, 1991-93; contbr. articles to profl. jours. Mem. AICPA, Am. Acctg. Assn., Ky. Soc. CPAs (mem. exec. com. 1992—, v.p. 1992—, bd. dirs.), Inst. Internal Auditors (pres. 1994), Inst. Mgmt. Accts. Republican. Office: U Louisville Coll Bus & Pub Adminstrn Louisville KY 40292

BROWN, BEULAH LOUISE, retired elementary educator; b. Warren County, Ohio, Feb. 21, 1917; d. Fred Austin and Roba E. (Doughman) Birmingham; m. William Dale Brown, Aug. 14, 1942 (dec. Apr. 1984). Student, Ohio U., 1937-39, BS in Edn. cum laude, 1957. Cert. tchr., Ohio. Tchr. 2d grade Bainbridge (Ohio) Village Sch., 1939-43; rsch. lab. asst. Mead Paper Corp., Chillicothe, Ohio, 1944-45; tchr. 2d grade Chillicothe City Schs., 1945-46, Marysville (Ohio) Schs., 1946-49; tchr. 1st grade Riley Twp. Sandusky County Schs., Fremont, Ohio, 1951-52; tchr. 2d grade Fremont City Schs., 1952-59; tchr. 2d grade Lancaster (Ohio) City Schs., 1959-64, tchr. 1st grade, 1966-75; tchr. 2d grade Ashland (Ohio) City Schs., 1964-66; supervising tchr. Bowling Green (Ohio) State U., 1955-59, Ohio U., Athens, 1960-64, 66-75, Ashland Coll., 1964-66. Vol. Lancaster Hosp., Meals on Wheels, Pub. Libr. Mem. AAUW, Farifield County Ret. Tchrs., Ohio Ret. Tchrs., Clionian Literary Club, Kappa Delta Pi, Delta Kappa Gamma. Republican. Methodist.

BROWN, BEVERLY MARIE, professional consultant; b. Kelly, N.C.; d. Homer and Dorothy D. (Thomas) B. ADN, Southeastern Community Coll., 1973; BSN, N.C. Cen. U., 1977; postgrad., Hampton Inst., 1979-80; MSN, Meharry Med. Coll., 1985. Advanced aide Episc. Hosp., Phila., 1972; staff nurse U. N.C., Chapel Hill, 1973-75; evening supr. Hillhaven Orange, Durham, N.C., 1975; office mgr., head nurse, supr. Cen. Family Practice, Durham, 1975-79; dir. staff devel. quality assurance Whittaker Meml. Hosp., Newport News, Va., 1979-82; patient care evaluator, staff devel. instr., relief supr. Meharry-HubbardHosp., Nashville, 1982-91, assoc. adminstr., v.p. nursing patient care svcs., 1991—; asst. prof. Tenn. State U., Nashville, 1988-93; DON Bethany Health Care Ctr., Nashville, 1991-92; relief supr., staffer Good Samaritan Health Care and Rehab. Ctr., Nashville, 1991, profl. cons., 1991—; dir./asst. dir. nursing Friendship Hospice Svc. of Nashville, 1992—. Circle leader, reporter, chairperson health care com. First Bapt. Ch. Capitol Hill, Nashville, 1985—; vol. Am. Cancer Soc., 1982—; advisory bd. United Way Middle Tenn. Community Partnership, 1990—; chairperson Minority AIDS Outreach, Nashville, 1988—; bd. dirs. AIDS Walk, Nashville, 1989-91; adv. bd. Vanderbilt AIDS and Vaccine, Nashville, 1989—; mem. NAACP, 1982—; vol. ARC, 1977—. Southeastern Community Coll. scholar, 1970-73. Mem. ANA, Tenn. Nurses Assn., Nat. League for Nursing, Peninsula Assn. Continuing Edn. (pres. 1980), Tenn. Soc. Health Care Risk Mgmt. (pres.-elect 1989, pres. 1991), Chi Eta Phi, Zeta Phi Beta. Home: 3026 Boulder Park Dr Nashville TN 37214-3802 Office: 2128 11th Ave North Nashville TN 37208

BROWN, BONNIE JOAN, human resources director; b. N.Y.C.; 1 child, Andrew Martin. BA in Psychology and Sociology, U. Okla., 1966; MBA, U. Mich., 1979. Rsch. assoc. Inst. for Social Rsch. U. Mich., Ann Arbor, 1971-74, dir. student svcs., 1974-77; human resources mgr. GE, Fairfield, Conn., 1979-90; dir. human resources Pub. Svc. Enterprise Group, Newark, 1990-94, Asea Brown Boveri Inc., Stamford, Conn., 1994—; cons. Dept. Human Svcs., Ann Arbor, 1978-79. Contbr. articles to profl. jours. Com. chair PTA, West Windsor, N.J., 1988; treas. Boy Scouts Am., Apalachin, N.Y., 1985; referee West Windsor Soccer Assn., 1989; peer arbitrator Mercer County Legal System, West Windsor, 1988; vol. Recording for the Blind, Princeton, N.J., 1992-94. Mem. Human Resources Planning Soc., Orgn. Devel. Network. Home: 187A Park St New Canaan CT 06840-5705 Office: Asea Brown Boveri Inc 501 Merritt 7 Norwalk CT 06851

BROWN, BONNIE LOUISE, state legislator; b. San Francisco, Oct. 5, 1942; d. Wilbert Lauren and Thelma (Asbury) Wonderley; m. Gary Leigh Brown, June 13, 1965; children—Mollie Shannon, Joel Alexander. Student, Oreg. State U., 1962-65, U. Idaho, 1965-69; B.A. in English, Morris Harvey Coll., 1971. Tchr. theatre Morris Harvey Coll., Charleston, W.Va., 1973; legis. coordinator W. Va. Citizen Action Group, Charleston, 1975-76; project dir. Com. for Humanities and Public Policy, Charleston, 1976-77; cons. Appalachian Ednl. Lab., Charleston, 1980; state legislator 23d Dist. Charleston, W.Va., 1982—; lobbyist W.Va. NOW, 1976-82; ERA field organizer, 1978-82. Contbr. articles to profl. jours. Chmn., South Charleston Human Rights Commn., 1976; advisor W.Va. Women's Commn., 1977—. Recipient 1st ann. Susan B. Anthony award, 1980; named Bus. and Profl. Women's Woman of Yr., 1987. Mem. Order Women Legislators. Democrat. Home: 2328 Woodland Ave SW Charleston WV 25303-2634

BROWN, BONNIE MARYETTA, lawyer; b. North Plainfield, N.J., Oct. 31, 1953; d. Robert Jeffrey and Diana (Parket) B. AB, Washington U., St. Louis, 1975; JD, U. Louisville, 1978. Bar: Ky. 1978, U.S. Dist. Ct. (we. dist.) Ky. 1979, U.S. Dist. Ct. (ea. dist.) Ky. 1993. Pvt. practice Louisville, 1978—; lectr., seminar leader various profl., ednl., govtl. and civic groups; cons. marital rape; registered lobbyist 1994 Ky. Gen. Assembly for Ky. Assn. Marriage and Family Therapy. Editor Ky. Appellate Handbook, 1985; contbr. articles to profl. jours. Vol. legal panel Ky. Civil Liberties Union, Louisville, 1984—; author, chief lobbyist Marital Rape Bill, Ky. Coalition Against Rape and Sexual Assault, 1982—; vol. advisor Louisville RAPE Relief Ctr., 1975—. Served USAR. Recipient Cert. Spl. Recognition RAPE Relief Ctr., 1980, Cert. Outstanding Contbn., Louisville YMCA, 1983, Cert. of Appreciation, James Graham Brown Cancer Ctr., 1984, Decade of Svc. award YMCA/Rape Relief Ctr., Outstanding Victim Adv. award Fayette County Govt., 1990. Mem. ABA (mem. family law sect., vice chair 1994-95, apptd. to appellate handbook com., jud. adminstrn. divsn. lawyers conf.), Ky. Bar Assn. (family law sect., seminar speaker, mem. task force solo practitioners and small law firms 1992, chairperson subcom. on law office automation and networking, Continuing Legl. Edn. award 1981, 93), Louisville Bar Assn. (liaison to mental health sect., organizer marital rape seminar, chmn. family law sect., mem. mediation com. property divsn., seminar speaker, organizer joint custody child abuse seminars, mem. solo practitioner and small law firm sect., chair 1995), Ky. Acad. Trial Attys. (spkr. seminar), Bus. and Profl. Women (pres. River City chpt.), Ky. Fedn. (legis. chair 1986-87, 90-92, legal counsel 1992, lobby corps chmn. 1993, 94, 95), Louisville Internat. Cultural Ctr., Women Lawyers Assn. Jefferson County. Republican. Office: Nat City Tower 101 S 5th St Ste 3850 Louisville KY 40202-3121

BROWN, CAROL ELIZABETH, educator; b. Boise, Idaho, Jan. 26, 1950; d. Mason Oliver Brown and Hazel (Metcalf) Henderson; m. Richard Bruce Wodtli, Aug. 16, 1989. BS in Art, U. Wis., 1972; MS in Acctg., U. Oreg., 1977; PhD in Computer Sci., Oreg. State U., 1989. CPA. Bookkeeper Stone Fence Inc., Madison, Wis., 1972-74; staff acct. Baillies, Denson, Erickson & Smith, Madison, 1974-75, Minihan, Kernutt, Stokes & Co., Eugene, 1977-78; instr. Oreg. State U., Corvallis, 1978-89, asst. prof., 1989-92, assoc. prof., 1992—. Assoc. editor Jour. Info. Sys., 1989-92; mem. editl. rev. bd. Internat. Jour. Intelligent Sys. in Acctg., Fin. and Mgmt., 1991—, Internat. Jour. Applied Expert Sys., 1994—; guest editor Expert Sys. With Applications, 1991; contbr. articles to profl. jours. Bd. dirs. United Way of Benton County, Corvallis, 1989—, sec.-treas., 1993—; vol. acct., 1982-86. Recipient Outstanding Vol. Svc. award United Way of Benton County, 1986, 93; rsch. grant Oreg. State U., 1988, 90, Scholarhsip award, 1992, 93; rsch. grant TIAA-CREF, 1990, 91. Mem. IEEE Computer Soc., Am. Acctg. Assn. (program adv. com. 1990-91, artificial intelligence/expert sys. sect., vice chairperson 1991-92, chairperson-elect 1992-93, chairperson 1993-94, Pioneer Svc. award 1994), Am. Assn. Artificial Intelligence, Inst. Mgmt. Accts. (dir. manuscripts Salem, Oreg. area 1990—, bd. dirs. 1990—, Merit cert. 1990-91, Rsch. grantee 1993), Oreg. Soc. CPA (com. mem. 1989—, vice chmn. computer svcs. com. 1990-91, Recognition cert. for Leadership Excellence 1989-90, Outstanding Svc. award 1990-91), Assn. Computer Machinery, others. Home: 1145 NW 20th St Corvallis OR 97330-2509 Office: Oreg State U Coll of Bus Bexell Hall # 200 Corvallis OR 97331-2601

BROWN, CAROL ROBERTSON, librarian; b. Anamosa, Iowa, Oct. 27, 1943; d. William Ferman and Grace Viola (Klumph) Robertson; m. Eric Ramsay Brown, Aug. 25, 1965 (div. July 1987); children: Ian Robertson, Kevin William. BA, Cornell Coll., Mt. Vernon, Iowa, 1965; MA, Ind. U., 1966. Reference librarian Undergrad. Library, Ind. U., Bloomington, 1966-68, asst. undergrad. librarian, 1968-70; adult materials specialist Houston Pub. Library, 1975-77, mgr. Jungman br., 1977-79, asst. chief br. svcs., 1979-88; cons. Carol Brown Assocs., Houston, 1988—; freelance cons., Houston, 1976-88. Author: Selecting Library Furniture, A Guide for Librarians, Designers and Architects, 1989, Planning Library Interiors, The Selection of Furnishings for the 21st Century, 1995; contbr. articles to profl. jours. Mem. AAUW, Library Adminstrn. and Mgmt. Assn., Pub. Library Assn., ALA, Tex. Library Assn., Phi Beta Kappa, Beta Phi Mu. Home and Office: Carol Brown Assocs 11706 S Kirkwood Stafford TX 77477

BROWN, CAROL WILLIAMS, computer consultant; b. Cleve., Apr. 8, 1941; d. Harter Whiting and Virginia Lambert (Templeman) Williams; m. Cyrus Winthrop Brown V, Sept. 26, 1964; 1 child, Laura Lambert Darby Brown. AB, Wellesley (Mass.) Coll., 1962; Cert. in Systems/Programming, NYU, 1970. Systems mgr. McKinsey & Co., Inc., N.Y.C., 1966-72; v.p. Winthrop, Brown & Co., Inc., N.Y.C., 1972-93; pres. Williams, Brown & Co., Inc., N.Y.C., 1993—. Author: The Minicomputer Simplified, 1980; co-author: Computer Security Handbook #2, 1983, #3, 1988. Vice pres. N.Y. Jr. League, N.Y.C., 1978-80; bd. dirs. Parents in Action, 1992—. Mem. ACM (Spl. Interest Group of Bus. Data Processors v.p.-treas. 1970-74). Republican. Presbyterian. Home: 315 W 86th St New York NY 10024-3180 Office: Williams Brown & Co Inc 19 W 44th St # 1108 New York NY 10036-5903

BROWN, CAROLYN THOMPSON, librarian; b. Bklyn., May 18, 1943; d. Frank L. and Martha Louise Thompson; children: Christopher Leslie, Michael Arthur. BA, Cornell U., 1965, MA, 1968; PhD, Am. U., 1978. Asst. prof. dept. English Howard U., Washington, 1978-84, assoc. prof., 1984-91, assoc. dean Humanities Coll. of Liberal Arts, 1988-90; dir. ednl. svcs. Libr. of Congress, Washington, 1990-92, assoc. libr. cultural affairs, 1992—. Writer: Goin' Home, 1981. Bd. dirs. Funds for the Communities Future, Washington, 1990—. Nat. Def. Fgn. Lang. Grad. Honor fellow Am. U., 1975-78, Postdoctoral fellow for minorities Ford Found., 1980-81, Woodrow Wilson Internat. Ctr. for Scholars fellow Smithsonian Instn., 1985-86; grantee Howard U., 1980, NEH, 1985. Mem. ALA (rep. 1990—), Assn. Asian Studies. Home: 1225 Edgevale Rd Silver Spring MD 20910

BROWN, CHERRY PAULETTE, architectural designer, design stylist; b. London, Eng., July 27, 1936; d. Herman and Sophie (Paul) Finer; m. Jerome Brown, 1965 (dec. June 1987). BA, MA in History of Art, U. Chgo., 1957; grad., Art Inst. of Chgo., 1957. Rsch. asst. U. Chgo., 1955-57, spl. asst. print collection, 1957; photography stylist Jim Brady Photography, Chgo., 1957-59; internat. housewares stylist Sears Roebuck & Co., Chgo., 1961-69; pres. Jerome Brown & Assocs., Ltd., Architects & Designers, Chgo., 1969—. Mem. Mus. of Contemporary Art. Recipient numerous product design awards, Indsl. Design mag., 1966-67, Architecture Soc. of Art Inst. of Chgo., 1992; sustaining fellow Art Inst. Chgo., 1987—. Mem. Arts Club of Chgo., Contemporary Arts Ctr. Democrat. Jewish. Office: Jerome Brown & Assocs Ltd 844 W Altgeld St Chicago IL 60614-2411

BROWN, CORRINE, congresswoman; b. Jacksonville, Fla., Nov. 11, 1946; married; 1 child, Shantrel. BS, Fla. A & M U., 1969; EdS, U. Fla., 1974. Former mem. Fla. Ho. of Reps; del. Nat. Dem. Conv., 1988; mem. 103rd-104th Congress from 3rd Fla. dist., 1993—. Mem. Sigma Gamma Rho. Baptist. Home: 815 S Main St Ste 275 Jacksonville FL 32207-8157 Office: US Ho of Reps 1037 Longworth House Office Bldg Washington DC 20515-0903

BROWN, D. ROBIN, elementary educator; b. Cleve., Oct. 31, 1949; d. William Michael and Darla G. (Carlson) Linsenmann; m. Ross H. Brown, Aug. 21, 1971. BA cum laude, W.Va. Wesleyan U., 1971; MA, Ashland U., 1988, postgrad., 1988-90; postgrad., Ohio State U., 1989-90. Cert. elem. tchr., Ohio, W.Va. Tchr. Lost Creek Elem. Sch., Clarksburg, W.Va., 1971-72, Leesburg (Va.) Middle Sch., 1972-75, Northmoor Elem. Sch., Dayton, Ohio, 1975-79, Jonathan Alder Lucas Local Schs., Plain City, Ohio, 1979—. Active TWIG # 158, Columbus, Ohio, 1990—, Salvation Army, Columbus, 1990—, Worthington Hills Women's Club, Columbus, 1985—. Recipient Sci. award Exxon, 1974. Mem. Internat. Reading Assn., Reading Recovery, Kappa Delta Pi, Sigma Eta Sigma, Pi Gamma Mu, Tri Beta. Home: 825 Highview Dr West Worthington OH 43235-1232 Office: Jonathan Alder Local Schs 4331 Kilbury Huber Rd Plain City OH 43064-9064

BROWN, DALE SUSAN, government administrator, writer; b. N.Y.C., May 27, 1954; d. Bertram S. and Beatrice Joy (Gilman) B. B.A., Antioch Coll., 1976. Research asst. Am. Occupational Therapy Assn., Rockville, Md., 1976-79; writer Pres.' Com. on Employment of People with Disabilities, Washington, 1979-82, program mgr., 1982—, program mgr. labor com., 1995; program mgr. work environment and tech. com. Ams. with Disabilities Act, 1986-94, new products devel. team, 1987-90, dir. 1991-93, with interagy. tech. assistance coordinating team, 1992-94, program mgr. Ams. with Disabilities Act, 1995—; cons. in field; gen. assembly speaker nat. conv. Gen. Fedn. Women's Clubs, 1981; mem. Rehab. Svcs. Adminstrn. Task Force on Learning Disabilities, 1981-83. Author: Steps to Independence for People with Learning Disabilities, 1980, Working Effectively with People Who Have Learning Disabilities and Attention Deficit Hyperactivity Disorder; writer film: They Could Have Saved Their Homes, 1982; dir. videotape Part of the Team People with Disabilities in the Workforce, 1990; editorial bd. Perceptions, 1981-83. Pres. Assn. Learning Disabled Adults, Washington, 1979-80; bd. dirs. Closer Look Nat. Info. Ctr., Washington, 1980-83, Am. Coalition of Citizens with Disabilities, 1985-86; chair 5th ann. conf. on Info. Tech. for User With Disabilities, 1989; spl. asst. for people with disabilites Federally Employed Women, 1991—; mem. congrl. task force Rights and Empowerment of Ams. with Disabilities, 1988-90; mem. editorial bd. Learning Disabilites Focus, 1988-90; cons. editor Learning Disabilites Rsch. and Practice, 1990—; co-editor Learning Disabilities and Employment; author: Pathways to Employment for People with Learning Disabilities, 1991.blue ribbon panel on Nat. Telecommunications Access for People with Disabilities, 1989—. Found. for Children with Learning Disabilities grantee, 1982; recipient Margaret Byrd Rawson award, 1989, Personal Achievement award, 1989, Individual Achievement award Nat. Coun. on Communication Disorders, 1991, Spl. Achievement award Pres.'s Com. on Employment of People with Disabilities, 1991, Gold Screen award Nat. Assn. Govt. Communicators, 1991, Arthur S. Fleming award, 1992, 94; named one of Ten Outstanding Young Ams., U.S. Jr. C. of C., 1994, Jaycees, 1994. Mem. Nat. Network of Learning Disabled Adults (founder, pres. 1980-81, rep. Interagy. com. on computer support handicapped employess 1988—), Nat. Assn. Govt. Communicators (Blue Pencil award 1986, rep. inter-agy. com. on handicapped employees 1989—, Learning Disabilities Assn. (bd. dirs. 1986-91), ALA. Democrat. Jewish. Office: Pres' Com Employment of People with Disabilities 1331 F St NW Washington DC 20004

BROWN, DARMAE JUDD, librarian; b. Jefferson City, Mo., Sept. 14, 1952; d. William Robert and Dorothy Judd (Curtis) B. BA, W.Va. Wesleyan Coll., 1974; MA, U. Denver, 1975; M of Computer Info. Systems, U. Denver, 1992. Searching assoc. Bibliog. Ctr. for Rsch., Denver, 1975-76; libr. N.E. Colo. Regional Libr., Wray, 1976-81; head tech. svcs. Ector County Libr., Odessa, Tex., 1981-84, Waterloo (Iowa) Pub. Libr., 1984-89; systems coord. Aurora (Colo.) Pub. Libr., 1989—. Mem. ALA, Iowa OCLC Users Group (pres. 1986-87), Colo. Libr. Assn., Libr. & Info. Tech. Assn., Beta Phi Mu, Sigma Alpha Iota. Home: 12010 E Harvard Ave Aurora CO 80014

BROWN, DEANNA DOLORES, state agency administrator; b. Sacramento, Dec. 31, 1964; d. George Clifton and Dolores Jean (Allen) B. BA in Communications, Calif. State U., Sacramento, 1988; postgrad., Golden Gate U., 1991-92. Intern March of Dimes Birth Defects Found., Sacramento, 1988; grad. student asst. Calif. State Lottery, Sacramento, 1988-89; asst. state safety coord. Calif. Dept. Personnel Adminstrn., Sacramento, 1989-90; assoc. govtl. program analyst Calif. Dept. Motor Vehicles, Sacramento, 1990—. Sec. adult Sunday sch. Ch. of God Pentecostal, Sacramento, soprano choir. Mem. Black Advocates in State Svc. Office: Calif Dept Motor Vehicles 2415 1st Ave Po Box 932345 Sacramento CA 94232-3820

BROWN, DEBORAH ELIZABETH, television producer; b. Aledo, Ill., Nov. 29, 1952; d. Kenneth M. and Mary Esther (Gilmore) B.; m. K. J. Lester, Nov. 28, 1975 (dec. Mar. 1982); children: Rebekah Jean, Aaron Mark, Jonathan Caleb. Student, Letourneau Coll., 1970; BA in Theater Arts, Sterling Coll., 1974; MA in Comm., Wheaton Coll., 1977. Producer, dir. Sta. WCFC-TV, Chgo., 1978-80; sales mgr. SNG Enterprises, St. Charles, Ill., 1980-82; pres., CEO Circle Family Video Stores, Niles, Mich., 1982-87; exec. producer Picture Radio Pictures, Lakeland, Fla., 1987-93; dir. prodn. and mgkt. Computer Keyboard, Portland, Oreg., 1993—; vis. prof. comm. Wheaton (Ill.) Coll., 1980; video cons. Spring Arbor Distbrs., Belleville, Mich., 1985, Gospel Films, Muskegan, Mich., 1985. Producer, dir., writer (TV program and book) Crafts With Emilie, 1979 (Spl. Emmy nomination); video contbg. editor Christian Booksellers Assn. jour., 1984-85; set decorator Cindy Williams Comedy Spl., 1993. Corp. sponsor Pregnancy Care Ctr., Niles, 1985-87; producer Four Flags Area Apple Festival, Niles, 1987. Mem. Fellowship of Christians in Arts, Media and Entertainment, Christian Video Retailers Assn. (exec. dir. 1985-87), Fla. Motion Picture and TV Assn. Baptist. Office: Computer Keyboard 12000 SE 82d Ste 1121 Portland OR 97266

BROWN, DELORES RUSSELL, health management company official; b. Phila., Sept. 20, 1947; d. William and Jean (Nichols) Russell; children: Brendell F., William A. Jr. Student, Temple U., 1969-71; BA, Antioch U., Phila., 1988; MSW, U. Pa., 1991. Lic. real estate salesperson, Pa.; cert. residential appraiser, Pa. Real estate cons. Ball Real Estate, Inc., Phila., 1976-86; publ. word processor Magnavox (GAC), Wymoor, Pa., 1982-83; real estate closing clk. Merrill Lynch Relocation, Bala Cynwyd, Pa., 1983-84; med. and tech. sec. U. Pa., Phila., 1984-86, adminstrv. asst., 1986-89; social worker for aged Episcopal Community Svcs., Phila., 1989-90, dir. social svc., 1991-92; sr. svc. coord., rsch. interviewer Phila. Health Mgmt. Corp., 1992—, facilitator, 1992. Mem. Phila. Mayor's Adv. Bd. on Aging, 1987; tutor Phila. Mayor's Literacy Program, 1988; asst. dir. social svcs. Zion Cares Ministry, Phila., 1991—; mem. Zion Bapt. Outreach Ministry, 1985—; mem. family planning bd. Temple U., 1970-76. Recipient svc. award Temple U., 1988, Rosa Wessell Outstanding MSW award, U. Pa., 1991. Mem. Nat. Assn. Real Estate Brokers (2d v.p. women's coun. Washington 1991-92, Disting. Local Chpt. Presdl. award 1993), Phila. Women's Coun. of Assn. Real Estate Brokers (pres. 1991-93, Outstanding Presdl. award 1993), Alliance of Black Social Workers, Women of Color Coalition. Home: 8101 Fayette St Philadelphia PA 19150-1214

BROWN, DENISE SCOTT, architect, urban planner; b. Nkana, Zambia, Oct. 3, 1931; came to U.S., 1958; d. Simon and Phyllis (Hepker) Lakofski; m. Robert Scott Brown, July 21, 1955 (dec. 1959); m. Robert Charles Venturi, July 23, 1967; 1 child, James C. Student, U. Witwatersrand, South Africa, 1948-51; diploma, Archtl. Assn., London, 1955; M of City Planning, U. Pa., 1960, MArch, 1965, DFA (hon.), 1994; DFA (hon.), Oberlin Coll., 1977, Phila. Coll. Art, 1985, Parsons Sch. Design, 1985; LHD (hon.), N.J. Inst. Tech., 1984, Phila. Coll. Textiles and Sci., 1992; DEng (hon.), Tech. U. N.S., 1991; HHD (hon.), Pratt Inst., 1992; DFA (hon.), U. Pa., 1994. Registered architect, U.K. Asst. prof. U. Pa., Phila., 1960-65; assoc. prof., head urban design program UCLA, 1965-68; with Venturi, Rauch and Scott Brown, Phila., 1967—, ptnr., 1969-89; prin. Venturi, Scott Brown and Assocs. Inc., Phila., 1989—; vis. prof. architecture U. Calif., Berkeley, 1965, Yale U., 1967-70; asst. prof. U. Pa., 1960-65, vis. prof. Sch. Fine Arts, 1982, 83; Eliot Noyes design critic in architecture Harvard U., Cambridge, Mass., 1989-90; mem. visitors com. MIT, 1973-83; mem. adv. com. dept. architecture Temple U., 1980—; cons. to dean search com. Sch. Architecture, Washington U., St. Louis, 1992; mem. adv. bd. dept. architecture Carnegie Mellon U., 1992—; mem. jury Prince of Wales Prize in Urban Design, Sch. Design Harvard U., Cambridge, Mass., 1993. Author: Urban Concepts, 1990; co-author: Learning from Las Vegas, 1972, rev. edit., 1977, A View from the Campidoglio: Selected Essays, 1953-84, 85, On Houses and Housing, 1992; contbr. numerous articles to profl. jours. Mem. curriculum com. Phila. Jewish Children's Folkshul, 1980-86; policy panelist design arts program NEA, 1981-83; mem. bd. advisors Architects, Designers and Planners for Social Responsibility, 1982—; mem. capitol preservation com. Commonwealth of Pa., Harrisburg, 1983-87; bd. dirs. Ctrl. Phila. Devel. Corp., 1985—, Urban Affairs Partnership, Phila., 1987-91; trustee Chestnut Hill Acad., Phila., 1985-89. Recipient numerous awards, citations, commendations for design and urban planning, including Commendatore Order of Merit (Italy), 1987, Chgo. Architecture award, 1987, U.S. Presdl. award Nat. Medal of Arts, 1992, Hall of Fame award Interior Design mag., 1992, (with Robert Venturi) The Phila. award, 1993, The Benjamin Franklin medal Royal Soc. for Encouragement of Arts, Mfr., and Commerce, 1993. Mem. Royal Inst. Brit. Archs., Am. Acad. Arts and Scis., Archs. Designers and Planners for Social Responsibility, Am. Planning Assn, Archtl. Assn. London, Internat. Women's Forum, Soc. Coll. and U. Planning, Soc. Archtl. Historians (bd. dirs. 1981-84), Carpenters Co. of City and County of Phila., Athenaeum of Phila., Royal Soc. Encouragement of Arts, Mfr. and Commerce. Democrat. Jewish. Office: Venturi Scott Brown & Assocs Inc 4236 Main St Philadelphia PA 19127-1696

BROWN, DIANA MARY, office manager, corporate officer; b. Waukegan, Ill., Jan. 10, 1940; d. George and Mary (Lamberti) Stefani; m. Gerald A. Brown, Sept. 26, 1959; 1 child, Kathleen Brown Speer. BA in Econs. and Sociology, Lake Forest Coll., 1980; MA in Social Svc. Adminstrn., U. Chgo., 1980. Ptnr. Musicland, Inc., Waukegan, 1967-79; planner Cook County Dept. Planning, Chgo., 1980-82; asst. to CEO Leaf, Inc., Bannockburn, Ill., 1984-86; office mgr., corp. officer, treas. Metzler & Assocs., Deerfield, Ill., 1986—. Mem. Phi Beta Kappa. Democrat. Roman Catholic. Office: Metzler & Assocs 520 Lake Cook Rd Deerfield IL 60015-5611

BROWN, DONNA MARIE, city official; b. Hopkinsville, Ky., Jan. 5, 1943; d. John William and Cola Marie (Hocker) B. BA, Western Ky. State Coll., 1965; MLS, U. Ky., 1970. Tchr. Logan County Pub. Schs., Russellville, Ky., 1965-66; libr. Albuquerque Pub. Schs., 1966-69; county libr. Amherst County Pub. Libr., Amherst, Va., 1970-73; pub. libr. cons. State of Va., Richmond, 1973-78; libr. III, Stockton (Calif.)-San Joaquin County Pub. Libr., 1978-79, coord. br. libr., 1979-81, dep. dir. libr. svc., 1981-92; dep. city mgr. City of Stockton, 1992—. Mem. ALA, LWV (pres. Stockton 1987-88), Calif. Inst. Librs. (pres. 1987-88), Calif. Libr. Assn. (councilor 1983-88, Rotary (pres. Stockton 1994-95). Democrat. Methodist. Home: 737 N Central Ave Stockton CA 95204 Office: City of Stockton 425 N El Dorado St Stockton CA 95202

BROWN, ELIZABETH ANN, foreign service officer; b. Portland, Oreg., Aug. 15, 1918; d. Edwin Keith and Grace Viola (Foss) B. A.B., Reed Coll., 1940; postgrad. (teaching fellow), Wash. State Coll., 1940-41; A.M., Columbia, 1943. Exec. asst. to chmn. 12th region WLB, Seattle, 1943-45; internat. affairs officer Dept. State, 1946-56; joined U.S. Fgn. Service, 1956; assigned Office UN Polit. Affairs, Dept. State, 1956-60; 1st sec. Am. embassy, Bonn, Germany, 1960-63; dep. dir. Office UN Polit. Affairs, 1963-65, dir., 1965-69; mem. State Dept. Sr. Seminar in Fgn. Policy, 1969-70; counselor for polit. affairs Am. embassy, Athens, Greece, 1970-75; dep. chief mission Am. embassy, The Hague, Netherlands, 1975-78; sr. insp. Dept. State, 1978-79, cons., 1980—; ret., 1979; adviser U.S. del. UN Gen. Assembly, 1946-50, 53, 55, 57-59, 64-65. Recipient 7th ann. Fed. Woman's award, 1967. Mem. Am. Fgn. Service Assn., Phi Beta Kappa. Home: 4848 Reservoir Rd NW Washington DC 20007-1561 Office: Dept State Washington DC 20007

BROWN, GERALDINE, nurse, freelance writer; b. Clemson, S.C.; d. Isaac and Gladys (Patterson) B. AS in Nursing, U. D.C., Washington, 1973; real estate cert., Long and Foster Inst., College Park, Md., 1984; cert. in TV broadcasting, Columbia Sch., Bailey's Crossroads, Va., 1987; BS in Nursing, Bowie State U., 1989, MA in Communications, 1991; PhD, Howard U., 1994. RN, D.C., FCC Third Class License. Supr. staff nurse Walter Reed Hosp., Washington, 1970-76; supr. clin. nurse Dept. Human Svcs., Washington, 1976-78, community health nurse, 1978-84; nursing instr. Phillips Bus. Sch., Alexandria, Va., 1984-85; pvt. nurse Washington, 1973—; dir. pub. affairs Bible Way Chs. Worldwide, Inc., Washington, 1978-91; society columnist As It Happens, Charlotte (N.C.) Post, 1964-66; society editor Washington Cafe. Soc. mag., 1971; contbr. feature stories Capital Spotlight newspaper, 1978—. Asst. organizer DC Mayor's United Nations Day, 1980; vol. Met. Boys and Girls Clubs, Washington, 1980—; vol. Nursing Instr., The Washington Saturday Coll., 1982-84; Co. ARC, 1973—, Big Sisters of the Washington Met. Area, 1988—. Recipient certs. of excellence Govt. of D.C., 1978-84; cert. of appreciation Mayor of D.C., 1980, meritorious pub. svc. award, 1980; svc. trophy Washington Saturday Coll., 1984. Mem. Am. Nurses Assn., Nat. Coun. Negro Women, Smithsonian Inst. (assoc.), NAACP, Nat. Black Nurses Assn., Washington Urban League, Chi Eta Phi. Democrat.

BROWN, GLENDA ANN WALTERS, ballet director; b. Buna, Tex., July 22, 1937; d. Jesse Olaf and Kathryn Jeanette (Rogers) Walters; m. David Dann Brown, Dec. 13, 1958 (div. Feb. 1994); children: Kathryn Jean, Vanessa Lea. Grad. high sch., Beaumont, Tex. Asst. tchr. Widman Sch., Beaumont, 1952-55; owner, tchr. Walters Sch. of Dance, Jasper, Tex., 1955-59; assoc. tchr. Emmamae Horn Sch., Houston, 1964-81; owner, tchr. Allegro Acad., Houston, 1981—; owner, dir. Allegro Ballet, Houston, 1974-81, artistic dir., 1981—; dir. Nat. Choreography Conf., 1987—. Mem. dance panel Cultural Arts Council, Houston, 1979, dance panel Tex. Commn. on the Arts, 1988-90; sec. Riedel Estates Civic Club, Houston, 1975-78; Rep. poll worker, Houston, 1970-81. Mem. Dance Masters Am. (exam. chmn. chpt. 3 1980-86), Southwestern Regional Ballet Assn. (exec. v.p. 1981—), Dance Am., Nat. Assn. Regional Ballet (bd. dirs. 1985-88), Regional Dance Am. (nat. bd. dirs., v.p. 1988-95, pres. 1995—). Methodist. Avocations: camping, singing, golf, travel. Office: Allegro Ballet and Allegro Acad Dance 1570 S Dairy Ashford St Ste 200 Houston TX 77077-3820

BROWN, HELEN GURLEY, writer, editor; b. Green Forest, Ark., Feb. 18, 1922; d. Ira M. and Cleo (Sisco) Gurley; m. David Brown, Sept. 25, 1959. Student, Tex. State Coll. for Women, 1939-41, Woodbury Coll., 1942; LLD, Woodbury U., 1987; DLitt, L.I. U., 1993. Exec. sec. Music Corp. Am., 1942-45, William Morris Agy., 1945-47; copywriter Foote, Cone & Belding (advt. agy.), Los Angeles, 1948-58; advt. writer, account exec. Kenyon & Eckhardt (advt. agy.), Hollywood, Calif., 1958-62; editor-in-chief Cosmopolitan mag., 1965—; editorial dir. Cosmopolitan internat. edits., 1972—. Author: Sex and the Single Girl, 1962, Sex and the Office, 1965, Outrageous Opinions, 1967, Helen Gurley Brown's Single Girl's Cook Book, 1969, Sex and the New Single Girl, 1970, Having It All, 1982, The Late Show, 1993. Named 1 of 25 most influential women in U.S., World Almanac, 1976-81; recipient Francis Holmes Achievement award for outstanding work in advt., 1956-59, Disting. Achievement award U. So. Calif. Sch. Journalism, 1971, Spl. award for editorial leadership Am. Newspaper Woman's Club, Washington, 1972, Disting. Achievement award in Journalism Stanford U., 1977, Matrix award in mag. category, N.Y. Women in Communications, 1985; Helen Gurley Brown Rsch. Professorship established in her name Northwestern U. Medill Sch. Journalism, 1986; inducted into Pubs.' Hall of Fame, 1988. Mem. Authors League Am., Am. Soc. Mag. Editors, AFTRA, Eta Upsilon Gamma. Office: Cosmopolitan The Hearst Corp 224 W 57th St New York NY 10019-3203

BROWN, HERMIONE KOPP, lawyer; b. Syracuse, N.Y., Sept. 29, 1915; d. Harold H. and Frances (Burger) Kopp; m. Louis M. Brown, May 30, 1937; children—Lawrence D., Marshall J., Harold A. BA, Wellesley Coll., 1934; LLB, U. So. Calif., 1947. Bar: Calif. 1947. Story analyst 20th Century-Fox Film Corp., 1935-42; assoc. Gang, Kopp & Tyre, Los Angeles, 1947-52; ptnr. to sr. ptnr. Gang, Tyre, Ramer & Brown, Inc., Los Angeles, 1952—; lectr. copyright and entertainment law U. So. Calif. Law Sch., 1974-77. Contbr. to profl. publs. Fellow Am. Coll. Trust and Estate Coun.; mem. Calif. Bar Assn. (chair probate law cons. group nd. legal specialization 1977-82, trust and probate law sect., exec. com. 1983-86, advisor 1986-89), L.A. Copyright Soc. (pres. 1979-80), Order of Coif, Phi Beta Kappa. Office: Gang Tyre Ramer & Brown Inc 132 S Rodeo Dr Beverly Hills CA 90212

BROWN, ILENE DE LOIS, special education educator; b. Wichita, Kans., Aug. 17, 1947; d. Homer DeWitt and Estella Lenora (Cleland) Rusco; m. Gale Robert Aaroe, Nov. 23, 1967 (div. July 1983); 1 child, Candice Yvonne. BEd in Elem. Edn., Washburn U., Topeka, 1969; MS, Nazareth Coll. Rochester, 1979. Cert. tchr. Idaho. Emotionally disturbed trainer Rochester Mental Health Ctr., Greece, N.Y., 1970-71, West Ridge, Greece, 1971-72; tutor kindergarten through grades 6 Craig Hill, Greece, 1978-79; resource rm. tchr. math. English Village, Greece, 1979-80; resource rm. tchr. grades 4-6 Lakeshore, Greece, 1980; tutor, translator Guadalajara, Mex., 1980-82; tchr. grade 1 English John F. Kennedy Sch., Guadalajara, 1982-83; tchr. various grades Greenleaf (Idaho) Friends Acad., 1983-89; resource tchr., high sch. spl. edn. community work coord. Middleton (Idaho) Primary Sch., 1989-91, tchr., 1991—, tchr. 2d grade, 1990—. Sunday sch. tchr. Mem. Coun. for Exceptional Children, Coun. for Children with Behavior Disorders and Learning Disabilities (officer, sec. state chpt. 1991-92), Middleton Profl. Devel. Com. (chairperson PDC 1992—), Idaho Edn. Assn., Middleton Edn. Assn. Office: Middleton Primary Sch 115 W Main St Middleton ID 83644-5565

BROWN, IRMA HUNTER, state legislator; b. Tampa, Fla., Jan. 5, 1939; d. Joseph Hartwell and Dovie Estoria (White) Hunter; m. Roosevelt Brown, 1962; chidren: Ramon Luture, Rosetta Carnita. BS magna cum laude, U. Ark., Pine Bluff, 1960; attended, Memphis State U., 1962, D.C. Tchrs. Coll., 1965-67. Tchr. Memphis Sch. Dist., 1961-64, Washington Sch. Dist., 1965-69; dir. nutrition edn. Model Cities Project, Little Rock, 1972-73; dir. differential day care placement Dept. Edn., Little Rock, 1974-75; chmn. Human Resource Com., Ark., 1978-80; mem. Ark. Ho. of Reps., 1981—; vice chmn. house affairs com., mem. joint com. pub. retirement & social security program, revenue & taxation com., state agys. and govt. affairs com. Pres. Little Rock PTA Coun., 1981—; mem. Little Rock Links Inc., Pulaski County Coun. on Aged, Union African Meth. Episcopal Ch. Recipient Disting. Citizen award Philander Smith Coll., 1981; fellow Inst. Polit., 1975. Mem. Alpha Kappa Alpha. Democrat. Home: 1920 S Summit St Little Rock AR 72202-6250*

BROWN, JAN WHITNEY, small business owner; b. Roundup, Mont., Mar. 16, 1942; d. John Estes and Janet Lillian (Snyder) Dahl; m. William A. Brown III; children: Erik Lane, Kimberly Elise. BA in Sociology, Social Work, Carroll Coll., 1976. Sec. 1st Nat. Bank, Bozeman, Mont., 1962, Office of Gov., Helena, Mont., 1963-69; pub. info. coord. Helena Model City Program, 1969-73; pub. relations and assn. mgmt. Mont. Bar Assn., Helena, 1973-76, Mont. Assn. Life Underwriters, Helena, 1973-76; legis. liaison Mont. Religious Legis. Coalition, Helena, 1975-81; exec. dir. Helena Food Share Inc., 1987; co-owner Jorud Photo and Gifts, Helena, 1971—; legislator Mont. St. Legislature, Helena, 1983-92; mem. legis. coun. Helena, 1989-92; bd. dirs. Helena Food Share, Inc., Bus. Improvement Dist.; chmn. state adminstrn. com. Mont. Ho. of Reps., 1989-92. Chmn. Mont. Medal of Valor Com., Helena, 1986-93; pres. United Way, Helena, 1982; bd. dirs. Mont. Area Health Edn. Ctr., Bozeman, 1988-93, Mont. Hunger Coalition, Helena, 1988-89, St. Peter's Cmty. Hosp., 1994—; Helena City Commr., 1993; vice chair Helena Citizens Coun., 1994. Recipient Disting. Svc. award Mental Health Assn., 1976, Disting. Community Svc. award Jaycees, 1982, Ann. Appreciation award Child Support Enforcement, 1985, United Way award, 1988, Community Svc. award VFW, 1988. Mem. Helena Unlimited. Democrat. Episcopalian. Office: Jorud Photo and Gifts 327 N Last Chance Gulch St Helena MT 59601-5013

BROWN, JANE ELIZABETH, dance/arts administrator; b. Spokane, Wash., Mar. 1, 1941; d. Paul Sterling Hoag and Betty Jane (Lochrie) McGlynn; m. Richard Fargo Brown, Feb. 18, 1968 (dec. Nov. 1979); children: Richard Setauket, Tracy Elizabeth, Lwyatt Keveney, Michael Fargo. Student, Oberlin Coll., 1958-59. Asst. pub. rels. dir. L.A. (Calif.) County Mus. Art, 1961-65; reporter Time/Life Bur., L.A., 1965-67, Newsweek, L.A., 1967-68; owner Amenities Unlimited, Ft. Worth, 1985-87; exec. dir., founder Ft. Worth (Tex.) Ballet, 1987-89; exec. dir. Karen Bamonte Dance Works, Phila., 1991—; dance panelist Tex. Commn. on the Arts, Austin, 1988-89; vol. cons. Bd. mem. Ft. Worth (Tex.) Symphony, Opera, Mus. of Modern Art, Ft. Worth, 1969-89; various coms. Jr. League, Ft. Worth, 1969-81; steering com. Stream Valleys Commn., Ft. Worth, 1976-82, Ft. Worth (Tex.) Bicentennial Com., 1978; bd. dir., mem. Soc. Hill Civic Assn., Phila., 1990-93. Mem. Phila. Dance Alliance (cons. 1993—, various coms.), Greater Phila. Cultural Alliance, Dance Theatre Workshop, Dance/USA, Phila. Chamber Music Soc. (bd. dirs.). Home: 261 S 3rd St Philadelphia PA 19106-3912 Office: Karen Bamonte Dance Works 3500 Lancaster Ave Philadelphia PA 19104-2434

BROWN, JANET MCNALLEY, retirement plan consultant; b. Denver, May 16, 1960; d. Michael Collins and Sharon Bess (Cook) McNalley. Student, Mt. Holyoke Coll., 1978-79; BA in Econs. with honors, Mills Coll., Oakland, Calif., 1982; MA in Social Scis., U. Calif., Irvine, 1987, elem. teaching credential, 1988. Teaching asst. U. Calif., Irvine, 1986-88; employee benefits adminstr. Western Co. N.Am., Ft. Worth, 1988-89; trust officer Ameritrust Tex. N.A., Ft. Worth, 1989-90; thrift and profit sharing analyst Burlington No. R.R., Ft. Worth, 1990-93; assoc. human resources group Coopers & Lybrand, Dallas, 1993-94; pension coord. Bell Helicopter Textron, Inc., Ft. Worth, 1994—. Dem. del., Ft. Worth, 1990; mem. Liberty Coalition, Bluebonnet Pl. Neighborhood Assn. (newsletter editor). Mem. AAUW (membership v.p. 1990-92, charter Eleanor Roosevelt Found. 1990—), Am. Soc. Pension Actuaries (qualified pension administr., cert. pension cons.). Home: 3408 Cockrell Ave Fort Worth TX 76109-3003 Office: Bell Helicopter Textron Inc PO Box 482 Fort Worth TX 76101

BROWN, JANIECE ALFREIDA, pilot; b. Ellensburg, Wash., May 23, 1956; d. Don Elmer and LaRhee Deloris (Montgomery) Lewis; m. David E. Brown, Oct. 10, 1993. AA, Big Bend Community Coll., Moses Lake, Wash., 1980-82; BS, Cen. Wash. U., 1982-84. Pilot AAR Western Skyways, Troutdale, Oreg., 1984-87; airline capt. N.P.A., Inc., Pasco, Wash., 1987-89; flight engr. airline pilot Alaska Airlines, Seattle, 1989-94, 1st officer Boeing 727 and MD-80; bus. mgr. David Brown & Assocs., 1994—. Lobbyist Save Our Watershed, Roslyn, Wash., 1978-80. Recipient Scholastic award CleElum (Wash.) High Sch., 1974. Mem. Airline Pilot Assn. (mem. dangerous goods com.), Alpha Eta Rho (pres. Ctrl. Wash. U. chpt. 1983-84). Home: 20912 NE Interlachen Ln Troutdale OR 97060-8731 Office: Alaska Airlines PO Box 61900 Seattle WA 98178

BROWN, JENNIFER MARIE, surgical assistant; b. Attleboro, Mass., Mar. 6, 1961; d. Philip Gaylord and Robert Nella (Croughwell) B. Automotive merchandiser K-Mart, Pittsfield, Mass., 1981-82; automotive mechanic Sears, Pittsfield, Mass., 1981-83; automotive transmission technician Discount Transmission, Pittsfield, Mass., 1984-86; auto parts store mgr. Reddington Auto Parts, Pittsfield, Mass., 1986-87; surg. technician Cooley Dickinson Hosp., Northampton, Mass., 1987-90, cert. surg. technologist, 1990-92, cert. surg. 1st asst., 1992—; materials mgr. Cooley Dickinson Hosp., Northampton, 1990-91. With U.S. Army, 1983-84, USAR, 1983-89. Mem. Assn. Surg. Technologists. Democrat. Roman Catholic. Home: 9 Mieczkowski Cir RR 1 Whatley MA 01373 Office: Cooley Dickinson Hosp Locust St Northampton MA 01060

BROWN, JOAN HALL, elementary school educator; b. Montgomery, Ala., Sept. 12; d. Leo Nathaniel and Bertha (Glaze) Hall; m. Tyrone Brown, Aug. 25, 1984. BS in Elem. Edn. cum laude, Ala. State U.; MEd cum laude, Auburn U., Montgomery, 1989. Cert. tchr., Ala. Tchr. Resurrection Sch., Montgomery, 1985-89, St. John the Bapt. Cath. Sch., Montgomery, 1989-91; tchr., former asst. prin. St. John Resurrection Cath. Sch., Montgomery, 1991-94; tchr. Highland Gardens Elem. Sch., Montgomery, 1994—; mem. sch. bd. Resurrection Sch., 1987-88, advisor, editor sch. newspaper; textbook com. Mobile Diocese, Montgomery, 1985-87, mem. English proficiency com., 1991-92; coord. State Spelling Bees, 1989, St. John the Bapt. Cath. Sch., 1990-91, St. John Resurrection Cath. Sch., 1991-94, textbook com. 1993-94. Mem. Resurrection Cath. Ch. Grantee Arts Coun. Montgomery, 1991, 93, 94. Mem. NEA, Ala. Edn. Assn., Nat. Honor Soc., Deka Philos Svc. Orgn. (v.p. 1985—), Kappa Delta Pi (honor soc. in edn.). Democrat. Roman Catholic. Home: 705 N Pass Rd Montgomery AL 36110-2906

BROWN, JOBETH GOODE, food products executive, lawyer; b. Oakdale, La., Sept. 15, 1950; d. Samuel C. Goode and Elizabeth E. (Twiner) Baker; m. H. William Brown, Aug. 4, 1973; 1 child, Kevin William. BA, Newcomb Coll. Tulane U., 1972; JD, Wash. U., 1979. Assoc. Coburn, Croft & Putzell, St. Louis, 1979-80; staff atty. Anheuser-Busch Cos. Inc., St. Louis, 1980-81, exec. asst. to v.p. sec., 1982-83, asst. sec., 1983-89, sec., v.p., 1989—. Trustee Anheuser-Busch Found., St. Louis, 1989—, Forsyth Sch., St. Louis, 1991; mem. adv. bd. Mo. Found. Women's Resources, St. Louis, 1990—; mem. devel. bd. St. Louis Children's Hosp., 1990—; dir. Girl Scout Coun. Greater St. Louis, 1991—. Mem. ABA, Mo. Bar Assn., Bar Assn. Met. St. Louis, Am. Soc. Corp. Secs. (pres. 1992), Algonquin Golf Club, Order of Coif. Republican. Presbyterian. Office: Anheuser-Busch Cos Inc 1 Busch Pl Saint Louis MO 63118-1849

BROWN, JUANITA RENNER, counselor, educator; b. Chandler, Okla., Jan. 23, 1934; d. Earl Franklin and Cecile Ruth (Gaither) Renner; m. Donald Gene Brown, Dec. 21, 1952; children: Donita Brown Kuykendell, William Dayton. BS in Elem. Edn., U. Ctrl. Okla., 1955; MEd in Guidance and Counseling, U. Okla., 1965. Cert. Okla. sch. counselor, nat. cert. counselor, elem. edn., Okla. Tchr. jr. h.s., girls basketball coach Deer Creek Bd. Edn., Edmond, Okla., 1954-55; tchr. elem. sch. Midwest City (Okla.) Bd. Edn., 1955-65; co-adminstr., co-counselor Southeastern Okla. Neighborhood Youth Corp. Eastern Okla. State Coll., Wilburton, 1965-66, instr. psychology, sociology, 1966-75; counselor, dir. spl. svcs. Piedmont (Okla.) Bd. Edn., 1978-86; counselor Upward Bound Redland C.C., El Reno, Okla., 1986-94; student tchr. supr., entry yr. tchr. supr. U. Ctrl. Okla., Edmond, 1994—; del. Internat. Conf. on Children with Learning Disabilities, San Francisco, 1977-78, White House Conf. on Children and Youth, Washington, 1970. Mem. Okla. Gov.'s Com. on Children and Youth, 1968-70. Mem. AAUW (pres. Wilburton chpt. 1972), S.W. Divsn. Student Assistance, Higher Edn. Alumni Coun., Am. Assn. Counseling and Devel., Okla. Assn. Children with Learning Disabilities (pres. 1988), NEA, Okla. Edn. Assn., Nat. Ret. Tchrs. Assn., Okla. Ret. Tchrs. Assn. Mem. United Meth. Ch. Home: 4605 NW 58th St Oklahoma City OK 73122 Office: U Ctrl Okla Dept Tchr Edn Edmond OK 73034

BROWN, JULIE M., state legislator; b. Worcester, Mass., Feb. 20, 1935; divorced; 4 children. Student, Worcester State Tchrs. Coll. Mem. N.H. Ho. of Reps.; mem. children, youth and juvenile justice com. 1st woman chairperson Rochester (N.H.) Rep. City Com., 1974-76, vice chairwoman, 1976-78; ward 2 selectman Rochester, 1986-92; mem. Rochester Planning Bd., 1985-89; bd. dirs. Rochester Red Cross, 1985-90, Strafford County Cmty. Action Program, 1983-90, chmn. bd., 1991—; crusade chair Am. Cancer Soc., 1976, bus. chair, 1977, profl. chair, 1978; dir 1st Ch. Congl. Youth Group, 1971-75. Home: 414 Lilac E Rochester NH 03867 Office: 414 Lilac City E Rochester NH 03867-4552*

BROWN, JUNE, journalist; b. Detroit, July 19, 1923; d. Simpson and Vela (Wilkerson) Malone; m. Warren C. Garner, June 28, 1961; 1 dau., Sylvia G. Mustonen. Student, Wayne State U., 1941. Columnist, classified advt. mgr. Mich. Chronicle, Detroit, 1945-74; columnist Detroit News, 1974-87, Mich. Chronicle, 1990-92; CFO Warner Garner Realty, Southfield, Mich., 1992—. Author: June Brown's Guide to Let's Read, 1981. Founder The Let's Read Summer Sch., 1980—. Recipient Best Column awards Detroit Press Club, 1971, 72, Nat. Newspaper Pubs. Assn., 1968, 69, Sch. Bell award Mich. Edn., Assn., 1989. Episcopalian. Home: PO Box 120 Holly MI 48442-0120 Office: care Warren Garner Realty 15565 Northland Dr E Ste 504-e Southfield MI 48075-5363

BROWN, JUNE GIBBS, government official; b. Cleve., Oct. 5, 1933; d. Thomas D. and Lorna M. Gibbs; children: Ellen Rosenthal, Linda Gibbs, Victor Janezic, Carol Janezic. B.B.A. summa cum laude, Cleve. State U., 1971, M.B.A., 1972; postgrad., Cleve. Marshall Law Sch., 1973-74; J.D., U. Denver, 1978; postgrad. Advanced Mgmt. Program, Harvard U., 1983. Real estate broker, officer mgr. N.E. Realty, Cleve., 1963-68; staff acct. Frank T. Cicirelli, C.P.A., Cleve., 1970-71; asst. to comptroller S.M. Hexter Co., Cleve., 1971; grad. teaching fellow Cleve. State U., 1971-72; dir. internal audit Navy Fin. Ctr., Cleve., 1972-75; dir. fin. systems design Bureau of Land Mgmt., Denver, 1975-76; project mgr. Bureau of Reclamation, 1976-79; insp. gen. Dept. Interior, Washington, 1979-81, NASA, Washington, 1981-85; v.p. fin. and adminstrn. Systems Devel. Corp., a Burroughs Co., 1985-86; assoc. adminstr. for mgmt. NASA, 1986-87; insp. gen. U.S. Dept. Def., Arlington, Va., 1987-90; dep. insp. gen. USN-CINCPACFLT, 1990; insp. gen. USN Pacific Fleet, Pearl Harbor, Hawaii, 1991-93; inspector gen. HHS, Washington, 1993—; bd. dirs. Fed. Law Enforcement Tng. Ctr., 1984-85, Interagy. Auditor Tng. program Dept. Agrl. Grad. Sch., 1983-85; chmn. interagy. com. on Ifon. Resource Mgmt., 1984-85; mem. bd. advs. Nat. Contract Mgmt. Assn., 1987-89. Mem. bd. advisors Howard U. Sch. Bus., 1987-89. Recipient award Am. Soc. Women Accts., 1969, 70, 71, Raulston award Cleve. State U., 1971, Pres.'s award Cleve. State U., 1971, Outstanding Achievement award U.S. Navy, 1973, Career Svc. award Chgo. region Fed. Exec. Bd., 1974, Outstanding Contbn. to Fin. Mgmt. award Denver region Fed. Exec. Bd., 1977, Donald L. Scantlebury award Joint Fin. Mgmt. Improvement Program, 1980, Outstanding Service award Nat. Assn. Minority CPA Firms, 1980, NASA exceptional service medal, 1985, Outstanding Achievement in Aerospace award, 1987, Woman of Yr. award, YWCA 1988, Bur. Land Mgmt., Dept. Interior, 1975, Disting. Pub. Svc. award Dept. Def., 1989, Meritorious Civilian Svc. award, U.S. Navy 1993, Nat. Capital Area chpt./Govt. Exec. Mag. award for leadership, 1994; named Disting. Alumni Cleve. State U., 1990. Fellow Nat. Acad. Pub. Adminstrn. (standing panel exec. orgn. and mgmt.); mem. AICPAs, Assn. Govt. Accts. (nat. pres. 1985-86, nat. exec. com. 1977-87, vice chmn. nat. ethics com. 1978-80, 90, chmn. fin. mgmt. standards bd. 1981-82, service award 1973, 76, 93, outstanding achievement award 1979, Robert W. King Meml. award 1988, nat. ethics com. 1990, dir. Hawaii chpt. 1991-93), Hawaii Soc. CPAs (bd. dirs. 1991-93), Am. Accts. Assn., Nat. Contract Mgmt. Assn. (bd. advisors 1988-90), NASA Alumni Assn., Women in Aerospace, Am. Soc. for Pub. Adminstrn. (at-large mem. nat. coun. 1994—, Profl. Responsibility Exemplery Practice award 1990, pres.-nat. capitol area chpt. 1989), Exec. Women in Govt., Beta Alpha Psi. Office: HHS Inspector Gen 330 Independence Ave SW Washington DC 20201

BROWN, JUNE WILCOXON, writer; b. W. Lafayette, Ohio, Aug. 14, 1914; d. Ralph Foster and Pearl Almeda (Marx) Wilcoxon; B.A., U. Md., 1935; m. Albert W. Brown, Nov. 3, 1938; 1 son, Peter Wilcoxon. Freelance writer, 1945-60, 81—; editor Select mag., Madison, Wis., 1959-65; radio script writer Beverly Stark Radio Show, 1963-68, John Doremus Show, 1971-72; sit-in hostess Mary Brooks Jackson radio show, St. Thomas, V.I., 1966-75, Louise Noble Radio Show, St. Thomas, 1975-81; author monthly column Caribbean Corner, 1977-78; author: Inside American Paradise, 1991 (hon. mention Internat. Literary awards 1988); author fiction and articles in nat. magazines. Mem. Nat. League Am. Pen Women (pres. Madison 1954), St. Thomas Community Music Assn. (v.p. 1970-71), Women in Communications (Writers cup Madison 1951), Kappa Kappa Gamma. Republican. Address: 2751 Regency Oaks Blvd # S301 Clearwater FL 34619-1524

BROWN, KAREN KENNEDY, bankruptcy judge, lawyer; b. Houston, May 23, 1947; d. Edwin Bland and Muriel Elizabeth (Dupuy) Kennedy; m. David Hurst Brown, Mar. 11, 1978 . B.A., U. Pa., 1970; J.D., U. Houston, 1973. Bar: Tex. 1974, U.S. Dist. Ct. (so. and we. dists.) Tex. 1975, U.S. Ct. Appeals (5th cir.) 1974, U.S. Ct. Appeals (11th cir.) 1981. Law clk. Judge John R. Brown, Houston, 1973-75, Judge Woodrow Seals, Houston, 1975-76; asst. fed. pub. defender So. Dist. Tex., Houston, 1976-82; pvt. practice, Houston, 1982-83; U.S. magistrate U.S. Cts. So. Dist. Tex., Houston, 1984-90; U.S. Bankruptcy Judge, 1990—. Mem. LWV. Episcopalian. Office: US District Court PO Box 61252 515 Rusk Ave Houston TX 77208*

BROWN, KAREN RIMA, orchestra manager, Spanish language educator; b. N.Y.C., Apr. 26, 1943; d. Alexander and Leona (Rosenfeld) Jaffe; m. Russell Vernon Brown, Aug. 13, 1966; children: Stephanie Leona and Gregory Russell. BA, Colby Coll., 1965; MA, U. Wis., 1966. Teaching asst. U. Wis., Madison, 1965-66; instr. Spanish U. Wis., Janesville, 1966-68, Baraboo, 1968-70, Eau Claire, 1970-71; instr. Spanish Ohio U., Zanesville, 1978—; mgr. Southeastern Ohio Symphony, New Concord, 1977—; lectr. Spanish Muskingum Coll., New Concord, 1984; mem., music panelist Ohio Arts Coun., Columbus, 1979-83, 90-93; pres. S.E. Ohio Regional Arts Coun., Zanesville, 1978-80. Bd. dirs. Muskingum County Visitors and Conv. Bur., Zanesville, 1987-90, bd. sec., 1989-90; bd. dirs. Assn. of Two Toledos, 1984-87, Ohio Citizens Com. for Arts, Canton, 1979-84. Mem. Am. Assn. Tchrs. Spanish and Portuguese, Ohio Valley Fgn. Lang. Assn., Bus. and Profl. Women, Phi Beta Kappa, Phi Sigma Iota, Sigma Delta Pi (hon.). Democrat. Office: Southeastern Ohio Sym Orch PO Box 42 New Concord OH 43762

BROWN, KAREN SMITH, telecommunications company executive; b. Memphis, June 20, 1962; d. Ray Lynn and Geneva Sue (Rial) Smith; m. Paul Kenneth Brown Jr., Nov. 17, 1990. BA, Union U., 1984. Registered comm. distbn. designer. City desk asst. Ft. Worth Star Telegram, 1984-86; editor Bapt. Sunday Sch. Bd., Nashville, 1986-88; tech. instr. bus. comm. systems AT&T, Nashville, 1988-89; mgr. field svcs. AT&T, Memphis, 1989-90; sr. distbn. design specialist distbn. techs. AT&T, Atlanta and Washington, 1991-93; sr. proposal mgr. outside plant systems AT&T, Atlanta, 1993—. Children's choir assoc., pianist Peachtree Corners Bapt. Ch., Norcross, Ga., 1992-94; active Christian Coalition, 1993-94. Office: AT&T 4725 River Green Pky Duluth GA 30136

BROWN, KATE, state legislator; b. Torrejon de Ardoth, Spain, 1960. BA, U. Colo.; JD, Lewis and Clark Northwestern. Mem. Oreg. Ho. of Reps., 1991—; atty. Democrat. Address: PO Box 82699 Portland OR 97282 Office: Oreg Ho of Reps State Capitol Salem OR 97310*

BROWN, KATHLEEN, state treasurer, lawyer; d. Edmund G. and Bernice Brown; m. George Rice (div. 1979); children: Hilary, Alexandra, Zebediah; m. Van Gordon Sauter, 1980; 2 stepsons. BA in History, Stanford U., 1969; grad., Fordham U. Sch. Law. Mem. L.A. Bd. Edn., 1975-80; with O'Melveny & Myers, N.Y.C., then L.A.; commr. L.A. Bd. Pub. Works, 1987-89; elected Treas. of Calif., 1990—. Democrat. Address: Office of State Treas PO Box 942809 Sacramento CA 94209-0001*

BROWN, KAY (MARY KATHRYN BROWN), state official; b. Ft. Worth, Tex., Dec. 19, 1950; d. H.C., Jr. and Dorothy Ruth (Ware) B.; m. William P. Dougherty, Dec. 15, 1978 (div. 1984); m. Mark A. Foster, Aug. 24, 1991. B.A., Baylor U., 1973. Reporter, UPI, Atlanta, 1973-76; reporter, feature writer Anchorage Daily Times (Alaska), 1976-77; reporter, co-owner Alaska Advocate, Anchorage, 1977; aide, researcher Alaska State Legislature, Juneau, 1979-80; dep. dir. div. of oil and gas (formerly div. minerals and energy mgmt.) Alaska Dept. Natural Resources, Anchorage, 1980-82, dir., 1982-86; elected Alaska Ho. of Reps., 1986; del. White House Conf. Libr. and Info. Svcs., 1991. Co-author: Geographic Information Systems: A Guide to the Technology, 1991. Office: House of Representatives State Capitol Juneau AK 99811*

BROWN, KAY, state legislator; b. Oct. 6, 1948; 3 children. BA in Edn., Dakota Wesleyan U. Ptnr. D.H. Gustafon, Kay Brown Assocs.; developer, cons.; mem. Minn. Ho. of Reps., 1992—. Home: 10714 Timberland Dr Northfield MN 55057 Office: 551 State Office Bldg Saint Paul MN 55155*

BROWN, KRISTI, principal. Prin. Holy Rosary Sch, Seattle. Recipient Elem. Sch. Recognition award U.S. Dept. Edn., 1989-90. Office: Holy Rosary Sch 4142 42nd Ave SW Seattle WA 98116

BROWN, LESLIE JEANNE, psychotherapist; b. Ada, Okla., Feb. 4, 1952; d. Wesley Elmo and Bonita (Pursiville) Hall; m. Alan Harry Brown, July 25, 1973; children: Matthew Alan, Lauren Elizabeth. BFA, S.W. Mo. State U., 1974, MS, 1985; MSW, U. Mo., 1987. Lic. profl. counselor, lic. clin. social worker; registered art therapist, registered play therapist-supr.; nat. cert. counselor; cert. social worker; cert. clin. mental health counselor; bd. cert. art therapist. Instr. art and design S.W. Mo. State U., Springfield, 1976-83, 85-86; psychotherapist Ozark Psychol. Assocs., Springfield, 1987—. Exhibited photographs in numerous one-woman shows including Kansas City, Mo., 1988, Hamburg, West Germany, 1989, Schwanenburg, Germany, 1991; contbr. articles to mags.; photographs represented in numerous permanent collections including U. Louisville, Springfield Art Mus. Grantee Mo. Arts Coun., 1983; recipient 1st place award Photo Spiva, 1987, East Tex. Internat., 1991, Best in Show award Photo Expo, 1988. Mem. Am. Art Therapy Assn., Am. Mental Health Counselor Assn., NASW, Am. Counseling Assn., Internat. Assn. Marriage & Family Counselors, Assn. for Play Therapy. Democrat. Home: 1304 E Cherry St Springfield MO 65802 Office: Ozark Psychol Assocs 2200 E Sunshine # 320 Springfield MO 65804

BROWN, LILLIE MCFALL, elementary school principal; b. Feb. 29; d. Clayton and Septertee (Dewberry) McFall; m. Charles Brown, Oct. 4, 1958; 1 child, Eric McFall. BA in Home Econ., Sci., Langston Univ., 1956; MA in Spl. Edn., Chgo. Tchrs. Coll., 1964; MA in Adminstrn., Seattle Univ., 1976. Home econ. tchr. Altue (Okla.) Separate Pub. Schs., 1955-56, first grade tchr., 1956-57, fourth grade tchr., 1957-60; middle sch. tchr. Chgo. Pub. Sch.s, 1960-64; spl. edn. primary tchr. Seattle Pub. Schs., 1966-67, spl. edn. intermediate tchr., 1967-68, program coord., 1968-71, elem. asst. prin., 1971-76, elem. prin., 1976—; Mem. Project READ, Seattle, 1968. Contbr. articles to profl. jours. Treas. African Am. Alliance, 1980—; historian Wash. Alliance Black Sch. Educators, 1991—; vol. Olympic Games, Seattle, 1990. Recipient Sears Found. grant., 1967. Mem. NAACP, Nat. Assn. Elem. Sch. Prins., Elem. Prins. Assn. Seattle Pub. Schs., Prins. Assn. Wash. State, Prin. Assn. Seattle Pub. Schs., Educational Leadership, Phi Delta Kappa, Kappa Delta Pi, Delta Sigma Theta. Democrat. Baptist. Home: 2736 34th Ave S Seattle WA 98144

BROWN, LINDA JOAN, psychotherapist, psychoanalyst; b. Mineola, N.Y., Feb. 18, 1941; d. Charles Harold and Helen (Golbach) B. Student, Smith Coll., Northampton, Mass., 1958-60; BA, Barnard Coll., N.Y.C., 1962; MPS in Art Therapy, Pratt Inst., Bklyn., 1973; MSW, Hunter Coll., N.Y.C., 1976. Cert. social worker, psychoanalyst, N.Y.; lic. clin. social worker, Calif.; diplomate clin. social work Am. Bd. Examiners in Clin. Social Work. Singer, actress Broadway theatres, N.Y.C., 1962-65, pub. rels./community rels. specialist, real estate, publicist/editor, pub., edn. cons., 1965-71; art therapist Bronx (N.Y.) Psychiat. Ctr., 1972-74; clin. social worker North Richmond Community Mental Health Ctr., S.I., N.Y., 1977-79; staff therapist Lincoln Inst. Psychotherapy, N.Y.C., 1978-80; sr. staff therapist Ctr. for Study Anorexia and Bulimia, N.Y.C., 1983-85; staff therapist Inst. Contemporary Psychotherapy, N.Y.C., 1988—; pvt. practice psychotherapy N.Y.C., 1978—; mem. human svc. faculty Tristate Inst. Traditional Chinese Acupuncture, N.Y.C., 1986-89; mem. faculty N.Y. Open Ctr., N.Y.C., 1987—; adj. faculty Health Choices Ctr. for Healing Arts, Princeton, N.J., 1987-90; clin. cons. Personal Performance Cons., EAP, 1988; human resources cons. industry, N.Y.C., 1988—; workshop leader seminars on stress mgmt., comm. and counseling skills, intimate relationship skills ; specialist in creative expression. Mem. NASW.

BROWN, LINDA JOYCE, nurse, administrator; b. Ft. Smith, Ark., June 2, 1943; d. James Warren and Drucilla Dot (Foster) Gholson; m. Billy Ray Brown, Feb. 28, 1968; children: Robin, David, Alan, Billy, Ray. BSN, Northwestern State U., 1970. Cert AIDS instr., La.; cert. BLS, ACLS. Staff nurse North Caddo Meml. Hosp., Vivian, La., 1970, staff nurse, discharge planner, 1987-89; staff nurse Morris Cafritz Meml. Hosp., Washington, 1971-72; dir. nurses Heritage Manor Nursing Home, Vivian, 1972-74; pub. health nurse Caddo Parish Health Unit, Shreveport, La., 1974-77; pub. health supr. Vivian br. Caddo Parish Health Unit, 1977-87; staff nurse La. State U. Med. Ctr., Shreveport, 1987; patient edn. nurse La. State U. Sch. Medicine, Shreveport, 1989-90, nurse mgr., clin. coord., 1990—. Tchr. Emmanuel Bapt. Ch., Vivian, 1972—. Mem. Shreveport Dist. Nurses' Assn. (past vice-chmn. community health sect.). Home: PO Box 471 Vivian LA 71082 Office: La State U Sch Medicine 1501 Kings Hwy Shreveport LA 71130

BROWN, LINDA LOCKETT, school food service administrator, nutrition consultant; b. Jacksonville, Fla., Jan. 8, 1954; d. Willie James and Katie Lee (Taylor) Lockett; m. Thomas Lee Brown, Dec. 18, 1982; children: Ashanti, William, Timothy. BS in Agr., U. Fla., 1975, M of Agr., 1981. Lic. profl. nutritionist; cert. food svc. dir. III; registered dietitian. Chemist/microbiologist Green Giant Co., Alachua, Fla., 1975-77; lab. technologist II U. Fla., Gainesville, 1977-81, extension agt. I, Ft. Myers, 1981-85, extension agt. II, 1985-87, West Palm Beach, 1987-88; pres. CINET, Inc., 1985—; area supr. Palm Beach County Sch. Food Svc., 1988-90; adj. prof. Palm Beach Community Coll., 1990; dir. sch. food svc. St. Johns County, 1990—; nutrition cons. Congregate Meals, Ft. Myers, 1984-87, Serenity House, Ft. Myers, 1985-87; cons. Performax, 1989—; treas. St. Augustine chpt. Internat. Food Svc. Execs. Assn., 1993—; apptd. by gov. Fla. Health and Human Svcs. Bd., elected vice chair, 1993-94, chair, 1994-95. Columnist Palm Beach Post, 1989—; contbr. articles to profl. jours. Mem. exec. bd. Community Coordinating Coun., Ft. Myers, 1985; Am. Heart Assn., Palm Beach, 1989-90; cofounder Friends of Hearing Impaired Youth, Gainesville, 1976; tutor-coord. Sampson, Gainesville, 1973; mem. Jr. League, Ft. Myers, 1987; mem. Jr. League, Palm Beach, Fla., 1987-90, mem. edn. tng. com., community rsch. com. 1989-90; mem. nutrition com. Am. Heart Assn., Palm Beach, 1989—. State U. System Bd. Regents grantee, 1980. Mem. NAFE, Soc. Nutrition Edn. (legis. network chmn.), Am. Dietetic Assn. (network of blacks in nutrition, chair legis. com. 1988-89, chair nominating 1989, sec. 1989-90, state profl. recruitment coord.), Fla. Dietetic Assn. (chair minority issues com., chair membership 1987-88, chair edn. and registration 1988-90, state profl. recruitment coord. rep. Fla. chpt., chair nominating com. 1994—), Palm Beach Dietetic Assn. (community nutrition chair 1988-89, chair legis. com. 1989-90), Caloosa Dietetic Assn. (sec.), Nat. Speakers Assn., Sch. Food Svcs. Assn. (1988—), Nat. Assn. Extension Home Econs. Agts., Internat. Platform Assn., Jacksonville Dietetic Assn., Nutrition Today Soc., Alpha Zeta, Epsilon Sigma Phi. Club: Greater Palm Beaches Bus. and Profl. Women (minority student mentor, role model mentor), Nat. Speakers Assn., N. Fla. Profl. Speakers Assn. Avocations: singing, violin. Office: 2234 George Wythe Rd Orange Park FL 32073

BROWN, LINDA PHILLIPS, educational program administrator; b. Goshen, N.Y., Feb. 7, 1941; d. Thomas James and Ethlyn Dana (Thompson) Phillips; m. Walter Armin Brown, Jan. 29, 1966; children: Karen Garlock, Gordon, Matthew. BA, So. Conn. State Coll., 1974; MS, Wheelock Coll., 1980. Adminstrv. supr., instr. Wheelock Coll., Boston, 1978-83, asst. dir. grad. admissions, 1985-86, acting dir. grad. admissions, 1986; childlife specialist R.I. Hosp., Providence, 1977-79, coord. Read-to-Me program, 1992—. Co-author: Birth Bond-Reunions Between Birth Parents and Adoptees...What Happens After, 1989 (Am. Adoption Congress award 1990). Bd. dirs. Tannerhill Foster Group Home, Providence, 1978-80, Fund for Community Progress, rep., 1993—; active ACLU, 1986—, Women for a Non-Nuclear Future, 1982—, Parents and Adoptees Liberty Movement (PALM), Providence, 1985—; New Eng. regional dir. Am. Adoption Congress, 1987-89, legis. dir., 1989-90. Recipient Appreciation award Am. Adoption Congress, 1989. Mem. Assn. for Care of Children in Hosps. Democrat. Episcopalian. Home and Office: 96 Everett Ave Providence RI 02906

BROWN, LOIS HEFFINGTON, health facility administrator; b. Little Rock, Mar. 28, 1940; d. Carl Otis and Opal (Shock) Heffington; M. Ivy Roy Brown, June 21, 1984; children: Carletta Jo Rice, Roby Lynn Rice, Pherby Allison Graham, Phelan Missy Graham. Student, Guilford Tech. Community Coll., Jamestown, N.C., 1974-75, 77, 80. Cert. hearing aid specialist. Sec. Berger Enterprises, West Memphis, Ark., 1962-65; office mgr. Beltone Hearing Care Ctr., Greensboro, N.C., 1975-81; owner Hearing Care Ctr., Cullman, Ala., 1982-85, Miracle-Ear Ctr., Cullman, Decatur, Fultondale, Jasper and Birmingham, Ala., 1985-87; pres. L&I Corp., Cullman, Decatur, Fultondale, Jasper and Birmingham, 1987-90, L & I Corp. dba Miracle Ear Ctr., Cullman, Decatur, Jasper, Ala., 1991-94; owner Conway (Ark.) Hearing Aid Ctr., 1994—. Gov.-appointed Ala. Bd. Hearing, chmn. of the bd., 1989-91. Mem. Nat. Hearing Aid Soc., Ala. Hearing Aid Dealers Assn. (sec. 1984-86, v.p. 1986-88, bd. dirs. 1988-91), Ark. Hearing Aid Dealers Assn., Women of the Moose. Republican. Baptist. Home: 199 Hwy 107 North Enola AR 72047

BROWN, LORENE B(YRON), library educator, educational administrator; b. Plant City, Fla., Nov. 9, 1933; d. Benjamin and Sallie (Barton) Byron; m. Paul L. Brown, Aug. 1, 1974. B.S., Fort Valley State Coll., 1955; M.S.L.S., Atlanta U., 1956; Ph.D., U. Wis., 1974. Cataloguer N.C. Central U., Durham, 1956-58, Gibbs Jr. Coll., St. Petersburg, Fla., 1958-60, Fort Valley State Coll., Ga., 1960-65, Norfolk State U., Va., 1965-70; assoc. prof., dean Atlanta U., 1970-89, prof., 1989—; dir. Info. Retrieval Workshops, Atlanta, 1976-78; evaluator Coop. Coll. Library Ctr., Atlanta, 1979-82; cons. United Bd. Coll. Devel., Atlanta, 1976-79. Mem. Friends of Library, Atlanta, 1982. Recipient Rachel Schenk award Library Sch. U. Wis., Madison, 1971; So. Fellowship Found. fellow Atlanta, 1972-74. Mem. ALA, Am. Soc. for Info. Sci., Assn. Library and Info. Sci. Edn., Ga. Library Assn., Met Atlanta Library Assn., Beta Phi Mu. Democrat. Baptist. Home: 855 Flamingo Dr SW Atlanta GA 30311-2402 Office: Atlanta U Sch Libr and Info Studies 223 James P Brawley Dr SW Atlanta GA 30314-4358

BROWN, LORI ANNE, graphic designer; b. Trenton, N.J., Mar. 14, 1963; d. Ronald and Peggy Ann (Eshelman) B. Grad. high sch., Hamilton Square, N.J. Secretarial trainee Hamilton Twp. Bd. Edn., Hamilton Square, N.J., 1981; sec. Agrl. Rsch. Ctr., Apopka, Fla., 1982; pres. USS Paegan-Starfleet, Winter Park, Fla., 1983—; graphic designer, bookkeeper Sunbelt Mktg. Svc. Duragreen Mktg. Inc., Mt. Dora, Fla., 1983—; co-owner TachyCon, Winter Park, 1989—, Pawtographics, Winter Park, 1989—; acad. dir., mem. exec. com. Starfleet, 1993-95. Home: PO Box 405 Winter Park FL 32790-0405 Office: Duragreen Mktg Inc 2600 Britt Rd PO Box 1485 Mount Dora FL 32757

BROWN, LORRAINE ANN, administrative services coordinator; b. Providence, Mar. 15, 1947; d. Leonard Francis and Elaine Frances (Pettis) Millen; m. Jeffrey Schofield Brown, May 22, 1976 (div. 1983); 1 child, Kaneeta Sage; m. Dieter Paul Wuennenberg, July 14, 1965; 1 child, Desiree Jacqueline Wuennenberg. Student, Manhattan Sch. Printing, 1972, L.A. Trade Tech. Coll., 1981-83. Communications rep. TransAmerica Occidental, Los Angeles, 1973-77; owner, jewelry designer The Lorraine Brown Co., El Segundo, Calif., 1979-83; mgr. Silk Lingerie Outlet, Sherman Oaks, Calif., 1982-83; office mgr. Am. Silk Label, L.A., 1984; asst. prodn. coordinator Pacific Coast Mills, L.A., 1984-85; asst. designer jr. wear Judy Knapp Inc., L.A., 1986-87; sales exec. Integrated Aquatic Systems, Marina Del Rey, Calif., 1987-88; adminstrv. svcs. coord. GTE Svcs., El Segundo, Calif., 1988—. Asst. leader Girl Scouts U.S., El Segundo, 1985-87; P.V.P. leader 4-H, 1991—; vol. Tree Muskateers and Swift Project. Mem. Svcs. Employees Assn. (pres.), Young Exec. Singles, Advanced Degrees, Sierra Singles. Home: 756 Main St El Segundo CA 90245-3051

BROWN, LULU BELLE DISSMORE, retired community health nurse; b. Blair, Wis., Nov. 20, 1926; d. Elbert David and Ellen Agusta (Salem) Dissmore; 1 child, Ellen Ann (dec.). Diploma, Meth. Hosp., 1947; postgrad., U. Dubuque. RN, Iowa; cert. tchr., Iowa. Staff nurse, head nurse Luth. Hosp., La Crosse, Wis., 1947-48, Wichita Falls (Tex.) Clinic, 1948-49, VA Hosp., Temple, Tex., 1949-62; sch. nurse Nora Springs (Iowa)-Rock Falls Community Sch., 1966-89; ret., 1989. Past mem. exec. bd., bd. dirs. N. Iowa chpt. ARC; hon. mem. program agy. United Presbyn. Ch. in U.S.A.; active Eden Presbyn. Ch., Rudd, Iowa; past mem. regional adv. coun. Easter Seal Soc. Mem. Am. Legion Aux. (treas. Nora Springs chpt., pres. Floyd County chpt.).

BROWN, LYNDA NELL, nursing educator; b. Humphreys County, Miss., Oct. 6, 1943; d. A. C. and Elizabeth (Holloway) Merchant; m. Walter U. Brown, Oct. 11, 1963; children: Rebecca E., Darren K., Sarah E. BSN, U. Miss., 1965; MS in Nursing, Boston U., 1974, EdD, 1977. Asst. prof. Boston Coll., Chestnut Hill, Mass., Vanderbilt U., Nashville; assoc. prof. U. Akron, Ohio, U. Ky., Lexington. Contbr. articles to profl. publs. Mem. ANA, Nat. League Nursing, ARN , Sigma Theta Tau (Excellence in Nursing award Delta Omega chpt., dist. lectr.).

BROWN, LYNETTE RALYA, journalist, publicist; b. Beloit, Wis., Dec. 15, 1926; d. Lynn Louis and Ethel Clara (Meeker) Ralya; m. Donald Adair Brown, Jr., Dec. 20, 1947; children: Donald Adair III, Alison Laura, Julia Carol. BA in Journalism, Mich. State U., 1948; MA in Journalism, Michigan State U., 1985; MA in Mass Comm., Wayne State U., 1983. Actress, publicist Grand Traverse Playhouse, Traverse City, Mich., 1946 (summer), N.Y. Summer Playhouse, Mackinac Island, Mich., 1947 (summer); writer WILS Radio, Lansing, Mich., 1947-48; writer, performer WJBK Radio, TV, Detroit, 1948-49; editor Denby Ctr. News, Detroit, 1949-51; freelance writer Oakland County, Mich., 1952-78; editor Henry Ford Mus., Dearborn, Mich., 1979-81; writer, reporter Legal Advertiser Newspaper, Detroit, 1983-85; publicist Bloomfield (Mich.) and Birmingham (Mich.) Pub. Librs., 1986-89; freelance writer, publicist Lynette Brown Comm., Birmingham, Mich., 1989—. Columnist: (newspaper) At the Libraries, 1986-89. Probation sponsor Dist. Ct. Mich., 1960-70; publicist Oakland County Vol. Bur., 1979-82; leader sr. high/jr. high youth group Drayton Ave. Presbyn. Ch., Oakland County, 1952-54, 62-66, Pine Hill Congl. Ch., Oakland County, 1968-71, Northbrook Presbyn. Ch., Oakland County, 1976-77; polit. campaign worker Rep. candidates and non-partisan jud. candidates, 1952—; Cub Scout leader Royal Oak Emerson Sch., Oakland County, 1961-64; Girl Scout troop leader Bloomfield Twp. Meadow Lake Sch., Oakland County, 1966-71. Mem. AAUW (chair women's issues, chair cultural interests). Home and Office: 6120 Westmoor Rd Bloomfield MI 48301

BROWN, LYNNE, artist; b. Dallas, Jan. 19, 1951; d. Raymond David and Rosalyn (Yaffie) B. BFA, U. Denver, 1972; MFA, Sch. of Art Inst. of Chgo., 1981, art history cert., 1982. Cons. photography and spl. programs Chgo. Coun. on Fine Arts, 1982; cons. arts apprenticeship program Sch. of Art Inst., Chgo., 1983-84, adminstrv. coord., 1985, 89; program faculty ACM Arts Program, Chgo., 1989-94; adj. instr. Elmhurst (Ill.) Coll., 1983-

85, adj. asst. prof., 1985-91; vis. artist Sch. of the Art Inst., 1992, 94—; vis. asst. prof. U. Ill., Chgo., 1994; vis. lectr. dept. of art theory and practice Northwestern U., Evanston, 1993; vis. faculty Colo. Coll., Colorado Springs, 1994; bd. dirs. Randolph St. Gallery, Chgo., pres. bd. 1989—. Exhibited in group show at Davenport Mus. of Art, 1993. Panelist, pub. art panel Pub. Art Program, Chgo., 1993; grant panelist Ill. Arts Coun., 1992-93; juror McKnight Found. Photo Fellowships, Mpls., 1992. Recipient Artist fellowship Ill. Arts Coun., 1994, fellowship, 1991, Purchase prize Ill. State Mus., 1987, 94, artist grant City of Chgo. Dept. Cultural Affairs, 1991, 94. Mem. Coll. Art Assn., Randolph St. Gallery (bd. pres. 1989—, chair exhbn. com. 1988-90), Arts Adv. Coun., Nat. Assn. of Arts Orgns., Soc. for Photographic Edn. (bd. dirs. 1990—, exec. com. 1991-93, nat. conf. co-chair 1993-94).

BROWN, MARCIA JOAN, author, artist, photographer; b. Rochester, N.Y., July 13, 1918; d. Clarence Edward and Adelaide Elizabeth (Zimber) B. Student, Woodstock Sch. Painting, summers 1938, 39; student painting, New Sch. Social Research, Art Students League; BA, N.Y. State Coll. Tchrs., 1940; student Chinese calligraphy, painting, Zhejiang Acad. Fine Arts, Hangzhou, Peoples Republic China, 1985, 87; studied painting with Judson Smith, Stuart Davis, Yasuo Kuniyoshi, Julian Levi. Tchr. English, dramatics Cornwall (N.Y.) High Sch., 1940-43; library asst. N.Y. Pub. Library, 1943-49; tchr. puppetry extra-mural dept. U. Coll. West Indies, Jamaica, B.W.I., 1953; tchr. workshop on picture book U. Minn.-Split Rock Arts Program, Duluth, 1986, workshop on Chinese brush painting Brush Artists Guild, 1988; sponsor Chinese landscape painting workshops with Zhuo HeJun, 1988-89; sponsored workshops Chinese caligraphy with Wong Dong Ling, 1989, 90, 92; invited speaker exhbn. illustrations, Japan, 1990, 94. Illustrator: The Trail of Courage (Virginia Watson), 1948, The Steadfast Tin Soldier (Hans Christian Andersen), 1953 (Caldecott Honor Book award), Anansi (Philip Sherlock), 1954, The Three Billy Goats Gruff (Asbjornsen and Moe), 1957, Peter Piper's Alphabet, 1959, The Wild Swans (Hans Christian Andersen), 1963, Giselle (Théophile Gautier), 1970, The Snow Queen (Hans Christian Andersen), 1972, Shadow (Blaise Cendrars), 1982 (Caldecott award 1983), How the Ostrich Got His Long Neck (Aardema), 1995, (with others) Sing a Song of Popcorn, 1988, Of Swans, Sugar Plums and Satin Slippers (Violette Verdy); author, illustrator: The Little Carousel, 1946, Stone Soup, 1947 (Caldecott Honor Book award), Henry Fisherman, 1949 (Caldecott Honor Book award), Dick Whittington and His Cat (retold), 1950 (Caldecott Honor Book award), Skipper John's Cook, 1951 (Caldecott Honor Book award), The Flying Carpet (retold), 1956, Felice, 1958, Tamarindo, 1960, Once a Mouse (retold), 1961 (Caldecott award), Backbone of the King, 1966, The Neighbors, 1967, The Bun (retold), 1972, All Butterflies, 1974 (Boston Globe Honor Book, Horn Book), The Blue Jackal (retold), 1977, Walk Through Your Eyes, 1979, (with photographs) Touch Will Tell, 1979, (with photographs) Listen to a Shape, 1979, Lotus Seeds; Children, Pictures and Books, 1985, (with others) From Sea to Shining Sea, 1993; translator. illustrator: Puss in Boots, 1952 (Caldecott Honor Book award), Cinderella (Charles Perrault), 1954 (Caldecott award 1955), How, Hippo!, 1969 (honor book Book World Spring Book Festival); author, photographer: film strip The Crystal Cavern, 1974; woodcut prints exhibited, Bklyn. Mus., Peridot Gallery, Hacker Gallery, Library Congress, Carnegie Inst., Phila. Print Club; Chinese brush painting and calligraphy exhibited at Hammond Mus., North Salem, N.Y., 1988; prints in permanent collection, Library of Congress, N.Y. Pub. Library, pvt. collections; art work in Mazza Gallery Findlay (Ohio) Coll.; traveling exhibition, lectrs. illustration Japan, 1990, 94. Recipient Disting. Svc. to Children's Lit. award, U. So. Miss., 1972, Regina medal Cath. Libr. Assn., 1977, Disting. Alumnus medal SUNY, 1969, Laura Ingalls Wilder award, 1992; U.S. nominee Internat. Hans Andersen award illustration, 1966, 76; career rsch. material in spl. libr. collection, SUNY, Albany, de Grummond Collection, U. So. Miss., Hattiesburg, Kerlan Collection, U. Minn. Fellow Internat. Inst. Arts and Letters (life); mem. Author's Guild, Print Coun. Am., Art Students League, Oriental Brush Artists Guild, Sumi-e Soc. Am, Am. Artists of Chinese Brush Painting.

BROWN, MARGARET DEBEERS, lawyer; b. Washington, Sept. 24, 1943; d. John Sterling and Marianna Hurd (Hill) deBeers; m. Timothy Nils, Aug. 28, 1965; children—Emeline Susan, Eric Franklin. BA magna cum laude, Radcliffe Coll., 1965; postgrad. Harvard U. Law Sch., 1965-67; JD, U. Calif.-Berkeley, 1968. Bar: Calif. 1969, U.S. Ct. Appeals (9th cir.) 1971, U.S. Supreme Ct. 1972, U.S. Ct. Appeals (D.C. cir.) 1986, U.S. Ct. Appeals (2d cir.) 1987. Assoc. White, Hamilton, Wyche, Shell & Pollard, Petersburg, Va., 1968-70, Heller, Ehrman, White & McAuliffe, San Francisco, 1970-73; sole practice, San Francisco, 1973-77; atty. Pacific Telephone (name changed to Pacific Bell 1984), San Francisco, 1977-83, sr. atty., 1983-85; sr. counsel Pacific Telesis Group, 1985—; speaker McGeorge Law Sch., Sacramento, 1983. Elder Calvary Presbyn. Ch., San Francisco. Mem. ABA, Am. Corp. Counsel Assn., Calif. State Bar (mem. com. bar examiners), San Francisco Bar Assn. (chmn. corp. law dept. sect. 1993, judiciary com. and nominating com. 1993), Phi Beta Kappa. Office: Pacific Telesis Group 130 Kearny St Ste 3659 San Francisco CA 94108-4866

BROWN, MARION LEPAGE, town clerk; b. Rochester, N.Y., July 19, 1928; d. Herbert J. and Catherine M. (McGrath) LePage; m. Allan J. Brown, Apr. 25, 1959; children: Deborah, Douglas, Jeffrey. BA, Nazareth Coll., 1950; postgrad., U. of State of N.Y., 1950-51. Tchr. Irondequoit Sch. Dist., Rochester, 1950-51; office mgr. Heldon Constrn. Corp., Rochester, 1951-53; corp. sec., office mgr. Le Page Motors, Inc., Rochester, 1953-59; councilwoman Town of Brighton, Rochester, 1978-89, town clk., receiver of taxes, 1989—; pres. Monroe County Long Term Care, Inc., Rochester, 1993—. Chmn. Judy Weis Meml. Edn. Scholarship Fund, Rochester, 1993-94; committeeman, past chmn. Brighton Rep. Town and County Com., Rochester, 1973—; bd. dir. Crestwood Children's Ctr., Rochester, 1981-91, Genesee Valley chpt. Arthritis Found., Rochester, 1982-89. Recipient Susan B. Anthony Civic award Susan B. Anthony Rep. Club, 1981, Citizen of Yr. award Brighton Rotary Club, 1993; Paul Harris fellow Brighton Rotary Club, 1993. Roman Catholic. Office: Town of Brighton 2300 Elmwood Ave Rochester NY 14618

BROWN, MARSHA ANN STOKES, lyricist, composer; b. Bryn Mawr, Pa., Apr. 17, 1952; d. Ophalina and Edith (Miller) Stokes; m. Norman Brown, 1970 (div. 1980); children: Anthony, Norman, Bryan, Joseph. Diploma med. asst., McCarrie Sch. Health and Tech., 1976; diploma in acctg., Community Coll. Phila., 1988; MA, 1992; grad., Computer Application Program, 1993. Psychiat. aide Phila. State Hosp.; now, freelance writer and lyricist Phila. Lyricist Nashville Music Co.; composer (Prayer Records) Prayer to God, 1986; author published poems, 1981—. Mem. Franciscan Mission Assocs. Recipient Iliad Lit. award 1990, Parent Teaching award, 1979; Named to World of Poetry Hall of Fame, 1990. Mem. AMA, RMT, ABI, BMI (N.Y. br.), Am. Bible Soc. Address: 2209 Edgley St Philadelphia PA 19121

BROWN, MARY CARNEY, state representative; b. Midland, Mich., Aug. 18, 1935; d. Sheldon and Wilma Carney; m. Donald J. Brown; children: Linda, Jeff, Jim. Student, Albion Coll., 1953-55; AB in Recreation, Syracuse U., 1957, MS in Phys. Edn., 1961. Tchr. various cos., camps and colls.; asst. prof. dept. phys. edn. for women Western Mich. U., 1965-76; state rep. State of Mich., 1976—; mem. legis. coms. Civil Rights and Women's Issues, Conservation, Environ. and the Great Lakrs, Human Svcs. and Children, Taxation; chmn. Ins. Com., Air Quality Subcommittee; chair House Dem. Caucus, 1983—. Mem. Friends of Kal-Haven Trail, Kalamazoo Womens Network; bd. dirs. Jobs for Mich. Grads., 1982-89; pres. Kalamazoo Area LWV, 1969-73, lobbyist, state bd. dirs., 1973-74; chairperson Kalamazoo County Dem. Party, 1975-76; founding mem. Kalamazoo Environ. Coun., 1991—; charter mem. Kalamazoo Nature Ctr.; mem. citizens adv. com. KRPH, 1987—; century club mem. Mich. Dem. Party, com. to assess need for constl. conv., 1977, co-chair policy com., 1986; spokesperson Mich. Dem. Women's Caucus, 1978-79,. Named Outstanding Freshman Legislator, State Capitol Bur. Booth newspapers, 1977, one of 10 Top Legislators, Detroit News poll, 1977, 79, Legislator of Yr., Mich. Assn. Children's Alliances, 1985, Woman of the Yr. NOW, 1982, Legislator of the Yr. Mich. Township Assn., 1989, Conservationist of the Yr. Sierra Club, 1990; recipient Cert. of Appreciation, Kalamazoo Alcohol and Drug Abuse Coun., Cert. of Svc. with distinction Assn. Student Govt. Western Mich. U., 1980; honored by Women Lawyers Assn. Mich., 1980, Community Svc. award Eagles Aerie 526 Kalamazoo, Cert. of Appreciation, County Rd. Assn. Mich., 1983, Woman of Achievement award Kalamazoo YWCA, 1993, The Brown Jacobs Equality in Edn. award Mich. NOW, 1994, Outstand Pub. Svc. award Planned Parenthood of Kalamazoo, 1994, Lifetime Achievement award Sierra Club, 1994. Mem. AAUW (co-winner Outstanding Mich. Legislator 1982), ACLU, ASTM, Am. Camping Assn. (bd. dirs. Mich. sect. 1972-76, 80-82), Am. Civil Liberties Union. Home: 1624 Grand Ave Kalamazoo MI 49006-4419 Office: Ho of Reps PO Box 30014 458 Roosevelt Bldg Lansing MI 48909-7514 also: Mich State Ho of Reps State Capitol Lansing MI 48909

BROWN, MARY ELEANOR, physical therapist, educator; b. Williamsport, Pa., Jan. 1, 1906; d. Sumner Locher and Mary Kate (Eagles) Brown. Student U. Wis.-Madison, 1927-28; B.A., Barnard Coll., 1931; M.A., NYU, 1941, postgrad., 1942-45, Western Reserve U., 1960-61; postgrad. U. Miami, Miami-Dade Jr. Coll., 1971-72, Cuesta Community Coll., 1977-79. Supervising phys. therapist, rsch. asst. Inst. for Crippled and Disabled, N.Y.C., 1941-46; instr. edn. N.Y.U., 1942-46; phys. therapist Childrens Rehab. Inst., Cockeysville, Md., 1946; organizing dir. phys. edn. State Rehab. Hosp., West Haverstraw, N.Y., 1946-47; phys. therapy cons. Nat. Soc. for Crippled Children and Adults, Chgo., 1947-49; physical therapy cons., dir. prof. svcs., dir. cerebral palsy sch. N.Y. State Dept. Health, Albany, N.Y. and Eastern N.Y. Orthopedic Hosp. Sch., Schenectady, N.Y., 1949-53; chief phys. therapist Bird S. Coler Hosp. for Chronic Diseases, N.Y.C., 1953-54; chief phys. therapist, instr. edn. St. Vincents Hosp. and N.Y.U., 1954-58; chief rsch. assoc. hand rsch. Highland View Hosp., Cleve., 1958-64, cons. on kinesiology, hand rsch., 1964-65; supr. continuing edn. for phys. therapists, asst. prof. phys. therapy Case Western Res. U., Cleve., 1964-68; dir. phys. therapy Margaret Wagner House of Benjamin Rose Inst., Cleve., 1968-70; free lance writer, 1970—; 1st Mary Eleanor Brown lectr. clin. phys. therapy rsch. Inst. Rehab. and Rsch., Tex. Med. Center, Houston, 1979; Adv. bd. Community Svcs. Dept. Cuesta Community Coll., San Luis Obispo, Calif., 1977-92; vol. UN and Univ. for Peace, Costa Rica, 1982—. Author: Therapeutic Recreation and Exercise: Range-of-Motion Activities for Health and Well-Being, 1990; contbr. articles in field to profl jours. Recipient Award of Merit, Case-Western Res. U., 1970; award for clin. rsch. Inst. Rehab. and Rsch., Tex. Med. Ctr., Houston, 1979; Lucy Blair Svc. award Am. Phys. Therapy Assn., 1984, Disting. Alumna award Lancaster Country Day Sch., 1987. Mem. Inst. Gen. Semantics, Internat. Soc. Gen. Semantics, Am. Phys. Therapy Assn. (Catherine Worthingham fellow 1990), Women for Internat. Peace and Arbitration, Found. for Global Community. Home: 1235 3rd St Apt B Los Osos CA 93402-1115

BROWN, MARY ELIZABETH, insurance agent; b. Ft. Worth, Oct. 12, 1956; d. J.W. and Barbara Joan (Brumley) B.; divorced; 1 child, Tierney Marie Epstein. BBA, So. Meth. U., 1980. Co-owner Atascocita Tennis Shop, Humble, Tex., 1981-86; sales rep., western region North Texas Cir. Bd., Grand Prairie, Tex., 1987-88; sales rep. Savin Corp., Dallas, 1988-91, G&K Svcs., Dallas, 1991-92, Nat. Auto Cellular, Dallas, 1992-93; agt. Northwestern Mut. Life, Dallas, 1993—. Mem. NALU, NAFE. Baptist. Office: Northwestern Mut Life 12221 Merit Dr Ste 1500 Dallas TX 75251

BROWN, MARY EVELYN, insurance agent; b. Hammond, Ind., Dec. 25, 1915; d. Frank and Mary Ann (Fuderich) Maglish; m. James Ward Brown, June 21, 1941. Grad. H.S., Griffith, Ind. Sec. Spitz & Miller Ins., Griffith, 1935-55; underwriter Spitz & Miller Ins. Inc., Griffith, 1955-75, sec., mgr., 1975—. Vol. Am. Cancer Soc., Griffith, 1986—. Recipient Ins. Woman of Yr. award Hammond Assn. Ins. Women, 1975. Mem. Nat. Assn. Ins. Women (regional dir. 1954-55, nat. rec. sec. 1955-56), Nat. Cath. Soc. Foresters, Ins. Women of Lake County (past pres. 1978, 86), Ind. Ins. Agts., Am. Legion. Republican. Roman Catholic. Home: 210 N Griffith Blvd Griffith IN 46319 Office: Spitz & Miller Ins Agy Inc 101 W Columbia St Griffith IN 46319

BROWN, MARY RAWSON, lawyer; b. Pitts., May 7, 1945; d. Daniel P. and Mary P. (Wilson) Brown; m. Earle M. Marsters, Aug. 30, 1986. AB with honors, Middlebury (Vt.) Coll., 1966; MA, Northwestern U., 1969; EdD, Cath. U. Am., 1980; JD cum laude, Harvard U., 1985. Bar: Mass. 1985. House dir. Northwestern U., 1968; dist. mgr., other positions New Eng. Telephone, AT&T, Boston, other locations, 1969-84; assoc. Bingham, Dana & Gould, Boston, 1985-86; lawyer, sole practice Mashpee, Mass., 1986—. Mem. Conservation Commn., Mashpee, 1985-89. Mem. Mass. Conveyancers Assn. (exec. com. 1992-94), Mortar Board. Office: PO Box 1 Mashpee MA 02649

BROWN, MAY WALE, script supervisor; b. Vienna, Austria, Apr. 22, 1918; came to U.S., 1936; d. Oskar and Julia (Figdor) Marmorek; m. F. Hamilton Wright, Aug. 1947 (div. 1962); m. Earl A. Brown, Apr. 24, 1965. Student, Konsular Acad., Vienna, Bucknell U., 1939. Visa interviewer Am. Consulate, Vienna, 1938; exec. sec. various cos. N.Y.C., 1938-41; polit. censor for Europe MGM Studios, Culver City, Calif., 1946-47; casting dir. OWI Voice of Am., N.Y.C., 1941-45; asst. mgr. Sta. KTTV-TV Studios, Hollywood, Calif., 1948-49; script supr. Fee Motion Picture Studios, Hollywood, 1953-86. Home: 30801 S Coast Hwy Trlr 749 Laguna Beach CA 92651-4204

BROWN, MELISSA ROSE, securities analyst; b. Manhasset, N.Y., Dec. 7, 1957; d. Frederick Robert and Cynthia (Barnett) B.; 2 children. BS in Econs., U. Pa., 1979; MBA, NYU, 1984. Tech. cons. Interactive Data Corp., N.Y.C., 1979-81; fin. analyst Nabisco Brands, N.Y.C., 1981-82; quantitative analyst Prudential Bache, N.Y.C., 1982-85; dir. quantitative rsch. Prudential Securities, N.Y.C., 1985—. Mem. Assn. for Investment Mgmt. Rsch. (chair subcom. Charlottesville Va. chpt. 1989-91), Chgo. Quantitative Alliance. Office: Prudential Securities 17th Fl 1 New York Plaza New York NY 10292

BROWN, NANCY J., state representative; b. Chgo., Sept. 3, 1942; d. Herman Hugo Becker (dec.) and Katherine Evelyn (Gralund) Johnson; m. Myron Douglass Brown, June 7, 1968; children: Derek Douglass, Jason Alan. BS, Barat Coll., 1978; postgrad., U. Mo., 1982—. Treas. Village of Riverwoods (Ill.), 1975-76, trustee, 1976-78, 79-80, plan commr., 1978; twp. trustee, mem. zoning bd. Oxford (Kans.) Twp. Johnson Co., 1981-84; mem. Kans. Ho. of Reps., 1984—; chair Ho. Local Govt. Com.; cons. TRW Credit Data, Chgo., 1978-80; extension asst. U. Kans., Lawrence, 1980-81, office mgr. Gubernatorial Campaign, Kans., 1981-82. Mem. Nat. Hazardous Material Transp. Adv. Coun., 1985-87, Kans. Task Force on Autism, Kans. Emergency Response Commn.; mem. adv. bd. Fed. Emergency Mgmt. Agy., 1992; past chmn. Kans. Community Devel. Block Task Force; governing bd. chair Alliance Pilot Project, 1993—; bd. dirs. Emergency Med. Svcs., 1991—; former mem. bd. dirs. LWV. Recipient Excellence in Edn. award Blue Valley Sch. Dist., 1984. Mem. Nat. Alliance HazMat Transp. (chair 1992-93), NAt. Conf. State legislators (mem. women's network bd. 992—, chair state/local/tribal rels. 1993—), Nat. Assn. Towns and Twps. (bd. dirs.), Kans. Assn. Twps. (exec. dir. 1983-90), Blue Valley Community Coun. (chmn.), The Mainstream Coalition (exec. dir.), Blue Valley Hist. Soc. Republican. Address: 15429 Overbrook Rd Stanley KS 66224-9798

BROWN, PAMELA SUE, accountant; b. Inglewood, Calif., Sept. 25, 1959; d. Bruce Kellner and Joyce (Wixom) B.; m. Victor Stanford Frake, Aug. 30, 1986; children: Emily Anne, Katie Nicole. AA, El Camino Coll., 1979; BS, Calif. State U., Long Beach, 1981. CPA, Calif. Staff acct. Richard H. O'Hara & Co., CPA, City of Industry, Calif., 1982-87; tax mgr. Fagan, Stiles & Co., CPA, Long Beach, Calif., 1987-88; pub. acct. Pamela Sue Brown, CPA, Long Beach, Calif., 1988—. Vol. Children's Miracle Network Telethon, Anaheim, Calif., 1988-89, Vol. Income Tax Assistance Program, Torrance, Calif., 1981. Mem. Am. Soc. Women Accts. (pres.-elect 1984-85, pres. 1985-87), Inst. Mgmt. Accts. (com. chairperson), Calif. Soc. CPAs, Long Beach Area C. of C. Democrat. Lutheran. Home and Office: 263 Belmont Ave Long Beach CA 90803-1523

BROWN, PATRICIA BERRY, state legislator; b. Concord, N.H., May 6, 1939; married; 3 children. BEd, Plymouth Tchrs. Coll., 1973; MALS, Dartmouth U., 1979. Ret. counselor; mem. N.H. Ho. of Reps.; mem. edn. com. Mem. Mascoma Sch. Bd., 1978-87, chair, 3 yrs.; chair SAU # 32, 1985; del. Constl. Conv., 1984; trustee, chair bylaw policy com. Mascoma Savings Bank, 1979-90, mem. salary com., 1991—; bd. dirs., personnel chair Hannah House, 1985-90; chair bd. program River City Arts, 1989-90; group mem., performer Shoestring Players, 1986—; cmty. liaison Twin Pine Housing Trust, 1992-93. Home: Canaan St PO Box 63 Canaan NH 03741 Office: NH Ho of Reps State Capitol Concord NH 03301*

BROWN, PATRICIA IRENE, lawyer, retired law librarian; b. Boston; d. Joseph Raymond and Harriet A. (Taylor) B. BA, Suffolk U., 1955, JD, 1965, MBA, 1970; MTS, Gordon Conwell Theol. Sem., 1977. Bar: Mass. 1965. Library asst. Suffolk U., Boston, 1951-60, asst. librarian, 1960-65, asst. law librarian, 1965-85, assoc. law libr., 1985-92; human resources counselor Winthrop (Mass.) Sr. Ctr., 1993—. Dir. Referral/Resource Ctr., Union Congl. Ch., Winthrop, Mass.; vol. health benefits counselor Mass. Dept. Elder Affairs, 1994—. First Woman inducted into Nat. Baseball Hall of Fame, Cooperstown, N.Y., 1988, All- Am. Girls Profl. Baseball League, 1950-51. Mem. Mass. Bar Assn., Assn. Am. Law Libraries, Am. Congl. Assn. (bd. dirs. 1992—).

BROWN, PAULA KINNEY, heating and air conditioning contractor; b. Portsmith, Va., June 19, 1953; d. Curtis Wade and Joan (Glascoe) Kinney; m. Wayne Howard Brown, Feb. 12, 1983; children: Rebecca Jo, Raina Jaye. AS, Lake Sumter Community Coll., 1973, 77; student Lake County Area Vocat. Ctr., 1979, 80. Cert. air conditioning and heating contrator. Pres. Kinney's Air Conditioning and Heating, Leesburg, Fla., 1981—; head computer system operator, 1986—, office mgr. Mem. adv. com. for Area Lake Air Conditioning and Heating Vo-Tech. Sch., Eustis, Fla., 1981-82, 1993—. Mem. Ch. of Christ. Home: #5 Lonesome Pine Trl Yalaha FL 34797 Office: Kinney's Air Conditioning & Heating Inc 409 N 13th St Leesburg FL 34748-4977

BROWN, RHEA A., nurse; b. Utica, N.Y., Sept. 25, 1941; d. Arthur and Catherine (Connelly) Rabatoy; m. Ronald D. Brown, Aug. 24, 1963; children: Roberta, Rory Ellen. Diploma, St. Peter's Hosp. Sch. Nursing, 1962; BSN, Fairleigh Dickinson U., 1978; sch. nurse cert., Seton Hall U., 1979; MS, Wagner U., 1985. Cert. sch. nurse. Staff nurse Visiting Nurse Assn., Crawford, N.J., staff school nurse coord.; nursing supr. Vis. Nurse and Health Svc., Elizabeth, N.J.; nursing order documentation specialist Vis. Nurse Affiliate, Elizabeth, N.J.; cons. nursing documentation specialist. Mem. profl. edn. com. Am. Cancer Soc. Union County; leader troop 23 Girl Scouts Am., 1973-77; pres. PTA Lincoln Sch., Cranford, N.J., 1975-76, past trustee; officer Cranford Jr. Women's Club, 1970's. Mem. ANA, N.J. State Nurses Assn. (sec. community health div. 1991-93, mem. com. health reorgn. com. 1993-94), LEARN (rec. sec. 1991-92, treas. 1992-93, pres. 1993-94), Am. Cancer Soc. Union County N.J. (profl. edn. com.), Sigma Theta Tau (rec. sec. chpt. 1987). Home: 212 Elm St Cranford NJ 07016-3011

BROWN, RHONDA ROCHELLE, chemist, health facility administrator; b. Shelbyville, Ky., July 13, 1956; d. Clifton Theophilus and Fannie Mae (Lawson) B. BA in Chemistry, U. Md., 1978; MA, Central Mich. U., 1983; JD, No. Va. Law Sch., 1992. Analytical chemist Dept. Health and Mental Hygiene, Annapolis, Md., 1978-83; epidemiologist Dept. Health and Mental Hygiene, Balt., 1983-88; patent examiner U.S. Patent and Trademark Office, Xtal City, Va., 1989-90; freelance researcher New Carrollton, Md., 1990—; mem. Am. Chem. Soc., Washington, 1978-82; mem., exec. bd. Nat. Lawyers Guild, Washington, 1987—; pres. Voucher Express, 1993—; mediator Superior Ct., Washington, 1993—; legal advt. mgr. Sentinel Newspaper. subcommittee chmn. Anne Arundel County Task Force for Drug and Alcohol Abuse, 1979-80; pres., bd. mem. Md. Ornithological Soc., 1979-82; mem., exec. bd. Md. Condominium and Homeowners Assn., Rockville, Md., 1988-91. Named Outstanding Young Women of Am., 1983. Mem. Nat. Intellectual Propery Law Assn., Anne Arundel County Tennis Assn., Sigma Iota Epsilon.

BROWN, ROBIN KENT, quality control development analyst; b. Ft. Leonard Wood, Mo., Jan. 22, 1955; d. Myron Sanger and Joyce Ellen (Kent) Helman; m. James A. Walker III, June 17, 1978 (div. 1981); m. Lawrence Robert Brown, May 23, 1982; children: Roger Barry, Eric Russell. BA in Math., SUNY, Binghamton, 1980; MBA, Rider Coll., 1990. Supr. Stow Mfg., Binghamton, 1978-79; load forecaster N.Y. State Electric and Gas, Binghamton, 1979-80; actuary Kwasha-Lipton, Ft. Lee, N.J., 1980-83; quality control development analyst Reuters, Stamford, Conn., 1994—. Pres. Edgemont Elem. PTA, Scarsdale, N.Y., 1992-94, 2d v.p., 1991-92; bd. dirs. Cotswold Civic Assn., Scarsdale, 1991—; mem. umbrella com. New Compact for Learning, Scarsdale, 1993-94. Home: 6 Chedworth Rd Scarsdale NY 10583 Office: Reuters 263 Tresser Blvd Stamford CT 06901

BROWN, (JERENE) ROXANNE, sales executive; b. L.A., July 5, 1947; d. John Phillip and Margaret Leona (Dalrymple) Ortiz; m. Terry Lee Wood, May 7, 1966 (div. Sept. 1969); 1 child, Tiffany Christine Wood Suraco; m. Christopher Corey Brown, July 17, 1984; children: Jason Michael and John Charles (twins). Student, Casper Coll., 1977. Info. operator Gen. Telephone, Baldwin Park, Calif., 1965-67; long distance operator Gen. Telephone, Santa Maria, Calif., 1967-69; office mgr. Monroe Calculator, Las Vegas, Nev., 1972-74; mgr. Exch. Club, Salt Lake City, 1977-81, Pouches Inc., Salt Lake City, 1981-82; asst. producer KSTU TV 20, Salt Lake City, 1982-84; sec. ADVO - System, Inc., Orange, Calif., 1984-85, terr. sales rep., 1985-88; major account exec. ADVO - System, Inc., Garden Grove, Calif., 1988—; cons. Rice - Urmana Advt., Huntington Beach, Calif., 1989-91. Bd. dirs. ACLU, Salt Lake City, 1977; precinct worker Voter Registrar, Huntington Beach, 1988, Long Beach, Calif., 1990. Mem. ACLU, Platform Speakers Assn., Ad Club Orange County. Home: 6119 E Seaside Walk Long Beach CA 90803-5654

BROWN, ROXIE AUSTIN, operational officer; b. Statesville, N.C., July 25, 1948; d. Ralph Gaston and Nola Jean (Austin) B.; m. John Michael Cly, Apr. 21, 1994; 1 child, Sammy Austin; 1 adopted child, Veronica Jean. BA in Bus. Mgmt. cum laude, U. Md., 1985; Diploma in Joint/Strategic Intelligence, Nat. Def. U., 1988. Cert. collection mgmt. specialist, cert. collection ops. technician. Vietnamese linguist Dept. Def., Ft. Meade, Md., 1968-74; Chinese linguist Dept. Def., Ft. Meade, 1974-77; detached svc. officer Dept. Def., Berlin, Germany, 1977-80; mission mgr. Dept. Def., Bad Aibling, Germany, 1980-85; mgmt. and ops. staff officer Dept. Def., Ft. Meade, 1985-88, mgmt. evaluations staff, 1989-90, chief sys. planning and mgmt., 1990-93, cross program mgr., 1993—; leadership mgmt. program staff Dept. Def., Ft. Meade, 1990-94; adj. faculty Nat. Cryptologic Sch., 1990-94. Mem. Coll. Assn. (pres. 1983-85). Home: 104 Oak Ln NW Glen Burnie MD 21061

BROWN, RUBYE GOLSBY, educator, artist; b. Youngstown, Ohio; d. Clifford and Augusta Bell (Blalock) Golsby; m. Robert L. Brown; children: Harlean J. Preston, Charles, Louis, Carson, Gloria, Robin, Debbie. BA in Edn., Youngstown (Ohio) State Coll., 1956, BS, 1979, MS in Sociology, Edn. and Adminstrn., 1981; Cert. in History and Govtl. Econs., Youngstown State U., 1989. Credit mgr. Klivan's, Youngstown, 1953-56; sec. City Hall, Treasurer's Office, Youngstown, 1956; substitute tchr. Chaney High Sch., Youngstown, 1981-92; tchr. Round Rock High Sch., 1992—; instr. Austin (Tex.) Community Coll., 1993—; owner Custom Craft, Austin, 1993—; instr. in art, pub. speaker on crime and drug abuse. Mem. Ohio State Bd. Health, 1980—; pres. Mahoning County Courtwatch, 1987—; ednl. specialist Police Dept. Task Force, Youngstown, 1989—; vol. Olin E. Teaque Detention Ctr. Recipient Health Care award, Columbus State Bd. Health, 1988. Mem. Am. Soc. Curriculum and Devel., Am. Univ. and Coll. Women. Democrat. Baptist.

BROWN, RUTH ELIZABETH, educator; b. Chgo., Oct. 5, 1964; d. Charles Malvern and Hiranush (Mucceret) B. BS, Eastern Mich. Univ., 1989. Cert. secondary tchr., Mich. Tchr. Davis Middle Sch., Hillsdale, Mich., 1991, Hillsdale County Intermediate Sch. Dist., 1989-91, 92—; bookkeeper Stadium Sports Centre, Inc., Hillsdale, 1983—. Mem. Rep. Women, Hillsdale, 1991—. Mem. AAUW (sec. Hillsdale br. 1991—), Bus. and Profl. Women (newsletter editor, Wonderful Woman award 1993), Profl. Substitute Tchrs., Roller Skating Assn., Sigma Sigma Sigma (pres. Mich. 1991—, Pearl award 1985, Laurel award 1987). Presbyterian. Home: 45 Apple Run Ln Hillsdale MI 49242 Office: Hillsdale County Intermediate Dist 3471 Beck Rd Hillsdale MI 49242

BROWN, SALLY ANN, research scientist; b. N.Y.C., Sept. 8, 1959; d. Richard Daniel and Joann Ellen (Detschel) B. BS in Biology, SUNY, Geneseo, 1981, MA in Biology, 1989. Grad. tchg. asst. biology dept. SUNY,

Geneseo, 1983; rsch. technician dept. neurology U. Rochester, N.Y., 1984-88; rsch. assoc. dept. neurogerontology U. So. Calif., L.A., 1989—; presenter in field. Co-author: The Busal Ganglia II Structure and Function, 1987, Aging: The Universal Human Experience, 1987; contbr. articles to profl. jours. Participant, tutor Literacy Vols./ESL, Rochester, 1978; active Big Bro.-Big Sister Program, Rochester, 1985-88. Leone-Haggerty Meml. scholar Miller Place (N.Y.) PTA, 1977, Regents scholar N.Y. State Bd. Regents, Albany, 1978, Mensa Soc. scholar, L.A., 1989; Sci. and Math. fellow N.Y. State Higher Edn., Albany, 1983. Mem. Zero Population Growth, Sierra Club (issue activist 1986-87), L.A. County Mus. Art (sponsor). Home: PO Box 1033 Hermosa Beach CA 90254 Office: Univ So Calif Dept Neurogerontology Main Campus 0191 Los Angeles CA 90089

BROWN, SANDRA LEE, educational consultant, watercolorist; b. Chgo., July 9, 1943; d. Arthur Willard and Erma Emily (Lange) Boettcher; m. Ronald Gregory Brown, June 21, 1983; 1 child, Jon Michael. BA in Art and Edn., N.E. Ill. U., 1966; postgrad., No. Ill. U. Cert. K-9 tchr., Ill. Travel agt. Weiss Travel Bur., Chgo., 1959-66; tchr. Chgo. Sch. System, 1966-68; tchr. Schaumburg (Ill.) Sch. Dist. 54, 1968-94, creator coord. peer mentoring program for 1st-yr. tchrs., 1992—; mem. adv. bd. Peer Coaching and Mentoring Network, Chgo. suburban region, 1992—;peer cons. Sch. Dist. 54; cons. Yardstick Ednl. Svcs., Lake County, Ill.; dir., cons. Yardstick Ednl. Svcs., Lake County. Exhibited in group shows Women's Exhibit, McHenry County, ill., 1992-93; representer by Gallerie Stephanie, Chgo. Campaign chmn. for mayoral candidate,Grayslake, Ill., 1989; campaign chmn. for trustee Citizens for Responsible Govt., Grayslake, 1991. Mem. Delta Kappa Gamma (chmn. women in arts Gamma Gamma chpt. Ill. 1992—). Home: PO Box 242 Grayslake IL 60030 Office: Yardstick Ednl Svcs PO Box 242 Grayslake IL 60030

BROWN, SANDRA LOUISE PALMER, small business owner, consultant; b. Royal Oak, Mich.; d. Michael Peter and Elizabeth Louis (Hampers) Palmer; m. Gregory Jacob Brown, June 9, 1990. BBA, Iowa State U., 1982; M in Human Resource Edn., Boston U., 1994. Transp. analyst Mass. Bay Transp. Authority, Boston, 1982-85; tech. support rep. Project Software & Devel., Cambridge, Mass., 1985-86; self-employed computer cons. Newton, Mass., 1986-87; account rep. IBM, Boston, 1987-92; pres. Am. Cons. and Tng., Concord, Mass., 1991-93; v.p. mktg. Drake Beam Morin, Inc., 1993-94; prin. Applied Intervention, Concord, 1994—; assoc. Human Resource Mgmt. Group. Mem. Mus. Fine Arts, Boston, 1987—, Jr. League Boston, 1985—; vol. Young Life, Westwood, Mass., 1984-86, Mass. Spl. Olympics, Boston, 1988. Mem. ASTD, NAFE, Am. Mgmt. Assn., New England Human Resource Assn., Boston Human Resource Assn., Boston Computer Soc., Lexington (Mass.) Club, Nat. Speakers Assn., New England Speakers Assn. Republican.

BROWN, SARA SLEE, artist, designer; b. St. Louis, July 13, 1945; d. Vergil Nelson and Beth Ellen (Stoke) Slee; m. Bruce Philson Brown, Aug. 22, 1968; children: Gillian Christine, Aaron Philson. BFA, U. Mich., 1968; MA, U. Iowa, 1980, MFA, 1981. Visual artist self-employed, Iowa City, Iowa, 1972-85; displays/graphics Iowa City Pub. Libr., Iowa City, 1985—; v.p. Iowa City/Johnson County Arts Coun., 1984-89; coord. Artsfest Steering Com., Iowa City, 1985-89. Artist, painting in oils. Recipient Patrons award McCook (Nebr.) C.C., 1984. Home: 108 Washington Park Rd Iowa City IA 52245-4828 Office: Iowa City Pub Libr 123 S Linn St Iowa City IA 52240-1803

BROWN, SHARON CAROLYN, psychotherapist, educator; b. Chgo., Mar. 11, 1944; d. Wallace Edward and Bernice Beatrice (Wurglitz) B. RN, Columbus Hosp. Sch. Nursing, 1965; BA, Mundelein Coll., 1972; MS, George Williams Coll., 1981. RN. Supr. nursing staff devel. Columbus Hosp., Chgo., 1976-78, supr. neurol. sci., 1978-79; counselor 1st Ch. Community Counseling Ctr., Lombard, Ill., 1981-82; tchr. Coll. of DuPage, Glen Ellyn, Ill., 1982—; pvt. practice psychotherapy Wheaton, Ill., 1982—; co-founder Phoenix Rising, Wheaton, 1984—. Co-author: Living On Purpose, 1988. Office: Phoenix Rising PO Box 3088 Glen Ellyn IL 60138-3088

BROWN, SHARON ELIZABETH, software engineer; b. Lynn, Mass., Nov. 23, 1960; d. Leland James Brown and Vail (Wilkinson) Bartelson. BSChemE, U. Mass., 1982. Software engr. K&L Automation div. Daniel Industry, Tucson, 1983-86, sr. software engr., 1986-87, asst. mgr. software systems, 1987; software mgr. Daniel Automation, Houston, 1987-91; sr. software engr. Praxis Instruments, Inc., Houston, 1991-93, Dresser Measurement, Houston, 1993—. Mem. NSPE. Republican. Home: 5735 Henniker Dr Houston TX 77041-6589 Office: Dresser Industries Inc PO Box 42176 Houston TX 77242-2176

BROWN, SHARON GAIL, company executive, consultant; b. Chgo., Dec. 25, 1941; d. Otto and Pauline (Lauer) Schumacher; B in Gen. Studies, Roosevelt U.; m. Robert B. Ringo, Aug. 2, 1984; 1 dau. by previous marriage, Susan Ann. Info. analyst Internat. Minerals & Chems., Northbrook, Ill., 1966-71, programmer analyst, 1971-74; programmer analyst Procon Internat. Inc. subs. UOP Inc., Des Plaines, Ill., 1974-76, systems analyst, 1976-77, project leader, 1977-78; mgr. adminstrv. services, 1978-82; spl. cons. to pres. IPS Internat., Ltd., 1982-83; spl. cons. to pres. CEI Supply Co. div. Sigma-Chapman, Inc., 1984-87, ptnr. and co-founder Brown, Ringo & Assocs., 1987—; data processing cons. Mem. Buffalo Grove (Ill.) Youth Commn., 1978-82; mem. adv. com. UOP Polit. Action Com., 1979-82; Mem. Rep. Senatorial Com. Inner Circle. Mem. Am. Mgmt. Assn., Chgo. Council on Fgn. Rels., Lake Forest-Lake Bluff Hist. Soc. Home: 90 Atteridge Rd Lake Forest IL 60045-1713

BROWN, SHIRLEY, state legislator; b. Oshkosh, Wis., Oct. 2, 1952; m. Jack W. Brown; children: Angela, Jack. Owner billing collection agy.; mem. Fla. Ho. of Reps., 1992—; mem. Fla. State Coordinating Coun. Early Childhood, 1991. Active Bay Haven Sch. Basics Plus, mem. exec. bd., 1987; active Boy Scouts Am.; bd. dirs. Sarasota Family Counseling Ctr., Sarasota Friends Unity in Cmty., 1990—. Mem. Am. Bus. Women's Assn., Fla. Collectors Assn., Bus. and Profl. Women. Democrat. Presbyterian. Office: Fla House of Reps State Capitol Tallahassee FL 32301*

BROWN, SHIRLEY ANN, speech and language pathologist; b. Bklyn., Oct. 9, 1935; d. Hyman and Lillian (Fuhrer) Rubak; m. Ronald Wallace Brown, Sept. 29, 1956; children: Abbie Howard, Daniel Mark. BA, Bklyn. Coll., 1956, MA, 1961. Lic. speech/lang. pathologist, N.Y., N.J. Speech pathologist Richmond County CP Treatment Ctr., S.I., N.Y., 1956-59, Coney Island Hosp., Bklyn., 1959-61, Mendham Boro Schs. and Chatham Twp. Schs., 1962-67; pvt. practice home care speech pathologist various hosps. and med. facilities, 1967-79; dir. speech pathology dept. Englewood (N.J.) Hosp., 1974-92; speech pathologist Holy Name Hosp., Teaneck, N.J., 1992—, Home Health Care Agys., Bergen County, 1992—; clin. supr. comm. disorders grad. program Hunter Coll., N.Y.C., 1993—, Kean Coll., N.J., 1993—. Chair svc. and rehab. Am. Cancer Soc., Hackensack, N.J. Recipient Nat. Honor citation for Profl. Edn., Am. Cancer Soc., 1985, Crimson Sword award Am. Cancer Soc., 1989. Mem. Am. Speech. Lang. and Hearing Assn. (cert., congl. action com., state chair career info., Continuing Edn. award 1983—, Outstanding Clin. Achievement award 1985), N.J. Speech, Lang. and Hearing Assn. Home: 6 Sisson Ter Tenafly NJ 07670-1810 Office: Holy Name Hosp Speech Pathology Dept 718 Teaneck Rd Teaneck NJ 07666-4281

BROWN, SHIRLEY MARK, retired science administrator; b. Phila., Apr. 25, 1924; d. Paul and Bertha Evelyn (Zucker) Mark; m. Bernard Beau, Sept. 1, 1947; children: Eric Joel, Aimee Susan. BA, Temple U., Phila., 1945, MA, 1947. Rsch. chemist U. Mich., Ann Arbor, 1947-50; instr. Upsala Coll., East Orange, 1960-74; acad. planner Rutgers U., New Brunswick, N.J., 1974-80, assoc. dir. Waksman Inst., 1980-88; exec. dir. Rutgers Rsch. and Ednl. Found., New Brunswick, 1980-94; assoc. dir. Office of Corp. Liaison and Technol. Transfer Rutgers U., 1988-91, adminstr. corp. contracts, 1991-94. sec. Joint Civic Com. Westfield 1962-66, Com. for Human Rights Westfield 1967-70; publicity chairperson. PTA Westfield 1963-67. Mem. LWV, Assn. Univ. Technol. Mgrs., Nat. Coun. Univ. Rsch. Adminstrs., Soc. Rsch. Adminstrs. Home: 146 Tudor Oval Westfield NJ 07090-2245

BROWN, SUSAN MARY, advertising executive; b. Chgo., Oct. 4, 1946; d. Jack William and Virginia Ruth (Porter) Baasel; m. Frank A. Brown, Feb. 12, 1966 (div.); 1 child, Kerry. Student, U. Kans., 1964-66. Supr. billing Mast. Advt. & Pub., Inc., Overland Park, Kans., 1973-78, mgr. nat. Yellow Pages svc., 1978-82, dir. nat. Yellow Pages sales, 1982-92; v.p., dir. ops. Ketchum Communications, Inc., 1992—. Vol. Am. Cancer Soc., Am. Heart Assn., Safehome. Republican. Lutheran. Office: Ketchum Communications Inc 7015 Coll Blvd Overland Park KS 66211

BROWN, SUSIE WARRINGTON, foundation executive; b. Lambert, Miss., Apr. 18, 1952; d. Richard Leon and Mary Josephine (White) Warrington; children: Melissa Jo, Ronny Leon. BBA, Delta State U., 1985; M of Health Sci., Wichita State U., 1987. Exec. dir. Harvey County United Way, Halstead, Kans., 1985-87, United Way Washington County, Greenville, Miss., 1987-90, United Way Kankakee (Ill.) County, 1991-94, United Way of Greater Utica, N.Y., 1994—; co-founder, dir. Christmas in Apr., Kankakee, 1991—; dir. Comty. Resource Ctr., Kankakee, 1992—; chmn. mayor's adv. com. Comty. Econ. Devel., Kankakee, 1994. Treas. Eastside Bus. Coun., Kankakee, 1991—. Recipient Point of Light award Pres. George Bush, 1990, Key to the City award Mayor Frank Self, 1992, Larry Power Comty. Excellence award Bourbonnais C. of C., 1994, Point of Light award Congressman Tom Ewing, 1992; Gus Shea Meml. scholar United Way Am., 1993. Mem. Manteno C. of C. (bd. dirs. 1992—), Kiwanis (com. chair 1991—). Baptist. Home: 97 Prospect St Utica NY 13501 Office: United Way Greater Utica 270 Genesee St Utica NY 13502-4617

BROWN, SUZANNE WILEY, museum director; b. Cheyenne, Wyo., Aug. 28, 1938; d. Robert James and Catharine Helen (Schroeder) Wiley; BS with honors, U. Wyo., 1960, MS, 1964; postgrad. U. Cin. Med. Sch., 1965-66, U. Ill., 1969-72; m. Ralph E. Brown, July 19, 1968; 1 dau., Nina M. Rsch. asst. Harvard Med. Sch., 1962-63; rsch. asst. U. Cin. Med. Sch., 1964-65; sr. lab. asst. U. Chgo., 1966-67; rsch. assoc. U. Colo. Med. Sch., 1968; teaching asst. U. Ill., 1971-73; exec. asst. Chgo. Acad. Scis., 1974-82, asst. dir., 1982-84, assoc. dir., 1984-90, ret.; mem. adv. bd. Mitchell Indian Mus., Evanston, Ill., Fechin Inst., Taos, N.Mex.; mem. collectors com. Field Mus., Chgo. NDEA fellow, 1960-62. Mem. Achievement Rewards Coll. Scis. (corr. sec.), Brookfield Zool. Soc. (bd. govs.), Phi Beta Kappa, Sigma Xi, Phi Kappa Phi.

BROWN, TERESA ELAINE, state legislator; b. Oct. 6, 1953; d. Waid Stanley and Elaine Agusta (Swift) Fosburg; children: Christopher, Delaine. Student, Alliance Coll., Edinboro U. Legis. aide 6th Legis. Dist., Meadville, Pa., 1979-86, 5th Legis. Dist., Meadville, 1987; per diem employee Crawford County, Meadville, 1988-89, asst. dir. tax claim bur., 1989-90; mem. Pa. Ho. of Reps., Titusville, 1991—; mem. appropriations com., transp. com.; sec. Legis. Office for Rsch. Liaison; co-chmn. Emergency Svcs. Outreach Group; active Fire Fighters Caucus, Task Force on Jobs and Bus. Expansion, Task Force on Environ., Task Force on Welfare Reform, Anti-gambling Caucus. Former editor Crawford County GOP Newsletter. Former asst. coord. Cambridge Springs (Pa.) Little League and Little Gridders; former mem. Miss Crawford County Pageant Scholarship Exec. Bd., Cambridge Springs Presbyn. Food Pantry; mem. adv. bd. U. Pitts., Titusville; past dist. leader GOP Cambridge Dist.; active Cambridge Springs Presbyn. Ch., also former mem. bd. deacons; active Meadville Med. Ctr. Aux., Pa. Ag Reps., Craford County GOP Exec. Bd., Northwest Coun. Rep. Women, Capitol Area Coun. Rep. Women in Govt. Mem. NRA, Bus. and Profl. Women, Meadville Sportsmen Club, Pa Ruffled Grouse Soc., Kiwanis Club of Cambridge Springs. Home: 209 S Franklin St Titusville PA 16354-1739 also: 697 Terrace St Apt 21 Meadville PA 16335 Office: Pa Ho of Reps State Capitol Harrisburg PA 17120

BROWN, TINA, magazine editor; b. Maidenhead, Eng., Nov. 21, 1953; d. George Hambley and Bettina Iris Mary (Kohr) B.; m. Harold Evans, Aug. 20, 1981; children: George Frederick, Isabel Harriet. M.A., Oxford U. Columnist Punch Mag., London, 1978; editor in chief Tatler Mag., London, 1979-83, Vanity Fair Mag., N.Y.C., 1984-92; editor New Yorker mag., N.Y.C., 1992—. Author: (play) Under the Bamboo Tree, 1973 (Sunday Times Drama award), (play) Happy Yellow, 1977, (book) Loose Talk, 1979, (book) Life As A Party, 1983. Named Most Promising Female Journalist, recipient Kathrine Pakenham prize Sunday London Times, 1973; named Young Journalist of Yr., 1978, Mag. Editor of Yr. Advt. Age mag., 1988. Office: The New Yorker 20 W 43rd St New York NY 10036-7440*

BROWN, TRINITA E., lawyer; b. N.Y.C., June 8, 1965. BA, Brown U., 1987; postgrad., Oxford U., 1988; JD, Am. U., 1990. Legis. aide to Rep. Donald Payne, 1993—; counsel Com. Pub. Works and Transp. Office: 2165 Rayburn House Office Bldg Washington DC 20515*

BROWN, TRISH EILEEN, artist; b. Tampa, Fla., Mar. 22, 1958; d. Burrell Joseph and Katharine Stowell (Weekly) B. BFA in Art History, U. South Fla., 1993. Photo asst. M&M Photo, Tampa, 1987-88, Silhouettes Studio, Tampa, 1989; flight attendant Pan Am. World Airways, N.Y.C., 1989-91; visual artist, sculptor; judge John's Seafood Festival, Maderia Beach, Fla., 1993; mem. artist alliance, Fla. Ctr. for Contemporary Art; presenter workshops in field. Artist: worked with HIV Women/AIDS Artreach phase 3, sculpture, 1994; group shows include Centre Gallery, U. So. Fla., 1994, U. Mobile Ala., 1994, Ctr. for Contemporary Art, Tampa, 1994, Fla. State U. Gallery and Mus., Tallahassee, 1994, Valencia C.C., Orlando, Fla., 1993, Tandemn Art Ctr., Venice, Fla., 1993, Punta Gorda (Fla.) Art Ctr., 1994, 4th Ann. Fla. Biennal, others; works included in pvt. collections; contbr. articles to profl. jours.; presenter festivals and confs. Vol. art/crafts instr. Substance Abused Mothers Against Drugs, Tampa, 1993; vol. docent Salvador Dali Mus., St. Petersburg, Fla., 1986-88; mem. Women's Caucus for Art, Nat. Women's Mus. Recipient Best of Show award for fibers/weaving, Fla. State Fair, 1988, 1st, 2nd and 3rd prizes, 1985-88, Hillsborough County Emerging Artist award. Democrat.

BROWN, TRISHA, dancer; b. Aberdeen, Wash., Nov. 25, 1936. B.A. in Dance, Mills Coll., Calif.; Ph.D. hon. in Fine Arts, Oberlin Coll. Founder, pres. Trisha Brown Dance Co., New York, NY, 1970—; founding mem. Judson Dance Theatre; choreographer Grand Union Improvisation Group, 1970-76; lectr. Mills Coll., Calif., Reed Coll., Oreg., NYU, Goucher Coll., Md., Carnegie Mellon U., Pa.; conductor workshops and seminars throughout world. Dancer worldwide; choreographer: Untitled, 1961, Trillium, 1962, Lightfall, 1963, Untitles Duet, 1963, Part of a Tango, 1963, Target, 1964, Rulegame Five, 1964, Motor, 1965, Homemade, 1965, Inside, 1966, Skunk Cabbage, 1967, Saltgrass and Waders, 1967, Medicine Dance, 1967, Snapshot, 1968, Ballet, 1968, Falling Duet, 1968, Sky Map, 1968, Dance with the Duck Head, 1968, Yellow Valley, 1968, Leaning Duets, 1970, The Stream, 1970, Man Walking Down the Side of a Building, 1970, Accumulation, 1971, Walking on the Wall, 1971, Leaning Duets II, 1971, Falling Duet II, 1971, Rummage Sale and the Floor of the Forest, 1971, Planes, 1971, Roof Piece, 1971, Primary Accumulation, 1972, Accumulating Pieces, 1973, Group Accumulation, 1973, Roof and Fire Piece, 1973, Spanish Dance, 1973, Structured Pieces, 1973, Figure 8, 1973, Drift, 1974, Spiral, 1974, Pamplona Stones, 1975, Locus, 1975, Line Up, 1976, Glacial Decoy, 1979, Opal Loop, 1980, Son of Gone Fishin', 1981, Set and Reset, 1984 (N.Y. Dance and Performance award 1984), Lateral Pass, 1985 (N.Y. Dance and Performance award 1986), Carmen, 1986, Newark, 1987, Astral Convertible, 1989, For M.G.: The Movie, 1991, Astral Converted, 1991, Another Story: As in Falling, 1993, If You Could See Me, 1994; featured TV show, Sta. WNET-TV, N.Y.C., Dance in America, Sta. WGBH-TV, Boston, Dancing on the Edge, Sta. WGBH-TV, Boston, Making Dances, Sta. WGBH-TVm Boston; drawings exhibited Venice Biennale, Toulon Museum; group exhibition: Numerals: Mathematical Concepts in Contemporary Art, Drawings: The Pluralist Decade, New Notes for New Dance, Art and Dance: Images From the Modern Dialogue; Avant-garde Theater and Dance Notes & Scores curated by Robert Rauschenberg; film Accumulation with Talking plus Watermotor, KCET, Los Angeles, and KTCA, Mpls. Fellow Guggenheim Found., 1975, 84, NEA Creative Artists Svc. Program, 1977, 81-84; MacArthur fellow, 1991; grantee NEA, N.Y. State Coun. on Arts, other founds. and corps.; recipient creative arts award Brandeis U., 1982, Dance Mag. award, 1987, Chevalier dans L'Ordre des Arts & des Lettres, Govt. France, 1988, Samuel H. Scripps Am. Dance Festival award, 1994. Home and Office: 225 Lafayette St Ste 807 New York NY 10012-4015

BROWN, VALERIE, state legislator; b. Kansas City, Mo., Oct. 30, 1945; divorced; 1 child, Lisa Davis. BS, U. Mo., 1972, MA, 1978. Former mayor City of Sonoma; mem. Calif. State Assembly, 1993—; marriage, family and child counselor. Mem. Sonoma Valley C. of C. (v.p.). Democrat. Presbyterian. Home: 299 1st St West Sonoma CA 95476 Office: Rm 2130 State Capital Sacramento CA 95814*

BROWN, VALERIE ANNE, psychiatric social worker, educator; b. Elizabeth, N.J., Feb. 28, 1951; d. William John and Adelaide Elizabeth (Krasa) B.; BA summa cum laude (fellow), C.W. Post Coll., 1972; MSW (Silberman scholar), Hunter Coll., 1975. Diplomate Am. Bd. Examiners, Am. Bd. Clin. Social Work, Nat. Assn. Soc. Work; cert. addictions specialist, cert. master hypnotherapist. Social work intern Greenwich House Counseling Center, N.Y.C., 1973-74, Metro Cons. Center, N.Y.C., 1974-75; sr. psychiat. social worker, co-adminstr. Saturday Clinic, Essex County Guidance Center, East Orange, N.J., 1975-80; pvt. practice psychiat. social work, psychotherapy, 1979—; sr. psychiat social worker John E. Runnells Hosp., Berkeley Heights, N.J., 1980-86; dir. social work Northfield Manor, West Orange, N.J., 1987; clin. coord. Project Portals East Orange Gen. Hosp., 1987-88; asst. dir. ARS/Century House Riverview Med. Ctr., Red Bank, N.J., 1988-93; sr. clin. case mgmt. specialist Prudential Ins. Co., Woodbridge, N.J., 1993-93; clin. dir. Greenhouse-KMC, Lakewood, N.J., 1994—; tech. advisor Nat. Comm. Network, 1988—; instr. Brookdale Coll., 1991—; co-founder Women's Growth Ctr., Cedar Grove, N.J., 1979; counselor Passaic Drug Clinic, 1978-80; field instr. Fairleigh Dickinson U., Madison, N.J., 1981-86, Brookdale Coll., 1989-92; field supr. Union Coll., Cranford, N.J., 1986; instr. Sch. Social Work, NYU, N.Y.C., 1980-83, asst. prof., 1983-85; evaluator Intoxicated Driver Resource Ctr., Essex County, N.J., 1987-88. Alt. Monmouth County profl. adv. bd. Mem. NASW, Psi Chi, Pi Gamma Mu, Sigma Tau Delta. Office: 20 Ellsworth Ct Red Bank NJ 07701-2002

BROWN, VANESSA, actress, journalist; b. Vienna, Austria, Mar. 24, 1928; d. Nah and Auna (Butterman) Brind; children: Cathy Lisa Sandrich, David Michael Sandrich. BA, UCLA, 1949. Journalist L.A. Times; exec. prodr., writer, documentary film maker; prodr. Career Awareness Audio and Video Current Prodns.; Roles in plays including The Seven Year Itch, The Prisoner of the Second Avenue, As You Like It, The Philanderer, Door to a Room, Pygmalion, Gigi; artist oil paintings and watercolors; internat. broadcaster Outlook, USIA's Voice of Am., 1962-82. Actress with roles in films including Bless the Beast and the Children, Rosie, The Bad and the Beautiful, The Fighter, The Basketball Fix, Three Husbands, The Heiress, Mother Wore Tights, The Late George Apley, The Ghost and Mrs. Muir, Girl of the Limberlost, Youth Runs Wild; roles in TV include True Colors, The Wonder Years, Murder She Wrote, Twilight Zone, Dallas, Call to Glory, General Hospital, All That Glitters, My Favorite Husband, Phantom of the Open Heart, Missing Heirs, others. Mem. TV, Radio, Newspaper Com. of Am. (chair 1990—). Democrat. Jewish.

BROWN, WARNELLA CHARLIE, speech and language pathologist; b. Summit, Miss., Jan. 4, 1960; d. Richard and Charlie B. (Lee) B. BS, U. So. Miss., 1980; MS, Columbia U., 1990; postgrad., L.I. U., 1993—. Speech therapist N.Y.C. Bd. Edn., 1982-83; elem. tchr. Redeemer Bapt. Sch., L.A., 1984-85; speech therapist N.Y.C. Bd. Edn., 1986—, St. Mary's Hosp. for Children, 1993—; speech therapist Vis. Nurses Assn., Bklyn., 1992. Active PTA United Fedn. of Tchrs. of N.Y.C. Mem. AAUW, Am. Speech and Hearing Assn., Nat. Assn. for Secondary Sch. Prins., Nat. Assn. Elem. Sch. Prins., Nat. Black Speech, Lang., and Hearing Assn., N.Y. State Speech, Lang. and Hearing Assn., N.Y.C. Black Speech, Lang. and Hearing Assn., ASCD, Univ. So. Miss. Alumni Assn., Tchrs. Coll. Alumni Assn., Phi Delta Kappa, Eagles (chpt. 68), Amanath Ct., Queen of South Palace, Alpha Kappa Alpha Sorority, Inc. Home: 2795 Shore Pkwy 4G Brooklyn NY 11223

BROWN, WENDY ELAINE, communications consultant; b. Los Alamos, N.Mex., Apr. 28, 1956; d. Leon J. and Dorothy (Stern) B.; m. Richard Swanson; 1 child, Tasmin Amanda Swanson. BA, Northwestern U., 1978. Software engr. Prime Computer Inc., Natick, Mass., 1978-80; systems programmer Dialcom, Silver Spring, Md., 1980-85; systems programmer, analyst APA, Falls Church, Va., 1985-86; mem. tech. staff Corp. for Open Systems, McLean, Va., 1986-89; cons. PSC Internat. Inc., McLean, 1989—. Author OSI Dictionary of Acronyms, 1992. Mem. IEEE Computer Soc., ACM, Assn. for Computing Machinery. Democrat. Jewish. Avocations: sewing, electronic networking. Home: 9417 Russell Rd Silver Spring MD 20910 Office: 8260 Greensboro Dr Ste 330 Mc Lean VA 22102

BROWN, WENDY WEINSTOCK, nephrologist; b. N.Y.C., Dec. 9, 1944; d. Irving and Pearl (Levack) Weinstock; m. Barry David Brown, May 2, 1971; children: Jennifer Faye, Joshua Reuben, Julie Aviva, Rachel Ann. BA, U. Mass., 1966; MD, Med. Coll. of Pa., 1970. Am. Bd. Internal Medicine, 1977. Intern U. Ill. Affiliated Hosps., Chgo., 1970-71; resident in internal medicine The Med. Coll. Wis. Affiliated Hosps., Milw., 1971-74; gen. practitioner Vogelweh (W. Germany) Health Clinics, 1975-76; fellow in nephrology Med. Coll. of Wis. Milw. County Med. Complex, Milw., 1976-78; staff physician St. Louis VA Med Ctr., 1978—, acting chief, hemodialysis sect., 1983-85, chief dialysis/renal sect., 1985-90; dir. clin. nephrology, 1990—; staff physician St. Louis U. Hosps., 1978—, St. Louis City Hosp., 1982-85, St Mary's Health Ctr., St. Louis, 1994—; assoc. prof. internal medicine St. Louis U. Health Sci. Ctr., 1985—. Reviewer Clin. Nephrology, Am. Jour. Kidney Disease, Jour Am. Geriatric Soc., Jour. Geriatric Nephrology and Urology, also mem. editl. bd.; contbr. articles to profl. jours. Mem. adv. coun. Mo. Kidney Program, 1985—, chmn., 1988-89; numerous positions Nat. Kidney Found., 1984—; bd. dirs. Nat. Kidney Found. Ea. Mo. and Metro East, Inc., 1980—; bd. dirs. Combined Health Appeal Greater St. Louis, Inc., 1988, pres., 1989—; bd. dirs. Combined Health Appeal Am., 1991—. Recipient Upjohn Achievement award Med. Coll. Wis. Affiliated Hosps. 1972, St. Louis YWCA Cert. of Leadership 1989, Chmn.'s award Nat. Kidney Found. of Ea. Mo. and Metro East 1990, Nat. Kidney Found., Washington 1990; named Casual Corner Career Woman of the Yr. 1986, Combined Health Appeal of Am. Vol. of Yr. 1991. Mem. Am. Soc. Nephrology, Internat. Soc. Nephrology, Am. Coll. Physicians, Coun. on the Kidney in Cardiovascular Disease, Am. Heart Assn., St. Louis Soc. Am. Med. Women's Assn., St. Louis Internists (v.p. 1983-84, pres. 1984-85), Women in Nephrology, Internat. Soc. for Peritoneal Dialysis, Am. Geriatrics Soc., Alpha Omega Alpha. Home: 100 Frontenac Frst Saint Louis MO 63131-3235 Office: Saint Louis VAMC 915 N Grand Blvd Saint Louis MO 63106-1621

BROWN-COCHRANE, ANDREA KANE, mortgage banking executive; b. Dhahran, Saudi Arabia, Jan. 30, 1962; came to U.S., 1963; d. Andrew Jackson and Elizabeth Jeannine (Kane) Brown; m. Mark Anthony Cochrane, June 29, 1985; 1 child, Dominic Mario. BS, Humboldt State U., 1985; MBA, U. Phoenix, 1990. Mgmt. trainee Western Fed. Savs., Marina Del Rey, Calif., 1985-86, computer systems and inventory control specialist, 1986-87; commitment coord. Calif. Fed. Bank., L.A., 1987-89, underwriter, 1989-90, assoc. underwriter, sales coord. secondary mktg., 1990-91, asst. sec., sect. head secondary mktg., 1991-92; asst. v.p., mgr. loan shipping dept. Calif. Fed. Bank, L.A., 1992-93; v.p., wholesale ops. mgr. BancBoston Mortgage Corp., 1994—. Mem. NAFE, Assn. Profl. Mortgage Women, Calif. Mortgage Bankers Assn. (edn. com.), Network for Profl. Devel., U. Phoenix Alumni Network (pres. 1991-92). Republican. Roman Catholic.

BROWNE, ANN APRIL, purchasing manager; b. Washington, Apr. 9, 1945; d. Benjamin and Sarah (Barr) Mudrick. BA in Bus. Mgmt., Eckerd Coll., 1987. Cert. purchasing mgr. Purchasing mgr. Gen. Kinetics, Rockville, Md., 1972-73; assoc. buyer Control Data Corp., Rockville, 1973-74; outside sales rep. Mid Atlantic Industries, Bladensburg, Md., 1974, U.S. C. of C., San Antonio, 1975; inside sales coord. Frabimore Equipment & Controls, Inc., Elk Grove Village, Ill., 1976-77; customer svc. rep. Viracon, Inc., Bensenville, Ill., 1977; purchasing mgr. Vectrol div. Westinghouse Elec. Corp., Oldsmar, Fla., 1978-83; purchasing agt. Helen Ellis Meml. Hosp., Tarpon Springs, Fla., 1987—. Mem. Material Mgmt. Assn. of Fla., Nat. Assn. Purchasing Mgmt. (cert.), Phi Theta Kappa.

BROWNE, JOY, psychologist; b. New Orleans, Oct. 24, 1950; d. Nelson and Ruth (Strauss) B.; Carter Thwaitt, June 9, 1966 (div. 1979); 1 child, Patience. BA, Rice U.; PhD, Northeastern U.; postgrad., Tufts U. Registered psychologist, Mass. With research/optics dept. Sperry Rand, Boston, 1966-68; engr. space program Itek, Boston, 1968-70; head social services dept. Boston Redevel. Authority, 1970-71; staff psychologist South Shore Counselling Assocs., Boston, 1971-82; on-the-air psychologist Sta. WITS, Boston, 1978-82, Sta. KGO, San Francisco, 1982-84; host, news Sta. KCBS, San Francisco, 1984-85; on-the-air psychologist Sta. WABC, N.Y.C., 1985-87, ABC Talkradio, N.Y.C., 1987—; dir. Town of Hull Adolescent Outreach Program. Author: The Used Car Game, 1971, The Research Experience, 1976, Nobody's Perfect, 1988, Why They Don't Call When They Say They Will and Other Mixed Signals, 1989. Mem. Am. Psychol. Assn., Phi Kappa Phi (Communicator of Yr.). Office: WOR Radio Network 1440 Broadway New York NY 10018

BROWNE, RENEE CELESTE, chemical engineer; b. Boston, May 29, 1963; d. Ralph Francis Jr. and Wilma Annette (Washington) B. BSChemE, U. So. Calif., 1985. Registered profl. engr., Tex. Govt. coord. Sungro Chemicals, L.A., 1986; environ. engr. Jacobs Engring. Group, Washington, 1987-88; process engr. Jacobs Engring., Houston, 1988—. Mem. AIChE.

BROWNE, SANDRA RAYE, counselor, consultant; b. Ft. Worth, Tex., Sept. 17, 1944; d. Thomas Leo and Willa Mae (Spencer) Raye; m. Stanley H. Browne, Feb. 28, 1987; children: William, Chandelle, Steven, Michael. BS in Liberal Studies, SUNY, 1987; MEd in Counseling and Guidance, U. Tex., 1992. Lic. prof. counselor. Pilot, wingrider, owner The Flying Pierces Airshow, Sebring, Fla., 1966-78; real estate broker El Paso, Tex., 1979-81; owner, cons./counselor Performance Consulting Assn., 1981—. Author poetry. Campaign mgr. Suzie Ayar for Mayor, El Paso, 1989; founder Amigo Airsho. Named Aviation Person of Yr., El Paso Aviation Assn., 1983, Outstanding Vol. of Yr., Insight Seminars, Santa Monica, Calif., 1985; named to El Paso Aviation Hall of Fame, 1993. Mem. The Exec. Forum, Am. Counseling Assn., Am. Mental Health Counselor's Assn., Kappa Delta Pi, others. Office: Performance Cons/Counseling Ste 103 4141 Pinnacle El Paso TX 79902

BROWNE-MCDONALD, GAIL KAY, accountant; b. Albany, Calif., Sept. 1, 1953; d. Floyd Edward and Marjorie Evelyn Browne; m. James Alan McDonald, Mar. 1, 1975 (div. Mar. 1977); 1 child, Brandon Casey. BBA in Acctg., U. Hawaii, Manoa, 1985; MS in Taxation, Golden Gate U., 1992. CPA, Calif. Adminstr., fiscal officer U. Hawaii, Manoa, Honolulu, 1985-87; CPA Schrambling and Assocs., San Francisco, 1987—. Treas. NOW, Honolulu, 1986-87. Mem. Commonwealth Club. Democrat. Office: Schrambling and Assocs One Market 1770 Steuart Tower San Francisco CA 94105

BROWNE-MILLER, ANGELA CHRISTINE, author, educator, social research association executive; b. Whittier, Calif., June 26, 1952; d. Lee Winston and Louisa Francesca (de Angelis) Browne; m. Richard Louis Miller, Feb. 22, 1986; 1 child, Evacheska. BA in Biology and Lit. with honors, U. Calif., Santa Cruz, 1976; postgrad. in spl. edn., Sonoma State U., 1976-77; MSW, U. Calif., Berkeley, 1981, MPH, 1983, Dr. Social Welfare, 1983, PhE in Edn., 1992. Lic. clin. social worker, Calif. Child and family counselor Clearwater Ranch Children's Home, Mendocino County, Calif., 1976-77; conselor, spl. edn. tchr. Bachman Hill Sch., Mendocino County, Calif., 1977-78; substitute tchr. Marin County (Calif.) Sch. Dist., 1978-79; founder Metatech/Metasome Corp. Services, 1982—; also bd. dirs. Whole Care Inst.; rsch. dir. Cokenders Alcohol and Drug Inst., Emeryville, Calif., 1983-89; exec. cons. Parkside Med. Svcs., Chgo., 1989-90; policy and program analyst White House Conf. on Families, Washington, summer 1980 to spring 1981; research analyst Office for Families, Adminstrn. for Children Youth and Families HHS, 1981, grant reader, 1982, 84, 85, 86; day care program evaluator, budget cons. care programs, San Francisco Bay area, summer 1983; lectr. Sch. Social Welfare, Haas Sch. Bus. U. Calif., Berkeley, 1984—; program cons. Wilbur Hot Springs Health Sanctuary, 1984-87; pres. Cokenders Alcohol and Drug Inst., Emeryville, 1986-90; lectr. Sch. Pub. Policy U. Calif., Berkeley, 1986-88; guest White House Conf. for a Drug-Free Am., 1987-88; lectr. in field. Author: The Day Care Dilemma, 1990, Working Dazed, 1991, Transcending Addiction, 1992, Gestalting Addiction, 1993, Learning to Learn, 1994; contbr. numerous articles to profl. jours.; panelist numerous nat. radio and TV appearances. Pub. dir. Californians for Drug Free Youth Conf., 1986; mem. Nat. Task Force on Drug Abuse, 1984. Recipient Presdl. Mgmt. Internship award, 1982; grantee Adminstrn. for Children Youth and Family Welfare, 1980; NIMH postdoctoral fellow, 197-89. Mem. Am. Pub. Health Assn., Nat. Assn. Social Workers, Edn. Adminstrs. and Rsch. Assn., Assn. Labor and Mgmt. Alcoholism Counselors and Adminstrs., Am. Acad. Psychotherapists, Mensa. Office: 98 Main St # 315 Belvedere Tiburon CA 94920-2566

BROWNER, CAROL, federal official; d. Michael Browner and Isabella Harty Hugues; m. Michael Podhorzer; 1 child, Zachary. Grad., U. Fla., 1977, JD, 1979. Gen. counsel govt. ops. com. Fla. Ho. of Reps.; with Citizen Action, Washington; chief legis. aide environ. issues to Sen. Lawton Chiles, legis. dir. to Sen. Al Gore, Jr., 1988-91; sec. Dept. Environ. Regulation, Fla., 1991-93; adminstr. EPA, Washington, 1993—. Office: Environmental Protection Agency Office of the Administrator 401 M St SW Washington DC 20460-0001*

BROWN-HEIGHT, PATRICIA ELLEN, English language educator; b. N.Y.C., Sept. 15, 1952; d. James Copeland and Alma Jean (Perry) Brown; 1 child, Omar Rasheem Brown-Height. BS, NYU, 1974; MS, CUNY, 1976. Grad. asst. NYU, N.Y.C., 1983-86; lectr. La Guardia C.C., Long Island City, N.Y., 1986—; dir. Am. social history jr. high sch. project CUNY, N.Y.C., 1990-92; learning disability counselor Coll. of S.I., CUNY, 1993—; mem. adv. coun. minority project on teaching profession curriculum devel. CUNY, 1990-92. Broadcaster radio program Good Reading from LaGuardia, WNYE, 1987; producer video: Conducting A Writing Conference for the Learning Disabled Student, 1989. Officer at large LaGuardia C.C. chpt. Profl. Staff Congress, N.Y.C., 1990—. Mem. MLA, Nat. Coun. Tchrs. English, N.Y. State English Coun., N.Y. Alliance of Black Sch. Educators. Liberal. Home: 102 Osgood Ave Staten Island NY 10304 Office: La Guardia CC 31-10 Thomson Ave Long Island City NY 11101

BROWNING, CAROL ANNE, pediatrician, educator; b. Appleton, Wis., June 1, 1936; d. Bertie Lee and Margaret (Loscher) B. BA, Oberlin Coll., 1958; MD, U. Wis., 1962. Diplomate Am. Bd. Pediatrics, Am. Bd. Neonatal-Perinatal Medicine. Intern Highland-Alameda County Hosp., Oakland, Calif., 1962-63; resident Children's Hosp. East Bay, Oakland, 1963-65; pediatrician Kaiser-Permanente Med. Ctr., Walnut Creek, Calif., 1965-68; fellow in neonatology Stanford U., 1968-70; neonatologist Med. Coll. Wis., Milw., 1970-89; mem. staff Sinai Samaritan Med. Ctr., Milw., 1970—; assoc. prof. pediatrics U. Wis. Sch. Medicine, Milw., 1989—; bd. dirs. Perinatal Found., Madison, Wis., 1988—; med. dir. NICU, 1991—. Bd. dirs. Unitarian Ch. North, Mequon, Wis., 1987-89, St. Francis Children's Ctr., Milw., 1987-90. Fellow Am. Acad. Pediatrics; mem. Nat. Perinatal Assn., Wis. Assn. for Perinatal Care (pres. 1976-77, Callon-Leonard award 1989). Democrat. Office: Sinai Samaritan Med Ctr 2000 W Kilbourn Milwaukee WI 53233

BROWNING, DEBORAH LEA, lawyer; b. Helena, Ark., Aug. 16, 1955; d. William Herman Jr. and Mildred Kate (York) B. BS, U. Ala., 1976; diploma, Oxford U., 1982; JD, U. Tex., 1984. Bar: Tex. 1984, D.C. 1985. Drug abuse counselor Aletheia House, Birmingham, Ala., 1972-76; in retail mgmt. Joskes of Houston, 1976-78; state parole officer Tex. Bd. Pardons and Parole, Houston, 1978-81; litigation clk. Harris County Dist. Attys. Office, Houston, 1983; appellate clk. Travis County Dist. Attys. Office, Austin, Tex., 1984; litigation assoc Hogan & Hartson, Washington, 1984—; pro bono atty. Internat. Human Rights Law Group, Washington, 1984-93, acting legal dir., 1986-89; pro bono atty. Lawyers Com. for Human Rights, 1993. Author: A Supplemental Report On The Chilean Plebiscite, 1988; co-author: Chile: The Plebiscite and Beyond, 1989, First Steps After Stroessner: An Analysis of the 1989 Paraguayan Elections, 1989; editor Am. Jour. Criminal Law, 1982-84. Vol. atty. Women's Legal Def. Fund., Washington, 1987-88; dir. Chile Election Observor Project, Paraguay Working Group; crime prevention coord. East End. Civic Assn., Houston, 1979-81. Mem. ABA (co-vice chair internat. human rights com., sect. internat. law and practice), Women's Bar Assn., Am. Soc. Internat. Law. Home: 7204 Central Ave Takoma Park MD 20912 Office: Hogan & Hartson 555 13th St NW Washington DC 20004-1109

BROWNING, NORMA LEE (MRS. RUSSELL JOYNER OGG), journalist; b. Spickard, Mo., Nov. 24, 1914; d. Howard R. and Grace (Kennedy) B.; m. Russell Joyner Ogg, June 12, 1938. A.B., B.J., U. Mo., 1937; M.A. in English, Radcliffe Coll., 1938. Reporter Los Angeles Herald-Express, 1942-43; with Chgo. Tribune, from 1944, Hollywood columnist, 1966-75; Vis. lectr. creative writing, editorial cons., mem. nat. adv. bd. Interlochen Arts Acad., Northwood Inst. Author: City Girl in the Country, 1955, Joe Maddy of Interlochen, 1963, (with W. Clement Stone) The Other Side of the Mind, 1965, The Psychic World of Peter Hurkos, 1970, (with Louella Dirksen) The Honorable Mr. Marigold, 1972, (with Ann Miller) Miller's High Life, 1972, Peter Hurkos: I Have Many Lives, 1976, Omarr: Astrology and the Man, 1977, (with George Masters) The Masters Way to Beauty, 1977, (with Russell Ogg) He Saw A Hummingbird, 1978, (with Florence Lowell) Be A Guest At Your Own Party, 1980, Face-Lifts: Everything You Always Wanted to Know, 1981, Joe Maddy Of Interlochen: Portrait of A Legend, 1991; Contbr. articles to nat. mags. Recipient E.S. Beck award Chgo Tribune. Mem. Theta Sigma Phi, Kappa Tau Alpha. Address: 226 Morongo Rd Palm Springs CA 92264

BROWNING, SARAH L., lawyer; b. Bourne, Mass., Jan. 23, 1952; d. Robert W. and Marjorie L. (Pike) B. BA, New Eng. Coll., 1973; JD, Franklin Pierce Law Ctr., 1990. Staff rschr. Ho. Rep. New Hampshire Gen. Ct., Concord, 1975-79; dir. devel. Eagle Square Marketplace, Concord, 1981-84; paralegal Sulloway & Hollis, Concord, 1986-90; counsel to house majority leader New Hampshire Gen. Ct., Concord, 1990—. Republican.

BROWNLEE, CHRISTENE, state legislator; b. Jonesboro, Ark., Oct. 16, 1955; m. Billy Earl Brownlee; 2 children. Grad., Turrell H.S., 1973. Mayor City of Gilmore; mem. Ark. Ho. of Reps.; sales Liquor Barrell. Republican. Mem. Christian-Disciples of Christ. Home: PO Box 27 Gilmore AR 72339-0027 Office: Ark House of Reps State Capitol Little Rock AR 72201*

BROWNLEE, PAULA PIMLOTT, association executive; b. London, June 23, 1934; came to U.S., 1959; d. John Richard and Alice A. (Ajamian) Pimlott; m. Thomas H. Brownlee, Feb. 10, 1961; children: Kenneth Gainsford, Elizabeth Ann, Clare Louise. BA with honors, Somerville Coll., Oxford (Eng.) U., 1957; PhD in Organic Chemistry, Oxford (Eng.) U., 1959. Postdoctoral fellow U. Rochester, N.Y., 1959-61; rsch. chemist Am. Cyanamid Co., Stamford, Conn., 1961-62; lectr. U. Bridgeport, Conn., 1968-70; asst. prof., then assoc. prof. Rutgers U., N.J., 1970-76, assoc. dean, then acting dean Douglass Coll., 1972-76; dean faculty, prof. chemistry Union Coll., Schenectady, N.Y., 1976-81; pres., prof. chemistry Hollins (Va.) Coll., 1981-90; pres. Assn. Am. Colls. and Univs., Washington, 1990—; bd. dirs. Ednl. Testing Svc., Bell Atlantic of Va. Author lab. manual; contbr. articles to profl. publs. Bd. dirs. U. Rochester, Assn. Religion in Intellectual Life, Nat. Humanities Ctr. Mem. Am. Chem. Soc., Royal Chm. Soc. London, Soc. Values in Higher Edn., Cosmos Club, Sigma Xi. Episcopalian. Office: Assn Am Colls and Univs 1818 R St NW Washington DC 20009-1692

BROWNMILLER, SUSAN, author, feminist activist; b. Bklyn., Feb. 15, 1935. Student, Cornell U., 1952-55. Asst. to mng. editor Coronet, N.Y., 1959-60; editor Albany Report, 1961-62; nat. affairs rschr. Newsweek, N.Y., 1963-64; staff writer Village Voice, N.Y., 1965; reporter NBC-TV, Phila., 1965; network newswriter ABC-TV, N.Y.C., 1966-68; free-lance journalist, 1968-70. Author: Shirley Chisholm, 1970, Against Our Will: Men, Women and Rape, 1975, Femininity, 1984, Waverly Place, 1989, Seeing Vietnam: Encounters of the Road and Heart, 1994. Mem. N.Y. Radical Feminists (co-founder). Office: care Grove Weidenfeld 841 Broadway New York NY 10003-4704*

BROWN-PAUL, BRENDA ELAINE, information engineer; b. Andrews AFB, Md., Aug. 3, 1959; d. Earl R. and Elouise J. (Grant) Borwn; m. Donald R. Paul, Sept. 21, 1985; children: Ariel E., Donald Jr. BFA, Howard U., 1981; postgrad., Md. U., 1990—. Office system coord. U.S. Postal Svc., Washington, 1984-89; systems adminstr. CKI, Rosslyn, Va., 1989-90; systems adminstr. GE Aerospace, Reston, Va., 1990-93, mem. Aerospace Diversity Coun., 1991; chair of communications com. diversity coun. GE, Reston, 1992-93; cons. Wang Labs., Bethesda, Md., 1993—; Pres. Glory To God, Inc., Forestville, Md., 1987—; ptnr., cons. Computer Tamers, Forestville, 1989. Author poems; creator paintings in several collections. Leader troop 343 Girl Scouts U.S., Washington, 1983-84; former sec., mem. Helping Hands Christian Fellowship, Inc., Washington, 1983—, Helping Hands Club, Springfield Baptist Ch., 1990—. Faculty scholar Howard U., 1977. Baptist.

BROWN PREMO, LISA ANN, mortgage securities executive; b. Reading, Pa., Aug. 30, 1956; d. Franklin George and Phyllis Mary (Fox) B.; m. Mark Premo, May 24, 1991; m. John Michael Millet, Aug. 8, 1981 (div. Feb. 1984). BS in Econs., U. Pa., 1978; MBA with honors, N.Y.U., 1981. Mktg. rep. NCR Corp., Ft. Washington, Pa., 1978-79; dealer sales rep. and analyst Exxon Co. USA, Linden, N.J., 1981-84; coord. bank relations Pennzoil Co., Houston, 1984-86; mgr. portfolio First Union Corp., Charlotte, N.C., 1986-90; mng. dir. First Union Capital Markets Corp., 1990—; ptnr. Options Trading Co., Houston, 1984-86. Fundraiser Am. Heart Assn., Houston, 1985. Recipient Exxon Excellence award, 1982. Mem. N.C. Bond Club, Wharton Alumni Assn. (sec. 1985-86), Wharton Women's Assn., Beta Gamma Sigma, Alpha Mu Alpha. Home: 3417 Meadow Bluff Dr Charlotte NC 28226 Office: First Union Corp One First Union Ctr Fnds Dc 8 # 0600 Charlotte NC 28288

BROWNRIGG, JUDITH HAMILTON, institutional sales executive; b. Roanoke, Va., June 14, 1950; d. Carl Cannaday and Mary Lee (Anderson) Hamilton; m. W. Grant Brownrigg, Apr. 28, 1984; children: Carter Grant, Taylor Hamilton. BS in Nursing, U. Va., 1972, MBA, 1982. RN, Va. Staff, charge nurse No. Va. Drs. Hosp., Falls Church, 1972; librarian John Hopkins Sch. Internat. Studies, Bologna, Italy, 1974-75; English instr. Politzer Sch. Langs., Bologna, 1975-76; staff, charge nurse Alexandria (Va.) Hosp., 1975, Roanoke (Va.) Meml. Hosp., 1972, 76-77; head nurse intensive care U. Va. Hosp., Charlottesville, 1972, 77-79, staff nurse clinic, 1979-80; mgmt. assoc. Equitable Life Assurance Soc., N.Y.C., 1982-84, product mgr., 1984-86; v.p. product devel. Equitable Real Estate Investment Mgmt., Inc., N.Y.C., 1986-87; v.p. instl. sales Equitable Real Estate, N.Y.C., 1987—. Baptist. Home: 305 N Mountain Ave Montclair NJ 07043-1021 Office: Equitable Real Estate Investment Mgmt Inc 787 7th Ave New York NY 10019-6018

BROWN-WAITE, VIRGINIA (GINNY BROWN-WAITE), state legislator; b. Albany, N.Y., Oct. 5, 1943; m. Harvey Waite; children: Jeannien Roxby Waite, Danene Mitchell, Sue Meaders. BS, SUNY, 1976; MS, Russell Sage Coll., 1984. Former commr. Hernando County; former legis. dir. N.Y. State Senate; mem. Fla. State Senate, 1992—. Active W Hernando GOP, United Way; bd. dirs. Habitat Humanity. Mem. Bus. and Profl. Women's Club, Suncoast MG Club, Rotary. Roman Catholic. Address: Fla State Senate State Capitol Tallahassee FL 32301*

BROYLES, BONITA EILEEN, nursing educator; b. Ross County, Ohio, Sept. 29, 1948; d. Arthur Runnels and Mary Elizabeth (Page) Brookie; m. Roger F. Broyles, Dec. 29, 1984; children: Michael Richard Brown, Jeffrey Allen Brown. BSN, Ohio State U., 1970; MA with honors, N.C. Cen. U., Durham, 1988; ADN, Piedmont Community Coll. CPR instr. Instr. nursing Watts Sch. Nursing, Durham; res. float staff nurse Durham County Gen. Hosp., Durham; dir. practical nursing edn., instr. Piedmont Community Coll., Roxboro, N.C.; maternity patient tchr. Mt. Carmel Med. Ctr., Columbus, Ohio; vice chmn. assoc. degree nursing faculty Piedmont Community Coll., 1990—. Contbr. articles to profl. jours. Named ADN Educator of Yr. N.C. Assoc. Degree Nursing Coun., 1993. Office: Piedmont C C College St Roxboro NC 27573

BROYLES, GLADYS BENITES, psychologist, hypnologist, hypnotherapist, counselor; b. Lima, Peru, June 3, 1959; came to U.S., 1982; d. Ernesto and Gladys Cayetana (Herrera) Benites; m. Spencer Barry Broyles, Apr. 21, 1984. Grad., Mater Admirabilis School, Lima, 1975; degree in teaching English, Inst. Cultural Peruano N.Am., Lima, 1975; student, U. Catholica del Peru, Lima, 1974-77, 76-78, Inst. Italiano de Cultura, Lima, 1976-77; B Gen. Psychology, Inca Garcilaso de La Vega U., Lima, 1982. QMRP Mental Health Profl. Audiologist, psychologist, translator Centro Peruano de Audicion y Lenguaje, Monterrico Lima, Peru, 1983-84; counselor Cen. Inst. for Deaf, St. Louis, 1984; substitute tchr. Archdioceses of St. Louis Cath. Schs., 1984-85; reservations and spl. svcs. sec., front desk rep. Rodeway Inn, St. Louis, 1985; front desk rep. Northwest Inn, St. Louis, 1985; counselor for mentally retarded and developmentally delayed Magdala Found., St. Louis, 1985-86; qualified mental retardation profl. Bellefontaine Habilitation Ctr., Dept. Mental Health, St. Louis, 1986-88; behavior coach Judevine Ctr. for Autism, St. Louis, 1988—, program mgr., 1991—; clin. caseworker asst. II St. Louis Mental Health Ctr., Dept. Mental Health, 1991; owner The Peruvian Image; founder Gladys Broyles Assn. Homes for mentally ill individuals; instr. CPA and First Aid ARC; pers. asst. British Consulate Offical in Lima, Peru, 1976; reservations mgr. Paracas Hotel, Lima, 1975; organizer Hosp . Mental Bravo Chico, Lima, 1979-80; founder Centro Medico Lince, Lima, 1979-82, Centro Medico Pucallpa, Peru, 1978-82, centro Peruano Audicion y Lenguaje, Lima, 1983-84. Mem. IACT, Pacer, Alliance Mentally Ill Assn. Roman Catholic. Avocations: reading, travel, music, indigenous arts. Home: 9835 Portage Dr Moline Acres MO 63136 Office: Judevine Ctr for Autism 5161 Washington Pl Saint Louis MO 63108

BROYLES, NORA AHERN, accountant; b. Panama City, Fla., July 3, 1960; d. Walter Smith and Doris Lane Ahern; m. Michael Lee Broyles, Jan. 18, 1992; 1 child, Michael. BBA in Acctg. cum laude, East Tenn. State U., 1988. CPA, Tenn. Word processing sec. Eastman Chem. Co., Kingsport, Tenn., 1978-85, chem. purchasing corr., 1985-90, mfg. cost acct., 1990—; acctg. lectr. East Tenn. State U., Johnson City, 1993-94. Treas., vol. John R. Hay House, Kingsport, 1991; audit vol. United Way, Kingsport, 1992-93. Mem. Inst. Mgmt. Accts. (dir., v.p. 1990-94), Tenn. Soc. CPAs. Methodist. Home: 208 Eastern Star Rd Kingsport TN 37663

BROYLES, RUTH RUTLEDGE, principal; b. Sullivan County, Tenn., July 15, 1912; d. Floyd Lylburn and Ethel Sally (Gross) Rutledge; m. David Lafayette Broyles, Aug. 15, 1937 (dec. Oct. 1980); children: Nancy Ann Broyles McCracken, Edwin Joseph, Dava Lee Broyles Russell. BS, East Tenn. State U., 1934, MA, 1968. Cert. English and biology tchr., Tenn., elem. edn. supr., supt. cert. Tchr. English Jonesborough (Tenn.) High Sch., 1934-38; tchr. 3d and 4th grades Telford (Tenn.) Elem. Sch., 1956-57; tchr. 3d grade Midway Elem. Sch., Jonesborough, 1957-62; tchr. 5th grade Jonesborough Elem. Sch., 1962-67; supr. tchr. corp. program East Tenn. State U., Johnson City, 1967-69; prin. Cherokee Elem. Sch., Johnson City, 1969-78, ret., 1978. County commr. Washington County Ct., 1980-90; chairperson Jonesborough Civic Trust, 1982-85, Watauga Regional Libr. Bd., Washington County, 1982-87, Washington County/Jonesborough Mus., Jonesborough, 1984—, Tenn. Homecoming 1986, 1985-86; mem. Washington County Libr. Bd., 1991—; mem. fin. com. Washington County Bd. Edn., 1991—; historian Washington County, 1991—; elder, Sunday sch. tchr., chair Christian edn. com. Jonesborough (Tenn.) Presbyn. Ch., 1989-91; moderator Presbyn. Women, chair adminstrv. com. Holston Presbytery, Kingsport, Tenn., 1989-94; historian Synod of Living Waters Presbyn. Women, Brentwood, Tenn., 1988-91; mem. Synod of Living Waters Ministry Divsn., Brentwood, 1988-93; mem. church coun. Tusculum Coll., Greenville, Tenn., 1991; mem. bicentennial com. for Washington County State of Tenn., 1993—. Named Woman of the Yr., Bus. and Profl. Women , Jonesborough, Tenn. 1975, Hon. Col., State of Tenn., 1989; Ruth Rutledge Broyles Scholarship Fund for tng. tchrs. named in her honor, 1994. Mem. Tenn. Ret. Tchrs. (state pres. 1985-86, Nashville 1978—, legis. asst. East Tenn. 1991—, Plaque 1985-86), N.E. Tenn. Tourism Coun. (chair, Silver Tray 1989, Outstanding Svc. award 1993), Tenn. Congress Parents and Tchrs. (v.p. Nashville 1984-69), Tenn. Libr. Assn. (trustee Nashville 1984-85), Washington County Ret. Tchrs. (chmn. scholarship com. 1991—), Tenn. Ret. Tchrs. Assn. Presbyterian.

BROZMAN, TINA L., federal judge; b. 1952. BA, NYU, 1973; JD, Fordham U., 1976. Ptnr. Anderson Russell Kill & Olick, 1976-85; bankruptcy judge U.S. Ct. So. Dist. N.Y., N.Y.C., 1985—; lectr. Practicing Law Inst., 1987. Mem. Assn. of Bar of City of N.Y. Office: US Dist Ct Alexander Hamilton Custom House 1 Bowling Grn New York NY 10004-1408*

BROZOWSKI, LAURA ADRIENNE, mechanical engineer; b. Yokohama, Japan, May 12, 1960; came to U.S., 1961; d. John and Muriel Sydney (Jackson) B. BSME, U. Calif., 1982; MS in Mech. Engring., Calif. State U., 1987; MBA, Pepperdine U., 1988. Registered profl. engr.; cert. profl. mgr. Mem. tech. staff Rocketdyne Divs. Rockwell Internat. Corp., Canoga Park, Calif., 1982—. Author in field. Fellow Inst. Advancement Engring.; mem. ASME, Nat. Soc. Profl. Engrs., Nat. Mgmt. Assn. Home: 22036 Collins St # 230-N Woodland Hills CA 91367-4713

BRUBAKER, KAREN SUE, manufacturing executive; b. Ashland, Ohio, Feb. 5, 1953; d. Robert Eugene and Dora Louise (Camp) B. BSBA, Ashland Coll., 1975; MBA, Bowling Green State U., 1976. Supr. tire ctr. ops. BF Goodrich Co., Akron, Ohio, 1976-77, supr. tire ctr. acctg., 1977-79, asst. product mgr. radial passenger tires, 1979-80, product mgr. broadline passenger tires, 1980-81, group product mgr. broadline passenger and light truck tires, 1981-83, mktg. mgr. T/A high tech radials, 1983-86; product mgr. B.F. Goodrich T/A radials The Uniroyal Goodrich Tire Co., Akron, Ohio, 1986-91; product mgr. Michelin performance tires Michelin Americas Small Tires, Akron, Ohio, 1991—. Sect. chmn. indsl. div. United Way, Akron, 1983-86; mem. adv. coun. to trustees Coll. Bus. and Econs., Ashland U., 1990-92. Recipient Alumni Disting. Service award Ashland Coll., 1986; Alpha Phi Clara Bradley Burdette scholar, 1975. Mem. Am. Mktg. Assn. (pres. Akron/Canton chpt. 1982-83, Highest Honors award 1983, nat. bd. dirs., v.p. bus. mktg. 1984-86, v.p. profl. chpts. 1987-89), Akron Women's Network, Zonta Internat., Beta Gamma Sigma, Omicron Delta Epsilon. Home: 822 Village Pkwy Fairlawn OH 44333 Office: Michelin Ams Small Tires 600 S Main St Akron OH 44397-0001

BRUBAKER, LOU ANN, advertising executive, consultant; b. Mansfield, Ohio, Apr. 29, 1957; d. Louis Stanley and Doris Ellen (Schneider) B. BA in Polit. Sci. and Urban Planning, Kent State U., 1981. Zoning adminstr. City of Cuyahoga Falls (Ohio), 1980-81; nat. sales trainer Nat. Mgmt. and Mktg., Columbus, Ohio, 1981-86; dir. advt. Drustar Drug Control Systems, Grove City, Ohio, 1986-88; advt. coord., STN Internat. Sci. and Tech. Network (STN) Internat. Chem. Abstract Svcs., Columbus, 1988-91; pres. Brubaker Advt. and Mktg., Laurel, Md., 1991—; bd. dirs. Woman Rising Inc., Balt. Home and Office: Brubaker Advt and Mktg 10422 Churchill Way Laurel MD 20723

BRUBAKER, NANCY SUSAN, physical therapist assistant; b. Amarillo, Tex., Feb. 6, 1959; d. John Leo and Frances Nadine (Hill) Smith; m. James Marcel Brubaker, Dec. 20, 1980; children: Maribeth Alexandra, Emma Abigail. AS, St. Petersburg Jr. Coll., 1982. Lic. phys. therapist asst., Fla. Computer audit clk. GE Co., Tampa, Fla., 1978-80; phys. therapist asst. Greene Rehab. Svcs., Sarasota, Fla., 1982-86, Rehab Works of Fla., Sarasota, 1986-92, Fla. Home Health, Bradenton, 1992-93, ResCare, Bradenton, 1992-93. Contbr. poetry to anthologies. Support facilitator Compassionate Friends, Bradenton, 1984-86; facilitator Empty Arms, Bradenton, 1984-85. Named Therapist Asst. of the Yr., Rehabworks, 1991. Republican. Baptist. Home: 3505 65th St W Bradenton FL 34209

BRUBECK, ANNE ELIZABETH DENTON, artist; b. Beardstown, Ill., Mar. 5, 1918; d. Harry B. and Helen Jean (Gibbs) Denton; m. William E. Brubeck, Dec. 14, 1940; children: Jean Denton Brubeck, William E. Student Christian Coll., 1935-36; B.Design, Newcomb Coll., Tulane U., 1939; postgrad. Art Inst. Chgo., 1939-40; A.A. (hon.), Wabash Valley Coll., 1981. Instr. painting Wabash Valley Coll., Mt. Carmel, Ill., 1962-67; painter; one-man shows include N.Y.C., 1961, 63-67, Evansville, Ind., 1963-69, Wabash Valley Coll., 1989, Risley's Gallery Wabash Valley Coll., Evansville, Ind., 1989, 91, Watercolor Exhibition Wabash Valley Coll., 1992; retrospective Wabash Valley Coll., 1980, 89, Risley's Gallery, 1989; juried exhbns. include Evansville Mus., 1963, 64, 65, Swopes Gallery, Terre Haute, Ind., 1964, 68, Nashville, 1967. Trustee Mt. Carmel Pub. Libr., 1954—, chmn., 1975-6; mem. cultural events com. Wabash Valley Coll., 1976-80. Brubeck Art Ctr.named in her and her husband's honor, 1976; named to Mt. Carmel High Sch. Centennial Hall of Fame, 1982. Mem. Ill. Libr. Assn., Nat. League Am. Penwomen, PEO. Methodist. Club: Reviewers Matinee. Home and Studio: 729 N Cherry St Mount Carmel IL 62863-2064

BRUCE, CLARA, pathologist; b. Chgo., Aug. 26; d. Frank A. and Bessie Pellegrino; children: Ted Bruce-Stokes, Darlene Bruce-Stokes. BS in Biology, Roosevelt U., Chgo.; MD, U. Ill. Fellow Coll. Am. Pathology, Internat. Acad. Pathology; mem. Chgo. Pathology Soc., Coll. Exec. Physicians. Home and Office: 459 Forest Trial Oak Brook IL 60521-1417

BRUCE, NADINE CECILE, internist, educator; b. Oak Park, Ill., Apr. 6, 1942; d. Roy Alford and Henrietta Hedwige (Denk) B. BS in Chemistry, Coll. St. Francis, 1964; MD, U. Ill., 1970. Diplomate Nat. Bd. Internal Medicine, Nat. Bd. Med. Examiners. Resident in internal medicine St. Francis Integrated Med. Program, Honolulu, 1970-74; pvt. practice Honolulu, 1974-77; assoc. program dir. med. residency program U. Hawaii, Honolulu, 1974-87, dep. program dir., 1987-90, program dir., 1990-91; cons. internist Rehab. Hosp. of the Pacific, 1992—. V.p. bd. trustees Hawaii Bound Sch., 1977-80; bd. govs. Hawaii Med. Libr., 1980-85, Hawaii Blood Bank, 1983; mem. drug product selection bd. State of Hawaii, 1984-92, chmn., 1987-89. Fellow ACP (bd. govs. 1989-93); mem. AMA, AAUP, Hawaii Med. Assn. (councilor 1978-82), Honolulu County Med. Soc. (pres. 1983-84), Am. Soc. Internal Medicine, N.Y. Acad. Scis., Soc. Gen. Internal Medicine. Republican. Roman Catholic. Office: Rehab Hosp of the Pacific 226 N Kuakini St Honolulu HI 96817-2498

BRUCE, RITA KAY, investment executive; b. Greencastle, Ind., Sept. 7, 1961; d. Earl Eugene and Phyllis Jean (Nelson) Clodfelter; div., 1984; 1 child, Kyle Nelson; m. R. Gregg Bruce, Apr. 14, 1990. Grad. high sch. Cert. fin. planner. Teller Lafayette (Ind.) Bank and Trust Co., 1981, investment clk., 1981-84, investment mgr. trust dept., 1984-87, investment officer, 1987-88, v.p. investments, 1993—. Home: 1909 Shenandoah Ct Lafayette IN 47905-4043 Office: Lafayette Bank & Trust Co PO Box 1130 Lafayette IN 47902-1130

BRUCE, SALLY SKIDMORE, physical scientist; b. Takoma Park, Md., Jan. 10, 1960; d. Robert Francis and Eleanor Jane (Jones) Skidmore; m. Thomas Allen Bruce, May 21, 1983; 1 child, Joseph Robert. AA in Electromech. Tech., Montgomery Coll., 1983; BS in Tech. and Mgmt., U. Md., 1993. Engring. technician Nat. Bur. Stds. Ctr. for Chem. Physics, Gaithersburg, Md., 1982-86; phys. sci. technician Nat. Inst. Stds. and Tech. Ctr. for Radiol. Rsch., Gaithersburg, 1986-90; phys. sci. technician NIST Physics Lab., Gaithersburg, 1990-94, phys. scientist, 1994—; mem. adv. com. for engring. systems Montgomery Coll., Germantown, Md., 1990-94. Democrat. Methodist. Office: NIST Rm B208 Gaithersburg MD 20899

BRUCK, ARLENE LORRAINE, secondary education educator; b. Kingston, N.Y., June 26, 1945; d. Machileo and Lillian (Turco) Forte; m. Laurence J. Bruck; children: Jennifer Lynn, Jason Scott. BA in Latin, Coll. Mt. St. Vincent, Riverdale, N.Y., 1967; MS in Psychology, SUNY, New Paltz, 1971. Cert. in social studies, Latin, elem. edn. Tchr. 2d grade Kingston Schs. Consol., 1967-74, tchr. Latin, psychology and sociology, 1984—; mem. Mid-Hudson Social Studies Coun., 1992—. Placement chair Jr. League, Kingston, 1982-84; vol. Girl Scouts, Tillson, N.Y., 1981-86, Athletes Against Drugs, Kingston, 1984-87. Recipient Mary Dodge McCarthy award for gen. excellence, 1967, Mid-Hudson Social Studies Coun. Excellence in Tchg. award, 1994; named Outstanding Young Woman, 1974; N.Y. State Regents scholar, 1963-67, AAUW scholar, 1963-67; NEH fellow, 1992. Mem. AAUW (v.p. 1970-74, sec. 1975-77, pres. program 1994), N.Y. State Assn. Fgn. Lang. Tchrs. Roman Catholic. Home: 39 Beth Dr Kingston NY 12401-6148 Office: Kingston High Sch 403 Broadway Kingston NY 12401-4617

BRUCK, PHOEBE ANN MASON, landscape architect; b. Highland Park, Ill., Nov. 26, 1928; d. George Allen and Louise Townsend (Barnard) Mason; m. F. Frederick Bruck, June 30, 1956. Student Bard Coll., 1946-49; BS, Ill. Inst. Tech., 1954; MLA, Harvard U., 1963. Trainee, Nat. Gallery of Art, Washington, 1947, Mus. Modern Art, N.Y.C., 1948; head design dept. Design Research Inc., Cambridge, Mass., 1955-60; cons. The Architects Collaborative & Sert, Jackson Assocs., Inc., 1960-63; v.p. F. Frederick Bruck, Architect & Assoc., Inc., Cambridge, pres., 1993; vis. design critic dept. landscape architecture Harvard U. Grad. Sch. Design, 1971-79; v.p. The Buccaneers Co., 1989—, also bd. dirs. Contbr. to New Landscapes for Living, 1980. Judge, New Eng. Flower Show, Mass. Hort. Soc., 1971-79, Thoreau Awards, Assn. Landscape Contractors, 1980; mem. Sci. Adv. Group for Edn., Cambridge Pub. Schs., 1981-82; chair Harvard Sq. Adv. Commn., 1987—; co-chair Quincy Sq. Design Com., 1991—, chair 1995. Mem. Mass. Bd. Registration of Landscape Architects (chair 1992-95), Am. Arbitration Assn., Am. Soc. Landscape Architects, Boston Soc. Landscape Architects (pres. 1973-75, examining bd. 1978-81), Mass. Soc. Mayflower Descendants, Harvard Sq. Def. Fund (chmn. adv. ocm. 1987, bd. dirs. 1984-85, pres. 1985-86), Harvard U. Grad. Sch. Design Alumni Assn. (officer 1972-78), Soc. for Protection of New Eng. Antiquities (design adv. com). Episcopalian. Home & Office: 148 Coolidge Hl Cambridge MA 02138-5521

BRUCK-LIEB, LILLY, retired consumer advisor, broadcaster, columnist; b. Vienna, Austria, May 13, 1918; came to U.S., 1941, naturalized, 1944; d. Max and Sophie M. Hahn; Ph.D. in Econs., U. Vienna; postgrad. Sorbonne, Paris, Sch. of Econs., London, Sch. of Bus., Columbia U., 1941-42, Sch. of Social Work, N.Y. U., 1964-66; m. Sandor Bruck, Mar. 7, 1943; 1 child, Sandra Lee (Mrs. John David Evans III); m. David L. Lieb, Dec. 7, 1985. Dir. consumer edn. Dept. Consumer Affairs, City of N.Y., 1969-78; project dir. Am. Coalition of Citizens with Disabilities, 1977-78; consumer advisor, broadcaster In Touch Networks, N.Y.C., 1978-90; consumer affairs commentator Nat. Public Radio, 1980-82; ret. Chmn. Westchester County, Bonds for Israel, 1960-64. V.p. Jewish Community Ctr., White Plains, N.Y. Recipient Eleanor Roosevelt award Bonds for Israel, 1963; Woman of Yr. award Anti Defamation League, 1972; Community Service award local council Girl Scouts U.S.A., 1974. Mem. Soc. of Consumer Affairs Profls. Democrat. Author: Access, The Guide to a Better Life for Disabled Americans, 1978; contbr. articles on disability and rehab. to books, ency., and mags. Home: 25 Murray Hill Rd Scarsdale NY 10583-2829

BRUCK-MUNRO, BETH ANNE, company executive; b. Richmond, Ind., Sept. 23, 1958; d. Edward Walter and Jayne Elizabeth (Dickerson) Bruck; m. Gregory D. Campbell, Sept. 20, 1980 (div. Feb. 1983); m. Arthur Duane Munro, May 25, 1986. AA in Bus. Adminstrn., St. Petersburg Jr. Coll., 1978; BA in Acctg., U. South Fla., 1980. CPA, Fla. Staff acct. Main Hurdman CPAs (now Peat Marwick & Co.), St. Petersburg, Fla., 1980-82; chief acct. Innova, Inc., Clearwater, Fla., 1982-83, controller, 1983-86; controller Med. High Tech. Internat., Inc., Clearwater, 1986—. Mem. Am. Inst. CPAs, Fla. Inst. CPA's, Phi Kappa Phi. Republican. Presbyterian. Office: Med High Tech Internat Inc 14155 58th St N Clearwater FL 34620-3739

BRUDERLE, EILEEN PATRICIA, realtor; b. Chgo., Sept. 14, 1959; d. Earl Francis Jr. and Mary Alice (Walsh) Murphy; m. Ken C. Bruderle, Dec. 28, 1991; children: K. Charles, Emma Lauren. BS in Mgmt. Info. Systems, Northeastern Ill. U., 1989. Lic. broker. Sr. systems cons. Automatic Data Processing, Chgo., 1979-87; programmer analyst, mgr. Nutra Sweet Co., Deerfield, Ill., 1987-91; cons. Elgin, Ill., 1991-93; owner Realty Execs. Advantage, Elgin, 1993—. Designer and writer: (software) Real Estate by Design, 1993. Office: Realty Execs Advantage 81 Market St Elgin IL 60123

BRUECKNER, BONNIE LICHTENSTEIN, security administrator; b. Chgo., Mar. 5, 1936; d. Ralph Henry and Hazel May (Mullens) Lichtenstein; m. Keith Allen Brueckner, June 18, 1988; children: Deborah Norwood, J. Patrick Klavas. BA in Psychology, San Diego State U., 1981. Security mgr. Phys. Dynamics, La Jolla, Calif., 1980-86, security cons., 1986—; sr. security coord. Lockheed, Burbank, Calif., 1986-87, United Tech., San Diego, 1987-89; div. adminstr. security Inst. for Def. Analyses Ctr. for Comm. Rsch. La Jolla, San Diego, 1989—. Mem. Nat. Classification Mgmt. Soc. Home: 3120 Almahurst Row La Jolla CA 92037-1162

BRUEGGER, BARBARA J., association executive; b. Medford, Oreg., May 11, 1940; d. Fred Marlow and Elizabeth (Smith) B. BS in Health, Phys. Edn. and Recreation, U. Oreg., 1962. Recreation aide ARC, Korea, 1962-63, Morocco, 1963-64; program dir., acting ctr. dir. ARC, Verdun, France, 1963-66; area program dir. ARC, Korea, 1966-68; asst. area dir. ARC, Vietnam, 1969-70; ctr. dir. YWCA Greater Atlanta, 1971-74; exec. dir. YWCA Cobb County, Marietta, Ga., 1974—. Recipient Franco/Am. award Verdun Woman's Club, 1964, Community Svc. award NAACP, 1986. Mem. Pilot Club Marietta (pres. 1986-87), Rotary. Home: 2068 Signal Ridge Chase Kennesaw GA 30144-3262 Office: YWCA of Cobb County 48 Henderson St Marietta GA 30064-3208

BRUEMMER, LORRAINE VENSKUNAS, funeral director, real estate broker, nurse; b. Waterbury, Conn., Jan. 25; d. Anthony George and Mary Agnes (Kritchman) Venskunas; m. Jay Porter Bruemmer, Oct. 28, 1973; 1 child by previous marriage: Linda L. Rocco Sovak. R.N., St. Francis Hosp. Sch. Nursing, 1950; B.S., Columbia U., 1958; M.Ed., U. Hartford, 1961. Head nurse pediatrics Cook Hosp., Hartford, Conn., 1953-56; instr. pediatrics Bellevue Hosp., N.Y.C., 1958-59; instr. med. surg. nursing New Britain Gen. Hosp., 1959-62; hosp. supr. New Britain Gen. Hosp., 1962-63; owner Venskunas Funeral Home, New Britain, 1962—; owner Bruemmer Venskunas Real Estate, New Britain, 1974—, Stanley Monumental Co., 1993—; commr. New Britain Health Dept., 1965-74; nurse blood bank ARC, N.Y.C., 1957-59, New Britain, 1960-69. Vol. Republican Party, New Britain. Mem. New Britain Funeral Dis. Assn. (pres. 1975-78), Conn. Funeral Dirs., Nat. Funeral Dirs., New Britain Bd. Realtors, Hartford Bd. Realtors, Nat. Bd. Realtors, Multiple Listing Service Greater Hartford. Roman Catholic. Clubs: Ladies Guild (pres. 1969), Shuttle Meadow Country. Avocations: antiques; golf; tennis; swimming; bicycling; gardening. Home: 36 Roslyn Dr New Britain CT 06052-1824 Office: Venskunas Funeral Home Ste 1612 665 Stanley St New Britain CT 06051-2736

BRUESEWITZ-LOPINTO, GAIL C., marketing professional; b. N.Y.C., May 17, 1956; d. Arthur George and Blanche Juliana (Dobos) Bruesewitz; m. Joseph LoPinto, Sept. 1990. BA in Eng. Lit., SUNY, Binghamton, 1978. Exec. sec. promotion and artist devel. Columbia Records/CBS Records, Inc., N.Y.C., 1979-82, dir. nat. dance music mktg., 1982-89; v.p., power station promotion Crossover Mktg. Inc., N.Y.C., 1989-90; pres. Brueser Prodns., 1990; nat. dir. promotion/artist devel. Ear Candy Records, 1990-91; prodn. coord. AIG Risk Mgmt., Inc. (divsn. Am. Internat. Group, Inc.), N.Y.C., 1991—; rep. record div. Women's Orgn. Coun. CBS, Inc., N.Y.C., 1980-82; adv. bd., dance/music, New Music Seminar, N.Y.C., 1989—. Editor newsletter Brueser's Boogie Backpage, 1983-90. Bd. dirs. Mt. Tremper (N.Y.) Lutheran Camp and Retreat Ctr., 1976-78, Camp Wilbur Herrlich, Pawling, N.Y., 1990; active Big Sisters, Binghamton (N.Y.) Social Svcs. dept., 1975-78. Named N.Y. rep. for Mademoiselle mag., 1975. Democrat. Lutheran. Office: Am Internat Group Inc 70 Pine St 3rd Fl New York NY 10270

BRUETT, KAREN DIESL, sales and fundraising consultant; b. N.Y.C., May 15, 1945; d. Francis J. and Dorothy (Peterson) Diesl; m. William H. Bruett, Jr., Mar. 18, 1967; 1 child, Lindsey Diesl. BA in English, St. Lawrence U., 1966; MA, Hunter Coll., 1971. Tchr. English Freeport (N.Y.) pub. schs., 1966-70; exec. interviewer, researcher Louis Harris & Assocs., N.Y.C., 1970-72; dir. adult edn. West Side YMCA, 1972-76, mem. bd. mgrs., 1978-83; v.p. new bus. devel. Gaylord Adams & Assocs., Inc., N.Y.C., 1976-81; account exec. John Blair Mktg., N.Y.C., 1981-83, v.p. sales, 1983-84, sr. v.p., gen. sales mgr., 1984-86; ind. sales and fundraising cons.; bd. dirs. Resolution, Inc., Winsooki, Vt. Trustee St. Lawrence U., 1978—, chmn. alumni fund, 1983-84, chmn. annual giving, 1984-88, chmn. planning com., 1987-88, mem. exec. com., 1987—, chmn. devel. com., 1988—; trustee Vt. Council on Arts, 1986-91, vice chmn. bd. trustees, chmn. devel. com., 1988-91; del. Am.-Soviet Youth Forum, Baku, USSR, 1974. Mem. Internat. Women's Forum, 1991—. Home and Office: 110 Mosle Rd Far Hills NJ 07931-2229

BRUFF, BEVERLY OLIVE, public relations consultant; b. San Antonio, Dec. 15, 1926; d. Albert Griffith and Hazel Olive (Smith) B. BA, Tulane U., 1948; postgrad. Our Lady of Lake Coll., 1956, Okla. Center for Continuing Edn., 1960-70. Asst. dir. New Orleans Theatre Guild, 1948-50; dist. dir. San Antonio Area coun. Girl Scouts Am., 1958-70, public rels. dir., 1970-83; free-lance pub. rels., 1983—; mem. Coun. of Pres., v.p., 1981-82, 84—; mem. Coun. of Internat. Rels. Zoning commr. Hill Country Village, Tex., 1973-76, 83-85, 88—; councilwoman Hill Country Village, 1985-88; bd. dirs. Animal Def. League, Camp Fire, Inc. Mem. Pub. Rels. Soc. Am., Tex. Pub. Rels. Assn. (Silver Spur award), Women in Communications (historian 1969-70, v.p. 1970-71, treas. 1971-73), Tex. Press Women (recipient state writing contest awards 1971, 72, 73, 74, mem. exec. bd. dirs. 1970-71, 73-74, dist. treas. 1972-73, dist. v.p. 1973), Nat. Fedn. Press Women, Internat. Assn. Bus. Communicators, Speech Arts of San Antonio (pres. 1964-66, 70-72, 84—, dir. 1964-72, 88—, chmn. bd. dirs. 1966-69), Am. Women in Radio and TV (dir. chpt. 1974, sec. 1975, pres. 1979-80), San Antonio Soc. Fund Raising Execs., Assn. Girl Scout Exec. Staff. (exec. bd. 1963-72, nat. bd. 1972-74). Home: 508 Tomahawk Trl San Antonio TX 78232-3620

BRUGGER, NANCY JO, counselor; b. Omaha, Mar. 6, 1949; d. Leonard E. Brugger and Gertrude E. (Ross) Wilson. BS, Creighton U., 1971; MS, U. Nebr., Omaha, 1981. Cert. profl. sch. counselor; nat. bd cert. counselor; nat. cert. sch. counselor. Sci. tchr. Westside Pub. Schs., Omaha, 1978-80; sci. tchr. Millard Pub. Schs., Omaha, 1980-82, counselor, 1982—; presenter, program developer in field. Softball coach Kingswood Athletic Assn., Millard, 1986-87; basketball referee for kids Millard (Nebr.) Lions Club, 1986-94; youth to youth coord. Millard (Nebr.) Drug Free Youth, Kiewit Middle Sch., 1988-92; leader Metro-Omaha Drug Free Youth, Fremont Conf., 1991. Named Outstanding Middle Sch. Counselor, Nebr. Profl. Counselors Assn., 1988. Mem. ACA, NEA, Am. Sch. Counselors Assn., Am. Assn. Christian Counselors, Nat. Mid. Sch. Assn., Nebr. Assn. for Med. Level Edn. (editor 1987-91), Nebr. Counselors Assn. (Outstanding Counselor 1988), Nebr. Sch. Counselors Assn. (v.p. 1985-86, 87-88), Phi Delta Kappa.

BRULO, SANDRA MARIE, psychiatric clinic administrator; b. Wilkes-Barre, Pa., May 17, 1952; d. Augustine Edward and Julie Ann (Wielgosz) B. BA in Sociology, Social Work, King's Coll., 1974; MPA, Marywood Coll., 1976, MSW, 1994. Lic. social worker; cert. qualified mental health/mental retardation profl.; cert. clin. hypnotherapist; cert. custody mediation. CLA housemgr. United Rehab. Svcs., Inc., Wilkes Barre, Pa., 1974, therapeutic activities worker, 1974; relief crisis caseworker Help Line, Wilkes Barre, 1975-76; evaluation cons. Dept. of Pub. Welfare OMR, Harrisburg, Pa., 1976-79; program coord. Luzerne County Parks and Recreation Dept., Harrisburg, 1976-77; mental retardation specialist Children's Svc. Ctr., Wilkes Barre, 1975-79, therapist, 1978-79, project dir. parent counselor program, 1979-82, partial hospitalization/BSU adminstrv. svcs. coord., 1982-83, dir. adminstrv. svcs., 1983—; instr. Coll. Misericordia, 1992—; adj. faculty instr. dept. social scis. Luzerne County Community Coll., Nanticoke, Pa., 1985—; bd. dirs. Luzerne County Children and Youth Svcs., Wilkes Barre, 1986—, Parenting Ctr. Task Force, Wilkes Barre, 1988—. Mem. Marywood Coll. Adv. Bd. for Pub. Adminstrn., St. Mary's Youth Ministry. Recipient Honor for Orgn. and Community Contbn., Luzerne County Mental Health Assn., 1987, Appreciation Honor fo rUnited Way Speakers' Bur., 1988. Mem. Pa. Mental Health/Mental Retardation Providers Assn., Mental Health Assn. of Luzerne County. Democrat. Roman Catholic. Office: Children's Svc Ctr 335 S Franklin St Wilkes Barre PA 18702-3808

BRUM, BRENDA, state legislator, librarian; b. Parkersburg, W.Va., Jan. 3, 1954; d. Carl Henry Ogilvie and Helen Mae (Camp) B. BS, W.Va. U., 1975, MA, 1978. Libr., tchr. English, Hamilton Jr. H.S., Parkersburg, 1976-85; libr. Parkersburg South H.S., 1985—; mem. W.Va. Ho. of Dels., 1991-92, 93-94. Bd. dirs. Wood County chpt. Am. Cancer Soc.; foster parent Try Again Homes; mem. adv. bd. Wood County Vocat. Nursing. Mem. LWV, Wood County Edn. Assn. (past treas., exec. com.). Democrat. Home: 2600 17th Ave Parkersburg WV 26101-6419

BRUMBACK PATTERSON, CATHY JEAN, psychologist; b. Birmingham, Ala., Oct. 15, 1953; d. Roy Clifton and Violet Lorraine (Wesley) Brumback; m. Louis Loomis Patterson, June 10, 1987; children: Catherine Elizabeth Patterson, Allyson Brumback Patterson. BA, U. Ala., Tuscaloosa, 1975; MA, U. Ala., Birmingham, 1977; EdS, Ga. State U., 1985, PhD, 1986. Lic. psychologist; cert. sch. psychologist. Tchr. Jefferson County Bd. Edn., Birmingham, 1975-76, Birmingham (Ala.) Bd. Edn., 1976-77, Baldwin County Bd. Edn., Bay Minette, Ala., 1977-79; psychometrist Regional Edn. Svc. Ctr., Bartlesville, Okla., 1979-81, Union Pub. Schs., Tulsa, 1981-82, Forsyth County Schs., 1982-84; sch. psychologist Atlanta (Ga.) Pub. Schs., 1984-87; pvt. practice psychologist Northport, Ala., 1987-94, Fairhope, Ala., 1994—; grad. rsch. asst. Ga. State U., Atlanta, 1982, 85, instr., 1986; instr. U. Ala., Tuscaloosa, 1988-90. Mem., Sunday sch. tchr. Christ Episcopal Ch., Tuscaloosa, 1989-93; mem. Tuscaloosa (Ala.) Arts Coun., 1991-93, Tuscaloosa (Ala.) County Preservation Soc., 1992-93, Women's Guild-Tuscaloosa (Ala.) Acad., 1992-93. Named Mrs. Ala., Mrs. Am. Assn., 1979, Outstanding Young Women of Am., 1982, 87, 89; recipient Outstanding Doctoral Student award Ga. Assn. Sch. Psychologists, 1987. Mem. AAUW, APA, Ala. Psychol. Assn., Tuscaloosa Area Psychologists, Nat. Register Health Svc. Providers, Northriver Yacht Club, West Ala. C. of C. (women's guild 1993), Phi Delta Kappa, Kappa Delta Pi. Home: PO Box 687 Montrose AL 36559 Office: Bldg A 22787 Hwy 98 Fairhope AL 36532

BRUMER, MIRIAM, artist, educator; b. N.Y.C., Oct. 7, 1939. B.A., U. Miami, 1960; M.F.A., Boston U., 1964. Mem. faculty N.Y. Inst. Tech., 1969-75, Five Towns Music and Art Found., 1977—, Hunter Coll., 1976-81, Marymount Manhattan Coll., 1976-86, NYU, 1983—, Queens Mus. Art, 1987—; artist-in-residence N.Y. Found. for Arts, 1985. One-woman shows include Hankook Gallery, N.Y.C., 1982; exhibited in group shows Fordham U., 1980, Boston City Hall, 1983, Leonardo di Mauro Gallery, 1987, Schneyer & Shen, 1987, Barnard-Biderman Gallery, N.Y., 1994, also others; represented in permanent collection Chase Manhattan Bank, Bell Labs., N.Y. Bank for Savs., also pvt. collections. Ludwig Vogelstein Found. grantee, 1976-77; Com. Visual Arts grantee, 1979, 80. Home: 250 W 94th St New York NY 10025-6954

BRUMMOND, TONI FRANCES, secondary education educator; b. Cody, Wyo., Dec. 8, 1949; d. Harold B. and Betty Jo (Dolce) B.; m. John D. Robinson, Oct. 27, 1973 (div. 1979). BA, U. No. Colo., 1972; MEd, U. South Fla., 1992. Cert. tchr. in lang. arts 7-12, ednl. leadership. English tchr. Sch. Dist. 60, Pueble, Colo., 1972-73; substitute tchr. Hillsborough County Schs., Tampa, Fla., 1972-75, English tchr., 1975—; active Ednl. Practices Commn., State of Fla., 1994—. Campaign worker Dem. Party, Tampa, 1984—. Mem. Hillsborough Classroom Tchrs. Assn. (mem. exec. bd.), Alpha Delta Kappa, Sigma Kappa Alum. Home: 5119 Corvette Dr Tampa FL 33624 Office: Gaither HS 16200 N Dale Mabry Tampa FL 33618

BRUNDAGE, DIANE NOEL, marketing professional; b. Oak Park, Ill., Dec. 14, 1954; d. Edwin Alonzo and Myra Jeanette (Simmons) B.; m. Scotland Christian Settle, June 23, 1984. BS, U. Ill., Chgo., 1978; MBA, Loyola U., 1979. Legis. aid Senator Soper, Chgo., 1976-78; acct. mgr. Digital Equipment Corp., L.A., 1979-83; acct. exec. Apple Computer, L.A., 1983-86; dist. mgr. Apple Computer, Phoenix, 1986-89; ops. mgr. Apple Computer, Irvine, Calif., 1989; regional sales mgr. Apple Computer, L.A., 1989-92; dir. mktg., dir. U.S. sales Apple Computer, Inc., Cupertino, Calif., 1992—. Home: 930 Meadow Rd Aptos CA 95003-9788 Office: 900 E Hamilton Campbell CA 95003

BRUNDAGE, SUSAN, art dealer, gallery director; b. Orange, N.J., June 18, 1949. BA, Smith Coll., 1971. Formerly with Paine Webber Inc., N.Y.C.; treas. White Columns, N.Y.C., 1978—; dir. Leo Castelli Gallery, N.Y.C.; exhbn. curator Sch. Visual Arts, N.Y.C., 1978-84. Office: 420 W Broadway New York NY 10012

BRUNDIDGE, NANCY CORINNE, social worker; b. Louisville, Miss., Sept. 27, 1920; d. Elijah and Roberta (May) Thompson; m. Roy Lee Brundidge, Dec. 24, 1937; children—Carlita J. Nickson, Adrienne Nickson. A.A., Ind. U., 1956; B.A., Roosevelt U., 1960, M.A., 1973. Caseworker I and II, Cook County Dept. Pub. Aid., Chgo., 1960-69; social worker Gary Sch. Corp., Ind., 1969-70; job specialist social worker Ind. State Employment, Hammond, 1970-73; social worker, attendance officer Hammond pub. schs., Ind., 1973—; cert. drug edn. cons. Hammond Sch. City, 1976—; guest lectr. Ind. State U., 1980-81. Chmn. adv. bd. Salvation Army program com. Named Ind. State Social Worker of Yr., Midwest Social Workers Council, 1983-84. Mem. AAUW (cultural chmn.). Home: 137 Porter St Gary IN 46406-1534

BRUNE, EVA, fundraiser; b. Bklyn., Apr. 20, 1952; d. Paul Mass and Edythe Siegel; m. David H. Brune, Oct. 30, 1988; children: Jared Alexander, Isaac Nicolai. BFA, Calif. Coll. Arts and Crafts, Oakland, 1979. Visual arts dir. Sonoma (Calif.) County Arts Commn., 1980-82; assoc. dir. Visual Arts Ctr. of Alaska, Anchorage, 1982-83; program dir. Internat. Sculpture Ctr., Washington, 1983; dir. Pro Arts, Oakland, 1983-85; devel. dir. A Traveling Jewish Theater, San Francisco, 1985-88; mng. dir. INTAR Hispanic Arts. Ctr., N.Y.C., 1988-94; dir. ann. fund The Big Apple Circus, N.Y.C., 1994—; instr. Calif. Coll. Arts and Crafts, Oakland, 1980-81. Past bd. dirs. Alliance Resident Theaters, N.Y.C., Cityarts, N.Y.C.; former panelist theater program Nat. Endowment for Arts, Washington. Recipient fellowships Nat. Endowment for the Arts, Washington, 1980, 82. Jewish.

BRUNELL, MELINDA ANN, communications executive; b. Seattle, Oct. 2, 1959; d. Richard Dwight and Colleen Constance (Chowning) McCorkle; m. Dan Brunell, Aug. 22, 1993. Student, U. Wash., 1978-80, Stirling (Scotland) U., 1981-82; BA in Communications, Wash. State U., Pullman, 1983. Account exec. Jay Rockey Pub. Rels., Seattle, 1983-86; asst. v.p., mgr. corp. communications Wash. Mut. Savs. Bank, Seattle, 1986-88; v.p., mgr. corp. communications and advt. Wash. Mutual Savs. Bank, Seattle, 1989-90; account supr. Pub. Communications, Inc., Chgo., 1990-91; sr. account dir. Lesnik Pub. Rels., Northbrook, Ill., 1991-92; exec. editor pub. group Grant/Jacoby Inc., Chgo., Ill., 1993—. Vol. Children's Hosp., Seattle, 1987-88. Mem. Pub. Relations Soc. Am. (2 Totem awards 1985, 1 Totem award 1987, 1 Bronze anvil 1994). Office: 4045 Northcott Ave Downers Grove IL 60515-1827

BRUNELLO-MCCAY, ROSANNE, sales executive; b. Cleve., Aug. 26, 1960; d. Carl Carmello and Vivan Lucille (Caranna) B.; divorced, 1991; m. Walter B. McCay, Feb. 26, 1994. Student, U. Cin., 1978-81, Cleve. State U., 1981-82. Indsl. sales engr. Alta Machine Tool, Denver, 1982; mem. sales./purchases Ford Tool & Machine, Denver, 1982-84; sales/ptnr. Mountain Rep. Enterprises, Denver, 1984-86; pres., owner Mountain Rep. Ariz., Phoenix, 1986—; pres. Mountain Rep. Oreg., Portland, 1990—, Mountain Rep. Wash., 1991—; sec. Computer & Automated Systems Assoc., 1987, vice chmn., 1988, chmn., 1989. Active mem. Rep. Party, 1985—; mem. Phoenix Art Mus., Grand Canyon Minority Coun., 1994. Mem. NAFE, Soc. Mfg. Engrs. (pres. award 1988), Computer Automated Assn. (sec. 1987, vice chmn. 1988 chmn. 1989), Nat. Hist. Soc., Italian Cultural Soc., Tempe C. of C., Vocat. Ednl. Club Am. (mem. exec. bd., pres. 1987—). Roman Catholic. Office: Mountain Rep Ariz 410 S Jay St Chandler AZ 85224

BRUNER, KAREN COLLEEN, financial planner; b. Livingston, Mont., Jan. 24, 1962; d. Kenneth J. and Rose Darlene (Lutz) B. BS, U. Idaho, 1984. Registered rep. Fin. planner Waddell & Reed, Boise, Idaho, 1984—. Mem. Bus. and Profl. Women, Lions. Office: Waddell & Reed 6156 Emerald St Boise ID 83704-8857

BRUNNER, ELIZABETH ANNE, anchor, reporter; b. Hartford, Conn., May 22, 1959; d. Galen Eames Jr. and Mary (Chacko) Russell. MusB, Lawrence U., 1981; postgrad., U. Ill., 1987. Dir. vocal music Rich South High Sch., Richton Pk., Ill., 1981-83; asst. mgr. U-S Splty. Retailing, Champaign, Ill., 1983-85; community svcs. rep. Sta. WCIA, Champaign, 1985-88, weather anchor, 1986-88; dir. community rels. Sta. WTVT, Tampa, Fla., 1988-93, news anchor, 1989-93; anchor Eye Opener Newscast, WCVB, Boston, 1993—; reporter, anchor Chronicle News Mag. Show, WCVB, Boston, 1993—; host live auction Sta. WILL Champaign, 1985-88; membership drive Sta. WEDU, Tampa, 1989-90. Mem. com. United Way of Greater Tampa, 1988-90; bd. dirs. Am. Cancer Soc., 1986-88, United Way of Champaign, 1987, Friends of Tampa Recreation, 1989-90, Boys and Girls Club of Tampa, 1990, In The Best Interests of the Children, 1994—, Germaine Lawrence Sch., 1994—. Recipient Up and Comers award Tampa Bus. Jour., 1990; media award Am. Cancer Soc., 1990, Pub. Rels. award Am. Women in Radio and TV, 1990, Cert. of Appreciation, United Way of Greater Tampa, 1990. Office: Sta WTVT PO Box 31113 Tampa FL 33631-3113

BRUNNER, LILLIAN SHOLTIS, nurse, author; b. Freeland, Pa.; d. Andrew J. and Anna (Tomasko) Sholtis; m. Mathias J. Brunner, Sept. 8, 1951; children: Janet Brunner Cramer, Carol Ann Brunner Burns, Douglas Mathias. RN, diploma, U. Pa., 1940, BS, 1945, LittD (hon.), 1985; MS in Nursing, Case-Western Res. U., 1947; ScD (hon.), Cedar Crest Coll., 1978. RN, Pa. Operating room supr. U. Pa. Hosp., Phila., 1942-45; head, fundamentals of nursing dept. U. Pa. Hosp., 1944-46; asst. prof. surgical nursing Yale U. Sch. Nursing, New Haven, Conn., 1947-51; surgical supr. Yale-New Haven Hosp., 1947-51; rsch. project dir. Sch. Nursing Bryn Mawr (Pa.) Hosp., 1973-77; co-founder History of Nursing Mus., Pa. Hosp., Phila., 1974; mem. bd. overseers Sch. Nursing, U. Pa., 1982-88, bd. overseers emeritus, 1988—; chmn. nursing adv. Presbyn.-U. Pa. Med. Ctr., Phila., 1970-88, 90-93, trustee, 1976-88, 90—, vice chmn. bd. trustees, 1985-88. Author: Manual of Operating Room Technology, 1966, (with others) Lippincott Manual of Nursing Practice, 1974, 4th edit., 1986, Textbook of Medical and Surgical Nursing, 1964, 6th edit., 1988; mem. editl. bd. Jour. Nursing and Health Care, Nusing '95, Nursing Photobook Series, 1978-90. Bd. dirs. Presbyn. Med. Ctr. Found., Phila., 1985-93, Presbyn. Med. Ctr., 1976—. Recipient Disting. Alumnus award Frances Payne Bolton Sch. Nursing, Case Western Res. U., 1980, Alumni award of merit Soc. Alumni Assns., U. Pa., 1995. Fellow Am. Acad. Nursing; mem. ANA, Nat. League for Nursing (judge nat. writing contest 1982-84, Disting. Svc. award 1979), Nat. League Am. Pen Women (sec. Phila. chpt. 1972-76, nat. sec. 1984-86), Assn. Oper. Rm. Nurses, Nurses Alumni Assn. U. Pa. Hosp., Ben Franklin Soc., Internat. Old Lacers Soc., Sigma Theta Tau, Pi Gamma Mu, Pi Lambda Theta. Home and Office: 1247 Berwyn Paoli Rd Berwyn PA 19312-1234

BRUNO, AUDREI ANN, nurse educator, administrator; b. Pitts., Oct. 31, 1946; d. Vincent Joseph and Julia Elizabeth (Karaffa) Mataya; m. Edward Orlando Bruno, Apr. 30, 1966; children: Brent Edward, Bradley Edward. AA, Community Coll. Alleghany County, 1976; BSN, Pa. State U., 1984; MSN, U. Pitts., 1988. Cert. nurse adminstr. Psychiat. nursing supr. Western Psychiat. Clinic and Inst., Pitts., 1976-81; staff charge nurse Magee Women's Hosp., Pitts., 1981-82; charge team leader Central Med. Pavillion, Pitts., 1982-84; clin. specialist Vis. Nurse Assn. of Alleghany County, Pitts., 1984-92; rschr. U. Pitts.; mem. speakers bur. Community Coll. Allegheny County; project developer WPIC Adolescent Module, 1980-81; CEO Psycho-Ednl. Cons., 1989. Chmn. North Huntington (Pa.) Suicide Awareness and Prevention Com., 1986-88; fieldworker Project Star, Pitts., 1986-88; mem. Pa. Task Force on Elder Abuse, Nurses Interest in Care of Elderly, Geriatric Ednl. Network; mem. adv. com. Nat. Project DART. Mem. Nursing Quality Assurance (cons.), Internat. Platform Assn., Sigma Theta Tau. Home: 14071 Ridge Rd North Huntingdon PA 15642

BRUNO, CAROL JEANETTE, gifted/talented education educator, innkeeper; b. Phila., Dec. 21, 1949; d. Everette Noble and Gertrude Mae (Weaver) Cliff; m. C. Gus Bruno, Aug. 28, 1971; children: Peter Everette, Jason Eugene. AA, Wesley Coll., 1969; BA, Davis & Elkins Coll., 1971; postgrad., St. Joseph's U., 1994—. Elem. tchr. Ocean City (N.J.) Primary Schs., 1971-72; instr. Atlantic C.C., Mays Landing, 1979-80; reading tchr. Egg Harbor Twp. (N.J.) Schs., 1980-82; coord. gifted edn. Sea Isle City (N.J.) Pub. Schs., 1982—, adviser student yearbook, Nat. Jr. Honor Soc. Local pres., county pres., mem. state bd. dirs. N.J. PTA, Trenton, 1978-90; founder After-Sch. Care Program, Ocean City, 1984, Ocean City Safe Homes Project, 1984; den mother Boy Scouts Am., Ocean City, 1980-82; mem. Mayor's Task Force on Drug and Alcohol Abuse, Ocean City; pres., bd. dirs. Cape Ednl. Fund, Cape May County, N.J., 1980—. Named Role Model, Sun Newspaper, 1988, Cape May County Tchr. of Yr., 1993. Mem. ASCD, Sea Isle City Edn. Assn. (sec.). Office: Sea Isle City Pub Sch 4501 Park Rd Sea Isle City NJ 08243

BRUNO, CATHY EILEEN, state official; b. Binghamton, N.Y. d. Martin Frank and Beverly Carolyn (Hamlin) Piza; m. Frank L. Delaney (div.); m. Paul R. Bruno, May 5, 1990. BA, SUNY, Binghamton; MSW, Syracuse U. Psychiat. social worker Willard (N.Y.) Psychiat. Ctr., 1968-73, Broome Devel. Ctr., Binghamton, 1973-74, 76; congl. legis. aide, 1975; asst. dir. bur. program and fiscal audits N.Y. State Office Mental Retardation and Devel. Disabilities, Albany, 1976-80, asst. dir. bur. program and fiscal audits, 1976-80, statewide coord. intermediate care facilities for developmentally disabled, 1980, cert. coord. Western County svc. group, 1980-83, Upstate unit dir. Bur. Cert. Control, 1983-85; dir. ICF/DD Survey and Rev., 1985-89; area dir. Bur. Program Cert., 1989—; adj. instr. SUNY Sch. Social Welfare, Albany, 1982-83. Grantee HEW, 1975-76. Mem. Am. Mgmt. Assn. Address: PO Box 3153 Albany NY 12203-0153 Office: 44 Holland Ave Albany NY 12229

BRUNO, GRACE ANGELIA, accountant, educator; b. St. Louis, Oct. 11, 1935; d. John E. and Rose (Goodwin) B. BA, Notre Dame Coll., 1966; MEd, So. Ill. U., 1972; MAS, Johns Hopkins U., 1983; PhD, Walden U., 1985. CPA, Mo., Md., N.J. Tchr. Sisters of Notre Dame, St. Louis, 1962-80; pres. Bruno-Potter, Inc., Avon By The Sea, N.J., 1981—; asst. treas., instr. acctg. Coll. of Notre Dame of Md., Balt., 1978-79, treas., 1979-80; asst. prof. acctg. Georgian Ct. Coll., Lakewood, N.J., 1985-91; fin. advisor James Harry Potter gold medal award ASME, N.Y.C., 1980—. Elected to Internat. Platform Assn., 1987. Mem. AICPA, N.J. Soc. CPAs, St. Louis Bus. Educators (treas. 1972-73), Inst. Bus. Appraisers, Inc., Johns Hopkins Univ. Faculty Club. Democrat. Roman Catholic. Home and Office: 419 3d Ave Avon By The Sea NJ 07717-1244

BRUNO, JUDYTH ANN, chiropractor; b. Eureka, Calif., Feb. 16, 1944; d. Harold Oscar and Shirley Alma (Farnsworth) Nelson; m. Thomas Glenn Bruno, June 1, 1968; 1 child, Christina Elizabeth. AS, Sierra Coll., 1982; D of Chiropractic, Palmer Coll. of Chiropractic West, Sunnyvale, Calif., 1986. Diplomate Nat. Bd. Chiropractic Examiners. Sec. Bank Am., San Jose, Calif., 1965-67; marketer Memorex, Santa Clara, Calif., 1967-74; order entry clk. John Deere, Milan, Ill., 1977; system analyst Four Phase, Cupertino, Calif., 1977-78; chiropractic asst. Dr. Thomas Bruno, Nevada City, Calif., 1978-81; chiropractor Chiropractic Health Care Ctr., Nevada City, 1987-91; pvt. practice Cedar Ridge, Calif., 1991—. Area dir. Cultural Awareness Coun., Grass Valley, Calif., 1977—; vol. Nevada County Libr., Nevada City, 1987-88, Decide Team III, Nevada County, 1987-92, Active Parenting of Teen Facilitator Nev. Union High Sch. Mem. Am. Chiropractic Assn., Women Health Practitioners of Nevada County (founder 1993—), Nevada County C. of C. (vol. task force health care 1993), Toastmasters (sec. 1988, pres. 1989, edn. v.p. 1990). Republican. Office: Chiropractor Health Care PO Box 1718 Cedar Ridge CA 95924-1718

BRUNO, KAY ANDERSON, public relations executive, speaker; b. Casper, Wyo., Aug. 4, 1941; d. James D. and Rhea (Wadsworth) Anderson; m. N.J. Bruno, Feb. 6, 1966 (div. 1985); children: James, Thomas, Michael. BS in Journalism, Northwestern U., 1963; cert. in advanced mgmt., Emory U., 1989. Assoc. editor Jour. Am. Med. Assn., Chgo., 1963-66; account exec. Gardner, Jones & Cowell, Chgo., 1966-69, Pub. Communications, Inc., Chgo., 1980; account supr. Hill & Knowlton, Chgo., 1981-85; sr. dir. pub. affairs Searle, Chgo., 1985-93; sr. cons. Marcy Monyek & Assoc., Chgo., 1993—; guest lectr. Medill Sch. Journalism Northwestern U., 1989; lectr. to various groups. Bd. dirs. Juvenile Protective Assn., 1983-92. Mem. Medill Sch. Journalism Alumni (pres., 1991-93). Office: 55 W Wacker Dr# 1110 Chicago IL 60601

BRUNO, MARILYN JOAN, foreign service officer, management consultant; b. Caracas, Venezuela, May 28, 1948; d. Philip Lee and Eugenia Alda (Micera) Bruno; m. Fernando Herrera (div. 1980); 1 child, Cynthia. BA, Mt. Holyoke Coll., 1969; MA, NYU, 1970, PhD, 1977; JD, N.Y. Law Sch., 1991. Lic. stockbroker, commodity broker, N.Y.; lic. real estate broker, Fla.; bar: N.Y., N.J., Fla., D.C. Adj. prof., asst. dir. NYU in Spain, Madrid, 1970-80; account exec. Dean Witter Reynolds/Shearson, N.Y.C. and Miami, 1980-82; v.p. Ace Am., Miami, Fla., 1982-84; v.p. precious metals dept. Capital Bancorp, Miami, Fla., 1983-84; pres. Bruno Cons. Co., Inc., Miami, Fla., 1984—; fgn. svc. officer Am. Embassy Dept. of State, Athens, Greece; lectr Tunderbird U., Mesa, Ariz., 1985—, Universidad de Los Andes, Bogota, 1984—. Author: Countertrade, 1984-86; columnist weekly col. in Jour. of Commerce, 1982-84; editorial asst.: Generally Accepted Accounting Principles, 1988; contbr. articles to profl. jours.; author travel guide. Named Woman Entrepreneur of the Yr., NOW, Palm Beach, 1986. Mem. Internat. Mgmt. Devel. Inst., Phi Alpha Delta. Office: Am Embassy-Athens PSC 108 Box 56 APO AE 09842-5009

BRUNO, MARY ANN T., health systems specialist; b. Altoona, Pa., May 14, 1953; d. Anthony J. Sr. and Theresa M. (Eder) B. BS, Pa. State U., 1975; MS, DePaul U., 1981. Recreation therapist Bayberry Psychiatric Hosp., Hampton, Va., 1975-76; therapeutic recreation specialist U.S. Dept. Vets. Affairs, Chgo., 1976-81, mgmt. analyst office of inspector gen., 1981-85; health systems specialist office of project mgmt. U.S. Dept. Vets. Affairs, Washington, 1985-86, mgmt. analyst office of planning and constrn., 1986-92, health systems specialist office of constrn. policy divsn., 1992—. Sec., bd. dirs. Fed. Women's Program Dept. Vets. Affairs, Washington, 1993—; v.p., bd. dirs. Our Lady of Good Counsel, Vienna, Va., 1985—; mem. Big Brothers and Big Sisters of Greater Washington, 1990—. Mem. Nat. Therapeutic Rec. Assn. (cert.), Pa. State Alumni Assn. (rising star award 1991). Roman Catholic. Home: 8702 Thunderbird Court Vienna VA 22182 Office: Dept Vets Affairs Constrn Policy 811 Vermont NW Washington DC 20420

BRUNO, SUSAN ELIZABETH, educator; b. Freeport, N.Y., June 19, 1946; d. Nicholas Stephen and May Elizabeth (McCarthy) B. BS in Edn., Fordham U., 1968; MA, Hofstra U., 1972. Cert. tchr., N.Y. Tchr. Massapequa (N.Y.) Sch. Dist. 23, 1968—. Office: Massapequa Sch Dist 23 4925 Merrick Rd Massapequa NY 11758-6201

BRUNO-GOLDEN, BARBARA, neuropsychologist. BS in Math. and Edn., Ursinus Coll., 1968; MEd, U. Del., 1969; EdD, Boston U., 1978. Postdoctoral fellow in clin. neuropsychology Boston Neurobehavioral Inst., 1986-89, staff neuropsychologist, 1989-94; pvt. practice, 1985—; tchr. Newton (Mass.) Pub. Schs., 1970-80; profl. trainer dept. sociology Boston U., 1977-78; dir. BEA-MOD Day Camp, Newton, 1971; head tchr. Fernald State Sch., Waltham, Mass., 1969-70; tchr. Marshallton (Del.) Pub. Schs., 1968-69; instr. Brandeis U., Waltham, 1970-73, Simmons Coll., Boston, 1975-76, Lesley Coll., Cambridge, Mass., 1973-75; guest lectr. Northeastern U., Boston, 1972-73; ednl. cons. to programs for autistic children and congenital or acquired central nervous sys. disorders, 1972—. Contbr. articles to profl. jours. Active area-wide human rights com. for mentally ill and mentally retarded Mass. Mental Health Ctr. Mem. Am. Psychol. Assn., Mass. Neuropsychol. Assn., Nat. Assn. Neuropsychologists. Home: 151 Sargent St Newton MA 02158-2338

BRUNS, LISA SLATER, marketing professional; b. Cin., Mar. 30, 1966; d. Charles Maclure and Rosemary Merele (Wilson) Slater; m. Robert George Bruns, Feb. 27, 1993. BS in Mktg., U. Ctrl. Fla., 1989. Asst. mgr. Enterprise Leasing, Orlando, Fla., 1989-91; sales and mktg. programs mgr. Dixon Ticonderoga Co., Maitland, Fla., 1991-93; bus. alliances mgr. IBAX Healthcare Systems, Longwood, Fla., 1994—. Home and Office: 604 Silver Birch Pl Longwood FL 32750

BRUNSVOLD, MARY HELEN SUSAN (CHICA BRUNSVOLD), artist; b. Ypsilanti, Mich., Mar. 6, 1940; d. Norman Leroy and Mary Helen (Norburn) Willey; m. Brian Garrett, Nov. 28, 1963; 1 child, Laura Ann. BS in Design, U. Mich., 1961, MA in Art, 1962. Cert. secondary tchr., Mich. Gen. illustrator Ctrl. Intelligence Agy., Langley, Va., 1962-67, Indsl. Coll. of Armed Forces, Washington, 1967-68; tchr. art Fairfax (Va.) County Adult Svc. and Recreation, 1969-71, Barcroft Recreation, Falls Church, 1974-82; Art tchr. studio, Falls Church, Va., 1976-80. One person shows include Shenandoah Valley Art Ctr., 1992, Lawrence Gallery, 1993; group shows include Nat. Watercolor Soc., 1993, Ala. Watercolor Soc., 1994, Okla. Watercolor Soc., 1994, Pitts. Watercolor Soc., 1994, Pa. Watercolor Soc., 1994. pres. Lake Barcroft Swim Team, Falls Church, 1965-69; membership chmn. Barcroft Recreation Ctr., Falls Church, 1975-88; pres. Lake Barcroft Woman's Club, Falls Church, 1975-76; tchr. Sunday sch. Faith Luth. Ch., Arlington, Va., 1976-80. Mem. Va. Watercolor Soc. (signature mem.), Potomac Valley Watercolorists (1st v.p. 1990-92, pres. 1993-95), Ala. Watercolor Soc., Okla. Watercolor Soc., Art League Va., Nat. Women's Mus. Art (charter mem.). Lutheran. Home: 3510 Wentworth Dr Falls Church VA 22044-1309

BRUNSWICK, CECILE RENEE, painter, photographer, editor; b. Antwerp, Belgium, July 26, 1930; came to U.S., 1939; d. Charles and Therese (Eckstein) Censor; m. Fred Curtis Brunswick, Mar. 3, 1958 (div. Aug. 1967); 1 child, Glen David. BA, Queens Coll., 1952; M of Internat. Affairs, Columbia U., 1954; cert. Film & TV, NYU, 1978. Asst. editor Coun. on Fgn. Rels., N.Y.C., 1957-58; Afghanistan del. to UN, N.Y.C., 1958-59; asst. editor Indonesian Consulate, N.Y.C., 1959-60; painter, water-colorist, 1964—; freelance photo rschr., photographer N.Y.C., 1978-90; comml. photography, advt., pub. rels., book pubs. , mags. including Nat. Geog. World, Forbes, N.Y. Mag., Interior Design, The Photo (Eng.). Group shows include Hudson River Mus., 1980 (prize), '81, Ted Bates 1981, Con Edison, 1979, Fotoforum, 1985, Kips Bay Decorator House, 1986, Jadite Galleries, 1988, Gensler and Assocs., L.A., 1992, Discoveries VI (prize) VII, 1991, 92, Del. Art Mus. Emerging Artists Gallery, 1992, Arts Etoiles, Montparnasse R.R., Paris, Paris-Washington Art Exch., 1993, Nour Found., N.Y.C., 1993, Itabashi Art Mus., Tokyo, 1994, Sano Art Mus., Shizuoka, 1994, Otani Meml. Art Mus., Hyogo, 1994; selected collections include World Children's Art Mus., Okazaki, Japan, Nestles, Can. Mus. Civilization, Que., Sumitomo Marine & Fire Ins. Co., others. Mem. Japan Soc., Art Initiatives, N.Y.C. C. of C. Studio: Artplace 419 Lafayette St New York NY 10003

BRUNTON, DONNA LEE, secretarial services manager; b. Denver, May 20, 1929; d. Harry Leroy and Myrtle Evelina (Wiswell) McCarthy; m. James Ewing Brunton, Aug. 20, 1948 (div. 1979); children: Mark Lionel, Valerie Lee Stotts. Student, Pasadena City Coll., 1963-64; cert. paralegal, U. So. Calif., 1979. Sec. Gray, White & Burkitt, Pasadena, Calif., 1964-79; office mgr. Hill, Gould & Pearson, L.A., 1979-81; owner Quick Response Secretarial Svc., Glendale, Calif., 1981—. Editor: (weekly bull.) Sunrise Rotary, 1993-94. Mem. Rotary Internat., Order of Ea. Star. Republican. Presbyterian. Office: Quick Response Sec Svc Ste 1190 700 N Brand Blvd Glendale CA 91203

BRUSHWOOD, ROWENA RUTH, accountant; b. Hamilton, Mo., Nov. 30, 1958; d. Calvin Raymond and Ruth Francis (Asher) Foss; m. John Otis Brushwood, Sept. 27, 1977; children: Steven Dallas, Johnathon Minor, Patrick Raymond, Rebecca Lee, Calvin Jason. BBA, Mo. Western State Coll., 1988. CPA, Mo. Staff acct. Clifton Gunderson & Co., St. Joseph, Mo., 1988-93; acctg. supr. Boehringer Ingelheim, St. Joseph, Mo., 1993—; instr. for women's fin. info. program AARP, St. Joseph, 1991. Sunday sch. tchr. Gower (Mo.) Bapt. Ch., 1989—; cub scout den leader Boy Scouts Am., Gower, 1988-90; girl scout troop leader Girl Scouts Am., Gower, 1991-92. Mem. AICPA, Mo. Soc. CPAs, Inst. Mgmt. Accts. (dir. student activities 1992-93,dir. ednl. seminars 1993-94, v.p. adminstrn. and fin. 1994-95). Republican. Baptist. Home: 201s169 Highway Gower MO 64454

BRYAN, ALICE RICCA, corporate risk manager; b. Kingman, Ariz., Sept. 17, 1940; d. Frank Alfred and Alice (Waters) Ricca; m. R.L. Bryan, July 26, 1956 (div. July 1969); children: Jesse Aaron II, Eleanore Alisa Gildersleeve. Grad. high sch., Lake Charles, La., 1959. CPCU; accredited residential mgr. Underwriting asst. Gen Conf. of Seventh Day Adventist Risk Mgmt., Riverside, Calif., 1964-72; risk mgmt. cons. Gen Conf. of Seventh Day Adventist Risk Mgmt., Washington, 1974-75, dir. ins. services, 1975-77; mgr. office Quinlan Ins., Newport Beach, Calif., 1972-73; comml. ins. underwriter CIMA, Washington, 1973-74; asst. dir. risk mgmt. Smithsonian Instn., Washington, 1977-82; ins. officer The World Bank, Washington, 1982-86; dir. risk mgmt. Adventist Health System West, Roseville, Calif., 1986-89; sr. v.p. Calif. Hosps. Affiliated Ins. Svcs., 1989-92; risk mgmt. cons., 1993—; dir. CHAIS workers compensation adv. bd., Sacramento, 1986-88; seminar developer Met. Mus. Edn. Program. Author, editor: Insurance and Risk Management for Museums and Historical Societies, 1985. Mem. Risk and Ins. Mgmt. Soc. (dep. San Francisco chpt., v.p. Washington chpt. 1978-84, pres. 1984-86, soc. dir. Sacramento chpt. 1990-92), Soc. of CPCU, Internat. Found. Employee Benefits. Republican. Adventist. Home: 118 Silverado Cir Roseville CA 95678-1023

BRYAN, BARBARA DAY, librarian; b. Livermore Falls, Maine, May 20, 1927; d. Lorey Clifford and Olga Elvira (Bergquist) Day; m. Robert S. Bryan, June 24, 1950. BA in Psychology, U. Maine, 1948; MS in Library Sci., So. Conn. State U., 1964. Catalog dept. asst. Yale U. Library, New Haven, 1948-49; departmental library cataloger Harvard U., Cambridge, Mass., 1949-51; descriptive cataloger Yale U. Library, New Haven, 1951-52; cataloger Fairfield (Conn.) Pub. Library, 1952-54, reference librarian, 1954-57, asst. librarian, order librarian, 1957-65; asst. dir. libraries Fairfield U., 1965-74, university librarian, 1974—; mem. Conn. State Libr. Bd., Hartford, 1978-82, chair, 1987-92; bd. dirs. Bibliomation, Inc., Stratford, Conn., 1987-91. Bd. dirs. Oak Lawn Cemetery Assn., 1994—. Recipient Disting. Alumnus award So. Conn. State U. Sch. of Libr. Sci., 1979; named Conn. Libr. Assn. Libr. of Yr., 1988. Mem. ALA (Conn. chpt. councilor 1977-80), Assn. Coll. and Rsch. Librs. (constn. and by-laws com. 1986-90, mem. coll. libr. sect. stds. com. 1991—), New Eng. Libr. Assn. (mem. com. 1981-85, coun. mem. 1975-77), Conn. Libr. Assn., Fairfield Hist. Soc., Conn. Audubon Soc., Oak Lawn Cemetery Assn. (bd. dirs.), Phi Beta Kappa, Phi Kappa Phi. Democrat. Home: 999 Merwins Ln Fairfield CT 06430-1919 Office: Fairfield U Fairfield CT 06430

BRYAN, CARLA WOLF, library director; b. Thomasville, Ga., Dec. 1, 1953; d. Harold William and Jean (Markus) Wolf; 1 child, Elizabeth Quinn Wolf Bryan. Student, Tex. A&M, 1971-73; BA, East Tex. State U., 1975; MLS, Tex. Women's U., 1983. Libr. clerk Selwyn Sch., Denton, Tex., 1975-76; libr. clerk Cedar Hill (Tex.) Publ. Libr., 1976-77, city libr., 1977-79; libr. dir. Northwood Inst., Cedar Hill, 1979-84, Duncanville (Tex.) Pub. Libr., 1984—; chair southwest geographic Northeast Tex. Libr. System, Garland, Tex., 1988—, awards com. chair, 1987-88, pub. libr. divsn./by-laws, 1993—; bd. dirs. Literacy Learning Ctr. Southwest Dallas County, 1994—. Mem. Tex. Libr. Assn., Pub. Libr. Adminstrn. N. Tex., Am. Libr. Assn. Democrat. Office: Duncanville Pub Libr 103 E Wheatland Rd Duncanville TX 75116-4822

BRYAN, CAROLINE ELIZABETH, quality assurance professional; b. Washington, Dec. 4, 1951; d. Carter Royston and Anna Maria (Schneider) B. BA, Vassar Coll., 1973. Programmer Santa Barbara Rsch. Ctr., Goleta, Calif., 1975-77; tester, software developer and sr. test technician Johnson Controls, Inc., Milw., 1977-85; cons. Cap Gemini Am., Cranford, N.J., 1986-90; quality assurance engr. PRC, Inc., McLean, Va., 1990-91; software quality assurance engr. Unify Corp., Sacramento, 1991-94; software engr. Objective Systems Integrators, Folsom, Calif., 1994—; cons. AT&T, Lincroft and Middletown, N.J., 1986-90. Editor (newsletter) Captain America, 1989. Fellow Murphy Ctr. for Codification of Human and Organizational Law; mem. IEEE (assoc.), Assn. for Computing Machinery, Am. Philatelic Soc., QuiltNet. Democrat. Roman Catholic. Home: 18 Freeman St Apt 1 Woodland CA 95695-3245 Office: Objective Systems Integrators 100 Blue Ravine Dr Folsom CA 95860

BRYAN, GAIL ANN, counselor; b. Dearborn, Mich., Jan. 16, 1947; d. James Paul and Blanche Alice (Sis) Hodde; m. John Charles Bryan, Sept. 6, 1968; children. Tara Marie, Darci Anne. AAS in Dental Hygiene, Ferris State Coll., 1969; B in Gen. Studies, Oakland U., Rochester, Mich., 1985, MA in Counseling, 1988. Lic. profl. counselor; registered dental hygiene. Dental hygienist James Bennett, DDS, Grand Rapids, Mich., 1969-71, William Love, DDS, Birmingham, Mich., 1971-74, Gary, Clarkston, Mich., 1976-78, Douglas Nyquist, DDS, Royal Oak, Mich., 1983-85; counselor Career & Family Counseling, Rochester Hills, Mich., 1988—; cons. Nat. Relocation Firms, Rochester Hills, 1989—, Ford Motor Co.-Pilot Project, Continuum Ctr.-Oakland U., Rochester Hills, 1993; adj. counselor, faculty Oakland C.C., Rochester, 1990—; assoc. staff Oakland U. Continuum Ctr. Mem. Nat. Career Devel. Assn., Am. Counselors Assn., Nat. Employment Counselors Assn., Mich. Employment Counselors Assn., Mich. Mental Health Counselors Assn. (sec. 1989-91), Mich. Career Devel. Assn. (membership 1992—, conf. co-chair 1994). Office: Career & Family Counseling 305 Barclay Circle 1001 Rochester Hills MI 48307

BRYAN, MARY ANN, interior designer; b. Dallas, Nov. 16, 1929; d. William C. and Harriet E. (Carter) Green; m. Frank Wingfield Bryan, Aug. 31, 1957; children: Frank Wingfield, Elizabeth F. BS in Interior Design U. Tex., 1950. Head of stock Foleys Dept. Store, Houston, 1952-53, asst. buyer, 1953-54, buyer, 1955-60, exec. tng. dir., 1960-61; owner, pres. The Bryan Design Assocs., Inc., Houston, 1961-94; mem. interior design mem. Tex. Bd. Archtl. Examiners, 1993—. Trustee Houston Art Inst.; mem. interior design adv. bd. Stephen F. Austin Coll.; U.S. del. Friendship Among Women. Mem. Am. Soc. Interior Designers (nat. bd. dirs. 1984-86, 91-92, pres. Gulf Coast chpt. 1975), Dover Club of Houston (pres. 1991-92), Chi Omega. Republican. Home: 10023 Locke Ln Houston TX 77042-3101 Office: The Bryan Design Assocs 1502 Augusta Dr Ste 100 Houston TX 77057-2454

BRYAN, MARY JO W., business manager, artist; b. Dumas, Tex., Apr. 12, 1944; d. Edwin Franklin and Martha Lou (Workman) Williams; m. Gary W. Bryan, June 4, 1966; children: Mark William, Stacy Lynn. BS in Edn., Tex. Tech U., 1966; MEd in Guidance and Counseling, North Tex. U., 1969; MA in Art, West Tex. A&M U., 1994. Cert. tchr., all-level counselor, Tex. Tchr. Lubbock (Tex.) Ind. Sch. Dist., 1966, Irving (Tex.) Ind. Sch. Dist., 1966-68; tchr. Dallas Ind. Sch. Dist., 1968-69, counselor, 1969-71; bus. mgr. Gary W. Bryan, M.D., P.A., Amarillo, Tex., 1977—; artist Amarillo, 1994—. Organizer Healthtreat, Med. Alliance, 1988; speakers chmn. Med. Alliance AIDS Program, 1992-94; mem. Leadership Amarillo, C. of C., 1989-90; Mem. Polk Street United Meth. Ch., program chmn. 1988, 90, 93. Mem. Med. Mgrs. (v.p. 1989-90, Svc. award 1989), Am. Med. Alliance, Tex. Med. Alliance, Potter-Randall County Med. Alliance (sec.-treas. healthreat, pres. 1988-89, Svc. award 1989). Office: Gary W Bryan MD PA 7305-B Wallace Amarillo TX 79106

BRYAN, TAMARA LEIGH, sales representative, engineer; b. Greenville, N.C., Aug. 6, 1959; d. Shirley Madara and Beverly Lou (Witherington) B. BS, East Carolina U., 1981, MA in Edn., 1985. Indsl./packaging engr. Owens-Ill., Pittston, Pa., 1981-84; teaching asst. East Carolina U., Greenville, N.C., 1984-85; sales rep. Techform, Inc., Mt. Airy, N.C., 1986-89, PMW Products, Inc., Raleigh, N.C., 1989-93, Creative Forming, Inc., Ripon, Wis., 1993-94, Ericsson Mobile Comm., Inc., 1995—. Mem. alumni bd. East Carolina U., 1991, mem. Wake County alumni bd., 1992. Mem. Inst. Packaging Profls. (exec. bd. 1987-89, 92-94, program dir. 1987—), Soc. Plastic Engrs. (bd. dirs. 1991-93, sec. 1992-93), Profl. Soc. Sch. of Industry and Tech./East Carolina U. (pres. 1991). Methodist.

BRYAN-PETERSON, MARGARET IRVING, research administrator; b. Keene Valley, N.Y., June 13, 1948; d. William Joseph and Dorothy Ellen (Whyte) Irving; m. Howard Maurice Bryan, June 13, 1970 (div. Oct. 1978); 1 child, Amanda Janel; m. Jeffrey Allan Peterson, Nov. 12, 1988. BA, SUNY, Potsdam, 1970; MA, Purdue U., 1975. Promotion/editl. asst. Instr. Publs. subs. Harcourt, Brace Jovanovich, Dansville, N.Y., 1971-74; rsch. asst. Jamestown (N.Y.) Planning Commn., 1977-78; project dir. devel. Downtown Bldg. Study, Jamestown, 1978-79; planning technician Chautauqua County Dept. Planning and Devel., Mayville, N.Y., 1979-80; asst. consortium dir. Chautauqua Consortium, Jamestown, 1980-81; exec. dir. C.O.D.E., Inc., Jamestown, 1982; grantsperson, planner Cattaraugus Comty. Action, Inc., Salamanca, N.Y., 1983-87; grantwriter, pub. rels. technician Chautauqua Opportunities, Inc., Mayville, 1987-89; ssoc. dir. sponsored programs, rsch. svcs. & econ. devel. SUNY, Fredonia, 1989-93, dir. Office of Grants Adminstrn./Rsch., 1993—; grantwriter Chautauqua County Dept. Social Svcs., Mayville, 1988, Chautauqua County Day Care Coord. Coun., Fredonia, 1988; sex equity coord. Cattaraugus-Allegany BOCES, Olean, N.Y., 1983; rschr., grantwriter RM Brown Engring., Jamestown, 1980; grantwriter Chautauqua Home Rehab. and Improvement Corp., Mayville, 1980. Past chair Jamestown Area Arts Coun., 1979; past bd. dirs. Jamestown Civic Ballet, 1980; past costume mistress Lucille Ball Little Theatre Jamestown, 1984; mus. dir. Southwestern Ctrl. Sch., Lakewood, N.Y., 1984-94; bd. dirs. Joint Neighborhood Project, Jamestown, 1988, Rsch. and Planning for Human Svcs. of Chautauqua Co., Inc., Jamestown, 1994, Fredonia Chamber Players, 1994; mem. ann. appeal com. Jamestown YWCA, 1993-94. Mem. Nat. Coun. Univ. Rsch. Adminstrs., Soc. Rsch. Adminstrs., Univ. Colls. Rsch. Coun. (chair 1993—). Democrat. Episcopalian. Home: 66 Spruce St Jamestown NY 14701 Office: SUNY Fredonia NY 14063

BRYANT, ANNE LINCOLN, association executive; b. Jamaica Plain, Mass., Nov. 26, 1949; d. John Winslow and Anne (Phillips) B.; m. Peter Harned Ross, June 15, 1986; stepchildren: Charlotte Ross, George Ross. BA in English, Secondary Edn., Simmons Coll., 1971; EdD in Higher Edn., U. Mass., 1978. Intern U. Mass., Amherst, 1972; asst. to dean Springfield Tech. C.C., 1972-74; dir. Nat. Assn. Bank Women Ednl. Found., Chgo., 1974-86; v.p. P.M. Haeger, Chgo., 1978-86; exec. dir. AAUW, Washington, 1986—, also exec. dir. Ednl. Found., Legal Advocacy Fund. Contbr. articles to profl. jours. Mem. exec. com. Simmons Coll., Boston, 1971—; adv. commr. Edn. Commn. States, 1986—; mem. bd. govs. UNA of U.S.A., 1991—, Ind. Sector, 1988-94, Hosp. Corp. Am., 1993-94. Recipient William H. Cosby Jr. award U. Mass., 1983; named Woman of Yr. for Edn., YWCA, 1976. Fellow Am. Soc. Assn. Execs. (bd. dirs. 1985-88, Key award 1992); mem. Am. Assn. for Higher Edn. (bd. dirs. 1980-87). Episcopalian. Office: AAUW 1111 16th St NW Washington DC 20036-4873

BRYANT, BARBARA EVERITT, academic researcher, market research consultant, former federal agency administrator; b. Ann Arbor, Mich., Apr. 5, 1926; d. William Littell and Dorothy (Wallace) Everitt; m. John H. Bryant, Aug. 14, 1948; children: Linda Bryant Valentine, Randal E., Lois Bryant Chen. AB, Cornell U., 1947; MA, Mich. State U., 1967, PhD, 1970. Editor art Chem. Engring. mag. McGraw-Hill Pub. Co., N.Y.C., 1947-48; editorial rsch. asst. U. Ill., Urbana, 1948-49; free-lance editor, writer, 1950-61; with continuing edn. adminstrn. dept. Oakland Univ., Rochester, Mich., 1961-66; grad. rsch. asst. Mich. State Univ., East Lansing, 1966-70; sr. analyst to v.p. Market Opinion Rsch., Detroit, 1970-77, sr. vp., 1977-89; dir. Bur. of the Census, U.S. Dept. of Commerce, 1989-93; rsch. scientist Sch. Bus. Adminstrn. U. Mich., 1993—. Author: High School Students Look at Their World, 1970, American Women Today & Tomorrow, 1977, Moving Power and Money: The Politics of Census Taking, 1995; contbr. articles to profl. jours. Mem. U.S. Census Adv. Com., Washington, 1980-86, Mich. Job Devel. Authority, Lansing, Mich., 1980-85; state editor LWV of Mich., 1959-61. Mem. Women in Communications, Inc. (pres. Detroit 1974-75, Nat. Headliner award 1980), Am. Mktg. Assn. (pres. Detroit 1976-77, midwestern v.p. 1978-80, v.p. mktg. rsch. 1982-84), Am. Statis. Assn., Am. Assn. Pub. Opinion Rsch., Population Assn. Am., Cosmos Club (Washington), Cornell Club N.Y. Republican. Presbyterian. Avocation: swimming. Home: 1505 Sheridan Dr Ann Arbor MI 48104-4051 Office: U Mich Sch Bus Adminstrn Ann Arbor MI 48109-1234

BRYANT, BERTHA ESTELLE, retired nurse; b. Va., Jan. 11, 1927; d. E.F. and Julia B. Diploma, Sibley Meml. Hosp., Washington, 1947; B.S., Am. U., 1948; M.A., Tchrs. Coll., Columbia U., 1962. Staff nurse, head nurse NIH, Bethesda, Md., 1954-59; asst. dir. nursing USPHS Alaska Native Hosp., Mt. Edgecumbe, 1959-61; instr. Sch. Nursing, U. Mich., 1962-64; chief div. clin. nursing Bur. Nursing, D.C. Dept. Public Health, Washington, 1964-65; commd. Nurse Corps, USPHS, 1965, nurse dir., capt., 1974—; nurse cons., hosp. facilities services br., div. hosps. and med. facilities Bur. Health Services, HEW, Silver Spring; nurse cons., social analysis br., div. health services research and analysis Nat. Center Health Services Research, Health Resources Adminstrn., HEW, Rockville, Md.; nurse cons. div. extramural research Nat. Center Health Services Research, Office Asst. Sec. Health, HHS, Hyattsville, Md., 1977-81. Contbr. articles to profl. jours. Mem. AAUW, Assn. Mil. Surgeons U.S., Commd. Officers Assn. USPHS. Home: 8004 Westover Rd Bethesda MD 20814-1147

BRYANT, EVELYN CHRISTINE, elementary education educator; b. Lakeview, S.C., Aug. 1, 1942; d. Jasper L. and Marcella (William) Page; m. James A. Bryant, Feb. 1, 1964; children: James Jr., Marc C., Linda E. AAS in Gen. Edn., Fayetteville Tech. C.C., Fayetteville, N.C., 1987; BS in Elem. Edn., Fayetteville State U., 1990, MA in Spl. Edn., 1994. Tchr.'s aide spl. edn. Ashley Sch., Fayetteville, 1976-81; substitute tchr. Cumberland County/Ft. Bragg, Fayetteville, 1989-90; data processor Census Bur., Fayetteville, 1990; tchr. chpt. I reading Midway Elem., Dunn, N.C., 1990—. Active Parents Autism Children, 1970—, Mother's Mar. Dimes, 1990-91. Mem. NEA, Order Eastern Star (asst. sec. 1986-87), Heroine Jericho, Daus. of Zion, Kappa Delta Pi. Baptist. Home: 725 Glensford Dr Fayetteville NC 28304

BRYANT, FRANCES JANE, newspaper editor; b. Cushing, Okla., Dec. 10, 1933; d. Edward Glahn and Dorothy Evelyn (McLean) B. AA, Christian Coll., Columbia, Mo., 1953; BJ, U. Mo., 1955. Reporter The Norman (Okla.) Transcript, 1955-57, wire editor, 1957-59, city editor, 1959-67, mng. editor, 1967—. Bd. dirs. Juvenile Svcs., Inc., Cleveland County, Okla., 1981-87, pres., 1984-85; bd. dirs. Cleveland County chpt. ARC, 1987-90. Named Oustanding Bus. Woman Bus. and Profl. Women, Norman, 1971, State Woman of Year Theta Sigma Phi, U. Okla., 1968; recipient Disting. Alumni award Columbia Coll. (formerly Christian Coll.), 1980; inducted Okla. Journalism Hall of Fame, 1994. Mem. AP Okla. News Execs. (pres. 1970-71, 91-92), Soc. Profl. Journalists, Altrusa Internat. (pres. Norman chpt. 1969-71). Democrat. Episcopalian. Home: 606 Sherwood Dr Norman OK 73071-4905 Office: The Norman Transcript 215 E Comanche St Norman OK 73069-6007

BRYANT, GAY, magazine editor, writer; b. Newcastle, Eng.; came to U.S., 1969; d. Richard King and Catherine (Shiel) B.; m. Charles Childs, Apr. 10, 1982. Student, St. Clare's Coll., Oxford, Eng., 1961-63. Sr. editor Penthouse Mag., N.Y.C., 1968-74; assoc. editor Oui mag., N.Y.C., 1974-75; founding editor New Dawn mag., N.Y.C., 1975-79; exec. editor Working Woman mag., N.Y.C., 1979-81, editor, 1981-84; editor, v.p. Family Circle mag., N.Y.C., 1984-86; editor-in-chief Infashion mag., N.Y.C., 1987-88, New Woman mag., N.Y.C., 1988-90, Mirabella mag., N.Y.C., 1990—; adj. prof. Sch. Journalism, NYU, 1982-87. Author: The Underground Travel Guide, 1973, How I Learned To Like Myself, 1975, The Working Woman Report, 1984. Recipient award Acad. Women Achievers, YMCA, N.Y.C., 1982. Mem. Women's Media Group, Am. Soc. Mag. Editors. Home: 34 Horatio St New York NY 10014-1622 Office: Mirabella Mag 200 Madison Ave 8th Fl New York NY 10016

BRYANT, JO ELIZABETH, state legislator; b. Aug. 6, 1937. AD, Cumberland Coll.; attended, St. Joseph Hosp. Sch. Med. Technology. Mem. Ky. Ho. of Reps. Mem. Med. Technologist Assn., Am. Soc. Clin. Pathologists, Ky. Real Estate Commn., Eastern Star. Republican. Baptist. Home: PO Box 536 Williamsburg KY 40769-0536 Office: Ky Ho of Reps State Capitol Frankfort KY 40601*

BRYANT, JOSEPHINE HARRIET, library executive; b. Oshawa, Ont., Can., Dec. 3, 1947; d. Donald Joseph and Margaret Mary (Quilty) B.; children: David Joseph, Michael Andrew. BA, U. Toronto, Ont., 1969, BLS, 1970, MLS, 1974; diploma in Pub. Adminstrn., U. Western Ont., London, 1988. Libr. Ont. Hydro, Toronto, 1970-74; libr. supr. Brampton (Ont.) Pub. Libr. and Art Gallery, 1974-77, branch head, 1977-79; regional dir. Fairview North York (Ont.) Pub. Libr., 1983-85, mgr. cen. libr., 1986, dep. dir., 1986-88, chief exec. officer, 1988—. Mem. ALA, Can. Libr. Assn., Ont. Libr. Assn., Inst. Pub. Adminstrn. Office: North York Pub Libr, 5120 Yonge St, North York, ON Canada M2N 5N9

BRYANT, KAREN WORSTELL, financial consultant; b. Cadillac, Mich., Sept. 7, 1942; d. Harley Orville and Rose Edith (Bell) Worstell; children: Lynda Jean, Tracey Jo, Cynthia Jill, Troy Thomas; m. Robert Melvin Bryant, Nov. 29, 1968. Student, Cen. Mich. U., 1963-67, Mich. State U., 1966, Johns Hopkins U., 1982-83. Sales rep. Xerox Corp., Southfield, Mich., 1972-74; cons. and employment contracts IBM World Trade Asia, The Policy Study Grp., Johnson & Johnson Internat., Tokyo, 1974-79; area sales mgr. Universal Plastics, McLean, Va., 1979-81; exec. product mgr. The Western Union Telegraph Co., Upper Saddle River, N.J., 1981-86; dir. mktg. and sales support The Nat. Guardian Corp., Greenwich, Conn., 1986-88; fin. cons. Smith Barney, Paramus, N.J., 1988—; guest lectr. for orgns.; fin. cons. to pastoral group Nyack (N.Y.) Hosp.; guest on TV documentaries. Contbr. articles to profl. jours. Mem. World Wildlife Fedn., N.Y. State Horse Coun., Nature Conservancy. Republican. Home: 19 Sky Meadow Rd Suffern NY 10901-2520 Office: Smith Barney Inc South Tower 140 E Ridgewood Ave 4th Fl Paramus NJ 07652-3919

BRYANT, MARY ELIZABETH, theatrical press agent; b. Apopka, Fla., Oct. 17; d. Theodore Alfred Bryant and Mabel Elizabeth (Eddy) Bryant-Decker. AB, U. Miami, 1953. Press and pub. rels. agt. Show Boat, Kiss of the Spider Woman, Grandchild of kings, Roza, Grind, A Doll's Life, Merrily We Roll Along, Sweeney Todd, Evita, Cabaret, Side by Side by Sondheim, A Little Night Music, Company, Follies, She Loves Me, Never Too Late, Zorba. Mem. Assn. Theatrical Press Agts. and Mgrs. Office: 165 W 46th St Ste 910 New York NY 10036-2501

BRYANT, NANCY WHITE, publishing executive; b. Columbus, Ohio, Sept. 1, 1957; d. Thomas Edward and Joan Carolyn (Olsen) White; m. George Frank Bryant Jr., July 9, 1983 (div. 1993). AB, Sweet Briar Coll., 1979; student, Pratt Inst., 1983. Catalog prodn. staff Sotheby's, N.Y.C., 1981-84; mgr. traffic dept. Dancer, Fitzgerald, Sample Direct, N.Y.C., 1985; devel. officer Sarah Lawrence Coll., Bronxville, N.Y., 1986; pres. White-Bryant Fine Arts Consulting, Croton-on-Hudson, N.Y., 1986-88; assoc. pub., editor The Aircraft Bulletin, N.Y.C., 1988-89; mktg., creative dir., co-founder Interview Images Inc, Port Chester, N.Y., 1989-90; U.S. sales mgr. Cahner's Marine Pubs., Stamford, Conn., 1990; pubs. dir. Designer Showhouses Internat. Ltd., N.Y.C., 1991-92; founder, pres. Showhouse Publs. Inc., N.Y.C., 1992—. Pub. Showhouse mag., 1994—. Pres., trustee Friends of Art, Sweet Briar Coll., 1985—; chmn. Alzhaimer's Disease Brochure, 1985-86. Season champion Internat. One Design Yachts, Long Island Sound Fleet, 1990, '91, Yacht Racing Assn. Long Island Sound, 1991. Mem. Jr. League on Hudson (trustee 1987), The Coffeehouse, Am. Yacht Club, Alumnae Assn. Sweet Briar Coll. (trustee 1988-91). Office: Showhouse Publs Inc 18 E 41st St New York NY 10017

BRYANT, PAMELA ANNE, military career officer; b. Detroit, July 15, 1950; d. Theodore Louis and Martha Marie (Nordstrom) Cogut; children: Tessa A. McGeaughay, Sean L. BS in Vocat. Indsl. Edn., U. Md., 1976; student, Mich. State U., East Lansing, 1969-71; MS, Troy (Ala.) State U., 1986. Commd. 2d lt. USAF, 1980, advanced through grades to maj., 1984; chief cargo ops., reports and systems div. 22d Air Force, Travis AFB, Calif., 1989-90; chief support div. directorate transp. Hdqrs USAF Res., Robins AFB, Ga., 1990-94; squadron commdr. 650th Transp. Squadron, Edwards AFB, Calif., 1994—; owner Bryant Enterprises, 1991—; lectr. Clifton-Morenci (Ariz.) Rotary Club, 1989. Soccer team coord. Am. Youth Assn., RAF Laken Heath, Eng., 1983; troop leader Girl Scouts U.S., RAF Laken Heath, 1982; membership chmn. Boy Scouts Am., RAF Laken Heath, 1983. U. Md. scholar, 1976. Mem. Nat. Def. Transp. Assn., NAFE, Air Force Assn. (life), Alpha Sigma Lambda.

BRYANT, PAMELA KAYE, nurse; b. Cullman, Ala., Aug. 19, 1953; d. James Franklin and Dorothy Marie (McAfee) Hancock; m. Patrick Dwight Bryant, Oct. 22, 1971; children: Joshua Patrick, Jody Lee. AAS in Nursing cum laude, Wallace State Community Coll., 1978; BS in Nursing with honors, U. Ala., Birmingham, 1982. RN, Ala. Nursing asst. Cullman Med. Ctr., 1975-76; staff nurse Ensor, Baccus, Williamson OB/GYN, Cullman, 1978-80; staff nurse Intermediate Care Unit Carraway Meth. Med. Ctr., Birmingham, 1982-85; staff nurse Cullman Internal Medicine, 1985-89; staff nurse, endoscopy svcs. Cullman Regional Med. Ctr., 1990—; nurse ARC, Birmingham, 1983. Recipient various awards Ala. State Fair, local county fairs for pen, ink and pencil drawings. Mem. Sigma Theta Tau. Democrat. Baptist. Home: 1400 E Hanceville Rd Cullman AL 35055-5306

BRYANT-CARTER, SHIRLEY M., school administrator; b. Chgo., Nov. 5, 1949; d. Charles and Minnie (Ferguson) Amerson; m. Naggie L. Carter Jr., Nov. 18, 1967 (dec. Aug. 1990); children: Kathryn Carter Jewell, Nycole L. Carter, Tiyaka A. Carter. BS in Edn. cum laude, Chgo. State U., 1974, MSEd in Counseling, 1978; postgrad., No. Ill. U., 1990—. Cert. sch. administr., counselor, Ill. Educator Chgo. Bd. Edn., 1975-88; dir. guidance Chgo. Vocat. High Sch., 1988—; pres., CEO Women on the Move Inc., Chgo., 1990—; instr. Harold Washington Coll., Chgo., 1989; lead counselor Northeastern Ill. U., 1990—; site supr. Am. Coll. Testing, Princeton, N.J., 1988—; mem. scholarship selection com. McDonald's Future Leader Program, Chgo., 1992. Author: Scholarship Hotline, 1989. Mem. tranfer adv. bd. Malcolm X Coll., 1993—; active Ill. Coun. Coll. Attendance, Chgo., 1989. Recipient Disting. Educator award Chgo. Assn. Asst. Prins., 1994. Mem. NAFE, ACA, Internat. Platform Assn., Chgo. Area Alliance Black Sch. Educators, Adult Continuing Edn. Assn., Phi Delta Kappa. Baptist. Home: 9400 S Hamilton Ave Chicago IL 60620-5613 Office: Chgo Vocat High Sch 2100 E 87th St Chicago IL 60617-3011

BRYANT EPPS, SHARON ELAINE, bank executive; b. Mesquite, Tex., June 25, 1962; m. Joel Epps, June 4, 1994; children: Katie, Jeremy, Marabeth. BBA, Abilene Christian U., 1983. V.p. corp. banking Bank One, Tex., N.A., Ft. Worth, 1986—; bd. dirs. Metro. Ft. Worth YMCA. Mem. Ft. Worth Profl. Women's Orgn., 1994. Mem. Ft. Worth C. of C. (local bus. devel. com. 1992—). Office: Bank One Tex NA 500 Throckmorton Fort Worth TX 76102

BRYERS, DIANE SARKISIAN, realtor, pianist; b. Phila., Nov. 10, 1949; d. Robert and Grace (Samuelian) Sarkisian; m. John J. Bryers, May 12, 1979; 1 child, Kira. MusB magna cum laude, Temple U., 1976, MusM, 1979; postgrad., Juilliard Sch. Music, 1979-81, Peabody Conservatory Music, 1981-86. Transcriber Ct. Reporters, Phila., 1967-70; legal sec., real estate paralegal Cohen, Shapiro, Polisher et al, atory Music, 1969-79; paralegal Eagan & Eagan, Willow Grove, Pa., 1980-83; owner, sales rep. Crawford Internat., Inc., Willow Grove, 1875-87; realtor Weichert Realtors, Spring House, Pa., 1987-88, RE/MAX Svcs., Inc., Blue Bell, Pa., 1988—; concert pianist, 1972—. Scholar Nat. Endowment for Arts, 1976-79. Mem. Nat. Assn. Realtors, Ctrl. Montgomery Bd. Realtors, North Penn Bd. Realtors (profl. standards com. 1988—), Ea. Montgomery Bd. Realtors, Pa. Bd. Realtors, Montgomery-Bucks County Builders Assn., Willow Grove C. of C. Republican. Office: RE/MAX Svcs Inc 794 Penllyn Pike Blue Bell PA 19422-1669

BRYFONSKI, DEDRIA ANNE, publishing company executive; b. Utica, N.Y., Aug. 21, 1947; d. Lewis Francis and Catherine Marie (Stevens) B.; m. Alexander Burgess Cruden, May 24, 1975. B.A., Nazareth Coll., Rochester, N.Y., 1969; M.A., Fordham U., 1970. Editorial asst. Dial Press, N.Y.C., 1970-71; editor Walker & Co., N.Y.C., 1971-73; editor Gale Research Co., Detroit, 1974-79, sr. editor, 1979, v.p., assoc. editorial dir., 1979-84, sr. v.p., editorial dir., 1984-86, exec. v.p., pub., 1986—. Author: The New England Beach Book, 1974; editor: Contemporary Literary Criticism, Vols. 7-14, 1977-80, Twentieth Century Literary Criticism, vols. 1-2, 1977-78, Contemporary Issues Criticism, vol. 1, 1982, Contemporary Authors Autobiography Series, vol. 1, 1984. Bd. dirs. Friends of Detroit Pub. Library, 1980-89, pres., 1984-86. Mem. ALA, Assn. Am. Pubs. (chmn. libraries com. 1983-85, exec. council gen. pub. div. 1985-87, co-chmn. joint com. resources and tech. services div. 1983-85). Home: 546 Lincoln Rd Grosse Pointe MI 48230-1218 Office: Gale Research Co 835 Penobscot Bldg Detroit MI 48226

BRYSON, DIXIE MARIE, psychological examiner, consultant; b. Little Rock, Sept. 5, 1959; d. Golden Daniel and Bernice Jane (Huggins) B. BS in Psychology, U. Ctrl. Ark., 1980, MS in Community Svc. Counseling, 1981. Cert. sch. psychology specialist, Ark. Psychol. examiner, clin. coord. adolescent treatment home East Ark. Regional Mental Health Ctr., Helena, 1981-83; psychol. examiner, adminstr. S.E. Ark. Human Devel. Ctr., Warren, 1983-84; psychol. examiner Conway (Ark.) Human Devel. Ctr., 1984-86; psychol. examiner, behavioral specialist Continuum Svcs., Conway, 1986-88; psychol. examiner, sch. psychology specialist Conway Pub. Schs., 1988—; cons. Conway Children's Clinic, 1990—, Counseling Assocs. Inc., Conway, 1993—. Chairperson Faulkner County Child Protection Team, Conway, 1984—, Faulkner County Child Abuse and Neglect Prevention Coun., Conway, 1992—; mem. Faulkner County Multidisciplinary Team, 1991—; vol. pre-post test counselor Ark. AIDS Found., Little Rock, 1991-93. Mem. Nat. Assn. Sch. Psychologists, Ark. Sch. Psychology Assn. (bd. dirs. 1993—, legis. chairperson 1993—). Home: 12 Kingspark Dr Maumelle AR 72113 Office: Conway Pub Sch 2220 Prince St Conway AR 72032

BRYSON, DOROTHY PRINTUP, retired educator; b. Britton, S.D., Dec. 2, 1894; d. David Lawrence and Marion Harland (Gamsby) Printup; m. Archer Butler Hulbert, June 16, 1923 (dec. Dec. 1933); children: Joanne Woodward, Nancy Printup; m. Franklin Fearing Wing, Oct. 15, 1938 (dec. Mar. 1942); m. Arthur Earl Bryson, Feb. 15, 1964 (dec. Apr. 1979). AB, Oberlin Coll., 1915; AM, Radcliffe Coll., 1916; LHD (hon.), Colo. Coll., 1989. Instr. Latin, Tenn. Coll., Murfreesboro, 1916-18; tchr. Latin, prin. high sch., Britton, 1918-20; instr. classics Colo. Coll., Colorado Springs, 1921-22, 23-25, sec., instr., head resident, 1951-60; tchr. latin San Luis Prep. Sch., Colorado Springs, 1934-36, 41-42, Sandia Sch., Albuquerque, 1937-39, Westlake Sch., L.A., 1946-49; exec. dir. YWCA, Colorado Springs, 1942-46, 49-51; editor western history Stewart Commn., Colorado Springs, 1934-41; ret., 1960. Editor: Overland to the Pacific, 5 vols., 1934-41. Bd. dirs. Day Nursery, Colorado Springs 1933-37. Fellow Aelioian Lit. Soc., 1920-21; scholar U. Chgo., 1920-21. Mem. LWV (v.p., bd. dirs. Colorado Springs 1943-45), Women's Edn. Soc. Colo. Coll. (pres., bd. dirs. 1955—), Reviewers Club, Tuesday Discussion Club, Pikes Peak Posse Westerners, Women's Literary Club, Phi Beta Kappa, Gamma Phi Beta. Republican. Episcopalian. Home: 107 W Cheyenne Rd Apt 610 Colorado Springs CO 80906-2509

BRZOSKA, DENISE JEANNE, paralegal, artist; b. Wilmington, Del., Mar. 21, 1945; d. Eugene Joseph and Marie Jeanette (Durr) B. Student, U. Del., 1971-84. Cert. graphic designer; cert. paralegal. Bookkeeping clk. Del. Div. of Revenue, Wilmington, 1963-66; tech. support personnel dept. physics and astronomy U. Del., Newark, 1966-91; paralegal Wilmington Trust Co./Trust Legal, 1992—. Artist representing Del. at Colliseum Arts Internat., World Trade Ctr., 1981. Campaign worker Joe Biden for U.S. Senate, Del., 1978, S.B. Woo for Lt. Gov., Del., 1984, S.B. Woo For U.S. Senate, Del., 1988. Mem. Del. Paralegal Assn., Wilmington Women in Bus., Pa. Horticultural Soc., Del. Art Mus., Wilmington Garden Day. Roman Catholic. Home: 422 Old Airport Rd New Castle DE 19720

BUC, NANCY LILLIAN, lawyer; b. Orange, N.J., July 27, 1944; d. George L. and Ethel (Rosenbaum) B. AB, Brown U., 1965, LLD (hon.), 1994; LLB, U. Va., 1969. Bar: Va. 1969, N.Y. 1977, D.C. 1978. Atty. Fed. Trade Commn., Washington, 1969-72, atty. adviser to chmn., 1970-71; asst. dir. Bureau of Consumer Protection, Washington, 1971-72; assoc. Weil, Gotshal & Manges, N.Y., 1972-77, ptnr., 1977-78; ptnr. Weil, Gotshal & Manges, Washington, 1978-80, 81-94, Buc Levitt & Beardsley, Washington, 1994—; chief counsel FDA, Rockville, Md., 1980-81; mem. recombinant DNA adv. com. NIH, 1990-94. Mem. editorial bd. Food Drug and Cosmetic Law Jour., 1981-87, Jour. of Products Liability, 1981-92, Health Span: The Jour. of Health, Bus. & Law, 1984—. Mem. adv. com. on new devels. in biotech. Office of Tech. Assessment, Washington, 1986-89, adv. com. on govt. policies and pharm. R & D, 1989-93; mem. Inst. of Medicine Com. to Study Medications Devel. and Rsch. at Nat. Inst. of Drug Abuse, 1993-95. Fellow Brown U., 1980-92; recipient Disting. Svc. award Fed. Trade Commn., Washington, 1972, Award of Merit FDA, Rockville, 1981, Sec.'s Spl. citation HHS, Washington, 1981, Ind. award Associated. Alumni of Brown U., 1991. Mem. ABA (spl. com. to study the FTC 1988-89), Com. of 200 Va. Law Sch. Found., Alan Guttmacher Inst. (bd. dirs.), Women's Legal Def. Fund (bd. dirs.). Office: Buc Levitt & Beardsley Ste 710 S 1800 M St NW Washington DC 20036-5800

BUCARO, KATHLEEN THERESE, creative director; b. Chgo., May 16, 1959; d. Martin Matthew and Catherine Madeleine (LaVerato) B. BA, Loyola U., Chgo., 1982; MS in Advt., Northwestern U., 1983. Copywriter Spiegel, Chgo., 1984-86; sr. writer BEC Advt., Chgo., 1986-87; copywriter UNISPOND Direct Response Mktg., Oak Brook, Ill., 1987-88, Haddon Advt., Chgo., 1988-89; copy supr. Foote, Cone, and Belding, Chgo., 1989-93; v.p., creative dir. Kobs & Draft Worldwide, Chgo., 1993—. Recipient Tempo award Chgo. Assn. Direct Marketers, Echo award Direct Mktg. Assn. Office: Kobs & Draft Worldwide 142 E Ontario Chicago IL 60611

BUCCI, ELAINE THERESA, lawyer, state legislator; b. Providence, Sept. 6, 1957; d. Anthony Joseph and Theresa (Garganese) B. BA in Elem. Edn. summa cum laude, Boston Coll., 1979; JD cum laude, Suffolk U., 1982. Bar: R.I. 1982, U.S. Dist. Ct. R.I. 1983. Atty. Bucci Law Offices, North Providence, R.I., 1982-94; mem R.I. Ho. of Reps., Providence, 1985-92; dep. majority leader R.I. Ho. of Reps., 1991-92; justice Dist. Ct. R.I., 1994—; clk. Providence Probate Ct., 1988-94. Active R.I. Legal/Ednl. Partnership Program, 1985—. Mem. R.I. Bar Assn., Sons of Italy. Home: 25 Prosper St Providence RI 02904-1120

BUCCI, MARY RUTH, primary education educator; b. New Castle, Pa., July 21, 1948; d. David Feyling and Mary Ann (Bintrim) Clausen; m. Richard Alan Bucci, May 24, 1975; children: Melissa Kay, Jeffrey Michael, Keren Ann. BS in Edn. cum laude, Slippery Rock U., 1971, MEd magna cum laude, 1974; MA in Edn. summa cum laude, Regents U., 1988. Ctr. tchr. and reading specialist, Pa. Tchr. lang. arts Shenango Elem. Sch., New Castle, 1971-76; tchr. kindergarten Rhema Christian Sch., Coraopolis, Pa., 1984—, curriculum specialist, 1988—, tchr. computer sci., 1991—; pvt. tutor, home sch. evaluator, cons. in field, Coraopolis, 1966—; mem. sec. Rhema Christian Sch. Bd., Aliquippa, Pa., 1986-89. Database developer Crisis Pregnancy Ctr., Coraopolis, 1986; active Prison Fellowship, Washington, 1994, Concerned Women for Am., 1994, Rutherford Inst., Charlottesville, Va., 1994. Mem. ASCD, His Schs. Assn., Alpha Xi Delta (chpt. dir. 1976-77, province collegiate dir. 1974-76). Republican. Home: 206 Windy Hill Dr Coraopolis PA 15108 Office: Rhema Christian Sch 601 Flaugherty Run Rd Coraopolis PA 15108

BUCHANAN, BEVERLY ANNE, pharmaceutical company executive; b. Chgo., Aug. 29, 1946; d. Jack Warren and Florence A. (Krey) Rexroat; m. Kenneth W. Stinnett, June 6, 1965 (div. June 1978); children: Debra A., Kenneth W. Jr.; m. Ronald Cyril Buchanan, Oct. 27, 1979. Student, Orange Coast Coll., Costa Mesa, Calif., 1976-78. Drug buyer Westfield Med. Co., Orange, Calif., 1980-82; pharm. exempte Park Lido Med. Co., Costa Mesa, 1982-86; pharm. exempte, head buyer Deckert Med. Co., Santa Ana, Calif., 1987-90; pharm. mgr. Physician Sales and Svc., Irvine, Calif., 1990—. Com. mem. Tustin (Calif.) Sch. Bd., 1979. Republican. Home: 12802 Dean St Santa Ana CA 92705

BUCHANAN, DEANNA RUDISILL, accounting administrator; b. Gastonia, N.C., Nov. 17, 1963; d. Harold Dean and Candace P. (Gates) Rudisill; m. Harold Van Buchanan, May 2, 1987; 1 child, Hillary Candace. BA, Lenoir Rhyne Coll., 1986. Staff acct. Hickory (N.C.) Springs Mfg. Co., 1986-88, cost acct., 1988-89, cost acctg. supr., 1989—. Mem. Inst. Mgmt. Accts. Baptist. Office: Hickory Springs Mfg Co 235 2d Ave NW Hickory NC 28603

BUCHANAN, DIANE KAY, pharmacist; b. Connersville, Ind., July 31, 1960; d. Everett and Wanda Lee (James) B. BS in Pharmacy, Purdue U., 1984. Registered pharmacist. Pharmacist, store mgr. Walgreen Co., Houston, 1984-86; staff pharmacist Randall's, Houston, 1986-88; staff pharmacist Osco Drug, Evansville, Ind., 1988-89, pharmacy mgr., 1989-92; cons. pharmacist Insta-Care, Decatur, Ga., 1992; asst. pharmacy mgr. Publix Super Markets, Norcross, Ga., 1992-94; pharmacy mgr. Publix Super Markets, Lawrenceville, Ga., 1994—; cmty. cons. Osco Drug, Evansville, Ind., 1988-92; part-time beauty cons. Mary Kay Cosmetics, 1993—. Mem., assoc. dir. Tri State Christian Singles, Evansville, 1988-91; mem. Evansville Mus. Contemporaries, 1989-92; mem. Mt. Carmel Christian Ch., Stone Mountain, Ga. Mem. Am. Pharm. Assn., Ind. Pharm. Assn. (D Pharmacy), Southwestern Ind. Pharmacist's Assn., Ga. Pharm. Assn., Gwinnett County Pharm. Assn., Purdue Alumni Assn. (life), Sigma Kappa (life). Home: 2533 Marcia Dr Lawrenceville GA 30244-5816 Office: 911 Ga Hwy 20 Lawrenceville GA 30243 Office: Publix Super Markets 911 Ga Hwy 120 Lawrenceville GA 30245

BUCHANAN, EDNA, journalist; b. Paterson, N.J.. Journalist Miami Beach (Fla.) Daily Sun, 1965-70; became journalist The Miami (Fla.) Herald, 1970. Author: Carr: Five Years of Rape and Murder, 1979, The Corpse Had a Familiar Face: Covering America's Hottest Beat, 1987, Nobody Lives Forever, 1990, Never Let Them See You Cry: More From Miami, America's Hottest Beat, 1992, Contents Under Pressure, 1992, Miami, It's Murder, 1994; contbr. articles to popular mags. Recipient Green Eye Shade award Soc. Profl. Journalists, 1982, Pulitzer prize for gen. reporting, 1986. Mem. United Ch. of Christ. *

BUCHANAN, GLORIA JEAN, retail executive; b. Bowling Green, Ky., Nov. 3, 1950; d. Albert M. and Lenora (Hayes)Paschal; m. Michael C.

Moonan (div.); 1 child, Shelly; m. Andrew George Buchnan. Mgr. Alexander Wallcovering, Falls Church, Va., 1976-81; decorator Duron Paints and Wallvocering, Beltsville, Md., 1982-84, sales rep., 1984-85, archtl. rep., 1985-86, dir., 1986-91; dir. archtl. sales dept. McCormick Paint Works Co., Rockville, Md., 1991—. Bd. govs. Washington Bldg. Congress, 1994—. Mem. NAFE, Constrn. Specification Inst. (industry dir. 1993-94, membership chmn. 1993-94), Interior Design Soc., Washington Sales and Mktg. Council. Republican. Episcopalian. Home: 9823 Arrowood Dr Manassas VA 22111 Office: McCormick Paint Works Co 7325 Lewis Ave Rockville MD 20705

BUCHANAN, LEE ANN, public relations executive; b. Albuquerque, July 6, 1955; d. William Henry Buchanan and Juanita Irene (Pilgrim) Wood; m. Charles Stanton Wood, Jan. 17, 1987. BA, U. Calif., Irvine, 1977. Exec. asst. to Congressman William Thomas, U.S. Ho. of Reps., Washington, 1979-83; dep. chief staff Gov. George Deukmejian, Sacramento, 1983-84; sr. v.p., ptnr. Nelson Comm., Costa Mesa, Calif., 1985-95. Bd. govs. Rep. Assocs. of Orange County, 1985—; founding sec. Orange County Young Reps., 1985. Mem. Internat. Assn. Bus. Communicators, Am. Assn. Polit. Cons., Pub. Relations Soc. Am., U. Calif.-Irvine Alumni Assn. Address: PO Box 1741 Mammoth Lakes CA 93546

BUCHANAN, LINDA PAULK, psychologist; b. Charleston, W.Va., May 20, 1958; d. Linton Auburn and Patricia Gwendolyn (McCulley) P.; m. William Lee Buchanan, Dec. 3, 1983. BA in Psychology, U. Ga., 1980; MEd in Cmty. Counseling, Ga. State U., 1983, PhD in Psychology, 1993. Instr. psychology Clayton (Ga.) Coll., 1983; dir. cmty. svcs. Psychol. Studies Inst., Atlanta, 1983-86; psychotherapist Presbyn. Hosp. Ctr., Oklahoma City, 1986-87; family therapist Moore (Okla.) Family Inst., 1986-87; staff therapist Atlanta Counseling Ctr., 1988-92; psychology resident Med. Coll. Ga./Augusta VA Med. Ctr., 1992-93; clin. dir., founder, owner Atlanta Ctr. for Eating Disorders, 1993—. Mem. APA, Ga. Psychol. Assn., Phi Kappa Phi, Psi Chi. Office: Atlanta Ctr for Eating Disorders 1 Dunwoody Pk Ste 112 Atlanta GA 30338

BUCHANAN, MARY ELLA, nurse; b. Hot Springs, Ark., July 19, 1950; d. Robert Glynn and Georgia Catherine (Dobson) B.; B.S. in Nursing, Vanderbilt U., 1972; M.S., U. Tenn., 1974. Staff nurse Met. Health Dept., Nashville, 1972-73; commd. lt. Nurse Corps, U.S. Army, 1973, advanced through grades to maj., 1983; ambulatory care nurse clinician Family Practice Clinic, Ft. Belvoir, Va., 1974-76, Robinson Barracks Army Health Clinic, Stuttgart, Germany, 1976-77, 5th Gen. Hosp., 1977-79, Acad. Health Scis., Ft. Sam Houston, Tex., 1979-80; ambulatory care nurse clinician Walter Reed Army Med. Center, Washington, 1980-81, nurse researcher Nursing Research Service, 1980-82, Nurse Ward 72, 1982-84; head nurse Ward 4A Irwin Army Community Hosp., Ft. Riley, Kans., 1984-85, evening and night supr., 1985-86, coordinator infection control, quality assurance, 1986-87; infection control cons. 18th MEDCOM, Seoul, 1988, infection control officer Silas B. Hays Army Community Hosp., Ft. Ord, Calif., 1989-91, nurse epidemiologist preventive medicine svc., Ft. Riley, Kans., 1991—; quality care cons. Manhattan, Ks., 1990—. Mem. Am. Nurses Assn. (cert. family nurse clinician, div. community health), Am. Pub. Health Assn., Assn. for Practitioners in Infection Control and Epidemiology (cert.), Sigma Theta Tau. Methodist. Clubs: Smithsonian Assocs. Home: 2010 Anderson Ave Manhattan KS 66502-3606 Office: USA MEDDAC Preventive Medicine Sv Fort Riley KS 66442

BUCHANAN, TERI BAILEY, communications agency owner; b. Long Beach, Calif., Feb. 24, 1946; d. Alton Hervey and Ruth Estelle (Thompson) Bailey; m. Robert Wayne Buchanan, Aug. 14, 1964 (div. May 1979). BA in English with highest honors, Ark. Poly. Coll., 1968. With employee communications AT&T, Kansas City, Mo., 1968-71; freelance writer Ottawa, Kans., 1971-73; publs. dir. Ottawa U., 1973-74; regional info. officer U.S. Dept. Labor, Kansas City, 1974; owner, operator PBT Communications, Kansas City, 1975-79; sr. pub. affairs rep., sr. editor, exhibit supr., communications specialist Standard Oil/Chevron, San Francisco, 1979-84; owner The Resource Group/Mktg. Comm., Yountville, Calif., 1984—; mem. faculty pub. rels. master's program Golden Gate U., San Francisco, 1987. Pub. rels. trainer Bus. Vols. for Arts, San Francisco, 1985-93; mem. Napa Conf. and Visitors Bur. Recipient Internat. Assn. Bus. Communicators Bay Area Gold and Silver awards, 1984. Mem. Napa C. of C., Yountville C. of C. (mktg. com.). Democrat. Episcopalian. Office: The Resource Group 6516 Yount St Yountville CA 94599

BUCHANAN, VALERIE RUSSO, nursing administrator, critical care nurse, entrepreneur, consultant; b. New Haven, Feb. 23, 1949; d. Alfred D. and Sherry (Florio) Russo; m. George F. Buchanan, 1966; children: George F. III, Gregory. AA, Middle Tenn. State U., 1980; BS, Ea. Ill. U., 1990; MPA, Albany State Coll., 1993. RN, Ill., Tenn., Ga.; cert. CCRN, nursing adminstr. Staff nurse U. Miss. Med. Ctr., Jackson, Rutherford Hosp., Murfreesboro, Tenn., S.E. Lackey Meml. Hosp., Forest, Miss.; staff nurse, asst. mgr., nurse mgr. Carle Found. Hosp., Urbana, Ill.; nurse mgr. surg. ICU, progressive care unit Phoebe Putney Meml. Hosp., Albany, Ga., 1990-92; dir. critical care nursing So. Ga. Med. Ctr., Valdosta, Ga., 1992-93; pres. The Buchanan Cos. Inc., Albany, Ga., 1994—; affiliate faculty Albany State Coll. Contbr. articles to profl. jours. Mem. AACN, Am. Heart Assn. (cardiopulmonary and critical care nursing couns.), Am. Trauma Soc., Am. Orgn. Nurses Execs., Am. Coll. Healthcare Execs., Soc. of Critical Care Medicine, Am. Soc. Pub. Adminstrs., Ga. Hosp. Assn., Ga. Orgn. Nurse Execs., Alpha Sigma Lambda, Sigma Theta Tau. Home: 1201 N Davis St Albany GA 31701-1843 Office: The Buchanan Cos Inc PO Box 491 Albany GA 31702

BUCHANAN-SOHRABI, JANICE LOUISE, finance administrator; b. Wichita, Kans., Oct. 23, 1961; d. Patric Vance and Mary Jane (Joyner) Buchanan; m. Jalil Sohrabi, Aug. 23, 1985. AB, U. Chgo., 1983; MBA, U. Okla., 1985. Fin. analyst Fed. Res. Bank, Oklahoma City, 1985-87; credit mgr. Mistletoe Freight, Oklahoma City, 1987-89; fiscal analyst Ho. Reps., State of Okla., Oklahoma City, 1989-91, asst. fiscal dir., 1991—; mem. fiscal affairs and oversight com. Nat. Conf. State Legislators, Denver, 1993. Editor: FY-93 Legislative Appropriations, 1992, FY-94 Legislative Appropriations, 1993. Vol. Children's Ctr., Bethany, Okla., 1990—. Mem. Assn. MBA Execs., Downtown Bus. Women's Assn. Democrat. Unitarian. Office: Okla State Ho Reps 305 State Capital Oklahoma City OK 73105

BUCHBINDER-GREEN, BARBARA JOYCE, art and architectural historian; b. Bronx, N.Y., Dec. 23, 1944; d. Michael and Esther Buchbinder; m. Raymond Jerome Green, Dec. 18, 1970. BA cum laude, Vanderbilt U., 1965; PhD, Northwestern U., 1974. Teaching asst. Northwestern U., Evanston, Ill., 1967-68; lectr. Northwestern U., Chgo., 1975; freelance researcher and writer Evanston, 1977—; editor GreenAssoc. Architects, Inc., Evanston, 1979—; cons. nomination forms Nat. Register of Historic Places, 1983—; mem. architecture adv. com. Mus. Sci. and Industry, Chgo., 1980-86; trustee Evanston Hist. Soc., 1986-92, pres., 1988-90, mem. house walk com. 1981-83, 88-90, chmn., 1988-90, mem. restoration planning com., 1980-91, editor newsletter TimeLines, 1989-92. Author: Lucy Fitch Perkins, 1984, Evanston: A Pictorial History, 1989; editor, compiler Evanstoniana, 1984; guest curator "Lucy Fitch Perkins" exhibit, 1983-84, "Photographs from Evanstoniana" exhibit, 1984-87; published photographer: Evanstoniana 1984, Evanston: A Pictorial History, 1989, Victorian Details, 1990; history editor Chgo. Yacht Club Blinker, 1993—; contbr. articles to profl. jours. Founding mem. Preservation League of Evanston, 1982; commr. Evanston Preservation Commn., 1981-89, chmn. preservations awards com., 1983-84, mem. evaluation com. 1978-92, chmn. 1985-89; mem. Citizen's Adv. Com. on Pub. Pl. Names, 1989-92. Univ. fellow Northwestern U., 1968-69, Dissertation Year fellow, 1969-70; Vanderbilt U. scholar, 1962-65. Mem. Victorian Soc. in Am. (bd. dirs. Chgo. chpt. 1978-81), Chgo. Architecture Found. Aux. Bd. (sec. 1990-91, exec. com. 1990-92, v.p. for community affairs 1991-92), Archtl. Soc. of Art Inst. Chgo., Soc. Archtl. Historians, Women's Archtl. League (v.p. 1980-82), Chgo. Maritime Soc., Nat. Trust for Hist. Preservation (bd. mem. Dewey Cmty. Conf. 1981-84, exec. com. 1981-82, rec. sec. 1982-83), Tibetan Terrier Club Am., Cliff Dwellers Club. Home and Office: 1026 Michigan Ave Evanston IL 60202-1436

BUCHERRE, VERONIQUE, environmental company executive; b. Casablanca, Morocco, Nov. 20, 1951; came to U.S., 1967; d. Maurice Daniel Bucherre and Lucette Jaqueline Piani; m. Douglas Lee Frazier; 1 child, Marc-Andrew. Diploma Para Profesores, Gregorio Maranon, Madrid, 1972; MA, San Francisco State U., 1974; PhD in Latin Am. Affairs, U. Paris-Sorbonne, 1980; diploma in conf. interpreting, London Sch. of Poly., 1983. Lic. real estate broker, Md. Instr. French Peace Corps, Baker, La., 1968; editorial asst. Newsweek mag., San Francisco, 1970-72; mem. faculty San Francisco State U., 1972-74, 77; conf. interpreter-translator France and U.S., 1974-85, rural developer, 1976-86; pres. Bucherre & Assocs., Washington, 1985-88; inventor The Rainbank System, 1985; bd. dirs. Rainbank System, 1986-88, CEO; pres. Rainbank Group Ltd., 1988—; vis. prof. Am. U., Washington, 1992, 93; student body rep. IHEAL, Sorbonne, Paris, 1974-75; mem. bd. mgmt. Inst. des Hautes Etudes del L'Amerique Latine, Paris, 1975-76; mem. Lab III, Centre Nat. de Recherche Scientifique, Paris, 1975-77; mem. civilian pers. rules editing com. Inter-Am. Def. Bd., 1991-94, pres. internat. civilian staff, 1987-92, bd. dirs., 1991-93. Author: Florence, 1979, Uruguay, 1980; co-author: Civilian Personnel Rules of the Inter-American Defense Board, Relief Ops. Manual. Named Hon. Citizen City of Mobile, Ala. Mem. Le Droit Humain (Paris), Droit Humain Club (Paris), GITE Club (Paris). Office: 6404 Western Ave Bethesda MD 20815-3307

BUCHHEIT, MELANIE FRANCIS, computer analyst; b. Savannah, Ga., Mar. 23, 1969; d. Frank A. and Brabara Joan (Watts) B. BS in Computer Sci., Armstrong State Coll., 1992. Adminstrv. computer analyst Armstrong State Coll., Savannah, 1990-92; small systems computer analyst Gulfstream Aerospace Co., Savannah, 1992-93; pvt. computer cons. Dallas, 1993-94; computing site ops. supr. Ariz. State U., Tempe, 1994—. 2d lt. Corps Engrs., USAR, 1992—. Home: 4425 N 78th St # 124B Scottsdale AZ 85251 Office: Ariz State U M/S # 0101 Scottsdale AZ 85251

BUCHHOLZ, BARBARA BALLINGER, free-lance writer; b. N.Y.C., Jan. 17, 1949; d. Joseph and Estelle Ruth (Cohen) Ballinger; m. Edward John Buchholz, Oct. 23, 1971; children: Joanna Emily, Lucy Rebecca. BA, Barnard Coll., 1971; MA, Hunter Coll., 1976; postgrad., NYU, 1978-80, Washington U., 1982-85. Editor House and Garden Guides mag., N.Y.C., 1972-80; reporter St. Louis Post-Dispatch, 1980-88; free-lance writer bus. and food publs. Chgo., 1988—. Co-author: Needlepoint Designs from Amish Quilts, 1977, Corporate Bloodlines: The Future of the Family Firm, 1989; author, editor: People's Emergency Guide, 1980, The Aviator's Source Book, 1982. Democrat.

BUCHHOLZ, KRISTI MICHELLE ATCHLEY, health and beauty aids executive; b. Knoxville, Tenn., May 6, 1962; d. Oliver Wendell and Montie Jane (Rogers) Atchley; m. James William Buchholz Jr., May 9, 1987; 1 child, James William III. BS in Advt., U. Tenn., 1985. Sales rep. Internat. Playtex, Dover, Del., 1985-87; mgr. key account ter. Shulton U.S.A., Collierville, Tenn., 1987-89, area mgr., 1989-90; 3 market dept. mgr., exec. HBA/GM Sales Mark Brokerage Co., Memphis, 1990—; speaker in field. Singer, soloist U. Tenn., 1980-83. Singer Friendship Ambassador Club, 1978-79; active local polit. campaigns. Mem. Women in Advt., Univ. Tenn. Advt. Club. Republican. Baptist. Office: 1727 Kirby Pkwy Memphis TN 38120-4367

BUCHMAN, MARION, poet, educator; b. Balt.; d. Jacob Solomon and Mildred (Valinski) Friedmond. Poetry reader Rider Coll., Trenton, N.J., 1963; instr. prosody Community Coll. Balt., 1970, Am. U., Washington, 1976, Johns Hopkins U., Balt., 1976-82, Balt. Free U., 1976-82. Author: A Voice in Ramah, 1960, America, 1976, In His Pavilion, 1986; contbr. numerous poems to mags., newspapers, anthologies, jours. including The N.Y. Times, Md. Eng. Jour., Ariz. Quar., Poet Lore, Stanza, Cats, Poetry View, Redbook; poems and books housed in Spl. Collection Dept. John Hopkins U. Recipient Cheltenham prize Arts Coun. Gt. Britain, John Masefield award, Al Di La prize Franklin Coll. Switzerland, Golden Poet award, 1st prize World of Poetry, 1989. Mem. Poetry Soc. Am. (awards 1978—), London Poetry Secretariat, Poetry Soc. G.B., N.Y. Poetry Forum, Nat. Fedn. State Poetry Socs., Md. Council English Tchrs. (hon.), Nat. Council Tchrs. English (affiliate), Author's Guild Am., Author's League Am. Home: 11 Slade Ave Apt 315 Baltimore MD 21208-5211

BUCHWALD, NAOMI REICE, federal magistrate judge; b. Kingston, N.Y., Feb. 14, 1944; BA cum laude, Brandeis U., 1965; LLB, cum laude, Columbia U., 1968. Bar: N.Y. 1968, U.S. Ct. Appeals (2d cir.) 1969, U.S. Dist. Ct. (so. and ea. dists.) N.Y. 1970, U.S. Supreme Ct. 1978. Litigation assoc. Marshall, Bratter, Greene, Allison & Tucker, N.Y.C., 1968-73; asst. U.S. atty. So. Dist. N.Y., 1973-80, dep. chief civil div., 1976-79, chief civil div., 1979-80; U.S. magistrate judge U.S. Dist. Ct. (so. dist.) N.Y., N.Y.C., 1980—, chief magistrate judge, 1994—. Editor Columbia Jour. Law and Social Problems, 1967-68. Recipient spl. citation FDA Commrs., 1978. Mem. ABA, Fed. Bar Coun. (v.p. 1982-84), Assn. of Bar of City of N.Y. (trademarks and unfair competition com. 1988-89, mem. long range planning com. 1993—, litigation com. 1994—), N.Y. State Bar Assn., Phi Beta Kappa, Omicron Delta Epsilon. Office: US Courthouse Rm 1602 Foley Sq New York NY 10007

BUCINSKI, JANICE KAY, secondary education educator; b. Poplar Bluff, Mo., Mar. 24, 1952; d. John Wiley and Sylvia (Brown) Smith; 1 child, Wesley Alexander. BA in History and Edn., U. Ark., 1974; MS in Edn., Ea. Ill. U., 1991. Lic. tchr., Ill., Mo. Social studies tchr. Bryant (Ark.) H.S., 1974-77, Meml. H.S., Evansville, Ind., 1981-82; market support rep. Van Ausdall and Farrar, Evansville, 1983-86; adminstrv. asst. Farm Credit Svcs., Effingham, Ill., 1986-87; social studies tchr. Effingham (Ill) H.S., 1987-92, Cmty. H.S. Dist. # 218, Oak Lawn, Ill., 1992—; girl's track and field coach Effingham H.S., 1989-92; girl's cross country coach Eisenhower H.S., Blue Island, Ill., 1992; yearbook advisor Polaris Sch., Oak Lawn, 1993—. Mem. Internat. Women's Pilot Assn., Phi Delta Kappa. Home: 15150 Quail Hollow Dr # 3-N Orland Park IL 60462

BUCIOR, JOYCE JOAN, elementary education educator; b. Lansing, Mich., Apr. 16, 1931; d. Ellis Lee and Ambra Mae (Updyke) Ward; m. Benjamin Bucior, June 13, 1957; 1 child, Julia Ann Bucior Hubbs. BA, Mich. State U., 1965, MA, 1968; postgrad., Ea. Mich. U., 1987. RN, Mich. Obstet. nurse Foote Hosp., Jackson, Mich., 1953-54; office nurse Earl E. Parker M.D., Leslie, Mich., 1954-66; tchr. 2d, 3rd and 4th grades Jackson (Mich.) Pub. Schs., 1965-92. Bd. dirs. Friends of Ella Sharp Mus., Jackson, 1993; active W.A. Foote Hosp. Aux., Jackson. Recipient Individual award Mich. Dept. of State Police Safety Planning, 1991. Mem. NEA, AAUW (bd. dirs. 1992-94), Mich. Edn. Assn., Jackson Edn. Assn., Jackson County Assn. of Ret. Sch. Pers., Delta Kappa Gamma (Omicron chpt.), Jackson City Women's Club. Methodist. Home: 2130 Ganton Dr Jackson MI 49203-3656

BUCK, ALISON JENNIFER, technical writer; b. Bangor, Maine, Dec. 11, 1952; d. George Hill and Anna (Komisaruk) B. BS, U. Maine, Orono, 1974; MA, Brigham Young U., 1978. Cert. tchr., Maine, Mass. Vol. program coordinator Head Start/Hampshire Community Action Commn., Northampton, Mass., 1980; career edn. specialist, job developer Hampshire Ednl. Collaborative, Northampton, 1981; documentation specialist Amherst (Mass.) Assocs., 1981-84; sr. tech. writer Visual Intelligence Corp., Amherst, 1984-85; tech. documentation specialist Video Communications Inc., Feeding Hills, Mass., 1986-87; contract tech. writer Digital Equipment Corp., Westfield, Mass., 1987; mktg. coordinator, tech. publs. mgr. Millitech Corp., South Deerfield, Mass., 1988; contract tech. writer Carrier Corp., Farmington, Conn., 1988-89; author computer-based tng. materials AMS Courseware Developers, Manchester, Conn., 1989-92; learning tech. Aetna Ins. Corp., Hartford, Conn., 1992-94; application developer Health New Eng., Springfield, Mass., 1994—. Co-author: The Coffee Maker Cookbook, 1988. Mem. Soc. for Tech. Communication. Democrat. Office: Health New England One Monarch Pl Springfield MA 01144

BUCK, ANNE MARIE, library director, consultant; b. Birmingham, Ala., Apr. 12, 1939; d. Blaine Alexander and Marie Reynolds (McGeorge) Davis; m. Evan Buck, June 17, 1961 (div. Apr. 1977); children: Susan Elizabeth Buck Rentko, Stephen Edward. BA, Wellesley (Mass.) Coll., 1961; MLS, U. Ky., 1977. Bus. mgr. Charleston (W.Va.) Chamber Music Soc., 1972-74; dir. Dunbar (W.Va.) Pub. Libr., 1974-76; tech. reference libr. AT&T Bell Labs., Naperville, Ill., 1977-79; group supr. libr. AT&T Bell Labs., Reading, Pa., 1979-83; group supr. support svcs. AT&T Bell Labs., North Andover, Mass., 1983; dir. libr. network Bell Communications Rsch. (Bellcore), Morristown, N.J., 1983-89; dir. human resources planning Bell Communications Rsch. (Bellcore), Livingston, N.J., 1989-91; univ. libr. N.J. Inst. Tech., Newark, 1991-95, Calif. Inst. of Tech., Pasadena, 1995—; adj. prof. Rutgers U., New Brunswick, N.J., 1989—; instr. U. Wis., Madison, 1988—; vice chmn. Engring. Info. Found., N.Y.C, 1994; mem. Engring. Info. Inc. (bd. dirs.), Castle-Point-on-the-Hudson, Hoboken, N.J., 1988—; speaker profl. assn. confs., 1982—; libr. cons. North Port (Fla.) Area Libr., 1990-91. Mem. editorial adv. bd. Highsmith Press, 1991—; contbr. articles to profl. jours. Sect. mgr. United Way of Morris County, Cedar Knolls, N.J., 1984—; advisor Family Svc. Transitions Coun., Morristown, 1987-90; libr. trustee Lisle (Ill.) Pub. Libr. Dist., 1978-80; bd. dirs. Kanawha County Bicentennial Commn., Charleston, W.Va., 1974-76. Recipient Vol.'s Gold award United Way, 1991. Mem. ALA (Grolier Nat. Libr. Week grantee 1975), Am. Soc. Info. Sci. (chpt. chmn. 1987-89, Chpt. of Yr. award 1988, treas. 1992—), Conf. Bd. Inc. (chmn. info. svcs. adv. coun. 1987-89), Spl. Libr. Assn., Am. Soc. Engring. Edn., Archons of Colophon, Indsl. Tech. Info. Mgrs. Group, Wellesley Coll. Alumni Assn. (class rep. 1986-91), N.J. Wellesley Club (regional chmn. 1986-89, corr. sec. 1994-95), Sierra Club, N.J. Schola Cantorum, Beta Phi Mu. Unitarian. Office: Calif Inst of Tech Mail Code 1-32 Pasadena CA 91125

BUCK, CAROL KATHLEEN, medical educator; b. London, Ont., Can., Apr. 2, 1925; d. Albert Henry and Evelyn Florence (Parsons) Whitlow; m. Robert Crawforth, June 22, 1946; children: Lucy Anne, Effie Louise. MD, U. Western Ont., 1947, PhD, 1950; DPH, London Sch. Hygiene and Tropical Medicine, 1951; LLD (hon.), Dalhousie U., 1989. Asst. prof. U. Western Ont., London, 1952-56, assoc. prof., 1956-62, prof. epidemiology, 1962-90, ret., 1990; mem. adv. com. Stats. Can., Ottawa, 1985—; mem. occupational disease panel Ministry of Labour, Toronto, Can., 1988—. Contbr. articles to profl. jours., chpts. to books. Fellow Royal Soc. Can., Am. Coll. Epidemiology; mem. Internat. Epidemiology Assn. (pres. 1981-84), John Howard Soc. Ont. (life), Univ. Club. Mem. New Dem. Party Can. Home: 181 Elmwood Ave, London, ON Canada N6C 1K1

BUCK, FRANCES MARKS, psychologist, consultant; b. Billings, Mont., June 2, 1953; d. Frederic Smith and Mary Elizabeth (Martin) Marks; m. Paul Buck III, Dec. 27, 1975; children: Maren Emily, Hollin Marie. BA with high honors in Psychology, U. Mont., 1975; MA in Psychology, U. Ariz., 1976, PhD in Psychology summa cum laude, 1980. Lic. clin. psychologist. Clin. psychologist VA Med. Ctr., Milw., 1980-85; clin. psychologist Rehab. Ctr. Community Med. Ctr., Missoula, Mont., 1985-89; dir. women's health focus Community Med. Ctr., Missoula, 1989-90, dir. women's and children's ctr., 1990-92, clin. psychologist, 1992-94; pvt. practice, 1994—; adj. instr. Sch. Nursing U. Wis., Milw., 1980; asst. prof. Med. Coll. Wis., Milw., 1980-85; sci. adv. bd. Paralyzed Vets. of Am., Washington, 1987—; founding mem. Jacobs Inst. Women's Health, 1991-93; pres. Am. Assn. Spinal Injury Psychologists, Jackson Heights, N.Y., 1991-92; peer reviewer Nat. Inst. of Disability Rehab. and Rsch., NIH, 1992—; presenter in field. Author: (patient edn. books) Chronic Fatigue Syndrome, 1992; psychosocial editor: Jour. Am. Paroplegia Soc., 1992—; contbr. chpts. to books and articles to profl. jours. Bd. mem. Mont. Mobility Impaired Housing, Missoula, 1988-91. Recipient YWCA Leadership award YWCA, Missoula, 1988, Clin. Excellence award Nat. Assn. Women's Health Profls., Chgo., 1992. Mem. APA, Am. Assn. Spinal Cord Injury Psychologists & Social Work (bd. dirs. 1987—, v.p. 1990, pres. 1991-92, pres. elect 1993-94), Phi Beta Kappa. Home: 6730 Gharrett Missoula MT 59803 Office: Health Focus 1018 Burlington Ste 101 Missoula MT 59801

BUCK, JANE LOUISE, psychology educator; b. Reading, Pa., Mar. 10, 1933; d. C. Robert and Viola Louise (Berger) B.; m. Leo Laskaris, Oct. 7, 1954 (div. Aug. 1978); 1 child, Julie. BA, U. Del., 1953, MA, 1959, MEd, 1966, PhD, 1971. Instr. U. Del., Newark, 1964-66; rsch. assoc. Rsch. for Better Schs., Phila., 1967-68; asst. prof. Del. State U., Dover, 1969-73, assoc. prof., 1973-77; prof. psychology Del. State Coll., Dover, 1977—; cons. in stats. E.I. duPont de Nemours, Wilmington, Del., 1983-93; vis. prof. Ctr. for Sci. and Culture, U. Del., 1986. Author: Specifying the Risk, 1985; contbr. articles to profl. jours. Speaker, evaluator Del. Humanities Forum, 1980-88; pres. Del. Gerontol. Soc., Newark, 1987-88. Mem. AAUP (coun. 1987-90, 93—, pres. Del. State U. chpt. 1976-80, chief negotiator 1982—, mem. com. on historically Black colls. and univs. and status of minorities in the profession 1988-90, interim sec. Del. Conf 1991-92, pres. Del. conf. 1993—, mem. com. govtl. rels. 1994—, Sternberg award for collective bargaining 1994), APA (Div. Two), Am. Psychol. Soc., Am. Statis. Assn., Danforth Assocs., Kappa Delta Pi, Psi Chi, Alpha Chi Omega. Office: Del State Univ Psychol Dept DuPont Pkwy Dover DE 19901

BUCK, LINDA DEE, recruiting company executive; b. San Francisco, Nov. 8, 1946; d. Sol and Shirley D. (Setterberg) Press; student Coll. San Mateo (Calif.), 1969-70; divorced. Head hearing and appeals br. Dept. Navy Employee Rels. Svc., Philippines, 1974-75; dir. human resources Homestead Savs. & Loan Assn., Burlingame, Calif., 1976-77; mgr. VIP Agy., Inc., Palo Alto, Calif., 1977-78; exec. v.p., dir. Sequent Personnel Svcs., Inc., Mountain View, Calif., 1978-83; founder, pres. Buck & Co., San Mateo, 1983-91. Publicity mgr. for No. Calif., Osteogenesis Imperfecta Found. Inc., 1970-72; cons. Am. Brittle Bone Soc., 1979-88; active Florence (Oreg.) Area Humane Soc., 1994—, Friends of Libr., Florence, 1994—; bd. dir. Women of Rhododendron Scholarship Program, Florence, Oreg., 1995—. Jewish.

BUCK, LORRAINE, sales representative; b. Columbus, Ohio, Sept. 15, 1968; d. Norman Whitney and Delphine Lorraine (Zelinski) B. BA in Journalism, Ind. U., 1990. Day care instr. Tabernacle Acad., Indpls., 1985-88; sales intern Sherwin-Williams, Indpls., 1989; sales rep. E.J. Brach, Inc., Cin., 1990-91, J.M. Smucker Co., North Canton, Ohio, 1991—. Mem. Women in Communications, Inc. (v.p. Ind. U. student affiliation 1988-90), Gamma Phi Beta. Republican. Methodist. Home: 707 W Commons St NE Canton OH 44721-3265

BUCKALEW, JUDITH ADELE, nurse, pharmaceutical industry executive; b. Paterson, N.J., July 2, 1947; d. Lester and Adele (Ryer) Ackerson; m. Robert Jay Buckalew, June 14, 1969 (div. Sept. 1975). B.S., William Paterson Coll., 1974; M.P.H., UCLA, 1979. R.N. Supr. med.-surg. unit Paterson Gen. Hosp., N.J., 1969-71; office mgr. pvt. physician Wayne, N.J., 1971-73; supr. pub. health dept. Englewood Hosp., N.J., 1973-75; pub. health adminstr. Vis. Nurse Assn., Santa Monica, Calif., 1975-77; dir. community resource planning office U. Calif. Med. Ctr., L.A., 1977-79; policy analyst, advisor office of policy and legislation Health Care Financing Adminstrn., U.S. HHS, Washington, 1979-80; mem. U.S. Senate Labor and Human Resources Com., Washington, 1980-81; legis. asst. U.S. Senator Dan Quayle, Washington, 1981-83; spl. asst. to Pres. U.S. for pub. liaison White House, Washington, 1983-85; v.p. govtl. affairs Internat. Assocs. for Fin. Planning, Washington, 1985-87; pres. Buckalew Assocs., Washington, 1987-89; v.p. govt. affairs Golden Rule Ins., 1987-88, Nat. Assn. Life Ins. Cos., 1988-89; mgr. govt. affairs Hoffmann-La Roche, Inc., 1989-92; dir. Washington govt. affairs Zeneca Pharms. Group, 1992—; cons., lectr. in field. Contbr. articles to profl. publs. Mem. Bush-Quayle campaign, 1988-89, Reagan-Bush Transition Team, 1980-81; bd. dirs. Hospice Action of L.A., Inc. Lt. (j.g.) USNR, 1985—. Recipient Disting. Alumnus of the Yr. award William Paterson Coll., 1986; named one of Outstanding Young Women in Am., 1985. Mem. Rotary. Republican. Home: 2406B S Walter Reed Dr Arlington VA 22206-1156 Office: Zeneca Pharms Group Ste 804 1250 Eye St NW Washington DC 20005

BUCKLER, MARILYN LEBOW, school psychologist, educational consultant; b. N.Y.C., Mar. 18, 1933; d. Herman and Gertrude (Abolitz) Lebow; m. Sheldon A. Buckler, June 1, 1952 (div. 1978); children: Julie, Eve, Sarah Buckler Welcome. BS cum laude, NYU, 1954; MEd in Counseling, Northeastern U., 1970. Cert. ednl. psychologist, Mass.; sch. guidance counselor, Mass., sch. psychologist, Mass. Kindergarten tchr. Washington Pub. Schs., 1955-56, Stamford (Conn.) Pub. Schs., 1956-58; guidance counselor Framingham (Mass.) Pub. Schs., 1969-70; sch. psychologist, guidance counselor Carlisle (Mass.) Pub. Schs., 1970—; parent workshop leader, mentor Wellesley Coll.-Stone Ctr., 1993—; tchr. parenting course Middlesex C.C., Bedford, Mass., 1990—, cons. LEAP program, 1992-93; workshop leader, creator parenting courses, various pvt. schs. and orgns., Mass., 1990—. Mem. ACA, Mass. Sch. Counselor Assn., Mass. Sch. Psychologists Assn., Pi Lambda Theta. Office: Carlisle Pub Schs 83 School St Carlisle MA 01741

BUCKLES, CANDACE SCHIMA, clinical instructor; b. Pamona, Calif., Feb. 16, 1964; d. Johnnie George and Glyness Dorthea (Barker) Schima; m. David Stanley Buckles, Sept. 23, 1989; stepchildren: Louisa Marie, Lynda Isabella. BSN, Med. U. S.C., 1986, MSN, 1991. RN, S.C.; cert. pediatric nurse Nat. Bd. Nurse Assocs. and Practitioners, ACLS, Pediatric Advanced Life Support cert. Am. Heart Assn. Staff nurse Med. U. S.C., Charleston, 1986-87, nurse clinician div. pediatric cardiology, 1987-90, nurse clinician dept. nursing, 1990-91, clin. instr. div. cardiothoracic surgery, 1992—; presenter at profl. confs. Contbr. articles, abstracts to profl. publs. Mem. Nat. Assn. Pediatric Nurse Assocs. and Practitioners, Assn. for Care of Children's Health, Am. Heart Assn. (coun. on cardiovascular nursing), Sigma Theta Tau. Office: Med U SC Div CT Surgery 171 Ashley Ave Charleston SC 29425-0001

BUCKLEW, SUSAN CAWTHON, federal judge; b. 1942. BA, Fla. State U., 1964; MA, U. So. Fla., 1968; JD, Stetson U., 1977; LLD (hon.), Stetson Coll. Law, 1994. Tchr. Plant High Sch., 1964-65, 70-72, Seminole High Sch., 1965-67, Chamberlain High Sch., 1969; instr. Hillsborough C.C., 1974-75; corp. legal counsel Jim Walter Corp., 1978-82; county ct. judge Hillsborough County, 1982-86; circuit ct. judge 13th Jud. Circuit, 1986-93; judge U.S. Dist. Ct. (mid. dist.) Fla., 1993—; mem. Gender Bias Study Commn., 1988-90, Fla. Bar Bench Bar Commn., 1990-92; bd. overseers Stetson Coll. Law, 1994—. Recipient award Disting Svc., Fla. Coun. Crime and Delinquincy, 1990, Disting. Alumnus award Stetson Lawyers Assn., 1994. Mem. ABA, Fla. Gar Assn., Fla. Assn. Women Lawyers, Hillsborough Assn. Women Lawyers (award Outstanding Pub. Svc. ADvancing Status Women 1991), Hillsborough County Bar Assn. (Robert W. Patton Outstanding Jursit award young lawyer's sect. 1990), Fla. State U. Alumni Assn., Am. Inns Ct. (LII, William Glenn Terrell chpt.), Athena Soc., Tampa Club, Delta, Delta, Delta Alumnae. Office: US Dist Ct 611 N Florida Ave Tampa FL 33602*

BUCKLEY, BETTY LYNN, actress; b. Ft. Worth, July 3, 1947; d. Ernest and Betty Bob (Diltz) B.; m. Peter Flood, 1972 (div. 1974). Actress: (Broadway debut) 1776, 1969, (London debut) Promises, Promises (stage prodns.) What's a Nice Country Like You Doing in a State Like This?, Pippin, 1973-75, I'm Getting My Act Together and Taking it on the Road, 1981, Cats, 1982-85 (Antoinette Perry award 1983), Juno's Swans, 1985, The Mystery of Edwin Drood, 1985-86, Song and Dance, 1986, Circle of Sound, Carrie, 1990, (London) Sunset Boulevard, 1994 (feature films) Carrie, 1976, Tender Mercies, 1983, Frantic, 1988, Another Woman, 1988, Rain without Thunder, 1993, Wyatt Earp, 1994, (TV movies) The Ordeal of Bill Carney, 1981, The Three Wishes of Billy Grier, 1984, Roses are For the Rich, 1987, Baby Cakes, 1989, Bonnie and Clyde: The True Story, 1992, The Devil's Work, (TV mini-series) Evergreen, 1985; regular (TV series) Eight is Enough, 1977-81; also cabaret and club performances; albums include Betty Buckley, 1987, Children will Listen, 1993, With One Look, 1994. Mem. Actors' Equity Assn., Screen Actors Guild, AFTRA. Office: Abrams Artists and Associates 9200 Sunset Blvd Ste 625 Los Angeles CA 90069

BUCKLEY, CAROL JOY, media specialist; b. Evanston, Wyo., Sept. 18, 1931; d. Frank Earl and Maude Annie (Hutchinson) Wirig; m. Jack H. Buckley, Mar. 18, 1930; children: John William, Jill, Heidi Ann, Mark Wirig, Michael Duke, Jay Harry. BS in Home Econs. with honors, U. Wyo., 1953, BS in Nursing with honors, 1954. Cert. elem. tchr.; RN. Grad. nurse Uinta County Meml. Hosp., Evanston, Wyo., 1954-55, Ivinson Meml. Hosp., Laramie, Wyo., 1956-57; asst. instr. U. of Wyo. Coll. of Nursing, Laramie, Wyo., 1955-57; elem. tchr. Daggett County Sch. Dist., Manila, Utah, 1958-59; acting health officer Daggett County, Manila, Utah, 1958-61; sch. nurse Uinta County Sch. Dist. 6, Lyman, Wyo., 1961-74, tchr. 5th grade, 1961-64; remedial reading kindergarten tchr. Reading Devel., Lyman, 1964-67; media specialist K-12 Remedial and Devel. Reading and English Lyman, 1972-83; libr., media specialist Lyman High Sch., 1983—. Contbg. author: Those Good Years at Wyoming U., 1965. Pres. Lyman PTA, 1964-65; chmn. Unita County Mental Health Adv. Bd., 1976; co-chmn. Uinta County Rep. Com.; mem. Wyo. Coun. for Children and Youth, 1977-82; mem. Wyo. Gov.'s Conf. on Libr. and Info. Svcs., 1978; mem. sec.'s adv. com. REgion VIII Health Edn. & Welfare, 1973; merit badge counselor Boy Scouts Am.; leader 4-H Club. Named Outstanding Young Educator, Evanston Jaycees, 1966, Wyo. Jaycees, 1966; Utah State U. grantee, 1971. Mem. Wyo. Libr. Assn. (constn. and by-pass com. 1977), Wyo. Ednl. Media Assn., Lyman Edn. Assn. (pres. 1969-70), Xadena Homemakers Club (v.p. 1965-87), Pi Beta Phi, Delta Kappa Gamma (pres. 1982-84), Sigma Theta Tau. Republican. Home: HC68 Box 1805 3991 N Hwy 414 Lyman WY 82937 Office: Uinta County Sch Dist 6 127 Franklin Lyman WY 82937

BUCKLEY, DEBORAH JEANNE MOREY, marketing manager; b. Bethesda, Feb. 26, 1952; d. Robert Earl and Carolyn Ann (Garrity) Morey; m. Robert Gill Buckley, Dec. 2, 1972; 1 child, Leigh Ann. AAS, Trident Tech. Coll., 1978; student, U. N.C., 1982-83. Nuclear chemistry specialist Duke Power Co., Charlotte, N.C., 1978-82; rsch. technician Graphic Arts Tech. Found., Pitts., 1984; sr. process technician U.S. Filter Corp., 1985-88, applications engr. in tech. svcs. group, 1988-92, market mgr. groundwater systems and sr. application engr., 1993—. Sec. Seneca Valley Acad. Games Parents Assn., Harmony, Pa., 1992-93. With USN, 1970-74. Mem. NAFE, Am. Elctroplaters Soc., Hazardous Materials Control Rsch. Inst. Republican. Office: US Filter Corp 181 Thorn Hill Rd Warrendale PA 15086-7527

BUCKLEY, ELIZABETH ANN, marketing executive; b. Duluth, Minn., Jan. 30, 1947; d. Robert Peers and Kate Wisdom (Holland) B.; m. Judson David Jones, Aug. 5, 1975 (div. Dec. 1981); 1 child, Felix David Buckley-Jones; m. Dennis Britton McGrath, Sept. 10, 1983. BA, St. Norbert Coll., 1969; MA, Mankato State U., 1978. Dep. commr. Minn. Dept. of Corrections, St. Paul, 1972-79; v.p. sales and mktg. City Venture, Mpls., 1979-83; exec. cons. Comml. Credit, Mpls., Balt., 1983-85; investment officer Dain Bosworth, Mpls., 1985-90; sr. v.p., chief mktg. officer Mona Meyer McGrath & Gavin, Mpls., 1990—; speaker in field. Chair bd. trustees Cricket Theatre, Mpls., 1989-91; chair Women's Polit. Caucus Outstanding Women, 1990-91. Mem. Am. Mktg. Assn. (chair pub. rels. com. Minn. chpt. 1992—), Minn. Speakers Assn., Minn. Sales and Mktg. Execs. (editor newsletter 1991-92). Home: 284 Pelham Blvd Saint Paul MN 55104-4935 Office: Mona Meyer McGrath & Gavin Ste 500 8400 Normandale Lake Blvd Minneapolis MN 55437-1080

BUCKLEY, ESTHER GONZALEZ-ARROYO, federal commissioner, educator; b. Laredo, Tex., Mar. 29, 1948; d. Hector and Amalia Margarita (Ayala) Gonzalez-Arroyo; m. Elmer Buckley; children: Trina, James, Catherine, Christopher, Rebecca, George, Jennifer. AA, Laredo Jr. Coll., 1965; BA in Math., U. Tex., 1967; postgrad., Southwestern Med. Sch., 1967-69; MS in Secondary Edn., Laredo State U., 1975. Tchr. math. Christen Jr. High Sch., Laredo, 1970, tchr. sci., 1971-74; tchr. adult basic edn. Laredo Jr. Coll., 1970-75, tchr. ESL, 1978-81; head sci. dept. Dr. Leo Cigarroa High Sch., Laredo, 1983-94, master tchr. sci. dept., 1994—; com. on civil rights U.S. Commn. on Civil Rights, Washington, 1983-92, Laredo, Tex., 1992—; sec., tchr. migrant youth program Laredo Ind. Sch. Dist., 1970, 71, 74, writer curricula for gifted and talented programs and English lang. devel., 1975, 82; presenter, presider in-svc. workshops, campus rep., 1978—, chmn. supr.'s tchr. adv. com., 1983—; mem. gov.'s Hispanic adv. com., 1987-91. AAUW rep. to Mi Laredo Edn. 2000 Goals Bd., 1990—; sec. Leadership Laredo, 1994—; mem. Tchr.'s Profl. Practices and Ethics Commn., Tex., 1982-83, Webb County Select Com. on Higher Edn., Laredo, 1986; mem. commn. on women State of Tex., Austin, 1987-89; mem. Tex. State task force on career ladder, 1987-90. Named Outstanding Hispanic Educator, Dept. Edn., 1984, Meritorious Tchr., Laredo C. of C., 1989, Outstanding Tandy Sci. Tchr., 1992; NSF fellow, 1992-95. Mem. Assn. for Supervision and Curriculum Devel., Assn. Tchrs. and Profl. Educators, Soc. Internat. Bus. Fellows, Phi Delta Kappa (charter mem. Laredo chpt.), Kappa Delta Pi (charter mem. Laredo chpt.), Webb County Reps. Women's Club (v.p. 1976-77). Republican. Roman Catholic. Home: 101 Century Cir Laredo TX 78043-6000 Office: US Commn on Civil Rights 2600 Zacatecas Laredo TX 78043

BUCKLEY, HELEN ANN, lawyer; b. San Francisco, June 12, 1926; d. Martin Joseph and Helen Bernice (Kuhl) B. AB, U. Calif., Berkeley, 1951; JD, U. Calif., 1954. Bar: Calif. 1955, D.C. 1956, Iowa 1977. Assoc. in law U. Calif., Berkeley, 1954-55; trial atty. tax div. U.S. Dept. Justice, Washington, 1955-60; tax counsel Hunt Foods, Fullerton, Calif., 1961-63; assoc., then ptnr. Pacht, Ross, Warne, Berhardt and Sears, Los Angeles, 1963-71; assoc. Norton Simon Inc., Los Angeles, 1971-74; prof. law U. Iowa Coll. Law, Iowa City, 1974-81; vis. prof. law Pepperdine U., Malibu, Calif., 1981-82; prof. law Temple U., Phila., 1982-83; spl. trial judge U.S. Tax Ct., Washington, 1983-94; D&L Straus disting. vis. prof. Pepperdine U. Sch. of Law, Malibu, Calif., 1994—; instr. law U. So. Calif. Law Ctr., 1973; vis. prof. law Hastings Coll., San Francisco, 1976. Mem. adv. com. Mus. Art, Iowa City, 1974-81. Mem. ABA, D.C. Bar Assn., Calif. Bar Assn., Nat. Assn. Women Judges. Office: US Tax Ct 400 2nd St NW Washington DC 20217-0002

BUCKLEY, LINDA ANNE, critical care, psychiatric-mental health, chemical dependency nurse; b. Kewanee, Ill., Sept. 11, 1945; d. Kenneth Leybourne and Rose Marie (Schlitz) B.; divorced; 1 child, Kael Damian Buckley. Lic. vocat. nurse diploma, Vocat. Nursing Sch. Calif., 1970; AA in Nursing, L.A. City Coll., 1978; BS, Calif. State U., Northridge, 1980, Ryan Credential Authorizing Service in California Public Schools, 1981; grad. in chem. dependency studies, L.A. Mission Coll., 1992. RN, Calif., Ill. Nurse pediatric and adult walk in clinic and emergency room Kaiser Hosp. West L.A., 1978-79; nurse operating room and perioperative unit Children's Hosp. L.A., 1978-80; hospice team nurse Vis. Nurses Assn., L.A., 1980; critical care nurse, charge nurse chem. dependency-psychiat. Henry Mayo Newhall Meml. Hosp., Valencia, Calif., 1982—; diabetes educator for endocrinologist Dr. Steven Baron, Newhall, Calif., 1990—; nurse adolescent psychiatry Olive View, UCLA Med. Ctr., 1991—.

BUCKLEY, LINDA TIBBETTS, public relations executive; b. Hartford, Conn., Dec. 2, 1954; d. Wesley Frederick and Noreen Philomena (Lowe) T.; m. Robert Bruce Buckley, Sr., Nov. 9, 1985; children: Brendan Patrick, Robert Bruce Jr. Student, U. South Fla., 1973-74. Office mgr. Inside Sports Mag. (divsn. Newsweek), L.A., 1979-80; sr. researcher, reporter Newsweek mag., L.A., 1980-92; dep. editor Newsweek on Campus, L.A., 1987-89; mgr. publicity and pub. rels. Universal Studios Fla., Orlando, 1992-94, dir. publicity and pub. rels., 1994—. Mem. L.A. Mayor's Christopher Columbus Bicentennial Com., 1990; bd. dirs. Reseda (Calif.) Homeowners Assn., 1987-91; asst. campaign mgr. L.A. City Coun. Candidate Peter Ireland, 1988; mem. adv. bd. Camp Good Days and Spl. Times. Recipient Spl. award Matsushita Pub. Rels. Competition, 1992, 2 Awards of Merit, Internat. Assn. Bus. Communicators, 1994. Mem. Pub. Rels. Soc. Am., Fla. Pub. Rels. Assn. Democrat. Roman Catholic. Home: 239 Lake Ellen Dr Casselberry FL 32707 Office: Universal Studios Fla 1000 Universal Studios Plz Orlando FL 32819

BUCKLEY, PRISCILLA LANGFORD, magazine editor; b. N.Y.C., Oct. 17, 1921; d. William Frank and Aloise (Steiner) B. BA, Smith Coll., 1943. Copy girl, sports writer UP, N.Y.C., 1944; radio rewrite staff mem. U.P., 1944-47; corr. U.P., Paris, France, 1953-56; news editor Sta. WACA, Camden, S.C., 1947-48; reports officer CIA, Washington, 1951-53; with Nat. Rev. Mag., N.Y.C., 1956—; mng. editor Nat. Rev. Mag., 1959-86, sr. editor, 1986—; mem. U.S. Adv. Commn. Pub. Diplomacy, 1984-91. Editor: The Joys of National Review, 1995; columnist One Woman's Voice Syndicate, 1976-80. Mem. Cosmopolitan Club, Sharon Country Club (Conn., sec. 1973-77, pres. 1978-80, 94-95). Home: Great Elm Sharon CT 06069 Office: Nat Review 150 E 35th St New York NY 10016-4178

BUCKLEY, REBECCA HATCHER, physician; b. Hamlet, N.C., Apr. 1, 1933; d. Martin Armstead and Nora (Langston) Hatcher; m. Charles Edward Buckley III, July 9, 1955; children: Charles Edward IV, Elizabeth Ann, Rebecca Kathryn, Sarah Margaret. BA, Duke U., 1954; MD, U. N.C., 1958. Intern Duke U. Med. Ctr., Durham, N.C., 1958-59, resident, 1959-61, practice medicine, specializing in pediatric allergy and immunology, 1961—; dir. Am. Bd. Allergy and Immunology, Phila., 1971-73, chmn. exam. com., 1971-73, co-chmn. bd. dirs., 1982-84; chmn. Diagnostic Lab. Immunology, 1984-88; mem. staff Duke U. Med. Ctr.; asst. prof. pediatrics and immunology, 1968-72, assoc. prof. pediatrics, 1972-76, assoc. prof. immunology, 1972-79, prof. immunology, 1979—, J. Buren Sidbury prof. pediatrics, 1979—. Contbr. numerous articles to med. publs. Recipient Allergic Diseases Acad. award Nat. Inst. Allergy and Infectious Diseases, 1974-79, Merit Rsch. award NIH, 1990, Nat. Bd. award Med. Coll. Pa., 1991, Clemens von Pirquet award Georgetown, 1993, Disting. Tchr. award Duke U. Med. Alumni Assn., 1993, Outstanding Achievement award Immune Deficiency Found., 1994. Fellow Am. Acad. Allergy (mem. exec. com. 1975-82, pres. 1979-80); mem. Am. Assn. Immunologists, Soc. Pediatric Rsch., Am. Acad. Pediatrics (Bret Ratner award 1992), Southeastern Allergy Assn. (pres. 1978-79), Am. Pediatric Soc. (coun. mem. 1991-97). Republican. Episcopalian. Home: 3621 Westover Rd Durham NC 27707-5032 Office: Duke U Med Ctr PO Box 2898 Durham NC 27710-0001

BUCKLEY, VIKKI, state official. Sec. of state State of Colo., 1995—. Office: Office of the Sec of State 1560 Broadway Ste 200 Denver CO 80202*

BUCKLEY, VIRGINIA LAURA, editor; b. N.Y.C., May 11, 1929; d. Alfred and Josephine Marie (Manetti) Iacuzzi; m. David Patrick Buckley, July 30, 1960; children: Laura Joyce, Brian Thomas. B.A., Wellesley Coll., 1950; M.A., Columbia U., 1952. Tchr. English Bennett Coll., Millbrook, N.Y., 1954-56, Berkeley Inst., Bklyn., 1956-58; copy editor World Pub. Co., N.Y.C., 1959-69; children's book editor Thomas Y. Crowell, N.Y.C., 1971-80; editorial dir. Lodestar Books, affiliate of Dutton Children's Books, div. Penguin Books USA, N.Y.C., 1980—. Author: State Birds; contbr. articles to profl. jours. Mem. ALA. Home: 33 Brook Ter Leonia NJ 07605-1504 Office: Lodestar Books 375 Hudson St New York NY 10014-3658

BUCKLEY-BRAWNER, KATHRYN YOLANDE, trading company administrator; b. Waltham, Mass., July 31, 1953; d. William Anthony and Yolande (Bredillet) Buckley; m. William Harrison Brawner, June 19, 1976; 1 child, Kyrsten Virginia. BA in Polit.Sci., Monterey Inst. Internat. Study, 1978. Gen. mgr. Photonic Systems, Santa Clara, 1986-87; internat. sales Christopher Ranch, Gilroy, Calif., 1987-91; mgr. Skan-Dutch Trading Co., Morgan Hill, Calif., 1991-92; v.p. Snow Pearl Internat., Inc., San Jose, Calif., 1992—. Graphic designer corp. identity package, 1985—. Trustee Monterey (Calif.) Inst. Internat. Studies, 1980-83. Mem. AAUW (graphic designer newsletter 1981-88, T-shirt 1984—), Commonwealth Club Calif. Roman Catholic. Home: 3147 Buena Vista Rd Hollister CA 95023 Office: Snow Pearl Internat Inc 6940 Claywood Way San Jose CA 95120

BUCKLO, ELAINE EDWARDS, federal judge; b. Boston, Oct. 1, 1944; married. AB, St. Louis U., 1966; JD, Northwestern U., 1972. Bar: Calif. 1973, U.S. Dist. Ct. (no. dist.) Calif. 1973, Ill. 1974, U.S. Dist. ct. (no. dist.) Ill. 1974, U.S. Ct. Appeals (7th cir.) 1983. Law clk. U.S. Ct. Appeals (7th cir.), Chgo., 1972-73; lectr. law Northwestern U., Chgo., 1973; assoc. Morrison & Foerster, San Francisco, 1973-74; assoc., then ptnr. Miller, Shakman (previously Devoe, Shadur & Drupp), Chgo., 1974-79; ptnr. Coin, Crowley & Nord, Chgo., 1980-83; ptnr., counsel Johnson & Schwartz, Chgo., 1983-85; U.S. magistrate judge U.S. Dist. Ct. (no. dist.) Ill., Chgo., 1985-94, judge, 1994—; vis. prof. law, U. Calif., Davis, 1978-80. Editor, Litigation, 1979-85; contbr. articles to profl. jours. Bd. dirs. Midwest Women's Ctr., Chgo., 1980-82. Mem. Fed. Bar Assn. (bd. dirs. 1987—, treas. 1988-89, sec. 1989-90, v.p. 1990—), Chgo. Bar Assn. (chairperson devel. of law com. 1989-90), Chgo. Coun. Lawyers (pres. 1977-78), Order of Coif. Office: US Dist Ct No Dist Everett McKinley Dirksen Bldg 2 S Dearborn St Rm 1764 Chicago IL 60606*

BUCKMAN, CATHY SMITH, accounting educator; b. Frankfort, Ky., Jan. 25, 1953; d. Ollie Tarleton and JoAnn (McConnell) Smith; m. Joseph Athel Buckman, July 8, 1989; 1 child, Laura. BA in Acctg. magna cum laude, Georgetown Coll., 1975; MS in Acctg., U. Ky., 1978. Acct. Ed Lynch, CPA, Georgetown, Ky., 1975-76; acctg. instr. Brescia Coll., Ownesboro, Ky., 1978-80, Georgetown (Ky.) Coll., 1980—. Mem. Inst. Mgmt. Accts. (v.p. edn. 1986-87, mem. Bluegrass chpt.). Office: Georgetown Coll Box 224 400 E College St Georgetown KY 40324

BUCKMAN, MERTIE W., retired corporate officer; b. Lyme, N.H., Oct. 19, 1904; d. Stephen Albert and Hattie Della (Dustin) Willigar; m. Stanley Joseph Buckman, Aug. 19, 1933 (dec. 1978); children: Robert Henry, John Dustin (dec.). BS, U. Wash., 1929, MS, 1930; HHD, Rhodes Coll., 1991, LeMoyne-Owen Coll., 1994. Instr. home econs. U. Minn., St. Paul, 1929-35, U. Ky., Lexington, 1935-36, U. Louisville, 1936-37; asst. sec.-treas. Bulab Holdings, Inc., Memphis, 1963-93; bd. dirs. Bulab Holdings, Inc. Active Civic Rsch. Com., Inc., 1949-59, Citizens Assn. Memphis and Shelby County, 1959-64, pres.; mem. advisor's coun. St. Mary's Episc. Sch., 1989—; session elder emeritus Raleigh Presbyn. Ch.; chmn. membership Ch. Women United Memphis and Shelby County, pres. 1976; bd. dirs. Nat. Conf. Christians and Jews, 1993—; mem. adv. bd. LeMoyne-Owen Coll., 1990—; trustee Christian Bros. U., 1988—, pres.' coun., 1992—; hon. trustee Rhodes Coll., 1983—. Recipient George L. Plimpton award Tilton (N.H.) Sch., 1967, Awards for Women YWCA Greater Memphis, 1988; named one of Ladies of Distinction Baddour Found., 1988, Citizen of Yr. Memphis and Shelby County Optimists, 1989-90, Outstanding Philanthropist Nat. Soc. Fund Raising Execs., 1990, Woman of Achievement for Steadfastness Women of Achievement, Inc., 1990, Person of Vision Alliance for Blind and Visually Impaired, 1991, many others. Mem. AAUW (life, treas. 1944-46, pres. 1946-48), YWCA (life, pres. 1950-52, 70-72), Weeders and Seeders Garden Club (pres. 1961), Sigma Xi. Republican. Presbyterian. Home: 3943 N Lakewood Dr Memphis TN 38128

BUCK-MOYER, SANDRA KAY, marriage and family therapist; b. Danville, Pa., Mar. 14, 1953; d. Franklin Adam and Martha (Bathurst) Moyer; m. David William Buck, Apr. 4, 1982; children: Lindsey, Paige. BS in English, Lock Haven U., 1975; MS in Edn. Exceptional Children, Pa. State U., 1976; Ma in Counseling, Calif. Poly U., 1985. Tchr. Santa Maria (Calif.) High Sch., 1976-85; tchr. St. Thomas (V.I.) Pub. Schs., 1982-83; counselor Calif. Poly U., San Luis Obispo, 1984-85; intern South County Mental Health Ctr., Arroyo Grande, Calif., 1985; counselor Paso Robles (Calif.) Schs., 1985—; therapist marraige & family pvt. practice, PAso Robles, 1993—; part-time tchr. Calif. Poly U., 1989-91; therapist Family Svcs. Ctr., San Luis Obispo, 1993—; cons. in field. Bd. dirs. Big Bros. Program, Paso Robles, 1994; mem. Santa Margarita (Calif.) PTA, 1988—; vol. Atascadero (Calif.) Youth Soccer, 1987—. Pacific Gas & Elec. Mini grantee, 1990. Mem. NOW, NEA (local sec. 1980), Calif. Assn. Marriage & Family Therapists. Home: 9547 Durango Rd Atascadero CA 93422-6128 Office: 819 12th St Paso Robles CA 93446-2214

BUCKNAM, MARY OLIVIA CASWELL, artist; b. Modesto, Calif., Feb. 6, 1914; d. Charles Henry and Helen Anne (Cross) Caswell; m. William Nelson Bucknam, June 22, 1946 (dec. 1966); children: William Nelson Jr., Charles Henry. BA, Calif. State U., San Jose, 1936; postgrad., U. Calif., Berkeley, 1938, Calif. State U., Stanislaus, 1968-75, U. San Francisco, 1968-75. Tchr. Stanislaus County (Calif.), 1936-38, Modesto (Calif.) Schs., 1938-43, San Bernardino (Calif.) City, 1943-46; art tchr. Klamath Union Schs., Klamath River, Calif., 1960-61; co-owner Bigfoot Ranch and Resort, Klamath River, 1960-66; art tchr., tchr. Riverbank (Calif.) City Schs., 1966-79; art cons. Riverbank Elem., 1986; gallery artist Cen. Calif. Art League, Modesto, 1986—. Group shows include Siskiyow Artists Assn., 1961-66 (best of show award, first award, other awards), Stanislaus County Shows, 1975-90 (best of show award, first award, other awards); over 150 paintings held by pvt. individuals and pub. orgns., Three Sisters Show Gallery tour, 1991-93, Travels with my Paintbrush Show Tour, 1991-92. Donor with Caswell family of land for Caswell State Park, San Joaquin County, Calif., 1955; pres. Caswell Sch. PTA, Ceres, Calif., 1956-57, Ceres Study Club, 1952-53; v.p. Siskiyou Artists Assn., Yreka, Calif., 1963-65; pres. Modesto Tchrs. Assn., 1940-41; vol. tchr. adult watercolor classes; active Trinity Singers Choir, 1990-95. Named Woman of Distinction Soroptimist Internat., Ceres, Calif., 1992, Outstanding Woman of Stanislaus County Stanislaus County Commn. for Women, 1994. Mem. Ctrl. Calif. Art League (chmn. bank shows Modesto 1988-94, co-chair young artists show Modesto 1986, 88, 89, 90, head docent 1994-95), Calif. Ret. Tchrs. Assn., Stanislaus County Hist. Soc., AAUW (Modesto br., fellowships chair 1959-60, historian 1956), Sierra Club, Tuolumne River Lodge, Delta Kappa Gamma (hist.-photography 1985-94, v.p. chpt. 1969-71), Kappa Delta Pi. Republican. Presbyterian. Home: 2704 La Palma Dr Modesto CA 95354-3229

BUCKNER, LINDA GALE, special agent; b. Dalton, Ga., Sept. 10, 1957; d. Malcolm T. and B. Ruth (Hayes) B. BS, Ga. State U., 1981; MPA, Brenau U., Gainesville, Ga., 1987; grad., FBI Nat. Acad., 1992. Sgt. Chatsworth (Ga.) Police Dept., 1978-81; adj. prof. Ga. State U., Atlanta, 1991—, Mercer U., 1994—; asst. spl. agt. in charge Ga. Bur. Investigation, Decatur, 1981—. Legis. liaison Ga. Bur. Investigation, Atlanta, 1994-95. Recipient Dirs. award Ga. Bur. Investigation, 1984. Mem. Internat. Assn. Women Police (pres. 1991-94), Ga. State U. Criminal Justice Alumni Orgn. (pres. 1992-93), Ga. Women in Law Enforcement (co-founder 1987, exec. dir. 1987-89), Nat. Alliance Non-Violent Programming (steering com. 1993-94), Coun. on Elder Abuse and Neglect (treas. 1992), Peace Officers Assn. Ga. (regional dir. 1992-93), Ga. League Families/POW-MIA, Ga. FBI Nat. Acad. Assocs. (conf. vice chair). Presbyterian. Office: Ga Bur Investigation 3121 Panthersville Rd Decatur GA 30037

BUCKNER, WANDA SUE, accountant; b. Tulsa, May 4, 1956; d. Leavy D. and Helen (McMurry) Clements; m. George W. Buckner, Dec. 27, 1974; children: Alicia Ann, Constance Christine. A.Acctg., Tulsa Jr. Coll., 1976. Cert. mgmt. acct., 1993. Internal auditor Homestead Savs. & Loan Assn., Woodward, Okla., 1978-81, corp. treas./controller, 1981-82, sr. v.p./CFO, 1985-86; acct./cons. Woodward, 1982-85; v.p., contr. Am. fed. Savs. and Loan, Oklahoma City, 1987-88; v.p. Cimarron Fed. Savs., Muskogee, Okla., 1988-92; acctg. supr. Tinker Credit Union, Midwest City, Okla., 1992-93, TMS, Inc., Stillwater, Okla., 1993-94; acct./cons. Stillwater, 1994—. Mem. Inst. Mgmt. Accts. Home: Rte 1 Box 27 Orlando OK 73073

BUCKNER-SHANAHAN, BETTY BONNIE, health products executive; b. Atlanta, Oct. 29, 1948; d. Gerald and Betty L. (Walker) Reynolds; m. David F. Shanahan, Feb. 28, 1992. BA, West Ga. Coll., 1970, MS, 1971. Indsl. engr. Milliken & Co., Spartanburg, S.C., 1975-76; mgr. indsl. engring. Burlingtin Industries, Bristol, Tenn., 1976-78; dir. indsl. engring. Arcata Corp., Kingsport, Tenn., 1978-81; dir. ops. Baxter, 1981-86; mgr. Ernst & Young, Chgo., 1986-87; dir. ops. Biotherapeutics, Franklin, Tenn., 1987-89; v.p. ops., COO Lifesource, Glenview, Ill., 1989—. Mem. NOW, Am. Assn. Blood Banks, Econ. Club of Chgo., Coun. of Community Blood (mem. bd. trustees 1991—), Inst. Indsl. Engrs. Republican. Home: 2510 Pebbleford Ln Glenview IL 60025 Office: Lifesource Blood Svcs 1205 N Milwaukee Ave Glenview IL 60025

BUCKRIDEE, PATRICIA ILONA, international marketing/strategy consultant; b. N.Y.C., Oct. 19, 1960; d. Laszlo Carl and Evelyn Liane (Schauer) Varhegyi; m. Winston D. Buckridee, Dec. 29, 1991; children: Karolyn Liane, Elizabeth Rachel. BS, Seton Hall U., 1982; MBA, Rutgers U., Newark, 1987. Statis. analyst UN, Vienna, Austria, 1983-85; cons., tutor, N.J., 1985-87; assoc. mgr. strategy and devel. AT&T, Basking Ridge, N.J., 1987-88; market mgr. microelectronics AT&T, Berkeley Heights, N.J., 1988-89; sr. product mgr. data systems group AT&T, Morristown, N.J., 1989; sr. fin. analyst Am. Express Travel Related Svcs. Co., N.Y.C., 1989-91; ind. cons. Scotch Plains, N.J., 1991—; internat. cons., N.J., 1985—; interpreter, translator, N.J., 1987—; pres. PIB Internat. Inc., 1991—. Mem. NAFE. Office: PIB Internat 14 King James Ct Scotch Plains NJ 07076-1111

BUDAK, MARY KAY, state legislator; b. Phila.; m. Michael S. Budak, 1953; children: Kathy Budak Norred, Michael S. III, Patricia A. Budak Jones. Student, Temple U., 1950-51, Purdue U., 1968, 80. Owner, mgr. Budak Memls. Inc., 1960-81; sec. to campaign coord. Michigan City Mayor Campaign, Ind., 1966-79; mem. Ind. Ho. of Reps., 1980—, mem. various coms., ranking majority mem. judiciary com., former ranking Rep. mem. family and children com., asst. Rep. whip. Pres. Miss Ind. Scholar Pageant, 1970-74, former mem. exec. bd.; mem. exec. bd. Michiana Sheltered Workshop, 1981-86, Parents & Friends of Handicapped; asst. Rep. WAIP; bd. dirs. Stepping Stone for Spousal Abuse. Named Outstanding Woman in Politics, 1982, Outstanding Legislator, Fraternal Order Police and State Employees, 1983. Mem. LWV, LaPorte County Grange, LaPorte GOP Women's Club (v.p. 1979-81), Bus. & Profl. Women's Club, LaPorte Rep. Women's Club, LaPorte Homemakers Ext. Club, VFW Aux., Kiwanis. Roman Catholic. Home: 5144 N Pawnee Trl La Porte IN 46350-8261 Office: Office State Senate State Capital Indianapolis IN 46204*

BUDD, BARBARA TEWS, sculptor; b. Milw., Jan. 4, 1935; d. Herbert Albert and Helen Estelle (Dieman) Tews; m. John Marshall Budd Jr., June 29, 1957; children: Elizabeth, John Marshall III, Peter, Benjamin. BA, Smith Coll., 1957; student of art, Yale U., 1958-59, Mpls. Inst. Art, 1960-73, Mpls. Sch. of Art, 1960-73, U. Minn., 1960-73. Co-author, illustrator: Uncommon Guide to Twin Cities, 1970, Uncommon Guide to Minnesota, 1971, Uncommon Guide to Dining, 1971; co-author: Colorado Springs Today, 1982, 2d edit., 1985; sculpture exhibits include The Tactile Gallery, Colo. Springs, Colo., 1990, Loveland Invitational Sculpture Show, Loveland, Colo., 1992-94, Pioneer Mus., Colo. Springs, Colo., 1993, New England Fine Arts Inst., Boston, 1993, Cottonwood Festival Sculpture Internat. Show, Hastings, Nebr., 1994, USAF Permanent Profs. Mus., 1995. Co-founder Minn. Children's Mus., 1971; bd. dirs. Colo. Springs Goals, 1975-84, Colo. Springs Sch., 1974-80, Cheyenne Village, Manitou Springs, Colo., 1974-80, Colo. chpt. Nat. Mus. Women in Art, Washington, D.C., 1988-94, Pikes Peak Art Council, 1991-94, St. Paul Arts and Sci. Coun., 1972, 1984-87, Penrose Hosp. Aux., 1984-87; mem. Pikes Peak Arts Commn., 1993—. Mem. Internat. Sculpture Ctr. (Washington), Colo. Artists Registry. Republican. Episcopalian. Home: 10 Thayer Rd Colorado Springs CO 80906

BUDD, BERNADETTE SMITH, newspaper executive, public relations consultant; b. N.Y.C., Feb. 23, 1948; d. Stanley Allen and Toby (Percak) Smith; children: Amanda Rose, Karen Wendy, Paige Elizabeth, Kelly Lyn Budd Tinsley; m. Thomas Witbeck Budd, July 4, 1988. BA in History and English, Bucknell U., 1964; MA in Liberal Studies, SUNY-Stony Brook, 1971; EdM, Columbia U., 1982; postgrad. Touro Coll. Tchr. history N.Y., 1964-69; innovator pre-sch. programs, Shoreham, N.Y., 1975-79; editor, pub. Cmty. Jour., Wading River, N.Y., 1978—, advt. mgr., 1978—; editor Shoreham-Wading River Newsletter, 1978-88; profl. breeder, shower A.K.C. golden retriever dogs; cons., workshop leader, 1979—; owner CJ Typesetting and Printing. Editor: C. of C. Directory, Shoreham, 1983, 84; contbr. articles N.Y. Times, Reader's Digest, Psychology Today Mag. Advisor Teen Recreation Adv. Com., Shoreham-Wading River, 1979-82; mem. Nuclear Emergency Evacuation Com., 1979-82; pres. PTA, Wading River, 1980-83; v.p. Spl. Edn. PTA, Wading River, 1979-80; active Com. Gifted and Talented Children, Wading River, 1979-80, Occupational Edn. Commn., 1979-80; mem. Suffolk County Human Rights Commn. Recipient Disting. Service award Am. Cancer Soc., 1982-83; award of merit N.Y. State Pub. Relations Assn., 1982-83; award of honor Nat. Sch. Pub. Relations Assn., 1981. Mem. Wading River C. of C. (bd. dirs. 1979-80), Suffolk County Bus. and Profl. Women's Assn., Women's Equal Rights Congress, East End Women's Network, N.Y.C. Press Assn., Rocky Point C. of C. (bd. dirs.), Soc. Profl. Journalists, Sigma Delta Chi, Kappa Kappa Gamma. Roman Catholic. Club: L.I. Press. Home and Office: Cmty Jour PO Box 619 Wading River NY 11792-0619

BUDDE, SANDRA CLAIRE, secondary school educator; b. San Jose, Calif., June 24, 1949; d. Calvin Edward and Geraldine Mary (Jurras) Thomas; m. David Cader Budde, June 19, 1971; children: Jason Cader, Benjamin Thomas, Kristen Milena. BA, U. Calif., Davis, 1970; postgrad., St. Mary's Coll. Lic. tchr., Calif. Spanish/French tchr. Los Cerros Middle Sch., Danville, Calif., 1972-84, chair fgn. lang. dept., 1979-83; French tchr. Monte Vista High Sch., Danville, Calif., 1984—, chair fgn. lang. dept., 1988-90, staff chair, G.A.T.E. coord., 1994—; mem. Monte Vista Site Coun., Danville, 1988-90; mem. San Ramon Dist. Curriculum Coun., Danville, 1988-91; mem. Calif. Sch. Leadership Acad., Pleasant Hill, 1992-94. Pres. Country Club Sch. PTA, San Ramon, Calif., 1991-92; elder St. Philip Ch., Dublin, 1991—. Named Tchr. of the Yr. San Ramon Valley Sch. Dist., 1989, Prin.'s award Ptnrs. in Edn.-Country Club Sch., San Ramon, 1992. Mem. AAUW (sect. leader 1986—), NEA, Calif. Tchrs. Assn., Am. Assn. Tchrs. French, Quicksilver Investment Club (sec. 1986—). Christian Ch. Office: Monte Vista High School 3131 Stone Valley Rd Danville CA 94526-1199

BUDDINGTON, PATRICIA ARRINGTON, engineer; b. Takoma Park, Md., Dec. 25, 1950; d. Warren and Elsie (Miller) B. BS, Northrop Inst. Tech., 1973; MS, Fla. Inst. Tech., 1986. With Air Force Systems Command, Edwards AFB, Calif., 1973-78; various positions Boeing Def. & Space Group, Huntsville, Ala., 1978-81, test engr. reaction control system inertial upper stage, 1981-86, lead engr. microgravity material processing facility, 1986-88, task leader advanced civil space systems, 1988—. Mem. AIAA (assoc. fellow). Office: Boeing Advanced Civil Space PO Box 240002 JW-21 499 Boeing Blvd Huntsville AL 35824-6402

BUDGE, MARCIA CHARLENE, family nurse practitioner; b. Goodland, Kans., Feb. 10, 1952; d. Edwin J. and Bonnie L. (Walker) Carleton; m. Marc R. Budge, May 7, 1977; 1 child, Steven R. ADN, Barton County Community Coll., 1983; cert. primary care nurse practitioner, U. Kans., 1986. RN, Kans., Tex.; cert. advanced RN practitioner, Kans.; cert. advanced nurse practitioner, Tex.; cert. nurse practitioner ANCC. Supr. and staff nurse St. John (Kans.) Dist. Hosp., 1983-85; staff nurse spl. care unit and obstetrics Pratt (Kans.) Regional Med. Ctr., 1986; advanced nurse practitioner, family nurse practitioner Med. Ctr. PA, Hutchinson, Kans., 1986-90; advanced nurse and family nurse practitioner Sterling (Kans.) Med. Ctr., 1990-92; advanced nurse practitioner Bapt. Hosp. Rural Health Clinic, Liberty, Tex., 1992-94; clinic dir. U. Tex. Med. Br. Regional Maternal and Child Health Program, Huntsville, 1994—, Walker County Health Dept., 1994—; mem. tech. adv. group Study of EACH/RPCH Concept in Kans., 1990-92. Chairperson bd. dirs. St. John Hosp. Dist. No. 1, 1991-92. Mem. Coun. Nurses in Advanced Practice, Am. Acad. Nurse Practitioners (cert. family nurse practitioner), Kans. Nurses Assn. (sec. advanced practice conf. group), Tex. Nurses Assn., Coastal Area Health Edn. Coop. (bd. dirs. 1993—). Home: 307 Brenda Ln Conroe TX 77385-9004 Office: U Tex Med Br UTMB-Huntsville 1411 11th St Huntsville TX 77340

BUDOFF, PENNY WISE, physician, author, researcher; b. Albany, N.Y., July 7, 1939; d. Louis and Goldene Wise. B.A., Syracuse U., 1959; M.D., SUNY-Upstate Med. Sch., 1963. Intern, St. Luke's Meml. Hosp., Utica, N.Y., 1963-64; practice medicine specializing in family practice and women's health, Woodbury, N.Y., 1964-85; clin. assoc. prof. family medicine SUNY at Stony Brook, 1980—; founder, med. dir. Penny Wise Budoff Women's Health Svcs. affiliated with North Shore U. Hosp. and Cornell U. Med. Coll., Bethpage, N.Y., 1992—; attending dept. ob/gyn North Shore U. Hosp., 1992—; asst. prof. ob/gyn family practice Cornell U. Medical Coll., 1993—; prin. investigator pilot study to determine heavy metal pesticides in breast cancer tissue from patients residing on Long Island 10 years or more North Shore Hosp. and Brookhaven Nat. Lab, 1994; lectr., TV guest on women's medicine and health issues; mem. panel menopause NIH, 1993; clin. rsch. on menstrual pain, premenstrual syndrome, menopause, breast cancer and osteoporosis. Author: No More Menstrual Cramps and Other Good News, 1980, No More Hot Flashes and Other Good News, 1983; author: (with others) World Book Health & Medical Annual, 1994; Contbr. articles to profl. jours. Bd. dirs. Coalition Against Domestic Violence. Named Women of Yr. C.W. Post Coll., 1981; recipient Nat. Consumers League award, 1983, Max Cheplove award Erie chpt. N.Y. State Acad. Family Physicians, 1983, Women of Distinction award Soroptomist Internat. of Nassau County, L.I., 1990, honoree Nassau County Coalition Against Domestic Violence, 1992, Fellow Nassau County Med. Soc., Am. Acad. Family Physicians (nat. com. on pub. rels.); mem. NOW (Equality Award in Health 1988, Unsung Heroine award), Am. Med. Women's Assn. (co-chmn. nat. women's health com., liaison), Nassau Acad. Family Physicians (past pres.). Home: 3 Seacreast Dr Huntington NY 11743 Office: Penny W Budoff MD Womens Health Service North Shore U Hosp/Cornell Med Ctr 4300 Hempstead Turnpike Bethpage NY 11714-5711

BUDREAU, TINA MARIE, psychiatric nurse practitioner; b. Des Moines, Oct. 8, 1956; d. Robert George and Mary Evelyn (Brebner) Shellady; m. John Robert Langenhan, Sept. 13, 1980; children: Trek Clyde, Pete William. BSN, U. Iowa, 1978, MA, 1985. Cert. psychiat./mental health nurse, ANA. Staff nurse St. Mary's Hosp., Rochester, Minn., 1978-79, Mercy Hosp., Davenport, Iowa, 1978-83; wellness cons. Creative Health Alternatives, Davenport, Iowa, 1985-89; staff nurse St. Lukes Hosp., Davenport, Iowa, 1984-85; nurse practitioner Vera French Mental Health Ctr., Davenport, Iowa, 1985-92, coord. homeless, elderly, family, 1991—; cons. Child Health Specialty Clinic, Iowa City, 1991-95, Salvation Army Homeless Women's Shelter, Davenport, 1985-92; mem. N.W. Child Care Adv. Bd., Davenport, 1990-95, sec. Vera French Joint Profl. Staff, Davenport, 1991. Author: (book chpt.) Homeless Mentally Ill, 1992; grantee Fed. Govt., 1990, 91, 92, 93, 94, grantee Crippled Children's Soc. Homeless Children, 1990. Chairperson John Lewis Coffee Shop for Homeless Davenport, 1991-92; advocate Quad-City Advocates for the Homeless, 1990-95. Recipient Nat. Search for Excellence award Iowa Nurses Assn., 1991, Spl. Recognition/Homeless Outreach, Vera French Mental Health Ctr., 1991, Spl. Recognition for Work with Homeless, Iowa Nurses Assn., 1991. Mem. Iowa Nurses Assn. (publicity chair 1991-92), Attention Deficit Disorder Group, Iowa Clin. Nurse Specialist Coun. Home: 209 W Oak St Long Grove IA 52756 Office: Vera French Mental Health 1441 W Central Park Ave Davenport IA 52804-1707

BUDZAK, KATHRYN SUE (MRS. ARTHUR BUDZAK), physician; b. Racine, Wis., May 6, 1940; d. Raymond Philip and Emma Kathryn (Sorensen) Myer; student Stephens Coll., 1957-58, Luther Coll., 1958-59; BS with honors, U. Wis. at Milw., 1962; MD, U. Wis., 1969; m. Arthur Budzak, Dec. 21, 1961; children: Ann Elizabeth, Lynn Marie. Intern, Madison (Wis.) Gen. Hosp., 1969-70; emergency physician, emergency suite St. Mary's Hosp., Madison, 1971-75; urgent care physician Dean Clinic, Madison, 1975—. Recipient Disting. Alumnae award Stephens Coll., 1979; named to Washington Park High Sch. Hall of Fame, 1985. Mem. AMA, Am. Acad. Family Physicians, Wis. Acad. Family Physicians (pres. south cen. chpt. 1979-81), Wis. Med. Soc., Dane County Med. Soc., Am. Med. Women's Assn. (sponsor U. Wis. student br., pres. 1989—), Wis. Med. Alumni Assn. (bd. dirs. 1979-82, pres. 1983-84, sec.-treas. 1994—), Wagon Trail Condo Assn. (dir., treas. 1990—, pres. 1993—), Sigma Sigma Sigma. Presbyterian. Home: 6110 Davenport Dr Madison WI 53711-2446 Office: 1313 Fish Hatchery Rd Madison WI 53715

BUECHNER, MARGARET, composer, music educator; b. Hannover, Germany, May 27, 1922; came to U.S., 1951, U.S. citizenship, 1961; d. Wilhelm and Martha Voss. MusM, U. Königsberg and U. Wuerzburg (Germany) and Conservatory, 1943; pvt. studies in composition and orch. with Otto Luening, Columbia U., 1954-55. Ind. composer, choir dir., 1956—; founder, pres. Mich. Composers League, Midland, 1960-66; mem. Composers Conf., Bennington, Vt., 1954, 55. Composer, librettist story ballets The Key, Phantomgreen, Mayerling, Elizabeth, The Erlking, also various symphonies, tone poems, other symphonic works, many chamber music works, various concert performances; recs. with the Nürnberger Symphoniker (German Symphony Orch.), including Ballet Suites of Phantomgreen and the complete music of the evening-length ballet Elizabeth and the tone poem The Old Swedes Church. Essay I and The Flight of the Am. Eagle, Symphonic Poem Erlkönig Symphonic Trilogy The Am. Civil War, Orchestral Choral Reminiscence The Liberty Bell, recorded with Royal Scottish Nat. Orch., (ballet music of evening length) La Belle et la Bête (Beauty and the Beast) performances, Bordeaux, France, Genova, Italy; other recs. include Five Symphonic Classics, Symphonic Ballet Music; many stage performances The Key, The Phantomgreen; TV broadcasts The Key. Home and Office: 4407 Gladding Ct Midland MI 48640-3383

BUEGELER, BARBARA STEPHANIE, accounting and business executive, consultant; b. Lawrence, Kans., Mar. 29, 1945; d. Kimball Drexel and Sara Patricia (Cook) Poland; m. Gregory E. Brown, Jan. 27, 1967 (div. Dec. 1981); 1 child, Katherine P.; m. David M. Buegeler, Feb. 14, 1986. BS magna cum laude, St. Edward's U., 1989, postgrad., 1989—. Acct., controller Schlotzsky's Lic. Corp. and Schlotzsky's, Inc., Austin, Tex., 1978-80; ind. ins. agt. New Eng. Life and Cen. Life, Austin, 1980-81; exec. v.p., controller, cons. Supreme Ct. Racquet Clubs, Inc., Austin and San Antonio, 1980-85; pvt. practice Austin, 1984—; asst. controller, cons. Bob Clark Builders Tex., Inc., Round Rock, 1985-87; cons., acct. D. Abernethy Constrn. Corp., Austin, 1987-93, Philanthroprises, Inc., Austin, 1987-93; controller C.D. Sprague Constrn. Corp., Austin, 1988-90; v.p., treas. Ribbons and Data Solutions, Inc., 1992-93; pres. Alexis' Dream, Inc., Austin, 1994—. Mem. NAFE, Inst. Internal Auditors, Assn. for Systems Mgmt. Democrat. Presbyterian. Office: Alexis' Dream Inc 1807 Slaughter Ln # 200-479 Austin TX 78748-6200

BUEHL, ELIZABETH ANNE, business owner, vocational educator; b. Phila., Feb. 3, 1950; d. John J. Jr. and Roselea (Wojack) Whirlein; m. Ernest H. Buehl Jr., May 12, 1979; children: Ryan Ernest, Trevor Ernest. BS, Pa. State U., 1971; MEd, Trenton (N.J.) State U., 1974; DEd, Widener U. Cert. secondary tchr., English and theatre arts, flight and written test examiner; lic. flight sch. ops, airport fixed base ops. V.p., owner Buehl Corp., Langhorne, Pa.; v.p., owner Flying Dutchman Air Svc., Inc., Langhorne, Pa., flight examiner; tchr., dept. head vocat. and tech. Neshaminy Sch. Dist., Langhorne, Pa., 1978-82; pres., owner Aerostats, Inc., Langhorne, Pa.; instrument, flight instr., flight examiner single and multi-engine airplanes. Bd. dirs. Bucks County Airport Authority; mem. Bucks County Sunset Rev. Bd., 1992. Recipient Spl. Achievement award FAA, 1991. Mem. Nat. Bus. and Profl. Women (hon., women in govt. award 1987), Nat. Fedn. of Tchrs., NAFE, Neshaminy Bus. and Profl. Women (past v.p.), Ninety-Nines, Inc., Internat. Soc. Poets. Home: Wood Ln Langhorne PA 19047

BUEHNER, CATHERINE MARY, gifted program administrator; b. Boston, Apr. 13, 1936; d. George Francis and Ann Marie (Meldody) Stanley; m. James John Buehner, Nov. 26, 1960; children: Audrey Mae, Paula Buehner Russell, James John. BA, Regis Coll., 1957; cert. in admisntrn. and supervision, Cleve. State U., 1987; MEd, John Caroll U., 1986. Cert. tch., supr. Claims rep. Social Security Adminstrn., Cleve., 1957-61; asst. tchr. Mentor (Ohio) Pub. Schs., 1972-76, tchr. grade 2, 1976-77, tchr. grade 3, 1977-80, tchr. of gifted, 1980-87, coord. of gifted program, 1987—; State Dept. Edn. continuing edn. unit provider Mentor Pub. Schs., 1990—; sec. Greater Cleve. Coords. of Gifted, 1993—. Author: (with others) Gifted in the Regular Classroom, 1993. Com. chairperson St. John Vianney Parish, Mentor, 1992—; mem Western Res. Neighborhood Assn., Mentor, 1970—. Mem. ASCD, Nat. Staff Devel. Coun., Nat. Assn. for Gifted Children, Phi Delta Kappa (chpt. 115). Home: 7201 Hayes Blvd Mentor OH 44060 Office: Mentor Pub Schs 6451 Center St Mentor OH 44060

BUELL, CARMEN D., state legislator. BS, Springfield Coll., 1966; MA, U. Mass., 1984. Mem. Mass. Ho. of Reps., 1985—, chair joint com. health care, mem. ways and means com., former chmn. spl. com. growth and change. Democrat. Home: 113 Beacon St Greenfield MA 01301-2603*

BUELL, LYNNDA LEE, writer, educator; b. Pontiac, Mich., May 11, 1940; d. Ewald George John and Lenore Amanda (Sprague) Berger; m. Phillip Lee Buell, JUne 23, 1962; children: Allison Lee, Jennifer Lynn (twins). Testamur of English, Lang. and Lit., Univ. Exeter, Eng., 1961; BA, Wittenberg U., 1962; MEd in Adminstrn. and Supervision, U. N.H., 1981. Cert. experienced educator. Tchr. of English Woodward High Sch., Toledo, 1962-64; tchr. of English, drama prodr., dir. Kingswood Regional H.S., Wolfeboro, N.H., 1964-69, Fitch Sr. H.S., Groton, Conn., 1969-70; drama dir., tchr. The Little Sch., Exeter, N.H., 1973-75; English dept. head Exeter Area Jr. H.S., 1975-86; mgr. Beach Club, Inc., Rye Beach, N.H., 1979-88; functions, promotions mgr. Sugarloaf USA, Carrabasset Valley, Maine, 1986-89; staff assoc. Advanced Systems in Measurement and Evaluation, Inc., Dover, N.H., 1988—; cons. Concord (N.H.) Sch. Dist., 1988-92, Wakefield (N.H.) Pub. Schs., 1988—, supervisory adminstrv. unit 52, Turner, Maine, 1988—, East Longmeadow (Mass.) Schs., 1990-92, Morehead State U., Ky., 1991—, Sea Cliff (N.Y.) Sch. Dist., 1991-93. Hudson Valley Bd. Contiuing Edn., White Plains, N.Y., 1993; project dir. Pa. Writing Assessment, Dept. Edn., Pa., 1990-92, Vt. Writing Assessment Program, 1990-92; test devel. cons. Maine Ednl. Assessment, 1988-91, Mass. Ednl. Assessment Program, 1988—, N.J. High Sch. Proficiency Test, 1990-93, Ky. KIRIS and Continuous Assessment Programs, 1991—, Hudson Inst. Modern Red Sch. House Project, 1993—. Author: Guidelines for Generating Student Work, 1992; (handbooks) The Registered Holistic Scoring Method: A Writing Handbook, 1991, Rsch. Data Analysis: Pa. Writing Assessment, 1992; (student brochure) The Writing Portfolio: Your History as a Writer, 1993; Writing Portfolio and Scoring Process, 1992. Mem. ASCD, Nat. Coun. Tchrs. of English, Am. Ednl. Rsch. Assn. Home: PO Box 292 Rye Beach NH 03871-0292 Office: Advanced Systems in Measurement & Evaluation 171 Watson Rd Dover NH 03820-5800

BUELOW, GRACE CARLSON, nurse, state agency surveyor; b. Mandan, N.D., Dec. 16, 1937; d. Ralph M. and Grace I. (Falkenstein) Carlson; m. Roger H. Buelow, Sept. 1, 1961; children: William Henry, Stephanie J. BSN, Jamestown (N.D.) Coll., 1960. RN, N.Mex., Utah, N.D. Staff nurse Jamestown Hosp., 1960-62; mem. staff Primary Children's Hosp., Salt Lake City, 1962-63, Pediatric Clinic, Jamestown, 1963-64, Thomas D. Meml. Hosp. and Ogden (Utah) Pub. Health, 1964; pub. health nurse Salt Lake County Health Dept., 1964-68; sch. nurse Granite Sch. Dist., Salt Lake City, 1964-68; staff nurse Dr. P. Harris, Santa Fe, 1969-71, Albuquerque Vis. Nurse Svcs., 1971-74; community health worker, educator Albuquerque Family Health Ctrs., 1974-75; dir. nursing svcs., and adminstr. Med. Personnel Pool, Albuquerque, 1982-86; program evaluator Medicare Blue Cross Blue Shield N.Mex., Albuquerque, 1987-91; health facility surveyor State N.Mex. Dept. of Health, Albuquerque, 1992—; part-time staff nurse St. Vincent Hosp., Santa Fe, 1969-71. Republican. Lutheran. Office: State of NMex Dept of Health Pub Health Divsn Bur Licensing & Cert 4111 Montgomery Blvd NE Albuquerque NM 87109

BUELOW, JEAN ELLEN, purchase order administrator; b. Milw., Aug. 1, 1956; d. Leonard Richard and Rosalie Jean (Rausch) Kwiecinski; divorced; children: Amy, Michael. BA, Alverno Coll., 1990. Cost acct. Iron Fireman, Milw., 1988-89; cost acct., gen. acct., accounts payable supr. Ampco Metal, Milw., 1989-91; accounts payable supr. Valve Merchants, Inc., Milw., 1991-92, mgr. purchase order control, 1992—; seminar instr., 1991-92. Vol. Boy and Girl Scouts, Milw., 1991—; music min. adult choir St. Rita Parish, West Allis, Wis., 1992-93, festival coord., 1993; mem. St. Rita Sch. Bd., West Allis, 1992—, fin. com., 1992—. Mem. Inst. Mgmt. Accts. Roman Catholic. Office: Value Mchts Inc 710 N Plankinton Ave Milwaukee WI 53203-2404

BUENDIA, IMELDA BERNARDO, clinical director, physician; b. Iloilo City, The Philippines, Nov. 12, 1944; d. Carlos P. and Coleta (De la Cruz) Bernardo; m. Arsenio G. Buendia, June 5, 1971; children: Mary Elaine, Joseph Carlo, Adrian Cesar. BS, U. The Philippines, 1964, MD, 1969. Resident in pediats. Philippine Gen. Hosp., Manila, 1969-71; resident in family practice St. Michael's Hosp., Milw., 1971-75; med. officer Talihina (Okla.) Hosp., 1975-78; med. officer Wewoka (Okla.) Indian Clinic, 1978-92, clin. dir., 1992—. Music dir. St. Joseph Cath. Ch., Wewoka, 1976—; active Phil-Am. Civic Orgn., Oklahoma City, 1978—. Recipient Dir. Excellence award USPHS, 1993. Fellow Am. Acad. Family Physicians; mem. Philippine Med. Assn. Okla. (treas. 1989, sec. 1990, pres.-elect 1994). Home: 7 Oakhurst Rd Wewoka OK 74884-3714 Office: Wewoka Indian Clinic Hwy 270 Wewoka OK 74884

BUESSING, MARJORIE B., state legislator; b. Kirkland, Wash., May 1, 1950; 4 children. Student, Bellevue (Wash.) C.C. Mem. N.H. Ho. of Reps., mem. edn. com. Sgt. CAP, Bellevue, 1966-68; vol. VISTA, Gary, Ind., 1970-71; treas., mem.-at-large Eastman PTO, 1989-92. Mem. Concord Contemporary Woman's Club. Republican. Mem. Unification Ch. Office: NH Ho of Reps State Capitol Concord NH 03301-1805*

BUETTNER, CAROL ANN, state legislator; b. Madison, Wis., Jan. 16, 1948; d. John J. and Lucile E. (Kraner) Murphy. BS, U. Wis., Oshkosh, 1972. Dir. nutrition program for older adults County of Winnebago, Wis., 1973-82; state rep. dist. 81 State of Wis., 1983-87, state senator, 1987—; instr. pre-retirement planning Fox Valley Tech. Inst., 1978-81. Bd. dirs. Oshkosh Found., 1976-82. Home: 232 Fulton Ave Oshkosh WI 54901-4506 Office: State Senate State Capital Madison WI 53707

BUETTNER, MARY E., lawyer; b. St. Louis, July 14, 1963; d. Edward B. Buettner and Joan Howard; m. Brian T. Christopher, July 20, 1984. AB, Washington U., 1984, JD, 1987. Bar: Mo. Staff counsel Citicorp Acceptance Co., Inc., St. Louis, 1986-89; atty. Peabody Holding Co., Inc., St. Louis, 1989-93; v.p., sec., gen. counsel Arch Coal Sales Co., Inc., St. Louis, 1993—. Mem. ABA, Bar Assn. Metro. St. Louis. Office: Arch Coal Sales Co Inc CityPlace One Ste 350 Saint Louis MO 63141

BUETTNER, VICKI JEAN, librarian; b. Oklahoma City, Dec. 12, 1951; d. Emil F. and Lorene C. (Bellinghausen) B. BA in History, Okla. State U., 1974; MLS, Okla. U., 1975. Collection libr. Ctr. for Econ. and Mgmt. Rsch., Norman, Okla., 1974-76; asst. dir. children's svcs. Pikes Peak Regional Libr., Colorado Springs, Colo., 1976-79; reference libr. Pikes Peak Regional Libr., Colorado Springs, 1979; reference coord. Western Plains Libr. System, Clinton, Okla., 1979-84; circulation libr. Southwest Okla. State U., Weatherford, 1984-90; libr. dir. Okla. State U. Oklahoma City Libr., 1990—. Bd. dirs. Southwest Playhouse, Inc., Clinton, 1989-90; vol. Libr. for the Blind. Mem. ALA, AAUW (state sec. 1991-93), Okla. Libr. Assn. (local arrangements chair 1992-93). Democrat. Roman Catholic. Office: Okla State U-Okla City Libr 900 N Portland Ave Oklahoma City OK 73107-6120

BUFFINGTON, LINDA BRICE, interior designer; b. Long Beach, Calif., June 21, 1936; d. Harry Bryce and Marguerite Leonora (Tucciarone) Van Bellehem; student El Camino Jr. Coll., 1955-58, U. Calif., Irvine, 1973-75; children: Lisa Ann, Phillip Lynn. Cert. interior designer and gen. contractor, Calif.; lic. gen. contractor, Calif. With Pub. Fin., Torrance, Calif., 1954-55, Beneficial Fin., Torrance and Hollywood, Calif., 1955-61; interior designer Vee Nisley Interiors, Newport Beach, Calif., 1964-65, Leon's Interiors, Newport Beach, 1965-69; ptnr. Marlind Interiors, Tustin, Calif., 1969-70; owner, designer Linda Buffington Interiors, Villa Park, Calif., 1970—, LBI, Contractors, 1993—; cons. builders, housing developments. Mem. Bldg. Industry Assn. (past pres. Orange County chpt. 1989, 90), Internat. Soc. Interior Designers, Nat. Assn. Home Builders. Republican. Office: 17853 Santiago Blvd Ste # 107 Villa Park CA 92667

BUFFTON, DEBORAH DARLENE, history educator; b. Valley City, N.D., Nov. 24, 1958; d. William George and Catherine Edith (Matthews) B.; m. Anthony George Massaros, June 27, 1987. BA, Ithaca Coll., 1979; MA, Binghamton U., 1981; PhD, U. Wis., 1987. Teaching asst. Binghamton (N.Y.) U., 1979-81, U. Wis., Madison, 1983-84, 86-87; asst. prof. U. Wis., LaCrosse, 1987-90, assoc. prof. history, 1990—, dir. history fair, 1989-93. Co-editor: A Gathering of Voices on the Asian American Experience, 1994; contbr. articles to profl. publs. Mem. exec. com. Wis. Inst., 1993—. Recipient Bourse Chateaubriand, French Govt., 1984-85; U. Wis.-LaCrosse rsch. grantee, 1990; U. Wis. System teaching fellow, 1994—; Disting. faculty scholar Wis. Inst., 1993. Mem. Am. History Assn., Am. Hist. Assn., Assn. Asian Scholars, French History Soc., Western Soc. French History, Amnesty Internat. Office: U Wis History Dept 401 North Hall La Crosse WI 54601

BUFFUM, ELIZABETH V., federal agency administrator; b. Washington, July 27, 1941; d. Harry Leo and Mary Ellen (Carnell) Veihmeyer; children: Stephen Wilder Buffum, Kathleen Carnell Buffum. BS, Akron U., 1972, MA, 1975; postgrad., Harvard U., 1985, Brookings Inst., 1990, 94, Fed. Exec. Inst., 1991. Cert. tchr. Owner small business, Washington, 1975-78; policy advisor Energy Rsch. and Devel. Administrn., Washington, 1975-77; analyst Exec. Office of the Pres., Washington, 1977-78; policy asst. to asst. sec. U.S. Dept. Energy, Washington, 1978-81; assoc.mgr. U.S. DOE Office of Sci. Tech. Information, Washington, 1981-85; dep. mgr. U.S. DOE Office of Sci. Tech. Information, Oak Ridge, Tenn., 1986-89, dir., 1990—; chief operating officer Sci. & Tech. Info. Office, Washington, 1993—; U.S. rep. Internat. Energy Agy., Paris, 1990—, Internat. Atomic Energy Agy., Vienna, Austria, 1990—; vice chair tech. adv. com. Internat. Coun. Sci. and Tech. Info. Pres. bd. dirs. Hope of Tenn., Oak Ridge, 1989-92; vol. FISH, Oak Ridge, 1988-94; fundraiser March of Dimes, 1989-94; fundraiser, tutor Norwood Elem. Sch., 1990-94. Recipient Administrv. and Mgmt. Excellence award Interagy. Com. on Info. Resources Mgmt., 1992, Orgnl. Excellence award Pub. Employees Round Table, 1992, Exceptional Svc. award Federally Employed Women, 1993. Mem. AAUW, NAFE, Am. Assn. Information Sci. (policy chair 1985), Assn. Politics and Life Scis., Federally Employed Women, Rotary Internat. Office: Dept Energy Sci & Tech Info Office 1000 Independence Ave SW Washington DC 20024

BUFORD, EVELYN CLAUDENE SHILLING, printing company executive, jewelry specialist; b. Fort Worth, Sept. 21, 1940; d. Claude and Winnie Evelyn (Mote) Hodges; student Hill Jr. Coll., 1975-76, Tarrant County (Tex.) Jr. Coll., 1992-93; m. William J. Buford, Mar. 1982; children by previous marriage: Vincent Shilling, Kathryn Lynn Shilling La Chappell. With Imperial Printing Co., Inc., Ft. Worth, 1964-70, 77-79, gen. sales mgr. comml. div., 1982-90, corp. sec., 1977-79; with Tarrant County Hosp. Dist., Fort Worth, 1973-77, asst. to asst. administr., 1981-84; merchandising asst. J.C. Penney Co., 1989—. Mem. adv. bd. Bus. Profls. Am., Ft. Worth Ind. Sch. Dist. Mem. Exec. Women Internat. (dir., publs. chmn., v.p. 1984, pres. 1985, chmn. adv. com. 1986, 87, scholarship dir. 1988-93, corp. publ. com. 1988-89, dir. S. ctrl. region 1993—). Republican. Methodist. Home: 1025 Kenneth Ln Burleson TX 76028-8375 Office: JC Penney Co Hurst TX 76053

BUGBEE, JOAN BARTHELME, corporate communications executive; b. Galveston, Tex., Dec. 31, 1932; d. Donald and Helen (Bechtold) Barthelme; m. George A. Bugbee, Apr. 2, 1966; children: Richard, John. BA in Journalism, U. Colo., 1955. Pub. rels. rep. Philco Corp., Phila., 1957-60; account exec. Jacobs Keeper Newell Assoc., Houston, 1960-63; pub. rels. rep. Tex. Ea. Corp., Houston, 1963-66; assoc. editor Oil and Gas Digest Mag., Houston, 1978-79; mgr. corp. communications Pennzoil Co., Houston, 1980-87, dir. corp. communications, 1987-90, v.p. corp. communication, 1990—. Mem. Pub. Rels. Soc. Am. (Outstanding Presentation award Phila. chpt. 1959), Forum Club of Houston (communications com.), Phi Beta Kappa.

BUGELLA, BARBARA, psychiatric nurse therapist; b. New Britain, Conn., July 22, 1962; d. Norman Almon and Claire Cecile (Boissonneau) Paradis; m. James Joseph Bugella, Jr., Aug. 19, 1988. BSN, St. Joseph Coll., West Hartford, Conn., 1984, MS in Nursing, 1990. RN, Conn.; cert. clin. nurse specialist ANA. Staff nurse VA Med. Ctr., Newington, Conn., 1985-87; staff nurse Inst. of Living, Hartford, Conn., 1984-85, 87-88, head nurse, 1988-90, nurse therapist, 1990-94; mgr. profl.'s program, 1994—; clin. assoc. faculty St. Jospeh Coll., West Hartford, Conn., 1990-92. Mem. Sigma Theta Tau.

BUHLER, JILL LORIE, editor, writer; b. Seattle, Dec. 7, 1945; d. Oscar John and Marcella Jane (Hearing) Younce; 1 child, Lori Jill Kelly; m. John Buhler, 1990; stepchildren: Christie, Cathie Vsetecka, Mike. AA in Gen. Edn., Am. River Coll., 1969; BA in Journalism with honors, Sacramento State U., 1973. Reporter Carmichael (Calif.) Courier, 1968-70; mng. editor Quarter Horse of the Pacific Coast, Sacramento, 1970-75, editor, 1975-84; editor Golden State Program Jour., 1978, Nat. Reined Cow Horse Assn. News, Sacramento, 1983-88, Pacific Coast Jour., Sacramento, 1984-88, Nat. Snaffle Bit Assn. News, Sacramento, 1988; pres., chief exec. officer Communications Plus, Port Townsend, Wash., 1988—; mag. cons., 1975—. Interviewer Pres. Ronald Regan, Washington, 1983; mng. editor Wash. Thoroughbred, 1989-90. Mem. 1st profl. communicators mission to USSR, 1988; bd. dirs. Carmichael Winding Way, Pasadena Homeowners Assn., 1985-87; mem. scholarship com. Thoroughbred Horse Racing's United Scholarship Trust; hosp. commr. Jefferson Gen. Hosp., 1995—. Recipient 1st pl. feature award, 1970, 1st pl. editorial award Jour. Assn. Jr. Colls., 1971, 1st pl. design award WCHB Yuba-Sutter Counties, Marysville, Calif., 1985. Mem. Am. River Jaycees (Speaking award 1982), Am. Horse Publs. (1st Pl. Editorial award 1983, 86), Port Townsend C. of C. (trustee, v.p. 1993, pres. 1994, officer 1995), Mensa (bd. dirs., asst. local sec., activities dir. 1987-88, membership chair 1988-90), Kiwanis Internat. (chair MEP com., treas. 1992—), 5th Wheel Touring Soc. (v.p. 1970). Republican. Roman Catholic. Home: 440 Adelma Beach Rd Port Townsend WA 98368-9605

BUHR, FLORENCE D., state senator; b. Strahan, Iowa, Apr. 7, 1933; d. Earnest G. and May (Brott) Wederquist; m. Glenn E. Buhr, 1955; children: Barbara, Lori Lynn, David. BA, U. No. Iowa, 1954. Precinct chair Polk County Dem. Ctrl. Com., Iowa, 1974-79; clerk, sec. Iowa Ho. Reps., 1974-79, 81-82; rep. dist. 85 State of Iowa, 1983-90, asst. majority leader Ho. Reps., 1985-90; now mem. Iowa State Senate, asst. majority leader, 1992-94. Democrat. Presbyterian. Home and Office: 4127 30th St Des Moines IA 50310-5946

BUHR, NANCY JEAN, secondary education educator; b. Detroit, May 19, 1950; d. William H. and Margaret (Little) Grettenberg; m. Daniel L. Buhr, June 21, 1975; children: Blake James, Brett William, Bryant Thomas. BS, U. Wis., Oshkosh, 1971, MSEd in Reading, 1973. Tchr. reading and English Elmbrook Schs., Brookfield, Wis., 1972-75; realtor Wauwatosa Realty, Sheboygan, Wis., 1977-78; adj. instr. Lakeland Coll., Sheboygan, 1988-89; reading specialist Sheboygan Area Sch. Dist., 1982—; mem. Dist. Strategic Planning Team, 1992-94; reviewer, coord. Wis. Sch. Evaluation Consortium, 1990, 92, 93; facilitator Dimensions of Learning, 1995—. Deacon 1st Congl. United Ch. of Christ, Sheboygan; organizer Sheboygan County Without Drugs, 1986-89. Fellow Herb Kohl Ednl. Found., 1993. Mem. NEA, AAUW (life, v.p., chmn. study group, editor newsletter, mem. scholarship selection and home tour coms., daycare, children, TV studies), Wis. State Reading Assn. (presenter workshops confs. 1989, 90, 91, 93, 95). Office: North High Sch 1042 School Ave Sheboygan WI 53083

BUIST, JEAN MACKERLEY, veterinarian; b. Newton, N.J., Dec. 24, 1919; d. Ackerson Jacob and Mary Morris (Morford) Mackerley; m. Richardson Buist, Oct. 2, 1948; children: Peter Richardson, Jean Morford Buist Earle, Mary Elizabeth Buist Lueth. DVM, Cornell U., 1942. Veterinarian Summit (N.J.) Dog and Cat Hosp., 1942-48; pvt. practice Sparta, N.J., 1948—. Mem. Sparta Twp. Bd. Health, 1962-82, chmn., 1972-82; mem., chmn., sec. N.J. State Bd. Vet. Med. Examiners. Recipient Gaines award Newton Kennel Club, 1970, Disting. Svc. award Assn. Women Veterinarians, 1989, Life Achievement award Baldwin Sch., 1992. Mem. Nat. Assn. State Bds. (pres.-elect 1984, pres. 1985-86), Am. Vet. Med. Assn. (nat. bd. exam. com. 1987-91, chmn. 1990-91), N.J. Vet. Med. Assn. (treas. 1982-92), N.J. Acad. Vet. Medicine and Surgery (bd. dirs. 1972-92, sec. 1975-82), Sussex County 4-H Horse Club Leaders Assn. (pres. 1970-76), Sussex County Horse Show Assn. (v.p. 1980-82, pres. 1982-90), Sussex County Farm and Horse Show Assn. (v.p. 1980-94). Home: 68 Sand Pond Rd Hamburg NJ 07419 Office: 143 Stanhope Rd Sparta NJ 07871

BUJOLD, LOIS MCMASTER, science fiction writer; b. Columbus, Ohio, Nov. 2, 1949; d. Robert Charles and Laura Elizabeth (Gerould) McMaster; m. John Fredric Bujold, Oct. 9, 1971 (div. Dec. 1992); children: Anne Elizabeth, Paul Andre. Author: (novels) Shards of Honor, 1986, The Warrior's Apprentice, 1986, Ethan of Athos, 1986, Falling Free, 1988 (Nebula award 1989), Brothers in Arms, 1989, Borders of Infinity, 1989, The Vor Game, 1990 (Hugo award 1991), Barrayar, 1991 (Hugo award 1992, Rickie award 1992, 1st place Locus Poll 1992), The Spirit Ring, 1992, Mirror Dance, 1994, Cetaganda, 1995; author: (novellas) The Borders of Infinity, 1987, The Mountains of Mourning, 1989 (Nebula and Hugo awards 1990), Labyrinth, 1989 (Best Novella/Novelette Analytical Lab. 1990), Weatherman, 1990 (Best Novella/Novelette Analytical Lab. 1991); contbr. short stories to sci. fiction mags., articles to profl. jours. Mem. Sic. Fiction and Fantasy Writers Am., Novelists, Inc. Office: Spectrum Literary Agency 111 8th Ave Ste 1501 New York NY 10011

BUKAR, MARGARET WITTY, administrator, civic leader; b. Evanston, Ill., June 21, 1950; d. LeRoy and Catherine Ann (Conrad) Witty; m. Gregory Bryce Bukar, June 5, 1971 (dec. 1989); children: Michael Bryce, Caroline Nicole. BS, DePaul U., 1972, MBA, 1981. Staff med. technologist The Evanston (Ill.) Hosp., 1972-75, immunopathology lab. supr., 1975-77, lab. mgr., 1977-84, dir. lab. adminstrn., 1984-85; bookkeeper Ronald Knox Montessori Sch., Wilmette, Ill., 1986-87; beauty cons. Mary Kay Cosmetics, 1990—; sec. Northwestern U., Evanston, 1991-94. Den leader Cub Scouts, Boy Scouts Am., Wilmette, 1985-87, den leader coach, 1987-88; active PTA of St. Francis Xavier Sch., 1985—, chair rummage sale, 1987-88, scouting coord., 1991-92, mem. sch. bd., 1986-87, sec. 1988-89, vice chmn., 1989-90; eucharistic min. sick St. Francis Xavier Ch., 1990—, liturgical song leader, 1993—; troop co-leader, song leader Girl Scouts Am., 1992—. Recipient Emily Withrow Stebbins award Evanston Hosp., 1985. Mem. NAFE, Am. Soc. Clin. Pathologists, Am. Acad. Physician Assts., Ill. Acad. Physician Assts., Wilmette Hist. Soc., Elms Social Club (pres. 1992). Avocations: knitting, interior design, reading.

BUKOWIECKI, SISTER ANGELINE BERNADETTE, nun; b. Edmonton, Alta., Can., Aug. 24, 1937; came to U.S. 1960; d. Felix Peter and Stella Isabelle (Yagos) B. BA, Marillac Coll., St. Louis, 1969; MA in Dogmatic/Systematic Theology, St. Louis U., 1971. Joined Hosp. Sisters of the Third Order of St. Francis, 1962; co-foundress Franciscan Sisters of New Covenant, Roman Cath. Ch., 1979. Provincial Franciscan Sisters of New Covenant, Denver, 1979—; founder, dir. Cath. Evangelization Tng. Ctr., Denver, 1983-91; internat. dir. Assn. of Coords. of Cath. Schs. Evangelization/2000, Rome, 1991-92, Cath. Evangelizaton Tng. Ctr., Denver, 1991—; adminstrv. bd. Immaculate Heart of Mary Parish Coun., Northglenn, Colo., 1983-85. Author or co-author 16 books, 1983-91. Mem. Nat. Coun. Cath. Evangelization (bd. dirs. 1983-85). Home: 10620 Livingston Dr Denver CO 80234-3732

BUKOWSKI, ELAINE LOUISE, physical therapist; b. Phila., Feb. 18, 1949; d. Edward Eugene and Melanja Josephine (Przyborowski) B. BS in Phys. Therapy, St. Louis U., 1972; MS, U. Nebr., 1977. Lic. phys. therapist, N.J. Clk. City of Phila., 1967; staff phys. therapist St. Louis Chronic Hosp., 1973, Cardinal Ritter Inst., St. Louis, 1973-74; dir. campus ministry musicals Creighton U., Omaha, 1974-75; teaching asst. U. Nebr. Med. Ctr., Omaha, 1975-76; lectr. in anatomy U. Sci. and Tech., Kumasi, Ghana, 1977-78; chief physical therapist Holy Family Hosp., Berekum, Ghana, 1978-79; coordinator info. & guidance The Am. Cancer Soc., Phila., 1979-81; staff phys. therapist Holy Redeemer Vis. Nurse Assn., Phila., 1981-83; rehab. supr. Holy Redeemer Vis. Nurse Assn., Swainton, N.J., 1983-87; asst. prof. phys. therapy Richard Stockton Coll. N.J., Pomona, N.J., 1987—; bd. dirs. The Bridge, Phila., 1979-80; vacation relief phys. therapist, N.J., summer 1988—; mem. profl. adv. coun. Holy Redeemer VNA, Swainton, N.J., 1982-93, chmn., 1985-91, mem. pers. com., cons. hospice program, 1985-87, rehab. cons., 1987-88; legis. adv. coun. subcom. on edn. and health care Cape May & Cumberland Counties, 1988-90; utilization rev. cons. rehab. svcs., 1990; mem. fitness screening team N.J. State Legislature, 1990; mem. geriatric rehab. del. Citizen Amb. Program, China, 1992. Co-author slide study program, 1976, (video) Going My Way? The Low Back Syndrome, 1976; contbr. articles to profl. jours. Vol. Am. Cancer Soc., Phila., 1979-82, Walk-a-Day-in-My Shoes prog. Girl Scouts Am., Cape May County, N.J., 1983-86; task force phys. therapy prog. Stockton State Coll., Pomona, N.J., 1985-88. U.S. Govt. trainee, 1971, 72; Physical Therapy Fund grantee, 1975, 76; recipient Vol. Achievement award Am. Cancer Soc., 1981. Mem. Am. Phys. Therapy Assn. (edn. sect., orthopedic sect., vice-chair So. sect.), N.J. Arthritis Health Professions Assn. (reader adv. network Arthritis Today, key contact voting dist. 1, legis. network State of N.J. 1989—, vice chairperson so. dist.), Smithsonian Assn., Phys. Therapy Club (sec. 1971-72). Office: Richard Stockton Coll NJ Phys Therapy Program Pomona NJ 08240

BULL, MARY MALEY, radio executive; b. Munich, Mar. 26, 1956; came to U.S., 1956; d. John David and Mary (Kline) M.; m. Steven Tremaine, May 23, 1981; children: Ellen, Emily, Stephanie. BA in History & Music, Trinity U., San Antonio, Tex., 1978. Exec. trainee Joskes' of Tex., San Antonio, 1978-79; office mgr. Advance Mktg., Dallas, 1979-80; acct. exec. Fisher Publs., San Antonio, 1980-82, asst. advt. mgr., advt. dir., 1982-88; sr. account mgr. KSMG-FM, San Antonio, 1988—. Actress Harlequin Theatres, San Antonio, 1979—, San Antonio Little Theatre, 1985—, St. Andrew's Players, 1982—; model various Tex. TV commls., mags., newspapers. Mem. adminstrv. bd., family ministries chmn., St. Andrews Meth. Ch., San Antonio, 1982-85, mem. applause support group, 1981-82, choir pres., 1989, mem. bell choir, dir. children's choir, 1993—; active Girl Scouts USA, 1992—, leader, 1994—. Recipient Nat. Presby. scholarship Nat. Presby. Ch., 1974-78, Dow Jones Writing award Dow Jones, 1974, Addy award, 1989; named Top Salesman Recorder-Times, 1982-84, one of Outstanding Young Women Am., 1983, 85, 87. Mem. San Antonio Advt. Fedn. (bd. dirs. 1988-94, 2d v.p. 1989-90, 1st v.p. 1990-91, pres. 1991-92, 10th dist. dir. 1992-93), Women in Comm., San Antonio Radio and Broadcast Execs., Suburban Newspaper Am. Club. Republican. Methodist. Office: KSMG-FM Radio 8930 Fourwinds Dr Ste 500 San Antonio TX 78239-1973

BULLARD, HELEN (MRS. JOSEPH MARSHALL KRECHNIAK), sculptor; b. Elgin, Ill., Aug. 15, 1902; d. Charles Wickliffe and Minnie (Cook) Bullard; student U. Chgo., 1921-29; m. Lloyd Ernst Rohrke, June 11, 1924 (div. Feb. 1931); children—Ann Louise (Mrs. Ross DeWitt Netherton), Barbara Jane (Mrs. Valtyr Emil Gudmundson); m. 2d, Joseph Marshall Krechniak, Jan. 30, 1932 (dec. Feb. 1964); 1 child, Mariana (Mrs. Wilfred Martin). With research dept. L.V. Estes, Inc., Chgo., 1920-22; operator Square D Co., Detroit, 1922-24; researcher Commerce and Adminstrn. library U. Chgo., Detroit, 1924-25, dir. Crossville (Tenn.) Play Ctr., 1949-50. Creator hand-carved dolls, 1949—, wood sculpture, 1959—; exhibited with Nat. Inst. Am. Doll Artists Exhbns., Los Angeles, 1963, Cin., 1964, Washington, 1965, Chgo., 1966, Boston, 1967, New Orleans, 1969, Detroit, 1970, Los Angeles, 1971, Omaha, 1972, Louisville, 1973, Miami, Fla., 1974, Milw., 1975, Watts Bar Dam, Tenn., 1976, Chgo., 1977, N.Y.C., 1979, others until 1987, also craftsmen's fairs, 1954-65, The Club, Birmingham, Ala., 1963, Oak Ridge Art Ctr., 1965, Children's Mus., Nashville, 1967, McClung Mus., Knoxville, 1969; one woman show Tenn. State Mus., 1972, Nashville, Knoxville, Asheville, N.C.; author: Dr. Woman of the Cumberlands, 1953, The American Doll Artist, 1965, Vol. II, 1974, A Bullard Family, 1966, Dorothy Heizer, the Artist and Her Dolls, 1972; Crafts and Craftsmen of the Tennesee Mountains, 1976, (monograph) My People in Wood, 1984, Faith Wick: Doll Artist Extraordinaire, 1986, Cumberland County, 1956-86, Vol. II, 1987, (with husband) Cumberland County's First Hundred Years, 1956. Campaign chmn. Cumberland County unit Am. Cancer Soc., 1947-52. Mem. So. Highland Handicraft Guild (dir. 1957-59), Highland Handicraft Guild, Nat. Inst. Am. Doll Artists (founder, pres. 1963-67, 69-71, chmn. bd. 1977-80), United Fedn. Doll Clubs (2d v.p. 1977-79), Am. Craftsmen's Coun., Tenn. Folklore Soc., Mensa. Democrat. Unitarian.

BULLARD, JUDITH EVE, psychologist, systems engineer; b. Oneonta, N.Y., Oct. 5, 1945; d. Kurt and Herta (Deutsch) Leeds; divorced; children: Nicholas A., Elizabeth A. BA in Polit. Sci., Spanish U., Oreg., 1966, MA in Psychology, 1973; MBA, George Washington U., 1994. Supr. residential program Skipworth Juvenile Home, Eugene, Oreg., 1966-68; research asst. Oreg. Research Inst., Eugene, 1968-69, 83-85; supr. residential program Ky. Correctional Facility, Lexington, 1969-70; research asst. U. Oreg., Eugene, 1970-73; asst. dir. Regional Mental Health Clinic, Frankfort, Ind., 1974-76; dir. mental health Lane County Mental Health, Eugene, 1977-80; cons. Managerial Communications, Eugene, 1980-83; systems engr. AT&T Bell Labs., Holmdel, N.J., 1985—; mem. strategic task force Globa Bus. Comm. Systems, mgr. tech. ptnr. program, 1993—, tech. and planning, 1993—, info. platform systems, 1993—, innovation, 1994—, mgr. forward looking work/tech. mgmt. group, 1993—, chair customer based panels edn. fourm, 1991—; planned and executed Globa Bus. Comm. Systems Rsch. Tech. Exchange Symposium; mem. Globa Bus. Comm. Systems Leadership Team Cultural Change Project. Producer video The World is Our Work Place, 1991. Bd. dirs. Asbury Park 10K, Jersey Shore 1/2 Marathon, 1985—, Women's Resource and Survival Ctr., Keyport, N.J., 1986—; chairperson Area Affirmative Action Com., 1990—; pres. Affirmative Action Diversity Coun. Recipient Affirmative Action award Bell Lab., Quality award Bus. Communication System, 1991, Continuous Improvement award, 1991, Diversity Improvement award 1991. Mem. Women's Profl. Network (trustee Holmdel br. 1987—), Partnership in Edn. & Bus., Corrections in Mental Health, Human Factors Soc. Office: AT&T BF409 200 Laurel Ave Middletown NJ 07748

BULLARD, JUDYANN DEPASQUALE, elementary education educator; b. Copaigue, N.Y., Oct. 7, 1952; d. Nicholas and Marie (Daole) DePasquale; married; 1 child, Robin Ann. AB in English, Ga. State U., 1973, postgrad., 1985—; MEd, Mercer U., Macon, Ga., 1984. Tchr. Robins AFB Sch. System, Warner Robins, Ga., summers 1980-84; tchr. grades 5, 7 and 8 Christ the King Sch., Atlanta, 1984-89; tchr. grade 5 Warren T. Jackson Sch., Atlanta Pub. Sch. System, 1989—; supervising tchr. Mercer U., Atlanta, 1992; dir. Rainbows for All Children: Support Program for Children in Grief, 1986-88. North Atlanta Parents for Pub. Schs. grantee, 1991. Mem. ASCD, Nat. Coun. Tchrs. English (workshop presenter 1991), Ga. Coun. Tchrs. English (workshop presenter 1989, 91, 92, 93), Profl. Assn. Ga. Educators, Atlanta Jr. C. of C., Ga. Assn. Educators, Kappa Delta Pi. Office: Warren T Jackson Sch 1325 Mount Paran Rd Atlanta GA 30327

BULLARD, LARCENIA J., state legislator; b. Allendale, S.C., July 21, 1947; m. Edward Bullard; children: Dwight M., Edwina Lynn, Vincent Brooker. BA, Antioch U., 1973; MA, Nova U., 1991. Former tchr., adminstr.; mem. Fla. Ho. of Reps., 1992—. Active South Dade Minority Cultural Arts Task Force, South Dade Alliance for Black Neighborhood Devel.; 1st v.p. Cmty. Concerts. Mem. Nat. Coun. Negro Women, Continental Soc., Inc., Greater South Dade-Miami C. of C., South Dade Civitan Club (bd. dirs. 1991-92). Democrat. Baptist. Office: Fla House of Reps State Capitol Tallahassee FL 32301*

BULLARD, MARCIA LYNN, weekly magazine editor; b. Springfield, Ill., Aug. 28, 1952; d. Clark Wesley and Eileen (Kloppenburg) B. AA, Springfield (Ill.) Coll., 1974; BS, So. Ill. U., 1974. Reporter Democrat and Chronicle newspaper, Rochester, N.Y., 1974-79, mag. editor, 1979-82; dep. mng. editor Life sect. USA Today, Washington, 1982-85; mng. editor USA Weekend mag., Washington, 1985-89, editor, 1989—. Tutor 2 schs. D.C., 1984-89, Literacy Vols., Washington, 1987. Mem. AP Mng. Editors. Office: USA Weekend 1000 Wilson Blvd Arlington VA 22229*

BULLARD, MARY ELLEN, retired religious study center administrator; b. Elkin, N.C., Jan. 12, 1926; d. Roy Brannoch and Mattie Reid (Doughton) H.; m. John Carson Bullard Sr., Apr. 27, 1957; children: John Carson Jr., Roy Harrell. BS, U. N.C., Greensboro, 1947; postgrad., Union Theol. Sem., N.Y.C., 1956; MA, Troy State U., Montgomery, Ala., 1979. Dir. women's and girls' work Gilvin Roth YMCA, Elkin, 1947-49; dir. Christian edn. 1st United Meth. Ch., Salisbury, N.C., 1949-51, Charlotte, N.C., 1951-55; dir. youth ministry United Meth. Ch., Western N.C. Conf., 1956-57; dir. ednl. ministries, div. continuing edn. Huntingdon Coll., 1979-88; dir. U.S. office Bibl. Resources Study Ctr., Inc., Jerusalem, 1988-92; bd. dirs. Church Women United Ala., 1970-71; del. World Meth. Coun., 13th World Meth. Conf., Dublin, 1976; mem. 15th World Meth. Conf., Nairobi, Kenya, 1986, 16th World Meth. Conf., Singapore, 1991, exec. com., 1991—, World Evangelism Com., 1991—; vice chair World Meth. Evangelism Inst., 1991—; del. Gen. Conf. United Meth. Ch., St. Louis, 1988, Louisville, 1992; mem. gen. coun. fin. and adminstrn. United Meth. Ch., 1992—. Bd. dirs. LWV, Montgomery, 1966-70, Am. Cancer Soc., Montgomery, 1975-81, Ala. Dept. Youth Svcs., Mt. Meigs Campus Chapel, 1984-85; mem. Montgomery Symphony League, 1984-94, Ala. World Affairs Coun., Montgomery, 1989-94. Recipient award of recognition Bd. Edn. We. N.C. Conf. The United Methodist Ch., 1956, Christian Higher Edn., Ala.-West Fla. Conf. United Meth. Ch., 1975, Conf. Coun. on Ministries, Ala. West Fla. Conf., 1987, Candler Sch. of Theology, Emory U., 1990. Mem. Christian Educators Fellowship, Kappa Delta Pi. Home: 3359 Warrenton Rd Montgomery AL 36111-1736

BULLARD, SHARON WELCH, librarian; b. San Diego, Nov. 4, 1943; d. Dale L. and Myrtle (Sampson) Welch; m. Donald H. Bullard, Aug. 1, 1969. B.S.Ed., U. Central Ark., 1965; M.A., U. Denver, 1967. Media specialist Adams County Sch. Dist. 12, Denver, 1967-69; tchr., libr. Humphrey pub. schs., Ark., 1965-66, libr., 1969-70; catalog libr. Ark. State U., Jonesboro, 1970-75; head documents cataloging Wash. State U., Pullman, 1979-83; head serials cataloging U. Calif.-Santa Barbara Davidson Libr., 1984-88, head circulation dept., 1988—; cons. Ctr. for Robotic Systems Microelectronics Rsch. Libr., Santa Barbara, 1986, Calif. State Libr. retrospective conversion project, 1987, Ombudsman's Office U. Calif., Santa Barbara, 1988; distributor Amway, 1985-91. Canvasser, Citizens for Goleta Valley, 1985-86. Mem. ALA, Calif. Libr. Assn. (tech. svcs. chpt. southern Calif. sect.), Libr. Assn. U. Calif.-Santa Barbara (mem. subcom. on advancement and promotion 1987-91), NAFE, So. Calif. Tech. Processes Group (membership com. 1987), Assn. Coll. and Rsch. Librs. (intern membership com. 1993-94), Libr. Adminstrn. and Mgmt. Assn. (mem. circulation/access svcs. systems and svcs. sect. 1993—, mem. equipment com. bldg. and equipment sect. 1993—), Notis Users Circulation Interest Group (presenter meeting 1992, mem. CIRC SIG steering com. 1993—, moderator meeting 1993—, vice chair elect 1994—), Pi Lambda Theta (exec. bd., sec. Santa Barbara chpt. 1990-91, hospitality com. 1991-92). Avocations: t'ai chi, walking, camping, boogey boarding, swimming.

BULLINGTON, KATHLEEN BURKE, educational consultant; b. Marshalltown, Iowa; d. Raphael Eggleston and Marjorie Narcissa (Busch) Burke; m. William August Bullington, July 25, 1954; children: Marjorie Anne, Mary Joan. BA magna cum laude, U. Iowa, 1948; MSE, Drake U., 1968. Permanent profl. teaching cert. Securities analyst investment dept. Bankers Life Co., Des Moines, 1948-57; arithmetic tchr. grades 4-6 Garton Elem. Sch., Des Moines, 1961-67; elem. tchr. grades 5-6 Windsor Elem. Sch., Des Moines, 1967-76; arithmetic tchr. grades K-6 various elem. schs., Des Moines, 1971-77; coord., cons. Des Moines Pub. Schs., 1976-90; instr. Grandview Coll., Des Moines, 1991, Drake U., Des Moines, 1992; project dir. Success Understanding Math. Program Des Moines Schs., 1985—; coord. Title 1/Chpt. 1 Math. Project Des Moines Schs., 1976-90; chair Des Moines Schs. Elem. Remediation Com., 1985-87; mem. Des Moines Schs. Math. Adv. Bd., 1983—; grant application reviewer Fund for Improvement and Reform Schs. and Teaching, Eisenhower Nat. Program Math. and Sci. Edn., 1990; panel mem. Blue Ribbon Schs. Office Ednl. Rsch. and Improvement, U.S. Office Edn., 1992; mem. North Ctrl. Assn. Evaluation team Iowa City (Iowa) Schs., 1993, comty. adv. bd. tchr. edn. Drake U., 1986. Co-author, editor: Pre/Post Test Items for Mathematics Objectives, 1979, 83, 85, Strategies for Teaching Computation Skills, 1978-79, revised edit., 1988-90, Handbook of Ideas for Parents, 1983, Strategies for Teaching Problem Solving, 1984, Manual for Certified Trainers, Success Understanding Mathematics, 1986-88. Team leader, Wales and China exchs. Friendship Force, Des Moines, 1981-83; bd. mem. Univ. Pl. Child Care Ctr. First Christian Ch., 1987-88, v.p. congregation, 1986-87, chair bd. elders, 1988-89. Recipient Leadership award curriculum dept. Des Moines Schs., 1986; exemplary status and dissemination grantee Nat. Diffusion Network, U.S. Dept. Edn., Washington, 1985-93. Mem. ASCD, AAUW (pres. Des Moines br. 1984-86, named gift honoree 1985), Nat. Coun. Tchrs. Math., Iowa Coun. Tchrs. Math. (editorial staff 1983-85), Nat. Diffusion Network Study Group, Phi Delta Kappa. Mem. Disciples of Christ. Home: 4100 Aurora Ave Des Moines IA 50310 Office: Des Moines Pub Schs 1800 Grand Ave Rm 343 Des Moines IA 50309

BULLOCK, IRENE P., bookkeeper, tax preparer; b. Chase City, Va., Apr. 10, 1922; d. William M. and Mamie L. (Harrington) Perry; m. Noel M. Bullock Jr., Jan. 26, 1941; children: Ann Bullock Arnold, Rae Bullock Creedle, Faye Bullock Cleaton. Student, USDA Grad. Sch. Office mgr. Std. Garments, Chase City, 1942-54; area clk. USDA Soil Conservancy Svc., Chase City, 1955-85, fed. woman's program mgr., 1980-85; bookkeeper, tax preparer Boswell Bookkeeping Svc., Chase City, 1987—; mem. EEO com. USDA-SCS, 1980-85, press corps USDA, 1960. Recipient Commendation award Soil Conservation Soc. Am., 1980. Mem. Nat. Assn. Retired Fed. Employees, Orgn. Profl. Employees USDA, Assn. Retired Soil Conservation Svc. Employees, Tanglewood Shores Club. Home: Rt 1 Box 1350 Chase City VA 23924 Office: Boswell Bookkeeping & Tax Svc 206 E Fifth St Chase City VA 23924

BULLOCK, JUDY ROESKE, executive benefits consultant, accountant; b. Monroe, Mich., Sept. 10, 1957; d. Ivan Kenneth and Nell Elizabeth (Giles) Roseke; m. Charles C. Bullock, Jr., Feb. 17, 1991; children: Charles Christopher Bullock, Catherine Christina Bullock. BA in Acctg., U. South Fla., 1982; postgrad., Keller, 1994—. ChFC, AICPA/PFS; CPA, Fla., Mo. Sr. tax specialist KPMG Peat Marwick, Tampa, Fla., 1982-84; tax/tech. design dir. CIGNA Fin. Svcs., Tampa, 1984-87; sr. mgr. tax/personal fin. svcs. Price Waterhouse, Tampa, St. Louis, 1987-93; exec. compensation practice leader, exec. benefits cons. Towers Perrin, St. Louis, 1994—; artist Innovative Solutions, St. Louis, 1991—. Loaned exec. United Way, Tampa, 1989. Mem. AICPA, Am. Compensation Assn., Am. Soc. CLU/ChFC, Mo. Soc. CPAs (mem. personal fin. svcs. com. 1993, mem. investment com. 1994). Republican. Roman Catholic. Home: 4003 Affirmed Dr Florissant MO 63034 Office: Towers Perrin 101 S Hanley Saint Louis MO 63105

BULLOCK, MARIE, real estate investment executive, educator; b. Washington, Aug. 18, 1941; d. Jerry John and Anna Marie (Horstkamp) McCarthy; m. Patrick Ettien, May 31, 1965 (div. Sept. 1969); m. 2d, Charles Edward Bullock, Mar. 3, 1973; children—Ryan, Bennett. BA in Spl. Edn., Marymount Coll., 1984, MA in Counseling, Trinity Coll., 1987; PhD in Counseling and Human Devel. Am. U., 1992. Cert. in spl. edn., Va. Sec., treas. McCarthy Mfg. Co. Inc., Alexandria, Va., 1969-82; v.p. EduTrainer, Inc., Alexandria, 1979-83; mng. ptnr. C&E Partnership, Alexandria, 1971—, dir. couns. svcs., 1992—. Pres. St. Andrew's Episcopal PTA, Bethesda, 1981; bd. dirs. Bethesda Acad. Arts. Mem. Montgomery County Assn. for

Children with Learning Disabilities (v.p. 1984), Council Exceptional Children, Am. Counseling Assn., Psi Chi. Democrat. Christian. Clubs: Kenwood Country (Bethesda, Md.); Zonta Internat. Avocations: reading; theater; cooking; biking; skiing. Home: 5118 Dalecarlia Dr Bethesda MD 20816-1802

BULLOCK, MOLLY, educator; d. Wiley and Annie M. Jordan; m. George Bullock; children: Myra A. Bauman, Dawn M. BS in Edn., No. Ariz. U., 1955, postgrad., 1958; postgrad., LaVerne U., 1962, Claremont Grad. Sch., 1963, Calif. State U. L.A., 1966. Tchr. Bur. Indian Affairs, Kaibeto, Ariz., 1955-56, Crystal, N.Mex., 1956-59; tchr. Covina (Calif.) Valley Unified Sch. Dist., 1961—, supervising master tchr. for trainees of LaVerne U. and Calif. State U. - L.A., 1961-71, mem. curriculum devel. adv. bd., 1977-79. Poet: A Tree (Golden Poet 1991), What is Love (Golden medal of honor). Mini grantee Hughes/Rotary Club/Foothill Ind. Bank, Covina, 1986-90. Mem. ASCD, NEA, NAFE, AAUW (treas. 1972), Internat. Platform Assn., Internat. Soc. Poets (hon. charter mem.), Calif. Tchrs. Assn. Home: 2175 Victoria Way Pomona CA 91767

BULMAHN, LYNN, journalist, free-lance writer; b. Waco, Tex., Feb. 18, 1955; d. Franklin Harrold and Louise (Stolte) B. BA, SW Tex. State U., 1977. Med., health, feature writer and gen. assignment reporter Waco Tribune Herald, 1977—; vis. journalist fellowship Duke U., 1991. Recipient Anson Jones Merit citation, Tex. Med. Assn., 1978, 91, Outstanding Contbn. award Nat. Found. March of Dimes, 1980, Pub. Health award for media excellence Tex. Pub. Health Assn., 1980, 85, 88, 89, 90, 91, 92, 93, 94, First Place award Readers Digest Mag. Workshop Tex. Competition, 1981, Feature Writing award North and East Tex. Press Assn., 1983, Media Appreciation award McLennan County Med. Assn., 1985, Journalism Excellence award Am. Cancer Soc., 1989, 91, Silver Star of Tex. award Tex. Hosp. Assn., 1989, 92, Newspaper award, Mental Health Assn., 1989, 90, 91, 94, Media award, 1985, Anson Jones award Tex. Med. Assn., 1992; co-recipient Tex. Katie award Press Club Dallas, 1993. Office: Waco Tribune-Herald 900 Franklin Ave Waco TX 76701-1906

BUMBRY, GRACE, soprano; b. St. Louis, Jan. 4, 1937; d. Benjamin and Melzia (Walker) B. Student, Boston U., 1954-55, Northwestern U., 1955-56, also fgn. countries, Music Acad. West, 1956-59; studied with, Lotte Lehmann, 1956-59; HHD (hon.), St. Louis U.; hon. doctorates in humanities, Rust Coll., Holly Spring, Miss., U. St. Louis, U. Mo.; MusD (hon.), Rockhurst Coll. Operatic debut, Paris Opera, 1960; debut Basel Opera, 1960, Bayreuth Festival, 1961, Vienna State Opera, 1963, Royal Opera House, Covent Garden, 1963, Salzburg Festival, 1964, Met. Opera, 1965, La Scala, 1966; has appeared other opera houses in Europe, S.Am., Japan, U.S.; command performances The White House and London; recs. for Deutsche Grammophon, Angel, London and RCA. Recipient John Hay Whitney award, Richard Wagner medal, 1963, Grammy award, 1979, Royal Opera House medal, 1988. Mem. Zeta Phi Beta, Sigma Alpha Iota. Office: Herbert H Breslin Inc 119 W 57th St New York NY 10019

BUMGARDNER, ROBERTA LYNN (ROBYN BUMGARDNER), human resources specialist; b. Lynchburg, Va., Aug. 1, 1957; d. Robert Lynwood and Naomi Missouri (Walker) B. BS with honors, Radford Coll., 1979; MS, Am. U., 1987. Tng. coord. A.T. Massey Coal Co., Richmond, Va., 1983-87, mgmt. devel. mgr., 1987-88, pers. dir., 1988-90, dir. human resource devel., 1990-91; client svcs. dir. The Execs. Exch., Glen Allen, Va., 1991-92; econ. dislocation and worker adjustment assistance Capital Area Tng. Consortium, County of Henrico, Va., 1992—; adj. faculty Averett Coll., Richmond, Va., 1992—. Treas. Ballet Petit, Richmond, 1989-91. Mem. Soc. for Human Resource Mgmt. Office: Capital Area Tng Consortium 7321 White Pine Rd Richmond VA 23237

BUMSTEAD, DAWN D., radio executive; b. Flint, Mich., July 15, 1965; d. Charles Stanley and Wanda June (Atchley) B. BA in Communications, Olivet Nazarene U., Kankakee, Ill., 1986. Lic. FCC radio telephone operator. Ops. mgr. Sta. WKOC-FM, Kankakee, 1986-88; news and community rels. dir. Sta. WUFL, Detroit, 1988—; pres. dawn bumstead communications, Mt. Clemens, Mich., 1989—; program dir. CV-one, Rochester Hills, Mich., 1989-91. Producer Information Plus, 1984-86, Single Walk, 1990-91, Kidminute, 1990-91. Instr. Brandon Community Edn., Ortonville, Mich., 1982; min. youth, dir. choir Lake Louise Ch. of Nazarene, Ortonville, 1990—. Mem. Nat. Religious Broadcasters, Concerned Women for Am., Nat. Right to Life, Rotary (hon.). Republican. Home: 699 W Magee Rd Apt 13102 Tucson AZ 85704-4654 Office: WUFL 42669 Garfield Rd Ste 328 Clinton Township MI 48038-5024

BUNCH, LUANN, marketing executive; b. Mpls., May 3, 1955; d. John F. and Theresa A. (Otten) Victory; m. Dennis Bunch, Dec. 24, 1986. AA, North Hennepin Community Coll., Brooklyn Park, Minn., 1975; BA magna cum laude, St. Cloud State U., 1976; MA with high honors, Southwestern Mo. State U., 1978. Dir. pub. rels. Park Cen. Hosp., Springfield, Mo., 1977-79; dir. community rels. and devel. Mt. Carmel Med. Ctr., Pittsburg, Kans., 1980-82; dir. physician mktg. and recruiting Coord. Svcs., Wichita, 1982-85; mgr. profl. rels. Rep. Health Corp., Dallas, 1985-86; dir. mktg. Timberlawn Psychiat. Hosp., Dallas, 1987-90; chief exec. officer, mktg. and pub. rels. cons. Victory Assocs., Plano, 1991—. Editor: Insight (Telestar award 1988), 1987, Direct Mail Piece (Telestar award 1988, Bronze Quill award of Excellence for Brown Bag lectr. series Internat. Assn. Bus. Communicators 1989), 1987, Inner View, 1977-78, Spectrum, 1980; host radio and TV talk shows, Pittsburg. Bd. dirs. ARC, Pittsburg, 1981; dir. Pittsburg Community Theatre, 1981; instr. Pittsburg Children's Theatre Workshop, 1981; pub. relations cons. Am. Diabetes Assn., Springfield, 1979. Recipient Applause award Tex. Soc. Mktg. and Pub. Rels., 1988-89, 90-91, Telestar award and merit award Brown Bay Series, 1990, First Pl. award Nat. Assn. Pvt. Psychiat. Hosps., 1990. Mem. Am. Mktg. Assn., Am. Soc. Mktg. and Pub. Rels., Am. Soc. Planning and Mktg., Women in Communications, Tex. Soc. Hosp. Mktg. and Pub. Rels. Roman Catholic. Home: 1087 Camellia Pl Fox River Grove IL 60021-1348 Office: Victory Assocs 569 Old Barn Rd Barrington IL 60010-6209

BUNDY, BLAKELY FETRIDGE, early childhood educator, advocate, writer; b. Chgo., Aug. 31, 1944; d. William Harrison and Bonnie Jean (Clark) Fetridge; m. Harvey Hollister Bundy III, Aug. 20, 1966; children: H. Hollister IV, Clark Harrison, Elizabeth Lowell, Reed Fetridge. BA cum laude, Wheaton Coll., Mass., 1966; MEd, Nat.-Louis U., 1985. Tchr. Norwich (Vt.) Kindergarten, 1966-67, Willow Wood Pre-Sch., Winnetka, Ill., 1983-93, bd. dirs., 1972-81, adv. bd., 1981-83, 93—; bd. dirs. North Ave. Day Nursery, Chgo., 1970-76, Ill. Family-to-Family Child Care Initiative, 1994-95; exec. dir. Winnetka Alliance for Early Childhood Edn., 1989—; accreditation system validator Nat. Acad. Early Childhood Programs, Washington, 1986—; mem. pres.'s commn. Wheaton Coll., Norton, Mass., 1987—; trustee Brooks Sch., North Andover, Mass., 1993—; cons. editor Nat. Assn. Edn. Young Children, 1991-95. Author pamphlets: What an Executive Should Know About Industry Sponsored Day Care, 1984, What an Executive Should Know About Child Care Services, 1985; contbr. articles to Chgo. Tribune, Redbook, Glamour mags., Early Childhood News, Dartnell Inst. Bus. Rsch. Jour., Child Care Ctr. Mag., Chgo. Sun-Times, Day Care and Early Education, Young Children, other publs. Mem. United Rep. Fund, Chgo., 1968-85; active N.E. Ill. coun. Boy Scouts Am., 1976-80, 85-88, Ill. Shore Coun. Girl Scouts U.S., 1981-89, World Found. for Girls Guides and Girl Scouts Friends of Our Cabaña Com., Cuernavaca, Mexico, 1986-94. Mem. Nat. Assn. for the Edn. Young Children (photographer publs.), World Assn. Girl Guides and Girl Scouts, Chgo. Assn. Edn. Young Children (steering com. Near North Suburban chpt. 1986—, commn. on salaries and working conditions, 1988-92, comm. adv. com. 1989-92, bd. dirs. 1992—, chair accreditation project mgmt. com. 1994—), Olive Baden-Powell Soc. (London). Episcopalian. Clubs: Indian Hill (Winnetka); Stevensville (Mich.) Yacht; Ocean Reef (Key Largo, Fla.). Avocations: golf, sailing. Office: Winnetka Alliance for Early Childhood 1235 Oak St Winnetka IL 60093-2168

BUNDY, HALLIE FLOWERS, biochemist, educator; b. Santa Monica, Calif., Apr. 2, 1925; d. Douglas and Phyllis (Flowers) B. BA in Chemistry, Mt. St. Mary's Coll., L.A., 1947; MS in Biochemistry, U. So. Calif., 1955, PhD in Biochemistry, 1958. Instr. sch. medicine U. So. Calif., L.A., 1959-60; asst. prof. Mt. St. Mary's Coll., 1960-63, assoc. prof., 1963-66, prof. biochemistry, 1966-90, emeritus prof., 1990—; asst. program dir. undergrad. rshc. participation NSF, Washington, 1965-66. Contbr. rsch. articles to profl. jours. USPHS predoctoral fellow, 1955-57; NSF Sci. Faculty fellow, 1969-70; grantee NIH, 1960-66, 86-89, NSF, 1961-78, 87-89, Grad. Women in Sci., 1974. Mem. Am. Chem. Soc., Pacific Slope Biochem. Conf., Sigma Xi. Office: Mt St Mary's Coll 12001 Chalon Rd Los Angeles CA 90049-1597

BUNDY, KELLY JANE, learning disabilities educator, consultant; b. Bedford, Ind., Nov. 15, 1958; d. Webster Herschel and Sarah Ann (Chambers) B. BA in Elem. Edn., Oral Roberts U., 1982, MA in Reading, 1986, postgrad. in Learning Disabilities, Psychometry, 1985-86. Tchr. 3rd grade St. Vincent Cath. Sch., Bedford, Ind., 1982-85; tchr. 4th grade Metro Christian Acad., Tulsa, Okla., 1986-87; elem. sch. tutor Diagnostic Instrn. Ctr., Tulsa, Okla., 1986-87; learning disabilities tchr. K-6 Parkview Primary, Intermediate Schs., Bedford, Ind., 1987-90; learning disabilities cons., tchr. OLJM Joint Svcs, Parkview Primary Sch., Bedford, 1990-92, OLJM Joint Svcs, Bedford Jr. High Sch., 1992—; co-presenter Conf. Okla. Assn. for Children and Adults with Learning Disabilities, Tulsa, 1987; presenter at in-service, meetings on Attention Deficit Disorder, Bedford, Ind., 1992-93. Mem. Learning Disabilities Assn., Children Having Attention Deficit Disorders, Read Coun., Coun. for Exceptional Children. Republican. Home: PO Box 1015 Bedford IN 47421-1015 Office: OLJM Joint Svcs 1501 N St Bedford IN 47421-3715

BUNDZA, MAIRA, librarian; b. Elizabeth, N.J., Jan. 23, 1955; d. Karlis Valters and Austra Ruta (Purvinska) B.; 1 child, Ansis. BA, Cornell U., 1976; MLS, Western Mich. U., 1984. Dir. libr. Latvian Studies Ctr., Kalamazoo, 1982—; lectr./cons. in exch. program Nat. Libr. Latvia, Riga, 1990-91. Editor: (newsletter) LSC Zinas, 1990; contbr. articles to profl. jours. Bd. dirs., sec. Whole Art Theater, Kalamazoo, 1989—; canvaser People's Ch., Kalamazoo, 1991-92, mem. events com., 1994—. Mem. ALA (nominating com. Slavic and East European sect.), Assn. for Advancement of Baltic Studies, Am. Latvian Assn., Beta Phi Mu. Unitarian. Office: Latvian Studies Ctr Libr 1702 Fraternity Village Dr Kalamazoo MI 49006-5941

BUNE, KAREN LOUISE, criminal justice official; b. Washington, Mar. 6, 1954; d. Harry and Eleanor Mary (White) B. BA in Am. Studies cum laude, Am. U., 1976, MS in Adminstrn. of Justice with distinction, 1978. Notary pub., Va. Case mgr. Arlington (Va.) Alcohol Safety Action Program, 1979-94; victim specialist Office of Commonwealth Atty., Arlington, Va., 1994—; case mgr. regional rep. of case mgmt. com. of Dirs. Assn. Commn. on Va. Alcohol Safety Action Program, Richmond, 1980-81, 84-85, 88-89, mem. subcom. studying treatment issues, 1988-94; chair career guidance subcom. alumni adv. com. Sch. Pub. Affairs Am. U., Washington, 1991-94. Sch. of Justice rep. alumni adv. com. Coll. Pub. Affairs, Am. U. Washington, 1982-86, chmn. student rels., 1982-86, mem. alumni steering com., 1991—. Recipient spl. achievement award Dept. Navy, 1973, merit award Arlington County, 1986, Woman of the Yr. Am. Biog. Inst., 1990, inducted into Hall of Fame for outstanding achievement in case management. Mem. AAUW, ASPA, NAFE, APHA, Nat. Assn. Chiefs Police (award of merit 1986), Nat. Criminal Justice Assn., Am. Police Hall of Fame (cert. of appreciation 1985), No. Va. Fraternal Order of Police, Acad. Criminal Justice Scis., So. Criminal Justice Assn., Am. Soc. Criminology, Va. Sheriffs Inst., Va. Assn. Female Execs., Internat. Platform Assn., Am. U. Alumni Assn. (pres. sch. pub. affairs chpt. 1994—), Women of Washington, Phi Kappa Phi, Phi Alpha Alpha, Phi Delta Gamma (1st v.p. 1981-82). Home: 926 16th St S Arlington VA 22202-2606 Office: Office of Commonwealth Atty 1425 N Courthouse Rd Arlington VA 22201

BUNIM, MARY-ELLIS, television producer; b. Northampton, Mass., July 9, 1946; d. Frank Roberts and Roslyn Dena (LaMontagne) Paxton; m. Robert Eric Bunim, Jan. 31, 1971; 1 dau., Juliana. Pres. Bunim-Murray Prodns., L.A., 1988—; exec. prodr. daily CBS-TV series Search for Tomorrow, 1976-81, As the World Turns, 1981-84, NBC-TV series Santa Barbara, 1984-86, syndicated Crime Diaries, 1988, ABC-TV series Loving, 1989-90, FBC series American Families, 1990; co-creator, exec. prodr. MTV series The Real World, 1992—, Road Rules, 1995—, NBC spl. Friends and Lovers, 1994.

BUNKER, BARBARA BENEDICT, psychology educator; b. Bklyn., June 26, 1931. BA in Psychology and Religion, Ohio Wesleyan U., 1953; DB in Religion and Art, U. Chgo., 1956; PhD in Social Psychology, Columbia U., 1970. Lic. psychologist, N.Y. Dir. religious life Women's Coll. Duke U., Durham, N.C., 1956-64; instr. dept. psychology and ednl. adminstrn. Tchrs. Coll. Columbia U., N.Y.C., 1968-70; asst. prof. psychology SUNY, Buffalo, 1970-75, assoc. prof., 1975—, dir. social psychology grad. program, 1977-83, dir. grad. studies and admissions dept. psychology, 1986-90; assoc. Ctr. for Policy Rsch., Columbia U., 1970-74; mem. Nat. Stds. and Admissions Com., 1972-76; chairperson policy com. faculty social scis. and adminstrn. SUNY, Buffalo, 1975-76, 82-83; NIMH psychology edn. rev. com., 1979-81; Fulbright lectr. Kobe (Japan) U. Sch. Bus. Adminstrn., 1990; Ken Benne scholar selection com. NTL Inst., 1992, 93, Otto Klineberg Intercultural and Internat. Rels. award selection com. SPSSI, 1994; Fulbright lectr. Keio U., Christian U., Tokyo, 1984. cons. editor Jour. Applied Behavioral Sci., 1971-74, High Sch. Behavioral Sci., 1976-77; author: (with others) Social Intervention: A Behavioral Science Approach, 1971, Student's Guide to Conducting Social Science Research, 1975, (tng. curricula) Psychology and You, 1971; contbr. articles to profl. jours., chpts. to books. Danforth Found. fellow, 1964-65, 65-66; recipient Disting. svc. award Erie County Mental Health Assn., 1988; grantee Instl. Funds for Precoll. Psychology Rsch., 1971, NTL Inst. for Applied Behavior Sci. for Women's Planning Conf. on Issues of Women in Orgns., 1973, Instl. Funds for Rsch. on Self-Disclosure, 1974, NIMH, 1979-84, Small Grup Rsch. Grant NTL Inst., 1986, Office Teaching Effectiveness Project award, 1988. Mem. APA, NTL Inst. (bd. dirs. 1976-82, chairperson bd. dirs. 1978-81), Soc. for Psychol. Study Social Issues, Orgn. Devel. Network, Internat. Assn. Applied Psychology, Internat. Assn. Conflict Resolution, Ea. Psychol. Assn., Sigma Xi. Home: 117 Highland Ave Buffalo NY 14222-1842

BUNN, BARBARA JEAN, state legislator; m. William Bunn; 2 children. BS, Kans. State U. Mem. Ga. Ho. of Reps., 1992—; mem. def. and vet affairs com., indsl. rels. com., reapportionment com., ret. educator. Republican. Presbyterian. Home: 2635 Stanton Rd Conyers GA 30208 Office: Ga House of Reps 411 Legis Office Bldg Atlanta GA*

BUNN, DOROTHY IRONS, court reporter; b. Trinidad, Colo., Apr. 30, 1948; d. Russell and Pauline Anna (Langowski) Irons; m. Peter Lynn Bunn; children: Kristy Lynn, Wade Allen, Russell Ahearn. Student No. Va. Community Coll., 1970-71, U. Va., Fairfax, 1971-72. Registered profl. reporter; cert. shorthand reporter. Pres., chief exec. officer Ahearn Ltd., Springfield, Va., 1970-81, Bunn & Assocs., Glenrock, Wyo., 1981—; cons. Bixby Hereford Co., Glenrock, 1981-89, co-mgr., 1989—. Del., White House Conf. on Small Bus., Washington, 1986, 94—. Mem. NAFE, Am. Indian Soc., Nat. Ct. Reporters Assn., Xcel Internat. (1st v.p., 1994—), Wyo. Shorthand Reporters Assn. (chmn. com. 1984-85), Nat. Cattlewomen, Wyo. Cattlewomen (Converse County), Nat. Fedn. Ind. Businesses (guardian 1991—), Nat. Fedn. Bus. and Profl. Women (1st v.p. Casper 1994—, pub. rels. chair, Choices chair), Nat. Cattlewomen. Avocations: art, music. Home: PO Box 1602 Bixby Hereford Co Glenrock WY 82637 Office: Bunn & Assocs 81 Bixby Rd Glenrock WY 82637

BUNT, LYNNE JOY, insurance broker; b. Corning, N.Y., Sept. 25, 1948; d. William Henry and Cleo Ann (Williams) Prentice. AA, Foothill Coll., 1969; ins. studies, IIAAC, IEA, WAIB, 1969. Account exec., v.p. Jardine Ins. Brokers, Inc., San Francisco, 1979—. Congregationalist. Democrat. Office: 333 Bush St San Francisco CA 94104-2806

BUNTEN, BRENDA ARLENE, geriatrics nurse; b. Paris, Ill., May 7, 1947; d. Arthur Ray Sr. and Maxine L. (Bacon) B. A in Arts and Scis., Lakeland Coll., Mattoon, Ill., 1968; ADN, Kapiolani C.C., Honolulu, 1992. Charge nurse Meml. Med. Ctr., Springfield, Ill., 1968-76, Mattoon Health Care Ctr., 1977-79; agy. nurse Kahu Malama, Inc., Honolulu, 1983; charge nurse, staff devel. coord., infection control officer Hale Nani Health Ctr., Honolulu, 1979-83, 83—, also nursing staff scheduler, supr., 1983-93; unit mgr. Randal Mill Manor, 1994—; fundraiser Challenger Run Hawaii, Honolulu, 1986—; co-owner, cons. retail sales Sunset Enterprises, Honolulu, 1982—. Mem. Alpha Kappa Psi, Beta Sigma Phi (pres. 1985-86). Home: 2009 Newbury Dr Arlington TX 76014

BUNTEN, JUDITH ANN, perinatal nurse, educator; b. Logan, Utah; d. Glenn and Bess Bunten. AA with honors, Antelope Valley Coll., 1963; BS with honors, UCLA, 1966; MS, U. Colo., 1968. RN, Calif.; cert. pub. health nurse, Calif.; cert. instr. community colls., Calif.; cert. basic cardiac life support; cert. neonatal resuscitation. Rsch. asst. U. Colo. Sch. of Nursing, Denver, 1969; instr. Mount St. Mary's Coll., L.A., 1973-76, St. John's Hosp., Santa Monica, 1974; instr., asst. dir. nursing edn. Cedars-Sinai Med. Ctr., L.A., 1976-78; clin. nurse, adminstrv. nurse UCLA Med. Ctr., L.A., 1966-68, 69-73, clin. nurse, 1978-83, adminstrv. nurse, 1983—; adj. faculty Coll. of the Canyons, Santa Clarita, Calif., 1986-91, 93; clin. nurse Holy Cross Hosp., Mission Hills, Calif., 1984-87; mgmt. preceptor UCLA Sch. of Nursing, 1990, Calif. State U., 1990; guest lectr. cmty. hosps., 1989-90; guest spkr. vocat. nurse graduation L.A. Sch. Dist., 1989. Contbr. to Maternity Nursing, 18th edit., 1995. Mem. ARC, Santa Clarita, 1990-91, co-organizer child's health fair, 1990. Regents scholar U. Calif., 1964-66. Mem. Perinatal Adv. Coun. of L.A. Office: UCLA Med Ctr Dept Nursing 10833 Le Conte Ave Los Angeles CA 90024

BUNYAN, ELLEN LACKEY SPOTZ, chemist, educator; b. Clarks Mills, Pa., Aug. 14, 1921; d. Scott Richard and Mary Ellen (Beal) Lackey; married; children: Mark Stephen Spotz, Leslie Claire Spotz, Elizabeth Grace O'Rourke. BS, U. Pitts., 1942; PhD, U. Wis., 1950. Sr. technologist Eastman Kodak Co., Kingsport, Tenn., 1942-44; instr. chemistry U. Wis., Milw., 1946-47; rsch. assoc. dept. chemistry U. Wis.-Madison, 1950-52; instr. physics St. Agnes Acad., Houston, 1965; Welch fellow chemistry Rice U., Houston, 1968-69; lectr. Montgomery Coll., Rockville, Md., 1970-72; asst. prof. chem. tech. U. D.C., Washington, 1972-78, assoc. prof., 1978-91, ret., 1991; adj. prof. continuing edn. Walter Reed Army Med. Ctr. U. D.C., 1991-94; adj. prof. U. D.C., 1995—; guest worker Nat. Bur. Standards, 1976. Curriculum developer Allied Health Chemistry; bd. dirs. Takoma Park Symphony, 1988-94; mem. adv. bd. Cambodian Children's Assn., Inc. Contbr. articles to profl. jours. Nat. Urban League fellow Eastman Kodak Co., 1976. Mem. NEA, Am. Chem. Soc., Am. Poolplayers Assn., Sigma Xi, Sigma Delta Epsilon. Methodist.

BUONO, KATHLEEN ANN CLEARY, nursing educator; b. Bklyn., Dec. 9, 1964; d. Sarah Murphy; m. James Gerard Buono, Jan. 9, 1988; 1 child, James Gerard. Diploma, Albany (N.Y.) Med. Ctr. Sch. Nursing, 1985; BSN, SUNY, New Paltz, 1988; student, Russell Sage Coll. RN, N.Y. Staff nurse oper. rm. Albany Med. Ctr.; staff nurse Benedictine Hosp., Kingston, N.Y.; now clin. instr. Albany Meml. Sch. Nursing. Home: PO Box 272 New Baltimore NY 12124-0272

BURACK, CYNTHIA, educator; b. Morgantown, W.Va., May 22, 1958; d. Charles Richard and Dwanda (Simmons) B. BA, W.Va. U., 1981; MA, U. Md., 1987, PhD, 1991. Instr. U. Md., College Park, 1986-91; asst. prof. George Washington U., Washington, 1991—. Author: The Problem of the Passions: Feminism, Psychoanalysis and Social Theory, 1994. Mem. U. Md. Chorus, 1986-94. Mem. Am. Polit. Sci. Assn., Internat. Soc. Polit. Psychology, Nat. Women's Studies Assn. Office: George Washington U 2201 G St NW Washington DC 20052

BURBANK, JANE RICHARDSON, Russian and European studies educator; b. Hartford, Conn., June 11, 1946; d. John and Helen Lee (West) B.; m. Frederick Cooper, Sept. 3, 1985. BA, Reed Coll., 1967; MLS, Simmons Coll., 1969; MA, Harvard U., 1971, PhD, 1981. Tchg. fellow Harvard U., Cambridge, Mass., 1976-80, asst. prof., 1981-85; asst. prof. U. Calif., Santa Barbara, 1985-86, assoc. prof., 1986-87; assoc. prof. U. Mich., Ann Arbor, 1987—, dir. Ctr. for Russian and East European Studies, 1992—; reviewer Kritika, 1983, Russian Rev., 1984, Am. Hist. Rev., 1988, 91, Jour. Modern History, 1989, 92, 93, Slavic Rev., 1990, Harvard Ukrainian Studies, 1991; presenter Comparative Study of Social Transformation seminar, U. Mich., 1990, Conf. on the Relationships between the State and Civil Soc. in Ea. Europe and Africa, Comparative Perspectives, Villa Serbelloni, Bellagio, Italy, 1990, L'viv U., Ukraine, 1990, U. Minn., 1990, Stanford (Calif.) U., 1990, 91, U. Mich., 1991, 92, 93, U. Iowa, 1991, Northwestern U., 1992. Author: Intelligentsia and Revolution: Russian Views of Bolshevism, 1917-1922, 1986; editor: Perestroika and Soviet Culture, 1989; editor Kritika, 1978-80; mem. editl. bd. Ind.-Mich. Series in Russian and East European Studies; contbr. articles to profl. jours. Fulbright-Hayes Rsch. award, 1991, Sheldon Traveling fellow Harvard U., 1977-78, Krupp Found. fellow, Ctr. for European Studies, Harvard U., 1977-78, AAUW fellow, 1980-81, Whiting fellow, 1980-81, Am. Coun. Learned Socs. fellow, 1983-84, Hoover Inst. Postdoctoral fellow, 1990-91; grantee NEH, 1984, Harvard U., 1982-84, Internat. Rsch. and Exchs. Bd., Acad. Exch. with the USSR, 1987-88, 91, U. Mich., 1990. Mem. Am. Hist. Assn., Am. Assn. for the Advancement of Slavic Studies, Social Sci. Rsch. Coun. (joint com. on Soviet studies 1988-93), Phi Beta Kappa. Office: U Mich Ctr Russian and East European Studies 204-220 Lane Hall Ann Arbor MI 48109-1290

BURBANK, NANCY ANN, artist, nurse; b. Flint, Mich., Mar. 17, 1930; d. Clarence E. Burgess and Sarah Martha (Hunt) Burgess-Warren; m. Rex James Burbank, Feb. 12, 1955; children: Jeffrey, Cynthia Burbank-Vandenberg, Scott. RN, Bronson Sch. of Nursing, 1951; BA in Art, San Jose State U., 1972; student, Queens Coll., U. Cambridge, Eng., 1993, 94. RN. Emergency rm. charge RN McLaren Hosp., Flint, 1951; head nurse Kapiolani Hosp., Honolulu, 1952, U. Mich. Hosp., Ann Arbor, 1956; instr. Sch. Pub. Health, Bangkok, 1969; nurse cons., RN Santa Clara County Mental Health, San Jose, Calif., 1974-82; hearing officer, RN Santa Clara County Health Dept., San Jose, Calif., 1984-88; artist Los Gatos, Calif., 1994—. One-woman shows include Town of Los Gatos, 1979-91, San Jose Mus. Art, 1983-94; exhibited in group shows at San Jose State U., 1983-94; card designer UNICEF, 1990; calendar designer AAUW, 1989 (Art Excellence award 1989). Art commr. Town of Los Gatos, 1984-90; founding mem., bd. dirs. San Jose Mus. Art, San Jose, 1972; art alumni bd. San Jose State U., 1984-89; founding mem. Friends of Art, Los Gatos, 1985; local action chair, bd. dirs. LWV, Los Gatos, 1993-94; program arts chair Los Gatos Unitarian Fellowship, 1993-94. Mem. AAUW (pro choice chair 1992, Nat. Art award 1989). Democrat. Home: 108 Belcrest Dr Los Gatos CA 95032

BURBIDGE, E. MARGARET, astronomer, educator; b. Davenport, Eng.; d. Stanley John and Marjorie (Stott) Peachey; m. Geoffrey Burbidge, Apr. 2, 1948; 1 child, Sarah. B.S., Ph.D., U. London; Sc.D. hon., Smith Coll., 1963, U. Sussex, 1970, U. Bristol, 1972, U. Leicester, 1972, City U., 1973, U. Mich., 1978, U. Mass., 1978, Williams Coll., 1979, SUNY, Stony Brook, 1985, Rensselaer Poly. Inst., 1986, U. Notre Dame, 1986, U. Chgo., 1991. Mem. staff U. London Obs., 1948-51; rsch. fellow Yerkes Obs. U. Chgo., 1951-53, Shirley Farr fellow Yerkes obs., 1957-59, assoc. prof. Yerkes Obs., 1959-62; rsch. fellow Calif. Inst. Tech., Pasadena, 1955-57; mem. Enrico Fermi Inst. for Nuclear Studies, 1957-62; prof. astronomy dept. physics U. Calif. San Diego, 1964—, univ. prof., 1984—; dir. Royal Greenwich Obs. (Herstmonceaux Castle), Hailsham, Sussex, Eng., 1984-90; rsch. prof. dept. physics U. Calif., San Diego, 1990—; Lindsay Meml. lectr. Goddard Space Flight Ctr., NASA, 1985; Abby Rockefeller Mauze prof. MIT, 1968; David Elder lectr. U. Strathclyde, 1972; V. Gildersleeve lectr. Barnard Coll., 1974; Jansky lectr. Nat. Radio Astronomy Observatory, 1977; Brode lectr. Whitman Coll., 1986. Author: (with G. Burbidge) Quasi-Stellar Objects, 1967; editor: Observatory mag., 1948-51; mem. editorial bd.: Astronomy and Astrophysics, 1969—. Recipient (with husband) Warner prize in Astronomy, 1959, Bruce Gold medal Astronomy Soc. Pacific, 1982; hon. fellow Univ. Coll., London, Girton Coll., Lucy Cavendish Coll., Cambridge; U.S. Nat. medal of sci., 1984; Sesquicentennial medal Mt. Holyoke Coll., 1987, Einstein medal World Cultural Coun., 1988. Fellow Royal Soc., Nat. Acad. Scis. (chmn. sect. 12 astronomy 1986), Am. Acad. Arts and Scis., Royal Astron. Soc.; mem. Am. Astron. Soc. (v.p. 1972-74, pres. 1976-78; Henry Norris Russell lectr. 1984), Internat. Astron. Union (pres. commn. 28 1970-73), Grad. Women Sci. (nat. hon. mem.). Office: U Calif-San Diego Ctr Astrophysics Space Scis Mail Code # 0111 La Jolla CA 92093

BURBRIDGE, ANN ARNOLD, elementary school educator; b. Galesburg, Ill., Sept. 13, 1947; d. Adis Michael and Janet Louise (Frymire) Arnold; m.

Robert Arthur Burbridge, June 27, 1970; children: Britt, Michael, Mark. BMEd, Augustana Coll., 1969; MMEd, Tex. Tech. U., 1987, postgrad.; Kodaly cert. levels 1, 2 and 3, Silver Lake Coll., 1990; Advanced Kodaly cert., U. North Tex., 1993; postgrad., Tex. Tech U.; Choral Music Experience Level I Cert., London. Cert. music tchr. Tchr. Washington Jr. High Sch., Chicago Heights, Ill.; music tchr. Mountain Home AFB (Idaho) Presch. and Kindergarten, Christ the King Cathedral Sch., Lubbock, Tex.; tchr. music Nat Williams Elem. Sch. Lubbock Ind. Sch. Dist.; music cons.; mem. campus performance objectives com., author curriculum materials for elem. music; dist. mentor; scorer Tex. Master Tchr. Exam.; clinician/presenter in field. Author: Fundamentals of Music, 1987; author, cons. Silver Burdett Ginn Publ. Co. Recipient Disting. Svc. award Lubbock Jaycees, Innovative Teaching Strategy award, LISD. Mem. Am. Choral Dirs. Assn., Am. Orff-Schulwerk Assn., Orgn. Am. Kodaly Educators, Music Educators Nat. Conf. (nat. registered and cert.), Kodaly Educators Tex., Tex. Music Educators Assn. (past chmn. elem. music region XVI), Tex. Classroom Tchrs. Assn. (rep.), Lubbock Elem. Music Tchrs. Assn. (treas.), Choristers Guild, Phi Delta Kappa (v.p. programs Llano Estacado chpt.).

BURCH, MARY LOU, housing advocate, executive; b. Billings, Mont., Apr. 4, 1930; d. Forrest Scott Sr. and Mary Edna (Hinshaw) Chilcott; m. J. Sheldon Robinson, June 18, 1949 (div. 1956); m. G. Howard Burch, Nov. 27, 1957 (div. 1984); children: Julie Lynne Scully, Donna Eileen, Carol Marie Kimball, Alan Robert, Christine Philips Spruill Enomoto. AA, Grant Tech. Coll., Sacramento, 1949; AB, Sacramento State Coll., 1955; student, U. Alaska, 1976-78, Santa Rosa (Calif.) Jr. Coll., 1987. Diagnostic tchr. Calif. Youth Authority, Perkins, 1955-57; com. chmn. on pub. info. Sequoia Union High Sch. Dist., So. San Mateo County, Calif., 1970-72; exec. dir. Presbyn. Hospitality House, Fairbanks, Alaska, 1979-80; realtor Century 21 Smith/Ring, Renton, Wash., 1980-81; cons. Fairbanks, Alaska, 1981-84; exec. dir. Habitat for Humanity of Sonoma County, Santa Rosa, Calif., 1986-89, Affordable Housing Assoc., Santa Rosa, Calif., 1989-90; pvt. cons. in housing and orgn. Scottsdale, Ariz., 1991-92, Prescott, Ariz., 1992—; bd. dirs. Hosp. Chaplainey Svcs, Santa Rosa, Villa Los Alamos Homeowners Assn.; cons. Access Alaska, Anchorage, 1983; contractor Alaka Siding, Fairbanks, 1982-83. Local coord. fgn. exch. student program Acad. Yr. in Am., 1993-94; acad. coord. fgn. exch. student program Cultural Homestay Internat., 1994. Named vol. of the year, Hosp. Chaplaincy Svcs., 1987. Democrat. United Ch. of Christ. Home and Office: 1288 Tapadero Dr # D-PCC Dewey AZ 86327-5823

BURCH, MARY SEELYE QUINN, law librarian, consultant; b. Worcester, Mass., Oct. 16, 1925; d. James Henry and Mary Seelye (O'Donnell) Quinn; m. Walter Douglas Burch, Aug. 18, 1972; children: Cathi, Andrew, David, John, Joan. BS, Suny, 1976; MLS, Pratt Inst., 1979. Law libr. N.Y. Supreme Ct., Troy, 1969-82; chief law libr. Office Ct. Adminstrn., Albany, N.Y., 1982-86; libr. N.Y. State Libr., 1986-89, ret., 1989; owner Mary S. Burch Law Libr. Svc., 1983—; instr. legal rsch. SUNY, 1981. Mem. N.Y. State Bar Assn. (lectr. 1980), Ulster County Bar Assn. (cons. 1980), Am. Assn. Law Librs., Assn. Law Librs. Upstate N.Y. (pres. 1971, v.p. 1981). Roman Catholic. Home: 946 Hoosick Rd Troy NY 12180-6635

BURCH, SARENA DICKERSON, lawyer; b. West Cola, S.C., Mar. 29, 1957; d. Curtis Howard and Linda (Blair) Dickerson; m. Preston Ratliff Burch, Oct. 19, 1985. BA, Converse Coll., 1978; JD, U. S.C., 1981. Bar: S.C. 1981. Jud. clk. Cir. ct. of S.C., Lexington, 1982-83; staff atty. Pub. Svc. Commn. S.C., Columbia, 1983-91; asst. gen. counsel S.C. Pipeline Corp., Columbia, 1991—. Bd. dirs. Trustus Theater, Columbia, 1993—; vol. Planned Parenthood, Columbia, 1994—. Mem. ABA, NAFE, AAUW, Am. Gas Assn., Mortar Bd. Methodist. Home: 225 Marabou Cir West Columbia SC 29169 Office: SC Pipeline Corp PO Box 102407 Columbia SC 29224

BURCHELL, JEANNE KATHLEEN, primary school educator; b. Queens, N.Y., May 14, 1930; d. Nicholas A. and Florence M. (Doscher) B. AB, Manhattanville Coll., 1951; MS, Fordham U., 1952, postgrad., 1952-58; postgrad., St. John's U., 1969. Cert. early childhood edn. tchr., sch. adminstr., supr., N.Y. Tchr. Gwendoline N. Alleyne Sch. Pub. Sch. 152, Queens, 1954-88, early childhood coord., 1988—. Assoc. editor Courier P.S. 152 PTA, 1960—. Recipient Award of Merit, Queensborough Fedn. Parents Clubs, Inc., Dist. 1, 1981, 92, Sch. of Edn. Alumni Achievement award Fordham U., 1994. Mem. Assn. Tchrs. N.Y. (Educator of Yr. 1988), Fordham U. Sch. Edn. Alumni Assn. (Achievement award 1994), Notre Dame Sch. Alumnae Assn. (pres. 1990—). Home: 84-09 35th Ave # 2E Jackson Heights NY 11372-5454 Office: Pub Sch 152 33-52 62d St Woodside NY 11377

BURCHER, HILDA BEASLEY, librarian; b. Va., June 5, 1938; d. Andrew and Virgie (Hall) Beasley; m. Eugene Stearns Burcher, June 18, 1960 (dec.); children: Eugene Andrew, Mark Eric. BA in English, U. Va., 1960; MSLS, U. Md., 1967. Tchr's. profl. cert., libr's. cert. Va. English tchr. Fairfax (Va.) County Pub. Schs., 1960-65, reference libr., 1969-75; head libr. St. Agnes Sch., Alexandria, Va., 1975-91; reference libr. part-time Fairfax Pub. Libr., 1987-95; libr. St. Stephens-St. Agnes Mid. Sch., Alexandria, 1991-95. Mem. Alexandria (Va.) Symphony League, 1987-95. Mem. AlA, Va. Edn'l. Media Assn., Met. Washington Ind. Sch. Libr.'s Assn., Va. Libr. Assn. (sch. chairperson 1994), Beta Phi Mu.

BURCHFIELD, PATRICIA CROSBY, mathematics educator; b. Bay Minette, Ala., July 24, 1930; d. Marshall Washington and Susie Vieva (Chason) Crosby; m. Thomas Edmund Lakeman, Sept. 15, 1950 (div. June 1984); children: Vieva L. Steele, Erin L. York, Jean Helms, Amelia M., Anne C., Thomas P.; m. Wilbur Manderson Burchfield, Dec. 27, 1986. BA, U. South Ala., 1967, MA, 1976; DEd, Auburn U., 1989. Cert. tchr. English, math., spl. edn. for gifted and talented, Ala. Math. tchr. Mobile County Pub. Schs., Mobile, Ala., 1968-70, honors/advanced placement math. tchr., 1972—; math. tchr. Gadsden (Ala.) City Schs., 1970-72; adj. instr. stats. U. South Ala., Mobile, 1982-84, 86—; chair math. dept. Murphy High Sch., Mobile, 1985—. Mem. Alcoa scholarship com., Mobile, 1983, 84. Recipient Space Orientation for Profl. Educators award NASA and U. Ala., 1989, 90, USSR, 1991, Innovative Teaching award South Cen. Bell Telephone, 1989, 91, Gov.'s Industry award, 1990, Presdl. Award for Excellence in Math., 1990; Tandy scholar, 1991, Woodrow Wilson Nat. fellow, 1993, Sci-Mat fellow, 1994. Mem. Coun. Presdl. Awardees, Nat. Coun. Tchrs. Math., Math. Assn. Am., Ala. Coun. Tchrs. Math., Ala. Coun. Computer Edn., Mensa, Intertel, Triple-Nine Soc., Delta Kappa Gamma. Republican. Episcopalian. Home: 862 Wendover Rd Mobile AL 36608-3543

BURDEN, JEAN (PRUSSING), poet, writer, editor; b. Waukegan, Ill., Sept. 1; d. Harry Frederick and Miriam (Biddlecom) Prussing; m. David Charles Burden, 1940 (div. 1949). BA, U. Chgo., 1936. Sec. John Hancock Mutual Life Ins. Co., Chgo., 1937-39, Young & Rubicam, Inc., Chgo., 1939-41; editor, copywriter Domestic Industries, Inc., Chgo., 1941-45; office mgr. O'Brion Russell & Co., Los Angeles, 1948-55; adminstr. pub. relations Meals for Millions Found., Los Angeles, 1955-65; editor Stanford Research Inst., South Pasadena, Calif., 1965-66; propr. Jean Burden & Assocs., Altadena, Calif., 1966-82; lectr. poetry to numerous colls. and univs., U.S., 1963—; supr. poetry workshop Pasadena City Coll., Calif., 1960-62, 66, U. Calif. at Irvine, 1975; also pvt. poetry workshops. Author: Naked as the Glass, 1963, Journey Toward Poetry, 1966, The Cat You Care For, 1968, The Dog You Care For, 1968, The Bird You Care For, 1970, The Fish You Care For, 1971, A Celebration of Cats, 1974, The Classic Cats, 1975, The Woman's Day Book of Hints for Cat Owners, 1980, 84, Taking Light from Each Other, 1992; poetry editor: Yankee Mag, 1955—; pet editor: Woman's Day Mag, 1973-82; contbr. numerous articles to various jours. and mags. MacDowell Colony fellow, 1973, 74, 76; Recipient Silver Anvil award Pub. Relations Soc. of Am., 1969, 1st prize Borestone Mountain Poetry award, 1963, Gold Crown award for lit. achievement, 1989. Mem. Poetry Soc. Am., Acad. Am. Poets, Authors Guild. Address: 1129 Beverly Way Altadena CA 91001

BURDETT, BARBRA ELAINE, biology educator; b. Lincoln, Ill., Mar. 18, 1947; d. Robert Marlin and Klaaska Johanna Baker; m. Gary Albert Burdett, Sept. 27, 1968; children: Bryan Robert, Heather Lea, Amanda Rose. AA, Lincoln Coll., 1981; postgrad., Ill. State U. Edn. Core, 1982-83; BS, Millikin U., 1985; postgrad., Western U., 1994—. Cert. tchr., Ill. Tchr. biology, botany and human physiology Brown County High Sch., Mt. Sterling, Ill., 1985—; dir. Drama Club, Brown County H.S., 1988-90, dir. sci. fairs; ednl. advisor Nat. Young Leaders Conf. Author: Misty White, 1991, Possums Sing, 1994. Sponsor Children, Inc., Richmond, Va., 1985—, Internat. Wildlife Coalition, North Falmouth, Mass., 1991—; vol. Vets. Hosp., St. Louis, 1988—. Mem. ASCD, Nat. Assn. Biology Tchrs. (Biology Tchr. of Yr. in Ill. 1994), Ill. Sci. Tchrs. Assn., Phi Delta Kappa (newsletter editor 1990), Phi Theta Kappa. Episcopalian.

BURDETTE, JANE ELIZABETH, association executive; b. Huntington, W.Va., Aug. 17, 1955; d. C. Richard and Jewel Kathryn (Wagner) B. AAS, Parkersburg Community Coll., W.Va., 1976; BA, Glenville State Coll., W.Va., 1978; MA, W.Va. U., 1984. Fund raiser, recruiter Muscular Dystrophy Assn., Charleston, W.Va., 1973, 74, 75; sec., bookkeeper Nationwide Ins. Co., Parkersburg, 1975; v.p. Burdette Funeral Home, Parkersburg, 1976-85; intake and referral specialist Wood County Sheltered Workshop, Parkersburg, 1984-85; exec. dir. YWCA, Parkersburg, 1985-91. Bd. dirs. Sheltered Workshop, Parkersburg, 1982-86, Western Dist. Guidance Ctr., Parkersburg, 1984-94; active Community Orgn. Disability, 1989—, vol. St. Joseph's Hosp., 1991—; mem. W.Va. Coun. Ind. Living, 1992-94; mem. W.Va Muscular Distrophy Assn. task force on disability issues, 1992—;bd. advisors Parkersburg Community Coll., 1980-89, Domestic Violence Interdisciplinary adv. com., 1987, Just Say No, 1987-91; chmn. Wood County Commn. on Crime, Delinquency and Corrections, Parkersburg, 1985—; chmn. Mid Ohio Valley United Fund Agy., 1986 Heads; v.p. Jr. League of Parkersburg, 1989—; mem. Sanctuary Soc., 1991—, All Saints Guild, 1991—, St. Margaret Mary Parish Coun., 1992—; bd. dirs. Community Svc. Coun., 1985—, Parkersburg Transit Authority, 1994—; liaison Gov. Commn. on Disabled Persons, Charleston, W.Va., 1981-85; mem. Career Adv. Network, 1987-91; treas. W.Va. Women's Conf., 1987; exec. com. W.Va. chpt. Muscular Dystrophy Assn., 1987—; mem. We've Been There Parent Support Group, 1987-90; v.p. A Spl. Wish Found., 1988—; mem. Parkersburg Consumer Adv. Group; mem. founding com. Banquet of Wealth, 1988-91; bd. dirs. Horizon's Ind. Living Ctr., v.p., 1990—; past transition plan team leader Wood County Bd. Edn.; past liason Internat. Yr. Disabled Persons; past treas. and program chmn. Gov.'s Conf.; former pres. Y Teen Club, YWCA; former adv. com. Mountwood Pk. White Oak Village, Organ Donor Com., 1989. Named Miss Wheelchair W.Va., 1981, Outstanding Young Woman of Yr. for W.Va., 1981, Outstanding Young Woman of the Yr, 1986; recipient Kenneth Hieges award Muscular Dystrophy Assn., 1982, Outstanding Citizen award Frat. Order of Police, 1984, Community Service award Moose Lodge, 1987, Cert. Appreciation State W.Va., Gov. Jay Rockefeller, Cert. Appreciation Am. Legion Aux., Trail of New Beginning award, Banquet of Wealth Trial Blazer award YWCA/Altrusa, 1989, Personal Achievement award for W.Va., MDA, 1993, 94, Mary Harriman Community Leadership award Jr. League Internat., 1994; named W.Va.'s Disabled Profl. Woman of Yr. Pilot Internats., 1989, Hometown Hero Sta. WSAZ-TV, 1993, One Who Makes a Difference, Sta. WTAP, 1994. Mem. NAFE, W.Va. Women in Higher Edn., W.Va. Funeral Dirs. Assn., Toastmasters (Communications and Leadership award 1989). Democrat. Roman Catholic. Avocation: designing. Home: 2500 Brooklyn Dr Parkersburg WV 26101-2913

BURDETTE-BRICKER, JULIA ANN, accountant; b. Owensboro, Ky., May 28, 1961; d. Donald Casley and Phyllis Ann (Cambron) B.; m. Donald R. Bricker, Nov. 23, 1994. BA, Ky. Wesleyan U., 1985. Office mgr. Norvac Svcs., Inc., Mercer Island, Wash., 1986-88; contr., acct. Dunkin & Bush, Inc., Redmond, Wash., 1988-92; bus. mgr. Sno-Country Ford, Inc., Monroe, Wash., 1992—. Republican. Home: PO Box 185 Fall City WA 98024

BURDSALL, DEBORAH PATTERSON, geriatrics nurse, educator; b. Meadville, Pa., Dec. 9, 1955; d. David B. and Darlene Jacqueline (Shipley) Patterson; m. Richard E. Burdsall, June 28, 1978; children: T. Scott Bentley, Steven David Spencer, James Stuart Taylor. Diploma, Evanston (Ill.) Hosp., 1981; BA in Psychology/Biology, Allegheny Coll., Meadville, 1978. Cert. gerontol. nurse. Oncology staff nurse Evanston Hosp., 1981-82; telemetry staff nurse Glenbrook Hosp., Glenview, Ill., 1982-84; weekend supr. Luth. Home and Svc. for Aged, Arlington Hts., Ill., 1985-90; coord. Omnibus Reconciliation Act 1987 Luth. Home and Svc. for Aged, Arlington Heights, Ill., 1990-91, minimum data set and care plan coord., 1991—, infection control/quality assurance coord., insvc. coord., 1993—. Office: Luth Home and Svcs for Aged 800 W Oakton St Arlington Heights IL 60004-4602

BURGER, CAROLYN S., financial executive; b. Abington, Pa., Jan. 11, 1940; d. Anne Nicholas Smithson; m. Allen W. Burger Jr. BA in Econs. and Polit. Sci., Wison Coll., 1962. With BPA, 1962-68, from comml. mgr. to asst. v.p., 1970-85; asst. v.p. econs. rsch. and fin. NSI, 1986; exec. dir. Bell Atlantic Corp., Phila., 1988, v.p., sec., treas., 1988-91; pres., CEO Diamond State Telephone divsn. Bell Atlantic Corp., Wilmington, Del., 1991—. Bd. dirs. Balch Inst. for Ethnic Studies, Phila., 1985—, The Phila. Orch., 1988—. Mem. Fin. Execs. Inst., Forum Exec. Women, Women's Way. Republican. Presbyterian. Office: Diamond State Telephone 911 N Tatnall St 2nd fl Wilmington DE 19801*

BURGER, JANETTE MARIE, librarian; b. Union City, Ind., July 9, 1958; d. William Bronson and Janet Sue (Boyle) B.; m. Dan Michael Mraz, Nov. 14, 1980 (div. May 1985). BA, Hanover Coll., 1980; M in Liberal Sci., Northern Ill. U., 1985. Subs. tchr. Dist. 300 Sch. Corp., Dundee, Ill., 1980-82; libr. Gail Borden Pub. Library, Elgin, Ill., 1982-83, Follett Software Co., 1984—. Democrat. Roman Catholic. Home: 1850 W Highland Ave # 203F Elgin IL 60123-5095 Office: Follett Software 1391 Corporate Dr McHenry IL 60050-7041

BURGER, PAULA, artist; b. Novogrvdek, Poland, July 27, 1934; came to U.S., 1949; d. Wolf and Sarah (Ginenski) Koladicki; m. David Zapiler, Nov. 25, 1951 (div. 1978); children: Susan, Freda, Steven; m. Samuel Burger, Apr. 5, 1981. Student, U. Denver, 1977-78, U. Colo., 1979, Art Students League, Denver, 1989-91. Lic. health care adminstr., real estate agt., Colo. Artist Denver, 1978—; Holocaust survivor lectr. One-woman and group shows include U. Denver Law Libr., 1992, 94, Town Hall Arts Ctr., Colo., 1993-94, Jewish Women & Art, Colo., 1994, Cross Currents Gallery, Ill., 1991, Creative Design Gallery, Colo., 1990, Art Zone, Colo., 1990-93; represented in permanent collections at U. Denver Law Sch. Libr., BMH Congregation, Colo., Landmark Edn., Colo., Zapiler & Ferris Attys. at Law, Colo. State Capitol. Mem. Denver Art Mus., Mus. Modern Art N.Y. Home: 160 S Monaco Pky Denver CO 80224-1125

BURGESON, JOYCE ANN, resource center official, travel agency official; b. Jamestown, N.Y., Sept. 10, 1936; d. Walter Edward and Marion (Cree) Van Horn; m. David G. Burgeson, Sept. 10, 1955; children: Kathalene, Donna, Jeffrey, Karen, Christine. AS, Empire State Coll., SUNY, Saratoga Springs, 1990. Bookkeeper Burgeson Wholesale, Jamestown, 1962-88; realtor assoc. Kote Realty, Jamestown, 1982-89; real estate appraiser Goldome Bank, Jamestown, 1986-89; travel saleswoman, tour escort Cert. Travel Tours, Jamestown, 1983-90, Travelhost of Jamestown, 1990—; payroll mgr. The Resource Ctr., Jamestown, 1988—; prin. Burgeson Bus. Seminars, Jamestown, N.Y., 1990—. Mem. bd. Maple Grove High Sch., Bemus Point, N.Y., 1979-82; mem. adminstrv. bd. 1st United Meth. Ch., Jamestown, 1985—; cert. lay speaker United Meth. Ch., 1987—; mem. investment com. Jamestown Audubon Soc. Mem. ASTD, NAFE, Am. Payroll Soc., Internat. Platform Assn., Toastmasters Internat., Order of Vikings. Home: 3280 W Oak Hill Rd Jamestown NY 14701-9791 Office: Burgeson Bus Seminars 3280 West Oak Hill Jamestown NY 14701-3824

BURGESON, KAREN SUE, accountant, educator; b. Jamestown, N.Y., Oct. 16, 1965; d. David G. and Joyce A. (VanHorn) B. AS in Bus. Adminstrn., Jamestown C.C., 1985; BA in Acctg., Grove City Coll., 1987; secondary cert., St. Bonaventure U., 1991, MBA in Acctg./Fin., 1995. Cert. tchr., N.Y. Adminstrv. asst. Burgeson Wholesale, Jamestown, 1981-87; accounts receivable/inventory control Crawford Furniture Mfg., Jamestown, 1987-90; acct. Zahm & Matson, Falconer, N.Y., 1990; bus. adminstrn. instr. Jamestown Bus. Coll., 1991-93; acct., clk. Manpower Temporary Svcs., Jamestown, 1987—; substitute tchr. Area Pub. Schs., Jamestown, 1993—. Mem. Inst. Mgmt. Accts., Kiwanis Internat.

BURGESS, EUNICE LESTER, psychologist, counselor, educator; b. Madison, Fla., Dec. 17, 1935; d. Thomas and Rebecca (Royal) Lester; m. Miller Burgess, Jr., Aug. 18, 1958; children—Brenda Joyce, Wanda Renee, Kenneth Bernard. B.S. in Elem. Edn., Tuskegee Inst., 1958, M.Ed. in Psychology and Guidance, 1963; postgrad. U. N.C., 1967-68, U. South Fla., 1980-83. Coordinator student affairs Tuskegee Inst., Ala., 1960-64; vocat. counselor Job Corps Ctr. for Women, St. Petersburg, Fla., 1964-66; vocat. rehab. counselor State Dept. Edn., St. Petersburg, 1966-68; elem. counselor Pinellas County Sch. System, Clearwater, Fla., 1968-77; guidance coordinator St. Petersburg Vocat.-Tech. Inst., 1977-80, coordinator outreach recruitment, 1980-86, dept. chair student svcs., 1992—; coordinator Evening Vocat. Guidance, 1986-91; cons. in career edn.; staff devel. tchr. in humanistic edn. Bd. dirs. NAACP, 1975-85; v.p. Pinellas County Black Polit. Caucus, 1976-77; co-chmn. St. Petersburg Community Alliance, 1974-75, mem. coun. elders, 1975—; mem. Guidance Adv. Bd. Pinellas County, 1975-76; sec., treas. St. Petersburg Fair Housing Bd., 1976-78; mem. Pinellas Profl. Dem. Women's Club, 1976—; v.p. Pinellas County Biracial Adv. Com., 1980-82; v.p. region IV Fla. Spl. Needs Assn., 1983-85, pres., 1986-87. Recipient Service Award Elem. div. of Fla. Sch. Counselor Assn., 1975, Service and Leadership award St. Petersburg C. of C., 1975, Outstanding Performance award City of St. Petersburg, 1973, Community Service awards Bethune Cookman Alumni Assn., 1976, St. Petersburg C. of C., 1977, Disting. Educator award Fla. Grand Lodge of Free and Accepted Masons, 1983, Outstanding Contbn. to Vocat. Edn. award Fla. Spl. Needs Assn., 1986, Outstanding Service to Vocat. Edn. plaque Am. Vocat. Assn./Spl. Needs div., 1986, Resolution of Dedication, State Dept. Edn. Fla. div. Spl. Needs, 1987, Alumni Merit award Tuskegee U., 1990, Alumni Leadership award, 1994; named Outstanding Educator of Yr., Pinellas County Sch. Bd., 1983, Nat. Parent, Tuskegee Inst., 1983; Fla. Sch. Counselor Human Rights award named in her honor, 1984. Mem. Am. Personnel and Guidance Assn., Fla. Personnel and Guidance Assn., Suncoast Personnel and Guidance Assn. (sec. 1981-82), Am. Sch. Counselor Assn. (human rights coordinator 1977-82), Fla. Sch. Counselor Assn. (v.p. post-secondary 1980-82), Suncoast Sch. Counselor Assn., NEA, Am. Vocat. Guidance Assn., Fla. Vocat. Assn. (v.p., bd. dirs. 1986-87), Assn. Non White Concerns, Sickle Cell Found. Pinellas County, Tuskegee U. Alumni Assn. (state dir. 1986—), Zeta Phi Beta (Woman of Yr. 1976, treas. 1980-82). Democrat. Baptist. Home: 3012 DeSoto Way S Saint Petersburg FL 33712 Office: Pinellas Tech Edn Ctr 901 34th St S Saint Petersburg FL 33711-2209

BURGESS, JANET HELEN, interior designer; b. Moline, Ill., Jan. 22, 1933; d. John Joseph and Helen Elizabeth (Johnson) B.; student Augustana Coll., Rock Island, Ill., 1950-51, U. Utah, Logan, 1951-52, Marycrest Coll., 1959-60; m. Richard Everett Guth, Aug. 25, 1951; children: John Joseph, Marshall Claude, Linnea Ann Guth Layman Sinclair; m. Milan Andrew Vodick, Feb. 16, 1980. One-person shows: El Pao, Bolívar, Venezuela, 1952-62; represented in pvt. collections, U.S., Europe, S.Am.; producer, designer Playcrafters Barn Theatre, Moline, Ill., 1963-65; designer, gen. mgr. Grilk Interiors, Davenport, Iowa, 1963-87; dir. Fine Arts Gallery, Davenport, 1978-84; chmn. bd. Product Handling, Inc., Davenport, 1981-88; owner, pres. mail order bus. Amazon Vinegar & Pickling Works Drygoods, Ltd., Davenport. Contbr. articles to profl. jours.; design work featured in Gift & Decorative Accessories mag., 1969, 80, Decor mag., 1979. Bd. dirs. Rock Island Art Guild, 1974-78, Quad Cities Arts Coun., 1980-84; bd. dirs. Village of East Davenport (Iowa) Assn., 1973-84, pres., 1981; bd. dirs. Neighborhood Housing Svcs., Davenport, Davenport Area Conv. and Tourism Bur., 1981; mem. adv. bd. interior design dept. Scott Community Coll., 1975-80; mem. Mayor's Com. Historic Preservation, Davenport, Iowa, 1976-77, 85—; bd. dirs. retail com. Operation Clean Davenport, 1981; mem. 16th Iowa Civil War Re-enactment Union. Mem. Gift and Decorative Accessories Assn. (nat. merit award 1969), Am. Soc. Interior Designers (profl.), Nat. Trust Hist. Preservation, Preservation Group, State Iowa Hist. Soc. Home: 2801 34th Avenue Rock Island IL 61201-6358 Office: 2218 E 11th St Davenport IA 52803-3705

BURGESS, JULIA EDITH, lawyer; b. Kingston, Ont., Can., Jan. 31, 1952; d. Charles Robert and Edith R. (Roselund) B.; m. Egidijus Kazimirus Marcinkevicius, Dec. 22, 1979; 1 child, Emily Victoria. BA with honors, U. Western Ont., 1976, LLB, 1979. Bar: Ohio 1980, U.S. Dist. Ct. (no. dist.) Ohio 1981. Asst. prosecutor Geauga County, Chardon, Ohio, 1979-83; v.p., atty. Nat. City Bank, Cleve., 1983—. Mem. Ohio Bar Assn., Cleve. Bar Assn. Office: Nat City Bank 1900 E 9th St Cleveland OH 44114-3303

BURGESS, MARY ALICE (MARY ALICE WICKIZER), publisher; b. San Bernardino, Calif., June 21, 1938; d. Russell Alger and Wilma Evelyn (Swisher) Wickizer; m. Michael Roy Burgess, Oct. 15, 1976; children from previous marriage: Richard Albert Rogers, Mary Louise Rogers Reynnells. AA, Valley Coll., San Bernardino, 1967; BA, Calif. State U., San Bernardino, 1975, postgrad., 1976-79; postgrad., U. Calif., Riverside, 1976-79. Lic. real estate salesman, Calif.; real estate broker, Calif. Sec.-treas. Lynwyck Realty & Investment, San Bernardino, 1963-75; libr. asst. Calif. State U., San Bernardino, 1974-76, purchasing agt., 1976-81; co-pub. The Borgo Press, San Bernardino, 1975—. Co-pub: (with Robert Reginald) Science Fiction and Fantasy Book Review, 1979-80; co-author (with M.R. Burgess) The Wickizer Annals: The Descendents of Conrad Wickizer of Luzerne County, Pennsylvania, 1983, (with Douglas Menville and Robert Reginald) Futurevisions: The New Golden Age of the Science Fiction Film, 1985, (with Jeffrey M. Elliot and Robert Reginald) The Arms Control, Disarmament and Military Science Dictionary, 1989, (with Michael Burgess) The House of the Burgesses, 2d edit., 1994; author: The Campbell Chronicles: A Genealogical History of the Descendants of Samuel Campbell of Chester County, Pennsylvania, 1989, (with Boden Clarke) The Work of Katherine Kurtz, 1992-93, (with Michael Burgess and Daryl F. Mallett) State and Province Vital Records Guide; editor: Cranberry Tea Room Cookbook, Still The Frame Holds, Defying the Holocaust, Risen from the Ashes: A Story of the Jewish Displaced Persons in the Aftermath of World War II, Being a Sequel to Survivors (Jacob Biber), 1989, Ray Bradbury: Dramatist (Ben P. Indick), 1989, Across the Wide Missouri: The Diary of a Journey from Virginia to Missouri in 1819 and Back Again in 1821, with a Description of the City of Cincinnati, (James Brown Campbell), Italian Theatre in San Francisco, Into the Flames: The Life Story of a Righteous Gentile, Jerzy Kosinski: The Literature of Violation, The Little Kitchen Cookbook, Victorian Criticism of American Writers, 1990, The Magic That Works: John W. Campbell and The American Response to Technology, 1993, Libido into Literature: The "Primera Época" of Benito Pérez Galdós, 1993, A Triumph of the Spirit: Stories of Holocaust Survivors, 1994, A Way Farer in a World in Upheaval, 1993, William Eastlake: High Desert Interlocutor, 1993, The Price of Paradise: The Magazine Career of F. Scott Fitgerald, 1993, The Little Kitchen Cookbook, rev. edit., 1994, An Irony of Fate: William March, 1994, Hard-Boiled Heretic: Ross Macdonald, 1994, We The People!, 1994; co-editor and pub. (with Robert Reginald) of all Borgo Press publs.; also reviewer, indexer, researcher and editor of scholarly manuscripts. Chmn. new citizens Rep. Women, San Bernardino, 1967; libr. San Bernardino Geneal. Soc., 1965-67; vol. Boy Scout Am., Girl Scouts U.S., Camp Fire Girls, 1960s. Recipient Real Estate Proficiency award Calif. Dept. Real Estate, San Bernardino, 1966. Mem. City of San Bernardino Hist. and Pioneer Soc., Calif. State U. Alumni Assn., Cecil County (Md.) Hist. Soc., Gallia County (Ohio) Hist. and Geneal. Soc., DAR (membership and geneal. records chmn. 1964-66, registrar and vice regent San Bernardino chpt. 1965-67). Office: The Borgo Press PO Box 2845 San Bernardino CA 92406-2845

BURGESS, MEREDITH NANCY STRANG, advertising agency executive; b. Rockland, Maine, Apr. 27, 1956; d. Walter P. and Charlene M. (Perkins) Strang; BS, U. Maine-Orono, 1978; m. James L. Burgess, June 24, 1978; children: Christopher James, Matthew Strang, Andrew Charles. Store activities rep. McDonald's Corp., Boston, 1978-79; account exec. Arnold & Co., Inc., Portland, Maine, 1979-80, field account supr., 1980-81, account supr. for McDonald's advt. in Maine, 1981-83, account svc. mgr., 1984, v.p., 1985-86; pres., co-owner Burgess, Brewer, Stanyon & Payne Inc., Portland, 1986-90; owner and pres. Burgess Advt. & Assocs., Inc., 1990—. Mem. Camden (Maine) Rep. Town Com., 1974-80, Cumberland (Maine) Rep. Town Com., 1980—, officer Cumberland County Rep. Com., 1990-94; del. Rep. Conv. Maine, 1974, 76, 78, 80, 88, 90, 92, 94; 1st alt. to Rep. Nat. Conv., 1976; com. woman from Knox County, Maine Rep. Com., 1980-81; bd. dirs. Ronald McDonald House, 1982-89, U. Maine Alumni Coun., 1986-92, Stand By Me, Inc., Greater Portland C. of C., 1992-93, Maine C. of C. and Industry. Recipient Conwell award 1992, Tribute to Women in Industry (TWIN) award 1993. Mem. Am. Assn. Advt. Agys. (bd. dirs., 1984-91),

Greater Portland Advt. Club (bd. dirs.), Soil Conservation Soc. Am. (1977-92), Natural Resource Coun. Maine, Maine Geneal. Soc., Maine Hist. Soc. (bd. dirs.), Soc. Mayflower Descendants (bd. dirs.), Alpha Phi. Home: 12 Country Charm Rd Cumberland Center ME 04021-9580 Office: Burgess Advt & Assocs Inc 1290 Congress St Portland ME 04102-2103

BURGESS, MYRTLE MARIE, retired lawyer; b. Brainerd, Minn., May 3, 1921; d. Charles Dana and Mary Elzaida (Thayer) Burgess. BA, San Francisco State U., 1947; JD, Hastings Coll. Law, 1950. Bar: Calif. 1951. Pvt. practice law, San Francisco, 1951-52, Reedley, Calif., 1952—; judge pro tem Fresno County Superior Ct., 1974-77; now owner/operator Hotel Burgess. Bd. dirs. Reedley Indsl. Site Devel. Found., 1970-81; dir., 2d v.p. Kings Canyon unit Calif. Republican Assembly, 1973-75; pres., bd. dirs. Sierra Community Concert Assn., Reedley council Girl Scouts U.S.A., 1955-56; commr. Fresno City-County Commn. Status of Women; bd. dirs., treas. Reedley Downtown Assn., 1983—; bd. dirs. Kinship Program, 1988; bd. dirs., sec. Kings View Found., bd. dirs. Calif. Hotel Motel Assn., 1993—. Recipient award for remodeling and preservation of old bldg. Fresno Hist. Soc., 1975, others. Mem. ABA, Calif. Bar Assn., Fresno County Bar Assn., World Jurist Assn., Am. Trial Lawyers, Reedley C. of C. (bd. dirs. 1958-63, 87-91, Woman of Yr. 1971, Athenian award 1988). Republican. Presbyterian. Clubs: Bus. and Profl. Women's (pres.). Lodge: Order Eastern Star. Office: 1107 G St Reedley CA 93654-3094

BURGESS, PATRICIA A., lawyer; b. Walla Walla, Wash., Mar. 14, 1951; d. Robert Baxter and Eleanor Patton (Anderson) B.; m. David C. Moore (div. April 1982); Douglas Curt Jeffries, June 12, 1986; Christopher, Alex. BA, Wash. State U., 1973; JD, U. San Francisco, 1976. Bar: Calif. Lawyer various small firms, 1977-83; assoc. counsel Stockman Law Corp., Sacramento, Calif., 1983-86, Stroock, Stroock & Lavan, N.Y., 1986-88, Bater & Mackenzie, San Francisco, 1988-90; v.p., counsel Foundation Health Corp., Calif., 1990—. Mem. bd. dirs. Humboldt County Hospice, 1981-83. Mem. Calif. Women Lawyers (mem. bd. dirs. 1979). Office: Found Health Corp 3400 Data Dr Rancho Cordova CA 95670

BURK, DANA PRAG, industrial engineer; b. Portland, Oreg., Apr. 13, 1960; d. John Allen Prag and Anne Elizabeth (Marshall) Jay; m. Alan E. Burk, Apr. 16, 1983. BS in Indsl. Engring., U. Portland, 1983. Scheduler Neltech Devel., Portland, 1981-82, mng. engr., 1982-83; dry storage supr. Gourmet Brands, Boardman, Oreg., 1983-86, quality assurance supr., 1986-87; indsl. engr. Lamb-Weston, Boardman, 1987-89; logistics project mgr. Lamb-Weston, Kennewick, 1989-91, warehouse svcs. mgr., 1991—.

BURK, SUSAN MARY, lawyer, engineer; b. Rockford, Ill., Feb. 27, 1952; d. Arthur J. and Thelma P. (James) McGinnis; children: Charles, Sally. BSEE, Milw. Sch. Engring., 1978; JD, Stetson Coll., 1993. Bar: Fla. 1993. Engr. in sales and mktg. Westinghouse, Milw., Austin (Tex.), Electric Machinery, Dresser Industries, Houston, N.Y.C., 1978-86; now pvt. practice St. Augustine, Fla. Mem. Am. Bus. Women's Assn., Fla. Bar Assn. Office: 19A McMillan St Saint Augustine FL 32095

BURK, SYLVIA JOAN, petroleum landman, freelance writer; b. Dallas, Oct. 16, 1928; d. Guy Thomas and Sylvia (Herrin) Ricketts; m. R. B. Murray, Jr., Sept. 7, 1951 (div. Jan. 1961); children: Jeffery Randolph, Brian BeVaughn; m. Bryan Burk, Apr. 26, 1973. B.A., So. Meth. U., Dallas, 1950, M.L.A., 1974; postgrad. U. So. Calif., 1973-74. Cert. profl. landman. Landman, E. B. Germany & Sons, Dallas, 1970-73; asst. mgr. real estate Atlantic Richfield Co., L.A., 1973-74; landman GoldKing Prodn. Co., Houston, 1974-76; oil and gas cons./landman, co-owner Burk Properties, Burk Ednl. Properties, Houston, 1976—. Author: Petroleum Lands and Leasing, 1983; contbr. articles and photographs to profl. jours.; photographer Author's Guild, 1984-93. Active Planning and Zoning Commn., Sugar Land, Tex., 1990-92; vol. media staff Economic Summit Industrialized Nations, Houston, 1990. Mem. Foremost Women 20th Century, Am. Assn. Petroleum Landmen (dir. 1980-82, 2d v.p. 1982-83, 71-94), Houston Assn. Petroleum Landmen (dir. 1978-79, 94-90), Dallas Woman's Club, Sweetwater Country Club, Huisache Club. Republican. Presbyterian.

BURK, YVONNE TURNER, artist, educator; b. Ames, Iowa, Jan. 11, 1928; d. Clarence George and Vida Selma (Zwiefel) Turner; m. Creighton A. Burk, June 3, 1949; children: Adrienne A., Laurie L., B. Diane. Student, Layton Sch. Art, 1946-48, U. Wyo., 1949-50, Arts Student League, 1960-62, Calif. Coll. Arts and Crafts, 1982-83. instr. The Visual Arts Sch. Princeton and Trenton, 1989; work has appeared at Tex. Fine Arts Citation Show, Austin, Hunterdon (N.J.) Art Ctr., N.J. City Mus., N.J. State Mus., Robinson Gallery, Houston, Laguna Gloria Art Mus.; commd. N.J. State Mus. One-woman shows include 1991 Retrospective R.G.K. Found., Austin. Recipient Art Chair award K.L.R.U. Auction, 1992. Home: 3837 Steck Ave Austin TX 78759

BURKE, BARBARA FLORENCE, university administrator; b. Norwood, Mass., Jan. 20, 1935; d. Walter Pryce and Florence Lorraine (Sullivan) B. AA, Fisher Jr. Coll., Boston, 1954; student, Northeastern U., 1967—. Legal sec. Hale and Dorr, Boston, 1954-56, Hoffman & Schwartz, Walpole, Mass., 1956-58; office mgr., bookkeeper George Iverson, Dedham, Mass., 1958-66; campaign sec. Dukakis for Atty. Gen., Boston, 1966; sec. Senate Pres. Maurice Donahue, Boston, 1967; campaign coord. Dukakis for Lt. Gov., Boston, 1969-70; dir. placement Sch. Law Northeastern U., Boston, 1967-69, 71-75, exec. asst. to pres., 1975-89, exec. dir. centennial celebration, 1989—; bd. dirs. Northeastern U. Fed. Credit Union, Boston. Pres. St. Jude Cath. Women's Club, Norfolk, Mass., 1958-59; v.p. Women on Wheels of Mass., 1965-66; chairperson Dem. Town Com., Norfolk, 1962-72. Roman Catholic. Office: Northeastern U 360 Huntington Ave Boston MA 02115-5096

BURKE, BETTY JANE, real estate manager; b. Houston, Dec. 30, 1918; d. Loren Joseph and Bess Eva (Bontz) Patton; m. Thomas Francis Vickers, Aug. 11, 1942 (dec. Aug. 1944); 1 child, Thomas Francis III; m. Elmo James Burke Jr., Oct. 7, 1955 (dec.); 1 child, Elmo James III. BS, U. Houston, 1940; MSW, Tulane U., 1953. Juvenile probation worker Harris County Probation, Houston, 1940-42; case worker Depelchin Faith Home, Houston, 1945-56; v.p. Burke Homes, San Antonio, 1966-83; pres. Burke Devel., San Antonio, 1983-92; v.p. Burke Properties, San Antonio, 1992—; bd. dirs. U. Tex. Sch. Social Work, Austin, 1965—. Mem. airport adv. com. City of San Antonio, 1970-72; mem. planning commn. City of San Antonio, 1986-89. Mem. NASW, AAUW (pres.). Democrat. Episcopalian. Office: Burke Properties 1922 Goliad Rd San Antonio TX 78223-2772

BURKE, DOROTHY DRECHSLER, accupunturist, nurse; b. Balt., Nov. 9, 1949; d. William Edward and Helen Roberta (Kirkpatrick) Drechsler; m. Thomas R. Burke, Feb. 14, 1993. BA in Am. Studies, U. Md., 1971, BSN, 1974, MS in Nursing, 1983, M of Acupuncture, 1992. RN, Md.; cert. BLS instr.-trainer; nat. bd. cert. in acupuncture. Med. intensive care nurse U. Md. Hosp., Balt., 1974-77, Johns Hopkins Hosp., Balt., 1977-78; coronary care nurse clinician Frances Scott Key Med. Ctr., Balt., 1978-80; cardiac clin. specialist Greater Balt. Med. Ctr., 1980-82; instr., cardiac rehab. nurse Union Meml. Hosp., Balt., 1982-87; cardiac clin. specialist Harbor Hosp. Ctr., Balt., 1987-92; instr. Howard C.C., 1992—; pvt. practice acupuncture Balt., 1992—; staff acupuncture and detox Sheppard Pratt Hosp.; instr. RN Sch. Nursing-Harbor Hosp. Ctr., 1989. Author: (with others) Myocardial Infarction: A Guide to Patient Education, 1988. Fellow Am. Soc. Acupuncture; mem. Am. Assn. Acupuncture and Oriental Medicine, Am. Holistic Nurses Assn., Sigma Theta Tau. Home: 3393 Canary Ct Ijamsville MD 21754-8929 Office: 3900 N Charles St Ste 103A Baltimore MD 21218-1755 Office: 3900 N Charles St # 103A Baltimore MD 21218-1755

BURKE, ELLEN VERONICA, primary education educator, school system administrator; b. Bklyn.; d. Paul Edward and Agnes Theresa (Hannan) B. BA, SUNY, Cortland, 1967; MA, Adelphi U., 1972. Cert. tchr. K-6, N.Y. Tchr. Sachem Sch. Dist., Holbrook, N.Y., 1967—; dir. Sachem Tchr. Ctr., 1991—. Mem. Sachem Ctrl. Tchrs. Assn. (pres. 1975-77, v.p. 1992—). Democrat. Roman Catholic. Office: Sachem Tchr Ctr Sachem High Sch N 212 Smith Rd Lake Ronkonkoma NY 11779

BURKE, JACQUELINE YVONNE, telecommunications executive; b. Newark, Apr. 10, 1949; d. Trim and Viola (Smith) Russell; m. Harry Clifford Burke Jr., Aug. 20, 1968 (div. 1977); 1 child, Terence Christopher. Student, Howard U., Washington, 1966-67; HHD, London Inst. Applied Rsch., 1993; Cert. of License for Gospel Ministry, Annointed Tabernacle, Greensboro, N.C., 1994. Ordained to ministry, Convent Ministries Internat. Teaching asst. Barringer High Sch., Newark, 1967; course developer Prudential Property and Casualty Ins., Newark, 1968-74; exec. Ad-A-System, Avenel, N.J., 1974-77; staff mgr. AT&T, Basking Ridge, N.J., 1977-83; quality assurance mgr. ops. and engring. Bell Communications Rsch., Morristown, N.J., 1984-86, dir. traffic routing adminstr., mem. tech. staff, 1986-91, tng./devel. specialist, 1991—; instr. Summer Tech. Edn. Program, Morristown, 1987; pres. Jacqueline Burke Enterprises, 1991—; dean Divine Healing Temple Bible Tng. Outreach Ctr., Plainfield, N.J., 1994—. Instr. Youth for Christ, Fanwood, N.J., 1984-86; cons., instr. Black Achievers/YMCA, Newark, 1985; pres. Archway Pregnancy Ctr., Elizabeth, N.J., 1985-89; mem. Faith Fellowship Ministries World Outreach Ctr., 1987—, tchr. neighborhood Bible study, 1989—; mem. bd. advisors Bros. and Sisters, Inc., 1989—; apptd. bd. advisors Am. Biog. Inst. Rsch., 1989; sec. Women Aglow, 1991-92, pres. Plainfield chpt. fellowship, 1992—; Am. del. to Africa African-Am. Summit, 1993; dean Divine Healing Temple Bible Tng. Outreach Ctr., Plainfield, N.J., 1994—. Recipient Tribute to Woman in Industry award YWCA, 1985, Black Achiever award, 1985, Sojourner Truth award Nat. Assn. Negro Bus. and Profl. Women, 1989, Bellcore Synergy III cert., 1989, Recognition award YWCA, 1986, Cert. of Recognition Urban Women's Ctr., 1990, Bellcore Software Devel. and Software Com. Quality award, 1991, Recognition award Woman Aglow Fellowship, Plainfield chpt., 1993; named Outstanding Young Woman Am., 1985; Proclamation from City Mayor of Plainfield, 1990. Mem. NAFE, Nat. Assn. Negro Bus. and Profl. Women's Club, Inc., Career Options/YWCA, Am. Mgmt. Assn., Tribute to Women and Industry (speaker, mem. mgmt. forum 1985—), Internat. Platform Assn., Am. Biog. Inst. (rsch. bd. advisors 1989—). Democrat. Home: 229 West Ave South Plainfield NJ 07080-1924 Office: Bell Comm Rsch 6 Corporate Pl Rm 1N177 Piscataway NJ 08855-1320

BURKE, KATHLEEN B., lawyer; b. Bklyn., Sept. 2, 1948. BA, St. John's U., 1969, JD, 1973. Bar: Ohio 1973. Ptnr. Jones, Day, Reavis & Pogue, Cleve. Mem. Ohio State Bar Assn. (pres. 1993-94). Office: Jones Day Reavis & Pogue North Point 901 Lakeside Ave Cleveland OH 44114

BURKE, KATHLEEN J., bank holding company executive. Exec. v.p., pers. rels. officer BankAmerica Corp., San Francisco. Office: BankAmerica Corp 555 California St San Francisco CA 94104*

BURKE, LILLIAN WALKER, retired judge; b. Thomaston, Ga., Aug. 2, 1917; d. George P. and Ozella (Daviston) Walker; m. Ralph Livingston Burke, July 8, 1948 (dec.); 1 son, R. Bruce. BS, Ohio State U., 1947; LLB, Cleve. State U., 1951, postgrad., 1963-64; grad., Nat. Coll. State Judiciary, U. Nev., 1974. Bar: Ohio 1951. Gen. practice law Cleve., 1952-62; asst. atty. gen. Ohio, 1962-66; mem., vice chmn. Ohio Indsl. Commn., 1966-69; judge Cleve. Mcpl. Ct., 1969-87, chief judge, 1981, 85, vis. judge, 1988—; guest lectr. Heidelburg Coll., Tiffin, Ohio, 1971; cons. Bur. Higher Edn., HEW, 1972. Pres. Cleve. chpt. Nat. Council Negro Women, 1955-57, recipient certificate of award, 1969; sec. East dist. Family Service Assn., 1959-60; mem. council human relations Cleve. Citizens League, 1959-79; mem. Gov.'s Com. on Status of Women, 1966-67; pres. Cleve. chpt. Jack and Jill of Am., Inc., 1960-61; v.p.-at-large Greater Cleve. Safety Council, 1969-79; mem. Cleve. Landmarks Commn., 1990—; woman ward leader 24th Ward Republican Club, 1957-67; mem. Cuyahoga County Central Com., 1958-68; sec. Cuyahoga County Exec. Com., 1962-63; alt. del. Rep. Nat. Conv., Chgo., 1960; bd. dirs., chmn. minority div. Nat. Fedn. Rep. Women, 1966-68; life mem., past bd. dirs. Cleve. chpt. NAACP; bd. dirs. Greater Cleve. Neighborhood Centers Assn., Catholic Youth Counselling Services; trustee Ohio Commn. on Status of Women, 1966-70, Consumers League Ohio, 1969-75, Cleve. Music Sch. Settlement; bd. mgmt. Glenville YWCA, 1960-70; mem. project com. Cleve. Orch. Recipient achievement award Parkwood Christian Meth. Episcopal Ch., 1968, Martin Luther King Citizen's award, 1969, outstanding achievement award Ta-Wa-Si Scholarship Club, 1969, Outstanding Svc. award Morning Star Grand chpt., Cleve., 1970, award of honor Cleve. Bus. League, 1970, svc. award St. Paul AME Ch., Lima, Ohio, 1972, Woman of Achievement award Inner Club Coun., Cleve., 1973, cert. of award Nat. Coun. Negro Women, 1969; named Career Woman of Yr., Cleve. Women's Career Clubs, 1969. Mem. ABA, Nat. Assn. Investment Clubs (pres. Dynasty Investors Club 1992—, bd. dirs. N.E. Ohio Coun. 1993—), Nat. Bar Assn., Ohio Bar Assn., Cuyahoga County Bar Assn., Cleve. Bar Assn., Am. Judicature Soc., Am. Judges Assn. (bd. govs. 1982-86, chmn. conv. agenda com. 1981-83), Phillis Wheatley Assn., Women Lawyers Assn. (hon. adviser), Ohio State U. Alumni Assn. (life), Am. Bridge Assn. (life), Women's City Club (Cleve.), Altrusa, Alpha Kappa Alpha. Episcopalian. Home: 1357 East Blvd Cleveland OH 44106-4018

BURKE, M. VIRGINIA, state legislator; b. Boston, Jan. 30, 1945; m. James G.; 2 children. Degree, Aquinas Coll., 1964. Roman Catholic. Home: 46 Meadowcrest Dr Bedford NH 03110 Office: NH Ho of Reps State Capitol Concord NH 03301*

BURKE, MARGARET ANN, computer and communications company specialist; b. N.Y.C., Feb. 25, 1961; d. David Joseph and Eileen Theresa (Falvey) B. BS in Computer Sci., St. John's U., Jamaica, N.Y., 1982; MBA, U. Md., 1994. Cert. data processor. Software specialist Bell Atlantic Corp., Washington, 1983—. Active Friends of Hillwood Mus., Washington. Mem. NAFE, Alliance Francaise, Nat. Fedn. Rep. Women, Am. Film Inst. Roman Catholic. Home: 6652 Hillandale Rd # A Bethesda MD 20815-6406 Office: Bell Atlantic 13100 Columbia Pike Silver Spring MD 20904

BURKE, MARGUERITE JODI LARCOMBE, writer, computer consultant; b. Pasadena, Calif.; d. Richard Albert and Marguerite (Colella) L.; m. M. Theodore Jockers, Dec. 5, 1954 (div. Nov. 1969); children: Richard Larcombe, Sir Blair; m. Roger Eugene Burke, Dec. 5, 1969. BA, Columbia U., 1949. Model Ford Agy., N.Y.C., 1949-54; freelance writer Savannah, Ga., 1969-80; pres. Jodi Larcombe Assocs., Murfreesboro, N.C., 1970—; freelance computer programmer Murfreesboro, 1981—; exec. asst. Resinall Corp., Severn, N.C., 1981—, computer programmer, 1981-89. Author: Sailing Cookbook, 1979; contbr. numerous articles to mags.; dir. Shotgun Theater Prodns., 1995. Dir. Shotgun Theater Prodns., N.Y. Mem. Met. Opera Oncore Soc., Am. Film Soc., Met Opera Patron Assn. (2d century cir.), Met. Opera Nat. Coun. Home: 306 Holly Hill Rd Murfreesboro NC 27855-2110 Office: Jodi Larcombe Assocs 306 Holly Hill Rd Murfreesboro NC 27855-2110

BURKE, MARIANNE KING, financial executive; b. Douglasville, Ga., May 30, 1938; d. William Horace and Evora (Morris) King; divorced; 1 child, Kelly Page. Student, Ga. Inst. Tech., 1956-59, Anchorage C.C., 1964-66, Portland State U., 1968-69; BBA, U. Alaska, 1976. CPA, Alaska. Sr. audit mgr. Price Waterhouse, 1982-90; v.p. fin., asst. sec. NANA Regional Corp., Inc., Anchorage, 1990—; v.p. fin. NANA Devel. Corp., Inc., Anchorage, 1990—; sec.-treas. Vanguard Industries, J.V., Anchorage, 1990—, Alaska United Drilling, Inc., Anchorage, 1990—; treas. NANA/Marriott Joint Venture, Anchorage, 1990—; v.p. fin. Arctic Utilities, Inc., Anchorage, 1990—, Tour Arctic, Inc., Anchorage, 1990—, Purcell Svcs., Ltd., Anchorage, 1990—, Arctic Caribou Inn, Anchorage, 1990—, NANA Oilfield Svcs., Inc., Anchorage, 1990—, NANA Corp. Svcs., Inc., Anchorage, 1992—; mem. State of Alaska Medicaid Rate Commn., 1985-88, State of Alaska Bd. Accountancy, 1984-87. Bd. dirs. Alaska Treatment Ctr., Anchorage, 1978, Alaska Hwy. Cruises; treas. Alaska Feminist Credit Union, Anchorage, 1979-80; mem. fund raising com. Anchorage Symphony, 1981. Mem. AICPA, Alaska Soc. CPAs, Govtl. Fin. Officers U.S. and Can., Fin. Execs. Inst. (bd. dirs.). Home: 7241 Foxridge Cir Anchorage AK 99518-2702 Office: NANA Regional Corp Inc 1001 E Benson Blvd Anchorage AK 99508-4256

BURKE, MARY GRIGGS (MRS. JACKSON BURKE), art collector; b. St. Paul. BA, Sarah Lawrence Coll.; MA in Clin. Psychology, Columbia U.; postgrad., New Sch. for Social Rsch. Pvt. collector Japanese art, St. Paul, 1966—; founder The Mary & Jackson Burke Found., N.Y.C., 1972—; mem. vis. com. Freer Gallery Art, Smithsonian Instn.; mem. Met. Mus. Art; pres. The Mary and Jackson Burke Found. Mem. nominating com., mem. membership com., mem. exec. com., mem. activities com. The Japan Soc., 1959-77, chmn. student and visitors com., 1957-63, chmn. art gallery adv. com., 1970-73, bd. dirs., 1968-77, also hon. life trustee; chmn. friend mem. Japan House Gallery, 1969-75, 87—; bd. dirs. The Cable (Wis.) Natural History Mus., 1968-92, also hon. life trustee, Sarah Lawrence Coll., Bronxville, N.Y., 1968-78, also hon. life trustee, The Internat. Crane Found., Baraboo, Wis., 1978-90, The Hobe Sound (Fla.) Nature Ctr., 1987—; mem. adv. coun. dept. art history and archeology Columbia U., N.Y.C., 1970—; mem. internat. coun. Mus. Modern Art, N.Y.C., 1970—; mem. vis. com. Freer Gallery of Art, Smithsonian Instn., Washington, 1971—, vice chmn., 1989-92; mem. vis. com. dept. Asiatic art Mus. Fine Arts, Boston, 1972-90, also friend, 1972-90; mem. vis. com. dept. Islamic art, mem. vis. com. dept. Asian art, mem. edn. com., mem. acquisitions com., bd. dirs. Met. Mus. Art, N.Y.C., 1976—, also friend Far Ea. dept., 1984—; mem. Smithsonian Assocs. nat. bd. Smithsonian Instn., Washington, 1977-83; mem. art gallery adv. com., mem. exec. com., mem. devel. com., bd. dirs. The Asia Soc., 1978-88, also hon. life trustee; friend Bklyn. Mus. Art, 1982—, Friends of Asian Art, Freer and Sackler Galleries, 1991—; William Beene fellows N.Y. Zool. Soc., 1986—. Decorated Order of The Sacred Treasure (Japan), Second Leve Gold and Silver Star (Japan). Home: 3 E 77th St New York NY 10021

BURKE, MARY THOMAS, university administrator, educator; b. Westport, County Mayo, Ireland, Nov. 28, 1930; d. Thomas T. and Anne T. (McGuire) B. BA, Belmont (N.C.) Abbey Coll., 1958; MA, Georgetown U., 1965; PhD, U. N.C., Chapel Hill, 1968. Tchr. elem. and jr. high schs. N.C., N.Y., 1952-58; guidance counselor, dir. guidance Our Lady of Mercy and Charlotte (N.C.) Cath. High Sch., 1960-64, tchr., 1958-64; instr. humanities Sacred Heart Coll., Belmont, N.C., 1963-65, assoc. prof., acad. dean, 1967-69, chmn., assoc. prof. edn. dept., 1969-70; assoc. prof. human devel. and learning U. N.C., Charlotte, 1970-76; prof. U. N.C., 1976-79, prof., area head support svcs., 1979-81, chmn. human svcs. dept., 1981—; chmn. State Adv. Coun. on Pupil Pers. Svcs., 1972-76. Co-editor: (with Judith Miranti) Ethical and Value Issues in Counseling, 1992. Bd. dirs. Mcklenburg chpt. and state divsn. Am. Cancer Soc., 1977-83, treas., 1983-86, crusade chmn., 1986; chairperson United Way, U. N.C., Charlotte, 1974; bd. dirs. St. Joseph Hosp., Asheville, Selwyn Life Ctr., Charlotte, 1986-90; bd. dirs. Nat. Bus. Forms, Greeneville, Tenn., 1973—, asst. sec., treas. bd. dirs., 1975-92, sec., treas., 1992—; mem. bd. trustees Belmont Abbey Coll., 1994—. Recipient Anti-Defamation award B'nai B'rith Women, 1978, Ray Thompson Human Relations award N.C. Assn. for Non-White Concerns, 1978, WBT Woman of Yr. award, 1979, Ella Stephen Barret Leadership award, 1983, AWO Good of Soc. award Am. Cancer Soc., 1981, Leadership award Am. Cancer Soc., 1988, Faculty Svc. award Gen. Alumni Assn. U. N.C., 1994. Mem. AACD (human rights com. 1992-93), N.C. Personnel and Guidance Assn. (exec. com. 1973-90, editorial bd. jour. 1975-78, pres. Metrolina chpt. 1973-74, state pres.-elect 1980-81, pres. 1981-82, leadership award 1983), N.C. Guidance Assn. (program com. 1974-75), Nat. Cath. Guidance Assn. (state rep. 1974-79), N.C. Assn. Religious and Value Issues in Counseling (chairperson 1974—, pres. 1985-86, 93-94, bd. dirs. 1986-94), N.C. Assn. Counselors Educators and Suprs., Am. Personnel and Guidance Assn., Am. Counselor Educators and Suprs. Assn., Assn. Religious Values in Counseling, Nat. Bd. Cert. Counselors, N.C. Assn. Group Work, N.C. Mental Health Assn., N.C. Sch. Counselors Assn. (Counselor Educator of Yr. award 1975), So. Assn. Counselor Educators and Suprs., Assn. for Religious Values in Counseling (bd. dirs. Metrolina AIDS Project 1989-90, pres. bd., 1990-92, pres. elect 1989-90, pres. 90-91, Pres.' award 1992), Coun. Accreditation of Counseling and Related Edn. Programs (bd. dirs. 1993—, vice chair 1994—, ACA liaison to Nat. Bd. Cert. Counselors 1994—), Phi Delta Kappa, Delta Kappa Gamma, Chi Sigma Iota, Mu Tau Beta (Devoted Svc. award 1994). Office: Univ of NC Dept Human Services Charlotte NC 28223

BURKE, N. LEE, health care consultant; b. Southbridge, Mass., May 1, 1945; d. Alfred and Germaine (Proulx) DeAngelis; m. Joseph H. Burke, Jr., Sept. 7, 1985. BS in Mgmt., Lesley Coll., Cambridge, Mass., 1989; post-grad., 1990—. Accredited profl. in human resources Am. Soc. Pers. Adminstrs.; cert. pers. cons. Nat. Assn. Pers. Cons. Pers. mgr. Emerson Pers., Boston, 1979-83; v.p. human resources Hunneman Real Estate Corp., Boston, 1983-93; health care cons. Bradford Barnes, Boston, 1993—. Mem. New Eng. Soc. for Human Resource Mgmt. (past v.p.), N.E. Human Resources Assn., Soc. for Human Resource Mgmt., Boston Human Resources Assn. Home: 20 Rowes Wharf Townhouse 11 Boston MA 02110 Office: Bradford Barnes 223 Lewis Wharf Boston MA 02110

BURKE, SHEILA P., legislative staff member; b. San Francisco, Jan. 10, 1951; d. George Abbott and Mary Joan (Winfield) B.; m. David Chew, Jan. 1983; children: Daniel, Kathleen, Sarah. BSN, U. San Francisco, 1973; MPA, Harvard U., 1982. Staff nurse Alta Bates Hosp., 1973-74; dir. student affairs Nat. Student Nurses Assn., 1974-75, dir. program and field svcs., 1975-77; legis. asst. Senator Robert J. Dole, 1977-78; mem. profl. staff Senate Com. Fin., 1979-82, dep. staff dir., 1983-84; dep. chief of staff Senate Majority Leader, 1985; chief of staff Senator Robert J. Dole, 1986—. Office: Office of the Rep Leader S-230 The Capitol Washington DC 20510*

BURKE, SUSAN ELIZABETH, marketing professional; b. Grand Rapids, Mich., Mar. 11, 1962; d. Edmund and Betty Jean (Smigiel) Faranski; m. John Steven Burke, May 2, 1992. B in Engring., Mich. State U., 1985; postgrad., DePaul U., 1991-95. Systems programmer Data Gen. Corp., Westboro, Mass., 1985-88; sr. tech. sales rep. Ingres Corp., Chgo., 1988-90; mktg. program mgr. Andersen Consulting, Chgo., 1990—. Mem. Soc. Competitive Intelligence, Soc. Women Engrs. Roman Catholic.

BURKE, YVONNE WATSON BRATHWAITE (MRS. WILLIAM A. BURKE), lawyer; b. L.A., Oct. 5, 1932; d. James A. and Lola (Moore) Watson; m. William A. Burke, June 14, 1972; 1 dau., Autumn Roxanne. A.A., U. Calif., 1951; B.A., UCLA, 1953; J.D., U. So. Calif., 1956. Bar: Calif. 1956. Mem. Calif. Assembly, 1966-72, chmn. urban devel. and housing com., 1971, 72; mem. 93d Congress from 37th Dist. Calif., 94th-95th Congresses from 28th Dist. Calif., House Appropriations Com.; chmn. Congl. Black Caucus, 1976; former ptnr. Jones, Day, Reavis & Pogue, L.A.; dep. corp. commr., hearing officer Police Commn., 1964-66; atty., staff McCone Commn. (investigation Watts riot), 1965; past chmn. L.A. Fed. Res. Bank; former U.S. adv. bd. Nestle. Vice chmn. 1984 U.S. Olympics Organizing Com.; bd. dirs. or bd. advisers numerous orgns.; former regent U. Calif., Bd. Ednl. Testing Svc.; Amateur Athletic Found.; former bd. dirs. Ford Found., Brookings Inst.; bd. supr's. 2d Dist., L.A. County Bd. of Supr's., 1992. Recipient Profl. Achievement award UCLA, 1974, 84; named one of 200 Future Leaders Time mag., 1974; recipient Achievement awards C.M.E. Chs.; numerous other awards, citations.; fellow Inst. Politics John F. Kennedy Sch. Govt. Harvard, 1971-72; Chubb fellow Yale, 1972. Office: Office Bd Suprs 383 Kenneth Hahn Hall Admn 500 W Temple St Los Angeles CA 90012-2713

BURKEN, RUTH MARIE, retail company executive; b. Kenosha, Wis., Sept. 25, 1956; d. Richard Stanley and Anne Theresa (Steplyk) Wojtak; m. James H. Burken, Oct. 15, 1988. AAS, Gateway Tech. Inst., 1976; BA, U. Wis.-Parkside, 1980. Transp. aide Kenosha Achievement Ctr. (Wis.), 1977; lifeguard U. Wis.-Parkside, Kenosha, 1980, library clk., 1978-80; asst. mgr. K Mart Corp., Troy, Mich., 1980-88, regional office supr., 1988, internal auditor, 1989-92, sr. field auditor, 1992—. Mem. NAFE, Distributive Edn. Clubs Am. (parliamentarian 1976), U. Wis.-Parkside Alumni Assn. Roman Catholic. Office: K Mart Internat Hdqs 3100 W Big Beaver Rd Troy MI 48084

BURKERT, DEBRA SUSAN, telecommunications marketing executive; b. Allentown, Pa., Dec. 16, 1962. BS in Computer Sci., Ind. U. of Pa., 1984. Product/tech. support Fin. Info. Svcs., Richardson, Tex., 1984-86; sr. product support DIALCOM, Rockville, Md., 1986-90; quality assurance team mgr. Digital Equipment Corp., Landover, Md., 1990; X.400/X.500 product mgr. MCI, Washington, 1990-93; program mgr. GE Info. Systems, Rockville, 1993—; rapporteur for internat. dir. svcs. Internat. Telecomm. Union (formerly CCITT), Geneva, Switzerland, 1993—; U.S. del. State Dept., 1993—. Adopt a family program leader GE Orgn., Rockville, 1993. Mem. N.Am. Dir. Forum (mktg. team leader), Electronic Messaging Assn. (adv. coun. 1993—), Elfun. Office: GE Info Svcs 401 N Washington St Rockville MD 20850

BURKES, LEISA JEANOTTA, company executive; b. Fairfield, Ohio, May 30, 1961; d. Will Robert and Rethel Jeanotta (Russell) Fights. BA in Chemistry, Miami U., Oxford, Ohio, 1982; BS in Med. Tech., Miami U., 1983; MBA, Duke U., 1991. Registered med. technologist. Med. technologist Mercy Hosp., Hamilton, Ohio, 1982-85; analytical chemist Procter & Gamble Co., Cin., 1985-87, products rsch. chemist, 1987-88; new products anlyst Glaxo Inc., Rsch. Triangle, N.C., 1988-90; internat. product mgr.-dermatology Glaxo Inc., Research Triangle Park, 1990-91, mgr. new product market devel., 1991—. Co-author: Supercritical Fluid Extraction and Chromatography, 1988; contbr. articles to profl. jours. Named Women of the Day, 1979; recipient many acad. scholarships, 1980-82. mem. Am. Soc. Med. Tech., Am. Soc. Clin. Pathology. Home: 130 Marquette Dr Cary NC 27513

BURKET, GAIL BROOK, author; b. Stronghurst, Ill., Nov. 1, 1905; d. John Cecil and Maud (Simonson) Brook; AB, U. Ill., 1926; MA in English Lit., Northwestern U., 1929; m. Walter Cleveland Burket, June 22, 1929; children: Elaine (Mrs. William L. Harwood), Anne, Margaret (Mrs. James Boyce). Pres. woman's aux. Internat. Coll. Surgeons, 1950-54, now bd. dirs. Mus.; nat. vice chmn. Am. Heritage of DAR, 1992—; pres. Northwestern U. Guild, 1976-78; sec. Evanston women's bd. Northwestern U. Settlement, 1979-81, pres., 1984-86; mem. cen. com., 1986—. Recipient Robert Ferguson Meml. award Friends of Lit., 1973. Mem. Nat. League Am. Pen Women (Ill. state pres. 1952-54, nat. v.p. 1958-60), Soc. Midland Authors, Poetry Soc. Am., Women in Communications Inc., AAUW (pres. N. Shore br. 1961-63), Ill. Opera Guild (bd. dirs. 1982—, 1st v.p. 1986-91, pres. 1991-93), Daus. Am. Colonists (state v.p. 1973-76), Colonial Dames Am. (chpt. regent 1974-80), Phi Beta Kappa, Delta Zeta. Author: Courage Beloved, 1949; Manners Please, 1949; Blueprint for Peace, 1951; Let's Be Popular, 1951; You Can Write a Poem, 1954; Far Meadows, 1955; This is My Country, 1960; From the Prairies, 1968. Contbr. articles, poems to lit. publs. Address: 1020 Lake Shore Dr Evanston IL 60202-1433

BURKETT, MARJORIE THERESA, nursing educator, gerontology nurse; b. Jamaica, West Indies, Mar. 21, 1931; d. David Cameron and Mabel Louise (McKenzie) Espeut; m. Leo A. Burkett, Apr. 4, 1962; 1 child, Catherine Ann. Diploma in Midwifery and Nursing, Kingston Sch. of Nursing, Kingston, Jamaica, 1953; diploma in Nursing Edn., U. Edinburgh (Scotland UK), 1963; diploma in Psychiat. Nursing, Royal Victoria Hosp., Montreal, Can., 1970; BA, U. West Indies, 1975; MSN Edn., U. Miami, 1977, PhD, 1990, adult health nurse practitioner, 1992. RN, Fla., Tenn., Eng. and Wales UK, Jamaica; cert. midwife, Jamaica. Asst. prof. Fla. Internat. U., North Miami, 1988—, coord. adult med. and surg. nursing, 1990, coord. Childbearing Nursing, 1992—; faculty mem. numerous community colls. and profl. coms. Contbr. articles to profl. jours. Mem. ANA, Nat. League Nursing, Fla. League Nursing, Fla. Nurses Assn., Transcultural Nursing Soc., Gerontol. Soc. Fla., Nat. Coun. on Aging, Sigma Theta Tau, Phi Lambda Pi, Phi Delta Kappa. Office: Fla Internat U Sch Nursing 3000 NE 145th St Miami FL 33181-3612

BURKHARDT, ANN, occupational therapist, clinical educator; b. Providence, Dec. 21, 1954; d. Kenneth Ralph and Betty Jane (Neale) B. BA in Psychobiology, Wheaton Coll., 1976; MA in Occupational Therapy, NYU, 1979. Lic. occupational therapist, N.Y., R.I., Mass.; cert. CPR, BLS, ARC.; cert. respirator tng. instr. Staff therapist Charlton Meml. Hosp., Fall River, Mass., 1979; staff therapist, sr. therapist Columbia U.-Harlem Hosp., N.Y.C., 1979-84; staff therapist, burn specialist Cornell Med. Ctr.-N.Y. Hosp., N.Y.C., 1984-86; dir. occupational therapy Greater Harlem Nursing Home, N.Y.C., 1986-87; chief occupational therapist Meml. Sloan-Kettering Cancer Ctr., N.Y.C., 1987-92; asst. dir. occupational therapy Columbia-Presbyn. Med. Ctr., N.Y.C., 1992—; clin. instr. Columbia U., N.Y.C., 1993—; pvt. practice N.Y.C., 1984—; del. World Fedn. Occupational Therapists, London, 1994; speaker in field. Author: (chpt.) Occupational Therapy Intervention in Recreational Settings in Acute Care, 1993, (pamphlet) Lymphedema: Self-Care and Treatment, 1992; contbr. articles to profl. jours. Mem. Am. Occupational Therapy Assn. (alt. rep. to rep. assembly 1992, polit. action com. 1994), N.Y. State Occupational Therapy Assn. (Merit award 1990, alt. rep. 1992—, pres. elect 1994), Metro N.Y. Dist. Occupational Therapy Assn. (bd. dirs., sec. 1990—), N.Am. Soc. Lymphology, Internat. Soc. Lymphology. Home: 160 E 91st St 4B New York City NY 10128

BURKHARDT, DOLORES ANN, library consultant; b. Meriden, Conn., July 28, 1932; d. Frederick Christian and Emily (Detels) Burkhardt; B.A., U. Conn., 1955; M.S., So. Conn. State Coll., 1960; postgrad. Cen. Wash. State Coll., 1962, Columbia, 1964—; 6th yr. diploma U. Conn., 1972. Asst. librarian So. Conn. State Coll. Library, summers 1960, 62; sch. library tchr. Farmington High Sch., Unionville, Conn., 1955-65; library cons.; media specialist East Farms Sch., Farmington, Conn., 1967-70; sch. library coordinator K-12, Durham-Middlefield, Conn., 1970-72; media specialist regional dist. 10, Burlington-Harwinton, Conn., 1972-78; ednl. media cons., 1978—. Instr. Boston U. Media Inst. Spl. cons. Conn. Dept. Edn., 1965—. Mem. AAUW (sec. 1956-58), NEA, Conn. Edn. Assn., New Eng. (pres. 1969-70), Conn. (2d v.p. 1965—, chmn. sch. library devel.; chmn. standards com. 1970-72, chmn. instructional materials selection policy com. Region 10) sch. library assns., Am. Assn. Sch. Librarians, New Eng. Sch. Devel. Council, Phi Delta Kappa. Lutheran. Home and Office: 812 Savage St Southington CT 06489-4629

BURKHART, JEAN LOUISE, customer service representative; b. Renton, Wash., Oct. 25, 1950; d. John Thomas and Lois Alice (Gramlich) Dawson; m. Thomas Hoff Burkhart, Aug. 17, 1974; children: Stephen Thomas (dec.), John William, Kate Elizabeth. BS in Home Econs. Edn., Wash. State U., 1973. Sales rep. Am. Hosp. Supply, Portland, Oreg., 1973-76; customer svc. rep. Mountain Bell, Denver, 1977-84; customer svc. rep./concierge United Airlines, Denver, 1985—. Active Jr. League of Denver, 1990—; vestry mem. St. Stephens Episcopal Ch., Aurora, Colo., 1991-94, sr. warden, 1994—; bd. mem. Polton Community Sch. Parent Tchr. Cmty. Orgn., 1993—. Mem. P.E.O. (pres. DT chpt. 1988-90). Republican. Home: 12371 E Bates Cir Aurora CO 80014

BURKHART, SANDRA MARIE, art gallery director; b. Cleve., Dec. 29, 1942; d. John Joseph Norris and Audrey Eleanor Kegg McGuire Marshall; m. Thomas Henry Burkhart, Oct. 29, 1960 (div. Sept. 26, 1979); children: Bryan, Brad, Lisa, Michelle. Student, Evergreen Valley Coll., San Jose, 1978-80, San Jose City Coll., 1978-80, West Valley Coll., Saratoga, Calif., 1978-79. Med. technician Eye Med. Clinic, San Jose, 1980-83; ind. corp. art salesperson San Jose, 1983-92; corp. sales dir. Phoenix Gallery, San Jose, 1986-88; v.p. mktg. Whittlers Mother, San Francisco, 1989-90; dir. Martin Lawrence Galleries, Santa Clara, Calif., 1990—. Home: 461 2nd St # 651 San Francisco CA 94107-1416

BURKHEAD, VIRGINIA RUTH, rehabilitation nurse; b. Marlow, Okla., Apr. 11, 1937; d. Norvin Woodrow Whitehead and Harriet Louise (Pittman) Mayes; m. Marvin Vern Foster, Oct. 16, 1956 (div. 1964); children: Deborah, Marcia, Marva, Laurie, Sheila; m. Robert Burdett Burkhead, Apr. 11, 1987. ADN, Casper Coll., 1971; BSN, Wash. State U., 1994. RN, Wash. Staff nurse, house supr., enterostomal therapy nurse Meml. Hosp. Natrona County, Casper, Wyo., 1971-79; enterostomal therapy nurse, coord. ostomy program Holy Family Hosp., Spokane, 1979—, coord. neurol. rehab. program, 1985—. Deaconess 1st Christian Ch., Spokane, 1986—. Mem. Assn. Rehab. Nurses, Wound, Ostomy and Contence Nurses Soc., Jacks and Jennys Square Dance Club (coun. del. 1992), Sigma Theta Tau. Mem. Christian Ch. (Disciples of Christ). : WA Home: 2116 E Lincoln Rd Spokane WA 99207 Office: Holy Family Hosp 5633 N Lidgerwood St Spokane WA 99207-1295

BURKHOLDER, GRACE ELEANOR, educator, archeologist; b. Sumas, Wash., Sept. 21, 1920; d. George Lewis and Leah (Benke) Welch; m. Warren Stanford Burkholder, June 4, 1938 (div. Apr. 1957); children: Warren Stanford, Carol Joyce Brackett. BEd cum laude, U. Miami, Fla., 1956; MEd, U. Okla., 1980. Tchr., Laurel Sch., Oceanside, Calif., 1956-58; elem. tchr. U.S. Navy, Kwajalein, M.I., 1958-59, Transport Co. Tex., Kwajalein, 1959-60, Arabian Am. Oil Co., Dhahran, Saudi Arabia, 1960-80. Author: An Arabian Collection: Artifacts from the Eastern Province, 1984, Perceptions of the Past: Solar Phenomena in Southern Nevada, 1995; author: (with others) Rock Art Papers, vol. 7, 1990, vol. 8, 1991, vol. 9, 1992, vol. 10, 1993, American Indian Rock Art, vol. 17, 1992; rsch., publs. on Ubaid sites and pottery in Saudi Arabia. Active San Diego Mus. Man, Mus. No. Ariz., Clark County Heritage Mus., Lost City Mus. Mem. Am. Rock Art Rsch. Assn., Nev. Archael. Assn.

BURKLAND, PAMELA RODGERS, company executive; b. San Mateo, Calif., Apr. 22, 1943; d. Robert Charles and Mary Ellen (McNerney) Rodgers; m. Melvin Elwyn Ohlson, Jan. 20, 1969 (div. 1976); children: Ingrid Anna, Arik Mikkel; m. Arthur Steven Rolon, Oct. 9, 1991. BA in Internat. Rels., Marylhurst Coll., 1965. Internat. mktg. adminstr. Varian Assocs., Santa Clara, Calif., 1978-85; export licensing supr. Varian Assocs., Palo Alto, Calif., 1985-87, internat. order adminstr. supr., 1987-90, mgr. internat. svcs. and transp., 1990—. Author of poetry. Mem. NAFE, Coun. Logistics Mgmt., Profl. Assn. Exporters and Importers (corp. sec. 1988-94, corp. pres. 1995—, founder, dir. 1986—), Internat. Soc. Poets. Republican. Office: Varian Assocs 3100 Hansen Way Palo Alto CA 94304-1030

BURKLE, PAMELA SUE, counselor; b. Toledo, Ohio, Dec. 7, 1948; d. Roy Loring and Ruth Kaye (Gabl) Kasch; m. Thomas D. Burkle, Sept. 12, 1970; children: Kristin Lynn, Brian Thomas. BS in Edn., Miami U., Oxford, Ohio, 1970; MS in Edn., No. Ill. U., 1992. Tchr. sci. Forest Park (Ohio) Mid. Sch., 1970-72, Jefferson Jr. H.S., Woodridge, Ill., 1972-94; counselor O'Neill Mid. Sch., Downers Grove, Ill., 1994—. Mem. ACA, NEA, Am. Sch. Counselors Assn., Ill. Counseling Assn., Ill. Sch. Counselors Assn., Ill. Sci. Tchrs. Assn. Methodist. Home: 1470 Coral Berry Ln Downers Grove IL 60515-1311 Office: O'Neill Mid Sch 635 59th St Downers Grove IL 60516-1436

BURKLEY, DIANE ELIZABETH, lawyer; b. Sendai, Japan, Jan. 16, 1952; d. Jsoeph Alan and Elizabeth J. (Root) B. BA, Duke U., 1973; JD, Georgetown U., 1977. Bar: Va. 1977, D.C. 1981, U.S. Supreme Ct. 1981. Staff atty. Office of Solicitor, U.S. Dept. Labor, Washington, 1977-80, asst. counsel for appellate litigation, 1980-81; spl. asst. to solicitor U.S. dept. Labor, Washington, 1981-83; cons. Exec. Office of the White House, Washington, 1983; assoc. Shaw, Pittnam, Potts & Trowbridge, Washington, 1983-84; assoc. Reed, Smith, Shaw & McClay, Washington, 1984-87, ptnr., 1987-89; deputy exec. dir., chief negotiator Pension Benefit Guaranty Corp., Washington, 1989-93; ptnr. Fried, Frank, Harris, Shriver & Jacobson, Washington, 1993—. Gen. counsel Atoka Country Supper Com., 1984-89; vol. Frank Wolfe Relection Campaign, 1986, Vote Am. Coalition and Vote Am. Found., Inc., 1986-89; coord. Reagan Revolution Reunion, 1987; Bush-Quayle com. Lawyers for Bush/Quayle, 1987-88; pres.-elect Bush's Transition, 1988. Mem. ABA, Am. Bankruptcy Inst., D.S. Bar Assn., Va. Bar Assn., Bush-Quayle SES Assn., Rep. Nat. Lawyers Assn., Reagan-Bush Alumni Assn. Roman Catholic. Office: Fried Frank Harris Shriver & Jacobson 1001 Pennsylvania Ave NW Washington DC 20004

BURKLOW, KAREN BETH, police officer; b. Limestone, Maine, Sept. 13, 1957; d. Paul Wayne and Hopesy Iris (Harvey) B. Grad. data processing, Thomas Tech., Thomasville, Ga., 1976; grad., Albany Regional Police Acad., 1980, FBI Nat. Acad., 1994. Patrol officer Thomasville (Ga.) Police, 1979-82, investigator, 1982-89, crime prevention officer, 1989-93, sgt. crime prevention unit, D.A.R.E. officer, 1993—. Named Officer of Yr. Exch. Club, Fairgrounds, 1990, Officer of Yr. Thomasville Police Dept., 1988; recipient 2d pl. comml. award Southeastern Model and Talent Conv., Atlanta, 1991, 1st pl. photogenic, 1991, 2 1st pl. awards comml. divsn. Mem. Ga. Crime Prevention Assn. (sec. 1989-92, regional dir. 1992-93), Ga. Women in Law Enforcement, Thomasville Jr. Svc. League, Kiwanis (pub. rels. chair 1992). Office: Thomasville Police Dept 921 Smith Ave Thomasville GA 31792-5623

BURKOW, JUDITH BETH, lawyer; b. L.A., Mar. 13, 1965; d. Ray Jerry and Lorraine Helene (Lowy) Friedman; m. Steven Howard Burkow, Aug. 28, 1993. BA, U. Calif., Berkeley, 1987; JD, UCLA, 1990. Assoc. Wyman, Bautzer, Kuchel & Silbert, L.A., 1990-91, Buchalter, Nemer, Fields & Younger, L.A., 1991-93; sr. atty. Paramount Pictures Corp., L.A., 1993—. Mem. Calif. State Bar Assn., L.A. County Bar Assn., Beverly Hills Bar Assn. Office: Paramount Pictures Corp 5555 Melrose Ave Hollywood CA 90038

BURLAGE, DOROTHY DAWSON, clinical psychologist; b. San Antonio, Sept. 13, 1937; d. Joseph M. and Virginia (Hendrix) Dawson. BA, U. Tex., 1959; EdM, Harvard U., 1972, PhD, 1978. Lic. psychologist, Mass. Horace Lentz lectr. Harvard Coll., 1972-73; rsch. assoc. in psychiatry Harvard Med. Sch., Cambridge, Mass., 1976-78; rsch. assoc. Children's Hosp. Med. Ctr., Boston, 1978-79; clin. fellow psychology Harvard Med. Sch., 1978-80; staff psychologist Eliot Community Mental Health Ctr., Concord, Mass., 1980-85; instr. dept. psychiatry Harvard Med. Sch., 1984-88; mem. staff dept. psychiatry Newton Wellesley Hosp., 1986-92; now with Harvard U. Health Svcs.; pvt. practice clin. psychologist Cambridge; clin. supr. Children's Hosp., Boston, 1994—. Contbr. articles to profl. jours. Bd. dirs. Children's Mus., Boston, 1988—, Profls. for Parents and Families, 1994; mem. scientist adv. bd. Mind Sci. Found., 1994. Grantee HEW, Bus. and Profl. Women's Found., 1976; fellow NIMH, 1972-73, 73-74, Zeta Tau Alpha, 1972-73; Woodrow Wilson fellow in Women's Studies, 1976-77. Mem. Am. Psychol. Assn., Mass. Psychol. Assn., AOA. Home: 10 Lancaster St Apt 5 Cambridge MA 02140-2816

BURLINGAME, BARBARA C., state legislator; b. Woonsocket, R.I., June 6, 1947; divorced; children: Gregory, Jeffery. BSBA, Bryant Coll., 1989. Rep. dist. 62 State of R.I., dep. majority leader, mem. finance com.; rep. R.I. House; mem. task force on domestic violence R.I. Supreme Court; mem. R.I. Port Authority, R.I. Human Resource Investment Coun., House Dem. Caucus on Bus. Issues; v.p. adminstrn. and small bus. svc. No. R.I. C. of C.; mem. Adv. Coun. of Options for Working Parents. Mem. NAACP, R.I. Women's Pol. Caucus (pres.), Woonsocket Rotary Club, Greater Woonsocket YMCA, Lambda Class Leadership R.I. Democrat. Home: 565 Fairmount St Woonsocket RI 02895-4157 Office: RI House of Reps State Capitol Providence RI 02903*

BURMAN, DIANE BERGER, organization development consultant; b. Pitts., Dec. 7, 1936; d. Morris Milton and Dorothy June (Barkin) Berger; m. Sheldon Oscar Burman, Dec. 15, 1926; children: Allison Beth, Jocelyn Holly, Harrison Emory Guy. BA, Vassar Coll., 1958; MA, Middlebury Coll., 1961. Tchr. of French Allderdice High Sch., Pitts., 1960-61, Mamaroneck (N.Y.) High Sch., 1961-64; personnel specialist G.D. Searle & Co., Skokie, Ill., 1972-77, orgn. devel. tng. cons., 1977-78; personnel and orgn. devel. cons. Abbott Labs., North Chgo., 1978-82; orgn. devel. cons., v.p., mgr. career devel. Harris Bank, Chgo., 1982—. Mem. edit. bd. Orgn. Devel. Jour., 1987. Bd. advisors Grad. Sch. Bus. No. Ill. U. Mem. ASTD (bd. dirs. Chgo. career devel. profl. practice area 1987—), Orgn. Devel. Network (exec. dir. Chgo. chpt. 1986-89), Assn. Psychol. Type-Nat. Conf., Orgn. Devel. Inst. (adv. bd. 1987—, chmn. nat. conf. 1990), Nat. Assn. Bank Women, Vassar Club (bd. dirs. 1975-80). Jewish. Home: 247 Prospect Ave Highland Park IL 60035-3357 Office: Harris Bank 111 W Monroe St Chicago IL 60603-4003

BURNETT, CAROL, actress, comedienne, singer; b. San Antonio, Apr. 26, 1933; d. Jody and Louise (Creighton) B.; m. Joseph Hamilton, 1963 (div.); children: Carrie Louise, Jody Ann, Erin Kate. Student, UCLA, 1952-54. Introduced comedy song I Made a Fool of Myself Over John Foster Dulles, 1957; Broadway debut in Once Upon a Mattress, 1959; regular performer in Garry Moore TV show, 1959-62; appeared several CBS-TV spls., 1962-63; star Carol Burnett Show, CBS-TV, 1966-77, Carol & Co., 1990-91; appeared on Broadway, play Once Upon a Mattress, 1960, play Plaza Suite, 1970, musical play I Do, I Do, 1973, Same Time Next Year, 1977, television miniseries Fresno; films include Pete 'n' Tillie, 1972, Front Page, 1974, A Wedding, 1977, Health, 1979, Four Seasons, 1981, Annie, 1982; TV movies Friendly Fire, 1978, The Grass is Always Greener Over the Septic Tank, 1979, The Tenth Month, 1979, Life of the Party, 1982, Between Friends, 1983, Hostage, 1988; club engagements, Harrah's Club, The Sands, Caesar's Palace, MGM Grand. Recipient outstanding comedienne award Am. Guild Variety Artists, 5 times; Emmy award for outstanding variety performance Acad. TV Arts and Scis., 5 times; TV Guide award for outstanding female performer, 1961, 62, 63; Peabody award, 1963; Golden Globe award for outstanding comedienne of year Fgn. Press Assn., 8 times; Woman of Year award Acad. TV Arts and Scis.; 12 People's Choice awards ; 1st ann. Nat. TV Critics Circle award for outstanding performance, 1977; San Sebastian Film Festival award for best actress for A Wedding, 1978; 1st Ace award Best Actress Between Friends, 1983, Horatio Alger award Horatio Alger Assn. Disting. Ams., 1988; named One of 20 Most Admired Women Gallup Poll, 1977. Address: Bill Robinson ICM 8942 Wilshire Blvd Fl 2 Beverly Hills CA 90211-1908

BURNETT, ELIZABETH BETSY, counselor; b. Columbus, Ohio, July 17, 1953; m. Gilbert C. Burnett, Jan. 2, 1973; children: Jeffrey, Stephanie. BS in Med. Tech. with honors, Rutgers U., 1976; MA in Counseling with honors, Denver Sem., 1992. Med. technologist various hosps., Denver and Plainfield, N.J., 1976-92; missions dir. Bear Creek Ch. and Family of Faith Ch., Denver, 1985-89; counseling dir. Providence Homes, Denver, 1989—; dir. Providence Counseling Ministry, Denver, 1993—; program cons. various urban counseling svcs. and rehabs., Denver, Colorado Springs, Mich., Calif., 1992—; urban ministry cons. Denver Sem., 1991—; contract counselor So. Gables Ch., Littleton, Colo., 1992—, presenter divorce recovery workshops, 1992—. Author: Handbook of Urban Christian Counseling, 1992. Children's dir. mothers of preschoolers, vacation Bible sch., and missions edn. program Bear Creek Ch., Denver, 1982-85; deaconess, lay leader So. Gables Ch., Littleton, 1992—. Recipient med. tech. award Muhlenberg Hosp., 1976. Mem. Am. Counseling Assn., Am. Assn. Christian Counselors, Christian Assn. Psychol. Studies, Christians for Bibl. Equality, Am. Soc. Clin. Pathologists, Mensa. Office: Providence Homes 801 Logan St Denver CO 80203-3114

BURNETT, IRIS JACOBSON, diplomat; b. Bklyn., Nov. 14, 1946; d. Milton and Rose (Dubroff) Groman; m. Allan Jacobson; 1 child, Seth Jacobson; m. David Burnett, Jan. 29, 1984; 1 child, Jordan Burnett. BS, Emerson Coll., 1968, Masters, 1971. Instr. Boston U., 1971-73; dir. press and pub. rels. Dept. Parks and Recreation, Boston, 1975-77; dir. internat. visitors U.S. Dept. State, Washington, 1977-80; dir. security Dem. Nat. Conv., N.Y.C., 1980; sr. v.p. Arrive Unltd., Washington, 1980-84; pres. In Advance, Arlington, 1984-87; asst. prof. Am. U., Washington, 1987-90; pres. Sound Remarks, Arlington, 1990-92; exec. dir. Debates '92, Washington, 1992; chief of staff U.S. Info. Agy., Washington, 1993—. Author: Hart for President, 1984, National Surrogate Schedule, 1984, Inauguration, Transition: Clinton Gore Campaign, 1992. Active McGovern presdl. campaign, Boston, 1972; mem. nat. staff Udall for Pres., Washington, 1974-76, Carter-Mondale '76, 1976-77; bd. dirs. Tap Am. Project, 1994—. Office: UN Info Agency 301 4th St SW Rm 800 Washington DC 20547

BURNETT, JUDITH JANE, foundation administrator, consultant; b. Muncie, Ind., Aug. 21, 1947; d. Albert Ward and Jane M. (Collins) Burnett; student public schs. Saleswoman, Collins Mobile Home Sales, Muncie, 1970-73; sales mgr. HiWay, Inc., Anderson, Ind., 1973-75; service dir., then ops. mgr. Indiana Homemakers, Inc., Indpls., 1975-80, exec. v.p., 1980-83, also dir.; corp. sec. Mgmt. Alternatives, Inc., Indpls., 1984-85; exec. v.p., dir. Three—I Homemakers, Inc., Illini Homemakers, Inc., 1980-83; dir. Home Care Med. Products Co., 1980-82; adminstr. ECF Med. Billing, 1987-88; adminstrv. Extended Med. Svcs., 1988-92; owner Projects and Promotions, 1988—; exec. dir. Ryan White Found., 1994—; mem. council Central Ind. Health Systems Agy., 1980-83; mgr. Eynon for Congress Campaign, 1985-86; mem. Homemaker, Handyman, Home Health Aide Task Force, 1980-83, sec., 1980-81, Marion County Council Rep. Women, Marion County GOP Strategy Team; vol. access control mgr. Tenth Pan An. Games, 1987. Mem. WINS, U.S. Tennis Writer's Assn., Nat. Fedn. Rep. Women. Baptist. Home: 9459 Timber View Dr Indianapolis IN 46250-1390

BURNETT, MARY PARHAM, lawyer, airline captain pilot; b. Jacksonville, Fla., Feb. 19, 1956; d. William Harold and Mary (Copeland) P.; m. Lane Thomas Burnett, Jan. 12, 1985. BA, Western State Coll., Colo., 1976; BS in Hotel-Restaurant Adminstrs., Fla. State U., 1977, JD, 1984. Bar: Fla. 1985, U.S. Dist. Ct. (mid. dist.) Fla. 1985; cert. arbitrator/mediator. Capt. Am. Airlines, 1985—; legal cons. Am. Airlines, Dallas/Ft. Worth, 1985; expert witness, legal cons.; prof. aviation law Jacksonville U. Mem. ABA, ATLA, Aircraft Owners and Pilots Assn. (panel atty. legal svcs. plan), Allied Pilots Assn., Fla. Bar (aviation law com. 1986-87, 90-95), Jacksonville Bar Assn., Jacksonville Bar Assn., Jacksonville Women Lawyers Assn., The Ninety-Nines Inc., Fla. State U. Alumni Assn., Jacksonville Seminole Boosters Club, Jacksonville Ski Club, Univ. Club,. Republican. Methodist. Home: 3745 Beauclerc Circle N Jacksonville FL 32257-4923 Office: Lane Burnett PA 331 E Union St Jacksonville FL 32202-2748

BURNETT, MONICA DOLORES, insurance company adminstrator; b. Providence, N.J., Sept. 20, 1958; d. Nicholas Victor and Dolores Monica (Zurovcik) C. RN, St. Joseph Hosp., 1979; BS, Post Coll., 1989; MBA, Rensselaer Poly. Inst., 1994. RN. RN St. Francis Hosp. and Med. Ctr., Hartford, 1979-86; HMO mktg./tng. cons. Travelers Ins., Hartford, 1986-88, disability tech. specialist, 1988-89, mgr. quality mgmt., 1989-91, dir. quality mgmt., tng., policy and procedure devel., 1991-93, dir. customer svc., 1993—; dir. product devel. Travelers Ins., Atlanta, 1993-95; account cons. Met Life Ins. Co., Glastonbury, Conn., 1995—. Author: (with others) Health Insurance Association of America, 1993, (manual) Disability Management, 1992. Pres. com. Employment of People with Disabilities, Washington, 1992—. Fellow Health Assn. of Am.; mem. NAFE. Home: 35 Sharon Dr South Windsor CT 06074 Office: Met Life Ins Co Hebron Ave Glastonbury CT 06033

BURNETTA-CARTER, PAULA WILCOX, principal; b. Kansas City, Mo., May 6, 1947; d. William Arthur and Mildred Louise (Roberts) Wilcox. BS, U. Kans., 1980, MS, 1988. Long distance operator AT&T, Kansas City, Mo., 1965-66; mgr. Allstate Ins. Co., Overland Park, Kans., 1966-76, Farmers Ins. Co., Overland Park, 1976-79; tchr. Rolling Ridge Elem. Sch., Olathe, Kans., 1980-86, Pioneer Trail Jr. High Sch., Olathe, 1986-89; asst. prin. of curriculum and instrn. Frontier Trail Jr. High Sch., Olathe, 1989-93; prin. Oskaloosa (Kans.) Mid. Sch., 1993—; dir. summer sch. Olathe Sch. Dist., 1988; presenter study skills Leavenworth (Kans.) Sch. Dist., 1988-89, Olathe Sch. Dist., 1988-89. Advisor Jr. Achievement, Overland Park, 1976; pres. Singles Group, Olathe, 1988-89; mem. City of Olathe Image Com., 1989-93. Mem. ASCD, Am. Rsch. Assn., Kans. Assn. Sch. Adminstrs., Kans. Assn. for Supervision and Curriculum, Kans. Assn. Mid. Sch., Phi Delta Kappa. Home: 1027 N Buchanan St Olathe KS 66061-2965 Office: Oskaloosa Sch Dist PO Box 345 Oskaloosa KS 66066

BURNEY, MARY ANN, mental health nurse; b. Feb. 19, 1947; d. William R. and Mary E. (Welborn) Pickett; m. Jack E. Burney (div.). ADN, Alvin Community Coll., Houston, 1984; LVN, Community Sch. Vocat., Houston, 1981; BSN, U. Tex., 1992, MSN in Psychiatric, 1994. Cert. psychiat.-mental health nurse, neuro-linguistic programmer, CNS. Staff nurse Spring Shadows Glen Psychiat. Hosp., Houston, 1984, DePelchin Children's Ctr., Houston, 1985-88; nursing supr. DePelchin Children's Ctr., Houston, 1989-92; primary care nurse geriatric unit Harris County Psychiat. Ctr., Houston, 1992—; Cons. in field. Producter tng. videos, audio visual aids in field; contbr. articles to profl. jours. Mem. ANA, Am. Psychiat. Nursing Assn., Phi Theta Kappa, Sigma Theta Tau.

BURNEY, VICTORIA KALGAARD, business consultant, civic worker; b. Los Angeles, Apr. 12, 1943; d. Oscar Albert and Dorothy Elizabeth (Peterson) Kalgaard; children: Kim Elizabeth, J. Hewett. BA with honors, U. Mont., 1965; MA, U. No. Colo., 1980; postgrad. Webster U., St. Louis, 1983-84. Exec. dir. Hill County Community Action, Havre, Mont., 1966-67; community orgn. specialist ACCESS, Escondido, Calif., 1967-68; program devel. and community orgn. specialist Community Action Programs, Inc., Pensacola, Fla., 1968-69; cons. Escambia County Sch. Bd., Fla., 1969-71; pres. Kal Kreations, Kailua, Hawaii, 1974-77; instr., dir. office human resources devel. Palomar Coll., San Marcos, Calif., 1978-81; chief exec. officer IDET Corp., San Marcos, 1981-87; cons. County of Riverside, Calif., 1983. Mem. San Diego County Com. on Handicapped, San Diego, 1979; cons. tribal resource devel., Escondido, Calif., 1979; mem. exec. com. Social Services Coordinating Council, San Diego, 1982-83; mem. pvt. sector com. and planning and rev. com. Calif. Employment and Tng. Adv. Council, Sacramento, 1982-83; bd. mgrs. Santa Margarita Family YMCA, Vista, Calif., 1984-86; bd. dirs. North County Community Action Program, Escondido, 1978, Casa de Amparo, San Luis Rey, Calif., 1980-83; mem. San

Diego County Pub. Welfare Adv. Bd., 1979-83, chairperson, 1981; mem. Calif. Rep. Cen. Com., Sacramento, 1989—; ofcl. San Diego County Rep. Cen. Com., 1985-93, exec. com., 1987-92, 2nd vice-chmn. 1991-92; chmn. 74th Assembly Dist. Rep. Caucus, 1989-90; chmn. Working Ptnrs., 1987-90; trustee Rancho Santa Fe Community Ctr., 1991-92; active Nat. Assistance League, 1993—; bd. dirs. Assistance League North County, 1994—, mem. 1993—. Mem. Nat. Assn. County Employment and Tng. Adminstrs. (chairperson econ. resources com. 1982-85), Calif. Assn. Local Econ. Devel., San Diego Econ. Devel. Corp., Oceanside Econ. devel. Council (bd. dirs. 1983-87), Oceanside C. of C., San Marcos C. of C. (bd. dirs. 1982-85), Carlsbad C. of C. (indsl. council 1982-85), Escondido C. of C. (comml. and indsl. devel. council 1982-87), Vista C. of C. (vice chairperson econ. devel. com. 1982-83), Vista Econ. Devel. Assn., Nat. Job Tng. Partnership, San Diego County Golden Eagle Club.

BURNHAM, PATRICIA WHITE, business executive, author; b. Omaha, July 30, 1933; d. William Max and Berniece Irene (Shockey) Orr; m. William L. White, June 18, 1955 (div. Nov. 1979); children: Lucinda, Christopher, Duncan; m. Robert A. Burnham, Feb. 23, 1980. BA in English, DePauw U., Greencastle, Ind., 1955; MA in English, Ill. State U., 1966, PhD in Adminstrn., 1977. Tchr. Morton Grove (Ill.) and Evansville (Ind.) pub. schs., 1955-60; instr. Ill. State U., Normal, 1963-71, dir. Nat. Student Exchange, 1971-74, dir. continuing edn., 1974-76, asst. dean, 1976-79; assoc. dir. Ill. Bd. Higher Edn., Springfield, 1979-80; assoc. vice provost Ohio State U., Columbus, 1980-81; specialist bus. ins. Nationwide Ins. Co., Columbus, 1981-83; v.p. pvt. banking Chase Manhattan Bank, N.A., N.Y.C., 1983-88; pres. Transitions Group, Inc., East Burke, Vt., 1986—. Author: Life's Third Act, 1994; contbr. articles to publs. and seminars on adult transitions. Bd. dirs. Mennonite Hosp., Bloomington, Ill., Ind. Coll. Fund, N.Y.; pres. Coun. Vt. Elders, 1994—. Mem. Am. Assn. Higher Edn., Am. Edn. Rsch. Assn., League of Women Voters (v.p. 1991-92), Am. Mktg. Assn., Fairfield County Exec. Women (bd. dirs. 1987-89), PEO (pres. Evansville 1959-61), Phi Beta Kappa, Phi Delta Kappa. Congregationalist. Office: Transitions Group Inc PO Box 239 East Burke VT 05832

BURNHAM, SOPHY, writer; b. Balt., Dec. 12, 1936; d. George Cochran and Sophy Tayloe (Snyder) Doub; m. David B. Burnham, Mar. 12, 1960 (div. 1984); children: Sarah Tayloe, Molly Bright. BA cum laude, Smith Coll., 1958. Aquisitions editor David McKay, Inc., N.Y.C., 1971-73; contbg. editor Town and Country mag., N.Y.C., 1975-80, New Art Examiner mag., Washington, 1985-86, Mus. & Arts/Washington, 1987-89, New Woman mag., 1984—; exec. dir. Fund for New American Plays, 1992—; author, playwright, Washington, 1970—. Author: (nonfiction) The Art Crowd (Book of Month Club alt. selection), 1973, The Landed Gentry, 1978, A Book of Angels, 1990, 1990, Angel Letters, 1991, For Writers Only, 1994; novelist: Buccaneer, 1977, The Dogwalker, 1979, Revelations, 1992, The President's Angel, 1993, For Writers Only, 1994; plays include The Study, The Nightingale, Beauty and the Beast, The Witch's Tale (winner Best Children's Radio Play 1980), Penelope (1st prize Women's Theatre, Seattle), Snowstorms (winner N.C. Festival of New Am. Plays 1993); films include The Smithsonian's Whale, The Leaf Thieves; contbr. articles, essays to mags. and jours. Mem. lit. panel D.C. Arts and Humanities Commn., 1986, 87; founding mem. The Studio Theatre, 1978-80, chmn. bd. dirs., 1979-80; founding mem. D.C. Community Humanities Coun., 1979-85, vice chair 1979-80. Recipient Daughter of Mark Twain award, 1974, Award of Excellence Communications Arts mag., 1980, Pub. Humanities award D.C. Community Humanities Coun., 1988; D.C. Arts and Humanities Coun. grantee, 1980-81, Helene Wurlitzer Found. of Taos grantee, 1981, 83, 91, Office of Advanced Drama Rsch. grantee U. Minn., 1976. Mem. Women's Internat. Theatre Alliance (sec. 1979-81), Octagon Com. (bd. dirs. 1984-89), Cosmos Club. Office: care Anne Edelstein 310 Riverside Dr # 1811 New York NY 10025

BURNHAM, VIRGINIA SCHROEDER, medical writer; b. Savannah, Ga., Dec. 9, 1908; d. Henry Alfred and Natalie Morris (Munde) Schroeder; children: Douglass L., Peter B., Gilliat S. (dec.), William W., Virginia L., Daniel B. Student, Smith Coll., Barnard Coll. V.p., sales mgr., bd. dirs. Conn. Mfg. Co. Inc., Waterbury, 1952-61, pres., chief exec. officer, bd. dirs., 1961-73; pres. Burnham Industries, Watertown, Conn., 1956-59; pres., bd. dirs. NuTip Corp., Waterbury, 1962-64, Maretta Inc., N.Y.C., 1963-65; pres., treas., bd. dirs. Tech., Inc., Waterbury, 1969-73; sec. The Gaylord Hosp., Wallingford, Conn., 1970-81; pres. Tech. Internat. Corp., 1973-75, Tech. Interaction, Med. Cons., Greenwich, Conn., 1975—, The Paper Mill, Inc., 1989-92; dir. Community Mental Health Ctr., Inc., Stamford, Conn., 1974-78; mem. nat. adv. food and drug com. FDA, Dept. Health, Edn., and Welfare, Washington, 1973-76; mem. health rsch. facilities coun. NIH, Washington, 1959-61, nat. adv. heart coun., 1957-60; mem. ad-hoc com. cons. on med. rsch. Subcom. Labor, Health and Welfare, U.S. Senate Appropriations Com., Washington, 1959-60. Co-author: Knowing Yourself, 1992, The Two-Edged Sword, 1990, The Lake With Two Dams, 1993, Since Time Began, 1994; contbr. articles to Am. Health Found. Newsletter, Jour. Sci. Health, Conn. Med. Jour. Mem. adv. coun. steering com. The Episc. Ch. Found., 1970-76, Commn. to Reform the Ct. System, Gen. Assembly, State of Conn., 1974-78, nat. adv. coun. SBA, Washington 1976-77, chmn. dist. adv. coun., Hartford, Conn., 1976-77; pres. Conn. Citizens for Judicial Modernization, Inc., Hartford, 1976-78; mem. Presdl. Task Force on Rehab. of Prisoners, Washington, 1969-70; bd. dirs. Assn. to Unite the Democracies, Washington, 1982—; chmn. dist. adv. coun. Small Bus. Adminstrn., Hartford, 1976-77; pres. Conn. chpt. Am. Health Found., N.Y.C., 1971-73; dir. exec. com. Greater N.Y. Safety Coun., N.Y.C., 1971-79, dir., 1964-79; vice-chmn., dir. Conn. Coun. of Nat. Coun. Crime and Delinquency, Hartford, 1965-73; mem. adv. com. Conn. Regional Med. Program, 1973-76, FDA, Washington and many more civic and health orgns. Decorated Knighthood of Honour and Merit, Sovereign Hospitaler Order of St. John of Jerusalem, Knights of Malta, 1985; recipient Ira V. Hiscock award Conn. Pub. Health Assn., 1986; Silver Key award The Gaylord Hosp., 1970, Disting. Svc. award Conn. Heart Assn., 1960, Conn. Mother of Yr. award Am. Mothers Com., 1951, Cert. of Honor, Conn. Cancer Soc., 1950, Merit award Am. Heart Assn., 1960. Mem. AAAS, APHA, Am. Cancer Soc., Am. Heart Assn., Am. Holistic Med. Found., Am. Women in Sci., Conn. Bus. & Industry Assn., Conn. Pub. Health Assn., Nat. Assn. Mfrs., N.Y. Acad. Sci. Republican. Episcopalian. Home and Office: 41 Duncan Dr Greenwich CT 06831-3616

BURNS, BARBARA, lawyer; b. Jersey City, May 12, 1951; d. Thomas Jr. and Regina (Trzanowska) Gangemi; m. Damon Williams, Jan. 4, 1977 (div. 1986); 1 child, Jacob Williams; m. Matthew Burns, Feb. 7, 1987; 1 child, Olivia Burns. BA, Newton Coll., 1973; JD cum laude, New Eng. Sch. Law, 1976. Bar: Mass. 1977, N.J., 1984, U.S. Dist. Ct. Mass. 1977, U.S. Dist. Ct. N.J. 1984, U.S. Supreme Ct. 1988. Corporate counsel Acton (Mass.) Corp., 1977-79; asst. gen. counsel Greater Media, Inc., East Brunswick, N.J., 1984-88, assoc. gen. counsel, 1988-93, v.p., gen. counsel, 1993—. Mem. Am. Corporate Counsel Assn., Fed. Comm. Bar Assn., N.J. Bar Assn. Office: Greater Media Inc Two Kennedy Blvd East Brunswick NJ 08816

BURNS, BARBARA BELTON, investment company executive; b. Fredericktown, Mo., Dec. 10, 1944; d. Clyde Monroe and Mary Celestial (Anderson) Belton; m. Larry J. Bohannon; Mar. 27, 1963 (div.); 1 child, Timothy Joseph; m. Donald Edward Burns, Nov. 1, 1980; stepchildren: Brian Edward, David Keone (dec.). Student, Ohio State U., 1970-75. Dir. nat. sales Am. Way, Chgo., 1976-77; recruiter Bell & Howell Schs., Columbus, Ohio, 1978-80; pres., founder Bardon Investment Corp., Naples, Fla., 1980-90; founder Cambridge Mgmt. Co., Columbus, 1983-86; pres., CEO Charter's Total Wardrobe Care, Columbus, 1984-89; founder, exec. Phoenix Bus. Group, Inc., 1990—. Treas. Vicace-Columbus Symphony, 1981-82; fundraiser Grant Hosp., Columbus, 1986; chmn. Impresarios/Opera Columbus, 1986-87; founding mem. Columbus Women's Bd., 1986-87; mem. devel. com. Babe Zaharias/Am. Cancer Soc.; auction chmn. Opera Ball-Opera/Columbus, 1989; tennis tournament chmn. NABOR Scholarship Fund, 1990, 91; mem. Philharmonic Chorale, Naples, Fla., 1992; spokesperson Diabetes Found. Collier Co., Fla., 1992—, pres., 1994; elder Vanderbilt Presbyn. Ch., 1994; prs. Diabetes Found., Inc., 1994—. Named Entrepreneur of Yr. Arthur Young/Venture mag., 1988, Outstanding Vol. Opera Columbus, 1986, Vol. of Yr. Diabetes Found., 1994; recipient Design award Reynoldsburg C. of C., 1988. Mem. Naples C. of C. (new bus. com. 1990—). Republican.

BURNS, B(ILLYE) JANE, museum director; b. Yeager, Okla., Nov. 1, 1940; d. William O. and Berniece (Floyd) French; m. Richard D. Burns, June 12, 1960 (div. 1990); children: Jennifer, Richard, Timothy, Daniel. AS, Okla. State U., 1960; BA in Bus., Goshen Coll., 1988. Treas. Woodlawn Nature Coun., Inc., Elkhart, Ind., 1975-82; cons. Am. art Midwest Mus. Am. Art, Elkhart, 1978-81, founding trustee, 1978—, dir., 1980-91; cons. Heritage Fine Arts, Elkhart; bd. dirs. Soc. Bank, Key Corp. Mem. Woodlaw Nature Coun., Inc., Elkhart, 4-Arts Club, Elkhart, Ind. Advs. for Art, Elkhart County Symphony. Mem. LWV (bd. dirs. 1985-91, v.p. 1990-91), Michiana Arts and Scis. Coun., Concert Club. Democrat. Methodist. Home: 2413 Greenleaf Blvd Elkhart IN 46514-4055 Office: MW Mus Am Art 429 S Main St Elkhart IN 46516-3210

BURNS, BRENDA, state legislator; b. LaGrange, Ga., Nov. 22, 1950; m. Bruce Burns; 3 children. Rep. dist. 17 State of Ariz.; vice chmn. judiciary com.; mem. econ. devel., internat. trade & tourism, ways & means, appropriations, edn. coms.; bus. mgr. Republican. Home: 8220 W Orange Dr Glendale AZ 85303-6006 Office: State Capitol 1700 W Washington St Phoenix AZ 85007-2812*

BURNS, CASSANDRA STROUD, prosecutor; b. Lynchburg, Va., May 22, 1960; d. James Wesley and Jeanette Lou (Garner) Stroud; m. Stephen Burns; 1 child, Leila Jeanette. BA, U. Va., 1982; JD, N.C. Cen. U., 1985. Bar: Va. 1986, N.J. 1986, U.S. Dist. Ct. (ea. dist.) Va. 1987, U.S. Ct. Appeals (4th cir.) 1987, U.S. Bankruptcy Ct. (ea. dist.) Va. 1987. Law clk. Office Atty. Gen. State of Va., Richmond, summer 1984; law intern Office Dist. Atty. State of N.C., Durham, 1985; staff atty. Tidewater Legal Aid Soc., Chesapeake, Va., 1987-89; asst. atty. Commonwealth of Va., Petersburg, 1989-90; assoc. atty. Bland and Stroud, Petersburg, 1990; asst. pub. defender City of Petersburg, 1990-91; Commonwealth's atty. City of Petersburg, Va., 1991—; founder BED Task Force on Babies Exposed to Drugs, 1991. Sec. Chesapeake Task Force Coun. on Youth Svcs., 1987-89; ch. directress and organist; mem. NAACP. Mem. Va. Bar Assn. (mem. coun. 1993—), Old Dominion Bar Assn., Va. Assn. Commonwealth Attys. (bd. dirs.), Legal Svcs. Corp. Va. (bd. dirs.), Soutside Va. Legal Aid Soc. (bd. dirs.), Petersburg Bar Assn., Petersburg Jaycees, Order Eastern Star, Peterburg C. of C., Phi Alpha Delta, Alpha Kappa Alpha. Democrat. Baptist. Club: Buddies (Lynchburg). Home: 326 N Park Dr Petersburg VA 23805 Office: Commonwealth's Atty 39 Bollingbrook St Petersburg VA 23805

BURNS, COLLEEN, federal procurement analyst; b. Dayton, Ohio, Apr. 7, 1960; d. Patrick Joseph and Harriet Marie (Ennis) B. Degree in Procurement and Materials Mgmt., Sinclair C.C., 1985; degree in Mgmt., Park Coll., 1988; degree in Gen. Adminstrn., Ctrl. Mich. U., 1991. Contract specialist USAF, San Antonio, 1985-88; supervisory contract adminstr. USAF, Dayton, 1988, contract specialist, 1989; supervisory contract specialist Army Corps. of Engrs., New Orleans, 1990-92; state procurement ctr. rep. U.S. SBA, New Orleans, 1992-94; dir. of contracting U.S. Army, El Paso, Tex., 1994—; facilitator U.S. Army, New Orleans, 1990-92, USAF, Dayton, 1991; instr. U.S. Army, New Orleans, 1990-92. Mem. Nat. Contract Mgmt. Assn. (v.p. 1991—, chair 1990-93, Cert. Honor 1989-90), Assn. Am. Mil. Engrs., Fed. Woman's Program (sec. 1980, scholar 1989).

BURNS, ELIZABETH MURPHY, media executive; b. Superior, Wis., Dec. 4, 1945; d. Morgan and Elizabeth (Beck) Murphy; m. Richard Ramsey Burns, June 24, 1984. Student U. Ariz., 1963-67. Promotion and programming sec. Sta. KGUN-TV, Tucson, 1967-68; programming and traffic sec. Sta. KFMB-TV, San Diego, 1968-69; owner, operator Sta. KKAR, Pomona, Calif., 1970-73; co-owner Evening Telegram Co. (parent co. Murphy Stas.); pres. Morgan Murphy Stas., Madison, Wis., 1976—; dir. Nat. Guardian Life Ins. Co., various media stas. and corps. Trustee Coll. St. Scholastica; bd. dirs. Republic Bank. Mem. Nat. Assn. Broadcasters (bd. dir.), Wis. Broadcasters Assn. Republican. Roman Catholic. Clubs: Madison, Nakoma Country; Northland Country (Duluth), Boulders Country (Carefree, Ariz.). Avocations: golf, tennis, travel. Home: 180 Paine Farm Rd Duluth MN 55804-2609 Office: Sta WISC-TV 7025 Raymond Rd Madison WI 53719-5098

BURNS, ELLEN BREE, federal judge; b. New Haven, Conn., Dec. 13, 1923; d. Vincent Thomas and Mildred Bridget (Bannon) Bree; m. Joseph Patrick Burns, Oct. 8, 1955 (dec.); children: Mary Ellen, Joseph Bree, Kevin James. BA, Albertus Magnus Coll., 1944, LLD (hon.), 1974; LLB, Yale U., 1947; LLD (hon.), U. New Haven, 1981, Sacred Heart U., 1986, Fairfield U., 1991. Bar: Conn. 1947. Dir. legis. legal svcs. State of Conn., 1949-73; judge Conn. Cir. Ct., 1973-74, Conn. Ct. of Common Pleas, 1974-76, Conn. Superior Ct., 1976-78; judge U.S. Dist. Ct. Conn., New Haven, 1978—, chief judge, 1988-92. Trustee Fairfield U., 1978-85, Albertus Magnus Coll., 1985—. Recipient John Carroll of Carrollton award John Barry Council K.C., 1973, Judiciary award Conn. Trial Lawyers Assn., 1978, Cross Pro Ecclesia et Pontifice, 1981, Law Rev. award U. Conn. Law Rev., 1987, Judiciary award Conn. Bar Assn., 1987, Raymond E. Baldwin Pub. Svc. award Bridgeport Law Sch., 1992. Mem. ABA, Am. Bar Found., New Haven County Bar Assn. Roman Catholic. Office: US Dist Ct 208 US Courthouse 141 Church St New Haven CT 06510-2030

BURNS, GLORIA M., judge. Bankruptcy judge U.S. Bankruptcy Ct. N.J., Camden, 1994—. Office: US Bankruptcy Court 15 North 7th St Camden NJ 08102-1104*

BURNS, SISTER JACQUELINE, college president; b. Kearny, N.J., Sept. 1, 1927; d. John Francis and Elizabeth Louise (Calmar) B. BA in History, Coll. St. Elizabeth, 1957; MA in History, Cath. U. Am., 1963, PhD in History, 1967; LHD (hon.), Seton Hall U., 1987. Secondary sch. tchr. St. John Cathedral High Sch., Paterson, N.J, 1957-64; instr., asst. prof. history Coll. of St. Elizabeth, Morristown, N.J., 1967-71, asst. dean of studies, 1971-76, dean of studies, 1976-81, pres., 1981—; bd. dirs. Chestnut Hill Coll., Phila., Am. Cath. Colls. and Univs.; del. Gen. Assemblies of Sisters of Charity, 1971, 75, 79, 84, 87, 91, 95, Provincial Assembly, 1967-77, 81, 85, 89, 93, Coun. So. Province, 1970-74. Trustee N.J. Ind. Coll. Fund, treas., 1985-87; mem. N.J. Com. for Humanities, New Brunswick, 1982-86; bd. dirs. N.J. Coun. on Econ. Edn., Trenton, 1984-88, Morris County Consumer Credit Union, 1984-88; mem. N.J. Bd. Higher Edn., Trenton, 1988-94, mem. exec. com., 1990-94, chair acad. affairs com., 1990-94; trustee St. Joseph Hosp. and Med. Ctr., Paterson, 1984-88; bd. dirs. Nat. Assn. Ind. Colls. and Univs., 1985-88; mem. Pub. Leadership Edn. Network; mem. exec. bd. N.J. Pres.'s Coun., 1994—. Recipient Pres.'s award for ednl. leadership Northeast Coalition of Ednl. Leaders, 1987, Woman of Achievement award Bus. and Profl. Women's Clubs N.J., Morris County, 1984, honoree Kearny Friends of Erin, 1986; Fulbright scholar, France, 1964. Mem. Am. Hist. Assn., Am. Cath. Hist. Assn., Am. Coun. on Edn. (nat. identification program for advancement of women in higher edn. adminstrn. 1976-82), Am. Cath. Colls. and Univs., Am. Assn. Higher Edn., Nat. Assn. Ind. Colls. and Univs. (bd. dirs. 1985-88), Assn. Ind. Colls. and Univs. N.J. (chair bd. dirs. 1985-87, bd. dirs. 1978—, exec. com. 1983—, chair acad. affairs com. 1978-81), Nat. Collegiate Honors Coun., Assn. Cath. Univs. and Colls. (bd. dirs. 1993—), Berkshire Conf. Women Historians, N.J. Coll. and Univ. Coalition on Women's Edn. (chair 1974-76), Morris County Hist. Soc., Women's Coll. Coalition, Morris County C. of C. (bd. dirs. 1988—). Office: Coll St Elizabeth Office of Pres 2 Convent Rd Morristown NJ 07960-6923

BURNS, JANICE WALKER, tea company executive; b. Little Rock, Apr. 10, 1939; d. Ambrose Taylor and Gladys (McKamie) Walker; m. Howard Marsh Burns, Dec. 27, 1962; 1 child, Cynthia Walker. AB, Randolph-Macon Woman's Coll., 1961. Mem. tng. program pub. Doubleday & Co., N.Y.C., 1961-62; copy editor Harcourt, Brace & World, N.Y.C., 1962-65; asst. editor McCormick-Mathers Pub. Co., N.Y.C., 1965-67; editor textbooks Holt, Rinehart & Winston, N.Y.C., 1967-69; CEO, owner Ea. Shore Tea Co., Inc., Church Hill, Md., 1983—. Product developer 4 specialty tea blends. Pres. West 200 Block Assn., N.Y.C., 1974-76; chmn. environ. com., chmn. police com. N.Y.C. Planning Bd., Zone 4, 1977-81; co-founder Friends for Church Hill Preservation, 1983, pres., 1983-85, 87-89; bd. mem. Church Hill Theatre, 1989-91; lector St. Luke's Episcopal Ch., 1984—. Mem. Nat. Assn. Specialty Food Trade, Church Hill Players (founder). Episcopalian. Home and Office: Ea Shore Tea Co Inc PO Box 84 Church Hill MD 21623

BURNS, MARIAN LAW, legal administrator; b. Drexel Hill, Pa., Jan. 10, 1954; d. Vincent Charles and Agatha M. (Paoletti) Law; m. Lawrence Joseph Burns, Sept. 29, 1979; children: Peter Andrew, Rita Marie. Paralegal, legal sec. Tuso & Gruccio, Vineland, N.J., 1972-74; legal sec. Swartz, Campbell & Detweiler, Phila., 1974-80; adminstrv. mgr. Drinker Biddle & Reath (formerly Smith, Lambert, Hicks & Beidler, P.C.), Princeton, N.J., 1980-88; legal adminstr. Sherr, Joffe & Zuckerman, P.C., West Conshohocken, Pa., 1988-90, Groen, Laveson, Goldberg & Rubenstone, Bensalem, Pa., 1990—. Mem. ABA (assoc., sect. econs. of law practice), Assn. Legal Adminstrs. (sec. Independence chpt. 1991-93, pres.-elect 1993—), Phila. Bar Assn. (assoc.). Office: Groen Laveson Goldberg & Rubenstone PO Box 8544 Ste 200 Bensalem PA 19020-8544

BURNS, MARIE T., secondary education educator; b. Nashua, N.H.; d. Charles Henry and Eleanor Agnes (Martin) O'Neil; m. Thomas M. Burns; children: Ann Burns Pelletier, Mary, Catherine Burns Patten. BA, Regis Coll.; postgrad., Rivier Coll. Cert. tchr., N.H. Tchr. English Pelham (N.H.) Sch. Dept., City of Nashua. Trustee, chmn. of house com., Mary A. Sweeney Home. Mem. Nat. Assn. Tchrs. English, New Eng. Assn. Tchrs. English, N.H. Assn. Tchrs. English, Nashua Tchrs. Union, Nashua Secondary Groping Practices Com.

BURNS, MARION G., management consultant, retired council executive; b. Tonawanda, N.Y., July 22, 1924; d. Herbert E. and Gertrude V. (Bristow) B. BA, Bethany Coll., W. Va., 1945; MS, Sch. Applied Social Sci. Western Res. U., 1948. Case worker family welfare dept. Salvation Army, Buffalo, 1945-46; dist. dir., functional dir. tng. and camping Akron (Ohio) Area Girl Scout Coun., 1948-53; exec. dir. Girl Scouts DuPage County Coun., Glen Ellyn, Ill., 1953-67, Seal of Ohio Girl Scout Coun., Columbus, 1967-71; mgmt. cons. Region V Girl Scouts U.S., Shawnee Mission, Kans., 1972-79; assoc. dir. ednl. svcs. Girl Scouts U.S., N.Y.C., 1979-82; interim exec. dir. Girl Scouts U.S., Tex. Wash., Ill., N.Y., 1983-87; exec. dir. Lake Erie Girl Scout Coun., Cleve., 1987-90; vol. mgmt. cons. Oklahoma City, 1991—. Mem. exec. com. coun. agy. execs. United Way Svcs., Cleve., 1989-90; mem. World Found. for Girl Guides and Girl Scouts, N.Y.C.; mem. Friends of Sangam Com., 1992—. Mem. NASW (cert. appreciation TEX 1984), Acad. Cert. Social Workers, Assn. Girl Scout Profl. Workers (pres. 1961-63, 64-66, v.p. 1957-60, Hall of Fame 1987), Zeta Tau Alpha. Mem. Christian Ch. Home: 3021 Willow Brook Rd Oklahoma City OK 73120-5724

BURNS, MARYANN MARGARET, elementary education educator; b. Portland, Maine, Mar. 4, 1944; d. William and Emma (Greco) B. BS in Edn. summa cum laude, U. Maine, 1974. Cert. elem. tchr., Maine. Pvt. sec. IBM, L.A., 1968-70; learning lab. tchr. Sch. Adminstrv. Dist. # 6, Bar Mills, Maine, 1974—. Mem. NEA, Maine Tchrs. Assn., U. Maine Alumni Assn., Polit. Action Com. Democrat. Roman Catholic. Home: 17 Wildrose Ave South Portland ME 04106-6619 Office: Sch Dist # 6 PO Box 38 Bar Mills ME 04004

BURNS, NANCY LEE, civil servant; b. Heathsville, Va., Mar. 12, 1945; d. Walter Harvey and Olive Ventry (Jones) Croxton; children: Robert Sanders, Paula Burns. Grad. vocat. course, Greene Vocat. Sch., Xenia, Ohio, 1980. Clk., transl. Nat. Air Intelligence Ctr., Wright Patterson AFB, Ohio, 1983—. Sec. NAACP, Wilberforce, Ohio, 1988-92; asst. tchr. ch., Xenia, 1976; vol. Spl. Olympics, Black Awareness Observance Com., Cox PTO, Combined Fed. Campaign Montgomery, Clark, Preble, Greene Counties; pres. Greene County Missionary, 1987, nurses aid Xenia Schs., 1982. Mem. Nat. Mgmt. Assn. Baptist. Home: 673 W 2nd St Xenia OH 45385-3613 Office: Nat Air Intelligence Ctr DXLP 4115 Hebble Creek Rd Dayton OH 45433-5613

BURNS, ROBIN, cosmetics company executive. Student, Syracuse U. Formerly with Bloomingdale's, N.Y.C., v.p.; pres. Calvin Klein Cosmetics; pres., CEO Estee Lauder USA, N.Y.C., 1990—. Office: Estee Lauder USA 767 5th Ave New York NY 10153-0001*

BURNS, SALLY ANN, medical association administrator; b. Findlay, Ohio, Dec. 13, 1959; d. Van Larson and Marian (Delia) B. Student, Findlay Coll., 1980-82, Bowling Green State U., 1982-83; AAS, Houston C.C., 1985. Lic. physical therapist asst., Tex. Intern in clin. studies various Hosps., Houston, 1984-85; patient care Spring Br. Meml. Hosp., Houston, 1985-86; pres. Burns Phys. Therapy Clinic, Inc., Houston, 1986—; pres., bd. dirs. Phys. Therapy Plus, Inc., Houston, 1988—; pres. FYI Med. Suppliers, Inc., 1991—, Pain Stop Inc., 1994—; pres. FYI Med. Suppliers, Inc., 1991—, FYI Med., Inc., 1991, Pain Stop, Inc., 1994—; mem. adv. com. Houston C.C. Sys. Physical Therapist Asst. Program. Author: Physical Therapy for Multiple Sclerosis. Mem. adv. com. Houston C.C. Sys. Phys. Therapist Asst. Program. Mem. Inst. for Profl. Health Svc. Administrs. (charter mem.), Am. Judicature Soc., Am. Phys. Therapy Assn., Tex. Phys. Therapy Assn., Community Health Administrn. Home: 1914 Potomac Houston TX 77057 Office: Phys Therapy Plus Inc 3303 Audley St Houston TX 77098-1921

BURNS, SANDRA, lawyer, educator; b. Bryan, Tex., Aug. 9, 1949; d. Clyde W. and Bert (Rychlik) B.; 1 son, Scott. BS, U. Houston, 1970; MA, U. Tex.-Austin, 1972, PhD, 1975; JD, St. Mary's U., 1978. Bar: Tex. 1978; cert. tchr., adminstr., supr. instrn., Tex. Tchr. Austin (Tex.) Ind. Sch. Dist., 1970-71; prof. child devel./family life and home econs. edn. Coll. Nutrition, Textiles and Human Devel. Tex. Woman's U., Denton, 1974-75; instrnl. devel. asst. Office of Ednl. Resources div. instrnl. devel. U. Tex. Health Sci. San Antonio, 1976-77; legis. aide William T. Moore, Tex. Senate, Austin, fall, 1978, com. clk.-counsel, spring, 1979; legal cons. Colombotti & Assocs., Aberdeen, Scotland, 1980; corp. counsel 1st Internat. Oil and Gas, Inc., 1983; contracted atty. Humble Exploration Co., Inc., Dallas, 1984; assoc. Smith, Underwood, Dallas, 1986-88; pvt. practice, Dallas, 1988—; atty. contracted to Republic Energy Inc., Bryan, Tex., 1981-82, ARCO, Dallas, 1985; vis. lectr. Tex. A&M U., fall 1981, summer, 1981; lectr. home econ. Our Lady of the Lake Coll., San Antonio, fall, 1975. Mem. ABA, State Bar of Tex., Phi Delta Kappa. Contbr. articles on law and edn. to profl. jours. Office: 8300 Douglas Ave Ste 800 Dallas TX 75225-5826

BURNS, YVONNE MARIE, systems programmer; b. Springfield, Ohio, Sept. 17, 1967; d. Carl Wesley and Agnes Louise (Miller) B. BS in Mgmt. Info. Systems, U. Dayton, 1992. Programmer analyst Mead Corp., Dayton, Ohio, 1989-92; assoc. cons. CSC Ptnrs., Cin., 1992-93; systems programmer Dean Witter Discover & Co., Riverwoods, Ill., 1993—. Vol. Big Bros., Big Sisters, Chgo., 1994, Burris for Gov. Campaign, Chgo., 1994; vol. com. chair Dean Witter Discover Co., 1994. Mem. Nat. Assn. Investment Clubs, Alpha Kappa Alpha (pres. 1989-91). Office: Dean Witter Discover & Co 2500 Lake Cook Rd Riverwoods IL 60015-3851

BURNSIDE, MARY BETH, biology educator, researcher; b. San Antonio, Apr. 23, 1943; d. Neil Delmont and Luella Nixon (Kenley) B. BA, U. Tex., 1965, MA, 1967, PhD in Zoology, 1968. Instr. med. sch. Harvard U., Boston, 1970-73; asst. prof. U. Pa., Phila., 1973-76; asst. prof. U. Calif., Berkeley, 1976-77, assoc. prof., 1977-82, prof., 1982—, dean biol. scis., 1984-90; mem. nat. adv. eye coun. NIH, 1990-94; mem. sci. adv. bd. Lawrence Hall of Sci., Berkeley, 1983—, Whitney Labs., St. Augustine, Fla., 1993—; mem. bd. sci. councillors Nat. Eye Inst., 1994—. Mem. editl. bd. Invest. Ophthalmol. Vis. Sci., 1992-94; contbr. numerous articles to profl. jours. Scientific adv. bd. Mills Coll., Oakland, Calif., 1986-90; trustee Bermuda Biol. Sta., St. George's, 1978-83; exec. bd. Miller Inst., Berkeley, Calif., 1993—. Recipient Merit award NIH, 1989—, rsch. grantee, 1972—; rsch. grantee NSF. Fellow AAAS; mem. Am. Soc. Cell Biology (coun. 1980-84). Office: U Calif Dept Molecular & Cell Biology 335 Life Scis Addn Berkeley CA 94720-3200

BURNSTEIN, FRANCES, chamber of commerce executive; b. N.Y.C., Oct. 13, 1935; d. Benny and Yetta Kirshenbaum; m. Barry Burnstein, Oct. 16, 1955; children: Steven, Barbara, Lori. Student, CCNY, 1953-55; grad., Insts. Orgn. Mgmt., 1983. Dep. mayor Twp. of Cherry Hill, N.J., 1975-77; exec. dir. Cherry Hill C. of C., 1977-88, pres., 1988—; commr. Camden County Parks, 1986-88. Trustee Cooper Found. Med. Ctr., Camden, N.J., 1980-89, Police Athletic League, 1976—; bd. dirs. ARC, Camden County, 1981—, Guidance Ctr., 1982-84; trustee Ronald McDonald House of Kids, Camden County United Way, 1981—, v.p., 1981-84, pres.'s cabinet, 1982-84; co-chair Del. River Region Tourism Council, 1983; exec. adv. coun. Rutgers

U. Sch.Bus., 1985—; bd. dirs. Disaster Appeal Com., 1981—. Named Newsmaker of Yr., Cherry Hill C. of C., 1984; Frances Burnstein Little League Softball Field dedicated to her, 1980; selected for cover of N.J. Woman Mag., 1986; named one of seven Women to Watch in 1986, State of N.J., Bus. Watch 1989 Bus. Jour. N.J. Mem. NAFE, N.J. Assn. C. of C. (v.p.), N.J. Assn. C. of C. Execs. (v.p. 1987—), Am. Assn. C. of C., Am. Assn. C. of C. Communications Coun., World Affairs Coun., Nat. Assn. Membership Dirs., Am. Mgmt. Assn., Am. Heart Assn. (bd. dirs. Cherry Hill chpt. 1987—). Republican. Jewish. Lodge: Garden State Rotary (Person of Yr. 1980). Office: Cherry Hill C of C 1060 Kings Hwy N Cherry Hill NJ 08034-1901

BURR, LAURIE DIANE, information technology consultant; b. Bath, N.Y., Jan. 29, 1953; d. Jonathan Williams and Dorothy Evelyn (Daines) B.; m. Jeffrey Howard Halpern. AB, Vassar Coll., 1974; MBA, U. Va., 1983. Fin. planner Burlington, Vt., 1975-76; mktg. rep. IBM, Burlington, 1976-80; fin. planner IBM/Lab.-Mfg., Poughkeepsie, N.Y., 1983-84; marketer, analyst IBM/Regional & Br. Offices, Balt., 1984-86; proposal mgr. IBM/Pub. Sector Group, Balt., 1986-88; cons. pub. sector industry IBM, Bethesda, Md., 1988-93; pres. Renaissance Consulting Co., Inc., Annapolis, Md., 1993—. Mem. Eastport Yacht Club.

BURRI, BETTY JANE, research chemist; b. San Francisco, Jan. 23, 1955; d. Paul Gene and Carleen Georgette (Meyers) B.; m. Kurt Randall Annweiler, Dec. 1, 1984. BA, San Francisco State U., 1976; MS, Calif. State U., Long Beach, 1978; PhD, U. Calif. San Diego, La Jolla, 1982. Research asst. Scripps Clinic, La Jolla, 1982-83, research assoc., 1983-85; research chemist Western Human Nutrition Rsch. Ctr., USDA, San Francisco, 1985—; adj. prof. nutrition dept. U. Nev., 1993—. Contbr. articles to profl. jours. Grantee NIH, 1982, 85, USDA, 1986-95; affiliate fellow Am. Heart Assn., 1983, 84. Mem. Assn. Women in Sci. (founding dir. San Diego chpt.), N.Y. Acad. Sci., Union Concerned Scientists, Am. Inst. Nutrition, Am. Soc. Clin. Nutrition. Office: Western Human Nutrition Rsch Ctr PO Box 29997 San Francisco CA 94129-0997

BURRIGHT-CROUCH, JANET ANN, association executive; b. Indianola, Iowa, Feb. 2, 1947; d. Eugene Blaine and Laura Edith (Pratt) Burright; m. William Michael Crouch, Aug. 19, 1967; children: Erin Gae, William Matthew. BA, Drake U., 1969; M of Edn. and Counseling Psychology, U. Mo., 1983. Lic. profl. counselor. Adminstrv. asst. United Ecumenical Ministries, Columbia, Mo., 1980-82; case mgr. Ctrl. Mo. Regional Ctr., Columbia, 1984-88, assoc. psychologist, 1988-89, trainer, 1990-91; lic. lay min. mid-Am. region Christian Ch. (Disciples of Christ), Mo., 1983-91; exec. dir. YWCA Oskaloosa, Iowa, 1991-94; parent specialist SIEDA Headstart, Ottumwa, Iowa, 1994—; cons. Kid's Corner, Oskaloosa, 1991—; facilitator abuse survivor support group Mahaska County Coalition Against Domestic Abuse, Oskaloosa, 1992—. Chair family selection com. Habitat for Humanity; mem. visioning task force Christian Ch. of the Upper Midwest. Mem. PEO, Phi Delta Kappa. Office: SIEDA Headstart 226 W Main Ottumwa IA 52501

BURRIS, CHRISTINE TUVE, association executive; b. Washington, Mar. 20, 1948; d. Richard Larsen and Maxine (Duvel) Tuve; m. James Frederick Burris, July 3, 1971; 1 child, Cameron William Tuve Burris. BA in Sociology, U. Md., 1971; MA in Rehab. Counseling, NYU, 1976. Social work intern Dept. Social Svcs., Montgomery County, Md., 1970; recreation leader Dept. Recreation, Montgomery County, Md., 1970-71; statis. asst. Nat. Soc. for Prevention of Blindness, N.Y.C., 1971-74; rehab. counseling intern Inst. for Crippled and Disabled, N.Y.C., 1975-76; rehab. counselor Fedn. Employment and Guidance Svc., Bronx, N.Y., 1976-77; rsch. asst. Indices, Inc., Falls Church, Va., 1977-79; sr. rsch. assoc. Rehab Group Inc., Falls Church, Va., 1979-82; staff assoc. Assn. Am. Med. Colls., Washington, 1984-87; exec. dir. D.C. Acad. Family Physicians, Washington, 1989—; cons. JWK Internat. Corp., Annandale, Va., 1984; Washington rep. Am. Fedn. for Clin. Rsch., Washington, 1984-87. Editor, pub. Newsletter of the D.C. Acad. of Family Physicians, 1989—, Newsletter of the Cove Point Beach Assoc., Inc., 1994—. Vol. Fondation de la Recherche des Maladies Cardiovasculaires, Lausanne, Switzerland, 1983, Nature Conservancy, Md. Chpt., Bethesda, 1988, Beavoir Sch., Washington, 1992—; bd. dirs. Cove Point Beach Assoc., Inc., 1993-96. Recipient traineeship U.S. Rehab. Svcs. Adminstrn., 1975-76, Ann. Svc. award Nature Conservancy, 1988. Mem. Am. Soc. Assn. Execs., Greater Washington Soc. Assn. Execs., Nat. Rehab. Counseling Assn. (legis. com. mem. N.Y. chpt. 1975-77). Democrat. Office: DC Acad Family Physicians 4803 Davenport St NW Washington DC 20016-4314

BURRIS, FRANCES WHITE, personnel director; b. Cuero, Tex., Oct. 18, 1933; d. Marian Cecil and Dorothy Christine (Pruetz) White; m. Berlie Burris Jr., Mar. 8, 1958 (div. 1982); children: William Alan, Joel Maurice. BA, Mary Hardin Baylor Coll., Belton, Tex., 1955; M in Eng., Trinity U., San Antonio, 1959. Cert. tchr., Tex. Elem. tchr. East and Mt. Houston Independent Sch. Dist., 1956, Edgewood Ind. Sch. Dist., San Antonio, 1956-57, 58-59; tchr. Edna (Tex.) Ind. Sch. Dist., 1957-58; elem. tchr. Northside Ind. Sch. Dist., San Antonio, 1960-62, Southside Schs., San Antonio, 1962-63; mgr. Michael's Dept. Store, Houston, 1980-81; eligibility worker Tex. Dept. Human Resources, Houston, 1981—. Mem. Meridith Manor Civic Club, Houston, 1966-78, Settlers Valley Civic Club, Katy, Tex., 1979-81. Mem. Tex. State Emplyees Union (exec. bd. 1984—, del. gen. assembly 1984-94, lobbyist 1985—). Democrat. Baptist. Club: Bridge (Houston).

BURRIS, HARRIET LOUISE, emergency physician; b. Alexandria Bay, N.Y., Apr. 7, 1949; d. Robert Barker and Harriet Louise (Dorman) Burtch; m. John Samuel Burris Jr., Nov. 30, 1974; children: Elizabeth Jane, Katherine Ann. SB, MIT, 1972; MD, SUNY, Syracuse, 1976. Diplomate Am. Bd. Family Practice, Am. Bd. Emergency Medicine, Nat. Bd. Med. Examiners. Resident in family practice St. Joseph's Hosp. Health Ctr., Syracuse, 1976-79; pvt. practice Cazenovia, N.Y., 1979-81; staff MD emergency dept. Middlesex Hosp., Middletown, Conn., 1982-83; staff MD family practice Cmty. Health Care Plan, Wallingford, Conn., 1983-84; staff MD emergency dept. Middlesex Med. Ctr.-Shoreline divsn. Middlesex Hosp., Essex, Conn., 1984—, acting med. dir., 1994—. Fellow Am. Assn. Family Physicians, Am. Coll. Emergency Physicians; mem. Handweavers Guild Conn. (libr.). Home: 422 Westland Ave Cheshire CT 06410-3142 Office: Middlesex Med Ctr-Shoreline 260 Westbrook Rd Essex CT 06426-1513

BURRIS, KATHRYN ANN, professional association administrator; b. Fredricksburg, Tex., Dec. 1, 1957; d. Bryon Curthburn and Sara Lee (Matthews) Rinehart; m. Charles Anthony Burris, Nov. 4, 1989. BS, Howard Payne U., 1979; diploma, Ranger Jr. Coll., 1982. Cert. Okla. Bd. Nurse Registration and Nursing Edn. Educator Brownwood (Tex.) Home and Sch., 1979-80; critical care nurse Brownwood Regional Hosp., 1981-83; home healthcare nurse Healthcare, Inc., Tulsa, 1983-85; staff nurse Broken Arrow (Okla.) Med. Ctr., 1984-85; state dir. Am. Chronic Pain Assn., Tulsa, 1987-93; exec. dir. Pain Tamers Support Network, Inc., Tulsa, 1993—; mem. Rehabilitative Adv. Coun. State Okla., 1993—; mem. Assistive Tech. Coun. Okla., 1994—. Feature columnist (newspaper) The Tulsa Tribune, 1988-92; contbg. writer (newsletters) Nat. Chronic Pain Outreach Assn. Lifeline, 1988, Am. Chronic Pain Assn. Chronicle, 1989-93, Pain Tamers Support Network, Inc., 1993—. Make-up artist Brownwood Theater Co., 1980-81, wardrobe dir., 1980; mem. State of Okla. Rehab. Adv. Coun., 1993—, State of Okla. Assistive Tech. Adv. Coun., 1994—. Mem. Reflex Sympathetic Dystrophy Syndrome Assn. (state dir. 1988—), Fibromyalgia Network. Mem. Reflex Sympathetic Dystrophy Syndrome Assn. (state dir. 1988-90). Democrat. Home: 5807 East 35th St Tulsa OK 74135 Office: Pain Tamers Support Network PO Box 55372 Tulsa OK 74155-1372

BURRIS, LAUREN BAYLERAN, business owner; b. Detroit, Mar. 30, 1952; d. Haig Aram and Dirouhi (Halajian) Bayleran; m. William James Burris, Feb. 14, 1981; children: Taron, Ian. BBA, U. Mich., 1973; MBA, Wayne State U., 1978. Sales rep. IBM Corp., Detroit, 1973-76; assoc. dir. U. Mich., Dearborn, 1976-78; owner Bayleran & Burris, Inc., Orchard Lake, Mich., 1978—, L.B. Burris & Co., Inc., Orchard Lake, 1982—, Servicelease, Inc., Orchard Lake, 1989—; cons. Rapidata, Southfield, Mich., 1980-82. Editor: A Practical Armenian & English Book, 1971. Head pub. rels. com. Oakland County C. of C., Pontiac, Mich., 1983. mem. Wayne State U. Alumnae Assn. (pres. Detroit chpt. 1981-83), Alpha Phi. Republican.

BURROUGHS, CAROL LOUISA STABEN, marriage and family therapist, educator; b. Philip, S.D., Feb. 24, 1960; d. Howard Arthur and Hazel Elaine (Stratton) Staben; m. Steven James Stickler, Feb. 14, 1977 (div. Feb. 1980); 1 child, Victoria Marie; m. Grant Smith Burroughs, Sept. 2, 1990. BS in Family Sci., Mont. State U., 1986, MS in Marriage and Family Therapy, 1988. Lic. clin. profl. counselor, Mont. Clk. Recklings Furniture & Hardware, Philip, 1975-81; cashier Kwik Way Inc., Belgrade Mont., 1981-83; work-study sec. Career Svcs. Mont. State U., Bozeman, 1983-86, adj. prof., tchg. asst. Health and Human Devel., 1987—; clin. profl. counselor N.W. Counseling Ctrs., Inc., Bozeman, 1988—. Clin. dir. Gallatin County Critical Incident Stress Mgmt. Team, Bozeman, 1991—; pub. rels. chair Sweet Pea Festival, Bozeman, 1992—; bd. deacons First Luth. Ch., 1990-93. Mem. ACA, Am. Clin. Mental Health Counselors Assn., Mont. Clin. Mental Health Counselors Assn. (area coord. 1991—, state legis. liaison 1994—), Mont. Counseling Assn. (dist. 9 senator 1991-93). Republican. Home: 407 W Lamme Bozeman MT 59715 Office: NW Counseling Ctrs Inc 104 E Main # 213 Bozeman MT 59715

BURROWS, BARBARA ANN, veterinarian; b. Columbia, S.C., Dec. 15, 1947; d. Robert Beck and Betty Elizabeth (Rabon) Burrows; m. Richard M. Duemmler, Aug. 31, 1968 (div. Aug. 1975); 1 child, Sandra Lynn. BA, Hartwick Coll., 1969; VMD, U. Pa., 1983. Bacteriologist Johnson & Johnson, North Brunswick, N.J., 1969-70; microbiologist Ciba-Geigy, Summit, N.J., 1973-79; veterinarian Amboy Ave Vet. Hosp., Metuchen, N.J., 1983-84, Black Horse Pike Animal Hosp., Turnersville, N.J., 1984-93, San Juan Animal Hosp., San Juan Capistrano, Calif., 1993-94; relief vet., 1994—; relief veterinarian Alicia Pet Clinic, Laguna Hills, Calif., Crown Valley Animal Hosp., Laguna Niguel, Calif. Capt. USAF. Mem. Am. Vet. Med. Assn., So. Calif. Vet. Med. Assn., Am. Assn. Feline Practitioners. Home: 25582 Breezewood St Dana Point CA 92629-2138

BURROWS, ELIZABETH MACDONALD, religious organization executive, educator; b. Portland, Oreg., Jan. 30, 1930; d. Leland R. and Ruth M. (Frew) MacDonald. Certificate, Chinmaya Trust Sandeepany, Bombay; PhD (hon.), Internat. U. Philosophy and Sci., 1975; ThD, Christian Coll. Universal Peace, 1992. Ordained to ministry First Christian Ch., 1976. Mgr. credit Home Utilities, Seattle, 1958, Montgomery Ward, Crescent City, Calif., 1963; supr. Oreg. Dist. Tng. West Coast Telephone, Beaverton, 1965; pres. Christian Ch. Universal Peace, Seattle, 1971—; prof. religion Christian Coll. Universal Peace, also bd. dirs.; pres. Archives Internat., Seattle, 1971—; v.p. James Tyler Kent Inst. Homeopathy, 1984—. Author: Crystal Planet, 1979, Pathway of the Immortal, 1980, Odyssey of the Apocalypse, 1981, Maya Sangh, 1981, Harp of Destiny, 1984, Commentary for Gospel of Peace of Jesus Christ According to John, 1986; author of poetry (Publisher's Choice award Poets of the New Era, Disting. Poets of Am.). Recipient Pres. award for literary excellence, 1994. Mem. Internat. Speakers Platform, Internat. New Thought Alliance, Cousteau Soc., Internat. Order of Chivalry, The Planetary Soc. Home: 10529 Ashworth Ave N Seattle WA 98133-8937

BURROWS, ENID YOUNG, technical writer; b. Providence, May 26, 1943; d. Murry J. and Libby Y. (Young) B. BS in Edn., Lesley Coll., 1965. Cert. tchr., Mass.; registered real estate salesperson, Mass. Tech. proposal coord. Northrop Corp. Precision Products Divsn., 1979-81; sr. prodn. editor documentation and tng. Wang Labs., Lawrence, Mass., 1983-84; sr. tech. proposal writer customer svc. Wang Labs., Lowell, Mass., 1984-85, sr. tech. writer corp. hqrs., 1985; cons., tech. writer Honeywell Bull., Waltham, Mass., 1986-87; sr. tech. writer Thomson Fin. Svcs., Boston, 1989-93; tchr. elem. and jr. h.s. Newton Pub. Schs., 1965-73; tchr. English and reading Duxbury (Mass.) Pub. Schs., 1974-76. Pres. Lesley Coll. B'nai B'rith Hillel, 1964; vol. Jewish Family and Children's Svc. Russian Resettlement Program, 1988—. Recipient Cmty. Svc. award Combined Jewish Philanthropies, 1994. Home: 205 Walden St Cambridge MA 02140

BURROWS, JANICE ELIZABETH HOWARD, human resources director; b. Boston, Oct. 24, 1944; d. Lloyd F. and Bernice E. (Cross) Howard; m. Quentin C. Burrows, June 25, 1966 (div. Nov. 1986); children: Matthew Howard, Christopher Lynch. BA cum laude, Harvard U., 1966; MBA, U. Calif., Berkeley, 1987. Mgr. employment, tng. U.S. Govt., Boston, 1966-72, Washington, 1966-72, N.Y.C., 1966-72; personnel specialist City of Berkeley, 1974-76; asst. dir. personnel Alta Bates Hosp., Berkeley, 1976-79; personel dir. Alta Bates Med. Ctr., Berkeley, 1979-86; human resources cons. JHB Assocs., Berkeley, 1986—; human resources dir. U. Calif. Libr., Berkeley, 1988—; dir. Humanities West, San Francisco, 1991—. Co-author: Minority Recruitment and Retention in ARL Libraries, 1990; author: Training Student Workers in Academic Libraries, 1994, Onward or Upward? Getting Ahead in an Unfair World, 1994. Docent Oakland Mus. Calif., 1992—; commr. personnel commn. Berkeley Unified Sch. Dist., chair, 1987-91. Nat. Merit scholar, 1962. Mem. Am. Libr. Assn., Nat. Forum Black Pub. Adminstrs., Indsl. Rels. Rsch. Assn., State Bar Calif. (assoc.). Home: PO Box 40073 Berkeley CA 94704-4073

BURSLEY, KATHLEEN A., lawyer; b. Washington, Mar. 20, 1954; d. G.H. Patrick and Claire (Mulvany) B. BA, Pomona Coll., 1976; JD, Cornell U., 1979. Bar: N.Y. 1980, U.S. Dist. Ct. (ea. and so. dists.) N.Y. 1980, U.S. Ct. Appeals (5th and 11th cirs.) 1981, Fla. 1984, U.S. Dist. Ct. (middle dist.) Fla. 1984., Tex. 1985. Assoc. Haight, Gardner, Poor & Havens, N.Y.C., 1979-81; counsel Harcourt Brace Jovanovich, Inc., N.Y.C. and Orlando, Fla., 1981-85; v.p. and counsel Harcourt Brace Jovanovich, Inc., San Antonio and Orlando, 1985-92; assoc. gen. counsel pub. Harcourt Gen., Inc., Chestnut Hill, Mass., 1992—; gen. counsel Harcourt Brace & Co., Chestnut Hill, Mass., 1994—. Mem. Maritime Law Assn. (proctor). Office: Harcourt Gen Inc 27 Boylston St Chestnut Hill MA 02167-1719

BURSON, ANNE TRIBBY, librarian, educator; b. St. Petersburg, Fla., Nov. 18, 1947; d. David Eugene and Ruth Louise (Mennen) Tribby; m. Ralph Taber Burson, Jan. 3, 1981. A.A., St. Petersburg Jr. Coll., 1967; B.A., U. S. Fla., 1969, M.A., 1974. Cert. tchr., Fla. Tchr., Clearwater Central Cath. High Sch., Fla., 1969-74; media specialist Dunedin Comprehensive High Sch., Fla., 1974-88, media specialist Ozona Elem. Sch., 1988—; cons. in field. Co-chmn. Dunedin High Sch. So. Assn. Evaluation, 1984—. Mem. Fla. Assn. Media in Edn., Pinellas Assn. Librarians and Media Specialists (sec. 1976-77, pres. 1990-91), Pinellas County Tchrs. Assn. (faculty rep. 1976-80), Delta Kappa Gamma (2d v.p. 1988—). Republican. Lutheran. Home: 2439 Indian Trl E Palm Harbor FL 34683-2806 Office: Ozona Elem Sch 525 Pennsylvania Ave Palm Harbor FL 34683-5298

BURSON, BETSY LEE, librarian; b. Olney, Tex., Dec. 16, 1942; d. James Hollis and Lora Elizabeth (Talbott) B.; m. Winston Rabb Henderson, June 26, 1976. BS in Edn., Kans. State Tchrs. Coll., 1964; MLS, Tex. Woman's U., 1967, PhD in Libr. Info. Studies, 1987. With Phoenix Pub. Libr., 1967-74; libr. dir. Glendale (Ariz.) Pub. Libr., 1974-75; project archivist Phoenix History Project, 1975-77; adj. faculty U. Ariz., Tucson, 1979, Tex. Woman's U., Denton, 1980; libr. cons. La. State Libr., Baton Rouge, 1982-85; libr. dir. El Paso (Tex.) Pub. Libr., 1987-90, Arlington (Tex.) Pub. Libr., 1990—. Office: Arlington Pub Libr 101 E Abram Arlington TX 76010-1004

BURSTEIN, SHARON ANN PALMA, corporate communications specialist; b. Schenectady, N.Y., July 18, 1952; d. Harold Edward and Lois Ida (Hesner) Rieck; m. Joseph Carmen Palma, May 17, 1975 (div. Sept. 1982); m. Richard Lyle Burstein, Sept. 8, 1985; 1 child, Alexandra Blaire. BA, Nat. Coll. Edn., 1974; postgrad., Russell Sage Coll., 1974-78, Union Coll., 1980. Cert. tchr., N.Y. Elem. tchr. Saratoga Springs (N.Y.) Schs., 1974-80; ednl. cons. Whitcomb Assocs., Boston, 1980-81; ednl. mktg. specialist Monroe Systems for Bus., Newington, Conn., 1981-83; nat. mktg. mgr. Victor Techs., Hartford, Conn., 1983, Exclusives, Boston, 1984-85; dir. pub. rels. Lawrence Group, Albany, N.Y., 1985-87, dir. corp. comm., 1987-88; v.p. Lawrence Group, Albany, 1988-89; v.p investors rels. Lawrence Group, N.Y.C., 1987-89; pres. S.A. Burstein & Assocs., Albany, 1989-94; adjunct prof. Russell Sage Coll., Troy, N.Y., 1994—; cons. N.Y. Assn. Bus. Ofcls., 1982-83. Editor: Helpline newspaper, 1985, 87; co-prodr. Playing It Safe, 1986 (Nori award 1987), To Be As Independent As You Can be (Nori award 1989), Cookbook Capital Connoisseur (Nori award 1989), Camp Ever Young (Nori award 1993); acted in TV comml., 1981 (Addy award 1982). Bd. dirs. Multiple Sclerosis Soc., Albany, 1986—, Mohawk Pathways Girl Scouts U.S.; active in N.Y. Spl. Olympics, 1987, Capital Women's Charity Found., Albany, 1987—. Mem. NAFE, Nat. Investor Relations Inst., Am. Mgmt. Assn., Assn. Profl. Communicators, Nat. Assn. Investment Clubs, Albany C. of C. (mem. women's bus. coun.), Kappa Delta Pi. Democrat. Clubs: Steuben, Womens Press. Home: 4 Birch Hill Rd Loudonville NY 12211-2004

BURSTYN, ELLEN (EDNA RAE GILLOOLY), actress; b. Detroit, Dec. 7, 1932; m. Paul Roberts; m. Neil Burstyn; 1 child, Jefferson. LHD (hon.), Dowling Coll.; DFA (hon.), Sch. Visual Arts. Artistic dir. The Actor's Studio, N.Y.C., 1982-88. Appeared regularly on Jackie Gleason TV show, 1956-57; Broadway debut in Fair Game, 1957-58, (summer stock) John Loves Mary, 1960, (Broadway prodns.) Same Time, Next Year, 1975 (Tony award for Best Actress, Drama Desk award, Outer Circle Critics award), 84 Charing Cross Road, 1982, Shirley Valentine, 1989, Shimada, 1992, (off-Broadway) Park Your Car in Harvard Yard with Burgess Meredith, (Chgo.) Driving Miss Daisy, 1988, Shirley Valentine, 1990; film appearances include Goodbye Charlie (under name Ellen McRae), 1964, For Those Who Think Young, 1965, Tropic of Cancer, 1969, Alex in Wonderland, 1971 (named Best Supporting Actress N.Y. Film Critics, Nat. Soc. Film Critics, Acad. Award nominee for Best Supporting Actress), The Last Picture Show, 1971 (Acad. award nominee Best Actress), The King of Marvin Gardens, 1972, The Exorcist, 1973 (Acad. Award nominee for Best Actress), Harry and Tonto, 1974, Alice Doesn't Live Here Anymore, 1974 (Acad. Award as Best Actress, Golden Globe award, Brit. Acad. award), Providence, 1977, Same Time Next Year, 1978, Dream of Passion, 1978, Resurrection, 1980, Silence of the North, 1980, The Ambassador, 1984, Twice in a Lifetime, 1986, Hannah's War, 1987, The Color of Evening, 1990, Grand Isle, 1990, Dying Young, 1990, The Cemetery Club, 1993, When a Man Loves A Woman, 1994; TV movies include Thursday's Game, 1974, The People vs. Jean Harris, 1981 (Emmy award nominee), Into Thin Air, 1985, Surviving, 1985, Act of Vengeance, 1986, Something in Common, 1986, Pack of Lies, 1987 (Emmy nomination) When you Remember Me, 1990, Mrs. Lambert Remembers Love, 1991, Taking Back My Life: The Nancy Ziegrenmeyer Story, 1992, Grand Isle, 1992, Shattered Trust: The Shari Karney Story, 1993, Getting Gotti, 1994, Trick of the Eye, 1994, Getting Out, 1994; TV series include: The Doctors, The Ellen Burstyn Show, 1986-87; dir. off-Broadway play Judgement, 1981, Into Thin Air, 1985, When You Remember Me, 1990, Running Out, 1991; star TV series The Ellen Burstyn Show, 1986; narrator segment TV show Dear America: Letters Home from Vietnam, 1988; appearance documentary film Balls of Grace; original photography work featured in Darkroom Photography mag., June, 1989. Mem. individual artists grants and policy overview panels Nat. Endowment for the Arts, Theater Adv. Council City of New York. Mem. Actors Equity Assn. (pres. 1982-85). Office: CAA 9830 Wilshire Blvd Beverly Hills CA 90212*

BURT, LISA MEFFORD, accountant, nurse; b. Niagara Falls, N.Y., Sept. 13, 1952; d. A. Jean and Dorothy N. (Hogg) Mefford; m. Lloyd Michael Burt, Sept. 17, 1983. Cert. in operating rm. tech. with honors, Miami (Fla.) Dade Community Coll., 1976, AA and ASN with honors, 1979; B in Acct. with honors, Fla. Internat. U., 1994. Lic. RN Fla. Loan teller First State Bank (now Barnett State Bank), Hialeah, Fla., 1971-75; surg. scrub nurse Mt. Sinai Med. Ctr., Miami Beach, Fla., 1976-78; coronary care nurse South Miami Hosp., Miami, 1979-83; real estate sales agt. Coldwell Banker, Miami, 1987-89; clin. nurse Dade Home Health Agy., Miami, 1989-90; comml. rsch. analyst Appraisal and Real Estate Assocs., Inc., Miami, 1990; quality assurance RN Kimberly Quality Care now Kimberly-Olsten Home Care, 1991-93; case mgr., quality care RN Staff Builders Home Health Care, Miami Lakes, Fla., 1993—; mem. operating rm. tech. program Miami Dade Community Coll., 1977-78. Mem. Palm Springs North Civic Assn., Hialeah, 1979—, Ctr. For The Fine Arts, Miami, 1986—; opera singer workshop Broward community Coll., 1985-86; singer, dancer, producing variety shows PROPS Cancer Rsch. Fund Raiser, 1987. Recipient Outstanding Acad. Achievements award Miami Dade Communty Coll., 1976, 78, 79, Nursing Leadership award, 1979, Excellence in Econs. award, 1988. Mem. ANA, Nat. Assn. Accts., Fla. Internat. U. Acctg. Assn., Fla. Pub. Interest Rsch. Group, Miami Amateur Computer Club, Wildlife Care Ctr., Phi Theta Kappa, Phi Kappa Phi.

BURT, MARJORIE LOMBARD, business manager; b. Stoughton, Mass., Feb. 25, 1956; d. John Joseph and Marie Josephine (Hopkins) Lombard; children: Katie Marie, Elizabeth Ann. BSBA with honors, Northeastern U., 1979. Acctg. trainee HEW Audit, Boston, 1976-78; staff acct. Etonic, Inc., Brockton, Mass., 1979-81; ops. acct. Foxboro Co., East Bridgewater, Mass., 1981-82, 86-87; chief acct. New Eng. Structures, Inc., Avon, Mass., 1983-84; bus. mgr. Mutron Corp., Brockton, Mass., 1988-92; contr. Connector Tech. Corp., Warwick, R.I., 1992-94; bus. mgr. Cath. Charities-Laboure Ctr., South Boston, Mass., 1994—. Tchr. confraternity Christian doctrine program St. Thomas Aquinas Ch., Bridgewater, 1988—; keyperson Old Colony United Way, Brockton, 1988-91, mem. funds allocation com., 1991—; vol. tchr. You and Me drug prevention program, Bridgewater, 1990-92, Parents for Edn., Bridgewater, 1990—; vol. Am. Electronics Assn.-Brockton Jr. High Sch. Alliance, 1990-92; mem. Bridgewater Parents Collaborative, 1991—. Mem. Am. Electronics Assn., Small Bus. Assn. New Eng. Roman Catholic.

BURTLE, DEBRA ANN, needlework and gift shop owner; b. Decatur, Ill., Oct. 24, 1953; d. Albert Eugene and Barbara Ann (Watson) Naab; m. Paul Walter Burtle, July 22, 1978; 1 child, Laura Rose. AA, Lincoln Land C.C., 1973; BS, Ea. Ill. U., 1975; cert., Martha Pullen Sch. Fashion, 1986, Margaret Boyle Sch. Needlework, 1989. Cert. tchr., Ill. Tchr. home econs. Athens (Ill.) Community Unit Sch. Dist., 1977-78, Waverly (Ill.) Community Unit Sch. Dist., 1978-80; instr. adult edn. Sew with Flo, Springfield, Ill., 1980-83, The Quilting Bee, Rochester, Ill., 1980-83, Springfield Crafts and Ceramics Club, 1987—; owner, mgr. Ruffles, Flourishes, and Satin Bows, Auburn, Ill., 1985—; textile judge Christian County Fair, Taylorville, Ill., 1974—, Ill. State Fair Springfield, 1992, 93, 94; demonstrator wool spinning Clayville Rural Life Ctr., Pleasant Plains, Ill., 1967-74, Ill. State Fair, Springfield, 1974-75; instr. wool spinning Lincoln's New Salem State Park, Petersburg, Ill., 1969; needlework demonstrator Winter Folk Fest, Blackburn Coll., Carlinville, Ill., 1992. Artisan exhibitor Springfield Art Assn. Fine Art Fair, 1989, others. Winner textile and garment awards Sangamon County Fair, New Berlin, Ill., 1971, Ill. State Fair 1988, 89, 91, 92, 93, 94; recipient Outstanding Farm Family award Ill. Farmers Union, 1993. Mem. Auburn Jr. Women's Club (sec. 1985), Elegant Stitchers Needlework Guild (v.p. 1986, pres. 1987-89). Home: RR 1 Box 145 Auburn IL 62615-9749 Office: Ruffles Flourishes and Satin Bows 115 N 4th St Auburn IL 62615-1451

BURTON, ANN MAPES, college administrator; b. Detroit, Mar. 4, 1933; d. Ralph James and Edith Blanch (Moore) B. BA in History, Duke U., 1954; MA in History, U. Mich., 1955; DPhil in History, Oxford U., 1960. Instr. Hunter Coll., CUNY, 1961-63; asst. prof. Bklyn. Coll., CUNY, 1964-71, assoc. prof., 1971-79, prof., 1979-84; assoc. dean faculty arts & scis. N.Y.U., 1981-86, dean arts & sci. adminstrn., 1986-93; v.p. acad. affairs Swiss Hosp. Inst., Washington, 1994, pres., 1995—; mem. doctoral faculty in history CUNY Grad. Sch., 1975-84; sec. univ. faculty senate CUNY, 1975-76, chmn. com. on funding alternatives, 1975, vice-chmn. univ. faculty senate, 1976-78, chmn. univ. faculty senate, trustee, 1978-81; chmn. coll. com. on master planning and ednl. policy Bklyn. Coll., 1975-76, chmn. curriculum com., 1974-76, dep. chmn. dept. history, 1969-71, chmn. dept. history, 1976-80; screening com. in history, Fulbright Commn., 1974-75. Contbr. articles to profl. jours. Trustee Grace Opportunity Project, 1985-93, Grace Ch. Sch., 1980-86, Gunn Meml. Libr., 1993—; chmn. music com. Grace Episcopal Ch., N.Y.C., 1979-89, treas., 1987-89, vestry mem., 1976-81; bd. dirs. N.Y. Chamber Soloists, 1980—; altar guild St. John's Ch., Washington, Conn., 1989—, vestry mem., 1991—, warden, 1994—. Mem. AAUW (fellow 1963-64), Am. Philos. Soc. (grantee 1963-64). Home: 7 South St Washington CT 06793

BURTON, BARBARA ABLE, psychotherapist; b. Columbia, S.C.; d. Eugene Walter Able and Mary Louise (Chadwick) Cantelou; 1 child, Stacia Louise. BA in Psychology, Ga. State U.; MSW, U. Ala., 1970. Diplomate Am. Bd. Examiners in Clin. Social Work, Internat. Acad. Behavioral Medicine, Counseling and Psychotherapy; cert. Am. Acad. Cert. Social Workers, NASW. Assoc. exec. dir. Positive Maturity, Inc., Birmingham, Ala., 1970-72; comm. org. planner Community Svc. Council, INc., Birmingham, Ala., 1972-75; adj. faculty U. Ala., Tuscaloosa, Ala., 1975-77; dir. Ensley Outpatient Drug Abuse Clinic, Birmingham, Ala., 1975-77, Sch.

of Social Work, Miles Coll., Birmingham, Ala., 1977-78; prog. mgr. and clin. cons. Goodwill Industries of Ala., Birmingham, Ala., 1977-81; pvt. practice New Orleans, 1983--; cons. Omega Internat. Inst., New Orleans, 1988--. Author: Love Me, Love Me Not, and Other Matters That Matter, 1990. Past chmn. Policy and Program Com. Birmingham Urban League; Ala. Adv. Com. on Social Svcs.; Ala. Com. for the Dev. of Higher Ed.; Ala. Conf. of Social Work. NIMH fellow Inst. on Human Sexuality, U. Hawaii, 1976. Mem. Am. Assn. Sex Educators, Counselors and Therapists, Nat. Assn. Social Workers, Pvt. Practitioners Unit of New Orleans, Acad. Cert. Social Workers, Internat. Platform Com., Psi Chi. Office: 1631 Constantinople St New Orleans LA 70115

BURTON, BARBARA ANNE, plumbing and heating company executive; b. Flushing, N.Y., Nov. 28, 1948; d. Victor Arthur and Anne (Inglima) Schettini; m. Maurice John Burton, Mar. 10, 1973; children: Anthony John, Christopher Maurice. Acad. diploma, Flushing High Sch., 1966. Loan payers. Household Fin. Corp., N.Y.C., 1966-67; sec. P.F. Collier Inc., London, 1968-69, exec. sec., 1969-70; sec. Bill Lutz Assocs., N.Y.C., 1970-72; exec. sec. merchandising Courtaulds N.Am., N.Y.C., 1972-75; sec.-treas. M. Burton Plumbing & Heating Corp., N.Y.C., 1975—. Republican. Roman Catholic. Home: 53-42 211 ST Bayside NY 11364 Office: M Burton Plumbing & Heating 206-01 48th Ave Bayside NY 11364

BURTON, BARBARA ELAINE, computer programmer analyst; b. Franklin, Va., Apr. 20, 1957; d. Oscar Banks Jr. and Maude Adlane (Jenkins) Banks Whitfield; m. Wellington M. Burton, May 12, 1979 (div. June 1993); children: Terra Marcellus, Essence Tineal. BS, Va. State U., Petersburg, 1978; MBPA, Howard U., 1984. Computer programmer Vitro Corp., Silver Spring, Md., 1978-85; software engr. MedLink Cons. Inc., Silver Spring, 1985-86; sr. programmer analyst Arbitron Rating Inc., Laurel, Md., 1986-87; programmer analyst Vitro Corp., Silver Spring, 1987—; mem. spkrs. bur. Vitro Corp., 1979—. Amb., Congl. Black Caucus Found., Wasington, 1993—; tutor Montgomery County Pub. Libr., Silver Spring, 1989-91; pub. speaker to jr. and sr. high sch. students. Mem. AAUW (role model), Va. State Alumni Assn., Howard U. Alumni Assn., Nat. Coun. Negro Women Inc., Toastmaster. Democrat. Baptist. Home: 17345 Moss Side Ln Olney MD 20832

BURTON, BETTY JUNE, minister, pastor; b. Muskegon, Mich., June 11, 1923; d. Bernard J. and Louise Ella (Weaver) Mulder; mem. Harold Ver Berkmoes, June 4, 1943 (div. 1966); children: Suzanne, James, Michael, William, Judith, David (dec.); m. Eldon Franklin Burton, June 27, 1971. Student of music, psychology and religion, Hope Coll., 1941-45; student, Garrett Evang. Theol. Sem., 1984-85. Ordained to ministry United Meth. Ch., 1986. Librarian Vassar Hosp. Sch. Nursing, Poughkeepsie, N.Y., 1958-60, Hackley Pub. Library, Muskegon, 1960-64, Boyne City (Mich.) Pub. Library, 1972-74; reporter Ludington (Mich.) Daily News, 1975-81; caseworker Aid to Dependent Children Mich. Dept. Social Services, Hart, 1974-78; pastor various Meth. Chs., Norwood, Barnard and Charlevoix, Mich., 1981-83, Mears (Mich.) United Meth. Ch., 1985, 86; assoc. pastor United Meth. Centenary, Pentwater, Mich., 1986-90; pastor First Congl. Ch. of Central Lake, Mich., 1990-92, Thompsonville (Mich.) Congl. Church, 1992-93; assoc. realtor Shaw Real Estate, Pentwater, 1975-81, Real Estate One, Traverse City, Mich., 1981-82, Century 21 Williams Real Estate, Pentwater, 1986-89. Sec. Pentwater Planning Commn., 1985. Mem. NAFE, International Platform Assn., Am. Assn. Christian Counselors, Nat. Christian Counselors Assn., Nat. Trust Hist. Preservation, Am. Museum Natural History, Nat. Audubon Soc., Am. Acad. Ministry, Hist. Soc. Mich., Oceana County Hist. Soc., Kappa Beta Phi (pres. 1943), Xi Gamma Beta (sec. 1970). Republican. Clubs: Women's of Pentwater (v.p. 1986—), Garden of Pentwater (pres. 1986—), Sierra. Home and Office: 4407 Daisy Ln Traverse City MI 49684-8761

BURTON, DIANE LOUISE, naval architect; b. Detroit, Aug. 5, 1954; d. Robert Walter and Anne Morley (Bishop) B. BS in Engring., U. Mich., 1979, MS in Engring., 1984. Engr. in tng. Naval Sea Sys. Command, Arlington, Va., 1980-82, engr., 1982-84, naval arch., 1984—. Mem. U.S. Sailing Assn. (chairwomen womens championships 1990-94, Olympic Team 1989, 91, 92), U.S. Europe Dinghy Class Assn., U.S. Olympic Yachting Comm. (class rep.), Severn Sailing Assn. Office: Navy Sea Sys Command 2531 Jefferson Davis Hwy Arlington VA 22242-5160

BURTON, DRENNA LEE O'REILLY, kindergarten educator; b. Advance, Mo., Apr. 22, 1948; d. Willard and Frances (Moore) Lee; m. Donald Gene Burton, May 25, 1987; children: Jennifer Anne, Heather Lee. BA in Edn., Lambuth U., 1970; MA in Edn., Southeast Mo. State U., 1984. Cert. tchr., Mo. Tchr. med.-dental assts. St. Louis Bus. Coll., 1970; tchr. Bell City (Mo.) R-2 Schs., 1971-74; tchr. 1st grade Delta (Mo.) R-5 Schs., 1974-81, tchr. kindergarten, 1981—; adv. bd. Parents as Tchrs.; adj. faculty Coll. Edn., Southeast Mo. State U., Cape Girardeau. Mem. Mo. State Tchrs. Assn., Community Tchrs. Assn. (sec., treas., v.p.), Mo. Assn. Rural Educators. Office: Delta R-5 Elem Sch PO Box 219 Delta MO 63744-0219

BURTON, KAREN, community health nurse; b. Rockford, Ill., Dec. 19, 1946; d. James Anthony and Malvina Signe (Hanson) Kenison; m. Larry P. Burton, Feb. 6, 1968; children: James, Brenda. Diploma, Swedish-Am. Hosp. Sch. Nursing, Rockford, 1967. Cert. RN Intravenous. Office nurse Rockford, 1967-84; skilled intermittent visit nurse, supplemental staff nurse Med. Pers. Pool, Rockford, 1984-88, home care supr., 1986-88; dir. mktg. Nihan's OPTION CARE, Rockford, 1988-90, IV specialist, on-call staff nurse, 1990—, pharmacy tech. and insvc. educator; long term care svcs. nurse cons., 1994—. Mem. Intravenous Nurses Soc., Oncology Nursing Soc. (nat. home care spl. interest group, NW Ill. chpt. sec. 1995—).

BURTON, KATHLEEN T., mental health professional; b. Lynn, Mass., Jan. 29, 1962; d. Charles W. and Mary L. (Mayer) B. BA in Psychology/Comms., Notre Dame Coll., South Euclid, Ohio, 1985; MEd in Counseling, Cleve. State U., 1990, EdS in Counseling Psychology, 1991; postgrad., Saybrook Inst., San Francisco, 1992—. Human rels. & devel. coord. Kaiser Permanente, Cleveland Heights, Ohio, 1984-87; counselor Cleve. Treatment Ctr., 1989-90; tchg. asst., counselor intern Cleve. State U., 1989-91; community trainer Woodland (Calif.) Community Options, 1991—; mental health profl., psychologist intern Davis, Calif., 1992—; group facilitator for human sexuality course dept. psychiatry Davis Med. Sch., 1994—; group leader, facilitator anxiety, phobias & panic Woodland Sr. Ctr., 1993—; lectr. anxiety, phobias, panic, drug addictions, Moscow, Kiev, 1994. Contbr. article to medical jour. Mem. ACA, Internat. Assn. for Addictions & Offender Counselors, Ohio Counseling Assn. (rep.), Am. Family Assn. Roman Catholic. Office: 2433 Creekhollow Ln Davis CA 95616

BURTON, NANETTE DARLENE, psychotherapist; b. Chgo., Feb. 27, 1950; d. Stephen P. and Inez M. (Moore) Mongelluzzo; 1 child, Bryan R. BA, Adams State Coll., 1972, MA, 1977. Cert. nat. bd. counselors; cert. family law mediater. Dir. San Luis Valley Devel. Evaluation Clinic, Alamosa, Colo., 1974-76; mental health therapist San Luis vAlley Comprehensive Community Mental Health Ctr., Alamosa, Colo., 1975-79; pvt. practice Monte Vista, Colo., 1979—, Sedona, Ariz., 1991—; child family therapist Kaiser Permanente, Portland, Oreg., 1990-91; dir. Village of Oak Creek Counseling Ctr., Sedona, 1992—. Author: Understanding Depression and Suicide, 1990. Mem. ACA, Am. Assn. Suicidology, Am. Assn. Mental Health Counselors, Amnesty Internat. Office: PO Box 20712 Sedona AZ 86341-0712

BURTON, SHEAROR FAY, educator, computer consultant; b. Eastpoint, Fla., Dec. 10, 1938; d. George Wilburn and Mary Virginia (Segree) Creamer; m. Thomas Eliot Gordon, Oct. 6, 1956 (div. Apr. 1969); children: Brenda Gale, Pamela Faith; m. Orlis Luell Burton, Dec. 25, 1969. AA, Gulf Coast Community Coll., Panama City, Fla., 1969; BA, Fla. State U., 1972; MA, U. West Fla., 1979. Cert. tchr., Fla. Tchr aide Chapman Elem. Sch., Apalachicola, Fla., 1966-67, sec., 1967-71; libr. Brown Elem. Sch., Eastpoint, Fla., 1972-73; media specialist Apalachicola High Sch., 1972-90; dist. adminstr. Franklin County Sch. Dist., Apalachicola, 1990—; adj. instr. Gulf Coast Community Coll., Panama City, 1987-89, Apalachicola coord., 1990-91; dir. Drug Free Schs. Adv. Coun., Apalachicola, 1989—; mem. Franklin County Literacy Bd., Apalachicola, 1989—; trainer Disadvantaged Youth Program, Apalachicola, 1990-91. Author: (computer program) Winner's Edge, 1989; editor: (newsletter) Good New's Report, 1991. Recipient Literacy Program Goal Achievement award Fla. Dept. Edn., Tallahassee, 1991. Mem. Fla. Assn. Sch. Adminstrs., Fla. Assn. Media in Edn., Fla. Literacy Coalition, Franklin County Literacy Bd., Philaco Woman's Club (parliamentarian 1988), Kappa Delta Pi, Delta Kappa Gamma (Alpha Lambda chpt. coor. sec. 1988). Baptist. Office: Franklin County Schs 155 Avenue E Apalachicola FL 32320-2099

BURTON, VALERIE DIANE, elementary school educator; b. East Orange, N.J., Aug. 5, 1947; d. Theodore R.and Elsie E. (Brown) Smith; m. Clifford R. Burton, Oct. 18, 1969; children: Celeste, Corey, Victoria. BA, U. Pitts., 1969. Cert. elem. edn. and social studies tchr., N.J. Employment counselor State of N.J., Newark, 1970-71; tchr. Morris Sch. Dist., Morris Twp., N.J., 1972—; multicultural specialist; adv. coun. rep. Morris Sch. Dist., Morristown, 1974-77, mem. negotiating team, 1981-85, elem. rep. social studies curriculum, 1985-86, gifted and talented rep., 1989—; master tchr. summer intern, 1993. Feature writer Long Beach (Calif.) Times Newspaper, 1988. Mem. edn. com. Jack & Jill, Inc., Morris County, 1982—mem. parent adv. com. Morristown (N.J.) H.S., 1992—; tutor, ednl. liaison Neighborhood House Vols., 1993—. Mem. ASCD, NAACP (edn. com. Morristown chpt. 1983-84), Urban League (edn. com. Morristown chpt. 1988-89), Delta Sigma Theta (mem. in-take com. 1990—, program com.). Democrat. Baptist. Home: 21 Stonehenge Rd Morristown NJ 07960-2649

BURZYNSKI, SUSAN MARIE, newspaper editor; b. Jackson, Mich., Jan. 1, 1953; d. Leon Walter and Claudia (Kulpinski) B.; m. James W. Bush, May 22, 1976 (div. 1989); children: Lisa M., Kevin J.; m. George K. Bullard, Jr., Mar. 21, 1992. AA, Jackson C.C., 1972; BA, Mich. State, 1974. Reporter Saratogian, Saratoga Springs, N.Y., 1974, Gongwer News Svc., Lansing, Mich., 1975, The State Jour., Lansing, 1975-79; Metro editor Port Huron (Mich.) Times Herald, 1979-82, mng. editor, 1982-86; asst. city editor Detroit News, 1986-87, Sunday news editor, 1987, news editor, 1988-91, asst. mng. editor/news, 1991—. Roman Catholic. Office: Detroit News 615 W Lafayette Blvd Detroit MI 48226-3197

BUSBY, MARJORIE JEAN (MARJEAN BUSBY), journalist; b. Kansas City, Mo., Jan. 31, 1931; d. Vivian Eric and Stella Mae (Lindley) Phillips; m. Robert Jackson Busby, Apr. 11, 1969 (dec. Feb. 1989). B.J., U. Mo., 1952. With Kansas City (Mo.) Star Co. (became div. Capital Cities Communications 1977, name changed to Capital Cities/ABC Inc.), 1952—, editor women's news, 1969-73, assoc. Sunday editor, People Sect. editor, 1973-77, fashion editor, 1978-81, feature and home writer, 1981—. Mem. Fashion Group (1st recipient Kansas City appreciation award 1978), Women in Communications, LSV, Mortar Board, Soc. Profl. Journalists, Kappa Alpha Theta (pres. Alpha Mu chpt. 1951-52). Presbyterian. Clubs: Leawood Country, Belle of Am. Royal Orgn. Home: 9804 Mercier St Kansas City MO 64114-3860 Office: 1729 Grand Ave Kansas City MO 64108-1413

BUSCH, ANN MARIE HERBAGE, medical/surgical clinical nurse specialist; b. Roseburg, Oreg., Jan. 24, 1958; d. Robert Canfield and Magdaline Mary (Tuchscherer) Herbage; m. John Patrick Busch, June 27, 1981; children: Rebecca Ann, Michael Robert. BSN summa cum laude, U. Portland, 1980; MSN, U. Calif., San Francisco, 1985. Cert. CPR instr., enterostomal therapy nurse. Staff nurse IV Stanford (Calif.) U. Hosp., 1981-88, acting nursing ednl. coord., 1986, 87; coord./educator RN refresher program De-Anza Coll., Cupertino, Calif., 1986-88; med-surg. clin. nurse specialist Community Hosp. Los Gatos (Calif.), 1988-92; surg. clin. nurse specialist Palo Alto VA Med. Ctr., 1992—; cons. for patient pathways U. So. Calif. Hosp., 1990-91; asst. clin. prof. dept. physiol. nursing U. Calif., San Francisco, 1993—. Mem. ANA (cert. clin. specialist in med./surg. nursing, mem. coun. nurses advanced practice), Wound, Ostomy, and Continence Nurses Soc. (cert. enterostomal therapy nurse), Am. Soc. of Parenteral and Enteral Nutrition, Nat. League Nursing, Oreg. Nurses' Assn., No. Calif. Clin. Nurse Specialist Group (pres.), Blue Key, Sigma Theta Tau, Delta Epsilon Sigma. Home: 1310 Stonehaven Dr West Linn OR 97068 Office: Palo Alto VA Med Ctr Surg Svc 112 3801 Miranda Ave Palo Alto CA 94304

BUSCH, JOYCE IDA, small business owner; b. Madera, Calif., Jan. 24, 1934; d. Bruno Harry and Ella Fae (Absher) Toschi; m. Fred O. Busch, Dec. 14, 1956; children: Karen, Kathryn, Kurt. BA in Indsl. Arts & Interior Design, Calif. State U., Fresno, 1991. Cert. interior designer Calif. Stewardess United Air Lines, San Francisco, 1955-57; prin. Art Coordinates, Fresno, 1982—, Busch Interior Design, Fresno, 1982—; art cons. Fresno Community Hosp., 1981-83; docent Fresno Met. Mus., 1981-84. Treas. Valley Children's Hosp. Guidance Clinic, 1975-79, Lone Star PTA, 1965-84; mem. Mothers Guild San Joaquin Mem. Hosp., 1984-88. Mem. Am. Soc. Interior Designers, Illuminating Engring. Soc. N.Am. Republican. Roman Catholic. Club: Sunnyside Garden (pres. 1987-88).

BUSCH, MARY SUZANNE, civil engineer; b. Stillwater, Okla., Dec. 31, 1958; d. Randall L. and Doris V. (Patton) Cain; m. Philip W. Dougharty, May 25, 1980 (div. June 1987); 1 child, Kristina Paige; m. Robert D. Busch, July 29, 1990; 1 child, Michelle M. BSCE, U. N.Mex., 1981. Registered profl. engr. Design engr. Wilson & Co., Albuquerque, 1981-82; engr. tech. U.S. Army Corps of Engrs., Albuquerque, 1983; design engr. Bovay Engrs., Albuquerque, 1985-88; transp. project mgr. City of Albuquerque, 1988-93, implementation mgr., 1993—. Mem. ASCE, N.Mex. Soc. Profl. Engrs. (Young Engr. of Yr. 1992, state dir. 1991-93, treas. 1994-95), Inst. Transp. Engr. Republican. Presbyterian. Office: City of Albuquerque PO Box 1293 Albuquerque NM 87103-1293

BUSCH, NANCY ELIZABETH, artist, educator; b. Manitowac, Wis. Sept. 7, 1944; d. Edgar Wilhelm and Dorothy Janette (Blust) Putz; m. Charles Nels Busch, Aug. 21, 1965; 1 son, Alexander. B.A. in Journalism, U. Mich., 1966, student Birmingham Bloomfield Art Assn., 1978-88, degree Ctr. for Creative Studies, 1985, post grad. U. Mich., 1987-88, MFA Wayne State U., 1990. Sales rep. Grosse Pointe News (Mich.), 1966-68; pres. Nels Advt. Co., Birmingham, Mich., 1968-75; pres., Busch & Morris, Birmingham, 1975-80, Busch & Assocs., Birmingham, 1980-88; prof. Instituto Federico Brandt, Caracas, Venezuela, 1991-93; cons. U. Mich. Devel. Bd., Ann Arbor, 1973-80. One Woman shows include Wayne State U., Mich. 1990, Sala Mendoza, Caracas, Venezuela, 1991, 93, Galeria Diners, Bogota, Columbia, 1993-94, Museo de Bellas Artes, Caracas, 1995; group shows include Creative Arts Ctr., Pontiac, Mich., 1990, Wayne State U., Mich., 1990, Willis Gallery, Detroit, 1990; pvt. collections include Aco Corp. Collection, Caracas, Univ. de los Andes, Bogota, Columbia, Museo de Arte Contemporaneo, Bogota. Recipient award of Excellence Nat. Public Rels. Soc. Am., 1975-80, Design award Internat. Graphis, 1980. Mem. Econs. Club of Detroit, Adcraft Club of Detroit, Am. Mktg. Assn., Southeastern Mich. Hosp. Assn. (awards for concept and creative devel. in reports, brochures and other collateral materials 1975-80), Am. Hosp. Assn., Mich. Hosp. Assn. (awards for reports, brochures and other materials 1975-80).

BUSELT, CLARA IRENE, religious organization administrator; b. Detroit, Jan. 30, 1921; d. Andrew and Bernice (Marcian) Kochanowski; m. Michael Leo Buselt, Apr. 18, 1940; children: Edwin, Nancy, Robert, John, Jane. Student, MacGregor Beauty Coll., Kansas City, 1939. Cosmetician various beauty shops, Leavenwoth, 1940-45; surp. dir. Sch. Lunch Program Sacred Heart Cafeteria, Immaculata High, Leavenworth, 1957-68; dietetic worker VA Med. Ctr., Leavenworth, 1968-81; office clk. Storage Box Inc., Leavenworth, 1987—; sr. Times corr., photographer Leavenworth Times, 1990—. Photographer (contest) Congress Americas, 1986. Mem. Sr. Coun. Park and Recreation, Leavenworth, 1988, Sr. Citizen Inc. Kitchen Band, 1993—. Recipient Gov. and First Lady Vol. award Gov. of Kans., 1990, Sr. Citizen of Yr. awrd Leavenworth County Coun. on Aging, 1994; named Silver Haired Legislator Leavenworth County, 1993. Mem. Women's Div. C. of C., Parish Council Sacred Heart Ch., Sacred Heart Alter Soc. (pres. 1977-87), Am. War Mothers (state pres. 1983-85, nat. color bearer 1985-87, nat. chaplain 1987-89), Cath. Literary Club (pres. 1983-85), Sch. Food Svc. Assn. (charter pres. 1958), St. John Hosp. Guild (pres. 1975-76), Loyal Christian Benefit Assn. (br. pres. 1977-88, nat. trustee 1981—), Daughters Isabella, Arch Diocese Coun. (pres. 1981-83), Nat. Assn. Ret. Fed. Employees, Loyal Christian Benefit Assn. (br. pres. 1977—), Ret. Eagles Activity Club (v.p. 1991-93, pres. 1993—). Home: 1413 S 16th St Leavenworth KS 66048-2914

BUSEMAN, KATHLEEN ANNE, ophthalmology nurse; b. Milbank, S.D., Nov. 4, 1954; m. Donald Ray Buseman, Aug. 21, 1976; children: Nicole, Sarah. RN, Sioux Valley Sch. of Nursing, Sioux Falls, S.D., 1976. RN, S.D.; cert. in ophthalmology. Staff RN Sioux Valley Hosp., Sioux Falls, S.D., 1976-78, asst. head nurse, 1978-81; surg. asst. Dr. Byron Hohm, Ophthalmology, Ltd., Sioux Falls, 1981-85; office nurse and insvc. coord. Ophthalmology, Ltd., Sioux Falls, 1985-92, nursing supr., 1993—; organizer, presenter insvcs. for area nursing homes and profl. mtgs. Mem. Am. Soc. Ophthalmic RNs. Home: 3909 S Fairhall Ave Sioux Falls SD 57106-1738 Office: Ophthalmology Ltd 1200 S Euclid Ave Sioux Falls SD 57105-0429

BUSH, BARBARA PIERCE, volunteer, wife of former President of the United States; b. Rye, N.Y., June 8, 1925; d. Marvin and Pauline (Robinson) Pierce; m. George Herbert Walker Bush, Jan. 6, 1945; children: George Walker, John Ellis, Neil Mallon, Marvin Pierce, Dorothy Walker. Student, Smith Coll., 1943-44; hon. degrees, Stritch Coll., Milw., 1981, Mt. Vernon Coll., Washington, 1981, Hood Coll., Frederick, Md., 1983, Howard U., Washington, 1987, Judson Coll., Marion, Ala., 1988, Bennett Coll., Greensboro, N.C., 1989, Smith Coll., 1989, Morehouse Sch. Medicine, 1989. Author: C. Fred Story; Millie's Book; Barbara Bush: A Memoir, 1994. Hon. chair adv. bd. Reading is Fundamental; hon. mem. Bus. Coun. for Effective Literacy; mem. adv. coun. Soc. of Meml. Sloan-Kettering Cancer Ctr.; hon. mem. bd. dirs. Children's Oncology Svcs. of Met. Washington, The Washington Home, The Kingsbury Ctr.; hon. chmn. nat. adv. coun. Literacy Vols. of Am., Nat. Sch. Vols. Program; sponsor Laubach Literacy Internat.; nat. hon. chmn. Leukemia Soc. of Am.; hon. mem. bd. trustees Morehouse Sch. of Medicine; hon. nat. chmn. Nat. Organ Donor Awareness Week, 1982-86; pres. Ladies of the Senate, 1981-88; mem. women's com. Smithsonian Assocs., Tex. Fedn. of Rep. Women, life mem., hon. mem.; hon. chairperson for the Nat. Com. on Literacy and Edn. United Way, Barbara Bush Found. for Family Literacy, Washington Parent Group Fund, Girls Clubs of Am., 10th anniversay Harvest Nat. Food Bank Network; hon. chmn. Nat. Com. for the Prevention of Child Abuse and Childhelp U.S.A.; hon. pres. Girl Scouts U.S; hon. chair Nat. Com. for Adoption; mem. bd. trustees Mayo Clinic Found.; hon. chair Read Am., Boarder Baby Project; mem. bd. visitors M. D. Anderson Cancer Ctr.; hon. chair Leukemia Soc. Am., Children's Literacy Initiative; hon. mem. Reading is Fundamental; ambassador at large Americares; honorary mem. Barbara Bush Found. for Family Literacy. Recipient Nat. Outstanding Mother of Yr. award, 1984, Woman of Yr. award USO, 1986, Disting. Leadership award United Negro Coll. Fund 1986, Disting. Am. Woman award Coll. Mt. St. Joseph, 1987. Mem. Tex. Fedn. Rep. Women (life), Internat. II Club (Washington), Magic Circle Rep. Women's Club (Houston), YWCA. Episcopalian. Office: 10000 Memorial Dr Houston TX 77024

BUSH, CRYSTAL REED, financial planner; b. Chgo., Dec. 14, 1957; d. Alonzo and Elmethra (Luster) Reed; m. Tony Bush, Aug. 12, 1989. BA in History, Roosevelt U., 1979; postgrad., DePaul U. Tchr. Chgo. Bd. Edn., 1979-90; pres. Buree Assocs., Chgo., 1990—. Fin. editor The Leguenet, 1991; contbr. articles to jours. Treas., chair program com. Women's Entrepreneur Network, Chgo., 1990-91; treas. League of Black Women, Chgo., 1991-92. Recipient Exceptional Contbn. award to Afro-Am. Cmty. AT&T, 1991, 92, 93. Home: 8644 S Kenwood Ave Chicago IL 60619 Office: Buree Assocs PO Box 6253 Chicago IL 60680-6253

BUSH, EMILY VAN DOREN, health and nutrition consultant; b. Portsmouth, Ohio, Oct. 30, 1941; d. John William and Mary Elizabeth (Van Doren) B.; m. Tom Bennett, Dec. 28, 1963 (div. Oct. 1975); 1 child, Matthew Terrance Bennett; m. Gary Zuckett, Aug. 5, 1976 (div. June 1992). BS, U. Mich., 1963. Lic. wholistic health educator, reflexologist, nutritional cons. Sec. to pres. Trailways of New Eng., Boston, 1963-64; sec. to Pres.'s asst. White House, Washington, 1965-66; dir. tutor Home Study Program, Wheaton, Md., 1966-68; tchr. Montgomery County Adult Edn., Rockville, Md., 1968-70; prodr., editor Change Newsletter, Boyds, Md., 1972-73; campaign mgr. Dem. com., Washington, 1967-71; prodr. Comty. Market Catalog, Louisa, Va., 1974-75; owner, mgr. The Lotus Shoppe, Pullman, W.Va., 1977-84; wholistic health consultant Wellness, Parkersburg, W.Va., 1984-88; dir. LIFE Conf. Ctr., Pullman, 1989-93; pres. bd., mgr. WEBS Women Ctr., Athens, Ohio, 1993—. Home: Rt 3 Box 452 Glouster OH 45732

BUSH, GAGE, ballet mistress. Ballet mistress Joffrey II Dancers, N.Y.C., 1990—. Office: The Joffrey Ballet 130 W 56th St New York NY 10019-3818*

BUSH, JOANNE TADEO, financial consultant; b. Norristown, Pa., May 17, 1947; d. I.C. and Anne (DeJohn) Arena; 1 child, Ryan J. Tadeo; m. David F. Bush, Oct. 15, 1989. BS in Acctg. cum laude, Villanova U., 1979; MBA in Taxation, Drexel U., 1982. Lic. securities broker, fin. cons. Adminstrv. asst. Cen. Montgomery Mental Health and Mental Retardation Ctr., Norristown, 1970-80; grad. teaching asst. Drexel U., Phila., 1981-82; lectr. Pa. State U., Abington, 1982-83; asst. prof. Ursinus Coll., Collegeville, Pa., 1883-84; fin. cons. Merrill Lynch, West Chester, Pa., 1984—. Active Bus. and Industry Coun., Exton, Pa., 1988—; program chair, charity ball com., West Chester; vol. YMCA. Mem. Rotary, Alpha Sigma Lambda, Beta Gamma Sigma, Phi Kappa Phi. Office: Merrill Lynch High And Market St West Chester PA 19382

BUSH, JUNE LEE, real estate executive; b. Philippi, W.Va., Sept. 20, 1942; d. Leland C. and Dolly Mary (Costello) Robinson; m. Jerry Lee Coffman, June 15, 1963 (div. 1970); 1 child, Jason Lance; m. Richard Alfred Bush, May 20, 1972. Grad., Fairmont State Coll., 1962, Dale Carnegie, Anaheim, Calif., 1988. Exec. sec. McDonnell Douglas, Huntington Beach, Calif., 1965-72; adminstrv. asst. Mgmt. Resources, Inc., Fullerton, Calif., 1978-80; bldg. mgr. Alfred Gobar Assocs., Brea, Calif., 1980—; treas. Craig Park East, Fullerton, 1982, bd. dirs., 1982-84. Author instrn. manual Quality Assurance Secretarial Manual, 1971. Sec. PTA, La Palma, 1974. Mem. Gamma Chi Chi. Home: 6600 E Canyon Hills Rd Anaheim Hills CA 92807-4239 Office: Alfred Gobar Assocs Inc 721 W Kimberly Ave Placentia CA 92670-6343

BUSH, KATE (CATHERINE BUSH), singer, songwriter; b. Bexley, Kent, England, July 30, 1958; d. Robert John and Hannah (Daly) B. Albums: The Kick Inside, 1978, Lionheart, 1979, Never For Ever, 1980, The Dreaming, 1982, Hounds of Love, 1985, The Whole Story, 1987, The Sensual World, 1989, The Red Shoes, 1993; videos: Live at the Hammersmith Odeon, 1980, The Whole Story, 1987. Office: Columbia Records 550 Madison Ave New York NY 10022-3211*

BUSH, MARJORIE EVELYNN TOWER-TOOKER, educator, media specialist, librarian; b. Atkinson, Nebr., Mar. 12, 1925; d. Albert Ralph and Vera Marie (Rickover) Tower-Tooker; m. Louis T. Genung, Feb. 2, 1944 (dec. Jan. 1982); 1 son, Louis Thompson; m. Laurence Scott Bush, Sept. 22, 1984; 1 stepson, Roger A. Bush. Student U. Nebr.,1951, Wayne State Coll., 1942-47; BA Colo. State Coll., 1966, U. No. Colo., 1970; postgrad. Doane Coll., 1967-68, U. Utah, 1973-74, PhD (hon.), 1973. Elem. tchr. Atkinson Public Schs., 1958-69; adminstr. libraries and audiovisual communications Clay County Dist. I-C, Fairfield, Nebr., 1972-81; media specialist Albion (Nebr.) City Schs., 1981—; mem. Neb. Gov.'s White House Conf. on Libraries. Chmn. edn. adminstrv. bd. Park Hill United Meth. Ch., Denver, also pres.; sec. Denver Symphony Guild. Mem. NEA (life), Nebr., Colo. edn. assns., Assn. Childhood Edn. Internat., ALA, Nebr., Mountain Plains library assns., Nat. Council Tchrs. English, AAUW, Nebr. Ednl. Media Assn., Assn. Supervision and Curriculum Devel., Assn. Ednl. Communications and Tech., Internat. Visual Literacy Assn., Nat. Council Exceptional Children, Alumni Assn. U. No. Colo. (life charter), Women Educators Nebr., United Meth. Women (pres.), Am. Legion Aux., Nebr. Lay Citizens Edn. Assn. (exec.), Am. Nat. Cowbelles, Nebr. Cowbelles, DAR (regent 1971, dist. treas. 1968-71), Internat. Platform Assn., LWV, Women's Soc. Christian Service, Ak-Sar-Ben. Club: Windsor Gardens (Denver). Lodges: Opti-Mrs. (pres.), Optimists Internat., Columbine Optimists (pres. 1987-88), Eastern Star. Home: 9655 E Center Ave Denver CO 80231-1276

BUSH, MELINDA JOHNSON, publisher; b. Champaign, Ill., June 14, 1942; d. Maurice R. and Margaret B. Johnson. BS, U. Colo., 1962; postgrad., NYU, 1962-64, London Sch. Econs. and Polit. Sci., 1962-64; postgrad.

Advanced Mgmt. Program, Harvard U., 1984; D (hon.), Johnson & Wales U., 1993. Cert. hotel adminstr. With J. Walter Thompson, Advt., N.Y.C., 1962-64; pub. rels. Paul Bradley Assns., N.Y.C., 1964-66; with Ziff-Davis Pub. Co., N.Y.C., 1966—, mktg. dir. photography div., 1966-74, asst. to pres., 1974-76; pub. Hotel & Travel Index, N.Y.C., 1976—, v.p. bus. div., 1983-85; v.p. Murdoch Mags. div., pub. Hotel & Travel Index, News Group Publs., Inc., N.Y.C., 1985—; sr. v.p., group pub. Murdoch Mags., News America, Inc., N.Y.C., 1987-89; exec. v.p. directories Reed Travel Group; mem. exec. bd. Reed Travel Group div. Reed Internat.; disting. lectr. Cornell Hotel Sch., 1989; advisor Cornell U. Hotel Sch., Lausanne Hotel Sch.; advisor tourism programs U. Mass., New Sch. for Social Rsch., Culinary Inst. Am. (also mem. corp. bd.); columnist, frequent speaker and panelist at industry assns. and convs.; chmn. N.Y.C. Real Estae Devel. Conf. Author articles in field. Pres.'s Coun. Model Cities Task Force, 1970-72; founder, chmn. Photography Youth Found., 1973-76; mem. nat. bd. dirs. Am. Univ., Washington., Sun Resorts Inc., Master Media, Inc. Recipient Albert E. Koehl award for Disting. Lifetime Svc. to Hospitality Industry, Am. Hotel Sales Mgmt. Assn., 1994; named Woman of Yr. in Travel, Travel Ind. Assn. Am., 1980. Fellow Inst. Cert. Travel Agts. (bd. dirs., trustee); mem. Hotel Sales Mgmt. Assn. Internat. (bd. dirs.), Am. Hotel and Motel Assn. (trustee, cert. hotel adminstr.), Ednl. Inst. (trustee), Com. of 200 Women Entrepreneurs. Office: Reed Travel Group Divsn Reed Internat PLC 500 Plaza Dr Secaucus NJ 07094-3602

BUSH, SARAH ANN, school administrator, entertainment company executive; b. Oblong, Ill.; d. Arthur Jack and Anna Fay (Herron) B. B of Music Edn., Ill. Wesleyan U., 1978; MS in Music Adminstrn., U. Ill., Champaign, 1986. Cert. specialist kindergarten-12th grade music. Music supr., computer tchr. and coord. Selmaville Sch., Salem, Ill., 1978—; with pub. rels./mktg., prodr. Raymond Prodns., Inc., Nashville, 1989-93; pres., prodr. Am. Prodns., Inc., Salem, 1994—; adjudicator IGSMA, State of Ill. Chairperson Marion County Talent Show, Salem; mem. music com. 1st Christian Ch., Salem; oboist Centralia Cultural Soc., 1978-88; counselor music and ch. camps; bd. dirs. SCIL Cmty. Concert Assn., N.Y., 1978-90. Recipient Those Who Excel award Ill. State Bd. Edn., 1989, Award of Excellence, So. Ill. U., 1989, 90; named Salem Citizen of Month, Toastmasters and Salem T-C Paper, 1989. Mem. NEA, NAFE, Music Educators Nat. Conf. (state officer Ill. chpt., state chair soc. gen. music 1990-92), Ill. Music Edn. Assn. (state v.p. 1990—, adjudicator), Selmaville Edn. Assn., Sigma Alpha Iota (life, chorus dir. frat. edn. 1977). Office: Am Prodns Inc 1111 W Boone Salem IL 62881

BUSH, SARAH LILLIAN, historian; b. Kansas City, Mo., Sept. 17, 1920; d. William Adam and Lettie Evelyn (Burrill) Lewis; m. Walter Nelson Bush, June 7, 1946 (dec.); children: William Read, Robert Nelson. AB, U. Kans., 1941; BS, U. Ill., 1943. Clk. circulation dept. Kansas City Pub. Library, 1941-42, asst. librarian Paseo br., 1943-44; librarian Kansas City Jr. Coll., 1944-46; substitute librarian San Mateo County Library, Woodside and Portola Valley, Calif., 1975-77; various temporary positions, 1979-87; owner Metriguide, Palo Alto, Calif., 1975-78. Author: Atherton Lands, 1979, rev. edition 1987. Editor: Atherton Recollections, 1973. Pres., v.p. Jr. Librarians, Kansas City, 1944-46; courtesy, yearbook & historian AAUW, Menlo-Atherton branch (Calif.) Br.; asst. Sunday sch. tchr., vol. Holy Trinity Ch., Menlo Park, 1955-78; v.p., membership com., libr. chairperson, English reading program, parent edn. chairperson Menlo Atherton High Sch. PTA, 1964-73; founder, bd. dirs. Friends of Atherton Community Library, 1967—, oral historian, 1968—, chair Bicentennial event, 1976; bd. dirs. Menlo Park Hist. Assn., 1979-82, oral historian, 1973—; bd. dirs. Civic Interest League, Atherton, 1978-81; mem. hist. county commn. Town of Atherton, 1980-87; vol. Allied Arts Palo Alto Aux. to Children's Hosp. at Stanford, 1967—, oral historian, 1978—, historian, 1980—; vol. United Crusade, Garfield Sch., Redwood City, 1957-61, 74-88, Encinal Sch., 1961-73, program dir., chmn. summer recreation, historian, sec.; vol. Stanford Mothers Club, 1977-81, others; historian, awards chairperson Cub Scouts Boy Scouts Am.; founder Atherton Heritage Assn. 1989, bd. dirs., 1989—; mem. Guild Gourmet, 1971—. Recipient Good Neighbor award Civic Interest League, 1992. Mem. PTA (life), Mid-Peninsula History Consortium. Episcopalian.

BUSHNELL, CAROLYN SUZANNE, bank executive; b. L.A., Sept. 1, 1940; d. William Commodore Bushnell and Mary (Kunellis) Oviatt. AA, Mt. San Antonio Jr. Coll., Walnut, Calif., 1961; BA, San Francisco State U., 1964; MEd, U. LaVerne, 1977. Cert. secondary tchr., Calif.; cert. elem. tchr., Calif.; lic. real estate agt., Calif. High sch. tchr. Santa Maria (Calif.) Union High Sch. Dist., 1965-67, Torrance (Calif.) Unified Sch. Dist., 1967-79; office leasing specialist Matlow-Kennedy Corp., Torrance, 1979-83; property mgr./leasing agt. Huntington Seacliff Corp., Torrance, 1983-85; v.p. comml. div. Lewis W. Ground & Assocs., San Diego, Calif., 1985-88; asset mgr. Travelers Ins. Cos., Santa Monica, Calif., 1988-90; v.p., corp. officer Home Savs. Am., Irwindale, Calif., 1990-92; asset mgr., dept. head Plus Investments, Inc., L.A., 1993-94; pres. Bushnell & Assocs. Comml. Real Estate, Glendora, Calif., 1994—; cons. and lectr., U.S., Can., 1978—; nat. alternate del. Nat. Network Women in Comml. Real Estate, L.A. chpt., 1992; selection com. Fulbright/Hays Internat. Ednl. and Cultural Exch. program, L.A., 1979—. Pres. bd. dirs. YWCA, Torrance, 1971-74; pres. So. Calif. Overseas Tchrs. Orgn., 1981-83, South Bay League of So. Calif. Forensic Assn., 1971-73. Scholarship Fulbright-Hays Internat. Ednl. and Cultural Exch. program, 1978-79; Coe fellowship Pepperdine U., 1973. Mem. AAUW (chpt. legis. com. chairperson 1989), Fulbright Alumni Assn., Nat. Soc. DAR (nat. resolutions com. 1990—, vice chmn. 1994—). Democrat. Greek Orthodox. Home and Office: PO Box 38 Glendora CA 91740-0038

BUSHNELL, CATHARINE, marketing consulting firm executive; b. Pullman, Wash, July 2, 1950; d. David and Catharine Howe (Goodfellow) B.; m. H. Michael Sisson, Oct. 31, 1975. BS in Speech, Northwestern U., 1972. Prodn. mgr. Mike White Advt., Chgo., 1972; stage actress, Chgo., 1972-73; ptnr., dir. photography Mome, Raths & Outgrabe, Chgo., 1973-75; exec. v.p. Sisson Assocs., N.Y.C., 1975—; pres. Illusion Gallery, Creative Resource Co., N.Y.C., 1981—, The Sisson Group Inc., 1986—; v.p. Ea. European Merchandising Corp., 1992—, also bd. dirs.; mem. bd. dirs. Digital Mktg. Assocs., 1993—; faculty New Sch.-Parsons Sch. of Design, 1985-86. Photographer motion picture stills for various films, N.Y.C., 1975—; author: Raggedy Ann and Andy in the Tunnel of Lost Toys, 1980; Raggedy Ann and Andy and the Pirates of Outgo Inlet, 1981; Linda's Magic Window, 1981; Frannie's Magic Kazoo, 1982. Judge ann. student photog. portfolio rev. High Sch. of Art and Design, N.Y.C., 1979-83. Mem. Licensing Industry Assn., Internat. Photographers Motion Picture Industry, Internat. Soc. Photography (charter), Actors Equity Assn., Northwestern U. Alumnae Assn., Delta Zeta. Office: The Sisson Group Inc 300 E 40th St New York NY 10016-2188

BUSHNELL, DANA EILEEN DORSEY, philosophy educator; b. L.A., Nov. 8, 1958; d. William Eugene and Margaret Delores (Dorsey) B.; m. Brian Powell Holtsclaw, Sept. 9, 1986. Student, U. Md., Balt., 1976-78; BA, U. New Orleans, 1983; MA, Tulane U., 1986, PhD, 1989. Asst. prof. U. New Orleans, 1985-90, Edinboro (Pa.) U., 1990—. Vol. Am. Cancer Assn., Erie, Pa., 1992. Mem. ACLU, Am. Philos. Assn., Soc. Women Philosophy, Soc. Legal & Social Philosophy. Office: Edinboro U Philosophy Dept Edinboro PA 16444

BUSHO, ELIZABETH MARY, nurse, educator; b. Ellendale, Minn., Feb. 26, 1927; d. Ruben Oscar and Lillian Katherine (Gahagan) B. RN, Kahler Hosps. Sch. of Nursing, 1948. RN, Minn. Oper. rm. staff nurse, Minn., Calif., Colo., 1948-53; oper. rm. head nurse, Mt. Sinai Hosp., Mpls., 1953-61; asst. supr. oper. rm. St. Barnabas Hosp., Mpls., 1961-71; asst. dir. surg. svcs. St. Mary's Hosp., Rochester, Minn., 1971-80, dir., 1980-90; sr. cons. oper. rms. Mayo Med. Ctr., Rochester, 1990-92; ind. cons. surg. svcs., 1992—; instr. Rochester Community Coll. Developer course in oper. rm. nursing. Mem. adv. bd. Rochester Area Vocat. Tech. Inst., Rochester Community Coll., Sigma Theta Tau. Republican. Methodist. Office: 2100 Valkyrie Dr # 415 Rochester MN 55901-2449

BUSK, SHARON LEE, accountant, cattle farmer; b. Ft. Campbell, Ky., Dec. 17, 1964; d. George Victor and Mary Ann (Michener) Francis; m. Robert Patrick Busk, Nov. 26, 1988. BBA, James Madison U., 1986. CPA, Va. Tax acct. Best Products Co., Inc., Richmond, Va., 1987; bank reconciliation acct. Ultimate Savings Bank, Richmond, 1987-88; instr. acctg. Dominion Bus. Sch., Harrisonburg, Va., 1989-90; contr.-truss divsn. Skyline Bldg. Sys., Harrisonburg, 1990-91; fixed asset acct. Wampler-Longacre, Inc., subs. WLR Foods, Inc., Hinton, Va. Mem. Inst. Mgmt. Accts. (dir. membership attendance 1992-94, v.p. membership 1994—), Young Farmers Assn. Republican. Episcopalian. Home: RR 1 Box 80-d Mount Solon VA 22843-9715 Office: Wampler-Longacre Inc PO Box 300 Hinton VA 22831-0300

BUSKIRK, PHYLLIS RICHARDSON, retired economist; b. Queens, N.Y., July 19, 1930; d. William Edward and Amy A. Richardson; m. Allen V. Buskirk, Sept. 13, 1950; children: Leslie Ann, William Allen, Carol Amy, Janet Helen. AB cum laude, William Smith Coll., 1951. Rsch. asst. W.E. Upjohn Inst. for Employment Rsch., Kalamazoo, 1970-75, rsch. assoc., 1976-83, sr. staff economist, 1983-87. Co-editor Bus. Conditions in the Kalamazoo Area, Quar. Rev., 1979-84, asst. editor Bus. Outlook for West Mich., 1984-87. Mem. Civil Svc. Bd. City of Kalamazoo, 1977-91, chmn., 1981-91; trustee First Presbyn. Ch., Kalamazoo, 1984-87, chmn., 1985, 86, mgr. adminstrn. and fin., 1987-92; trustee Sr. Citizens Fund, Kalamazoo, 1984-88, corp. restructuring com. 1985-86. exec. bd. 1986-88; bd. dirs. Heritage Community Kalamazoo, 1988—; pres., bd. dirs. Westland Meadows, 1988-89, Golden Age, 1989-92, continuous quality improvement com., 1992—; bd. dirs. Kalamazoo County Futures Coms., 1987-89. Fellow Presbyn. Ch. Bus. Adminstrn. Assn.; mem. Nat. Assn. Ch. Bus. Adminstrn., P.E.O., Kalamazoo Network, YWCA. Home: 3324 Saint Antoine Ave Kalamazoo MI 49006-5522

BUSSEY, PATRICIA JEAN, interior designer, real estate company executive; b. Long Beach, Calif., Nov. 10, 1923; d. Charles Davenport and Nora Augustine (Bills) Hamilton; m. Henry Dillon, July 15, 1945 (dec. 1957); children: Patrick H., Michael C.; m. Frederick Ernest Bussey, Sept. 16, 1961. Student, U. Calif., San Francisco, 1963; real estate cert., Anthony's Sch., 1982. Sec. N. Am. Aviation, Inglewood, Calif., 1942-44, Juvenile and Adult Probation, Oakland, Calif., 1946-50; model May Co., Los Angeles, 1944-45; stenographer Los Angeles Hall Records, 1944-45; adminstrv. asst. ABMA Werner Von Braun, Oakland, 1950-52, Piper and Aero Commander Sales, Oakland, 1953-57; owner, pres. Paticia Bussey Interior Design, Oakland Castro Valley, Calif., 1957—; sales agt. Peter Mattie Co., San Francisco, 1982—; owner, mgr., apt. bldgs., restaurants. Bd. dirs. 4,000,000 Coop, Castro Valley, 1975-76. Republican. Clubs: Blackhawk (Danville, Calif.), Lakes (Palm Desert, Calif.).

BUSTEED, BEATRICE, financial planner; b. L.A., Jan. 8, 1938; d. Ignacio and Clemencia (Armijo) Val Verde; m. Donald J. Busteed, Jan. 23, 1982. AA, Trade Tech. Jr. Coll., 1957; BA, Calif. State U., L.A., 1974; MBA, Pepperdine U., 1983. Pvt. sec., bookkeeper E.S. Dulin, L.A., 1962-72, Neil Petree, 1968-73; sec., paralegal O'Melveny & Myers, 1973-86, personal fin. mgr., 1980-89; rep. Fin. Network Investment Corp., 1984—; conservator of person and estate of Alice N. O'Melveny, 1989—; trust administrator and co-trustee of John O'Melveny Lifetime Trust, 1989—. Rockwell Internat. fellow Pepperdine U., 1982. Mem. Internat. Assn. for Fin. Planning, Inst. Cert. Fin. Planners, Mensa (bd. dirs. greater L.A. area 1975-78), Phi Kappa Phi. Republican. Roman Catholic. Home: 5530 Thornburn St Apt 204 Los Angeles CA 90045-2140 Office: 3250 Wilshire Blvd Ste 900 Los Angeles CA 90010-1511

BUSTER, CAROLYN, owner, operator; b. Hammond, Ind., Feb. 28, 1942; d. Ernest Latin and Ada Mae (Brook) Forsythe. D of Culinary Arts, Johnson & Wales, Providence, 1991. Exec. sec. Youngstown Sheet & Tube Co., East Chgo., Ind., 1959-70; home economist, chef asst. The Bakery Restaurant, Chgo., 1970-75; co-owner The Cottage Restaurant, Calumet City, Ill., 1975-93; nat. food coord. Great Chefs TV Prodn., 1994—; bd. dirs. Les Dames Internat. Chgo. Chpt., 1980—, Am. Inst. Wine & Food, Chgo., 1985—; adv. bd. Lexington Inst., Chgo., 1986—. Mem. Am. Inst. Wine & Food, Les Dames d'Escoffier Internat., Internat. assn. Culinary Profls., Cert. Culinary Profls.

BUSTIN, BEVERLY MINER, state senator; b. Morrisville, Vt., Feb. 14, 1936; d. Donald Haze and Della Mae (Kenfield) Miner; children: Catherine Margaret, David Wayne. BS, Thomas Coll. Maine state senator, 1979—, chair joint select com. on alcoholism services, 1982-84, chair instl. services com., 1983-84, chair bus. and commerce commn., 1985-87. Mem. Kennebec County (Maine) Dem. Com., Hollowell (Maine) Dem. Com.; treas. Uplift, Inc., 1980-86; vice chair Kennebec County Regional Health Agy., 1984-88, chair audit program rev., 1987—, mem. banking and ins. com., 1987—, chair joint select com. on corrections, 1987—, chair Commn. on Overcrowding at AMHI-BMHI, 1987-89. Office: Maine State Senate State Capital Augusta ME 04330*

BUSWELL, DEBRA SUE, small business owner, programmer, analyst; b. Salt Lake City, Apr. 8, 1957; d. John Edward Ross and Marilyn Sue (Patterson) Potter; m. Randy James Buswell, AUg. 17, 1985; 1 child, Trevor Ryan. BA, U. Colo., Denver, 1978. Programmer, analyst Trail Blazer Systems, Palo Alto, Calif., 1980-83; data processing mgr. Innovative Concepts, Inc., San Jose, Calif., 1983-86; owner Egret Software, Milpitas, Calif., 1986—. Mem. IEEE, No. Calif. Pick Users. Home and Office: 883 Del Vaile Ct Milpitas CA 95035-4518

BUTA, MARY OPRITZA, retired business education educator; b. Youngstown, Ohio, Jan. 2, 1913; d. Daniel Pamfilie and Marina (Neaga) Opritza; m. Serafin Simon Buta, Mar. 5, 1949 (dec. 1989); 1 child, Mary Jeanette Buta Lomuscio. BS in Edn., Miami U., Oxford, Ohio, 1935; MA in Edn., NYU, 1940; postgrad., Youngstown (Ohio) State U., 1932-33, 73, Westminster Coll., New Wilmington, Pa., 1962. Cert. apprentice pharmacist, Ohio State Bd. Tchr. Bryan High Sch., Yellow Springs, Ohio, 1935-37, Meml. High Sch., Campbell, Ohio, 1937-43, Bliss Coll., Columbus, Ohio, 1944, Struthers (Ohio) High Sch., 1946-49, 53-81; tchr., treas. North High Sch., Youngstown, Ohio, 1952-53; confidential sec. Am. Embassy U.S. State Dept., Bucharest, Romania, 1949-50; dept. chmn. Struthers High Sch., 1976-81. Sponsor Nat. Honor Soc., Struthers High Sch.; active Struthers Girl Scouts, 1962-65. Named One of Outstanding Secondary Educators by Outstanding Secondary Educators of Am., 1973. Mem. AAUW (editor Youngstown chpt. bull. 1968-70), NEA (life), Mahoning Ret. Tchrs. Assn. (sec. 1981-83), Salem Hist. Soc. (life), Ohio Ret. Tchrs. Assn. (life), Nat. Ret. Tchrs. Assn., Office Strategic Svcs. Vets. (life), Raymond Molyneaux Hughes Soc. (personal accomplishments recognition cert. Miami U.), FDR Pensioners Club, Carmen Sylva Aux., Frat. Bus. Edn. (hon.), Delta Kappa Gamma Internat. Soc. (Gamma Epsilon chpt. honoring women educators 1974), Delta Pi Epsilon (life, hon. grad. bus. edn. 1948). Mem. Holy Trinity Romanian Orthodox Ch.

BUTCHER, AMANDA KAY, university administrator; b. Lansing, Mich., Oct. 25, 1936; d. Foster Eli and Mayme Lenore (Taft) Stuart; m. Claude J. Butcher, Aug. 24, 1957; 1 child, Mary Beth. BS in Bus., Cen. Mich. U., 1981. Office asst. Dept. Dairy Sci., East Lansing, Mich., 1966-76; bus. mgr. dept. pathology Coll. Vet. Medicine Mich. State U., East Lansing, 1976—. Mem. Adminstrv. Profl. Suprs. Assn. (v.p. 1982), Adminstrv. Profl. Assn. East Lansing (pres. 1976-80). Democrat. Home: 610 Emily Ave Lansing MI 48910-5404 Office: Mich State U Coll Vet Medicine A59 Vet Teaching Hosp East Lansing MI 48824-1314

BUTCHER, SUSAN HOWLET, dog kennel owner, sled dog racer; b. Boston, Dec. 26, 1954; d. Charles and Agnes (Young) B.; m. David Lee Monson. Driver 1st dog team to summit Mt. KcKinley, Alaska, 1979; winner among top 10 finishers Long Distance Sled Dog Races, Alaska and Minn., 1978-87; 5th pl. Iditarod Race, Anchorage and Nome, Alaska, 1980, 81, 2d pl., 1986, 87,88, 90, champion, winner 1st pl., 1986, 87, world record holder, 1986-87; champion, winner 1st pl. Coldfoot Classic Race, Brooks Range, Alaska, 1985; winner Iditarod, Alaska, 1988, Kusho 300, Bethel, Alaska, 1988, Portage 250, Alaska, 1988; bd. dirs. Iditarod Trail Com., Wasilla, Alaska, 1980-86, ambassador of good will Iditarod Sport of Sled Dog Racing, 1982—; mem. nutrition adv. panel Purina Pro Plan, St. Louis, 1986—; tech. advisor Allied Fibers, N.Y.C., 1985—. Contbr. articles to profl. jours. Hon. chmn. March of Dimes, Anchorage, 1986, Spl. Olympics, Anchorage, 1987. Named Musher of Yr. Team and Trail, N.H., 1987, one of Profl. Sports Women of Yr. Womens Sports Found., N.Y.C., 1987, Sports Woman of Yr., W.S.F, 1988, Sportswomen of Yr. U.S. Sports Acad.; recipient Victor award, Las Vegas, Nev., 1987, 88, legis. commendation States of Alaska and Mass., 1986-87, Moniqo Bedeaux prize French Sport Acad., 1989, Athletic Achievement award Tanguray, N.Y., 1989. Mem. Iditarod Trail Com., Iditarod Trail Blazers (life), Beargrease Race Com., Kuskokwim 300 Race Com. Club: Interior Dog Mushers (Manley, Alaska); Nome Kennel; Norton Sound Sled Dog. Office: Iditarod Trail Com PO Box 870800 Wasilla AK 99687*

BUTEAU, MICHELLE DIANE, energy company executive; b. Oakland, Calif., Mar. 6, 1952; d. Bernard Lamonthe and June (Dowler) B.; m. Barry Crawford Anderson, Nov. 1974 (div. 1982); 1 child, Damon Buteau-Anderson. BA in Liberal Arts, Cath. U. Am., 1974, MBA, Loyola/Notre Dame Coll., 1989. Dir. U.S. Summer Sch. Inst., U.S. Dept. State/USIA, Posnan, Poland, 1975-76; bookkeeper Internat. Energy Assocs. Ltd., Washington, 1980-83, rsch. assoc., 1983-85, project mgr., 1984-92, sr. cons., 1987-89, mgr. emergency planning, 1992—, sr. project mgr., prin. cons. hydroelectric plant, New Martinsville, W. Va. Actress and dir. dinner theatres, 1974—. Intern to Senator Everett M. Dirksen, Washington, 1968; pres. Cath. Youth Orgn., Bethesda, Md., 1968-70. Mem. NAFE, Am. Mgmt. Assn., Nat. Emergency Mgmt. Agy., Women's Coun. on Energy and the Environment. Buddhist. Avocations: acting, dancing, singing, writing. Office: Ogden Power Corp 3211 Jermantown Rd Fairfax VA 22030-2807

BUTERA, ANN MICHELE, consulting company executive; b. Bayside, N.Y., Apr. 27, 1958; d. Gaetano Thomas and Josephine (Inserro) B. BA, L.I. U., 1979; MBA, Adelphi U., 1982. Dept. mgr. Abraham & Straus Stores, Huntington, N.Y., 1978-80; mgmt. cons. Chase Manhattan Bank N.A., Lake Success, N.Y., 1980-83, Nat. Bankcard Corp., Melville, N.Y., 1983-84; pres. Whole Person Project, Inc., Elmont, N.Y., 1984—. Bd. dirs. Nassau County coun. Girl Scouts U.S., 1985—. Recipient Bus. Achievement award Women on the Job, 1990. Mem. NAFE, ASTD, Fin. Women Internat., L.I. Networking Entrepreneurs (pres. 1984—), North Shore Bus. Forum, L.I. Ctr. for Bus. and Profl. Women. Republican. Roman Catholic. Home and Office: Whole Person Project Inc. 82 Cerenzia Blvd Elmont NY 11003-3631

BUTERAKOS, KATHLEEN ANN, assistant principal; b. Jamaica, N.Y., Feb. 28, 1951; d. William Michael and Ann Marilyn (Parrucci) Maurer; m. James Nicholas Buterakos, Aug. 18, 1973; 1 child, Sophia Anndrina. BA in English and Edn., Queens Coll., 1972, MS in Edn., 1977; postgrad., SUNY, Albany, 1978, Brigham Young U., 1978, McPherson Coll., 1978; Profl. Diploma in Ednl. Supervision, St. John's U., Jamaica, N.Y., 1982; postgrad., Adelphi U., 1983, U. Mont., 1986. Cert. tchr., adminstr., supr., N.Y. Tchr. Elijah Clark Jr. High Sch., South Bronx, N.Y., 1972-75, Intermediate Sch. 291, Bklyn., 1975; tchr., dean, asst. prin. Jean Nuzzi Jr. High Sch., Queens Village, N.Y., 1975-83; asst. prin. William Cowper Intermediate Sch., Maspeth, N.Y., 1983-94; asst. prin.-in-charge William Cowper Intermediate Sch. Annex, Elmhurst, N.Y., 1994—. Doctoral fellow Hofstra U., 1990. Mem. ASCD, Nat. Sci. Tchrs. Assn., Nat. Coun. Tchrs. English, Internat. Reading Assn., Phi Delta Kappa. Roman Catholic. Office: William Cowper Intermediate Sch Annex 76-05 51st Ave Elmhurst NY 11373

BUTLER, ADRIENNE BUUCK, pediatrician; b. Cambridge, Mass., Sept. 12, 1946; d. Winfried Paul and Eileen Ann (Redmond) Buuck; m. John E. Butler, Dec. 27, 1970; children: John E. Jr., Carole L., Michael R. AB in Chemistry summa cum laude, Regis Coll., 1968; MD, U. Vt., 1972. Diplomate Am. Bd. Pediats. Commd. U.S. Army, 1971, advanced through grades to lt. col.; pediatrician U.S. Army, various locations, 1972-82; pvt. practice Waycross, Ga., 1982—; dep. health dir. Southeast Health Unit, Waycross, 1984—. Fellow Am. Acad. Pediats. (mem. Ga. chpt., regional facilitator CATCH 1992—, chair adolescent com. 1994—). Roman Catholic. Office: Southeast Health Unit 1101 Church St Waycross GA 31501

BUTLER, ALICE CLAIRE, rehabilitation nurse; b. Lander, Wyo., Sept. 9, 1925; d. Donald A. and Violet C. (Carney) Sherlock; m. Harry Wallace Butler, July 25, 1958 (wid. Feb. 1994); children: Gladys Norene, Linda Marie, Janet Christine, Mary Alice, David Paul, Anna Louise, Rebecca Ruth, Philip Clyde, John Glenn, James Sheldon. ADN, Penn Valley Community Coll., 1976; AA, Kansas City (Mo.) Jr. Coll., 1949; BA in Elem. Edn., U. Mo., Kansas City, 1986. RN, Mo.; cert. rehab. nurse. Charge nurse Rehab. Inst., Kansas City; asst. dir. nursing Children's Mercy Hosp., Kansas City, 1977-81; staff relief nurse Clara Manor Nursing Home, Kansas City; part-time nursing coord. Park Lane Med. Ctr., Kansas City. Mem. Assn. Rehab. Nurses, Mo. League for Nursing. Home: 4311 Campbell St Kansas City MO 64110-1621

BUTLER, ANNE LAWRASON, writer, bed and breakfast operator; b. New Orleans, Apr. 5, 1944; d. Charles Mathews and Katharine Minor (Pipes) B.; m. Miles Poindexter III, May 1, 1968 (div. 1978); 1 child, Chase Mathews; m. Charles Murray Henderson, Aug. 20, 1990; 1 child, Charles Stewart Hamilton. BA, Sweet Briar Coll., 1965; MA, Humboldt State U., 1970. Asst. editor AAA Tour Books, Washington, 1965-68, Calif. Living Mag., Monterey, 1968-70; editor Country Roads Mag., St. Francisville, La., 1985-90; owner/operator Butler Greenwood Plantation, St. Francisville, Calif., 1992—; guest lectr. on crime various univs. Author: Angola - Louisiana State Penitentiary, 1991, Dying to Tell - Crime and Consequence, 1992, The Little Chase and Big Fat Aunt May books, 1978, 80 (1st place for juvenile fiction Deep South Writers Comp., U. S.W. La.), More than a Cookbook. Vol. docent Audubon Pilgrimage, St. Francisville, 1970—; mem., vol. West Feliciana Hist. Soc., 1970—; bd. dirs. West Feliciana Civic Club, 1970—, West Feliciana Hosp., 1975; pres. St. Francisville Overnight, 1993-94; active West Feliciana Parish Tourist Comm., 1995. Mem. La. Bed and Breakfast Assn., St. Francisville C. of C. Democrat. Episcopalian. Home: 8345 US Hwy 61 Saint Francisville LA 70775

BUTLER, BRETT, comedian, actress; b. Montgomery, AL, 1958; d. Roland Decatur Anderson, Jr. and Carol; adoptive parent Bob Butler; m. Charles Wilson, 1978 (div. 1981); m. Ken Ziegler, 1987. Waitress Houston, TX, 1981-82; stand-up comedian, 1982—. star of Grace Under Fire, 1992—. Office: ABC 2020 Ave of the Stars Los Angeles CA 90067*

BUTLER, CAROL KING, advertising executive; b. Charlotte, N.C., May 29, 1952; d. Charles Snowden Watts and Marion (Thomas) King; m. James Rodney Butler, Aug. 12, 1972 (div. 1975). Student U. N.C., Greensboro, 1970-72. Sales rep. Sta.-WKIX, Raleigh, N.C., 1978-82, N.C. Box, Inc., Raleigh, 1982-84; radio sales account exec. WRAL-FM, Raleigh, 1984-88, team sales mgr., 1989; prin. Butler-Smith Assocs., Raleigh, 1988-89; ind. programming and video producer, Raleigh, 1989-90; prin., freelance presentation/video script writer, producer and sales person, Carol Butler Sales Writer, 1991—. Mem. NAFE. Democrat. Mem. Unity Ch. Avocations: water skiing, golf, tennis, boating, bicycling. Home: 6616 English Ivy Ln Raleigh NC 27615

BUTLER, GLORIA FAY, elementary education educator; b. Alexandria, Va., Oct. 4, 1948; d. Thomas Alfred and Shirley Mae (Waggy) B. BS, James Madison U., 1970; MEd, U. Va., 1977. Tchr. Prince William County Schs., Manassas, Va., 1970—; grade level chairperson Dale City Elem., Woodbridge, Va., 1992-94, quality mgmt. chairperson, 1993-94; mem. curriculum restructuring team in math. Prince William County Sch., Manassas, 1992-93. Reviewer, cons.: (tchr.'s manual) Virginia, 1991. Treas. Historic Prince William, Manassas, 1992. Mem. NEA, Va. Edn. Assn., Prince William Edn. Assn., Nat. Coun. Math. Tchrs., Greater Washington Reading Coun., Phi Delta Kappa. Baptist. Home: 15449 Windsong Ln Dumfries VA 22026 Office: Dale City Elem 14550 N Brook Dr Woodbridge VA 22193

BUTLER, GRACE CAROLINE, medical administrator; b. Lima, Peru, Dec. 19, 1937; (parents Am. citizens); d. Everett Lyle and Mary Isabella (Sloatman) Gage; m. William Langdon Butler, Dec. 28, 1961; children: Mary Dyer, William Langdon Jr. AA, Stephens Coll., 1957; BS in Nursing, Columbia U., 1960; postgrad., Union County Coll., 1984. Head nurse N.Y. State Psychiat. Inst., N.Y.C., 1960-61; clin. instr. Columbia U., N.Y.C., 1960-61; staff nurse, educator Vis. Nurse Service, Summit, N.J., 1962-63; health adminstr. Eagle Island Girl Scout Camp, Tupper Lake, N.Y., 1964; evening supr. Ashbrook Nursing Home, Scotch Plains, N.J., 1968-72;

teaching asst. Scotch Plains-Fanwood (N.J.) Sch. System, 1975-78; staff nurse Westfield (N.J.) Med. Group, 1980-82, head nurse, 1982-83, supr., 1983-84; office adminstr. Harris S. Vernick, MD, PA, Westfield, 1984-86, corp. v.p., office adminstr., 1986-88; corp. v.p., office adminstr. Assocs. in Medicine, Westfield, 1988-90; pvt. researcher, 1990—; diabetes educator Boehringer Manneheim Diagnostics, 1984—, Eli Lilly and Co., Indpls., 1984—; microbiologist tester Med. Technol. Corp., Somerset, N.J., 1984—; computer advisor Cordis Corp., Miami, 1985—. Asst. leader Girl Scouts of America, Fanwood, N.J., 1970-73; religious educator All Saints Episcopal Ch., Scotch Plains, 1967-82; bd. dirs. PTA, Scotch Plains, Fanwood, 1973-79; social dir. Highland Swim Club, Scotch Plains, 1973-78. Mem. League For Ednl. Advancement for Registered Nurses, Am. Soc. of Notaries, Columbia U./Presbyn. Hosp. Sch. of Nursing Alumni Assn. Republican. Episcopalian. Home: 125 Russell Rd Fanwood NJ 07023-1063

BUTLER, JILL D., accountant; b. Lawton, Okla., Oct. 25, 1962; d. Bliss P. and Ramona J. (Rheam) Sheldon; m. Paul A. Butler, Aug. 17, 1985. BS in Bus. Acctg., Okla. State U., 1985. Staff acct. Tracy Luckey Co., Harlem, Ga., 1986-90; cost acct. Club Car, Inc., Harlem, Ga., 1990—. Mem. Inst. Mgmt. Accts. (dir. newsletter 1993-94, v.p. comm. 1994—). Republican. Office: Club Car Inc 4152 Washington Rd Augusta GA 30907

BUTLER, JOAN MARIE, physical education educator; b. Hanover, N.H., Jan. 22, 1958; d. James Francis and M. Jean (Chagnon) B. BS in Phys. Edn. magna cum laude, Keene State Coll., 1980. Cert. tchr., N.H. Phys. edn. instr. Keene (N.H.) State Coll. Lab. Sch., 1981; phys. edn. instr. and athletic dir. Chesterfield (N.H.) Cen. and Westmoreland Elem. Schs., 1981-82; phys. edn, instr. Hanover St. and Sch. St. Schs., Lebanon, N.H., 1983-87; phys. edn. instr. Prince William County Sch. Dist., Dumfries, Va., 1987-89, Grantham Village (N.H.) Sch., 1989-90, Canaan (N.H.) Elem. Sch. and Enfield (N.H.) Village Sch., 1990—; children's daycare programmer and waterfront supr., LaSalette, Enfield, summer, 1981-84; water safety swimming instr. Lebanon Meml. Pool, summer, 1985-87, S. Run Recreation Ctr., Burke, Va., Jan.-July, 1989; cultural arts activity com. chair person, Hanover Str. Elem. Sch., Lebanon, 1985-87; cross-country ski instr. Eastman Ski Touring Ctr., Grantham (N.H.), Dec.-Mar., 1989—; water safety swimming instr., swim team coach, Eastman Recreation Dept., Grantham, June-Aug., 1989-93; water safety instr. Colby Sawyer Coll., New London, 1993—. Sec. Lebanon Recreation Adv. Bd., Lebanon, N.H., 1987. Recipient Golden Apple Tchr. award, Enfield Village Sch., 1992. Mem. AAHPERD, N.H. Assn. Health, Phys. Edn., Recreation and Dance (Tchr. Merit award 1992). Home: PO Box 45 Georges Mills NH 03751-0045 Office: Canaan Elem Sch School St Canaan NH 03741

BUTLER, JODY TALLEY, gifted education educator; b. Columbus, Ga., Mar. 14, 1958; d. Bill Ray and Jacqueline (Hay) T.; m. Danny Butler. BS in Edn., West Ga. Coll., 1979, MEd, 1982; EdD, Auburn U., 1988. Cert. tchr., Ga. Tchr. Cen. Primary Sch., Carrollton, 1979-88; tchr. gifted student program QUEST Cen. Middle Sch., Carrollton, 1988—; co-owner Hay's Mill Antiques, Ga., 1994—. Named Finalist for Outstanding Dissertation award, 1989. Mem. Internat. Reading Assn., Ga. Ptnrs. in Edn. Coun., Carroll County Community Chorus, Phi Delta Kappa (Dissertation of Yr. award 1989), Phi Kappa Phi, Alpha Gamma Delta. Presbyterian. Office: Ctrl Middle Sch 155 Whooping Creek Rd Carrollton GA 30116-8999

BUTLER, LINDA RAE AXELSON, recreational facility manager; b. Statesboro, Ga., May 22, 1959; d. Joseph Allen and Malcolm Rae (Smith) Axelson; m. Aug. 29, 1981 (div. Feb. 1989). BA in Spanish, Baker U., 1981. Acct. Lois A. Brozey, CPA, San Diego, 1981-82; bus. mgr. San Diego Chicken, Inc., 1983; discount brokerage mgr. Union Bank and Trust, Bartlesville, Okla., 1984; bus. mgr. ARCO Arena, Sacramento, 1985-86, box office mgr., 1987-91; box office mgr. San Diego Sports Arena, 1991-92, Arrowhead Pond of Anaheim, Calif., 1993—; cons. Don Chargin Boxing Prodns., L.A., 1987—. Recipient scholarship Baker Univ., 1981. Mem. Box Office Mgrs. Internat., Alpha Chi Omega (sch. com. chmn. 1981), Sigma Delta Pi, Alpha Mu Gamma. Republican. Presbyterian. Home: 1105 Woodside Dr Placentia CA 92670-3719 Office: Arrowhead Pond of Anaheim 2695 E Katella Ave Anaheim CA 92806-5904

BUTLER, MARGARET KAMPSCHAEFER, retired computer scientist; b. Evansville, Ind., Mar. 7, 1924; d. Otto Louis and Lou Etta (Rehsteiner) Kampschaefer; m. James W. Butler, Sept. 30, 1951; 1 child, Jay. AB, Ind. U., 1944; postgrad., U.S. Dept. Agr. Grad. Sch., 1945, U. Chgo., 1949, U. Minn., 1950. Statistician U.S. Bur. Labor Statistics, Washington, 1945-46, U.S. Air Forces in Europe, Erlangen and Wiesbaden, Germany, 1946-48; statistician U.S. Bur. Labor Statistics, St. Paul, 1949-51; mathematician Argonne (Ill.) Nat. Lab., 1948-49, 51-80, sr. computer scientist, 1980-92; dir. Argonne Code Ctr. and Nat. Energy Software Ctr. Dept. Energy Computer Program Exch., 1960-91; spl. term appointee Indsl. Tech. Devel. Ctr. Argonne Nat. Lab.; cons. AMF Corp., 1956-57, OECD, 1964, Poole Bros., 1967. Author: Careers for Women in Nuclear Science and Technology, 1992; editor Computer Physics Communications, 1969-80; contbr. (chpt.) The Application of Digital Computers to Problems in Reactor Physics, 1968, Advances in Nuclear Sci. and Technology, 1976; contbr. articles to profl. publs. Treas. Timberlake Civic Assn., 1958; rep. mem. nomination coml Hinsdale (Ill.) Caucus, 1961-62; coord. 6th dist. ERA, 1973-80; del. Rep. Nat. Conv., 1980; bd. mgr. DuPage dist. YWCA Met. Chgo, 1987-90; mem. computer and info systems adv. bd. Coll. DuPage, 1987—; mem. industry adv. bd. computer sci. dept. Bradley U., 1988-91; vice-chair Ill. Women's Polit. Caucus, 1987-90; chair voter's svc. LWV, Burr-Ridge-Willowbrook, 1991-93. Recipient Cert. Leadership, Met. YWCA, Chgo., 1985, Merit award Chgo. Assn. Technol. Socs., 1988; named to Fed. 100, 1991; named Outstanding Woman Leader of DuPage County Sci., Tech. and Health Care, 1992; recipient spl. award Am. Nuclear Soc. Math and Comp. divsn., 1992. Fellow Am. Nuclear Soc. (mem. publs. com. 1965-71, bd. dirs. 1976-79, exec. com. 1977-78, chmn. bylaws and rules com., 1979-82, profl. women in ANS com. 1991-93, reviewer for publs.); mem. Assn. Computing Machinery (exec. com., sec. Chgo. chpt. 1963-65, publs. chmn. nat. conf. 1968, reviewer for publs.), Assn. Women in Sci. (pres. Chgo. area chpt. 1982, exec. bd. 1985-87), Nat. Computer Conf. (chmn. Pioneer Day com. 1985, tech. program chmn. 1987). Republican. Home: 17w139 Hillside Ln Hinsdale IL 60521-6062

BUTLER, MARTHA L., state official, accountant; b. Wilmington, Ohio, Sept. 15, 1952; d. William Delbert and Stella Mae (Farmer) B. BS, Ohio State U., 1986. CPA, Ohio. Bookkeeper Sta. WMWM Radio, Wilmington, Ohio, 1970-71; legal sec. Dennis & Cartwright, LPA, Wilmington, 1971-72; com. sec. Ohio Senate, Columbus, 1973-76, legis. aide, 1977-80, asst. clk., 1981-84, clk., 1985—. Acct., mgr. Rep. Senate Campaign Com., Columbus, 1983—; newsletter editor Clintonville Bapt. Ch., Columbus, 1989-94; mem. Ohio W.Va. YMCA Youth in Govt. Com., St. George, W.Va., 1985-95, chair scholarship com., 1994-95; vol. Whetstone Park of Roses, Columbus, 1993-94. Scholar Kellogg Found., 1991. Mem. Am. Soc. Legis. Clks. and Secs. (chair membership 1992), Ohio Soc. CPAs. Office: Ohio Senate State House Columbus OH 43215

BUTLER, MARY LOU, artist; b. La Crosse, Wis., Oct. 9, 1943; d. Winston Burnette and Mary Louise (Hengel) Reider; m. John D. Johnson, Aug. 19 (div. 1971); children: John David, Stephen Andrew; m. Rolland Paul Butler, June 3 (dec. June 9, 1993); 1 stepchild: Bonnie Ann Kennedy. Student, Can. Coll., Woodside, Calif., 1969-70, Foothill Coll., Los Altos Hills, Calif., 1973-74, DeAnza Coll., Cupertino, Calif., 1974-75. Sec. Gateway Transp. Co., La Crosse, 1962; asst. supr. Allis Chalmers Mfg. Co., La Crosse, 1962-66; keypunch operator Dalmo Victor, Belmont, Calif., 1966-68; bookkeeper J.D. Johnson, 1968-70; elec. data processing Hubbard & Johnson Lumber Co., Redwood City, Calif., 1970-73; from computer operator to systems analyst, programmer Farinon Electric, San Carlos, 1973—. Exhibited in group shows at Sidestreet Gallery, Sandpoint, Idaho, Many Hands Gallery, Missoula, Mont., Maries Art-eries, Missoula, MONAC Western Art Show, Spokane, Wash., Libby (Mont.) C. of C., Wilderness Art Coun., The Rose Petaler, Sandpont, Missoula Mus. Arts, Tumalo Creek Gallery, Bend, Oreg. Recipient best of show award WAC Spring Art Show, 1986; winner Sanders County Task Force logo contest. Mem. Wilderness Arts Coun., Nat. Mus. Women in Arts. Republican. Home: 231 Klakken Rd Noxon MT 29853

BUTLER, NANCY TAYLOR, gender equity specialist, program director; b. Newport, R.I., Oct. 31, 1942; d. Robert Lee and Roberta Claire (Brown) Taylor; m. Edward M. Butler, Aug. 22, 1964; children: Jeffrey, Gregory, Katherine. AB, Cornell U., 1964. Asst. dir. Equity Tng. Ctr. Project TIDE Trenton (N.J.) State Coll., 1990—; owner Equity Resources, Tinton Falls, N.J., 1993—. Editor: Go for It! A Role Model Directory, 1991; editor Equity Exch., 1991—. Mem. Monmouth County dist. ethics com. Supreme Ct. N.J., 1987-91; pres. Vol. Ctr. Monmouth County, Red Bank, 1985-89; mem. Cornell U. Coun., Ithaca, N.Y., 1987-91, 94—; dir. Cornell Assn. Class Officers, 1991—. Named one of Woman of Achievement Commn. on Status of Women, 1988. Mem. AAUW (life; pres. N.J. chpt. 1988-90, Edn. Found. Named Gift 1982, 83, 84, 86, 87, 89, 91), Nat. Coalition for Sex Equity in Edn. Home: 20 Cedar Pl Tinton Falls NJ 07724-2807 Office: Trenton State Coll Project TIDE CN4700 Trenton NJ 08650-4700

BUTLER, PATRICIA O., management consultant; b. Liberty, N.Y., Feb. 3, 1953; d. Paul Stephen and Florence (Dunn) Obuhanich; m. William Reiley Butler, Aug. 4, 1984; 1 child, William Paul Langley. BA, Elmira (N.Y.) Coll., 1977. Mgr. product adminstrn. Savin Corp., Binghamton, N.Y., 1979-83; master scheduler Codman & Shurtleff, Randolph, Mass., 1983; mgr. ops. systems USCI div. C.R. Bard, Billerica, Mass., 1983-86; sr. cons./project mgr. Digital Corp., Maynard, Mass., 1986-87; cons. Coopers & Lybrand, Boston, 1987-89; pres., cons. MBC, Westboro, Mass., 1989—; cons. Coopers & Lybrand, 1987-89. Author tng. manuals: Cycle Counting, 1988, System Implementation, 1985. Vol. Food Bank, Westboro, Mass., 1989-91. Mem. Data Processing Mgmt. Assn., Am. Prodn. Inventory Control Soc. (bd. dirs. 1986-87), Profl. Women's Network, Newcomers Club (interest group coord. for golf and skiing 1987-91), Psi Chi.

BUTLER, SUSAN LOWELL, association executive, writer; b. Bklyn., Feb. 10, 1944; d. John William and Catherine (Mauro) Yost; m. Horace Hamilton Lowell (div. 1982); m. James Thomas Butler, Feb. 12, 1983; stepchildren: James, Kevin, Michael. BA, Lycoming Coll., 1965; postgrad., U. Pa., 1965-67. Tchr. English and Journalism Bristol Twp. Schs., Levittown, Pa., 1967-70; field rep. Nat. Edn. Assn., Washington, 1970-74, dir. communications, 1974-80; dir. western states region Nat. Edn. Assn., Austin (Tex.) and Denver, 1980-84; account supr. Dale Chrisman & Assocs., Austin, 1984-86; pvt. cons. Austin, 1986-88; exec. v.p. Women in Comm., Inc., Washington, 1988-91; nat. exec. dir. Nat. Women's Hall of Fame, Seneca Falls, N.Y., 1991—; mem. bd. The Media Inst., Washington, 1989-91. Author: National Education Association: A Special Mission, 1987, Handbook of Association Communications, 1987. V.p. pub. affairs Mental Health Assn. of Tex., Austin, 1987-88; bd. dirs.Nat. Women's Hall of Fame. Mem. Am. Soc. Assn. Execs., Pub. Rels. Soc. Am. (accredited), Nat. Press Club, Women, Men and Media (exec. com.), Women in Communications Inc. Episcopalian. Home: 406 Skyhill Rd Alexandria VA 22314-4920 Office: Nat Womens Hall of Fame 76 Fall St Seneca Falls NY 13148-1409

BUTLER, TCHININA BENFADENE, insurance adjuster; b. Henryetta, Okla., Mar. 7, 1955; d. Noel Elgin and Dorothy Francis (Palmer) Rayburn; m. Michael Terrance Latham,Aug. 5, 1977 (div. Jan. 1982); 1 child, Rose Marie Latham; m. David Charles Butler, July 1, 1992; 1 child, Stacie Lynn. A in Claims, Ins. Inst. Am., 1990; A in Engrng. Tech., Okla. State U., 1992; A in Mcpl. Fire Protection, Sch. of Engrng. Tech. Life, health, accident agt. Liberty Nat. Life Ins., Oklahoma City, 1976-78; gen. ins. agt. Franklin Life, Oklahoma City, 1979-81; multi-line adjuster Shelter Ins. Cos., Oklahoma City, 1981-92, Johnson Claim Svc., Moore, Okla., 1992—; sec./treas. Okla. Arson Adv. Coun., Oklahoma City, 1993-94. Co-chairperson Com. to Elect John Shorty Barnett for Gov., Okla., 1990. Recipient Best All Around Community Project award Okla. Jaycees, 1988. Mem. Internat. Assn. Arson Investigators (Okla. chpt.), Fire Marshall Assn. (Okla. chpt. mem. com. 1992—), Civil Air Patrol (sr.), Edmond Jaycees (community svc. v.p. 1988, chpt. pres. 1989), Toastmasters Internat. (participant success leadership program 1989). Republican. Office: Johnson Claim Svc 840 SE 4th St Moore OK 73160

BUTLER, TONI JEAN, transportation executive; b. Beufort, S.C., July 14, 1963; d. Tony Lee and Betty Joe (Tramel) B. BS in Acctg., Akron U., 1986. CPA, Ohio. Gen. acct. Rail Van Consol., Inc., Twinsburg, Ohio, 1987-88, fin. analysts, 1988, asst. controller, 1988-90; contr. Ellindor Devel. Corp., Worthington, Ohio, 1990-92; project mgr. info. systems, 1993—; Rail Van, Inc.; advisor Lamberts CPA Rev. Course, Columbus, Ohio, 1990. Chair subcom. Arthritis Found., Columbus, 1990-94; treas. Columbus chpt. Star Fleet, 1993, v.p., 1994; asst. to prodr. CareCon Found., Columbus, 1994. Mem. AICPA, Ohio Soc. CPAs.

BUTLER, VICKIE BURKHART, college official; b. Knoxville, Tenn., May 22, 1955; d. James Claude and Ruth Adelia (Pratt) B.; m. Benjamin Larry Butler, Jan. 7, 1984; 1 stepson, Benjamin Brent. BS, Carson-Newman Coll., 1976; MS, U. Tenn., 1979. Cert. tchr. Tchr. Knox County Sch. System, Knoxville, 1976-82; state vol. coord. Tenn. Dept. Human Svcs., Nashville, 1982-89; dir. alumni rels. Carson-Newman Coll., Jefferson City, Tenn., 1989—; mem. Tenn. Advancement Resources Coun., 1989—; cons.; workshop leader; program builder; grad. Tenn. Leadership, 1990. Author: (manual) DHS Volunteer Services, 1982. Pianist, dir. bell choir 1st United Meth. Ch., Newport, 1985—, sec. nominations and personnel com. mem. Fellow Lab. for Learning; mem. Gamma Sigma Sigma, Phi Lambda Theta, Kappa Delta Pi. Office: Carson Newman Coll Russell Ave Jefferson City TN 37760

BUTLER-THOMAS, JANNETTE SUE, human resources professional; b. Eugene, Oreg., Mar. 15, 1960; d. Robert Eugene and Dorothy Marilyn (Irvin) Butler; m. Robert Alan Thomas, Oct. 3, 1992. BS in Hotel Adminstrn., U. Nev., Las Vegas, 1982. Cert. health promotion dir., sr. profl. in human resources. Pers. mgmt. trainee The Sheraton Corp., San Diego, 1982-83; dir. pers. The Sheraton Corp., Palm Coast, Fla., 1983-85; dir. human resources The Sheraton Corp., Dallas, 1985-89; corp. dir. human resources Hilton Reservations Worldwide, Carrollton, Tex., 1989—. Mem., vol. The 500, Inc., Dallas, 1992—, Nat. Multiple Sclerosis Soc., Dallas, 1991—; mem., vol. youth sponsor Episcopal Youth Community, Dallas, 1993—. Recipient Volunteerism award Lodging Industry Tng. Ctr., 1988. Mem. Soc. for Human Resource Mgmt., Dallas Human Resource Mgmt. Assn., Tex. Hotel/Motel Pers. Assn. (membership chair 1987). Episcopalian. Office: Hilton Reservations Worldwide 2050 Chennault Rd Carrollton TX 75007-3506

BUTRYN, SUE ANN, quality assurance engineer; b. Jamestown, N.Y., Sept. 12, 1958; d. Harry Nathaniel and Shirley Ann (Beardsley) Holt; m. Walter Michael Butryn, Nov. 20, 1993. Grad. high sch., Falconer, N.Y. Assemblier Cummins Engine, Lakewood, N.Y., 1981-83, trainer, 1983-86, team leader, 1986-91, quality assurance engr., 1991—. Mem. Am. Soc. Quality Control. Home: 1437 Goshen Rd Panama NY 14767-9757 Office: Cummins Engine Co 4720 Baker Street Ext Lakewood NY 14750-9762

BUTTERBRODT, JANET ANN, psychotherapist; b. Marshfield, Wis., Sept. 27, 1953; d. William E.H. and Luella Cecila (Young) B.; m. Dennis Knickelbein, June 20, 1975; children: Blake Allison, Bryce Aaron. BS, U. Wis., Stevens Point, 1975; MS, U. Wis., Oshkosh, 1984; student, Loyola U. Med. Ctr., 1990. Student Outagamie County Human Svcs., Appleton, Wis., 1983-84; ptnr. Associated Counselors, Sheboygan, Wis., 1984-86; family trainer Family Tng. Program, Winnebago, Wis., 1984-86; marriage and family therapist St. Elizabeth Hosp., Appleton, 1985-88; drug/alcohol counselor New Horizons, Oshkosh, 1989; psychotherapist Valley Counseling Ctr., Appleton, 1989-90, Associated Counselors, Appleton, 1990—; bd. dirs. E. B. Davis Found./Davis Day Care, Oshkosh, 1993—. Del. Dem. Party, Winnebago County, 1984. Mem. Am. Counseling Assn., Internat. Assn. Marriage & Family Counselors, Am. Mental Health Counselors, Assocs. For Specialists in Group Work, Wis. Assn. for Drug and Alcohol Abuse, Wis. Outpatient Mental Health Clinics, Am. Soc. Clin. Hypnosis, EMDR Network. Democrat. Methodist. Office: Associated Counselors Zuelke Bldg Ste 525 103 W College Ave Appleton WI 54911-5744

BUTTERFIELD, DEANNE, public administrator; b. The Dalles, Oreg., Apr. 20, 1951; d. L. Curt B. and Colleen (McCarton) Graham; m. John S. Huyler Jr., 1980; 1 child, Jesse. BS in Urban Studies, Portland State U.; MPA, Harvard U., 1979. Dir. legis. affairs Gov. Richard Lamm, Denver, 1984-86; dist. dir. Congressman David Skaggs, Westminster, Colo., 1986-87; prin. DeAnne Butterfield Cons., Boulder, Colo., 1982-92; co-dir. Rocky Flats Local Impacts Initiative, Arvada, Colo., 1992—; coun. mem. Gov.'s Defense Conversion Coun., Colo., 1993—. City coun. mem. Boulder City Coun., 1989-92; commr. Colo. Air Quality Control Commn., 1986-87; mem. Dem. State Exec. Com., 1984-87. Mem. Soc. of Friends. Home: 810 Yellow Pine Ave Boulder CO 80304-4313 Office: Rocky Flats Impact Initiative 5460 Ward Rd #205 Arvada CO 80002

BUTTERFIELD, DIANE MARIE, financial executive, accountant, consultant; b. Albert Lea, Minn., Aug. 24, 1950; d. William Roland and Genevieve Elaine (Mahowald) B. BA in Acctg., S.W. State U., Minn., 1972. CPA, Minn. Various positions Peat Marwick Mitchell and Co., Mpls., 1972-80; sr. mgr. Peat Marwick Mitchell and Co., N.Y.C., 1980-83; cons. Edmond, Okla., 1983-84; dir. acctg. Policy and Rsch. dept. Household Internat., Prospect Heights, Ill., 1984-89; dep. contr. Mfrs. Hanover Trust Co., N.Y.C., 1989-92; mgr. fin. acctg. and reporting Fleet Fin. Group, Providence, 1992; fin. dir. Chem. Bank, N.Y.C., 1992—; alt. mem. emerging issues task force Fin. Acctg. Standards Bd., 1984-87; mem. fn. instruments dept., 1986-89. Mem. AICPA, Inst. Mgmt. Accts.

BUTTERWORTH, JANE ROGERS FITCH, physician; b. Louisville, Aug. 3, 1937; d. Howard Mercer and Jane Rogers (McCaw) Fitch; m. William Butterworth, Sept. 5, 1958 (div. Feb. 1968); children: Jane Rogers, William Stoddard, Robert Mercer, Benjamin Richard Mallory, Anne Lewis. BS, U. Louisville, 1971, MD, 1974. Rotating intern Humana Hosp. Audubon (formerly St. Joseph's Hosp.), Louisville, 1974-75, resident in radiology, 1975-76; resident in phys. medicine and rehab. Frasier Rehab. (formerly Inst. of Phys. Medicine and Rehab.), Louisville, 1976-80; staff physiatrist Rockford (Ill.) Meml. Hosp., 1980-83; clin. instr. Rockford Sch. Medicine, 1980-83; med. dir. phys. medicine and rehab. Western Res. Care System, Youngstown, Ohio, 1983—, mem. teaching staff residency program, 1983—; clin. instr. Northeastern Ohio U. Coll. of Medicine, Rootstown, 1983—, chairperson phys. medicine subcoun., mem. acad. rev. and promotions com., 1985-95; adj. faculty Youngstown State U., 1984—; regional med. advisor Rehab. div. Ohio Indsl. Commn., Youngstown, 1985—; mem. admissions com. Northeastern Ohio U. Coll. Medicine, 1988. Mem. choir St. John's Episcopal Ch., Youngstown, vestrywoman, 1989-91; bd. dirs. Goodwill Industries, Youngstown, 1985-92, advisor rehab. div., 1986—, bd. advisors, 1993—; mem. med. rev. staff Hospice, Youngstown, 1984—; dir. med. svcs. Easter Seals Soc., Youngstown, 1987—; mem. med. bd. pub. TV, Youngstown, 1986—; violinist Youngstown State U. Community Orch., 1985; mem. Youngstown Musica Sacra, 1989—. Recipient Community Svc. award St. John's Episcopal Ch., 1988. Mem. AMA, Ohio Med. Assn., Mahoning County Med. Soc. (coun. 1989, alt. del to Ohio Med. Assn. 1990, pres. 1992), Ky. Med. Assn., Jefferson County Med. Soc., Am. Congress Rehab. Medicine, Colonial Dames Soc. Am., Phi Beta, Chi Delta Phi, Kappa Alpha Theta. Republican. Home: 186 Rockland Dr Boardman OH 44512 Office: Western Res Care System Southside Hosp 345 Oak Ave Youngstown OH 44512-6124

BUTTI, LINDA, visual artist, educator; b. Bklyn., Jan. 15, 1951; d. Vincent and Philomena (Canobbio) B. BA cum laude, CUNY, 1972, MFA, 1975. Asst. prof. art LaGuardia C.C., CUNY, Seton Coll., Yonkers, N.Y., St. John's U., N.Y.C., Molloy Coll., 1994—; lectr. S.I. Mus., 1991-94, 95, also others; guest artist, speaker Women in History Month, SUNY, Stonybrook, Kean Coll., 1994, Snug Harbor Cultural Ctr., 1995—; instr. art workshops, N.Y., 1994. One-woman shows include Ward Nasse Gallery, N.Y.C., 1984, 86, Newhouse Ctr. for Contemporary Art, N.Y.C., 1985, Princeton (N.J.) U., 1989, Whitehall Gallery, N.Y.C., 1991, St. John's U., N.Y.C., 1993, Cheng Chung Gallery, N.Y.C., 1993, S.I. Cable TV, 1994; exhibited in group shows at Bklyn. Mus., 1986, Pace U., 1989, 88, Nancy Stein Gallery, 1989, Guild Hall Mus. , E. Hampton, N.Y., 1989, Nabisco Brands Gallery, N.J., 1989, Lincoln Ctr., N.Y.C., 1987, Newhouse Gallery, 1987, Marywood Coll., Pa., 1987, S.I. Mus., 1988, Paul VI Inst., 1988, Phoenix Gallery, N.Y.C., 1988, Aart Vark Gallery, Phila., 1990, Lever House, N.Y,C., 1990, St. John's U., N.Y.C., 1990, Broome St. Gallery, N.Y.C., 1991, Paul VI Inst. for Arts, Washington, 1991, Snug Harbor Cultural Ctr., N.Y.C., 1991, Iona-Seton Faculty Exhibit, Yonkers, N.Y., 1991; represented in permanent collections Bell Atlanta, Smith Barney, Upham and Harris, N.Y.C., NBC Studios, N.Y.C., Brenau Coll., Ga., Cath. Telecommunications Ctr. of Am., N.Y.C., Sterling Drug Art Collection, Pa., Mitsubish Capital, N.Y.C., Iona Coll., The Art Network S.I., N.Y., Rhone-Paulene Rover, Inc., Pa., Shneyer & Shen, N.Y.C., S.I. U. Hosp. South. Recipient Creative Artist award CAM Competition, 1979, Guild Hall Mus. Honorable award, 1989; grantee Com. for Visual Arts, 1980, 85, 89, Chase Manhattan Bank, 1981, S.I. Coun. on Arts, 1991, N.Y.C. Dept. Cultural Affairs, 1993, N.Y. State Coun. on the Arts, 1993, 94; honoree Woman of Achievement award Nat. Orgn. Italian-Am. Women, 1992. Mem. Women in the Arts (sec. 1984—), Cath. Artists of the 80's (coord. spl. projects 1985—), Cath. Fine Artists Assn. (v.p. exhbns. 1995), Women Caucus for Art.

BUTTON, CHRISTINA MILLS, art consultant; b. Phila., Dec. 17, 1941; d. James Arthur and Geraldine Evelyn (Huffman) Mills; m. Alan Frederick Button, Jan. 27, 1962; children: Alan Frederick II, Angela Dawn. BA, U. Wis., Oshkosh, 1977. Asst. to dir. Priebe Gallery, U. Wis., Oshkosh, 1976-77; gallery rep. Hang Up Gallery, Neenah, Wis., 1977-79; owner, mgr., artist rep. Christina Button Gallery, Oxford, Ohio, 1982-85; self-employed artist rep. Ramsey, N.J., 1986-88; self-employed art cons. Appleton, Wis., 1988—. Bd. dirs. AGA-Ctr. for Visual Arts, 1989-91. Mem. AAUW (scholar 1976-77), Fox Valley Arts Alliances. Home and Office: 8 S Inverness Cir Appleton WI 54914-4138

BUTTON, RENA PRITSKER, public relations company executive; b. Providence, Feb. 15, 1925; d. Isadore and Esther (Kay) Pritsker; m. Daniel E. Button, Aug. 16, 1969; children by previous marriage: Joshua, Bruce, David Posner. Student, Pembroke Coll., 1942-45; B.S., Simmons Coll., 1948; postgrad., Albany Law Sch., Union U., 1968-69. Spl. asst. to U.S. Rep., 1967-69; spl. projects coordinator United Jewish Appeal, 1971-74; exec. dir. Nat. Council Jewish Women, Inc., N.Y.C., 1974-76; pres. Button Assos., N.Y.C., 1976—; exec. v.p. Catalyst, N.Y.C., 1980-82; pres. Button & Button, Albany, N.Y., 1982—; mem. adv. coun. N.Y. State Senate Minority, 1980—; exec. dir. N.Y. State Coun. on Alcoholism and Other Drug Addictions, 1990-93. Co-producer, moderator: TV pub. affairs program Speak For Yourself, Albany, N.Y., 1963-66. Past mem. Mohawk-Hudson Council on Ednl. TV.; chmn. pub. affairs com. Marymount Manhattan Coll.; Past bd. dirs. Albany YWCA, Albany Council Chs. Devel. Corp., World Affairs Council, Planned Parenthood Assn. Albany; trustee Jerusalem Women's Seminar, Citizen's for Family Planning, N.Y. Com. Integrated Housing, Hist. Albany Found. Ctr. for Counselling; pres. Sr. Service Ctr. Albany Area.; Bd. dirs. Com. Modern Cts.; exec. dir. N.Y. Head Injury Assn., 1993—. Clubs: Siasconset Casino (Siasconset, Mass.), Univ. (Albany). Home and Office: 16 Spruce Ct Delmar NY 12054-2614

BUTTRAM, DEBRA DORIS, fashion vendor and consultant, English educator, trainer for service and therapy dogs; b. Port St. Joe, Fla., Aug. 22, 1954; d. Wayne Morrison Sr. and Doris Mae (Amos) B.; m. David Cheuk Lun Kong, Dec. 29, 1979 (div. 1989); m. Marcello Galimberti, June 12, 1993. BS in Early Childhood Edn., Fla. State U., 1978. English tchr. Metta Found. for Refugees, Sydney, Australia, 1979; exec. asst. East West Freight Ltd., Hong Kong, 1981-82; boutique dir. Diane Fries Ltd., Hong Kong, 1985; buyer, boutique dir. Joyce Boutique Ltd., Hong Kong, 1985-87; mktg., sales exec. Icarus Ltd. (Chanel), Hong Kong, 1988-90; freelance wholesale fashion vender Milan, Italy; trainer, sec. Italian Assn. for Use of Assistance Dogs, Bosisio Parini, Italy, 1991—. Home and Office: Via IV Novembre 26, 22040 Bosisio Parini Italy

BUTTS, VIRGINIA, corporate public relations executive; b. Chgo.. BA, U. Chgo. Writer Dave Garroway radio show NBC, N.Y.C., 1953; writer, producer, talent Sta. WBBM-TV, Chgo.; midwest dir. pub. relations for mags. Time, Fortune, Life and Sports Illustrated, Time Inc., 1956-63; dir. pub. relations Chgo. Sun-Times and Chgo. Daily News, 1963-74; v.p. pub. relations Field Enterprises, Chgo., 1974-84; v.p. pub. rels. The Field Corp., 1984-90; pub. rels. counsel Marshall Field V, Chgo., 1991—; mem. pub. affairs com. Art Inst. Chgo. Contbr. Lesly's Public Relations Handbook, 1978, 83, World Book Ency. Recipient Clarion award Women in

Communications, Inc., 1975, 76, Businesswoman of the Yr. award Lewis U., 1976. Mem. Pub. Rels. Soc. Am. (nat. bd. ethics 1987-93), Publicity Club Chgo. (Golden Trumpet award 1968, 69, 75, 76, 80), Nat. Acad. TV Arts and Scis., The Chgo. Network.

BUURMAN, ELOISE BERNHOFT, guidance counselor, retired; b. Tacoma, Wash., July 17, 1915; d. Georg Kristian and Ellen Victoria (Ekman) Bernhoft; m. Gerrit Buurman, Nov. 25, 1943 (dec. Oct. 1990); children: Gerrit B., Ellen J. Buurman Hulse. AA, Skagit Valley Jr. Coll., 1934; BA in Phys. Edn., U. Wash., 1936, cert. in teaching, 1937; cert. in counseling, Western Wash. U., Bellingham, 1970. Cert. tchr., Wash. Phys. edn. and sci. tchr. Monroe (Wash.) High Sch., 1937-43; phys. edn. tchr. Clover Park Sr. High Sch., Tacoma, 1943-44; phys. edn. and history tchr. Lynden (Wash.) High Sch., 1952-68; counselor Lynden High Sch., 1968-75; ret. Lynden (Wash.) High Sch., 1975; coach boy's basketball Monroe High Sch., 1943. Tournament chmn. Ladies Golf Club at Grandview, Custer, Wash., 1975-85. Mem. AAUW, Delta Kappa Gamma, Pi Lambda Theta. Lutheran. Home: 6911 Holeman Ave Blaine WA 98230-9005

BUUS, LINDA LEE PANNETIER, educator; b. Rapid City, S.D., Aug. 23, 1949; d. Max Pannetier and Pansy A. (Francisco) Robison; m. David V. Buus, Aug. 1, 1970 (div. Apr. 1988); children: Baend J., Yuri D. BS in Secondary Edn., Black Hills State, 1973; MEd, Lesley Coll., 1988. Cert. tchr. English, social studies, libr.-media specialist, Wyo. Tchr.'s aide Taipei (Republic of China) Am. Sch., 1971-72; 7th and 8th grade social studies tchr. Our Lady of Perpetual Help Sch., Rapid City, 1973-74; 7th and 8th grade English and spelling tchr. Newcastle (Wyo.) Jr. High Sch., 1974-75; 9th grade social studies, English tchr. Campbell County Jr. High Sch., Gillette, Wyo., 1975-76; 9th grade social studies tchr. Twin Spruce Jr. High Sch., Gillette, 1976-81, Sage Valley Jr. High Sch., Gillette, 1982—; social studies dept. chairwoman Twin Spruce and Sage Valley Jr. High Schs., Gillette, 1979-91, 94—; mem. liaison task force Campbell County Sch. Dist., Gillette, 1983-86, mem. curriculum coordinating coun., 1987-90; student tchr. supr. U. Wyo., Laramie, 1980-93. Mem. Sigma Kappa svc. sorority, Spearfish, S.D., 1968, pres., 1970; participant Wyo. Gov.'s Youth Conf./Legis. Youth Forum, Cheyenne, 1979-81. Fellow Taft Inst. Govt., 1985, Nat. Humanities Summer History, 1991. Mem. NEA (de.-rep. assembly 1986), Campbell County Edn. Assn. (faculty rep. 1983-88, v.p. 1986-87, Leadership Team 1994—), Wyo. Edn. Assn. (senate liaison legis. dinner, 1985, Profl. Stds. and Practices Commn. 1994—), Wyo. Coun. of the Social Studies, Nat. Coun. of the Social Studies, Kappa Delta Pi. Roman Catholic. Home: 415 Sisson Ave Moorcroft WY 82721 Office: Sage Valley Jr H S 1000 W Lakeway Rd Gillette WY 82718-5692

BUVINGER, JAN, library director; b. Lampasas, Tex., Oct. 4, 1943; parents Orville Layne and Myriam (Hamer) Rogers. BS, Coll. Charleston, N.C., 1965; MLS, Emory U., 1970. Childrens asst. libr. Charleston (S.C.) County Libr., 1970-71, reference libr., 1972-75, head reference dept., 1976-77, dep. dir., 1977-79, dir., 1979—. Mem. Am. Libr. Assn., S.C. Libr. Assn., S.E. Libr. Assn. Office: Charleston County Libr 404 King St Charleston SC 29403-6466

BUXTON, LUCINDA CATHERINE, wildlife film maker, writer, lecturer; b. Epping, Essex, Eng., Aug. 21, 1950; came to U.S., 1993; d. Aubrey Leland and Pamela Mary (Birkin) B. Grad. pvt. sch. Freelance wildlife film maker Survival Anglia Ltd., Norwich, Eng., 1971-93; appearances on TV programs and numerous radio shows, Eng. Author: Survival in the Wild, 1980, Survival: South Atlantic, 1983; films include Last Kingdom of the Elephants, 1977, Penguin Island, 1979, Falkland Summer, 1980, Wideawake Island, 1983, The Fall of Squirrel Nutkin, 1985, The Mother Who Never Dies, 1986, Mountains of Water, 1987, White Water, Blue Duck, 1987, Fire Demons, 1988, The Last Call for the Corncrake, 1989, Devil Islands, 1990, Leopards & Hyeanas-Armies of the Night, 1992, Armies of the Night, 1992; contbr. articles to wildlife mags. Recipient media award Variety Club Gt. Britain, 1982, best of category award for Stranded Beyond the Falklands, San Francisco Internat. Film Festival, 1984. Fellow Royal Geog. Soc. (Cherry Kearton award 1983); mem. Internat. Assn. Wildlife Film-Makers, Royal Soc. for Protection Birds, Worldlife Fund for Nature, Falkland Islands Found., Brit. Sub-Aqua Club. Roman Catholic. Home: 1800 Hoyt St Lakewood CO 80215-2950 also: The Old House, Langham, Holt, Norfolk NR25 7DG, England

BUYSE, MARYLOU, pediatrician, clinical geneticist, medical administrator; b. N.Y.C., June 27, 1946; d. George J. and Barbara M. (Sauer) B.; A.B., Hunter Coll., 1966; M.D., Med. Coll. Pa., 1970; MS in Med. Adminstrn. U. Wis., 1993; m. Carl N. Edwards, Jan. 22, 1982. Intern, U. Mich., 1970-71; resident in pediatrics Los Angeles County-U. So. Calif. Med. Center, 1971-73, fellow, 1973-75; instr. Boston U., 1975; asst. prof. pediatrics U. So. Calif., 1973-75, Tufts U., 1976-84; coordinator Myelodysplasia Clinic, Tufts-New Eng. Med. Center, Boston, 1976-79, dir. Cystic Fibrosis Clinic and staff pediatrician Center for Genetic Counseling and Birth Defects Evaluation, 1975-82, med. dir. Center for Birth Defects Info. Service, 1978-82, dir. center, 1982-94; pres. Medx, Ltd., 1985—; pres. Ctr. for Birth Defects Info. Scis., Inc., 1985—; dir. clin. genetics Children's Hosp., Boston, 1985-86; mem. med. adv. bd. Mass. Cystic Fibrosis Found., 1977-79; med. dir. Ferald State Sch., 1988-94; assoc. med. dir. MassPRO, 1993—; mem. Mass. Bd. Registration in Medicine, 1994—; cons. in field. Recipient Physicians Recognition award AMA, 1975, Alumni Achievement award Med. Coll. Pa., 1987. Diplomate Am. Bd. Med. Genetics. Fellow Am. Acad. Pediatrics, Mass. Med. Soc. (asst. sec.-treas. 1991-94, trustee 1991—, sec.-treas. 1994—); mem. Am. Med. Woman's Assn. (pres. Mass. br. 39 1986-91), Am. Mgmt. Assn., Am. Soc. Human Genetics, AAAS, Am. Med. Writers Assn., Soc. Craniofacial Genetics (pres. 1986), Am. Coll. Physician Execs., Teratology Soc., Charles River Dist. Med. Soc. (pres. 1993—), Alpha Omega Alpha. Asso. editor Birth Defects Compendium, 2d edit., 1979; assoc. editor Syndrome Identification Jour., 1977-82, editor, 1982; editor Jour. Clin. Dysmorphology, 1982-86, Dysmorphology and Clinical Genetics, 1986-94; editor-in-chief Birth Defects Encyclopedia, 1990. Office: Ctr Birth Defects Info Svcs Inc Dover Med Bldg Box 1776 Dover MA 02030

BUZALJKO, GRACE WILSON, editor, writer; b. Cambridge, Mass., Nov. 4, 1922; d. Charles and Elizabeth (Douglas) Wilson; m. Ahmed Buzaljko, Mar. 9, 1963 (div. Mar. 1980). BA cum laude, St. Mary Coll., Leavenworth, Kans., 1944; postgrad., U. Pitts., 1946-47, New Sch. for Social Rsch., 1949-50. Promotions asst. Pitts. Press, 1945-48; manuscript editor John Wiley & Sons, N.Y.C., 1948-52, Harcourt Brace Jovanovich, N.Y.C., 1952-60, U. Calif. Press, Berkeley, 1960-67; adminstrv. editor Harcourt Brace Jovanovich, San Francisco, 1967-72; editor dept. anthropology U. Calif., Berkeley, 1973-88, ret., 1988. Editor: Yurok Myths (A.L. Kroeber), 1976, Karok Myths (A.L. Kroeber and E.W. Gifford), 1980; contbr. articles to profl. jours. Co-clk. Berkeley Soc. of Friends Meeting, 1988-90. Mem. AAUW (v.p., program chmn. Berkeley br. 1981-83, legis. chmn. 1988-94), Miwok Archeol. Preserve of Marin, Am. Anthrop. Assn. Home: 612 Albemarle St El Cerrito CA 94530-3217

BUZBY, MARIANNE, pediatric nurse, educator; b. Norfolk, Va., Nov. 25, 1959; d. John Schofield and Ruthe Carolyn (Tauber) B. BSN, U. Delaware, 1981; MSN, cert. pediatric nurse practitioner, U. Pa., 1987. RN, Pa., N.J. Staff nurse The Children's Hosp. of Phila., 1981-83, primary nurse, 1983-84, nursing supr., 1984-86, pediatric nurse practitioner, GI/nutrition coord. outpatient liver transplant, 1987-94; liver transplant coord., 1994—; lectr. grad. program U. Pa. Sch. Nursing, Phila., 1988—; steering com. Nursing of Children Network, 1987-88, treas., 1988-89, mem.-at-large, 1989-90; facilitator Hepatitis B Found./Am. Liver Found., Phila., 1992—; presenter U. Pa. Sch. Nursing, Phila., 1988, Dept. Youth and Family Svcs., Princeton, N.J., 1991, Endoscopy Seminars Internat., Atlanta, 1992, Newborn Nurses, Moorestown, N.J., 1992, others. Co-author: (book chpt.) Child Health Care: Process and Practice, 1992; contbr. articles to profl. jours. Educator, Organ Donor Awareness, Pa. and N.J., 1988-93; nurse Nat. Immunization Campaign, Phila., 1991-93; mem. Am. Liver Found., 1991—, Crohn's and Colitis Found. Am., 1991—; presenter sibling workshop Children's Hosp. of Phila., 1992. Fellow Nat. Assn. Pediatric Nurse Assocs. and Practitioners; mem. ANA (cert.), Am. Acad. Nurse Practitioners, Soc. Gastroenterology Nurses and Assocs. (co-chair pediatric spl. interest group 1990-92, editorial com. 1991-92, chair pediatric spl. interest group 1992-93, editorial bd. 1992—, presenter 1990, 92, grantee 1990), Assn. Pediatric Gastroenterology and Nutrition Nurses (pres.-elect 1989-91, pres. 1991—, presenter 1991, 92), Alumni Soc. U. Pa. (bd. dirs. 1991-93), Sigma Theta Tau. Episcopalian. Office: Children's Hosp Phila 34th St & Civic Center Blvd Philadelphia PA 19104

BUZZELL, BARBARA FEDER, public relations executive; b. Bethesda, Md., Apr. 4, 1953; d. Harold William and Edith (Herman) Feder; m. F. Scott Buzzell, Sept. 19, 1981. BA, U. Pa., 1975. Fashion coord. Bloomingdale's, Tysons Corner, Va., 1976-78; dir. pub. rels. I. Magnin, Rockville, Md., 1979-81; exec. v.p. Laurey Peat & Assocs., Dallas, 1982—. Bd. dirs. SPCA of Tex., Dallas, 1989—, Diffa, Dallas, 1990-93, Friends of Fair Park, Dallas, 1986-88; active AIDS Arms, 1995—. Recipient Matrix award Women in Comm., Achievement award Tex. Pub. Rels. Soc. Am. Mem. Pub. Rels. Soc. Am. Office: Laurey Peat & Assocs Inc 2001 Ross Ave # 3020 Dallas TX 75201

BYARS, BETSY (CROMER), author; b. Charlotte, Aug. 7, 1928; d. George Guy and Nan (Rugheimer) Cromer; m. Edward Ford Byars, June 24, 1950; children: Laurie, Betsy Ann, Nan, Guy. Author: Clementine, 1962, The Dancing Camel, 1965, Rama, the Gypsy Cat, 1966, The Groober, 1967, The Midnight Fox, 1968 (Am. Book of Yr. selection Child Study Assn. 1968, Lewis Carroll Shelf award 1970), Trouble River, 1969 (Am. Book of Yr. selection Child Study Assn. 1969), The Summer of the Swans, 1970 (Am. Book of Yr. selection Child Study Assn. 1970, John Newbery medal 1971), Go and Hush the Baby, 1971, The House of Wings, 1972 (Am. Book of Yr. selection Child Study Assn. 1972, Nat. Book award nomination 1973), The 18th Emergency, 1973 (Am. Book of Yr. selection Child Study Assn. 1973, New York Times Outstanding Book of Yr. 1973, Dorothy Canfield Fisher Meml. Book award Vt. Conress of Parents and Teachers 1975), The Winged Colt of Casa Mia, 1973 (Am. Book of Yr. selection Child Study Assn. 1973, New York Times Outstanding Book of Yr. 1973), After the Goat Man, 1974 (Am. Book of Yr. selection Child Study Assn. 1974), The Lace Snail, 1975 (Am. Book of Yr. selection Child Study Assn. 1975), The TV Kid, 1976 (Am. Book of Yr. selection Child Study Assn. 1976), The Pinballs, 1977 (Woodward Park School Annual Book award 1977, Child Study Children's Book award Child Study Children's Book Com. at Bank Street Coll. of Edn. 1977, Ga. Children's Book award 1979, Charlie May Simon Book award Ark. Elem. School Coun. 1980, Surrey School Book of Yr. award Surrey School Librs. of Surrey 1980, Mark Twain award Mo. Assn. of School Librs. 1980, William Allen White Children's Book award Emporia State Univ. 1980, Young Reader medal Calif. Reading Assn. 1980, Golden Archer award Dept. Libr. Sci. Univ. of Wis.-Oskosh 1982), The Cartoonist, 1978, Good-bye Chicken Little, 1979 (New York Times Outstanding Book of Yr. 1979), The Night Swimmers, 1980 (Am. Book of Yr. selection Child Study Assn. 1980, Best Book of Yr. School Libr. Jour. 1980, Am. Book award for Children's Fiction 1981), The Cybil War, 1981 (Tenn. Children's Choice Book award Tenn. Libr. Assn. 1983, Sequoyah Children's Book award 1984), The Animal, the Vegetable, and John D. Jones, 1982 (Parents' Choice award for Lit. Parents' Choice Found. 1982, Best Children's Book Sch. Libr. Jour. 1982, CRABbery award Oxon Hill Br. of Prince George's County Libr. 1983, Mark Twain award Mo. Assn. of School Librs. 1985), The Two-Thousand-Pound Goldfish, 1982 (New York Times Outstanding Book of Yr. 1982), The Glory Girl, 1983, The Computer Nut, 1984 (Charlie May Simon award 1987), Cracker Jackson, 1985 (S.C. Children's Book award 1988, Md. Children's Book award 1988), The Not-Just-Anybody Family, 1986, The Golly Sisters Go West, 1986, The Blossoms Meet the Vulture Lady, 1986, The Blossoms and the Green Phantom, 1987, A Blossom Promise, 1987, Beans on the Roof, 1988, The Burning Questions of Bingo Brown, 1988, Bingo Brown and the Language of Love, 1989, Hooray for the Golly Sisters, 1990, Bingo Brown, Gypsy Lover, 1990, Seven Treasure Hunts, 1991, Wanted...Mud Blossom, 1991, The Moon & I, 1992, Bingo Brown's Guide to Romance, 1992, McMummy, 1993, The Golly Sisters Ride Again, 1994, The Dark Stairs: A Herculeah Jones Mystery, 1994, Coast to Coast, 1994; editor: Growing Up Stories, 1995. Recipient Regina medal Catholic Libr. Assn., 1987. Home: 126 Riverpoint Dr Clemson SC 29631-1049*

BYARS, DONNA, artist, sculptor, educator; b. Rock Island, Ill.; d. Percy and Helen (Mactier) Byars; 1 child, Eric Byars Freeman. BA, State U. Iowa; student, Parsons Sch. Design, N.Y.C. Instr. collage New Sch. for Social Rsch., N.Y.C., 1980; dir. gallery Parsons Sch. Design, N.Y.C., 1984-86, instr. drawing, 1980—; artist-in-residence Palisades Interstate Park, N.Y., 1976; presentor Nat. Sculpture Conf., Cin., 1987; panelist N.Y. Found. for the Arts, Inc., 1990. Solo exhbns. at 55 Mercer St., N.Y.C., A.I.R. Gallery, N.Y.C., Hudson River Mus., Yonkers, N.Y., U. So. Maine, Portland; group shows include Stephens Coll., Columbia, Mo., A.I.R. Gallery, N.Y. Feminist Art Inst., Va. Mus. Fine Arts, Richmond, Parsons Sch. Design, N.Y.C., Hudson River Mus., Fine Arts Mus. of L.I., Max Hutchinson's Sculpture Fields, Kenoza Lake, N.Y., Katonah (N.Y.) Mus., Hillwood Mus., Long Island U.-C.W. Post, Franklin Furnace, N.Y.C., Sculpture Ctr., N.Y.C.; commns. include Wave Hill, Bronx, N.Y., 1979, Long Island U.-C.W. Post, 1993, (site sculptures) Bard Coll., Annandale-on-Hudson, N.Y., Max Hutchinson's Sculpture Fields; subject of articles. Mem. A.I.R. Gallery, N.Y.C., 1979-89. Mem. Coll. Art Assn. Home: 5 Woodworth Ave Yonkers NY 10701-2725

BYAS, TERESA ANN URANGA, medical clerical administrator; b. Plainview, Tex., Mar. 20, 1955; d. Adam T. and Lucy (Sandoval) Uranga; m. Wesley W. Byas, Sept. 11, 1972 (div. 1992); children: Chad W., Christina Ann. Student, Tex. Wesleyan U., 1987-88, Tarrant County Jr. Coll., Ft. Worth. Cert. home health svc. Teller Allied Nat. Bank (now named 1st Interstate), Ft. Worth, 1985-87, Nowlin Savs. and Loans (now named Comerica), Ft. Worth, 1987-88; missionary United Meth. Ch. Global Bd. World Missions, Brazil, 1988-91; asst. mgr. Bag 'n Baggage, Ft. Worth, 1991-92, store mgr., 1992-93; med. record clerical coord. Total Home Health Svcs., Inc., Ft. Worth, 1993—. Mem. Women's Polit. Caucus, Ft. Worth, United Meth. Women's Group; hon. mem. Westcliff United Meth. Women's Group (chpt. named in her honor 1991). Mem. Am. Bus. Women's Assn. Democrat. Home: PO Box 26805 Fort Worth TX 76126-0805 Office: Total Home Health Svcs Inc 170 Sycamore Sch Rd Fort Worth TX 76134

BYER, DIANA, performing arts company executive; b. Trenton, N.J., Aug. 31, 1946; d. Fred and Norma (Handis) B. Grad. high sch., Trenton. Soloist Manhattan Festival Ballet, N.Y.C., 1972, Les Grands Ballet Canadiens, Montreal, Can., 1975; dir. Ballet Sch. of N.Y., N.Y.C., 1978—, N.Y. Theatre Ballet, 1978—; dir., founder Project LIFT scholarship program for children living N.Y.C. homeless shelters, 1989—. Helen Weiselberg scholar Nat. Arts Club, 1988, 90, 93. Office: NY Theatre Ballet 30 E 31st St New York NY 10016-6716

BYFIELD, RITA RAE, nursing educator, operating room nurse; b. Bartlesville, Okla., Mar. 30, 1950; d. Bill R. and Beverly A. (Loper) Nichols; m. Michael U. Byfield, May 31, 1969; children: Sean, Kristi, Katee. ADN, Tulsa Jr. Coll., 1977; BSN, Pittsburg (Kans.) State U., 1989; MEd in Health Occupations, U. Cen. Okla., 1993. RN, Okla.; cert. nurse oper. rm., CPR instr. Operating room nurse Jane Phillips Med. Ctr., Bartlesville, 1976; nursing asst. III St. Francis Hosp., Tulsa, 1974; allied health instr. Tri-County Vocat. Sch., Bartlesville, Okla., 1990, practical nursing instr., 1991-94; prof. nursing Bartlesville Wesleyan Coll., 1994—. Named New Health Profl. of Yr. Okla. Vo-Tech. System, 1994. Mem. Assn. Oper. Rm. Nurses (bd. dirs.), Okla. Nursing Assn., Okla. Vocat. Edn. Assn., Pittsburg State U. Nursing Alumni (sec. bd. dirs., bd. dirs. 1992—), Sigma Theta Tau, Gamma Upsilon Nursing Honor Soc., Kappa Delta. Home: 912 S Cherokee Ave Bartlesville OK 74003-5024

BYINGTON, DIANE B., social work educator; b. Atlanta, Sept. 5, 1951; d. Claude H. and Ruth (Singleton) B.; 1 child, Joel Blum. BA, Calif. State U., 1974; MSW, Fla. State U., 1977, PhD, 1982. Clin. counselor Med. U. of S.C., Charleston, 1974-75; program evaluator Apalachee Mental Health, Tallahassee, 1977-80; program adminstr. Dept. Adminstrn., Tallahassee, 1982-83; rsch. assoc. Fla. State U., Tallahassee, 1983-84; program mgr. Health & Rehabilitative Svcs., Tallahassee, 1984-86; asst. prof. East Carolina U., Greenville, N.C., 1986-89; assoc. prof. U. Denver, 1989—. Democrat. Mem. Unity Ch.

BYINGTON, SALLY RUTH, association administrator, writer, consultant; b. Grand Rapids, Mich., Apr. 16, 1935; d. George and Evangeline (Boerma) Meyer; m. S. John Byington, Nov. 27, 1964 (div. Dec. 1988); children: Nancy Lee Rhodes, Barbra Ann. BA, Western Mich. U., 1957; MA, U. Md., 1962. Cert. tchr. k-8, Md. Grad. asst. U. Md., College Pk., 1959-60; tchr. U. Chgo. Lab. Sch., 1963-64, Grand Rapids, Mich., 1957-59. 64-65, Montgomery County Md. Pub. Schs., Rockville, Md., 1961-63; learning specialist Endeavor Learning Ctr., Rockville, 1987-88; asst. to pres. Women in Militry Svc., Arlington, Va., 1988-89; exec. asst. Korean War Vets. Meml. Adv. Bd., Washington, 1989-91; pub. safety cons., civic activist, 1991-93; cons. Children Early Edn. Program, Bur. Edn. for Handicapped, Dept. edn., Washington, 1975-80; diagnostician pvt. practice. Author: Marriage Through Divorce and Beyond. Pres. Greater Springfield (Va.) Rep. Women's Clubs, 1980s, v.p., 1980s; dist. dir. Fairfax County Rep. Com., 1988; vol. Fairfax County Pub. Schs. Enrollment Study, 1985; coord. Capitol Hill Cmty. Policing Coun.; mem. MPD's Chief of Police Citizens Adv. Coun.; project dir. Guns into Plowshares Sculpture Project; mem. Ward 6 Crime Task Force. Recipient vol. recognition award Fairfax Pub. Schs., 1985. Mem. LWV (study rep. 1980's), Capitol Hill Restoration Soc. (pub. safety issues chair). Home and Office: 1231 Maryland Ave NE Washington DC 20002-5335

BYMEL, SUZAN YVETTE, talent manager, film producer; b. Chgo.; d. Howard Behr and Jacqueline Shirley (Richards) B. Student, U. Ill., Chgo. Exec. asst. Kenny Rogers Prodns., 1981; prodn. exec. Pinehurst Prodns., 1982; music mgmt. assoc. Frontline Mgmt., 1983; pres. Suzan Bymel & Assocs., 1985—; oper. ptnr. Meg Ryan Prodns. (a.k.a. Fandango Films), 1988-93; freelance screenwriter, actress. Mem. Hollywood Woman's Polit. Com., L.A. Office: 1724 N Vista St Los Angeles CA 90046

BYNE, ANN MENDELSOHN, graphic designer; b. Queens, N.Y., Mar. 10, 1950; d. George and Gloria (Feldman) Mendelsohn; m. Eric Harvey Byne, Sept. 3, 1972; children: Scott, Heather. BFA, Pratt Inst., 1972. Art judge On My Own Time exhibit, Rockland County, N.Y., 1989; mem. com. Mount Aramis art exhibit, Orange County, N.Y., 1987, 94; mem. selection com. County Exec. art awards, Rockland County, 1990, 94. Active Art in Pub. Places Com., Rockland County, 1991—; mem. edn. bd. Reform Temple Suffern, Rockland County, 1987-88; mem. Leadership Rockland, 1993-94. Mem. Communication Profls. Rockland, Hudson Valley Mktg. Assn. (Eclat design award 1991, 92, 93), Rockland Bus. Assn.

BYNUM, HENRI SUE, education and French educator; b. Columbia, Miss., Feb. 7, 1944; d. George Milton and Lois Marie (Newsom) Dearing; m. James Lamar Bynum Jr., Feb. 28, 1965; children: James Wesley, Charles Drew. BA, U. So. Miss., 1967, MEd, 1977, PhD, 1979. Cert. tchr., Fla. Tchr. French, Spanish, modern dance Natchez (Miss.) Adams Pub. Schs., 1972-76; tchr. ESL U. So. Miss., Hattiesburg, 1977-79, coord. academic programs English Lang. Inst., 1979-81, adj. prof., 1980-81; dir. internat. edn. So. Ctr. for Rsch. and Innovation, Hattiesburg, 1981-82; chmn., asst. prof. dept. ESL U. So. Ala., Mobile, 1982-85; tchr. French, Spanish Moss Point (Miss.) High Sch., 1985-86; tchr. French Vero Beach (Fla.) Jr. High, 1986-87; prof. edn., French, Indian River Community Coll., Ft. Pierce, Fla., 1987—; adj. prof. Mobile Coll., 1986; cons. for curriculum devel. Colegio LaCruz, Puerto LaCruz, Venezuela, Escuela Anaco (Venezuela); co-dir. ESL curriculum Workshop, Assn. Venezuelan Am. Schs., Anaco. Cons. Safe Space, Inc., Vero Beach, 1989—. Mem. Phi Delta Kappa, Kappa Delta Pi. Republican. : 4261 Deuce Ct Vero Beach FL 32968 Office: Indian River Community Coll 3209 Virginia Ave Fort Pierce FL 34981-5541

BYRAM, ELIZABETH NYE, photographer; b. Worcester, Mass., Sept. 29, 1943; d. Joseph Gibson and Nancy (Nye) B. Student, U. Conn., 1961-63, Art Student League, 1963-66; student of photography, Parson's Sch. of Design, 1965, 90, 91; student of lighting, Sch. of Visual Arts, N.Y.C., 1989. Outer space painting exhibitor Art Rental Program, Phila. Mus., 1968-69; photo montage exhibitor East Hampton Gallery, N.Y.C., 1968, Woodruff Art Ctr., Atlanta, 1988; outer space painting exhibitor Lord & Taylor, N.Y.C., 1970, Sindin Harris Gallery, Hartsdale, N.Y., 1970; ann. competition Alexandria (La.) Mus., 1988; exhibitor Contemporary Am. Painting Soc. of the Four Arts Mus., Palm Beach, Fla., 1989; one woman show The Marine Mus., Amagansett, N.Y., 1989; seascape photo exhbn. The Picture Emporium, Westhampton, N.Y., 1991, Photographer's Forum Mag., 1991; landscape photography European Art, N.Y.C., 1992; photography Parrish Art Mus., Southampton, N.Y., 1992. Exhibited in group shows at Del Mar (Calif.) Fair, 1991, Water Tower Gallery, Louisville, 1991-93, Art 1 Gallery, Southampton, N.Y., 1991, Smith Nautical Gallery, N.Y.C., 1992, L.A. County Fair, 1992, Md. Fedn. of Art, Annapolis, 1994, Soc. Contemporary Photography, Kansas City, Mo., 1994, Eastman Kodak and Cornell Capa sponsored Juried Exhbn., Freeport, N.Y., 1994, Millenium Gallery, East Hampton, N.Y., 1994, Imaging New Jersey, 1995-96; represented in permanent collection Mus. of City of N.Y., numerous corp. collections in N.Y. area. Participating photographer The Partnership for the Homeless Benefit Auction, Christies Auction House, N.Y.C., 1990. Recipient Photography award Long Beach Mus., 1984, Robert May Photo award Mamaroneck Artists' Guild, N.Y., 1986, Ann. Photo Search award Barclay Graphics, Hollywood, Fla., 1989, Photo award Akron Art Mus., 1992, Best in Show in Photography award Three River Arts Festival The Carnegie Inst. of Pitts., 1991, Marine Art Photo award Sea Heritage Found., N.Y.C., 1992. Mem. NAFE, Am. Soc. Picture Profls. Home and Studio: 200 E 58th St New York NY 10022

BYRD, CHRISTINE WATERMAN SWENT, lawyer; b. Oakland, Calif., Apr. 11, 1951; d. Langan Waterman and Eleanor (Herz) Swent; m. Gary Lee Byrd, June 20, 1981; children: Amy, George. BA, Stanford U., 1972; JD, U. Va., 1975. Bar: Calif. 1976, U.S. Dist. Ct. (ctrl., so. no., ea. dists.) Calif., U.S. Ct. appeals (9th cir.). Law clk. to Hon. William P. Gray, U.S. Dist. Ct., L.A., 1975-76; assoc. Jones, Day, Reavis & Pogue, L.A., 1976-82, ptnr., 1987—; asst. U.S. atty. criminal divsn. U.S. Atty.'s Office-Cen. Dist. Calif., L.A., 1982-87. Author: The Future of the U.S. Multinational Corporation, 1975; contbr. articles to profl. jours. Mem. Am. Arbitration Assn. (Calif. adv. com., large and complex cases 1992—), Fed. Bar Assn., Calif. State Bar (com. fed. cts. 1985-88), L.A. County Bar Assn., Women Lawyers Assn. L.A. County, Stanford Profl. Women L.A. County, Stanford Alumni Assn., Ninth Jud. Cir. Hist. Soc. (bd. dirs. 1986—). Republican. Office: Jones Day Reavis & Pogue 555 W 5th St Fl 46 Los Angeles CA 90013-1010

BYRD, D. TONI, lawyer; b. Ft. Wayne, Ind., July 20, 1954; d. Milton Bruce and Susanne J. (Schwerin) B. BA, U. Tulsa, 1978; JD, Northeastern U., 1986. Bar: Pa. 1986, U.S. Dist. Ct. (mid. dist.) Pa. 1988, U.S. Ct. Appeals (3d cir.) 1989, U.S. Ct. Appeals (D.C. cir.) 1989, U.S. Supreme Ct. 1991. Exec. dir. Lewisburg (Pa.) Prison Project, 1982-83; pub. housing coord. Union County Housing Authority, Lewisburg, 1980-83; fed. jud. law clk. U.S. Dist. Ct., Williamsport, Pa., 1986-88; asst. fed. pub. defender Fed. Pub. Defenders, Williamsport, 1988—; bd. dirs. Lewisburg Prison Project, Susquehanna Valley Women in Transition, Lewisburg. Recipient Recognition of Leadership award NAACP, Lewisburg, 1982, 83. Mem. ABA, Fed. Bar Assn. (treas. 1994), Nat. Assn. Criminal Def. Attys., Pa. Bar Assn., Pa. Assn. Criminal Def. Attys. Office: Fed Pub Defenders 1 Executive Plz Ste 302 330 Pine St Williamsport PA 17701

BYRD, GISÈLE MARIE, publishing executive, book designer; b. Dothan, Ala., June 10, 1956; d. John Edwin and Yvonne Caroline (Mertz) B. BS in Journalism, U. Md., 1979; Diplome, U. Sorbonne, Paris, 1986. Design mgr. Nat. Telephone Coop. Assn., Washington, 1980-83; freelance designer Paris, 1983-87; art dir. Univ. Press Am., Lanham, Md., 1987-89, v.p. design, 1991—. Mem. organizing com. Mardi Gras Masquerade Ball for charity, Balt., 1992, 93, 94. Mem. Washington Book Pubs. (book jacket design award 1992, 93). Democrat. Office: Univ Press Am 4720 Boston Way Lanham Seabrook MD 20706-4310

BYRD, MARY JANE, education educator; b. Topeka, Apr. 21, 1946; d. Vernon Thomas and Mary Elizabeth (Caldwell) Wharton; m. Gerald David Byrd, June 24, 1965; children: Kari, Juli, Cori. BS, U. So. Ala., 1980, MBA, 1984; D of Bus. Adminstrn., Nova Southeastern U., 1991. Dental asst. Gerald E. Berger, DMD, Mobile, Ala., 1963-65; dental hygenist Robert P. Hall, DMD, Mobile, Ala., 1965-66; teller Am. Nat. Bank, Mobile, Ala., 1972-75; office mgr. Byrd Surveying, Inc., Mobile, Ala., 1975-80; div. acct. cafeteria Morrison, Inc., Mobile, Ala., 1980-82; mgmt. cons. pvt. practice Mobile, Ala., 1982-84; lectr. acctg. U. South Ala., Mobile, Ala., 1984; asst.

prof. acctg. & mgmt. Univ. Mobile, Mobile, Ala., 1984-89; assoc. prof. acctg. & mgmt. Mobile Coll., 1989—; reviewer Internat. Jour. Pub. Adminstrn., 1991—; dir. Nat. Assn. Accts., Mobile, 1986-89. Author: Supervisory Management Study Guide/Southwestern, 1993, Small Business Management: An Entrepreneur's Guide to Success/Irwin, 1994; contbr. articles to profl. jours. Named Assoc. of the Month, Home Builders Assn., 1986, Charles S. Dismukes Outstanding Mem., Nat. Assn. Accts. Mem. AAUW, Acad. Mgmt., Am. Bus. Women Assn., Assn. for Bus. Grad. Dirs., Mortgage Lenders Assn., So. Acad. Mgmt. Office: Univ Mobile PO Box 13220 Mobile AL 36663-0220

BYRD, MYONA SUE, library media specialist; b. Oak Ridge, Tenn., Oct. 6, 1947; d. Paul Eugene Sr. and Dorothy Ophelia (Driver) Gipson; children: Robert Kevin, Brian Lee. BS, Cumberland Coll., 1968; MA in Edn., Ea. Ky. U., 1978. Cert. elem. tchr. 1-8; cert. sch. libr. K-12. Sec. Cumberland Coll., Williamsburg, Ky., 1965-68; cert. social worker Ky. Dept. of Social Svcs., Corbin and Williamsburg, 1968-73; elem. tchr. Williamsburg Ind. Sch., 1975-84, libr., media technology specialist, 1984—; co-organizer Hug-A-Book Project, Williamsburg Ind. Sch., 1989-90, initiated celebrity reader program, 1991—, Libr. Power Program, 1994—; treas. UCEA Librs., Ky., 1991-92. Mem. 1st Bapt. Ch., Williamsburg, 1990—, PTA; tech. com. Williamsburg Ind. Sch., 1992—. Mem. Upper Cumberland Edn. Assn. Librs., Ky. Libr. Assn., Am. Libr. Assn., Ky. Sch. Media Assn., Phi Delta Kappa. Republican. Baptist. Home: 144 N 9th St Williamsburg KY 40769-1703

BYRD, SANDRA JUDITH, computer specialist; b. Detroit, July 14, 1960; d. Brian Kenneth and Ruth (Jocius) Paukstys; m. Michael Keith Byrd, Nov. 23, 1985; children: Kristin Michelle, Adam Keith. BA, So. Ill. U., 1994. Asst. mgr. Colony West Swim Club, 1979, mgr., summers, 1980-82; aquatic supr. So. Ill. U., Carbondale, 1982; asst. mgr. Body Shop, Vero Beach, Fla., 1984; office mgr. Insta-Med Clinics, Inc., Vero Beach, 1984; receptionist Redgate Communications Corp., Vero Beach, 1985, circulation asst., 1985-87, circulation mgr., 1987-88; circulation dir. TT Pubs., Inc., Longwood, Fla., 1988-89; supr. of nursing payroll Orlando (Fla.) Regional Med. Ctr., 1989—, computer specialist nursing adminstrn. computer support, 1990-91; info. specialist dept. ops. improvement Orlando Regional Healthcare System, 1993—; bus. mgr. Treasure Coast Diagnostics, Inc., 1987-88. Ill. State scholar, 1979-82. Mem. NAFE. Home: 19429 Spring Oak Dr Eustis FL 32726-7238 Office: Orlando Regional Med Ctr 1414 Kuhl Ave Orlando FL 32806-2008

BYRD, VERA LEE, university counselor; b. Barberton, Ohio, Apr. 25, 1960; d. Betty Jane (Brown) B. BA in Sociology, Mt. Union Coll., 1983; MA in Coll. Student Pers., Bowling Green State U., 1985. Asst. dean of student Denison U., Granville, Ohio, 1985-86; counselor minority student programs Behrend Coll. Pa. State U., Erie, 1987-88; youth svcs. adminstr., drug and alcohol therapeutic worker Erie County Youth Diversion Program John K. Kennedy Ctr., Inc., 1988-90; treatment specialist II, drug and alcohol outpatient therapeutic counselor Greater Erie Cmty. Action Com. Drug and Alcohol Svcs. Network; Act 101 counselor, higher edn. equal opportunity program Dept. Acad. Support Svcs. Edinboro U. Pa., 1990-93, Dept. Acad. Svcs. Shippensburg (Pa.) U., 1993—. Bd. dirs. Cumberland Valley Links, Mont Alto, Pa., 1994—; cons. Striving to Educate People, Chambersburg, Pa., 1993—. Honored by United Way Erie County for vol. svc., 1991, Holy Trinity Cmty. Ctr., 1990. Mem. Pa. Assn. Devel. Educators, Tri-State Consortium Equal Opportunity Programs in Higher Edn. Democrat. Mem. Ch. of God in Christ. Office: Shippensburg U 1871 Old Main Dr 304 Wright Hall Shippensburg PA 17257

BYRD-LAWLER, BARBARA ANN, association executive; b. Martinsburg, W.Va., Aug. 31, 1952; d. James Leonard and Elizabeth (Somerfield) Byrd; m. R. Michael Lawler, Jan. 24, 1981; 1 child, Marjorie Lynn. BS, Old Dominion U., 1973, MS, 1975; postgrad., U. Maryland, 1976. Cert. assn. exec. Instr. Old Dominion U., Norfolk, Va., 1972-75; asst. prof. U. Maryland, Balt., 1975-76; assoc. dir. Am. Dental Hygienists Assn., Chgo., 1976-79; dir. edn. Am. Coll. Preventive Medicine, Washington, 1979-81; dir. profl. affairs Tex. Pharm. Assn., Austin, 1981-83; dir. edn. and research Tex. Med. Assn., Austin, 1983-86; exec. v.p. Internat. Assn. Hospitality Accts., Austin, 1986-90, Community Assns. Inst., Alexandria, Va., 1990—; chair Assns. Advance Am. Com., 1994—. Bd. dirs. Nat. Bd. Cardiopulmonary Credentialing, Gaitersburg, N.D., 1981-82, mem. exec. com. 1982; bd. dirs. South Tex. Arthritis Found., San Antonio, 1987-89, Capital Area Arthritis Found., Austin, 1986-89; founding chmn. Travis County Adult Literacy Coun., Austin, 1984-90, chmn. emeritus 1990—; bd. dirs. Am. Hotel and Motel Assn. Research Found., 1988-90. Recipient award Internat. Assn. Bus. Communicators, 1988; named one of Outstanding Young Women Am., 1981, Top 10 Bus. Women of Yr., Am. Bus. Women's Assn., 1986, Greater Washington Soc. of Assn. Execs. Monument award in edn., 1992. Fellow Am. Soc. Assn. Execs. (charter, vice chmn. 1991-92, planning com. 1985-88, 91-92, Assn. Advance Am. and planning com. 1991—, chair Assn. Advance Am. com. 1994, bd. dirs. 1985-86, 88—, chmn. edn. sect. 1985-86, chmn. task force on social responsibility 1989—, chair fellows 1989-90, Excellence award 1985, 88, 94, CAE commr. 1991-93, Mgmt. Achievement award 1983, sec.-treas. 1993-94, gov. task force 1992-93); mem. Town Lake Bus. Women's Assn. (Woman of Yr. 1986), Tex. Soc. Assn. Execs. (com. chair 1981—), Greater Washington Soc. Assn. Execs. (CAE cert. com., instr. and tutor 1991-92), Leadership Austin, Leadership Tex. (bd. dirs., tng. group 1987—), World Future Soc., Internat. Assn. Hosp. Accts. (hon. 1990). Home: 4203 Wilton Woods Ln Alexandria VA 22310-2942 Office: Community Assns Inst 1630 Duke St Alexandria VA 22314-3426

BYRNE, BARBARA MOAKLER, investment banker; b. Holyoke, Mass., Aug. 23, 1954; d. Howard William Moakler and Margaret Hazel (Mulligan) O'Donnell; m. Brendan Thomas Byrne Jr., Sept. 28, 1985; children: Meaghan, Erin, Brendan. BA, Mt. Holyoke Coll., 1976; MBA, NYU, 1980. Various positions, then supply analyst Mobil Corp., N.Y.C., 1976-80; assoc. Lehman Bros., N.Y.C., 1980-83, v.p., 1983-85, sr. v.p., 1985-88, mng. dir., 1988—. Contbr. articles on corp. fin. to profl. jours. and books. Mem. Jr. League N.Y. Democrat. Roman Catholic. Home: 101 Hun Rd Princeton NJ 08540-6723 Office: Lehman Bros 200 Vesey St New York NY 10285*

BYRNE, JAMIE MARIA, communications educator; b. Belleville, Ill., July 31, 1961; d. Charles Henry III and Betty Jean (Stokes) Doerge ; m. Charles Alan Byrne, Oct. 10, 1987. BS in English and Journalism, Murray (Ky.) State U., 1983, MS in Comm., 1985; postgrad., Pa. State U. Sys. mgr. Murray State News, 1983-84; asst. prof. U. Wis., Platteville, 1984-88, Elizabethtown Coll., 1988-91, Millersville U. of Pa., 1991—; adj. prof. Millersville U. of Pa., 1989-91. Big Sister Grant County (Wis.) Dept. Family Svcs., 1985-88; dir. Platteville Community Players, 1986; pub. rels. specialist Theatre of the Seventh Sister, Lancaster, Pa., 1990-91; publicity com. mem. Jamison Mus. Assn., Platteville, 1987-88. Faculty Devel. grantee Pa. State Sys. Higher Edn., 1992; Journalism Edn. grantee Gannett Found., 1990; grantee U. Wis., 1986-87; Jesse Stuart fellow Murray State U., 1983. Mem. NAFE, Pub. Rels. Soc. Am. (sec. Cen. Pa. chpt. 1990-91, pres. 1993, bd. dirs. 1990-91, 94—), Nat. Broadcasting Soc. (nat. v.p. regional devel. 1986-92, nat. pres. 1993—, Outstanding Profl. mem. U. Wis., Platteville chpt. 1987), Coll. Media Advisors, Am. Culture Assn. Roman Catholic.

BYRNE, OLIVIA SHERRILL, lawyer; b. Trenton, N.J., Aug. 14, 1957; d. Stewart and Elizabeth (Sherrill) B. Student, Vanderbilt U., 1975-76; BA, Bowdoin Coll., 1979; JD, U. Toledo, 1982; LLM in Taxation, Georgetown U., 1987. Bar: Tex. 1982, Ohio 1984, Md. 1985. Assoc. Whiteford, Taylor & Preston, Balt., 1984-87, Linowes & Blocher, Silver Spring, Md., 1987-90, Weinberg & Jacobs, Rockville, Md., 1990—. Author: The At-Risk Rules Under the Tax Reform Act of 1986, The Door Closes on Tax Motivated Investments, IRS Issues New Guidelines for Management Contracts Used for Facilities Financed with Tax Exempt Bonds, 1993, RRA '93 Loosens Real Estate Rules for Exempt Organizations, 1993. Mem. Tax Coun. for State of Md. Mem. ABA (exempt orgn. com. taxation sect. 1991—), Md. Bar Assn. (coun. taxation sect.), Balt. City Bar Assn. (chmn. speakers bur. young lawyers sect.), Lawyers for Arts Washington, Comml. Real Estate Woman (bd. dirs., pres.-elect), Profls. for Strathmore Hall (co-chmn.), D.C. Bowdoin Coll. Alumni Assn. (pres. 1992—), Howard County C. of C. (legis. com. 1989), Rotary. Home: 107 N Brook Ln Bethesda MD Office: Weinberg & Jacobs One Ctrl Plz Ste 1200 11300 Rockville Pike Rockville MD 20852

BYRNES, CHRISTINE ANN, internist; b. Darby, Pa., Dec. 18, 1951; d. John Edward and Olga (Rebechi) B. BA, U. Del., Newark, 1974; MD, Jefferson Med. Coll., Phila., 1978. Diplomate Am. Bd. Internal Medicine. Resident internal medicine Thomas Jefferson U. Hosp., Phila., 1978-81; coord. internal medicine residency program U. Med. & Dentistry of N.J./ Cooper Med. Ctr., Camden, 1981-82; attending physician Thomas Jefferson U. Hosp., 1982-87, instr. medicine, 1982-85, clin. asst. prof. medicine, 1985-87; assoc. dir. Merck Human Health, West Point, Pa., 1987-89; sr. assoc. dir. Merck Human Health, 1989-91, dir., 1991-92, sr. dir., 1992—. Mem. ACP, Soc. Gen. Internal Medicine, Am. Soc. Internal Medicine, Am. Soc. Clin. Pharmacology and Therapeutics, Am. Geriatrics Soc.

BYRON, BEVERLY BUTCHER, congresswoman; b. Balt., July 27, 1932; d. Harry C. and Ruth Butcher; m. Goodloe E. Byron, 1952 (dec.); children: Goodloe E. Jr., Barton Kimball, Mary McComas; m. B. Kirk Walsh, 1986. Student, Hood Coll., 1962-64. Mem. 96th-102nd Congresses from 6th Md. dist., 1979-93; Presdl. appt. to base closing and realignment commn., 1993. State treas. Md. Young Dems., 1962, 65; bd. assocs. Hood Coll.; bd. visitors USAF Acad., 1980-87; trustee Mt. St. Mary's Coll.; bd. dirs. Frederick County chpt. ARC; sec. Frederick Heart Assn., 1974-79; mem. Frederick Phys. Fitness Commn.; chmn. Md. Phys. Fitness Commn., 1979-89; mem. Frederick County Landmarks Found.; bd. dirs. Am. Hiking Soc.; bd. dirs. Adventure Sports Inst., 1992—; bd. advisors Internat. Studies Frostburg State U., 1990—, Am. Volkssport Assn., 1991—. Episcopalian. Home: 306 Grove Blvd Frederick MD 21701-4813

BYRON, CINDI HANSEN, executive; b. Glendive, Mont., Feb. 9, 1954; d. Bernie Lawrence Jr. and Lois Marie (Rilla) Hansen; m. Dennis Dean Byron, July 3, 1992. Grad. high sch., Glendive, Mont. Bookkeeper Robert Fladmo CPA, Glendive, Mont., 1972-75; deputy to treas. Dawson County, Glendive, Mont., 1975-87, county treas., 1987—. Leader 4-H, Glendive, 1973—; mem. Vets. Nursing Home Com., Glendive, 1992—; treas. Our Savior Luth. Ch., Glendive, 1988-92; mem. Dawson County Dem. Ctr. Com., 1987—. Mem. Mont. County Treas. Assn. (sec./treas. 1992-93, v.p. 1993-94, pres. 1994-95), Burlington No. Credit Union (bd. dirs. 1990—), Women of Moose. Office: Dawson County Treas 207 W Bell St Glendive MT 59330-1616

BYRON, RITA ELLEN COONEY, travel executive, publisher, real estate agent, photojournalist, writer; b. Cleve.; d. Harry James and Marie (Hakey) Cooney; m. Carl James Byron Jr., Nov. 27, 1954 (dec.); children: Carey Lewis, Carl James, Bradford William. Student Cleve. Coll., 1954, Western Res. U., 1955, John Carroll U., 1956; PhD (hon.), Colo. State Christian Coll., 1972. Mgr. European Immigration dept. U.S. Steamship Lines, Cleve., 1956; real estate agt. W.I. White Realtor Inc., Shaker Heights, Ohio, 1965-67, J.P. Malone Realtors Inc., Shaker Heights, 1967-70, Thomas Murray & Assocs., 1971-76, Mary Anderson Realty, Shaker Heights, 1978-79, Barth Brad & Andrews Realtors Inc., Shaker Heights, 1979—, Heights Realty, 1986—; v.p., co-owner Your Connection To Travel, Kent, Ohio, 1980—; v.p., gen. mgr. World Class Travel Agy., 1985—; dir. Travel One div. Quaker Sq., Akron, Travel Trends for Singles, 1985, Playhouse Sq. Travel, 1986, World Class Internat., 1986. Mem. U.S. Figure Skating Assn., 1960—, Wightman Cup Women's Com., 1965—; mem. women's com. Cleve. Mus. of Art, 1969—, Friendship Force Ohio, 1986 ; co-chmn. Cleve. Invitational Figure Skating Competition, 1972—; chmn. Gold Rush Rush, U.S. Ski Team, 1982, Cleve. benefit U.S. Olympic Teams, Midas Touch, 1983, Gran Apres-Ski Prix, 1981, blue ribbon ball Hunt Club for Handicapped; patron Cleve. 500, 1983; originator Benefits Unltd., Exceptional Single Person's, Connections Unltd., 1983; founder, coordinator Singled Out Club, 1983; coptnr., adv. bd. The Service Service, 1984; benefit chmn., patroness various balls and fund-raising events; vol. Foster Parents Inc., 1983; vol. Council on World Affairs, 1983, Bellefaire Home for Spl. Children, 1983, Big Sisters Greater Cleve., 1983, Camp Cheerful, 1983, Chisholm Ctr., 1983, Children's Diabetic Camp Ho Mita Koda, 1984, Young Audiences, 1985; adv. trustee Friends of Fairmount Theatre of the Deaf, 1983; mem. Greater Cleve. Growth Assn., 1983. Mem. Western Res. Hist. Soc., Garden Ctr. Greater Cleve., Friends Cleve. Pub. Library, UN Assn. of U.S., Cleve. Council World Affairs, U.S. Ski Ednl. Fund (chmn. benefits), English Speaking Union (jr. bd.), Travel Age Exchange, Globetrotters Internat. Fedn. Women's Travel Orgns., North Coast Exec. Women's Network, Growth Assn., Council on Small Enterprises. Cleve. Real Estate Bd., Cleve. Photographic Soc. (bd. dirs. 1989—), Camera Guild (exec. bd. trustees 1989), Associated Photographers, Photographic Soc. Am. Clubs: Cleve. Skating, Broadmoor World Arena Figure Skating, Colony Beach and Racquet, Suburban Ski, Cleve. Advertising, Communicator's, Towne Hall, Women's City, Gilmour Acad. Women's, Mid-Day, Cleve. Wellesley, Arctic Circle, Intrepid Traveler, Tibet, Mongolia and China Explorers', Himalaya Yeti (1987 Nepal Expdn.), Internat. Chagrin Valley Camera, Nat. Hist. Mus. Photo Soc., Kodochromse Adventure Soc., Nature Artists Soc., Cleve. Astronomical Soc., Archeol. Soc., Holden Aborteum Soc., East Berlin Photo Club, Chagrin Valley Photo Club, Shaker Lakes Nature Club, Met. Parks, Photography Club, Photocrafters, Sanctuary Marsh Photo, Cuyahoga Valley Nat. Pk. Photo Club (assoc. photographer, various photography awards). Co-pub., exec. editor The Single Register (pub. documentary book The Fall of the Wall 1989), other publs.; featured in numerous publs. Home: 18126 Lomond Blvd Cleveland OH 44122-5012 Office: World Class Travel 3520 Ingleside Rd Cleveland OH 44122-5002 also: Es Turo Edificio, Kontiki, Majorica Balearic Islands Spain

BYRUM, DIANNE, state legislator; b. Mar. 18, 1954; d. Cecil Dershem and Mary D.; m. James E. Byrum; children: Barbara Anne, James Richard. AA, Lansing Cmty. Coll.; BS cum laude, Mich. State U. Rep. dist. 68 State of Mich., 1991—; owner Blackhawk Hardware, Leslie, Mich., 1983—; vice chmn. transp. com. State of Mich., chair liquor control com., mem. conservation, environment & great lakes, edn. & local govt. coms. Recipient Disting. Citizen award Ingham County Soil Conservation Dist., 1991, Disting. Alumnus award Lansing Cmty. Coll., 1993. Mem. Am. Cancer Soc. (Ingham-Delta branch mem. bd. dirs.), Mich. Retail Hardware Assn., Ingham County Farm Bur., Lansing Regional C. of C., Greater Lansing Safety Coun., S. Lansing Bus. Assn., S. Lansing-Everett Kiwanis, Women Bus. Owners. Democrat. Home: 4933 Bellevue Onondaga MI 49264*

BYSIEWICZ, SUSAN, state legislator; b. New Haven, Conn.. BA magna cum laude, Yale Coll., 1983; JD, Duke U., 1986. Pol. reporter N.Y. Times, Washington, 1985; campaign mgr., issues dir. White & Case, N.Y., 1986-88, Blumenthal, Hartford & Stamford, Conn., 1990, Robinson & Cole, Hartford, Conn., 1988—; mem. Middletown Dem. Com., 1989—; rep. dist. 100 State of Conn., 1993—; atty. Author: Ella: A Biography of Governor Ella T. Grasso, 1984; contbr. chpt. to book. Conn. Bar Assn., N.Y. Bar Assn. Democrat. Address: Conn House of Reps State Capitol Hartford CT 06106*

CAADERS, CATHERINE, counselor; b. Yonkers, N.Y.; d. Ambrose Victor Jr. and Bette (Flynn) McCall; m. Marc Caaders, Feb. 14, 1985. B in Elem. Edn., U. Dayton, 1967; M in Spl. Edn., Manhattan Coll., 1972; M in Counseling, Fordham U., 1978, profl. diploma, 1989. Cert. sch. counselor, spl. educator, elem. tchr., N.Y. Elem. tchr. Pub. Schs., Yonkers, N.Y., 1968-77, tchr. of learning disabled, 1977-86; high sch. counselor Saunders Trade and Tech. High Sch., Yonkers, 1986-90, Rome (N.Y.) Free Acad., 1992—; counselor Staley Jr. High Sch., Rome, 1990-92; part time family counselor Cath. Archdiocese N.Y., Bronx and Spring Valley, 1978-82; part time acad. advisor Pace U., Briarcliff, Pleasantville, N.Y., 1979-83.ž. N.Y. State Occupational Equity Ctr. grantee, 1990-91; N.Y. State Dept. Labor fellow, 1992. Mem. Assn. Counseling and Devel., N.Y. State Assn. Counseling and Devel., N.Y. Assn. Coll. Admission Counselors, Mohawk Valley Counselors Assn. Republican. Office: Rome Free Acad 500 Turin St Rome NY 13440-3398

CAAMANO, KATHLEEN ANN FOLZ, gifted education professional; b. Rozellville, Wis., Dec. 20, 1944; d. Joseph and Isabel Ann (Brost) Folz; m. Gerald J. Caamano, Aug. 10, 1968; children: Michelle, David. BS, U. Wis., Stevens Point, 1968; MA, Cen. Mich. U., 1971. Cert. tchr., Ill. Tchr. Midland (Mich.) Pub. Schs., 1968-74, Newark (Ohio) City Schs., 1974-77; tchr. Minooka (Ill.) Sch. Dist., 1986—, coord. gifted edn., 1986—. Pres. Camelot Homeowners Assn., Joliet, Ill., 1985; tutor Big Bros./Big Sisters Assn. Will County, 1990; voter registrar Will County, Joliet, 1992—. Recipient Those Who Excel award Ill State Bd. Edn., 1992. Mem. Internat. Reading Assn., Ill. Edn. Assn. (tchr. rep. 1992—), Gifted Edn. Coun., Ill. Assn. Ednl. Rsch. and Evaluation, Will County Reading Coun., Delta Kappa Gamma (v.p.), Beta Sigma Phi (pres.). Roman Catholic. Home: 22257 S Galahad Dr Joliet IL 60436-7611

CABANAS, ELIZABETH ANN, nutritionist; b. Port Arthur, Tex., Oct. 27, 1948; d. William Rosser and Frances Merle (Block) Thornton. BS, U. Tex., 1971; MPH, U. Hawaii, 1973. Registered dietitian. Clin. nutritionist Family Planning Inst., Honolulu, 1972-74; dietitian Kauikeolani Hosp., Honolulu, 1974-75; dietitian San Antonio Ind. Schs., 1975-84, asst. food service adminstr., 1984-89; coord. equipment and facilities Dallas Ind. Sch., 1990-91; nutritionist div. endocrinology, metabolism and hypertension, clin. studies unit rsch. nutritionist, asst. prof. dept. health related scis. U. Tex. Med. Br., Galveston, 1991—; lectr. nutrition U. Hawaii, Honolulu, 1974-75; lectr. St. Mary's U., San Antonio Coll., 1984-90; mem. adj. faculty Tex. Woman's U., 1994—; cons. dietitian, 1980-92; presenter in field. Contbr. articles to profl. jours. Mem. Allegro San Antonio Symphony Orch., 1984—, Galveston Symphony; patron The Grand 1894 Opera House, Galveston Island, Knights of Regina Krewe, Galveston Hist. Found. Recipient diabetes educator recognition Eli Lilly & Co., 1994. Mem. Am. Diabetes Assn., Am. Assn. Diabetes Educators, Assn. Sch. Bus. Ofcls. Internat., Nutrition and Food Svc. Mgmt. Com., Am. Dietetic Assn., Coun. Nutritional Scis. and Metabolism (profl. sect., non-peer rev. com. 1993—), Tex. Sch. Food Svc. Assn. (dist. bd. dirs. 1977-78), Tex. State Nutrition Coun. (sports and cardiovascular nutritionists practice group, Tex. gerontologists practice group), San Antonio Sch. Food Svc. Assn. (com. chmn. 1975-89), Tex. Assn. Sch. Bus. Ofcls., Tex. Restaurant Assn., San Antonio Area Food Svc. Adminstrs. Assn. (pres. 1989-90), Assn. Profls. in Positions Leadership in Edn., Dallas Dietetic Assn. (cons. nutritionists practice group, chair 1990-91), San Antonio Mus. Assn., Randolph C. of C., Galveston Art League, Space City Ski Club, Sierra Club, Hawaii Club (chmn. entertainment com. 1983). Republican. Methodist. Home: 711 Holiday Dr Apt 75 Galveston TX 77550-5579 Office: U Tex Med Br Rte M-40 301 University Blvd Galveston TX 77550-2708

CABANYA, MARY LOUISE, software development executive, rancher; b. Denver, Nov. 3, 1947; d. Dareo and Hellen Etta (Charley) Mattivi; m. Robert L. Cabanya, Jan. 6, 1978. BS in Math., U. So. Colo., 1969; postgrad., Regis U., 1985. Flight test engr. Boeing Co., Seattle, 1969-75; computer scientist Telephone Computing Service, Seattle, 1975-77; support engr. Digital Equipment Corp., Denver, 1977-79; cons. computer systems Colorado Springs, Colo., 1979-92; program mgr. Digital Equipment Corp., Colorado Springs, 1980-92; owner, operator ostrich ranch Little Pines Ranch, Colorado Springs. Mem. Rocky Mountain Ratite Assn., Am. Ostrich Assn., Aircraft Owners Pilots Assn. Republican. Roman Catholic.

CABLE, MABEL ELIZABETH, urban planner, artist; b. Sewickley, Pa., May 23, 1935; d. Andrew Lee and Josephine (James) Yeck; m. Charles Allen Cable, Dec. 19, 1955; children: Christopher A., Carolyn E. BS, Edinboro U., 1958; M in Urban-Rural Planning, U. Pitts., 1982. Tchr. Mount Union (Pa.) Jr.-Sr. High Sch., 1964-69; graphics illustrator Crawford County Planning Commn., Meadville, Pa., 1974-79, planner, 1979-86; asst. dir. planning Crawford County Planning Commn., Meadville, 1987-94. Exhibitor Foothills Art Gallery, Golden, Colo., 1986-87, Pastimes Gallery, Meadville, Pa., 1987—. Bd. dirs. Penn Lakes coun. Girl Scouts U.S.A., Meadville, 1974-79; pres. John Brown Heritage Assn., Meadville, 1985-88; mem. adv. coun. Pa. Community Devel. Block Grant Com., Harrisburg, 1987-94, chmn., 1990-94. Mem. Am. Inst. of Cert. Planners, Am. Planning Assn., Pa. Planning Assn. Home: 199 Jefferson St Meadville PA 16335-1108

CABOT, JANE FENDERSON, public relations executive; b. Biddeford, Maine; d. Charles Warren and Janet Clare (Hazelton) Fenderson; m. Edward S. Cabot, June 8, 1981; stepchildren: Edward S. Jr., Eliot, Elizabeth. AB magna cum laude, Mt. Holyoke Coll., 1965. Legis. asst. to Sen. Edmund S. Muskie U.S. Senate, Washington, 1965-72, counsel subcomm. on intergovtl. rels., 1972-76; appointments sec., dir. scheduling to First Lady Rosalynn Carter White House, Washington, 1976-81; exec. v.p. M Booth & Assocs., N.Y.C., 1987—. Exec. com. Women's Commn. Refugee Women and Children, 1990—. Office: M Booth & Assocs 470 Park Ave S New York NY 10016

CABOT, LINDA ANN, management information systems adminstrator, educator; b. Charlottesville, Va., Apr. 11, 1947; d. Thomas Edwin and Lillian Mae (Mullen) Grinels; m. John McElroy Cabot, Aug. 25, 1968 (div. 1980); children: Christiane Ann, Lauren McElroy. A.A., John Wood Coll., Quincy, Ill., 1976; BA, Quincy Coll., 1977; MS, George Williams Coll., Downers Grove, Ill., 1979. Juvenile probation officer DuPage County, Wheaton, Ill., 1979-80; career guidance specialist San Juan Coll., Farmington, N.Mex., 1980-81; counselor San Juan Mental Health Ctr., Farmington, 1981-82; counselor U. Albuquerque, 1983-83, dir. career planning/placement, 1983-85; specialist career planning Am. Coll. Testing, 1985-87; mgr. mktg. Ga. Tech., 1987-89, mgr. user svcs., 1989-92, assoc. dir. client svcs., 1992—, instr. campus quality initiative, 1994—. Presentor Profl. workshops N.Mex. Mental Health Conf., 1981, computer programs Ga. Ann. Computing Conf., 1986-93; counselor trainer Nat. Indian Youth Council, Albuquerque, 1981; career program facilitator CETA, 1981. Mem. New Futures Adv. Bd., Albuquerque, 1983-84; planner N.Mex. Commn. on Status of Women, 1984; Mem. Am. Coll. Personnel Assn., Helpdesk Inst. (pres. Atlanta chpt. 1994, 95). Democrat. Office: Ga Inst Tech OIT Client Svcs Atlanta GA 30332-0710

CABRERA, CARMEN, educational administrator, educator; b. Havana, Cuba, Dec. 31, 1948; came to U.S., 1962; d. Armando and Carmen (Gomez) C. AA, East L.A. Coll., 1970; BA, Calif. State U., L.A., 1972; MA, Calif. State U., 1975. Cert. tchr. Tchr. Sacred Heart of Mary H.S., Montebello, Calif., 1973-91, acad. dean, 1989-91; tchr., curriculum dir. Cantwell Sacred Heart of Mary H.S., Montebello, 1991—; instr. East L.A. Coll., Monterey Park, Calif., 1974-77; chairperson dept. fgn. lang. Sacred Heart of Mary H.S., 1980-91, Cantwell Sacred Heart of Mary H.S., 1991-93. Assoc. Beverly Hosp. Found., Montebello, 1990—. Mem. ASCD, Am. Assn. Tchrs. Spanish and Portuguese (contest dir. 1987-89), Am. Coun. on Teaching Fgn. Langs., Nat. Cath. Ednl. Assn., Phi Kappa Phi. Office: Cantwell Sacred Heart Mary 329 N Garfield Ave Montebello CA 90640-3803

CACCAMISE, GENEVRA LOUISE BALL (MRS. ALFRED E. CACCAMISE), retired librarian; b. Mayville, N.Y., July 22, 1934; d. Herbert Oscar and Genevra (Green) Ball; m. Alfred E. Caccamise, July 7, 1974. BA, Stetson U., DeLand, Fla., 1956; MLS, Syracuse U., 1967. Tchr. grammar sch., Sanford, Fla., 1956-57, elem. sch., Longwood, Fla., 1957-58; tchr., libr. Enterprise (Fla.) Sch., 1958-63; libr., media specialist Boston Ave. Sch., DeLand, 1963-82; head media specialist Blue Lake Sch., DeLand, 1982-87, ret., 1987. Author Volusia County manual Instructing the Library Assistant, 1965. Charter mem. West Volusia Meml. Hosp. aux., DeLand, 1962-81; leader Girl Scout U.S., 1955-56; area dir. Fla. Edn. Assn., Volusia county, 1963-65; bd. dirs. Alhambra Villas Home Owners Assn., 1972-75; bd. trustees DeLand Pub. Library, 1977-86, sec., 1978-80, v.p., 1980-82, pres. 1982-84; v.p. Friends of DeLand Pub. Library, 1987, pres., 1989, 90, 95, bd. dirs., 1991—, newsletter editor 1992-95; charter mem. Guild of the DeLand Mus. Art, v.p., 1990, pres. 1991-92, bd. dirs. 1991—; co-orgn. chmn. Friends DeLand Mus. Art, 1993; bd. dir. West Volusia Hist. Soc., 1995. Mem. AAUW (2d v.p. chpt. 1965-67, rec. sec. 1961-65, 78-80, pres. 1980-82, parliamentarian 1982-84), Assn. Childhood Edn. (1st v.p. 1965-66, corr. sec. 1963-65), DAR (chpt. registrar 1969-80, asst. chief page Continental Congress, Washington 1962-65), Fla. Libr. Assn., Bus. & Profl. Women's Club (corr. sec. DeLand 1968-71, 2d v.p. 1969-70), Stetson U. Alumni Assn. (class chmn. for ann. fund drive 1968), Volusia County Assn. Media in Edn. (treas. 1977), Volusia County Retired Educators Assn. (pres. Unit II 1988-90, scholarship chmn. 1992—), Soc. of Mayflower Descendants (lt. gov. Francis Cook Colony 1988-90), Pilgrim John Howland Soc., Colonial Dames XVII Century, Magna Charta Dames, Nat. Soc. New Eng. Women (v.p. Daytona Beach Colony 1990-91), Hibiscus Garden Circle (treas. 1988-89, v.p. 1990-93), Delta Kappa Gamma (pres. Beta Psi chpt. 1982-84), Nat. Soc. of U.S. Daus. of 1812. (rec. sec. Peacock chpt. 1989-90), DeLand Garden Club (corresponding sec. 1993—, editor newsletter 1993—). Democrat. Episcopalian. Address: PO Box 241 Deland FL 32721

CACCIATORE SINNOTT, ANN FRANCES, special education educator; b. Phila., Mar. 26, 1953; m. Frank I. Cacciatore, Sept. 12, 1975; 1 child, Alice C. BS, U. Tampa, 1974; postgrad., U. South Fla., 1976-78, Fla. Co. U., 1979-81, U. Cen. Fla., 1988. Cert. tchr., Fla. Remedial tchr. Hillsborough County Pub. Schs., Tampa, Fla., 1975; lead tchr. gifted edn. program Polk County Pub. Schs., Winter Haven, Fla., 1976-79; tchr. of emotionally handicapped Polk County Pub. Schs., Dundee, Fla., 1979-80; tchr. spl. edn. Polk County Pub. Schs., Lakeland, Fla., 1980-82; lead tchr. spl. edn. Palm Beach County Pub. Schs., Lake Worth, Fla., 1983-85; behavior specialist, instrnl. support tchr., program asst. Orange County Pub. Schs., Orlando, Fla., 1990—. Co-author: Resource Manual for Emotionally-Handicapped Teachers, 1982; author learning games; developer Affective Curriculum Guide, Grades K-12. Grantee FDLRS, 1980, Coun. Exceptional Children, 1991-92; Found. Computer grante, 1992-93. Fellow Coun. Exceptional Children, Coun. for Children with Behavior Disorders; mem. PTA, Peace Found., Autistic Soc. Office: Orange County Pub Schs 445 W Amelia St Orlando FL 32801

CACHIA, JULIA CYBELE, systems programmer; b. Newport, R.I., Oct. 18, 1952; d. John Leslie Jr. and Shirley Anne (Smith) Bell; m. Myr C. Cachia, Dec. 24, 1981 (div. Nov. 1991). BA in Polit. Sci., Towson State U., 1976. Computer operator Balt. County Govt., Towson, Md., 1978-82, asst. data processing ops. supr. office of budget, 1982-86, asst. data processing ops. supr. health dept., 1986-89, systems programmer tech. support, 1989—; counselor, cons. various groups and informal networks, 1990—. Fellow Internat. Soc. Philos. Enquiry (sr. rsch. fellow, dir. testing 1979-81); mem. NAFE, Am. Ednl. Gender Info. Svc., Mensa, Wisdom Soc. Home: # 2400 28 Allegheny Ave Towson MD 21204-3921 Office: Balt County Govt Budget Off MS 3012 400 Washington Ave Towson MD 21204-4606

CADORETTE, LISA ROBERTS, medical/surgical nurse; b. Johnson City, N.Y., June 12, 1966; d. John Lawrence and Dorothy Ellen (Ace) Roberts; m. Jeffrey Cadorette, May 31,1991; children: Jessica Renee, Jacqueline Elyse. BSN magna cum laude, Neumann Coll., 1989. RN, Pa.; cert. ACLS Am. Heart Assn. Commd. lt. USAF Nurse Corps., 1989; staff nurse USAF Nurse Corps., Andrews AFB, Md., 1989-90, Dover AFB, Del., 1990-91; asst. to chair divsn. nursing and health scis. Neumann Coll., Aston, Pa., 1992—; vol. emergency med. technician Lima (Pa.) Fire Co., 1988-91, Media (Pa.) Fire Co., 1988-91. Mem. Nightingale Soc., Sigma Theta Tau, Delta Epsilon Sigma. Office: Neumann Coll Divsn Nursing and Hlth Scis Aston PA 19014

CADWALLADER, ESTELLE M., small business owner; b. Phila., July 16, 1945; d. Samuel and Mary Schultz; m. Forrest Scot Cadwallader. BA in History and Bus., Temple U. Owner Altair Enterprises, N.Y.C., New Hope, Pa. Mem. City Council Indsl. Devel. Orgn., N.J. Mem. Nat. Watch and Clock Club. Home: PO Box 105 Solebury PA 18963-0105 Office: PO Box 533 Stockton NJ 08530-0242

CADWELL, FRANCHELLIE MARGARET, advertising agency executive, writer; b. Hamilton, Bermuda, Apr. 23, 1937; came to U.S., 1938; d. Margaret (Roulston) C.;. B.S., Cornell U., 1955. Pres. Cadwell Davis Ptnrs., N.Y.C., 1975—. Author: The Un-Supermarkets, 1969. Mem. Pres. Coun. Cornell Women; bd. dirs. N.Y. Humane Soc.; bd. govs. N.Y. Arthritis Found., N.Y.C.; bd. mem. Nat. Parks; mem. Pres.'s Com. Employment of People with Disabilities. Recipient Nat. Humanitarian award, YWCA award, Entrepreneurial award Women Bus. Owners of N.Y., 1983, Girl Scouts USA award. Mem. Advt. Women N.Y., Fashion Group, Cosmetic Toiletry and Fragrance Assn., Non-Prescription Drug Mfrs., Women in Comm. (Matrix award 1980). Home: 7 E 94th St New York NY 10128-1912 Office: Cadwell Davis Ptnrs (USA) Advt 375 Hudson St New York NY 10014-3658

CADY, DIANE MARIE, investor relations executive; b. Hackensack, N.J., Jan. 8, 1955; d. Herbert C. and Margaret A. (Heinsman) Jacobsen; m. Dean E. Cady, May 11, 1980 (div. June 1993); 1 child, Elizabeth C. Student, Prescott Coll., 1972-74, U. Calif., Santa Barbara, 1974-75. Dir. investor rels. Am. Stock Exch., N.Y.C., 1981-87; v.p. investor rels. Ply Gem Industries, Inc., N.Y.C., 1987—. Recipient Gold medal Internat. Ann. Report Competition, 1993, Bronze medal Fin. World Ann. Report awards, 1993. Mem. Nat. Investor Rels. Inst. Democrat. Unitarian. Office: Ply Gem Industries Inc 777 Third Ave New York NY 10017

CAFFEE, VIRGINIA MAUREEN, secretary; b. Kansas City, Mo., Feb. 25, 1948; d. Frederick Arthur Gladden and Ethel Elizabeth (Keithly) Courier; m. Jack B. Todd Jr., May 13, 1967 (div. Dec. 1973); m. Marcus Pat Caffee, May 31, 1975; 1 child, Katheryn Elizabeth. Student, Ctrl. Mo. State U., 1966-73, Okla. State U., 1977-78; BBA in Bus. Edn., Sam Houston State U., 1985. Cert. profl. sec., 1975. Land abstractor Johnson County Title Co., Warrensburg, Mo., 1967-68; dept. sec., bus. placement office Ctrl. Mo. State U., Warrensburg, 1968-69; exec. sec. European Exchange System, Giessen, Germany, 1969-70; confidential sec. Consolidated Freightways, Kansas City, 1972-73; exec. sec. Behring Internat., Houston, 1974-75; sr. sec. Tenneco Oil Co.-E&P, Houston, 1979-84; exec. sec. St. Petersburg (Fla.) Hilton & Towers, 1989-90; adminstrv. mgr. Tampa Bay Engring., Clearwater, Fla., 1990-92; office mgr., WP trainer Marcus Caffee, Consulting, Largo, Fla., 1992—; ad hoc instr. St. Petersburg (Fla.) Jr. Coll., 1993, Profl. Secs. Internat. chpt. liaison for CPS rev. course, 1993-94; presenter in field. Editor (performance programs) Suncoast Singers, 1991— (Community Svc. award Arts Coun. Co-op 1993), Clearwater Community Chorus, 1993—, (newsletters) Clearwater Sparkler, 1992-93 (1st pl. award 1993), Fla. Divsn. The Secretariat, 1993-94. Sec. Montgomery County Choral Soc., Conroe, Tex., 1986-88, publicity co-chmn., 1987-89; pres. Anona Meth. Ch. Choir, Largo, 1990-91. Recipient Mo. State Tchrs. scholarship Mo. Congress Parents and Tchrs., 1966. Mem. NAFE, AAUW, Nat. Assn. Exec. Secs., Profl. Secs. Internat. (chmn. secs. week, sec. Clearwater chpt. 1992-93, pres., 1994chmn. seminar and v.p. Clearwater chpt. 1992-93, workshop spkr. Fla. divsn. 1993, program spkr. St. Petersburg chpt. 1993, alternate del. to internat. conv. 1993, alternate del. to divsn. meeting 1993, 94, del. dist. conv. 1994, Sec. of Yr. 1994-95), CPS Soc. Tex. (roster chmn. 1983-85). Republican. Methodist. Office: Marcus Caffee Consulting 13985 105th Terr North Largo FL 34644-5303

CAFFERATA, PATRICIA ANN, advertising executive; b. Smithville, Mo., Sept. 6, 1944; d. Jack and E. Agnes (Sims) Shepherd; m. D. Michael Cafferata, Mar. 27, 1976; 1 child, Diane L. BS in Home Econs. cum laude, N.W. Mo. State U., 1969. Research assoc. Barickman Advt., Kansas City, Mo., 1969-73; research assoc. Needham, Harper and Steers, Chgo., 1973-74, assoc. research dir., 1974-82, sr. v.p., research dir., 1982-87; pres., chief exec. officer Young and Rubicam, Chgo., 1987—. Mem. The Adv. Council J.L. Kellogg Grad. Sch. Mgmt. Northwestern U., Evanston, Ill., 1987, pres. council Museum Sci. and Industry, Chgo., 1987; bd. dirs. James Webb Young Fund U. Ill., 1987, Chgo. Area Council Boy Scouts Am., 1987, Mus. Broadcast Communicatins, Chgo., 1987. Named Woman of Yr., Women's Advt. Club Chgo., 1986. Mem. Am. Psychol. Assn., Am. Mktg. Assn., The Chgo. Network. Clubs: Chgo. Advt. (bd. dirs. 1986-87), Women's Advt., Econ. of Chgo. Office: Young & Rubicam/Chgo 1 S Wacker Dr Ste 1800 Chicago IL 60606*

CAFFIN, LOUISE ANNE, library media educator; b. N.Y.C., Feb. 15, 1943; d. Milton D. and Tinette C. Caffin. BS, NYU, 1964; MLS, L.I. U., 1966. Tchr. N.Y.C. Bd. Edn., 1966—. Author: (manuscripts) Outward Bound, 1985, California Vs. Caryl Chessman, 1948-60 and Beyond, 1984, The Untrammelled Road He Chose: William O. Douglas, 1983, Invictus, 1985, Automobiles, Alcohol Abuse and Traffic Safety Curriculum, 1986, Tribute to Anne Frank, Private Letters and Public Works, 1987, If...Covert Operations in World War II, 1988. Member B'nai B'rith. Mem. Schoolmen and Schoolwomen's Lodge. Office: Frank D Whalen Middle Sch 135 2441 Wallace Ave Bronx NY 10467-9215

CAGGINS, RUTH PORTER, nurse, educator; b. Natchez, Miss., July 11, 1945; d. Henry Chapelle and Corinne Sadie (Baines) Porter; m. Don Randolph Caggins, July 1, 1978; children: Elva Rene, Don Randolph, Myles Thomas Chapelle. BS, Dillard U., New Orleans, 1967; MA, NYU, 1973; PhD Tex. Woman's U., 1992. Staff nurse Montefiore Hosp., Bronx, 1968-70, head nurse, 1970-72; nurse clinician Met. Hosp., N.Y.C., 1973-74, clin. supr., 1974-76; asst. prof. U. So. La., Lafayette, 1976-78; assoc. prof. Prairie View A&M U. Coll. Nursing, Houston, 1978—, apptd. project dir. LIFT Ctr. Active The Links Inc., Houston, 1982—, Cultural Arts Coun., Houston, Nat. Black Leadership Initiative on Cancer, Houston. Recipient Tchg. award Nat. Inst. Staff and Orgnl. Devel., 1992-93. Mem. ANA (clin. ethnic/racial minority fellow 1989-91), Nat. Black Nurses Assn., A.K. Rice Inst. (assoc. Ctrl. States Ctr., Tex. Ctr.), Assn. Black Nursing Faculty in Higher Edn. (Dissertation award 1990), Sigma Theta Tau, Delta Sigma Theta, Chi Eta Phi. Democrat. Baptist. Avocations: singing, sewing, traveling, aerobics, writing. Home: 5602 Goettee Cir Houston TX 77091-4523 Office: Prairie View A&M U Coll Nursing 6436 Fannin St Houston TX 77030-1519

CAGLE, PAULETTE BERNICE, mental health administrator and psychologist; b. Ft. Worth, July 14, 1944; d. James Frank and Cordelia Pauline (Bourke) C. BS, North Tex. State U., 1972; MA, So. Meth. U., 1976. Lic. chem. dependency counselor; cert. diagnostic and evaluation psychologist; qualified mental health profl. Part-time psychometrist Jack Waxler, Psychologist, Richardson, Tex., 1973-77; social worker Vernon (Tex.) State Hosp., 1977-78, psychologist, 1978-88; adminstr. tech. programs Wichita Falls (Tex.) State Hosp., 1988-91, assoc. dir. mgmt. and support, 1991—; cons. mem. quality improvement coun. Vernon State Hosp., 1992-94. Co-founder and mem. Cmty. Svcs. Quality Assurance Dirs. of Tex., 1993-94; designated contact Metnal Health Disaster Assistance, Austin, 1994; mem. Wichita County Mental Health Assn., 1992—. Named Sister of the Yr. Sisterhood of Freedom, 1991. Mem. Am. Counseling Assn., Am. Mental Health Counselors Assn., Tex. Assn. Alcoholism and Drug Abuse Counselors, Internat. Assn. of Marriage and Family Counselors. Office: Texas Dept Mental Health Wichita Falls State Hosp PO Box 300 Wichita Falls TX 76307-0300

CAHILL, CATHERINE M., orchestra executive. Gen. mgr. N.Y. Philharmonic, N.Y.C. Office: New York Philharmonic Avery Fisher Hall 10 Lincoln Ctr Plz New York NY 10023-6973*

CAHILL, MARY-CAROL, psychologist; b. N.Y.C.; d. Harold Daniel and Mildred Eva (Gessler) C. A.B. (N.Y. State Regents scholar) Coll. New Rochelle; A.M., Fordham U., Ph.D., 1967. Licensed psychologist, N.Y. Human factors engr. Grumman Aerospace Corp., Bethpage, N.Y., 1967-70; asst. prof. Rensselaer Poly. Inst., Troy, N.Y. 1970-74, psychology, Fordham U., Bronx, N.Y., 1974-76, assoc. prof., 1976-78; cons. in human factors engring. and environ. design, 1967—. Contbr. articles to profl. jours.; editorial cons. textbooks. N.Y. State Regents scholar; NSF fellow Fordham U., N.Y. State Regents fellow. Mem. Human Factors Soc. (pres. Metropolitan chpt. 1979), Soc. for Info. Display (vice-chmn. Mid-Atlantic chpt. 1976, 77), Am. Psychol. Assn., Am. Psychol. Soc., Eastern Psychol. Assn., N.Y. State Psychol. Assn., N.Y. Acad. Scis., Assn. for Women in Sci., Sigma Xi. Office: PO Box 536 Scarsdale NY 10583-0536

CAHILL, PAMELA LEE, state legislator; b. Belfast, Maine, Apr. 22, 1953; d. B.D. and Catherine (Snow) Sanborn; m. Bradley W. Cahill; children: Veronica Lynn, Brandon. Student, U. Maine. Former mem. Maine Ho. of Reps.; mem. Maine State Senate. Exec. dir. Reagan-Busch campaign, Maine, 1984. Republican. Office: Maine State Senate Capitol State Augusta ME 04330 Address: Box 796 R R 3 Wiscasset ME 04578*

CAHOON, SUSAN ALICE, lawyer; b. Jacksonville, Fla., Oct. 14, 1948; d. Robert Harold and Alice (Dubberly) C. BA, Emory U., 1968; JD, Harvard U., 1971. Bar: Ga. 1971, U.S. Dist. Ct. (no. dist.) Ga. 1971, U.S. Dist. Ct. (no. & ea. dists.) Tex. 1977, U.S. Dist. Ct. (mid. dist.) Ga. 1978, U.S. Dist. Ct. (we. dist.) Wis. 1979, U.S. Supreme Ct. 1979, U.S. Ct. Appeals (4th cir.) 1980, U.S. Dist. Ct. (so. dist.) Ga. 1981, U.S. Ct. Appeals (5th, 11th & D.C. cirs.) 1981, U.S. Ct. Appeals (6th cir.) 1983. Assoc. Kilpatrick & Cody, Atlanta, 1971-76, ptnr., 1977—. Contbr. articles to law revs., chpts. to books. Chmn. Stone Mountain Park Authority, Atlanta, 1984—; v.p. Fulton County Divsn. Am. Heart Assn., Atlanta, 1992-93, pres. 1993—; v.p. USO Coun. Ga., Inc., Atlanta, 1992—; bd. dirs. Atlanta Conv. & Visitors Bur., 1992—, Metro Atlanta Crime Commn., 1990-92, Fed. Defender Program, 1987-92; pres. Atlanta Area Alumni Club, 1975; mem. Leadership Atlanta, 1982, Leadership Ga., 1989. Mem. ABA (litigation sect. com. chair 1986-88), Ga. Bar Assn. (com. chair 1980-81), Atlanta Bar Assn. (bd. dirs. 1981-87, leadership award 1991), D.C. Bar Assn., Am. Law Inst., Phi Beta Kappa, Omicron Delta Kappa. Baptist. Home: 2040 Old Dominion Rd Atlanta GA 30350-4619 Office: Kilpatrick & Cody 1100 Peachtree St Ste 2800 Atlanta GA 30309*

CAIN, BECKY C., association executive; married; 1 child. BA in Polit. Sci., W.Va. U., 1969. Social studies tchr. Suttle Sch., Perry County, Ala., 1969-70; Am. govt., econs. tchr. Selma (Ala.) High Sch., 1970-72; nat. pres. League of Women Voters, Washington, 1992—; guest editorial columnist Charleston (W.Va.) Gazette Newspaper, 1984-88. Campaign coord. Citizens for Progress Through Edn., 1987-88, People for Better Govt., 1989; facilitator effectiveness program W.Va. Sch. Bd., 1989-91; active local League of Women Voters, W.Va., from 1975, mem. local bd. dirs., 1975-84, mem. state league bd. dirs., 1977-81, mem. legis. action com., 1977-81, local league pres., 1981-83, state league pres., 1983-87, chair League Women Voters W.Va. Endowment Trust, 1983-92, nominating com. chair, 1984-85, off-bd. dirs. League Women Voters U.S. Agrl. Study Com., 1986-88, mem. nominating com., 1986-87, bd. dirs. nat. league, 1988-92, trustee league edn. fund, 1988-92, chair nat. league program planning, 1989-90, chair nat. coun. planning, 1990-91, co-chair nat. 75th anniversary, 1991-92.; chair City of St. Albans Charter Rev. Com., 1979-80, W.Va. Citizens for Passage Constl. Amendment # 2, 1987; active City of St. Albans Parks and Recreation Com., 1982-86, Kanawha County Metro Govt. Com., 1985-86, W.Va. Legis. Higher Edn. Study Commn., 1986-87, Dept. Natural Resources Dir. Groundwater Policy and Tech. Adv. Com., 1986-87, State Bd. Edn. Blue Ribbon Commn. on Ednl. Reform, 1987, W.Va. Solid Waste Mgmt. Bd. Solid Waste Mgmt. Task Force, 1991-92, W.Va. C. of C. Health Care Task Force, 1990-92, W.Va. Election Commn., 1990—, W.Va. Divsn. Environ. Reorganization Adv. Bd., 1992-93, Nat. Recycling Adv. Coun., 1992—; mem. adv. bd. Ctr. Environ. Learning, Region III EPA, 1987-93; bd. dirs. Leadership W.Va., Inc., 1990—, Citizens for Tax Justice, 1993—; mem. adv. commn. on election law ABA, 1992-95; mem. exec. com. Leadership Conf. on Civil Rights, 1992—, U.S. EPA Safe Drinking Water adv. com., 1993—, nat. adv. com. UNICEF, 1994—, bd. dirs. Health Alliance, 1994-95. Recipient Common Cause Pub. Svc. award, 1988, W.Va. Celebrate Women Outstanding Achievement award, 1988, Corma A. Mowrey Meml. award W.Va. Edn. Assn., 1992, W.Va. U. Polit. Sci. Disting. Alumna award, 1994. Mem. League Women Voters U.S., Common Cause. Office: League of Women Voters 1730 M St NW Washington DC 20036-4505

CAIN, LYNNE DEE ANNE GILLEN, mental health advocate, educator; b. San Antonio, Dec. 3, 1953; d. Donald Martin and Dorothy Mae (Jira) Gillen; m. Lamont Clark Cain Sr., Jan. 30, 1976; 1 child, Robin Rene Cain Garness. AS with high honors, Presentation Coll., 1974; BA cum laude, Yankton Coll., 1976. Cert. mental health advocate, S.D. Adv. Svcs. Dir. social svcs. Shalom Health Ctrs., Yankton, S.D., 1977-80; psychol. tecnician Custer (S.D.) State Hosp., 1981-83; vol. VISTA Custer-South Hills Advocacy, 1983-84; cons. citizen advocacy S.D. Advocacy Svcs., Pierre, 1985-87, mental health advocate, 1987—; tchr. adult edn. Springfield (S.D.) Correction Facility, 1990-93; bd. dirs. Handicapped Advocacy Program of Yankton, advocate assoc., 1986—; mem. adv. bd. Presentation Coll., Aberdeen, S.D., 1976-80; cons. Citizen Advocacy Network, 1987—; dir. Harmony Notes, Yankton, 1992—, co-chmn., 1991—. Author (plays): Harmony Tales, 1989, The Homecoming in Short, 1982. Chair mother's march Svcs. March of Dimes, S.D., 1981; vol. various civic orgns., 1972—; active Child Network, 1993-94, S.D. Coalition Citizen's With Disabilities, 1991—; founder Custer Area Svc. Alliance, 1984. Recipient Sunflower award S.D. Volunteerism, 1984; Adult Edn. grantee S.D. Dept. Edn., 1993. Fellow Konechan Soc.; mem. Am. Legion Auxillary, St. Vincent's Ch., Phi Theta Kappa. Democrat. Roman Catholic. Home: PO Box 573 Springfield SD 57062-0573 Office: Patient Advocacy Program PO Box 885 Yankton SD 57078-0885

CAIN, MADELINE ANN, state representative; b. Cleve., Nov. 21, 1949; d. Edward Vincent and Mary Rita (Quinn) C. BA, Ursuline Coll., 1973; MPA, Cleve. State U., 1985. Tchr. St. Augustine Acad., Lakewood, Ohio, 1973-75; clk. coun. legis. aide Lakewood City Coun., 1981-85; legis. liaison Cuyahoga County Bd. Commrs., Cleve., 1985-88; mem. Ohio Ho. of Reps., Columbus, 1989—. Mem. Cudell Neighborhood Improvement Corp., West Blvd. Neighborhood Assn.; trustee Malachi House. Mem. Lakewood Bus. and Profl. Women, Lakewood C. of C., City Club. Democrat. Roman Catholic. Home: 2169 Glenbury Ave Cleveland OH 44107-3849 Office: Ohio Ho of Reps State House Columbus OH 43215

CAIN, PATRICIA JEAN, accountant; b. Decatur, Ill., Sept. 28, 1931; d. Paul George and Jean Margaret (Horne) Jacka; m. Dan Louis Cain, July 12, 1952; children: Mary Ann, Timothy George, Paul Louis. Student, U. Mich., 1949-52, Pasadena (Calif.) City Coll., 1975-76; BS in Acctg., Calif. State U., L.A., 1977, MBA, 1978; M in Taxation, Golden Gate U., Los Angeles, 1988; Diploma in Pastry, Hotel Ritz, France, 1991. CPA, Calif.; cert. personal fin. planner; cert. advanced fin. planner. Tax supr. Stonefield & Josephson, L.A., 1979-87; chief fin. officer Loubella Extendables, Inc., L.A., 1987—; participant program in bus. ethics U. So. Calif., L.A., 1986; trainer for A-Plus in house tax Arthur Andersen & Co., 1989-90; instr. Becker CPA Rev. Course, 1989-93. Bd. dirs. Sierra Madre coun. Girl Scouts U.S.A., 1968-73, treas., 1973-75, nat. del., 1975; mem. Town Hall, L.A., 1987—, L.A. Bus. Forum, 1991—. Listed as one of top six tax experts in L.A. by Money mag., 1987. Mem. AICPA (chair nat. tax teleconf. 1988, taxation com./forms subcom. 1994—), Am. Women's Soc. CPAs (bd. dirs. 1986-87, v.p. 1987-90), Calif. Soc. CPAs (chair free tax assistance program 1983-85, high road com. 1985-86, chair pub. rels. com. 1985-89, microcomputer users discussion group taxation com., fin. com./speaker computer show and conf. 1987-93, planning com. and speaker San Francisco Tax and Microcomputer show 1988, state com. on taxation 1991—, speaker Tax Update 1992, dir. L.A. chpt. 1993-95, v.p. 1995—), Internat. Arabian Horse Assn., Wrightwood Country Club, Beta Alpha Psi. Democrat. Episcopalian. Office: Loubella Extendables Inc 5540 Harbor St Commerce CA 90040-1419

CAIRNS, MARION GRACE HUEY, former state legislator; b. Sparta, Ill., June 8, 1928; d. Frank McClellan and Pertie (Boyington) Huey; m. Donald F. Cairns, Sept. 2, 1950; 1 child, Douglas Scott. BA, Monmouth Coll., 1950; LLD (hon.), Webster U., 1989; DHL (hon.), Monmouth Coll. Prin. Ellis Grove (Ill.) Elem. Sch., 1951-52; tchr. Nebr. High Sch., Falls City, 1952-54; layout designer Hallmark Corp., Kansas City, Mo., 1954-55; instr. evening sch. Washington U., St. Louis, 1959; substitute tchr. Webster Groves (Mo.) High Sch., 1960-66; instr. Hickey Bus. Sch., St. Louis, 1966-70; mem. Mo. Ho. of Reps., Jefferson City, 1977-90; adj. prof. Webster U., Webster Groves, 1978-90, adv. bd. to paralegal studies; mem. adv. com. to Children's Svcs. Commn., State of Mo., Jefferson City, 1980-90; bd. dirs. Edgewood Children's Ctr., Webster Groves. Advocate crime victims Mo. Victim Assistance Network; active Mo. Humanities Coun. Named Citizen of Yr. Webster Groves C. of C., 1984, Child Advocate of Yr. Mo. Child Care Assn., 1985, St. Louis Coun. Child Abuse and Neglect 1987, Citizens for Mo. Children, 1990; recipient YWCA Women in Leadership award, 1989. Mem. Nat. Fedn. Rep. Women. Presbyterian. Home: 17 E Swon Ave Saint Louis MO 63119-3010

CAIRNS, SARA ALBERTSON, physical education educator; b. Bloomsburg, Pa., July 18, 1939; d. Robert Wilson and Sara (Porter) Albertson; m. Thomas Cairns, Apr. 13, 1968. BS in Edn., Pa. State U., 1961; MS in Edn., West Chester U., 1965. Cert. tchr., Pa., Del., prin., Del.; adaptive p.e. specialist. Phys. edn. tchr., coach Cen. Columbia County High Sch., Bloomsburg, Pa., 1961-64; phys. edn. tchr. Christina Sch. Dist., Newark, Del., 1964—; cons. U. Del., Newark, 1984—, coop. tchr., 1965—; area coord. New Castle (Del.) County Parks and Recreation, 1973—; presenter in field. Contbr. articles to profl. publs. Chair Leasure Elem. Sch. campaign United Fund, 1987-91. Recipient Outstanding Svc. award New CAstle County Parks and Recreation, 1985. Mem. NEA, AAHPERD, Del. Assn. Health, Phys. Edn., Recreation and Dance (v.p. dance 1991-94, exec. bd.), Del. State Edn. Assn. Democrat. Presbyterian. Home: 40 Vansant Rd Newark DE 19711-4839 Office: Leasure Elem Sch 925 Bear Corbitt Rd Bear DE 19701-1324

CAJERO, CARMEN, state legislator; b. Morenci, Ariz.. State rep. dist. 10 Ariz. Ho. of Reps.; mem. appropriations com., natural resources com., agr. and rules com.; businesswoman. Democrat. Home: 104 W District St Tucson AZ 85714-2528 Office: Office of State Senate 1700 W Washington St Phoenix AZ 85007-2812*

CALABRESE, MARYLYN E. JONES, writing consultant; b. Scranton, Pa., Nov. 12, 1935; 1 child, David. AB, Bryn Mawr Coll.; MAT, Wesleyan U.; MA in English, U. Pa., PhD in Edn. Tchr., workshop leader, cons. Conestoga Sr. High Sch., Berwyn, Pa., 1967-76; chair English dept. Conestoga Sr. High Sch., 1982-91; writing cons. pvt. practice Malvern, Pa., 1991—. Contbr. articles to profl. jours. and papers to pubs. Recipient Decade of Equity award Mid-Atlantic Ctr. Sex Equity, Am. U., 1982. Home and office: 9 Madeline Dr Malvern PA 19355

CALABRESE, ROSALIE SUE, arts management consultant, writer; b. N.Y.C., Feb. 17, 1938; d. Julius and Florence (Tuck) Hochman; m. Anthony J. Calabrese, June 15, 1960 (div.); 1 child, Christopher. BA in Journalism, CCNY, 1959. Asst. news editor Electronic News, N.Y.C., 1960; asst. to publicist Abner Klipstein, N.Y.C., 1963; asst. to producer Leonard Field, N.Y.C., 1964; mgr. Am. Composers Alliance, N.Y.C., 1969-85, exec. dir., gen. mgr., 1985-94; dir. Rosalie Calabrese Mgmt., N.Y.C., 1983—; music advisor Phillis Rose Dance Co., N.Y.C., 1987—; also bd. dirs.; sec. bd. dirs. Am. Composers Orch., N.Y.C., 1987-93; bd. dirs. 1st Ave. Ensemble, Golden Fleece Ltd., Friends Am. Composers, treas., 1991-94; mem. adv. bd. Downtown Music Prodns., Joan Miller's Dance Players, N.Y.C. Author, lyricist: (musicals) A Hell of An Angel, Simone, Not in Earnest, Murdering MacBeth, Pop Life, Does Anyone Here Speak Arabic?, Friends and Relations, Double-Play; assoc. producer, treas. box office: (play) Courtyard, 1959, The Mime and Me; co-producer: various plays at White Lake (N.Y.) Playhouse, also packaged tours for Prodn. Assocs.; dir. night club acts for Florence Hayle; lyricist with various composers; contbr. short stories and poetry to lit. and nat. mags. Mem. Dramatists Guild, Broadcast Music Inc., Am. Music Ctr., St. Agnes Poetry Unit. Office: Rosalie Calabrese Mgmt Box 20580 W Sta New York NY 10025-1521

CALABRO, JOANNA JOAN SONDRA, artist; b. Waterbury, Conn., Dec. 2, 1938; d. Theodore Gruwien and Madeleine Elizabeth (Raynor) Reinhard; m. John Paul Calabro, Oct. 15, 1960; 1 child, Victor Theodore. Student, Paier Sch. Art, 1965-66, Mus. of Fine Arts Sch., 1976, Rice U., 1977; student of sculpture with, Bruno Lucchesi, Pietrasanta, Italy, 1982. Art instr. at gallery workshops Houston, 1975-78; co-owner Archway Gallery, Houston, 1975-78, Fine Arts of Rockport, Mass., 1989—. One woman shows include Five Star Gallery, Houston, 1974-75, Roberts Gallery, Houston, 1977, Dayton (Ohio) Soc. of Painters, 1983, Wilmington (Ohio) Coll., 1983, Rockport Art Assn., 1989, 92; represented in permanent collections at Am. Embassy, Bratislava, Slovak Republic. Sculpture instr. for merit badge San Houston Area coun. Boy Scouts Am., Houston, 1978; juror for scholastic art shows, Tex., 1975, Ohio, 1982, numerous other art shows, Conn., Tex., Ohio, Mass., 1970—; mem. art coun. Bd. Selectmen, Rockport, 1994. Recipient numerous awards including 1st Place award Champions Art, 1974, Am. Pen & Brush Women, 1975, Conn. Classic Art, 1978, Martha Moore Meml. award, 1989, Richard Ricchia Meml. award, 1990, R.V. T. Steeves award, 1990, William N. Ryan award, 1991. Mem. Am. Artist Profl. League, Rockport Art Assn. (bd. dirs. 1992-93), Guild Boston Artists, The Copley Soc. of Boston, Am. Medallic Sculpture Assn., Federation Internat. de la Me'daille. Studio: 74 Main St Rockport MA 01966

CALAMITA, KATHRYN ELIZABETH, nursing administrator; b. Portland, Maine, Oct. 12, 1943; d. Maurice Daniel and Eleanor Elizabeth (Sullivan) Casey; m. John Joseph Calamita, Jan. 9, 1965; children: Angela Marie, Carla Anne, Daniel John. RN, Mercy Hosp. Sch. Nursing, Springfield, Mass., 1964; student, Midwestern State U., Wichita Falls, Tex., 1979-86, Vernon Regional Coll., 1987; BS in Bus., St. Joseph's Coll., Windham, Maine, 1992. Cert. CPR, ACLS. Staff nurse Mercy Hosp., Springfield, 1964; med/surg. nurse Wichita Gen. Hosp., Wichita Falls, Tex., 1976-77, nurse ICU, 1977-79, supr. dept. nursing, 1979-86, assoc. adminstr. nursing dept., 1986-92; health facility adminstr. Wichita Falls Rehab. Hosp., 1992; rehab. nurse Bay Convalescent and Rehab. Ctr., Panama City, Fla., 1993-94;

supr. L.A. Wagner Rehab. and Nursing Ctr., Panama City, Fla., 1994—. Contbr. articles to newsletters. Vol. United Way. Mem. ANA, FNA. Democrat. Roman Catholic.

CALDERWOOD, BETTY LOUISE, library director; b. Grove City, Pa., Sept. 1, 1937; d. Ernest and Bessie Eileen (Gibson) Bott; m. William James Calderwood, June 11, 1960; children: Shelley Calderwood Adams, Melinda L., Melissa S., Elizabeth J. Student, Slippery Rock State U., 1956; BA, Sterling (Kans.) Coll., 1959; postgrad., U. N.Mex., 1963; ME, U. Kans., 1964; MSLS, Emporia State U., 1968; postgrad., Rensselaer Poly. Inst., 1968, Bemidji State U., 1972, Wichita State U., 1987-89. Lic. tchr. early childhood edn., elem. edn., secondary edn., spl. edn., mental retardation, behavioral disorders, gifted, media specialist, researcher. Tchr. Topeka Pub. Schs., 1959-61, 63-67; tchr., libr. Menninger Found., Topeka, 1961-62; tchr. Albuquerque Pub. Schs., 1962-63; libr. dir. Sterling (Kans.) Coll., 1967-73; dir., tchr. Country Acres Presch., Sterling, 1974-76; media specialist Sterling Pub. Schs., 1979-92, gifted coord., 1987—, dist. libr. dir. Unified Sch. Dist. 376, 1992—; cert. examiner Myers-Briggs Type Indicator, 1993—. Editor: Sterling Community Cemetery Directory, 1986, Sterling College: A Prairie Light, 1989, 92, Mid-Kansas Guide Book, 1991; creator/developer historic preservation Sterling College Alumni House, 1987,. Sunday sch. coord. U. Presbyn. Ch., Sterling, 1991—; mem., elder Cemetery Adv. Bd., Sterling, 1990—; conservator Community Cemetery Records, 1984—; hospice vol., 1993—. Named Outstanding Alumni Sterling Coll. Alumni Assn., 1987. Mem. Rice County Hist. Soc., P.E.O., Kans. Libr. Assn., Scots Heritage Soc. Republican. Office: 308 E Washington Ave Sterling KS 67579-1725

CALDINI, MARIA PIA, physician; b. Florence, Italy, Aug. 8, 1931; d. Alessandro and Laura (Fornari) Poltri-Tanucci; m. Paolo Caldini, Apr. 11, 1956; children: Carolina, Filippo. MD, Florence U., 1956. Diplomate Am. Bd. Anesthesiologists. Intern U. Hosp., Florence, 1955-56; resident in anesthesiology U. Padua (Italy) Med. Sch., 1958-59, Winnipeg (Can.) Hosp., 1960-61, Denver Gen. Hosp., 1964; intern Mercy Hosp., Balt., 1965-66; resident instr., asst. prof. Johns Hopkins Hosp., Balt., 1967-72; anesthesiologist Lahey Clinic Found., Boston, 1972-81, New England Bapt. Hosp., Boston, 1981—. Fellow Am. Coll. Anesthesiologists; mem. Mass. Med. Soc., Mass. Soc. Anesthesiologists, Suffolk Med. Soc., Am. Soc. Anesthesiologists, Internat. Anesthesia Rsch. Soc., Smithsonian Inst., Am. Orchids Soc., Mass. Orchids Soc. Office: New England Bapt Hosp 92 Parker Hill Ave Roxbury MA 02120-3216

CALDWELL, CAREY TERESA, museum curator; b. McMinnville, Tenn., July 24, 1954; d. Harold Glenn Caldwell and Nancy Perkins (Bragg) Caldwell-Tedesco. BA in History, Queens Coll., Charlotte, N.C., 1974; postgrad., U. S.C., 1974-75, U. N.C., 1976; MA in Anthropology/Museology, U. Wash., 1987. Archaeology, field, lab. and rsch. asst. Ninety Six (S.C.) Hist. Site, 1974-75; tribal curator Suquamish (Wash.) Indian Tribe, 1977-78, dir. Suquamish Tribal Cultural Ctr. and Mus., 1979-85; cons. Bainbridge Island (Wash.) Japanese-Am. Heritage Project, 1986-87; cons. Fed. Cylinder Project Am. Folklife Ctr., Libr. of Congress, Washington, 1986-87; sr. curator of history The Oakland (Calif.) Mus., 1987—; cons., strategic planner, advisor to numerous mus., orgns., Indian tribes and community groups including Nat. Mus. of Am. Indian, Smithsonian Instn., NEH, Wash. State Heritage Coun., 1978—; panelist, reviewer NEH, 1986—; grants reviewer Inst. Mus. Svcs., 1986; cons. United Indians of All Tribes Found., Seattle, 1992-93; evaluator, cons. Osage Tribal Mus., 1993; cons. Native Am. Archives Project, 1981-82. Contbr. articles to profl. publs. Mem. Am. Assn. Mus., Western Mus. Conf. (v.p. 1990-92), Am. Anthropol. Assn., Coun. for Mus. Anthropology (bd. dirs. 1988-89), Internat. Coun. Mus., Am. Assn. for State and Local History (edn. com. 1981-82, publs. com. 1987-92, program com. 1989 ann. meeting, common agenda adv. bd. 1990-92, Award of Merit 1993), Wash. Mus. Assn. Democrat. Office: The Oakland Mus 1000 Oak St Oakland CA 94607-4820

CALDWELL, COURTNEY LYNN, lawyer, real estate consultant; b. Washington, Mar. 5, 1948; d. Joseph Morton and Moselle (Smith) C. Student, Duke U., 1966-68, U. Calif., Berkeley, 1967, 1968-69; BA, U. Calif., Santa Barbara, 1970, MA, 1975; JD with highest honors, George Washington U., 1982. Bar: D.C. 1984, Wash. 1986, Calif. 1989. Jud. clk. U.S. Ct. Appeals for 9th Cir., Seattle, 1982-83; assoc. Arnold & Porter, Washington, 1983-85, Perkins Coie, Seattle, 1985-88; dir. western ops., assoc. gen. counsel MPC Assocs., Inc., Irvine, Calif., 1988-91, sr. v.p., 1991—. Bd. dirs. Univ. Town Ctr. Assn., 1994, Habitat for Humanity, Orange County, 1993-94, chair, legal com., 1994. Named Nat. Law Ctr. Law Rev. Scholar, 1981-82. Mem. Calif. Bar Assn., Wash. State Bar Assn., D.C. Bar Assn., Urban Land Inst., Univ. Town Ctr. Assn. (bd. dirs. 1994), Habitat for Humanity Orange County (bd. dirs. 1993-94, chair legal com. 1994). Office: MPC Assocs Inc 1451 Quail St Ste 212 Newport Beach CA 92660

CALDWELL, DONNA LYNN, radiologic technologist; b. Memphis, Sept. 8, 1960; d. D.P. and Margret Quinn (Wingo) C. Cert. in radiologic tech., St. Vincent Infirmary, Little Rock, 1983; BS, U. Cen. Ark., 1983; MEd, U. Ark., Little Rock, 1994. Registered, cert. in radiography and cardiovasc. interventional tech., Am. Registry Radiologic Technologists. Technologist John L. McClellan Meml. VA Hosp., Little Rock, 1983-91; part-time cardiovasc. interventional technologist U. Ark. for Med. Scis. Med. Ctr., Little Rock, 1991—; instr. radiologic tech. U. Ark. for Med. Scis., Little Rock, 1992—. Mem. Am. Soc. Radiologic Technologists, Ark. Soc. Radiologic Technologists (Cen. dist.), Sigma Sigma Sigma (chpt. adv., Alumnae Recognition award 1992). Baptist. Home: 100 Donna Dr Little Rock AR 72205 Office: Univ Ark for Med Scis Dept Radiologic Tech 4301 W Markham Slot 563 Little Rock AR 72205

CALDWELL, ETHEL LOUISE LYNCH, academic administrator; b. Chgo., July 16, 1938; d. Samuel Thomas and Louise (Brown) Lynch; m. Robert Caldwell Jr., Sept. 7, 1957 (div. 1968). BS in Bus. Edn., DePaul U., 1976; MS in Counseling Psychology, George Williams Coll., Downers Grove, Ill., 1979, MS in Adminstrn., 1979. Lic. tchr., Ill. Sec. Inland Steel Co., Chgo., 1957-68; adminstrv. asst. 1st Nat. City Bank, St. Thomas, V.I., 1968-71; pers./purchasing mgr. Peoples Bank of V.I., St. Thomas, 1971-73; bus. edn. tchr. Ctrl. YMCA Coll., Chgo., 1976, Chgo. Profl. Coll., 1976-78; rsch. asst. U. Ill., Chgo., 1978-79, rsch. assoc., 1980-81, asst. dir. early outreach, 1981-83, dir. early outreach, 1983—; pres. Lynch Enterprises, Summit, Ill., 1987—; mem. adv. bd. Ctr. for Ednl. Rsch. and Devel. U. Ill., Chgo., 1989—; mem. exec. bd. Chgo. Coun. Postsecondary Edn., 1989-91; mem. adv. bd. Project Canal, Chgo. Pub. Schs., 1990—; lectr. African-Am. Studies Ctr., Smithsonian Inst., Washington, 1992; mem. counselor articulation bd. DePaul U., 1993—; field reader U.S. Dept. Edn., 1993—; mem. adv. coun. Greater Chgo. Youth Behavior Project, 1993—. Active Chgo. Urban League, Lulac Coun. # 5201, 1988—, Ill. Com. on Black Concerns in Higher Edn., 1989—. Recipient Health Careers Opportunity Program award U.S. Dept. Health and Human Svcs., 1987-80, 93—, Disting. Alumna award Argo Community High Sch., 1993. Mem. Am. Assn. for Higher Edn. (Achievement award 1991), Nat. Assn. for Coll. Admissions Counselors, Assn. Black Women in Higher Edn. (founding mem. Chgo. chpt.). Baptist. Office: U Ill 1919 W Taylor St M/C 969 Chicago IL 60612-7246

CALDWELL, GAIL, book critic; b. Amarillo, Tex., Jan. 20, 1951; d. Bill M. and Ruby C. BA, U. Tex., 1978, MA in Am. Studies, 1980. Instr. U. Tex., Austin, to 1981; book critic, book editor Boston Globe, 1985—; judge Radcliffe Bunting Fiction Fellowship; nominator Irish-Times/Aer Lingus Internat. Fiction Prize; mem. Pulitzer jury fiction, 1991. Mem. PEN New Eng. (bd. dirs.), Nat. Book Critics Circle. Office: The Boston Globe 135 Morrissey Blvd Boston MA 02107*

CALDWELL, JOAN MARIE, artist, educator; b. Lancaster, Pa., Dec. 17, 1927; d. George Joseph and Doris (Fay) Brouillette; m. Richard Holmes Caldwell, Dec. 24, 1970 (div. Jan. 8, 1987); children: Toni Lauren, Wendy Ann, Andrea Joy, Richard Blake, Spencer Edward. Diploma, Mus. Fine Arts Sch., Boston, 1949; BA magna cum laude, U. Calif., San Diego, 1988; MFA in Studio Painting, Calif. State U., Fullerton, 1993. Tchr. Sch. Organic Edn., Fairhope, Ala., 1950-52, Mobile (Ala.) H.S., 1952, Monteverde Sch., Costa Rica, 1955-60; ceramics vol. La. Palma Continuation Sch., Carlsbad, Calif., 1978-80; dir. art program Magnolia Sch., Carlsbad, Calif., 1978-80; instr. Calif. State U., Fullerton, 1993; artist, 1952—. Exhbns. include Orlando Gallery, Sherman Oaks, Calif., 1993-94. Mem. Healing Racism/Dialogue, San Diego, 1993-94. Home: 3675 Bernard Dr # 120 Oceanside CA 92056

CALDWELL, JUDY CAROL, advertising executive, public relations executive; b. Nashville, Dec. 28, 1946; d. Thomas and Sarah Elizabeth Carter; m. John Cope Caldwell; 1 child, Jessica. BS, Wayne State U., 1969. Tchr. Bailey Mid. Sch., West Haven, Conn., 1969-72; editorial asst. Vanderbilt U., Nashville, 1973-74; editor, graphics designer, field researcher Urban Observatory of Met. Nashville, 1974-77; account exec. Holden and Co., Nashville, 1977-79; bus. tchr. Federated States of Micronesia, 1979-80; dir. advt. Am. Assn. for State and Local History, Nashville, 1980-81; dir. prodn. Mktg. Communications Co., Nashville, 1981-83; ptnr. Victory Images of Tenn., Inc., Nashville, 1990-92; owner, pres. Ridge Hill Corp., Nashville, 1983—.

CALDWELL, L. SCOTT, actress. Mem. Milw. Repertory Theatre, 1981-82; mem. Negro Ensemble Co. Appeared in The Daughters of the Mock, 1978, A Season to Unravel, 1979, Old Phantoms, 1979, Plays from Africa, 1979, Home, 1979, 80, Boesman and Lena, 1981, Colored People's Time, 1982, About Heaven and Earth, 1983; other theater appearances include A Raisin in the Sun, Buffalo, 1982, A Play of Giants, 1984, Joe Turner's Come and Gone, New Haven, 1985, Boston, 1986, N.Y.C., 1988 (Antoinette Perry award for best featured actress in a play 1988), A Month of Sundays, N.Y.C., 1987; appeared in films Without a Trace, 1983, Exterminator 2, 1984, Dutch, 1991, The Fugitive, 1993; TV movies: God Bless the Child, 1988, Dangerous Passion, 1990, Love, Lies and Murder, 1991, Baby of the Bride, 1991, Extreme Justice, 1993, Darkness Before Dawn, 1993, For the Love of My Child: The Anissa Ayala Story, 1993; TV series The Outsiders, 1990. Office: J Michael Bloom Ltd 9200 Sunset Blvd Ste 710 Los Angeles CA 90069*

CALDWELL, LINDA E., critical care nurse; b. Spencer, Iowa, June 23, 1954; d. George W. and Elaine Wava (Parks) D.; m. Bill Caldwell, June 25, 1988. ADN, Cumberland County Coll., 1984; EMT, Cumberland Adult Edn., 1986. RN; cert. EMT. Staff nurse Newcomb Med. Ctr., Vineland, N.J.; head nurse Leesburg State Prison, Delmont, N.J.; charge nurse, ICU South Jersey Hosp. Division, Millville, N.J., 1991—; emergency med. tech. Bridgeton Ambulance Svc. Mem. EOF (past pres.), AACN. Home: 33 Walnut St Bridgeton NJ 08302-2049

CALDWELL, MAMIE B., principal; b. Elloree, S.C., June 2, 1943; d. Johnny Miller and Alicess (Bradley) Pearsall; m. Richard Caldwell, July 11, 1970; 1 child, Madeline Rose. BS, Allen U., 1968; MEd, S.C. State U., 1978, 6-yr. cert., 1990. Cert. in bus. edn., S.C. Tchr. Dantzler Elem. Sch., Holly Hill, S.C., 1968-69; Elloree (S.C.) Tng. Sch., 1969-70; Elloree (S.C.) Tng. Sch. Elloree High Sch., 1970-82, asst. prin., 1982-92, interim prin., 1992-93, asst. prin., 1993—; instr. Orangeburg-Calhoun Tech. Coll., Orangeburg, S.C., 1982; spl. needs coord. Elloree High Sch., 1988—; dir. fed. programs Orangeburg Sch. Dist. 7, 1994—. Author 3 plays in mag., 1990. Voting poll mgr. Orangeburg County, 1974; Orangeburg area promotion educator The AME Chs., Orangeburg, 1987—; dir. Christian edn. Brown Chapel AME Ch., Cameron, S.C., 1990—, tutorial program dir., 1991—. Recipient Outstanding Svc. award Elloree High Student Coun., 1987, Community Svc. award NAACP-Santee/Elloree Br., 1993; named Prin. Apprentice, S.C. Dept. Edn., 1991-92. Mem. Iota Tau Zeta, Zeta Phi Beta, Phi Delta Kappa. Democrat. Methodist.

CALDWELL, MARY ELLEN, English language educator; b. El Paso, Ark., Aug. 6, 1908; d. Clay and Mabel Grace (Coe) Fulks; m. Robert Atchison Caldwell, Feb. 22, 1936; 1 child, Elizabeth. PhB, U. Chgo., 1931, MA, 1933. Instr. English U. Ark., Fayetteville, 1940-42, U. Toledo, 1946-48; from instr. to asst. prof. to assoc. prof. U. N.D., Grand Forks, 1966-79; assoc. prof. emeritus U. N.C., Grand Forks, 1979—, prof. ext. divsn., 1979—. Author: North Dakota Division of the American Association of University Women, 1930-63, A History, 1964; co-author: The North Dakota Division of the American Association of University Women, 1964-84, 2d vol., 1984; contbr. revs. and articles to scholarly jours. Sec. citizen's com. Grand Forks Symphony Assn., 1960-66. Mem. AAUW (life, N.D. state pres. 1968-70), P.E.O., MLA (life), Soc. for Study of Midwestern Lit. (bibliography staff 1973—), Linguistic Cir. of Manitoba and N.D. (pres. 1981), Melville Soc. Democrat. Episcopalian. Home: 514 Oxford St Grand Forks ND 58203

CALDWELL, PATRICIA FRANCES, management consultant, lecturer; b. Columbus, Ohio, Aug. 21, 1942; d. Richard and Elizabeth Frances (McQuiniff) Smith; m. Terry Edward Caldwell, Dec. 19, 1970; children: Carrie Elizabeth, Christina Leigh. BS, Otterbein Coll., 1964; MEd, U. Okla., 1967; PhD, U. Calif., Riverside, 1981. Cert. secondary edn. tchr., Calif., OHio. Secondary tchr. Copley (Ohio) Jr. High Sch., 1964-65, Apple Valley (Calif.) Jr. High Sch., 1967-68; tchr., counselor Victor Valley Community Coll., Victorville, Calif., 1968-74; asst. dean of students San Bernardino (Calif.) Valley Coll., 1974-78; lectr. Calif. State U., San Bernardino, 1979-82, 85-86, La Verne U., Victorville, 1983-84, U. Redlands, Calif., 1988—; pvt. practice mgmt. cons. Victorville, 1987—; cons. John Deere Corp., Moline, Ill., 1992—, Victor Valley Coll., Victorville, Palomar Coll., San Marcos, Calif., San Bernardino Valley Coll., 1992—, John Deere Corp., Moline, Ill., 1992—, Allan Hancock Coll., Santa Maria, Calif., 1993—, Victor Valley Union High Sch. Dist., Victorville, 1993—, Pacific Oaks Coll., 1994—, Harbor Coll., 1995—, Barstow Coll., 1995—, Network Calif. C.C. Founds., 1995—, Western Fairs Assn., 1989—, Western Wash. Fair, 1992—, Pacific Nat. Exhbn., Vancouver, B.C., 1990—, Calif. Assn. Racing Fairs, 1993-94, Calif. Constrn. Authority, 1994, numerous county, state fairs. Leader Girl Scouts U.S., Victorville, 1980-94; pres. San Gorgonio Girl Scout coun., 1984-87; bd. dirs. Oro Grande Found., Victorville, 1984—, Desert Communities United Way, Victorville, 1983-93, Victor Valley Coll. Found., 1994, pres., 1994-95, Victorville, 1988—; pres. Victor Elem. Dist. Bd. Trustees, 1980-90; founder High Desert Early Childhood Ctr. and Found., 1972, v.p., 1994-95. Recipient Lifetime Achievement award United Way, 1993—; named Soroptimist Woman of Distinction, 1992. Mem. Rotary, Victorville C. of C. (v.p. bd. dirs. 1994-95). Republican. Presbyterian. Home: 13993 Burning Tree Dr Victorville CA 92392-4353 Office: 15476 W Sand St Victorville CA 92392-2314

CALDWELL, ROBERTA LEE, organizational development consultant; b. L.A., Jan. 20, 1949; d. Harry and Ruth (Newby) Goodman; children: Chandra, Tiffany. BA in Psychology, Antioch Coll., 1985; M in Human Resources and Orgnl. Devel., U. San Francisco, 1989. Regional mgr., cons. N.R.A.C., L.A., 1972-78; mgmt. cons. in pvt. prctice, L.A., 1978-81; regional mgr./cons. Merrill Lynch, L.A., 1981-83; mgmt. cons. Corp. Competitive Edge, San Francisco, 1983-90; in tng. and devel. Amoco Oil, Chgo., 1991-92; orgnl. devel. cons. Community Mut. Blue Cross/Blue Shield, Cin., 1992—. Mem. ASTD, Orgnl. Devel. Network, Soc. for Human Resources Mgmt. Home: 943 Falling Water Dr Fort Lauderdale FL 33326

CALDWELL, SARAH, opera producer, conductor, stage director and administrator; b. Maryville, Mo., Mar. 6, 1924. Student, U. Ark., Hendrix Coll., New Eng. Conservatory, Berkshire Music Ctr., Tanglewood, Mass.; D. Mus. (hon.), Harvard U., Simmons Coll., Bates Coll., Bowdoin Coll. Mem. faculty Berkshire Music Ctr.; dir. Boston U. Opera Workshop, 1953-57; created dept. music theater Boston U.; founded Boston Opera Group (later became Opera Co. of Boston), 1957, sinced served as artistic dir. and condr. Asst. to Boris Goldovsky in direction of New Eng. Opera Co.; operatic directorial debut with Rake's Progress, Opera Workshop, 1953; operatic debut as condr. with Opera Group of Boston, 1957, Carnegie Hall debut with Am. Symphony Orch., 1974; condr. and/or dir. maj. opera cos. in U.S., including N.Y. Met. Opera, Dallas Civic Opera, Houston Grand Opera, N.Y.C. Opera; condr. with maj. orchs. including: Indpls. Symphony, Milw. Symphony, Am. Symphony, N.Y. Philharmonic; condr. at Ravinia Festival, 1976. Recipient Rogers and Hammerstein award. Office: Opera Co Boston Inc PO Box 50 Newton MA 02258-0001*

CALDWELL, SUSAN HAVENS, art history educator; b. Clinton, Okla., June 9, 1938; d. Charles Hayes and Mary Jane (Oberer) Havens; m. Peter Richard Caldwell, Aug. 30, 1961; children: Margaret Elizabeth Caldwell Mesander, Peter Charles. BA, Washburn U., 1961; PhD, Cornell U., 1974. Asst. prof. art history dept. art Boise (Idaho) State U., 1974-76; asst. prof. art history Sch. of Art U. Okla., Norman, 1976-81, assoc. prof. art history Sch. of Art, 1981—. Script writer, co-prodr. (video) And They Sang a New Song: 24 Musical Elders at Santiago de Compostela, 1989; contbr. articles to profl. jours. Fellow Samuel H. Kress Found., Cornell U., 1968-69; grantee NEH/Okla. Found. for Humanities, 1986-87, U.S.-Spanish Joint Com. for Cultural Cooperation, 1986-87. Mem. NOW, Coll. Art Assn. Am., Internat. Ctr. Medieval Art, Soc. Hispanic Art Hist. Studies in U.S., Feminist Medieval Art History Project. Democrat. Office: Univ Okla Sch of Art 520 Parrington Oval Norman OK 73019

CALDWELL, ZOE, actress, director; b. Hawthorn, Victoria, Australia, Sept. 14, 1933; m. Robert Whitehead, 1968; 2 sons: Sam, Charlie. Attended, Meth. Ladies Coll., Melbourne, Australia. Dorothy F. Schmidt Vis. Eminent Scholar in Theatre, Fla. Atlantic U., 1989-93. Theater debut as mem. of Union Theatre Repertory Co., Melbourne, 1953; other appearances in The Madwoman of Chaillot, Goodman Theatre, Chgo., 1964, The Way of the World, The Caucasian Chalk Circle, Mpls., Slapstick Tragedy, N.Y.C., 1966 (Best Supporting Actress Tony award 1966), Antony and Cleopatra, Richard III, The Merry Wives of Windsor, Stratford, Ont., Can., Shakespeare Festival, 1967, The Prime of Miss Jean Brodie, 1967 (Best Actress Tony award 1968), Colette, N.Y.C., 1970, A Bequest to the Nation, London, 1970, The Creation of the World and Other Business, N.Y.C., 1972, Love and Master Will, Washington, 1973, The Dance of Death, N.Y.C., 1974, Long Day's Journey Into Night, N.Y.C., Washington, 1976, Medea, N.Y.C., 1982 (Best Actress Tony award), Lillian, 1986, Come A-Waltzing With Me, A Perfect Ganesh, 1993, Master Class, 1995; dir. (plays): An Almost Perfect Person, N.Y.C., 1977, Richard II, Stratford, Ont., 1979, These Men, off-Broadway, 1980, The Taming of the Shrew, Hamlet, Am. Shakespeare Theatre, 1985, Vita and Virginia, N.Y.C., 1994. Decorated Order Brit. Empire; recipient Theatre World award, 1966. Address: 1501 Broadway New York NY 10036-5502

CALDWELL-PORTENIER, PATTY JEAN GROSSKOPF, advocate, educator; b. Davenport, Iowa, Sept. 28, 1937; d. Bernhard August and Leontine Virginia (Carver) Grosskopf; m. Donald Eugene Caldwell Mar. 29, 1956 (dec. Feb. 1985); children: John Alan, Jennifer Lynn Caldwell Lear; m. Walter J. Portenier, Oct. 3, 1992. BA, State U. Iowa, 1959. Hearing officer Ill. State Bd. Edn., Springfield, 1979-91, Appellate Court, 1986-91; pres., bd. dirs. Tri-County Assn. for Children With Learning Disabilities, Moline, Ill., 1972-79; adv. vol., Iowa and Ill., 1979-91; mem. adv. coun. Prairie State Legal Svcs., Inc., Rock Island, Ill., 1984-91; mem. profl. svcs. com. United Cerebral Palsy N.W. Ill., Rock Island, 1986-88; arbitrator Am. Arbitration Assn., Chgo., 1986-91, Better Bus. Bur., Davenport, 1986-91. Founder, pres. Quad Cities Diabetes Assn., Moline, 1969-72, bd. dirs., 1973—; mem. com. Moline Internat. Yr. Disabled, 1981; mem. Assn. for Retarded Citizens, Rock Island, 1987; mem. vol. Coun. on Children at Risk, Moline, 1988-91; reader for the blind Sta. WVIK, Rock Island, 1989-91. Mem. Ill. Assn. for Children with Learning Disabilities (bd. dirs., adv. 1980-83). Methodist. Home and Office: 2443 La Condessa Dr Los Angeles CA 90049-1221

CALDWELL-WOOD, NAOMI RACHEL, library media specialist; b. Providence, Mar. 31, 1958; d. Atwood Alexander II and Juanita (Johnson) Caldwell; m. Patrick William Wood, July 25, 1980; 1 child, William Earl Wood. BS, Clarion State Coll., 1980; MSLS, Clarion U. Pa., 1982; postgrad., Tex. A&M U., 1986-87, Providence Coll., 1990-92, U. Pitts., 1992—. Cert. teaching libr. Asst. dir., adult svcs. libr. Oil City (Pa.) Pub. Libr., 1984-85; microtest reference libr. Sterling C. Evans Libr., Tex. A&M U., College Station, 1985-87; libr. media specialist Nathan Bishop Mid. Sch., Providence, 1987-92; libr. sci. doctoral fellow dept. libr. sci. Sch. Libr. and Info. Sci. U. Pitts., 1992—; sch. library media specialist Feinstein H.S. for Pub. Svc., Providence, 1994—; mem. discovery award com. U.S. Bd. on Books for Young People, 1994; mem. com. R.I. Children's Book Award, 1990-92, R.I. Read-Aloud, 1990-92; participant Native Am. and Alaskan Native Pre-Conf. to White House Conf. on Librs. and Info. Scis., Washington, 1991, George Washington U. Nat. Indian Policy Ctr. Forum on Native Am. Librs. and Info. Svcs., Washington, 1991; hon. del. White House Conf. on Libr. and Info. Svcs., Washington, 1991; mem. U.S. nat. sect. Internat. Bd. on Books for Young People; presenter in field. Mem. editorial adv. bd., reviewer Multicultural Rev., 1991—; mem. adv. bd. Native Ams. Info. Dir., 1992, OYATE, 1992—, Gale Ency. Multicultural Am.. Native N.Am. Ref. Libr.; reviewer Clarion Books, Greenwood Press, Random House, Harcourt Brace Trade Divsn., Browndeer Press, Oryx Press; contbr. articles to profl. jours. Mem. Am. Indian Libr. Assn. (NMRT publicity com. 1986, NMRT minority recruitment com. 1986-88, OLOS libr. svcs. for Am. Indian people subcom. 1986-88, 90-91, chmn. 1992—, ALCTS micropub. com., 1988-90, mem. coun. com. on minority concerns 1991-92, 94-96, councilor-at-large 1992—), Am. Assn. Sch. Librs., Spl. Librs. Assn., Libr. Adminstrn. Mgmt. Assn. Home: 475 Sowams Rd Barrington RI 02806 Office: Feinstein HS for Pub Svc 544 Elmwood Ave Providence RI 02907

CALEGARI, MARIA, ballerina; b. N.Y.C., Mar. 30, 1957; d. Richard A. and Marion (Gentile) C. Student, DuPons Dance Sch., Queens., 5 yrs., Ballet Acad., Queens, 6 yrs., Sch. Am. Ballet, 3 yrs. Mem. corps de ballet N.Y.C. Ballet, 1974-82, soloist, 1982-83, prin., 1983-94. Dancer in N.Y.C. Ballet's Balanchine Celebration, 1993. Recipient Alumni award Profl. Children's Sch., 1986.

CALHOUN, CLAYNE MARSH, law librarian; b. Orange, N.J., July 22, 1950; d. John Clayton and Anne (Jack) Marsh; m. Thomas Sidney Calhoun, Aug. 26, 1972; 1 child, Samuel Clayton. BA, Stratford Coll., 1972; MSLS, Cath. U. Am., 1976. Asst. libr. Caplin & Drysdale, Washington, 1975-77; libr. Roanoke (Va.) Law Libr., 1977—; lectr. Va. Western Community Coll., Roanoke. Pres. Roanoke Valley Swimming, Inc., 1991—. Mem. Am. Assn. Law Librs., Roanoke Valley Swimming, Inc. (pres. 1991). Office: Roanoke Law Libr 315 Church Ave SW Roanoke VA 24016-5007

CALHOUN, ESSIE LEE, public relations executive; b. Granada, Miss., June 17, 1947; d. James Arthur and Sammie Louise (Glover) Dickerson; m. Lee Arthur Calhoun, Dec. 1969 (div. 1978); 1 child, Kwame Mandulo. BE, U. Toledo, 1970; MEd, Bowis State U. Basic skills instr. South Bend (Ind.) Skills Ctr., 1970-71; cons., spl. programs Washtenaw Intermediate Sch. Dist., Ann Arbor, 1971-73; tchr., adminstr. Prince George's City Schs., Upper Marlboro, Md., 1973-81; sales rep. Eastman Kodak Co., Balt., 1982-84; mktg. specialist Eastman Kodak Co., Rochester, N.Y., 1984-86; sales mgr. Eastman Kodak Co., Washington, 1987-88; dir. pub. affairs planning Eastman Kodak Co., Rochester, 1988-89, dir. cmty. rels., 1989-93, dir. corporate contbns. and cmty. rels., 1994—; mem. adv. bd. Ctr. Corporate Cmty. Rels., Boston, 1990—; mem. conf. bd. Contbns. Coun., 1994—. Mem. exec. com. United Way of Greater Rochester, N.Y., 1989—chair African-Am. Leadership Devel. Program, Rochester, 1991-94; mem. corporate adv. coun. Congl. Black Caucus Found., Washington, 1992—; vice chair bd. dirs. Urban League of Rochester, 1993—; corporate assoc. United Way of Am., Arlington, Va., 1994—; mem. human rels. com. Monroe County, Rochester, 1994. Recipient Disting. Svc. award Nat. Capital Big Bros., Washington, Vol. Svc. award African-Am. Leadership Devel. Program, Rochester, 1992-94, Appreciation award The East L.A. Cmty. Union. Mem. Pub. Rels. Soc. Am., Nat. Corporate Women's Network, Bus. Policy Rev. Coun., Kodak Women's Mgmt. Forum. Baptist. Home: 32 Braunston Dr Fairport NY 14450 Office: Eastman Kodak Co 343 State St Rochester NY 14650-0517

CALHOUN, EVELYN WILLIAMS, social worker; b. Tyler, Tex., Sept. 12, 1921; d. James Stanley and Norma (Skelton) Williams; m. William Benjamin Calhoun, Jr., Mar. 15, 1942 (div. Mar. 1949); children: William Benjamin III, Anne Stanley (Mrs. Donald Elliot Loyd). B.A., Baylor U., 1941; M.S.W., Worden Sch. Social Work, 1960; postgrad., U. Chgo., 1955-56. Lic. social psychotherapist, Tex.; cert. social worker, advanced clin. practitioner, Tex. Field worker Tex. Dept. Pub. Welfare, Tyler, 1953-55; field placement Salvation Army Family Svc., Chgo., 1955-56; child welfare worker Tyler-Smith County Child Welfare Unit, 1957-59; field placement Tex. Inst. Rehab. and Research, Baylor U., Houston, 1959-60, med. social worker, 1960-64; research social worker pre-natal research project dept. ob-gyn. U. Tex. Med. Br., Galveston, 1964-66, supr. social svc. dept. ob-gyn., 1966-74, cons. satellite clinics, 1967-74, cons. family planning project, 1969-74, cons., supr. head and neck cancer svc., ear, nose and throat, chest surgery and neurosurgery, 1974-78, cons., supr. plastic surgery and oral surgery svc., 1975-78, supr. internal medicine svcs., otolaryngology, ophthalmology and dermatology, 1978-81; field instr. U. Houston Grad. Sch. Social Work, 1968-81. Bd. dirs. Galveston County Community Action Coun., 1966-68, Galveston chpt. Am. Cancer Soc., 1974-81; trustee Houston Intergroup Assn., 1974-76. Mem. Nat. Assn. Social Workers (chmn. research coun. San Jacinto chpt. 1963-64, dir. chpt. 1964-67, chmn. Galveston br. 1964-67, sec. 1967-68; group leader so. regional inst. 1966, alt. Tex. del. 1969-71, Tex. del. 1971-73, dir. 1969-73; alt. del. Tex. state coun. 1967), Acad. Cert. Social Workers, Galveston County Soc. Social Svc. Dirs. (sec. 1979-80), AAUW, Baylor Alumnae Assn., Daus. King (pres. 1976-78), Order De Moley, Toastmistress, Delta Alpha Pi. Episcopalian. Home: 405 Hodencamp Rd Hillcrest Inn #230 Thousand Oaks CA 91306 also: PO Box 7662 Thousand Oaks CA 91359-7662

CALHOUN, NANCY, state legislator; b. Suffern, N.Y., July 10, 1944; d. Andrew Felix and Paula Mathilda (Kusmitsch) Coleman; children: Richard, Cathy Calhoun Wells, Glenn. Student, Empire State Coll., 1981—. Tax collector Washingtonville (N.Y.) Sch. Dist., 1976-84; adminstrv. aide Office of the Assessor, Town of Blooming Grove, 1978-81; mem. Council, Town of Blooming Grove, 1982-85, supr., 1986-90; assemblywoman N.Y. State Assembly, Albany, 1991—. State committeewoman N.Y. State Rep. Com., 1985-91. Named Citizen of Yr., Monell Engine Co., 1988. Office: NY State Assembly State Capitol Albany NY 12224*

CALHOUN, SIMONE TERESA, women's health nurse; b. Hartford, Conn., Aug. 31, 1939; d. Leo and Marie (Desbiens) Amirault; m. William J. Calhoun, Oct. 22, 1960; children: Paige, William J. II, Pamela, Alison. RN, Hartford, 1960; BSN with acad. honors, St. Joseph Coll., 1982. RNC. Staff nurse Manchester (Conn.) Meml. Hosp., 1960-62; staff nurse labor and delivery St. Francis Hosp., Hartford, 1963-82; perinatal nurse clinician St. Francis Hosp. and Med. Ctr., Hartford, 1982—. Contbr. articles to profl. jours. Active nursing com. March of Dimes, West Hartford, Conn., 1982—; active St. James Ch., Manchester; facilitator, founder Pregnancy and Infant Loss Group, Hartford, 1982—, Subsequent Pregnancy Support Group, Hartford, 1986—. Recipient Bishop McAuliffe award St. Francis Sch. Nursing, 1960, Wyeth-Ayerst award, 1989; Stuart Hamilton fellow Greater Hartford Consortium, 1992. Mem. NAACOG (chairperson 1987-90, 90-93, com. nursing practice 1990-92), AWHONN (instr., trainer EFM 1992—), ACOG Conn. Adv. Coun., Sigma Theta Tau. Home: 250 Ferguson Rd Manchester CT 06040-4535 Office: Saint Francis Hosp Med Ctr 114 Woodland St Hartford CT 06105-1200

CALHOUN-REUTER, MARY KAY, realtor; b. Bellevue, Ohio, July 30, 1944; d. Newton William and Esther Frances (Baehr) Calhoun; m. G. Wynn Reuter, May 21, 1977; children: Alyssa Newton, Alexander William. BSW, Ohio State U., 1966. Social worker Franklin County, Columbus, Ohio, 1966-82; realtor Kerrigan Realty, Columbus, 1982-86, Cam Taylor Co., Columbus, 1986-93, King Thompson Holzer Wollam, Gahanna, Ohio, 1993—. Mem. Bexley Eastmoor Berwick Realty Assn. (pres. 1991-92), East Area Realty Assn. (pres. 1989-90), Gahanna Area Realty Assn., Bexley C. of C. (charter, Bexley Women's Club, Columbus Bd. Realtors (One Million Dollar Club 1989, Five Million Dollar Club 1991, Ten Million Dollar Club 1994), Ohio State U. Alumna Club. Home: 140 N Merkle Rd Bexley OH 43209 Office: King Thompson Holzer Wollam 107 N Hamilton Rd Gahanna OH 43230

CALINESCU, ADRIANA GABRIELA, museum curator, art historian; b. Bucharest, Romania, Dec. 30, 1941; came to U.S., 1973; d. Nicolae and Tamara Gane; m. Matei Alexe Calinescu, Apr. 29, 1963; children: Irena, Matthew. BA, Cen. Lyceé, Bucharest, 1959; MA in English, U. Bucharest, 1964; MLS, Ind. U., 1976, MA in Art History, 1983. Asst. prof. Inst. Theater and Cinema, Bucharest, 1967-73; rsch. asst. Ind. U. Art Mus., Bloomington, 1976-79, rsch. assoc., 1979-83, curator ancient art, 1983—; vis. assoc. mem. Am. Sch. Classical Studies, Athens, Greece, 1984. Author: The Art of Ancient Jewelry: An Introduction to the Burton T. Berry Collection, 1994; author, co-editor: Ancient Art from the V. G. Simkhovitch Collection, 1988. NEA fellow, 1984; grantee Salzburg Seminar, 1970, NEA, 1987, 93, Kress Found., 1991, Internat. Rsch. and Exchanges Bd., 1991. Mem. Archaeol. Inst. Am., Classical Art Soc., Beta Phi Mu. Office: Ind U Art Mus E 7th St Bloomington IN 47405

CALISHER, HORTENSE (MRS. CURTIS HARNACK), writer; b. N.Y.C., Dec. 20, 1911; d. Joseph Henry and Hedvig (Lichtstern) C.; m. Curtis Harnack, Mar. 23, 1959; children by previous marriage: Bennet Hughes, Peter Heffelfinger. A.B., Barnard Coll., 1932; LittD (hon.), Skidmore Coll., 1980, Grinnell Coll., 1986; LittD, Hofstra U., 1988. Adj. prof. English Barnard Coll., N.Y.C., 1956-57; vis. lectr. State U. Iowa, 1957, 59-60, Stanford U., 1958, Sarah Lawrence Coll., Bronxville, N.Y., 1962, 67; adj. prof. Columbia U., N.Y.C., 1968-70, CCNY, 1969; vis. prof. lit. SUNY, Purchase, 1971-72, Brandeis U., 1963-64, U. Pa., 1965; Regent's prof. U. Calif., 1976; vis. prof. Bennington Coll., 1978, Washington U., St. Louis, 1979, Brown U., spring 1986; lectr., Fed. Republic of Germany, Yugoslavia, Rumania, Hungary, 1978; guest lectr. U.S./China Arts Exch., Republic of China, 1986. Author: (novels) False Entry, 1961, Textures of Life, 1962, The New Yorkers, 1969, Journal from Ellipsia, 1965, Queenie, 1971, Standard Dreaming, 1972, Eagle Eye, 1973, On Keeping Women, 1977, Mysteries of Motion, 1984, The Bobby-Soxer, 1986 (Kafka prize U. Rochester 1987), Age, 1987, (under pseudonym Jack Fenno) The Small Bang, 1992, In the Palace of the Movie-King, 1994; (novellas) The Railway Police, 1966, The Last Trolley Ride, 1966; short stories include In The Absence of Angels, 1951, Tale for the Mirror, 1962, Extreme Magic, 1963, Collected Stories, 1975, Saratoga Hot, 1985; autobiography: Herself, 1972; memoir: Kissing Cousins, 1988; contbr. short stories, articles, revs. to Am. Scholar, N.Y. Times, Harpers, Yale Rev., New Criterion, others. Guggenheim fellow, 1952, 55; Dept. of State Am. Specialists's grantee to S.E. Asia, 1958; recipient Acad. of Arts and Letters award, 1967, Nat. Council Arts award, 1967, Lifetime Achievement award Nat. Endowment for the Arts, 1989. Mem. Am. Acad. Arts and Letters (pres. 1987-90), PEN (pres. 1986-87). Office: care Donadio & Assocs 121 W 27th St Ste 704 New York NY 10001

CALKINS, JOANN RUBY, nursing administrator; b. Mich., June 28, 1934; d. William Russell and Imajean (Dunkle) Armentrout; m. James W. Calkins, 1952; children: Russell, Jill, Cindy; m. W. Arthur Brindle, May 7, 1983. AS, Delta Coll., 1964, BS, Cen. Mich. U., 1972, MA, 1977. Staff nurse, L.P.N. clin. instr., asst. dir. Sch. Nursing, Midland (Mich.) Hosp., 1964-71; dir. nursing, dir. substance abuse unit Gladwin (Mich.) Hosp., 1972-76; prin. Calkins Profl. Counseling & Cons., Harrison, Mich., 1976-78, part-time, 1978-83; dir. nursing service Central Mich. Community Hosp., Mt. Pleasant, 1978-83; dir. nursing Oaklawn Hosp., Marshall, Mich., 1983-87; asst. adminstr. profl. svcs. DON Betsy Johnson Meml. Hosp., Dunn, N.C., 1987-93, v.p. profl. svcs., 1993—; part-time prin. W. Arthur and Assocs. Cons.; conducted workshops Mich. Dept. Public Health, Mich. Hosp. Assn.; exec. dir. Holistic Health Agy., 1977-82. Trustee Mid-Mich. Community Coll.; vol. counselor student nurses Cen. Carolina Coll., 1988-93; mem. adv. bd. to schs. of nursing Johnston Community Coll., Sampson Community Coll., Cen. Carolina Community Coll.; mem. adv. bd. St. Joseph of the Pines Home Health Agy., 1988-93; cert. layity speaker Meth. Ch., 1994. Recipient Murial A. Grimmason Nursing Scholarship award, 1962; Cert. nursing adminstr. Mem. Mich. Soc. Hosp. Nursing Adminstrs. (mem. steering com. 1979-80, dir., 14 county rep. 1980-83, pres. 1983-84, chmn. devel. com.), Mich. Nurses Assn., Am. Orgn. Nurse Execs., N.C. Orgn. Nurse Execs. (exec. bd. dirs. 1990-93). Lodge: Lioness Internat. (3d v.p. 1985). Office: 800 Tilghman Dr Dunn NC 28334-5510

CALKINS, JUDITH MORITZ, financial executive; b. New Haven, May 31, 1942; d. George Carl and Amelia Elinor (Pluta) Moritz; m. Peter W. Calkins, May 4, 1974; children: David Stone, Adam, Seth, Rachel. AA, Concordia Coll., Bronxville, N.Y., 1962; BS in Acctg. cum laude, N.H. Coll., 1994. Staff adminstr. Treas. Office, Carling Brewing Co., Waltham, Mass., 1971-76; bus. mgr. PR Pub. Co. Inc., Exeter, N.H., 1977-90; fin. mgr. Jackson, Jackson & Wagner, Exeter, 1987—. Dist. and coun. leadership trainer Boy Scouts Am., scoutmaster, Exeter. Mem. NAFE, Inst. Mgmt. Accts., Am. Mgmt. Assn. Lutheran. Office: Jackson Jackson & Wagner 14 Front St Exeter NH 03833-2747

CALLAGHAN, GEORGANN MARY, management consultant; b. Bklyn., June 25, 1944; d. George Louis and Jean (Russo) Carpenito; m. Matthew John Callaghan, June 7, 1969; children: Matthew, Michael, Christian. BS in Hist. Studies, SUNY Empire State Coll., 1994. Asst. to dir. pers. Kemder Ins., N.Y.C., 19622-65, asst. to assoc. gen. counsel, 1965; asst. to pres. Kalvin Miller, Meyer & Sacks, N.Y.C., 1969-70; asst. to ptnr. Dewey, Ballantine Bushby Palmer & Wood, N.Y.C., 1970-74; fashion cons. Bonwit Teller, Scarsdale, N.Y., 1979-91; self-employed office mgmt. cons. Scarsdale, 1980—. Mem. PTA, Town and Village Club; bd. dirs. Maroon and White; den mother exec. com. Boy Scouts Am. Mem. Maroon & White Athletic Assn. (bd. dirs.), PTA, Town and Village Club. Home and Office: 49 Carman Rd Scarsdale NY 10583-6328

CALLAHAM, BETTY ELGIN, librarian; b. Honea Path, S.C., Oct. 8, 1929; d. John Winfred and Alice (Dodson) C. B.A., Duke U., 1950; M.A., Emory U., 1954, Master Librarianship, 1961. Tchr. pub. schs. N.C., Ga. and S.C., 1951-60; field svcs. libr. S.C. State Libr., 1961-64, adult cons., 1964-65, dir. field svcs., 1965-74, dep. libr., 1974-79, dir., 1979-90, ret., 1990; Conf. coord. Gov.'s Conf. on Pub. Librs., 1965, S.C. White House Conf. Libr. and Info. Svcs., 1978-79; del. White House Conf. Libr. and Info. Svcs., 1979; mem. OCLC Users Coun., 1982-84, 86-87; chair del. SOLINET, 1983-84; bd. dirs. Southeastern Libr. Network, 1984-88, vice chmn., 1985-86, chmn. bd. 1986-87. Active S.C. Hist. Soc. Mem. ALA (coun. 1977-80), S.C. Libr. Assn. (fed. rels. coord. 1976-80, chmn. pub. libr. sect. 1985, mem. legis. com. 1984-90, v.p., pres.-elect 1987-88, pres. 1988-89, Intellectual Freedom award 1986, Educator of Yr. award 1987), Nat. Trust Hist. Preservation, S.C. Soc., Riverbanks Zool. Soc., Hist. Columbia Soc., Friends S.C. State Mus., Friends McKissick Mus., Friends Richland County Pub. Libr., S.C. Wildlife Fedn., Nat. Wildlife Fedn. Home: 733 Poinsettia St Columbia SC 29205-2067

CALLAHAM, BRENDA MARIE JEFFERIES, medical association administrator; b. Roanoke Rapids, N.C., Nov. 5, 1953; d. John Ellis and Anna Mae (Phipps) Jefferies; children: Jeffrey Ian, Tanisha Denise. Grad., Washington Sch. for Secs., 1974; cert. computer info. sys., Strayer Coll., 1993. With AMA, Washington, 1974—, adminstrv. sec., exec. sec., word processing coord., staff asst., computer sys. adminstr., now sys. adminstr. Mem. Am. Assn. Med. Soc. Execs., Capital Personal Computer User Group, Capital Area Novell Users Group, AT&T Sys. 75 Users. Democrat. Baptist. Office: AMA 1101 Vermont Ave NW Washington DC 20005

CALLAHAN, CHRISTINE H., state legislator; b. N.Y.C., Oct. 19, 1944; divorced; children: Mary, James. AA, Centenary Coll., 1964; BS, U. R.I., 1989. Rep. dist. 99 R.I. Ho. of Reps.; mem. fin. com., joint com. on small bus. Acct. R.I. Philharmonic Orch. Home: 651 Indian Ave Middletown RI 02842-5717 Office: RI House of Reps State House Providence RI 02903*

CALLAHAN, KATHLEEN ELISABETH, artist; b. Woburn, Mass., Dec. 20, 1957; d. Robert Filmore and Dorothy Elisabeth (Sellar) Sheerin; m. Glenn Thomas Callahan, Aug. 17, 1984; 1 child, Justin Dean. AS, Endicott Coll., 1978; BA, Syracuse U., 1980. Tech. illustrator Ford Aerospace and Communications MIT Lincoln Labs., Lexington, 1981-88; freelance artist Fitchburg, Mass., 1986-91; artist, pres., co-founder Celebrity Fine Art Co., Fitchburg, 1991-94. Numerous exhibits in permanent collections, corp. collections, and gallery shows. Home: 226 Birchcroft Rd Leominster MA 01453-4666 Office: KC Creations Inc 226 Birchcroft Rd Leominster MA 01453

CALLAHAN, LEEANN LUCILLE, psychologist; b. San Diego, Calif., Dec. 7, 1950; d. Charlie A. Olsen and Delores A. (Libke) Turner; m. Chuck Callahan, Oct. 31, 1970; children: Clint, Devin, Chet. BS/MS in Psychology, San Diego State U., 1983; PhD in Psychology, USIU, San Diego, 1990. Lic. clin. psychologist. Clin. dir. Sharp Cabrillo Hosp., San Diego, 1989-91, Charter Hosp., San Diego, 1991-93; psychologist San Diego, 1989—; preferred provider Charter Hosp., San Diego, 1990—, speakers bur., 1990—; staff psychologist Sharp Cabrillo Hosp., San Diego, 1989-92. Contbr. articles to profl. jours. Pres. PTA, San Diego, 1985; citizen adv./city coun. City of San Diego, 1987; vol. Poway Unified Sch. Dist., San Diego, 1975—; speaker Rotary, San Diego, 1994. Mem. APA, Calif. State Psychol. Assn. Office: 9320 Carmel Mountain Rd Ste D San Diego CA 92129-2159

CALLAHAN, MARILYN JOY, social worker; b. Portland, Oreg., Oct. 11, 1934; d. Douglas Q. and Anona Helen (Bergemann) Maynard; m. Lynn J. Callahan, Feb. 27, 1960 (dec.); children: Barbara Callahan Baer, Susan Callahan Sewell, Jeffrey Lynn. BA, Mills Coll., 1955; MSW, Portland State U., 1971, secondary teaching cert., 1963. Bd. cert. diplomate in clin. social work. Developer, adminstr. ednl. program Oreg. Women's Correctional Ctr., Oreg. State Prison, Salem, 1966-67; mental health counselor Benton County Mental Health, Corvallis, Oreg., 1970-71; inst. tchr. Hillcrest Sch., Salem, Oreg., 1975-81; social worker protective svcs. Mid Willamette Valley Sr. Svcs. Agy., Salem, 1981-88; psychiat. social worker dept. forensics Oreg. State Hosp., 1988-93; pvt. practice specializing of adult sexual offenders Salem, 1993—; pvt. practice in care/mgmt. of elderly, 1993—; panel mem. Surgeon Gen.'s N.W. Regional Conf. on Interpersonal Violence, 1987; speaker in field; planner, organizer Seminar on Age Discrimination, 1985. Mem. NASW (bd. dirs. Oreg. chpt.), Acad. Cert. Social Workers (lic. clin. social worker), Oreg. Gerontol. Assn., Catalina 22 Nat. Sailing Assn. Office: Ste 304 780 Commercial St SE Salem OR 97301-3455

CALLAIS, ELAINE DENISE ROGERS, accountant; b. Cleveland, Tenn., Dec. 30, 1962; d. Eddie L. and Dennie Jo (Richards) R.; m. Edwin T. Callais Jr.; 1 child, Rachel Savannah. BS cum laude, Tenn. Wesleyan Coll., 1985. CPA, Tenn. Asst. contr. Luesing Group, Inc., Atlanta, 1985-90; reimbursement specialist Life Care Ctrs. Am., Cleveland, 1990—. Co-author: (manual) Policies and Procedures of the Luesing Group, Inc., 1988, Life Care Centers of America Accounts Receivable Financial Manual, 1993. Vol. United Way, Cleveland, 1991, ARC, Cleveland, 1978-82. Mem. AICPA, Inst. Mgmt. Accts., Beta Sigma Phi, Sigma Kappa (pres. 1984-85). Republican. Presbyterian. Home: 1111 Cookdale Trl NW Cleveland TN 37312-3610 Office: Life Care Ctrs Am 3570 Keith St NW Cleveland TN 37312-4309

CALLAN, CLAIR MARIE, physician, laboratory director, educator; b. Sleaford, Lincolnshire, Eng., May 18, 1940; d. Joseph Edward and Margaret Mary (Hart) Mills; m. John Patrick Callan, Apr. 4, 1964; children: Eoin, Grainne, Colm, Maeve. M.B., B.Surgery, B. in Art of Obstetrics, Univ. Coll., Dublin, Ireland, 1963, MBA U. Phoenix, 1993. Intern Mater Hosp., Dublin, 1963-64, resident in anesthesia, 1964-65; staff physician State of Conn., Middletown, 1966-68; anesthesiologist St. Francis Hosp., Hartford, Conn., 1972-76; med. dir. Dept. of Income Maintenance, State of Conn., Hartford, 1978-84; v.p. med. and regulatory affairs, dir. med. affairs Abbott Labs., Abbott Park, Ill., 1985-92, venture head, 1992-93, v.p. med. and regulatory affairs and advanced rsch. hosp. products divsn., 1993—; clin. asst. prof. med., Chgo. Med. Sch./U. Health Scis., 1987—. Contbr. articles to profl. jours. Pres. PTA, Wethersfield, Conn., 1974, Capitol Region Assn. of Pvt. Swim Clubs, Hartford, 1978. Mem. Am. Med. Women's Assn. (pres. 1984-85, councillor 1981-83), AMA (pres. Conn. aux. 1979-81), Am. Acad. Med. Dirs. Republican. Roman Catholic. Avocations: tennis; golf; needlework. Home: 1835 W North Pond Ln Lake Forest IL 60045 Office: Abbott Labs D97V 1 Abbott Park Rd North Chicago IL 60064-3500

CALLANAN, KATHLEEN JOAN, electrical engineer, airplane company executive; b. Detroit, Feb. 10, 1940; d. John Michael and Grace Marie (Kleehammer) C. BSE in Physics, U. Mich., 1963; postgrad. in physics Northeastern U., 1963-65; MSEE, U. Hawaii, 1971; diploma in Japanese lang. St. Joseph Inst. Japanese Studies, Tokyo, 1973; cert. in mgmt. Boeing Mil. Airplane Co. Employee Devel., 1985. Vis. scholar Sophia U., Tokyo, 1976-79; elec.-electronic components engr. Boeing Mil. Airplane Co. (named changed to Boeing Def. and Space Group-Product Support Div.), Wichita, Kans., 1979-83, instrumentation design engr., 1983-85, strategic planner for tech., 1985-86, research and engring. tech. supr., 1986-87, electromagnetic effects avionics mgr., 1987-89, elec. and electronics mgr., 1989, design tech. support mgr., 1990-92, engring. leader, 1992—. Contbr. articles to profl. jours. Mem. Rose Hill Planning Commn., Kans., 1982-85; coord. Boeing Employees Amateur Radio Soc., Wichita, 1982-83, sec., 1991. Fellow Soc. Women Engrs. (sr. mem., sect. rep. 1981-83, sec. treas. 1985-86, regional bd. dirs. 1983-85, sect. pres. 1987-88); mem. Bus. and Profl. Women, Quarter Century Wireless Assn. (communications com. 1985-86), Assn. of Old Crows (bd. dirs. 1988-91, chpt. pres. 1991). Lodge: Toastmasters (local pre pres. 1985-86, competent toastmaster 1985). Avocations: amateur radio, singing, bowling. Home: 1201 N West St Rose Hill KS 67133-9333 Office: PO Box 7730 M/S K 86-71 Wichita KS 67277-7730

CALLANDER, KAY EILEEN PAISLEY, business owner, retired gifted talented education educator, writer; b. Coshocton, Ohio, Oct. 15, 1938; d. Dalton Olas and Dorothy Pauline (Davis) Paisley; m. Don Larry Callander, Nov. 18, 1977. BSE, Muskingum Coll., 1960; MA in Speech Edn., Ohio State U., 1964, postgrad., 1964-84. Cert. elem., gifted, drama, theater tchr., Ohio. Tchr. Columbus (Ohio) Pub. Schs., 1960-70, 80-88, drama specialist, 1970-80, classroom, gifted/talented tchr., 1986-90, ret., 1990; sole prop. The Ali Group, Kay Kards, 1992—; coord. Artists-in-the Schs., 1977-88; cons., presenter numerous ednl. confs. and sems., 1971—; mem., ednl. cons. Innovation Alliance Youth Adv. Coun., 1992—. producer-dir., Shady Lane Music Festival, 1980-88; dir. tchr. (nat. distbr. video) The Trial of Gold E. Locks, 1983-84; rep., media pub. relations liason Sch. News., 1983-88; author, creator Trivia Game About Black Americans (TGABA), exhibitor of TGABA game at L.A. County Office Edn. Conf., 1990; presenter for workshop by Human Svc. Group and Creative Edn. Coop., Columbus, Ohio, 1989. Benefactor, Columbus Jazz Arts Group; v.p., bd. dirs. Neoteric Dance and Theater Co., Columbus, 1985-87; tchr., participant Future Stars sculpture exhibit, Ft. Hayes Ctr., Columbus Pub. Schs., 1988; tchr. advisor Columbus Coun. PTA's, 1983-86, ch-chmn. reflections com., 1984-87; mem. Columbus Mus. Art, Families U.S., Citizens for Humane Action, Inc.; supt.'s adv. coun., Columbus Pub. Schs., 1967-68; presenter Young Author Sem., Ohio Dept. Edn., 1988; cons. and workshop leader for sem./workshop Teaching about the Constitution in Elem. Schs., Franklin County Ednl. Coun., 1988; presenter for Illustrating Methods for Young Authors' Books, 1986-87; sponsor Minority Youth Recognition Awards, 1994. Named Educator of Yr., Shady Lane PTA, 1982, Columbus Coun. PTAs, 1989, winner Colour Columbus Landscape Design Competition, 1990; Sch. Excellence grantee Columbus Pub. Schs.; Commendation Columbus Bd. Edn. and Ohio Ho. of Reps. for Child Assault Prevention project, 1986-87; first place winner statewide photo contest Ohio Vet. Assn., 1991. Mem. ASCD, AAUW, Assn. for Childhood Edn. Internat., Ohio Coun. for the Social Studies, Franklin County Ret. Tchrs. Assn., Nat. Mus. Women in the Arts, Ohio State U. Alumni Assn., U.S. Army Officers' Club (def. constrn. supply ctr., Columbus), The Navy League, Liturgical Art Guild Ohio, Columbus Jazz Arts Group, Columbus Mus. of Art, Nat. Coun. for the Social Studies, The Columbus Art League, Columbus Maennerchor (Damen sect.). Republican. Home: 2323 Colts Neck Rd Blacklick OH 43004-9648 Office: The Ali Group Kay Kards PO Box 13093 Columbus OH 43213-0093

CALLARD, CAROLE CRAWFORD, librarian, educator; b. Charleston, W.Va., Aug. 8, 1941; d. William O. and Helen (Shay) Crawford; m. Donald Pope Callard, Apr. 20, 1966; children: Susan Lynne, Annie Laurie. BA in Am. History, U. Charleston, 1963; MLS, U. Pitts., 1966; MA in Social Founds., Ea. Mich. U., 1978. Tchr. Blessed Sacrament Sch., South Charleston, W.Va., 1962-64; grad. trainee W.Va. Libr. Commn., Charleston, 1964-65; reference libr. Tompkins County Pub. Libr., Ithaca, N.Y., 1966-69; head libr. U.S. Embassy, Addis Ababa, Ethiopia, 1969-70; head govt. documents Haile Sellassie U., Addis Ababa, 1970-71; br. libr. Ann Arbor (Mich.) Pub. Libr., 1973-83; documents libr. U. Mich., Ann Arbor, 1983-84; pub. svcs. supr. Libr. of Mich., Lansing, 1986-95; depository libr. inspector Govt. Printing Office, 1995—; chair around the world, around the campus U. Mich. Faculty Women's Club, Ann Arbor, 1974-76; tchr. genealogy Holt Pub. Schs., Okemos Pub. Schs., 1990-92; judge Mich. History Day, 1991, 93, 94. Author: Index to 150th Anniversary Issue Ithaca Jour., 1967, Guide to Local History, Sources in the Huron Valley, 1980; editor: Sourcebook of Michigan, 1986, Michigan Cemetery Atlas, 1991, Michigan 1870 Census Index, 1991-95, Michigan Cemetery Sourcebook, 1994; column editor Mich. History Mag. and Chronicle; contbr. articles to profl. jours. Membership chair LWV, Ann Arbor; v.p. Geneal. Soc. Washtenaw County, Mich., 1993, pres., 1993-94; v.p. Palatines to Am., 1987-90, Washtenaw Libr. Club, 1982-83; pres. Mich. Staff Assn., Lansing, 1985-86; pres. Govt. Documents Roundtable of Mich., pres., 1992-93; pres. Mich. Data Base Users Group, 1992-93; chmn. book sale Friends of Ann Arbor Pub. Libr. Recipient Notable Document award Govt. Documents Roundtable of Mich., 1991, Paul Thurston Documents award Govt. Documents Roundtable of Mich., 1993; grantee U. Pitts., 1966, prof. staff grantee Ann Arbor Pub. Schs., 1980, edn. found. grantee Mich. Libr. Assn., 1982. Mem. ALA (state and local documents com.), AAUW (corr. sec., historian 1973-74, 82-83), DAR, Internat. Soc. Brit. Genealogy (trustee 1994), Mich. Libr. Assn. (chmn. govt. documents sect. 1982-84, leadership acad. 1991-93), Spl. Librs. Assn., Fedn. Genealogy Socs. (del., corr. sec. 1986-87, v.p. regional affairs 1989-92), Nat. Genealogy Soc. (instr. devel. com. 1988-90, chair instns. com. 1992—, chair archives & libr. com. 1993-94), Mich. Geneal. Coun.

CALLAWAY, KAREN A(LICE), journalist; b. Daytona Beach, Fla., Sept. 5, 1946; d. Robert Clayton III and Alice Johnston (Webb) C. BS in Journalism, Northwestern U., 1968. Copy editor Detroit Free Press, 1968-69; asst. woman's editor, features copy editor, news copy editor, asst. makeup editor Chgo. Am. and Chgo. Today, 1969-74; asst. makeup editor Chgo. Tribune, 1974-76, asst. news editor, 1976-81, assoc. news editor spl. sect., 1981—, assoc. news editor vertical publs., 1993—; adviser Jr. Achievement Tribune sponsored co., Chgo., 1976-77; editor Infant Mortality sect., 1989; vis. prof. student chpt. Soc. Profl. Journalists, Northwestern U., 1989. Chmn. class of 1968 20th reunion Northwestern U., 1989, mem. seminar day com., 1989-90, chmn., 1991, mem. alumni bd. dirs. Medill Sch. Journalaism, 1991—; vol. Northwestern U. Settlement House. Mem. Soc. of Profl. Journalists, Sigma Delta Chi, Kappa Delta. Methodist. Office: Chicago Tribune 435 N Michigan Ave Ste 573 Chicago IL 60611-4001

CALLBECK, CATHERINE S., Canadian government official; b. Central Bedeque, P.E.I., Can., July 25, 1939; d. Ralph and Ruth Callbeck. B Commerce, Mt. Allison U., Can., 1960; BEd, Dalhousie U., 1963; postgrad., Syracuse U. Mem. from 4th dist. of Prince P.E.I. Legislative Assembly, 1974-78, min. health and social svcs., min. responsible for disabled, 1974-78; with Callbeck's Ltd., Ctrl. Bedeque, 1978-88; M.P. from Malpeque dist. Ho. of Commons, Ottawa, Ont., Can., 1988-93; leader Liberal Party of P.E.I., Can., 1993—; 1st elected woman premier, pres. exec. coun. P.E.I., Can., 1993—; mem. legis. assembly 1st Dist. Queens, 1993—. Chair bd. dirs. Confedn. Ctr. of Arts; bd. regents Mt. Allison U.; bd. govs. U. P.E.I.; mem. Maritime Provinces Higher Edn. Commn.; bd. dirs. Inst. for Rsch. in Pub. Policy, P.E.I. United Fund, P.E.I. divsn. Can. Heart Found.; mem. provincial com. Internat. Yr. of the Disabled. Liberal. Mem. United Ch. of Can. Office: Office of the Premier, Shaw Bldg PO Box 2000, Charlottetown, PE Canada C1A 7N8

CALLEN, ELNORA STOLLER, nurse, mental retardation professional; b. Lewistown, Mont., Feb. 11, 1935; d. Edward T. and Hilja Alice (Hannula) Stoller; (div. 1965); children: Susan M., John M., Shirley A., Thomas E., William F., Katherine E. Student, Great Falls (Mont.), Sch. Practical Nursing, 1966; ADN, No. Mont. Coll., 1970; BA in Psychology and Health Scis., Ft. Wright Coll. Holy Names, 1974. RN, Wash. LPN Deaconess Hosp., Great Falls, Mont., 1966-68; RN staff nurse Deaconess Hosp., Great Falls, 1970; staff nurse Deaconess Hosp., Spokane, 1970-72, Holy Family Hosp., Spokane, 1972-74; RN therapist Community Mental Health Ctr., Spokane, 1975; alcoholism counselor, nurse Community Personal Guidance Ctr., Community Alcohol Bd., Spokane, 1977; skilled lab. instr. ADN nursing program Lewis-Clark State Coll., Lewiston, Idaho, 1978-79; RN II, qualified mental retardation profl. State of Wash., Dept. Social and Health Svcs., Medical Lake, 1982—; coll. health ctr. RN Fort Wright Coll. of the Holy Names, Spokane, 1971-74; part time RN charge nurse newborn/premature nursery St. Joseph's Hosp., Lewiston, summer 1978, part time RN float, summer 1979; mem. bd. dirs. Am. Heart Assn., Spokane, 1980-82; RN cons. Social Detoxification Ctr., Spokane (Wash.) Alcoholism Care Ctr., 1981-82. vol. RN disaster nursing Washington Red Cross, 1978-82; visual and hearing screening, vol. worker ARC-Pub. Elem. Schs., Spokane, 1982; campaign worker Rep. Party, Spokane, 1985-86. Recipient scholarship No. Mont. Coll., 1969, George B. Boland Nurses scholarship Gonzaga U., 1979. Mem. Eagles Aux., Alpha Chi. Roman Catholic. Home: 2010 E 12th Ave Spokane WA 99202-3519

CALLENDER, NORMA ANNE, education educator; b. Huntsville, Tex., May 10, 1933; d. C. W. Carswell and Nell Ruth (Collard) Hughes Bost; m. B.G. Callender, 1951 (div. 1964); remarried 1967 (div. 1973); children: Teresa Elizabeth, Leslie Gemey, Shannah Hughes, Kelly Mari; m. E. Purfurst, June 1965 (div. Aug. 1965). BS, U. Houston, 1969; MA, U. Houston at Clear Lake, 1977; postgrad. U. Houston, 1970, Lamar U., 1972-73, Tex. So. U., 1971, St. Thomas U., 1985, 86, U. Houston-Clear Lake, 1979, 87, 89-93, San Jacinto Coll., 1988, 89, 94. Aerospace Inst., NASA, Johnson Space Ctr., 1986. Cert. profl. reading specialist, Tex. Tchr., Houston Ind. Schs., 1969-70; co-counselor and instr. Ellington AFB, Houston, 1971; tchr. Clear Creek Schs., League City, Tex., 1970-86; counselor, LPC intern Guidance Ctr., Pasadena (Tex.) Ind. Sch. Dist., 1993—, coord. group counseling, 1994—; part-time instr. San Jacinto Coll., Pasadena, Tex., 1980-81, 91-93; univ. adj., U. Houston, Clear Lake, 1986-91; owner, dir. Bay Area Tutoring and Reading Clinic, Clear Lake City, Tex., 1970—, Bay Area Tng. Assocs, 1982—; cons. in field, 1994—. Contbr. poetry to profl. jours. State advisor U.S. Congl. Adv. Bd., 1985-87; vol., bd. dirs. Family Outreach Ctr., 1989-92; vol. Bay Area Coun. on Drugs and Alcohol, Nassau Bay, Tex., 1993-94; bd. dirs. Ballet San Jacinto, 1985-87; adv. bd. Community Ednl. TV, 1990-92. Recipient Franklin award U. Houston, 1965-67; Delta Kappa Gamma/Beta Omicron scholar, 1967-68; PTA scholar, 1973; Berwin scholar, 1976; Mary Gibbs Jones scholar, 1976-77; Found. Econ. Edn. scholar, 1976; Insts. Achievement Human Potential scholar, Phila., 1987. Mem. APA (student mem. 1990—, assoc.), ACA, Clear Creek Educators Assn. (past, honorarium 1976, 77, 85), Assn. Bus. and Profl. Women, Internat. Reading Assn., U. Houston Alumni Assn. (life), Leadership Clear Lake Alumni Assn. (charter, program and projects com mem. 1986-87, edn. com. 1985), Charles F. Menninger Soc., Houston Mental Health Assn., Houston Psychol. Assn. (student mem. 1991—), Kappa Delta Pi, Phi Delta Kappa, Phi Kappa Phi (life), Psi Chi (life). Mem. Life Tabernacle Ch. Home: 963 Seagate Ln Houston TX 77062-4312 Office: 1234 Bay Area Blvd Ste R Houston TX 77058

CALLOWAY, CLEOLIUS BEATRICE, rehabilitation nurse; b. Yukon, W.Va., June 10, 1943; d. George Sr. and Mattie Lee (Johnson) C.; m. Ulysses Turnage, July 24, 1981. AA, SUNY, Buffalo, 1973; BA, SUNY, 1981; AAS, Trocaire Coll., 1977; BSN, D'Youville Coll., 1980; postgrad., SUNY, Buffalo. Registered nuclear med. technician. Radiation therapy technician Buffalo Gen. Hosp., 1966-74, nuclear med. technician, 1969-77, chief technologist nuclear med., clin. instr., 1977-82; health account exec. Johnhill Enterprises Inc., Buffalo, 1986-89; nuclear medicine technician Roswell Park Cancer Ins., Buffalo, 1989—; mem. steering com. Health Com. of WNY, Buffalo, 1987. Vol. Roswell Alliance Found., Buffalo, 1990-91, Campfresh Horizons, Buffalo, 1991, Kevin House, 1992—; mem. steering com. United Negro Coll. Fund, Buffalo, 1986-90. Mem. ANA, Soc. of Nuclear Medicine, N.Y. State Nurses Assn. (dist. 1). Baptist. Home: PO Box 934 Buffalo NY 14205-0934 Office: Buffalo Vets Adminstrn Med Ctr 3495 Bailey Ave Buffalo NY 14215-1129

CALLOWAY, DORIS HOWES, nutrition educator; b. Canton, Ohio, Feb. 14, 1923; d. Earl John and Lillian Ann (Roberts) Howes; m. Nathaniel O. Calloway, Feb. 14, 1946 (div. 1956); children: David Karl, Candace; m. Robert O. Nesheim, July 4, 1981. BS, Ohio State U., 1943; PhD, U. Chgo., 1947; DSc (Hon.), Tufts U., 1992. Head metabolism lab., nutritionist, chief div. QM Food and Container Inst., Chgo., 1951-61; chmn. dept. food sci. and nutrition Stanford Rsch. Inst., Menlo Park, Calif., 1961-63; prof. U. Calif., Berkeley, 1963-91, provost profl. schs. and colls., 1981-87; mem. expert adv. panel on nutrition WHO, Geneva, 1972-92, tech. adv. com. Consultative Group on Internat. Agrl. Rsch., 1989-93, Internat. Commn. on Health Rsch. for Devel., 1987-90, adv. coun. Nat. Inst. Arthritis, Metabolic and Digestive Diseases, Nat. Inst. Aging, NIH, Bethesda, Md., 1974-77, 78-82; trustee Internat. Maize and Wheat Improvement Ctr., 1983-88; trustee, bd. dirs. Winrock Internat. Inst.; cons. FAO, UN, Rome, 1971, 74-75, 81-83; lectr. Cooper Meml., 1983, Roberts Meml., 1985. Author: Nutrition and Health, 1981, Nutrition and Physical Fitness 11th edit., 1984; mem. editorial bd. Am. Dietetic Assn. Jour., 1974-77, Environmental Biology and Medicine, 1969-79. Recipient Meritorious Civilian Svc. Dept. Army, 1959, Disting. Achievement in Nutrition Rsch. award Bristol-Myers Squibb, 1994; named Disting. Alumna Ohio State U., 1974, Wellcome vis. prof. Fedn. Am. Soc. Exptl. Biol., U. Mo., 1980. Fellow Internat. Union of Nutritional Scis., Am. Inst. Nutrition (pres. 1982-83, sec. 1969-72, editorial bd. 1967-72, Conrad A. Elvehjem award 1986); mem. Inst. Medicine NAS, Sigma Xi. Office: U Calif Morgan Hall Berkeley CA 94720

CALVERT, LINDA DARNELL, women's health nurse, educator; b. Huntsville, Tex., Nov. 5, 1960; d. Gary Mac and Jimmie Jo (Park) C. BSN, Harding U., Searcy, Ark., 1983; MS in Nursing, West Tex. State U., 1988. RN, Tex.; cert. in perinatal nursing. Charge nurse, labor and delivery Huntsville (Tex.) Meml. Hosp., 1983-84; staff nurse, relief charge nurse in labor and delivery Scott and White Meml. Hosp., Temple, Tex., 1984-86; staff nurse, relief charge nurse Meth. Hosp. of Lubbock, Tex., 1986-88; jr. med.-surg. instr. Meth. Hosp. Sch. Nursing, Lubbock, 1988-91; instr. Abilene (Tex.) Intercollegiate Sch. Nursing, 1991-93, asst. prof., 1993—. Mem. health profl. adv. com. March of Dimes, Abilene; USPHS trainee, 1987-88. Named one of Outstanding Young Women of Am., 1987. Mem. Assn. Women's Health Obstetrical Neonatal Nursing, Nat. League for Nursing, Tex. Perinatal Assn., Health Educators Resource Network Abilene, Sigma Theta Tau, Alpha Chi. Home: 1519 Yeomans Rd Abilene TX 79602-7458

CALVERT, LOIS PRINCE, geriatrics nurse; b. Lawrenceburg, Tenn., June 27, 1948; d. Virgil Miller and Beulah Mae (Fox) Prince; m. Albert Sidney Johnson, Sept. 26, 1970 (div. 1985); children: Kelley Nicole, Kristopher Scott; m. Malon Sherman Calvert, Oct. 19, 1990. Student, Bapt. Hosp. Sch. Nursing, 1966-67, Belmont Coll., 1966-67; ADN cum laude, Columbia State C.C., 1970; cert. in nursing home adminstrn., George Washington U., 1985. RN, Ala., Tenn. Psychiat. nurse, staff RN Bapt. Meml. Hosp., Memphis, 1970-71; staff RN, psychiat. staff nurse VA Hosp., Memphis, 1971-73; DON svc. Lawrenceburg (Tenn.) Health Care Ctr., 1975-80, nursing home adminstr., 1980-85; case mgr., aide supr., staff RN Lawrenceburg (Tenn.) Home Health Agy., 1985-86; staff RN, case mgr. home health patients, coord. home health Mid-South Home Health Agy., Florence, Ala., 1986-87; DON svcs. Lawrenceburg (Tenn.) Manor, Inc., 1987—; paramed. examiner ASB-Meditest, Nashville, 1989—; mem. NCLEX panel, item reviewer LPN State Bds., 1993. Sustaining membership chmn. Lawrence County coun. Girl Scouts U.S., 1977-78; pianist, dir. youth choir East End Meth. Ch., 1985-94. Fellow Am. Coll. Health Care Adminstrs. (profl. cert.); mem. Tenn. Employee Rels. Com., NADONA (founding mem. Tenn. chpt., state corr. sec. 1995), Beta Sigma Phi (Girl of Yr. 1973, 76). Baptist. Home: 1613 Ann Rd Lawrenceburg TN 38464 Office: Lawrenceburg Manor 3051 Buffalo Rd Lawrenceburg TN 38464

CALVERT, LOIS WILSON, civic worker; b. Hartford, Conn., Sept. 12, 1924; d. Royal Wouldhave and Evelyn Charlotte (Danielson) Wilson; m. Wallace Erdix Calvert, Mar. 29, 1947; children: Pamela, Gary, Craig and David (twins). Grad., Bryant Coll., 1943. Registrar of voters Town of Simsbury, Conn., 1982—. Hist. columnist Imprint Publs., West Hartford, Conn., 1986-87. Bd. dirs., mng. dir. Simsbury Hist. Soc., 1978—; mem. Simsbury Com. on Aging, 1980-89, Dem. Town Com., Simsbury, 1982—; archivist Simsbury Cemetery Assn., 1987—, Friends of Simsbury Libr.; del. 6th dist. Dem. Conv., Bristol, Conn., 1984, 86; trustee Simsbury Land Trust, 1984-88; justice of the peace Town of Simsbury, 1985—, mem. design rev. bd., 1989-93; mem. constl. conv. bicentennial commn. Hometown Hero, 1986; alt. Conn. Dem. Conv. for Gov., Hartford, 1986; del. State Dem. Conv., 1990, 92.; mem. tourism com. Town of Simsbury, 1994, annual report com., 1994; judge Regional History Day, 1993-94. Named a Simsbury Woman Hartford Woman mag., 1987. Mem. Registrar of Voters Assn. Conn., Soc. of Mary and John. Congregationalist. Home: 28 Riverside Rd Simsbury CT 06070-2517

CALVIN, DOROTHY VER STRATE, computer company executive; b. Grand Rapids, Mich., Dec. 22, 1929; d. Herman and Christina (Plakmyer) Ver Strate; m. Allen D. Calvin, Oct. 5, 1953; children: Jamie, Kris, Bufo, Scott. BS magna cum laude, Mich. State U., 1951; MA, U. San Francisco, 1988; EdD, U. San Francisco, 1991. Mgr. data processing. Behavioral Rsch. Labs., Menlo Park, Calif., 1972-75; dir. Mgmt. Info. Systems Inst. for Prof. Devel., San Jose, Calif. 1975-76; systems analyst, programmer Pacific Bell Info. Systems, San Francisco, 1976-81; staff mgr., 1981-84; mgr. applications devel. Data Architects Inc., San Francisco, 1984-86; pres. Ver Strate Press, San Francisco, 1986—. Instr., Downtown C.C., San Francisco, 1980-84, Cañada C.C., 1986-92, Skyline Coll., 1988-92, City Coll. of San Francisco, 1992—; mem. computer curriculum adv. coun. San Francisco City Coll., 1982-84. V.p. LWV, Roanoke, Va., 1956-58; pres. Bulliss Purissima Parents Group, Los Altos, Calif., 1962-64; bd. dirs. Vols. for Israel, 1986-87. Mem. NAFE, ACM, IEEE Computer Soc., Assn. Systems Mgmt., Assn. Women in Computing, Phi Delta Kappa. Democrat. Avocations: computing, gardening, jogging, reading. Office: Ver Strate Press 1645 15th Ave San Francisco CA 94122-3523

CALVIN, ROCHELLE ANN, development association adminstrator; b. St. Paul, Feb. 28, 1936; d. Peter Herbert and Leah (Noun) Schaffer; m. Arnold Orloff, 1958 (div. 1982); children: Robin, Nadine, Steven; m. Stafford R. Calvin, Nov. 25, 1989. BA, U. Minn., 1957. Dir. woman's divsn. United Jewish Fund, St. Paul, 1977-91, devel. dir., 1991—. Pres. Hadassah, St. Paul, 1977. Jewish. Office: United Jewish Fund 790 S Cleveland Saint Paul MN 55116

CALVIN, SHIRLEY ANN, claims representative; b. Clarksdale, Miss., Sept. 28, 1952; d. Marshall Jackson, Sr. and Lillie Beatrice (Hall) Keys; children: Dmitric, Tandiwe, Algernon. BS in Social Welfare, Tenn. State U., 1974. Field crew leader U.S. Census Bur., Nashville, 1980; claim rep. Kemper Ins. Co., Nashville, 1981-83; claim specialist State Farm Ins. Co., Nashville, 1983—. Tchr. Children's Ch. Sch. Pilgrim Emanuel Bapt. Ch., choir mem., sec. music coun., Nashville, 1991—. Mem. Tenn. State U. Alumni Assn. (corr. sec. 1993-94), Alpha Kappa Alpha (asst. sec. 1994-96, ednl. advancement found. rep. 1989—). Democrat. Home: 4814 Shshone Dr Old Hickory TN 37138-4110 Office: 3024 Business Park Cir Goodlettsville TN 37072-3132

CAMAC, MARGARET VICTORIA, construction company executive; b. Wellington, New Zealand, Mar. 26, 1946; came to U.S., 1981; d. Paul and Cavel (d'Durnett) Leonard; m. Barry John Camac, June 1, 1968; children: Bianca, Karla, Paula, Victoria. BA, U. Manitoba, Winnipeg, Manitoba, Can., 1977; MEd, U. Manitoba, Winnipeg, Can., 1978. Tchr. New Zealand, 1966-69, Can., 1969-76; vol. set up parent programs for handicapped children various bus., Rio Grande Valley, Tex., 1981-86; v.p. Wellington Constrn. Co., 1991—; child advocate. Vol. Ga. Coun. Child Abuse, Atlanta, 1990-91. Mem. Jr. League Atlanta (named one of Twelve Outstanding Vols. in Atlanta, 1990-91, mem. fidelity trust 1991). Home: 335 Mount Paran Rd NW Atlanta GA 30327-4605

CAMASTRO-PRITCHETT, ROSE, artist, educator, business owner; b. Chgo., May 16, 1942; d. Mario and Maria (Michelinl) Camastro; m. David Conway Pritchett, June 2, 1972; children: Jenny, Jesse. BFA, Quincy (Ill.) U., 1964; MS, Western Ill. U., 1972. Art tchr., dept. chair Elizabeth Seton High Sch., South Holland, Ill., 1967-69; art tchr. Quincy Pub. Schs., 1969-71, sch. counselor, 1972-77; art tchr. John Wood C.C., Quincy, 1977-81; entrepreneur Camastro-Pritchett Enterprises, Quincy, 1977-81; sch. counselor Aramco Oil Co. Schs., Ras Tanura, Saudi Arabia, 1981-87; freelance artist Camastro-Pritchett Enterprises, Ras Tanura, 1984-87; pres. Camastro-Pritchett Art Internat., Quincy, 1987—. Counselor, Adams County Suicide Prevention, Quincy, 1975-76, Operation Rainbow, Quincy, 1993-94; campaigner for Dem. candidates in Adams County, 1972-73. Recipient Outstanding Artist award City of Quincy Arts Awards, 1989, Grumbacher Gold medal Quincy Art Ctr., 1988. Mem. Nat. Assn. Women Artists (Gehner award 1991, 92), Phi Delta Kappa. Office: Camastro-Pritchett Art Internat Inc 1310 Washington Quincy IL 62301

CAMBIO, BAMBILYN BREECE, state legislator; b. Johnston, R.I., Dec. 14, 1956; m. James V. Cambio. Cert. Am. Inst. Paralegal Studies. State rep. dist. 11 R.I. Ho. of Reps.; mem. HEW com., joint com. on environment and energy; freelance paralegal, title examiner. Mem. Am. Political Item Collectors, R.I. Cuacus Women Legis. Office: RI Ho of Reps State Capitol Providence RI 02903*

CAMDESSUS, BRIGITTE D'ARCY, family therapist; b. Paris, Dec. 18, 1933; came to U.S., 1987; d. Jacques Henri and Genevieve Marie (Lestre) D'Arcy; m. Michel Jean Camdessus, Dec. 6, 1957; children: Francois, Marie-Odile, Christine, Thibaut, Claire, Marie-Genevieve. MA in Polit. Sci., Institut d'Etudes Politiques, 1954; MA in Clin. Psychology, Paris U., 1976; cert. in marital counseling, French Assn.Marital Counseling, 1979; postgrad. in family therapy, Ecole des Parents, Paris, 1979-82. Clinician Convalescent Nat. Hosp., Le Vesinet, France, 1974-80; ind. trainer, cons. Paris, 1981-82; trainer, cons. marital and family therapy Ctr. Etudes Cliniques des Communications Familiales, Paris, 1983-89; cons. Internat. Counseling Ctr., Washington, 1987-90; chmn. bd. dirs. Ctr. Etudes Cliniques des Communications Familiales, Paris, 1989—. Editor: Quand les Grands Parents s'en melent, 1993, L'Enfance Violentee, 1993, others; contbr. articles to profl. jours. Home: 4515 W St NW Washington DC 20007-1513 Office: Ctr Etudes Cliniques des Comm Familiales, 96 Ave de la Republique, 75011 Paris France

CAMERON, IRMA KYLLIKKI, small business owner, consultant; b. Rovaniemi, Finland, Dec. 25, 1948; came to U.S., 1967; d. Antti Antero Napankangas and Laura Vappu (Karvonen) Makkyla; m. Matt Kullervo Kosola, Dec. 24, 1964 (div. July 1972); 1 child, Jari; m. Jerry Lee Massmann, Aug. 25, 1984. BA in Mid Mgmt., Hennepin County Community Coll., 1982; postgrad. in bus. mgmt., Coll. of St. Thomas, 1983-85. Supr. sales Gen. Mills, Inc., Mpls., 1970-75; mgr. sales office Gen. Mills, Inc., Tampa, Fla., 1975-77; mgr. customer svc. Gen. Mills, Inc., Mpls., 1977-80, mgr. consumer rels., 1980-88; prin. Customer Rels. Cons., Plymouth, Minn., 1988—. Contbg. author: Business Communication Today, 1986. Arbitrator Better Bus. Bur. Minn., Mpls., 1981-92; mem. exec. com. Community Action team. Gen. Mills., Mpls., 1985-88, chmn. Adopt-A-Highrise Project, 1986-88. Recipient Leadership award Mpls. YWCA, 1981. Mem. NAFE. Republican.

CAMERON, JANICE CAROL, marketing administrator; b. Pitcairn, N.Y., Feb. 16, 1940; d. Lawrence Baird and Alice Irene (Manchester) Morgan; m. Albert A. Cameron, III, June 11, 1960 (div. Oct. 26, 1967); children: Albert A. IV, Richard D. AA, Jefferson C.C., Watertown, 1978; BA in Mgmt., St. Mary's Coll., Moraga, Calif., 1984. Stenographer/sr. typist Jefferson C.C., Watertown, 1969-78; dept. sec. Brigham Young U., Provo, Utah, 1978-80; nat. dir. Howard Ruff Cmty. Forums Target, Inc., 1982-86; exec. sec. Merrill Lynch Realty, San Francisco, 1986-88, San Francisco Progress, 1988-89; sr. mktg. adminstr. IPF Divsn., Prouzdzan Bancorp, The Pacific Bank N.A., San Francisco, 1989—; notary public. Contbr. articles to profl. jorus.; asst. dir. play: Of Quiet Desperation, Margetts Arena Theatre, Brigham Young U., 1980. Founder, chair First Support Group for Mormons LDS, Social Svcs. Divsn., Fremont, Calif., 1986-94; chair Parents, Families and Friends of Lesbians and Gays, Danville-San Ramon, Calif., 1993-94. Democrat. Home: 9200 Alcosta Blvd Apt H-3 San Ramon CA 94583-4131 Office: HELP PO Box 3315 San Ramon CA 94583-8315

CAMERON, JOANNA, actress, director; b. Greeley, Colo.; d. Harold and Erna (Borgens) C. Student, U. Calif., 1967-68, Pasadena Playhouse, 1968. media cons. to Cath. Bishops on Papal Visit of Pope John Paul II, Calif., 1987. Starred in: weekly TV series The Shazam-ISIS hour, CBS, 1976-78; host, dir.: for TV equipped ships USN Closed Circuit Network Program, 1977, 78, 79, 80; guest star: numerous network TV shows, including Merv Griffin Show, The Survivors, Love American Style, Mission Impossible, The Tonight Show; appeared in numerous commls.; network prime time shows including Name of the Game, Medical Center, Bob Hope Special, The Bold Ones, Marcus Welby, Columbo, High Risk, Switch; motion picture debut in How to Commit Marriage, 1969; other film appearances include The Amazing Spiderman; dir. various commls., CBS Preview Spl.; producer, dir. documentaries include Razor Sharp, 1981, El Camino Real, 1987; discovered by Walt Disney while spl. tour guide at Disneyland; named in Guiness Book of Records for most nat. network programmed commls. Mem. Dirs. Guild Am., Acad. TV Arts and Scis., AFTRA, Screen Actors Guild, Delta Delta Delta. Club: Los Angeles Athletic. Address: Cameron Prodns PO Box 1011 Pebble Beach CA 93953-1011

CAMERON, JUDITH LYNNE, secondary education educator, hypnotherapist; b. Oakland, Calif., Apr. 29, 1945; d. Alfred Joseph and June Estelle (Faul) Moe; m. Richard Irwin Cameron, Dec. 17, 1967; 1 child, Kevin Dale. AA in Psychol., Sacramento City Coll., 1965; BA in Psychol., German, Calif. State U., 1967; MA in Reading Specialization, San Francisco State U., 1972; postgrad., Chapman Coll.; PhD, Am. Inst. Hypnotherapy, 1987. Cert. tchr., Calif. Tchr. St. Vincent's Catholic Sch., San Jose, Calif., 1969-70, Fremont (Calif.) Elem. Sch., 1970-72, LeRoy Boys Home, LaVerne, Calif., 1972-73; tchr. Grace Miller Elem. Sch., LaVerne, Calif., 1973-80, resource specialist, 1980-84; owner, mgr. Pioneer Take-out Franchises, Alhambra and San Gabriel, Calif., 1979-85; resource specialist, dept. chmn. Bonita High Sch., LaVerne, Calif., 1984—; mentor tchr. in space sci. Bonita Unified Sch. Dist., 1988—, rep. LVTV; owner, therapist So. Calif. Clin. Hypnotherapy, Claremont, Calif., 1988—; bd. dirs., recommending tchr., asst. dir. Project Turnabout, Claremont, Calif.; Teacher-in-Space cons. Bonita Unified Sch. Dist., LaVerne, 1987—; advisor Peer Counseling Program, Bonita High Sch., 1987—; advisor Air Explorers/Edwards Test Pilot Sch., LaVerne, 1987—; mem. Civil Air Patrol, Squadron 68, Aerospace Office, 1988—; selected amb. U.S. Space Acad.-U.S. Space Camp Acad., Huntsville, Ala., 1990; named to national (now internat.) teaching faculty challenger Ctr. for Space Edn., Alexandria, Va., 1990; regional coord. East San Gabiel Valley Future Scientists and Engrs. of Am.; amb. to U.S. Space Camp, 1990; mem. adj. faculty challenger learning ctr. Calif. State U., Dominguez Hills, 1994; rep. ceremony to honor astronauts Apollo 11, White House, 1994. Vol. advisor Children's Home Soc., Santa Ana, 1980-81; dist. rep. LVTV Channel 29, 1991; regional coord. East San Gabriel Valley chpt. Future Scientists and Engrs. of Am., 1992; mem. internat. investigation Commn. UFOs, 1991. Recipient Tchr. of Yr., Bonita H.S., 1989, continuing svc. award, 1992; named Toyolaa Tchr. of Yr., 1994. Mem. NEA, AAUW, Internat. Investigations Com. on UFOs, Coun. Exceptional Children, Calif. Assn. Resource Specialists, Calif. Elem. Edn. Assn., Calif. Tchrs. Assn., Calif. Assn. Marriage and Family Therapists, Planetary Soc., Mutual UFO Network, Com. Sci. Investigation L5 Soc., Challenger Ctr. Space Edn., Calif. Challenger Ctr. Crew for Space Edn., Orange County Astronomers, Chinese Shar-Pei Am., Concord Club, Rare Breed Dog Club (L.A.). Republican. Home: 3257 N La Travesia Dr Fullerton CA 92635-1455 Office: Bonita High Sch 115 W Allen Ave San Dimas CA 91773-1437

CAMERON, KAREN ANN, marketing executive; b. Detroit, Jan. 7, 1958; d. Anthony Thomas and Christine Ann (Tylawski) Paonessa; m. James L. Cameron, Sept. 1, 1990. BA, Wayne State U., 1981; MS, Purdue U., 1983. With GM, Detroit, 1977—, sec. pers. Cadillac div., 1978-79, sr. clk. material mgmt. Cadillac div., 1979-81; comm. coord. Fisher Body divsn. GM, Warren, 1983-84, asst. mgr. comm. rsch. Chevrolet-Pontiac-Can. Group, 1984-86; mgr. communication Cadillac div. GM, Detroit, 1986-88; market rsch. mgr. Cadillac div., Detroit, 1988-91; mgr. competitive intelligence activity Cadillac Divsn. GM, Detroit, 1991—, 1991-94; mgr. product rsch. group Cadillac Divsn. GM, Detroit, 1994—; instr. in communication Purdue U., West Lafayette, Ind., 1981-83; instr. in bus. writing Warren (Mich.) Consol. Schs., 1983-86; part-time mem. faculty Wayne State U., Detroit, 1991—. Editor Upfront, 1984-86, Voice and Vision, 1986-88, Competitive Intelligence newsletter, 1993-94; mem. editl. bd. Jour. Managerial Issues, 1988—. Vol. Detroit Children's Hosp., 1983; solicitor March of Dimes, 1989. Recipient Labor Studies Scholarship, United Auto Workers, Detroit, 1985.

CAMERON, LUCILLE WILSON, retired dean of libraries; b. Nashua, N.H., Dec. 21, 1932; d. Hugh Alexander and Louise Perham (Baldwin) C.; m. James Robert Doris, Aug. 19, 1976; children: Glenn A. Browning, Gail W. Browning, Valerie B. Cruickshank. BA, U. R.I., 1964, MLS, 1972. Social case worker R.I. Dept. Pub. Assistance, Providence, 1964-70; asst. circulation libr. U. R.I. Libr., Kingston, 1970-72, reserve libr., 1972-73, reference/bibliographer, 1973-88, head reference unit, 1983-86, chair pub. svcs., 1988-89, interim dean, 1989-90, dean, 1990-92. Co-author: Labor and Industrial Relations Journals and Serials, 1989; contbr. articles to profl. jours. Recipient Computerized Intergrated Libr. System award Champlin Founds., Providence, 1989, 90, 91, Coll. Tech. Libr. Program award U.S. Dept. Edn., Washington, 1990, Disting. Alumna award Grad. Sch. Libr. and Info. Studies, U. R.I., Kingston, 1991. Mem. ALA, Assn. Coll. and Rsch. Librs., Consortium R.I. Acad. and Rsch. Librs., Higher Edn. Libr. Info. Network (chair), Univ. Press New England (gov.), Alpha Kappa Delta.

CAMERON, MARY EMILY, pediatrics nurse, nursing researcher; b. Newark, Mar. 22, 1948; d. Donald Eugene and Clara Preston (Zink) C. BSN, Duke U., 1970; pediatric nurse practioner cert., Ind. U., Indpls., 1973; MS, Boston U., 1985; PhD, U. Pa., 1994. RN, Pa. Nurse practioner United Health Svcs., Clairfield, Tenn., 1973-74; insvc. dir. Jellico (Tenn.) Community Hosp., 1974-75; instr., nurse practioner East Tenn. State U. Coll. Medicine, Johnson City, 1975-76, 79-82; staff nurse Holston Valley Med. Ctr., Kingsport, Tenn., 1976-79; charge nurse Boston City Hosp., 1982-86; sect. chair Boston City Hosp. Sch. Practical Nursing, 1984-85; instr. U. Mass Sch. Nursing, Boston, 1985-86; teaching and rsch. asst. U. Pa. Sch. Nursing, Phila., 1986-91, clin. rsch. coord., 1991-94; asst. prof. pediatric nursing Temple U., Phila., 1994—; lectr. Mass. Emergency Med. Svcs., Boston, 1983-85; cons. U. Pa. Sch. Nursing, 1991-94. Contbr. articles to profl. jours. Ch. instr., choir mem. Springfield, Pa., 1987-94. Fellow Nat. Assn. Pediatric Nurse Assocs. and Practitioners (hon., CPNA); mem. ANA (cert. maternal-child health nurse, pediatric nurse), Pa. Nurses Assn., Nat. League Nursing. Methodist. Office: Temple Univ Coll Allied Health Professions 3307 N Broad St Philadelphia PA 19140

CAMERON, MINDY, newspaper editor; m. Bill Berg; 2 children; 1 stepchild. B in Journalism, Pacific U. Exec. prodr./anchor, writer pub. TV Rochester, N.Y. and Boise, Idaho; newspaper reporter Boise and Lewiston, Idaho; assoc. city editor Seattle Times, 1981-83, city editor, 1983-89, dep. editorial page editor, 1989-90, editorial page editor, 1990—; leader workshops Am. Press Inst.; writer, reporter PBS documentary, 1978. Bd. dirs. Pacific U., Northwest Pub. Affairs Network. Mem. Nat. Conf. Editorial Writers (bd. dirs. 1993—), Am. Soc. Newspaper Editors, Soc. Profl. Journalists. Office: Seattle Times Fairview Ave N & John PO Box 70 Seattle WA 98111-0070*

CAMERON, NAN, nurse; b. Washington, Pa., Sept. 15, 1953; d. Wilfred Robert and Nan (James) C.; 1 child, Dewayne Cameron. BSN, U. Ky., 1977; MSN, Gwynedd Mercy Coll., 1987. RN, W.Va. Dir. staff devel. Guiffre' Med. Ctr., Phila., 1980-83; clin., editor Springhouse (Pa.) Corp., 1983-84; patient care coord. Albert Einstein Med. Ctr., Phila., 1984-86; div. dir. St. Mary Hosp., Phila., 1986-88; adminstrv. asst. inpatient nursing St. Patrick Hosp., Lake Charles, La., 1988-90; nurse adminstr. Drs. Hosp., Healthtrust, Inc., Moblie, Ala., 1990; asst. adminstr. nursing USA Drs. Hosp., Moblie, Ala., 1990-93; v.p. nursing Greenbrier Valley Med. Ctr., Ronceverte, W.Va., 1993—; mem. faculty Thomas Jefferson U., Phila., 1988. Clin. editor: Emergencies, 1985, Neoplastic Disorders, 1985. Mem. ANA (cert. nursing adminstr., advanced), Am. Orgn. Nurse Execs., Oncology Nursing Soc., Am. Coll. Healthcare Execs. Home: 409 S Lafayette St Lewisburg WV 24901-1548 Office: Greenbrier Valley Med Ctr Ronceverte WV 24970

CAMERON, NINA RAO, lawyer; b. N.Y.C., Apr. 28, 1925; d. Paul and Grace (Malatino) Rao; m. John D. Cameron, Jan. 9, 1950 (div.); 1 child, Scott; m. Robert M. Gewald. BA, Manhattanville, 1945; LLB, Bklyn. Law Sch., 1950; JD, U. Mex., 1968. Bar: N.Y. 1951, U.S. Ct. Appeals (2nd cir.) 1962, U.S. Supreme Ct. 1966. Pvt. practice N.Y.C., 1951, 55, 90—; atty. adviser U.S. Immigration and Naturalization Svc., N.Y.C., 1952-54, dist. counsel, 1968-84, spl. counsel, 1985-90; asst. dir. commerce City of N.Y., 1956-58; asst. commr. dept. pub. events, dir. UN Consular Corps Coms. N.Y.C., 1958-65; law sec. Supreme Ct. State of N.Y., 1967. Chmn. govt. officials com. Internat. Debutante Ball, 1980—. Decorated Orden de Ruben Dario (Nicaragua), Order Nacional al Merito (Ecuador), Order of Merit (Italy), Officers Cross of Merit (Germany), Order of the Brilliant Star (China), Officer of the Natural Order of the Cedar (Lebanon); recipient Amita award to Women of Outstanding Achievement of Italian Ancestry, 1956, Vespu CCI award to Outstanding Ams. of Italian Ancestry, 1957, award Soc. Fgn. Consuls in N.Y., 1961, 63, award for community svc. JFK Libr. for Minorities of Am. Heritage, 1972. Mem. Am. Soc. Italian Legions of Merit (bd. dirs., officer), Am. Immigration Lawyers' Assn. Republican. Roman Catholic. Office: 58 W 58th St New York NY 10019

CAMERON, RITA GIOVANNETTI, writer, publisher; b. Washington; d. Joseph Angelo and Adeline Katherine (Fochett) C. BS with honors, U. Md., 1957; MEd, Am. U., Washington, 1962; DEd, Nova U., 1978. Tchr. D.C. pub. schs., Washington, 1959-64; prin. Prince George's County (Md.) Pub. Schs., 1964-73, 76-84; supr. instrn. K-12 Prince George's County pub. schs., 1973-76; free-lance writer ednl. materials Media, Materials Inc., Balt., 1965-75; free-lance writer travel articles AAA, Washington, 1978-83; owner, pub. Sch. House Global Enterprises, Fort Washington, Md., 1980—; presenter, cons. to sch. systems and ednl. orgns., 1985—. Author: Let's Learn About Maryland and Prince George's County, 1970, Let's Learn About Maryland, 1972, Super Sub! Or How to Substitute Teach in Elementary School, 1974, AAA Traffic Safety Teacher Guide Grades 4-6, 1982, 83; author, pub.: The Master Teacher's Plan and Record Book, 1985, The School House Encyclopedia of Educational Programs and Activities, 1991; also author numerous sci. and social studies kits and student programs, travel articles. Food preparer So Others Might Eat, Washington, 1985—, Missions of Charity Home for AIDS Victims, Washington, 1992—. Recipient Outstanding Citizenship award DAR, 1954, Nat. Tchr. award Expedition Nat. Tchr. Awards Program, 1960-61, Outstanding Tchr. Sci. award D.C. Coun. Engring. and Archtl. Soc. and Washington Acad. Scis., 1964, Outstanding Educator of Yr. award Prince George's County Bd. Edn., 1982-83, Am. Hist. award DAR, 1987, Outstanding Contbn. to Bicentennial Leadership Project award Couns. for Advancement of Citizenship, 1989. Mem. Md., Fla., N.Y., Pa., N.J., Va., Tex., Ga., Gt. Lakes, Mid. States, S.E., and N.E. Regional Coun. for Studies, U. Md. Alumni Assn., Am. U. Alumni Assn., Nova U. Alumni Assn., Nat. Press Club, Phi Kappa Phi. Roman Catholic. Office: Sch House Global Enterprises PO Box 441028 Fort Washington MD 20749-1028

CAMERON, SUSAN KAY, public relations executive; b. Storm Lake, Iowa, Mar. 15, 1960; d. Charles William and Lois JoAnn (Reser) Hutchins; m. Michael J. Cameron, Aug. 12, 1989. BA, Buena Vista Coll., Storm lake, Iowa, 1982. Asst. dir. pub. rels. Buena Vista Coll., Storm Lake, 1982-84; mgr. news and editorial svcs. Drake U., Des Moines, 1984-85; dir. pub. rels. Buena Vista Coll., Storm Lake, 1985—; presenter Conf. for Women in Higher Edn., Cedar Rapids, 1988; chair Coun. for Advancement Support of Edn. com. for career advancement for minorities and women, Mid-Am. dist., 1989, presenter leadership conf., 1990, sec., 1990, student scholarship chair, 1992, conf. program track chair, 1992-93, conf. program chair, 1994-95. Alumni bd. dirs. St. Mary's Cath. Sch., Storm Lake, 1991-93. Mem. Storm Lake C. of C. (pub. rels. com. chair 1986-87, amb. 1990—, bd. dirs. 1992, Profl. Leadership award 1993). Roman Catholic. Office: Buena Vista Coll 610 W 4th St Storm Lake IA 50588-1798

CAMMARATA, JOAN FRANCES, Spanish language and literature educator; b. Bklyn., Dec. 22, 1950; d. John and Angelina Mary (Guarnera) Cammarata; m. Richard Montemarano, Aug. 9, 1975. BA summa cum laude, Fordham U., 1972; MA, Columbia U., 1974, MPhil., 1977, PhD, 1982. Preceptor, Columbia Coll., N.Y.C., 1974-82; adj. instr. Fordham U., N.Y.C., 1980-81; adj. asst. prof. Iona Coll., New Rochelle, N.Y., Manhattan Coll., 1982-84; asst. prof. Manhattan Coll., Riverdale, N.Y., 1982-90, assoc. prof., 1990—. Author: Mythological Themes in the Works of Garcilaso de la Vega, 1983; editl. reviewer D.C. Heath; contbr. articles and revs. to profl. jours. Fellow arts and sci Columbia U., 1972-75; grantee Manhattan Coll., 1985, 91, NEH, 1987, 88; named univ. assoc. Faculty Resources Network Program NYU, 1985—, Andrew Mellon Found. vis. scholar, 1990; scholar-in-residence NYU, 1991-92; mem. adv. bd. Centro de Idiomas del Sureste, Mex. Mem. Cervantes Soc. Am., Am. Council Teaching of Fgn. Langs., N.E. MLA (Rsch. Fellowship grantee 1991), South Atlantic, South Ctrl. and Midwest MLA, Inst. Internat. de Lit. Iberoamericana, Renaissance Soc. of Am., Assn. Internat. de Hispanistas, MLA, Am. Assn. Tchrs. Spanish and Portugese, Hispanic Inst., N.Y. State Assn. Fgn. Lang. Tchrs. Roman Catholic. Avocations: piano, gardening, writing, needlework. Home: 135 Lawrence Pl New Rochelle NY 10801-1108 Office: Manhattan Coll Riverdale NY 10471

CAMMERMEYER, MARGARETHE, nurse; b. Oslo, Mar. 24, 1942; came to U.S., 1951; d. Jan and Margrethe (Grimsgaard) C.; m. Harvey H. Hawken, Aug. 1965 (div. 1980); children: Matthew, David, Andrew, Thomas. BS, U. Md., 1963; MA, U. Wash., 1976, PhD, 1991. RN, Wash. Enlisted U.S. Army, 1961, advanced through grades to capt., 1965, resigned, 1968; staff nurse VA Hosp., Seattle, 1970-73, clin. nurse specialist in neurology, epilepsy, 1976-81; clin. nurse specialist in neuro-oncology VA Med. Ctr., San Francisco, 1981-86; clin. nurse specialist in neuroscis., nurse rschr., col. VA Med. Ctr., Tacoma, Wash., 1986—; asst. chief nurse, supr. Army Res. Hosp., Oakland, Calif., 1985-88, Wash. Army N.G. and N.G. Hosp., Tacoma, 1988-94. Co-author: Neurological Assessment for Nursing Practice, 1984 (named Book of Yr. ANA), Serving in Silence, 1994; co-editor, contbg. author: Core Curriculum for Neuroscience Nursing, 1990; contbr. articles to profl. publs. Decorated Bronze Star medal; recipient presdl. cert. for outstanding community achievement of Vietnam era vets., 1979, "A" Proficiency designation Office of Surgeon Gen. Dept. of Army, 1986; named Woman of Yr. Woman's Army Corps Vets. Assn., 1984, Nurse of Yr. VA, 1985. Mem. NOW (women of power award 1993), Feminist Majority Found., Am. Assn. Neurosci. Nursing (chair core task force), Am. Nurses Assn. (hon. human rights award 1994), Wash. State Nurses Assn., Assn. Mil. Surgeons of U.S., Sigma Theta Tau. Home: 1715 S 234th St Seattle WA 98198-7522 Office: Am Lake VA Med Ctr Dept Neuroscience Tacoma WA 98493

CAMP, ALETHEA TAYLOR, federal agency administrator; b. Wingo, Ky., Nov. 12, 1938; d. Wayne Thomas and Ethel Virginia (Austin) Taylor; children: Donna Paul, Sean Richard. BA, Murray State U., 1961; MA, So. Ill. U., 1975. Tchr. McClean and Hopkins (Ky.) County Schs., 1961-64; instr. homebound Harrisburg (Ill.) Community Sch. Dist., 1971-73; counselor evaluation Coleman Rehab. Ctr., Shawneetown, Ill., 1974-75; counselor corrections and parole Dept. Corrections, State Ill., Springfield, 1975-77, supr. casework, 1977, supr. parole, 1977-80; asst. warden programs Dept. Corrections, State Ill., Hillsboro, 1980-84, warden, 1984-91; correctional program specialist Nat. Inst. Corrections, Washington, 1991—. Mem. Am. Correctional Assn., Ill. Correctional Assn., N. Am. Wardens Assn. Office: Nat Inst Corrections 320 1st St NW Washington DC 20534-0002

CAMP, BARBARA ANN, municipal government official; b. Lancaster, Pa., Feb. 13, 1943; d. Linton Ferguson and Anna (Wills) Mennig; m. Nils Victor Anderson, Nov. 25, 1961 (div. 1972); children: Barbara Jean, Susan Michelle, Jennifer Eileen; m. Robert Tomlin Camp, Dec. 29, 1973. Cert. mcpl. clk., Sun Oil Corp., Phila., 1960-61; sales clk. Thomas Jewelers, Ocean City, N.J., 1969-71; composite typist Avalon Herald, N.J., 1971-72; exec. sec. Publs. Press., Pleasantville, N.J., 1972-74; clk.-typist Twp. of Upper Tuckahoe, N.J., 1977-78, mcpl. clk., 1978—. Editor twp. calendar, 1984-86. Mem. Mcpl. Clks. Assn. of N.J. (asst. treas. 1985-87, treas. 1987, asst. sec. 1988, sec. 1989, 2d v.p. 1990, 1st v.p. 1991, pres. 1992), Internat. Inst. Mcpl. Clks. (bd. dirs. region II 1994), Cape May County Clks. Assn. (past sec., past v.p., past pres.), Assn. Twps. (sec.). Avocations: snow skiing, boating. Home: 210 Pacific Ave # A Marmora NJ 08223-1039

CAMP, HAZEL LEE BURT, artist; b. Gainesville, Ga., Nov. 28, 1922; d. William Ernest and Annie Mae (Ramsey) Burt; m. William Oliver Camp, Jan. 24, 1942; children: William Oliver, David Byron. Student, Md. Inst. Art, 1957-58, 62-63. One-woman shows at Ga. Mus. Art, Rockville Art Mus., Coll. Notre Dame (Balt.), U. Md., Balt. Vertical Gallery, Cleveland Meml. Gallery (Balt.), Unicorn Gallery, 1982, Hampton Ctr. for Arts and Humanities (Va.), 1985, Bendann Art Gallery, Balt., 1980, others; exhibited in juried shows at Peale Mus., Balt., Wilmington (Del.) Fine Arts Ctr., Smithsonian Instn., Bendann Art Gallery, Balt., 1990, City Hall Gallery, Balt., 1982, Balt. Watercolor Soc., 1983, 94, Miniature Painters, Sculptors and Gravers Soc. at the Arts Club, Washington, 1987, 88, 89, 90, 91, 92, 93, 94 (Honorable Mention award 1991), Hampton Bay Days Raddison Hotel Gallery, 1988, Twentieth Century Gallery, Williamsburg, Va., 1989, 90, 91, 92, 93, 94, D'Art Ctr., Norfolk, Va., 1989, Va. Watercolor Soc. at Va. Beach Ctr. for Arts, 1990, at Verona, Va., 1991, William King Regional Arts Ctr., Abingdon, Va., 1992, Yorktown Cultural Arts Ctr. Va., 1991, 92, 93, 94, Goucher Coll. (1st prize in watercolor Nat. League Am. Pen Women Md. Juried Exhibit 1993, 94), Hermitage Found. Mus., Norfolk, 1994, Francis Land House, Va. Beach, 1994, Cork Gallery Lincoln Ctr., N.Y.C., 1994, Nat. Juried Exhibit of Nat. League Am. Pen Women, Turner Gallery, Balt., 1994, Balt. Watercolor Soc., Pa. Watercolor Soc., 1994, Suffolk Art League, 1994, Susquehanna U. Lore A. Degenstein Gallery, 1994, others; represented in permanent collections Ga. Mus. Art, Athens, Peabody Inst., Balt., Rehoboth Art League, Del., numerous pvt. collections; works publ. in Artists of Mid-Atlantic, 1991; contbr. illustrations to mags., booklets. Recipient 1st prize Md. chpt. Artists' Equity, 1967, St. Marys County Art Assn., 1964, 67, 1st prize still life Cape May, N.J., 1969, Catonsville (Md.) Community Coll., 1969, Nat. League Am. Pen Women Exhibit at St. John's Coll., 1969, Best in Show York (Pa.) Art Assn. Gallery, 1972, 2d award Md. Inst. Alumni Founding Chpt., Balt., 1976, Best in Show Three Arts Club, Balt., 1978, Honorable Mention, Rehoboth Art League, Del., 1983, 93, Purchase award Old Point Nat. Bank, Hampton, Va., 1985, Merit award Hampton (Va.) City Hall, 1986, Juror's Choice award Twentieth Century Gallery, Williamsburg, Va., 1987, Award of Excellence Md. State Biennial Eliminations of Nat. League Am. Pen Women at Essex Community Coll., 1989, Montgomery Coll., Rockville, Md., 1987, Honorable Mention award Nat. Miniature Show, Jackson, Tenn., 1991, Honorable Mention award Suffolk Art League, 1992. Mem. Nat. League Am. Pen Women (pres. Carroll bd. 1968-70, editor The Quill 1975-76, editor Carroll br. 1982-83, rec. sec. nat. exec. bd. 1979-80, nat. nominating com. 1982, Md. art chmn. 1982, 3d prize oil Nat. Biennial exhibit Tulsa, Okla., 1966, miniature exhibit at Furman U., 1992, 1st prize Nat. Show, Excellence award and honorable mention 1993), Rehoboth Art League, Hampton Arts League, Va. Watercolor Soc. (signature artist mem), Balt. Watercolor Soc. (signature artist mem., hon. mention 1982, sec. 1978-80), Peninsula Fine Arts Ctr., 20th Century Gallery, Yorktown Cultural Arts Ctr., Tidewater Art Assn., Miniature Painters, Sculptors and Gravers Soc. Washington, D.C. (assoc.), Pa. Watercolor Soc. Methodist. Home: 2 Bayberry Dr Newport News VA 23601-1006

CAMP, JANE (JANE BARTELMAY), artist, educator; b. Delavan, Wis., Jan. 23, 1963; d. Walter Russell and Anna Marie (Levick) C.; m. Laurin Gene Bartelmay, June 16, 1990. BFA, Ill. Wesleyan U., 1985; MS, Ill. State U., 1990, MFA, 1993. Office asst. Ill. Wesleyan U., Bloomington, 1982-85; art. coord. Apostolic Christain Restmar, Morton, Ill., 1986-89; instr. art Ill. State U., Normal, 1988-92, McLean County Art Ctr., Bloomington, 1991-94; composing artist, camera lab operator The Pantagraph Newspaper, Bloomington, 1992-93; instr. art Tenn. State U., Nashville, 1994; art instr. Heartland C.C., Bloomington, Ill., 1994—, Richland C.C., Decatur, Ill., 1994—; printing cons. Instant Copy of Md., Rockville, 1984; coord., designer Heyworth (Ill.) Sch. Mural Project, 1993, 94. One woman shows include Univ. Galleries, Normal, Ill., 1990, 92; exhibited in group shows at Bergner's Scholastic Art Exhibit, Peoria, Ill., 1981, Ill. County Fair, Peoria, 1981, Ill. Wesleyan Holmes Exhbn., Bloomington, 1983, Ill. Wesleyan Advanced Painting Show, Bloomington, 1984, Wakely Gallery Exhibit, Bloomington, 1985, Univ. Galleries, Normal, 1989, 90, 92, Ill. State Fair, Springfield, 1992, Watercolor USA, Springfield, Mo. 1992, Greenview Arts Ctr., Chgo., 1993, Layman Gallery, Lincoln, Ill., 1994, 510 Gallery, Decatur, Ill., 1994, Artworks Gallery, Peoria, Ill., 1994, Flushing (N.Y.) Coun. on Culture and the Arts, 1994, We. Ill. U., 1995; represented in permanent collections Tenn. State U., Nashville, Peoria Tool Co., pvt. collections. co-sponsor Alateen, Peoria, 1987-88. Mem. Artist Coalition Ctrl. Ill., Alpha Lamba Delta. Home: RR 2 Heyworth IL 61745-9802

CAMP, LINDA JOYCE, local government official; b. Plattsburgh, N.Y.; d. Maurice B. and Katherine E. (Trombley) C. BS, Cornell U., 1973, M of Pub. Sci., 1977. Media specialist N.Y. Sea Grant Program, Ithaca, 1973-76; mgr. comm., cable comm. officer City of St. Paul, 1980-87, purchasing systems mgr., 1988—; mem. met. coun. telecom. task force, St. Paul, 1982-85; mem. Minn. Telecom. Coun., St. Paul, 1984-85. Vol. Big Sister Program, St. Paul, 1980-83; bd. dirs. Minn. Ctr. for Women in Govt. Bush fellow, 1987. Mem. Nat. Assn. Telecom. Officers (pres. 1983, Pres.'s award 1985), Am. Mgmt. Assn., Am. Soc. for Pub. Adminstrn. (bd. dirs.), St. Paul Women in City Mgmt., Cornell U. Club (Minn.). Office: City of St Paul 515 City Hall Saint Paul MN 55102

CAMPANELLI, PAULINE EBLE, artist; b. N.Y.C., Jan. 25, 1943; d. Joseph and Dorothy Eble; m. Dan Campanelli, May 24, 1969. Grad., Ridgewood Sch. of Art, 1964; student, Art Students League, 1965-67. fine arts pub. N.Y. Graphic Soc. Exhibited in group shows including Am. Art Gallery, Greenwich, Conn., Temple U., Lever House; represented in pub., corp. and pvt. collections throughout U.S.; author: Wheel of the Year, 1989, Ancient Ways, 1991, Circles, Groves and Sanctuaries, 1992, Rites of Passage, 1994, Halloween Collectibles, 1995, Art of Pauline and Dan Campanelli, 1995; art work and home featured in Colonial Homes, Country Living, Country Almanac, Country Collectibles.

CAMPBELL, ALICE SHAW, retired accountant, poet; b. Crawfordsville, Ind., Aug. 29, 1918; d. Chester Monroe and Amy Susan (Peck) Shaw; m. George A. Campbell, Aug. 29, 1936. Student, Ind. U., 1958-74. With State and USDA Soil Conservation Svc., 1952-57, Dept. HEW-Social Security Adminstrn., 1957-59; acct. Lafayette Motor Parts Co., West Lafayette, Ind., 1959-88. Author: (poetry) Kaleidoscope, 1989; contbr. poetry to publs. including Best Poems of 1995, Treasured Poems of Am., The Desert Sun, In the West of Ireland. Tchr., counselor Hanging Rock Christian Assembly, Ind. Named Golden Poet, World of Poetry, 1989; recipient L.A. Poetry Acad. award presented by Milton Berle, 1993.

CAMPBELL, ALMA JACQUELINE PORTER, educator; b. Savannah, Ga., Jan. 5, 1948; d. William W. and Gladys B. Porter. BS in Elem. Edn., Savannah State Coll., 1969; MEd, SUNY, Brockport, 1971, cert. advanced study in adminstrn. magna cum laude, 1988. Cert. permanent elem. tchr., N.Y. Elem. tchr. Savannah, 1969-70, 71-74; tchr. intern project unique Rochester (N.Y.) City Sch. Dist., 1970-71, tchr., 1974-88, adminstrv. intern chpt. 1 office, 1988; mem. student progress task force, 1994, mem. coun. elem. leadership, mem. instrnl. com.; basic skills cadre Francis Parker Sch., Rochester, 1988—, lead tchr. mentor, 1991—; lead tchr., mentor tchr., basic skills cadre John Walton Spencer Elem. Sch., 1992-93; vice prin. Theodore Roosevelt Sch # 43, 1993-94; Distar demonstration tchr. Rochester City Sch. Dist., 1976-78, curriculum writer, 1987, 88, tchr. rsch. linker, demonstration tchr., 1987-88; active Effective Parenting Info. and Children program, 1987-89; active coop. tchr. program Nazareth Coll. and Rochester City Sch. Dist., 1987; mem. policy bd. Rochester Tchr. Ctr., 1994; adv. com. N.Y. State Systemic Iniative, 1994, sch. quality reviewer; coord., presenter ednl. workshops; apptd. mem. Student Progress Task Force, 1995; asst. WXXI Broadcasting Partnership and Sch. Number 43. Author: (with McGriff) Quick Reference Manual for Teachers, 1989-90; co-author: A Quick Reference Manual for Teachers and Absolutely Jam-Packed With Super Teaching Tips, 1991-92. Mem. Martin Luther King Commn. on Edn., Rochester, 1988-89, Francis Parker Sch. PTA, 1988—; mental health asst. Curriculum Task Force, Rochester City Sch. Dist., 1991, coop. learning tchr., trainer, 1990, 91-92; asst. dir. Meml. A.M.E. Zion Ch., 1979-82, dir. summer camp, 1982-85, asst. sec. bd. Christian edn., 1987-89; bd. dirs. Hamm House, Jefferson Area Child Devel. Ctr., 1990-91; active United Way; mem steering com. African Am. Devel. Program. Mem. ASCD (assoc.), NAFE (sub-adv. com. Strong Mus. sch. programs), Am. Assn. Sch. Adminstrs., Internat. Reading Assn., Rochester Coun. Elem. Leadership, Phi Delta Kappa, Alpha Kappa Alpha (chair nominating com. 1988-89, Ivy Leaf reporter 1992—, Cert. of Achievement 1988). Democrat. Home: 40 Menlo Pl Rochester NY 14620-2718 also: Meml AME Zion Ch Clarissa St Rochester NY 14604

CAMPBELL, ALMIRA TAYLOR, retired librarian; b. Hyde Park, Mass., May 26, 1920; d. Arthur Balcom and Mildred Victoria (Fuller) Taylor; m. Vincent Alexander Douglas Argyle Campbell, June 26, 1953 (dec. 1985); 1 child, Faith Campbell Bacastow. AA, Colby Jr. Coll., 1940; BA, Mt. Holyoke Coll., 1942; BS Sch. Libr. Sci., Simmons Coll., 1943. Acquisitions asst. Yale Law Sch. Libr., New Haven, 1943-45; prof. asst. accessions dept. Williston Meml. Libr./Mt. Holyoke Coll., South Hadley, Mass., 1945-48; head libr. Mt. Hermon (Mass.) Sch.,, 1948-53; head libr., tchr. French Stoneleigh Prospect Hill Sch., Greenfield, Mass., 1961-70; cataloguer F.L. Boyden Libr./Deerfield (Mass.) Acad., 1970-79; now ret.; vol. Ormond Beach (Fla.) Pub. Libr., 1983-89. Vol. Meml. Hosp., Ormond Beach, 1981—, Halifax Humane Soc., Ormond Beach, 1988—; Circle leader, mem. choir Christ Presbyn. Ch., Ormond Beach, 1986—; leader Alzheimer Support Group, Daytona Beach, Fla., 1987-92. Mem. AAUW. Republican. Home: 28 Niagara Falls Cir Ormond Beach FL 32174-8222

CAMPBELL, ANITA JOYCE, computer company executive; b. Jefferson City, Mo., Sept. 24, 1953; d. George Rigsby and Betty Jean (Heade) Sanders; m. Michael Joseph Campbell (div. 1986); children: Kim Erik Seaver, Daniel Joseph Campbell. AAS, Lincoln U., Jefferson City, 1985. Student lab. mgr. Lincoln U., 1985; integrated systems analyst Xerox Corp., St. Louis, 1988-89, ins. industry project mgr., western region ops. mgmt. staff, 1990-91, advanced product specialist, western regions ops. mgmt., 1991, advanced solutions tech. mgr., western region ops. mgmt., 1992-93, tech. market project mgr., rsch. & engring, integrated systems orgn., 1993-94, tech. mktg. mgr. integrated solutions, systems sales and support, 1994-95; tech. con., integrated document solutions Integrated Document Solutions, 1995—. Co-developer Delta Plan, 1988. Office staff campaign mgr. for Carter-Mondale Reelection Com., Washington, 1989-90; waterfront dir. Spl. Olympics, Lake of the Ozarks, Mo., 1987; bd. dirs. ARC, Jefferson City, 1986. Home: 912 Leawood Dr Saint Louis MO 63126-1114 Office: Xerox Corp 11885 Lackland Rd Saint Louis MO 63146-4236

CAMPBELL, BONNIE JEAN, former state attorney general; b. Norwich, N.Y., Apr. 9, 1948; d. Thomas Glenn and Helen Henrietta (Slater) Pierce; m. Edward Leo Campbell, Dec. 24, 1974. BA summa cum laude, Drake U., 1982, JD, 1984. Bar: Iowa 1985, U.S. Dist. (no. and so. dist.) Iowa 1985, U.S. Ct. Appeals (8th cir.) 1989, U.S. Supreme Ct. 1989. Clk. U.S. Dept. Housing and Urban Devel., Washington, 1965-67, U.S. Senate Subcom. on Inter Govtl. Relations, Washington, 1967-69; case worker Hon. Harold E. Hughes, Washington, 1969-74; field rep. U.S. Senator John C. Culver, Des Moines, 1974-80; assoc. Wimer, Hudson, Flynn & Neugent, P.C., Des Moines, 1984-89; of counsel Belin, Harris, Helmick, Des Moines, 1989-91; atty. gen. State of Iowa, 1991-94. Mem. awareness com. Powell III, Iowa Meth. Hosp., Des Moines, 1984; mem. adv. com. Des Moines Community Coll., Ankeny, Iowa, 1985; state chmn. Iowa Dems., Des Moines, 1987-89. Mem. Iowa Bar Assn. (lawyers helping lawyers 1985—), Phi Beta Kappa. Home: 300 Walnut St #187 Des Moines IA 50309 Office: Office Atty Gen Hoover State Office Bldg 2nd Fl Des Moines IA 50319

CAMPBELL, CLAIR GILLILAND, lawyer; b. Aberdeen, Md., Nov. 27, 1961; d. Bobby Eugene and Sara Frances (Matkins) G. BA, U. Ala., 1982; JD, Cumberland U., 1985. Bar: N.C. 1985, U.S. Dist. Ct. (we. and mid. dists.) N.C. 1985, S.C. 1986. Ptnr. Karney, Campbell & Karney, Charlotte, N.C., 1985-91, Charlotte, 1991—; instr. Paralegal Inst., Queens, Coll., 1990; participant Wild Dolphin Project. Author: Twas the Night Before the Orange Bowl, 1988. Mem. ABA, Assn. Trial Lawyers Am., Mecklenburg County Bar Assn. (program coord. edn. com. 1986-88, panel televised lawyers discussion 1991, mem. speakers forum com. 1992, silent ptnr.), N.C. Acad. Trial Lawyers, Ducks Unltd., Cumberland Alumni Assn. (reunion com. 1989-90), DAR (vice regent 1993-94), Nat. Soc. Colonial Dames, Alpha Omicron Pi (sec. 1994—). Home: 3915 Pomfret Ln Charlotte NC 28211 Office: Karney Campbell & Karney 1208 S Tyron St Charlotte NC 28203

CAMPBELL, CLAIRE PATRICIA, nurse, educator; b. Jan. 10, 1933; d. Hugh Paul and Clara Louise (Bell) Campbell. Student So. Meth. U., 1956-57; BS in Nursing, U. Tex. Sch. Nursing-Galveston, 1959, Family Nurse Practitioner, 1979, cert., 1984, 89; MS in Nursing, Tex. Woman's U. Sch. Nursing, 1971. Staff nurse Parkland Meml. Hosp., Dallas County Hosp. Dist., 1955-70, head nurse gen. surgery, chest surgery, neurosurgery, orthopedics, and internal medicine, until 1970; instr. nursing Tex. Woman's U. Sch. Nursing, Dallas, 1971-72; rschr. nursing diagnosis, Dallas, 1972-77; family nurse practitioner Otis Engring. Health Service, Dallas, 1979-86, nurse practitioner pain mgmt. program Dallas Rehab. Inst., 1986—; adj. asst. prof. U. Tex. Sch. Nursing, Arlington, 1976—; cons. nursing diagnosis. Author: Nursing Diagnosis and Intervention in Nursing Practice, 1st edit., 1978, 2d edit., 1984. Mem. Am. Nurses Assn., Tex. Nurses Assn. - Dist. 4, North Am. Nursing Diagnosis Assn., Sigma Theta Tau. Roman Catholic.

CAMPBELL, DANA MARIE, prosecuting attorney; b. Portland, Oreg., Feb. 16, 1961; d. John Donald and Anita Louise (Brosinsky) C.; m. Alan Ross Oratz, May 23, 1993. BS, Oreg. State U., 1983; JD, Lewis and Clark Coll., 1988. Bar: Oreg. 1989, Hawaii 1990. Mng. editor Oreg. State U. Daily Barometer Newspaper, Corvallis, 1981-83; news editor Junction City (Oreg.) Times, 1983-84; asst. editor Home Computer Mag., Eugene, Oreg., 1984-85; head law clk. U.S. Atty.'s Office, Portland, 1987-88; dep. dist. atty. Marion County Dist. Atty., Salem, Oreg., 1989-91; instr. sex harassment Visitor Industry Family & Edn. Ctr. Maui C.C., Kihei, Hawaii, 1994—; dep. pros. atty. Maui County Pros. Office, Wailuku, 1991—; rsch. and writing cons. Campbell Cons., Kihei, 1994—. Founding mem. Maui County Domestic Violence Task Force, Wailuku, 1992-93; vol. atty. Women Helping Women Shelter, Paia, Maui, 1992-93; vol. fundraisers YMCA, Wailuku, 1993. Mem. Hawaii State Bar Assn., Oreg. State Bar, Hui Na Po'okela Canoe Club. Democrat. Office: Office Pros Atty 200 High St Wailuku HI 96793

CAMPBELL, DEBRA LYNN, marketing and new venture consultant; b. Phoenix, Apr. 8, 1954; d. Joseph David and Elaine Lucinda (Krueger) C.; m. J. Frederick Stillman III, Oct. 26, 1985; 1 child, J. Frederick Stillman IV. BS, U. Ariz., 1975; MBA, Harvard U., 1980. Brand mgr. Procter & Gamble Co., Cin., 1975-78; project mgr. Dunham & Marcus, N.Y.C., 1980-81; v.p. Cox, Lloyd Assocs., N.Y.C., 1981-83; cons. Am. Cons. Corp., N.Y.C., 1983-85, dir., 1985-87, dir., chief fin. officer, 1987-88, pres., chief operating officer, 1988-90; pres. DCA, 1990—; bd. dirs. Amarillo Grill, Inc. Treasurer Phoenix Theatre Co., N.Y.C. Recipient Reggie award Promotion Mktg. Assn. Am. (Reggie award 1986, 87, 90). Mem. Am. Mktg. Assn. Office: DCA 175 Riverside Dr New York NY 10024-1616

CAMPBELL, DEMAREST LINDSAY, artist, designer, writer; b. N.Y.C.; d. Peter Stephen III and Mary Elizabeth (Edwards) C.; m. Dale Gordon Haugo. BFA in Art History, MFA in S.E. Asian Art History, MFA in Theatre Design. Art dir., designer murals and residential interiors Campbell & Haugo, 1975—. Designed, painted and sculpted over 200 prodns. for Broadway, internat. opera, motion pictures. Mem. NOW, Asian Art Mus. Soc., San Francisco. Mem. United Scenic Artists, Scenic & Title Artists and Theatrical Stage Designers., Sherlock Holmes Soc. London, Amnesty Internat., Nat. Trust for Hist. Preservation (Gt. Brit. and U.S.A. chpt.), Shavian Malthus Soc. (charter Gt. Brit. chpt.).

CAMPBELL, DONNA MARIE, telecommunications executive; b. Somerville, N.J., Oct. 7, 1949; d. Howard E. and Joyce E. Bilbee; m. Charles Edward Campbell, Mar. 28, 1969; children: Carla Marie, Bradley James. Student, Eckerd Coll. Bus. Mgmt., St. Petersburg. Personnel adminstr. The Bradenton Herald, 1979-82; dir. telecommunications HCA Blake Hosp., Bradenton, Fla., 1982-88; corp. mgr. telecomm. Snelling & Snelling Internat., Sarasota, Fla., 1988-90; mgr. telecomm. and ops. mgr. Health Resource Network Sarasota (Fla.) Meml. Hosp., 1990-94; dir. The Health Resource Network, 1994—; mem. SunHealth Alliance Task Force, 1991. Mem. Am. Bus. Women's Assn. (sec. 1983, pres. 1984, woman of yr. 1985), West Fla. Hosp. Comm. Assn. (sec. 1984-85, pres. 1986-87), Am. Hosp. Assn. (guest speaker nat. conf. 1991), IBX Users' Group (attendant console foucs com. 1993-94, nat. conf. hostess 1995), Fla. Pub. Interest Rsch. Group, Am. Coalition for the Homeless. Republican. Baptist. Office: Sarasota Meml Hosp 1700 S Tamiami Trl Sarasota FL 34239-3555

CAMPBELL, DORIS KLEIN, retired psychology educator; b. Tazewell County, Ill.; d. Emil L. and Cora May (Osterdock) Klein. AB, Augustana Coll., 1930; MA, U. Ill., 1931; EdD, U. Fla., 1962. Instr. Arlington Hall, Washington, 1931-33, Cen. Coll., Mc Pherson, Kans., 1933-37; supr. student teaching Seattle (Wash.) Pacific Coll., 1937-39; tchr. The Harris Schs., Chgo., 1939-41; instr. to full prof. East Tenn. State Univ., Johnson City, 1960-77; Fulbright prof. psychology Silliman Univ., Dumaguete, Philippines, 1977-80; cons. Philippine-Am. Ednl. Found., Manila, 1968-69. Recipient Fulbright grant Coun. for Internat. Exchange of Scholars, Washington, 1968-69. Mem. APA, Am. Assn. Ret. Persons, Am. Coun. for the Blind, Fulbright Alumni Assn., Phi Kappa Phi, Delta Kappa Gamma, Tau Kappa Alpha, Kappa

Delta Pi, Psi Chi. Methodist. Home: Presbyn Homes Apt B212 16 Lake Hunter Dr Lakeland FL 33803

CAMPBELL, ELIZABETH TODD, judge; b. Russellville, Ala., Mar. 5, 1952; d. A. W. and Robbie L. (Smith) Todd; m. Andrew P. Campbell, Nov. 25, 1978; 3 children. BA, Auburn Univ., 1974; JD, Univ. of Ala. Law Sch., 1977. Bar: Ala. 1977. Clk. Ala. Legis., 1974; law clk. Ala. Atty. Gen.'s Office, 1975, Jefferson County Dist. Atty.'s Office, 1976; law clk. to Judge Inzer B. Wyatt U.S. Dist. Ct. (so. dist.) N.Y., 1977-78; asst. U.S. atty., 1978-85; magistrate judge U.S. Dist. Ct. (no. dist.) Ala., Birmingham, 1985—. Recipient John Morrisette Constitutional Law award, M. Leigh Harrison award. Mem. Birmingham Bar Assn., Fed. Bar Assn., Birmingham Women's Network, League of Women Voters. Office: Hugo L Black US Courthouse 1729 5th Ave N Rm 274 Birmingham AL 35203*

CAMPBELL, ELLEN LANGAS, marketing executive; b. Pitts., July 31, 1958; d. George William and Angie (Nefoplaus) Langas; m. Clayton Joseph Campbell, Apr. 30, 1988; children: Stephanie Alexis, Veronica Kelly. BS summa cum laude, Robert Morris Coll., Coraopolis, Pa., 1979; MBA, U. Pitts., 1980. Rsch. specialist Westinghouse Elec., Pitts., 1979-80; mkt. specialist Corning Glass Wks., Corning, N.Y., 1980-82; regional sales mgr. Corning Glass Wks., Phila., 1982-84; sr. account exec. Schubert Advt., Exton, Pa., 1984-86; show host, v.p. consumer affairs and pub. rels. QVC Network, Inc., West Chester, Pa., 1986-93; owner Campbell & Co. Comm., Exton, 1993—; corp. advisor Freedom Valley Girl Scouts; freelance voice-over and commercial actress. Author (book of poetry): Memories of Melodies, 1985. Named Mrs. Pa. U.S. Internat., 1994-95. Mem. Better Bus. Bur. Ea. Pa. (bd. dirs. 1991-92), West Chester C. of C. (bd. dirs. 1991-92), Direct Mktg. Assn. Office: Campbell & Co 443 Spruce Dr Exton PA 19341

CAMPBELL, FRANCES HARVELL, foundation administrator; b. Goldston, N.C.; d. George Henry and Evelyn (Meggs) Harvell; m. John T. Campbell, Jr., Apr. 27, 1968 (div. Aug. 1973). BS magna cum laude, U. Md., 1982. Asst. to Congressman Claude Pepper, U.S. Ho. of Reps., 1968-80, staff dir., 1980-89; exec. dir., curator Mildred and Claude Pepper Libr.; chmn. bd., pres. Mildred and Claude Pepper Found., 1989—; exec. dir. Franklin D. Roosevelt Meml. Commn., 1988-92; Author: Young America Speaks, 1957. V.p. Dem. Women of Capitol Hill, 1982-83. Mem. NAFE, ACLU, Fla. State Soc. (bd. dirs. 1982-85), Greenpeace, Rotary Club, Econ. Club, Phi Kappa Phi, Alpha Sigma Lambda. Avocations: orchid culture, reading, traveling. Home: 3711 Shamrock St W # 144 Tallahassee FL 32308-2658 Office: 101 S Monroe St Tallahassee FL 32301-1529

CAMPBELL, GWENDOLYN JONES, quality management manager; b. Orlando, Fla., Nov. 14, 1946; d. Samuel Jones and Lucy Myrtle (Campbell) Jackson; m. Marvin L. Campbell, June 12, 1976 (div. Feb. 1982). BA, Fisk U., 1967; postgrad., Atlanta U., 1967-68, 78-79, U. Ga., 1977-78, Ga. State U., 1979-81. Svc. rep. Social Security Adminstrn., Atlanta, 1967; claims rep. Social Security Adminstrn., Nashville, 1968-72; mgmt. intern Social Security Adminstrn., Atlanta, 1972-73, ops. supr., 1973, state rels. specialist, 1974-77, programs specialist, 1978-80, br. mgr., 1980, tng. officer, specialist, 1981-90, supr. programs br., 1990-91, total quality mgmt. project mgr., 1991—. Author numerous tng. pkgs. on leadership, quality, effective staff work; contbg. author: (textbook) Cases in Public Management, 1979, (pamphlet) Worship Guide on AIDS, 1990. Exec. bd. So. Christian Leadership Conf./Women, Atlanta, 1972—; leadership team United Negro Coll. Fund, Atlanta, 1979—; adv. bd. humanities Clark-Atlanta U., Atlanta, 1993—; adv. bd. Friends of Gammon Seminary, Atlanta, 1993—. Recipient Disting. Leadership award United Negro Coll. Fund, Atlanta, 1991, Dept. Health and Human Svcs. Sec.'s Disting. Vol. Svc. award, 1991, Thousand Points of Light award, 1991. Mem. NAFE, Am. Soc. for Quality Control. Methodist. Home: 3341 Glenview Cir SW Atlanta GA 30331-2407 Office: Social Security Adminstrn 101 Marietta St NW Ste 1904 Atlanta GA 30323-1801

CAMPBELL, H.R. CADE, mathematics and science educator, researcher; b. Washington, D.C., July 9, 1943; d. Jesse Boddie and Mary Campbell. BSc in Tchr. Edn., D.C. Tchrs. Coll., 1976. Sci. and math. tchr. Peace Corps., Nuku Alofa, Tonga, 1975-77; grad. rsch. asst. in pacific island studies U. Hawaii, Honolulu, Hawaii, 1979-81; English instr. Ecole Adept, Paris, 1982-84; science tchr. Hine Jr. H.S., Washington, D.C., 1988-89; science and math tchr., founder Khemit Math and Science Program, Washington, D.C., 1989—; science and math lectr. various colls., univs., pub. schs., 1989—. Contbr. articles to profl. jours.; host (talk show) A Woman's View WDCU-FM, 1989—. Recipient Outstanding Svc. award The Inst. Healing and Happiness, 1992; grantee D.C. Commn. on the Arts, Washington D.C., 1991. Mem. Innerlight Women's Club (radio liaison 1994—). Home: PO Box 43311 Washington DC 20010

CAMPBELL, JANE TURNER, former realtor; b. Macon, Mo., July 8, 1931; d. Thomas Freeman and Rena Ellen (Vandiver) Turner; m. Duard Ray McDonald, Aug. 25, 1952 (div. 1955); m. Ian MacCallum Campbell, Mar. 28, 1958; children; Colin Turner, Clay Ian. BS in Edn., U. Mo., 1953; postgrad., San Diego State Coll., 1955-57, UCLA, 1958. Cert. secondary sch. tchr., Calif., Ill., N.J.; lic. real estate salesperson, broker, N.J., lic. real estate salesperson, Pa. Tchr. Hallsville (Mo.) High Sch., 1953-54; co-owner McDonalds' Clothiers, Wewoka, Okla., 1954-55; tchr., class advisor Imperial (Calif.) High Sch., 1955-58, Temple City (Calif.) High Sch., 1958-59; prof. Coll. San Mateo, Calif., 1965-70, McHenry County Coll., Crystal Lake, Ill., 1972-76, Waubonsee Coll., Aurora, Ill., 1976-79; tchr., adminstr. Purnell Sch., Pottersville, N.J., 1980-86; realtor Sig Kuhne Realtors, Milford, N.J., 1986-89, Burgdorff Realtors, Inc., Pittstown, N.J., 1989-94; ret., 1994; co-founder Audio, Verbal, & Tutorial Ctr. McHenry County Coll., 1975-77. Chairperson Del. Valley Autumn Antique Show, Holland Twp., N.J., 1988-93, Holland Twp. Hist. Preservation Commn., 1989—, Christmas Project, Hunterdon County, N.J., 1988—. Mem. Hunterdon County Bd. Realtors (Community Svc. award 1988), N.J. Assn. Realtors, Holland Twp. Women's Club (chairperson Clarence Carter Night 1988), Golden Talents (pres., v.p., trustee 1988-91), Pi Beta Phi. Republican. Episcopalian. Home: RR 2 Box 2672-6 Aitken Ln RR 2 Box 2572-2 Edwards MD 65326

CAMPBELL, JANET CORAL, architect; b. Albuquerque, Nov. 24, 1953; d. Ovid Sylvester Campbell II and Evelyn Grace (Kistler) London; m. Rodney Lee Pope, June 12, 1977 (div. 1991). BS, Ga. Inst. Tech., 1975, MArch, 1977; MS in Real Estate, Ga. State U., 1989. Registered arch., Ga. Assoc. planner Metro Atlanta Rapid Transp. Authority, 1977-78; project designer Toombs, Amisano & Wells, Atlanta, 1978-80; project arch., designer Thompson, Ventielett & Steinback, Atlanta, 1980-84; project arch. Dimery, Corbet & West, Atlanta, 1984; arch., renderer Dan Harmon & Assocs., Atlanta, 1984-85; pres. Chantilly Properties, Inc., Atlanta, 1985-91; prin. Campbell Pope & Assocs., Atlanta, 1985-91; arch. J.D. & Assocs., Burlingame, Ga., 1991; sr. arch. U. Calif., San Francisco, 1991—; pvt. practice San Francisco, 1992—. Mem. AIA (bd. dirs. Ga. chpt. 1989-91, Excellence of Studies award 1977). Republican. Mem. Plymouth Brethren Ch. Home: 2 Parker Ave # 302 San Francisco CA 94118

CAMPBELL, JEAN, retired human services organization administrator; b. Fairhaven, Mass., Mar. 4, 1925; d. Elwyn Gilbert and Marion Hicks (Dexter) C. AA, Lasell Coll., Auburndale, Mass., 1944; BA, Brown U., 1946; MEd, U. Hartford, 1963. Field dir. Waterbury (Conn.) Area Coun. Girl Scouts, Inc., 1946-52; exec. dir. Manchester (Conn.) Girl Scouts, Inc., 1952-60; dist. dir. Conn. Valley Girl Scout Coun., Inc., Hartford, 1961-63; dir. field svcs. Plymouth Bay Girl Scout Coun., Taunton, Mass., 1963-64, exec. dir., 1964-68; exec. dir. New Bedford (Mass.) YWCA, 1968-87. Trustee Millicent Libr., Fairhaven, 1970—; corporator Compass Bank for Savs., 1976—, St. Luke's Health Found., 1986—; bd. dirs. Greater New Bedford Concert Series, 1978—; com. mem., past pres. Interchurch Coun. of Greater New Bedford, 1973—; bd. dirs., former treas. ICC Svcs. Corp., 1973—; bd. dirs. ICC Congregate Housing, Inc., 1991—, Fairhaven Improvement Assn., 1990-93; mem. 1st Congl. Ch. Fairhaven, chair history com., 1990-94; mem. Fairhaven/New Bedford--Tosashimizu (Japan) Sister City Com., 1991-94; asst. treas. Ladies Br. of the N.B. Port Soc., 1990-94, treas., 1994—. Recipient Sidney Adams Community Service award Interchurch Council of Greater New Bedford, 1984, AAUW Achievement award, 1987, Thanks badge Girl Scouts U.S., 1956; named Woman of Yr., Internat. Women's Day Com., 1987. Mem. AAUW (3d v.p. New Bedford club 1991-93), Moneta Assocs. Investment Club (pres. 1982-84, 86-91), Fairhaven Hist. Soc. (investment com. 1992—), Lasell Coll. Alumnae Inc. (bd. mgmt. 1994—), Delta Kappa Gamma (pres. Eta chpt. 1986-88, chair family lit. project 1991—, mem. state lit. coun. 1991—, Alpha Upsilon State Achievement award 1992).

CAMPBELL, JILL FROST, academic administrator; b. Buffalo, July 29, 1948; d. Jack and Elaine Mary (Hamilton) Frost; m. Gregory H. Campbell, May 31, 1969; children: Geoffrey, Kimberly, Kristina. BS, SUNY, Brockport, 1970, MS in Edn., 1981; postgrad., SUNY, Buffalo, 1989—. Acct. clk. bursar's office SUNY, Brockport, 1974-75, sr. acct. clk., 1975-78, instl. rsch. asst., 1978-82, asst. dir. instl. rsch. office, 1982-86, acting assoc. pers. office, 1986-87, dir. contract and grant adminstrn. Rsch. Found., 1987—. Mem. exec. com. Nativity Home Sch. Assn., Nativity Blessed Virgin Sch., Brockport, 1985-87, mem. sch. pub. rels. and mktg. com., 1985-88; mem. Frineds of Brockport Athletics, 1985—; coach Brockport Youth Summer Soccer, 1989-91; mem. com. Chancellor's Award for Excellence in Profl. Svc., Brockport, 1989, 90, 94, 95. Grantee United Univ. Professions, 1985, 90, 93, 94. Mem. NAFE, Nat. Assn. Instl. Rsch. (mem. exec. com., co-originator and discussion leader books and current issues 1985-87, co-author profl. file, presenter papers, presenter panels 1979-87), SUNY Assn. Instl. Rsch. and Planning Officers (mem. exec. com., presenter papers, presenter panels 1984-87), Nat. Coun. Univ. Rsch. Adminstrs., North East Assn. Instl. Rsch. (mem. exec. com., sec. 1985-87, presenter papers, presenter panels 1978-87), Internat. Conf. for Women in Higher Edn. (presenter 1992), SUNY Brockport Alumni Assn., Brockport Profl. Women's Group, Rsch. Found. Cen. Office (users group 1987-90, sponsored program comm. com. 1990—, 4-yr. rsch. coun. vice chair 1991, chair 1992), N.Y. State/United Univ. Professions (Excellence award 1990). Home: 5129 Redman Rd Brockport NY 14420-9601 Office: SUNY Rsch Found 350 New Campus Dr Brockport NY 14420-2932

CAMPBELL, JOAN BROWN, religious organization executive. BA, U. Mich., MA; DDiv (hon.), Bethany Coll., Coe Coll., Lynchburg Coll., Doane Coll. Ordained, Christian Ch., also Am. Bapt. Churches (USA). Assoc. exec. dir. Communited United Headstart, 1967-69; exec. sec. Welfare Action Coalition, Cleve., 1969-71; exec. dir. Coun. for Action in Pub. Edn., Ohio, 1971-73; program developer Roman Cath. Diocese, N.Y.C., Cleve., 1973; assoc. exec. dir. Greater Cleve. Interch. Coun., 1973-79; asst. gen. sec. Commn. Regional and Local Ecumenism, Nat. Coun. Chs., 1979-85; exec. dir. U.S. office World Coun. Chs., 1985-91; gen. sec. Nat. Coun. Chs. Christ in U.S.A., N.Y.C., 1991—. Founder, 1st pres. WomenSpace, Cleve. Women's Ctr., 1974-76; v.p. Cleve. Urban League, 1975-79; pres. Nat. Assn. Ecumenical Staff, 1976-78; mem. steering com. U.S. Ch. Leaders, 1989—; bd. dirs. Ind. Sector, 1993—, Union Theol. Sem., 1993—; mem. adv. com. Pew Global Stewardchip Initiative, 1993—; trustee Nat. Religious Partnership for Environment, 1993—. Named to Women of Achievement, YWCA, Leadership Cleve., Martin Luther King Jr. Bd. Preachers, Sponsors and Collegium of Scholars, Morehouse Coll. Mem. NAAPC (life, bd. dirs.), Coun. on Christian Unity, Christian Ch. (Disciples of Christ) (life), Mortar Bd., Phi Beta Kappa. Office: Nat Coun Chs of Christ in USA 475 Riverside Dr Ste 1062 New York NY 10115-0001

CAMPBELL, JUDITH LOWE, child psychiatrist; b. Indpls., Jan. 21, 1946; d. Albert St. Clair and Adele V. (Lobraico) Lowe; m. Robert Frank Campbell, Nov. 30, 1968; children: Christiaan Robert, Kevin Lowe, Geoffrey Ford. BS in Zoology, Butler U., 1967; MD, Ind. U., 1971. Resident in psychiatry Ind. U. Sch. Medicine, 1971-73, fellow in child psychiatry 1973-75; asst. dir. Riley Child Guidance Clinic, Indpls., 1975-79, dir. child psychiatry consultation, liaison svc. to pediatrics, 1975-79; dir. child psychiatry svcs. Riley Hosp. for Children, 1979-85; pvt. practice child psychiatry, Indpls., 1985—; child psychiatry cons. Ctr. for Mental Health of Madison County, Anderson, Ind., 1975-77, Lutheran Child Welfare Assn., Indpls., 1974—, Lutherwood Children's Home, Indpls., 1974—, Jewish Family and Children's Svcs., 1983-84, child and adolescent div. Midtown Cmty. Mental Health Ctr., 1983-85; assoc. med. dir. child and adolescent psychiat. svcs. Cmty. Hosps. of Indpls., Inc., 1989-90; med. dir. outreach svcs. Arbor Hosp. of Greater Indpls., 1990, med. dir. children's unit, 1990-92, pres. med. staff, 1990-92; med. dir. Arbor Hosp., 1992-94. instr. Ind. U. Sch. Medicine, Indpls., 1974-75, asst. prof. dept psychiatry, 1975-89, clin. assoc. prof., 1989-94. Vice-precinct committeeman Rep. Party, 1990-94; mem. parent's adv. coun. Butler U., 1989-93, pres., 1990-93. Recipient Physician's Recognition award in Continuing Edn. AMA, 1974, 77; Helen McQuiston award in sci., 1967. Fellow Am. Psychiat. Assn., Ind. Psychiat. Soc. (councilor 1978-80, 90-91, sec. 1981-83, editor newsletter 1981-83, chmn. com. women 1983-92, mem. ethics com. 1992—), Am. Acad. Pediatrics (Ind. br.), Am. Acad. Child and Adolescent Psychiatry, Ind. Coun. Child and Adolescent Psychiatry (sec. 1986-87, pres.-elect 1987-88, pres. 1988-89, Smithsonian Assocs., Indpls. Mus. Art, Indpls. Zool. Soc., Pi Beta Phi. Clubs: Eastern Star, Woodland Country. Contbr. articles on child psychiatry to profl. jours. Research on emotional aspects of burns in children, craniofacial anomalies in children, also sex differences in child and adolescent population groups. Office: 11075 N Pennsylvania St Indianapolis IN 46280-1091

CAMPBELL, JUDITH MAY, physical education educator; b. Terre Haute, Ind., May 13, 1938; d. O.H. and D. Juanita C. B.S. in Phys. Edn., Ind. State U., 1960, M.S., 1963; D.Phys. Edn., Ind. U., 1978. Recreational dir. Terre Haute Park Dept., summers 1958-60; tchr. St. Louis pub. schs., 1960-61; instr. dept. phys. edn. Ind. State U., Terre Haute, 1961-66, asst. prof., 1968-75, assoc. prof., 1975-79, prof., 1979—, dir. undergrad. preparation; coach volleyball and basketball teams Univ. Sch., 1970-74, girl sports dir., 1974-78; founder Ind. Spl. Olympics, Inc., 1970; chmn. basketball Wabash Valley Bd. Women Ofcls., 1963-65, 68-74; nat. adv. bd. Spl. Olympics, Inc.; mem. nat. adv. bd. Joseph P. Kennedy, Jr. Found., 1972-74, chmn. Contbr. articles to profl. publs.; developer phys. edn. program in sch. curriculums. Bd. dirs. Ind. Spl. Olympics, 1968-74, state co-dir., 1970-74; bd. dirs. State Girls Sports Adv. Bd., 1975-77, Leadership Terre Haute, 1989—; mem. Air Pollution Bd. Vigo County, 1987-90; trustee Vigo Country Sch. Bd., 1986-94. Recipient Lambert award Ind. State U., 1960; recipient Outstanding Phys. Fitness Leadership award Vigo County Jaycees, 1968, Service award Vigo County Assn. for Retarded Citizens, 1971, Community Service award Vigo County Jaycees, 1974, Eleanor St. John Disting. Alumni award, 1977, Katherine Hamilton Vol. award, 1989; Lilly Found. grantee, 1974; Chismar Found. grantee, 1972; Internat. Leadership Scholar; selected grand marshall Homecoming Parade Ind. State U., 1985. Mem. AAUP (pres. 1981—), Ind. Assn. Health, Phys. Edn. & Recreation (program devel. leadership award 1972, leadership award 1974), Mental Health Assn. Vigo County (bd. dirs. 1985-93), LWV (bd. dirs. Vigo County chpt. 1987-89), Delta Kappa Gamma (pres. 1980-82, grantee 1978), Phi Delta Kappa, Delta Psi Kappa. Home: 6745 E Manor Dr Terre Haute IN 47802

CAMPBELL, KRISTA ANN, arts administrator; b. Newark, Jan. 15, 1963; d. Larry Lee and Patricia Ann (Pyle) C. BA, Wittenberg U., 1985; MA in Mgmt., Carnegie Mellon U., 1992. Mktg. mgr. The Rouse Co., Columbia, Md., 1985-88; devel. asst. Columbus (Ohio) Mus. Art, 1989-90; gallery asst. Carnegie Mellon Art Gallery, Pitts., 1990-91; intern, registrar dept. Whitney Mus. of Am. Art, N.Y.C., 1991; exec. dir. Cin. Artists' Group Effort, 1992-94. Vol. Cin. Mus. Natural History, 1993. Recipient Pub. Svc. Career Opportunities award 1992, Barbara Jenkins Meml. scholarship, 1990, Art in the Marketplace grant for Arts Programming, 1987.

CAMPBELL, MARGARET M., social work educator; b. New Orleans, Dec. 1, 1928; d. Walter and Caroline Louise (Seither) C. BA, St. Mary's Dominican Coll., 1950; MSW, Boston Coll., 1952; 3d yr. cert. clin. practice, N.Y. Sch. Social Work, 1959; DSW, Columbia U., 1970. Caseworker Charity Hosp., New Orleans, 1951-53, Cath. Social Services, San Francisco, 1953-55; supr. Spl. Service Club sect. U.S. Army Europe, 1956-58; caseworker Children's Bur., New Orleans, 1959-60, Associated Cath. Charities, New Orleans, 1960-63; lectr. Dominican Coll., New Orleans, 1961-66; spl. projects worker Associated Cath. Charities, New Orleans, 1964-65; dir. Fla. Family Ctr., New Orleans, 1965-67; asst. prof. Tulane U. Sch. Social Work, New Orleans, 1968, assoc. prof., 1971; dir. continuing edn. programs Tulane U., New Orleans, 1976-80; dir. Child Welfare Svcs. Tng. Ctr. Region VI, New Orleans, 1979-82; dean Tulane U. Sch. Social Work, New Orleans, 1982-94, prof., 1986—; dir. Ctr. on Aging, 1993—; chmn. various coms. sch. social work including Advanced Programs Admissions, Continuing Edn., Family and Children Task Report, Library, Ednl. Policy, Direct Services to Individuals Sequence, NASW Student Liaison, Priorities Com. Author numerous publications and articles in profl. jours. in field. Mem. Kingsley House Bd., 1985, Area Agy. on Aging, 1988; bd. dirs. Tulane Ctr. of Aging, Rsch. and Svcs., 1993. Recipient Alumnae award Dominican Coll., 1970, Dominican Coll. Torchbearer award, 1985. Mem. NASW (chpt. pres. 1973-75, bd. dirs., treas., program dir., membership com., 1955-85; social worker of yr. Southeastern La. chpt. 1976; La. chpt. award 1978, La. chpt. Lifetime Achievement award 1992), Acad. Cert. Social Workers, Internat. Conf. on Social Welfare, New Orleans Children's Council, Child Welfare Info. Exchange Panel for La., Task Force on Adolescent Treatment Ctr., New Orleans Collaborative Tng. Program, Child Welfare League (chmn. southeastern conf. 1980-83), Council on Social Work Edn. (steering com. 1980-81, coordinator 1985), La. State Med. Soc. (geriatrics subcom. 1985-86), Nat. Council on Aging, Gerontological Soc. Am. (conf. com. 1985), Southern Gerontology Soc., Adult Protection Services Network, Coun. on Social Work Edn. (planning com. ann. meeting 1990-91), Am. Pub. Welfare Assn. (regional conf. com. 1989-90), Nat. Assn. Deans and Dirs. Schs. Social Work (chair 1991 meeting). Office: Tulane U Sch of Social Work New Orleans LA 70118

CAMPBELL, MARIA BOUCHELLE, lawyer; b. Mullins, S.C., Jan. 23, 1944; d. Colin Reid and Margaret Minor (Perry) C. Student, Agnes Scott Coll., 1961-63; AB, U. Ga., 1965, JD, 1967. Bar: Ga. 1967, Fla. 1968, Ala. 1969. Pvt. practice law Birmingham, Ala., 1968-94; law clk. U.S. Cir. Ct. Appeals, Miami, Fla., 1967-68; assoc. Cabaniss, Johnston and Gardner, 1968-73; sec., counsel Ala. Bancorp., Birmingham, 1973-79; sr. v.p., sec., gen. counsel AmSouth Bancorp., 1979-84, exec. v.p., gen. counsel, 1984-94; exec. v.p., gen. counsel AmSouth Bank, 1984-94; exec. asst. to rector Parish of Trinity Ch., N.Y.C., 1994—; lectr. continuing legal edn. programs; cons. to charitable orgns. Exec. editor Ga. Law Rev, 1966-67. Bd. dirs. St. Anne's Home, Birmingham, 1969-74, chancellor, 1969-74; bd. dirs. Children's Aid Soc., Birmingham, 1970-94, 1st v.p., 1988-90, pres., 1990-92; trustee Canterbury Cathedral Trust in Am., 1992—, Discovery 2000 Children's Mus., 1991-94, Soc. for Propagation of Christian Knowledge, 1991-93; bd. dirs. NCCJ, 1985-94, state chair, 1990-93; bd. dirs. Positive Maturity, 1976-78, Mental Health Assn., 1978-81, YWCA, 1979-80, Op. New Birmingham, 1985-87, pers. com., 1987-90, v.p., 1990-94; bd. dirs. Soc. for the Fine Arts U. Ala., 1986-89, Baptist Hospital Found. of Birmingham Inc., 1994—; commr. Housing Authority, Birmingham Dist., 1980-85, Birmingham Partnership, 1985-86, Leadership Birmingham, 1986—, program com., 1989-90, co-chair program com., 1990-91; mem. pres. adv. coun. Birmingham So. Coll, 1988-92, chair bd. overseers Masters Program, 1990-94; mem. pres.'s cabinet U. Ala., 1990—; trustee Ala. Diocese Episcopal Ch., 1971-72, 74-75, mem. canonical revision com., 1973-75, 89-91, liturg. commn., 1976-78, treas., chmn. dept. fin., 1979-83, mem. coun., 1983-87, chancellor, 1987-91, cons. on stewardship edn., 1981-94, dep. to gen. conv., 1985, 88, 91; mem. Standing Commn. on Constn. and Canons, 1988—; vestryman St. Luke's Episcopal Ch., 1991-94; bd. advisors So. region of Am. Soc. Corp. Secs., pres., 1992-94; community advisor Jr. League Birmingham, 1992-93; mem. adv. bd. Cahaba River Soc., 1991-94. Named One of Top 10 Women in Birmingham, 1989, One of Top 5 Women in Bus., 1993. Mem. ABA, State Bar Ga., Fla. Bar, Ala. Bar Assn., Birmingham Bar Assn., Am. Corp. Counsel Assn. (bd. dirs. Ala. 1984-89), Assn. Bank Holding Cos. (chmn. lawyers com. 1986-87), Greater Birmingham C. of C. (bd. dirs. 1988-94, exec. com. 1992-94, vice chmn., gen. counsel 1993-94), Summit Club, Kiwanis. Home: 200 Rector Pl Apt 36E New York NY 10280 Office: The Parish of Trinity Ch 74 Trinity Pl New York NY 10006

CAMPBELL, MARILYN R., state legislator; b. Salem, N.H., July 31, 1932; married; 3 children. BS, U. N.H., 1954. Registered occupational therapy. Former dir. Salemhaven, Inc.; farmer, pres. Turner Homestead, Inc., Salem; dir. Granite State Electric Co.; mem. N.H. Ho. of Reps.; mem. environment and agriculture com. V.p. N.H. Farm Bur., 1984-88; pres. N.H. Farm Bur. Assoc. Women, 1980-84; mem. women's com. Am. Farm Bur., 1984-90. Methodist. Home: 79 Brady Ave Salem NH 03079-4004 Office: 7B Mallard Ct Derry NH 03038-1812*

CAMPBELL, MARY MARGARET STINECIPHER, research chemist, educator; b. Chattanooga, Feb. 26, 1940; d. Jesse Franklin and Florence Gladys (Marshall) S.; m. John David Fowler Jr. (div. Mar. 1979); children: John Christopher, Jesse David; m. Billy M. Campbell, Jan. 1995. BA, Earlham Coll., 1962; PhD, U. N.C., 1967. Postdoctoral researcher Research Triangle Inst., Research Triangle Park, N.C., 1966-68, 74-76; mem. staff Los Alamos (N.Mex.) Nat. Lab., 1976—; adj. prof. organic, inorganic and phys. chemistry U. N.Mex. Grad. Ctr., Los Alamos, 1989—; instr. chemistry lab., 1989; vis. scientist AFOSR (AFATL), Eglin AFB, Fla., 1980-81. Contbr. articles to profl. jours.; inventor ammonium nitrate explosive systems and other explosive salts, fruit grower using organic methods. Mem. AAUW (sec. 1972-74), Am. Chem. Soc., N.Mex. Network Women in Sci. and Engring. (v.p. 1985-86, pres. 1986-87), Los Alamos Women in Sci. (pres. 1983-85), Toastmasters Internat. (pres. 1988, 696 Club), Los Alamos Folkdancers (treas. 1991-93), Bio-Integral Rsch. Ctr., N.Mex. Apple Coun. Democrat. Unitarian. Office: Los Alamos Nat Lab Ms C920 Group Dx-16 Los Alamos NM 87545

CAMPBELL, MARY RITA, research psychologist, educator; b. Louisville, May 26, 1961; d. Michael Patrick and Elizabeth (Fanning) C.; m. Allen Dodson Ford, Dec. 20, 1986; children: William Campbell Ford, Christian Allen Ford. BA in Psychology, U. Louisville, 1985, MA in Exptl. Psychology, 1991. Rsch. asst. Mercer-Meidinger, Louisville, 1986-87; lectr. U. Louisville, 1988-89; behavioral rsch. scientist BDM Internat., Ft. Knox, Ky., 1989-90; rsch. psychologist BDM Fed., Inc., Ft. Chaffee, Ark., 1990-93, Ft. Polk, La., 1993-94; rsch. psychologist BDM Engring. Svcs. Co., Alexandria, Va., 1994—; adj. prof. Northwwester State U., Leesville, La., 1993—. Vol. ARC, Louisville. Recipient Cert. of Commendation, Joint Readiness Tng. Ctr., 1992, BDM Excellence award, 1994. Mem. APA (assoc., assoc. mem. divsn. mil. psychology, assoc. mem. divsn. exptl. analysis and behavior), Human Factors and Ergonomics Soc. (assoc.), Psi Chi. Office: BDM Engring Svcs Inc 4401 Ford Ave Ste 402 Alexandria VA 22302

CAMPBELL, SISTER MAURA, religious studies and philosophy educator; b. Bayonne, N.J.; d. Patrick John and Helena Marie (Collins) C. BS, Seton Hall U., 1940, MA, 1945; MA, Providence Coll., 1953; PhD, St. Mary's Sch. Theology, Notre Dame, Ind., 1955; hon. doctorate in religious edn., Providence Coll., 1985; postgrad. Marquette U, Ottawa U., 1969, Cath. U. Am., 1970-71. Joined Dominican Order, Roman Cath. Ch., 1927. Tchr. elem. and secondary schs., 1930-42; dir. postulants Mt. St. Dominic, Caldwell, N.J., 1955-59, dir. scholastics, 1959-69; mem. faculty Caldwell Coll., 1955—, prof. religious studies, 1957-86, prof. emerita, 1986—, chmn. dept., 1969-86; permanent rep. internat. Cath. edn. office UN Non-Govtl. Orgns., 1969—; cons. Thomas Edison State Coll., 1982—; v.p. internat. Cath. orgns. N.Y. Info. Ctr., 1978, pres., 1982-87; permanent rep. World Assembly Internat. Cath. Edn. Office, Bangkok, 1982; participant Women's Forum, Nairobi, Kenya, 1985, Mexico City, 1986, Madrid, 1993, Rome, 1994; participant World Congress of OIEC, Rome, 1994. Recipient Recognition award for outstanding achievement in higher edn. State of N.J., 1989, Award for Svc. Caldwell Coll., 1989, Jubilee medal Archdiocese of Newark, 1994, Svc. award Thomas Edison State Coll., 1994, Disting. Svc. award Sacred Heart Inst., 1994. Mem. editorial bd. The Cath. Adv. Mem. Ecumenical/Interfaith Commn. Archdiocese of Newark, 1986-90; elected mem. exec. bd. NGO/DPI at UN, 1988-90. Recipient 40th Anniversary Faculty award Caldwell Coll., 1979. Mem. Dominican Edn. Assn. (past pres.), Coll. Theology Soc. (past v.p., sec.), Am. Acad. Religion, Religious Edn. Assn., Cath. Theology Soc., Council Religion and World Affairs, Theta Alpha Kappa (hon. mem. alumnus 1989, Veritas award 1989, Outstanding Prof. Religion award 1989). Office: Caldwell Coll 9 Ryerson Ave Caldwell NJ 07006

CAMPBELL, MILDRED CORUM, business owner, nurse; b. Warfield, Va., Feb. 24, 1934; d. Oliver Lee and Hazel King (Young) Corum; m. Hugh Stuart Campbell, Dec. 2, 1972. BSN, U. Va., 1956; operating rm. mgr. cert., U.S. Army Med. Svcs. Sch., San Antonio, 1967; gen. mgr. cert., Cedars of Lebanon Med. Ctr., L.A., 1968. Head nurse plastic surgery U. Va. Med. Ctr., Charlottesville, 1956-58, head nurse cardio-surg., 1958-61; staff nurs operating rm. NIH Heart Inst., Bethesda, Md., 1961-62; supr. operating and recovery rms. Med. Univ. of S.C., Charleston, 1962-64; head nurse cardio operating rms. Meth. Hosp., Tex. Med. Ctr., Houston, 1964-67; supr. operating and recovery rms. Cedars of Lebanon Med. Ctr., L.A., 1967-68; product-nurse cons. Ethicon, Inc., Somerville, N.J., 1968-69; nurse cons. Johnson & Johnson, New Brunswick, N.J., 1969-70; gen. mgr. Ariz. Heart Inst., Phoenix, 1970-72; owner, pres., bd. dirs. Highland Packaging Labs., Inc., Somerville, 1983—. Mem., moderator Nat. Ass. Operating Rm. Nurses, Denver, 1963-76; pres. Aux. Orgn., Muhlenberg Hosp., Plainfield, N.J., 1979-80; chmn. Assn. for Retarded Citizens Fund Raising Ball, Somerset County, N.J., 1982. Mem. Inst. Packaging Profls. Home: 58 Westcott Rd Princeton NJ 08540-3071 Office: Highland Packaging Labs Inc 1181 US Highway 202 S Somerville NJ 08876-3909

CAMPBELL, NANCY EDINGER, nuclear engineer; b. Washington, May 9, 1957; d. Ralph Joseph and Eleanor (Brabble) Edinger; m. Larry Alan Campbell, Feb. 25, 1984. BS in Nuclear Engrng. with honors, Ga. Inst. of Tech., 1978; MBA, U. Pitts., 1985. Nuclear safety engr. Westinghouse Nuclear Tech. Div., Monroeville, Pa., 1978-81; nuclear fuel proposal engr. Westinghouse Nuclear Fuel Div., Monroeville, 1981-86; nuclear fuel project engr. Westinghouse Comml. Nuclear Fuel Div., Monroeville, 1986-90; reactor engr. U.S. Nuclear Regulatory Commn., Washington, 1990—; chmn. hospitality, rep. nuclear fuel div. Westinghouse Women's Career Devel. Com., Pitts., 1985-87. Mem. DAR, Am. Nuclear Soc., Federally Employed Women, Nat. Trust Hist. Preservation, Engrng. Soc. Balt., Phi Kappa Phi, Tau Beta Pi, Phi Eta Sigma. Republican. Episcopalian. Office: US Nuclear Regulatory Commn Washington DC 20555

CAMPBELL, PATRICIA ELAINE, elementary education educator; b. Cin., Dec. 3, 1943; d. Jake T. and Margaret O. (Hunter) C.; 1 child, Andre. BA in Elem. Edn., Andrews U., 1968; MA in Edn., U. Cin., 1978. Cert. elem tchr., prin. and supr., Ohio. Tchr. elem. Cin. Pub. Schs., 1968—, consulting tchr. Math. Assessment Devel., 1988—; curriculum writer gifted and talented, career edn., programs in math. and sci.; mentor; youth program leader. Chair bd. Pvt. Parochial Sch., Cin., 1991—. Mem. Ohio Maths. Group., Cin. Maths. Groupg, Nat. Coun. Tchrs. Maths. Adventist. Office: Cin Pub Schs 230 E 9th St Cincinnati OH 45202

CAMPBELL, PATRICIA K., public relations executive, writer, journalist; b. Rock Rapids, Iowa, Nov. 2, 1956; d. Charles Wayne and Virginia Louise (Skidmore) C.; 1 child. Julia Noelle. AA in Liberal Arts, Ellsworth C.C., Iowa Falls, Iowa, 1976; BA in Speech Radio TV, U. No. Iowa, 1979. Editorial asst., news reader, program host KUNI-KHKE, affiliate of NPR, Cedar Falls, Iowa, 1976-80; editor, newsletter Commodities Report, Oster Comm., Inc., Cedar Falls, Iowa, 1980-83; pub. rels. writer Chgo. Mercantile Exchange, Ill., 1983-84, pub. rels. specialist, 1985-86, mgr. pub. rels., 1986-87; journalist, coor. Reuters Am., Inc., Chgo., 1987-88, filing editor, 1988-90; dir. media rels. Chgo. Bd. Options Exchange, 1990—. Mem. United Church of Christ. Home: 2909 N Sheridan Rd Chicago IL 60657 Office: Chgo Board Options Exchange 400 S LaSalle Chicago IL 60605

CAMPBELL, POLLYANN S., lawyer; b. Zanesville, Ohio, Oct. 26, 1949; d. Walter Frederick and and Ann Marie (Heiss) Stuenkel; m. John William Campbell II, Apr. 3, 1970 (div. Oct. 1990); children: Georgia Ann, John William III. BA cum laude, Shorter Coll., 1970; JD magna cum laude, Woodrow Wilson Coll. of Law, 1981. Bar: Ga. 1981, U.S. Dist. Ct. (no. dist.) Ga. 1981. Assoc. Lipshutz, Frankel, Greenblatt, King and Cohen, Atlanta, 1982-85; dist. underwriter, counsel Stewart Title Guaranty Co., Atlanta, 1985-87; state counsel Transamerica Title Ins. Co., Atlanta, 1987-90; appointed div. counsel Commonwealth Land Title Ins. Co. and Transamerica Title Ins. Co., Atlanta, 1990—; presenter Ga. Real Estate Closing Attys. Assn. seminar, 1991, Commonwealth Land Title Ins. Co. seminar, 1992. Editor-in-chief Woodrow Wilson Jour. Law, 1979-81. Mem. coun. Luth. Ch. of Nativity, Austell, Ga., 1982, 89-91, pres., 1990-91; mem. Rudisill Meml. Handbell Choir. Mem. ABA, Ga. Bar Assn., Atlanta Bar Assn., Am. Land Title Assn. (state ct. mem. of judiciary com.), Dixie Land Title Assn. (edn. com.). Office: Commonwealth Land Title Ins Co Transam Title Ins Co 990 Hammond Dr NE Ste 770 Atlanta GA 30328-5510

CAMPBELL, RENODA GISELE, personal management executive; b. L.A., May 4, 1963; d. Rumby D. and Margarete (Alexander) C. BA, Loyola Marymount U., L.A., 1985. Exec. sec. Warner Brothers Records, Burbank, Calif., 1987-89; mgmt. exec. Direct Mgmt. Group, L.A., 1989-90, media coord., 1990-91, assoc. mgr., 1991—. Office: Direct Mgmt Group 947 N La Cienega Blvd Ste G West Hollywood CA 90069-4700

CAMPBELL, RUTH ANN, budget analyst; b. La Plata, Md., Aug. 25, 1948; d. Lawrence Gilbert Pilkerton and Eleanor Garretter (Swann) Pilkerton-Grimm; m. Joseph Harvey Campbell, May 22, 1970 (wid. Oct. 1989); children: Joseph Lawrence, Timothy Craig. Clk.-stenographer Gen. Svcs. Adminstrn., Washington, 1966-68, sec., stenographer, 1968-70, program asst., 1970-71; adminstrv. asst. Gen. Svcs. Adminstrn., Mpls., 1971-72; adminstrv. asst. Gen. Svcs. Adminstrn., Washington, 1974-75, program analyst, 1975-78, corr. specialist, 1978-79, program analyst, 1979, budget analyst, 1979—. Sec. Fed. Women's Program/Gen. Svcs. Adminstrn., Washington, 1981-82, PTA, Waldorf, Md., 1981-83, Sch Adv. Coun., Waldorf, 1982-83; treas. Cub Scout Pack, La Plata, Md., 1982-87; mem. vestry Christ Ch., Wayside, 1990—, treas. Woman's Guild, 1990—; treas. Athletic Boosters Club, 1993-94; sec. Warrior Stadium Steering Com.; team capt. Thursday Nite Mixed Bowling League, 1976—. Mem. Am. Assn. Budget and Program Analysis. Episcopalian. Home: 7305 St Marys Ave La Plata MD 20646 Office: Gen Svcs Adminstrn Rm 1105 Bldg 4 Washington DC 20406

CAMPBELL, RUTH ANN, secretary; b. Madisonville, Ky., Dec. 22, 1950; d. Charles Persey and Lillian Marie (May) C.; 1 child, Christopher James. Cert. in word processing, Ill. Ctrl. Coll., 1987, cert. in typing, 1987. Cashier Super-X Drug Store, East Peoria, Ill., 1989-90, Tri-Star Mkgt., Inc., Washington, Ill., 1990-91; Title IV sec. student support svcs. program Ill. Ctrl. Coll., Peoria, 1991—. Home: 225 Stewart St Apt 2 East Peoria IL 61611 Office: Ill Ctrl Coll 115 SW Adams Peoria IL 61602

CAMPBELL, SALLY WORTHINGTON, public relations executive; b. Pitts., Jan. 3, 1947; d. Aubrey Walter and Marie Ruth (Henningsen) Worthington; BA in Journalism, Auburn U., 1968; m. John Jette Campbell, Aug. 31, 1968 (div. 1991); children: Ashley, Heather, John Jette, Jr. Reporter-intern Montgomery, Ala. Jour., 1968; asst. editor Auburn (Ala.) Extension Service, 1968-69; tchr. lang. arts Nichols Jr. High Sch., Tuskegee, Ala., 1969-70; editor Where Mag., Houston, 1971-79, southwestern editorial supr., 1979; dir. public relations Austin (Tex.) Civic Ballet, 1980-82, v.p. Ballet Austin, 1983-84, also bd. dirs.; publs. and info. officer St. Edward's U., Austin, 1987-88; dir. comm. North Tex. Commn., Dallas, 1988-92, v.p. comm. 1992—; cons. public relations Retinitis Pigmentosa Found., Houston, 1979. V.p. Austin Jr. Forum, 1980-82; writer for KTBC-TV 1st place award Region II public svc. announcement competition, Tex. Broadcasters Assn., 1981, Leadership Austin, 1983-84. Mem. Women in Communications, Laguna Gloria Mus. Women's Art Guild, Alpha Omicron Pi. Republican. Presbyterian. Recipient Best of Austin award Internat. Assn. Bus. Communicators, 1988. Home: 3119 Milton Ave Dallas TX 75205-1449 Office: North Tex Commn PO Box 610246 Dallas TX 75261-0246

CAMPBELL, SANDRA J., state legislator. State rep. dist. 53 R.I. Ho. of Reps.; dep. minority leader, mem. fin. com. Republican. Office: RI House of Reps State House Providence RI 02903*

CAMPBELL, SELAURA JOY, lawyer; b. Oklahoma City, Mar. 25, 1944; d. John Moore III and Gyda (Hallum) C. AA, Stephens Coll., 1963; BA, U. Okla., 1965; MEd, Chapel Hill U., 1974; JD, N.C. Cen. U., 1978; postgrad. atty. mediation courses, South Tex. Sch. of Law, Houston, 1991, Atty. Mediators Inst./Dallas, Dallas, 1992. Bar: Ariz 1983; lic. real estate broker, N.C.; cert. tchr. N.C. With flight svc. dept. Pan Am. World Airways, N.Y.C., 1966-91; lawyer Am. Women's Legal Clinic, Phoenix, 1987; charter mem. Sony Corp. Indsl. Mgmt. Seminar, 1981; guest del. Rep. Nat. Conv., Houston, 1992; judge all-law sch. mediation competition for Tex., South Tex. Sch. Law, Houston, 1994. Mem. N.C. Cen. U. Law Rev., 1977-78. People-to-People del. People's Republic of China, 1987; guest del. Rep. Nat. Conv., Houston, 1992. Mem. Ariz. Bar Assn., Humane Soc. U.S., Nat. Wildlife Fedn., People for the Ethical Treatment of Animals, Amnesty Internat., Phi Alpha Delta. Republican. Episcopalian. Home: 206 Taft Ave Cleveland TX 77327-4539

CAMPBELL, SUSAN CARRIGG, teacher; b. Copaigue, N.Y., Dec. 8, 1946; d. Richard Carrigg and Mildred Josephine (Schneider) C. BS cum laude, SUNY, Oswego, 1968; MA, Adelphi U., 1992. Cert. secondary tchr., N.Y. Tchr. Brentwood (N.Y.) Pub. Schs., 1968—; co-developer learning skills program Brentwood (N.Y.) Pub. Schs., 1985-89, co-chairperson sch. improvement team, 1990-92, 93-94, mem. summer curriculum writing project, 1993, adv. program com., 1993-94, conflict resolution trainee, 1994; adv. Student Leaders Club, Brentwood, N.Y., 1991; coord. Art Enrichment Show, 1986-91. Mem. L.I. Coun. Social Studies, Brentwood Tchrs. Assn., Kappa Delta Pi, Pi Gamma Mu. Democrat. Lutheran.

CAMPBELL, SUSAN PANNILL, banker; b. Richmond, Va., May 28, 1947; d. Raymond Brodie and Lucie Courtice (McDonald) C.; m. William F. Stutts Jr., May 16, 1992. A.B., Coll. William and Mary, 1969; M.Ed., U. Va., 1970, postgrad., 1974-75; postgrad. Summer Inst. of Coll. Admissions, Harvard U., 1972. Counselor, instr. Thomas Nelson Community Coll., Hampton, Va., 1970-71; asst. dean admissions U. Va., Charlottesville, 1971-78; banking officer, asst. v.p. Tex. Commerce Bank, Houston, 1978-82; asst. v.p. First City Tex., Houston, 1982-85, v.p., 1985-92; v.p. Franklin Fed. Bancorp, Austin, 1993-94; v.p. Nations Bank, 1994—. Loaned exec. United Way, Houston, 1978; v.p. EnCorps, div. Houston Symphony League, 1981-82, pres., 1982-83, bd. dirs., 1983-85; bd. dirs. Houston Symphony League, 1982-83, Austin Lyric Opera, 1993—; bd. advisors Houston Symphony Soc., 1982-94. Honor award scholar Mary Baldwin Coll., Staunton, Va., 1965-66. Mem. Coll. William and Mary Alumni Assn., U. Va. Alumni Assn. (bd. dirs. Houston and Austin chpts.), Kappa Alpha Theta. Democrat. Methodist. Office: Nations Bank PO Box 908 Austin TX 78781

CAMPBELL, SUSAN REBECCA, psychotherapist, educator; b. Anderson, S.C., Jan. 8, 1957; d. Alvin Lamar Sr. and Wallie Ann (English) C. BA, Clemson U., 1980; MA, Mid. Tenn. State U., 1985. Instr. Tri-County Tech. Coll., Pendleton, S.C., 1985-86, 89; psychotherapist Aiken (S.C.) Barnwell Mental Health Ctr., 1986-88; counselor Anderson Oconee Pickens Mental Health Ctr., 1988-89; clin. coord. Anderson Area Med. Ctr., 1989—; psychotherapist Don Chung, MD, Anderson, 1990-91, Anderson Psychiatric Assocs., 1994—. Office: Anderson Area Med Ctr 800 N Fant St Anderson SC 29621

CAMPBELL, VIRGINIA KOLNICK, rehabilitation counselor; b. Smelterville, Idaho, Feb. 21, 1934; d. Dolph and Ruberta Rhoda (Hunt) Towles; m. Phillip Kolnick, Dec. 30, 1953 (div. Apr. 1963); children: Jo Ann, Phyllis Ann, Betty Sue; m. Robert Lloyd Campbell, Sept. 18, 1993. AA in Nursing, Phoenix Coll., 1961; BS in Sociology, Ariz. State U., 1966, MA in Edn., 1968, M of Counseling, 1971. RN Ariz.; cert. rehab. counselor. Coord. pvt. duty nursing Med. Personnel Pool, Phoenix, 1971-72; nurse health evaluation Ariz. Health Plan, Phoenix, 1973; instr. continuing edn. program Phoenix Coll., Maricopa County C.C. Dist., 1973-75; vocat. rehab. counselor III, cardio-pulmonary specialist State of Ariz., Phoenix, 1974-92, ret., 1992. Mem. ANA, Am. Assn. Cardiovascular Pulmonary Rehab. (fellow), Ariz. Cardiovascular Pulmonary Reahb. Assn., Ariz. Nurses Assn., Kappa Delta Phi. Home: 9224 E Bighorn Dr Prescott Valley AZ 86314-7302

CAMPBELL-SMITH, MARY LOVE, medical-surgical nurse; b. St. James, Jamaica, May 18, 1963; came to U.S., 1984; d. Melford W. and Phyllis M. (Pennycooke) Campbell; m. Winston Anthony Smith, June 22, 1991. AA, Cuyahoga Community Coll., 1987, ADN, 1988; BSN, Cleve. State U., 1993. UBQA rep. St. Lukes Med. Ctr. Sr. pres. Nursing Student Orgn., Warrensville Heights, 1987-88. Mem. ANA. Home: 860 Montford Rd Cleveland Heights OH 44121

CAMPBELL-WHITE, ANNETTE JANE, venture capitalist; b. Dunedin, Otago, New Zealand, Jan. 28, 1947; came to U.S., 1975; d. Charles and Patricia Gwendolyn Ann (Pratt) C.; m. Ruediger Naumann-Etienne, Aug. 22, 1985. BSChemE, U. Capetown, South Africa, 1968; MSc in Phys. Chemistry, U. Capetown, Republic of South Africa, 1970. Market devel. exec. Brit. Oxygen, London, 1973-74; health economist SRI Internat. (formerly Stanford Rsch. Inst.), Menlo Park, Calif., 1975-76; prin. and owner ECCO Cons. Group, Berkeley, Calif., 1976-79; sr. analyst Hambrecht & Quist, San Francisco, 1979-81, gen. ptnr., 1981-83; spl. ltd. ptnr. L.F. Rothschild, Unterberg, Towbin, San Francisco, 1983-85; founder, mng. gen. ptnr. MedVenture Assoc., San Francisco, 1986—; bd. dirs. Physiometrix, Inc., AmCell, Inc., Cardiac Pathways Corp., ArthroCare, Inc., Intelliwire, Inc. Bd. dirs. San Francisco Opera, 1993—. Mem. Western Assn. Venture Capitalists. Office: MedVenture Assoc 4 Orinda Way Ste 150 Orinda CA 94563-2515

CAMPER, GALE DIANA, critical care nurse, consultant; b. Detroit, Sept. 14, 1955; d. Isaac Melvin Jr. and Lilie Mamilone; children: Corey, Canden. BSN, Mercy Coll. Detroit, 1978. RN, Mich.; CCRN; cert. ACLS. Staff nurse ICCU Sinai Hosp. Detroit, 1978-79; staff nurse Cardiac Care Unit/Cardiac Surg. Unit Providence Hosp., Southfield, Mich., 1980—; arbitrator Mich. Med. Arbitration program, Detroit, 1985—. Mem. AACN (cert. critical care nurse), Am. Assn. Legal Nurse Cons., Mich. Nurses Assn.

CAMPFIELD, KRISTEN MARGARET, lawyer; b. Battle Creek, Mich., Jan. 26, 1960; d. Wayne William and Catherine Patricia (Howe) C. BA, Stephens Coll., 1981; JD, U. Notre Dame, 1984; LLM, U. London, 1990. Bar: Calif., Pa. Assoc. Parkinson, Wolf, Lazar & Leo, L.A., 1984-87, Baker & McKenzie (formerly MacDonald, Halsted & Laybourne), L.A., 1987-89; pvt. practice L.A., 1990-93; asst. counsel Dept. Environ. Resources, Harrisburg, Pa., 1993—. Speaker Heal the Bay, Santa Monica, Calif., 1992-93; co-founder Stephens Coll. Alumnae Club of So. Calif., L.A., 1992. Mem. State Bar of Calif., State Bar of Pa. Office: Pa Dept Environ Resources 400 Market St Harrisburg PA 17055

CAMPION, JANE, director, screenwriter; b. Wellington, New Zealand; d. Richard and Edith Campion. Dir., screenwriter Peel: An Exercise in Discipline, 1982 (also editor, Palme d'Or short film category Cannes Internat. Film Festival 1986), A Girl's Own Story, 1983, Passionless Moments, 1984 (also prodr., cinematographer, camer operator), After Hours, 1984, Sweetie, 1989, The Piano, 1993 (Palme d'Or Cannes Internat. Film Festival 1993, Academy Award Best Original Screenplay 1994); dir. An Angel at my Table, 1990, (TV) Two Friends, 1986; composer: Feel the Cold (from A Girl's Own Story), 1983. Office: Creative Artists Agy 9830 Wilshire Blvd Beverly Hills CA 90212-1825*

CAMPIONE, MARY ELLEN, software consultant, writer; b. Salinas, Calif., Aug. 30, 1963; d. David Arthur Sr. and Ellen Loraine (Loughran) McNabb; m. Richard James Campione, Oct. 2, 1993. BS in Computer Sci., Calif. Poly., 1985. Programmer Ford Aerospace, Palo Alto, Calif., 1985-88; software engr. Sun Microsystems, Mountain View, Calif., 1988-89; developer support engr. Next Computer Inc., Redwood City, Calif., 1990-91; ind. software cons., writer San Francisco, 1991—. Author: Typesetting Tables on The Unix System, 1990, Postcript By Example, 1992.

CAMPOLI, ELLA FRANCES, mortgage company executive; b. New Castle, Pa., Nov. 5, 1906; d. Domenico and Michelina (Perretta) Faraone; m. James Campoli, May 4, 1925. Student, New Castle Bus. Coll., 1923. Office, traffic mgr. Harper Furniture Co., Cinn., 1948-50; asst. to pres. Harper Furniture co., Cinn., 1951-62; ptnr. Campoli Partnership, Oldsmar, Fla., 1968--. Mem. Oldsmar City Coun., 1971-76; vice mayor City of Oldsmar, 1975. Mem. AAUW, Am. Bus. Women's Assn. (Women of the Yr. award 1989), Oldmar Civic Club, Pilot Internat. (pres. Cin. chpt. 1961-62, publicity, chairperson 1962—). Democrat. Roman Catholic. Home and Office: 327 Shore Dr E Oldsmar FL 34677-3915

CAMPOS, CATHERINE RITA, association administrator; b. Boston, Nov. 9, 1960; d. Lorenzo Drake and Klara H. (Straut) C. BA, Bates Coll., 1982; MBA, Northeastern U., 1990. Cert. cash mgr. Bank teller Worcester (Mass.) County Instn. for Savs., 1983-84; from asst. head teller to asst. treas. cash mgmt. State St. Bank and Trust Co., Boston, 1984-93; fin. mgr. AAAS, Directorate for Edn. and Human Resources Programs, Washington, 1993—. Mem. Washington Cash Mgmt. Assn. Office: AAAS Directorate Edn and Human Resources 1333 H St NW Washington DC 20005

CAMPOS MONTEIRO, JULIETA, psychologist; b. Fortaleza, Ceara, Brazil, Apr. 25, 1956; came to U.S., 1985; d. Paulo Martins and Maria Angelita (Campos) M. BA in Psychology, U. Ceara, 1980; MS in Edn., So. Ill. U., 1988, PhD, 1994. Nat. cert. counselor. Coord. sch. counseling Colegio Christus, Fortaleza, 1981-85; psychodramatist therapist Inst. do Homem, Fortaleza, 1988—; assoc. prof. U. Fortaleza, 1988—. Recipient PEO Internat. Peace scholarship, PEO Internat. Sisterhood, Des Moines, 1990-92, fellowship for doctorate studies, Brazilian Ministry of Edn., Capes, Brasilia, Brazil, 1990-94; Ambassador of Good Will, Rotary Internat. Club Found., Evanston, Ill., 1985-86. Fellow Inst. Homem-Fortaleza (therapist); mem. Assn. for Specialists in Group Work (chair internat. rels. com. 1991-94, cert. appreciation 1991, 92), Nat. Coun. Psychology, Phi Delta Kappa. Democrat. Roman Catholic.

CANADA, KARYN E., communications executive; b. Dallas, Jan. 27, 1948; d. Jene Victor and Mary Eleanor (Jensen) Oberholtzer; m. Charles Glenn Canada, June 10, 1972; children: Kara Elizabeth, Charla Glynn. Student, Eastfield Jr. Coll., Mesquite, Tex., 1986-87. Buyer Sammons Communications, Inc., Dallas, 1978-90; owner Hiring Info. Resources Exchange, Tex., 1993—. Bd. dirs. Mesquite ISD sch., 1992—, pres. sch. bd., 1993—, master trustee grad. leadership TASB, 1994—. Mem. VFW Auxiliary (pres. local chpt. 1981-82, award 1981-82).

CANADA, MARY WHITFIELD, librarian; b. Richmond, Va., June 13, 1919; d. Waverly Thomas and Ruth Bradshaw (Smith) C. B.A. magna cum laude, Emory and Henry Coll., 1940; M.A. in English, Duke U., 1942; B.S. in L.S., U. N.C., 1956. Asst. circulation dept. Duke U. Library, 1942-45, undergrad. librarian, 1945-55, reference librarian, 1956-85, asst. head reference dept., 1967-79, head dept., 1979-85. Contbr. articles to profl. jours. Mem. exec. com. Friends of Duke U. Library. Duke U. grantee Can., 1979, 81. Mem. ALA (life; initiated performance evaluation discussion group), Southeastern Library Assn. (sec. coll. and univ. sect., chmn. nominating com. reference services div., also chmn. div.), N.C. Library Assn. (chmn. nominating com., chmn. newspaper com., chmn. coll. and univ. sect.), Alumni Assn. Sch. Library Sci. U. N.C. (pres.), Va. Hist. Soc. (life), Va. Geneal. Soc., DAR (chpt. regent), Friends of Va. State Archives, Campus club (Duke U.), Planning Adv. Com. N. Cen. Durham, Va. Mus. Beta Phi Mu. Methodist. Home: 1312 Lancaster St Durham NC 27701-1132

CANADY, HORTENSE G., foundation director; b. Chgo., Aug. 18, 1927; d. Alexander H. Golden and Essie M. (Atwater) Perry; m. Clinton Canady, Jr., Aug. 18, 1945; children: Clinton III, Alexa Canady-Davis, Alan L., Mark H. BA, Fisk U., 1947; MA, Mich. State U., 1975. Rschr. Mich. State Health Dept., Lansing, 1947; dir. Community Nursery Sch., Lansing, 1947-48; asst. dir. fin. aid Lansing C.C., 1975-89; dir. Lansing C.C. Found., 1989—. Edn. chair NAACP, Lansing, 1962-69; mem. women's commn. State of Mich., Lansing, 1969-71, bd. edn. Lansing Sch. Dist., 1969-72, nat. bd. YWCA, N.Y.C., 1977-83, exec. com. United Negro Coll. Fund, Detroit, 1978—; trustee Kalamazoo (Mich.) Coll., 1986—; regional v.p. Athena Found., Lansing, 1992—. Recipient Diana award YWCA, 1977, Pres.'s award Nat. Dental Assn., 1979, Black Book award Dollars and Sense Mag., 1984, Regional Athena award Lansing C. of C., 1989; named Citizen of Yr., NAACP, 1980. Mem. LWV, Nat. Soc. Fund Raising Execs., Nat. Coun. Rsch. Devel., Lansing/ East Lansing Chpt. Links (pres.), Lansing Woman's Club (program chair), Delta Sigma Theta (nat. pres. 1983-88). Baptist. Home: 3808 W Holmes Lansing MI 48911-2171

CANAVAN, CHRISTINE ESTELLE, state legislator; b. Dorchestor, Mass., Jan. 25, 1950; m. Paul Canavan; 2 children. Grad., Massasoit C.C., 1983; BS summa cum laude, U. Mass. RN, Mass. Rep. dist. 10 Mass. Ho. of Reps., Boston, mem. personnel and adminstrn. com., ins. com., housing and urban devel. com.; mem. Stockton Sch. Com., 1990—, vice chair, 1992—. Mem. Am. Nephrology Nurses' Assn., Amvets, Polish White Eagles Inc. Democrat. Roman Catholic. Home: 29 Mystic St Brockton MA 02402 Office: Mass Ho of Reps Mass State House Boston MA 02133*

CANDON, MARY EVA, lawyer; b. Washington, May 15, 1950; d. Charles Vincent Candon and Mary Therese (Sanker) Maloy. BA, Emmanuel Coll., 1972; JD, Georgetown U., 1983. Bar: Pa. 1987, D.C. 1988. Program dir. U.S. Youth Coun., Washington, 1972-75, dir., 1975-77; exec. dir. D.C. Dem. Party, Washington, 1978-84; spl. asst. to chmn. Dem. Nat. Com., Washington, 1984-85; exec. dir. Am. Coun. Young Polit. Leaders, Washington, 1985-88, Legal Aid Soc. of D.C., Washington, 1988-94; chmn. Alcoholic Beverage Control Bd., Washington, 1991—. Mem. D.C. Dem. State Com., Washington, 1988—, co-chair del. selection com., 1992; v.p. Washington-Moscow Exch. Ctr., Washington, 1989-92; pres. Assn. State Dem. Exec. Dirs., Washington, 1982-85. Roman Catholic. Home: 2122 California St NW Washington DC 20008-1803 Office: Alcohol & Beverage Control Bd 614 H St NW Rm 807 Washington DC 20001-4542

CANDRIS, LAURA A., lawyer; b. Frankfort, Ky., Apr. 5, 1955; d. Charles M. and Dorothy (King) Sutton; m. Aris S. Candris, Dec. 22, 1974. AB with distinction in polit. sci., Transylvania Coll., 1975; postgrad., U. Pitts., 1975-77, U. Fla., 1977-78; JD, U. Pitts., 1978. Bar: Fla. 1978, U.S. Dist. Ct. (mid. dist.) Fla. 1978, U.S. Ct. Appeals (4th and 5th cirs.) 1980, Pa. 1981, U.S. Dist. Ct. (we. dist.) Pa. 1982, U.S. Ct. Appeals (3d cir.) 1983. Assoc. Coffman, Coleman, Andrews & Grogan, Jacksonville, Fla., 1978-80, Manion, Alder & Cohen, Pitts., 1981-85; assoc. Eckert, Seamans, Cherin & Mellott, Pitts., 1985-86, ptnr., 1987—, vice chmn. labor and employment law dept, mem. practice mgmt. com.; counsel Nat. Assn. Women in Constrn. (chpt. 161), Pitts., 1985-86. Contbr. articles to profl. jours. Coun. mem. O'Hara Twp. Planning Commn., 1990; bd. dirs. Tri-State Employers Assn., 1991-93, Parent and Child Guidance Ctr., 1991—; treas., mem. exec. com. TEC/Pa. Small Bus., 1992-94, bd. dirs., 1993—. Nat. Merit Found. scholar 1972-75; named Ky. Col., 1974. Mem. ABA (EEO com. labor sect., labor and employment law com. litigation sect.), Fla. Bar, Pa. Bar Assn. (CLE com. employment and litigation sect.), Allegheny County Bar Assn. (CLE com., coun. on professionalism, employment and fed. cts. sect., hdqs. com. and pers. subcom.), Soc. Hosp. Attys. Western Pa., Pitts. Pers. Assn., Strategic Plannign Comm. Republican. Office: Eckert Seamans Cherin & Mellott Fl 42D 600 Grant St Pittsburgh PA 15219-2701

CANE, PAULA P., speech and language pathologist, scriptwriter, actor; b. Cin., Feb. 16, 1945; d. Paul J. and Pauline Albia (Patti) Weber; children: Adam, Miguel. BS, Purdue U., 1967, MS, 1971; postgrad., Harvard U., 1991. Lic. speech and lang. pathologist, Fla., Conn. Instr. comm. U. Bridgeport, Conn., 1974-75; speech and lang. pathologist Lee County Bd. Edn., Ft. Myers, Fla., 1986; cons. Cedar Montessori Schs., Naples, Fla., 1986-87; with casting, prodn. mgmt. Suncoast Films, Inc., Clearwater, Fla., 1989; choreographer, casting CPN Prodn. Co., Clearwater, Fla., 1991; pvt. practice speech and lang. pathology St. Petersburg Beach, Fla., 1967—; speech pathologist Nova Care, 1992—, Premier Rehab., 1993—; screenwriter, playwright St. Petersburg, Fla., 1986—, Premier Rehab., 1993—; actor, voice instr. Pass-A-Grille Actors Studio, St. Petersburg, co-founder, 1989; mem. bd. dirs. St. Petersburg-Clearwater (Pinellas Co.) Film Commn., 1994—; condr. numerous workshops on spl. needs of gifted and talented children. Contbr. numerous articles to publs.; appeared in (films) Electra (Crystal Reel award for best supporting actress in feature film 1992), Edward Scissorhands, Problem Child II, Coupe de Ville, With Hostile Intent (CBS), also commls. and industrial films. Bd. dirs. St. Petersburg/Clearwater (Pinellas County) Film Commn.; co-founder, pres. Parents and Friends Gifted and Talented Children. Recipient Ind. Speech and Hearing Found. awards, 1966-67, grad. teaching fellow Purdue U., 1970-71, Tampa Bay FMPTA, 1992. Mem. Am. Speech-Lang.-Hearing Assn. (cert. clin. competence 1972—), Fla. Motion Picture and TV Assn., ActNet, Ind. Film Project. Home and Office: 1404 Pass A Grille Way Saint Petersburg FL 33706-4236

CANELAS, DALE BRUNELLE, library director; b. Chgo., Jan. 13, 1938; d. Ralph Everley and Margaret Barbara (Clark) Brunelle; m. L. Marcelo Canelas, June 17, 1961; 1 child, Cathryn Margaret. BS in Humanities, Loyola U., Chgo., 1960; MLS, Rosary Coll., 1966; cert. in mgmt., U. Md.,

1971. Asst. dir. Palatine (Ill.) Pub. Libr., 1966-68; asst. dir. adminstrv. svcs. Northwestern U. Libr., Evanston, Ill., 1969-75; assoc. dir. Stanford (Calif.) U. Libr., 1975-84; dir. U. Fla. Librs., Gainesville, 1985—. Vice pres. Freedom to Read Found., Chgo., 1977-78. Mem. ALA (various coms. and offices), Libr. Adminstrn. and Mgmt. Assn. (pres. 1978-80), Assn. Rsch. Librs. (bd. dirs. 1992—, various coms. 1985—). Office: U Fla Librs 210 Library W Gainesville FL 32611

CANETTO, SILVIA SARA, psychology researcher, educator; b. Ferrara, Italy, July 18, 1955; came to U.S., 1981; d. Amalio and Edda (Succi Leonelli) C. D. Psychology, U. Padua (Italy), 1977; MA, Hebrew U. of Jerusalem, 1983; PhD in Clin. Psychology, Northwestern U., 1987. Lic. psychologist. Family psychologist Martha Washington Hosp., Chgo., 1986-88; asst. prof. dept. psychology Colo. State U., Ft. Collins, 1991—; vis. asst. prof. dept. psychology U. Vt., Burlington, 1989-91; vis. asst. prof. dept. psychology U. Mont., Missoula, 1988-89. Author: Developmental Psychobiology, 1985, Suicide and Life-Threatening Behavior, 1989, 92, 95, Death Studies, 1994; author, editor: (with Lester) Women and Suicidal Behavior, 1995; cons. editor Suicide and Life-Threatening Behavior, 1988—, Omega, 1992-93, Death Studies, 1994—, Jour. Integrative and Eclectic Psychotherapy, 1990, Psych of Women Quarterly, 1994, Internat. Jour. Aging and Human Devel., 1995, Pscyhologia, 1995; contbr. chpts. to books. Active The Italian Program, Mont. Pub. Radio, 1988-89. Internat. scholar Min. Fgn. Affairs, Italy, Israel, 1977-80; grantee Israeli Ctr. for Psychobiology, Rotary Internat., APA, Adminstrn. on Aging, European Chemoreception Rsch. Orgn. Mem. APA, Am. Assn. Suicidology, Gerontol. Soc. Am., Assn. for Women in Psychology, Internat. Coun. Psychologists. Office: Colo State U Dept Psychology Fort Collins CO 80523

CANFIELD, CONSTANCE DALE, accountant, nurse; b. Fairmont, W.Va., May 2, 1940; d. Robert Alman and Dorothy Jane (Motter) C. RN, Fairmont Gen. Hosp., 1961; Flight Nurse Diploma, Sch. Aerospace Med., 1967; BS in Acctg., Rollins Coll., Winter Park, Fla., 1979; student, Stetson U., 1975-76, Fla. Inst. Tech., 1976-77; grad., Army Comd. Gen. Staff Coll., Ft. Levenworth Kans., 1991. RN, Fla. Prin. C. D. Canfield, Acct., Melbourne, Fla., 1979-90; acct. C.D. Canfield, Acct., Melbourne, Fla., 1991—. Gov.'s appointee Women in Mil. for Am. Meml. Found., Washington, 1991; gov.'s escort Fla. Freedom Festival, Inc., Tallahassee, 1991; state coord. VietNam Women's Meml. Project, Inc., Washington, 1986—; bd. dirs. Space Coast Philharmonic Orch., Cocoa, Fla., 1989—; adminstrv. bd. United Meth. Ch., Melbourne, 1987—; musician Melbourne Mcpl. Band, 1980-90, Space Coast Philharmonic Orch., 1986-87; vol. attendant Harbor City Ambulance Squad., 1991. With USAF, 1963-70, U.S. Army, 1970-75, maj. USAR, N.G., 1989—. Decorated Air Force Commendation medal, VietNam Campaign Medal with four bronze stars, Vietnam Service Medal, Vietnam Medal of Honor 1st class, Cross Gallantry. Mem. AACN, Nat. Soc. Tax Profls., Nat. Soc. Pub. Accts., Fla. Assn. Ind. Accts. (sec. space coast chpt. 1992-93), Internat. Biog. Assn. (life), VFW (life), Vietnam Vets. of Brevard, Inc. (life), Emergency Rm. Nurses Assn., N.G. Officers Assn., Fla. Hist. Soc., U. S. C. of C., Fla. Home Builders Assn., Internat. Lions Club, Soc. Brevard Profl. Womens Network. Republican. Methodist. Office: CD Canfield Acct 834 Sarno Rd Melbourne FL 32935-5028

CANFIELD, JUDY OHLBAUM, psychologist; b. N.Y.C., May 15, 1947; d. Arthur and Ada (Werner) Ohlbaum; m. John T. Canfield (div.); children: Oran David, Kyle Danya. BA, Grinnell Coll., 1963; MA, New Sch. Social Rsch., 1967; PhD, U.S. Internat. U., 1970. Psychologist Mendocino State Hosp., Talmage, Calif., 1968-69, Douglas Coll., New Westminster, BC, Can., 1971-72, Family & Childrens Clinic, Burnaby, BC, Can., 1971-72; psychologist, trainer, cons. VA Hosp., Northampton, Mass., 1972-75; dir. New England Ctr., Amherst, Mass., 1972-76; dir., psychologist Gateways, Lansdale, Pa., 1977-78; asst. prof., psychologist Hahnemann Med. Ctr., Phila., 1978-84; pres., dir. Inst. Holistic Health, Phila., 1978-85; psychologist, cons. Berkeley, Calif., 1986—. Mem. task force, tng. com. Berkeley Dispute Resolution Svc., 1986-89; mem. measure H com. Berkeley United Sch. Dist., 1987-88. Mem. APA, Nat. Register Health Svc. Providers in Psychology, Nat. Assn. Advancement Gestalt Therapy (steering com. 1990), Calif. Psychol. Assn., Alameda County Psychol. Assn. (info.-referral svc. 1989—), Assn. Humanistic Psychology. Office: 2031 Delaware St Berkeley CA 94709-2121

CANFIELD, LYNDA RAE, writer, spiritual director; b. Elmira, N.Y., June 15, 1947; d. Raymond Frank and Doris Rae (Kilbourne) C.; m. William U. Hensel, IV, Sept. 10, 1967 (div. Oct. 1975); children—Jason William, Aaron David. B.A., Albany State U., 1969; M.S., Pa. State U., 1972. Cert. psychologist, Wis. Psychologist. assoc. Madison Pub. Schs., 1972-77; realtor Lyons Romo Inc., Tucson, 1978-83; writer bus. publs., Tucson, 1978—; spiritual dir., retreat dir. Redemptorists Picture Rocks Retreat, Tucson, 1991—. Contbr. articles on tourism, sci., bus., religion to mags. Pres. bd. Avra Water Coop., Avra Valley, Tucson, 1982-88; pres. Picture Rocks Fire Aux., 1978-80. Recipient Merit award Met. Tucson C. of C. Rodeo Com., 1985. Democrat. Roman Catholic. Avocations: tennis, banjo. Home: PO Box 569 Cortaro AZ 85652-0569

CANGEMI, LISA LYNNE, art director, graphic designer; b. Bklyn., May 20, 1963; d. Robert A. and Elizabeth J. (Kopter) C. BFA in Graphic Design with honors, Sch. Visual Arts, N.Y.C., 1985. Art dir. Grey Advt., N.Y.C., 1985-86; asst. art dir. Conde Nast Publs., N.Y.C., 1986-87, Geyer McAllister Publs., N.Y.C., 1986-87, Walker and Co., N.Y.C., 1987-88; art dir. Earnshaw Publs., N.Y.C., 1988-89; asst. art dir. CMP Publs., Manhasset, N.Y., 1989-90; art dir. McKeefry and Co., Richmond Hill, N.Y., 1990—. Recipient 1st place award N.Y./N.J. Advt. Club, 1992, 93. Office: PO Box 782 Lynbrook NY 11563

CANGIAMILLA, BETTE FRANCES, accounting executive; b. Hanford, Calif., Apr. 16, 1957; d. Boyd Lowell Sharp and Janet (Praria) Judd; m. Clyde Jon Nold, May 4, 1974 (div. 1987); children: Mandolin P., Christopher J.; m. James Frank Cangiamilla, Aug. 27, 1988. AA in Bus., Gavilan Coll., Gilroy, Calif., 1992; BS in Bus./Acctg., San Jose State U., 1994, postgrad., 1994—. Fin. controller Hollister (Calif.) Disposal, Inc., 1984-92; owner, operator Hollister Bookkeeping and Tax Svc., 1985—; acct. mgr. Ridgemark Golf & Country Club, Hollister, 1992—; fin. controller John Smith Landfill, Inc., Hollister, 1986-92, Ajax Portable Svc., Hollister, 1987-92. Supporter Monterey County (Calif.) Symphony Guild, 1991—; parent mem. Calif. High Sch. Rodeo Assn., Hollister, 1991—; dir. 33rd Dist. Agrl. Assn., San Benito County Fair Bd., 1992-94; asst. fin. chmn. AT&T Pebble Beach Nat. Pro-Am. Mem. Internat. Assn. Hospitality Accts., El Gabilan Young Ladies Inst., NAFE. Republican. Roman Catholic. Office: Hollister Bookkeeping Tax PO Box 1352 Hollister CA 95024-1352

CANGUREL, SUSAN STONE, personnel executive; b. Madison, Wis., Sept. 11, 1946; d. John Mather and Lois Marie (Wiessinger) Murray; m. Mel Cangurel; children: Lora Rae, Julie Lynn. Student U. Wis., 1964-66; BS, U. Wis., Milw., 1978; MBA, Century U., Albuquerque, 1990; PhD, Century U., 1994. Adminstrv. asst. Madison C. of C., 1967-72; v.p. loan adminstrn.Kensington Mortgage & Fin. Corp., Milw., 1972-79; v.p. adminstrn. Mortgage Investment Co., El Paso, 1979-85; mgr. personnel svcs. Summa Corp., Las Vegas, 1985-88, v.p. MGM Desert Inn, 1988-91; human resources dir. The Miles Group, El Paso, 1991—. Mem. Soc. Human Resource Mgrs., Am. Soc. for Tng. & Devel. (cert. profl. human resources 1992, cert. sr. profl. human resources 1993). Author poems and short stories. Home: 731 Espolon Dr El Paso TX 79912-1706

CANIGLIA, SHARON W., secondary education educator; b. Washington; d. Joseph Francis and Joanne Mary Weingarden; m. Kenneth U. Caniglia, July 31, 1976; children: Catherine Mary, Jill Christine, Christopher Joseph. AA, Tallahassee C.C., 1973; BS, U. Md., 1975; MA in Elem. Edn., George Washington U., 1977. Cert. secondary tchr., Md. Tchr. St. Peter's Sch., Waldorf, Md., 1975-78, Piccowaxen Mid. Sch., Bel Alton, Md., 1979; pvt. practice cons., tutor Waldorf, 1982-86; mem. bd. edn. Charles County Pub. Schs., LaPlata, Md., 1990—. Tchr. First Bapt. Ch., Waldorf, 1990—; mem. Willis Com., Annapolis, Md., 1992—. Recipient Svc. award Huntington Neighborhood Assn., 1991. Mem. Nat. Assn. for Edn. of Young Children, Md. Sch. Bd. Assn., Nat. Sch. Bd. Assn., PTA (hon. life), New Horizon Homemakers. Republican. Roman Catholic. Home: 3141 Franklin Ct Waldorf MD 20602 Office: Charles County Pub Schs PO Box D LaPlata MD 20646

CANINO, SYLVIA JOSEFINA, metallurgical engineer; b. Santurce, P.R., July 15, 1955; d. Alfredo and Aida Canino. BS in Chemistry, Ga. Inst. Tech., 1977; MS in Materials Sci., Northeastern U., 1986. Metallurgical engr. Bethlehem Steel Corp., Sparrows Point, Md., 1977-79; extrusion metallurgist Consolidated Aluminum Corp., Madison, Ill., 1979-82; project engr. Nuclear Metals, Inc., Concord, Mass., 1982-87; product devel. engr. Lanxide Corp., Newark, Del., 1987-93; metallurg. project engr. Price Pfister, Inc., Pacoima, Calif., 1993—; mem. electrical conductivity task team Aluminum Assn., Washington, 1981. Co-patentee protective coating for ceramic matrix composite. Mem. Am. Foundrymen's Soc. (mem. permanent mold tech. com.). Office: Price Pfister Inc 13500 Paxton St Pacoima CA 91331

CANJAR, PATRICIA MCWADE, psychologist; b. Pitts., Mar. 14, 1932; d. Robert Malachai McWade and Lillian Kathryn (Seidenstricker) Robb; m. Lawrence N. Canjar, Aug. 4, 1951 (dec. Nov. 1972); 1 son, R. Michael; m. James M. McDonald, Sept. 24, 1977. A.A., Carlow Coll., 1951; B.A., U. Detroit, 1973, M.A., 1975. Lic. psychologist, Mich. Psychologist, Robinwood Clinic, Detroit, 1973-77, Psychol. Resources, Birmingham, Mich., 1977-80, Realistic Living Ctr., Warren, Mich., 1983-85, Behavior Ctr., Birmingham, 1980-84; with Eastwood Cmty. Clinic, Big Beaver, Mich., 1984-94; ret. 1994. Mem. Nat. YWCA Spl. Commn., Boston, N.Y.C. and Washington, 1967; bd. dirs. YWCA, Pitts., 1961-65, Detroit, 1965-67; asst. coordinator United We Sing, Pitts. Music Festival, 1955-65; pres. Carnegie Mellon Women's Club, Pitts., 1963-65, U. Detroit Faculty Wives' Club, 1968-70; mem. State of Mich. Fair Campaign Practices Commn., 1968-70; treas. Grandview Beach Assn., 1982-84, pres., 1984-87. Fellow Am. Psychol. Assn.; mem. Mich. Assn. Profl. Psychologist, Mich. Assn. Alcohol and Drug Abuse Counselors. Democrat. Roman Catholic.

CANN, NANCY TIMANUS, retail yacht sales executive; b. Balt.; d. E. Frank Timanus and Ruth F. (Herman) Schell; m. Jerrold R. Cann, Mar. 25, 1967; 1 child, Justin Ronald. Grad., Balt. Bus. Coll., 1967. Pres. Crusader Yacht Sales, Inc., Annapolis, Md., 1982—; bd. dirs. Bayfarers. Mem. Yacht Architects and Brokers Assn. (v.p. 1989-91, 92—, chmn. membership com. 1989-92, bd. dirs. 1992—, pres. 1994—). Home and Office: 7078 Bembe Beach Rd Annapolis MD 21403-3616

CANN, SHARON LEE, health science librarian; b. Ft. Riley, Kans., Aug. 14, 1935; d. Roman S. and Cora Elon (George) Foote; m. Donald Clair Cann, May 16, 1964. Student Sophia U., Tokyo, 1955-57; BA, Calif. State U., Sacramento, 1959; MSLS, Atlanta U., 1977. Cert. health scis. librarian. Recreation worker ARC, Korea, Morocco, France, 1960-64; shelflister Library Congress Washington, 1967-69; tchr. Lang. Ctr., Taipei, Taiwan, 1971-73; library tech. asst. Emory U., Atlanta, 1974-76; health sci. librarian Northside Hosp., Atlanta, 1977-85; library cons., 1985-86; librarian area health edn. ctr., learning resource ctr. Morehouse Sch. Medicine, 1985-86; edn. librarian Ga. State U., 1986-93; head libr. Ga. Bapt. Coll. Nursing, 1993—. Editor Update, publ. Ga. Health Scis. Library Assn., 1981; contbr. articles to publs. Chmn. Calif. Christian Youth in Govt Seminar, 1958. Named Alumni Top Twenty Calif. State U.Sacramento, 1959. Mem. ALA, ASCD, Med. Library Assn., Spl. Library Assn. (dir. South Atlantic chpt. 1985-87), Ga. Library Assn. (spl. library div. chmn. 1983-85), Ga. Health Scis. Library Assn. (chmn. 1981-82), Atlanta Health Sci. Library Com. (chmn. 1979, 95), Am. Numis. Assn., ARC Overseas Assn. Home: 5520 Morning Creek Cir Atlanta GA 30349-3538

CANNELL, NORI TRAUTMAN, business and technology educator; b. Brookings, S.D., Oct. 30, 1953; d. Carl Gottlieb and Silva Pearl (Phillips) Trautman; m. Larry Rugg Cannell, May 12, 1973; children: Paige, Megan. BEd, No. State U., Aberdeen, S.D., 1975; MEd, U. Louisville, 1986. Cert. tchr., Kans., Nebr., Ariz., Ky. K-8 tchr. Dist. 89, Albion, Nebr., 1975-77; bus. edn. tchr. Leavenworth (Kans.) High Sch., 1978-85, Sacred Heart Acad., Louisville, 1985-88; clerical and computer instr. Phoenix Urban League, 1988-90; bus. edn. tchr. Xavier Coll. Prep., Phoenix, 1990-91; vocat. counselor Ednl. Svc. Unit 13, Scottsbluff, Nebr., 1991-92; tech. prep. coord. Western Nebr. C.C., Scottsbluff, 1992-94; bus. edn./computer tchr. South Mountain H.S., Phoenix, 1994—; Perkins grant cons. Ednl. Svc. Unit 13, Scottsbluff, 1991—; cons. Nat. Ctr. Rsch. Vocat. Edn. Nat. Roster for Tech. Prep. Mem. adv. com. Chadron State Coll., 1992-93; mem. strategic planning com. Western Nebr. C.C., 1991-93, adopt-a-sch. com., 1992-93; mem. indsl. tech. adv. com. Gering City Schs., 1992-93. Econ. Edn. scholarship U. Louisville, 1985-86. Mem. AAUW, Nat. Tech. Prep. Network, Bus. and Profl. Women (2d v.p. 1991-93). Republican. Address: 1250 W Maden Aven Mesa AZ 85209

CANNELLA, DEBORAH FABBRI, elementary school educator; b. Statesville, N.C., Sept. 7, 1949; d. Raymond Joseph and Sylvia (Sides) Fabbri; m. S.J. Garciga, Apr. 16, 1970 (div. 1990); children: Jennifer, Melissa, Bryan; m. Frank Cannella, July 1, 1994. Student, U. So. Fla., 1970, 91—; Presch. Edn. degree, Montessori Inst. Am., 1984. Cert. Montessori Presch. Edn., Kansas City, Mo. Tchr. presch. Montessori Acad. of Temple Terr., Fla., 1982-87; tchr. 1st grade St. John's Parish Day Sch., Tampa, Fla., 1987—. Facilitator Bay Area Assn. Ind. Schs. Profl. Day, 1990, mem. program com., 1990-92; bd. dirs. Tampa Prep. Parent's, grad. reception, 1987-88. Mem. Assn. for Childhood Edn., Tampa Mus. of Art, Tampa Bay Performing Arts Ctr., Mus. Sci. and Tech. Episcopalian. Office: St John's Parish Day Sch 906 S Orleans Ave Tampa FL 33606-2941

CANNELLA, KATHLEEN ANN SILVA, nursing educator, researcher; b. Durham, N.C., Apr. 1, 1949; d. Joseph Andrew Silva and Lurene (Chapman) Brinser; m. Sam Chris Cannella, May 1, 1971; 1 child, Elizabeth Karen. Diploma, Md. Gen. Hosp. Sch. Nursing, 1970; BS cum laude, Ga. State U., 1974; MN, Emory U., 1975; MS in Community Counseling, PhD, Ga. State U., 1987. Instr. Piedmont Hosp. Sch. Nursing, Atlanta, 1976-83, Ga. Bapt. Hosp. Sch. Nursing, Atlanta, 1983-85; clin. examiner, cons. So. Performance Assessment Ctr., Univ. State N.Y., 1989—; rsch. health scientist, rehab. rsch. and devel. unit VA Med. Ctr., Atlanta, 1990-91; assoc. prof. North Ga. Coll., Dahlonega, Ga., 1988-91; assoc. prof. Nell Hodgson Sch. Nursing Emory U., 1992-94; nurse rschr. Vets. Affairs Med. Ctr., Atlanta, 1992-94; clin. specialist pulmonary and critical care medicine Atlanta Vets. Affairs Med. Ctr., 1994—. Contbr. articles to profl. jours. Grantee in field. Mem. ANA, So. Nursing Rsch. Soc., Am. Ednl. Rsch. Assn., Ga. Ednl. Rsch. Assn., Am. Urol. Assn. Allied Inc., Am. Heart Assn., Ga. Heart Assn., Sigma Theta Tau (Alpha Epsilon and Epsilon Alpha chpts.). Home: 2016 Fisher Trl NE Atlanta GA 30345-3429

CANNELLA, NANCY ANNE, administrator; b. Franklin Square, N.Y., Feb. 26, 1951; d. Philip and Nina (Vecchiano) Calabrese; m. Joseph L. Cannella, Jan. 10, 1950; children: Kimberly, Jonathan, Ashley. BS in Elem. Edn., St. John's U., 1973, MS in Curriculum Devel., 1975. Tchr. elem. sch. Bklyn. Dioceses, 1972-76; program devel. specialist Farifax County (Va.) Pub. Schs., 1976-80; dir. Armonk (N.Y.) Children's Corner, 1982—; coll. field supr. Manhattanville Coll., Harrison, N.Y., 1990-94; bd. dirs., v.p. Harrison Youth Coun., Westchester. Co-pres. Louis M. Klein Mid. Sch. PTA, Harrison, 1990-93; treas. Harrison Ave. Sch. PTA, 1986-88, v.p. ways 'n means, 1984-86; bd. dirs. Harrison Day Ctr., 1993. Mem. Westchester Assn. Edn. Young Children (bd. dirs. 1989-92, sec. 1991-92), Westchester Dist. Parent Tchr. Assn. (co-pres. 1990-93), Harrison Youth Coun. (bd. dirs. 1990—, v.p. 1992-94, co-pres. 1994—), Harrison Parent Tchr. Coun. (v.p. 1993, co-pres. 1994), Sch. Age Dir.'s Network (pres. 1988-90, v.p. 1991-93). Home: 26 Sunny Ridge Rd Harrison NY 10528-2206 Office: Armonk Children's Corner PO Box 601 Armonk NY 10504-0601

CANNIZZARO, LINDA ANN, geneticist, researcher; b. S.I., N.Y., Aug. 4, 1953. BS, St. Peter's Coll., 1975; MS, Fordham U., 1977, PhD, 1981. Postdoctoral fellow Dartmouth U. Med. Sch., Hanover, N.H., 1981-83; fellow in human genetics Children's Hosp. Phila., 1983-84; co-dir. cytogenetics Milton S. Hershey (Pa.) Med. Ctr., 1984-86; dir. gene mapping S.W. Biomed. Rsch. Inst., Scottsdale, Ariz., 1986-89; asst. prof. Fels Inst. Temple U. Med. Sch., Phila., 1989-91; assoc. prof. Albert Einstein Coll. Medicine, Bronx, N.Y., 1993—; dir. clin. and molecular cytogenetics Albert Einstein Coll. Medicine and Montefiore Hosp., Bronx, N.Y., 1993—. Assoc. editor Cytogenetics Cell Genetics, 1993—; contbr. articles to profl. jours. Grantee Am. Cancer Soc., 1989-90, 94—. Mem. AAAS, AAUW, Am. Soc. Human Genetics. Office: Albert Einstein Coll Med Dept Pathology F538 1300 Morris Park Ave Bronx NY 10461-1975

CANNON, BROOKE JANA, clinical neuropsychologist; b. Sioux Falls, S.D., Dec. 31, 1962; d. Joseph Alexander and Joy Naomi (Youppi) Szuhay; m. J. Timothy Cannon, Nov. 17, 1984; 1 child, Jaye Alexandra. BS, U. Scranton, 1984, MS, 1985; MA, SUNY, Binghamton, 1987, PhD, 1989. Lic. psychologist, Pa.; cert. rehab. counselor. Psychology intern West L.A. VA Med. Ctr., 1988-89; postdoctoral fellow Norwalk (Conn.) Hosp., 1989-90; clin. neuropsychologist Wilkes-Barre (Pa.) VA Med. Ctr., 1990—; pvt. practice Clarks Summit, Pa., 1991—. Contbr. articles to profl. jours. Mem. APA, Northeastern Pa. Psychol. Assn. Democrat. Lutheran. Office: Wilkes-Barre VA Med Clinic 1111 E End Blvd Wilkes-Barre PA 18711

CANNON, CHRISTINE ANNE, veterinarian; b. Chgo., Nov. 13, 1952; d. Joseph Phillip and Mildred Eileen (Toll) C.; m. Robert L. Van Grinsven, Mar. 25, 1989. BS in Animal Sci., Purdue U., 1974; BS in Vet. Medicine, U. Ill., 1975, DVM, 1977. Vet. Bellemore Animal Hosp., Granite City, Ill., 1977-79, Humane Soc. of Mo., St. Louis, 1979-81, Wheaton Way Vet. Hosp., Bremerton, Wash., 1981-82, Rose Hill Animal and Bird Hosp., Kirkland, Wash., 1982-83; relief vet. Wash., 1983-87; vet., owner Bird and Exotic Pet Care Clinic, Lynnwood, Wash., 1987-92; vet. owner A Pet Care Clinic, Mountlake Terrace, Wash., 1992—. Asst. editor Avian Emergency Care A Manual for Emergency Clinics, 1990. Group leader Canine Coll., Kirkland, 1986-87; mentor Project Discovery, Edmonds, Wash., 1989; leader explorer scouts troop Boy Scouts Am., St. Louis, 1981; chair King County Animal Control Citizens Adv. Com., 1991—. Mem. Assn. Avian Veterinarians (pub. rels. com., chair client edn. com.), Am. Vet. Med. Assn., Wash. State Vet. Med. Assn. (eds. and pubs. com. newsletter), Seattle-King County Vet. Med. Assn. (rep. South Snohomish chpt. 1990—, chair ethics com. 1991-94, pres. 1995), Finch Lovers of Puget Sound (co-founder, sec.-treas. 1987-91), Avicultural Soc. Puget Sound, N.W. Exotic Bird Soc., Pacific N.W. Herpetological Soc. Office: A Pet Care Clinic 23502 56th Ave W Mountlake Terrace WA 98043

CANNON, GRACE BERT, immunologist; b. Chambersburg, Pa., Jan. 29, 1937; d. Charles Wesley and Gladys (Raff) Bert; m. W. Dilworth Cannon, June 3, 1961 (div. 1972); children: Michael Quayle, Susan Radcliffe, Peter Bert Cannon. AB, Goucher Coll., 1958; PhD, Washington U., St. Louis, 1962. Fellow Columbia U., N.Y.C., 1962-64, Columbia U. Coll. Physicians and Surgeons, N.Y.C., 1964-65; staff fellow NIH Nat. Cancer Inst., Bethesda, Md., 1966-67; cell biologist Litton Bionetics, Inc., Kensington, Md., 1972-80, head immunology sect., 1980-85; dir. sci. ImmuQuest Labs., Inc., Rockville, Md., 1985-88; pres. Biomedical Analytics, Inc., Rockville, Md., 1988-94; mgr. ATLIS Fed. Svcs., Inc., Rockville, Md., 1991—; Mem. contract rev. coms. Nat. Cancer Inst., 1983-87. Contbr. articles to profl. jours. Mem. Pub. Svc. Health Club, Bethesda, Md., 1984—, sec., 1990—. Grantee USPHS, 1959-65, NSF, 1959. Mem. AAAS, Am. Assn. for Cancer Rsch., N.Y. Acad. Sci., Sigma Xi. Republican. Presbyterian (deacon). Home and Office: 4905 Ertter Dr Rockville MD 20852-2203

CANNON, ISABELLA WALTON, mayor; b. Dunfermline, Scotland, May 12, 1904; came to U.S., 1916; d. James and Helen Bett (Seaman) Walton; m. Claude M. Cannon. BA, Elon Coll., 1924, LLD (hon.), 1978. Tchr. pub. schs.; head dept. stats. French Purchase Commn., Washington; fin. officer UN, Washington; with N.C. State U. Library; mayor of Raleigh, N.C., 1977-79. V.p. Women in Bus. Adv. Council, N.C. Conservation Council, Women's Polit. Caucus; charter mem. Wake County Dem. Women; organizer, pres. Univ. Park Assn., Raleigh; civic sponsor, mem. bldg. com. Raleigh Little Theatre; mem. Univ. Neighborhood Planning Council, N.C. Child Advocacy, N.C. Commn. Bicentennial of U.S.; bd. dirs. Mordecai Sq. Hist. Soc.; chmn. Wade CAC; mem. devel. bd. YWCA Acad. of Women; chairperson Keep Am. Clean Sweep; bd. dirs. Raleigh Symphony Orch.; mem. Women's Forum of N.C.; mem. Coll. Presdl. Electors, Centennial Com.; bd. dirs., historian St. Luke's Home, Raleigh liaison RSVP bd., Raleigh Bicentennial Task Force 1988-92, Martin Luther King Jr. Celebration Com., 1989-92; precinct chair numerous polit. orgns. Recipient. Disting. Alumnus award Elon Coll., 1983, Medallion award, 1991, Isabella Cannon Rm. named in her honor Elon Coll., 1987, Isabella Cannon Leadership Fellows Program established in 1991, Lifetime Achievement award Theatre in the Park, Govt. award YWCA Acad. Women, 1988, Role Model Leader award N.C. State U., 1991, Mentor of Distinction award Women Bus. Adv. Coun., 1994; Isabella Cannon Arboretum Intership established in her honor N.C. State U., 1991. Mem. N.C. Sr. Citizens Assn. (pres.), Elon Coll. Alumni Assn., Delta Kappa Gamma. Mem. United Ch. of Christ.

CANNON, NANCY GLADSTEIN, insurance agent; b. San Francisco; d. Richard and Caroline (Decker) Gladstein; m. Robert L. Cannon; 1 child, Richard Michael. BA, San Francisco State U., 1964; JD, U. West Los Angeles, 1980. Tchr. San Bruno (Calif.) Park Schs., Inglewood (Calif.) Unified Schs.; exec. dir. Henrico Edn. Assn., Richmond, Va., 1975-76; agt. Blue Cross So. Calif., 1981-84, State Farm Ins. Co., Pacific Palisades, Calif., 1984—; pres. Cannon Ins. Agy. Inc., Pacific Palisades, 1984—. Del. Dem. Nat. Conv., Chgo., 1968; bd. govs. Pacific Palisades Civic League, 1987-91, Community Coun., 1988-89; bd. dirs. YMCA, Pacific Palisades, 1989-93, Sunset Mesa Property Owners Assn., 1991-93. Mem. Pacific Palisades C. of C., Santa Monica C. of C., Malibu C. of C., L.A. Athletic Club. Republican. Office: Cannon Ins Agy Inc 15415 Sunset Blvd Pacific Palisades CA 90272

CANNON, SAMANTHA KARRIE, entrepreneur, management consultant; b. Dayton, Ohio, Aug. 27, 1948; d. Emerson Lee and Elizabeth Ann (Riecken) Poppler; m. Peter Marcellus Cannon, Oct. 30, 1988. BA in Psychology, Calif. State U., Sacramento, 1977, MPA, MSW, 1982. Editor, pub. Equitable Life, Sacramento, 1972-76; mgmt. cons. State of Calif., Sacramento, 1976—; pvt. practice mgmt. cons. Sacramento, 1990—; founder, owner Your Best Friend, Sacramento, 1991—; mgmt. cons. United Way, Sacramento, 1985-88. Editor, pub.: (jour.) The Westerner, 1972-76. Past bd. dirs. Aquarian Effort; vol. comty. rape, suicide, family crisis, substance abuse and ex-offender programs; bd. dirs. Diogenes Youth Svcs., 1992-94. Recipient numerous local, state and nat. poetry awards. Lutheran. Office: Calif Dept Alcohol & Drug Programs 1700 K St Sacramento CA 95814

CANNON, STACEY MARGARET, lawyer; b. Long Branch, N.J., June 16, 1955; d. Bruno Yancerelli and Eunice (Mabb) Cannon; m. Joseph B. Schlam, May 25, 1980 (div. Dec. 1994); children: Alexandra, Mark. BA, Rutgers U., 1975; JD, Boston U., 1979. Atty. Bailey, Donovan & Cannon, Boston, 1981-83; pvt. practice Malden, Mass., 1983-85; atty. Digital Equip Corp., Maynard, Mass., 1985-87; asst. gen. counsel Sun Microsystems, Billerica (Mass.), Mountain View (Calif.), 1987-90; gen. counsel Logica North Am., Waltham, Mass., 1990-93; atty., cons. Proteon and Signature Fin., Boston, 1993; corp. counsel Kendall Sq. Rsch. Inc., Waltham, 1993—; dir. Kendall Sq. Rsch. Realty Corp., Boston, Kendall Sq. Rsch. SARL, Paris, Kendall Sq. Rsch. Ltd., London; mng. dir. Kendall Sq. Rsch. GmbH, Munich, Germany, 1993—. Democrat. Jewish. Home: 53 Spring St Lexington MA 02173

CANNON, VALERIE LYNN, medical laboratory professional; b. Gary, Ind., Jan. 11, 1957; d. Lawrence Wendell and Ruth (Augustus) C. BS, St. Mary's Coll., 1979; cert. med. technologist, Evanston Hosp. Sch. Med. Tech., Ill., 1980; MPA, Ind. U., Gary, 1990. Med. technologist St. Catherine's Hosp., East Chicago, Ind., 1980-82; lab. supr. Meth. Hosp., Merrillville, Ind., 1982-86, phlebotomy supr., 1986-90; lab. mgr. Loyola U. Med. Ctr., Maywood, Ill., 1990—. Named one of Outstanding Young Women Am., 1991. Mem. Am. Soc. Clin. Pathologists, Am. Coll. Healthcare Execs., Soc. Ambulatory Care Profls., Clin. Lab Mgmt. Assn. Methodist. Office: Loyola U Med Ctr 2160 S 1st Ave Maywood IL 60153-3304

CANOVA-DAVIS, ELEANOR, biochemist, researcher; b. San Francisco, Jan. 18, 1938; d. Gaudenzio Enzio and Catherine (Bordisso) Canova; m. Kenneth Roy Davis, Feb. 10, 1957; children: Kenneth Roy Jr., Jeffrey Stephen. BA, San Francisco State U., 1968, MS, 1971; PhD, U. Calif., San Francisco, 1977. Lab. asst. Frederick Burk Found. for Edn., San Francisco, 1969-71; rsch., tchg. asst. U. Calif., San Francisco, 1972-77, asst. rsch. biochemist, 1980-84; NIH postdoctoral fellow U. Calif., Berkeley, 1977-80; sr. scientist Liposome Tech., Menlo Park, Calif., 1984-85, Genentech, Inc.,

South San Francisco, 1985—. Contbr. articles to profl. jours. Recipient Nat. Rsch. Svc. award NIH, 1977-80; grantee Chancellor's Patent Fund, U. Calif., San Francisco, 1976, Earl C. Anthony Trust, 1975; grad. div. fellow U. Calif., San Francisco, 1972-73. Mem. Am. Chem. Soc., Calif. Scholarship Fedn., Sequoia Woods Country Club, Protein Soc., Am. Peptide Soc., Am. Soc. Mass Spectrometry. Roman Catholic. Home: 2305 Bourbon Ct South San Francisco CA 94080-5367 Office: Genentech Inc 460 Point San Bruno Blvd South San Francisco CA 94080-4918

CANTILENA, MARY ANN, psychologist; b. N.Y.C., Nov. 4, 1951; d. Charles Anthony and Girolama Josephine (Romano) C. BA, Hunter Coll., 1973; MS, Pace U., 1978; D in Psychology, Rutgers U., 1990. Lic. psychologist; RN. Tchr. St. Joseph's Sch., N.Y.C., 1973-76; nurse practitioner, coord. Mt. Sinai Med. Ctr., Milw., 1979-84; asst. nursing coord. Isabella Geriatric Ctr., N.Y.C., 1984-88; psychology technician FDR VA Hosp., Montrose, N.Y., 1988-89; assoc. psychologist South Beach Psychiat. Ctr., S.I., 1989—; pvt. practice clin. psychologist S.I., 1991—; cons. psychologist Episcopal Ch. of L.I., Garden City, N.Y., 1993—. Mem. APA, NOW. Democrat. Roman Catholic. Home: 157 Giffords Ln Staten Island NY 10308-2012

CANTLIFFE, JERI MILLER, artist, art educator; b. Alliance, N.C., Nov. 25, 1927; d. Rufus Faye Miller and Viola Elizabeth (Ireland) Miller Smith; m. Lawrence R. Cantliffe Jr., Sept.1, 1949; children: Eileen M., David L., Geri Lyn, Lisa Ann, Jonathan M. BA, Meredith Coll., 1949; M in Art Teaching, Wesleyan U., 1967; postgrad., Paier Sch. Art, New Haven, 1974-76. Designer Stephenson Appliance Co., Raleigh, N.C., 1949-50; lab. asst. N.C. State Coll., Raleigh, 1950, Hoffman-LaRoche Pharms., Clifton, N.J., 1951-52; art tchr. Horace Wilcox Tech. Sch., Meriden, Conn., 1962-66; workshop tchr. Park & Recreation Dept., Haddam and Wallingford, Conn., 1970-84, YWCA, Meriden, 1970-85, Middletown (Conn.) Art Guild, 1970-90, instr. in arts and crafts, 1989; workshop tchr. Community Art Ctr., Kensington, Conn., 1977-79; freelance artist specializing in home portraits, 1980—. One-woman shows include Cen. Bank, Meriden, 1977, 79, 82, Meriden Pub. Libr., 1981, 84 (commd. artists, Woman of Yr. in Arts award 1979), Cheshire (Conn.) Pub. Libr., 1982, Phoenix Mut. Life Inst. Co., Hartford, Conn., 1982, New Haven Pub. Libr., 1983, 86, Greene Art Gallery, Guilford, Conn., 1984, Meredith Coll., Raleigh, 1984, Lord Proprietor's Inn, Edenton, N.C.; juried mem. shows include Salamagundi, N.Y.C., New Haven Paint & Clay, Friends of New Britain (Conn.) Mus., Meriden Arts & Crafts (Frederick Flatow award 1979, Butler Paint award 1980, Alan Reid Meml. prize watercolor 1986), Middletown (Conn.) Art Guild (1st prize watercolor 1977, 78, 92, 93), Guilford Art League, 1994, Brush & Palette, New Haven, Milford (Conn.) Fine Arts, Mt. Carmel Art Assn., Hamden, Conn., Wis. Watercolor Show, Glastonbury (Conn.) Art Guild, The New Group, New Haven, Conn. Classic Arts, Conn. Acad. Fine Arts, Am. Penwomen, Fairfield, Conn.; invitational shows include Jewish Home for the Aged, New Haven, Art-on-the-Mountain, Wilmington, Vt., Wesleyan Showcase, Middletown Showcase (Most Popular award 1979), Glastonbury C. of C., AAUW Art Show, Soundview Ann. Art Show, Greeley Nat. Art Show, 1990, Brownstone Group, Meriden, 1990-94, Art Cache Gallery, Vt., 1990-94, Ariz. Arts & Crafts Market Gallery, 1990-92; illustrator Meriden Calendar, Meriden City Hall Christmas Card, Meriden Centennial Quilt. Co-chmn. Commn. on the Arts, Meriden, 1975-76. Recipient Redstone Mfg. award Mum Art Festival, Bristol, Conn., 1978, Best in Show award Middletown Annual Winter Show, 1978, Judges Tri-color award Community Art League, Kensington, 1978, Most Popular Vote award Middletown Showcase, 1979, Middletown Art Guild, 1992, Rick Ciburi 1st prize award Cheshire Art League, 1981, Best in Show (watercolor) Bridgeport Art League, 1982, Women in Leadership award Middlesex County C. of C., 1992, Women in Leadership award YMCA, 1993; named Woman Yr. in Arts Meriden-Record Jour., 1981, Meriden Girls Club, 1982, Meredith Coll., 1984, Meriden YWCA, 1992, 100 Exceptional Women 1893-1993, 1993. Mem. Nat. League Am. PEN Women (nat. asst. membership for the arts 1990-94, bd. dirs., sec. 1990-92, 92-94, nat. art show com. 1990-94, nat. asst. membership chair for arts, br. membership chair 1993-94, pres. Fairfield County br. 1988-92, corr. sec. 1992, v.p. 1986-88, 1st prize watercolor 1993, nat. art bd. 1990-94), PEN Women (state art co-chair 1988-89), Colo. Artists Assn., Rotary (youth exch. com., internat. com. chair youth exch. officer Meriden club, club svc. chair 1993, mem. scholarship com. 1993-94, dist. internat. com. 1993-94, Paul Harris fellow Meriden Rotary 1992). Congregationalist.

CANTOR, ALEXANDRA, professional society administrator; b. N.Y.C., Nov. 22, 1961; d. Murray A. and Lois (Van Arsdel) C. BA, William Smith Coll., 1983. Exec. sec. Nissel & Nissel, CPAs, N.Y.C., 1983-85, Am. Soc. Journalists and Authors Charitable Trust, N.Y.C., 1986—; exec. dir. Am. Soc. Journalists and Authors, N.Y.C., 1985—. Contbg. author: Tools of the Writer's Trade, 1990; editor Sitzmark newsletter of High Life Ski Club, Rockaway, N.J., 1994—. Office: Am Soc of Journalists 1501 Broadway Ste 302 New York NY 10036-5503

CANTOR, ELEANOR WESCHLER, medical association executive; b. N.Y.C., Dec. 30, 1913; d. Samuel Peter and Anna (Rauchwerger) W.; m. Alfred Joseph Cantor, June 9, 1938; children—Pamela Corliss, Alfred Jay. B.A., Hunter Coll., N.Y.C., 1938. Producer radio quiz show CBS, N.Y.C., 1936-41; exec. officer Internat. Acad. Proctology, N.Y.C., 1948—, Internat. Bd. Proctology, 1950—; co-founder Acad. Psychosomatic Medicine, 1954.

CANTOR, KATHY JO, respiratory therapy educator; b. Weirton, W.Va., Mar. 24, 1959; d. Frederick Eugene and Virginia Aileen (Welshans) C. BS, Wheeling (W.Va.) Jesuit Coll, 1981; MS in Edn., U. Dayton, 1992. Credentialed perinatal/pediatrics respiratory care specialist. Respiratory technician St. John Med. Ctr., Steubenville, Ohio, 1979-80; respiratory therapy intern Duke U. Med. Ctr., Durham, N.C., 1981-82; staff respiratory therapist Duke U. Med. Ctr., Durham, 1982-84, clin. instr. respiratory therapy, 1984-85, physiol. monitoring pool supr., 1985, staff respiratory therapist, 1985-86; contingent staff respiratory therapist Ohio Valley Med. Ctr., Wheeling, W.Va., 1986-93; casual staff respiratory therapist Mercy Hosp., Pitts., 1992—; asst. prof., clin. coord. respiratory therapy program Jefferson Tech. Coll., Steubenville, Ohio, 1987—; mem. Tech. Prep Course of Study Com. Jefferson County Sch. Dist. and Jefferson Tech. Coll., 1990—. Mem. Am. Assn. Respiratory Care, Weirton Bus. and Profl. Women's Soc. Democrat. Methodist. Home: RD # 1 Box 91 Colliers WV 26035 Office: Jefferson Tech Coll 4000 Sunset Blvd Steubenville OH 43952-3598

CANTOR, MURIEL GOLDSMAN, sociologist, educator; b. Mpls., Mar. 2, 1923; d. Leo and Bess Goldsman; m. Joel M. Cantor, Aug. 6, 1944 (Nov. 1988); children: Murray Robert, Jane Cantor Shefler, James Leo. B.A., UCLA, 1964, M.A., 1966, Ph.D., 1969. Lectr. dept. econs. and sociology Immaculate Heart Coll., L.A., 1966-68; faculty Am. U., Washington, 1968-93, instr., 1968-69, asst. prof. sociology, 1969-72, assoc. prof., 1972-76, prof., 1976—, prof. emerita, 1993—, chmn. dept., 1973-75, 77-79, dir. women's studies, 1989-93; vis. prof. communication studies UCLA, 1982; cons. agys. including NIMH; cons. Corp. for Pub. Broadcasting, 1974-75, 80-81, Women, Men and Media, U. S.C., 1990-91. Author: The Hollywood TV Producer: His Work and His Audience, 1971, 2d edit. with new intro., 1987, Prime Time Television: Content and Control, 1980, (with Joel M. Cantor) 2d edit. rev. and enlarged, 1992, (with Phyllis L. Stewart) Varieties of Work Experience, 1974, 82, (with Suzanne Pingree) The Soap Opera, 1983, (with Sandra Ball-Rokeach) Media, Audiences and Social Structure, 1986, (with Cheryl Zollors) Creators of Culture: Descriptions and Professions in Culture Industries, 1993; editor Nat. SWS newsletter, 1977-78. Bd. dirs. Population Inst., 1978-80; trustee WETA, 1972-76. NIMH grantee, 1979-81; recipient Premio Diego Fabbri for Soap Opera in Rome, 1988. Mem. Am. Sociol. Assn. (chair soc. culture sect. 1990-91, co-editor newsletter 1991-93), D.c. Sociol. Soc. (pres. 1977-78, Stewart A. Rice Merit award 1987), Sociologists for Women in Soc. (pres.-elect 1994, pres. 1995), Ea. Sociol. Soc. (exec. coun. 1981-83, 89-92), So. Sociol. Soc. (exec. coun. 1991-93), Internat. Sociol. Assn., Internat. Inst. Sociology. Home: 8408 Whitman Dr Bethesda MD 20817-6823 Office: Am U Dept Sociology Washington DC 20016

CANTOR, PAMELA CORLISS, psychologist; b. N.Y.C., Apr. 23, 1944; d. Alfred Joseph and Eleanor (Weschler) C.; m. Howard Feldman, Sept. 11, 1969; children: Lauren Jaye, Jeffrey Lee. BS cum laude, Syracuse U., 1965; postgrad. in medicine, Johns Hopkins U., 1969-70; MA, Columbia U., 1967, PhD, 1972; postgrad., Harvard U.-Children's Hosp. Med. Ctr., 1973-74. Instr. Radcliffe Inst., Harvard U., 1977-78; assoc. prof. psychology Boston U., 1970-80; pvt. practice clin. psychology, Needham, Mass., 1980—; faculty Med. Sch., Harvard U.; lectr. in field, also TV and radio appearances. Author: Understanding A Child's World- Reading in Infancy through Adolescence, 1977; cons. editor: Suicide and Life-Threatening Behavior; columnist: For Parents Only; contbr. chpts. to handbooks and numerous articles to profl. jours. Apptd. mem. Mass. Gov.'s Office for Children Statewide Adv. Bd., 1980—; adv. bd. Samaritans of Boston; pres. Nat. Com. Youth Suicide Prevention; mem. HHS Presdl. Task Force on Youth Suicide. Mem. Am. Psychol. Assn., Am. Assn. Suicidology (pres. 1985-86), Am. Orthopsychiat. Assn., Mass. Psychol. Assn., Am. Assn. Suicidology (bd. dirs.). Home: 11 Parkman Way Needham MA 02192

CANTRELL, ANDREA E., library administrator; b. Springfield, Mo., Jan. 1, 1948; d. A.J. Cantrell and Wilma (Snowden) Cave; m. Stephen J. Chism, 1989. BA, Am. U., 1970; MLS, U. Md., College Park, 1971. Young adult svcs. libr. Thomas Jefferson Regional Libr., Jefferson City, Mo., 1971-72; reference libr. Springfield-Greene County Libr. (Mo.), 1972-74; coord. Libr. resources Mo. State Libr., Jefferson City, 1974-78; chief cons. svc. Wash. State Library, Olympia, 1978-79; dir. Joplin Pub. Libr. (Mo.), 1979-81; dir. libr. resources div. Okla. Hist. Soc., Oklahoma City, 1981-85; spl. collections libr. U. Ark., Fayetteville, 1985—. Author: Manuscript Resources for Women's Studies, 1989; contbr. articles to profl. jours. Mem. ALA (chmn. staff devel. com. 1977-78; genealogy com. 1983-85), Ark. Libr. Assn. (chmn. Coll. and Univ. div. 1986-87), Assn. Specialized and Coop. Libr. Agys. (chmn. 1978-79), Ark. & Mo. Libr. Assns. (mem. various coms.), Zeta Tau Alpha. Office: U Ark Librs Spl Collections Dept Fayetteville AR 72701

CANTRELL, LANA, actress, singer; b. Sydney, Australia, Aug. 7, 1943; d. Hubert Clarence and Dorothy Jean (Thistlethwaite) C. JD, Fordham Law Sch., 1993. Singer supper clubs, TV programs, Australia, 1958-62; U.S. debut: TV show The Tonight Show, NBC, 1962; rec. artist RCA and Polydor Records, 1967—(Grammy award as Most Promising New Female Artist, Nat. Assn. Rec. Arts and Scis. 1967); recs. include Lana!, Act III, And Then There Was Lana, The Now of Then!. Pres. Thrush, Inc.; U.S. rep. Internat. Song Festival, Poland, 1966, UN Internat. Women's Year Concert, Paris, France, 1975. Recipient 1st prize Internat. Song Festival Poland, 1966; 1st Internat. Woman of Yr. award Feminist Party, 1973. Office: 300 E 71st St New York NY 10021-5234

CANTRELL, LINDA MAXINE, counselor; b. Ann Arbor, Mich., June 20, 1938; d. Donald LaVerne and Lila Maxine (Crull) Katz; m. Douglas D. Cantrell, Dec. 28, 1963; children: Douglas David Jr., Warren Vincent, Bryan LaVerne. BA, U. Mich., 1960, MA, 1963, postgrad., 1963-65. Cert. secondary tchr., Mich.; lic. ins. salesperson, lic. profl. counselor Mich. Caseworker Cook County Dept. Pub. Aid, Chgo., 1960; psychometrist Evanston (Ill.) Schs., 1960-61; rsch. assoc. U. Mich., Ann Arbor, 1961-64; guidance counselor Radcliff Mid. Sch., Garden City, Mich., 1964-66; dir. guidance and counseling St. Mary Acad., Monroe, Mich., 1985-87; counselor, head counselor Ypsilanti (Mich.) Adult Edn., 1987—; sales leader Primerica Fin. Svcs., 1993—. Rep. precinct leader Ann Arbor, 1971; clk., marker, rec. sec. Thrift Shop of Ann Arbor, 1981—; bd. dirs. Ypsilanti Adult/Cmty. Edn. Adv. Com., 1990—; treas. Burns Park Sch., Ann Arbor, 1978-79; rec. sec. Chapel of Love Ch., 1989—; co-chmn. benefits Ann Arbor Chamber Orch., 1981-82; chmn. ann. benefit Rudolf Steiner Sch. Ann Arbor, 1984-85; treas. Burns Park PTO, 1978-79; vol. Greenhills Schs., 1978-81, St. Paul's Luth. Sch., 1972-73, among others. Recipient Gil Bursley award Rep. Party, 1972, scholarship Chi Omega, 1957. Mem. AAUW (fellowship chmn. 1971-73), Mich. Assn. for Counseling and Devel. (membership chmn. Monroe County chpt. 1986-87), Ypsilanti Fedn. Tchrs. (rec. sec. 1989-91), Mich. Assn. for Acad. Advisors Community Edn., Washtenaw Counselors Assn., Monroe County Counselors Assn. (membership chmn. 1985-87), Ann Arbor Women's City Club (membership com. 1985-87), Ea. Mich. U. Coll. Bus. Wives (program chmn. 1974, pres. 1975), Phi Kappa Phi, Pi Lambda Theta. Republican.

CANTRELL, SHARRON CAULK, secondary education educator; b. Columbia, Tenn., Oct. 2, 1947; d. Tom English and Beulah (Goodin) Caulk; m. William Terry Cantrell, Mar. 18, 1989; 1 child, Jordan; children from previous marriage: Christopher, George English, Steffenee Copley. BA George Peabody Coll. Tchrs., 1970; MS Vanderbilt U., 1980; EdS Mid. Tenn. State U., 1986. Tchr., Ft. Campbell Jr. High Sch., Ky., 1970-71, Whitthorne Jr. High Sch., Columbia, Tenn., 1977-86, Spring Hill (Tenn.) High Sch., 1986—; chmn. edn. Homecoming '86 Maury County Schs., Columbia, 1984-86. Mem. NEA, AAUW (pres. Tenn. div. 1983-85), Maury County Edn. Assn. (pres. 1983-84), Tenn. Edn. Assn., Assn. for Preservation Tenn. Antiquities, Maury County C. of C., Friends of Children's Hosp., Phi Delta Kappa. Mem. Ch. of Christ. Home: 5299 Main St Spring Hill TN 37174 Office: Spring Hill High Sch 1 Raider Lane Columbia TN 38401

CANTÚ, NORMA V., federal official; b. Brownsville, Tex., Nov. 2, 1954. BS summa cum laude, Pan Am. U., 1973; JD, Harvard U., 1977. Bar: Tex. 1978, U.S. Dist. Ct. (so. dist.) Tex. 1979, U.S. Dist. Ct. (we. dist.) Tex. 1981, U.S. Ct. Appeals (5th and 11th cirs.) 1982, Calif. 1985, U.S. Ct. Appeals (10th cir.) 1986, U.S. Dist. Ct. (no. dist.) Tex. 1992. Tchr. English Brownsville, 1974, San Antonio, 1979; intern nursing home task force Office of Atty. Gen. Tex., 1977-78; staff atty. Chicana rights project Mex. Am. Legal Def. and Ednl. Fund, 1979-83, nat. dir., 1983-92, regional counsel, 1985-93; asst. sec. for civil rights Office for Civil Rights U.S. Dept. of Edn., Washington, 1993—; cons. NEA, Nat. Assn. Sch. Lawyers, Dept. of Edn., CRESST ctr. testing UCLA. Mem. exec. com. Avance Parent Child Tng. Program, 1990, 92, bd. dirs., 1990—; pro bono legal counsel YWCA San Antonio; mem. City San Antonio Health Facilities Commn., City of San Antonio Com. Drafting Regulations, Tex. Human Rights Commn., 1992, Ctr. Hispanic Health Policy Devel., 1992. Recipient Appreciation award Tex. Senate, 1993, Leadership award Hispanic Mag., 1993, Reynaldo G. Garza award Hispanic issues sect. State Bar Tex., 1993. Office: Dept of Education Office for Civil Rights 330 C St SW Washington DC 20202

CANTUS, JANE SCOTT, management consultant; b. Phila., Aug. 31, 1965; d. H. Hollister and Barbara Jane (Park) C. BA in History, Duke U., 1987; MBA, U. Va., 1990. Lyndon B. Johnson intern U.S. Congress, Washington, summer 1986; Dwight D. Eisenhower intern Rep. Nat. Com., Washington, summer 1986; legal asst. Crowell & Moring, Washington, 1987-88; fin. mgmt. asst. Martin Marietta Corp., Bethesda, Md., summer 1989; bus. devel. rep. def. and space div. Bechtel Nat., Inc., San Francisco, 1990-91; project control engr. Bechtel Savannah River Site, S.C., 1991; market analyst; bus. devel. rep. def. and space divsn. Bechtel Power Corp., Gaithersburg, Md., 1992-93; sr. assoc. Bechtel Financing Svcs., Inc., Gaithersburg, 1993-94, Korn/Ferry Internat., Washington, 1994—. Active Jr. League, 1987—. Recipient Sr. Leadership award, Duke U., 1987; named to Outstanding Young Women of Am., 1988. Mem. DAR (insignia com. chmn. McLean, Va. chpt., 1983—). Republican. Episcopalian.

CANTWELL, LOIS, editor-in-chief; b. Jersey City, June 16; m. Robert Sefcik, Oct. 3, 1981; children: Teddy, Zoe. BA, U. Wis., 1973. Editor Ideal Pub., N.Y.C., 1977-78; editor-in-chief children's div. Parents mag., N.Y.C., 1978-81; editor-in-chief Careers mag. E.M. Guild Inc., N.Y.C., 1987-89; freelance writer N.Y.C., 1981-87; v.p., dir. internal comm. Kidder, Peabody and Co., Inc., N.Y.C., 1989-90; mgr. internal comm. Sony Corp. Am., Park Ridge, N.J., 1990-93; editor-in-chief Inside Mag., Whippany, N.Y., 1993—; cons. AT&T, Morristown, N.J., 1985, CNR Ptnrs., N.Y.C., 1987. Author: Money and Banking, 1984, Freedom, 1985, Modeling, 1986, Blackstone's Magic Adventures, 1986. Pres. Midtown Manor Coop., N.Y.C., 1985, treas., 1986. Mem. Soc. Profl. Jours., Nat. Acad. TV Arts and Scis., Internat. Assn. Bus. Communicators, Fred Lewis Allen Room, Writers Room, Sigma Delta Chi. Home: 42 Walnut Ave Millburn NJ 07041-1512

CANTWELL, MARIA E., congresswoman. Grad., Miami U. Former rep. Dist. 44 State of Wash.; mem. 103rd Congress from 1st Wash. dist., Washington, D.C., 1993—; owner pub. rels. firm. Office: US Ho Reps Office Ho Mems Washington DC 20515

CANTWELL, MARY, journalist; b. Providence; d. I. Leo and Mary G. (Lonergan) C.; m. Robert Lescher, Dec. 19, 1953 (div.); children: Katherine, Margaret. B.A., Conn. Coll., 1953. Copywriter Mademoiselle, N.Y.C., 1953-58; chief copywriter Mademoiselle, 1962-67, mng. and features editor, 1968-77, sr. editor features, 1978-80; mem. editiorial bd. N.Y. Times, 1980—, columnist, 1988-90. Author: American Girl, 1992; contbr. articles and fiction to mags. Recipient Conn. Coll. medal, 1983, Walker Stone Editorial Writing award Scripps Howard, 1987. Office: NY Times 229 W 43rd St New York NY 10036-3913

CANTY, HENRIETTA MATHIS, state legislator; b. Oct. 23; widowed; 4 children. MA, U. Pa. State rep. dist. 38 Ga. Ho. of Reps., 1990-92, state rep. dist. 52, 1993—; sec. govt. affairs com., mem. ins. com., state inst. and property com. Democrat. Home: 487 Lynn Valley Rd SW Atlanta GA 30311-2358*

CAPALDI, ELIZABETH ANN DEUTSCH, psychological sciences educator; b. N.Y.C., May 13, 1945; d. Frederick and Nettie (Tarasuck) Deutsch; m. Egidio J. Capaldi, Jan. 20, 1968 (div. May 1985). A.B., U. Rochester, 1965; Ph.D., U. Tex., 1969. Asst. prof. dept. psychol. scis. Purdue U., West Lafayette, Ind., 1969-74, assoc. prof., 1974-78, prof., 1979-86, asst. dean Grad. Sch., 1982-86, head dept. psychol. scis., 1983-88, sec.-treas. council of grad. dept. psychology, 1986-88; prof. U. Fla., Gainesville, 1988—; mem. basic behavioral neuroscis. fellowship rev. panel NIH, reviewer's res. NIMH, 1991; spl. asst. to pres., U. Fla. Author: Psychology, 1984, 3d edit., 1991; cons. editor Jour. Exptl. Psychology, 1991; assoc. editor Psychonomic Bull. Rev., 1993; contbr. articles to profl. jours. NIMH grantee, 1984-94, NSF grantee, 1995—. Fellow AAAS, APA, Am. Psychol. Soc. (mem. governing bd. 1991—); mem. Psychonomic Soc. (mem. governing bd. 1992—), Midwestern Psychol. Assn. (sec.-treas. 1988-90, pres. 1991), Sigma Xi. Home: 4140 NW 44th Ave Gainesville FL 32606-4518 Office: U Fla Dept Psychology Gainesville FL 32611

CAPELL, CYDNEY LYNN, editor; b. Jacksonville, Fla., Dec. 20, 1956; d. Ernest Clary and Alice Rae (McGinnis) Capell; m. Garrick Philip Martin, July 16, 1983 (div. Jan. 1988). BA, Furman U., 1977. Mktg. rep. E.C. Capell & Assocs., Greenville, S.C., 1977-80; sales rep. Prentice-Hall Publs., Cin., 1980-81; sales, mktg. rep. Benjamin/Cummings, Houston, 1981-83; sales rep. McGraw-Hill Book Co., Houston, 1983-85, engring. editor, N.Y.C., 1985-87; acctg. and infosystems editor Bus. Pubs., Inc., Plano, Tex., 1988-89; sr. editor Gorsuch Scarisbrick Pubs., Scottsdale, Ariz., 1989-90; editor-in-chief rsch. dept. Rauscher, Pierce, Refsnes Stock Brokers, 1990-94; editor-in-chief Marshall & Swift, L.A., 1994—; editor lit. mag. Talon, 1972; news editor Paladin newspaper, 1977. Named Rookie of Yr., McGraw-Hill Book Co., 1985. Mem. NOW, NAFE, Women in Pub., Women in Communications, Mensa. Republican. Avocations: tennis, ballet.

CAPELLA, PAULA MARIE, occupational therapist; b. Pequannock, N.J., Sept. 4, 1957; d. Robert Ottavio and Norma Mary (Piantanida) C. BS, Kean Coll., 1980; cert. in grad. studies, Dallas Theol. Sem., 1992. Registered occupational therapist. Staff occupational therapist Beth Israel Hosp., Passaic, N.J., 1980-83, pediatric supr., 1984-86; staff occupational therapist United Cerebral Palsy of North Jersey, East Orange, 1983-84; pvt. practice, 1986—; instr. occupational therapy Kean Coll., Union, N.J. Team participant, team leader non-denominational Christian group mission to Guatemala, 1986, 88, 89, 90, 91, 92, 93. Named Clinician of Yr., N.J. Early Intervention Coalition, 1993. Mem. Am. Occupational Therapy Assn., N.J. Occpational Therapy Assn., N.J. Early Intervention Coalition, Phi Kappa Phi.

CAPELLE, MADELENE CAROLE, opera singer, educator, music therapist; b. Las Vegas, Nev., July 29, 1950; d. Curtis and Madelene Glenna (Healy) C. BA, Mills Coll., 1971; MusM, U. Tex., 1976; postgrad., Ind. U., 1976-77; diploma cert., U. Vienna, Austria, 1978; postgrad. in creative arts, Union Coll. Cert. K-12 music specialist, Nev. Prof. voice U. Nev. Clark County C.C., Las Vegas, 1986—; music therapist Charter Hosp., Las Vegas, 1987—; pvt. practice music therapy, Las Vegas, 1989—; music specialist Clark County Sch. Dist., Las Vegas, 1989—; contract music therapist Nev. Assn. for Handicapped, Las Vegas, 1990; guest voice coach U. Basel, Switzerland, 1992; presenter concerts in Kenya, self-esteem workshops for children and adult women; artist-in-residence, Nev., Wyo., S.D., Oreg., Idaho, N.D., Utah, 1988—; mem. cons. roster Wyo. Arts Cou., 1988—; cons. U.S. rep. Princess Margaret of Romania Found.; workshops in music therapy and humor therapy Germany, Austria, Switzerland; workshop day treatment program dir. Harmony Health Care; judge Leontyne Price Nat. Voice Competition. Opera singer, Europe, Asia, S.Am., U.S., Can., Australia, 1978—; roles include Cio Cio San in Madama Butterly, Tosca, Turandot and Fidelio, Salome Electra; community concerts artist; featured PBS artist Guess Who's Playing the Classics; featured guest All Things Considered PBS radio, 1985; co-writer (one-woman show) The Fat Lady Sings, 1991 (Women's Awareness award); concerts Africa, Kenya, Somalia; concerts for Jugaslavian Relief throughout Europe; guest soloist national anthem San Francisco 49ers. Pres., founder, cons. Children's Opera Outreach, Las Vegas, 1985—; artist Musicians Emergency Found., N.Y.C., 1978-82; vol. Zoo Assn., Allied Arts, Ziegfeld Club (first Junior Ziegfeld Young Woman of Yr.), Las Vegas, 1979—; clown Very Spl. Arts, Nev., Oreg., S.D., 1989-90; goodwill and cultural amb. City of Las Vegas, 1983; panelist Kennedy Ctr., Washington, 1982; artist Benefit Concerts for Children with AIDS; mem. Nev. Arts Alliance, Make a Wish Found., Lyric Opera of Las Vegas. Named Musician of Yr. Swiss Music Alliance, 1993. Mem. Internat. Platform Assn., Nat. Assn. Tchrs. Singing (featured guest speaker), Performing Arts Soc. Nev., Brown Bag Concert Assn. (bd. dirs.), Make a Wish Found., Las Vegas Lyric Opera (bd. dirs.). Democrat. Home: 3266 Brentwood St Las Vegas NV 89121-3316

CAPLAN, ELINOR, Canadian provincial legislator, former cabinet minister; b. Toronto, Ont., Can., 1944; m. Wilf Caplan; children: David, Mark, Zane, Meredith. Pres. Elinor Caplan and Assocs., 1973-78; alderman Ward 13 City of North York, 1978-85; mem. Ont. Legislature, 1985—; minister Ministry of Health, Toronto, 1987-90; chmn. Mgmt. Bd. of Cabinet, chmn. of cabinet Peterson Govt.; minister Govt. Svcs. Past chmn. North York Coun. Com., Human Resources Adv. Coun., Rapid Transit Subcom.; past mem. North York Bd. of Health; past vice chmn. North York Interagy. Coun. Mem. North York Bus. Assn. (founder, past chmn. devel. and econ. growth com.). Office: Ont Legis Assembly, Legis Bldg, Toronto, ON Canada M7A 1A4

CAPO, HELENA FRANCES, comedienne; b. N.Y.C., July 29, 1959; d. Frank Remo Capo and Rose Nellie (Aguilar) Richards; m. William Patterson, Oct. 18, 1986; 1 child, W. Spencer Patterson. BA, Queens Coll., 1981. Engr., disc jockey Sta WQMC-AM, N.Y.C., 1980; writer Sta. WBLS-FM, N.Y.C., 1984-86; assoc. editor Laugh Factory Mag., Los Angeles, 1985-87; pres. Precision Production Inc., N.Y.C., 1985—; producer N.Y.C. 1st Official Comedy Day, 1984; tchr. Learning Annex, N.Y.C., 1984; creator Availiabilities Hotline, N.Y.C., 1985. Author: Training Your Pet Flea, 1984, Dogslapping, 1987, Fast Talking for Fun and Profit, 1990; (audio tape) Fran's Fast Fractured Fairy Tales, 1991; (record album) Rappin' Mae, 1985; producer: Stand-Up for Animals, 1988. Named Worlds Fastest Talker Guinness Book World Records, N.Y.C. and London, 1989, 91. Roman Catholic. Office: Precision Prodns Inc PO Box 314 Flushing NY 11358

CAPODILUPO, ELIZABETH JEANNE HATTON, public relations executive; b. McRae, Ga., May 3, 1940; d. Lewis Irby and Essee Elizabeth (Parker) Hatton; m. Raphael S. Capodilupo, Jan. 21, 1967. Grad., Dale Carnegie Inst., 1976. Sec. A.R. Clark Acct., Fernandina Beach, Fla., 1958-59; receptionist, girl Friday Sta. WNDT-TV, N.Y.C., 1960-62, Coy Hunt and Co., N.Y.C., 1962-69; clk. Woodlawn Cemetery, Bronx, N.Y., 1969-71, historian, community affairs coord., 1971—, editor newsletter, 1979—, asst. to pres., 1984, dir. pub. rels., 1984; grad. asst. Dale Carnegie Inst., 1977-78. Researcher Woodlawn Cemetery's Hall of Fame; contbr. articles to profl. jours. Chmn. ann. Adm. Farragut Honor Ceremony, Bronx, 1976—; founder, chmn. Toys for Needy Children, 1983-91; bd. dirs. Bronx Mus. Arts, v.p., 1983-84; pres. Bronx Coun. Arts, 1987-90; mem. adv. bd. Salvation Army, 1985, Bronx Arts Ensemble, 1985; bd. mgrs. Bronx YMCA, 1985, life mem., vice chmn., 1989—; bd. dirs. Bronx Urban League, 1985; bd. dirs. Bronx Coun. on Arts, 1985, pres., 1987-90; mem. Bronx Landmarks Task Force, 1994—. Recipient award citation VFW, 1976, Voice of Democracy Program judge's citation, 1980, Disting. Community Svc. award N.Y.C. Council, II Leone di Sanmarco award Italian Heritage & Culture

Com. Bronx, 1989; named Woman of Yr., YMCA, Bronx, 1986, Woman of Yr., Network Orgn. of Bronx Women, 1986, Jeanne and Ray Capodilupo named as Mr. & Mrs. Bronx 1989-90 proclaimed by Borough Pres., named Pioneer of the Bronx, 1992; cert. appreciation Dale Carnegie Inst., 1977; Outstanding Citizenship award Bronx N.E. Kiwanis Club, 1981; Service to Youth award YMCA of Bronx, 1983; recipient proclamation City Council of N.Y., Italian Heritage and Culture Com. of the Bronx, 1989; Outstanding Cemeterian award Am. Cemetery Assn., 1987-88; Citation of Merit Bronx Borough Pres.'s Office, 1988; Spl. Hons. for Outstanding Vol. Work Ladies Aux. Our Lady of Mercy Med. Ctr.; named Hon. Grand Marshall Bronx Columbus Day Parade, 1987-89, Bronx Meml. Day Parade, 1989; apptd. to commn. celebrating 350 yrs. of the Bronx by Borough Pres., recipient Pioneer award for Women's History Month for Outstanding Humanitarian Svcs., 1991. Mem. Bronx County Hist. Soc., Network Orgn. Bronx Women, Women in Communication, Bronx C. of C. (sec. 1988), YMCA (life mem.), N.Y. Press Club, Italian Big Sisters Club, Women's City Club, Order Eastern Star. Methodist. Office: Woodlawn Cemetery PO Box 75 Bronx NY 10470-0075

CAPONE, MARGARET LYNCH, civic worker, parliamentarian; b. Wilkinsburg, Pa., May 21, 1907; d. John Edward and Anna Freda (Dunstrup) Lynch; m. Carmen R. Capone, July 21, 1936 (dec. May 1983); children: David Michael, Mary Ann Capone Sperling, Donald William. Student U. Pitts., 1925-33, 1949-53, Carnegie Inst. Tech., 1955-56. Parliamentarian Pa. Nurses Assn., 1960-68, Allegheny County Law Wives, Pa., 1975-89; treas. Allegheny County LWV, 1965-69, v.p., 1969-73, pres., 1973-79, parliamentarian, 1979—, historian, 1980; parliamentarian St. Lucy Guild to Blind, Pitts., Allegheny County Lawyers Aux., Diocese Coun. Cath. Women, Marian Manor Guild; cons. parliamentarian. Author: So You've Joined A Club, 1954; Parliamentary Pointers, 1972; editor Clea News, 1954-72. Named Woman of Yr., Clea News, 1973; Personality of Yr., Pitts. chpt. K.C., 1979. Mem. Nat. Assn. Parliamentarians (profl. registered parliamentarian, local pres. 1959-61, state pres. 1963-64, nat. v.p. 1977-79), Am. Inst. Parliamentarians (cert. profl. parliamentarian), Duquesne U. Women's Guild. Republican. Roman Catholic. Lodges: K.C. Women's Guild, Toastmistresses (pres. local club 1950-51, nat. bd. dirs. 1953-63, nat. sec. 1954-56, nat. v.p. 1956-57, editor Toastmistress Mag. 1958-62). Home: 6530 Zupancic Dr Pittsburgh PA 15236-3652

CAPORINO, GRACE CONNOLLY, English educator, consultant; b. Red Bank, N.J., Aug. 8, 1940; d. Daniel Joseph and Mary Agnes (Martinez) Connolly; m. Gabriel Anthony Caporino, July 19, 1960 (dec. Mar. 1974); children: Melanie Brezovsky, Pamela. BA in Lit., Purchase Coll., 1974; MA in Teaching, Manhattanville Coll., 1978. Cert. H.S. English tchr., N.Y. H.S. English tchr. Carmel (N.Y.) H.S., 1974—; adj. prof. English Westchester C.C., Valhalla, N.Y., 1990; lit. cons. Advanced Placement English Lit. Exam Reader, The Coll. Bd., Princeton, N.J., 1988—; cons. tchr. task force U.S. Holocaust Meml. Mus., Washington, 1990—; project dir. NEH masterwork grant CUNY Grad. Ctr., N.Y.C., 1989-91; mem. edn. outreach com. Westchester Holocaust Commn., White Plains, N.Y., 1994—; judge nat. essay contest U.S. Holocaust Meml. Mus., Washington, 1990. Contbg. editor: (pamphlets) Guidelines for Teaching the Holocaust, 1993, Teacher's Guide for Artifact Poster Series, 1993. Summer fellow Haifa U. and Yad Vashem, Jerusalem, Israel, 1987, summer NEH fellow Hollins Coll., Roanoke, Va., 1988; recipient Louis Yavner Teaching award Regents of SUNY, 1991. Mem. Nat. Coun. Tchrs. English (mem. teaching about genocide and intolerance com. 1994—), Internat. Consortium Nat. Coun. Tchrs. English (host European profs. English U.S. visit 1994), N.Y. State United Tchrs., Westchester Coun. English Tchrs. Home: 213 California Rd Yorktown Heights NY 10598 Office: Carmel HS Fair St Carmel NY 10512

CAPOZZI, LISABETH EAMES, human resources specialist; b. Balt., July 23, 1960; d. Robert Frederick and Patricia Ann (Stern) Eames; m. Louis J. Capozzi Jr., July 28, 1990. BA cum laude, Bucknell U., 1982; postgrad., Villanova U., 1984. Asst. v.p. human resources Chem. Banking Corp., East Brunswick, N.J., 1986-91; human resources quality mgr. AMP Inc., Harrisburg, Pa., 1992—. Vol. Children's Playroom, Harrisburg, 1992—. Mem. Nat. Soc. Human Resource Mgmt. (pres. Capital area chpt. 1993—), Jr. League Harrisburg (chair cmty. rsch. 1993—).

CAPOZZOLI-HADLAND, VALENTINA C., health care management consultant; b. N.Y.C., Mar. 9, 1957; d. Louis Gerald and Olympia (DiBona) Capozzoli; m. David P. Hadland, Mar. 10, 1989. Student, Randolph-Macon Women's Coll., 1975-76, Hofstra U., 1976-77; ADN, Coll. Misericordia, Bronx, N.Y., 1979; BSN, U. Parma, Italy, 1980. RN, N.Y.; cert. ALS Am. Heart Assn. Staff nurse Cen. Suffolk Hosp., Riverhead, N.Y., 1979-80, Hosp. for Spl. Surgery, N.Y.C., 1981-82; freelance nurse Greater N.Y. Nursing Svc., N.Y.C., 1982-84; adminstr. Best Care, Garden City, N.Y., 1984-86; dir. Alternative Care Systems, Inc., N.Y.C., 1986-87; dir. of nursing Unity Healthcare Holding Co., N.Y.C., 1987-89, v.p. ops., 1989-90; pres. V.C.H. Cons., Inc., West Islip, N.Y., 1990—; cons. Animal Hosp. East Islip, 1988—, Lymphedema Svcs., N.Y.C., 1989-90, Animal Assocs., Safety Harbor, Fla., 1989—, Fin. Med. Group, Nesconset, N.Y., 1990—. Author treatment of lithisis in cats, 1991. Mem. ANA, NAFE, Nat. League Nursing, Am. Assn. Permanent Color Technicians, N.Y. State Assn. Registered Profl. Nurses. Republican. Home: 75 Beatrice Ave West Islip NY 11795 Office: VCH Cons Inc 75 Beatrice Ave West Islip NY 11795

CAPPELLA, ELENA A., lawyer, legal association administrator; b. Bklyn., June 17, 1947; d. Damian F. Galbo and Helen A. (Zammataro) Galbo DiNapoli; m. Joseph N. Cappella, 1970; children: Jeffrey, Elise. AB in Math. magna cum laude, LeMoyne Coll., 1969; MA in Comm., Mich. State U., 1974; JD magna cum laude, U. Wis., 1979. Bar: Wis. 1979, Pa. 1992. Law clk. to Hon. Alfred T. Goodwin U.S. Ct. Appeals (9th cir.), 1979-80; lectr. Law Sch. and Women Studies Program U. Wis., Madison, 1980-81; asst. state pub. defender State of Wis., 1981-84; exec. dir. Wis. Jud. Commn., 1984-90; dep. to exec. v.p. Am. Law Inst., Phila., 1990-92, dep. dir., 1993—; speaker on jud. ethics and discipline; program chairperson Legal Assn. Women, Madison, 1983-90; mem. comm. com. State Bar Wis., 1987-89. Mem. task force on women and criminal justice sys. Wis. Women's Network, 1982-86, chairperson, 1983-84; mem. adv. com. Ctr. for Jud. Conduct Orgns., Am. Judicature Soc., 1985-86, chairperson, 1986; lawyer-coach mock trial tournament area H.S; bd. dirs. Madison chpt. NOW, 1974, chpt. coord., 1975-76. Mem. Am. Law Inst., Order of Coif. Office: Am Law Inst 4025 Chestnut St Philadelphia PA 19104-3054

CAPPELLO, EVE, business educator, writer, international business consultant; b. Sydney, Australia; d. Nem and Ethel Shapira; children: Frances Soskins, Alan Kazdin. AA, Santa Monica City Coll., 1972; BA, Calif. State U.-Dominguez Hills, 1974; MA, Pacific Western U., 1977, PhD, 1978. Singer, pianist, L.A., 1956-76; profl. devel., mgmt./staff tng., 1976-85; instr. Calif. State U. Extension, Dominguez Hills, 1977-90; counselor Associated Tech. Coll., L.A., 1994—. instr. Mt. St. Mary's Coll., U. of Judaism, U. So. Calif., Loyola Marymount U.; founder, pres. A-C-T Internat.; invited speaker World Congress Behavior Therapy, Israel, Melbourne U., Australia. Mem. Internat. Platform Assn., Book Publicists So. Calif., Profl. Women Toastmasters, Zonta Internat., Alpha Gamma. Author: Let's Get Growing, 1979, The New Professional Touch, 1988, 2d edit., 1988, Dr. Eve's Garden, 1984, Act, Don't React, 1985, 3d edit., 1988, The Game of the Name, 1985, The Perfectionist Syndrome, 1990, Why Aren't More Women Running The Show?, 1994; newspaper columnist, 1976—; contbr. articles to profl. jours. Home: 10600 Eastborne Ave Apt 16 Los Angeles CA 90024-5971 Office: PO Box 25544 Los Angeles CA 90025-0544

CAPPETTA, ANNA MARIA, art educator; b. New Haven, Feb. 14, 1949; d. Alfonso M. and Elvira (Bove) Cavaliere; m. Vincent John Cappetta, July 17, 1971. BS in Art Edn., So. Conn. State U., 1971, MS in Spl. Edn., 1973, MS in Supervision/Adminstrn., 1980, MS in Art Edn., 1981. Sub. tchr. West Haven (Conn.) Sch. System, 1971; art educator/coord. North Haven (Conn.) Sch. System, 1971—; adj. prof. art So. Conn. State U., New Haven, 1984-92; cons. Area Coop. Ednl. Svcs., Conn., 1987—. Co-author: (mag.) Art Education, 1990, School Arts, 1986—, Impace II Experienced Teachers Handbook, 1992; contbg. editor School Arts mag., 1991—. Recipient North Haven Tchr. of Yr. award, 1986, Conn. Celebration of Excellence award, 1987, 90, 92, Nat. Art Educator award, 1988, 89, Conn. Art Educator award, 1989, North Haven Tchr. of Yr. award, 1989. Fellow Nat. Coun. Basic Edn.; mem. Nat. Art Edn. Assn. (nat. elem. dir. 1991-95, Nat. Art Educator award 1988, 89, advisory 1994, Briefing Paper Series 1993), Conn. Art Edn. Assn. (Conn. Art Educator award 1989), Nat. Women's Art Caucus, Phi Delta Kappa (co-editor newsletter 1987-89), Delta Kappa Gamma. Home: PO Box 1399 19 Johnson Ln Madison CT 06443

CAPPIELLO, ANGELA, conference and meeting planner; b. New Hyde Park, N.Y., July 6, 1954; d. Augustine and Angela (Tamburello) C. Cert. meeting and conv. mgmt., NYU, 1988, cert. assn. mgmt., 1989, cert. food and beverage mgmt., 1989, cert. travel mgmt., 1990, cert. hotel and motel mgmt., 1991; cert. in fin. controls, NYU, 1992. Cert. meeting profl. Mgr. meetings and convs. N.Y. Libr. Assn., N.Y.C., 1987-89; conf. coord. ASCE, N.Y.C., 1989; mgr. meetings and confs. Coun. Cons. Orgns., N.Y.C., 1990-91; asst. to pres. Goodstein Devel. Corp., N.Y.C., 1991-93; asst. meetings mgr. Nat. Episcopal Ch., N.Y.C., 1993—. Mem. NAFE, Am. Soc. Assn. Execs., Meeting Planners Internat. (bd. dirs. N.Y. chpt. 1991-93), N.Y. Soc. Assn. Execs., Profl. Conf. Mgrs. Assn., Internat. Soc. Meeting Planners, Religious Conf. Mgrs. Assn., Nat. Assn. for Advancement Fat Acceptance (bd. dirs. 1983-86). Home: 36 New Hyde Park Rd New Hyde Park NY 11040-4935 Office: Nat Episcopal Church 815 2nd Ave New York NY 10017-4503

CAPPS, PATRICIA, communications and psychology educator, counselor; b. Greenville, Miss., Dec. 21, 1951; d. John A. and Mary Frances (Baker) C. BA, U. West Fla., 1972; MS, Ind. U., 1975. Exec. asst. Gov's. Office/Bus. Assistance, Tallahassee, Fla., 1980-81; legis. officer St. Petersburg Jr. Coll., Clearwater, Fla., 1981-82, instr., program coord. Bus. Adminstrn., 1982-85; exec. dir. Bay Area Consortium for Bus. and Higher Edn., Clearwater, 1985-86; asst. prof., dir. entrepreneurship program St. Petersburg Jr. Coll., 1986-89, assoc. prof., counselor, 1989—. Appointee Gov.'s Commn. on Status of Women, Tallahassee, 1978-80; bd. dirs. Mental Health Assn. Pinellas County, St. Petersburg, 1985-86; active Nat. Conf./Citizen Involvement, L.A., 1985; cons. trainer Woman to Woman alcohol awareness program Assn. Jr. Leagues Internat., 1987-90; community v.p. Jr. League Clearwater-Dunedin, 1991-92. Mem. Internat. Assn. of Bus. Communicators. Democrat. Office: St Petersburg Jr Coll 2465 Drew St Clearwater FL 34625-2898

CAPPUCCIO, NANCY ELLEN, management consultant; b. Salem, Mass., July 18, 1962; d. John S. and Bertha L. (Masse) C. BS in Fin., Bentley Coll., 1984; MBA, Babson Coll., 1992. Fin. analyst Bolt Beranek and Newman Inc., Cambridge, Mass., 1985-89; contr. Marsoft Inc., Cambridge, Mass., 1989-91; cons. KPMG Peat Marwick, Boston, 1992—. Recipient Presdl. scholarship Bentley Coll., 1983. Mem. Coll. Club, Beta Gamma Sigma.

CAPRONI, KATHLEEN JEAN, psychologist; b. Lynn, Mass., Oct. 14, 1966; d. Albert J. and Karin L. (Anderson) C. BA summa cum laude, Brandeis U., 1988; PhD, SUNY, Buffalo, 1993. Lic. psychologist, N.Y. Tchr. Lemberg Children's Ctr./Brandeis, Waltham, Mass., 1985-88, head tchr., 1988 summer; rsch. asst. Brandeis U., Waltham, 1986-88, SUNY, Buffalo, 1988-90; rsch. asst. Rsch. Inst. on the Addiction, Buffalo, 1990-91, group therapist, 1991-93; therapist Jewish Family Svcs., Buffalo, 1992-93; psychology intern Ulster County Mental Health, Kingston, N.Y., 1993, resident in psychology, 1994-95; psychologist, 1995—; adj. instr. Marist Coll., Poughkeepsie, N.Y., 1994—; cons. Windsor Counseling, New Windsor, N.Y., 1993—. Vol., caregiver support group leader Amherst (N.Y.) Sr. Ctr., 1990-92; cons. Girl Scouts Am., Buffalo, 1991-92. Mem. NOW, Am. Psychol. Assn., Phi Beta Kappa. Office: Ulster County Mental Health PO Box 1800 Golden Hill Dr Kingston NY 12401-0800

CAPSOURAS, BARBARA ELLEN, college official; b. Niagara Falls, N.Y., Nov. 10, 1951; d. Joseph John and Wanda M. (Szczepanska) Horvath; m. John David Capsouras, Nov. 20, 1981; children: Cristina, Alexi. Student, Trenton State Coll., 1969-70; AA in Bus. Adminstrn. with high honors, County Coll. of Morris, 1982; postgrad., Fairleigh Dickinson U., 1983-84. Cert. family day care provider, N.J. Adminstrv. asst. tech. ops. Warner-Lambert Co., Morris Plains, N.J., 1970-79, adminstrv. asst. internat. mfg., 1979-80, adminstrv. asst. internat. mktg., 1980-83, pub. affairs coord., 1983-89; dir. alumni rels. County Coll. Morris, Randolph, N.J., 1990—, bd. dirs., mem. adv. bd. Child Care Ctr., 1990-93. Mem. AAUW, N.J. Consortium Alumni Profls., County Coll. of Morris Alumni Assn. (adv. bd. 1990—, mgr. campaign steering com. 1990—), High Life Ski Club (officer 1972—, mem. race team, recipient various tennis and skiing awards). Office: County Coll Morris 214 Center Grove Rd Randolph NJ 07869-2086

CAPSTICK, WENDY KEY, accountant; b. Atlanta, Nov. 9, 1964; d. Woodrow Earl and Janie Belle (Shepherd) Key; m. Lincoln S. Capstick III, July 5, 1994. BBA in Acctg., Ga. So. Coll., 1987. CPA, Ga., Alaska. Audit staff Price Waterhouse, Savannah, Ga., 1987-90; audit sr. Price Waterhouse, Anchorage, Alaska, 1990-93; audit mgr. Price Waterhouse, Atlanta, 1993—. Mem. AICPAs, Ga. Soc. CPAs, Inst. Mgmt. Accts. Office: Price Waterhouse 50 Hurt Plz Ste 1700 Atlanta GA 30303

CAPUTO, ANNE SPENCER, academic program director; b. Eugene, Oreg., Jan. 14, 1947; d. Richard J. and Adelaide Bernice (Marsh) Spencer; m. Richard Philip Caputo, July 15, 1977; 1 child, Christopher Spencer Caputo. BA in History, Lewis and Clark Coll., Portland, Oreg., 1969; MA, U. Oreg., 1971; MALS, San Jose State U., 1976. Librarian San Jose State U., Calif., 1972-76; online instr. DIALOG Info. Services, Palo Alto, Calif., 1976-77, chief info. scientist, Washington, 1977-85, mgr. classroom instrn. program, 1986-89, dir. acad. programs, 1990—; asst. prof. info. sci. Catholic U. Am., Washington, 1978—; online cons. Nat. Com. Library-Info. Sci., Washington, 1980-82; bd. dirs. ASK!, Washington, 1981—. Author: Brief Guide to DIALOG Searching, 1979. Contbr. articles to profl. jours. Named Info. Sci. Tchr. of Yr., Catholic U. Am., 1983. Mem. Am. Soc. for Info. Sci. (officer, chair Potomac Valley chpt. 1985-86), ALA, Spl. Library Assn., D.C. Library Assn., Am. Assn. Sch. Librarians. Episcopalian. Avocation: photographing architectural details on National Trust buildings. Home: 4113 Orleans Pl Arlington VA 22304 Office: Knight-Ridder Info Inc 1525 Wilson Blvd # 640 Arlington VA 22209-1760

CAPUTO, JANETTE SUSAN, clinical neuropsychologist, educator; b. Detroit, Nov. 16, 1946; d. Anthony John and Sarah Rose (Mancuso) C.; m. Thomas Aloysius Closurdo, Oct. 29, 1971 (div. Jan. 1981); m. Kenneth Joseph Bruza, Aug. 4, 1981. BA, Wayne State U., 1968, MLS, 1969, PhD, 1976; MA, Ctrl. Mich. U., 1985, D in Psychology, 1989. Dir. librs. St. Joseph Mercy Hosp., Pontiac, Mich., 1971-77; libr., head. sci. libr. Wayne State U., Detroit, 1977-81; dir. Saginaw Health Sci. Libr. Saginaw (Mich.) Coop Hosps., 1981-83; contract psychologist Midland (Mich.) Mental Health, 1985, Dow Chem. Co., Midland, 1985-87; predoctoral fellow Rusk Inst. Rehab. Medicine, N.Y.C., 1987-88; clin. neuropsychologist Mid. Mich. Regional Med. Ctr., Midland, 1988-90; staff neuropsychologist Mary Free Bed Hosp., Grand Rapids, Mich., 1990-91; pres. Rehab. Strategies, P.C., Alma, Mich., 1991—. Author: The Assertive Librarian, 1984, Stress and Burnout in Library Service, 1990; contbr. articles to profl. jours. Mem. APA, Am. Viola Soc., Am. Congress Rehab. Medicine, Nat. Acad. Neuropsychology, Internat. Neuropsychology Soc., Rotary (Alma-St. Louis). Home: 5651 N Luce Rd Alma MI 48801 Office: Rehab Strategies PC 255 Warwick Alma MI 48801

CAPUTO, KATHRYN MARY, paralegal; b. Bklyn., June 29, 1948; d. Fortunato and Agnes (Iovino) Villacci; m. Joseph John Caputo, Apr. 4, 1976. AS in Bus. Adminstrn., Nassau Community Coll., Garden City, N.Y., 1989. Legal asst. Jacob Jacobson, Oceanside, N.Y., 1973-77; legal asst., office mgr. Joseph Kaldor, P.C., Franklin Square, N.Y., 1978-82, William H. George, Valley Stream, N.Y., 1983-89; exec. legal asst., office adminstr. Katz & Bernstein, Westbury, N.Y., 1990-93; sr. paralegal and office adminstr. Blaustein & Weinick, Garden City, N.Y., 1993—; instr. adult continuing edn. Lawrence (N.Y.) High Sch., legal sec. procedures, 1992—. Spl. events coord. Bklyn.-Queens (N.Y.) Marriage Encounter, 1981, 82, 83, 85, 86. Mem. NAFE, L.I. Paralegal Assn. Office: Blaustein & Weinick 1205 Franklin Ave Garden City NY 11530-1629

CAPUTO, LISA M., White House staff member; b. Wilkes-Barre, Pa.; d. A. Richard and Rosemary (Shea) C. BA in French and Polit. Sci. magna cum laude, Brown U., 1986; MS in Journalism with highest honors, Northwestern U., 1987. Press sec., fed. grants coord. U.S. Rep. Bob Traxler, Washington, 1987-89; press sec. nat. issues Dukakis-Bentsen Campaign, Boston, 1988; press sec. U.S. Senator Tim Wirth, Washington, 1989-92; dir. vice presdl. media ops. Dem. Nat. Conv., N.Y.C., 1992; press sec. to Hillary Rodham Clinton Clinton-Gore Campaign and Presdl. Transition, Little Rock, 1992; dep. asst. to Pres., press sec. to First Lady The White House, Washington, 1993—. Office: Office of the First Lady 1600 Pennsylvania Ave NW Washington DC 20500

CARABILLO, VIRGINIA ANNE (TONI CARABILLO), writer, editor, graphic designer; b. Bklyn., Mar. 26, 1926; d. Anthony S. and Anne Virginia (Woods) C. AB cum laude, Middlebury Coll., 1948; MA, Columbia U., 1949; postgrad., UCLA, 1960-61. Dir. pub. relations Vassar Coll., Poughkeepsie, N.Y., 1949-51; pub. relations and publs. editor Daystrom Electric Corp, 1952-54, Daystrom Western Indsl. div., 1954-59; mng. editor Empire Mag., Los Angeles, 1959; adminstrv. asst. System Devel. Corp., Santa Monica, Calif., 1959-61, employee publs. editor, 1961-62, head corp. publs. office, 1962-66, asst. mgr. corp. communications, 1966-70, head corp. publs., 1966-68, head graphic design, 1968-70, editorial cons., 1964-70; pres. Graphic Communications Cons., Los Angeles, 1971—; editor Nat. NOW Times, Washington and Los Angeles, 1977-85; assoc. editor Eleanor Smeal Report, Washington and Los Angeles, 1985-91. Author: Poetry of Personhood, 1971, (with Eleanor Smeal) Why and How Women Will Elect the Next President, 1984, (with Judith Meuli) A Passion For The Possible, 1985, The Feminization of Power, 1988, A Guide to the Videotape, Abortion: For Survival, 1989 (with Meuli and June Bundy Csida) The Feminist Chronicles, 1953-1993, 1993; contbr. articles to profl. jours; designer, writer almanac, calendar; exec. producer: (videotape) Abortion: For Survival, 1989; co-producer, writer: (videotape) Abortion Denied: Shattering Young Women's Lives, 1990. Founding mem. Calif. chpt. NOW, 1966, pres. L.A. chpt., 1968-70, 80-82, v.p. L.A. chpt., 1988—, nat. bd. dirs. 1968-77, nat. v.p., 1971-74, chmn. Nat. Adv. Com., 1975-77; dir. Nat. ERA Countdown Campaign Office, L.A., 1982; del. Dem. Conv., 1984; v.p. The Fund for the Feminist Majority, 1987—. Recipient multiple awards Internat. Indsl. Editors Assn., 1960-70 Leadership awards NOW, 1982, 94. Mem. Feminist Found. (v.p.). Democrat. Roman Catholic. Home: 1126 Hi Point St Los Angeles CA 90035-2610 Office: Graphic Communications Cons 1126 Hi Point St Los Angeles CA 90035-2610

CARACCI, LISA CHRISTINE, clinical psychologist; b. Chgo., Mar. 9, 1964; d. Michael C. and Barbara Mary (Angelini) C. BA, San Diego State U., 1987; postgrad. in Psychology, Forest Inst. Profl. Psychology, Wheeling, Ill., 1988—. Mental health counselor Luth. Gen. Hosp., Park Ridge, Ill., 1990-93; intern St. Therese Med. Ctr., Waukegan, Ill., 1992-93; psychometrist J.D. & Assocs., South Holland, Ill., 1993—. Mem. APA, Ill. Psychol. Assn., Mental Health Assn. Ill., Chgo. Psychoanalytic Soc., Am. Civil Liberties Union. Democrat. Roman Catholic. Home: 17w115 White Pine Rd Chicago IL 60106-2868

CARADJA, PRINCESS CATHERINE, speaker to veterans organizations; b. Romania, 1893; came to U.S. 1955; d. Prince Kretulesco and Princess Cantacuzene; m. Prince Caradja, 1914; children. Proprietor hosp. for typhus cases, Romania, 1916-19, St. Catherine's Crib found. for orphan children, Romania, 1919-49; speaker on life behind Iron Curtain and the value of freedom France, England, Algeria, Morocco, Canada, U.S., 1952—; speaker variuos POW and vet. groups. Recipient Freedom award of the Order of Lafayette, 1966, award Valley Forge Freedom Found., 1977. Home and Office: care Armour Home PO Box 564 Comfort TX 78013-0564

CARAHER, EVA MARIA, counselor, educator; b. Pasadena, Calif., July 25, 1964; d. James Michael and Anna Elizabeth (Hubrich) C.; m. Renato Patrick Almanzor, Jr., Apr. 6, 1991. BA in French, San Diego U., 1985, MS in Counseling, 1990. Instr. ESL various pvt. and pub. orgns., Tapei, Taiwan, 1987—; human rels. trainer, cons., ptnr. Empower Perspectives, Berkeley, Calif., 1989—; coord., advisor, instr. liberal studies program Patten Coll., Oakland, Calif., 1993-94; ESL instr. Patten Coll., Oakland, 1993-94; tchr. cons. Spectrum, Berkeley, Calif., 1994—; facilitator, camp counseling coord. Nat. Conf., L.A., 1989—; chair Task Force on Diversity, Patten Coll., 1993-94; vol. Berkeley showing NAMES project, 1993. Mem. ACA, Assn. for Multicultural Counseling and Devel., Third World Counselors Assn. Office: Empower Perspectives PO Box 14925 Berkeley CA 94701-5925

CARAMELLO, JANET ENDRES, travel company executive; b. Naples, Fla., Sept. 27, 1966; d. Wallace Hurst and Rakel Hilda (Taavitsainen) E.; m. James Caramello, Feb. 16, 1992. AA, U. Fla., 1986, 1986; BS, U. Fla., 1988. Mktg. dir. SunCoast Travel, Naples, 1982-84; soft lines mgr. Wal-Mart, Cape Coral, Fla., 1988-89; pres. Travel Connection, Naples, 1989—; bd. dirs. Mad Mushroom Pizza, Bloomington, Ind., Wallace Constrn., Inc., Naples; cons. Gumby's Pizza, Raleigh, N.C., 1988-92. Editor: (newsletter) Travel Times, 1989-92. Mem. AAUW (bd. dirs. 1991-92, grad. chmn. 1989-92), NAFE, Profl. Organized for Leadership Opportunity (social com. 1988-92), S.W. Travel Internat. Assn., Naples Panhellenic Assn., Naples C. of C. (membership com. 1989-91), Kappa Alpha Theta. Home: 4595 25th Ct SW Naples FL 33999-7815

CARASIG-MANALO, JUDY, mechanical engineer; b. Manila, Philippines, Nov. 2, 1966; came to U.S., 1974; d. Edgardo DeJesus and Sonia Aurora (Gonzalvo) Carasig; m. Antonio Tagle Manalo, Oct. 6, 1990; 1 child, Julianne Aurora. BSME, Stony Brook (N.Y.) U., 1988; MSME, Stevens Inst. Tech., 1990. Intern engr. Grumman Space Systems, Bethpage, N.Y., 1987; rsch. asst. Stony Brook (N.Y.) U., 1987-88; mech. engr. ARDEC, Picatinny Arsenal, N.J., 1988-89; project engr. ARDEC, Picatinny Arsenal, 1989-91, program mgmt. engr., 1991—; facilitator Total Quality Mgmt. Office, ARDEC, 1990-91, chairperson Asian-Pacific Employee Program Com., 1991-93. project engr.: (prodn. and design) Desert Storm Mortar, 1990-91 (Appreciation award 1992). Fellow Tau Beta Pi. Roman Catholic. Home: 70 Rustic Ave Medford NY 11763-4446 Office: Ardec Smcar Eg Picatinny Arsenal NJ 07806

CARBONELLO, KAREN DELSPINA, administrator, consultant, educator; b. Orange, N.J., Sept. 16, 1956; d. Anthony C. and Frances A. (De Rosa) DelSpina; m. Gary Allen Carbonello, Dec. 10, 1978; children: Justin, Lyndsey. BA in Sociology, Seton Hall U., 1977; MA in Sociology, Fordham U., 1984. Dir. criminal justice planning County of Morris, Morristown, N.J., 1978-82, asst. trial ct. adminstr., 1982-88; prof. sociology Caldwell (N.J.) Coll., 1984-85, Seton Hall U., South Orange, N.J., 1986-88, 92—, Fairleigh Dickinson U., Madison, N.J, 1988; exec. adminstrv. asst. to dep. dir. N.J. Adminstrv. Office of the Cts., Trenton, 1988-91; mem. Supreme Ct. com. minority affairs, Morris County Mental Health adv. bd. Past trustee Jersey Battered Women Svcs., Morristown; past mem. social detoxification adv. bd. St. Clare's Hosp., Denville, N.J.; mem. adv. com. N.J. Judiciary EEO/AA, 1988-91. Recipient Resolution award Morris County Bd. Freeholders, 1988. Fellow Inst. for Ct. Mgmt.; mem. Nat. Assn. Ct. Mgrs., Am. Sociol. Assn., Children's Def. Fund, N.J. Assn. for Children. Republican. Roman Catholic.

CARD, ELIZABETH STROBEL, import company executive, journalist; b. N.Y.C., Apr. 12, 1932; d. Josef Alois and Bertje (Slieker) Strobel; m. J.S. Schoenfeld, June 5, 1952 (div. Nov. 21, 1989); children: Jamie Elizabeth Schoenfeld Naylor, Marilee Elizabeth Schoenfeld Nickelson; m. William C. Card, Mar. 1, 1991. BS in Journalism, U. Utah, 1953, postgrad. Reporter Deseret News, Salt Lake City, 1971-85; freelance journalist Netherlands, Czechoslovakia, U.S.A., Wales, 1985-91; v.p. Archtl. Specialities, Salt Lake City, 1992—; pres., founder Czech Crystal by Eliska, Salt Lake City, 1994—; lectr. numerous orgns. in field of glass cutting and genealogy. Author 7 books for LDS readers; author: Blood of My Blood-The Czech Glassmakers, 1994, New York, Birthplace of Utah (History of Mormon Church 1830-1950), 1994 (Utah Arts Coun. award). Chmn. Class of '53, U. Utah, 1993-94; vol. Czech Mormon Ch., Czech Republic, 1980—. Recipient award Utah Bicentennial Commn., 1976, award Utah Heritage Found., 1980, Utah Hist. Soc., 1981, Czech Freedom Revolution Moravian and Bohemian Univs., 1990. Home: 2927 Millicent Dr Salt Lake City UT 84108-2019

CARDELLINO, DONNA, personal manager; b. Phila., June 8, 1958; d. William John and Helen Marie (Kelly) C. Student in rec. arts and scis.,

UCLA. Fin. control mgr., pub. rels. div. L.A. Olympic Organizing Com., Westwood, Calif., 1980-84; freelancer various entertainment cos., 1984-85; agt., co-owner Pegasus Entertainment, West Hollywood, Calif., 1985-86, 87—; pers. mgr. D.C. Mgmt. Co., Hollywood, Calif., 1986—. Vol. Muscular Dystrophy Assn., Richstone Child Abuse Ctr. Roman Catholic. Office: DC Mgmt Co 7095 Hollywood Blvd Ste 504 Los Angeles CA 90028-8903

CARDEN, JOY CABBAGE, educational consultant; b. Livermore, Ky., Dec. 15, 1932; d. Henry L. and Lillie (Richardson) Cabbage; m. Donald G. Carden, Dec. 19, 1954; children: Lynn Kehlenbeck, Tom Carden, Bob Carden, Jan Blount, Jim Carden. BA, Ky. Wesleyan, 1955; MA, U. Ky., 1975. Instr. music Owensboro (Ky.) City Schs., 1955-57; founder, dir. Musical Arts Ctr., Lexington, Ky., 1980-88; edn. specialist Roland Corp., L.A., 1989, dir. edn., 1990-94, edn. cons., 1994—. Author: Music in Lexington Before 1840, 1980, Guide to Electronic Keyboards, 1988; composer ensembles for electronic keyboards. Mem. Music Tchrs Nat. Assn. (commd. composer 1987), Nat. Guild Piano Tchrs. (state chmn. 1980-88), Nat. Conf. Piano Pedagogy (com. chmn. 1990), Ky. Music Tchrs. Assn. (state chmn. 1980-88), Music Tchrs. Calif. Home and Office: 112 La Fontenay Ct Louisville KY 40223-3020

CARDENAS, DIANA DELIA, physician, educator; b. San Antonio, Tex., Apr. 10, 1947; d. Ralph Roman and Rosa (Garza) C.; m. Thomas McKenzie Hooton, Aug. 20, 1971; children: Angela, Jessica. BA with highest honors, U. Tex., 1969; MD, U. Tex., Dallas, 1973; MS, U. Wash., 1976. Diplomate Nat. Bd. Med. Examiners, Am. Bd. Phys. Medicine & Rehab., Am. Bd. Electrodiagnostic Medicine. Asst. prof. dept. rehab. medicine Emory U., Atlanta, 1976-81; instr. dept. rehab. medicine U. Wash., Seattle, 1981-82, asst. prof. dept. rehab. medicine, 1982-86, assoc. prof. dept. rehab. medicine, 1986-92, prof. rehab. medicine, 1992—; med. dir. rehab. medicine clinic U. Wash. Med. Ctr., Seattle, 1982; project dir. N.W. Regional Spinal Cord Injury System, Seattle, 1990—. Editor: Rehabilitation & The Chronic Renal Disease Patient, 1985, Maximizing Rehabilitation in Chronic Renal Disease, 1989; contbr. articles to profl. jours. Co-chairperson Lakeside Sch. Auction Student Vols., Seattle, 1991; bd. dirs. CONSEJO Counseling & Referral Svc., 1994. Mem. Am. Spinal Injury Assn. (chairperson rsch. com. 1991), Am. Acad. Phys. Medicine and Rehab., Am. Congress of Rehab. Medicine (chairperson rehab. practice com. 1980-84, Ann. Essay Contest winner 1976), Am. Assn. Electrodiagnostic Medicine. Office: Univ Wash RJ-30 Dept Rehab Medicine 1959 NE Pacific St Seattle WA 98195-0004

CARDENAS, LETICIA HELENA, speech pathologist, special education educator; b. San Antonio, Apr. 22, 1958; d. Andy Cardenas and Rose (Villarreal) Penaloza; m. Ramiro A. Sanchez, July 12, 1983 (div. May 1989). BA, Our Lady of the Lake U., San Antonio, 1980; postgrad., Oud Lady of the Lake U., San Antonio, 1993—. Speech pathologist San Antonio Ind. Sch. Dist., 1980-82, autism tchr., 1982-90, autism tchr. cons., autism evaluator, 1990—. Named Tchr. of Yr. Trinity U., San Antonio, 1988; recipient Tchr. award Mental Health Assn., San Antonio, 1988. Mem. Coun. Exceptional Children, Nat. Soc. Autistic Children, Tex. Speech and Hearing Assn. Home: 415 Tophill Rd San Antonio TX 78209-3447 Office: San Antonio Ind Sch Dist 1811 S Laredo St San Antonio TX 78207-7019

CARDENAS, LYNDA LEIGH, pediatrics nurse; b. Van Nuys, Calif., Apr. 17, 1959; d. Jack Thomas and June Lee (Smith) Strayer; m. Ramon A. Cardenas, Jan. 21, 1988 (div. 1991). Diploma in med. assisting, Western Tech. Coll., 1983; lic. vocat. nurse, Simi Valley Adult Edn., 1991. LVN, Calif. Med. asst. La Serena Retirement Village, Thousand Oaks, Calif., 1982-84, Registry/Pvt. Geriatrics, Simi Valley, Calif., 1984-88; nurse, staff coord. Valley Children's Home, Inc., Simi Valley, 1988—. Office: Valley Childrens Home Inc 3224 E Wilmot St Simi Valley CA 93063

CARDIN, SUZETTE, nurse manager; b. Attleboro, Mass., Feb. 4, 1950; d. Wilfred W. and Vera E. (Broadbent) C.; m. Edward R. Barden, May 10, 1986; children: Luke Edward, Helen Elizabeth. Diploma, Children's Hosp. Sch. Nursing, Boston, 1970; BSN, Southeastern Mass. U., 1974; MS, U. Md., 1978; postgrad., UCLA, 1990—. RN, Calif. Nursing instr. Fall River (Mass.) Diploma Sch. Nursing, 1974-76; staff nurse SICU Johns Hopkins Hosp., Balt., 1977-78; dir. critical care nursing Med. Ctr. Hosp. Vt., Burlington, 1978-83; nurse mgr. UCLA Med. Ctr., 1984—; editorial cons. Dimensions of Critical Care Nursing, 1989—, Clin. Issues in Critical Care Nursing, 1989-92, Am. Orgn. Nurse Execs. Leadership Prospectives, 1993—. Co-editor: Personnel Management in Critical Care Nursing, 1989, Critical Care Nursing, 1992. Recipient award Profl. Businesswomen, 1973, award Maxicare Ednl. & Rsch. Found, 1993, Nurse Mgr. Leadership Excellence award Am. Orgn. Nurse Execs., 1994. Mem. AACN (chair various coms., co-editor CCRN newsletter 1985-86, mem. cert. com. 1984-85, liaison AANN cert. bd. 1986-88, pres. Vt. chpt. 1979-81, mem. program com. 1987-88, NTI com. 1987-88, L.A.-AACN scholar, 1992), Am. Heart Assn., Children's Hosp. Alumnae Assn. (scholarship, 1992), Sigma Theta Tau (co-editor newsletter Gamma Tau chpt. 1987-89). Home: 2102 Farrell Ave Redondo Beach CA 90278-1819

CARDINA, CLAIRE ARMSTRONG, archivist, records manager; b. Montclair, N.J., June 13, 1931; d. Cole Alexander and Florence Maida (Brown) Armstrong; m. William John Johnson, June 9, 1951 (div. 1980); children: James Benjamin, Glenn Alexander; m. Daniel John Cardina, Oct. 5, 1985. BA, Gettysburg Coll., 1951; MLS, Rutgers U., 1970. Cert. archivist, records mgr. Svc. rep. C&P Telephone Co., Hyattsville, Md., 1951-54, N.J. Bell Telephone Co., East Orange, 1954-56; coorespondent AT&T, N.Y.C., 1956-60; librarian Madison Jr. Sch., Madison, N.J., 1970-72; media specialist Miles Elem. Sch., Tampa, Fla., 1972-82; records Mgr. City of Tampa, 1982-87, archivist, records mgr., 1987—; adj. prof. Hillsborough C.C., Tampa, 1984—, mem. office sys. tech. adv. com., 1986-91; adj. prof. U. South Fla. Schy. Libr. & Info. Sci., Tampa, 1992-93; mem. Fla. Hist. Records Adv. Bd., Tallahassee, 1983-86. Author records management manuals, leaflets for govtl. and profl. orgns. Bd. dirs., pres. Friends of Tampa/Hillsborough County Pub. Libr., Tampa, 1978—; mem. Pres.'s Round Table Orgns. Greater Tampa, 1983-84; mem. adv. com. City of Tampa Archives, 1989—; mem. adv. coun. Tampa Bay History Ctr., 1993—; del. Tampa Sister Cities Com., 1993. Mem. Assn. Records Mgrs. and Adminstrs. (internat. conf. program com. 1987—, asst. chair 1993, chair 1994, co-chair mcpl. and county govt. industry action com. 1990-94, internat. chair micrographics subcom. 1986-88, chmn. bd. dirs. Tampa Bay chpt. 1986-87, pres. 1985-86, Mem. of the Yr. 1986, 92), Inst. Cert. Records Mgrs., Soc. Am. Archivists, Soc. Fla. Archivists (founding bd. dirs. 1988-90, 92-93, v.p. 1990-91, pres. 1991-92), Nat. Assn. Govt. Archivists and Records Adminstrs. (local govt. records com. 1986-91, mem. com. 1994—), Fla. Records Mgmt. Assn. (bd. dirs. 1993-94, pres. 1994—), Assn. for Info. and Image Mgmt., Network Exec. Women (historian 1991—, bd. dirs. Compass Project 1991—), Acad. Cert. Archivists, Toastmasters Internat. (Able Toastmaster), Tampa Bay Rutgers Club (sec. 1990-94). Republican. Presbyterian. Office: City of Tampa 1104 E Twiggs St Tampa FL 33602-3118

CARDINAL, SHIRLEY MAE, education educator; b. Morann, Pa., May 6, 1944; d. Thomas Joseph and Mary Louise (Nemish) Giza; m. Charles Edward Cardinal, June 11, 1966; children: Julie Ann, Karen Lee. BS, Lock Haven U., 1966; MEd, Pa. State U., 1970. Tchr. Bald Eagle Nittany Corp., Mill Hall, Pa., 1966-68; tchr., supr. Pa. State U., University Park, 1968-76; tchr., chairperson State Coll. (Pa.) Area Schs., 1968-76; primetime educator Oregon-Davis Corp., Hamlet, Ind., 1984—; instr., cons. Dept. Edn., Indpls., 1979—, cons. energy edn., 1980-85, educator linker, 1981—, rep. prime time, 1987—; instr. Ancilla Coll., Donaldson, Ind., 1976—; chair for evaluation North Ctrl. Accreditation Assn., 1988-89; mem. leadership team North Ctrl. Regional Ednl. Lab., 1991-92, 93-94, 94—, Fermi Nat. Accelerator Lab., 1994—. Author: Energy Activities with Learning Skills, 1980. Chmn. publicity com. Rep. Orgn. Plymouth, Ind., 1983—; mem. Teacher Talk, Ind. Gov's. Com., 1988-89. Recipient Mankind and Edn. award U.S. Jaycees and Ind. Jaycees, 1981. Mem. Ind. State Tchr. Assn., Marshall County Reading Assn., Pa. State U. Club, Phi Delta Kappa (v.p. programs South Bend chpt. 1992-93, v.p. membership 1994-95), Pi Lambda Theta, Sigma Kappa (chmn. Parent Club), Tri Kappa. Roman Catholic. Home: 10101 Turf Ct Plymouth IN 46563-9494

CARDONA, LORRAINE MARIE, human services administrator; b. N.Y.C., Dec. 20, 1956; d. Claudio Jorge and Carmen Antoñia (Ricoy) C.; m. C. Martinez-Parente, Apr. 18, 1992. BA in Psychology, U. S.C., Spartanburg, 1984; M in Human Devel. and Learning, U. N.C., Charlotte, 1990. Program dir. Piedmont Alternate Living, Greenville, S.C., 1983-86; behavior specialist Ctr. for Human Devel., Charlotte, N.C., 1986-88; dir. client svcs. Metrolina AIDS Project, Charlotte, N.C., 1988-92; instr. Broward C.C., Ft. Lauderdale, Fla., 1993—; br. adminstr. Henderson Mental Health Ctr., Pompano Beach, Fla., 1993—; pub. speaker community edn. Metrolina AIDS Project, Charlotte, 1988-92; cons., program developer AIDS Health Adv., Seattle, 1992-93. Author: (anthology) Speaking Heart to Heart, 1992; contbr. numerous articles to profl. jours. Mem. Am. Counseling Assn., Assn. Specialists in Group Work.

CARDWELL, NANCY LEE, editor, writer; b. Norfolk, Va., Apr. 2, 1947; d. Joseph Thomas Cardwell and Martha (Bailey) Underwood. B.A. in Econs., Duke U., 1969; M.S. in Journalism, Columbia U., 1971. Copy editor Wall Street Jour., N.Y.C., 1971-73, reporter, 1973-76, editor fgn. dept. and Washington bur., 1977-80, night news editor, 1981-83, nat. news editor, 1983-87, asst. mng. editor, 1987-89; sr. editor Bus. Week mag., N.Y.C., 1989-91; editor Habitat World, Habitat for Humanity Internat., Americus, Ga., 1991-94; dir. comms. Craver, Matthews, Smith & Co., Falls Church, Va., 1994-95; freelance editor/writer, 1994—. Episcopalian. Home: 1529 N Kenilworth St Arlington VA 22205

CARDWELL, SANDRA GAYLE BAVIDO, real estate broker; b. Vinita, Okla., July 14, 1943; d. Amos Calvin Wilkins and Gretta Odell (Pool) Wilkins Kudlemyer; m. Phillip Patrick Bavido, Nov. 26, 1964 (div. Dec. 1973); 1 child, Phillip Patrick Bavido Jr.; m. Max Loyd Cardwell, Jan. 18, 1979 (div. Apr. 1992). AA, Tulsa Jr. Coll., 1973; BS cum laude, U. Tulsa, 1975. Sec. with various cos., 1966-69; sec. U.S. Dept. Fgn. Langs., West Point, N.Y., 1969-70; dep. ct. clk. civil div. Tulsa County Dist. Ct., Tulsa, 1975-76, dep. ct. clk. U.S. Passport Office, 1976-77; broker-assoc. Gordona Duca, Inc., Realtors, Tulsa, 1977—. Mem. Polit. Action Com., Tulsa, 1980—; vol. in children's rights and child abuse legis. and statutes. Mem. AAUW, Tulsa Met. Bd. Realtors, Okla. Bd. Realtors, Tulsa Christian Women's Club (contact advisor 1988-89), Stonecroft Ministries (life publs. 1987-88), United Meth. Women (bd. dirs. 1986-87), Phi Theta Kappa (pres.), Pi Sigma Alpha (treas. 1974). Republican. Methodist. Home: RR 4 Box 253-1 Vinita OK 74301-9585 Office: Gordona Duca Inc Realtors 7103 S Yale Ave Tulsa OK 74136-6308

CAREY, ERNESTINE GILBRETH (MRS. CHARLES E. CAREY), writer, lecturer; b. N.Y.C., Apr. 5, 1908; d. Frank Bunker and Lillian (Moller) Gilbreth; m. Charles Everett Carey, Sept. 13, 1930; children: Lillian Carey Barley, Charles Everett. B.A., Smith Coll., 1929. Buyer R. H. Macy & Co., N.Y.C., 1930-44, James McCreery, N.Y.C., 1947-49; Carey writer and lectr. Book reviewer, 1949—, syndicated newspaper articles, 1951, (with Lillian Moller Gilbreth) (McElligott medallion Assn. Marquette U. Women 1966); author: Jumping Jupiter, 1952, Rings Around Us, 1956, Giddy Moment, 1958, (with Frank B. Gilbreth, Jr.) Cheaper by the Dozen, 1949 (Prix Scarron French Internat. Humor award 1951, over 50 translations), Belles on Their Toes, 1951; contbg. author: Smith Voices—Selected Works by Smith College Women, 1990; lifetime papers represented in collections at Smith Coll.; also mag. articles and book revs. Bd. dirs. Right to Read, Inc., 1968—, co-chmn., 1967; lay adv. com. Manhasset (N.Y.) Bd. Edn.; trustee Manhasset Pub. Libr., 1953-59, v.p., 1956-59; trustee Smith Coll., 1967-72; active in care/preservation and current student use of Frank B. and Lillian M. Gilbreth lifetime papers at various worldwide librs. and univs.; honored guest ann. meeting Ariz. Libr. Friends, 1994. Montgomery award Friends of Phoenix Pub. Libr., 1981, honored guest Ariz. Lib. Friends, 1994. Mem. Authors Guild Am. (life mem., mem. guild council 1955-60), P.E.N. Republican. Conglist. Clubs: North Shore, Smith College (L.I.) (asst. chmn. scholarship com. 1950-59); Smith Coll. (N.Y.); Smith College Phoenix (Phoenix) (vice chmn. scholarship com. 1967), 7 College Conf. Council (Phoenix). Home: 6148 E Lincoln Dr Paradise Valley AZ 85253

CAREY, JEAN LEBEIS, management consulting executive; b. Charleston, W.Va., June 2, 1943; d. Edward H. and Marian (Lendved) Lebeis; m. Robert W. Carey, Nov. 1971 (dec. Mar. 1990); 1 child, Megan Rose. BA, Pa. State U., 1965. Programmer Penn Mut. Life Ins., Phila., 1967-68; sr. analyst/programmer U. Pa., Phila., 1969-72; sr. systems analyst Acme Markets, Phila., 1972-74; programming mgr. Bryn Mawr Coll., Pa., 1976-77; project adminstr. Smith Kline Beckman, Phila., 1977-83; project mgmt. cons. Arco Chem. Co., Phila., 1983-87; chief exec. officer Carey Project Orgn., Ardmore, Pa., 1987—; chmn. Sys. Methodology Users Mid-Atlantic, 1984-86, PMI Sys. Tech. Papers, 1983; co-dir. Cobol project U. Pa., Phila., 1969-72; lectr. in field. Author: Quality Management and Performance Measurement in Information Services, 1991, Making Quality Happen in Information Services, 1992, Project Manager's Handbook, 1993; contbr. articles to profl. jours. Bd. dirs. Scan/Child Abuse Treatment Ctr., Phila., 1983-94, Danceteller/Dance Theater, Phila., 1985-88, Self Help Crafts of the World/Phila., Inc., 1994—, chmn. bd. dirs., 1995—; mem. Leadership, Phila. vol. svcs. group, 1985-91; exec. com. SCAN Devel. Fund, Inc., 1989—. Recipient Excel award, Arco, 1986. Mem. Project Mgmt. Inst. Soc. of Friends. Home and Office: Carey Project Orgn 663 Cricket Ave Ardmore PA 19003-1806

CAREY, KATHRYN ANN, advertising and public relations executive, editor, consultant; b. Los Angeles, Oct. 18, 1949; d. Frank Randall and Evelyn Mae (Walmsley) C.; m. Richard Kenneth Sundt, Dec. 28, 1980. BA in Am. Studies with honors, Calif. State U., L.A., 1971. Cert. commercial pilot instrument rated. Tutor Calif. Dept. Vocat. Rehab., L.A., 1970; teaching asst. U. So. Calif., 1974-75, UCLA, 1974-75; claims adjuster Auto Club So. Calif., San Gabriel, 1971-73; corp. pub. rels. cons. Carnation Co., L.A., 1973-78; cons., adminstr. Carnation Community Svc. Award Program, 1973-78; pub. rels. cons. Vivitar Corp., 1978; sr. advt. asst. Am. Honda Motor Co., Torrance, Calif., 1978-84; exec. dir. Am. Honda Found., 1984—; adminstr. Honda Matching Gift and Vol. Program, Honda Involvement Program; mgr. Honda Dealer Advt. Assns., 1978-84; cons. advt., pub. rels., promotions. Editor: Vivitar Voice, Santa Monica, Calif., 1978, Rod Machado's Instrument Pilots' Survival Manual, c. 1991; editor Honda Views, 1978-84, Found. Focus, 1984—; asst. editor Friskies Research Digest, 1973-78; contbg. editor Newsbriefs and Momentum, 1978—, Am. Honda Motor Co., Inc. employees publs. Calif. Life Scholarship Found. scholar, 1967. Mem. Advt. Club L.A., Pub. Rels. Soc. Am., So. Calif. Assn. Philanthropy, Coun. on Founds., Affinity Group on Japanese Philanthropy (pres.), Ninety-Nines, Am. Quarter Horse Assn., Aircraft Owners and Pilots Assn., Los Angeles Soc. for Prevention Cruelty to Animals, Greenpeace, Ocicats Internat., Am. Humane Assn., Humane Soc. U.S., Elsa Wild Animal Appeal. Office: Am Honda Found 1919 Torrance Blvd Torrance CA 90501-1486

CAREY, MARIAH, vocalist, songwriter; b. N.Y.C., 1969; d. Alfred Roy and Patricia Carey; m. Thomas Mottola, June 5, 1993. Back up vocalist with Brenda K. Starr. Albums: Mariah Carey, 1990, Emotions, 1991, Mariah Carey MTV Unplugged, 1992, Music Box, 1993 (Grammy nomination, Best Pop Female Vocal for "Dreamlover"), Merry Christmas, 1994. Recipient Grammy awards Best New Artist of 1990, Best Pop Vocal Performance by Female, 1990. Office: Columbia Records 51 W 52nd St New York NY 10019-6119*

CAREY, SHIRLEY ANNE, nursing consultant; b. Syracuse, N.Y., Sept. 27, 1939; d. John Crotty and Eva Mae (Pratt) Walsh; m. John Paul Carey, July 23, 1966; children: Jason Leo, Jonathan Paul, Jennifer Anne. BSN, Nazareth Coll., 1961. RN, Calif. Charge nurse surg. svcs. L.A. County Hosp., 1962-64; instr. nursing L.A. County-U. So. Calif. Med. Ctr. Sch. Nursing, 1964-70; rschr./developer nursing edn. films Concept Media, Irvine, Calif., 1971-78; comty. health educator Huntington Beach (Calif.) Med. Ctr., 1983-93; nursing cons., health educator, writer Huntington Beach, 1988—; instr. basics of babysitting Huntington Beach Med. Ctr., 1986-93; instr. basic life support Am. Heart Assn., Huntington Beach, 1986—; HIV/AIDS educator ARC, Tustin, Calif., 1991—; bd. dirs. West Orange County Consortium Spl. Edn., Huntington Beach, 1991-92, clk., 1992, alt., 1993; bd. trustees Huntington Beach City Sch. Dist., 1990-94, 94—, clk., 1992, pres., 1993. Author, educator: (film series) Impaired Mobility, 1993, Basic Patient Care, 1994; film coord.: (film series) Human Development: Conception to Neonate, 1992, Human Development: First 2 1/2 Years, 1992, Human Development 2 1/2 to 6 Years, 1993. Pres., bd. dirs. Harry W. Montague Basketball Meml. Scholarship Com., Huntington Beach, 1989-94; sec., bd. dirs. Huntington Beach Sister City Assn., 1993-94; mem., past officer Orange County (Calif.) Adoptive Parents, 1975-94; active Girl Scouts Am., Costa Mesa, 1984-94, PTA, Huntington Beach, 1976-94; commr. Huntington Beach Comty. Svcs. Commn., 1994. Recipient Hon. Svc. award PTA, 1989. Mem. No On Drugs in Schs., Nat. Sch. Bd. Assn. (mem. fed. rels. network 1993-94), Calif. Sch. Bd. Assn. (mem. legis. network 1990-94, del. assembly 1994). Home and Office: 21142 Brookhurst St Huntington Beach CA 92646

CARFORA, JEANNE BAXTER, educator; b. Joliet, Ill., Nov. 5, 1947; d. William Arphax and Edna Mae (Stone) Baxter; m. Santo Carfora, Aug. 22, 1970; children: Christina Marie, Sara Elizabeth. BA in Elem. Edn., Culver Stockton Coll., 1969; MS in Learning Disabilities, U. Wis., 1975. Elem. tchr. Janesville (Wis.) Bd. Edn., 1969-80, educator, parent liaison, 1992—; adult and child tutor Janesville Literary Coun., 1986-88; Orton/Gillingham tchr. Orton/Dyslexia Found., Janesville, 1988-92; tchr., co-founder Time Traveler, Janesville, 1991; developer, coord. Family Resource Ctr., Janesville, 1992—; workshop leader Mega Skills, Janesville, 1994—; creator, coord. Parent/Child Reading program, 1994; creator Parent/Child Reading Game, 1994. Bd. dirs. ECHO Cmty. Food and Clothing, Janesville, 1984-86, Janesville Lit. Coun., 1986-88; co-chair, founder Cmty. Awareness Com., 1988-90; mem. 1st Christian Disciples of Christ Ch., 1957—, elder, 1989-90, 94—, outreach chmn., 1985-86. Mem. AAUW (sec. Janesville chpt. 1981-82). Home: 531 Greendale Janesville WI 53546 Office: Chapter I Family Resource 811 N Pine Janesville WI 53545

CARGILL, CLAIRE PATRICE, dentist; b. Kingston, Jamaica, W.I., Aug. 16, 1963; d. Eric Charles and Monica Vandeline (Brown) C. BS in Zoology cum laude, Howard U., 1986, DDS, 1991. Microfiche technician United Svcs. Life Ins. Co., Arlington, Va., 1985-90; dental asst. Wheaton, Md., 1991-92; dental asst., hygienist Hygiene Assocs., Rockville, Md., 1991—; gen. dentist Dr. Walter J. Ross, Washington, 1992-94; pvt. practice dentistry Washington, 1994—; dental cons. Software Dynamics, Hyattsville, Md., 1990-93; presenter in field. Recipient Table Clinic award D.C. Dental Soc., 1990, 2 awards Howard U. Coll. Dentistry, 1991. Mem. Acad. Gen. Dentistry, Am. Assn. Women Dentists, Robert T. Freeman Dental Soc., Oral Cancer Soc., Omicron Kappa Upsilon. Roman Catholic. Office: 1241 Pennsylvania Ave SE Washington DC 20003

CARIGNAN, DENNISE A., career counselor; student San Francisco State U., 1977-78, Ron Bailie Sch. Broadcast, San Francisco, 1981-82. With Gibraltar Savs. & Loan Assn., San Francisco, 1972-74; pub. rels. rep. Washington Bros. Distbg. Co., San Leandro, Calif., 1974-76; adminstrv. asst. Teleport Oil Co., San Francisco, 1977-79; case mgr. Project New Pride, ARC, San Francisco, 1980-83; intern news dept. Sta. KBLX-KRE Radio, Berkeley, 1983; career counselor Inner City Outpatient Svcs., San Francisco, 1983—. Mem., sec. audience devel. com. Oakland Symphony; mem. Chancel Choir; fundraiser S.C.A.R.E.; vol. ARC. Home: PO Box 10573 Oakland CA 94610-0573

CARINO, AURORA LAO, psychiatrist, hospital administrator; b. Angeles, The Philippines, Jan. 11, 1940; came to U.S., 1967; d. Pedro Samson and Hilaria Sanchez (Paras) Lao; m. Rosalito Aldecoa Carino, Dec. 2, 1967; children: Robert, Edwin, Antoinette. AA, U. of the East, Manila, 1961; degree in medicine, U. of the East, Quezon City, The Philippines, 1966. Lic. psychiatrist N.Y., Conn., Fla.; cert. Am. Bd. Psychiatry and Neurology. Resident in pediatrics U. of the East-R.M. Meml. Hosp., Quezon City, 1966-67; rotating intern Stamford (Conn.) Hosp., 1967-68; resident in psychiatry Norwich (Conn.) Hosp., 1968-71, staff psychiatrist, 1971-75; staff psychiatrist, unit chief, acting clin. dir. Harlem Valley Psychiat. Ctr., Wingdale, N.Y., 1975-80; svc. chief Fla. State Hosp., Chattahoochee, 1982-83; unit chief Hudson River Psychiat. Ctr., Poughkeepsie, N.Y., 1980-82, unit chief, acting clin. dir., 1983-90, asst. to clin. dir., 1990-93, dep. med. dir.-admissions, 1993—; cons. Dept. Mental Hygiene, Dutchess County, Poughkeepsie, 1976—. Active N.Y. State Psychiat. Polit. Action Com., 1990—. Mem. Am. Psychiat. Assn., Am. Acad. Psychiatry and Law. Republican. Roman Catholic. Home: 10 Millbank Rd Poughkeepsie NY 12603

CARINO, LINDA SUSAN, financial software company executive; b. San Diego, Nov. 4, 1954; d. DeVona (Clarke) Dungan. Student, San Diego Mesa Coll., 1972-74, 89-90. Various positions Calif. Can. Bank, San Diego, 1974-77, ops. supr., 1977-80, ops. mgr., 1980-82; asst. v.p. ops. mgr. First Comml. Bank (formerly Calif. Can. Bank), San Diego, 1982-84; v.p. data processing mgr. First Nat. Bank, San Diego, 1984-91; v.p. conversion adminstr. Item Processing Ctr. Svc. Corp., Denver, 1991-92; mgr. computer ops. FIserv, Inc., Van Nuys, Calif., 1992-93; v.p., data processing mgr. So. Calif. Bank, La Mirada, Calif., 1993-94, v.p. tech. support mgr., 1994—. Democrat. Home: 255 So Vista Del Monte Anaheim Hills CA 92807 Office: So Calif Bank PO Box 588 La Mirada CA 90637-0588

CARITHERS, JEANINE RUTHERFORD, veterinary educator; b. Boone, Iowa, Sept. 26, 1933; d. John Twedt Rutherford and Catherine Elizabeth (Rutherford); m. Robert William Carithers, Sept. 23, 1953; children: Jeffrey Scott, Brian Reid, Douglas Sean. B.S. Iowa State U. in Zoology, 1956; M.A. in Physiology, Iowa State U., 1965; Ph.D. in Anatomy, U. Mo., 1968. Tchr. sci. Union pub. schs., Iowa, 1964-65; asst. prof. vet. anatomy Iowa State U., Ames, 1968-72, assoc. prof., 1972-76, prof., 1976—, chairperson vet. anatomy, 1979-89, intern asst. v.p. acad. affairs, 1987-88, asst. dean grad. coll., 1988-89; professeur associe Ministre del'Education Nationale, France, 1976. Contbr. articles to profl. jours. Mem. Soc. of Neurosci., Am. Assn. Anatomists, AAAS, Am. Assn. Vet Medicine Colls., Congress of European Comparative Endocrinologists, N.Y. Acad. Scis., World Assn. Vet. Anatomists, Sigma Xi, Gamma Sigma Delta. Office: Iowa State U 1092 Vet Medicine Dept Anatomy Ames IA 50011

CARLCANO, CARLOTTA MIGUELINA (CARLOTTA BOTOE), educator, reading specialist; b. N.Y.C.; d. Carl and Marietta (Guilyard) C. BA, St. John's U., 1969; MS, L.I. U., 1973; postgrad., St. John's U. Cert. tchr., guidance counselor, N.Y. Mktg. rep. IBM Corp., N.Y.C., 1963-71; tchr. Bklyn., 1971-75; reading specialist Title I, Chpt. 1, Bklyn., 1975-77; coord. Open Enrollment, Bklyn., 1977; tchr., reading specialist N.Y.C. Pub. Schs., Bklyn., 1977—. Chairperson Community Sch. Improvement Project, 1984-85. Mem. ASCD, NAFE, Nat. Inst. Bus. Mgmt. Democrat. Roman Catholic.

CARLEN, SISTER CLAUDIA, librarian; b. Detroit, July 24, 1906; d. Albert B. and Theresa Mary (Ternes) C. AB in Library Sci., U. Mich., 1928, MA in Library Sci., 1938; LHD (hon.), Marygrove Coll., 1981, Loyola U., Chgo., 1983, Sacred Heart Major Sem., 1989; LittD (hon.), Cath. U. of Am., 1983. Asst. librarian St. Mary Acad., Monroe, Mich., 1928-29; asst. librarian Marygrove Coll., Detroit, 1929-44, librarian, 1944-69, library cons., 1970-71; on leave as index editor New Cath. Ency., 1963-67, Cath. Theol. Ency., 1968-70; library cons. grad. div. Casa Santa Maria, N.Am. Coll., Rome, 1971-72; libr. St. John's Provincial Sem., Plymouth, Mich., 1972-80, libr. emeritus, 1980-82, scholar-in-residence, 1982-85, archivist, 1985-88; rsch. affiliate Bentley Hist. Libr., U. Mich., Ann Arbor, 1989—; supr. orgn. and servicing Community Ctr. Libraries staffed by vols.; bd. dirs. Corpus Instrumentorum, Inc., v.p., 1969-70; mem. instructional materials com. Mich. Curriculum Study; cons. McGraw Hill Ency. World Biography, 1968-72, World Book Ency., 1969-70; mem. working group on uniform headings for liturgical works Internat. Fedn. of Libr. Assns., 1972-75. Author: Guide to Encyclicals of the Roman Pontiffs, 1939, Guide to the Documents of Pius XII, 1951, Dictionary of Papal Pronouncements, 1958; editor: Papal Encyclicals, 1740-1981, 1981, Papal Pronouncements, 1991; editor: column At Your Service, Cath. Library World, 1950-52; Reference Book Rev. Sect., 1952-64, 66-72; Books for the Home column; monthly news release, Nat. Cath. Rural Life Conf., 1952-61; adv. bd.: The Pope Speaks, 1953-88, Pierian Press; contbr.: Catholic Bookman's Guide, 1961, Dictionary Western Chs, 1969, Ency. Dictionary of Religion, 1979, Translatio Studii, 1973. Trustee Marygrove Coll., Detroit, 1976-79, vice chmn. bd., 1977-79. Recipient Disting. Alumna award U. Mich. Sch. Libr. Sci., 1974, Domitilla award Marygrove Coll., 1991. Mem. ALA (coun. 1958-61, 68-71), Cath. Libr. Assn. (chmn. com. membership 1946-49, chmn. Mich. unit 1952-54, chmn. coll. and univ. sect. 1954-56, chmn. publs. com. 1961-62, pres. 1965-67, Jerome award 1993), Mich. Libr. Assn. (chmn. coll. sect. 1956-57, chmn. recruiting com. 1959-60), Accademia Olubrense (charter), Am. Friends of

Vatican Libr. (co-founder, v.p.), Phi Beta Kappa, Phi Kappa Phi, Beta Phi Mu. Home: 2301 Sandalwood Cir # 215A Ann Arbor MI 48105-1352

CARLETON, MARY RUTH, television news anchor, consultant; b. Sacramento, Feb. 2, 1948; d. Warren Alfred and Mary Gertrude (Clark) Case; m. Bruce A. Hunt, Jan. 21, 1989. BA in Polit. Sci., U. Calif.-Berkeley, 1970, MJ, 1974. TV news anchorwoman, reporter Sta. KXAS-TV, Ft. Worth, 1974-78, Sta. KING-TV, Seattle, 1978-80, Sta. KOCO-TV, Oklahoma City, 1980-84; news anchor, reporter Sta. KTTV-TV, L.A., 1984-87; news anchor Sta. KLAS-TV, Las Vegas, Nev., 1987-91, KTNV-TV, 1991-93, Sta. UNLV-TV, 1993—; broadcast instr. Okla. Christian Coll., 1981-84, UCLA, 1985-87, U. Nev.-Las Vegas, 1991—; pub. speaking cons.; dir. UNLV Women's Ctr., 1991—; news dir. univ. news Sta. UNLV-TV, 1992—. Bd. dirs. World Neighbors, Oklahoma City, 1984-89, Allied Arts Coun. So. Nev.-Las Vegas, 1988—, Nev. Inst. for Contemporary Art, 1988—; bd. dirs. United Way, Las Vegas, 1991—, secret witness bd., 1991—, Las Vegas Women's Coun., 1993—, Friends of Channel 10, 1991—. Named Best Environ. Reporter, Okla. Wildlife Fedn., 1983, Disting. Woman of So. Nev., Woman of Achievement Las Vegas Women's Coun., 1990; recipient Broadcasting award UPI, 1981, Nat. award for best documentary, 1990, Tri-State award for best newscast, 1990, Emmy award, L.A., 1986, L.A. Press Club award 1986, 90, Nat. award for documentaries UPI, 1990, Woman of Achievement Media award Las Vegas C. of C., 1990. Mem. AARP (mem. nat. econ. issues team 1992—, state legis. com.)Women in Comm. (Clarion award 1981, Best Newscaster 1990), Soc. Prol. Journalists, Press Women, Investigative Reporters, Sigma Delta Chi. Democrat. Roman Catholic. Avocations: tennis, gourmet cooking. Office: Sta KTNV-TV 3355 S Valley View Blvd Las Vegas NV 89102-8216

CARLI, LINDA LORENE, psychology educator; b. Willimantic, Conn., Jan. 25, 1956; d. Victor Batista and Mary Bessie (Dominique) C.; m. Michael William Dorsey, June 14, 1980; 1 child, Alexander Lawrence Carli-Dorsey. BA, U. Conn., 1977; MA, U. Mass., 1980, PhD, 1984. Asst. prof. Mount Holyoke Coll., South Hadley, Mass., 1984-85, Holy Cross Coll., Worcester, Mass., 1985-91; asst. prof. Wellesley (Mass.) Coll., 1991-93, assoc. prof., 1993—; vis. scholar Harvard U., Cambridge, Mass., 1991-92; rsch. assoc. U. Mass., Lowell, 1993—; reviewer chpts., articles and grant applications APA and NSF; lectr. and cons. in field. Contbr. articles to profl. jours. Dupont grantee Women's Coll. Coalition, 1993. Mem. APA, Assn. Women in Psychology, Acad. Mgmt., Soc. for the Advancement Social Psychology. Democrat. Unitarian-Universalist. Office: Wellesley Coll Dept Psychology Wellesley MA 02181

CARLILE, JANET LOUISE, artist, educator; b. Denver, Apr. 26, 1942; d. Jessie Crawford and Alice Essie (Locker) C.; m. David Hildebrand, Sept. 1, 1963 (div. 1968). BFA, Cooper Union, 1966; MFA, Pratt Inst., 1971. Prof., dep. chmn. art dept., chmn. printmaking dept. Bklyn. Coll., CUNY, 1971—; founder Incline Village (Nev.) Fine Arts Ctr., 1966-68; instr. Sch. Visual Arts, N.Y.C., 1968-70, Printmaking Workshop, N.Y.C., 1971, Scarsdale (N.Y.) Studio Workshop, 1971-73, SUNY-Stony Brook, L.I., 1976, Bard Winter Coll., Rhinebeck, N.Y., 1980; head printmaking, asst. dir. Bklyn. (N.Y.) Mus. Art Sch., 1971-77; dir. Bklyn. (N.Y.) Coll. Press, 1977—; cons. Woodstock (N.Y.) Sch. Art, 1980-84; judge Alpine Artists Show, Ouray, Colo., 1989. One woman shows include Blue Mt. Gallery, N.Y.C., 1980; exhibited in group shows at Associated Am. Artists Gallery, N.Y., 1971-81, Bklyn. Mus., 1976, Ulster County Artists Show, N.Y. State Coun. Show, 1984, Alpine Artists Show Ouray County, 1987; design for IRT Bklyn. Mus. Sta. Sec. San Juan Vista Landowners Assn., Ridgway, Colo., 1980-86. Recipient full scholarship Cooper Union, N.Y.C., 1962-66, Hirshorn Purchase prize, Soc. Am. Graphic Artists, 1969, Grad. fellowship Pratt Inst., Bklyn., 1971, Best of Show award, Alpine Artists Show Ouray County, 1987, NEA Workshop grant Colo. Coun. Arts, 1991, Creative Incentive award CUNY, 1992. Mem. Ouray (Colo.) County Arts Assn. (pres. 1991-93). Home: PO Box 1805 Ouray CO 81427-1805 also: 12 Bellows Ln Woodstock NY 12498-1204 Office: Brooklyn Coll Art Dept Bedford at Ave H Brooklyn NY 11210

CARLILE, LORI ANN, insurance examiner; b. Oklahoma City, Feb. 11, 1964; d. Robert Edwin and Beverly June (Thomas) C. AAS, BS in Indsl. Electronic Tech., Cameron Univ., 1993. Receptionist Vet. Affairs, Lawton, Okla., 1992-93; customer svc. examiner Dan and Bradstreet Corp., Oklahoma City, 1993-94, HealthPlan Svcs., Oklahoma City, 1994—. Vol. AMBUCS, Lawton, 1992. Sgt. USAF, 1987-91. Mem. AAUW, Okla. Karate Assn. (awards 1993), Cameron U. Alumni Assn. Republican. Baptist. Office: HealthPlan Svcs 525 Central Park Dr Ste 400 Oklahoma City OK 73105-1703

CARLIN, BETTY, educator; b. N.Y.C., Sept. 20, 1931; d. Samuel and Rose Sara (Bernstein) Grossberg; m. Arthur S. Carlin, July 18, 1953 (dec. Mar. 1988); children: Lisa Anne Skinner, James Howard. BA, UCLA, 1952; MA, U. Calif., Berkeley, 1955. Educator L.A. Sch. Dist., 1952-55; owner Carlins Shoes, L.A., 1952-68; educator Berkeley (Calif.) Sch. Dist., 1957-58, Castro Valley (Calif.) Sch. Dist., 1967—; master tchr. spl. programs Calif. State Coll., Hayward, 1967-84; educator U. Calif., Berkeley, 1984-86; co-owner Art-Car Corp., 1978-88. Mem. Nat. Tchrs. Assn., Calif. Tchrs. Assn., Commonwealth Club, San Francisco Opera Guild.

CARLISLE, LILIAN MATAROSE BAKER (MRS. E. GRAFTON CARLISLE, JR.), author, lecturer; b. Meridian, Miss., Jan. 1, 1912; d. Joseph and Lilian (Flournoy) Baker; student Dickinson Coll., 1929-30, Pierce Coll. Bus. Adminstrn., 1930-31; B.A., U. Vt., 1981, M.A., 1986; m. E. Grafton Carlisle, Jr., Jan. 9, 1933; children: Diana, Penelope. Adminstrv. sec. RAF Ferry Command, Montreal, Can., 1942; exec. staff mem. in charge collections, research Shelburne (Vt.) Mus., 1951-61; exec. sec. Burlington Area Community Health Study, 1963, coordinator, 1964; asst. coordinator Vt. Mental Retardation Planning Project, 1965; project dir. 4-county Champlain Valley Medicare Alert, 1966; dir. public relations Champlain Valley Agrl. Fair, 1968-77; lectr. U. Vt. Elder Hostel program, 1976-77, mem. faculty Vacation Coll., 1980-83. Pres., Burlington Community Council for Social Welfare, 59-61, 71-73; chmn. bd. Interfaith Sr. Citizens, 1977-79; justice of peace, 1979-81; pres. Chittenden County Extension Adv. Com., 1977-78; chmn. publs. com. Vt. Bicentennial Commn., 1974-77; mem. Vt. Ho. of Reps., 1968-70. Recipient Community Council Disting. Citizen award, 1978. Mem. Vt. (trustee, chmn. mus. com. 1967), N.Y. (faculty seminar) Chittenden (pres. 1969-72, editor Heritage Series of 10 books about Chittenden County towns 1972-76) hist. socs., Vt. Old Cemetery Assn., Vt. Folklore Soc., League Vt. Writers (dir. 1962; v.p., pres. 1967-69). Am. Pen Women (pres. Green Mountain br. 1980-82), Order Women Legislators (pres. Vt. br. 1972-74), Meml. Soc. Vt. (pres. 1989-94), Chi Omega. Conglist. Club: Zonta (pres. 1964-65). Co-author: The Story of the Shelburne Museum, 1955; Profile of the Community, 1964; Environmental and Personal Health of the Community, 1964; Vermont Clock and Watchmakers, Silversmiths and Jewelers, 1970; also numerous catalogs on collections at Shelburne Mus.; editorial cons. Burlington Social Survey, 1967; editor: Historic Guide to Burlington Neighborhoods, 1991; contbr. articles to profl. jours. Home: 117 Lakeview Ter Burlington VT 05401-2906

CARLISLE, MARGO DUER BLACK, chief senatorial staff; b. Providence; d. Thomas F. Jr. and Margaret MacCormick Black; m. Miles Carlisle; children: Mary Hamilton, Tristram Coffin. BA, Manhattanville Coll. Legis. asst. Senator James A. McClure, Washington, 1973; staff mem. budget comm. task force U.S. Senate, Washington, 1974-75, exec. dir. steering com., 1975-80; staff dir. Senate Rep. Conf., Washington, 1981-84; exec. dir. Coun. for Nat. Policy, Washington, 1985-86; asst. sec. for legis. affairs Dept. Def., Washington, 1986-89; v.p. for govt. rels. The Heritage Found., Washington, 1989-90; chief staff Senator Thad Cochran, Washington, 1991—; staff dir. nat. security and fgn. policy subcoms. for Rep. platform, 1984, Washington. Contbr. articles on govt. policy to profl. jours. Trustee Phila. Soc., Washington, 1987-88, 93—. Catholic. Home: 3221 Garfield St NW Washington DC 20008 Office: Office of Sen Thad Cochran Senate Office Bldg 326 Russell Washington DC 20510

CARLISLE, PATRICIA KINLEY, mortgage company executive, paralegal; b. Royston, Ga., Sept. 21, 1949; d. Luther Clark Kinley and Ann Busby Carey; children: Angela Renee, William Clark, Matthew Vincent. Grad., Suburban Inst. Real Estate, Tucker, Ga., 1978; grad. with honors, Lanier Tech. Sch., Oakwood, Ga., 1983; postgrad., Gainesville Coll., 1986, Maryville Coll., 1986. Lic. real estate salesperson, Ga. Fin. analyst, then pers. mgr. Citicorp Acceptance Co., Inc., St. Louis, 1983-89; exec. v.p., v.p. purchasing, regional sales mgr. George-Ingraham Corp., Stone Mountain, Ga., 1989-90; sr. loan officer Terrace Mortgage Co., Atlanta, 1990-92; dir. client svcs. Paynter and Everett, P.C., 1992—; dir. of client rels. Paynter & Everett, P.C., 1993—; rsch. bd. advisors Am. Biog. Inst., Inc. Mem. NAFE, Forsyth County Bd. Realtors, Aircraft Owners and Pilots Assn., Female Execs. North Atlanta. Home: PO Box 467364 Atlanta GA 31146-7364

CARLISLE, VIVIAN RUTH, science educator; b. Birmingham, Ala., Dec. 2, 1933; d. Fred Edward and Ethel Chamblee (Johnson) C. BS, Jacksonville State U., 1955; MS, Nova U., 1981; postgrad., U. Tampa, U. Fla., U. So. Fla. Tchr. Calhoun County Edn., Anniston, Ala., 1955-56; tchr. Hillsborough County Sch. Bd., Tampa, Fla., 1956-59, sci. dept. chair, 1959-74, tchr., 1974—, mid. sch. team leader gifted students, 1994—; supr. and tchr. Hillsborough County Summer Program, 1957-67; dir. Project Discovery, Tampa, 1970; coord. Tchrs. as Advisors, Webb Jr. High Sch., Tampa, 1988. Author practicum, 1981, tchr.'s manual, 1988; editor: Life Sci. Curriculum, 1984; co-author: Earth Sci. Curriculum, 1982. Recipient Tchrs. as Advisors grantee Fla. State Bd. Edn., 1988, Tchr. of Yr. award, 1989-90; project discovery grantee Hillsborough County Sch. Bd., 1970. Mem. Hillsborough Classroom Tchrs. Assn., NEA, nat., state and county tchr. assns., Phi Mu, Chi Beta (hon.). Home: 5761 Colonial Dr New Port Richey FL 34652

CARLOZZI, CATHERINE L., public relations, communications consultant; b. Berea, Ohio, July 25, 1953; d. Charles Henry and Carol Louise (Jones) Bader; m. Nicholas Carlozzi, Jan. 4, 1975. BA in English summa cum laude, Denison U., 1975; MA in English with distinction, U. Wis., 1976. Teaching asst. U. Wis., Madison, 1976-77; editor Visual Edn. Cons., Madison, 1977-78; copywriter advt. Walnut Equipment Leasing, Ardmore, Pa., 1978-79; assoc. nat. dir. publications Laventhol & Horwith, Phila., 1979-84; sr. assoc., mgr. spl. projects, v.p. Brown Boxenbaum, N.Y.C., 1984-91; prin. Carlozzi Comm. Cons., Cedar Grove, N.J., 1991—. Trustee Montclair, N.J. Art Mus., 1993—, co-chmn. audience devel. com., mem. nominating com., exec. com. Recipient Dir.'s award Montclair Art Mus., 1994. Mem. N.Y. Women in Comm. (Cert. Appreciation 1993, 94, comm. com. 1992—), Editl. Freelancers Assn., Phi Beta Kappa. Office: Carlozzi Comms Cons 334 Crestmont Rd Cedar Grove NJ 07009-1908

CARLS, JUDITH MARIE, physical education educator, golf coach; b. Moline, Ill., Aug. 16, 1940; d. Orville Allen and Eleanor Lou (Shollenberger) Meyers; m. Larry Michael, Dec. 21, 1966 (div. June 1971). BA in Phys. Edn., U. No. Iowa, 1962; MA, Western Ill. U., 1982. Cert. educator/adminstr. K-14, Ill. Phys. edn. instr. John Deere Jr. High, Moline; dep. chmn. phys. edn. Moline High Sch., 1965-93; dir. golf schs. Recreation Park Golf Course, Long Beach, Calif., 1993—; part-time instr., student tchr. supr. Calif. State U., Fullerton, 1994—; cons. LPGA Jr. Golf Program, L.A., 1993-94. Campaign, fundraiser Tim Bell State Rep., Moline, 1980-84. Named to Ill. Coaches Hall of Fame, 1993. Mem. NEA, Ladies Profl. Golf Assn. (mid-west sect. 1982—), Ill. Phys. Edn. Assn. (govt. affairs office 1989-93), Phi Kappa Phi. Republican. Lutheran. Home: 2814 32nd Avenue Dr Moline IL 61265-6956

CARLSEN, JANET HAWS, insurance company owner, mayor; b. Bellingham, Wash., June 16, 1927; d. Lyle F. and Mary Elizabeth (Preble) Haws; m. Kenneth M. Carlsen, July 26, 1952; children: Stephanie L. Chambers, Scott Lyle, Sean Preble, Stacy K., Spencer J. Cert., Armstrong Bus. Sch., 1945; student, Golden Gate Coll., 1945-46. Office mgr. Cornwall Warehouse Co., Salt Lake City, 1950-55, Hansen's Ins., Newman, Calif., 1969-77; owner Carlsen Ins., Gustine, Calif., 1978—. Mem. city coun. City of Newman, 1980-82, mayor, 1982-94; bd. dirs. ARC, Stanislaus, Calif., 1982-83; grand marshall Newman Fall Festival, 1989; v.p. cen. div. League of Calif. Cities, 1989-90, pres., 1990, 91; dir. Ctrl. Valley Opportunity Ctr., 1990—, Sr. Opportunity Svc. Ctr., 1993—. Named Soroptimist Woman of Achievement, 1987, Soroptimist Woman of Distinction, 1988, Outstanding Woman, Stanislaus County Commn. for Women, 1989, Newman Rotary Club Citizen of Yr., 1993-94, Woman of Yr. Calif. State Assembly Dist. 26, 1994. Morman. Club: Booster (Newman). Lodge: Soroptimist. Home: 1215 Amy Dr Newman CA 95360-1003 Office: 377 5th St Gustine CA 95322-1126

CARLSEN, LINDA ELAINE, school superintendent; b. Sidney, Mont., June 6, 1951; d. Gilbert W. and Aileen P. (Painter) Lightfield; m. Dewaine C. Carlsen, Apr. 22, 1972; 1 child, Deneata. BS with high honors, Ea. Mont. Coll., 1975, MS magna cum laude, 1985; EdD, U. Mont., 1993. Cert. supt. K-12, prin. 7-12. Tchr. Circle (Mont.) Pub. Schs., 1975-86; supt.-prin. Custer (Mont.) Pub. Schs., 1986-90; supt. St. Regis (Mont.) Pub. Schs., 1990—. Mem. VFW Ladies Aux., Richey, 1975-93. Mem. ASCD, Am. Assn. of Sch. Adminstrs., Mont. Assn. Sch. Supts., Mont. Assn. of Sch. Bus. Ofcls., Western Mont. Sch. Adminstrs., Delta Kappa Gamma. Home: PO Box 219 5 Tiger St St Regis MT 59866 Office: St Regis Schs 6 Tiger St St Regis MT 59866

CARLSON, BELA MAE, medical nurse, consultant; b. Wilmington, N.C., July 15, 1923; m. Charles E.K. Carlson. RN diploma, Mercy Coll. Nursing, Detroit, 1945; ob-gyn. nurse practitioner, Ob-Gyn. Group of Manchester, 1973, Mt. Sinai Hosp., Hartford, Conn., 1975. Cert. Lamaze instr., 1967, sex educator, 1978, nurse practitioner, 1980. Head nurse obstetrics and nursery Charlesgate Hosp., Cambridge, Mass., 1946-48; pvt. practice Manchester, Conn., 1965-72; nurse practitioner Ob-Gyn. Group of Manchester, 1973-89; retired, 1989; monitricing nurse Manchester Monitrice Associated, Inc., 1969-78; pvt. lamaze instr., 1967-89, ednl. coord. Manchester Meml. Hosp., 1967-89, instr. NAACOG, 1975-79; lectr. in field; cons. schs. in and around Manchester, Growth Facilitators, Inc., 1986-89, Meriden Wallingford Sch. Nursing, 1973-75, U. Conn. Sch. Nursing, 1975-89, U. Hartford Nursing Program, 1979-89, U. Conn. Pub. Interest Rsch. Group, 1980-81, Manchester C.C., 1981-82, Ednl. Community Assocs., Inc., 1976-89. Contbr. articles and reviews to profl. jours. Mem. NAACOG, Internat. Childbirth Edn. Assn., Internat. Soc. Psychosomatics in Ob-Gyn., Am. Soc. Psychoprophylactics in Obstetrics, Nurses Assn. of Am. Coll. of Ob-Gyn., Am. Assn. Sex Educators, Counselors and Therapists, Nurse Practitioner Conf. Group of Conn., Nurse Practitioner Assocs. for Continuing Edn., Ob-Gyn. Nurse Practitioners Conn., Manchester Monitrice Assocs., Inc., Family Oriented Childbirth Info. Svc. Home: PO Box 2417 Shallotte NC 28459-2417

CARLSON, CAROLIN MCCORMICK FURST, civic worker; b. Williamsport, Pa., Apr. 20, 1934; d. S. Dale and Esther Caroline (McCormick) Furst O'Brien; m. Elton Frederic Carlson, Sept. 15, 1956 (dec. 1970); children: Eric Dale, Margaret Cora, Dwight Leonard. BA, Smith Coll., 1955. Dir. First Nat. Bank of Port Allegany, Pa.; class fund sec. Abbot class Phillips Acad., Andover, Mass., 1951—; chmn. Abbot 40th Reunion, 1991. Contbr. articles to weekly paper Reporter-Argus, 1961-87. Jr. choir dir. Gethsemane Evang. Luth. Ch., Port Allegany, 1971-82, charter lay asst., 1972-74, 84-90, congl. sec., 1973-93, Theos chpt. exec. dir. and grief counselor, 1972-76, chmn. bicentennial celebration com., 1975-76, pres. Luth Ch. Women, 1959-61, treas., 1962-65, 84-85, program chmn., 1976-80, sr. choir, 1983-86, Emporium Ministerium grief counselor, 1984-87; chmn. noon hour cultural series S.W. Smith Meml. Pub. Libr., 1972-74, 77-78, bd. dirs., 1977-89, v.p. spl. events, 1978-82, book selection, 1977-82, 94—, pres., 1985-88, adv. bd. McKean Literacy Team, 1991-94; active Port Area Community TV, 1981-92; den mother Allegany Highland coun. Boy Scouts Am., Port Allegany, 1967-70, 76-79, sec., 1976-79, merit badge counselor, 1984-92; asst. troop leader Keystone Tall Tree coun. Girl Scouts U.S., 1969-74; charter driver Meals on Wheels, 1972-92; adv. bd. Charles Cole Meml. Hosp., 1988—, long-range planning, 1990-91; adv. bd. dirs. McKean County Children & Youth Svcs., 1980-83; v.p. Port Allegany High Sch. Band Boosters, 1982-85; chmn. United Way, 1984, 85; bd. dirs. Port Allegany Area Econ. Devel. Corp., 1984—, solicitation chmn. capital funds drive, 1987-90; grants com. McKean County Coun. of Arts, 1990-93. Recipient award Luth. Ch. Am., 1975. Mem. Smith Coll. Alumnae Assn., Abbot Acad. Alumnae Assn., Indian Echo County Club, Port Allegany Woman's Club (treas. 1957-60, 66-67, 94—, auditor 1965, 82, sec. 1963-65, 70-71, 2d v.p. 1967-68, 17-72, pres. 1977-79, choir 1961—), McKean County Women's Club (sec. 1958-60, 66-68, treas. 1970-72, 1st v.p. 1972-76), Order Ea. Star. Republican. Home: 45 Church St Port Allegany PA 16743-1133

CARLSON, CLARE, state legislator; b. Grand Forks, N.D., Apr. 27, 1956. BS, N.D. State U. Rep. dist. 18 N.D. Ho. of Reps.; farmer. Republican. Lutheran. Home: 201 Chestnut St Grand Forks ND 58201-4661 Office: ND Ho of Reps State Capitol Bismarck ND 58505*

CARLSON, DALE BICK, writer; b. N.Y.C., May 24, 1935; d. Edgar M. and Estelle (Cohen) Bick; children: Daniel, Hannah. BA, Wellesley Coll., 1957. Lic. wildlife rehabilitator, 1991. Pres. Bick Pub. House, 1993—. Author children's books, adult books 1961—, including: Perkins the Brain, 1964, The House of Perkins, 1965, Miss Maloo, 1966, The Brainstormers, 1966, Frankenstein, 1968, Counting Is Easy, 1969, Your Country, 1969, Arithmetic 1, 2, 3, 1969, The Electronic Teabowl, 1969, Warlord of the Genji, 1970, The Beggar King of China, 1971, The Mountain of Truth (Spring Festival Honor book, named Am. Library Assn. Notable Book), 1972, Good Morning Danny, 1972, Good Morning, Hannah, 1972, The Human Apes, 1973 (named Am. Library Assn. Notable Book), Girls Are Equal Too, 1973 (named Am. Library Assn. Notable Book), Baby Needs Shoes, 1974, Triple Boy, 1976, Where's Your Head?, 1977, The Plant People, 1977, The Wild Heart, 1977, The Shining Pool, 1979, Lovingsex for Both Sexes, 1979, Boys Have Feelings Too, 1980, Call Me Amanda, 1981, Manners That Matter, 1982, The Frog People, 1982, Charlie the Hero, 1983, 1984-85: The Jenny Dean Science Fiction Mysteries, The Mystery of the Shining Children, The Mystery of the Hidden Trap, The Secret of the Third Eye, The James Budd Mysteries, The Mystery of Galaxy Games, The Mystery of Operation Brain, 1985, Miss Mary's Husbands, 1988, Basic Manuals in Wildlife Rehabilitation Series (6 vols.), 1993-94, others. Mem. Authors League Am., Authors Guild, Wind Over Wings. Address: 307 Neck Rd Madison CT 06443

CARLSON, DESIREE ANICE, pathologist; b. Clinton, Iowa, June 10, 1950; d. Donald Richard and Bernice Elfriede (Jacobs) C.; m. Helmut Gunther Rennke; stepchildren: Stephanie Rennke, Christianne Rennke. MD, Duke U., 1975. Resident in pathology U. Wash., Seattle, 1975-76, N.E. Deaconess Hosp., Boston, 1976-77, Peter Bent Brigham Hosp., Boston, 1977-79; pathologist W. Roxbury VA Med. Ctr., Boston, 1979-82; med. dir. blood bank Univ. Hosp., Boston, 1982-90; assoc. chief pathology N.E. Meml. Hosp., Stoneham, Mass., 1990-93; chief pathology Brockton (Mass.) Hosp., 1993—; asst. prof. pathology Boston U. Sch. Med., 1982—; cons. pathology Brigham and Women's Hosp., Boston, 1984—; mem. adv. bd. ARC, Dedham, 1982—. Contbr. articles to profl. jours., book chpts. Recipient Outstanding Contbd. Article award Med. Lab. Observer, 1988. Mem. Coll. Am. Pathologists (N.E. regional commr. 1991—), Am. Med. Women's Assn., Am. Assn. Blood Banks, Mass. Med. Soc. (coms.), Mass. Pathology Soc., N.E. Pathology Soc. Republican. Presbyterian. Office: Brockton Hosp 680 Centre St Brockton MA 02402

CARLSON, GRACE-ELIZABETH, pediatrics nurse; b. Chgo.; d. Claud Charles and Marcella (Pierce) Ruch; m. Hal George Carlson (dec. Oct. 1994); children: Laura K. Helmuth, Kristina M. Helmuth Uddenberg, John G. Carlson. B in Music Edn., Northwestern U., 1966; AAS in Phys. Therapy, Oakton Community Coll., 1983, AAS in RN, 1986; MS in Parent/Child Health, Rush U., 1989. RNC. Staff nurse, mem. cardiac team neonatal intensive care Luth. Gen. Hosp., Park Ridge, Ill., 1986-89, unit educator neonatal intensive care, 1989-90, ednl. specialist, 1990—; cons. resource ctr. Luth. Gen. Hosp., 1992. Contbr. articles to profl. jours. Mem. NAACOG, Nat. Assn. Neonatal Nurses, Chgo. Area Assn. Neonatal Nurses, Sigma Theta Tau. Office: Luth Gen Hosp 1775 Dempster St Park Ridge IL 60025

CARLSON, JANET FRANCES, psychologist, educator; b. Newport, R.I., Oct. 3, 1957; d. Robert Carl and Alice Marion (Orina) C.; m. Kurt Francis Geisinger, Sept. 22, 1984. BS summa cum laude, Union Coll., Schenectady, 1979; MA in Clin. Psychology, Fordham U., 1982, PhD in Clin. Psychology, 1987. Lic. psychologist, N.Y.; cert. sch. psychologist, N.Y., Conn. Clin. psychology intern Conn. Valley Hosp., Middletown, Conn., 1983-84; research fellow Schering-Plough Found., Bronx, N.Y., 1984-85; psychologist I Creedmoor Psychiat. Ctr., Queens Village, N.Y., 1985-86; psychologist Hallen Sch., Mamaroneck, N.Y., 1986-88; asst. prof. psychology Fordham U., Bronx, N.Y., 1988-89; asst. prof. sch. and applied psychology Fairfield (Conn.) U., 1989-93, dir. sch. and applied psychology programs, 1989-90; asst. prof. counseling and psychol. svcs. SUNY, Oswego, 1993—; vis. asst. prof. psychology LeMoyne Coll., Syracuse, N.Y., 1992-93. Recipient Sugar-free scholarship, 1984-85, Sigma Xi Grant-in-Aid of Research, 1984-85. Mem. Am. Ednl. Rsch. Assn., APA, Nat. Assn. Sch. Psychologists, Ea. Psychol. Assn., N.Y. State Psychol. Assn., Northeastern Ednl. Rsch. Assn. (pres. 1995—, bd. dirs. 1990-93, editor newsletter 1988-91), N.Y. Assn. Sch. Psychologists, Sigma Xi, Psi Chi (charter), Phi Kappa Phi.

CARLSON, JEANNIE ANN, writer; b. Bklyn., Jan. 13, 1955; d. Lloyd Arthur and Ruth Frances (Riley) C.; m. Kenneth D. Williams, May 15, 1976 (div. 1981); 1 child, Carl Philip; m. H. Daniel Hopkins, Dec. 16, 1987 (div. 1994). BA, Randolph-Macon Woman's Coll., 1977. Mktg./editing rep. Harris Pub., White Plains, N.Y., 1982; adminstrv. asst. Ray Fried Assocs., Inc., Eastchester, N.Y., 1980-84; proofreader Nat. Pennysaver, Elmsford, N.Y., 1983-84; chief writer Profl. Resume and Writing Service, St. Petersburg, Fla., 1984-87; exec. writer, pres. Viking Comm., Inc., 1987—; feature writer Asbury News, Crestwood, N.Y., 1983-84; editorial asst. Children's Rights Am., Largo, Fla., 1984; pub. rels. coord. The Renaissance Cultural Ctr., Clearwater, Fla., 1985; com. mem. work area on comm. Pasadena Community Ch., St. Petersburg, Fla., 1986-88, Christian edn. bd. Our Savior Luth. Ch., St. Petersburg, 1991-93; editorial advisor Grief Recovery Ctrs. Fla., 1992. Recipient Golden Poet award World of Poetry, 1985, 88, 89, 91, 92, Silver Poet award, 1986, 90, Recognition award Nat. Soc. Poets, 1979, poetry awards Internat. Publs., 1976-77, Achievement Certs. Profl. Resume and Writing Service, 1985, 86, 87, World of Poetry awards of merit, 1983 (2), 85, 87, 88 (2), 91, 92, Editor's Choice award Nat. Libr. Poetry, 1994. Mem. City News Service (affiliate writer), Profl. Assn. Resume Writers, Phi Beta Gamma. Methodist. Avocations: theatre, culinary arts, music. Office: Viking Communications Inc 300 31st St N Ste 212 Saint Petersburg FL 33713-7624

CARLSON, JENNIE PEASLACK, lawyer; b. Ft. Thomas, Ky., June 11, 1960; d. Roland A. and Shirley (Willen) Peaslack; m. Charles I. Michaels, Aug. 13, 1983 (div. May 1989); m. Richard A. Carlson, May 2, 1992. BA in English, Centre Coll., 1982; JD, Vanderbilt U., 1985. Bar: Ohio 1985. Atty. Taft, Stettinius & Hollister, Cin., 1985-91; v.p., dep. gen. counsel Star Banc Corp., Cin., 1991—. Home: 8 Elmhurst Pl Cincinnati OH 45208 Office: Star Banc Corp 425 Walnut St 9th Fl Cincinnati OH 45202

CARLSON, JOAN HOGAN, municipal official; b. Hartford, Conn., Aug. 5, 1922; d. Emil Ludwig and Josephine (Purcell) Marzano; m. Matthew J. Hogan, Oct. 13, 1945 (div. Jan. 1977); children: Ann, Matthew Jr., Lawrence, Joan Jr., Laura, Thomas; m. Carl F. Carlson, Aug. 12, 1989. Student, Cornell U., 1943; BS, St. Joseph Coll., 1944; MEd, Springfield (Mass.) Coll., 1978. Draftsman Curtiss-Wright Corp., Buffalo, 1944, Standard-Knapp Co., Portland, Conn., 1945-48; substitute tchr. Bd. Edn., Avon, Conn., 1958; field rep. Cmty. Renewal Team, Hartford, Conn., 1965-67; field rep., supr. Conn. Dept. of Cmty. Affairs, Hartford, Conn., 1967-79; mcpl. svcs. coord. Conn. Dept. Human Resources, Hartford, Conn., 1979-89; mcpl. agt. for elderly Youth & Family Svcs., Old Saybrook, Conn., 1991—. Mem. Dem. Town Com., Westbrook, Conn., 1976-83, chairperson, 1980-83; mem. Bd. Tax Appeals, Westbrook, 1990—; exec. dir. Lower Valley ARC, Westbrook, 1990—. Mem. Conn. Assn. Mcpl. Agts. for Elderly (treas. 1993-94), Conn. State Employees Union (treas. Coun. 400, chpt. 413 1990-96), St. Mark's Ladies Guild. Democrat. Roman Catholic. Home: 3 Marvin Dr Westbrook CT 06498-2156 Office: Youth & Family Svcs 322 Main St Old Saybrook CT 06475-2350

CARLSON, KATHLEEN BUSSART, law librarian; b. Charlotte, N.C., June 25, 1956; d. Dean Allyn and Joan (Parlette) Bussart; m. Gerald Mark Carlson, Aug. 15, 1987. BA in Polit. Sci., Ohio State U., 1977; JD, Capital U., 1980; MA in Libr. and Info. Sci., U. Iowa, 1986. Bar: Ohio 1980 (inactive). Editor Lawyers Coop. Pub. Co., Rochester, N.Y., 1980-83; asst. state law libr. State of Wyo., Cheyenne, 1987-88, state law libr., 1988—. Elder Highlands Presbyn. Ch., Cheyenne, 1990-93; 2d v.p. bd. dirs. Wyo. coun. Girl Scouts U.S., Casper, 1990-92, 1st v.p. bd. dirs., 1993—. Mem.

Am. Assn. Law Librs. (sec., treas. state, ct. and county SIS 1992-95, edn. com. 1991-92, indexing legal periodical lit. adv. com. 1993—, chair 1994-95), We. Pacific Assn. Law Librs., Wyo. Libr. Assn. (sec. acad. and spl. librs. sect. 1990-92, pres. 1994-95), Bibliographic Ctr. for Rsch. (trustee 1991-95), Kappa Delta, Beta Phi Mu. Home: 911 E 18th St Cheyenne WY 82001-4722 Office: State Law Libr Supreme Ct Bldg Cheyenne WY 82002

CARLSON, KATHY A., librarian; b. San Antonio, Oct. 27, 1946; d. Fred and Allien (Alder) Hardin; m. Charles A. Carlson, Aug. 27, 1966; children: Grady, Andy. BS in Elem. Edn., Sam Houston U., 1968. Cert. elem. tchr., libr., Tex. Elem. tchr. Aldine Ind. Sch. Dist., Houston, 1968, Del Rio (Tex.) Ind. Sch. Dist., 1968-71; elem. tchr. San Felipe Del Rio Ind. Sch. Dist., Del Rio, 1971-73, 74-76, libr., 1977-81; elem. tchr. Hondo (Tex.) Ind. Sch. Dist., 1981-85, libr., 1985—. Pres. Medina Community Hosp. Aux., Hondo, 1995; treas. Family Community Coun., Hondo, 1990-92, sec., 1990-92; 1st v.p. Aggie Moms. Mem. Tex. Libr. Assn. Home: 1309 Acorn Rd Hondo TX 78861-1003 Office: Hondo Ind Sch Dist 2603 Avenue H Hondo TX 78861

CARLSON, MARIANNE RIRIE, speech pathologist; b. Hamilton, New Zealand, Oct. 7, 1957; d. David and Ruth Joanne (Irwin) Ririe; m. David Martin Carlson, June 18, 1982; children: Elizabeth Melissa, David Wayne. BS in Communications Disorders, Brigham Young U., 1980; MS in Speech Pathology, U. Utah, 1983. Cert. clin. competence in speech pathology. Speech language pathologist Jordan Sch. Dist., Sandy, Utah, 1983—, mem. social and inservice coms. Mem. Am. Speech and Hearing Assn., Utah Speech and Hearing Assn. Home: 2848 Adams St Salt Lake City UT 84115-3312

CARLSON, MARILYN A., English language educator; b. Gothenburg, Nebr., July 24, 1938; d. Harold N. and Verma Elnora (Granlund) C.; m. Paul E. Carlson, July 31, 1959 (dec. Sept. 1988); 1 child, Andrea Joy. BS in Edn., English and Psychology, Sioux Falls Coll., 1960; MA in History, U. S.D., 1973, MA in English, 1992. English and social scis. instr., curriculum coord. Beresford (S.D.) Pub. Sch., 1960-78; English and social scis. instr. Sioux Empire Coll., Hawarden, Iowa, 1979-85; instr. of English and ESL Midwest Inst. for Internat. Studies, Sioux Falls, 1985-89; asst. prof. English Augustana Coll., Sioux Falls, 1989—; part time instr. psychology Northwestern Coll., 1985; part time instr. English and lit. Nat. Coll., 1985-88; part time instr. English and history Augustana Coll., 1986-89; presenter in field. Author: Visions of Light: Flannery O'Connor's Themes and Narrative Method, also rev.; author critiques. Named Tchr. of Yr., 1976; S.D. Humanities scholar, 1993; Bush mini-grantee, 1993; Internat. Studies grantee, 1994. Mem. AAUP, Nat. Coun. Tchrs. English, Nat. Fedn. Music Clubs, Am. Assn. Univ. Profs. Home: RR 3 Box 14 Beresford SD 57004-9205 Office: Augustana Coll Dept English 29th St and Summit Ave Sioux Falls SD 57197

CARLSON, MARY ANN, state legislator, hotel executive; b. Palo Alto, Calif., Jan. 22, 1944; m. Wesley H. Carlson; 5 children. BA, Marquette U., 1965; postgrad., Fordham U., 1977; MA in Psychology, Lesley Coll., 1991. Co-owner, operator West Mountain Inn, Arlington, Vt.; mem. Vt. State Senate, Montpelier, 1989—; Dem. leader rules/joint fiscal com. U.S. Senate, mem. appropriations com., chair gen. affairs and housing com., chair jud. nominating bd. Chair., coord. Coun. of Vt. Interactive Television; adv. bd. Healthcare 2000; gen. affairs and housing com., mem. appropriations com. United Way of Bennington County. Mem. Vt. Businesses for Social Responsibility, Arlington Townscapes, Bennington, Arlington, Manches C. of C. Democrat. Home: PO Box 481 Arlington VT 05250-0465 Office: Vt State Senate State Capitol Montpelier VT 05602*

CARLSON, NATALIE SAVAGE, author; b. Winchester, Va., Oct. 3, 1906; d. Joseph Hamilton and Natalie Marie (Villeneuve dit Vallar) Savage; m. Daniel Carlson, Dec. 7, 1929; children: Stephanie Natalie (Mrs. Robert David Sullivan), Julie Ann (Mrs. Walter Erskine McAlpine). Student parochial schs., Calif. Newspaper reporter Long Beach (Calif.) Sun, 1926-29; writer, children's books, 1929—. Author: The Talking Cat and Other Stories of French Canada, 1952 (N.Y. Herald Tribune Children's Spring Book Festival award 1952), Alphonse, That Bearded One, 1954 (N.Y. Herald Tribune Children's Spring Book Festival award 1954, Boys' Club of Am. Jr. Book award 1955), Wings Against the Wind, 1955 (Honor Book award 1955, Boys' Club of Am. Book award 1956), Sashes Red and Blue, 1956, Hortense: The Cow for a Queen, 1957 (Honor Book award 1957), The Happy Orpheline, 1957, The Family Under the Bridge, 1958 (Newbery honor book 1959), A Brother for the Orphelines, 1959, Evangeline: Pigeon of Paris, 1960, The Tomahawk Family, 1960, The Song of The Lop-eared Mule, 1961, A Pet for the Orphelines, 1962, Carnival in Paris, 1962, School Bell in the Valley, 1963, Jean-Claude's Island, 1963, The Orphelines in the Enchanted Castle, 1964, The Letter on the Tree, 1964, The Empty Schoolhouse, 1965 (Children's Book award Child Study Assn. of Am. 1965), Sailor's Choice, 1966, Chalou, 1967, Luigi of the Streets, 1967, Ann Aurelia and Dorothy, 1968, Befana's Gift, 1969, Marchers for the Dream, 1969, The Half-Sisters, 1970, Luvvy and the Girls, 1971, Marie Louise and Christophe, 1974, Mary Louise's Heyday, 1975, Runaway Marie Louise, 1977, Jaky or Dodo?, 1978, Time for the White Egret, 1978, The Night the Scarecrow Walked, 1979, King of the Cats and Other Tales, 1980, A Grandmother for the Orphelines, 1980, Spooky and the Witch's Goat, 1980, Marie Louise and Christophe at the Carnival, 1981, Spooky Night, 1982, Surprise in the Mountains, 1983, The Ghost at the Lagoon, 1984, Spooky and the Ghost Cat, 1985, Spooky and the Wizard's Bats, 1986, Spooky and the Bad Luck Raven, 1988. Republican. Roman Catholic. Address: 29250 Hwy 19 N Lot 17 Clearwater FL 34621*

CARLSON, NATALIE TRAYLOR, publisher; b. St. Paul, Feb. 15, 1938; d. Howard Ripley and Maxine (Johnson) Smith; m. James S. Carlson, Oct. 6, 1990; children: Drew Michael, Dacia Lyn, Dana Ann. BA, Jacksonville (Ala.) State U., 1975. Dir. Madison County Assn. of Mental Health, Huntsville, Ala., 1966-67; campaign mgr. U.S. Senatorial Race, No. Ala., 1968; pub. rels. Anniston Acad., 1970-76; journalist The Anniston Star, 1970-74, The Birmingham News, 1972-76; dir. Ala. affiliate, Am. Heart Assn., Birmingham, 1976-77; mgr. San Vincent New Home div., San Diego County Estates Realty, 1978-79; dir. sales Blake Pub. Co., San Diego, 1980-86; pres. Century Publ., San Diego, 1986—. Alternate del. at large Rep. Nat. Conv., San Francisco, 1964; fin. chmn. Madison County Rep. Exec. Com., Huntsville, Ala., 1966-69; pres. Madison County Rep. Women, Huntsville, 1967, 68; Diocesan Conv. del. Grace Episcopal Ch., Ala., 1975; active Nat. Rep. Party, 1962—; mem. St. James Episcopal Ch., Newport Beach, 1990—. Recipient 1st Pl. Newswriting award AP, 1971, 72, 73; nominee Outstanding Woman of Yr., Huntsville Area Jaycees, 1967. Mem. Long Beach Area C. of C., Palm Springs C. of C., Greater Del Mar C. of C., Huntington Beach C. of C., Kappa Kappa Gamma.

CARLSON, P(ATRICIA) M(CELROY), writer; b. Guatemala City, Guatemala, Feb. 3, 1940; (parents Am. citizens); d. James Benjamin and Alene (Jones) McElroy; m. M.A. Carlson, Aug. 20, 1960; children: Geoffrey, Richard. BA, Cornell U., 1961; MA, Cornell, 1966, PhD, 1974. Instr., lectr. psychology and human development Cornell U., Ithaca, N.Y., 1973-78; mem. bd. dirs. Bloomington Restorations, Inc., 1982-84. Author: (with M. Potts, R. Cocking and C. Copple) Structure and Development in Child Language, 1979, Audition for Murder, 1985, Murder is Academic, 1985, Murder if Pathological, 1986, (with Richard Darlington) Behavioral Statistics, 1987, Murder Unrenovated, 1988, Rehersal for Murder, 1988, Murder in Dog Days, 1991, Murder Misread, 1991, Bad Blood, 1991, Gravestone, 1993, Bloodstream, 1995, eight short stories. Chair Ithaca Environ. Commn., 1975-78; bd. dirs. Historic Ithaca, 1976-77. Mem. Mystery Writers Am. (bd. dirs. 1990-92), Sisters in Crime (internat. sec. 1990-91, v.p. 1991-92, pres. 1992-93). Address: Vicky Bijur Literary Agy 333 West End Ave New York NY 10023

CARLSON, SALLY P., town clerk; b. Jamestown, N.Y.; d. Julius Pickett and Marjorie (Fenton) Hough; m. Robert J. Carlson, June 29, 1968; children: Kelly C., Brooke Carlson Norris. BS in Secondary English, State U. Coll., Geneseo, 1965; postgrad., Syracuse U., 1966-67, Fredonia, 1969-71. Tchr. Randolph (N.Y.) Ctrl. Sch., 1965-68; town clk.-tax collector, tax collector Town of North Harmony, Stow, N.Y., 1972—; tax collector Chautauqua Sch. Dist., 1986-92. Trustee Ashville (N.Y.) Free Libr., 1980-93, pres. bd., 1992, 93, pres. 1994—. Tech. grantee N.Y. State Archives and Records, 1992-93, Indexing grantee N.Y. State Archives, 1994-95. Mem. N.Y. State Town Clks. Assn., Mcpl. Clks. of Chautauqua County (pres. 1982). Republican. Methodist. Home: PO Box 176 Stow NY 14785-0176 Office: Town of North Harmony PO Box 167 Stow NY 14785-0167

CARLSON, STACY, legislative staff member; b. Burbank, Calif., Sept. 6, 1960. BA in Econ., Calif. State U., 1982; MBA, Stanford U., 1988. Legis. asst. to Rep. Bill Thomas, 1982-84; chief of staff Kern County Bd. Suprs., 1984-86; various positions including sr. v.p. strategic planning and spl. projects Silicon Valley Bank, Santa Clara, Calif., 1989-93; minority staff dir. Com. House Adminstrn., 1993—. Office: Com on House Administration H-330 The Capitol Washington DC 20515*

CARLSON, SUZANNE OLIVE, architect; b. Worcester, Mass., Aug. 20, 1939; d. Sigfrid and Helga (Larson) C. BS, R.I. Sch. Design, 1963. Jr. ptnr. Dingnam-Fauteux & Partners, Worcester, 1969-70; ptnr. Richard Lamoureux Asso., Worcester, 1970-75, Herron & Carlson (AIA), Worcester, 1975—; Guest lectr. Holy Cross Coll., 1969-70. Chmn. Worcester Hist. Commn., 1976-88; trustee Worcester Heritage Soc., 1982-88, Park Spirit of Worcester Inc., 1987—; trustee Worcester Girls Inc. of Worcester, pres. 1989-92, sec. 1994—; trustee Performing Arts Sch. Worcester, 1977-86, v.p. 1980-85; trustee Cultural Assembly Greater Worcester, 1981-86, v.p., 1982-83. Recipient European Honors Program grant Rome, Italy, 1961-62; recipient AIA School medal for excellence, 1963. Mem. AIA (exec. bd. Ctrl. Mass. chpt. 1969-71, sec.-treas. 1970-71, v.p. 1971-72, pres. 1972-73), Mass. Soc. Architects (exec. bd. 1972-74, v.p. 1975, pres. 1976), New Eng. Regional Coun. Architects (pres. 1977), New Eng. Antiquities Rsch. Assn. (membership chair 1982-84, 90-94, resource devel. chair 1994—, graphics dir. jours. 1982—, trustee 1990—). Home and Office: Herron & Carlson 2 Oxford Pl Worcester MA 01609-2008

CARLSON-PICKERING, JANE, educator; b. Providence, Sept. 17, 1954; d. Arthur Julius and Laura Helen (Extovicz) Carlson; m. Allan Thomas Pickering, Nov. 2, 1980; children: Lauren, Taylor. BS in Art Edn., R.I. Coll., 1976, MEd in Art and Indsl. Arts Edn., 1983. Cert. elem. tchr. (life), R.I., gifted edn. tchr., NASA Lunar Disc tchr. Profl. photographer Ted Pickering Studios, Warwick, R.I., 1973—; calligraphy tchr. Warwick Adult Edn., 1978; secondary tchr. graphics arts Warwick Sch. Dept., 1976-78, secondary tchr. gifted program, 1978-83; elem. gifted program coordinator and tchr. Chariho Sch. System, Wyoming, R.I., 1983—; mem. Commr.'s Task Force on Vocat. and Insl. Arts Edn., Providence, 1984-85, Commr.'s Task Force on Gifted and Talented Edn., 1991-92, Chariho K-12 Curriculum Coun., 1992—, tech. com., 1993—; aerial photographer for Aerovisions, 1988-92. Recipient First Pl. award photography contest Warwick Arts Found., 1984, Tchr. award Invent Am., 1991, Lunar Disc Program Tchr. Tng. Cert. NASA, 1991. Mem. NEA, ASCD, State Advs. Gifted Edn., Nat. Student Art Edn. Assn. Club (treas. 1971-72), Epsilon Pi Tau. Home: 209 Blueberry Ln West Kingston RI 02892-1818 Office: Chariho Sch Dept Switch Rd Wood River Junction RI 02894

CARLTON, CAROL LEE, librarian; b. Williamson, W.Va., Mar. 19, 1941; d. Samuel Howard and Edna Lorraine (Moore) C. AS in Med. Tech., Bluefield Coll., 1961; BS in Secondary Edn., Pikeville Coll., 1966; MS in Community Devel., U. Louisville, 1972; MLS, U. Ky., 1978. Supr. bacteriology dept. Appalachian Regional Hosp., Harlan, Ky., 1963-64; social worker, juvenile ct. worker Ky. Dept. Child Welfare, Pikeville, Ky., 1966-67; asst. chief technologist ARC Regional Blood Ctr., Louisville, 1967-68; social svc. worker W.Va. Dept. Welfare, Williamson, 1968-73, supr. family svcs., 1974-77; quality control reviewer, state hearing officer W.Va. Dept. Welfare, Charleston, 1973-74; grad. asst. U. Ky., Lexington (Ky.) Tech. Inst., 1977-78; asst. libr. S.E. Community Coll., Cumberland, K.Y., 1978-80; libr. So. W.Va. Community Coll., Williamson, 1980-90, dir. libr. svcs., 1990—. Named to Ky. Cols., 1980; Devel. Faculty Mini-grantee Ky. Coun. Higher Edn., 1980, Coll. Libr. Tech. and Cooperation Networking grantee U.S. Dept. Edn., 1990. Mem. AAUW (chair scholarship com. 1982—), Ky. Libr. Assn., W.Va. Libr. Assn., W.Va. Cmty. Coll. Assn., Nat. Rlwy. Hist. Soc., Women of the Moose, Am. Soc. Clin. Pathologists (registered med. technologist), Beta Phi Mu, Phi Alpha Theta, Phi Theta Kappa. Democrat. Baptist. Office: So W Va Community Coll Armory Rd Williamson WV 25661-3400

CARLTON, DIANE V., county official; b. Dobbs Ferry, N.Y.. BA in History, SUNY, Geneseo, 1981; MPA, U. Del., 1983. Asst. planner Westchester County Dept. Planning, White Plains, N.Y., 1982-84; from planner to sr. planner Sullivan County Dept. Planning, Monticello, N.Y., 1984-89; dir. land use Town of Naugatuck, Conn., 1989-90; dir. planning Otsego County Dept. Planning, Cooperstown, N.Y., 1990—; cons. in field, 1990—; adj. prof. SUNY, Oneonta, 1994—. Author/editor: (handbooks) Planning and Zoning Handbook, 1990, SEQR Handbook, 1991, Subdivision Handbook, 1992, ZEO Handbook, 1994, Site Plan Handbook, 1994. Active Am. Cancer Soc., Oneonta, 1991-93; big sister Big Buddies Program, Delhi, N.Y., 1992—. Mem. N.Y. State Assn. Environ. Mgmt. Couns. (sec. 1992—), N.Y. State Assn. of Planning Dirs. (sec. treas. 1993—). Office: Otsego County Dept Planning 197 Main St Cooperstown NY 13326

CARLTON, KIMBERLY SUSAN, human resources manager; b. Ft. Riley, Kans., Aug. 10, 1965; d. Kenneth Lawrence and Barbara Dorothy (Nichol) Kunz; m. Arthur Fred Carlton, Oct. 14, 1989; 1 child, Jessica Megan. BBA, Idaho State U., 1987. Personnel generalist Casa Grande (Ariz.) Regional Med. Ctr., 1988-91, asst. dir. human resources, 1991-92; mgr. human resources Cen. Ariz. Med. Ctr., Florence, 1992—. Mem. Am. Bus. Women's Assn. (past pres., current v.p. Casa Grande Valley chpt.), Soc. Human Resource Mgmt. (Ctrl. Ariz. human resource mgmt. assoc., current pres.). Home: 1898 S Private Dr Casa Grande AZ 85222 Office: Cen Ariz Med Ctr 450 W Adamsville Rd Florence AZ 85232

CARLTON, PATRICIA PALETSKY, marketing professional; b. Ashland, Pa., Sept. 29, 1941; d. Vincent Edward and Natalie Joan (Sedar) Paletsky; m. John B.K. LaBarre, June 13, 1964 (div. Oct. 1980); children: Sedar M.T., Deirdre A.P.; m. Robert Elsworth Carlton, Apr. 12, 1983. BA, Rutgers U., 1963; postgrad., various. Customer engr. NCR, Trenton, N.J., 1963-64; computer programmer Inst. Social Rsch., Ann Arbor, Mich., 1964-66; systems analyst Ypsilanti (Mich.) State Hosp., 1966-67, U. Mich. Hosp., Ann Arbor, 1967-69; asst. data processing mgr. City of Rockville, Md., 1981-82; project mgr. Victor O. Schinnerer, Washington, 1982-84, Dialcom, Rockville, 1984-86; X.400 program mgr. BT Tymnet/Dialcom, Rockville, 1986-90; EDI product mgr. GE Info. Svcs., Rockville, 1990-93, X.400 product mgr., 1993—. Recipient scholarship Douglass Coll., New Brunswick, Md., 1959-63. Mem. AAUW (pres., v.p., scholarship named in honor 1991), Knights of Lithuania (treas., trustee 1974—), Douglass Coll. Alumni (pres. 1983—). Home: 5321 Trailway Dr Rockville MD 20853-1574 Office: GE Info Svcs 401 N Washington St Rockville MD 20850-1706

CARLTON, SARA BOEHLKE, rehabilitation services administrator; b. Black River Falls, Wis., July 1, 1937; d. Ralph William and Hazel Olive (Drecktrah) Boehlke; m. Mason Gant Carlton, Sept. 9, 1961 (div.); children: Holly Gant, John Frederick. BS, U. Wis., 1959; MEd, Rutgers U., 1981, EdD, 1988. Occupational therapist VA Hosp., Lyons, N.J., 1960-65; occupational therapist Hunterdon Med. Ctr., Flemington, N.J., 1968-71, dir. occupational therapy, 1971-73, dir. child evaluation & treatment, 1973-85, adminstrv. rehab. coord., 1985-88; asst. v.p. Mt. Washington Pediat. Hosp., Balt., 1988—; mem. adj. faculty Rutgers U., 1981, Johns Hopkins U., Balt., 1991—. Mem. Holland Twp. Red. Fdn., Hunterdon County, N.J., 1972-78, v.p., 1974-78; trustee Hunterdon Occupational Tng. Ctr., Flemington, 1972-80, pres. 1978; trustee Hunterdon County Bd. Mental Health, 1975-77; mem. adv. bd. Inst. for Study of Exceptional Children, Ednl. Testing Svc., Princeton, N.J., 1978-80; trustee Upton Sch. Found., Balt., 1988—, sec. 1990—; mem. Md. State Interagy. Coordinating Coun., 1989—; bd. deacons Second Presbyn. Ch., Balt. Mem. Am. Coll. Healthcare Execs., Am. Occupational Therapy Assn., Md. Occupational Therapy Assn. Presbyterian (deacon 2d Presbyn Ch., Balt.). Home: 113 Fireside Cir Baltimore MD 21212

CARLTON-ADAMS, GEORGIA M., psychotherapist; b. Kansas City, Mo.; d. George Randolph Carlton and Harriett Marie (Smith) Carlton-Witt; m. John Adams; 1 child, J.J. II. Student, Kansas City (Mo.) Jr. Coll., Rockhill Coll., Trinity Coll., Dublin, Ireland, 1973, City U. of London (Eng.), 1978. Owner Pure White Electric Light and Magic, Lakewood, Calif., 1985—; dir., owner Trauma Buddy's, Lakewood, 1988—; clin. hypotherapist Inner Group Mgmt., Cerritos, Calif., 1989—; cons. Rockwell, McDonnell Douglas, Long Beach, Calif., 1987-90; owner In Print mag., 1990—; staff counselor FHP. Author: Who Calls on Pandora, 1969, Jupiter in Scorpio, 1974, Burma Route, 1989, Counterstrike: Dimitri Manulski, 1990, Kitty Morphis, 1982, Mouse Tails, 1991, Bookish Miss Emma, 1993, A Little Trip Through the Universe, 1993, Handbook for the Living, 1990. Adv. Greater Attention Victims Violent Crimes; active Animal Rights Pet Protection Soc., Calif. Preventive Child Abuse Orgn., Sierra Club. Mem. Calif. Astronomy Assn., Acoustic Brain Rsch., Inner Group Mgmt., NLP Integration Soc. (pres. 1988-89), British Psychol. Assn., C. of C. Home and Office: 744 Chestnut Ave Apt 11 Long Beach CA 90813-4157

CARLUCCI, MARIE ANN, nursing administrator, nurse; b. N.Y.C., Apr. 22, 1953; d. Clarence Hugh and Anna Rebecca (Mills) McNamee; m. Paul Pasquale Carlucci, Aug. 18, 1973; children: Christine, Patricia. Diploma in nursing, Mt. Vernon Hosp. Sch. Nursing, N.Y., 1974; BS in Behavioral Sci. summa cum laude, Mercy Coll., 1991; postgrad., N.Y. Med. Coll., 1991—. Cert. emergency nurse. Staff nurse Mt. Vernon (N.Y.) Hosp., 1974-82, Lawrence Hosp., Bronxville, N.Y., 1982-84; staff nurse No. Westchester Hosp., Mt. Kisco, N.Y., 1984-91, asst. dir. nursing, mem. nurse mgmt. and ethics coms., 1991-94; asst. dir. nursing Ferncliff Manor, Yonkers, N.Y., 1994—. Religious edn. tchr. St. John and St. Mary's Ch., Chappagua, N.Y., 1984-94; campaign mgr. Com. to Elect Paul P. Carlucci, Chappagua, 1990; mem. surrogate decision making com. N.Y. Commn. Quality Care for Mentally Disabled; mem. Hastings Ctr. Mem. N.Y. Orgn. Nurse Execs., St. John and St. Mary's Women's Assn., Psi Chi, Phi Gamma Mu. Roman Catholic. Home: 23 Pine View Rd # 5 Mount Kisco NY 10549-3336 Office: Ferncliff Manor 1154 Saw Mill River Rd Yonkers NY 10710

CARLYON, DIANE CLAIRE, nurse; b. Butte, Mont., Nov. 5, 1950; d. Roy and Claire Jenny (Madison) C.; (div.); children: Michael Wade Jr., Tammy Michelle. BSN, U. Tenn., 1987. Staff nurse Oakland Naval Hosp., Calif., Kimberly Nurses, Memphis; staff nurse, staff nurse Meth. Cen. Hosp., Memphis; utilization mgmt. Qual-Med Health Plan, Bellevue, Wash.; utilization mgmt./quality assurance coord. Gen. Hosp. of Everett; IV infusion specialist Homedco, Redmond, Wash.; clin. field coord. Vis. Nurse's of N.W. Everett, Everett, Wash. Mem. Meth. Hosp. staff adv. bd., Assistance Impaired Nursing Students com., IMHOTEP, Snohomish County Aids Task Force, Ryan White Care Funds Planning Coun. Mem. ANA, Tenn. Nurses Assn. (task force HIV), Wash. Nurses Assn. Home: 11605 Hwy 99 # A201 Everett WA 98204

CARMAN, RENEE LOU, accountant; b. Spokane, Wash., Nov. 2, 1951; d. Jack P. Manning and Marjorie L. Rogers; m. Gary L. Carman, Mar. 10, 1972 (div. Dec. 1988); children: Stacy, Trevor, Meagan. BA in Bus. Adminstrn., U. Mont., 1977; MBA, Ea. Wash. U., 1989. CPA, Wash. Tax acct. LeMaster & Daniels, Spokane, 1977-84, Cominco Am., Spokane, 1984-88; tax mgr. McDirmid, Mikkelsen & Secrest, Spokane, 1988—. Mem. AICPA, Inst. Mgmt. Accts. (dir. tech. meetings 1989-94), Estate Planning Coun., Wash. Soc. CPAs, Exec. Women Internt. (asst. treas. 1989-94). Roman Catholic. Office: McDirmid Mikkelsen Secrest Ste 300 926 W Sprague Spokane WA 99204

CARMICHAEL, JUDY LEA, record industry executive, concert jazz pianist; b. Lynwood, Calif., Nov. 27, 1952; d. John Alvin and Jeanne Pauline (Boock) Hohenstein. Student, Calif. State U., Long Beach, 1970-73, Calif. State U., Fullerton. Pianist, lectr. L.A., 1972-82, Steinway Artist, N.Y.C., 1984, USIA, L.A., N.Y.C., Zurich, Paris, and, Cannes, France, 1987-88, Carnegie Hall Concert, N.Y.C., 1988, Rio de Janiero, 1989; owner C&D Prodns., N.Y.C., 1989—; pianist, lectr. Peggy Guggenheim Concert, Venice, Italy, 1990, Concert Am. Acad. in Rome, 1990, 91, USIA Tour of Portugal & Spain, 1991; chmn. jazz fellowships com. NEA, Washington, 1990-91; pianist USIA Tour of India, Tour of China, 1992, Singapore, 1994; featured on (TV programs) Marian McPortland's Piano Jazz, 1990, Morning Edition Nat. Pub. Radio, Entertainment Tonight, CBS, CBS Sunday Morning with Charles Kuralt, 1993. Author (music) Judy Carmichael's Complete Book of Stride Piano, 1987; producer, artist (LP's) Jazz Piano, 1983, Two Handed Stride, 1980, (CD's) Trio, 1989, Old Friends, 1991, Pearls, 1985, ...And Basie Caller Her Stride, 1993, Judy, 1994; jazz editor Sheet Music mag., 1989-90; contbr. numerous articles to profl. jours. NEA fellow, grantee; Grammy award nominee. Mem. Musician's Union.

CARMICLE, LINDA HARPER, psychotherapist; b. Westmore, Tenn., Oct. 20, 1937; d. Noel Franklin and Mary Frank (Caldwell) Harper; m. Jerrel B. Carmicle, June 2, 1956; children: Roxanna Linn Carmicle Lynch, Jerry Noel. AA, St. Petersburg Jr. Coll., 1968; BSW with honors, Tex. Women's U., 1975, MA, 1977; PhD in Psychology, Fielding Inst., Santa Barbara, Calif., 1992. Lic. profl. counselor, marriage and family therapist; cert. eating disorder specialist, chem. dependency specialist; cert. group psychotherapist; cert. clin. group therapist; supr. for LPCs. Dir. Galaxy Ctr., Garland, Tex., 1975-78; counselor Saudi Arabia Internat. Sch., Daharan, 1978, Dallas County Family Ct. Counselors, Dallas, 1979-83; pvt. practice psychotherapy Dallas and Plano, Tex., 1983—; adj. faculty Tex. Women's U., Denton, 1976-78, rep. Coun. on Social Work Edn., 1977. Active Custer Rd. United Meth. Ch. Mem. Am. Group Psychotherapy Assn., Am. Assn. Marriage and Family Therapy, Tex. Assn. Counseling Devel., Tex. Assn. Marriage and Family Therapy, Dallas Group Psychotherapy Soc. (newsletter staff), Internat. Assn. Transactional Analysis, Internat. Assn. Eating Disorder Profls. Democrat. Methodist. Home: 3005 Saddlehead Dr Plano TX 75075-1529 Office: 2301 Ohio Dr # 215 Plano TX 75093

CARMONA, LAURA GRACE, systems analyst; b. San Francisco, Sept. 9, 1959; d. Louis Stephen and Carole Louise (Pellechi) C. BA in Studio Art, Wellesley Coll., 1981. Rsch. assoc. Nat. Computer Graphics Assn., Washington and Fairfax, Va., 1982; programmer, analyst U.S. Ho. Reps., Washington, 1982-84; cons. Peppertree Software Cons., Washington, 1984-86, Battelle Meml. Inst., Washington and Arlington, Va., 1986-89; sys. analyst, project leader Mgmt. Action Corp., Manassas, Va., 1989-94; tech. support engr. Telecomm. Mgmt. Assocs., Manassas, 1995—; bookkeeper B.L. Osborn, Inc., Manassas, Va., 1990-94. Home: 10043 Irongate Way Manassas VA 22110 Office: Telecomm Mgmt Assocs 10530 Linden Lake Plz Ste 200 Manassas VA 22110

CARNES, JULIE E., federal judge; b. Atlanta, Oct. 31, 1950; m. Stephen S. Cowen. AB, U. Ga., 1972, JD, 1975. Bar: Ga. 1975. Law clk. to Hon. Lewis R. Morgan U.S. Ct. Appeals (5th cir.), 1975-77; asst. U.S. Atty. U.S. Dist. Ct. (no. dist.), Ga., 1978-90; spl. counsel U.S. Sentencing Commn., 1989, commr., 1990—; judge U.S. Dist. Ct. (no. dist.), 1992—. Office: US Courthouse 75 Spring St Ste 2167 Atlanta GA 30303

CARNEY, ANN VINCENT, secondary education educator; b. Slippery Rock, Pa., Feb. 17, 1933; d. Arthur Porter and Leila Felicia (Watson) Vincent; m. Charles Lucien Carney Jr., Dec. 15, 1954 (div. 1974); children: Adrienne Ann, Stephen Vincent. BS, Drexel Inst. Tech., 1955; MEd, U. Pitts., 1972. Cert. tchr., reading specialist, Pa. Tchr. English Allegheny Valley Sch. Dist., Springdale, Pa., 1957-62; reading specialist Gateway Sch. Dist., Monroeville, Pa., 1972—. Mem. AAUW, Internat. Reading Assn., Keystone State Reading Assn., Three Rivers Reading Coun., Phi Kappa Phi, Omicron Nu. Republican. Home: 4013 Impala Dr Pittsburgh PA 15239-2705 Office: Gateway Sch Dist 2609 Mosside Blvd Monroeville PA 15146-3378

CARNEY, DEBORAH LEAH TURNER, lawyer; b. Great Bend, Kans., Aug. 19, 1952; d. Harold Lee and Elizabeth Lura (Dillon) Turner; m. Thomas J.T. Carney, Mar. 20, 1976; children: Amber Blythe, Sonia Briana, Ross Dillon. BA in Human Biology, Stanford U., 1974; JD, U. Denver, 1976. Bar: Kans. 1977, U.S. Dist. Ct. Kans. 1977, U.S. Ct. Appeals (10th cir.) 1982, Colo. 1984, U.S. Dist. Ct. Colo. 1984, U.S. Supreme Ct. 1989, U.S. Claims Ct. 1990. With Turner & Boisseau, Great Bend, 1976-84, of counsel, 1984-93; assoc. Lutz & Oliver, Arvada, Colo., 1984-85; prin. Deborah Turner Carney, P.C., Golden and Lakewood, Colo., 1985-92; shareholder Deborah & T.J. Carney, P.C., Golden, Colo., 1992—. Author (newsletter) Profl. Solutions, 1984; editor Apple Law newsletter, 1984-86; contbr. articles to profl. jours. Mem. ABA (computer divsn.), Kans. Bar

Assn., Colo. Trial Lawyers Assn., 1st Jud. Dist. Bar Assn. (Colo.), Barton County Bar Assn. (Kans.), Kiwanis (bd. dirs. Denver club 1988-90, trustee 1990-92, sec. 1992-93). Republican.

CARNEY, JEAN KATHRYN, psychologist; b. Ft. Dodge, Iowa, Nov. 10, 1948; d. Eugene James and Lucy (Devlin) C.; m. Mark Krupnick, Jan. 1, 1977; 1 child, Joseph Carney Krupnick. BA, Marquette U., Milw., 1970; MA, U. Chgo., Chgo., 1984; PhD, U. Chgo., 1986. Registered Clin. Psychologist, Ill. Reporter Milw. Jour., 1971-76, editorial writer, 1976-79; asst. prof. psychology St. Xavier Coll., Chgo., 1985-86; dir. Lincoln Park Clinic, Chgo., 1986-87; pvt. practice psychotherapist Chgo., 1987—; mem. sci. staff Michael Reese Hosp. Med. Ctr., Chgo., 1987—; instr. Northwestern U. Med. Sch., 1991—; lectr. U. Ill. Coll. Medicine, 1993—. Recipient Best Series Articles, 1975, Best Editorial, 1978, Milw. Press Club, William Allen White Nat. Award for Editorial Writing, 1978, Robert Kahn Meml. Award for Research on Aging, Univ. Chgo., 1985. Mem. APA, Ill. Psychol. Assn., Chgo. Assn. Psychoanalytic Psychology. Home: 915 Burns Ave Flossmoor IL 60422-1107 Office: 55 E Washington St Ste 1219 Chicago IL 60602

CARNEY, JUDITH, occupational therapist, school system adminstrator; b. Indpls., Oct. 30, 1949; d. Isadore and Luba Nisenbaum; m. Stephen M. Carney, Mar. 4, 1979; children: Matt, Johanna. BS, Ind. U., Indpls., 1971. Registered occupational therapist. Head occupational therapist Cedars Sinai Med. Ctr.; dir. devel. nursery Children's Hosp., Oakland, Calif.; mem. Sch. Dist. Governing Bd., Lafayette, Calif.; leader program for distrubed and devel. disabled children U. Calif.-Irvine Med. Ctr.; nursery sch. tchr. Wilshire YMCA; docent Babes in the Woods; tchr. environ. sci. Heald Bus. Coll.; legis. rep., sch. bd. rep. Burton Valley Elem. Pres. Burton Valley PTA; mem. RAPPORT; campaign chair for sch. funds; active numerous coms. Burton Valley and Lafayette Sch. Dist.; 1st v.p. Del Valle PTA Coun. Mem. AAUW (Lamorinda br., chair kid phone program, chair edn. equity program). Home: 3203 Lucas Dr Lafayette CA 94549-5546

CARNEY, KATE, actress, director, educator; b. Rice Lake, Wis., Aug. 2, 1933; d. Rexford Hugh and Margot Caroline (Haanstad) C. BS, U. Wis., 1955; MA, Mt. Holyoke Coll., 1958; postgrad., Centre du Théâtre Nationale, 1970, Columbia U. and Case-Western Res. U., 1957-63; Creative Arts fellow U. Colo., 1963. Actress performing in London, Paris, Istanbul, Ankara, Tel Aviv and Nicosia, 1970-72, Off Off-Broadway! An Anthology with Kay Carney, N.Y.C., Boston, Chgo., San Francisco, Vancouver, Balt., Phila., Boston and various U.S. colls., 1973—; performed Tonques, 1985, Camptown Ladies, 1986, Age of Enlightenment, 1986, Vacancy, 1987, Taste of Honey, 1988, N.Y.C., And A Nightingale Sang, 1992, My Fair Lady, 1992, Boston, Washed Up Middle Aged Women, 1993, Dr. Owens-Adair, 1994; dir. Mourning Pictures, Broadway and Lenox Arts Ctr., 1974, A Pretty Passion, Interart Theatre, N.Y.C., 1982, Quilt Pieces, Theatre of Open Eye, N.Y.C., 1983, Superwoman Bites the Dust, Playwright's Platform, Boston, 1984, The Mothers, Ubu Repetory Theatre, 1987, Airport, Theater at St. Peter's, 1988, A Good Time, Playwright's Horizons, 1988, Sleep Disturbances, Am. Renaissance Theatre, 1989, Man with the Killer Pen, New Dramatists, 1991, numerous others; tchr. acting, directing and psychophys. work Hunter Coll., Henry St. Playhouse, SUNY, Purchase, U. Calif.-Santa Cruz, 1977-80; assoc. prof. dept. theatre Smith Coll., Northampton, Mass., 1980-82, Bklyn. Coll., 1983-87; tchr. Ensemble Studio Theatre Inst., 1987, Brandeis U., 1989-92, Pine Manor Coll., 1993—; condr. workshops for profls. in U.S. and abroad, Coll. of Charleston, 1989, Marymount Manhattan Coll., 1988; organizer, trainer La Mama theatre groups, Paris and Tel Aviv; bd. dirs. Bear Rep. Theatre, 1977-79; performed with Open Theater, 1965-67; seminarian with Jerzy Grotowski, 1970. Moratorium organizer, performer Angry Artists Against the War, 1966-70; mem. Performing Artists for Nuclear Disarmament, 1981—, St. Clements Arts in Religious Action Com., 1972-75; organizer Bay Area Women in Theatre Orgn., 1978-80; contbr. articles to profl. jours. Kosciuszko Found. grantee, 1979, SUNY Rsch. Found. grantee, 1976. Mem. Soc. Stage Dirs. and Choreographers, Actors Equity, AFTRA, New England Theatre Conf., Women and Theatre Program, Assn. for Theatre in Higher Edn. (presenter nat. convs.), League Profl. Theatre Women/N.Y. Democrat. Unitarian. Office: Pine Manor Coll Theatre Dept 400 Heath St Chestnut Hill MA 02167

CARNEY, KATHLEEN L., interior designer; b. Cleve., Dec. 19, 1947; d. Joseph Smythe and Irene (Smith) Walsh; m. James A. Carney, July 18, 1970; 1 child, James Kenneth. BA, Barat Coll. Sacred Heart, Lake Forest, Ill., 1969. Cert. interior designer, Ohio, Ill. Tchr. Cleve. Bd. Edn., 1969-71; owner The Mart - Antiques & Interiors, Rocky River, Ohio, 1985—. Jr. League Cleve., 1978—; fundraiser, liaison Malachi House Cleve., 1987—; patron mem. women's com. Cleve. Orch.; active Pioneer Womens bd. Western Res. Acad., Hudson, Ohio, 1987-88; bd. dirs. Cleve. Montessori Assn. Cleve., 1977—; active ARC. Mem. Am. women's Econ. Devel. Corp., Allied Bd. Trade, Nat. Fedn. Ind. Bus., Am. Soc. Interior Designers (allied practitioner), Interior Design Soc. (assoc. mem.), Westwood Country Club. Democrat. Roman Catholic. Home: 65 Kensington Oval Cleveland OH 44116-1504 Office: The Mart 28691 Center Ridge Rd Cleveland OH 44145-3810

CARNEY, PATRICIA ANNE, educator, researcher; b. Cambridge, Mass., July 7, 1958; d. William James and Ellen Gloria (Morehouse) C.; m. Robert Carey Gersten, Jan. 5, 1985 (div. Nov. 1992). BS, St. Anselm Coll., 1980; MS, U. N.H., 1989; PhD, U. Wash., 1994. RN Dartmouth Hitchcock Med. Ctr., Hanover, N.H., 1980-81, asst. head nurse, 1981-85; project coord. Dartmouth Med. Sch., Hanover, N.H., 1986-89, instr., 1989-90; rsch. asst. U. Wash., Seattle, 1990-94; rsch. asst. prof. dept community and family medicine Dartmouth Med. Sch., Hanover, N.H., 1994—; cons. Midwest Consortium for Clin. Assessment, Seattle, 1992-93, Mercy Hosp. Found., Des Moines, 1991-93. Contbr. articles to profl. jours. Vol. Downtown Emergency Svc. Ctr., Seattle, 1990-91, Am. Cancer Soc., Manchester, N.J., 1985-90. Recipient award Innovation in Edn., 1992, rsch. award Agy. for Health Care Policy and Rsch., 1993. Mem. AAAS, Soc. for Med. Decision Making, Nightengale Soc., Toastmasters Internat., Sigma Theta Tau.

CARNEY, PHILLITA TOYIA, marketing communications management company executive, business and ministry consultant; b. Chgo., Apr. 18, 1952; d. Phillip Leon Carney and Margaret Clarice (Ewing) Brown. Student, U. Utah, 1971-74; BS in Bus., Westminster Coll., 1976. Ordanined to ministry Full Gospel Ch., 1989; state cert. sexual assault advocate counselor and tgn., Chgo., Ill. Corp. tng. dir. U&I Sugar Corp., Salt Lake City, also Moses Lake, Wash., 1976-77; program coord. Div. on Aging, Seattle, 1977-78; bus. devel. officer Del Green Assoc., Foster City, Calif., 1978-79; regional v.p. Equitec Fin. Group, San Francisco, Irvine and Oakland, Calif., 1979-84, United Resources, Oakland, San Francisco, Nev., 1984-86; owner, mgr. Carney & Assocs., Oakland, 1986; regional v.p. Eastcoast Ops. Benefits Communications Corp. div. Great West Life Insurance Co., Washington, 1986-87; nat. dir. enrollment services, nat. plan adminstr. U.S. Conf. Mayors Fringe Benefits Program, MCW Internat., Ltd., 1988—; dir. pub. rels. nat./internat. Liberty Temple Full Gospel Ch. and World Out Reach Ministries, Chgo., 1989—; dep. dir. Ams., Internat. Biog. Centre, 1992; dir. Total One, San Francisco; corp. cons., advisor Am. Intermediation Services, San Francisco, 1986; cons. Washington Literacy Council; sr. bus. cons., ptnr. Performance Strategies Inc., San Diego, 1986; ministry cons. Crusaders Ch., Chgo., 1991—; assoc. pastor Higher Love Ministries, Chgo., 1993—; bus. and ministry cons., 1989—; ch. elder, cons. New Covenant Life Ch., Chgo., 1994—; bd. dirs. Pastors Englewood, 1993—; exec. prodr., host "Focus" Radio Broadcast, Chgo., 1994—; moderator, creator pub. affairs radio program, 1975-76 (Best Pub. Affairs Program award Nat. Pub. Radio 1976); del. White House Conf. on Small Bus., Washington, 1986; mem., lobbyist Concerned Women for Am., 1987—; founder Eaglewood Cares, Inc., Chgo., 1994—; appointed chairperson media rels. Chgo. Legis. for Chgo. Alternative Policy Strategies, 1995—; colomist CAPS Newsletter Chgo. Defender Citizens Newspaper, 1995— . Recipient award Am. Legion, 1970, DAR, 1970; named Most Admired Woman of Decade, Am. Biog. Inst. Fellow Am. Biog. Inst. Rsch. Assn. (assoc., nat. advisor); mem. Internat. Assn. Fin. Planning, Women Entrepreneurs, Internat. Biog. Ctr. (del. 1992), Bus. and Profl. Women, Sales Mktg. Exec. Assn., Zonta Internat. (pres. 1985—). Avocations: jogging, swimming, reading, writing. Home: 10925 S Wood St Chicago IL 60643-3419

CARO, MELANIE DARLEEN, lawyer; b. Fairborn, Ohio, Dec. 12, 1956; d. Eugene Campbell and Bonnie Jean (Beall) Parkerson; m. Frank Anthony Caro, Jr., May 12, 1984; children: Tracy Hedberg, Alexandra Caro. BA summa cum laude, Washburn U., 1981, JD with honors, 1985. Legal intern Kans. Dept. Revenue, Topeka, 1983-85, atty., 1985-90; asst. U.S. atty. Dept. of Justice/U.S. Atty.'s Office, Topeka, 1990—. Leader Daisy/Girl Scouts U.S., Topeka, 1993; bd. dirs. Washburn Rural Mid. Sch. Parents Orgn., Topeka, 1992, 93, Topeka Gifted Orgn./501 Sch. Dist., 1987-89. Mem. Topeka Women Attys. (bd. dirs. 1989—), Am. Inns. of Ct., Topeka Inns of Ct., Topeka Bar Assn. (bd. dirs. 1986-90), Phi Kappa Phi. Republican. Office: US Attys Office 444 SE Quincy St Topeka KS 66683-0001

CARON, DENISE DEBORA, insurance and financial agent/broker; b. N.Y.C., Nov. 11, 1959; d. Arthur Strettle and Micheline (Rozene) C. BSN, Adelphi U., 1981, MSN, 1989; postgrad. in Bus. Adminstrn., Columbia U., 1993—. RN, N.Y.; CNOR, CNAA. CCRN Winthrop Univ. Hosp., Mineola, N.Y., 1981-83; asst. nursing care oper. rm. coord. L.I. Jewish Med. Ctr., New Hyde Park, N.Y., 1983-86, clin. nurse specialist, 1986-89; asst. dir. oper. rm. Lenox Hill Hosp., N.Y.C., 1989-92; sr. mgmt. cons. Deloitte and Touche, Parsippany, N.J., 1992; dir. surg. svcs. Beth Israel Med. Ctr., N.Y.C., 1992-94; broker/agt. Equitable Life Assurance Soc. and Equico Securities, N.Y.C., 1994—; guest faculty cert. program Adelphi U., Garden City, N.Y., 1986. Recipient scholarship Adelphi U., 1978-81, 89. Mem. Am. Assn. Oper. Rm. Nurses, Met. Assn. Health Care Execs., Sigma Theta Tau. Office: Equitable Life Assurance 1221 Avenue Of The Americas New York NY 10020-1001

CARONE, PATRICIA, state legislator; b. Greenville, Pa., Mar. 21, 1943. BA, George Washington U.; MA, Georgetown U. Rep. dist. 12 Pa. Ho. of Reps.; tchr. Home: 2700 Rochester Rd Mars PA 16046-9115 Office: Pa Ho of Reps State Capitol Harrisburg PA 17120*

CARONIA, LYNETTE MARIE, chemical engineer; b. New Orleans, Nov. 12, 1963; d. Frank James and Bertha Anita (Campos) C. BSChemE, La. State U., 1986. Registered engr.-in-tng., La. From assoc. process engr. to foreman utilities & fine chems. Occidental Chem. Corp., Hahnville, La., 1988-93; process safety coord. Basic Chems. group Occidental Chem. Corp., Hahnville, 1993—.

CAROSA, ROSINA M., nun, artist; b. Bklyn., July 1, 1940; d. Giocondo Jack and Carmela Lily Carosa. Student, Marymount Coll., 1958-60, Caldwell (N.J.) Coll., 1971-72. Joined Order of St. Clare, 1960. Head art dept. Monastery of St. Clare, Bordentown, N.J., 1973-74, mem. liturgy com., 1981—; retreat dir., novice mistress Monastery of St. Clare, Bolivia, 1975-80; mem. Holy Name Fedn. of Poor Clares, vocation dir., 1988—; instr. Monastery of St. Clare, 1988—; guest spkr., cons. One-woman show The Upstairs Gallery, Bordentown, N.J., 1994; group shows include St. Joseph's Coll., Phila., 1992, Assn. Uniting Religion and Art, Phila., 1992, Engrs. Armory, Phila., 1992, Midwestern Franciscan Fedn., Viterbo Coll., La Crosse, Wis., 1993, Trenton (N.J.) City Mus., 1993, 94, Peter Madero Gallery, N.Y.C., 1994, Smithville Mansion Festival '94, Easthampton, N.J., 1994 (Merit award 1994), N.J. Network, Trenton, 1995, numerous others; contbr. poetry to pubs. Recipient numerous grants; recipient painting awards Gardenstate Water Color Soc. Mems. Show, 1991, 16th Ann. Juried Art Show, Burlington County (N.J.) Cultural and Heritage Dept., 1992, 17th Ann. Juried Art Show, 1993. Mem. Gardenstate Watercolor Soc., Assn. Uniting Religion and Art, Trenton Artist Workshop Assn., New Arts Program. Roman Catholic. Home: Monastery of St Clare 201 Crosswicks St Bordentown NJ 08505

CAROZZA, SHIRLEY CAVINESS, government department administrator; b. Taylorsville, N.C., Jan. 8, 1936; d. Howard D. and Kathleen Brooks; m. Caviness, Aug. 20, 1960 (div. Aug. 1980); children: Thomas Raynard, Gregory Caviness, Craig Caviness; m. Michael Carozza. Student, Morgan State U. Dir. budget Health & Human Svcs., Washington, 1986-91; from dep. asst. to asst. sec. Veteran Affairs, Washington, 1991-92, dep. asst. sec. for budget, 1992—. Home: 9217 Midwood Dr Silver Spring MD 20910 Office: Dept of Veterans Affairs 810 Vermont Ave NW Washington DC 20420

CARPENTER, ANGELICA SHIRLEY, librarian, author; b. St. Louis, Mar. 28, 1945; d. James Grafton and Jean (Starkel) Shirley; m. Richard Allen Carpenter, June 22, 1968; 1 child, Carey Anne. AB in French, U. Ill., 1967, MS in LS, 1977, MEd, 1974. Br. mgr. Springfield (Mo.)-Greene County Libr., 1979-82; dir. Palm Springs (Fla.) Libr., 1982—. Co-author: Frances Hodgson Burnett, 1990, L. Frank Baum, 1992. Founding exec. dir. BookFest of Palm Beaches, West Palm Beach, 1990-92, chmn. authors' com., 1993-94. Mem. ALA, Soc. Children's Book Writers and Illustrators, Fla. Libr. Assn., Fla. Pub. Libr. Assn. (pres. 1993), Palm Beach County Libr. Assn. (pres. 1990-91), Internat. Wizard of Oz Club. Office: Palm Springs Libr 217 Cypress Ln Palm Springs FL 33461-1698

CARPENTER, CAROL MAUREEN, instructional developer, writer; b. Highland Park, Mich., Nov. 9, 1943; d. Eugene Reginald and Ione L. (Simpson) Boggess; m. Mack Lee Carpenter; children: Robert Lee, Cheryl Anne. BS, Wayne State U., 1966, MEd, 1972, EdD, 1984. Cert. tchr., Mich. Eng. tchr. Detroit Pub. Schs., 1966-71; Eng. instr. Oakland C.C., Auburn Hills, Mich., 1971-73; program coord. Detroit Inst. Tech., 1974-80; curriculum devel. Oakland U., Troy, Mich., 1980-81; newspaper reporter Observer and Eccentric Newspaper, Livonia, Mich., 1981-82; creative mgr. planning Sandy Corp., Troy, 1982-85; prin., v.p., bd. dirs. The High Performance Group, Inc., Southfield, Mich., 1985—; Eng. instr. Wayne State U., Detroit, 1979-80, Henry Ford C.C., Dearborn, Mich., 1980-81; workshop presenter Nat. Order Women Legislators Ann. Conf., Mackinac Island, Mich., 1991. Author: (poem) The Envelope Please, 1992. Recipient Tompkins award, 1980, Judith Siegel Pearson Writing award Wayne State U., 1984; Ropewalk scholar U. So. Ind., 1993, Cranbrook Writers Conf. scholar, Birmingham, Mich., 1980. Mem. ASTD (awards com. automotive group 1992—). Office: The High Performance Group 17117 W 9 Mile Rd Ste 1545 Southfield MI 48075-4521

CARPENTER, CAROL SETTLE, audio text business executive; b. Schenectady, Oct. 22, 1953; d. Carl Oscar and Ursula Elsen (McEldowney) Settle; m. R. Jay Carpenter, May 4, 1985; children: Reilly, Evie. BBA, Rochester Inst. Tech., 1975, postgrad. Inst. Children's Lit., 1988-91. Mgmt. trainee Lincoln First Bank, Rochester, N.Y., 1976-77; investment sec. Blyth Eastman Dillon, Scottsdale, Ariz., 1977-79; stockbroker E.F. Hutton, Scottsdale, 1979; stockbroker Rauscher Pierce Refsnes, Scottsdale, 1979-81; exec. v.p. RL Kotrozo Inc., Scottsdale, Ariz., 1981-85; asst. v.p. United Bank Ariz., Phoenix, 1985-88; asst. v.p. investments Citibank, Phoenix, 1988-91; freelance greeting card designer, Phoenix, 1991; CFO Warning Comm., Inc. Phoenix, 1992—. Staff vol. Crisis Nursery, Phoenix, 1987; co-pres. Khalsa Sch. Parent Coun., 1994—; mem. Contemporary Art Forum. Mem. Phi Gamma Nu. Republican. Presbyterian. Clubs: Plaza (Phoenix) (promotion chmn. 1986-87 , membership devel. 1988), Phoenix Country. Avocations: music, art, writing for children. Home: 374 E Verde Ln Phoenix AZ 85012-3012

CARPENTER, DOROTHY FULTON, former state legislator; b. Ismay, Mont., Mar. 13, 1933; d. Daniel A. and Mary Ann (George) Fulton; m. Thomas W. Carpenter, June 12, 1955; children: Mary Ione, James Thomas. BA, Grinnell Coll., 1955. Tchr. elem. schs., Houston, and Iowa City, 1955-58; mem. Iowa Ho. Reps., 1980-94, asst. minority floor leader, 1982-88, chair ethics and state govt. coms., 1992-94; ret., 1994. Pres. Planned Parenthood of Iowa, 1970; bd. dirs. Planned Parenthood Fedn. Am., 1977-80; fin. chmn. Episcopal Diocese of Iowa, 1979-80. Recipient Grinnell Coll. Alumni award, 1980. Mem. NOW, Common Cause. Republican.

CARPENTER, ELIZABETH JANE, digital equipment company communications executive, operations manager; b. Cleve., Mar. 29, 1949; d. Robert E. and Joan Jaffe. BA, Western Coll., Oxford, Ohio, 1970. Pub. rels. asst. Lennen & Newell/Pacific, Honolulu, 1970-73; account exec. Marschalk Advt., Cleve., 1973-76; cons. Carpenter Advt. & Pub. Rels., Cleve., 1976-80; internat. pub. rels. mgr. Wang Labs., Inc., Boston, 1980-82, advt. mgr., 1982-87; mgr. worldwide comm. CSS Digital Equipment Corp., Merrimack, N.H., 1987-92, advt. mgr. U.S. Svcs. group, 1992—; assoc. producer Am. Treasure, TV spl., 1986, The Entrepreneurs, TV spl., 1986-87; owner Carpenter Antiques, Dennis, Mass. Mem. Cape Cod Antiques Dealers Assn., Boston Advt. Club, Boston Club. Office: Digital Equipment Corp 3 Results Way Marlboro MA 01752-3080

CARPENTER, ESTHER, biological science educator; b. Meriden, Conn., June 4, 1903; d.. Ernest Charles and Nettie Jane (Hale) C. BA, Ohio Wesleyan U., 1925; MS, U. Wis., 1927; PhD, Yale U., 1932; DSc (hon.), Ohio Wesleyan U., 1956. Adj. instr. zoology Smith Coll., Northampton, Mass., 1933-34; from instr. to prof. Smith Coll., Northampton, 1934-54, prof., 1954-66, Myra M. Sampson prof., 1966-68. Republican. Congregationalist. Home: L209 Pennswood Village Newtown PA 18940

CARPENTER, JUDITH LEIDNER, counselor; b. Bklyn., Dec. 23, 1950; d. Jack and Selma (Paris) Leidner; m. Lucas Adams Carpenter, Sept. 2, 1972; 1 child, Meredith Lauren. BA, SUNY, Stony Brook, 1971; MA, U. N.C., 1973; MSc, C.W. Post Coll., 1981; cert. edn. specialist, West Ga. Coll., 1989. Cert. sch. counselor. Tchr. English Charleston (S.C.) County Schs., 1972-74, Middle Island (N.Y.) Schs., 1974-81; counselor Midles Island (N.Y.) Schs., 1981-85, Henry County Schs., McDonough, Ga., 1985-88, Rockdale County Schs., Conyers, Ga., 1988—. Mem. com. to evaluate health and human sexuality com. Newton County Bd. Edn., Covington, Ga., 1994. Mem. NEA, Ga. Assn. Educators, Ga. Sch. Counselors Assn. (Counselor of Yr. award 1992-93, 93-94, workship presenter 1991-94), Student Assitance Profls. Ga. (workshop presnter 1993-94), Rockdale County Assn. Educators. Democrat. Jewish. Office: Conyers Mid Sch 335 Sigman Rd Conyers GA 30207

CARPENTER, MARJ COLLIER, news director; b. Mercedes, Tex., Aug. 23, 1926; d. Walter Downs and Beatrice Catherine (Diehl) Collier; m. C.T. Carpenter Jr., Aug. 8, 1946 (dec. May 1965); children: Catherine, Carolyn Stewart, Jim Bob. BM magna cum laude, Tex. A&I U., 1946; DHL, Austin Coll., 1992. Reporter Mercedes (Tex.) Enterprise, 1943-44; tchr. Kingsville (Tex.) High Sch., 1946-47, Shelton Elem. Sch., Odem, Tex., 1947-49; reporter, news editor Pecos (Tex.) Ind., 1958-65; news editor Andrews (Tex.) News, 1965-72; daily columnist, area editor Big Spring (Tex.) Herald, 1972-78; news dir. Presbyn. Ch. U.S.A., Atlanta, 1978-87; news dir Presbyn. Ch. U.S.A., Lousiville, 1987—; ruling elder Presbyn. Ch. U.S.A., Big Spring, 1976, North Decatur Presbyn. Ch., Decatur, Ga., 1982. Editor Assembly in Brief, Presbyn. News Briefs, 1978—. Mem. bd. Permian Basin Girl Scouts U.S.A., Odessa, Tex., 1963-69. Recipient Citizen of Yr. award Big Spring C. of C., 1978, Bell-Mackay award Presbyns. for Renewal, 1992, numerous awards AP, Nat. Fedn. Press Women, Ky. Press Women, Ga. Press Women, Tex. Press Women, West Tex. Press. Mem. Nat. Fedn. Press Women (pres. 1991-93, Communicator of Achievement 1984), Soc. Profl. Journalists, Presbyn. Print Partnership, Bus. and Profl. Women (pres. 1969), Modern Study Club (pres. 1960). Home: 8917 Marksfield Cir # 6 Louisville KY 40222-7222 Office: Presbyn Ch USA 100 Witherspoon St Louisville KY 40202-1396

CARPENTER, MARY CHAPIN, country music singer; b. Princeton, N.J., 1959; d. Chapin and Bowie C. BA, Brown U., 1981. Admin. asst. R. J. Reynolds, Washington, 1983-83; owner GETAREALJOB Music. Albums: Hometown Girl, 1987, State of the Heart, 1989, Shooting Straight in the Dark, 1990, Come On Come On, 1992, Stones in the Road, 1994; recs. on CBS, 1987—. Named Top New Female Vocalist by Acad. Country Music, 1990, Female Vocalist of Yr. by Country Music Assn., 1992; recipient Washington Area Music awards 1986, 87, 89, Grammy award Best Country Performance, Female, 1992, 93, 94. Mem. ASCAP. Office: care Studio One Artists 7010 Westmoreland Ave Ste 100 Takoma Park MD 20912*

CARPENTER, MARY LAURE, hospital administrator; b. South Bend, Ind., Oct. 17, 1953; d. Daniel Pierre and Elizabeth Ann (Arigan) Laure; m. Gregory John Ingrassia, Oct. 26, 1974 (div. 1981); m. David James Carpenter, Dec. 30, 1983. Exch. student, France, 1970; student, U. Mo., St. Louis, 1972-74; BA, DePaul U., Chgo., 1988. With Christian Hosp. N.E., St. Louis, 1974-78; patient account mgr. Faith Hosp., Creve Coeur, Mo., 1978-81; telephone collector Tri-County Accounts Bur., Wheaton, Ill., 1981; Medicaid supr. Ingalls Meml. Hosp., Harvey, Ill., 1981-82; owner Medicare Claims Svc., Berkeley, Ill., 1982-84; ops. mgr. Superior Med. Supply, Elmhurst, Ill., 1984-85; bus. mgr. Forest Health Sys.-Forest Hosp., Des Plaines, Ill., 1985-86; asst. adminstr. Vencor/Sycamore (Ill.) Hosp., 1986-89; patient accounts mgr. Linden Oaks Hosp., Naperville, Ill., 1989-91; bus. office mgr. Vencor Hosp. Chgo., Northlake, Ill., 1991—; lectr. in field. Mem. Am. Guild Patient Acctg. Mgrs. (v.p. 1979-80, Pres.'s award, 1980, Journalism award 1979), Health Care Fin. Mgmt. Assn., Midwest Hosp. Credit Mgr. Assn. (bd. dirs. 1976-79). Office: Vencor Hosp 365 E North Ave Melrose Park IL 60164-2628

CARPENTER, ROXANNE SUE, realtor; b. Lebanon, Pa., Mar. 16, 1952; d. John Harold and Viola Helen (Miller) Ristenbatt; m. Richard Lee Carpenter, Jan. 30, 1971 (div. May 1989); children: Keith Scott, Jeffrey Alan. Lic. real estate salesperson, Pa. Computer operator Good Samaritan Hosp., Lebanon, 1969-82; legal sec. Allen H. Krause, Esquire, Lebanon, 1982; personal sec. Judge John Walter, Lebanon County Courthouse, Lebanon, 1983-87; realtor Suburban Realty, Annville, Pa., 1986—. Deaconess, mem. consistory St. Mark's United Ch. of Christ, Lebanon, 1990-93; solicitor United Way Lebanon County, 1985-92; pres. Lebanon Women of Today, 1986-87, chmn. Today's Woman, 1985, 86; mem. Lebanon County Dem. Com., 1988—; mem. adv. bd. Big Bros. and Big Sisters, sec.-treas., 1984-86; project chmn. Muscular Dystrophy Lebanon County, 1982-86. Recipient various awards, including Outstanding Officer of Yr. award Lebanon Women of Today, 1987, Pa. Assn. Realtors Excellence Club award, 1988, 89, 90, Pa. Assn. Realtors Excellence Club "Gold" award, 1990. Mem. Nat. Assn. Realtors, Pa. Assn. Realtors (excellence club life mem. 1990), Lebanon County Bd. Realtors, Lebanon Jaycee Women (chmn. Serena Lodge auction 1985), Lebanon Jaycettes (v.p. 1982, pres. 1984, project chmn. 1985, 86, Jaycete of Yr. award 1983, Pres. of Yr. award 1984). Democrat. Home: 670 Prescott Dr Lebanon PA 17046-8710 Office: Suburban Realty 30 W Main St Annville PA 17003-1318

CARPENTER, SUSAN KAREN, lawyer; b. New Orleans, May 6, 1951; d. Donald Jack and Elise Ann (Diehl) C. BA magna cum laude with honors in English, Smith Coll., 1973; JD, Ind. U., 1976. Bar: Ind. 1976. Dep. pub. defender of Ind. State of Ind., Indpls., 1976-81, pub. defender of Ind., 1981—; chief pub. defender Wayne County, Richmond, Ind., 1981; bd. dirs. Ind. Pub. Defender Coun., Indpls., 1981—; Ind. Lawyers Comm., Indpls., 1984-89; trustee Ind. Criminal Justice Inst., INdpls., 1983—. Mem. Criminal Code Study Commn., Indpls., 1981—, Supreme Ct. Records Mgmt. Com., Indpls., 1983—. Mem. Ind. State Bar Assn. (criminal justice sect.), Nat. Legal Aid and Defender Assn., Nat. Assn. Defense Lawyers, Phi Beta Kappa. Office: State Pub Defender 1 N Capitol Ave # 800 Indianapolis IN 46204-2026

CARPENTER, SYLVIA JO, surgical nurse; b. Mt. Airy, N.C., Mar. 13, 1957; d. Billy Grey and Peggy L. (Beck) Smith; m. Christopher Lee Carpenter, Aug. 6, 1988; children: Adrianne Brooke, Stephen Clarke. AAS, Miss. Gulf Coast Jr. Coll., 1978. RN, N.C. Staff nurse oper. rm. No. Surry Hosp., Mt. Airy, 1979-91; staff nurse cardiothoracic surgery N.C. Bapt. Hosp., Winston-Salem, 1992-93; pub. health nurse Surry County Health Dept., 1993—. Assn. dir. Girls in Action, Surry County, N.C., 1987-90; dir. Women's Missionary Union, Mt. Airy, 1990-92. Recipient N.C. Nurse Gt. 100 award, 1994. Mem. Assn. Oper. Rm. Nurses (cert., bd. dirs. Cen. N.C. chpt. 1988-89, sec., 1989-91, pres., 1992-93), N.C. Bapt. Nurse Fellowship. Democrat. Baptist. Home: 2187 W Pine St Mount Airy NC 27030

CARPENTER, VIRGIE MAE, librarian; b. Pine Bluff, Ark., Oct. 3, 1934; d. William Clyde Clemons and Martha Pearl (Murdock) Jones; m. Bruce McKinley Tipton, Dec. 16, 1960 (dec. May 1979); m. Thomas F. Carpenter, Feb. 15, 1980. BS, Henderson State U., 1959; MLS, Tex. Woman's U., 1960. Tchr. Social Hill Elem. Sch., Malvern, Ark., 1956-59; libr. Malvern Jr. High Sch., 1960—; sponsor Libr. Club, Malvern, 1960—, Student Coun., Malvern, 1961-84. Mem. NEA, Ark. Edn. Assn., Ark. Libr. Assn., Malvern Edn. Assn. Baptist. Home: 925 Clardy St Malvern AR 72104-4448 Office: Malvern Jr High Sch 1910 Roosevelt St Malvern AR 72104

CARPENTER-MASON, BEVERLY NADINE, executive health care quality assurance nurse; b. Pitts., May 23, 1933; d. Frank Carpenter and Thelma Deresa (Williams) Carpenter Smith; m. Sherman Robert Robinson Jr., Dec. 26, 1953 (div. Jan. 1959); 1 child, Keith Michael; m. David Solomon Mason Jr., Sept. 10, 1960; 1 child, Tamara Nadina. Grad. in nursing, Shadyside Hosp. Sch. Nursing, Pitts.; BS, St. Joseph's Coll., North Windham, Maine, 1979; MS, So. Ill. U., 1981; postgrad., Columbia Pacific U., 1989—. RN, Pa., D.C., Md., Fla. Staff nurse med. surgery, ob-gyn neontology and pediatrics Pa., N.Y., Wyo., Colo. and Washington, 1954-68; mgr. clinician dermatol. svcs. Malcolm Grow Med. Ctr., Camp Spring, Md., 1968-71; pediatric nurse practitioner Dept. Human Resources, Washington, 1971-73; asst. dir. nursing Glenn Dale Hosp., Md., 1973-81; nursing coord. medicaid div. Forest Haven Ctr., Laurel, Md., 1981-83, spl. asst. to supr. for med. svcs., 1983-84; spl. asst. to supt. for quality assurance Burr. Habilitation Svcs., Laurel, 1984-89; exec. asst. quality assurance coord. Mental Retardation Devel. Disabilities Adminstrn., Washington, 1989-91; also bd. dirs., 1989—; asst. treas. Am. Bd. Quality Assurance Utilization Rev. Physicians, 1988-94, chair exam. com., 1990-93; ret. Mental Retardation Devel. Disabilities Adminstrn., Washington, 1991; bd. dirs. Quality Mgmt. Audits, Inc., 1991-94; coord. quality assurance health svcs. div. UPARC, Clearwater, Fla., 1993-94; cons., lectr. in field; case study editor, mem. jour. editorial bd. Am. Coll. Med. Quality, 1985—, chmn. publs. com., 1987—, asst. treas., 1988—; mem. Am. Bd. Quality Assurance and Utilization Rev. Physicians, 1984—; owner, prin. BCM Assocs., 1992—. Contbr. articles to profl. jours. Mem., star donor ARC Blood Drive, Washington, Md., 1975-91; chair nominations com. Prince Georges Nat. Coun. Negro Women, Md., 1984-85. Recipient awards Dept. Air Force and D.C. Govt., 1966-92, Della Robbia Gold medallion Am. Acad. Pediatrics, 1972, John P. Lamb Jr. Meml. Lectureship awrd East Tenn. State U., 1988, Woman of Yr., 1990. Mem. NAFE, Am. Assn. Mental Retardation (conf. lectr. 1988), Am. Coll. Utilization Rev. Physicians, Assn. Retarded Citizens, Healthcare Quality Inst., Top Ladies of Distinction (1st v.p. 1986-91), Internat. Platform Assn., Order Ea. Star (Achievement award Deborah chpt. 1991), Am. Bd. Quality Assurance Utilization Rev. Physicians (Chmn. of Yr. award 1992, presdl. citation, Calvin R. Openshaw Svc. award 1993). Democrat.

CARPENTER-MORALES, JANET LYNNE, education educator; b. Ontario, Oreg., Oct. 29, 1959; d. Keith Phil and Lois Imogene (Edens) Carpenter; m. John C. Morales, Mar. 17, 1990; 1 child, Carson Carpenter. BA in English, U. Hawaii, Hilo, 1987. Producer, writer, editor, technician KHBC-TV, Hilo, 1987-88; freelance writer Creative Resources Ink, Hilo, 1988-92; comm. coord. Greenwich U., Hilo, 1990-92; instr. basic skills Dept. Edn., Hilo, 1990—; instr. ESL Job Tng. Partnership Act, Hilo, 1991—; ind. producer Creative Video & Media, Hilo, 1992—; cons. Big Island Lit., Hilo, 1990—. Author: (play) Near Missus, 1985 (award 1985); (children's books) A Chance to Dance, Fish Hook-y, 1992; (screenplay) Kapu, 1993; writer, editor: (TV series) Shelf Life, 1988. Home: PO Box 515 Pahala HI 96777

CARPENTIERI, PAULA A., materials engineer; b. Pitts., July 14, 1954; d. Angelo Santo and Carmela Marie (Silvestri) C.; m. Eugene Joseph Shiamone. BA, Seton Hill Coll., 1976. Sr. materials engr. GM Packard Electric Divsn., Warren, Ohio, 1976—. Pres. Warren Jr. Women's League, 1978—; bd. dirs. Children's Rehab. Ctr., Warren, 1984-91. Mem. Am. Chem. Soc. Roman Catholic. Home: 420 Quarry Ln Warren OH 44483

CARPER, GERTRUDE ESTHER, artist, marina owner; b. Jamestown, N.Y., Apr. 13, 1921; d. Zenas Mills and Virgie (Lytton) Hanks; m. J. Dennis Carper, Apr. 5, 1942; children: David Hanks, John Michael Dennis. Student violinist, Nat. Acad. Mus., 1931-41; diploma fine arts, Md. Inst. of Art, 1950; voice student, Frazier Gange, Peabody Inst. Music, 1952-55. Interior decorator O'Neill's (Importers), Balt., 1942-44; auditor Citizens Nat. Bank, Covington, Va., 1945-46; owner, developer Essex Yacht Harbour Marina, Balt., 1955—, owner, developer St. Michael's Sanctuary wildlife preserve, 1965—. Jewelry designer, 1987—; portrait artist, 1947—; exhibited one-woman shows Ferdinand Roten Gallery, Balt., 1963, Highfield Salon, Balt., 1967, Le Salon des Nations a Paris, 1985, Ducks and Geese of North Am., 1986, Series of Lighthouses, 1991; exhibited group shows Md. Inst. Alumni Show, 1964, Essex Libr., 1981, Hist. Preservation of Am., Hall of Fame, 1989, others; works included in collections including Prestige de la Peinture d'Aujourd'hos dans le Monde, 1990, Artists and Masters of the Twentieth Century, 1991; author: Expressions for Children, 1985, Fidere, 1993, Mentation, 1993; contbr. articles and poetry to ch. publs. and newspapers. Vol. tchr. of retarded persons, 1942—; leader Women's Circle at local Presbyn. chs., 1952-87, mem. 40 yrs. of choir svc. Mem. Md. Inst. Art Alumni Assn. (life), Grand Coun. World Parliament of Chivalry (Nobless of Humanity citation). Office: Essex Yacht Harbour Marina 500 Sandalwood Rd Baltimore MD 21221-5830

CARR, ANNE ELIZABETH, real estate and mortgage broker, metaphysician; b. Ithaca, N.Y., May 24, 1939; d. John Franklin II and Helen Louise (Ziegler) C.; m. Robert Kern Mansur, Sept. 7, 1980 (div. 1982). Student U. Rochester, 1957-60; BA, U. Edinburgh, Scotland, 1962, MA in English Lit., 1962; postgrad. NYU, 1966, 77; grad. Realtors Inst. Lic. real estate broker, Fla.; cert. residential specialist. With various advt. and pub. rels. firms, N.Y.C., 1962-72; dir. comm. Unishield, Inc., N.Y.C., 1972-74; dir. pub. rels. Thermasol Ltd., N.Y.C., 1974-76; v.p., CFO Sports Mktg., Inc., N.Y.C., 1976-80; sales dir. Found. Investments, Highland Beach, Fla., 1980-85; dir. mktg. Concordia Properties, Highland Beach, 1985-86; pres. Sunstone Realty, Inc., Boca Raton, 1987—; chmn. bd. dirs. Inner Circle Soc., Inc., 1994—. Mem. NRA, NAFE, AULV Nat. Assn. Realtors, Fla. Assn. Realtors, Women's Coun. Realtors, South Palm Beach Assn. Realtors, Mensa, Intertel, Harley Owners Group Club. Avocations: motorcycling, scuba diving, pistol/rifle shooting, crystals, healing. Home: 8705 Eagle Run Dr Boca Raton FL 33434-5433

CARR, BESSIE, retired education educator; b. Nathalie, Va., Oct. 10, 1920; d. Henry C. and Sirlena (Ewell) C. BS, Elizabeth City Coll., N.C., 1942; MA, Columbia U. Tchrs. Coll., 1948, PhD, 1950, EdD, 1952. Cert. adminstr., supr., tchr. Prin. pub. sch., Halifax, Va., 1942-47, Nathalie-Halifax County, Va., 1947-51; prof. edn. So. U., Baton Rouge, 1952-53; supr. schs. Lackland Schs., Cin., 1953-54; prof. edn. Wilberforce U., Ohio, 1954-55; tchr. Leland Sch., Pittsfield, Mass., 1956-60; chair math. dept., tchr. Lakeland Mid. Sch., N.Y., 1961-83. Founder, organizer, sponsor 1st Math Bowl and Math Forum in area, 1970-76; founder Dr. Bessie Carr award Halifax County Sr. High Sch., 1962. Mem. AAUW (auditor 1970-85), Delta Kappa Gamma (auditor internat. 1970-76), Assn. Suprs. of Math. (chair coordinating council 1976-80), Ret. Tchrs. Assn., Black Women Bus. and Profl. Assn. (charter mem. Senegal, Africa chpt.). Democrat. Avocations: travel, photography, souvenirs.

CARR, BONNIE JEAN, professional ice skater; b. Chgo., Sept. 29, 1947; d. Nicholas and Agnes Marie (Moran) Musashe; m. James Bradley Carr, Dec. 8, 1984; children: Brittany Jean, James Bradley II, Brooke Anderson. BS, Northwestern U., 1969; JD (hon.), Loyola U., Chgo., 1978. Skater Adventures on Ice, Mpls., 1961; prin. skater Jamboree on Ice, Chgo., 1961-68; society editor The Free Press, Colorado Springs, Colo., 1969; prin. skater, publicist on tour, asst. lighting dir., tour ednl. tutor Holiday on Ice Internat., 1970-74; skating dir. William McFetridge Sports Ctr., Chgo., 1975-86; choreographer, prin. skater Ice Time, USA, Mundelein, Ill., 1975—; skating coach St. Bronislava Athletic Club, Chgo., 1967-69; publicity dir. Amateur Skating Assn. Ill., Chgo., 1968; founder, dir. skating programs for blind, hearing impaired and mentally handicapped, Chgo., 1975-85; physical fitness advisor Exec. Health Seminars, Chgo., 1979; founder, dir. skating programs Fred Hutchinson Cancer Rsch. Ctr., Seattle, 1985-86; guest speaker Am. Cancer Soc., Columbia, S.C., 1973; conditioning coach Riverside Wellness and Fitness Ctr., Richmond, Va., 1989-91, Southampton Rec. Assn., Richmond, 1991-94; figure & speed skating coach Va. Spl. Olympics, 1991—. Recipient Key to City, Mobile, Ala., 1973, Service Recognition award Special Olympics, Chgo., 1984. Mem. Am. Guild Variety Artists, Am. Coun. on Exercise (cert. 1990). Methodist. Home: 1931 Albion Rd Midlothian VA 23113-4148 Office: Ice Time USA 28800 N Gilmer Rd Mundelein IL 60060-9538

CARR, DOLEEN PELLETT, computer and environmental specialist, consultant; b. Alameda, Calif., Sept. 23, 1950; d. Charles Joseph Ziegler and Dola Faye (Cushing) Peterson; m. Glen Allwin Pellett, June 26, 1971 (div. 1986); children: Mark D., Michael J.; m. Danny Lynn Carr, Dec. 29, 1986. BA, U. Wis., Madison, 1973. Notary Pub., Mich. Budget analyst Ednl. Testing Svc., Princeton, N.J., 1979-80; tech. recruiter Uniforce Svcs., Inc., Rock Hill, S.C., 1983-84; mgr. tng. and documentation Electronic Data Systems Corp., Troy, Mich., 1985-87; tech. writer, trainer, analyst cons. CES, Inc., Troy, 1989-92; pres. D'Carr Co., Inc., Roseville, Mich., 1988—; tech. writer, trainer, cons. Eaton Corp., Southfield, Mich., 1992-93; installer Gt. Plains Acctg., Fargo, N.D., 1990—; cons. Hazardous Materials Info. Exch., Washington, 1989—; cons., tech. writer Saturn Corp., 1991-92, Blue Cross Blue Shield, Southfield, Mich., 1992-93: tech. writer FANUC Robotics, N.A., Inc., Auburn Hills, Mich., 1993—. Co-author: CIW-Weld Monitor, 1990, 93. Active Roseville Dem. Com. Mem. AAUP, ASTD, NAFE, Internat. Platform Assn., Greater Trenton Musicians Union, Profl. Bus. Women Assn., Macintosh Users' Club, Macom County Democrats, Roseville Kiwanis (treas., clown 1994—). Democrat. Roman Catholic. Office: 2000 S Adams Rd Auburn Hills MI 48326

CARR, GWENN CLAIRE, instructional technology consultant, educator; b. Darby, Pa., Jan. 7, 1950; d. Donald f. and Anna Marie (Murphy) Phillips; m. Martin Carr; children: Tara, Rebecca. BS in Elem. Edn., St. Joseph's U., 1974; MEd, Chestnut Hill Coll., 1983. Cert. educator, Pa. Vision therapist Drs. Marcus & Seiderman, King of Prussia, Pa., 1986-88; computer tchr. Compu-Tech, Mt. Laurel, N.J., 1986-88; tchr. Archdiocese of Phila., 1968-92; computer instr. Ctr. for Tech. Studies, Norristown, Pa., 1990—; acad. instr. PECO Energy Co., Plymouth Meeting, Pa., 1992-94; project mgr., instrnl. tech. cons. The Learning Ctr., Norristown, 1994—; resident resource assoc. Temple U., 1993—; adj. prof. Allentown Coll., 1994—; mem. benefit com. Montgomery County Libr., Norristown, 1986-88; mem. middle states rev. com. Archdiocese of Phila., 1988-92; cons. on CES Compu-Tech, Mt. Laurel, 1986-88. Author: (jour.) Technology & Learning, 1991. Sec. Peter Wentz Farmstead Soc., Worcester, Pa., 1991-94. Edn. Alumni-St. Joseph's U., Phila., 1992-94. Mem. Peter Wentz Farmstead Soc., Edn. Chpt. Alumni St. Joseph's U. Roman Catholic. Home: 2104 3rd St Norristown PA 19401-1931 Office: The Learning Ctr One Lafayette Pl Norristown PA 19401

CARR, JACQUELYN B., psychologist, educator; b. Oakland, Calif., Feb. 22, 1923; d. Frank G. and Betty (Kreiss) Corker; children: Terry, John, Richard, Linda, Michael, David. BA, U. Calif., Berkeley, 1958; MA, Stanford U., 1961; PhD, U. So. Calif., 1973. Lic. psychologist, Calif; lic. secondary tchr., Calif. Tchr. Hillsdale High Sch., San Mateo, Calif., 1958-69, Foothill Coll., Los Altos Hills, Calif., 1969—; cons. Silicon Valley Companies, U.S. Air Force, Interpersonal Support Network, Santa Clara County Child Abuse Council, San Mateo County Suicide Prevention Inc.,Parental Stress Hotline, Hotel/Motel Owners Assn.; co-dir. Individual Study Ctr.; supr. Tchr. Edn.; adminstr. Peer Counseling Ctr.; led numerous workshops and confs. in field. Author: Learning is Living, 1970, Equal Partners: The Art of Creative Marriage, 1986, The Crisis in Intimacy, 1988, Communicating and Relating, 1984, 3d edit., 1991, Communicating with Myself: A Journal, 1984, 3d edit., 1991; contbr. articles to profl. jours. Mem. Mensa. Club: Commonwealth. Home: 837 Miller Ave Cupertino CA 95014-4642 Office: Foothill College 12345 El Monte Ave Los Altos CA 94022

CARR, JANICE HANEY, microbiologist; b. Atlanta, June 20, 1951; d. Elbert Carlton and Mary Katheryn (Frazier) H.; m. John Wood Carr, May 4, 1985. BS, Oglethorpe U., 1973; postgrad., Ga. State U., 1981. Respiratory therapy technician Northside Hosp., Atlanta, 1974-75; animal care technician Briarcliff Animal Hosp., Atlanta, 1975-76; lab. technician br. of data and specimen handling Ctr. for Disease Control, Atlanta, 1976-77, lab. technician enteric diseases lab., 1977-81, microbiologist, 1981—. Contbr. articles to profl. jours. Mem. Nat. Trust for Historic Preservation, Decatur Cemetery Task Force, Humane Soc. Am.; 1st v.p, 2d v.p. Oglethorpe U. Alumni Bd. Mem. Southeastern Electron Microscopy Soc., Electron Microscopy Soc. Am., Am. Soc. for Microbiology. Office: Nat Ctrs Disease Control and Prevention 1600 Clifton Rd Ms # C01 Atlanta GA 30333

CARR, MARCELLA IRENE, medical-surgical nurse; b. McCook, Nebr., Oct. 9, 1938; d. Carl Oscar and Ruby Marcella (Miller) Peterson; m. Robert Connell Carr, Aug. 20, 1957; children: Brenda Irene Bell, Robert Carl Carr, David Alan Carr. LPN diploma, Mid Plains C.C., 1977; ADN, Dakota Wesleyan U., 1985; BS, U. Nebr., 1987. RN, Kans., Nebr., Fla.; cert. BLS, Am. Heart Assn. Stenographer, clk. Frontier County Welfare Office, Curtis, Nebr., 1956-66; office asst. Charles E. Hranac, M.D., Cozad, Nebr., 1967-75; staff nurse Cozad (Nebr.) Community Hosp., 1977-87; staff nurse part-time Richard Young Hosp., Kearney, Nebr., 1989-93; pool nurse Great Plains Health Alliance, Phillipsburg, Kans., 1987-93; home health nurse Cozad (Nebr.) Cmty. Hosp., 1993-94; house supr. Southview Manor Care Ctr., Cozad, 1994—. Mem. ANA, Nat. League Nursing, Kans. Nurses Assn., Am. Assn. Ret. Persons, Royal Neighbors Am. (oracle 1964-66), Maccabees, Psi Chi. Republican. Mem. Ch. of Christ. Home: 512 W 11th St Cozad NE 69130-1306 Office: Southview Manor Care Ctr 318 W 18th St Cozad NE 69130

CARR, MARIE PINAK, book distribution company executive; b. Buffalo, June 17, 1954; d. Henry and Hildegard (Poech) Pinak; m. Richard Wallace Carr, Oct. 18, 1980; children: Katharine Marie, Ann Louise, Elizabeth Ashby. BS, Syracuse U., 1976. Cancer microbiologist Nat. Cancer Inst., Rockville, Md., 1976-78; mktg. specialist Precision Sci., Washington, 1978-80; art importer Dicmar Trading Co., Inc., Washington, 1981-83; book dist. Dicmar Trading Co., Inc., Silver Spring, Md., 1983—. Co-author: The Willard Hotel, 1986. Bd. dirs. Salvation Army Women's Aux., Washington, 1982-94, pres., 1990-91; bd. dirs. Am. Cancer Soc., Washington, 1988-90; co-chmn. Nat. Cancer Ball, 1989, 90; active Jr. League Washington, 1987-90. Mem. Washington Club. Republican. Roman Catholic. Office: Dicmar Trading Co Inc 8850 Brookville Rd Silver Spring MD 20910-1803

CARR, PATRICIA WARREN, adult education educator; b. Mobile, Ala., Mar. 24, 1947; d. Bedford Forrest and Mary Catherine (Warren) Slaughter; m. John Lyle Carr, Sept. 26, 1970; children: Caroline Elise, Joshua Bedford. BS in Edn., Auburn U., 1968, MEd, 1971. Tchr. DeKalb County Schs., Atlanta, 1969-70; counselor Dept. Defense Schs., Okinawa, Japan, 1972-75; tchr. Jefferson County Schs., Jefferson, Ga., 1975-76; counselor Clarke County Schs., Athens, Ga., 1976-78; tchr. Fairfax County Schs., Adult and Community Edn., Fairfax, Va., 1980—; resource specialist Vol. Learning Program; coord. Enrichment for Srs. Program Fairfax Area Agy. on Aging and Adult and Community Edn., 1985-89; cons. State Va. Dept. Edn., 1984—, Va. Assn. Adult and Community Edn., 1987, Commn. on Adult Basic Edn., 1988; instr. George Mason U., Fairfax, 1985. Tchr. Met. Meml. United Meth. Ch., Washington, 1981—; co-leader McClean, Va. troop Girl Scouts U.S., 1985-88. Mem. Am. Assn. Adult and Community Edn., Smithsonian Nat. Assocs., No. Va. Assn. Vol. Adminstrs., Va. Assn. Adult and Community Edn. Methodist. Office: Fairfax County Adult & Community Edn 7510 Lisle Ave Falls Church VA 22043-1099

CARR, RUTH ELLEN, marketing executive; b. Concord, N.H., July 20, 1950; d. Collins F. and Roberta M. (Hatch) C. BA, Plymouth State Coll., 1974; MS, Ind. U., 1981. Rsch. scientist Mich. Tech. U., Houghton-Hancock, 1974; environ. scientist Ind. Water Pollution Control Div., Indpls., 1975-78; water quality planner Ind. Heartland Coord. Commn., Indpls., 1978-79; project scientist Mid-States Engring., Indpls., 1980-82; mgr. and sales assoc. Mony Fin. Svcs., South Portland, Maine, 1983-87; project mgr. environ. DuBois & King, Inc., Saco, Maine, 1987-88; assoc. mktg. mgr. Dufresne-Henry, Inc., Portland, 1988—. Bd. regents Econ. Devel. Coun. Maine, Augusta, 1992-93. Mem. Soc. Mktg. Profl. Svcs. (v.p., bd. dirs. Maine chpt. 1991-93), Maine Water Pollution Control Divsn. (mem. publ. staff 1991-93), Women's Transp. Seminar. Home: 20 Ocean View Rd Scarborough ME 04074 Office: Dufresne-Henry Inc 22 Free St Portland ME 04101-3900

CARRA-TACHIKAWA, LUCILLE, documentary film producer and director; b. N.Y.C., Oct. 3; d. Sal C. and Rose (DiBona) Carra; m. Kazutoshi Tachikawa, Sept. 27, 1987. BFA in Film Prodn., NYU, 1973, MA in Cinema Studies, 1976. Film programmer Toho Internat., N.Y.C., 1974-86; prin. Travelfilm Co., N.Y.C., 1986—. Producer, dir. (film) The Inland Sea, 1991 (Nat. Geographic Earthwatch Film award 1993, Black Maria Film Festival Dir.'s Choice award 1993, Best Documentary award The Hawaii Internat. Film Festival 1991); assoc. producer (video) Sri Lanka: Children in War, 1993; producer, dir. (documentary film) Dvorak and America, 1994. Recipient film awards The Japan Found., Tokyo, 1989, Iowa Humanities Bd., 1991, Ill. Humanities Coun., Chgo., 1993, NEH, 1994; script writing award Minn. Humanities Coun., St. Paul, 1993. Office: Travelfilm Co 35 E 10th St New York NY 10003

CARRELL, HEATHER DEMARIS, educational consultant; b. Bryn Mawr, Pa., Jan. 4, 1951; d. Jeptha J. and J. Demaris (Affleck) C.; m. Peter F. Brazitis, June 27, 1981; children, Evan, Victoria. BA, Oberlin Coll., 1973; MEd, U. Wash., 1976, PhD, 1982. Cert. tchr., Wash. Head tchr., trainer Exptl. Edn. Unit U. Wash., Seattle, 1976-80, tchr. trainer, 1976-80, supr. early childhood and spl. edn. tchrs. in tng., 1980, coord. classrooms behavior disorders, 1980-81, coord. interdisciplinary tng., 1979-82, asst. prin., 1981-82, cons. Transition Rsch. Problems Handicapped Youth, 1986-88; self-employed cons., 1983—; cons. North Kitsap Sch. Dist., Poulsbo, Wash., 1984; presenter edn. and spl. edn. various groups from U.S., Can., Australia, 1977-82; pres., co-founder Hansville (Wash.) Coop. Presch., 1982, 84-89; mem. diversity and multicultural advocacy team Wash. State Sch. Dirs. Assn.; rep. to U. Wash. Tchr. Profl. Edn. Adv. Bd., 1992—; mem. WSSDA Fin. Task Force, 1994; mem. Intertribal Coun. Com. on Racism, North Kitsap, Wash., 1993—. Author: (with others) The Experimental Education Training Program, 1977; contbr. articles to profl. publs. Commr. North Kitsap Dept. Parks and Recreation, 1983-84; dir. North Kitsap Sch. Bd., 1990—, v.p., 1992-93, pres., 1993—; trustee North Kitsap Tchr. of Yr. Found., 1989-90; bd. dirs. North Kitsap Juvenile Diversion Bd., 1987-91; co-founder, v.p. Kitsap Cmty. Found., 1993—. Bur. Edn. Handicapped fellow, 1974-75, 77-78.

CARRICK, KATHLEEN MICHELE, law librarian; b. Cleve., June 11, 1950; d. Michael James and Genevieve (Wenger) C. BA, Duquesne U., Pitts., 1972; MLS, U. Pitts., 1973; JD, Cleve.-Marshall U., 1977. Bar: Ohio 1977, U.S. Ct. Internat. Trade 1983. Rsch. asst. The Plain Dealer, Cleve., 1973-75; head reference SUNY, Buffalo, 1977-78, assoc. dir., 1978-80, dir., asst. prof., 1980-83; dir., assoc. prof. law Case Western Res. U., Cleve., 1983—; cons. Mead Data Central, Dayton, Ohio, 1987-91. Author: Lexis: A Research Manual, 1989; contbr. articles to profl. jours. Fellow Am. Bar Found.; mem. ABA, Am. Law Inst., Am. Assn. Law Librs., Assn. Am. Law Schs., Scribes. Home: 1317 Burlington Rd Cleveland OH 44118-1212 Office: Case Western Res U 11075 East Blvd Cleveland OH 44106-5409

CARRICO, DEBORAH JEAN, special education teacher; b. East St. Louis, Ill., Dec. 6, 1948; d. Leo Anthony and Edna Linda (Willett) C. BS, Murray State U., 1972; MA, Calif. State U., L.A., 1978. Cert. tchr., Calif. Tchr. Bonita Unified Sch. Dist., San Dimas, Calif., 1973-74, L.A. County Office Edn., Downey, 1974—; mentor L.A. County Office of Edn., 1989—. Bd. dirs. Hope House, Anaheim, Calif., 1988—. Mem. Coun. for Exceptional Children, Phi Kappa Phi. Democrat. Roman Catholic. Office: LA County Office Edn 9300 Imperial Hwy Downey CA 90242-2813

CARRIER, JOYCE H., federal agency administrator; b. Schenectady, N.Y.; d. James A. and Norma A. (Dedrick) C.; m. Steven J. Akey, July 30, 1988; 1 child, Kendall Wood Akey. BSBA, U. S.C., 1978. Pub. rep. McGraw-Hill, Memphis, 1978-81; account exec. Arrive Unlimited, Washington, 1982-84; nat. advance Mondale for Pres., Washington, 1984; sr. account exec. Jasculea/Terman & Assocs., Chgo., 1985-86; dir. scheduling and advance Brock Adams for Senate, Seattle, 1986-87; dep. dir. scheduling, dir. advance Dukakis for Pres., Boston, 1987-88; dep. comm. dir. Office for Environ. Affairs, State of Mass., Boston, 1989-90; mgr. corporate comm. Bill Info. Sys., Boston, 1990-93; dep. asst. sec. for pub. liaison U.S. Dept. Treasury, Washington, 1993—. Office: US Dept of Treasury Office Pub Liaison 1500 Pennsylvania Ave NW Rm 3418 Washington DC 20220

CARRILLO, JOAN ALICE, clinical psychologist; b. San Juan, P.R., Aug. 1, 1955; d. Clifford Aloysius and Dorothy Erna (Silvera) C. BA in Psychology magna cum laude, U. Pa., 1979; PhD in Clin. Psychology, Columbia U., 1990. Lic. psychologist, Fla. Researcher Anxiety Disorders Clinic N.Y. State Psychiat. Inst., N.Y.C., 1986-87, clin. researcher, supr. biometrics dept., 1987-88; clin intern Wilford Hall Med. Ctr., San Antonio, 1988-89; staff psychologist Mental Health Clinic Homestead (Fla.) AFB Hosp., 1989-91, partnership provider Mental Health Clinic, 1991-92; pvt. practice Homestead & Coral Gables, 1991—; staff tchr. psychol. testing and diagnostics South Miami (Fla.) Hosp. Addiction Treatment Program, 1992—; group svcs. provider Neurocare, Inc., North Miami Beach, Fla., 1993—. Capt. USAF, 1988-91. Decorated Air Force Achievement medal, 1991. Mem. APA. Office: 139 NE 15th St Homestead FL 33030 also: 1570 Madruga Ave Ste 305 Miami FL 33146-3013

CARRINGTON, BETTY WATTS, nurse-midwife, educator; b. W.Va., Mar. 14, 1936; d. James Henry and Odessa E. Watts; m. Homer S.I. Carrington, Aug. 17, 1958; children: Michael S., Lynn Ellen. BSN, U. Mich., 1958; MS, Columbia U., 1971, EdD, 1986. Cert. nurse-midwife. Dir. nurse-midwifery svc. Maternity-Infant Care Project/Brookdale Hosp. Affiliation, Bklyn.; assoc. prof. nurse-midwifery SUNY Health Sci. Ctr., Bklyn.; dir. grad. program in nurse-midwifery Columbia U. Sch. Nursing, N.Y.C.; nurse-midwife rsch. assoc. dept. obstetrics and gynecology Harlem Hosp. Ctr.; cons. minority recruitment and retention. Contbr. articles to profl. jours. WHO fellow, Tanzania, 1983. Fellow Am. Coll. Nurse Midwives (nat. v.p. 1973-74); mem. NAUW (L.I. br. pres. 1986-90), Sigma Theta Tau. Home: 11931 220th St Jamaica NY 11411-2010

CARRINGTON, ILDIKÓ DE PAPP, literary critic; b. Windsor, Ont., Can., Dec. 6, 1929; came to U.S., 1940; d. John Ladislas and Emmy Vilma (Birgling) de Papp; m. George Cabell Carrington Jr., June 26, 1954 (dec. Sept. 1990); 1 child, John Cabell Carrington. BA, Wellesley Coll., 1951; MA, Harvard U., 1952. Instr. Valparaiso (Ind.) U., 1952-53, Ohio State U., Columbus, Ohio, 1953-59; lectr. Ohio State U., Lakewood, Ohio, 1963-66; instr. Nat. U. of Iran, Tehran, 1966-67, No. Ill. U., DeKalb, 1967—. Author: Margaret Atwood and Her Works, 1987, Controlling the Uncontrollable, 1989; co-author: Plots and Characters in the Fiction of William Dean Howells, 1976; guest editor spl. issue Essays on Canadian Writing on Canadian-Am. Literary Rels., 1981; contbr. articles to profl. jours. Recipient Award for Outstanding Short Fiction Ill. Arts Coun., 1973, Winner Novella Contest Sou'wester Mag., 1979. Home: 1724 Judy Ln De Kalb IL 60115-1802

CARRINGTON, JILL EMILEE, art historian; b. San Francisco, Mar. 1, 1953; d. Alan Wallace and Jean Vivian (Bedore) C.; m. Mark V. Sheffield Jr., July 15, 1972 (div. Feb. 1980); 1 child, David M. BA, Pomona Coll., Claremont, Calif., 1979; MA, Syracuse U., 1985, MPhil, 1986, PhD, 1995. Instr., grad. teaching asst. fine arts Syracuse (N.Y.) U., 1980-86, 88-89; asst. prof. art Stephen F. Austin State U., Nacogdoches, Tex., 1989—. Contbr. articles to profl. jours. Cons. stained glass Christ Episcopal Ch., Nacogdoches, 1990—; treas., literacy bd. Nacogdoches Adult Literacy Ctr., 1992-93; vol. PTA, Nacogdoches, 1993-94; tchr. Christ Episocpal Ch., Nacogdoches, 1991—. Fellow Samuel H. Kress Found., 1986-87, grad. fellow Syracue U., 1986-87, 87-88; grantee Gladys Krieble Delmas Found., 1987-88, Stepehn F. Austin State U., 1991-93. Mem. Medieval Soc. Am., Italian Art Soc., Coll. Art Assn. Democrat. Episcopalian. Home: 320 E Austin St Nacogdoches TX 75961-2868 Office: Stephen F Austin State U Art Dept PO Box 13001 SFA Sta Nacogdoches TX 75962-3001

CARRINGTON, MARY MARGARET, small business owner; b. Milw., June 30, 1934; d. John J. and Marie A. (Van Ermen) Sullivan; m. Richard H. Carrington, Aug. 6, 1960 (dec. Mar. 1989); 1 child, Christina M. Carrington Riley. BS, Marquette U., 1956, MA, 1957; postgrad., U. Wis., 1957, 58; PhD, Interam. U., 1959. Asst. prof. St. Mary's Coll., South Bend, Ind., 1958-60; instr. Bradford H.S., Kenosha, Wis., 1961-62, U. Wis., Parkside, 1963-73; elected ofcl. Racine (Wis.) County Bd., 1966-70, Mt. Pleasant Bd., 1975-91; owner Carma Farms, 1967—; dir., sec. Southeastern Wis. Health Sys. Agy., Milw., 1976-81; advisor Heritage Bank Women's Fin. Coun., Racine, 1981-86. Author: (booklet) History of Town of Mt. Pleasant, 1976, (jour.) Wis. Speech Comm. Jour., 1958; co-author: (booklet) Homesite in the Country, 1968. Gov. Wis. Coastal Mgmt. Coun., Madison, 1988—; membership co-chair Racine County Econ. Devel. Corp., Racine, 1987—;

bd. dirs. Racine County Health-Human Svcs., 1991—; active Racine County Women's Commn., 1995—. Named Woman of Yr., Women's Civic Coun., 1971, Woman of Distinction-Govt., YWCA, 1991; recipient citation, Senate State of Wis., 1991. Mem. AAUW (pres. investment study group 1994-95), Wis. Communities for Econ. Devel. (bd. dirs., pres. 1987-90), Wis. Women Entrepreneurs (v.p. Racine br. 1983-85, state bd. dirs. 1991-94), Point West Bus. Assn. (program chair 1993-94), Racine Mfg. and Commerce Assn. (amb. 1991—), Racine Rotary (Paul Harris fellow 1989). Republican. Roman Catholic. Home: 8930 Washington Ave Racine WI 53406

CARRIS, JOAN DAVENPORT, writer; b. Toledo, Aug. 18, 1938; d. Roy and Gertrude Elfrid (Nichols) Davenport; m. Barr Tupper Carris, Dec. 28, 1960; children: Minda Sue, Leigh Ann, Bradley. BS in English, Iowa State U., 1960. Cert. tchr. in English, French, and speech. Classroom tchr. Iowa Pub. Schs., 1960-65; pvt. practice as writer, journalist, author, 1976—; tutor, ednl. cons., 1966—; instr. Ti-IN Ednl. Network, San Antonio; N.J. Coun. on Children's Lit.: Authors and Illustrators Ann. Symposiums, 1986-95; instr. SAT-PSAT preparation, 1988-90; appeared on nat. radio and TV shows for interviews about edn., test preparation, and children's lit. Author: SAT Success, 1982, rev. edit., 1994, Hedgehogs in the Closet, 1987, Success with Words: Vocabulary for College, Tests and Life, 1988, rev. edit., 1994, Just a Little Ham, 1989, The Greatest Idea Ever, 1990. Aunt Morbelia and the Screaming Skulls, 1990, Panic Plan for SATs, 1990, Howling for Home, 1992, A Ghost of a Chance, 1992, S.A.T. Word Flash, 1993, Stolen Bones, 1993, Beware the Ravens, Aunt Morbelia, 1994, others. Recipient Reader's Choice award State of Ind., 1986, Tenn., 1986, Iowa, 1985. Mem. Children's Book Guild Washington D.C. (pres. 1992-93), Nat. League Am. Pen Women (pres. Princeton br. 1980-83), Soc. Children's Book Writers. Home: 1639 Cecile St McLean VA 22101-5002

CARROLL, ADORNA OCCHIALINI, real estate executive; b. New Britain, Conn., Aug. 24, 1952; d. Antonio and Mary Ida (Reney) Occhialini; m. Christoper P. Buchas, Sept. 7, 1974 (div. Nov. 1982); 1 child, Jenna Rebecca; m. John Francis Carroll, Oct. 15, 1983; children: Jordan Ashley, Sean William. BA in Philosophy, Cen. Conn. State U., 1975; grad., Realtors Inst., 1989. Lic. real estate broker, real estate agt. Dir. therapeutic recreation program Ridgeview Rest Home, Cromwell, Conn., 1974, Meadows Convalescent Home, Manchester, Conn., 1975, Andrew House Health Care, New Britain, 1976; owner, mgr. Liquor Locker, Newington, Conn., 1977-87; owner, broker A.O. Carroll & Co., Newington, 1985-93, A. O. Carroll & Agostini Co., Kensington, Conn., 1994—; ptnr. Marco Realty & Devel. Co., Newington, 1978—. Mem. Nat. Assn. Realtors (multiple listing policy forum 1993, legis./polit. forum 1993, mem. svcs. com. 1994, mem. recruitment and retention forum 1994, mem. state fiscal affairs com. 1995, personal asst. working group 1995, promotion & devel. forum 1995, edn. forum 1995), Conn. Assn. Realtors (v.p.-at-large 1992, 93, 94, vice-chair legislation 1991, mem. legis. policy & RPAC coms. 1991, conv. com. 1990, polit. affairs com. 1988, 89, chair state MLS task force 1994, chair agy. task force 1994, chair personal assts. 1995, chair agy. 1995, chair comms./tech. com. 1995), Greater New Britain Assn. Realtors (local dir. 1991, 92, chair legislation & nominating coms. 1991-92, pres. 1990, 93, chair bylaws com. & state conv. 1990, pres.-elect 1989, chair programs & polit. affairs 1991, sec. 1988, chair polit. affairs & AM HM WK 1988, speaker 1989—, Realtor of Yr. 1991, state dir. 1995), Nat. Package Store Assn., Conn. Package Store Assn. (legis. lobbyist 1984-88, pres. 1986-88, Disting. Svc. award 1985), Greater Hartford Package Store Assn. (pres. 1981-82), Marchegian Soc. New Britain (pres. 1992, corr. sec. & chair budget 1991), Newington C. of C. (bd. dirs. 1987-88, chmn. legis. 1988). Home: 23 Occhialini Ct Newington CT 06111-4754 Office: AO Carroll & Agostini Co 742 Worthington Ridge Berlin CT 06037

CARROLL, AILEEN, retired librarian; b. Mason, Wis., Aug. 7, 1914; d. John P. and Mary (Noonan) C. BA, De Paul U., 1938; MA, Northwestern U., 1940; MLS, Rosary Coll., 1965. Tchr. Chgo. Pub. Schs., 1940-52; systems media dir., libr. organizer Cook County Pub. Schs., 1952—. Author and pub. of children's poetry. Vol. St. Vincent's Orphanage, Chgo., Sacred Heart Home for the Aged, Chgo. Recipient scholarship AAUW, 1991. Mem. AAUW (Western Springs, Ill.), LWV, Rep. Club of Oak Park, Art Group of Western Springs. Home: 712 Courtland Cir Western Springs IL 60558-1945

CARROLL, AMY M., graphic designer; b. Juneau, Alaska, May 1, 1967; d. James Edward and Denise Marie (Bolduc) C.; m. David P. Gregovich, Dec. 23, 1992. BFA, No. Ariz. U., 1989. Graphic artist intern No. Ariz. U., Flagstaff, 1988-89; print shop asst. Miner Pub., Juneau, 1989-90; typesetter Juneau Empire, 1990; graphic designer U. Alaska S.E.-Juneau Campus, 1990—. Mem. NOW. Home: PO Box 22041 Juneau AK 99802

CARROLL, BONNIE, publisher, editor; b. Salt Lake City, Nov. 20, 1941. Grad. high sch., Ogden, Utah. Owner The Peer Group, San Francisco, 1976-78; pub., editor The Reel Directory, Cotati, Calif., 1978—. Pub., editor The Reel Thing newsletter, San Francisco, 1977-78. Mem. Assn. Visual Communicators (bd. dirs. 1987-90), No. Calif. Women in Film, San Francisco Film Tape Council (exec. dir. 1979-81). Office: The Reel Directory PO Box 866 Cotati CA 94931-0866

CARROLL, JANE HAMMOND, artist, author, poet; b. Greenville, S.C., May 15, 1946; d. Charles Kirby and Margaret (Cooper) Hammond; m. Robert Lindsay Carroll Jr., Feb. 3, 1968; children: Jane-Gower, Robert Lindsay III. BA, U. S.C., 1968. Tchr. A.C. Flora High Sch., Columbia, S.C., 1968-70; exec. field dir. N.E. Ga. Girl Scout Coun., Athens, 1970-71; asst. dir. AID-Vol. Greenville, 1971-73; author, artist Winston Derek Pubs., Nashville, 1985—. Author, artist: Grace, 1987 (Gov.'s Collection 1988), Intimate Moments, 1987 (Gov.'s Collection), Dayspring Art Body, 1989, Beyond the Wall, 1991; group shows at Fine Art Mus. of the South, Mobile, Williams Salon, Atlanta, 1989, 92, 93, 94, Mus. Archives, Washington, 1992, Internat. Pastel Show, Ga., 1991, 95, Fine Arts Mus. South, 1990; permanent collections Greenville Meml. Hosp., S.C., Embassy Suites, Ill., Macan Motor Cars, Ga., Jenny Pruitt Reality, Ga. and others. Bd. mgr. Greenville Jr. League, 1971-73; artist for fundraiser Rehab. Edn. for Handicapped Adults and Children, Atlanta, 1992; vol. artist Arts in the Atlanta Project, 1993. Mem. Nat. League Am. Pen Women (chair art's program 1984—, Achievement award 1987, 89, 93, 94, 95), Atlanta Artist Club (v.p. 1984-85, Merit award 1990). Presbyterian. Home and Office: 2979 Majestic Circle Atlanta GA 30002

CARROLL, JEANNE, public relations executive; b. Oak Park, Ill., May 20, 1929; d. John P. and Mary (Noonan) Carroll; BA, U. London, 1950; MA, Northwestern U., 1951; m. Harold M. Kass, Apr. 1966. Bus. girls editor Charm Mag., N.Y.C., 1951-53; pub. relations dir. Rosary Coll., River Forest, Ill., 1953-66; chmn. publicity Am. Cancer Soc., bd. dirs. W. and S.W. Suburban Unit, 1967—; med. adminstr., asst. to Dr. Harold Kass, Oak Park, Ill., 1969—; pub. rels. cons., 1993—. Pub. relations counselor in Midwest for Brown U., 1962; dir. pub. relations Mundelein Coll., 1968; producer radio show for teen-agers, Chgo., 1954; lectr. sci. devels. Bell Labs. for AT&T, 1954; participant annual Sun-Times seminars for coll. journalists MacMurray Coll., Jacksonville Ill. Chmn. March of Dimes campaign for Chgo., ednl. TV Channel 11, River Forest, 1963; trustee DePaul U., Chgo., chmn. Soc. Fellows dinner; chmn. Oak Park Hosp. Ben Din Dan, 1971-80; mem. com. library Internat. Relations, 1975-82; mem. bd. Arden Shores, sch. for boys, 1984—; bd. dirs. Globe Theatre Ctr.; mem. adv. bd. USO, mem. com. USO Celebration D-Day Activities, Chgo., 1994. Recipient Excellence award for coll. brochures Am. Coll. Pubs. Com., 1957; medal of recognition for work in pub. relations Bishop Fulton Sheen, 1960; Humanitarian award Performing Arts Ctr. and Citizens Com., Chgo., 1976; award DuSable Mus., 1978. Mem. Ill. Assn. Coll. Admissions Counsellors (pres.), Assn. Coll. Pub. Relations Assn., Family Service Assn. Am. (past bd. dirs.), Acad. Hosp., Pub. Relations, Ill. (pres.), Chgo. (pub. relations dir., med. soc. auxs.), Oak Park Hosp. (pres. women's aux. 1986-89), West Suburban Hosp. Med. Ctr. Aux. (life). Home: 712 Courtland Circle Springdale Western Springs IL 60558

CARROLL, KAREN COLLEEN, physician, infectious disease educator; b. Balt., Nov. 7, 1953; d. Charles Edward and Ida May (Simms) C.; m. Bruce Cameron Marshall, Feb. 13, 1982; children: Kevin Charles Marshall, Brian Thomas Marshall. BA, Coll. Notre Dame of Md., 1975; MD, U. Md., 1979. Diplomate Am. Bd. Internal Medicine, Am. Bd. Infectious Diseases, Am. Bd. Pathology. Intern internal medicine U. Md., 1979-80; intern primary care internal medicine U. Rochester, AHP, 1980-82, chief med. resident internal medicine, 1982-83; fellow infectious diseases U. Mass., 1984-86; fellow med. microbiology Health Svcs. Ctr. U. Utah, 1989-90; asst. prof. pathology U. Utah Med. Ctr., Salt Lake City, 1990—, adj. asst. prof. infectious diseases, 1990—; dir. microbiology lab. Associated Regional and Univ. Pathologists, Inc., Salt Lake City, 1990—. Contbr. articles to profl. jours. Fellow Am. Coll. Pathologists; mem. Am. Soc. Microbiologists, Infectious Diseases Soc. Am. Office: U Utah Med Ctr Dept Pathology 50 N Medical Dr Salt Lake City UT 84132

CARROLL, KAREN JEORGIANNA, portfolio administrator; b. Morristown, N.J.; d. Leonard Joseph and Gladys Louise (Lemanski) Kalechitz; m. James Douglas Carroll, Oct. 21, 1973 (div. Dec. 1984). Grad., Gibson Career/Finishing Sch., Phila., 1967. Asst. to pres. H. Lane Enterprises, West Caldwell, N.J., 1967-68; adminstrv. asst. Titanium Metals Corp., Caldwell, N.J., 1968-69; libr. USAF Base, Udornthai, Thailand, 1969-70; asst. to libr. U. of Calif., Rohnert Park, 1970-71; pres.'s asst. Gordon Labs., Mass., 1971-72; corp. sec. Titanium Industries, Fairfield, N.J., 1972-86; asst. to chmn. CBA Industries, Paramus, N.J., 1986-89; portfolio adminstr., asst. to chmn. Firemark Group, Parsippany, N.J., 1989—.

CARROLL, KIM MARIE, nurse; b. Ottawa, Ill., Feb. 13, 1958; d. John J. and Charin E. (Reilley) Marmion; m. Thomas Christopher Carroll, Aug. 25, 1979; children: Christopher John, Meaghan Elizabeth. B.S.N., U. Denver, 1983; diploma Copley Meml. Hosp. Sch. Nursing, Aurora, Ill., 1979. R.N., Ill., Ind., Colo.; critical care practitioner. Staff nurse Penrose Hosp., Colorado Springs, Colo., 1979-83, asst. head nurse cardiac floor, 1983-84; asst. dir. nurses Big Meadows Nursing Home, Savanna, Ill., 1985-86, dir. nurses, 1986-88; clin. dir. Ind. Heart Physicians, Inc., Beech Grove, Ind., 1989—. Mem. NAFE, Am. Heart Assn., Am. Orgn. Nurse Execs., Ind. Coun. on Cardiovascular Nursing, Beta Sigma Phi (chpt. pres. 1988-89, rec. sec. 1991-92), Sigma Theta Tau. Roman Catholic. Avocation: skiing. Home: 8229 Autumn Mill Ln Indianapolis IN 46256-3444 Office: Ind Heart Physicians Inc 112 N 17th Ave # 300 Beech Grove IN 46107-1228

CARROLL, LILLIAN ESTHER, librarian, elementary school educator; b. West Union, W.Va., June 13, 1942; d. P.R. and L.G. (Gaskins) Pitts; m. James Wetzel Carroll, June 22, 1967. BA, Glenville St., 1965; MA, W.Va. U., 1977. Cert. elem. tchr., W.Va. Tchr., libr. Wood County Schs., Parkersburg, W.Va., 1964—; cons. Nat. Evaluation Systems, 1990. V.p. Living Heritage Mus. Project, 1992—. Mem. NEA, W.Va. Edn. Assn., W.Va. Ednl. Media Assn., Wood County Libr. Media Assn. (Wood County Media Specialist of Yr. 1993, W.Va. Media Specialist of Yr. 1994). Office: Mineral Wells Sch RR 1 Box 40 Mineralwells WV 26150-9710

CARROLL, LUCY ELLEN, choral director, music coordinator, educator; b. N.Y.C., Oct. 11; d. Edward Joseph and Lucy Sophie (Czapszys) C. B in Music Edn., Temple U., 1968; MA, Trenton State Coll., 1973; D in Musical Arts, Combs Coll. Music, Phila., 1982. Cert. tchr. music, N.J., Pa., Nat. Cert., 1991. Tchr. music Log Coll. Jr. High Sch., Pa., 1968-72, Ind. (Pa.) High Sch., 1972-73; tchr. music William Tennent High Sch., Warminster, Pa., 1973—, dir. mus. theater, 1973—; music coord. Centennial Schs., 1991; founder, dir. Madrigal Singers, Warminster, Pa., 1971—; choral dir. Cabrini Coll., Radnor, Pa., 1974-77, First Day Singers, Phila., 1979-83, Combs Coll. of Music, Phila., 1981-84, 87-88; choral adjudicator various Music festivals, 1973—; guest lectr. mus. seminars, convs., and writers' confs.; del. Internat. Arts Conf., Cambridge, Eng., 1992. Singer (operas Ambler Festival) Street Scene, 1970, Death of Bishop of Brindisi (premiere); (Robin Hood Dell) La Boheme; dir. (jazz theater piece N.Y.C.) Murder of Agamemnon, 1980, (musi. drama) Power of Love (1705), 1986, (outdoor music theater) Vorspiel (Pa. Historic Commn. 1989); contbr. articles to profl. jours., also sci. fiction to sci. fiction mags. and anthologies. Recipient awards Writers of the Future, 1985, 87, Andrew Ferraro award Combs Coll. of Music, 1989, Internat. Order of Merit IBA, 1991, plaque for Svc. to Music Bucks County Commr., 1991, Disting. Citizen medal Southampton Township, 1994; finalist Pa. State Tchr. of Yr., 1995. Mem. Am. Choral Dirs. Assn., Theatre Assn. Pa., Del. Valley Composers (choral cons. 1988-90), Pa. Edn. Assn. Centennial Edn. Assn., Bucks County Music Educators Assn., Hist. Soc. Pa., Smithsonian Assocs., Music Fund Soc. of Phila., The Sonneck Soc. for Am. Music, Pa. Music Educators Assn. (adv. bd. 1986-87), Friends of Pa. Hist. and Mus. Commn., Sigma Alpha Iota. Republican. Roman Catholic. Home: 712 High Ave Hatboro PA 19040-2418 Office: William Tennent High Sch Music Dept 333 Centennial Rd Warminster PA 18974-5400

CARROLL, MARIE-JEAN GREVE, educator, artist; b. Paterson, N.J., Dec. 19, 1930; d. William John and Charlotte Marie (Kranich) McGill; m. Theodore R. Greve, Nov. 4, 1950 (div. Oct. 1979); children: Richard W. Greve, Helen E. Greve Beard, Theodore A. Greve; m. William P. Carroll, 1981 (div. 1989). BA in Art Edn., William Paterson Coll., Wayne, N.J., 1971; MA in Visual Art, 1976. Cert. art tchr., N.J. Art tchr. Pequannock (N.J.) Elem. Sch., 1971-72, Passaic Valley High Sch., Little Falls, N.J., 1972-77, 85-86, Ramapo High Sch., Franklin Lakes, N.J., 1986—. Works exhibited at shows in Fla. galleries, 1983, Longboat Key Art Gallery, 1983,. 84, Manatee Art Gallery, 1984, others. Den mother Boy Scouts Am., Ridgewood, N.J., 1960. Recipient art awards. Mem. NEA, Bergen County Edn. Assn., N.J. Edn. Assn., Nat. Art Edn. Assn. Office: Ramapo Regional High Sch George St Franklin Lakes NJ 07417

CARROLL, MARY DAVIS, physician; b. Chgo., Aug. 15, 1921; d. William James and Mary Ellen (O'Hagen) Davis; m. William F. Carroll Jr.; children: William James, Mary Ellen, Catherine. BS, U. Chgo., 1943, MS, 1944, MD, 1948. Diplomate Am. Bd. Family Practice. Intern Passavant Meml. Hosp., Chgo., 1949; pvt. practice Crown Point, Ind., 1950—; chief of staff St. Anthony Med. Ctr., Crown Point, 1976-77; med. dir. Nursing Home, Crown Point, 1976—. Pres. home and sch. assn. St. Mary's Sch., Crown Point, 1962-63; mem. parish coun. St. Matthias Ch., Crown Point, 1970s. Mem. AMA, Am. Acad. Family Practice, Ind. Acad. Family Practice (past bd. dirs.), Lake County Med. Soc. (bd. dirs. 1972-93, pres. 1981-82). Office: 124 N Main St Crown Point IN 46307-4049

CARROLL, MEGAN ELIZABETH, lawyer; b. Lake Forest, Ill., Sept. 7, 1967; d. Barry Joseph and Barbara (Pehrson) C. Student, Middlebury Coll., Paris, 1987-88; BA in Philosophy, French Lit., Boston Coll., 1989, JD, 1992. Bar: Mass., 1993, Ill. 1994, D.C. 1994. Law clk. Middlesex County Probate & Family Ct., Cambridge, Mass., 1990-91; assoc. Powers & Hall, Boston, 1991; asst. dist. atty. Norfolk County, Mass., 1992; prin., owner Carroll Assocs., Lake Forest, Ill.; bd. dirs. Carroll Internat. Corp. Arts review writer various publs. Mem. Am. Ireland Fund, Boston, Chgo., 1985—, DAR, Chgo., 1985—, Phillips Acad. Alumni Coun., Andover, Mass., 1991—; trustee Regency Pk. Condominiums, Brookline, Mass., 1989-91; sec. Phillips Acad. Alumni Class of 1985, Andover, 1989—. Recipient Golden Key Nat. Honor Soc., Boston Coll., 1989, Order of the Cross and Crown, Scholar of the Coll. Mem. ABA, Arts and Media Law Assn. of Boston Coll. (pres., founder), Woman's Athletic Club of Chgo., Order of Malta Aux., Phi Delta Phi. Republican. Roman Catholic. Home: 24 Columbia St Wellesley MA 02181 also: 55 Mayflower Rd Lake Forest IL 60045

CARROLL, PAT, actress; b. Shreveport, La., May 5, 1927; d. Maurice Clifton and Kathryn Angela (Meagher) C.; children: Sean, Kerry, Tara. Student, Immaculate Heart Coll., 1944-47, Catholic U., 1950; Litt.D. (hon.), Barry Coll., Miami, Fla., 1969. pres. Sea-Ker, Inc., Beverly Hills, Calif., 1979—; pres. CARPA Prodns., Inc., N.Y.C. Profl. debut in stock prodn. A Goose for the Gander, 1947; supper club debut at Le Ruban Bleu, N.Y.C., 1950; appeared on numerous television shows, 1950—, including: Red Buttons Show, 1951, Caesar's Hour, 1956-57 (Emmy award), Danny Thomas Show, 1961-63, The Ted Knight Show, 1985, She's the Sheriff, 1987-1988; Broadway debut in Catch a Star, 1955 (Tony nomination); appeared in motion picture With Six You Get Eggroll, 1968; producer, actress: Gertrude Stein Gertrude Stein Gertrude Stein for colls. and univs. (Grammy award 1980, Drama Desk award, Outer Critics Circle award); Shakespeare debut as nurse in Romeo and Juliet and Falstaff in The Merry Wives of Windsor (Helen Hayes award, 1990), Shakespeare Theater at the Folger, 1986 (Helen Hayes award 1987); voice of Ursula, the Wicked Squidwitch, in The Little Mermaid, 1989; appeared in The Show-Off, 1992, Roundabout Theater Company. Pres. Center of Films for Children, 1971-73; bd. regents Immaculate Heart Coll., Hollywood, Calif., 1970. Mem. AFTRA, SAG, Actors Studio, Actors Fund (life), Actors Equity Assn., Acad. TV Arts and Scis. (trustee 1958-59), Am. Youth Hostel (life), Del. and Hudson Canal Hist. Soc., The Players, George Heller Meml. Fund. Office: care Judy Schoen and Assoc 606 N Larchmont Blvd Ste 309 Los Angeles CA 90004

CARROLL, PATRICIA MARY, marketing and sales executive; b. N.Y.C., Dec. 5, 1939; d. Patrick Michael and Bridget Patricia (Ginnelly) Curran; m. Thomas Michael Carroll, Jan. 26, 1963; children: Matthew Thomas, Jeanne Anastasia. BS, Fordham U., 1961; MS, Coll. New Rochelle, 1975; postgrad., NYU, 1972, CUNY, 1983—. Cert. tchr. spl. edn. and English, N.Y. Exec. confidential sec. N.Y. Daily News, 1961-66; tchr. White Plains (N.Y.) Adult Edn. Ctr. and Westchester Devel. Ctr., 1975; asst. dir. nursing and allied health edn. March of Dimes Birth Defects Found., White Plains, 1976-84; sales/mktg. mgr. Stoffel Seals Corp., Nyack, N.Y., 1984-87; mgr. mktg. McGraw-Hill, N.Y.C. and Washington, 1988-89, Faulkner & Gray, Inc., 1989-91; sales promotion mgr. Pennysaver Group, Elmsford, N.Y., 1991—; copy editor Pergamon Press, Elmsford, N.Y., 1979; editor texts A. Liss. Editor, assoc. editor The First Six Hours of Life series, 1978-82, Prenatal Care series, 1978-82, 1978-85, Intrapartal Care series, 1980-82, The Birth Defects Original Article Series, 3 vols., 1984; contbr. articles to profl. jours. and newspapers. Mem. legis. adv. com. N.Y. State Assembly, 1980-84; mem. Mamaroneck (N.Y.) Beautification Com., 1983; nominating com. for assoc. mems. Internat. Festivals Assn., 1986-87. Coll. scholar, 1957; program dir. Am. Cancer Soc.'s Rd. to Recovery, 1992. Mem. AAUW, Women In Communications (program com. 1980-91), Women's Nat. Book Assn., Am. Coll. Healthcare Mktg. Inst., Direct Mail Assn., Women's Direct Response Group, Healthcare Pub. Rels and Mktg. Soc. Roman Catholic. Home: 171 Maple Ave Mamaroneck NY 10543-3530 Office: Pennysaver Group 101 Executive Blvd Elmsford NY 10523

CARROLL, SHIRLEY DEVAUX STRONG, realtor; b. La Jolla, Calif., June 30, 1930; d. Fred Buhl and Leoda Carolyn (Hissong) Strong; m. Dorrence Coney Talbut, June 19, 1954 (div. Sept. 1969); children: Gregory Harrison Mack, Jeffrey Mitchell Strong, March Foster Chad; m. John Lawrence Carroll, Aug. 16, 1973. Student, Stephens Coll., 1948-49; BEd, U. Toledo, 1951; cert. in land use planning and devel., Am. Planning Assn., 1979. Lic. real estate sales broker, Tex. Tchr. Monroe (Mich.) Pub. Schs., 1951-52, Columbus (Ohio) City Schs., 1952-55, Greenwich (Conn.) Pub. Schs., 1955-56; producer Young People's Concert Series, Toledo, 1968-70; realtor Danberry Real Estate and Ins., Toledo, 1970-73; v.p., mgr. Rilco Mfg. Inc., Clute, Tex., 1974-76; coord. Sandusky County Econ. Devel., Fremont, Ohio, 1984-85; realtor Bolte Real Estate and Ins., Fremont, 1987—; exec. dir. Arts Coun. Sandusky County, Fremont, 1988-91; Treas. Internat. Energy Conservation Soc., Houston, 1977-82; commr. Planning and Zoning Commn., Missouri City, 1979-84, Ballville Zoning Commn., Fremont, 1984-89; dir. devel. Tex. Solar Energy Soc., Austin, 1982-84. Dir., writer, producer: (tv shows) Music for Young People, 1968-70. Campaign mgr. Bette (Graham White) for Mayor, Houston, 1976; mem. Tax Equalization Bd., Missouri City, Tex., 1980. Recipient appreciation award Am. Solar Energy Soc., Boulder, Colo., 1982. Mem. NAFE, Women in Networking, Fremont Area Artists and Fireland Artists, Fremont Country Club Women's Assn. (pres. 1989-90), Friends of Birchard Libr. (pres. 1988-90), Firelands Assn. of Realtors, Spectrum Gallery (Toledo). Home: 1829 Buckland Ave Fremont OH 43420-3503 Office: Bolte Real Estate 2378 W State St Fremont OH 43420-1441

CARROZZELLA, LOUISE BAILEY, government affairs consultant; b. Boston, Dec. 16, 1934; d. John Moran and Barbara (Leary) Bailey; m. Conrad J. Kronholm, Nov. 7, 1959 (div. 1978); children: Eric, Justin, John, Bailey; m. John A. Carrozzella, 1991. BA, Marymount Coll., Tarrytown, N.Y., 1956; postgrad., Boston U. Sch. of Law, 1956-57, Conn. State U., New Britian, 1957-58. Lic. ins. broker. Agt. John Hancock Ins. Co., Rocky Hill, Conn., 1985—; special events coord. Hartford Arts Council, Conn., 1984—. Staff mem. Dukakis Campaign, Hartford, Conn., 1988; sec. Conn. Law Enforcement Found., 1980—; trustee U. of Conn. Bd. of Trustees, 1978—; pres Hartford Ballet, 1974; lobbyist Masonic Home and Hosp., 1989. Recipient Alumnae Svc. award U. Conn., 1992, Yr. of the Women medal U. Conn. Mem. World Affairs Ctr., University Club, Hartford Club, March of Dimes. Democrat. Roman Catholic. Home: 11 Walbridge Rd West Hartford CT 06119-1344

CARSCH, RUTH ELIZABETH, consulting librarian; b. London, May 3, 1945; came to U.S., 1949; d. Harry and Ellen Margot (Adler) C.; 1 child, Zachariah Robert. BA, CUNY, 1967; MS, Columbia U., 1968. Cert. libr., N.Y., Calif. Reference libr. N.Y. Pub. Libr., 1968-70; tech. info. specialist Bechtel, Inc., San Francisco, 1972-75; rsch. assoc. Erick & Lavidge Mkt. Rsch., San Francisco, 1980-86; cons. Met. Mus. Art, 1992, Calif. Conservation Corps, 1992, Port Authority N.Y. and N.J., 1982-84, Camp, Dresser, McKee Engrs., Boston, 1988; info. assoc. Foudn. Ctr., 1991—; reference libr. Skyline Coll., 1988—. Mem. Art Librs. Soc., No. Calif. Bus. Librs. Roundtable, Bay Area Architecture-Engring. Librs. Roundtable.

CARSON, GAIL MARIA, fashion designer, marketing consultant; b. Detroit, Nov. 27, 1954; d. Samuel Salvador and Dorothy Marie (Mallard) Dasher; m. Calvin Jerome Carson, Feb. 15, 1975; 1 child, Meredith Jojuan. Student, U. Detroit, 1972-74, Siena Heights Coll., 1982-83; cert. in merchandising, Fashion Inst. Am., 1986. Hostess coffee shop J.C. Penney Co., Southfield, Mich., 1975-78; exec. dir. office ethnic minority higher edn. Wayne State U., Detroit, 1982-86; fashion show coord. Prodns. Plus, Inc., Birmingham, Mich., 1986-91; internat. mktg. cons. Internat. Mktg. Assn., Southfield, 1976—; designer knitwear Needle Classics, Detroit, 1986—, Rio Boutique, Detroit, 1993—. Mem. Winship Cmty. Coun., Detroit, 1976-80; fundraiser, campaigner Judge Bruce Morrow, Detroit, 1992; co-chairperson Mumford High Sch. Alumni, Detroit, 1992—; co-chairperson coun. Scott Meml. United Methodist Ch., Detroit, 1989-91. Recipient Outstanding Leadership award E.B.O.N. Assocs., 1980, Outstanding Achievement award Amway Corp., 1981, Outstanding Young Woman of Am. award, 1983. Mem. Knitter's Guild Am., Mumford H.S. Alumni Assn. and Endowment (co-chairperson 1992—, Outstanding Leadership award 1992), Mom and Dad Club Gesu Sch.

CARSON, LINDA FRANCES, gynecologic oncologist; b. Manchester, Conn., Feb. 8, 1952; d. Culley Clyde and Dorothy (Scarbourough) C.; m. Bruce Allen MacFarlane, June 2, 1974 (div. 1988); children: Megan Carson, Ian Scarbourough; m. Roderick Allen Barke, Jan. 13, 1989. BA, Conn. Coll., 1974; MD, George Washington U., 1978. Intern and resident Sinai Hosp. Balt., 1978-82; fellow in gynecologic oncology Barnes Hosp., St. Louis, 1982-83, U. Minn., 1983-86; dir. gynecologic oncology Hennepin County Med. Ctr., Mpls., 1986-89; dir. VA Gynecologic Svc., Mpls., 1989-90, dir. gynecol., 1990—, v.p. ob/gyn., 1994—; dir. div. gynecologic oncology U. Minn., Mpls., 1990—, assoc. prof. div. gynecologic oncology, 1991—; co-prin. investigator Gynecologic Oncology Group, 1990—; co-dir. Upper Midwest Trophoblastic Diseases Ctr. U. Minn., 1986—; dir. Women's Cancer Ctr., 1988—. Reviewer: Am. Jour. Obstetrics and Gynecology, 1989—, Gynecologic Oncology, Cancer, 1989—; contbr. articles to profl. jours. Fellow Am. Cancer Soc.; mem. AMA, Hennepin County Med. Soc., Internat. Soc. for Study Vulvar Disease, Mpls. Coun. Obstetrics and Gynecology, Minn. State Med. Soc., Minn. Women's Med. Soc., Soc. of Gynecologic Oncologists, Western Assn. Gynecologic Oncologists. Office: U Minn Dept Ob/Gyn Box 395 Mayo 420 Delaware St SE Minneapolis MN 55455

CARSON, MARGARET ANN, environmental engineer; b. Providence, June 13, 1956; d. William Oldham and Ann Patricia (Toye) C. BS in Biology magna cum laude, Franklin Pierce Coll., 1978; MS in Environ. Engring., U. Lowell, 1991. Jr. chemist K.J. Quinn, Seabrook, N.H., 1978-80; grad. teaching asst. in chemistry, engring. design U. Lowell, Mass., 1980-82; jr. sanitary engr. Mass. Dept. Environ. Quality Engring., Woburn, 1983-84, sr. sanitary engr., 1984-88; engr. IV, prin. Mass. Dept. Environ. Protection, Woburn, 1988—, compliance inspection supr., 1988-93, multimedia compliance and enforcement supr., 1993—; mem. Mass. Hazardous Waste Adv. Com., Boston, 1990-93. Conservation commr. Town of Wilmington, Mass., 1988-89. Roman Catholic. Home: 314 Riverside Ave Medford MA 02155

CARSON, MARGARET MARIE, gas industry executive, marketing professional; b. Windber, Pa., Dec. 30, 1944; d. Peter and Margaret (Olenik) Buben; m. Claude Carson, Dec. 30, 1967 (div. 1974); m. Brian Charles Scruby, June 6, 1975; stepchildren: Debbie, Victor, Chris, Kenneth. BA, U. Pitts., 1971; MS in Mgmt., Houston Bapt. U., 1985. Petroleum analyst Gulf Oil Co., Pitts., 1973-75, crude oil analyst, 1971-74, environ. coordinator, 1974-79, mgr. oil acquistition, Houston, 1980-84, mktg. dir., 1985; sales dir. Cabot Cons. Group, Houston, 1985-86; dir. competitor analysis and corporate planning dept., Enron Corp., Houston, 1987—; adj. prof. bus tech. Houston Community Coll., 1985-91. Columnist: The Collegian, 1984-85. Bd. dirs. Indiana U., Pa., 1980-81. Mem. Am. Competitiveness Soc. (bd. dirs.), Internat. Energy Economists, Gas Processors Assn. (speaker tech. sessions 1985-94), Gas Rsch. Inst., Univ. Club.

CARSON, MARY SILVANO, career counselor, educator,; b. Mass.; d. Joseph and Alice V. (Sherwood) Silvano; m. Paul E. Carson (dec.); children: Jan Ellen, Jeffrey Paul, Amy Jayne. BS, Simmons Coll., Boston; MA, U. Chgo., 1961; postgrad., Ctr. Urban Studies, 1970, U. Chgo., 1970, 72, DePaul U., Chgo., 1980. Cert. acad. counselor, Ill. Mgr. S.W. Youth Opportunity Ctr., Dept. Labor, Chgo., 1965-67; careers' counselor Gordon Tech. High Sch., Chgo., 1971-74; dir. Career and Assessment Ctr., YMCA C.C., Chgo., 1974-81; project coord. Career Ctr., Loop Coll., Chgo., 1981-82; mem. adv. bd. City-Wide Coll. Career Ctr. Bd. dirs. Loop YWCA, Chgo., coord. employment project, 1985-87; ESL tchr., Greece, 1990. Mem. ACA, TESOL, Internat. Counseling Assn., Internat. Lyceum (London), Am. Ednl. Rsch. Assn., Nat. Vocat. Guidance Assn., Chgo. Bus. and Profl. Women's Club, Met. Club (San Francisco), World Affairs Coun., Browning Soc., World Coun., English Speaking Union, Pi Lambda Theta (chpt. pres. 1975).

CARSON, REGINA EDWARDS, healthcare administrator, educator; b. Washington; d. Reginald Billy and Arcola (Gold) Edwards; m. Marcus T. Carson; children: Marcus Reginald, Ellis K., Imani R. BS in Pharmacy, Howard U., 1973; MBA in Mktg., Loyola Coll., Balt., 1987, MBA in Health Care Adminstrn., 1987. Asst. prof., asst. dir. pharmacy U. Md., Balt., 1986-88; assoc. prof., coord. profl. practice Howard U., Washington, 1988—; exec. v.p. Marrell Inc., Randallstown, Md., 1985-93; drug utilization rev. cons. Md. Pharmacy Assn., Balt., 1986—; pharmacist, cons. Balt. County Adv. Coun. Drug Abuse, Towson, 1984-86; adv. com. longterm care com. Nat. Assn. Retail Druggists; prin. Marrell Consulting, 1993—. Bd. dirs. Balt. County Hosp. Aux., Randallstown, Joshua Johnson Coun. Balt. Mus. Art., NW Hosp. Ctr., Randallstown. Fellow Am. Soc. Cons. Pharmacists; mem. Nat. Assn. Retail Druggists, Am. Assn. Colls. Pharmacy, Nat. Pharm. Assn. (life, Outstanding Women in Pharmacy 1984). Office: Howard U Coll Pharmacy 2300 4th St NE Washington DC 20002-1220

CARSTEN, ARLENE DESMET, financial executive; b. Paterson, N.J., Dec. 5, 1937; d. Albert F. and Ann (Greutert) Desmet; m. Alfred John Carsten, Feb. 11, 1956; children: Christopher Dale, Jonathan Glenn. Student Alfred U., 1955-56; Exec. dir. Inst. for Burn Medicine, San Diego, 1972-81, adv. bd. mem., 1981-92; founding trustee, bd. dirs. Nat. Burn Fedn., 1975-83; chief fin. officer A.J. Carsten Co. Inc., San Diego, 1981-91; chief fin. officer A.J. Carsten Co., Ltd., Powell River, B.C., Can., 1992—. Contbr. articles to profl. jours. Organizer, mem. numerous community groups; chmn. San Diego County Mental Health Adv. Bd., 1972-74, mem., 1971-75; chmn. community relations subcom., mem. exec. com. Emergency Med. Care Com., San Diego, Riverside and Imperial Counties, 1973-75; pub. mem. psychology exam. com. Calif. State Bd. Med. Quality Assurance, 1976-80, chmn., 1977; mem. rep. to Health Services Agy. San Diego County Govt., 1980; mem. Calif. Dem. Cen. Com., 1968-74, exec. com., 1971-72, 73-74; treas. San Diego Dem. County Cen. Com., 1972-74; chmn. edn. for legislation com. women's div. So. Calif. Dem. Com., 1972; dir. Muskie for Pres. Campaign, San Diego, 1972; organizer, dir. numerous local campaigns; councilwoman City of Del Mar, Calif., 1982-86, mayor, 1985-86; bd. dirs. Gentry-Watts Planned Indsl. Devel. Assn., 1986-90, pres., 1987-90; commencement speaker Alfred U., 1984. Recipient Key Woman award Dem. Party, 1968, 72, 1st Ann. Community award Belles for Mental Health, Mental Health Assn. San Diego, 1974, citation Alfred U. Alumni Assn., 1979. Office: RR# 2 Malaspina Rd C-13, Powell River, BC Canada V8A 4Z3

CARSTENS, JANE ELLEN, retired library science educator; b. New Iberia, La., Apr. 19, 1922; d. Charles John and Marie Claudia (Blanchet) C. BA in Elem. Edn., U. Southwestern La., 1942; BS in LS, La. State U., 1945; MS in LS, Columbia U., 1955, DLS, 1975. Asst. libr. Hamilton Lab. sch. and instr. libr. sci. U. Southwestern La., Lafayette, 1942-66; assoc. prof. library sci. U. Southwestern La., 1969-75; children's librarian/storyteller N.Y. Pub. Libr., N.Y.C., 1947-49, summers 53 and 55; vis. lectr. U. Minn., Mpls., 1955-56, summer 59, La. State U., Baton Rouge, summer 1958, State Coll. Iowa, Cedar Falls, summer 1963; prof. libr. sci. U. Southwestern La., Lafayette, 1975-94; vis. lectr. Syracuse U., summers 1962, 64, U. Tex., Austin, summers 1976-86, 89. Named Tchr. of Yr. Amoco, 1982, Outstanding Alumna U. Southwestern La., 1986, Faculty Adv. of Yr., U. Southwestern La. Student Govt. Assn., 1992; recipient Essae Culver Disting. Svc. award La. Libr. Assn., 1987, Blue Key Alumni Faculty Excellence award, 1990, Point of Excellence award Kappa Kelta Pi, 1992, Outstanding Tchr. award USL Found., 1994; dedicatee Blue Key Faculty/Student Staff Directory, 1994-95. Mem. ALA, Assn. Libr. and Info. Sci. Edn., Assn. Libr. Svc. to Children (mem. Newbery award com. 1989-90), Am. Assn. Sch. Librs., La. Libr. Assn. (pres. 1959-60), Young Adult Libr. Svc. Assn., Phi Kappa Phi (pres. USL chpt. 1984-85), Delta Kappa Gamma (pres. Alpha chpt. 1988-90). Roman Catholic. Home: 214 St Joseph St Lafayette LA 70506-4535 Office: U Southwestern La PO Box 40298 Lafayette LA 70504-0298

CARSWELL, LOIS MALAKOFF, botanical gardens executive, consultant; b. N.Y.C., Mar. 2, 1932; d. Arthur and Dora (Krechevsky) Malakoff; m. Donald Carswell, Oct. 12, 1957; children: Anne Carswell Tang, Alexander, Robert Ian. AB magna cum laude, Radcliffe Coll., 1953; cert. in bus. adminstrn., Harvard U. and Radcliffe Coll., 1954. Editor Dell Pub. Co., N.Y.C., 1954-56; publicist Ruth E. Pepper Co., N.Y.C., 1957-58; vol. Bklyn. Botanic Garden, 1964—, co-chmn. plant sales, 1967—, co-chmn. capital campaign, 1984-88, chmn. bd. dirs., 1989—; chmn. Coalition Living Mus. N.Y. State, N.Y.C., 1980—; cons. N.Y. State Natural Heritage Trust, 1982—. Office: Bklyn Botanic Garden 1000 Washington Ave Brooklyn NY 11225-1099

CARTAINO, CAROL ANN, editor; b. N.Y.C., Dec. 7, 1944; d. Pietro Michael and Ann Wanda (Scotch) C.; 1 child, Clayton Collier-Cartaino. BA, Rutgers U., 1966; postgrad., NYU, 1967-68. Cert. English tchr., N.J. Prodn. editor trade book Prentice-Hall, Inc., Englewood Cliffs, N.J., 1966-68, from asst. to assoc. editor trade book, 1968-72, editor trade book, 1972-77; editor-in-chief Writer's Digest Books, Cin., 1978-86, freelance editor and collaborator, 1986-87; editl. dir. Don Aslett, Inc., Pocatello, Idaho, 1987-93, Marsh Creek Press, Pocatello, Idaho, 1993—; assoc. Collier Assoc. Literary Agy., Seaman, Ohio, 1987-94; proprietor White Oak Edits., 1987—; speaker in field; instr. in writing So. State C.C., Hillsboro and Wilmington, Ohio, 1989—. Vol. nurses aide Hackensack (N.J.) Hosp. State of N.J. scholar, 1962-66, Emerson (N.J.) PTA scholar, 1962. Roman Catholic. Home and Office: 2000 Flat Run Rd Seaman OH 45679-9551

CARTER, ANNETTE WHEELER, state legislator; b. May 24, 1941; divorced. Grad., Ala. State Coll. Mem. Conn. Ho. of Reps.; mem. pub. safety, cmty. and exportation coms., vice chmn. appropriations com., asst. majority leader; housing advisor Capitol Region Conf. Chs.; mem. nat. black Caucus, State Legis. Recipient Outstanding Accomplishments award Hope SDA Ch., 1990, Crispus A. Tucks award, 1991, Conn. State Black Dem. award, 1992. Mem. NAACP (award 1993), Greater Hartford Black Dem. Club. Episcopalian. Home: 207 Branford St Hartford CT 06112-1406 Office: Office of State Senate State Capital Bldg Hartford CT 06106*

CARTER, ARLENE MAE, psychiatric nurse; b. Alliance, Nebr., Oct. 8, 1947; d. Louis and Alice Abigail (Davis) Zahradnick; m. William Frank Carter, Oct. 11, 1983 (div. 1988); m. Charles Ray Cravens, Aug. 18, 1989. BS, Union Coll., 1970; MS, Loma Linda U., 1974. RN, Colo. Staff nurse ICU, CCU Porter Meml. Hosp., Denver, 1970; staff nurse St. Anthony's Hosp., O'Neill, Nebr., 1970-72; staff nurse ICU, CCU St. Bernadine's Hosp., San Bernardino, Calif., 1972-74; staff nurse West Holt Meml. Hosp., Atkinson, Nebr., 1973-75, N.T. Enloe Meml. Hosp., Chico, Calif., 1977-78; commd. capt. U.S. Army, 1978, advanced through grades to lt. col., 1986; staff nurse, clin. nurse specialist in psychiatry Fitzsimmons Army Med. Ctr., Aurora, Colo., 1978-82; psychiat. clin. nurse specialist U.S. Army MEDDAC, Ft. Campbell, Ky., 1982-87; clin. nurse mgr. residential treatment facility 2d Gen. Hosp., Landstuhl, Germany, 1987-90; clin. nurse specialist psychiatry U.S. Army MEDDAC, Ft. Polk, La., 1990-92; psychiat. case mgr. Gateway to Care, Ft. Polk, 1992-93, U.S. Army MEDDAC, Ft. Leavenworth, Kans., 1993—; instr. Morningside Coll., Sioux City, Iowa, 1975-76, asst. prof. nursing, 1976-77; mental health cons. Cherry County Hosp., Valentine, Nebr., 1974-75; presenter chem. dependency awareness programs, programs at profl. confs., grief resolution work and women's issues, mental health case mgmt. in the mil. Contbr. to profl. pubis. Mem. Nat. League Nursing (cert. addictions nurse), Nat. Assn. Alcohol/Drug Abuse Counselors, Nurses Soc. on Addictions. Office: CMHS MACH Cmty Mental Health Fort Leavenworth KS 66027

CARTER, BARBARA ANN PHLEGAR, home health nursing executive; b. Anderson, Ind., July 23, 1954; d. Carl Leslie and Thelma Virginia (Morgan) Phlegar; m. Steven Anderson Carter, Apr. 8, 1979; children: Morgan Elizabeth, Leslie Ann. ADN, U. S.C., Aiken, 1974, BSN, 1992. Cert. home health nurse. Pvt. scrub and office nurse Carolina ENT, West Columbia, S.C., 1974-78; charge nurse operating rm. Lexington County Hosp., West Columbia, 1978-79; sr. pub. health nurse Colleton County Home Health, Walterboro, S.C., 1979-85; staff nurse emergency rm. Colleton Regional Hosp., Walterboro, 1986-88; staff/charge nurse Med. Coll. Ga., Augusta, 1988-89; documentation coord. St. Joseph Home Health Care, Augusta, 1989-91, nurse mgr., 1991—. Mem. nominating com. First Bapt. Ch., Walterboro, 1984-87, dir. adult Sunday sch., 1987. Mem. Assn. Oper. Rm. Nurses (bd. dirs. 1979), BSN Honor Soc. of U. S.C., Home Health Nurses Assn., Omicron Theta Alpha (sec. 1973-74).

CARTER, BARBARA JOANNE, floral shop owner; b. Springfield, Ill., Apr. 30, 1955; d. William Earl and Louise C. (Cooper) O.; m. Paul Eugene Carter. Cert. profl. florist, Ill. Clk. claims Franklin Life Ins. Co., Springfield, 1982-83; mgr. Nino's Steakhouse, Milw., 1983-87, The Landscape Ctr., Springfield, 1980-87; owner CID Floral, Springfield, 1987—; bd. dirs. Brinkerhoff Inc., Springfield. Bd. dirs. Brinkerhoff Aux., Springfield, 1986-87; decorator Ill. State Park Dist., Lincoln's Home, 1989-90, 91-93. Mem. Ill. State Florists Assn., Greater Springfield C. of C., Women in Mgmt. Office: CID Floral 3351 S 6th St Springfield IL 62703-4709

CARTER, BRENDA MASON, interior deisgner; b. Vernon, Tex., Aug. 8, 1941; d. Emory Dallas and Minerva Price (Rhoads) Hollar; m. Wesley Reilly Mason III, June 28, 1963 (div. Nov. 1967); m. Everitt Adelbert Carter, Mar. 28, 1980. BA, UCLA, 1963. Head of design Southwest Office, San Diego, 1963-65, E.M.I. Inc., $, 1965-66; pres. Brenda Mason Design Assocs., Inc., $, 1966—; dir. Vantage Controls, Salt Lake City. Recipient AIA Orchid award, 1980, 82, award of Excellence, 1967; Sacramento Hist. Soc. award, 1971. Republican. Home and Office: 1440 Puterbaugh St San Diego CA 92103-3710

CARTER, CARLA CIFELLI, management consultant; b. Chicago Heights, Ill., June 2, 1949; d. John Louis and Irene Frances (Romandine) Cifelli. BA, Western Mich. U., 1971; MBA, Ariz. State U., 1985. Tchr. Limestone (Maine) High Sch., 1971-75; mgr. employment and tng. Chubb Life Ins., Concord, N.H., 1975-78; employee relations supr. TRW, Inc., Plainville, Conn., 1978-79; asst. dir. corp. tng. Cigna, Bloomfield, Conn., 1979-82; cons. to human resources dept. Sentry Ins. Co., Scottsdale, Ariz., 1983-84; asst. v.p. Bank of Am., Phoenix, 1984-87; employee devel. adminstr. City of Phoenix, 1987-90; dir. Am. Productivity and Quality Ctr., Houston, 1990—; regional mgr. Reading and Learning Internat., Mesa, Ariz., 1987—; bd. dirs. Cert. Pub. Mgr. Program, Phoenix, 1988-89; sr. examiner Ariz. Quality Award, 1994, 95. Author: Human Resources and the Total Quality Imperative, 1994, Understanding the Organization, 1982, The Responsive City, Am. Productivity and Quality Ctr., 1990, Seven Basic Tools, HR mag., 1992, Measuring and Improving the HR Function Continous Journey, 1993. Advisor Literary Vols., Phoenix, 1989; mem. Gov.'s Conf. on Quality, Ariz., 1993-94. Mem. ASTD (govtl. affairs dir. 1988-89), Am. Quality and Participation Soc. (nat. presenter 1992), Orgn. Devel. Network (nat. presenter 1989), Soc. Human Resource Mgmt. (regional presenter 1992, nat. presenter 1994), The Conf. Bd. Home: 6040 N Camelback Manor Dr Paradise Valley AZ 85253-5148 Office: Am Productivity & Quality Ctr 123 N Post Oak Ln Ste 430 Houston TX 77024-7719

CARTER, CAROLYN HOUCHIN, advertising agency executive; b. Louisville, Nov. 2, 1952; d. Paul Clayton and Georgia Houchin C.; m. Jeffrey Starr, Dec. 8, 1988. BSJ, Northwestern U., 1974, MSJ, 1975. Asst. account exec. SSC&B Advt., Inc., N.Y.C., 1975-76, account exec., 1976-77; account exec. Grey Advt., Inc., N.Y.C., 1977-79, account supr., 1979-81, v.p., account supr., 1981-82, v.p., mgmt. supr., 1982-85, v.p., group mgmt. supr., 1985-87, sr. v.p., 1987-92, exec. v.p., 1992—; mem. Nat. Advt. Rev. Bd., 1983-87; mem. adv. bd. advt. history Smithsonian Nat. Mus. Am. History, 1988-94. Chair March of Dimes Media Adv. Council, 1981-86; mem. U.S. Coun. World Comm. Yr., 1983; active YMCA Acad. Women Achievers, 1992. Recipient Clairol Mentor award Clairol, Inc., 1991. Mem. Women in Communications (pres. N.Y. chpt. 1982-83, N.Y. Matrix award in Advt. 1988, Nat. Headliner award 1991), Advt. Women of N.Y. (bd. dirs. 1987-88), Internat. Womens Forum (bd. dirs. N.Y. chpt. 1994). Office: Grey Advt Inc 777 3rd Ave New York NY 10017-1301

CARTER, CATHERINE LOUISE, educator; b. Oakland, Calif., Mar. 31, 1947; d. Robert Collidge and Mae (Reidy) C. BA, Ohio Wesleyan U. Tchr. Barclay Elem. Sch., Cherry Hill, N.J., 1969-72, Malberg Elem. Sch., Cherry Hill, N.J., 1972-80, Beck Mid. Sch., Cherry Hill, N.J., 1980-89, 94—, Carusi Jr. High Sch., Cherry Hill, N.J., 1989-94; coord. Nat. Women's History Month Cherry Hill Jr. Schs., 1993-94. Mem. dist. Recycling Program Cherry Hill Pub. Schs., 1990-94. Mem. NEA, NOW, N.J. Edn. Assn., Camden County Edn. Assn., Cherry Hill Edn. Assn., World Wildlife Fedn., Global Fund for Women, Planned Parenthood, Alice Paul Centenial Found., Seeking Edn. Equity and Diversity (study group 1994), Freedom from Hunger, Population Comms. Internat. Home: 1015 Oaklyn Ct Voorhees NJ 08043 Office: Beck Mid Sch Cropwell Rd Cherry Hill NJ 08003

CARTER, CHARLENE A., psychologist; b. Marshall, Mich., Apr. 7, 1941; d. Charles V. F. and Eva L. (Hesling) Hampton.; m. Ross E. Carter, Jan. 15, 1966; children: Laura, Paul. BA in Psychology and Sociology, Albion Coll., 1962; MA in Clin. Pharmacology, Mich. State U., 1964, PhD in Clin. Pharmacology, 1968. Lic. psychologist, Wis. Clin. intern VA Hosp., Battle Creek, Mich., 1963-65, Psychol. Clinic, Mich. State U., East Lansing, 1965-66; clin. intern Counseling Ctr., Mich. State U., East Lansing, 1966-68, asst. prof., 1968-69; asst. clin. prof. dept. psychiatry and mental health scis. Med. Coll. Wis., Milw., 1983—; clin. asst. prof. dept. psychology U. Wis., Milw., 1993—; pvt. practice Bangor, Maine, 1971, Media, Pa., 1974-75, Milw., 1988—; dir. clin. tng. Wis. Sch. for Girls, Oregon, Wis., 1969-70; staff psychologist The Counseling Ctr., Cmty. Mental Health Ctr., Bangor, Maine, 1971, Adult Cmty. Svc. Child Guidance and Mental Health Clinics Delaware County, Media, Pa., 1971-75; mem. staff Milw. Psychiat. Hosp., 1989—, Waukesha (Wis.) Meml. Hosp., 1992—; psychologist cons. Office of Hearings and Appeals Social Security Adminstrn., Milw., 1986-91; lectr. in field. Contbr. articles to profl. jours. USPHS fellow, 1962, 65, 66. Mem. APA, Am. Assn. Cancer Edn., Milw. Area Women Psychologists. Office: Mayfair North Tower 2600 North Mayfair Rd Ste 310 Milwaukee WI 53226

CARTER, DENISE EVETT, grant administrator; b. Lake Worth, Fla., Oct. 30, 1959; d. Joe Edward and Ruth Elvira (Frederick) Dorsey; m. Tyrone Carter, Nov. 24, 1984. BA in Am. Studies, U. Fla., 1982. Rsch. analyst Palm Beach County Housing & Community Devel., West Palm Beach, Fla., 1984, planner, 1984-85; planning analyst City of Cocoa, Fla., 1985-86; planner Brevard County Community Devel. Block Grant Program, Merritt Island, Fla., 1986-87, sr. planner, 1987-89; compliance coord. Brevard County Community Devel. Block Grant Program, Cocoa, 1989-91; supr. Brevard County Community Devel. Block Grant Program, Melbourne, 1991—. Capt. 24 hr. relay team Easter Seal Soc., Melbourne, 1993; vol., high fundraiser achiever March of Dimes, Melbourne, 1991-93; Bible sch. tchr. Melbourne Ch. of Christ, 1990-93; bd. dirs. Fla. Community Devel., 1993-94; ex-officio mem. Community Devel. Block Grant Adv. Bd., sec., 1989—; sec. Brevard County Housing Authority, mem. Family Self-Sufficiency Adv. Bd., 1992-93; co-chmn. vol. com. Very Spl. Arts, 1993—. Named to Historic Women of Brevard, Brevard Culture Alliance, 1992; recipient Cert. of Appreciation, Brevard County Child Care Assn., 1992; Cmty. Devel. Block Grant Prepares, 1987—. Home: 151 Kristi Dr Indian Harbour Beach FL 32937

CARTER, EDITH HOUSTON, statistician, educator; b. Charlotte, N.C., Oct. 12, 1936; d. Z. and Ellie (Hartsell) Houston; BS, Appalachian State U., 1959, MA, 1960; PhD, Va. Poly. Inst. and State U., 1976; m. Fletcher F. Carter, Apr. 2, 1961. Transcript analyst Fla. Dept. Edn., Tallahassee, 1961-65; instr. Radford U., 1969-70, 91-94, asst. prof., 1994—; prof. New River C.C., Dublin, Va., 1970—, dir. instl. research, 1974-78, asst. dean Coll. Arts and Scis., 1978-79, statistician, 1979-83. Violist Va. Poly. Inst. and State U. Orch., Radford U. Orch., S.W. Va. Opera Soc. Orch.; sec./treas. Radford New River Valley chpt. Am. Sewing Guild, 1991-94, pres., 1994-95. Mem. Am. Ednl. Research Assn., State and Regional Ednl. Rsch. Assn. (sec./treas. 1989-93, pres. 1993—), Assn. Instl. Research (exec. bd. 1976-78), Southeastern Assn. C.C. Research (exec. bd. 1976-78, Outstanding Service award, Disting. Service award 1981), Nat. Council Research and Planning, Coll. Music Soc. (Outstanding Svc. award 1992), Am. String Tchrs. Assn., Va. Fedn. Women's Clubs (dir. 1968-70), Va. Tech. U. Alumni (pres. New River Valley chpt. 1982-83), Radford Jr. Woman's Club (pres. 1967-68). Methodist. Clubs: Radford Garden. Editor Community Coll. Jour. Research and Planning, 1981-93, Am. Assn. Community Colls. Jour., 1991—, Newsletter Southeastern Assn. C.C. Research, 1972—; mem. editorial bd. C.C. Rev., 1990-93. Home: 6924 Radford Univ Radford VA 24142 Office: Radford U Russell Hall Radford VA 24142

CARTER, ELEANOR ELIZABETH, business manager; b. Durham, N.C., July 16, 1954; d. Joseph William Jr. and Sheila Dale (Swartz) C. BS in Social Work, N.C. State U., 1977. Field worker family planning Wake County Health Dept., Raleigh, N.C., 1975-76; sales rep. Bristol-Myers Products, N.C., 1977-80; regional adminstn. asst. Bristol-Myers Products, Dallas, Tex., 1980; regional trainer Bristol-Myers Products, Washington, N.C., Va., 1980; sales adminstrn. mgr. corp. hdqrs. Bristol-Myers Products, N.Y.C., 1980-81; dist. supr. Bristol-Myers Products, Cin., 1981-82; account rep. Fuji Photo Film U.S.A., Inc., Cin., 1982-83; spl. account mgr. Fuji Photo Film U.S.A., Inc., Chgo., 1983-90; nat. account mgr. Fuji Photo Film U.S.A., Itasca, Ill., 1991—. Mem. Nat. Assn. Female Execs., Alpha Kappa Delta. Presbyterian. Office: Fuji Photo Film USA Inc 1285 Hamilton Pky Itasca IL 60143-1147

CARTER, ELIZABETH NORMAN, economics consultant, educator; b. Amarillo, Tex., Apr. 12, 1935; d. Gordon Alexander and Florence Ann (Binns) MacInnes; m. Reynold Gail Green, July 7, 1956 (div. July 1970); children: David Ian, Stacia Alexandria, Christopher Reynold; m. Donald Lee Carter, June 17, 1973. BA, Westminster Coll., 1958; M of Instrn., U. Del., 1989. Cert. secondary edn. tchr., Alaska, Calif. Tchr. Garden Grove (Calif.) Unified Sch. Dist., 1968-73, Anchorage Sch. Dist., 1974-76, 80-93; owner Alaska Book Co., Anchorage, 1976-79; pres. EMC Cons., Anchorage, 1993—; bd. dirs. Alaska Model UN, Anchorage; cons., bd. trustees Alaska Coun. Econ. Edn., Anchorage, 1985-94; mem. Alaska Coun. Social Studies, 1976-93. Bd. dirs. Anchorage Comty. Schs., 1976-77; del. Anchorage Dem. Caucus, 1976, Gov.'s Econ. Summit, Anchorage, 1993. Named Presdl. Disting. Tchr., Presdl. Scholars Program, 1993; recipient Teaching Excellence award Anchorage Coun. Social Studies, 1993; econ. edn. grantee U. Del., 1987, 88. Mem. Alaska World Affairs Coun. (bd. dirs. chair edn. 1993-94), UN Assn.-USA. Presbyterian. Home: 5341 Country Club Ln Anchorage AK 99516-3013

CARTER, GALE DENISE, elementary education educator; b. N.Y.C., Sept. 5, 1953; d. Albert Edward and Josephine (Hernandez) D'Ambrosio; m. David Samuel Carter, Apr. 3, 1976; children: Stephanie, David, Jennifer, Michelle. BS, U. Md., 1975, MEd, 1992. Tchr. 7th grade Mt. Calvary Sch., Forestville, Md., 1975-77; tchr. 6th and 7th grades Mother Catherine Spaulding Sch., Helen, Md., 1986-87; substitute tchr. St. Mary's County Pub. Schs., Leonardtown, Md., 1987-88, tchr. 3rd grade, 1988-90, tchr. 6th grade, 1990—, reading specialist Margaret Brent Middle Sch., 1995—. Leader Girl Scouts U.S., Washington. Recipient Marian Medal award Archdiocese of Washington/Cath. Girl Scouting, 1968. Mem. PTA, Md. Tchrs. Assn., Internat. Reading Assn. (Md. chpt.). Democrat. Roman Catholic. Home: 1480 King Rd Mechanicsville MD 20659-3735 Office: St Marys County Pub Schs Leonardtown MD 20650

CARTER, GEORGIAN L., minister; b. St. Mary's, Ga., July 3, 1939; d. Leroy Sr. and Abbie (Myers) Logan; m. Calvin L. Carter, Mar. 26, 1956; children: Janice Carter Slocumb, Arlette Carter Fletcher, Eric. AA, Prince Georges Community Coll., Largo, Md., 1973; cert., Dale Carnegie Sch., 1980. Ordained to ministry Deliverance Ch. of Christ, 1983. Clk., trustee Deliverance Ch. of Christ, Seat Pleasant, Md., 1968-87, Bible class tchr., 1983-89; sec., sick and shut-in ministry Full Gospel A.M.E. Zion Ch., Temple Hills, Md., 1989-92; mem. Live Oak Ch. of God, Hinesville, 1992, Sunday sch. tchr. of adult class, 1993—; with HUD, Washington, 1967-89; tchr. noon-time Bible study U.S. State Dept. Fellowship, 1989-91; lay min. and leader Hines Estates Bible Study Group, 1993—. Asst. dir. Glenarden (Md.) Housing Authority, 1973-75. Democrat. Home: 909 Byrum Dr Hinesville GA 31313-5752

CARTER, HARRIET VANESSA, public relations specialist, congressional aide; b. N.Y.C.; d. Gerard Frederick and Eugenia Carter. BA in Spanish magna cum laude, Tulane U., 1969; MEd in Spanish, U. Ill., 1974; postgrad., U. D'Aix en Provence, France, 1972, U. Nice, France, 1974, U. Montreal, 1979, U. Vienna, 1980. Spanish tchr. King Philip Jr. High Sch., West Hartford, Conn., 1971-76, Irvington (N.Y.) High Sch., 1976-77, Closter (N.J.) Village Sch., 1977-78; Spanish tchr., coordinator academic awards program Benjamin Sch., North Palm Beach, Fla., 1978-81; asst. to clin. dean, pub. relations coordinator, med. residency coordinator Am. U. of Caribbean Sch. of Medicine, Miami, Fla., 1981-84; asst. dir. admissions Ross U. Sch. of Medicine, N.Y.C., 1984; coord. ednl. tng., asst. to pres. United Schs. of Am., Miami, 1985-86; pvt. practice pub. relations specialist in edn., medicine, polit. govt. and travel Miami, 1986—; coord. div. of Latino studies Fla. Internat. U., Miami, 1987-88, promotions cons. in broadcasting, 1989-90, TV prodr., exec. asst. to program dir., 1990-91; TV prodr., co-host series Volunteer Miami, Sta. WLRN-TV, 1991-92; congl. aide, 1993—; Pub. rels. mgr. Voyager mag., Lake Park, Fla., 1981-82; instr. med. Spanish U. Conn. Med. Sch., Farmington, 1974, Mt. Sinai Hosp., Hartford, 1973; teaching asst. in Spanish U. Ill., Urbana, 1970-71, fellow, 1970. Founder, editor (newsletter) Focus on Multi-Cultural Happenings, 1975-76; editor (newsletter) American University of the Caribbean School of Medicine, 1981-84; contbr. articles to profl. jours. Participant Hispanic leadership tng. program Cuban-Am. Nat. Coun., Miami, 1988; mem. pub. rels. and comms. com. Leadership Miami, 1989—; vol. Miracle Telethon, Miami Children's Hosp., 1986, Jerry Lewis Labor Day Telethon, 1989, 93, 94, auction Sta. WLRN-TV, Miami, 1990-94, vol.-a-thon for United Way Dade County, Sta. WPLG-TV, 1991; guide So. Gov.'s Conf., Miami, 1995; active Greater Miami Ambs. Corps, 1985-92, Coun. Internat. Visitors Greater Miami. Semi-finalist Miss Teenage Am. Contest; recipient recognition award U.S. Ho. of Reps., 1991, cert. of merit for commitment to cmty. svc. Pres. of U.S., 1991; fellow U. Ill., 1969-70; scholar Govt. of Austria, 1980. Mem. NATAS, AAUW (co-chmn. com. on women 1980-81), Phi Beta Kappa, Phi Delta Kappa. Office: Ste 202 9357 Fontainebleau Miami FL 33172-4210

CARTER, HELEN R., small business owner, telecommunications executive; b. Hot Springs, Ark., May 20, 1939; d. Hugh Benjamin and Caroline (Yeager) Davis; widow; 1 child, Terri Lynne. Student, Richland Coll., 1973-74, Trinity Valley Coll., Athens, Tex., 1980,81. Acct. Norris Dispensers, Hot Springs, Ark., 1961-63; sec. to controller Southland Corp., Dallas, 1965-70; co-owner Carter Comm., Dallas, Gun Barrel, Tex., 1970—. Pres. Bus. and Profl. Women, Cedar Creek Lake Area, 1981, 93, Avanti Soc., Cedar Creek Lake Area, 1983-87; bd. dirs. Zonta Internat., Dallas, 1974-75. Nmed Citizen of Yr. Cedar Creek Lake C. of C., 1984. Mem. TeleProbes (sec.-treas 1981—), N. Am. Telecomm. Assn. (sec.-treas. Dallas 1970-74, Svc. award

1990). Office: Carter Mobile Comm PO Box 968 N Hwy 90 GBCI Gun Barrel TX 75147

CARTER, JANE FOSTER, agriculture industry executive; b. Stockton, Calif., Jan. 14, 1927; d. Chester William and Bertha Emily Foster; m. Robert Buffington Carter, Feb. 25, 1952 (wid. Dec. 1994); children: Ann Claire Carter Palmer, Benjamin Foster. BA, Stanford U., 1948; MS, NYU, 1949. Pres. Colusa (Calif.) Properties, Inc., 1953—; owner Carter Land and Livestock, Colusa, 1965—; sec.-treas. Carter Farms, Inc., Colusa, 1975-94, pres., 1994—. Author: If the Walls Could Talk, Colusa's Architectural Heritage, 1988; author, editor: Colusa County Survey and Plan for the Arts, 1981, 82, 83, Implementing the Colusa County Arts Plan, 1984, 85, 86. Mem. Calif. Gov.'s Commn. on Agr., Sacramento, 1979-82, Calif. Rep. Cen. Com., 1976—; del. Rep. Nat. Conv., Kansas City, Mo., 1976, Detroit, 1980, Dallas, 1984; trustee Calif. Hist. Soc., 1979-89, regional v.p., 1984-89; mem. Calif. Reclamation Bd., 1983—, sec. 1986—; mem. Calif. Historical Resources Comm., 1994—; Heritage Preservation Com. City of Colusa, 1976—, chmn., 1977-83, vice chmn., 1983-91; bd. dirs. Colusa Community Theatre Found., 1980—, English Speaking Union, San Francisco, 1992—, pres., 1993—; bd. dirs. Leland Stanford Mansion Found., Sacramento, 1992—; trustee Calif. Preservation Found., 1989—. Recipient award of Merit for Historic Preservation Calif. Hist. Soc., 1989, Design award Calif. Preservation Found., 1990. Mem. Sacramento River Water Contractors Assn. (sec. 1992—), Francisca Club, Kappa Alpha Theta. Episcopalian. Home and Office: 4746 River Rd Colusa CA 95932-4200

CARTER, JANICE JOENE, telecommunications executive; b. Portland, Oreg., Apr. 17, 1948; d. William George and Charline Betty (Gilbert) P.; m. Ronald Thomas Carter, June 13, 1968; children: Christopher Scott, Jill Suzanne. Student, U. Calif., Berkeley, 1964, U. Portland, 1966-67, U. Colo., Boulder, 1967-68; BA in Math, U. Guam, 1970. Computer programmer Ga.-Pacific Co., Portland, 1972-74; systems analyst ProData, Seattle, 1974-79; systems analyst, mgr. Pacific Northwest Bell, Seattle, 1979-80; data ctr. mgr. Austin Co., Renton, Wash., 1980-83; developer shared tenent svcs. Wright-Runstad, Seattle, 1983-84; system adminstr. Hewlett-Packard, Bellevue, Wash., 1984; telecom. dir. Nordstrom, Inc., Seattle, 1984—; mem. large customer panel AT&T, Seattle, 1987—. Ski instr. Alpental, Snoqualmie Pass, Wash., 1984-87; bd. dirs. Educationally Gifted Children, Mercer Island, Wash., 1978-80; mem. curriculum com. Mercer Island Sch. Bd., 1992—; mem. Sweet Adelines. Mem. Telecom. Assn., Internat. Comm. Assn., System 85/ETN User Group. Office: Nordstrom Inc 1904 3rd Ave Seattle WA 98101

CARTER, JEAN GORDON, lawyer; b. Fort Belvior, Va., July 30, 1955; d. Thomas Laney and Cleone (Hunter) Gordon; m. Michael L. Carter, Sept. 17, 1977; children: Christina Jean, William Gordon. BS magna cum laude with honors in Accountancy, Wake Forest U., 1977; JD with high honors, Duke U., 1983. Bar: N.C. 1983; CPA; bd. cert. specialist in estates. Acct. Arthur Andersen & Co., Charlotte, N.C., 1977-80; atty. Moore & Van Allen, Raleigh, N.C., 1983-90; ptnr. Hunton & Williams, Raleigh, N.C., 1990—; councilor tax sect. N.C. Bar Assn., 1993—; coun. Estates sect. N.Y. Bar Assn., 1990-92; pres. Wake County Estates Coun., Raleigh, 1991-92; v.p. N.C. Planned Giving Coun., Raleigh, 1991-92. Mem. Order of the Coif, Phi Beta Kappa. Democrat. Methodist. Home: 8612 Seagate Dr Raleigh NC 27615 Office: Hunton & Williams 1 Hannover Sq Raleigh NC 27601

CARTER, JOY EATON, electrical engineer, consultant; b. Comanche, Tex., Feb. 8, 1923; d. Robert Lee and Carrie (Knudson) Eaton; m. Clarence J. Carter, Aug. 22, 1959; 1 child, Kathy Jean. Student, John Tarleton Agrl. Coll., 1939-40; B Music cum laude, N. Tex. State Tchrs. Coll., 1943, postgrad., 1944-45; postgrad., U. Tex., 1945; MSEE, Ohio State U., 1949, PhDEE and Radio Astronomy, 1957. Engr. aide Civil Service Wright Field, Dayton, Ohio, 1945-46; instr. math. Ohio State U., Columbus, 1946-48, asst., then assoc. Rsch. Found., 1947-49, from instr. to asst. prof. elec. engring., 1949-58; rsch. engr. N.Am. Aviation, Columbus, 1955-56; mem. tech. staff Space Tech. Labs. (later TRW Inc.), Redondo Beach, Calif., 1958-68; sect. head, staff engr. electronics rsch. labs. The Aerospace Corp., El Segundo, 1968-72, staff engr. and mgr. system and terminals, USAF Satellite Communications System Program Office, 1972-77, mgr. communications subsystem Def. Satellite Communications System III Program Office, 1978-79; cons. Mayhill, N.Mex., 1979—. Active Mayhill Vol. Fire Dept.; bd. dirs. Mayhill Cmty. Assn., 1988—, sec. bd. dirs., 1988—; co-chair music com. Mayhill Bapt. Ch., 1988—, trustee, 1989-92, 94—; bd. dirs. Otero County Farm Bur., 1987—. Named Cow Belle of Yr. Otero Cow Belles, 1988. Mem. IEEE (sr., life), Am. Astron. Soc., Am. Nat. Cattle Women (sec. otero CowBelles chpt. 1986-87, 1st v.p. 1988, historian 1989), Calif. Rare Fruit Growers, Native Plant Soc. N.Mex., Sacramento Mountains Hist. Soc. (bd. dirs. 1986—), High Country Horseman's Assn., Sigma Xi (life), Eta Kappa Nu (life), Sigma Alpha Iota (life), Alpha Chi, Kappa Delta Pi, Pi Mu Epsilon, Sigma Delta Epsilon. Home and Office: PO Box 23 Mayhill NM 88339-0023

CARTER, JOYE MAUREEN, pathologist, consultant; b. June 3, 1957; d. Russell Eugene and Marjorie Bernice (Hart) C. BA cum laude, Wittenberg U., 1979; MD, Howard U., 1983. Diplomate Am. Bd. Medicine, Am. Bd. Pathology. Intern Booth Meml. Hosp., N.Y.C., 1983-84; Resident Howard U. Hosp., Washington, 1984-88; chief resident in pathology Howard U. Hosp., 1988-89; fellow in forensic pathology Dade County, Miami, Fla., 1988-89; dir. forensic sci. master's program Armed Forces Inst. Pathology, George Washington U., Washington, 1989-92; dep. chief med. examiner Armed Forces Inst. Pathology, George Washington U., 1991-92; assoc. prof. George Washington U., Washington, 1989—; asst. clin. prof. George Washington U., 1992—, Howard U., 1991—; chief med. examiner D.C., 1993—; cons. Office of U.S. Atty., Washington, 1990—; mem. D.C. Anatomical Bd. Contbr. articles profl. jours. Mem. Mayor's Com. on Child Abuse, Mayor's Com. on Infant Mortality. Maj. USAF, 1989-92. Recipient Nat. Def. Svc. medal, 1991; Health Professions scholar USAF, 1980. Fellow Coll. Am. Pathologists; mem. D.C. Med. Soc., Am. Acad. Forensic Scis., Nat. Assn. Med. Examiners, Aerospace Med. Assn., So. Med. Assn., Nat. Med. Assn. (sec. pathology sect. 1992-94), Medico-Chirugical Soc. of D.C., Mid-Atlantic Forensic Pathology Assn. Democrat. Office: Office Chief Med Examiner 1910 Massachusetts Ave SE Washington DC 20003

CARTER, KAREN SUZANNE, city manager; b. Chester, S.C., Aug. 27, 1960; d. Howell Ernest Jr. and Frances (Rockholt) C. BA in Polit. Sci., Winthrop U., 1982; MPA, U. S.C., 1984. Asst. v.p. adminstrv. svcs. Security Fed. Savs. & Loan, Columbia, S.C., 1985-87; pers. dir., asst. to city mgr. City of Camden, S.C., 1987-90; city mgr. City of York, 1990—; cons. Burkhold Planning & Mgmt., Columbia, 1993—. Named Young Career Woman of Yr., S.C. Bus. and Profl. Women's Clubs, 1992. Mem. S.C. Assn. City and County Mgrs., Internat. City Mgrs. Assn., Internat. Pers. Mgmt. Assn. ((Excellence in Pers. award 1988), Greater York C. of C. (bd. dirs. 1991-94), United Way (Western York County pres.-elect 1994), Local Govt. Assurance (bd. dirs., v.p. 1990—), Rotary (bd. dirs. York club 1990—). Home: 9 Brookwood Dr York SC 29745-2009 Office: City of York 10 N Roosevelt St York SC 29745-1533

CARTER, LENA SMITH, music specialist, singer; b. Chattanooga, Jan. 5, 1946; d. Percy Smith and Martha Aileen Paris Briggs; m. David George Carter, Aug. 14, 1965; children: Ehrika, Jessica, David Jr. BS in Music Edn., Ctrl. State U., Wilberforce, Ohio, 1966; M. in Music Performance and Repertory, Miami U., Oxford, Ohio, 1968; Diploma Music/Humanities, Paris Am. Acad., 1977; postgrad., Pa. State U., 1975-77. Music specialist Dayton (Ohio) Pub. Schs., 1967-72; music specialist, head tchr. Hartford (Conn.) Pub. Schs., 1979-85, music specialist, 1987—; assoc. dept. community rels. United Tech. Corp., Hartford, 1985-86; text processor dept. corp. comm. N.E. Utilities, Hartford, 1986-87; artist-in-residence dept. music Universidade Federal de Paraiba, Joao, Pessoa, Brazil, 1988, master tchr., 1990, 91. Co-author chpt. in book: Bilingually Prepared Teachers and Students: In Search of Diversity, 1991. Mem. Hartford Pub. High Sch./Conn. Mut. Alliance, 1985; edn. adv. coun. Willimantic Textile History Mus., 1989; bd. dirs. Greater Hartford Acad. Performing Arts, 1985, Conn. Inst. for Arts, 1989; mem. Mansfield Tng. Sch. Bd., Conn., 1989. Leadership Am. Conf./Nat. Found. for Women's Resources fellow, 1990. Mem. NAFE, Am. Guild Mus. Artists, Coll. Music Soc., Companeiros das Americas (pres. Conn./Paraiba com. 1988-92), Alpha Kappa Alpha. Democrat. Pentecostal Ch. Home and Office: PO Box 2566 Hartford CT 06146-2566

CARTER, LINDA WHITEHEAD, oncology nurse, educator, consultant, researcher; b. Bluefield, W.Va., Dec. 20, 1941; d. Lee Joseph and Kathleen (Witherspoon) Whitehead; m. J. Stephen Carter, Mar. 11, 1961; children: Paul Scott, Kristin Hope. Student, Westmoreland Coll., Youngwood, Pa., 1980-83, St. Vincent Coll., Latrobe, Pa., 1984-85; BSN, Carlow Coll., Pitts., 1986; MSN, U. Pitts., 1992. RN, Pa.; cert. oncology nurse; clin. nurse specialist. Oncology staff nurse Westmoreland Hosp., Greensburg, Pa., 1986-93, facilitator support group, 1988-93, oncology educator, 1990-93; clin. nurse specialist Magee Women's Hosp., Pitts., 1993-94; faculty Carlow Coll. Divsn. Nursing, Pitts., 1993—; grad. asst. Pitts. Cancer Inst., 1990; grad. clin. nurse specialist Allegheny Gen. Hosp., Pitts., 1991-92; nurse of hope Am. Cancer Soc., 1987, mem. pub. edn. com. Westmoreland Unit, 1987-88, mem. nursing edn. com., 1987—, mem. profl. edn. com., 1990—, bd. dirs., 1989-92. Mem. editorial rev. bd. Oncology Nursing Forum, 1994-95. Named Vol. of Yr., Am. Cancer Soc., 1988, Pa. Div. scholar, 1987, Nat. scholar, 1989-91. Mem. ANA, Pa. Nurses Assn., Nat. League for Nursing, Oncology Nursing Soc. (nominating com. Greater Pitts. chpt. 1990-91, newsletter com. 1992-93), Internat. Soc. Nurses in Cancer Care, Sigma Theta Tau. Home: 2922 Bryer Ridge Dr Export PA 15632-9393 Office: Carlow Coll Curran Hall 3333 5th Ave Pittsburgh PA 15213

CARTER, LOU ANN ROSE, human services planner, nurse; b. Everett, Wash., Jan. 27, 1957; d. George Eugene and Virginia Ann (Jones) Carpenter; children: Amanda Lee, Rosalie Ann. Cert. practical nursing, Everett C.C., 1976, Assoc. in Arts & Scis., 1988; BA in Human Svcs., Western Wash. U., 1991, postgrad., 1994—. LPN Parkway Nursing Home, Snohomish, Wash., 1977-78, Providence Hosp., Everett, 1979-80; clin. LPN Tulalip Tribes, Marysville, Wash., 1981-90, Indian student social worker, 1991-92, svcs. planner, 1993—. Bd. dirs. ARC, sec., 1993-94; v.p. Arlington Middle Sch. PTSA. Democrat. Office: Tulalip Tribes 6326 33rd Ave NE Marysville WA 98271-7433

CARTER, MAE RIEDY, retired college official, consultant; b. Berkeley, Calif., May 20, 1921; d. Carl Joseph and Avis Blanche (Rodehaver) Riedy; BS, U. Calif., Berkeley, 1943; m. Robert C. Carter, Aug. 19, 1944; children: Catherine, Christin Ann. Ednl. adv., then program specialist div. continuing edn. U. Del., Newark, 1968-78, asst. provost for women's affairs, exec. dir. commn. status women Office Women's Affairs, 1978-86; adv. bd. Rockefeller Family grant project, 1979-83. Regional v.p. Del. PTA, 1960-62; pres. Friends Newark Free Library, 1968-69; mem. fiscal planning com. Newark Spl. Sch. Dist., 1972. Recipient Outstanding Service award Women's Coordinating Council, 1977, 79; Spl. Recognition award, Nat. U. Extension Assn., 1977, award for credit programs, 1971, Creative Programming award, 1971; AAUW grantee, 1968; Fulbright grantee, 1976; named to Delaware Women Hall of Fame, 1995. Mem. AAUW (past br. pres.), LWV, NOW, Nat. Assn. for Women Edn., Women's Legal Def. Fund, Nat. Women's Polit. Caucus. Republican. Author: Research on Seeing and Evaluating People, 1982, (with Geis and Butler) Seeing and Evaluating People, 1982, revised, 1986, (with Haslett and Geis) The Organizational Woman: Power and Paradox, 1992; also papers, reports in field. Home: 604 Dallam Rd Newark DE 19711-3110

CARTER, MARGARET L., legislator; b. La., Dec. 29, 1935; d. Emma Carter; 9 children. BA, Portland State U., 1972; MEd, Oreg. State U., 1973; postgrad., Washington State U. Community organizer, asst. dir. Community Action Agy., Shreveport, La.; tchr. Albina Youth Opportunity Sch., Portland; counselor Portland Community Coll.; mem. Oreg. Ho. of Reps., Salem, 1984—; mem. Joint Trade and Econ. Devel. com., 1985—, co-chair 1989—, Human Resources com., 1985, vice chair, 87, Edn. com., 1985, 87, 89, Conf. com. on Dr. Martin Luther King State Holiday, co-chair, 1985, Joint Health Care com. 1986. Founder, mus. dir. Joyful Sound Singers Piedmont Ch. Christ; vol. counselor various juvenile detention ctrs. and women's prisons, voter registration drives in Portland's black neighborhoods, Project Pride; organizer Oreg. chpt. of Sickle Cell Anemia Found.; founder Oreg. Black Leadership Conf.; mem. Oreg. State Commn. on Post Secondary Edn. and the Oreg. Alliance for Black Sch. Educators, Spl. Commn. for the Parole Bd. on the Matrix System; mem. Gov.'s Task Force on Pregnancy and Substance Abuse, 1989—, Coun. on Alcohol and Drugs, 1989—, bd. dirs. ARC, Emanuel Med. Ctr. Found. Recipient Jeanette Rankin award Oreg. Women's Polit. Caucus, 1985. Mem. Nat. Organ. Black Legis. Elected Women (v.p. 1985), Nat. Black Caucus (exec. com.), Blacks in Gov. (regional pres.), Alpha Kappa Alpha. Democrat. Home: 2948 NE 10th Ave Portland OR 97212-3240 Office: Oreg State Legis H-478 State Capitol Salem OR 97310

CARTER, MARY EDDIE, government administrator; b. Americus, Ga., Mar. 14, 1925; d. Walker G. and Esther (Stewart) C. B.A., LaGrange Coll., 1946; M.S., U. Fla., 1949; Ph.D., U. Edinburgh, 1956. Tchr. LaGrange (Ga.) Coll., 1946-47; chemist Callaway Mills, LaGrange, 1947-48; microscopist So. Research Inst., Birmingham, Ala., 1949-51; chemist West Point Mfg. Co., Shawmut, Ala., 1951-53; research assoc. FMC Corp., Am. Viscose div., Marcus Hook, Pa., 1956-71; lab chief textiles and clothing lab. U.S. Dept. Agr., Knoxville, Tenn., 1971-73; dir. So. Regional Research Ctr, 1973-80; asso. adminstr. Agrl. Research Service, Washington, 1980-92; area dir. Agrl. Rsch. Svc., Athens, Ga., 1992—. Recipient Herty medal Ga. sect. of Am. Chem. Soc., 1979, Meritorious Presdl. Rank award, 1982, 87; Named Fed. Woman of Yr. City Wide Fed. Exec. Bd., 1977. Fellow AAAS, Cellulose, Paper and Textile Div. of Am. Chem. Soc.; mem. Am. Chem. Soc., Am. Assn. Textile Chemists and Colorists, Inter-Soc. Color Coun., Fiber Soc., Inst. Food Technologists, Am. Assn. Cereal Chemists, Sigma Xi. Office: USDA Agrl Rsch Svc PO Box 5677 Athens GA 30604-5677

CARTER, MICHELLE ADAIR, editor; b. El Paso, Tex., Dec. 2, 1944; d. Theodore Edwin and Dorothy (Terwilliger) Grimm; m. Laurence Roy Carter, Jan. 28, 1967; children: Robyn Adair, David Brian. BJ, U. Mo., 1966. Copy editor Kansas City (Mo.) Star, 1966-67; reporter San Mateo (Calif.) Times, 1967-82, news editor, 1982-88, mng. editor, 1988—. Coauthor: Children of Chernobyl: Raising Hope From The Ashes, 1993. Bd. dirs. San Mateo County Gen. Hosp. Found., 1990—, bd. exec., 1991—; founder Children of Chernobyl Project, Belmont, Calif., 1990—. Recipient numerous writing awards AP, UPI, San Francisco Bar Assn., Calif. Tchrs. Assn. Mem. Am. Soc. Newspaper Editors, Nat. Fedn. Press. Women, Soc. Profl. Journalists, Peninsula Press Club. Mem. United Ch. Christ. Office: San Mateo Times PO Box 5400 San Mateo CA 94402-0400

CARTER, OLIVIA, psychiatric nurse; b. Carthage, Tenn., Jan. 30, 1950; d. Willie Roy and Robbie Key (Garrett) C. AA in nursing, Mid. Tenn. State U., 1975; BS in nursing, Tenn. Tech. U., 1992. RN, Tenn.; cert. psychiatry and mental health nurse. Nurse supr. Blvd. Terr. Nursing Home, Murfreesboro, Tenn., 1975-76; charge nurse Murfreesboro Health Care Corp., 1976-77; nurse mgr., geriopsych. Alvin C. York VA Med. Ctr., Murfreesboro, 1977—, nurse mgr. chronic mentally ill, 1994—; equal opportunity counselor. Vol. nurse ARC; vol. Teen Drug and Alcohol Rehab. Recipient commendation Vanderbilt Child and Adolescent Psychiat. Hosp., Nashville, 1989. Mem. ANA, Nat. Black Nurse's Assn., Alpha Kappa Alpha. Methodist. Home: 1819 Florence Rd Murfreesboro TN 37129 Office: Ward 7A 3400 Lebanon Rd Murfreesboro TN 37129

CARTER, PAMELA LEE, school system administrator; b. Indpls., Sept. 29, 1949; d. Bernard Marsh and Virginia Lee (Rigsby) Fisher; m. Michael Carter, Aug. 19, 1975. BS in Elem. Edn., Ball State U., 1971, MA, 1973; postgrad., various univs. Cert. tchr., Mich. Kindergarten tchr. Lynn (Ind.) Elem. Sch., 1971-74, Padgett Elem. Sch., Lakeland, Fla., 1974; substitute tchr. Farmington (Mich.) and Clarenceville (Mich.) Pub. Schs., 1975-76; kindergarten tchr. Waverly Community Schs., Lansing, Mich., 1976-86, K-12 curriculum coord., 1985—; nat. lecture staff Gesell Inst. Human Devel., New Haven, Conn., 1986—; resource counselor Willoway Summer Day Camp, Wixom, Mich., 1976; assoc. dir. Meadowbrook Woods Learning Ctr., Novi, Mich., 1975; child devel. cons. Northland Pioneer Coll., Holbrook, Ariz., 1975. Contbr. articles to profl. jours. Named Outstanding Early Childhood Specialist Cen. Mich. Assn. for Edn. Young Children, 1985, Outstanding Young Educator Waverly Jaycees, 1980. Mem. ASCD, Nat. Staff Devel. Coun., Nat. Assn. Edn. Young Children, Assn. for Childhood Edn. Internat., Sierra Club. Office: Waverly Community Schs 620 Snow Rd Lansing MI 48917

CARTER, PAMELA LYNN, state attorney general; b. South Haven, Mich., Aug. 20, 1949; d. Roscoe Hollis and Dorothy Elizabeth (Hadley) Fanning; m. Michael Anthony Carter, Aug. 26, 1971; children: Michael Anthony Jr., Marcya Alicia. BA cum laude, U. Detroit, 1971; MSW, U. Mich., 1973; JD, Ind. U., 1984. Bar: Ind. 1984, U.S. Dist. Ct. (no. dist.) Ind. 1984, U.S. Dist. Ct. (so. dist.) Ind. 1984. Rsch. analyst, treatment dir. U. Mich. Sch. Pub. Health and UAW, Detroit, 1973-75; exec. dir. Mental Health Ctr. for Women and Children, Detroit, 1975-77; consumer litigation atty. UAW-Gen. Motors Legal Svcs., Indpls., 1983-87; securities atty. Sec. of State, Indpls., 1987-89; Gov.'s exec. asst. for health and human svcs. Gov.'s Office, Indpls., 1989-91, dep. chief of staff to Gov., 1991-92; with firm Baker & Daniels, 1992-93; atty. gen. State of Ind., Indpls., 1993—. Author poems. mem. Cath. Social Svcs., Indpls., Jr. League, Indpls., Dem. Precinct, Indpls. Recipient Outstanding Svc. award Indiana Perinatal Assn., 1991, Community Svc. Coun. Ctrl. Ind., 1991, non-profl. healthcare award Family Health Conf. Bd. Dirs., 1991, award for excellence Women of the Rainbow, 1991; named Outstanding Young Woman of America, 1977, Breakthrough Woman of the Year, 1989. Mem. Nat. Bar Assn., Ind. Bar Assn., Coalition of 100 Black Women. Democrat. Office: 402 W Washington St Rm C553 Indianapolis IN 46204-2739*

CARTER, PAULENE, chemist, youth advisory consultant; b. Richmond, Ind., Oct. 26, 1951; d. Woodrow General and Odessa Prince (Ernestine) Smith; m. David Carter, Jan. 6, 1974; children: Byron, Kelly, Derrick. BA, Ind. U., 1974; MA, Ball State U., 1993. Chem. analyst Dana, Richmond, 1974—; cons. various youth orgns., Richmond, 1980—. state trustee Ind. Tech. Coll.; fundraiser United Way Wayne County. Mem. Am. Chem. Soc. Baptist. Office: Dana Corp 1400 Dana Pky Richmond IN 47374-1354

CARTER, ROBERTA ECCLESTON, educator, therapist; b. Pitts.; d. Robert E. and Emily B. (Bucar) Carter; divorced; children: David Michael Kiewlich, Daniel Michael Kiewlich. Student Edinboro State U., 1962-63; BS, California State U. of Pa., 1966; MEd, U. Pitts., 1969; MA, Rosebridge Grad. Sch., Walnut Creek, Calif., 1987. Tchr., Bethel Park Sch. Dist., Pa., 1966-69; writer, media asst. Field Ednl. Pub., San Francisco, 1969-70; educator, counselor, specialist Alameda Unified Sch. Dist., Calif., 1970—; master trainer Calif. State Dept. Edn., Sacramento, 1984—; personal growth cons., Alameda, 1983—. Author: People, Places and Products, 1970, Teaching/Learning Units, 1969; co-author: Teacher's Manual Let's Read, 1968. Mem. AAUW, NEA, Calif. Fedn. Bus. and Profl. Women (legis. chair Alameda br. 1984-85, membership chair 1985), Calif. Edn. Assn., Alameda Edn. Assn., Charter Planetary Soc., Oakland Mus., Exploratorium, Big Bros. of East Bay, Alameda C. of C. (svc. award 1985). Avocations: aerobics, gardening, travel. Home: 1516 Eastshore Dr Alameda CA 94501-3118

CARTER, ROSALYNN SMITH, wife of former President of U.S.; b. Plains, Ga., Aug. 18, 1927; d. Edgar and Allie (Murray) Smith; m. James Earl Carter, Jr., July 7, 1946; children: John William, James Earl III, Donnel Jeffrey, Amy Lynn. Grad., Ga. Southwestern Coll.; DHL (hon.), Morehouse Coll., 1980; LLD (hon.), U. Notre Dame, 1987. Disting. fellow Inst. Women's Studies Emory U., Atlanta, 1990—; vice chair, bd. dirs. The Carter Ctr., chair Mental Health Task Force Carter Ctr.; vice chair Global 2000; hon. chair, bd. dirs. Rosalynn Carter Inst. of Ga. Southwestern Coll.; cofounder Every Child By Two Campaign for Early Immunization. Author: First Lady from Plains, 1984, (with Jimmy Carter) Everything to Gain: Making the Most of the Rest of Your Life, 1987, Helping Yourself Help Others: A Book for Caregivers, 1994. Hon. chair Project Interconnections; bd. dirs. Friendship Force, Gannett Co., Crested Butte Physically Challenged Ski Program; bd. advisors Habitat for Humanity; sponsor Nat. Alliance for Rsch. on Schizophrenia and Depression; trustee Menninger Found.; hon. trustee Scottish Rite Children's Med. Ctr.; mem. Ga. Gov.'s Commn. to Improve Svcs. for Mentally and Emotionally Handicapped, 1971; hon. chair Pres.'s Commn. on Mental Health, 1977-78. Recipient Vol. of Decade award Nat. Mental Health Assn., 1980, Presdl. Citation APA, 1982, Nathan S. Kline medal of merit Internat. Com. Against Mental Illness, 1984, Disting. Alumnus award Am. Assn. State Colls. and Univs., 1987, Dorothea Dix award Mental Illness Found., 1988, Dean's award Columbia U. Coll. Physicians and Surgeons, 1991, Notre Dame award for internat. humanitarian svc., 1992, Eleanor Roosevelt Living World award Peace Links, 1992. Hon. fellow Am. Psychiat. Assn.

CARTER, RUTH B. (MRS. JOSEPH C. CARTER), association executive; b. Charlotte, Vt.; d. Ira E. and Sadie M. (Congdon) Burroughs; m. Joseph C. Carter, June 28, 1935. PhB, U. Vt., 1931. Prin. Newton Acad., Shoreham, Vt., 1931-35; substitute tchr. Spaulding High Sch., Barre, Vt., 1931-35, Woodbury (Vt.) High Sch., 1935-36; tchr. Craftsbury Acad., Craftsbury Common, Vt., 1936-38; sales mgr., buyer Vt. Music Co., Barre, 1939-44; statistician Syracuse U., 1944-46; instr. English Temple U., Phila., 1946-47; records clk. sec. Phila., 1947-56; tchr. English Cen. High Sch., Phila., 1957, Springfield Twp. Sr. High Sch., Montgomery County, Pa., 1964-65; exec. dir. White-Williams Found., 1966-82, trustee, 1982—. Author: (with Joseph C. Carter) Anchors Aweigh Around the World with Ernest Vail Burroughs, 1960, Pilgrimage to the Lovely Lands of our Ancestors, 1984. Recipient Humanitarian award Chapel of Four Chaplains, 1981; city coun. citation City of Phila., 1982. Mem. AAUW (admissions chmn. Phila. chpt. 1959-61, sec. 1961-64, treas. 1965-67), DAR (treas., historian, com. chmn., budget dir., treas., historian, com. chmn., regent Germantown chpt., 1983-86, 89-92, treas. 1992—, registrar 1986-89, pub. rels. chmn. 1986—), Women for Greater Phila., New Eng. Historic Geneal. Soc., Geneal. Soc. Vt., Soc. Mayflower Descs. (bd. dirs. 1983-84, sec. 1985-91)., Temple U. Faculty Wives Club (rec. sec. 1983-86, pres. Old York group), Temple U. Women's Club, The English Speaking Union, Regent's Club (Phila. chaplain 1986-88). Republican. Methodist. Home: 40 W Mt Carmel Ave D2 Glenside PA 19038-3438

CARTER, SALLY PACKLETT, elementary education educator; b. Clovis, N.Mex., May 15, 1948; d. Charles Everett and Marion Jamie (Pippin) Gee; m. Leonard Gene Carter, Mar. 7, 1969; 1 child, Dale Lee. BS in Edn., Ctrl. Mo. State U., 1969, MS in Edn., 1981. Cert. vocat. home econs. grades 7-12, elem. edn. grades K-6, Mo., K-8 elem. edn., home econs. grades 7-12, Ariz. Home econ. tchr. Deepwater (Mo.) High Sch., 1969-71; tchr. grade 7 Deepwater (Mo.) Sch., 1971-73; tchr. grades 1 and 2 Davis R-12, Clinton, Mo., 1974-80; tchr. grade 5 Southeast Elem., Clinton, 1980—. Mem. Nat. Coun. Tchrs. Math., Mo. State Tchrs. (pres. ctrl. dist. 1989-90), Clinton Tchrs. Assn. (pres. 1985, 90, 92), Clinton C. of C., VFW Ladies Aux. Post 1894, Delta Kappa Gamma (1st v.p. Mu. chpt. 1992-94, pres. Mu. chpt. 1994—), Phi Kappa Phi. Home: 248 NE 251 Clinton MO 64735

CARTER, SARAH ANNE, internist, educator; b. Dover, Ark., Dec. 15, 1940; d. Wallace Graham and Ruth Eva (Forrest) Jennings; m. Michael Allen Carter, July 4, 1969; 1 child, Elizabeth Ruth. BS, Ark. Tech. U., 1961; MD, U. Ark., Little Rock, 1965. Diplomate Am. Bd. Internal Medicine, Am. Bd. Geriatrics. Rotating intern Bapt. Med. Ctr., Little Rock, 1965-66; resident medicine U. Ark. and Little Rock VA Med. Ctr., 1966-69; physician Holt-Krock Clinic, Ft. Smith, Ark., 1969-71; physician asst. chief addiction unit North Little Rock (Ark.) VA Med. Ctr., 1971-73; asst. chief medicine dept. Bedford (Mass.) VA Med. Ctr., 1973-76; from lectr. to sr. lectr. Northeastern U., Boston, 1973-76; asst. chief ambulatory care sec. Denver VA Med. Ctr., 1976-82; from instr. to asst. prof. U. Colo., Denver, 1976-82; staff MD, assoc. chief of staff ambulatory care Memphis VA Med. Ctr., 1982—; from asst. to assoc. prof. U. Tenn., Memphis, 1982—. Recipient Mgrs. award Fed. Execs. Assn., 1993. Mem. ACP, Nat. Assn. VA Physician Ambulatory Mgrs., Memphis Internal Medicine Acad., Soc. Gen. Internal Medicine. Office: Memphis VA Med Ctr 1030 Jefferson Ave Memphis TN 38104

CARTER, SARALEE LESSMAN, immunologist, microbiologist; b. Chgo., Feb. 19, 1951; d. Julius A. and Ida (Oiring) Lessman; B.A., National Coll., 1971; m. John B. Carter, Oct. 7, 1979; children: Robert Oiring, Mollie. Supr. lab. immunology Weiss Meml. Hosp., Chgo., 1973-80; lab. immunology supr. Henrotin Hosp., Chgo., 1980-84; tech. dir. Lexington Med. Labs., West Columbia, S.C., 1984—; mem. nat. workshop faculty Am. Soc. Clin. Pathologists; clin. instr. faculty Med. U. S.C. Mem. Am. Soc. Clin. Pathologists (subspecialty cert. in microbiology and immunology, cert. med. technologist). Researcher Legionnaires Disease and mycoplasma pneumonia World Soc. Pathologists, Jerusalem, Israel, 1980. Contbr. articles to profl. jours.; Mem. Rep. Senoritorial Inner Circle, co-chmn. S.C. Young Profls. for George Bush. Office: 110 Medical Ln E Ste 100 West Columbia SC 29169

CARTER, SHEENA LAFAYE, psychologist, educator; b. Savannah, Ga., July 22, 1959; d. Bryant and Susie Isabella (Sellers) C.; m. Thomas Anthony Gatch, May 26, 1984; 1 child, Daniel Chaney Gatch. BA in Psychology, Armstrong State Coll., 1981; MS in Clin. Psychology, Northwestern State U., 1984; PhD in Applied Developmental Psychology, U. New Orleans, 1989; postgrad., La. State U., 1989-91. Lic. psychologist, Ga. Psychology intern Ga. Regional Hosp., Savannah, 1983-84; learning disabilities specialist The Royce Ctr. for S.L.D., Savannah, 1984-85; rsch. asst. U. New Orleans, 1986-87; rsch. assoc. La. State U. Sch. Medicine, New Orleans, 1987-89, clin. asst. prof., 1991-92; asst. prof. pediats. divsn. neonatology Emory Sch. Medicine, Atlanta, 1993—; cons. psychology S.E. La. Hosp., Mandeville, 1991-92, Atlanta Area Psychol. Assocs., 1992-94; adj. faculty U. New Orleans, 1991-92, Oglethorpe U., Atlanta, 1992-93. Author: Infant Affect Manual, 1989; contbr. articles to profl. jours. Mem. sch. bd. Jefferson (La.) Presbyn. Day Sch., 1991-92; mem. Agenda for Children, New Orleans, 1991-92; mem. com. family life adv. bd. Covenant House of New orleans, 1992; vol. Nat. Coun. of Negro Women Adolescent Mother's Initiative Program, New Orleans, 1991-92; invited guest speaker on infancy to various civic and pvt. orgns. Mem. APA, Internat. Soc. Infant Studies, Ga. Psychol. Assn. Office: Emory Regional Perinatal Ct Neonatal Sect PO Box 26015 80 Butler St SE Atlanta GA 30335

CARTER, SUSAN D., state legislator; b. Salt Lake City, May 23, 1949; m. Gary S. Carter; 4 children. BA, Stanford U., 1971; MAT, Harvard U., 1971. Mem. N.H. Ho. of Reps. Bd. dirs. Parent Info. Ctr.; co-chair Bow Sch. Dist. Curriculum Com., 1991-92; sec.-treas. Boy Scout Troop 386. Republican. Mem. LDS Ch. Office: NH State Senate State Capitol Concord NH 03301*

CARTER, SYLVIA, journalist; b. Keokuk, Iowa; d. Charles Sylvester and Frances Elizabeth (Smith) C. B of Journalism, U. Mo., 1968. Intern Quincy (Ill.) Herald-Whig, 1966, Detroit Free Press, 1967; reporter The N.Y. Daily News, 1968-70; successively gen. assignment reporter, edn. reporter, food writer, restaurant critic Newsday, Melville, N.Y., 1970—, N.Y. Newsday, N.Y.C., 1985—; founder, editor Kidsday Newsday, Melville. Author: Eats: The Best Little Restaurants in New York, 1988. Trustee Anne O'Hare McCormick Scholarship Fund, N.Y.C., 1988—. Mem. Newswomen's Club N.Y. (pres. 1990-92, bd. dirs., Front Page award 1982). Democrat. Presbyterian. Home: 111 Waverly Pl New York NY 10011 also: 46 Crescent Bow Ridge NY 11961 Office: NY Newsday 2 Park Ave New York NY 10016

CARTER, THERESA (TERI) ANN, paralegal; b. Tonawanda, N.Y., Mar. 27, 1959; d. Norman Richard and Mary Joan (Bell) Schalk; m. Christopher Troy Barbour, June 26, 1982 (div. Mar. 1989); children: Joni Elizabeth, Matthew Allen; m. David Mark Carter, Jan. 1, 1990. Student, Calif. State U., Fresno, 1976-79. Screening paralegal Legal Svcs. Mid. Tenn., Clarksville, 1983-88; paralegal, legal sec. Christine Zellar, Clarksville, 1984-89, Bagwell, Bagwell, Parker, Riggins & Kennedy, Clarksville, 1989-92; paralegal Kennedy, Zellar & Assocs., Clarksville, 1992—. Parent coord. Project Tiger Recycling East Montgomery Elem. Sch., Clarksville, 1992-94; asst. den leader cub scouts Boy Scouts Am., 1993—; co-organized support rallies Operation Desert Storm, Clarksville, 1991. With U.S. Army, 1979-82. Mem. Jaycees. Democrat. Home: 1317 Old Gratton Rd Clarksville TN 37043-2517 Office: Kennedy Zellar & Assocs 127 S 3rd St Clarksville TN 37040-3403

CARTIER, CELINE PAULE, librarian, administrator, consultant; b. Lacolle, Que., Can., May 10, 1930; d. Henri Rodolphe and Irene (Boudreau) Robitaille; m. Georges Cartier, Nov. 29, 1952; children: Nathalie, Guillaume. Diplome superieur en pedagogie, U. Montreal, 1948, certificats en litterature et linguistique, 1952; diplome de bibliothecaire-documentaliste, Inst. Catholique, Paris, 1962; maîtrise en adminstrn. publique, Ecole Nationale d'Adminstrn. Publique, 1976; maîtrise en bibliothéconomie, U. Montreal, 1982. Dir. Bibliotheque Centrale, Commn. des ecoles catholiques, Montreal, 1964-73; dir. spl. collections U. Quebec, 1973-76, dir. sector librs., 1976-77; chief gen. librs. U. Laval, Que., 1977-78; gen. dir. libraries U. Laval, 1978-89; cons. Conseil CRC Cons., 1989—. Contbr. articles to profl. jours. Mem. Corp. des Bibliothecaires Profs. de Quebec.

CARTLAND, BARBARA, author; b. Eng., July 9, 1901; d. Bertram and Polly (Scobell) C.; m. Alexander George McCorquodale, 1927 (div. 1933); m. Hugh McCorquodale, Dec. 28, 1936 (dec. 1963); children: Raine (Countess Spencer), Ian, Glen. Student pvt. girls' schs. in, Eng. Lectr., polit. speaker; TV personality (2 lecture tours), Can., 1940. Author hist. novels, biographies, material on health and phys. fitness; books include: (history) The Outrageous Queen: A Biography of Christina of Sweden, 1956, The Scandalous Life of King Carol, 1957, The Private Life of Charles II: The Woman He Loved, 1958, The Private Life of Elizabeth, Empress of Austria, 1959, Josephine, Empress of France, 1961, Diane de Poitiers, 1962, Metternich: The Passionate Diplomat, 1964; (biography) Ronald Cartland, 1942, Bewitching Women, 1955, Polly: The Story of My Wonderful Mother, 1956; (autobiography) The Isthmus Years: Reminiscences of the Years 1919-1939, 1943, The Years of Opportunity 1939-1945, 1948, I Search for Rainbows 1946-1966, 1967, We Danced All Night 1919-1929, 1970, I Seek the Miraculous, 1978; (non-fiction) Touch the Stars: A Clue to Happiness, 1935, You-in the Home, 1946, The Fascinating Forties: A Book for the Over-Forties, 1954, Marriage for the Moderns, 1955, Be Vivid, Be Vital, 1956, Love, Life and Sex, 1957, Look Lovely, Be Lovely, 1958, Vitamins For Vitality, 1959, Husbands and Wives, 1971, Etiquette Handbook, 1962, The Many Facets of Love, 1963, Sex and the Teenager, 1964, Living Together, 1965, The Pan Book of Charm, 1965, Woman, The Enigma, 1965, The Youth Secret, 1968, The Magic of Honey, 1970, Barbara Cartland's Book of Beauty and Health, 1972, Men Are Wonderful, 1973, Food For Love, 1975, Recipes for Lovers, 1977, Barbara Cartland's Book of Useless Information, 1977, Barbara Cartland's Book of Love and Lovers, 1978, Romantic Royal Marriages, 1981, Barbara Cartland's Etiquette for Love and Romance, 1984, Getting Older, Growing Younger, 1984, The Romance of Food, 1984, Barbara Cartland's Book of Health, 1985, A Year of Royal Days, 1988; (novels) Jigsaw, 1925, Sawdust, 1926, If The Tree Is Saved, 1929, For What?, 1930, Sweet Punishment, 1931, A Virgin in Mayfair, 1932, Just Off Piccadily, 1933, Not Love Alone, 1933, A Beggar Wished, 1934, Passionate Attainment, 1935, First Class, Lady?, 1935, Dangerous Experiment, 1936, Desperate Defiance, 1936, The Forgotten City, 1936, The Forgotten City, 1936, Saga at Forty, 1937, But Never Free, 1937, Broken Barriers, 1938, Bitter Winds, 1938, The Gods Forget, 1939, The Black Panther, 1939, Stolen Halo, 1940, Now Rough, Now Smooth, 1941, Open Wings, A Twenty-Third Novel, 1942, The Leaping Flame, 1942, The Dark Stream, 1944, After The Night, 1944, Yet She Follows, 1945, Escape From Passion, 1945, Armour Against Love, 1945, Out Of Reach, 1945, The Hidden Heart, 1946, Against The Stream, 1946, The Dream Within, 1947, If We Will, 1947, Against This Rapture, 1947, No Heart Is Free, 1948, No Heart Is Free, 1948, A Hazard of Hearts, 1949, The Enchanted Moment, 1949, A Duel of Hearts, 1949, The Knave of Hearts, 1950, The Little Pretender, 1950, Love Is An Eagle, 1951, A Ghost In Monte Carlo, 1951, Love Is The Enemy, 1952, Cupid Rides Pillion, 1952, Elizabethan Lover, 1953, Love Me For Ever, 1954, Desire of the Heart, 1954, The Enchanted Waltz, 1955, The Kiss of the Devil, 1955, The Captive Heart, 1956, The Coin of Love, 1956, Sweet Adventure, 1957, Stars In My Heart, 1957, The Golden Gondola, 1958, Love In Hiding, 1959, The Smuggled Heart, 1959, Love Under Fire, 1960, Messenger of Love, 1961, The Wings of Love, 1962, The Hidden Evil, 1963, The Fire of Love, 1964, The Unpredictable Bride, 1964, Love Holds the Cards, 1965, A Virgin in Paris, 1966, Love to the Rescue, 1967, Love is Contraband, 1968, The Enchanting Evil, 1968, The Unknown Heart, 1969, The Innocent Heiress, 1970, The Reluctant Bride, 1970, The Secret Fear, 1970, The Pretty Horse-Breakers, 1971, The Queen's Messenger, 1971, Stars in Her Eyes, 1971, Lost Enchantment, 1972, A Halo for the Devil, 1972, The Wicked Marquis, 1973, The Odious Duke, 1973, The Glittering Lights, 1974, A Sword to the Heart, 1974, Fire on the Snow, 1975, Bewitched, 1975, Call of the Heart, 1975, The Frightened Bride, 1975, The Impetuous Duchess, 1975, The Karma of Love, 1975, Love Is Innocent, 1975, The Husband Hunters, 1976, The Incredible Honeymoon, 1976, A Kiss for the King, 1976, Love in Hiding, 1976, Moon Over Eden, 1976, Never Laugh at Love, 1976, No Time for Love, 1976, Passions in the Sand, 1976, The Secret of the Glen, 1976, The Slaves of Love, 1976, The Wild Cry of Love, 1976, Conquered by Love, 1976, Love Locked In, 1977, The Mysterious Maid-Servant, 1977, The Wild Unwilling Wife, 1977, The Castle Made for Love, 1977, The Hell-cat and the King, 1977, Love and the Loathsome Leopard, 1977, The Love Pirate, 1977, The Marquis Who Hated Women, 1977, The Naked Battle, 1977, No Escape From Love, 1977, Punishment of a Vixen, 1977, The Saint and the Sinner, 1977, The Temptation of Torilla, 1977, A Touch of Love, 1977, A Duel with Destiny, 1977, The Magic of Love, 1977, A Rhapsody of Love, 1977, The Disgraceful Duke, 1977, Love at the Helm, 1977, The Chieftain without a Heart, 1978, A Fugitive from Love, 1978, The Ghost Who Fell in Love, 1978, Love Leaves at Midnight, 1978, Love, Lords and Lady-Birds, 1978, The Passion and the Flower, 1978, The Twists and Turns of Love, 1978, The Irresistible Force, 1978, The Judgement of Love, 1978, Lord Ravenscar's Revenge, 1978, Lovers in Paradise, 1978, A Princess in Distress, 1978, The Race for Love, 1978, A Runaway Star, 1978, Magic or Mirage?, 1978, Alone in Paris, 1978, Flowers for the God of Love, 1978, The Problems of Love, 1978, The Drums of Love, 1979, The Duke and the Preacher's Daughter, 1979, Imperial Splendor, 1979, Light of the Moon, 1979, Love in the Clouds, 1979, Love in the Dark, 1979, The Prince and the Pekinese, 1979, Love Climbs In, 1979, The Prisoner of Love, 1979, A Serpent of Satan, 1979, The Treasure of Love, 1979, The Dutchess Disappeared, 1979, A Nightingale Sang, 1979, The Dawn of Love, 1979, A Gentleman in Love, 1979, Only Love, 1979, Bride to the King, 1979. Women Have Hearts, 1979. Terror in the Sun, 1979, Who Can Deny Love?, 1979, Love Has His Way, 1979, The Explosion of Love, 1979, A Song of Love, 1980, Love for Sale, 1980, Lost Laughter, 1980, Free from Fear, 1980, The Goddess and the Gaiety Girl, 1980, Little White Doves of Love, 1980, Ola and the Sea Wolf, 1980, The Perfection of Love, 1980, The Prude and the Prodigal, 1980, Punished with Love, 1980, The Power and the Prince, 1980, Lucifer and the Angel, 1980, Signpost to Love, 1980, From Hell to Heaven, 1981, Pride and the Poor Princess, 1981, Count the Stars, 1981, Dollars for the Duke, 1981, Dreams Do Come True, 1981, The Heart of the Clan, 1981, In the Arms of Love, 1981, Touch a Star, 1981, Love in the Moon, 1981, A Night of Gaiety, 1981, The Waltz of Hearts, 1981, The Wings of Ecstasy, 1981, For All Eternity, 1981, For All Eternity, 1981, Afraid, 1981, Love in the Moon, 1981, Enchanted, 1981, Winged Magic, 1981, A Portrait of Love, 1981, The River of Love, 1981, Gift of the Gods, 1981, An Innocent in Russia, 1981, A Shaft of Sunlight, Pure and Untouched, 1981, Love Wins, 1982, Secret Harbor, 1982, Looking for Love, 1982, The Vibrations of Love, 1982, Lies for Love, 1982, Love Rules, 1982, Moments of Love, 1982, Riding to the Moon, 1982, Diona and a Dalmation, 1983, Wish for Love, 1983, A Very Unusual Wife, 1984, White Lilac, 1984, Temptation for a Teacher, 1985, A Witch's Spell, 1985, The Love Trap, 1986, Secret of the Mosque, 1986, Wanted: A Wedding Ring, 1987, A World of Love, 1987, Lovers in Lisbon, 1988, The Goddess of Love, 1988, Paradise in Penang, 1989, A Game of Love, 1989, Love is the Key, 1990, The Marquis Wins, 1990, Heaven in Hong Kong, 1990, Seek the Stars, 1991, Escape, 1991, Drena and the Duke, 1992, Love Strikes a Devil, 1992, The Windmill of Love, 1992, A Dynasty of Love, 1993, To Scotland and Love, 1993, Hidden by Love, 1992, The Queen of Hearts, 1993, The Cave of Love, 1993, Walking to Wonderland, 1993, A Duel of Jewels, 1993, and many, many others; series include "Camfield Romance" series, (editor only) "Barbara Cartland's Library of Love" series; novels also published under pseud. County councillor, Hertfordshire, chmn. St. John Coun., pres. Br. Royal Coll. Midwives, dep. pres. St. John Ambulance Brigade; chief lady welfare officer, Bedfordshire, 1941-45; founder Cartland Onslow Romany Trust. Decorated Dame Order of Brit. Empire, Dame of Grace St. John of Jerusalem; recipient Bishop Wright Air Industry award for contbn. to devel. aviation, 1984, Gold Medal of City of Paris for Achievement La Maire de la Ville, 1988; named Woman of Yr. by Nat. Home Furnishings Assn., 1981. Mem. Nat. Assn. Health (founder, pres. 1965), Oxfam (v.p.). Office: care Berkley Pubs Inc 200 Madison Ave New York NY 10016-3901*

CART-ROGERS, KATHERINE COOPER, emergency nurse; b. Jacksonville, Tex., Aug. 7, 1948; d. Raymond Jesse and June (Walker) Cooper; m. Frank E. Rogers, Sept. 25, 1981; 1 child, Natalie Christine Cart. Med. Technologist, St. Mary's, Galveston, Tex., 1967; BS in Nursing, Stephen F. Austin U., Nacogdoches, Tex., 1989; postgrad., Regent U., Virginia Beach, Va. Cert. CPR, Emergency Nurse, ACLS, instr. trauma nurse core course. Pharmacology-toxicology researcher U. Tex. Med. Br., Galveston, 1967-68, Ohio State U., Columbus, 1968-72; physicians asst., lab. supr. Newborn Meml. Hosp., Jacksonville, 1975-78; lab. mgr. East Tex. Med. Ctr., Rusk, 1978-87; lab. supr. Nacogdoches Meml. Hosp., 1987-89, emergency rm. nurse, 1989-91; emergency rm. chrge nurse Kingwood (Tex.) Pla. Hosp., 1991-92; nursing cons. Thorstenson Eye Clinic, Nacogdoches, 1991-92; dir. emergency svcs., trauma coord., employee health dir. Nan Travis Hosp., Jacksonville, Tex., 1992—; dir. surg. svcs. Thorstenson Ambulatory Surgery Ctr., Nacogdoches, 1992-93. Mem. AACCN, Emergency Nurses Assn., Tex. Trauma Coords., Tex. Regional Adv. Coun. for Trauma Area G. Home: 310 N Mound St Nacogdoches TX 75961-5032

CARTWRIGHT, MARY LOU, laboratory scientist; b. Payette, Idaho, Apr. 5, 1923; d. Ray J. and Nellie Mae (Sherer) Decker; B.S., U. Houston, 1958; M.A., Central Mich. U., 1976; m. Chadwick Louis Cartwright, Sept. 13, 1947. Med. technologist Methodist Hosp., Houston, 1957-59, VA Hosp., Livermore, Calif., 1960-67, Kaiser Permanente Med. Center, Hayward, Calif., 1967-71, United Med. Lab., San Mateo, Calif., 1972-73; sr. med. technologist Oakland (Calif.) Hosp., 1974-86; cons. med. lab. tech. Oakland Public Schs. Chmn., Congressional Dist. 11 steering com. Common Cause, 1974-77; consumer mem. Alameda County (Calif.) Health Systems Agy., 1977-78. Served with USNR, 1945-53. Mem. Calif. Soc. Med. Tech., Calif. Assn. Med. Lab. Tech. (Technologist of Yr. award 1968, 78, Pres.'s award 1977, Service award chpt. 1978, 79), Am. Soc. Med. Tech. (by-laws chmn. 1981-83), Disabled Am. Veterans (adjutant treas. of chpt. 122, 1993-95), Am. Bus. Women's Assn., Nat. Assn. Female Execs. Democrat. Home and Office: 350 Bennett St Apt 9 Grass Valley CA 95945-6870

CARTWRIGHT, RHONDA DELRIE, banker; b. Alexandria, La., June 28, 1952; d. Willis and Betty (Holt) Delrie; m. David Owen Cartwright, Jan. 1, 1972; children: Regan Treece, Anthony Holt. BSBA, U. Southwestern La., 1974; MBA, Northwestern State U., Natchitoches, La., 1987. Mgmt. acct. Caterpillar Tractor Co., Peoria, Il., 1974-75; staff acct. Everitt, Knight & Masden CPAs, Alexandria, 1975-76; revenue agt. III La. Dept. Revenue & Taxation, Baton Rouge, 1976-80; internal auditor Rapides Bank & Trust, Alexandria, 1980-83; dept. head acctg. Rapides Bank & Trust, 1983-87, sr. v.p. fin. ops. and cash mgmt. div., 1987—; tchr. St. Leo Coll., St. Leo, Fla., 1989—. Mem. Am. Inst. Bankers, Bank Adminstrn. Inst., Alexandria-Pineville C. of C., Cath. Daugs., Phi Kappa Phi, Alpha Beta. Roman Catholic. Office: Rapides Bank & Trust 400 Murray St Alexandria LA 71301-8398

CARUANA, JOAN, educator, psychotherapist, nurse; b. Bklyn., Dec. 11, 1941; d. Gaetano and Fanny Caruana. RN, St. Vincent Hosp. Sch. Nursing, 1961; BS, Boston Coll., 1964; MA, NYU, 1975; grad., Psychoanalytic Psychotherapy Study Ctr., 1992. Cert. clin. specialist in adult psychiat. mental health nursing. Instr. St. Vincent's Hosp. Sch. Nursing, N.Y.C., 1965—; psychotherapist N.Y.C., 1987—; Editor St. Vincent's Hosp. Alumnae Assn. Newsletter, 1978—. Office: St Vincents Hosp Sch Nursing 27 Christopher St New York NY 10014-3596

CARUSO, CHERYL ANNE, accountant, accounting company executive; b. Oregon City, Oreg., June 20, 1948; d. John Everett Harding and Juanita Jewell (Taylor) Saxon; m. Joseph Paul Caruso, Jun. 17, 1968 (div. Sept. 1977); 1 child, Joelle Maria Caruso. BS in Acctg., San Diego State U., 1985. Asst. contr. Frye & Smith LTD, divsn of Am. Standard, San Diego, 1980-85; owner, cons. CAC's Acctg. Svcs., San Diego, 1986—; CFO Pacific Southwest Bio Svcs., National City, Calif., 1990—. Pioneer girls leader Coll. Ave. Baptist Ch., San Diego, Calif., 1990—; sec. AWANAS, Coll. Ave. Baptist Ch., 1994—. Mem. Inst. Mgmt. Accts. Republican. Home: 302 Stone Edge Dr El Cajon CA 92021

CARUSO, DEBRA ANN, primary special education educator; b. Providence, Oct. 26, 1956; d. Anthony Carl and Gloria Marie (Ricci) C.; 1 child, Tyler John. BA in Elem. Edn. and Psychology, R.I. Coll., 1978; MEd in Spl. Edn., Providence Coll., 1983. Cert. preK-8 resource tchr., R.I. Elem. tchr. Cranston (R.I.)-Johnston Cath. Regional Sch., 1978-86; tchr. primary spl. edn. Thornton Sch., Johnston, R.I., 1986—. Mem. Am. Fedn. Tchrs. Roman Catholic. Home: 6 Kern Acre Dr Johnston RI 02919

CARVER, BALA BANSAL, physician; b. Kasauli, India, May 22, 1945; came to U.S., 1968; d. Rameswar Dass and Lila Wati (Garg) Bansal; m. Kewal Krishan Sawhney, Feb. 17, 1972 (div. Dec. 1975); m. Earl Chadwick Carver Jr., Aug. 5, 1978; 1 child, Christopher Chadwick. MD, Christian Med. Coll., India, 1967. Diplomate Am. Bd. Pathology, Am. Bd. Hematology, Am. Bd. Blood Banking, Am. Bd. Histocompatibility and Immunogenetics. Med. dir. hematology and blood bank Med. Coll. Pa., Phila., 1976-77; med. dir. transfusion medicine Lehigh Valley Hosp., Allentown, Pa., 1977—; asst. clin. prof. Hahnemann U., Phila., 1989—; mem. med. adv. com. Samuel Miller Meml. Blood Ctr., Bethlehem, Pa., 1977—. Mem. Am. Soc. Clin. Pathologists, Am. Assn. Blood Banks, Am. Soc. Aphresis, Am. Soc. Histocompatibility and Immunogenetics, Pa. Assn. Blood Banks. Republican. Methodist. Office: Lehigh Valley Hosp 1200 S Cedar Crest Blvd Allentown PA 18105

CARVER, JOAN SACKNITZ, university dean; b. Spokane, Wash., Jan. 22, 1931; d. Weldon and Mabel (Swanson) S.; m. Jay Randall Carver, June 25, 1955; 1 child, James Randall (dec.). BA, Barnard Coll., 1953; MA, U. N.C., 1957; PhD, U. Fla., 1965. Exec. sec. Iranian del. to UN, N.Y.C., 1953-55; tchr. Lake Shore Jr. High Sch., Jacksonville, Fla., 1956-57; office mgr. Bartram Sch., Jacksonville, 1957-58; from asst. to assoc. prof. Jacksonville U., 1958-60, 63-75, prof., 1975—, chmn. div. social scis., 1982-83, dean Coll. Arts and Scis., 1983—, dir. Taft Seminars in Practical Politics, 1968-78; instr. employee seminars City of Jacksonville, 1969-82; evaluator ABT Assocs., Boston, 1975; mem. reaffirmation coms. So. Assn. Colls., Atlanta, 1983-94. Contbr. articles to profl. jours. Sec., bd. dirs. Jacksonville Cmty. Coun., Inc., 1976-80; commr. 1st Appellate dist. Jud. Nominating Commn., Tallahassee, 1983-87; commr. Jacksonville Mayor's Com. on Status of Women, 1984-88; bd. trustees St. John's Country Day Sch., Orange Park, Fla., 1984—, pres., 1993-95; chair career opportunities subcom. Def. Adv. Com. on Women in Svc., Washington, 1991-93. Recipient Prof. of Yr. award Jacksonville, U., 1972, EVE award for achievement in edn. Fla. Times Union, Jacksonville, 1982; Seven Coll. Conf. nat. scholar Barnard Coll., 1949-53; grad. fellow U. Fla., 1960-63. Mem. Fla. Polit. Sci. Assn. (pres. 1975-76), Am. Soc. for Pub. Adminstrn. (pres. N.E. Fla. chpt. 1987-88), Women's Caucus for Polit. Sci.-South (pres. 1981-82), So. Polit. Sci. Assn. (membership chmn. 1983-91, rec. sec. 1993-94), Jacksonville Women's Network (pres. 1987-90), Phi Beta Kappa. Democrat. Episcopalian. Home: 46 15th St Jacksonville FL 32233-5722 Office: Jacksonville U 2800 University Blvd N Jacksonville FL 32211-3321

CARVER, JUANITA ASH, plastic company executive; b. Indpls., Apr. 8, 1929; d. Willard H. and Golda M. Ashe; children: Daniel Charles, Robin Lewis, Scott Alan. Cons. MOBIUS, 1983— ; pres. Carver Corp., Phoenix, 1977—. Bd. dirs. Scottsdale Meml. Hosp. Aux., 1964-65, now assoc. Organizer Pressure Lift. Republican. Methodist. Patentee latch hook rug yarn, pressure lift. Home: 9866 Reagan Rd # 126 San Diego CA 92126

CARVER, PATRICIA ANN PULLEN, accountant; b. Louisville, Oct. 13, 1954; d. Carsue Sr. and Agnes I. (Elery) Pullen; m. Richard L. Carver, Aug. 5, 1972; children: Toni R., Michael A. BS in Commerce, U. Louisville, 1982. CPA, Ky. Revenue field auditor Ky. Revenue Cabinet, Louisville, 1983-87; acct. Met. Sewer Dist., Louisville, 1987-88, accts. payable supr., 1988-89, revenue adminstr., 1989-90, fin. analyst, 1990-91, chief internal auditor, 1991—. V.p safe place oversight com. Ctr. Youth Alternatives, Louisville, 1994—; bd. dirs. African Am. Cath. Ministries, Louisville, 1994—; acct. Ky. Edn. Reform All at Risk Childrens Caucus, Louisville, 1994—. Recipient Black Achiever award YMCA, Louisville, 1990. Mem. AICPAs, Ky. Soc. CPAs, Bellarmine Coll. African-Am. Leadership Inst., River City Bus. and Profl. Women, Delta Sigma Theta (alumni chpt.). Democrat. Office: Louisville & Jefferson Co Met Sewer Dist 400 S 6th St Louisville KY 40202

CARY, ARLENE D., retired hotel company sales executive; b. Chgo., Dec. 19, 1930; d. Seymour S. and Shirley L. (Land) C.; student U. Wis., 1949-52; B.A., U. Miami, 1953; m. Elliot D. Hagle, Dec. 30, 1972 (div.). Public relations account exec. Robert Howe & Co., 1953-55; sales mgr. Martin B. Iger & Co., 1955-57; sales mgr., gen. mgr. Sorrento Hotel, Miami Beach, Fla., 1957-59; gen. mgr. Mayflower Hotel, Manomet, Mass., 1959-60; various positions Aristocrat Inns of Am., 1960-72; v.p. mktg., McCormick Center Hotel, Chgo., 1972-93; ret. 1993. Active Nat. Women's Polit. Caucus, Internat. Orgn. Women Execs., membership promotion chmn., 1979-80, bd. dirs., 1980-81. Recipient disting. salesman award Sales and Mktg. Execs. Internat., 1977. Mem. Profl. Conv. Mgmt. Assn., Nat. Assn. Exposition Mgrs., Internat. Assn. Exposition Magmt., Hospitality Sales and Mktg. Assn. Internat., Hotel Sales Mgmt. Assn., Meeting Planners Internat., Am. Soc. Assn. Execs., N.Y. Soc. Assn. Execs., Chgo. Soc. Assn. Execs., Ind. Hotel Alliance (sec. 1986—). Jewish. Home: 1130 S Michigan Ave Apt 3203 Chicago IL 60605-2322

CASABELLA, SUSAN LYNN, aerospace engineer; b. Cranston, R.I., July 16, 1961; d. Philip Anthony and Ruth M. E. (Johnston) C.; m. Craig Alan Henderson, Aug. 25, 1990. AS in Engring. Sci., Hudson Valley C.C., 1982; BSME, Rensselaer Poly. Inst., 1984. Cert. EMT, L.A. County. Engr. McDonnell Douglas Helicopter Co., Culver City, Calif., 1984-85; engr. II Northrop B-2 Divsn., Pico Rivera, Calif., 1985-88; engr. cons. AdTek Co. at Rockwell Internat., Downey, Calif., 1988; engr., design cons. Butler Svc. Group at Rockwell Internat., Downey, 1988-90; program adminstr., coord. City of Carson, Calif., 1990—; engring. cons. Inconen Corp. at Northrop Aircraft Divsn., Hawthorne, Calif., 1993-94; sr. engr. Northrop Aircraft Divsn., Hawthorne, 1994—; fitness/wellness cons., Lakewood, Calif., 1990—. Editor newsletters At the Vet, 1992—, Crossroads Crier, 1992—; columnist for newsletter Fitness Assocs. West, 1994, Reserve News. Advisor explorer post Boy Scouts Am., Carson, Calif., 1993—; res. dep. sheriff L.A. County Sheriff's Dept., Long Beach, Calif., 1987—, Carson, Calif.; vol. CPR/1st aid instr. ARC, Long Beach, 1993—; mem. legal compliance rev. bd. L.A. County Dept. Edn., Downey, Calif., 1991-92; vice moderator Cross Rds. Cmty. Ch., Lakewood, Calif., 1994, 95; presenter pilot youth program "Fun2BFit," Am. Coun. on Exercise, L.A., 1993. Mem. AAUW, NAFE, AAHPERD, Soc. Advancement of Material and Process Engring., Calif. Res. Peace Officers Assn., Internat. Dance Exercise Assn. Democrat. Mem. United Ch. of Christ. Home: 5725 Tanglewood St Lakewood CA 90713-2533 Office: Northrop Aircraft Divsn 1 Northrop Ave 3855/63 Hawthorne CA 90250-3277

CASANOVA-LUCENA, MARIA ANTONIA, computer engineer; b. Cienfuegos, Las Villas, Cuba, Jan. 1, 1954; came to U.S., 1979; d. Manuel José and Loida Eugenia (Ojeda) Casanova; m. Angel de Jesus Lucena, Aug. 12, 1978; 1 child, Ingrid. BSEE cum laude, U. Miami, 1985. Software engr. Martin Marietta Corp., Orlando, Fla., 1986-89; computer engr., mgr. software acquisition, Tng. Sys. divsn. Naval Air Warfare Ctr., Orlando, 1989—. Mem. IEEE, Golden Key, Sigma Xi, Tau Beta Pi, Eta Kappa Nu, Phi Kappa Phi. Home: 3212 Lake George Cove Dr Orlando FL 32812-6844 Office: Naval Air Warfare Ctr Tng Sys Divsn Code 242 12350 Research Pky Orlando FL 32826

CASCIANO, NANCY ANN, cytotechnologist; b. Phila., Dec. 17, 1947; d. Edward Walter and Alma Irene (Neidert) Pienta; m. Joseph Christian Casciano, June 6, 1970; 1 child, Lisa Ann. AA, Atlantic C.C., 1969; diploma, Thomas Jefferson U., 1969; BA in Natural Sci., Thomas Edison Coll., 1991. Cytotechnologist Nazareth Hosp., Phila., 1970-71, Shore Meml. Hosp., Somers Point, N.J., 1974-89; cytology supr. Newcomb Med. Ctr., Vineland, N.J., 1989-91; cytotechnologist Nat. Health Labs, Northfield, N.J., 1991—. Eucharistic min. Our Lady of Sorrow Ch., 1984—, Shore Meml. Hosp., 1985—; vol. Atlantic County Parks; mem. Friends of the Park. Named Atlantic County's Outstanding Person with a Disability, 1990. Roman Catholic. Office: Nat Health Labs Cytology Dept Zion and New Rds Northfield NJ 08225

CASCIO, ANA MARIA MELO, stockbroker; b. Camp Maior, Piaui, Brazil, July 9, 1946; came to the U.S., 1973; d. Niomar De Carvalho Goncalves and step-father Mauricio Tauil; m. Joseph Anthony Cascio, Mar. 19, 1975 (div. 1989); 1 child, Anthony Joseph Melo. B in Econs., Brazilian U., Rio de Janeiro, 1968; M in Econs., Getulio Vargas Found., Rio de Janeiro, 1970. Economist Banco do Brazil, N.Y.C., 1975-76; trainee Gillette, Boston, 1973-74; salesperson Alex Joseph, Syracuse, N.Y., 1977-78, John Hancock Ins., Syracuse, 1979-80, GM Olds Divsn., Syracuse, 1981-83, Jules J. Karp, N.Y.C., 1986-89; stockbroker Paragon, N.Y.C., 1990-91, Josephthal Lyon & Ross, N.Y.C., 1992—. Roman Catholic. Office: Josephthal Lyon & Ross 380 Madison Ave New York NY 10017

CASCIO, DONNA LEE, secondary education educator; b. Elizabeth, N.J., Mar. 11, 1948; d. Gerald and Doris Ethel Cascio. BS in Biology and Chemistry, Fairleigh Dickinson U., 1970; MA in Environ. Studies, Montclair State Coll., 1976. Cert. elem. tchr., supr., N.J. Secondary tchr. Woodbridge (N.J.) High Sch., 1972—; ednl. programming cons. Metlar House Mus., Piscataway, N.J., 1990—. Marine Sci. Consortium tchr. exch. grantee, Russia, 1992. Democrat. Roman Catholic. Home: 29 Keith Jeffries Ave Cranford NJ 07016 Office: Woodbridge High Sch St George and Kelly St Woodbridge NJ 07095

CASE, ANDRA BETH, gifted students education administrator; b. Dallas, June 24, 1947; d. A.J. Ingram and Nita Faye (Garrison) Perry; m. Sammy N. Williams, May 8, 1967 (div. Aug. 31, 1987); m. James H. Case, March 12, 1993. BS in Elem. Edn., Ea. Tex. U., 1969, MEd, 1974. Fourth grade tchr. Dallas Independent Sch. Dist., 1969-71; first and fifth grade tchrs. Castleberry Independent Sch. Dist., Ft. Worth, 1971-72; fourth grade tchr., team chmn. Plano (Tex.) Independent Sch. Dist., 1972-80; elem. gifted students tchr. Richardson (Tex.) Independent Sch. Dist., 1980-82, coord. secondary gifted programs, 1982-87, adminstrv. dir. K-12 gifted programs, 1987—. Co-author: NHA Resource of Creative & Inventive Activities!. Pres.-elect, pres. Exch. Club of Richardson, editor Texchange 1985-88. Mem. Richardson Edn. Assn., Tex. Assn. Gifted and Talented (exec. bd., region 10 dir.), Nat. Assn. Gifted Children, Coun. Exceptional Children (TAG div.), Richardson Assn. Tex. Profl. Educators, Assn. Tex. Profl. Educators, No. Cen. Tex. Assn. Supervision and Curriculum Development, Tex. Assn. Supervision and Curriculum Devel., ASCD, Phi Delta Kappa, Delata Kappa Gamma, Beta Sigma Phi (pres. 1976-79), Nat. Inventive Thinking Assn. (exec. bd.), Tex. Odyssey of the Mind State Assn. (exec. bd., past assoc. dir., past treas., past sec.), Kiwanis (bd. dirs., past sec.), Leadership Richardson Alumna Assn. Office: Richardson Ind Sch Dist 1700 Gateway Blvd Richardson TX 75080-3558

CASE, KAREN ANN, social worker; b. Fresno, Calif., May 15, 1947; d. Wendell and Lora-Lee (Edwards) Bell; m. Gary Richard Case, Apr. 17, 1970; children: Nancy, Noelle, Kevin. BA in Social Welfare, Calif. State U., Fresno, 1969; MSW, Va. Commonwealth U., 1990. Flight attendant United Air Lines, Washington, 1969-70; social work intern Prince William County Cooperative Ext., Manassas, Va., 1988-89; social work intern/therapist Women's Ctr., Vienna, Va., 1989-91; social worker, therapist The Ctr., Pleasanton, Calif., 1992-93; psychiat. social worker CPC Fremont (Calif.) Hosp., 1992—. Vol., dir. hotline High Desert Child Abuse Coun., 1982-84. Mem. Nat. Com. for Prevention Child Abuse (pres. No. Va. chpt. 1987-89, bd. dirs. Va. chpt. 1987-89), Calif. Clin. Social Work Soc., Am. Orthopsychiat. Assn., NASW, Alpha Xi Delta. Democrat. Roman Catholic. Office: CPC Fremont Hosp 39001 Sundale Dr Fremont CA 94538-2005

CASEBIER, LINDY, state legislator; b. Dec. 27, 1960. BMEd, ME, U. Louisville. Rep. dist. 29 Ky. State Ho. of Reps., 1987-92; senator dist. 7 Ky. State Senate, 1993—; del. Rep. Nat. Conv., 1984; chmn. Jefferson County Rep. Party, 1991. Mem. Am. Cancer Soc. (former bd. dirs.), Ky. Edn. Assn., Jefferson County Tchrs. Assn., Valley Optimist Club. Baptist. Address: 9116 Wooddale Dr Louisville KY 40272-2755 Office: Ky State Senate State Capitol Frankfort KY 40601*

CASERTA, C. DANA, writer and marketing consultant; married. Nat. sales dir. Relocation Mortgage, Inc., Wilton, Conn., 1980-87; jewelry designer, cons. Namely Art Designs, Huntington, Conn., 1987—; writer/composer children's songs. Author: (children's books) The Little Broken Ornament, 1991, Peck Peck LaBeck's Adventures, 1991, Pie in the Sky! 1992, Haganizer Geezer! No More Ground Hog Day!, 1992, The Party At The Pound!, 1992, The Day Lenny the Leopard Lost his Spots!, 1992, The Dump Truck Story, 1993, Sneeze! Sneeze! Sneeze! Why Does Furball-Furcania Make Everyone Sneeze?, 1993, Clown's Purpose?, 1993, Horace's Birthday Cake, 1993; co-author (children's books) The Dog Ate My Homework, 1990, Mookie & Mitzi, 1990, They Walked the World!, 1994, Children's Banking, 1994; inventor (game board) Good Egg! Rotten Egg! or Chicken Feathers!, 1994; character creator Millie Millipede, 1993, Furball-Furcania, 1993; author: The Life and Art Works of a Genious: Sir Nicolaus, 1994. Recipient Spl. Mktg. award Social Security Dept., Washington, D.C., 1992. Office: 341 Booth Hill Rd Huntington CT 06484-3402

CASEY, BARBARA A. PEREA, state representative, educator; b. Las Vegas, N.Mex., Dec. 21, 1951; d. Joe D. and Julia A. (Armijo) Perea; m. Frank J. Casey, Aug. 5, 1978. BA, N.Mex. U., 1972; MA, Highland U., Las Vegas, N.Mex., 1973. Instr. N.Mex. Highlands U., Las Vegas, 1972-74; tchr. Roswell Ind. Schs., Roswell, N.Mex., 1974—; mem. N.Mex. Ho. of Reps., 1984—; instr. N.Mex. Mil. Inst., Roswell, 1977-82, Roswell Police Acad., 1984. Mem. NEA (Adv. of of Yr.), AAUW, Am. Bus. Women's Assn., N.Mex. Endowment for Humanities. Democrat. Roman Catholic. Home: 1214 E 1st St Roswell NM 88201-7960

CASEY, BEVERLY ANN, postmaster; b. Decaturville, Tenn., Aug. 6, 1949; d. Willie Hugh and Lillian Blanche (Ivy) Tillman; m. John Robert Casey, Jan. 19, 1969 (div. 1982); children—John Gary, Kimberly Jean. Student Jackson State Community Coll., 1982-84. Sec. State of Tenn., Western Institute, 1969-76; post office clk. U.S. Postal Service, Western Institute, 1977-82, postmaster, 1982-84; postmaster U.S. Postal Service, Pickwick Dam, Tenn., 1984—; officer-in-charge U.S. Postal Service, Michie, Tenn., 1984. Bd. dirs. Pickwick Med. Clinic, 1986; vol. Hardeman chpt. Saint Jude, Bolivar, Tenn., 1983; mem. parents advancement com. Wesleyan Coll., 1991-94; town chmn. Reelfoot council Girl Scouts U.S., 1980-84, activities chmn., 1980-84, recipient Appreciation award, 1983. Named Outstanding 3d Class Postmaster 380 area U.S. Postal Service, 1984; recipient Vol. Service award Cystic Fibrosis Found., Tenn. Chpt., 1982, Vol. Appreciation Cert. Western Mental Health, 1984. Mem. Nat. League of Postmasters (v.p. Tenn. br. 1984-86), 380 Postmasters Assn. (pres. 1983-84), U.S. Postal Service (dir.-at-large women's adv. coun. 1983-88). Baptist. Avocations: walking; tennis. Home: PO Box 363 Pickwick Dam TN 38365-0363 Office: US Postal Service Pickwick Dam TN 38365

CASEY, BONNIE LYNN, school counselor; b. Cleve., Aug. 8, 1950; d. Michael Edward and Christine Marie (Juliano) C. BS in Edn., Kent State U., 1972; MEd, Cleve. State U., 1976, EdS, 1994. Cert. elem. edn., sch. counseling, prin., staff pers., pupil pers. adminstr. Tchr. Warren Heights, Ohio, 1973-78, Wickliffe, Ohio, 1979-89; counselor Buhrer Sch., Cleve. Pub. Schs., 1990—; intervention assistance team Cleve. Pub. Sch., 1992-94, guidance com., 1990-94; coord. sch. Mediation Program, 1991-95. Mem. ACA. Home: 818 S Green St South Euclid OH 44121 Office: Cleveland Pub Schs Buhrer Sch 1600 Buhrer Ave Cleveland OH 44109

CASEY, ELBERTA, secondary education educator; b. Frankfort, Ky., Feb. 20, 1956; d. James Vernon and Meta Bush (Dowden) C. BA, Transylvania U., Lexington, Ky., 1978; M in Secondary Edn., U. Ky., 1986. Tchr. sci. at middle sch. level Fayette County Schs., Lexington, 1978—. Mem. NEA, Ky. Edn. Assn., Nat. Middle Sch. Assn., Nat. Sci. Tchrs. Assn., Nat. Middle Level Sci. Assn., Fayette County Edn. Assn. Christian. Office: Crawford Middle Sch 1813 Charleston Dr Lexington KY 40505

CASEY, ELLEN PATRICIA, obstetric/gynecological nurse; b. Cambridge, Mass., Nov. 10, 1960; d. John Michael and Ellen Louise (Clark) O'Connor; m. Thomas Allen Casey, Apr. 4, 1987. BSN, Boston Coll., 1982. Staff nurse med. surgery The Cambridge Hosp., 1982-85, staff nurse ob-gyn. and newborn nursery, 1985-86, staff nurse ICU, 1986-87, staff nurse ob-gyn. NBN, 1987—; CPR instr. The Cambridge Hosp., 1983—, unit preceptor, 1987—; instr. neonatal resuscitation program, 1992. Mem. Mass. Nurses' Assn. Roman Catholic. Home: 56 Wheeler St Malden MA 02148

CASEY, ETHEL LAUGHLIN, concert and opera singer; b. Tarboro, N.C., Jan. 14, 1926; d. Maurice Lee and Mary Irene (Williams) Laughlin; m. Willis Robert Casey, May 23, 1946; children: Willis Robert, Walker Laughlin. Student, Va. Intermont Coll., 1944-45; BA, Greensboro Coll, 1946-47; postgrad., U. N.C., 1948, 62, Meredith Coll., 1949, Northwestern U., 1961. Founder, owner Carolina Records Co.; founder concert series N.C. State Art Mus. Performed at numerous convs. and festivals; oratorio soloist, conv. and mus. comedy performer; author: Claude de France, 1963, Psalms (160 psalm poems), 1987; composer Christmas Night, 1971, America Will Endure, 1972, U.S.A., 1972; N.Y. debut Town Hall, 1961; concert singer performing at Carnegie Hall, all-Debussy concert, 1961, Tribute to Galli-Curci, 1965, Composer's Showcase, N.Y., 1965, Electronic Concert, Ann Arbor, Mich., 1966, Webern World Premieres Internat. Webern Festivals, Seattle, Buffalo, 1962-66, World Premieres of Graphic Music, 1965, command performance Greek Royal Princess, 1966, New Vistas, World Premieres of Am. Music, 1968; performance of Babbitt's electronic opera Philomel, 1968; Gov.'s Concerts, Judson Hall, N.Y., 1969, 70, Nat. Congress, Constn. Hall, Washington, 1970; World Premieres Webern and Earls Music Carnegie Hall, 1971, world premieres own music and Webern Lincoln Ctr., N.Y.C., 1971, Internat. Platform Assn., Washington, 1972, performed in Leningrad, USSR, 1975; TV and radio performer, 1936—. Founder, God's Ministry, Christian Broadcast Network, 1981-82. Named Alumna of Year, Va. Intermont Coll., 1967, Singer of Year, Nat. Assn. Tchrs. Singing, 1963; honored as singer All-Am. City Celebrations, Tarboro, N.C., 1978; recipient award Greensboro Coll. Concert, 1980. Mem. N.C. State Music Soc. (founder). Home and Office: 1605 Park Dr Raleigh NC 27605-1608

CASEY, KAREN ANNE, banker; b. Bklyn., Oct. 5, 1955; d. Stanley Joseph and Helen Katherine (Kosowski) Mozeleski; m. Dennis Joseph Casey, May 14, 1977; children: Christopher Sean, Erin Michelle. BBA, Baruch Coll., CUNY, 1977. CPA, N.Y., CFP. Jr. acct. Coopers & Lybrand, N.Y.C., 1977-78, sr. acct., 1978-79, supr., 1979-81; asst. fin. contr. Gulf Internat. Bank, N.Y.C., 1981-82, fin. contr., 1982; v.p., fin. contr. Allied Irish Banks plc, N.Y.C., 1982-87, sr. v.p., fin. contr., 1988-89, sr. v.p. mgmt. support svcs., 1989-92, sr. v.p., CFO, Allied Irish Bank, 1992-94, sr. v.p., head pvt. fin. svcs., 1994—; bank rep. to Bank Adminstrn. Inst., 1983—, Inst. Fgn. Bankers, 1984—, Com. of Banking Insts. on Taxation, 1984—. Mem. Am. Inst. CPAs. Roman Catholic. Avocations: gardening, golf, tennis, reading. Office: Allied Irish Banks Plc 405 Park Ave New York NY 10022-4405

CASEY, PATRICIA ANN, secretarial company owner; b. Plant City, Fla., Oct. 6, 1949; d. Cecil Theo and Martha Irene (Williams) Roberts; m. Duane Earl Casey, June 14, 1991. AA in Bus., Hillsborough C.C., Tampa, Fla., 1982. Clk. Land O'Lakes (Fla.) Svc. Sta., 1979-82; asst. to staff adminstr. Pitts Chiropractic Clinic, Tampa, Fla., 1982-83; customer svc. Groff Industries, Inc., Tampa, 1983-87; sec. Schreuder & Davis, Inc., Tampa, 1987-88; office mgr. Racetrack Rd. Nursery, Odessa, Fla., 1989-91; owner, operator Words-to-Go, Lutz, Fla., 1990—; sales rep. Avon Products, Inc., Lutz, 1985—, Tupperware, Tampa, 1993-94. Historian Phi Beta Lambda, Tampa, 1982; Sunday sch. tchr. Sunlake Bapt. Ch., 1990-94. Sgt. USAF, 1975-79. Recipient Svc. award Phi Beta Lambda, Tampa, 1982. Mem. Am. Legion Aux. (sgt. at arms 1992-93, asst. sgt. at arms 1993-94), Women's Missionary Union (group leader 1991-94, girls-in-action leader 1992-93, girls-in-action asst. leader 1993-94), Phi Theta Kappa (Outstanding mem. 1982). Home: 19106 Alice Circle Lutz FL 33549 Office: Words-to-Go 19106 Alice Circle Lutz FL 33549

CASEY, PATRICIA LEE, film producer; b. N.Y.C.; d. Joseph and Johanna Lina (Tanner) C.; m. Judd Bernard, Feb. 18, 1972; 1 child, Alicia; stepchildren: Adrianna, Michael. Student, L.A. City Coll. Ballet dancer Radio City Music Hall, N.Y.C.; ballerina L.A. Ballet Co., 1959-64; producer Kettledrums Films, Valley Village, Calif. Dancer, choreographer (film) Double Trouble, 1965; assoc. prodr. Blue, 1967, Man Who Had Power Over Women, 1969, Glad All Over, 1970, Inside Out, 1973, Marseilles Contract, 1975, The Class of Miss MacMichaels, 1979; asst. prodr. Point Blank, 1966; co-star Fade In, 1967; prodr. Monty Python's And Now For Something Completely Different, 1971, The Playboy Guide to Amsterdam, 1980, Blood Red, 1989. Office: Kettledrum Films 4961 Agnes Ave Valley Village CA 91607

CASEY, PHYLLIS MARIE, educational administrator; b. Raleigh, N.C., June 12, 1951; d. L.C. and Mabel Elizabeth (Powell) C. BA in English cum laude, Va. State U., 1973; MEd in Ednl. Adminstrn., Pa. State U., 1981. English tchr. Garner (N.C.) Sr. High Sch., 1976-80, Washington and Lee High Sch., Montross, Va., 1982-85; asst. dir. Office of Minority Affairs Frostburg State U., 1985-86, asst. dir. Aux. Svcs. and Office of Confs., 1986-92, assoc. dir. Aux. Svcs. and Ctr. for Profl. and Extended Edn., 1992-94, dir. Continuing and Profl. Edn., 1995—; active numerous univ. coms., 1985—. Mem. AAUW, NAACP, LWV, NAFE, Assn. of Conf. and Events Dirs. Internat., Nat. Fedn. of Bus. and Profl. Women, Nat. Univ. Continuing Edn. Assn., Rotary, Alpha Kappa Alpha, Alpha Kappa Mu. Home: 316 Braddock Rd Apt 331 Frostburg MD 21532-2322 Office: Frostburg State Univ 20 Braddock St Frostburg MD 21532-2302

CASH, AUDREY SUTTON, secondary school educator; b. Ellenton, Ga., Mar. 16, 1926; d. James Young and Martha Anne (Baker) Sutton; m. Thomas Bell, Dec. 24, 1948; children: Thomas M., Martha C. Reubert, Melanie C. Hill, Richard J. Diploma, Baldwin Jr. Coll., 1944; BS, U. Ga., 1947, MS, 1950; postgrad., Va. Commonwealth U., 1967-68, Fla. State U., 1969. Tchr. Moultrie (Ga.) High Sch., 1947-49, Cook High Sch., Adel, Ga., 1950-52, Juliette Lowe Sch., Savannah, Ga., 1955-57, Terry Parker High Sch., Jacksonville, Fla., 1968-88; ret., 1988; pres. Hope Enterprises of Jacksonville, Fla. Inc., 1977-87; lectr. Elderhostel, 1994. Author: (cookbook) Southern Literary, 1978. Active Jacksonville Rep. Com., 1968-88; tchr. adult Sunday sch. class Bapt. Ch., 1987—; active Salvation Army Aux., poverty relief, community recreation for sr. citizens, 1989—. Mem. AAUW (v.p. Jacksonville chpt. 1986-87, pres. 1988-89), Phi Kappa Phi, Phi Upsilon Omicron. Baptist. Home: 7210 White Birch Dr Jacksonville FL 32211-2820

CASH, CAROL VIVIAN, sociologist; b. Port Arthur, Tex., Jan. 22, 1929; d. Mano Nathan and Floris Duval (Akin) C.; m. Robert Morrow Welch, Dec. 21, 1951 (div. 1966); children: Catherine Carol, Robert M. III, Candice Claire. AA, Lamar Jr. Coll., 1951; BS in Sociology, U. Houston, 1971. Sec. Port Arthur SS Co., 1948-50; with Gov's Office State of Tex., Austin, 1951-52; legal sec. Wesley W. West, Houston, 1953-55. Author numerous children's books. Active Houston area Boy Scouts Am., Girl Scouts U.S., 1960-76, Port Arthur Hist. Soc.; mem. Tex. Sesquicentennial Com., 1986; active in restoration of Tex. historic homes. Mem. AAUW (chmn. Port Arthur fund raiser 1982), Tex. Artist Mus. Soc., Planetary Soc., Fed. Women's Clubs, Writer's Club (v.p. 1983-84, pres. 1984-85, treas. 1985-90), U. Houston Alumni Assn.

CASH, JENNIFER WOEHLK, oncology nurse; b. Tampa, Fla., Sept. 18, 1962; d. August Henry and Betty Jean (Cardova) Woehlk; children: Jessica Michele, Cody Alan; m. Jeffrey Scott Cash. BSN, U. So. Fla., 1987, BA in Eng. Lit., 1986, MSN, 1992. Clin. nurse specialist in radiation oncology Univ. Community Hosp., Tampa. Med. editor: Health and Vitality jour. Bd. dirs. Am. Cancer Soc. Mem. Oncology Nurses Soc. (cert.), Sigma Theta Tau. Home: 17020 Shady Pines Dr Lutz FL 33549-6185

CASH, JUNE CARTER, singer; b. Maces Springs, Va., June 23, 1929; d. Ezra and Maybelle (Addington) Carter; m. John R. Cash; children: Rebecca Carlene, Rozanna Lea, John Carter. Student, Neighborhood Playhouse Sch. Dramatics, 1955-56; HHD (hon.), Nat. U., San Diego, 1977. Propr. June Carter Cash Antiques and Gift Shop, Hendersonville, Tenn. Singer with, Carter Family, 1939-43, with Carter Sisters (and mother), after 1943; performed on, Sta. XERF, Del Rio Tex., Sta. KWTO, Springfield, Mo.; mem. Grand Ole Opry, Sta. WSM, Nashville; TV appearances include John Davidson Show, Tennessee Ernie Show, Johnny Cash Show, others; films include: Thaddeus, Rose and Eddie, Country Music Holiday; TV movies: Stage Coach, Murder Coweta Country, The Baron, The Last Days of Frank and Jessie James, Keep on The Sunny Side, Appalachian Pride, Gospel Road, Country Music Caravan, Road to Nashville, Tennessee Jamboree, Gospel Road; TV spl. The Best of The Carter Family; songs recorded include: Baby It's Cold Outside, Music Music Music, Love Oh Crazy Love, Let Me Go Lover, Leftover Loving; contbr. to album Johnny Cash is Coming to Town, 1987; author: Among My Klediments, 1979, From the Heart, 1986, Mother Maybelle's Cookbook, 1989; co-author: Ring of Fire. Address: House of Cash Inc PO Box 508 Hendersonville TN 37077-0508*

CASH, (CYNTHIA) LAVERNE, physicist; b. Statesville, N.C., Oct. 7, 1956; d. William J. and Martha Lee (Stroud) C. BS, Appalachian State U., 1979; MS, Clemson U., 1982; AA, Mitchell Community Coll., 1976; postgrad., Johns Hopkins U. Physicist U.S. Army Material Systems Analysis Activity, Aberdeen Proving Ground, Md., 1984-88; rsch. physicist U.S. Army Edgewood Rsch., Devel. and Engring. Ctr., Aberdeen Proving Ground, 1988—. Contbr. articles to profl. publs. Mem. Oak Grove Bapt. Ch, Bel Air, Md., singer in choir, sound engr., numerous others. Mem. Am. Phys. Soc., Sigma Phi Sigma, Pi Mu Epsilon, Phi Theta Kappa, Gamma Beta Phi. Baptist. Home: 100 Drexel Dr Bel Air MD 21014-2002

CASH, ROSANNE, country singer, songwriter; b. Memphis, May 24, 1955; b. May 1955; d. John R. Cash and Vivian (Liberto) Distin; m. Rodnay J. Crowell, Apr. 7, 1979 (div. 1992); children: Caitlin Rivers, Chelsea Jane, Carrie Kathleen. Student, Vol. State C.C., 1974, Vanderbilt U., 1976, Lee Strasberg Theatre Inst., 1977. Rec. artist Ariola Records, Europe, 1978-84, CBS Records, worldwide, 1979—. Songwriter Blue Moon with Heartache, 1979, Seven Year Ache, 1980 (Gold Record award Rec. Industry Assn. Am. 1981), I Don't Know Why You Don't Want Me, 1984, (Grammy award 1985), Hold On (Robert J. Burton award 1987), others; Albums: Right Or Wrong, Seven Year Ache, 1980, Somewhere in the Stars, Rythym & Romance, 1985, King's Record Shop, 1987, Hits 1979-89, 1989, Interiors, 1990. Bd. advisors Nashvillians for Nuclear Arms Freeze, 1987-90. Mem. AFTRA, Nat. Acad. Rec. Arts and Scis. (Grammy award 1985), Am. Fedn. Musicians, Screen Actors Guild, Broadcast Music, Inc. (Spl. Achievement awards), Nashville Songwriters Assn. Internat. Democrat. Office: Side One Mgmt #1A 373 W 49th St # 1A New York NY 10019-7316*

CASHIER-CORSO, MARIA ANNE, university administrator; b. Syracuse, N.Y., May 1, 1946; d. Emelio Ernest and Manuela (Biancardi) Cashier; m. Samuel Frank Corso, May 2, 1970. BS, Syracuse U., 1982, MBA, 1985, postgrad., 1989—. Adminstrv. asst. to dean Syracuse U. Sch. Mgmt., 1980-87; mgr. Info. Ctr. CIS Corp., Syracuse, 1987-88; adj. instr. LeMoyne Coll., Syracuse, 1988—; lectr., dir. Bus. Adminstrn. Student Adv. Ctr. SUNY, Oswego, 1990—; cons., trainer Bristol-Myers Squibb Co., Syracuse, 1988-92. Contbr. articles for ednl. confs. in field. Vol. Loretto Rest Nursing Home, 1977-87. Mem. NAFE, ASCD, Assn. Computing Machinery (chmn. 1990-91, profl. devel. chair 1991—, publicity chair 1988—), Soc. Applied Learning Tech., Assn. Edn. and Computer Tech., Internat. Mgmt. Coun. (student liaison com. 1991), Syracuse Microcomputer Club, Beta Gamma Sigma, Phi Lambda Theta, Delta Mu Delta. Roman Catholic. Office: SUNY-Oswego Bus Adminstrn Student Adv Ctr 16 Swetman Hall Oswego NY 13126

CASHMAN, MELISSA, psychologist; b. San Antonio, Nov. 28, 1958; d. Patrick Joseph Cashman and Harryette (Lowenstein) Boone. BA in Psychology, U. Okla., 1980; MA in Psychology, Calif. Sch. Profl. Psychology, 1985, PhD in Clin. Psychology, 1991. Lic. psychologist, Calif.; limited lic., Mich. Psychol. trainee U. Okla., Norman, 1978-80; counselor Youth Svcs. for Oklahoma County, Oklahoma City, 1981-83; psychol. trainee primary mental health program Fresno (Calif.) Unified Sch. Dist., 1984; psychol. trainee permary mental health program Calif. Mens Colony, San Luis Obispo, 1984-85; psychology intern Hathaway Home for Children, Lake View Terrace, Calif., 1986-87; therapist E. Ross Clark, Modesto, Calif., 1988, Family Svc. Agy., Modesto, 1988; mental health clinician Stanislaus County Mental Health, Modesto, 1989-93; psychologist Bay Mills Indian Community, Brimley, Mich., 1993—; cons. The Children's Shelter, Ardmore, Okla., 1988. Mem. APA, Mich. Assn. Childrens Alliances Inc., Psi Chi. Home: 494 Sheridan Dr Sault Sainte Marie MI 49783

CASHMORE, PATSY JOY, speechwriter, editor, author, consultant, educator; b. Milw., July 20, 1943; d. Anthony J. and Eva Irene (Arseneau) Peters; m. Gary Roy Cashmore, July 5, 1963 (div. Feb. 1983); children: Jay Allen, Jeffery Scott. Student U. Ill.-Chgo., 1961-62, Inst. Broadcast Arts, Milw., 1966-67, U. Wis.-Milw., 1970, U. Wis.-Madison, 1971-76,labor studies N.Y.C. Grad. Ctr., 1978. Copy writer H. Vincent Allen & Assocs., Chgo., 1961-63; asst. program coord. Sta.-WRIT, Milw., 1967-69; asst. news assignment editor WITI-TV, Milw., 1969-72; pub. rels. asst. Deaconess Hosp., Milw., 1972-73; asst. editor Milw. Labor Press, 1973-81, editor, 1981-90, coord. spl. comm. United Assocs., Washington, 1990—; voice talent on radio and TV commls.; instr., mem. faculty adv. com. U. Wis. Extension-Sch. for Workers, Madison; panelist NEH; guest Israeli govt., 1976, Govt. Fed. Republic Germany, 1980, pre-NATO talks Friedrich Ebert Found., 1981, 87, Peoples Republic of China, 1983, All Union Cen. Coun. of Trade Unions of Soviet Union, 1985; studied in East Africa, 1987. Contbr. articles to nat. publs. Chmn. comm. com., treas. Milw. Coun. on Drug Abuse, 1981-83, bd. dirs., 1984-87, Milw. Coun. on Alcoholism, 1985-88; mem. community affairs com. United Way, 1983-86; active Variety Club, 1983-87; chmn. community adv. bd. Sta.-WVTV pub. TV, 1982-85; bd. dirs. Goals 2000 Comm.tions Com., 1983; participant U.S. Del. to observe elections in El Salvador, 1989; ednl. specialist U.S. State Dept., Lesotho, 1990; vol. Earthwatch, Borneo, 1988. Mem. Internat. Labor Comm. Assn. (v.p. 1985, 87, 89, Best Signed Column award 1973, Best Feature Story award 1975, award of Merit for best use of art 1982, Best Headline award 1982, First award for gen. excellence newspaper 1982, 83, 87, 88, 1st award Labor History best instl. profile 1986, 87, 88, Best Graphics award 1987, Best Original Cartoon 1987, 88), U.S. Treasury Dept. (Liberty Bell award, 1986), Midwest Labor Press Assn. (pres.), Wis. Labor Press Assn. (treas.), Indsl. Rels. Rsch. Assn. (bd. dirs.), Milw. Jr. Acd. Club (past sec.-treas.). NAFE, Sigma Delta Chi, Wapatule Ski Club (newsletter editor 1984-85), Nat. Press Club, Milw. Press Club, Milw. Pen and Mike Club (Milw.). Avocations: travel, skiing, golf, swimming. Office: United Assn Journeymen & Apprentices 901 Massachusetts Ave NW Washington DC 20001-4307

CASON, JUNE MACNABB, musician, educator, arts administrator; b. Phila., June 21, 1930; d. Vernon C. and Eleanor (Scarlet) Macnabb; m. Roger Lee Cason, June 12, 1952; children: David Alan, Diane Louise, Nancy Lynn. Student, Eastman Sch. Music, Rochester, N.Y., 1948-52; grad., U. Houston, 1965-69; postgrad. in bus., U. Pa., 1984. Dir. youth chorus St. John's Episcopal Ch., Charleston, W.Va., 1956-63; soloist ch. and music groups, Charleston, 1957-63; founder, dir. music summer camp Episcopal Diocese W.Va., 1961-62; soloist Christ Ch. Cathedral, Houston, 1963-71, Gilbert and Sullivan Soc., Houston, 1970; pvt. tchr. voice, Houston, 1965-71, Wilmington, Del., 1971—; tchr. voice San Jacinto Coll., Pasadena, Tex., 1969-71; founder, gen. mgr., soloist Minikin Opera Co., Wilmington, 1972-87; mem. faculty Wilmington Music Sch., 1973-77; mem. Del. Pro Musica, Wilmington, 1973-77, chmn., 1975-77; dir. music Immanuel Episcopal Ch., Wilmington, 1973-75; instr. music Albert Einstein Acad., Wilmington, 1975-76; v.p. Resource Ctr. for Performing Arts, 1982-86; chmn. Music Consortium New Castle County, 1982-84; devel. dir. Opera Delaware, 1988-92; trainer, cons. Nonprofit Mgmt. Devel. Ctr., La Salle U., 1989—; dir. devel. arts and humanities U. Del., 1992—. Contbr. articles to profl. jours. Recipient Theta Eta award U. Rochester, 1952. Mem. Music Tchrs. Nat. Assn. (nat. conv. chmn. vocal programs 1989—), Nat. Assn. Tchrs. Singing, Del. Music Tchrs. Nat. Assn., Nat. Soc. Fundraising Execs., Coun. Advancement and Support of Edn., Met. Opera Guild, Sigma Alpha Iota (Sword of Honor 1971). Republican. Home: 1125 Grinnell Rd Wilmington DE 19803-5125 Office: Univ Del Devel Office Academy Bldg Newark DE 19716

CASON, MARILYNN JEAN, technological education institute executive; b. Denver, May 18, 1943; d. Eugene Martin and Evelyn Lucille (Clark) C.; married. BA in Polit. Sci., Stanford U., 1965; JD, U. Mich., 1969; MBA, Roosevelt U., 1977. Bar: Colo. 1969, Ill. 1973. Assoc. Dawson, Nagel, Sherman & Howard, Denver, 1969-73; atty. Kraft, Inc., Glenview, Ill., 1973-75; corp. counsel Johnson Products Co., Inc., Chgo., 1975-86, v.p., 1977-86; mng. dir. Johnson Products Co., Inc., Lagos, Nigeria, 1980-83; v.p. internat. Johnson Products Co., Inc., Chgo., 1986-88; v.p., gen. counsel DeVry, Inc., Chgo., 1989—. Bd. dirs. Ill. chpt. Arthritis Found., Chgo., 1979—, chmn., 1991-93; bd. dirs. Internat. House, Chgo., 1986-92, Ill. Humanities Coun.,

Chgo., 1987—, chmn., 1993—. Mem. ABA, Nat. Bar Assn., Cook County Bar Assn. (pres. community law project 1986-88). Club: Stanford (Chgo.) (pres. 1985-87). Home: 3108 Colfax St Evanston IL 60201-1842 Office: DeVry Inc One Tower Ln Ste 1000 Oakbrook Terrace IL 60181

CASON, NICA VIRGINIA, nursing educator; b. Edna, Tex.; 1 child, Cynthia Diane. Diploma, Lillie Jolly Sch. Nursing, 1965; BSN, U. Tex. Med. Br., Galveston, 1967; MSN, U. So. Miss., 1981. RN, Miss. Pub. health nurse Miss. State Dept. Health, Pascagoula; nursing instr. Miss. Gulf Coast Community Coll.-Jackson County Campus, Gautier, chair ADN program; comdr. 403d Aeromed. Staging Squadron, Keesler AFB, Miss. Col. USAFR, 1968—. Mem. NOADN, Nat. League Nursing, Sigma Theta Tau, Phi Kappa Phi.

CASPER, MARIE LENORE, middle school educator; b. Honesdale, Pa., Mar. 26, 1954; d. Frank J. and Ellenore L. (Austin) Shedlock; m. Gerald Joseph Casper, Oct. 9, 1976; children: Julia Anne, Jennifer Marie. BA, Marywood Coll., 1976. Cert. elem. and secondary social studies tchr., Pa. Substitute tchr. Western Wayne Sch. Dist., South Canaan, Pa., 1976-81, secondary and elem. tchr., 1981-86, chpt. 1 math. specialist, 1986-90, middle sch. social studies tchr., 1990—; social studies tchr. Wallenpaupack Area Sch. Dist., Hawley, Pa., 1980-81; corp. sec. Simply Elegant Homes & Constrn., Inc., Kresgeville and South Canaan, Pa.; coord. Western Wayne Middle Sch. (WW II commemorative com.). Contbr. articles to profl. publs. Mem. AAUW (treas. Hawley-Honesdale br. 1981-83), Pa. Geog. Alliance, Nat. Geog. Soc., Wayne County Hist. Soc., Western Wayne Edn. Assn., Smithsonian Inst., Audobon Soc., Am. Legion Auxiliary. Republican. Roman Catholic. Home: PO Box 31 Salem Mt Rd South Canaan PA 18459-0031 Office: Western Wayne Med Sch Box 376B Lake Ariel PA 18436 also: Simply Elegant Homes & Cnst PO Box 937 Kresgeville PA 18333

CASPERS, CORLYN MARIE, adult nurse practitioner; b. Breckenridge, Minn., Aug. 24, 1964; d. Wilbur Richard Caspers and Coralee Meredith (Warner) Fries; m. Rodney Ralph Kolkow, May 1, 1993; children: Megan, Laura. BSN, Oreg. Inst. Tech., 1986; MS, U. Portland (Oreg.), 1994. RN, registered adult nurse practitioner. Hospice primary care nurse Klamath (Oreg.) Hospice, 1985-93; clin. mgr. Merle West Med. Ctr., Klamath Falls, 1989, primary care nurse, 1986-94; home health nurse Merle West Med. Ctr., 1988-94; clinician at coll. health svcs. Oreg. Inst. Tech., Klamath Falls, 1994—; sub-chmn. quality assurance and standards com., 1989, nursing edn. coun., preceptor Merle West Med. Ctr., 1988-94.

CASSEDAY, ELIZABETH JUNE, pediatrics nurse; b. Saint Paul, Feb. 15, 1967; d. George F. Casseday and Laura L. Schultz. BSN, Aurora U., 1989. Staff nurse level C Rush-Presbyn. St. Luke's Med. Ctr., Chgo., 1989—, supr. ancillary staff pediatric adolescent svcs., 1990—. Vol. nurse Grace Youth Camp, Mich., 1988—; vol. Spl. Olympics, Ill., 1989, Kane County Health Dept., Aurora, Ill., 1986-89. Mem. ANA, Ill. Nursing Assn. Home: 3222 Oak Ave Brookfield IL 60513 Office: Rush Presbyn Saint Lukes 1750 W Harrison Chicago IL 60613

CASSEL, SYLVIA ANN, market research company executive; b. Potsdam, N.Y., June 28, 1938; d. Fredrick Mott and Lillian (Walker) C. BS, SUNY, Potsdam, 1960; postgrad., NYU, 1960-61; MBA, CUNY, 1980. Systems engr. IBM, 1961-63; mgr. systems, programming Diners Club, 1963-64; mgr. data processing Katz Agy., 1965-69; mgr. spl. projects Arbitron, N.Y.C., 1970-72; mgr. computer client service Axiom/Simmons Market Research Bur., N.Y.C., 1972-78; sr. v.p. Mediamark Rsch. Inc., N.Y.C., 1978—. SUNY fellow, 1960-61; Alcoa Found. scholar, 1956-60. Mem. Advt. Data Processing Assn. (pres. 1979-80), Am. Mktg. Assn., Advt. Women N.Y., Internat. Advt. Assn. Republican. Club: Advt. of N.Y. Office: Mediamark Rsch Inc 400 Madison Ave Bldg 3 New York NY 10017-1909

CASSELL, KAY ANN, librarian; b. Van Wert, Ohio, Sept. 24, 1941; d. Kenneth Miller and Pauline (Zimmerman) C. B.A., Carnegie-Mellon U., 1963; M.L.S., Rutgers U., 1965; M.A., Bklyn. Coll., 1969. Reference librarian Bklyn. Coll. Library, 1965-68; adult svcs. cons. N.J. State Libr., Trenton, 1968-71; libr. cons.-vol. Peace Corps, Rabat, Morocco, 1971-73; adult svcs. cons. Westchester Libr. System, White Plains, N.Y., 1973-75; dir. Bethlehem Pub. Libr., Delmar, N.Y., 1975-81, Huntington (N.Y.) Pub. Libr., 1982-85; exec. dir. Coordinating Coun. Lit. Mags., N.Y.C., 1985-87; univ. libr. New Sch. for Social Rsch., 1987-88; assoc. dir. programs and svcs. br. libro. N.Y. Pub. Libr., 1989—; adj. faculty Grad. Sch. L.S., SUNY, Albany, 1976-78, Palmer Sch. Libr. and Info. Scis., L.I. U., 1986-90; chmn. cmty. adv. com. Capital Dist. Humanities Program, Albany, 1980-81; bd. dirs. Literacy Vols. of Suffolk, Bellport, n.Y., 1981-85; chair N.Y.C. Sch. Libr. Sys. Coun., 1991-94; treas. Libr. Pub. Rels. Coun., 1993—. Mem. ALA (pres. reference and adult svcs. divsn. 1983-84, chair membership com. 1991—, coun. 1991—), N.Y. Libr. Assn. (pres. reference and adult svcs. sect. 1975-76), Feminist Press (bd. dirs. 1994—), Beta Phi Mu. Office: NY Pub Libr Office Programs & Svcs 455 5th Ave New York NY 10016-0109

CASSENS, SUSAN FORGET, artist; b. Ft. Pierce, Fla., May 11, 1956; d. Louis Conrad and Joan Hancock Forget; m. Steven Dale Cassens, Mar. 4, 1979; children: Christopher, Michael, Scott. AA, U. Fla., 1976; BA in Edn. with honors, Fla. Atlantic U., 1978. Tchr. Garden City Elem., Ft. Pierce, 1978-79; owner Brush Strokes Art Gallery, Ft. Pierce, 1993—; bd. mem. St. Lucie County Cultural Affairs Coun., Ft. Pierce, 1993. Cover artist: Cracker Cuisine, 1993; exhbns. include A.E. Backus Gallery, Ft. Pierce, Treasure Coast Art Gallery, Ft. Pierce. Chpt. sec. Philanthropic Ednl. Orgn., Ft. Pierce, 1987, chpt. pres., 1989; mem. Vero Beach Ctr. for the Arts, A.E. Backus Art Gallery, Mainstreet (Ft. Pierce) Inc., St. Lucie Hist. Soc.; chair St. Lucie Mural Soc., Ft. Pierce, 1994—. Mem. Nat. Mus. of Women in the Arts (charter mem.), Vero Beach Art Club, Heathcote Botanical Gardens (charter mem.). Presbyterian. Office: Brush Strokes Art Gallery 218 Orange Ave Fort Pierce FL 34954

CASSIDY, ESTHER CHRISTMAS, federal agency administrator; b. Upper Marlboro, Md., Aug. 5, 1933; d. Donelson and Esther (Brooke) Christmas; divorced; children: William Keeling K., Carroll Cassidy Drewyer, Daniel Clark. BA, Manhattanville Coll., 1955. Phys. scientist, R&D Nat. Bur. Standards, Gaithersburg, Md., 1955-73; sci. advisor U.S. Congressman Teno Roncalio, Washington, 1973-74; asst. dir. congl. affairs Energy R&D Adminstrn. Dept. Energy, Washington, 1974-78; dir. congl. and legis. affairs Nat. Inst. Standards and Tech., Gaithersburg, 1978—. Contbr. articles to profl. jours. Mem. IEEE (sr.). Office: Nat Inst Standards and Tech Adminstrv Bldg Rm A-1111 Gaithersburg MD 20899

CASSIDY, JUDITH, accounting educator; b. Bogalusa, La., Jan. 17, 1943; d. Joseph Peter Jr. and Leila (Russ) C.; m. John Thomas Sullivan, Feb. 26, 1963 (dec.); children: Michael Sullivan, Sean Sullivan. BA in Econ., Tulane U., 1963; MBA, U. Tex., 1982; PhD in Acctg., Tex. Tech, 1986. CPA, Miss., CMA. Asst. prof. La. State U., Baton Rouge, 1985-88; assoc. prof. U. Miss., University, 1989—; cons. healthcare cost containment, activity based costing for manufacturing. Contbr. articles to profl. jours. NSF fellow, 1960. Mem. Miss. Soc. CPAs, Inst. Mgmt. Accts. (chpt. pres. 1992-93), Inst. Internal Auditors, Info. Sys. Audit and Control Assn., Am. Acctg. Assn., Rotary (Oxford, Miss., sec. 1994—). Home: PO Box 3158 University MS 38677 Office: U Miss Sch Accountancy University MS 38677

CASSIN, KIMBERLEY JEAN, private school educator; b. Chgo., Sept. 16, 1954; d. William Francis and Beverley Jean (Wilkerson) Bowen; m. Michael Joseph Cassin, Aug. 6, 1979; children: Kathleen Michelle, Pamela Christine. BS in Biology, Christian Bros. Coll., 1976; EMT, Shelby State Coll., 1977. EMT Crittenden Emergency Med. Svcs., West Memphis, Ark., 1977-80; lab. technician St. Jude's Children's Rsch. Hosp., Memphis, 1980-81, Genetics Ctr., Scottsdale, Ariz., 1986-87; educator Cathedral High Sch., Natchez, Miss., 1981-86, Tyler (Tex.) Cath. Schs., 1988—. Grantee Univ. Tex. Health Sci. Ctr., Tyler, 1988. Mem. Am. Inst. Biol. Scis., Am. Soc. Biochemists and Molecular Biologists (grantee 1989), Nat. Sci. Tchrs. Assn. Home: 210 Driftwood White Oak TX 75693

CASSTEVENS, KAY L., federal official; b. Ft. Worth, July 4, 1949; d. Floyd C. and Shirley D. (Jackson) C. BJ cum laude, U. Tex., 1971; JD, George Washington U., 1979. Bar: D.C. 1980. Legis. aide Senator George McGovern, S.D., 1973-77; legis. dir. Rep. John F. Seiberling, Ohio, 1977-85; legis. dir. Sen. Tom Harkin, Iowa, 1986-91, chief of staff, 1991-92; asst. sec. legis. and congrl. affairs Dept. of Edn., Washington, 1993—; dep. issues dir. to Geraldine Ferraro, Mondale-Ferraro Campaign, fall 1984; mem. rsch. staff Dukakis for Pres. Campaign, fall 1988; dep. campaign mgr. Ams. for Harkin Presdl. Campaign, 1991-92. Office: Dept of Education Legislative & Congressional Affairs 600 Independence Ave SW Washington DC 20202-0001

CASSY, CATHERINE MARY, elementary school educator; b. Granite City, Ill., Aug. 12, 1949; d. George Joseph and Margaret Mary (Pieper) Crawshaw; m. Gene Herschel Cassy, June 5, 1971. BS in Edn., So. Ill. U., 1971; MS, Lindenwood Coll., 1987. Cert. lifetime elem., instrumental music, vocal music tchr., reading specialist, Mo., elem. tchr., Ill. Tchr. music Fowler Elem. Sch., Phoenix, 1972-73; tchr. 5th grade Parkview Elem. Sch., Granite City, 1973-82; tchr. of gifted Maryville Sch., Granite City, 1982-83; tchr. 6th grade and vocal music Henderson Jr. High Sch., St. Charles, 1984-86; tchr. 6th grade, tchr. vocal music Barnwell Jr. High Sch., St. Charles, Mo., 1986-87; tchr. 6th grade M.G. Henderson Elem. Sch., St. Charles, 1987—; cycle chairperson Henderson Sch., 1991—. Choral dir. Holy Family Ch., Granite City, 1974—; mus. dir., performer Showtime Express, Inc., Granite City, 1989—; chair Great Rivers Environ. Edn. Network. Named Tchr. of Yr. Barnwell Jr. High Sch., 1987; recipient Travis Hack Meml. award, 1993, Excellence in Teaching award Emerson Electric, 1993; Nat. Elem. Sci. Leadership grantee Nat. Sci. Resource Ctr., 1993. Mem. NSTA, NEA, Nat. Coun. Tchrs. Math., Mo. Coun. Tchrs. Math., Mo. Sci. Tchrs. Assn., Acad. Sci. St. Louis, Nature Conservancy, Phi Delta Kappa. Home: 2191 Shirlene Dr Granite City IL 62040-2564 Office: Henderson Elem Sch 2501 Hackmann Rd Saint Charles MO 63303-5452

CAST, ANITA HURSH, small business owner; b. Columbus, Ohio, July 11, 1939; d. Charles Walter and Hulda Marie (Ramsey) Hursh; m. William R. Cast, Apr. 1, 1961; children: Jennifer, Carter, Meghan. BA, DePauw U., 1961. Ptnr. Cast Hursh and Assocs., Ft. Wayne, Ind., 1982—; pianist Words and Music, Ft. Wayne, 1983—; owner Anita Cast's Wearable Art, Ft. Wayne, 1986—; cons. for bd. tng. Bd. dirs., pres. Am. Symphony Orch. League, vol., v.p., 1985-86; bd. dirs. WBNI Nat. Pub. Radio, Ft. Wayne; commr. Ind. Gov.'s Mansion Commn., 1987, Ind. Arts Commn., 1979-87; chmn., bd. dirs. Fine Arts Found., Ft. Wayne, 1988; pres. Ft. Wayne Philharmonic, 1977-79; v.p. Friends of Music, Indiana U., Leadership Ft. Wayne Adv. Bd.; v.p., then pres. Ind. Endowment of the Arts, Ft. Wayne, 1985—; chmn. bd. Arts United of Greater Ft. Wayne, 1988-90; pres. Met. YMCA, Ft. Wayne, 1986—; mem. Mayor's Bicentennial Exec. Bd., 1989—; mem. Ind. Cultural Congress Hon. Com. Lily Endowment Leadership fellow. Republican. Episcopalian. Home and Office: Anita Cast Wearable Art 4401 Taylor Rd Fort Wayne IN 46804-1913

CASTALDI, MARILYN LEE, public relations executive; b. Phila., Jan. 24, 1946; d. Felix Vincent and Rena Margaret Castaldi; m. Howard A. Singer, Feb. 14, 1981. BA, Syracuse U., 1967; MBA in Mktg., NYU, 1986. Reporter/editor Gannett Suburban News Group, Cherry Hill, N.J., 1967-69; dir., pub. rels. Hosp. of U. of Pa., Phila., 1969-76; mgr. consumer affairs Johnson & Johnson Personal Products Co., Milltown, N.J., 1977-79; corp. comm./merchandising mgr. Avon Products, N.Y.C., 1979-81; account supr. Hill & Knowlton, L.A., N.Y.C., 1982-84; sr. v.p., U.S. practice dir. health care Hill & Knowlton, N.Y.C., 1992-93; from account supr. to exec. v.p. Burson-Marsteller, N.Y.C., 1984-92; sr. v.p., dir. health care group Fleishman-Hillard, N.Y.C., 1993—. Mktg. adv. com. Multiple Sclerosis Soc., N.Y.C.,a 1992-93. Recipient Silver Anvils, Pub. Rels Soc. Am., 1991, Big Apple awards, 1990, 91, MacEachern awards Am. Hosp. Assn., 1970-75, 84. Mem. Women Execs. in Pub. Rels. (bd. dirs. 1992-94, pres. 1994-95), Pharm. Advt. Coun. Democrat.

CASTANO, ELVIRA PALMERIO, art gallery director, art historian; b. Cin., July 23, 1929; d. John and Josephine C.; m. Carlo Palmerio, June 1, 1958 (dec.); 1 child, Marina. B Lit. Interpretation, Emerson Coll., 1950; postgrad., Pius XII Inst., Florence, Italy, 1954-55; student opera with Cesare Sturani. Curator Castano Art Gallery, Boston, 1965-78; dir. Castano Art Gallery, Needham, Mass., 1978—; researcher Archives of Am. Art Smithsonian Instn., Boston, 1988-89; Vatican translator; interpreter Italian art, specialist in Macchiaioli art; Italian lang. translator. Mem. Rep. Presdl. Task Force, Nat. Rep. Senatorial Com., Presdl. Inner Circle; bd. dirs. Needham Hist. Soc.; vol. Sail Boston, 1992; del. Presdl. Trust, 1992; aapptd. Gov.'s Com. on Women's Issues. Cardinal Spellman scholar. Mem. Boston Mus. Fine Arts, Fogg Art Mus. of Harvard U., Friends of Needham Libr., Archives Am. Art Boston, Alliance Francaise Boston, World Affairs Coun. Boston, Nat. Mus. Women in Arts, Needham Hist. Soc. (mem. bd. dirs.). Address: 245 Hunnewell St Needham MA 02194-1425

CASTANO, MARY LINDA, educator; b. Warren, Pa., May 15, 1951; d. Dominic Joseph and Angeline Susan (Gorfida) C. BS Edn. in Sci. and Psychology, Edinboro (Pa.) U., 1973. Tchr. Port Allegany (Pa.) Sch. Dist., 1973-74; tchr. Coudersport (Pa.) Sch. Dist., 1974—, coach girls basketball, 1974-89, coach varsity track, 1976-92. Democrat. Roman Catholic. Home: 105 W 4th St Coudersport PA 16915-1147

CASTEEL, ANGELA MICHELE, editor-in-chief; b. Little Rock, Apr. 8, 1960; d. Charles Walter and Joann (Moore) C. BA, U. Ark., Little Rock, 1983. Editor, art dir. Sagely Advt., Little Rock, 1981-82; promotion dept. editor Ark. Democrat, Little Rock, 1983-89; editor Falcon Publs., Little Rock, 1989-93; editor-in-chief Connell Publs., Little Rock, 1993—. Artist in field of design works, painting, and drawing. Named one of Women in Bus. Adv. of Yr., U.S. Small Bus. Adminstrn., 1990. Mem. Internat. Assn. Bus. Communicators, Ark. Advt. Fedn. Republican. Mem. Ch. of Christ. Office: Home Entertainment Group Ste 201 10801 Executive Center Dr Little Rock AR 72211

CASTEEL, DIANN BROWN, elementary school educator; b. Greeneville, Tenn., Dec. 16, 1953; d. Harold James Brown and Clara Ruth (Phillips) Johnston; m. Everette Kenneth Casteel, Oct. 7, 1972; children: Trisha DiAnn, Mary Camille, Cheyenne James. BS, East Tenn. State U., 1973, MA, 1976, EdD, 1994. Cert. tchr., Tenn. Tchr. Greene County Bd. Edn., Greeneville, 1973-90; dir. Project Choice, Greeneville-Greene County Ctr. for Tech., 1990-91; tchr. Doak Sch., Tusculum Sta., Tenn., 1992—; founder Iowa-Tenn. Student Exch. Program, Dayton and Greeneville, 1986-87; secondary educator, evening instr. Tusculum Coll., Greenville, Tenn., Guidance and Assessment for Single Parent/Displaced Homemaker Program, 1989-90. Founder, conor Hay Relief Program, Tenn., 1986-87; leader 4-H Club, Baileyton Elem. Sch., 1985-88; mem. Ottway United Meth. Ch., Greenville, 1985-92; v.p. Ottway United Meth. Women, Greeneville, pres., 1976; mem. women's group study exch. to India, Rotary Internat., 1989; mem. 1st Christian Ch., Greenville, Tenn., 1992—. Recipient Horse of Yr. award Appalachian Horse Show Assn., 1967, Outstanding Citizen award Ruritan Nat., 1986, 4-H Emerald Club Leader award, 1987, DIANA award Epsilon Sigma Alpha, 1990, Book of Golden Deeds award Greeneville (Tenn.) Exchange Club, 1992. Mem. NEA, Greene County Edn. Assn., East Tenn. Edn. Assn., Tenn. Edn. Assn., Internat. Platform Assn., U.S.S. Greenville, Inc., Kappa Delta Pi, Phi Delta Kappa. Democrat. Home: 2545 Flatwoods Rd Greeneville TN 37745 Office: Doak Sch Tusculum Sta Greeneville TN 37743

CASTEEN, MARSHA FIELDS, pharmaceutical executive; b. Kinston, N.C., Feb. 1, 1952; d. Marshall Holt and Leora Evelyn (Swanson) Fields; m. Linwood Allen Casteen, May 15, 1970 (div. Feb. 1993); children: James Holt, Taylor Dawn. AD, Cape Fear C.C., Wilmington, N.C., 1972; ADN, U. N.C., Wilmington, 1981, BA in English, 1991. RN, N.C. Sec. First Fed. Savs. and Loan of Tarpon Springs, Holiday, Fla., 1972-74, Integon Ins., Wilmington, N.C., 1974-76; staff nurse New Hanover Regional Med. Ctr., Wilmington, 1981-93; clin. rsch. assoc. Pharm. Product Devel. Inc., Wilmington, 1993-94; asst. project mgr., 1992—. Office: Pharm Product Devel Inc 115 N 3d St 5th Fl Wilmington NC 28409

CASTELLANO, ELIZABETH CHRISTINE, administrative analyst; b. Oława, Poland, Apr. 9, 1950; came to U.S., 1961; d. Roman and Emilia (Pawliszyn) Midera; m. Michael Castellano, Oct. 17, 1971; children: Christopher, Peter. AA in Liberal Arts, Coll. of Staten Island, 1971; AAS in Data Processing, Mercer County C.C., West Windsor, N.J., 1986; BA in Humanities, Thomas A. Edison State Coll., 1991; MPA, Rutgers U., 1994. Data processing programmer N.J. Dept. Treasury, Trenton, 1986-88; adminstrv. analyst N.J. Dept. Transp., Trenton, 1988—. Past trustee Mercer County C.C. Mem. Am. Soc. for Pub. Adminstrn., Data Processing Mgmt. Assn. (past pres., v.p. Mercer County C.C. chpt.), Pi Alpha Alpha, Phi Theta Kappa. Office: NJ Dept Transportation 1035 Parkway Ave Trenton NJ 08625

CASTELLANO, MARY ANN, software engineer; b. Bklyn., Sept. 8, 1962; d. Louis and Mary (Casino) C. BA, Cornell U., 1983; MS, Dartmouth Coll., 1988. Instr. computer Empire Blue Cross Blue Shield, N.Y.C., 1984-86; cons. info. systems Digital Equipment Corp., Concord, Mass., 1988-90; prin. software engr. Digital Equipment Corp., Boxboro, Mass., 1990—; Co-author articles to profl. publs. Mem. Boston chpt. Cornell Alumni Assn. Office: Digital Equipment Corp 85 Swanson Rd Boxboro MA 01719-1367

CASTELLINI, MARY MERCER, author; b. Portland, Oreg., Apr. 4, 1923; d. Reuben Howard and Alma Evangeline (Holmes) Mercer; m. Edgar Aldo Castellini, Aug. 25, 1946 (wid. Febb. 1983); children: Edgar M., Anita M. BA in Am. Civilization, Dominican Coll., 1974. Author; botanical researcher at Herbarium Calif. Acad. Scis., San Francisco, 1984-87. Author: A Victorian Heritage in Old Cow Hollow, 1977, Herbarium Messages from California Flora, 1978, Herbarium: A Noetic Herbal Expedition, 1979; editor: An Anthology of American Women Writers, 1979; exhibitor/lectr./artist San Francisco Pub. Libr., 1977, Marin (Calif.) Pub. Libr./Marin Civic Ctr., 1977, Tiburon Pub. Libr., 1991, Golden Gate Theol. Seminary, Mill Valley, Calif., 1992—. Den leader Boy Scouts Am., Stuart Hall Sch. for Boys, San Francisco, 1955-57; leader Girl Scouts U.S., Convent of the Sacred Heart, San Francisco, 1957-59; mem. Mothers' March on Polio, Polio Soc., San Francisco, 1955; freshman YWCA pres. U. Wash., Seattle, 1943; mem. chorus Emeritus Coll. of Maria. Named Outstanding Californian, Rare Books and Calif. History, The Bancroft Libr., U. Calif. Berkeley, 1993—. Mem. Ina Coolbrith Cir. (life), AAUW (Washington, life, Individual grant Ednl. Found. 1977-78, 78-79), Calif. Botanical Soc., Alpha Chi Omega. Home and Office: 465 Ridge Rd Tiburon CA 94920

CASTELLINI, PATRICIA BENNETT, business management educator; b. Park River, N.D., Mar. 25, 1935; d. Benjamin Beekman Bennett and Alice Catherine (Peerboom) Bennett Breckinridge; m. William McGregor Castellini; children: Bruce Bennett Subhani, Barbara Lea Ragland. AA, Allan Hancock Coll., Santa Maria, Calif., 1964; BS magna cum laude, Coll. Great Falls, 1966; MS, U. N.D., 1967, PhD, 1971. Fiscal acct. USIA, Washington, 1954-56; pub. acct., Bremerton, Wash., 1956; statistician USN, Bremerton, 1957-59; med. svcs. accounts officer U.S. Air Force, Vandenberg AFB, Calif., 1962-64; instr. bus. adminstrn. Western New Eng. Coll., 1967-69; vis. prof. econs. Chapman Coll., 1970; vis. prof. U. So. Calif. systems Griffith AFB, N.Y., 1971-72; assoc. prof., dir. adminstrv. mgmt. program Va. State U., 1973-74; assoc. prof. bus. adminstrn. Oreg. State U., Corvallis, 1974-81, prof. mgmt., 1982-90, emeritus prof. mgmt., 1990—, univ. curriculum coord., 1984-86, dir. adminstrv. mgmt. program, 1974-81, pres. Faculty Senate, 1981, Interinstl. Faculty Senate, 1986-90, pres., 1989-90; exec. dir. Bus. Enterprise Ctr., 1990-92, Enterprise Ctr. L.A., Inc., 1992—; commr. Lafayette Econ. Devel. Authority, 1994—; cons. process tech. devel. Digital Equipment Corp., 1982. Pres., chmn. bd. dirs. Adminstrv. Orgnl. Svcs., Inc., Corvallis, 1976-83, Dynamic Achievement, Inc., 1983-92; bd. dirs. Oreg. State U. Bookstores, Inc., 1987-90, Internat. Trade Adv. Group, 1992—, BBB of Acadiana, 1994—, sec., 1995—, Internat. Trade Devel. Group; exec. dir. Bus. Enterprise Ctr., Inc., 1990-92; dir., cons. Oregonians in Action, 1990-91; commr. Lafayette Econ. Devel. Authority, 1994—. Cert. adminstrv. mgr. Pres. TYEE Mobil Home Park, Inc., 1987-92. Fellow Assn. Bus. Communication (mem. internat. bd. 1980-83, v.p. Northwest 1981, 2d v.p. 1982-83, 1st v.p. 1983-84, pres. 1984-85); mem. Am. Bus. Women's Assn. (chpt. v.p. 1979, pres. 1980, named Top Businesswoman in Nation 1980, Bus. Assoc. Yr. 1986), Assn. Info. Systems Profls., Adminstrv. Mgmt. Soc., AAUP (chpt. sec. 1973, chpt. bd. dirs. 1982, 84-89, pres. Oreg. conf. 1983-85), Am. Vocat. Assn. (nominating com. 1976), Associated Oreg. Faculties, Nat. Bus. Edn. Assn., Nat. Assn. Tchr. Edn. for Bus. Office Edn. (pres. 1976-77, chmn. public relations com. 1978-81), La. Bus. Incubation Assn. (sec.-treas. 1993—), Corvallis Area C. of C. (v.p. chamber devel. 1987-88, pres. 1988-89, chmn. bd. 1989-90, Pres.' award 1986), Boys and Girls Club of Corvallis (pres. 1991-92), Sigma Kappa, Rotary (bd. dirs. 1990-92, 94—, pres.-elect 1992, treas. 1995—). Roman Catholic. Contbr. numerous articles to profl. jours. Office: Enterprise Ctr of La Inc 3419 NW Evangeline Thruway Carencro LA 70520-9000

CASTELLON, CHRISTINE NEW, real estate professional; b. Pittsfield, Mass., June 22, 1957; d. Edward Francis Jr. and Helen Patricia (Cordes) New; m. John Arthur Castellon, Oct. 1, 1988. BS in Elec. and Computer Engring., U. Mass., 1979; MBA, Northeastern U., 1986. Engr. microwave radio system design New Eng. Telephone Co., Framingham, Mass., 1979-82; mgr. minicomputer support group New Eng. Telephone Co., Dorchester, Mass., 1982-85; mgr. current systems planning/network svcs. NYNEX Svc. Co., Boston, 1985-87; mem. tech. staff computing environments Bellcore, Piscataway, N.J., 1987-90; assoc. dir. info. systems provisioning NYNEX Telesector Resources Group, N.Y.C., 1990-93; speaker New Eng. Telephone Careers-In-Engring. Program, 1980-82. Leader 2d violin sect. Cen. Jersey Symphony Orch., Raritan Valley Community Coll., N.J., 1988—; prin. 1st violinist New Eng. Conservatory Extension Div., Boston, 1979-87; violinist Civic Symphony Orch., Boston, 1982-87; active UMASS Coll./Industry Adv. Com. Named Monument Mountain High Sch. valedictorian, 1975; recipient Arion Music award, 1975, cert. Applied Music and Theory Pittsfield Community Music Sch., 1975, Exceptional Merit award NYNEX, 1987. Mem. IEEE, U. Mass. Alumni Assn. (coll./industry adv. com. for women), Northeastern U. MBA Alumni Assn. Roman Catholic. Home: 622 Old York Rd Neshanic Station NJ 08853-3600

CASTELNUOVO-TEDESCO, DIANA, public relations executive; b. L.A., June 22, 1960; d. Pietro and Lisbeth (Stone) C-T. BA, Smith Coll., 1982. Acct. exec. Joanne Creveling, Inc., N.Y.C., 1983-85; publicity mgr. Vogue/Butterick, N.Y.C., 1986-88; sr. acct. exec. Porter/Novelli, N.Y.C., 1988-90, acct. supr., 1990-91, v.p., 1992; exec. dir. pub. rels. Lancaster Group Worldwide, N.Y.C., 1993—. Mem. Pub. Rels. Soc. Am., Fashion Group. Office: Lancaster Group Worldwide 1285 Ave of the Americas New York NY 10019

CASTIGLIONE, KATHIE ANNE, accountant; b. Patchogue, N.Y., Aug. 20, 1951; d. William Arthur and Rosemary Anne (Falvey) Rogers; m James M. Castiglione, Sept. 27, 1969; children: James W., John S. AAS, Suffolk C.C., Riverhead, N.Y., 1982; BBA, Dowling Coll., 1984; MST, L.I. U., 1990. CPA, N.Y. Acct. Center Moriches (N.Y.) Libr., 1983—; adj. asst. prof. Suffolk C.C., Riverhead, 1987-94; instr., lectr. L.I.U.-C.W. Post Campus, Brookville, N.Y., 1992-94; instr. St. Francis Coll., Brooklyn Heights, N.Y., 1994—. Mem. AICPA, N.Y. State Soc. CPAs. Home: 28 Ocean Ave Center Moriches NY 11934-3614

CASTLEBERRY, ARLINE ALRICK, architect; b. Mpls., Sept. 19, 1919; d. Bannona Gerhardt and Meta Emily (Veit) Alrick; m. Donald Montgomery Castleberry, Dec. 25, 1941; children: Karen, Marvin. B in Interior Architecture, U. Minn., 1941; postgrad., U. Tex., 1947-48. Designer, draftsman Elizabeth & Winston Close, Architects, Mpls., 1940-41, Northwest Airlines, Mpls., 1942-43, Cerny & Assocs., Mpls., 1944-46; archtl. draftsman Dominick and Van Benscotten, Washington, 1946-47; ptnr. Castleberry & Davis Bldg. Designers, Burlingame, Calif., 1960-65; prin. Burlingame, 1965-90. Recipient Smith Coll. scholarship. Mem. AIA, Am. Inst. Bldg. Designers (chpt. pres. 1971-72), Commaisini, Alpha Alpha Gamma, Chi Omega. Democrat. Lutheran. Home and Office: 3004 Canyon Rd Burlingame CA 94010-6019

CASTLEBERRY, MAY LEWIS, librarian,curator,editor; b. Midland, Tex., Sept. 26, 1954; d. Frank Petit and Katharine Elizabeth (Egan) Castleberry; m. Michael C. FitzGerald, June 11, 1976. Student, U. Tex.-Austin, 1972-74; BFA, BA, So. Meth. U., Dallas, 1974-76; MS, Columbia U., 1977-78; MA, NYU, 1987. Libr. Whitney Mus., N.Y.C., 1978—. Pub. artists and writers series, Whitney Mus. Am. Arts; dir.: Dal Vero, 1983, Could I Ask You Something?, 1984, The View, 1985, Annie, Gwen, Lilly, Pam and Tulip, 1986, Hiddenness, 1987, My Pretty Pony, 1988, Heat, 1989, Swimming,

1991, Ghost of Chance, 1991, The First Picture Book, 1991. Mem. Art Librs. Soc. N.Am. (George Wittenborn award 1979). Home: 41 5th Ave New York NY 10003 Office: Whitney Mus of Am Art 945 Madison Ave New York NY 10021-2705

CASTLE-JAMES, ELIZABETH ELIZA, religious organization administrator; b. Balt., Nov. 1, 1950; d. John Thomas and Elizabeth Eliza (Wilson) Castle; m. Osborne Samuel James, Jr., Dec. 20, 1980 (div. Nov. 1993); children: Claudia C. Boulware, Richsharia D. Boulware, Kurtson E. Boulware, Curtis R. Boulware II. AA in Criminal Justice, Valencia Community Coll., 1982; DD in Systematic Theology, U. Theology and Theism, 1990; D (Hon), Internat. Theological Seminary, Coll of Theism, 1994. Account exec. Sta. WEBB, Balt., 1975-77; liaison coord. Balt. City Jail, 1977-79; case mgr. Health and Rehabilitative Svcs., Cocoa, Fla., 1980-88; CEO Yissakar Ministries, Gainesville, Fla., 1989-94, Jabbok Ministries, Gainesville, 1991-94, Resurrected Life Ministries, Inc., Sarasota, Fla., 1994—; pres. The House of La E'Shika, Sarasota, 1992—; CEO Resurrected Life Ministries Inc., 1994—; bd. dirs. Jay Ministries, West Palm Beach, Fla., 1993. Co-author: Reflections in Lace, 1992; author: (poetry) Power, 1990 (honorary mention 1990); columnist, religious editor Mahogany Revue, Ocala, Fla., 1992-93; author short story, 1987 (honorary mention 1987); contbr. articles to newspaper. Chairperson Com. for Aged and Disabled Persons, Gainesville, 1993; chmn. grant com. Student Adv. Com. of Howard Bishop Mid. Sch., Gainesville, 1993; candidate City Commr. Dist. I, Gainesville, 1993, 95; mem. leadership bd. Homeless Coalition, Sarasota, 1994—; mem. exec. com. Democratic Club, Sarasota, 1994; bd. dirs. Family Self-Sufficiency Project, Sarasota, 1994—, Common Ground Cmty. Assn. Recipient 1st Willie Bruton award U. Ctrl. Fla., 1982, Dr. Martin L. King scholarship, 1982. Mem. NAFE, God's Women of Power (pres. 1993), Gainesville Women's Network, Phi Beta Kappa, Chi Epsilon. Democrat. Office: House of La E'Shika PO Box 49796 Sarasota FL 34230-6796

CASTLEN, PEGGY LOU, insurance company executive; b. Parkersburg, W.Va., Sept. 7, 1939; d. Ted and Nina Leone (Wehler) Swartz; m. Tom Mefford Castlen, June 16, 1962 (div. Oct. 30, 1987); children: Michael Alan, Thomas Matthew, Cynthia Anne. BS in Edn., Miami U., 1961; M of Human Resource Devel., Univ. Assocs., San Diego, 1983. Lic. personal lines ins. agt.; CPCU. Elem. tchr. various sch. systems, Dearborn, Mich., 1961-62, Chgo., 1962-64, Oxford, Bluffton, Ohio, 1964-65, 65-66; dir. Bluffton (Ohio) Community Nursery Sch., 1969-71; coord. Assn. for Effectiveness Trainers, Columbus, Ohio, 1974-77; ind. tng. cons. Columbus and Portland, Oreg., 1971-80; office svcs. supr. NERCO, Inc., Portland, Oreg., 1980-85; personnel div. mgr. Nationwide Mut. Ins. Co., Portland, Oreg., 1985-89, field sales mgr., 1989-90; life co. human resources officer Nationwide Ins., Columbus, 1990—; cons., com. bd. mem. Jr. Achievement, Portland, 1981-85; assessor-cons., bd. dirs. Employment Connection, Beaverton, Oreg., 1980-85. Chairperson United Way Campaign Nationwide Regional Office, Portland, 1989; chairperson adv. com. Lake Oswego (Oreg.) Sch. Dist., 1985-88; elder, trustee United Presbyn. Ch., Beaverton, 1978-81, Columbus, 1975-77; mem. adv. bd. Downtown Cmty. Based Program, 1993—. Recipient Vol. of Yr. award Nationwide Civic Action Program, 1989; named to Drummer's Soc., 1990. Mem. Soc. for Human Resource Mgmt., Am. Mgmt. Assn., Profl. Ins. Pers. Adminstrs., CPCU Soc. (editor newsletter), Nationwide Ins. Enterprise Human Resources Coun. Presbyterian. Office: Nationwide Ins Co One Nationwide Pla Columbus OH 43216

CASTO, DONNA GAY, librarian, media specialist; b. Las Crucas, N.Mex., Aug. 13, 1953; d. Donald LeRoy and Gayle Beatrice (Johnson) Wood; m. Verlan Casto, Dec. 31, 1970; children: Jarrett Neil, Marissa Diane, Bethany Janelle. BS in Bus. Edn., Ark. Tech. U., Russellville, 1990; MS in Edn. Media/Libr. Sci., U. Ctrl. Ark., 1992. Bus. edn. instr. North Ctrl. Vo-Tech., Leslie, Ark., 1992; libr. media specialist Witts Springs (Ark.) Sch., 1990—. Vice-chair Dem. Election Com., Van Buren County, Ark., 1990—; treas. Witts Springs PTA, 1990—. Recipient Wall Street Jour. award, 1990. Mem. NEA/Ark. Edn. Assn. (pres. local dist. 1992—).

CASTOR, CAROL JEAN, artist, teacher; b. Bend, Oreg., Feb. 3, 1944; d. Keith and Lena (Morara) Morrison; m. William Harold Castor, Aug. 28, 1965; 1 child, William Franklin. BFA, U. Okla., 1967; postgrad., U. Tulsa, summer 1976, Art Student's League of N.Y., N.Y.C., summer 1984. Dir. art dept. Jefferson Jr. High Sch., Oklahoma City, 1967-68; art instr. Vinita (Okla.) High Sch., 1976-80; profl. artist specializing in commd. portraiture Carol Castor Art Studio, Vinita, 1980—, profl. artist commd. for portraits of Native Ams. & Cowboys, 1980—; maintains Window Gallery on Mainstreet Vinita. Exhibited in permanent colls.: Vinita Pub. Libr., 1st Nat. Bank & Trust, Vinita, Cowgirl Hall of Fame and Western Heritage Ctr., Hereford, Tex., Okla. Hall of Fame, Oklahoma City; featured in 2d edit. of American Artists: An Illustrated Survey of Leading Contemporaries; portraits represented by Grand Cen. Galleries, N.Y.; represented in permanent collection of Okla. U. Med. Sch., Okla. City. Mem. Mayor's Adv. Com., Vinita, 1972-74, Vinita Pub. Libr. Bldg. Com., 1974-75; charter mem. Vinita chpt. Okla. Alliance for Mentally Ill, 1986—; organizer, mem. com. Young Life, Vinita, 1987—, chronically and mentally ill Vinita Day Ctr. Inc., 1987—; organizer Ea. Trails Art Assn., 1972—. Recipient Best Banner award Nat. Conv. AAUW, Albuquerque, 1979, AAUW Women of Acheivement award, Vinita, 1985, Community Svc. award Vinita C. of C., 1984, Hall of Fame, 1993. Mem. AAUW (pres. Vinita chpt. 1972-74), P.E.O. Am. Soc. Portrait Artists. Democrat. Episcopalian. Home and Studio: 121 Jennie Ln Vinita OK 74301

CASTOR, PAMELA L., principal; b. Osceola, Ark., Jan. 1, 1958; d. C. L. Shoemaker; m. Jerry L. Castor, Dec. 22, 1984. BS, Ark. State U., 1979, MEd, 1987. Tchr., trainer Manila (Ark.) Pub. Schs., 1980-89; elem. sch. prin. Manila Pub. Schs., 1990—. Bd. dirs. Northeast Ark. Disabilities Coun., Manila, 1989-91. Mem. ASCD, Alpha Delta Kappa (pres. 1987-88), Phi Delta Kappa. Methodist. Office: Manila Elem Sch PO Box 670 Manila AR 72442-0670

CASTORINO, SUE, communications executive; b. Columbus, Ohio, May 5, 1953; m. Randy Minkoff, Oct. 29, 1983. BS in Speech, Northwestern U., Evanston, Ill., 1975. Grad. fellow Ohio Gov.'s Sch., Columbus, 1975; producer, community affairs WBBM-TV (CBS all-news)), Chgo., 1975; news anchor, reporter Sta. WBBM, Chgo., 1981-86; news reporter WHTH-AM/FM, Newark, Ohio, 1975; news anchor, reporter WERE-AM (NBC all-news), Cleve., 1975-78, WWWE-AM (ABC), Cleve., 1978-81; founder, pres. Sue Castorino: The Speaking Specialist, Chgo., 1986—; guest lectr. various groups in bus., medicine, govt., law, sports, fin., worldwide, 1986—; leader media and presentation skills seminars; pvt. voice coach, 1986—. Author: North Shore Mag., 1987—; voice-over and on-camera talent, 1986—. Recipient Golden Gavel award Chgo. Soc. Assn. Execs., 1991, various news reporting awards AP, UPI, Chgo., 1981-86. Mem. Sigma Delta Chi. Office: The Speaking Specialist 435 N Michigan Ave Ste 2700 Chicago IL 60611-4009

CASTRO, AMUERFINA TANTIONGCO, geriatrics nurse; b. Morong, Rizal, Philippines, July 30, 1942; d. Eusebio and Juana (Victorio) Tantiongco; m. El B. Castro, Apr. 6, 1966; children: Cesar, El Jr., Christopher. BSN, U. East, Quezon City, Philippines, 1963; MA in Nursing, NYU, 1975. Cert. in oncology and gerontology nursing. Mem. staff U. East Ramon Magsaysay Meml. Med. Ctr., Quezon City, 1963-64; mem. faculty St. Catherine Sch. Nursing, Quezon City, 1964-65; operating room nurse Fordham Hosp. and Union Hosp., Bronx, N.Y., 1966-69; staff nurse in chemotherapy rsch. Meml. Hosp.-Sloan Kettering, N.Y.C., 1969-74; charge nurse Greenbrook (N.J.) Manor Nursing Home, 1989—. Vice-chmn., trustee Found. Philippine-Am. Med. Soc. N.J., 1990—. Mem. ANA, N.J. Nurses Assn., Philippine Nurses Assn. Am. (bd. dirs., nat. svc. award 1988-90), Philippine Nurses Assn. N.J. (pres., adv. bd., outstanding mem. award 1986—), U. East Ramon Magsaysay Meml. Med. Ctr. Nursing Alumni Assn. U.S.A. (pres. 1988-92, mem. adv. bd., Outstanding Alumni in Cmty. Svc. award 1993), Sigma Theta Tau Internat. (Mu Theta chpt.).

CASTRO, JAN GARDEN, author, arts consultant, educator; b. St. Louis, June 8, 1945; d. Harold and Estelle (Fischer) Garden; 1 child, Jomo Jemal. Student, Cornell U., 1963-65; B.A. in English, U. Wis., 1967; publishing cert., Radcliffe Coll., 1967; M.A.T., Washington U., St. Louis, 1974, MA, 1994. Life cert. tchr. secondary English, speech, drama and social studies, Mo. Tchr., writer St. Louis, 1970—; dir. Big River Assn., St. Louis, 1975-85; lectr. Lindenwood Coll., 1980—; co-founder, dir. Duff's Poetry Series, St. Louis, 1975-81; founder, dir. River Styx P.M. Series, St. Louis, 1981-83; arts cons. Harris-Stowe State Coll., 1986-87. Contbg. author: San Francisco Rev. Books, 1982-85, Am. Book Rev., 1990—, Mo. Rev., 1991, Newsletters, 1993, Tampa Rev., 1994—, The Nation, Am. Poetry Rev.; author books including Mandala of the Five Senses, 1975, The Art and Life of Georgia O'Keeffe, 1985, paperback edit., 1995; editor: River Styx mag., 1975-86; co-editor: Margaret Atwood: Vision and Forms, 1988; TV host and co-prodr. The Writers Circle, Double Helix, St. Louis, 1987-89. Mem. University City Arts and Letters Commn., Mo., 1983-84. Recipient Arts and Letters award St. Louis Mag., 1985, Editor's award and editor during G.E. Younger Writer's award to River Styx Mag., Coordinating Coun. for Literary Mags., 1986, Arts award Mandrake Soc. Charity Ball, 1988, Leadership award YWCA St. Louis, 1988; NEH fellow UCLA, 1988, Johns Hopkins U., 1990. Mem. MLA, Margaret Atwood Soc. (founder). Home: 7420 Cornell Ave Saint Louis MO 63130-2914 Office: Lindenwood College Saint Charles MO 63301

CASTRO, MARJORIE ELLEN, assistant superintendent; b. N.Y.C.; d. Adam Wilkens and Beatrice (Summers) Merle; m. Ray John Castro, Sept. 9, 1967; children: Thomas Scott, Daniel John, Christine Lynne. BS, Bucknell U., 1964; MA, Columbia U., 1967, EdD, 1990. Tchr. Newton (Mass.) Pub. Schs., 1964-66; fed. reading cons. Prince Georges County Pub. Schs., Marlboro, Md., 1967-69; tchr., reading specialist, dist. reading coord. Valhalla (N.Y.) Pub. Schs., 1969-82; from elem. sch. prin. to mid. sch. prin. Dobbs Ferry (N.Y.) Pub. Schs., 1982-93; asst. supt. curriculum and instrn. Bedford Ctrl. Schs., Mount Kisco, N.Y., 1993—; mentor Assn. Women Adminstrs. of Westchester, 1987-90, Coll. of New Rochelle (N.Y.) Mentor Program, 1986-87. Co-author: (children's book) We Must Say "No!", 1990. Recipient Sivak Premier Contbn. award Dobbs Ferry Sivak Award Com., Nat. Coun. of Adminstrv. Women in Edn., 1990, Leadership and Rsch. award Nat. Coun. of Women in Edn., Assn. Women Adminstrs. of Westchester Rsch. award, 1989. Mem. Nat. Coun. Adminstrv. Women in Edn. (v.p. 1994—), Assn. Women Adminstrs. Westchester (pres. 1992-93), N.Y. State Assn. Women Adminstrs. (exec. bd.), Phi Delta Kappa (Kappan of Yr. Pace U. chpt. 1990). Unitarian. Home: 36 Easton Ave White Plains NY 10605 Office: Bedford Ctrl Schs Adminstrv Office Fox Ln Campus PO Box 180 Mount Kisco NY 10549

CASWALL DEVEY, EMILY JANE, organization administrator; b. Cleve., Apr. 17, 1954; d. Edward L. and Virginia (Reynolds) C.; children: Hannah, Cas. BA in English, Ursuline Coll., Cleve., 1979. Group mgr. Halle's Dept. Store, Mentor, Ohio, 1973-81; asst. store mgr. T.J. Maxx, Mentor, 1981-82; store mgr. Lane Bryant, West Palm Beach, Fla., 1983-84; asst. store mgr. J. Bryon's, Miami, Fla., 1984-86; tchr. phys. edn. Laurel Sch., Shaker Heights, Ohio, 1986-89; dir. Mall Network Publs., Beachwood, Ohio, 1989; asst. dir. Falcon Camp, Cleve., 1991—; co-chmn. Cleve. mag., 1988. Chmn. playground fund raising Temple Emmanuel, University Heights, Ohio, 1989-91; mem. Hadassah, Cleve., 1984—; ofcl. OHSA. Mem. Fashion Group Cleve., U.S. Field Hockey Assn. (NE Ohio Field Hockey Coach of Yr. 1988). Republican. Office: Falcon Camp 4251 Delta Rd SW Carrollton OH 44615 also: Delta Rd SW Carrollton OH 44615

CASWELL, DOROTHY ANN COTTRELL, arts administrator; b. N.Y.C., Dec. 18, 1938; d. Donald Peery and Eleanor Hildaborg (Westberg) Cottrell; m. Allen Edward Caswell, Oct. 24, 1959; children: David Alan, Bruce Leland. Student, Carleton Coll., Northfield, MN., 1956-59; AB in Psych., George Wash. U., 1960-61; postgrad., SUNY, Oneonta, 1971-76. Sec. U.S. Fgn. Service, Tunis, Tunisia, 1959-61; mng. dir. Glimmerglass Opera, Inc., Cooperstown, N.Y., 1975-78; exec. dir. Upper Catskill Community Council on the Arts, Oneonta, N.Y., 1978-80; devel. officer Catskill Arts Consortium, Oneonta, 1981-83; devel. cons. Otsego Urban Rural Self-Devel. Assocs., Inc., Oneonta, 1982-83; co-founder, pres. Catskill Choral Soc., 1970-76, 81-84; assoc. producer Orpheus Theatre, Inc., Oneonta, 1984-91; voice tchr. Oneonta, 1984—; ptnr., co-owner OnStage Prodn. Svcs., 1991—; cons., arts adminstrv. Doroothy Caswell Assocs., Oneonta, 1981—; past pres., mem. sub-area coun. Health Sys. Agy. N.E. N.Y., also mem. planning adv. group and rev. adv. Singer/actress with Orpheus Theatre, 1984—; actress WSKG-TV Pub. TV film series Susquehanna Stories, 1990. Vol., mem. chorus Glimmerglass Opera Cooperstown, 1974—; mem. mil. acad. selection com. for Congressman Sherwood Boehlert of N.Y.; mem. Otsego County Health Planning Adv. Coun.; bd. dirs. Otsego County Tourism Bur., 1987-90, Oneonta Downtown Coalition, 1982-84. Honored for outstanding performance and svcs. to the community, SUNY, 1975. Mem. Ostego County C. of C., Oneonta Profl. Women's Network. Democrat. Protestant.

CASWELL, FRANCES PRATT, retired English language educator; b. Brunswick, Maine, June 25, 1929; d. Harold Edward and Marian Elizabeth (Nicoll) Pratt; m. Forrest Wilbur Caswell, June 30, 1956; children: Lucy Caswell Hilburn, Helen Caswell Watts, Harold F. BA, U. Maine, 1951; MA, U. Mich., 1955. Tchr. English, Bridgton (Maine) High Sch., 1951-54, Grosse Point (Mich.) High Sch., 1955-56; instr. South Maine Tech. Coll., South Portland, 1968-84, chmn. dept., 1984-93; bd. dirs. Maine Vocat. Region 10. Contbg. author: Brunswick, Maine, 250 Years A Town, 1989. Pres. United Pejepscot Housing Inc., Brunswick, 1987-93. Mem. AAUW, Nat. Coun. Tchrs. English, Casco Bay Art League. Republican. Methodist.

CASWELL, LINDA KAY, insurance agency executive; b. Canton, Ohio, Sept. 29, 1952; d. Lloyd Norman and Eva Mae (Clark) C. Grad. high sch., Canton, Ohio. Office mgr., sec. Harold Dickinson Architect, Canton, 1970-73; dist. mgr., sec., clk. Met. Life Ins., Canton, 1973-80, office mgr., 1980-86; brokerage assoc. Met. Brokerage, Canton, 1986-89; owner, pres. Golden Horizons Ins. Agy., Canton, 1987—. Office: Golden Horizons Ins Agy 5874 Fulton Dr NW Canton OH 44718-1735

CATALANO, JANE DONNA, lawyer; b. Schenectady, N.Y., Feb. 21, 1957; d. Alfred and Joan (Futscher) Martini; m. Peter Catalano, June 18, 1988. BA, SUNY, Plattsburgh, 1979; JD, Albany Law Sch., 1982. Bar: N.Y. 1983, U.S. Dist. Ct. 1983. Atty. Pentak, Brown & Tobin, Albany, N.Y., 1982-87, Niagara Mohawk Power Corp., Albany, 1987—. Mem. N.Y. State Bar Assn., Albany County Bar Assn. Home: 7 Blackburn Way Latham NY 12110-1943 Office: Niagara Mohawk Power Corp PO Box 591 111 Washington Ave Albany NY 12201

CATALFAMO, JANICE STELLA, financial consultant; b. Rochester, N.Y., Mar. 21, 1936; d. Anthony R. and Josephine (Di Sano) Barone; m. Carmen J. Catalfamo; children: Jomaine, Kenneth, Anthony, Kevin. Student, Monroe Community Coll. Lic. ins. agt., N.Y.; cert. real estate, N.Y.; notary pub., N.Y. Rep. customer svc. Rochester Community Savs. Bank, 1976-86; dist. rep. Prudential Fin. Svcs., 1988—; owner, ptnr. Richmond Precision Mfg., Inc., 1990—; fin. cons. telecommunications co. start-up, Rochester, 1989—. Active Boy Scouts Am.; former troup leader Girl Scouts U.S.A.; active various polit. campaigns; mem. adv. com. N.Y. State Legislature; coord. family ct. judge campaign; sec., treas. Pop Warner Football League. Mem. NAFE, Life Underwriters Assn., Nat. Assn. Profl. Sales Women, Women of Round Table. Republican. Roman Catholic. Home: 11 Neville Ln Rochester NY 14618 Office: Prudential Fin Svcs 1701 Lac Deville Blvd Rochester NY 14618

CATALFO, BETTY MARIE, health service executive, nutritionist; b. N.Y.C., Nov. 2, 1942; d. Lawrence Santo and Gemma (Patrone) Lorefice; children—Anthony, Lawrence, Donna Marie. Grad. Newtown High Sch., Elmhurst, N.Y., 1958. Sec., clk. ABC-TV, N.Y.C., 1957-60; lectr., nutritionist Weight Watchers, Manhasset, N.Y., 1965-76; founder, pres. Every-Bodys Diet, Inc. dba Stay Slim, Queens, N.Y., 1976—; dir. in-home program N.Y. State Dept. Health, N.Y.C., 1985—; founder, pres. Delitegul Diet Foods, Inc., 1988—; lectr. in field. Author: 101 Stay-Slim Recipes, 1983, Get Slim and Stay Slim Diet Cook Book, rev. ed., 1987, Diet Revolution, 1991, Holiday Cookbook, 1992, Eating Out, 1994, Change or Select, 1994, Calories Do Count!, 1994, Fat Free Receipes, 1994; Author, dir., producer: (video) Dancersize for Overweight, 1986, Get Slim and Stay Slim Diet Cook Book, Eating Right for Your Life, Hello It's Me and I'm Slim; author, editor: (video) Eating Right For Life, 1985, Isometric Techniques for Weight Reduction, Dance Your Calories A-Weigh; author, producer: (video) Eating Habits, 1986—; (video) Isometric Techniques for Weight Reduction, 1986, Patience Is a Virtue When Weight Loss is the Goal, 1986, Slow Down you Eat to Fast, 1994, Always Giving Never Receiving, 1994, Relax and Don't You Worry, 1994; producer, dir.: (video) Positive and Negative Diet Forces, 1987, (video) Hello It's Me and I'm Thin, 1987, (video) Dance Your Calories A-Weigh, 1987, (video) Positive and Negative Diet Forces, 1987. Sponsor, lectr. St. Pauls Ctr., Bklyn., 1981—, Throgs Neck Assn. Retarded Children, Bronx, 1985—; active ARC, LWV, Am. Italian Assn., United Way Greenwich, Council Chs. and Synagogues, Heart Assn., N.Y. Meals on Wheels, 1985—, Health Assn. Fairfield County, Food Svcs. for Homeless People, 1993, 94, 95; chairperson, sponsor Battered Women, 1994—. Named Woman of Yr., Bayside Womens Club, N.Y., 1983, O, PK Woman of Yr., 1986—, Woman of Yr. Richmond Boys Club, 1987, Woman of Yr. Bronx Press Club Assn., 1987; recipient Merit award for Svc. Cath. Archdiocese of Bklyn., 1985, Merit award Svcs. Cath. Archdioces of Bklyn. and Queens, 1992, 93, 94, Community Service award Sr. Citizens Sacred Heart League Bklyn./Queens Archdiocese. N.Y. State Nutritional Guidance for Children Nat. Assn. Scis. Mem. Nat. C. of C. for Women (Woman of Yr. 1987, 90), Pres.'s Coun. on Nutrition, Roundtable for Women in Food Service, Bus. and Profl. Women's Club, Pres. Council for Phys. Fitness, Nat. Assn. Female Execs., Assn. for Fitness in Bus. Inc., Nat. Assn. Female Bus. Owners. Democrat. Roman Catholic. Club: Mothers Sacred Heart Sch. (chairperson 1979-82). Avocations: reading; travel, golf, family. Home: 21422 27th Ave Flushing NY 11360-2608 also: 58 Riverview Ct Greenwich CT 06831-4127 Office: 10005 101st Ave Ozone Park NY 11416-2610

CATANESE, KATHLEEN SMITH, art educator; b. Trenton, N.J., Apr. 21, 1949; d. Peter Joseph and Mabel Marie (Smith) C.; m. Frank John Bitetto, Dec. 27, 1975; children: Mary Anne, Tricia Megan. BS, Trenton State Coll., 1972. Cert. art tchr. grades K-12, elem. edn. tchr. grades K-8, N.J. Asst. dir. young printmakers workshop Trenton (N.J.) State Coll., 1972-73; art tchr. Summit (N.J.) Bd. Edn., 1972-75, Union (N.J.) Twp. Bd. Edn., 1975-76, Hamilton Twp. (N.J.) Bd. Edn., 1977-84, 88—; chairperson Am. Edn. Week Com., Hamilton Twp., 1992—; workshop presenter in field. Author, illustrator: The Sun Sent Streaks, 1991 (N.J. Bell award 1991); artist for various books; exhibited in group shows at Morris Mus., Morristown, N.J., 1994, Phillips Mill, New Hope, Pa., 1994. Organizer Active Citizens for the Environment, East Amwell, N.J., 1992—. Recipient Gov.'s Tchr. Recognition award State of N.J., 1991; grantee Geraldine R. Dodge Found., Morristown, N.J., 1993. Mem. NEA, N.J. Edn. Assn., Nat. Art Edn. Assn., Art Educators N.J. (corr. sec./publicity youth art month asst.), Seminar For Rsch. in Art Edn., Ctr. for Book Arts, Printmaking Coun. N.J. Democrat. Roman Catholic. Home: PO Box 387 Ringoes NJ 08551 Office: Hamilton Twp Bd Edn 90 Park Ave Hamilton Square NJ 08690

CATE, JEAN MCGREGOR, school system administrator; b. Batlesville, Okla., Nov. 23, 1946; d. James Wilson and Dorothy (Ellis) McGregor; m. John Griffin Cate, Aug. 24, 1968; children: Jeffrey, Steven. BS in Zoology, U. Okla., 1970, MEd in Sci. Edn., 1982, secondary adminstrn. cert., 1984. Tchr. sci. Dist 73 1/2 Schs., Skokie, Ill., 1970-71, Southport High Sch., Indpls., 1971-72; tchr. sci. Norman (Okla.) Pub. Schs., 1972-76, tchr. biology, 1978-84, elem. sci. cons., 1985-86, drug, bus. and computer dir., 1986-92, dir. health curriculum, 1992—. Author: Investigations in Natural Science: Biology, 1984; contbr. articles to profl. jours. Treas. Norman Dem. Women, 1983-86; county chmn. March of Dimes, Norman, 1977; pres. Lincoln Elem. Sch. PTA, Norman, 1983, 87; bd. dirs. Juvenile Svcs. Inc., Norman; chmn. edn. com. Okla. Drug and Alcohol Policy Bd., 1993-94. Recipient Patron of Yr. award Lincoln Elem. Sch., 1987, Four-Way Test award Norman Rotary Club, 1992, prevention advocacy award Okla. Prevention Network, 1992. Mem. ASCD, Okla. Acad. for State Goals (co-chmn. curriculum 1989-90), Phi Delta Kappa. Presbyterian. Office: Norman Pub Schs 131 S Flood Ave Norman OK 73069

CATELL, PADMA JOY, psychologist, educator, dean; b. N.Y.C., Jan. 17, 1944; d. Joseph Cicatelli and Belle (Mishkind) Diamond; m. Peter Lampell, Mar. 4, 1965 (div. July 1971). BA in Biology, CUNY-Hunter Coll., 1969; MA in Biology, CUNY, 1971; PhD in Psychology, Calif. Inst. Integral Studies, 1984. Lic. psychologist, lic. marriage, family and child counselor, Calif. Biomed. rsch. grad. fellow CUNY-Hunter Coll., 1971; counselor Cathedral Hill Hosp., San Francisco, 1971-75; co-founder, dir. Buena Vista Women's Svcs., San Francisco, 1975-81; dir. Buena Vista Counseling Ctr., San Francisco, 1979—; asst. prof. psychology Calif. Inst. Integral Studies, San Francisco, 1984—, dean Sch. Healing Arts, 1993—; ptnr./therapist Mariposa Counseling Ctr., San Rafael, Calif., 1992—. Pres. Coalition for Med. Rights of Women, San Francisco, 1974-76. Mem. APA, Calif. Assn. Marriage and Family Therapists. Office: Buena Vista Counseling Ctr 801 Portola Dr San Francisco CA 94127-1234

CATES, JO ANN, librarian, management consultant; b. Ft. Worth, June 25, 1958; d. Charles Kimbrough and Lydia Joe (Sachse) C.; m. Joseph Daniel Frank, Oct. 28, 1989; 1 child, Jacob Abraham Frank, Dec. 9, 1993. BS in Journalism, Boston U., 1980; MLS, Simmons Coll., 1984. Advt. asst. Boston Phoenix, 1978-79; med. serials asst. Mass. Gen. Hosp., Boston, 1979-80; editorial asst. Exceptional Parent Mag., Boston, 1980-81; libr. reference asst. Lesley Coll., Cambridge, Mass., 1981-84; head reference libr. Lamont Libr., Harvard U., Cambridge, Mass., 1984-85; chief libr. Poynter Inst. for Media Studies, St. Petersburg, Fla., 1985-91; head transp. libr. Northwestern U., Evanston, Ill., 1991-94; tchr. News Libr. and Newsroom Seminars Poynter Inst., 1990-91; mem. Harvard Com. on Instrn. Libr. Use, 1984, mem. adv. com. on book and serial budgets, 1991-94; cons. journalism orgns. Calif., Fla., Mass., 1984—; book reviewer Libr. Jour., Choice, 1985—, Am. Reference Book Annual, 1993—. Author: Journalism: A Guide to the Reference Literature, 1990; editor Transp. Divsn. Bull., 1992-94; mem. editorial bd. Footnotes, 1991-94; contbr. articles to profl. jours. Mem. Transp. Rsch. Bd. Info. Svcs. Com., 1991-94; media intern Dem. Nat. Com., Boston, 1979-80. Scholar Women in Comm., 1976-78; Trustee scholar Boston U., 1978-80; Simmons Coll. grantee, 1982-84. Mem. Spl. Librs. Assn., Assn. for Edn. in Journalism and Mass Comm., Suncoast Info. Specialists (pres. 1990-91). Home: 500 Sheridan Rd # 1E Evanston IL 60202

CATES, Z. VIRGINIA GRUYE, interior designer; b. Mpls., July 24, 1937; d. Raymond C. and Florence (Tiden) Gruye; m. Dennis M. Cates, Aug. 1, 1981; children: Michelle, Douglas, Ginger, Laural. Student, U. Minn., 1959-63; cert. in interior design, West Valley Coll., 1991. Cert. interior designer, Calif. Prin. designer Nouveaux Design, San Jose, Calif., 1984-87; prin. designer, pres. Nouveaux Design, Inc., San Jose, 1987—; mem. discover design adv. coun. Showplace Sq. Group, San Francisco, 1992-94; bd. dirs. Found. Mind/Being-Rsch. Orgn., Los Altos, Calif., 1980—. Mem. Am. Soc. Interior Designers, Interior Design Guild of Saratoga. Democrat. Unitarian. Office: Nouveaux Design Inc 860 Hampswood Way San Jose CA 95120

CATHER, PHYLLIS BAKER, pediatrics nurse; b. Bubbling Springs, Capon Bridge, W.Va., Aug. 7; d. Burzie Carmelias Sr. and Daisy Violet (Rowland) Baker; m. George William Cather Sr., Apr. 23, 1960; children: George William Cather, Jr., Natalie Jo Cather Miller, Marietta Dale Cather Walls, Edwin Baker Cather, Brian Lee Cather. Diploma, Winchester (Va.) Meml. Hosp., 1957; student, Med. Coll. Va., 1956; BSN, Richmond (Va.) Profl. Inst., 1960. RN, Va.; cert. pediatric nurse. Staff nurse Stuart Circle Hosp., Richmond, 1957-58; staff nurse pediatrics Med. Coll. Va., Richmond, 1958-60; staff nurse pediatrics Winchester Med. Ctr., 1960—, pediatric and nursery nurse, 1979—; pediatric nurse, 1984-94. Vol. substitute sch. nurse, 1973-84.

CATHEY, MARY ELLEN JACKSON, religious studies educator; b. Florence, S.C., Jan. 12, 1926; d. John William and Mary Ellen (Heinrich) Jackson; m. Henry Marcellus Cathey, May 31, 1958; children: Mary Emily Cathey Ewell, Henry Marcellus Jr. AB, Winthrop Coll., 1947; MRE, Presbyn. Sch. Christian Edn., Richmond, Va., 1953. Cert. Christian educator. Tchr. English, drama Jenkins Jr. High Sch., Spartanburg, S.C., 1947-51; dir. Christian edn. First Presbyn. Ch., Anderson, S.C., 1953-56, Bethesda (Md.) Presbyn. Ch., 1956-59; organizer, dir. Co-op Nursery Sch., Bethesda Presbyn. Ch., 1967-70; dir. Christian edn. Potomac Presbyn. Ch., Potomac, Md., 1977-83, Bethesda Presbyn. Ch., 1983-85, Nat. Presbyn. Ch., Washington, 1985-88; freelance cons. and educator Nat. Capital Presbytery, Washington, 1988—; edn. cons. Covenant Presbyn. Ch., Arlington, Va., 1987, First Presbyn. Ch., Arlington, 1989-91, Lewinsville Presbyn. Ch.,

McLean, 1990; elder Nat. Presbyn. Ch., 1990—; elder commr. Gen. Assy., Presbyn. Ch., Milw., 1992. Author hymn text: God Almighty, God Eternal, 1956, others, numerous poems; co-author: Confirmation Guidebook, 1988, The Circle of Wholeness, 1991. Active in past various civic orgns. Recipient Sparkler Award Presbyn. Sch. of Christian Edn. Alumni/ae Coun., 1991. Mem. Hymn Soc., Presbyn. Writers' Guild, Presbyn. Assn. Musicians, Assn. Presbyn. Ch. Educators, Nat. Capital Presbytery Educators. Home and Office: 1817 Bart Dr Silver Spring MD 20905

CATHOU, RENATA EGONE, chemist, consultant; b. Milan, Italy, June 21, 1935; d. Egon and Stella Mary Egone; m. Pierre-Yves Cathou, June 21, 1959. BS, MIT, 1957, PhD, 1963. Postdoctoral fellow, research assoc. in chemistry MIT, Cambridge, 1962-65; research assoc. Harvard U. Med. Sch., Cambridge, 1965-69, instr., 1969-70; research assoc. Mass. Gen. Hosp., 1965-69, instr., 1969-70; asst. prof. dept. biochemistry Sch. Medicine, Tufts U., 1970-73, assoc. prof., 1973-78, prof., 1978-81; pres. Tech. Evaluations, Lexington, Mass., 1983—; sr. cons. SRC Assocs., Park Ridge, N.J., 1984-93; sr. investigator Arthritis Found., 1970-75; vis. prof. dept. chemistry UCLA, 1976-77; mem. adv. panel NSF, 1974-75; mem. bd. sci. counselors Nat. Cancer Inst., 1979-83; ind. cons. and writer. Mem. editorial bd. Immunochemistry, 1972-75; contbr. chpts. to books and articles to profl. jours. MIT Company Founders citation, 1989; NIH predoctoral fellow, 1958-62; grantee Am. Heart Assn., 1969-81, USPHS, 1970-81. Mem. AAAS, Am. Soc. for Biochemistry and Molecular Biology, Am. Assn. Immunologists, U.S. Power Squadron (dist. lt. comdr.), Charles River Squadron (past comdr.). Office: Tech Evaluations PO Box 23 Lexington MA 02173

CATLETT, ELIZABETH, sculptor, printmaker, educator; b. Washington, Apr. 15, 1919; d. John and Mary (Carson) C.; m. Francisco Mora, Oct. 31, 1946; children: Francisco Mora, Juan Mora, David Mora. BS Art cum laude, Howard U., 1936; MFA, State U. Iowa, 1940; studied with Ossip Zadkine, N.Y.C., 1943; HLD (hon.), Morgan State U., 1993, Tulane U., 1995; PhD (hon.), Spellman Coll., 1995; DFA (hon.), Parsons Sch. Design, 1995. Art dept. head Dillard U., New Orleans, 1940-42; instr., promotions dir. G.W. Carver Sch., N.Y.C., 1944-45; prof. sculpture Nat. Sch. Fine Arts, Mexico City, 1958-76; head sculpture coll. Nat. Autonomous U. Mex., 1959-76; artist in residence U. Mich., Ann Arbor, 1990. One woman shows include Barnett Aden Gallery, Washington, 1947-48, Nat. Sch. Fine Arts, Mexico City, 1962, Modern Art Mus., Mexico City, 1970, Studio Mus. Harlem, 1971-72, Tobey Moss Gallery, L.A., 1981, New Orleans Mus. Art, 1983, Main Pub. Libr., Miami, Fla., 1984, Howard U., Washington, 1984, Miss. Mus. Art, 1986, Ariz. State U., 1987, Montgomery (Ala.) Mus. Art, 1991, Montclair (N.J.) Mus. Art, 1991, Time Warner Gallery, N.Y.C., 1992, June Kelly Gallery, N.Y.C., 1993, Isobel Neal Gallery-1 Space, Chgo., 1994, others; exhibited in group shows at Taller de Grafica Popular, Salon de la Plastica Mexicana, Mex., N.Y., Chgo., Washington, Balt., L.A., Atlanta, others, internationally in Moscow, Paris, Prague, Leipzig, Tokyo, Warsaw, Peking, Belgrade, Montreal, Berlin, Havana, others, 1951-89; represented in permanent collections Atlanta Univ., Balt. Mus. Art, City New Orleans, Cleve. Mus. Art, Colgate-Palmolive, Fisk U., Hampton U., High Mus., Howard U., Inst. Politecnico Nacional, Mex., Libr. Congress, Met. Mus., Miss. Mus. Art, Museo de Arte Moderno, Mex., Mus. Modern Art, Nat. Inst. Fine Arts, Mex., Narodniko Musea, Prague, Nat. Mus. Am. Art, New Orleans Mus. Art, Schomburg Ctr. Rsch. Black Culture, Secretaria de Educacion Publica, Mex., Studio Mus., Harlem, Wadsworth Atheneum. Recipient 1st prize sculpture Golden Jubilee Nat. Exposition, 1941, Tlatlico prize 1st Sculpture Biannual, 1962, Xipe Totec prize 2d Sculpture Biannual, 1964, 1st Prize sculpture Atlanta U. Annual, 1965, 1st Purchase prize Nat. Print Salon, 1969, Alumni award Howard U. Washington, 1979, Honor award Outstanding Achievement Visual Arts Nat. Women's Caucus Art Conf., San Francisco, 1981, James Van der Zee award Phila. Mus. Art, 1983, award Amistad Rsch. Ctr., New Orleans, 1990, Candace award Art Nat. Coalition 100 Black Women, N.Y.C., 1991, numerous commns., 1966-92; named honoree Nat. Sculpture Conf., Ohio, 1987; scholar awards Howard U., State U. Iowa, grants Julius Rosenwald Found., 1945-47, Brit. Coun. Great Britain, 1971.

CATLEY-CARLSON, MARGARET, association executive; b. Nelson, B.C., Oct. 6, 1942; d. George Lorne and Helen Margaret (Hughes) Catley; m. Stanley F. Carlson, Oct. 30, 1970. BA with honors, U. B.C., 1966; postgrad., Inst. Internat. Relations, U. W.I., St. Augustine, Trinidad and Tobago, 1970; LLD (hon.), U. Regina, 1985; LittD (hon.), St. Mary's U., 1985; Fellow, Ryerson Poly. Inst. Concordia U., 1986, Mt. St. Vincent U., 1990. Joined Dept. External Affairs., Can., 1966; second sec. Can. High Commn., Colombo, Sri Lanka, 1968; with aid and devel. div. Dept. External Affairs, 1970-74; econ. counsellor Can. High Commn., London, 1975-77; v.p. Can. Internat. Devel. Agy., 1978, sr. v.p., acting pres., 1979-80; asst. undersec. Dept. External Affairs, 1981-82; asst. sec. gen. UN; dep. exec. dir. ops. UNICEF; pres. Can. Internat. Devel. Agy., 1983-89; dep. minister Health and Welfare Country of Canada, 1989-92; pres. The Population Coun., N.Y.C., 1993—. Office: The Population Coun 1 Dag Hammarskjold Plz New York NY 10017-2201

CATLIN, SUSAN LYNN, alcohol and drug abuse psychotherapist; b. Chgo., Dec. 15, 1954; d. Charles Sexton and Dorothy Mary (Good) C. BA, U. Ill., 1977; postgrad., George Williams Coll., 1983, Roosevelt U., 1992—. Cert. alcohol and drug counselor. Psychiat. tech. Forest Hosp., Des Plaines, Ill., 1979-85; alcohol counselor Ptnrs. in Psychiatry, Des Plaines, 1985-90; dir., pres. S.L. Catlin and Assocs., Des Plaines, Schaumburg, Ill., 1990—; cons. Advanced Psychiat. Svcs., 1990-94. Fellow Div. of Ill. Addictions, Nat. Assn. Alcoholism and Drug Abuse Counselors. Republican. Methodist. Home: 1300 Pennwood Ct Schaumburg IL 60193-5206

CATOE, BETTE LORRINA, physician, health educator; b. Washington, Apr. 7, 1926; d. John Booker and Laura Beola (Adams) C.; B.S. cum laude, Howard U., 1948, M.D., 1951; m. Warren J. Strudwick, Sept. 17, 1949; children—Laura Christina, Warren J., William J. Intern, Freedmen's Hosp., Washington, 1951-52; pediatric resident Howard U. Freedman's Hosp., 1952-55; practice medicine specializing in pediatrics, Washington, 1956—; instr. bacteriology Howard U., 1955-57; mem. staff Providence Hosp., Columbia Hosp., Howard U. Hosp., Washington Hosp. Center; sch. health officer Dept. Health, Washington, 1960-64; clin. instr. Howard U., 1956-58. Mem. D.C. Health Planning Adv. Council, 1967-77, chmn., 1973-77; chmn. D.C. Devel. Disabilities Adv. Council, 1970-74; mem. D.C. Mayor's Commn. on Food and Nutrition, 1971-72, Mayor's Commn. on Maternal and Child Health. 1978-84; mem. D.C. Commn. Jud. Tenure and Disabilities, 1977—, chair, 1984—; bd. dirs. United Way of Nat. Capital Area, 1974-76, chmn. social planning com., 1974-75; bd. govs. St. Alban's Sch., 1978-84; bd. dirs. D.C. Health and Welfare Council, 1968-73, pres., 1973-74; del. Democratic Nat. Conv., 1976; bd. dirs. Met. Washington Health and Welfare Council, 1970-72, Parent Council of Washington, 1974-75, Met. Med. Founds., Inc., Silver Spring YMCA, 1977-80. Mem. AMA, D.C. Chirurg. Soc., D.C. Med. Soc., Nat. Med. Assn. (chmn. pediatric sect. 1981-83), Am. Med. Women's Assn., NAACP, Urban League, Assn. Comprehensive Health Planners (dir. 1975-77), Women's Aux. Medico-Chirurg. Soc., Jack and Jill Am., Century Club of Nat. Assn. Negro Bus. and Profl. Women's Clubs (pres. 1985-89), Alpha Kappa Alpha. Baptist. Clubs: Links, Carrousels (nat. v.p. 1986-88, nat. pres. 1988-90), Women's Nat. Dem. Home: 1748 Sycamore St NW Washington DC 20012-1031 Office: 5505 5th St NW Washington DC 20011

CATOLINE, PAULINE DESSIE, small business owner; b. Ft. Worth, Dec. 17, 1937; d. Byron Hillis and Dessie Elizabeth (Plumlee) Doggett; children: Sherry Lou, Brenda Lynn; m. Donald Ralph Ackerman, Feb. 19, 1993. BA in Bus. Mgmt. (labor rels. specialty), Hiram Coll., 1989. Notary public, Ohio. Sec. Gen. Am. Life Ins. Co., Ft. Worth, 1956-57, Kelly Girl Svcs., Youngstown, Ohio, 1965-69; legal sec. Burgstaller, Schwartz & Moore, Youngstown, 1962-65, Green, Schiavoni, Murphy & Haines, Youngstown, 1969-71, Flask & Policy, Youngstown, 1971-83; sec. Western Res. Care System, Youngstown, 1983-87, exec. sec., 1987-90; owner, mgr. Pauline's Place, Youngstown, 1993—; legal sec. Henderson, Covington, Stein, Donchess & Messenger Law Firm. Pres. PTA, Cottage Hills, Ill., 1968-69, brownie and scout leader, 1968-69. Mem. Mahoning County Legal Secs. Assn. (v.p. 1973-74, editor monthly booklet 1974-75), Exec. Link, Missionary Group Club. Democrat. Methodist. Home: 3961 Cannon Rd Youngstown OH 44515-4604

CATOR, DONNA MARIE, human resources total quality professional; b. Bangor, Maine, July 28, 1945; d. Robert Earle and Marjorie Emma (Bennett) Fuller; m. Donald L. Wolf Jr., 1965 (div. 1980); children: Joseph Philip Wolf, James Aubrey Wolf; m. Patrick W. Cator, Sept. 1, 1981; 1 child, Stephen P. BS in Mgmt. of Human Resources, Cen. Wesleyan Coll., Central, S.C., 1990. Adminstrv. asst. H. Putsch & Co., Fletcher, N.C., 1975-77; pers. mgr. Dia-Compe, Inc., Fletcher, 1977-81; mgr. employee rels. Ralph Wilson Plastics Co., Fletcher, 1981-84, mgr. human resources, 1984-92, mgr. human resources and total quality, 1992—; conf. speaker Nolan Co., San Antonio, 1993. Chairperson Mayor's Com. for Employment of Disabled Persons, Asheville, N.C., 1986; mem. adv. bd. Employment Security Commn., 1991—; participant scholarship selection com. Duke Power Co., 1993; bd. dirs. Jr. Achievement, Western N.C., 1989-91, Quality Forward, Asheville, 1987-89; mem. Buncombe County Rep. Women's Club; del. Rep. party, 1988, 90. Mem. Soc. for Human Resource Mgmt., Western N.C. Human Resource Assn., Henderson County C. of C. (indsl. divsn.). Episcopalian. Office: Ralph Wilson Plastics Co PO Box 249 Fletcher NC 28732-0249

CATROPPA, COLLEEN JEANETTE, food service executive; b. Newton, Kans., Dec. 27, 1953; d. Kenneth Duane and Dorine (Stelljes) Hand; m. Anthony Catroppa, Aug. 7, 1977; 1 child, Anthony Kenneth. Student, Kans. State U., 1971-74. From asst. buyer to buyer Macy's, Kansas City, Kans.; dept. mgr. Macy's, Wichita, Kans.; sales staff IBM, Wichita, Kans.; prin. K.C. Art Gallery, Rogers, Ark.; owner Tony-Cs Restaurant, Rogers, Ark., 1993—; owner South Roads Shopping Ctr., Tulsa, Okla., 1982-84, Dixieland Mall Rogers, Ark., 1986-87, K.C. Gallery Metcalf Shopping Ctr., Kansas City, 1982-86. Sec. Rogers Jr. Aux., 1987-92. Recipient Best New Restaurant award Ark. Times, 1988, Best Italian Restaurant, 1988. Mem. Rogers Jr. Aux. (charter). Republican. Lutheran. Home: 8391 S Lakeshore Dr Rogers AR 72756 Office: Tony Cs Restaurant 14528 E Highway 12 Rogers AR 72756

CATTANEO, JACQUELYN ANNETTE KAMMERER, artist, educator; b. Gallup, N.Mex., June 1, 1944; d. Ralph John and Gladys Agnes (O'Sullivan) Kammer; m. John Leo Cattaneo, Apr. 25, 1964; children: John Auro, Paul Anthony. Student Tex. Woman's U., 1962-64. Portrait artist, tchr. Gallup, N. Mex., 1972; coord. Works Progress Adminstrn. art project renovation McKinley County, Gallup, Octavia Fellin Performing Arts wing dedication, Gallup Pub. Library; formation com. mem. Multi-modal/Multi-Cultural Ctr. for Gallup, N.Mex.; exch. with Soviet Women's Com., USSR Women Artists del., Moscow, Kiev, Leningrad, 1990; Women Artists del. and exch. Jerusalem, Tel Aviv, Cairo, Israel; mem. Artists Del. to Prague, Vienna and Budapest.; mem. Women Artists Del. to Egypt, Israel and Italy, 1992, Artist Del. Brazil, 1994. One-woman shows include Gallup Pub. Libr., 1963, 66, 77, 78, 81, 87, Gallup Lovelace Med. Clinic, Santa Fe Station Open House, 1981, Gallery 20, Farmington, N.Mex., 1985—, Red Mesa Art Gallery, 1989, Soviet Restrospect Carol's Art & Antiques Gallery, Liverpool, N.Y., 1992, N.Mex. State Capitol Bldg., Santa Fe, 1992, Lt. Govt. Casey Luna-Office Complex, Women Artists N.Mex. Mus. Fine Arts, Carlsbad, 1992, Rio Rancho Country Club, N.Mex., 1995; group shows include: Navajo Nation Library Invitational, 1978, Santa Fe Festival of the Arts Invitational, 1979, N.Mex. State Fair, 1978, 79, 80, Catharine Lorillard Wolfe, N.Y.C., 1980, 81, 84, 85, 86, 87, 88, 89, 91, 92, 4th ann. exhbn. Salmagundi Club, 1984, 90, 3d ann. Palm Beach Internat., New Orleans, 1984, Fine Arts Ctr. Taos, 1984, The Best and the Brightest O'Brien's Art Emporium, Scottsdale, Ariz., 1986, Gov.'s Gallery, 1989, N.Mex. State Capitol, Santa Fe, 1987, Pastel Soc. West Coast Ann. Exhbn. Sacramento Ctr. for Arts, Calif., 1986-90, gov.'s invitational Magnifico Fest. of the Arts, Albuquerque, 1991, Assn. Pour La Promotion Du Patrimone Artistique Français, Paris, Nat. Mus. of the Arts for Women, Washington, 1991, Artists of N.Mex., Internat. Nexus '92 Fine Art Exhbn., Trammell Corw Pavilion, Dallas, Carlsbad (N.Mex.) Mus. Fine Art; represented in permanent collections: Zuni Arts and Crafts Ednl. Bldg., U. N.Mex., C.J. Wiemar Collection, McKinley Manor, Gov.'s Office, State Capitol Bldg., Santa Fe, Historic El Rancho Hotel, Gallup, N.Mex., Sunwest Bank. Fine Arts Ctr., En Taos, N.Mex., Armand Hammer Pvt. Collection, Wilcox Canyon Collections, Sadona, Ariz., Galaria Impi, Netherlands, Woods Art and Antiques, Liverpool, N.Y., Stewarts Fine Art, Taos, N.Mex. Mem. Dora Cox del. to Soviet Union-U.S. Exchange, 1990. Recipient Cert. of Recognition for Contbn. and Participation Assn. Pour La Patrinome Du Artistique Français, 1991, N.Mex. State Senate 14th Legislature Session Meml. # 101 for Artistic Achievements award, 1992, Award of Merit, Pastel Soc. West Coast Ann. Membership Exhbn., 1993. Mem. Internat. Fine Arts Guild, Am. Portrait Soc. (cert.), Pastel Soc. of W. Coast (cert.), Mus. N.Mex. Found., Mus. Women in the Arts, Fechin Inst., Artists' Co-op. (co-chair), Gallup C. of C., Gallup Area Arts and Crafts Council, Am. Portrait Soc. Am., Pastel Soc. N.Mex., Catharine Lorillard Wolfe Art Club of N.Y.C. (oil and pastel juried membership), Chautauqua Art Club, Soroptimists (Internat. Woman of Distinction 1990). Address: 210 E Green St Gallup NM 87301-6130

CATTANI, MARYELLEN B., lawyer; b. Bakersfield, Calif., Dec. 1, 1943; d. Arnold Theodore and Corinne Marilyn (Kovacevich) C.; m. Frank C. Herringer; children: Sarah, Julia. AB, Vassar Coll., Poughkeepsie, N.Y., 1965; JD, U. Calif. (Boalt Hall), 1968. Assoc. Davis Polk & Wardwell, N.Y.C., 1968-69; assoc. Orrick, Herrington & Sutcliffe, San Francisco, 1970-74, ptnr., 1975-81; v.p., gen. counsel Transamerica Corp., San Francisco, 1981-83, sr. v.p., gen. counsel, 1983-89; ptnr. Morrison & Foerster, San Francisco, 1989-91; sr. v.p. gen. counsel Am. Pres. Cos., Ltd., 1991—; bd. dirs. Bank the West, ABM Industries Inc. Author: Calif. Corp. Practice Guide, 1977, Corp. Counselors, 1982. Regent St. Mary's Coll., Morega, Calif., 1986—, pres., 1990-92, trustee, 1990—, chmn., 1993—; trustee Vassar Coll., 1985-93, The Head-Royce Sch., 1993—; bd. dirs. The Exploratorium, 1988-93; active Ctr. Pub. Resources San Francisco. Mem. ABA, State Bar Calif. (chmn. bus. law sect. 1980-81), Bar Assn. San Francisco (co-chair com. on women 1989-91), Calif. Women Lawyers, San Francisco C. of C. (bd. dirs. 1987-91, gen. counsel 1990-91), Am. Corp. Counsel Assn. (bd. dirs. 1982-87), Women's Forum West (bd. dirs. 1984-87). Democrat. Roman Catholic. Club: Women's Forum West.

CATTELL, HEATHER BIRKETT, psychologist; b. Carlisle, eng., Dec. 16, 1936; came to U.S., 1955; d. Wilfred B. and Anne Birkett; m. Russel B. Shields, June 10, 1953 (div. 1963); children: Vaughn, Gary, Heather Luanne; m. Raymond B. Cattell, May 9, 1981. BA, U. Hawaii, 1974, MA, 1977, PhD, 1979. Lic. clin. psychologist, Hawaii. Dir. rsch. Salvation Army, Honolulu, 1979-81; pvt. practice Honolulu, 1981—; lectr., workshop leader, U.S., Australia, Can., and United Kingdom, 1989—. Author: The 16PF: Personality in Depth, 1989. Mem. Phi Beta Kappa. Office: 1188 Bishop St Ste 1702 Honolulu HI 96813-3307

CATTERALL, MARLENE, Canadian legislator; b. Ottawa, Ont., Can., Mar. 1, 1939; d. Paul and Isobel Petzold; m. Ron Catterall, July 14, 1962; children: Karen, Chris, Cheryl. Ed., Carleton U. Alderman City of Ottawa, 1976-85; coun. mem. Regional Municipality Ottawa-Carleton, 1976-85; mem. from Ottawa West Ho. of Commons, 1988—, apptd. parliamentary sec. to pres. of treasury bd. Mem. Ottawa Women's Network, Bus. and Profl. Women's Club. Liberal. Roman Catholic. Office: House of Commons, Rm 451-S Centre Block, Ottawa, ON Canada K1A 0A6

CATTERTON, MARIANNE ROSE, occupational therapist; b. St. Paul, Feb. 3, 1922; d. Melvin Joseph and Katherine Marion (Bole) Maas; m. Elmer John Wood, Jan. 16, 1943 (dec.); m. Robert Lee Catterton, Nov. 20, 1951 (div. 1981); children: Jenifer Ann Dawson, Cynthia Lea Uthus. Student, Carleton Coll., 1939-41, U. Md., 1941-42; BA in English, U. Wis., 1944; MA in Counseling Psychology, Bowie State Coll., 1980; postgrad., No. Ariz. U., 1987-91. Registered occupational therapist, Occupational Therapy Cert. Bd. Occupational therapist VA, N.Y.C., 1946-50; cons. occupational therapist Fondo del Seguro del Estado, Puerto Rico, 1950-51; dir. rehab. therapies Spring Grove State Hosp., Catonsville, Md., 1953-56; occupational therapist Anne Arundel County Health Dept., Annapolis, Md., 1967-78; dir. occupational therapy Eastern Shore Hosp. Ctr., Cambridge, Md., 1979-85; cons. occupational therapist Kachina Point Health Ctr., Sedona, Ariz., 1986; regional chmn. Conf. on revising Psychiat. Occupational Therapy Edn., 1958-59; instr. report writing Anne Arundel Community Coll., Annapolis, 1974-78. Editor Am. Jour. Occupational Therapy, 1962-67. Active Md. Heart Assn., 1959-60; mem. task force on occupational therapy Md. Dept. of Health, 1971-72; chmn. Anne Arundel Gov. Com. on Employment of Handicapped, 1959-63; mem. gov.'s com. to study vocat. rehab., Md., 1960; com. mem. Annapolis Youth Ctr., 1976-78; mem. ministerial search com. Unitarian Ch. Anne Arundel County, 1962; curator Dorchester County Heritage Mus., Cambridge, 1982-83; v.p., officer Unitarian-Universalist Fellowship Flagstaff, 1988-93; co-moderator, founder Unitarian-Universalist Fellowship of Sedona, 1994—, respite care vol., 1994—; citizen interviewer Sedona Acad. Forum, 1993, 94. Mem. P.R. Occupational Therapy Assn. (co-founder 1950), Am. Occupational Therapy Assn. (chmn. history com. 1958-61), Md. Occupational Therapy Assn. (del. 1953-59), Ariz. Occupational Therapy Assn., Pathfinder Internat., Dorchester County Mental Health Assn. (pres. 1981-84), Internat. Platform Assn., Ret. Officers Assn., Air Force Assn. (Barry Goldwater chpt., sec. 1991-92), Severn Town Club (treas. 1965), Internat. Club (Annapolis, publicity chmn. 1966), Toastmasters, Newcomers (Sedona, pres. 1986), Zero Population Growth, Delta Delta Delta. Republican. Home: 415 Windsong Dr Sedona AZ 86336-3745

CAUDILL, MAUREEN, computer consultant; b. Portsmouth, Ohio, July 14, 1951; d. Elmon C. and Harriet L. (Sisler) C. BA, U. Conn., 1973; MA in Teaching, Cornell U., 1974. Customer engr. Raytheon Data Systems, Wellesley, Mass., 1975-78; mem. tech. sales support staff Hewlett-Packard Co., Wallingford, Conn., 1978-81; project programmer Gould Ocean Systems div., Cleve., 1982-83; sr. software engr. Data Systems div. Gen. Dynamics Co., San Diego, 1983-85; computer cons. Rockwell Internat., Hughes Aircraft Corp., Honeywell Corp., other corps., 1985-89; founder, computer cons. Adaptics, San Diego, 1987-89; engrng. specialist space systems div. Gen. Dynamics, San Diego, 1989-90; mgr. tech. and applications support Sci. Applications Internat. Corp., 1990-91; owner, cons., writer NeuWorld Svcs., San Diego, 1991-93; co-founder, dir. rsch. NeuWorld Fin., San Diego, 1993—; organizer ann. meetings on neural networks, San Diego, Boston, Washington, Seattle, 1987-90; instr. San Diego Extension in Intelligent Systems Technologies U. Calif., 1990—; presenter on neural networks, U.S., Japan, Mex., also others, 1987—. Author: Neural Network Primer, 1989, Naturally Intelligent Systems, 1990, Understanding Neural Networks: Computer Exploration, 1992, In Our Own Image, 1992, Using Neural Networks, 1994; contbg. editor Finance mag., 1994—. Mem. IEEE (chair publs. Neural Networks Coun.), Internat. Neural Network Soc. (adviser to exec. bd. 1988-90), Assn. Computing Machinery.

CAUDLE, DIANE ISABEL, insurance agent; b. Toronto, Ont., Can., June 29, 1950; came to U.S., 1965; d. Albert Gordon and Ann (Taylor) Steels; m. Joe Everett Caudle, Dec. 15, 1973. BA in Edn., U. Fla., 1972. Ins. clk. Conlon Ins. Agy., Hollywood, Fla., 1972-73; ins. clk., underwriter Hanover Ins. Co., Jacksonville, Fla., 1973-83; ins. customer svc. rep. Heston-Fielding & Assocs., Jacksonville, Fla., 1983-86; ins. customer svc., agt. Herbie Wiles Ins., St. Augustine, Fla., 1986—. Bd. dirs. St. Augustine Humane Soc., 1991—, Habitat for Humanity, St. Augustine, St. Johns County, 1994—, mem. family sel. com., 1992—. Mem. Nat. Assn. Ins. Women. Office: Herbie Wiles Ins 400 N Ponce De Leon Blvd Saint Augustine FL 32084-3587

CAUGHLIN, STEPHENIE JANE, organic farmer; b. McAllen, Tex., July 23, 1948; d. James Daniel and Betty Jane (Warnock) C. BA in Family Econs., San Diego State U., 1972, MEd, 1973; M. in Psychology, U.S. Internat. U., San Diego, 1979. Cert. secondary life tchr., Calif. Owner, mgr. Minute Maid Svc., San Diego, 1970-75; prin. Rainbow Fin. Svcs., San Diego, 1975-78; tchr. San Diego Unified Sch. Dist., 1973-80; mortgage broker Santa Fe Mortgage Co., San Diego, 1980-81; commodity broker Premex Commodities, San Diego, 1981-84; pres., owner Nationwide Futures Corp., San Diego, 1984-88; owner, sec. Nationwide Metals Corp.; owner, gen. mgr. Seabreeze Organic Farm, 1984—. Sec. Arroyo Sorrento Assn., Del Mar, Calif., 1978—. Mem. Greenpeace Nature Conservancy, DAR, Sierra Club, Jobs Daus. Republican. Avocations: horseback riding, swimming, skiing, gardening. Home and Office: 3909 Arroyo Sorrento Rd San Diego CA 92130-2610

CAULFIELD, BARBARA ANN, lawyer; b. Oak Park, Ill., Dec. 2, 1947; d. Edward F. and Lucille M. (Kloth) C.; children: Alexander, Elizabeth. BS, Northwestern U., 1969, JD, 1972. Bar: Ill. 1972, Calif. 1982, Alaska 1983. Dir. research Chgo. Law Enforcement Group, 1972-73; instr. law Northwestern U., Chgo., 1973-74; assoc. prof. U. Oreg., Eugene, 1974-78; prof. U. Calif. Hastings, San Francisco, 1978-83, dean acad. affairs, 1980-81; ptnr. Brobeck, Phleger & Harrison, San Francisco, 1983-90; sr. counsel Pacific Bell, 1991; judge U.S. Dist. Ct. (no. dist.) Calif., San Francisco, 1991-94; ptnr. Latham & Watkins, San Francisco, 1994—; assoc. dir. Nat. Inst. for Trial Advocacy, San Francisco, 1979-82; lawyer rep. U.S. Ct. Appeals (9th cir.), San Francisco, 1984-87; Brendan Brown lectr. Cath. U. Am., Washington, 1984. Author: Questions Raised by Privacy, 1977, Child Abuse and Neglect, 1979, California Criminal Evidence, 1980, Civil RICO, 1987. Founder Child Advs. Assn., Chgo., 1972; bd. dirs. Nat. Com. to Prevent Child Abuse, Chgo., 1974-83, Lawyer's Com. for Urban Affairs, Chgo., 1986—. Named Citizen of Yr., Chgo. C. of C., 1974; recipient spl. commendation U. Calif. San Francisco, 1982. Mem. ABA (coun. criminal justice sect. 1980-84, chmn. litigation sect. com. 1983-86), Calif. Bar Assn., Alaska Bar Assn., Am. Law Inst., Queen's Bench, Assn. Trial Lawyers Am. Office: Latham & Watkins Ste 1900 505 Montgomery St San Francisco CA 94111

CAULFIELD, JOAN, academic relations coordinator, educator; b. St. Joseph, Mo., July 17, 1943; d. Joseph A. and Jane (Lisenby) Caulfield; BS in Edn. cum laude, U. Mo., 1963, MA in Spanish, 1965, PhD, 1978; postgrad. (Mexican Govt. scholar) Nat. U. Mexico, 1962-63. TV tchr. Spanish, Kansas City (Mo.) pub. schs., 1963-68; tchr. Spanish, French Bingham Jr. High Schs., Kansas City, 1968-78; asst. prin. S.E. High Sch., Kansas City, 1984; prin. Nowlin Jr. High Sch., Independence, Mo., 1984-86, Lincoln Coll. Preparatory Acad., Kansas City, Mo., 1986-88, asst. supt., Kansas City, 1988-89; part-time instr. U. Mo.-Kansas City; dir. English Inst., Rockhurst Coll., summers, 1972-75, coord. sch. coll. rels., 1989—; mem. nat. steering com. Brain-Based Learning Network; assessor dept. elem. and secondary edn. State Mo. Mem. Sister City Commn., Kansas City, 1980—, Kans.' Quality Performance Assessment Team; ofcl. translator to mayor on trip to Seville, Spain, 1969; bd. dirs. Kansas City chpt. NCCJ, Expo '92 World's Fair, Seville, Spain (translator 1992), St. Theresa's Acad., 1991-94, Kansas City Acad. of Learning; selected leadership training Greater Mo.; trainer Harmony in a World of Difference, 1989-93; mem. task force C. of C. Named Outstanding Secondary Educator, 1973. Mem. Romance Lang. Assn., Assn. for Supervision and Curriculum Devel., Nat. Assn. Secondary Sch. Prins., Modern Lang. Assn. (contbr. jour.), Am. Assn. Tchrs. Spanish & Portuguese, Friends of Seville, Friends of Art, Magnet Schs. Am. (contbr. jour.), Mo. Mid. Sch. Assn. (contbr. jour.), Phi Sigma Iota, Phi Delta Kappa, Delta Kappa Gamma (state scholar 1977-78, contbr. jour. Bulletin), Phi Kappa Phi, Sigma Delta Pi. Presbyterian. Home: 431 W 70th St Kansas City MO 64113-2022 Office: 5225 Troost Ave Kansas City MO 64110-2545

CAUSEY, ANNETTE DENISE, librarian; b. Macon, Ga., May 20, 1960; d. Tom Wilson Sr. and Betty Mae (Evans) C. BA, Wesleyan Coll., Macon, Ga., 1982; MLS, Atlanta U., 1985. Audio technician Macon (Ga.) Talking Book Ctr., 1982-84; grad. libr. asst. Atlanta U. SLIS, Trevor Arnett Library, Atlanta, 1984-85; libr. technician U.S. Ct. Appeals, Atlanta, 1985-86; libr. Salvation Army SFOT, Atlanta, 1986-87; reference, circulation libr. Life Chiropractic Coll., Ga., 1988—; internship The Bibb County Dept. Family and Children Services, Macon, Ga., 1882, v.p. Student Govt. Assn., 1985, colloquium com. mem. Atlanta U. SLIS, 1985; part-time reference libr. Ga. State U. Big sister Links Wesleyan Coll. Davis Homes, Macon, Ga. Mem. Met. Atlanta Library Assn., American Theo. Library Assn., Nat. Assn. Female Execs., Atlanta Hawks, Booster Club. Democrat. Methodist. Home: 2080 Bent Creek Way SW Atlanta GA 30311-3871 Office: Life Chiropractic Coll 1269 Barclay Cir Marietta GA 30060-2996

CAUTHEN, CARMEN WIMBERLEY, state government assistant, jewelry designer; b. Raleigh, N.C., Aug. 4, 1959; d. William Peele and Cliffornia (Grady) Wimberley; m. Ricky Leon Cauthen, May 26, 1990. Student, Ga. Inst. Tech., 1977-78; BA in Polit. Sci., N.C. State U., Raleigh, 1986. Asst. sgt.-at-arms N.C. Ho. of Reps., Raleigh, 1981, 82, computer calendar clk., various yrs.; owner, jewelry designer Accessories and Things, Raleigh, 1984—; sec. Coll. Humanities/Social Sci. N.C. State U., Raleigh, 1989-91; owner bookkeeping/typing svc. CTYPE, Raleigh, 1990—; jour. clk. N.C.

Ho. of Reps., Raleigh, 1992-94, adminstrv. clk., 1992—. Mem. Am. Soc. Legis. Clks. and Secs. Democrat. Christian. Home: 703 Latta St Raleigh NC 27607 Office: NC Gen Assembly House Prin Clks Office Legis Bldg/ Jones St Raleigh NC 27603-5924

CAUTHORNE-BURNETTE, TAMERA DIANNE, family nurse practitioner, healthcare consultant; b. Richmond, Va., Apr. 13, 1961; d. Robert Francis Cauthorne and Lois Avery (Lloyd) Cumashot; m. William Nichols Burnette, Dec. 3, 1983. BSN, U. Va., 1983; postgrad., Med. U. S.C., 1988; MSN, Old Dominion U., 1993, grad. cert. in women's studies, 1994; postgrad., Med. Coll. Va., 1994—. RN, Va.; family nurse practitioner. Staff nurse, charge nurse gynecology-oncology unit U. Va. Med. Ctr., Charlottesville, 1983, staff nurse, charge nurse high-risk labor and delivery, ICU, 1984-85; staff nurse, charge nurse, preceptor med. ICU Med. U. S.C., 1985-87, staff nurse ICU, 1988; staff nurse, charge nurse med.-surg. ICU, progressive care Stuart Cir. Hosp., Richmond, Va., 1988-90; staff nurse pediatric and neonatal ICU CHildrens' Hosp. of the King's Dau., Norfolk, Va., 1990, staff nurse, team leader neonatal ICU, 1990-91; pvt. health care cons., 1993—; cons. Old Dominion U. Coll. Health Sci., Sch. Nursing, 1993—, undergrad. clin. facility, 1994—; condr. analysis of Russian and Ukrainian health care system; breast self-exam instr. Am. Cancer Soc., 1982—; presenter at profl. confs. Contbr. author for med. texts Delmar Pub. Vol. Ronald McDonald House, 1980-83; docent Spoleto Festival USA, 1984—, MacArthur Meml. Mus., 1991; vol. receptionist info. ctr. Gibbes Art Gallery, 1987-89; vol. ARC Blood Donation Ctr., 1986—; mem. coll. health sci. coun. U. Va. Fellow Internat. Pedigogical Acad./Moswoc, Order of Omega Nat. Honor Soc.; mem. AACN (mem. coms.) Va. Coalition for Nurse Practitioners, DAR, U. Va. Alumnae Assn., Jr. League Norfolk and Virginia Beach, Daus. of Confederacy, Carolina Art Assn., S.C. Hist. Soc., Confederate Meml. Lit. Soc., U. Va. Sch. Nursing Alumnae Assn. (pres.), U. Va. Coll. Health Scis. Coun., Alpha Delta Pi (chmn. nat. panhellenic rels. com.), Sigma Theta Tau.

CAUTHRON, ROBIN J., federal judge; b. Edmond, Okla., July 14, 1950; d. Austin W. and Mary Louise (Adamson) Johnson. BA, U. Okla., 1970, JD, 1977; MEd, Cen. State U., Edmond, Okla., 1974. Bar: Okla. 1977. Law clk to Hon. Ralph G. Thompson U.S. Dist. Ct. (we. dist.) Okla., 1977-81; staff atty. Legal Svcs. Ea. Okla., 1981-82; pvt. practice law, 1982-83; spl. judge 17th Jud. Dist. State Okla., 1983-86; magistrate U.S. Dist. Ct. (we. dist.) Okla., Oklahoma City, 1986-91, judge, 1991—. Editor Okla. Law Rev. Bd. dirs. Juvenile Diabetes Found. Internat., 1989—; mem. nominating com. Frontier Coun. Boy Scouts Am., 1987, Edmond Ednl. Endowment; trustee, sec. First United Meth. Ch., 1988-90. Mem. ABA, Okla. Bar Assn. (vice chmn. 1990), Okla. County Bar Assn. (bd. dirs. 1990— bench and bar com.), McCurtain County Bar Assn. (pres. 1986), Am. Judicature Soc., Nat. Assn. Women Judges, Fed. Bar Assn., Okla Assn. Women Lawyers, Nat. Coun. Women Magistrates (bd. dirs. 1990-91), Okla. Jud. Conf. (v.p. 1985), Am. Inns of Ct. (pres. elect 1990-91), Order of Coif, Phi Delta Phi. Office: US Courthouse 200 NW 4th St Rm 3122 Oklahoma City OK 73102-3003*

CAVALIERE, TERRI ANGELA, neonatal nurse practitioner; b. Bklyn.; d. Antonio and Anna (Bonica) Salerno; m. Anthony J. Cavaliere, Dec. 11, 1982. BSN, Hunter Coll., 1970; MS, U. Calif., San Francisco, 1973. RN, N.Y.; cert. neonatal nurse practitioner. Staff nurse King's County Hosp., Bklyn., 1970-72; staff nurse U. Calif.-San Francisco Moffett Hosp., 1973-74, sr. staff nurse, 1974-75; asst. head nurse NICU-North Shore U. Hosp., Manhasset, N.Y., 1976-77; clin. nurse specialist Winthrop U. Hosp., Mineola, N.Y., 1977-80; neonatal practitioner North Shore U. Hosp., Manhasset, 1982—; mem. NCC test com. for neonatal nurse practitioner cert. exam 1990—; faculty/cons. nurse practitioner program Harlem Hosp., N.Y.C., 1991—; clin. preceptor Grad. program in Nursing, SUNY, Stony Brook, 1988, Adelphi U., Garden City, N.Y., 1984—, asst. adj. prof. Sch. Continuing Edn. in Nursing, 1978-80, asst. clin. prof. perinatal nurse clinician program, 1976-77; lectr. in field; cons. in field.; asst. clin. prof. Sch. Nursing NNP Program SUNY, Stony Brook, 1994. Book reviewer Nurses' Book Club, 1984; videotape reviewer Am. Jour. Nursing, 1985; manuscript reviewer W. B. Saunders Nursing Texts, 1990-91, Neonatal Network, 1991—; contbr. articles to profl. jours. Recipient Diana Dolgin Nurse of Yr. award March of Dimes, 1992. Mem. N.Y. State Nurses Assn. (coun. on ethical practice in nursing 1987-91), Nat. Assn. Neonatal Nurses, L.I. Assn. Neonatal Nurses (pres. 1994), N.Y. State Perinatal Assn., Sigma Theta Tau. Office: North Shore Univ Hosp 300 Community Dr Manhasset NY 11030-3876

CAVALLARO, MARY CAROLINE, retired physics educator; b. Everett, Mass., Feb. 2, 1932; d. Joseph and Domenica Cavallaro. BS, Simmons Coll., 1954, MS, 1956; EdD, Ind. U., 1972; postgrad., Tufts U., 1980-81. Inst. math. and physics Sweet Briar (Va.) Coll., 1955-56; instr. physics Simmons Coll., Boston, 1956-58, Randolph-Macon Woman's Coll., Lynchburg, Va., 1958-59; lectr. Boston U., 1960-61; asst. prof. physics Framingham (Mass.) State Coll., 1961-63; prof. physics Salem (Mass.) State Coll., 1963—, coord. secondary edn., 1963-94; ret.; cons. Instroductory Phys. Scis. group Edn. Devel. Ctr., Newton, 1966; asst. to dean grad. studies Salem State Coll., 1971-78, coord. pre-engring. program, 1980-89, coord. secondary edn. program, 1989-90; vis. scholar Harvard U. Grad. Sch. Edn., Cambridge, Mass., 1989-90. Grantee NSF, 1962. Mem. AAUW, NEA, Am. Phys. Soc., Am. Assn. Physics Tchrs., Nat. Sci. Tchrs. Assn., Am. Inst. Physics, Soc. Coll. Sci. Tchrs., Mass. Tchrs. Assn., Simmons Coll. Alumnae Assn., Ind. U. Alumnae Assn., Pi Lambda Theta.

CAVALLERO, HAZEL HELEN, properties corporation executive; b. Burntmill, Colo., Mar. 18, 1913; d. Walter Merwin and Elizabeth Belle (Donley) Heller; m. John Walter Miller, June 4, 1937 (dec. Dec. 1943); m. Robert Angelo Cavallero, May 10, 1950; 1 child, Robert Clive. BA, U. Ill., 1941; MA, Stanford U., 1950. Pres. CSI, Inc., San Mateo, Calif., 1979—. Bd. dirs. Peninsula Vols., Menlo Park, Calif., 1962-74. Lt. (j.g.) USN, 1943-45. Republican. Episcopalian. Home: One Baldwin Ave # 323 San Mateo CA 94401 Office: 181 2nd Ave Ste 314 San Mateo CA 94401-3815

CAVALLON, BETTY GABLER, interior designer; b. Waverly, N.Y., July 17, 1918; d. Wallace Frederick and Harriet (Heaton) Gabler; grad. Parisien Sch. Design, Detroit, 1939; m. Michel Francis Cavallon, Dec. 26, 1946 (dec. 1981); children: Claire, Carol (dec.); stepchildren: Michael, Mary; m. John W. Crist, Nov. 20, 1982. Lic. interior designer, Conn. Fabric coordinator Montgomery Ward, 1940-46; interior designer Betty Cavallon Interiors Ltd., Stamford, Conn., 1946—. Mem. Am. Soc. Interior Designers (corp.). Republican. Episcopalian. Home and Office: 69 Riverside Ave Stamford CT 06905-4413

CAVANAGH, SHIRLEY BICKOFF, librarian; b. New Haven, Aug. 5, 1952; d. Sidney and Sylvia (Weinstein) Bickoff; m. Thomas E. Cavanagh, Aug. 16, 1991. BS, Southern Conn. State Univ., 1974, MLS, 1982. Pub. svcs. asst. Yale U. Libr., New Haven, 1975-82; staff libr. So. Conn. State U., New Haven, 1982-85, assoc. libr., head govt. documents dept., 1985—. Mem. ALA, Assn. Coll. and Rsch. Libraries, Conn. Library Assn. (exec. bd.), Gov. Documents Orgn. of Conn. (chair 1994-95, mem. ednl. tech. adv. com. 1994—). Democrat. Jewish. Home: 3230 Whitney Ave # 803 Hamden CT 06518-2129 Office: So Conn State U 501 Crescent St New Haven CT 06515-1330

CAVASINA, MARY MAGDALENE, surgeon; b. Canonsburg, Pa., Dec. 26, 1927; d. Joseph Edward and Rose (Staffen) C. BS, U. Pitts., 1948; MD, Women's Med. Coll. of Pa., 1952. Diplomate Am. Bd. Surgery. Intern Mercy Hosp., Pitts., 1952-53, resident in gen. surgery, 1953-57; teaching fellow U. Pitts., 1953-57; sr. surg. staff mem. Canonsburg Gen. Hosp., 1957-92, chief surgery, 1962-75. Asst. chief and fire surgeon Canonsburg Vol. Fire Dept. Mem. Cath. Daus. of Am., Bus. and Profl. Women's Club, Pitts. Surg. Soc., Am. Coll. Surgeons. Republican. Roman Catholic. Office: 160 W Pike St Canonsburg PA 15317-1328

CAVEN, NANCY JO, nursing administrator; b. Aberdeen, S.D., Mar. 12, 1961; d. James L. and Joan C. (Cochrane) C. BA in Nursing, Coll. of St. Catherine, 1983. Cert. ins. rehab. specialist, case mgr.; qualified rehab. cons. RN-surg. and transplant intensive care VA Med. Ctr., Mpls., 1983-90; qualified rehab. cons.-disability mgmt. specialist Intracorp., Minnetonka, Minn., 1990-92; developer, coordinator, mgr. catastrophic injury mgmt. program Intracorp., Minnetonka, 1992—, supr. catastrophic injury mgmt. program, 1992-93, field svc. mgr., 1993—, managed care mgr., 1994—; cons. Health Staff Nursing Agy., Mpls., 1993-94; chair employee rels. coun. Intracorp., 1991-93. Mem. Am. Assn. for Continuity of Care, Am. Assn. Rehab. Providers, Sigma Theta Tau (officer Chi chpt. 1986-88). Republican. Roman Catholic. Home: 3921 Upton Ave S Minneapolis MN 55410 Office: Intracorp 5700 Smetana Dr Ste 200 Minnetonka MN 55343

CAVERS-HUFF, DASIEA YVONNE, philosopher; b. Cleve., Oct. 24, 1961; d. Lawrence Benjamin and Yvonne (Warner) Cavers; m. Brian Jay Huff, July 26, 1986. BA, Cleve. State U., 1984, MA, 1988; postgrad., U. Md., 1986-90. Teaching asst. Cleve. State U., 1983-86; instr. Upward Bound program Case Western Res. U., Cleve., 1986; instr. U. Md., Coll. Park, Md., 1987-89; mem. faculty Charles County Community Coll., 1989-90; asst. prof. Riverside Community Col., 1990—. U. Md. grad. fellow, 1986-87; Ford Found. predoctoral fellow, 1987-89. Mem. Am. Philos. Assn., Minority Grad. Student Assn. (co-chmn. U. Md. 1987-88). Democrat. Home: 25969 Andre Ct Moreno Valley CA 92553 Office: Riverside City Coll Humanities and Social Scis Div Riverside CA 92506

CAVES, PEGGY, medical, surgical nurse; b. Lodi, Calif., July 19, 1945; d. Burnerd Clette and Thelma Jean (Humphrey) Hamilton; m. Virgil Wayne Caves, Feb. 14, 1978; children: Rhonda Pilcher Miller, Kelly Pilcher Rainwater, Shelly Pilcher Dennis; stepchildren: Shelly Deanne White, Leo Wayne, Karrie Ausbrooks, Billy. LPN, Kiamichi Vo-Tech, Hugo, Okla., 1982. Staff nurse Pushmataha Hosp., Antlers, Okla., Texoma Med. Ctr., Denison; dr. nursing Antlers (Okla.) Nursing Home; staff nurse Presby. Hosp., Oklahoma City; dr. nursing Choctaw Nursing Home, Antlers, Okla., 1991—; staff nurse Med. Ctr. of Southeastern Okla., Durant, Okla., 1992-93; staff nurse outpatient dept., emergency room Choctaw Nation Hosp., Talihina, Okla., 1993-94; pvt. duty nurse Superior Home Health, Talihina, 1994—; dir. nurses Choctaw Nation Nursing Home, 1994—; dir. nursing Choctaw Nation Nursing Home. Home: PO Box 872 Antlers OK 74523-0872

CAVISH, JACQUELYN ANN, artist, educator; b. Riverside, Calif., Mar. 28, 1944; d. John Angus and Hope Florence (Franson) Ross; m. John David Richards, Apr. 1969 (div. 1973); 1 child, Clayton Andrew; m. Carl Walter Cavish, Nov. 10, 1979 (div. Aug. 1992). Student, U. Ariz., 1962-66; BA in Spanish, UCLA, 1968; MFA, U. Calif., Santa Barbara, 1988. Instr. art Wright Cultural Ctr., Port Hueneme, Calif., 1990—, Oxnard (Calif.) Coll., 1990—. One-woman shows Ojai (Calif.) Valley Arts Ctr., 1989, Ventura (Calif.) Arts Commn., 1990, Wheeler Hot Springs Gallery, Ojai, 1991, Danica House, Ventura, 1992, Calif. Gold Coast Watercolor Soc., Ventura, 1993, Moorpark (Calif.) Coll., 1993, Alley Gallery, Carpinteria, Calif., 1994, State of the Arts Gallery, Olympia, Wash., 1994, others; group shows include Ventura County Mus. History and Art, 1992, Conejo Valley Art Mus., Thousand Oaks, Calif., 1989-93, Santa Barbara (Calif.) Mus. Natural History, 1992, Midwest Watercolor Soc., Green Bay, Wis., 1993, N.E. Watercolor Soc., Goshen, N.Y., 1993, East Wash. Watercolor Soc., Richland, 1993, Clymer Mus. & Gallery, Ellensburg, Wash., 1993, Fremont Arts & Crafts Fair, Seattle, 1994, Yosemite Nat. Park, Calif., 1995. Chmn. Arts and Crafts Harbor Days, Port Hueneme, 1991-93. Recipient 2d place award Art Walk, Thousand Oaks, 1991, hon. mention Yosemite (Calif.) Renaissance Exhibit, 1991, Best of Show award Allied Artists Santa Monica Mountains, 1991, visual arts award Oxnard Cultural and Fine Arts Commn., 1992. Mem. Coll. Art Assn., Calif. Gold Coast Watercolor Soc. (founding), Oxnard Art Assn. (pres. 1989). Democrat. Studio: PO Box 2005 Port Hueneme CA 93044-2005

CAVNAR, MARGARET MARY (PEGGY CAVNAR), business executive, former state legislator, nurse, consultant; b. Buffalo, July 29, 1945; d. James John and Margaret Mary Murtha Nightengale; BS in Nursing, D'Youville Coll., 1967; MBA, Nat. U., 1989; m. Samuel M. Cavnar, 1977; children: Heather Anne Hicks, Heide Lynn, Dona Cavnar Hambly, Judy Cavnar Bentrim. Utilization rev. coord. South Nev. Meml. Hosp., Las Vegas, 1975-77; v.p. Ranvac Publs., Las Vegas, 1976—; ptnr. Cavnar & Assocs., Reseda, Calif., 1976—, C & A Mgmt., Las Vegas, 1977—; pres. PS Computer Svc., Las Vegas, 1978—; bd. mem. Nev. Eye Bank, 1987-89, exec. dir., 1990-91; dir. of health fairs Centel & CH13TV, 1991-94; pres., bd. dirs. Bridge Counseling Assocs. Mem. Clark County Republican Cen. Com., 1977-87, Nev. Rep. Cen. Com., 1978-80; mem. Nev. Assembly, 1979-81; Rep. nominee for Nev. Senate, 1980; Rep. nominee for Congress from Nev. 1st dist., 1982, 84; bd. dirs., treas. Nev. Med. Fed. Credit Union; v.p. Community Youth Activities Found., Inc., Civic Assn. Am.; mem. utilization rev. bd. Easter Seals; trustee Nev. Sch. Arts, 1980-87; nat. adviser Project Prayer, 1978—; co-chmn. P.R.I.D.E. Com., 1983—; co-chmn. Tax Limitation Com., 1983, Personal Property Tax Elimination Com., 1979-82, Self-Help Against Food Tax Elimination Denial Com., 1980; mem. nat. bd. dirs., co-chmn. Nev. Pres. Reagan's Citizens for Tax Reform Com., 1985-88; mem. Nev. Profl. Standards Rev. Orgn., 1984; co-chmn. People Against Tax Hikes, 1983-84; bd. dirs. Nev. Eye Bank, 1988-90. Mem. Nev. Order Women Legislators (charter, parliamentarian 1980—), Cosmopolitanly Hers Info. (pres.), Sigma Theta Tau. Office: PO Box 26073 Las Vegas NV 89126-0073

CAWEIN, KATHRIN (MRS. SEABURY CONE MASTICK), artist; b. New London, Conn., May 9, 1895; d. Henry and Barbara (Franz) Cawein; M.A. (hon.), Oberlin Coll., 1966; D.F.A. (hon.), Pacific U., 1980, Forest Grove, Oreg.; student Art Students League; m. Seabury Cone Mastick, Apr. 3, 1964. Music roll editor, music interpreter with various musicians, 1911-32; tchr. County Center Work Shop, 1935-36; owner studio for children, 1950-55; one man shows; County Center, White Plains, N.Y., 1935, Village Art Center, N.Y.C., 1945, Town Hall, N.Y.C., 1950, 8th St. Playhouse, N.Y.C., 1953, Sarasota, Fla., 1973, U. Tampa (Fla.), 1973, Oberlin (Ohio) Coll., 1975, St. John's Ch., Pleasantville, N.Y., 1976, Berea (Ky.) Coll., 1977, Pacific U., Forest Grove, Oreg., 1979, 80, 81, 83, 85 , 90, Mt. Kisco (Ky.) Libr., 1991, Internat. Kisco Libr., 1991; exhibited group shows U.S., Eng., France, Italy, Ecuador, including Century of Progress, 1934, Tex. Centennial, 1937, World's Fair, 1939; represented in permanent collections at Met. Mus., Nat. Mus., Washington, Pa. State U., Tampa U., Oberlin Coll.; illuminated books St. Marks Ch., Van Nuys, Calif.; illuminated manuscripts Pacific U., The Life of Christ Congl. Ch., Portland. Oreg., 1991, The 13 Steps of Christ, 1991 now in permanent collection Cmty. Ch., Portland. Recipient Frank Talcott Non-Mem. prize Soc. Am. Etchers, 1936, prize for lithography Village Art Center, 1944, prize for etching Nat. Assn. Women Artists, 1947, prize for dry point Pleasantville Woman's Club, 1950, prize for etching, 1952, prize for dry point Westchester Fedn. Women's Clubs, 1951, others; Kathrin Cawein Gallery of Art named in her honor Pacific U., 1985. Mem. Nat. Assn. Women Artists, Art Students League (life), Chgo. Soc. Etchers, Soc. Graphic Artists. Home and Studio: 35 Mountain Rd Pleasantville NY 10570

CAYLEFF, SUSAN EVELYN, educator; b. Boston, Mar. 4, 1954; d. Nathan and Frieda (Kates) C. BA, U. Mass., 1976; MA, Sarah Lawrence Coll., 1978, Brown U., 1979; PhD, Brown U., 1983. Teaching fellow Brown U., Providence, 1981-83; asst. prof. Inst. for the Med. Humanities, U. Tex. Med. Br., Galveston, 1983-87; assoc. prof. dept. women's studies San Diego State U., 1987—; faculty advisor varsity women's crew team, 1988—; mem. adj. faculty Inst. for the Med. Humanities, U. Tex. Med. Br., 1987—; humanities rep. com. for the protection of human subjects San Diego State U., 1988—. Author: Wash and Healed...., 1987, Wings of Gauze: Women of Color and The Experience of Health & Illness, 1993, Babe: The Life and Legend of Babe Didrikson Zahanos, 1995; editorial cons. Tex. Medicine, 1985-87; mem. editorial bd. Med. Humanities Rev., 1986-87; contbr. articles to profl. jours. Nat. Endowment for Humanities grantee, 1984, Babe Didrikson Zaharias Meml. Found. grantee, 1986, San Diego State U. Found. grantee, 1988, Kennedy Inst. for Bioethics scholar Georgetown U., 1984, Calif. State U. scholar, 1989—; named Outstanding Prof. San Diego State U. Assoc. Students, 1993, prof. nominee San Diego State U. Trustees, 1994. Nat. Endowment for Humanities grantee, 1984, Babe Didrikson Zaharias Meml. Found. grantee, 1986, San Diego State U. Found. grantee, 1988, Kennedy Inst. for Bioethics scholar Georgetown U., 1984, Calif. State U. scholar, 1989—; named Outstanding Prof. San Diego State U. Assoc. Students, 1993, San Diego State U. Trustees, 1994. Mem. Am. Assn. for the History of Medicine, Nat. Women's Studies Assn., Coordinating Group for Women in the Hist. Profession, Western Assn. for Women's Historians, Soc. for Menstrual Cycle Rsch., Brown U. Alumni Assn., Phi Kappa Phi. Democrat. Jewish. Office: San Diego State U Dept Womens Studies San Diego CA 92182

CAYLOR, DEE JERLYN, accountant; b. Calhoun, Ga., Dec. 22, 1942; d. George Herbert and Annie Mae (Shirley) Darnell; widowed; children: Mark Gerald, George Alexander, Gregory Wayne. Student, Am. Inst. Banking, 1961, Dalton Jr. Coll., 1979, Continual Learning Inst., Nashville, 1985. Asst. mgr. Holidy Inn, Calhoun, Ga., 1969-72; asst. gen. mgr. Gentry Inn, Nashville, 1973-74; resident mgr. Am. Homes, Nashville, 1975-77; office mgr. Liberty Carpets, Dalton, Ga., 1978-79; owner, operator Age Olde Traditions, Antiques, Calhoun, 1980-83; resident mgr. Allied Mgmt. Co., Nashville, 1984-85; acct. Vawter, Gammon, Norris & Collins, Nashville, 1986, Robert Half & Accountemps, Nashville, 1987-88; resident mgr. Carter Co., Nashville, 1989—; office mgr. Bridal Path Wedding Chapel, Nashville, 1991—; acct. Gaddy, Gaydou & Assoc., 1993; pvt. practice acct. Nashville, 1994—. Exec. dir. spl. TV musical Tribute to Women in Country Music, 1990. Mem. Women of Music and Entertainment Network (founder, pres. 1988-94), Nashville Apt. Assn. (community svc. com. 1990). Republican. Baptist.

CAYTON, MARY EVELYN, clergyman; b. Morgantown, W. Va., July 7, 1926; d. Adam Johnson and Dorothy Ena (Bigler) C. Student, Internat. Bible Coll., San Antonio, Tex., 1955. Ordained minister Full Gospel Denomination, 1958. Founder, pastor Morgantown (W.Va.) Revival Ctr., 1956-92; staff, controller's office W.Va. U., Morgantown, 1951-55, '58-84; chmn. Morgantown Revival Ctr. Assn., 1956—. Home and Office: Morgantown Revival Ctr RR 3 Box 542A Morgantown WV 26505-9803

CAZALAS, MARY REBECCA WILLIAMS, lawyer, nurse; b. Atlanta, Nov. 11, 1927; d. George Edgar and Mary Annie (Slappey) Williams; m. Albert Joseph Cazalas (dec.). R.N., St. Joseph's Infirmary Sch. Nursing, Atlanta, 1948; BS in Pre-medicine, Oglethorpe U., 1954; MS in Anatomy, Emory U., 1960; JD, Loyola U., 1967. Gen. duty nurse, 1948-68; instr. maternity nursing St. Joseph's Infirmary Sch. Nursing, 1954-59; med. researcher in urology Tulane U. Sch. Medicine, 1961-65; legal researcher for presiding judge La. Ct. Appeals (4th cir.), 1965-71; sole practice, 1967-71; asst. U.S. atty., New Orleans, 1971-79; sr. trial atty. EEOC, New Orleans, 1979-84; owner Cazalas Apts., New Orleans, 1962—; lectr. in field. Contbr. articles to med. and legal pubs. Bd. advisors Loyola U. Sch. Law, New Orleans, 1974, v.p. adv. bd., 1975; mem. New Orleans Drug Abuse Adv. Com., 1976-80, task force Area Agy. on Aging, 1976-80, pres.'s coun. Loyola U., 1978—, adv. bd. Odyssey House, Inc., New Orleans, 1973; chmn. women's com. Fed. Exec. Bd., 1974; bd. dirs. Bethlehem House of Bread, 1975-79. Named Hon. La. State Senator, 1974; recipient Superior Performance award U.S. Dept. Justice, 1974, Cert. Appreciation Fed. Exec. Bd., 1975, 76, 77, 78, Rev. E.A. Doyle award, 1976, commendation for teaching Guam Legislature, 1977. Mem. Am. Judicature Soc., La. State Bar Assn., Fed. Bus. Assn. (v.p. 1976—, pres. 1976-78, bd. dirs. 1972-75), Fed. Bar Assn. (1st v.p. 1973, pres. New Orleans chpt. 1974-75, nat. coun. 1974-79), Assn. Women Lawyers, Nat. Health Lawyers Assn., DAR, Bus. and Profl. Women's Club, Am. Heart Assn., Emory Alumni Assn., Oglethorpe U. Alumni Assn., Loyola U. Alumni Assn. (bd. dirs. 1974-75, 1977, v.p. 1976), Jefferson Parish Hist. Soc., Phi Delta Delta (merged with Phi Alpha Delta, pres. 1970-72, bd. dirs., vice justice 1974-75), Sierra Club, Zonta, Alpha Epsilon Delta, Phi Sigma, Leconte Hon. Sci. Soc. Democrat.

CAZDEN, COURTNEY B(ORDEN), education educator; b. Chgo., Nov. 30, 1925; d. John and Courtney (Letts) Borden; m. Norman Cazden (div. 1971); children: Elizabeth, Joanna. BA, Radcliffe Coll., 1946; MEd, U. Ill., 1953; EdD, Harvard U., 1965. Elem. tchr. pub. schs., N.Y., Conn., Calif., 1947-49, 54-61, 74-75; asst. prof. edn. Harvard U., Cambridge, Mass., 1965-68, assoc. prof., 1968-71, prof., 1971—; vis. prof. U. N.Mex. summer 1980, U. Alaska, Fairbanks, summer 1982, U. Auckland, N.Z., spring 1983, Bread Loaf Sch. of English, Vt., 1986—; chairperson bd. trustees Ctr. Applied Linguistics, Washington, 1981-85. Author: Child Language and Education, 1972, Classroom Discourse: The Language of Teaching and Learning, 1988, Whole Language plus Essays on Literacy in the US and New Zealand, 1992; co-editor: Functions of Language in the Classroom, 1972, English Plus: Issues in Bilingual Education, 1990; editor: Language in Early Childhood Education, rev. edit., 1981. Trustee Highland Ednl. and Rsch. Ctr., New Market, Tenn., 1982-84; bd. dirs. Feminist Press, Old Westbury, N.Y., 1982-84; clk. New Eng. regional office Am. Friends Svc. Com., Cambridge, 1989-92. Recipient Alumna Recognition award Radcliffe Coll., 1988; fellow Ctr. Advanced Study in Behavioral Scis., Stanford, Calif., 1978-79; Fulbright research fellow, New Zealand, 1987. Mem. Nat. Acad. Edn., Coun. on Anthropology and Edn. (pres. 1981, George & Louise Spindler award 1994), Am. Assn. Applied Linguistics (pres. 1985), Nat. Conf. on Rsch. in English (pres. 1993-94), Am. Ednl. Rsch. Assn. (exec. com. 1981-84, award for disting. contbns. to ednl. rsch. 1986). Quaker. Office: Harvard U Grad Sch Edn Appian Way Cambridge MA 02138

CECIL, DORCAS ANN, property management executive; b. Greensboro, N.C., Mar. 31, 1945; d. George Joseph and Marianne Elizabeth (Zimmerman) Ernst; m. Richard Lee Cecil, June 8, 1968; children: Sarah, Matthew. BA, U. Ark., 1967. Pres. B & C Enterprises Property Mgmt., Ltd., O'Fallon, Ill., 1977-93, Cecil Mgmt. Group, Inc., O'Fallon and St. Louis, 1993—. Bd. dirs. O'Fallon Pub. Libr., 1983—, v.p., 1986-87, pres., 1987—; sec. St. Vincent de Paul Soc., 1987—; bd. dirs. Leadership Coun. Southwestern Ill., 1994—. Mem. Inst. Real Estate Mgmt. (cert., v.p. 1987, pres. St Louis chpt. 1990, vice chmn. Nat. IREM standard coms. 1991—, regional v.p. 1992-93, governing councillor 1994—, mem. nat. ethics and discipline hearing bd. 1994—), Nat. Apt. Assn., St. Louis Multi-Housing Coun., Profl. Housing Mgmt. Assn., Community Assns. Inst., Nat. Assn. Realtors, Ill. Assn. Realtors (housing com. 1994—), Belleville Assn. Realtors (bd. dirs. 1991-94), Belleville Bd. Realtors (chmn. multi-family com. 1990-94), O'Fallon C. of C. (bd. dirs. 1987—, v.p. 1988—, pres. 1992-93). Office: Cecil Mgmt Group Inc PO Box 459 O'Fallon IL 62269-0459

CECIL, MAXINE, critical care nurse; b. Healdton, Okla., Sept. 25, 1921; d. James Albert and Clara (Phelps) Metz; children: Harold E. Seals, James Michael Seals, David Ray Smith. LPN, Seventh Day Adventist Hosp., Ardmore, Okla., 1954; ADN cum laude, No. Okla. Coll., Tonkawa, Okla., 1979. RN, Okla. LPN Seventh Day Adventist Hosp., Ardmore, 1953-66; LPN, charge nurse at nursing homes Ardmore, 1966-74; LPN and RN Johnston Meml. Hosp., Tishomingo, Okla., 1974-80; RN Meml. Hosp. So. Okla., Ardmore, Okla., 1980-84; charge nurse Love County Med. Ctr., Marietta, Okla., 1988-90; charge nurse, RN Lakeland Manor, Inc., Ardmore, 1982—; nurse Meml. Convalescent Home, Ardmore, 1990—; pres. LPN Assn for Carter, Love, Johnston and Marshall Counties, 1963-70; mem. state bd. LPNs, 1968. Instr. first aid ARC, Ardmore, 1960-62; pathfinder dir. Seventh Day Adventist Ch., Ardmore.

CECIL, SHARON VIRGINIA, psychiatric nurse; b. Thomasville, Ga., July 16, 1946; d. Robert S. and Lillie (Horne) Justice; m. James M. Cecil, Dec. 20, 1980; 1 child, Michelle Pickens. Student, U. Louisville, 1979-81; A. Degree in Art, Jefferson Community Coll., Louisville, 1987, ADN, 1990. Pharmacy technician Jones Apothecary, Louisville, 1985-88; nurse extern Alliant-Norton Hosp., Louisville, 1989, nurse registry, 1989-91; mem. staff, tutor and para profl. counselor Jefferson C.C., 1990-94; nurse Bapt. Hosp. East, Louisville, 1991—; staff Alliant Norton, 1993—. Life mem. Kosair-Children's Hosp. Aux., bd. dirs., 1984-88; bd. dirs. Friends for Life, 1992—; vol. Cancer Support Network, 1991—; active Am. Cancer Soc. Mem. Am. Nurses Credentialing Ctr. (cert. psychiatrist and mental health nurse 1993), Ky. Nurses Assn., Chas F. Menninger Soc., Phi Theta Kappa, Psi Beta.

CEDARBAUM, MIRIAM GOLDMAN, federal judge; b. N.Y.C., Sept. 16, 1929; d. Louis Albert and Sarah (Shapiro) Goldman; m. Bernard Cedarbaum, Aug. 25, 1957; children: Daniel Goldman C., Jonathan Goldman C. BA, Barnard Coll., 1950; LLB, Columbia U., 1953. Bar: N.Y. 1954, U.S. Dist. Ct. (so. dist.) N.Y. 1956 U.S. Ct. Appeals (2d cir.) 1956, U.S. Ct. Claims 1958, U.S. Supreme Ct. 1958, U.S. Dist. Ct. (ea. dist.) N.Y. 1980, U.S. Ct. Appeals (5th and 11th cirs.) 1981. Law clk. to judge Edward Jordan Dimock U.S. Dist. Ct. (so. dist.) N.Y., 1953-54, asst. U.S. atty., 1954-57; atty. Dept. Justice, Washington, 1958-59; part-time cons. to law firms in litigation matters, 1959-62; 1st asst. counsel N.Y. State Moreland Act Commn., 1963-64; assoc. counsel Mus. Modern Art, N.Y.C., 1965-79;

assoc. litigation dept. Davis, Polk & Wardwell, N.Y.C., 1979-83, sr. atty., 1983-86; acting justice Village of Scarsdale, N.Y., 1978-82, justice, 1982-86; judge U.S. Dist. Ct. (so. dist.) N.Y., 1986—; mem. com. defender svcs. Jud. Conf. U.S., 1993—; trustee Barnard Coll.; co-counsel Scarsdale Open Soc. Assn., 1968-86. Mem. adv. com. on labor rels. Scarsdale Bd. Edn., 1976-77; mem. Scarsdale Bd. Archtl. Rev., 1977-78. Recipient Medal of Distinction Barnard Coll., 1991. Mem. Am. Law Inst., ABA (chmn. com. on pictorial graphic sculptural and choreographic works 1979-81), N.Y. State Bar Assn. (chmn. com. on fed. legislation 1978-80), Assn. of Bar of City of N.Y. (com. on copyright and literary property, 1982-84, com. on the Bicentennial 1988-92), Fed. Bar Coun., Copyright Soc. U.S.A. (trustee, mem. exec. com. 1979-82), Supreme Ct. Hist. Soc. Jewish. Office: US Dist Ct US Courthouse 40 Foley Sq New York NY 10007-1581

CEDEL, MELINDA IRENE, secondary school educator, violinist; b. Ft. Worth, July 31, 1957; d. Albert and Emilia Florence (Sylvester) C. Student, N.C. Sch. Arts, 1974-77; MusB Edn., U. S.C., 1979. Cert. tchr., S.C. Tchr. music Charleston (S.C.) County Pub. Schs., 1979-92; pvt. tchr. music, 1983—. Performed with Florence Symphony, Columbia Philharm., S.C. Chamber Orch., Augusta Symphony, Savannah (Ga.) Symphony, Hilton Head (S.C.) Symphony, Jacksonville Summer Symphonetta; concertmaster Brunswick (Ga.) Civic Orch.; musician Charleston Symphony, 1979—, Charleston Symphony Chamber Orch., 1985-92, Long Bay (S.C.) Symphony, Savannah Symphony Orch.; musician, mgr. Charlestowne String Quartet, 1983-92; condr. Charleston County Prep. Orch., 1983-84; performer Piccolo Spoleto, 1980; co-dir. Charleston County Strolling Strings. Mem. Am. Fedn. Musicians, Am. String Tchrs. Assn., Suzuki Assn. of the Ams., Inc., Mensa, Kappa Phi Kappa. Home: 1011 Greenwillow Dr Saint Marys GA 31558-6303

CEKAUSKAS, CYNTHIA DANUTE, social worker; b. Detroit, Mar. 24, 1954; d. Vladas Algimantas and Isabel Gana (Stasiulis) C. BA in Sociology, Madonna Coll., Livonia, Mich., 1976; MSW, U. Mich., 1979. Bd. cert. social worker, La.; lic. clin. social worker, Fla. Psychiat. social worker Charity Hosp. New Orleans, 1982-84; social worker child and adolescent svc. DePaul Hosp., New Orleans, 1986-87; social worker, family advocacy programmgr. Army Community Svcs., Friedberg, Fed. Republic Germany, 1988-89; social worker, mgr. family adv. program, chmn. family adv. case mgmt. team Community Counseling Ctr., Camp Zama, Japan, 1989-90; social worker, exceptional family mem. program mgr. Army Community Svcs., Bamberg, Germany, 1990-91; alt. family adv., on-call crisis counselor Desert Storm Army Community Svcs., Bamberg, Fed. Republic Germany, 1990-91; social worker, family advocacy rep., head dept. family adv. Naval Med. Clinic, New Orleans, 1991—; presenter child abuse prevention Bad Nauheim Elem. Sch., 1988-89. Contbr. articles to newspapers. Hosp. corpsman USN, 1979-82. Recipient Customer Svc. award Giessen Mil. Cmty., 1988-89, Friend Bad Nauheim Elem. Sch. award, 1989, commendation for exceptional svc. Cam Zama, 1990, Scroll of Appreciation for Desert Storm/Desert Shield, Bamberg, Germany, 1990-91, Outstanding Performance award, 1993, 94. Mem. NAFE, NOW, Acad. Cert. Social Workers, Federally Employed Women. Democrat. Roman Catholic. Home: Rue Parc Fontaine Apt 3110 New Orleans LA 70131-6906 Office: Naval Med Clinic Family Advocacy Dept New Orleans LA 70142

CELENTANO, LINDA NANCY, industrial designer; b. Englewood, N.J., May 11, 1958; d. Edward and Ruth (Meyers) C. Student design, U. Copenhagen, 1978; B Indsl. Design, Pratt Inst., 1980. Indsl. designer Lebowitz/Gould Design, N.Y.C., 1979-81; indusl. designer Smart Design, N.Y.C., 1981-85; product design dir. Medin Corp., Wallington, N.J., 1985—; lectr. Pratt Inst. Alumni Series, Bklyn., 1986-87. Designer Product Design, 1987, Indsl. Design Mag., 1986, 90, Product Design II, 1987, Product Design VI, 1994, Internat. Design Yearbook, 1988, 89, N.Y. Times, 1990, New and Notable Product Design, 1991, also salad servers; represented in permanent collection Cooper-Hewitt Collection, N.Y.C. Vol. Libr. for Recording for Blind, N.Y.C., 1990; co-founder Rowena Reed Kostellow Fund, 1990—, active exec. com.. Recipient Excellence award Indsl. Design Mag., 1986. Mem. Indsl. Designer Soc. Am. Lutheran. Home: 325 Haywood Dr Paramus NJ 07652-3329 Office: 555 B Shaler Blvd Ridgefield NJ 07657

CELENTINO, ANNE ELIZABETH, lawyer; b. Columbus, Ohio, July 25, 1961; d. William and Judith Lee (Adams) Joseph; m. Christopher Celentino, Sept. 5, 1987; 1 child, Joseph. BA in History, U. Calif., Santa Barbara, 1983; JD, Georgetown U., 1987. Atty. Sheppard, Mullin, Richter & Hampton, San Diego, 1987-91; sr. employment coun. Cubic Corp., San Diego, 1991—; frequent spkr. on employment law topics. Contbr. articles to profl. jours. Mem. ABA (mem. labor and employment law sect.), Am. Corporate Coun. Assn., San Diego County Bar Assn., Indsl. Rels. Rsch. Assn., Calif. Employment Law Counsel, Lawyers Club (mem. sexual harassment task force). Office: Cubic Corp 9333 Balboa Ave San Diego CA 92186

CELLI, MARY JANE, city councilwoman; b. Hartford, Conn., Aug. 18, 1934; d. John Welles and Dorothea (Fraser) Baxter; m. Michael G. Celli, Sr., May 18, 1962; 1 child, Michael G. Jr. AA, Brookdale Coll., 1978; BS, Kean Coll., 1982; MA, U. Va., 1983; EdD, Temple U., 1988. Cert. profl. mgr., tchr. C Programs Product Assurance, Ft. Monmouth, N.J., 1978-83; C, PMB Program Mgmt. Br. PM TMDE, Ft. Monmouth, N.J., 1983-85; sr. program analyst JTC3A, Ft. Monmouth, N.J., 1985-89; C, strategic programs PMSATCOM, Ft. Monmouth, N.J., 1989-94; owner, Celli's Antiques, Long Branch, N.J., 1958—. Mem. Long Branch Planning Bd., 1988-93; sec. Long Brand Libr. Bd., 1986-88. With USAF, 1952-55, Washington. Recipient Mid-Career fellowship U.S. Govt., U. Va., 1982-83. Mem. Am. Contr. Soc., N.J. Elected Woman's Ofcls., Armed Forces-Comm. Elec. Assn., VFW. Roman Catholic. Home: 382 Morris Ave Long Branch NJ 07740-6518

CELMER, VIRGINIA, psychologist; b. Detroit, June 26, 1945; d. Charles and Stella (Kopicko) C. BA in English, Marygrove Coll., 1968; MA in Theological Studies, St. Louis U., 1977; PhD in Counseling Psychology, Tex. Tech. U., 1986. Lic. psychologist; lic. chem. dependency counselor; cert. alcoholism and drug abuse counselor. Chaplain Mercy Ctr. for Health Care Svcs., Aurora, Ill., 1977-81; grad. asst. counselor U. Counseling Ctr., Tex. Tech. U., Lubbock, 1982-86, pre-doctoral intern in counseling psychology, 1985-86; post-doctoral intern Consultation Ctr., San Antonio, 1986-89, staff psychologist, 1989-90; pvt. practice psychologist San Antonio, 1989—; instr. dept. psychology Tex. Tech. U., Lubbock, 1981-85, Oblate Sch. Theology, San Antonio, 1989-90. Contbr. articles to profl. jours. Mem. APA, Tex. Psychol. Assn., Bexar County Psychol. Assn., Am. Group Psychotherapy Assn., San Antonio Group Psychotherapy Assn., Nat. Assn. Alcoholism and Drug Abuse Counselors, Tex. Assn. Alcoholism and Drug Abuse Counselors, Leadership Conf. Women Religious (region XII), Intercongregational Leadership Group San Antonio. Office: 1603 Babcock Rd Ste 270 San Antonio TX 78229-4750

CENTRACCHIO, CHARLENE JOAN, social science educator; b. Providence, July 27, 1958; d. Giovanni Ferivante and Lucille Marie (Antonelli) C. BA, R.I. Coll., 1980, Cert. education gifted children, 1984, MEd, 1985, CAGS in Curriculum, 1992. Substitute tchr. North Providence (R.I.) Sch. Dept, 1980-87, tchr., 1987—; mem. curriculum resources adv. bd. R.I. Coll., 1989—; developer, scorer R.I. Social Studies Merit Test, 1991—; team mem. Presdl. award for excellecne U.S. Dept. Edn., 1990; presenter in field. Mem. Supter-Team for Drug and Alcohol Prevention, coord. substance-abuse prevention program, 1993—. Mem. Super-Team for Drug and Alcohol Prevention. Recipient Key to the Town of North Providence for Substance Abuse Prevention, 1989. Mem. R.I. Social Studies Assn. (bd. dirs., v.p. membership, sec. 1994—), R.I. Cheerleading Coaches Assn., North Providence Boosters Assn. (corr. sec. 1987—). Roman Catholic. Home: 185 Chenango Ave Providence RI 02904-4310

CEPAITIS, ELIZABETH A., state legislator; b. Lowell, Mass., Apr. 22, 1943; 3 children. BS in Edn., Salem State Coll., 1964; MBA, Rivier Coll., 1978. Mem. N.H. Ho. of Reps.; mem. mcpl. com. and county govt. com.; fin. controller. Former treas., bd. dirs. Nashua Children's Assn.; former vol. Humane Soc. New England. Office: NH Ho of Reps State Capitol Concord NH 03301*

CERAVOLO, DONNA L., association executive; b. Birmingham, Ala., Mar. 23, 1951; d. Joseph Anthony and Flora Mae (Hull) C.; m. Frank Ippolito, Jr., Aug. 20, 1971 (div. 1977); m. Wells B. Jones, July 26, 1980; 1 child, Jake Christian Jones. BA, U. Ala., Tuscaloosa, 1973; MPA, Auburn U., 1976. Planner Ala. Dept. Mental Health, Montgomery, 1973-76; dir. Ala. devel. disabilities advocacy program U. Ala. Law Sch., Tuscaloosa, 1976-78; exec. dir. Evanston (Ill.) Youth Commn., 1978-81; interim exec. dir. YWCA, Evanston, 1985; dep. dir. Pathways for Youth, N.Y.C., 1986-88; exec. dir. YWCA, Bklyn., 1988—; dir. Queens (N.Y.) Svcs. for Autistic Citizens, 1987—, Women and AIDS Resource Network, Bklyn., 1992—; mem. bd. dirs. Lutheran Social Svcs. of Metro. N.Y., 1994; active Leadership N.Y., 1994-95. Mem. Nat. Assn. YWCA Execs. Democrat. Episcopalian. Home: 211 Grand Ave Freeport NY 11520 Office: YWCA Bklyn 30 3rd Ave Brooklyn NY 11217-1897

CEREMSAK, KAREN MARIE, communications executive, public relations and marketing communications executive; b. Norfolk, Va., Nov. 2, 1959; d. Thomas Joseph and Lula June (Meekins) C. BA in Comm., Va. Tech., 1981. Asst. editor, asst. to dir. USIA, Washington, 1981-83; mgr., dir. corp. comm. Eastern Airlines, 1984-90, staff v.p. comm., 1990-91; dir. comm. Air Transport Assn., Washington, 1991-92; cons. comm. USAir and British Airways, Washington, 1993; dir. comm. Unisys Govt. Sys. Group, McLean, Va., 1993-94, v.p. comm., 1994—. Mem. Internat. Assn. Bus. Communicators, Pub. Rels. Soc. Am., Fairfax County C. of C. (bd. dirs. 1994—). Home: 801 S Pitt St Alexandria VA 22314 Office: Unisys Corp 8201 Greensboro Dr Ste 1100 Mc Lean VA 22102

CERENOV, ELIZABETH, food products executive; b. Neptune, N.J., July 28, 1958; d. Oka and Elisabeth T. (Bujanics) C. Grad. high sch., Howell, N.J., 1976. Cashier Atlantic and Pacific Tea Co., Edison, N.J., 1975-78, front end mgr., 1978-79, head cashier, 1979-84; retail sales rep. frozen divsn. Food Enterprises N.Y., Fairfield, N.J., 1984-85, mem. deployment team, 1986, retail supr., 1986-87, retail sales rep. grocery divsn., 1987, retail supr., 1988-90, jr. account mgr., 1990-92, account mgr., 1992—. Mem. NAFE. Home: PO Box 218 Howell NJ 07731

CEREZO, CARMEN CONSUELO, federal judge; b. 1940. BA, U. P.R., 1963, LLB, 1966. Pvt. practice, 1966-67; law clk. U.S. Dist. Ct., San Juan, 1967-72; judge Superior Ct., P.R., 1972-76, Ct. Intermediate Appeals, 1976-80; judge U.S. Dist. Ct., P.R., 1980-93, chief judge, 1993—. Office: Federico Degetau Fed Bldg Rm CH-131 150 Carlos Chardon Ave Hato Rey San Juan PR 00918-1761*

CERNA, CHRISTINA MONICA, lawyer; b. Munich, Germany, Oct. 9, 1946; came to U.S., 1951; d. Eduardo Joseph and Marija (Vogel) C. BA, NYU, 1967; MA, U. Munich, 1970; JD, Am. U., 1973; LLM, Columbia U., 1974. Bar: D.C., U.S. Ct. Appeals (D.C. cir.), U.S. Supreme Ct. With Fried, Frank Harris, Shriver and Kampelman, Washington, 1974; with solicitor's office U.S. Dept. Labor, Washington, 1976-79; human rights specialist Inter Am. Commn. on Human Rights, OAS, Washington, 1979-94; sr. specialist Inter-Am. Drug Abuse Control Commn., OAS, Washington, 1994—; vis. fellow St. Antony's Coll., Oxford U., 1989-90. Mem. Am. Soc. Internat. Law. Democrat. Office: OAS 1889 F St NW Washington DC 20006-4493

CERNY, CHARLENE ANN, museum director; b. Jamaica, N.Y., Jan. 12, 1947; d. Albert Joseph and Charlotte Ann (Novy) Cerny; children: Elizabeth Brett Cerny-Chipman, Kathryn Rose Cerny-Chipman. BA, SUNY, Binghamton, 1969. Curator Latin-Am. folk art Mus. Internat. Folk Art, Santa Fe, 1972-84, mus. dir., 1984—; adv. bd. C.G. Jung Inst., Santa Fe, 1990—. Mem. Mayor's Commn. on Children and Youth, Santa Fe, 1990-93, adv. bd. Recipient Exemplary Performance award State of N.Mex., 1982, Internat. Ptnr. Among Mus. award Am. Assn. Mus./Internat. Coun. Mus., 1991; Smithsonian Instn. travel grantee, 1976; Florence Dibell Bartlett Meml. scholar, 1979; Kellogg fellow, 1983. Mem. Am. Assn. Mus., Internat. Coun. Mus. (bd. dirs. 1991—), Am. Folklore Soc., Mountain-Plains Mus. Assn., N.Mex. Assn. Mus. (chair membership com. 1975-77). Office: Mus Internat Folk Art PO Box 2087 Santa Fe NM 87504-2087

CERULO, KAREN A., sociologist; b. Perth Amboy, N.J., Jan. 25, 1957; d. Albert Joseph and Michelina (Nicastro) C. BA, Rutgers U., 1980; MA, Princeton U., 1983, PhD, 1985. Asst. prof. SUNY, Stony Brook, 1985-88, Rutgers U., New Brunswick, N.J., 1990—; vis. asst. prof. Rutgers U., 1988-90. Author: Identity Designs: The Sights and Sounds of a Nation; mem. editorial bd. Sociol. Inquiry, 1989-93; contbr. articles to profl. jours. Mem. Rutgers Univ. Internat. Friendship Program, 1993—. Mem. Am. Sociol. Assn. (sec.-treas. culture sect. 1993-94), Internat. Comms. Assn. (sec.-treas. popular culture sect. 1987-89), Ea. Sociol. Soc., North Ctr. Sociol. Soc. Office: Rutgers Univ Dept M Sociology Lucy Stone Hall New Brunswick NJ 08903-5072

CERVILLA, CONSTANCE MARLENE, marketing consultant; b. Lafayette, Ind., Dec. 28, 1951; d. Norman Cimmino and Marilyn Jane (Stonebraker) C. AB, Harvard U., 1974, postgrad., 1974-75. Mktg. asst. Gen. Mills, Inc., Mpls., 1975-76; product dir. Pillsbury Co., Mpls., 1976-78; asst. v.p. Citicorp, N.A., Rochester, N.Y., 1978-80; cons. Bain & Co., Boston, 1980-81; owner, pres. Core Group Mktg., Inc., Mpls., 1981—; co-founder, v.p. Mil. Communications Ctr., Inc., Mpls., 1983-89; co-founder Gift Certificate Ctrs., Inc., 1990—; speaker to bank mktg. orgns. Mem. Bank Mktg. Assn., Harvard/Radcliffe Club Minn., Mpls. Inst. Arts, Wilderness Soc., Nat. Rowing Assn., Harvard Club (N.Y.C.). Office: Core Group Mktg Inc 6436 City West Pky Eden Prairie MN 55344-7712

CESEÑA, CARMEN, education educator, education administrator; b. Ensenada, Calif., July 16, 1947; d. Teodoro L. Ceseña and Guadalupe (Miranda) Carrillo; m. Rogelio A. Cardenas, Feb. 16, 1978; children: Maya-Ixel Ceseña-Cardenas. BA, San Jose State, 1969, standard elem. credential, 1972, MA, 1975; postgrad., Claremont Grad. Sch., 1986—. Cert. community coll. life credential. Lectr. U. Calif., Berkeley, 1975-86; lectr., supr. Sonoma State U., Rhonert Park, Calif., 1978-79; instr. Stanislaus State U., Turlock, Calif., 1982-84, Victor Valley Coll., Victorville, Calif., 1990—; mem. acad. senate Victor Valley Coll., Victorville, 1991—; dist. advisory mem. Victor Elem. Sch. Dist., Victorville, 1990—; chairperson dept. Victor Valley Coll. Gain Program, Victorville, 1991-93; site coun. chair Del Rey Elem. Sch., Victorville, 1990—. Founding mem. Calif. Assn. Bilingual Edn., San Jose, 1970, High Desert Latino Coalition, 1993; mem. Victor Valley Little League, 1988—. Kellogg fellow Univ. Austin, 1993-94. Mem. AAUW, Assn. for Study of Higher Edn., Nat. Assn. Pers. Adminstrs., Am. Assn. Women in Community and Jr. Colls., Pi Lambda Theta. Home: 15852 Inyo Ct Victorville CA 92392-3479 Office: Victor Valley Coll 18422 Bear Valley Rd Victorville CA 92392-5849

CESINGER, JOAN, author; b. Oswego, N.Y., July 2, 1936; d. Guy Wesley and Gladys Matildia (Redlinger) Wagner; m. John Robert Cesinger, July 7, 1956; children: Michael, Richard, Steven. BA in Edn., Northwestern U., 1957. Asst. editor, feature writer Frontier Enterprise, Vernon Town Crier, Mundelein News, Lake Zurich, Ill., 1966-69; editor Lamp of Learning, Lake Zurich, 1967-68; mag. columnist Allen Raymond Inc., Darien, Conn., 1972-77; treas., office mgr., editor Dynamic Resources, La Verne, Calif., 1980-92. Author: Games and Activites for Early Childhood Education, 1967, If I Were . . ., 1975, Kindling Patriotism with Challenging Activties, 1976, Fostering Spelling Achievement with Challenging Games, 1980, American Government: Puzzles, Games, and Individual Activities, 1982, World Cultures: Puzzles, Games, and Individual Activities, 1985, The Plant Kingdom, 1985, Earth and Its Surface, 1985, Air and Weather, 1985, Civics and Citizenship, 1986, World Geography: Puzzles, Games, and Individual Activities, 1985, World History: From the Fall of Rome to Modern Times, 1986, Let's Learn About Dinosaurs, 1987, Holiday Sparklers, 1988, Book 2, 1989. Mem. Brookfield West Garden (v.p. 1978-79), P.E.O., Kappa Kappa Gamma, San Vincente Valley Club, Book Marks Club, Conversations Club (chmn.). Home and Office: 23347 Barona Mesa Rd Ramona CA 92065-4345

CEYER, SYLVIA T., chemistry educator. Grad. summa cum laude, Hope Coll., Holland, Mich.; PhD, U. Calif., Berkeley. Postdoctoral fellow Nat. Bur. Standards; faculty mem. dept. chemistry MIT, Cambridge, Mass., 1981—, asst. prof., now prof. and Keck Found. prof. of energy. Recipient Recognition award for young scholars AAUW Ednl. Found., 1988, Nobel Laureate Signature awd. for Graduate Education in Chemistry, Am. Chemical Soc., 1993. Fellow Am. Acad. Arts and Scis. Office: MIT Dept Chemistry 77 Massachusetts Ave Cambridge MA 02139-3594

CHABOT, DOROTHY ANN, sales manager; b. Lewiston, Maine, Dec. 27, 1970; d. Julien Honore and Lucy Agnes (Moore) C. BFA in Painting and Drawing, U. of the Arts, 1993. Cashier Lane Bryant, Phila., 1990-93, mgr., 1993-94; ind. cons. Mary Kay, Phila., 1993—; visual merchandiser Fashion Bug, 1994—; bookseller Waldenbooks, 1994—. Office: Fashion Bug Lewiston Mall Lewiston ME 04240

CHACE, REGINA GRACE, clinical psychologist; b. Mineola, N.Y., July 25, 1955; d. Gordon Lyon and Ruth Evelyn (Kornicker) C. BA in Psychology, U. So. Calif., 1985; MA in Clin. Psychology, Calif. Sch. of Profl. Psychol., L.A., 1987, PhD in Clin. Psychology, 1992. Lic. clin. psychologist. Coord. Ctrl. City Hotel Project, L.A., 1986-88; commd. 2d lt. USAF, 1989, advanced through grades to capt.; psychologist USAF, Washington, 1989, Edwards AFB, Calif., 1990-92, Wiesbaden, Germany, 1992-94; cons. NASA, L.A., 1990-92, Edwards Test Pilot Sch., 1990-92, Dept. of Def. Schs., Wiesbaden, 1992—. Author: Stress and Burnout, 1992. Coord. homeless outreach team Skid Row Mental Health, L.A., 1986-88. Mem. APA, Air Force Psychologists. Home: 81-100 Ave 53 Thermal CA 92274 Office: 2011 Cerro Gordo Los Angeles CA 90039

CHADWICK, JOANNE, church administrator. Exec. dir. Commn. for Women of the Evangelical Lutheran Church in America, Chicago, Ill. Office: Evangelical Lutheran Church Am 8765 W Higgins Rd Chicago IL 60631

CHADWICK, SHARON STEVENS, librarian; b. Syracuse, N.Y., June 1, 1951; d. Robert Harold and Melba Frances (Hurlburt) Stevens; m. Gary Robert Chadwick, May 27, 1972. BS in Chemistry, Clarkson Coll. Tech., 1973; MSLS, Syracuse U., 1975; MS in Chemistry, SUNY, Oswego, 1980. Asst. librarian SUNY, Oswego, 1977-78; chemistry, physics bibliographer Syracuse U., 1978-79; sci. librarian Humboldt State U., Arcata, Calif., 1980—. Mem. ALA, Am. Chem. Soc., Med. Libr. Assn., N.Y. Acad. Scis., Self-Help for Hard of Hearing, Nat. Captioning Inst., Humane Soc. U.S. Home: 190 Willow Ln Arcata CA 95521-9210 Office: Humboldt State U The Libr Arcata CA 95521

CHAET, VICKY ISABEL, visual artist; b. Chgo., Dec. 27, 1941; d. Louis and Rose Chaet; m. John R. Manning. BFA in Ceramics, U. Chgo., 1963; MFA in Sculpture, Ceramics, U. Mass., 1971; MFA in Computer Graphics, Sculpture, Stanford U., 1973. pvt. cons., art critiques for artists, 1979—; field instr. Antioch U. West, 1981; faculty visual thinking Coll. Engring., Boston U., 1978-79; guest lectr. Mass. Coll. of Art, 1978; instr. pottery Mudflat Sch., Cambridge, Mass., 1976-77; tchg. assoc. dept. art Stanford U., 1972-73. One-person shows include Bergman Gallery, Chgo., 1968, Herter Gallery, Amherst, Mass., 1971, Sumner Gallery, Palo Alto, Calif., 1974, 75, 86, Live Art Gallery, San Francisco, 1992, 93; group exhbns. include Allen Art Mus., Oberlin, Ohio, 1973, Allyne Gallery, 1977, Riskin-Sinow Gallery, 1989-90, Nelson Morales Gallery, 1990 (all San Francisco), Dow and Frosini Art Gallery, Berkeley, 1991, Artreach, San Francisco, 1995; works in pvt. collections at William Bonifas Fine Arts Ctr., Escanaba, Mich., Sundown Design Ltd., San Francisco, DeAnza Coll., Cupertino, Calif. Calif. State U. rsch. grantee, 1969, Women Artists History through Mudflat Sch. teaching grantee, 1977; Stanford U. fellow, 1971-73, vis. scholar, 1973-75; The Ragdale Found. artist residency, Lake Forest, Ill., 1988, 89; contbr. articles to profl. jours.; illustrator: Unravelling Smoke, 1975. Office: 339 Frederick St San Francisco CA 94117-3913

CHAFEE, JUDITH DAVIDSON, architect; b. Chgo., Aug. 18, 1932; d. Percy Bernard and Christina (Affeld) D.; adopted d. Benson Bloom; m. Richard Spofford Chafee, 1959 (div. 1964). BA, Bennington Coll., 1954; BArch, Yale U., 1960, MArch, 1960. Lic. architect, Conn., N.Y., Ariz.; cert. Nat. Coun. Archtl. Registration Bds. Draftsperson Paul M. Rudolph, Architect, New Haven, 1960-61; draftsperson, design The Architects Collaborative, Cambridge, Mass., 1962-63; job capt., design Eero Saarinen and Assocs., Hamden, Conn., 1963-65; project architect Edward Larrabee Barnes, Architect, New Haven, 1965-69; prin. Judith Chafee, Architect, Hamden, Conn., 1966-69, Tucson, 1969—; vis. critic U. Ariz. Coll. Architecture, 1973-76, adj. prof., 1977—; guest architect, critic to advanced students U. Tex. Coll. Architecture, 1976; vis. prof. disting. visitor's studio, advanced studio MIT Dept. Architecture, fall semesters, 1986, 88, advanced design studio Washington U. Sch. Architecture, St. Louis, spring semester, 1988; mem. jury We. Home awards Sunset mag., 1979, Ariz. Solar Energy Commn. Western Solar Utilization Network, Ariz. Passive Solar Design Competition, 1981, Design and Environ. awards program Dept. of Navy, 1983, Rancho San Miguel Design Competition, Sante Fe, 1987, Ariz. Homes of Yr. Competition, 1992, The Environ. Showcase Home, 1992; guest speaker Princeton U., 1989, Mont. State U., 1990, S.W. Ctr. U. Ariz., 1990; mem. vis. com. MIT Sch. Architecture and Planning, 1990—. Contbr. numerous articles to jours. and mags. in field. Nat. Endowment for the arts/Am. Acad. in Rome mid-career fellow, 1977; recipient award of excellence Archtl. Record mag., 1970, 75, 79, Outstanding Use of Concrete award Am. Concrete Inst. 1978, 84, Mortar Bd. Citation award for archtl. edn. Ariz. Mortar Bd., 1988. Fellow AIA (First Honor award Housing mag. 1978, com. on design 1986-89, jury mem. Honor awards, N.Mex. Soc. Architects, Concrete Masonry Design awards Calif. Coun., Concrete Masonry Assn. Calif., Nev. 1988, Ariz. Homes of Yr. awards 1989, Orange County Ann. Design awards 1989, del. to Internat. Conf. on Architecture, Urban Planning and Design, Finland, 1989), Amer. Acad. in Rome; mem. Nature Conservancy, Nat. Trust for Hist. Preservation, Old Fort Lowell Neighborhood Assn., El Presidio Neighborhood Assn., Tucson Mountain Assn. Office: Judith Chafee Architect 317 N Court Ave Tucson AZ 85701-1016

CHAFFEE, DORCAS DIXON, educational curriculum developer; b. Portsmouth, N.H., Mar. 13, 1915; d. James Payson and Mary (Russell) Dixon; m. Robert Gibson Chaffee, Aug. 24, 1938 (dec. Oct. 1986); children: Jenifer Dixon Pears, Jonathan Knowlton, Deborah, Daniel Dixon, Sara. AB, Smith Coll., 1936. Cert. pub. libr. Rsch. asst. Children's Hosp., Phila., 1938-42; libr. Lyme (N.H.) Town Libr., 1956-71; office mgr. Lyme Med. Assn., 1956-66; dir. MOVE (Mus. Ongoing Venture in Edn.), Hanover and Lebanon, N.H., 1966-83; asst. dir. Regional Ctr. Edn. Tng., 1977-83. Co-editor: Perspectives '76, 1976. Mem. bd. incorporators Montshire Mus., Norwich, Vt., 1980—; bd. dirs. Lyme Home Health Agy., 1988-94; com. mem. Lyme Found.; vol. Lyme Elem. Sch., 1990—, Lyme Libr., 1952—; mem. Lyme Dem. Com., 1990—, Hospice of Upper Valley, Lebanon, 1975—, Lyme Historians Inc., 1980—. Mem. N.H. Libr. Trustees Assn., Utility Club, Phi Beta Kappa, Sigma Xi, Delta Kappa Gamma (hon.). Mem. United Ch. of Christ. Home: 2 on the Common Lyme NH 03768

CHAGNON, LUCILLE TESSIER, literacy and developmental learning specialist; b. Gardner, Mass., June 1, 1936; d. Fred G. Tessier and Alfreda C. (Ross) Noel; m. Richard J. Chagnon, Sept. 16, 1978; children: Daniel, David. BMus, Rivier Coll., Nashua, N.H.; adv. cert. in Human Resource Mgmt. and Cmty. Devel., Inst. Cultural Affairs, Chicago, 1969; MEd, Boston Coll., 1972. Edn. specialist, N.H., 1960-73; internat. cons. Inst. Cultural Affairs, Chgo., 1973-79; staff tng. dir. CO-MHAR, Inc., Phila., 1979-81; pres., owner Chagnon Assocs., Collingswood, N.J., 1981-86; prin. Sacred Heart Sch., Camden, N.J., 1986-87; founder, dir. Lifeline Literacy Project, Phila., 1988—; sr. project staff Right Assocs., Phila., 1983-93; literacy and learning specialist Rutgers U., Camden, 1989—; adj. grad. faculty dept. counseling psychology Temple U. Sch. Edn., Phila., 1985-90. Author: (with Richard J. Chagnon) The Best is Yet to Be: A Pre-Retirememt Program, 1994, Easy Reader, Learner, Writer, 1994. Bd. dirs. Camden County Literacy Vols. of Am., 1987-91, Handicapped Advocates for Ind. Living, 1988—; mem. Collingswood Bd. Edn., 1985-89. Mem. Internat. Reading Assn., Nat. Coun. Tchrs. English, Nat. Learning Found., Brain-Based Edn. Network, Inst. Noetic Scis., Inst. Cultural Affairs, New Horizons for Learning, Internat. Alliance for Learning. Home and Office: 1 Courtland Ln Willingboro NJ 08046-3405

CHAIN, BEVERLY JEAN, communications executive; b. Greenfield, Ohio, June 20, 1933; d. Edwin Clifton and Ursel (Penwell) C. BS in Journalism,

Ohio U., 1955; MA, NYU, 1964; EdD, Columbia U., 1974. Dir. pub. rels. CAVE, Sao Paulo, Brazil, 1955-59; dir. pub. rels. intermedia NCCCUSA, N.Y.C., 1959-66; exec. for communications in Latin Am. Nat. Coun. Chs., USA, N.Y.C., 1966-72; assoc. dir. audio-visual dept. United Meth. Ch., N.Y.C., 1972-74; assoc. gen. sec. Bd. Global Ministries United Meth. Ch., 1974-83; dir. office communications United Ch. of Christ, N.Y.C., 1983—; bd. dirs. Nat. Coun. Chs., N.Y.C., 1986—. Contbr. articles to profl. jours. Pub. interest adv. Telecommunication Consumer Coalition, N.Y.C., 1984—. Mem. Associated Ch. Press, Women in Comms., Religious Pub. Rels. Coun., World Assn. Christian Comms. (bd. dirs. London 1979-90, pres. N.Am. region 1979-85). Democrat.

CHALBERG-PLUNKETT, SHERRI LINELL, construction executive; b. Leavenworth, Kans., Mar. 10, 1960; d. Larry Allen and Esther Louise (Martin) C.; m. James Davidson Plunkett, Oct. 25, 1986. BSBA, William Jewell Coll., 1984; MBA, Rockhurst Coll., 1988. Personnel dir. Belger Cartage Service, Kansas City, Mo., 1984-86; v.p. Jim Plunkett, Inc., Kansas City, Kans., 1986—; chief exec. officer Wall Systems Corp., Kansas City, Kans., 1986—. Mem. Home Builders Assn., Assoc. Builders and Contractors, Nat. Assn. Women in Constrn. (dir., recording sec. 1990-91). Republican. Mem. Unity Ch. Home: 7511 NW Tomahawk Ln Kansas City MO 64151-1427 Office: Jim Plunkett Inc 1304 Argentine Blvd Kansas City KS 66105-1537

CHALKLEY, JACQUELINE ANN, retail company executive; b. Benson, Minn., Jan. 3, 1946; d. Vincent Otto and Dorothy Mildred (Alsaker) Kaehler. BA in Art History cum laude, Brown U., 1967; MA, Columbia U., 1968; postgrad. in Contemporary Art, New Sch. for Social Rsch., N.Y.C., 1968-70; postgrad. in Ceramics, U. Md., 1970-72. Art tchr. Summit (N.J.) High Sch., 1968-70, Rockville (Md.) High Sch., 1970-74; adj. prof. ceramics Montgomery Coll., Rockville, 1974-78; owner Jackie Chalkley at Foxhall Square, Washington, 1978—, Jackie Chalkley at Willard Collection, Washington, 1986—, Jackie Chalkley at Chevy Chase Plz., Washington, 1989—; juror Rhinebeck Craft Fair, 1981, New Eng. Buyers Market, Boston, 1982, Craft Art '82, Richmond, Va. Craft Show, 1983, Smithsonian Crafts Exhbn. '83, Smithsonian Instn. Women's Com. Craft Show, 1984, Annie Albers fashion show at Renwick Gallery, 1984, Morristown Craft Fair, 1984, Washington Craft Show, 1986, Potomac Craftsmen's Guild Show, 1987, Harrisburg Arts Festival, 1987, Ceramic Guild Washington, 1987, Washington Guild Goldsmiths, 1987, 18th Bienniel Exhbn. Creative Crafts Coun., 1988, others; appointee screening com. Piedmont Craftsman's Guild, Winston-Salem, N.C., 1983-86, D.C. Commn. Arts, 1983-85; mem. hon. com. Brandeis Art Exhbn., 1984; mem. hon. com. various exhbns. and fundraisers Textile Mus., 1984-86. Mem. hon. com. 2d Ann. 34th St. Art Fair, John Eaton Sch., 1985; mem. benefit com. Washington Charitable Fund, 1989; hon. bd. trustees D.C. chpt. Design Industries Found. for AIDS, 1989, 90; mem. auction ann. benefit com. Washington Project for Arts, 1989, 90. Appeared on cover of Forecast Mag., 1978; recipient Best Taste in Washington award Washingtonian Mag., 1982, 1st Ann. Outstanding Accessories Merchandising award Accessories Mag., 1985; named one of 23 People to Watch in 1983, Washingtonian Mag., 1982; her apt. chosen as Residential Interior of Yr., Am. Soc. Interior Designers, 1985, 92; her store named 1986 Comml. Interior of Yr., Am. Soc. Interior Designers; nat. award for logo design Am. Corp. Identity, 1988, 91. Mem. Am. Craft Coun., Washington Fashion Group, James Renwick Craft Leaders Caucus. Office: Jackie Chalkley 5301 Wisconsin Ave NW Washington DC 20015-2015

CHALMERS, ANNE, direct marketing consultant. Dir. membership devel. Common Cause, 1972-75; dir. devel. Nat. Right to Work Found., 1975-76; asst. exec. dir. North Tex. affiliate Am. Diabetes Assn., 1977; programmer/analyst Data Processing Dept., Dallas Ind. Sch. Dist., 1978-80; mgr. direct mktg. Environ. Educators, Inc., 1980-83; account exec. Saturn Corp., 1983-86; account supr. Mktg. Gen., Inc., 1986-90; pres. Chalmers Mktg. Group, Inc., Alexandria, Va., 1990—; speaker in field. Mem. Women's Direct Response Group (bd. dirs. 1994—), Direct Mktg. Assn. Washington (bd. dirs. 1983-88). Office: Chalmers Mktg Group 103 W Monroe Ave Alexandria VA 22301-1921

CHALMERS, DIANA JENA, association administrator; b. Harvey, Ill., Aug. 25, 1955; d. Melvin Earl and Rita Caroline (Zulfer) Besse; Michael Jon Chalmers, Mar. 18, 1972; children: Mikki Lynn, Robert Michael. Mgr. Pizza Hut, Richton Park, Ill., 1975-77; owner, operator D-Dusters, Hazel Crest, Ill., 1985-91; trustee Village of Hazel Crest, 1987-94; adminstrv. dir. Hazel Crest Area C. of C., 1990—. Author of poems. Founder Neighbors United Party, Hazel Crest, 1989; chmn. Hazel Crest Hazelnut Festival, 1986-90; coord. Hazel Crest Blood Donor Program, 1990-93; pres. Hazel Crest Girl's Softball. Mem. Chgo. Southland Chamber. Home: 2746 174th St Hazel Crest IL 60429-1730 Office: Hazel Crest Area C of C 3649 183rd St Hazel Crest IL 60429-2400

CHAMBERLAIN, BARBARA KAYE, small business owner; b. Lewiston, Idaho, Nov. 6, 1962; d. William Arthur and Gladys Marie (Humphrey) Greene; m. Dean Andrew Chamberlain, Sept. 13, 1986; children: Kathleen Marie, Laura Kaye. BA in English cum laude, BA in Linguistics cum laude, Wash. State U., 1984. Temp. sec. various svcs., Spokane, Wash., 1984-86; office mgr. Futurepast, Spokane, 1986-87; dir. mktg. and prodn. Futurepast: The History Co., Melior Publs., Spokane, 1987-88, v.p., 1988-89; founder, owner PageWorks Publ. Svcs., Post Falls, Idaho, 1989—; mem. dist. 2 Idaho State Ho. of Reps., 1990-92; mem. Idaho State Senate, 1992-94; adj. faculty North Idaho Coll., 1995. Author North Idaho's Centennial, 1990; editor Washington Songs and Lore, 1988. Bd. dirs. Mus. North Idaho, Coeur d'Alene, 1990-91, Ct. Apptd. Spl. Advocates, 1993—, Northwest Water Watch, 1992-94. Named Child Advocate Legislator of Yr., Idaho Alliance for Children, Youth and Families, 1993. Mem. AAUW, NOW, LWV, Nat. Women's Polit. Caucus, Idaho Women's Network, No. Idaho Pro-Choice Network, Idaho Conservation League, Mensa, Post Falls C. of C. Democrat. Office: PO Box 1893 Post Falls ID 83854

CHAMBERLAIN, JILL FRANCES, financial services executive; b. Chgo., Mar. 25, 1954; d. Chester Emery and Mary Edythe (Hurd) C. B.A. in Math. with honors, Ill. State U., 1975; M.B.A., U. Chgo., 1981. Programmer Arthur Andersen, Chgo., 1975-76; cons. Laventhol & Horwath, Chgo., 1976-77; fin. systems analyst U. Chgo. Hosp., 1978-80; v.p. CHI/COR Info. Mgmt., Inc., Chgo., 1980-87; systems designer GECC, Stamford, 1987-88; mgr. GE Capital Corp., 1988—; cons. RMS Bus. Systems, Chgo., 1976-77. Mem. NAFE. Libertarian. Methodist. Avocations: reading, traveling, needlework. Office: GE Capital 1600 Summer St Stamford CT 06905-5125

CHAMBERLAIN, KATHRYN BURNS BROWNING, retired naval officer; b. Rapid City, S.D., Jan. 17, 1951; d. George Alfred III and Mildred Doty Browning; m. Thomas Richard Masker, Apr. 19, 1975 (widowed Sept. 1978); m. Guy Caldwell Chamberlain III, Mar. 25, 1981 (div. Oct. 1988); children: Burns Doty, Anne Caldwell. BA, La. Tech. U., 1973; postgrad., Naval Postgrad. Sch., Monteray, Calif., 1978-79; MA, Auburn U., 1984; postgrad., U. Ill., 1994-95. Ensign USN, 1974, ltjg., 1976, lt., 1978, advanced through grades to lt. comdr., 1983, surface warfare designation, 1980, joint staff officer, 1986; comdg. officer Mil. Sealift Command Office USN, Alaska, 1986-88; comdr., exec. officer USNAVFAC USNAVFAC, Newfoundland, Nfld., Can., 1991-94; mem. Armed Svcs. YMCA. Mem. Am. Mgmt. Assn., Internat. City/County Mgmt. Assn., Lions Internat. Home and Office: PO Box 6586 Champaign IL 61826-6586

CHAMBERLAIN, PATRICIA ANN, environmental manager, land use planner; b. Haskell, Tex., Sept. 30, 1941; d. James Franklin Kennedy and Roberta Marie; m. Herbert F. Chamberlain, July 20, 1962 (div. Oct. 1967); children: Norma Ann Marie, Catherine Denise; m. Clayton C. Wright, Mar. 5, 1994. AA, Odessa (Tex.) Jr. Coll., 1970; BS in Secondary Edn., Tex. Tech. U., 1971, PhD in Land Use Planning, Mgmt. & Design, 1984. Cert. wildlife biologist. Lab. and x-ray tech. Med. Ctr. Hosp. and Drs. offices, Odessa, 1964-68; supr. urban wildlife program Tex. Rodent & Predatory Animal Control Svc., San Antonio, 1972-80; rsch. wildlife biologist USDA U.S. Forest Svc., Lubbock, Tex., 1981-84; community planner USAF San Antonio Real Property Maintenance Agy., 1985-87; environ. engr. USAF SARPMA, San Antonio, 1987-88; br. chief USAF Environ. Br., Brooks AFB, Tex., 1988-91; community planner USAF Ctr. Environ. Excellence, San Antonio, Brooks AFB, 1991-94, natural resources specialist, 1994—; mem. USAF Graphics Working Group, Washington, 1987-91. Mem. Target '90 Goals for San Antonio, 1986-87. With U.S. Army, 1960-62. Caesar Kleberg Wildlife Rsch. Found. grantee, 1980-84; named to San Antonio Women's Hall of Fame, 1992. Mem. Am. Planning Assn. (regional treas. 1986, 87), Soc. Am. Mil. Engrs., Wildlife Soc. (nat. urban wildlife and regional planning com. mem. 1980-82), Phi Kappa Phi, Sigma Tau Delta, Beta Beta Beta. Office: USAF Ctr Environ Excellence Brooks AFB San Antonio TX 78235

CHAMBERS, ANNE COX, newspaper executive, former diplomat; b. Dayton, Ohio. Student Finch Coll., N.Y.C.; hon. degrees: D Pub. Service, Wesleyan Coll., 1982; DHL, Spelman Coll., 1983; LLD, Oglethorpe U., 1983, DHL, Brenau Coll., 1989, LLD, Clark Atlanta U., 1989. Chmn. bd. Atlanta Jour.-Constn.; Am. ambassador to Belgium, 1977-81; bd. dirs. Cox Enterprises, Inc. Bd. dirs. Atlanta Arts Alliance, High Mus. Art, Cities in Schs., Am. Ditchley Found., MacDowell Colony, Forward Arts Found., Emory Mus. Art and Archaeology, N.Y. Bot. Garden, Coun. Am. Ambs., Chairman's Coun., Met. Mus. Art; trustee Mus. Modern Art; mem. internat. council Mus. Modern Art, nat. com. Whitney Mus. Am. Art. Decorated Legion of Honor (France). Mem. Council Fgn. Relations. Home: 426 W Paces Ferry Rd NW Atlanta GA 30305-1003 Office: Atlanta Newspapers 1400 Lake Hearn Dr NE Atlanta GA 30319-1464

CHAMBERS, CAROL TOBEY, elementary school educator; b. L.A., July 17, 1947; d. Joseph Richard and Jean Doris (Neal) Tobey; m. Joseph Price Chambers, June 8, 1973; 1 child, Ryan Leigh. Student, Ohio State U., 1965-67; BS in Edn., George Peabody Coll. Tchrs., 1969; postgrad., U. Tenn., 1971, Belmont U., 1971, 88, Tenn. State U., 1980-83; Vanderbilt U., 1986, 92, Trevecca Coll., 1978, 89, 90; postgrad., Tenn. Arts Acad., 1989, 94. Cert. tchr. elem. edn., elem. art, Tenn. Tchr. 4th grade Metro-Nashville Pub. Sch., Nashville, 1969-70, tchr. art, music, 1970-71; tchr. 5th grade Harding Acad., Nashville, 1971-75, tchr. art, 1977—; presenter workshops Mid-So. Assn. Ind. Schs., Nashville, 1986; mem. vis. com. oak Hill Sch., So. Assn. Colls. and Schs. Nashville, 1990, St. Bernard Acad., 1991; chair planning com. Harding Acad., Nashville, 1992-94; fine arts chair St. Cecilia Acad. Parent's Club, Nashville, 1991-93, mem. parent's club; co-founder Art Tchr.'s Guild, Nashville; organizer Youth Art Month Exhbit, Nashville, 1992, 93, 94, 95. V.p. in charge of art Children's Internat. Edn. Ctr., Nashville, 1985-90; cons. Cheekwood Fine Arts Ctr. and Bot. Gardens Edn. Dept., Nashville, 1987—; prodr. parent's seminar 1st Bapt. Ch., 1986. Outstanding Tchr. of Humanities grantee Tenn. Humanities Couns., 1988; selected for Tenn. Arts Acad., 1994. Mem. Nat. Art Edn. Assn., Tenn. Art Edn. Assn., Nat. Mus. Women in the Arts (charter). Baptist. Home: 722 Starlit Rd Nashville TN 37205-1210 Office: 170 Windsor Dr Nashville TN 37205-3764

CHAMBERS, CAROLYN SILVA, communications company executive; b. Portland, Oreg., Sept. 15, 1931; d. Julio and Elizabeth (McDonnell) Silva; widowed; children: William, Scott, Elizabeth, Silva, Clark. BBA, U. Oreg. V.p., treas. Liberty Comm., Inc., Eugene, Oreg., 1960-83; pres. Chambers Comm. Corp., Eugene, 1983—; chmn., bd. dirs. Chambers Constrn. Co., 1986—; bd. dirs., dep. chair bd. Fed. Res. Bank, San Francisco, 1982-92; bd. dirs. Portland Gen. Corp.; bd. dirs. U.S. Bancorp. Mem. Sacred Heart Med. Found., 1980—; mem. Sacred Heart Gov. Bd., 1987-92; mem. U. Oreg. Found., 1980—, pres., 1992-93; chair U. Oreg. Found. The Campaign for Oreg., 1988-89; pres., bd. dirs. Eugene Arts Found.; bd. dirs., treas., dir. search com. Eugene Symphony; mem. adv. bd. Eugene Hearing and Speech Ctr., Alton Baker Park Commn., Pleasant Hill Sch. Bd.; chmn., pres., treas. Civic Theatre, Very Little Theatre; negotiator, treas., bd. dirs., mem. thrift shop Jr. League of Eugene. Recipient Webfoot award U. Oreg., 1986, Pres.'s medal, 1991, Disting. Svc. award, 1992, Pioneer award, 1983, Woman Who Made a Difference award Internat. Women's Forum, 1989. Mem. Nat. Cable TV Assn. (mem. fin. com., chmn. election and by-laws com., chmn. awards com., bd. dirs. 1987—, Vanguard award for Leadership 1982), Pacific Northwest Cable Comm. Assn. (conv. chmn., pres.), Oreg. Cable TV Assn. (v.p., pres., chmn. edn. com., conv. chmn., Pres.'s award 1986), Calif. Cable TV Assn. (bd. dirs., conv. chmn., conv. panelist), Women in Cable (charter mem., treas., v.p., pres., recipient star of cable recognition), Wash. State Cable Comm. Assn., Idaho Cable TV Assn., Community Antenna TV Assn., Cable TV Pioneers, Eugene C. of C. (first citizen award, 1985). Home: PO Box 640 Pleasant Hill OR 97455-0640 Office: Chambers Comm Corp PO Box 7009 Eugene OR 97401-0009

CHAMBERS, CLYTIA MONTLLOR, public relations consultant; b. Rochester, N.Y., Oct. 23, 1922; d. Anthony and Marie (Bambace) Capraro; m. Joseph John Montllor, July 2, 1941 (div. 1958); children: Michele, Thomas, Clytia; m. Robert Chambers, May 28, 1965. BA, Barnard Coll., N.Y.C., 1942; Licence en droit, Faculte de Droit, U. Lyon, France, 1948; MA, Howard U., Washington, 1958. Assoc. dir. dept. rsch. Coun. for Fin. Aid to Edn., N.Y.C., 1958-60; asst. to v.p. indsl. rels. Sinclair Oil Corp., N.Y.C., 1961-65; writer pub. rels. dept. Am. Oil Co., Chgo., 1965-67; dir. editorial svcs., v.p. Hill & Knowlton Inc., N.Y.C., 1967-77; sr. v.p., dir. spl. svcs. Hill & Knowlton Inc., L.A., 1977-90; sr. cons. Hill & Knowlton Inc., 1990—; cons. and trustee Childen's Inst. Internat., L.A., 1988-93. Co-author: The News Twisters, 1971; editor: Critical Issues in Public Relations, 1975. Mem. Calif. Rare Fruit Growers (editor Fruit Gardener 1979—). Home: 11439 Laurelcrest Dr Studio City CA 91604-3872

CHAMBERS, DOROTHY ROSE, special education educator; b. Yakima, Wash., May 8, 1941; d. George Milford and Blance Mary (McCarthy) Hollenbeck; BS in Speech and Lang. Therapy, Marquette U., 1964; MA in Spl. Edn., San Francisco State U., 1969; m. Thomas M. Chambers, Aug. 14, 1971; adopted children—David, Monique, Christopher, George, Elizabeth. Speech pathologist Mpls. Pub. Schs., 1964-65, Milbrae (Calif.) Sch. Dist., 1965-68; reading specialist Dept. Def., Landstuhl, Germany, 1970-71; tchr. children with extreme learning problems Portland (Oreg.) Public Schs., 1971-80, dept. chmn. spl. edn., 1980-84, program specialist program devel., 1984-86, diagnostic specialist assessment program spl. edn., 1986-94, speech and lang. pathologist, 1994—; cert. instr. develop. therapy U. Ga., 1982; instr. Portland State U., D.C.E., 1982, 83. HEW Dept. Rehab. fellow, 1969. Mem. Am. Speech and Hearing Assn. (cert. in clin. competence), Common Cause, Cousteau Soc., NEA, Oreg. Edn. Assn., Nat. Council Exceptional Children (presenter nat. conv. 1984). Democrat. Roman Catholic. Author: PEACHES (Pre-Sch. Ednl. Adaptation for Children Who Are Handicapped), 1978. Home: 12414 SE Oatfield Rd Portland OR 97222-6956 Office: Portland Pub Schs 501 N Dixon St Portland OR 97227-1804

CHAMBERS, IMOGENE KLUTTS, school system administrator, financial consultant; b. Paden, Okla., Aug. 6, 1928; d. Odes and Lillie (Southard) Klutts; BA, East Central State U., 1948; MS, Okla. State U., 1974, EdD, 1980; m. Richard Lee Chambers, May 27, 1949. High sch. math. tchr. Marlow (Okla.) Sch. Dist., 1948-49; with Bartlesville (Okla.) Sch. Dist., 1950-94, asst. supt. bus. affairs, treas. Ind. Sch. Dist. 30, 1977-87, treas., 1985-94; fin. acctg. cons. Okla. State Dept. Edn., 1987-92; dir. Plaza Nat. Bank, 1984-94; adv. dir. Bank Okla., 1994—. Bd. dirs. Mutual Girls Club, 1981—; treas. Okla. Schs. Ins. Assn., 1982—, adminstr., 1993—. Mem. Okla. Assn. Sch. Bus. Ofcls., Assn. Sch. Bus. Ofcls. Internat., Okla. Assn. Retired Sch. Adminstrs., Okla. State U. Alumni Assn., E. Ctrl. Univ. Alumni Assn. (bd. dirs. 1994—), Rotary, Phi Delta Kappa. Democrat. Methodist. Home: 911 SE Greystone Pl Bartlesville OK 74006-5141 Office: Bartlesville Ind Sch Dist 30 1100 S Jennings St Bartlesville OK 74005

CHAMBERS, JOAN LOUISE, library director; b. Denver, Mar. 22, 1937; d. Joseph Harvey and Clara Elizabeth (Carleton) Baker; m. Donald Ray Chambers, Aug. 17, 1958. B.A. in English Lit., U. No. Colo., Greeley, 1958; M.S. in Library Sci., U. Calif.-Berkeley, 1970; M.S. in Systems Mgmt., U. So. Calif., 1985. Librarian U. Nev., Reno, 1970-79; asst. univ. librarian U. Calif., San Diego, 1979-81; univ. librarian U. Calif., Riverside, 1981-85; dir. libraries Colo. State U., 1985—; mgmt. intern. Duke U. Libr., Durham, N.C., 1978-79; sr. fellow UCLAA summer, 1982; cons. tng. program Assn. of Rsch. Libraries, Washington, 1981; libr. cons. Calif. State U., Sacramento, 1982-83, U. Wyo., 1985-86, U. Nebr., 1991-92, Calif. State U. System, 1993-94. Contbr. articles to profl. jours., chpts. to books. U. Calif. instl. improvement grantee, 1980-81; State of Nev. grantee, 1976, ARL grantee, 1983-84. Mem. ALA, Assn. Coll. and Rsch. Librs. IFLA (com. mem.) CNI, Libr. Adminstrn. and Mgmt. Assn., Colo. Libr. Assn., Assn. Rsch. Librs., United Way, Sierra Club, Beta Phi Mu, Phi Lambda Theta, Kappa Delta Phi. Home: 4470 S Lemay Ave Apt 1305 Fort Collins CO 80525-4844 Office: Colo State U William E Morgan Libr Fort Collins CO 80523

CHAMBERS, LINDA DIANNE THOMPSON, social worker; b. Mexia, Tex., Apr. 21, 1953; d. Lee and Essie Mae (Hopes) Thompson; m. George Edward Chambers, Nov. 30, 1978; 1 child, Brandon. AS cum laude, Navarro Coll., Tex., 1974; B in Social Work magna cum laude, Tex. Woman's U., 1976; cert. gerontology and Human Svcs. Mgmt., Sam Houston U., 1982; M in Social Work, U. Tex.-Arlington, 1990. Lic. marriage and family therapist. Mem. social work staff Dept. Human Resources, Ft. Worth, Tex., 1975, Children's Med. Ctr., Dallas, 1976, Mexia State Sch., Tex., 1976-93, Methodist Home, Waco, Tex., 1993—. Pres., Raven Exquisites, Mexia, 1983-84, sec.-treas., 1984-85; bd. dirs. Limestone County Child Welfare Bd., Hospice, Inc.; pres. bd. dirs. Limestone County unit Am. Cancer Soc.; bd. dirs. Gibbs Meml. Libr.; mem. Tex. Dem. Women; vol. McLennon County Pub. Health Dist. AIDS Clinic; coord., founder Limestone County Teen Parent Program; co-founder Limestone County Parenting Coalition; mem. Limestone County Youth Adv. Com.; PTO sec. Ctrl. Tex. Literacy Coalition, 1992—; vol. Ctr. for Action Against Sexual Assault, Family Abuse Ctr.; mem. Tex. Hist. Found., Nat. Mus. Women in Arts, 1985—; Recipient numerous awards for scholarship and profl. excellence. Fellow Internat. Biog. Assn. (dep. bd. gov., life); mem. Am. Sociol. Soc. (sec. 1975-76), Univ. Woman's Assn., Am. Childhood Edn. Internat., Nat. Assn. Social Workers, NAFE, Am. Assn. Mental Retardation, Nat. Assn. Future Women, Am. Soc. Profl. and Exec. Women, Nat. Assn. Negro Bus. and Profl. Women's Clubs, AAUW, Tex. Woman's U. Nat. Alumnae Assn., Mortar Bd. Honor Soc. (sec.-treas. 1975-76), Tex. Soc. Clin. Social Workers, Internat. Platform Assn., Internat. Assn. Bus. and Profl. Women, Tex. Assn. Clin. Social Workers, Am. Biog. Assn. (dep. bd. govs.), Nat. Mus. Women Arts, Los Amigos, Limestone County Parenting Coalition (co-founder), Phi Theta Kappa, Alpha Kappa Delta, Alpha Delta Mu, Young Dems. Club. Avocations: reading, gardening, gourmet cooking. Home: 102 Harding Mexia TX 76667

CHAMBERS, LOIS IRENE, insurance automation consultant; b. Omaha, Nov. 24, 1935; d. Edward J. and Evelyn B. (Davidson) Morrison; m. Peter A. Mscichowski, Aug. 16, 1952 (div. 1980); 1 child, Peter Edward; m. Frederick G. Chambers, Apr. 17, 1981. Clk. Gross-Wilson Ins. Agy., Portland, Oreg., 1955-57; sec., bookkeeper Reed-Paulsen Ins. Agy., Portland, 1957-58; office mgr., asst. sec., agt. Don Biggs & Assocs., Vancouver, Wash., 1958-88, v.p. ops., 1988-89, automation mgr., 1989-91, mktg. mgr., 1991-94; automation cons. Chambers & Assocs., Tualatin, Oreg., 1985—; chmn. adv. com. Clark Community Coll., Vancouver, 1985-93, adv. com., 1993-94. Mem. citizens com. task force City of Vancouver, 1976-78, mem. Block Grant rev. task force, 1978—. Mem. Ins. Women of S.W. Wash. (pres. 1978, Ins. Woman of Yr. 1979), Nat. Assn. Ins. Women, Nat. Users Agena Systems (charter; pres. 1987-89), Soroptimist Internat. (Vancouver)(pres. 1978-79, Soroptimist of the Year 1979-80). Democrat. Roman Catholic. Office: Chambers & Assocs 8770 SW Umatilla St Tualatin OR 97062-9338

CHAMBERS, MARGARET WARNER, lawyer; b. West Chester, Pa., Oct. 12, 1959; d. Samuel Lippincott and Margaret Ewing (Warner) C.; m. Bruce Wayne Nifong, June 21, 1986. BS in Edn., Pa. State U., 1980; JD, Suffolk U., 1983. Bar: Mass. 1983. Staff atty. pub. records div. Mass. Sec. of State's Office, Boston, 1983-84, staff atty. securities div., 1984-86; assoc. Ropes & Gray, Boston, 1986—. Mem. ABA (state regulation of securities com., investment-advisers/investment co. subcom., sec. state regulation of securities com. 1991—), Mass. Bar Assn. (sect. coun. bus. law sect. 1990-92, mem. securities law com.), Boston Bar Assn. (securities com.). Mem. Soc. of Friends. Office: Ropes & Gray 1 International Pl Boston MA 02110-2624

CHAMBERS, MARJORIE BELL, historian; b. N.Y.C., Mar. 11, 1923; d. Kenneth Carter and Katherine (Totman) Bell; m. William Hyland Chambers, Aug. 8, 1945; children: Lee Chambers-Schiller, William Bell, Leslie Chambers Trujillo, Kenneth Carter. AB cum laude, Mt. Holyoke Coll., South Hadley, Mass., 1943; MA, Cornell U., 1948; PhD, U. N.Mex., 1974; LLD honoris causa, Ctrl. Mich. U., 1977; LHD (hon.), Wilson Coll., 1980, Northern Michigan U., 1982. Staff asst. Am. Assn. UN, League of Nations Assn., N.Y.C., 1944-45; program specialist dept. rural sociology Cornell U., Ithaca, N.Y., 1945-46, rsch. asst. dept. speech and drama, 1946-48; substitute tchr. Los Alamos (N.Mex.) Pub. Schs., 1962-65; project historian U.S. AEC, Los Alamos, 1965-69; adj. prof. U. N.Mex., Los Alamos, 1970-76, 84-85; pres. Colo. Women's Coll., Denver, 1976-78; dean Grad. Sch. Union Inst., Cin., 1979-82, mem. core faculty Grad. Sch., 1979—; interim pres. Colby-Sawyer Coll., New London, N.H., 1985-86; vis. prof. Cameron U., Lawton, Okla., 1974; commr., vice-chair N.Mex. Commn. on Higher Edn., Santa Fe, 1987-91; chair citizen adv. bd. U.S. Army Command and Gen. Staff Coll., Ft. Leavenworth, Kans., 1990—; mem. bd. dirs. Coun. Ind. Colls. and Univs., Santa Fe, 1991—; rep. Los Alamos County Labor Mgmt. Bd. Contbr. articles to profl. jours. Chair Los Alamos County Coun., 1976, councilor, 1975-76, 79; candidate N.Mex. 3d Congl. Dist., 1982, lt. gov. N.Mex., 1986; chair Sec. of Navy's Advisory Bd. on Edn. and Tng., Washington and Pensacola, Fla., 1987-89; acting chair, vice-chair adminstrn. Pres. Carter's Com. for Women, Washington, 1977-80; chair Los Alamos County Pers. Bd., 1983-90; mem. nat. adv. coun. U.S. SBA, 1990—; mem., editor Los Alamos and N.Mex. Rep. Ctrl. com., 1982—; trustee Colby-Sawyer Coll., New London, N.H., 1980-89. Recipient Teresa d'Avila award Coll. St. Teresa, Winona, Minn., 1978, Disting. Woman award U. N.Mex. Alumni Assn., Albuquerque, 1990, N.Mex. Disting. Pub. Svc. award Gov. and Awards Coun., Albuquerque, 1991; named Outstanding N.Mex. Woman Gov. and Com. on Status of Women, Albuquerque, 1988, 89. Mem. AAUW (life, nat. pres. 1975-79, pres. Edn. Found.), DAR, Bus. and Profl. Women (Los Alamos parliamentarian and dist. parliamentarian 1991-93), Women's Polit. Caucus (gov. bd., conv. keynoter, vice-chair Rep. caucus 1971—), Internat. Women's Forum, N.Mex. Hist. Soc., Los Alamos Hist. Soc. (pres.). Presbyterian.

CHAMBLISS, CHARLOTTE MARIE, secondary education educator; b. Dallas, May 4, 1956; d. Wallace C. and Betty H. (Duncan) C. BFA cum laude, U. North Tex., 1984. Supr., dispatcher Direct Couriers Am., Dallas, 1978-85; instr. visual arts B.T. Washington High Sch., Dallas, 1989-94; visual art instr. Hillcrest H.S., Dallas, 1994—. O'Donnell Found. grantee, 1994—. Home: 2547 Valwood Pkwy Farmers Branch TX 75234

CHAMBLISS, TONJA NIKITA, electrical engineer; b. Nashville, Oct. 31, 1962; d. Rufus Steve Jr. and Barbara Jean (Garrett) Crawford. Cert. in ub. Mgmt., Ind. U.-Purdue U. Inst., 1993. Apprentice draftsman Williams, Russell & Johnson, Inc., Atlanta, 1983; elec. engr. Saginaw (Mich.) Div. GM, Inc., 1984-86, Naval Surface Warfare Ctr. Crane Div., Crane, Ind., 1989—. Mem. Blacks in Govt. Home: 726 Ridge Crest Ct Bloomington IN 47401-4567

CHAMINGS, PATRICIA ANN, nurse, educator; b. Lakeland, Fla., June 21, 1940; d. Roy John and Esther Delilah (O'Steen) C. Diploma, Orange Meml. Hosp., 1961; BSN, U. Fla., 1964, M of Nursing, 1965; PhD, George Peabody Coll., 1978. Cert. nurse adminstr. advanced. Dir., assoc. prof. grad. program Vanderbilt U., Nashville, 1976-84; asst. dean Emory U., Atlanta, 1984-85; prof. U. N.C., Greensboro, 1985—, dean, 1985-90, dir. anesthesia edn. project, 1989-92; bd. trustees Wesley Long Cmty. Hosp., 1989-91; bd. dirs. N.C. Ctr. for Nursing, Health Svc. Ministry, N.C. Commn. on Mental Health, Devel. Disabilities and Substance Abuse Svcs., 1993-96. Col. Nurse Corps USAFR. Trustee Wesley Long Cmty. Hosp., 1989-95; bd. dirs. N.C. Ctr. for Nursing; active N.C. Commn. on Mental Health, Devel. Disabilities and Substance Abuse Svcs., 1993-96. Col. Nurse Corps, USAFR. Named N.C. Nurse Educator of Yr., 1988; advanced nurse tng. grantee USPHS, 1989-91. Fellow Am. acad. Nursing; mem. Sigma Theta Tau Internat.

CHAMIS, ALICE YANOSKO, information management consultant; b. Arvida, Quebec, Can.; d. Andy and Anna (Michalcik) Yanosko; m. Christos C. Chamis; children: Chrysanthie Diane, Anna Lisa, Constantinos Andy. BS, McGill U., Montreal, Can., 1959; M.S.L.S., Case Western Res. U., 1962, PhD, 1984. Lit. chemist Alcan, Arvida, 1959-61; libr. mgr. B.F. Goodrich Co., Brecksville, Ohio, 1962-69; asst. dir. Cuyahoga County Pub. Libr., Cleve., 1970-80; project mgr. Case Western Res. U., Cleve., 1985-86;

asst. prof. Kent State U., Kent, Ohio, 1986-88; pres. Info. Mgmt. Consultants, Westlake, Ohio, 1980—. Author: Vocabulary Control and Search Strategies in Online Searching, 1991; contbr. 15 articles to profl. jours. Plenum scholar. Mem. Spl. Librs. Assn., Am. Soc. for Info. Sci. (Best Paper award), Soc. Competitive Intelligence Profls. Office: Info Mgmt Consultants 24534 Framingham Dr Cleveland OH 44145-4902

CHAMP, LAURNA JANE, marriage and family therapist; b. Aug. 13, 1951; d. Laurn R. and Janet Isabella Champ. BS, Kans. State U., 1973.; MEd, Ctrl. State U., Edmond, Okla., 1980; PhD, Okla. State U., 1986. Lic. marital and family therapist, Okla.; reg. play therapist. Preschool tchr. Keystone and Sch. Creative Play, Oklahoma City, 1974-76; adminstr. YWCA, Oklahoma City, 1976-78, Northwest Christian Ch., Oklahoma City, 1978-80; adminstr., therapist U. Okla. Health Sci. Ctr., Oklahoma City, 1980-83; instr., adminstr. Rose State Coll., Midwest City, Okla., 1981-94; instr., specialist child devel. Okla. State U., Stillwater, 1983-85; child and family therapist Child and Family Ctr., Oklahoma City, 1983—, Red Rock Mental Health Ctr., Oklahoma City, 1987-88; specialist child devel. Region IV Head Start, Dallas, 1983-94; with vocat.-tech. system State of Okla., 1983—, Dept. Mental Health, 1991-94; cons. child devel. & parenting. Author: (training manual) Orientation to Head Start Caregiver Book, 1984 (Excellence award Soc. Tech. Comm. 1984), Instant Training Guide Series, 1987, (book) Resolving Behavior Problems, 1989. Bd. dirs. St. Paul's Episc. Christian Women, Oklahoma City, 1993-94. Mem. Am. Assn. Marriage and Family Therapist, Am. Assn. Counseling and Devel., Nat. Assn. Edn. Young Children, So. Assn. Children Under Six, Okla. Assn. Edn. Young Children, Okla. Family Resource Coalition. Democrat. Office: Child and Family Ctr 5100 N Brookline 625 Oklahoma City OK 73112

CHAMPAGNE, CECILE BELISLE, nursing educator, maternal/child health nurse; b. Worcester, Mass., Jan. 7, 1941; d. Alfred N. and Blanche (Poissant) B.; m. Raymond W. Champagne, Jr., Aug. 20, 1967; 1 child, Robert Raymond. BS, Salve Regina Coll., Newport, R.I., 1962; MS, Boston U., 1964; DNSc, Widener U., Chester, Pa., 1992. Instr. Salve Regina Coll., Newport, R.I.; asst. prof. Wilkes Coll., Wilkes-Barre, Pa., Coll. Misericordia, Dallas, Pa.; assoc. prof. East Stroudsburg (Pa.) U. Active March of Dimes HPAC. Mem. Sigma Theta Tau, Kappa Gamma Pi. Home: 117 Donny Dr Taylor PA 18517-9707

CHAMPION, MARY ELLEN, architect; b. Lexington, Ky., Dec. 9, 1946; d. Bennie Wise and Lannis Victoria (Coldiron) C.; m. Everett Lee Champion, Aug. 15, 1988. BA, U. Ky., 1971, BArch, 1976. Registered Nat. Coun. Archtl. Registration Bds., Ky., Ohio. Project architect McCloskey, John Morgan, Al Harmon, Lexington, Ky., 1971-78; prin. architect Mary Ellen Craft, Architect, Lexington, 1978-79; project architect Camargo Assocs., Inc., Cin., 1979-85, project/dept. mgr., 1986-88; project mgr. Camargo Assocs. (div. Jacobs Engring. Group), Cin., 1989-90, mgr. quality, 1990-91, regional mgr. quality, 1991-92; sr. project mgr. Belcan Engring. Group, Cin., 1992—. Big Brothers, Big Sisters Am., Lexington, 1974-78. Mem. Project Mgmt. Inst., Internat. Soc. Pharm. Engrs. (speaker 1992, founding sec. Gt. Lakes chpt. 1993, v.p. 1994). Office: Belcan Engring Group 10200 Anderson Way Cincinnati OH 45242

CHAMPION, MAXINE CHRISTINA, lawyer, business executive; b. N.Y.C.; d. Max and Mimi (Ravashiere) Sokol; 1 child, Christina Anne. BA, Pa. State U., 1967; JD, Am. U., 1977. Bar: Pa. 1977, U.S. Ct. Appeals (D.C. cir.) 1977, U.S. Tax Ct. 1977, U.S. Ct. Appeals (fed. cir.) 1978, U.S. Ct. Claims 1978, U.S. Supreme Ct. 1980. Devel. specialist IRS, Washington, 1973-76; atty./advisor to chief judge U.S. Tax Ct., Washington, 1976-78; trial atty. tax div. Dept. Justice, Washington, 1978-84; tax counsel Ways and Means Com. Ho. Reps., Washington, 1984-88; v.p. govt. rels. LTV Corp., Washington, 1988-92; v.p. govt. and internat. rels. Nestle U.S.A., Inc., 1992—; bd. dirs. Am. Coun. for Capital Formation Ctr. for Policy Rsch., Bulgarian-Am. Friendship Soc., Inc., Washington, 1992—; mem. Tax Coalition, Washington, 1984—, former chmn. bd.; commr. adv. group Internal Revenue, 1988-90. Co-chair Nat. Race for the Cure, 1994. EEC fellow, 1983. Mem. ABA (tax. and corp. sects. 1977—, editor ann. report 1980), Fed. Bar Assn. (officer 1990—), Capitol Forum. Office: Nestle USA Inc Ste 310 1133 Connecticut Ave NW Washington DC 20036

CHAMPION, NORMA JEAN, communications educator, state legislator; b. Oklahoma City, Jan. 21, 1933; d. Aubra Dell and Beuleah Beatrice (Flanagan) Black; m. Richard Gordon Champion, Oct. 3, 1953; children: Jeffery Bruce, Ashley Brooke. BA in Religious Edn., Cen. Bible Coll., Springfield, Mo., 1971; MA in Comm., S.W. Mo. State U., 1978; PhD in Ednl. Comm., U. Okla., 1986. Producer, hostess The Children's Hour, Sta. KYTV-TV, NBC, Springfield, 1957-86; asst. prof. Cen. Bible Coll., 1968-84; prof. broadcasting Evangel Coll., Springfield, 1978—; mem. Springfield City Coun., 1987-92, Mo. Ho. of Reps., Jefferson City, 1992—; mem. adj. faculty Assemblies of God Theol. Sem., Springfield, 1987—; frequent lectr. to svc. clubs, ednl. seminars; seminar speaker Internat. Pentecostal Press Assn. World Conf., Singapore, 1989; announcer various TV commls. Contbr. numerous articles to religious publs. Mem. bd Mo. Access to Higher Edn. Trust, 1990—; regional rep. Muscular Dystrophy Assn.; mem. adv. bd. Chameleon Puppet Theater, 1987; mem. exec. bd. Univ. Child Care Ctr., 1987; hon. chmn. fund raising Salvation Army, 1986; also numerous other bds., hon. chairmanships.; judge Springfield City Schs. Recipient commendation resolution Mo. Ho. of Reps., 1988; numerous award for The Children's Hour; Aunt Norma Day named in her honor City of Springfield, 1976. Mem. Nat. Broadcast Edn. Assn., Mo. Broadcast Edn. Assn., Nat. League Cities, Mo. Mcpl. League (human resource com. 1989, intergovtl. rels. com. 1990), Nat. Assn. Telecom. Officers and Advisors, Internat. Pentesostal Press Assn., Josephson Inst. for Advancement Ethics, Springfield C. of C., Mo. PTA (life). Republican. Mem. Assemblies of God Ch. Home: 3609 S Broadway Ave Springfield MO 65807-4505 Office: Evangel Coll 1111 N Glenstone Ave Springfield MO 65802-2191

CHAMPLIN, CAROLYN RENEE, administrator, accountant; b. Hamilton, Ohio, Aug. 15, 1954; d. Stanley Dewey Le Master, Jr.; m. Franklin Ross Champlin, Aug. 15, 1975 (div.); children: Bryan Ross, Carissa Jo, Benjamin Scott. Student, Okla. State U., 1978-81; B in Profl. Accountancy, Miss. State U., 1987. Adminstr. Miss. State U. Devel. Found., Starkville, 1983-90; acct. Miss. State U. Coll. Vet. Medicine, Starkville, 1983-90; asst. Miss. State U. Sch. of Accountancy, 1983-90; bus. adminstr. Advanced Microelectronics div. Inst. for Tech. Devel., Jackson, Miss., 1991—; mem. Inst. for Tech. Devel. Money Purchase Pension Plan Com., Jackson, 1992—. Bd. dirs. Madison County Ednl. Found., 1992—, chair grant solicitations com., membership and corp. membership coms., 1992—. Recipient scholarship Inst. for Mgmt. Accts., Miss. State U., 1987. Mem. Inst. Mgmt. Accts. (bd. dirs. Jackson chpt., dir. spl. events 1992—), Phi Kappa Phi, Beta Alpha Psi. Methodist. Office: Inst for Tech Devel Advanced Microelectronics 1080 River Oaks Dr Ste A250 Jackson MS 39208-9779

CHAN, GRACE P, industrial designer; b. Auburn, Wash., Apr. 11, 1962; d. Ming C. and Fan Wong; m. Philip Y. Chan, Aug. 31, 1991. BFA, U. Washington, 1985; AAS, Green River Community Coll., Auburn, Wash., 1987. Facilities planner, interior designer Boeing, Seattle, 1987-89, indsl. design lead, 777 flight deck, 1989-93, indsl. designer, ctrl. flight deck rsch., 1994—; mentor adv. indsl. design Western Washington U., Bellingham, Wash., 1992. dir. art fair Boeing Arts and Crafts, Seattle, 1992-93. Recipient Design Aire award Design Aire, Fla., 1992, Indsl. Design Excellence award Indsl. Designer's Soc. Am., Va., 1993, Indsl. Design Invitational award Northwest Indsl. Design, Wash., 1994. Home: 7940 B Seward Park Ave South Seattle WA 98118 Office: Boeing Ctrl Flight Deck Engring PO Box 3707 M/S 6H-TX Seattle WA 98124

CHAN, JULIE YU-CHIUNG, internal revenue agent; b. Canton, China, Aug. 19, 1944; came to U.S., 1967; d. Feng and Jin-Sha (Chan) C. BA, Nat. Taiwan U., Taipei, 1966; MBA, Appalachian State U., 1968. Internal revenue agt. IRS, Monterey Park, Calif., 1983—. Mem. Inst. Mgmt. Accts. Home: 7000 S La Cienega Blvd # 12 Inglewood CA 90302

CHANCELLOR, DORIS ANN, librarian, secondary education educator; b. Malvern, Ark., Apr. 12, 1947; d. Floyd Wesley and Doris Maxine (Selph) Thomas; m. Harold Wayne Chancellor, Dec. 21, 1968; children: Brett Wayne, Jill Lindsay. BSE, Henderson State U., 1968, MSE, 1973. English tchr. Poyen (Ark.) Pub. Schs., 1968-70; libr., English tchr., grant writer Ouachita Pub. Schs., Donaldson, Ark., 1970—. Mem. Ark. Assn. Sch. Librs. and Media Educators. Democrat. Baptist. Office: Ouachita Sch Dist RR 1 Box 33 Donaldson AR 71941-9706

CHANDLER, CLAIRE ELIZABETH, business consultant, applications engineer; b. Lafayette, Ind., Apr. 29, 1960; d. Arthur Alan and Jane Anne (Johnson) C. BSChemE, Purdue U., 1982. Chem. engr. E.I. DuPont DeNemours & Co., Phila. and Troy, Mich., 1982-84; systems engr., industry mktg. rep. IBM Corp., L.A., 1984-88; internat. systems cons. FileNet Corp., Costa Mesa, Calif., 1988-90, Munich, Germany, 1988-90; sr. product mkgt. mgr. NCR Corp., Pacific Mktg. Group, Dayton, Ohio, 1991-92; cons. Dayton, 1992; sr. applications engr. Kofax Image Products, Irvine, Calif., 1993-94; sr. cons. Ascent Bus. Devel., 1994—. Del. Ind. Dem. State Conv., 1978; camp counselor Camp Ronald McDonald for Good Times, L.A., 1989—; vol. Make a Wish Found., Irvine, 1993. Mem. Assn. for Info. and Image Mgmt., Omicron Delta Kappa. Office: Kofax Image Products 3 Jenner Irvine CA 92718-3807

CHANDLER, ELISABETH GORDON (MRS. LACI DE GERENDAY), sculptor, harpist; b. St. Louis, June 10, 1913; d. Henry Brace and Sara Ellen (Sallee) Gordon; m. Robert Kirkland Chandler, May 27, 1946 (dec.); m. Laci de Gerenday, May 12, 1979. Grad., Lenox Sch., 1931; pvt. study sculpture and harp. Mem. Mildred Dilling Harp Ensemble, 1934-45; instr. portrait sculpture Lyme Acad. Fine Arts, 1976—; dir. Abbott Coin Counter Co., Inc., 1941-55. Exhibited sculpture NAD, Nat. Sculpture Soc., Allied Artists Am., Nat. Arts Club, Pen and Brush, Lyme Art Assn., Mattatuck Mus., Catherine Lorillard Wolfe Art Club, Am. Artists Profl. League, Hudson Valley Art Assn., USIA, 1976-78, Lyme Art Ctr., 1979, retrospective exhbn. Lyme Acad. Fine Arts, 1987, Madison Gallery, 1987, Old State House, Hartford, Conn., 1989, Mellon Art Ctr., Wallingford, Conn., 1989, Fairfield U. Walsh Gallery, 1991, Brit. Mus., London, Am. Medallic Sculptors Assn. Traveling Exhbn., 1994; represented in permanent collections Aircraft Carrier USS Forrestal, Gov. Dummer Acad., James Forrestal Research Ctr. of Princeton U., Lenox Sch., James L. Collins Parochial Sch., Tex., Storm King Art Ctr., Columbia U., Pace U., White Plains, N.Y., St. Patrick's Cathedral, N.Y.C., McAuley Ctr., St. Joseph's Coll., West Hartford, Conn., Forrestal Meml. Medal, Timoschenko Medal for Applied Mechanics, Benjamin Franklin Medal, Albert A. Michelson Medal, Jonathan Edwards Medal, Shafto Broadcasting Award Medal, Woodrow Wilson Sch. of Princeton U., Ga. Pacific Bldg., Atlanta, Messiah Coll., Grantham, Pa., Adlai E. Stevenson High Sch., Ill., Queen Anne's County Courthouse Square, Md., pvt. collections. With mus. therapy div. Am. Theatre Wing, 1942-45; trustee The Lenox Sch., 1953-55; chmn. Associated Taxpayers Old Lyme, 1969-72; mem., trustee Brookgreen Gardens, S.C., 1989—. Recipient 1st prize Bklyn. War Meml. competition, 1945; 1st prize sculpture Catherine Lorillard Wolfe Art Club, 1951, 58, 63, Gold medal, 1969; Founders prize Pen & Brush, 1954, 76, 78, Gold medal, 1957, 61, 63, 69, 74, 76, Am. Heritage award, 1968, Solo Show award, 1961, 69, 75; Thomas R. Proctor prize NAD, 1956, Dessie Greer prize, 1960, 79, 85; Sculpture prize Nat. Arts Club, 1959, 60, 62, Gold medal, 1971; Gold medal Am. Artists Profl. League, 1960, 69, 73, 75, prize, 1981, Anna Hyatt Huntington prize, 1970, 76, Harriet Mayer Meml. prize, 1961; Gold medal Hudson Valley Art Assn., 1956, 69, 74, Mrs. John Newington award, 1976, 78; Lindsey Morris Meml. prize Allied Artists Am., 1973, Gold medal, 1982; sculpture prize Acad. Artists, 1974; Sydney Taylor Meml. prize Knickerbocker Artists, 1975; New Netherlands DAR Bicentennial medal, 1976, named Citizen of Yr., Town of Old Lyme, Conn., 1985. Fellow NAD (academician), Nat. Sculpture Soc. (council 1976-85, Tallix Foundry award 1979, John Spring Founder's award 1986, John Cavanaugh Meml. prize 1991, Silver medal, citation 1992), Am. Artists Profl. League, Internat. Inst. Arts and Letters; mem. Federation International de la Medaille, Nat. Arts Club, Allied Artists Am., Am. Medallic Art Soc., Pen and Brush, Catherine Lorillard Wolf Art Club, Lyme Art Assn. (pres. 1973-75), Council Am. Artists Socs. (dir. 1970-73), Am. Artists Profl. League (dir. 1970-73), Lyme Acad. Fine Arts (trustee 1976—, chair sculpture dept.). Home and Studio: 2 Mill Pond Ln Old Lyme CT 06371

CHANDLER, JONI ANN, commercial insurance agent; b. Milford, Del., Sept. 22, 1962; d. Charles Delano and JoAnne (Bliss) C.; 1 child, Heath Thomas Northam. AS in Edn. magna cum laude, Tidewater C.C., Virginia Beach, Va., 1994. Cert. profl. ins. woman; accredited customer svc. rep. Various positions to svc. technician Gt. Am. Ins. Co., Richmond, Va., 1982-85; life, accident and health ins. agt. Bankers Life & Casualty Ins. Co., Florence, S.C., 1986; comml. ins. agt. Butler-Hartsell Ins. Agy., Virginia Beach, 1987-91, INSCO Group, Inc., Virginia Beach, 1991-93, S.L. Nusbaum Ins. Agy., Norfolk, Va., 1993—. Mem. PTA, Virginia Beach, 1992—. Mem. Nat. Assn. Ins. Women, Ins. Women of Virginia Beach (rec. sec., chmn. fundraising com. 1994—). Home: 4335 Atwater Arch Virginia Beach VA 23456-1441 Office: SL Nusbaum Ins Agy Inc 234 Monticello Ave Ste 1218 Norfolk VA 23510-2309

CHANDLER, KRIS, computer consultant, educator; b. Cleveland Heights, Ohio, June 26, 1948; d. Gerhard A. and Hanna R. (Rittmeyer) Hoffmann; children: Karen, Heidi. BSBA with honors and spl. distinction U. So. Colo., 1984, postgrad., 1984-85; MBA, U. Ark., 1987; PhD in C.C. Adminstrn. Colo. State U, 1993. Owner, mgr. V&W Fgn. Car Svc., Canon City, Colo., 1970-80; prin. The Chandlers, Computer Cons., Pueblo, Colo., 1982-88; ptnr. Jak Rabbit Software, 1989—; faculty Pikes Peak Community Coll., chair dept. computer info. systems, U. So. Colo., also mgr. Sch. Bus. microcomputer lab. Bd. dirs. Canon City Community Svc. Ctr., 1978-80, Canon City chpt. ARC, 1978-81. Mem. Assn. for Computing Machinery, Data Processing Mgmt. Assn. (advisor student chpt. Pikes Peak Community Coll. 1989—), U. So. Colo. Honors Soc. (pres.), U. So. Colo. Grad. Assn. (founder), Alpha Chi, Sigma Iota Epsilon. Home and Office: 401 S Neilson Ave Pueblo CO 81001-4238

CHANDLER, MARCIA SHAW BARNARD, farmer; b. Arlington, Mass., Aug. 22, 1934; d. John Alden and Grace Winifred (Copeland) Barnard; m. Samuel Butler Chandler, Aug. 31, 1952 (dec. 1986); children: Shawn Chandler Seddinger, Mark Thurmond, Matthew Butler. BA, Francis Marion Coll., Florence, S.C., 1976; MEd, U. S.C., 1985. Resource person United Cerebral Palsy of S.C., Dillon, 1976-79; instr. English Horry-Georgetown Tech. Coll., Conway, S.C., 1980-81; farm owner, mgr. Dillon. Author: (with others) Best of Old Farmer's Almanac, First 200 Years, 1991; cover artist So. Bell Telephone Directory, 1988, 90. Bd. dirs., publicist, artist Dillon County Theatre, Inc., 1985—; publicist, bd. dirs., artist MacArthur Ave. Players, Dillon, 1990—; bd. dirs. Friends of Francis Marion U., 1985—; pres. Dillon Area Arts Coun., 1980-85, Jr. Charity League of Dillon, 1960-75; nat. poetry judge DAR, 1982. Recipient Honorable Commendation for civic involvement S.C. Ho. Reps., Mar. 22, 1990. Mem. Cousteau Soc., Ctr. Environ. Edn., Internat. Fund Animal Welfare, World Wildlife Fund, Nature Conservancy. Home: 203 Reaves Ave Dillon SC 29536-1919

CHANDLER, MARGUERITE NELLA, real estate corporation executive; b. New Brunswick, N.J., May 16, 1943; d. Edward A. and Marguerite (Moore) C.; m. Ronald Wilson, May 30, 1964 (div. Nov. 1973); children: Mark, Adam; m. Richmond Shreve, Nov. 22, 1979; 1 child, Laura. BS in Acctg., Syracuse U., 1964, MS in Polit. Mgmt., 1988. Tax acct. Peat Marwick Mitchell, Providence, 1964; grant adminstr., psychology dept. Brown U., Providence, 1965; intern in devel. cons. Washington, 1973-75; prin., tng. cons. M. Chandler Assocs., 1975-76; mgmt. cons. Edmar Corp., Bound Brook, N.J., 1976-78, pres., chief exec. officer, 1978-90, pres., 1991—. Peace Corps vol., 1966-68; established Food Bank Network of Somerset County, 1982, pres., 1982-85; established Worldworks Found., Inc., 1983; founder PeopleCare Ctr., 1984, pres., 1984-86; bd. dirs. N.J. Coun. for Arts, 1986-87; pres. bd. trustees N.J. Coun. of Chs., 1985-90; bd. dirs. United Way Somerset Valley, 1984-91, gen. campaign chmn., 1985-86; recorder Blue Ribbon Com. on Ending Hunger in N.J., 1984-86; vol. Somerset Community Action Program, 1969-71, Missionaries of Charity, Calcutta, India, 1981; treas. Somerset County Day Care Assn., 1969-71; mem. N.J. Gov.'s Task Force on Pub./Pvt. Sector Initiatives, 1986-91; Dem. candidate for U.S. Congress Dist. 12, 1990; mem. adv. bd. US-USSR Youth Exchange, Ptnrs. in Peacemaking, The Giraffe Project; mem. Gov.'s Adv. Coun. on Solid Waste Mgmt., 1991-92; chairperson numerous fund-raising events to combat world hunger. Named Woman of Yr., Women's Resource Ctr. Somerset County, 1983, Citizen of Yr., Somerset County C. of C., 1985, N.J. Chpt. Nat. Assn. Soc. Workers, 1986, Bus. and Profl. Women's Club, 1987, Person of Decade, Courier-News, 1989, Bus. Person of Year, Bus. for Ctrl. N.J. mag., 1993; recipient People's Champion award Somerset Family Planning Service, 1985, Disting. Service award N.J. Speech-Language-Hearing Assn., 1986, N.J. Women of Achievement award Douglass Coll. and N.J. Fedn. Women's Clubs, 1986, Brotherhood award Central Jersey chpt. Nat. Conf. Christians and Jews, 1986, Presdl. End Hunger award, 1987. Mem. Assn. N.J. Recyclers (pres. 1991-93), Somerset C. of C. (chmn. bd. 1989-90, chmn. strategic planning cultural and heritage com.), World Bus. Acad. (bd. dirs. 1988-89), Rotary (pres. Bound Brook-Middlesex club 1993-94), Regional Plan Assn. (bd. dirs. 1994—). Mem. Soc. of Friends. Home: 6 Lisa Ter Somerville NJ 08876-2515 Office: PO Box 149 Bound Brook NJ 08805-0149

CHANDLER, MARLENE MERRITT, construction executive; b. Greenville, S.C., Dec. 13, 1949; d. Harvey Allen and Gladys Iona (Stewart) Merritt; m. Charles Mack Owens, June 8, 1968 (div. Oct. 1984); 1 child, Heather Michelle; m. Ray Lewis Chandler, Apr. 25, 1985. Grad. high sch., Piedmont, S.C. Asst. billing and computer operator Dillard Paper Co., Greenville, 1968-70; exec. asst. Daniel Constrn. Co., Greenville, 1970-74; co. sec., pres. asst. M.L. Garrett Constrn. Co., Greenville, 1974-78; asst. to purchasing mgr. P.Y.A. Monarch Co., Inc., Greenville, 1978-83; mgr., owner, pres. RAM Builders, Easley, S.C., 1985—; owner, pres. RAM Builders of Greenville, Inc., Greenville, 1986—. Author poem: Poetry Contest, 1989. Tutor Greenville Lit. Assocs., Inc., 1988-90; dir. S.C.'s Living Doll Pageant, S.C.'s Most Beautiful Girl Pageant, S.C.'s Baby of the Yr., S.C.'s Baby Bumpkin Contest. Named Mrs. I Love You Greenville, Greenville Bus. Assn., 1981, Mrs. S.C., S.C. Little Miss/Beauty Pageant, Greenville, 1982. Republican. Baptist. Home and Office: RAM Builders Greenville Inc 10129 Anderson Rd Easley SC 29642-9303

CHANG, BARBARA KAREN, medical educator; b. Milltown, Ind., Jan. 6, 1946; m. M.F. Joseph Chang-Wai-Ling, Oct. 6, 1967; children: Carla Marie Yvonnette, Nolanne Arlette. BA, Ind. U., 1968; MA, Brandeis U., 1970; MD, Albert Einstein Coll. Medicine, 1973. Diplomate Am. Bd. Internal Medicine, Am. Bd. Med. Oncology, Am. Bd. Hematology. Resident in internal medicine Montefiore Med. Ctr., Bronx, N.Y., 1973-75; fellow in hematology/oncology med. ctr. Duke U., Durham, N.C., 1975-78; staff physician VA Med. Ctr., Augusta, Ga., 1978—, chief hematology/oncology, 1980-89, assoc. chief of staff edn., 1990-95; prof. medicine Med. Coll. Ga., Augusta, 1978—; chief of staff VA Med. Ctr., Albuquerque, 1995—; prof., asst. dean U. N.Mex. Sch. Medicine, Albuquerque, 1995—; mem. Sci. Adv. Bd., Washington, 1983-88; mem. expert panels computer applications Dept. Vets. Affairs, Washington, 1988—. Contbr. numerous articles on cancer rsch. to profl. jours. Youth coord. Am. Hemerocallis Soc., Augusta, 1993-95. Grantee Nat. Cancer Inst., Am. Cancer Soc., 1978-93. Fellow ACP, Am. Soc. Hematology, Am. Assn. Cancer Rsch., Am. Soc. Clin. Oncology, Bioelectromagnetic Soc. (bd. dirs. 1983-86). Office: Dept Vets Affairs Med Ctr 1 Freedom Way Augusta GA 30904-6285

CHANG, LING WEI, sales executive; b. Taiwan, China, July 27, 1960; came to U.S., 1976; d. Thomas T.P. and Hou Hsin (Wang) C. BE, Cooper Union, 1982; MS, Syracuse U., 1989. Engr. Data Systems div. IBM Corp., Poughkeepsie, N.Y., 1982-83; assoc. engr. IBM Corp., 1983-85; systems engr. Nat. Accounts div. IBM Corp., N.Y.C., 1985-87, account systems engr. North Ctrl. Mktg. div., 1987-89, adv. systems engr. U.S. mktg. and svcs., 1990; adv. mktg. rep. N.Y. gov. br. IBM U.S., N.Y.C., 1991-92, acct. mgr. N.Y. Pub. Svcs., 1993-94; br. mgr. LEXIS-NEXIS, N.Y.C., 1994—. Vol. City Hosp. Ctr. at Elmhurst, N.Y., 1978; jr. judge Nat. Energy Found., 1979-82; bd. mgrs. Queens Ctr. Pla. Condominium, 1990-92. Mem. Jaycees, Tau Beta Pi, Eta Kappa Nu. Home: 87-08 Justice Ave 10D Elmhurst NY 11373 Office: LEXIS-NEXIS 200 Park Ave New York NY 10166

CHANG, SHIRLEY LIN (HSIU-CHU CHANG), librarian; b. Chia-yi, Taiwan, June 22, 1937; came to U.S., 1962, naturalized, 1977; d. Tzu-kun and Ying (Chang) Lin; m. Parris H. Chang, Aug. 3, 1963; children: Yvette Y., Elaine Y., Bohdan P. BA, Nat. Taiwan U., Taipei, 1960; postgrad. U. Wash., 1962-63; MLS, Columbia U., 1967; MA, Pa. State U., 1988. Libr. asst. Yale U., New Haven, 1964, Columbia U., N.Y.C., 1964-67; asst. ref. libr. Pa. State U., University Park, 1971-75; cataloguer Australian Nat. U., Canberra, 1978; catalog/ref. libr. Lock Haven U., 1979—, asst. prof., 1982-88, assoc. prof., 1988—. Mem. ALA, Chinese-Am. Librs. Assn. (chmn. awards com. 1982-83), Asian/Pacific Am. Librs. Assn., Assn. for Asian Studies, Phi Beta Delta Honor Soc. Home: 1221 Edwards St State College PA 16801-6930 Office: Lock Haven U Stevenson Libr Lock Haven PA 17745

CHANG, SYLVIA TAN, health facility administrator, educator; b. Bandung, Indonesia, Dec. 18, 1940; came to U.S., 1963.; d. Philip Harry and Lydia Shui-Yu (Ou) Tan; m. Belden Shiu-Wah Chang, Aug. 30, 1964; children: Donald Steven, Janice May. Diploma in nursing, Rumah Sakit Advent, Indonesia, 1960; BS, Philippine Union Coll., 1962; MS, Loma Linda (Calif.) U., 1967; PhD, Columbia Pacific U., 1987. Cert. RN, PHN, ACLS, BLS Instr., IV, TPN, Blood Withdrawal. Head nurse Rumah Sakit Advent, Bandung, Indonesia, 1960-61; critical care, spl. duty and medicine nurse, team leader White Meml. Med. Ctr., L.A., 1963-64; nursing coord. Loma Linda U. Med. Ctr., 1964-66; team leader, critical care nurse, relief head nurse Pomona (Calif.) Valley Hosp. Med. Ctr., 1966-67; evening supr. Loma Linda U. Med. Ctr., 1967-69, night supr., 1969-79, adminstrv. supr., 1979-94; sr. faculty Columbia Pacific U., San Rafael, Calif., 1986-94; dir. health svc. La Sierra U., Riverside, Calif., 1988—; site coord. Health Fair Expo La Sierra U., 1988-89; adv. coun. Family Planning Clinic, Riverside, 1988-94; blood drive coord. La Sierra U., 1988—. Counselor Pathfinder Club Campus Hill Ch., Loma Linda, 1979-85, crafts instr., 1979-85, music dir., 1979-85; asst. organist U. Ch., 1982-88. Named one of Women of Achievement, YWCA, Greater Riverside Cs. of C., The Press Enterprise, 1991. Mem. Am. Coll. Health Assn., Assn. Seventh-day Adventist Nurses, Pacific Coast Coll. Health Assn., Adventist Student Pers. Assn., Sigma Theta Tau Internat. Republican. Seventh-day Adventist. Home: 11466 Richmont Rd Loma Linda CA 92354 Office: La Sierra U Health Svc 4700 Pierce St Riverside CA 92515

CHANG, TAIPING, marketing executive, magazine publisher; b. Tainan, Taiwan, Apr. 20, 1949; came to U.S., 1975; d. Lanfeng Chang and Shuchun Liu; m. David R. Knechtges, June 7, 1976; 1 child, Jeanne Y. BA, Tunghai U., 1971, MA, 1974; PhD, U. Wash., 1981. Lectr. Tunghai U., Taichung, Taiwan, 1974-75; asst. prof. Pacific Luth. U., Tacoma, 1986-88; pub. Asia Pacific Bus. Jour., Seattle, 1988-94; pres. Asia Media Group, Inc., Seattle, 1989-94; asst. prof. Asian studies program U. Puget Sound, Tacoma, Wash., 1994—; bd. dirs. Chong-Wa Benevolent Assn., Seattle, No. Seattle (Wash.) C.C.; chmn. World Trade Club-Taiwan Forum, Seattle, 1991—. Editor: Editor-in-Chief, 1988. Named Woman of Yr., Asia Am. Soc., Seattle, 1990. Mem. Rotary Club. Office: U Puget Sound Pac-Rim Studies Tacoma WA 98416 also: U Puget Sound Asian Studies Program Tacoma WA 98416-0110

CHANIN, LEAH FARB, law library administrator, lawyer, consultant, law educator; b. Galveston, Tex., Nov. 29, 1929; d. A. C. and Celia (Rubenstein) Farb; m. Louis Chanin, Feb. 4, 1951 (dec. Jan. 1991); children: Scott, Leonard, Johanna, Rebecca. BA, So. Meth. U., 1950; LLB, Mercer U., 1954. Bar: Ga. 1954, U.S. Dist. Ct. (mid. dist.) Ga. 1954. Practice, Macon, Ga., 1959-63; mem. Kenmore & Culpepper, 1959-63; mem. faculty Walter F George Sch Law, Mercer U., 1964-92, asst. prof. law, 1969-72, assoc. prof., 1972-77, prof., 1977-92, dir. Law Libr., 1964-92, dean pro tem, 1986-87; prof., dir. libr. D.C. Sch. Law, 1992—. mem. Fed. Merit Rev. Com., 1979-81. Author: Specialized Legal Research, 1987, Georgia Legal Research, 1990, Legal Research in D.C., Maryland and Virginia, 1995; contbr. articles to profl. jours. Mem. State Bar Ga. (adv. ethics opinions bd., pres. author's ct. 1985-86), Am. Assn. Law Librs. (pres. 1982-83), Internat. Assn. Jewish Lawyers. Democrat. Jewish. Home: 3001 Veazey Ter NW Apt 1027 Washington DC 20008-5405 Office: DC Sch Law 719 13th St NW Washington DC 20005-3997

CHANNER, LISA EILEEN, theatre artist; b. Detroit, May 5, 1966; d. Harold Hudson and Eileen (Maclanaghan) C.; life ptnr. Maureen Futtner. BA in Theatre, U. Mass., 1989. Cert. tchr. of dance, London. Tchr. The Arts Cmty., New Paltz, N.Y., 1980-84; co-artistic dir. Sleeveless Theatre, Inc., Northampton, Mass., 1989—, co-founder, 1989—. Co-author: (plays) Womb for Rent: A Pro Choice Comedy, 1989, The F Word: A Fresh

Look at Feminism, 1991. Mem. NOW. Democrat. Unitarian. Office: Sleeveless Theatre Inc PO Box 2 Northampton MA 01061

CHANNING, CAROL, actress; b. Seattle, Jan. 31, 1923; d. George and Adelaide (Glaser) C.; m. Charles F. Lowe, Sept. 5, 1956; 1 son, Channing George. Student, Bennington Coll. Actress: (Broadway prodns.) No for an Answer, 1941, Let's Face It, 1941, Proof Through the Night, 1942, So Proudly We Hail, Lend an Ear, 1948 (Theatre World award, Critic's Circle award), Gentlemen Prefer Blondes, 1949, 51-53, Wonderful Town, 1953, Pygmalian, 1953, The Vamp, 1955, Show Business, 1959, Show Girl, 1961, George Burns-Carol Channing Musical Revue, 1962, The Millionairess, 1963, Hello Dolly, 1964-67, also revivial (Tony award for Best Actress, N.Y. Drama Critics Cir. award for Best Actress), Carol Channing with Her Stout-Hearted Men, 1970 (London Critics award), Four on a Garden, 1971, Cabaret, 1972, Festival at Ford's, 1972, Carol Channing and Her Gentlemen Who Prefer Blondes Revue, 1972, Jerry's Girls, 1984-85, Legends, 1986, (theatre tours) Lorelei, 1973-75, Carol's Broadway Revue; (films) First Travelling Saleslady, 1956, Thoroughly Modern Millie, 1967 (Golden Globe award as Best Supporting Actress 1967), Skidoo, 1968, Shinbone Alley (voice), 1971, Sgt. Peppers Lonely Hearts Club Band, 1978, Happily Ever After (voice), 1990, Hans Christian Andersen's Thumbelina (voice), 1994, others; (TV prodns.) Svengali and the Blonde, Three Men on a Horse, Crescendo; (TV appearences) The Love Boat, 1977, Alice in Wonderland, 1985, Where's Waldo? (voice), 1991, Addams Family (voice), 1992, The Magic School Bus (voice), 1994. Recipient Best Night Club Act award, 1957, 64, Spl. Tony award, 1968, Theatre World award for Bronze medallion City of N.Y., 1978. Christian Scientist. Office: William Morris Agy 151 El Camino Beverly Hills CA 90212-2704*

CHAO, ELAINE L., philanthropic organization executive; d. James S.C. and Ruth M.L. (Chu) C.; m. Mitch McConnell, 1993. AB, Mt. Holyoke Coll., 1975; MBA, Harvard U., 1979; LLD (hon.), Villanova U., 1989, Sacred Heart U., 1991; DLD (hon.), St. John's U., 1991; DHL (hon.), Niagara U., 1992; DHum (hon.), Drexel U., 1992, St. John's U., 1991, Thomas More Coll., 1994. Assoc. Gulf Oil Corp., Pitts., summer 1978; sr. lending officer Citicorp, NA, N.Y.C., 1979-83; v.p. capital markets group BankAmerica, San Francisco, 1984-86; dep. maritime adminstr. U.S. Dept. Transp., Washington, 1986-88; chmn. Fed. Maritime Commn., Washington, 1988; dep. sec. U.S. Dept. Transp., Washington, 1989-91; pres. United Way Am., Alexandria, Va., 1992—; White House fellow, 1983-84; adj. asst. prof. Grad. Sch. Bus. Adminstrn., St. John's U., 1984. Recipient Young Achiever award Nat. Coun. Women U.S., Inc., 1986; Eisenhower Fellow Assn. fellow, 1984; named. one of 10 Outstanding Women of Am., 1988. Mem. Coun. on Fgn. Rels., Inc., Am. Coun. Young Polit. Leaders (bd. dirs. 1989), Harvard Bus. Sch. (vis. com. 1989, Outstanding Alumni award 1993), Harvard Club. Office: United Way of America 701 N Fairfax St Alexandria VA 22314

CHAPARRO, JENNIFER NICHOLS, graphic designer; b. St. Joseph, Mich., Jan. 10, 1962; d. Michael Kent and Carolyn (Stinson) Nichols; m. Michael Joseph Chaparro, July 14, 1984; 1 child, Mercedes Alicia. BA in Design, UCLA, 1984. Graphic designer Associated Students, UCLA, 1982-84; freelance designer Variety Arts, Inc., N.Y.C., 1983-86; art dir. Domino's Pizza Emporium, Ann Arbor, Mich., 1985-87; graphic designer supr. Life Fitness, Inc., Irvine, Calif., 1987-92; freelance designer Design for the Future, Dayton, Ohio, 1992—; cons. in field. Bd. dirs. Ronald McDonald House, Dayton, 1994—. Recipient Clairemont Art Guild Student Merit award, 1980. Mem. Dayton Visual Arts Ctr. (bd. dirs. 1994—), Dayton Advt. Club. Home: 7274 Caribou Trl Dayton OH 45459-4865

CHAPEY, ROBERTA, speech pathology educator; b. Bklyn., Dec. 9, 1942; d. Robert J. and Geraldine (Donnelly) Chapey; m. Kris Thiruvillakkat; stepchildren: Kris, Michael, David. BA, Marymount Manhattan Coll., 1964; MA, NYU, 1965; EdD, Columbia U., 1974. Prof. speech pathology Bklyn. Coll., 1974—. Editor: Language Intervention Strategies in Adult Aphasia, 3d edit., 1994; contbr. articles to profl. jours. Mem. Am. Speech and Hearing Lang. Assn., N.Y. State Speech Hearing Lang. Assn. (mem. neurologic comm. disorders com. 1993, 94), N.Y.C. Speech Hearing Lang. Assn., Jr. League No. Westchester, Lewisboro Garden Club. Roman Catholic. Home and Office: 225 E 66th St 5D New York NY 10021

CHAPIN, CAROL LOUISE, accountant, insurance company executive; b. Cleve., Dec. 17, 1950; d. Daniel William and Janice Dawn (Baird) Baskette; m. Dan Herbert Eiler, Mar. 1970 (div. 1974); 1 child, Laura Monique; m. Raymond Bruce Chapin, June, 1980. BS summa cum laude in Acctg., U. Akron, 1979; MBA, Baldwin Wallace Coll., 1992. CPA, Ohio; cert. mgmt. acct. Sr. acct. Coopers & Lybrand, Akron, Ohio, 1979-83; supr. gen. acctg. Med. Mut. Cleve., 1983-84; mgr. alternative delivery systems acctg. Blue Cross and Blue Shield of Ohio, Cleve., 1984-93, dir. corp. acctg., 1994—. Editor (column) The Ohio CPA Jour., 1992-94. Mem. AICPA, Cleve. chpt. Ohio Soc. CPAs (chmn. mems. in industry com. 1993-94), Inst. Cert. Mgmt. Accts. Democrat. Office: Blue Cross and Blue Shield of Ohio 2060 E 9th St Cleveland OH 44115-1355

CHAPIN, DEBORAH ANNE, lawyer; b. N.Y.; d. Victor and Mia (Gumpert) Baum; m. Richard S. Chapin (div.); 1 child, Joshua. BA, Skidmore, 1972; MPA, U. Cin., 1974; JD, NYU, 1984. Mgmt. analyst Office of Rsch., Evaluation & Budget, Cin., 1974-76; investigator, city mgr. Spl. Investigation Unit, Cin., 1976-79; dir. planning & mgmt. support systems City Planning Commn., Cin., 1978-79, cons., 1979; spl. asst. to the counsel pres., fiscal matters Office of the Council Pres., N.Y., 1979-81; assoc. Squadron, Ellenoff, Plesent & Lehrer, N.Y., 1984-89; v.p., corp. counsel Viacom Internat., N.Y., 1989—; dep. gen. counsel Viacom Interactive Media, N.Y., 1994—. Office: Viacom Internat Inc 1515 Broadway New York NY 10036

CHAPIN, DIANE LOUISE, cardiac care nurse; b. Berwick, Pa., Oct. 8, 1952; d. A. Richard and Esther Elizabeth (Remphrey) C.; m. James Yeatts, June 11, 1977 (div. Mar. 1983). Diploma, Williamsport (Pa.) Sch. Nursing, 1973; BS in Edn., Bloomsburg State Coll., 1975. CCRN; cert. provider/instr. BCLS and ACLS. Charge nurse orthopedics Geisinger Med. Ctr., Danville, Pa., 1974-77, charge nurse urology, 1980-81; charge nurse psychiatry DePaul Hosp., Norfolk, Va., 1977-78; home health nurse John D. Archibald Meml. Hosp., Thomasville, Ga., 1982-83; med. staff/charge nurse Tallahassee Community Hosp., 1981-82, supr., 1984-86, nurse educator ICU, 1986-87, asst. nurse mgr. ICU, 1987-90; nurse mgr. critical care unit HCA Palmyra Med. Ctr., Albany, Ga., 1990-93; dir. critical care Palmyra Med. Ctr., Albany, 1993—; grad. cons. area 4 Student Nurse Assn. Pa., 1973-74; developer restorative nurse program in home health, 1981; co-developer critical care internship program, 1991. Mem. AACN. Methodist. Home: 2503B Doncaster Dr Albany GA 31707-1711

CHAPIN, LINDA MARI, principal; b. Detroit, Apr. 15, 1949; d. Jack and Edith (Lacoff) C. BA, U. Mich., 1970, Ednl. Specialist degree, 1978; MA, Wayne State U., 1974. Cert. tchr., guidance counselor, prin., supr., supt., Mich., Md. Tchr., counselor Warren Woods (Mich.) Pub. Schs., 1970-79; dir. gifted and talented programs Ingham Intermediate Sch. Dist., Mason, Mich., 1979-84; prin. Frederick (Md.) County Bd. Edn., 1984-88; head Roeper Sch. for the Gifted, Bloomfield Hills, Mich., 1988-89; prin. Christina Sch. Dist./Bayard Intermediate Sch., Newark, Del., 1989-91; acad. dean Am. Sch. in London, 1991-93; prin. Middle River Middle Sch. Baltimore County Pub. Schs., Towson, Md., 1993—. Mem. ASCD, Assn. for the Gifted (treas. 1984-87), Nat. Assn. Secondary Sch. Prins. Democrat. Jewish.

CHAPIN, SUZANNE PHILLIPS, retired psychologist; b. Syracuse, N.Y., Aug. 9, 1930; d. Harold Bridge and Charlotte Virginia (Warner) Phillips; m. Richard Hilton Chapin, June 13, 1953 (div. 1964); children: Bruce Phillips Chapin, Linda Chapin Fry. BA, Syracuse U., 1952; MA, Columbia U., 1965. Statis. asst. Syracuse Bd. of Edn., 1952-53; psychol. examiner Stamford (Conn.) Pub. Schs., 1965-68, psychologist Head Start program, 1967-68; psychologist Southbury (Conn.) Tng. Sch., 1968-74, Onondaga Assn. for the Retarded, Syracuse, 1974, Harlem Valley Psychiatric Ctr., Wingdale, N.Y., 1974-93, Mid-Hudson Psychiat. Ctr., New Hampton, 1993; ret., 1993. Mem. Danbury Women's Ctr., Sierra Club, Audubon Soc. Democrat. Home: 29 Cornell Rd Danbury CT 06811-3717

CHAPLIN, GERALDINE, actress; b. Santa Monica, Calif., July 3, 1944; d. Charles and Oona (O'Neill) C.; 1 child, Shane. Ed. pvt. schs., Royal Ballet Sch., London. Motion pictures include Doctor Zhivago, 1965, Stranger in the House, 1967, I Killed Rasputin, 1968, The Hawaiians, 1970, Innocent Bystanders, 1973, Buffalo Bill and the Indians or Sitting Bull's History Lesson, The Three Musketeers, 1974, The Four Musketeers, 1975, Nashville, 1975, Welcome to L.A, 1977, Cria, 1977, Roseland, 1977, Remember My Name, 1978, A Wedding, 1978, The Mirror Crack'd, 1980, Voyage en Douce, 1981, Bolero, 1982, Corsican Brothers, The Word, L'Amour Par Terre, White Mischief, 1988, The Moderns, 1988, Chaplin, 1992; TV appearances My Cousin Rachel. Office: William Morris Agy 151 El Camino Beverly Hills CA 90212*

CHAPLIN, VIRGINIA TUFTS, volunteer; b. Lewiston, Maine, Aug. 3, 1925; d. George W. and Annie M. (Hellen) Tufts; m. Joseph B. Chaplin, Jr., June 22, 1946 (dec. Dec. 1992); children: James, William, Anne, Sarah. BS, U. Maine, 1946; postgrad., Yale U., 1984-87. Social worker State of Maine, Augusta, 1946-49. Pres. YWCA Lewiston-Auburn, Maine, 1958-62; nat. bd. dirs. YWCA, 1970-82, v.p., 1979-82, mem. world coun., Athens, 1979; trustee Ctrl. Maine Med. Ctr., Lewiston-Auburn, 1971-77, hon. bd. dirs., 1977; trustee Bangor (Maine) Theol.Sem., 1992—; pres. Woman's Hosp. Assn., Lewiston-Auburn, 1963-65; mem. World Svc. Coun. YWCA, 1982—; mem. fin. adv. com. Town of Georgetown, 1993—. Mem. U. Maine Alumni Assn. (hon. bd. dirs., Black Bear award 1971). Home: PO Box 468 Georgetown ME 04548

CHAPLINE, CLAUDIA BEECHUM, artist, art dealer; b. Oak Park, Ill., May 23, 1930; d. Jacob Burwell and Lillian Estella (Schell) C.; m. James Nicol Hood, Nov. 1956 (div. 1972); children: Craig Chapline Hood, Randall Jameson Hood; m. Harold Chambers Schwarm, Feb. 14, 1989. BA in Drawing and Painting cum laude with spl. honors, George Washington U., 1953; MA in Dance Therapy, Washington U., St. Louis, 1956. Instr. dance Washington U., St. Louis, 1953-56, U. Mo., Columbia, 1956-57, Alhambra (Calif.) High Sch., 1959-60, El Camino Coll., L.A., 1960-61; dir. Shatto Drama Ctr., L.A., 1958-59; assoc. prof. dance UCLA, 1960-67; asst. prof. dance Calif. State U., Northridge, 1961-64; founder, dir. Inst. for Design/Dance and Exptl. Art, Santa Monica/Sacramento, 1974-88; lectr. dance U. Calif. ext., L.A., 1981-82; owner Claudia Chapline Gallery & Sculpture Garden, Stinson Beach, Calif., 1987—; coord. Artists in Social Instns., Calif. Arts Coun., 1982-84, program mgr. Art in Pub. Bldgs., 1984-90; dir. Bolinas (Calif.) Mus. Devel., 1989. One-woman shows include Humanist Ctr., St. Louis, 1956, Hobart Gallery, 1966, 67, E.B. Crocker Art Gallery, Sacramento, 1967, Humboldt Galleries, San Francisco, 1969, Jacqueline Anhalt Gallery, L.A., 1973, Palos Verdes Mus. Art, 1975, Inst. for Dance and Experimental Art, Santa Monica, Calif., 1976, 78, 79, Shackelford and Sears Gallery, Davis, Calif., 1986, IDEA, Sacramento, 1990, Wilder Gallery, Los Gatos, Calif., 1992, Claudia Chapline Gallery, Stinson Beach, Calif., 1994, JFK U., Orinda, Calif., 1994, Met. Club, San Francisco, 1995, Galerie Im Gabla, Erlangen, Germany, 1995, Anagma Arte Contemporaneo, Valencia, Spain, 1995; exhibited in group shows at Corcoran Gallery of Art, Washington, 1952, Hobart Gallery, 1965, Ryder Gallery, L.A., 1967, Zachary Waller Gallery, L.A., 1970, Long Beach Mus. Art, 1971, L.A. County Mus. Art, 1973, L.A. Inst. Contemporary Art, 1975, Pasadena Artists Concern, 1976, Gray Whale, Sacramento, 1985, Bolinas Mus., Calif., 1990, 92, 93, 94, Marin Arts Coun., 1993, 94, Artisan's Gallery, Mill Valley, Calif., 1994, Somar Gallery, San Francisco, 1994; represented in numerous pub. and pvt. collections. Mem. San Francisco Art Dealers Assn., ArtTable (bd. dirs. 1993-95). Office: Claudia Chapline Gallery & Sculpture Garden PO Box 946 3445 Shoreline Stinson Beach CA 94970

CHAPMAN, CANDACE, investment consultant professional; b. Tuscaloosa, Ala., May 20, 1956; d. James Emory and Betty Jean (Gaston) C. BBA in Finance, U. Ga., 1978, M in Accountancy, 1981. CPA, Ga. Tax acct. Ernst & Whinney, N.Y.C., 1981-83; tax sr. Price Waterhouse, Atlanta, 1983-85; fin. cons. Peterson Co., Atlanta, 1985-87; investment mgmt. sales First Am. Bank, Atlanta, 1987-91, Atlanta Capital Mgmt., 1991-94; cons. Wyatt Investment Consulting, Inc., Atlanta, 1994—; bd. dirs. Cagle's Inc., Atlanta, 1993—, chairperson audit com., 1994—. Mem. pub. rels. AIDS Walk, Atlanta, 1991, 92; vol. Project Open Hand, Atlanta, 1991—; dir., vol. fundraising Cool Girls, Atlanta, 1993—. Recipient Outstanding Voluntary Svc. to Cmty. award Martin Luther King Ctr., 1994. Mem. Nat. Assn. Securities Profls., Ga. Govtl. Fin. Officers Assn. (mem. comm. com. 1993—), Internat. Found. Employee Benefits, Nat. Assn. Securities Profls., Health Care Fin. Mgmt. Assn., Women in Pensions. Democrat. Office: Wyatt Investment Cons Inc Ste 432 4170 Ashford Dunwoody Rd NE Atlanta GA 30319

CHAPMAN, JUDITH COSTE, charitable institution volunteer administrator; b. St. Louis, Nov. 22, 1934; d. Felix Wilkins Coste and Dorothy (Cramer) Coste Gale; m. Gilbert Whipple Chapman Jr., June 14, 1956; 1 child, Gilbert Whipple III. BA, Sarah Lawrence Coll., 1956. Mgr. North Country Garden Club of L.I., N.Y., 1975-78, 2d v.p., 1981-83, treas., 1983-86, pres., 1989-91; bd. dirs. Raynham Hall Mus., Oyster Bay, N.Y., 1991-94, treas., 1994—; bd. dirs. North Shore Wildlife Sanctuary, Mill Neck, N.Y., 1988—, pres., 1991—. Co-chair Jane B. Francke Sanctuary, Brookville, N.Y., 1977—; bd. dirs. Planned Parenthood Nassau County, 1972-76, pres.'s adv. com., 1977-94. Recipient Medal of Merit, Garden Club of Am., 1994. Episcopalian. Home: 121 Factory Pond Rd Locust Valley NY 11560

CHAPMAN, KAREN LOUISE, lawyer; b. Denver, Apr. 1, 1954; d. Arthur Alec and Kathleen Joan (Weiss) C.; m. Stuart Donovan Jenkins, June 30, 1984. BS, U. Colo., 1976; JD, Stanford U., 1979. Bar: Colo. 1979, D.C. 1980. Atty. bur. competition FTC, Washington, 1972-82; assoc. Morrison & Foerster, Denver, 1982-84; assoc. Kirkland & Ellis, Denver, 1984-85, ptnr., 1875-94; ptnr. Bartlit Beck Herman Palenchar & Scott, Denver, 1994—. Pres. Stanford Pub. Interest Law Found., Calif., 1978-79. Regents scholar, 1972-73, Boettcher scholar, 1972-76; recipient Wall Street Journal award, 1976. Mem. ABA, D.C. Bar Assn., Colo. Bar Assn. Office: Bartlit Beck Herman et al 511 16th St Ste 700 Denver CO 80202-4232

CHAPMAN, KATHLEEN HALLORAN, state legislator, lawyer; b. Estherville, Iowa, Jan. 19, 1937; d. Edward E. and Meryl (McConoughey) Halloran; m. Allen Ray Chapman, Apr. 29, 1961; children: Christopher, Stuart. BA, U. Iowa, 1959, JD, 1974. Bar: Iowa 1974, U.S. Ct. Appeals (8th cir.) 1974. Prin. Booth & Chapman, Cedar Rapids, Iowa, 1974—; mem. Iowa Ho. of Reps., Des Moines, 1983-92, vice chmn. judiciary com., 1983-86, vice chmn. ethics com., 1985-88, vice chmn. ways and means com., 1987-88, chmn. rules and adminstrn. com., 1987-88, asst. majority leader, 1989-90, chmn. edn. appropriations, 1991—; Legis. Coun. Iowa Gen. Assembly, 1987—; participant Atlantic Exch., 1989. Trustee East Cen. Regional Libr., Cedar Rapids, 1974-80, Tanager Place, Cedar Rapids, 1978—. Toll fellow Coun. State Govts., 1988. Mem. Iowa Bar Assn. Democrat. Roman Catholic. Office: 1010 The Ctr Cedar Rapids IA 52401

CHAPMAN, KRISTIN HEILIG, public relations consultant; b. New Orleans, Nov. 4, 1966; d. Brady Alexander and Margaret Faye (Fisher) Heilig; m. Mark Richard Chapman, Sept. 16, 1989. BA in Journalism and Pub. Rels., Auburn U., 1988. Acct. exec. Ketchum Pub. Rels., Atlanta, 1988-90; mktg. coord. IBM, El Paso, Tex., 1991; acct. supr. The Randolph Partnership, Atlanta, 1992—. Vol. The Atlanta Project, 1992-94, Jr. League Gwinnett and North Fulton Counties, Duluth, Ga., 1992—. Recipient Gold Touchstone award Am. Hospice Assn., 1993-94, Gold Flame award Internat. Assn. Bus. Communicators, 1990, 93, Clarion award Women in Comm., 1994. Mem. Pub. Rels. Soc. Am. (com. 1989—, Phoenix award 1990, 91, 92, 93, 94, Silver Anvil award 1994). Republican.

CHAPMAN, PAULA ANNE, cultural organization administrator; b. Tiffin, Ohio, Sept. 15, 1960; d. Paul Everett and Mary Virginia (Brosious) Young; m. James Nelson Cook, Sept. 16, 1977 (div. Dec. 1981); children: Nichole Adele, Jessica Theresa, Samantha Rebekah; m. Harry N. Chapman, Dec. 10, 1988. BS in Psychology, Heidelberg Coll., 1982; MA in Polit. Sci., Bowling Green (Ohio) State U., 1987; postgrad., Ball State U., 1994—. Child therapist Sandusky (Ohio) Youth Referral Svc., 1982-83; parole officer State of Ohio, Columbus, 1983-86; dep. dir. Seneca, Sandusky and Wyandot Commn. Mental Health Bd., Tiffin, 1986-87; program dir. WSOS Cmty. Action Commn., Fremont, Ohio, 1987-88; dir. community devel. Seneca Indsl. and Econ. Devel. Corp., Tiffin, 1988-90; exec. dir. Tiffin Area C. of C./Seneca Indsl. & Econ. Devel. Corp., Tiffin, 1988-90; pres. Chapman Cmty. Devel. Cons., Tiffin, 1990-93; dir. devel. St. Francis Health Care Ctr., Green Springs, Ohio, 1993-94, St. Francis Coll., Ft. Wayne, Ind., 1994—; adj. prof. econs. Tiffin U., 1987-94; mem. ednl. adv. bd. Vanguard/Sentinel Vocat. Sch., Fremont, 1989-90; chmn. Tiffin Fair Housing Bd., 1985-90; bd. dirs. Ohio Indsl. Tng. Program, Sandusky, 1988-90, Pvt. Industry Coun., Fremont, Seneca County Revolving Loan Fund, Tiffin; chairperson adv. bd. WSOS. Candidate Seneca County Commr., 1992; docent Ft. Wayne Children's Zoo; active Ft. Wayne Women's Bur.; vol. Legal Svcs. Maumee Valley, Ft. Wayne; mem. fin./devel. com. Ft. Wayne YWCA; mem. mktg. com. Sci. Ctrl., Ft. Wayne; mem. Grad. Ft. Wayne Leadership Works, 1994; vol. house mgr. Ft. Wayne Civic Theatre. Mem. NAFE, Nat. Soc. Fundraising Execs. (mem. Ind. chpt. steering com.), Bus. and Profl. Women's Assn. (Young Career Woman 1987, 89), Ft. Wayne C. of C. (mem. VIP com., Ambs. Club), Kiwanis Internat. (mem. Ind. dist. steering com., Iodine Deficiency Disease project, bd. dirs. Ft. Wayne Downtown chpt.). Home: 1721 Woodland Xing Fort Wayne IN 46825-7228

CHAPMAN, SARA SIMMONS, academic administrator, English educator; b. Charleston, W.Va., Apr. 24, 1940; d. Maxwell E. and Billie Morrison Simmons. BA, Morris Harvey Coll., Charleston, W.Va., 1962; MA, Marshall U., Huntington, W.Va., 1966; DHL (hon.), Mount Vernon Coll., 1992; PhD, Ohio U., 1970; MLS, Ball State U., 1977; D Pedagogy (hon.), U. Charleston, W.Va., 1989. Instr. English Morris Harvey Coll., Charleston, W.Va., 1965-66; instr. English Marshall U., Huntington, W.Va., 1966-67, asst. prof. English, 1969-72, assoc. prof. English, 1972-76, dir. acad. planning, 1975; asst. dean Colls. Arts and Scis., dir. U. Honors Program Kansas State U., Manhattan, 1976-79; assoc. vice chancellor for acad. affairs State U. System Minn., St. Paul, 1979-81; prof. English Newcomb Coll., Tulane U., New Orleans, 1982-86, dean, 1982-86; asst. dir., edn. programs NEH, Washington, 1985-87; vis. prof. dept. English Princeton U., Princeton, N.J., 1987-88; pres., prof. English The Sage Colls., Troy, N.Y., 1988-95; bd. dirs. N.Y. State Coun. on Econ. Edn., N.Y.C., Hudson Mohawk Assn. Colls. & Univs. Exec. Com., Coun. Ind. Colls. and Univs. N.Y.; nat. cons. Am. Coun. on Edn., Office of Women in Higher Edn. Nat. Forum, Washington, 1989, 90, 93; mem. Ready to Learn project Corp. Pub. Broadcasting. Author: Henry James's Portrait of the Writer as Hero, 1989. Bd. dirs. Emma Willard Sch., 1988—; mem. hon. adv. com. N.Y. LWV, 1989; mem. adv. coun. Hudson Valley coun. Girl Scouts U.S.; bd. dirs., mem. adv. com. higher edn. rsch. WAMC Pub. Broadcasting and Spenser Found.; mem. com. edn. prin. Corp. Pub. Broadcasting. Recipient Leadership award Women's Bus. Devel. Ctr., Albany, 1989; Harvard Grad. Sch. Edn. fellow, 1982; Adminstrv. grantee Rockefeller Found., 1974; grantee NEH, 1979-82, Nat. Endowment for Arts, 1984. Mem. Troy (N.Y.) Country Club, Ft. Orange Club (Albany). Home: 46 1st St Troy NY 12180-3811 Office: The Sage Colls Office of the President 45 Ferry St Troy NY 12180-4115

CHAPMAN, SUSAN LYNN, veterinarian; b. Slayton, Minn., Nov. 12, 1964; d. Robert George and Marcella Mae (Wahl) C. BS in Animal Sci., S.D. State U., 1987; DVM, U. Minn., 1991. Dairy farmer Robert Chapman Farm, Westbrook, Minn., 1989; lab animal technician U. Minn., St. Paul, 1989-91; vet. Cold Spring (Minn.) Vet. Clinic, 1991-93, Watertown (Minn.) Vet. Clinic, 1993-94, Animal Med. Ctr., Hutchinson, Minn., 1994—. Mem. Am. Vet. Med. Assn., Minn. Vet. Med. Assn., Am. Assn. Bovine Practioners, Phi Kappa Phi, Gamma Sigma Delta. Lutheran. Home: 987 Echo Dr # 306 Hutchinson MN 55350

CHAPMAN-SZMAL, ELIZABETH, communications/advertising professional; b. Syracuse, N.Y., Oct. 24, 1960; d. Donald Warren and Olga C. (Chester) Schulenberg; m. Paul-Michael Szmal, Oct. 30, 1993. BA in Psychology, Mt. Holyoke, 1982; MA in Mass Communication, Emerson Coll., 1984; postgrad., Boston U., 1982. Sales asst. WHTT/CBS, Inc., Boston, 1984; program dir. WMRE/Mariner Comm., Boston, 1985; talk show host WIBX Radio/Teamworx, Inc., Utica, N.Y., 1986; disc jockey, rsch. dept. mgr. WAQX Radio, Syracuse, N.Y., 1987; air personality WHEN Radio, Syracuse, 1987-92; creative assoc. Norwak Assocs., Syracuse, 1990-92; pub. rels. assoc. Nowak Assocs., Syracuse, 1993—. Vol. Am. Cancer Soc., Dewitt, 1992, March of Dimes, Dewitt, 1993. Mem. AAUW, WICI, Franciscan Secular Order. Republican. Roman Catholic. Office: Nowak Assocs 6075 E Molloy Rd Bldg 7 Syracuse NY 13211

CHAPO, ROBIN GAYLE, manufacturing clerk; b. North Tonawanda, N.Y., Apr. 28, 1962; d. John Robert Chapo and Catherine Leah Harp. BS in Mgmt., Canisius Coll., 1986. Data entry coord. Am. Lung Assn., Buffalo, 1986-88; office clk. Tops Markets, Tonawanda, N.Y., 1989-91; packager IIMAK, Amherst, N.Y., 1991, mfg. clk., 1991—. Mem. IIMAK Social Com. (treas. 1992—, pres. 1993—). Republican. Presbyterian. Home: 93 Cleveland Ave Tonawanda NY 14150-2401 Office: IIMAK 310 Commerce Dr Amherst NY 14228-2303

CHAPPELEAR, VIRGINIA, counselor, educator; b. Mechanicsburg, Ohio, Oct. 28, 1944; d. Edward A. and Martha Jean (Pitts) Hunt; m. Albert S. Chappelear III, July 23, 1964; children: Nancy Noël, Jean Juliet, Albert S. IV, Virginia Vanessa. BA in Psychology, Muskingum Coll., 1975; MEd in Counseling, Ohio U., 1983. Lic. social worker; cert. grief counselor; cert. death educator. Child welfare caseworker Guernsey County Children's Bd., Cambridge, Ohio, 1976-79; social worker Cambridge (Ohio)-Guernsey County Health Dept., 1979-83, social svc. supv., 1984-86; asst. prof., coord. mental health Muskingum Area Tech. Coll., Zanesville, Ohio, 1986-94; social worker, trainer Hospice of Guernsey, Cambridge, 1989—; pvt. practice Counseling Assocs., Zanesville, 1994—; ednl. cons. Ohio Dept. Aging, Columbus, Ohio, 1991—; mem. adv. bd. Social Worker Asst. Tech., Zanesville, 1991—, Hospice Care of Bethesda, Zanesville, 1994—. Mem. ACA, Assn. Death Edn. and Counseling, Chi Sigma Iota. Home: 2 Yorkshire Dr Cambridge OH 43725

CHAPPELL, BARBARA KELLY, child welfare consultant; b. Columbia, S.C., Oct. 17, 1940; d. Arthur Lee and Katherine (Martin) Kelly; 1 child, Kelly Katherine. BA in English and Edn., U. S.C., 1962, MSW, 1974. Tchr. English, Dept. Edn., Honolulu, 1962-65, Alamo Heights High Sch., San Antonio, 1965-67; caseworker Dept. Social Services, Columbia, S.C., 1969-70; supr. Juvenile Placement and Aftercare, Columbia, 1970-72; child welfare cons. Edna McConnell Clark Found., N.Y.C., 1974-75; dir. Children's Foster Care Rev. Bd. System, Columbia, 1975-85; child welfare cons., 1985-89; adminstr. Dept. Human Resources and Juvenile Svcs., Balt., 1989-92; exec. dir. New Pathways, Inc., Balt., 1992—; lectr. in field. Contbr. articles to profl. jours. Coordinator Child's Rights to Parents, Columbia, 1970-75. Episcopalian. Home and Office: 3215 Girardeau Ave Columbia SC 29204-3314

CHAR, CARLENE, writer, publisher, editor; b. Honolulu, Oct. 21, 1954; d. Richard Y. and Betty S.M. (Fo) C. BA in Econs., U. Hawaii, 1977; MA in Bus. Adminstrn., Columbia Pacific U., 1984, PhD in Journalism, 1985, B in Gen. Studies in Computer Sci., Roosevelt U., 1986. Freelance writer, Honolulu, 1982—; editor Computer Book Rev., Honolulu, 1983—; info. developer Sprint, 1988—.

CHARANIS, STEPHANIE DIANE, accountant; b. Balt., Sept. 2, 1965; d. Melvin Norman and Phyllis Rona (Sindler) Rubin; m. James Anthony Charanis, May 4, 1991. Student, U. Md., 1987. CPA; cert. mgmt. acct. Sr. acct. Ernst & Young, Balt., 1987-90; asst. mgr. fin. reporting CSX Intermodal, Hunt Valley, Md., 1990—. Com. chmn. young adult div. Jewish Community Fedn. Balt., 1988—. Mem. AICPAs, Md. Assn. CPAs, Inst. Mgmt. Accts. Office: CSX Intermodal 200 International Cir Hunt Valley MD 21030

CHARBAUSKI, COLLEEN ANNE, accountant; b. Geneva, Ill., Apr. 11, 1959; d. Joseph Raymond and Marlene Josephine (Schramer) Murphy; m. David Michael Charbauski, Sept. 16, 1989; 1 child, Kevin Michael. AA, Coll. DuPage, 1979; BA, Aurora U., 1993. Acct. Caterpillar, Inc., Aurora, Ill., 1979—; officer Murphy Laundries, Inc., Oswego, Ill., 1989-94; bd. dirs. Giving Employees Meaningful Svc. (GEMS), Aurora. Cmty. girls and boys basketball coach, Sugar Grove, Ill., 1991-95; bd. dirs. Sugar Grove Athletic Assn., 1993-94; den leader Boy Scouts Am., Sugar Grove, 1993-95; mem. St. Anne's Women's Club, Oswego, 1977—; pres. Bus. Resources Social Club, Aurora, 1983-85, 88-89, 93-94. Mem. Inst. Mgmt. Accts., Omicron Delta

Kappa, Phi Theta Kappa. Republican. Roman Catholic. Home: 169 Meadows Ct Sugar Grove IL 60554-5009 Office: Caterpillar Inc PO Box 348 Aurora IL 60507-0348

CHAREST, GABRIELLE MARYA, educational administrator; b. Westfield, Mass., Jan. 3, 1943; m. Leonard Kenneth Charest, Aug. 21, 1965; children: Leonard Kenneth Jr., Douglas John. BA, St. Joseph Coll., West Hartford, Conn., 1964; MEd, Westfield State Coll., 1978; postgrad., U. Mass., 1989—. Cert. tchr., adminstr., Mass. Tchr. French, West Springfield (Mass.) Jr. High Sch., 1964-65, Agawam (Mass.) Jr. High Sch., 1967-69; tchr. French, Latin, Spanish, and English, Agawam High Sch., 1973-81, chmn. dept. fgn. langs., 1981, asst. prin., 1981—; mem. adj. faculty Westfield State Coll., 1986—; rsch. asst. U. Mass., Amherst, 1991-92; workshop presenter on mentoring, 1990; chmn. steering com. for re-evaluation by N. Eng. Assn. Schs. and Colls., 1986-88; presenter profl. devel. workshops Agawam Pub. Schs., 1992-93;. Sec. West Springfield Conservation Commn., 1971-73; mem. Friends West Springfield Libr., 1990—, Springfield Libr. and Mus., 1994. Grantee New Eng. Assn. Schs. and Colls., 1991-92. Mem. ASCD, NEA, Nat. Assn. Secondary Sch. Prins., Mass. Tchrs. Assn., Mass. Secondary Sch. Adminstrs. Assn., Connecticut Valley Prins. Assn., New Eng. Native Am. Inst., Phi Delta Kappa. Home: 241 Valley View Cir West Springfield MA 01089 Office: Agawam High Sch 760 Cooper St Agawam MA 01001

CHARLES, ISABEL, university administrator; b. Bklyn., Mar. 10, 1926; d. James Patrick and Isabel (Roney) C. B.A., Manhattan Coll., 1954; M.A., U. Notre Dame, 1960, Ph.D., 1965; postgrad., U. Mich., 1968-69. Chmn. dept. English Bishop Watterson High Sch., Columbus, Ohio, 1954-59, St. Mary of the Springs Acad., Columbus, 1959-62; asst. prof. English Ohio Dominican Coll., Columbus, 1965-68; acad. dean, exec. v.p. Ohio Dominican Coll., 1969-73; asst. dean Coll. Arts and Letters, U. Notre Dame, 1973-75, acting dean, 1975, dean, 1976-82, asst. provost, 1982-87, assoc. provost, 1987—. Contbr. articles to profl. jours. Mem. MLA, Assn. Am. Colls. Home: 1802 Stonehedge Ln South Bend IN 46614-6341

CHARLES, JUDITH KOREY, professional association executive; b. N.Y.C., Feb. 23, 1925; d. Harold Richard and Rose Kay (Boren) Korey; m. Alfred W. Charles, July 1, 1962; 1 child, Frederic Korey Charles. AB, Brown U., 1945. Advt. copy chief Sears, Roebuck and Co., N.Y.C., 1952-59, Saks 34th St, N.Y.C., 1959-61; account exec. Jesse Kram Advt., N.Y.C., 1961-63, Markland Advt., N.Y.C., 1963-65; pres. Creative Communication, N.Y.C., 1965-89; exec. dir. Roundtable for Women in Foodservice Inc., N.Y.C., 1989—; guest lectr. NYU Inst. Retail Mgmt., Women's Food Svc. Inst.; adj. prof. Barbizon Sch. Fashion Merchandising, N.Y.C., NYU Sch. Continuing Edn. Recipient Brown Bear award Associated Alumni of Brown U., 1991. Mem. Brown U. Club. Democrat. Office: Roundtable Women in Foodservice 425 Central Park W New York NY 10025

CHARLES, KATHLEEN J., federal agency official; b. Washington, Jan. 30, 1950; d. Joseph Stanislaus and Jane Marie (Coogan) Foley; m. Keith Charles, Jan. 13, 1979 (div. Dec. 1987); children: Sarah, Emily. BA in Secondary Edn., U Dayton, 1971; MA in Secondary Edn., U. Md., 1976. Mgmt. intern NASA, Washington, 1971-73, program analyst, 1973-81; dep. comptroller Goddard Space Flight Ctr., Greenbelt, Md., 1981-84, Nat. Oceanic & Atmospheric Adminstrn., Washington, 1984-87; asst. inspector gen. Office of Inspector Gen., Dept. State, Washington, 1987-92; dep. asst. sec. Bur. Diplomatic Security, Washington, 1992-95, Fin. and Mgmt. Policy, Washington, 1995—. Chmn. membership PTA, Alexandria, 1989-92; bd. dirs. Jr. Auxiliary Alexandria Hosp., 1989—. Mem. Am. Astronautical Soc. (v.p. fin. 1984-86). Home: 1124 Francis Hammond Pky Alexandria VA 22302-3404 Office: Dept State 2201 C St NW Washington DC 20522-1003

CHARLES, LYN ELLEN, marketing executive, commercial artist, photographer; b. Little Falls, N.Y., Sept. 1, 1951; d. Searle and Barbara (Yount) C. Student So. Conn. State U., 1969-70, Lake Placid Sch. Art, 1975-76; BA, U. Conn., 1970-73; A.I.S., Art Instrn. Schs., Inc., 1974-76. Vanda beauty counselor, divsn. Dart Industries, Orlando, Fla., 1972-73; rsch. asst. Conn. State U., New Britain, 1974; comml. artist Conn. Community Colls., Hartford, 1978; market researcher Karen Assocs., Farmington Valley Mall, Simsbury, Conn., 1981; market research operator Consumer Surveys Telemarketing, Inc., Dedham, Mass., 1981-87; receptionist and file clerk Jobpro Temp. Svcs., 1987-88; field rep. Actnow, Westhampton Beach, N.Y., 1987-88; with Inventory Control Co., S. Hasckensack, N.J., 1988—; artist, vol. Farmington Valley Arts, Avon, Conn., 1982-84; freelance artist West Hartford Art League, 1978-81, Northwestern Conn. Art Assn., 1979-81, Wadsworth Atheneum, 1980-82. Vol. med. receptionist Hosp. and Clinical Info. Desk, U. Conn. Health Ctr., 1976-78, 75, Office Cultural Affairs, Pub. Survey to Select Artist for Art Work at Coliseum, Hartford Civic Ctr., 1979; mem. Childreach Sponsorship of PLAN Internat. USA, 1992—. Recipient Alice Collins Dunham prize, 69th Ann. Exhbn. of Conn. Acad. Fine Arts, 1980. Mem. Christian Ch. Avocations: hiking, swimming, bicycling, horseback riding, skiing, ballet, skating. Office: Inventory Control Co PO Box 23 South Hackensack NJ 07606-0023

CHARLES, MARY LOUISE, newspaper columnist, photographer, editor; b. L.A., Jan. 24, 1922; d. Louis Edward and Mabel Inez (Lyon) Kusel; m. Henry Loewy Charles, June 19, 1946; children: Susan, Henry, Robert, Carol. AA, L.A. City Coll., 1941; BA, San Jose (Calif.) State U., 1964. Salesperson Bullock's, L.A., 1940-42, Roos Bros., Berkeley, Calif., 1945-46; ptnr. Charles-Martin Motors, Marysville, Calif., 1950-54; farm editor Indep. Herald, Yuba City, Calif., 1954-55; social worker Sutter County, Yuba City, 1955-57; social worker Santa Clara County, San Jose, 1957-61, manual coordinator, 1961-73, community planning specialist; 1973-81; columnist Sr. Grapevine various weekly newspapers, Santa Clara County, 1981-86; editor Bay area Sr. Spectrum Newspapers, Santa Clara, 1986-90; columnist, 1990-94; columnist Santa Clara Valley edit. Senior Mag., 1994—; columnist San Jose Mercury News, 1994—; founder, pres. Triple-A Coun. Calif., 1978-80. Vice chmn. Santa Clara County Sr. Care Commn., 1987-89, chmn., 1989-91, mem. social svcs. com., 1993—; mem. Calif. Legis. Roundtable, 1975—. Served with WAVES, USNR, 1942-45. Recipient Social Welfare award Daniel E. Koshland Found., 1973, Friends of Santa Clara County Human Rels. Commn. award, 1992; named 24th State Assembly Dist. Woman of Yr., 1990. Mem. NASW, LWV (San Jose/Santa Clara Bd. 1993—), Nat. Coun. Sr. Citizens (bd. dirs. 1988—), Svc. Employees Internat. Union (mem. local 535, state exec. bd. dirs. 1973—, pres. sr. mems. and retiree chpt. 1982—), Congress of Calif. Srs. (bd. dirs. 1987—, region IV pres. 1992—, trustee 1993—), Older Women's League (bd. dirs. 1980-84), Older Women's League of Calif. (edn./resource coord. 1987-89, pres. 1990-91), Am. Soc. on Aging (co-chair women's concerns com. 1985-86, awards com. 1990-93), Nat. Coun. on Aging., Calif. Specialists on Aging (treas. 1985-93), Calif. Srs. Coalition (chmn. 1986, treas. 1993—), Calif. Writers Club. Home and Office: 2527 Forbes Ave Santa Clara CA 95050-5547

CHARLETON, MARGARET ANN, child care administrator, consultant; b. Orange, Calif., Aug. 3, 1947; d. Arthur Mitchell and Isabelle Margaret (Esser) C.; (div. Sept. 1985). AA in Liberal Arts, Orange Coast Coll., 1968; BA in Psychology, Chapman Coll., 1984. Head tchr. Presbyn. Ch. of the Master, Mission Viejo, Calif., 1977-81; child care program adminstr. Crystal Stairs, Inc., L.A., 1981—; mem. adv. bd. Children's Home Soc., Santa Ana, Calif., 1982-83; trainer Sesame St. Presch. Edn. Program with PBS, 1994; cons. Calif. Sch. Age Consortium, Coast Mesa, 1987, Calif. State Dept. of Edn., 1988; lectr. in field. Trainer Sesame St. Presch. Edn. Program with PBS, 1994; contbr. articles to profl. jours. Mem. South Orange County Community Svc., Mission Viejo, 1983—; liaison Family Svcs.-Marine Base, El Toro, Calif., 1989—. Recipient Plaque of Recognition, Vietnamese Community of Orange County, 1984. Mem. NAFE. Roman Catholic. Office: Crystal Stairs Inc 5105 W Goldleaf Cir Ste 200 Los Angeles CA 90056-1272

CHARLTON, BETTY JO, state legislator; b. Reno County, Kans., June 15, 1923; d. Joseph and Elma (Johnson) Canning; BA, U. Kans., 1970, MA, 1976; m. Robert Sansom Charlton, Feb. 24, 1946 (dec. 1984); children: John Robert, Richard Bruce. Asst. instr. polit. sci. and western civiliation U. Kans., Lawrence, 1970-73; legis. adminstrv. svcs. employee State of Kans., Topeka, 1977-78, legis. aide gov's. office, 1979; mem. Kans. Ho. of Reps., 1980-95.

CHARNAS, FRAN ELKA, theatre director, educator; b. Cleve.; d. Morris and Zelda (Wymor) C. BFA in Theatre, Ohio U., 1968; MA in Theatre, Emerson Coll., 1981. Producer, dir. East Cleveland (Ohio) Music Theatre, 1972-74; mem. faculty Boston Conservatory, 1980—; adminstrv. dir. Summer Inst. in Mus. Theatre, Boston, 1984; presenter and cons. in field. Dir., choreographer (mus.) The All Night Strut, 1975—, (TV spl.), 1988; dir. (mus.) Party of One, 1989, (opera) Look What A Wonder Jesus Has Done, 1990; co-author, dir. (mus.) Sheboppin, 1987; dir. various plays and mus. Mem. New Eng. Theatre Conf. Office: The Boston Conservatory 8 The Fenway Boston MA 02115

CHARNEY, PATTI KAY, engineering company executive; b. Fresno, Calif., Dec. 28, 1956; d. Donald Edward and Frances Mae (Samson) Diblin; m. Mark Richard Charney, Aug. 8, 1987; children: Candace Kristen, Alexandra Anne, Patrick Mitchell. BS, Calif. State Poly. U., Pomona, 1983. Contracts adminstr., space systems divsn. Gen. Dynamics, San Diego, 1989-92; sr. contracts adminstr. Maxwell Labs., Inc., San Diego, 1992-93; dir. contracts Applied Remote Tech., Inc., Scripps Ranch, Calif., 1993—. Mem. Nat. Contracts Mgmt. Assn. Republican. Home: 4894 Alondra Way Carlsbad CA 92008

CHARNIN, JADE HOBSON, magazine executive; b. N.Y.C., Mar. 12, 1945; d. John Louis Campo and Elizabeth (Anne) Stanton; m. David Alan Hobson, Dec. 30 (div. 1972); m. Martin Charnin, Dec. 18, 1984. BA, NYU, 1967. Asst. editor Glamour mag., N.Y.C., 1970; accessory editor Vogue mag., N.Y.C., 1970-78, fashion editor, 1978-81, fashion dir., 1981-86, creative dir. fashion, 1987-88; v.p., dir. creative svcs. for fashion and design group Revlon, Inc., 1988; exec. creative dir. Mirabella Mag., 1988-94; fashion dir.. N.Y. Mag., 1994—; cons. editor Self mag., N.Y.C., 1979-81. Costumer coord. for off broadway shows Laughing Matters, 1989, Martin Charnin, the Hits and the M.S.'s, 1990. Mem. NAFE, ASPCA, Am. Horticultural Soc., Nat. Mus. Women in the Arts, Horticultural Soc. N.Y. (bd. dirs.), Internat. Platform Assn., Humane Soc., Animal Protection Inst. Democrat. Avocations: gardening, opera, ballet, theater, skiing. Office: NY Mag 755 2d Ave New York NY 10017

CHARPENTIER, GAIL WIGUTOW, private school executive director; b. N.Y.C., Mar. 10, 1946; d. Jacob M. and Ethel (Israel) Wigutow; m. Peter Jon Charpentier; children: Elisabeth Marie, Matthew Kyle. BA, CUNY, 1967; MA, New Sch. Social Research, N.Y.C., 1976. Lic. social worker; cert. adminstr. of spl. edn. Tchr. Spl. Service Pub. Sch., Bronx, N.Y., 1967-73; adminstr. Boston City Hosp., 1973-76; dir. Monson Devel. Ctr., Palmer, Mass., 1976; residential dir. Kolburne Sch., New Marlboro, Mass., 1976-79; exec. dir. Berkshire Meadows, Housatonic, Mass., 1979—; researcher Nat. Opinion Research Ctr., N.Y.C. and Boston, 1973-76; trainer residential child care, Mass., 1978—; mem. human rights bd. Oakdale Found., Great Barrington, 1980—. Recipient Community Criminal Justice award Justice Resource Inst., 1984. Mem. Am. Assn. Mental Retardation, Mass. Assn. Approved Pvt. Schs. (bd. dirs. 1982-84, ins. trustee 1983-87, svc. award 1982), New Eng. Assn. for Child Care, Internat. Assn. for Retts Syndrome, Berkshire Profl. Women, Hop Brook Club (v.p.). Home: Orchard House PO Box 406 Tyringham MA 01264-0406 Office: Berkshire Meadows 249 N Plain Rd Housatonic MA 01236-9736

CHARROW, CYD BETH, municipal official, psychotherapist; b. Chgo., Apr. 13, 1947; d. Manuel and Ruthe (Liebling) Nepon; m. Fred Charrow, Dec. 27, 1987. BS, U. Ill., 1968; MSW, Tulane U., 1970. Social worker Dept. Child Welfare, San Francisco, 1971-73; exec. dir. Alameda County YWCA, 1973-78; mgmt. cons. No. Calif., 1978-80; dir. social svc. Bronx (N.Y.) Jewish Community Coun., 1980-82; dir. Storefront Svc. to Older Adults, Bklyn., 1982-84; asst. dir. mental health clinic Copay Inc., Great Neck, N.Y., 1984-85; pvt. practice psychotherapy Baldwin, N.Y., 1980—; dir. dept. sr. svcs. Inc. Village of Rockville Centre, N.Y., 1985—, dir. employee devel., 1991—; psychotherapist Oceanside (N.Y.) Counseling Ctr., 1989-93; faculty, cons. Molloy Coll., Rockville Centre, 1990—; tng. cons. Am. Jewish Com., San Francisco, 1992; cons. City of Berkeley, Calif., 1979-80. Author: Senior Citizens Alcohol and Substance Abuse Prevention, 1990 (grantee 1990), Communication Skills for Managers, 1990. Chairperson Bronx Neighborhood Coalition, 1981, Interagency Coordinating Coun., Bklyn., 1983; advisor Sr. Citizens Adv. Coun., Bronx, 1981-82. Recipient Innovations award Nat. League of Cities, 1989, 1st pl. award N.Y. Conf. of Mayors, 1993, cert. of merit Nassau County Exec., 1990, proclamation Mayor of Rockville Centre, 1992; NIMH grantee, 1969-70. Mem. NASW, NAFE, Am. Psychol. Mgmt., L.I. Sr. Ctr. Dirs. Assn. (cons. 1990), Rockville Centre Woman's Club (rec. sec. 1992—). Jewish. Home: 930-5 Merrick Rd Baldwin NY 11510 Office: Inc Village of Rockville Centre 1 College Pl Rockville Centre NY 11571

CHARTERS, KAREN ANN ELLIOTT, critical care nurse, health facility administrator; b. Chelsea, Mass., Apr. 3, 1946; d. Albert Charles and Hazelle Marie (Kraus) Elliott; m. Byron James Charters, Feb. 4, 1972. Diploma, Grace New Haven Sch. Nursing, New Haven, Conn., 1967; student, So. Conn. State Coll., 1968, U. New Haven, 1974; CCRN, St. Leo Coll., 1993. Cert. CCRN. Asst. head nurse Yale New Haven (Conn.) Hosp., 1972-76; staff nurse critical care unit Hosp. Corp. Am., 1982—; relief clin. coord. Columbia New Port Richey (Fla.) Hosp., 1987—. Mem. AACN (bd. dirs. Gulf Coast chpt. 1990-91, treas. 1991-93), Am. Heart Assn. (past bd. dirs.). Home: 13318 Hillwood Cir Hudson FL 34667-1421 Office: Columbia New Port Richey Hosp 5637 Marine Pkwy New Port Richey FL 34653

CHARTIER, JANELLEN OLSEN, airline service coordinator; b. Chgo., Sept. 12, 1951; d. Roger Carl and Genevieve Ann (McCormick) Olsen; m. Lionel Pierre-Paul Chartier, Nov. 6, 1982; 1 child, Régine Anne. B.A. in French and Home Econs., U. Ill., 1973, M.A. in Teaching French, 1974; student U. Rouen (France), 1971-72. Cert. tchr., Ill. Flight attendant Delta Airlines, Atlanta, 1974—, French qualified, 1974—, Spanish qualified, 1977-82, German qualified, 1980—, in-flight svc. coord., 1980—, European in flight svc. coord., 1983—; French examiner In-Flight Svc., 1984—; interpreter Formax, Inc., Mokena, Ill., 1976-82; staff interpreter Acad. Legal and Tech. Translation, Ltd., 1991—. Bd. dirs. One Plus One Dance Co., Champaign, Ill., 1977-78. Mem. Alliance Maison Francaise de Chgo., Phi Delta Kappa, Alpha Lambda Delta. Roman Catholic. Home: 155 N Harbor Dr Apt 3506 Chicago IL 60601-7323

CHASANOW, DEBORAH K., federal judge; b. 1948. BA, RUtgers U., 1970; JD, Stanford U., 1973. Pvt. practice atty. COle & Groner, Washington, 1975; asst. atty. gen. State of Md., 1975-79; chief criminal appeals divsn. Md. Atty. Gen.'s Office, 1979-87; U.S. magistrate judge U.S. Dist. Ct. Md., 1987-93, dist. judge, 1993—; instr. law schs. U. Balt., U. Md., 1978-84. Mem. Fed. Magistrate Judges Assn., Md. Bar Assn., Prince George's County Bar Assn., Montgomery County Bar Assn., Women's Bar Assn., Marlborough Am. Inn. Ct. (pres. 1988=90), Wrangler's Law Club, Phi Beta Kappa. Office: US Courthouse Rm 465A 6500 Cherrywood Ln Greenbelt MD 20770

CHASE, ALISON BECKER, modern dancer, choreographer, teacher; b. Eolia, Mo.. Studied dance, Washington U., St. Louis, UCLA; with Murray Louis, Mia Slavenska. Former modern dance tchr. Dartmouth Coll., Dartmouth; dancer, choreographer, co-artistic dir. Pilobolus Dance. Office: Pilobolus Dance PO Box 388 Washington Depot CT 06794 also: Sheldon Soffer Mgt Inc 130W 56th St New York NY 10019*

CHASE, CHARLENE ANN, social services executive; b. Long Beach, Calif., Dec. 30, 1941; d. Ernest Leo and Ruth Sultana (Cole) Miles; m. Amos J. Chase, Dec. 22, 1968 (dec. Apr. 1994); children: Amos John II, Joshua Miles. BA, L.A. Pacific, 1965; MA, Sierra U., 1989. Cert. social worker. Social worker L.A. County Social Svcs., Southgate, Calif., 1968-70; supr. L.A. County Social Svcs., L.A., 1970-72; staff developer L.A. County Social Svcs., L.A., 1972-77; adminstr. L.A. County Social Svcs., El Monte, Calif., 1977-82; dep. dir. Santa Barbara (Calif.) Social Svcs., 1982-88, dir., 1988—; instr. Hancock C.C., Santa Maria, Calif., 1984-87; 1st v.p. Calif. Child Welfare Strategic Planning, 1990-91; bd. dirs. Santa Barbara Regional Health Initiative, 1989—, Area Agy. on Aging, Santa Barbara, 1990—. Mem. bd. ARC, Santa Barbara, 1982-89. Mem. Calif. County Welfare Dirs. Assn. (pres. 1991-92). Mem. Unity Ch. Home: PO Box 55 Los Alamos CA 93440 Office: Santa Barbara County Social Svcs 234 Camino del Remedio Santa Barbara CA 93110

CHASE, DORIS TOTTEN, sculptor, video artist, filmmaker; b. Seattle, 1923; d. William Phelps and Helen (Feeney) Totten; m. Elmo Chase, Oct. 20, 1943 (div. 1972); children: Gregary Totten, Randall Jarvis Totten. Student, U. Wash., 1941-43. lectr. tours for USIA in S.Am., 1975, Europe, 1978, India, 1972, Australia, 1986, Eastern Europe, 1987. One-woman shows include Seligmann Gallery, Seattle, 1959, 61, Gallery Numero, Florence, Italy, 1961, Internat. Gallery, Italy, 1962, Hall Coleman Gallery, Seattle, 1962, Gallery Numero, Rome, 1962, 66, Formes Gallery, Tokyo, 1963, 70, Bangkok Ctr. Mus., Thailand, 1963, Bolles Gallery, San Francisco, 1964, Collectors Gallery, Seattle, 1964, 66, 69, Suffolk (N.Y.) Mus., 1965, Smolin Gallery, N.Y.C., 1965, Tacoma Art Mus., 1967, Ruth White Gallery, N.Y.C., 1967, 69, 70, Fountain Gallery, Portland, Oreg., 1970, U. Wash. Henry Gallery, 1971, 77, Wadsworth Athenum, Hartford, Conn., 1973, Hirshhorn Mus., Washington, 1974, 77, Anthology Film Archives, N.Y.C., 1975, 80, 83, Donnell Libr., N.Y.C., 1976, 79, 83, 92, Performing Arts Mus. at Lincoln Ctr., 1976, Mus. Modern Art, N.Y.C., 1978, 80, 87, 93, High Mus., Atlanta, 1978, Herbert Johnson Mus., 1982, A.I.R. Gallery, N.Y.C., 1983-85, Art in Embassies, USIS, 1984-88, Inst. Contemporary Art, London, 1989, Woodside/Braseth Gallery, 1990, 92, John F. Kennedy Ctr., 1990, Seattle Arts Mus., 1990, 92, 95; circulating exhibit Western Mus. Assn., 1970-71, Am. Inst. Archs., Seattle, 1994; represented in permanent collections Finch Coll. Mus., N.Y.C., Mus. Modern Art, N.Y.C., Seattle Art Mus., Ashai Shimbum, Tokyo, Georges Pompidou Ctr., Paris, Battelle Inst., Mus. Fine Arts Boston, Milw. Art Inst., Art Inst. Chgo., Mus. Fine Arts Houston, Frye Art Mus., Seattle, Nat. Collection Fine Arts, Smithsonian Instn., Washington, Wadsworth Athenum, N.C. Mus. Art, Raleigh, Mus. Modern Art, Kobe, Japan, Pa. Acad. Art, Phila., Portland Art Mus., Vancouver (B.C.) Art Gallery, Montgomery (Ala.) Mus. Fine Art, Hudson River Mus., N.Y.C.; works represented in archival collections Ctr. for Film and Theatre Rsch., U. Wis., Madison, U. Wash., Seattle; works reproduced in various art mags. & books; executed monumental kinetic sculpture Kerry Park, Seattle, Anderson, Ind., Expo '70, Osaka, Japan, Sculpture Park, Atlanta, Lake Park, Ind., Met. Mus. Art, N.Y.C., Montgomery Mus. Fine Arts, Seattle Ctr. Theater; multi-media sculpture for 4 ballets, Opera Assn. Seattle; included in Sculpture in Park program N.Y.C., Playground of Tomorrow ABC-TV, L.A.; work in video TV Exptl. Lab., Sta. WNET-TV; TV prodn. Lies, 1980, Window, 1980; Doris Chase Dance Series produced at Bklyn. Coll., U. Mich., Ann Arbor, Sta. RTSI-TV, Switzerland, Sta. WCET-Cin., Sta. WGBH-TV, Boston, Sta. WNYC, N.Y.C., NET; prodr. Doris Chase Dance Series, 1971-81, Concept Series, 1980-84; prodr. By Herself Series: Table for One (with Geraldine Page), 1985, (with Anne Jackson) Dear Papa, 1986, (with Luise Rainer) A Dancer, 1987, (with Priscilla Pointer) Still Frame, 1988, (with Joan Plowright) Sophie, 1989, The Chelsea, 1994. Recipient honors and awards at numerous festivals in U.S. and fgn. countries; grantee Nat. Endowment for Arts, Seattle Arts Commn., Am. Film Inst., 1988, N.Y. State Coun. for Arts, Mich. Arts Coun., Seattle Art Commn., 1992, Jerusalem Film Festival, 1987, Berlin Film Festival, 1985, 87, London Film Festival, 1986, Am. Film Inst. Festival, 1987, 94, Retirement Rsch. Found., 1994; subject of documentary Doris Chase: Portrait of the Artist, PBS, 1985, book & video Doris Chase: Artist in Motion (by Patricia Failing), 1992; recipient Wash. Gov.'s Art award, 1992. Mem. Actors Studio (writer, dirs. wing 1986, bd. dirs. 911, Art media Ctr. 1990-94). Address: Chelsea Hotel 222 W 23rd St New York NY 10011-2393

CHASE, JEAN COX, retired educator; b. Charlottesville, Va., July 2, 1925; d. Joseph Lee and Wirt (Davidson) Cox; m. John Bryant Chase Jr., June 16, 1951 (dec. June 1978); children: Nancy Davidson Chase, Jean Cox Chase. BA magna cum laude, U. N.C. Woman's Coll., 1946; MA in Eng. Lang. and Lit., U. Mich., 1947; postgrad., U. Va., 1950, 53, various univs. Cert. tchr., Va., N.C. Instr. English Carroll Coll., Waukesha, Wis., 1947-49, housemother, 1948-49; teaching asst. English U. Wis., Madison, 1949; editorial proof reader Michie Legal Publs., Charlottesville, Va., 1951; tchr. of English and Latin Lane High Sch., Charlottesville, Va., 1950-53; critic tchr. for sch. edn. in English U. Va., Charlottesville, Va., 1951; tutor Chapel Hill, N.C., 1958-66; teaching English, gifted, remedial Jordan High Sch., Durham, N.C., 1966; tchr. English, Orange County High Sch., Hillsborough, N.C., 1966-67; instr. Cen. Piedmont Community Coll., Charlotte, N.C., 1970-87; co-chmn. fall faculty conf., Cen. Piedmont Community Coll., 1974, vice-chmn. faculty senate, 1976-77, chmn., 1977-78, chmn. writing across the curriculum, 1980-84 and others; judge Charlotte Writers Club Contest, 1984. Co-editor, author: The Communication Course, 1974; contbg. author, The Jane Doe Papers, 1977, Women of Mecklenburg: Making a Difference, 1980. Active N.C. state legis. coun., N.C. Coun. Women's Orgns., World Affairs Conf. Planning Com., Univ. League, Jr. Svc. League, Creative Retirement Hilton Head, others; vol. English, Latin tutor. Recipient scholarship U. Mich., Ann Arbor, 1946-47, fellowship Nat. Endowment for Humanities, Carnegie Mellon Univ., Pitts., 1981. Mem. MLA, AAUW (various offices, coms. Hilton Head br.), Nat. Coun. Tchrs. English, Great Books Study Group, Phi Beta Kappa, Kappa Delta Pi, Chi Omega (advisor local chpt. 1959-69), others. Democrat. Episcopalian. Home: 300 Woodhaven Dr Apt 3405 Hilton Head Island SC 29928-7516

CHASE, JEANNE NORMAN, artist, educator; b. Spokane, Wash., Feb. 15, 1929; d. John Henry and Violet Inez (Crosby) Norman; m. David Carl Chase, July 4, 1964. BFA in Painting, Calif. State U., Northridge, 1959. Instr. painting and drawing Ringling Sch. Art and Design, Sarasota, Fla., 1978-94, chmn. fine arts dept., 1983-85; condr. workshops Ringling Workshop Series, Wildacres Retreat, N.C., 1984, 85; lectr. in field. Group and one-woman shows include Rauchbach Gallery, Bal Harbour, Fla., 1981, 83, Boca Grande (Fla.) Gallery, 1982, Tatem Gallery, Ft. Lauderdale, 1986, 87, St. Boniface Conservatory of Arts, Sarasota, 1988, Helios Gallery, Naples, Fla., 1989, Manatee C.C. Fine Arts Gallery, 1988, Phillips Gallery, Sanibel, Fla., 1991, Mickelson Gallery, Washington, 1989-94, others; nat. and internat. juried competitions Ridge Crest Art Assn., Winter Haven, Fla., 1980, Mason Keane Gallery, N.Y.C., 1981 (Best of Show), Tampa (Fla.) Mus. of Arts, 1982, El Paso Mus. Art, 1982, Columbia-Greene C.C., Hudson, N.Y., 1982, Edison C.C., Ft. Myers, Fla., 1982, 85, The Soc. of the Four Arts, Palm Beach, Fla., 1982, 87, The Capitol Gallery, Tallahassee, Fla., 1986, Tampa Mus., 1988, Binnewater Arts Ctr., N.Y.C., 1988, others.; represented in permanent collections former Pres. Jimmy and Roslyn Carter, Grace Lemon (collector), Indonesia, Bendix Avionies, Dr. and Mrs. Victor Maitland, Fla., Ringling Sch. Art and Design, Mr. and Mrs. E. Howland Swift III, Va., Chatahoochie Mus. Art, Ga., Dr. Artine Artinian, Fla., George Whitman, Shakespeare and Co., Paris, Veroingue Rabin Le Gall E'cole des Beaux-Arts, Paris, Donahoe Swift Assn., N.Y.C.; works published in book American Artists, an Illustrated Survey of Leading Contemporary Americans, 1986; subject in books: Female Artists in the United States: a Research and Resource File, 1986, 88, Artists and Their Cats, 1990; subject numerous newspaper articles; TV and video interviews: Focus on the Arts, Channel 4, 1980, A Fabric of Our Own Making, Ga. State U., 1981, Introduction to Jeanne Norman Chase, local sta., St. Augustine, Fla., 1991. Mem. Fla. Artists Group. Recipient Merit award Foster Harmon Gallery, Sarasota, 1991. Mem. Fla. Artists Group. Studio: 1602 Bay Rd Sarasota FL 34239-6808

CHASE, LINDA JOANN, lawyer; b. Bklyn., July 1, 1948; d. Richard George and Jeannette (Mogilnicki) C.; m. Warren F. Luther, Oct. 6, 1973 (dec. 1977). B.A., SUNY-Albany, 1969; J.D., Fordham U., 1982. Bar: N.Y. 1983, U.S. Dist. Ct. (so. and ea. dists.) N.Y. 1983, Ill. 1985, U.S. Dist. Ct. (no. dist.) Ill. 1985, U.S. Ct. Appeals (7th cir.) 1985. Tchr., St. Kevin's Sch., Flushing, N.Y., 1970-73; program asst. Young Pres.'s Orgn., Inc., N.Y.C., 1973-75; paraprofl. Paul, Weiss, Rifkind, Wharton & Garrison, N.Y.C., 1976; program dir. Practising Law Inst., N.Y.C., 1977-82; assoc. Chadbourne, Parke, Whiteside & Wolff, N.Y.C., 1982-84, Phelan, Pope & John Ltd., Chgo., 1984-91; chief counsel Subcom. Oversight and Investigations, Ho. Com. Natural Resources, 1991—. Recipient U.S. Law award, U.S. Law Week, 1982. Mem. ABA, Chgo. Bar Assn. Democrat. Office: Subcom on Oversight & Investigations 305 O'Neill House Office Bldg Washington DC 20515*

CHASE, MARY ANN, physician; b. Boston, Aug. 15, 1945; d. Roscoe Moses and Dorothy Elinor (Carney) C.; m. John R. Vinton, July 18, 1964; children: Nathaniel, Andrew. BA, NYU, 1970; MD, Med. Coll. Pa., 1974. Diplomate Am. Bd. Internal Medicine. Intern Montefiore Hosp. and Med.

Ctr., N.Y.C., 1974-75, resident, 1975-77; physician FHP, Salt Lake City, 1977—. Mem. ACEP, Utah Med. Assn. Democrat. Episcopalian. Office: FHP 2500 S State St Salt Lake City UT 84115

CHASE, SYLVIA B., journalist; b. St. Paul, Feb. 23, 1938; d. Kelsey David and Sylvia (Bennett) C. B.A., UCLA, 1961. Aide to Calif. State Assembly Com. on Fin. and to Senator Thomas Rees, 1961-65; active polit. campaigns Calif., 1961-68; coordinator Kennedy for Pres., 1968; advance person Atty. Gen. Tom Lynch of Calif., 1966; action reporter Sta. KNX Los Angeles, 1969-71; corr. and anchorwoman CBS News, N.Y.C., 1971-77; corr. 20/20 ABC News, N.Y.C., 1977-86; anchorwoman Sta. KRON-TV News, San Francisco, 1986-90; corr. Primetime Live ABC News, N.Y.C., 1990—. Recipient Emmy award 1978, 80, 86, 87; Headliners award, 1979, 83, 94; Front Page award, 1979; Gainsbrugh award, 1979; consumer award Nat. Press Club, 1982; Pinnacle award, 1983; Russell L. Cecil award, 1983; Communications award Better Health and Living Mag., 1986, Award of Courage, NOW, 1987; Peabody award, 1989, Robert F. Kennedy award, 1989, Matrix award Women in Communications, 1992, AWRT award, 1994. Office: PrimeTime Live 147 Columbus Ave 3rd Fl New York NY 10023-5900*

CHASEK, ARLENE SHATSKY, academic director; b. Newark, N.J., June 1, 1934; d. Herman and Rose (Sporn) Shatsky; m. Marvin B. Chasek, Apr. 10, 1960; children: Pamela S., Laura N., Daniel J. BA, Cornell U., 1956; MA, Columbia U., 1957; postgrad., U. N.D., 1972-74, Rutgers U., 1981-91. Tchr. English and journalism Elizabeth (N.J.) Pub. Schs., 1978-80, Summit (N.J.) Pub. Schs., 1978-80; coord. MA program Fairleigh Dickinson U., Teaneck, N.J., 1979-81; editor AT&T, Murray Hill, N.J., 1980-81; project coord. Consortium for Ednl. Equity Rutgers U., New Brunswick, 1981-85; project dir. Rutgers Consortium for Ednl. Equity, New Brunswick, 1985-88, dir. spl. projects, 1988-93; dir. family involvement programs in math., sci. and tech. Rutgers Consortium for Ednl. Equity, 1993—. Author, editor: Rutgers Family Tools and Technology, 1994, Rutgers Family Science, 1993, Mathematics in Art/Art in Mathematics, 1986 (U.S. Dept. Edn. award 1987), From Jumping Genes to Red Giants: A Guide to High School Science Research; author: The Recruitment and Retention Challenge, 1982, Futures Unlimited, 1985 (Curriculum award am. Ednl. Rsch. Assn. 1986). Mem. AAUW, LWV, NSTA, Nat. Assn. Equity Educators, Coop. Learning Assn., Internat. Tech. Edn. Assn., Assn. Math. Tchrs. N.J. Home: 9 Schindler Pl New Providence NJ 07974-1738 Office: Rutgers Univ Consortium for Ednl Equity 4090 Livingston Campus New Brunswick NJ 08903

CHASE-RIBOUD, BARBARA DEWAYNE, sculptor, writer; b. Phila., June 26, 1939; d. Charles Edward and Vivian May (West) C.; m. Marc Eugene Riboud, Dec. 25, 1961 (dec. 1981); children: David, Alexis; m. S.G. Tosi, July 4, 1981. M.F.A., Yale U., 1960; PhD (hon.), Temple U., 1981, Muhlenberg Coll., 1993. Exhibited in one-woman shows Berkeley (Calif.) Mus., 1973, Mass. Inst. Tech., 1973, Detroit Art Inst., 1973, Indpls. Art Mus., 1973, Mus. Modern Art, Paris, 1974, Kunstmuseum Dusseldorf, 1974, Bronx Mus., 1979, Pasadena Coll., Calif., 1990, Kiron Arts and Comm., Paris, 1994; exhibited in group shows Whitney Mus., N.Y.C., Smithsonian Mus., Washington, Mus. Modern Art, N.Y.C., Carnegie Inst., Pitts., Centre Pompidou, Paris; represented in permanent collections Met. Mus., Mus. Modern Art, Lannan Found., Los Angeles, Centre Pompidou, Nat. Collections, France, others; author: From Memphis and Peking, Poems, 1974, Sally Hemings, 1979, new edit., 1994, Study of a Nude Woman as Cleopatra, Verse, 1987, Valide, 1986, Echo of Lions, 1989 (citation State Legislature, Gov. Conn., 1989), The President's Daughter, 1994, Egypt's Nights, 1994. John Hay Whitney Found. fellow, 1958; Nat. Endowment for Arts fellow, 1973; recipient Kafka prize for best fiction written by an Am. women, 1979, Academic of Italy with Gold medal, 1979, The Carl Sandburg Poetry prize, 1988. Mem. PEN, The Century Assn., Yale Alumni Assn., Am. Ctr. N.Y.

CHASEY, JACQUELINE, lawyer. Formerly counsel Bertelsmann, Inc.; sr. counsel Bertelsman, Inc., 1990-93; v.p., legal affairs, 1994—. Office: Bertelsmann Inc 1540 Broadway New York NY 10036-4094

CHASKI, HILDA CECELIA, public health administrator, epidemiologist; b. Balt., Apr. 14, 1951; d. Milton Sylvester and Marylee (Evans) C.; m. H. Douglas Adams, 1994. BA in Biology, Manhattanville Coll., 1973; MPH, Yale U., 1987. Pub. health sanitarian Del. Dept. Health and Social Svcs., Georgetown, 1974-85; pub. health cons., New Haven, 1987; dep. dir. div. environ. health and epidemiology Mo. Dept. Health, Jefferson City, 1987-94; dir. environ. health Kansas City (Mo.) Dept. Health, 1990—; instr. anatomy and physiology Del. Tech. and C.C., Georgetown, 1981-85; adj. faculty St. Louis U. Sch. Pub. Health, 1992—; mem. Show Me Health Reform Commn., 1993; presenter in field. Contbr. articles to profl. jours. Pres. Del. Environ. Assn., 1977; mem. Columbia (Mo.) Bd. Plumbing Examiners, 1988-90, Columbia Commn. on Bicycling, 1988-91. Recipient letter of commendation State of Del., 1981, 84, Young Careerist award DeVries Bus. and Profl. Women's Club, 1980, cert of appreciation Del. Tech. and C.C.-Calif. Coll. Respiratory Therapy, 1981, Strategic Leadership for State Execs. award Duke U., 1991, Mo. Gov.'s award for productivity, 1993. Mem. APHA, Nat. Environ. Health Assn. (exec. coun. 1977), Mo. Pub. Health Assn. (v.p. Ctrl. Mo. chpt. 1988-89, pres. 1989-90, chair legis. com. 1993).

CHASSE, EMILY SCHUDER, librarian, educator, storyteller; b. Paducah, Ky., June 10, 1953; d. Charles Bernard and Ann (Sidwell) Schuder; m. William Chasse, Aug. 30, 1980; 1 child, Sarah Ann Schuder Chasse. Student, Iowa State U., 1972-74; BA in Elem. Edn., Antioch Coll., 1976; MLS, U. R.I., 1979. Cert. tchr., Conn. Child care worker Walker Home & Sch., Needham, Mass., 1975-78; children's libr. Plainville (Conn.) Pub. Libr., 1979-82; part-time instr. in children's lit. Manchester (Conn.) Community Coll., 1981-83; asst. curriculum lab. libr. Cen. Conn. State U., New Britain, 1982-89, libr. on-line search svcs., 1989—; freelance storyteller, 1980—. Contbr. articles to profl. jours. Mem. ALA, Conn. Libr. Assn., Conn. Storytelling Assn., Hither & Yon Storytellers. Democrat. Mem. Soc. of Friends. Office: Cen Conn State U Burritt Libr 1615 Stanley St New Britain CT 06050

CHASTAIN, DENISE JEAN, process improvement engineer; b. Casper, Wyo., Dec. 12, 1961; d. Jerry and Nancy Gayle (Stewart) C. BAChemE, Ga. Inst. Tech., 1986. Registered profl. engr., Ga. Product devel. engr. Ga. Pacific, Atlanta, 1986-89; process improvement engr. Lockwood Greene Engrs., Atlanta, 1989-94, Ga. Pacific, Atlanta, 1994—. Named Young Engr. of Yr., Ga., 1994. Mem. AIChE (sec. 1989-90, vice chmn. 1990-91, chmn. 1991-93), Engrs. for Edn. (nat. profl. devel. com. and subcom. for profl. standards).

CHASTAIN, KELLY D., consumer advocate, columnist; b. Kansas City, Mo., Aug. 4, 1956; d. David Lee Lawson and Sally Marie (Boyer) Moore; m. Jack T. Chastain, Oct. 10, 1980 (div. Apr. 1988); children: John B. Carter, Misty M., Candice E. Real estate agent Century 21, Kansas City, 1984-86; auto wholesaler Family Auto Consulting Svcs., Kansas City, 1988-90, auto cons., appraiser, 1990—. Author, tech. dir. Women's Auto Adv. newsletter, 1993—; designer bus. plan for completely automated Car Mktg. Sys. Mem. Women's Resource Network, Clay County Women's Exch. (editor newsletter 1994), Platte County Women's Exch., Home Bus. Connection, Gladstone J.C.'s, Toastmasters. Home: 5408 NW Foxhill Rd Parkville MO 64152-3426

CHATARY, PATRICIA ANN, educator, artist; b. Camden, N.J., Apr. 28, 1953; d. Paul Ralph and Helen Julia (Peschko) C.; m. Robert Wayne Clauss, Oct. 20, 1971 (div. Nov. 1983); children: Benjamin Robert, Season Emily. BA in English and Creative Writing, BFA in Ceramics, Grand Valley State U., 1991. Instr. ceramics Holland (Mich.) Area Arts Coun., 1991—; vis. instr. ceramics Dept. Art, Hope Coll., Holland, 1992—; adj. instr. Grand Valley State U., 1994—. Vol. Holland Area Arts Coun., 1991—. Penland Sch. Crafts scholar, 1989;, Grand Valley State U., 1988; recipient Outstanding Student award Mich. Assn. Governing Bds. Univs., Lansing, 1991. Mem. AAUW, Nat. Coun. Educators Ceramic Arts, Urban Inst. Contemporary Art, Phi Kappa Phi.

CHATFIELD, CHERYL ANN, non profit organization executive, educator; b. King's Park, N.Y., Jan. 24, 1946; d. William David and Mildred Ruth (King) C.; m. Gene Allen Chasser, Feb. 17, 1968 (div. 1979); m. James Bernard Arkebauer, Apr. 16, 1983 (div. 1987). BS, Cen. Conn. Coll., 1968, MS, 1972; PhD, U. Conn., 1976. Cert. gen. prin. securities. Tchr. Bristol East High Sch., Conn., 1968-77; adminstr. New Britain Schs., Conn., 1977-79; prof. Ariz. State U., Phoenix, 1979; stockbroker J. Daniel Bell, Denver, 1980-83, Hyder and Co., Denver, 1983-84; stockbroker; chief exec. officer Chatfield Dean & Co., Denver, 1984-90, Women Securities Internat., 1990-92; exec. dir. Visitor Hospitality Ctr., Santa Fe, N.Mex.; instr. Ctr. Entrepreneurship U. N.Mex., 1992—; tchr. investment seminars Front Range Community Coll., Denver, 1984-86; speaker women's groups, Denver, 1983-86. Author: Low-Priced Riches, 1985, Selling Low-Priced Riches, 1986, (newspaper columns) For Women Investors, 1982-84, Commentary, 1985-86; editor, founder (newsletter) Women in Securities. Project bus. cons. Jr. Achievement, Denver, 1986; exec. dir., visitor Hopitality Ctr. at State Penitentary. Mem. NAFE, AAUW, Aircraft Owners and Pilots Assn., Internat. Women's Forum, Kappa Delta Pi. Republican. Roman Catholic. Avocation: flying. Office: 2801 Rodeo Rd Ste B-217 Santa Fe NM 87505

CHATFIELD, MARY VAN ABSHOVEN, librarian; b. Bay Shore, N.Y.; d. Cornelius and Elma Elizabeth (Sumner) van Abshoven; m. Robert W. Chatfield, June 22, 1963 (div. 1981); 1 child, Robert Warner, Jr. A.B., Radcliffe Coll., 1958; S.M., Columbia U., 1961; M.B.A., Harvard U., 1972. With library system Harvard U., Cambridge, Mass., 1961-92, librarian Bus. Sch., 1963-78, head libr., 1978-92; acting libr. Countway Libr. Harvard Med. Sch., 1988-89; head libr. Angelo State U., San Angelo, Tex., 1992—. Mem. Daughters of Brit. Empire, Rotary. Episcopalian. Home: 1701 Wilshire Pl San Angelo TX 76901-2111 Office: Angelo State U Porter Henderson Libr San Angelo TX 76909

CHATFIELD-TAYLOR, ADELE, arts administrator, historic preservationist; b. Washington, Jan. 29, 1945; d. Hobart Chatfield-Taylor and Mary Owen (Lyon) C.-T.; m. John Guare, May 20, 1981. BA, Manhattanville Coll., 1966; MS in Historic Preservation, Columbia U., 1974; postgrad. (Loeb fellow), Harvard U., 1978-79. Archtl. historian Historic Am. Bldg. Survey, Washington, 1967; co-founder, dir. Urban Deadline Architects, Inc., 1968-73; landmarks preservation specialist N.Y.C. Landmarks Preservation Commn., 1973-74, asst. to chmn., 1974-79, dir. policy and programs, 1979-80; adj. prof. historic preservation program Grad. Sch. Architecture and Planning, Columbia U., 1976-84; exec. dir. N.Y. Landmarks Preservation Found., 1980-84; dir. design arts program Nat. Endowment for Arts, 1984-88; pres. Am. Acad. in Rome, N.Y.C., 1988—; bd. dirs. Preservation ACTION, 1976-84, regional v.p., 1978-83, sec., 1983-84; trustee Ctr. for Bldg. Conservation, 1978-84; mem. U.S. del. to China, Women in Architecture, 1977, 80, U.S. del. to China, Historic Preservationists, 1982; mem. exec. com. U.S./Internat. Coun. on Monuments and Sites, 1979-84; mem. China adv. com. Nat. Endowment Arts, 1980-84, vice chmn. design arts policy panel, 1978-82; bd. dirs. Nat. Alliance of Preservation Commns., 1983-84; trustee Tiber Island History Mus., 1983—; guest lectr. Harvard U., MIT, Columbia U., NYU, U. Va. Contbr. articles to profl. jours. Mem. restoration com. South Street Seaport Mus., 1975-84; mem. Nat. Com. on U.S.-China Relations, 1982—; mem. lawn adv. bd. U. Va., 1982-86; mem. adv. bd. Jeffersonian Restoration, 1989—, Law and the Arts, 1989—; bd. dirs. Greenwich Village Trust for Historic Preservation, 1983-84, Internat. Design Conf. Aspen, 1986-90, Nat. Bldg. Mus., 1989—; mem. adv. bd. Jeffersonian Restoration, 1989—; mem. Commn. Fine Arts, 1990-94. Archtl. fellow Ednl. Facilities Lab Acad. Ednl. Devel., 1982-83; Rome prize Am. Acad. in Rome, 1983-84; fellow N.Y. Inst. Humanities, 1983-89. Mem. Nat. Trust Historic Preservation, Friends of Cast Iron Architecture, Preservation League N.Y. State, Met. Mus. Art, Centurion Assn. Club: Pug Dog of Greater N.Y. Office: Am Acad in Rome 7 E 60th St New York NY 10022-1001

CHATTORAJ, APARNA, gynecologist, educator; b. Calcutta, India, Dec. 1, 1935; came to U.S., 1962; d. Tarak N. and Kashi Bhattacharya; m. Sati. C. Chattoraj, July 31, 1961; 1 child, Partha P. MD, U. Calcutta, 1958; PhD, Boston U., 1965. Diplomate Am. Bd. Ob-Gyn. Asst. prof. Boston U. Med. Sch., 1965—; pvt. practice Needham, Mass., 1983—; clin. instr. Harvard Med. Sch., Boston, 1978-90; gynecologist Boston U. Student Health, 1975-93, U. Mass. Student Health, Boston Harbor campus, 1983—; practicing and attending physician Deaconess Glover Hosp., Needham, 1978—; cons. gynecologist Curry Coll., Milton, Mass., 1980-90, Wheaton Coll., Norton, Mass., 1975-83, Babson Coll., Wellesley, Mass., 1978-82. Contbr. over 220 sci. articles to profl. jours. Active Prabasi, Inc., Boston, 1963—. Recipient award Leukemia Found., 1966-68. Mem. Fedn. Am. Socs. Exptl. Biology. Home: 5 Bryant Ln Dover MA 02030 Office: 20 Chestnut St Needham MA 02192

CHATWANI, ANSUYA A., anesthesiologist, educator; b. India, Feb. 16, 1948; came to U.S., 1975; d. Mulji M. and Gangabai (Ramaiya) Babla; m. Ashwin J. Chatwani, Feb. 5, 1977; children: Nita, Amit. MD, T.N. Med. Coll., Bombay, 1971. Diplomate Am. Bd. Anesthesiology. Intern Nair Hosp., Bombay, 1972, resident, 1973-74; resident Temple Hosp., Phila., 1975-77; asst. prof. Temple U. Sch. Medicine, Phila., 1978-87, assoc. prof., 1987—; dir. preanesthesia assessment unit Temple Hosp., Phila., 1994—. Mem. Am. Soc. Anesthesiologists, Internat. Anesthesia Rsch. Soc. Hindu. Office: Temple U Hosp 3401 N Broad St Philadelphia PA 19002

CHAUDHRY, PEGGY ELLEN, business educator; b. LaCrosse, Wis., Nov. 5, 1957; d. Dayton Irving and Evelyn Marie (Slaback) Pertzsch; m. Sohail Siddique Chaudhry, July 7, 1990; children: Matthew, Aeysha. BSBA, Stout U., 1980; MBA, U. Wis., La Crosse, 1985; PhD in Internat. Bus., U. Wis., Madison, 1992. Teaching asst. U. Wis., Madison, 1988, lectr., 1989-91; asst. prof. Villanova (Pa.) U., 1991—. Contbr. articles to profl. jours. European Cmty. fellow Danish Summer Rsch. Inst., 1990, 91, 92. Mem. Acad. Internat. Bus., MBA Assn. (pres. 1984-85). Lutheran. Home: 1126 Prescott Rd Berwyn PA 19312 Office: Villanova U Coll Commerce Finance Dept Mgmt Villanova PA 19085-1678

CHAUSSEE, LORRAINE ANN, municipal official; b. Rockford, Ill., Jan. 16, 1938; d. John Stanley and Victoria Frances (Podgorski) Pastuska; m. Barry D. Chaussee, May 10, 1956; children: John Barry, Jeffrey Allen, Mark Andrew, Mary Lorraine. Registered mcpl. clk., Ill. Adminstr. ins. and pensions Glaziers Local 1355, Rockford, 1964-81; adminstr. elections County of Winnebago, Rockford, 1977-78; elected city clk. City Loves Park, Ill., 1981—. Bd. dirs. GPAC Sr. Citizen Ctr., Loves Park, 1984—; chair Leader Luncheon YWCA, 1984-85; sec. Women in Dem. Politics, Rockford, 1984-85; Dem. candidate Ill. State Senate, 1994. Mem. Am. Bus. Women (Sinnissippi chpt. Woman of Yr. 1986), Internat. Inst. Mcpl. Clks. (cert., Quill award 1992), Women Electing Women, Ill. Dem. Women, Mcpl. Clks. Ill. (dist. bd. dirs. 1983-84, 91-92, treas. 1986-88, v.p. 1988-89, pres. 1990-91, sec.). Roman Catholic. Home: 6225 Browns Pky Loves Park IL 61111

CHAVARRIA, DOLORES ESPARZA, financial service executive; b. Levelland, Tex., Nov. 13, 1952; d. Thomas Medina and Hermenejilda (Estrada) Esparza; m. Margarito R. Grimaldo (div. Feb. 1975); children: Maurice Patrick, Margarito; m. Frank Sedillo Chavarria; 1 child, Mecca Esparza. AS, South Plains C.C., 1977; student, Tex. Tech U., 1977-78. Notary public, Tex. Supr. cen. supply South Park Med. Ctr., Lubbock, Tex., 1980-84, dir. materials mgmt. dept., 1984-90; buyer City of Lubbock, 1990-94, recruiter, 1994—; prin. D.E.E. Enterprises, Lubbock, 1992—. Chmn. S.W. Voter's Registration, Lubbock, 1988. Mem. Nat. Assn. Purchasing Mgmt. (2d v.p. South Plains chpt.), Am. Bus. Women's Assn., Tex. Purchasing Mgmt. Assn., Hispanic Assn. of Women. Democrat. Roman Catholic. Home: PO Box 195 Rte 5 Smyer TX 79367 Office: 1625 13th St Lubbock TX 79457-0001

CHAVE, CAROLYN MARGARET, lawyer, arbitrator; b. Chgo., Jan. 30, 1948; d. Grant Carruthers and Priscilla Morrison (Shaw) C.; m. Robert Edmund Hand; children: Joshua, Chloe, Robert, Grant. BA, U. Chgo., 1970; MAT, Oakland U., 1971; JD, Loyola U., Chgo., 1976. Bar: Ill. 1976, N.Y. 1979. Tchr. corps intern Pontiac (Mich.) Pub. Schs., 1970-71; sec., receptionist Grad. Sch. Bus., U. Chgo., 1971; counselor Sonia Shankman Orthogenic Sch., Chgo., 1972; pvt. practice Chgo., 1976-78; asst. v.p., assoc. counsel Bank of Tokyo, N.Y.C., 1978-85; substitute tchr. N.Y.C. Pub. Schs., 1986-88; with Breckenridge Law Offices, 1986-88; sr. v.p., counsel, mgr. human resources Tokai Bank, N.Y.C., 1988—; arbitrator Am. Arbitration Assn., N.Y.C., 1986—. Vol. lawyer Chgo. Vol. Legal Svcs., 1977-78; designer playground PS 41 Parent Assn., Greenwich Village, N.Y., 1987. Mem. N.Y. County Lawyers Assn. Office: Tokai Bank Ltd 55 E 52nd St New York NY 10055-0002

CHAVERS, BLANCHE MARIE, pediatrician, educator, researcher; b. Clarksdale, Miss., Aug. 2, 1949; d. Andrew and Mildred Louise (Cox) C.; m. Gubare Robert Mpambara, May 21, 1982; 1 child, Kaita. B.S. in Zoology, U. Wash., 1971, M.D., 1975. Diplomate Am. Bd. Pediatrics. Intern, U. Wash., Seattle, 1975-76, resident in pediatrics, 1976-78; fellow in pediatric nephrology U. Minn., Mpls., 1978-81, instr., 1981-82, asst. prof. pediatrics, 1983—, assoc. prof. pediatrics, 1990—; attending physician dept. pediatrics, U. Minn. Sch. Medicine, Mpls., 1981—. Contbr. articles to profl. jours. Recipient Clin. Investigator award NIH, 1982. Mem. Am. Acad. Pediatrics, Am. Soc. Nephrology, Am. Soc. Pediatric Nephrology, Internat. Soc. Nephrology. Democrat. Mem. African Methodist Episcopal Zion Ch. Avocations: tennis; reading; collecting African artifacts; art. Home: 9218 Fawnridge Cir S Bloomington MN 55437-1825 Office: Univ Minn Box 491 Mayo 515 Delaware St SE Minneapolis MN 55455-0348

CHAVEZ, DOROTHY VAUGHAN, elementary school educator, environmental educator; b. Columbus, Miss., Jan. 13, 1942; d. Robert Clayton and Sara (Harris) Vaughan; m. Samuel Patrick Chavez, Nov. 18, 1961; children: Sarah Rose Chavez Brundage, Samuel Clayton. BS, Miss. U. for Women, 1962; MEd, U. North Tex., 1968; postgrad., Tex. A&M U., 1987—. Cert. tchr., supr., Tex. Tchr. Littleton (Colo.) Ind. Sch. Dist., 1962-64, Albuquerque Ind. Sch. Dist., 1964-65, Richardson (Tex.) Ind. Sch. Dist., 1965-69, Austin (Tex.) Ind. Sch. Dist., 1973-89, 92, Round Rock (Tex.) Ind. Sch. Dist., 1992—; mem. Tex. environ. edn. adv. com. Tex. Edn. Agy./Tex. Senate Bill 1340. Author: Nature's Classroom: Locations and Programs in Texas, 1991; editor: Directory of Environmental Education and Interpretive Centers, 1992, Take Children to the Wilds... to Discover Wildflowers and Native Plants, 1993; contbr. articles to environ. pubs. Dir. vol. usher staff Austin Symphony Orch. Soc., 1971-94. Mem. Tex. Assn. Environ. Edn. (editor 1991-93, bd. dirs., Outstanding Contbns. award 1992), Tex. Edn. Agy. (environ. edn. adv. com.), Tex. Outdoor Edn. Assn., Nat. Sci. Tchrs. Assn., Tex. Sci. Tchrs. Assn., N.Am. Environ. Edn. Assn., Am. Nature Study Soc., Inst. Earth Edn., Roger Tory Peterson Inst., Tex. PTA (hon. life), Alpha Delta Kappa, Delta Kappa Gamma, Gamma Sigma Delta. Home: 4107 Mark Rae St Austin TX 78727 Office: Gattis Elem Sch 2920 Round Rock Ranch Blvd Round Rock TX 78664

CHAVEZ, NELBA, federal agency administrator. BA in Sociology and Psychology, U. Ariz.; MSW, UCLA; PhD in Social Work, U. Denver; student sr. exec. program in state and local govt., Harvard U. From clin. dir. to exec. dir., COO La Frontera Ctr., Tuscon, 1972-89; prin. Chavez and Assocs., 1989-90; dir. juvenile probation svcs. City and County of San Francisco, 1990-92; adminstr. Substance Abuse and Mental Health Svcs. Adminstrn., USPHS, U.S. Dept. Health and Human Svcs., Washington, 1993—; bd. dirs. Nat. Coalition of Hispanic Mental Health and Human Svc. Orgns.; active U.S. Senate Hispanic Adv. Com., Pres. Nat. Coun. on Handicapped, White House Prevention Com. on Drug-Free Am. Active Tuscon Mayor's Task Force on Children. Office: Dept Health and Human Svcs Substance Abuse Svcs Adminstrn 5600 Fishers Ln Rm 13C-05 Rockville MD 20857*

CHÁVEZ-SILVERMAN, SUZANNE, Chicano/Latino and Latin American literature educator; b. L.A., Mar. 21, 1956; d. Joseph Herman and June Audrey (Chávez) Silverman; 1 child, Etienne Joseph Strauss. BA magna cum laude, U. Calif., Irvine, 1977; MA, Harvard U., 1979; PhD, U. Calif., Davis, 1991. Permanent lectr. U. South Africa, Pretoria, 1982-84; asst. prof. Spanish and L.Am. lit. Pomona Coll., Claremont, Calif., 1989—. Contbr. articles to profl. jours. and anthologies. NEH rsch. asst. grantee Pomona Coll., summers 1992, 93. Mem. MLA, Am. Studies Assn., Nat. Assn. for Chicano Studies, Am. Lit. Assn., Am. Assn. Tchrs. Spanish and Portuguese, Latin Am. Studies Assn. Office: Pomona Coll Modern Langs Dept 550 N Harvard Ave Claremont CA 91711

CHAVOOSHIAN, MARGE, artist, educator; b. N.Y.C., Jan. 8, 1925; d. Harry Mesrob and Anna (Tashjian) Kurkjian; m. Barkev Budd Chavooshian, Aug. 11, 1946; children: J. Dean, Nora Ann. Student Art Students League, 1943, Reginald Marsh, N.Y.C., 1943, Mario Cooper, N.Y.C., 1977. Designer Needlework Arts Co., N.Y.C., 1943-44; illustrator John David Men's Store, N.Y.C., 1944-45; illustrator, layout artist Fawcett Publs., N.Y.C., 1945-47; designer, illustrator Pa. State U., University Park, 1947-49; art tchr. Trenton pub. schs., N.J., 1958-68, art cons. Title One Program, 1968-74; painting instr. Princeton Art Assn., N.J., 1974-77, Jewish Community Ctr., Ewing, N.J., 1974-85, Contemporary Club, Trenton, 1974-85, YMCA, YWCA, Trent Ctr., Trenton, 1974—; artist-at-large Alliance For Arts Edn., N.J., 1979-80; adj. asst. prof. art instr. Mercer County Coll., West Windsor, N.J., 1985—; tchr. watercolor workshops Chalfonte, Cape May, N.J. One woman shows include Rider Coll., 1974, Jersey City Mus., 1980, N.J. State Mus., 1981, Trenton City Mus., 1984, 87, Arts Club, Washington, D.C., 1991, Coryell Gallery, Lambertville, N.J., 1993; exhibited in group shows at Douglas Coll., N.J., 1977, Bergen Mus., Paramus, N.J., 1980, 81, 82, Hunterdon Art Ctr., Clinton, N.J., 1982, Morris Mus., Morristown, N.J., 1984, Allied Artists of Am., 1984, 86, 89, 91, 92, 93, 94, Salmagundi Club, N.Y.C., 1988, 91, 92, Barron Art Ctr., Woodbridge, N.J. (Ida Wells and Clara Stroud award 1993), Ridgewood (N.J.) Art Inst. (Ruth Ratay Meml. Fund award 1994); represented in permanent collections Mercer County Cultural and Heritage Commn., Arts Club of Washington, N.J. State Mus., Jersey City Mus., Trenton City Mus., Morris Mus., Rider Coll., Art Mus. San Lazarre, Italy, corp. offices Bristol Myers Squibb, Schering Plough Corp, Pub. Svc. Electric and Gas, Co. Recipient numerous awards Union Coll., Mercer County Cultural and Heritage Commn., Phillips Mill (Walter E. Martin Meml. award 1992, Patrons award for watercolor 1994), Am. Watercolor Soc., Phila. Watercolor Club, Ligorno and Solansky award Hunterdon County Cultural and Heritage Commn., 1991, Cynthia Goodgal Meml. award Ridgewood Art Inst., 1992, Ruth Ratay award Cmty. Arts Assn. Mid Atlantic Show, 1994; named Woman of Month Woman's Newspaper of Princeton, 1984. N.J. State Council Arts fellow, 1979. Fellow Am. Artists Profl. League (Am. Arts Clon. award 1973, Winsor Newton award 1980, Gold medal, Barron Art Ctr. award 1991, 93, Merit award 1992, Am. Artists Profl League award 1994, others); mem. Nat. Assn. Women Artists (two yr. nat. travel award 1985, recipient S. Winston Meml. award 1988), Catherine Lorillard Wolfe Art Club (Bee Paper Co. award 1977, Anna Hyatt Huntington Bronze medal 1979), Allied Artists Am. (elected mem., Henry Gasser Meml. award 1992), N.J. Watercolor Soc. (Newton Art Ctr. award 1972, Helen K. Bermel award 1984, Howard Savs. Bank award 1986-87), Painters and Sculptors Soc. (Medal of Honor, Digby Chandler medal, others), Garden State Watercolor Soc. (Triangle Art Ctr. award 1976, 89, 94, Grumbacher Silver medal 1981, Merit award 1982, Trust Co. award 1987, Triangle award 1994), Midwest Watercolor Soc., Nat. Arts Club (John Elliott award 1988), Phila. Watercolor Club (Village Art award 1991). Filmed Watercolr Workshop aired on State of the Arts N.J. Workshop. Democrat. Mem. Apostolic Ch. Armenia. Home: 222 Morningside Dr Trenton NJ 08618-4914

CHAVOUS, BARBARA, social welfare administrator; b. Phila., May 16, 1951; d. Leon Monroe and Lois Jean (Brock) Miller; children: Tiffany Jean, Dawn Terece. BSW, Temple U., 1981, MSW, 1982; postgrad., Columbia Pacific U. Assoc. dir. Red Shield Emergency Ctr. Salvation Army, Phila., 1983-84; exec. dir. S.W. Task Force, Phila., 1984-85, Children, Youth and Family Coun. of Del. Valley, Phila., 1986-87; assoc. dir. Russell Conwell Ednl. Svc. Ctr. Temple U., Phila., 1988-89; dir. Realizing Econ. Achievement, Phila., 1989-90; housing and mgmt. staff analyst Phila. Housing Authority, 1990-93, dir. resident svcs., 1990-93; prin. Advantage Unlimited, Phila., 1993—; cons. Pa. State Senate, 1993, Black Family Reunion Inst., Phila., 1993. Cons. 2d senatorial race, Phila., 1993, 2d Congl. race, Phila., 1993, mayoral race, Phila., 1987, 93; active African Am. Health Coalition, Phila., 1993, YWCA, Phila., 1993. Mem. NAFE, NAHRO, NASW, NBCDI, Black Family Svcs. Seventh Day Adventist. Office: Advantage Unlimited 3624 Market St One E Philadelphia PA 19104

CHAZAN, ELLA FAYE, psychotherapist; b. Romania, July 23, 1945; arrived in Can., 1948; came to U.S., 1971; d. Morris and Ruth (Sosnowicz) Steen; m. Larry L. Chazan, June 9, 1968 (div. 1978); 1 child, Jennifer Elise. B Human Resource Mgmt. magna cum laude, Palm Beach Atlantic

Coll., 1991; M Profl. Studies in Human Rels., N.Y. Inst. Tech., 1993. With regional sales office Grant Industries divsn. Eddy Match Co., Winnipeg, Man., Can., 1963-68; exec. asst. to Can. sales mgr. John Deere Ltd., Hamilton, Ont., 1968-71; owner, mgr. JELCO Mgmt., property mgmt. con., small bus. cons., Upland, Calif., 1971-85; exec. asst. to regional v.p. Chandler Corp., Fontana, Calif., 1979-82; adminstrv. asst. to v.p. Schostak Bros. & Co., Inc., Southfield, Mich., 1986-93; adminstr. Family Medicine Assocs., Deerfield Beach, Fla., 1993; resident psychotherapist Omega Psychology Ctr., Inc., Boca Raton, Fla., 1993—, Ctr. for Psychology and Behavioral Medicine, Inc., Boca Raton, 1994—. Mem. ACA, NAFE, Palm Beach County Mental Health Assn. Home: 20513 Via Marisa Boca Raton FL 33498-6754 Office: 9033 Glades Rd Boca Raton FL 33434

CHEATHAM, VALERIE MEADOR, clinical dietitian; b. Huntington, W.Va., June 17, 1957; d. Phillip Jarrell and Anna Lee (Law) Meador; m. Edward Lee McCallum, May 13, 1978 (div. 1990); children: Shaun Jeffrey, Briana Marie; m. Miles W. Cheatham III, Oct. 26, 1990. BS in Biology, James Madison U., 1979; MS in Nutrition, Clemson U., 1986. Registered dietitian, 1987. Cytotechnologist Roanoke (Va.) Meml. Hosp., 1979-80; greenhouse mgr. Greenwood Nurseries, Princeton, W.Va., 1980-81; vet. technician Lewisburg (W.Va.) Animal Hosp., 1981-82; rsch. asst. Clemson (S.C.) U., 1984-86; clin. dietician Anderson (S.C.) Meml. Hosp., 1986-87, asst. food svc. dir., 1987-91, nutritionist III dept. health and environ. control, 1994—; nutritionist Dept. Health and Environ. Control Anderson County (S.C.) Health Dept., 1994—. Mem. Am. Dietetic Assn., Am. Soc. Hosp. Food Svc. Adminstrs. (pres. Palmetto chpt. 1991—), Piedmont Dist. Dietetics Assn. (sec.), S.C. Dietetics Assn. Home: 712 Loblolly Dr Anderson SC 29625-2612 Office: Anderson Meml Hosp Dept Health Environ Control 220 McGee Rd Anderson SC 29625

CHEE, SHIRLEY, real estate broker; b. Ridley Park, Pa., Dec. 29, 1941; d. Richard E. and Lillian G. (Laudeman) Foehl; married, Nov. 26, 1967 (div. Nov. 1976). BS, Susquehanna U., 1963; grad., Real Estate Inst., 1975, postgrad., 1976-77. Music tchr. Nether Providence (Pa.) Sch. System, 1963-65, Anne Arundel Sch. System, Annapolis, Md., 1965-67; 1st cellist Annapolis Symphony Orch., 1967; bank teller Guaranty Bank & Trust Co., Morgan City, La., 1967-68; real estate agt. Joe J. Relle, Inc., Gretna, La., 1969-71; real estate broker Clyde Casey Real Estate, Inc., Gretna, 1972-75; pres. Chee, Inc. Realtors, 1976—, Harvey, La., 1976—; pres. West Bank Profl. Real Estate Sch., Inc., Gretna, 1976-87; mem. merger task force New Orleans and Jefferson Bds. Realtors, 1992. Chmn. small bus. Am. Cancer Soc., New Orleans, 1978, 79; pres. West Bank Rep. Women's Club, Gretna, 1976; mem. Harvey Canal Indsl. Assn., 1988. Mem. Jefferson Bd. Realtors (chmn. edn. 1979, dir. 1989-90, chmn. profl. standards 1989, 91), La. Realtors Assn., Nat. Assn. Realtors, ERA-S.E. La. Brokers Coun. (pres. 1990, sec. 1989-90, treas. 1990, Multi-Million Dollar award 1989), New Orleans Met. Assn. Realtors (bd. dirs. 1993-94). Home: 728 Hickory St Terrytown LA 70056-5113 Office: Chee Inc Realtors 1600 4th St Harvey LA 70058-4410

CHEEK, BARBARA LEE, college reading program director, educator; b. Springfield, Mo., Oct. 25, 1935; d. Curtis Earl and Gertrude Helen (Ahonen) Nelson; m. Lee Roy Clyde, June 16, 1961; children: Michael, Paul, Daniel. BA in Edn. cum laude, Pacific Luth. U., 1957; postgrad., U. Wash., Seattle, 1961-62; MA in Elem. Reading Edn., Boise (Idaho) State U., 1982; postgrad., Ea. Oreg. U., 1983, Seattle U., 1989. Cert. elem. and secondary edn. tchr., Wash. Sec. engring. dept. Boeing Aircraft Co., Seattle, 1957; instr. Edmonds (Wash.) Sch. Dist., 1957-61, Clover Pk. Sch. Dist., Tacoma, Wash., 1961-62, Payette (Idaho) Sch. Dist., 1970-74; bookkeeper Cheek Dairy Supply, Payette, 1970-71; instr. Ontario (Oreg.) Sch. Dist., 1975-79; prof. Treasure Valley Community Coll., Ontario, 1979-89; prof. Pierce Coll., Tacoma, 1989—, dir. reading dept., 1989—; instr. Profl. Excellence Program Tacoma (Wash.) Sch. Dist., 1994; sec. Malheur Reading Coun., Ontario, 1986-87; faculty exec. bd. Treasure Valley Community Coll. Faculty, Ontario, 1986-88; mem. Peer Evaluation Oreg. Devel. Edn., Ontario, 1986; cons. Tacoma Sch. Dist. Profl. Excellence Program 1993—. Moderator Ont. candiate's fair AAUW, 1985, state sec., Payette, 1972-74, sec. N.W. region, 1974, br. pres., 1970-72, 75-77; bd. dirs. Boy Scouts Am., Oregon, Idaho, 1971-84; deacon, v.p. Luth. Ch., 1986; mem. basic literacy steering com. Tacoma, 1992; mem. Pierce County Literacy Coalition (bd. dirs. Tacoma). Recipient Faculty Devel. award Higher Edn. State of Wash., 1990-91. Mem. AAUW (chpt. pres. 1970-72), ASCD, Western Coll. Reading Assn., Wash. State Community Coll. Faculty Devel. (state com.), Wash. Devel. Edn. Assn., Am. Assn. Women in Community and Jr. Colls., Coll. Reading and Learning Assn., Tchr. English to Speakers of Other Langs., Alpha Delta Kappa (v.p. 1986). Republican. Office: Pierce Coll 9401 Farwest Dr SW Tacoma WA 98498-1999

CHEEVER, SUSAN LILEY, writer; b. N.Y.C., July 31, 1943; d. John and Mary Watson (Winternitz) C.; m. Robert Cowley, May, 1967 (div. 1975); m. Calvin Tomkins, II, Oct. 1, 1982; m. Warren James Hinckle III, June 10, 1989; children: Sarah Liley Cheever Tomkins, Warren James Hinckle IV. BA, Brown U., 1965. Tchr., Colo. Rocky Mountain Sch., Colo., 1965-67, Scarborough Sch., N.Y., 1968-69; writer Westchester-Rockland Newspapers, N.Y., 1970-72; editor, writer Newsweek Mag., N.Y., 1974-78; free lance writer, N.Y., 1978—; council mem. Authors Guild. Author: Looking for Work, 1980, A Handsome Man, 1981, The Cage, 1982, Home Before Dark, 1984, Doctors and Women, 1987, Elizabeth Cole, 1989, Treetops: A Famiy Memoir, 1991, A Woman's Life, 1994. Guggenheim Found. fellow, 1984, nominee Nat. Book Critics Circle, 1984. Mem. Pen/Am. Ctr., Authors League. Democrat. Episcopalian.

CHELEMER, JOAN HIRSH, art dealer; b. Pitts., Dec. 23, 1932; d. Manuel and Sophia S. (Cohen) Hirsh; m. Harold Chelemer, June 30, 1957; children: Marc Jason, Scott Brian, Bruce Noah. BA, U. Pitts., 1954. Copywriter Gimbels Dept. Store, Pitts., 1954-56; assoc. editor The Jewish Criterion-Anglo Jewish Weekly, Pitts., 1956-58; pub. rels. officer Pitts. Post-Gazette, 1958-60; project adminstr. Allegheny County Contrs. Office, Pitts., 1980-88; dir. pub. rels. and devel. Pitts. Civic Garden Ctr., 1988; Israeli art dealer, co-owner Aviva Art, Pitts., 1990—; indexer, photographer, writer Pitts. Index for Judaic Art, 1991—. Host Pitts. Coun. Internat. Visitors; support vol., hosp. coord. Reach to Recovery, Am. Cancer Soc., Pitts., 1981—; mem. adv. coun. Internat. Poetry Forum, Pitts., 1988—; bd. mem. Pitts. Fund for Arts Edn., 1987-93; vol., mem. Western Pa. Hist. Soc. Jewish Archives, Pitts., 1993; fundraiser U. Pitts. Alumni, 1975—; vol. The Carnegie, Pitts., 1992—; fundraiser United Jewish Appeal, Pitts., 1990—; bd. mem. Jewish Community Ctr., 1977-79; active Frick Art and Hist. Ctr. Mem. ACLU (mem. program com.), Ams. for Dem. Action, Amnesty Internat., Audubon Soc. of Western Pa., Hadassah, Handgun Control Inc. Democrat. Jewish. Home: 5800 Wayne Rd Pittsburgh PA 15206-2110 Office: Aviva Art PO Box 81212 Pittsburgh PA 15217-4212

CHELL, BEVERLY C., lawyer; b. Phila., Aug. 12, 1942; d. Max M. and Cecelia (Portney) C.; m. Robert M. Chell, June 21, 1964. BA, U. Pa., 1964; JD, N.Y. Law Sch., 1967; LLM, NYU, 1973. Bar: N.Y. 1967. Assoc. Polur & Polur, N.Y.C., 1967-68, Thomas V. Kingham Esq., N.Y.C., 1968-69; v.p., sec., asst. gen. counsel, dir. Athlone Industries Inc., Parsippany, N.J., 1969-81; asst. v.p., asst. sec., assoc. gen. counsel Macmillan Inc., N.Y.C., 1981-85, v.p., sec., gen. counsel, 1985-90; vice chmn., gen. counsel K-III Holdings, N.Y.C., 1990-92, K-III Comm. Corp., N.Y.C., 1992—. Mem. Assn. of Bar of City of N.Y., Am. Soc. Corp. Secs. Home: 1050 Fifth Ave New York NY 10028-0110 Office: K-III Comm Corp 745 5th Ave Fl 23 New York NY 10151-2298

CHELSTROM, MARILYN ANN, political education consultant; b. Mpls., Dec. 5; d. Arthur Rudolph and Signe (Johnson) C. BA, U. Minn., 1950; LHD, Oklahoma City U., 1981. Staff asst. Mpls. Citizens Com. Public Edn., 1950-57; coord. policies and procedures Lithium Corp. Am., Inc., Mpls., N.Y.C., 1957-62; exec. dir. The Robert A. Taft Inst. Govt., N.Y.C., 1962-77, exec. v.p., 1977-78, pres., 1978-89, pres. emeritus, 1990—; polit. edn. cons., 1990—; pres. Chelstrom Connection, 1992—. Editor: Teaching the Excitement of Politics in America, 1984, Political Parties, Two Party Goverment and Democracy in United States, 1988. Active LWV, Mpls., 1950-60, N.Y.C., 1972—; charter mem. Citizens League Greater Mpls., 1952-60; del. White House Conf. on Edn., 1955; vice chmn. Minn. Women for Humphrey, 1954; treas. councilman Luth. Ch. Recipient Cert. of Recognition for Svc. to Mpls. Pub. Schs., Mpls. Citizens Com., 1957; named Town Topper, Mpls. Star, 1958. Mem. Am. Polit. Sci. Assn., Minn. Alumni Assn. (gov. N.Y. 1963—, pres. 1971-73, nat. dir. 1971-75), Minn. Alumni Club (Mpls.). Lutheran. Home: 9600 Portland Ave Minneapolis MN 55420-4564 Office: 155 E 38th St New York NY 10016

CHEN, BARBARA MARIE, anesthesiologist; b. Youngstown, Ohio, May 17, 1960; d. Ching Chi and Kim Lian (Wong) C. BS summa cum laude, Youngstown State U., 1981; MD, St. Louis U., 1985. Diplomate Am. Soc. Anesthesiologists. Resident in surgery Bklyn.-Caledonian Hosp., Bklyn., 1985-88; resident in anesthesia Georgetown U. Hosp., Washington, 1989-92; staff anesthesiologist NIH, Bethesda, Md., 1992—; staff anesthesiologist, researcher Georgetown U. Hosp., Washington, 1992—. Vol. Spl. Olympics, Arlington, Va., 1992, Community for a Creative Nonviolence, Washington, 1989—, Holiday Project, 1989—, Martha's Table, 1994—. Recipient Robert Dripps Meml. award Janssen Pharm., 1991. Mem. AMA, Am. Soc. Anesthesiologists, Am. Regional Soc. Anesthesiologists, Am. Heart Assn., Am. Med. Women's Assn., Soc. Cardiovascular Anesthesiologists. Methodist. Office: Georgetown U Hosp 3800 Reservoir Rd NW Washington DC 20007-2196

CHEN, CECILIA AHYAN, dermatologist; b. Hlaingdet, Thazi, Burma, Dec. 23, 1940; came to U.S., 1969; m. Henry Chen, Oct. 18, 1965; children: Amy Jo, Jean Marie, Susie Ellen, Edward Scott. MB BChir, Rangoon (Burma) U., 1965. Resident in dermatology U. Md. Hosp., Balt., 1971-74; pvt. practice Balt., 1974—. Mem. Am. Acad. Dermatology, Med. and Chirugical Faculty of Md., Md. Dermatology Soc. Roman Catholic.

CHEN, CHING-CHIH, information science educator, consultant; b. Foochow, Fukien, China, Sept. 3, 1937; came to U.S, 1959; d. Han-chia and May-ying (Liu) Liu; m. Sow-Hsin Chen, Aug. 19, 1961; children: Anne, Catherine, John. BA, Nat. Taiwan U., Taipei, 1959; MLS, U. Mich., 1961; PhD, Case Western Res. U., 1974. Asst. Sch. Libr. Sci. U. Mich., Ann Arbor, 1960-61, svc. libr., 1961-62; sci. reference libr. McMaster U., Hamilton, Ont., Can., 1962-63, head sci. libr., 1963-64; sr. sci. libr. U. Waterloo, Ont., Can., 1964-65; head engring., math. and sci. libr. U. Waterloo, Can., 1965-68; assoc. sci. libr. MIT, Cambridge, Mass., 1968-71; asst. prof. Sch. Libr. and Info. Sci. Simmons Coll., Boston, 1971-76, asst. dean for acad. affaris Sch. Libr. and Info. Sci., 1977-79, assoc. dean, prof. Sch. Libr. and Info. Sci., 1979—; cons. Am. Soc. Info. Sci./Cath. U. of Am., 1976-77, Chung-Shan Inst. Sci. Rsch., Taiwan, 1977-87, Abt .Assocs., Inc. 1980-82, Sci. and Tech. Info. Ctr. Nat. Sci. Coun., Taiwan, 1973-77, S.E. Asia region WHO, 1980, 81, Western Pacific region, 1981-82, Engring. Info. Inc., 1982, Unesco, Paris, 1984, Nat. Geographic Soc., 1985, Norman Bethuen U. Med. Scis. Libr., 1986, Getty Trust, 1988, USIA, 1988, Ont. Coun. Gradual Studies, 1989, FID, 1989, World Bank, 1990, UNESCO, 1991, DataConsult, Mex., 1991, Soros Found., 1992-93, USIA, 93-94. Author, editor 25 books including Biomedical, Scientific and Technical Book Reviewing, 1976, Sourcebook on Health Sciences Librarianship 1977, Quantitative Measurement and Dynamic Library Service, 1978, Scientific & Technical Information Sources, 2d edit., 1987, (with others) Numeric Databases, 1984, HyperSource on Hypermedia/Multimedia Technologies, 1989, HyperSource on Optical Technologies, 1989, Optical Technologies in Libraries: Use & Trends, 1991; editor-in-chief Microcomputers for Information Management, 1983—; also editor numerous conf. proceedings.; contbr. over 100 articles to profl. jours. Barbour scholar U. Mich., 1959-61, Case Western Res. U. fellow, 1973-74, NATO fellow, 1975, AAAS fellow, 1985; Emily Hollowell Rsch. grantee, 1972—, Simmons Coll. Fund Rsch. grantee, 1972-81; recipient Disting. Svc. award Chinese-Am. Librs. Assn., 1982, Cert. of Appreciation, Asian-Pacific-Am. Librs. Assn., 1983, Disting. Alumni award U. Mich., 1983, Outstanding Svc. award Nat. Cen. Libr., 1986, Disting. Svc. award Asian-Am. Libr. Assn, 1992, Cindy award Assn. Visual Comm., 1992. Fellow AAAS; mem. ALA (disting. svc. award 1989), AAUP, Am. Soc. for Info. Sci. (best Info. Sci. Tchr. award 1983), Assn. Am. Libr. Schs., Assn. Coll. and Rsch. Librs., Libr. Info. Tech. Assn. (Gaylord Libr. and Info. Tech. Achievement award 1990, Outstanding Achievement Libr Hi Tech. award 1994), New Eng. Libr. Assn. (Emily Galloway award 1994). Home: 1400 Commonwealth Ave Newton MA 02165-2830 Office: Simmons Coll 300 The Fenway Boston MA 02115

CHEN, CONCORDIA CHAO, mathematician; b. Peiping, China; came to U.S., 1955, naturalized, 1969; d. Chun-fu and Kwie Hwa (Wong) Chao; BA in Bus. Adminstrn., Nat. Taiwan U., 1954; MS in Math., Marquette U., 1958; postgrad. Purdue U., 1958-60, M.I.T., 1961-62; m. Chin Chen, July 2, 1960; children: Marie Hui-mei, Albert Chao. Teaching asst. Purdue U., Lafayette, Ind., 1958-60; system analysis engr. electronic data processing div. Mpls.-Honeywell, Newton Highlands, Mass., 1960-63; mgmt. planning asst. Lederle Labs., Am. Cyanamid Co., Pearl River, N.Y., 1964, computer applications specialist, 1967, ops. analyst, 1967; staff programmer IBM, Sterling Forest, N.Y., 1968-73, adv. programmer Data Processing Mktg. Group, Poughkeepsie, 1973-80, mgr. systems programming and systems architecture, Princeton, N.J., 1980-82, sr. systems analyst, 1982-83, data processing mktg. cons., Beijing, 1983-88 ; sr. planner IBM DSD, Poughkeepsie, 1988-92; program mgr. Chiang Indsl. Charity Found Ltd., 1993—. Chmn. ednl. council Hudson region MIT. Mem. Am. Math. Soc., Soc. Indsl. and Applied Maths., MIT Club Hudson Valley (pres.). Home: 85 Moulton St Newton Lower Falls MA 02162-1407 Office: Chiang Indsl Charity Found Ltd, 7/F Chinaweal Ctr 414-424 Jaffe Rd, Wanchai Hong Kong Hong Kong

CHENAULT, MARILYN MATHIS, legal administrator; b. Mt. Vernon, Ill., Oct. 21, 1949; d. Nathan Bullock and Marguerite (Woodberry) Chenault; m. Tom Dee McFall, Aug. 29, 1969; children: Shannon, Nathan; m. Troy David Phillips, Aug. 14, 1981; stepchildren: Todd, Brittany. BS with honors, Okla. State U., 1970. Adminstrv. asst. Opticks, Inc. div. G. D. Searle, Dallas, 1977-78; office adminstr. Glast, Phillips and Murray, Dallas, 1978-81; exec. dir. Haynes and Boone L.L.P., Dallas, 1981—; bd. dirs. Law Net., Inc.; lectr. law So. Meth. U. Sch. Law, Dallas, 1981—; instr. paralegal program So. Meth. U., 1981-85; legal adv. coun. Wang Labs., 1985-91, Pitney Bowes, 1991—; mem. Tech. Task Force, 1989—; chair Practicing Law Profitability Conf., 1984, Large Law Firm Tech. Conf., 1990; co-chair Law Net Inc. Conf., 1988. Contbr. articles to Nat. Law Jour. Lou Wentz scholar Coll. Bus., Okla. State U., Stillwater, 1969-70, also C.V. Richardson scholar, 1969-70; named Outstanding Office Mgmt. Grad., 1970. Mem. NAFE, State Bar Tex. (law office mgmt. com.), Dallas Bar Assn. (strategic planning com. 1990—, chair mktg. subcom.) Tex. Lawyer Law Tech. Planning Com. 1992, Nat. Assn. Legal Adminstrs. (dir. of adminstrn. sect. 1979-85, mem. large firm adminstrn. sect. 1985-91, com. mem. 1986-88, vice-chmn. 1989-90, chmn., 1990-91, chair in-house tng. task force, 1990-91, communication/governance/structure issues task force 1988-89, instr. law office adminstrn. course 1984, 87, pres. Dallas chpt. 1985-86, prin. adminstrs. team 1991—, nat. nominating co. 1992-93). Home: 1002 Morningstar Trail Richardson TX 75081 Office: Haynes and Boone 3100 Nationsbank Plz Dallas TX 75202

CHENEY, CAROL, endocrinologist; b. St. Louis, June 29, 1948; d. Robert Simpson and Nancy Ann (Bisel) C.; m. Joshua Aaron Bardin, June 9, 1979; children: Joseph, Jonathan. BA summa cum laude, Oberlin Coll., 1970; MD, U. Calif., San Diego, 1976. Diplomate Am. Bd. Internal Medicine, Am. Bd. Endocrinology. Asst. clin. prof. medicine U. Calif., San Diego, 1982-83; pvt. practice endocrinology Encinitas, Calif., 1984-86; endocrinologist Scripps Clinic and Rsch. Found., La Jolla, Calif., 1986—; assoc. clin. prof. U. Calif., San Diego, 1986—. NSF fellow, 1970-71, Woodrow Wilson Found. fellow, 1970-71. Fellow ACP; mem. Am. Diabetes Assn. (chair patient edn. 1987-91, bd. dirs. 1987-93), Juvenile Diabetes Assn. (bd. dirs. 1994—), Endocrine Soc., N.Am. Menopause Soc., Jacobs Inst. for Women's Health. Democrat. Office: Scripps Clinic 10666 N Torrey Pines Rd La Jolla CA 92037

CHENEY, ELEANORA LOUISE, retired educator; b. Seneca Falls, N.Y., June 3, 1923; d. Guy Darrell and Alice Augusta (McCoy) Stevenson; m. John C. Dinsmore, Jan. 13, 1941 (div. 1953); children: Patricia Walter, Nancy Shannon, Jon Dinsmore; m. Daniel Laverne Cheney, Aug. 8, 1959. BA, Rutgers U., 1966; MA, U. Glassboro, 1971. Account clk. GE, Auburn, N.Y., 1953-58; supr. accounts payable Sylvania Electric, Camillus, N.Y., 1958-60; cost acctg. clk. RCA, Cherry Hill, N.J., 1960-64; honors English tchr. Lenape Regional High Sch., Medford, N.J., 1966-74; guidance counselor Shawnee High Sch., 1974-81; owner Another World of Travel, Marlton, N.J., 1981-86; part-time travel agt., 1986—; notary pub., 1983—. Counselor Contact Ministries, Moorestown, N.J., 1976—; mem. fin. com., nominating com. Haddonfield (N.J.) United Meth. Ch., 1987-92, supr. ch. sch., 1980-82; bd. dirs. Fellowship House, Camden, N.J. Named to Nat. Woman's Hall of Fame, 1994. Mem. AAUW. Republican. Methodist. Home: 445 Westminster Ave Haddonfield NJ 08033

CHENEY, LOIS SWEET, infection control nurse; b. Clifton Springs, N.Y., Oct. 26, 1933; d. Jennie M. (Smith) Sweet; divorced; children: Linda Cheney Thorpe, Susan Cheney Post, Douglas A. Cheney. Diploma in nursing, Rochester (N.Y.) Gen. Hosp., 1954; BS in Edn. with high honors, Mansfield (Pa.) State Coll., 1973; MS, Columbia Pacific U., Mill Valley, Calif., 1982. RN, N.Y. Coord. infection control and employee health Clifton Springs Hosp. and Clinic; now infection control officer Monroe Community Hosp., Rochester; speaker on mgmt. AIDS in long term care, 1987, 88, 89, 92; speaker and cons. in infection control. Contbr. articles to profl. jours. Mem. Assn. Profls. in Infection Control and Epidemiology (cert., Rochester-Finger Lakes chpt.), Bus. and Profls. Women's Club, Toastmasters Internat., Intravenous Nurses Soc.

CHENG, DEBRA SHU PAO, consultant; b. Madrid, Dec. 15, 1962; d. Sheldon S.D. and Lan-Hsiang (Lee) C. AB, Columbia U., Barnard Coll., 1983; MA in Internat. Affairs, Columbia U., 1991. Clk. U.S. Dept. of State, Washington, 1983-84; dir., membership British-Am. C. of C., N.Y.C., 1984-86; mktg. officer Nat. Westminster Bank PLC, N.Y.C., 1986-88; exec. asst. to pres. Endispute Inc., Washington, 1988-89; cons. Bus. Internat., N.Y.C., 1990; cadre Elf Aquitaine, Paris, 1992-93. Buttenweiser fellow Columbia U., 1991. Home: 8704 Irvington Ave Bethesda MD 20817-3606

CHENHALLS, ANNE MARIE, nurse, educator; b. Detroit, May 26, 1929; d. Peter and Beatrice Mary (Elliston) McLeod; m. Horacio Chenhalls, 1953 (dec.); children: Mark, Anne Marie Chenhalls Delamater. Student Detroit Conservatory Music, 1946-47; grad. Grace Hosp. Sch. Nursing, 1951; B. Vocat. Edn., Calif. State U.-Los Angeles, 1967, B.S. in Nursing, 1968; M.A., Calif. State U.-Long Beach, 1985. R.N., Calif. Nurse, Grace Hosp., Detroit, 1951-52; pvt. duty nurse, Mexico City, 1953-54; nurse St. Francis Hosp., Lynwood, Calif., 1957-63; assoc. prof. nursing Compton Coll. (Calif.), 1964-72; health educator, sch. nurse Santa Ana Unified Sch. Dist. (Calif.), 1972-76, 79—; med. coord., internat. health cons. Agape Movement, San Bernardino, Calif., 1976-79; instr. community health, Uganda, 1982; med. evaluator Athletes in Action, 1979; pub. health nurse Orange County Health Dept., Calif., 1990—. Assoc. staff mem. Campus Crusade for Christ. Solo vocalist, Santa Ana, Orange, Seal Beach, Dinner Theater, Calif., Civic Light Opera, Buena Park, Calif.; acting Master's Repertory Theater, 1990—, Santa Ana. U.S. govt. grantee, 1968. Mem. Calif. Sch. Nurses Assn., Nat. Educators Assn., Calif. Tchrs. Assn., Internat. Platform Assn. Democrat. Home: 30802 S Coast Hwy Trlr A2 Laguna Beach CA 92651-4207 Office: Santa Ana Unified Sch Dist 1405 French St Santa Ana CA 92701-2414

CHENNAULT, ANNA CHEN, aviation executive, author, lecturer; b. Peking, China, June 23, 1925; d. P.Y. and Isabel (Liao) Chen; m. Claire Lee Chennault, Dec. 21, 1947 (dec. July 1958); children: Claire Anna, Cynthia Louise. BA in Journalism, Lingnan U., Hong Kong, 1944; LittD, Chungang, Seoul, Korea, 1967; LLD (hon.), Lincoln U., 1970; HHD (hon.), Manahath Ednl. Center, 1970, St. Johns U., 1982, Am. U. of Caribbean, 1982; D Bus. Admin. (hon.), John Dewey U. Consortium, Ednl. Affiliations, 1983. War corr. Central News Agy., 1944-48; spl. Washington corr. Ctrl. News Agy., 1965—; with Civil Air Transp., Taipei, Taiwan, 1946-57, editor bull., 1946-57, pub. relations officer, 1947-57; chief Chinese Sect. Machine Translation Research, Georgetown U., 1958-63; broadcaster Voice of Am., 1963-66; U.S. corr. Hsin Shen Daily News, Washington, 1958—; v.p. internat. affairs Flying Tiger Line, Inc., Washington, 1968-76; pres. TAC Internat., 1976—; chmn. bd. dirs. CIC, Inc.; bd. dirs. Nations Bank. Feature writer: Hsin Ming Daily News, Shanghai, 1944-49; Author: Chennault and the Flying Tigers: Way of a Fighter, 1963; best seller A Thousand Springs, 1962; Education of Anna, 1980; also numerous books in Chinese including Song of Yesterday, 1961, M.E.E, 1963, My Two Worlds, 1965, The Other Half, 1966, Letters from U.S.A, 1967, Journey Among Friends and Strangers, Chinese edit, 1978, China Times, Chinese-English Dictionaries. Mem. Pres.'s adv. com. arts John F. Kennedy Center Performing Arts, 1970—; Pres. Nixon's spl. rep. Philippine Aviation Week Celebration, 1973; mem. women's adv. com. on aviation to sec. transp.; v.p. Air and Space Bicentennial Organizing Com.; spl. asst. to chmn. Asian-Pacific council AmChams, mem. spl. com. transp. to sec. transp., 1972, chmn. com. for spl. transp. activities, 1972; mem. U.S. nat. com. for UNESCO, 1970—; mem. adv. council Am. Revolution Bicentennial Adminstrn., 1975-77, also mem. ethnic racial council; advisor Nat. League Families of Am. Prisoners and Missing in S.E. Asia; presdl. appointee Pres.'s Export Council, 1981, vice chmn., 1981-85; pres. Chinese Refugee Relief, Washington, 1962-70, Gen. Claire Chennault Found., 1960—; hon. chmn. Chinese-Am. Nat. Fedn., 1974—; committeewoman Washington Republican Party, 1960—; mem. Nat. Rep. Finance Com., 1969—; cons. heritage groups, nationalites div. Asian affairs Rep. Nat. Com., 1969—; chmn. Nat. Rep. Heritage Council, 1979, 87; bd. govs. Am. Acad. Achievement, Dallas; appointee Take Pride in Am. Adv. Bd., 1991—; trustee Center Study Presidency, Library Presdl. Papers, 1970—, Helping Hand Found.; bd. visitors Civil Air Patrol; presdl. appointee Presdl. Scholars Commn., 1985—; bd. dirs. People to People Internat; founder, chmn. Nat. Rep. Asian Assembly; internat. fin. chmn. FDR Meml. Commn., 1993—. Recipient Woman of Distinction award Tex. Tech U., 1966, Freedom award Order of Lafayette, 1966, Freedom award Free-China Assn., 1966, Lady of Mercy award, 1972, Rep. of Yr. award D.C. Rep. Fedn., 1974, award of honor Chinese-Am. Citizens Alliance, 1972, Mother Gerard Phelan award Marymount Coll., 1985, award Ams. by Choice, 1987, Capital Press Women's award, Women of Achievement Internat. award. Fellow Aerospace Med. Assn. (hon.); mem. Nat. Aero. Assn. (bd. dirs.), Nat. League Am., PEN Women, Writers Assn., Free China Writers Assn., 14th Air Force Assn. (chmn. awards com. 1969—), USAF Wives Club, Flying Tiger Assn., U.S. C. of C. (coun. on trends and perspective), Am. Newspaper Women's Club Washington, Nat. Mil. Families Assn. (founder, chmn.), Theta Sigma Phi, others. Clubs: Overseas Press (N.Y.C.); Pisces, 1925 F Street, International, Capitol Hill, National Press, Aero, George Town, Army-Navy (Washington). Home: 2510 Virginia Ave NW Washington DC 20037-1904 Office: TAC Internat Chennault Bldg 1049 30th St NW Washington DC 20007-3823

CHENOWETH, HELEN, congresswoman; b. Topeka, Kans., Jan. 27, 1938; 2 children. Attended, Whitworth Coll., 1975-79; cert. in law office mgmt., U. Minn., 1974; student, Rep. Nat. Com. Mgmt. Coll., 1977. Bus. mgr. Northside Med. Ctr., 1964-75; state exec. dir. Idaho Rep. Party, 1975-77; chief of staff Congressman Steve Symms, 1977-78; campaign mgr. Symms for Congress Campaign, 1978, Leroy for Gov., 1985-86; v.p. Consulting Assocs., Inc., 1978—; bd. dirs. Ctr. Study of Market Alternatives. Deacon Capitol Christian Ctr., Boise. Office: US Ho of Reps Office House Mem Washington DC 20515*

CHENOWETH, MARY MURPHY, nursing educator; b. Elkins, W.Va., Jan. 27, 1953; d. Wyatt W. and Emma Loretta (Bohan) Murphy; m. Gary Owen Chenoweth, Jan. 18, 1984; children: Bridget Allyn, Kelley M. Poling. Diploma, Upshur County Sch. Nursing, Buckhannon, W.Va., 1982; ADN, Davis and Elkins Coll., 1984, BSN magna cum laude, 1986; postgrad., W.Va. U. Cert. correctional health profl. Nurse, asst head nurse in ob-gyn. Meml. Gen. Hosp., Elkins, W.Va.; staff nurse, resource pool in ob-gyn. W.Va. U., Morgantown; DON Correctional Med. Systems, Huttonsville, W.Va.; lectr. in nursing Davis and Elkins Coll. Mem. ANA, W.Va. Nursing Assn., Inst. Noetic Scis., So. States Correctional Assn., Alpha Chi.

CHER (CHERILYN SARKISIAN), singer, actress; b. El Centro, Calif., May 20, 1946; d. Gilbert and Georgia LaPiere; m. Sonny Bono, Oct. 27, 1964 (div.); 1 child, Chastity; m. Gregg Allman, June 1975 (div.); 1 child, Elijah Blue. Student drama coach, Jeff Corey. Singer with husband as team, Sonny and Cher, 1964-74; star TV shows: Cher, 1975-76, The Sonny and Cher Show, 1976-77; concert appearances with husband, 1977, numerous recs., TV, concert and benefit appearances with Sonny Bono; TV appearances, ABC-TV, 1978, appearance with Sonny Bono in motion pictures, Good Times, 1966, Chastity, 1969; film appearances include Silkwood, 1983,

Mask, 1985 (Best Actress, Cannes Internat. Film Festival), The Witches of Eastwick, 1987, Suspect, 1987, Moonstruck (Golden Globe award 1988, Acad. award for best actress 1988), 1987, Mermaids, 1990; helped form rock band, Black Rose, 1979; recorded albums Black Rose, 1980, Cher, 1987, Heart of Stone, 1989 (Double Platinum and 3 Gold Singles), Love Hurts, 1991. Office: Bill Sammeth Orgn PO Box 960 Beverly Hills CA 90213-0960 also: care Creative Artists Agy 9830 Wilshire Blvd Beverly Hills CA 90212-1804*

CHERNAY, GLORIA JEAN, association executive; b. Cleve., Oct. 14, 1938; d. Joseph and Angela M. (Fiorelli) Iuliano; m. Terry A. Chernay, July 11, 1959 (div. 1973); children: Debbie Jean, Vickie Ann. BS, Ind. State U., 1959; MS, Ind. U., South Bend, 1971; PhD, Mich. State U., 1977. Tchr. Mishawaka (Ind.) Pub. Schs., 1960-74; instr. Mich. State U., E. Lansing, 1974-76; asst. prof. George Mason U., Fairfax, Va., 1976-82; dep. dir. Nat. Coun. for Accreditation of Tchr. Edn., Washington, 1982-86; dir. constituent svcs. Coun. on Postsec. Accreditation, Washington, 1986-90; exec. dir. Assn. of Tchr. Educators, Reston, Va., 1990—; ednl. cons. fed., state, local edn. agencies and higher edn. instns. Contbr. articles to profl. jours. Pres. Hawthorne Village, Fairfax, 1987-88, bd. dirs. 1988-92. Mem. Phi Delta Kappa (area coord. 1988-90). Office: Assn Tchr Educators 1900 Association Dr Reston VA 22091-1502

CHERNESKY, MARY ELEANOR, extension director; b. Bryn Mawr, Pa., Sept. 14, 1943; d. Lewis J. and Ruth T. (Tomkins) Yost; m. George J. Chernesky, July 25, 1964; 1 child, Robert Mark. BS in Home Econs., U. Nebr., Omaha, 1965; MS of Edn., Iowa State U., 1979. Adminstrv. dietitian Clarinda (Iowa) Mcpl. Hosp., 1967-69; instr. art Turkey Valley Schs., Waucoma, Iowa, 1986-94; ext. agt. home econs. Iowa State U. Coop. Ext. Svc., Fayette, 1970-76, Mason City, 1976-86; ext. agt. home econs. U. Fla. Coop. Ext. Svc., Seffner, 1986-94, ext. dir., 1994—. Co-author: (teaching module) Enviro Shopping, 1991; prodr.: (instrnl. videos) Enviroshopping, 1992, Food Safety, 1993 (Nat. State award 1993). Pres. Condominium Assn., Treasure Island, 1988-94. Recipient Disting. Svc. award Nat. Assn. Ext. Home Economists, 1979, Continued Excellence award Nat. Assn. Ext. Home Economists, 1992; grantee Hillsborough Co. Dept. Solid Waste, 1991-95. Mem. Fla. Assn. Ext. Home Economists (1st v.p. 1990-92, state sec. 1992-93), Am. Assn. Home Economists, Epsilom Sigma Phi (State Team award 1991). Home: 13610 S Village Dr Apt 205 Tampa FL 33624-4384 Office: Hillsborough County Coop Ex Coop Ex 5339 County Rd 597 S Seffner FL 33584-3334

CHERNIK, BARBARA EISENLOHR, librarian; b. Washington, Feb. 18, 1938; d. William Stewart Jr. and Pauline (Fortney) Eisenlohr; m. Glenn Edwin Chernik, Sept. 5, 1964; 1 child, Lee Glenn. BA, Dickinson Coll., 1959; MLS, U. Ill., 1960. Children's libr. Arlington (Va.) County Pub. Libr., 1960-62; U.S. Army libr. U.S. Army Europe, Metz, France, 1962-64; asst. head boys and girls libr. Kenosha (Wis.) Pub. Libr., 1965-66; libr. educator Gateway Tech. Coll., Kenosha, 1967-80; libr. dir. Warren-Newport Pub. Libr., Gurnee, Ill., 1980-90; libr. cons. Chernik Cons. Svcs., Kenosha, 1988—; libr. dir. Coun. Bluffs (Iowa) Pub. Libr., 1992—. Author: Library Resources I, 1979, Introduction to Library Services for Library Technicians, 1982, Library Procedures for LMTAs, 1983, Introduction to Library Services, 1992. Pres. Kenosha br. AAUW, 1968-70, Lake County Human Svc. Coun., 1988-90; trustee Kenosha Pub. Libr., 1972-78; sec. Kenosha Human Rels. Commn., 1978-81; active Leadership Council Bluffs, Council Bluffs Mayor's Task Force on Youth, Network Council Bluffs. Mem. ALA, Pub. Libr. Assn., Iowa Libr. Assn., AAUW, Rotary. Home: Apt 19 255 Oakland Ave Council Bluffs IA 51503

CHERNOFF-PATE, DIANA, interior designer, small business owner; b. San Mateo, Calif., Apr. 7, 1942; d. Fred Eugene and Nadine (Chernoff) Pate; 1 child, Kim Renee. BA in Design, U. Calif., Berkeley. Lic. cosmetologist, Calif. Owner, mgr. Diana Interiors, Napa, Calif.; co-owner, v.p., mgr. ops. Stickney Enterprises, Redwood, Calif., Stickney Restaurants and Bakeries, Redwood; pub. rels. specialist, coord. passenger svc. tng. TWA, San Francisco; adminstr. Internat. Fed. Employees Benefits, 1973, Pension Funds, 1982. Author: Cooking for Profit. Co-sponsor Stanford Athletic Fund, Stanford U.; mem. Frank Lloyd Wright Found. Mem. LWV (Carmel br.), NAFE, Internat. Platform Assn., Am. Soc. Phys. Rsch., Am. Assn. Ret. Persons, Embroiderers Guild Am. (founder San Mateo and Santa Clara chpts.), World Affairs Coun., Designers Lighting Forum, Inst. Noetic Scis., San Francisco De Young Mus., San Francisco Asian Mus., San Francisco Ballet, Commonwealth Club Calif. Home: 1220 Cayetano Dr Napa CA 94559-4263

CHERRY, ELIZABETH KATE, agent, auditor; b. Meridian, Miss., Nov. 15, 1955; d. William Bryant and Gladys Inez (Covington) Rhaly; m. Terry Cherry, May 26, 1974. BS in Sci. with distinction, Miss. State U., 1978. Auditor U.S. Fidelity and Guaranty, Meridian, Miss., 1979-92; artist mgr. Cherry Art, Porterville, Miss., 1992—. Tchr. Scooba Presbyn. Ch. Scooba, Miss., 1975—. Recipient Ins. Woman of the Yr. award Ins. Women of Meridian, Miss., 1985. Mem. Miss. Coun. Nat. Assn. Ins. Women Internat. (state Dir. 1988-89), Ins. Women Meridian (pres. 1983-84). Presbyterian. Home: RR 1 Box 170A Porterville MS 39352-9801

CHERRY, LINDA LEA, deputy United States marshal; b. Davenport, Iowa, Apr. 6, 1956; d. Francis Eugene and Joan Grace (Rottman) Johnson; m. Bradley Scott Cherry, Mar. 1, 1980; children: Jacob Carl, Lucas Andrew. AA, Des Moines Area Community Coll, 1981; BS, Upper Iowa U., 1992. Cert. peace officer; cert. sex crimes investigator. Cashier Frontier Grocery Store, Polk City, Iowa, 1976; clk. typist Deere Employees Credit Union, Ankeny, Iowa, 1974-76; gas sta. attendant Go-Tane, Ankeny, 1977; radio operator Ankeny Police Dept., 1976-78, detective, 1980-85, 89-90, patrol officer, 1978-80, 85-89; guard U.S. Marshals Svc., Des Moines, 1983-90, dep. U.S. marshal, 1990—, recruiter, pub. info. officer, spl. emphasis program mgr., 1990—, student intern coord., 1992—; seized asset specialist, 1994—; instr. Ankeny Police Dept., 1980-90; apptd. mem. coun. Iowa Law Enforcement Acad., 1988-90; apptd. mem. E-911 Commn., 1986-88. Named Officer of Yr., Optimist Club, Ankeny, 1981. Mem. NRA (life), Iowa Assn. Women Police (pres. 1982-88, Officer of Yr. 1989, fundraising/publicity officer 1992—), Iowa State Policeman's Assn. (del. 1989), Iowa Assn. Chiefs and Police Officers (legis. com. 1989-90), Internat. Assn. Women Police (life, regional coord. 1986-88, chmn. membership com. 1991-94, rec. sec. 1992-94, pres. 1994—, Officer of Yr. 1989). Republican. Lutheran. Home: RR 2 Box 30 Elkhart IA 50073-9802 Office: US Marshals Svc 208 US Courthouse Des Moines IA 50309

CHERRY, RONA BEATRICE, magazine editor, writer; b. N.Y.C., Apr. 26, 1948; d. Manuel M. and Sylvia Zelda C. B.A., Am. U., 1968; M.S., Columbia U., 1971. Reporter No. Va. Sun, Arlington, 1968; reporter Akron Beacon Jour., Ohio, 1969-70, Wall St. Jour., N.Y.C., 1971-72; assoc. editor Newsweek mag., N.Y.C., 1972-74; reporter N.Y. Times, N.Y.C., 1976-77; exec. editor Glamour mag., N.Y.C., 1977-88; editor-in-chief Longevity mag., v.p., dir. new mag. devel. Gen. Media Internat., N.Y.C., 1988-92; editor-in-chief Fitness Mag., N.Y.C., 1992—; lectr. New Sch. Social Rsch., 1978, Sch. Continuing Edn., NYU, 1980; faculty Summer Pub. Inst., 1980, 83, Reader's Digest Writer's Workshops; mem. screening com. Nat. Mag. awards, 1980-82, 90-92, judge, 1991-92, 94; judge Nat. Media awards Am. Speech-Lang.-Hearing Assn., 1988. Co-author: The World of American Business, 1977; contbg. author: Woman in the Year 2000; contbr. articles to publs. including N.Y. Times Sunday mag., Parade, Ms. mag., Christian Sci. Monitor; contbr. book revs. to Sunday N.Y. Times. Mem. nat. comms. coun. March of Dimes, 1981-92; v.p. Newswomen's Club N.Y., 1985-87. Recipient Media award Nat. Assn. Recycling Industries, 1973, Bus. Journalism award U. Mo., 1977, Am. Coll. Radiology, 1986, Writer's award Am. Soc. Anesthesiologists, 1983, Maggie award Planned Parenthood Fedn. Am., 1985, Media award Am. Coll. Radiology, 1986. Mem. Am. Soc. Mag. Editors (bd. dirs. 1990-92). Home: 140 Riverside Dr # 8J New York NY 10024-2605 Office: Fitness Gruner & Jahr USA Publ 110 Fifth Ave New York NY 10011

CHERRYH, C. J., writer; b. St. Louis, Sept. 1, 1942; d. Basil L. and Lois Ruth (Van Deventer) C. BA in Latin, U. Okla., 1964; MA in Classics, Johns Hopkins U., 1965. Cert. tchr., Okla. Tchr. Oklahoma City Pub. Schs., 1965-77; lectr. in field. Author: novel Gate of Ivrel, 1976, Well of Shiuan, 1978, Brothers of Earth, 1976, Hunter of Worlds, 1976, The Faded Sun: Kresrith, 1977, The Faded Sun: Shon'Jir, 1978, Fires of Azeroth, 1979, The Faded Sun: Kutath, 1979, Hestia, 1979, Sunfall, 1981, Downbelow Station, 1981 (Hugo award for best novel 1982), Wave Without a Shore, 1981, The Pride of Chanur, 1982, Merchanter's Luck, 1982, Port Eternity, 1982, Forty Thousand in Gehenna, 1983, The Dreamstone, 1983, The Tree of Swords and Jewels, 1983, Chanur's Venture, 1984, Cuckoo's Egg, 1985, Visible Light, 1985, The Kif Strike Back, 1985, Angel with the Sword, 1985, Chanur's Homecoming, 1986, Exile's Gate, 1988, Cyteen, 1988 (Hugo award 1988, 89), Smuggler's Gold, 1988, Rimrunners, 1989, Rusalka, 1989, Chernevog, 1990, Yvgenie, 1991, Heavy Time, 1991, Rumrunners, 1991, Hellburner, 1992, Chanur's Legacy, 1992, Goblin Mirror, 1993, Faery in Shadow, 1993, Tripoint, 1994, Foreigner, 1994, Rider at the Gate, 1995, Invader, 1995; editor: Flood Tide, 1990; translator: Stellar Crusade by Pierre Barbet, 1980, The Green Gods by Nathalie & Charles Henneberg, 1980, The Book of Shai by Daniel Walther, 1982; contbr. short stories to numerous mags. Woodrow Wilson fellow, 1965; recipient John W. Campbell award for best new writer, 1977, Hugo award for short story, 1979, for novel, 1982, 89, Locus award for best sci. fiction novel, 1988. Mem. Sci. Fiction Writers Assn. (v.p.), Alpha Lambda Delta, Phi beta Kappa.

CHERTOK, BARBARA LISS, special education educator; b. Boston, Nov. 7, 1935; d. Wolf and Pauline (Garber) Liss; m. Benson T. Chertok, June 4, 1961 (dec. 1981); children: Victoria Chertok May, Maxwell Benjamin. Student, Boston U., Am. U. Cert. oral interpreter: visible to spoken. Speechreading (lipreading) instr. Montgomery Coll., Rockville, Md., 1986—; pvt. practice Bethesda, Md., 1986—; coord. oral interpreting workshops Bethesda; bd. dirs. Am. Hearing Rsch. Found., Sta. WRC-TV Deaf and Hard of Hearing Cmty. Adv. Bd., SHHH Montgomery County Chpt. Bd.; spkr., presenter in field; cons. in field. Contbr. articles to profl. jours. Vol. Clinton Campaign, Washington, 1992. Featured in numerous newspaper and jour. articles and on TV. Mem. Alexander Graham Bell Assn. for Deaf (mem. Oral Hearing Impaired Sect., Internat. Orgn. Edn. Hearing Impaired), Self Help for Hard of Hearing People, Auditory-Verbal Internat., Assn. Late Deafened Adults, Washington Area Group Hard of Hearing, Telecommunications for Deaf, Inc., League for Hard of Hearing. Home and Office: 4940 Sentinel Dr Apt 205 Bethesda MD 20816

CHESHIRE, SANDRA KAY, lawyer; b. Akron, Ohio, Sept. 4, 1958; d. Clarence and Pauline Patricia (Kriener) C. BA in History, Polit. Sci., Capital U., 1979; MBA, Ohio State U., 1982, JD, 1982. Bar: Ind. 1982, Ohio 1982, U.S. Dist. Ct. (no., and so. dists.) Ind. 1982, Nebr. 1988; CLU; chartered fin. cons. Asst. counsel Lincoln Nat. Corp., Ft. Wayne, Ind., 1982-87; gen. counsel Universal Assurors Inc, Omaha, 1987-93; pres. Cheshire Law Office, Omaha, 1993—; adj. faculty Ind.-Purdue U., 1983-87; pres. faculty Nebr. Coll. of Bus., 1993—. Fellow Life Mgmt. Inst.; mem. ABA, Nebr. Bar Assn., Omaha Bar Assn. Lutheran. Home: 10682 Lafayette Plz # 107 Omaha NE 68114 Office: Cheshire Law Office 7701 Pacific St Ste 122 Omaha NE 68114

CHESKY, EVELYN G., state legislator. Chmn. bd. Hoyoke Pub. Works, 1978; alderman-at-large, 1985; state rep. dist. 5 Mass. Ho. of Reps., Boston, mem. counties com., pub. safety and fed. fin. assistance com. Mem., bd. dirs. Holyoke Boys and Girls Club. Recipient Polish Heritage Citizens award Holyoke Hosp. Aux. Democrat. Office: Mass Ho of Reps State Capitol Boston MA 02133*

CHESKY, PAMELA BOSZE, school system administrator; b. Perth Amboy, N.J., June 17, 1942; d. Joseph John and Irene (Konazeski) Bosze; m. Frederick Alan Chesky, Aug. 20, 1966; children: Rick, Scott. BA, Coll. Notre Dame, Balt., 1964; MLS, Rutgers U., 1992. Cert. ednl. media specialist. Tchr. social studies Woodbridge (N.J.) Bd. Edn., 1964-69, ednl. media specialist, 1969-93, supr. librs. guidance and nursing svcs., 1993—; mem. membership com. Infolink, Piscataway, N.J., 1994; mem. adv. com. Sch. Comm., Info. Libr. Svc. Rutgers U., 1994. Contbr. articles to profl. jours. Commr. Woodbridge Cultural Arts Commn., 1992—; vice-chairlady Middlesex County Dem. Orgn., New Brunswick, N.J., 1992—; parliamentarian Woodbridge Dem. Orgn., 1993—. Mem. ALA (affiliate assembly), Am. Assn. Sch. Librs. (membership com. 1993—), N.J. Assn. Sch. Counselors, N.J. Sch. Nurses Assn., Edn. Media Assn. N.J. (pres. 1993-94, scholarship 1992), Gamma Phi Beta. Democrat. Roman Catholic. Home: 135 Midwood Way Colonia NJ 07067 Office: Woodbridge Bd Edn PO Box 428 School St Woodbridge NJ 07095

CHESLER, DORIS ADELLE, real estate professional; b. Lincoln, Ill., Sept. 23, 1924; d. Harry and Esther Pearl (Campbell) Schoth; m. Eugene Albert Aughenbaugh, May 23, 1943 (div. Sept. 1970); children: Judith C. Wallace, Rodney E., Paula Sue Pask; m. Arthur Bernard Chesler, Oct. 16, 1972. Realtor, assoc. Kilgore Real Estate, Brandon, Fla., 1969-76; broker Doris A. Chesler, Realtor, Brandon, 1976—. Den mother Cub Scouts Am., Tampa, 1961-62; leader 4-H Club, Decatur, Ill., 1956. Mem. Nat. Bd. Realtors, Fla. Assn. Realtors, Greater Tampa Assn. Realtors, Inc. Republican. Presbyterian. Office: 1104 N Parsons Ave Ste A Brandon FL 33510-3112

CHESLEY, THEA BRICETTE, librarian, consultant, writer; b. Chgo., June 10, 1952; d. Theodore B. and Selma M. (Soltner) C.; m. Curtis G. Neitzke, July 23, 1981 (div. Jan. 1994). BA, U. Ill., Chgo., 1977, MA, 1979; MS, U. Ill., Urbana, 1986. Libr. paraprofl. U. Ill. Libr. Health Scis., Chgo., 1975-80; advt. copywriter Squires Advt., Springfield, Ill., 1981-82; head acquisitions and serials Sangamon State U. Libr., Springfield, 1982-86; sr. libr. Ill. Dept. Corrections, Springfield, 1986—. Contbr. articles to profl. jours. Mem. ALA (various coms. 1985—), Ill. Libr. Assn. (various coms. 1982—), Am. Correctional Assn. (chmn. librs. com. 1986—), Ill. Correctional Assn. (bd. dirs. 1989—). Office: Ill Dept Corrections 1301 Concordia Ct Springfield IL 62794-9277

CHESNA-SERINO, EDNA MAE, nurse; b. Chelsea, Mass.; d. John 1st and Edna Winifred (Daly) Chesna; m. Robert E. Serino Sr., May 1, 1960; children: Robert Jr., Marie Elena, Susan Olivia. Assoc. Nursing, North Shore C.C., 1977; BSN, Salem State Coll., 1995. RN. Med./surg. nurse Mass. Soldiers Home, Chelsea, 1973-82; allergy nurse cons. Respiratory Care Physicians, Lynn, Mass., 1983-88, Allergy Assocs., Lynn, 1983-88; sch. nurse Abraham Lincoln Elem. Sch., Revere, Mass., 1988-89; adult day health nurse Cmty. Family Adult Care, Everett, Mass., 1990-91; assessment/evaluation nurse Chelsea, Revere, Winthrop Home Care, 1992-93; founder, CEO The Vital View Corp., Revere, 1983-88; substitute sch. nurse, Winthrop and Revere, Mass. Mem. Rep. Presdl. Task Force, Washington, 1985—; treas. Friends of Revere Pub. Libr., 1993-94. Mem. Mass. Nurses Assn. (bd. dirs. dist. IV 1984-89), Revere C. of C. (bd. dirs. 1985-86), Rotary (disting. svc. award 1991-94, nurse and women rep., London and Paris 1989). Roman Catholic. Office: PO Box 92 Revere MA 02151

CHESNEY, SUSAN TALMADGE, human resources specialist; b. N.Y.C., Aug. 12, 1943; d. Morton and Tillie (Talmadge) Chesney; m. Donald Lewis Freitas, Sept. 17, 1967 (div. May 1976); m. Robert Martin Rosenblatt, Apr. 9, 1980. AB, U. Calif., Berkeley, 1967. Placement interviewer U. Calif., Berkeley, 1972-74, program coord., 1974-79; pers. adminstr. Hewlett-Packard Co., Santa Rosa, Calif., 1982-84; pres. Mgmt. Resources, Santa Rosa, 1984—; human resources mgr. BioBottoms Inc., Petaluna, Calif., 1990-91; human resources adminstr. Parker Compumotor, Rohnert Park, Calif., 1991-93; cons. Kensington Electronics Group, Healdsburg, Calif., 1984-85, Behavioral Medicine Assocs., Santa Rosa, 1985-86, M.C.A.I., Santa Rosa, 1986-87, Bowdon Designs, Santa Rosa, 1987-88, Bass & Ingram, Santa Rosa, 1988—. Mem. Nat. Soc. Performance Instrn., No. Calif. Human Resources Coun., Pers. Assn. Sonoma County. Avocations: cooking, gardening, music.

CHESNICK, JOYCE BAILES, retail executive; b. Memphis, June 6, 1925; d. George W. and Jean (Goldberg) Bailes; m. Joseph Chesnick, Feb. 28, 1945; children: Joan Chesnick Dinerstein, Joseph Jr., Robert G. Student, U. Tex., 1943-45, U. Houston, 1954-56. Co-chmn. Robert Joseph Interiors, Inc., Corpus Christi, Tex., 1981—, Robert Joseph, Inc., Houston, 1982—; prin., co-chmn. Georgetown Manor, Houston, 1968—, San Antonio, 1971—, Beaumont, Tex., 1974—; adv. bd. mem. Ethan Allen, Inc., Danbury, Conn. Bd. govs. Congregation Beth Israel, 1982—; contbg. mem. Mus. Fine Arts, Houston. Mem. Am. Soc. Interior Designers (assoc.), United Daus. Confederacy, S.W. Home Furnishings Assn., Houston Retail Furnishings Assn., Westwood Country Club (gov. 1977-81). Home and Office: 8353 Kempwood Dr Houston TX 77055-1031

CHESNUT, CAROL FITTING, economist; b. Pecos, Tex., June 17, 1937; d. Ralph Ulf and Carol (Lowe) Fitting; m. Dwayne A. Chesnut, Dec. 27, 1955; children: Carol Marie, Stephanie Michelle, Mark Steven. BA magna cum laude, U. Colo., 1971; JD, U. Calif., San Francisco, 1994. Rsch. asst. U. Colo., 1972; head quality controller Mathematica, Inc., Denver, 1973-74; cons. Mincome Man., Winnipeg, Can., 1974; cons. economist Energy Cons. Assocs. Inc., Denver, 1974-79; exec. v.p. tng. ECA Intercomp, 1980-81; gen. ptnr. Chestnut Consortium, S.F., 1981—; sec., bd. dirs. Critical Resources, Inc., 1981-83. Rep. Lakehurst Civic Assn., 1968; staff aide Senator Gary Hart, 1978; Dem. precinct capt., 1982-88. Mem. ABA, ACLU, AAUW (1st v.p. 1989-90), Am. Mgmt. Assn., Soc. Petroleum Engrs., Am. Nuclear Soc. (chmn. conv. space activities for 1989, chair of spouse activities 1989), Am. Geophys. Union, Assn. Women Geoscientists (treas. Denver 1983-85), Associated Students of Hastings (rep. 1994), Calif. State Bar, Century Club, Phi Beta Kappa, Phi Chi Theta, Phi Delta Phi. Unitarian. Office: 100 McAllister St Apt 2101 San Francisco CA 94102-4944

CHESNUT, NONDIS LORINE, English language educator, writer, consultant; b. Hagerstown, Md., June 29, 1941; d. Anthony Valentine and Myrtle Marie (Allen) Campbell; m. Raymond Otho Chesnut, Aug. 25, 1962; 1 child, Starlina Mintina Chesnut Kladler. BS in English and Speech, Concord Coll., 1962; postgrad., Frostburg U., 1967; MEd, Shippensburg U., 1972; postgrad., W.Va. U., 1972; Advanced Grad. Specialist Degree, U. Md., 1974. Cert. administr., secondary prin., elem. prin., reading specialist, tchr. Tchr. English and speech Harpers Ferry (W.Va.) High Sch., 1962-64; libr. Great Mills (Md.) High Sch., 1968-69; tchr. English and reading North Hagerstown High Sch., Hagerstown, Md., 1964-73; tchr. South Hagerstown High Sch., Hagerstown, 1974-77; reading resource tchr. Woodland Way Elem. Sch., Hagerstown, 1977-83; adj. instr. grad. sch. Hood Coll., Frederick, Md., 1982-83; reading specialist Fountain Rock Elem. Sch., Hagerstown, 1983-85; tchr. Williamsport (Md.) High Sch., 1985—; reading and lang. arts cons., Md., 1973—; speaker, presenter local, nat. and internat. workshops, 1973—. Writer for radio programs and advertisements for reading, 1986—, TV programs, 1974-78, 90-91; appeared on TV programs, 1974-78; co-editor column Beckley Post Herald, 1957-59; contbr. articles to newspapers and mags., 1964—; appeared in film Guarding Tess, 1993. Mem. Concord Coll. Debating Team, 1961-62, Concord's newspaper staff, 1959-61, Disabled Learners Interest Group, 1972-75, masterly learning IRA Interest Group, 1975-81, Internat. Rsch. coms., 1976-77, 1985-84, Washington County Network of Orgns., 1984-88; co-dir. Billy Bud, 1962; v.p. Women's Ind. Club, 1962, treas., 1961; sec.-treas. Fgn. Lang. Club, 1961, Debate Club, 1961-62; treas. Meth. Youth Fellowship, 1961; pres. Tri-Hi-Y, 1959; legis. chair State of Md. Reading Coun., 1977-78; active Life in Spirit Group St. Ann's Roman Catholic Ch., 1994, Grace United Meth. Ch. Recipient Pres.'s award State of Md. Reading Coun., 1981, Pres.'s award Washington County Reading Coun., numerous others; W.Va. Legislature scholar, 1959-62, Voice of Democracy award VFW/Ladies Aux., 1992. Mem. AAUW (ednl. chair 1983-85, legis. v.p. 1986-87, community chair 1987-89), NEA (Washington County Tchrs. Assn. (publicity and scholarship coms., bldg. rep. 1989—, del.), ASCD, VFW (chairperson Voice of Democracy 1989-94, VFW award 1989-94), State of Md. Tchrs. Assn., Md. State Tchrs. Assn., State of Md. Internat. Reading Assn. Coun. (sec. 1975-77, v.p.-elect. 1979-80, v.p. 1980-81, pres. 1981-82, nominating chair 1982-83), Washington County Tchrs. Assn., Internat. Reading Assn. (sec.-treas. sex differences in reading 1976-77, 83-85, gender differences in reading 1985-86, readability interest group, mastery learning interest group, del. convs., internat. rsch. com. 1976-77, disabled learners 1975-82), Assn. Rsch. and Enlightenment (Guidance Helping award 1989), Md. Supervision and Curriculum Devel., Coll. Reading Assn., Md. Assn. English Tchrs., United Dem. Assn., Internat. Platform Assn., Am. Legion (chair oratorial contest 1989-94, speech coach). Democrat. Home: 13615 Rockcliff Dr Hagerstown MD 21742-2350 Office: Williamsport High Sch 5 S Clifton Dr Williamsport MD 21795-1197

CHESNUTT, JANE, publishing executive; b. Kenedy, Tex., Oct. 10, 1950; m. W. Mallory Rintoul. BJ, U. Tex., 1973. Editorial asst. Am. Jour. Nursing, N.Y.C., 1975-78; asst. editor Woman's Day mag., N.Y.C., 1978-82, health editor, 1982-89, beauty, health, fashion editor, 1989-91, editor-in-chief, 1991—. Mem. Am. Soc. Mag. Editors, Women in Communication (Clarion award 1985). Office: Woman's Day Mag 1633 Broadway New York NY 10019-6708

CHESSMAN, REBECCA LEE, librarian; b. Balt., Nov. 8, 1945; d. Robert Lee and Hazel Rebecca (Pearce) Hildenbrand; m. Robert Blakley, Oct. 22, 1977. AB in Teaching, Colo. State Coll., 1967; MA, U. Denver, 1974. Tchr. English Astoria (Oreg.) High Sch., 1967-73; ref. and tech. svc. libr. Fresno (Calif.) County Office Edn., 1974-77; jr. high sch. libr. Fremont Jr. High Sch., Seaside, Calif., 1977-83; elem. sch. libr. Patton Sch. Mt. Penin Unified Sch.Dist., Marina, Calif., 1983-84; dist. libr. Belmont (Calif.) Sch. Dist., 1983-94; sch. libr. Buchser Mid. Sch., Santa Clara (Calif.) Unified Sch. Dist., 1994—. Editor: (newsletters) Lymphad, 1989—, Coracle, 1989-91, BFA Update, 1992-94. Mem. com. English/Lang. Arts Task Force, Belmont, 1991-93. Mem. ALA, NEA, Calif. Libr. Media Educators (treas. 1990-92), Calif. Tchrs. Assn. (sec. Golden Gate svc. ctr. coun. 1990-92), Belmont Faculty Assn. (pres. 1989-91), Clan Donald USA (editor regional newsletter 1989—). Democrat. Episcopalian. Home: 1720 Halford Ave # 322 Santa Clara CA 95051 Office: Belmont Sch Dist 2960 Hallmark Dr Belmont CA 94002

CHESTER, NIA LANE, psychology educator; b. L.A., Dec. 8, 1945; d. Thomas Henry and Virginia (Chalmers) Lane; m. C. Ronald Chester, Aug. 9, 1969 (div. July 1988); children: Caben Paul, Ian Thomas. BA magna cum laude, Smith Coll., 1967; MA, Columbia U., 1968; PhD, Boston U., 1981. Tchr. Elmont (N.Y.) Meml. High Sch., 1967-70; master tchr. Ednl. Collaborative Greater Boston, Cambridge, Mass., 1971-75; teaching fellow Harvard U., Cambridge, 1976-78; rsch. assoc. Boston U., 1981-83, 88—; rsch. scholar Radcliffe Coll., Cambridge, 1983-84; assoc. prof. psychology Pine Manor Coll., Chestnut Hill, Mass., 1983—, Lindsey prof., 1990, chair divsn. Natural and Beharioral Scis., 1993-94, dir. internship program, 1994—; reviewer Jour. Personality and Social Psychology, 1985—; vis. prof. Boston U., 1986-88. Editor: Experience and Meaning of Work in Women's Lives, 1990; contbr. articles to profl. jours., chpts. to books. Bd. dirs. Peabody Aftersch. Program, Cambridge, 1983-85, Tobin Aftersch. Program, Cambridge, 1989—. NIMH fellow, 1979; recipient Ruth Allinger Gibson '26 Teaching award, 1992; Women's Coll. Coalition grantee, 1992. Mem. APA, Ea. Psychol. Asn. (program com. 1989-93). Office: Pine Manor Coll Dept Psych 400 Heath St Chestnut Hill MA 02167-2332

CHESTER, SHARON ROSE, photographer, natural history educator; b. Chgo., July 12, 1942; d. Joseph Thomas and Lucia Barbara (Urban) C. BA, U. Wis., 1964; grad., Coll. San Mateo, 1972-74; postgrad., U. Calif., Berkeley, 1977; grad., San Francisco State U., 1989. Flight attendant Pan Am. World Airways Inc., San Francisco, 1965; free lance photographer San Mateo, Calif., 1983—; stock photographer Comstock, N.Y.C., 1987—; lectr. Soc. Expdns., Seattle, 1985-91, Abercrombie & Kent, Chgo., 1992-94, Seven Seas Cruise Line, San Francisco, 1994—; owner Wandering Albatross, 1993. Author (checklist) Birds of the Antarctic and Sub-Antarctic, 1986, revised, 1994, Antarctic Birds and Seals: A Pocket Guide, 1993, South to Antarctica, 1994, The Northwest Passage, 1994; translator: Field Guide to the Birds of Chile, 1989; co-author: The Birds of Chile, 1993; photos featured in Sierra Club Book: Mother Earth Through the Eyes of Women Photographers and Writers, 1992; photographer mag. cover King Penguin and Chick for Internat. Wildlife Mag., 1985, Sierra Club Calendar, 1986; exhibited photos at Royal Geog. Soc., London, 1985. Mem. Calif. Acad. Sci. Home: 724 Laurel Ave Apt 211 San Mateo CA 94401-4131

CHESTER, STEPHANIE ANN, lawyer, banker; b. Mpls., Oct. 8, 1951; d. Alden Runge and Nina Lavina (Hanson) C.; divorced. B.A. magna cum laude, Augustana Coll., 1973; J.D., U. S.D., 1977; postgrad. C.F.S.C., ABA Nat. Grad. Trust Sch., Evanston, Ill., 1984. Bar: S.D. 1977, Minn. 1979. Asst. counselor Minnehaha County Juvenile Ct. Ctr., Sioux Falls, S.D., 1972-73; child care worker Project Threshold, Sioux Falls, 1973-74; legal intern Davenport, Evans, Hurwitz & Smith, Sioux Falls, 1976; law clk. S.D.

Supreme Ct., Pierre, 1977-78; originations dept. buyer Dain Bosworth, Inc., Mpls., 1978-79; v.p., trust officer 1st Bank of S.D., N.A., Sioux Falls, 1979-86; v.p. First Trust Co., Inc., St. Paul, 1986-93; cons. Chester & Stoffels, Inc., St. Paul, 1993-94; lawyer Westby, Chester & Lees, P.A., 1994—; pres. Sioux Falls Estate Planning Coun., 1983-85. Projects and research editor S.D. Law Rev., 1977; author law rev. comment. Mem. fund raising coms. S.D. Symphony, Sioux Falls Community Playhouse, Augustana Coll., 1982-83; mem. S.D. div. Nat. Women's Polit. Caucus; mem. events com. Augustana Coll. Fellows, Sioux Falls, 1984; bd. dirs. YWCA, Sioux Falls, 1984, Sioux Falls Arena/Coliseum, 1985; mem. Sioux Falls Jr. Service League, 1984. Augustana Coll. scholar, 1969-73; Augustana Coll. Bd. Regents scholar, 1973. Mem. S.D. Bar Assn., Minn. Bar Assn., ABA, 2d S.D. Jud. Circuit Bar Assn., Nat. Assn. Bank Women (state conv. com. 1983-85), Phi Delta Phi, Chi Epsilon. Democrat. Lutheran. Clubs: Network, Portia (Sioux Falls). Office: 79 Western Ave N Ste C Saint Paul MN 55102

CHESTERFIELD, RHYDONIA RUTH EPPERSON, financial company executive; b. Dallas, Tex., Apr. 23, 1919; d. Leonard Lee and Sally E. (Stevenson) Griswold; m. Chad Chesterfield, Apr. 21, 1979. BS Southwestern U., 1952; BS, North Tex. U., 1954, ME, 1956; PhD, Bernardean U., 1974, Calif. Christian U., 1974, LLD (hon.), 1974. Evangelist with Griswold Trio, 1940-58; tchr., counselor Dallas public schs., 1952-58, L.A. pub. schs., 1958-74; pres. Griswold-Epperson Fin. Enterprise, L.A., 1974—; pres. GEC Enterprises, 1979—; guest speaker various schs., chs. and civic orgns. in U.S. and Can. Author: Little Citizens series, Cathedral Films; contbr. articles on bus. to profl. pubis. Fellow Internat. Naturopathic Assn.; mem. L.A. Inst. Fine Arts, Assn. of Women in Edn. (hon.), Internat. Bus. and Profl. Women, Calif. C. of C., L.A. C. of C., Pi Lambda Theta (hon.), Kappa Delta Pi (hon.). Office: 10790 Wilshire Blvd Apt 202 Los Angeles CA 90024-4426

CHESTNUT, CYNTHIA MOORE, state legislator; b. Tallahassee, July 25, 1949; m. Charles S. Chestnut; 1 child, Christopher Moore. BS, Fla. A&M U., 1970; MS, Fla. State U., 1971; PhD, Nova U., 1981. Comnr. Gainesville City, 1987-90, mayor-comnr., 1989-90; state rep. dist. 23 Fla. Ho. of Reps.; tchr.; dir. student affairs Alachua County Sch. Bd. Mem. NAACP, LINKS (pres. 1989), Jr. League, Alpha Kappa Alpha. Democrat. Methodist. Home: 101 SE 2nd Pl Ste 108 Gainesville FL 32601 Office: Fla House of Reps State Capitol Tallahassee FL 32301*

CHESTNUT, KATHI LYNNE, lawyer; b. Springfield, Mo., Nov. 7, 1959; d. Stanley Carl and Onita Faye (Weir) C. BA in Polit. Sci. summa cum laude, William Woods Coll., 1980; JD, Washington U., St. Louis, 1983. Bar: Mo. 1983, U.S. Dist. Ct. (ea. dist.) Mo. 1983, Ill. 1984, (so. dist.) Ill. 1991, U.S. Ct. Appeals (8th cir.) 1984, U.S. Supreme Ct., 1991. Assoc. Evans and Dixon, St. Louis, 1983-89, ptnr., 1990—; reviewer Mo. Jud. Edn. Com., Jud. Desk Book, Civil Procedure. Mem. Mo. Bar Assn. (contbg. author Mo. Civil Procedure publ. 1988, 90), Ill. Bar Assn., Met. Bar Assn., St. Louis, Order of Coif, Alpha Chi Omega (Sigma Sigma Psi chpt. sec. 1985-86). Republican. Presbyterian. Home: 5318 Kenrick Parke Dr Saint Louis MO 63114-9999 Office: Evans & Dixon 1200 Saint Louis Pl 200 No Broadway Saint Louis MO 63102-2035

CHEUNG, JUDY HARDIN, education educator; b. Santa Rosa, Calif., Feb. 3, 1945; d. Robert Stephens and Edna Rozella Hardin. BA, Calif. State U. at Sonoma, Rohnert Park, Calif., 1966; MA, U. San Francisco, 1981. Tchr. St. Thomas (V.I.) Dept. Edn., 1967-71, Sonoma Devel. Ctr., Eldridge, Calif., 1971—; co-chairperson Ednl. Svcs. Profl. Practice Group, Eldridge, Calif., 1989-90, 93-94; co-owner BJ Records, Santa Rosa. Author, pub.: Acorn to Embers, 1987, Welcome to the Inside, 1984; author, photographer, pub. Captions, 1986. Recipient awards Silver Pegasus, 1983, Poets of the Vineyard, 1986, 87, Ark. Writers Conf., 1988. Mem. Calif. Fedn. Chaparral Poets (pres. 1989-91, 93-95), Ina Coolbrith Cir. (pres. 1988-90), Calif. Writers Club (treas. Redwood writers br. 1985-86), Bay Area Poets Coalition, Artists Embassy Internat. (Amb. of Arts award 1992), World Congress of Cultures and Poetry (internat. bd. dirs. 1993—, Grand Cultures medal 1993). Home and Office: 704 Brigham Ave Santa Rosa CA 95404-5245

CHEUNG, LING CHANG, medical technologist, researcher; b. Nanjing, Jiang-su, China, July 31, 1934; came to U.S., 1977; d. Chong De and Fong Ying (Liu) C.; m. Gene K.H. Cheung, May 8, 1962; children: David Fong, May Mei, Nancy Nan. MD, Beijing Med. U., 1956, MPH, 1959; postgrad., Howard U., 1982. Lectr. Henan Med. Coll., Zhen-zhow, China, 1959-75; rsch. assoc. Hong Kong U., 1975-77; rsch. fellow NIH, Bethesda, Md., 1978-81; scientist Bethesda Rsch. Labs., Gaithersburg, Md., 1981-82; rsch. assoc. Howard U., Washington, 1982-83; rsch. instr. Uniformed Svcs. U. of Health Scis., Bethesda, 1983-89; med. technologist NIH, Bethesda, 1989—; cons. Henan Med. Inst., Zhen-Zhow, 1986—, Tien-Jing (China) Liver Disease Inst., 1992—; vis. prof. Henan Med. U., 1987—; teaching dir. Potomac (Md.) Chinese Sch., 1990-92. Author: Life and Nutrition, 1964. Vice pres. Assn. Ethnic Chinese in Met. Washington, Chinese Culture and Cmty. Svc. Ctr. Mem. NIH Chinese Am. Assn. (sci. com. 1980—), Alumni Assn. Beijing Med. U. in Met. Washington (founder, pres.), Shanxian Province Assn. (founder). Home: 11608 Milbern Dr Potomac MD 20854 Office: Nat Inst Health 9000 Rockville Pike Bethesda MD 20892

CHEVERS, WILDA ANITA YARDE, probation officer; b. N.Y.C.,; d. Wilsey Ivan and HerbertLee (Perry) Yarde; m. Kenneth Chevers, May 14, 1950; 1 child, Pamela Anita. BA, CUNY, 1947; MSW, Columbia, 1959; PhD, NYU, 1981. Probation officer, 1947-55; supr. probation officer, 1955-65; br. chief Office Probation for Cts. N.Y.C., 1965-72, asst. dir. probation, 1972-77, dep. commr. dept. probation, 1978-86; prof. pub. adminstrn. John Jay Coll. Criminal Justice CUNY, 1986-91; conf. faculty mem. Nat. Council Juvenile and Family Ct. Judges; mem. faculty N.Y.C. Tech. Coll., Nat. Coll. Juvenile Justice; mem. adv. com. Family Ct., First Dept. Sec. Susan E. Wagner Adv. Bd., 1966-70. Sec., bd. dirs. Allen Community Day Care Ctr., 1971-75; bd. dirs. Allen Sr. Citizens Housing, Queensboro Soc. for Prevention Cruelty to Children; chairperson, bd. dir. Allen Christian Sch., 1987—. Named to Hunter Coll. Hall of Fame, 1983. Mem. ABA (assoc.), N.Y. Acad. Pub. Edn., Nat. Council on Crime and Delinquency, Nat. Assn. Social Workers, Acad. Cert. Social Workers. Middle Atlantic States Conf. Correction, Alumni Assn. Columbia Sch. Social Work, NAACP, Am. Soc. Pub. Adminstrn. (mem. council), Counseliers, Hansel and Gretel Club (pres. 1967-69, Queens, N.Y.). Delta Sigma Theta. Home: 9012 Covered Wagon Ave Las Vegas NV 89117-7010

CHEW, LINDA LEE, fundraising management consultant; b. Riverside, Calif., Mar. 3, 1941; d. LeRoy S. and Grace (Ham) Olson; m. Dennis W. Chew, July 23, 1965; children—Stephanie, Erica. B.Mus., U. Redlands, 1962. Cert. fund raising exec. Dir. pub. events U. Redlands (Calif.), 1962-69; dir. fin. and communications San Gorgonio council Girl Scouts U.S.A., Colton, Calif., 1969-71; exec. dir. United Cerebral Palsy Assn. Sacramento-Yolo Counties, 1972-73; fin. devel. dir. San Francisco Bay coun. Girl Scouts U.S.A., 1973-76; chief devel. and pub. info. East Bay Regional Park Dist., Oakland, Calif., 1976-86; cons. Chew & Assocs., Alamo, Calif., 1986—; pres. Providence Hosp. Found., Oakland, 1991-92. Bd. dirs. Planned Parenthood Contra Costa County, 1980-82, San Ramon Valley Edn. Found., 1984-88; Calif. Conservation Corps Bay Area Ctr. Adv. Bd., 1988-89; Mem. AAUW (pres. Redlands br. 1968-69), Nat. Soc. Fund Raising Execs. (nat. bd. dirs. 1981-90, nat. vice chmn. 1982-84, pres. Golden Gate chpt. 1979-80, bd. dirs. 1987-90, Abel Hanson Meml. award 1977, Outstanding Fund Raising Exec. 1988), Assn. Healthcare Philanthropy (Region 11 cabinet mem. 1991—), Am. Guild Organists (dean Riverside-San Bernardino chpt. 1969-71), Pub. Rels. Soc., Alamo Rotary, Lamorinda Volleyball Club (pres. 1994). Office: 170F Alamo Plz Ste 400 Alamo CA 94507-1550

CHEW, LYNDA CASBEER, elementary school educator; b. Corpus Christi, Tex., Oct. 1, 1947; d. Joseph Olen and Ethel Jean (Milam) Casbeer; m. Jack H. Chew, Aug. 28, 1976; children: Doise Elizabeth, Charlotte Lee. BA, U. Tex., 1974; MA, S.W. Bapt. Sem., 1975; MEd, U. Tex., El Paso, 1988. Elem. tchr. Sierra Blanca (Tex.) Ind. Sch. Dist., 1979-80, Orange Grove (Tex.) Ind. Sch. Dist., 1987-88, Socorro Ind. Sch. Dist., El Paso, 1988-94, Leander (Tex.) Ind. Sch. Dist., 1994—. Pres. Horizon Heights PTA, El Paso, 1989-90; v.p. Hueco PTO, El Paso, 1990-91, chmn. Dist. PTO/PTA Counc., El Paso, 1989-91. Recipient 4 Regional Ctr. for Minorities sci. grants. Mem. ASCD, Assn. Tex. Profl. Educators (bldg. rep., adv. com. 1990-92), Assn. for Compensatory Educators Tex., Sci. Tchrs. Assn. Tex., Elem. Sci. Tchrs., U. Tex. Alumni Assn. Baptist. Home: 1901 Honeysuckle Round Rock TX 78664 Office: Whitestone Sch 2000 Crystal Falls Leander TX 78641

CHEW, MARGARET SARAH, geography educator, retired; b. Evanston, Ill., Aug. 20, 1909; d. Nathaniel Durbin and Nettie Jane (Trumbauer) C. BS, Northwestern U., 1930, MS, 1936; PhD with distinction, Clark U., 1960. Maths. and social studies tchr. Iron Belt (Wis.) High Sch., 1930-36; geography tchr. SUNY, Buffalo, 1937-38; social studies tchr. Haven Sch., Evanston, 1938-45; profl. geography U. Wis., La Crosse, 1945-79, chmn. geography dept., 1952-65; emeritus prof. geography U. Wis., 1979—; geography tchr. St. Teresa Coll., Winona, Minn., summer 1939; leader geography credit earning tours U. Wis., La Crosse, summers 1963-80; lectr. in field. Contbr. articles to profl. jours. Recipient fellowships in geog. Clark U., Worcester, 1936-37, 50-51; named fellowship grant presented to outstanding women La Crosse Br. AAUW, 1976. Mem. AAUW, Am. Assn. Geographers, Nat. Coun. Geography (chmn. map com. 1952-54), Wis. Geog. Soc. (founder, several offices), Delta Kappa Gamma (state scholarship chair, summer scholarship award 1951), Philanthropic Ednl. Orgn. (sec., many coms.).

CHEYNE, VALORIE E., psychologist; b. Bloomfield Hills, Mich., Apr. 28, 1944; d. Cyril Gordon Browne and Dorothy Ellenor (Neel) Van Kempen; m. Kenneth McLean, July 22, 1967; 1 child, Casey. BA, Mich. State U., 1966; MEd, Wayne State U., 1978; Psy. S., Ctr. for Humanistic Studies, 1983; PhD, Union Inst., 1988. Lic. psychologist, Mich.; cert. tchr., Mich.; cert. social worker, Mich. Tchr. multiply physically hadicapped and learning disabled Farmington (Mich.) Pub. Schs., 1966-72; counselor, psychotherapist, coordinator attention deficit ctr. Human Potential Counseling Ctr., Southfield, Mich., 1968-92; dir. clin. svcs. Human Potential Counseling Ctr., Southfield, 1988—; mem. adj. faculty Ctrl. Mich. U., Mt. Pleasant, Oakland C.C., Union Inst. Pres. bd. Women's Survival Ctr., Pontiac, Mich., 1985—; bd. dirs. Jr. League, Birmingham, Mich., Jr. Women's Assn. for Detroit Symphony Orch. Mem. APA, Mich. Psychol. Assn. (women's issues com.), Mich. Women Psychologists (pres.), Am. Orthopsychiat. Assn., Assn. Humanistic Psychology, Mich. Inter-Profl. Assn., Internat. Coun. Psychologists, Profl. Acad. Custody Evaluators. Congregationalist. Club: Hill and Dale Garden (Farmington) (Pres. 1977-78). Office: 31000 Telegraph Rd Ste 130 Bingham Farms MI 48025

CHIAPPERINI, PATRICIA BIGNOLI, real estate appraiser, consultant; b. N.Y.C., Jan. 16, 1946; d. Gennaro and Giovanna (Resburgo) Bignoli; m. Joseph M. Chiapperini, Dec. 14, 1968. BS in Acctg. and Econs., St. John's U., 1968; postgrad., U. Ala., 1969, Rutgers U., 1980, Am. Inst. Real Estate Appraisers, 1983. Cert. gen. real property appraiser, N.J., instr. real property appraising, N.J., gen. real property appraiser, N.J. Staff acct. Cleary, During & Co., N.Y.C., 1967-69; chief acct. Montgomery Bapt. Hosp. (Ala.), 1969-70; internal auditor Scottex Corp., N.Y.C., 1970-73; office mgr. Mid-Jersey Realty, East Brunswick, N.J., 1973-79; self-employed real estate appraiser, North Brunswick, N.J., 1979—; guest lect. Middlesex County Coll., 1979—; adj. prof. Jersey City State Coll. Chmn. Arts and Cultural Com., Milltown, N.J., 1979-83; active Am. Legion Aux., Milltown, 1973—. Recipient John Marshall award St. John's U., 1968. Mem. Nat. Assn. Ind. Fee Appraisers, Cen. Jersey Ind. Fee Appraisers (treas., 1982-83, v.p., 1984), Milltown C. of C. (v.p. 1987). Roman Catholic. Office: 735 Georges Rd North Brunswick NJ 08902-3314

CHIASSON, MARCELLE CAMILLE, physician; b. Lameque, Can., Sept. 16, 1933; came to U.S., 1970; d. Azade and Stella (Robichaud) C.; m. Marcello Zurita, 1982 (div. 1983); 1 child, Kevin. Degree in Pub. Health Nursing, McGill U., Montreal, 1955; MD, U. Ottawa, Can., 1962; Cert. Acupuncturist, NCCA, 1992. Diplomate Am. Bd. Anesthesiology. Intern St. Paul's Hosp., Vancouver, B.C., 1962-63; resident in anesthesiology U. B.C. Hosps., Vancouver, 1968-69, 70-72; resident in medicine Shaughnessy Hosp., Vancouver, 1969-70; gen. practice B.C., 1963-68; anesthesiologist chief East Portland Hosp., Oreg., 1973-74; med. dir. Acupuncture Pain Control and Rehab. Ctr., Portland, Oreg., 1974—; instr. Oreg. Health Scis. U., 1976-85, clin. asst. prof., 1985-89, asst. prof., 1989—. Fencing Champion of B.C., Fencing Assn. of B.C., 1968. Home: 8030 SW 57th Ave Portland OR 97219-3154 Office: Acupuncture Pain Control 4055 SW Garden Home Rd Portland OR 97219-3543

CHIAVARIO, NANCY ANNE, business and community relations executive; b. Centralia, Ill., Aug. 17, 1947; d. Victor Jr. and Alma Maria (Arsenault) C. Asst. mgr. rent supplement B.C. Housing Mgmt. Commn., Vancouver, 1975-81, adminstrv. asst., 1981-84, mgr. tenants and ops. svc., 1985-86, adminstrv. asst., 1986-87; commr., vice chmn. Vancouver Park Bd., 1986-90, chair, 1991-93; city councillor Vancouver, 1993—. Pres. B.C. Recreation and Parks Assn., 1989-90; exec. dir. B.C. Sport and Fitness Coun. for the Disabled, 1989-90; dir. B.C. Wheelchair Sports Assn., 1991-92; mem. Non-Partisan Assn. Mem. Inst. Housing Mgmt. (cert. adminstr. 1983, cert. finance 1985), West End Commn. Ctr. Assn. (pres. 1985-86), Mt. Pleasant Commn. Ctr. Assn. (pres. 1981-83). Democrat. Home: 205-90 E 11th Ave, Vancouver, BC Canada V5T 2B8 Office: Vancouver City Coun, 453 W 12th Ave, Vancouver, BC Canada V5Y 1V4

CHICAGO, JUDY, artist; b. Chgo., July 20, 1939; d. Arthur M. and May (Levenson) Cohen. B.A., U. Calif. at Los Angeles, 1962, M.A., 1964. Cofounder Feminist Studio Workshop, Los Angeles, 1973, Through the Flower Corp., 1977. Author: Through the Flower: My Struggle as a Woman Artist, 1975, The Dinner Party: A Symbol of Our Heritage, 1979, Embroidering Our Heritage: The Dinner Party Needlework, 1980, The Birth Project, 1985, Holocaust Project: From Darkness Into Light, 1993; one-woman exhbns. include, Pasadena (Calif.) Mus. Art, 1969, Jack Glenn Gallery, Corona del Mar, Calif., 1972, JPL Fine Arts, London, 1975, Quay Ceramics, San Francisco, 1976, San Francisco Mus. Modern Art, 1979, Bklyn. Mus., 1980, Parco Galleries, Japan, 1980, Fine Arts Gallery, Irvine, Calif., 1981, Musee d'Art Contemporain, Montreal, 1982, ACA Galleries, N.Y.C., 1984, 85, 86; group exhbns. include Jewish Mus., N.Y.C., 1966, 67, Whitney Mus., 1972, Winnipeg Art Gallery, 1975; represented in permanent collections Bklyn. Mus., San Francisco Mus. Modern Art, Oakland Mus. Art, Pa. Acad. Fine Arts, L.A. County Mus. Art, also numerous pvt. collections. Office: PO Box 1327 Belen NM 87002

CHIECHI, CAROLYN PHYLLIS, federal judge; b. Newark, Dec. 6, 1943; d. Michele A. and Dominica (DeFilippis) C. BS magna cum laude, Georgetown U., 1965, JD, 1969, LLM in Taxation, 1971. Bar: D.C. 1969, U.S. Dist. Ct. D.C., U.S. Ct. Fed. Claims, U.S. Tax Ct., U.S. Ct. Appeals (D.C. cir., Fed. cir., 5th cir., 6th cir., and 9th cirs.), U.S. Supreme Ct. Atty., advisor to judge Leo H. Irwin U.S. Tax Ct., Washington, 1969-71; assoc. Sutherland, Asbill & Brennan, Washington, 1971-76, ptnr., 1976-92; judge U.S. Tax Ct., 1992—; bd. regents Georgetown U., Washington, 1988—, nat. law alumni bd., 1986-93; bd. dirs. Stuart Stiller Meml. Found., Washingotn, 1986—; prin. Coun. for Excellence in Govt., Washington, 1990-92. Dept. editor Jour. of Taxation, 1986-92; contbr. articles to profl. jours. Fellow Am. Bar Found., Am. Coll. of Tax Counsel; mem. ABA, D.C. Bar Assn., U.S. Ct. Fed. Claims Bar Assn., Fed. Cir. Bar Assn., Fed. Bar Assn. Office: US Tax Ct 400 2nd St NW Washington DC 20217-0002*

CHIKI, GINA MARIE, accounting administrator; b. Brownsville, Pa., Mar. 11, 1960; d. Romualdo Gino and Pearl Ann (Todaro) Gallo; m. Albert Louis Chiki, Oct. 2, 1981. Degree in computer programming, Computer Tech., Pitts., 1983. Receptionist Dr. Richard Stevenson VMD, Fayette City, Pa., 1978-79; blue print operator McGraw Edison, Canonsburg, Pa., 1979-83; sales profl. Troutmans/Pomeroy's, Washington, Pa., 1983-84; ins. sec. Erie Ins. Co., Washington, 1984-86; asst. bookkeeper Ceisler, Richman Law Firm, Washington, Pa., 1986-88; acct. mgr. asst. Siegfried, Rivera et al, Coral Gables, Fla., 1988—. Mem. Elkettes (treas. 1991-92, corr. sec. 1992-93, rec. sec. 1993-94, v.p. 1994—). Democrat. Roman Catholic. Home: 14038 SW 67 Ter Miami FL 33183 Office: Siegfried Rivera et al Ste 1102 201 Alhambra Cir Coral Gables FL 33134

CHILCUTT, DORTHE MARGARET, art educator, artist; b. Fond du Lac, Wis., Jan. 29, 1915; d. John William and Pearl Evelyn (Burnett) Trummer. BS, U. Wis., 1940, MS, 1952; postgrad. NYU, 1975-78, Instituto Allende, Mex., summer 1958, La Romita Sch. Art, Italy, 1978-93, Schohegan Sch. Painting and Sculpture, 1959; m. Booth Chilcutt, Feb. 14, 1942; children—Karen Chilcutt Hulett, Booth, Cindy Jo Chilcutt Underhill, Debra Ann Chilcutt-Flippo. Layout artist DeVry Corp., Chgo., 1941-42; tchr. art St. Louis pub. schs., 1951-53, Monroe County Schs., Key West, Fla., 1957-62, Okeechobee Jr. High Sch. (Fla.), 1963-84, Indian River C.C., 1984-94. One woman shows Little Gallery, Key West, 1960, Martello Gallery, Key West, 1963, Ft. Pierce Art Gallery (Fla.), 1970; exhibited in group shows Jacksonville Art Mus. (Fla.), 1959, Tampa Art Mus., 1960, Norton Art Gallery, West Palm Beach, Fla., 1960, Backus Gallery, Ft. Pierce, 1977-94, St. Louis Art Mus., 1951, Wis. Salon of Art, Madison, 1947, Key West Art and Hist. Soc., 1957-90, Key West Art Ctr., 1959; represented in permanent collections Ft. Pierce Art Gallery, Martello Galleries. Recipient Best of Show awards Fla. Fedn. Art, 1974, Ft. Pierce Art Gallery, 1977, Ybor City Ann. Fiesta Day, 1980, Backus Festival, 1992, 1st pl. awards Highlands Art League 8th Ann., 1974, Jensen Beach Ann., Elliot Mus., 1974, 84, Ft. Pierce Scholarship Show, 1972-75, Four-County Art Show, Ft. Pierce, 1972-94, Tchr. of Yr. award Okeechobee County Sch. Bd., 1976, others. Mem. Fla. Watercolor Soc. (sec. 1974-84, bd. dirs. 1984-86), Gold Coast Water Color Soc., Nat. Art Edn. Assn., Fla. Art Edn. Assn. (Career Service award 1986), Miami Watercolor Soc., Treasure Coast Art Soc., Palm Beach Water Color Soc. Democrat. Contbr. articles to profl. jours. Home: 506 SW 15th St Okeechobee FL 34974-5264

CHILD, JULIA MCWILLIAMS (MRS. PAUL CHILD), cooking expert, television personality, author; b. Pasadena, Calif., Aug. 15, 1912; d. John and Julia Carolyn (Weston) McWilliams; m. Paul Child, Sept. 1, 1945. BA, Smith Coll., 1934. With advt. dept. W.&J. Sloane, N.Y.C., 1939-40; with OSS, Washington, Ceylon, China, 1941-45; co-founder Am. Inst. Wine & Food, 1982. Hostess TV program The French Chef, WGBH-TV, Boston, from 1962, Julia Child & Co., 1978-79, Julia Child & More Co., 1980, Dinner at Julia's, PBS, 1983; occasional cooking segment Good Morning America, ABC-TV, 1980—; video cassettes The Way to Cook, 1982; author: (with Simone Beck and Louisette Bertholle) Mastering the Art of French Cooking, 1961, The French Chef Cookbook, 1968, Mastering the Art of French Cooking, Vol. II, 1970, (with Simone Beck) From Julia Child's Kitchen, 1975, Julia Child & Company, 1978, Julia Child & More Company, 1979, Mastering the Art of French Cooking I & II, 1983, The Way to Cook, 1989; columnist McCall's mag., 1975-82, Parade mag., 1982-86. Recipient Peabody award, 1964, Emmy award, 1966, French Ordre de Merite Agricole, 1967, Ordre National de Merite, 1974. Office: Good Morning Am 147 Columbus Ave New York NY 10023 also: care Knopf Inc 201 E 50th St New York NY 10022-7703*

CHILDERS, NANCY COPE, art educator; b. Balt., Feb. 10, 1966; d. Davis Kelly and Margie Catherine (Rogers) Cope; m. Wright Latimer Childers Jr., Dec. 28, 1990. BFA, U. Tenn., Chattanooga, 1989. Cert. elem. tchr., Ala. Art tchr. Chattanooga Middle Sch., 1990; art tchr., liaison S.E. Inst. for Edn. in the Visual Arts, Chattanooga, 1990-91; art tchr. Coun. on Aging, Ft. Payne, Ala., 1991-92; artist in residence Ft. Payne H.S., 1993—, cmty. edn. coord., 1994-95; art instr. N.E. Ala. State C.C., Rainsville, 1993—; commd. artist Compass Bank, Ft. Payne, 1993—, Plainview H.S. Alumnae Assn.; artist in field. Recipient 1st pl. award Gadsden Art Assn., 1993. Mem. Nat. Art Edn. Assn., Ala. Art Edn. Assn., Assn. for Visual Artists, Artists Guild (co-founder, treas. 1993—), Big Wills Art Coun. (bd. dirs.), DeKalb County Tourist Assn. (bd. dirs.). Home: 311 8th St NW Fort Payne AL 35967

CHILDERS, PAMELA BARNARD, educator; b. Mt. Holly, N.J., Oct. 11, 1943; d. George W. and Audrey (Clerihue) Barnard; m. Malcolm G. Childers, 1993. BA, Radford Coll., Radford, 1965; MS, Radford U., Radford, 1975; MA, Northeastern U., Boston, 1988; ABD, Nova U., 1993. Poetry tchr./cons. Geraldine R. Dodge Found., Morristown, N.J., 1986—; coll. tchr. Woodrow Wilson Nat'l Fellowship Found., Princeton, N.J., 1987-88; Caldwell chair composition The McCallie Sch., Chattanooga, 1991—; English tchr. Red Bank Regional High Sch., Little Silver, N.J., 1966-91, McCallie Sch., Chattanooga, 1991—; editor The Grapevine Northeastern U. Writing Newsletter, Boston, 1986-90; mem. editorial bd. The Writing Ctr. Jour., Mich. Tech. U., 1987—, Computers and Composition, Purdue U., 1987-90; treas. Assembly on Computers in English; pres. Nat. Writing Ctrs. Assn. Author: Waking Dreams, 1989, The High School Writing Center, 1989, Nat. Directory of Writing Centers, 1992, Programs and Practices, 1994, Waking Dreams II, 1990. Mem. MLA, Nat. Coun. Tchrs. English (com. instructional tech.), Nat. Writing Ctrs. Assn. (pres.). Dem. Presbyterian.

CHILDERS, SHERYL GRACE, public relations professional; b. Pontiac, Mich., Oct. 31, 1962; d. Allen Leonard and Tonya Elizabeth (Hurst) Tunny; m. Robert C. Childers, Oct. 11, 1985; children: Jeremy Robert, Kyle Allen. BA, Oakland U., 1985. Pub. rels. Pontiac (Mich.) Motors; communications coord. GM, Pontiac; staff asst. Pontiac Divsn. GM, GM Powertrain, Brighton, Mich.; adminstr. GM N.Am. Truck, Pontiac, 1993—. Mem. Pub. Rels. Soc. Am. Roman Catholic. Office: NAm Truck Platforms 31 E Judson Mc # 160304 Pontiac MI 48342

CHILDERS, SHIRLEY RUTH, vocational education educator, behavior science; b. Statham, Ga., Mar. 10, 1951; d. Rosevelt and Lucille (Barnette) Thurmond; m. James Douglas Childers, Jan. 2, 1971; children: Tyrish, Miranda. Master Lic. Cosmetology, Minosa Sch. Beauty, 1970-71; AA, Gainesville (Ga.) Coll., 1971-73; BS, Brenau Coll., 1973-75; MEd, Ga. State U., 1980-83. Cert. tchr., Ga. Owner, mgr. Shirley's Beauty Salon, Gainesville, 1971-79; vocat. tchr. Lanier Tech. Inst., Oakwood, Ga., 1977—; faculty steering com. Lanier Tech. Sch., Oakwood, 1986-91, sec. adv. bd., 1991, insvc. com., 1992. Author: Positional Papers Hair, 1981. Chmn. AKA Cotillion, Gainesville, 1975, AKA Scholarship Com., Gainesville, 1985-90; coord. Gen. Missionary Bapt. Ch., Ga., 1980-89; pres. PTO, Gainesville, 1990; vol. Project Find, 1972 (cert.), Summer Reading Program, 1974 (cert.); acitve Leadership Hall County, 1992, Exec. Leadership Ga. State U., 1990-91, Coalition on Teenage Pregnancy, Hall County, 1986; v.p. Angelic Voices Choir St. John Bapt. Ch., 1971—. Recipient Cert. of Merit award Kiwanis, Gainesville, 1969, Outstanding Svc. award St. John Bapt. Ch., Gainesville, 1986, Cert. of Appreciation award Girl Scouts, Gainesville, 1987. Mem. Ga. Vocat. Assn., Cultural Ednl. Tour Inst. (pres., cons.), Alpha Kappa Alpha (Soror of Yr. 1989, 90). Democrat. Baptist. Home: 2079 Garden Rd Gainesville GA 30507-5019

CHILDERS, SUSAN LYNN BOHN, special education educator, human resources and transition specialist; b. Zanesville, Ohio, Mar. 1, 1948; m. Lawrence J. Childers; 1 child, Jeffrey Scott. AA, Ohio U., 1978, BS in Edn. cum laude, 1982; MEd in Supervision, Ashland U., 1991. Profl. cert. 1-8 elem. tchr., K-12 edn. handicapped and supervision; spl. edn. tchr., Ohio. Educator learning disabilities, developmentally handicapped Maysville Local Sch. Dist., South Zanesville, Ohio, 1982-89; work-study coord. Holmes County Office Edn., Millersburg, Ohio, 1990, editor spl. edn. newsletter, 1990-93, cons., supervisor work-study programming, 1991-93; mem. spl. edn. life skills task force West Holmes Local Sch. Dist., Millersburg, 1991-93; spl. edn. supr. Wayne County Bd. Edn., Wooster, Ohio, 1993-94; adminstr. severe behavior handicapped program, supr. special edn. Ashland-Wayne County Bd. Edn., Wooster, 1994—; mem. Holmes County Spl. Edn. Adv. Coun., 1990-93 , E. Holmes Local Sch. Dist. Strategic Planning Action Team Job/Life Skills, 1993, Regional Adv. Coun. for Ohio's Employability Skills Project, Holmes County Job Placement adv. bd., 1991-93; speaker in field; rep. Ohio Devel. Handicapped Issues Forum; mem. steering com. Ohio Speaks, 1991-94; developer ednl. programs. Editor Spl. Edn. Newsletter Holmes County Office Edn., 1990-93. Mem. adv. bd. Holmes County Job Placement, Holmes County Litter Prevention and Recycling edn. rep., Holmes County Abuse Prevention Community Action Plan com., 1993; vol. Ohio Buckeye Book Fair, 1991, 92, 93, Holmes County Spl. Olympics, 1990-93, chairperson of vols., 1993; mem. jr. assembly Bethesda Hosp., 1970-78; mem. Beaux Arts Zanesville Art Ctr., 1972-78; mem. spl. needs adv. bd. Ashland-West Holmes Career Ctr., 1990-93; mem. Transition and Communication Consortium on Learning Disabilities, Ohio U. Alumni Career Resource Network, Holmes County Abuse Prevention Community Action Plan com., 1993, Ohio Buckeye Book Fair Vol. 1991, 92, 93; mem. Ohio Staff Devel. Coun.; co-chair fundraising com. Creating Connections Symposium, Akron, Ohio, 1994; active Ohio Children and Family First Clin. Cluster, Wooster, Ohio, 1994—. Recipient award Muskingum County Office Litter Prevention, 1988, Kids Care Project, 1989, Maysville Bd. Edn., 1989, Merit award Keep Ohio Beautiful program, 1991, Ohio Future Forum's Exemplary Transition from Sch.-to-Work Model award, 1993, Model Program designation Ohio's Employability Skills Project, 1987. Mem. ASCD, Career Edn. Assn., Coun. Exceptional Children, Ohio Rural Edn. Assn., Ohio Sch. Suprs. Assn., Ohio Assn. Vocat. Edn. Spl. Needs Pers., Ohio Assn. Suprs. and Work-Study coords. (award of Excellence 1992, reg. pres. 1993-94), Am. Assn. Univ. Women, Wayne-Holmes Elem. Adminstrs. Assn., Phi Delta Kappa. Home: PO Box 192 Millersburg OH 44654-0192 Office: Kinney Meml Bldg 2534 Burbank Rd Wooster OH 44691-1675

CHILDRESS, DORI ELIZABETH, nurse consultant; b. Chgo., Jan. 25, 1945; d. John Fredrick and Doris Eleanor (Clark) Klafin; m. Larry Dunn, May 3, 1969 (div. Aug. 21, 1975); m. Terry Childress, May 17, 1986. BSN, Calif. State U., Chico, 1976; MSN, Calif. State U., Chica, 1983. Cert. prof. in healthcare quality; RN, Calif. Critical care nurse Kaiser Permanente, Sacramento, 1977-82; dir. nursing edn. Rancho Arroyo Vocat. Tech., Sacramento, 1979-86; nurse cons. State of Calif. Dept. Health, Sacramento, 1986—. With USAF, 1984-88. Recipient State Pub. Health award Dept. Health Svcs., State of Calif., Sacramento, 1994. Mem. Nat. Assn. Healthcare Quality Profls., Calif. Assn. Healthcare Quality Profls., Toastmasters Internat. (area gov. 1992-93, dist. sgt.-at-arms 1989-90, Outstanding Area Gov. award 1993), Sigma Theta Tau. Home: 2510 Auburn Rd Lincoln CA 95648 Office: State of Calif Dept Health Medi-Cal Managed Care Divsn 714 P St Rm 692 Sacramento CA 95814

CHILDRESS, FAY ALICE, university administrator; b. Annapolis, Md., Nov. 23, 1929; d. John Douglas and Winifred Lee (Stevens) Howard; m. Larry Brownlow Childress, June 7, 1949; children: Patricia, Peter, Mary, Charles. AA, Montgomery Coll., Takoma Park, Md., 1979; BS, U. Md., 1982, M of Gen. Adminstrn., 1992. Program technician NSF, Washington, 1972-78, sr. program technician, 1978-82, adminstrv. officer, 1982-86; asst. to exec. v.p. and equal opportunity officer Cath. U. Am., Washington, 1986—. Contbr. articles to profl. jours. Mem. steering com. Washington Area Affirmative Action Group, 1988—; mem. Washington Area Higher Edn. Liaison Group, 1989—; chief election judge Montgomery County Election Bd., Silver Spring, 1986-92; mem. Seven Oaks-Evanswood Citizens Assn., Silver Spring, 1980—; vol. Montgomery County Mental Health Assn., Rockville, 1982-84. Mem. Coll. and Univ. Pers. Assn., Montgomery Coll. Alumni Assn. (bd. govs. 1985-87), U. Md. Coll. Alumni Assn. (govt. rels. com. 1992—), Soc. Human Resource Mgmt., Alpha Sigma Lambda (pres. Tau chpt. 1988-90). Office: The Cath U of Am 620 Michigan Ave NE Washington DC 20064-0001

CHILDRESS, KERRI J., federal agency administrator; b. Sydney, Nebr.; d. Jack L. and Florence (Paris) Lindley; children: Kelly Nicole, Patrick Tyler. BA in History and Polit. Sci. summa cum laude, U. Md., 1983. Assoc. editor Navy Times newspaper, Springfield, Va., 1977-80; tchr. history and journalism Dept. Def. High Sch., Wuerzburg, Germany, 1982-84; historian Mt. Vernon Ladies' Assn., Va., 1984-85, Arlington Nat. Cemetery, 1985-89; media rels. officer Mil. Dist. of Washington, Ft. McNair, 1989-91; pub. affairs officer Office Gov. U.S. Soldiers' and Airmen's Home, Washington, 1991—; mem. pub. affairs staff Presdl. Inaugural Com., 1977. Contbr. articles to profl. jours. With USN, 1973-77, lt. Res. Recipient Hon. Tomb Guard ID Badge from sentinels, Tomb of the Unknowns, Arlington Cemetery, Achievement medal, Dept. Army, 1990; named Sailor of Yr., Naval Res. Unit, 1978. Mem. Phi Kappa Phi, Phi Alpha Theta. Office: Office of the Gov US Solidiers & Airmen's Home Washington DC 20317*

CHILDS, ELAINE JARCZYNSKI, nurse educator; b. Rockledge, Fla., Aug. 14, 1957; d. Joseph Francis Jarczynski and Patricia Ann Sturrock; m. Stephen Mark Childs, Jan. 26, 1980. RN, Brevard Community Coll. Nursing, 1977; BSN, U. Cen. Fla., 1985; postgrad., U. Fla., 1991—. RN, Fla. Mgr. clin. outcomes HILL-ROM, Batesville, Ind., 1987—; lectr./educator on wound mgmt. and issues related to immobility. Author: (with Oscar Alvarez) Pressure Ulcers: Physical, Supportive and Local Aspects of Management, 1991. Mem. AACN, Am. Assn. Geriatric Nursing, Wound Healing Soc. (assoc.), Wound, Ostomy and Continence Nurses Soc., Sigma Theta Tau.

CHILDS, MARY ELLEN CRABTREE, occupational health nurse; b. Mobile, Ala., Oct. 11, 1940; d. Edward Beauregard and Annie Irene (Barton) O'Rourke; divorced; children: Claude Vincent, Marley Barton, Milissa Mayrene Crabtree, Mary Angelique Flannagan. Student, 20th Century Bus. Coll., 1960, Southwest State Coll., 1970, George Wallace Coll., 1975, U. Auburn, 1978. RN, Ala., Calif.; ACLS. Staff nurse, ICN, NBN, CCU U. South Ala., Mobile; nurse Home Health Svcs., Enterprise, Ala.; relief house supr. Crenshaw County Hosp., Luverne, Ala.; vocat. educator practical nursing Trenholm Tech. Coll., Montgomery, Ala.; dir. insvc. edn. Wiregrass Hosp. & Nursing Home, Geneva, Ala.; psychiatric house supr. Charter Woods Hosp., Dothan, Ala.; nurse emergency rm. Edge Meml. Hosp., Troy, Ala.; nurse coronary care Flower Hosp., Dothan, Ala.; charge nurse, quality assurance Lyster Army Hosp, Ft. Rucker, Ala.; insvc. educator, house supr. Linda Vista Hosp., L.A.; supr. Edgemont Psychiat. Hosp., L.A., 1991-92; charge nurse Naval Clinic, Port Hueneme, Calif., 1992—; occupational health nurse specialist U.S. Naval Clinic, 1992-93, Woodland Community Hosp., 1993-94; occupational health nurse specialist, workers comp. claims specialist Wrangler, Inc., Oneonta, Ala., 1994—. Author: A Babe in the Woods, 1989. Mem. Ala. Nurses Assn., Am. Heart Assn. (BLS-C instr.), Tri-State Quality Assurance Assn., Ala. Safety Coun., Occupational Health Nurse Assn., Kiwanis Club of Ala. (past pres.). Home: PO Box 842 Hanceville AL 35077

CHILDS, RHONDA LOUISE, medical insurance company executive; b. Albany, N.Y., Sept. 29, 1946; d. David Cornelius and Rhoda Louise (Rodeniser) Curley; m. Lindsay N. Childs, July 22, 1972; children: Ashley Louise, Nathan Shreeve David Curley, Justin David Curley. BA in Sociology and Anthropology, Cath. Convent Coll., Buffalo, 1966; cert. proficiency exam, McGill U., Montreal, Que., Can., 1968; student, Siena Coll., Loudonville, N.Y., Russell Sage Coll. Adminstrv. asst. Hypersonic Lab., McGill U., 1966-68; adminstrv. asst. dept. comparative religions Sir George Williams U., Montreal, 1966-68; with various community svc. orgns., Europe, Can., Africa, 1968-71; researcher N.Y. State Mental Hygiene Dept., Albany, 1971-72; non-teaching profl. SUNY, Albany, 1973-75; community liaison Collins Bay Penitentiary, Kingston, Ont., Can., 1976-77; ct. monitor Family Ct., 1975-78; pres. Concerned Citizens Against Crossgates, Guilderland, N.Y., 1978-80; adminstrv. asst. St. Catherine's Ctr. for Children, Albany, 1980-85; dir. govt. and community affairs Empire Blue Cross and Blue Shield, Albany, 1985-94; devel. counsel St. Peter's Hosp., Albany, 1994—; cons. to numerous nonprofit orgns.; founder, coord. Family Agys. Committed To Svc., 1983-86; founder, pres. Corp. Vol. Coun.; lectr. numerous ednl. and exec. seminars; speaker in field. Author: My Own Telephone Book, 1988. Bd. dirs. Salvation Army, Sr. Svc. Ctrs. Albany County, Albany Symphony Orch., Northeastern N.Y. chpt. Arthritis Found., March of Dimes; mem. br. coun. Am. Heart Assn.; bd. dirs., mktg. cons. Annie Schaffer Sr. Ctr.; grad. Capital Leadership, 1988-94; pres. Child Abuse and Neglect Coun., 1987-90; trustee Capital Dist. chpt., mem. pub. rels. com. Nat. Multiple Sclerosis Soc.; mem. devel. com. N.Y. State Mus. Inst.; mem. adv. bd. Ret. Sr. Vol. Programs; trustee, pres. St. Anne Inst.; pres. N.Y. State Legis. Forum, 1993—; numerous others. Recipient Outstanding Svc. award Family Agys. Committed to Svc., 1985, Community Svc. award Cystic Fibrosis Found., 1988, Tribute to Women award, YWCA, 1991, Franklin D. Roosevelt Vol. award March of Dimes, 1991, June A. Bonneau award Sr. Svc. Ctrs. Albany, Citizen of Yr. award Samaritans, 1994, Golden Rule award, 1994, Lifetime Achievement award Women of Excellence, 1994, Outstanding Svc. award St. Anne Inst., 1994. Mem. APHA, Nat. Soc. Fund Raising Execs., Albany-Colonie Regional C. of C. (numerous coms., guest lectr.), Corp. Vol. Couns. Am., NAFE, SUNY Women's Club, Women's Press Club, Enterprising Women's Leadership Inst., Rotary (coms., Dist. 719 Citizen of Yr. award 1990, Airport Citizen of Yr. award, 1990, Paul Harris fellow 1990). Democrat. Roman Catholic. Home: 308 Quidor Ct Slingerlands NY 12159-9554 Office: St Peter's Hosp 315 S Manning Blvd Albany NY 12208

CHILDS, SADIE L., mathematician, chemist, patent agent; b. Winston Salem, N.C., May 18, 1952; d. Robert Hubert and Pollie (James) C. BS, Howard U., 1974; MS, U. D.C., 1993. Patent examiner U.S. Patent and Trademark Office, Washington, 1974-90; cons. Washington, 1990—. Trustee Sargent Meml. Presbyn. Ch., Washington, 1978-84, deacon, 1984—; vol. Children's Hosp., Washington. Mem. Nat. Coun. Negro Women (svc. award 1983, educator 1982—), Phi Delta Kappa (educator 1989—), Delta Sigma Theta Sorority Inc. Home and Office: 1814 Bryant St NE Washington DC 20018-3626

CHILDS, SHIRLE MOONE, educational administrator; b. N.Y.C., Aug. 2, 1936; d. Harold McDaniel and Bessie Mary (Batts) Moone; m. William Childs, Sept. 5, 1971; children by previous marriage: Duane Kelby Milner, David Kent Milner. BS, U. Hartford, 1968, MS, 1970; PhD, U. Conn., 1978. Tchr., Hartford (Conn.) Public Schs., 1968-71, vice prin., acting prin. Mark Twain Elem. Sch., 1973-77, early childhood edn. specialist, 1978-84; asst. supt. instrnl. svcs. East Orange (N.J.) Pub. Schs., 1984-87; adminstrv. asst. for instruction Teaneck (N.J.) Pub. Schs., 1987-89; dir. curriculum, instrn. evaluation Windham (Conn.) Pub. Schs., 1990-94; assoc. cons. early childhood edn. Conn. State Dept. Edn., 1994—; dir. curriculum, instrn. lectr., adj. prof., instr. Conn. Coll. for Women, Eastern Conn. State Coll., U. Hartford. Past pres. bd. dirs. Women's League Day Care; trustee Hartford ConservatoryTeaneck Libr. Coun., 1987-89; trustee Windham History and Textile Mus., 1990—; bd. dir. Windham Heights Day Care Ctr., Windham United Way; assessor State of Conn.; mem. Windsor Dem. Club; mem. Commr.'s Task Force on High Sch. Graduation Requirements N.J. Dept. Edn., 1987; assessor Md. and N.J. Assessment Ctrs., 1987; bd. dirs. Assault on Illiteracy, 1980—. Rockefeller Found. fellow, 1977-78; Kettering Found. fellow, 1976-85. Mem. Nat. Assn. Edn. Young Children, Am. Assn. Sch. Adminstrs., Assn. Supervision and Curriculum Devel. (facilitator early childhood edn. network 1988—), Hartford Assn. Edn. Young Children, Conn. Assn. Suprs./Instrs. in Spl. Edn., Urban League, NAACP, Nat. Council Negro Women, Delta Sigma Theta (nat. sec. 1979-83), Phi Delta Kappa, Pi Lambda Theta. Methodist. Lodge: Order Eastern Star. Avocations: Chinese cooking, needlepoint, quilting. Home: 26 Regency Dr Windsor CT 06095-3844 Office: 322 Prospect St Willimantic CT 06226-2208

CHILTON, ALICE PLEASANCE HUNTER (MRS. ST. JOHN POINDEXTER CHILTON), former state official, vocational counselor; b. Boyce, La., Apr. 16, 1911; d. Albert Eugene and Maggie (Texada) Hunter; BA, La. Coll., 1930; MS, La. State U., 1934, PhD, 1982, Guidance Counselor certificate, 1954; m. St. John Poindexter Chilton, Mar. 2, 1935. Tchr. secondary sch., Glenmora, La., 1931-35; with La. Div. Employment Security and USES, Baton Rouge, 1937-74, employment interviewer and supr., 1937-43, personnel officer, 1943-46, ops. analyst, 1946-55, supr. counseling and tech. svcs., 1955-74. Mem. curriculum study com. East Baton Rouge, Parish Sch. Bd., 1968; rec. sec. Quota Internat., Baton Rouge, 1961-62, 2d v.p., 1963-64. Bd. dirs. YWCO. Recipient certificate of merit La. Acad. Sci., 1960. Mem. Nat. Trust Historic Preservation, La. Geneal. and Hist. Soc. (pres. 1957), La. Landmarks Soc., Found. for Hist. La., Kent Plantation House, Inc. (sec.1979-81), Preservation Resource Ctr., La. Preservation Alliance (dir. 1984-86), Hist. Assn. of Cen. La. (bd. dirs. 1980-86, 89—), Alexandria Hist. and Geneal. Library and Mus. (bd. dirs. 1986—), Ctrl. La. Geneal. Soc., DAR, Phi Kappa Phi. Methodist. Address: 431 Belgard Bnd Boyce LA 71409-9238

CHIN, CECILIA HUI-HSIN, librarian; b. Tientsin, China; came to U.S., 1961; d. Yu-lin and Ti-yu (Fan) C. B.A., Nat. Taiwan U., Taipei, 1961; M.S.L.S., U. Ill., 1963. Cataloger, reference librarian Roosevelt U., Chgo., 1963; reference librarian, indexer Ryerson & Burnham Libraries, Art Inst. Chgo., 1963-70, head reference dept. indexer,, 1970-75; acting dir. libraries Art Inst. Chgo., 1976-77, assoc. librarian, head reference dept., 1975-82; chief librarian Nat. Mus. Am. Art and Nat. Portrait Gallery, Smithsonian Inst., Washington, 1982—. Compiler: The Art Institute of Chicago Index to Art Periodicals, 1975. Reciipent awards Nat. Portrait Gallery, Smithsonian Instn., 1984, 89. Mem. Art Librs. Soc., D.C. Libr. Assn., Washington Rare Book Group. Office: Nat Mus Am Art & Nat Portrait Gallery Smithsonian Instn Washington DC 20560

CHIN, CINDY LAI, accountant; b. Kowloon, Hong Kong, Dec. 2, 1957; came to U.S., 1964; d. Sau Kuen and Koon On C. BS in Acctg., CUNY, 1980; grad., Real Estate Inst., 1987-90. Real estate acct. Milford Mgmt., Inc., N.Y.C., 1980-82; staff acct. Occidental Petroleum Corp., N.Y.C., 1983-85; portfolio acct. Yarmouth Group Inc., N.Y.C., 1985-91; sr. portfolio acct. CPC, N.Y.C., 1993—; cons. C&M Real Estate Joint Venture, N.Y.C., 1985-89. Mem. China Inst., N.Y.C., 1986. Mem. NAFE, Hunter Coll. Acctg. Alumni Assn. Home: 32 Gary Ct Staten Island NY 10314-1616 Office: CPC 5 W 37th St New York NY 10018-6222

CHIN, JANET SAU-YING, data processing executive, consultant; b. Hong Kong, July 27, 1949; came to U.S., 1959; d. Arthur Quock-Ming and Jenny (Loo) C. BS in Math, U. Ill., Chgo., 1970; MS in Computer Sci., U. Ill., Urbana, 1973. System programmer Lawrence Livermore (Calif.) Lab., 1972-79; sect. mgr. Tymshare Inc., Cupertino, Calif., 1979-83, Fortune Systems, Redwood City, Calif., 1983-85; div. mgr. Impell Corp, Berkeley, Calif., 1985; pres. Chin Assocs., Oakland, Calif., 1985-88; bus. devel. mgr. Sun Microsystems, Mountain View, Calif., 1988-92; engrng. dir. Cadence Design Systems, San Jose, Calif., 1992-94, quality dir., 1994—; Vice-chmn. Am. Nat. Standards Inst. X3H3, N.Y.C., 1979-82, internat. rep. X3H3, 1982-88. Coauthor: The Computer Graphics Interface, 1991; contbr. tech. papers to profl. publs. Mem. Assn. Computing Machinery, Sigma Xi.

CHIN, JENNIFER YOUNG, public health educator; b. Honolulu, June 22, 1946; d. Michael W.T. and Sylvia (Chang) Young; BA, San Francisco State Coll., 1969; M.P.H., U. Calif., Berkeley, 1971; m. Benny Chin, Nov. 16, 1975; children: Kenneth Michael, Lauren Marie, Catherine Rose. Edn. asst. Am. Cancer Soc., San Francisco, 1969-70; intern Lutheran Med. Ctr., Bklyn., 1971; community health educator Md. Dept. Health and Mental Hygiene, Balt., 1971-74; community health educator Northeast Med. Svcs., San Francisco, 1975; pub. health educator Child Health and Disability Prevention, San Francisco Public Health Dept., 1975-83; health educator maternal and child health, 1991—. USPHS grantee, 1970-71. Mem. Soc. No. Calif. Pub. Health Edn. (treas. 1976, 77), Am. Public Health Assn. Office: 680 8th Ste 200 San Francisco CA 94103

CHIN, MARJORIE SCARLETT YEE, controller, business executive; b. Reno, Mar. 24, 1941; d. Wing Yee and Jessie (Wong) Echavia; m. Manford Jeffrey Chin, Dec. 26, 1969. AA, Contra Costa Coll., 1969; BS, John F. Kennedy U., 1988. Treas., contr. Maya Corp., South San Francisco, 1977-78; fin. and pers. coord. Garretson-Elmendorf-Zinov, San Francisco, 1978-82; bus. mgr. Cyclotomics, Berkeley, Calif., 1982-85; contr. JTS Leasing Corp., South San Francisco, 1985-88; contr., office mgr. Barbary Coast Steel Corp., Emeryville, Calif., 1988-90; cons. WAM, 1990-91, U. Calif., Berkeley, 1992-94; sr. acct. San Francisco, 1993—; contr. X.Clusiv Vending Corp., San Francisco, 1994—; bd. dirs. Experience Unlimited, Pleasant Hill, Calif. Vol. driver ARC, Richmond, Calif., 1978; vol. UNICEF, San Francisco, 1980. Mem. NAFE, AAUW, Nat. Assn. Accts. (bd. dir.), Calif. Fedn., Bus. & Profl. Women Club (sec. 1980—). Home: Two Embarcadero Ctr San Francisco CA 94111

CHIN, SUE SOONE MARIAN (SUCHIN CHIN), conceptual artist, portraitist, photographer, community affairs activist; b. San Francisco; d. William W. and Soo-Up (Swebe) C. Grad. Calif. Coll. Art, Mpls. Art Inst., (scholar) Schaeffer Design Ctr.; student, Yasuo Kuniyoshi, Louis Hamon, Rico LeBrun. Photojournalist, All Together Now show, 1973, East-West News, Third World Newscasting, 1975-78, Sta. KNBC Sunday Show, L.A., 1975, 76, Live on 4, 1981, Bay Area Scene, 1981; graphics printer, exhbns. include Kaiser Ctr., Zellerbach Pla., Chinese Culture Ctr. Galleries, Capricorn Asunder Art Commn. Gallery (all San Francisco), Newspace Galleries, New Coll. of Calif., L.A. County Mus. Art, Peace Pla. Japan Ctr., Congress Arts Communication, Washington, 1989; SFWA Galleries, Inner Focus Show, 1989—, Calif. Mus. Sci. and Industry, Lucien Labaudt Gallery, Salon de Medici, Madrid, Salon Renacimento, Madrid, Life Is a Circus, SFWA Gallery, 1991, 94, Sacramento State Fair, AFL-CIO Labor Studies Ctr., Washington, Asian Women Artists (1st prize for conceptual painting, 1st prize photography), 1978, Yerba Buena Arts Ctr. for the Arts Festival, 1994; represented in permanent collections L.A. County Fedn. Labor, Calif. Mus. Sci. and Industry, AFL-CIO Labor Studies Ctr., Australian Trades Coun., Hazeland and Co., also pvt. collections; author (poetry) Yuri and Malcolm, The Desert Sun. 1994 (Editors Choice award 1993-94). Del. nat., state convs. Nat. Women's Polit. Caucus, 1977-83, San Francisco chpt. affirmative action chairperson, 1978-82, nat. conv. del., 1978-81, Calif. del., 1976-81. Recipient Honorarium AFL-CIO Labor Studies Ctr., Washington, 1975-76; award Centro Studi Ricerche delle Nazioni, Italy, 1985; bd. advisors Psycho Neurology Found. Bicentennial award L.A. County Mus. Art, 1976, 77, 78. Mem. Asian Women Artists (founding v.p., award 1978-79, 1st award in photography of Orient 1978-79), Calif. Chinese Artists (sec.-treas. 1978-81), Japanese Am. Art Coun. (chairperson 1978-84, dir.), San Francisco Women Artists, San Francisco Graphics Guild, Pacific/Asian Women Coalition Bay Area, Chinatown Coun. Performing and Visual Arts. Chmn., Full Moon Products; pres., bd. dir. Aumni Oracle Inc. Address: PO Box 421415 San Francisco CA 94142-1415

CHING, JULIA, religion educator; b. Shanghai, China, Oct. 15, 1934; came to Can., 1951; d. William Ching and Christina Ching Tsao; m. Willard G. Oxtoby, 1981. PhD, Australian Nat. U., Canberra, 1972. Prof. U. Toronto, Ont., Can., 1978—; univ. prof., 1994—. Author: Confucianism and Christianity, 1977 (Outstanding Acad. Book of Yr., Choice), Probing China's Soul, 1990; co-author: Christianity and Chinese Religions, 1989. Trustee United Bd. for Christian Higher Edn. in Asia, N.Y., 1977-86; co-organizer Spirit of Asia Pacific Gala, Toronto, 1990; co-pres. 33d Internat. Congress for Asian and N.African Studies, Toronto, 1990. Fellow Royal Soc. Can.; mem. Am. Soc. for Study of Religion. Office: U Toronto, Victoria Coll, Toronto, ON Canada M5S 1K7

CHING, STEFANIE W., realtor; b. Honolulu, Oct. 29, 1966; d. Norman K.H. and Jocelyn C. H. (Lee) C. BBA in Fin., U. Hawaii at Manoa, 1988; postgrad., U. Hawaii, Manoa, 1992—. Realtor Grad. Realtor Inst. Fin. analyst Am. Savs. Bank, F.S.B., Honolulu, 1988-89; realtor Herbert K. Horita Realty, Inc., Honolulu, 1989—; part-time auditor Kahala Hilton, Honolulu, 1990-92; mem. project sales team Herbert K. Horita Realty, Inc., Honolulu, 1993—. Mem. NAFE, NAR, HAR, Honolulu Bd. Realtors, Internat. Platform Assn., Million Dollar Club, Phi Kappa Phi, Beta Gamma Sigma, Phi Eta Sigma. Home: 5339 Manauwea St Honolulu HI 96821-1917 Office: Herbert K Horita Realty Inc 2024 N King St Ste 200 Honolulu HI 96819-3493

CHINITZ, JODY ANNE KOLB, data processing executive; b. Bay City, Mich., July 8, 1953; d. Adam H. and Evelyn I. (Sylvester) Kolb; m. William A. Chinitz, Feb. 11, 1979. Student Saginaw Valley State Coll., 1972, Bklyn. Coll., 1973-76; BA in Russian Lang. and Lit. summa cum laude, CUNY, 1980. With personnel dept. N.Y. Life Ins. Co., N.Y.C., 1972-77, computer programmer, 1977-80; computer systems cons. Soroban Data Systems, Inc., N.Y.C., 1980-82; project leader Midlantic Nat. Bank, West Orange, N.J., 1982-89, asst. v.p., 1989—. Home: 31 Norwood Ave Montclair NJ 07043-1921 Office: 95 Old Short Hills Rd West Orange NJ 07052-1088

CHINN, APRIL LOUISE, accounting clerk; b. Howell, Mich., Apr. 28, 1972; d. Jerald Edward and Marjorie Ann (Wright) C. BBA in Acctg., Western Mich. U., 1994. Purchasing clk., sec. Bradhart Products, Inc., Howell, Mich., 1988-90; acctg. clk. Gilreath Mfg., Inc., Howell, Mich., 1992-93; vol. tutor North Parchment Elem. Sch., 1993-94, Park Place Residential Ctr., Kalamazoo, 1993-94; vol. ARC, Kalamazoo, 1993. Treas. Western Mich. Univ. Residence Hall Floor Coun., Kalamazoo, 1990-91. Western Mich. U. Medallion scholar, Kalamazoo, 1990, Ames Dept. Store scholar, Howell, 1990, Ctrl. Mich. U. scholar, 1990; recipient Freshman Hon. award Western Mich. U., 1990. Mem. Inst. Mgmt. Accts. (com. svc. dir. 1993-94), Golden Key Nat. Honor Soc.

CHINN, PEGGY LOIS, nursing educator, editor; b. Columbia, S.C., Feb. 25, 1941; d. Hubert R. and Margaret (Gasteiger) Tatum; m. Philip C. Chinn, June 15, 1964 (div. 1974); children: Kelleth Roger, Jonathan Mark (dec.). AA, Mars Hill Coll., 1960; BS, U. Hawaii, 1964; MS, U. Utah, 1970, PhD, 1971. From instr. to asst. prof. U. Utah, Salt Lake City, 1971-74; assoc. dir., prof. Tex. Woman's U., Denton, 1974-78; prof. Wright State U., Dayton, Ohio, 1978-81, SUNY, Buffalo, 1981-90, U. Colo., Denver, 1990—; founder, editor Advances in Nursing Sci., Rockville, Md., 1978—; cons., lectr. in field. Author: Child Health Maintenance, 1974, 2d edit., 1978, Theory in Nursing, 1983, 4th edit., 1995, Peace and Power, 3d edit., 1991; contbr. articles to profl. jours. Co-founder Cassandra: Radical Feminist Nurses Network, nationwide 1982, Margaret Daughters Inc., Buffalo, 1984. Fellow Am. Acad. Nursing (governing coun. 1987-90); mem. Am. Nurses Assn., Nat. League for Nursing, Sigma Theta Tau. Office: U Colo Health Sci Ctr 4200 E 9th Ave Box C288 Denver CO 80262

CHINN-HECHTER, MAMIE MAY, non-profit organization executive; b. Oakland, Calif., Aug. 20, 1951; d. Bing T. and Georgia S. (Ong) C.; m. Marc S. Hechter. BS in Bus., U. Nev., 1974. Loan processor First Fed. Savs. and Loan, Reno, 1974-75, loan processor supr., 1975-76, sr. loan counselor, affirmative action officer, 1977-78; jr. loan officer First Fed. Savs. and Loan, Carson City, Nev., 1976-77; loan officer State of Nev. Housing Divsn., Carson City, 1978-79, loan adminstr., 1979-83, dep. adminstr., 1983-93; pres., CEO Nev. Comty. Reinvestment Corp., Las Vegas, 1993—; mem. exec. com. Housing and Devel. Fin., Ethics Com., Media and Comms. Com., Carson City, 1987-93. Mem. Carson City Women's Polit. Caucus, Nev. Women's Polit. Caucus; bd. mem. Nev. Community Reinvestment Corp., 1991—. Mem. NAFE, Capitol City (Carson City sec. 1984-88), Women's Bowling Assn. (bd. dirs. 1983-84), Nat. 600. Office: Nev Comty Reinvestment Corp Ste 8 5920 W Flamingo Rd Las Vegas NV 89103

CHINSAMY, ANUSUYA, paleobiologist, researcher; b. Pretoria, Transvaal, South Africa, Aug. 27, 1962; came to U.S., 1992; d. Krishna and Sushilla (Pillay) C.; m. Yunus Nadi Turan, July 2, 1992. Higher diploma in Edn., Westville U., Durban, South Africa, 1985; BSc with honors, U. Witwatersrand, Johannesburg, South Africa, 1984, MSc, 1988, PhD, 1991. Jr. lectr. U. Witwatersrand, 1988-90, lectr., 1991-92; postdoctoral fellow U. Pa., Phila., 1992. Editor: Palaeontological Newsletter of PSSA, 1991-92, co-editor, 1990; contbr. articles to profl. jours. Rsch. grantee NSF, 1992-94, Coun. for Sci. and Indsl. Rsch., 1984, 86, 87. Mem. Palaeontological Soc. of S.A. (recipient Lystrosaurus shield 1986), Soc. Vertebrate Palaeontology. Office: Univ of Pennsylvania 3800 Spruce St Philadelphia PA 19104

CHINTALA, MAUREEN JULIA, reading educator, administrator; b. Jersey City, N.J., July 14, 1949; d. Cyril Francis and Marguerite Helen (Ryan) McGranahan; m. George Michael Chintala, Jr., Aug. 3, 1985; stepchildren: George M., Judith Anne, Michael J. BA, Caldwell (N.J.) Coll., 1971; MEd, William Paterson Coll., 1977. Cert. elem. tchr. K-8; cert. prin. Grade 3 tchr. Vernon (N.J.) Twp. Bd. of Edn. Rolling Hills Sch., 1971-82, reading tchr., 1982—; adminstrv. coord. Rolling Hills Sch. Vernon Bd. Edn., 1977—, dir. adult continuing edn., 1977—. Bldg. rep. N.W. Jersey Reading Coun., Sussex County, 1992, 93. Recipient Gov.'s Tchr. Recognition award 1986. Mem. ASCD, NEA, Assn. for Community Edn., Vernon Twp. Edn. Assn., Sussex County Edn. Assn., N.J. Edn. Assn. Office: Rolling Hills Sch PO Box 769 Vernon NJ 07462-0769

CHIOCCHI, ADRIANA GUEVARA, lawyer; b. L.A., July 10, 1962; d. Adrian and Gloria De River Guevara; m. William A. Chiocchi, May 17, 1986; 2 children. BA in English and Econs., U. Calif., San Diego, 1984; JD, U. So. Calif., L.A., 1987, MBA, 1987. Atty. Loeb & Loeb, Century City, Calif., 1987-88, Troy Casden Gould, Century City, 1988-90; gen. counsel, asst. v.p., sec. Com Sys., Inc., Westlake Village, Calif., 1990-92; corporate coun. Advanced MicroDevices, Inc., Sunnyvale, Calif., 1992—. Office: Advanced Micro Devices Inc Mail Stop 68 1 AMD Pl PO Box 3453 Sunnyvale CA 94088-3453

CHIORAZZI, MARY LORRAINE, psychiatrist; b. New York. BS, Marymount Manhattan Coll., 1966; MD, Georgetown U., 1970. Diplomate Am. Bd. Psychiatry. Pvt. practice child, adolescent, adult psychiatry Englewood, N.J., 1975—. Office: 163 Engle St Englewood NJ 07631-2530

CHIPMAN, DEBRA DECKER, paralegal; b. Oneonta, N.Y., Sept. 21, 1959; d. Leon Hannibal and Patricia Elizabeth (Ainsworth) Decker; m. Michael A. Chipman, May 24, 1980 (div. Sept. 1990); 1 child, Amanda Michelle. Student, Robert Morris Coll., 1988-94. Sec., receptionist Power

Engring. Corp., Binghamton, N.Y., 1977-78; accounts payable clk. Old Dominion U. Rsch. Found., Norfolk, Va., 1978-80; adminstrv. asst. U. Pitts., 1980-81; paralegal Papernick & Gefsky, Attys. at Law, Pitts., 1981-93; mgr. Preferred Settlement Svcs., Inc., Pitts., 1993—. Recipient award Otsego County Bankers Assn., 1977. Mem. Nat. Assn. Legal Assts, Pitts. Paralegal Assn. (co-chair fundraising com. 1990), Pa. Assn. Notaries, Pa. Land Title Assn., Pa. Land Title Inst. (western Pa. chpt. edn. com.). Methodist. Home: 2688 Hunters Point Dr Wexford PA 15090-7991 Office: 9401 Mcknight Rd Ste 305A Pittsburgh PA 15237-6000

CHISHOLM, MARGARET ELIZABETH, retired library education administrator; b. Grey Eagle, Minn., July 25, 1921; d. Henry D. and Alice (Thomas) Bergman; children: Nancy Diane, Janice Marie Lane. BA, U. Washington, 1957, MLS, 1958, PhD, 1966. Libr. Everett (Wash.) C.C., 1961-63; asst. and assoc. prof. edn. U. Oreg., Eugene, 1963-67; assoc. prof. edn. U. N.Mex., Albuquerque, 1967-69; prof., dean Coll. Libr. and Info. Svcs. U. Md., College Park, 1969-75; v.p. univ. relations and devel. U. Washington, Seattle, 1975-81; dir. and prof. Grad. Sch. Libr. and Info. Sci., U. Wash., Seattle, 1981-92; ret., 1992; adv. com. White House Conf. on Libr. and Info. Sci., 1989-91, Pub. Broadcasting Svc. Archive; commr. Western Interstate Commn. Higher Edn., Colo., 1981-85. Author: Information Technology: Design and Applications (with Nancy Lane), 1990. Mem. USIA del. to Mexican-Am. Commn. on Cultural Coop., 1990. Civilian aide U.S. Army, 1978-88. Recipient Ruth Worden award U. Wash., Seattle, 1957, Disting. Alumni award St. Cloud (Minn.) U., 1977, Disting. Alumni award U. Wash., 1979, John Brubaker award Cath. Libr. Assn., 1987, Pres.'s award Wash. Libr. Assn., 1991. Mem. ALA (exec. bd. 1989-90, pres. 1988-89, v.p. 1986-87), Assn. Pub. TV Stas. (trustee 1975-84, 87-93), White House Conf. on Libr. and Info. Svcs. (adv. com. 1989-91). Home: 5892 NE Park Point Pl Seattle WA 98115-7845

CHISHOLM, SHIRLEY ANITA ST. HILL, former congresswoman, educator, lecturer; b. Bklyn., Nov. 30, 1924; d. Charles Christopher and Ruby (Seale) St. Hill; m. Conrad Chisholm, Oct. 8, 1949 (div. Feb. 1977); m. Arthur Hardwick, Jr., Nov. 26, 1977. B.A. cum laude, Bklyn. Coll.; M.A., Columbia U.; LL.D. (hon.), Talladega (Ala.) Coll., Hampton (Va.) Inst., LaSalle Coll., Phila., U. Maine, Portland, Capital U., William Patterson Coll., Pratt Inst., Coppin State Coll., N.C. Coll., Kenyon Coll., Wilmington (Ohio) Coll., Acquinas Coll., Grand Rapids, Mich., Reed Coll., Portland, Oreg., U. Cin., Smith Coll., Northampton, Mass. Former nursery sch. tchr., dir. nursery sch.; ednl. cons. Div. Day Care, Bur. Child Welfare, N.Y.C.; mem. N.Y. State Assembly, 1964-68, 91st-98th Congresses from 12th Dist. N.Y., 1969-83; Purington chair Mount Holyoke Coll., South Hadley, Mass., 1983-87; Lectr. Spellman Coll., Atlanta. Author: Unbought and Unbossed, 1970, The Good Fight, 1973. Hon. mem. bd. dirs. Cosmopolitan Young People's Symphony Orch., N.Y.C.; adv. bd. Fund. for Research and Edn. in Sickle Cell Disease; bd dirs. Bklyn. Home for Aged; mem. Central Bklyn. Coordinating Council; mem. nat. adv. council Inst. for Studies in Edn., Notre Dame; mem. adv. com. Washington Workshops; nat. bd. dirs. Ams. for Democratic Action; mem. adv. council NOW; hon. com. mem. United Negro Coll. Fund.; Presdl. candidate Dem. Party, 1972. Named Alumna of Year Bklyn. Coll. Alumni Bull., 1957; recipient award for outstanding work in field of child welfare Women's Council of Bklyn., 1957, Key Woman of Year award, 1963, Woman of Achievement award Key Women, Inc., 1965. Mem. Nat. Assn. Coll. Women, Bklyn. Coll. Alumni, LWV, Key Women, NAACP, Delta Sigma Theta. Methodist. *

CHISWICK, NANCY ROSE, psychologist; b. East Orange, N.J., May 8, 1945; d. Haim Hershel and Beatrice May (Levinson) C.; m. Arthur Howard Patterson, Aug. 5, 1973; children: Michael Chiswick-Patterson, Emily Chiswick-Patterson. AB, Smith Coll., 1966; MA, U. Ill., Chgo. Circle, 1970; PhD, U. Ill., 1973. Lic. psychologist, Pa. Intern Northwestern U. Med. Sch., Chgo., 1973; mental retardation specialist The Counseling Svc., Bellefonte, Pa., 1973-75; clin. staff psychologist Pa. State U., 1975-80; dir. clin. psychologist Child, Adult and Family Psychol. Ctr., State College, PA., 1980—; adj. prof. psychology and human devel. Pa. State U., 1974—; mem. allied staff Ctr. Community Hosp., State Coll., 1985—; staff Meadows Psychiat. Hosp., Centre Hall, Pa., 1985—. Creator, co-host pub. TV Series About Women, 1979-80. Del. White House Conf. Families, 1980, bd. dirs. Meadows Psychiat. Hosp., 1983-85, Jewish Community Ctr., 1989—. Named Guest in Residence W. Marlin Butts Com. Oberlin (Ohio) Coll., 1978. Fellow Cen. Pa. Psychol. Assn. (sec. 1987-89), mem. APA, Pa. Psychol. Assn. Home: 2443 Hickory Hill Dr State College PA 16803 Office: Child Adult & Family Psychol Ctr 315 S Allen St Ste 218 State College PA 16801-4832

CHITTENDEN, CONSTANCE THIAS, software engineering executive; b. Oxnard, Calif., Jan. 16, 1940; d. Edwin Paul and Virginia Way (Hertzog) Thias; m. Robert Leon Warmke, Apr. 15, 1961 (div. July 1975); children: Douglas William Warmke, Teresa Diane Warmke, Richard Earl Warmke; m. Wayne King Chittenden, Jan. 26, 1980. BS with distinction, Stanford U., 1961. Dynamicist Lockheed Missiles and Space Corp., Sunnyvale, Calif., 1961-64; sr. sci. programmer Stanford U., Palo Alto, Calif., 1970-72; math. tchr. Escola Maria Immaculata High Sch., São Paolo, Brazil, 1972-74; sr. software engr., asst. lab. dir. SRI Internat. (formerly Stanford Rsch. Inst.), Menlo Park, Calif., 1974—; dir. Neural Systems Corp., Los Altos Hills, Calif., 1989—; cons. in field, 1965-69. Inventor automatic blood pressure measurement, systolic slope as indicator of heart disease, adaptive tree neural network; contbr. articles to profl. jours. Elder Valley Presbyn. Ch., Portola Valley, Calif., 1991-93. Recipient Tech. Excellence award Soc. for Women Engrs., 1985; named Outstanding Engr. Info. Systems AIAA, 1987. Mem. IEEE, Phi Beta Kappa. Republican. Presbyterian. Office: SRI International 333 Ravenswood Ave Menlo Park CA 94025

CHITTICK, ELIZABETH LANCASTER, association executive, women's rights activist; b. Bangor, Pa., Nov. 11, 1918; d. George and Flora Mae (Mann) Lancaster. Student, Columbia U., 1944-45, N.Y. Inst. Fin., 1950-51, Hunter Coll., 1952-56, Upper Iowa U., Fayette, 1976. Adminstrv. asst., chief clk U.S. Naval Air Stas., Seattle and Banana River, Fla., 1941-45; v.p. treas. W.A. Chittick & Co., MAnila, 1945-52; 31062Smith; real estate salesperson La Jolla, Calif., 1949; registered rep. Bache & Co., N.Y. Stock Exch., N.Y.C., 1950-62, Shearson & Hamil, 1962-63; investment adviser, 1962-65; revenue officer IRS, N.Y.C., 1965-72; pres. Nat. Woman's Party, Washington, 1971-89, Woman's Party Corp., 1978-91; commr. Washington Commn. on Status of Women, 1982-86; pres., adminstr. Sewall-Belmont House; bd. dirs. Wexita Corp., N.Y.C., Pan Am. Liason Com. of Women's Orgns. Inc.; 1st v.p., bd. dirs. Nat. Coun. Women U.S. Lectr., TV and radio commentator on Equal Rights Amendment; author: Answers to Questions About the Equal Rights Amendment, 1973, 76. Mem. Coalition for Women in Internat. Devel., Internat. Women's Yr. Continuing Com., 1978-81, Women's Campaign Fund, Washington, 1975-80, Women's Nat. Rep. Club, N.Y.C., Women Govt. Rels., Washington; mem. U.S. com. of cooperation to Inter-Am. Commn. of Women, OAS, 1974-80; del. U.S. World Conf. of Internat. Women's Yr., Mexico City, 1975; mem. women's history ctr. task force Am. Revolution Bicentennial Adminstrn., 1973-76; mem. adv. com. U.S. Ctr. for Internat. Women's Yr., 1973-76; vice convenor com. on law and status of women Internat. Coun. of Women; chmn. UN Drive for war orphans and widows, Manila, 1949;. Mem. Greater Washington Soc. Assn. Execs., Internat. Coun. Women (Paris), Nat. Fedn. Bus. and Profl. Women's Clubs, Gen. Fedn. Women's Clubs, Women's Press Club (N.Y.C.), Am. Newswomen's Club, Nat. Press Club, Order Eastern Star. Home and Office: 3590 S Ocean Blvd #107 Palm Beach FL 33480-5742

CHITTISTER, JOAN DAUGHERTY, writer, lecturer; b. Dubois, Pa., Apr. 26, 1936; d. Harold C. and Loretta (Cuneo) C. BA, Mercyhurst Coll., 1962; MA, U. Notre Dame, 1968; PhD, Pa. State U., 1971; LLD (hon.), Chestnut Hill Coll., 1986, Villa Maria Coll., 1988, Loyola U., Chgo., 1989, St. Leo (Fla.) Coll., 1990, Loyola U., New Orleans, 1990, Santa Clara U., 1994; HHD (hon.), St. Mary's Coll., Notre Dame, Ind., 1989. Tchr. elem. sch. Diocese of Erie (Pa.), 1955-59, tchr. secondary sch., 1959-74; pres. Fedn. St. Scholastica Benedictine Sisters, 1971-78, Conf. Am. Benedictine Prioresses, 1974-90; prioress Benedictine Sisters of Erie, 1978-90; exec. dir. Benetivision, Erie, 1990—; bd. dirs. Nat. Cath. Reporter, Kansas City; bd. trustees Global Edn. Assn., N.Y., 1988-94; mem. exec. bd. Ecumenical/Cultural Rsch. Ctr., Collegeville, Minn., 1976—. Author: Women, Church and Ministry, 1983, Winds of Change: Women Challenge Church, 1986, Wisdom Distilled from the Daily, 1990, Job's Daughters: Women & Power, 1990, Womanstrength, 1990, Insights for the Ages, 1992; co-author: Faith and Ferment: Study of Christian Beliefs and Practices, 1983; co-author, editor: Climb Along the Cutting Edge, 1977; columnist (newspaper) Nat. Cath. Reporter; contbr. articles to profl. jours. Bd. dirs. Emmaus Ministries, Inc., Erie, 1990—; bd. corporators St. Vincent Health Ctr., Erie, 1986—; bd. trustees Erie Community Found., 1993—. Recipient U.S. Cath. award U.S. Cath. mag., 1992, St. Catherine of Sienna award Dominican Sisters, Springfield, Ill., 1992; named Disting. Pennsylvanian Gannon U., Erie, 1984, Disting. Alumna of Yr. Mercyhurst Coll., Erie, 1986, Woman of Yr. The Erie 80 Club, 1989, Disting. Daughter Pa., Harrisburg, 1991, Pope Paul VI Tchr. pf Peace Pax Christi USA, 1990. Mem. Speech Communication Assn. Roman Catholic. Home: 355 E 9th St Erie PA 16503

CHITTY, (MARY) ELIZABETH NICKINSON, university historian; b. Balt., Apr. 27, 1920; d. Edward Phillips and Em Turner (Merritt) Nickinson; m. Arthur Benjamin Chitty, June 16, 1946; children: Arthur Benjamin, John Abercrombie, Em Turner, Nathan Harsh Brown. BA cum laude, Fla. State U., 1941, MA, 1942; D in Civil Law, U. of South, 1988. Tchr. Fla. Indsl. Sch. for Girls, Ocala, 1942-43; psychometrist neuropsychiat. dept. Sch. Aviation Medicine, Pensacola (Fla.) Naval Air Sta., 1943-46; assoc. editor Sewanee (Tenn.) Alumni News, U. of South, 1946-62; bus. mgr., mng. editor Sewanee Review, 1962-65, dir. fin. aid and career services, 1970-80, assoc. univ. historiographer, 1980—; freelance editor. Editor: (with H.A. Petry) Sewanee Centennial Alumni Directory, 1954-62; Centennial Report of the Registrar of the University of the South, 1959; (with Arthur Ben Chitty) Too Black, Too White (Ely Green), 1970; author: (with Moultrie Guerry and Arthur Ben Chitty) Men Who Made Sewanee, 1981, (with A.B. Chitty and W. Givens) Ninety-Nine Iron, 1992; columnist Sewanee Mountain Messenger, 1985—. Bd. dirs. Sewanee Civic Assn., 1979-80, 86-88; CONTACT-Lifeline of Coffee and Franklin Counties, 1981-84; mem. adv. coun. St. Andrew's Sewanee Sch., 1988—. Mem. Assn. Preservation Tenn. Antiquities (trustee 1985-88), AAUW (pres. Sewanee br. 1975-77), Fla. State U. Alumni Assn. (dir. 1941—, permanent pres. Class of 1941), Mortar Bd., Phi Beta Kappa, Phi Kappa Phi, Phi Alpha Theta, Kappa Delta. Democrat. Episcopalian. Home: 100 South Carolina Ave Sewanee TN 37375-2045 Office: U of the South Sewanee TN 37385-1000

CHITWOOD, LERA CATHERINE, information professional, manufacturing company manager; b. Columbiana, Ala., Sept. 14, 1942; d. Roy P. and Lizzie Hearn (Erwin) C.; m. John N. Mathys, Mar. 17, 1984 (div. 1992); 1 child, Jonathan Roy Chitwood Mathys. BA in English, Carson-Newman Coll., 1964; MLS, Emory U., 1967; MBA, DePaul U., 1985. Asst. head dept. bus. and sci. Atlanta Pub. Libr., 1964, 66-69; tchr. English, Sequoyah High Sch., Doraville, Ga., 1965; libr. Ill. Inst. Tech. Stuart Sch. Mgmt. and Fin., Chgo., 1970-79; sr. reference libr., asst. prof. bibliography U. Ala., Huntsville, 1979-82; mgr. bus. rsch. Motorola Inc., Schaumburg, Ill., 1985—. Libr. sch. scholar Atlanta Pub. Libr., 1966. Mem. Soc. Competitive Intelligence (CI Rev. columnist, 1991—), Assn. Global Strategic Info. Home: 208 E Crescent Ave Elmhurst IL 60126-4054 Office: Motorola Inc 1303 E Algonquin Rd Schaumburg IL 60196

CHIU, DOROTHY, pediatrician; b. Hong Kong, Aug. 8, 1917; came to U.S., 1946; d. Yan Tse and Connie Kwai-Ching Wan; m. Kitman Au, Aug. 7, 1918; children: Katherine, Margo, Doris, James, Richard. BS, Lingnan U., 1939; MD, Nat. Shanghai Med. Coll., 1945. Diplomate Am. Bd. Pediats. Sch. physician L.A. Sch. Dist., 1954-55; pvt. practice Burbank, Calif., 1954-55, San Fernando, Calif., 1955—; staff pediatrician Holy Cross Med. Ctr., Mission Hills, Calif., 1961—. Bd. dirs. Burbank Cmty. Concert, 1970-80. Fellow Am. Acad. Pediats.; mem. Calif. Med. Assn., L.A. County Med. Assn. Republican. Office: 11273 Laurel Canyon Blvd San Fernando CA 91340

CHIU, LILY WAI PING, administrative assistant; b. Hong Kong, July 16, 1967; d. Yue Ling and Mo Lan (Lam) C.; m. Michael Pinzon, Apr. 15, 1989; 1 child, Lena Wai Ling Pinzon. BA in Psychology cum laude, NYU, 1988. Adminstrv. asst. NYU, N.Y.C., 1988—. Mem. Psi Chi, Phi Beta Kappa. Democrat. Roman Catholic. Office: NYU 6 Washington Pl New York City NY 10003

CHIU, MARGARET CHI YUAN LIU, real estate broker; b. Quanzhou, Quangdong, China, Nov. 3, 1926; d. Chien Shan and Wen Bing Liu; m. Wan-Cheng Chiu, Feb. 6, 1954; children: Linda, Ellen, Elaine Amy. BA, Nat. Taiwan U., 1950; MBA, N.Y.U., 1956. Clk. Taiwan Supply Bur., Taipei, Taiwan, 1950-53; realtor assoc. Tropic Shore Realty, Honolulu, 1973-79; realtor broker Urner & Assocs., Inc., Honolulu, 1979-93; realtro broker Hale Koa Realty, Honolulu, 1993—. Chinese paintings shown in various exhibitions, 1990—. Joint U.S. and Republic of China fellow, 1951-52. Mem. Nat. Assn. Realtors, Hawaii Assn. Realtors, Honolulu Bd. Realtors, Chinese Women's Benevolent Assn. Hawaii (pres. 1987-91), Hawaii Chinese Assn. (v.p. 1985), Lung Kong Kung Shaw Soc. (sec. 1990-92). Home: 216 Kalalau St Honolulu HI 96825

CHIZAUSKAS, CATHLEEN JO, manufacturing company executive; b. Little Rock, Dec. 26, 1954; d. Daniel John and Marilyn (Wolff) Quigley; m. Alan Michael Chizauskas, Nov. 11, 1978; children: Marc Alan, Danielle Kelley. Diploma in Mgmt., Simmons Coll., Boston, 1981. Clk. typist to direct materials buyer Gillette Safety Razor Co., Boston, 1972-79, buyer capital equipment, 1979, mgr. MRO and purchasing svcs., 1979-85, adminstrv. asst. to v.p. mktg., 1985-87, exec. asst. to pres., 1987-88, assoc. brand mgr. shave creams, 1988-89, bus. mgr., 1989-91, product mgr., 1991-94, nat. trade mktg. mgr. grooming products, 1994—. Mem. Am. Mgmt. Assn., Simmons Coll. Grad. Sch. Alumnae Assn. Roman Catholic. Home: 14 St Lawrence St Braintree MA 02184-8244 Office: Gillette Co Gillette NAm Blade/Razor div Gillette Park Boston MA 02106

CHO, MARCIANA ROSALIND, office manager, controller; b. Honolulu, Feb. 11, 1951; d. Ponciano Gonzales and Blanche (Baldwin) Galera; m. George Kita Cho, June 26, 1970 (div. June 1990); children: Cassandra Lokelani, George Kita. Grad., high sch., 1969. Receptionist Kelso, Spencer, Snyder & Stirling, Honolulu, 1975; sec. Bacon Co. Inc., Honolulu, 1975-76, Shatzer & Gaillard Inc., Honolulu, 1976-77; office mgr. Charles Pankow Assocs., Honolulu, 1978-84; project coord. Albert C. Kobayashi, Inc., Honolulu, 1984-86; office mgr. Hygrade Electric, Kailua-Kona, Hawaii, 1986-89, Landscape Svcs. Corp., Honolulu, 1989-90; office mgr. Hawaii divsn. Am. Techs., Inc., Kapolei, 1990—. Mem. Nat. Assn. Women in Constrn. (treas. 1990-91, dir. 1991-93, v.p. 1993-94). Office: Am Techs Inc Hawaii Divsn 91-220 Kalaeloa Blvd Kapolei HI 96707-1820

CHOAT, DOLORES ANNE WILLOUGHBY, educator, computer consultant; b. Chickasha, Okla., Jan. 6, 1938; d. Loranzie Dawl and Anna Mae (Montgomery) Wilkes; m. Don Jeral Willoughby, Apr. 8, 1956 (dec. Apr. 1975); children: Danny Michael, Melissa Dawn Willoughby Cunningham; m. Arthur James Choat, Jr., May 30, 1977; stepchildren: Aleisa Choat Morrow, Keith. BS, U. Sci. and Arts Okla., 1969; MEd, Southwestern Okla. State U., 1976; postgrad. Okla. State U., 1985-90, Ctrl. State U., Edmond., 1975; postgrad., U. Okla., 1985-89, 92. Cert. K-8 sci., math., reading, and social studies tchr., Okla. Teller Okla. Nat. Bank, Chickasha, 1957-66; tchr. Verden (Okla.) Pub. Schs., 1969-82, Amber-Pocasset (Okla.) Schs., 1982-89; tchr. sci., computer coord. Chickasha Intermediate Sch., 1989-92; elem. tchr. Grand Avenue Sch., Chickasha, 1992—; mem. evaluation com. North Ctrl. Accreditation, Oklahoma City, 1993; mem. sci. curriculum alignment com. Chickasha Schs., 1992-93, site chmn. for sci. and computer programs, 1993-94; reviewer CHIME newsletter, 1986. Contbr. articles to profl. publs. Mem. adv. bd. Chickasha Pub. Libr., 1993—. Mem. NSTA (space adv. bd. 1990-94, gen. rev. panel 1994-96, NASA Educators' Workshop Math and Sci. Tchrs. award 1990), Nat. Mid. Level Sci. Tchrs. Assn. (state chmn. 1992-93), Okla. Sci. Tchrs. Assn. (bd. dirs. 1993-95), Okla. Reading Coun. (grantee 1993), Okla. Aerospace Educators Assn. (sec. 1994—), AAUW (editor Okla. newsletter 1993—, bylaws com. 1993, mem. local com. creative writing project), Lace Guild Okla. (sec. 1992-93), U. Sci. and Arts Okla. Alumni Assn. (past dist. bd. dirs.), Delta Kappa Gamma (chmn. nominating com. 1993-94), Kappa Kappa Iota. Democrat. Presbyterian. Home: 727 S 16th St Chickasha OK 73018-3901 Office: Chickasha Schs 900 W Choctaw Ave Chickasha OK 73018-2213

CHOATE, LESLEY JEANNE, accountant; b. Deer Island, Oreg., Mar. 10, 1935; d. Edward Leroy and Lesley Frances (Saunders) Howe; m. William Calvin Choate, Jan. 28, 1955; children: Julia Casandra Nettiecris, Jerome Vincent Alexander. Student, Pacific U., 1952-53; BSBA, U. Nev. Las Vegas, 1974; postgrad., Portland (Oreg.) State U., 1977-79. Jr. acct. Walter J. Frenz P.A., Portland, 1974-75, Holdner Backstrom & Co., Portland, 1975-76; acct. Portland Iron Works, 1976-78; staff acct. Tube Forgings Am., Portland, 1978-79; inventory cost supr. Bingham Internat., Inc., Portland, 1979-87; accounts payable supr. Metra Steel Co., Portland, 1988-90; acctg. supr. North Lincoln Hosp., Lincoln City, Oreg., 1990—. Mem. Nat. Assn. Accts., Nat. Soc. Pub. Accts., Oreg. Assn. Pub. Accts., Healthcare Fin. Mgmt. Republican. Lodge: Rebekahs. Office: North Lincoln Hosp 3043 NE 28th St Lincoln City OR 97367

CHODOROW, JOAN, psychoanalyst, dance therapist; b. N.Y.C., May 29, 1937; d. Eugene Aaronovitch and Lillian (Kleidman) C.; m. Louis H. Stewart, June 23, 1985; step-children: Daniel Stewart, Sarah Stewart Hawklyn. MA in Psychology, Dance Therapy, Goddard Coll., 1972; Diploma in Analytical Psychology, C. G. Jung Inst. Los Angeles, 1983; PhD in Psychology, Union Grad. Sch., 1988. Registered dance therapist; lic. MFCC, Calif. Founder, tchr. Community Dance Studio, Los Angeles, 1957-64; dance therapist Child Psychiat. County Hosp., Los Angeles, 1964-66, Lawrence Sch., Van Nuys, Calif., 1965-67; dance therapist, psychotherapist Psychiat. Med. Group, Santa Barbara, Calif., 1968-73; lectr. U. Calif., Santa Barbara, 1967-79, Community Coll., Santa Barbara, 1967-79; dance therapist Psychiat. Dept. Cottage Hosp., Santa Barbara, 1968-83; practicing psychotherapist Santa Barbara, 1973-83; practicing Jungian analyst Fairfax, Calif., 1983—; tchr. C.G. Jung Inst., San Francisco, 1983—; visiting faculty Insts. Los Angeles, Houston,Israel 1976—; dir., tchr. Dance Therapy, Santa Barbara 1975-83; faculty Active Imagination course Geneva, 1984, 90, Zurich 1985-86. Author: Dance Therapy and Depth Psychology, 1990; editor: What is Dance Therapy, Really?, 1973; keynote speaker Internat. Dance Therapy Conf. in Berlin, 1994; contbr. articles to profl. jours. Mem. Am. Dance Therapy Assn. (pres. 1974-76, keynote speaker 1983, 91), Internat. Assn. Analytical Psychol., Am. Psychol. Assn., Calif. Assn. Marriage and Family Therapists, C.G. Jung Inst. San Francisco. Jewish.

CHOICE, PRISCILLA KATHRYN MEANS (PENNY CHOICE), gifted education educator, international consultant; b. Rockford, Ill., Nov. 8, 1939; d. John Z. and Margaret A. (Haines) Means; m. Jack R. Choice, Nov. 14, 1964; children: William Kenneth, Margaret Meta. BA, U. Wis., 1963; MEd, Nat.-Louis U., 1990; MA, N.E. Ill. U., 1995. Field rsch. dir. Tatham-Laird and Kudner Advt., Chgo., 1964-69; drama specialist Children's Theatre Western Springs (Ill.), 1969-81; gifted teaching asst. Sch. Dist. 181, Hinsdale, Ill., 1980-84; tchr. Sch. Dist. 99, Cicero, Ill., 1984-85; gifted edn. program coord. Community Consolidated Sch. Dist. 93, Carol Stream, Ill., 1985—; drama specialist, cons. Choice Dramatics, Hinsdale and Clarendon Hills, Ill., 1976—; producing dir. Mirror Image Youth Theatre, Hinsdale, 1986-88; adj. prof. Coll. DuPage, Glen Ellyn, Ill., 1990-92, Nat.-Louis U., Evanston, Ill., 1991—, Govs. State U., University Park, Ill., 1992—; internat. cons. in gifted edn. and drame-in-edn., 1989—. Contbg. author Gifted/Arts Resource Guide, 1990; contbg. editor Ill. Theatre Assn., Followspot News, 1992—. Bd. dirs. Ill. Theatre Assn., Chgo., 1983-87; mem. gifted adv. com. Ednl. Svc. Ctr., Wheaton, Ill., 1987-90, 92—, Northeastern Ill. U., Chgo., 1993—. Recipient Ill. State Bd. Edn. gifted edn. fellowship, 1988, AAUW continuing edn. scholarship, 1986, 90, Excellence award Ill. Theatre Assn., 1991, Excellence award Ill. Math. and Sci. Acad., 1990, Recognition of Excellence, No. Ill. Planning Commn. Gifted Edn., 1990. Mem. ASCD, World Coun. on Gifted Edn., Nat. Assn. Gifted Children, Ill. Assn. Gifted Children (membership chair 1992—), Ill. Coun. Gifted, Am. Assn. Theatre in Edn., Ill. Theatre Assn. (bd. dirs. 1983-87, Outstanding Achievement award 1991), Inst. for Global Ethics, Ill. Alliance Arts Edn., Theatre Western Springs, Phi Delta Kappa. Home: 113 S Prospect Ave Clarendon Hills IL 60514-1422 Office: Cmty Consol Sch Dist 93 Jay Stream Sch 283 El Paso Ln Carol Stream IL 60188-1736

CHOLDIN, MARIANNA TAX, librarian, educator; b. Chgo., Feb. 26, 1942; d. Sol and Gertrude (Katz) Tax; m. Harvey Myron Choldin, Aug. 28, 1962; children: Kate and Mary (twins). BA, U. Chgo., 1962, MA, 1967, PhD, 1979. Slavic bibliographer Mich. State U., East Lansing, 1967-69; Slavic bibliographer, instr. U. Ill., Urbana, 1969-73, Slavic bibliographer, asst. prof., 1973-76, Slavic bibliographer, assoc. prof., 1976-84, head Slavic and East European Libr., 1982-89, head, prof., 1984—, dir. Russian and East European Ctr., 1987-89, C. Walter and Gerda B. Mortenson Disting. prof., 1989—. Author: Fence Around the Empire: Russian Censorship, 1985; editor: Red Pencil: Artists, Scholars and Censors in the USSR, 1989, Books, Libraries and Information in Slavic and East European Studies, 1986. Mem. ALA, Am. Assn. for the Advancement of Slavic Studies (pres. 1995), Phi Beta Kappa. Jewish. Home: 1111 S Pine St Champaign IL 61820-6334 Office: U Ill Libr 1408 W Gregory Dr Urbana IL 61801-3692

CHOLETTE, MAUREEN THERESA, geriatrics nurse, nursing administrator; b. Lakewood, N.J., Feb. 20, 1949; d. I. James and Clare E. (French) Kress; m. Viateur Cholette; children: Pierre, Paul. AD, Middlesex County Coll., Edison, N.J., 1969; student, St. Joseph's Coll., Windham, Maine, 1993—. RN, N.J.; cert. in nursing adminstrn. Staff, charge nurse Birchwood Convalescent Ctr., Edison; charge nurse, ADON, DON Burlington Woods Convalescent Ctr., Burlington, N.J.; dir. nursing svcs. Medford (N.J.) Convalescent and Nursing Ctr., 1980—. Mem. Nat. Assn. Dirs. Nursing Adminstrn. in Long Term Care (cert. dir. nursing adminstrn. in long term care), Assn. Nursing Adminstrs. of Long Term Care Facilities in N.J., Inc., Nat. Gerontol. Nursing Assn., N.J. Assn. Dirs. Nursing Adminstrn./Long Term Care (bd. mem.). Home: 301 Magnolia St Browns Mills NJ 08015-2642

CHONKO, LORRAINE NANCY, state legislator; b. Brunswick, Maine, Dec. 31, 1936; d. Philip J. and Rosalva M. (Pinnette) Lachance; m. John J. Chonko, June 8, 1957; children: Eva Marie Chonko Ross, John J. Jr., Jolene. Grad. high sch., Brunswick. Mem. Maine Ho. of Reps., mem. joint standing com. appropriation and fin. affairs. Home: 266A New Lewiston Rd Pejepscot ME 04067*

CHOPIN, SUSAN GARDINER, lawyer; b. Miami, Fla., Feb. 23, 1947; d. Maurice and Judith (Warden) Gardiner; m. L. Frank Chopin, Sept. 4, 1964; children: Philip, Alexandra, Christopher. BBA, Loyola U., New Orleans, 1966; JD cum laude, U. Miami, 1972; MLitt (Law), Oxford U., Eng., 1983. Bar: Fla. 1972, Iowa 1979. Sr. law clk. to judge U.S. Dist. Ct. (so. dist.) Fla., Miami, 1972-73; ptnr. Chopin & Chopin, Miami, 1973-77; assoc. prof. law sch. Drake U., Des Moines, 1979-80; pvt. practice law Palm Beach, Fla., 1981—. Mem. editorial bd. Fla. Bar Jour., 1975—; contbr. articles to profl. jours., legal revs. Trustee Preservation Found. of Palm Beach, 1986-89. Mem. ABA, Fla. Bar Assn., Iowa Bar Assn., Fed. Bar Assn., Internat. Bar Assn., Fla. Assn. Women Lawyers, Soc. Wig and Robe, Palm Beach County Bar Assn., English Speaking Union, Phi Kappa Phi, Phi Alpha Delta. Office: Nations Bank Tower Ste 810 1555 Palm Beach Lakes Blvd West Plam Beach FL 33401

CHORAZY, SANDRA MARIE, advertising agency executive; b. Bristol, Pa., May 12, 1957; d. Sam and Rose (Monico) Fiorelli; m. Steve Michael Chorazy, Aug. 13, 1984. BS in Commerce, Rider Coll., 1979. Asst. buyer J. Walter Thompson, N.Y.C., 1980-84, sr. buyer, 1984-88, v.p. broadcast negotiation, 1988—. Office: J Walter Thompson USA Inc 466 Lexington Ave New York NY 10017-3140

CHORAZY LYJAK, ANNA JULIA, pediatrician, medical administrator, educator; b. Braddock, Pa., Feb. 25, 1936; d. Walter and Cecilia (Swiatkowski) Lyjak; m. Chester John Chorazy, May 6, 1961; children: Paula Ann Chorazy, Mary Ellen Chorazy-Cuccaro, Mark Edward Chorazy. BS, Waynesburg Coll., 1958; MD, Women's Med. Coll. Pa., 1960. Diplomate Am. Bd. Pediats. Intern St. Francis Gen. Hosp., Pitts., 1960-61; resident in pediats., tchg. fellow Children's Hosp. of Pitts., 1961-63, pediatrician, devel. clinic, 1966-75; pediat. house physician Western Pa. Hosp., Pitts., 1963-66; med. dir. Rehab. Instn. Pitts., 1975—; clin. asst. prof. pediats. Children's Hosp. Pitts. and U. Pitts. Sch. Medicine, 1971-94, clin. assoc. prof. pediats., 1994—; pediat. cons. Children's Home Pitts., 1985—. Author chpts. to books. Co-chmn. EACH Joint Planning and Assessment, Pitts., 1980-85;

mem. adv. com. 10th Nat. Conf. on Child Abuse, Pitts., 1993. Fellow Am. Acad. Pediats.; mem. AMA, Pa. Med. Soc., Pitts. Pediat. Soc., Allegheny County Med. Soc. Home: 131 Washington Rd Pittsburgh PA 15221-4437 Office: Rehab Inst Pitts 6301 Northumberland Ave Pittsburgh PA 15217

CHORPENNING, SUSAN BETH, visual artist; b. Marietta, Ohio, Sept. 5, 1948; d. Harry Row and Margaret Ellen (Hayes) C. AB, U. Calif., Berkeley, 1976, MA, 1978, MFA, 1979. Asst. prof. Calif. State U., Arcata, 1979-80; visual artist N.Y.C., 1982—; lectr. sculpture U. Calif., Berkeley, 1980, Calif. Coll. Arts and Crafts, Oakland, 1981, 82; vis. artist Hampshire Coll., Amherst, Mass., 1984, Claremont Coll., L.A., 1986, CUNY, 1993. Exhibited sitework at Fulton Ferry Landing State Park, N.Y.C., 1990; exhibited in group shows at Prospect Park, N.Y.C., 1990, FGIC Corp. Hdqs., N.Y.C., 1993; art performance at The Knitting Factory, N.Y.C., 1990. Panel moderator, organizer Women's Caucus for Art, San Francisco, 1981, mem., 1980-87; mem. Brklyn. Waterfront Artist's Coalition, 1989-91; mem. coord. com. Women's Action Coalition, N.Y.C., 1992-93. Materials grantee GE, 1979; Gottlieb Found. fellow, 1989, Artist's Fellowship fellow, 1989. Mem. Orgn. Ind. Artists, Art Initiatives. Home: 351 Court St # 2 Brooklyn NY 11231

CHOSTNER, CHRYSTAL LEA, manufacturing company professional; b. San Diego, Feb. 1, 1963; d. Gilbert E. Chostner and Sheila I. Radley. BA, Lindenwood Coll., 1984. Sr. estimator Teledyne Ryan Aero., San Diego, 1985-89; sr. contract pricing adminstr. Sundstrand Power Systems, San Diego, 1989-91, sr. supplier cost analyst, 1991-93; contracts mgr. Photon Rsch. Assocs., Inc., La Jolla, Calif., 1993—; cons. CLC Enterprises, San Diego, 1992—. Advisor Jr. Achievement, San Diego, 1985. Mem. Soc. Cost Estimating and Analysis (dir. edn. 1987, 88, v.p. 1989, treas. 1990), Nat. Contract Mgmt. Assn., Nat. Mgmt. Assn. (co-chair scholarship fund 1985). Republican. Seventh-day Adventist. Office: Photon Rsch Assocs Inc Ste 300 10350 N Torrey Pines Rd La Jolla CA 92037-1020

CHOU, YUAN L., industrial engineer; b. Singapore, Republic of Singapore, Mar. 10, 1966; came to U.S., 1982; d. Tai Yun and Tzen Min (Lee) C. BS in Indsl. Engring., Cornell U., 1987, M of Engring., 1988. Hardware quality engr. Hewlett-Packard Co., Boise, Idaho, 1988-90, mfg. engr., 1990-93; product mktg. engr. AT&T-Microelectronics, Allentown, Pa., 1993-94, product line prodn. contr., 1994—. Mem. Soc. Women Engrs. (sec. S.W. Idaho sect. 1991-92, pres. 1992-93), Inst. Elec. Engrs., Mensa. Office: AT&T-Microelectronics 555 Union Blvd Allentown PA 18103

CHOUDHURY, SHARMIN AHMAD, elementary education educator; b. Dhaka, Bangladesh, Feb. 29, 1960; came to U.S., 1984; d. Tajuddin Ahmad and Zohra (Khatun) Ahmad; m. Munirul Islam Choudhury, Oct. 24, 1977; children: Taj C., Aumrita. B in Liberal Arts, Navran Coll., 1980; MA, George Washington U., 1990. Tchr. Maple Leaf Internat. Sch., Dhaka, 1980-84; head counsellor Green Acre Sch. Summer Camp, Rockville, Md., 1986; v.p. Aegean Maritime Shipping and Trading Co., Washington, 1987-90; elem. tchr. Muslim Community Sch., Potomac, Md., 1990—; advisor Primary Sch., Dhaka, 1987—; sponsor, co-dir. Dardaria Primary Sch., Dhaka, 1987—. Author 2 books; contbr. poetry to lit. jours. Mem., advisor Mohila Parishad, women's orgn., Dhaka, 1987—; mem. SamHati, women's orgn., Bethesda, Md., 1987—. Fellow George Washington U., 1987, grantee, 1988. Mem. N.Am. Coun. for Muslim Women, Soc. for Internat. Devel./Women in Devel., Lifeline Network: World Alliance for Humanitarian Assistance for Bosnia. Office: Muslim Cmty Sch 7917 Montrose Rd Potomac MD 20852

CHOW, CATHY K., finance controller; b. Taipei, Taiwan, Dec. 7, 1954; d. Ching Swun and Yue Jee (Ma) Chou; m. David Chow, June 28, 1980; 1 child, Sarah. BA, Shi-Lee Coll., Taipei, 1976; student, Keller Grad. Sch. of Mgmt., UCLA. Jr. acct. Lou-I Food Co., Taipei, 1972-77; acct. Curtis-Dodd Group, Chgo., 1980-81; budget specialist ITT Barton, City of Commerce, Calif., 1982-83; acctg. specialist FDIC, Costa Mesa, Calif., 1983-84; fin. contr. Dimerco Express (USA) Corp., Wood Dale, Ill., 1984—. Mem. NAFE. Home: 403 Banbury Ter Roselle IL 60172 Office: Dimerco Express USA Corp 955 Dillon Dr Wood Dale IL 60191

CHOW, DONNA LYNNE, librarian, educator; b. Montgomery, Ala., Nov. 18, 1945; d. George Vernon Stambaugh and Mildred Dimple (Brown) Holman; m. Terrence Jun On Kee Chow, May 29, 1970 (div. Sept. 1974); children: Christianne Margaret Hanners Bennington, Mildred Dimple Mei Lin Leialohalani Chow. BA, U. Md., 1969; MLS, U. Hawaii, 1971. Cert. child devel. assoc. Law librarian Anthony, Hoddick, Reinwald & O'Connor, Honolulu, 1974-75; editor, indexer, model Honolulu, 1975-78; pre-sch. tchr., adminstr. The Early Sch., Honolulu, 1980-86; cataloger, spl. librarian U. Hawaii at Manoa, Honolulu, 1986-89; elem. librarian St. Andrew's Priory, Honolulu, 1990-91; libr. dir. Autauga-Prattville Pub. Libr., Prattville, Ala., 1992-94; supr. ACTMEDIA, 1994—. Cataloger: (book) Tsuzaki/Reinecke Pidgin Creole Collection, 1990. Voter registrar State of Hawaii, Honolulu, 1990-91; class registrar Model Mugging Hawaii, Honolulu, 1987-91; singer Honolulu Symphony Chorus, 1989-91. Mem. ALA, Hawaii Assn. Sch. Librs., Ala. Libr. Assn., S.E. Libr. Assn. Home: 3069 Pinehill Rd Montgomery AL 36109

CHOW, RITA KATHLEEN, nursing administrator; b. San Francisco, Aug. 19, 1926; d. Peter and May (Chan) C. BS, Stanford U., 1950, nursing diploma, 1950; MS, Case Western Res. U., 1955; profl. diploma in nursing edn. adminstrn, Columbia U., 1961, EdD, 1968; B of Individualized Studies, George Mason U., 1983. Asst. in teaching Stanford U., Calif., 1951-52; instr., dir. student health Fresno (Calif.) Gen. Hosp. Sch. Nursing, 1952-54; instr. Wayne State U. Coll. Nursing, Detroit, 1957-58; rsch. assoc., project dir. cardiovascular nursing rsch. Ohio State U., Columbus, 1965-68; commd. officer USPHS, 1968, advanced through grades to nurse dir., 1974; spl. asst. to dep. dir. Nat. Ctr. Health Svcs. Rsch., Health Svcs. and Mental Health Adminstrn., HEW, Rockville, Md., 1969-73; dep. dir. manpower utilization br., 1970-73; dep. dir. Office Long Term Care; dep. chief nurse officer USPHS, Rockville, 1973-77; chief quality assurance br. div. long-term care Office of Standards and Certification, Health Standards and Quality Bur., Health Care Fin. Adminstrn., HHS, 1977-82; supervisory clin. nurse and spl. asst. to health systems adminstr. USPHS Indian Hosp., HRSA, HHS, Rosebud, S.D., 1982-83; dir. patient edn., asst. dir. nursing G.W. Long Hansen's Disease Ctr., USPHS, Carville, La., 1984-89; dir. nursing Federal Correctional Institution, Fort Worth, Tex., 1989—. Author: Identifying Nursing Action with the Care of Cardiovascular Patients, 1967, Cardiosurgical Nursing Care: Understandings, Concepts, and Principles for Practice, 1975; mem. editorial bd. Nursing and Health Care, 1983—; contbr. to publs. in field. Served with Nurse Corps U.S. Army, 1954-57. AAUW scholar; Nat. League Nursing fellow, 1959-61; recipient research grant Sigma Theta Tau, 1966; recipient Fed. Nursing Service award Assn. Mil. Surgeons U.S., 1969, citation for outstanding contbn. to cardiovascular nursing Am. Heart Assn., 1972, 79, Nursing Edn. Alumni Assn. award for distinguished achievement in nursing research Columbia U. Tchrs. Coll., 1973, Meritorious Service medal USPHS, 1977, Disting. Alumnus award Case Western Res. U. Sch. Nursing, 1979, Disting. Service medal USPHS, 1987, Artist of Life award Internat. Women's Writing Guild, 1987, Women's Honors in Pub. Svcs. award Am. Nurses' Assn. 1988.

CHOYKE, PHYLLIS MAY FORD (MRS. ARTHUR DAVIS CHOYKE, JR.), management executive, editor, poet; b. Buffalo, Oct. 25, 1921; d. Thomas Cecil and Vera (Buchanan) Ford; m. Arthur Davis Choyke Jr., Aug. 18, 1945; children: Christopher Ford, Tyler Van. BS summa cum laude, Northwestern U., 1942. Reporter City News Bur., Chgo., 1942-43, Met. sect. Chgo. Tribune, Chgo., 1943-44; feature writer OWI, N.Y.C., 1944-45; sec. corp. Artcrest Products Co., Inc., Chgo., 1958-88, v.p., 1964-88; pres. The Partford Corp., Chgo., 1988-90; founder, dir. Harper Sq. Press div., 1966—. Author: (under name Phyllis Ford) (with others) (poetry) Apertures to Anywhere, 1979; editor: Gallery Series One, Poets, 1967, Gallery Series Two, Poets—Poems of the Inner World, 1968, Gallery Series Three: Poets: Levitations and Observations, 1970, Gallery Series Four, Poets, I am Talking About Revolution, 1973, Gallery Series Five/Poets—To An Aging Nation (with occult overtones), 1977; (manuscripts and papers in Brown U. Library). Bonbright scholar, 1942. Mem. DAR (corr. sec. Gen. Henry Dearborn chpt. 1991-92, treas. 1992-94), Soc. Midland Authors (bd. dirs. 1987-94, treas. 1988-93, pres. 1993-94), Mystery Writers Am. (assoc.), Chgo. Press Vets. Assn., Arts Club Chgo., John Evans Club (Northwestern U.), Poetry Soc. Am. (N.Y.C.), Friends of Lit., Acad. Am. Poets (N.Y.C.). Home: 29 E Division St Chicago IL 60610-2316

CHOY-KWONG, MARIA, neurologist; b. Lima, Peru, Mar. 14, 1959; came to U.S., 1970; d. Ernesto Sheung and Lily Kee (Chong) Choy; m. David C. Kwong, May 27, 1984; 1 child, Elizabeth Choy. BA, MD, Boston U., 1984. Diplomate Bd. Psychiatry and Neurology. Intern Harlem Hosp. Columbia U., N.Y.C., 1984-85; neurology resident Albert Einstein Coll. Medicine, Bronx, N.Y., 1985-88; electromyography fellow Hosp. Spl. Surgery Cornell Med. Ctr., N.Y.C., 1988-89; pvt. practice Edison, N.J., 1991—; presenter nat. conf. Am. Acad. Neurology, 1988, nat. conf. Am. Headache Assn., 1989. Office: Ctrl. Jersey Neurol Inst 470 Hwy 79 Morganville NJ 07751

CHRAPKOWSKI, ROSEMARIE, chemical dependence therapist, art therapist; b. Chgo., Dec. 8, 1935; d. Andrew H. and Charlotte D. (Potrackie) C. BFA, U. Chgo. and Sch. Art Inst. Chgo., 1959, postgrad., 1962-63, 78; student Inst. Psychiatry, Chgo., C.G. Jung Inst., Chgo.; grad. alcoholism counselor tng. program Grant Hosp., Chgo., 1981. Cert. alcoholism counselor, Ill.; cert sr. addictions counselor, Ill. Artist various studios and agys., from 1963; dir. art and prodn. J.L. Dow Advt. and Pub. Rels. Co., Chgo., 1963-65; staff artist Soc. for Visual Edn., Chgo., 1965-66; supr. picture acquisitions Ency. Brit., Inc., Chgo., 1969-71; alcoholism counselor U. Ill. Alcohol Program, Chgo., 1978; sr. chem. dependence counselor Northwestern Meml. Hosp. Inst. Psychiatry, Chgo., 1979-86, expressive arts therapist, 1986—; pvt. practice therapy, Chgo., 1981—; therapist Assocs. in Jungian Psychology and Creative Therapies, Chgo., 1987—; cons., workshop presenter; instr., lectr. Interventions, Inc., Cen. State Inst. Addictions, 1986—. Exhibited paintings various galleries, from 1958. Mem. Nat. Assn. Alcoholism and Drug Abuse Counselors, Ill. Addictions Counselors Assn., Ill. Alcoholism and Drug Dependence Assn., Ill. Women's Substance Abuse Coalition, Inc., Am. Art Therapy Assn., Ill. Art Therapy Assn., C.G. Jung Inst., Alumni Assn. Sch. Art Inst. Chgo. (life), NOW, Sierra Club, Lincoln Park Zool. Soc., Nat. Anti-Vivisection Soc. (life), Humane Soc. U.S., World Wildlife Fund, African Wildlife Found. Office: 6415 N Sheridan Rd Apt 1208 Chicago IL 60626-5304

CHRISCO, SUZANNE ELAINE, nurse, employment recruiter; b. Milw., Feb. 1, 1955; d. Irvin Robert and Colleen Sue (Stivers) Rinehart; m. Gary Steven Chrisco, June 24, 1978 (div. Mar. 1992); children: Adam Carl, Luke Irvin, Thomas Andrew. AS in Nursing, Mesa State Coll., 1978; BS with Distinction in Mgmt. Human Resources, Colo. Christian U., 1992. Critical care nurse numerous hosps., Denver, 1978-84; musician, pres. Zion Flight, Inc., Englewood, Colo., 1984—; perinatal nurse specialist Healthdyne Perinatal Svcs. Inc., Atlanta, Ga., 1992—; mgr. hosp. accts. Med. Express, Inc., Boulder, 1994; voice coach, 1984-94. Mem. adv. bd. Project C.U.R.E., Evergreen, Colo., 1991—; bd. dirs. March of Dimes, Grand Junction, Colo., 1992-93. Mem. Vineyard Christian Fellowship Ch. Office: Med Express Inc 3850 38th St Boulder CO 80301

CHRISCOE, CHRISTINE FAUST, industrial trainer; b. Atlanta, Oct. 29, 1950; d. Henry Charles and Shirley Faye (Birdwell) Faust; B.A., Spring Hill Coll., 1973; postgrad. Ga. State U., 1974—; m. Ralph D. Chriscoe, June 25, 1983. Trainer, Fed. Res. Bank, Atlanta, 1973-77; project mgr., tng. dept. Coca Cola U.S.A., Atlanta, 1977-79, sr. project mgr., 1979-81, mgr. tech. tng., 1981-84, mgr. sales, mgmt. and mktg. tng., 1984-85, mgr. bottler tng., 1984-85; mgr. human resources devel., 1986-88; mgr. tng. and devel., 1988-90; pres. Christine Chriscoe and Assocs., 1990—, Ga. Pacific Corp., 1990—, dir. human resources devel., 1990-92, dir. human resources devel. and planning, 1992—; speaker Best of Am. Human Resource Conf., Ga. State U., Nat. Soc. Performance Improvement. Trustee Ga. Shakespeare Festival. Mem. ASTD (speaker), Internat. TV and Video Assn., Soc. for Applied Learning Techs., Tng. Dirs.' Forum (bd. dirs.), Human Resources Planning Soc. Roman Catholic.

CHRISMAN, DIANE J., librarian; b. Lackawanna, N.Y., June 20, 1937; d. Floyd R. and Elizabeth R. (Nowakowski) Schutta. B.A., U. Vt., 1959; M.S.L.S., Simmons Coll., 1960. Asst. head Crane br. Buffalo & Erie County Pub. Library, 1961-64, asst. head young adult dept., 1964-65, asst. head order dept., 1965-68, coordinator children div., 1968-79, dep. dir., 1979—; lectr. SUNY-Buffalo, 1966-68, 80, 90-94. Contbr. articles to profl. jours. Mem. ALA, N.Y. Libr. Assn., Zonta (past pres.). Home: 78 Rainbow Ter Orchard Park NY 14127-2517 Office: Buffalo & Erie County Pub Libr Lafayette Sq Buffalo NY 14203-1821

CHRIST, BARBARA HELEN, accountant; b. Wilmington, Del., 1958. BS in Acctg., U. Del., 1980. CPA, Pa.; CPCU; cert. mgmt. acct.; assoc. in ins. acctg. and fin.; cert. fin. examiner. Audit supr. Price Waterhouse, Zurich, Switzerland, 1980-85; audit sr. Price Waterhouse, Phila., 1985-86; audit supr. Coopers & Lybrand, Phila., 1986-87; account specialist CIGNA Cos., Phila., 1988-91; exam. mgr. Pa. Dept. Ins., Harrisburg, 1991—. Instr. ARC, West Chester, Pa., 1976-91; treas. Fairmount Park Coun. for Historic Sites, Phila., 1991-94. Mem. AICPA, Pa. Inst. CPAs, Inst. Cert. Mgmt. Accts., Soc. Fin. Examiners, Ins. Data Mgmt. Assn.

CHRIST, KATHY SCOTT, advertising executive; b. Hartford, Conn., July 6, 1951; d. Arthur Herman and Elizabeth M. (McCombe) C.; m. Paul J. Arnini, Jan. 17, 1969 (div. Apr. 1970); 1 child, June Elizabeth. Diploma, U. Conn., 1972. Asst. to v.p. adminstrn. Nat. Telephone Co., East Hartford, Conn., 1972-74; adminstrv. asst. Downtown Council, Hartford, 1974-76; exec. asst. to chmn. Imaginetics Internat., Unionville, Conn., 1977-78; mgr. sales and mktg. Info-Dial Corp., Bloomfield, Conn., 1979-80; mktg. dir. Southerby Prodns., Long Beach, Calif., 1982; account exec. to advt. sales mgr. King Videocable Co., Lake Elsinore, Calif., 1982—. Dir. pub. relations Hartford Easter Seals Rehab. Softball Marathon, 1980; mem. Students at Risk Adv. Com. Elsinore Union High Sch. Dist., 1987—; bd. dirs. Substance Abuse Council, SW Riverside County, 1987—; media coord. United Way telethon, 1989. Mem. Cable Advt. Bur., Bus. and Profl. Women, Lake Elsinore Valley C. of C., Temecula Valley C. of C., Greater Hartford Women's Softball Club (spokesman, mgr. 1978-80). Republican. Office: King Videocable Co 556 Birch St Lake Elsinore CA 92530-2725

CHRISTEL, MARY TERESE, secondary school educator; b. Chgo., July 18, 1957; d. Walter L. and Isabel M. (Ritter) C. BSS, Northwestern U., 1979; MA, Columbia Coll., 1988. Tchr. Adlai E. Stevenson High Sch., Lincolnshire, Ill., 1979—. Contbr. articles to profl. jours.; co-editor Scriptor, 1991—. Recipient fellowship NEH, Bloomington, Ill. 1989, Kenosha, Wis., 1990, Chgo., 1992; named Educator of Month Coca Cola Bottlers, Nov., 1992. Mem. NEA, Ill. Edn. Assn., Nat. Coun. Tchrs. of English (commn. on media edn. 1994), Ctr. for Media Literacy. Office: 1 Stevenson Dr Lincolnshire IL 60069-2824

CHRISTEN, LYNNE ROBBINS, banking officer, public relations specialist; b. Opp, Ala., Jan. 9, 1946; d. Farrell Gaston and MaryNell (Woodham) R.; m. Johnny David Hughes, July 15, 1971 (div. Feb. 1974); m. Henry Tiffany Christen Jr., Jan. 26, 1975; children: Eric Robbins, Ryan Gallagher. Student, Auburn U., 1964-65; AA, Clayton State U., 1975; interior design cons. designation, ICS Inst., Scranton, Pa., 1981. Accredited pub. rels. profl. Flight attendent, supr. Eastern Air Lines, Atlanta, 1965-86; career devel. cons. Careers Plus, Mary Esther, Fla., 1987—; pvt. banking officer for Okaloosa-Walton County AmSouth Bank of Fla., Ft. Walton Beach; prof. pub. speaker N.W. Fla., 1988—. Author: (manual) Be Your Own Decorator, 1984; columnist local periodical, 1988; contbr. bus. related articles to various jours. Mem. adv. bd. Ft. Walton Beach H.S., Okaloosa Med. Assistance Clinic, Okaloosa Econ. Devel. Program Com.; bd. dirs. ARC, Emerald Coast chpt. Recipient award of distinction N.W. Fla. Pub. Rels. Assn., 1990. Mem. NAFE, Ft. Walton Beach C. of C. (editor Coast Lines mag. 1990-93, Outstanding Mem. of Yr. 1989), Leadership C. of C. (grad. 1989). Republican. Methodist. Home: 390 Angela Ln Mary Esther FL 32569-1612 Office: AmSouth Bank 25 NE Beal Pkwy PO Box 4069 Fort Walton Beach FL 32548

CHRISTENSEN, BARBARA, amusement ride company executive; b. Passaic, N.J., Jan. 31, 1938; d. Edward V.N. and Adriana (Van Gurp) Myers; m. Robert D. Christensen, June 15, 1968 (div. Sept. 1978); 1 child, Darryl Lee. BS, Trenton State Coll., 1959. Client svc. rep. Leo Burnett Advt. Agy., Chgo., 1970-73; adminstr. Mich. State Assessors Bd., Lansing, 1973-83; judge State of Mich. Tax Tribunal, Lansing, 1983-87; dir. Coopers & Lybrand, Detroit, 1987-91; corp. pres. Etcetera, Inc., Las Vegas, Nev., 1991—; speaker in field; cert. instr. U. Mich. and community colls. Contbr. articles to profl. jours., newspapers, mags.; author: Michigan Assessors Training Manual, 1975, Assessing Made Simple, 1977, Historical Book, 1971. Named Mich. Woman Newspaper Columnist of Yr. Mem. Nat. Assn. Rev. Appraisers, Inst. Property Taxation, Internat. Assn. Assessing Officers, Soc. Real Estate Appraisers, Assn. Equalization Dirs., Woman's Press Club. Office: Etcetera Inc 2620 S Maryland Pky Ste 361 Las Vegas NV 89109-1673

CHRISTENSEN, CAROLINE, vocational educator; b. Lehi, Utah, Oct. 5, 1936; d. Byam Heber and Ruth (Gardner) Curtis; m. Marvin Christensen, June 16, 1961; children: Ronald, Roger, Robert, Corlyn, Richard, Chad. BS, Brigham Young U., 1958, MS, 1964. Sec. Brigham Young U., Provo, Utah, 1954-58; instr. bus. Richfield (Utah) High Sch., 1958-61, Sevier Valley Applied Tech. Ctr., Richfield, 1970-92. Historian, Sevier Sch. Dist. PTA, 1968, 69; chmn. Heart Fund Dist., 1983, Voting Dist., 1988-90; dist. chmn. Am. Cancer Drive, 1994. Mem. Utah Edn. Assn., Am. Vocat. Assn., Utah Vocat. Assn., Nat. Bus. Edn. Utah Bus. Edn. Assn. (sec. 1986-87), NEA, Western Bus. Edn. Assn., Sevier Valley Tech. Tchrs. Assn. (sec. 1971-92, pres. 1986-87), Delta Pi Epsilon (historian), Delta Kappa Gamma (treas. 1975-90, pres. 1990-92, state nominating com. 1993—, state treas. 1993—), Phi Beta Lambda (advisor 1988-92).

CHRISTENSEN, DONNA RADOVICH, crafts consultant, educator; b. Midvale, Utah, Sept. 16, 1925; d. Daniel and Clara Ellen (Turley) Radovich; B.A., U. Utah, 1947; M.A. Columbia U., 1951; m. John Whittaker Christensen, Feb. 2, 1952; children: Carlyn M. Christensen Szalanski, John Chipman, Craig Whittaker. Tchr. and guidance counselor Jordan High Sch., Sandy, Utah, 1947-50; sec. Placement Bur. of Columbia U. Tchr.'s Coll., N.Y.C., 1950-51; free-lance designer of needlecrafts, 1970—; tchr. of needlecraft, 1965—; tchr. 18th Century painted finishes Isabel O'Neil Found. for Art of Painted Finish, N.Y.C., 1975-77; cons. in crafts, 1965—. V.p. Silvermine Guild of Artists, 1965-68, hospitality chmn., 1958-65. Recipient Service award Silvermine Guild, 1963, Journeyman's medallion O'Neil Studio, 1974. Mem. Embroider's Guild of Am., Needle and Bobbin Club (v.p. 1977-82, pres. 1982-89, bd. dirs. 1989-91), New Canaan Sewing Group (exec. bd. 1977-81), Phi Kappa Phi, Pi Lambda Theta, Kappa Delta Pi. Mormon. Club: New Canaan Garden (exec. bd. 1972-77, v.p. 1987-89, pres. 1989-91), Federated Garden of Conn. Inc. (asst. civic devel. chmn. 1991-93). Home: 788 Ponus Ridge New Canaan CT 06840-3412

CHRISTENSEN, IRENE, artist; b. Oslo, Apr. 12, 1945; came to the U.S., 1968; d. Frank Marlow and Gerd (Nicelaysen) C.; m. Nicholas V. Steiner, Apr. 19, 1968 (div. 1988); children: Mark, Nadine; m. Finn Fjeldberg, July 29, 1988. Student, Oslo Engring. Sch., 1967, Art Student League, N.Y.C., 1978-81. One-person shows include Norwegische Tage, Ingelheim am Rhein, Germany, 1983, Goldome Bank, N.Y.C., 1983, Royal Norwegian Consulate, N.Y.C., 1987, Ward-Nasse Gallery, N.Y.C., 1992, Carlos Williams Ctr. for Arts, Rutherford, N.J., 1993, Kristal Gallery, Warren, Vt., 1994, Union Camp Corp., N.J., 1994; exhibited in numerous group shows including Art Ctr. No. N.J., 1977, Art Expo 89, N.Y.C., Dallas City Hall, 1990, Bergen Mus. Art and Sci., N.J., 1991, LNM Gallery, Oslo, Norway, 1992, Lever House, N.Y.C., 1992, Centro Cultural Recoleta, Buenos Aires, Argentina, 1992, Emerging Collector, N.Y.C., 1993, Brooke Alexander Gallery, N.Y.C., 1993, Barn Gallery, N.J., 1993, City Without Walls, Newark, 1993, Behn Shahn Gallery, N.J., 1993, Johnson & Johnson Corp. Art Gallery, N.J., 1993, Nabisco Gallery, N.J., 1993, Seton Hall U., N.J., 1994, Fairleigh Dickinson U., N.J., 1994, Jain Marunouchi Gallery, N.Y.C., 1994, Ctr. Gallery, Demarest, N.J., 1994, Cork Gallery, N.Y.C., 1994. Mem. Assn. Norwegian Visual Artists. Home: 99 Palmer Ave Tenafly NJ 07670-2639

CHRISTENSEN, JEAN KANESKI, counselor; b. Detroit, Dec. 6, 1934; d. Vincent John and Anne Hendricka (Zackiewicz) Kaneski; m. Leon Ross Christensen, June 18, 1955 (div. Dec. 1979); children: Holly Anne, Laurel Kay, Bari Lee, Peter Vincent. BA, Wayne State U., 1956; MA, U. Mich., 1973. Lic. counselor, Mich. Counselor freshman studies Detroit Inst. Tech., 1973-74; dir. women's resource ctr. Schoolcraft Coll., Livonia, Mich., 1974-82, asst. dean comty. svc., 1982-85; dir. human resources Lake Mich. Coll., Benton Harbor, 1985-86, v.p. student svcs. and human resources, 1987-89, v.p. student and comty. resources, 1989-91, counselor, coord. spl. populations, 1993—; pres., sec., treas. Mich. C.C. Cmty. Svcs. Assn., Livonia, 1975-85. Bd. dirs. Am. Cancer Soc., Benton Harbor, 1987-88, Girl Scouts Am., Sturgis, Mich., 1987-89; mem. Dedicated Orgns. Now United to Serve, Benton Harbor, 1993—, Animal Aid, Benton Harbor, 1986—; founder Mich. Women's Hall of Fame. Recipient Salute to Women award AAUW, 1985; named Woman of Yr., Bus. and Profl. Women, 1984. Mem. Nat. Bd. Cert. Counselors (cert.), Mich. Counseling Assn., Mich. Occupational Spl. Populations Assn., Mich. Women's Studies Assn., Mich. Coll. Pers. Assn., Tri County Coalition on Alcohol and Other Drugs (bd. dirs., treas. 1986-94). Home: 5660 Woodland Watervliet MI 49098 Office: Lake Mich Coll 2155 E Napier Benton Harbor MI 49022

CHRISTENSEN, JOAN K., state legislator; children: Cara, David, Laura, Michael. Grad., Met. Bus. Coll., Chgo.; student, Syracuse U. Mem. N.Y. State Assembly, 1990—; mem. local govt., cities, small bus., labor and aging coms.; hon. mem. N.Y. State Assembly P.R./Hispanic Task Force. Liaison to Mayor's Syracuse Commn. for Women; mem. City of Syracuse (N.Y.) Bd. of Assessment Rev., 1984, Syracuse Common Coun., chair fin., taxation and assessment com., Vets. Airport, Pub. Safety, Pub. Works and Transp. Coms.; bd. dirs. Am. Heart Assn., Meals on Wheels, Paul Robeson Performing Arts Co., Eric Trust Meml. Found.; bd. dirs., vice chair Neighborhood Watch Groups of Syracuse; hon. co-chair Pregnancy Hotline Task Force; active Thursday Morning Roundtable. Recipient Svc. award Greater Eastwood C. of C., 1990, Valley Dem. of Yr. award, 1991, Onondaga County Dem. of Yr. award, 1992, Jeannette Rankin award Onondaga County Women's Polit. Caucus, 1992. Democrat. Office: NY State Assembly State Capitol Albany NY 12224*

CHRISTENSEN, KAREN KAY, lawyer; b. Ann Arbor, Mich., Mar. 9, 1947; d. Jack Edward and Evangeline (Pitsch) C.; m. Kenneth Robert Kay, Sept. 2, 1977; children: Jeffrey Smithson, Braden, Bergen. BS, U. Mich., 1969; JD, U. Denver, 1975. Bar: Colo. 1975, D.C. 1976, U.S. Supreme Ct. 1979. Atty., advisor office of dep. atty. gen. U.S. Dept. of Justice, Washington, 1975-76, trial atty. civil rights div., 1976-79; legis. counsel ACLU, Washington, 1979-80; staff atty. D.C. Pub. Defender Service, Washington, 1980-85; asst. gen. counsel Nat. Pub. Radio, Washington, 1985-93; gen. counsel Nat. Endowment Arts, Washington, 1993—; mem. D.C. Bd. Profl. Responsibility, 1990—. Mem. D.C. Bar Assn., NCA/ACLU (exec. bd. 1986-93, chair 1993), Phi Beta Kappa. Office: 1100 Pennsylvania Ave NW Washington DC 20530

CHRISTENSEN, KAREN MARIE, insurance company official, marketing consultant; b. Chgo.; d. A.W. and Charlotte (Johnson) C.; children: Cheryl Christensen, Matthew D. MacConnel. BA, U. South Fla., MBA, 1983. Mem. faculty mktg. dept. U. South Fla., Tampa, 1983-86; advanced mktg. cons. MetLife, Tampa, 1987-92; regional tng. dir. MetLife, Charlotte, N.C., 1992—. Mem. Audubon Soc. Lutheran. Office: MetLife 6100 Fairview Rd Ste 525 Charlotte NC 28210

CHRISTENSEN, LISA ANN, metallurgical engineer; b. Flint, Mich., Apr. 16, 1963; d. Robert Charles and Joan Nancy Christensen. BSMetE, Mich. Tech. U., 1985. Metall. engr. Delphi Automotive Sys. divsn. Gen. Motors, Grand Rapids, Mich., 1985—. Violinist Grand Rapids (Mich.) Parks & Recreation Orch., 1991-95. Mem. Am. Soc. Metals Internat., Minerals Metals Materials Soc. Office: Delphi Automotive Sys 2100 Burlingame Ave SW Grand Rapids MI 49509

CHRISTENSEN, MARTHA, mycologist, educator; b. Ames, Iowa, Jan. 4, 1932; d. Leo Martin and Eva (Patterson) C. BS, U. Nebr., 1953; MS, U. Wis., 1956, PhD, 1960. High sch. sci. tchr. Ralston (Nebr.) Pub. Schs., 1953-54; research assoc. U. Wis. Dept. Botany, Madison, 1960-62; asst. prof. U. Wyo. Dept. Botany, 1963-68, assoc. prof., 1968-76, prof., 1976-89, prof.

emerita, 1989—. Mem. Ecol. Soc. Am., Brit. Mycol. Soc., Mycol. Soc. Am. (pres. 1987-88). Office: U Wyoming Dept Botany Laramie WY 82071

CHRISTENSEN, SALLY HAYDEN, government executive; b. Washington, Apr. 25, 1935; d. Sharp Adolphus and Grayce Elizabeth (Long) Hayden; m. John William Christensen, Mar. 24, 1969; children—John Stephen, Donna Isabelle. Student Dunbarton Coll. of Holy Cross, 1953-54, Am. U., U. Va. Chief higher edn. br. U.S. Office Edn., 1966-68, dep. dir. budget office, 1968-72, chief budget rev. br., 1974-80, dep. asst. sec., 1980-81, acting asst. sec., 1981, dep. asst. sec., dir. budget service, 1981—, cons. to rules and regulations task force, 1972-74. Author Congl. reports. Recipient Spl. citations Sec. Edn. and U.S. Commr. Edn., 1972, 1980, 81, 84; Pres.'s Disting. Exec. award, 1982, 88; HEW Superior Service award, 1965. Club: Arlington County Com. of 100. Home: 5415 18th St N Arlington VA 22205-3032 Office: US Dept Edn 400 Maryland Ave SW Washington DC 20202

CHRISTENSON, LYNNE ELLEN, media consultant; b. Alton, Ill., Jan. 23, 1956; d. Harlan Esterbrook and Jacqueline Ursula (Joehl) Bartlett; m. Ted Allen Christenson, Feb. 10, 1984. BS, Ea. Ill. U., Charleston, 1978. Tchr. English, Cowden (Ill.)-Herrick High Sch., 1978-80; adminstrv. asst. instrnl. TV, So. Ill. U., Carbondale, 1980-82; asst. to assoc. dean and registrar So. Ill. U. Law Sch., Carbondale, 1982-84; media asst. Group Nine Mktg., Louisville, 1984-86; media dir. Sharp Advt., Louisville, 1986-89; media cons., ptnr. ImMEDIAte, Inc., Louisville, 1989—. Mem. rape crisis team Women's Ctr., Carbondale, 1981-84; rape counselor Rape Relief Ctr., Louisville, 1984-85. Mem. Am. Women in Radio and TV (bd. dirs. Louisville chpt. 1985—, chpt. pres. 1986-87, chmn. nat. bylaws and policies com. 1989-91, area v.p. nat. bd. dirs. 1991-93), NOW (legis. watch violence against women Louisville 1989-91). Office: ImMEDIAte Inc 756 S 1st St Ste A-2 Louisville KY 40202

CHRISTIAN, LINDA MARIE, county government official; b. Helena, Mont., Sept. 22, 1949; d. Lawrence Eugene and Mary Ceona (Price) Smith; m. Dennis J. Willis Sr., July 6, 1968 (div. 1972); children: Dennis John Willis Jr., Andrew Bonnell Christian. Cert. Paralegal, Kennesaw Coll., Marietta, Ga., 1986-88; Cert. Pub. Mgmt., U. Ga. Reservations mgr. Guest Travel, Mpls., 1968-74; sales staff North Cen. Airlines, Mpls., 1974-76; mktg. and sales mgr. Internat. Travel, Tampa, Fla., 1981-82; asst. dir. ops. and maintenance Cobb Community Transit, Marietta, Ga., 1989—. Author (poetry): Battle of the Clouds, 1991 (Golden Poet award 1991). Civic leader East Cobb Civic Assn./Alpine Lakes Homeowners, Marietta, 1983-89; campaign mgr. Com. to Elect Thea Powell County Commr., Marietta, 1985-86; planning commr. Cobb County, Marietta, 1986-89; legis. liaison Cobb County Rep. Party, 1988-89; exec. com. Cobb County Rep. Party, 1988-89; legis. liaison Ga. Transit Assocs., 1991—; active mgmt.-edn. EXCEL-Cobb County. Recipient Award for Service as Planning Commr. Cobb County Bd. Commrs., 1989. Mem. Women's Transp. Seminar, Am. Planning Assn., Assn. County Commrs. (policy com. 1986-88), Am. Pub. Transp. Assn. Republican. Office: Cobb Cmty Transit 10 E Park Sq Fl 4 Marietta GA 30090

CHRISTIAN, SUZANNE HALL, financial planner; b. Hollywood, Calif., Apr. 28, 1935; d. Peirson M. and Gertrude (Engel) Hall; children: Colleen, Carolyn, Claudia, Cynthia. BA, UCLA, 1956; Master's, Redlands U., 1979; cert. in fin. planning, U. So. Calif., 1986. Cert. fin. planner. Instr. L.A. City Schs., 1958-59; instr. Claremont (Calif.) Unified Schs., 1972-84, dept. chair, 1981-84; fin. planner Waddell & Reed, Upland, Calif., 1982—, sr. account exec., 1986; corp. mem. Pilgrim Place Found., Claremont; lectr. on fin., estate and tax planning for civic and profl. groups. Author: Strands in Composition, 1979; host Money Talks with Suzanne Christian on local TV cable, 1993—. Mem. legal and estate planning com. Am. Cancer Soc., 1988—; profl. adv. com. YWCA-Inland Empire, 1987; treas. Fine Arts Scripps Coll. Recipient Silver Crest award Torchmark, 1985-87, 93, 94. Mem. Inst. Cert. Fin. Planners, Internat. Assn. Fin. Planners, Planned Giving Roundtable, Estate Planning Coun. Pomona Valley, Claremont C. of C. (pres., bd. dirs.), Curtain Raisers Club of Garrison (pres. 1972-75), Circle of Champions, Rotary (bd. dirs.), Kappa Kappa Gamma (pres. 1970-74). Home: PO Box 1237 Claremont CA 91711-1237 Office: Waddell & Reed Ste 222 1317 W Foothill Blvd Upland CA 91786-3673

CHRISTIANSON, ELIN BALLANTYNE, librarian, civic worker; b. Gary, Ind., Nov. 11, 1936; d. Donald B. and Dorothy May (Dunning) Ballantyne; m. Stanley David Christianson, July 26, 1959; children: Erica, David. BA, U. Chgo., 1958, MA, 1961, Cert. advanced studies, 1974. Asst. librarian, then librarian J. Walter Thompson Co., Chgo., 1959-68; libr. cons., 1968—; asst. prof. Grad. Libr. Sch., U. Chgo., 1981-90, Sch. Libr. and Info. Sci., Ind. U., 1982—, libr., info. svcs. cons., 1968—; editor The Libr. Quarterly Grad. Library Sch. U. Chgo., 1988-90. Chmn. Hobart Am. Revolution Bicentennial Commn., 1974-76; bd. dirs. Hobart Hist. Soc., 1973—, pres., 1980-85, 89—; pres. LWV, Hobart, 1977-79. Recipient Laura Bracken award Hobart Jaycees, 1976, Cert. Achievement Ind. Am. Revolution Bicentennial Commn., 1975; Woman of Yr. award Hobart Bus. and Profl. Women, 1985, Resident Recognition award Northwest Ind. Forum, 1988. Mem. AAUW (pres. Hobart br. 1975-77), ALA, Ind. Libr. Assn., Spl. Libs. Assn. (chmn. advt. and mktg. div. 1967-68), Assn. Library and Info. Sci. Edn., U. Chgo. Grad. Libr. Sch. Alumni Assn. (v.p. 1971-74, 76-77, pres. 1977-79). Unitarian. Author: Non-Professional and Paraprofessional Staff in Special Libraries, 1973; Directory of Library Resources in Northwest Indiana, 1976; Old Settlers Cemetery, 1976; New Special Libraries: A Summary of Research, 1980; Daniel Nash Handy and the Special Library Movement, 1980; co-author: Subject Headings in Advertising, Marketing and Communications Media, 1964; Special Libraries: A Guide for Management, 1981, rev. 3d edit., 1991; mem. editorial adv. bd. New Standard Encyclopedia, 1986—. Home: 141 Beverly Blvd Hobart IN 46342-4346

CHRISTIE, HELEN GABRIELLE, Indian tribal council official; b. Fairland, Okla., May 9, 1948; d. Kenneth Eugene and Kathe (Klein) Hill; m. George Christie, Apr. 12, 1973 (div. Apr. 1993); children: Matthew, David. AA, N.E. Okla. A&M Coll., 1968; BS in Edn., Northeastern State U., Tahlequah, Okla., 1970, postgrad., 1971-88; postgrad., U. Okla., 1991, 93. Cert. tchr., Okla.; cert. life tchr., Mo. Elem. tchr. Seneca (Mo.) R-7 Sch. Dist., 1970-78; tchr. adult edn. Inter-Tribal Coun., Inc., Miami, OKla., 1988-93, dir. Kumon math., 1990-93, dir. edn., employment and tng. programs, 1993—; curriculum designer Cultural Curriculum Guide for Communities, 1989, Four Circles of Learning, 1990. Chmn. parent com. Indian edn. programs Fairland (Okla.) Schs., 1988-93. Recipient scholarship award Mo. Congress Parents and Tchrs., 1971; grantee Wider Opportunities for Women, 1993. Mem. NAFE, Nat. Indian Adult Edn. Assn., Nat. Indian Edn. Assn., Cherokee Nation Okla., Okla. Coun. Indian Edn., Rho Theta Sigma. Democrat. Roman Catholic. Office: Inter-Tribal Coun Inc Box 1308 Miami OK 74355

CHRISTIE, JANE T., association executive; b. Stamford, Conn., Oct. 14, 1935; d. Walter Hutton Tyler and Janet Mary Roome; m. Alden Bradford Christie, June 21, 1958 (dec. Mar. 1983). BA cum laude, Radcliffe Coll., 1957; MA, Harvard U., 1958. Asst. dir. teens YWCA, Cambridge, Mass., 1958-61, dir. teens, 1962-68; transcriber Mass. Hist. Soc., Boston, 1961-62; coord. Job Corps Programs, YWCA, Balt., 1968-69, counselor, adminstr., 1969-74, assoc. exec. dir., 1974-75, exec. dir., 1976—; cons. Fuel Fund of Ctrl. Md., Balt., 1993; cons. to YWCA of U.S.A., 1990-92; mem. faculty YWCA Nat. Pres. and Exec. Dirs. Tng., 1994—. Co-author: Breakthrough: A Handbook on Racial Justice, 1975. Bd. dirs. Balt. Neighborhoods, Inc., 1991-93; mem. adv. com. on prevailing wage rates State of Md., 1992-93; mem. CHAS, Baltimore County, 1992—; chair United Way Agy. Execs. Adv. Com., 1980-84. Named Outstanding Woman Mgr. U. Balt., 1983. Mem. NAFE, Nat. Assn. YWCA Exec. Dirs., Harvard-Radcliffe Club, Hamilton St. Club. Democrat. Home: 1519 Roundhill Rd Baltimore MD 21218 Office: YWCA of the Greater Baltimore Area 128 W Franklin St Baltimore MD 21218

CHRISTINE, VIRGINIA FELD, actress; b. Stanton, Iowa, Mar. 5, 1920; d. George Allen Ricketts and Helga (Ossian) Kraft; m. Fritz Feld, Nov. 10, 1940; children: Steven, Danny. Student, UCLA, 1939-40. Actress appearing in Edge of Darkness, Mission to Moscow, The Killers, Cover Up, High Noon, The Mummy's Curse, Not as a Stranger, Cyrano, The Men, Three Brave Men, Cobweb, Body Snatchers, The Spirit of St. Louis, Johnny Tremaine, Judgement at Nuremberg, Guess Who's Coming to Dinner?, The Prize, Rage to Live, Four for Texas, 300 TV shows; spokeswoman, role of Mrs. Olson TV comml. Proctor & Gamble (Folgers), Cin., 1964-85. Hon. mayor, Brentwood, Calif.; bd. dirs. Family Planning Ctrs. Greater Los Angeles; judge Am. Coll. Theatre Festival. Recipient 1st place award Forensic League, 1937, Hall of Fame award Long Beach City Coll., 1977, citation-cultural award City of Los Angeles, 1979. Democrat.

CHRISTMAN, HELEN DOROTHY NELSON, resort executive; b. Denver, Nov. 25, 1922; d. Hector C. and Dorothy C. (Hansen) Russell; m. James Ray Christman, Aug. 7, 1942 (dec. June 1986); children: J. Randol, Linda Rae. Student, Colo. U., 1940-42. Producer Sta. KRMA-TV, Denver, 1960-62; resident mgr. Mana Kai Maui, Maui, Hawaii, 1974-76, exec. coord., 1976-78; pres. Resort Apts., Inc., 1986—; bd. dirs. Kihei Community Assn. Pres. Stephen Knight PTA, Denver, 1957; radio and TV chmn. Colo. PTA, 1958-59; producer ednl. TV programs for PTA, Denver County, 1960-61; bd. dirs. Maui United Way, 1983—, Am. Lung Assn. Hawaii, Maui; precinct pres. Maui Reps.; chmn. Maui County Rep. Com., 1989-91; mem. adv. bd. State of Hawaii Reapportionment Com., Maui, 1991—. Mem. Delta Delta Delta, Women's Golf Club (chmn. Silverswood chpt.), Maui Country Club (chmn. women's golf assn. 1987), Waiehu Women's Golf Assn. (pres. 1992-93), Maui Liquor Commn. Address: 3448 Hookipa Pl Kihei HI 96753-9216

CHRISTMAN, ODELLA FERN, special education educator; b. Kiowa, Okla., Aug. 25, 1949; d. Jake and Tommie H. (Griffin) Lambert; m. James Pete Christman, Mar. 5, 1968; children: Kacey Danielle, Bambi Michelle. BS in Elem. Edn., South Okla. State U., 1986, MEd, 1991. Tchr. spl. edn., coord. Pittsburg (Okla.) Pub. Sch., 1986—. Mem. Laubauch Literacy Coun. (cert. adult tchr.). Democrat. Baptist. Home: PO Box 148 Pittsburg OK 74560-0148 Office: Pittsburg Pub Sch PO Box 200 Pittsburg OK 74560-0200

CHRISTMAN, SHARON ANN, elementary school educator; b. Greenville, Pa., Sept. 28, 1957; d. Ronald Paul and Dorothy Janet (Ramsey) C. BS in Art Edn., Edinboro State Coll., 1979; MA, U. Ala., Tuscaloosa, 1992. Tchr. art K-6th grade Mountain Brook Schs., Birmingham, Ala., 1980—. Designer: (craft book) Christmas Is Coming, 1986, 87, 88, 90, 94. Mem. Nat. Art Edn. Assn., Internat. Soc. Edn. through Art, Kappa Delta Pi. Office: Mountain Brook Elem 3020 Cambridge Rd Birmingham AL 35223-1225

CHRISTOFFEL, KATHERINE KAUFER, pediatrician, educator; b. N.Y.C., June 28, 1948; d. George and Sonya (Firstenberg) Kaufer; m. Tom Christoffel, Oct. 11, 1970 (div. Dec. 1992); children: Kevin, Kimberly. BA, Radcliffe Coll., 1969; MD, Tufts U., 1973; MPH, Northwestern U., 1981. Diplomate Am. Bd. Med. Examiners; bd. cert. pediatrics. Asst. prof. Sch. Medicine U. Chgo., 1976-79; from asst. prof. to assoc. prof. Med. Sch. Northwestern U., Chgo., 1979-91, prof. Med. Sch., 1991—; dir. Nutrition Evaluation Clinic Children's Meml. Hosp., Chgo., 1982—; med. dir. Violent Injury Prevention Ctr. CMMC, Chgo., 1993—; chair steering com. Handgun Epidemic Lowering Plan, Chgo., 1993—; dir. Pediatric Practice Rsch. Group, Chgo., 1984—. Contbr. numerous articles to med. jours. Rsch. grantee Nat. Insts. Child Health and Human Devel., 1989-94. Fellow Am. Acad. Pediatrics (spokesperson on firearms 1985—, injury com. 1985-93, chair adolescent violence task force 1994, 1st Injury Control award 1992); mem. APHA (Disting. Career award 1991), Am. Coll. Epidemiology, Soc. for Pediatric Rsch., Ambulatory Pediatric Assn. Office: Children's Meml Hosp 2300 Children's Plz # 46 Chicago IL 60614

CHRISTOFFERSEN, SUSAN GRAY, small business owner; b. Oakland, Calif., Aug. 11, 1942; d. Edward Kiley Gray and Mabel Genevieve (Griffiths) Lee; m. Timothy Robert Christoffersen, July 24, 1965; children: Jenny, Shannon. BA, Stanford U., 1964, MA, 1965. U.S. history tchr. Leonia High Sch., N.J., 1965-67; frontier intern Nat. and World Coun. Chs., Brazil, India, Switzerland, 1967-68; U.S. history tchr. Pacifica High Sch., West Pittsburg, Calif., 1969-70; advt. chairwoman Kennedy-King Found.; bus. officer Pacific Sch. Religion, Berkeley, Calif., 1977-78; tax preparer Expatriate Tax Dept. Chevron Corp., San Francisco, 1983; from engrng. dept. to quality cons. AT&T, San Francisco, Pleasanton, Calif., 1983-88; pres. Quality Efficiency, Alamo, Calif., 1988—; substitute tchr., counselor Juvenile Hall, Martinez, Calif., 1969-75; mgr. rental properties, 1977—. Chairwoman land use subcom. East Bay Regional Parks Adv. Com., 1978-80; co-founder Las Trampas Ridgelands Assn., 1980-82; singer Gospel Choir, Community Presbyn. Ch., Danville, 1989-92. Mem. AAUW (bd. dirs. Danville, Calif. br. 1992-93), Stanford Women of East Bay. Democrat. Episcopal. Home: 234 Via Bonita Alamo CA 94507-1840

CHRISTOPHER, SHARON A. BROWN, bishop; b. Corpus Christi, Tex., July 24, 1944; d. Fred L. and Mavis Lorraine (Krueger) Brown; m. Charles Edmond Logsdon Christopher, June 17, 1973. BA, Southwestern U., Georgetown, Tex., 1966; MDiv, Perkins Sch. Theology, 1969; DD, Southwestern U., 1990. Ordained to ministry United Meth. Ch., 1970; elected bishop 1988. Dir. Christian Edn. First United Meth. Ch., Appleton, Wis., 1969-70, assoc. pastor, 1970-72; pastor Butler United Meth. Ch., Butler, Wis., 1972-76, Calvary United Meth. Ch., Germantown, Wis., 1972-76, Aldersgate United Meth. Ch., Milw., 1976-80; dist. supt. Ea. Dist. Wis. Conf. United Meth. Ch., 1980-85; asst. to bishop Wis. Conf. Wis. Confs. United Meth. Ch., Sun Prairie, Wis., 1986-88; bishop North Cen. jurisdiction United Meth. Ch., Minn., 1988—. Contbr. articles and papers to religious publs. Bd. dirs. Nat. Coun. Chs. of Christ, 1988—, United Meth. Ch. Bd. of Ch. & Soc., 1988-92, bd. discipleship, 1992—; bd. dirs. Walker Meth. Health Ctr., Mpls., 1988—, Meth. Hosp., Mpls., 1988—, Nat. United Meth. Clergywomen, 1992—; trustee Hamline U., St. Paul, 1988—; gen. and jurisdictional conf. del., 1976, 80, 84, 88; mem. N. Cen. Jurisdiction Com. on Episcopacy, 1984-88, Com. on Investigation, 1980-88, Gen. Bd. Global Ministries, 1980-88, chmn. Mission Pers. Resources Program Dept., 1984-88. Named one of Eighty for the Eighties, Milw. Jour., 1980.

CHRISTY, AUDREY MEYER, public relations consultant; b. N.Y.C., Mar. 11, 1933; d. Mathias J. and Harriet Meyer; m. James R. Christy, Apr. 19, 1952; children: James R., III, Kathryn M. Smith, John T., Alysia A. Coleman, William J. BA, U. Buffalo, 1967. Pub. rels. officer Turgeon Bros., Buffalo, 1968-69; mem. pub. rels. staff Sch. Fine Arts, U. Nebr., Omaha, 1972; pub. rels. exec. Mathews & Clark Advt., Sarasota, Fla., 1974-75; profiles editor Tampa Bay mag., Tampa, Fla., 1972; pub. rels. cons. Bildex Corp., 1973-79; owner, operator Christy & Assocs., Venice, Fla., 1976-94; dir. mktg. comm. Northern Trust Bank, Naples, 1994—. Trustee Big Bros./Big Sisters of Sarasota; vice chmn. Erie County March of Dimes, 1970; bd. dirs. Sarasota chpt. Am. Cancer Soc., Manasota (Pvt.) Industry Coun., 1987-89; mem. S.W. Fla. Ambulance Adv. Com., 1981; pres. Community Health Edn. Coun. Recipient various advt. awards. Mem. Pub. Rels. Soc. Am. (Outstanding Pub. Svc. award 1984), Fla. Hosp. Assn., Nat. Assn. Women Bus. Owners (charter mem. Sarasota chpt.), Sarasota County C. of C. (v.p., bd. dirs. 1990-91, vice chmn. mktg. 1984-85, 85-86, 86-87, 88-90, 90, vice chmn. 1989-90), Sarasota Manatee Press Club, LWV (editor Sarasota publ. 1978-79). Home: 216 Bayshore Cir Venice FL 34285-1407 Office: Christy & Assoc 100 W Venice Ave Ste L Venice FL 34285-1928

CHRONISTER, CONNIE SUE, critical care nurse; b. Massillon, Ohio, Apr. 30, 1959; d. Gene Lee and Norma Jean (Harrold) Bender; m. Bret Charles Chronister, Oct. 10, 1981; children: Tyler Charles, Nathan Bret. BSN cum laude, Kent State U., 1981; MSN, Case Western Res. U., 1992. RN, Ohio; cert. ALS provider, Am. Heart Assn.; cert. critical care nurse, AACN. Staff nurse med.-surg. Doctor's Hosp., Massillon, Ohio, 1981-83, staff nurse critical care, 1984-87; office nurse Primary Stark Med. Specialties, Massillon, Ohio, 1984-87; staff nurse critical care Medina (Ohio) Gen. Hosp., 1986—; rsch. asst. Case Western Res. U., 1992-93. Contbr. articles to profl. jours. Recipient Eight and Forty Nurses' scholarship The Am. Legion, 1991, The Heritage scholarship Massillon Community Hosp., 1991, Mellen scholarship Case Western Res. U., 1990-91, Ind. scholarship Case Western Res. U., 1990; grantee in field. Mem. AACN, Ohio Nurses' Assn., Respiratory Nursing Soc., Ohio Coalition Nurses with Specialty Certification, Sigma Theta Tau, Delta Xi. Home: 2825 Sharon Copley Rd Medina OH 44256-7409

CHRONISTER, ROCHELLE BEACH, state legislator; b. Neodesha, Kans., Aug. 27, 1939; m. Bert Chronister, 1961; children: Pam, Phillip. AB, U. Kans. State rep. dist. 13 Kans. Ho. of Reps.; former asst. majority leader; chmn. Kans. Rep. Party, 1989—. Named Woman of Yr., Neodesha C. of C. Mem. AMA (aux.), Bus. and Profl. Women. Methodist. Home: RR 2 Box 321 A Neodesha KS 66757-9562 Office: Kans Ho of Reps State Capitol Topeka KS 66612*

CHRONISTER, VIRGINIA ANN, school nurse, educator; b. York, Pa., Sept. 25, 1940; d. Ernest B. and Mary L. (Anderson) Stokes; m. Burton F. Chronister, June 13, 1964; children: Scott E., Karen A. Student, York Jr. Coll., Millersville (Pa.) Coll.; diploma, Harrisburg (Pa.) Hosp., 1961; BS in Profl. Arts, St. Joseph's Coll., North Windham, Maine, 1985; M. (equivalency), Pa. State U., 1989; postgrad., St. Joseph's Coll., North windham, Maine. RN, Pa.; cert. sch. nurse (edn. specialist II), Pa. Charge nurse Harrisburg Hosp., 1961-64; instr., practical nurses York Cty Sch. Dist., 1964-68; instr., med. secs. Yorktowne Bus. Inst., York, 1985; sch. nurse West York Sch. Dist., York, 1985—; substitute sch. nurse, 1972-85. Recipient Cardiac Nursing award. Mem. NEA, AAUW, Pa. State Edn. Assn. (sch. nurse sect.), Pa. Sch. Health Assn., Nat. Assn. Sch. Nurses, Harrisburg Hosp. Alumnae Assn., Yourk County Sch. Nurse Assn. (pres. 1991-92), United Ostomy Assn. (charter mem.), West York Area Edn. Assn. (pres. 1993—), York County Coord. Coun., Beta Sigma Phi. Home: 2090 Loman Ave York PA 17404-4214

CHRYSSA, sculptor; b. Athens, Greece, 1933. Student, Academie de la Grande Chaumiere, Paris, France, 1953-54, Calif. Sch. Fine Arts, 1954-55. One-woman shows include, Guggenheim Mus., N.Y.C., 1961, Cordier and Ekstrom Gallery, N.Y.C., 1962, Betty Parsons Gallery, N.Y.C., 1961, Mus. Modern Art, N.Y.C., 1963, Inst. Contemporary Arts, Phila., 1965, Pace Gallery, N.Y.C., 1966, 68, Walker Art Ctr., Mpls., 1968, Harvard, 1968, Obelisk Gallery, Boston, 1969, Gallery der Spiegel, Cologne, Germany, 1969, Gallery Rive-Droite, Paris, 1969, Whitney Mus., N.Y.C., 1972, Mus. d'Art Contemporain, Montreal, 1974, Mus. d'Art Modern de la Ville de Paris, 1979; group shows include exhbns., Whitney Mus. Am. Art, N.Y.C., 1960, 61, 62, 64, 66, 69, Mus. Modern Art, 1960-61, 63, 64, 66, 67, 72, Carnegie Instn., 1961, 64, Seattle World's Fair, 1963, VII Biennial, São Paulo, Brazil, 1963, 1963, Stedjlik van Abbemuseum, Eindhoven, Holland, 1966, Inst. Contemporary Art, Boston, 1966, Art Inst. Chgo., 1966, Yale Art Gallery, 1967, Los Angeles County Mus., Phila. Art Mus., 1967, Documenta, Kassel, Germany, 1968 Albright-Knox Art Gallery, Buffalo, 1982, Leo Castelli Gallery, 1988, 91; represented in permanent collections, Mus. Modern Art, Whitney Mus., Guggenheim Mus., Chase Manhattan Bank, Met. Mus. Art, all N.Y.C., Albright-Knox Gallery, Buffalo, Walker Art Ctr., Mpls., Boise Cascade Corp., Idaho, Hirshhorn Mus., Corcoran Gallery of Art, both Washington, Tate Gallery, London. *

CHRYSSIKOS, ALEXANDRA G., secondary education educator; b. Welch, W.Va., Jan. 22, 1924; d. James and Virginia (Farasly) G.; m. Paul Nicholas Chryssikos, Dec. 5, 1944; children: Telemac P., Virginia A. BS in Edn., Concord State Tchrs. Coll., 1953; Masters, W.Va. U., 1962. 6th grade tchr. Ramsey Elem. Sch., Bluefield, W.Va., 1953-56; 4th-6th grade tchr. Cumberland Heights Elem. Sch., Bluefield, W.Va., 1956-68, Whitethorn Elem. Sch., Bluefield, W.Va., 1968-83; jr. high-high sch. tchr. Windy Mountain Learning Ctr., Bluefield, W.Va., 1983—. Contbr. articles to profl. jours. Pres. Bluefield Jr. Woman's Club, 1959-60. Mem. AAUW (pres. 1966-68), Assn. Tchr. Edn. (pres. 1971-72), Alpha Delta Kappa. Home: 1236 College Ave Bluefield WV 24701

CHU, ESTHER BRINEY, retired educator; b. Bluff City, Ill., Jan. 27, 1911; d. John and Charlotte (Shaw) Briney; m. H.T. Chu, Apr. 19, 1935 (dec. May 1983); children: David S.C., Edna S.C., George S.T. BA, U. Ill., 1935, MA, 1936; PhD, Northwestern U., 1942. Prof. history Hunter Coll., N.Y.C., 1943-45, 55-58; prof. history Jersey City (N.J.) State Coll., 1959-75, prof. emeritus, 1976; pres., faculty assoc. day coun., exec. com. Jersey City State Coll., 1960-75; founder Can. studies program, New Jersey Colls. Author: Briney Families, 1976, Briney Patriots Pioneers and Families, 1979, Briney Families Coast to Coast, 1989. Past pres. YWCA, Mt. Vernon, N.Y.; bd. dirs. Pilgrim Place, Claremont, Calif., 1984-92; chmn. Young People's Dem. Club, Schuyler County, Ill., 1932-33, UN Women's Guild, Westchester County, N.Y., 1951-60. Named Outstanding Educator of Am., 1971, Ill. Coll. scholar, 1931; Northwestern U. fellow, 1938. Mem. Am. Hist. Assn. (life), AAUP (pres. coll. chpt. 1970-72, nat. com. W 1972-75), AAUW, Assn. Can. Studies in U.S., LWV (pres. 1982-83), Phi Alpha Theta. Democrat. Episcopalian. Home: 2734 Mountain View Dr La Verne CA 91750-4312

CHUA, CHRISTINA YEE-WAI, financial advisor; b. Hong Kong, Hong Kong, Aug. 9, 1959; arrived in U.S., 1976; d. Hung-Tih Hendrick and Mai-King (Lam) C. B in Nursing, U. New Brunswick, 1982. Primary nurse Dr. Everett Chalmer's Hosp., Fredericton, N.B., Can., 1982, Dr. Rafik Sarkissian, Beverly Hills, Calif., 1983-84; sales asst. Shearson Lehman Brothers, Inc., L.A., 1984-86, fin. cons., 1986-87; fin. cons. Shearson Lehman Hutton, Inc., Century City, Calif., 1987-88; fin. advisor Great Western Fin. Securities, San Gabriel, Calif., 1989-90; v.p. Calif. One Investment Corp., Pasadena, 1990-91; exec. dir. Linsco/Pvt. Ledger/Grattan Fin. Strategies, Glendale, Calif., 1991—; CEO C.J. Rockwell, Inc., Glendale, Calif., 1991—; chmn., CEO Y.W. Rockwell, Glendale, Calif., 1993—, Y.W. Rockworld Inc., Glendale, Calif., 1994—; ceo C.J. Rockwell, Inc., Glendale, 1991—; lectr. in field, 1991—. Dir., lectr. fin. seminar United Community Ch. Glendale, 1991—, vice-chmn. women fellowship 1992-93), Pasadena Chinese Am. Assn. Office: YW Rockwell 1147 E Broadway St Ste 517 Glendale CA 91205 also: CJ Rockwell Inc 1280 Terminal Way Ste 3 Reno NV 89502 also: Rockworld Inc 1130 E Broadway Ste 128 Glendale CA 91205

CHUBB-HALE, VIRGINIA MIGNON, adult education educator; b. Roanoke, Va., Nov. 3, 1942; d. Leon and Perneller (Delaney) Chubb; m. David Lee Hale; 1 child, Brian. BS, Bluefield State Coll., 1966; MEd, U. Va., 1972. Tchr. Amherst (Va.) County Sch. Bd., 1966-67; tchr. Roanoke City Schs., 1967-85, 86—, tchr. adult edn., 1971-75, tchr. gifted program, 1979; coordinator elementary social studies Roanoke City Sch. Bd., 1985-86. Author: Outstanding Blacks in Roanoke Past and Present, 1983. Mem. Roanoke Cath. Sch. Bd., 1970-74, Comm. on Christian Edn., 1979-82; chmn. Christian Edn., 1975-77; sponsor Safety Patrol, 1970-87, Y-Teens, 1979-81; pres., founder NW Investor; bd. dirs. Harrison Heritage and Cultural Ctr. Named Outstanding Woman SW Va., Times and World News, 1983. Mem. Roanoke Edn. Assn., Va. Edn. Assn. (Mary Hatwood Futrell award 1988), Nat. Edn. Assn., Va. Council for the Social Studies (Tchr. of Yr. award 1980), Roanoke Valley Hist. Soc., Am. Assn. for Univ. Women, Bluefield State Coll. Alumni Assn. (past pres.), NAACP, Cath. Hist. Soc., Delta Kappa Gamma. Home: 2721 Cove Rd NW Roanoke VA 24017-3015

CHUNG, CONSTANCE YU-HWA (CONNIE CHUNG), broadcast journalist; b. Washington, Aug. 20, 1946; d. William Ling and Margaret (Ma) C.; m. Maurice Richard Povich. B.S., U. Md., 1969; D.J. (hon.), Norwich U., Northfield, Vt., 1974; LHD, Brown U., 1987. TV news reporter WTTG-TV, Metromedia Channel 5, Washington, 1969-71; corr. CBS News, Washington, 1971-76; TV news anchor sta. KNXT-TV, CBS, L.A., 1976-83; anchor NBC News, NBC News at Sunrise, NBC Nightly News (Saturday), NBC News Digests, NBC News, N.Y.C., 1983-86, NBC News Digest, NBC Nightly News (Saturday), NBC News Mag. 1986, 1986-87, NBC News Digests, NBC Nightly News (Saturday), NBC News Spls., 1987-89, Saturday Night With Connie Chung (CBS-TV), CBS Evening News (Sunday ed.), from 1989, CBS Evening News With Connie Chung (Sundays), 1992-93; co-anchor CBS Evening News, 1993—; host Eye to Eye, CBS News, 1993—. Recipient Emmy award for individual achievement Nat. Acad. TV Arts and Scis., 1978, 80, 87; Metro Area Mass Media award AAUW, 1971; cert. of achievement for series of broadcasts which enhanced pub. awareness of cruelties of seal harvesting U.S. Humane Soc., 1969; award Atlanta chpt. Nat. Assn. Media Women, 1973; Outstanding Excellence in News Reporting and Pub. Service award Chinese-Am. Citizens Alliance, 1973; nominated for Woman of Yr. award Ladies Home Jour., 1975; named Outstanding Young Woman of Yr., 1975; recipient award for best TV reporting Los Angeles Press Club, 1977; award for outstanding TV broadcasting Valley Press Club, 1977; Women in Communications award Calif. State U., L.A., 1979; George Foster Peabody award for programs on environment Md. Center Public Broadcasting, 1980; hon. mem. Pepperdine U.

Broadcast Club, 1981; Newscaster of Yr. award Temple Emanuel Brotherhood, 1981; Portraits of Excellence award B'nai B'rith, Pacific S.W. Region, 1980; First Amendment award Anti-Defamation League of B'nai B'rith, 1981. Office: CBS News Eye To Eye With Connie Chung 524 W 57th St Studio 47 New York NY 10019*

CHUNG, CYNTHIA NORTON, communications specialist; b. Milton, Mass., Apr. 14, 1955; d. Ralph Arnold and Mary Elizabeth (McDonald) N.; m. Chinsoo Chung; children: Sara Jane, Steven Joonmok. BFA in Archtl. and Graphic Design, U. Mass., 1977. Graphic designer Garber Travel, Inc., Brookline, Mass., 1977-78; graphic and exhibit designer Rust Craft, Inc., Dedham, Mass., 1978-80; corp. advt. artist Morse, Inc., Canton, Mass., 1980-83; pvt. practice designer Boston, 1983-84; asst. art dir. Cahners Pub. Co., Newton, Mass., 1984-86, art dir., 1986-87; art dir. Knapp, Inc., Brockton, Mass., 1987-89; customer svc. rep. TWA, Boston, 1990; communications specialist Boston Fin. Data Svcs., Quincy, Mass., 1992—. Designer graphs and charts for Vols. I and II State Budget Commonwealth of Mass., 1982; art dir. Mini Micro Systems, 1984-87. Mem. Kappa Kappa Gamma (pres. 1975-76). Roman Catholic. Home: 134 Samoset Ave Quincy MA 02169-2452 Office: Boston Fin Data Svcs Inc Two Heritage Dr Quincy MA

CHUNG, SANDRA L., healthcare facility administrator; b. Cleve., June 2, 1938; d. Gustave and Ruth (Davis) Donner; m. Charles Chung, Apr. 12, 1966 (dec. July 1994). AAS in Nursing, Cuyahoga Community Coll.; postgrad., U. Hawaii. Staff nurse emergency dept. Kaiser Permanente Med. Care Program, Honolulu, supr., grant coord. family practice program, supr. med. subspecialty clinics, clin. supr., clinic supr. Hawaii Kai Clinic; clinic supr. Kaiser Permanente Med. Care Program, Hawaii Kai Clinic, 1984—. Past. pres. Am. Cancer Soc.; rsch. bd. dirs. Am. Biog. Inst. Mem. ANA (cert. nursing adminstr., Nat. Disting. Svc. Registry), Hawaii Nurses Assn. (past pres.), Hawaii Kai Bus. and Profl. Women (past pres.), East Honolulu Pub. Health Nurses (chair adv. com.), Hawaii Horse Show Assn. (bd. dirs.), Hawaii Combined Tng. Assn. (bd. dirs.), Oahu Quarter Horse Assn. (pres.). Home: 2499 Kapiolani Blvd Apt 1803 Honolulu HI 96826-5311 Office: 333 Keahole St Honolulu HI 96825-3406

CHUN OAKLAND, SUZANNE NYUK JUN, state legislator; b. Honolulu, June 27, 1961; d. Philip Sing and Mei-Chih (Chung) Chun; m. Michael Sands Chun Oakland, June 11, 1994; 1 child, Mailene Nohea Pua Oakland. BA in Psychology and Comm., U. Hawaii, 1983. Adminstrv. asst. Au's Plumbing and Metal Works, Hawaii, 1979-90; community svc. specialist Senator Anthony Chang, Hawaii, 1984; adminstrv. asst. Smolenski and Woodell, Hawaii, 1984-86; rsch. asst., office mgr. City Coun. Mem. Gary Gill, Hawaii, 1987-90; mem. Hawaii Ho. of Reps., 1990—. Named Legis. of the Yr. Hawaii Long Term Care Assn., 1993, Healthcare Assn. Hawaii, 1993, Hawaii Psychiatric Med. Assn., 1994, Autism Soc. Hawaii, 1994. Democrat. Episcopalian. Office: State House Reps State Capitol Honolulu HI 96813-2437

CHUPELA, DOLORES CAROLE, children's librarian; b. New Brunswick, N.J., Dec. 25, 1952; d. John Joseph and Cecilia Dolores (Pazdon) C. BS, Douglass Coll., 1975; MLS, Rutgers U., 1984. Cert. tchr., N.J. Libr., Edison Pub. Libr. (N.J.), 1979—. Author: Gates to Lands of Pleasure, 1986, Thomas Alva Edison, the Wizard of Menlo Park ... his New Jersey Years, 1991; contbg. author 1984 Summer Reading Club Manual. Speaker civic orgns. Recipient Presdl. sports award in figure skating, 1980, Pub. Rels. award, Spl. Recognition award Del. Raritan Girl Scout Coun., 1990, 91; named Tercentennial Citizen-of-Week, Middlesex County, N.J., New Brunswick, 1983, named to Edison High Sch's. Hall of Honor, 1990. Mem. ALA and Assn. Libr. Svc. to Children, N.J. Libr. Assn. (1st place award 1989, pub. rels. award 1992), Rutgers Alumnae Assn. (speaker radio program), Children's Book Coun., U.S. Figure Skating Assn., Libr. Pub. Rels. Coun. (Share the Wealth award 1990), Princeton Skating Club. Democrat. Roman Catholic. Home: 51 Latonia St Edison NJ 08817-4252 Office: Edison Pub Libr 340 Plainfield Ave Edison NJ 08817-3147

CHURCH, IRENE ZABOLY, personnel services company executive; b. Cleve., Feb. 18, 1947; d. Bela Paul and Irene Elizabeth (Chandas) Zaboly; children: Irene Elizabeth, Elizabeth Anne, Lauren Alexandria Gadd, John Dale Gadd II. Grad. high sch. Pers. cons., recruiter, Cleve., 1965-70; chief exec. officer, pres. Oxford Pers., Pepper Pike, Ohio, 1973-89, Oxford Temporaries, Pepper Pike, 1979—, Oxford Group Ltd., Inc., 1989—; guest lectr. in field, 1974—; expert witness for ct. testimony, 1982—. Troop leader Lake Erie coun. Girl Scouts U.S., 1980-81; mem. Christian action com. Federated Ch., United Ch. Christ, 1981-85, sub-com. to study violence in rels. to women, 1983, creator, presenter programs How Work Affects Family Life and Re-entering the Job Market, 1981, mem. Women's Fellowship Martha-Mary Circle, 1980—, program dir., 1982-84, 87—; chpt. leader Nat. Coalition on TV Violence, 1983—; mem. The Federated Ch., United Ch. of Christ, Chagrin Falls, Ohio, program dir Mary-Martha Circle, 1982—, christian action com. 1981-85, mem. Mary-Martha Circle, Women's fellowship, 1980—; mem Better Bus. Bur., 1973-82. Mem. Nat. Assn. Pers. Cons. (cert., mem. ethics com. 1976-77, co-chairperson ethics com. 1977-78, mem. bus. practices and ethics com. 1980-82, mem. cert. pers. cons. soc. 1980-82, regional leader for membership 1987—, Pres.'s award 1988), Ohio Assn. Pers. Cons. (trustee 1975-80, 85—, sec. 1976-77, 85-87, chairperson bus. practices and ethics com. 1976-77, 81-82, 1st v.p., chairperson resolutions com. 1981-82, chairperson membership com. 1985-89, 2d v.p. 1987—, Outstanding Svc. award 1987, pres. 1988-89), Greater Cleve. Assn. Pers. Cons. (2nd then 1st v.p., 1974-76, state trustee 1975-80, pres. 1976-77, bd. advisor 1977-78, chairperson bus. practices and ethics com. 1974-76, chmn. nominating com., 1983-88, membership com. 1987-87, arbitration com., 1980, 85-87, fundraising, 1980-89, bd. dirs. 1980-89, trustee 1985-89, program chair 1987-89, Vi Pender Outstanding Svc. award 1977), Euclid C. of C. (small bus. com. 1981, chairperson task force com. evaluating funding in social security and vet.'s benefits 1981), Internat. Platform Assn., Am. Bus. Women's Assn., Nat. Assn. Temp. Svcs., Chagrin Valley C. of C. (leader Chagrin Blvd./East chpt. 1987—, Pres.'s award for Outstanding Contbns. 1988, pres. bd. dirs 1990—), Greater Cleve. Growth Assn. Coun. Small Enterprises, Rotary (vocat. svc. chairperson, program com. 1987—, membership chairperson 1988-89). Home: 8 Ridgecrest Dr Chagrin Falls OH 44022-4218

CHURCH, LORENE KEMMERER, retired government official; b. Jordan, Mont., Oct. 18, 1929; d. Harry F. and Laura (Stoller) Kemmerer; m. Scott Johnston, Sept. 8, 1948 (div. 1953); children: Linda M., Theodore O.; m. Fred C. Church, May 9, 1956; children: Ned B., Nia J. Student, Portland Community Coll., 1973-76, Portland State U., 1978-79. Sec. intelligence div. IRS, Portland, Oreg., 1973-75; trade asst. Internat. Trade Adminstrn., U.S. Dept. Commerce, Portland, 1975-84, internat. trade specialist, 1984-94; ret., 1994. Mem. NAFE, World Affairs Coun., N.W. China Coun., Portland C. of C. (Europe 1992 com. 1988-89, internat. trade adv. bd. 1988-89). Democrat. Roman Catholic. Home: 19725 SW Pike St Beaverton OR 97007-1446 Office: US Dept Commerce US&FCS 121 SW Salmon St Portland OR 97204

CHURCH, MARTHA ELEANOR, former college president; b. Pitts., Nov. 17, 1930; d. Walter Seward and Eleanor (Boyer) C. BA, Wellesley Coll., 1952; PhD, U. Pitts., 1954, U. Chgo., 1960; DSc (hon.), Lake Erie Coll., 1975; LittD (hon.), Houghton Coll., 1980; LHD (hon.), Queens Coll., 1981, Ursinus Coll., 1981, St. Joseph Coll., 1982, Towson State U., 1983, Dickinson Coll., 1987. Instr. geography Mt. Holyoke Coll., South Hadley, Mass., 1953-57; lectr. geography Ind. U. Gary Center, 1958; instr., then asst. prof. geography Wellesley Coll., 1958-59; dean coll., prof. geography Wilson Coll., 1965-71; assoc. exec. sec. Commn. Higher Edn., Middle States Assn. Coll. and Secondary Sch., 1971-75; pres. Hood Coll., Frederick, Md., 1975-95; bd. dirs. Farmers and Mechanics Nat. Bank, 1982—, Montgomery Mut. Ins. Co., 1989-90; cons. for Choice: Books for Coll. Librs.; co-chmn. nat. adv. panel nat. Ctr. for Rsch. to Improve Postsecondary Teaching and Learning, U. Mich., 1985-90; mem. bd. vis. Def. Intelligence Coll., 1988-91; mem. adv. bd. dirs. Automobile Club Md., 1991—. Author: The Spatial Organization of Electric Power Territories in Massachusetts, 1960; Co-editor: A Basic Geographical Library: A Selected and Annotated Book List for Am. Colls, 1966; cons. editor, Change mag., 1980—. Bd. dirs. Coun. for Internat. Exchange of Scholars, 1979-80, Japan Internat. Christian U. Found., 1977-91, Nat. Center for Higher Edn. Mgmt. Systems, 1980-83; bd. dirs. Am. Coun. on Edn., 1976-79, vice chmn., 1978-79, mem. nat. identification panel, 1977—, Nat. Rsch. Com., 1993—; bd. advisors Fund for Improvement of Postsecondary Edn., HEW, 1976-79; mem. Sec. of Navy's Adv. Bd. on Edn. and Tng., 1976-80; chmn. Md. commn. on Civil Rights, 1981-82; trustee Bradford Coll., Mass., 1982-87, Peddie Sch., N.J., 1982—, Carnegie Found. for the Advancement of Teaching, 1986—, vice chairperson 1990-92, chairperson, 1992-94; trustee Nat. Geographic Soc., 1989—, chair audit review com., 1993—; trustee Nat. Geographic Soc. Edn. Found., 1989—; chmn. bd. dirs. Medici Found., Princeton, N.J., 1985—; mem. Md. Humanities Coun., 1985-86, Md. Jud. Disabilities Commn., 1985-94; commr. Edn. Commn. States, Md., 1981—; exec. com. Campus Compact: Project for Pub. and Community Svc., 1986-89. Recipient Christian R. and Mary F. Lindback Found., Disting. Teaching award Wilson Coll., 1971. Mem. AAUW, Am. Assn. Advancement of Humanities (dir. 1979-81), Am. Assn. Higher Edn. (chmn. 1980-81, bd. dirs. 1979-83), Assn. Am. Geographers, Nat. Assn. Ind. Colls. and Univs. (bd. dirs. 1983-86), Md. Ind. Colls. and Univs. Assn. (pres. 1979-81, exec. com. 1988-92), Assn. Am. Colls. and Univs. (adv. com. project on status and edn. of women 1980-85), Women's Coll. Coalition (exec. com. 1976-80, 87-89), Am. Conf. Acad. Deans (sec., editor 1969-71), Council Protestant Colls. and Univs. (bd. dirs. 1969-71), Soc. Coll. and Univ. Planning (editorial bd. 1979—), Cosmos Club, (jour. editorial bd., 1990-94), Inst. Ednl. Leadership (bd. dirs. 1982-87), Rotary Club of Frederick, Sigma Delta Epsilon. Office: Hood Coll Office of President 401 Rosemont Ave Frederick MD 21701-8575

CHURCH, MARY MITCHELL, English as second language educator; b. Highland Park, Ill., July 14, 1939; d. Robert Roy and Dania (Mavor) Mitchell; m. William Lawrence Church, June 14, 1960 (div. Jan. 1977); children: Laurel Mavor, Emily Ryan, Gwynne Dania; m. Charles A. Doehlert, June 12, 1983. BA, U. Wis., 1961. Cert tchr. elem., ESL k-12. Vol. tchr. U.S. Peace Corps, Addis Ababa, Ethiopia, 1963-65, Ahlman Acad., Kabul, Afghanistan, 1971-72; ESL tchr. Internat. Sch. of Lusaka, Zambia, 1972-74, Madison (Wis.) Met. Sch. Dist., 1977—; adj. instr. Sch. Edn. U. Wis., Madison, 1982—. Author: (textbooks) Interactions Two: A Communicative Grammar, 1985, A New Beginning, 1988, Beyond the Beginning, 1991; contbr. book. Mem. bilingual-bicultural com. Madison Sch. Bd., 1979; mem. budget com. Middleton (Wis.) Cross Plains Sch. Bd., 1981-82; vol. Afghan Relief Com., Madison, Ethiopia II. Recipient finalist Ernest L. Boyer award for Edn. Excellence, Madison Bd. Edn., 1988; named Disting. Tchr. of Tchrs., U. Wis., 1990. Mem. Tchrs. of English as a Second Operative Lang. Office: James Madison Meml HS 201 S Gammon Rd Madison WI 53717

CHURCH, MONICA DELIMA, artist, educator; b. Middlebury, Vt., Nov. 21, 1964; d. Lloyd Maurice Jr. and Anita Church; m. Robert K. Brigham. BA in Visual Arts, Bennington Coll., 1987; MFA, U. Ky., 1993. Dir. Ctr. for Contemporary Art U. Ky., Lexington, 1993-94; instr. Transylvania U., Lexington, 1994—. One-woman shows include The Cafe Joseph-Beth, Lexington, Ky., 1993, Bluegrass Airport Gallery, Lexington, 1993. Recipient Purchase award, Liquitex Excellence in Art Students Program, Binney & Smith, 1992, Merit award Anderson Fine Art Ctr., 1992, San Jacinto Coll. South, 1993. Mem. Lexington Art League, Coll. Art Assn. Office: 12 Vassar St Poughkeepsie NY 12601 Office: Box 64 Vassar Coll 124 Raymond Ave Poughkeepsie NY 12601

CHURCH, SONIA JANE SHUTTER, librarian; b. York, Pa., Dec. 15, 1940; d. Robert Benjamin and Eva Alverta (Horn) Shutter; m. Ernest Layton Church, May 20, 1966; children: Robert Bruce, Jennifer Grace. BS in Edn., Millersville Coll. 1962; MLS, U. Pitts., 1978. Playground supr. York City Sch. Dist., Pa., 1961; officer USMC, 1962-66; children's libr. Prunedale br. Monterey County Libr., Calif., 1978-79; youth svcs. coord. Monterey County Libr., 1979-83, 85-88, head libr. Prunedale br., 1983-85; children's svcs. mgr. Ventura (Calif.) County Libr., 1988—; writer Book Beat Column for Fortnighter Newspaper, Salinas 1983-85. Editor pamphlet: What Will we do with the Baby? a collection of nursery rhymes and finger plays, 1977. Mem. Deferred Comp. Task Force, Monterey County, 1983-88, Mgmt. Coun., Monterey County, 1983-88; chmn. adminstrv. com. Social Svcs. Commn., Monterey County, 1983-85, chmn. ad hoc com., 1983-88; coordinating com. Boy Scouts Am., Salinas, 1983-85; Children's Svcs. Mgmt. Consortium, 1986-87; tchr. Sun. Sch., Luth. Ch. Good Shepherd, Salinas, 1982-88; chmn. latchkey com. Child Care Task Force, Ventura County; chmn. childrens com. Black Gold Libr. System, Calif., 1991; mem. children's coord. coun. Ventura County, 1993—. Served to capt., USMC 1962-66. Recipient Celebrate Literacy award Internat. Reading Assn., 1994—, Margaret Lunch Exemplary Svc. award Calif. Reading Assn.; Sico scholar, 1958-62. Mem. ALA, Assn. Libr. Svc. to Children (liaison with nat. orgns. serving child com.), Calif. Libr. Assn. (pres. children's svcs. chpt. 1989-90, Beatty award com. 1990-92, chair Beatty com. 1993-95, children's svcs. mgmt. chpt., assembly 1991—, planning com. 1992—), Assn. Children's Librs. of No. Calif., Sch. and Pub. Librs. Assn. Monterey Bay Area (pres. 1979-80, 1985-86), Assn. Childhood Edn. Internat., Nat. Story League (co-founder Ventura County storytellers group), Calif. Reading Assn., Internat. Reading Assn., Ventura County Reading Assn. (pres. 1991-92), Ventura County Lit. Coun., So. Calif. Coun. Lit. for Children and Young People, Soc. Children's Book Writers, Am. Legion (comdr. 1984-85), Women's Internat. Bowling Congress, Women's Bowling Assn., U. Pitts. Alumni Assn., Millersville Univ. Alumni Assn., Beta Phi Mu, Beta Sigma Phi. Democrat. Lutheran. Home: 5110 W Wooley Rd Apt 2 Oxnard CA 93035-1858 Office: Ventura County Libr 651 E Main St Ventura CA 93001-2814

CHURCHILL, MARILYN J., special education program coordinator; b. Lawrence, Mass., Aug. 2, 1932; d. Ernest Lees and Doris (Adams) Chase; m. Philip Baker Churchill, June 21, 1953 (dec.); children: Wendy Louise, Jeffrey Adams. AB, Harvard U., 1968; MEd, Boston U., 1968-69. Coord. spl. needs programs Medford (Mass.) Pub. Schs. Named Horace Mann Teacher Medford (Mass.) Public Schs., 1986-87, 87-88. Mem. AAUW, NEA, MTA. Home: 55 Orchard Ln Melrose MA 02176 Office: Medford Pub Schs Winthrop St Medford MA 02155-5314

CHWATSKY, ANN, photographer, educator; b. Phila., Jan. 11, 1942; BS in Art Edn., Hofstra U., 1965, MS, 1971; postgrad. L.I. U., 1973-74. Cert. tchr. Photography editor L.I. mag., 1976-80; instr. Internat. Ctr. Photography, N.Y.C., 1979-80, Parrish Art Mus., Southampton, N.Y., 1984—; mem. faculty L.I. U., Greenvale, N.Y., 1982—; dir. master art workshop Southampton Coll., 1985—; mem. art faculty NYU, 1991—. Author, photgrapher The Man In The Street, 1989; photographer The Four Seasons of Shaker Life; photographs featured in Time, Newsweek, Newsday, Manchete, N.Y. Times, MD Medical Times; one person shows include Photographers Gallery, London, 1985, Shakers, Nassau County Mus. Fine Arts, 1987, Greater Lafayette (Ind.) Mus. Art, 1988, Brooklyn Coll., 1990, Kiev, USSR Exhibition Hall, 1991, Brooklyn Coll., Lincoln Ctr., Buenos Aires, 1993; group shows include The Other, Houston Ctr. Photography, 1988, L.I. Fine Arts Mus., 1984, Women's Interart Ctr., N.Y.C., 1976, 80, Parrish Art Mus., Southampton, 1979, Internat. Ctr. Photography, N.Y.C., 1980, 82, Nassau County Mus. Fine Arts, 1983, Soho 20 Gallery, N.Y.C., 1984, New Orleans World's Fair, 1984, Southampton Gallery, 1988, 89, Lizan Tops Gallery, L.I., 1994; represented in permanent collections: Forbes N.Y.C. Midtown YWCA, Nassau County Mus. Fine Arts, Susan Rothenberg, others. Bd. dirs. Rosa Lee Young Day Care Ctr., Rockville Centre, 1982—. Recipient Estabrook Disting. Alumni award Hofstra U., 1984; Kodak Profl. Photographers award, 1984; Eastman Found. grantee, 1981-82; Polaroid grantee, 1980. Mem. Assn. Am. Mag. Profls., Picture Profls. Am., Profl. Women Photographers N.Y.C. Democrat. Jewish. Avocations: tennis, gardening. Home: 111 4th Ave # 7C New York NY 10003 also: 29 E 22nd St # 3N New York NY 10010

CHYPRE, ELIZABETH, silversmith, business owner; b. N.Y.C., July 30, 1938; d. Henry and Irma Mendez; m. John R. Petrak, June 1, 1957 (div. 1972); children: John H. Petrak, James E. Petrak; m. Louis J. Chypre, Mar. 13, 1977. AA, Dutchess Community Coll., Poughkeepsie, N.Y., 1973; BS in Human & Community Svc., Empire State Coll., 1976; MS in Criminal Justice, L.I. U., 1979. Ceramist Chypre & Chypre Assocs., Rhinebeck, N.Y., 1981-87; designer, silversmith The Wordsmiths, Rhinebeck, 1988—. Editor newsletter Hudson Valley Artisan's Guild, 1991—; contbr. Against the Night, 1969, Hudson Valley Arts Rev., 1993; author: Business Sense for Craftsmen, 1992. Intern vol. Dutchess County Dept. Probation, Poughkeepsie, 1976; vol. judo instr. YMCA, 1969-71; mem. Hope Lodge Cancer Support Group, 1988—. Scholar Fashion Inst. Tech., 1955; recipient Disting. Svc. award YMCA, 1971, Freddie award Hudson Valley Ceramic Assn., 1981, 17 Blue Ribbons, 1982-86. Mem. Hudson Valley Artisan's Guild (v.p. 1991-93). Office: Chypre & Chypre PO Box 484 Rhinebeck NY 12572-0484

CIAK, BRENDA SUSAN, nurse; b. Springfield, Mass., Jan. 29, 1955; d. Stanley Peter and Jessica Evelyn (Jorkowski) Ciak; divorced, 1989. BS in Pub. Health, U. Mass., 1976, BSN, 1979, RN, 1979; MSN, Boston U., 1986. RN, Mass.; cert. in infection control; cert. gerontological nurse. Staff nurse Miriam Hosp., Providence, 1979-80; head nurse Western Mass. Kidney Ctr., Springfield, 1980-85; nurse epidemiologist Providence Hosp., Holyoke, Mass., 1985-86; infection control nurse VA Med. Ctr., Northampton, Mass., 1986—; presenter at profl. confs. Contbr. to profl. publs. Co-founder, co-chair AIDS/HIV Positive Support Group VA Med. Ctr., Northampton, 1989-92. Featured in article in Women Unltd. mag., 1991; contbr. articles to profl. jours. Mem. NAFE, Assn. Practitioners in Infection Control (elected mem. New England chpt. nominating com. 1993-94), Advanced Nursing Practice Group of Western Mass. (chairperson 1989—), Zonta Club Internat. (bd. dirs. 1992-94), Springfield Mus. and Libr. Assn., Sigma Theta Tau (chpt. archivist 1990-92). Home: 102 Wolcott St Springfield MA 01104-2418 Office: VA Med Ctr Rte 9 Northampton MA 01060

CIANCIOLO, ELIZABETH PEELER, clinical psychologist; b. Staunton, Va., Feb. 10, 1959; d. Clayton Samuel and Suzanne Elliot (Lovern) Peeler; m. Joseph Jude Cianciolo, Sept. 12, 1987; children: Catherine Grace, Joseph Clayton. BA, Mary Baldwin Coll., 1982; MA, Hofstra U., 1985, PhD, 1988. Lic. psychologist, Va.; cert. sch. psychologist, N.Y. Family and community worker Woodrow Wilson Rehab. Ctr., Fishersville, Va., 1981-83; psychometrician William Floyd Sch. Dist., Mastic Beach, N.Y., 1985; sch. psycholgoist Massapequa (N.Y.) Sch. Dist., 1986-88; neuropsychology coord. Ctr. for Rehab., Caninack, N.Y., 1988; clin. psychologist Neurol. Rehab. Assocs., Waynesboro, Va., 1988-90; sr. clin. psychologist Woodrow Wilson Rehab. Hosp., Fishersville, Va., 1990—, spinal cord rsch. com., 1991—; pvt. practice Staunton, Va., 1990—; presenter Spinal Cord Injury Rehab. Confs., Va., 1991-94; adj. prof. Mary Baldwin Coll., Staunton, 1989. Contbr. articles to profl. jours. Outreach com. Trinity Episcopal Ch., Staunton, 1989—, Christian edn. com., 1989—. Mem. AAUW, APA, Am. Assn. Spinal Cord Injury Psychologists, Psi Chi. Episcopalian. Office: Woodrow Wilson Rehab Ctr Fishersville VA 22939

CIANFLONE, JANICE LUCY, artist, educator; b. White Plains, N.Y., Dec. 13, 1952; d. Edmund John and Lucy Gloria (Casarella) C. BFA, Manhattanville Coll., 1975. Cert. art tchr., Mass. Textile/repeat artist Brewster Finishing and Designing Corp., N.Y.C., 1975-77; textile designer P. Kaufmann, Inc., N.Y.C., 1977-78; art tchr. Lura A. White Sch., Shirley, Mass., 1978—; painter on ceramics The Potting Shed, West Concord, Mass., 1979-81; children's illustrator, poet, painter. Mem. Women's Caucus for the Arts, Mass. Tchrs. Assn., NEA.

CIANGIO, CYNTHIA M., communications executive; b. Montclair, N.J., Mar. 6, 1953; d. Nicholas Gabriel and Elizabeth (Cwikla) C. AB in English, Muhlenberg Coll., 1975. Dir. pub. rels. Caldwell Coll., 1976-77; asst. dir. Libr. of the Chathams, 1977-79; freelance writer, artist Perth Amboy, N.J., 1979-81; art dir. E&B Marine, Inc., Edison, N.J., 1981-83, v.p. mktg., 1983-85; dir. advt. and communications Bell Atlantic Bus. Supplies, Exton, Pa., 1985-89; mgr. corp. media relations Bell Atlantic Corp., Phila., 1989—. Mem. Direct Mktg. Assn., Third Class Mail Assn., Bus. to Bus. Users Group, Original Equipment Mfrs. Exch., Internat. Assn. Bus. Communicators. Home: One Victorian Ct Wayne PA 19087 Office: Bell Atlantic Corp 1717 Arch St Philadelphia PA 19103-4201

CIARALDI, ANN MARIE, university official; b. Amesbury, Mass., Jan. 22, 1962; d. Edward Joseph and Janice Lee (Greaney) C. BA in Polit. Sci. and Psychology, Plymouth (N.H.) State Coll., 1984, MEd in Guidance and Counseling, 1989. Dir. residence hall Plymouth State Coll., 1984-87; area dir. U. Tampa, Fla., 1987-90; asst. dir. residence life U. Mass., Lowell, 1990—, adminstrv. jud. hearing officer, 1991—, coord. residential orientation, 1991—; workshop presenter in field; plaacement coord. New Eng. Student Affairs Placement Conf., 1992, conf. chmn., 1993, 94. Mem. Assn. Coll. Pers. Adminstrs., Assn. Coll. and Univ. Housing Officers, Nat. Assn. Student Pers. Adminstrs., Mass. Coll. Pers. Assn., Boston Area Coll. Housing Assn., NOW, Amnesty Internat. Democrat. Roman Catholic. Office: U Mass 1 University Ave Lowell MA 01854

CIAVOLA, LOUISE ARLENE, foundation executive; b. Summit Station, Ohio, July 16, 1933; d. Orus Allen and Marie Elizabeth (White) Helser; m. Rex George Ciavola, May 20, 1961; children: Rex George Jr., Todd Colby, Christina Adelina. BS in Edn. with honors, Ohio U., 1954; postgrad., U. Mich., 1959-60, 84, Western Mich U., 1960, Wayne State U., 1984. Cert. elem. and secondary tcr., Ill., Ohio, Mich. Tchr. pub. schs., Northlake, Ill., 1954-55, Cuyahoga Falls, Ohio, 1955-57, Newark, Ohio, 1957-59, Kalamazoo, 1959-60, Grosse Pointe, Mich., 1960-85; asst. dir. vols. Children's Hosp. Mich., Detroit, 1978-82; assoc. exec. dir. Cystic Fibrosis Found., Grand Rapids, Mich., 1988-89, assoc. exec. dir., Greater Mich. Chpt., 1989-92. Bd. dirs., officer Jr. Women's Assn. for Detroit Symphony Orch., 1964-70, Tennis and Crumpets, Inc., Detroit, 1975-82; bd. dirs. Midland (Mich.) Hosp. Ctr., 1985-87, Mother's Club Grosse Pointe South High Sch., 1983-84; co-founder, bd. dirs. Grosse Pointe Found. for Acad. Enrichment, 1970-85; chmn. United Found., Grosse Pointe Park, Mich., 1968; deacon Grosse Pointe Meml. Ch., Grosse Pointe Farms, Mich., 1970. Recipient award for devoted svc. Children's Hosp. Mich., 1982. Mem. NAFE, Cen. U.S. Ski Assn. (bd. dirs. 1977-81), Spring Lake Country Club, 20th Century Club (Midland), Contemporary Rev. Club (Midland), Otsego Ski Club (Gaylord, Mich.), Chimes, Silver Creek Valley C.C., Kappa Delta Pi, Phi Alpha Theta, Tau Beta. Republican. Presbyterian. Home: 6113 Country Club Pky San Jose CA 95138-2307 Office: Cystic Fibrosis Found 404 Mckay Towers Grand Rapids MI 49503

CICCONE, MADONNA LOUISE VERONICA See MADONNA

CICHOWSKI, MARYANN EMILY, tool and die executive; b. Deep River, Conn., July 6, 1918; d. Anthony C. and Zofia (Pryga) Wolak; m. Frank A. Cichowski, July 4, 1939; children: Francis A., Ronald J. Diploma in bus., New Britain Secretarial Sch., Conn., 1936; student, St. Joseph Coll., West Hartford, Conn., 1938, Newport (R.I.) Secretarial Sch., 1942. Quality control-office clk. Fafnir Bearing Co., New Britain, 1936-39; clk. typist Naval Torpedo Sta., Newport, 1942-43; office mgr. Fame Tool & Die Co., Plainville, Conn., 1955-77; treas. Fame Tool & Die Co., Inc., Plainville, Conn., 1977-82, pres., 1983—; mem. adv. bd. for New Britain/Hartford region Derby Savs.-DS Bancorp, 1993—. Treas. St. Paul's Ladies Guild, Kensington, Conn., 1970-71, v.p., 1972-73, pres., 1974-75. Mem. Conn. Bus. and Industry Assn., Polonaise Club, Inc. (treas. New Britain chpt. 1985—). Home: 28 1/2 Sunset Ln Berlin CT 06037 Office: Fame Tool & Die Co Inc 387 Woodford Avenue Ext Plainville CT 06062-2523

CIELINSKI-KESSLER, AUDREY ANN, technical writer, publisher, small business owner; b. Cleve., Sept. 10, 1957; d. Joseph and Dorothy Antoinette (Hanna) Cielinski. BJ with high honors, U. Tex., 1979. Reporter, writer Med. World News mag., N.Y.C., 1979; asst. copy chief Med. World News mag., Houston, 1983-84; free-lance writer, editor, 1984—; editorial asst. Jour Health and Social Behavior, Houston, 1980-81; sec. dept. psychiatry Baylor Coll. Medicine, Houston, 1980-81; procedures analyst, tech. writer, tech. librarian Harris County Data Processing Dept., Houston, 1981-83; communications specialist III, Wang systems adminstr. office of planning and rsch. Houston Police Dept.; tchr. tech. writing class, 1985-89; tech. writer Chevron Exploration and Prodn. Svcs. Co., Houston, 1990-92; freelance tech. writer, 1992—; owner The Write Hand, Silver Spring, Md., 1992—. Contbr. stories and articles newspapers and mags.; editor newsletters Signals, CEPS Synergy, PCLIBtm Letter, Insights. Vol. writer, graphic designer, office religious edn. St. Ambrose Roman Cath. Ch., Houston, 1983-92; vol. editor newsletters Greater Houston area Am. Cancer Soc. and VGS, Inc. Recipient Commendation award Chief of Police, Houston, Chief's Command Employee of Month award June, 1989. Mem. NAFE, Women in Comms., Nat. Assn. Desktop Pubs., Am. Med. Writers Assn., Soc. for Tech. Comm., Soc. Children's Book Writers (assoc.), Sigma Delta Chi, Phi Kappa Phi, Alpha

Lambda Delta. Home and Office: 2112 Bucknell Terr Silver Spring MD 20902-4322

CIMAROSSA, DEBORAH KAY, training supervisor, human resource consultant; b. Springfield, Ill., Feb. 14, 1956; d. Andon Theodore and Lillian Berneice (Hall) Davis; m. James Theodore Cimarossa, May 2, 1987; children: Nicholas James, Mark Joseph. BA in Mgmt. with honors, Sangamon State U., 1993. Sec. Marine Bank/Bank One, Springfield, 1974-75; pers. asst. Ill. Dept. Pub. Health, Springfield, 1975-79; adminstrv. asst. Dasher Mktg., Inc., Springfield, 1979-80; pers. mgr. City Water, Light & Power, Springfield, 1980-85, tng. supr., 1985—; pres., owner CIMCO Security and Mgmt. Cons., Springfield, 1992—. Instr., tutor in CPR, ARC, Springfield, 1988—; precinct committeewoman Sangamon County Rep. Ctrl. Com., Springfield, 1990—; county bd. mem. Sangamon County Bd., Springfield, 1993; ptnr. in edn. Hazel Dell Elem. Sch., Springfield, 1993. Mem. ASTD, Am. Pub. Power Assn., Profl. Tng. Assn. Ill., Ctrl. Ill. Tng. and Mgmt. Profls. (pres. 1994—), Women in Mgmt. (pres. 1991-92, Women of Achievement award 1988). Roman Catholic. Office: City Water Light & Power 200 E Lake Dr Springfield IL 62707-8988

CINO, MARIA, legislative staff member; b. Buffalo, Apr. 19, 1957; d. Richard J. and Lucy M. (Tripi) C. BA in Polit. Sci., St. John Fisher Coll. Project supr. Rep. Nat. Com., 1981-82, dir. local programs, 1983-84, exec. asst. field dir., 1985-86; rsch. analyst Am. Viewpoint, Inc., 1986-88; adminstrv. asst. Rep. L. William Paxon, 1989-93; exec. dir. Nat. Rep. Congl. Com., 1993—. Mem. Ho. Adminstrv. Assts. Assn., Pi Gamma Mu. Office: Nat Rep Congl Com 320 1st St SE Rm 203 Washington DC 20003*

CIOCIOLA, CECILIA MARY, educational specialist; b. Chester, Pa., Feb. 9, 1946; d. Donato Francis Pasqual and Mary Theresa (Dugan) C. BA, Immaculata Coll., 1975; MA, West Chester U., 1984. Tchr. Archdiocese of Phila., 1964-72, Harrisburg (Pa.) Diocese, 1972-74, Camden (N.J.) Diocese, 1974-76; tchr., elem. sci. chairperson Archdiocese of Phila., 1976-86; ednl. cons. Macmillan Pub. Co., Delran, N.J., 1986-88; program officer PATHS/PRISM, Phila., 1988-90; asst. exec. dir. minority engring., math., sci. program Prime, Inc., Phila., 1988—; instr. edn. dept. Chestnut Hill Coll., Phila.; cons. Delaware County Intermediate Unit, Media, Pa., 1986-87; chairperson elem. (grades 1-8) sci. com. Phila. Archdiocese, 1985-86, mem., 1984-86; coord. Chester County Cath. Schs.: Computer Edn., Pa., 1982-84, Fed. Nutrition Program, St. Agnes Sch., West Chester, Pa., 1982-84, Justice Edn. Teaching Strategies, St. Agnes Sch., West Chester, 1983-84. Author, editor: (curriculum) Elementary Life and Earth Science, 1984. Mem. Nat. Sci. Tchrs. Assn. Office: Prime Inc The Wellington 135 S 19th St Ste 250 Philadelphia PA 19103-4907

CIOE, EILEEN, financial advisor; b. Providence, Sept. 5, 1943; d. Joseph and Brigida Evelyn (Macerone) C.; m. Marcelino R. Jaramillo. BS, Bryant Coll., 1969; MA, Memphis State U., 1973. Cert. fin. planner. Engring. technician R.I. Dept. Transp., Providence, 1976-79; gen. mgr. R.I. Pub. Transit Authority, 1979-81, M.A.R.T.A., Atlanta, 1981-84, Westinghouse Broadcasting Co., N.Y.C., 1984-86; fin. advisor Am. Express Fin. Advisors, Inc., Boca Raton, Fla., 1986—. Sec. Leukemia Soc. Am., 1987. Named Transp. Woman of Yr. Woman's Transp. Group, 1980, First Woman of R.I. State of R.I., 1980, Outstanding Alumni Bryant Coll., 1984. Mem. Am. Businesswomen's Assn. (pres. 1987-89, Am. Businesswoman of Yr. 1988-89, Women of Yr. 1989-90), IDS Gold Team, Torch Club. Roman Catholic. Home: 6461 NW 2nd Ave Boca Raton FL 33487-2007

CIOLLI, ANTOINETTE, librarian, retired educator; b. N.Y.C., Aug. 20, 1915; d. Pietro and Mary (Palumbo) C.; A.B., Bklyn. Coll., 1937, M.A., 1940; B.S. in L.S., Columbia U., 1943. Tchr. history and civics Bklyn. high schs., 1943-44; circulation librarian Bklyn. Coll. Library, 1944-46; instr. history Sch. Gen. Studies, Bklyn. Coll., 1944-50, asst. prof. library dept., 1965-73, assoc. prof., 1973-81, prof. emerita, 1981—; reference librarian Bklyn. Coll. Library, 1947-59, chief sci. librarian, 1959-70, chief spl. collections div., 1970-81, hon. archivist, 1981—. Mem. ALA, Am. Hist. Assn., Spl. Libraries Assn. (museum group chpt. sec. 1950-51, 52-54), N.Y. Library Club, Beta Phi Mu. Author: (with Alexander S. Preminger and Lillian Lester) Urban Educator: Harry D. Gideonse, Brooklyn College and the City University of New York, 1970; contbr. articles to profl. jours. Home: 1129 Bay Ridge Pky Brooklyn NY 11228-2337

CIOPPA, CAROL ANN, architect; b. Bklyn., Dec. 10, 1944; d. Edward T. and Gladys (Maguire) Martin. BFA, Pratt Inst., 1966. Lic. architect, N.Y. Space planner Becker & Becker Assocs., N.Y.C., 1966-68; design asst. Unimark Internat., N.Y.C., 1968-72; sr. designer Harper & George, N.Y.C., 1972-74; sr. design mgr. ISD Inc., N.Y.C., 1974-80; pres. Cioppa Rosen Architects PC, N.Y.C., 1980—; mem. com. Internat. Design Ctr. N.Y., L.I., 1991—. Project designer for mags. Advt. Age, 1985, Progressive Architecture, 1988, Profl. Office Design, 1988, Contract Design, 1992. Recipient Internat. Cert. of Honor, Women in Design Internat., 1981, Lumen award Internat. Soc. Lighting Designers, 1980. Mem. AIA (mem. mktg. com. 1993—). Roman Catholic. Office: Cioppa Rosen Architects PC 72 Madison Ave New York NY 10016-8704

CIOPPA, MARSHA SUZANNE, air traffic control specialist; b. Edinburgh, Scotland, Sept. 8, 1962; came to U.S., 1963; d. Donald Sr. and Sandra Lee (Neal) Agee; m. Anthony Paul Cioppa Jr., Oct. 11, 1990. Cert., Mike Monroney Aero. Ctr., 1985. Cert. air traffic control specialist. Waitress, cook, restaurant mgr. Agee's Airport Restaurant, Williamstown, 1976-84; air traffic contr. DOT/FAA Miami Air Rt. Traffic Control Ctr., Miami, 1985—, quality assurance specialist, 1992-93. Republican. Baptist. Home: 1018 SW 113th Ter Pembroke Pnes FL 33025-4310

CIPLIJAUSKAITE, BIRUTE, humanities educator; b. Kaunas, Lithuania, Apr. 11, 1929; came to U.S., 1957; d. Juozas and Elena (Stelmokaite) C. B.A., Lycee Lithuanien Tubingen, 1947; M.A., U. Montreal, 1956; Ph.D., Bryn Mawr Coll., 1960. Permanent mem. Inst. Rsch. in Humanities U. Wis., Madison, 1974, asst. prof., 1961-65, assoc. prof., 1965-68, prof., 1968-73, John Bascom prof., 1973—. Author: La Soledad y la poesía española contemporánea, 1962, El poeta y la poesía, 1966, Baroja, un estilo, 1972, Deber de plenitud: La poesía de Jorge Guillén, 1973, Los noventayochistas y la historia, 1981, La mujer insatisfecha, 1984, La novela femenina contemporánea (1970-85), 1988, Literaturos eskizai, 1992; editor: Luis de Gongora, Sonetos completos, 1969, critical edit., 1981, Jorge Guillén, 1975, (with C. Maurer) La voluntad de humanismo: Homenaje a Juan Marichal, 1990, Novísimos, postnovísimos, clásicos: la poesía de los 80 en España, 1991; translator: Juan Ramón Jiménez, Sidabrinukas ir as, 1982, María Victoria Atencia, Svenciausios Karalienes Ekstazes, 1989, Voces en el silencio: Poesía lituana contemporánea, 1991, Birute Pukeleviciute, Planto, 1994. Guggenheim fellow, 1968. Mem. Assn. For Advancement Baltic Studies (v.p. 1981), Asociación Internacional de Hispanistas. Office: U Wis Dept Spanish 1220 Linden Dr Madison WI 53706-1557

CIPRIANO, PATRICIA ANN, educator, consultant; b. San Francisco, Apr. 24, 1946; d. Ernest Peter and Claire Patricia (Croak) C. BA in English, Holy Names Coll., Oakland, Calif., 1967; MA in Edn. of Gifted, Calif. State U.-L.A., 1980. Cert. tchr., tchr. gifted, adminstrv. svc., lang. devel. specialist, Calif. Tchr. English, math. Bancroft Jr. High Sch., San Leandro, Calif., 1968-79, 83-85, coord. gifted edn., 1971-79; tchr. English, math., computers San Leandro High Sch., 1979-83, 85—, mentor tchr., 1991-94, chmn. English dept., 1992—, coord. gifted and talented edn., 1981-83; cons. Calif. State Dept. Edn., various Calif. sch. dists.; dir. Calif. Lit. Project Policy Bd. Recipient Hon. Svc. award Tchr. of Yr., Bancroft Jr. High Sch. PTA, 1973; bd. dirs. Calif. Curriculum Correlating Coun. Mem. NEA, Calif. Assn. for Gifted, World Coun. Gifted and Talented, Cen. Calif. Coun. Tchrs. English (past pres.), Calif. Assn. Tchrs. English (bd. dirs., past pres.), Nat. Coun. Tchr. English (bd. dirs.), San Leandro Tchrs. Assn., Calif. Tchrs. Assn., Computer Using Educators, Assn. for Supervision and Curriculum Devel., Calif. Math. Coun., Nat. Coun. Tchrs. Math., Curriculum Study Commn., Delta Kappa Gamma (past pres.). Roman Catholic. Avocations: reading, piano, calligraphy, tennis, photography. Contbr. articles to profl. jours. Office: San Leandro HS 2200 Bancroft Ave San Leandro CA 94577-6198

CIRILO, AMELIA MEDINA, educational consultant, supervisor; b. Parks, Tex., May 23, 1925; d. Constancio and Guadalupe (Guerra) C.; m. Arturo Medina, May 31, 1953 (div. June 1979); children: Dennis Glenn, Keith Allen, Sheryl Amelia, Jacqueline Kim. B.S. in Chemistry, North Tex. State U., 1950; M.Ed., U. Houston, 1954; Ph.D. in Edn. and Nuclear Engring., Tex. A&M U., 1975; cert. in radioisotope tech. Tex. Woman's U., Denton, 1962; cert. in Pub. Speaking Dale Carnegie, 1993. Cert. in supervision, bilingual Spanish, Tex.; cert. permanent profl. tchr., Tex. Tchr. sci., dept. Starr County Schs., Rio Grande City, Tex., 1950-53; elem. tchr. San Benito-Brownsville, Tex., 1953-54, Kingsville (Tex.) Schs., 1954-56; tchr. sci. dept. head chem. physics LaJoya (Tex.) Pub. Schs., 1956-70; teaching asst. Tex. A&M U., College Station, 1970-74; instr. fire chemistry Del Mar Jr. Coll., Corpus Christi, Tex., 1974-75; exec. dir Hispanic Ednl. Research Mgmt. Analysis Nat. Assn., Inc., Corpus Christi, 1975-79; head dept. chem. physics San Isidro (Tex.) High Sch., 1979-82; tchr. chemistry W.H. Adamson High Sch., Dallas, 1982-84, Skyline High Sch. 1984-92; ednl. cons., 1992—; chmn. faculty adv. com., 1983-84; tchr. high intensity lang. sci. Skyline High Sch., Dallas, 1984-86, chem. tchr. 1986-92; mem. core faculty Union Grad. Coll., Cin., P.R., Ft. Lauderdale, and San Diego, 1975-79; mathematician Well Instrument Devel. Co., Houston, summers 1950-54; panelist, program evaluator Dept. of Edn., Washington, 1977-79; program evaluator, Robstown, Tex., 1975-79; tchr. trainer Edn. 20 and 2 Region Ctrs., Corpus Christi and San Antonio, 1975-79; researcher, writer Coll. Edn. and Urban Studies, Harvard U., Cambridge, Mass., 1978-80; vis. prof. bilingual dept. East Tex. State Coll., Commerce, 1978; ednl. cons. and supv. Adult Basic Edn. Lincoln Ctr., Dallas Ind. Sch. Dist., 1994—; conf. presenter program evaluation, 1977-79. Author: Comparative Evaluation of Bilingual Programs (named one of best U.S. books), 1978; Reflections (poetry), 1983; contbr. chpt. to book. NSF grantee Boston U., 1963-65; grantee Harvard U., 1983; bd. dirs. Meth. Home for Elderly, Weslaco, Tex., 1968, Am. Cancer Soc. fund drive, College Station, 1971-74; Brazos County advisor Tex. Constl. Revision Commn., 1973-74; sec. Goals for Corpus Christi Com. of 100; Corpus Christi rep. Southwestern Ednl. Authority, Edinburg, Tex., 1977-79; co-founder, bd. dirs. Women's Shelter, Corpus Christi, 1977-78; exec. bd. Nat. Com. Domestic Violence, 1978-80; pres. Elem. PTA, 1972-75; mem. Women's Polit. Caucus, Mex. Am. Democrats; Mem. Tex. Tchrs. Assn., NEA, Tex. Assn. Bilingual Educators, AAUW, Chem. Soc., Pan Am. Round Table, So. Sociol. Assn., Rocky Mountain Sociol. Assn., Metroplex Educators Sci. Assn., League United Latin Am. Citizens (pres. College Station 1973-74, past dist. dir. Corpus Christi). Avocation: ballroom dancing, comedy. Home and Office: 4959 Lomax Dr Dallas TX 75227-2711

CIRONA, JANE CALLAHAN, investment executive; b. Detroit, Feb. 23, 1949; d. Earl J. and Madeline Katherine (Freihaut) Callahan; children from previous marriage: Christopher Randall, Elisabeth Anne; m. James M. Cirona, Aug. 29, 1992. BA, Albion Coll., 1970; postgrad., Aquinas Coll., 1989—. Asst. mgr. Nat. Bank of Detroit, 1971-75; program coord. Muskegon (Mich.) Community Coll., 1978-79; services coord. Muskegon (Mich.) County Community Mental Health, 1979-81; supr. engring. services Teledyne Continental Motors, Muskegon; v.p. investment PaineWebber Inc., Muskegon, Mich., 1982—. Dir. Muskegon Econ. Growth Alliance, 1987—, Every Woman's Place, Muskegon, 1979-86; mem. Albion Coll. Planned Giving Adv. Bd., 1989—; mem. Commn. on Growth and Devel. Episcopal Diocese of Western Mich., 1985-88, Consumers Power Citizen Adv. Panel, Muskegon, 1983-84; bd. dirs. Mercy Hosp., Muskegon. Mem. Zonta Internat. Office: PaineWebber Inc PO Box 959 Muskegon WI 49443-0959

CIRRITO, KIMBERLEE MICHELE, critical care nurse; b. North Tonawanda, N.Y., July 11, 1962; d. Samuel and Joan (Newhart) Cirrito; (div.); children: Joshua, Kaylee. AS, Niagara County Community Coll., Sanborn, N.Y., 1982; student, U. Buffalo, 1984. Staff and relief charge nurse, preceptor Erie County Med. Ctr., Buffalo; staff and relief charge nurse Lawnwood Regional Hosp., Ft. Pierce, Fla., Sebastian Humana Hosp., Roseland, Fla.; staff nurse surg. ICU Buffalo Gen. Hosp.; staff nurse Sisters of Charity, Buffalo; spl. care nurse DeGraff Meml. Hosp., North Tonawanda. Mem. AACN. Home: 2714 Stenzel Rd North Tonawanda NY 14120

CISLER, THERESA ANN, osteopath; b. Tucson, Dec. 20, 1951; d. William George and Lucille (Seeber) C.; 1 child, Daniel Collin. BSN, U. Ariz., 1974; DO, Kirksville Coll. Osteopathy, 1983. Operating room technician St. Joseph's Hosp., Tucson, 1973-74, operating room nurse, 1974-78, operating room inservice coordinator, 1978-79; intern Tucson Gen. Hosp., 1983-84; family practice and manipulation Assoc. Jane J. Beregi, D.O., Tucson, 1984-87; practice medicine specializing in osteo. manipulation Tucson, 1987—; active med. staff Tucson Gen. Hosp., 1984—, med. records chmn., 1985-87; part time med. staff Westcenter Drug & Rehab., Tucson, 1984-88; vol. med. staff St. Elizabeth Hugary Clinic, 1984-87; mem. substance abuse com. Westcenter - Tucson Gen. Hosp., 1986-88, osteo. concepts com., 1986—, osteo. manipulative cons., 1986—. Eucharistic minister St. Pius X Ch., Tucson, 1984-86, eucharistic minister coordinator, 1987—. Mem. Am. Osteo. Assn., Am. Acad. Osteopathy, Ariz. Osteo. Med. Assn. (at-large ho. of dels. 1985—), Kirksville Coll. Osteopathy-Century Club, Cranial Acad. Roman Catholic. Home and Office: 4002 E Grant Rd Ste D Tucson AZ 85712-2549

CISMARU, PAT KLEIN, municipal official; b. N.Y.C., Sept. 27, 1933; children: Jay, David. BBA, CCNY, 1958; MEd, CUNY, 1960; MS, Tex. Tech U., 1985, PhD, 1991. Cert. social worker, Tex., CEMR, OAMT mgmt. Owner Masonry Constrn. Co., Lubbock, Tex., 1980—; dir. respite unit LRMHMR Ctr., Lubbock, 1980-89; acad. dir. Park Coll., Lubbock, 1985-90; programs adminstr. RRIP Lubbock Housing Authority, 1989-93; owner rental property, N.J., Vt., Tex., Colo., 1972—; owner residential and comml. laundromats, Colo., 1991; convenience store, Colo., 1993—; tanning salons, Tex., 1993—. Mem. NAFE, AARP, LWV, NASW, Goodwill Industries. Home: 5108 79th Dr Lubbock TX 79424-3022 Office: 2812 Weber Dr Lubbock TX 79404-1222

CISNEROS, EVELYN, dancer; b. Long Beach, Calif., 1955. Mem. San Francisco Ballet Co., 1977—. Performances include Scherzo, Mozart's C Minor Mass, Romeo and Juliet, Medea, The Tempest, 1980, Stars and Stripes, In the Night, A Midsummer Nights Dream, Cinderella, A Song for Dead Warriors, 1984, Confidences, 1986, Sleeping Beauty, 1992, Swan Lake, 1993. Office: San Francisco Ballet 455 Franklin St San Francisco CA 94102-4471 also: Peter S Diggins Assocs 133 W 71st St New York NY 10023-3834

CITRINO, MARY ANNE, investment banker; b. Newark, N.J., Apr. 24, 1959; d. Robert Joseph Jr. and Jean (Coraci) C.; m. Todd Wakelee Smith, Aug. 9, 1986. BA in Econs., Princeton U., 1981; MBA, Harvard U., 1986. Assoc. Morgan Stanley & Co., N.Y.C., 1986-91, v.p. mergers and acquisitions, 1991-94; prin., 1994—. Home: 152 E 74th St New York NY 10021-3542

CITRON, BEATRICE SALLY, law librarian, lawyer, educator; b. Phila., May 19, 1929; d. Morris Meyer and Frances (Teplitsky) Levinson; m. Joel P. Citron, Aug. 7, 1955 (dec. Sept. 1977); children: Deborah Ann, Victor Ephraim. BA in Econs. with honors, U. Pa., 1950; MLS, Our Lady of the Lake U., 1978; JD, U. Tex., 1984. Bar: Tex. 1985; cert. all-level sch. libr., secondary level tchr., Tex. Claims examiner Social Security Adminstrn., Pa., Fla. and N.C., 1951-59; head libr. St. Mary's Hall, San Antonio, 1979-80; media, reference and rare book libr., asst. and assoc. prof. St. Mary's U. Law Libr., San Antonio, 1984-89; asst. dir., head pub. svcs. St. Thomas U. Law Libr., Miami, Fla., 1989—. Mem. ABA, Am. Assn. Law Librs. (publs. com. 1987-88, com. on rels. with info. vendors 1991-93, bylaws com. 1994—), S.W. Assn. Law Librs. (continuing edn. com. 1986-88, chmn. local arrangements 1987-88), S.E. Assn. Law Librs. (newsletter, program and edn. coms. 1991-94), South Fla. Assn. Law Librs. (treas. 1992-94, v.p. 1994-95, pres. 1995—). Office: St Thomas U Law Libr 16400 NE 32nd Ave Miami FL 33160

CITRON, DIANE, lawyer; b. Cin., Oct. 9, 1953; d. Carl and Georgia (Reid) C. B.A., Franklin and Marshall Coll., 1975; J.D., Case Western Res. U., 1978. Bar: D.C. 1978, Calif 1985. Assoc. Wasserman, Orlow, Ginsberg & Rubin, Washington, 1978-80; staff atty. U.S. SEC, Washington, 1980-83; sr. counsel Freddie Mac, Washington, 1983-84; assoc. Orrick, Herrington & Sutcliffe, San Francisco, 1984-85; assoc. Brown & Wood, San Francisco, 1985-87; spl. counsel Skadden, Arps, Slate, Meagher & Flom, San Francisco, 1987-92; ptnr. Mayer, Brown & Platt, Chgo., 1992—. Mem. ABA (bus. law sect., real property sect., subcom. securitization), Fed. Bar Assn., Women's Bar Assn. D.C., Bar Assn. D.C., Pi Gamma Mu. Democrat. Jewish. Office: Mayer Brown & Platt 190 S La Salle St Chicago IL 60603-3410*

CITROWSKE, PAULA ELIZABETH, manufacturing engineer; b. Norman, Okla., Apr. 12, 1967; d. William Andrew and Peggy O'Neal (Whittaker) Munter; m. Clair Donald Citrowske Jr., July 25, 1992; 1 child, Jeffry David. BSME, U. Okla., 1989; postgrad., Okla. State U., 1990—. Registered profl. engr. intern, Okla. Summer engr. Mobil Pipeline, Dallas, 1987, 88; Summer engr. Halliburton Svcs., Duncan, Okla., 1990, engr., 1990, sr. engr., 1991; sr. engr. H.S. Mfg., Duncan, Okla., 1992, mfg. engr. II, 1993-95, prodn. specialist, 1995—; host plant tours Halliburton Energy Svcs., 1991—, leader product coord. team, 1991-93, mem. project coord. team, 1993, project coord. new system, 1993-94. 2d violinist Lawton (Okla.) Philharmonic Orch., 1990-92. Mem. ASME (assoc.). Republican. Baptist. Home: 1001 N Harville Rd Duncan OK 73533-1507 Office: Halliburton Energy Svcs PO Box 1431 Duncan OK 73536-0342

CIULLO, ROSEMARY, psychologist; b. Chgo.. BA, U. Ill., Chgo., 1974; MA, Gov.'s State U., University Park, Ill., 1977; PsyD, Forest Inst. Profl. Psychology, 1986. Psychologist Madden Mental Health Ctr. Mem. APA, Ill. Psychol. Assn. Office: 1200 S 1st Ave Hines IL 60141

CIURCZAK, ALEXIS, librarian; b. Long Island, N.Y., Feb. 13, 1950; d. Alexander Daniel and Catherine Ann (Frangipane) C. BA Art History magna cum laude, U. Calif., L.A., 1971; MA Libr. Sci., San Jose State U., 1975; cert. tchr. ESL, U. Calif., Irvine, 1985. Intern IBM Rsch. Libr., San Jose, Calif., 1974-75; tech. asst. San Bernardino Valley Coll. Libr., Calif., 1975; tech. svcs. librarian Palomar Coll., San Marcos, Calif., 1975-78, pub. svcs. librarian, 1978-81, libr. dir., 1981-86, pub. svcs. librarian, 1987—, instr. Libr. Technology Cert. Program, 1975—; exchange librarian Fulham Pub. Libr., London, 1986-87; coord. San Diego C.C. Consortium Semester-in-London Am. Inst. Fgn. Study, 1988-89. Mem. ALA, San Diego Libr. Svcs. com., Calif. Libr. Media Educators Assn., Patronato por Niños, Kosciuszko Found., So. Calif. Tech. Processes Group, Pacific Coast Coun. Latin Am. Studies, Libros, Reforma, Libr. Assn. (British), Calif. Libr. Assn., Calif. Tchrs. Assn., Phi Beta Kappa, Beta Phi Mu. Office: Palomar CC 1140 W Mission Rd San Marcos CA 92069-1487

CIUREA, LUCIA E., physician; b. Romania, June 21, 1928; came to U.S., 1967; MD, U. Romania, 1953. Diplomate Am. Bd. Psychiatry. Staff psychiatrist VA Hosp., Mass., 1981—; instr. in field. Mem. Am. Psychiat. Assn. Home: 274 Clarendon St Apt 2 Boston MA 02116

CIURRIA, IARA, management consultant; b. Campinas, Sao Paulo, Brazil, Aug. 24, 1952; came to the U.S., 1982; d. Humberto and Mafalda (Pavan) C.; m. Konstantinos Stavropoulos, Feb. 2, 1980 (div.). BS in Math., Sao Paulo State U., São José do Rio Preto, 1974; MS in Applied Math., Campinas State U., Campinas, 1982; PhD in Ops. Rsch., Stanford U., 1989. H.S. tchr. Colegio Santo Andre, São Jose'do Rio Preto, 1974; grad. asst. UNESP-Brazil, São Jose'do Rio Preto, 1974; asst. prof. Bus. Sch.-Brazil, São Jose'do Rio Preto, 1973-75, UNICAMP-Brazil, Campinas, 1978-82; sr. cons. Bender Mgmt. Cons., Arlington, Va., 1989—. Mem. INFORMS Inst. Office: Bender Mgmt Cons 2231 Crystal Dr Arlington VA 22202

CIVISH, GAYLE ANN, psychologist; b. Lynnwood, Calif., Sept. 29, 1948; d. Leland and Arline (Frazer) Civish; children: Nathan Morrow, Shane Morrow. BA, U. Nev., Reno, 1970; MA, U. Colo., 1973, PhD, 1983. Lic. psychologist, Colo.; cert. sch. psychologist, Colo. Sch. psychologist Jefferson County (Colo.) Schs., 1983-89; psychologist in pvt. practice Lakewood, Colo., 1983—. Contbr. articles to profl. jours. Mem. APA, Colo. Psychol. Assn. (bd. dirs. 1990-93), Colo. Women Psychologists (past external liaison), Am. Soc. Clin. Hypnosis, Feminist Therapy Inst. (steering com. 1994—), Assn. for Women in Psychology, Phi Kappa Phi, Phi Delta Kappa. Democrat. Office: 3000 Youngfield St Ste 376 Lakewood CO 80215-6552

CLAASSEN, SHERIDA DILL, newspaper executive; b. Columbia, Mo., Nov. 27, 1948; d. Wilben Hubert and Dorothy Louise (Richardson) Dill; m. Arthur Norman Claassen, June 22, 1985; children: April Dill, Christopher Wilben. BJ, U. Mo., 1970; MBA, Pepperdine U., 1981. Editor Graphic Herald, Downers Grove, Ill., 1970-73; area editor Suburban Trib/Chgo. Tribune, 1973-78; copy editor San Jose (Calif.) Mercury, 1978-79, asst. metro. editor, 1979-81; city editor Wichita (Kans.) Eagle, 1981-82, asst. mng. editor, news, 1982-85, dir., R & D, 1985-91, exec. editor, 1991-94, v.p., assoc. pub., 1995—. V.p., bd. dirs. Wichita Festivals, Inc., 1988-91; bd. dirs. Roots & Wings, Wichita, 1989-91; active Leadership Kans. Class 1989, Topeka, 1989, Leadership 2000 Class 1991, Wichita, 1991. Recipient Excellence in Entrepreneurship award Knight-Ridder, Inc., 1990. Office: Wichita Eagle PO Box 820 Wichita KS 67201-0820

CLABAUGH-DICK, LORI, financial planner; b. Roaring Spring, Pa., June 27, 1964; d. Charles J. and Shirley J. (Gorsuch) Clabaugh; m. Lance A. Dick, May 16, 1987; children: Cameron Z., Jordan C. BS in Fin., Pa. State U., 1986. Cert. mgmt. acct. Fin. planner, analysis mgr. Mid-State Bank & Trust Co., Altoona, Pa., 1986-94; electronic svcs. mgr. Keystone Fin. Inc., Altoona, 1995—. Mem. Inst. Mgmt. Accts. (sec. 1990-92, Most Valuable Member 1991), Nat. Assn. Bank Cost & Mgmt. Acctg., Bank Adminstrn. Inst. Home: RR3 Box 289 Hollidaysburg PA 16648 Office: Keystone Fin Inc PO Box 708 Altoona PA 16603

CLAGETT, ANDREA MARQUIT, art dealer, appraiser; b. Bklyn., Apr. 16, 1954; d. Harold and Gloria J. (Weinstein) Marquit; m. Gordon Jell Clagett, Oct. 1, 1988. BA in Art and Archaeology, Washington U., St. Louis, 1975. Exec. asst. to gallery dir. Marlborough Gallery Inc., N.Y.C., 1975-78; sr. cataloguer Sotheby Parke Bernet, Inc., N.Y.C., 1978-82; prin. Andrea Marquit Fine Arts, N.Y.C., 1982-91, Boston, 1989—. Mem. Boston Art Dealers Assn., Appraisers Assn. Am., New Eng. Appraisers Assn., Boston Soc. Architects (affiliate), Artcetera '92 (hon. bd. mem.), Artcetera '94, Design Finds (dir., co-mgr.), Art Adv. Svc. (co-founder), Boston Area Womens Art Dealers Group (co-founder), Contemporary Art Support Group the Mus. Fine Arts, Newbury St. League, Nat. Coun. Jewish Women.

CLAGETT, LESLIE PLUMMER, editor; b. Providence, Apr. 30, 1956; d. Robert Eugene and Peg (Hassett) Plummer; m. John Stephen Clagett, June 10, 1982. BA in English, Denison U., 1978. Mng. editor N.Y. Arts Jour., N.Y.C., 1978-81, Arts & Architecture, L.A., 1981-85; assoc. editor architecture Home mag., L.A., 1985—. Mem. Archtl. League, Nat. Trust for Hist. Preservation. Office: Home Mag 5900 Wilshire Blvd Fl 15 Los Angeles CA 90036-5013

CLAIBORNE, LIZ (ELISABETH CLAIBORNE ORTENBERG), fashion designer; b. Brussels, Mar. 31, 1929; came to U.S., 1939; d. Omer Villere and Louise Carol (Fenner) C.; m. Arthur Ortenberg, July 5, 1954; 1 son by previous marriage, Alexander G. Schultz. Student, Art Sch., Brussels, 1948-49, Academie, Nice, France, 1950; DFA, R.I. Sch. Design, 1991. Asst. Tina Lesser, N.Y.C., 1951-52, Omar Khayam, Ben Reig, Inc., N.Y.C., 1953; designer Juniorite, N.Y.C., 1954-60, Dan Keller, N.Y.C., 1960-76, Youth Guild Inc., N.Y.C., 1976-89; designer, pres., chmn. Liz Claiborne Inc., N.Y.C., 1985-89, pres., 1976-89, chmn., chief oper. officer, until 1989; chmn. Liz Claiborne Cosmetics, 1985-89; guest lectr. Fashion Inst. Tech., Parsons Sch. Design; bd. dirs. Coun. of Am. Fashion Designers, Fire Island Lighthouse Restoration Com. Recipient Designer of Yr. award Palciode Hierro, Mexico City, 1976, Designer of Yr. award Dayton Co., Mpls., 1978, Ann. Disting. in Design award Marshall Field's, 1985, One Co. Makes a Difference award Fashion Inst. Tech., 1985, award Coun. Fashion Designers, 1986, Gordon Grand Fellowship award Yale U., 1989, Jr. Achievement award Nat. Bus. Hall of Fame, 1990, Frederick A.P. Barnard award Barnard Coll., 1991, Hon. Doctorate, R.I. Sch. of Design, 1991; named to Nat. Sales Hall of Fame, 1991. Mem. Fashion Group. Roman Catholic.

CLAIRE, ELIZABETH, writer; b. Bronx, N.Y., Apr. 6, 1939; d. Albert Rudolph and Anna Eardley; m. Edward J. Simms, Dec. 2, 1957 (div. 1962); children: Jon Arthur Simms, James Albert Simms. BA in Edn., CCNY,

1966; MS in TESOL, NYU, 1968. Cert. English, Spanish, ESOL, N.J. Tchr. N.Y.C. Bd. Edn., 1966-75, Ft. Lee (N.J.) Pub. Schs., 1977-87; freelance materials writer Saddle Brook, N.J., 1987—; tchr. Dwight-Englewood (N.J.) Sch., summers, 1993, 94; pres. Eardley Publs., Saddle Brook, N.J., 1980—; cons. N.J. and N.Y. Pub. Schs., 1988—. Author: ESL Teachers Activities Kit, 1989, Dangerous English, 1990, Classroom Teachers ESL Survival Kit # 1, 1994, Where Is Taro?, 1994, Classroom Teachers ESL Survival Kit # 2, 1995. Mem. Results!, 1989—; candidate Saddle Brook Town Coun., 1990. Mem. TESOL (asst. newsletter editor 1990-91), N.J. TESOL, Mensa (exec. com. 1982-83), Toastmasters (pres. Elmwood Park chpt. 1994-95, Best Speaker Div. A 1992), Phi Beta Kappa. Home: 302 Nedellec Dr Saddle Brook NJ 07662

CLAMAR, APHRODITE J., psychologist; b. Hartford, Conn., Sept. 26, 1933; d. James John and Georgia (Panas) Clamar; m. Richard Cohen, June 24, 1973. BA, CCNY, 1953; MA, Columbia U., 1955; PhD, NYU, 1978; student, Stella Adler Conservatory of Acting and Playwrights Horizon Thetare Sch., 1987-91. Mgmt. cons., psychologist Milla Alihan Assocs., N.Y.C., 1957-62; rsch. psychologist coord. Inst. Devel. Studies N.Y. Med. Coll., N.Y.C., 1964; intern psychologist Bellevue Psychiat. Hosp., N.Y.C., 1964-66; assoc. prof. Fashion Inst. Tech., N.Y.C., 1966-69; supervising psychologist Lifeline Ctr. Child Devel., N.Y.C., 1966-67; chief psychologist I Spy Health Program Beth Israel Med. Ctr., N.Y.C., 1967-70; dir. community-sch. mental health programs Soundview Community Svcs., Albert Einstein Coll. Medicine Yeshiva U., N.Y.C., 1970-73; dir. treatment program court-related children, dept. child psychiatry Harlem Hosp.; mem. faculty dept. psychiatry Coll. Physicians and Surgeons Columbia U., N.Y.C., 1973-76; pvt. practice psychotherapy N.Y.C., 1976-95; pres. Richard Cohen Assocs. Pub. Rels., N.Y.C., 1995—; cons. to pub. health and mental health agys., N.Y.C., 1976-91; mem. faculty Lenox Hill Hosp. Psychoanalytic and Psychotherapy Tng. Program, 1982-88; theater producer, artistic dir. Tom Cat Cohen Prodns., Inc., 1990—. Author: (with Budd Hopkins) Missing Time, 1981; contbr. articles to profl. jours. Fellow AAAS; mem. APA, Dramatists Guild, Authors Guild. Democrat. Greek Orthodox. Home: 162 E 80th St New York NY 10021-0454 Office: 30 E 60th St New York NY 10022-1008

CLAMON, HARLEYNE DIANNE, retired social service supervisor; b. Camden, Tex., Feb. 12, 1940; d. Harley and Ada Virginia (Handley) C. BA, Sam Houston U., 1961. Lic. master social worker, Tex. Tchr. Big Sandy Ind. Sch., Dallardsville, Tex., 1961-62; social worker Tex. Dept. Human Svcs., Tex. City, 1962-75; social service supr. Tex. Dept. Human Svcs., Galveston, 1975-79, Tex. City, 1979-80, Livingston, 1980-92. Mem. adv. com. Mental Health, Mental Retardation, Livingston, Tex., 1980-87, chmn. 1982-87; vol. Polk County Meml. Hosp., 1982—; adult ladies Sun. sch. tchr. Leggett Bapt. Ch., 1984—, song leader, 1994—. Mem. AAUW (pres. Livingston, Tex. 1984-86), DAR (Indian chmn. 1984-86, chaplain Livingston chpt. 1992-94), Bus. and Profl. Women (pres. Livingston 1983-85, Woman of Yr. 1982-83), Am. Pub. Welfare Assn., Tex. Pub. Employees Assn. (bd. dirs. 1970-75), Polk County Hist. Commn. (v.p. 1994—), Sam Houston State U. Alumni. Democrat. Baptist. Home: 616 W Calhoun St Livingston TX 77351-2751

CLAMPITT, AMY KATHLEEN, writer, editor; b. New Providence, Iowa, June 15, 1920; d. Roy Justin and Lutie Pauline (Felt) C. B.A. with honors in English, Grinnell Coll., 1941, DHL (hon.), 1984; DHL (hon.), Bowdoin Coll., 1992. Sec., writer Oxford Univ. Press, N.Y.C., 1943-51; reference libr. Nat. Audubon Soc., N.Y.C., 1952-59; free-lance writer, N.Y.C., 1960-77; editor E.P. Dutton, N.Y.C., 1977-82; writer-in-residence Coll. William & Mary, Williamsburg, Va., 1984-85; vis. writer Amherst Coll., 1986-87; Grace Hazard Conkling disting. writer Smith Coll., 1993. Author (poetry) The Kingfisher, 1983, What the Light Was Like, 1985, Archaic Figure, 1987, Westward, 1990, A Silence Opens, 1994, (essays) Predecessors, Et Cetera, 1991. Recipient Lit. award Am. Acad. Arts and Letters, 1984, Writer's award Lila Wallace-Reader's Digest, 1991; Guggenheim fellow, 1982-83, Acad. Am. Poets fellow, 1984, MacArthur fellow, 1992. Mem. AAAL, PEN, Authors Guild. Democrat.

CLANCY, JUDITH MEYER, health facility administrator; b. Columbus, Ohio, Feb. 26, 1952; d. John Sherman and Aldyth Louise (Barber) Meyer; m. Michael James Clancy, Jan. 12, 1979 (div. 1991); children: Corinne Renee, Joannna Michelle. BSN, Ohio State U., 1975; cert., R.B. Turnbull Sch., 1977; MA, Cen. Mich. U., 1981; student, Ohio Wesleyan U., 1970-72. RN, Ohio. Staff nurse, charge nurse Children's Hosp., Columbus, 1977, enterostomal nurse clinician, 1977-89, dir. surg. nursing, 1981-89; dir. clin. ops. Nova Home Health Svcs., Phoenix, 1989-90, coord. programs and spl. projects corp. office, 1990-92; enterostomal nurse clinician Good Samaritan Regional Med. Ctr., Phoenix, 1992—. Named to Outstanding Young Women Am., 1982. Mem. Internat. Assn. Enterstomal Therapy, Sigma Theta Tau, Sigma Iota Epsilon. Home: 7106 N Via Nueva Scottsdale AZ 85258

CLANCY, MARY CATHERINE, Canadian Parliament member; b. Halifax, N.S., Can., Jan. 13, 1948; d. Douglas and Catherine (Casey) C. BA with honors, Mt. St. Vincent U., Halifax, 1970; LLB, Dalhousie U., Halifax, 1974; LLM, U. London. Lawyer, broadcaster, univ. lectr., columnist; mem. Parliament, Ottawa, Ont., Can., 1988—; apptd. parliamentary sec. Min. of Citizenship & Immigration, Ottawa, 1993—. Bd. govs. Dalhousie U.; bd. govs. Mt. St. Vincent U., pres. nat. bd. alumni; v.p. Atlantic region Nat. Women's Liberal Commn.; pres. St. Joseph's Children's Ctr.; bd. dirs. YWCA, Atlantic Ballet Co., Home of Guardian Angel, Seaweed Theatre. Mem. N.S. Barristers Soc. Liberal. Roman Catholic. Home: 6064 Coburg Rd, Halifax, NS Canada B3H 1Z2 Office: House of Commons, 461 Confederation Bldg, Ottawa, ON Canada K1A 0A6 also: 2131 Gottingen St Ste 210, Halifax, NS Canada B3K 5Z7

CLAPPER, CYNTHIA RAE, mental health services professional; b. Everett, Wash., Apr. 28, 1955; d. Duane and Harriet Waneta (Olson) Duncan; m. James Clapper, July 21, 1973 (div. Dec. 1977); 1 child, Nicholas James. BS in Counseling, Western Wash. U., 1978, MS in Counseling Psychology, 1981; human svcs. mgmt. cert., U. Wash., 1989. Lic. counselor, Wash., Idaho. Sr. counselor, supr. Victoria Village, Stanwood, Wash., 1981-83; day treatment dir., caseworker Turning Point Youth Svcs., Arlington, Wash., 1983-84; mental health therapist Island County Mental Health, Camano Island, Wash., 1983-85, Mental Health Svcs., Stanwood, 1984-85; clin. dir. Adams County Community Counseling, Othello, Wash., 1985-89; programs dir. Hays Shelter Home, Boise, Idaho, 1989-90; staff psychologist Region III Mental Health Ctr., Caldwell, Idaho, 1990-91; program specialist Divsn. Family and Community Svcs., Boise, 1991—; cons. on day treatment in Idaho Bur. Mental Health, Boise, 1993; liaison to state and local family and mental health consumer self-help groups in Idaho, 1991—, grant monitor for Leadership Acad., 1991—; ctrl. office state contact Adult Svcs. and Idaho fed. block grant application for mental health; state contact adult svcs., Idaho. Mem. ACA. Home: 3663 Collister Ct Boise ID 83703 Office: Bur Mental Health & Adult Svcs Divsn Family & Cmty 450 W State St 7th Fl Boise ID 83720-0036

CLAPPER, MARIE ANNE, magazine publisher; b. Chgo., Nov. 21, 1942; d. Chester William and Hazel Alice (Gilso) Reinke; m. William Neil Petersen, Aug. 17, 1963 (div. 1975); children: Elaine Myrtice, Edward William; m. Lyle N. Clapper, Jan. 1, 1980; children: Jeffrey Leland, Anne Reinke; stepchildren: John Scott, Susan Louise. Student, Augustana Coll., Rock Island, Ill., 1960-63; EdB, Northeastern U., 1964. Writer Pack-o-Fun mag., Park Ridge, Ill., 1976-77; editor Pack-o-Fun mag., Des Plaines, Ill., 1977-78, pub., 1990—; asst. to pub., circulation dir. Crafts 'n Things mag., Des Plaines, Ill., 1978-82, pub., 1982—; pub. Decorative Arts Painting mag., Des Plaines, 1990—, The Cross Stitcher mag., Des Plaines, 1991—, Bridal Crafts mag., Des Plaines, 1991—. Host TV show The Crafts 'n Things Show, 1984-86, Crafting for the 90s, 1990-94. Mem. Mag. Publishers Am. (bd. dirs.), Hobby Industry Am., Soc. Craft Designers. Office: Crafts 'n Things Ste 375 2400 Devon Des Plaines IL 60018-4618

CLAPSADDLE, PATRICIA LEE, art educator; b. Cleveland, Dec. 13, 1950; d. George Thomas and Jean (Sweet) Fuller; m. William Harold Clapsaddle, Apr. 13, 1974; children: Sarah Aubrey, Eben Weston. BFA, U. Cin., 1973; MFA, Kent State U., 1990. Art educator Ipswich (Mass.) Sch. Dist., 1973-77, West Geauga Sch. Dist., Chesterland, Ohio, 1979-82, Chardon (Ohio) Sch. Dist., 1982—. Mem. N.E. Ohio Edn. Assn., Ohio Art Edn. Assn., Nat. Art Edn. Assn. Office: Chardon HS 151 Chardon Ave Chardon OH 44024-1089

CLARDY, JANET LYNN, human resources manager; b. Anaheim, Calif., Feb. 27, 1964; d. Edward Emmart and Betty Jean (Milhollin) Rice; m. Ross Steven Clardy, May 28, 1988. BA, Calif. State U., Fullerton, 1987, MBA, 1990. From compensation analyst to field human resources mgr. Taco Bell Corp., Irvine, Calif., 1987-91; corp. human resources mgr. Taco Bell Corp., Irvine, 1991-94; mgr. employment and employee rels. St. Joseph Hosp., Orange, Calif., 1994—. Vol. Vol. Ctr. of Orange County, Calif., 1991—; active mem. Ch. of Christ. Mem. Soc. for Human Resources Mgmt. Republican. Home: 14135 Elystan Cir Westminster CA 92683-4823 Office: St Joseph Hosp 110 W Stewart Dr Orange CA 92668

CLARDY, MARY JOANNE, educator; b. Kansas City, Mo., Sept. 11, 1955; d. Norris Alger and Mary Jane (Brewster) Smith. AA, Miss. County Coll., 1985; BA, Gov.'s State U., University Park, Ill., 1988, MA in English, 1992. Cert. tchr, Ill., Mo.; cert. gifted students tchr., Ill. Tchr. Sch. Dist. #160, Country Club Hills, 1989-94; tchr., coord. gifted program Sch. Dist. #159, 1994—; instr. Joliet Jr. Coll. Home: 301 Robin Hill Dr Shorewood IL 60435-9642

CLARE, CHRISTINE ANNE, nursing adminstrator; b. Arcadia, Calif., June 7, 1962; d. John Dean and Patricia Elizabeth (Cronshey) Hallock; m. Richard Edward Clare, July 12, 1986; children: Rachel Nicole, Jeffrey Dean. AS in Nursing, San Bernardino Valley Coll., 1984; BSN, Calif. State U., 1988; MSN, U. Calif., 1992. RN, Calif.; cert. nurse adminstr. Charge nurse Buena Park Doctor's Hosp., Buena Park, Calif., 1984-87; staff nurse Long Beach Meml. Med. Ctr., Long Beach, 1987-89; ho. supr. Los Alamitos (Calif.) Med. Ctr., 1989-92, dir. nursing dept. emergency, 1992-94, clin. dir. dept. med./surg., 1994—. Mem. Orgn. Nurse Execs. Calif. Republican. Home: 9621 Random Dr Anaheim CA 92804 Office: Los Alamitos Med Ctr 3751 Katella Ave Los Alamitos CA 90720

CLARK, BARBARA MARLENE, state legislator; b. Beckley, W.Va., June 12, 1939; m. Thomas Clark; children: Jan, Crystal, Thomas II, Brian. Mem. N.Y. State Assembly, 1986—; past mem. assembly standing com. on aging, housing, small bus., and social svcs.; mem. standing com. on children and families, corps., authorities and commns. edn. and labor. V.p. Parents Assn.; mem. exec. bd., prin. consultative coun. Andrew Jackson H.S., Sprinfield Garden Jr. H.S., P.S. 176, Cambria Heights, N.Y.; mem. adv. coun. Teen Pregnancy Prevention Program; active NAACP, Nat. Coun. Negro Women. Democrat. Home: 12056 224th St Jamaica NY 11411-2141 Office: NY State Assembly State Capitol Albany NY 12224*

CLARK, BETH, minister; b. Bradford, N.H., Apr. 15, 1914; d. John Scott and Bessie (Murdock) Pendleton; m. John Guill Clark, June 20, 1940 (dec. 1955); children: John Guill Jr., Beverly Estelle Clark Daggett. BA, Colby Coll., 1935; BD, Andover Newton Theol. Sch., 1938; MDiv, Ea. Bapt. Theol. Sem., 1967; D Ministry, Lancaster Theol. Sem., 1981; postgrad., U. Athens, 1970, Jungian Inst., Zurich, 1980, Mansfield Coll., Oxford, Eng., 1982, 85, Caribbean Inst., 1989. Ordained to ministry United Ch. of Christ, 1967. Exec. dir. YWCA, Bristol, Tenn., 1955-59, Asheville, N.C., 1959-60; dean of women Anderson (S.C.) Coll., 1960-61, Eastern Coll., St. Davids, Pa., 1961-65; vol. rsch. coord. Selinsgrove (Pa.) State Sch., 1965-78; interim min. various chs. Penn. Ctrl. Conf., United Ch. of Christ, Harrisburg, 1968—. Author: Grief in the Loss of a Pastor, 1981; editor: Meditations on the Lord's Supper (John G. Clark), 1958. Bd. mgr. Bethany Children's Home, Womelsdorf, Pa., 1982-88; mem. adv. com. Sun Home Nursing Svcs., Northumberland, Pa., 1982—, sec., bd. dirs., 1989—. Mem. Interim Network (steering com. 1978-80), Assn. Ret. State Employees, Alban Inst., Interagy. Club (pres. 1966-68), Triangle Club (v.p. 1970-74), Phi Mu. Democrat. Home: 709 9th St Selinsgrove PA 17870-1707

CLARK, BEVERLY ANN, lawyer; b. Davenport, Iowa, Dec. 9, 1944; d. F. Henry and Arlene F. (Meyer) C.; m. Richard Floss; children: Amy and Barry (twins). Student, Mich. State U., 1963-65; BA, Calif. State U.-Fullerton, 1967; MSW, U. Iowa, 1975, JD, 1980. Bar: Iowa 1980; lic. social worker. Probation officer County of San Bernardino, San Bernardino, Calif., 1968, County of Riverside, Riverside, Calif., 1968-69; social worker Skiff Hosp., Newton, Iowa, 1971-73; social worker State of Iowa, Mitchellville, 1973-74, planner, Des Moines, 1976-77, law clk., Des Moines, 1980-81; instr. Des Moines Area Community Coll., Ankeny, Iowa, 1974-75; corp. counsel Pioneer Hi-Bred Internat., Inc., Des Moines, 1981—; adj. prof. Drake Law Sch. Editor: Proceedings: Bicentennial Symposium on New Directions in Juvenile Justice, 1975. Founder Mothers of Twins Club, Newton, Iowa, 1971; co-chmn. Juvenile Justice Symposium, Des Moines, 1974-75; mem. Juvenile Justice Com., Des Moines, 1974-75; mem. Nat. Offender Based State Corrections Info. System Com., Ia. rep., 1976-78; incorporator, dir. Iowa Dance Theatre, Des Moines, 1981; mem. Pesticide User's Adv. Com., Fort Collins, Colo., 1981-88; co-developer Iowa Migrant Ombudsmen Project, Pioneer, Inc. and Proteus, Inc. Recipient Disting. Alumni award U. Iowa, 1990, Nat. award Ctr. for Pub. Resources. Mem. ABA (subcom. on devel. individual rights in work place, termination-at-will subcom. 1982—), Iowa Bar Assn., Polk County Bar Assn., Polk County Women Atty.'s Assn., Am. Trial Lawyers Assn., Am. Assn. Agrl. Lawyers, Am. Seed Trade Assn., Am. Corp. Counsel Assn., Ctr. for Pub. Resource. Home: 7750 Hwy F-24 West Baxter IA 50028-9801 Office: Pioneer Hi-Bred Internat Inc 700 Capital Sq 400 Locust St # 700 Des Moines IA 50309-2340

CLARK, BEVERLY JEAN, lawyer; b. Detroit, May 21, 1939; d. Harry and Evelyn Blanche (Mabin) C. BA, U. Mich., 1961, MA, 1963; JD, Wayne State U., 1972. Bar: Mich. 1973, U.S. Dist. Ct. (ea. dist.) Mich. 1973, (we. dist.) Mich. 1990, U.S. Ct. Appeals (6th dist.) 1973. Pvt. practice Detroit, 1973—; bd. dirs. Mich. Indian Legal Services, Traverse City. Co-founder Mich. Women's Campaign Fund, Detroit; mem. Mich. Civil Rights Commn., 1981-91, chmn., 1991. Named Ford Scholar, Ford Motor Co., 1957-61. Fellow Am. Acad. Matrimonial Lawyers; mem. Acad. Family Mediators, Mich. Trial Lawyers Assn. (pres. 1983-84), Women Lawyers Assn. (pres. 1978-79, First in Leadership 1987), Nat. Lawyers Guild (bd. dirs.). Democrat. Office: 440 E Congress Ste 4R Detroit MI 48226

CLARK, BEVERLY MOLL ANN, health facility administrator; b. Lebanon, Pa., Jan. 20, 1947; d. Oscar S. Sr. and Bettylou Spotts (Shay) M. Diploma, Lebanon Sch. Nursing, 1965; Assocs., Helene Fuld Sch. Nursing, 1972. Staff nurse Lebanon Valley Gen. Hosp., Lebanon, charge nurse ICU, head nurse ICU, CCU; supr. Hyman S. Caplan Pavilion, Lebanon.

CLARK, BONNIE DAWN, counselor; b. Winston-Salem, N.C., Feb. 11, 1955; d. Douglas Copeland and Tomasue (Anderson) C.; m. Patricia Lee Davis, Sept. 4, 1981 (div. Sept. 1988); m. Mary Elizabeth Harrison, Apr. 24, 1993. BA, U. N.C., 1980; MS in Edn., Old Dominion U., 1986; MA in Counseling, N.C. Ctrl. U., 1992. Nationally cert. counselor; lic. profl. counselor, N.C.; cert. moderator Women for Sobriety; cert. substance abuse counselor; master hypnotist. Sexual minorities counselor Switchboard Crisis Ctr., Greensboro, 1977-80; vol. coord., outreach specialist Drug Action Coun., Greensboro, N.C., 1979-80; substance abuse edn. specialist Durham County Substance Abuse Svcs., Durham, N.C., 1991-92; dual-diagnosis counselor Duke U. Med. Ctr., Durham, 1992-93; family counselor Three Springs Treatment Ctr., Siler City, N.C., 1993-94; dual-diagnosis counselor Vance County Mental Health Clinic, Henderson, N.C., 1994—; pvt. practice counselor Durham, 1992—; owner, mgr., pres. Dawn's Light Landscaping, Ltd., Norfolk, 1987-90; selection bd. mem. enlisted edn. advancement program USN, Pensacola, Fla., 1990. V.p. Nat. Clearinghouse for Social Change in Mil., Chapel Hill, 1991-92; pub. affairs officer N.C. Vets. Coalition, Durham, 1992-93, pres., 1994—. Lt. USN, 1981-90. Mem. ACA, NOW, NAFE, Nat. Women's Studies Assn., N.C. Counselor's Assn., Elizabeth Kuber-Ross Ctr., N.C Addiction Profls., Triangle Bus. and Profl. Guild. Office: VGWF County MH/DD/SAS 125 Charles Rollins Rd Henderson NC 27536

CLARK, CANDY, actress; b. Norman, Okla.; d. Thomas Prest and Ella Lee (Padberg) C. Student public schs., Ft. Worth. Appeared in movies Fat City, 1971, American Graffiti, 1973 (nominated for best supporting actress), The Man Who Fell To Earth, 1975, Citizens Band, 1976, The Big Sleep, 1977, When Ya' Coming Back Red Ryder, 1978, More American Graffiti, 1978, National Lampoon Goes To The Movies, 1981, Blue Thunder, 1981, Amityville 3-D, 1983, Stephen King's Cat's Eye, 1984, At Close Range, 1986, The Blob, 1988, Cool-As-Ice, 1991, Buffy the Vampire Slayer, 1992, Radioland Murders, 1994; appeared in TV movies Amateur Night at the Dixie Bar and Grill, 1978, Where The Ladies Go, 1980, Rodeo Girl, 1980, Popeye Doyle, 1986, Plan of Attack, 1992; appeared in off-Broadway show A Coupla White Chicks Sitting Around Talking, 1981, play It's Raining on Hope Street, 1988.

CLARK, CAROLYN ARCHER, technologist, scientist; b. Leon County, Tex., Feb. 16, 1944; d. Ray Brooks and Dena Mae (Green) Archer; m. Frank Ray Clark, Nov. 20, 1960 (div. Oct. 1979); children: Frank Ray, Valerie Lynn, Bruce Layne; m. Jack G. Simpson, May 1993. BA, Sam Houston State U., 1961; MS, Tex. A&M U., 1973, PhD, 1977. Supr., bookkeeper Rep. Sewing Machine Distbrs., Dallas, 1961-65; door-to-door sales Avon Products, Inc., Bryan, Tex., 1965-72; lectr. Tex. A&M U., College Station, Tex., 1977, rsch. assoc., 1977-79; sr. sci. Lockheed Emsco., Houston, 1979-82, prin. scientist, 1983-85; aerospace technologist, phys. scientist NASA Stennis Space Ctr., Miss., 1985-87; staff scientist Lockheed EMSCO, Houston, 1987-88; sr. project mgr., office mgr. Ctr. for Space and Advanced Tech., Houston, 1988-91; staff scientist Lockheed Engrng. and Scis. Co., Houston, 1991—; cons. in field. Contbr. articles to profl. publs. Recipient Commendation for Outstanding Contbns. Lockheed, 1979-80, 91, Commendation for Excellence, 1984; Cert. of Merit U.S. Dept. Agr. 1980; Grad. Rsch. fellow Tex. A&M, 1975-76; NSF co-grantee Tex. A&M, 1976-77. Mem. Am. Soc. Plant Taxonomists, Bot. Soc. Am., Sigma Xi, Phi Sigma, Alpha Chi, Kappa Delta Pi. Republican. Office: Lockheed Engring/Scis Co 2400 Nasa Rd 1 Houston TX 77058-3799

CLARK, CAROLYN CHAMBERS, nurse, author, educator; b. Superior, Wis., Mar. 25, 1941; d. John and Phyllis (Olsen) Stark. BS, U. Wis., 1964; MS, Rutgers U., Newark, 1966; EdD, Columbia U., 1976. RN, Fla.; cert. advanced registered nurse practitioner, Fla. Instr. Bergen Community Coll., Paramus, N.J., 1972-74; pvt. practice wellness nursing, 1972—; founder, dir. The Wellness Inst., Sloatsburg, 1979-84; assoc. prof. Pace U., Pleasantville, N.Y., 1983-84; cons. VA Med. Ctr., Bay Pines, Fla., 1988-89, provider continuing programs for nurses, 1990—; alt. healing specialist/cons. Bay Area Psychol. Svcs, 1994—; dir. Women's Wellness Ctr. of the Resource Ctr. of Women. Author: Nursing Concepts and Processes, 1977, The Nurse as Group Leader, 1977, 3rd edit., 1994 (also pub. in Swedish, German), Mental Health Aspects of Community Health Nursing, 1978, Classroom Skills for Nurse Educators, 1978, Assertive Skills for Nurses, 1978, Management in Nursing, 1979, The Nurse as Continuing Educator, 1979, Enhancing Wellness: A Guide for Self-Care, 1981, Wellness Nursing: Concepts, Theory, Research and Practice, 1986, Deadlier than Death, 1993, Dangerous Alibis, Cast Into The Fire, 1994; editor, pub. The Wellness Newsletter, 1980-95; editor Alternative Health Practitioner: The Jour. of Complimentary and Natural Care, 1995—; pres. Wellness Resources, 1992—; contbr. articles to profl. jours.; mem. editorial bd. Am. Jour. Holistic Nursing, 1985-88, Women's Health Care Internat., 1985—. Grantee, N.J. Blue Cross, 1982, Robert Wood Johnson Found., 1983; recipient award Fla. Free Lance Writers Assn., 1988, 92. Fellow Am. Acad. Nursing; mem. Mystery Writers Am., Sisters in Crime. Office: 3451 Central Ave Saint Petersburg FL 33713-8522

CLARK, CHRISTINE MAY, editor, author; b. Peoria, Ill., Apr. 25, 1957; d. Darrell Ronald and Alice Venita (Burkitt) French; m. Terry Randolph Clark, Aug. 28, 1982. B.A., Judson Coll., 1978. Assoc. editor David C. Cook Pub., Elgin, Ill., 1978-80; editor Humpty Dumpty, 1980-94; editor Children's Digest, 1980-83, Jack and Jill , 1983-86, Turtle mag., 1990—; editorial dir. Children's Better Health Inst., Indpls.; assoc. editor Highlights for Children, Honesdale, Pa., 1994—; speaker Pacific Northwest Writers' Conf., 1986, Soc. Children's Book Writers Confs., Tex., 1987, 88, Reader's Digest Writers' Confs., S.C., 1989, W.Va., 1990, Seattle Pacific U., 1991, Highlights Found. Writers Workshop at Chautauqua, 1993. Author: (religious curriculum) Come, Follow Me, 1983, Living in Covenant, 1985. Contbr. articles and stories to children's and adult religious mags., also to Indpls. Monthly, Indpls. Woman, This Is Indianapolis, Key Horizons. Asst. scout leader Fox Valley Council Girl Scouts U.S., 1972; vol. Elgin Mental Health Ctr., 1975-76; big sister Big Sister-Little Sister Program, Elgin, 1980. Recipientjournalism award EDPRESS, 1986, 87, 88, 89, 90, 92, Outstanding Reporting award Soc. Profl. Journalists, 1990; Aurora Found. scholar, 1975. Mem. Soc. Children's Book Writers and Illustrators, Ednl. Press Assn., Judson Coll. Alumni Assn. Reorganized Ch. of Jesus Christ of Latter-day Saints. Avocations: Piano; travel. Home: 309 18th St Honesdale PA 18431 Office: Highlights for Children 803 Church St Honesdale PA 18431

CLARK, DEBRA FEIOCK, marketing professional; b. Frankfurt, Fed. Republic Germany, June 19, 1958; came to U.S., 1960; d. Ray Donald Feiock and Joanne (Hackler) MacNiven; m. Steven D. Clark, Sept. 5, 1981 (div. 1986). BA in Communications, Calif. State U., Fullerton, 1981; cert. in mktg., U. Calif., Berkeley. Mgr. Foto Hall, Inc., Tustin, Calif., 1979-82; copy products sales rep. Kodak Copy Products, Los Angeles, 1982-85; electronic pub. sales Kodak Copy Products, Whittier, Calif., 1985-88; comml. mktg. Kodak Electronic Photography, Fremont, Calif., 1988—; regional account mgr. Thermal Printing Systems Eastman Kodak Co., 1990-92, bus. devel. mgr. Printer Producers Divsn., 1992—; guest speaker Fullerton (Calif.) Community Coll., 1988. Vol. Internat. Spl. Olympics, Reno, 1989, Girl Scouts U.S., 1989-90; socials dir. YAF Fellowship. Mem. Sigma Kappa Sorority Alumni Assn. (pres. 1987-88). Presbyterian. Office: Eastman Kodak 37741 Madera Ct Fremont CA 94536-6637

CLARK, DESMOND LAVERNE (MISS DESMOND CLARK), editor, entertainer, minister; b. Omaha, May 4, 1951; d. Thomas Edward and Louise Gwendolyn (Jackson) C. BS, Tenn. State U., 1973. Sec. Atlanta (Ga.) Housing Authority, 1973, modernization asst., 1974, contract coord., 1977; word processor, proof reader Touche Ross & Co., Miami, 1981, word processing supr., 1989; asst. editor Innerself Publs., Hollywood, Fla., 1991—, editor, 1994—; interfaith minister Interfaith Seminary, N.Y.C., 1993; profl. entertainer Curtain Call Prodns., Ft. Lauderdale, Fla., 1990—. Mem. exec. com. Dem. Party, Miami, 1980-88. Mem. Asn. Interfaith Ministry. Home: 3150 NW 135th St # 1 Opa Locka FL 33054-4884 Office: Inner Self Publs 915 S 21st Ave Apt 2A Hollywood FL 33020-6950

CLARK, DIANNA LEA, broadcast executive; b. Lincoln, Ill., June 27, 1956; d. Raymond Burnell and Patricia JoAnn (Bartle) Kirby; m. Robert Allen Clark, Nov. 25, 1978. AA, Springfield (Ill.) Coll., 1976; BA, Sangamon State U., Springfield, 1979. With broadcast svcs. Sangamon State U., 1977-80; traffic dir. Sta. WIL-FM, St. Louis, 1980-85; ops. dir. Sta. KCLC Lindenwood Coll., St. Charles, Mo., 1985-86; radio sta. mgr. St. Louis Community Coll. at Flo Valley, St. Louis, 1986—. Dir. St. Charles Women's Bowling Assn., 1993—. Mem. NAFE, Am. Bus. Women's Assn. (regional conf. sec. 1990-92, Woman of Yr. 1986, 92), Am. Legion Aux., Nat. Broadcasting Soc., W.I.N.O.S. Bowling Club (sec., bd. dirs. 1983—), Alpha Epsilon Rho (nat. conv. coord. 1987, 93, nat. project chmn. Tourette syndrome 1984-92, regional conv. dir. 1989-91, Nat. Outstanding Mem. 1986, Nat. Honor Lifetime Mem. 1990). Office: St Louis CC Sta KCFV 3400 Pershall Rd Saint Louis MO 63135-1408

CLARK, DONNA MARIA, college registrar; b. Galveston, Tex., June 16, 1958; d. Frederick William Jr. and Joann Judith (Clause) C. B Gen. Studies, U. S.W. La., 1981, MS, 1983; postgrad., La. State U., 1991-93. Lic. rehab. counselor. Residence counselor Student Pers. Office U. Southwestern La., Lafayette, 1978-81, acad. counselor/advisor Coll. Gen. Studies, 1981-83; rehab. coord. Underwriters Adjusting Co., Lafayette, 1983-85, Continental Rehab., Metairie, La., 1985-86; ins. and securities agt. Primerica/ALW, Chalmette, La., 1986-90; spl. needs instr. Job Tng. Partnership Act, Chalmette, 1988-91; devel. edn. instr. Nunez Tech. Inst., Chalmette, 1988-91, student pers. svcs. officer, 1991-92; fin. aid admissions Nunez C.C., Chalmette, 1992—; cons., presenter La. Office of Vocat. Edn. Sex Equity Conf., Baton Rouge, 1992. Editor catalog Nunez C.C., 1993, 94;

photographer. Bd. dirs. Jimmy's Kids, Chalmette, 1987-88; mem. statewide com. to study minority affairs, 1994. Mem. NOW, So. and La. Assn. Coll. Registrars and Admissions Officers, La. Asst. Student Fin. Aid Adminstrs., Nat. Displaced Homemaker Network, U. S.W. La. Alumni Assn. Democrat. Roman Catholic. Office: Nunez CC 3700 La Fontaine St Chalmette LA 70043-1249

CLARK, ELEANOR M., federal agency administrator; b. Columbus, Ohio, Feb. 22, 1940; d. John Douglas and Mary Elizabeth Clark. BBA, George Washington U., 1964. CPA. Sr. auditor Stanton, Minter and Bruner, 1964-68; sys. acct. Office of Sec. of Commerce, 1968-71; acctg. mgr. Nat. Found. Arts and Humanities, 1971-75; assoc. dir. Nat. Tech. Info. Svc., 1975-82; dir. Office of Sec. Dept. Commerce, 1982-84; dir. Price Waterhouse, 1984-90; comptr. Fed. Housing Adminstrn., Washington, 1990—. Author: (with others) Handbook on Governmental Accounting and Auditing. Mem. AICPA, D.C. Inst. CPAs, Assn. Govt. Accts., Brookings Instn. Accts. Roundtable. Office: Fed Housing Adminstrn 451 7th St SW Rm 5132 Washington DC 20410*

CLARK, ELIZABETH ADAMS (LIZ CLARK), genealogy educator; b. Arcadia, Fla., Jan. 16, 1944; d. Calvin Emmett and Ruth Gertrude (Paxton) Adams; m. Eugene Corry Clark, Apr. 27, 1963; children: Mary Corry Clark-Cross, Walter Emmett. BS in History, Ga. Coll., 1971. Tchr. spl. reading Washington County Schs., Sandersville, Ga., 1971-72; tchr. spl. needs Adairsville (Ga.) Sch., 1973-75; instr. genealogy Blue Ridge Community Coll., Flat Rock, N.C., 1977-85; property mistress, set decorator Flat Rock Playhouse, State Theatre N.C., 1979-85; software specialist, computer cons. Fonda Corp., St. Albans, Vt., 1985-87; pub., editor Cane Break Pub., Spartanburg, S.C., 1985—; cons. in arts State Theatre N.C., 1984. Author: Cane Break Cooking, 1990; also articles. Organizing corr. sec. Henderson County Dem. Women, 1978-80, bd. dirs., 1991—; bd. dirs. Henderson Little Theatre, 1977-85, exec. v.p., 1985; bd. dirs. Spartanburg Coalition for Choice, 1989; active NOW, 1992—, coord. Spartanburg chpt., 1992-93, coord. S.C., 1993—; active ACLU, 1992—, Voters United for Equality, 1993—; mem. Spartanburg Nat. Women's Polit. Caucus, 1992—. Recipient Scnow award, 1994, Geraldine Ferraro Woman of Yr. award, 1994. Mem. AAUW, ACLU, DAR (award as Woman of Yr. for Adairsville, Ga. 1974), Western Carolina Geneal. Soc., Carolina Alliance for Fair Employment, Corry Family Soc., Clark Family Soc. (bd. dirs., editor newsletter 1989-93), Nat. Women's Polit. Caucus. Episcopalian. Home and Office: 1009 Oak Creek Dr Spartanburg SC 29302-2981

CLARK, ELIZABETH ANNETTE, insurance company administrator; b. Mpls., Oct. 6, 1934; d. Walter Burdette and Daveda Marguerite (Hansen) Garver; m. Forrest Halter, May 17, 1958 (div. Feb. 1973); children: Gregory, Linda Halter Balsiger; m. Leslie Matthew Clark, Sept. 28, 1976. AA, Montgomery Coll., 1954; AAS, Greenville (S.C.) Tech. Coll., 1973; B in Gen. Studies, Furman U., 1979; MBA, Clemson (S.C.) U., 1987. CLU. Data processor Liberty Life Ins. Co., Greenville, 1973-84, mgr. quality improvement dept., 1984-88, dir. project mgmt., 1989, asst. v.p. policy forms, 1989—; instr. computer programming part-time Greenville Tech. Coll., 1980-81. Sec. S.C./Piedmont chpt. Nat. Multiple Sclerosis Soc., Greenville, 1974-76; bd. dirs. Greenville Little Theatre, 1974-76; chmn. invitation com. Bicentennial Ball, Greenville, 1976; mem. Speakers' Bur., Family Counseling Ctr., 1991—. Fellow Life Mgmt. Inst.; mem. Life Office Mgmt. Assn. (rep. so. systems devel. commn. 1985-90, program chmn. 1987-88, sec. 1988-89, chmn. 1989-90), EFS Users (v.p, 1992-95), Life and Health Compliance Assn. (mem. exec. com.), Am. Coun. Life Ins. (task force on policy forms filing 1994-95), Mensa, Beta Sigma Phi (pres. Greenville chpt. 1975-76, 93-94, v.p. coun. 1975-76, Woman of Yr. 1975, 89, 90, 93, Alpha-Omega award 1977). Unitarian. Home: 121 Rockwood Dr Greenville SC 29605-1942 Office: Liberty Life Ins Co PO Box 789 Greenville SC 29602-0789

CLARK, EUGENIE, zoologist, educator; b. N.Y.C., May 4, 1922; m. Hideo Umaki, 1942; m. Ilias Konstantinou, 1949; 4 children; m. Chandler Brossard, 1966; m. Igor Klatzo, 1969. BA, Hunter Coll., 1942; MA, NYU, 1946, PhD (Pacific Sci. Bd. fellow 1949), 1950; DSc (hon.), U. Mass., Dartmouth, 1990. Rsch. asst. in ichthyology Scripps Instn. Oceanography, 1946-47; with N.Y. Zool. Soc., 1947-48; research asst. in animal behavior Am. Museum Nat. History, N.Y.C., 1948-49; research assoc. Am. Museum Nat. History, 1950-80; instr. Hunter Coll., 1954; exec. dir. Cape Haze Marine Lab., Sarasota, Fla., 1955-67; asso. prof. biology City U. N.Y., 1966-67; asso. prof. zoology U. Md., 1968-73, prof. zoology, 1973-92, prof. emerita, sr. rsch. scientist, 1992—; vis. prof. Hebrew U., 1972. Author: Lady with a Spear, 1953, The Lady and the Sharks, 1969, Desert Beneath the Sea, 1991; subject of biography, Shark Lady (Ann McGovern), 1978. Recipient Myrtle Wreath award in sci. Hadassah, 1964, Nogi award in art Underwater Soc. Am., 1965, Dugan award in aquatic sci. Am. Littoral Soc., 1969, Diver of Yr. award Boston Sea Rovers, 1978, David Stone medal, 1984, Stoneman Conservation award, 1982, Gov. of S. Sinai medal, 1985, Lowell Thomas award Explorers Club, 1986, Wildscreen Internat. Film Festival award, 1986, medal Gov. Red Sea, Egypt, 1988, Nogi award in Sci., 1988, Women's Hall of Fame award State of Md., 1989, Women Educators award, 1990, Alumnae award, Franklin Burr award Nat. Geographic Soc., 1993; named to Hunter Coll. Hall of Fame Nat. Assn. Underwater Instrs., 1990, DEMA Hall of Fame, 1993; Fellow AEC, 1950; Saxton Fellow, 1952; Breadloaf Writer's fellow; Fulbright scholar Egypt, 1951 . Fellow AAAS; mem. Am. Soc. Ichthyology and Herpetology (life), Soc. Woman Geographers (Gold medal 1975, U. Md. Pres.'s medal 1993), Internat. Soc. Profl. Diving Scientists, Nat. Pks. and Conservation Assn. (vice chmn. 1976), Am. Littoral Soc. (v.p. 1970-89), Am. Elasmobranch Soc. Home: 7817 Hampden Ln Bethesda MD 20814-1108 Office: Univ Md Dept Zoology College Park MD 20742

CLARK, FAYE LOUISE, drama and speech educator; b. La., Oct. 9, 1936; student Centenary Coll., 1954-55; B.A. with honor, U. Southwestern La., 1962; M.A., U. Ga., 1966; PhD, Ga. State U., 1992; m. Warren James Clark, Aug. 8, 1969; children—Roy, Kay Natalie. Tchr., Nova Exptl. Schs., Fort Lauderdale, Fla., 1963-65; faculty dept. drama and speech DeKalb Community Coll., Atlanta, 1967—, chmn. dept., 1977-81. Pres. Hawthorne Sch. PTA, 1983-84. Mem. Ga. Theatre Conf. (sec. 1968-69, rep. to Southeastern Theatre Conf. 1969), Ga. Psychol. Assn., Ga. Speech Assn., Atlanta Ballet Guild, Friends of the Atlanta Opera, Southeastern Theatre Conf., Atlanta Hist. Soc., Atlanta Artists Club (sec. 1981-83, dir. 1983-89), Young Women of Arts, Speech Communication Assn., High Mus. Art, Phi Kappa Phi, Pi Kappa Delta, Sigma Delta Pi, Kappa Delta Pi, Thalian-Blackfriars. Presbyterian. Club: Lake Lanier Sailing. Home: 2521 Melinda Dr NE Atlanta GA 30345-1918 Office: DeKalb Community Coll Humanities div North Campus Dunwoody GA 30338

CLARK, GEORGIANNA MAE (GEORGI CLARK), actress, producer, director; b. Mackinaw City, Mich., Nov. 10, 1940; d. George Alvin and Edna S. (Sailler) Ranville; m. Dennis R. Clark, 1961; children: Michele Marie, Tracey Lynn. Student, No. Mich. Coll., 1972, Grand Rapids Jr. Coll., 1977—; 10 acting certs.. Lic. cosmetologist, Mich. Actress TV and film prodns. including Dallas, Target, NBC Today, Getting Even, In High Cotton, Texasfest, Killing In A Small Town, Touch & Die, J.F.K.; celebrity model On Location Big D Ranch, Patricia Stevens Modeling; dir., camera operator prodns. for Heritage Cablevision including Cattle Baron's Ball, Gerald Ford's Race for the Cure, Joan Collins Fund Raiser, USA Film Festival, Hands Across America, Tex. Women's News; producer, hostess cable TV show Georgi's Psychic Awareness, Dallas, 1985-95; agent, owner Georgi's Entertainment, Inc., USA, Can., 1985-92; extra's agent T.A.L.E.N.T., 1985-92; CEO Concept I Comm., 1992-95; officer Premier Productions; owner Coiffures by Georgi, 1970-77; v.p. Phoenix Bldg., Inc., 1968-83, One Day Automotives, Inc.; dir. modeling, promotions and entertainment David Payne Agy., Dallas, 1985; dir., mistress of ceremonies various Queen Pageants, Miss Teen Pageants, Art Shows, Faces Internat. Makeup/Hair Stylist Yr. Book, Dallas, 1987. Writer (screenplays) The Neighbor; 2, 6, 7, 3, 4 (exec. producer, dir.), The Exoneration, Balloon, The Book & 36, Man Rehind the Wheel, Symbolic Syndrome, Trash, Treasures & Trouble; columnist Cheboygan Daily News, 1972, producer, dir., hostess, writer (made for TV) The Art of Acupuncture; dir. Tex. Swindle's Medicine Show; exec. dir., exec. prodr. Dallas Alive; contbr. articles and poems to National Enquirer, Redbook, American Peotry Anthology. Mem. Nat. Assn. Broadcasting Engrs. and Technicians (sec.-treas. 1990), Country Music Assn., United Fedn. Musicians (agt.), Tex. Film and Tape Profls., Dallas Screenwriters Assn. (treas.), Dallas Communication Coun., Dallas C. of C. Mem. Burt Lake Band of Ottawa and Chippewa Indians, Inc.

CLARK, JACQUELINE HUNT, university program administrator; b. Lumberton, N.C., Mar. 29, 1956; d. Grady and Parnell (Cummings) Hunt; m. Dexter Clark, Dec. 21, 1975; children: Jessica, Tara. BA in Sociology, Pembroke (N.C.) State U., 1977; MEd in Guidance and Counseling, Campbell U., Buies Creek, N.C., 1986. Counselor Indian Edn. program Lumberton Jr. High Sch., 1984-87, Lumberton Sr. High Sch., 1977-87; cousnelor student support svcs. Pembroke State U., 1987-89; mgr. family advocacy program Hohenfels Tng. Area, Germany, 1989-90, dir. army community svc., 1990-91; counselor student support svcs., instr. univ. orientation Pembroke State U., 1991-93, program coord. Title III grant, 1993—. Mem. Lumberton Planning Bd.; mem. adv. coun. Lumberton Sr. High Sch.; HIV/AIDS community health advisor. Mem. AAUW, ACA, N.C. Assn. Counseling and Devel., Phi Delta Kappa. Baptist. Home: 565 Caton Rd Lumberton NC 28358-0453

CLARK, JANE ANGELA, medical group administrator, educator; b. Linton, Ind., Sept. 18, 1955; d. Frank William and Doris Louise (French) Barlich; m. William H. Clark, June 4, 1977; children: William Daniel, Stephanie Lynne. BA, Purdue U., 1976; postgrad., U. Wis., 1978-79, U. Pa., 1985-90. Cert. employee benefits specialist. Rsch. asst. Purdue U., West Lafayette, Ind., 1977; pers. specialist Sentry Ins., Stevens Point, Wis., 1977-81; adminstr. Indianhead Med. Group, Rice Lake, Wis., 1981-88, Emergency Room Physicians Group, Rice Lake, 1985—; instr. mgmt. Wis. Indianhead Tech. Coll., Rice Lake, 1985—; cert. instr. Zenger-Miller courses; mem. suprs. mgmt. adv. com. Wis. Indianhead Tech. Coll., 1985-87. Chairperson Am. Heart Assn., Shell Lake, Wis., 1989; bd. dirs. United Way, Rice Lake, 1987-88. Mem. After Five Club (bd. dirs.), Alpha Lambda Delta, Phi Alpha Theta, Kappa Delta Pi. Republican. Baptist. Home: Rt 1 Box 267A Shell Lake WI 54871

CLARK, JANET EILEEN, political scientist, educator; b. Kansas City, Kans., June 5, 1940; d. Edward Francis and Mildred Lois (Mack) Morrissey; AA, Kansas City Jr. Coll., 1960; AB, George Washington U., Washington, 1962, MA, 1964; PhD, U. Ill., 1973; m. Caleb M. Clark, Sept. 28, 1968; children: Emily Claire, Grace Ellen, Evelyn Adair. Staff, U.S. Dept. Labor, Washington, 1962-64; instr. social sci. Kansas City (Kans.) Jr. Coll., 1964-67; instr. polit. sci. Parkland Coll., 1970-71; asst. prof. govt., N.Mex. State U., Las Cruces, 1971-77, assoc. prof., 1977-80; assoc. prof. polit. sci. U. Wyo., 1981-84, prof., 1984-94; prof. polit. sci., head dept. West Georgia Coll., Carrollton, Ga., 1994—. Co-author: Women, Elections and Representation, 1987, The Equality State, 1988, Women in Taiwan Politics: Overcoming Barriers to Women's Participation in a Modernizing Society, 1990; editor Women & Politics, 1991—. Wolcott fellow, 1963-64, NDEA Title IV fellow, 1967-69. Mem. Internat. Soc. Polit. Psychology Gov. Coun., 1987-89. Mem. NEA (pres. chpt. 1978-79), Am. Polit. Sci. Assn., Western Polit. Sci. Assn. (exec. coun. 1984-87), Western Social Sci. Assn. (exec. coun. 1978-81, v.p. 1982, pres. 1985), Women's Caucus for Polit. Sci. (treas. 1982, pres. 1987), LWV (exec. bd. 1980-83, treas. 1986-90, pres. 1991-93), Women's Polit. Caucus, Beta Sigma Phi (v.p. chpt. 1978-79, sec. 1987-88, treas. 1988-89, v.p. 1989-90, pres. 1990-91), Phi Beta Kappa, Chi Omega (prize 1962), Phi Kappa Phi. Democrat. Lutheran. Book rev. editor Social Sci. Jour., 1982-87. Contbr. articles to profl. jours. Home: 333 Foster St D-23 Carrollton GA 30117 Offiice: West Ga Coll Dept Polit Sci Carrollton GA 30118

CLARK, JEANNE (BARBARA), police commander; b. Chgo., Nov. 15, 1948; d. James John and Margaret Jessilyn (Sullivan) McGough; m. Patrick M. Clark, May 15, 1992. BA, St. Xavier U., Chgo., 1971; MA, U. Ill., 1975; cert. police mgmt., Northwestern U., 1982. Officer Chgo. Police Dept., 1975-78, youth officer, 1978-80, sgt., 1980-88, lt., 1988-89, comdr., 1989—; sec.-treas. Comdg. Officers and Sgts. Chgo. police Dept. Credit Union, 1986-88; chmn. Ill. Anti Car Theft Com., Chgo., 1989-91; v.p. St. Jude Police League, 1994—. Office: Chgo Police Dept 021 Dist 300 E 29th St Chicago IL 60616

CLARK, JEANNIE SPERRY, clinical psychologist; b. Philippi, W.Va., Sept. 11, 1962; d. Clarence Everett and Josephine Leila (Haught) Sperry; children: Danielle Ashley, Joshua Braden. BA, W.Va. U., 1983; MS, Ohio U., 1987, PhD, 1990. Lic. psychologist, W.Va. Supervised psychologist Fred Krieg, PhD and Assocs., Vienna, W.Va., 1990-91; psychologist Valley Community Mental Health, Fairmont, W.Va., 1991-92, United Hosp. Ctr., Clarksburg, W.Va., 1992-93; asst. prof., dir. psychology, Weston divsn. Dept. Behavioral Medicine/Psychiatry W.Va. U. Sch. Medicine, 1993—; vis. asst. prof. W.Va. U., Morgantown, 1991-92. Mem. APA, W.Va. Psychol. Assn.

CLARK, JESSIE DONA, social worker; b. Rochester, N.Y., Feb. 28, 1922; d. Robert Edward and Florence Virginia (Nelson) Bray; m. James Governeau Banks, Jan. 23, 1943 (div. Nov. 1972); children: James Governeau, Franklin Frazier, David Robert; m. Paul Andrews Clark, Jan. 21, 1973. BA, Howard U., 1947, MSW, 1960. Psychiat. social worker St. Elizabeths Hosp., Washington, 1960-65; family relocation officer D.C. Redey, Land Agy., 1965-73; supr. social worker Dept. Community Mental Health, St. Thomas, V.I., 1975; spl. asst. to comptroller V.I. Housing Auth., St. Thomas, 1975-85; evaluator, vice chmn. Operation Sisters United, St. Thomas, 1975-83; cons. V.I. Labor Mgmt. Com., St. Thomas, 1984—; cons. human resources dept. U. V.I., 1992—. Bd. dirs. YWCA (Phyllis Wheatley Br.), Washington; commr. Youth Coun., Washington, Vis. Nurses Assn., Washington, Ptnrs. for Health, St. Thomas (editor mo. newsletter 1988-89). Recipient Disting. Lady award Plymouth Congl. Ch., 1967, Outstanding Performance award D.C. Redevelopment Agy., 1971; NIMH fellow 1957-60. Mem. Internat. Assn. Pers. Mgrs. (v.p.), Nat. Assn. Housing & Renewal Officials, Nat. Assn. Social Workers (V.I. chpt., pres. 1985-87, Social Worker of Yr. 1983), Eta Phi Beta (v.p. 1988-89). Home: PO Box 8485 Charlotte Amalie VI 00801-1485

CLARK, JOYCE NAOMI JOHNSON, nurse; b. Corpus Christi, Tex., Oct. 4, 1936; d. Chester Fletcher and Ermal Olita (Bailey) Johnson; m. William Boyd Clark, Jan. 4, 1958; (div. 1967); 1 child, Sherene Joyce. Student, Corpus Christi State U., 1975-77. RN; cert. instrument flight instr. Staff nurse Van Nuys (Calif.) Community Hosp., 1963-64, U.S. Naval Hosp., Corpus Christi, 1964-68; patient care coord. Meml. Med. Ctr., Corpus Christi, 1968—. Leader Paisano Council Girl Scouts U.S.A., Corpus Christi, 1968-74. Recipient Charles A. Mella award Meml. Med. Ctr., 1981, Paul E. Garber award CAP, 1986, cert. of appreciation in recognition of Support Child Guard Missing Children Edn. Program Nat. Assn. Chiefs of Police, Washington, 1987, Charles E. Yeager Aerospace Edn. Achievement award, 1985, Grover Loenig Aerospace award, 1986, Cert. of World Leadership Internat. Biographical Ctr., Cambridge, Eng., 1987, Gill Robb Wilson award # 1021, 1988, Merit award Drug Free Am. Through Enforcement, Edn., Intelligence Nat. Assn. Chiefs of Police. Mem. USAF Aux, CAP Air Search and Rescue (past comdr. 3rd group, wing chief pilot, Sr. Mem. of Yr 1986), Am. Assn. Oper. Rm. Nurses (v.p. 1969), Soc. Nursing Profls., Am. Fed. Police, Aircraft Owners and Pilots Assn., Smithsonian Instn. Home: 1001 Carmel Pky Apt 33 Corpus Christi TX 78411-2152 Office: Meml Med Ctr Oper Rm 4606 Hospital Blvd Corpus Christi TX 78405-1818

CLARK, KAREN, state legislator. BS, Coll. St. Teresa, Winona, Minn. Mem. Minn. Ho. of Reps., 1981—, chmn. housing com., mem. various coms. Recipient Martin Luther King, Jr. award, 1987, Minn. Alliance Progressive Leadership award, 1991, Leadership award Nat. Gay & Lesbian Task Force. Home: 503 State Office Bldg Saint Paul MN 55155 Office: Minn State Senate State Capitol Saint Paul MN 55155*

CLARK, KAREN HEATH, lawyer; b. Pasadena, Calif., Dec. 17, 1944; d. Wesley Pelton and Lois (Ellenberger) Heath; m. Bruce Robert Clark,Dec. 30, 1967; children: Adam Heath, Andrea Pelton. Student, Pomona Coll., Claremont, Calif., 1962-64; BA, Stanford U., 1964-66; MA in History, U. Wash., 1968; JD, U. Mich., 1977. Bar: Calif. 1978. Instr. Henry Ford Community Coll., Dearborn, Mich., 1968-72; assoc. Gibson, Dunn & Crutcher, Irvine, Calif., 1977-86, ptnr., 1986—. Bd. dirs. Dem. Found. Orange County, 1989-91, 94—, Planned Parenthood Orange County, Santa Ana, Calif., 1979-82, New Directions for Women, Newport Beach, 1986-91, Women in Leadership, 1993—. Mem. Women in Leadership (founding mem. 1993), Women in Comml. Real Estate, Bldg. Industries Assn. So. Calif., Calif. Mortgage Bankers Assn. Office: Gibson Dunn & Crutcher 4 Park Plz Irvine CA 92714

CLARK, KATHLEEN MULHERN, foreign language and literature educator; b. Phila., Oct. 10, 1948; d. John Joseph Jr. and Rosalie (Callahan) Mulhern; m. Robert Lee Clark, Oct. 7, 1972; children: Matthew, Kelly. AB, Immaculata Coll., 1970; MA, Villanova U., 1981; postgrad., U. Laval, Que., Can., 1969, Ecole Francaise des Attachés de Presse, Paris, 1991. Cert. French tchr. French tchr. Great Valley High Sch., Devault, Pa., 1971-72, Conestoga Sr. High Sch., Berwyn, Pa., 1970-71, 72-78; lectr. fgn. lang. Immaculata (Pa.) Coll., 1973-89, prof. fgn. lang., lit., 1989—; translator Burroughs Corp., Paoli, Pa., 1976-78; translator, cons. Smith, Kline Animal Health Products, West Chester, Pa., 1985; co-developer, designer Leadership Core Curriculum, Immaculata, 1990—. Class rep. Immaculata Coll. Alumnae Assn., 1970—; mem. Phoenixville (Pa.) Sch. & Home Assn., 1984—. Recipient grant U. Laval, 1969, Pew Meml. Trust, 1990. Mem. AAUP, MLA, Am. Assn. Tchrs. French, Am. Coun. on Teaching of Fgn. Langs., Alliance Française, Pi Delta Phi. Roman Catholic. Home: 65 Rossiter Ave Phoenixville PA 19460-2509 Office: Immaculata Coll Faculty Ctr # 17 Immaculata PA 19345

CLARK, KELLY, small business owner; b. Grosse Pointe, Mich., Apr. 19, 1953; d. Leo James and Marie Victoria Magdeline (Ulanowicz) Kelly; m. William Lee Clark, June 22, 1973 (dec. Jan. 1986). Student, Boston U., 1975; BA in Sociology, Wayne State U., 1976. Tchr. Community Action Program for Juvenile Offenders, South Boston, Mass., 1976; prodn. artist Reporter Pub. Co., Marblehead, Mass., 1977; copywriter McDougall Assocs., Salem, Mass., 1977-79; v.p., creative dir. Andrew Curcio Inc., Boston, 1980-86, account supr., 1982-86, exec. v.p., 1983-86; pres., co-founder Alden & Clark, Inc., Boston, 1986—, Kelly Clark Advt. and Comms., Boston, 1988—. Pres. William Lee Clark Meml. Found., 1986—; mem. Women Affirming Life, Birghton, Mass.; chair Cotting League of Athletic and Sci. Ptnrs., Cotting Sch. for Spl. Needs Students, Lexington, Mass.; chair William Lee Clark Sci. Edn. Fund, Lexington; mem., sec. Ward Rep. Com., City of Boston; cons. Jr. Achievement Spl. Program for borderline students Boston High Sch.; exec. dir. DIME Borrowers Assn. Mass., 1993—; bd. dirs. Mass. chpt. Am. Right Coalition. Mem. Nat. Bus. Owners (chair speakers bur.), Friends of Mass. Coll. of Art, Women of Wayne, Wayne State U. Alumni Assn., Amnesty Internat., Am. Women Entrepreneurs, Women's Ednl. and Industrial Union. Roman Catholic. Office: Alden & Clark Inc 110 W Concord St Boston MA 02118-1508

CLARK, LETITIA Z., federal judge; b. 1945. BA, Rice U., 1967; MA, Rutgers U., 1970; JD, Syracuse U., 1973. Atty. EPA, Dallas, 1974-76; asst. U.S. atty. Southern District of Texas, 1982-85; bankruptcy judge Southern District of Texas, Houston, 1985—. Office: US Bankruptcy Ct PO Box 61010 515 Rusk St Houston TX 77002*

CLARK, LOYAL FRANCES, public affairs specialist; b. Salt Lake City, July 16, 1958; d. Lloyd Grant and Zina (Okelberry) C. Student, Utah State U., 1976-78. Human resource coord. U.S. Forest Svc., Provo, Utah, 1984—, fire info. officer, 1987—, pub. affairs officer, interpretive svcs. coord., edn. coord., 1988—; mem. Take Pride in Utah Task Force, Salt Lake City, 1989—; chairperson Utah Wildlife Ethics Com., Provo, 1989—. Instr. Emergency Svcs., Orem, Utah, 1990—. Recipient Presdl. award for outstanding leadership in youth conservation programs Pres. Ronald Reagan, 1985, Superior Svc. award USDA, 1987, Exemplary Svc. award U.S. Forest Svc., 1992, Nat. Eyes on Wildlife Achievement award USDA Forest Svc., 1993. Mem. Nat. Wildlife Fedn., Nat. Assn. Interpretation, Utah Soc. Environ. Educators, Utah Wildlife Fedn. (bd. dirs. 1981-85, v.p. 1985-87, Achievement award 1983, 85, 87), Utah Wilderness Assn., Am. Forestry Assn., Nature Conservancy, Women in Mgmt. Coun. Office: Uinta Nat Forest 88 W 100th N Provo UT 84601

CLARK, LYNN, mental health administrator, counselor; b. Chgo., Oct. 13, 1946. BA in Speech and English Edn., U. South Fla., 1970, MA in Early Childhood Edn., 1974, MA in Gerontology, 1978; PhD in Family Rels., Fla. State U., 1983. Lic. counselor, Fla. Adminstrv. asst., therapist Chgo. Assn. Rehab. & Ednl. Svcs., 1983-84; rehab. therapist Cognitive Rehab. Inst., Tampa, Fla., 1984-85; program dir. Cognitive Rehab. & Family Support Svcs., Dunedin, Fla., 1985—; pres., founder CRAFSS & HIS. Mem. Am. Assn. for Counseling and Devel., Am. Assn. Marriage and Family Therapy, Nat. Rehab. Assn., Nat. Coun. Family Rels., Nat. Assn. Rehab. Providers to the Pvt. Sector. Home: 12501 Vonn Rd Largo FL 34644

CLARK, LYNN FIORDALISI, accountant; b. Glen Cove, N.Y., Feb. 29, 1964; d. Frank George and Martha Walker (Ferguson) Fiordalisi; m. Mark Walter Clark, Jan. 5, 1994. BBA in Acctg., Adelphi U., 1987. CPA N.Y., Ariz. Sr. auditor Ernst & Young, N.Y.C., 1987-91; controller Banco Bamerindus, N.Y.C., 1991-93; fin. analyst Cigna Health Care Ariz., Phoenix, 1993-94; pvt. practice as CPA, 1994—. Dir. vol. ctr. United Way, Phoenix, 1994—. Mem. AICPA, Ariz. Soc. CPA's, N.Y. State Soc. CPA's, Scottsdale C. of C., Scottsdale Jaycees. Home: 14428 N 91st St Scottsdale AZ 85260

CLARK, MARCIA RACHEL, prosecutor; b. Berkeley, Calif., 1953; d. Abraham I. Kleks; m. Gabriel Horowitz, 1976 (div. 1980); m. Gordon Clark (div. 1994); 2 children. BA in Polit. Sci., UCLA, 1974; JD, Southwestern U., 1979. With Brodey and Price, L.A., 1979-81; with L.A. County Dist. Atty.'s Office, 1981—, now dep. dist. atty.; prosecuting atty. trial of Robert Bardo, 1991, O.J. Simpson, 1994-95. Office: Office of the Dist Atty 18-000 Criminal Courts Bldg 210 W Temple St Los Angeles CA 90012*

CLARK, MARGARET PRUITT, think tank executive administrator; b. Eau Clair, Wis., May 9, 1946; d. Robert Earl and Gladys (Taylor) Pruitt; m. Kenneth Hall Clark, Aug. 14, 1966; children: Deborah Margaret, Robert James (dec.). BA in Sociology, Beloit Coll., 1966; MA in Sociology, U. Ill., Chgo., 1970; PhD in Sociology, U. Tex., 1976. Instr. U. Md., 1977-79, George Mason U., Fairfax, Va., 1979-80; asst. prof. sociology Bowdoin Coll., Brunswick, Maine, 1980-83; instr. U. Maine, Augusta, 1983; mediator Maine Ct. Mediation Svc., Brunswick, 1985-87; mem. Maine Ho. of Reps., Augusta, 1986-92; exec. dir. Adolescent Pregnancy Coalition, 1988-90, Advocates for Youth (formerly Ctr. for Population Options), Washington, 1992—. Vol. coord. steering com. ERA, 1984; coord. Maine chpt. NOW, 1984-86; mem. Gov. Brennen's Task Force on Adolescent Pregnancy and Parenting, 1985-86, Commn. to Study Health Svcs. in Pub. Schs., 1987-88, Blue Ribbon Commn. on Health Care Expenditures, 1987-89, Commn. to Study Status of Nursing and Health Care Professions in Maine, 1988-89; bd. dirs. Family Planning Assn. Maine, 1980-88, chmn. nominating com. 1985-86, v.p., 1987; bd. dirs. pub. policy com. Nat. Coun. on Alcoholism, 1985-88, others. Mem. Northeast Network Progressive Elected Ofcls., Nat. Order Women Legislators, Am. Sociol. Assn., Assn. Clin. Sociologists, Sociologists for Women in Soc., NOW. Office: Advocates for Youth 1025 Vermont Ave NW Ste 200 Washington DC 20005

CLARK, MARSHA KOHLENBERGER, service association administrator; b. Belleville, Ill., Mar. 13, 1955; d. Harvey Charles and Eulalia Pearl (Schifferdecker) Kohlenberger; m. James L. Clark, Sept. 12, 1982. BS in Elem. Edn., S.E. Mo. State U., 1977; MBA, Maryville U., 1990. Cert. cash mgr., instr. Elem. instr. R-II Schs., Elsberry, Mo., 1977-79; bank officer Boatmen's Bank, St. Louis, 1979-91; exec. dir. Foster Care Coalition, St. Louis, 1992-93; dir. older adult svc. info. system OASIS, 1993—. Vol., mem. advocacy team YWCA, St. Louis, Leadership Ladder Women's Consortium, St. Louis; mem. Community Devel. Adv. Commn., Kirkwood, Mo., 1992-94; bd. dirs. Kids in the Middle, St. Louis, 1990—. Recipient Women in Leadership award Coro Found., 1990. Mem. LWV (bd. dirs. 1988-92). Methodist. Office: OASIS 601 Olive St Saint Louis MO 63101-1717

CLARK, MARTHA FULLER, state legislator, architectural historian, preservation consultant; b. York, Maine, Mar. 14, 1942; m. Geoffrey Clark; 2 children. BA, Mills Coll., 1964; MA, Boston U., 1977. Mem. N.H. Ho. of Reps. Bd. dirs. Strawbery Banke, 1976-92; founder, pres. Inherit N.H.; bd. trustees Friends of Music Hall; preservation cons. Preservation Action, Plan, N.H., 1992—; active Hist. Dist. Commn., 1977-80, Portsmouth Mus.

Commn., 1985—, Gov. Commn. on 21st Century Living Landscape Task Force, 1989-90. Mem. N.H. Hist. Soc. (bd. trustees 1992—). Demcrat. Office: NH House of Reps State Capitol Concord NH 03301*

CLARK, MARTHA J., insurance company executive; b. Glen Ridge, N.J., May 31, 1949; d. David Ormiston and Marion Jane (Drury) C.; children: Christopher, Alexis. AB, Brown U., 1971; MBA, Harvard U., 1978. CLU, 1986, chartered fin. cons., 1987. Asst. treas., trainee Chase Manhattan Bank, N.Y.C., 1971-74, 2d v.p. corp. fin., 1974-76, v.p., team leader corp. lending, 1978-81; v.p. corp. fin. Prudential Ins. Co., Newark, 1981-83, v.p., treas., 1983-89; pres., chief exec. officer Prudential Power Funding Assocs., Newark, 1989-92; pres. Prudential Asset Mgmt. Co., 1992—; bd. dirs., mem. audit com., compensation com. Dexter Corp.; bd. dirs., mem. audit com., pension com., contract rev. com. Foster Wheeler Corp. Treas., trustee Corp. of Brown U., 1987—, mem. budget and fin. com., audit and investment com., bd. dirs. Third Century Fund; bd. dirs. Ind. Coll. Fund. N.J., 1988—, chmn. fin./audit com.; trustee Stuart Country Day Sch. of Sacred Heart, Princeton, N.J., 1989—. Recipient Alumni Svc. award Brown U., Providence, R.I., 1984. Mem. Fin. Women's Assn., Com. of 200, Assn. Alumni Brown U. (bd. dirs., mem. exec. com. 1982-87, treas. 1982-84), Women's Campaign Fund. Republican. Presbyterian. Office: Prudential Asset Mgmt Co Prudential Plz 751 Broad St Newark NJ 07102-3777

CLARK, MARY HIGGINS, author, business executive; b. N.Y.C., Dec. 24, 1931; d. Luke J. and Nora C. (Durkin) Higgins; m. Warren Clark, Dec. 26, 1949 (dec. Sept. 1964); children: Marilyn, Warren, David, Carol, Patricia. BA, Fordham U., 1979; hon. doctorate, Villanova U., 1983, Rider Coll., 1986, Stonehill Coll., 1992, Marymount Manhattan Coll., 1992, Chestnut Hill, 1993, Manhattan Coll., 1993, St. Peter's Coll., 1993. Advt. asst. Remington Rand, 1946; stewardess Pan Am., 1949-50; radio scriptwriter, producer Robert G. Jennings, 1965-70; v.p., partner creative dir., producer radio programming Aerial Communications, N.Y.C., 1970-80; chmn. bd., creative dir. D. J. Clark Enterprises, N.Y.C., 1980—. Author: Aspire to the Heavens, A Biography of George Washington, 1969 (N.J. Author award 1969), Where Are the Children, 1976 (N.J. Author award 1977), A Stranger Is Watching, 1978 (N.J. Author award 1978), The Cradle Will Fall, 1980, A Cry in the Night, 1982, Stillwatch, 1984, Weep No More, My Lady, 1987, While My Pretty One Sleeps, 1989, The Anastasia Syndrome, 1989, Loves Music, Loves to Dance, 1991, All Around the Town, 1992, I'll Be Seeing You, 1993, Remember Me, 1994, The Lottery Winner, 1994; author: (with Thomas Chastain, others) Murder in Manhattan, 1986; editor: Murder on the Aisle: The 1987 Mystery Writers Anthology, 1987. Recipient Grand Prix de Litterature Policiere France, 1980. Mem. Mystery Writers Am. (pres. 1987, dir.), Authors League, Am. Soc. Journalists and Authors, Acad. Arts and Scis. Republican. Roman Catholic. *

CLARK, NANCEE FLESHER, painter, educator; b. Bloomington, Ill., May 23, 1948; d. Robert Herberth and Mary Major (Morris) Flesher; married; 1 child, Lalenya Judyth McMann. BAA, U. Fla., 1975, MFA, 1979. Asst. to editor-in-chief Infection and Immunity dept. medicine U. Fla., Gainesville, 1979-87; instr. art Santa Fe Community Coll., Gainesville, 1980-93; coord. cultural programs Santa Fe C.C., Gainesville, 1987-91; prof. drawing Ringling Sch. Art and Design, Orlando, Fla.; adj. instr. U. Fla., 1979, 84; painting resident Studio Art Ctrs. Internat., Florence, Italy, 1994. Exhibited in one-person shows at U. Fla., 1979, U. Cen. Fla., 1984, Lake City Community Coll., 1987, Swanston Fine Arts Gallery, 1989, others; exhibited in group shows at Thomas Ctr. for Arts, Gainesville, 1981, 87, 90, Japan Internat. Arts Soc., Tokyo, 1981-82, U. Tex., Tyler, 1983, U. Fla., 1985, Joan Hodgell Gallery, Sarasota, Fla., 1985, Valencia Community Coll., 1986, 88, Foster Harmon Gallery, Sarasota, 1992, Jacksonville Art Mus., 1987, Ringling Mus., 1992, Polk Mus., 1992, others; works in collections at U. Fla., Jacksonville Art Mus., Barnett Bank, Tampa, So. Bell. Guest artist Artists-in-Schs. Program, Alachua County, Fla., 1986-89; mem. Alachua County Arts Adminstrs., 1988-90. State of Fla. artist fellow, 1982-83, 91-92. Home: 5104 73rd St E Bradenton FL 34203-7922

CLARK, OUIDA OUIJELLA, public relations executive, educator; b. Birmingham, Ala., Dec. 7, 1949; d. Fred and Johnnie (Norrington) C. BA in Spanish Edn., Dillard U., New Orleans, 1971; grad. cert. pub. relations Am. U., 1973, U. Valencia (Spain), 1974; cert. journalism NYU, 1972; postgrad. U. Chgo., 1980. Fgn. Svc. intern USIA, 1971; freelance pub. relations cons., 1972-76; tchr. English as 2d lang. Arlington (Va.) Pub. Schs., 1976-78; founder, pres. Clark Prodns., Ltd., Inc., Little Rock, 1981—; pres., founder Global Pub. Rels., Inc., Washington, 1976, and Little Rock, 1981-95; multilingual free-lance pub. rels. cons.; rsch. assoc. Philander Smith Coll., 1980-81; active Africare Project, Senagal, Upper Volta, Mauritania, Niger, Chad, Sierra Leone, 1973; founder Internat. Ptnr. Sch., Vienna, Austria. Recipient Pub. Rels. award Nat. Powderly Alumni Assn., 1977, NEA support funds, 1987; Ark. Endowment Humanities grantee, 1982. Musical composer, dir. Children of the 21st Century; author (radio play) Bon Voyage, Everything Has Its Place, You Just Can't Drift, Culture is Never Tasteless, various dramas for Horizons of Success series, Everything Has Its Place, On Life of James Weldon Johnson, You Just Can't Drift, Culture Is Never Tasteless, It Comes From Within Life of J.C. Penny, Controlled By the Stars The Life of the Founders of Sears and Roebuck, You Must Make a Decision Life of Mahalia Jackson, A Mixed Blessing Life of W.C. Handy, A Passion to Succeed-A Story on the Life Milton Hershey, A Vision of Tomorrow-A Story of Ralph Bunche; project dir. radio programs. Mem. Pub. Rels. Soc. Am., Am. Film Inst., Capital Press Club, Dillard U. Alumni Assn. (co-founder, Ark. chpt.). Baptist. Contbr. articles to profl. jours.; patent Nat. Directory of Music and Dance Studios, 1978, rev., 1980. Office: PO Box 583 Little Rock AR 72203-0583

CLARK, PATRICIA ANN, federal judge; b. Buffalo, July 26, 1936; d. Andrew A. and Mary (Gardner) Zacher; m. James A. Clark, Mar. 25, 1960; B.A., Goucher Coll., Towson, Md., 1958; postgrad. Duke U., 1958-60; LL.B., U. Colo., 1961. Bar: Colo. 1961, U.S. Dist. Ct. D.C. 1961. With Transamerica Title Ins. Co., 1962-65; assoc. Holme, Roberts and Owen, 1965-70, ptnr., 1970-74; judge U.S. Bankruptcy Ct., Denver, 1974—. Commr., Colo. Civil Rights Commn., 1969-72; trustee Waterman Fund, 1978—; mem. transition adv. com. U.S. Cts., 1980-84, com. jud. resources, 1987-91. Recipient Disting. Alumni award U. Colo. Sch. Law, 1984. Mem. Colo. Bar Assn., Denver Bar Assn. Office: US Bankruptcy Ct US Custom House 721 19th St Denver CO 80202-2513

CLARK, PATRICIA K., federal agency administrator; b. York, Pa., 1951; d. Robert H. and Esther M. (Gladfelter) C. BS in Biology, Ursinus Coll., 1973; MSc in Environ. Sci., Drexel U., 1975. Indsl. hygienist area and regional offices Dept. Labor, dist. office supr., asst. regional adminstr. fed.-state ops., dep. regional adminstr., dir. compliance programs, dir. Directorate Tech. Support, OSHA. Mem. Am. Conf. Govtl. Indsl. Hygienists, Am. Indsl. Hygiene Assn. Office: Dept Labor Tech Support 200 Constitution Ave NW Rm N3653 Washington DC 20210*

CLARK, SANDRA MARIE, school administrator; b. Hanover, Pa., Feb. 17, 1942; d. Charles Raymond Clark and Mary Josephine (Snyder) Clark Wierman. BS in Elem. Edn., Chestnut Hill Coll., 1980; MS in Child Care Adminstrn., Nova U., 1985; MS in Ednl. Adminstrn., Western Md. Coll., 1992. Cert. elem. tchr., elem. prin., Pa. Tchr. various elem. schs., Pa., 1962-75; asst. vocation directress Mt. St. Joseph Motherhouse, Chestnut Hill, Pa., 1975-76; tchr. St. Catharine's Sch., Spring Lake, N.J., 1976-77; asst. mgr. Jim's Truck Stop, New Oxford, Pa., 1977-81; adminstr. Little People Day Care Sch., Hanover, 1981-88, sec., treas. bd. dirs., 1985-86; coord. regional resource Magic Yrs. Child Care & Learning Ctrs., Inc., Hanover, 1987-88; prin. St. Vincent de Paul Sch., Hanover, Pa., 1988—; presenter Hanover Area Seminar for Day Care Employees, 1983-86. coord. sch. safety patrols St. Vincent's Sch., Hanover, 1969-75, vice-chmn. bd., 1982-84; multi-media instr. first aid ARC, Hanover, 1983-86, bd. dirs., 1984-88; exec. sec. of bd. of dirs. ARC, Hanover, 1988; 1st v.p. Hanover Area Coun. of Chs., 1988, pres., 1989; validator accreditation program Nat. Acad. Early Childhood Programs, Washington, 1987—; bd. dirs. Life Skills Unltd. Handicapped Adults, 1988—; facilitator Harrisburg Diocesan Synod, Hanover, 1985-88, parish del., 1988. Pa. Dept. Pub. Welfare tng. grantee, 1986. Mem. NAFE, Nat. Cath. Ednl. Assn. Democrat. Roman Catholic. Club: Internat. Assn. Turtles (London). Home: 348 Barberry Dr Hanover PA 17331-1302 Office: St Vincent De Paul Sch Hanover PA 17331

CLARK, SARA JANE, accounting company executive; b. South Bend, Ind., Aug. 28, 1948; d. Robert F. and Maxine (Walker) Bennett; m. William H. Clark, Oct. 2, 1976; 1 child, Kristen Marie. Adminstrv. asst. Doherty Zable & Co., Chgo., 1975-77; gen. ptnr. Bennett Clark Co., Valparaiso, Ind., 1977-92, Bennett Clark Inc., 1992—; mem. LaSalle St. Cashiers, Chgo., 1979-85, 87-88, outing com. chmn., 1982, correspondence com. chmn., 1987-88. Treas. Porter County Children's Choir. Republican. Presbyterian. Avocations: reading, traveling, needlework.

CLARK, SARA MOTT, retired home economics educator; b. Mahaffey, Pa., Sept. 19, 1915; d. William Benjamin and Anna Pearl (Murray) M.; m. Maximilian Steineger, Dec. 13, 1941; children: Max III, Benjamin Alan, Betsy Ann, Kathryn Louise. BS, Juniata Coll., Huntingdon, Pa., 1933-37, Ind. U. Pa., 1940-41. Dietician, Home Econ. Tchr., Internat. Porcelain Art Tchr. Dietician Adrian Hosp., Punxsutawney, Pa., 1937-40; home econs. tchr. Scio High Sch., Ohio., 1941-42, Punxsutawney (Pa.) Area Dist. Sch., 1960-77; artist, tchr. Internat. Porcelain Artist, Bradenton, Fla.; pres. NW Pa. Hosp. Dietetics Orgn., Punxsutawney, 1938-40; chmn. Am. Home Econs. Central We. Dist., Punxsutawney, 1967-68. Vol. Art Display Internat. Porcelain Artist Atlanta Ga. 1986, Art in Action Festival Arts State Coll. 1981-82; Author: Various Porcelain Paintings China and Fla. 1986. Den mother Boy Scouts Am., Punxsutawney, 1951-56; Brownie leader Girl Scouts U.S., Punxsutawney, 1959; Sunday Sch. tchr. First Bapt. Ch., Punxsutawney, 1957-60. Recipient Tribute to Porcelain Artist award Punxsutawney Spirit, 1987. Mem. AAUW (historian Bradenton 1991-93, chair bridge group 1993-94), Progressive Study Club (pres. 1953-54, 75-76, farewell luncheon award), Treasures of Porcelain Artists, Gulf Coast Porcelain Artists, New Floridians Club (1st v.p. 1994). Republican. Home: 4270 Coquina Cir Apt B Bradenton FL 34208-5127

CLARK, SHARON ENID, principal; b. Houston, Aug. 7, 1940; d. Olen Otto and Mavis Marie (Godkin) Peterson; m. Philip Blair Crow (div.); 1 child, Shannon Lee Crow; m. Ross Daryl Clark; 1 child, Shelley Enid. BS in Edn., Sam Houston State U., 1961; MEd, Prairie View A&M U., 1976; postgrad., U. St. Thomas, Houston, 1988-92. Cert. elem. and high sch. tchr., adminstr., supr., Tex. Tchr. Spring Br. Ind. Sch. Dist., Houston, 1961-68, 72-73, dir. summer program, 1968; tchr. Albuquerque Pub. Schs., 1969-71; tchr. Waller (Tex.) Ind. Sch. Dist., 1973-74, tchr., team leader, 1976-92, sci. advisor, 1989-92, prin., 1992—; team leader Nat. Tchr. Corps Cycle IX, Waller, 1974-76; facilitator Tex. Elem. Sci. Insvc. Program; trainer Tactics for Thinking, Tex.; presenter in field; staff developer for numerous profl. orgns., Tex., 1976—; co-chair state com. on svc. learning; mentor prin. Tex. Middle Sch. Network, 1993. Contbr. articles to prof. jours. Recipient Tchrs. Make a Difference award Channel 13/Harris County Dept. Edn., 1988, Tchr. of Yr. award Waller Ind. Sch. Dist., 1988, Outstanding LIfe Sci. Tchr. award Harris County Med. Soc., 1990. Mem. ASCD, Nat. Sci. Tchrs. Assn., Nat. Mid. Sch. Assn., Internat. Reading Assn., Nat. Coun. Social Studies, Tex. Elem. Prins. and Suprs. Assn., Phi Delta Kappa (v.p.). Office: Jones Intermediate Sch Waller Ind Sch Dist PO Box 2877 Univ Dr/Owens Prairie View TX 77484

CLARK, SUSAN (NORA GOULDING), actress; b. Sarnia, Ont., Can., Mar. 8, 1943; d. George Raymond and Eleanor Almond (McNaughton) C. Student, Toronto (Ont.) Children's Players, 1956-59; student (Acad. scholar), Royal Acad. Dramatic Art, London. partner Georgian Bay Prodns. Producer: Jimmy B. and Andre, 1979, Word of Honor, 1980, Maid in America, 1982; star Webster, ABC-TV, 1983-89; appeared in Brit. TV prodns., repertory theatre; appeared in Brit. premiere of play Poor Bitos; appeared in Can. TV prodns., including Heloise and Abelard, Hedda Gabler; starred in Taming of the Shrew; appeared in Sherlock Holmes, Williamstown Theatre Festival, (taped for HBO), 1981, Meetin's on the Porch, Canon Theater, Beverly Hills, 1990, Lion in Winter, Walnut St. Theater, Phila., 1992; Getting Out, Mark Taper Forum, Los Angeles, 1978, The Vortex, Walnut Street Theatre, 1994; films include The Apple Dumpling Gang, Night Moves, The North Avenue Irregulars, Airport '75, Midnight Man, Porky's, Murder by Decree, Tell Them Willie Boy is Here, Skin Game, City on Fire, Madigan, Coogan's Bluff, Skullduggery, Promises in the Dark, Valdez is Coming, Showdown, Double Negative, Nobody's Perfekt; appeared in segments of TV series Columbo, Marcus Welby, Barnaby Jones; appeared in Double Solitaire, Pub. Broadcasting System; TV films include: Something for a Lonely Man, 1968, The Astronaut, 1972, Trapped, 1973, Babe, 1975 (Emmy award), McNaughton's Daughter, 1976, Amelia Earhart, 1976 (Emmy nom.), Jimmy B. & Andre, 1980 (also co-prodr.), The Choice, 1981, Maid in America, 1982 (also co-prodr.), Snowbound, The Jim and Jennifer Stolpa Story, 1993, Tonya and Nancy, The Inside Story, 1994, The Butterbox Babies, 1994. Mem. ACLU, Am. Film Inst. Office: care Georgian Bay Prodns 3815 W Olive Ave Ste 101 Burbank CA 91505-4648

CLARK, SUSAN LESLEY, research analyst; b. Melrose, Mass., Oct. 4, 1959; d. Robert Spencer and Ruth Norma (Griffin) C. BA in Russian Studies, Middlebury Coll., 1981; MA in Nat. Security, Georgetown U., 1986. Rsch. asst. Ctr. for Naval Analyses, Alexandria, Va., 1982-86; rsch. analyst Inst. for Def. Analyses, Alexandria, 1986—; participant MIT Seminar XXI Program, 1994—. Editor, contbr.: Gorbachev's Agenda, 1989, Soviet Military Power in a Changing World, 1991; contbr. articles to profl. jours. Mem. Am. Assn. for Advancement Slavic Studies, Coun. Fgn. Rels. (term mem.), Geographic Soc. Lisbon (corr. 1990—), Ctr. for Strategic and Internat. Studies (mem. Am. working group Am.-Ukrainian adv. com. 1993—). Office: Inst for Def Analyses 1801 N Beauregard St Alexandria VA 22311-1733

CLARK, SUSAN MATTHEWS, psychologist; b. Newton, Kans., Aug. 5, 1950; d. Glenn Wesley Matthews and Jane Buckles; m. S. Bruce Clark, Aug. 14, 1971; children: Casandra Jane, Ryan Matthews. BME, Wichita State U., 1971, MME, 1975, MA, 1982; PhD, North Tex. State U., 1985. Elem. tchr. Derby (Kans.) Pub. Schs., 1972-74; profl. musician Amarillo (Tex.) Symphony, 1974-77; psychol. cons. Achenbach Ctr., Hardtner, Kans., 1983-85; psychologist VA Med. Ctr., Wichita, Kans., 1984-85, St. Francis Acad., Inc., Salina, Kans., 1986-89, Psychiat. Clinic Wichita, 1989-93; gen. mgr. Affiliated Psychiat. Svcs., Wichita, 1993—; bd. dirs. Salina Coalition for the Prevention of Child Abuse, 1986-87. Author: Grant, 1987. Bd. deacons Plymouth Congl. Ch., Wichita, 1989-92, mem. bd. Christian Edn., 1993—. Recipient: Phi Kappa Phi, Mu Phi Epsilon, Psi Chi. Mem. APA, Nat. Acad. Neuropsychology, Southwestern Psychol. Assn., Kans. Psychol. Assn., Wichita Area Psychol. Assn., Kans. Assn. Profl. Psychologists, Beta Sigma Phi. Republican. Congregationalist. Office: Affiliated Psychiat Svcs 1148 S Hillside St Ste 104 Wichita KS 67211-4005

CLARK, SUSAN RAE WINTERHALTER, reading educator; b. Toledo, Ohio, Oct. 13, 1945; d. James Reinold and Mildred Evelyn (Bricker) Winterhalter; m. William Charles Clark, Aug. 22, 1970; children: James Jason, Jeffrey Allen. BS in Edn. with honors, U. Del., 1967, MS in Edn. and Reading with honors, 1969; PhD with honors, U. Mo., Kansas City, 1992. Cert. tchr. Tchr. 5th grade Franklin Sch., Westfield, N.J., 1967-68; instr. reading Study Ctr. U. Del., Newark, 1968-69; reading improvement specialist Dept. Defense, Torrejon Air Base, Madrid, 1969-70; tchr. educationally handicapped Franklin Sch., Burlingame, Calif., 1970-73; dir. reading Watchung Hills Regional High Sch., Warren, N.J., 1973-74; edn. cons. State Dept. N.J., Somerville, 1974-75; instr. Licking County/Ohio State Vo Tech, Newark, 1975-76, Met. C.C.-Longview, Lee's Summit, Mo., 1976—; adj. instr. Avila Coll., Kansas City, 1992-93, U. Mo., Kansas City, 1992—; cons. in edn., Lee's Summit, Mo., 1988—; researcher Longview C.C., Lee's Summit, 1992—; dir., cons. Lindamood-Bell Learning Processes, Kansas City, 1988—. Mem. NAt. Assn. Devel. Edn., Nat. Reading Conf., Internat. Reading Assn., Volksmarch, Phi Kappa Phi. Republican. Presbyterian. Home: 1405 Gulfport Ave Lees Summit MO 64081 Office: Longview CC 500 Longview Rd Lees Summit MO 64081

CLARK, TERESA WATKINS, psychotherapist, clinical counselor; b. Hobart, Okla., Dec. 18, 1953; d. Aaron Jack Watkins and Patricia Ann (Flurry) Greer and Ralph Gordon Greer; m. Philip Winston Clark, Dec. 29, 1979; children: Philip Aaron, Alisa Lauren. BA in Psychology, U. N.Mex., 1979, MA in Counseling and Family Studies, 1989. Lic. profl. clin. counselor, N.Mex. Child care worker social svcs. divsn. Family Resource Ctr., Albuquerque, 1978-79; head tchr., asst. dir. Kinder Care Learning Ctr., Albuquerque, 1979-80; psychiat. asst. Vista Sandia Psychiat. Hosp., Albuquerque, 1980-87; psychotherapist outpatient clinic Bernalillo County Mental Health Ctr.-Heights, 1989-91; therapist adolescent program Heights Psychiat. Hosp., Albuquerque, 1991—. Mem. ACA, Am. Assn. Multicultural Counseling and Devel., N.Mex. Health Counselors Assn. (ctrl. regional rep. bd. dirs., bd. dirs.), Phi Kappa Phi. Democrat. Office: Heights Psychiat Hosp 103 Hospital Loop NE Albuquerque NM 87109

CLARK, THREESE ANNE, occupational therapist; b. Bath, N.Y., Jan. 16, 1946; d. Frank George and Beulah Irene (Harris) Brown; m. Jacob Clark, Mar. 11, 1966 (div. Mar. 1977); 1 child, Jayson Todd. BS in Occupational Therapy, U. N.D., 1967, MS in Counseling and Guidance, 1977. Lic. occupational therapist, Pa., Md. Occupational therapist U. N.D. Med. Ctr., 1968; chief occupational therapist, program developer Corning (N.Y.) Hosp., 1968-69, Arnot-Ogden Hosp., Elmira, N.Y., 1969-71; staff occupational therapist VA Ctr., Bath, N.Y., 1971-74; instr. occupational therapy U. N.D., Grand Forks, 1974-77; prin. investigator occupational therapy Ohio State U., 1977-79; occupational therapist Regional Ednl. Assessment and Cons. Team, Hillsboro, Ohio, 1979-81; occupational therapist, phys. medicine and rehab. Saint Mary's Hosp., West Palm Beach, Fla., 1981-82; chief occupational therapist Mercy Med. Ctr., Oshkosh, Wis., 1982-87; dir. occupational therapy, clin. dir. spinal injury program HealthSouth Rehab. Hosp. Altoona, 1987—; pres. and owner Life Care Planning and Mgmt. Inc., Altoona, 1993—; cons. Founders Pavillion, Corning, 1969, Grafton (N.D.) State Sch. for the Retarded, 1975-76, Heart of Am. Rehab. Ctr., Rugby, N.D., 1976-77, Andrea Clifford program, 1978; guest lectr. support groups, community groups, ednl. programs, 1987—; presented numerous papers on occupational therapy. Contbr. articles to profl. jours. Pres. adv. bd. Occupational Therapy Asst. Program, Mt. Aloysius Jr. Coll., 1988-92, 94—; mem. adv. profl. com. Home Nursing Agy., Altoona, 1988-93; mem. com. Health Care Adv. Com., 1994—; bd. dirs. Ctr. for Internat. Living of South Ctrl. Pa., 1992—; mem. med. svc. com. Evergreen Manor, Oshkosh, 1985-87; chair home/family life and human rels. Northtowne Elem. Sch. PTA, Columbus, Ohio, 1978, others. Mem. Am. Occupational Therapy Assn. (coun. edn. 1974-76, coun. affiliate pres. 1976), Nat. Rehab. Assn., Ohio Occupational Therapy Assn., Columbus Dist. Occupational Therapy Assn., Pa. Occupational Therapy Assn., Am. Assn. Hand Therapists. Baptist. Home: 5300 5th Ave Altoona PA 16602-1312 Office: HealthSouth Rehab Hosp 2005 Valley View Blvd Altoona PA 16602-4598 also: Life Care Planning Mgmt Inc 5300 5th Ave Altoona PA 16602

CLARK, TONI ANDERSON, accountant, controller; b. Atlanta, Sept. 1, 1959; d. Edward Ray and Dorothy Ann (Leininger) Anderson; m. Randall Corwyn Clark, Oct. 17, 1987. BS in Acctg., Auburn U., 1982. Jr. acct. West Point (Ga.) Pepperell, Inc., 1982-83, acct., 1983-86, cost acct., 1986-87, sr. cost acct., 1987; acctg. coord Great Am. Knitting Mills, Burlington, N.C., 1987-90, cost and budget mgr., 1990-94, asst. contr., 1994—. Mem. Inst. Mgmt. Accts. (co-dir. mem. acquisition 1984-85, v.p. membership 1985-86, v.p. adminstrn. 1986-87). Baptist. Home: 1920 Bradbury Dr Burlington NC 27215 Office: Great Am Knitting Mills PO Drawer 1359 Burlington NC 27215

CLARKE, ALYCE GRIFFIN, state legislator; b. Yazoo City, Miss.; m. L.W. Clarke Jr.; 1 child, DeMarquis Johntrell. BS, Alcorn State U.; MS, Tuskegee Inst.; postgrad., Jackson State U., Miss. Coll. Nutritionist; mem. Miss. Ho. of Reps., 1985—, vice chmn. interstate coop com., mem. various coms. Active Econ. Devel. Com., Exec. Dem. Commn., New Hope Found. Mem. Nat. Assn. Cmty. Health Ctrs., Pub. Health Assn., Jack & Jill Am., Alcorn Alumni, Alpha Kappa Alpha. Democrat. Baptist. Home: 1053 Arbor Vista Blvd Jackson MS 39209-7135 Office: Miss State Senate State Capitol Jackson MS 39201*

CLARKE, CORDELIA KAY KNIGHT MAZUY, management executive; b. Springfield, Mo., Nov. 22, 1938; d. William Horace and Charline (Bentley) Knight; m. Logan Clarke, Jr., July 22, 1978; children by previous marriage—Katharine Michelle Mazuy, Christopher Knight Mazuy. A.B. with honors in English, U. N.C., 1960; M.S. in Statistics, N.C. State U., 1962. Statistician Research Triangle Inst., Durham, N.C., 1960-63; statis. cons. Arthur D. Little, Inc., Cambridge, Mass., 1963-67; dir. mktg. planning and analysis Polaroid Corp., Cambridge, 1967-70; dir. mktg. and bus. planning Transaction Tech. Inc., Cambridge, 1970-72; pres. Mazuy Assos., Boston, 1972-73; v.p. Nat. Shawmut Bank, Boston, 1973-74; sr. v.p., dir. mktg. Shawmut Corp., 1974-78; sr. v.p., dir. retail banking Shawmut Bank, 1976-78; v.p. corp. devel. Arthur D. Little, Inc., 1978-79; v.p. Conn. Gen. Life Ins. Co., 1979-85; pres. CIGNA Securities, 1983-85; chmn. Templeton, Inc., 1985-92; exec. v.p. McGraw-Hill Inc., 1985-90; pres. micromarketing divsn. ADVO, 1990—; faculty Williams Sch. Banking; adv. com. Bur. of Census, 1978-84; bd. dirs. Guardian Life Ins. Co., Colt Mfg., CLS Corp.; tchr. Amos Tuck Grad. Sch. Bus., Dartmouth Coll., 1964-65, exec.-in-residence, 1978, 80; bd. overseers, 1979-85; exec.-in-residence Wheaton Coll., 1978; vis. prof. Simmons Grad. Sch. Mgmt., 1978; mem. schs. adv .council Bank Mktg. Assn., 1976-78; mem. corp. adv. bd. Hartford Nat. Bank & Trust Co., 1980-87. Columnist Am. Banker, 1976-78. Mem. Mass. Gov.'s Commn. on Status of Women, 1977-79; bd. corporators Babson Coll., 1977-80; adv. bd. Boston Mayor's Office Cultural Affairs, 1977-79; bd. dirs. Blue Shield of Mass., 1976-79, Greater Hartford Arts Council, 1979-93; trustee Children's Mus. Hartford, 1980-82; corporator Inst. of Living, 1981-92; regent U. Hartford, 1982-94; bd. dirs. Hartford Art Sch., 1982-94, Hartford Stage Co., 1985—, Manhattan Theatre Club, 1988-91, Inst. for Future, 1988-92, N.Y. Internat. Festival of Arts, 1989-91; trustee Goodspeed Opera, 1988—. Mem. Am. Mktg. Assn., Phi Beta Kappa, Phi Kappa Phi, Kappa Alpha Theta. Home: 89 River Rd East Haddam CT 06423-1402 Office: 1 Univac Ln Windsor CT 06095-2629

CLARKE, DOROTHY HOFF, lawyer; b. Louisville, Dec. 17, 1943; d. John A. and Carol (Stillwell) Hoff; m. Frederic B. Clarke III; children: Fredric B. IV, Claire E., Peter E. Stambaugh, Elisabeth M. Stambaugh. BS in Fgn. Svc., Georgetown U., Washington, 1966, JD, 1981. Bar: Va. 1982, U.S. Dist. Ct. (ea. dist.) Va., U.S. Ct. Appeals (4th cir.). Mem., chmn. Arlington (Va.) Sch. Bd., 1984-92; del. Dem. Nat. Conv., Atlanta, 1988; mem. Dem. State Cen. Com., Va., 1980-82; past chmn. Va. Dept. for Children; mem. No. Va. Juvenile Detention Commn. Mem. ABA, AAUW (pres. 1974-76), Va. Women Attys. Assn., Va. Bar Assn., Arlington Bar Assn. Roman Catholic. Office: 2060 14th St N # 206 Arlington VA 22201-2519

CLARKE, HEIDI CHRISTINE, physical therapist; b. Montreal, Que., Can., July 6, 1963; came to U.S., 1983; d. Horst Adolf and Maiga (Dorn) Freier; m. George Allan Clarke, Aug. 21, 1983; children: George Allan Jr., G. Andrew Thomas. BS in Anatomy and Physiology, Andrews U., 1987, MS in Phys. Therapy, 1988. Cert. phys. therapist, Ohio. Staff phys. therapist Kettering (Ohio) Med. Ctr., 1988-90, coord. back program, 1990-91, supr. phys. therapy, 1991-93, asst. chief phys. therapy, 1993-94; assoc. prof., acad. coord. clin. edn. Andrews U., Dayton, Ohio, 1994—. Cons. in devel. fitness room Sr. Ctr., Miamisburg, Ohio, 1992. Home: 509 Schuyler Dr Kettering OH 45429

CLARKE, INGRID GADWAY, academic ombudsman, consultant; b. Bad Homburg, Hesse, Fed. Republic Germany, Sept. 21, 1942; came to U.S., 1964, naturalized, 1982; d. Johann Kajetan and Irmgard (Schneider) Rebholz; m. David Scott Clarke, Dec. 24, 1984. B.A. equivalent, Johann Wolfgang Goethe Universität, Frankfurt, Fed. Republic Germany, 1964; M.A., Memphis State U., 1965; postgrad. Tulane U., 1965-69; Ph.D., So. Ill. U., 1984. Instr. So. Ill. U., Carbondale, 1969-74, univ. ombudsman, 1974—, also chairperson bd. dirs. students' legal assistance program, 1980-86 . Mem. Carbondale Human Relations Com., 1974-76; chairperson Carbondale Fair Housing Bd., 1978-82. Fulbright scholar, 1964-67. Mem. Fulbright Alumni Assn., Univ. and Coll. Ombudsman Assn. (founder and first pres. 1985-86), Soc. Profls. in Dispute Resolution Delta Phi Alpha. Avocations: opera; tennis; skiing. Office: So Ill U Office Univ Ombudsman Carbondale IL 62901

CLARKE, JANICE CESSNA, principal; b. Inglewood, Calif., Sept. 8, 1936; d. Eldon W. and Helen V. (Parcels) Cessna; m. Jack F. Clarke, Mar. 30, 1958; children: Scott Alan, Kristin Ann, Kerry Suzanne. BA, U. of Redlands, 1958; MA in Teaching, Reed Coll., 1963; EdD, U. Nev., Reno, 1993. Cert. tchr., adminstr., Nev. Elem. tchr. Portland (Oreg.) Pub. Schs., 1959-62, Eugene (Oreg.) Pub. Schs., 1964-66; music tchr. Tempe (Ariz.) Pub. Schs., 1969-70; music tchr. Washoe County Sch. Dist., Reno, 1971-80, tchr.

gifted and talented program, 1980-89, coord. gifted and talented program, 1989-93; prin. Brown Elem. Sch., Reno, 1993—; bd. dirs. Far West Lab. for Ednl. Rsch., San Francisco, 1983-90. Mem. Nev. State Bd. Edn., 1982-90, pres., 1984-86. Recipient Disting. Svc. award Washoe County Tchr. Assn., 1974, Tchr. of Month award Reno/Sparks C. of C., 1984; named to El Segundo High Sch. Hall of Fame, 1989. Mem. NEA, NSEA, Nev. Assn. Sch. Adminstrs., Nev. Sch. Bds. Assn. (bd. dirs. 1982-90), Nat. Assn. Elem. Sch. Prins., Phi Delta Kappa, Delta Kappa Gamma. Office: Brown Sch 13815 Spelling Ct Reno NV 89511

CLARKE, JOYCE ANNE, biochemist; b. Sheffield, Eng., Sept. 17, 1947; came to U.S., 1968; d. Fred A. and Annie (Johnson) C.; m. Frank Ogawa, 1982. BA with honors, Girton Coll., Cambridge U., Eng., 1968, MA, 1972; PhD (fellow) in Biochemistry, U. Calif., Riverside, 1974. Research asst. dept. biochemistry U. Calif.-Riverside, 1968-73; lectr. dept. life scis. Middle East Tech. U., Ankara, Turkey, 1974-76; Dept. Energy research asso. Plant Research Lab., Mich. State U., East Lansing, 1976-78; assoc. biochemist dept. plant scis. U. Calif., Riverside, 1979-82, comm. coord. Internat. Club, 1979-82; biochemist Sci. Applications Internat. Corp., 1982-85, 91—; lectr. dept. biochemistry Va. Polytech. Inst. and State U., Blacksburg, 1986-89. Exec.-on-loan to Rebuild L.A., 1992-93. NSF fellow, 1976-78; Phi Beta Kappa scholar, 1972-73. Mem. Brit. Film Inst., Anglo-Am. Friendship Club, Oxford and Cambridge Clubs of L.A. (treas. 1992—). Episcopalian. Contbr. articles on plant psysiology and jojoba biochemistry to profl. jours. Home: 14901 Newport # 101 Tustin CA 92680

CLARKE, KATHERINE M., psychologist, educator; b. Vancouver, B.C., Oct. 29, 1953; d. R. Alex and Nancy M. (Graves) C. BA, U. B.C., 1975, MA, 1977; PhD, Loyola U., Chgo., 1981. Registered psychologist, Ont. Assoc. prof. St. Paul U., Ottawa, 1981-92, Weston Jesuit Sch. Theology, Cambridge, Mass., 1992—. Mem. APA, Soc. for Psychotherapy Rsch. Office: Weston Jesuit Sch Theology 3 Phillips Pl Cambridge MA 02138-3495

CLARKE, KIT HANSEN, radiologist; b. Louisville, May 24, 1944; d. Hans Peter and Katie (Jones) Hansen; AB, Randolph-Macon Woman's Coll., 1966; MD, U. Louisville, 1969; m. Dr. John M. Clarke, Feb. 14, 1976; children: Brett Bonnett, Blair Hansen, Brandon Chamberlain; stepchildren: Gray Campbell, Jeffrey William John M. Intern, Louisville Gen. Hosp., 1969-70; resident in internal medicine and radiology U. Tenn., Knoxville, 1970-73; resident in radiology U.S. Fla., Tampa, 1973-74; staff radiologist, chief spl. procedures Palms of Pasadena, St. Petersburg, Fla., 1974—, chmn. radiology dept., 1992—. Active Fla. Competitive Swim Assn. of AAU. Diplomate Am. Bd. Radiology. Fellow Am. Coll. Radiology; mem. AMA, Fla. West Coast Radiology Soc., Radiol. Soc. N.Am., Fla. Med. Assn., Pinellas County Med. Soc., Fla. Radiology Soc., Am. Horse Show Assn. (hunter, jumper divsn). Episcopalian. Home: 7171 9th St S Saint Petersburg FL 33705-6218 Office: 1609 Pasadena Ave S Saint Petersburg FL 33707-4565

CLARKE, LOUISE LEHTOLA, educational association administrator; b. Worcester, Mass., Mar. 27, 1952; d. Wilho and Helmi (Tarkiainen) Lehtola; m. Jeffrey Roland Clarke, June 22, 1974; children: Erica, John. BA, U. Mass., 1974; MA, Anna Maria Coll., 1976. Grants dir. Alliance for Edn., Worcester, 1986-88, dir. devel., 1988-92, dir. profl. devel. inst., 1992—; dir. Urban Math. Collaborative, Phila., 1990-94; cons. Greater Worcester (Mass.) Cmty. Found., 1993—. Pres. Jr. League, Worcester, 1985-86; bd. mem. Visiting Nurse Assn., Worcester, 1989—; founding bd. mem. Accord-Ctr. for Diversity, Worcester, 1991—, Advs. for Excellence in Edn., Worcester. Recipient Friend of Edn. award Ednl. Assn. Worcester, Mass., 1987, Literacy award Ctrl. Mass. Reading Coun., 1988. Mem. ASCD, Phi Delta Kappa. Baptist. Office: Alliance for Edn 405 Grove St Worcester MA 01605

CLARKE, LOUISE RIGDON, gifted student program administrator; b. Kansas City, Mo., July 23, 1936; d. Raymond Harrison and Margret (Britt) Rigdon; children: Michael Terrell, Steven Harrison. BA, Agnes Scott Coll., 1954-58; postgrad., U. Va.; M in Adminstrn. and Supervision, Radford U., 1986; CAGS in Adminstrv. Leadership, Va. Tech., 1994. Cert. middle sch. supr., prin. Arborvirus serologist Ctr. for Disease Control, Atlanta, 1958-64; English tchr. Chinese Middle Sch., Taipei, Taiwan, 1965-67; dir. Navy Relief Soc. for Marine Base Camp LeJeune, Jacksonville, N.C., 1975-76; sci. tchr. jr. high sch., 1980-84; hons. resource tchr. jr. high programs for gifted, 1984-86; coord. programs for gifted, talented and highly motivated Roanoke (Va.) City Pub. Schs., 1986—; adj. faculty Hollins (Va.) Coll., 1989—; past pres. Roanoke Regional Coun. Edn. of the Gifted. Mem. ASCD, Va. Assn. Supervision and Curriculum Devel., Nat. Assn. Gifted Children (pres.), Va. Assn. for Edn. Gifted, Am. Ednl. Rsch. Assn., Phi Dela Kappa. Avocations: tennis, bird watching, hiking. Home: 3362 Forest Ct Roanoke VA 24018 Office: Roanoke City Pub Sch PO Box 13145 Roanoke VA 24031-3145

CLARKE, MARGARET ANNE, maternal-child nurse; b. Rockville Centre, N.Y., July 28, 1954; d. Walter Joseph and Eda Rose (Brandimarte) Meyer; m. Jeffrey Clarke, Sept. 12, 1987 (div. Nov. 1990); 1 child, Katherine Marie. BSN, Mt. St. Mary Coll., 1977. Cert. perinatal nurse specialist, ANA; cert. lactation educator, UCLA. Staff nurse, charge relief med.-surg. Scott adn White Hosp., Temple, Tex., 1977-79; staff nurse, charge relief med.-surg. nursing Community Hosp., Monterey, Calif., 1979-80; med.-surg. nurse Good Samaritan Med. Ctr., West Palm Beach, Fla., 1982-86, maternity staff nurse, charge relief, 1986-88, perinatal educator edn. dept., 1988-90; chairperson Women's Health Seminar, 1989; staff RN perinatal svcs. Good Samaritan Med. Ctr., West Palm Beach, Fla., 1990-91; staff educator New Medico, Neurol. Rehab., West Palm Beach, 1991-92; intake nurse Women's Health Svcs., West Palm Beach, 1992—; chairperson Women's Health Seminar, 1989; mem. Palm Beach County Breastfeeding Task Force, 1993—. Roman Catholic. Home: 211-B Foxtail Dr West Palm Beach FL 33415

CLARKE, MARIE ELSIE, apparel design educator; b. Vineland, N.J., Aug. 22, 1927; d. John George and Adeline (Mazzi) Vraila; m. Joseph H. Clarke, Jan. 28, 1950 (div. 1986); children: Andrew, Helene. Cert., Pratt Inst., 1948. Stylist Bancroft Sporting Goods, Woonsocket, R.I., 1973-74; asst. dir. design India Imports of R.I., Providence, 1974-76, dir. of design, 1976-80; assoc. prof. apparel design RISD, Providence, 1981-94, prof. apparel design, 1994—; part-time instr. apparel design dept. RISD, 1978-80; cons. Bennett & Co., Newburyport, Mass. and Hong Kong, 1989—, GJM, Newburyport and Hong Kong, 1986-89, New Eng. Mfrs., 1985-87. Guest curator exhibit Newport Hist. Soc., 1985. Mem. Fashion Group Internat., Costume Soc. Democrat. Office: RISD Apparel Design Dept 2 College St Providence RI 02903-2717

CLARKE, MARJORIE JANE, environmental consultant, author, researcher; b. Miami, Fla., July 14, 1953; d. Garnet Winston Clarke and Janice Marie (Platt) Johnson. BA in Geology, Smith Coll., 1975; MA in Environ. Sci., Johns Hopkins U., 1978; MS in Energy Tech., NYU, 1982; doctoral program in earth/environ. sci., CUNY, 1991—. Cert. qualified environ. profl. Intern EPA, Washington, 1974-75, 76; phys. scientist U.S. EPA, N.Y.C., 1978; sr. economist Tri-State Regional Planning Commn., N.Y.C., 1979-81; policy coord. N.Y. Power Authority, N.Y.C., 1981-83; environ. scientist N.Y.C. Dept. Sanitation, 1984-88; dir. solid waste rsch. INFORM, Inc., N.Y.C., 1988-90; tech. rsch. cons. WNET-Channel 13, N.Y.C., 1990; environ. cons. Natural Resouce Def. Coun., N.Y.C., 1990—; sr. solid waste cons. INFORM, 1990—; cons. Air and Waste Mgmt. Assn., 1993-94; mem. steering com. Citywide Recycling Adv. Bd., N.Y.C., 1991—; mem. Camden County Environ. Tech. Adv. Com., 1993—; mem. N.J. Dept. Environ. Protection and Energy Mercury Emission Standard-Setting Task Force, 1992—; mem. N.Y. State Adv. Bd. on Ops. Requirements, Albany, 1988-92; examiner Qualified Environ. Profls. Program, 1995—; peer reviewer Environ. Def. Fund, N.Y.C., 1988—, Nat. Resources Def. Coun., N.Y.C., 1988-90; chmn. Manhattan Waste Prevention Adv. Com., 1991—. Author: Burning Garbage in the U.S., 1991; contbr. articles to profl. jours., 1983—. Chmn. Manhattan Citizens' Solid Waste Adv. Bd., N.Y.C., 1992-94, vice chair, 1994—. Recipient citation Dartmouth Coll., 1974; featured on cover Money Mag., 1981; U.S. EPA grantee, 1991—; Gilleece fellow CUNY, 1991-95. Mem. ASME (indsl. and mcpl. waste rsch. com. 1986—, operator cert. com. 1988—), Air and Waste Mgmt. Assn. (sec. 1988-89, vice chair 1989-90, chmn. solid waste and thermal treatment com. 1990-92, vice chair solid waste intercom. task force 1992-94, chair integrated waste mgmt. com. 1994—, tech. dir. video 1993-94), N.Y. State Solid Waste Combustion Inst. (tech. adv. com. 1988-92), Riverside-Inwood Neighborhood Gardens (founder, pres. 1984—), N.Y. Cycle Club (ride leader 1982—). Democrat. Home and Office: 1795 Riverside Dr Apt 5F New York NY 10034-5334

CLARKE, MARY ELIZABETH, retired army officer; b. Rochester, N.Y., Dec. 3, 1924; d. James M. and Lillian E. (Young) Kennedy. Student U. Md., 1962; D.Mil.Sci., Norwich U., Northfield, Vt., 1978. Joined U.S. Army as pvt., 1945, advanced through grades to maj. gen., 1978; exec. asst. to Chief of Plans and Policies, Office of Econ. Opportunity, 1966-67; comdr. WAC Tng. Bn., 1967-68; office dep. chief of staff for pers., 1968-71; WAC staff adviser 6th Army, 1971-72; comdr., comdt. U.S. Women's Army Corps Ctr. and Sch., 1972-74; chief WAC Adv. Office, U.S. Army Mil. Pers. Ctr., Washington, 1974-75, dir. Women's Army Corps, Washington, 1975-78; comdr. U.S. Army Mil. Police and Chem. Sch. Tng. Ctr., Ft. McClellan, Ala., 1978-80; dir. human resources devel. Office of Dep. Chief of Staff for Personnel, Washington, 1980-81, ret., 1981; hon. prof. mil. sci. Jacksonville (Ala.) State U. Mem. Def. Adv. Com. on Women in the Svcs., 1984—, vice chmn., 1986—; mem. adv. com. Women Veterans, 1989—, chmn., 1991; mem. The Presidential Commn. on the Assignment of Women in the Armed Forces. Decorated D.S.M.; recipient Toastmasters Internat. award, 1984, Nat. Veteran's award, 1994. Mem. Assn. of U.S. Army (coun. trustees), United States Automobile Assn. (bd. dirs. 1978-88), WAC Assn., WAC Mus. Found., Bus. and Profl. Women's Club. Address: 514 Fairway Dr SW Jacksonville AL 36265-3301

CLARKE, MARY PATRICIA, sports league communications executive; b. N.Y.C., May 31, 1966; d. Peter Francis and Ellen Marie (Murphy) C. BA, Fordham U., 1988; MS, Syracuse U., 1991. Asst. prodr. Good Morning Am. ABC/Capital Cities, N.Y.C., 1986-89; acct. supr. Edelman Pub. Rels., N.Y.C., 1991-92, Cohn & Wolfe Pub. Rels., N.Y.C., 1992-93; dir. corporate comm. NHL, N.Y.C., 1993—. Recipient Outstanding Tchg. Asst. award Syracuse U., 1991. Roman Catholic. Office: NHL Enterprises 1251 6th Ave New York NY 10019

CLARKE, URANA, musician, writer, educator; b. Wickliffe-on-the-Lake, Ohio, Sept. 8, 1902; d. Graham Warren and Grace Urana (Olsaver) C.; artists and tchrs. diploma Mannes Music Sch., N.Y.C., 1925; cert. Dalcroze Sch. Music, N.Y.C., 1950; student Pembroke Coll., Brown U.; BS, Mont. State U., 1967, M of Applied Sci., 1970. Mem. faculty Mannes Music Sch., 1922-49, Dalcroze Sch. Music, 1949-54; adv. editor in music The Book of Knowledge, 1949-65; v.p., dir. Saugatuck Circle Housing Devel.; guest lectr. Hayden Planetarium, 1945; guest lectr., bd. dirs. Roger Williams Park Planetarium, Providence; radio show New Eng. Skies, Providence, 1961-64, Skies Over the Big Sky Country, Livingston, Mont., 1964-79, Birds of the Big Sky Country, 1972-79, Great Music of Religion, 1974-79; mem. adv. com. Nat. Rivers and Harbors Congress, 1947-58; instr. continuing edn. Mont. State U. Chmn. Park County chpt. ARC, 1967-92, chmn. emeritus 1992—, co-chmn. county blood program, first aid instr. trainer, 1941-93; instr. ARC cardio-pulmonary resuscitation, 1976-84; mem. Mont. Commn. Nursing and Nursing Edn., 1974-76; mem. Park County Local Govt. Study Com., 1974-76, 93-94, chmn., 1984-86, 94—; mem. Greater Yellowstone Coalition. Mem. Am. Acad. Polit. Sci., Am. Musicol. Soc., Royal Astron. Soc. Can., Inst. Nav., Maria Mitchell Soc. Nantucket, N.Am. Yacht Racing Union, AAAS, Meteoritical Soc., Internat. Soc. Mus. Research, Skyscrapers (sec.-treas. 1960-63), Am. Guild Organists, Park County Wilderness Assn. (treas.), Trout Unlimited, Nature Conservancy, Big Sky Astron. Soc. (dir. 1965—), Sierra Club. Lutheran. Club: Cedar Point Yacht. Author: The Heavens are Telling (astronomy), 1951; Skies Over the Big Sky Country, 1965; also astron. news-letter, View It Yourself, weekly column Big Skies, 1981—; contbr. to mags. on music, nav. and astronomy. Pub. Five Chorale Preludes for Organ, 1975; also elem. two-piano pieces. Inventor, builder of Clarke Adjustable Piano Stool. Address: Log-A-Rhythm 9th St Island Livingston MT 59047

CLARK-HUSMANN, JANET, health services executive; b. Detroit, Oct. 3, 1941; d. John Francis Bullock and Martha Barbara (Bauer) Clark; m. Donald Bruce Tyson, Feb. 29, 1964; children: William John, Barbara June; m. Herman John Husmann, Nov. 11, 1988. AAS in Dental Hygiene, Broome C.C., 1961; BS in Health Edn., SUNY, Cortland, 1963; MPA in Mgmt., SUNY, Albany, 1993. Dental hygiene tchr. West Genessee Ctrl. Schs., Camillus, N.Y., 1964-65; health educator N.Y. State Dept. of Health, Syracuse, 1965-70; sr. sanitarian N.Y. State Dept. of Health, Monticello, 1977-80; prin. sanitarian N.Y. State Dept. of Health, N.Y.C., 1980-86; field ops. rep. N.Y. State Dept. of Health, Albany, 1986-89, mgr. Indian health, 1990—; sanitarian, health educator Onondaga County Health Dept., Syracuse, 1970-77; chmn., CEO Ha'awi Found. for Econ. Devel. in Indigenous Nations, 1994—. Mem. Nat. Environ. Health Assn., N.Y. Soc. Profl. Sanitarians (sec. 1970-84), N.Y. State Registry of Sanitarians (treas. 1987-90, pres. 1990—, Meritorious Svc. award 1986). Home: 355 Manning Blvd Albany NY 12206 Office: NY State Dept Health Rm 612 Empire State Plaza Tower Albany NY 12237

CLARKSON, CAROLE LAWRENCE, insurance company professional; b. Fredericksburg, Va., Dec. 18, 1942; d. Jerry Allen and Gladys Mae (Eubank) Lawrence; m. David Wendell Morris, Aug. 14, 1965 (div. 1977); 1 child, Peyton Lawrence; m. Lawrence Herbert Clarkson, Aug. 14, 1982. BA, Purdue U., 1965; postgrad., Ind. U., Indpls., 1970, U. Ill., 1971-73, U. Louisville Sch. of Bus., 1980-82. Pub. sch. tchr. various, Ind., Okla., Ill., N.C., Italy, 1965-75; librarian documentation U. Louisville Computing Ctr., 1980-82, IBM Corp., Austin, Tex., 1983-85; ins. mgr. Ohio State Life Ins. Co., Columbus, 1985-88, Community Life Ins. Co., Columbus, 1988-90; hosp. audit/stop loss coord. Health Adminstrn. Svcs., Houston, 1991—; supervisory mgr. Ins. Inst. of Am., 1987—. Mem. Internat. Claims Assn. (assoc. life and health claims 1987), Nat. Assn. Female Execs., Purdue U. Alumni Assn. Home: 2006 Kelona Dr Spring TX 77386

CLARKSON, ELISABETH ANN HUDNUT, civic worker; b. Youngstown, Ohio, Apr. 20, 1925; d. Herbert Beecher and Edith (Schaaf) Hudnut; A.B., Wilson Coll., 1947; M.A., State U. N.Y., 1973, also postgrad.; LH.D. (hon.), Wilson Coll., 1985; m. William M.E. Clarkson, Sept. 23, 1950; children: Alison H., David B., Andrew E. With J.L. Hudson Co., Detroit, 1947-50; writer The Minute Parade, daily Sta. WGR, Detroit, 1948-50; trustee Wilson Coll., Chambersburg, Pa., 1970-83, chmn. bd. trustees, 1979-82; bd. dirs. Buffalo Mus. Sci., 1972-87, 90—; mem. Trinity Episcopal Ch., 1950—, Racism Commn. Episcopal Diocese of W. N.Y., 1989-92, Cultural Leadership Group, 1994—; bd. dirs., companion in charge Soc. Companion of the Holy Cross, 1986-90, N.Y. State Mus., 1985-90; past chmn. jr. group Alright Knox Art Gallery; collector, curator Graphic Controls Corp. collection art, 1976-83; bd. dirs. Bischoff Clarkson Hudnut Corp., North Creek, N.Y., 1973-83; bd. trustees Clarkson Ctr. for Human Svcs., 1995—. Author: You Can Always Tell a Freshman, 1949, An Adirondack Archive: The Trail to Windover, 1993; also articles, dramatic presentations, archival materials Adirondack Mus., 1950-77. Recipient Trustee award for disting. svc. Wilson Coll., 1983, trustee emeritus. Mem. Buffalo Art Commn., 1983—, chmn. 1990—; mem. community adv. panel Niagara Frontier Transp. Authority, 1991-94; mem. exec. bd. arts adv. council SUNY at Buffalo, 1985-95; bd. dirs. N.Y. State Mus. Assn., Albany, 1985-90; mem. Garret Club, Buffalo Tennis and Squash Club. Episcopalian. Home: 156 Bryant St Buffalo NY 14222-2003 also: Windover North Creek NY 12853

CLARKSON, JOCELYN ADRENE, medical technologist; b. Bennettsville, S.C., July 9, 1952; d. Henry Louis and Frankie Allene (Carter) C. BA in Biology, Columbia (S.C.) Coll., 1973; cert. med. tech., Presbyn. Hosp., Charlotte, N.C., 1975. Coll. tutor of Germanic language Columbia Coll., 1970-73, switchboard operator, 1972-73; lab aide Richland Meml. Hosp., Columbia, 1974, now, med. technologist; profl. model. Appeared (TV commls.) Back Porch Restaurant and Meat Market, 1992, (film) The Chasers; author: poems, compilation, short stories, Messages from Hijac, 1989. Mem. Am. Soc. Clin. Pathologists (assoc.), Assn. for Studies of Classical African Civilization, African Am. Resource Inst. Roman Catholic. Home: 201 H L Clarkson Rd Hopkins SC 29061-9723

CLARNO, BEVERLY ANN, state legislator, farmer; b. Langlois, Oreg., Mar. 29, 1936; d. Howard William and Evelyn June (Young) Boice; m. Roy Clarno, July 15, 1991; children: Dan, Don, Randy, Cindi. Student, Marleherst Coll., 1985, Lewis & Clark Law Sch., 1985-87. Real estate broker Lake Realty and Hatfield & Skopil, Lake Osewego, Oreg., 1984-85; pres. T & H Hog Farms, Wasco, Oreg., 1973-76; securities examiner State of Oreg., Salem, 1981-83; circuit ct. clerk Deschutes County, Bend, Oreg., 1987-88; state legislator State of Oreg., 1988—. Recipient Cost Cutting award, Citizens for Cost Effective Govt., Portland, 1991. Mem. Boys & Girls Aid Soc., Kiwanis Club, Lions Club, High Desert Mus., Eastern Star. Republican. Methodist. Home: 25325 Dodds Rd Bend OR 97701-9370 Office: Oregon House Reps State Capitol Salem OR 97310*

CLARO, DEBRA LYNN, paralegal; b. Washington, Sept. 10, 1964; d. Frank Santos and Marion Joyce (Medeiros) Claro. B in Criminal Justice, U. Md., 1988; AD in Paralegal, Prince George's C.C., Largo, Md., 1992. Dirs. sec. Comptr. of the Currency, Washington, 1983-92, paralegal, 1992—. Republican. Roman Catholic. Home: 13138 Grand View Ct Upper Marlboro MD 20772 Office: Comptr of the Currency 250 East St SW Washington DC 20219

CLARY, ALEXIA BARBARA, management company executive; b. Waterbury, Conn., Sept. 17, 1954; d. John Joseph and Veza (Mandzik) Zurlis; 1 child, Jason Farrell. BBA, U. Miami, Coral Gables, Fla., 1976; postgrad., U. New Haven, 1978-80, Mercer U., 1988-89. Buyer Hewlett Packard, Cupeztino, Calif., 1981-83; sr. buyer Mannesman Tally, Seattle, 1983; purchase mgr. ICI, Redmond, Wash., 1983-84; commodity mgr. No. Telecom, St. Mountain, Ga., 1985-88; mfg. rep. Montgomery Mktg., Norcross, Ga., 1988-90; internat. purchasing agt. Sci. Atlanta, Norcross, Ga., 1990-91; pres. Farrell Mgmt. Group, Lawrenceville, Ga., 1991-92; sr. buyer Amphenol, Danbury, Conn., 1992-94; purchasing mgr. Danaher-Gulton Graphic, East Greenwhich, R.I., 1994—. U. Miami scholar, 1974-75. Mem. Women in Electronics (v.p. sponsors 1989-90, guest speaker 1989), Nat. Assn. Female Execs., Nat. Assn. Purchasing Mgrs. Republican. Roman Catholic. Home: 37 River Farms Rd West Warwick RI 02893

CLARY, ROSALIE BRANDON STANTON, timber farm executive, civic worker; b. Evanston, Ill., Aug. 3, 1928; d. Frederick Charles Hite-Smith and Rose Cecile (Liebich) Stanton; BS, Northwestern U., 1950, MA, 1954; m. Virgil Vincent Clary, Oct. 17, 1959; children: Rosalie Marian Hawley, Frederick Stanton, Virgil Vincent, Kathleen Elizabeth. Tchr., Chgo. Public Schs., 1951-55, adjustment tchr., 1956-61; faculty Loyola U., Chgo., 1963; v.p. Stanton Enterprises, Inc., Adams County, Miss., 1971-89; author Family History Record, genealogy record book, Kenilworth, Ill., 1977—. also lectr. Leader Girl Scouts U.S., Winnetka, Ill., 1969-71, 78-86, Cub Scouts, 1972-77; badge counselor Boy Scouts Am., 1978-87; election judge Rep. Com., 1977—. Mem. Nat. Soc. DAR (Ill. rec. sec. 1979-81, nat. vice chmn. program com. 1980-83, state vice regent 1986-88, state regent 1989-91, rec. sec. gen., 1992—), Am. Forestry Assn., Forest Farmers Assn., North Suburban Geneal. Soc. (governing bd. 1979-86), Winnetka Hist. Soc. (governing bd. 1978-90), Internat. Platform Assn., Delta Gamma (mem. nat. cabinet 1985-89). Roman Catholic. Home: 509 Elder Ln Winnetka IL 60093-4122 Office: PO Box 401 Kenilworth IL 60043-0401

CLASTER, BARBARA LEINER, psychologist; b. Cleve., Feb. 11, 1931; d. Philip A. and Della Florence (Berkowitz) Leiner; m. Jay B. Claster, Apr. 28, 1963 (div. Mar. 1990); 1 child, Saundra Margaret. AB, Ohio U., 1953; MA, Northwestern U., 1954, PhD, 1966. Licensed psychologist, Pa., Mass. Psychologist Div. Counseling Penn. State U., University Park, 1961-64; practicing psychology State College, Pa., 1966-68, 1975-87; staff asst. to v.p. student affairs Penn. State U., University Park, 1968-71, coordinator tutoring Edn. Opportunity Program., 1971; psychotherapist, assoc. staff mem. Postgrad. Cen. Mental Health, N.Y.C., 1973-86. Convenor, bd. dirs. task force Mental Health Profl. Cen. Pa. 1978-79, chmn. interdisciplinary com. 1982-84; organizer, chmn. Women's Forum State Coll. 1977-79; mem. mental health/mental retardation adv. com. State of Pa., 1979-89; bd. dirs. task force Centre County Legal Svcs. Inc. 1971-72; chairwoman N.Y.C. Coalition for Women's Mental Health, 1985-86, bd. dirs. 1987-90, recognition award 1988. Recipient Susan B. Anthony award N.Y.C. chpt. NOW, 1990. Fellow APA, Am. Orthopsychiat. Assn., Mass. Psychol. Assn., Pa. Psychol. Assn.; mem. AAAS, Assn. Women Sci., Feminist Therapy Inst. Inc., N.Y. Acad. Sci., N.Y. State Psychol. Assn. (recognition award 1989), Soc. Advancement Self-Psychology, Soc. Psychotherapy Rsch., Pi Lambda Theta. Democrat. Jewish. Home and Office: 1065 Park Ave New York NY 10128-1001

CLAUDE, MARCIA MCCAULLEY, public relations executive; b. Charleston, S.C., July 5, 1961; d. Thomas Thorpe and Mary Carolyn (Crook) McCaulley; m. Richard James Claude, June 10, 1989; children: James Adam, Sarah Carolyn. BS in Comms., U. Tenn., 1983. Anchor weekend weather Sta. WTVK-TV, Knoxville, 1984-85, promotion asst., 1985-88; with pub. rels. and media Tennessee Valley Fair, Knoxville, 1989; with pub. rels. and spl. events Ober Gatlinburg (Tenn.) Resort, 1989-91; owner, dir. Nancy Watson Model and Talent Agency, Knoxville, 1992-94; freelance pub. rels. specialist Knoxville, 1994—; instr. snow skiing Rolf Lanz Ski Sch., Gatlinburg, 1982—; dir. regional youth talent contest Tennessee Valley Fair, 1989—; dir. media, VIP and publicity Tenn. Spl. Olympics-Winter Games, Gatlinburg, 1989, 90, 91. Adminstr., fundraiser AIDS Response Knoxville-Heartstrings, 1992; with pub. rels., fundraiser Children with Attention Deficit Disorder of East Tenn., Knoxville, 1992-93; grant adminstr. Westview Community Action Group, Knoxville, 1993-94. Recipient Gold Addy, Knoxville Ad Club, 1989, Gold medallion Broadcast Promotion/Mktg. Execs., 1989. Mem. Profl. Ski Instrs. Am. (assoc. cert.). Home and Office: 1525 Fay St Knoxville TN 37921

CLAUS, CAROL JEAN, small business owner; b. Uniondale, N.Y., Dec. 17, 1959; d. Charles Joseph and Frances Meta (Fichter) C.; m. Armand Joseph Gasperetti, Jr., July 7, 1985. Student pub. schs., Uniondale. Asst. mgr. Record World, L.I., N.Y., 1977-82, mgr. Info. Builders Inc., N.Y.C., 1982-92; pres. Carol's Creations, Belen, N.Mex. Mem. NAFE, Nat. Organization for Women. Democrat. Roman Catholic.

CLAUSEN, BETTY JANE HANSEN, travel consultant; b. Brooklyn, Wis., Oct. 25, 1925; d. Arthur John and Kathryn (Hefty) Hansen; m. Henry Albert Clausen, Jan. 31, 1948 (div. 1976); 1 child, Scott Alyn. BA, Beloit Coll., 1947. Psychometric sec. Vocat. Counseling Bur., Rockford (Ill.) Coll., 1947-48; classified ad-taker Beloit (Wis.) Daily News, 1948-49; copy-writer WROK, Rockford, 1955-60; tchr. elementary schs., Rockford, Elmhurst, Ill., 1960-61; exec. mgr. Melrose Park (Ill.) C. of C., 1961-67; mng. dir. S.W. Sr. Center, Parma Heights, Ohio, 1967-77; exec. dir. Sr. Citizens, Inc., Hamilton, Ohio, 1977-90, ret. 1990. Founder, pres. Easter Seal Parents Group Rockford, 1957-60, project chmn. Villa Park, Ill., 1963-65; treas. Easter Seal Aux., 1965-66; treas. United Cerebral Palsy, Rockford, 1959-60, bd. dirs. Ill. Soc., 1959-60; co-chmn. 53-Minute March, Elmhurst, 1963; pres. Freeman Sch. PTA., Rockford, 1959-60; chmn. exceptional child PTA, Elmhurst, 1962-66; hon. life mem. Ill. PTA.; mem. S.W. Community Resource Coun., 1968-77, Butler County Coun. on Aging, 1977-83; bd. dirs. Coun. Exceptional Children, New Neighbors League, S.W. Cleveland chpt., 1967; mem. coun. on aging Cin. Area Adv. Coun., 1979-83, coun. task force on aging Butler County Human Svcs. Named Citizen of Week, Elmhurst Press, 1966, Outstanding Sr. Citizen of Butler County by Cin. Area Coun. on Aging, 1991. Mem. Ill. C. of C., Ill. Assn. C. of C. Execs., West Suburban Coun. Chambers, Ohio Assn. Sr. Citizens Ctrs., Altrusa, Delta Delta Delta. Methodist. Home: 1224 Beissinger Rd Hamilton OH 45013-1106

CLAUSER, ANGELA FRANCES, medical/surgical, pediatrics and geriatrics nurse; b. Leavenworth, Kans., June 25, 1955; d. Donald F. Sr. and Agnes Angela (Forge) C. AA, Kansas City (Kans.) Jr. Coll., 1984; BSN, Pitts. State U., 1986. RN, Kans.; cert. provider CPR, Am. Heart Assn. Sec. U.S. Army, Ft. Leavenworth, Kans., USAF Acad., Colorado Springs, Colo., VA, Leavenworth; staff nurse St. John's Hosp., Leavenworth. Mem. NAFE, Nurses Svc. Orgn., U. Kans. Alumni Assn., Pitts. State U. Alumni Assn., Kans. City Jr. Coll. Alumni Assn.

CLAUSS, SUSAN H., youth center administrator; b. St. Louis, Apr. 2, 1946; d. William Davis and Norma Eleanor (Tiemann) Hawker; m. Michael Charles Cross, Apr. 19, 1974 (dec. May 1986); m. Luther L. Clauss III, Oct. 20, 1990. MAT in Music Edn., Washington U., St. Louis, 1969, postgrad., 1972-75, data processing cert., 1983; MEd in Gen. Counseling, U. Mo., St. Louis, 1988. Music dir. Florissant (Mo.) Presbyn. Ch., 1973-78, 81-92; field exec. Girl Scout Coun. Greater St. Louis, 1978-79, tng. dir., 1979-81; tng. specialist Nat. Gen. Ins. Co., St. Louis, 1981-82, documentation specialist, 1982-83, statis. programmer, 1983-87; trainer, cons. Luth. Family & Children's Svcs. of Mo., St. Louis, 1987-89; assoc. counselor In-Glow Christian Counseling, St. Louis, 1988-89; project coord. Progressive Youth Ctr., St. Louis, 1989-92, dir. prevention svcs., 1992—; ind. tng. cons., St. Louis, 1981-89. Co-author: Birth Crisis Intervention, 1990. Coun. instr. Girl Scouts Coun. Greater St. Louis, 1981-93; bd. dirs. Joint Neighborhood Ministry, St. Louis, 1993—. Recipient Thanks badge Girl Scouts Coun. Greater St. Louis, 1987. Mem. ACA, ASTD (bd. dirs. St. Louis chpt. 1981-85), Assn. for Specialists in Group Work, Mo. Counseling Assn., Mo. Assn. Alcohol & Drug Abuse Programs, Chi Sigma Iota. Office: Progressive Youth Ctr 8630 Olive Blvd Saint Louis MO 63132

CLAUSSEN, DANIELLIA DELYNN, juvenile probation officer; b. Lampasas, Tex., June 28, 1966; d. Lester Eugene Sr. and Shirley Laverne (O'Neal) Cavness; m. Daniel Ray Claussen, Sept. 3, 1988. BS in Criminology and Corrections, Sam Houston State U., 1988. Eligibility specialist Tex. Dept. Human Svcs., Texas City, 1988-89; probation officer Brazoria County Juv. Probation, Angleton, Tex., 1989—. Author poetry. Mem. Tex. Probation Assn.

CLAUSSEN, EILEEN BARBARA, federal agency administrator; b. N.Y.C., June 9, 1945; d. Louis and Elsie (Young) Lerner; children: Hillary Anne, Geoffrey David. BA, George Washington U., 1966; MA, U. Va., 1967. Systems analyst USN, Washington, 1967-68; cons. Booz, Allen & Hamilton, Inc., Washington, 1968-69; asst. dir. ctr. for comml. devel. Boise Cascade Corp., Washington, 1969-72; various mgmt. positions Office of Solid Waste U.S. EPA, Washington, 1972-83, dir. characterization and assessment div., 1984-87, acting dep. asst. adminstr. air and radiation, 1988-89, dir. atmospheric and indoor air programs, 1987-93; spl. asst. to pres., sr. dir. global environ. affairs Nat. Security Coun., Washington, 1993—. Home: 4712 Chesapeake St NW Washington DC 20016-4466 Office: Nat Security Coun 1600 Pennsylvania Ave NW Washington DC 20500*

CLAUSSEN, KELLI, artist; b. Virginia, Minn., Oct. 30, 1943; d. Luke O'Farrell and Sarah (Haryn) Suihkonen; m. Paul Kelly, Nov. 1964 (div. 1969); children: Christopher, Stephanie, Mechelle; m. Howard Boyd Claussen, Nov. 17, 1989. BS in Visual Arts, Ind. State U., 1990. Artist Arlington, Wash., 1990—; owner Watermelon Patch Antiques and Art, Sandstone, Minn., 1994—. Exhibited in group shows at Salmon Days Art Show, 1990, Bellevue, Wash., 1992, Everett, Wash., 1992, 3 juried shows at Ind. U., 1987-90. Mem. Woman Artist Mus., Washington, 1990-91, Seattle Art Mus., 1991-92, Mpls. Inst. Art. Roman Catholic. Home and Office: RR 3 Box 15K Sandstone MN 55072

CLAWSON, ROXANN ELOISE, college administrator, computer company executive; b. Dallas, Oct. 15, 1945; d. Robert Wellington Clawson and Jeannette Irene (Rodenhauser) Clawson Clayton. BFA, Mich. State U., 1968. Library asst. Cooper Union, N.Y.C., 1970-75, asst. librarian, 1976-82, asst. to dean, 1985—; pres. Standing By Wordprocessing, N.Y.C., 1982—; v.p. Word Group, N.Y.C., 1984—; computer cons., 1986—. Acting appearance in The Dragon's Nest, La MaMa Theatre, 1989. Mem. Nat. Assn. Female Execs., N.Y. Personal Computer Group. Democrat. Lutheran. Avocation: administration.

CLAX, FREDA MARIE, publication designer; b. Red Bank, N.J., Nov. 19, 1959; d. Joseph and Anita (Desbordes) C. Assoc. Specialized Tech., Art Inst. Pitts., 1981; BFA, Sch. Visual Arts, N.Y.C., 1987. Freelance graphic designer and illustrator various cos. various cos., N.Y.C., 1981-85; freelance designer Self Mag., Conde Nast Publs., N.Y.C., 1987; freelance designer communications design dept. Citicorp, N.Y.C., 1987, Weight Watchers Mag., N.Y.C., 1987; freelance designer Boating Mag., 1987; jr. designer Prima Mag., Gruner and Jahr Publs., N.Y.C., 1987-88; freelance designer In Fashion and Internat. Sportswear Mag., Murdoch Publs., N.Y.C., 1988, Mademoiselle mag., 1989, Episodes mag., 1990; asst. art dir. Footwear News mag. and newspaper Fairchild Publs., N.Y.C., 1988-89; sr. designer Essence Mag., N.Y.C., 1989-90; freelance cons. Mademoiselle mag., 1990—; freelance designer various clients, Hackensack, N.J., 1991—; owner, creative dir. Sandbox Designs, Tinton Falls, N.J., 1994—; freelance creative dir. Liquid mag., 1995. Mem. NAFE, Am. Inst. Graphic Arts.

CLAXTON, HARRIETT MAROY JONES, retired English language educator; b. Dublin, Ga., Aug. 27, 1930; d. Paul Jackson and Maroy Athalia (Chappell) Jones; m. Edward B. Claxton, Jr., May 27, 1953; children—E. B. III, Paula Jones. AA, Bethel Woman's Coll., 1949; AB magna cum laude, Mercer U., 1951; MEd, Ga. Coll., 1965. Social worker Laurens County Welfare Bd., Dublin, 1951-56; high sch. tchr., Dublin, 1961-66; instr. Middle Ga. Coll., Cochran, 1966-71, asst. prof. English, lit. and speech, 1971-85, assoc. prof. 1985-86; research tchr. Trinity Christian Sch., 1986, 92, sr. English tchr., 1986-87; part-time tchr., Ga. Coll., 1987, Emanuel County Jr. Coll., 1988-93, Middle Ga. Coll., 1985-93. Contbr. articles to profl. jours. and newspapers; editor Laurens County History, II, 1987. Pres. bd. Dublin Assn. Fine Arts, 1974-76, 82-84, Dublin Hist. Soc., 1976-78; mem. Laurens County Library Bd., 1960-68; chmn. Dublin Hist. Rev. Bd., 1980—; sec. Am. Assn. Ret. Persons, 1987—; v.p. Dublin community Concert, 1991—. Named Woman of Yr., St. Patrick's Festival, Dublin, 1979, Most Popular tchr., Dublin Ctr., 1985; recipient Outstanding Service award Cancer Soc., Dublin, 1985, 93. Mem. DAR (regent, state, dist. and nat. awards), Sigma Mu, Alpha Delta Pi, Phi Theta Kappa, Chi Delta Phi, Delta Kappa Gamma. Democrat. Baptist. Clubs: Woman's Study (pres.), Erin Garden (pres.) (Dublin). Home: 101 Rosewood Dr Dublin GA 31021-4129

CLAY, JUANITA LOUNDMON, foundation administrator; b. Charleston, W.Va., Aug. 11; d. Albert D. and Mattie L. (Collins) L.; children: Pamela Clay-Mitchell, Kimberly Clay, Dana Clay-Braddock. BA, W.Va. State U.; MSW, W.Va. U.; MA, Ind. U.; PhD, Fla. State U., 1978. Psychologist Navistar Corp., Indpls., 1978-80; pvt. practice psychology, Indpls., 1980-84; clin. psychologist Lakeview Mental Health Ctr., Pensacola, Fla., 1984-85; pvt. practice A Better Way Christian Counseling Ministry, Tallahassee, Fla., 1985-88; prof. Christian Broadcast Network U., Va. Beach, Va., 1988-89; assoc. prof. Am. U. of Les Cayes, Haiti, 1989-91; cons. Washington Project, 1989—, Haiti Mins. Conf., Port-Au-Prince, 1989, Rock Ch. Internat., Va. Beach, 1989—, Reconciliation Community Ch., Alexandria, Va., 1988-89; founder, dir. first group treatment home for girls in the Ind.; founder A Better Way. Precinct chmn. Rep. Exec. Com., Tallahassee, 1987-88; bd. mem. City Coun. EEO Commn., Tallahassee, 1987-89; pres. Ind. Conf. Social Welfare, Indpls., 1970-73. Fla. U. Systems grantee, 1976; named one of Outstanding Young Women Am., 1968; recipient Community Service award City of Pensacola, 1974, YMCA, C. of C., Ft. Wayne, Ind., 1970. Mem. Am. Assn. Counseling and Devel., Va. Assn. Counseling and Devel., Ind. Psychology Assn. Office: 916 S Calhoun St Fort Wayne IN 46802

CLAY, SUSAN JOSE, lobbyist; b. Lowell, Mass., Oct. 13, 1946; d. John Laughton and Maria Dolores (Abreu) C.; children: Jeffrey Alan, Dana Anthony Demers. BS, U. N.H., 1968. Pub. rels. cons. Clay-Wells Assocs., Durham, N.H., 1968-71; career/life counselor Women for Higher Edn., Hooksett, N.H., 1975-76; assoc. dir. St. Joseph Community Svcs., Merrimack, N.H., 1976-78; community rels. dir. Social Welfare Coun., Concord, N.H., 1978-80; lobbyist, exec. dir. Common Cause/N.H., Concord, 1981—; owner, cons. Granite Profiles, Concord, 1992—. Editor: (rules handbook) Learning the Legislative Ropes, 1984, (commn. report) Committee on Legislative Reform, 1986; contbr. poetry to N.H. Profile mag., 1963-64. Mem. LWV, Concord, 1982-84, N.H. Bipartisan Comm. on Voter Participation, Concord, 1988, Commn. on Legis. Reform, Concord, 1986. Named Young Poet of Yr., N.H. Poetry Soc., 1964, Outstanding Young Woman in Am., 1984. Mem. Nat. Abortion and Reproductive Rights Action League, ACLU, N.H. Women's Lobby. Republican. Roman Catholic. Home: 150 Bunker Hill Rd New Boston NH 03070 Office: Common Cause of NH 4 Park St Concord NH 03301-6313

CLAYBURGH, JILL, actress; b. N.Y.C., Apr. 30, 1944; d. Albert Henry and Julia (Door) C.; m. David Rabe, Mar., 1979. B.A., Sarah Lawrence Coll., 1966. Former mem., Charles Playhouse, Boston; Off-Broadway plays include The Nest; Broadway debut in The Rothschilds, 1970; stage appearances include In the Boom Boom Room (David Rabe), Design for Living (Noel Coward); film appearances include The Wedding Party, 1969, The Telephone Book, 1971, Portnoy's Complaint, 1972, The Thief Who Came to Dinner, 1973, The Terminal Man, 1974, Gable and Lombard, 1976, Silver Streak, 1976, Semi-Tough, 1977, An Unmarried Woman, 1978, Luna, 1979, Starting Over, 1979, It's My Turn, 1980, First Monday in October, 1981, I'm Dancing as Fast as I Can, 1982, Hannah K, 1983, Where Are The Children, 1986, Shy People, 1987, Whispers in the Dark, 1992, Rich in Love, 1993, Naked in New York, 1994; appeared in TV films The Art of Crime, 1975, Hustling, 1975, Griffin and Phoenix, 1976, Miles to Go..., 1986, Who Gets the Friends?, 1988, Fear Stalk, 1989, Unspeakable Acts, 1990, Firestorm: A Catastrophe in Oakland, 1993, Honor Thy Father and Mother: The True Story of the Menendez Brothers, 1994; TV documentary: Ask Me Anything: How to Talk to Kids About Sex, 1989. Recipient Best Actress award for An Unmarried Woman, Cannes Film Festival; Golden Apple award for best film actress in An Unmarried Woman. Office: care William Morris Agy 151 S El Camino Dr Beverly Hills CA 90212-2704*

CLAYMAN, LILLIAN DUDKIEWICZ, mayor; b. Trenton, N.J., Mar. 25, 1953; d. Adam Stanislaus and Rozalia (Strutyaska) Dudkiewicz; m. Roger Clayman, Aug. 10, 1980; children: David, Rebecca. AB in Am. History, Rutgers U., PhD in Am. History; MA in Am. History, SUNY, Binghamton, 1976. Elem. sch. tchr. St. Hedweg's Sch., Trenton, 1974-75; teaching asst. Am. History SUNY, Binghamton, 1975-76; teaching asst., rsch. asst. Rutgers U., New Brunswick, N.J., 1976-78; instr., rsch. asst. Inst. Mgmt. and Labor Rels. Rutgers U., New Brunswick, 1978-80; lectr. Am. History Post Coll., Waterbury, Conn., 1980-82; coord. labor studies for women U. Conn., Storrs, 1982-83, lectr. labor studies, 1983-88; mayor Town of Hamden, Conn., 1991—; adj. coord. commuter programs Livingston Coll., Rutgers U., New Brunswick, 1979; adj. instr. Am. History, Post Coll., Waterbury, 1989-91; adj. instr. Pub. Adminstrn., The Grad. Sch., Univ. New Haven, Conn., 1989-91. Press sec. Greco for state senate; Hamden coord. Morrison for Congress; state coord. Richard Gephardt for Pres.; clk. Parks and Recreation Commn., Hamden, 1983, Hamden Libr. Bd., 1983; mem. S. Ctrl. Conn. Nat. Orgn. for Women Exec. Bd.; coordinating com., press rels com. March of Dimes Walk-a-thon, Hamden, 1988, 89; appointed Hamden Coun., 1986, elected 1987, reelected 1989, chmn. fin. and adminstrn. com., vice chmn. labor com.; bd. dirs. Hamden-North Haven YMCA; exec. Hamden LWV. Cartoonist: contbr. numerous cartoons political and humourous to various pubs.; author: A Selcted Bibliography on Educational Programs, Inst. Mgmt. and Labor Rels. New Brunswick, 1979. Home: 163 Four Rod Rd Hamden CT 06514 Office: Hamden Town Hall 2372 Whitney Ave Hamden CT 06518-3207

CLAYPOOL, NANCY, social worker; b. Monterey, Calif., Aug. 6, 1957; d. Harold Herbert and Nancy Jeanne (Klohe) C.; 1 child, James Paul. BA in Social Welfare, San Francisco State U., 1980; M Social Work, U. Calif., Berkeley, 1985. Program developer Women's Found., San Francisco; foster care coord., house supr. Charila Svcs. for Girls, San Francisco; therapist Sierra Clinic, San Francisco; clin. social worker Youth Homes, Inc., Walnut Creek, Calif.; homebased early childhood devel. tchr. Thurgood Marshall Family Resource Ctr., Oakland, Calif., 1992; psychiat. social worker Eden Med. Ctr., Castro Valley, Calif., 1992—. Contbr. articles to profl. publs. Mem. Alameda County Mental Health Bd., 1992—, chair, 1993-94, vice chair, 1994-95. Named Regional Clinician of Yr., Horizon Mental Health Svcs., 1994; Health-Social Networking grantee, 1984. Mem. Nat. Assn. Social Workers. Home: 3946 35th Ave Oakland CA 94619-1435

CLAYTON, EVA M., congresswoman, former county commissioner. Former commr. Warren County, N.C.; mem. 103rd Congress from 1st N.C. dist., Washington, D.C., 1993—. Democrat. Office: US Ho of Reps 222 CHOB Washington DC 20515

CLAYTON, GEORGIA LOU, media specialist; b. Cherokee, Iowa, June 4, 1950; d. George Weber and Flora May (Warnke) C. BA, U. No. Iowa, 1972; MS in Edn., U. Western Ill., 1978. Cert. prin., kindergarten-12th; cert. educator, media specialist, tchr., ednl. specialist. Sch. libr. elem./secondary sch. Lone Tree (Iowa) Schs., 1972-74; media specialist elem. sch. Washington Elem., Davenport, Iowa, 1974-86, Lincoln Fundamental Sch., Davenport, 1986—; contact person phase III staff devel. Lincoln Fundamental Sch., 1988—; mem. multi-cultural non-sexist com. Davenport Cmty. Sch. Dist., staff devel. com. Active Lincoln Sch. PTA, 1986—, tchr. rep., 1986-92. Chpt. II grantee State of Iowa Dept. Edn., 1992-93. Mem. NEA, ASCD, Iowa Ednl. Media Assn., Iowa State Edn. Assn., Davenport Edn. Assn. (chair instrnl. and profl. devel. 1988—), U. Iowa Alumni Assn., Phi Delta Kappa (life, pres. Quad City chpt.), Pi Lamda Theta. Lutheran. Home: 1107 E Central Park Ave Davenport IA 52803 Office: Lincoln Fundamental Sch 318 E 7th St Davenport IA 52803

CLAYTON, NORMA TOWNE, rape crisis program director, retired secondary education educator; b. Naples, Maine, Aug. 16, 1941; d. Norman Pingree and Elsie Adeline (Treadwell) Towne; m. John Middleton Clayton Jr., Aug. 17, 1968; 1 child, Signe Louisa. BA in Math., U. Maine, 1963; MEd in Natural Scis., U. Del., 1969, MBA, 1982. Cert. profl. secondary math. tchr., Del. Tchr. math. Alexis I. duPont High Sch., Red Clay Consol. Sch. Dist., Wilmington, Del., 1963-91; ret., 1991; program director Rape Crisis CONTACT Del., Wilmington. Deacon First and Cen. Presbyn. Ch., 1970-74, ruling elder, 1977-81, chairperson mission study and pastor search, 1989-90; mem. ministry unit New Castle Presbytery, 1990—, mem. new ch. devel. com., 1991— (chair 1993-94); mem. adminstrv. commn., 1992—, vice-moderator, 1992-93, moderator 1993-94. Mem. NEA (del. to assembly 1963—), Del. State Edn. Assn. (legis. liaison 1990), Nat. Coun. Tchrs. of Math., Del. Coun. Tchrs. of Math., Red Clay Edn. Assn. Home: 234 Cheltenham Rd Newark DE 19711-3682 Office: CONTACT Del PO Box 9525 Wilmington DE 19809

CLAYTON, REBECCA KILGO, educator, artist; b. Givhans, S.C., Sept. 25, 1916; d. Middleton Samuel and Catherine Rebecca (Green) C. BS, Coll. Charleston, S.C., 1944; MA, U. Mich., 1959; postgrad., Pa. State U., The Citadel, U. N.C., U. S.C., LaVerne Coll., U. Ala. Tchr. elem. sch. Dorchester County, S.C., 1939-43, Charleston County, S.C., 1944-53; tchr., prin. 1st Orthopedic Sch., Charleston, 1953-55; spl. edn. tchr. U.S. Army Schs., Verdun, France, Frankfurt and Munich, Fed. Republic Germany, 1955-59; tchr. class for retarded Mitchell Elem. Sch., Charleston, 1959-60; tchr. elem. and spl. edn., remedial instr. Panama Canal Co., Balboa, C.Z., Republic of Panama, 1960-80, prin. migrant summer sch. program; missionary tchr. TEAM Missions, Venezuela, Evangel. Christian Acad., Madrid. Artistic works exhibited in galleries throughout C.Z. and Republic of Panama. Devotions chmn. Fellowship of the Concerned; jr. dept. pianist Balboa Union Ch. and Pedregal Meth. Mission Ch., Republic of Panama; mem. The Charleston Mus. Recipient Panama Canal Hon. Pub. Svc. award, 1981. Mem. NEA, AAUW, Coun. Exceptional Children (treas. C.Z. br.), Internat. Reading Assn., S.C. Hist. Soc., S.C. Coastal Conservation League, Nat. League Am. Pen Women, Japan Internat. Christian Univ. Found. (women's com.), Nat. Trust Hist. Preservation, Nat. Hist. Soc., Internat. Soc. Artists, Phi Delta Kappa, Delta Kappa Gamma, Interam. Women's Club. Home: Rfd Givhans Ridgeville SC 29472

CLAYTON, VERNA LEWIS, state legislator; b. Hamden, Ohio, Feb. 28, 1937; d. Matthews L. and Yail (Miller) Lewis; m. Frank R. Clayton, Feb. 4, 1956; children: Valerie Clayton Euneman, Barry L. Office mgr., Village of Buffalo Grove, Ill., 1972-78, village clk., 1971-79, village pres., 1979-91; mem. Ill. Ho. of Reps., Springfield, 1993—. Mem. Lake County Solid Waste Planning Agy. (chmn. tech. com., chmn. agy.), Nat. League of Cities (chmn. transp. and communications steering com.). Recipient Disting. Service award Amvets, 1981. Mem. Northwest Mcpl. Conf. (pres. 1983-84), Chgo. Area Transp. Study Council Mayors (vice chmn. 1981-83, chmn. 1985-91), Mcpl. Clks. Ill. (treas. 1978-79), Mcpl. Clks. Lake County (pres. 1977-78), Ill. Mcpl. League (bd. dirs., v.p. 1985-90, pres. 1989-90), Buffalo Grove Rotary Club (hon. mem.), Buffalo Grove C. of C. (bd. dirs.). Republican. Methodist. Home: 2831 Acacia Ter Buffalo Grove IL 60089-6634 Office: 314 Mchenry Rd Ste D-1 Buffalo Grove IL 60089-6749 also: 2119 N Stratton Bldg Springfield IL 62706

CLAYTON, XERNONA, media executive; b. Muskogee, Okla., Aug. 30, 1930; m. Paul L. Brady. BS with honors, Tenn. State U., 1952; postgrad., U. Chgo. Cert. tchr. Ill., Calif. Tchr. pub. schs. Chgo., Los Angeles; with So. Christian Leadership Conf., Atlanta; host Sta. WAGA-TV, Atlanta, 1967-79; with Sta. WTBS-TV, Atlanta, 1979—, host, producer, 1981-82, coordinator of minority affairs, 1982—, now corp. v.p. of urban affairs; guest lectr. Harvard U.; appointed Motion Picture and TV Commn., Ga., commr. Bd. Review, Appellate Bd. of unemployment compensation. Author: (with Ed Clayton) The Peaceful Warrior. Coordinated Doctors' Com. for Implementation, Atlanta; bd. trustees Martin Luther King, Jr. Ctr.; bd. dirs Nat. Assn. Advancement Colored People, Multiple Sclerosis Soc., Sci. and Tech. Mus. Atlanta, Nat Assn Sickle Cell Disease; mem. Nat. Issues Forum of Jimmy Carter Presidential Library. U. Chgo. scholar; recipient numerous awards including Bronze Woman of the Year, 1969, President's award Nat. Conf. Mayors, 1983, Communications Woman of Achievement award Am. Women in Radio and TV, 1984-85, The Kizzy award, 1979, Humanitarian award, Hillside Internat. Truth Ctr., 1986, Acad. Women Achievers, YWCA, 1986, American Spirit award USAF Recruiting Service, 1987; Xernona Clayton Scholarship named in her honor by the Am. Intercultural Student Exchange, 1987-90; featured on cover of The New York Time Mag.; cited for her accomplishments by Ebony, Town & Country, Georgia Mags. Mem. Nat. Assn. Media Women (pres.), Alpha Kappa Alpha. Baptist. Office: Turner Broadcasting One CNN Center Atlanta GA 30303

CLAYTOR, HELEN NATALIE JACKSON, association executive; b. Mpls., Apr. 12, 1907; d. Madison Sycamore and Amy Brown (Wood) Jackson; m. Earl Williams Wilkins, Aug. 19, 1929 (dec. Jan. 1941); 1 child, Roger Wood; m. Robert White Claytor, Oct. 2, 1943; children: Judith Amy, Sharon Anne. BA cum laude, U. Minn., 1928; HHD (hon.), Ea. Mich. U., 1968; D of Pub. Svc. (hon.), Western Mich. U., 1972; HHD (hon.), Aquinas Coll., 1985. Social worker group work YWCA, Trenton, N.J., 1928-30; social worker case work Provident Assn., Kansas City, Mo., 1930-32; social casework supr. Fed. Emergency Relief Adminstrn., Kansas City, 1932-35; social worker group work YWCA, Kansas City, 1935-40; race rels. specialist YWCA of the U.S.A., N.Y.C., 1940-44, pres., 1967-73; mem. Nat. Women's Adv. Com. on Civil Rights, Washington, 1967-70; vice chair Nat. Women's Adv. Com. to Office of Econ. Opportunity, Washington, 1968-70. Mem. Human Rels. Commn., Grand Rapids, 1955-68; hon. mem. nat. bd. YWCA of the U.S.A., 1975—, YWCA of Grand Rapids, 1975—. Recipient Community Svc. award Mayor of Grand Rapids, 1956, Nat. Women's Svc. award Alpha Kappa Alpha, 1970, Ambassador award YWCA of the U.S.A., 1993; named to Mich. Women's Hall of Fame, Mich. Women's Studies Assn., Lansing, 1985. Mem. NAACP (life), Grand Rapids Urban League (Community Svc. award 1982). Home: 2032 Coit Ave NE Grand Rapids MI 49505-6218

CLAYTOR, KATHARINE DRANEY, human resources executive; b. Ft. Monmouth, N.J., Nov. 2, 1959; d. Edward P. and Margaret (Heliker) Draney; m. Stephen M. Claytor, June 1, 1985; children: Emily G., William M. BA in Bus./Econ., Emory & Henry Coll., 1981; postgrad., Lynchburg Coll. Accredited profl. human resources. Pers. analyst County of Roanoke, Va., 1983-89, asst. dir. human resources, 1989—. Subcom. chair Am. Heart Assn., Roanoke; mem. alive and well bd. Coun. Community Svcs.; com. chair Christ Episcopal Ch. Mem. Soc. Human Resource Mgmt., Internat. Pers. Mgmt. Assn., Salem Jr. Women's Club (pres. 1991-92). Office: County of Roanoke PO Box 29800 Roanoke VA 24018

CLEARY, AUDREY, state legislator, nurse volunteer; b. Menominee, Mich., June 1, 1930; d. Edmund James and Laura Elizabeth (Mushynski) Boucher; m. Joseph Wolter Cleary, June 19, 1954; children: Patrick, Susan, Barbara, Paul, William, Philip, Richard, David, Mary, Peter, Steve. BSN, Marquette U., 1952. Staff nurse obstetrics St. Joseph's Hosp., Milw., 1952-55; state legislator State of N.D., Bismarck, 1991—. Coord. Birthright Bismarck, 1972—; city chairperson Cancer Crusade, Bismarck, 1982; vice chmn. dist. 49 Dem. Non-partisan League, Bismack, 1988—; bd. dirs. Friends of N.D. Gov.'s Residence, Bismarck, 1988—, St. Vincent's Nursing Home, Bismarck, 1991—; pres. gov.'s counsel Commn. on Status of Women, Bicmarck, 1989-92, Bishop's Commn. on Cath. Schs., Bismarck, 1989—; mem. Bismarck-Mandan Symphony League. Mem. Cath. Daughters of the Ams., N.D. Mental Health Assn., 6th Dist. Med. Aux., Toastmasters (pres. # 581 1992—), Kiwanis (Golden "K"). Home: 104 Seminole Ave Bismarck ND 58501-3544

CLEARY, BEVERLY ATLEE (MRS. CLARENCE T. CLEARY), author; b. McMinnville, Oreg., 1916; d. Chester Lloyd and Mable (Atlee) Bunn; m. Clarence T. Cleary, Oct. 6, 1940; children: Marianne Elisabeth, Malcolm James. BA, U. Calif., 1938; BA in Librarianship, U. Wash., 1939. Children's librarian Pub. Libr., Yakima, Wash., 1939-40; post librarian U.S. Army Regional Hosp., Oakland, Calif., 1942-45. Author: Henry Huggins, 1950, Ellen Tebbits, 1951, Henry and Beezus, 1952, Otis Spofford, 1953, Henry and Ribsy, 1954, Beezus and Ramona, 1955, Fifteen, 1956 (Dorothy Canfield Fisher Meml. Children's Book award 1958), Henry and the Paper Route, 1957, The Luckiest Girl, 1958, Jean and Johnny, 1959 (ALA Notable Book citation 1961), The Real Mole, 1960, Hullabaloo ABC, 1960, Two Dog Biscuits, 1961, Emily's Runaway Imagination, 1961, Henry and the Clubhouse, 1962, Sister of the Bride, 1963, Ribsy, 1964 (Dorothy Canfield Fisher Meml. Children's Book award 1961), The Mouse and the Motorcycle, 1965 (ALA Notable Book citation 1966), Mitch and Amy, 1967, Ramona the Pest, 1968, Runaway Ralph, 1970, Socks, 1973 (Golden Archer award U. Wis. 1977), (play) The Sausage at the End of the Nose, 1974, Ramona the Brave, 1975 (Golden Archer award U. Wis. 1977), Ramona and her Father, 1977 (ALA Notable Book citation 1978, Newbery Honor Book award ALA 1978, Boston Globe/Horn Book Honor award 1978), Ramona and Her Mother, 1979, Ramona Quimby, Age 8, 1981 (Newbery Honor Book award ALA 1982, Am. Book award nominee 1982), Ralph S. Mouse, 1982 (Calif. Assn. Tchrs. English award 1983, Golden Kite award Soc. Children's Book Writers 1983), Dear Mr. Henshaw, 1983 (Dorothy Canfield Fisher Meml. Children's Book award 1985, ALA Notable Book citation 1984, N.Y. Times Notable Book 1983, Horn Book's Honor list 1984, Best Books list Sch. Libr. Jour. 1983, Christopher award 1983, Newbery medal ALA 1984, Commonwealth Silver medal Commonwealth Club Calif. 1984), Ramona Forever, 1984, Lucky Chuck, 1984, The Ramona Quimby Diary, 1984, Beezus and Ramona Diary, 1986, Janet's Thingamajigs, 1987, The Growing Up Feet, 1987, A Girl from Yamhill: A Memoir, 1988, Muggie Maggie, 1990, Strider, 1991, Petey's Bedtime Story, 1993. Recipient Laura Ingalls Wilder award ALA, 1975, Children's Choice Election 2nd Place award, 1978, Regina medal Cath. Libr. Assn., 1980, de Grummond award U. Miss., 1982, U. So. Miss. medallion, 1982, George C. Stone award Claremont Colls., 1983, Newbery medal, 1984, Hans Christian Andersen medal nominee, 1984, Everychild Honor citation Children's Book Coun., 1985, Ludington award Ednl. Paperback Assn., 1987. Mem. Authors Guild of Authors League Am. Office: William Morrow & Co 1350 Ave Of The Americas New York NY 10019

CLEARY, KAY A., actuary, educator; b. Springfield, Ill., May 7, 1951; d. Howard H. Hoogesteger and Lenore A. Cudnik Moley; m. Thomas M. Cleary, Sept. 1, 1970 (div. Mar. 1972); 1 child, Jennifer A. Cleary; m. Patrick J. Murphy. BA, Northwestern U., 1978. ESL and GED tchr. Mundelein (Ill.) High Sch., 1976-84; vocat. counselor The Lambs, Inc., Libertyville, Ill., 1978-81; data quality mgr. Kemper Group, Long Grove, Ill., 1981-86; comml. pricing mgr. Allstate Ins., Barrington, Ill., 1986-89; rsch. mgr. Allstate Ins., Menlo Park, Calif., 1989—. Election ofcl., various locations, 1975—. Mem. Casualty Actuarial Soc. (assoc.), Mensa, Toastmasters (pres. Menlo Park club 1993—).

CLEARY, LYNDA WOODS, financial account executive , consultant; b. Birmingham, Ala., June 18, 1950; d. Eugene and Elizabeth (Wright) Woods; m. George Cassius Riley, Nov. 29, 1975 (div. 1979); m. Richard Charles Cleary, Dec. 12, 1987. Student, Dartmouth Coll., 1970-71; BA, Tougaloo (Miss.) Coll., 1972; postgrad., Rutgers U., 1981-83; MBA, N.Y. Inst. Tech., 1992. Comml. underwriter Continental Ins. Co., N.Y.C., 1973-74; lectr. John Ericson Sch., Ostersund, Sweden, 1974; asst. underwriting cons. Prudential Property and Casualty, Holmdel, N.J., 1975-80; market rsch. analyst Continental Ins. Co., Piscataway, N.J., 1981-86; bus. systems analyst Am. Internat. Group, N.Y.C., 1986-87; ins. agt. Equitable Fin. Cos., N.Y.C., 1988; spl. agt. Northwestern Mut. Life, Princeton, N.J., 1988-89; cons. Cleary Woods Cons., Princeton, 1989—; account exec. Dean Witter, N.Y.C., 1992-93; fin. cons. Fahnestock & Co., Inc., Red Bank, N.J., 1993—; cons. Nat. Torque Tech. Labs., Piscataway, 1989—. Fin. com. mem. Princeton

Walk Homeowners Assn., 1988—; fundraiser Crossroads Theatre, New Brunswick, N.J., 1988—; asst. troop leader, Girl Scouts USA, West Windsor. Recipient Cert. of Appreciation Concerned Community Women of Jersey City, Inc., 1990. Mem. Women Life Underwriters Confedn., Am. Mgmt. Assn., NAFE, Nat. Assn. Life Underwriters. Democrat. Baptist. Office: 3 Harding Rd Red Bank NJ 07701

CLEARY, MANON CATHERINE, artist, educator; b. St. Louis, Nov. 14, 1942; d. Frank and Crystal (Maret) C. BFA, Washington U., St. Louis, 1964; MFA, Tyler Sch. Art, Temple U., 1968. Instr. fine arts SUNY, Oswego, 1968-70; from instr. to assoc. prof. D.C. Tchrs. Coll., Washington, 1970-78; from assoc. prof. to prof. art U. D.C., Washington, 1978—, acting chmn. dept., 1985-86, 90-91; assoc. dean Coll. Liberal and Fine Arts U. D.C., 1992-94, acting coord. art program, 1994—. One woman shows include Mus. Modern Art Gulbenkian Found., Lisbon, Portugal, 1985, Iolas/Jackson Gallery, N.Y.C., 1982, Osuna Gallery, Washington, 1974, 77, 80, 84, 89, Univ. D.C., 1987, Tyler Gallery SUNY at Oswego, 1987, J. Rosenthal Fine Arts, Washington, 1991, Ripley Gallery, Washington, 1994, others; group exhibits include Twentieth Century Am. Drawings: The Figure in Context, Traveled Nat. Acad. Design, 1984-85, others. Artist-in-residence Herning Hojskole, Denmark, 1980, Ucross Found., Wyo., 1984. Recipient Faculty Rsch. award, U. D.C., 1983, 89. Mem. Coll. Art Assn., Pi Beta Phi. Democrat. Presbyterian. Home: 1736 Columbia Rd NW Washington DC 20009-2833 Office: UDC Art Dept Rm 7812 4200 Connecticut Ave NW Bldg 48 Washington DC 20008-1174

CLEAVER, KATHLEEN NEAL, law educator, writer; b. Dallas, May 13, 1945; d. Ernest Eugene and Pearl Juette (Johnson) Neal; m. Eldridge Cleaver, Dec. 27, 1967 (div. Sept. 1987); children: Maceo Eldridge, Jojuyounghi. Student, Oberlin Coll., 1963-64; student, Barnard Coll., 1965-66; BA in History summa cum laude, Yale U., 1984, JD, 1988. Bar: N.Y. 1990. Faculty rsch. asst. (part-time) Yale U. Law Sch., New Haven, Conn., 1984-85, 85-87; summer assoc. Fried, Frank, Harris, Shriver and Jacobson, N.Y.C., 1985; summer law clk. Office of the Gen. Counsel and Fed. Rels., Yale U., 1986; summer assoc. Cravath, Swaine & Moore, N.Y.C., 1987; part-time assoc. Cravath, Swaine & Moore, 1987-89, assoc., 1989-91; rsch. fellow Yale U. Law Sch., 1991; law clk. to Hon. A. Leon Higginbotham Jr. U.S. Ct. Appeals (3rd. cir.), Phila., 1991-92; asst. prof. Law Emory U. Sch. Law, Atlanta, 1992—; fellow Bunting Inst., Cambridge, Mass., 1994-95; guest speaker on TV, radio; participant in pub. and univ. programs in Switzerland, U. Heidelberg, U. Frankfort in Germany, various U.S. colls. and univs.; speaker at numerous civic, svc. and ch. groups, schs. and colls. in San Francisco Bay Area, 1976-80. Contbr. articles to various publs. Film appearances in The Family Gone Wild, 1979, The Eldridge Cleaver Story, 1978, Zabriskie Point, 1969. Comms. sec. Black Panther Party, Oakland, Calif., 1967-69. Recipient Civil Liberties award ACLU, 1993. Mem. ABA, Phi Beta Kappa. Office: Bunting Inst 34 Concord Ave Cambridge MA 02138

CLEAVES, MARGARET BEAR, agricultural administrator; b. Cloverdale, Ohio, Dec. 19, 1932; d. Leo Joseph Eickholt and Thelma Adeline (Martin) Weaver; m. Jacob Daniel Bear, Nov. 21, 1953 (dec. 1974); children: Margo Dorene Bear, Jason William Bear; m. Raymond Herbert Cleaves, Aug. 28, 1976. Student, Felt and Tarrant, Toledo, 1950, Ohio State U., 1965. Billing acct. Libby Glass Co., Toledo, 1950; payroll acct. Champion Spark Plug, Toledo, 1950-54; acct. Colonial Finance Co., Lima, Ohio, 1954-55; office mgr., acct. McMahan-Heidt Hosp., Lima, 1956-68; agrl. and fin. mgr. Cleaves Farms, Continental and Elida, Ohio, 1976—. Active Child Conservation League, pres., 1986-87; coord., tax preparer Tax Cons. for Elderly, Lima, 1987-91. Mem. Ohio Oil and Gas Assn., Nat. Assn. Investors Corp. (assoc. dir. n.e. buckeye coun. 1984—). Mem. Ch. Brethren.

CLECAK, DVERA VIVIAN BOZMAN, psychotherapist; b. Denver, Jan. 15, 1944; d. Joseph Shalom and Annette Rose (Dveirin) Bozman; m. Pete Emmett Clecak, Feb. 26, 1966; children: Aimée, Lisa. BA, Stanford U., 1965; postgrad., U. Chgo., 1965; MSW, UCLA, 1969. Lic. clin. social worker, Calif.; lic. marriage, family and child counselor, Calif. Social work supr. Harbor City (Calif.) Parent Child Ctr., 1969-71; therapist Orange County Mental Health Dept., Laguna Beach, Calif., 1971-75, area coordinator, 1975-79; pvt. practice psychotherapy Mission Viejo, Calif., 1979—; founder, exec. dir. Human Options, Laguna Beach, 1981—; mem, co-chmn. domestic violence com. Orange County Commn. on Status of Women, 1979-81; mem. mental health adv. com. extension U. Calif., Irvine, 1983, counseling psychologist, 1980, lectr., 1984-85; lectr. Saddleback Community Coll., Mission Viejo, 1981-82, Chapman Coll., Orange, 1979; field instr. UCLA, 1970-71, 77-78. Recipient Women Helping Women award Saddleback Community Coll., 1987, Cert. for child abuse prevention Commendation State of Calif. Dept. Social Svcs., 1988, Community Svc. award Irvine Valley Coll. Found., 1989; named Orange County Non-profit Exec. of Yr., 1994. Mem. NASW, Calif. Marriage Family and Child Counselors' Assn., Phi Beta Kappa. Office: 303 Broadway #204 Laguna Beach CA 92651

CLEGHORN, CHEREE BRIGGS, healthcare executive, consultant; b. Phoenix, June 25, 1945; d. Dale Sheaffer and Jeannetta Jeanne (Sebaugh) Briggs; m. George Reese Cleghorn, Mar. 15, 1975; stepchildren: Nona Elizabeth, John Michael. BA, Newcomb Coll., 1966; BJ, U. Mo., 1969. Reporter The Charlotte (N.C.) Observer, 1969-72; dir. pub. affairs Sch. Medicine U. N.C., Chapel Hill, 1972-75; spl. asst. to pres. Queens Coll., Charlotte, 1975-76; dir. pub. affairs WSU Health Care Inst., Detroit, 1976-79; cons. pub. affairs Detroit Med. Ctr. Corp., 1979-81, Johns Hopkins Sch. Pub. Health, Balt., 1982-83; v.p. pub. affairs Washington Healthcare Corp., 1983-86; pres. Cleghorn Health Communications, Bethesda, Md., 1986-88; pres. pub. rels. div. Rosenthal, Greene & Campbell, Bethesda, 1988-90; pres. Cleghorn & Assocs., Bethesda, 1990-94; v.p. corporate affairs Loudoun Healthcare, Inc., Leesburg, Va., 1994—. Mem. communications com. Greater Washington Bd. Trade, 1988-90. Mem. Soc. Profl. Journalists, Am. News Women's Club, Pub. Rels. Soc. Am., Assn. Am. Med. Coll.'s Group on Pub. Affairs. Democrat. Presbyterian. Office: Loudoun Healthcare Inc 224 Cornwall St NW Leesburg VA 22075-0600

CLEGHORN, GWENDOLYN MICHAEL, principal, educator. AB, Miss. U. for Women, 1952; MA, Emory U., 1953. Instr. dept. English So. Meth. U., Dallas, 1953-54; tchr. dept. English The Westminster Schs, Atlanta, 1954-55, 60-61; tchr. dept. English The Westminster Schs., Atlanta, 1967-94, chmn. dept. English, 1967-82, assoc. prin., 1986—; tchr. dept. English Packer Collegiate Inst., Brooklyn Heights, N.Y., 1955-58; asst. prof. dept. English Ga. State U., Atlanta, 1963-67; coll. counselor, sr. class adviser, grade chmn. The Westminster Schs., 1973-86; instr. div. continuing edn. The U. Ala., 1982; instr. grad. edn. Converse Coll., 1983; ind. schs. rep. Profl. Standards Commn.; examination reader, cons. Advanced Placement English; mem., chair Coun. on Entrance Svcs. of Coll. Bd.; mem. vis. com. So. Assn. Colls. and Schs.; presenter in field. Mem. Nat. Assn. Coll. Admission Counselors (mem. pres.' coun.), So. Assn. Coll. Admission Counselors (pres., chmn. admission practices com.). Home: 51 Peachtree Way NE Atlanta GA 30305-3735

CLEINO, BARBARA CLAIRE, orthopaedic nurse; b. Tuscaloosa, Ala., Apr. 14, 1958; d. Edward Henry and Elizabeth Anne (White) Cleino. BSN, U. Ala., Tuscaloosa, 1982; MSN, U. Ala., Birmingham, 1993. Cert. orthopaedic nurse. Staff nurse DCH Regional Med. Ctr., Tuscaloosa, 1982-91, orthopaedic case mgr., 1991—. Pres. Bama Skydivers, Tuscaloosa, 1987—. Mem. Nat. Assn. Orthopaedic Nurses (pres. elect Birmingham chpt. 1994), Sigma Theta Tau. Episcopalian.

CLELAND, GLADYS LEE, university administrator; b. Schenectady, Feb. 27, 1959; d. Anthony John and Anna Mae (Feight) Campana; m. Michael Joseph Cleland, Aug. 4, 1984. BA in Communications and Edn. cum laude, SUNY, Plattsburgh, 1981; MA summa cum laude, U. Fla., 1986. Asst. instr. communications SUNY, Plattsburgh, 1982-83, admissions/media rels. advisor, 1987-88; asst. instr. communications U. Fla., Gainesville, 1985-86; instr. English and communications Clinton Community Coll., Plattsburgh, 1986-87; news cons., acad. liaison Sta. WCFE-TV, Plattsburgh, 1987-88; pub. info. dir. Syracuse (N.Y.) U., 1989-93, pub. rels. coord., 1993-94; spl. projects mgr. SUNY Health Sci. Ctr., Syracuse, 1994—; news. cons. Sta. WCFE-TV 57, Plattsburgh, 1987-88; producer, rschr. CVPH Med. Ctr., Plattsburgh, 1982-87; freelance talent Sta. WIXT-TV 9, Syracuse, 1988—; press steward Winter Olympic Games, lake Placid, N.Y., 1980; radio announcer, news reporter, sales rep. Sta. WIRY-AM, Plattsburgh, 1980-83; freelance producer, news reporter Sta. WPBT-TV, Miami, Fla., 1983-84. Author: Satellite News Gathering, 1986. Recipient broadcast awards N.Y. State Broadcast Assn., Plattsburgh, 1982-84, Outstanding Talent award Internat. TV Assn., Gainesville, 1986. Mem. Women in Comms., Pub. Rels. Soc. Am., Syracuse Press Club, Omicron Delta Kappa, Phi Kappa Phi. Roman Catholic. Home: 4239 Mill Run Rd Liverpool NY 13090-1813 Office: SUNY Health Sci Ctr 750 E Adams St Syracuse NY 13210

CLEM, ELIZABETH ANN STUMPF, music educator; b. San Antonio, July 9, 1945; d. David Joseph and Elizabeth Burch (Wathen) Stumpf; m. D. Bruce Clem, June 17, 1972; children: Sean David, Jeremy Andrew. BA in Music Edn., St. Mary-of-the-Woods (Ind.) Coll., 1970; MEd, Drury Coll., Springfield, Mo., 1979. Elem. tchr. St. Christopher Sch., Speedway, Ind., 1970-71; elem. and jr. high sch. tchr. Indpls. Sch. System, 1971-72; elem. tchr. Augusta (Ga.) Sch. System, 1972-73, Wabash (Ind.) Sch. System, 1976-77; pvt. practice piano tchr. Wabash, Ind., 1975-77, Honolulu, 1983-86, Burke, Va., 1986-90, Manhattan, Kans., 1990-93, Fayetteville, N.C., 1993—; pvt. practice piano tchr. Meth. Coll. Performing Arts, 1993—; co-chmn. Manhattan Musicianship Auditions, 1991, chmn., 1992. Dist. fund raiser rep. Wabash chpt. Am. Cancer Soc., 1975; leadership coord. Wabash coun. Girl Scouts U.S.A., 1976; music coord. Ft. Shafter Sacred Heart Chapel, Honolulu, 1985-86; mem. exec. bd. Little Apple Invitational Soccer Tournament, 1992. Mem. Nat. Guild Piano Tchrs., Music Tchrs. Nat. Assn. (cert.), N.C. Music Tchrs. Assn., Raleigh Piano Tchrs. Assn., Fayetteville Piano Tchrs. Assn. (v.p.). Republican. Roman Catholic.

CLEMENT, CHARLENE MARIE, community health nurse; b. Pontiac, Mich., June 26, 1951; d. Clyde F. and Cathleen Marcia C. ADN, Mott C.C., Flint, Mich., 1976; BS, U. Mich., Flint, 1987. RN, Mich. Sec. Fre-Bar, Inc., Holly, Mich., 1969-76; staff nurse Flint Osteo. Hosp., 1976-88; supr. obstetrics Tolfree Meml. Hosp., West Branch, Mich., 1988; staff nurse U. Mich. Med. Ctr., Ann Arbor, 1988—; childbirth educator St. Joseph Hosp., Flint, 1987. Health and safety instr. ARC, Detroit, 1992—. Mem. Mich. Nurses Assn. Methodist.

CLEMENT, EDITH BROWN, federal judge; b. Birmingham, Ala., Apr. 29, 1948; d. Erskine John and Edith (Burrus) Brown; m. Rutledge Carter Clement Jr., Sept. 3, 1972; children: Rutledge Carter III, Catherine Lanier. BA, U. Ala., 1969; JD, Tulane U., 1972. Bar: La. 1973, U.S. Dist. Ct. (ea., mid. and we. dists.) 1973, U.S. Ct. Appeals (5th cir.) 1975, U.S. Supreme Ct. 1978, U.S. Ct. Appeals (11th cir.) 1981. Law clk. to Hon. H.W. Christenberry U.S. Dist. Ct., New Orleans, 1973-75; assoc. Jones, Walker, Waechter, Poitevent, Carrere & Denegre, New Orleans, 1975-91; judge U.S. Dist. Ct. (ea. dist.) La., New Orleans, 1991—; speaker at seminars and profl. meetings. Mem. dean's coun. Tulane U. Law Sch., 1991—. Life fellow La. Bar Found.; mem. ABA, La. State Bar Assn., Maritime Law Assn. U.S., Fed. Bar Assn. (pres. New Orleans chpt. 1990-91), New Orleans Bar Assn. (v.p. 1980-81). Roman Catholic. Office: US Dist Ct RM C-455 500 Camp St Rm C-455 New Orleans LA 70130-3313

CLEMENT, EVELYN GEER, library educator; b. Springfield, Mass., Sept. 1, 1926; d. Elihu and Helen (Schenck) Geer; m. J.R. Clement, Sept. 9, 1946 (div. 1972); children: James Randall, Timothy B., Susan Henson, Marc W., Audrey Ethriedge. BA with honors, U. Tulsa, 1965; MLS, U. Okla., 1966; PhD, Ind. U., 1975. Librarian Tulsa City-County Library, 1960-66; learning resources librarian Oral Roberts U., Tulsa, 1966-68; spl. instr. U. Okla., Norman, 1966-70; prof., chmn. library sci. Memphis State U., 1972-85, dir. Ctr. for Instructional Service and Research, 1985—, chmn. acad. senate, 1979-80, mem. faculty tenure and promotion appeals com., 1980-82, mem. standing univ. com. on libraries, 1975-80, 86-87, chmn. women's task force, 1984-85. Editor: Bibliographic Control of Nonprint Media, 1972; contbr. articles to profl. jours. Doctoral fellow U.S. Office Edn., Title II-B, Ind. U., 1968-71. Mem. ALA, Tenn. Library Assn., Memphis Library Council (chmn. 1974-75), Memphis Area Librarians' Assn., Memphis State U. Libraries Assn. (pres. 1986), Pi Gamma Mu, Phi Alpha Theta, Beta Phi Mu. Republican. Avocations: microcomputer, needlepoint, exercise, reading. Home: 280 Patterson St Memphis TN 38111-6014

CLEMENT, HOPE ELIZABETH ANNA, librarian; b. North Sydney, N.S., Can., Dec. 29, 1930; d. Harry Wells and Lana (Perkins) C. BA, U. of King's Coll., 1951; MA, Dalhousie U., 1953; BLS, U. Toronto, 1955; D of Civil Law (hon.), U. King's Coll., 1992. With Nat. Library of Can., Ottawa, Ont., 1955-92; chief nat. bibliography div. Nat. Library of Can., 1966-70, asst. dir. research and planning br., 1970-73, dir. research and planning br., 1973-77, assoc. nat. librarian, 1977-92. Editor: Canadiana, 1966-69. Mem. Can. Libr. Assn. (Outstanding Svc. to Librarianship award 1992), Internat. Fedn. Libr. Assns. (medal 1991).

CLEMENT, KATHERINE ROBINSON, social worker; b. Balt., Dec. 19, 1918; d. Alphonso Pitts and Sue Seymour (Ashby) Robinson; m. Harry George Clement, Dec. 5, 1941 (div. 1948). BA, Coll. of Wooster, Wooster, Ohio, 1940; MS in Social Work, Smith Coll., 1953; post grad., Washington Sch. of Psychiatry, 1951. Lic. clin. social worker, Calif. Social worker Family Svc., Cin., 1953-55, Hamilton, Ohio, 1955-57; social worker Family Svc. Orange County, Santa Ana, Calif., 1957-60; counselor pvt. practice, Fullerton, Calif., 1959-63; social worker Family Svc., Long Beach, Calif., 1961-1963, San Mateo (Calif.) County Welfare Dept., 1963-1967; supr. child protection Yolo County Dept. Social Svcs., Woodland, Calif., 1967-79; pvt. practice Woodland, Calif., 1980—; cons. psychiatric social svc. State Dept. Social Svcs., Sacramento, 1984—. Active Yolo County Dem. Cen. Com.; treas. Feminist Legal Svcs.; bd. dirs. Yolo County ARC; mem. Yolo County Health Coun. Mem. NASW, NOW, LWV, Mensa, Toastmasters, Soroptimist Internat. Democrat. Unitarian. Home: 205 Modoc Pl Woodland CA 95695-6662

CLEMENT, MAUREEN CLYNE, fine arts consultant, artist; b. N.Y.C., Aug. 8, 1957; d. John Patrick and Sheila Mary (Doherty) Clyne; m. Richard William Clement, June 2, 1990. Student, Am. U. in Paris, 1975-76; BFA, Boston U., 1980, MFA, 1982; MBA, Georgetown U., 1992. Freelance artist, arts. mktg. Boston, N.Y.C., Washington, 1982—; acting pub. affairs officer Corcoran Gallery of Art, Washington, 1992; mktg. dir. STUDIOS, Washington, 1992-93; fine arts cons. Arlington, Va., 1993—; pres. Grad. Women in Bus. at Georgetown U., Washington, 1991-92; script cons. Nat. Found. for Women Bus. Owners, Washington, 1993. Solo exhbns. include Pastels, 1984, From the End of the World, 1986, Provincetown Dreams, 1987, Cities in Dust, 1989. The MacDowell Colony fellow Petersborough, N.H., 1984, Va. Ctr. for the Creative Arts fellow Sweet Briar, Va., 1985, N.Y. Benefit Patrons fellow Fine Arts Work Ctr., Provincetown, Mass., 1985-86. Mem. Nat. Mus. of Women in the Arts, Coll. Art Assn., Cultural Alliance of Greater Washington. Office: 1400 S Barton St #408 Arlington VA 22204

CLEMENT, SHIRLEY GEORGE, educational services executive; b. El Paso, Tex., Feb. 14, 1926; d. Claude Samuel and Elizabeth Estelle (Mattice) Gillett; m. Paul Vincent Clement, Mar. 23, 1946; children: Brian Frank, Robert Vincent, Carol Elizabeth, Rosemary Adele. BA in English, Tex. Western Coll., 1963; postgrad. U. Tex., El Paso, N.Mex. State U.; MEd in Reading, Sul Ross State U., 1987. Tchr. lang. arts Ysleta Ind. Schs., El Paso, 1960-62; tchr. adult edn., 1962-64, tchr. reading/lang. arts, 1964-77; owner, dir. Crestline Learning Systems, Inc., El Paso, 1980-90; dir. Crestline Internat. Schs. (formerly Crestline Learning Systems, Inc., now Internat. Acad. Tex. at El Paso), 1987-90; instr. Park Coll., Ft. Bliss, Tex., 1992-94, U. Phoenix, 1995; dir. tutorial for sports teams U. Tex., El Paso, 1984; bd. dirs. Southwest Inst., pres., 1993; dir. continuing edn. program El Paso Community Coll., 1985; mem. curriculum com. Ysleta Ind. Schs., El Paso, 1974; mem. Right to Read Task Force, 1975-77; mem. Bi-Centennial Steering Com., El Paso, 1975-76; presenter Poetry in the Arts, Austin, Tex., 1992; Poetry Soc. Tex. program presenter Mesilla Valley Writers, 1993-94, El Paso Writers, 1994-95, Poetry Soc. Tex., 1993; instr. writing Paris Am. Acad., summer 1994, 95; cons. Ysleta Schs. 1995; instr. Paris Am. Acad., 1995—; lectr. on reading in 4 states. Author: Beginning the Search, 1979; contbr. articles to profl. jours.; contbr. poems to Behold Texas, 1983. Treas. El Paso Rep. Women, 1956; facilitator Goals for El Paso, 1975; mem. hospitality com. Sun Carnival, 1974, Cotton Festival, 1975. Mem. Internat. Reading Assn. (pres. El Paso County council 1973-74, presentor 1977-87), Assn. Children with Learning Disabilities (tchr. 1980), Poetry Soc. Tex. (Panhandle Penwomen's first place award 1981, David Atamian Meml. award 1991), Nat. Fedn. State Poetry Soc. (1st place award ann. contest 1988, 1st prize El Paso Historical Essay contest 1991), Chi Omega Alumnae (pres. 1952-53). Home: PO Box 1645 114 Casas Bellas Ln Santa Teresa NM 88008-1645

CLEMENTS, LYNNE FLEMING, family therapist, programmer; b. Bklyn., Aug. 8, 1945; d. Daniel Gillies and Dorothy Frances (Zitzmann) Fleming; m. Louis Myrick Clements, Feb. 19, 1972; children: Ryan Louis, Glenn Fleming. BA in Sociology, Bradley U., 1967; MSW, Fordham U., 1973; postgrad. studies, Columbia U., 1970-71; cert. family therapy, Inst. for Mental Health Edn., 1990. Computer programmer Employer's Comml. Union Group Ins. Cos., Boston, 1967-69, Harvard Bus. Sch., Cambridge, Mass., 1969-70, Volkswagon of Am., Englewood Cliffs, N.J., 1971; psychiatric social worker Associated Cath. Charities Family and Children's Svcs., Paramus, N.J., 1973-74, Christian Health Ctr., Wyckoff, N.J., 1976; owner, mgr. Wicker Wagon, Bergenfield, N.J., 1977-85; psychotherapist The Psychotherapy Counseling Ctr., Bergenfield, N.J., 1982-89; programmer analyst Atlas Computing Svcs., Secaucus, N.J., 1984-86; program coord., family therapist Div. of Family Guidance, Hackensack, N.J., 1986-91; pres. Corp. Family Resources, Ridgewood, N.J., 1989—; part-time family therapist N.J. Ctr. for Psychotherapy Inc., Ridgefield Park, 1990; family therapist cons. Family Recovery of Valley View, White Plains, N.Y., 1992—. Sunday sch. tchr. All Saints Ch., 1982-89, chmn. bd. community play ctr., 1977-78; mem. Twin-Boro Youth Ministry Coun., 1989—, Bergen County Family Day Care Coalition, 1989—; apptd. sec. Mayor's Beautify Bergenfield Com., 1991—; chmn. entertainment Bergen County Children's Festival, 1993; apptd. chmn., designer Bergenfield's Coun. for Arts, 1993—; chmn. curriculum enhancement com. Bergen County Acad. for Advancement of Sci. and Tech., 1992—. Recipient 1st and 2nd pl. awards Bergenfield 1980 Art Contest; NIMH grantee, 1973. Mem. AAUW, Gifted Child Soc. (parent workshop coord. 1989—, bd. dirs. 1991—), Nat. Assn. Social Workers, Acad. Cert. Social Workers, Am. Orthopsychiat. Assn., Fordham U. Alumni Assn., N.J. Commerce and Industry Assn. (child care com. 1990—, human resources com. 1990—), N.J. Soc. Clin. Social Workers, Zonta (Amelia Earhart chmn. 1987-88), Women of Accomplishment (founder, pres. 1991—, chmn. women's coalition conf. 1993—). Episcopalian. Home: 148 Harcourt Ave Bergenfield NJ 07621-1917 Office: Corp Family Resources Ste 1 15 Godwin Ave Ridgewood NJ 07450-3817

CLEMENTS, MARY MARGARET, retired educator; b. Glasgow, Scotland, Dec. 23, 1925; came to U.S., 1928; d. Peter MacIntyre and Margaret Service (Mackay) Somerville; m. Carl Emery Clements, Aug. 28, 1954; children: Robert Peter, Margaret Ann Clements Fleming. BA in Edn., U. Akron, 1946; MA in History, U. Mich., 1950. Permanent cert. tchr., Ohio. Tchr. English, history and Spanish, Brunswick (Ohio) H.S., 1946-47, Covington (Ohio) H.S., 1947-51, Xenia (Ohio) Ctrl. H.S., 1951-58, Notre Dame Acad., Chardon, Ohio, 1970-74; tchr. Spanish, Villa Angela Acad., Cleve., 1968-70; tutor for pupil pers. Euclid (Ohio) Sch. System, 1963-67, 91-94, chmn. English dept. summer sch., 1980-91; ret., 1994. Sec., coord. united thank offering Diocesan Episcopal Ch. Women, 1981-94; editor Episcopal Ch. Women's News Notes, 1984-94; mem., host family Am. Field Svc., Euclid, 1961-94; pres. PTA Coun., Euclid, 1974-76; provost Deanery Episcopal Ch., Cleve., 1993-95; trustee Ctr. for Human Svcs., Cleve., 1976-86; mem., past pres. Meridia Euclid Hosp., 1976-94; mem. Women's Caucus, Euclid, 1978-82. Recipient award for civic leadership Du Pont, 1980. Mem. AAUW (pres. 1978-80, Faculty Wives Assn. (pres. 1963-65). Home: 55 E 213th St Euclid OH 44123

CLEMENTZ, MARINA CATHERINE, counselor; b. Minneola, N.Y., Aug. 17, 1961; d. John Jr. and Nancy Catherine (Villani) DeAngelis; m. Michael Lee Clementz, Dec. 5, 1987; 1 child, Andrew Robert. B in Social Work, Fla. State U., 1983; MEd, Fla. Atlantic U., 1988. Social worker St. John's Nursing Home, Lauderhill, Fla., 1983-85, Sunrise (Fla.) Rehab. Hosp., 1985-88; dir. social work Tiffany House, Ft. Lauderdale, Fla., 1988-89; guidance counselor Mirimar (Fla.) H.S., 1989-90; dir. social work Ft. Pierce (Fla.) Infectious Disease Ctr., 1990-91; guidance counselor Ft. Pierce (Fla.) Ctrl. H.S., 1991—; drop-out prevention counselor Performance-Based Diploma Program-Ft. Pierce (Fla.) Ctrl. H.S., 1991—. Recipient Schear's award Fla. State U. Sch. Social Work, Tallahassee, 1983. Mem. Am. Counseling Assn., Am. Sch. Counselors Assn., Phi Theta Kappa Alumni Assn. Democrat. Lutheran. Office: Ft Pierce Ctrl HS 1101 Edwards Rd Fort Pierce FL 34982-4399

CLEMONS, JANE ANDREA, state legislator; b. Poughkeepsie, N.Y., Apr. 2, 1946; d. Mary (Longendyke) Martin; m. Michael R. Clemons, Oct. 15, 1966; children: Bret, Nick, Benjamin. Student, Moore Gen. Hosp., Grasmere, N.H., 1966. Nurse various orgns., Nashua, N.H., 1967-89; accounts mgr. D & M Cleaning Co., Nashua, 1989-92; mem. N.H. Ho. of Reps., Nashua, 1990-92. Sponsor Sr. Citizen Computer Health Care Program, Nashua, 1983-84; ward chair Dem. City Com., Nashua, 1988; del. Dem. State Conv., Nashua, 1988; vol. Merrimack (N.H.) Friars Club, 1990-92; del. State Dem. Pary, 1993. Greek Orthodox. Home: 177 Kinsley St Nashua NH 03060 Office: NH House Reps State House Concord NH 03301*

CLEMONS, JULIE PAYNE, telephone company manager; b. Attleboro, Mass., June 13, 1948; d. John Gordon and Claire (Paquin) P.; m. W. Richard Johnson, Oct. 10, 1970 (div. Oct. 1980); m. E.L. Clemons, Apr. 23, 1988. BBA, U. R.I., 1970. Svc. rep. New England Telephone, East Greenwich, R.I., 1970-71; svc. rep. So. Bell, Jacksonville, Fla., 1971-73, bus. office supr., 1973-77, bus. office mgr., 1978-84, staff mgr. assessment, 1984-86, mgr. assessment ctr., 1987-89; dir. human resource assessment State of Fla., Jacksonville, Fla., 1987-89; dir. human resource assessment Customer Svcs. Revenue Recovery Ctr., 1989-93, mgr. small bus. sales and svc., 1994-95, br. mgr. small bus. No. Fla., 1995—; br. mgr. Small Bus. North Fla., 1994—. Vol. Learn to Read; bd. dirs. Duval Assn. of Retarded Citizens, Jacksonville, 1981-86, treas. 1983-84. Mem. NAFE, Am. Mgmt. Assn., Pioneers of Am., Jacksonville C. of C. Roman Catholic. Office: So Bell Tower 301 W Bay St 15BB1 Jacksonville FL 32202

CLEMONS, NANCY LONG, telephone company executive; b. LaGrange, Tex., Sept. 8, 1948; d. Andrew E. and Helen Margaret (Albert) Schmidt; m. Joseph Michael Long, Nov. 20, 1970 (div. Oct. 1991); m. Harold William Clemons, May 8, 1993. AA, San Jacinto Jr. Coll., Houston, 1987; BA, U. Houston, 1989, MA, 1991. Mgr. Southwestern Bell Tel. Co., Houston, 1970—. Counselor Crisis Intervention, Inc., Houston, 1987—, dir. 1987-88; pres. Crime Stopper of the Bay Area, Seabrook, Tex., 1992-93. Mem. Clear Lake C. of C. (dir. memberships 1989), South Shore Harbour Homeowners Assn. (pres. 1987-91). Home: 203 Empress Dr Houston TX 77034-1501

CLENDANIEL, FONTAINE COWAN, design educator, graphic designer; b. Takoma Pk., Md., July 26, 1951; d. Thomas Warner Cowan and Lois (Jackson) Cowan-Rische; m. Charles Elwood Clendaniel III, Jan. 3, 1981. BFA, U. Tex., 1976; cert., Am. Inst. Graphic Arts, 1986. Prodn. artist Naylor Type and Mats, Houston, 1974-76; graphic artist C-E Lummus, Houston, 1976-77; graphic designer Exxon Co., U.S.A., Houston, 1977-80; art dir. Unified Graphics, Houston, 1980; lead artist Houston Lighting and Power, 1980-81; sr. designer CPS Group - Bozell, Jacobs, Kenyon & Eckhardt, Houston, 1981-83; owner, designer Clendaniel & Assocs. Graphic Design, Houston, 1983-88; sales rep., designer MicroType, Inc., Houston, 1988-89; sales rep. Typografiks, Inc., Houston, 1989; design instr. Art Inst. Houston, 1990—. Designer, art dir. (print media) U.S. Home Annual Report 1981; designer, prodn. mgr. (print media) U.S. Home Annual Report 1982, McFaddin Ventures Annual Report 1986, (print media and specialty items) Flagship Hotel Logo 1988. Mem. Magnolia Grove Civic Club, Houston, 1988—. Recipient Cert. of Excellence Grand Prix Houston Advt. Fedn., 1982, Cert. of Merit Grand Prix, 1984; work pub. in Regional Annual Print mag. 1984; work exhibited in Mead Annual Report Show, 1986. Assoc. mem. Art Dirs. Club Houston, Houston Prodn. Mgrs. Assn. Episcopalian. Office: Art Inst Houston 1900 Yorktown Houston TX 77056

CLEVELAND, ANNE C(ATHERINE), home economics educator; BS, Syracuse U., 1941; MS, SUNY-Albany, 1947; postgrad. St. Rose Coll., 1954, Russell Sage Coll., 1968, Tex. Technol. U., 1969, Cornell U., 1964, Syracuse U., SUNY-Plattsburg. Tchr. various elem. schs., 1941-46, 50-59; tchr. Albany (N.Y.) Pub. Schs., 1959-77; home econs. coord. Glens Falls (N.Y.) City Schs., 1959-77. Bd. dirs. ARC chpt.; bd. dirs., chmn. Glens Falls Literacy Vols.; chmn. vols. Adirondack chpt. ARC; pres. Glen Falls Study Group.; chair fundraising L.T. Recipient American Red Cross Chapter award, 1988. Mem. AAUW (bd. dirs., award 1977, co-pres. Adirondack chpt. 1990-92, pres.), Home Econs. Tchrs. Assn. (numerous activities, including coord. and founder Job Index Service 1977-79, N.Y. State pres. 1970-72, N.Y. State White Orchid award 1982), Am. Home Econs. Assn. (N.Y. State membership promotion chmn., state co-chmn. conv., pres. N.Y. State ea. dist., Betty Lamp award) N.Y. State Tchrs.' Assn. (chmn. ways and means, chmn. membership, gen. chmn. chmn. zone conf. home econs. conf.), Nat. Assn. Vocat. Home Econs. Tchrs., Nat. Econs. Assn., Home Econs. Edn. Assn., N.Y. State Home Econs. Assn. (Service award 1982), Delta Kappa Gamma (numerous activities, including v.p. Alpha Epsilon chpt., pres. chpt., 1st v.p., state pres., Ruth Frasier scholar, N.Y. State achievement award, Achievement award N.Y. state chpt., awards com., com. tolerance, 1st v.p. vol. for literacy scholarship com.), Soc. Mayflower Descs. (sec. Albany County), Catholic Daus. Am. (chmn. edn. 1966-79, 1st vice regent chpt. 1979-81, regent 1979-83, dist. deputy, 1988-92), DAR (sec. Jane McGrew chpt., recording sec.), New Eng. Women (v.p. colony 25, chaplain GF chpt., pres.).

CLEVELAND, EDNA CHARLOTTE, writer, typist; b. Kidder, Mo., Aug. 20, 1930; d. Alexander Roger and Lola Elizabeth (Milstead) Short; m. Newcomb Lee Cleveland, Aug. 5, 1950; children: Kathy, Joe, Margo, Karen, Harvey, Don, Roger. BA in English, U. Mo., Kansas City, 1953; MA in English, N.W. Mo. State U., 1990. Cert. tchr. English and Spanish, Mo. Rural elem. tchr. Cameron, Mo., 1948-50; elem. tchr. 2d grade Independence, Mo., 1950-54; tchr. secondary Spanish Fairfax, Mo., 1984-87; instr. writing Tarkio (Mo.) Coll., 1988-90; profl. writer, researcher and typist Mo. Writer, Fairfax, 1990—. Vol., gift shop buyer Community Hosp. Fairfax, 1973-78, cookbook com., Meth. Ch.; reader Iowa Commn. for Blind. Named Vol. of the Yr., Iowa Commn. for Blind, 1987. Mem. AAUW. Home: RR 1 Box 130 Fairfax MO 64446-9760

CLEVELAND, JULIA LYNN, elementary educator; b. Ft. Dodge, Iowa, May 1, 1952; d. Euzema Hendrix and Mildred Helen (Harris) C. BS, Berry Coll., Mt. Berry, Ga., 1973, MEd, 1978. Cert. tchr. in early childhood and middle grades. Tchr. Cloverleaf Elem. Sch., Cartersville, Ga., 1973-85, Cass Middle Sch., Cartersville, 1985—; team leader Cass Middle Sch., Cartersville, Ga., 1989—; mem. site based mgmt. com. Cass Mid. Sch., 1993—, mem. tech. com., 1993—. Editor Casszine jour., 1989—. Mem. People for the Ethical Treatment of Animals, Nat. Mus. of Women in the Arts, Greenpeace. Named Tchr. of the Yr., Cass Middle Sch., 1992. Mem. NEA, Ga. Assn. Educators, Profl. Assn. of Ga. Educators, Cousteau Soc. Republican. Methodist. Home: PO Box 313 Armuchee GA 30105 Office: Cass Middle School 195 Fire Tower Rd Cartersville GA 30120

CLEVELAND, PEGGY ROSE RICHEY, cytotechnologist; b. Cannelton, Ind., Dec. 9, 1929; d. "Pat" Clarence Francis and Alice Marie (Hall) Richey; cert. U. Louisville, 1956; B. Health Sci., U. Louisville, 1984; m. Peter Leslie Cleveland, Nov. 25, 1948 (dec. 1973); children: Pamela Cleveland Litch, Paula Cleveland Bertloff, Peter L. Cytotechnologist cancer survey project NIH, Louisville, 1956-59; chief cytotechnologist Parker Cytology Lab., Inc., Louisville, 1959-75; mgr. cytology dept. Am. Biomed. Corp., 1976-78, Nat. Health Labs., Inc., Louisville, 1978-89; clin. instr. cytology Sch. Allied Health U. Louisville, 1989—; leader cytotechnologist del. to People's Republic of China, 1986; with various hosps. and labs., 1990—; ptnr. Sham Star Stable thoroughbred horse breeding and racing. Mem. Am. Soc. Clin. Pathologist (cert. cytotechnologist), Internat. Acad. Cytology (cert. cytotechnologist), Am. Soc. Cytology (del.-person to person cytology delegation, amb. USSR, 1990), Kentuckiana Cytology Soc., Cytology Soc. Ind., Horseman's Benevolent and Protective Assn. Democrat. Roman Catholic. Home: 8774 Lieber Hausz Rd Lanesville IN 47136

CLEVELAND, SUSAN ELIZABETH, library administrator, researcher; b. Plainfield, N.J., Mar. 14, 1946; d. Robert Astbury and Grace Ann (Long) Williamson; m. Stuart Craig Cleveland, Aug. 21, 1971; children: Heather Elizabeth, Catherine Elisa. BA, Douglass Coll., Rutgers U., 1968; MLS, Rutgers U., 1969. Acquisitions libr. Jefferson U., Phila., 1970-71; biomed. libr. VA Hosp., Hines, Ill., 1972; med. cataloger U. Ariz., Tucson, 1973-74; dir. U. Pa. Hosp. Libr., Phila., 1974-87; exec. dir. Cleveland, Lamb, Urban Assocs., 1987-89; libr. dir. Mt. Sinai Hosp., Phila., 1989, West Jersey Health System, Voorhees, N.J., 1990—; cons. in field, Phila. USPHS fellow, Detroit, 1969-70; recipient Chapel of 4 Chaplains Legion of Honor. Mem. Med. Libr. Assn. (Phila. chpt.), Spl. Libr. Assn., Basic Health Sci. Libr. Consortium, S.W. N.J. Consortium for Health Info. Svcs., Health Scis. Libr. Assn. N.J., Acad. Health Info. Profls., Caravan Club. Home: 9 Sylvan Ct Laurel Springs NJ 08021

CLEVEN, CAROL CHAPMAN, state legislator; b. Hanover, Ill., Nov. 2, 1928; d. Edward William and Vivian (Strasser) Chapman; m. Walter Arnold Cleven; children: Kern W., Jeffrey P. BS, U. Ill., 1950, postgrad., 1950-56. Elem. sch. tchr. Derinda Ctr., Ill., 1946-47; with rsch. staff U. Ill., Urbana, 1950-56; exec. dir. Crittenton Hasting House, Brighton, Mass., 1975-86; mem. Ho. of Reps. of Mass. Great and Gen. Ct., Boston, 1987—; mem. edn. com., fed. fin. assistance com., com. pub. svcs. edn. com., HUD com., fed. fin. assistance com., Commn. on Indoor Air Pollution; mem. Rep. Task Force on AIDS, Mass. Caucus of Women Legislators, Spl. Commn. on Worker Availability in Human Svcs. Professions, Commn. on Mobile Home Parks, Adolscent Health Adv. Coun., Spl. Commn. on Pub. Assiatance, Spl. Com. on Women and th eCriminal Justice System, LEgis. Caucus on Older Citizens' Concerns. Mem. Chelmsford (Mass.) Sch. Com., 1969-87, mem. elem. needs com., 1969-71, mem. sch. bldg. com., 1971-76; bd. dirs. Camp Paul for Exceptional Children, 1987—; past pres. Lowell (Mass.) YMCA, Lowell Coll. Club; mem. Merrimack River Watershed Coun., Mass. Coalition for Pregnant and Parenting Teens, Alliance for Young Families; 1st v.p. Boston Ctr. Blind Children; bd. dirs. Chelmsford Ednl. Found. Mem. Mass. Assn. Sch. Coms. (life), Friends of the Library, Chelmsford Hist. Soc., Chelmsford LWV, Florence Crittenton League of Lowell, Phi Sigma, Sigma Delta Epsilon. Congregationalist. Home: 4 Arbutus Ave Chelmsford MA 01824-1113 Office: State House Rm 36 State Capitol Boston MA 02133

CLEVEN, CHERYL ANN, school psychologist; b. Lincoln, Nebr., Nov. 18, 1954; d. Bertil R. and Bernetta M. (Leyden) C.; m. Norman D. Farley, May 23, 1987; children: Adam C., Laura C. BS, U. Nebr., 1976, MA, 1983, MS, 1984, PhD, 1987. Tchr. Wahoo (Nebr.) Pub. Schs., 1980-81, Lincoln (Nebr.) Pub. Schs., 1981-83; psychol. cons. Head Start, Lincoln, 1983-86; psychol. intern Ralston (Nebr.) Pub. Schs., 1986, Meyer Children's Rehab. Inst., Omaha, 1987; psychology resident Mary Bridge Children's Hosp., Tacoma, Wash., 1989-90; sch. psychologist Peninsula Sch. Dist., Gig Harbor, Wash., 1987—. Contbr. articles to profl. jours. Named Sch. Psychology Student of Yr. N.E. Sch. Psychology Assn., 1986.

CLEVENGER, PENELOPE, international business consultant; b. Denver, Dec. 6, 1940; d. Harold Friedland and Charlotte (Glatt) Friedland Beskin; m. Willie K. Clevenger, Oct. 15, 1961 (div.). AA, Stephens Coll., 1960. Office mgr. Malcolm S. Gerald, Chgo., 1977-79; pers. mgr. Rolm/Midwest, Chgo., 1979-82; office adminstr. Nutech Engrs., Chgo., 1982-83; office mgr. Am. Acad. Orthopaedic Surgeons, Chgo., 1983-85; dir. adminstrn. Telecommunications Industry Assn. (formerly U.S. Telecommunications Suppliers Assn.), Chgo., 1985-88; pres. InterWorld Svcs., Ltd., 1988—. Bd. dirs. Ctr. Tng. and Rehab. of Disabled, Chgo., 1981-84; vol. Northwestern Meml. Hosp., 1985-87, Christian Industrial League, 1992—. Mem. Meeting Profls. Internat. (Chgo. chpt.), Meeting Profls. Internat. (nat. orgn.), Soc. for Human Resource Mgmt., Japanese Am. Soc. Chgo. Democrat. Jewish. Home and Office: 233 E Wacker Dr Apt 3913 Chicago IL 60601-5116

CLEVENGER, SARAH, botanist, computer consultant; b. Indpls., Dec. 19, 1926; d. Cyrus Raymond and Mary Beth (Stevens) C. A.B., Miami U., 1947; Ph.D., Ind. U., 1957. Tchr sci. Radford Sch., El Paso, Tex., 1949-51, Hillsdale Sch., Cin., 1951-52; asst. prof. Berea (Ky.) Coll., 1957-59, 61-63, Wittenberg U., Springfield, Ohio, 1959-60, Eastern Ill. U., 1960-61, Ind. State U., Terre Haute, 1963-66; assoc. prof. Ind. State U., 1966-78, prof., 1978-85, prof. emerita, 1985—. Mem. Am. Inst. Biol. Sci., Am. Soc. Plant Taxonomists, Bot. Soc. Am., Internat. Assn. Plant Taxonomy, Phytochem. Soc. N.Am. (past sec.). Home: 717 S Henderson St Bloomington IN 47401-4838

CLEVER, LINDA HAWES, physician; b. Seattle; d. Nathan Harrison and Evelyn Lorraine (Johnson) Hawes; m. James Alexander Clever, Aug. 20, 1960; 1 child, Sarah Lou. AB with distinction, Stanford U., 1962, MD, 1965. Diplomate Am. Bd. Internal Medicine, Am. Bd. Preventive Medicine in Occupational Medicine. Intern Stanford U. Hosp., Palo Alto, Calif., 1965-66; resident Stanford U. Hosp., Palo Alto, 1966-67, fellow in infectious disease, 1967-68; fellow in community medicine U. Calif., San Francisco, 1968-69, resident, 1969-70; med. dir. Sister Mary Philippa Diagonostic and Treatment Ctr. St. Mary's Hosp., San Francisco, 1970-77; chmn. dept. occupational health Calif. Pacific Med. Ctr., San Francisco, 1977—; clin. prof. medicine Med. Sch., U. Calif., San Francisco; NIH rsch. fellow Sch. Medicine, Stanford U., 1967-68; mem. San Francisco Comprehensive Health Planning Coun., 1971-76, bd. dir.; mem. Calif.-OSHA Adv. Com. on Hazard Evaluation System and Info. Svc., 1979-85, Calif. Statewide Profl. Standards Rev. Coun., 1977-81, San Francisco Regional Commn. on White House Fellows, 1978-81, 83-89, chmn., 1979-81. Editor Western Jour. Medicine, 1990—; contbr. articles to profl. jours. Trustee Stanford U., 1972-76, 81-91, v.p., 1985-91; trustee Marin Country Day Sch., 1978-85; bd. dirs. Sta. KQED, 1976-83, chmn., 1979-81; bd. dirs. Independent Sector, 1980-86, vice chmn., 1985-86; bd. dirs. San Francisco U. High Sch., 1983-90, chmn. 1987-88; active Womens Forum West, 1980—, bd. dirs. 1993. Fellow ACP (gov. No. Calif. region 1984-89, chmn. bd. govs. 1989-90, regent 1990—, vice chair bd. regents 1994-95), Am. Coll. Occupational and Environ. Medicine; mem. Inst. Medicine NAS, Calif. Med. Assn., Calif. Acad. Medicine, Am. Pub. Health Assn., We. Occupational Medicine Assn., We. Assn. Physicians, Stanford U. Women's Club (bd. dirs. 1971-80), Chi Omega. Office: 2351 Clay St San Francisco CA 94115-1931

CLEVER, MARCIA SUE, psychiatrist; b. Natrona Heights, Pa., Aug. 13, 1956; d. John Stacy and Marjorie Mae (DeBay) Clever; m. James Paul Hickey, June 27, 1987; 1 child, Blair. BS, U. Pitts., 1977; MD, Cornell U., 1981. Diplomate Am. Bd. Psychiatry and Neurology. Intern in surgery U. Calif.-Davis Med. Ctr., Sacramento, 1981-82, resident in surgery, 1982-83, resident in psychiatry, 1983-85; sr. resident in geropsychiatry U. Calif.-San Francisco, Langley Porter Neuropsychiat. Inst., 1985-86; assoc. psychiatrist Timberlawn Psychiat. Hosp., Dallas, 1986-87; pvt. practice Johannesburg, S.Africa, and Rome, 1987-91; asst. clin. prof. U. Ill., Chgo., 1989; med. dir. psychiat. emergency screening svc. Kimball Med. Ctr., Lakewood, N.J., 1992-95; asst. clin. prof. psychiatry U. Medicine and Dentistry N.J., Piscataway, N.J., 1995—; psychiat. cons. U.S. Dept. State, Johannesburg, 1987-89. Burroughs-Wellcome fellow, 1984-86. Mem. Am. Psychiat. Assn.

CLEWIS, CHARLOTTE WRIGHT STAUB, teacher; b. Pitts., Aug. 20, 1935; d. Schirmer Chalfant and Charlotte Wright (Rodgers) Staub; student Memphis State Coll., 1953-54, U. Wis., 1957-59; BA, Newark State Coll., 1963; MAT, Loyola Marymount U., 1974; m. John Edward Clewis, Aug. 11, 1954; 1 dau., Charlotte Wright. Asst. to dir., housemother Leota Sch. and Camp, Evansville, Wis., 1957-59; tchr. math. Rahway Jr. High Sch. (N.J.), 1963-70; tchr. math. Torrance (Calif.) Unified Sch. Dist., 1970—, coord. math. dept., 1977—, mem. math. steering com., 1978-83, 86-89, mem. proficiency exam writing com., 1977-91; mem. instructional materials rev. panel State of Calif., 1986; instr. Weekend Coll. Marymount-Palos Verdes, 1992—; coach math. teams. Sec., pres. Larga Vista Property Owners Assn., 1975-84; mem. Rolling Hills Estates City Celebration Com., 1975-81; treas. adult leaders YMCA, Metuchen, N.J., 1967-69; bd. dirs. Peninsula Symphony Assn., 1978-84, sec., 1993; commr. Rolling Hills Estates Parks and Activities, 1981—, chmn., 1985, 90. Named Tchr. of Yr., Rahway Jr. High Sch., 1966; recipient Appreciation award PTA, 1984, Hon. Service award PTA, 1986. Mem. Nat. Coun. Tchrs. Math., Calif. Math. Coun. Avocations: bicycling, camping, reading, horseback riding, computers. Home: 1 Gaucho Dr Rllng Hls Est CA 90274-5113 Office: Calle Mayor Mid Sch 4800 Calle Mayor Torrance CA 90505-4401

CLICK, CHARLCIE HENRY, systems analyst; b. Chattanooga, Aug. 12, 1948; d. Charles Sutton and Charlcie Estelle (Webb) Henry; (div.); children: Laura Amberly Click, LeAnna Elizabeth Click. BA in Math., U. Tenn., 1978, MS in Engring. Mgmt., 1983. Engring. aide Tenn. Valley Authority, Chattanooga, 1967-69, programming technician, 1969-74, power supply engr., 1974-80, programmer analyst, 1980-83, sys. analyst, 1983—, project leader, 1988—. Democrat. Presbyterian. Home: 7702 Lasata Ln Harrison TN 37341

CLICK, MARIANNE JANE, credit manager; b. Marion, Ohio, Aug. 2, 1949; d. Raymond E. and Martha C. (Robinson) C. BS in Edn., Ohio State U., 1971. Various positions Western Auto Supply, Delaware, Ohio, 1973-87; dept. mgr. Western Auto Supply, Kansas City, Mo., 1988-89, dir. revolving ops., 1989—. Bd. dirs. Consumer Credit Counseling Svcs., Kansas City, 1992—. Mem. Internat. Credit Assn., Credit Assn. Greater Kansas City (bd. dirs. 1991—), Internat. Assn. Credit Card Investigators, Merchants Rsch. Coun., Alpha Lambda Delta. Republican. Office: Western Auto Supply Co 5777 Deramus Ave Kansas City MO 64120-1261

CLIFF, JOHNNIE MARIE, mathematics and chemistry educator; b. Lamkin, Miss., May 10, 1935; d. John and Modest Alma (Lewis) Walton; m. William Henry Cliff, Apr. 1, 1961 (dec. 1983); 1 child, Karen Marie. BA in Chemistry, Math., U. Indpls., 1956; postgrad., NSF Inst., Butler U., 1960; MA in Chemistry, Ind. U., 1964; MS in Math., U. Notre Dame, 1980. Cert. tchr., Ind. Rsch. chemist Ind. U. Med. Ctr., Indpls., 1956-59; tchr. sci. and math. Indpls. Pub. Schs., 1960-88; tchr. chemistry, math. Martin U., Indpls., 1989—, chmn. math. dept., 1990—, divsn. chmn. depts. sci. and math., 1993—; adj. instr. math. U. Indpls., 1991. Contbr. rsch. papers to sci. jours. Grantee NSF, 1961-64, 73-76, 78-79, Woodrow Wilson Found., 1987-88; scholarship U. Indpls., 1952-56, NSF Inst. Reed Coll., 1961, C. of C., 1963. Mem. AAUW, NAACP, NEA, Assn. Women in Sci., Urban League, N.Y. Acad. Scis., Am. Chem. Soc., Nat. Coun. Math. Tchrs., Am. Assn. Physics Tchrs., Nat. Sci. Tchrs. Assn., Am. Statis. Assn., Am. Assn. Ret. Persons, Neal-Marshall-Ind. U. Alumni Assn., U. Indpls. Alumni Assn., U. Notre Dame Alumni Assn., Ind. U. Chemist Assn., Notre Dame Club Indpls., Kappa Delta Pi, Delta Sigma Theta. Democrat. Baptist. Home: 405 Golf Ln Indianapolis IN 46260-4108 Office: Martin U 2171 Avondale Pl Indianapolis IN 46218-3867

CLIFFORD, ELIZABETH ANNE, marketing professional; b. Des Moines, Feb. 22, 1961; d. Robert Edward Jackson and Sandra Lee (Mullenberg) Mickesh; m. Justin Burns Clifford, Sept. 12, 1987. BA, Iowa State U., 1983. Directory advt. cons. U S WEST Direct, West Des Moines, 1984-86; product devel. mgr. U S WEST Direct, Aurora, Colo., 1986-89; strategic mktg. mgr. U S WEST Direct, Englewood, Colo., 1989-94; mkt. devel. specialist U S WEST Mktg. Resources Group, Englewood, Colo., 1994—. Contbn. articles to profl. jours. Mem. Iowa State U. Alumni Assn., Rocky Mt. Direct Mktg. Assn. Republican. Office: U S WEST Mktg Resources Group 198 Inverness Dr West 3rd Flr Englewood CO 80112

CLIFFORD, RITA KAY, nursing school administrator; b. Ashland, Kans., Oct. 1, 1940; d. Ernest Leslie and E. Regina (Carleton) Harris; m. Jack Carter, Dec. 23, 1968; 1 child, Christina Lee. BSN, U. Kans., 1962, PhD, 1981; MS in Psychiat. Nursing, Boston U., 1964. Staff nurse Peter Bent Brigham Hosp., Boston, 1962-64; instr. U. Kans. Sch. Nursing, Kansas City, 1964-67, asst. prof., 1967-71, assoc. prof., 1971—, asst. dean, 1974-92, assoc. dean, 1992—; mem. adv. bd. Nursing and Health Careers Resource Ctr., Kansas City, 1989—. Contbr. articles to profl. jours. and chpts. to books. Planning com. Women's Concern Conf. II, Kansas City, 1982, Women's Agenda II Nat. Conf., Kansas City, 1988; phone capt. Johnson County (Kans.) Humane Soc., 1990. Named Disting. Alumnus U. Kans. Nurses Alumni Assn., 1992. Mem. ANA, NLN, Midwest Nursing Rsch. Soc., Kans. State Nurses Assn. (pres. dist. II 1988-90, steering com. 1989-91), Sigma Theta Tau (internat. del. 1991, pres. Delta chpt. 1992—), Phi Delta Kappa. Office: U Kans Sch Nursing 3901 Rainbow Blvd Kansas City KS 66160-7501

CLIFTON, JUDY RAELENE, association administrator; b. Safford, Ariz., Nov. 8, 1946; d. Ralph Newton and Fayrene (Goodner) Johnson; student Biola Coll., 1964-65; BA in Christian Edn., Southwestern Coll., 1970; married. Editl. asst. Accent Publications, Denver, 1970-73; expediter Phelps Dodge Corp., Douglas, Ariz., 1974-78; exec. asst. So. Ariz. Internat. Livestock Assn., Inc., Tucson, 1978-81; supt.'s sec. Phelps Dodge Corp., 1981—; sec. exec. bd. PAC, Phelps Dodge, 1985-90. Mem. adv. bd. Ariz. Lung Assn.; mem. Silver City Arts Coun., 1986-90; mem. Am. Security Council, 1979-85; leader 4-H, Douglas; mem. Rep. Nat. Com., 1978—, Conservative Caucus, 1979-85; del. Quadrennial N.Mex. State Rep. Con., 1988, 92. Recipient Am. Legion Good Citizen award, 1964, DAR award, 1964. Mem. NAFE, DAR, Nat. Assn. Evangelicals, U.S. Tennis Assn., So. Ariz. Internat. Livestock Assn., AAUW, Eagle Forum, Freedom Found., N.Mex. Eagle Forum, Mus. N.Mex. Found., Lordsburg/Hidalgo County C. of C. (1st v.p bd. dirs. 1990-93), Sigma Lambda Delta. Baptist. Clubs: Trunk & Tusk, Pima County Republican, Centre Ct., Westerners Internat., So. Ariz. Depression Glass, Tucson Tennis, Rep. Senatorial. Home: Drawer M Playas NM 88009

CLIFTON, LAURI ANN, accountant, administrator; b. Janesville, Wis., Aug. 5, 1960; d. Lawrence H. and Deanna M. (Neprud) Tunks; m. Kevin L. Clifton, Sept. 22, 1984; children: Alexandria, Elizabeth. BBA in Acctg., U. Wis., Whitewater, 1983. CPA. Acct. Virchow, Krause & Co., Elkhorn, Wis., 1985-87; supr., acct. Virchow, Krause & Co., Janesville, 1987-91; mgr. budgeting and acctg. Sch. Dist. Janesville, 1991—; tax preparer Janesville, 1991—. Mem. Wis. Cert. Pub. Accts., Zonta Club Janesville (bd. dirs. 1991—). Lutheran. Office: Sch Dist Janesville 527 S Franklin St Janesville WI 53545-4899

CLINE, CAROLYN JOAN, plastic and reconstructive surgeon; b. Boston; d. Paul S. and Elizabeth (Flom) Cline. BA, Wellesley Coll., 1962; MA, U. Cin., 1966; PhD, Washington U., 1970; diploma Washington Sch. Psychiatry, 1972; MD, U. Miami (Fla.) 1975. Diplomate Am. Bd. Plastic and Reconstructive Surgery. Rsch. asst. Harvard Dental Sch., Boston, 1962-64; rsch. asst. physiology Laser Lab., Children's Hosp. Research Found., Cin., 1964, psychology dept. U. Cin., 1964-65; intern in clin. psychology St. Elizabeth's Hosp., Washington, 1966-67; psychologist Alexandria (Va.) Community Mental Health Ctr., 1967-68; research fellow NIH, Washington, 1968-69; chief psychologist Kingsbury Ctr. for Children, Washington, 1969-73; sole practice clin. psychology, Washington, 1970-73; intern internal medicine U. Wis. Hosps., Ctr. for Health Sci., Madison, 1975-76; resident in surgery Stanford U. Med. Ctr., 1976-78; fellow microvascular surgery dept. surgery U. Calif.-San Francisco, 1978-79; resident in plastic surgery St. Francis Hosp., San Francisco, 1979-82; practice medicine, specializing in plastic and reconstructive surgery, San Francisco, 1982—. Contbr. chpt. to plastic surgery textbook, articles to profl. jours. Mem. Am. Bd. Plastic and Reconstructive Surgeons (cert. 1986), Royal Soc. Medicine, Calif. Medicine Assn., Calif. Soc. Plastic and Reconstructive Surgeons, San Francisco Med. Soc. Address: 490 Post St Ste 735 San Francisco CA 94102

CLINE, CATHIE B., hospital administrator; b. Detroit, Jan. 2, 1943; d. Harold Norman Brodie and Fannie Bokatuik; m. Ted Allen Bingham, June 11, 1983; children: John, Peter, Fannie. BSN, Ohio State U., 1964, MHA, 1981. Staff nurse Tb facility Means Hall Ohio State U. Hosps., Columbus, 1964-65, head nurse Columbus Cancer Clinic, 1965-66, staff nurse coronary care step-down unit, 1972-75, asst. head nurse, constant care nursing, 1975-76, asst. dir., surg. nursing, 1978-79, interim assoc. hosp. adminstr./nursing, 1979, dir. critical care nursing, 1979-81; assoc. v.p. Cuyahoga County Hosp. System, 1981-82; v.p. patient svcs. MetroHealth Med. Ctr., Cleve., 1982-89, v.p. inpatient/hosp. based svc., 1989-92, sr. v.p. ops., 1992—; interim pres. MHS, 1993-94, sr.v.p., cOO, 1993; clin. instr. nursing Frances Payne Bolton Sch. Nursing Case Western Reserve U., Cleve., 1982, mem. exec. com. BSN consortium, 1989, asst. dean, 1990; vice chmn. nursing com. Ctr. Health Affairs, Greater Cleve. Hosp. Assn., 1983, chair nursing com., 1989-91; mem. nursing adv. com. Nursing Edn. Program Cuyahoga C.C., Cleve., 1983; lectr. continuing edn. Cleve. State U., 1984; clin. instr. dept. nursing Cleve. State U., 1990; bd. dirs. Vis. Nurses Assn. Hospice, Cleve., 1990; apptd. Opportunity for Change com. State of Ohio Health Care Access Com., Columbus, 1991; chair Cleve. State U./Metrohealth Acad. Com., 1991; membership com. Midwest Alliance Nursing, Indpls., 1992; chair steering com. Robert Wood Johnson Grant, 1993. Bd. dirs. Cleve. Area Citizen's League of Nursing, 1985-87; mem. task force clinical reimbursement, Cuyahoga C.C., Cleve., 1985; chair Greater Cleve. Nursing Roundtable, 1986-88; mem. steering com. United Way, 1990, rep. to campaign for health affairs, 1991-93; mem. adv. com. MSNMBA program Case Western Reserve U., 1990; apptd. by mayor City Tree Commn., City of Westlake, 1993. Johnson & Johnson Wharton fellow, 1986; recipient spl. recognition contbns. and support nursing edn. MetroHealth Sch. Nursing, 1989. Mem. Lake Erie Orgn. Nurse Execs. (charter, pres.-elect), Ohio State U. Alumni Assn. (life), Alpha Delta Pi, Sigma Theta Tau. Office: MetroHealth Med Ctr 2500 Metro Health Dr Cleveland OH 44109

CLINE, DOROTHY MAY STAMMERJOHN (MRS. EDWARD WILBURN CLINE), educator; b. Boonville, Mo., Oct. 19, 1915; d. Benjamin Franklin and Lottie (Walther) Stammerjohn; grad. nurse U. Mo., 1937; BS in Edn., 1939, postgrad., 1966-67; MS, Ark. State U., 1964; m. Edward Wilburn Cline, Aug. 16, 1938 (dec. May 1962); children: Margaret Ann (Mrs. Rodger Orville Bell), Susan Elizabeth (Mrs. Gary Lee Burns), Dorothy Jean. Dir. Christian Coll. Infirmary, Columbia, Mo., 1936-37; asst. chief nursing svc. VA Hosp., Poplar Bluff, Mo., 1950-58; tchr.-in-charge staff State Tng. Ctr. No. 4, Poplar Bluff, 1959-66, Dorothy S. Cline State Sch. #53, Boonville, 1967-85; instr. U. Mo., Columbia, 1973-74; cons. for workshops for new tchrs., curriculum revision Mo. Dept. Edn. Mem. Butler County Council Retarded Children, 1959-66; v.p. Boonslick Assn. Retarded Children, 1969-72; sec.-treas. Mo. chpt. Am. Assn. on Mental Deficiency, 1973-75. Mem. NEA, Mo. Tchrs. Assn., Am. Assn. on Mental Deficiency, Council for Exceptional Children, AAUW (v.p. Boonville br. 1968-70, 75-77), Mo. Writers Guild, Creative Writer's Group (pres. 1974—), Columbia Creative Writers Group, Eastern Center Poetry Soc., Laura Speed Elliott High Sch. Alumni Assn., Bus. and Profl. Women's Club, Smithsonian Assn., U. Mo. Alumni Assn., Ark. State U. Alumni Assn., Internat. Platform Assn., Mo. Hist. Soc., Boonslick Hist. Soc., Friends Historic Boonville, Delta Kappa Gamma, PEO. Mem. Christian Ch. Home: 603 High St Boonville MO 65233-1212

CLINE, JANE LYNN, state official; b. Kingwood, W.Va., June 25, 1956; d. Robert Denzil and Helen Jane (Phillips) C. BSBA, W.Va. U., 1978, MBA, 1986. Acct. W.Va. Dept. Hwys., Charleston, 1978-79, comptr., 1979-89; dep. commr. W.Va. Divsn. Motor Vehicles, Charleston, 1989, commr., 1989—. Field rep. Caperton for Gov., 1987-88, 92-93; active W.Va. Young Dems., 1980-87, Caperton Inaugural Com., Charleston, 1988, 93. Named Outstanding Young Dem., W.Va. Young Dems., 1983. Mem. Am. Assn. Motor Vehicle Adminstrn. (Region III v.p. 1993-94, pres. 1994—), Internat. Pers. Mgmt. Assn., Bus. and Profl. Women. Methodist. Office: WVa Divsn Motor Vehicles State Capitol Complex Bldg 3 Rm 113 Charleston WV 25317

CLINE, JANICE CLAIRE, educator; b. Wausau, Wis., Aug. 22, 1945; d. George Leroy Cline and Irma Olga (Brummond) Doering; m. Brent Buell, Jan. 28, 1979. BS, U. Wis., 1967; MA, NYU, 1972; student of Eli Siegel, 1978; student of Ellen Reiss, Aesthetic Realism Found., N.Y.C., 1977—; student of Aesthetic Realism Teaching Method, 1977—. Tchr. Hyde Park High Sch., Chgo., 1967-69; instr. Chase Manhattan Bank JOB Tng. Program, N.Y.C., 1969-71; evaluator York Coll. Title I Evaluation Team, Jamaica, N.Y., 1972; adj. lectr. N.Y.C. Community Coll., CUNY, Bklyn., 1971-72; lectr. York Coll., CUNY, Jamaica, 1972—; Aesthetic Realism cons.-in-tng., N.Y.C., 1977—; guest speaker WVON, Chgo., 1980. Contbr. articles to profl. jours. Coord. Conf. in Support of the Liberation of S. Africa and Namibia, York Coll., Jamaica, N.Y., 1985, Student/Faculty Consortium on Central Am., York Coll., 1986. Recipient Outstanding Contribution award Afro-Am. Club, York Coll., 1985, Outstanding Contribution award Conf. of African People, Jamaica, N.Y., 1986. Mem. AAUP, Profl. Staff Congress, Internat. Reading Assn. (Manhattan coun.), CUNY Women's Coalition. Office: CUNY York Coll 94-20 Guy R Brewer Blvd Jamaica NY 11451

CLINE, LINDA JEAN, reading educator; b. Salem, Ohio, July 18, 1948; d. Henry Richard and Elsie Louise (Boor) C. BS, Ind. State U., 1970; MEd, Ashland U., 1984. Cert. elem. tchr., secondary tchr., supr. Tchr. English, journalism, newspaper advisor Galion (Ohio) High Sch., 1970-72; tchr. 4th and 5th grade Colonel Crawford Schs., Bucyrus/North Robinson, Ohio, 1973-74; tchr. chpt. 1 reading Plymouth Local Schs., Plymouth/Shiloh, Ohio, 1975—, coord. right-to-read program, 1983—, coord. chpt. 1, 1989-90, mem. supt.'s master planning com., 1990-92, mem. prin.'s adv. com., 1992-93. Pres. United Meth. Women 1st United Meth. Ch., Shelby, Ohio, 1985-87, 94, lay speaker, 1988—. Scholar State of Ind., 1966. Mem. NEA, Ohio Edn. Assn., Plymouth Edn. Assn. (pres. 1979-81), Order Ea. Star (Worthy Matron 1977, 81, 95, Grand Rep. N.H. 1979), Alpha Sigma Alpha (corr. sec. 1966—), Sigma Tau Delta. Republican.

CLINE, PATRICIA ANN, mathematics educator; b. Pitts., Jan. 18, 1941; d. Charles R. and Ruth Marilyn (Hinish) C.; m. Abraham J. Al-Arnasi, June 1, 1963 (div. Dec. 1985); children: Eve, Abraham Jr. BS in Math., Geneva Coll., Beaver Falls, Pa., 1961; MA in Math., NYU, N.Y.C., 1971; MS in Computer Sci., Fairleigh Dickenson U., 1982. Cert. math. tchr., N.J. Tchr. Monroe-Woodbury High Sch., Central Valley, N.Y., 1961-62; actuarial trainee Met. Life, N.Y.C., 1962-64; math. tchr. Lincoln High Sch., Jersey City, 1964-71, No. Highlands High Sch., Allendale, N.J., 1972—. Leader Brownies, Girl Scouts U.S.A., Montvale, N.J., 1970-72. NSF grad. study grantee NYU, 1968-71, NSF Summer Insts. grantee San Diego State U., 1970, Indiana U. Pa., 1988, Rutgers U., 1990, 91, William Paterson Coll., 1992. Mem. NEA, AAUW, Nat. Coun. Math. Tchrs., N.J. Edn. Assn., Assn. Math. Tchrs. N.J., Bergen County Edn. Assn., No. Highlands Edn. Assn. (negotiation 1976-77, 90-92, pres. 1978-80, 88-92, v.p. 1987, del. convs. 1980, 86, 87, 93), Garden State Ski Club. Home: 62 Rolling Ridge Rd Upper Saddle River NJ 07458

CLINE, PAULINE M., educational administrator; b. Seattle, Aug. 25, 1947; d. Paul A. and Margaret V. (Reinhart) C. BA in Edn., Seattle U., 1969, MEd, 1975, EdD, 1983. Cert. tchr., prin., supt., Wash. Tchr., Marysville High Sch., Wash., 1969-70; tchr./adminstr. Blanchet High Sch., Seattle, 1970-78; asst. prin. Edmonds High Sch., Wash., 1978-84; prin. College Place Middle Sch., Edmonds, 1984-85, Mountlake Terrace High Sch., Wash., 1985-93; asst. supr., Mount Vernon Sch. Dist., 1993—. Recipient Washington award for excellence in edn. Gov. and Supt. Pub. Instruction, 1992. IDEA Kettering fellow, 1984, 86, 87, 90, 92, 93, 94. Mem. Am. Assn. Sch. Adminstr., Assn. Supervision and Curriculum Devel., Phi Delta Kappa. Roman Catholic. Club: Women's University (Seattle). Lodge: Rotary (charter mem., past pres. Alderwood club). Avocations: skiing; kayaking; backpacking. Office: Mount Vernon Sch Dist 124 East Lawrence Mount Vernon WA 98273

CLINE, SANDRA BROCK, publisher; b. Peru, Ind., July 28, 1946; d. James Edward and Betty L. (Jenkins) Brock; m. Stephen Carr Cline, Apr. 4, 1980; children: Eleanor Cline Trent, Emily D. Cline, Margaret Cline Curl. BA, St. Mary-of-the Woods Coll., 1993. Regional mktg. dir. M.S. Mgmt. Assocs., Inc., Indpls.; founder, v.p., gen. ptnr. Letter Set, Inc., Indpls., 1976-82; founder, gen. ptnr. Lilith Assocs., Inc., Indpls., 1976-82; founder, pres. CFE, Inc., Indpls., 1982-84; pres. Cline Pub. Co., Inc., Zionsville, Ind., 1984—. Bd. dirs. Patrick Henry Sullivan Mus., Miracle on Main St., Part II Corp.; founder, bd. dirs. Boone County Leadership, Inc., 1990-91; founding dir. Cmty. Found. Boone County; founder advisor Endowment for First Amendment Freedom; , Network of Women in Bus., Indpls., 1976-81, pres. 1981. Mem. Nat. Newspaper Assn. (First Pl. Investigative and Indepth Reporting 1992, Honorable Mention Best Writing 1992, Best Column Serious Subject 1991, Best Family Life/Living Pages 1991, 2d Pl. Gen. Excellence 1991, Best Coverage of Environ. News 1990, 2d Pl. Freedom of Info. 1991), Hoosier State Press Assn. (bd. dirs. 1988-93, first woman pres. 1991-92, numerous awards), Inland Press Assn., Greater Zionsville C. of C., Women in Comms. (Indpls. profl. chpt. Frances Wright award 1991). Home and Office: PO Box 483 Zionsville IN 46077

CLINE, SANDRA WILLIAMSON, elementary education educator; b. San Francisco, Dec. 10, 1944; d. Wilburn Woodrow and Hazel Stewart (Cochrane) Williamson; m. Charles William Cline, June 11, 1966; 1 child, Jeffrey Charles. BA, Western Mich. U., 1970, MA, 1973; MA, Western Mich. U., 1986. Cert. tchr., Mich. 1st-3rd grade tchr. Portage Mich. Pub. Schs., 1971—, mem. sch. effectiveness team and report card rev. com., 1988-92, mem. sci. writing team, 1989—; mus. co-dir. Lake Ctr. Elem. Sch., Portage, 1982-83, student tchr. supr., safety patrol advisor, 1st grade chairperson, state com. for social studies, writing chairperson, 1988-94. Vol. Portage Police, 1992—. Mem. NEA, ASCD, Nat. Coun. Tchrs. English, Nat. Sci. Tchrs. Assn., Assn. for Study of Cooperation in Edn., Mich. Edn. Assn., Portage Edn. Assn. (exec. bd., membership chairperson, elem. grievance chair), Mich. Assn. Supervision and Curriculum Devel. (conf. com.), Am. Fedn. Police (Nat. Patriotism award 1994), Phi Kappa Kappa. Home: 2170 Sanibel Island B-4 Portage MI 49002-0425 Office: Lake Ctr Elem Sch 10011 Portage Rd Kalamazoo MI 49002-7249

CLINE, VIVIAN MELINDA, lawyer; b. Seneca, S.C., Oct. 6, 1953; d. Kenneth H. and Wanda F. (Simmons) Fuller; m. Terry S. Cline, June 15, 1974 (div. Oct. 1986); 1 child, Alicia C. BSBA, Calif. State U., Northridge, 1974; JD, Southwestern U., L.A., 1983. Bar: Calif. 1983, Tex., 1990. Paralegla Internat. House Pancakes, North Hollywood, Calif., 1976-78; assoc. Tuohey & Prasse, Santa Ana, Calif., 1983-85; paralegal Smith Internat., inc., Newport Beach, Calif., 1978-83; corp. counsel Smith Internat., inc., Houston, 1985—. Bus. cons. Jr. Achievement, Houston, 1992-94. Mem. Exec. Women's Network (sec. 1993, pres. 1994, dir. programs 1995). Republican. Presbyterian. Office: Smith Internat Inc 16740 Hardy St Houston TX 77032

CLINEFELTER, RUTH ELIZABETH WRIGHT, historian, educator; b. Akron, Ohio, Nov. 2, 1930; d. Cyril and Ruth Elizabeth (Dresher) Wright. BA, U. Akron, 1952, MA, 1953; MLS, Kent State U., 1956. Serials libr. U. Akron, 1953-61, social scis. rsch. libr., 1961-76, humanities rsch. libr., 1977-83, social scis. humanities bibliographer, 1983—; lectr. in gen. studies U. Akron, 1960, instr. bibliography, 1956-59, asst. prof. bibliography, 1959-77, assoc. prof. bibliography, 1977-84, prof. bibliography 1984—; resource person NEH, Ohio; mem. joint study com. Am. History Rsch. in Ohio Ohio Hist. Soc., 1969-70; mem. acad. affairs com. Ohio Faculty Senate, 1971-72; mem. hist. abstracts bibliographic svc. ABC Clio Users Bd., 1978-79. Contbr. articles to profl. jours. Trustee, treas. Akron Area Women's History Project; active Citizens Against Sys. Abuse, Humane Soc. Greater Akron, Nat. Trust for Hist. Preservation, Progress Through Preservation, Summit County Hist. Soc., Cascade Locks Park Assn., Pet Guards Shelter. Mem. Acad. Libr. Assn. Ohio, AAUP, Am. Hist. Assn., Assn. for Bibliography of History, North Am. Conf. British Studies, North Cen. Women's Studies Assn., Ohio Acad. History, Ohio Classical Assn. Democrat. Episcopalian. Home: 1377 Hadden Cir Akron OH 44313-6505 Office: U Akron Bierce Libr Akron OH 44325

CLINTON, HILLARY RODHAM, First Lady of United States, lawyer; b. Chgo., Oct. 26, 1947; d. Hugh Ellsworth and Dorothy (Howell) Rodham; m. William J. Clinton, Oct. 11, 1975; 1 child, Chelsea Victoria. BA with high honors, Wellesley Coll., 1969; JD, Yale U., 1973; LLD (hon.), U. Ark., Little Rock, 1985, U. Pa., 1993, U. Mich., 1993, U. Ill., 1994; D Pub. Svc. (hon.), George Washington U., 1994. Bar: Ark. 1973, U.S. Dist. Ct. (ea. and we. dists.) Ark. 1973, U.S. Ct. Appeals (8th cir.) 1973, U.S. Supreme Ct. 1975. Atty. Children's Def. Fund, Cambridge, Mass. and Washington, 1973-74; legal cons. Carnegie Coun. on Children, New Haven, 1973-74; counsel, impeachment inquiry staff Judiciary Com. U.S. Ho. of Reps., Washington, 1974; asst. prof. law U. Ark., Fayetteville, 1974-77; reporter fed. ct. speedy trial planning group U.S. Dist. Ct. (ea. dist.) Ark., 1975-79; ptnr. Rose Law Firm, Little Rock, 1977-92; headed Com. on Health Care, Washington, D.C., 1993—; bd. dirs. Legal Svcs. Corp., Washington, 1978-81, chmn., 1978-80; bd. dirs. Wal-Mart Stores, Inc., 1986-92, TCBY Enterprises, Inc., 1989-92, Lafarge Corp., 1990-92; lectr. U. Ark. Law Sch., Little Rock, 1979-80. Author: Handbook on Legal Rights for Arkansas Women. Bd. dirs. Childrens Def. Fund, Washington, Child Care Action Campaign, Nat. Ctr. on Edn. and the Economy, Children's TV Workshop, Pub./Pvt. Ventures, Ark. Children's Hosp., Franklin and Eleanor Roosevelt Inst.; mem. commn. on quality edn. So. Regional Edn. Bd.; chmn. Ark. Edn. Stds. Com., 1983-84. Named Outstanding Layman of Yr. Phi Delta Kappa, 1984, One of 100 Most Influential Lawyers in Am., Nat. Law Jour., 1988, 91; recipient Lewis Hine award Nat. Child Labor Law Com., 1993, Albert Schweitzer Leadership award Hugh O'Brian Youth Found., 1993, Iris Cantor Humanitarian award UCLA Med. Ctr., 1993, Friend of Family award Am. Home Econs. Assn., 1993, Charles Wilson Lee Citizen Svc. award Com. for Edn. Funding, 1993, Claude D. Pepper award Nat. Assn. for Home Care, 1993, Commitment to Life award AIDS Project L.A., 1994, Disting. Svc., Health Edn. and Prevention award Nat. Ctr. for Health Edn., 1994, Cerviel Corp. Achievement award Vista mag., 1994, Social Justice award United Auto Workers, 1994, Ernie Banks Positivism trophy Emil Verban Meml. Soc., 1994, Humanitarian award Alzheimer's Assn., 1994, Elie Wiesel Found., 1994, Internat. Broadcasting award Hollywood Radio and TV Soc., 1994, Ellen Browning Scripps medal Scripps Coll., 1994, Disting. Pro Bono Svc. award San Diego Vol. Lawyer Program, 1994, Spl. Achievement award Hispanic Pub. Corp., 1994, Hippy U.S.A. award, 1994, Disting. Citizen award Coalition Citizens with Disabilities in Ill., 1994, AIDS Awareness award, 1994, Ellington Shield Against Helplessness, Duke Ellington Sch. for the Performing Arts, 1994. Fellow Am. Bar Found.; mem. ABA (chmn. commn. women in the profession 1987-91), Ark. Bar Assn. Home and Office: White House 1600 Pennsylvania Ave NW Washington DC 20500-0002

CLINTON, MARIANN HANCOCK, association executive; b. Dyersburg, Tenn., Dec. 7, 1933; d. John Bowen and Nell Maurine (Johnson) Hancock; m. Harry Everett Clinton, Aug. 25, 1956; children—Carol, John Everett. B.Mus., Cin. Conservatory Music, 1956; B.S., U. Cin., 1956; M.Mus., Miami U., Oxford, Ohio, 1971. Tchr. music public schs. Hamilton County, Ohio, 1956-57; tchr. voice and piano Butler County, Ohio, 1964—; instr. music Miami U., 1972-75; exec. dir. Music Tchrs. Nat. Assn., Cin., 1977-86; mng. dir. Am. Music Tchr., 1977-86. Mem. adminstrv. bd. Middletown (Ohio) 1st United Methodist Ch., 1968-72; bd. dirs. Friends of the Sorg Opera House. Mem. Music Educators Nat. Conf., Am. Ednl. Research Assn., Am. Soc. Assn. Execs., Nat. Fedn. Music Clubs, Pi Kappa Lambda, Kappa Delta Pi, Mu Phi Epsilon, Phi Mu. Republican. Home: 6543 Niderdale Way Middletown OH 45042-9400

CLINTON, MARY ELLEN, neurosurgeon; b. Evanston, Ill., Feb. 15, 1950; d. Merle P. and Carmine E. (Wolfe) C.; m. William J. Wade Jr. BS, Loyola/Marymount U., 1972; MD, U. So. Calif., 1976. Intern internal medicine Vanderbilt U. Hosp., Nashville, 1976-77, resident in neurology, 1979-81, chief resident, 1981-82, fellow in neuromuscular disease and electrodiagnostics, 1982-83, asst. prof. neurology, 1983-91; staff physician emergency medicine Donelson Hosp., St. Thomas Hosp., Nashville, 1977-79; asst. clin. prof. Vanderbilt U., N~shville, 1991—; dir. electrodiagnostic testing Neurosurg. Assocs., Na: ville, 1991—; reviewing physician Mid South Found. for Med. Care, Inc., Memphis, 1991—; med. expert Social Security and Disability Determination State of Tenn., 1987—; dir. Vanderbilt Muscle Biopsy Lab., 1984-89; dir. neurodiagnostic labs. Nashville VA Hosp., 1989-91; mem. staff Parkview/West Side HCA Hosps., Nashville, So. Hills Med. Ctr.; cons. staff Bapt. Hosp., Nashville; consultant Williamson Med. Ctr., Franklin, Tenn. Contbr. articles and abstracts to profl. jours. Co-dir. Nashville br. Muscular Dystrophy Assn., 1983-91. Recipient Physician's Recognition award AMA, 1984, 88. Mem. Am. Soc. for Internal Medicine, Soc. for Neurosci., Am. Med. Women's Assn., Nashville Acad. Medicine, Tenn. Med. Assn., AMA, So. Clin. Neurol. Soc., Am. Acad. Clin. Neurophysiology, Am. Assn. for Electrodiagnostic Medicine, Am. Acad. Neurology, Kappa Gamma Pi. Office: Neurosurg Assocs 4230 Harding Rd Nashville TN 37205

CLOONEY, ROSEMARY, singer; b. Maysville, Ky., May 23, 1928; d. Andrew and Frances (Guilfoyle) C.; m. Jose Ferrer, 1953 (div. 1961), remarried, 1961 (div. 1967); children: Miguel Jose, Maria Providencia, Gabriel Vincente, Monsita, Rafael. Singer Columbia Records, 1950-53, Concord Jazz, 1977—. Performed with Betty Clooney as The Clooney Sisters, Sta. WLW, Cin.; toured with Tony Pastor Orch., 1945-48; songs include Come On-a My House, 1951 (Gold record), Tenderly, 1952 (Gold record), Botcha Me, 1953 (Gold record), Half as Much, 1953 (Gold record), Hey There, 1954 (Gold record); albums include Rosie Sings Bing, Everything's Rosie!, 1952, (with Duke Ellington) Blue Rose, Everything's Coming Up Rosie, With Love, 1980, Sings the Music of Cole Porter, 1982, Sings Harold Arlen, 1983, (with Woody Herman) My Budy, 1983, Sings Irving Berlin, 1985, Sings Ballads, 1985, Sings the Music of Johnny Mercer, 1987, Sings the Music of Jimmy Van Heusen, 1987, 1951-1952, 1988, Sings Show Tunes, 1988, Sixteen Most Requested Songs, 1989, Sings Rodgers, Hart and Hammerstein, 1990, Sings the Lyrics of Ira Gershwin, 1990, For the Duration, 1991, Girl Singer, 1992, Tribute to Billy Holiday, 1992, Do You Miss New York?, 1993 (Grammy award nominee for Best Traditional Vocal), 1993, The Essence of Rosemary Clooney, 1993, Still On the Road, 1994; film appearences include The Stars are Singing, 1953, Here Come the Girls, 1953, White Christmas, 1954, Red Garters, 1954, Deep in my Heart, 1954; TV appearences include The Rosemary Clooney Show, 1956-57, Lux Music Hall, 1957; appeared Bing Crosby's 50th Anniversary tour; author: (autobiography) This For Remembrance, 1977. Recipient Spl. award Look Mag., 1954; James Smithson Bicentennial Medal for contbn. to arts, 1992. Office: Concord Jazz Inc PO Box 845 Concord CA 94522*

CLOPINE, MARJORIE SHOWERS, librarian; b. N.Y.C., June 25, 1914; d. Ralph Walter and Angelina (Jackson) Showers; m. John Junior Clopine, June 19, 1948 (div.); m. Frank Mason Storck, Sept. 14, 1985. BA, Pa. State U., 1935; MS, Drexel U., 1936; MS, Columbia U., 1949. Gen. asst. Libr., Drexel U., Phila., 1937-42; asst. libr. Gen. Chem. Div., Allied Chem. Corp., Morristown, N.J., 1943-46; bibliographer U.S. Office Tech. Svcs., Washington, 1946; med. libr. VA Hosp., Washington, 1946-49; asst. libr. U.S. Naval Obs., Washington, 1949-52, libr., 1952-63; assoc. libr. Bethany (W.Va.) Coll., 1967-69; assoc. libr. Marine Rsch. Lab. Fla. Dept. Natural Resources, St. Petersburg, 1971-73; cons. in astronomy Dewey Decimal Classification Editorial Office, Library of Congress, Washington, 1956. Chmn., Community Improvement program, Fla. Dist. 14, Gen. Fedn. Women's Clubs, 1980-82; libr. cons. Garden Ctr., Oglebay Park, Wheeling, W.Va., 1965-69. Alice B. Kroeger Meml. scholar, 1935-36. Mem. AAUW, LWV, Inst. Retired Execs. and Profls., Women's Resource Ctr. of Sarasota, Friends of the Arts and Scis., Nat. Assn. Ret. Fed. Employees, Spl. Libraries Assn., Beta Phi Mu. Clubs: Woman's Club of Sarasota. Contbr. articles to profl. jours. Home and Office: 8400 Vamo Rd Apt 540 Sarasota FL 34231-7811

CLOPINE, SANDRA LOU, religious organization administrator; b. Ft. Wayne, Ind., May 12, 1936; d. Clarence Melvin and Gwendola Louise (Copp) Burry; m. Sidney Ray Goodwin, July 12, 1957 (dec. 1963); 1 child, Gwenda Lynn Goodwin Stewart; m. Myron Stanley Clopine, Aug 7, 1982; stepchildren: Charles, Dan, Linda Clopine Palser, Lynnette Clopine Blackstone. BA, Southwestern Assemblies of God, Waxahachie, Tex., 1958; BS, West Tex. State U., 1968; MA, Assemblies of God Theol. Sem., Springfield, Mo., 1979. Ordained to ministry West Tex. Assemblies of God, 1971. Fgn. missionary Assemblies of God Ch., Ghana, West Africa, 1961-65; social worker Tex. Ctr. Human Devel., Amarillo, 1968-69, dir. vol. svcs., 1969-70; instr. Arusha Bible Sch., Tanzania, East Africa, 1970-80; instr. sociology Evang. Coll. Assemblies of God, Springfield, 1979-80; office of info. coord. Internat. Corr. Inst., Brussels, 1980-82; state dir. Women's Ministries, Nebr., 1984-85; nat. sec., dept. head for denomination Assemblies of God Women's Ministries, Springfield, Mo., 1986-94, coord. Nat. Prayer Ctr., 1994—; speaker women's convs., leadership seminars, other orgns. Recipient Outstanding Contbn. award Internat. Corr. Inst., 1983, Leadership Friend of Yr. award Highland Child Placement Ctr., Kansas City, Mo., 1989; named Disting. Alumnus Southwestern Assemblies of God Coll., 1989. Mem. Nat. Assn. Evangs. Women's Commn. (chair 1992-95, bd. adminstrs. 1992—), Evang. Press Assn., Nat. Women's Leadership Task Force (steering com. 1990-92), Internat. Pentecostal Press Assn., Delta Epsilon Chi. Republican. Office: Assemblies of God 1445 N Boonville Ave Springfield MO 65802-1805

CLOSE, GLENN, actress; b. Greenwich, Conn., Mar. 19, 1947; d. William and Bettine Close; m. Cabot Wade (div.); m. James Marlas, 1984 (div.); 1 child, Annie Maude Starke. B.A., Coll. William and Mary, 1974. Profl. actress, also accomplished mus. performer (lyric soprano); co-owner The Leaf and Bean Coffee House, Bozeman, Montana, 1991—. Joined New Phoenix Repertory Co., 1974; made Broadway debut in Love for Love; other Broadway appearences include The Rules of the Game, The Member of the Wedding, 1974-75, Rex, Barnum, 1980-81 (Tony award nominee), The Real Thing, 1984-85 (Tony award for Best Actress in Drama), Benefactors, 1986, Wine Untouched, Death and the Maiden, 1992 (Drama League N.Y. Distinguished Performance award, 1992, Tony award for Best Actress in Drama, 1992), Sunset Boulevard, 1994-95; other theatre appearences include Uncommon Women and Others, The Singular Life of Albert Nobbs, 1982 (Obie award), Childhood, 1985, one performance oratorio Joan of Arc at the Stake, 1985, Sunset Boulevard (L.A.), 1993-94, and other repertory and regional theatres; films include The World According to Garp, 1982 (Acad. award nominee), The Big Chill, 1983 (Acad. award nominee), The Natural, 1984 (Acad. award nominee), Greystoke: The Legend of Tarzan, Lord of the Apes (voice), 1984, The Stone Boy, 1984, Maxie, 1985, Jagged Edge, 1985, Fatal Attraction, 1987, Light Years (voice), 1988, Dangerous Liaisons, 1988, Immediate Family, 1989, Reversal of Fortune, 1990, Hamlet, 1990, Hook (cameo), 1991, Meeting Venus, 1991, The House of the Spirits, 1994, The Paper, 1994; TV films include Too Far To Go, 1979, Orphan Train, 1979, The Elephant Man, 1982, Something about Amelia, 1984 (Emmy award nominee), The Elephant's Child (host), 1987, The Emperor's New Clothes (host), 1987, The Legend of Sleepy Hollow (narrator), 1988, Stones for Ibarra, 1988, (also exec. prodr.) Sarah, Plain and Tall, 1991, Skylark, 1993 (Emmy award nomine for Lead Actress in a Miniseries, 1993), Serving in Silence: The Margarethe Cammermeyer Story, 1995. Recipient Woman of Yr. award Hasty Pudding Theatricals, 1990, Dartmouth Film Soc. award, 1990. Mem. Phi Beta Kappa. Office: CAA 9830 Wilshire Blvd Beverly Hills CA 90212*

CLOT, ARCHLYN ANN, medical technologist; b. Miami, Mar. 9, 1931; d. Charles Edward and Neil Thelma (Hamlett) Buker; m. William A. Clot, June 14, 1958; 1 child, Stephen Joshua. BS, U. Miami, 1954; MT, Emory U., 1955. Registered Med. Technologist. Head technician Roberts Meml. Clinic, Atlanta, 1955-57, Cardio-Pulmonary Lab. at Jackson Meml. Hosp., Miami, 1957-59. Pres. Woman's Cancer Assn. of Univ. of Miami, 1975-77, S. Fla. Kidney Found., 1978-80; mem. Exec. Subcom. for the Protection of Human Subjects in Research, 1978-82; pres. Miami/Bogota/CAli Sister Cities Inc., 1980-81; mem. Fla. Task Force on AIDS, 1980, Bd. Govs. U. Miami Hosps and Clinics, 1978—; chairperson Fla. Statewide Human Rights Advocacy Com., 1985-88; mem. Child Abuse Task Force Dist. XI, 1984—. Mem. Am. Contract Bridge League (life master), Mensa Internat., Afghan Hound Club Am. (pres. 1989, 90, 91), Am. Kennel Club (judge, del.), Am. Sighthound Field Assn. (judge), Zeta Tau Alpha. Democrat. Presbyterian. Home: 6840 SW 119th St Miami FL 33156-4778

CLOUD, LINDA BEAL, retired secondary school educator; b. Jay, Fla., Dec. 4, 1937; d. Charles Rockwood and Agnes (Diamond) Beal; m. Robert Vincent Cloud (Aug. 15, 1959 (dec. 1985). BA, Miss. Coll., 1959; MEd, U. So. Fla., 1976; EdS, Nova U., 1982; postgrad., Walden U., 1983. Cert. tchr., Fla. Tchr. Ft. Meade (Fla.) Jr.-Sr. High Sch., 1959-67, 80-89, Lake Wales (Fla.) High Sch., 1967-80; pres. Cloud Aero Svcs., Inc., Babson Park, Fla., 1992—; part-time tchr. Spanish, English, Polk County Adult Schs., 1960-76; instr. Spanish Warner So. Coll., Lake Wales, 1974; instr. vocal music, drama, composition Webber Coll., Babson Park, Fla.; cons., pvt. tutor in field. Contbr. articles to profl. and equine publs.; author, dir. numerous pageants for schs. Charter mem., bd. dirs. Lake Wales Little Theatre, Inc., 1976; dir. Four Sq. swing choir; entertainer for various local orgns.; ring announcer Fla. State Fair, 1987-88; judge poetry and essay contests; bd. dirs. Defenders of Crooked Lake. Recipient Best Actress award Lake Wales Little Theatre, Inc., 1978-79. Mem. AAUW, Nat. Coun. Tchrs. English, Fla. Coun. Tchrs. English, Polk Coun. Tchrs. English, Polk Fgn. Lang. Assn., Lake Wales Little Theatre (charter), Ye Mystic Krewe de Peru, Sassy Singers, Southeastern Peruvian Horse Club (life). Republican. Mem. Babson Park Community Ch. Home: 1654 Seminole Rd Babson Park FL 33827-9793

CLOUDMAN, RUTH HOWARD, museum curator; b. Oklahoma City, June 11, 1948; d. Harry Howard and Hazel Marcellus (Clay) C. BA, Washington U., St. Louis, 1970; MA, Bryn Mawr Coll., 1973. Asst. curator Joslyn Art Mus., Omaha, 1973-75, chief curator, 1975-78; guest curator Sheldon Meml. Art Gallery/U. Nebr., Lincoln, 1978-79; assoc. Newhouse Galleries, N.Y.C., 1980-84; sr. curator Portland (Oreg.) Art Mus., 1984-90; Mary and Barry Bingham, Sr. curator European and Am. Art J.B. Speed Art Mus., Louisville, 1990—, chief curator, 1990—. Author mus. catalogs and articles. Mem. Coll. Art Assn., Am. Assn. Museums. Office: JB Speed Art Mus 2035 S 3rd St Louisville KY 40208-1812

CLOUGHERTY, ANNE MARIE, foreign language educator; b. Brighton, Mass.; d. Joseph Francis and Anne Lucille (de Bettencourt) C. BA, Boston Coll., 1974; MA, Ind. U., 1976, MPA, 1984; Etudes de Gestion, U Paris, 1982. Assoc. instr. dept. French Ind. U., Bloomington, 1974-78; vis. lectr. dept. English U. Lille, France, 1979-82; assoc. instr. Sch. Pub. & Environ. Affairs, Ind. U., 1982-84; asst. prof. Mass. Bay Community Coll., Wellesley, 1985-87; lectr. Latin, coord. lang. lab. Regis Coll., Weston, Mass., 1987-88; case mgr. Delta Projects, 1990—; program dir. Riverside Community Health and Mental Retardation Ctr., Arlington, Mass., 1991; asst. trilingual office Broadway Chiropractic, Somerville, Mass., 1991; telemarketer Neighborhood Readers Svc., Boston, 1991-92; prof. Med. English Centro Hispano and Employment Connections Inc., Chelsea, Mass., 1992-93; pre-vocat., instr. ESL, med. termininology and med. English, Centro Hispano, Chelsea, 1993—. Mem. Mass. Fgn. Lang. Assn., NOW, ACLU, Phi Beta Kappa. Office: Centro Hispano 248 Broadway Chelsea MA 02150

CLOVER-LEE, SHEVONNE JONES, geriatrics nurse; b. Richmond, Va., Oct. 9, 1962; d. Lonnie Jr. and Ann T. (Jones) Clover; m. Larry S. Lee, Feb. 8, 1986 (dec.). Diploma in nursing, Petersburg (Va.) Gen. Hosp., 1984; student, John Tyler Community Coll., Chester, Va., 1990—. RN, Va. Cert. IV, venipuncture therapy. Pvt. duty nurse Petersburg, Va.; staff nurse John Randolph Hosp., Hopewell, Va., 1985—; charge nurse/supr. Battlefield Park Convalescent Ctr., Petersburg, Va., 1983-88, Waverly (Va.) Health Care Ctr., 1991—.

CLOVSKY, JUDITH HARTENSTINE, association executive; b. Washington, Aug. 1, 1943; d. Olin Cyrus and Sara Ellen (Brassington) H.; m. David Joel Clovsky, Dec. 19, 1969. Diploma, Meth. Hosp. Sch. Nursing, 1965; BSN, Pa. State U., 1969, MN, 1980. RN. Community mental health nurse Coun. House, Inc., Pitts., 1969-70; behavioral sci. staff nurse W.Va. Med. Ctr., Morgantown, 1970-72; head nurse Polyclinic Med. Ctr., Harrisburg, Pa., 1972-74, nurse liaison, 1976; adolescent community mental health nurse Elmira (N.Y.) Psychiat. Ctr., 1976-78; nursing educator Corning (N.Y.) Community Coll., 1978-86; exec. dir. YWCA of Chemung County, Elmira, 1986—. Recipient 4 Way Test award Elmira Rotary, 1990; named Woman of Achievement Chemung County Coun. Women, 1984; Paul Harris fellow, 1992. Mem. N.Y. State Bus. and Profl. Women (com. chair 1992—), Fingerlakes Health Systems Agy. (chair Subarea Coun. 1988-94, chair 1994—, bd. dirs.), Rotary, BPW (past pres. 1981-82, past dist. dir., 1984-87 N.Y. Dist VI). Mem. United Ch. Christ. Office: YWCA of Chemung County 211 Lake St Elmira NY 14901-3108

CLOYD, HELEN MARY, accountant, educator; b. Austria-Hungary, 1918; d. Valentine and Elizabeth (Kretschmar von Kienbusch) Yuhasz; came to U.S. 1922, naturalized, 1928; BS, Eastern Mich. U., 1953; MA, Wayne State U., 1956; PhD, Mich. State U., 1963; m. George S. Smith, Mar. 4, 1939 (dec.); children: George, Nora; m. Chester L. Cloyd, Apr. 16, 1960 (dec.). Pub. accounting Haskins & Sells, Detroit, 1945-53; tchr. Marine City (Mich.) High Sch., 1954-59; instr. acctg. Central Mich. U., Mt. Pleasant, 1959-60; asst. prof. Wayne State U., Detroit, 1960-61; tchr. Grosse Pointe (Mich.) High Sch., 1961-64; assoc. prof. acctg. Ball State U., Muncie, Ind., 1964-71; prof. Shepherd Coll., Shepherdstown, W.Va., 1971-76; assoc. prof. George Mason U., Fairfax, Va. Recipient McClintock Writing award CPA, Mich., Ind., W.Va. Mem. AICPA, Am. Acctg. Assn., Am. Econs. Assn., AAAS, Assn. Sch. Bus. Ofcls., Delta Pi Epsilon, Pi Omega Pi, Pi Gamma Mu. Clubs: Order Eastern Star, White Shrine. Contbr. numerous articles to publs. Home: PO Box 186 Inwood WV 25428-0186

CLUETT, HELEN CATHERINE, nursing educator; b. Quincy, Mass., Mar. 31, 1935; d. William Patrick and Mary Louise (Foley) C. Diploma in nursing, Whidden Meml. Hosp. Sch., Everett, Mass., 1956; BSN, Boston Coll., 1975; MSN, Boston U., 1979. Staff nurse med.-surg. unit Milton (Mass.) Hosp., 1956-57, asst. head nurse med.-surg. unit, 1957-58; pvt. duty nurse Mass. State Nurses Registry, Boston, 1958-60; intravenous nurse Mass. Gen. Hosp., Boston, 1961-66; staff nurse oper. rm. Boston Floating Hosp.,

Tufts New Eng. Med. Ctr., 1966-67; instr. oper. rm. nursing Peter Bent Brigham Hosp. Sch. Nursing, Boston, 1967-73, instr. med.-surg. nursing, 1975-85; perioperative nurse educator Brigham and Women's Hosp., Boston, 1985—; facilitator, lectr. Cmty. High Schs., Boston; provider lecture to nursing students from Simmons Coll., Quincy Coll., Roxbury C.C., Bunker Hill C.C., Boston and Quincy, Mass., U. Mass., Boston, 1989—; coord. clin. experience cardiopulmonary vascular sci. dept. Northeastern U., Boston, 1986—; clin. assoc. U. Mass. Coll. Nursing, Boston, 1990—; presenter in field. Treas. Nursing Rsch. Network Boston, 1988-92; mem. capital devel. campaign Sacred Heart Parish, Weymouth, Mass., 1992. Mem. ANA, Brigham and Women's Nursing Orgn. (coord. nursing grand rounds 1986—), Assn. Oper. Rm. Nurses (chair project Alpha com. Mass. chpt. I 1988—, nominating com. 1991-92, chair 1992-93, editorial com. 1987-88, del. 1987-92, 95, Excellence in Perioperative Nursing award 1992, bd. dirs. 1994-96), Sigma Theta Tau. Home: 466 Front St Weymouth MA 02188-2804 Office: Brigham and Women's Hosp 75 Francis St Boston MA 02115-6195

CLUFF, MARIELLEN SMITH, gerontology and rehabilitation nurse; b. Greenfield, Ohio, Dec. 21, 1945; d. William DeWitt and Elizabeth Belle (Hamilton) Smith; m. James Edward Cluff, Jan. 23, 1970; children: James Edward Jr., Jerry R., Jennifer Diane. Diploma, Community Hosp Sch. Nursing, Springfield, Ohio, 1983; AA, AS, So. State Community Coll., Hillsboro, Ohio, 1980; BSN, Ohio U., 1990. RN, Ohio; cert. gerontology nurse. Med.-surg. staff nurse Greenfield Area Med. Ctr., dir. rehab.; staff nurse VA Med. Ctr., Chillicothe, Ohio, 1992—. Mem. ANA, Ohio Nurses Assn., Assn. Rehab. Nurses. Named Employee of Yr., Greenfield Area Med. Ctr., 1989. Home: 7766 Keplinger Rd Hillsboro OH 45133-9790

CLUM, CHERI CANDACE, management analyst; b. Lansing, Mich., Oct. 7, 1950; d. Floyd Myron and Elizabeth Victoria (Bell) C.; divorced. AA with honors, No. Va. C.C., 1989; BA with honors, Nat.-Louis U., 1992, MS, 1995. Sec. U.S. Fed. Govt., various locations, 1978; classifier U.S. Army Civilian Pers., Ft. Myer, Va., 1988-92; mgmt. analyst U.S. Army Material Command, Alexandria, Va., 1992—; owner, mgr. Cherished Creations, Falls Church, Va., 1980—; tchr. Fairfax County Adult Edn., Fairfax, Va., 1980—; lectr. in field. Designer quilt, needlework, Smithsonian Mus., also counted thread designs. Chmn. Meridian Park Community Watch. Mem. Am. Needlepoint Guild (v.p. 1981-83), Quilters Unltd. (programs com., hospitality com. 1989—), Embroiderers Guild, Internat. Tng. and Comm., Cookie Cutter Collector Club. Home: 810 N West St Falls Church VA 22046-2322 Office: US Army Material Command 5001 Eisenhower Ave Alexandria VA 22333-0003

CLURFELD, ANDREA, editor, food critic; b. N.Y.C., Mar. 13, 1954; d. Jerome and Geraldine R. Clurfeld. BA in Art History, Wells Coll., 1976. Reporter, arts editor Hunterdon County Democrat, Flemington, N.J., 1977-82; night and Sunday editor New Jersey Herald, Newton, N.J., 1982-86; restaurant critic/food editor Asbury Park Press, Neptune, N.J, 1986—; tchr. minority journalism workshop Rider Coll., Lawrenceville, 1987-88. Recipient award N.J. Press Assn., 1978-94, Nat. Newspaper Assn., 1981, Soc. Profl. Journalists, 1991, 94. Mem. Internat. Assn. Culinary Profls., Assn. Food Journalists, James Beard Found., Monmouth County Cooks Coop. (founding). Avocations: fine American crafts, travel, gardening. Home: Jolly Cackle Farm 103 Bowne Rd Locust NJ 07760 Office: Asbury Park Press Inc PO Box 1550 3601 Hwy 66 Neptune NJ 07754-1550

CLUSE-TOLAR, THERESA SUE, social worker; b. Lancaster, Ohio, June 27, 1959; d. Lewis R. and Patricia L. (Schnapp) C.; m. James A. Tolar, July 18, 1987; children: Nathan Dennis, Lucas Jamal. AB, Ohio U., 1981; MSW, Ohio State U., 1985, PhD, 1994. Lic. ind. social worker, Ohio., cert. clin. social worker. Dir. Ctr. for Visually Impaired, Lancaster, 1981-85; caseworker Franklin County Children's Svcs., Columbus, Ohio, 1985-88; div. specialist Tri-County Mental Health, Logan, Ohio, 1988; outpatient therapist New Horizons, Lancaster, 1988; counselor emergency svc. Fairfield Family Counseling, Lancaster, 1988-89; grad. adminstrv. asst. Ohio State U., Columbus, 1988-90, grad. teaching asst., 1991; psychiat. social worker Riverside Meth. Hosp., Columbus, 1989-93; asst. prof. Rio Grande (Ohio) U., 1991-93; lectr. U. N.C., Wilmington, 1994—; co-chair Student Faculty Liaison Com. Ohio State U., Columbus, 1989-90; rep. practice teaching unit com. Ohio State U., Columbus, 1988-89; mem. bd. dirs. Yahweh Ctr., 1994, faculty senate, 1994. Bd. dirs. Fairfield County Coun. for Disabled, Lancaster, 1981-84, treas. 1983-84; voting mem. Ohio Soc. to Prevent Blindness, Columbus, 1982-85. Mem. NASW, Coun. Social Work Edn., Alpha Delta Mu. Home: 106 W Bedford Rd Wilmington NC 28403 Office: U NC Dept Sociology 601 S College Rd Wilmington NC 28403

CLYNE, PATRICIA EDWARDS, author and editor; b. N.Y.C., May 2, 1935; d. Ray Augustus and Neta Helen (Bohnsack) Edwards; m. Francis Gabriel Clyne, June 11, 1960; children: Stephen Paul De Villo, Christopher Jason, Francis Joseph, Ray Augustus. BA, Hunter Coll., N.Y.C., 1959. Editorial asst. various mags., book pubs., 1959-75; contbg. editor Hudson Valley Mag., 1990—. Author: Orange County: A Chronicle of Three Centuries, 1993, Hudson Valley Tales and Trails, 1990, Caves for Kids in Historic New York, 1980, 2d edit. 1992, The Curse of Camp Gray Owl, 1981, Strange and Supernatural Animals, 1979, Ghostly Animals of America, 1977, Patriots in Petticoats, 1976, Tunnels of Terror, 1975, 2d edit. 1993, The Corduroy Road, 1973, 2d edit. 1984; asst. to editor: The Collected Works of Edgar Allan Poe, Vol. I, 1969, II and III, 1978; contbr. numerous articles to jours. Mem. Orange Heritage. Home and Office: PO Box 147 Circleville NY 10919

CMAR, JANICE BUTKO, special education educator; b. Pitts., Nov. 10, 1954; d. Edward Michael and Ruth Lillian (Pickard) Butko; m. Dennis Paul Cmar, children: Michael, Nicole. BS, Mansfield U., 1976; MS, Duquesne U., 1990. Cert. home economist. Home econ. tchr. Duquesne (Pa.) Sch. Dist., 1978-83; special edn. tchr. Allegheny Intermediate Unit, Pitts., 1985-; sponsor Duquesne High Sch., Y-Teens and Future Homemakers Am., 1979-83, Pathfinder Student Coun., Bethel Park, Pa., Mon-Valley Secondary Sch. Yearbook and Prom, Jefferson, Pa. Vol. Allegheny County Dept. Cmty. Svcs., Pitts., 1986—; mem. com. Allegheny County Dem. Orgn. Mem. Am. Fedn. Tchrs., Am. Home Econs. Assn., Pa. Home Econs. Assn., Allegheny County Home Econs. Assn. (pres. 1991-92), Phi Delta Kappa, Alpha Sigma Tau. Democrat. Home: Jefferson Borough 918 Old Hickory Ln Clairton PA 15025-3437 Office: 4 Station Sq Fl 2 Pittsburgh PA 15219-1119

COAKES, MICHELLE DENISE, art educator, potter; b. Ft. Worth, Dec. 10, 1959; d. Raynor Eugene and Shirley Ann (Johnson) C. BFA in Ceramics, No. Ill. U., 1982, MA in Ceramics, 1985, MFA in Ceramics, 1987; postgrad., Wichita State U., 1987-88. Apprentice Eckel's Pot Shop, Bayfield, Wis., 1982-83; instr. Highland C.C., Freeport, Ill., 1986-87; ceramics technician Wichita (Kans.) State U., 1988-89; artist-in-residence Fla. Gulf Coast Art Ctr., Belleair, 1989-91; asst. prof. art, mem. honors and grad. faculties Western Ky. U., Bowling Green, 1991—; demonstrating artist Artrain Nat. Travelling Art Mus., 1986; studio asst. Penland (N.C.) Sch., 1988; studio asst. Arrowmont Sch. Arts and Crafts, Gatlinburg, Tenn., summers 1989-90, instr., 1992; juror scholastic art awards Regional High Sch. Exhbn., Tampa, Fla., 1990; curator Nat. Exhibit Fla. Craftsmen Gallery, St. Petersburg, 1990, Nat. Crafts Invitational Fine Arts Gallery, Western Ky. U., 1993, Ky. Mus., Bowling Green, 1993; monitor Haystack Mountain Sch. Crafts, Deer Isle, Maine, 1992. One-woman show Fine Arts Gallery, Bowling Green, 1993; exhibited in group shows, including Arrowmont Sch. Arts and Crafts, 1990, Everson Mus. Art, Syracuse, N.Y., 1990, San Angelo (Tex.) Mus. Fine Art, 1990, 91, Miss. Mus. Art, Jackson, 1991, Wichita Falls (Tex.) Art Mus., 1991, Auckland (New Zealand) Inst. and Mus., 1992, Newport Harbor Art Mus., Newport Beach, Calif., 1993, Evansville (Ind.) Art Mus., 1993, Headley-Whitney Mus., Lexington, Ky., 1993, Nat. Ceramics Exhbn., New Haven, Conn., 1993. Vol. Meals on Wheels, Largo, Fla., 1990-91. Recipient purchase award TransFinancial Art Exhibit, Bowling Green, 1993; artist grantee Pinellas County Arts Coun., Clearwater, Fla., 1991. Mem. Nat. Coun. on Edn. for Ceramic Arts, Am. Craft Coun. Democrat. Mem. Ba'hai Faith. Home: 1267 Cabell Dr Bowling Green KY 42104 Office: Western Ky U Art Dept Bowling Green KY 42104

COATS, THERESA ANN, data analyst; b. Tullahoma, Tenn., Oct. 27, 1960; d. Jack Darwin and Mary Kay (Schenk) C.; m. Timothy Wayne Long, Oct. 22, 1994. BS, Mid. Tenn. State U., 1982. Quality control technician Mike Rose Foods, Nashville, 1982-85; processor Dominion Bank, Nashville, 1985-88; data analyst Grumman Tech. Svcs., Kennedy Space Ctr., 1988—. Coach Spl. Olympics, Titusville, Fla., 1993-94. Recipient Prins. award Riverview Elem. Sch., 1994. Mem. Nat. Mgmt. Assn. (sec. 1994-95), Space Coast Paddlers Canoe and Kayak (v.p. 1993-94).

COBB, CECELIA ANNETTE, counselor; b. Dayton, Ohio, June 22, 1944; d. Fred E. and Margaret Laverne (Ogle) C.; m. Robert A. Fackler, June 25, 1966 (div. Mar. 1981); m. James A. McCluskey, June 18, 1983; 1 child, James Christian. BS, Ohio U., 1967; MA in Teaching, Saginaw Valley State Coll., 1978; MA in Counseling, Oakland U., 1993. Lic. profl. counselor, Mich.; cert. tchr., Mich. Tchr. L'Anse Creuse Pub. Schs., Mt. Clemens, Mich., 1966-91, counselor, 1993—; cons. Establishment Crisis Ctr., Mt. Clemens, 1968-70; supr. tchr. Mich. State U., Lansing, 1970-72; leader pilot project Quest Inc., Findlay, Ohio, 1982-83. Provider shelter for homeless, Mt. Clements, 1983-93. Mem. ACA, NEA, Mich. Edn. Assn., Mich. Counseling Assn., Macomb County Assn. Counseling and Devel., Chi Sigma Iota. Democrat. Home: 38098 Lakeshore Dr Harrison Township MI 48045-2855 Office: L'Anse Creuse Pub Schs 36727 Jefferson Ave Harrison Township MI 48045-2917

COBB, JANE OVERTON, legislative staff member; b. Charleston, S.C., July 23, 1962; d. Dolphin Dunnaha and Sue (Hagood) Overton; m. Robert Watson Cobb, July 15, 1989; children: Robert Watson, Jr., Johnson Hagood. BA, Vanderbilt U., 1984, MEd, 1985. Cert. secondary tchr., Ga. Tchr. English Columbia High Sch., Atlanta, 1985-86; tchr. ESL Hangzhou, China, 1986-87; govt. affairs asst. Hewlett Packard Co., Washington, 1987-89; mem. congrl. staff U.S. Ho. Reps., Washington, 1989—. Office: US Ho Reps Govt Ops Com B-350 Rayburn House Office Bldg Washington DC 20515

COBB, KAY, state legislator; m. Larry Cobb; children: Barbara Cobb Murphy, Elizabeth Cobb DeBusk. BS, U. Miss., JD. Atty.; mem. Miss. State Senate, mem. elections com., chairwoman various coms. Mem. Miss. Prosecutors Assn., C. of C., Am. Legion. Democrat. Baptist. Office: Mississippi State Senate State Capital Jackson MS 39201 Address: PO Box 1173 Oxford MS 38655-1173*

COBB, LORENE POZYC, physical therapist; b. Newark, Aug. 31, 1963; d. Stanley Joseph and Marie Josephine (Dante) Pozyc; m. David James Cobb, Apr. 25, 1987; 1 child, Owen David. BS, Russell Sage Coll., 1985. Cert. neurodevel. treatment pediatric clients. Staff therapist John F. Kennedy Med. Ctr., Edison, N.J., 1985-88; cons. therapist early intervention program Monmouth and Ocean Counties, Inc., Wall, N.J., 1988-89; cons. therapist Lisa Leifer Phys. Therapy/Pediatric Therapy, Edison, 1988-89; co-owner, v.p., sec. 1 Step Up, Inc., Little Silver, N.J., 1989—. Contbr. articles to profl. jours. Mem. Am. Phys. Therapy Assn., Neurodevel. Treatment Assn., Phi Kappa Phi. Roman Catholic. Home: 1485 Garrett Dr Wall NJ 07719 Office: 1 Step Up Inc 200 White Rd Apt 101 Little Silver NJ 07739-1160

COBB, MARGARET MARY, research physician; b. Binghamton, N.Y., Nov. 7, 1948; d. John William and Margaret Mary (Jones) Menta; m. Fredrick Donald Cobb, June 5, 1971; 1 child, Heather Edith. MS, Syracuse U., 1977; PhD, Cornell U., 1981; MD, N.Y. Med. Coll., 1985; MPH with distinction, Yale U., 1990. Diplomate Nat. Bd. Med. Examiners. Rsch. assoc. E.R. Squibb & Sons, Princeton, N.J., 1970-73; rsch. asst. Syracuse (N.Y.) U., 1973-77; sr. rsch. assoc. Cornell U., Ithaca, N.Y., 1977-79; postdoctoral fellow Upstate Med. Ctr., Syracuse, 1980-81; med. intern Yale U. Affiliate, New Haven, Conn., 1985-86, postdoctoral fellow, resident pub. health, 1986-87; rsch. assoc., physician Rockefeller U., N.Y.C., 1987-90; assoc. dir. profl. med. svcs. Am. Cyanamid Corp., Pearl River, N.Y., 1990-93; sr. assoc. med. dir. Pfizer Inc., N.Y.C., 1993-94; pvt. practice N.Y.C.; sr. med. dir. Warner Lambert Co., N.J., 1994—. Eucharistic minister St. Catherine's Ch., Riverside, Conn. Mem. AAAS, AMA, APHA, N.Y. Lipid Club, Sigma Xi. Roman Catholic. Home: 2 Glen Rd Greenwich CT 06830-4632 Office: 1735 York Ave Ste 2F New York NY 10128-6855

COBB, SHIRLEY ANN, public relations specialist, journalist; b. Oklahoma City, Jan. 1, 1936; d. William Ray and Irene (Fewell) Dodson; m. Roy Lampkin Cobb, Jr., June 21, 1958; children: Kendra Leigh, Cary William, Paul Alan. BA in Journalism with distinction, U. Okla., 1958, postgrad., 1972; postgrad., Jacksonville U., 1962. Info. specialist Pacific Missle Test Ctr., Point Mugu, Calif., 1975-76; corr. Religious News Svc., N.Y.C., 1979-81; spltу. editor fashion and religion Thousand Oaks (Calif.) News Chronicle, 1977-81; pub. rels. cons., Camarillo, Calif., 1977—; media mgr. pub. info City of Thousand Oaks, 1983—. Contbr. articles to profl. jours. Trustee Ocean View Sch. Bd., 1976-79; pres. Point Mugu Officers' Wives Club, 1975-76, 90—, Calif. Assn. Pub. Info. Ofcls. (pres. 1989-90, Paul Clark Lifetime Achievement award 1993); bd. dirs. Camarillo Hospice, 1983-85; sec. Conejo Valley Hist. Soc., 1993-95. Recipient Spot News award San Fernando Valley Press Club, 1979. Mem. Pub. Rels. Soc. Am. (L.A. chpt. liaison 1991), Sigma Delta Chi, Phi Beta Kappa, Chi Omega. Republican. Clubs: Las Posas Country, Spanish Hills Country, Town Hall of Calif. Home: 2481 Brookhill Dr Camarillo CA 93010-2112 Office: 2100 Thousand Oaks Blvd Thousand Oaks CA 91362

COBB, TERRI R. (CECI COBB), film and video producer; b. N.Y.C., Feb. 18, 1934; d. Leo Odell and Jean (Wister) Gruber; m. Ira Reamer, July 4, 1954 (div. May 1975); children: Jeff, David, Ellen; m. David G. Cobb, Aug. 2, 1975. Student, U. Miami, 1953-54, Miami Dade C.C., 1970-72. Vocalist The Girlfriends, N.Y.C., 1952-53; dental asst. Miami, Fla., 1953-56, med. asst., 1956-58; prodr., host TV talk show People and Places, Tampa, Fla., 1981—; freelance film and video prodr., prodn. coord. Encore Film & Video Prodn., Tampa, 1984—; freelance model, actress, Fla.; seminar leader Tom Kirby Assocs., Fla., 1986—; cons. U. South Fla. Dept. Edn., Tampa, 1980—. Health educator, fund raiser, speaker Fla. March of Dimes, 1974—; bd. dirs. Fla. Healthy Mother-Healthy Baby Coalition. Recipient Jone Intercable Golden Cassette award, 1989, Crystal Reel award Fla. Motion Picture & TV Assn., 1990. Mem. Fla. Perinatal Assn. (bd. dirs.), Fla. Womens' Alliance, Fla. Motion Picture and TV Assn. (bd. dirs.), Fla. Soc. Assn. Execs. (bd. dirs.). Home: 16612 Hutchinson Rd Odessa FL 33556-2327

COBBAN, HELENA, columnist; b. Abingdon, U.K., Oct. 31, 1952; came to the U.S., 1982; d. James Macdonald and Lorna Mary (Marlow) C.; m. Sohel Rached (div. 1983); children: Tarek Rached, Leila Rached; m. William Bauer Quandt, Apr. 21, 1984; 1 child, Lorna. BA, Oxford (Eng.) U., 1973, MA, 1977. Corr. in Middle East Christian Sci. Monitor, Boston, 1976-81; social sci. rsch. coun., fellow internat. peace & security, 1986-88; dir. initiative for peace and cooperation in the Middle East Washington, 1991-93; columnist Christian Sci. Monitor, Boston, 1990—. Author: The Palestinian Liberation Organization, 1984, The Making of Modern Lebanon, 1985, The Superpowers and the Syrian-Israeli Conflict, 1991. Recipient Outstanding Academic Book award Choice Mag., 1985. Mem. Internat. Inst. for Strategic Studies, Middle East Studies Assn., Middle East Watch Chpt. of Human Rights Watch. Home: 2318 44th St NW Washington DC 20007

COBLE, CAROL DELORIS, accounting executive; b. Lafayette, Ind., Oct. 6, 1946; d. Fred and Edna Marie (Wolf) Marsh; m. William Albert Coble, July 15, 1964; children: Frederic Kelly, Michelle Marie, Melissa Lee. AS, Ind. Vocat. Tech., 1987. Cashier The Andersons, Delphi, Ind., 1978-79; data entry The Andersons, Delphi, 1979-86, head clk., 1987; acct. Inweld Corp., Lafayette, 1987-91, acctg. mgr., 1991—. Mem. Inst. Mgmt. Accts. (sec. 1991-92, treas. 1992-93, employment dir. 1994—), Tippecanoe Area Pers. Assn. (legis. rep. 1992-93). Republican. Office: Inweld Corp PO Box 7208 Lafayette IN 47903

COBURN, FRANCES GULLETT, retired elementary school educator; b. Princess, Ky., Apr. 20, 1919; d. Gilbert G. and Lula (Kitchen) Gullett; m. Ralph L. Coburn, Dec. 20, 1941 (dec. Feb. 1966). BS cum laude, Morris Harvey Coll., 1950; MA in Adminstrn., Marshall U., 1952. Tchr. Braeholm (W.Va.) Elem. Sch., 1938-49; tchr. Amherstdale (W.Va.) Elem. Sch., 1949-51; prin. King Fuel Elem. Sch., Emmett, W.Va., 1951-53; tchr. Peyton Elem. Sch., Huntington, W.Va., 1953-78; supervising tchr. Marshall U., Huntington, 1953-78. Contbr. articles to profl. jours. Vol. Huntington Mus. Art; asst. with crafts at 2 Huntington nursing homes; sec. adminstrv. bd. Johnson Meml. Ch., 1981-94, sec. coun. on ministries, 1990-92; mem. Circle 7; donor rm. asst. ARC (recipient 35 yr. pin); mem. Logan County coun. Girl Scouts U.S., Logan, W.Va. Named Outstanding Elem. Tchr. of Am., 1972, Ky. Col., Gov. of Ky., 1991; recipient cert. of excellent svc. as vol. Presbyn. Manor Nursing Home, 1990-94, 35-yr. pin as vol. blood ctr. ARC, 1990. Mem. AAUW, Woman's Club Huntington, Huntington Garden Club, Women Builders of Univ. of Charleston, W.Va., Panhellenic, Delta Kappa Gamma, Kappa Delta Phi, Phi Mu. Methodist. Home: 1034 12th Ave Huntington WV 25701-3422

COBURN, MARJORIE FOSTER, psychologist, educator; b. Salt Lake City, Feb. 28, 1939; d. Harlan A. and Alma (Ballinger) Polk; m. Robert Byron Coburn, July 2, 1977; children: Polly Klea Foster, Matthew Ryan Foster, Robert Scott Coburn, Kelly Anne Coburn. B.A. in Sociology, UCLA, 1960; Montessori Internat. Diploma honor grad. Washington Montessori Inst., 1968; M.A. in Psychology, U. No. Colo., 1979; Ph.D. in Counseling Psychology, U. Denver, 1983. Licensed clin. psychologist. Probation officer Alameda County (Calif.), Oakland, 1960-62, Contra Costa County (Calif.), El Cerrito, 1966, Fairfax County (Va.), Fairfax, 1967; dir. Friendship Club, Orlando, Fla., 1963-65; tchr. Va. Montessori Sch., Fairfax, 1968-70; spl. edn. tchr. Leary Sch., Falls Church, Va., 1970-72, sch. adminstr., 1973-76; tchr. Aseltine Sch., San Diego, 1976-77, Coburn Montessori Sch., Colorado Springs, Colo., 1977-79; pvt. practice psychotherapy, Colorado Springs, 1979-82, San Diego, 1982—; cons. spl. edn., agoraphobia, women in transition. Mem. Am. Psychol. Assn., Am. Orthopsychiat. Assn., Phobia Soc., Council Exceptional Children, Calif. Psychol. Assn., San Diego Psychological Assn., The Charter 100, Mensa. Episcopalian. Lodge: Rotary. Contbr. articles to profl. jours.; author: (with R.C. Orem) Montessori: Prescription for Children with Learning Disabilities, 1977. Office: 826 Prospect St Ste 101 La Jolla CA 92037-4206

COCCHIARELLA, VICKI MARSHALL, state legislator; b. Livingston, Mont., Dec. 19, 1949; d. James and Ruth E. (Officer) Marshall; m. Larry Ray Cocchiarella, 1973; children: Cara Jo, Michael James. BA, U. Mont., 1978, MA, 1985. Property mgr., 1975—; teaching asst. U. Mont., 1979-80, adminstrv. clk., 1981—; mem. Mont. Ho. of Reps., 1989—, mem. interim com. state employee compensation. Bd. dirs. Child & Family Resource Coun. Mem. Mont. Pub. Employees Assn. (former bd. dirs., former 1st v.p., pres. 1987—). Democrat. Home: 535 Livingston Ave Missoula MT 59801-8003 Office: Mont State Senate State Capitol Helena MT 59620*

COCCO, JACQUELINE M., state legislator; b. Bridgeport, Conn.. Grad., St. Vincent's Sch. Nursing. State rep. dist. 127 Conn. Ho. of Reps., 1987—; chmn. family and workplace com., mem. labor and pub. employees com., pub. health com., asst. majority leader; mem. Dem. Town Com., 1984—; mem. Bd. Humane Affairs, 1986-90; mem. Charter Rev. Com., 1988-89; vis. nurse. Home: 93 Heppenstall Dr Bridgeport CT 06604-1007 Office: Office of State Senate State Senate Bldg Hartford CT 06106*

COCCO, MARIE ELIZABETH, journalist; b. Malden, Mass., Jan. 15, 1956; d. Morris Alfred and Dorothy Anne (Colameta) C.; m. Thomas Neal Burrows, Sept. 4, 1982; children: Matthew C. Burrows., Michael C. Burrows. BA, Tufts U., 1978; MS, Columbia U., 1979. Journalist Daily Register, Shrewsbury, N.J., 1979-80, Newsday, L.I., N.Y., 1980—. Recipient Excellence in Editorial Writing award N.Y. State Pubs. Assn., 1992, Nat. Reporting award Sigma Delta Chi, 1991. Mem. White House Corrs. Assn. (Barnet Nover award 1991), Nat. Press Club (Washington Corr. award 1991). Office: Newsday Washington Bur 1001 Pennsylvania Ave NW Washington DC 20004-2505

COCHÉ, JUDITH, psychologist, educator; b. Phila., Sept. 2, 1942; d. Louis and Miriam (Nerenberg) Milner; m. Erich Coché, Oct. 16, 1966 (dec.); 1 child, Juliette Laura; m. John Anderson, Jan. 1, 1994. BA, Colby Coll., 1964; MA, Temple U., 1966; PhD, Bryn Mawr Coll., 1975. Diplomate Am. Bd. Profl. Psychology. Rsch. asst. Jefferson Med. Coll., 1965-66; diagnostician Law Ct., Aachen, Germany, 1967-68; staff psychologist N.E. Community Mental Health Ctr., Phila., 1969-74; family clinician Inst. Pa. Hosp., 1974-76; instr. psychology Drexel U., 1976-77; lectr. Med. Coll. Pa., 1977-78; asst. clin. prof. Hahnemann Med. Coll., Phila., 1979—; pvt. practice Phila., 1974—, N.J., 1985—; assoc. prof. psychiatry U. Pa., 1985—; mem. faculty Family Inst. of Phila., 1990—; sr. cons. Phila. Child Guidance Clinic, 1992—; clin. cons. Hilltop Prep Sch., 1977-86; clin. supr. Am. Assn. Marriage and Family Therapy. Co-author: Couples Group Psychotherapy, A Clinical Practice Model, 1990; contbr. chpts. to books, articles to profl. jours. Bd. dirs. Whitemarsh Art Ctr., 1977-78, Please Touch Museum, 1982-89; mem. prof. adv. bd. Parents Without Ptnrs., 1977-86; mem. adv. com. Pa. Ballet/Shirley Rock. Grantee Del. Children's Bur. Bryn Mawr Coll., 1974-75, Pa. Hosp., 1975-77. Fellow Am. Group Psychotherapy Assn.; mem. APA, Am. Assn. Marriage and Family Therapy (approved supr.), Am. Family Therapy Assn., Phila. Soc. Clin. Psychologists (pres. 1980-81), Family Inst. Phila., Pa. Psychol. Assn. (chmn. legis. com. 1982), Soc. Rsch. in Psychotherapy. Address: 2037 Delancey Pl Philadelphia PA 19103-6509

COCHRAN, CAROLYN, library director; b. Tyler, Tex., July 13, 1934; d. Sidney Allen and Eudelle (Frazier) C.; m. Guy Milford Eley, June 1, 1963 (div.). BA, Beaver Coll., 1956; MA, U. Tex., 1960; MLS, Tex. Woman's U., 1970. Libr., Canadian (Tex.) High Sch., 1970-71; rep. United Food Co., Amarillo, Tex., 1971-72; libr. Bishop Coll., Dallas, 1972-74; interviewer Tex. Employment Commn., Dallas, 1975-76; libr. St. Mary's Dominican, New Orleans, 1976-77, DeVry Inst. Tech., Irving, Tex., 1978—; with Database Searching Handicapped Individuals, Irving, 1983—; vol. bibliographer Assn. Individuals with Disabilities, Dallas, 1982-85. Mem. Am. Coalition of Citizens with Disabilities, 1982-85, Assn. Individuals with Disabilities, 1982-86, Vols. in Tech. Assistance, 1985—, Radio Amateur Satellite Corp., 1985-86; sponsor 500, Inc., 1988—. HEW fellow, 1967; honored Black History Collection, Dallas Morning News, Bishop Coll., Dallas, 1973. Mem. ALA, Spl. Libr. Assn., Am. Coun. of Blind and Coun. Citizens with Low Vision. Club: Toastmistress (pres. 1982-83) (Irving). Reviewer Library Jour., 1974, Dallas Morning News, 1972-74, Amarillo Globe-News, 1970-71. Office: DeVry Inst Tech 4801 Regent Blvd Irving TX 75063-2440

COCHRAN, JACQUELINE LOUISE, general management executive; b. Franklin, Ind., Mar. 12, 1953; d. Charles Morris and Marjorie Elizabeth (Rohrbaugh) C. BA, DePauw U., 1975; MBA, U. Chgo., 1977. Fin. analyst Pan Am World Airways, N.Y.C., 1977-79, Gen. Bus. Group W. R. Grace & Co., N.Y.C., 1979-80; sr. fin. analyst Gen. Bus. Group div. W. R. Grace & Co., N.Y.C., 1980-81, mgr. fin. analysis, 1981-82; dir. fin. planning and analysis Gen. Bus. Group div. W. R. Grace & Co., N.Y.C., 1982-85; v.p. fin. Am. Breeders Svc. div. W. R. Grace & Co., DeForest, Wis., 1985-87, v.p. feed ops. Grace Animal Svc. div., 1987-89; gen. mgr., chief ops. officer SoftKat div. W. R. Grace & Co., Chatsworth, Calif., 1990; pres. SoftKat div. W.R. Grace & Co., Chatsworth, Calif., 1990-92; vice-chmn., chief adminstrv. officer Baker & Taylor, Inc., Thousand Oaks, Calif., 1992, pres. SoftKat div., 1992; exec. cons. Jacqueline Cochran Cons., Westlake Village, Calif., 1993—. Bd. visitors DePauw U., 1993—. Recipient Women of Distinction award Madison (Wis.) YWCA, 1987; named to Acad. Women Achievers YWCA N.Y., 1984. Mem. Nat. Assn. Corp. Dirs., ABCD, The Microcomputer Industry Assn. (adv. coun. 1992), AAUW, Phi Beta Kappa, Alpha Lambda Delta, Delta Delta Delta (advisor scholarship com. Madison chpt. 1985-89, treas. 1986-89, ho. corp. bd. dirs. 1986-89, fin. advisor 1986-89). Republican. Methodist.

COCHRAN, JERI LYNN, entrepreneur; b. Bethesda, Md., Jan. 3, 1961; d. Carl R. and Mildred (Tanaka) C. BA in Edn., U. Guam, 1985. Cert. tchr., Guam. Substitute tchr. Dept. Edn., Guam, 1979, tchr., 1985-89; disc jockey Sta. KGUM 567, Guam, 1989; office mgr. PSI Guam, 1989; tchr. L.A. Unified Sch. Dist., 1990-93; distr. Amway, L.A., 1993—; chief of staff Motivational Seminar, Guam, 1989; fashion cons. Designs on You, L.A., 1992; leadership coun. Berendo Middle Sch., L.A., 1992-93. L.A. Tchrs. Union rep. for Belmont Cluster # 12 Instrnl. Cabinet. Regent scholar U. Guam, 1985, Tchr. Tng. scholar, 1985. Mem. Berendo Family Orgn., Sierra Club. Home: 4545 San Andreas Ave Los Angeles CA 90065

COCHRAN, JILL TEAGUE, legislative staff member; b. Waco, Tex., May 3, 1946; d. Olin E. and Freddie (Dunman) Teague. BA, U. Tex., 1971. Med. illustrator's asst. U. Tex., San Antonio, 1972-74; staff asst. Ho. Vets.'

Affairs Com., 1974-81, mem. profl. staff Subcom. Edn., Tng. and Employment, 1981—. Office: Subcom Edn Tng & Employment Rm 337A Cannon House Office Bldg Washington DC 20515*

COCHRAN, MARY ANN, nurse, educator; b. Chgo., Dec. 12, 1951; d. Lawrence Donovan and Mary Gracz (Capizzi) Lee; m. Thomas Lee Cochran, Mar. 12, 1971; 1 child, Nathan Edgar. Diploma in nursing, St. Joseph's Hosp., Joliet, Ill., 1973. RN, Ill.; cert. post anesthesia nurse. Staff nurse Silver Cross Hosp., Joliet, 1973—, stafff nurse ICU, 1979—, in-svc. educator post anesthesia care unit, 1987-92, BLS instr., 1987—. Mem. AACN, Am. Soc. Post Anesthesia Nurses, Ill. Soc. Post Anesthesia Nurses (membership chair 1990-92, ways & means chair 1992—). Office: Silver Cross Hosp 1200 Maple Rd Joliet IL 60432-1497

COCHRAN, SHIRLEY JEAN, accountant; b. Franklin, Tenn., Sept. 28, 1943; d. Leslie O. and N. Pearl (Henson) Layne; m. John F. Cochran, Aug. 30, 1963; children: Karla Jean, John Gregory. Cert. in Acctg., Columbia State U., 1982, Athens State U., 1990. CPA, Tenn. Sr. clk. Prudential Ins. Co., Nashville, 1961-65; comm. and quality control E.I. DuPont DeNemours Co., Columbia, Tenn., 1965-66; legal sec./paralegal Courtney and Fleming, Columbia, Tenn., 1974-83; CPA, mgr. Kraft CPA's, Columbia, Tenn., 1983—. Mem. Exch. Club, Columbia, 1993; mem. exec. com. Frank Cochran for Gov. Campaign, Maury County, 1994; grad. Leadership Maury Class, 1992-93. Recipient Outstanding Mem. award Nat. Assn. Accts., 1989. Mem. Inst. Mgmt. Accts. (pres., v.p. edn., bd. dirs. 1991—, Past Pres. award 1990), Tenn. Soc. CPA, Maury-Lawrence Legal Secs. Assn. (charter), Columbia State Alumni Assn. (bd. dirs., scholarship com. 1990—, Am. Preservation Tenn. Antiquities (tour hostess 1991—), Maury County C. of C. (small bus. com. 1994, home tour com. 1994), Gamma Beta Phi. Mem. Ch. of Christ. Office: Kraft Bros Esstman Patton & Harrell 610 N Garden Columbia TN 38401

COCHRANE, ALISON LEE, gas pipeline company marketing manager; b. Superior, Wis., Feb. 4, 1961; d. Wesley Charles and Mary (Hoch) C. BS in Petroleum Engring., U. Okla., 1984; MBA, U. Tex. Permian Basin, Odessa, 1988. Registered profl. engr., Okla. Prodn. engr. BP Exploration, Inc., Midland, Tex., 1984-87; prodn. engr. BP Exploration, Inc., Houston, 1987-89, gas coord., 1989-90; sr. rep. for mktg. Panhandle Eastern Pipe Line Co., Houston, 1990-91, coord. mktg., 1991-93; mgr. mktg., 1993—. Mem. Soc. Petroleum Engrs., Natural Gas Transp. Assn., Natural Gas Assn. Houston. Roman Catholic. Office: Panhandle Eastern Pipe Line 5400 Westheimer Ct Houston TX 77056-5310

COCHRANE, BETSY LANE, state senator; b. Asheboro, N.C.; d. William Jennings and Bobbie (Campbell) Lane; m. Joe Kenneth Cochrane, 1958; children: Lisa, Craig. BA, Meredith Coll., 1958. Mem. N.C. Ho. of Reps., Raleigh, 1980-88; house minority leader N.C. Ho. of Reps., Raleigh, N.C., 1985-88; mem. N.C. Senate, Raleigh, 1988—, chmn. Commn. on Aging, 1989—, vice chmn. higher edn. com., 1991-92; senate minority whip, 1993—, senate minority leader, 1995-96; mem. Nat. Rep. Platform Com.; chmn. Joint Legis. Ethics Com., 1991. Trustee Davie County Hosp. Recipient Woman in Govt. award N.C. Jaycees, 1985; named one of 10 Outstanding Legislators in Nation, 1987, Disting. Citizen of Yr. N.C. Libr. Dirs., 1991, Legislator of Yr. N.C. Divsn. Aging, 1991, N.C. Assn. for Home Care, 1992, Citizen of Yr. N.C. Health Facilities Assn., 1993. Baptist. Office: 122 Azalea Cir Advance NC 27006

COCKER, BARBARA JOAN, marine artist, interior designer; b. Uxbridge, Mass.; A.A., Becker Jr. Coll., 1943; student Mt. St. Mary Coll., 1944-45, Clark U., 1945, N.Y. Sch. Interior Design, 1965-67. Owner, operator Barbara J. Cocker, Interior Design, Rumson, N.J., 1966—; owner Barbara J. Cocker Paintings of the Sea Gallery, Nantucket, Mass., 1975-86, 91, 95; tchr. adult edn. courses in interior design, 1965-68; artist, pvt. instr. marine art; pres. Maximus Praetorius Corp., Nantucket, Mass., 1979—; one-man shows marine paintings: Little Gallery, Barbizon, N.Y., 1971, Old Mill Assn., 1971, Pacem en Terris Gallery, N.Y.C., 1972, Central Jersey Bank & Trust Co., Rumson, 1971, 72, 74, 77, 79, Little Gallery, Nantucket Art Assn., 1975, 77, 79, 81, 84, 87, 89, 91, 92, Caravan House Galleries, N.Y.C., 1975, 79, Guild of Creative Art, Shrewsbury, N.J., 1976, 81, 85, 88, 93, IBM Corp., N.J., 1977, South St. Seaport Mus., N.Y., 1977, 80, Provident Nat. Bank, Phila., 1978, Gallery 100, Princeton, 1978, Bell Telephone Research Labs., 1982, 86, AT&T, 87, Midlantic Bank, N.J., 1988, 93, 94, Art Alliance N.J., 1983, 91, Gilpin House Gallery (Va.), Swain Art Gallery, N.J., 1984, Oceanic Libr., N.J., 1989, 91, 93, Red Bank Libr., N.J, 1989, 91, Captiva (Fla.) Civic Assn., 1994, Captiva Community Ctr., 1994; group shows include: Guild Creative Art N.J., Composers, Authors and Artists Am. NAD, Salmagundi Club N.Y.C., Monmouth Coll. Festival of Arts, Caravan House Galleries, Pen and Brush Club, N.Y.C., N.Y.C., Lever House Galleries, N.Y.C., Nat. Arts Club, N.Y.C., Ocean County Artists Guild, N.J., Chelsea Gardens Gallery, Fla., Frank Lewis, Killarney, Ireland; painting selection for publication Clean Ocean Action, N.J., 1994. Named Woman of Yr. Zonta Internat., 1986. Mem. Catharine Lorillard Wolfe Arts Club, Am. Artists Profl. League, N.Y. Guild Creative Arts, Nantucket Art Assn., Art League Marco Island, Fla. Composers, Authors and Artists Am., Allied Artists Am., Monmouth Arts Found. (N.J.), So. Vt. Artists Inc., Pen and Brush Club (N.Y.C.), Big Arts Ctr. (Sanibel, Fla.), Sanibel-Captiva Art League. Address: 3 Rumson Rd Rumson NJ 07760 also: Paintings Of Sea Studio 10 Old South Wharf Box 574 Nantucket MA 02554

COCKREL, TERESA LYNN, laboratory technician; b. Leitchfield, Ky., Jan. 20, 1960; d. Edward Carl and Freeda Mae (Jackson) C. BS, Western Ky. U., 1984. Med. records typist Barren River Comprehensive Care Ctr., Bowling Green, Ky., 1982-84; community svc. worker Tri-County Community Action Agy., LaGrange, Ky., 1985-88; sr. rsch. tech. U. Ky., Lexington, 1988-90, prin. lab. tech., 1990—; Bacteriology div. rep. Livestock Disease Diagnostic Ctr. Christmas com., 1990-92, blood drive coord., 1990. Youth worker Cumberland Presbyn. Ch., Caneyville, Ky., 1982—, youth coord., 1992-94, editor newsletter, 1993; 4-H fair judge 1984, 85, 88; vol. Western Ky. U. Future Farmers Am. Field Days, 1982-84; food exhibit judge Spencer County Fair, 1981; vol. Grayson County Day Camps, 1976, Henry County Day Camps, 1974-78, Health Fair Exhibit Crestwood Sta. Sr. Citizens Coun., 1985-87. Mem. NRA, Order of Eastern Star, Gamma Sigma Sigma (recording sec. 1981-83). Republican. Home: 1242 Summitt Dr Lexington KY 40502-2273 Office: Livestock Disease Diagnostic Ctr 1428 Newtown Rd Lexington KY 40511-1220

COCKRILL, ANN TERESA, lawyer; b. Spokane, Wash., Sept. 4, 1953; d. Leonard Marshall and Joan Mary (Ledwich) C. BA, Seattle U., 1975; JD, Gonzaga U., 1980. Bar: Wash. 1980. Atty. Evergreen Legal Svcs., Yakima, Wash., 1980-81; law clk. Wash. State Ct. Appeals, Tacoma, 1981-83; atty. Atty. Gen. Office State of Wash., Olympia, 1983; atty. The Boeing Co., Seattle, 1985—. Mem. Wash. State Bar Assn.

CODERRE, ELAINE ANN, state representative; b. Providence, Oct. 11, 1947; d. Henry N. and Mary A. (McDonald) Daigneault; m. Raymond Russen Coderre, Feb. 3, 1967; children: Robert, Thomas, Karen. Student, U. R.I., 1965-68. Bank teller Pawtucket (R.I.) Inst. for Savs., 1970-82; pres. Dano USA, Pawtucket, 1982—; rep. R.I. Ho. Reps., 1985—; bd. dirs. Sr. Inn., Pawtucket, 1985—. Mem. Heart Fund Drive, Pawtucket, 1985, Pawtucket Tenants Affairs Bd., 1985—; sec. Child Support Enforcement Commn., 1985—. Named one of Outstanding Young Women in America, 1981. Mem. Vis. Nurses Assn. (bd. dirs. 1986—), VFW Aux. (sr. v.p. 1984-87, legisl. chair 1986-87), Jaycee Women. Democrat. Roman Catholic. Home: 18 Angle St Pawtucket RI 02860-3006 also: RI House Reps Office House Mems Providence RI 02903*

CODERRE, NANCY ADELE, financial analyst; b. Cleve., Aug. 21, 1962; d. Richard Alfred and Julia (Viedt) C. BA, U. Colo., 1984; MBA with high honors, Babson Coll., 1986. Cert. mgmt. acct. Asst. contr. Boston Ch. Christ, Lexington, Mass., 1987; sr. cost acct. M/A Com., Omni Spectra, Waltham, Mass., 1987-88; fin. analyst Analogic Corp., Peabody, Mass., 1988-93, Carrier Corp., Syracuse, N.Y., 1994—. Mem. Inst. Mgmt. Accts., Beta Gamma Sigma. Home: 313 E Willow St # 526 Syracuse NY 13203

CODY, MARY BETH, medical-surgical nurse; b. Bklyn., Oct. 23, 1954; d. John Peter and Helen Joan (Van Jones) Ianno; m. James Francis Cody, June 19, 1977; children: James Patrick, Kristen Mary, Brian Lawrence. BS in Biology and Psychology, SUNY, Oswego, 1975; AAS in Nursing summa cum laude, SUNY, Farmingdale, 1981. Cert. in med.-surg. nursing ANA. Nurse's aide Mercy Hosp., Rockville Centre, N.Y., 1979-81; charge nurse Nassau County Med. Ctr., East Meadow, N.Y., 1981-85, Brunswick Hosp. Ctr., Amityville, N.Y., 1985—. Active St. Kilian Mothers Club, Farmingdale, N.Y., 1986—, Forest Ave. Sch. PTA, West Babylon, N.Y., 1989—, Girl Scouts U.S.A., West Babylon, 1991—, LaSalle Parent Assn., 1992—, Santapogue PTA, 1993—, Boy Scouts Am., 1993—. Mem. ANA, Phi Beta Kappa. Republican. Roman Catholic. Home: 414 18th St West Babylon NY 11704

COE, ELIZABETH ANN, elementary education educator; b. El Paso, Tex., Feb. 25, 1944; d. Charles William Murray and Jeanne (Roman) Moore; children: Christopher E. Sanchez, Christine Angela Sanchez. BS in Edn., N.Mex. State U., 1968; postgrad., U. N.Mex., 1987-88; MA in Edn., N.Mex. State U., 1992; postgrad., East N.Mex. U., 1970-92. Cert. elem. educator, lang. arts. educator Kindergarten thru grade 12, social studies educator Kindergarten thru grade 12, N.Mex. Tchr. Hatch (N.Mex.) Schs., 1968-70, Ruidoso (N.Mex.) Mcpl. Schs., 1970-84; real estate agt., 1978-88; tchr. Tularosa (N.Mex.) Schs., 1988—; workshop leader Region IX, Ruidoso, 1989, 90; rep. Project L.E.A.D., U. N.Mex., Albuquerque, 1991, N.Mex. State BA Restructuring Conf., Albuquerque, 1990, Mesilla Valley Regional Coun. on Bilingual Edn., 1968-70; co-chair Internat. Reading Assn. Young Authors Conf., Tularosa, 1990-91; cons. N.Mex. State Writing Project, 1993; mem. task force on writing and portfolio assessment N.Mex. State Dept. Edn., 1993—. Author: (short story) Los Desesperados, 1989 (1st prize Tri-State award), Tortillitas Quemaditas, 1991 (Honorable Mention). Mem. N.Mex. State Dept. Edn. Task Force on Writing. Mem. NEA, LWV, Phi Kappa Phi. Home: PO Box 929 Ruidoso NM 88345-0929

COE, MARGARET LOUISE SHAW, community service volunteer; b. Cody, Wyo., Dec. 25, 1917; d. Ernest Francis and Effie Victoria (Abrahamson) Shaw; m. Henry Huttleston Rogers Coe, Oct. 8, 1943 (dec. Aug. 1966); children: Anne Rogers Hayes, Henry H.R., Jr., Robert Douglas II. AA, Stephens Coll., 1937; BA, U. Wyo., 1939. Asst. to editor The Cody Enterprise, 1939-42, editor, 1968-71. Chmn. bd. trustees Buffalo Bill Hist. Ctr., Cody, 1966—, Cody Med. Found., 1964—; commr. Wyo. Centenniel Commn., Cheyenne, 1986-91. Recipient The Westerner award Old West Trails Found., 1980, Gold Medallion award Nat. Assn. Sec. of State, 1982, disting alumni award U. Wyo., 1984, exemplary alumni award, 1994, Gov.'s award for arts, 1988; inducted Nat. Cowgirl Hall of Fame, 1983. Mem. P.E.O., Delta Delta Delta. Republican. Episcopalian. Home: 1400 11th St Cody WY 82414-4206

COERVER, ELIZABETH ANN, data base consultant; b. St. Louis, Sept. 4, 1941; d. Harrison Fredrick and Virginia (Marks) C. BA, Fontbonne Coll., St. Louis, 1963. Supr. McDonnell Douglas, St. Louis, 1969-71, cons., 1971-74; sr. cons. McDonnell Douglas, Washington, 1974-75, Phoenix, 1975-77; sr. cons. Mcauto Internat., London, 1977-79; prin. cons. Mcauto Internat., Bonn, Germany, 1979-80; prin. cons. Mcauto Benelux, Hilversum, The Netherlands, 1980-82, Dublin, Ireland, 1982-84; sr. cons. McDonnell Douglas, St. Louis, 1984-93, prin. specialist IS tech., 1993—. Author: (class) IMS Application Programming, 1971, Data Base Design, 1972, Master Terminal Operations, 1972. Mem. AAUW. Office: McDonnell Douglas PO Box 516 Saint Louis MO 63166-0516

COFFEE, VIRGINIA CLAIRE, civic worker, former mayor; b. Alliance, Nebr., Dec. 8, 1920; d. James Maddigan and Adelaide Mary (Forde) Kennedy; BS, Chadron State Coll., 1942; m. Bill Brown Coffee, June 21, 1942; children: Claire, Sara, Virginia Anne, Sue. High sch. prin., Whitman, Nebr., 1942; bookkeeper Coffee & Son, Inc., Harrison, Nebr., 1965—, officer, 1967—, pres., 1987—; dir. Friends of Agate Fossil BEOS, Inc., 1988, v.p. 1988—; mayor City of Harrison, 1978-80. Leader, Girl Scouts U.S.A., 1953-63; mem. Harrison Elem. Sch. bd., 1958-64; mem. liaison com. Chadron State Coll., 1975; pub. rels. chmn. Nebr. Cowbelles, 1968; sec. NW Stock Growers, 1971-73; corp. officer Ft. Robinson Centennial, 1973-88; officer Gov.'s Ft. Robinson Centennial Commn., 1973-75; hon. gov. Nebr. Centennial, 1967; chmn. Sioux County Bicentennial, 1973-77; trustee Nebr. State Hist. Soc. Found., 1975—, Village of Harrison, 1973-80; bd. dirs. Harrison Community Club, Inc., 1983-86, officer, 1984-86; apptd. Sioux County Vis. com. 1989—; apptd. adm. Nebr. Navy, 1992. Recipient Disting. Svc. award Chadron State Coll., 1994. Mem. Nebr. State Hist. Soc. (life, dir. 1979-85, 2d v.p. 1982-84, 1st v.p. 1984-85, com. for marker to honor Harrison centennial 1985-86), Wyo. State Hist. Soc., Cardinal Key Honor Frat., Sioux County Hist. Soc. (bd. dirs. 1975-81, 83-84, 87-90, pres. 1988-90, co-pres., sec., v.p.) Sioux county history book com. 1985-86, contbr. articles. Roman Catholic. Clubs: Nebr. Cattle Women, Ladies Community, Westerners Corral Internat., United C. of C. (we. Nebr. chpt.), Harrison Community Inc. Contbr. articles to area newspapers; chmn. compilation com. book Sioux County Memoirs of Its Pioneers, 1967; coordinator Harrison sect. book Nebraska Our Towns, 1988. Address: PO Box 336 Harrison NE 69346-0336

COFFEL, PATRICIA K., clinical social worker; b. Bismarck, N.D., Sept. 14, 1934; m. Raymond A. Kobe, 1956; children: Anne, Elizabeth, Colleen, Denise, Tim, Heidi; m. Mitchel D. Coffel, 1983. Student, U. N.D., 1954-55; BA in Sociology, Coll. St. Benedict, 1956; MSW, Wayne State U., 1981. Cert. social worker, Mich. Dir. social svcs. dept. Pontiac Nursing Ctr., 1978-84; dir. of med. social work dept. Advanced Profl. Home Health Care, Troy, Mich., 1985-86; med. social worker Visiting Nurses of Met. Detroit, 1987; family worker, therapist Camp Oakland Youth Svcs., Oxford, Mich., 1987-89; client svcs. case mgr. Macomb-Oakland Regional Ctr., Mt. Clemens, Mich., 1989-90; clin. social worker, case mgr. Oakdale Regional Ctr., Lapeer, Mich., 1990-91; social worker Clinton Valley Ctr., Pontiac, Mich., 1991—; counselor Suicide Prevention, Inc., St. Louis, 1971-72, Macomb County Crisis Ctr., Warren, Mich., 1973-74; geriatric counselor Beverly Enterprises, Pontiac and Novi, Mich., 1981-83; grief and loss counselor Hospice SE Mich., Southfield, 1982-83. Grad. profl. scholar Wayne State U. Sch. Social Work, 1980. Mem. NASW (qualified clin. social worker), Acad. Cert. Social Workers (diplomate in clin. social work). Home: 645 Oakwood Rd Ortonville MI 48462-8589 Office: Clinton Valley Ctr Mich Dept Mental Health 140 Elizabeth Lake Rd Pontiac MI 48341

COFFELT, SHERRI KAY, marketing professional; b. Missouri Valley, Iowa, July 3, 1962; d. Joseph Jene Coffelt and Karen Kay (Earleywine) Siemer. BA in Bus. Adminstrn., Iowa State U., 1984; MBA, Creighton U., 1994. Asst. project dir. Information Resources, Inc., Chgo., 1984-85, assoc. project dir., 1985, project dir., 1985-86, sr. project dir., 1986, acct. exec., 1987; assoc. product mgr. ConAgra Frozen Foods, Omaha, 1987-89, product mgr., 1989-91, sr. product mgr., 1991-93, group product mgr., 1993—. Vol. Children's Hosp., Omaha, 1989-91. Mem. Am. Mktg. Assn., Phi Kappa Phi, Beta Gamma Sigma.

COFFEY, JOANNE CHRISTINE, dietitian; b. Cambridge, Mass., Aug. 18, 1942; d. Timothy Patrick and Helen (Stevens) C. BS in Nutrition, Simmons Coll., 1964, M in Libr. and Info. Sci., 1994; MPH, U. Calif., Berkeley, 1966. Registered dietitian. Dietitian, clin. sect. chief VA Med. Ctr., Manchester, N.H., 1976-80; chief dietetic svc. VA Med. Ctr., Altoona, Pa., 1980-82, Providence, 1982-89; asst. chief dietetic svc. VA Med. Ctr., Boston, 1989—. Mem. Nature Conservancy, Nat. Trust for Hist. Preservation, Smithsonian. Mem. ALA, Am. Dietetic Assn. Democrat. Roman Catholic. Office: VA Med Ctr 150 Huntington Ave Boston MA 02130-4830

COFFEY, KELLY ANN, food products executive; b. Superior, Nebr., June 7, 1954; d. John Gerald and Shirley May (Tincher) C.; m. Dale Edward Graves, Nov. 18, 1983; 1 child, Eric John Graves. BA in Advt., U. Nebr., 1976, MBA in Mktg., 1981. V.p. mktg. TMS Corp., First Fed. Lincoln, Nebr., 1977-82; account exec. Sta. KSYZ, Grand Island, Nebr., 1982-83; assoc. Rasmussen & Assocs. Advt. Agy., Grand Island, 1983-86; sales promotion mgr. Comml. Fed. Savs. & Loan, Omaha, 1986-88; mgr. mktg. svcs. Armour/Con Agra, Omaha, 1988-90; mgr. sales promotion/prodn. ConAgra Frozen Foods, Omaha, 1990—; staff presenter U. Nebr. Entrepreneurial Devel. Series, 1992. Bd. dirs. United Way, Grand Island, 1985, campaign chmn., 1985, loaned exec., 1987, co. campaign co-chair 1994; capt. women's athletic fund drive U. Nebr., Omaha, 1988-93; drive capt. Omaha Girls Inc., 1987, co-chmn., 1989-90, Pathfinder mentor program, 1989-90, pub. rels. com., 1989-93, bd. dirs., 1991-93; bd. dirs. Child Savs. Inst., 1991-93; amb. Gov. of Nebr.'s Women in Samll Bus. Com. Mem. Bus. and Profl. Women (pres. Lincoln chpt. 1983, Young Career Woman 1988), Am. Mktg. Assn. (v.p. membership 1988-90, pres. 1990-91, bd. dirs. 1991-92), Grand Island C. of C. (indsl. devel. com., small bus. coun., judge parade queen pageant/float), Omaha Women's Network Club, Toastmasters (state conv. chmn., past pres.). Republican. Roman Catholic. Home: 4819 Douglas St Omaha NE 68132-3218 Office: ConAgra Frozen Foods 5 Conagra Dr Omaha NE 68102-5005

COFFEY, NANCY ANN, commercial real estate broker, model; b. Palm Springs, Calif.; d. Arthur Johnson and Joan (Hunter) C. BA, Stanford U., MS in Engring. Indsl. real estate broker Coldwell Banker, Houston, 1977-79; comml. broker Coldwell Banker, San Francisco, 1980-87, Cushman & Wakefield, N.Y.C., 1987-90; model Gilla Roos, N.Y.C., 1991—. Active Jr. League, San Francisco, 1981-87, N.Y.C., 1987-92; mem. spl. project bd., mem. Sloan Kettering Cancer Ctr., N.Y.C.

COFFIELD, SHIRLEY A., lawyer; b. Portland, Oreg., Mar. 31, 1945. BA, Willamette U., 1967; MA, U. Wisc.-Madison, 1969; JD, George Washington U., 1974. Bar: D.C. 1975. Formerly ptnr. Baker & Hostetler, Washington; ptnr. Keller & Heckman, Washington, 1994—; adj. prof. internat. econ. law Georgetown U. Law Sch., 1982—. Mem. ABA, Fed. Bar Assn., Am. Soc. Internat. Law, D.C. Bar, Pi Gamma Mu, Phi Delta Phi. Office: Keller & Heckman Ste 500 West 1001 G St NW Washington DC 20001

COFFILL, MARJORIE LOUISE, civic leader; b. Sonora, Calif., June 11, 1917; d. Eric J. and Pearl (Needham) Segerstrom; A.B. with distinction in Social Sci., Stanford U., 1938, M.A. in Edn., 1941; m. William Charles Coffill, Jan. 25, 1948, (dec.); children: William James, Eric John. Asst. mgr. Sonora Abstract & Title Co. (Calif.), 1938-39; mem. dean of women's staff Stanford, 1939-41; social dir. women's campus Pomona Coll., 1941-43, instr. psychology, 1941-43; asst. to field dir. ARC, Lee Moore AFB, Calif., 1944-46; partner Riverbank Water Co., Riverbank and Hughson, Calif., 1950-68. Mem. Tuolumne County Mental Health Adv. Com., 1963-70; mem. central advisory coun. Supplementary Edn. Ctr., Stockton, Calif., 1966-70; mem. advisory com. Columbia Jr. Coll., 1972-89, pres., 1980—; pres. Columbia Found., 1972-74, bd. dirs., 1974-77; mem. Tuolumne County Bicentennial Com., 1974—; active PTA, ARC. Pres., Tuolumne County Rep. Women, 1952—, assoc. mem. Calif. Rep. Central Com., 1950. Trustee Sonora Union High Sch., 1969-73, Salvation Army Tuolumne County, 1973—; bd. dirs. Lung Assn. Valley Lode Counties, 1974—, life 1986—. Recipient Pi Lambda Theta award, 1940, Outstanding Citizen award C. of C., 1974, Citizen of Yr. award, 1987; named to Columbia Coll. Hall of Fame, 1990; named Alumnus of Yr., Sonora Union High Sch., 1994. Mem. AAUW (charter mem. Tuolumne County br., pres. Sonora br. 1965-66). Episcopalian (mem. vestry 1968, 75). Home: 376 Summit Ave Sonora CA 95370-5728

COFFIN, BERTHA LOUISE, telephone company executive; b. Atlanta, Aug. 19, 1919; d. William Wesley and Bertha Louise (Marsh) Mendenhall; m. J. Donald Coffin, Feb. 14, 1943 (dec. Sept. 1978). BA, U. Kans., 1940. Med. technologist Midwest Research Lab., Emporia, Kans., 1940-43; ins. agt. Coffin Ins. Agy., Council Grove, Kans., 1943—, sole owner, mgr., 1978-82; treas. Council Grove Telephone Co., 1947-50, sec.-treas., 1950-78, pres., gen. mgr., chmn. bd., 1978—; del. legis. confs. Nat. Telephone Coop. Assn., 1986, 88, 91, 92, 94, mem. comml. co. com., 1987-91, mem. govt. affairs com., 1991—; bd. dirs. Am. Wireless Comm. Corp., Kans. Telecomm. Assn.; founder, pres. Kans. Personal Comm. Svcs., Ltd., 1995—. Copy preparation for book The Story of the Santa Fe Trail, 1982; author: History of Council Grove Telephone Company, 1991; ann. civic sects. tel. directory. Pres. various lit. clubs, Council Grove, 1945-72; speaker various civic, polit. and religious groups, 1962—; mem. adv. coun. Manhattan Christian Coll., 1983-86, trustee, 1986-92, 93—, chmn., 1991-92. Mem. Kans. Telecom. Assn. (bd. dirs. 1992—), Independent Tel. Pioneers (dir. 1984—). Democrat. Office: PO Box 272 Council Grove KS 66846-0272

COFFIN, JUDY SUE, lawyer; b. Beaumont, Tex., Aug. 17, 1953; d. Richard Wilson and Genie (Mouton) C.; m. Gary P. Scholick, Nov. 10, 1983; children: Jennie Sue, Kate Frances. BA, U. Tex., 1974; JD, So. Meth. U., 1976. Bar: Tex. 1977, Calif. 1982. Atty. NLRB, Tex., 1977-80; shareholder Littler, Mendelson, Fastiff, Tichy & Mathiason, San Francisco, 1980—, also bd. dirs. Office: Littler Mendelson Fastiff Tichy & Mathiason 20th Fl 650 California St San Francisco CA 94108-2693

COFFIN, LORI ANN, desk officer; b. Gardner, Mass., Apr. 26, 1959; d. Leslie Gordon Jr. and Lucille (Allain) C. Dispatcher Rindge (N.H.) Police Dept., 1976-82, Peterborough (N.H.) Police Dept., 1982-89; patrol officer Greenfield (N.H.) Police Dept., 1990-92; desk officer Jaffrey (N.H.) Police Dept., 1992—. Firefighter Rindge Fire Dept., 1986-93; assoc. advisor Pub. Safety Explorer Post #308, Rindge, 1983-86. Mem. N.H. Police Assn., Jaffrey Police Assn. Home: 633 Route 119 Rindge NH 03461-4100 Office: Jaffrey Police Dept 15 River St Jaffrey NH 03452-1313

COFFINDAFFER BURKETT, SANDRA LOUISE, pastoral counselor; b. Marion, Ohio, Jan. 8, 1947; d. Dane Leo Coffindaffer and Thelma Louise (Richardson) Saylor; m. Lester Roger Hudson, July 1973 (div.); m. Gregory Eldon Burkett, Oct. 6, 1990; 1 child, Dane Roger Hudson; 1 stepchild, Chad Gregory Burkett. BS in Home Econs., Ohio U., 1969; MA in Bibl. Counseling, Trinity Seminary, Newbourgh, Ind., 1993. Lic. Christian counselor. Dept. mgr. Lazarus, Columbus, Ohio, 1969-70; tchr. Westerville (Ohio) Schs., 1970-80; dir., counselor Christ the King Ch., Columbus, 1980—; directorship Christ the King, 1988—; internat. speaker on healing the broken-hearted. Author/tchr.: (tng. program) Breakthrough. Pres., program dir. Parents Without Ptnrs., Columbus, 1974-76; sec. Come Alive in '85, Columbus, 1984-85. Mem. Assn. Christian Counselors, Am. Assn. Christian Counselors. Office: Christ the King Counseling 1050 Polaris Pky Columbus OH 43240-2005

COFFINGER, MARALIN KATHARYNE, retired air force officer, consultant; b. Ogden, Iowa, July 5, 1935; d. Cleo Russell and Katharyne Frances (McGovern) Morse. BA, Ariz. State U., 1957, MA, 1961; diploma, Armed Forces Staff Coll., 1972, Nat. War Coll., 1977; postgrad., Inst. for Higher Def. Studies, 1985. Commd. 2nd lt. USAF, 1963, advanced through grades to brig. gen., 1985; base comdr., dep. base comdr. Elmendorf AFB, Anchorage, Alaska, 1977-79; base comdr. Norton AFB, San Bernardino, Calif., 1979-82; chmn. spl. and incentive pays Office of Sec. Def., Pentagon, Washington, 1982-83; dep. dir. pers. programs USAF Hdqrs., Pentagon, Washington, 1983-85; command dir. NORAD, Combat Ops., Cheyenne Mountain Complex, Colo., 1985-86; dir. pers. plans USAF Hdqrs., Pentagon, Washington, 1986-89; ret. USAF, 1989. Key note speaker, mem., dedication ceremonies Vietnam Meml. Com., Phoenix, 1990; mem. sheriff's exec. posse Maricopa County. Decorated Air Force D.S.M., Def. Superior Svc. medal, Legion of Merit, Bronze Star.; recipient Nat. Medal of Merit. Mem. NAFE, Air Force Assn. (vet./retiree coun., pres. Sky Harbor chpt. 1990), Nat. Officers Assn., Ret. Officers Assn., Internat. Platform Assn., Maricopa County Sheriff's Exec. Posse, Ariz. State U. Alumni Assn. (Profl. Excellence award 1981). Roman Catholic. Home: 8531 E San Bruno Dr Scottsdale AZ 85258-2577

COFFMAN, JENNIFER B., federal judge; b. 1948. BA, U. Ky., 1969, MA, 1971, JD, 1978. Ref. libr. Newport News (Va.) Pub. Libr., 1972-74, U. Ky., 1974-76; atty. Law Offices Arthur L. Brooks, Lexington, Ky., 1978-82; ptnr. Brooks, Coffman and Fitzpatrick, Lexington, 1982-92, Newberry, Hargrove & Rambicure, Lexington, 1992-93; judge U.S. Dist. Ct. (ea. dist.) Ky., London, 1993—; adj. prof. Coll. Law, U. Ky., 1979-81. Bd. dirs. YWCA Lexington, 1986-92; elder, chair stewardship com. Second Presbyn. Ch., 1993. Mem. ABA, Ky. Bar Assn., Fayette County Bar Assn., U. Ky. Alumni Assn. Office: 207 US Courthouse 300 S Main St London KY 40741

COFFMAN, (ANNA) LOUISE M., retired elementary education educator; b. Turlock, Calif., Aug. 11, 1924; d. Christopher Ezekial and Annie Laurie (Curtice) Mann; m. Dean Wilton Coffman, Feb. 10, 1945; children: Dane Wilbur, Nancy J. Coffman Hildreth, Janet L. Coffman Dempsey. AA,

Modesto Jr. Coll., 1944; BS, Millersville State U., 1961; MEd, Western Md. Coll., 1966. Elem. tchr. Laird Sch. Stanislaus County, Modesto, Calif., 1944-45; tchr. 4th grade Cen. Sch. Dist., York, Pa., 1957-66; tchr. 3d grade Spring Grove (Pa.) Sch. Dist., 1966-84, ret., 1984; part-time tchr. Grace Acad. Christian Discipleship, York, 1985—; free-lance writer, 1979—; columnist "Notes From the Country," York Sunday News, 1977-88. Vol. Bell Shelter, York, 1985—, Access-Shelter for Abused Women, York, 1985—; tchr. rep. ARC, York, 1966-84; v.p. women's fellowship St. Paul's-Wolf's United Ch. of Christ, York, 1990-92, editor newsletter, mem. consistory; del. Pa. Ctrl. Conf., 1995. Mem. AAUW (sec. Invest-Hers group 1994-95), Women in Comm., Inc., Delta Kappa Gamma (Eta chpt., parliamentarian 1987-89, 2d v.p. 1990-92). Republican. Mem. United Ch. of Christ. Home: 3897 Barachel Dr York PA 17402

COFFMAN, ORENE BURTON, hotel executive; b. Fluvanna, Va., Mar. 13, 1938; d. John C. and Adele (Melton) Burton; m. John H. Emerson, Aug. 5, 1955 (div. 1972); 1 child, Norman Jay; m. Mack H. Coffman, Oct. 26, 1986. Degree in hotel and motel mgmt., Michigan State U., 1966-70. Cert. hotel mgr., Mich. State U., 1970. Telephone operator Colonial Williamsburg (Va.) Hotel, 1962-64; room clk. Colonial Williamsburg (Va.) Hotel, 1964-68; mgr. front office Colonial Williamsburg (Va.) Hotel, 1968-83; asst. mgr. Williamsburg Inn, 1983—; pres. Colonial Williamsburg Employees Fed. Credit Union, 1980-85. Mem. Am. Hotel Motel Assn. (nat. acctg. award 1970). Democrat. Baptist. Office: Williamsburg Inn PO Box B Williamsburg VA 23187-3704

COFFMAN, WILMA MARTIN, women's health nurse, educator; b. Washington County, Tenn., Dec. 29, 1939; d. Oval Earnest and Buena (Light) Martin; m. Niles Lee Coffman, Aug. 26, 1961; children: Stephen Lee, Ruth Marie, Andrew William. BSN, East Tenn. State U., 1962; MS, U. Tenn., Knoxville, 1987. RN, Tenn. Staff nurse in maternal-child health Holston Valley Hosp. and Med. Ctr., Kingsport, Tenn.; instr. Kingsport City Schs., Johnson City Schs. Organist, pianist Beulah Bapt. Ch., Greenvale Bapt. Ch. Mem. Toonie Cash Evangelist Assn., Pi Lambda Theta. Home: 410 Lakeridge St Kingsport TN 37663-3760

COGAN, KAREN DIANE, psychologist educator; b. Redondo Beach, Calif., Sept. 20, 1963; d. William Dean and Betsy Alice (Rosselot) C.; m. Trent Anthony Petrie, Sept. 2, 1989. BA in Psyhology, UCLA, 1985, MS in Kinesiology, 1987; PhD in Psychology, Ohio State U., 1991. Lic. psychologist, Tex. Intern psychology U. Calif., San Diego, 1990-91; psychologist So. Meth. Univ., Dallas, 1991-92; prof., psychologist U. North Tex., Denton, 1992—; pvt. practice Denton, 1992—; cons. sport psychology U. North Tex. and other univs., 1988—. Mem. APA (counseling divsn., sport psychology divsn.), Assn. for Advancement of Applied Sport Psychology (cert. cons.). Home: 2212 Brooklake W Denton TX 76207 Office: Univ North Tex Testing Ctr PO Box 13487 Denton TX 76203

COGGIN, CHARLOTTE JOAN, cardiologist, educator; b. Takoma Park, Md., Aug. 6, 1928; d. Charles Benjamin and Nanette (McDonald) Coggin; BA, Columbia Union Coll., 1948; MD, Loma Linda U., 1952, MPH, 1987; D in Sci. (hon.), Andrews U., 1994. Intern, Los Angeles County Gen. Hosp., Los Angeles, 1952-53, resident in medicine, 1953-55; fellow in cardiology Children's Hosp., Los Angeles, 1955-56, White Meml. Hosp., Los Angeles., 1955-56; research assoc. in cardiology, house physician Hammersmith Hosp., London, 1956-57; resident in pediatrics and pediatric cardiology Hosp. for Sick Children, Toronto, Ont., Can., 1965-67; cardiologist, co-dir. heart surgery team Loma Linda (Calif.) U., asst. prof. medicine , 1961-73, assoc. prof., 1973-91, prof. medicine, 1991—, asst. dean Sch. Medicine Internat. Programs, 1973-75, assoc. dean, 1975—, spl. asst. to univ. pres. for internat. affairs, 1991, co-dir., cardiologist heart surgery team missions to Pakistan and Asia, 1963, Greece, 67, 69, Saigon, Vietnam, 1974, 75, to Saudi Arabia, 1976-87, People's Republic China, 1984, 89-91, Hong Kong, 1985, Zimbabwe, 1988, Kenya, 1988, Nepal, 1992, 93, China, 1992, Zimbabwe, 1993; mem. Pres's. Advisory Panel on Heart Disease, 1972—; hon. prof. U. Manchuria, Harbin, People's Republic China, 1989, hon. dir. 1st People's Hosp. of Mundanjiang, Heilongjiang Province, 1989. Apptd. mem. Med. Quality Rev. Com.-Dist. 12, 1976-80. Recipient award for service to people of Pakistan City of Karachi, 1963, Medallion award Evangelismos Hosp., Athens, Greece, 1967, Gold medal of health South Vietnam Ministry of Health, 1974, Charles Elliott Weinger award for excellence, 1976, Wall Street Jour. Achievement award, 1987, Disting. Univ. Svc. award Loma Linda U., 1990; named Honored Alumnus Loma Linda U. Sch. Medicine, 1973, Outstanding Women in Gen. Conf. Seventh-day Adventists, 1975, Alumnus of Yr., Columbia Union Coll., 1984. Diplomate Am. Bd. Pediatrics. Mem. Am. Coll. Cardiology, AMA (physicians adv. com. 1969—) Calif. Med. Assn. (com. on med. schs., com. on member services), San Bernardino County Med. Soc. (chmn. communications com. 1975-77, mem. communications com. 1987-88, editor bull. 1975-76), Am. Heart Assn., AAUP, Med. Research Assn. Calif., Calif. Heart Assn., AAUW, Am. Acad. Pediatrics, World Affairs Council, Internat. Platform Assn., Calif. Museum Sci. and Industry MUSES (Outstanding Woman of Year in Sci. 1969), Am. Med. Women's Assn., Loma Linda Sch. Medicine Alumni Assn. (pres. 1978), Alpha Omega Alpha, Delta Omega. Author: Atrial Septal Defects, motion picture (Golden Eagle Cine award and 1st prize Venice Film Festival 1964); contbr. articles to med. jours. Democrat. Home: 11495 Benton St Loma Linda CA 92354-3682 Office: Loma Linda U Magan Hall Rm 105 11060 Anderson St Loma Linda CA 92350

COGGINS, REBECCA LEONIA, accountant; b. Greenville, S.C., Dec. 26, 1951; d. Harry E. and Hazel L. (Edwards) C. BA in Econ. and Bus. Adminstrn., Furman U., 1974; MBA, Clemson/Furman U., 1981. CPA, S.C. Pers. asst. County of Greenville, 1974-75, asst. pers. dir., 1975-81, pers. dir., 1981-84; alumni dir. Furman U., Greenville, 1984-88; acct. Saunders & Co., CPAs, Simpsonville, S.C., 1988-91, Bradshaw, Gordon & Clinkscales, Greenville, 1991-93; supr. Elliott Davis & Co., Greenville, 1994—. Mem. Inst. Mgmt. Accts., Am. Soc. Women Accts. (most valuable mem. 1993), Greenville C. of C. (leadership Greenville class XX 1993-94), Foothills Quilting Guild (treas. 1994—). Home: 120 Keith Dr Greenville SC 29607

COGGS-JONES, ELIZABETH, county official; b. Milw., Dec. 2, 1956; d. Isaac N. and Marcia P. Coggs; m. Wendell Jones; children: Priscilla, Chloe, Devona. Student, U. Wis., Milw. Milw. County Dem. com.-woman 6th Aldermanic Dist.; 10th dist. supr. Milw. County Bd., 1988—; mem. fin. com. Milw. County Bd., mem. human needs and svcs., mem. pks., recreation and cultural com., mem. com. on coms., former mem. long term support planning, re-apportionment/re-districting com.; chair Combined Community Svcs. Bd., 1988—, Commn. Handicapped and Disabled Persons, 1988-90, Milw. County South African Pension Divestment Task Force Commn., 1990—, Housing & Community Devel., Social Devel. Commn., 1993—. Vol. United Negro Coll. Fund; mem. PTA Brown St. Acad., Milw. Edn. Ctr.; past mem. Task Force Children's Ct. Ctr., Preschool to 5th Grade Adv. Coun., North Divsn. Neighborhood Ujima Housing Coop. Team, Habitat Humanity, Hon. Com. Pres. Carter Project, Inner City Arts Coun., Gov.'s Adv. Bd. Bicycle Safety; past chair Prevention Task Force Fighting Back, Social Ministry Com., Downtown Child Care Devel. Adv. Com., TEACH Adv. Coun.; former chair adv. bd. Welfare Alternative Project; former v.p. Harambee Ombudsman Project, Inc.; active Dem. Party-North Side Unit, Girl Scouts Milw. Area, Inc., various local, state and nat. civil rights campaigns and issues; former bd. dirs. East Side Housing Action Coalition, Inc. Mem. Orgn. Black County Ofcls., Wis. Counties Assn. Bd., Nat. Assn. Counties (mem. steering com. on employment 1988-93). Address: 901 N 9th St Milwaukee WI 53233-1425

COGNETTO, ANNA MARIE, social worker; b. Herkimer, N.Y., May 25, 1957; d. Anthony N. and Margaret J. (Williams) C. AS with honors, Herkimer County C.C., 1977; BS with honors, Cornell U., 1979; MSW, Syracuse U., 1981. Cert. social worker, N.Y.; diplomate in clin. social work. Social worker The Ctr. for Youth Svcs., Rochester, N.Y., 1981-82; psychiat. social worker Rockland Children's Psychiat. Ctr., Newburgh, N.Y., 1982-88; pvt. practice Poughkeepsie, N.Y., 1983—; social worker CHP Alcohol Clinic, Poughkeepsie, 1988-90; social worker II Dutchess City Dept. Mental Hygiene, Poughkeepsie, 1990-92; adj. lectr. Dutchess C.C., Poughkeepsie, 1985—; social worker, evaluator N.Y. State DWI Program, Poughkeepsie, 1991—; guest lectr. Sanctuary/N.Y. State Spl. Edn. Tng. Resource Ctr., Poughkeepsie, 1993—; cons. Hudson Valley Cons., Poughkeepsie, 1993—. Mem. NASW, Am. Bd. Clin. Social Workers (diplomate), Chronic Fatigue and Immune Dysfunction Syndrome Assn. Am., N.Y. Assn. Social Workers (gay and lesbian issues com. 1994—). Office: 24 Davis Ave Poughkeepsie NY 12603-2408

COHAN, CAROLE, advertising agency executive. Former v.p. and exec. v.p. Saatchi & Saatchi Compton, Inc., N.Y.C.; now sr. v.p. and broadcast creative dir. McCann-Erickson N.Y., N.Y.C. Office: McCann-Erickson NY 750 3d Ave New York NY 10017

COHEN, ANNETTE LOUISE, nurse; b. Bangor, Maine, Apr. 13, 1955; d. Kelsey Eugene and Nancy Eva (Bolduc) Patten; m. Edward Vincent Callahan, Jr., July 8, 1979 (div. Apr. 1991); m. Gerald Cohen, July 16, 1994. Grad., St. Mary's Sch. Nursing, Lewiston, Maine, 1978. LPN, Maine. Staff nurse St. Mary's Hosp., Lewiston, Maine, 1978-90, St. Joseph's Hosp., Bangor, 1980-87; pvt. duty nurse New Eng. Home Health Care, Bangor, 1990—; staff nurse Elizabeth Levinson Ctr., Bangor, 1992—. Vol. fund-raiser United Cerebral Palsy, Bangor, 1987—. Mem. Maine State Employee's Assn. Home: 219 Center St Brewer ME 04412

COHEN, AUDREY C., college president; b. May 14; d. Abe and Esther (Morgan) C.; children: Dawn Jennifer, Winifred Alisa. BA magna cum laude, U. Pitts., 1953; postgrad. in polit. sci. and edn. George Washington U., 1957-58; DHL (hon.), U. New Eng., 1988; D of Sci. (hon.), Coll. Human Svcs., 1988. Founder, pres. Part-Time Rsch. Assocs., 1958-64; exec. dir. Women's Talent Corps., 1964-68; founder, pres. Audrey Cohen Coll (formerly Coll. Human Svcs.), N.Y.C., 1964—; creator of new entry level career categories Audrey Cohen Coll., 1964; participant pres. owner mgmt. program Harvard Grad. Sch. Bus. Adminstrn., 1982; lectr. in field; cons. Commn. Occupational Status Women in Nat. Vocat. Guidance Assn.; founder Am. Coun. Human Svcs., 1974; key speaker X Triennial Conf. Internat. Assn. U. Pres., Kobe, Japan, 1993. Developer ednl. paradigm Purpose-Centered System of Edn., 1970-74; speaker in field; contbr. articles to profl. jours.; adv. bd. Glamour Mag.'s Woman of Yr. Awards, 1990-91. Active subcom. higher edn. N.Y.C. Partnership; chmn. Com. on Yr. 2000, N.Y. World Future Soc.; nat. adv. com. Horizons-Bicentennial Commn.; mem. planning com. Hemispheric Congress Women, Miami, Fla., 1975-76; chairperson Nat. Task Force on Women, Edn. and Work, 1975; active Manhattan Borough Pres.'s Adv. Com. on Health Careers for Disadvantaged, Pub. Edn. Assn. Project for Restructured Edn. System N.Y.C.; mem. exec. com. Assn. Better N.Y. Recipient Stanley M. Isaacs award Am. Jewish Com., 1959, George Champion award Chase Manhattan Bank, 1970, Disting. Vis. prof. award U. Mass., 1975, Ednl. Devel. Cert. of Achievement award Atlantic Richfield Co., 1979; Otty award Our Town newspaper, 1981; Mina Shaughnessy scholarship award U.S. Office Edn., 1983; Empire State award, 1984-85; Outstanding Leadership in Higher Edn. award Commn. Ind. Colls. and Univs., 1984-85; Giraffe Club award, 1989; Pres.'s award Nat. Orgn. Human Svcs. Edn., 1993; Anti-bias award Nat. Westminister Bancorp and N.Y.C. Job and Career Ctr., 1993; named in a Commending Resolution N.Y. State Legis., 1994. Mem. Support Services Alliance, Inc. (bd. dirs.), Fin. Women's Assn., Am. Jewish Com. (exec. com., bd. dirs.), Council Higher Edn. Instns. Clubs: Economic, Harvard, Lotos, Women's Forum. Home: 37 E 67th St New York NY 10021-5929 Office: Audrey Cohen Coll Office of the President 345 Hudson St New York NY 10014-4502

COHEN, BARBARA ANN, artist; b. Milw., Feb. 18, 1953; d. Joseph and Irene Marion (Brown) C. BS in Art, U. Wis., 1975. One-woman shows include 1st Wis. Nat. Bank, 1981; exhibited in group shows at San Francisco State, 1975-76, Comprehensive Employment Tng. Act, Milw., 1979, San Dieguito Art Guild, 1981, Imperial Valley Art Show, 1982, La Jolla Light Photo Contest, 1986, Clairemont Art Guild, 1993. Recipient 1st Pl. award for oil painting Imperial Valley Art Show. Mem. Clairemont Art Guild. Democrat. Jewish. Home: 6455 La Jolla Blvd # 357 La Jolla CA 92037

COHEN, BONNIE R., government official; b. Brockton, Mass., Dec. 11, 1942; d. Harold I. and Irma (Sims) Rubenstein; m. Louis R. Cohen, Sept. 29, 1965; children: Amanda, Eli. BA, Smith Coll., 1964; EdM, Harvard U., 1965; MBA, Harvard Bus. Sch., 1967. Analyst RMC, Inc., Washington, 1967-71; asst. to vice supt. Washington Pub. Schs., 1971-72; sr. cons. Levin & Assocs., Washington, 1972-76; treas. UMWA Funds, Washington, 1976-81; advisor Stanford U. Treas., Palo Alto, Calif., 1981; sr. v.p. Nat. Trust for Historic Preservation, Washington, 1981-93; asst. sec. of interior Dept. of the Interior, Washington, 1993—; trustee ARC Retirement System, Washington, 1986-89; investment chair DC Retirement System, 1984-87. Bd. dirs. Beauvoir Sch., Washington, 1985-88, Nat. Cathedral Sch., Washington, 1985-88, Environ. Defense Fund, Washington, 1982-86, Ctr. for Marine Conservation, Washington, 1987-93. Mem. City Club. Democrat. Home: 3060 Garrison St NW Washington DC 20008-1050 Office: Dept of the Interior 1849 C St NW Washington DC 20240-0001

COHEN, CARLA LYNN, publisher; b. N.Y.C., Feb. 27, 1937; d. Barnet and Florence (Skolnick) Ellowis; children—Beth Diane, Jeffrey. Student Clark U., Adelphi U. Editor, Oceanside (N.Y.) Beacon, 1975-77; adminstrv. asst. pub. relations Bd. Suprs. Nassau County, 1977-78; pres. Carla Cohen Communications, Oceanside, N.Y., pres. Cotar Publs., Nassau Borders Papers, Floral Park, N.Y., 1981—; editor Voters Guide, Lawrence, N.Y., 1979-80. Grand Marshall Meml. Day parade, 1986; panelist weekly Town Meeting radio talk show Sta. WGBB. Recipient Patriotic Service award VFW, 1976; Outstanding Achievement award Am. Cancer Soc., 1976-77; Pub. Service award USAF, 1983; named Woman of Yr., B'nai B'rith, 1985, Sons of Italy, 1985, Businessperson of the Yr. Nassau County Coun. C. of C., 1989-90. Mem. C. of C. (v.p. 1982—), LWV (v.p. 1979), Internat. Platform Assn. Republican. Jewish. Office: PO Box 155 Franklin Square NY 11010-0513

COHEN, CLAUDIA, journalist; b. Englewood, N.J., Dec. 16, 1950; d. Robert B. and Harriet (Brandwein) C. BA, U. Pa., 1972. Mng. editor The Daily Pennsylvanian; with More Mag., N.Y.C., 1973-76, mng. editor, 1976-77; reporter N.Y. Post, N.Y.C., 1977-78, editor Page Six, 1978-80; daily columnist N.Y. Daily News, N.Y.C., 1980-81; TV entertainment reporter Live with Regis and Kathie Lee, Sta. WABC-TV, 1983—, Eyewitness News, WABC 1984-89. Trustee Sch. of Arts and Scis., U. Pa.; mem. adv. bd. N.Y. Hosp. Cornell Med. Ctr. Office: Sta WABC 7 Lincoln Square Plz New York NY 10023-5998

COHEN, CONNIE POLLACK, artist, social worker; b. Phila., Nov. 1, 1933; d. Jacob Kugelman and Ruth Brill Kugelman Pollack; stepfather, Herbert H. Pollack; m. Kenneth Richard Frankl, Sept. 2, 1955 (div. Sept. 1965); 1 child, Keith Evan; m. Richard Warren Cohen, June 3, 1966; stepchildren: Daniel Arthur, Lisa Cohen Lowy. BA, Smith Coll., 1955. Artist, 1945—; art tchr. pvt., N.Y.C. and Scottsdale, Ariz., 1992-93; represented by Images Art Gallery, N.Y.C., Internat. Design Corp., Washington. Exhibited in solo shows at Arsenal Gallery, N.Y.C., 1976, Gallery Madison 90, N.Y.C., 1984, Ward Nasse Gallery, N.Y.C., 1984, Graham Hall Gallery/Smith Coll., Northampton, Mass., 1985, Spaso House Gallery, Moscow, 1989, Elaine Benson Gallery, Bridgehampton, N.Y., 1989, Images Show, 1995, also numerous group shows; sculptor and photographer; author articles. Founding dir., pres. Friends of P.S. 169, The R.F. Kennedy Sch., N.Y.C., 1958-90; mem. youth and the law com. Women's City Club, N.Y.C., 1956-59; mem. Task Force to Revise Spl. Edn. in N.Y.C., 1982-84; mem. Chancellors Adv. Com. Spl. Edn., 1980-85. Mem. N.Y. Soc. Women Artists (bd. dirs., rec. sec.), N.Y. Artists Equity Assn., Katonah Gallery Mus. Art (exhibiting mem.). Home: 1125 Park Ave New York NY 10128

COHEN, CYNTHIA MARYLYN, lawyer; b. Bklyn., Sept. 5, 1945. AB, Cornell U., 1967; JD cum laude, NYU, 1970. Bar: N.Y. 1971, U.S. Ct. Appeals (2d cir.) 1972, U.S. Supreme Ct. 1975, U.S. Dist. Ct. (so. and ea. dists.) N.Y. 1972, (cen. and no. dists.) Calif. 1980, U.S. Ct. Appeals (9th cir.) 1980, U.S. Dist. Ct. (so. dist.) Calif. 1981, U.S. Dist. Ct. (ea. dist.) Calif. 1986. Assoc. Simpson Thacher & Bartlett, N.Y.C., 1970-76, Kaye, Scholer, Fierman, Hayes & Handler, N.Y.C., 1976-80; assoc. Stutman, Treister & Glatt, P.C., L.A., 1980-81, ptnr., 1981-87; ptnr. Hughes Hubbard & Reed, N.Y.C. and L.A., 1987-93, Morgan, Lewis & Bockius, L.A., Phila., N.Y.C., 1993—. Bd. dirs. N.Y. chpt. Am. Cancer Soc., 1977-80. Recipient Am. Jurisprudence award for evidence, torts and legal instns., 1968-69; John Norton Pomeroy scholar NYU, 1968-70, Founders Day Cert., 1969. Mem. ABA (antitrust and litigation sects.), Assn. of Bar of City of N.Y. (trade regulations com. 1976-79), L.A. County Bar Assn. (antitrust, comml. law and bankruptcy sects.), Assn. Bus. Trial Lawyers, Fin. Lawyers Conf., N.Y. State Bar Assn. (chmn. class-action com. 1979), State Bar Calif. (antitrust and bus. law sects.), Delta Gamma, Order of Coif. Home: 4818 Bonvue Ave Los Angeles CA 90027-1105 Office: Morgan Lewis & Bockius 801 S Grand Ave Fl 22 Los Angeles CA 90017-4613

COHEN, D. ASHLEY, clinical psychologist, assessment specialist; b. Omaha, Oct. 2, 1952; d. Cenek and Dorothy A. (Bilek) Hrabik; m. Donald I. Cohen, 1968 (div. 1976); m. Lyn J. Mangiameli, June 12, 1985. BA in Psychology, U. Nebr., Omaha, 1975, MA in Psychology, 1979; PhD in Clin. Psychology, Calif. Coast U., 1988. Lic. psychologist, Calif.; lic. marriage and family therapist, Nev.; cert. substance abuse counselor, Nev. Team mgr. Ea. Nebr. Human Svcs. Agy., 1976-79; family specialist Ea. Nebr. Human Svcs. Agy. Consultation & Edn., 1979-80; psychotherapist Washoe Tribe, Gardnerville, Nev., 1980; therapist Family Counseling Svc., Carson City, Nev., 1980-93; psychotherapist Alpine County Mental Health, Markleeville, Calif., 1981-89, dir., 1990-93; psychologist Golden Gate Med. Examiners, San Francisco, 1993—; conf. presenter and spkr. in field; presenter rsch. findings 7th European Conf. Personality, Madrid, 1994, Oxford (Eng.) U. ISSID Conf., 1991; site coord. nat. standardization Kaufmann brief intelligence test A.G.S., 1988-90. Vol. EMT, Alpine County, 1983-93. Recipient Svc. to Youth award Office Edn., 1991. Mem. APA, Internat. Neuropsychol. Soc., Internat. Soc. Study Individual Differences, Am. Psychol. Soc., Western Psychol. Assn., Calif. Psychol. Assn., Am. Critical Incident Stress Found. Office: PO Box 60501 Sunnyvale CA 94088-0501

COHEN, DIANA LOUISE, mental health administrator, psychology, educator, psychotherapist; b. Phila., Apr. 8, 1942; d. Nathan and Dorothy (Rubin) Blasberg; m. Jules L. Frankel, July 3, 1987; 1 child, Jennifer. BA, Temple U., 1964, MEd, 1969. Lic. psychologist, Pa., N.J.; nat. cert. mental health counselor. Caseworker Phila. Gen. Hosp., 1964-69, staff psychologist, 1969-70; staff psychologist Atlantic Mental Health Ctr., McKee City, N.J., 1970-80, unit dir., 1980-87, v.p. profl. svcs., 1987-91; pvt. practice Pa., N.J., 1991—; mem. adj. faculty Glassboro (N.J.) State Coll., 1988—; community mediator Community Justice Inst., Atlantic County, N.J., 1990—. Com. chmn. Atlantic County Commn. for Missing and Abused Children, 1984-89. Grantee N.J. Dept. Edn., 1988-89, N.J. Job Tng. Partnership Act, 1990. Mem. AACD, APA (assoc.), Pa. Psychol. Assn., N.J. Psychol. Assn. (assoc.). Home: 569 Gravelly Run Rd Mays Landing NJ 08330-1654 Office: 2106 New Rd Linwood NJ 08221 also: 1718 Welsh Rd Philadelphia PA 19115

COHEN, ELAINE HELENA, pediatrician, pediatric cardiologist; b. Boston, Oct. 14, 1941; d. Samuel Clive and Lillian (Stocklan) C.; m. Marvin Leon Gale, May 7, 1972; 1 child, Pamela Beth Gale. AB, Conn. Coll., 1963; postgrad., Tufts U., 1963-64; MD, Med. Coll. Pa., 1969. Diplomate Am. Bd. Pediats. Intern in pediats. Children's Hosp. of L.A., 1969-70, resident in pediats., 1970-71; fellow in pediat. cardiology UCLA Ctr. Health Scis., 1971-72, L.A. County/U. So. Calif. Med. Ctr., L.A., 1972-74; pediatrician Children's Med. Group of South Bay, Chula Vista, Calif., 1974—; clin. instr. dept. pediats. UCLA Sch. Medicine, 1971-72, U. So. Calif., L.A., 1972-74; clin. asst. prof. dept. pediats. U. Calif., San Diego, 1974—, preceptor dept. pediats., 1992-94. Fellow Am. Acad. Pediats.; mem. Calif. Med. Assn., San Diego County Med. Soc. Office: Children's Med Group South Bay 280 E St Chula Vista CA 91910

COHEN, ELIZABETH ANN, construction worker; b. Queens Astoria, N.Y., July 18, 1960; d. Kenneth Walter and Ina Pauline (Beutel) C. BMus cum laude, Crane Sch. Music, Potsdam, N.Y., 1982; studied with Elly Ameling, Munich, 1984; MS, C.W. Post Coll., 1989. Tchr. music BOCES II, Patchogue, N.Y., 1984-86, Massapequa Sch. Dist., Massapequa Park, N.Y., 1988-89; steamfitter Local 638, 1989—. Recital tour, Germany, 1984. Republican. Lutheran. Home: PO Box 567 Shawnee On Delaware PA 18356

COHEN, ELIZABETH G., education and sociology educator, researcher; b. Worcester, Mass., May 1, 1931; d. Jacob and Anita (Asher) Ginsburg; m. Bernard P. Cohen, Sept. 20, 1953; children: Anita Cohen Williams, Lewis Samuel. B.A., Clark U., Worcester, 1953; M.A., Harvard U., 1955, Ph.D., 1958. Lectr. sociology Boston U., 1957-58; lectr. sociology and edu. Stanford U., 1962-66, asst. prof., 1966-69, assoc. prof., 1969-75, prof., 1975—, dir. Environ. for Teaching, 1970-76, chmn. social sci. in edu., 1970-93, dir. program for complex instruction, 1982—. Author: A New Approach to Applied Research, 1968, Designing Groupwork: Strategies for Heterogeneous Classrooms, 2d edit., 1994; contbr. chpts. in books and articles in field to profl. jours. Trustee Clark U., 1986—. Woodrow Wilson fellow, 1954-55; AAUW fellow, 1956-57; Fulbright fellow, 1972. Mem. Pacific Sociol. Assn. (v.p. 1981-82), Sociology of Edn. Assn. (v.p. 1982-83), Am. Sociol. Assn. (sect. chmn. 1979-80), Am. Ednl. Research Assn., Sociol. Research Assn. Democrat. Jewish. Home: 851 Sonoma Ter Palo Alto CA 94305-1024 Office: Stanford Univ Sch Of Edn Palo Alto CA 94305

COHEN, ESTA HARRIS, calligrapher and educator; b. Bklyn., Mar. 24, 1940; d. Louis and Dorothy (Soloff) Harris; m. George M. Cohen, Oct. 8, 1972; children: Nathan Michael, Rachel Susan. BA U. Mass., 1961. Tchr. Fairfield (Conn.) Sch. System, 1961-65; tchr. White Plains (N.Y.) Schs., 1965-69; asst. prin. White Plaine (N.Y.) Schs., 1969-73; tchr. calligraphy White Plains Adult Edn., 1980—; owner Esta Cohen Calligraphy, White Plains, 1980—; cons. in field. Bd. dirs. Student Advocacy, White Plains, 1991; mem. Com. on Handicapped, Elmsford, N.Y., 1984-91. Mem. Soc. Scribes, Westchester Calligraphers Guild. Democrat. Jewish. Home and office: 22 Lenroc Dr White Plains NY 10607-2420

COHEN, FRANCES DOROTHY, volunteer; b. Cin., July 31, 1927; d. Israel and Rebecca Lehrner; m. Stanley Cohen, Dec. 16, 1951; children: Ronald Alan, Martha Anne. BS in Applied Arts, U. Cin., 1950. Active Friends of U. Cin. Coll. Conservatory of Music Fund Raiser, 1994; chair Big Sale VIII and IX, Cin. Art Mus., 1993, mem. capital campaign steering com. and cmty. chair, 1991, chair membership subcom., 1988—, docent, 1990—, gallery aide, 1986; trustee U. Cin. Found., 1993—, many other activities. Recipient Fanny Smith award Cin. Art Mus., 1993, Vol. award WCET, 1982, 87, 91, Trustees' award U. Cin., 1994; named Enquirer Woman of Yr., 1987, Woman of Yr. N.E. Suburban Life, 1984; honoree ORT Bonds for Israel, 1978. Home: 2301 Royal Oak Ct Cincinnati OH 45237

COHEN, HELEN HERZ, camp owner, director; b. N.Y.C., Oct. 29, 1912; d. Fred W. and Florence (Hirsch) H.; m. Albert F. Schliefer, Sept. 22, 1933 (dec. Nov. 1941); m. Edwin S. Cohen, Aug. 31, 1944; children: Edwin C., Roger, Wendy. PhB, Brown U., 1933; MA, Columbia U., 1934; postgrad., NYU, Columbia. Counselor Camp Walden, Denmark, Maine, 1930-38, owner, 1939—; tchr. social studies Alcuin Prep. Sch., 1935; office mgr. Lewis P. Weil Importer, 1935-40; founder, pres. Main Idea, Inc., 1969—. Active alumni coun. Pembroke Coll., 1960; chmn. camp divns. Bridgton (Maine) Hosp. Fund, 1962—; trustee Fund for Advancement Camping, 1980-90. Recipient Gold Key award Columbia Scholastic Press, 1972, award Fund for Advancement of Camping Patron, 1982. Mem. Am. Camping Assn. (regional bd. dirs. 1947-50, 52-55, 56-59, 60-63, standards visitor 1957-93, chmn. pvt. camps 1961, bd. dirs. 1963—, v.p. N.Y. 1963-75, Va. sect. 1975), Pioneers of Camping, Maine Camp Dirs. Assn. (legis. com. 1960-63, bd. dirs. 1963—, Halsey Gulick award 1991), Pembroke Coll. Club (co-founder), Cosmopolitan Club, Cornell Club, Farmington Country Club, Boar's Head Sports Club. Home: Ednam Forest 104 Stuart Pl Charlottesville VA 22903-4740 Office: Camp Walden Berry Rd Denmark ME 04022-9708

COHEN, HOLLACE T., lawyer; b. Bklyn., May 10, 1948; d. Benjamin Carl and Esther (Abramowitz) Topol; m. Steven L. Cohen, June 22, 1969; children: Harlan Grant, Lauren Cecily. BA, CCNY, 1969; JD, NYU, 1972. Bar: N.Y. 1973. Assoc. Whitman & Ransom, N.Y.C., 1972-81, ptnr., 1981—. Mem. ABA, Am. Bankruptcy Inst., N.Y. State Bar Assn., Assn. Bar City N.Y., Sky Club. Office: Whitman Breed Abbott Morgan 200 Park Ave New York NY 10166

COHEN, IDA BOGIN (MRS. SAVIN COHEN), import and export executive; b. Bklyn.; d. Joseph and Yetta (Harris) Bogin; student St. Johns U.; B.S., N.Y.U.; m. Barnet Gaster, June 26, 1941 (div. May 1955); m. 2d, Savin Cohen, Aug. 30, 1964. Sec.-treas. J. Gerber & Co., Inc., N.Y.C., 1942-54, v.p., dir., 1954-73; pres., dir. Austracan U.S.A., Inc., N.Y.C., 1960-73; v.p. Parts Warehouse, Inc., Woodside, N.Y., 1970-72, sec.-treas., 1972-83; also engaged in pvt. investments. Contbr. articles to South African Outspan, newspapers. Home: 12 Shorewood Dr Sands Point NY 11050

COHEN, JOYCE E., state senator, investment executive; b. McIntosh, S.D., Mar. 27, 1937; d. Joseph and Evelyn (Sampson) Petik; children: Julia Jo, Aaron J. Grad., Coll. Med. Tech., Minn., 1955; student, UCLA, 1957-58, Santa Ana Coll., 1957-62. Med. rsch. technician dept. surgery U. Minn., 1955-58; dept. immunology UCLA, 1958-59; dept. bacteriology U. Calif., 1959-61; med. rsch. scientist Allergan Pharms., Santa Ana, Calif., 1961-70; ptnr. Co-Fo Investments, Lake Oswego, Oreg., 1978-84; mem. Oreg. Ho. of Reps., 1979-81, Oreg. State Senate, 1983-94. Chmn. trade amd econ. devel., govt. reorgn. and reinvention com., senate judiciary com.; mem. senate revenue and sch. fin. com.; vice-chair agr. & natural resources com., health care & bio-ethics com.; mem. bus., housing & fin. com., rules com.; co-chair joint task force on lottery oversight; mem. joint com. on asset forfeiture oversight adv.; mem. Senate Exec. Appointments; mem. joint com. on land use, alt. joint com. legis. audit; mem. Energy Policy Rev. Bd.; appointed to Oreg. Coun. Econ. Edn., Oreg. Criminal Justice Coun., adv. com. Ctr. for Rsch. on Occupational and Environ. Toxicology; mem. Jud. Br. State Energy Policy Rev. Com., 1979, Gov's. Commn. on Child Support. Woodrow Wilson Lecture series fellow, 1988. Mem. LWV, Assn. Family Conciliation Cts. (founding mem.), Oreg. Environ. Coun., Oreg. Women's Polit. Caucus. Democrat. Office: Oreg State Senate State Capitol Bldg Rm S218 Salem OR 97310

COHEN, JUDITH LYNNE, healthcare administrator; b. N.Y.C., July 25, 1951; d. Everett Herbert and Rose (Schulman) C. BS with distinction, Simmons Coll., 1973; MBA, NYU, 1984. CPA, N.Y. Staff and rsch. therapist NYU Med. Ctr., 1974-79; clin. specialist U. Mich. Med. Ctr., Ann Arbor, 1979-81; audit staff Ernst & Whinney, N.Y.C., 1984-85; cons. Peat, Marwick, Mitchell & Co., N.Y.C., 1985-86; healthcare cons. Loeb & Troper, Inc., N.Y.C., 1986-89; adminstr. dept. psychiatry Mt. Sinai Med. Ctr., N.Y.C., 1990—. Mem. AICPA, Am. Hosp. Assn., N.Y. Soc. CPA's, Greater N.Y. Hosp. Assn., Healthcare Fin. Mgmt. Assn., Beta Gamma Sigma. Home: 2185 Lemoine Ave Fort Lee NJ 07024-6030 Office: Mt Sinai Med Ctr Dept Psychiatry Box 1228 1 Gustave L Levy Pl New York NY 10029

COHEN, JUNE LAURA, financial analyst; b. D.C., Aug. 20, 1946; d. Bernard and Anne (Wald) Silkes; m. David Jack Cohen, Sept. 1, 1968; children: Cheryl Lynn, Amy Beth. BS, Pa. State U., 1968, MEd, 1973. Tchr. Juniata Mifflin VoTech., Lewistown, Pa., 1969-71; instr. Fairfax (Va.) County Adult Edn., 1974-75; tchr. Anne Arundel County, Annapolis, Md., 1976-84; jr. acct. Annapolis Fed. Savs. Bank, 1985-86, sr. acct., 1986-87; fin. adminstr. Juvenile Justice Adv. Coun., Balt., 1987-91; fin. analyst Gov.'s Office for Children, Youth and Families, Balt., 1991—. Author: (instrnl. material) UNIPAC, 1971, (handbook) Financial Management Handbook, 1991, instrnl. guide for video, 1989. PTA corr. sec. Broadneck El. Sch., Arnold, Md., 1978-80; rec. sec. Colonial Nursery Sch., Annapolis, 1981-83; fin. sec. Hadassah, Annapolis, 1985-88; chair edn. com. Temple Solel, Bowie, Md., 1992-93. Democrat. Office: Govs Office for Children Youth & Families 300 W Lexington St Baltimore MD 21201

COHEN, LAUREL, nursing administrator; b. Chgo., Dec. 1, 1943; d. Carl Eugene and Joan Adele (Arenz) Patterson; m. Sidney Henry Cohen, June 29, 1968 (div. Nov. 1981); children: Elizabeth Ann Cohen Jonsson, David Arthur, Douglas Edward, Deborah Sue; m. Frederick Joseph Foti, Jan. 19, 1985 (div. June 1994). Diploma in nursing, Swedish Covenant, 1967; BS, Moody Bible Inst., 1976. RN, N.J. Staff nurse Overlook Hosp., Summit, N.J., 1980-82; pub. health nurse Patient Care Svc., West Orange, N.J., 1982-83; hospice nurse The Hospice, Inc., Montclair, N.J., 1984-87; fin. svc. rep. Primerica Fin. Svcs., Duluth, Ga., 1985-89; coord. home care Vis. Nurse Assn. Essex Valley, East Orange, N.J., 1994—. State coord. La Leche League, N.J., 1976-78; hospice vol. The Hospice, Inc., 1987—; mem. MADD, Rep. Presdl. Task Force, 1989. Lt. (j.g.) USNR, 1967-69. Mem. Adoptees Liberty Movement Assn. (spokesman 1977-83), DAR. Republican. Presbyterian. Home: 79 Broad St Summit NJ 07901-3621 Office: Primerica Fin Svcs 40 Galesi Dr Wayne NJ 07470-4841

COHEN, LINDA CAROL, city official; b. Saco, Maine, May 7, 1955; d. Max Cohen and Kate Evalena (Fraley) Masters; 1 child, April Dawn. A in Law Enforcement, So. Maine Vocat. Tech. Coll., 1976; BBA, U. So. Maine, 1983. Sec. ERA Home Sellers, South Portland, Maine, 1978-84; code enforcement sec. City South Portland, 1987-88, asst. to the assessor, 1988-89, city clk., 1989—; election adv. com. mem. Sec. of State, Augusta, Maine, 1992—, citizen bee steering com. mem., 1993—. Vol. Peoples Regional Opportunity Program, South Portland, 1984-86; pres. Cumberland County Mcpl. Clks. Assn., Maine, 1991-92. Mem. Internat. Inst. Mcpl. Clks., New. Eng. Town & City Clks. Assn., Maine Town & City Clks. Assn. (legis. policy com. chair 1991—), Cumberland County Mcpl. Clks. Assn. Democrat. Office: City of South Portland 25 Cottage Rd S Portland ME 04106-3699

COHEN, LITA INDZEL, state legislator; m. Stanley S. Cohen; children: Reuven, Shoshana. AB in Polit. Sci. cum laude, U. Pa., 1962, postgrad., JD, 1965. Bar: Pa. 1965. Clk. Henderson, Wetherill & O'Hey, Norristown, 1964, Levi, Mandel & Miller, Phila., 1965; asst. regional counsel HUD, 1966-67; asst. counsel Sch. Dist. Phila., 1967-71; pvt. practice Merion, Pa., 1971-76; exec. v.p., gen. counsel, COO Ind. Broadcasting Co., Inc. and Banks Broadcasting Co., 1976-82; pres. Orange Prodns., Inc.-Nat. Radio Syndication Co., 1983-87, Lita Cohen Radio Svcs., Merion, Pa., 1987-93; mem. Ho. of Reps., Conshohocken, Pa., 1992—. Bd. dirs. Merion Civic Assn.; mem. citizens fire prevention com. Phila. Fire Dept.; active Lower Merion/Narberth Watershed Assn., Lower Merion Twp. Police Pension Assn., Har Zion Temple; v.p. bd. dirs. Phila. Child Guidance Ctr.; Lower Merion Twp. commr., 1986-93; capt. Heart Fund Block; mem. women's adv. com. Montemery County C.C.; hon. pres. Golda Meir Profl. Women's Hadassah; past bd. dirs. Kaiserman JYC, Atwater Kent Mus. Mem. Pa. Bar Assn., Phila. Bar Assn., Montgomery County Bar Assn.

COHEN, LIZABETH ANN, historian. AB, Princeton U., 1973; MA, U. Calif., Berkeley, 1981, PhD, 1986. Asst. curator Fine Arts Mus. San Francisco, 1975-77; dir. Camron-Stanford House Mus., Oakland, Calif., 1976-78; mus., pub. history cons.; with Dept. History Carnegie-Mellon U., from 1986; now assoc. prof. NYU Dept. History. Author: Making A New Deal: Industrial Workers in Chicago 1919-1939, 1990; contbr. numerous articles in profl. jours. Recipient Philip Toft Labor History award, Cornell U., 1990, Bancroft prize in Am. History award, Columbia U., 1991; fellow NEH, 1993, Am. Coun. Learned Socs., 1994, Guggenheim Found., 1995. Office: NYU Dept History 19 University Pl New York NY 10003-4501

COHEN, LIZZ, medical intensive care nurse; b. Boston, May 15, 1956; d. Sydney Meyer and Barbara Rosalyn (Lerman) C. AAS in Nursing, Rockland Community Coll., Suffern, N.Y., 1985; student, Dominican Coll. BLS Am. Heart Assn. Clk. typist Rockland Jour. News, West Nyack, N.Y., 1977-79; therapy aide Letchworth Village, Thiells, N.Y., 1979-81; sec. Bocour Artist Colors, Garnerville, N.Y., 1982-83; med. office asst. Dr. Brian Holt, New City, N.Y., 1983-84; LPN Helen Hayes Hosp., Haverstraw, N.Y., 1985; RN Nyack (N.Y.) Hosp., 1985—. Mem. AACN (CCRN), N.Y. State Nurses Assn., Rockland Community Coll. Alumni Assn.

COHEN, LOIS RUTH KUSHNER, research institute administrator; b. Phila., May 31, 1938; d. Joseph George and Doris (Bronstein) Kushner. Tchr.'s diploma, Gratz Coll., Phila., 1957; BA, U. Pa., 1960; MS, Purdue U., 1961, PhD, 1963, LittD (hon.), 1989. Rsch. coord. dept. sociology Purdue U., 1963-64; social sci. analyst div. dental health USPHS, Washington, 1964-70; chief applied behavioral studies div. dental health USPHS, NIH, Bethesda, Md., 1970-71; chief Office Social and Behavioral Analysis, 1971-74; spl. asst. to dir. Div. Dentistry, 1974-76, Nat. Inst. Dental Rsch., 1976—; vis. lectr. Howard U., spring 1964, health policy and social medicine Harvard U., 1981-88; Percy T. Phillips vis. prof. Columbia U. Sch. Dental and Oral Surgery, N.Y.C., 1988; cons. WHO, 1970, 74, 75, dental health unit WHO, 1970—, Inst. Medicine Nat. Acad. Sci., 1977-80; co-dir. Internat. Collaborative Study Dental Manpower Systems in Relation to Oral Health Status, 1970-84. Co-editor: Toward a Sociology of Dentistry, 1971, Social Sciences and Dentistry, Vol. I, 1971, Vol. II, 1984; editorial reviewer Social Sci. and Medicine, 1975—, Jour. Preventive Dentistry, 1973—, Scandinavian Jour. Dental Rsch., 1973—; contbr. numerous articles to profl. jours., books. Recipient Phila. High Sch. for Girls Rowen stipend, 1956, Superior Svc. awards Pub. Health Svc., 1988, 93; Senatorial scholar U. Pa., 1960; David Ross Fellow NSF, 1963. Fellow AAAS (gov. coun. 1971), Am. Coll. Dentists (hon.), Internat. Coll. Dentists (hon.); mem. Am. Pub. Health Assn, Am. Dental Assn. (hon.), Am. Sociol. Assn., Behavioral Scientists in Dental Rsch. (founder, pres. 1971-72), Federation Dentaire Internationale (cons.), Internat. Assn. Dental Rsch. (dir. 1976-77, chmn. internat. rels. com. 1979-83, disting. sr. scientist award 1987), Am. Assn. Dental Rsch. (dir. 1980-81). Office: DHHS USPHS NIH NIDR Westwood Bldg Rm 503 5333 Wesbard Ave Bethesda MD 20892*

COHEN, LORI, computer software developer; b. Bklyn., Feb. 25, 1958; d. Arnold and Rhoda (Gingold) Newman; children: Melanie Sue, Justin Marc, Tyler Philip. BA in Computer Sci., SUNY, Oswego, 1979. Jr. programmer Fedn. Employment and Guidance, N.Y.C., 1979-81; programmer/analyst Lehman Bros. Kuhn Loeb, N.Y.C., 1981-84; sr. programmer/analyst Merrill Lynch, N.Y.C., 1984-86; mgr. mortgage-backed securities devel. Shearson/Lehman, N.Y.C., 1986-88; mgr. workstation devel. Magna Software, N.Y.C., 1988-90; project mgr. Instinet, N.Y.C., 1990—. Office: Instinet 875 3rd Ave New York NY 10022-6225

COHEN, MADELINE, optometrist; b. Bklyn., Aug. 7, 1958; d. Murray and Isabel (Herman) C. AAS in Ornamental Horticulture, SUNY, Farmingdale, 1980; BS in Plant Sci. with honors, Rutgers, 1981; MS in Spl. Edn., Adelphi U., 1986; D in Optometry, SUNY, N.Y.C., 1994. Cert. tchr. spl. edn.; lic. optometrist, N.Y. Sr. instr. Helen Keller Nat. Ctr., Sands Point, N.Y., 1982-90; optometrist Stahl Eye Assoc., Hauppauge, N.Y., 1994—. Recipient Award of Excellence contact lens patient care Vistakon, 1994. Mem. Am. Optometric Assn., Am. Acad. Optometry, N.Y. State Optometric Assn., Optometric Ext. Program, Coll. Optometrists in Vision Devel., Omega Epsilon Phi, Phi Theta Kappa, Beta Beta Beta. Office: Stahl Eye Assocs 140 Adams Ave Hauppauge NY 11788

COHEN, MARCY SHARON, lawyer, banker; b. N.Y.C., Apr. 29, 1957; d. Morton G. and Sue (Krumstock) C.; m. Lawrence Liebs. BA, Lehman Coll., 1975; JD, NYU, 1978. Assoc. Marcus & Marcus, N.Y.C., 1978-80; asst. gen. counsel Bank Leumi Trust Co., N.Y.C., 1980-84; gen. counsel, corp. sec. Atlantic Bank of N.Y., N.Y.C., 1984-93; dep. gen. counsel Republic Nat. Bank, N.Y.C., 1993—. Mem. ABA, N.Y. State Bar Assn. (exec. com. corp. counsel sect. 1990—), N.Y. County Bar Assn. Office: Republic Nat Bank 452 Fifth Ave New York NY 10018

COHEN, MARILYN SAMMA, vice principal; b. Balt., Aug. 24, 1947; d. Samuel William and Rose Frances (Hack) Zell; m. Barry David Cohen, June 9, 1968; children: Isaac, Hoble. BA in Sociology, U. Md., 1969, MEd in Elem. Sch. Counseling, 1972. Cert. guidance counselor. Guidance counselor Am. Coop. Sch., Liberia, West Africa, 1983-86, Anglo-Am. Sch., Moscow, 1987-93; vice-prin. New Hope Acad., Landover Hills, Md., 1993—; community workshop leader, Moscow, Russia, and Md. Mem. mental health com. for fgn. community U.S. Embassy, Moscow, 1990-93. Mem. ACA, Am. Sch. Counseling Assn., Women's Fedn. for World Peace. Mem. Unification Ch. Office: New Hope Acad 7009 Varnum St Landover Hills MD 20784-2109

COHEN, MARY ANN, judge; b. Albuquerque, July 16, 1943; d. Gus R. and Mary Carolyn (Avriette) C. BS, UCLA, 1964; JD, U. So. Calif., 1967. Bar: Calif. 1967. Ptnr. Abbott & Cohen, P.C. and predecessors, Los Angeles, 1967-82; judge U.S. Tax Ct., Washington 1982—. Mem. ABA (sect. taxation), Legion Lex. Republican. Office: US Tax Ct 400 2nd St NW Washington DC 20217

COHEN, MICHELLE, programmer, analyst; b. Jerusalem, Israel, May 24, 1962; came to U.S., 1963; d. Joseph Benjamin and Ruth (Arusi) C. Student, Cope Vocat. Inst., N.Y.C., 1982; BA in Econs., Bklyn. Coll., 1989. Vol. programmer Human Resource Adminstrn., N.Y.C., 1982; cons. programmer Datronics, Inc., N.Y.C., 1982-83; programmer, analyst Chase Manhattan Bank, N.Y.C., 1983—. Active CAMERA, Bklyn., 1990. Home: 1462 E 17th St Brooklyn NY 11230

COHEN, MIRIAM, writer, educator; b. N.Y.C., Oct. 14, 1926; d. Jacob and Bessie (Gilman) Echelman; m. Sid Grossman, Mar. 31, 1949 (dec. 1955); 1 child, Adam; m. Monroe D. Cohen, May 31, 1959; children: Gabriel, Jem. Grad., Newburgh Free Acad., N.Y., 1943. tchr. writing Queens Coll., Writer's Voice, N.Y.C., 1990-94. Author 24 books for children and young adults. Recipient 10 Best Books of 1985 award Parents Choice, 1985. Mem. Soc. Children's Books Writers, Author's Guild. Home: Sunnyside 39-16 49th St Long Island City NY 11104 Office: care Greenwillow Books 105 Madison Ave New York NY 10016-7418

COHEN, NANCY JEAN, curator; b. Watertown, N.Y., Feb. 9, 1944; d. Irving and Dorothy Elizabeth (Slavin) Mendelsohn; m. Lawrence Phillip Cohen, Aug. 21, 1966; children: Lisa, Allyson, Celia. BA, Syracuse U., 1965, MA, 1966; MLitt, Drew U., 1988. Tchr. English Hackettstown (N.J.) High Sch., 1967-68; curator contemporary art N.J. Ctr. Visual Arts, Summit, 1984—, head curator, 1989-92, asst. curator, 1993-94. Contbr. essays to exhbn. catalogues. Mem. Skating Club Morris (Morristown, N.J., bd. dirs.). Home: 29 Coventry Rd Mendham NJ 07945 Office: NJ Ctr Visual Arts 68 Elm St Summit NJ 07901

COHEN, RACHELLE SHARON, journalist; b. Phila., Oct. 21, 1946; d. Hyman and Diane Doris (Schultz) Goldberg; m. Stanley Martin Cohen, June 22, 1968; 1 dau., Avril Heather. BS, Temple U., 1968. Editor, Somerville Jour. (Mass.), 1968-70; reporter Lowell Sun (Mass.), 1970-72, AP, Boston, 1972-79; state house bur. chief Boston Herald Am., 1979-80, editorial page editor, 1980-82; editorial page editor, columnist Boston Herald, 1982—. Mem. Mass. Bar Assn. (bench, bar, press com.), Mass. Assn. Mental Health (bd. dirs. 1993—). Office: Boston Herald 1 Herald Sq Boston MA 02118-2297

COHEN, SARA RUTH, volunteer, social service consultant; b. Chgo., June 10, 1944; d. Nathan and Faye (Levitt) Bofman; m. Leonard Cohen, May 10, 1969; 1 child, Nava. BA, Roosevelt U., 1967. Vocat. counselor Mcpl. Tb Sanitarium, Chgo., 1967-71. Chair student tutoring Solomon Sch., Chgo., 1982-85; beat, block watch capt. Neighborhood Watch Program, Chgo., 1985—; v.p. Peterson Park Improvement Assn., Chgo., 1989, 90; social action chair Shaare Tikvah, Chgo., 1986-92; cons., field rep. The Ark, Chgo., 1989-94; donation coord. Deborah's Place, Chgo., 1988-94; cmty. outreach worker Good News Ptnrs., Chgo., 1992-94; vol svc. Rest Shelter, 1992, Project Head Start, 1992; coord. neighbors helping neighbors projects Irving Park Food Pantry, 1994. Recipient Humanitarian award Raoul Wallenberg Com., 1990, Pub. Svc. for Homeless award Mental Health Assn., 1987; named Citizen of Month, Lerner Newspaper, 1981, Citizen of Yr., 1982. Jewish. Home: 6122 N Lawndale Chicago IL 60659

COHEN, SELMA, reference librarian, researcher; b. N.Y.C., Mar. 14, 1930; d. George and Rose (Cohen) Unger; m. Irwin H. Cohen, Nov. 19, 1950; children: Barbara Katzeff, Joel. Grad. high sch., William Howard Taft High Sch., 1948. Asst. bookkeeper acctg. dept. Severud, Perrone et al, N.Y.C., 1970-75; asst. bookkeeper acctg. dept. Russell Reynolds Assocs., Inc., N.Y.C., 1976-77, rsch. asst., 1977—, reference libr., 1985—. Chairwoman Scott Tower Charity Com., Bronx, 1976-84, Scott Tower Property Improvement Com., Bronx, 1983-84. Home: 3400J Paul Ave Bronx NY 10468-1002 Office: Russell Reynolds Assocs 200 Park Ave New York NY 10166-0002

COHEN, SELMA JEANNE, dance historian; b. Chgo., Sept. 18, 1920; d. Frank A. and Minna (Skud) C. A.B., U. Chgo., 1941, M.A., 1942, Ph.D., 1946. Free lance writer, 1949—; editor Dance Perspectives, N.Y.C., 1959-76; founder, dir. Dance Critics Conf., Am. Dance Festival, 1970-72, U. Chgo. Seminars in Dance History, 1974-76; disting. vis. prof. Five Colls., Inc., 1976-77; editor Internat. Ency. Dance, N.Y.C., 1981—; dance editor World Ency. Contemporary Theatre, 1985—; adj. prof. U. Calif., Riverside, 1983-89, disting. scholar, 1990—. Author: The Modern Dance: Seven Statements of Belief, 1966, Doris Humphrey, An Artist First, 1972, Dance as a Theatre Art, 1974, Next Week, Swan Lake: Reflections on Dance and Dances, 1982. Rockefeller Found. grantee, 1969; Am. Dance Guild award, 1976; Guggenheim fellow, 1980; recipient Profl. Achievement award U. Chgo., 1974; award Dance mag., 1981. Mem. Am. Soc. Aesthetics, Am. Soc. Theatre Rsch., Dance History Scholars, Am. Coun. Learned Socs., Internat. Fedn. for Theatre Rsch., World Dance Alliance. Home: 29 E 9th St New York NY 10003-6350

COHEN, SUSAN LOIS, author; b. Chgo., Mar. 27, 1938; d. Martin and Ida Handler; m. Daniel E. Cohen, Feb. 2, 1958; 1 child, Theodora (dec.). BA, New Sch. for Social Rsch., 1960; MA in Social Work, Adelphi U., 1962. Social worker N.Y.C., 1962-67; various social work positions in N.Y.C., 1962-68. Author: The Liberated Couple, 1969, reassued under title Liberated Marriage, 1973; (under name Elizabeth St. Clair) Stonehaven, 1974, The Singing Harp, 1975, Secret of the Locket, 1975, Provenance House, 1976, Mansion in Miniature, 1977, Dewitt Manor, 1977, The Jeweled Secret, 1978, Murder in the Act, 1978, Sandcastle Murder, 1979, Trek or Treat, 1980, Sealed with a Kiss, 1981; (with Daniel Cohen) The Kids' Guide to Home Computers, 1983, The Kids' Guide to Home Video, 1984, Teenage Stress, 1984, Screen Goddesses, 1984, Rock Video Superstars, 1985, Wrestling Superstars, Vol. 1, 1985, Vol. 2, 1986, Hollywood Hunks and Heroes, 1985, Heroes of the Challenger, 1986, A Six-Pack and a Fake ID, 1986, The Encyclopedia of Movie Stars, 1986, A History of the Oscars, 1986, Teenage Competition: A Survival Guide, 1987, Young and Famous: Hollywood's Newest Superstars, 1987, Going for the Gold, 1987, What You Can Believe about Drugs, 1988, What Kind of Dog is That, 1989, When Someone You Know Is Gay, 1989, Zoo Superstars, 1989, Zoos, 1992, Where to Find Dinosaurs Today, 1992, Going for the Gold: Medal Hopefuls for Winter '92, 1992. Mem. Wodehouse Soc., Watson's Erroneous Deductions, Chapter One, The Capers of Sherlock Holmes, Clumber Spaniel Club of Am. Address: 877 Hand Ave Cape May Court House NJ 08210

COHEN-STRATYNER, BARBARA NAOMI, curator; b. N.Y.C., Mar. 5, 1951; d. Maxwell Tillman and Cecelia (Spivakowsky) Cohen. AB, Barnard Coll., N.Y.C., 1972; MFA, NYU, 1974, PhD, 1980. Profl. costumer opera cos., N.Y.C., 1972-77; costume coord. Theatre Devel. Fund, N.Y.C., 1974-76; editor Dance Data Dance Horizons, N.Y.C., 1976-78; editor The Bookwoman Women's Nat. Book Assn., 1987-88; editor Performing Arts Resources Theatre Libr. Assn., 1980—; freelance exhibition curator, 1986—; curator of exhibitions N.Y. Pub. Library for the Performing Arts, N.Y.C., 1987—; mem. faculty fashion history Parsons Sch. Design, N.Y.C., 1987—; cons. Shubert Archive, N.Y.C., 1987—; cons. Barnard Coll. Centennial, N.Y.C., 1988—, Carnegie Hall Centennial, N.Y.C., 1989—. Author: Biographical Dictionary of Dance, 1982, Popular Music: 1900-1919, 1988; contbg. editor Contemporary musicians, 1989—. Pub. svc. writer Gay Men's Health Crisis, N.Y.C. Shubert Found. fellow, 1977-78. Mem. Am. Assn. Muss., Internat. Coun. Muss., N.Y. Muss. Coun., Mus. Edn. Roundtable (bd. dirs. 1993—, vice chair pubs. 1994—), Theatre Libr. Assn. (editor 1980—). Democrat. Jewish.

COHN, JANE SHAPIRO, public relations executive; b. N.Y.C., May 19, 1935; d. Harry I. and Ann (Safanie) Shapiro; m. Albert M. Cohn, June 30, 1957 (div. 1972); children: Theodore David, William Alan. BA, Brandeis U., 1956; postgrad., Coll. of New Rochelle, 1974-76. Dir. pub. rels. Hudson River Mus., Yonkers, N.Y., 1976-79; account exec. Dudley-Anderson Yutzy Pub. Rels. Agy. subs. Ogilvy Mather, N.Y.C., 1979-81; dir. communications Haines Lundberg Waehler, N.Y.C., 1981-91; prin. Jane Cohn Pub. Rels., Sherman, Conn., 1991—; cons. Inst. Contemporary Art, Phila., 1983; speaker, mktg. promotion strategies conf., 1989. Contbr. articles to profl. jours. Fellow Soc. Mktg. Profl. Svcs. (bd. dirs. N.Y. chpt. 1988-89, 92—, spkr. 1994 annual convention, Gold Medal award 1994); mem. AIA (assoc. 1988, speaker annual conv.), Am. Mktg. Assn. (panelist ann. conv. 1987, moderator profl. services sect. ann. conv. 1988, exec. mem.), Practice Mgmt. Assn. (speaker promotion strategies conf. 1989). Democrat. Jewish. Office: Jane Cohn Pub Rels 31 Spring Lake Rd. Sherman CT 06784

COHN, JUDITH, pulmonologist, educator; b. Chgo., Jan. 3, 1950; d. Lawrence Fishel and Helen (Rothschild) C.; m. Neal Jeffrey Taslitz, June 15, 1986; 1 child, Aaron Mayer. BS, U. Wis., 1971; PhD, U. Pa., 1977; MD, Northwestern U., Chgo., 1983. USPHS predoctoral fellow U. Pa., Phila., 1971-76; Muscular Dystrophy Found. postdoctoral fellow Yale U. Sch. Medicine, New Haven, 1977-79; postdoctoral rsch. fellow Northwestern U. Sch. Medicine, 1980, extern, 1982; intern in internal medicine Hines (Ill.) VA Hosp., 1983-84; resident Robert Wood Johnson Med. Ctr., U. Medicine-Dentistry N.J., New Brunswick, 1985-87; fellow in pulmonary medicine Rush-Presbyn.-St. Luke's Med. Ctr., Chgo., 1987-90, asst. prof., 1990—; pvt. practice, Chgo., 1990—; assoc. dir. immunosci. venture pharm. products divsn. Abbott Labs, Abbott Park, Ill., 1991-93, med. dir. immunosci. venture pharm. products divsn., 1993—. Contbr. articles to med. jours., chpt. to book. James Kemper scholar Northwestern U., 1979-83. Mem. AMA (reviewer Jour. 1990—), Am. Thoracic Soc., Chgo. Lung Assn., Chgo. Med. Soc. (continuing med. edn. com. 1982-83), N.Y. Acad. Scis., Sigma Xi. Democrat. Jewish. Home: 984 Oak Dr Glencoe IL 60022-1427 Office: Abbot Labs Dept 048K Bldg AP6A-1 1 Abbot Park Rd Abbott Park IL 60064-3500

COHN, LUCIE SCHMIDTMANN, engineer; b. Jamaica, N.Y., Oct. 22, 1963; d. Otto Stanislaus and Nancy Dorothy (Koonmen) S.; m. Randy B. Cohn, Sept. 4, 1994. BS in Computer Sci., Siena Coll., Loudonville, N.Y., 1985; MS in Computer Sci., Stevens Inst. Tech., Hoboken, N.J., 1989; student, U.S. Coast Guard Acad., New London, Conn., 1981-82, St. John's U., 1980-81, 83; Degree in Systems Engring., Polytech U. Bklyn., Bklyn., 1994. Computer cons. dept. computer sci. Siena Coll., Loudonville, N.Y., 1984-85; figure clk. King Kullen Grocery Co., Westbury, N.Y., 1983-85; project mgr. AT&T Bell Labs., Whippany, N.J., 1985-88; asst. to rsch. and devel. mgr. AT&T Bell Labs., 1988-89, system/software engr., 1990-93, systems test engr., 1993—; source selection cons. Highpoint Codominium Assn., Stanhope, N.J., 1989-92, bd. dirs., 1990-92; copmuter cons. Champcare Inc., Davenport, Iowa, 1989-91; head math judge North Jersey Regional Sci. Fair, 1990, head math and computer sci. judge, 1992, math. and computer sci. judge, 1991-94. Contbr. articles to profl. jours. Vol. N.J. Spl. Olympics, Area 3, Flanders, N.J., 1985-93, vol. coord., 1985-93, design/graphic artist, 1989. Recipient Vol. award, N.J. Spl. Olympics Area 3, 1989. Mem. ACM (vice chmn. 1984-85, capt. programming team 1984-85), IEEE, IEEE Computer Soc. Math. Assn. Am., Performance Mgmt. Assn. (mem. North Jersey chpt. planning com. 1990, sec. 1990-91), Profl. Assn. Diving Instrs., N.J. Skin Diving Club (sec. 1994), On The Bottom Dive Club, Upsilon Pi Epsilon. Republican. Roman Catholic. Home: 42 Yorkshire Ave West Mildord NJ 07480 Office: AT&T Bell Labs PO Box 903 67 Whippany Rd Whippany NJ 07981-0903

COHN, MARIANNE WINTER MILLER, civic activist; b. Denver, Jan. 15, 1928; d. Henry Abraham II and Esther (Sheflan) Winter; m. Benjamin K. Miller, Dec. 29, 1948 (dec. Dec. 1972); children: Judy Ellen, Philip Henry; m. Isidore Cohn Jr., Jan. 3, 1976; children: Ian Jeffrey, Lauren Kerry. Student, Colo. U., 1946-47. Mem. exec. bd. Greater New Orleans Tourist and Conv. Commn., 1985; chmn. spouse program arrangements Am. Coll. Surgeons, La., 1985; mem. exec. bd. NCCJ, New Orleans, 1987—, sec., 1991-92, treas., 1993-94, nat. bd. dirs., 1993; bd. dirs. Jewish Endowment Found., New Orleans, 1987-88; mem. Arts Coun. of New Orleans, 1988—, v.p. devel. 1991-92, v.p. grants, exec. bd., 1995; pres. La. Mus. Found. of La. State Mus., 1989-90, bd. dirs., 1994—; mem. Sisterhood of Temple Emanuel Denver (pres. 1957-60); women's bd. dirs. Nat. Jewish Hosp. at Denver, 1951-80, pres. women's div., 1960-61, mem., sec. gov. bd., 1972-76; bd. dirs. New Orleans Symphony Aux., 1980; mem. nat. bd. Nat. Jewish Ctr., 1976—; chmn. Odyssey Ball of New Orleans Mus. Art, 1992; bd. dirs. La. Coun. for Music and Performing Arts, 1991-92; mem. exec. bd. New Orleans Arts Coun., 1991-92, 95—; mem. governing bd. La. State Mus., 1992—; exec. bd. Arts Coun. 95' V.P. Grants, 1995. Recipient Woman of Fashion award Men of Fashion, 1989. Republican.

COHN, MARILYN BARBARA (LYNNE COHN), library director; b. Bklyn., Nov. 13, 1936; d. Elias and Clara Rose (Greenfield) Yellin; m. Jerry Cohn, Dec. 22, 1957; children: Candace, Mitchel, Sharron. BS in Pharmacy magna cum laude, L.I. U., 1958; MLS, Columbia U., 1962. Reference libr. Carrier Found., Belle Mead, N.J., 1985-88, dir. med. libr., 1988—. Mem. Nat. Network Med. Librs. (rep. regional adv. com. N.Y.C. chpt. 1990-94), Health Sci. Librs. of N.J. (sec. Princeton chpt. 1988-90). Jewish. Home: 24 Layne Rd Somerset NJ 08873-2920 Office: Carrier Found Rte 601 Belle Mead NJ 08502

COHN, MARJORIE BENEDICT, curator, art historian, educator; b. N.Y.C., Jan. 10, 1939; d. Manson and Marjorie (Allen) Benedict; m. Martin Cohn, Dec. 19, 1960. BA, Mt. Holyoke Coll., 1960; AM, Radcliffe Coll., 1961. Conservator works of art on paper Art Mus. Harvard U., Cambridge, Mass., 1963-89, lectr. fine arts, 1974-77, sr. lectr., 1977—, print curator, 1989—, acting dir., 1990-91; vis. lectr. Boston U., 1972, 73, Wellesley (Mass.) Coll., 1973; vis. asst. prof. Brown U., Providence, 1975. Author: Wash & Gouache, 1977, A Noble Collection: The Spencer Albums of Old Master Prints, 1992, (with S.L. Siegfried) Works by J.A.D. Ingres in Collection of the Fogg Art Museum, 1980, Francis Calley Gray and Art Collecting for America, 1986. Sec. Arlington (Mass.) Hist. Commn., 1972-85. Mem. Am. Acad. Arts and Scis., Print Coun. Am. Democrat. Office: Harvard U Fogg Art Mus 32 Quincy St Cambridge MA 02138-3845

COHN, MILDRED, biochemist, educator; b. N.Y.C., July 12, 1913; d. Isidore M. and Bertha (Klein) Cohn; m. Henry Primakoff, May 31, 1938; children: Nina, Paul, Laura. BA, Hunter Coll., 1931, ScD (hon.), 1984; MA, Columbia U., 1932, PhD, 1938; ScD (hon.), Women's Med. Coll., 1966, Radcliffe Coll., 1978, Washington U., St. Louis, 1981, Brandeis U., 1984, U. Pa., Phila., 1984, U. N.C., 1985; PhD (hon.), Weizmann Inst. Sci., Israel, 1988; ScD (hon.), U. Miami, 1990. Rsch. asst. biochemistry George Washington U. Sch. Medicine, 1937-38; rsch. assoc. Cornell U., 1938-46; research assoc. Washington U., 1946-50, 51-58, assoc. prof. biol. chemistry, 1958-60; assoc. prof. biophysics and phys. biochemistry U. Pa. Med. Sch., 1960-61, prof., 1961-78, emeritus, 1982—, Benjamin Rush prof. physiol. chemistry, 1978-82; sr. mem. Inst. Cancer Research, Phila., 1982-85; Chancellor's disting. prof. biophysics U. Calif., Berkeley, spring 1981; vis. prof. biol. chemistry Johns Hopkins U. Med. Sch., 1985-91; research assoc. Harvard U., 1950-51; established investigator Am. Heart Assn., 1953-59, career investigator, 1964-78. Editorial bd. jour. Biol. Chemistry, 1958-63, 67-72. Recipient Cresson medal Franklin Inst., 1976, award Internat. Assn. Women Biochemists, 1979, Nat. Medal Sci., 1982, Chandler medal Columbia U., 1986, Disting. Svc. award Coll. Physicians, 1987, Women in Sci. award N.Y. Acad. Sci., 1992, Gov.'s award for excellence in sci., Pa., 1993. Mem. NAS, Am. Philos. Soc. (v.p. 1994—), Am. Chem. Soc. (Garvan medal 1963, Remsen award Md. sect. 1988), Harvey Soc., Am. Soc. Biol. Chemists (pres. 1978-79), Am. Biophys. Soc., Am. Acad. Arts and Scis., Phi Beta Kappa, Sigma Xi, Iota Sigma Pi (hon. nat. mem. 1988). Office: U Pa Med Sch Dept Biochemistry Philadelphia PA 19104

COIN, SHEILA REGAN, management consultant; b. Columbus, Ohio, Feb. 17, 1942; d. James Daniel and Jean (Hodgson) Cook; m. Tasso H. Coin, Sept. 17, 1967 (div.); children: Tasso, Alison Regan. BS, U. Iowa, 1964. RN Staff nurse VA Hosp., Boston, 1964-66; field rep. ARC, Chgo., 1966-67, adminstr., 1967; asst. div. dir. Am. Hosp. Assn., sec. Am. Soc. Hosp. Dirs. Nursing, Chgo., 1967-69; owner Coin & Assocs., Chgo., 1975-77; ptnr. Coin, Newell & Assocs., Chgo., 1977—; instr. dept. continuing edn. Loyola U., Chgo., 1975-77, Rock Valley Coll. Mgmt. Inst., Rockford, Ill., 1978-80, Ill. Central Coll. Inst. Personal and Profl. Devel., Peoria, 1979-85, Triton Coll. Continuing Edn., River Grove, Ill., 1983-86, No. Ill. U. Continuing Edn., DeKalb, 1983-86; mem. editorial bd. Tng. Today mag., 1992-94, assoc. editor, 1994—. Vol. Art Inst., Chgo., 1968-69; mem. Chgo. Beautiful Com., 1968-73; chmn. Mayor Daley's Chgo. Beautiful Awards Project, 1972; mem. jr. bd. Girl Scouts Assn., Chgo., 1975-76; mem. jr. governing bd. Chgo. Symphony Orch., 1971—, pres., 1977-78; governing mem. Orchestral Assn., Chgo., 1977-81; bd. dirs. Mid-Am. chpt. ARC, Chgo., 1979-81, 91—, vice chmn. 1986-89, mem. planning & evaluation subcom., 1991—, chmn. quality mgmt. steering com., 1992—, bd. dirs. Chgo. dist., 1981-89, chmn. fin. devel. com., 1982-85, vice chmn. dist. bd., 1986-89; bd. dirs. Ill. chpt. Lupus Found. Am., 1991-93; bd. dirs., mem. Survive Alive House Found., 1989—; dir. Com. for Thalossemia Chgo. Bd., 1981-82; mem. Women's bd. Nat. Com. Prevention Child Abuse, Chgo., 1981-82; mem. State of Ill. Disabled Persons Adv. Coun. , 1988—; academic specialist in mgmt. devel. U.S. Info. Agy., 1994. Mem. ASTD (exec. com. of mgmt. devel. profl. practice area 1992—), Ill. Tng. and Devel. Assn., Organizational Devel. Network Chgo. Democrat. Roman Catholic. Office: Coin Newell & Assocs 919 N Michigan Ave Chicago IL 60611-1601

COIT, MARGARET LOUISE, writer; b. Norwich, Conn., May 30, 1919; d. Archa Willoughby and Grace (Leland) C.; m. Albert E. Elwell, Jan. 28, 1978 (dec.). A.B. (Weil scholar), U. N.C., Greensboro, 1941; Litt.D., Woman's Coll., 1959. With Lawrence (Mass.) Daily Eagle, 1941, Newburyport (Mass.) Daily News, 1944, Haverhill (Mass.) Gazette, 1946; book reviewer Greensboro Daily News, Boston Globe, N.Y. Times, N.Y. Post, Saturday Rev., etc.; mem. staff U. N.H. Writers Conf., 1950-63, U. Colo. Writers Conf., 1958—; author-in-residence Fairleigh Dickinson U., Rutherford, N.J., 1954; prof. Fairleigh Dicksinson U., Rutherford, N.J., 1955-84; prof. Bunker Hill C.C., Charlestown, Mass., 1973-75. Author: John C. Calhoun: American Portrait, 1950, reprinted 1989, 93, Mr. Baruch (biography), 1957, The Fight for Union, 1961 (Thomas Edison award), reprinted in Spanish 1965, (with others) The Growing Years, The Sweep Westward, 1964, Husband Served in Mass House, 1971-75, Andrew Jackson, 1965, reprinted 1991, Massachusetts, 1968, Calhoun: Great Lives Observed, 1970, (with others) The Courage to Grow Old, 1990, From Dawn to Harvest, 1989, The Spirit of New England, 1991. Moderator West Newbury Town Meeting; sec. West Newbury Rep. Town Com. Breadloaf fellow Breadloaf Writers Conf., 1948; Book award of Nat. Council of Women U.S., 1958; named vice adm. Confederate Navy of U.S. Mem. Soc. Am. Historians, Am. Hist. Assn., Nat. Arts Club of N.Y.C., Phi Beta Kappa. Congregationalist. Home: Berry Hill Farm 109 Moulton St West Newbury MA 01985-2212*

COKER, GURNELLE SHEELY, retired secondary education educator; b. Ballentine, S.C., Nov. 17, 1915; d. George Johnston and Vennie Blanche (Amick) S.; m. Theron Hemingway Coker, Sr., Apr. 10, 1938; 1 child, Theron Hemingway Jr. BA, Winthrop Coll., 1936; M Edn., U. S.C., 1953. Cert. tchr., S.C. Tchr. 5th grade Hebron Consolidated Sch., Cades, S.C., 1936-38; elem. prin. Lexington County, Gilbert, S.C., 1938-41; jr. stock tracer 21st Sub Depot, Columbia (S.C.) Army Air Base, 1942-43; med. technician Station Hosp. Lab., Ft. Jackson, S.C., 1944-46; English tchr. Chapin (S.C.) High Sch., 1948-55; English tchr. Brookland-Cayce High Sch., West Columbia, S.C., 1955-69, English tchr., counselor, 1958-69, dir. guidance, 1969-81, ret., 1981. Sec. Earlwood Little Boys Baseball League, Columbia, 1954-55; mem. Lexington (S.C.) County Mental Health, 1970-75; active fund dr. Am. Heart Assn., Columbia, 1975—. Recipient Life Svc. award Ascension Luth. Ch. Women, 1955, Our Saviour Luth. Ch. Women of Evang. Luth. Ch. Am., 1990; appreciation So. Interscholastic Press Assn., 1964, Meritorious Svc. award Brookland-Cayce Sch. Bd. Trustees, 1981; Spl. Study scholar Lexington Sch. Dist. II, 1959; named Tchr. Yr. Lexington County Dist. II, 1968. Mem. Lexington County Retired Educators Assn. (pres. 1985-87), S.C. Retired Educators Assn. (council dels. 1981—, sec. 1989-90), Gen. Fedn. of Women's Clubs of S.C. (v.p. Women's Club of W. Columbia 1992-94, pres 1994—); U. S.C. Alumni Assn., Winthrop Coll. Alumni Assn., Alpha Delta Kappa (pres. Epsilon chpt. 1984-86), Delta Kappa Gamma (contbr. article and editorials to Alpha Eta state digest 1966-71, Svc. award 1971, 2d v.p. Alpha Eta state S.C. 1987-89, Internat. Svc. award 1989, pres. Rho chpt. 1994—). Republican. Lutheran. Lodge: Order Ea. Star (worthy matron Earlwood chpt. 1959-60). Home: 1440 Cardinal Dr West Columbia SC 29169-6016

COKER, LYNDA, state legislator; b. Oct. 2, 1946; m. Gene V. Coker; 2 children. BS, Fla. State U., 1969; MEd, Ga. State U., 1982. Exec. asst. Cobb County Sheriff; mem. Ga. Ho. Reps., 1990-92, 1993—, mem. agrl. and consumer affairs com., mem. game, fish and parks com., mem. pub. safety com., mem. indsl. rels. com. Mem. Ga. Sheridd's Assn., Legal Sec. Assn., Civitan. Republican. Home: 4560 Ponte Verda Dr Marietta GA 30067 Office: Ga House of Reps State Capitol Atlanta GA 30334*

COLACECCHI, MARY BETH, editor; b. Corning, N.Y., Aug. 15, 1961; d. Joseph John and Mary Louise (Alotto) C.; m. James Stuart Hamilton, Oct. 8, 1988. AB, Cornell U., 1983. Freelance writer-editor daily newspapers and mags., newsletters and wire svc. daily newspapers, East Coast area, 1984-95; copy desk paginator News-Jour., Daytona Beach, Fla., 1984; reporter Press and Sun-Bull., Binghamton, N.Y., 1984-86; copy editor So. Conn. Newspapers, Greenwich, Stamford, 1986-89; asst. metro editor for layout Gannett Westchester Newspapers, White Plains, N.Y., 1989; assoc. editor Catalog Age Mag. div. Cowles Bus. Media, Stamford, 1990-94. Freelance writer St. Petersburg (Fla.) Times, 1984, Daytona Beach (Fla.) News-Jour., 1984, Greenwich (Conn.) Time, 1986-89; freelance editor Stamford (Conn.) Advocate, 1990. Mem. Emmaus Cmty., Stamford, 1986—; soup kitch coord. New Covenant House, Stamford, 1993—. Fellow Poynter Inst. for Media Studies, 1984, ethics fellow, 1988. Mem. Investigative Reporters and Editors, Nat. Fedn. Press Women, Conn. Press Club (bd. dirs. 1993—, newsletter editor 1993—, Comm. Excellence award 1991-94).

COLAMARINO, KATRIN BELENKY, lawyer; b. N.Y.C., Apr. 29, 1951; d. Allen Abram and Selma (Burwasser) Belenky Lang; m. Leonard J. Colamarino, Mar. 20, 1982; m. Barry E. Brenner, June 1, 1974 (div. June 1979); 1 child, Rachel Erin. BA, Vassar Coll., 1972; JD, U. Richmond, 1976. Bar: Ohio 1976, U.S. Ct. Apls. (Fed. cir.), 1982. Staff atty. AM Internat. Inc., Cleve., 1976-78; atty. Lipkowitz & Plaut, N.Y.C., 1980-81; atty. Docutel Olivetti Corp., Tarrytown, N.Y., 1981-84; atty. NYNEX Bus. Info. Systems, White Plains, N.Y., 1984-85; corp. counsel, sec. Logica Data Architects, Inc., N.Y.C., 1986-90; corp. counsel SEER Technologies, Inc., N.Y.C., 1990-91; v.p. tech. divsn. counsel Citibank N.A., N.Y.C., 1991—. Class agt. Fieldston Sch., N.Y.C., 1980—, exec. bd. Ethical Fieldston Alumni Assn., 1980-90, 92—, v.p. 1987-90; alumnae coun. rep. Vassar Coll., 1982-86. Mem. ABA, Computer Law Assn. Office: Citibank NA 909 3d Ave 32/1 New York NY 10043

COLBURN, JULIA KATHERINE LEE, volunteer, educator; b. Columbus, Ohio, Feb. 8, 1927; d. Fred Merritt and Lillian May (Getrost) Lee; m. Joseph Linn Colburn, Sept. 5, 1947; children—Joseph Linn, Jr., David Laird, Andrew Lee, Julia LeeAnne. B.S. in Edn., Ohio State U., 1948. Libr. asst. Columbus Pub. Libr., 1945-48, Ohio State U. Libr., Columbus, 1945-47; life ins. acct. Nationwide Ins., Columbus, 1949-50; substitute tchr. Columbus Pub. Schs., 1965-69, 79-81, vol. resource person, 1979—. Author: The Six Who Signed, Christmas at Valley Forge; editor, compiler (state pub.) Ohio Daughters of 1812, Star and Anchor, 1983-85 (nat. first award, 1984, 85). Presiding judge Franklin County Bd. Elections, Columbus, 1959—; pres. Linden Jr. Civic Club, Columbus, 1953, Rhapsody Unit, Columbus Symphony, 1975-77, Arlington Park PTA, Columbus, 1963-64, Linden-McKinley Jr.-Sr. High PTA, Columbus, 1964-66, Northland High PTA, Columbus, 1972-73; organizing pres. Lazarus Cancer Ray, Columbus, 1953; leader Northland council Girl Scouts U.S., 1968-70; vol. Vision Ctr., Columbus, 1969-72 (Named Vol. of Yr. 1971); v.p. Linden United Meth. Women, Columbus, 1965-66, pres. 1966-68, various coms. 1963—; pres. Meth. Youth Fellowship, Columbus, 1944-45; adminstrv. bd. Linden United Meth. Ch., Columbus, 1944-45, 52—, choir soloist, mem., 1945—, Sunday sch. tchr., 1959—, spl. membership awards 1971, 77; dist. chmn. Christian Global Concerns Columbus North Dist. United Meth. Women, 1973-77. Recipient Silver Good Citizenship medal Ohio Soc. SAR, 1978, Medal of Appreciation, Benjamin Franklin chpt. SAR, 1978, Martha Washington meda. Ohio SAR, 1989. Mem. Ohio Geneal. Soc. (speakers staff 1978—), First Families of Ohio, DAR (Good Citizenship cert. 1945, state rec. sec. 1983-86, state vice regent 1986-89, state regent 1989-92, v.p. gen., 1992—, various offices and coms. 1976—), NSDAR (speakers staff 1983—, chaplain vice pres. club 1993-94, parliamentarian nat. vice chmn. club 1994—), Children of Am. Revolution (sr. pres. state 1976-78, sr. nat. rec. sec. 1982-84, various coms. 1974—, Ohio Service award, 1979, maj. benefactor 1986, nat. vice chmn. 1980-83), U.S. Daus. of 1812 (parliamentarian, chmn. nat. membership 1985-88, state pres. 1983-85, treas. Nat. Hdqrs. Endowment Trust Fund, 1988-91, assn. pres., state pres. 1991-93), Colonial Dames of Am., Dames of the Ct. of Honor, Colonial Dames XVII Century (state first v.p. 1985-87, 95—), Daus. Colonial Wars (state historian 1984-86, nat. vice chmn. 1989-92, state custodian 1992—), Women Desc. Ancient and Honorable Arty. Co. (state rec. sec. 1983-86, state pres. 1986-89, nat. parliamentarian 1989-92, chaplain nat. 1992-95, nat. organizing sec. 1995—), Daus. Am. Colonists (Old Trails chpt. treas. 1981-85, vice regent 1985-87, regent 1987-89), New Eng. Women (pres. Columbus colony 1984-87, nat. chmn. 1987—), Colonial Daus. Seventeenth Century, Daus. Union Vets., Zeta Phi Eta. Republican. Club: Ohio Fedn. Women's (trustee, chmn. 1974-83), Noreast Women's (v.p. 1994—). Lodges: Order of Eastern Star (star point 1961-62), Linden Lawanis (Kiwanis Aux. pres. 1964). Avocations: genealogy; music; writing. Home: 1887 Northcliff Dr Columbus OH 43229-5332

COLBURN, KATHLEEN ANN, hospice administrator, psychologist; b. Clinton, Mass., Sept. 23, 1950; d. Clinton Franklin and Kathryn (Melanson) C. BA in English Lit., U. Mass., 1973; MA in Psychology, Drake U., 1976. Supr. of psychol. svcs. Polk County Juvenile Home, Des Moines, 1977-79; clin. dir. Survival, Inc., Quincy, Mass., 1979-80; dir. resident svcs. Broadlawns Med. Ctr., Des Moines, 1980-81; legis. analyst Legis. Fiscal Bur., Des Moines, 1981-84; chief of adminstrn. Iowa Dept. of Substance Abuse, Des Moines, 1984-86; exec. dir. Hospice of Ctrl. Iowa, Des Moines, 1986—; bd. dirs. AIDS of Greater Des Moines, 1991-94, sec. bd., 1993-94; keynote spkr. 1st East/West Internat. Hospice Conf., Tianjin, China, 1992. Contbr. articles to profl. jours. Vol. Bernie Lorenz Recovery House, Des Moines, 1986-87, Sherman Hill Neighborhood Assn., Des Moines, 1989—; vol. mental health adv. coun. Broadlawns Med. Ctr., Des Moines, 1991-92; vol. speaker United Way of Cen. Iowa, Des Moines, 1987—. Grantee Iowa Pharmacy Assn., 1989, Aetna Ins. Co., 1991, Kresge Found., 1992, Mid-Iowa Health Found., 1993. Mem. Nat. Assn. Home Care (bd. dirs. Washington chpt. 1991—, Spl. Contbn. to Hospice Field award 1993), Hospice Assn. Am. (bd. dirs. Washington chpt. 1990—, chmn. bd. dirs. 1991—), Greater Des Moines Rotary. Office: Hospice of Ctrl Iowa 3609 1/2 Douglas Ave Des Moines IA 50310-5345

COLBY, BARBARA DIANE, interior designer, consultant; b. Chgo., Dec. 6, 1932; d. Raymond R. and Mertyl Shirley (Jackson) C.; 1 son, Lawrence James. Student Wright Jr. Coll., 1950, Art Inst. Chgo., UCLA. Owner, F.L.S., Los Angeles, 1971-77; ptnr. Ambiance Inc., Los Angeles, 1976-77; owner Barbara Colby, Ltd., Los Angeles, 1977-81; bus. adminstr. Internat. Soc. Interior Designers, Los Angeles, 1982—; owner Chromanetics, Glendale, Calif., 1981—; instr. Otis/Parsons Sch. Design, Los Angeles Fashion Inst. Design and Merchandising; dir. color Calif. Coll. Interior Design, Costa Mesa, Calif., 1987; also lectr. in field. Author: Color and Light Influences and Impact, 1990; contbg. editor Giftware News. Instr. L.A. County Regional Occupation Program, 1990-94; tng. cons. United Edn. Inst., 1994—. Recipient award for Best Children's Room, Chgo. Furniture Show, 1969, award Calif. Design Show '76, 1976. Mem. Am. Soc. Interior Designers (cert.), Color Mktg. Group of U.S. (chairholder). Author: Color and Light: Influences and Impact, 1990; contbr. articles to profl. jours. Office: 245 W Loraine St Apt 309 Glendale CA 91202-1849

COLBY, JOY HAKANSON, art critic; b. Detroit; d. Alva Hilliard and Eleanor (Radtke) Hakanson; m. Raymond L. Colby, Apr. 11, 1953; children: Sarah, Katherine, Lisa. Student, Detroit Soc. Arts and Crafts, 1945; B.F.A., Wayne State U., 1946. Art critic Detroit News, 1947—; originator exhibit Arts and Crafts in Detroit, 1906-1976; at Detroit Inst. Arts, 1976; Mem. visual arts adv. panel Mich. Council for Arts, 1974-79; mayor's appointment Detroit Council for Arts, 1974; mem. Bloomfield Hills Arts Council, 1974. Author: Art and A City, 1956, lead essay in Arts and Crafts in Detroit catalog, 1976; Contbr. articles to art periodicals. Recipient Alumni award Wayne State U., 1967, Art Achievement award, 1983, Headliner award, 1984, award for arts reporting Detroit Press Club, 1984, Art Leadership award Ctr. for Creative Studies, 1989. Office: 615 W Lafayette Blvd Detroit MI 48226-3124

COLBY, KAREN LYNN See WEINER, KAREN COLBY

COLBY, LESTINA LARSEN, secondary education educator; b. Mt. Sterling, Ky., Apr. 19, 1937; d. Harold L. and Opal Kearney (Caudel) Larsen; m. Bruce Redfearn Colby, Dec. 28, 1962; children: Charles, Harold, Pamela. BS, U. Chgo., 1958, postgrad., 1958-62. Sci. tchr., debate coach Community High Sch., Midlothian, Ill., 1958-61; biology tchr., debate coach U. Chgo. Lab. Sch., 1961-66; sci. tchr. Springer Jr. High Sch., Wilmington, Del., 1977; biology and math. tchr. McKean High Sch., Wilmington, 1978; biology tchr., debate coach, student coun. advisor U. Liggett Sch., Grosse Pointe, Mich., 1979-93, Edsel B. Ford endowed sci. chair, 1990; biology tchr., chmn. sci. dept. Episcopal High Sch., Jacksonville, Fla., 1993—. Author: Teacher's Manual for Encyclopaedia Britannica's Evolution Unit, 1966, Plants and Animals, 1968. Mem. Nat. Assn. Biology Tchrs. (Mich. Outstanding Biology Tchr. 1990), Nat. Sci. Tchrs. Assn., Fla. Assn. Sci. Tchrs. Baptist. Office: Episcopal HS Jacksonville 4455 Atlantic Blvd Jacksonville FL 32207-2197

COLBY, MARVELLE SEITMAN, business management educator, administrator; b. N.Y.C., Oct. 31, 1932; d. Charles Edward and Lily (Zimmerman) Seitman; m. Robert S. Colby, Apr. 11, 1954 (div. Apr. 1979); children: Lisa, Eric; m. Selig J. Alkon, Dec. 6, 1986. BA, Hunter Coll., 1954; MA, U. N.Colo., 1973; PhD in Pub. Adminstrn., Nova U., 1977; cert., Harvard Grad. Sch. Bus., 1979. V.p. SE Region URC Mgmt. Services Corp., Washington, 1972-77; dir. devel. Hunter Coll. Woman's Ctr. Community Leadership, N.Y.C., 1977-78; dir. tng. and career devel. Girl Scouts U.S., N.Y.C., 1978-79; dir. Overseas Tour Ops. Am. Jewish Congress, N.Y.C., 1979-81; chief exec. officer Girl Scout Council Greater N.Y.C., 1981-82; prof. bus. mgmt. Marymount Manhattan Coll., N.Y.C., 1982—, chmn. bus. mgmt. and acctg. div., 1982-89, 93—; adj. prof. NYU, 1986-92; mem. exec. com. Assn. Recreation Mgmt., N.Y.C., 1982; cons. Rockport Mgmt., Washington, 1974-78. Author: Test Your Management IQ, 1984; co-author: Lovejoy's Four Year College Guide for the Learning Disabled, 1985, Introduction to Business, 1991; contbr. articles to profl. jours. Chmn. Met. Dade County Commn. Status Women, Miami, 1975-77; chief planner Met. Dade County U.S. SBA 1st annual conf. Future Women Bus., 1977. Named to Hunter Coll. Hall of Fame, 1986. Mem. Acad. Mgmt., Hunter Coll. Alumni Assn. (bd. dirs. 1978-79), Phi Delta Kappa. Club: Lotos (mem. literary com. 1983-89). Home: 242 E 72nd St New York NY 10021-4574 Office: Marymount Manhattan Coll 221 E 71st St New York NY 10021-4501

COLBY, VIRGINIA LITTLE, former educator; b. Saugus, Mass., May 1, 1917; d. Guy L. and Alberta M. (Chadwick) Little; m. Robert G. Colby, Dec. 25, 1951. AB, U. Mass., 1940. Svc. rep. N.E.T. and T. Co. Bus. Office, Lynn, Mass., 1940-63, N.E.T. and T. Co., Concord, N.H., 1963-67; tchr. Shaker Regional Sch. Dist., Belmont, N.H., 1967-77. Co-author: Concord Eastside: A History of East Concord, New Hampshire; contbr. articles to profl. publs. Mem. AAUW (past pres. Concord br.), Lakes Region Retired Tchrs. Assn. (past pres.), No. N.H. Telephone Pioneers Am. (past pres.), Boscawen Hist. Soc., Inc. (sec., libr.), Concord Ch. Women United (past pres., v.p.), Delta Kappa Gamma (hon. mem. Beta chpt.). Home: 134 Mountain Rd Concord NH 03301-6931

COLBY-HALL, ALICE MARY, Romance studies educator; b. Portland, Maine, Feb. 25, 1932; d. Frederick Eugene and Angie Fraser (Drown) C.; m. Robert A. Hall, Jr., May 8, 1976; stepchildren: Philip, Diana Hall Goodall, Carol Hall Erickson. B.A., Colby Coll., 1953; M.A., Middlebury Coll., 1954; Ph.D., Columbia U., 1962. Tchr. French, Latin Orono (Maine) High Sch., 1954-55; tchr. French Gould Acad., Bethel, Maine, 1955-57; lectr. French Columbia U., 1959-60; instr. Romance lit. Cornell U., Ithaca, N.Y., 1962-63, asst. prof., 1963-66, assoc. prof., 1966-75, prof. Romance studies, 1975—, chair Romance studies, 1990—. Author: The Portrait in Twelfth Century French Literature: An Example of the Stylistic Originality of Chrétien de Troyes, 1965; mem. editorial bd.: Speculum, 1976-79, Olifant, 1974—. Fulbright grantee, 1953-54; NEH fellow, 1984-85; recipient Médaille des Amis d'Orange, 1985. Mem. Modern Lang. Assn., Medieval Acad. Am. (councillor 1983-86), Internat. Arthurian Soc., Société Rencesvals, Académie de Vaucluse, Phi Beta Kappa. Republican. Congregationalist. Home: 308 Cayuga Heights Rd Ithaca NY 14850-2107 Office: Cornell U Dept Romance Studies Ithaca NY 14853

COLDIRON, VICKI IRENE, farm owner; b. Whittier, Calif., May 1, 1945; d. Victor Ivan and Nell Eunice (Wetzel) C. BA in English, U. So. Calif., 1965. Cert. tchr. Tchr. Dept. Edn., L.A., 1965-66, Kahului, Hawaii, 1966-72; bartender Royal Lahaina (Hawaii) Hotel, 1973-90; ind. real estate speculator/developer Lahaina, 1986-90; owner/mgr. Maui Farms, Purcell, Okla., 1990—. Mem. Am. Quarter Horse Assn., Okla. Thoroughbred Assn., Tex. Thoroughbred Assn., Okla. Quarter Horse Racing Assn., Thoroughbred Owners/Breeders Assn. Democrat. Presbyterian. Home and Office: Maui Farms Rt 2 Box 26 Purcell OK 73080

COLE, ANN DALBY, sales representative; b. Texarkana, Tex., Nov. 1, 1945; d. Howard Hampton and Mary Bailey (Andrews) Dalby; m. Charles Northen Cole, Aug. 2, 1969. Student, Mary Washington Coll., 1963-66; BS in Med. Tech., Med. Coll. Va., 1967; postgrad., Rollins Coll., 1984-86. Cert. med. tech. Am. Soc. Clin. Pathologists. Med. tech. Med. Coll. Va., Richmond, 1967-68, Halifax Dist. Hosp., Daytona Beach, Fla., 1968-69, Seminole Meml. Hosp., Sanford, Fla., 1969-73; chemistry lab. supr. Seminole Meml. Hosp., Sanford, 1973-78, lab. mgr., 1978-82; lab. mgr. Ctrl. Fla. Regional Hosp., Sanford, 1982-86; sales/territory mgr. B/R Instrument Corp., Easton, Md., 1987—; med. lab. tech. adv. com. Valencia C.C., Orlando, Fla., 1976-86; med. lab. edn. adv. com. State of Fla., Tallahassee, 1978-86; med. lab. aide adv. com. Seminole County Sch. System, Altamonte Springs, Fla., 1980-86. Leader Girl Scouts USA, 1993—. Mem. AAUW (program v.p. 1992-94), Clin. Lab. Mgmt. Assn. (chpt. treas. 1992—, ednl. scholarship 1986). Episcopalian. Home: 12861 Hamlet Ave Apple Valley MN 55124

COLE, BETTY LOU MCDONEL SHELTON (MRS. DEWEY G. COLE, JR.), judge; b. Elwood, Ind., June 5, 1926; d. Bernard Miller and Vee Marie (Robertson) McDonel; m. Elbert Shelton, Dec. 13, 1944; children: Steven Elbert, Jeanette Louise; m. 2d, Dewey G. Cole, Jr., Dec. 24, 1975. Student, Ind. U., 1947-50, LLB, 1969; student, Ball State U., 1964-65. Bar: Ind. 1969, Fed. Cts., 1969. Pvt. practice, Muncie, Ind., 1969—, Betty L. Shelton Law Office, 1970-78; sr. ptnr. firm Dunnuck, Cole, Rankin and Wyrick, Muncie, 1978-80; judge Delaware County Superior Ct., 1980—. Mem. ABA, Ind. Bar Assn., Muncie Bar Assn., Ind. Judges Assn., Am. Trial Lawyers, Ind. U. Law Alumni Assn., Nat. Assn. Women Judges, LWV (league pres. 1963-64), Bus. and Profl. Women., Riley-Jones Club, Columbia Club. Office: Del County Justice Ctr 100 W Washington St Muncie IN 47305-2810

COLE, CAROLYN JO, brokerage house executive; b. Carmel, Calif.; d. Joseph Michael, Jr., and Dorothea Wagner (James) C.; A.B., Vassar Coll., 1965. Mgr. tech. services Aims Group, N.Y.C., 1965-67; editor Standard & Poor's Corp., N.Y.C., 1968-74; sr. v.p. PaineWebber, Inc., N.Y.C., 1975-95; exec. v.p. Tucker Anthony Inc., Boston, 1995—; guest lectr. Harvard U. Bus. Sch.; chmn. bd. dirs. N.Y. Women's Bldg. Named to YWCA Acad. Women Achievers. Mem. NOW, DAR, N.Y. Soc. Security Analysts (past bd. dirs.), Assn. for Investment Mgmt. and Rsch., Soc. Fgn. Analysts, Aspen Inst. Humanistic Studies, Fin. Women's Assn., Women's Econ. Roundtable, Econ. Club N.Y., Women in Need (past bd. dirs.). Democrat. Episcopalian. Club: Vassar (N.Y.C.). Contbr. to Ency. Americana. Office: Tucker Anthony Inc One Beacon St Boston MA 02108

COLE, ELMA PHILLIPSON (MRS. JOHN STRICKLER COLE), social welfare executive; b. Piqua, Ohio, Aug. 9, 1909; d. Brice Leroy and Mabel (Gale) Phillipson; m. John Strickler Cole, Oct. 3, 1959. AB, Berea Coll., 1930; MA, U. Chgo., 1938. Various positions in social work, 1930-42; dir. dept. social svc. Children's Hosp. D.C., Washington, 1942-49; cons. pub. coop. Midcentury White House Conf. on Children and Youth, Washington, 1949-51; exec. sec. Nat. Midcentury Com. on Children and Youth, N.Y.C., 1951-53; cons. recruitment Am. Assn. Med. Social Workers, 1953; assoc. dir. Nat. Legal Aid and Defender Assn., 1953-56; exec. sec. Marshall Field Awards, Inc., 1956-57; dir. assoc. orgns. Nat. Assembly Social Policy and Devel., 1957-73; assoc. exec. dir. Nat. Assembly Nat. Vol. Health and Social Welfare Orgns., 1974; dir. edn. parenthood project Salvation Army, 1974-76, asst. sec. dept. women's and children's social svcs., 1976-78, dir. rsch. project devel. bur., 1978-92, ind. cons., 1993—; mem. Manhattan adv. bd., 1975—, sec., 1984—, mem. hist. commn., 1976—, exec. com., 1988-94; cons. nat. orgns. Golden Anniversary White House Conf. on Children and Youth,

1959-60; mem. adv. coun. pub. svc. Nat. Assn. Life Underwriters and Inst. Life Ins.; judges com. Louis I. Dublin Pub. Svc. awards, 1961-74; v.p. Blue Ridge Inst. So. Cmty. Svc. Execs., 1977-79, exec. com., 1979-81; mem. awards jury Girls Clubs Am., 1981-93; adv. bd. Nat. Family Life Edn. Network, 1982—. Mem. com. pub. rels. and fundraising Am. Found. for Blind Commn. on Accreditation, 1964-67; mem. task force on vol. accreditation Coun. Nat. Orgns. for Adult Edn., 1974-78; adv. bd. sexuality edn. project Ctr. for Population Options, 1977-86; bd. dirs., sec. James Lenox House, 1985-89, pres., 1989-94, treas., 1994—; bd. dirs., sec. James Lenox House Assn., 1985-89, pres., 1989-94, sec., 1994—; bd. dirs. Values and Human Sexuality Inst., 1980-85, Sexuality Info. and Edn. Coun. of U.S., 1993—. Mem. Pub. Rels. Soc. Am. (cert.), Nat. Assn. Social Workers (cert.), Nat. Conf. Social Welfare (mem. pub. rels. com. 1961-66, 69-82, chair adminstrn. sect. 1966-67), Jr. League N.Y., Women's Club of N.Y., Pi Gamma Mu, Phi Kappa Phi. Home: 19 Washington Sq N New York NY 10011-9170

COLE, GRACE V., painter, art educator; b. Chgo.; d. Peter S. and Katherine Marie (Hill) Ellis. Student, Prairie State Coll., Ecole Albert du Fois, Vihiers, France. Tchr. for pvt. apprentices Chgo., 1979—; tchr. Prairie State Coll., Chicago Heights, Ill., 1986—, Old Town Triangle, Chgo., 1990—; cons. in field, juror, gallery asst., lectr., curator, sales rep., mentor and dir. numerous orgns. Exhibited in group shows at Portraits, Inc., N.Y. Jayson Gallery, Chgo., Clementi House Gallery, London; commd. portraits include Coe Coll., Iowa, Ill. Coll., Medinah Country Club (10 works), Ill., Bank of Louisville (2 works), Bristol Meyers, Ind., Epsicopal Diocese of Chgo. (2 works), numerous other pvt. and pub. collections. Featured in article in the Artist's Mag., 1984; recipient Golden Apple award Prarie State Coll., 1994. Mem. New Group/Mus. Contemporary Art, Chgo. Artist's Coalition (bd. dirs. 1979—). Studio: AN Art Place 10th Fl 847 W Jackson Chicago IL 60607

COLE, GRETCHEN BORNOR, distribution and service executive; b. Detroit, Nov. 12, 1927; d. Maurice Frank and Dora Levina (Richardson) Bornor; m. Ernest James Cole, Mar. 31, 1951; (div. May, 1981); children: Cynthia, Sara Ann. BA, DePauw U., 1949; MSW, Wayne State U., 1980. Cert. social worker, Mich. Regional sec. Kenyon and Eckhardt, Detroit, 1951-52; office mgr. W.O. Earl Assocs., Detroit, 1952-54; social worker St. Joseph Mercy Hosp., Pontiac, Mich., 1981-82; with Detroit Air Compressor and Pump Co., Ferndale, Mich., 1963-80, sec., 1981, v.p., 1982, chmn., pres., 1990—, also chmn. bd. dirs.; regional dir., v.p. Atlas Copco Distbr. Assn., 1987-90; mem. Atlas Copco Compressors Coun. Bd., 1990-92. Named one of Top 50 Woman Bus. Owners State of Mich., 1986, 94. Mem. Women's Econ. Club, Nat. Assn. Women Bus. Owners, Econ. Club Detroit, Founder's Soc., Detroit Inst. Arts, Alpha Chi Omega. Republican. Episcopalian. Office: Detroit Air Compressor & Pump Co 3205 Bermuda St Ferndale MI 48220-1060

COLE, HEATHER ELLEN, librarian; b. Rochester, N.Y., Nov. 7, 1942; d. Donald M. and Muriel Agnes (Kimball) C.; m. Stratis Haviaras; 1 child, Elektra Maria Muriel. BA, Cornell U., 1964; MS, Simmons Coll., 1973. Mgr. Brentano's, Boston, 1968-70; intern Harvard Coll. Libr., Cambridge, Mass., 1970-73, reference libr., 1973-77, libr., 1977—; libr. Hilles and Lamont Librs., 1977—. Mem. AAUW, ALA, Am. Soc. Info. Sci. (New England chpt.), Assn. Coll. Rsch. Librs. Democrat. Episcopalian. Home: 19 Clinton St Cambridge MA 02139-2303 Office: Harvard Coll Lamont Library Cambridge MA 02138

COLE, HELEN, state legislator; b. Tishomingo, Okla., July 13, 1922; m. John Cole; 2 children. Former mayor, Moore, Okla., mem. Okla. Ho. of Reps., 37-39th sessions; mem. Okla. Senate, 1984—. Active Cleveland County Republican Women's Club. Mem. Yukon C. of C., Am. Legion Aux. Office: Okla Senate State Capital Oklahoma City OK 73105 also: 3026 SW 89th St Apt A Oklahoma City OK 73159-6351*

COLE, JANE BAGBY, librarian; b. Tulsa, May 23, 1931; d. Walter James and Mary Frances (Eakin) Bagby; m. Bruce Herman Cole, June 7, 1953; children—Rosemary Neilsen, Dorothy Domrzalski, Robert Bagby, Frances. B.A., Grinnell Coll., 1953; M.A., U. Chgo., 1977. Library asst. Elem. Dist. 101, Western Springs, Ill., 1961-71, library aide, 1973-75; librarian Elem. Dist. 102, La Grange, Ill., 1975-77, River Forest Jr. High Sch., Ill., 1977-79; audio-visual dir. Elem. Dist. 7, Phoenix, 1980-83; library dir., curator Desert Bot. Garden, Phoenix, 1983—. Mem. Spl. Librs. Assn. (treas. Ariz. chpt. 1992-94), Coun. Bot. and Hort. Librs. (pres. 1994—). Office: Desert Bot Garden 1201 N Galvin Pky Phoenix AZ 85008-3437

COLE, JANET See **HUNTER, KIM**

COLE, JOAN HAYS, social worker, clinical psychologist; b. Pitts., Sept. 4, 1929; d. Frank L. Wertheimer and Edith H. Einstein; BA, Western Res. U., 1951; MSSA in Social Work, Case Western Res. U., 1962; PhD, Wright Inst., 1975; m. Robert M. Wendlinger, June 1984; children: Geoffrey F. Cole, Douglas R. Cole, Peter Hays Cole. Cert. clin. social worker; diplomate Am. Bd. Orthopsychiat. Social group worker Alta House Settlement House, Cleve., 1958-59; housing dir. Cleve. Urban League, 1961-62; dir. Citizens for Safe Housing, Cleve., 1963; housing dir. United Planning Orgn., Washington, 1963-68; asst. prof. community orgn. U. Md., Balt., 1968-72; asso. prof. Lone Mountain Coll., San Francisco, 1975-78; psychotherapist, supr., organizational cons., Berkeley, Calif., 1977—; cons. various public and vol. social welfare, health and housing agys., 1969—; mem. adj. faculty Union Grad. Sch. and Antioch West Coll., 1978-80; lectr. U. Calif. Sch. Social Welfare, Berkeley, 1980-84; mem. faculty Berkeley Psychotherapy Inst., 1981—, pres., 1983-85. NIMH grantee, 1971-72, Sr. Social Work Career Devel. grantee, 1973-75. Fellow Soc. Clin. Social Work (diplomate), Am. Orthopsychiat. Assn.; mem. NASW, ACLU, Soc. Study of Social Issues, Acad. Cert. Social Workers, Nat. Conf. on Social Welfare and Psychotherapists for Social Responsibility. Home: 535 Pierce St Apt 355 Albany CA 94706-1058 Office: 6239 College Ave Oakland CA 94618-1329

COLE, JOHNNETTA BETSCH, academic administrator; b. Jacksonville, Fla., Oct. 19, 1936; d. John Thomas and Mary Frances (Lewis) Betsch; m. Robert Eugene Cole (div. 1982); children: David, Aaron, Ethan; m. Arthur J. Robinson, Jr., 1988. Student, Fisk U., 1953; BA in Sociology, Oberlin Coll., 1957; MA in Anthropology, Northwestern U., Evanston, Ill., 1959, PhD, 1967. Instr. U. Calif., Los Angeles, 1964; dir. black studies Wash. State U., Pullman, 1969-70; prof. anthropology U. Mass., Amherst, 1970-83, assoc. provost undergrad. edn., 1981-83; vis. prof. Hunter Coll., N.Y.C., 1983-84, prof. anthropology, 1983-87, dir. Inter-Am. Affairs Program, 1984-87; pres. Spelman Coll., Atlanta, 1987—; corp. bd. dirs. Coca Cola Enterprises, Nations Bank Ga., Mgmt. Tng. Corp., Merck & Co., Inc.; trustee Rockefeller Found. Author, editor: Anthropology for the Eighties, 1982, All American Women, 1986, Anthropology for the Nineties, 1988, Conversations: Straight Talk with America's Sister President, 1993; mem. editorial bd. The Black Scholar. Recipient Women First award YWCA, 1993. Fellow Am. Anthrop. Assn.; mem. Assn. Black Anthropologists (past pres.). Baptist. Office: Spelman Coll Office of the President 350 Spelman Ln SW Atlanta GA 30314-4398

COLE, JULIE PARSONS, social worker; b. Pasadena, Calif., Jan. 10, 1946; d. Winchell Monroe and Elisabeth Loreen (Moss) Parsons; m. Carter Lee Cole, May 10, 1975; children: Katherine E., Craig A. Smith. BA with honors, U. of the Pacific, 1967; MSW, UCLA, 1970. Lic. clin. social worker; bd. cert. diplomate; cert. Acad. Cert. Social Workers. Case worker II San Joaquin County Bur. Pub. Assistance, Stockton, Calif., 1967-68; caseworker I and II L.A. County Dept. Pub. Social Svcs., Pasadena, Calif., 1968, L.A. Dept. Adoptions, Compton, Calif., 1970-74; caseworker III Family Svcs. of L.A., Calif., 1974-80; pvt. practice lic. clin. social worker, 1981—; chairperson San Fernando Valley Child Abuse Resource Com., 1978-80; cons., lic. clin. social worker Villa Esperanga, Apoura, Calif., 1987-94. Chairperson, editor: San Fernando Valley Child Abuse Resource Directory, 1979. Founder The Elisabeth M. and Winchell M. Parsons Scholarship, ASME Aux., N.Y.C., 1985; bd. mem. ASME Aux., L.A., 1989-94, chairperson, 1994. Recipient Vol. of the Yr. award Family Svcs. L.A., 1980, United Way Vol. award United Way San Fernando Valley, 1980; fellow HEW, Washington, 1968-70. Mem. NASW, Soc. for Clin. Social Workers, Acad. Cert. Social Workers, Am. Bd. Examiners in Clin. Social Workers, C.G. Jung Inst. (life), Elisabeth K. Ross Ctr. (life), UCLA Sch. Social Welfare Alumni, Phi Kappa Phi. Home: 1736 Upper Ranch Rd Westlake Village CA 91362 Office: 21103 Vanowen St Canoga Park CA 91303

COLE, JUNE ROBERTSON, psychotherapist; b. Dothan, Ala., Sept. 29, 1931; d. C. Pete and Mary (Danzey) Robertson; m. Robert Walker Cole, Jr., Feb. 11, 1956; children: Robert Pete, Mary Cathlyn. AA, Del Mar Coll., 1974; BA, Tex. A&I U., 1976; MA, Corpus Christi State U., 1978; postgrad Fielding Inst., Santa Barbara, 1985—. Lic. marriage and family therapist, profl. counselor. Actress, singer, radio, films, TV, stage, 1933-55; rec. artist Gold Label Records, 1951-55; pres. Coastal Bend Security Co., Corpus Christi, 1969-71; dir. Reality Therapy Ctr., Corpus Christi, 1975—; co-dir. Counseling and Psychology Resource Ctr., Corpus Christi, 1984—; pvt. practice psychotherapy, 1976—; mem. mental health staff Bayview Psychiatric Hosp., Corpus Christi, 1986—, Southside Community Hosp., Corpus Christi, 1989—, Charter Psychiatr. Hosp., Corpus Christi, 1990—; faculty Park Coll., Naval Air Sta., Corpus Christi, 1987-92. Bd. dirs. Coastal Bend Jazz Soc., 1978-79; presenter papers on Post Traumatic Stress Disorder, Compatibility Psychotherapy & 12 Step Programs in alcohol, drug addictions. Mem. AACD, APA, NOW, Am. Assn. for Mental Health Counselors, Am. Assn. Behavior Therapists, Tex. Psychol. Assn., Internat. Assn. for Group Psychotherapists, Corpus Christi Council Women, Nueces County Psychol. Assn., Tex. Assn. Counseling and Devel., Gulf Coast Assn. Counseling and Devel., Tex. Mental Health Counselors Assn., Coastal Bend Marriage and Family Therapists Assn., Internat. Inst. Reality Therapists. Office: 5934 S Staples St Ste 216 Corpus Christi TX 78413-3842

COLE, KATHLEEN ANN, social worker, advertising agency executive; b. Cin., Nov. 22, 1946; d. James Scott and Kathryn Gertrude (Borisch) Cole; B.A., Miami U., 1968; M.S.W., U. Mich., 1972; M.M., Northwestern U., 1978; m. Brian Brandt, Mar. 21, 1970. Social worker Hamilton County Welfare Dept., Cin., 1969-70, Lucas County Children Services Bd., Toledo, 1970-74, East Maine Sch. Dist., Niles, Ill., 1974-77; account supr. Leo Burnett Advt. Agy., Chgo., 1978-93; primary therapist, Lifeline, Chgo., 1994—; field instr. Loyola U., Chgo., 1976-77. Mem. Acad. Cert. Social Workers, Nat. Assn. Social Workers, Miami U. Alumni Assn. (dir. 1976—), Northwestern U. Prof. Women's Assn., Kellogg Alumni Assn., North Shore United Meth. Congregation. Home: 414 Kelling Ln Glencoe IL 60022-1113

COLE, KELLIE BIRDGETT ARNDT, artist; b. Detroit, Sept. 15, 1964; d. Glenn Earl and Phyllis Karen (Paulson) Arndt; m. Robert Preston Cole, June 11, 1988; 1 child, Morgan Christian. Student, Stetson U., 1982-83, Internat. Acad. Merchandising and Design, 1983-86, Oakland Community Coll., 1989-90. Interior designer Roberts' Interior Design, Inc., Largo, Fla., 1984-88, 90-91; with Dickinson, Wright, Moon, Van Dusen & Freeman, counselors at law, Royal Oak, Mich., 1988-89; cons. in field. Mem. NOW, ASPCA, Greenpeace, People for the Ethical Treatment of Animals. Republican. Lutheran. Home: 3607 Dubsdread Circle Orlando FL 32804

COLE, MARILYN BUSH, occupational therapy educator; b. N.Y.C., Jan. 29, 1945; d. George Lyman and Theis Odette (Maurer) Bush; m. Carl E. Cole, Aug. 31, 1968 (div. June 1981); children: Charlot E. Cole, Bradley Eric Cole; m. Martin M. Schiraldi Sr., July 3, 1982. BA, U. Conn., 1966; grad. cert., U. Pa., 1969; MS, U. Bridgeport, 1982. Registered occupational therapist, Conn. Staff occupational therapy Ea. Pa. Psychiat. Inst., Phila., 1968-69; dir. occupational therapy Middlesex Meml. Hosp., Middletown, Conn., 1973-76; supervising occupational therapist Lawrence & Meml. Hosps. Day Treatment Ctr., New London, Conn., 1976-79; staff occupational therapist Newington Children's Hosp., Newington, Conn., 1980-82; asst. prof. occupational therapy Quinnipiac Coll., Hamden, Conn., 1982—; cons. psychiat. svcs. VA Med. Ctr., West Haven, Conn., 1983-91; cons. Fairfield Hills Hosp., Newtown, Conn., 1989-91. Author: (textbook) Group Dynamics in Occupational Therapy, 1993; co-author Structured Group Experiences, 1982, chpt. in Group Process and Structure, 1988; contbr. articles to profl. jours. Grantee Quinnipiac Coll, 1986. Mem. Am. Occupational Therapy Assn. (Communications award 1976, cert.), Conn. Occupational Therapy Assn. (sec. 1878, nominations chair 1982-89), World Fedn. Occupational Therapists, AAUW (cultural chair 1972, publicity chair 1973-76, edn. chair 1989-91, nominations 1993—), Ctr. for Study Sensory Integrative Dysfunction (cert. 1979). Republican. Episcopalian. Office: Quinnipiac Coll Dept Occupl Therapy Mount Carmel Ave Hamden CT 06518

COLE, MAX, artist; b. Hodgeman County, Kans., Feb. 14, 1937; d. Jack Delmont C. and Bertha (Law) Fakes; m. Richard Cole, Sept. 4, 1955 (dec. April 1958); children: Douglas, Janet, Cindy. B.A., Fort Hays State U., 1961; M.F.A., U. Ariz., 1964. Asst. prof. Pasadena (Calif.) City Coll., 1967-78; guest lectr. Claremont (Calif.) Grad. Sch., 1978, Coll. Creative Studies, U. Calif., Santa Barbara, 1977, 79, Contemporary Arts Council, Los Angeles County Mus. Art, 1979, Miami Dade Coll., 1982. Exhibited group shows: Los Angeles County Mus. Art, 1976, Corcoran Gallery Art, Washington, 1977, La Jolla Mus., 1980, Santa Barbara Mus., 1980, Mus. Fine Arts of N.Mex., 1984, Neuberger Mus., Purchase, N.Y., 1984, Marilyn Pearl Gallery, N.Y.C., 1985, Pratt Manhattan Ctr. Gallery, 1985, UCLA, 1988, Nat. Gallery Modern Art, New Delhi, 1988; one-man shows: Louver Gallery, L.A., 1979, 80, Sidney Janis Gallery, N.Y.C., 1977, 80, Oscarsson Siegeltuch Gallery, N.Y.C., 1986, Zabriskie Gallery, N.Y., 1987, Haines Gallery, San Francisco, 1988, 93, Mus. Folkwang, Essen, Germany, 1993, Kunstraum Kassel, Kassel, Germany, 1992, Kiyo Higashi Gallery, L.A., 1991, 93, 94; represented in permanent collections: Los Angeles County Mus. Art, Newport Harbor Mus. Art, La Jolla Mus. Contemporary Art, Mus. N.Mex., Dallas Mus. Art, Santa Barbara Mus., Everson Mus., Tel Aviv Mus., La. Mus., Denmark. Address: 195 E 3rd St New York NY 10009-7424

COLE, NANCY JANE, art educator; b. Dallas, Dec. 28, 1941; d. Thomas Clifton and Margaret (Morrow) Cole; children: Debra Earnest, Jason Earnest. BS, U. North Tex., 1964; M in Liberal Arts, So. Meth. U., 1974; postgrad., Mechosin Internat. Summer Sch. of Art, 1993. Cert. tchr., Tex. Tchr. elem. art Dallas Ind. Sch. Dist., 1964-74; tchr. jr. high art De Soto (Tex.) Ind. Sch. Dist., 1974-82; tchr. art De Soto (Tex.) H.S., 1982—, art dept. chair, 1986—; instr. painting Mountain View Coll., Dallas, 1975-76. Author: (high sch. curriculum guides) Art I, Art II, Art III, Art IV, 1985; illustrator: Junior High Biology Work Book, 1982. Recommendation chmn. Southwest Dallas County Panhellenic Assn., 1990-95; sponsor De Soto High Sch. Art Club, 1991—. Mem. Nat. Art Edn. Assn., Nat. Coun. Edn. for the Ceramic Arts, Dallas Women's Caucus for Art, Dallas Artists Rsch. and Exhbn., De Soto Art League. Methodist. Home: 832 Vince Ln De Soto TX 75115 Office: De Soto HS 600 Eagle Dr De Soto TX 75115

COLE, NATALIE MARIA, singer; b. L.A., Feb. 6, 1950; d. Nathaniel Adam and Maria (Hawkins) C.; m. Marvin J. Yancy, July 30, 1976 (div.); m. Andre Fisher (div.). B.A. in Psychology, U. Mass., 1972. Rec. singles and albums, 1975—; albums include Dangerous, 1985, Everlasting, 1987, Inseparable, Thankful, Good To Be Back, 1989, Unforgettable, 1991 (4 grammys, 3 grammys 1992), Too Much Weekend, 1992, Take A Look, 1993 (Grammy award nominee best jazz vocal 1994), Holly and Ivy, 1994; television appearances include Lily in Winter, USA, 1994. Recipient Grammy award for best new artist, best Rhythm and Blues female vocalist 1975, 76; recipient 1 gold single, 3 gold albums; recipient 2 Image awards NAACP 1976, 77; Am. Music award 1978, other awards. Mem. AFTRA, Nat. Assn. Rec. Arts and Scis., Delta Sigma Delta. Democrat. Baptist. Office: care Don Fischel Triad Artists 16th Fl 10100 Santa Monica Blvd Los Angeles CA 90067*

COLE, RUTH ELIZABETH, nursing educator; b. Murray, Ky., Oct. 15, 1920; d. Ory Leander and Rema (Boyd) C. Diploma in Nursing, Nazareth Sch. Nursing, Lexington, Ky., 1944; BS, U. Tex., 1949; MA, Columbia U., 1954; EdD, Ind. U., 1972. Staff nurse Houston-McDevitt Clinic Hosp., Murray, Ky., 1944-45; office nurse Dr. A.D. Butterworth, Murray, Ky., 1947; DON Murray State Coll., 1949-51; chair dept. nursing Murray State U., 1954-77; prof. nursing Harding U., Searcy, Ark., 1978-80; program dir. Murray Calloway County Hosp. Hospice Program, Murray, 1980-81; chair emeritus Murray State U. Mem. Hospice Adv. Coun., Murray, 1980—, Pres.'s Adv. Coun. on Sci. and Nursing, Harding U., 1973—; bd. dirs. ARC, Murray, 1971—. Capt. USNR, 1945-46, 51-53, to 80. Named Nurse Educator of the Yr. Ky. League for Nursing, 1977; Ruth E. Cole Hon. Nursing scholar, Sigma Theta Tau, 1977; Ky. Col. Commonwealth of Ky.; inducted Hall of Fame Sch. of Nursing U. Tex. Med. Br., Galveston, 1994. Mem. Murray Woman's Club (chair Delta cept. 1991-92, lifetime achievement award 1993), Sigma Theta Tau, Pi Lambda Theta, Delta Kappa Gamma. Home: 812 Main Murray KY 42071

COLE, SUSAN MERLE, city official; b. Hamilton, Mont., Oct. 2, 1943; d. Merlin Everett and Laura Taft (Dean) Bickell; m. George Arthur Cole, July 3, 1965; children: Francine Ruth Tageant, Spencer Everett. BA in Math. with honors, U. Mont., 1965; MPA, San Diego State U., 1992. Tchr. math. and physics U.S. Peace Corps, Tapah, Perek, Malaysia, 1965-66; engr. Pacific N.W. Bell, Spokane, Wash., 1972-74; adminstrv. asst. Gov.'s Office State Commn. on Local Govt., Helena, Mont., 1974-76; computer programmer City of Spokane, 1976-77, supervisory data processing analyst, 1979-88; analyst, programmer Am. Sign & Indicator, Spokane, 1978; systems and program mgr. City of Chula Vista, Calif., 1988-91, prin. mgmt. asst., 1991-94, asst. dir. fin., 1994—; v.p. Media West, Inc., Spokane, 1978—; sec.-treas. Trapper Cole Radio Inc., San Diego, 1988-92. Precint committeeperson Dem. party, Spokane, 1982-84; vol. ESL aid City Coll., San Diego, 1993; vol. Aqualink, San Diego, Tijuana, Mexico, 1991—. Recipient Presdl. Commendation award U.S. Pres., 1972. Mem. Data Processing Mgmt. Assn. (bd. mem. 1981-91), Nat. Mgmt. Assn. (pres. 1982-83), Am. Soc. Pub. Adminstrn. Unitarian-Universalist. Home: 2445 Brant St # 206 San Diego CA 92101 Office: City of Chula Vista Engring 276 4th Ave Chula Vista CA 91910

COLE, SUSIE CLEORA, retired government employee relations official; b. Bloomsburg, Pa.; d. Harry E. and Chloe Ann (McKinstry) Cole; m. Richard Edward Miller, July 31, 1959 (div. Aug. 1977); 1 child, Terri Lee Miller; m. Gerald Edward Nelson, Feb. 18, 1978 (div. June 1982). Student in history No. Va. Community Coll., 1982; also govt. courses. With Dept. Navy, Washington, 1957-74, clk., technician U.S. Dept. Navy, Washington, 1957-67, Navy mil. pay regulations specialist, 1962-71; mgr. error detection and reduction program for mil. pay, allowances and travel, 1967-71, fiscal acct. 1971-74, fiscal clk. Dept. State, Washington, 1975-77, sr. retirement claims examiner, 1977-83, employee rels. officer, 1983-94, also mgr. fed. health benefits program and mgr. fed. life ins. program, 1983-94, ret., 1994. Active Citizen's Band Radio Club, Fairfax, Va., 1974-82, Retarded Children's Ctr., Fairfax, 1981-82. Recipient various govt. awards, including Sustained Exceptional Achievement award Dept. State, 1983-93. Democrat. Avocations: reading, travel, history, music, art. Home: 4605 John Tyler Ct Apt 104 Annandale VA 22003-6524 Office: US Dept State Bur Pers Office Employee Rels 2201 C St NW Washington DC 20520-0001

COLECCHIA, FRANCESCA MARIA, educator; b. Pitts.; d. Albert and Ambrosina (Donatelli) C. B.E., Duquesne U.; M.Litt., Ph.D., U. Pitts.; postgrad., Universidad Autonoma Mex.; fellow, Universidad Central del Educador, 1962. Prof. modern langs. Duquesne U., Pitts.; chmn. dept. Duquesne U., 1977-86, dir. lang. lab. programs, 1960-72; asso. editor Duquesne Hispanic Rev., 1961-72, Estudios (Duquesne U.); co-dir. cert. program in internat. bus. Duquesne U., 1985-90; Fulbright lectr., Colombia, 1963-64; vis. prof. Mt. Mercy Coll., Pitts., spring 1968; lectr. East Carolina U., 1969; Commonwealth speaker Pa. Council on the Humanities, 1984-86; reader NEH Transl. Program, 1983-84, 85-86, oral proficiency tests Am. Coun. Teaching Fgn. Langs./ Ednl. Testing Service, 1985-89; reader, cons. Choice Mag., 1979—; mem. nat. selection com. Fulbright awards, 1988, 89, 90, 92; mem. review panel NEH, 1994. Author: Repaso Breve, 1962, Repaso Oral, 1967, Paisajes y Personajes Latinoamericanos, 1971, Selected Latin American One-Act Plays, 1972, Federico Garcia Lorca: An Annotated Bibliography of Criticism, 1979, Federico Garcia Lorca: An Annotated Primary Bibliography, 1981, (with L.G. Cruz) Cuban Theater in the U.S. A Critical Anthology, 1990, (with M. Durán) Lorca's Legacy, 1991, Crossroads and Other Plays of Carlos Solorrano, 1992; co-editor Garcia Lorca Rev., 1973-83; book rev. editor Hispanic Jour., 1987-88; contbr. articles to profl. publs. Mem. Atty. Gen.'s Task Force design regional treatment center for women, 1969; bd. dirs., corp. sec., Western regional v.p. Pa. Program for Women and Girl Offenders, Inc.; bd. dirs., corp. sec. Female Offenders Program; mem. Pa. Humanities Coun., 1987-95; bd. dirs. Renewal Inc., 1988-92. Western Pa. recipient commendation scroll Asociacion Colombiana de Profesores de Ingles, 1964; Amita nat. award for contbns. to edn., 1969; U.S. Office Edn. Inst. grantee, 1971; Pa. Cen. for Internat. Edn. grantee, 1985. Mem. AAUW (Pitts. 1st v.p. 1965-67, dir. 1961-63, co-chmn. coll. faculty program Pitts. br., pres. br. 1968-70, coll. faculty program com. Pa. div., mem. fellowship com. Pa. div. 1969-70), MLA (v.p. Pitts., mem. Del. Assembly 1978-80), NEMLA (sec./treas. women's caucus 1993-94, v.p. 1994-95), Nat. Assn. Lang. Lab. Dirs. (editor secondary sch. directory), Latin Am. Studies Assn., Am. Assn. Tchrs. Spanish and Portuguese, Inst. Internacional de Literatura Iberoamericana, Asociacion Internacional de Hispanistas, Adminstrv. Women Edn., Zonta Club (pres. Pitts. 1981-82), Delta Kappa Gamma (Pa. profl. affairs com. 1977-79), Sigma Kappa Phi, Phi Kappa Phi, Sigma Tau Delta, Phi Sigma Iota. Home: 401 Lexington Ave Pittsburgh PA 15215-3222

COLEMAN, ARLENE FLORENCE, nurse practitioner; b. Braham, Minn., Apr. 8, 1926; d. William and Christine (Judin) C.; m. John Dunkerken, May 30, 1987. Diploma in nursing, U. Minn., 1947, BS, 1953; MPH, Loma Linda (Calif.) U., 1974. RN, Calif. Operating room scrub nurse Calif. Luth. Hosp., L.A., 1947-48; indsl. staff nurse Good Samaritan Hosp., L.A., 1948-49; staff nurse Passavant Hosp., Chgo., 1950-51; student health nurse Moody Bible Inst., Chgo., 1950-51; staff nurse St. Andrews Hosp., Mpls., 1951-53; pub. health nurse Bapt. Gen. Conf. Bd. of World Missions, Ethiopia, Africa, 1954-66; staff pub. health nurse County of San Bernadino, Calif., 1966-68, sr. pub. health nurse, 1968-73, pediatric nurse practitioner, 1973—. Contbr. articles to profl. jours. Mem. bd. dist. missions Bapt. Gen. Conf., Calif., 1978-84; mem. adv. coun. Kaiser Hosp., Fontana, Calif., 1969-85, Bethel Sem. West, San Diego, 1987—; bd. dirs. Casa Verdugo Retirement Home, Hemet, Calif., 1985—; active Calvary Bapt. Ch., Redlands, Calif., 1974—; mem. S.W. Bapt. Conf. Social Ministries, 1993—. With USPHS, 1944-47. Calif. State Dept. Health grantee, 1973. Fellow Nat. Assn. Pediatric Nurse Assocs. and Practitioners; mem. Calif. Nurses Assn. (state nursing coun. 1974-76). Democrat.

COLEMAN, BRENDA FORBIS, gifted and talented educator; b. Dallas, May 17, 1951; d. Thomas Carlyle and Dorothy Jean (Tillerson) Forbis; m. Rufus Andrew Coleman, July 2, 1971; 1 child, Christopher Andrew. BS, Dallas Bapt. U., 1972; MEd, East Tex. State U., 1979; cert. gifted and talented, Tex. Woman's U., 1990. Elem. tchr. Plano (Tex.) Ind. Sch. Dist., 1972-79; elem. tchr. Lewisville (Tex.) Ind. Sch. Dist., 1983-86, gifted and talented facilitator, 1986-89; elem. tchr. Lake Dallas (Tex.) Ind. Sch. Dist., 1989-91, gifted and talented EXCEL program coord., 1991—; presenter in field. Organizer canned food dr. Lake Dallas Families, 1989. Mem. Tex. Assn. for Gifted and Talented, Assn. of Tex. Profl. Educators, Phi Delta Kappa. Republican. Methodist. Home: 109 Woody Trl Lake Dallas TX 75065-3123 Office: Lake Dallas Ind Sch Dist 190 Falcon Dr Lake Dallas TX 75065

COLEMAN, CAROLYN, state legislator; b. Oklahoma City, Oct. 15, 1952; d. Irwin Arthur and Beulah Wyatt; m. Richard E. Coleman; children: Mary Rachel, Sarah Elizabeth. Student, Rose State Coll., Southwestern Bible Coll. Mem. Okla. Ho. of Reps., Oklahoma City, 1990—. Mem. Metro South Crisis Ctr., Okla. Fedn. Rep. Women. Home: 1617 SE 5th St Moore OK 73160-8337 Office: Okla Ho of Reps State Capitol Oklahoma City OK 73105*

COLEMAN, CATHERINE AMELIA, market analyst; b. Augusta, Ga., Mar. 12, 1963; d. Thomas Gerald and Carole (Garrett) C. Student, Livingston U., 1981-84; BS in Computer Sci., Bus. Mgmt., U. South Ala., 1989. Fin. adviser Citicorp Retail Services, Mobile, Ala., 1985-86; market analyst QMS Inc., Mobile, 1986-90; sales rep. Premier Indsl. Corp., Mobile, 1990-93; acct. exec. Household Fin. Corp., Mobile, 1993—. Home: 6050 Grelot Rd Apt 101 Mobile AL 36609-3664 Office: 3725 Airport Blvd Ste 139 Mobile AL 36608

COLEMAN, CHERYL ANTON, sales executive; b. Toledo, Nov. 3, 1953; d. Ralph Herbert Snyder and Coletta Marie Nickerson; 1 child, John Daniel; m. Rodgers A. Coleman, Jan. 11, 1992; stepchildren: Benjamin Scott, Christi

Shelaine. Student U. Toledo, 1971-73. With Kroger Co., Toledo, 1972-80, dept. supr. merchandising; sales dir. Growth Unltd., Toledo, 1979-80; owner CJ's Bar, Toledo, 1980-82; sales rep. Armour Food Co., Orlando, Fla., 1983-85; dist. sales mgr. Jones Dairy Farm, 1985-87; regional sales mgr. Southland Corp., 1987-92. Mem. NAFE (network dir. 1979—), Nat. Assn. for Women. Democrat. Home: PO Box 1115 Rockwall TX 75087 Office: Southland Corp 2711 N Haskell Ave Dallas TX 75204

COLEMAN, CLAIRE KOHN, public relations executive; b. New Castle, Pa., Nov. 19, 1924; d. Louis and Florence (Frank) K.; BA, Pa. State U., 1945; m. Frederick H. Coleman, Mar. 10, 1957; children: Franklin, Elliot. Market editor Fairchild Publs., N.Y.C., 1945-48; asst. home editor N.Y. Times, 1949-50; public relations dir. United Wallpaper, Chgo., 1950-53; public relations dir. Asso. Am. Artists, N.Y.C., 1953-54; dir. Wallpaper Info. Bur., N.Y.C., 1954; dept. head Roy Bernard, Inc., N.Y.C., 1955-58; public relations dir. The Siesel Co., N.Y.C., 1972—, sr. v.p., 1981-88; pres. Tisch Trask Comm. Resources Pub. Rels. Group, 1988-89; sr. v.p. Anthony M. Franco, N.Y.C., 1989-90; pres. Coleman Comm., N.Y., 1990—. Mem. central steering com., Sch. Dist. Critical Assessments, New Rochelle, N.Y., 1969-71; bd. dirs., v.p. Beechmont Assn., 1960-74; mem. Mayor's Adv. Council on Aging, 1966; mem. Mayor's Adv. Com. on Bd. Edn. Appointments, 1969; v.p. Council of PTAs, 1969-70; chmn. women's div. United Jewish Appeal, New Rochelle, 1971. Fellow Internat. Furnishings and Design Assn. (formerly Nat. Home Fashions League: founder 1947, nat. treas. 1977-78, nat. pres. 1980-81, N.Y. chpt. v.p. 1994, Cir. of Excecllence award 1994); mem. Women Execs. Pub. Rels. (bd. dirs. 1983-84, sec. 86-87, found. pres. 1993-94, v.p. 1994-95), Woman Execs. Pub. Rels. Found. (v.p. 1992-93, pres. 1993-94.

COLEMAN, DEBORAH ANN, electronics company executive; b. Central Falls, R.I., Jan. 22, 1953; d. John Austin and Joan Mary Coleman. BA, Brown U., 1974; MBA, Stanford U., 1978; PhD in Engring. (hon.), Worcester (Mass.) Poly., 1987. Mfg. supr. Tex. Instruments, Attleboro, Mass., 1974; with fin. mgmt. tng. program Gen. Electric, Providence, 1975-76; with fin. mgmt. Hewlett-Packard, Cupertino, Calif., 1978-81; contr. Macintosh/Apple 32 group Apple Computer, Cupertino, 1981-84, dir. ops., 1984-85, v.p. worldwide mfg., 1985-87, CFO, 1987-89, CIO, 1990-92; v.p. materials ops. Tektronix Inc., Wilsonville, OR, 1992-94; chmn., CEO Merix Corp., Forest Grove, OR, 1994—; Mem. U.S. Dept. Def. Mfg. Sci. Tech. Bd., 1988-91; bd. dirs. VMX, Inc., Software Pub Corp., Octel. Mem. adv. coun. Stanford Inst. Mfg. Automation, 1985-87; mem. Harvard U. Bus. Sch. Vis. Com., 1987—, Com. of 200, 1987—; trustee San Jose/Cleve. Ballet, 1989-92, Brown U., 1994—. Mem. Internat. Women's Forum. Democrat. Roman Catholic. Office: Merix Corp 1521 Poplar Ln PO Box 3000 FI-385 Forest Grove OR 97116

COLEMAN, ELISABETH CHARLOTTE, corporate communications executive; b. Woking, Surrey, Eng., May 26, 1945; came to U.S., 1949; d. David and Anne Lise (Bojesen) C.; m. Rock Brynner, Dec. 24, 1978 (div. Jan. 1984). BA, Vassar Coll., 1966. Researcher Newsweek Mag., N.Y.C., 1967-70; corr. Newsweek Mag., San Francisco, 1970-73; reporter Sta. KQED-TV, San Francisco, 1973; radio-TV reporter ABC News, N.Y.C., 1973-74; reporter Sta. KABC-TV News, L.A., 1974-76; press sec. to Gov. Edmund G. Brown, Jr. Sacramento, 1976-78; producer Inside Story, PBS series, N.Y.C., 1980-82, Jack Hilton Prodns., N.Y.C., 1982-85; pres. Coleman Prodns., N.Y.C., 1985-88; dir. pub. rels. Ernst & Whinney, N.Y.C., 1988-90; v.p. internat. pub. affairs Am. Express, N.Y.C., 1990—. Contbr. articles to N.Y. Sunday Times Mag., Columbia Journalism Review, Family Weekly, N.Y. Daily News. Mem. PRSA, AFTRA. Office: Am Express Travel Related Svcs American Express Tower New York NY 10285

COLEMAN, FRANCES MCLEAN, secondary school educator; b. Jackson, Miss., Feb. 17, 1940; d. Robert Beatty and Dorothy Trotter (Witty) McLean.; m. Thomas Allen Coleman, Aug. 29, 1964; children: James Plemon, Robert McLean, Dorothy Witty McLean, Josiah Dennis, Leonidas McLean. BA, U. Miss., Oxford, 1962; MS, U. Miss., Jackson, 1964, PhD, 1970. Cert. tchr., Miss. Coord. Title I ESEA Choctaw County, Ackerman, Miss., 1970-73; instr. anatomy and physiology Wood Jr. Coll., Mathiston, Miss., 1977-78; instr. math. Miss. State U., Starkville, 1978-81; tchr. Choctaw City Sch. Dist., Ackerman, 1982—. Author: (jour.) Surgery, 1966. Active Miss. State Bd. of Health, Jackson, 1980-94. Recipient Presdl. award for Excellence in Sci. Teaching NSF, 1990, Sci. Tchr. awards Disney, 1993; Coun. for Basic Edn. Sci.-Math. fellow, 1994; named Educator of Yr. Milken Family Founds., 1991; Tandy scholar, 1991. Mem. Nat. Sci. Tchrs. Assn., Am. Assn. German Tchrs., Am. Assn. French Tchrs., Am. Assn. Physics Tchrs., Nat. Assn. Biology Tchrs., Miss. Edn. Computer Assn. (Miss. Computer Educator of Yr. 1990), Miss. Fgn. Lang. Assn. (pres. secondary sect. 1992-94). Episcopalian. Home: Box 268 Ackerman MS 39735 Office: Choctaw County Sch Dist Box 398 Ackerman MS 39735

COLEMAN, GLORIA JEAN, chemical manufacturing company professional; b. Hannibal, Mo., May 9, 1952; d. Gene Hughes and Joan (Wiley) Carroll; m. Larry Dean Coleman, Nov. 25, 1971. BBA, Culver-Stockton Coll., Canton, Mo., 1992. Cert. profl. sec. Sec., bookkeeper, cashier Western-So. Life Ins., Hannibal, Mo., 1970-77; exec. sec. Marion County Mut. Savs. and Loan, Hannibal, 1977; acctg./info. svcs. dept. sec. Am. Cyanamid, Hannibal, 1977-85, users svcs. coordinator, 1985-88, analyst office systems, 1988-90, analyst computer edn. and tng., 1990—; mem. adv. bd. Hannibal area Vocat. Tech. Sch. Bus. Edn. Com., 1985-91; pub. speaker area schs. and svc. orgns., Quincy, Ill., Hannibal, Springfield, Mo., 1986—. Bd. dirs. ARC, Hannibal; mentor Bus. and Profl. Women's Club, Hannibal, 1985-86,also coord. individual devel. program for pub. speaking; fundraiser Convocom Pub. Broadcasting Sta., Quincy, 1986, Hannibal, 1988. Mem. Cert. Profl. Sec. Acad., Profl. Secs. Internat. (sec. Quinsippi chpt. 1984-85, v.p. Heartland chpt. 1988-89, pres. 1989-91, parliamentarian 1991-93, pres. Mo. div. 1993-94, Sec. of Yr. 1985), Kiwanis (Early Bird 1990-94). Mem. Assembly of God Ch. Home: 106 Butternut Dr Hannibal MO 63401 Office: Am Cyanamid PO Box 817 Hannibal MO 63401-0817

COLEMAN, JEAN BLACK, nurse, physician assistant; b. Sharon, Pa., Jan. 11, 1925; d. Charles B. and Sue E. (Dougherty) Black; m. Donald A. Coleman, July 3, 1946; children: Sue Ann Lopez, Donald Ashley. RN, Spencer Hosp. Sch. Nursing, Meadville, Pa., 1945; student Vanderbilt U., 1952-54. Nurse, dir. nursing Bulloch Meml. Hosp., Statesboro, Ga., 1948-51, nurse supr. surgery, 1954-67, dir. nursing, 1967-71; physicians asst., nurse anesthetist to Robert H. Swint, Statesboro, 1971—; mem. physician assts. adv. com. Bd. Med. Examiners Ga., 1987—. Named Woman of Yr. in Med. Field, Bus. and Profl. Women, 1980. Mem. ANA, Ga. Nurses Assn., Am. Acad. Physicians Assts., Ga. Assn. Physicians Assts. (bd. dirs. 1975-79, v.p. 1979-80, pres. 1980-81), Ga. Bd. Med. Examiners (ex-officio mem. 1994). Democrat. Roman Catholic.

COLEMAN, JULIE KATHRYN, middle school educator; b. Peoria, Ill., Sept. 18, 1955; d. John Edward and Mary Ann (Koch) Birdoes Jr.; m. Richard Lee Coleman, Aug. 14, 1976; children: William Casey, Jaime Lee. BS in Edn., Ill. State U., 1977, MS in English, 1986. Cert. elem. educator, secondary English tchr., Ill., Ala., Fla. Tchr. English Norwood Sch., Peoria, Ill., 1977-85; tchr. Saint Pius X Sch., Mobile, Ala., 1985-86, Cora Castlen Elem. Sch., Grand Bay, Ala., 1986-87; tchr. Dr. W. J. Creel Elem. Sch., Melbourne, Fla., 1987-89, tchr., team chairperson, 1989-93; 7th and 9th grade lit. tchr. DeLaura Jr. High Sch., Satellite Beach, Fla., 1993—; adv. bd. Limestone Area Curriculum Adv. Com., Peoria, 1977-85; adv. com. mem. Peoria County Inst. Curriculum Com., 1982-85; presenter in field. Mem. Metro-Mobile Reading Coun., Brevard Reading Coun., Delta Kappa Gamma-Beta Sigma. Democrat. Roman Catholic. Home: 305 Park Ave Satellite Beach FL 32937

COLEMAN, K(ATHERINE) ANN, educator; b. Plattsburg, N.Y.; d. John and Anna C. BS, Elms Coll., 1963; MS, Springfield Coll., 1964; PhD, Boston Coll., 1971; MPH, Harvard U., 1978. Psychologist Exec. Office of the Pres., Washington, 1964-66; research assoc. Harvard U., Cambridge, Mass., 1970-71; asst. prof. SUNY, Stony Brook, 1971-75, asst. prof., 1975-78; assoc. prof. Boston U., 1978—; owner, pres. La Di Da Properties, Cambridge, 1986—. Co-author: (with others) Behavioral Statistics: The Core, 1994; contbr. articles to profl. jours. Mem. New Eng. Ednl. Rsch. Orgn. (bd. dirs. 1974-86, v.p. 1985-86, pres. 1986-87), Ea. Ednl. Rsch. Orgn. (div. chmn. 1979-91, bd. dirs. 1985-91). Home: 32 Shepard St Cambridge MA 02138-1519 Office: Boston U Dept Psychology 64 Cummington St Boston MA 02215-2407

COLEMAN, KATHY WRAY, science educator; b. Louisville, July 14, 1960; d. James M. and Gertrude (White) C. BS in Biology, Ky. State U., 1983; MAT, Spalding U., 1986. Cert. tchr., Ohio. Tchr. sci. Cleve. Pub. Schs., 1986—, tutor, 1989—; tchr. sci. Case Western Res. U., Cleve., 1990—; staff reporter Call and Post Newspaper, Cleve., 1993—; advisor Summer Youth Employment Tng. Program, Cleve., 1987; rsch. asst. Case Western Res. U. Med. Sch., Cleve., summer 1991; program coord. CTV Steel Summer Inst., Cleve., 1992—. Founder African Am. Women's Polit. Action Com., 1993—; active NAACP, Grass Roots Poets Polit. Action Com., 1990—, 11th Dist. Congl. Caucus, 1989—. Recipient Ednl. Activist award The Grass Roots Polit. Action Com., 1990, Tchr. Par Excellence award Cleve. Sch. Budget Coalition, 1989. Mem. NOW (Woman of Yr. 1993). Democrat. Home: 3901 Silsby Rd University Heights OH 44118 Office: Cleve Pub Schs 1380 E 6th St Cleveland OH 44144

COLEMAN, LILLIAN SIMONS, editor, writer; b. Atlanta, Jan. 26, 1955; d. Henry Mazyck and Martha Jane (Mack) Simons; m. John Dozier Coleman III, Nov. 29, 1975; children: Keating Simons, Lillian Marshall, John Dozier IV. BA in English, Columbia (S.C.) Coll., 1977; M in Mass Communications, U. S.C., 1980. Instr. journalism U. S.C., Sumter, 1979-82; communications mgr. Assn. for Edn. in Journalism and Mass Communication, Columbia, 1982-84, asst. editor, 1984-87, editor AEJMC News and Journalism and Mass Communication Directory, 1987—; freelance writer, photographer Sandlapper mag., Columbia, 1980-82, Carolina Lifestyle mag., Columbia, 1983. Office: Assn Edn in Journalism & Mass Comm 1621 College St Columbia SC 29208-0251

COLEMAN, LINDA, state legislator. BA, U. Miss.; JD, Miss. Coll. State rep., mem. penitentiary com., vice chairwoman county affairs, judiciary, pub. bldgs., grounds & lands coms. Miss. Ho. of Reps., Jackson. Mem. Nat. Bar Assn., Magnolia Bar Assn. Democrat. Baptist. Office: Miss Ho of Reps State Capitol Jackson MS 39205*

COLEMAN, NANCY CATHERINE, actress; b. Everett, Wash., Dec. 30, 1912; d. Charles Sumner Coleman and Grace Sharpless; m. Whitney French Bolton, Sept. 16, 1943 (dec. Nov. 1969); children: Charla Elizabeth, Grania Theresa. BA, U. Wash., 1934. Appeared in films including King's Row, 1941, Dangerously They Live, 1941, The Gay Sisters, 1942, Desperate Journey, 1942, The Edge of Darkness, 1943, In Our Time, 1944, Devotion, 1946, Her Sister's Secret, 1947, That Man From Tangier, 1953, Slaves, 1968; various TV shows including Valiant Lady, 1954-55; plays include Susan and God with Gertrude Lawrence, 1938, The Desperate Hours, 1955. Mem. AFTRA, SAG, N.Y. TV Acad., Actors' Equity, Motion Picture Arts and Scis.

COLEMAN, PATRICIA BARRY, chemist; b. Richmond, Va., May 29, 1952; d. Thomas Byrnes and Marie Elizabeth (Sauerwald) Barry; m. David Michael Roush, June 23, 1973 (div. 1982); 1 child, Jennifer Marie; m. David Manley Coleman, Oct. 14, 1990. BS, Coll. William and Mary, 1973; PhD, U. Calif., Davis, 1977. Rsch. staff Western Electric, Princeton, N.J., 1977-81; spectroscopist Internat. Minerals & Chems., Terre Haute, Ind., 1981-83; sr. applications chemist Perkin-Elmer, Norwalk, Conn., 1983-87; sr. tech. specialist Perkin-Elmer, Norwalk, 1987-91, sr. engr., 1991-92; prin. rsch. sci. assoc. Ford Motor Co., Dearborn, Mich., 1992—. Editor: The Design, Sample Handling & Applications of Infrared Microscopes, 1987, Practical Sampling Techniques for Infrared Analysis, 1993; co-editor-in-chief: Critical Reviews in Analytical Chemistry, 1991-94. Mem. ASTM (sec. 1982-85), ANACHEM (pres. 1994), E-13 Molecular Spectroscopy (sec.), Fedn. Analytical Chemistry & Spectroscopy Socs. (long range planning chair 1991-94, governing bd. chmn. 1987, program chair 1984), Soc. for Applied Spectroscopy (pres. 1986). Office: Ford Motor Co Mail Drop 3061/SRL 20000 Rotunda Dearborn MI 48121-2053

COLEMAN, VICTORIA ALLEN, small business owner, horticulturist; b. Mooresville, N.C., Apr. 21, 1952; d. Charles Gray Allen and Betty Jean (Webster) Canty; m. Oscar Gene Colemam III, May 28, 1971; children: April Ann, Amie Jean, Oscar Gene IV. Owner, designer Coleman's Indoor Plants, Charlotte, N.C., 1974-78; part-owner, sec., treas. B&B Greenhouses, Midland, N.C., 1978-81; part owner, mgr. Coleman's Greehouses, Inc., West Palm Beach, Fla., 1981-87; owner Coleman's Greenhouses, Midland, N.C., 1987—.

COLEMAN, WINIFRED ELLEN, administrator; b. Syracuse, N.Y., Oct. 3, 1932; d. Peter Andrew and Josephine (Fahey) C. BA, Lemoyne Coll., Syracuse, N.Y., 1954; MA, Marquette U., 1956. Dean of students Cazenovia (N.Y.) Coll., 1957-71; dean of students Trinity Coll., Washington, 1971-81; exec. dir. Nat. Coun. Catholic Women, Washington, 1981-85; pres. St. Joseph Coll., West Hartford, Conn., 1991—; bd. trustees, Lemoyne Coll., Syracuse, 1980-86, Loretto Geriatric Ctr, Syracuse, 1987—, St. Vincent DePaul Soc., Syracuse; mem. Nat. Assn. Women Deans, Washington, 1957-81. Vice chmn. Syracuse Commn. for Women, 1986—; commr. Metro Commn. for Aging, Syracuse, 1987—; bd. dirs. Cen City Girl Scout Coun. Hon. Trinity Coll. Alumnae, Washington, 1978, Cazenovia (N.Y.) Coll. Alumnae, 1968, Naming of Winifred E. Coleman Student Union, Cazenovia Coll., 1961; recipeint Chantal Award, Catholic Daughters of the Am. 1963. Mem. Alpha Sigma Nu (nat. bd. dirs. 1980-82). Roman Catholic. Home: 27 Buckingham Ln West Hartford CT 06117-2758 Office: St Joseph Coll 1678 Asylum Ave West Hartford CT 06117

COLEMAN-JOHNSON, DEBRA LYNN, electrical engineer; b. Mobile, Ala., Apr. 7, 1966; d. Fred and Mattie Lois (Carter) C.; married, June 2, 1990. BSEE, Boston U., 1988. Test engr. Raytheon Corp., Andover, Mass., 1987-88; liaison design engr. Boeing Co., Everett, Wash., 1988-89; software engr. Boeing Co., Seattle, 1989-90; sr. sys. engr. Boeing Co., Renton, Wash., 1990—; pres., owner Beacon Pub. and Media House, Seattle, 1994—; lectr. Math., Engring. and Sci. Achievement Orgn., 1989—; v.p. Seattle City Tours, 1990-93. Vol. MATHCOUNTS, Seattle, YMCA Black Achievers Program, 1994—. Mem. Nat. Soc. Black Engrs. Home: 3020 21st Ave S Seattle WA 98144-5906 Office: Beacon Pub and Media House 3020 21st Ave S Seattle WA 98124-2207

COLEMAN-RICE, JANIE LOU, elementary teacher; b. Pikeville, Ky., July 6, 1966; d. John Ellis and Fern (Justice) Coleman; m. James Claude Rice, July 25, 1992. BS in Edn., Pikeville Coll., 1989; MA in Edn., Morehead State U., 1993. Cert. elem. sch. counselor, Ky. Elem. tchr. Pike County Bd. Edn., Pikeville, Ky., 1990—; coach high sch. softball, Mullins High Sch., Pikeville, 1990-93, jr. high basketball, Mullins Jr. High Sch., 1993—; mem. sight-based decision making coun., Mullins Sch., 1993—. Named Ky. Col., State Gov. Mem. Am. Counseling Assn., Am. Sch. Counselors Assn., Nat. Edn. Assn.,Ky. Counseling Assn., Ky. Edn. Assn., Pike County Edn. Assn. Mem. Church of Christ. Home: RR 3 Box 594A Pikeville KY 41501-8281 Office: Mullins Sch 1265 N Mayo Trl Pikeville KY 41501-8299

COLEMAN WOOD, KRISTA ANN, physical therapy educator; b. Decatur, Ill., July 28, 1956; d. Wayne Dudley and Shirley Margaret (Doner) Coleman; m. Earl Andrew Wood, Mar. 21, 1987; 1 child, Karolyn Christine. BS, Eastern Ill. U., Charleston, 1978; BS in Phys. Therapy, U. Ill., Peoria, 1980; MSc in Bioengring., U. Strathclyde, Glasgow, Scotland, 1986; MS in Phys. Therapy, U. Minn., Mpls., 1988, PhD in Biomechanics, 1994. Lic. phys. therapist, Minn., Wis. Staff phys. therapist Bellin Meml. Hosp., Green Bay, Wis., 1980-82, Rehab. Specialists, Anoka, Minn., 1982-83, Fairview Hosp., Mpls., 1983-85; grad. rsch. and teaching asst. U. Minn., Mpls., 1984-85, 86-89, instr. phys. therapy curriculum, dept. phys. medicine, 1989-92, clin. specialist faculty phys. therapy curriculum, 1992—; cons. Recreational Opportunities for Physically Disabled, Green Bay, Wis., 1980-82; mem. survey team Green Bay Area Accessibility Guide, 1982. Mem. Robbinsdale (Minn.) Crime Prevention Assn., 1989. Rotary Found. grad. fellow, 1985-86, Charles and Constance Murcott Found. scholar Found. Phys. Therapy, 1988-89. Mem. WISE, Am. Phys. Therapy Assn., Am. Coll. Sports Medicine, Rehab. Engring. Soc. N.Am., Internat. Soc. Biomechanics, Soc. Orthopedic Medicine, Minn. Orthopedic Phys. Therapy Study Group (pres. 1994—), Phi Sigma. Methodist. Office: Univ Minn Minneapolis MN 55455

COLES, ANNA LOUISE BAILEY, university official, nurse; b. Kansas City, Kans., Jan. 16, 1925; d. Gordon Alonzo and Lillie Mai (Buchanan) Bailey; children: Margot, Michelle, Gina. Diploma, Freedmen's Hosp. Sch. Nursing, 1948; B.S. in Nursing, Avila Coll., Kansas City, Mo., 1958; M.S. in Nursing, Cath. U. Am., 1960, Ph.D. in Higher Edn., 1967. Instr. VA Hosp., Topeka, 1950-52; supr. VA Hosp., Kansas City, Mo., 1952-58; asst. dir. in-service edn. Freedmen's Hosp., Washington, 1960-61; adminstrv. asst. to dir. nursing Freedmen's Hosp., 1961-66, assoc. dir. nursing services, 1966-67, dir. nursing, 1967-69; dean Howard U. Coll. Nursing, Washington, 1968-86, dean emeritus, 1986—; cons. pvt. practice, Kansas City, Kans.; dir. minority devel. U. Kans., 1991—; cons. Gen. Research Support Program, NIH, 1972-76, VA health care com. NRC-Nat. Acad. Scis., 1975-76, VA Central Office continuing edn. com., 1976—; pres. Nurses Examining Bd., 1967-68; mem. Inst. Medicine, Nat. Acad. Scis., 1974—; Mem. D.C. Health Planning Adv. Com., 1968-71, Tri-State Regional Planning Com. for Nursing Edn., 1969, Health Adv. Council, Nat. Urban Coalition, 1971-73. Contbr. articles to profl. jours. Bd. dirs. Iona Whipper Home for Unwed Mothers, 1970-72; bd. dirs. Nursing Edn. Opportunities, 1970-72; trustee Community Group Health Found., 1976-77, cons., 1977—; bd. regents State Univ. System Fla., 1977; adv. bd. Am. Assn. Med. Vols., 1970-72. Recipient sustained superior performance award HEW, 1962, Meritorious Pub. Svc. award Govt. of D.C., 1968, medal of honor Avila Coll., 1969, Disting. Alumni award Howard U. Nat. Assn. for Equal Opportunity in Higher Edn., 1990, cmty. svc. award Black Profl. Nurses Kansas City, 1991, lifetime achievement award Assn. Black Nursing Faculty in Higher Edn., 1993, svc. award Midwest Regional Conf. on Black Families and Children, 1994. Mem. Nat. League Nursing (dir.), Am. Nurses Assn., Freedmen's Hosp. Nursing Alumni Assn., Am. Congress Rehab. Medicine, Am. Assn. Colls. of Nursing (sec. 1975-76), Societas Docta, Inc., Sigma Theta Tau, Alpha Kappa Alpha. Home: 6841 Garfield Dr Kansas City KS 66102-1038

COLETTA, HALLIE ADRIENNE, scenic artist, illustrator; b. N.Y.C., Sept. 8, 1951; d. Harold Robert and Irene Ann (Mozdzier) C. Student, Acad. di Belle Arti, Venice, 1970-71. Scenic artist United Scenic Artists, N.Y.C., 1986—; jewelry designer Coronet Jewelry Mfg., N.Y. and N.J., 1972-90; freelance artist Coletta Design Co., New City, N.Y., 1980—; scenic artist Penquin Repertory Co., Stony Point, N.Y., 1985—. Illustrator (children's book) From A to Z, 1980 (Art Dirs. Club award), The Illustrated Treasury of Humor for Children, 1980. Bd. dirs. West Br. Conservation Assn., New City, 1975—. Recipient Merit award Art Dirs. Club N.Y., 1980, Creative Arts Honor award Nat. Poetry Press, 1969, Regents Art award N.Y. Bd. Regents, 1969, Hon. Mention award Nat. Comml. Sign Design Contest, 1986. Mem. United Scenic Artists Union (local 829). Democrat. Home: 232-242 Zukor Rd New City NY 10956

COLETTA, NANCY JOY, vision scientist, educator; b. Pawtucket, R.I., Sept. 3, 1955; d. Armand Anthony and Nora Afton C. BS, Providence Coll., 1977; OD, Pa. Coll. Optometry, 1981; PhD, U. Calif., Berkeley, 1985. Guest worker Nat. Eye Inst., Bethesda, Md., 1980-81; rsch. assoc. Ctr. for Visual Sci. U. Rochester, N.Y., 1985-87; asst. prof. optometry U. Houston, 1988-94, assoc. prof. optometry, 1994—; grant referee NSF, 1988-90; jour. referee Vision Rsch., 1985—, Jour. Physiology, 1990, Jour. Optical Soc., 1987—, Investigative Ophthalmology and Visual Sci., 1989—, Visual Neurosci., 1991—, Optometry and Vision Sci., 1994—. Contbr. articles to Applied Optics, Archives of Ophthalmology, Investigative Opththalmology and Visual Sci., Jour. Optical Soc. Am., Ophthalmic and Physiol. Optics, Vision Rsch. Recipient Harold Kohn award Am. Optometric Found., 1981, Chancellor's Patent Fund award U. Calif., Berkeley, 1985, Best Post award Houston Soc. for Engring. in Medicine and Biology, 1991; grantee SPIE, 1988, NIH, 1989, 91, Nat. Eye Inst., 1992—. Fellow Am. Acad. Optometry; mem. Optical Soc. Am., Assn. for Rsch. in Vision and Ophthalmology, Sigma Xi, Beta Sigma Kappa. Office: U Houston 4901 Calhoun Rd Houston TX 77004-2612

COLFACK, ANDREA HECKELMAN, elementary education educator; b. Yreka, Calif., July 17, 1945; d. Robert A. Davis and June (Reynolds) Butler; m. David Lee Heckelman, Sept. 5, 1965 (div. Nov. 1982); children: Barbara, Julie; m. Neal Cleve, Jan. 1, 1984; 1 stepchild, Karl. AB, Calif. State U., L.A., 1966; MA, Calif. State U., Fresno, 1969. Life standard elem. credential, Calif. cert. competencs: Spanish, Calif.; ordained to ministry Faith Christian Fellowship Internat., 1987. Tchr. Tulare (Calif.) City Schs., 1966-67, Palo Verde Union Sch. Dist., 1967-70, Cutler-Orosi (Calif.) Union Sch. Dist., 1979-82, Hornbrook (Calif.) Union Sch. Dist., 1982-84; sales mgr. Tupperware, Fresno, Calif., 1973-79; bilingual tchr. Richmond (Calif.) Unified Sch. Dist., 1984—; site mentor Bayview Elem. Sch., Richmond, 1990-91; ELD mentor, Richmond, 1992-94; elected to dist. Mentor Selection Com., 1994-95. Co-author: Project Mind Expansion, 1974. Mem. United Tchrs. Richmond, Calif. Assn. Bilingual Educators (sec. Richmond 1990-91), AAUW (pres. Tulare br. 1967-68). Democrat. Pentecostal. Home: 875 Redwood Ct Crockett CA 94525-1442 Office: Grant Elem Sch ELD/Bilingual Resource 2400 Downer Ave Richmond CA 94804-1458

COLFLESH, TRUDY PATTERSON, psychotherapist, author; b. Steubenville, Ohio, June 6, 1939; d. Robert Mead and Gertrude (Lippencott) Patterson; m. George William Colflesh, Aug. 5, 1961; children: Michael, Christopher, Karen. BA in Religious Studies, Coll. Wooster, 1961; postgrad., Oberlin Sch. Theology, 1962; MA in Counseling and Human Devel., Montclair State U., 1990. Dir. Christian Edn. Calvary Presbyn. Ch., Canton, Ohio, 1961-63; counselor Christian Counseling Ctr., Clifton, N.J., 1990—; founder women's support groups St. Andrew's Presbyn. Ch., Berea, Ohio, 1966-72, elder, 1972; founding v.p. Women's Aglow Fellowship Internat., Miami, Fla., 1973-75, area v.p. Outreach and Retreats, No. N.J., 1980-86. Author: Too Precious to Die, 1984. Mem. Am. Assn. Christian Counselors, Am. Counseling Assn., Nat. Assn. for Christian Recovery, Phi Kappa Phi. Home: 33 Northwood Dr West Milford NJ 07480-3724 Office: Christian Counseling Ctr 352 Clifton Ave Clifton NJ 07011-2619

COLGATE, DORIS ELEANOR, retailer, sailing school administrator; b. Washington, May 12, 1941; d. Bernard Leonard and Frances Lillian (Goldstein) Horecker; m. Richard G. Buchanan, Sept. 6, 1959 (div. Aug. 1967); m. Stephen Colgate, Dec. 17, 1969. Student Antioch Coll., 1958-60, NYU, 1960-62. Rsch. supr. Geyer Moyer Ballard, N.Y.C., 1962-64; adminstrv. asst. Yachting Mag., N.Y.C., 1964-68; v.p. Offshore Sailing Sch. Ltd., Inc., N.Y.C., 1968-78, pres., Ft. Myers, Fla., 1978—; pres., CEO On and Offshore, Inc., Ft. Myers, 1984—; v.p. Offshore Travel, Inc., City Island, 1978-88. Author: The Bareboat Gourmet, 1983; contbr. articles to profl. jours. Mem. Royal Ocean Racing Club (London chpt.), Nat. Women's Sailing Assn. (chair nat. women's adv. bd. 1990-94, chair, 1991-94, pres. 1994—), Am. Women's Econ. Devel. Corp. (adv. bd. 1980-86, Betty Cook Meml. Lifetime Achievement award 1994), Internat. Women Boating (bd. dirs.). Avocations: sailing, photography, writing, cooking. Home: 1555 San Carlos Bay Dr Sanibel FL 33957-3423 Office: Offshore Inc 16731 McGregor Blvd Fort Myers FL 33908-3876

COLGATE, JESSIE M., insurance company executive, lawyer; b. Buffalo, N.Y., May 13, 1950; d. Richard M. Colgate and Rosemary (Hall) Evans. AB, Harvard U., 1972; JD, Georgetown U., 1977. Bar: D.C. 1977. Assoc. Shea Gould, Washington, 1977-79, Steptoe & Johnson, Washington, 1979-86, Miller & Chevalier, Washington, 1986; v.p. N.Y. Life Ins. Co., Washington, 1987—. Bd. dirs. Columbia Hosp. for Women, Washington, 1986—. Mem. ABA, D.C. Bar Assn. Episcopalian. Office: NY Life Ins Co 1001 Pennsylvania Ave NW Washington DC 20004-2505

COLIN, KIM RENEE, financial advisor; b. Hardin, Mont., Oct. 7, 1957; d. Raymond and Doris C. Student, Wash. State U., 1976-77. Cert. fin. planner. Registered rep. Investor's Diversified Services, Honolulu, 1978-79, Portland, Oreg., 1979-80; registered rep. Waddell & Reed, Inc., Portland, 1980-81; fin. advisor, pres. Diversified Fin. Planning, Inc., Portland, Oreg., 1981—; cons. Money Mag., Parent Mag., Working Mother, Oregonian Newspaper, Self Mag., USA Today newspaper; continuing edn. tchr. Portland State U., 1987. Author, editor Fin. Perspectives, 1987—. Named One of 200 Top Fin. Planners, Money Mag., 1987. Mem. Inst. Cert. Fin. Planners (pres. Oreg. 1988-89, exec. dir. regional coun.), Internat. Assn. Fin.

Planning (v.p. pub. relations Portland chpt. 1986-87). Office: Diversified Fin Planning 2235 SW Butn Hlsdl Hwy Portland OR 97201

COLISH, MARCIA LILLIAN, history educator; b. Bklyn., July 27, 1937; d. Samuel and Daisy (Kartch) C. B.A. magna cum laude, Smith Coll., 1958; M.A., Yale U., 1959, Ph.D., 1965. Instr. history Skidmore Coll., Saratoga Springs, N.Y., 1962-63; instr. Oberlin Coll., Ohio, 1963-65, asst. prof., 1965-69; assoc. prof. Oberlin Coll, Ohio, 1969-75; prof. history Oberlin Coll., Ohio, 1975—; Frederick B. Artz prof. history Oberlin Coll., 1985—, chmn. dept. history, 1973-74, 78-81, 85-86; vis. scholar Am. Acad. Rome, 1968-69; lectr. history Case Western Res. U., Cleve., 1966-67; editorial cons. W.W. Norton & Co., 1973, John Wiley & Sons, Inc., 1981, SUNY Press, 1983, 85, U. Chgo. Press, 1988, U. Calif. Press, 1988, Princeton U. Press, 1988, U. Notre Dame Press, 1991, 92, 94, U. Ill. Press, 1995, U. Pa. Press, 1995; cons. dept. history Grinnell Coll., 1974, Knox Coll., 1981, St. John's U., 1981, Whitman Coll., 1982, Hope Coll., 1995; mem. exec. bd. Ohio Program Humanities, 1976-81, exec. bd., 1978-81, vice chmn., 1979-81; writing residency, Villa Serbellonia, Bellagio, 1995. Author: The Mirror of Language: A Study in the Medieval Theory of Knowledge, 2d rev. edit., 1983, The Stoic Tradition from Antiquity to the Early Middle Ages, 1985, enlarged paperback edit., 1990, Peter Lombard, 1994. Mem. exec. bd. Oberlin ACLU, 1970-74, chmn., 1972-74, rec. sec., 1976-77, vice chmn., 1979-80; mem. exec. bd. Oberlin YWCA, 1966-70. Samuel S. Fels fellow Yale U., 1961-62, Younger Scholar fellow NEH, 1968-69, sr. fellow, 1981-82, fellow Inst. for Rsch. in Humanities, U. Wis., 1974-75, Nat. Humanities Ctr. fellow, 1981-82, Guggenheim fellow, 1989-90, fellow Woodrow Wilson Ctr., 1994-95; mem. Princeton Inst. Advanced Study, 1986-87; NEH summer grantee U. Calif. Santa Barbara, 1993; recipient Wilbur Cross medal Yale Grad. Sch. Alumni Assn., 1993. Fellow Medieval Acad. Am. (coun. 1987-89, 2d v.p. 1989-90, 1st v.p. 1990-91, pres. 1991-92); mem. Am. Hist. Assn., Medieval Assn. Midwest (coun. 1978-81), Midwest Medieval Conf. (pres. 1978-79), Renaissance Soc. Am., Ctrl. Renaissance Conf., Soc. Internat. pour Etude Philosophie Medievale, Phi Beta Kappa. Home: 143 E College St Apt 310 Oberlin OH 44074-1759 Office: Oberlin Coll Dept History Oberlin OH 44074

COLLADO, CAROL BUTLER, international health consultant, nursing educator; b. N.Y.C., Aug. 28, 1940. BS, Nazareth Coll. of Rochester, 1962; MN, U. Wash., 1968. RN, N.Y., Md. Staff nurse various N.Y.C. hosps., 1962-64; asst. clin. instr. Bellevue-Mills Sch. Nursing, N.Y.C., 1964-65; asst. instr., staff nurse II Cornell U. N.Y. Hosp., N.Y.C., 1965-67; nurse educator (Mex. and Dominican Republic) Pan Am. Health Orgn., WHO, Washington, 1969-76; asst. prof. Coll. Human Devel., Pa. State U., University Park, 1977-79, Duke U., Durham, N.C., 1981-83; staff nurse med.-surg. unit Raleigh (N.C.) Community Hosp., 1981-87; project dir. PINCAP, NEWH, Nursing Consortium, Rocky Mount, N.C., 1983-86; mem. adj. faculty Sch. Nursing George Mason U., Fairfax, Va., 1989—; cons. World Bank, 1988—, Pan Am. Health Organ., 1977—, Coll. of Nursing, Madrid, 1989-90, U. Ill., 1989—, NIH, 1991. Contbr. articles to profl. jours. Mem. ANA, Am. Pub. Health Assn., Nat. League for Nursing (N.C. League for Nursing bd. dirs. 1984-87, program com. 1984-85, membership chmn. 1985-87), Sigma Theta Tau. Home: 13211 Collingwood Ter Silver Spring MD 20904-1419

COLLAZO, VERONICA O., federal agency administrator; b. San Antonio. BA, Am. U., MS in Adminstrn. of Justice; PhD, U. Denver. Dep. dir. internat. mcpl. devel. Internat. City Mgmt. Assn., Washington; dep. dir. Office Human Resource Devel., Washington; dep. chief, pers. liaison and tng., civil divsn. Dept. Justice; dir. Office of Tng. Sys. U.S. Postal Svc., Washington, 1991-92, v.p. diversity devel., 1992—. Office: US Postal Svcs 475 L'Enfant Plz SW Rm 3641 Washington DC 20260-5600*

COLLETTE, FRANCES MADELYN, tax consultant, lawyer; b. Yonkers, N.Y., Aug. 5, 1947; d. Morris Aaron and Esther (Gang) Volbert; m. Roger Warren Collette, Dec. 25, 1971; children: Darren Roger, Bonnie Frances. BEd summa cum laude, SUNY-Buffalo, 1969; JD, cum laude, U. Miami, 1980. Bar: Fla. 1980. Employment counselor Fla. Bur. Employment Security, Miami, 1969-73; unemployment claims adjudicator Fla. Bur. Unemployment Claims, Miami, 1973-77; Fla. unemployment tax and personnel cons.; owner Unemployment Svcs. Fla., Inc., Miami, 1977-93; lectr. in field. Mem. BBB S. Fla. (1st v.p. 1980-81, bd. govs., 2d vice chmn. 1990-91). Jewish.

COLLEY, MARJORIE, association executive; b. Boyne City, Mich., Jan. 3, 1939; d. Ralph Elwood and Lois Louise Brooks; children: Monte, Lori, Terry, Timothy. BA, Western Ill. U., 1985; MS, Aurora U., 1987. Program dir. YMCA, Macomb, Ill., 1975-79; exec. dir. YWCA, Canton, Ill., 1979-85, Aurora, Ill., 1985—; mem. exec. com. Coun. Ill./St. Louis YWCAs, past pres. 1984-85. Chair City of Aurora Youth Study Com., 1992-93; bd. dirs., mem. exec. com. Mercy Ctr. for Health Care Svcs., Aurora, 1992—; mem. adv. com. Riverboat, Aurora, 1993—. Named Career Women of Yr., Daily Ledger, Canton Ill., 1984. Mem. Nat. Assn. YWCA Dirs. (chair nominating com., bd. dirs.), Exch. Club (pres. 1994—), Aurora C. of C. (ambs. 1986-94, bd. dirs. 1987-89). Office: YWCA 201 N River St Aurora IL 60506-4163

COLLIER, BEVERLY JOANNE, elementary education educator; b. Grand Haven, Mich., Oct. 28, 1936; d. Joseph Frank and Anne (Mary) Snyder; divorced; children: Ann, Cindy. Student, U. Mich., 1955-57; BA, Western Mich. U., 1965. Cert. elem. tchr., Mich. 1st grade tchr. Fruitport (Mich.) Community Schs., 1965-93; retired, 1993. Contbr. articles to local newspapers. Active Grand Haven (Mich.) Presbyn. Ch. Mem. ASCD, NEA, Muskegon Edn. Assn., Mich. Edn. Assn. (past regional rep.). Home: 1235 Washington Ave Grand Haven MI 49417-1627 Office: Fruitport Community Sch 305 Pontaluna Rd Fruitport MI 49415-9652

COLLIER, GAIL TARBOX, artist; b. Ithaca, N.Y., June 7, 1946; d. John William and Audrey Anne (Shirey) Tarbox; m. Joe Marvin Collier, Mar. 6, 1971; children: Kendra Seelye, Joel Henderson. BA, Allegheny Coll., 1968; MA, No. Ill. U., 1987. Tchr. watercolor painting South Barrington Park Dist., Barrington, Ill., 1983-86; freelance artist Barrington, Ill., 1983—. Contbg. artist (book) Whetstone, 1987. Showcase chmn. Grove Ave PTO, Barrington, 1983, chmn. picture lady program, 1984-85; mem. PTO bd. Barrington Mid. Sch., 1986-87; mem. fine arts boosters bd. Barrington High Sch., 1988-90. Recipient award excellence North Shore Art League, 1984, Jurors' Choice Purchase award Harper Coll., 1989, Honorable Mention award, Merit award Norris Cultural Ctr., 1988, 89. Mem. Colored Pencil Soc. Am., Profl. Picture Framers Am., Barrington Area Arts Coun. (gallery & sel. com. 1987-89, gallery chmn. 1989, sel. com. 1992), Chgo. Artists Coalition, Deer Path Art League (award for Drawing 1989). Home: 788 Golf Ct Barrington IL 60010-3869

COLLIER-EVANS, DEMETRA FRANCES, veterans benefits counselor; b. Nashville, Dec. 18, 1937; d. Oscar Collier and Earllee Elizabeth (Williams) Collier-Sheffield; m. George Perry Evans, Dec. 21, 1966; 1 child, Richard Edward. AA in Social Sci., Solano Community Coll., Suisun City, Calif., 1974; BA in Social Sci., Chapman Coll., Orange, Calif., 1981. Cert. tchr., Calif. Specialist placement, case responsible person employment devel. dept. City of San Diego, 1975-82; vocat. tchr. San Diego Community Coll., 1982-83; specialist placement N.J. Job Service, Camden, 1984-86, mgr. job bank, 1985; specialist placement Abilities Ctr., Westville, N.J., 1987-88; veteran's benefits counselor VA, Phila. 1988—; mem. bd. dirs. Welfare Rights; cons. Bumble Bee Canning Co., San Diego, 1982. Developer women's seminar Women's Opportunity Week, City of San Diego, 1982, network seminar Fed. Women's Week, City of Phila., 1986. Bd. dirs. Welfare Rights Orgn., San Diego, 1982; mem. Internat. YWCA. Served with USAF, 1956-59. Recipient Excellence cert. San Diego Employer Adv. Bd., 1981, Leadership cert. Nat. U., San Diego, 1981. Mem. Black Advs. State Service (charter, corr. sec. San Diego chpt. 1981-82), Nat. Assn. Female Execs., AAUW, NAACP (life, rec. sec. San Diego 1982), Chapman Coll. Alumni Assn., Alpha Gamma Sigma. Democrat. Avocation: calligraphy. Office: VA 5000 Wissahickon Ave Philadelphia PA 19144-4867

COLLINE, MARGUERITE RICHNAVSKY, maternal/women's health and pediatrics nurse; b. Bayonne, N.J., Nov. 30, 1953; d. John P. and Margaret M. (Conaghan) Richnavsky; m. Richard L. Colline, Oct. 8, 1977; children: Jennifer, Nicole, Danielle, James Michael. Diploma in practical nurse, Union County Tech. Inst., Scotch Plains, N.J., 1973; BSN, Seton Hall U., 1978. RN, N.J., Md. Practical nurse oncology unit John E. Runnell's Hosp., Berkley Heights, N.J.; staff nurse infant unit Johns Hopkins Hosp., Balt.; staff nurse neonatal unit Overlook Hosp., Summit, N.J. Mem. Nat. Assn. Neonatal Nurses, Sigma Theta Tau. Home: 8 Overlook Dr Bridgewater NJ 08807-2105

COLLING, CATHARINE MARY, nurse, hospital administrator; b. Broomfield, Colo., Jan. 15, 1909; d. Patrick and Margaret Mary (Ryan) Kirby; m. Anthony Joseph Colling; 1 child, Mary Helen Colling Nightingale. BA, Ursuline Coll., 1934. RN, Calif. Supr. Mary's Help Hosp., 1945-50; adminstrv. indsl. nurse Standard Oil Co. of Calif., San Francisco, 1951-62; ward conservator Bank of Am. Trust Dept., 1964-67; instr. indsl. nursing Univ. San Francisco, 1954-69; adminstr. White Sands Convalescent Hosp., Pleasant Hill, Calif., 1967-70, Hillhaven Lawton Convalescent Hosp., San Francisco, 1970-91; mktg. dir. Hillhaven, San Francisco, 1991—. Recipient numerous nursing awards. Mem. Am. Coll. Nursing Home Adminstrs., No. Calif. Assn. Indsl. Nurses, Western Indsl. Nurses, Calif. Nurses Assn., Catholic Nurses Assn., Mary's Help Hosp. Alumni Assn., Calif. Assn. Hosp. Facilities. Republican. Roman Catholic. Office: 1359 Pine St San Francisco CA 94109

COLLINGS, CELESTE LOUISE (SHORTY VASSALLI), marketing executive, professional artist; b. Highland Park, Ill., Dec. 9, 1948; d. Robert Zane Jr. and Laura (Vasaly) C.; m. John Austin Darden III, July 17, 1971 (div. July 1975); 1 child, Desiree Anne; m. John Cochran Barber, Dec. 13, 1984. BA, U. Ariz., 1970; postgrad., N.Mex. State U., 1975; completed mktg. mgr. seminar, U. Calif., Irvine, 1978; cert. of achievement, Wilson Learning Course, 1983. Art tchr. Devargas Jr. High Sch., Santa Fe, 1971; artist, pvt. tchr. Las Cruces, N.Mex., 1971-75; sales rep. Helpmates Temp. Services, Santa Ana, Calif., 1975-76; sales account mgr. Bristol-Myers Products, N.Y.C., 1976-82; sales mgr. Profl. Med. Products, Greenwood, S.C., 1982-85; mktg. mgr. med. products Paper-Pak Products, La Verne, Calif., 1985-88; owner Multi-Media West, Newport Beach, Calif., 1988—; mgmt. trainee Bristol-Myers, Kansas City, Mo., 1978; sales trainee Profl. Med. Products, Greenwood, 1983, product strategy, 1984, chmn. nat. adv. com., 1983-84; owner and pres. Accent Shoji Screens, Newport Beach, Calif., 1981—. Exhibited in one-woman shows at Nancy Dunn Studio and Gallery, San Clemente, Calif., 1980, The Collectables, San Francisco, 1980, Breeden Gallery, Orange Calif., 1992, Orange County Cen. for Contemporary Art, Santa Ana, Calif., Laguna Beach (Calif.) Festival of the Arts Art-A-Fair, 1981, Ariz. Inter-Scholastic Hon. Exhibit, 1st place award, 1962-66, Glendale Fed. Savs. Art Exhitibition, 1982; numerous others; represented by Patricia Corriea Art Gallery, Santa Monica, Calif., Breeden Gallery, Orange, Calif., L.A. Artcore. Mem. Orange County Performing Arts Ctr., Colona Del Mar, Calif., 1981, Orange County Visual Artists, 1990, Orange County Ctr. for Contemporary Art, 1993; asst. dir. Orange County Satelittle, Womens Caucus for Art, organizer, 1993. Recipient 10 sales awards Bristol-Meyers, 1976-82, Western Zone Sales Rep. award Profl. Med. Products, 1984, Gainers Club award, 1984; named Nat. Sales Rep. of Yr. Profl. Med. Products, 1984. Mem. Humanities Assocs., U. Ariz. Alumni Assn., Kappa Alpha Theta Alumni.

COLLINS, AUDREY B., judge. BA, Howard U., 1967; MA, Am. U., 1969; JD, UCLA, 1977. Asst. atty. Legal Aid Found. L.A., 1977-78; with Office L.A. County Dist. Atty., 1978-94, dept. dist. atty., 1978-94, head dep. Torrance br. office, 1987-88, asst. dir. burs. ctrl. ops. and spl. ops., 1988-92, asst. dir. atty., 1992-94; judge. U.S. Dist. Ct. (Ctrl. Dist.) Calif., 1994—; dep. gen. counsel Office Spl. Advisor, L.A. Police Dept. Bd. Commrs., 1992. Advisor Spl. Assistance to Victims in Emergency, 1992-93; pres. L.A. Dist. Atty.'s Crimie Prevention Found., 1993. Acad. scholar Howard U.; named Lawyer of Yr., Langston Bar Assn., 1988; honoree Howard U. Alumni Club So. Calif., 1989. Mem. Nat. Bar Assn., Calif. Women Lawyers, State Bar Com. Bar Examiners (chair subcom. on moral character 1992-93, co-chair 1993-94), L.A. County Bar Assn., L.A. County Bar Judiciary Com., Assn. L.A. County Dist. Attys. (pres. 1983), Black Women Lawyers L.A. County, L.A. County Dist. Atty.'s Conf. (sec. 1993), Women Lawyers L.A., Order of Coif, Phi Beta Kappa. Office: Edward R Roybal Fed Bldg 255 E Temple St Rm 680 Los Angeles CA 90012*

COLLINS, BARBARA-ROSE, congresswoman; b. Detroit, Apr. 13, 1939; d. Lamar N. Sr. and Versa (Jones) R.; widowed; children: Cynthia Lynn, Christopher Loren. Student, Wayne State U. Commr. Human Rights Commn., Detroit, 1974-75; Mich. state rep., 1975-81; councilwoman City of Detroit, from 1982; mem. 102nd-103rd Congresses from 13th (now 15th) Mich. dist., 1991—, mem. govt. ops. com., mem. post office and civil svc. com., mem. pub. works and transp. com.; regional coord. Nat. Black Caucus of Local Elected Officials, 1984. Chmn. Detroit City Coun. Task Force on Teenage Violence, 1985. Recipient Dist. Community Svc. award Shrines of the Black Madonna Pan African Orthodox Christian Ch., 1981, Devoted Svc. award Metro Boy Scouts Am., 1984, Invaluable Svc. award Pershing High Sch., Detroit, 1985. Office: 1108 Longworth HOB Washington DC 20515-2215 also: Dist Office 1543 E Lafayette Detroit MI 48207

COLLINS, BETH ANNE, clinical nurse specialist, researcher; b. Harrisonburg, Va., Dec. 8, 1958; d. Verne Edman and Charlotte Anna (Hahne) Collins. BS in Psychology, Shenandoah Coll., Winchester, Va., 1980; BSN, Med. Coll. Va., 1981, MSN, 1982; PhD in Nursing, U. Tex., 1988. Cert. in inpatient obstetric nursing, neonatal nursing. Staff nurse Winchester Meml. Hosp., 1979-81; teaching asst. Med. Coll. Va. Sch. Nursing, Richmond, 1982; staff nurse U. Va. Hosp., Charlottesville, 1982-83; instr. nursing U. Va. Hosp. Sch. Nursing, 1982-85; teaching asst., acad. asst. U. TEx., Austin, 1985-88; asst. prof. Med. Coll. Va. Sch. Nursing, 1986-91, assoc. prof., 1991—; rsch. coord. Med. Coll. Va./Va. Commonwealth U. NIH MEM Network, Richmond, 1991—; cons. Healty Start Mortality Initiative, Richmond, 1991; manuscript reviewer Jour. Ob-Gyn. Neonatal Nursing, 1992—. Contbr. articles to profl. jours. Booth organizer HealthFest, Austin, 1987. A.D. Williams Found. grantee Med. Coll. Va., 1980-90. Mem. So. Nursing Rsch. Soc. (bd. dirs. 1991—), Nursing Assn. of Am. Coll. Ob-Gyn. (program com. 1992—, chair rsch. com. 1989), chpt. coord. Dist. IV 1984-85, chpt. sec.-treas. 1983-84), Med. Coll. Va. Alumni Assn. (bd. dirs. nursing 1991—, Alumni Star 1992). Office: Med U SC 171 Ashley Ave Charleston SC 29425-2233

COLLINS, CARDISS, congresswoman; b. St. Louis, Sept. 24, 1931; m. George W. Collins (dec.); 1 child, Kevin. Ed., Northwestern U.; hon. degree, Winston-Salem State U., Spelman Coll. Barber Scotia Coll.; sec. Ill. Dept. Revenue, then acct., revenue auditor; mem. 93d-103d Congresses from 7th Ill. Dist., 1973—; mem. govt. ops. com., energy and commerce com., chair subcom. on commerce, consumer protection and competitiveness, subcom. on legis. and nat. security; former chair. govt. activity and transp. subcom.; former majority whip-at-large; former chair Congl. Black Caucus, sec.; former chair Mems. Congress for Peace through Law. Mem. NAACP, The Chgo. Network, The Links. Mem. Nat. Coun. Negro Women, Chgo. Urban League, Black Women's Agenda, Alpha Gamma Pi, Alpha Kappa Alpha. Democrat. Baptist. Office: US Ho of Reps 2308 Rayburn Washington DC 20515

COLLINS, CHRISTINE M., occupational health nurse; b. Long Beach, Calif., Apr. 29, 1952; d. Owen Ward and Marion Almy (Maltby) Collins; m. Robert Blair Reynolds, July 1, 1973 (div. 1985); stepchildren: Pamela Jean, Yvonne Kay; 1 child, Edwin Blair (dec.). BSN, Calif. State U., 1980; postgrad. in Nursing, U. Pa. Staff nurse ICU Marshall Hosp., Placerville, Calif., 1980-83; FNP Sierra Family Clinic, Placerville, 1983-84; occupational nurse, nurse practitioner Hewlett Packard, Roseville, Calif., 1984-85; mgr. employee health svc. U. Calif. Davis Med. Ctr., Sacramento, 1985-86; nurse practitioner Children's Hosp. Pitts., 1987-88; dir. employee health Med. Ctr. Del., Wilmington, 1988—. Mem. AAHEP, Assn. Occupational Health Nurses, Sigma Theta Tau. Office: Med Ctr Del 501 W 14th St Wilmington DE 19899

COLLINS, DORIS MARTIN, city official; b. Roanoke, Va., Mar. 16, 1945; d. William Norris and Nina Canary (Moore) Martin; m. Cecil Livingston Collins, Feb. 5, 1990; children: Melanie Rose Wharton, Oliver Seth Wharton. BS, Va. Commonwealth U., 1969; MPA, Fla. State U., 1987. Adminstrv. asst. City of Tallahassee, 1984-89; town recorder Town of Jonesborough, Tenn., 1989-90; revenue adminstr. City of Knoxville, 1990—. Mem. Am. Soc. Pub. Adminstrn., Internat. City Mgmt. Assn., Govt. Fin. Officers Assn. Office: City of Knoxville 400 E Main St Knoxville TN 37902

COLLINS, DOROTHY SMITH, librarian; b. Nacogdoches, Tex., July 25, 1934; d. A.V. and Betty (Yarborough) Smith; m. Julius A. Collins, Aug. 14, 1954 (dec.). BA in Sociology, Prairie View (Tex.) A&M U.; MA in Elem. Edn., Tex. So. U.; MLS, U. So. Calif. Tchr. U.S. Dependant Sch., Schwabisch, Fed. Republic Germany; tchr., librarian Cleve. Pub. Schs.; tchr. Westside Elem. Sch. Dist., Lancaster, Calif.; librarian Antelope Valley/Palmdale High Sch. Dist., Lancaster; coordinator research and reference ctr. San Diego County Office Edn. Pres. bd. dirs. San Diego chpt. United Scleroderma Found., 1983-94; alumni Leadership Edn. Awareness Devel., 1986—; bus. vol. for the arts, 1993—. Mem. Am. Ednl. Research Assn., Delta Kappa Gamma, Delta Sigma Theta. Home: 6267 Rockhurst Dr San Diego CA 92120-4607 Office: San Diego County Office Edn 6401 Linda Vista Rd San Diego CA 92111-7319

COLLINS, EARLEAN, state legislator; b. Rolling Fork, Miss.; m. John Grant, July 31, 1978; 1 child, Dwarrye. BA in Sociology, U. Ill., Chgo. Social service adminstr. State of Ill., Chgo., 1972-76, elected state senator, 1977—, asst. majority leader; bd. dirs. Nat. Caucus of Black Legislators, Westside Bus. Assn. of Chgo., Nat. Conf. State Legislators. Sponsor Unwed Mothers United, Chgo., 1977—, Collins Queenettes, Chgo., 1977—, Westside Progressive Women's Orgn., Chgo., 1980—. Numerous best legislator & recognition awards from profl. & civic groups. Mem. Intergovtl. Coop. Council, Operation PUSH, Ill. Job Tng. Council, NAACP, Conf. Women Legislators. Democrat. Baptist. Office: Ill State Senate State Capitol Springfield IL 62706*

COLLINS, EILEEN MARIE, astronaut; b. Elmira, N.Y., Nov. 19, 1956; d. James Edward and Rose Marie (O'Hara) C.; m. James Patrick Youngs, Aug. 1, 1987. AS in Math., Sci., Corning C.C., 1976; BA in Math., Econs., Syracuse U., 1978; grad., USAF Undergrad. Pilot Tng., Vance AFB, Okla., 1979, USAF Test Pilot Sch., Edwards AFB, Calif., 1990; MS in Ops. Rsch., Stanford U., 1986; student, USAF Inst. Tech., 1986; MA in Space Systems Mgmt., Webster U., 1989. Commd. 2d lt. USAF, 1978, advanced through grades to lt. col., 1993; instr. pilot 71st flight tng. wing USAF, Vance AFB, 1979-82; aircraft comdr. 86th mil. airlift squadron USAF, Travis AFB, Calif., 1983-85; asst. prof. math. USAF Acad., Colorado Springs, Colo., 1986-89; astronaut Johnson Space Ctr. NASA, Houston, 1990—; second in command, space shuttle Discovery, 1995. Decorated Air Force Commendation medal with one oak leaf cluster, Meritorious svc. medal with one oak leaf cluster, Air Force Expeditionary medal. Mem. U.S. Space Found., Am. Inst. Aeronautics and Astronautics, Air Force Assn., Women Mil. Aviators, Order Daedalians.

COLLINS, GLADYS IRENE, university counselor; b. Dallas; d. Benjamin and Elizabeth (Banks) Thomas; m. Richard Conner Collins, Nov. 8, 1945 (dec. July 1970); 1 dau., Marrian Ruth Lacy. BS, Prairie View U., 1939; MEd, U. Minn., 1960. Elem. art tchr. Dallas Ind. Sch. Dist., 1939-60, high sch. art tchr., 1960-65, high sch. adv. guidance counselor, 1965-79; career counselor So. Meth. U., Dallas, 1979, 84—; bldg. rep. J.W. Ray Sch., Dallas, 1941-45; sch. coordinator Project Upward Bound, Lincoln High Sch., Dallas, 1965-69, adv. guidance counselor, chmn. pupil personnel com., 1965-77; adv. guidance counselor, chmn. pupil personnel com. Arts Magnet Sch., Dallas, 1977-79. Trustee Dallas Mus. Art, 1980-1984, Mus. African-Am. Life and Culture, Dallas, 1978—; bd. dirs. Maria Morgan Br. YWCA; leader Girl Scouts U.S.A., 1940-45; eucharistic min. St. James Cath. Ch.; chairperson Rite Christian Initiation of Adults; donor, benefactor African Am. Mus., Dallas Fair Park, chair spkrs. bur. Recipient Disting. Ednl. Service award Dallas Classroom Tchrs., 1967; Cmty. Svc. award South Dallas Bus. and Profl. Women, 1968, Outstanding Tchr. of Yr. award Lincoln High Sch., Dallas, 1970; appreciation award Maria Morgan YWCA, Dallas, 1981, South Oak Cliff High Sch., Dallas, 1979. Mem. Dallas Negro Art Assn. (pres. 1943-46), Dallas Assn. Counselors (pres. 1966-68), Dallas Tchrs. Council (pres. 1952-66, appreciation award 1966), Delta Sigma Theta (Golden life mem., past v.p.. mem. housing bd. scholarship com.), Phi Delta Kappa (charter). Roman Catholic. Clubs: Wednesday Morning Study (pres.), Cedar Crest Neighborhood Assn. (sec. 1980, rec. sec.) (Dallas).

COLLINS, GWENDOLYN BETH, health administrator; b. Akron, Ohio, Dec. 28, 1943; d. Emmert Samuel and Lillice Elizabeth (Matthews) Shaffer; m. Charles F. Collins, Feb. 10, 1969 (div. 1976); 1 child, Holly Marie. BA, Case Western Res. U., 1971. Social worker Ohio Div. Pub. Welfare, Akron, Cleve., 1970-72; social services dir. Smithville-Western Care Ctr., Wooster, Ohio, 1975-76, social work cons., 1976; social worker Edwin Shaw Hosp., Akron, 1976-78; clin. treatment services coordinator The Blick Clinic for Devel. Disabilities, Tallmadge, Ohio, 1978; co-adminstr. The Sun Ctr. Inc., Akron, 1979-81; exec. dir. Canton Area Regional Health Edn. Network, 1981-88; project dir. Region VII Cancer Registry, Canton, Ohio, 1984-88; program dir. Diabetes Mgmt. Ctr., St. Petersburg, Fla., 1988-89, 92-94, Pasadena Sr. Health Ctr. and St. Petersburg Health Ctr., St. Petersburg, 1995—; health program devel. cons., 1986-88; mem. continuing med. edn. com. Aultman Hosp., 1983-88; planner and evaluator Directions for Mental Health, Inc., Clearwater, Fla., 1990-92. Mem. adv. com. Camp Y-Noah, 1985-86. HHS grantee, Canton, 1986-88. Mem. Cancer Control Consortium Ohio (mem. cancer incidence mgmt. com. 1986-87). Republican. Home: 13013 89th Ave N Largo FL 34646-2706

COLLINS, JOAN HENRIETTA, actress; b. London, May 23, 1933; came to U.S., 1938; d. Joseph William and Elsa (Bessant) C.; m. Anthony Newley (div.); children: Tara, Sacha; m. Ronald S. Kass, Mar., 1972 (div.); 1 child, Katy; m. Peter Holm (div.); m. Maxwell Reed. Ed., Francis Holland Sch., London; student, Royal Acad. of Dramatic Art. Films include: I Believe in You, Girl in the Red Velvet Swing, Rally Round the Flag Boys, Island in the Sun, Seven Thieves, Road to Hong Kong, Sunburn, The Stud, Game for Vultures, The Bitch, The Big Sleep, The Good Die Young, Land of the Pharoahs, The Bravados, Esther and the King, Warning Shot, The Executioner, Tales from the Crypt, The Bawdy Adventures of Tom Jones, The Skin of Our Teeth, Claudia, The Opposite Sex, The Virgin Queen, Quest for Love; theater appearances include: The Last of Mrs. Cheyney, The 7th Veil, A Doll's House, Private Lives (London, Broadway, also tour); TV films include: Drive Hard, Drive Fast, 1973, The Man Who Came to Dinner, Paper Dolls, 1982, The Wild Women of Chastity Gulch, 1982, The Cartier Affair, The Making of a Male Model, 1983, Her Life as a Man, 1984; miniseries: The Moneychangers, 1976, Sins, 1986, Monte Carlo, 1986, Tonight at 8:30, 1991, Decadence, 1994; appeared in Faerie Tale Theater (Showtime TV), 1982; star TV series: Dynasty, 1981-89; other TV appearences Roseanne (ABC), 1993, Mama's Back spl., 1993; video spl. Secrets of Fitness and Beauty, 1994; author: Past Imperfect (autobiography), 1978, Katy, A Fight for Life, Joan Collins Beauty Book, (novels) Prime Time, 1988, Love & Desire & Hate, 1991, My Secrets, 1994, Too Damn Famous, 1995. Recipient Emmy nomination, Golden Globe award, Ace award, People's Choice award.

COLLINS, JUDY MARJORIE, singer, composer; b. Seattle, May 1, 1939; d. Charles T. and Marjorie (Byrd) C.; m. Peter A. Taylor, Apr., 1958 (div.); 1 son, Clark Taylor. Pvt. study piano, 1953-56. Debut as profl. folk singer, Boulder, Colo., 1959; has since appeared in numerous clubs, U.S. and around world; performer concerts including Newport Folk Festival, maj. concert halls and summer theatres, throughout U.S. and Europe; also appeared radio and TV, including HBO TV spl. Judy Collins: From the Heart, 1989; recording artist, Elektra; profl. acting debut as Solveig in N.Y. Shakespeare Festival prodn. of Peer Gynt, 1969; producer, dir. documentary movie Antonia: A Portrait of the Woman, 1974; composer songs including Albatross, 1967, Since You've Asked, 1967, My Father, 1968, Secret Gardens, 1972, Born to the Breed, 1975; albums include Bread & Roses, Colors of the Day, So Early in the Spring/The First Fifteen Years, 1977, Hard Times for Lovers, 1979, Running for My Life, 1980, Trust Your Heart, 1987, Sanity and Grace, 1989, Recollections, Fires of Eden, 1990, Judy Sings Dylan: Just Like a Woman, 1993; author autobiography Trust Your Heart, 1987. Recipient Grammy award, 1968, 6 Gold Lps., Silver medal Atlanta Film Festival, Blue Ribbon award Am. Film Festival, N.Y.C., Christopher award. Office: care Charles R Rothschild Prodns Inc 330 E 48th St New York NY 10017-1729*

COLLINS, KATHLEEN, writer; b. Lowell, Mass., Nov. 10, 1953; d. John Joseph and Barbara Ann (McCarthy) C. BA, Mich. State U., 1975. Sr. researcher Cen. States, S.E. and S.W. Areas Health & Welfare Fund, Chgo., 1976-79; steward Teamster Local 743, Chgo., 1978-79; tchr. religious edn. Roman Cath. Ch., Chgo., 1976-77, 81, eucharistic min., 1985—; data and info. coord. Roman Cath. Ch., Schooley's Mt., N.J., 1980-84; English lang. tutor for fgn. students Mich. State U., East Lansing, 1971-74, entertainment and movie coord., 1972-74; church organist, E. Brunswick, N.J., 1967-69. Author: (with Mary E. Collins): A People Worth Saving, 1981, Treasures, 1983, Israel--Destroyed?, 1986, NOW, 1987, He's Coming, 1987, The Azume, 1991, Alexin and the Bear, 1992, Yatahay-Okay! 1993; co-author, editor booklets. Dem. election judge Washington Twp., N.J., 1985; election clk. 1984-88, election inspector 1988, 89; advisor to bd. trustees Mich. State U., 1975; invited Patriot's Day marcher, Lexington, Mass., 1962-66. Mem. DAR, Internat. Platform Assn. Republican. Home: 57 Nestlingwood Dr Long Valley NJ 07853-3528

COLLINS, KATHLEEN A., artistic director; b. Elmira, N.Y., Dec. 20, 1951; d. James G. and Joyce (Balmer) C.; m. Andrew Stephon Elston, May 28, 1977; children: Megan, Kate. BA, SUNY, Albany, 1974; MA in Theatre, U. Wash., 1976, MFA in Theatre, 1979. Dir. edn. Seattle Children's Theatre, 1975-78; instr. drama Lakeside Sch., Seattle, 1978-79; artistic dir. Honolulu Theatre for Youth, 1979-83, Fulton Opera House, Lancaster, Pa., 1983—; guest lectr. U. Wash., Seattle, 1979, U. Hawaii, Honolulu, 1981. Contbg. author: Drama With Children, 1979. Bd. dirs. PTO, Lancaster, 1990—. Mem. Am. Assn. Theatre Educators, Assn. and Soc. for Theatre and Children. Democrat. Roman Catholic. Office: Fulton Theatre Co Box 1865 Lancaster PA 17603-1865

COLLINS, LISA DIANE, art educator; b. Long Beach, Calif., Sept. 20, 1967; d. Jimmy Royce and Cloa Mae (Westbrook) C. BS Art Edn., BA Comml. Art, Kennesaw State Coll., Marietta, Ga., 1991; student, U. Ga. Studies Abroad, Cortona, Italy, 1988, Kennesaw State Coll. Studies, San Miguel, Mex., 1989; postgrad., W. Ga. Coll., Carrollton. Instr. studio art for children Kennesaw State Coll., 1988—; art educator Josh Powell Camp, Kennesaw, 1990-92; art tchr. Floyd Middle Sch., Mableton, Ga., 1991—; freelance artist; prodn. asst. Share Mag., Kennesaw State Coll., 1990-91, coop. tchr. to upcoming art tchrs., 1993—; dir. Floyd Celebrates Arts at Marble House Gallery, 1991—; judge Paulding County Fine Arts Assn. Exhibit, 1993. Mem. Profl. Assn. Ga. Educators. Home: 3800 Parks Dr Powder Springs GA 30073

COLLINS, MARIBETH WILSON, foundation president; b. Portland, Oreg., Oct. 27, 1918; d. Clarence True and Maude (Akin) Wilson; m. Truman Wesley Collins, Mar. 12, 1943; children: Timothy Wilson and Terry Stanton (twins), Cherida Lynne, Truman Wesley Jr. BA, U. Oreg., 1940. Pres. Collins Found., Portland, Oreg., 1964—; dir. Collins Pine Co., Collins Holding Co., Ostrander Resource Co. Mem. exec. com., sec. bd. trustees Willamette U., Salem, Oreg., also mem. coms. on orgn. and campus religious life. Mem. Univ. Club, Internat. Club, Gamma Phi Beta. Republican. Methodist. Home: 2275 SW Mayfield Ave Portland OR 97225-4400 Office: Collins Found Ste 305 1618 SW 1st Ave Portland OR 97201-5708

COLLINS, MARTHA, English educator, writer; b. Omaha, Nov. 25, 1940; d. William E. and Katheryn (Essick) C.; m. Theodore M. Space, Apr. 1991. AB, Stanford U., 1962; MA, U. Iowa, 1965, PhD, 1971. Asst. prof. N.E. Mo. U., Kirksville, Kirksville, 1965-66; instr. U. Mass., Boston, 1966-71, asst. prof. English, 1971-75, assoc. prof., 1975-85, prof. English, 1985—, co-dir. creative writing, 1979—, co-chair English, 1994—; dir. Martha's Vineyard Writers' Workshop, Vineyard Haven, Mass., summer 1984. Author (poetry): The Catastrophe of Rainbows, 1985, The Arrangement of Space, 1991, A History of Small Life on a Windy Planet, 1993. Fellow Bunting Inst., 1982-83, Ingram Merrill Found., 1988, NEA, 1990; recipient Pushcart prize, 1985, De Castagnola award, 1990, others. Mem. Poetry Soc. Am., Assoc. Writing Programs. Democrat. Office: U Mass-Boston Dept English Boston MA 02125

COLLINS, MARTHA LAYNE, college president, former governor; b. Shelby County, Ky., Dec. 7, 1936; d. Everett Larkin and Mary Lorena (Taylor) Hall; m. Bill Collins, July 3, 1959; children: Stephen Louis, Marla Ann. Student, Lindenwood Coll.; B.S., U. Ky., 1959. Former tchr. Fairdale High Sch., Louisville, Seneca High Sch., Louisville, Woodford County Jr. High Sch., Versailles; lt. gov. State of Ky., 1979-83, gov., 1983-87; exec. in residence U. Louisville Sch. of Bus., from 1988; pres. St. Catherine Coll., St. Catherine, Ky., 1990—; pres. Martha Layne Collins & Assocs., Lexington, 1988—; sec. Ky. Edn. and Humanities Cabinet, 1984-87; chmn. Nat. Conf. Lt. Govs., 1982-83, So. Growth Policies Bd., 1986-87, So. Regional Edn. Bd., 1986, Nat. Gov.'s Task Force on Drug ans Substance Abuse, 1987, So. Growth Policies Bd., 1986; bd. dirs. Eastman-Kodak Co., Inc., Rochester, N.Y., R.R. Donnelley & Sons, Chgo., Bank of Louisville. Mem. Woodford County (Ky.) Democratic Exec. Com.; mem. Dem. Nat. Com., 1972-76; chmn. Dem. Nat. Conv., San Francisco, 1984; former coordinator Women's Activities for State Dem. Hdqrs.; del. Dem. Nat. Conv., Miami, 1972, Midterm charter Conf., Kansas City, 1974; mem. credentials com. Dem. Nat. Com. Vice Presdl. Selection Process Commn., co-chair credentials com. Dem. Nat. Conv., Atlanta, 1988; Ky. chairwoman 51.3 Com. for Carter, 1976; mem. Ky. Dem. Central Exec. Com.; sec. Ky. Dem. Party; elected clk. Ct. of Appeals, 1975; clk. Supreme Ct. Ky., 1975; past tchr. Sunday sch.; mem. Ky. Commn. on Women; exec. dir. Ky. Friendship Force; mem. Dem. Nat. Com. Policy Commn. and Fairness Commn.; hon. chmn. bd. USO of Ky. Inc.; hon. co-chmn. Parents Against Child Exploitation; mem. adv. bd. Lexington Child Abuse Council; bd. govs. Dream Factory; organized first Woodford County Jr. Miss Pageant. Fellow Harvard U. Inst.; mem. So. Gov.'s Assn. (chmn. 1987), Woodford County Jaycee-ettes (past pres.), U. Ky. Alumni Assn., Women's Missionary Union (past pres.), Nat. Conf. Appellate Ct. Clks., Leukemia Soc. Am. (hon. chairperson), Young Writer's Contest Found. (hon. bd. advs.), Ky. Alliance for Arts Edn. (hon. bd. dirs.), Leadership Ky. (bd. dirs.) Japan Am. Soc. Ky., Internat. Women's Forum, Hope for Drug-Free Am. (statesmen com.), Psi Omega Dental Aux. (past pres.). Baptist. Clubs: Bus. and Profl, Women's, Order Eastern Star. Office: St Catharine Coll Office of the President Saint Catherine KY 40061*

COLLINS, MARTHA TRAUDT, lawyer; b. Colorado Springs, Colo., July 23, 1952; d. Verne O.M. and Helen Louise (Post) Traudt; m. Alexander F. Rolle; children: Joseph T. Collins, Alexander S. Rolle. BS in Math., U. Nebr., 1974; JD, U. Colo., 1977. Bar: Colo. 1977. Assoc. Holme Roberts & Owen LLC, Denver, 1977-82, ptnr., 1983—. Contbg. author: Rocky Mountain Mineral Law Foundation's Law of Federal Oil and Gas Leases, 1988; also articles. Bd. dirs. Human Svcs., Inc., Denver, 1988-92, pres. bd., 1993; mem. Law Alumni Bd., U. Colo. Sch. Law, 1987-91; Leadership Denver, 1993-94. Mem. Colo. Bar Assn., Denver Bar Assn., Women's Bar Assn., Order of Coif, Phi Beta Kappa. Office: Holme Roberts & Owen LLC Ste 4100 1700 Lincoln Denver CO 80203

COLLINS, MARY, health association executive, former Canadian legislator; b. Vancouver, B.C., Can., Sept. 26, 1940; d. Fredrick Claude and Isabel Margaret (Copp) Wilkins; children: David, Robert, Sarah. Student, U. B.C., Queen's U., Kingston, Ont., Can.; LLD (hon.), Royal Rds. Mil. Coll., 1994. Mem. Can. Ho. of Commons, 1984-93; pres., CEO B.C. Health Assn., 1994—; mem. fed. cabinet Can., assoc. min. nat. def., 1989-92, min. Western econ. diversification, 1993, min. state environ., 1993, min. responsible for status of women, 1990-93, min. of health, 1993; dir. Vancouver Bd. Trade. Mem. Progressive Conservative Party. Home: 201-1315 W 7th Ave, Vancouver, BC Canada V6H 1B8

COLLINS, MARY ALICE, psychiatric social worker, educator; b. Everett, Wash., Apr. 20, 1937; d. Harry Edward and Mary (Yates) Caton; BA in Sociology, Seattle Pacific Coll., 1959; MSW, U. Mich., 1966; PhD, Mich. State U., 1974; m. Gerald C. Brocker, Mar. 24, 1980. Diplomate Am. Bd. Social Workers. Dir. teenage, adult and counseling depts. YWCA, Flint, Mich., 1959-64, 66-68; social worker Catholic Social Services, Flint, 1969-71, Ingham Med. Mental Health Center, Lansing, Mich., 1971-73; clin. social worker Genesee Psychiat. Center, Flint, 1974-82, Psychol. Evaluation and Treatment Ctr., East Lansing, Mich., 1982-84; pvt. practice, East Lansing, 1984—; instr. social work Lansing C.C.; lectr. Mich. State U., 1974, 87-93, part-time adj. asst. prof., 1993—; vis. prof. Hurley Med. Center, 1979-84; v.p. Brief Psychotherapy Coalition, 1994; cons. Ingham County Dept. Social Services, 1971-73. Advisor human relations Youth League, Flint Council Chs., 1964-65; sec. Genesee County Young Democrats, 1960-61, pres. Round Lake Improvement Assn., 1984-87. Mem. NASW, Acad. Cert. Social Workers, Phi Kappa Phi, Alpha Kappa Sigma. Contbr. articles to profl. jours. Home: 5945 Round Lake Rd Laingsburg MI 48848-9454

COLLINS, MARY ELLEN, human resources executive; b. Indpls., Jan. 24, 1949; d. Carl William and Hester (Dawson) McConn; m. Thomas N. Wininger, June 19, 1971 (div. 1981); m. Larry Wayne Collins, Dec. 15, 1983; 1 child, Ann Marie. Diploma in nursing, Holy Cross Coll., 1969; BS, Coll. of St. Francis, 1981; MS, Ind. U., 1984; PhD in Orgnl. Behavior, Union Inst., Cin., 1993. Edn. coord. Cmty. Hosp., Indpls., 1969-84; dir. tng. Middletown (Ohio) Regional Hosp., 1984-87; pres. People Power Cons. Svc., Cin., 1987—; adj. prof. Coll. Mt. St. Joseph, Ohio, 1988-93. Adminstrv. chair Deerfield Ch., Maineville, 1987-89. Mem. ASTD (bd. dirs. Cin. chpt. 1988-89), Assn. for Psychol. Type (pres., founder Greater Cin. chpt. 1992—, bd. dirs. Gt. Lakes region, Internat. New Leader award 1993), Assn. Quality Participation (healthcare adv. bd., Disting. Faculty mem.), Internat. Visitors Ctr., Women Entrepreneurs, Inc. Methodist.

COLLINS, MARY ELLEN KENNEDY, librarian, educator; b. Pitts., Feb. 28, 1939; d. Joseph Michael and Stella Marie (Kane) Kennedy; m. Orpha Collins. BA, Villa Maria Coll., 1961; MLS, U. Pitts., 1970, PhD, 1980. Tchr., Pitts. Catholic Schs., 1962-65; tchr., Anne Arundel County Schs., Annapolis, 1965-67; legal sec., firm Joseph M. Kennedy, Pitts., 1967-70; cataloger Newport News (Va.) Libr. System, 1970-71; reference librarian Glenville (W.Va.) State Coll., 1971-80; asst. prof. libr. sci. Ball State U., Muncie, Ind., 1980-83; reference librarian, asst. prof. Purdue U., West Lafayette, Ind., 1983-88, assoc. prof., 1988—. Author: Education Journals and Serials: An Analytical Guide, 1988; contbr. articles to profl. jours. Sec. Presbyn. Ch., 1973-74, pres., 1974-76, bd. deacons, 1979-80; chmn. library com., Muncie, 1981-83; mem. belle com. W.Va. Folk Festival, 1973-80. Recipient Title III advanced study grant, 1977-78, Disting. Edn. and Behavioral Scis. Libr. award Assn. Coll. and Rsch. Librs., ALA, 1994. Mem. ALA (reference books rev. com. 1979-82, profl. devel. com. 1983-87, mem. Ednl. Behavioral Scis. (sect.-problems of access and control of ednl. materials 1984-88, curriculum materials com. 1988—, adult libr. materials com. 1988—), Ind. Library Assn., Spl. Libraries Assn., Assn. Coll. and Rsch. Libraries, Am. Assn. U. Profs., Assn. Ind. Media Educators, Assn. Am. Libr. Schs., AAUW (corr. sec. 1981-82), Delta Kappa Gamma, Sigma Sigma Sigma, Beta Phi Mu. Republican. Office: Purdue U HSSE Libr West Lafayette IN 47907

COLLINS, MOIRA ANN, graphics and communications company executive, calligrapher; b. Washington, Dec. 16, 1942; d. Peter William and Louise (Carroll) Collins; m. Andrew Joseph Griffin, Aug. 21, 1965; children: Andrew Fitzgerald, Timothy Collins. BA, U. Toronto (Ont., Can.), 1964; MA in Teaching, Northwestern U., 1965; MEd in Urban Studies, Northeastern U., Chgo., 1968. Tchr., Chgo. Bd. Edn., 1965-68; studied with profl. calligraphers, scribes and illuminators, Haystack Mountain Sch., Deer Isle, Maine, 1973, U. Calif. Santa Cruz, 1973-74; freelance calligrapher, 1974-78; mem. publicity and promotional staff Swallow Press, Chgo., 1978-79; owner Letters, Chgo., 1979—; pres. Astrogram, Chgo. 1986; intern Gestalt Inst. of Toronto & Oasis Ctr, Chgo., 1986-87. HEW fellow Northeastern U., 1967-68. Author, contbr.; Celebration: Anais Nin, 1975; contbr. to Goodfellow Rev. of Crafts, 1979. Calligrapher: Erotica, 1976, Chgo. Rev., 1978. Chmn. fund-raising Van Gorder Walden Sch., Chgo., 1979-80. Mem. Chgo. Calligraphy Collective (co-founder, chmn. 1976-77, pres. 1978-79, hon. mem.), Soc. Scribes N.Y., Soc. Scribes and Illuminators (Eng.), Friends Calligraphy Calif. Democrat. Roman Catholic. Home: 3920 N Lake Shore Dr # 9N Chicago IL 60613-3447 Office: 3600 N Lake Shore Dr Ste 1817 Chicago IL 60613-4625

COLLINS, MONICA ANN, journalist; b. Rockville Center, N.Y., June 21, 1951; d. Louis Andrew and Eileen Ann (Hellawell) C. B.A., Vassar Coll., 1973. Writer, editor The Real Paper, Cambridge, Mass., 1975-79; TV critic Boston Herald Am., 1979-83, USA Today, Arlington, Va., 1983-89; columnist Boston Mag., 1983-85, TV Guide, 1989—; TV critic Boston Herald, 1989—. Roman Catholic. Office: The Boston Herald 1 Herald Sq Boston MA 02106-2096

COLLINS, PATRICIA A., lawyer, judge; b. Camp Lejeune, N.C., Mar. 12, 1954; d. Thomas and Margaret (Parrish) C. BA, U. Va., 1976; JD, Gonzaga U., 1982. Bar: Alaska 1982, U.S. Dist. Ct. Alaska, U.S. Ct. Appeals (9th cir.) 1982. Assoc. Guess & Rudd, Anchorage and Juneau, 1982-84, 85-87; asst. pub. defender Alaska Pub. Defender's Office, Ketchikan, 1984-85; prin. Collins Law Office, Juneau, 1987—; part time fed. magistrate judge U.S. Cts., Juneau, 1988—; adj. prof. U. Alaska, Juneau, 1991—. Mem. Alaska Bar Assn., Juneau Sailing Club. Office: Collins Law Office 326 4th St # 804 Juneau AK 99801 also: US Dist Ct 318 4th Ave Juneau AK 99801*

COLLINS, RENEE, realtor; b. Germany, May 11, 1941; came to U.S., 1961; children: Michael, Roland. Cert. residential specialist; grad. sr. appraiser. With distbn. cost acctg. dept. Procter & Gamble Co., Cin., 1968-72; teller Fifth Third Bank, Cin., 1973-77; residential real estate agt. RE/MAX Unltd., Cin., 1977—. Mem. Realtors Nat. Mktg. Inst. (residential sales coun.), Home Builders Assn. Cin. (sales and mktg. coun., silver award), Nat. REsidential Appraisal Inst., Cin. Bd. Realtors (Multi Million Dollar Producer award 1983-93), President's Sales Club (Ohio award), RE/MAX 100% Club. Home: 1009 Anderson Hills Dr Cincinnati OH 45230-4018 Office: REMAX Unltd 8291 Beechmont Ave Cincinnati OH 45255-3189

COLLINS, SARAH RUTH, education educator; b. Northumberland, Pa., May 13, 1939; d. Walter Brown and Alice Marie (Neighbour) Knight; m. Frank Gibson Collins, June 13, 1960; children: James, Pamela Collins Williams. BA, Wheaton Coll., 1960; MA, U. Tex., Austin, 1974; PhD, Vanderbilt U., 1980. Tchr. various levels Evanston, Ill., 1960-61, Berkeley, Calif., 1961-71; tchr. pre-sch. and kindergarten Austin, Tex., 1969-73; tchr. in early childhood U. Tex., Austin, 1972-74; tchr. reading Motlow State C.C., Tullahoma, Tenn., 1977-91, prof. edn., 1982-93, coord. social scis., 1986-93; mem. state-wide adv. coun. for tchr. edn. and cert., 1987-90, state-wide adv. coun. for minorities in tchr. edn., 1990-91; tchr. edn. Mid. Tenn. State U., 1979—; presenter at profl. confs. Columnist feature articles for local newspaper. Actress Community Playhouse, Tullahoma, 1973-87; storyteller various librs. and pub. schs., 1974—; violinist Mid. Tenn. Symphony Orch., Murfreesboro, 1987-89; presenter programs on grief and loss at various profl. confs. and community orgns.; v.p. in charge of programs Unitarian Universalist Ch. of Tullahoma. Recipient Gov. Ned McWherter's cert. of recognition Tenn. Collaborative Leadership Acad., 1991. Mem. AAUP (v.p. 1986-87, sec. 1990-91), Assn. Tchr. Educators, Bus. and Profl. Women's Club, Phi Delta Kappa, Kappa Delta Pi. Home: 1703 Country Club Dr Tullahoma TN 37388-4831 Office: Motlow State CC Lynchburg Hwy Tullahoma TN 37388

COLLINS, SHARON MCCOY, producer, correspondent; b. Charlottesville, Va., Apr. 27, 1952. Dir. news Sta. WDVA Radio, Danville, Va., 1978-81; dir. news, reporter Sta. WAKG-FM Radio, Danville, 1981-83; reporter Sta. WVTM-AM Radio, Danville, 1981-83; reporter Sta. WSET-TV, Lynchburg, Va., 1979-91, bur. chief, 1983-89, mng. editor, 1989-91; prodr. weekly environ. mag. programs, correspondent Sta. CNN/TBS, Atlanta, 1991—. Prodr., correspondent Flood Spl. (Emmy award 1994), Earth Summit Spl. (ACE award 1992), Save the Earth Spl. (EMA award 1992). Pres. Danville Devel. Coun., 1990; bd. dirs. Crimestoppers, Danville. Recipient AP awards including Radio Best News Operation award, 1981, Radio Continuing Story award, 1981, Radio Outstanding Effort by Reporter award, 1981, 82, Feature award, 1987, Best In-Depth Report award, 1986, Best Documentary award, 1990, Douglas Freeman award, 1990; recipient Best In-Depth Report award UPI, 1985, Continuing Story award, UPI, 1987, Crimestoppers Prodn. of Yr. award SE Conv., 1985; named BPW Woman of Yr., 1982, Jaycees Woman of Yr., 1990. Mem. Danville C. of C. (bd. dirs.). Home: 1331 Briers Dr Stone Mountain GA 30083 Office: CNN Earth Matters 1 CNN Ctr Atlanta GA 30303

COLLINS, SHIRLEY DEAN, medical facility administrator, small business owner; b. Joplin, Mo., June 21, 1947; d. Edward Christian and Anna Belle (Gandy) Beyer; divorced; 1 child, Florence Anne. Student, Mo. So. State Coll., 1965-67. With pers. office Milligan Air Conditioning and Heating, Joplin, Mo., 1968-69; with payroll and ins. Independent Gravel, Joplin, 1969-70; matron and cook Cherokee County Courthouse, Columbus, Kans., 1973-74; clk., tchr. art Stuff 'n Thangs, Baxter Springs, Kans., 1975-77, House of Gifts, Miami, Okla., 1979-81; owner, tchr. art Nuthin' Much, Galena, Kans., 1977—; admitting registrar, registrations St. John's Regional Med. Ctr., Joplin, 1982—. Committeewoman Rep. Party, 1972-74; leader Girl Scouts Troop, 1981-83. Home: RR 2 Box 502 Galena KS 66739-9446 Office: St John's Regional Med Ctr 2727 Mc Clelland Blvd Joplin MO 64804-1626

COLLINS, SUSAN MARGARET, archaeologist; b. Trenton, N.J., June 26, 1948; d. Thomas Raymond and Marjorie Ann (Lakness) C. BA cum laude, U. Colo., 1969, MA, 1971, PhD, 1975. Spl. researcher Sch. Am. Rsch., Santa Fe, N.Mex., 1972-73; teaching assoc. U. Colo., Denver, 1973-75, instr., 1975; instr. U. Colo., Boulder, 1974; vis. asst. prof. U. Colo., Denver, 1978-79; asst. prof. Western Carolina U., Cullowhee, N.C., 1975-78; acting dir. lab. pub. archaeology Colo. State U., Ft. Collins, 1980-82; dir. archaeology program Pueblo of Zuni, N.Mex., 1982-84; state archaeologist Colo. Hist. Soc., Denver, 1988—; dep. state historic preservation officer Colo. Hist. Soc., Denver, 1989—; adj. assoc. prof. U. Colo., Denver, 1990—. Contbr. articles to profl. jours. Mem. Lt. Gov.'s Task Force Ute Mountain Pk., Ute Indian Reservation, 1990—. Mem. Nat. Assn. State Archaeologists (sec.-treas. 1990-92), Soc. Am. Archaeology, Colo. Coun. Profl. Archaeologists (pres. 1985-86), Col. Archaeol. Soc., Soc. for Hist. Archaeology. Democrat. Office: Colo Hist Soc 1300 Broadway Denver CO 80203-2137

COLLINS, VICKI TICHENÉ, critical care and emergency room nurse; b. Germany, Dec. 1, 1944; children: David, Michael, Amy. Diploma, St. Anthony Sch. Nursing, Columbus, Ohio, 1968. Cert. advanced trauma life support. Night nurse Fairfax Hosp., Falls Church, Va., 1977—. Mem. No. Va. Emergency Nurses Assn. Home: 11 Edgecliff Ln Stafford VA 22554-5118

COLLINS, WINIFRED QUICK (MRS. HOWARD LYMAN COLLINS), organizational executive, retired navy officer; b. Great Falls, Mont.; m. Howard Lyman Collins (dec.). B.S., U. So. Calif., 1935; grad. Harvard-Radcliffe Program in Bus. Adminstrn., 1938; M.A., Stanford U., 1952. Commd. ensign U.S. Navy, 1942, advanced through grades to capt. 1957; personnel dir. Midshipman's Sch., Smith Coll., 1942-43; asst. chief Naval Personnel for Women, 1957-62; ret.; nat. v.p. U.S. Navy League, 1964-70, nat. dir. and chmn. nat. awards com., 1964—; nat. dir. Ret. Officers Assn.; former cons. HEW; former trustee Helping Hand Found.; former mem. Sec. Navy's Bd. Advs. and Tng. of Naval Personnel; dir. CPC Internat., Inc., 1977-84, chmn. employee investment com., mem. audit, exec. compensation and exec. coms.; bd. dirs. Leadership Found.; trustee U.S. Naval Acad. Found., 1977—. 1st v.p. Republican Women of D.C.; sec. USN Commendation Medal. Decorated Legion of Merit, Bronze Star; recipient Navy's Disting. Civilian Pub. Service award, 1971, Disting. Service award Navy League of U.S., 1973; named to Hall of Fame Internat. Bus. and Profl. Women's Assn., 1994. Mem. Harvard Grad. Bus. Sch. Washington Club (past dir.), Army Navy Town Club, Army Navy Country Club, Chevy Chase Club. Home: Harbour Sq 540 N St SW Washington DC 20024-4557

COLMAN, WENDY, psychoanalyst; b. Flushing, N.Y., July 6, 1950; d. Leo M. and Ray (Fine) C. BS, Tufts U., 1972; MA, NYU, 1977, PhD in Occupational Therapy, 1984; postgrad., Phila. Sch. of Psychoanalysis, 1988-92. Cert. psychoanalyst. Occupational therapist Extended Family Ctr., San Francisco, 1973-74; cons. child abuse San Francisco, 1974-75; sr. occupational therapist Roosevelt Hosp., N.Y.C., 1975-77; adj. instr. occupational therapy dept. NYU, N.Y.C., 1977-80; asst. prof. occupational therapy dept. Boston U., 1980-83; dir. grad. edn. occupational therapy, dept. assoc. prof. Temple U., Phila., 1984-87; cons. curriculum design Kean Coll. N.J., Union, 1985-88; cons. spl. projects, vice provost for rsch.- grad. studies Temple U., Phila., 1987-88; evaluation rsch. coord. Nat. Inst. Adolescent Pregnancy, Phila., 1986-90; pvt. practice psychotherapy and psychoanalysis, 1989—; assoc. tng. analyst, assoc. supr. Phila. Sch. of Psychoanalysis. Contbr. articles to profl. jours. and texts in occupational therapy and psychoanalysis. Fellow Am. Occupational Therapy Assn.; mem. Nat. Assn. Advancement Psychoanalysis. Office: The Benson East 100 Old York Rd Ste 1208 Jenkintown PA 19046-3251

COLON, PHYLLIS JANET, city official; b. Taylor, Tex., Sept. 1, 1938; d. Jack and Lydia Windmeyer; m. Henry J. Colon, Feb. 12, 1977; children: Walter N. Barnes III, Bradley H. Barnes, Mark A. Barnes. AA in Pub. Adminstrn., Del Mar Coll.; postgrad. in Acctg., Durham Jr. Coll.; BAAS in Pub. Adminstrn., Tex. A&I U., 1987; postgrad., Art Inst. Dayton. Registered profl. appraiser, Tex., assessor, Tex.; cert. tax adminstr., Tex.; lic. real estate borker, Tex. Mgr. info. Med. Arts Lab., Dayton, Ohio, 1970-73; appraiser Nueces County Appraisal Dist., Corpus Christi, 1973-82; tax assessor, collector Flour Bluff Ind. Sch. Dist., Corpus Christi, 1982, dir. spl. svcs., 1992-93; tax assessor, collector City of Laredo, Tex., 1993—; mem. profl. stds. com. Bd. Tax Profl. Examiners, 1991, vice chmn., 1992, chmn. 1994—. Mem. advance planning bd. Corpus Christi Libr.; chmn. ad hoc planning com. Del Mar Coll., 1989—. Recipient achievement award State of Tex., Hero award City of Corpus Christi. Mem. NAFE, AAUW (bd. dirs. Corpus Christi br.), Tex. Assn. Assessing Officers, Tex. Sch. Assessors Assn., Inst. Cert. Tax Adminstrs., Am. Soc. Notaries, Corpus Christi C. of C., Art Mus. South Tex., Kiwanis (treas. Corpus Christi 1989-90, pres. 1990—). Republican. Lutheran. Home: 8728 Martinique Dr Laredo TX 78041-8008 Office: City of Laredo PO Box 329 1110 Houston St Laredo TX 78040-8019

COLONEL, SHERI LYNN, advertising agency executive; b. Bklyn., Sept. 3, 1955; d. Irwin Murray Glaser and Rosalind (Mendelson) Krasik; m. Peter T. Colonel, Sept. 20, 1981 (dec.). B.A. in Psychology, SUNY-Cortland, 1977. Account exec. Ted Bates Co., N.Y.C., 1978-80; account exec. SSC&B Advt. (name now Ammirati & Puris/LINTAS), Inc., N.Y.C., 1980-82, v.p. account supr., 1982-83, v.p. mgmt. supr., 1983-84, sr. v.p. mgmt. supr., 1984-88, exec. v.p., 1988—, bd. dirs. 1990-94, pres. Gotham Group, 1994—. Mem. Advt. Women N.Y., NAFE. Home: 280 Park Ave S New York NY 10010 Office: The Gotham Group 79 5th Ave New York NY 10003-3034

COLONNA, ELIZABETH ALICE, anesthesiologist; b. Hampton, Va., Sept. 24, 1959; d. Shepherd Waller Jr. and Betty T. (Hammond) C.; m. Keith E. Eyre, Apr. 25, 1987. BS in Microbiology cum laude, Tex. Tech. U., 1981, MD, 1985. Diplomate Am. Bd. Anesthesiology; lic. anesthesiologist, Tex. Intern dept. gen. surgery Tex. Tech. Sch. Medicine, Lubbock, 1985-86; emergency rm. physician Arlington (Tex.) Meml. Hosp., 1986; resident in anesthesiology Ochsner Found. Hosp., New Orleans, 1987-90; pvt. practice San Antonio, 1990—; chmn. med. ethics com. Met. Hosp., San Antonio, 1994; surg. asst., office aid Dr. Bohn D. Allen, M.D., Arlington, summer 1980; surg. asst. All Sts. Episcopal Hosp., Ft. Worth, summer 1981; anesthesia technician Tex. Tech. Sch. Medicine, Lubbock, summer 1982, 83; pres. Pre-Med. Soc., 1980; chmn. Resident's Standards Bd., 1980; mem. Tex. Tech. Med. Sch. Admissions Com., 1981; vice-chmn. anesthesia dept. Met. Hosp., 1993; mem. operating rm. com. Bapt. Hosp. System, 1993; med. dir. of bloodless medicine surgery program Metro. Hosp., 1994—; mem. credentials com. Baptist Hosp., 1994—. Mem. Tex. Tech. and Ch. Choirs, 1978-81; music dir., adv. bd. Christ Wesleyan Ch., 1989-90. Named Outstanding Young Woman Am., 1982, 87. Mem. Am. Soc. Anesthesiologists, Soc. Cardiovascular Anesthesiologists, Christian Med. and Dental Soc., Tex. Med. Assn., San Antonio Soc. Anesthesiologists, Bexar County Med. Soc., Phi Kappa Phi, Alpha Epsilon (pres., historian 1979-80, Sr. ward 1981). Republican.

COLONNA, ISABEL WILLETT, marketing professional; b. Atlantic City, N.J., Sept. 5, 1961; d. Francis Merrill and Faith Bernadette Honsberger Willett; m. Joseph Peter Colonna, Aug. 8, 1987. BA in Mktg., Boston Coll., 1987; JD, Suffolk Law Sch., 1993. Mktg. profl. So. N.J. Devel. Coun., Atlantic City, 1985-86; real estate salesperson Coldwell Banker Realtors, Brigantine, N.J., 1983-86; managerial asst. Kelly Svcs., Inc., Boston, 1986-87; mktg. and sales profl. The Patriot Group, Inc., Boston, 1987-92; v.p. John Hancock Funds, Boston, 1992—. Democrat. Roman Catholic. Home: 2 Hillcrest Ave Nahant MA 01908-1113

COLONNELLO, DIANE THERESA, social worker, psychotherapist; b. Rockville Centre, N.Y., July 31, 1959; d. John Charles and Joan Francis (Curtin) C.; m. John F. Oldenborg, Sept. 10, 1983. BA in Psychology, SUNY, Stony Brook, 1981; MSW, Adelphi U., 1983. Lic. clin. social worker Fla., N.Y. Clin. social worker Cath. Charities, Patchogue, N.Y., 1983-84, Alternatives Counseling Ctr., Southampton, N.Y., 1984-86, Project Outreach, West Hempstead, N.Y., 1984-86; crisis intervention specialist David Lawrence Mental Health Ctr., Naples, Fla., 1986-88; clin. social worker Psychiat. Ctr. of Med. Ctr. Hosp., Punta Gorda, Fla., 1988-93; pvt. practice counselor Affiliated Psychologist, Ft. Myers, Fla., 1992-95; clin. supr. Human Svcs. Found., Ft. Myers, 1994—; pvt. practice counselor Neuropsychiat. Assocs. SW Fla., Ft. Myers, 1995—. Mem. Tri County Critical Incident Debriefing Team of S.W. Fla., Ft. Myers, 1988. Mem. NASW (diplomate), Internat. Critical Incident Stress Found., Inc. Office: Neuropsychiat Assocs SW Fla 12700 Creekside Lake Ste 1301 Fort Myers FL 33919

COLONY-COKELY, PAMELA CAMERON, medical researcher; b. Boston, Apr. 18, 1947; d. Donald Gifford Colony and Priscilla (Adams) Pratley; m. E. Paul Cokely Jr., Apr. 26, 1986; children: Daniel Patrick, John Travis. BA, Wellesley (Mass.) Coll., 1969; PhD, Boston U., 1976. Rsch. asst. sch. medicine Boston U., 1969-71, U. Hosp., 1971-73, Peter Bent Brigham Hosp., Boston, 1973-75; instr. dept. anatomy Harvard Med. Sch., 1975-77; assoc. staff in medicine Peter Bent Brigham Hosp., Boston, 1976-79; sr. fellow, instr. Harvard Med. Sch., Boston, 1979-81; asst. prof. anatomy and medicine Pa. State Coll. Medicine, Hershey, Pa., 1981-88; assoc. prof. rsch., pre-health advisor Franklin and Marshall Coll., Lancaster, 1988-91; adj. assoc. prof. of surgery Pa. State Coll. Medicine, Hershey, 1988-91, sr. rsch. support assoc. dept. surgery, 1991—; ind. assessor Nat. Health and Med. Rsch. Coun., Australia, 1985—; ad-hoc reviewer NIH, Nat. Cancer Inst., Bethesda, Md., 1986; lectr., adj. instr. Harrisburg Area Cmty. Coll., 1991—. Contbr. articles to profl. jours. Fellow Nat. Found. Ileitis and Colitis, 1979-81; grantee Fed. Republic Germany, 1978, Cancer Rsch. Ctr., 1982-83, NIH, 1982-91. Mem. AAAS, Am. Soc. Cell Biology, N.Y. Acad. Sci., Am. Gastroent. Assn., Nat. Assn. Advisors Health Profls. Home: Shamrock Farm RR 2 Box 1760 Lebanon PA 17046-9254 Office: Pa State Coll Medicine Dept Surgery Divsn Gen Surgery PO Box 850 Hershey PA 17033

COLOSIMO, ANN MARIE, orthopaedic nurse; b. Red Bank, N.J., May 19, 1939; d. Donald and Anna Veronica (Kelly) Hickey; m. Anthony Colosimo, June 28, 1958 (div. 1985); children: Lynn Marie, Susan. AAS, Brookdale Community Coll., 1975; BSN, Trenton State Coll., 1983. Cert. Nat. Orthopaedic nurse, 1990. Staff and charge nurse Perth Amboy (N.J.) Gen. Hosp., 1975-77; staff nurse othopaedics Riverview Med. Ctr., Red Bank, N.J., 1977-83, asst. clin. coord. othopaedics, 1983-86, staff nurse orthopaedics, 1986-90, nurse case mgr. orthopaedics, 1990—. Mem. Nat. Assn. Orthopaedic Nurses (pres. 1984-85, 92-93, pres.-elect 1991-92), Collaborative Practice Com., Sigma Theta Tau (Lambda Delta chpt., community leader award 1992). Home: 409 Knollwood Dr Middletown NJ 07748

COLOSIMO, MARY LYNN SUKURS, psychology educator; b. Chgo., Aug. 14, 1950; d. Charles Paul and Charlotte Pearl (Bartkus) S.; m. Ronald Alfred Colosimo, Nov. 26, 1977; children: Elizabeth Catherine, Victoria Carmella, Christina Charlotte, Diana Clare. BA, Bradley U., 1972, MA, 1974; PhD, U. Chgo., 1981. Cert. tchr., Ill. Tchr. Lincoln (Ill.) High Sch., 1973-75; counselor Lyle Elem. Sch., Bridgeview, Ill., 1975-78; prof. St. Xavier Coll., Chgo., 1984-86; prof. psychology Trinity Christian Coll., Palos Heights, Ill., 1988—; pvt. practice as counselor, cons., Orland Park, Ill., 1983-90; educator, dir. summer program for gifted elem. students, after-sch. enrichment program women's ministry, retreat work, small group leader Cmty. Life Ch., Lockport, Ill.; researcher in field. Contbr. articles to profl. jours. Mem. ACA, ASCD, AAUW, Am. Edni. Rsch. Assn., Assn. Rsch. Value Issues in Counseling, Assn. Christian Therapists, Am. Assn. Christian Counselors, Nat. Assn. Guidance Counselors, Ill. Assn. Guidance Counselors, Phi Kappa Phi.

COLSMITH, MARCIA JOY, secondary education educator; b. Milw., Sept. 21, 1959; d. Charles Gordon and Marcella Katherine (Niemuth) Vlach; m. James Stephen Smith, May 10, 1986. BS in Computer Sci., U. Wis., Milw., 1984, MS in Computer Sci., 1986. Cert. secondary tchr., Ill. Supr. computers Coll. Engring., Milw., 1983-84; cons. Computing Svcs. Divsn., Milw., 1984-85; chief programmer Data Transit, Brown Deer, Wis., 1984; teaching asst. Coll. Engring., Milw., 1985-86; mem. tech. staff AT&T Bell Labs., Naperville, Ill., 1985-92; tchr. Ind. Sch. Dist. 200, Wheaton, Ill., 1993-94, Sch. Dist. 101, Batavia, Ill., 1994—. Co-author book revs. Reading Edge, 1992; contbr. articles to profl. jours. Chair Indian Hill Women's Com., Naperville, 1990-92; campaign activist Emily's List Dem. Com., Naperville, 1990—; chair Violence Against Women Task Force; mem. DuPage County NOW Edn. Task Force. Recipient Outstanding Contbn. awards Affirmative Action Com., 1988, Indian Hill West Resource Coun., 1989; Cert. of Appreciation, Women of 7783 Info. Group, 1989. Mem. NOW, ACLU, AAUW, LWV, Ill. Pro-Choice Alliance, League No. Ill., People for the Am. Way, Nature Conservancy, Phi Theta Kappa (Phi Beta chpt.). Democrat. Office: Violence Against Women Task Force PO Box 1106 Wheaton IL 60189-1106

COLSON, ELIZABETH FLORENCE, anthropologist; b. Hewitt, Minn., June 15, 1917; d. Louis H. and Metta (Damon) C. BA, U. Minn., 1938, MA, 1940; MA, Radcliffe Coll., 1941, PhD, 1945; PhD (hon.), Brown U., 1978, D of Sociology, 1979; D.Sc., U. Rochester, 1985, U. Zambia, 1992. Asst. social sci. analyst War Relocation Authority, 1942-43; research asst. Harvard, 1944-45; research officer Rhodes-Livingstone Inst., 1946-47, dir., 1948-51; sr. lectr. Manchester U., 1951-53; assoc. prof. Goucher Coll., 1954-55; research assoc., assoc. prof. African Research Program, Boston U., 1955-59, part-time, 1959-63; prof. anthropology Brandeis U., 1959-63; prof. anthropology U. Calif.-Berkeley, 1964-84, prof. emeritus, 1984—; vis. prof. U. Zambia, 1987; Lewis Henry Morgan lectr. U. Rochester, 1973; vis. rsch. assoc. Refugee Studies Program Queen Elizabeth House, Oxford, 1988-89. Author: The Makah, 1953, Marriage and the Family Among The Plateau Tonga, 1958, Social Organization of the Gwembe Tonga, 1960, The Plateau Tonga, 1962, The Social Consequences of Resettlement, 1971, Tradition and Contract, 1974; jr. author Secondary Education and the Formation of an Elite, 1980, Voluntary Efforts in Decentralized Management, 1983, sr. author For Prayer and Profit, 1988; sr. editor: Seven Tribes of British Central Africa, 1951; jr. editor People in Upheaval, 1987. AAUW travelling fellow, 1941-42, fellow Ctr. Advanced Study Behavioral Scis., 1967-68, Fairchild fellow Calif. Inst. Tech., 1975-76. Fellow Am. Anthrop. Assn., Brit. Assn. Social Anthropologists, Royal Anthrop. Inst. (hon.); mem. Nat. Acad. Sci., Am. Acad. Arts and Scis., Am. Assn. African Studies (Disting. Africanist award 1988), Soc. Applied Anthropology, Soc. Woman Geographers, Phi Beta Kappa. Office: U Calif Dept Anthropology Berkeley CA 94720

COLTON, DEBORAH G., federal government official; b. Nashville, May 14, 1954; d. Dudley T. and Sylvia (Hall) C. BA, Syracuse U., 1975, MSW, 1977. Rsch. and devel. specialist Peace, Inc., Syracuse, N.Y., 1975-77; assoc. dir. Nat. Inst. Pub. Mgmt., Washington, 1977-78; project mgr., sr. rsch. analyst Am. Pub. Welfare Assn., Washington, 1978-80, policy assoc., 1980-84; profl. asst. Subcom. on Human Resources Com. on Ways and Means, U.S. Congress, Washington, 1984-87, staff dir. Subcom. on Human Resources, 1987-91, asst. to chmn., 1991-94, dep. staff dir., 1994—. Mem. The Tax Coalition. Democrat. Home: 1718 Crestwood Dr Alexandria VA 22302 Office: Com on Ways and Means 1102 Longworth House Office Bldg Washington DC 20515

COLTON, MARIE W., state legislator; m. Henry E. Colton; 4 children. Grad., U. N.C., postgrad.; postgrad., Mars Hill Coll. State rep., speaker pro tempore N.C. Senate, Raleigh, 1991—, past chmn. ethics com., now vice chmn. rules, appointments & calendar coms., mem. fin., environ., human resources, transp., govt. ops. coms. With Signal Corps, U.S. Army, WWII. Recipient Spl. Legis. award N.C. chpt. Am. Acad. Pediat., 1987, Gertrude Carraway award Hist. Preservation Found.; named Legislator of Yr., Sierra Club. Mem. AAUW, LWV, Bus. and Profl. Women's Club, Children's Welfare League. Democrat. Episcopalian. Home: 392 Charlotte St Asheville NC 28801-1432 Office: NC State Senate State Capital Raleigh NC 27611*

COLTRANE, TAMARA CARLEANE, intravenous therapy nurse; b. Greensboro, N.C., Oct. 18, 1963; d. Charles Floyd and Nancy Jane (Lemons) C. BS in Nursing, U. N.C., 1986. RN, N.C.; cert. in intravenous therapy. Nursing asst. (summer) Mary Field Nursing Home, High Point, N.C., 1984; med.-surgical nurse Wesley Long Cmty. Hosp., Greensboro, 1986-88, IV team nurse, 1988—; mem. nursing policy com. Wesley Long Cmty. Hosp., Greensboro, 1987-88, nursing adv. com. 1987-89, 91-93. Mem. coun. on ministries, pianist, coord. comm. Sandy Ridge United Meth. Ch., High Point, N.C., 1990—, mem. adminstrv. bd., 1986-88, 90—; vol. worker Starmount Villa Nursing Home, Greensboro, 1984. Mem. Nat. Intravenous Nurses Soc. (N.C. chpt.), Sigma Theta Tau. Office: Wesley Long Cmty Hosp 501 N Elam Ave Greensboro NC 27402

COLVIN, GRETA WILMOTH, entrepreneur; b. Odessa, Tex., Mar. 24, 1962; d. Charles Hayden and Sherry Beth (Browning) Wilmoth; m. Michael Anthony Colvin, Aug. 16, 1986; 1 child, Michael Anthony Jr. AA in Radio-TV-Film, San Antonio Coll.; BS, U. Tex.; grad., Dale Carnegie, 1993. Lic. broadcaster, paralegal. Various media positions W.M. Entertainment, San Antonio, 1978-86; co-owner Image Nightclubs, San Antonio, 1986-88; owner W.C. Advt., San Antonio, 1980-88; retail mgr. Hastings, San Antonio, 1989-94; pres. Paradigm Enterprises, Flagstaff, Ariz., 1994—. Democrat. Home: 2845 N Prescott Flagstaff AZ 86001 also: 2800 Cerrillos Santa Fe NM 87501 also: 11623 Whisper Valley San Antonio TX 78230

COLVIN-PHILLIPS, GAYLE ANN, psychotherapist; b. L.A., Sept. 21, 1953; d. Robert Owen Sr. and Rachel Rebecca (Lemley) Colvin; m. Frederick Randale Phillips Sr., July 28, 1970; children: Frederick Andrew Phillips, Brian Scott Phillips. AA in Psychology, Okla. City Community Coll., Oklahoma City, 1986; BS in Sociology, Okla. State U., 1990, BS in Psychology, 1991, MS in Counseling, 1993. Adminstr., fin. cons. Security Fin. Cons., Oklahoma City, 1980-88; case worker Big Bros./Big Sisters, Stillwater, Okla., 1988-89; counselor Payne County Family Practices, Stillwater, 1989; social worker Dept. Human Svcs. Child Welfare, Stillwater, 1990; instr. Langston (Okla.) U., 1992; counselor Payne County Dept. Guidance Clinics and Health, Stillwater and Cushing, Okla., 1992-93, Church of Jesus Christ of Latter Day Saints, Stillwater, 1993—. Disaster vol. ARC, Oklahoma City, 1987-88; vita site coord. IRS, Oklahoma City, 1982-84. Mem. ACA, APA, Am. Assn. for Christian Counselors, Okla. Psychol. Assn., Okla. Assn. Counseling and Devel., Assn. for Humanist Psychology, Phi Theta Kappa, Psi Chi. Republican. Mem. LDS Ch. Home: 812 S Willis Ave Stillwater OK 74074 Office: PO Box 1906 Stillwater OK 74076-1906

COLWELL, RITA ROSSI, microbiologist, molecular biologist; b. Nov. 23, 1934; m. Jack H. Colwell, May 31, 1956; children: Alison E.L., Stacie A. BS in Bacteriology with distinction, Purdue U., 1956, MS in Genetics, 1958; PhD, U. Wash., 1961; DSc, Heriot-Watt U., Edinburgh, Scotland, 1987; DSc (hon.), Hood Coll., 1991; DSc, Purdue U., 1993; LLD, Notre Dame Coll., 1994. Rsch. asst. genetics lab. Purdue U., West Lafayette, Ind., 1956-57; rsch. asst. U. Wash., Seattle, 1957-58, predoctoral assoc., 1959-60, asst. rsch. prof., 1961-64; asst. prof. biology Georgetown U., Washington, 1964-66, assoc. prof. biology, 1966-72; prof. microbiology U. Md., 1972—, v.p. for acad. affairs, 1983-87; dir. Ctr. Marine Biotech., 1987-91; pres. Md. Biotech. Inst. U. Md., 1991—; hon. prof. U. Queensland, Brisbane, Australia, 1988; cons., advisor Washington area comms. media, congressman, legislators, 1978—; external examiner various univs. abroad, 1964—; mem. coastal resources adv. com. dept. natural resources State of Md., 1979; NAS ocean scis. bd., 1977-80, vice-chair polar rsch. bd., 1990-94; mem. Nat. Sci. Bd., 1984-90, sci. adv. bd. Oak Ridge Nat. Labs., 1988-90, 93-96, adv. com. FDA, 1991-92, food adv. com., 1993-96. Author 16 books including (manual numerical taxonomy) Collecting the Data, 1970, (with M. Zambruski) Rodina-Methods in Aquatic Microbiology, 1972, (with L. H. Stevenson) Estuarine Microbial Ecology, 1973, (with R. Y. Morita) Effect of the Ocean Environment on Microbial Activities, 1974, (with A. Sinsky and N. Pariser) Marine Biotechnology, 1983, Vibrios in the Environment, 1985, Nucleic Acid Sequence Data, 1988; mem. editorial bd. Microbial Ecology, 1972-91, Applied and Environ. Microbiology, 1969-81, Oil and Petrochemical Pollution, 1980-91, Jour. Washington Acad. Scis., 1981-87, Johns Hopkins U. Oceanographic Series, 1981-84, Revue de la Fondation Oceanographique Ricard, 1981-92, Estuaries, 1983-89, Zentralblatt fur Bacteriologie, 1985—, Jour. Aquatic Living Resources, 1987—, System. Applied Microbiology, 1985—, World Jour. Microbiology and Biotechnology, 1988—; contbr. articles and revs. to profl. jours. including Can. Jour. Fisheries and Aquatic Scis., Soc. Gen. Microbiology, Jour. Bacteriology, others. Recipient Gold medal Internat. Biotech. Inst., 1990, Purkinje Gold medal Achievement in Scis. Czechoslavakian Acad. Scis., 1991, Civic award Gov. Md., 1990, Cert. Recognition, NASA, 1984, Alice Evans award Am. Soc. Microbiol. Com. on Status of Women, 1988, Andrew White medal Loyola Coll., 1994; named Phi Kappa Phi Scholar of Yr., 1992, Outstanding Women on Campus U. Md., 1979. Fellow AAAS (chmn. sect. biol. scis. 1993-94, pres.-elect 1994) , Grad. Women Sci., Can. Coll. Microbiologists, Am. Acad. Microbiology (chmn. bd. govs. 1989-94), Washington Acad. Scis. (bd. mgrs. 1976-79), Marine Tech. Soc., (exec. com. 1982-88), Sigma Delta Epsilon; mem. Am. Soc. Microbiology (various sci. coms. 1961—, pres. 1985, chmn. program com. REGEM-1 1988, Fisher award 1985), World Fedn. Culture Collections, Internat. Union Microbiol. Soc. (v.p. 1986-90, pres. 1990-94), Am. Inst. Biol. Scis. (bd. govs. 1976-82), Am. Soc. Limnology and Oceanography, Internat. Coun. Sci. Unions (gen com., exec. bd. 1993—), U.S. Fedn. Culture Collections (governing bd. 1978-88), Soc. Indsl. Microbiology (bd. govs. 1976-79), Classification Rsch. Group Eng. (charter), Soc. Gen. Microbiology, Phi Beta Kappa, Sigma Xi (Ann. Achievement award 1981, Rsch. award 1984, nat. pres. 1991—), Omicron Delta Kappa, Delta Gamma. Office: U Md Biotech Inst Office Pres Ste 550 4321 Hartwick Rd College Park MD 20740

COLY, LISETTE, foundation executive; b. N.Y.C., Apr. 6, 1950; d. Robert Raymond and Eileen (Lyttle-Garrett) C.; children: George Robert Damalas, Anastasia Eileen Damalas. BA cum laude, Hunter Coll., 1973. Sec. Parapsychology Found., Inc., N.Y.C., 1972-75, assoc. editor, 1975—, v.p., 1978—. Assoc. editor Parapsychology Rev. and Procs. Ann. Internat. Parapsychology Found. Confs., 1978—; editor, conf. coord. Proceedings Ann. Internat. Confs., 1989—. Office: 1 Parapsychology Found Inc 228 E 71st St New York NY 10021-5136

COMBIE, JOAN DIANE, biotechnology researcher; b. New London, N.H., June 30, 1946. BS, Colby-Sawyer Coll., 1968; MS, U. Ky., 1978, PhD, 1982. Toxicologist, med. toxicologist, 1982-87; dir. rsch., v.p., co-owner J.K. Rsch., Bozeman, Mont., 1987—. Contbr. 42 articles to profl. jours.; patentee in field. Mem. Am. Soc. Microbiology, Soc. Indsl. Microbiology. Office: JK Rsch 210 S Wallace Ave Bozeman MT 59715-4857

COMBS, LINDA JONES, management company executive, researcher; b. Jonesboro, Ark., Apr. 12, 1948; d. Dale Jones and Neva (Craig) Green; 1 child, Nathan Isaac. BSBA, U. Ark., 1971, MBA, 1972, PhD in Bus. Adminstrn., 1983. Assoc. economist Bur. Bus. and Econ. Rsch., Fayetteville, Ark., 1973-76; pres. Combs Mgmt. Co., Springdale, Ark., 1976-83; asst. prof. fin. U. Ark., Fayetteville, 1983-87; asst. prof. fin. and mktg. Western Ill. U., Macomb, 1987-88; asst. prof. bus. adminstrn. Cen. Mo. State U., Warrensburg, 1988-94; assoc. prof. bus. adminstrn. N.E. State U., Tahlequah, Okla., 1989-94; pres. Combs Mgmt. Co., Fayetteville; cons. in credit and polit. rsch. Sears, Roebuck, Chgo., 1973-74, Fayetteville Adv. Coun., 1975-76; cons. in fin. and banking, Fayetteville, 1973-76. Contbr. articles to profl. jours. Mem. Ark. Gov.'s Inaugural Com., Little Rock, 1985; county co-chmn. Clinton for Gov., Washington County, Ark., 1984, 86, 90; bd. dirs. Shiloh Mus., Am. Cancer Soc., South Washington County, North Ark. Symphony Soc.; bd. dirs. Ark. State Hosp. System, sec., chmn., 1993-94; active numerous polit. campaigns for candidates and issues. Mem. Am. Mktg. Assn. (health care mktg.), Transp. Rsch. Forum. Office: Combs Mgmt Co PO Box 1452 Fayetteville AR 72702-1452

COMBS, MAXINE SOLOW, English language educator; b. Dallas, June 14, 1937; d. Eugene Maxwell and Sayd Frances Solow; m. Edouard Gauthier; m. 2d Bruce Combs; children: Bella, Wayne; m. 3d Martin Bernstein, Feb. 20, 1992. BA, Mills Coll., 1958; MA, Wayne State U., 1961; PhD, U. Oreg., 1968. Instr. English Idaho State U., Pocatello, 1963-65; lectr. English Lane C.C., Eugene, Oreg., 1966-69, Am. U., Washington, 1970-74; asst. prof. English George Mason U., Fairfax, Va., 1979-88; instr. English Howard U., Washington, 1988-89; asst. prof. English U. of D.C., Washington, 1972-77, 81-88, 90—. Author: (chapbook of poems) Swimming out of the Collective Unconscious, 1988, (chapbook of stories) Foam of Perilous Seas, 1989 (Slough Press Fiction award), (short stories and novella) Handbook of the Strange, 1995. Home: 2216 King Pl NW Washington DC 20007

COMBS, SANDRA LYNN, state board official; b. Lancaster, Pa., Aug. 31, 1946; d. Clyde Robert and Violet (Sensenig) Boose; m. Allen Evans Combs, Aug. 30, 1969; children: Evan McKenzie, Leslie Ann. AAS in Nursing, Thomas Nelson C.C., Hampton, Va., 1980; BS in Psychology, Juniata Coll., 1968. RN, Va. Dir. vols. in probation Yorktown (Va.) Juvenile Ct., 1973-74; emergency nurse assoc. to pvt. practice physician Hampton, Va., 1980-82; chmn. bd. dirs., CEO Hampton Rds. Admirals Profl. Hockey Team, Hampton, 1981-82; mem. sch. bd. York County Pub. Schs., Yorktown, 1985-94; vice chmn. Va. Parole Bd., Richmond, 1994—; mem. supt.'s adv. coun. York County Pub. Schs., 1984-94, mem. long range strategic planning com., 1989-94; trustee New Horizons Tech. Ctr., Gov.'s Sch., Hampton, 1991-94; mem. Va. edn. tech. adv. com. Va. Dept. Edn., 1992—. Pres. Hampton Med. Soc. Aux, 1977-78, Dare Elem. PTA, York County, 1979-81, York County Coun. PTA, 1983-84; chmn. York County Rep. Com., 1984-90, 1st Dist. Rep. Congl. Com., Va., 1990-94; adviser edn. policy George Allen for Gov., Richmond, 1992-93. Capt. USAF, 1968-73, Vietnam. Decorated Bronze Star medal, Cross of Gallantry (Vietnam), Air Force Commendation medal. Mem. ASCD, VFW, Va. Sch. Bds. Assn. (bd. dirs. 1990-94, award of Excellence 1990, 91, 92), Mil. Order World Wars. Methodist. Home: 9925 Groundhog Dr Richmond VA 23235 Office: Va Parole Bd 6900 Atmore Dr Richmond VA 23225

COMDEN, BETTY, writer, dramatist, lyricist, performer; b. Bklyn., May 3, 1919; d. Leo and Rebecca (Sadvoransky) C.; m. Steven Kyle, Jan. 4, 1942; children: Susanna, Alan. Student, Bklyn. Ethical Culture Sch., Erasmus Hall High Sch.; B.S., N.Y. U. Writer, performer nightclub act, Revuers; writer: (with Adolph Green) book and lyrics Broadway shows On The Town, 1944-45, Billion Dollar Baby, Two on the Aisle, Bells are Ringing, Fade-Out-Fade-In, Subways are for Sleeping, On the Twentieth Century, A Doll's Life, 1982 (Tony award nomination), lyrics for Peter Pan, lyrics for Hallelujah, Baby!, lyrics for The Will Rogers Follies, 1991 (Tony award); screenplays Auntie Mame, Good News, The Barkleys of Broadway, Singin' in the Rain, The Band Wagon, others; screenplay and lyrics for On the Town, Bells are Ringing, Fade-Out-Fade-In, Subways are for Sleeping, It's Always Fair Weather, What a Way to Go; co-author: book for Applause, 1970; co-author (with Adolph Green) book for Lorelei, 1973, book and lyrics On the 20th Century, 1978; appeared in: On the Town, 1944; performed with Adolph Green, 1959, 77; also appeared in play Isn't it Romantic, 1983, in movie Garbo Talks, 1985, The Band Wagon; author: Off Stage, 1995. Recipient Donaldson award and Tony award for Wonderful Town, as co-lyricist Best Score 1983; Tony award for Hallelujah, Baby, as co-writer Best Score 1968, Tony award Applause 1970, Tony award Lyrics and Book On the 20th Century, A Doll's Life, Tony award for Best Original lyrics The Will Rogers Follies, 1991; Woman of Achievement award NYU Alumnae Assn. 1978; N.Y.C. Mayor's award Art and Culture 1978, Lifetime Achievement award Kennedy Ctr., 1991, Grammy award for Will Roger Follies, 1992; named to Songwriters Hall of Fame 1980, Theatre Hall of Fame. Mem. Dramatists Guild (council, v.p. Dramatists Guild Fund). Office: care The Dramatists Guild 234 W 44th St New York NY 10036-3909

COMEAU, LORENE ANITA EMERSON, real estate developer; b. Haverhill, Mass., Sept. 6, 1952; d. Russell Paul and Jeannette (La Course) Emerson; m. Peter Robert Comeau, May 6, 1950; children: Stephen David, Michelle Patricia. BA with honors, Northeastern U., 1975. Lic. real estate broker. Housing rep., pub. liaison U.S. Dept. HUD, Boston, 1975-78; devel. mgr. John M. Corcoran & Co., Milton, Mass., 1978-84, v.p., 1984-94; ptnr. Corcoran Realty Assocs., Milton, 1994—; bd. dirs. Stoneham Coop. Bank, 1992—, mem. bd. affairs com., 1992-93, mem. security com., 1993—; v.p. Merrimack Valley Housing Partnership, Lowell, Mass., 1986-89. Treas. Andover (Mass.) br. Merrimack Valley YMCA, 1986-88, vice chair, 1988-90, chair, 1990-92; assoc. mem. Andover Zoning Bd. Appeals, 1984-87; mem. Andover Fair Housing Com., 1982-87, Andover Housing Partnership Com., 1990—, Andover Planning Bd., 1993—; mem. Andover Master Plan Com., 1982-84, chmn. com. housing component and master plan, 1989-90; mem. fin. com., corp. bd. Merrimack Valley YMCA, Lawrence, Mass., 1984-86, 91-94, treas. corp. fin. com., 1992-95, mem. low income housing subcom. corp. bd.; mem. adv. bd. Caritas Cmtys., 1994—. Mem. LWV (fin. chmn. Andover chpt. 1981-83, budget chmn. 1983-84, 86-87), New England Women in Real Estate (seminars com., cmty. rels. com., program com.), Developers Coun.-Builders Assn. Greater Boston, Nat. Leased Housing Assn. Washington, Urban Land Inst. (assoc.), Internat. Coun. Shopping Ctrs., Nat. Assn. Indsl. and Office Properties (pub. affairs com.), Svc. Club of Andover, Sanborn Sch. PTO (curriculum enrichment com.), West Middle Sch. PAC (curriculum enrichment com., women's history month). Republican. Episcopalian. Home: PO Box 4108bv Andover MA 01810 Office: John M Corcoran & Co 500 Granite Ave Milton MA 02186-5626

COMEAU, SUSAN, bank executive. Exec. v.p. State St. Boston Corp., Boston. Office: State St Boston Corp 225 Franklin St Boston MA 02110*

COMEAUX, KATHARINE JEANNE, realtor; b. Richland, Wash., Jan. 18, 1949; d. Warren William and Ruth Irma (Remington) Gonder; m. Jack Goldwasser, May 25, 1992; 1 child, Thelma Morrow. AA, West Valley Coll., 1970; student, San Jose State U., 1970-71. Cert. realtor. Realtor Value Realty, Cupertino, Calif., 1975-79, Valley of Calif., Cupertino, 1979-81, Coldwell Banker, Cupertino, 1981-82, Fox & Carskadon, Saratoga, Calif., 1984-90. With Los Gatos-Saratoga Bd. Realtors Polit. Action, 1984-89; v.p. Hospice of Valley Svc. League, Saratoga, 1984-89; big sister Big Bros./Big Sisters, San Jose, Calif., 1976-90. Home: 4330 Fish Hatchery Rd Grants Pass OR 97527

COMEAUX, TINA BOISSEY, school board executive, civic worker; b. Groves, Tex., Mar. 21, 1956; d. Robert Oliver and Jim Marie (Glenn) Boissey; m. Charles Allen Comeaux, Jan. 3, 1976; children: Candice Lynn, Christy Ann. Student, Lamar U., 1974-76. Saleswoman Burkett's Jewelry, Port Neches, Tex., 1974-78. Trustee Port Neches Ind. Sch. Dist., 1987—, sec., 1991-92, v.p., 1992-93, pres. 1993—; co-chmn. summer reading program Groves Pub. Libr., 1984-89, founder, tchr. presch. reading program, 1986-89; del. area coun. Van Buren Sch. PTA, Groves, 1984-90, parent. vol., 1990; treas. Grove Elem. Sch. PTA, 1988-92, mem. exec. bd., 1990—; libr. vol. Grove Elem. LOVE Program, 1991-92; mem. exec. bd. Port Neches-Groves Area Coun. PTA, 1993—, Port Neches Mid. Sch. PTA, 1993—; vol. computer coord. Woodcrest Elem., 1993-94; treas. Groves Mid. Sch. PTA, 1992-93; pres. Groves Pub. Libr., 1986-89; others. Presdl. scholar Lamar U., 1974. Mem. Nat. Sch. Bds. Assn., Tex. Assn. Sch. Bds. (rep. 1989-91), Tex. Vols. in Pub. Schs., Sabine-Neches Adminstrs. and Sch. Bd. Mems. Assn. (co-chmn. 1989-91), Van Buren Sch. PTA (life), S.E. Tex. Art Mus. Roman Catholic. Home: 1723 Llano St Port Neches TX 77651

COMER, DEBRA RUTH, management educator; b. Phila., Apr. 11, 1960; d. Nathan Lawrence and Rita (Ellis) C.; m. James Michael Maloney. BA, Swarthmore Coll., 1982; MA, Yale U., 1984, MPhil, 1985, PhD, 1986. Instr. Yale U., New Haven, 1984; orgnl. devel. cons. Port Authority of N.Y. & N.J., N.Y.C., 1984-87; asst. prof. mgmt. Hofstra U., Hempstead, N.Y., 1987-93; assoc. prof. mgmt. Hofstra U., Hempstead, 1993—, chairperson dept. mgmt. and GB, 1995—. Contbr. articles to profl. jours. Yale U. fellow, 1982-86, Joshua B. Lippincott fellow Swarthmore Coll., 1982; Hofstra U. grantee, 1988, 89, 90, 91, 92, 93, 94. Mem. APA, Acad. Mgmt., Ea. Acad. Mgmt., Organizational Behavior Teaching Soc. Jewish. Office: Hofstra U Dept Mgmt and GB 228 Weller Hall Hempstead NY 11550

COMERFORD, ELLEN MAJOR SHAPLEY, artist, critic; b. Buffalo, June 6, 1938; d. John Martin and Florence Anna (Bolton) Shapley; m. Thomas Edison Comerford, July 1, 1961; children: Mary M., Thomas E. III, John Patrick, Matthew M. BA in English, U. Buffalo, 1960; MA in Art/Art History, SUNY, Buffalo, 1987. Freelance arts critic, columnist Niagara Gazette, Niagara Falls, N.Y., 1986—; artist-in-residence DeVeaux campus U. Niagara Falls, 1992—. Bd. dirs. Friends of Niagara U. Theatre, 1988—.

Mem. Niagara Coun. of Arts, Mem.'s Gallery of Albright-Knox Art Gallery, Coll. Club Niagara Falls. Democrat. Home: 205 S 4th St Lewiston NY 14092

COMET, CATHERINE, conductor; m. Michael Aiken; 1 child, Caroline. MusM in Orch. Conducting, Juilliard Sch. Music; studied with Pierre Boulez, Nadia Boulanger, Igor Markevich. Former music dir., condr. U. Wis. Symphony & Chamber Orch.; EXXON-Arts Endowment condr. St. Louis Symphony Orch., 1981-84; music dir. St. Louis Youth Orch.; assoc. condr. Balt. Symphony Orch., 1984-86; music dir. Grand Rapids (Mich.) Symphony Orch., 1986-90, 91—, Am. Symphony Orch., N.Y.C., 1990-91; guest condr. Pasadena Symphony, Buffalo Philharm., Ala. Symphony, Nat. Symphony, others. Recipient 1st prize Internat. Young Condrs.' Competition, France, 1966, Dmitri Mitropoulos Internat. Contest prize, 1968. Office: Grand Rapids Symphony Orch 220 Lyon St NW Ste 415 Grand Rapids MI 49503*

COMFORT, PRISCILLA MARIA, college official, human resources professional; b. Ft. Dix, N.J., Feb. 20, 1947; d. Jennie Rita (Manes) McGuire; children: James, Aimee. BS, Montclair State Coll., 1969; MEd, Trenton State Coll., 1980. Cert. tchr., guidance counselor, pub. mgr., N.J. Tchr. Burlington (N.J.) Twp. and City Schs., 1969-72; employment svc. interviewer N.J. Dept. Labor and Industry, Trenton, 1972-74; prin. career devel. specialist N.J. Dept. Civil Svc., Trenton, 1974-76, prin. pers. technician, 1976-79; dir. pers. svcs. Stockton State Coll., Pomona, N.J., 1979-89; asst. v.p. human resources Stockton State Coll., Pomona, 1990; with N.J. Gov.'s task force on sexual harassment, 1993. Mem. Betty Bacharach Rehab. Hosp. Found. Bd., 1993; tchr. CCD Assumption Ch., Pomona, 1981-84, mem. CCD adv. bd., 1983-84; active Little League, PTO, 1977-84; mem. pers. com. Big Bors./Big Sisters Adv. Com., 1988; mem. community adv. bd. Jewish Family Svcs., 1991—; mem. adv. bd. pers. com. Atlantic City C. of C., 1985. Recipient Tribute to Women in Industry award YWCA (twin), 1987, Mgmt. Merit award, 1986, 88, SUN Mag. award, 1988, Community Recognition award Chapel of the Four Chaplains, 1988. Mem. ASPA, Cert. Pub. Mgrs. Assn., N.J. Atlantic County Pers. Assn., Assn. Affirmative Action in Higher Edn. (panelist), N.J. Pers. Adv. Bd., N.J. Coll. and Univ. Pers. Assn. (chmn., sec.-treas., chmn. mem. sect.), Coll. and Univ. Pers. Assn. (nat. bd. dirs. 1993, nat. legis. com. 1989-93, bd. dirs. ea. region 1990—, sec. 1990-93, active other coms.), CUPA Ea. Acad. for Human Resource Excellence (chair-elect 1994). Roman Catholic. Office: Stockton State Coll Jim Leeds Rd Pomona NJ 08240

COMINI, ALESSANDRA, art historian, educator; b. Winona, Minn., Nov. 24, 1934; d. Raiberto and Megan (Laird) C. BA, Barnard Coll., 1956; MA, U. Calif., Berkeley, 1964; PhD with distinction, Columbia U., 1969. Teaching asst. U. Calif., Berkeley, 1964; vis. instr. U. Calif., 1967; preceptor Columbia U., 1965-66, 67-68, instr., 1968-69, asst. prof., 1969-74; vis. asst. prof. So. Methodist U., summers 1970, 72, assoc. prof. art history, 1974-75, prof., 1975—, Univ. disting. prof., 1983—; Alfred Hodder resident humanist Princeton U., 1972-73; vis. asst. prof. Yale U., 1973; vis. humanist various univs.; lectr. in English, German and Italian at various univs. and museums in U.S., Eng., Italy, Germany, and Austria; keynote speaker Gewandhaus Symposia, Leipzig, Dem. Republic Germany, 1983, 85, 87, 89, Mahler Internat. Congress, Amsterdam, 1988, 95, Hamburg, 1989; featured speaker Purchase, N.Y., 1989, Leningrad, 1990, Stockholm, 1991, Berlin, 1993, Beethoven Extravaganza, Milw., 1994, Schiele Symposium, Indpls., 1994; panelist NEH Museums and Public Programs, 1978—. Author: Schiele in Prison, 1973, Egon Schiele's Portraits, 1974 (Nat. Book award nominee 1975, reissued 1990, Charles Rufus Morey Book award 1975), Gustav Klimt, 1975, reissued 1986, 90, 93, also German, French and Dutch edits, Egon Schiele, 1976, reissued 1986, 94, also German, French and Dutch edits, The Fantastic Art of Vienna, 1978, The Changing Image of Beethoven, 1987; contbg. author: World Impressionism, 1990, Käthe Kollwitz, 1992, Egon Schiele, 1994, Violetta and her Sisters, 1994; contbr. numerous articles to Stagebill, Arts Mag., also; author various catalogue and book introductions, also book revs. for N.Y. Times, Women's Art Jour. Awarded Grand Decoration of Honor for svcs. to Republic of Austria, 1990; recipient Charles Rufus Morey Book award Coll. Art Assn. Am., 1976, Laural award AAUW, 1979; named Outstanding Prof., 1977, 79, 83, 85, 86, 87, 88, 90; AAUW travel fellow, 1966-87; NEH grantee, 1975; named Meadows Disting. Teaching Prof., 1986-87. Mem. ASCAP, Coll. Art Assn. Am. (bd. dirs. 1980-84), Women's Caucus for Art (bd. dirs. 1974-78, Life Achievement award 1995), Tex. Inst. Letters. Democrat. Home: 2900 McFarlin Blvd Dallas TX 75205-1920 Office: So Meth U Dept Art History Dallas TX 75275

COMISKY, HOPE A., lawyer; b. Phila., Apr. 23, 1953; married; three children. BA with distinction, Cornell U., 1974; JD, U. Pa., 1977. Bar: Pa. 1977, U.S. Dist. Ct. (ea. dist.) Pa. 1978, D.C. 1979, U.S. Ct. Appeals (3d cir.) 1979, U.S. Supreme Ct. 1987, U.S. Dist. Ct. (mid. dist.) Pa. 1991, N.Y. 1993. Law clerk ea dist. U.S. Dist. Ct., Pa., 1977-78; assoc. Dilworth, Paxson, Kalish & Kauffman, Phila., 1978-84, ptnr., 1985-91; ptnr. Anderson Kill Olick & Oshinsky P.C., Phila., 1992—; spkr. in field. Contbr. articles to profl. jours. Bd. dirs. Phila. Sch.; hon. bd. dirs. Fedn. Day Care Svcs., mem. exec. com., chmn. pers. practices com., 1985-91. Mem. Phi Beta Kappa, Mortar Bd. Office: Anderson Kill Olick & Oshinsky PC 1600 Market St Fl 14 Philadelphia PA 19103-7240

COMMANDER, JOANNA, health, physical education and athletics director; b. Bklyn., May 8, 1948; d. Constantine Frank and Pauline (Coronges) C. BS, So. Conn. State U., 1970; MA, Adelphi U., 1974; PD, St. John's U., Jamaica, N.Y., 1982. Cert. health, phys. edn. K-12 sch. dist. supr. Tchr. health and phys. edn. Sewanhaka Ctrl. High Sch. Dist., Elmont, N.Y., 1970-86, dist. coord. health edn., 1982-86; dist. dir. health, phys. edn. and athletics Lynbrook (N.Y.) Schs., 1986—; conductor parent workshops communication and sexuality Lynbrook Pub. Schs. Named Coach of Yr. Newsday, 1986. Mem. AAHPERD, AAUW, NOW, N.Y. State Assn. Health, Phys. Edn., Recreation and Dance, N.Y. State Profl. Health Educators, Nassau County Athletic Assn. (v.p. women sports 1990—). Home: 98 Powell Ave Rockville Centre NY 11570-3034

COMMIRE, ANNE, playwright; b. Wyandotte, Mich.; d. Robert and Shirley (Moore) C. BS, Eastern Mich. U., 1961; postgrad., Wayne State U., NYU. Author: (plays) Shay, 1973, Put Them All Together, 1978, Transatlantic Bridge, 1977, Sunday's Red, 1980, Melody Sisters, 1983, Starting Monday, 1988; (book) (with Mariette Hartley) Breaking the Silence, 1990, (teleplays) Rebel for God, 1980, Hayward's, 1980; editor: Something About the Author, 1970-90, Yesterday's Authors of Books for Children, 1977-78, Historic World Leaders, 1994. Recipient Eugene O'Neill Theatre award, 1973, 78, 83, 88; Creative Artists Program grantee, 1975; Rockefeller grantee for playwriting, 1979. Mem. PEN, Authors Guild, Dramatists Guild, Writers Guild Am. Democrat. Home: 11 Stanton St Waterford CT 06385-1439 also: 274 W 95th St New York NY 10025

COMOSS, PATRICIA B., cardiac rehabilitation nurse, consultant; b. Shamokin, Pa., Apr. 20, 1947; d. William J. and Lucille M. (Shipulski) McCall; m. Eugene J. Comoss, Nov. 25, 1970. Diploma, St. Joseph's Hosp., Reading, Pa., 1968; BS in Health Care Mgmt., Pa. State U., Harrisburg, 1982. CCU staff nurse Polyclinic Med. Ctr., Harrisburg; head nurse, cardiac rehab. Rehab. Hosp., Mechanicsburg, Pa.; dir. edn. AMSCO/Rehab., Mechanicsburg; founder, pres. Nursing Enrichment Consultants, Harrisburg. Co-author: Cardiac Rehabilitation: A Comprehensive Nursing Approach, 1979; contbr. articles to profl. jours. Fellow Am. Assn. Cardiovascular and Pulmonary Rehab. (bd. dirs. 1986-88, v.p. 1988-90, pres.-elect 1990-91, pres. 1992, chair fed. project on clin. practice guidelines on cardiac rehab. 1992—); mem. ANA, AACCN, Am. Coll. Sports Medicine, Am. Heart Assn. Home: 4100 Elmerton Ave Harrisburg PA 17109-1327

COMPAIN, RITA, librarian; b. N.Y.C., Dec. 4, 1926; d. Benjamin and Sara (Modell) Romer; m. Ernest A. Compain, Apr. 17, 1948 (div. 1987); children: Michael, Daniel, Andrew. BS, CUNY, 1947; MLS, L.I. U., 1963; Profl. Dipl., St. John's U., N.Y.C., 1975; postgrad., Columbia U., 1969-70, Lang. & Lit. Inst. Genosee, 1985. Children's librarian Bklyn. Pub. Library, 1947-49; library coordinator Oceanside (N.Y.) pub. schs., 1959-61; librarian Franklin Sq. (N.Y.) pub. schs., 1961-71; staff developer BOCES Nassau, Jericho, N.Y., 1974-76; serials librarian Am. Mus. Natural History, N.Y.C., 1977-79; library cons. Rita Compain Agy., N.Y.C., 1980-85; project dir. "Open Sesame" Am. Reading Council, N.Y.C., 1985-88; staff developer library media Kingston (N.Y.) pub. schs., 1988-93; asst. prof. L.I. U., Greenvale, 1969-75; library cons. Great Neck pub. schs., 1975-76; adj. prof. SUNY, New Paltz, 1988-94; ednl. cons.; lectr. in field; mem. com. Nassau County Jail Library Pilot Prog., E. Meadow, 1979. Contbg. author: Open Sesame Guide to Implementation, 1987; contbg. author, dir. video: Teacher Training Film, 1986; author: New Connections: An Integrated Approach to Literacy, 1994, Giants a Thematic Guide, 1992. Mem. ALA, Internat. Reading Assn., N.Y. State Reading Assn., Nassau-Suffolk Sch. Libr. Assn. (pres. 1969-70), N.Y. State Libr. Assn., Amnesty Internat., Delta Kappa Gamma. Home: 7742 Whitebridge Glen University Park FL 34201

COMPTON, ANN WOODRUFF, news correspondent; b. Chgo., Jan. 19, 1947; d. Charles Edward and Barbara (Ortlund) C.; m. William Stevenson Hughes, Nov. 25, 1978; children: William Compton, Edward Opie, Ann Woodruff, Michael Stevenson. BA, Hollins (Va.) Coll., 1969. Reporter, anchorwoman WDBJ-TV (CBS), Roanoke, Va., 1969-70; polit. reporter, state capitol bur. chief WDBJ-TV (CBS), Richmond, Va., 1971-73; fellow Washington Journalism Center, 1970, trustee, 1978-93; corr. ABC News, N.Y.C., 1973-74; White House corr. ABC News, Washington, 1974-79, 81-84, 89—, congl. corr., 1979-81, 84-86, chief Ho. of Reps. corr., 1987-88. Trustee Hollins Coll., 1987-93; bd. dirs. Freedom Forum Ctr. for Media Studies, Columbia U., 1984—. Named Mother of Yr., Nat. Mother's Day Com., 1987. Mem. White House Corrs. Assn. (dir. 1977-79), Radio-TV Corrs. Bd. (chmn. 1987). Office: ABC News Washington Bur 1717 Desales St NW Washington DC 20036-4407

COMPTON, MARY BEATRICE BROWN (MRS. RALPH THEODORE COMPTON), public relations executive, writer; b. Washington, May 25, 1923; d. Robert James and Abia Eliza (Stone) Brown; m. Ralph Theodore Compton, Mar. 18, 1961. Grad. Thayer Acad., Chandler Sch., Leland Powers Sch. Radio, TV and Theatre, Boston, 1942. Radio program dir. Converse Co., Malden, Mass., 1942-45; head radio continuity dept. Sta. WAAB, Yankee Network, Worcester, Mass., 1945-46; asst. dir. radio Leland Powers Sch. Radio, TV and Theatre, Boston, 1946-49, dir., 1949-51; program asst. Sta. KNBH, Hollywood, Calif., 1951-52; v.p. Acorn Film Co., Boston, 1953-54; dir. women's communications, editor Program Notes, radio interviewer NAM, N.Y.C., 1954-61. Celebrities pub. rels. Nat. Citizens for Nixon, 1968, Kennedy Ctr. Pub. Info., 1985-89, Washington Nat. Cathedral Visitor's Svcs., 1989—. Mem. Soc. Old Plymouth Colony Descs., Magna Carta Dames, Congl. Country Club (Bethesda, Md.). Home: 15300 Wallbrook Ct Apt 3F Silver Spring MD 20906-1455

COMPTON, NORMA HAYNES, retired university dean; b. Washington, Nov. 16, 1924; d. Thomas N. and Lillian (Laffin) Haynes; m. William Randall Compton, Mar. 27, 1946; children: William Randall, Anne Elizabeth. AB, George Washington U., 1950; MS, U. Md., 1957, PhD, 1962. Rschr. Julius Garfinckel & Co., Washington, 1955; tchr. Montgomery Blair High Sch., Silver Spring, Md., 1955-57; instr. U. Md., 1957-60, teaching and rsch. fellow Inst. Child Study, 1960-61, assoc. prof., 1962-63; psychology extern St. Elizabeths Hosp., Washington, 1962-63; assoc. prof. Utah State U., 1963-64, prof., 1964-68, head dept. clothing and textiles, 1963-68, dir. Inst. for Rsch. on Man and His Personal Environment, 1967-68; dean Sch. Home Econs. Auburn (Ala.) U., 1968-73; dean Sch. Consumer and Family Scis. Purdue U., 1973-87, prof. family studies, 1987-90; faculty The Edn. Ctr., Longboat Key, Fla., 1991—; cons. Burgess Pub. Co., Mpls., 1975-81, Nat. Advt. Rev. Bd., N.Y.C., 1978-82; bd. dirs. Armour & Co., Phoenix, 1976-82, Home Hosp., Lafayette, Ind., 1983-89; chair Adv. Commn. Status Women, Sarasota, Fla., 1993—. Author: (with Olive Hall) Foundations of Home Economics Research, 1972, (with John Touliatos) Approaches to Child Study, 1983, Research Methods in Human Ecology/Home Economics, 1988; contbr. articles to profl. jours. Bd. deacons Congl. United Ch. of Christ. Mem. APA, AAUW, P.E.O., Assn. Women in Psychology, Am. Home Econs. Assn., Phi Beta Kappa, Sigma Xi, Phi Kappa Phi, Omicron Nu, Psi Chi.

COMPTON, SUSAN LANELL, retired librarian; b. Batesville, Ark., Aug. 20, 1917; d. Thomas Smith and Susan (Whitlow) Compton. BS in Edn., Ark. State Tchrs. Coll., 1939; BS in Libr. Sci., Peabody Coll. Tchrs., 1948. Asst. cataloger U. Ark. Gen. Libr., Fayetteville, 1948-49; head catalog dept. Ark. Libr. Commn., Little Rock, 1949-77, chief cataloger, bibliographer, indexer, 1977-79; free-lance writer. Author: Beauty Transient & Other Poems, 1969, Looking Forward to a New Day, 1984, Ozark Sketches: A Family Chronicle, 1991; contbr. to Collier's Ency., 1970-76; editor quar. libr. bull. Ark. Librs., 1949-74. Mem. AAUW, Nat. League Am. Pen Women (v.p., program chmn. Ark. Pioneer br. 1972-74, pres. 1974-76), Am. Libr. Assn. (life), Ark. Hist. Assn., Ark. Fedn. Women's Clubs. Christadelphian. Home: 620 N Oak St Little Rock AR 72205-4156

COMSTOCK, MARGOT MARY, editor, writer, graphic designer, consultant; b. Paterson, N.J., Oct. 11, 1940; d. Kenneth Franklin and Phyllis Abigail (Taylor) C.; m. Allan Richard Tommervik, Oct. 14, 1972; children: Roberta Ann, Kirin Lee. BA, Heidelberg Coll., Tiffin, Ohio. Crossword puzzle constructor Daily Variety, L.A., 1987-91, editorial desk, 1989-92; co-founder, pres., editor Softalk Pub. Inc., North Hollywood, Calif., 1980-84; mgr. creativity ctr. Broderbund Software, Novato, Calif., 1992-93; founder, owner MC ART Design & Graphics, Fairfax, Calif., 1994—; co-founder Digital Sports Network, Fairfax, Calif., 1994—; cons. Origin Systems, Austin Tex., 1981-88, Sirtech Software, 1986-87; cons., reviewer San Luis Revue, San Luis Obispo, Calif., 1986-88; cons. columnist II Computing, San Francisco, 1985-86. Founder, editor periodical Softalk, 1980-84. Tchr. of literacy Laubach Literacy Action, Arroyo Grande, Calif., 1986-89; foster parent Childreach Plan Internat., 1985—. Named Microcomputer Pioneer, Smithsonian Instn., 1987. Mem. NOW (newsletter editor Marin chpt. 1993—, bd. dirs.), Computer Game Developers Assn., Assn. for Software Design, Hackers Conf. Office: Digital Sports Network 6 School St Box 598 Fairfax CA 94978

COMSTOCK, REBECCA ANN, lawyer; b. Mpls., Mar. 13, 1950; d. Clark Franklin and Ruth Carolyn (Sundt) C.; m. John A. Aronld, Mar. 2, 1991. Student, Conn. Coll., 1968-70; BA summa cum laude, U. Minn., 1973; JD Order of St. Ives, U. Denver, 1977. Bar: Minn. 1978, U.S. Dist. Ct. Minn. 1978. Atty. Dorsey & Whitney, Mpls., 1982—. Mem. ABA, Minn. State Bar Assn. (chmn. adminstrv. law sect. 1989-90, exec. coun. environ. and natural resources sect. 1992-94), Hennepin County Bar Assn., Legal Aid Soc. Minn. (bd. dirs. 1988-93), Minn. Women Lawyers Assn. (bd. dirs. 1979-81), Mpls. Athletic Club. Office: Dorsey & Whitney 220 S 6th St Minneapolis MN 55402

CONATY, LUANN WILDER, volunteer, author; b. Borger, Tex., Jan. 20, 1934; d. Billy O. and C. Hazel (Nave) Wilder; m. Lyman T. Black, May 29, 1953 (div. May 1977); children: Andrew L. Black, Kevin J. Black, Linda Black Tritch; m. Frank X Conaty, Sept. 29, 1978; stepchildren: Dorothy A. Conaty, Frank X Conaty Jr., Marian M. Conaty. Student, Tulsa U., 1951-53, Butler U., Indpls., 1979-80. Exec. sec. Carter Oil Co., Tulsa, 1953-56; exec. recruiter Brown Efficiency Employment Agy., Indpls., 1977-79; benefits adminstr. Boehringer Mannheim, Indpls., 1979-81; author Northboro, Mass. Co-author: Each In Our Own Voice, 1994. Chair Republican Town Com., Northboro; mem. Mass. Gov.'s Commn. on Gay and Lesbian Youth, 1993-94; buddy vol. AIDS Project, Worcester, Mass., 1987-94, buddy coord., 1991-94; mem. steering com. Aid Support Svcs. com. Shrewsbury (Mass.) Congl. Ch., 1992-94; counselor Crisis Ctr. for Rape Victims and Battered Women, Nashua, N.H., 1983-86; discussion leader Bible Study Fellowship, Indpls., 1969-76; elder Windham (N.H.) Prsbyn. Ch., 1983-86.

CONAWAY, JANE ELLEN, elementary education educator; b. Fostoria, Ohio, July 9, 1941; d. Robert and Virginia Conaway; B.A. in Elem. Edn., Mary Manse Coll., Toledo, 1966; M.Ed. in Elem. Edn., U. Ariz., 1969; postgrad. in reading, U. Toledo, 1975-77; postgrad. U. Wis., 1987—. Tchr. Sandusky pub. schs., Ohio, 1966-67, Bellevue City Schs., Ohio, 1969-70; coord. 1st grade small group instrn. program St. Mary's Grade Sch., Sandusky, 1970-71; tchr. Chpt. I remedial reading Eastwood Local schs., Pemberville, Ohio, 1971-87, also dist. dir. Right to Read program; reading specialist Middleton-Cross Plains (Wis.) Area Sch. Dist., 1987—. Mem. NEA, Wis. Edn. Assn., Middleton Edn. Assn., Madison Area Reading Coun., Delta Kappa Gamma. Cert. as reading specialist in diagnostic and remedial reading, Wis. Home: 1302 Wexford Dr Waunakee WI 53597-1842 Office: Middleton Cross Plains Sch Dist 6701 Woodgate Rd Middleton WI 53562-3818

CONDE, MARILYN T., nursing administrator; b. L.A., Dec. 4, 1947; d. Paul C. and Edith G. (Sherman) McHugh; 1 child, Joshua Paul. LVN, El Camino Coll., Torrance, Calif., 1970; BSBA, U. O.P., 1994. Cert. gastrointestinal technician, cen. svc. technician. Gastrointestinal lab. technician/infection control Costa Mesa Meml. Hosp.; supr. cen. svc., emergency room staff, gastrointestinal lab. Chino (Calif.) Community Hosp.; mgr. svc. pers. St. Jude Hosp. and Rehab. Ctr., Fullerton, Calif., St. Francis Med. Ctr., Lynwood, Calif. Mem. Am. Soc. Healthcare Cen. Svc. Pers., Calif. Cen. Svc. Assn., San Diego County Assn. Med. Cen. Svc. Material Mgmt.

CONDIC, KRISTINE SALOMON, librarian, educator; b. Battle Creek, Mich., Dec. 18, 1955; d. John and Helen Salomon; m. Eric Condic, Oct. 6, 1990; 1 child, Amanda Condic. BA, Western Mich. U., 1979, MSL, 1980. Reference libr. Univ. Nebr., Omaha, 1981-84; coord. computer search svcs. Kresge Libr. Oakland U., Rochester, Mich., 1984-93; reference libr. Oakland U., Rochester, 1993—. Contbr. articles to libr. sci. jours. Mem. ALA. Office: Oakland U Kresge Libr Rochester MI 48309-4401

CONDRAN, CYNTHIA MARIE, gospel musician; b. Avon Park, Fla., Apr. 29, 1953; d. Kenneth Dale and Ruth Mae (Garber) Grubb; m. Lee Light Condran, July 3, 1971. Student, Lebanon Valley Coll., 1970-72. Piano tchr. Sebring, Fla., 1968-70, Annville, Pa., 1971—; gospel musician, writer, arranger Condran Music Co., Annville, Pa., 1972—, also recording engr.; writer comml. jingles. Sang by spl. invitation at Elipse of The White House, 1982; composer The Only Thing Holding You Back, 1977, Just A Few More Rivers, 1975, The Patchwork Quilt, 1978, Freedom, 1976, The Little Things, 1980, We're America, Heavens Fiesta, He's the Lord of Everyday, 1989, I've Never Known Such Love, 1990, I Just Want To Talk To You, 1990, Sweep Our Sins, 1990, Eternal Friends, 1991, The Precious Jewels At Christmas Time, 1992, Lost On My Way Back Home, 1993, I Believe in the Power of Love, 1993, To Speak Your Name, 1994, Forever, 1994, We Praise You Lord, 1994. Mem. Gospel Music Assn., Broadcast Music Inc., Christian Bus. and Prof. Women (music chmn.). Republican. Home: RR 3 Box 602 Annville PA 17003-9590

CONDRILL, JO ELLARESA, logistics executive, speaker; b. Hull, Tex., Oct. 25, 1935; d. Freddie (dec.) and Ida (Donatto) Founteno; m. Edwin Leon Ellis, Jan. 9, 1955 (div. 1979); children: Michael Edwin, James Alcia, Resa Ann, Thomas Matthew; m. Donald Richard Condrill, Sept. 21, 1980 (div. 1985). BS in Bus. Adminstrn., Our Lady of the Lake U., 1982; grad. Logistics Exec. Devel. Course, Army Logistics Mgmt. Ctr., 1985; MS in Pub. Adminstrn., Cen. Mich. U., 1987; grad. Program Mgmt. Course, Def. Systems Mgmt. Coll., 1989; grad., U.S. Army War Coll., 1993. Cert. seminar coord. Sec. USAF, Wiesbaden, Fed. Republic Germany, 1968-73; sec. mil. tng. ctr. USAF, San Antonio, 1973-77; editorial asst. Airman Mag., San Antonio, 1978; mgmt. analyst San Antonio Air Logistics Ctr., San Antonio, 1979-82; inventory mgr. ground fuels Detachment 29, Alexandria, Va., 1982-83; logistics plans officer Mil. Dist. Washington, 1983-85, chief logistics plans ops. and mgmt., 1985-88, hdqrs. dept. of the army staff Office of the Dep. Chief of Staff for Logistics, 1988—; chief integration br. Office of the Dep. Chief of Staff for Logistics, 1990—; owner Seminars by Jo, Alexandria, Va., 1984-86; field instr. Golden State U., L.A., 1985-86; instr. Fairfax County Adult Edn., Springfield, Va., 1984; vol. aide ARC Wilford Hall Hosp., San Antonio, 1978; constn. drafter KC Women's Aux., San Antonio, 1977; den mother Boy Scouts Am., San Antonio, 1967; docent Nat. Mus. Am. History, 1988. Civilian v.p. student coun. Army War Coll., Carlisle, Pa. Recipient Achievement medal for civilian svc. Dept. Army, 1984; Best Speaker award Def. Logistics Agy. Mem. Federally Employed Women (treas. Pentagon I chpt. 1987-88), Toastmasters (area gov. 1984-85, adminstrv. lt. gov. 1989-90, dist. 27 ednl. gov. 1990-91, dist. 27 gov. 1991-92, top ranking dist. gov. in internat. orgn. 1991-92, Internat. Pres. Disting. Dist. award 1991-92, internat. dir. 1994-96). Roman Catholic. Home: 6138 Talavera Ct Alexandria VA 22310-1887

CONDRON, BARBARA O'GUINN, metaphysics school administrator, publisher; b. New Orleans, May 1, 1953; d. Bill Gene O'Guinn and Marie Gladys (Newbill) Jackson; m. Daniel Ralph Condron, Feb. 29, 1992; 1 child, Hezekiah Daniel. BJ, U. Mo., 1973; MA, Coll. Metaphysics, Springfield, Mo., 1977, DD, D Metaphysics, 1979. Field rep. Sch. Metaphysics, New Orleans, 1978-80; dir. Interfaith Ch. Metaphysics, 1884-89; pres. Nat. Hdqs. Sch. Metaphysics, Windyville, Mo., 1980-84, chmn. bd., mem. faculty, 1989—; CEO SOM Pub., Windyville, 1989—; guest lectr., instr. Kans. Dept. Social Svcs. Conf., Topeka, 1986, U. Mo., Columbia and St. Louis, 1986, Mo. Tchrs. Conf., St. Louis, 1991, U. Okla., Norman, 1988-89, Parliament of World's Religions, Chgo., 1993; creator Sch. of Metaphysics Assocs., 1992; initiator, advisor Nat. Dream Hotline, 1988—. Author: What Will I Do Tomorrow? Probing Depression, 1977, Search for a Satisfying Relationship, 1980, Strangers in My Dreams, 1987, Kundalini Rising, 1992, Dreamers Dictionary, 1994, Spiritual Renaissance, 1995; editor-in-chief Thresholds Jour., 1990—; editor Wholistic Health and Healing Guide, 1992—. Office: Sch Metaphysics Nat Hdqs Windyville MO 65783

CONE, FRANCES MCFADDEN, data processing consultant; b. Columbia, S.C., Oct. 20, 1938; d. Joseph Means and Francis (Graham) McFadden: m. Charles Cone Jr., May 1962 (div. Sept. 1964); 1 child, Deborah Ann Cone Craytor. BS, U. S.C., 1960, MEd, 1973, M Math., 1977. Systems svc. rep. IBM, 1960-62; programmer/analyst Ga. Power Co., Atlanta, 1964-68, S.C. Fin. and Data Processing, Columbia, 1968-69; instr., head dept. Midlands Tech. Coll., Columbia, 1969-75; tng. coord. S.C. Nat. Bank, Columbia, 1975-79; systems analyst S.C. Dept. Health and Environ. Control, Columbia, 1979-80; project analyst So. Co. Svcs., Atlanta, 1980-89; cons. George Martin Assocs., Atlanta, 1989-93; sr. programmer, analyst Emory U., Decatur, Ga., 1993—; adj. prof. Golden Gate U., Sumter, S.C., 1976-80. Mem. Nat. Mgmt. Assn. (sec., treas., awards comn. 1981-89). Republican. Episcopalian. Office: Emory U Computing Ctr Decatur GA 30322

CONE, SUSAN LADELL, chemical company executive; b. Nashville, Tenn., May 1, 1967; d. Thomas Fite and Charlotte Ladell (Huskey) C. BA in English Lit., U. Tampa, 1990; postgrad studies, Vanderbilt U., 1992—. Office staff Cone Solvents, Inc., Nashville, 1990, sales rep., 1990-91; gen. mgr., v.p. Tennessee Adhesives Co., Mt. Juliet, Tenn., 1991-92; exec. v.p. Cone Solvents, Cone Oil Co., B & C Aviation, Nashville, 1992—, Tenn. Adhesives, Inc., Mt. Juliet, 1992—; new generation com., bd. dirs. Tenn. Oil Marketers Assn., Nashville, 1993-95; mem., chair membership com. Region IV Nat. Assn. Chem. Distributors, Washington, 1993-95. Mem. fin. com. Phil Bredesen for Gov., Tenn., 1994, Jim Cooper for Senate, Tenn.; host for Elephant Stomp, Bill Frist for Congress, Tenn., 1994; bd. alumni Battle Ground Acad. 1992-95. bd. visitors, 1993-97. Mem. Tenn. Leadership, Jr. League of Nashville (membership coun. 1993-94), Nashville Rotary Club (life). Home: 107 Chatsworth Dr Nashville TN 37215-2432 Office: Cone Solvents Inc 240 Great Circle Rd Ste 320 Nashville TN 37228-1707

CONE, VIRGIE HORNE HYMAN, former educator, civic worker; b. Brooksville, Fla.; d. George G. and Virgie (Horne) Hyman; m. Edward Elbert Cone, Dec. 20, 1930 (dec. Feb. 1962); children: Molly Gentile (dec. Jan. 1989), Edward Elbert. BS, Fla. State Coll. Women; MEd, U. Fla., 1956. Tchr., Meml. Jr. High Sch., Hillsborough County, 1929-31; tchr. Duval County Robert E. Lee Sr. High Sch., Jacksonville, Fla., 1943-55, dean, 1955-70; prin. Lee High Sch. (1st woman secondary sch. prin. in county), 1971-74; owner Cone's Antiques. Chmn., ARC night vols. St. Vincent's Hosp., 1969-71; mem. task force Mayor's Community Planning Coun., 1969; pres. Hamilton County unit Am. Cancer Soc., 1974-76; v.p. Hamilton County Meml. Hosp. Aux., 1975-76; mem. adv. coun. Health and Rehab. Svcs., Dist. 3, Fla.; dir. Area Agy. on Aging, 1977-82, bd. dirs., 1982—; del. White House Conf. on Aging, 1981; mem. adv. coun. Social Security; mem. state legis. com. Am. Assn. Retired Persons, 1983-87, chmn., 1986-87; mem. State Longterm Care Ombudsman Coun., 1983-87, chmn. 1985-87 mem. adv. coun. State Civil Rights Commn.; pres. North Fla. Mental Health Bd., 1978-80; mem. Hamilton County Planning Coun., Gov.'s Commn. on Status Women, 1978-80; mem. exec. bd. North Central Fla. Health Planning Coun., 1979-80; bd. dirs. Mid. Fla. Area Agy. on Aging,

State Comprehensive Health Assn., State Nursing Home Adv. Com.; mem. pub. issues com. Am. Cancer Soc.; mem. Banking Sunset Task Force, Fla., 1990-91; mem. aging commn. Fla. Med. Assn., 1988-93; mem. state com. to rewrite rating scale for nursing homes. Health ctr. named in her honor, Jasper, Fla., 1993. Mem. Fla. Coun. Tchrs. Math. (curriculum chmn. 1952, sec. 1949), AAUW (Jacksonville v.p. 1953), Duval Tchrs. Assn. (chmn. profl. rights and responsibilities com. 1965-66), Jacksonville Panhellenic Assn. (pres. 1959-60, mem. scholarship com. 1963-68), Duval Personnel and Guidance Assn. (organizing chmn. 1966-69), Nat. Assn. Secondary Prins., Fla. Assn. Secondary Prins., Hamilton Ret. Tchrs., Fla. Assn. Area Agy. Dirs. (pres.), Fla. Ret. Educators Assn. (state legis. chair 1990-92), Am. Assn. Ret. Persons (capitol city task force, state legis. com.), Pilot Club of Jacksonville, Suwanee Valley Country Club (dir. 1978-80), Delta Kappa Gamma (chpt. pres. 1959-61), Sigma Kappa (nat. scholarship chmn. 1963-77). Home: 3D NW St Jasper FL 32052

CONERLY-PERKS, ERLENE BRINSON, retired chemist; b. Jackson, Miss., Nov. 16, 1938; d. Alvin Bryan and Erlene (Brinson) Conerly; m. Paul Allen Perks, May 4, 1991. BS, Millsaps Coll., 1959; MS in Tech. Mgmt., Am. U., 1978. Chemist NIH, Bethesda, Md., 1962-78; research biologist Dynamac, Rockville, Md., 1979-80; chemist EPA, Washington, 1980-94; ret., 1994. Democrat. Episcopalian.

CONEY, CAROLE ANNE, accountant; b. Berkeley, Calif., Aug. 11, 1944; d. Martin James and Ida Constance (Ditora) Skuce; m. David Michael Coney, June 20, 1964; children: Kristine Marie, Kenneth Michael. BS cum laude, Calif. State Poly. U., 1985, MBA, 1988. Tax cons., instr. H&R Block, Portland, Oreg., 1969-71; acct., asst. sec.-treas. Surety Ins. Co., La Habra, Calif., 1973-76; bookkeeper Homemakers Furniture, Downers Grove, Ill., 1976-79; office mgr., acct. Helen's Pl. Printing, Upland, 1979-80; bookkeeper Vanguard Cos., Upland, 1980-82; dir. acctg. Coll. Osteopathic Medicine of Pacific, Pomona, Calif., 1982-89; acctg. mgr. City of Ontario, Calif., 1989—. Pres. Brea/La Habra Newcomers, 1975; treas. Alta Loma (Calif.) Com. to Elect Robert Neufeld, 1981. Mem. NAFE, Nat. Assn. Coll. and Univ. Bus. Officers, Calif. Soc. Mcpl. Fin. Officers, Govt. Fin. Officers Assn., Assn. Coll. and Univ. Auditors, Coun. Fiscal Officers, Soroptimists, Ontario Kiwanis, Delta Mu Delta, Alpha Iota. Democrat. Roman Catholic. Home: PO Box 4910 24581 San Moritz Dr Crestline CA 92325-4910 Office: City of Ontario 303 E B St Ontario CA 91764-4196

CONEY, ELAINE MARIE, English and foreign languages educator; b. Magnolia, Miss., Aug. 9, 1952; d. Allen Leroy and Katie Jane (McLeod) C. BA in Spanish, Millsaps Coll., 1974; MA in Spanish, U. Interam. Saltillo Coahuila, Mex., 1975, PhD, 1977; MEd, U. So. Miss., 1979. Tchr. fgn. langs. South Pike High Sch., Magnolia, Miss., 1977-91; tchr. English Amite County Schs., Liberty, Miss.; instr. Jackson (Miss.) State U.; GED instr. South Pike Schs., Magnolia, Miss.; instr. Spanish, French and English composition S.W. Miss. Community Coll., Summit, 1989—. Mem. NEA (del. conv. 1986, 88), Am. Assn. Tchrs. French, Am. Assn. Tchrs. Spanish and Portuguese, Miss. Assn. Educators (instructional profl. devel. com.), Nat. Coun. Tchrs. English, Miss. Fgn. Lang. Assn. (pres. 1991-93), SPAE (treas.). Home: PO Box 208 Magnolia MS 39652-0208

CONGER, CYNTHIA LYNNE, financial planner; b. Omaha, Dec. 8, 1948; d. Bob Bruce Ashton and Cleo (Artz) Ashton Taplin; m. Terry H. Conger, Dec. 21, 1969 (div. June 1989); children: Cynthia T., Scott A. BA in Acctg., U. Ark., Little Rock, 1980, MBA in Fin. and Econ., 1983. CPA, Ark.; cert. fin. planner. Staff acct. Leaseway Ark., Inc., Little Rock, 1981-83; rsch. asst. Indls. Rsch. and Econ. Com., Little Rock, 1983; agt. Conn. Mutual Life, Little Rock, 1983-84; v.p., fin. planner Ark. Fin. Group, Inc., Little Rock, 1984—; pres. Cynthia L. Conger, CPA, PA, Little Rock, 1989—. Mem. Civitan, Little Rock, 1985-89. Mem. Internat. Assn. Fin. Planning (Ark. chpt., v.p. 1986-87, pres. 1987-89, bd. dirs. 1994—, Delphi rsch. task force 1991), Registry Fin. Planning Practitioners. Methodist. Office: Ark Fin Group Inc Ste 375 225 E Markham Little Rock AR 72201-1643

CONGER, LUCINDA, librarian; b. Ft. Bragg, N.C., June 11, 1941; d. Meredith Moore and Ann Oliver (Mumford) Dickinson; m. Bruce C. Conger, June 25, 1966. BA, Radcliffe Coll., 1963; MLS, Rutgers U., 1964; student, Wesley Sem., Washington, 1990. Reference libr. U. Calif., Davis, 1964-65; cataloger Libr. of Congress, Washington, 1965, reference libr., 1966; compact storage libr. Princeton (N.J.) U., 1966-70; dir. reclassification Albion (Mich.) Coll., 1970-71, serials libr., 1971-73; reference libr. Yale U., New Haven, 1973-75, U.S. Dept. State, Washington, 1976—; chief Reader Svcs. Br., 1994—. Author: Online Command Chart, 1977, 91; columnist Database Mag., 1980-90; contbr. articles to profl. jours. Vol., Washington Cathedral, 1976—. Recipient Govt. Computer News award, 1992. Mem. Harvard Club of Washington at the Nat. Press Club, D.C. Online Users Group (chair 1981-83). Democrat. Episcopalian. Home: 4906 Jamestown Rd Bethesda MD 20816-2709 Office: State Dept Libr 2201 C St NW Washington DC 20520-2442

CONGETT, SYLVIA MONICA, psychologist; b. Queens, N.Y., Nov. 5, 1965; d. Norberto Raul and Lidia Rosa (Falzone) C.; m. Richard Norman Shadick, June 12, 1993. BS magna cum laude, Tufts U., 1987; MA, Pa. State U., 1989, PhD, 1992; postgrad., NYU. Lic. psychologist, N.Y. Staff therapist Psychol. Clinic, University Park, Pa., 1989-91; neuropsychology cons. Nittany Valley Rehab. Hosp., Pleasant Gap, Pa., 1990-91; psychology intern Bellevue Hosp. Ctr., N.Y.C., 1991-92; postdoctoral fellow in neuropsychology Hosp. for Joint Diseases-NYU Med. Ctr., 1992-94; staff psychologist Bellevue Hosp., 1992—, Rusk Inst., N.Y.C., 1994—. Author: (with others) Minority Mental Health Perspectives, 1990, Neurology Clinics, 1994; contbr. articles to profl. jours. Grantee NIMH, 1987-90. Mem. APA (divsn. 39, 40, 45, 49), N.Y. Neuropsychology Group, Nat. Acad. Neuropsychology. Office: Rusk Inst Rehab Medicine 400 E 34th St Rm 811-C New York NY 10016

CONGLETON, LAURA HELEN, freelance writer, film editor; b. Stamford, Conn., Jan. 14, 1962; d. Edward Blackburn and Lois Helen (Foster) C. BA, Mt. Holyoke Coll., S. Hadley, Mass., 1984; cert. in film prodn., NYU, 1992. Mgr. svc. stds. Chase Manhattan Bank, N.Y.C., 1984-87; mng. editor Sci. DataLink, N.Y.C., 1987-89; multimedia cons. N.Y.C., 1989-93. Film editor The Original Cast Album, 1992; 2d. asst. editor The West Film Project, 1993—. vol. The Pearl Theatre Co., N.Y.C., 1988—, InTouch Networks, N.Y.C., 1990-92; audio describer for visually-impaired theatre goers, 1992—. mem. N.Y. Acad. TV Arts and Scis., IATSE (Local 771).

CONIGILARO, PHYLLIS ANN, retired educator; b. Ilion, N.Y., Nov. 27, 1932; d. Gus Carl and Jennie Margaret (Marine) Denapole; m. Paul Anthony Conigilaro, July 16, 1983. BS cum laude, SUNY, Cortland, 1955; MA in Edn., Psychology, Cornell U., 1961. Cert. tchr., N.Y. Elem. classroom tchr. Mohawk (N.Y.) Central Sch., 1955-88. Contbr. articles to profl. jours. Bd. dirs. United Fund of Ilion, Herkimer, Mohawk and Frankfort, 1984-86, pres., 1986; pres. bd. edn. St. Mary's Parochial Sch., 1978; mem. Herkimer County Hist. Soc., 1988—, bd. dirs., 1994—. Mem. N.Y. State United Tchrs., Mohawk Tchrs. Assn. (past pres.), AAUW (pres. Herkimer chpt. 1981-82), N.Y. State Ret. Tchrs. Assn. (past legis. chmn. Herkimer County chpt.), Rep. Women's Club, Kappa Delta Pi. Republican. Roman Catholic. Home: RR 1 Box 285 Frankfort NY 13340-9557

CONKLIN, ANNA IMMACULATA ZOTTI, mathematics and language arts educator; b. N.Y.C., Aug. 9, 1951; d. Cosimo Phillip and Josephine Ann (D'Andria) Zotti; m. Joseph Dennis Conklin. BA in Early Childhood Edn, Jersey City State U., 1973; MA in ESL, Kean Coll., Union, N.J., 1984; postgrad., Rutgers U., 1984—. Tchr. sci. and math. St. Michael's, Jersey City, 1973-74; tchr. math. and lang. arts Union City (N.J.) Bd. Edn., 1974—; box office mgr., treas. Pk. Players Theater Orgn., Union City, 1984—; environ. sci. and environ. edn. educator Rutgers U., 1984—, Montclair State U., 1984—; active Passion Play, Union City, 1974—. Vol. ARC, Am. Cancer Soc.; environmentalist work on oilspill, Veldez, Alaska; participant Bermuda Biol. Rsch. Sta.; active with county and state sci. fairs N.J.; N.J. Agrl. Soc. Tchr. Workshop Participant. Mem. N.J. Edn. Assn., World Wildlife Fedn., Am. Cetacean Assn., Internat. Wildlife Coalition, Marine Sci. Coalition, Audubon Soc., Greenpeace, EArthwatch, Liberty Sci. Ctr. of N.J., Phi Delta Kappa. Democrat. Roman Catholic. Home: 24 Green Valley Ct Secaucus NJ 07094 Office: Union City Bd Edn 3912 Bergen Tpke Union City NJ 07087-2599

CONKLIN, MARA LORAINE, public relations executive; b. Vallejo, Calif., July 28, 1962; d. Kenneth J. and Laura T. (Siegrist) Cichosz; m. Rex D. Conklin, Sept. 6, 1986; children: Elisabeth, Emily. BA, Marquette U., 1984. Nat. news editl. staff Nat. Safety Coun., Chgo., 1984-85; corp. comm. specialist Household Internat., Prospect Hgts., Ill., 1985-86; acct. supr. Posner McGrath Ltd., Lincolnshire, Ill., 1986-90, v.p., 1990-92, sr. v.p., 1992-94, exec. v.p., 1994—. Recipient Spectra award Internat. Assn. Bus. Communicators, 1992, 94, Silver Trumpet award Publicity Club Chgo., 1993. Mem. Marquette Club Chgo. (chair alumni com. 1986-94, pres. 1994—). Office: Posner McGrath Ltd 300 Tri-State Internat Lincolnshire IL 60069

CONKLIN, SUSAN JOAN, psychotherapist; b. Bklyn., Feb. 7, 1950; d. Joseph Thomas Hallek and Stella Joan (Kubis) Kuceluk; m. John Lariviere Conklin, July 25, 1981; children: Genevieve Therese, Michelle Therese. BA, CCNY, 1972; MSW, CUNY, 1975. Lic. ind. clin. social worker; cert. diplomat. Shop counselor Assn. for Help of Retarded Citizens, N.y.C., 1971-75; dir. social svcs., acting exec. dir. North Berkshire Assn. for Retarded Citizens, North Adams, Mass., 1975-77; project dir. Title XX tng. grant State of Mass., North Adams, 1978-79; pvt. practice psychotherapy Williamstown, Mass., 1979—; asst. prof. North Adams State Coll., 1977-85, Berkshire C.C., Pittsfield, Mass., 1985-86; therapeutic touch practitioner, 1978—. Pres. Williamstown PTO, 1989-91; bd. dirs., edn. com., spl. events coord. Hospice No. Berkshire, Inc., 1989—. Mem. NASW (bd. dirs. 1981-83, regional coun. mem. 1980-83, 93—), Nurse Healers-Profl. Assn., Inc. (editor-in-chief Coop. Connection newsletter 1983-88), LWV, Nurse Healer-Prof. Assoc., Inc. Coop. Democrat. Episcopalian. Home and Office: 85 Hawthorne Rd Williamstown MA 01267-2700

CONKLIN, WENDY ANN, communications consultant; b. Seattle, Feb. 19, 1957; d. Edwin Roscoe Jr. and Lucille Munsell (Freeman) C.; m. Jeffrey K. Robertson. AA in Edn., Union Coll., 1977; BA in Psychology, U. Conn., 1979. Adminstr. U. Miami Sch. Medicine, 1980-84; mgr. pub. rels. Community Savs., Riviera Beach, Fla., 1984-86; mgr. comms. Bristol-Myers Squibb, Princeton, N.J., 1986-91; comms. cons. Strategic Comms., Hopewell, N.J., 1991—. Mng. editor columns for internal newspaper, 1991 (Silver Quill award 1991, 2 Apex awards 1991); mng. editor: (internal mag.) Clear Images, 1990 (Iris award 1990); contbr. articles to profl. publs. Chairperson bd. dirs. Hand to Hand of N.J., 1989—. Mem. Internat. Assn. Bus. Communicators (mem. Iris award com. 1986—), Coun. Comm. Mgmt. Home and Office: Strategic Comms PO Box 183 Hopewell NJ 08525

CONLEY, KATHERINE LOGAN, religious studies educator; b. Rutherford, N.C., Sept. 3, 1911; d. Claude Joseph and Mary (Beam) Logan; m. Jesse William Conley, Dec. 26, 1942. BS in Edn., Asheville (N.C.) Coll., 1936; postgrad., Presbyn. Ch. Christian Edn., Richmond, Va., 1939-40. Dir Christian edn. Presbyn. Ch., Spartanburg, S.C., 1940-41, Knoxville, 1941—; chmn. bldg. com. Seventh-Day Adventist Ch., Rutherford, N.C., 1963; lay speaker United Meth. Ch., Rutherfordton, 1973-91. Mem. Genealogical Soc., DAR (regent 1976-78), Amnesty Internat., Am. Bible Soc. (silver). Democrat. Home: RR 2 Box 138 Rutherfordton NC 28139-9435

CONLEY, MARY THERESE, perioperative nurse; b. Sandusky, Ohio, Mar. 15, 1955; d. Elmer J. and Adelaide C. (Tremper) C. Diploma, Providence Hosp. Sch. Nursing, 1976; BSN cum laude (Ruth E. Kelly award), Bowling Green (Ohio) State U., 1986; MA in Pastoral Ministries summa cum laude, St. Mary's Coll. of Minn., Winona, 1990. RN, Ohio, CNOR. Nurse surgery dept. Providence Hosp., Sandusky, 1976—. Active in parish bereavement svcs. Mem. Assn. Operating Rm. Nurses (past bd. dirs. Sandusky chpt., scholarship), Golden Key Nat. Honor Soc., Phi Kappa Phi, Phi Eta Sigma, Sigma Theta Tau (Zeta Theta chpt.).

CONLEY, THERESA R., library director; b. New London, Conn., Oct. 3, 1956; d. Robert James and Cecelia Rose (Massad) C. Student, Clark U., 1974-76; BA, Conn. Coll., 1978; MLS, U. R.I., 1980. Libr. asst. Gales Ferry (Conn.) Pub. Libr., 1980-81; libr. dir. Lyme (Conn.) Pub. Libr., 1986—; grad. asst. Grad. Libr. Sch., U. R.I., Kingston, 1979-80; del. to Conn. Gov.'s Conf. on Libr. and Info. Svcs., 1990. Mem. ACLU, Conn. Libr. Assn., Southeastern Conn. Libr. Assn. (trustee 1989—, sec. 1991-92, pres. 1992-93), Amnesty Internat. Office: Lyme Pub Libr 482 Hamburg Rd Lyme CT 06371-3109

CONLIN, ROXANNE BARTON, lawyer; b. Huron, S.D., June 30, 1944; d. Marion William and Alyce Muraine (Madden) Barton; m. James Clyde Conlin, Mar. 21, 1964; children: Jacalyn Rae, James Barton, Deborah Ann, Douglas Benton. BA, Drake U., 1964, JD, 1966, MPA, 1979; LLD (hon.), U. Dubuque, 1975. Bar: Iowa 1966. Assoc. firm Davis, Huebner, Johnson & Burt, Des Moines, 1966-67; dep. indsl. commr. State of Iowa, 1967-68, asst. atty. gen., 1969-76; U.S. atty. So. Dist. Iowa, 1977-81; ptnr. Conlin, P.C., Des Moines, 1983—; adj. prof. law U. Iowa, 1977-79; guest lectr. numerous univs. Chmn. Iowa Women's Polit. Caucus, 1973-75, del. nat. steering com., 1973-77; cons. U.S. Commn. on Internat. Women's Year, 1976-77; gen. counsel NOW Legal Def. and Edn. Fund, 1985-88, pres., 1986-88. Contbr. articles to profl. publs. Nat. committeewoman Iowa Young Dems.; also pres. Polk County Young Dems., 1965-66; del. Iowa Presdl. Conv., 1972; Dem. candidate for gov. of Iowa, 1982; bd. dirs. Riverhills Day Care Ctr., YWCA; chmn. Drake U. Law Sch. Endowment Trust, 1985-86; bd. counselors Drake U., 1982-86; pres. Civil Justice Found., 1986-88, Roscoe Pound Found., 1994—. Recipient award Iowa ACLU, 1974, Iowa Citizen's Action Network, 1987, Alumnus ofYr. award Drake U. Law Sch., 1989, ann. award Young Women's Resource Ctr., 1989, Verne Lawyer award as Outstanding Mem. Iowa Trial Lawyers Assn., 1994; named one of Top Ten Litigators Nat. Law Jour., 1989, 100 Most Influential Attys., 1991; inductee Iowa Women's Hall of Fame, 1981; scholar Reader's Digest, 1963-64, Fischer Found., 1965-66. Mem. NOW (bd. dirs. 1986-88), ABA, ATLA (chmn. consumer and victims coalition com. 1985-87, chmn. edn. dept. 1987-88, parliamentarian 1988-89, sec. 1989-90, v.p. 1990-91, pres.-elect 1991-92, pres. 1992-93), Iowa Bar Assn., Assn. Trial Lawyers Iowa (bd. dirs.), Internat. Acad. Trial Lawyers, Iowa Acad. Trial Lawyers, Higher Edn. Commn. Iowa (co-chmn. 1988-90), Phi Beta Kappa, Alpha Lambda Delta, Chi Omega (Social Svc. award). Office: 300 Walnut St Ste 5 Des Moines IA 50309-2239

CONLON, KATHLYN ANN, sales manager; b. Newark, N.J., June 29; d. Charles Joseph Sr. and Kathlyn Claire (Stevens) C.; divorced; children: Brian J., Terence R. Student, Fairleigh Dickinson U., 1971-73, William Paterson Coll., 1979-81. Lic. broker. Prin. office mgr. County Clk./County of Passaic, Paterson, N.J., 1974-82; children's theatrical agent, 1985—; adminstrv. asst. to surrogate judge County of Passaic, 1982-85; adminstrv. asst., benefits coord. AT&T, Short Hills, N.J., 1992-93; regional sales mgr., broker Grinspec, Inc., New Providence, N.J., 1994—; small bus. owner Originals by Kathi, 1985—; appeared in TV shows, commls. and movies. Pres. Little Falls (N.J.) Dem. Orgn., 1978-81, mcpl. dem. chairwoman, 1980-83; county committeewoman, 1978-83; v.p. Little Falls Tenants Orgn., 1979; state spokeswoman for U.S. Sen. John Glenn's Presdl. campaign, 1980; chmn. United Way for County of Passaic, 1984; bd. dirs. Colonial Hill Condo Assn., 1987—; mem. Passaic County Marine Corp. League, 1980—, A.W. Roberts PTA, 1991—. N.J. State scholar, 1971; recipient Passaic County Elks scholarship, 1971, Little Falls VFW scholarship, 1971; named to Outstanding Young Women of Am., 1984, Miss Eagle Rescue Squad, Little Falls, 1970. Roman Catholic.

CONLON, KATHRYN ANN, county official; b. Mankato, Minn., July 30, 1958; d. Ralph Raymond and Joan Margaret (Meyer) Walter; m. James Alan Conlon, Oct. 1, 1977; children: Jessica Marie, Brian Michael. Student, Mankato Vocat. Sch., 1976-77. Teller Minn. Valley Fed. Credit Union, 1977; clk. Nicollet County Credit Bur., 1977-78; abstracter Lorna Holmquist, St. Peter, Minn., 1978-82; dep. recorder, abstracter Nicollet County, 1982-84, county recorder, abstracter, 1984—, sec. to dept. heads, 1985, chmn. dept. heads, 1986. Mem. Spina Bifida Assn. Minn., 1981—, Spina Bifida Assn. S.W. Minn., 1983—; bd. dirs. Children's Cen. Child Care, 1985-87, United Way, 1990-91. Mem. Minn. Assn. County Recorders (2nd v.p. 1994, pres. 1995), VFW Aux., Am. Legion Aux., St. Peter Lions. Avocations: handcrafting, camping, volleyball. Home: RR 3 Box 116 Saint Peter MN 56082-9542 Office: Nicollet County Recorder PO Box 493 Saint Peter MN 56082-0493

CONLON, SUZANNE B., federal judge; b. 1939. AB, Mundelein Coll., 1963; JD, Loyola U., Chgo., 1968; postgrad., U. London, 1971. Law clk. to judge U.S. Dist. Ct. (no. dist.) Ill., 1968-71; assoc. Pattishall, McAuliffe & Hostetter, 1972-73, Schiff Hardin & Waite, 1973-75; asst. U.S. atty. U.S. Dist. Ct. (no. dist.) Ill., 1976-77, 82-86, U.S. Dist. Ct. (cen. dist.) Calif., 1978-82; exec. dir. U.S. Sentencing Commn., 1986-88; spl. counsel to assoc. atty. gen., 1988; judge U.S. Dist. Ct. (no. dist.) Ill., 1988—; asst. prof. law De Paul U., Chgo., 1972-73, lectr., 1973-75; adj. prof. Northwestern U. Sch. Law, 1991—; vice chmn. U. Coll. Dublin Internat. Inst., 1993-94. Mem. ABA, Fed. Bar Assn., Chgo. Bar Assn., Nat. Assn. Women Judges, Am. Judicature Soc. Office: US Dist Ct No Dist Everett McKinley Dirksen Bldg 219 S Dearborn St Rm 2356 Chicago IL 60604*

CONN, BARBARA BRADY, photographer; b. Orange, N.J., May 17, 1941; d. H. Neill and Marion Louise (Jacobus) Brady; children: Sarah Landick Conn, Stephen Brady Conn. BA, U. Wis., 1965; MEd, William and Mary Coll., 1980; AD of Completion, Hallmark Inst. Photography, Turners Falls, Mass., 1988. Cert. middle sch. tchr. English, Mass. Wife, mother Fgn. Svc., U.S. Govt., 1966-85; tchr., tutor Frontier Regional Sch., South Deerfield, Mass., 1989—; owner Yes! Photography, South Deerfield, Mass., 1988—. Contbg. photographer to mag. covers and calendars, Berkshire Mag., 1990-94, greeting cards, Red Oak Pubs., 1990-94. Recipient Hon. mention Nat. Geog. Traveler Photo Contest, 1993. Mem. Profl. Photographers of Am., Brattlebora Camera Club. Home and Office: 8B Duncan Dr South Deerfield MA 01373-9743

CONNALLY, SANDRA JANE OPPY, art educator; b. Crawfordsville, Ind., Feb. 10, 1941; d. Thomas Jay and Helen Louise (Lane) Oppy; m. Thomas Maurice Connally, Nov. 9, 1962; children: Leslie Erin Connally Hosier, Tyler Maurice. BS, Ball State U., 1963, MA, 1981. Freelance writer Muncie, Ind., 1971-76, art/freelance, 1964-81; substitute tchr. Muncie (Ind.) Community Schs., 1980-81, art tchr., 1981—. Two women shows include Emens Auditorium, Ball State U., 1983; juried shows include Ball State U. Small Drawing and Sculpture, 1964, Alford House/Anderson (Ind.) Fine Arts Ctr., Winter Show, 1979, 80, 81, Summer Show, 1981, Historic 8th St. Exhbn., 1981, Patrons Watercolor Gala, Oklahoma City, 1983, Whitewater Valley Annual Drawing, Painting and Printmaking Competition, Richmond, Ind., 1983; represented in numerous pvt. collections; contbr. short stories to profl. publs. Recipient Monetary award Container Corp. Am., 1981, Spl. Achievement award Ind. Dept. Edn., 1992-93, 94, Nat. Gallery Videodisc Competition award, 1993; named Disting. UniverCitizen Ball State U., 1992; Ball State U. Mus. Art and Margaret Ball Meml. Fund grantee, 1992, Robert P. Bell grantee, 1993. Mem. Ind. State Tchr. Assn., Muncie Tchrs. Assn., Internat. Platform Assn., Nat. Art Edn. Assn., Art Edn. Assn. Ind. Republican. Methodist. Home: 2351 W Warwick Rd Muncie IN 47304-3346

CONNELL, JANICE T., lawyer, author, arbitrator, business executive. BS in Fgn. Service, Georgetown U., 1961; M in Polit. and Internat. Adminstrn., U. Pitts., 1976; JD, Duquesne U., 1979. Bar: U.S. Dist. Ct. (we. dist.) Pa. 1979, U.S. Ct. Appeals (3d cir.) 1979, U.S. Supreme Ct. 1983. Pres. Regency Advertising, Jacksonville, Fla. and Pitts., 1968-74, Connell Leasing of Fla., Jacksonville and Pitts., 1970-80; v.p., sec. Nat. Motor Leasing Inc., Pitts., 1980-86; ptnr. Connell & Connell, Pitts., 1980-1986; arbitrator N.Y. Stock Exchange, 1981—, Am. Arbitration Assn., 1985—, Nat. Assn. Securities Dealers, 1983—. Author: Queen of the Cosmos, 1990, Visions of the Children, 1992, The Triumps, 1993. Founder Pitts. Ctr. for Peace, Inc., 1988—, Marion Ctr. World Peace, 1990—, Ctr. for Peace Ams., 1991; bd. dirs. Assn. Jr. Leagues Am., Wheeling, W.Va., Pitts., 1964—, Salvation Army, Wheeling, 1967-68, United Way, Jacksonville, 1971, YMCA, Jacksonville, 1992, Legal Aid Soc., Pitts., 1985—; bd. dirs. women's adv. bd. Duquesne U., Pitts., 1980—; founding dir. Inst. for World Concern, 1981—. Mem. ABA (real property sect.), Pa. Bar Assn., Allegheny County Bar Assn., Epiphany Assn. Office: 2 Gateway Ctr Ste 620 Pittsburgh PA 15222-1450 also: 3 Bethesda Metro Ctr Ste 750 Bethesda MD 20814-6300 also: 112 SE 10th St Delray Beach FL 33483-3426

CONNELL, MARY ELLEN, diplomat; b. Laconia, N.H., Jan. 20, 1943; d. Howard Benjamin and Jessie Louise Smith Naylor; m. O. J. Connell III, Nov. 4, 1969 (div. Aug. 1988); 1 child, Piers Andrew. BA, Smith Coll., Northampton, Mass., 1964; MPhil, U. Kans., 1969; MS, Nat. War Coll., 1992. Info. ctr. dir. U.S. Fgn. Svc., Nairobi, Kenya, 1978-80; pub. affairs officer U.S. Fgn. Svc., Bujumbura, Burundi, 1980-82; officer African affairs USIA, Washington, 1982-85, exec. asst. to assoc. dir. for policy, 1985-86; counselor pub. affairs U.S. Fgn. Svc., Copenhagen, 1986-90; vis. scholar St. Deiniol's Wales, 1991; exec. sec. USIA, Washington, U.K., 1992—. Mem. Am. Fgn. Svc. Assn., Atlantic Coun., Army and Navy Club. Episcopalian. Office: USIA 301 4th St SW Washington DC 20547

CONNELL, SHIRLEY HUDGINS, public relations professional; b. Washington, Oct. 5, 1946; d. Orville Thomas and Mary (Beran) H.; m. David Day Connell, Dec. 13, 1980 (div. 1985). BA, U. R.I., 1968, MA, 1970. Clk., editor MGM Studios, Culver City, Calif., 1970-72; scriptor, talent Monarch Records, Studio City, 1972-73; communications specialist U. So. Calif., L.A., 1973-81; dir. pub. rels. Six Flags Movieland, Buena Park, Calif., 1981-82; dir. pub. rels. Donald J. Fager & Assocs., N.Y.C., 1982-93, dir. policy holder/pub. rels., 1993—; cons. Children's TV Workshop, N.Y.C., 1978; ind. beauty cons. Mary Kay Cosmetics, 1991—; instr. Princeton Rev., 1990-91. Contbr. articles to profl. jours.; contbg. editor Greater N.Y. Doctor's Shopper mag., 1987—. Pres. bd. trustees Oaks at North Brunswick Condominium Assn., 1987—; founding mem. Mcpl. Svcs. Com., North Brunswick; mgr. Animal Rescue Force, 1988—; chair environ. com. Twp. of North Brunswick, 1994—; water quality monitor Stony Brook Millstone Watershed Assn., 1994—; snuggler pediat. and neonatal units St. Peter's Hosp. Mem. NAFE, Marine Tech. Soc. (vice chmn. 1980-81), Mensa (pub. rels. adv. com. 1989—, pub. rels. coord. Ctrl. N.J. chpt. 1992—, bd. dirs. 1992—), Oceanic Soc. (bd. dirs. 1979-81).

CONNELLY, BETTY FEES, lay ministries consultant; b. L.A., Apr. 13, 1924; d. Ferdinand R. and Margaret (Lewis) Fees; m. Daniel Snyder Connelly, Apr. 20, 1946; children: Richard, Kathleen, Patrick. BA, Pomona Coll., Claremont, Calif., 1945; BS in Edn., U. Minn., 1947; postgrad., Claremont Grad. Sch., 1962-63. Pres. officer Women of Episcopal Ch. Triennial, Denver, 1977-80; lay min. cons. St. James Episcopal Ch., Newport Beach., Calif., 1981-83, dir. lay ministries and evang. svc. and outreach, 1988-93; mem. Coun. for Devel. Ministry, 1988-94; mem. exec. com. Anglican Fellowship of Prayer, dep. gen. conv. Episcopal Ch., 1982, 85, 88, 94; trustee Pension Group Episcopal Ch. With USN, 1944-46. Republican. Home: 3706 S Sea Breeze Santa Ana CA 92704-7141

CONNELLY, DENISE MARIE, marketing professional; b. Phila., Oct. 7, 1958; d. Joseph Calvin and Leonore Regina (Norton) C. BA in Biology, Bloomsburg U., 1980. Market mgr. IMS Am., Inc., Ambler, Pa., 1982-86; sr. analyst Wyeth Labs., Radner, Pa., 1986-88; sr. analyst, new products Zenecz Pharms., Wilmington, Del., 1988-89, new product planner, 1989-90, markets promotions mgr., 1990-93, promos mgr., 1993—. Mem. Healthcare Providers Coalition of Del., Dover, 1993. Mem. Pharm. Advt. Coun. Office: Zeneca Pharms Group 1800 Concord Pike Wilmington DE 19897

CONNELLY, DIANE MAUREEN, urology service coordinator; b. Springfield, Mass., Sept. 29, 1943; d. Paul A. and Catherine C. Connelly. Diploma, Framingham (Mass.) Union Hosp., 1964; BA, Am. Internat. Coll., 1967; MEd, Springfield Coll., 1971; MSN, U. San Diego, 1993. Emergency rm. nurse, utilization rev. nurse Wesson Meml. Hosp., Springfield, 1965-74; oper. rm. nurse Alvarado Community Hosp., San Diego, 1974-76; cardiac lab. nurse, oper. rm. nurse Beth Israel Hosp., Boston, 1976-83; from oper. rm. nurse to outpatient dept. nurse Children's Hosp., San Diego, 1989-93, oper. rm. nurse, 1993—. Mem. Assn. Oper. Rm. Nurses, Emergency Nurses Assn., Am. Heart Assn., Sigma Theta Tau. Home: 7974 Mission Center Ct # A San Diego CA 92108-1464

CONNELLY, ELIZABETH ANN, state legislator; b. N.Y.C.; d. John Walter and Alice Marie (Mallon) Keresey; m. Robert Vincent Connelly; children: Alice, Robert, Margaret, Therese. Grad. high sch., Bronx. Telephone sales Pan Am. World Airways, N.Y.C., 1946-54; mem. N.Y. State Assembly, Albany, 1973—, chair com. on mental health, retardation/devel. disabilities, 1977-92, chair com. on standing coms., 1993-95, speaker pro tem, 1995—; chair Legis. Women's Caucus, N.Y. State, 1993—. Recipient over 100 awards, honors 1972-92 including Staten Island Hosp. Vol. Yr.award, 1972-73, Cert. Appreciation Willowbrook Chpt. Benevolent Soc. Retarded Children, 1978, Staten Island Alzheimers Family Support Group award, 1983, Legislator of Yr. award N.Y.S. Coun. Alcoholism, 1983, Staten Island Lighthouse award svcs. to blind and handicapped, 1984, Woman of Yr. award Epilepsy Ctr., 1984, Disting. Citizenship award Wagner Coll., 1984, N.Y.S. Psychological Assn. award, 1986, Humanitarian of Yr. award Staten Island Ctr. Independent Living, 1987, Alliance for Mentally Ill of N.Y.S. award, 1988, Thomas G. GIlbert Meml. award N.Y.S. Head Injury Assn., 1992; honored by Staten Island Mental Health Soc., 1989, NAt. Barrier Awareness Found., 1990, Irish Am. Heritage Mus., 1991, Staten Island Head Injury Assn., 1991, Family Svc. League Suffolk County, 1992. Democrat. Office: NY State Assembly LOB 826 Albany NY 12248*

CONNELLY, KATHLEEN FITZGERALD, public relations executive; b. Springfield, Mass., Dec. 26, 1949. BA, Newton Coll.; MA in Polit. Sci., Rutgers U.; postgrad., U. Chgo. Legis. aide Mass. State Legis.; officer, corp. comm. and bond dept. Continental Bank & Trust Co. of Chgo., 1972-78; acct. exec. Hill & Knowlton, 1978, v.p., 1979-81, sr. v.p. group dir., 1981-86; mng. dir., sr. v.p. Hill & Knowlton, Inc., 1987-89, dep. gen. mgr., sr. v.p., 1990, exec. v.p., dir. worldwide bus. devel., bd. dir., 1990-92; pres. Dilenschneider Group, 1991—. Office: Dilenschneider Group 3 First Nat Plz 70 West Madison St Chicago IL 60603*

CONNELLY, PATRICIA ANN, mediator, lawyer, educator; b. Montevideo, Minn., June 30, 1946; d. Ellis Edwin and Mytrie Viola (Holtan) C.; m. Christoph O. Steinbruchel, Mar. 24, 1973; children: Justin Ellis, Erin Christine. BA cum laude, Macalester Coll., 1968; MA, U. Minn., 1970, JD, 1974. Bar: Minn. 1975, Ill. 1977, U.S. Dist. Ct. (no. dist.) Ill. 1977. Rsch. lawyer Am. Bar Found., Chgo., 1975-76; lawyer Montgomery Ward Life Ins., Chgo., 1976-78, pvt. practice, Chgo., 1978-81; faculty Cmty. Coll., Zurich, Switzerland, 1982-88; lawyer, mediator Saratoga Mediation, Saratoga Springs, N.Y., 1989-90; dir. Mediation Ctr., Clifton Park, N.Y., 1991—; adj. faculty Marist Coll., Poughkeepsie, N.Y., 1991—, Hudson Valley Com. Coll., Troy, N.Y., 1991—; arbitrator Matrimonial Disputes N.Y. State 3rd, 4th Judicial Dists. Contbr. articles to profl. jours. bd. dirs. Family Resource Coalition of N.Y., treas., 1993—. Mem. Acad. Family Mediators, Assn. of Family & Conciliation Courts. Office: Mediation Ctr Clifton Exec Park 1741 Rte 9 Clifton Park NY 12065-2420

CONNELLY, PATRICIA LORRAINE, travel executive; b. Phila., Mar. 29, 1948; d. Robert H. and Helen (Kinsley) Nickerson; m. Joseph J. Connelly, Jan. 10, 1986. BA, Western State U., 1987; postgrad., Holy Family Coll., 1988. Mgr. Trainseair Travel Inc., Phila.; assn. tax acct. Gen. Refractories Co., Phila.; travel mgr. Morgan, Lewis, Bockius, Phila.; adv. bd. Four Seasons Hotel. Mem. Nat. Passenger Traffic Assn., Delaware Valley Corp. Travel Mgrs. Assn. (asst. v.p.), Am. Soc. Travel Agts. (cert.), Meeting Planners Internat., Internat. Soc. Meeting Planners (cert. meeting planner).

CONNER, CANDICE CLARICE, student services professional, consulting psychotherapist; b. Houston, Sept. 25, 1955; d. Bill W. and Dovie (Jones) C. BS in Criminology & Corrections, Sam Houston State U., 1979; postgrad., U. Okla., 1983; MEd in Counseling & Student Svcs., U. North Tex., 1993. Student svcs. profl. DeSoto Ind. Sch. Dist., 1986-87, cons., 1987-89; student svcs. specialist Garland (Tex.) Ind. Sch. Dist., 1989—. Mem. Am. Counselors Assn., Tex. Counselors Assn., Chi Omega, Phi Delta Kappa. Republican. Home: PO Box 822365 Dallas TX 75382-2365 Office: North Garland HS 2109 W Buckingham Rd Garland TX 75042-5031

CONNER, JEANNE WILLIAMS, retired educator; b. Pitts., Aug. 10, 1930; d. John Scouten and Jean (Haggenjos) Williams; m. James Beynon Conner, Aug. 9, 1952; children: James Beynon Jr., David Hardwick, William Scouten. BS, Northwestern U., Evanston, 1952; postgrad., U. Calif., Santa Barbara, 1966-68. Rsch. asst. AMA, Chgo., 1952-54; tchr. The Harris Sch., Chgo., 1961-63, Laguna Blanca Sch., Santa Barbara, Calif., 1965-76; spl. edn. tchr. Santa Barbara Ctr. Ednl. Therapy, 1977-79; pvt. tutor Santa Barbara, 1979-80. writer Am. Jour. of Forensic Psychiatry, reviewer; writer Bur. of Med. Econ. Rsch. of AMA, 1952-54. Mem. AAUW, Phi Beta Kappa. Republican. Congregationalist. Home: 14409 W Futura Dr Sun City West AZ 85375-5931

CONNER, PATRICIA LORETTA, computer programmer, analyst; b. Akron, Ohio, Mar. 9, 1958; d. Ralph Herman and Mildred P. Stewart; m. Paul D. Conner, Oct. 13, 1990; 1 child, Jennifer. BBA, Kent State U., 1983; MBA, Case Western Res. U., 1986. CPA, Tex. Data processing instr. So. Ohio Coll., Akron, 1984-86; sr. sys. analyst Gen. Dynamics, Ft. Worth, 1986-89; sys. analyst City of Dallas, 1991; computer programmer Texas Instruments, Inc., Plano, Tex., 1991—. Mem. Nat. Assn. Accts. Office: Texas Instruments Inc M/S 8418 PO Box 869305 Plano TX 75086-9305

CONNERLY, DIANNA JEAN, business official; b. Urbana, Ill., June 7, 1947; d. Ellsworth Wayne and Imogene (Sundermeyer) Connerly. Student Ill. Comml. Coll., 1967. Bookkeeper, Jerry Earl Pontiac, 1968-72; officer mgr. Jack Nicklaus Pontiac, 1972-76; office mgr. Simon Motors Inc., Palm Springs, Calif., 1977-83; bus. mgr., 1983—. Vol. counselor How Found., 1992. Mem. Am. Bus. Women's Assn. (pub. rels. dir. Trendsetter chpt. 1983—). Office: 78611 US Highway 111 La Quinta CA 92253

CONNERY, CAROL JEAN, foundation director; b. Amarillo, Tex., Oct. 22, 1948; d. William Wayne and Joyce Jean (Forney) Connery. AA, Christian Coll., 1969; BJ, U. Tex., Austin, 1971. Asst. dir. admissions Columbia (Mo.) Coll., 1971-80; exec. dir. nat. office Teenworld Scholarship Program, Overland Park, Kan., 1980-82; account exec. Mktg. Comm., Inc., Lenexa, Kans., 1983-86; account supr. Krupp/Taylor USA, Dallas, 1986-90; mktg. cons., 1990-93; dir. devel. St. Anthony's Found., Amarillo, Tex., 1994—. Trustee Columbia Coll. Mem. Assn. Healthcare Philanthropy (mem. regional bd.), Nat. Soc. Fund Raising Execs., United Way, Ctr. City Bus. and Profl. Women, Zeta Tau Alpha, Phi Theta Kappa (past nat. v.p.). Methodist. Home: 3203 Janet Dr Amarillo TX 79109-3253

CONNOLLY, COLLEEN MARIE, software engineer; b. Boston, Mar. 1, 1961; d. James A. and Marie F. (Mula) C. BA, Stonehill Coll., 1982; BSEE, U. Notre Dame, 1983. Software engr. Imlac Corp., Needham, Mass., 1983-84; sr. software engr. Prime Computer, Bedford, Mass., 1984-89, Lotus Devel. Corp., Cambridge, Mass., 1989—. Home: 39 Russell St Arlington MA 02174-3017 Office: Lotus Devel Rogers St Cambridge MA 02142

CONNOLLY, R. SUE, banker, business owner; b. Evanston, Ill., Oct. 13, 1947; d. Robert Joel and Margaret J. (Castor) Berndtson; 1 child, J. Erik. BA in Econs., Wittenberg U., 1969; MBA in Fin., Loyola U., Chgo., 1977. Examiner FDIC, Chgo., 1969-73; with No. Trust Bank Corp., Chgo., 1976—; sr. v.p., credit policy officer Spl. Industry and Met. Groups, Chgo., 1994—; pres., owner R.S.C. Group indsl. caterers, Elk Grove, Ill., 1984—; chair internat. com. Robert Morris Assocs., Chgo., 1985-86, mem. loan rev. round table, 1987—, 2d v.p., 1989-90. Career adv. coun. Elk Grove H.S., 1989—; contbg. mem. Nat. Dem. Com.; active Chgo. House. Mem. Nat. Assn. Bank Women. Episcopalian. Home: 29 Grange Pl Elk Grove Village IL 60007 Office: No Trust Bank 50 S La Salle St Chicago IL 60603-1003

CONNOLLY, RUTH CAROL, critical care nurse; b. Pitts., Oct. 2, 1944; d. Chester John and Mary Elizabeth (Sansbury) Williams; separated; children: Patrick L., Sean M. Diploma in nursing, Allegheny Gen. Hosp., Pitts., 1965; cert. nurse practitioner, Allegheny Gen. Hosp., 1983, La Roche Coll., Pitts., 1983. RN, Pa. Staff nurse critical care Divine Providence Hosp., Pitts.; asst. clin. supr. Allegheny Gen. Hosp., clin. supr. neuroscis. unit; nurse practitioner Triangle Urol. Group, Pitts. Contbr. articles to nursing jours. Mem. AACCN, Am. Assn. Urology Allied Nurses, Am. Urol. Assn. Allied (founding mem. and pres.-elect Pitts. chpt.), Am. Assn. Office Nurses. Home: 5549 Pocusset St Pittsburgh PA 15217

CONNOLLY-O'NEILL, BARRIE JANE, interior designer; b. San Francisco, Dec. 22, 1943; d. Harry Jr. and Jane Isabelle (Barr) Wallach; m. Peter Smith O'Neill, Nov. 27, 1983. Cert. of design, N.Y. Sch. Interior Design, 1975; BAF in Environ. Design, Calif. Coll. Arts and Crafts, 1978. Profl. model Brebner Agy., San Francisco, 1963-72; TV personality KGO TV, San Francisco, 1969-72; interior designer Barrie Connolly & Assocs., Boise, Idaho, 1978—; bd. dirs. Zoo Boise. Bd. dirs. Zoo Boise. Recipient Best Interior Design award Mktg. and Merchandising Excellence, 1981, 84, 91, Best Interior Design award Sales and Mktg. Coun., 1985, 86, Best Residential Design award Boise Design Revue Com., 1983, Grand award Best in Am. Living, Nat. Assn. Home Builders, 1986, 89, 2 Gold Nuggett Merit awards, 1990, Street of Dreams, People's Choice award, 1991, Award for Best Interior Merchandising MAME, Portland, 1991, Nat. Merit award, 1992. Mem. Nat. Assn. Home Builders (Nat. Silver award for best interior design 1991), Am. Soc. Interior Designers (affiliate), Inst. Residential Mktg. (Silver awrd 1991).

CONNOR, CRISTINA PEREZ, nurse manager; b. Manila, Philippines, Nov. 10, 1960; came to U.S., 1983; d. Jose DeLeon and Zenaida (Baltazar) Perez; m. John Thomas Connor, Mar. 17, 1989; 1 child, John Christopher. BSN, Far. Eastern U., 1981. RN N.J., N.Y. Nurse Far Eastern U. Hosp., Manila, 1981-83; staff nurse Bellevue Hosp. Ctr., N.Y.C., 1983-84; nurse Elizabeth (N.J.) Gen. Med. Ctr., 1984, practical nurse, 1984-85, nurse, 1985-91, nurse mgr., 1991—. Mem. Am. Soc. Post-Anesthesia Nurses, N.J. Soc. Post-Anesthesia Nurses, Pacu Leaders Actively Networking. Roman Catholic. Home: 111 Exeter Ct Piscataway NJ 08854 Office: Elizabeth Gen Med Ctr 925 E Jersey St Elizabeth NJ 07201

CONNOR, FRANCES PARTRIDGE, education educator; b. Bklyn., May 4, 1919; d. Horace K. and Sybil V. (Rafters) P.; m. Leo E. Connor, June 7, 1952. BA, St. Joseph's Coll., 1940; MA, Columbia U., 1948, EdD, 1953; LLD (hon.), Coll. New Rochelle, 1976. Cert. history, social studies tchr., spl. edn. tchr., N.Y. Tchr. history/econs. Haverstraw (N.Y.) Schs., 1940-42; tchr. N.Y. State Rehab. Hosp., West Haverstraw, 1942-49; lectr. Hunter Coll., CCNY, N.Y.C., 1946-54; tchr. spl. edn Ramapo Ctrl. Schs., Suffern, N.Y., 1949-53; coord. spl. edn. U. Ga., Athens, summers 1952-53; rsch. assoc. U.S. Office of Edn., Washington, 1954-58; survey assoc. Tchrs. Coll., Columbia U., N.Y.C., 1953-54, prof., dir. Rsch. and Demonstration Ctr./ Inst. for LD, 1955-87, dept. chair, 1962-85, Richard March Hoe prof. emeritus, 1987—; mem. profl. adv. bd. Willowbrook Consent Decree, N.Y. State Dept. of Mental Retardation/Devel. Disabilities, Albany, 1977—; mem. bd. dirs. Family Resource Assocs., Shrewsbury, N.J. Author: Education of Homebound and Hospitalized Children, 1964, Experimental Curriculum for Young Mentally Retard Children, 1964; editor: Critical Issues for Low Incidence Populations, 1987. Mem. bd. trustees Mt. Saint Mary Coll., Newburgh, N.Y., 1970—, Human Resources Schs., Albertson, N.Y., 1984—; mem. Pres.'s Com. on Employment of Handicapped, Washington, 1972-89; del., mem. steering com. White House Conf. on the Handicapped, Washington, 1975-78; mem. Coalition of Disabled Women and Their Advocates, Ocean County, N.J., 1990—. Recipient Behavioral Sci. award Nat. Hemophilia Found., 1968, Pioneer in Spl. Edn. award Hofstra U., 1986. Fellow Am. Assn. on Mental Retardation; mem. Coun. for Exceptional Children (pres. 1964-65, Wallin award 1982, Outstanding Contbr. award 1992), Com. Rehab. Internat. Roman Catholic. Home: 200 4th Ave Spring Lake NJ 07762-1014

CONNOR, MARY RODDIS, foundation administrator; b. Marshfield, Wis., May 14, 1909; d. Hamilton and Catherine S. (Prindle) Roddis; m. Gordon R. Connor, July 20, 1929 (dec. 1986); children: Mary I. Pierce, Gordon P., Catherine Dellin, David (dec.), Sara W. Connor. Student, Wellesley Coll., 1927-28; student, U. Wis., 1929. Corp. sec. Connor Lumber and Land Co., Connor Forest Industries, Wausau, Wis., 1954-78; co-founder, exec. dir. Camp Five Mus. Found., Inc., Laona, 1968—; bd. dirs., v.p. Hamilton Roddis Found.; pres. Connor Found., Forest History Assn. Wis., 1975-87; v.p. Gordon R. Connor Charitable Found.; mem. Nat. Women's Adv. Coun., Am. Forest Products Inst., 1960-78; active Mary Roddis Connor U. Wis. Endowment Fund, 1992. Author: A Century with Connor Timber, 1972, Forestry Futures and Conservation Misconcepts, 1946, 2d rev. edition, 1947; contbr. articles to various publs. Legis. chmn. 7th Dist. Wis. Fedn. Rep. Women, 1963-65, bd. dirs., 1955-65, vice chmn. 1955-59; del. Rep. county, state, nat. conventions, 1962; vice chmn. Marathon County; Rep. vice chmn. Recipient Gov.'s Wis. Heritage Tourism award, 1993, State Hist. Soc. Wis. Award of merit, 1970, 90, Outstanding Achievement in Environ. Protection Svcs. award U.S. EPA, 1987, Forest History Assn. Wis. Mus. award, 1978, Nat. Award in Edn. Arbor Day Found., 1975. Mem. Wis. Mayflower Soc., Colonial Dames (Wis. Soc.), The Hugenot Soc. of Wis., Bascom Hill Soc. (U. Wis.), Lake States Resource Alliance, Inc., Lake States Women in Timber, Inc., Forest History Assn. of Wis., State Hist. Soc. of Wis., Nat. Trust for Hist. Preservation, Wausau chpt. DAR (nat. vice chmn. resolutions 1965-68, Wis. state chmn. nat. def., 1962-65, conservation chmn. 1974-77, recipient many awards). Home: 1011 8th St Wausau WI 54403

CONNOR, WILDA, government health agency administrator; b. Pleasantville, N.J., Apr. 9, 1947; d. Herman Smith and Rubina (Miraglio) Cooney; m. James J. Connor Jr., Nov. 5, 1966; 1 child, James J. III. BSBA cum laude, Glassboro (N.J.) State Coll., 1985; postgrad., U. Pa., 1988—. Employee services coord. Turning Point Drug Outpatient Program, Collingswood, N.J., 1976-78; mgmt. specialist Camden County Ctr. Addictive Diseases, Lakeland, N.J., 1978-87; adminstr. Family Practice Ctrs. Camden (N.J.) County Health Dept., 1988—. Com. fund raiser Camden County Dem. Congl. Campaign, Stratford, N.J., 1986; mem. Solid Waste Adv. Coun., Camden County; mem. Coastal Resources Adv. Commn. Dept. Environ. Protection. Mem. N.J. Assn. Alcoholism Counselors, N.J. Substance Abuse Cert. Bd. (cert. 1987, 89 MSA), LWV, Solid Waste Adv. Council. Roman Catholic. Home: PO Box 226 228 E Vasey Ave Clementon NJ 08021 Office: Camden County Dept Policy Planning & Devel Bldg 6981 N Park Dr E 3d Fl Pennsauken NJ 08109

CONNORS, DORSEY, television and radio commentator, newspaper columnist; b. Chgo.; d. William J. and Sarah (MacLain) C.; m. John E. Forbes; 1 dau., Stephanie. BA cum laude, U. Ill. Fl. reporter WGN-TV Rep. Nat. Conv., Chgo., Dem. Nat. Conv., L.A., 1960. Conducted: Personality Profiles, WGN-TV, Chgo., 1948-49, Dorsey Connors Show, WMAQ-TV, Chgo., 1949-58, 61-63, Armchair Travels, WMAQ-TV, 1952-55, Homeshow, NBC, 1954-57, NBC Today Show, Dorsey Connors program, WGN, 1958-61, Tempo Nine, WGN-TV, 1961, Society in Chgo, WMAQ-TV, 1964; writer: column Hi! I'm Dorsey Connors, Chgo. Sun Times, 1965—; Author: Gadgets Galore, 1953, Save Time, Save Money, Save Yourself, 1972, Helpful Hints for Hurried Homemakers, 1988. Founder Ill. Epilepsy League; mem. woman's bd. Children's Home and Aid Soc., mem. women's bd. USO. Mem. AFTRA, NATAS, Screen Actor's Guild, Mus. Broadcast Communications (founding mem.), Soc. Midland Authors, Chgo. Hist. Soc. (guild com., costume com.), Chi Omega. Roman Catholic. Office: Chgo Sun Times 401 N Wabash Ave Chicago IL 60611-3532

CONNORS, MICHELE PERROTT, wholesale beverage company executive; b. Ft. Lauderdale, Fla., June 28, 1952; d. Samuel R. and Mariette (Larouche) Perrott; m. Robert Gary Connors, Apr. 14, 1973; children: Eva Marie, Colleen Elizabeth. AA, Daytona Beach Community Coll., Fla., 1972. Legal sec. Richard Krause, Ormond Beach, Fla., 1972-74; sec. S.R. Perrott, Inc., Ormond Beach, 1974-79, v.p., ops. mgr., 1979-83, pres., chief exec. officer, 1983—; prin., pres. Michele & Group Modeling Talent Agy., 1989—. Bd. dirs. Daytona Beach Easter Seals Soc., 1985—, chmn. fundraising, 1983-86; bd. dirs. Am. Cancer Soc., 1989—. Mem. Beer Industry Fla., Nat. Beer Wholesalers, Ormond Beach C. of C. (pres. 1984), Oceanside Country Club, Trails Racquet Club. Republican. Roman Catholic. Office: S R Perrott Inc PO Box 836 Ormond Beach FL 32175-0836

CONOVER, CAROLE ANN, small business owner; b. Hackensack, N.J., Jan. 28, 1941; d. Harry Sayles Conover and Gloria Belle (Dalton) Reed; m. Henry Meursinge Duys Jr., May 30, 1964 (div. 1969); children: Henry M. III, Lizabeth Conover, Noah Ogden. BA in Lit. and Journalism, Smith Coll., 1963. Assoc. Carl Byoir and Assocs., N.Y.C., 1979-81; pub. affairs specialist MasterCard Internat., N.Y.C., 1981-82; pres. Conover Assocs. Pub. Rels. Firm, N.Y.C., 1982—; chmn., creative dir. Conover Models and Talent Internat., N.Y.C., 1985—. Author: (book and play) Cover Girls: A Biography of Harry Conover, 1978; writer 10th and 11th Daytime Emmies Award Show for NATAS, 1982-83. Adoption chmn. Wilton (Conn.) Animals in Distress, 1965-68. Named Best Young Writer Winter Park (Fla.) Bulletin, 1952. Mem. NAFE, Authors and Writers League, Dramatists Guild, Wilton Riding Club. Democrat. Roman Catholic. Office: 30 Park Ave New York NY 10016

CONOVER, MONA LEE, retired educator; b. Lincoln, Nebr., Nov. 9, 1929; d. William Cyril and Susan Ferne (Floyd) C.; m. Elmer Kenneth Johnson, June 14, 1953 (div. 1975); children: Michael David, Susan Amy, Sharon Ann, Jennifer Lynne. AB, Nebr. Wesleyan U., 1952; student, Ariz. State U., 1973-75; MA in Edn., No. Ariz. U., 1985. Cert. tchr., Colo., Ariz. Tchr. Jefferson County R-1 Sch., Wheat Ridge, Colo., 1952-56, Glendale (Ariz.) Elem. Sch. # 40, 1972-92; dir. Glendale Adult Edn., 1987-92; ret., 1992. Author: ABC's of Naturalization, 1989. Mem. AAUW, Am. Assn. Adult Community and Continuing Edn., Ariz. Edn. Assn., Phoenix Botanical Gardens, Tchrs. English to Speaker of Other Langs., Mountain Plains Adult Edn. Assn., Heard Mus., Phoenix Zoo, Order of Ea. Star, Phi Kappa Delta. Republican. Methodist.

CONOVER, NANCY ANDERSON, secondary school counselor; b. Manhattan, Kans., July 8, 1943; d. Howard Julius and Wilma June (Katz) Anderson; m. Gary Hites Conover, Aug. 10, 1968; children: Chad Anderson, Cary Hites. BS in Edn., Kans. State U., 1965; MEd, Wichita State U., 1991. Cert. sch. counselor, tchr., Kans. Tchr. Flint (Mich.) Sch. Dist., 1965-66, Unified Sch. Dist. 259, Wichita, Kans., 1967-68, Overland Park (Kans.) Sch. Dist., 1968-70; bus. mgr., sec.-treas. Gary Conover, D.D.S., Wichita, 1985-94; sch. counselor United Sch. Dist. 259, Wichita, 1991-94; secondary sch. counselor Unified Sch. Dist. 385, Andover, Kans., 1994—. Mem. Am. Counselors Assn., Kans. Assn. Counselors, Kans. Dental Aux. (sec. 1970-74), Wichita Dist. Dental Aux. (pres. 1970-75), Jr. League Wichita (adminstrv. v.p. 1978-82), Gamma Phi Beta, Phi Kappa Phi Honor Soc. Republican. Lutheran.

CONOVER, NELLIE COBURN, retail furniture company executive; b. Lebanon, Ohio, Dec. 21, 1921; d. Frank C. and Isabel (Murphy) Coburn; student public schs.; m. Lawrence E. Conover, Jan. 11, 1941; children—Lawrence R., Carol, David C., Constance, Christina. Co-founder, 1949, since exec. sec.-treas. Larry Conover Furniture & Appliance, Inc., and predecessor, Milford, Ohio, also trustee co. pension fund. Mem. Milford C. of C., Cin. Hist. Soc., Milford Hist. Soc., DAR. Democrat. Roman Catholic. Address: 438 Main St Milford OH 45150

CONRAD, JUDY L., insurance company executive; b. Reading, Pa., May 22, 1952; d. Willard Martin and Mary Eleanor (Strecker) Conrad; m. Mark A. Stead, Feb. 14, 1988 (dec. 1990); stepchildren: Matthew, Mark Jr., Adrian, Angela. BS in Edn., West Chester (Pa.) U., 1974. CFP, CLU. Tchr. Auscilla Christian Acad., Monticello, Fla., 1980-82; sales agt. Alden Levin Assocs., Phila., 1977-80, John Hunt Assocs., Tallahassee, Fla., 1982-84; life and employee benefits mgr. Corp. Risk Assocs., Tallahassee, Fla., 1982-84; acct. exec. Cigna/INA Cos., Phila., 1985-86; fin. svcs. rep. The Travelers Ins. Cos., Orlando, Fla., 1986-90; fin. svcs. mgr. The Travelers Ins. Cos., Orlando and Tampa, 1990—; pub. speaker, lectr. in field. With Free Fin. Clinics, Orlando Sentinel sponsored hotline 1992, local TV show St. Petersburg, Clearwater area 1992-94. Recipient Life Citation award INA/CIGNA, 1984. Mem. Am. Soc. CLU, Ctrl. Fla. Soc. ICFP (edn. dir. 1991—, v.p. 1992—, pres.-elect 1993, pres. 1994), Am. Coll. CLU & ChFC, Nat. Assn. Life Underwriters, Gen. Agts. and Mgrs. Assn., Internat. Assn. Fin. Planners. Republican. Office: The Travelers Ins Cos 1000 Legion Pl Ste 1400 Orlando FL 32801-1057

CONRAD, KAY ANN, reference librarian; b. Wabash, Ind., Mar. 18, 1945; d. Frank Robert and Helen A. (Little) C. BA, Manchester Coll., North Manchester, Ind., 1967; MLS, Ind. U., 1968. Cert. permanent grade I pub. libr., Wis. Asst. prof. Valley City (N.D.) State Coll., 1968-72; head reference libr. Fond du Lac (Wis.) Pub. Libr., 1972—. Compiler: Index of 1854 History of Fond du Lac County, Wisconsin, 1988. Mem. Fond du Lac Sesquicentennial Com., 1986. Mem. ALA, AAUW, Wis. Libr. Assn. (bd. dirs. reference and adult svcs. sect. 1985-90), Fond du Lac County Hist. Soc., Fond du Lac Community Theatre Assn. Office: Fond du Lac Pub Libr 32 Sheboygan St Fond Du Lac WI 54935-4220

CONRAD, SISTER LINDA, elementary school educator; b. Lorain, Ohio, Apr. 26, 1951; d. Chester Clifford and Virginia Ann (Smith) C. BA, Notre Dame Coll., Cleve., 1987. Cert. tchr., Ohio; mem. Sisters of Notre Dame. Tchr. Julie Billiart Sch., Lyndhurst, Ohio, 1977-85, St. Francis Sch., Cleve., 1987-92, Gesu Sch., Cleve., 1992-94; dir. ctr. for excellence in edn. Notre Dame Coll. Ohio, South Euclid, 1994—; dir. Project Stars Grant, Cleve., 1991-92, Tchr. Thinking in Art Curriculum Grant, Cleve., 1993-94; moderator Student Coun., Cleve., 1988-92. Roman Catholic. Office: Notre Dame Coll 4545 College Rd South Euclid OH 44121

CONRAD, MARIAN SUE (SUSAN CONRAD), special education educator; b. Columbus, Ohio, May 3, 1946; d. Harold Marion Griffith and Susie Belle (House) Goheen; m. Richard Lee Conrad, Jan. 23 1971. BS, Ohio State U., 1967. Tchr. spl. edn. West High Sch., Columbus, Ohio, 1967-70; spl. edn. work study coord. North High Sch., Columbus, 1974-79, Whetstone High Sch., Columbus, 1979-80, Briggs High Sch., Columbus, 1980—, West High Sch., Columbus, 1970—. Bd. dirs. Jr. Div., The Columbus Symphony Club, 1972-79; vice chmn. Zoofari, Columbus, 1978—; bd. dirs., life mem. Wazoo, Columbus, 1974-87; bd. dirs., chair coms. Jr. League, Columbus, 1982—; vice chmn. devel. com. Dublin (Ohio) Counseling Ctr., 1987—; trustee Columbus Zoo, 1991—. Recipient Mayors Award for Vol. Svc., Columbus, 1988. Mem. Am. Bus. Women's Assn. (v.p. 1979-80, bd. dirs., Woman of Yr. 1980), Coun. Exceptional Children (pres. 1988-89, Educator of Yr. 1989), Ohio Assn. Suprs. and Work Study Coords., Dublin Women in Bus. and Professions, Country Club at Muirfield, Iota Lambda Sigma (Alpha Gamma chpt.). Republican. Methodist. Home: 5842 Moray Ct Dublin OH 43017-9747 Office: West HS 179 S Powell Ave Columbus OH 43204-3099

CONRAD, PAM, author; b. N.Y.C., June 18, 1947; d. Robert Fredrick and Doris Elizabeth (Dowling) Stampf; m. Robert Raymond Conrad, June 25, 1967 (div. 1982); children: Johanna, Sarah Loretta. BA, New Sch. Social Rsch., N.Y.C., 1984. Author: I Don't Live Here!, 1984, Prairie Songs, 1985 (Spur award Western Writers Am. 1985, Internat. Reading Assn. award 1986, Boston Globe-Horn Book award 1986, Judy Lopez Meml. award Women's Nat. Book Assn. 1986), Holding Me Here, 1986, What I Did for Roman, 1987, Seven Silly Circles, 1987, Taking the Ferry Home, 1988, Staying Nine, 1988, My Daniel, 1989 (Spur award Western Writers Am. 1989), The Tub People, 1989, Stonewords: A Ghost Story, 1990 (Edgar award Mystery Writer's Am. 1991, Boston Globe-Horn Book award 1990), Prairie Vision: The Life and Times of Solomon Butcher, 1991, Pedro's Journal, 1991, The Lost Sailor, 1992, The Tub Grandfather, 1993, Pumpkin Moon, 1994, Molly and the Strawberry Day, 1994, Doll Face Has a Party!, 1994, The Rooster's Gift, 1995, Call Me Ahnighito, 1995, Animal Lingo, 1995. Mem. Authors Guild, Soc. Childrens Book Writers. Home: 61 Cedar Ave Rockville Centre NY 11570-2926 Address: care Maria Carvainis Agy 235 W End Ave New York NY 10023*

CONRAD-ENGLAND, ROBERTA LEE, pathologist; b. Meriden, Conn., Aug. 25, 1950; d. Hans and Emma Ann (Bort) Conrad; m. Gary Thomas England, June 6, 1976; children: Eric Bryan, Christopher Ryan. BS in Microbiology, U. Ky., 1972, MD, 1976. Diplomate Nat. Bd. Med. Examiners, Bd. Am. Pathologists. Resident anatomic and clin. pathology Emory U. Affiliated Hosps., Atlanta, 1976-80; pathologist Western Bapt. Hosp., Padurah, Ky., 1980—; cons. Marshall County Hosp., Benton, Ky., 1985—. Mem., com. chairperson PTA, Poducah, Ky., 1993-94; mother's asst. Boy Scouts Am., Poducah, 1991-94. Fellow Coll. Am. Pathologists, Am. Soc. Clin. Pathologists; mem. Ky. Med. Assn., Ky. Mentors Women in Sci., Alpha Omega Alpha, Phi Beta Kappa. Office: 625 Whitney Dr Paducah KY 42001

CONRATH, VIVIAN CAROLINE COSIO, investment company executive; b. Camagüey, Cuba, June 4, 1956; came to the U.S., 1967; d. Julio Elio Cosio and Maria Carolina Castellanos; m. Ron Haskamp, March 23, 1982 (div. Dec. 1984); m. William J. Conrath (separated). Degree in Cytotechnology, U. Louisville; attended, Spalding Coll., 1974-77. Cytotechnologist U. Hosp., Louisville, Ky., 1977-79; mgr. company, Louisville, 1979-81; owner Tristar Distbg., Cinn., 1981-82; sales rep. John Hancock, Cinn., 1982-87; reg. investment advisor, sales agent N.Y. Life, Cinn., 1987—; owner Cosio Fin. Svcs. Mem. Nat. Assn. Life Underwriters (Nat. Sales Achievement award 1989, 90, Nat. Sales Quality award 1994). Republican. Roman Catholic. Home: 1077 Stratford Ct Loveland OH 45140

CONRON, SHANA RIMEL, lawyer; b. St. Louis; m. Michael Conron, Jan. 22, 1964; 1 child, Rachel. AB, Washington U., 1960; MA, U. Ill., 1961; JD, Columbia U., 1978. Assoc. editor Polit. Sci. quar., N.Y.C., 1969-72; editor Parker Sch., Columbia U. Law Sch., N.Y.C., 1972-74; assoc. Chadbourne & Parke, N.Y.C., 1978-83; v.p., divsn. counsel Citibank, N.A., N.Y.C., 1983—. Mem. ABA, Assn. Bar City of N.Y. Office: Citibank NA 153 E 53d St New York NY 10043

CONROY, CATHERINE MARTIN, public relations executive; b. Bklyn., Dec. 29, 1948; m. Robert Ellsworth Conroy, 1972; 1 child, Amy Elizabeth. BA, Bklyn. Coll., 1970. Adminstrv. dir. Met. Golf Assn., N.Y.C., 1970-74; v.p. Blyth, Eastman Dillon & Co., Inc., N.Y.C., 1975-78; asst. v.p. Merrill Lynch, N.Y.C., 1978-83; sr. v.p. Donaldson, Lufkin & Jenrette, Inc., N.Y.C., 1983—. Mem. Pub. Rels. Soc. Am., Fin. Comm. Soc. Office: Donaldson Lufkin & Jenrette Inc 140 Broadway New York NY 10005-1101

CONROY, MARY A., state legislator. Mem. ways & means com., joint com. health care cost containment Md. House of Dels., Annapolis, 1987—. Democrat. Office: 208 Lowe House Office Bldg 6 Government Bladen Blvd Annapolis MD 21401-1991 also: Md State Senate State Capital Annapolis MD 21401*

CONROY, SARAH BOOTH, columnist, novelist, speaker, editor; b. Valdosta, Ga., Feb. 16, 1927; d. Weston Anthony and Ruth (Proctor) Booth; m. Richard Timothy Conroy, Dec. 31, 1949; children: Camille Booth, Sarah Claire. B.S., U. Tenn., 1950. Continuity writer Sta. WNOX, 1945-48; commentator, writer Sta. WATO, 1948-49; reporter, architecture columnist Knoxville News Sentinel, 1949-56; assoc. editor The Diplomat mag., 1956-58; columnist Washington Post, 1957-58, design editor, columnist, 1970-82, feature writer, columnist, 1982—; reporter, art critic Washington Daily News, 1968-70; regular contbr. N.Y. Times, 1968-70; mem. adv. bd. Horizon mag., 1978-85. Author: Refinements of Love A Novel about Clover and Henry Adams, 1993. Recipient Raven award Mystery Writers Am., 1990, Mass Media award Am. Assn. U. Women, 1992. Mem. AIA (hon.). Home: 5016 16th St NW Washington DC 20011-3842 Office: The Washington Post 1150 15th St NW Washington DC 20071-0001*

CONROY, TAMARA BOKS, business executive; b. Most, Bohemia, Czechoslovakia; came to U.S., 1947; d. Alois and Tatiana (Shapilova) Boks; m. John P. Conroy, Aug. 19, 1950 (dec. Oct. 1973); 1 child, Michael Thomas (dec.). Student, U. Graz, Austria, 1945-47; RN, New Rochelle (N.Y.) Med. Ctr., 1950; student, Coll. of William & Mary, 1958, 59, Cath. U. Am., 1960; BS in Nursing Edn., Columbia U., 1963, MA in Spl. Edn., 1965. RN, N.Y.; cert. spl. edn. tchr., N.Y. Nurse accident rm. New Rochelle Hosp./Med. Ctr., 1950-51; pub. health nurse Va. Dept. of Health, Richmond, 1958-59; tchr. spl. edn. Southern Westchester Bd. Coop. Edn. Svcs., Portchester, N.Y., 1965-83; freelance artist and painter N.Y.C. and Pelham, N.Y., 1969—; asst. to chmn. math. dept. Columbia U., N.Y.C., 1975-76. Author math. program Learning Numbers-Step by Step, 1977. Pres., founder Classical Music Lovers' Exch., Pelham, 1980—. Mem. Am. Fedn. Tchrs., N.Y. State United Tchrs., BOCES Tchrs. Assn. (profl.), Women's Mus. Group, Mamaroneck Artists Guild, Silvermine Artists Guild, Westchester Musicians Guild (assoc.), Kappa Delta Pi. Office: Classical Music Lovers' Exch PO Box 31 Pelham NY 10803

CONSAGRA, SOPHIE CHANDLER, academy administrator; b. Radnor, Pa., Apr. 28, 1927; d. Alfred D. and Carol (Ramsay) Chandler; children: Maria, Pierluigi, Francesca, George. B.A., Smith Coll., 1949; M.A., Cambridge (Eng.) U., 1952. Exec. dir. Del. Arts Council, 1972-78; dir. visual arts and architecture N.Y. State Council Arts, 1978-80; dir. Am. Acad. in Rome, 1980-84, pres., 1984-88, pres. emerita, vice chmn./spl. projects, 1988-90; cons. Nat. Endowment Arts. Recipient Smith Coll. award, 1986. Address: 955 Lexington Ave New York NY 10021-5101

CONSIDINE, SUSAN MARY, entrepreneur; b. Queens, N.Y., Jan. 21, 1958; d. Richard Thomas and Mary Michael (Zappulo) C.; 1 child, Shane Anthony. Diploma in Nursing, Samaritan Hosp., Troy, N.Y., 1979; BS, SUNY, Utica, 1981; MBA, Rensselaer Poly. Inst., 1989. RN. Nurse St. Elizabeth Hosp., Utica, 1980-81, Marcy Psychiat. Ctr., Utica, 1981-84; sales mgr. Lincoln Logs Ltd., Chestertown, N.Y., 1984-86, v.p. dealer devel., 1986-87, v.p. customer svc., 1987-90, exec. v.p., 1990-92, also bd. dirs.; owner Tokens of Friendship, Bolton Landing, N.Y., 1992—. Home: RR # 1 Box 60 Horicon Ave Bolton Landing NY 12814 Office: Tokens of Friendship Main St Bolton Landing NY 12814

CONSILIO, BARBARA ANN, legal administrator, management consultant; b. Cleve., June 22, 1938; d. Joseph B. and Anna E. (Ford) C. BS, Kent State U., 1962; MA, U. Detroit, 1973. Cert. social worker, Mich. Tchr. Chagrin Falls (Ohio) High Sch., 1962-64; probation officer Macomb County Juvenile Ct., Mt. Clemens, Mich., 1965-68, casework supr., 1968-74; dir. children's svcs. Macomb County Juvenile Ct., Mt. Clemens, 1974-79; mgr. foster care and instns. Oakland County Juvenile Ct., Pontiac, Mich., 1979-83; ct. adminstr. Oakland County Probate Ct., Pontiac, 1983-93, ret., 1993. Bd. dirs. Children's Charter Cts. of Mich., Lansing, Statewide Adv. Bd. on Sexual Abuse, Lansing, Havenwyck Hosp., Auburn Hills, Orchards Children's Svcs., Southfield, Oakland County Coun. Children at Risk, Pontiac; mem. Nat. Women's Polit. Caucus, N.Y.C.; bd. dirs. Care House, Pontiac. Mem. Nat. Coun. Juvenile and Family Ct. Adminstrs. Group, Mich. Probate and Juvenile Register's Assn., Mich. Juvenile Ct. Adminstrs. Assn., Nat. Assn. Ct. Mgrs., Supreme Ct. Task Force on Racial and Ethnic Bias, Office of Children and Youth Svcs. (state foster care system rev. com.), Nat. Coun. Juvenile and Family Ct. Judges (Outstanding Ct. Adminstr. award, 1993). Home: 4045 Chestnut Hill Dr Troy MI 48098-4205

CONSOR, JENNETTE ESTELLE, lawyer, consultant and fundraiser; b. N.Y.C., Nov. 4, 1948; d. Hediberto and Estelle (Ortiz De Carballo) Morales Irrizary; children: Brice Nathaniel, Simone Ronit. BA, U. Houston, 1974; JD, So. Meth. U., 1978. Bar: Tex. 1980. Law clerk., atty. Bates, Tibbals & Lee, Dallas, 1978-81; corp. atty. Hunt Oil Corp., Dallas, 1981-84; corp./bus. atty. in sole practice Dallas, 1984-89; legal svcs. mgr. Resolution Trust Corp., Dallas, 1990-93, sr. atty. in litigation, 1993—; cons. Women in Film/Dallas, 1985-92, Crescent club Social Com., Dallas, 1989—, Walt Garrison Rodeo Com. Multiple Sclerosis, Dallas, 1991-93. Fundraiser for polit. campaigns, 1985-94; apptd. mem. Motion Picture Commn. Classification Bd., Dallas, 1983-85, Human and Health Svcs. Commn., Dallas, 1987-89, Cultural Affairs Commn., 1992-93; mem. Walt Garrison Rodeo com. Multiple Sclerosis, Dallas, 1991-93; acting exec. dir. S.W./Tradefest, 1994; chmn. vol. task force Dallas Tradefest, 1993; bd. dirs. Mexican Cultural Ctr., 1995—, West Dallas Cmty. Ctrs., 1995. Mem. State Bar Tex., Dallas Bar Assn., Dallas Women's Bar Assn., Women in Firm/Dallas (bd. dirs. and editor newsletter 1989-90), Hispanic C. of C. of Dallas, Dallas Women's Found., Dallas Friday Group, Dallas World Salute Young Profl. League. Home: 2808 McKinney Ave Apt 607 Dallas TX 75204 Office: Resolution Trust Corp 3500 Maple Ave 12th Fl Dallas TX 75219

CONSTABLE, ELINOR GREER, federal official, diplomat; b. San Diego, Feb. 8, 1934; d. Marshall Raymond and Katherine (French) Greer; m. Peter Dalton Constable, Mar. 8, 1958; children: Robert, Philip, Julia. B.A., Wellesley Coll., 1955. Mem. staff Dept. Interior, 1955-57, Dept. State, 1957-58, OEO, 1964-68; sr. assoc. Transcentury Corp., Washington, 1971-72; with Dept. State, Washington, 1973—, dir. investment affairs, 1978-80; dep. asst. sec. Internat. Fin. and Devel., 1980-83; dep. asst. sec. for econ. and bus. affairs Dept. State, from 1983-93, asst. secr. for Oceans, International Environmental and Scientific Affairs Bureau, 1993—; ambassador to Kenya, 1986-89; rsch. prof. diplomacy Georgetown U., Washington, 1989-91; capital devel. officer US AID, Pakistan, 1977-78; sr. inspector Office Inspector Gen., 1992; asst. sec. Oceans, Environ., Sci. and Tech., 1993—. Office: Oceans Internat Environ Sci Affairs Office of Asst Secr 2201 C St NW Washington DC 20520-0001*

CONSTANCE, BARBARA ANN, financial planner, small business owner, consultant; b. Springfield, Mass., Dec. 24, 1945; d. Edward F. and Margaret E. (Price) Corcoran; m. Thomas F. Tiedgen, Apr. 27, 1968 (div. 1975); m. G. Lawrence Gadsby Jr., May 5, 1978 (div. 1991); m. F. David Constance, Dec. 6, 1991. AA, Vt. Coll., Montpelier, 1965. CLU; chartered fin. cons. Adminstrv. asst. Mass. Mut. Life Co., Springfield and Hartford, Conn., 1965-75; office mgr. Am. Nat. Life Ins. Co., Springfield, 1976; traveling trainee Conn. Gen. Life Ins. Co., Bloomfield, 1976; sales rep. Conn. Gen. Life Ins. Co., Springfield, 1976-77; dir. mktg. NN Life Ins. Services, Johnston, R.I., 1978-80; sales rep. New Eng. Mut. Life Co., Providence, 1980-82; pvt. practice fin. planner Tiverton, R.I., 1982—; pres., founder Heritage Prodns., Ltd., Tiverton, R.I., 1988-91; cons. Northwestern Mutual Life Ins. Co., Providence, 1986-87; co-founder, bd. dirs. Career Connections, Inc. Bd. dirs. YWCA of Greater R.I., Big Sister Assn. of R.I. Mem. Am. Soc. CLUs and ChFC (past pres. R.I. chpt.), Nat. Assn. Life Underwriters, R.I. Life Underwriters, Assn. Health Ins. Agts., Newport County Women's Network (co-founder), R.I. Woman's Career Network, R.I. Bus. Exch., R.I. Estate Planning Coun. Republican. Episcopalian. Home and Office: 177 Highland Rd Tiverton RI 02878-4003

CONSTANT, HOLLY ANN, administrator; b. Muskego, Wis., Sept. 2, 1965; d. Robert Andrew and Nancy Ann (Gingrich) C. BA in Econs., Am. U., 1987, BS in Polit. Sci., 1987; MPA, Columbia U., 1989, MPH, 1990. Grad. intern Congl. Budget Office, Washington, 1988; adminstrv. resident The Presbyn. Hosp., N.Y.C., 1988-89; ops. analyst Columbia Hosp. Women, Washington, 1990; dir. health resources D.C. Hosp. Assn., Washington, 1990—; bd. dirs. Community Healthcare Inc., Washington; coun. mem. Health & Human Svcs. Acad., Washington, 1993—; speaker in field. Vol. Race for the Cure, Washington, 1990—; grad. mentor U. Md., College Park, 1991-92; tech. cons. Mayor's Task Force on Health Care Reform, Washington, 1993-94, Mayor's Transition Team, Washington, 1990. Pub. Affairs fellow Columbia U., 1987, Grad. Teaching fellow, 1989; recipient Stafford H. Cassell award Am. U., 1987. Mem. Am. Guild Patient Account Mgmt. Am. Pub. Health Assn., Met. Washington Pub. Health Assn. (bd. dirs. 1992—), Healthcare Fin. Mgmt. Assn. (bd. dirs. 1991—), Citizen Amb. Program (Del. mem. 1993). Home: 6519 Major St Alexandria VA 22312

CONSTANTINE, JAN FRIEDMAN, lawyer; b. N.Y.C., Jan. 22, 1948; d. Howard J. and Elayne (Sercus) Friedman; m. Lawrence Levien, Oct. 11, 1970 (div. Sept. 1974); m. Lloyd E. Constantine, June 22, 1975; children: Isaac, Sarah, Elizabeth. BA, Smith Coll., Northampton, Mass., 1970; JD, George Washington U., 1973. Bar: N.Y. 1974, U.S. Dist. Ct. (so. and ea. dists.) N.Y. 1975, U.S. Ct. Appeals (2d cir.) 1975. Staff atty. div. spl. projects FTC, Washington, 1973-75; staff atty. N.Y. office FTC, N.Y.C., 1975-77; asst. atty. U.S. Dist. Ct. (ea. dist.) N.Y., Bklyn., 1977-82; litigation counsel Macmillan, Inc., N.Y.C., 1982-84, assoc. gen. counsel, 1985-90, dep. gen. counsel, 1990-91; dep. gen. counsel The News Corp. Ltd., N.Y.C., 1991-92; gen. counsel News Am. Pub. Inc., N.Y.C., 1992—; vis. asst. prof. George Washington U. Law Sch., Washington, 1974. Mem. Assn. of Bar of City of N.Y. (mem. consumer protection com. 1981-84, corp. law com. 1987-90, media law com. 1991—). Home: 10 W 66th St New York NY 10023 Office: The News Corp Ltd 1211 Ave Of The Americas New York NY 10036-8701

CONSTANTINE, VIRGINIA, state legislator. State rep., mem. bus. legis. com., marine resources com. Maine Ho. of Reps., Augusta. Democrat. Home: Box 3560 RR 1 Box 3560 Bar Harbor ME 04609-9743 Office: Maine Ho of Reps State Capital Augusta ME 04333*

CONSTANTINEAU, CONSTANCE JULIETTE, banker; b. Lowell, Mass., Feb. 18, 1937; d. Henry Goulet and Germaine (Turner) Goulet-Lamarre; m. Edward Joseph Constantineau; children: Glen Edward, Alan Henry. Student, Bank Adminstrn. Inst. and Am. Inst. Banking, 1975-87. Mortgage sec. The Cen. Savs. Bank, Lowell, 1955-57; head teller First Fed. Savs. & Loan, Lowell, 1957-59, Lowell Bank & Trust Co., Lowell, 1973-74; br. mgr. Century Bank & Trust Co., Malden, Mass., 1975-78; v.p. purchasing, mgr. support svcs. First Security Bank of N.Mex. (formerly First Nat. Bank Albuquerque), 1983—; mem. planning purchasing mgr.'s conf. Bank Adminstrn. Inst., San Antonio, Orlando, Fla., New Orleans; treas. polit. action com. First Nat. Bank, 1986. Bd. dirs., historian Indian Pueblo Cultural Ctr., Albuquerque, 1986-89. Mem. Fin. Women Internat., In-Plant Mgmt. Assn. (charter). Home: 13015 Deer Dancer Tr NE Albuquerque NM 87112 Office: 1st Security Bank NMex 40 1st Plz Ctr NW Albuquerque NM 87102-3338

CONSTANTINI, JOANN M., information management consultant, speaker; b. Danbury, Conn., July 30, 1948; d. William J. and Mathilda J. (Ressler) C. BA, Coll. White Plains, N.Y., 1970; postgrad. Central Conn. State Coll., 1977-78, U. Hartford, 1985-88, U. Jacksonville, 1991, Nova U. Sch. Psychology, 1992—. Cert. records mgr., 1987; lic realtor, N.C. Psychiat. social worker N.Y. State Dept. Mental Hygiene, Wassaic, 1970-73; with Northeast Utilities, Hartford, Conn., 1973-88, methods analyst, 1979-82, records and procedures mgmt. adminstr., 1982-88; document contr., mgr. Ralph M. Parsons Co., Fairfield, Ohio, 1990-91, St. Johns River Power Park, Jacksonville, 1991—; dir. Meriden (Conn.) YWCA, 1976-77, My Sisters Place, 1984-87; mem. faculty Cen. Piedmont Community Coll., 1989-90, Fla. C.C., Jacksonville, 1993—. Bd. dirs. Meriden YWCA, Conn., 1978-79; vol., 1984—, Queen City Friends, Charlotte, 1988-89; mem. Greater Charlotte Bd. Realtors; mem. adv. coun. Clermont Coll., Cin., 1990-91, Jacksonville C.C. 1991—, Greater Hartford C.C., 1986. Mem. AAUW, Assn. Record Mgmt. and Adminstrs. (sec. 1984-85, bd. dirs., 1984-86, internat. chair industry action program 1989-93, chair industry action com. for pub. utilities, 1986-89), Assn. Image and Info. Mgmt. (dir. 1984-86), Electric Council New Eng. (chair records mgmt. com. 1985-87), Coll. White Plains Alumnae Assn., Nat. Trust for Hist. Preservation, Inst. Cert. Records Mgrs., Am. Platform Assn., Am. Assn. Ind. Investors, Beta Sigma Phi. Democrat. Roman Catholic. Club: Northeast Utilities Women's Forum. (treas. 1983-88). Avocations: antiques, fund raising, traveling, collecting cookbooks. Home: 11538 Jonathan Rd Jacksonville FL 32225-1314

CONSTANTINO-BANA, ROSE EVA, nursing educator, researcher; b. Labangan Zamboanga del Sur, Philippines, Dec. 25, 1940; came to U.S., 1964; naturalized, 1982; d. Norberto C. and Rosalia (Torres) Bana; m. Abraham Antonio Constantino, Jr., Dec. 13, 1964; children: Charles Edward, Kenneth Richard, Abraham Anthony III. B.S. in Nursing, Philippine Union Coll., Manila, 1962; M.Nursing, U. Pitts., 1971, Ph.D., 1979; J.D., Duquesne U., Pitts., 1984. Lic. clin. specialist in psychiatric-mental health nursing; registered nurse. Instr. Philippine Union Co., 1963-65, Spring Grove State Hosp., Balt., 1965-67, Montefiore Sch. Nursing, Pitts., 1967-70; instr. U. Pitts., 1971-74, asst. prof., 1974-83, assoc. prof., 1983—, chmn. Senate Athletic Com., 1985-86, 89-90, univ. senate sec., 1991-92, univ. senate v.p., 1993—; project dir. grant div. of nursing HHS, Washington, 1983-85; prin. investigator NIH NCNR, 1991—; bd. dirs. Internat. Council on Women's Health Issues, 1986—. Author: (with others) Principles and Practice of Psychiatric Nursing, 1982; contbr. chpts. to books and articles to profl. jours. Mem. Republican Presdl. Task Force, Washington, 1980, Rep. Senatorial Com., Washington, 1980. Mem. ABA, Pa. Bar Assn., Women's Bar Assn., Assn. Trial Lawyers Am., Am. Assn. Nurse Attys., Am. Nurses Assn., Pa. Nurses Assn., Nat. League Nursing, Pa. League Nursing (chairperson area 6), U. Pitts. Sch. Nursing Alumni Assn., U. Duquesne Law Alumni Assn., Sigma Theta Tau, Phi Alpha Delta. Seventh-Day Adventist. Avocations: cooking, playing the piano. Home: 6 Carmel Ct Pittsburgh PA 15221-3618 Office: U Pitts Sch Nursing 415 Victoria St Pittsburgh PA 15261

CONTI, ISABELLA, psychologist, consultant; b. Torino, Italy, Jan. 1, 1942; came to U.S., 1964; d. Giuseppe and Zaira (Melis) Ferro; m. Ugo Conti, Sept. 5, 1964; 1 child, Maurice. J.D., U. Rome, 1966; Ph.D. in Psychology, U. Calif.-Berkeley, 1975. Lic. psychologist. Sr. analyst Rsch. Inst. for Study of Man, Berkeley, Calif., 1967-68; postgrad. rsch. psychologist Personality Assessment and Rsch. Inst., U. Calif.-Berkeley, 1968-71; intern U. Calif.-Berkeley and VA Hosp., San Francisco, 1969-75; asst. prof. St. Mary's Coll., Moraga, Calif., 1978-84; cons. psychologist Conti Resources, Berkeley, Calif., 1977-85; v.p. Barnes & Conti Assocs., Inc., Berkeley, 1985-90; pres. Lisardco, El Cerrito, Calif., 1989—; v.p. ElectroMagnetic Instruments, Inc., El Cerrito, Calif., 1985—. Author: (with Alfonso Montuori) From Power to Partnership, 1993; contbr. articles on creativity and mgmt. cons. to profl. jours. Regents fellow U. Calif.-Berkeley, 1972; NIMH predoctoral rsch. fellow, 1972-73. Mem. Am. Psychol. Assn. Office: Lisardco 1318 Brewster Dr El Cerrito CA 94530

CONTRERAS-TAYLOR, ROSE CATHLEEN, quality improvement professional; b. Riverside, Calif., Nov. 25, 1956; d. Ramón and Pauline (Fonseca) Contreras; m. William Steve Taylor, July 9, 1983; 1 child, Ramón Cuahutémoc Taylor. Bachelor's degree, Pitzer Coll., 1979; MBA, U. Chgo., 1988. Health coord. Peace Corps, Tegucigalpa, Honduras, 1979-83; dir. Assn. Ho. Substance Abuse Program, Chgo., 1983-85; adminstrv. resident Mt. Sinai, Chgo., 1986-87; mgmt. analyst, budget mgr. Univ. Hosp., Albuquerque, 1988-91, quality improvement coord., 1991-94; hosp. adminstr. and CEO Guadalupe County Hosp., Santa Rosa, N.Mex., 1994—. Mem. Mayor's Health Task Force, Chgo., 1984. Recipient Merit of Honor, Ministry of Health, Honduras, 1981. Mem. Am. Soc. Quality Control (bd. dirs., sec. 1993—), Assn. Quality and Participation, Albuquerque Quality Network. Home: 607 High St NE Albuquerque NM 87102

CONVERSE, JOYCE ELLEN, obstetrical nurse; b. Grand Rapids, Minn., Oct. 8, 1947; d. Arnold Emil and Ellen Marie (Calkins) Strom; m. Gerald Lee Converse, June 21, 1968; children: Lisa Joy, Scott Gerald. Diploma of nursing, St. Luke's Hosp. Sch. Nursing, 1968; student, U. Wis., 1976, BSN, 1986, MSN, 1989. RN, Wis.; cert. Neonatal Resuscitation Program instr. Staff nurse St. Mary's Hosp., Duluth, Minn., 1968-69, Madison Gen. Hosp., Madison, Wis., 1969-77; maternal nurse clinician Madison Gen. Hosp., Madison, 1977-84, Meriter-Madison Gen. Hosp., Madison, 1984-90; nurse mgr. Meriter-Park Hosp., Madison, 1990-93; cons. Higman Healthcare, 1993—; lectr. U. Wis. Sch. Nursing, Madison, 1990-91; lectr. various profl. orgns. Contbr. articles to profl. jours. Mem. Assn. Women's Health, Obstetric and Neonatal Nurses (NCC inpatient obstetric nursing cert.), Nat. Perinatal Assn., Wis. Assn. for Perinatal Care, Sigma Theta Tau. Home: 5112 Denton Pl Madison WI 53711

CONWAY, ANNE CALLAGHAN, federal judge; b. Cleve., July 30, 1950. AB, John Carroll U., 1972; JD, U. Fla., 1975. Bar: Fla. 1975, U.S. Supreme Ct. 1981, U.S. Ct. Appeals (5th and 11th cirs.), U.S. Dist. Ct. (mid., no. and so. dists.) Fla. Law clk. to justice U.S. Dist. Ct., Orlando, Fla., 1975-77; from assoc. to ptnr. Wells, Gattis & Hallowes, Orlando, 1978-81; assoc. Carlton, Fields, Ward, Emmanuel, Smith & Cutler, P.A., Orlando, 1982-85, ptnr., 1985-91; judge U.S. Dist. (Mid. Dist.) Fla., Jacksonville, 1991—; mem. adv. com. on local rules U.S. Dist. Ct., Orlando, 1990-91, grievance com. Orlando div., mid. dist., 1986-91. Bd. dirs. So. Ballet Theatre, Winter Park, Fla., 1985-89, adv. bd., 1985-89; bd. dirs. Greater Orlando Area Legal Svcs., 1978-85. Mem. ABA, Orange County Bar Assn. (chairperson state and fed. trial practice com. 1989-90). Office: US Courthouse 80 N Hughey Ave Rm 646 Orlando FL 32801-2207*

CONWAY, JILL KATHRYN KER, former college president; b. Hillston, New South Wales, Australia, Oct. 9, 1934; d. William Innis and Evelyn Mary (Adames) Ker; m. John James Conway, Dec. 22, 1962. B.A., U. Sydney, Australia, 1958; Ph.D., Harvard U., 1969; hon. degree, St. Thomas (N.B.) U., 1974; hon. degrees, Mt. Holyoke Coll., 1975, Amherst Coll., 1976, York U., Toronto, 1977, U. N.H., 1977, Westfield State Coll., 1979, Mt. St. Vincent U., Halifax, N.S., 1980, Wesleyan U., 1980, U. Mass., 1981, Williams Coll., 1982, Queen's U., 1983, U. Toronto, 1984, McGill U., 1984, Potsdam Coll., SUNY, 1986, Providence Coll., 1987, Smith Coll., 1988, Miami U., 1989, U. Rochester, 1990, Dartmouth Coll., 1990, Notre Dame U., 1990, Manhattanville Coll., 1991, Elms Coll., 1991, Keene State U., 1991, Lake Forest Coll., 1992, Tufts U., 1992, Brock U., 1992, Bentley Coll., 1993. Lectr. history U. Toronto, Ont., Can., 1964-68, asst. prof., 1968-70, assoc. prof., 1970-75, v.p., 1973-75; pres. Smith Coll., Northampton, Mass., 1975-85, Sophia Smith prof., 1975-85; vis. scholar MIT, Boston, 1985—; bd. dirs. Merrill Lynch Co., Arthur D. Little, Inc., Colgate-Palmolive Co., Nike, Inc., Allen Group Inc. Author: The Female Experience in Eighteenth-and Nineteenth-Century America: A Guide to the History of American Women, 1982, Women Reformers and American Culture, 1987, Autobiographies of American Women: An Anthology, 1992, True North, 1994; co-author: The Road From Coorain, 1989; editor: (with Joan Scott and Susan Bourque) Learning About Women, 1989, 1992, (with Susan Bourque) The Politics of Women's Education, 1993; rschr. numerous publs. on Am. social and intellectual history, history of family life and sex roles, and history of edn. Trustee Mt. Holyoke Coll., The Kresge Found., The Knight Found., New Eng. Med. Ctr.; former trustee Clarke Sch. for Deaf, Coll. Retirement Equities Fund, Acad. of Music, Northampton, Hampshire Coll., Northfield Mt. Hermon Sch.; bd. dirs. Ctr. Communications. Mem. Am. Hist. Assn., Can. Hist. Assn., Am. Antiquarian Soc. Home: 65 Commonwealth Ave Boston MA 02116 Office: MIT Program Sci Tech & Soc Cambridge MA 02139

CONWAY, M. MARGARET, political science educator; b. Terre Haute, Ind., May 14, 1935; d. Frank Joseph and Mary Kathryn C. BS in Econs., Purdue U., 1957; MA in Polit. Sci., U. Calif., Berkeley, 1960; PhD in Polit. Sci., Ind. U., 1965. Lectr. to prof. U. Md., College Park, Md., 1963-89; prof. U. Fla., Gainesville, Fla., 1989—. Recipient Disting. Scholar/Tchr. award U.Md., 1985. Mem. Am. Polit. Sci. Assn. (v.p. 1991-92), So. Polit. Sci. Assn. (pres. 1986-87). Office: U Fla PO Box 117325 Gainesville FL 32611-7325

CONWAY, NANCY ANN, publisher, editor; b. Foxboro, Mass., Oct. 15, 1941; d. Leo T. and Alma (Goodwin) C.; children: Ana Lucia DaSilva, Kara Ann Martin. Cert. in med. tech., Carnegie Inst., 1962; BA in English, U. Mass., 1976, cert. in secondary edn., 1978. Tchr. Brazil-Am. Inst., Rio de Janeiro, 1963-68; freelance writer, editor Amherst, Mass., 1972-76; staff writer Daily Hampshire Gazette, North Hampton, Mass., 1976-77; editor Amherst Bull., 1977-80, Amherst Record, 1980-83; features editor Holyoke (Mass.) Transcript/Telegram, 1983-84; gen. mgr. Monday-Thursday Newspapers, Boca Raton, Fla., 1984-87; dir. editorial South Fla. Newspaper Network, Deerfield Beach, 1987-90; pub., editor York (Pa.) Newspapers, Inc., 1990—. Bd. dirs. Math.: Opportunities in Engring., Sci. and Tech.-Pa. State, York, 1991—. Recipient writing awards, state newspaper assns. Mem. Am. Soc. Newspaper Editors, Soc. Profl. Journalists, Pa. Newspaper Pub. Assn. Office: York Newspapers Inc 205 N George St York PA 17401-1107

CONWAY, VIRGINIA MARIE, bank officer; b. Buffalo, Nov. 10, 1961; d. Henry Bernard and Lois Ann (Schneggenburger) McWilliams; m. Vance Philip Conway, Apr. 26, 1986. BS in Acctg. magna cum laude, Canisius Coll., 1983, MBA, 1988. CPA, Md.; cert. mgmt. acct. Staff acct. Goldome Realty Credit Corp., Buffalo, 1983-86; sr. mgmt. acctg. officer Marine Midland Bank, Buffalo, 1986-93, sr. fin. MIS officer, 1993-94, asst. v.p., 1994—. Mem. Inst. Mgmt. Accts., Inst. Cert. Mgmt. Accts., Beta Gamma Sigma, Phi Gamma Nu. Home: 165 Lyndhurst Rd Williamsville NY 14221-6872 Office: Marine Midland Bank 1 Marine Midland Ctr 22nd fl Buffalo NY 14203

CONWELL, ESTHER MARLY, physicist; b. N.Y.C., May 23, 1922; d. Charles and Ida (Korn) C.; m. Abraham A. Rothberg, Sept. 30, 1945; 1 son, Lewis J. B.A., Bklyn. Coll., 1942; M.S., U. Rochester, N.Y., 1945; Ph.D., U. Chgo., 1948; DSc, Bklyn. Coll., 1992. Lectr. Bklyn. Coll., 1946-51; mem. tech. staff Bell Telephone Labs., 1951-52; physicist GTE Labs., Bayside, N.Y., 1952-61; mgr. physics dept. GTE Labs., 1961-72; vis. prof. U. Paris, 1962-63; Abby Rockefeller Mauze prof. M.I.T., 1972; prin. scientist Xerox Corp., Webster, N.Y., 1972-80; research fellow Xerox Corp., 1981—; adj. prof. U. Rochester, 1990—; cons., mem. adv. com. engring. NSF, 1978-81. Author: High Field Transport in Semiconductors, 1967, also research papers; mem. editorial bd. Jour. Applied Physics; Proc. of IEEE; patentee in field. Fellow IEEE, Am. Phys. Soc. (sec.-treas. div. condensed matter physics 1977-82); mem. AAAS, Nat. Acad. Scis., Soc. Women Engrs. (Achievement award 1960), Nat. Acad. Engring. Office: 800 Phillips Rd Webster NY 14580-9720

CONWELL, THERESA GALLO, financial services representative; b. Utica, N.Y., Mar. 6, 1947; d. Ernest and Anna (Caiazzo) Gallo; m. Charles Ray Conwell, Aug. 19, 1978. BS in Edn., SUNY-Potsdam, 1968; MA in Edn., SUNY-Cortland, 1978; Cert. tchr., N.Y.; CLU; chartered fin. cons., registered rep.; ChFc. Tchr. pub. schs., Clinton, N.Y., 1969-78, Portland, Conn., 1978-80; supr. mktg. services Phoenix Mut. Life Ins. Co. (now Home Life Ins. Co.), Hartford, Conn., 1980-82, assoc. mgr. agt. tng., 1982-84, mgr. agt. tng., 1984-85, dir. agt./mgmt. devel., 1985-88, fin. svcs. rep., 1988—; speaker to small bus. orgns., women's groups, N.Y., New Eng., 1986—. Mem. NAFE, NOW, Am. Soc. CLU, Nat. Assn. Life Underwriters, Internat. Assn. Fin. Planners, Hartford Assn. Life Underwriters, Conn. Assn. Life Underwriters, Nat. Assn. Securities Dealers, Nat. Assn. Profl. Saleswomen, Bus. and Profl. Women of Glastonbury (pres.), Pres. Club (assoc. 1991). Democrat. Avocations: tennis, golf, swimming, aerobics, reading. Home: 191 Knollwood Dr Glastonbury CT 06033-1821 Office: Phoenix Home Life Ins Co Commerce Ctr One 333 E River Dr East Hartford CT 06108

CONYARD, SHIRLEY JEAN, college dean; b. Mebane, N.C., Feb. 17, 1940; d. William N. and Thelma (Holt) C. BA, St. John's U., Jamaica, N.Y., 1968; MSW, Fordham U., 1971; MPA, NYU, 1978; DSW, Adelphi U., 1981. Lic. social worker. Rsch. technologist Downstate Med. Ctr., Bklyn., 1959-65; supr. community svcs. Angel Guardian Home, Bklyn., 1968-73; researcher, psychotherapist Jewish Hosp. and Med. Ctr., Bklyn., 1973-79; acad. dean Audrey Cohen Coll., N.Y.C., 1981—; asst. prof. N.Y.C. Tech. Coll., 1982—; cons. Fordham-Tremont Community Mental Health Ctr., Bronx, 1982-90, Dept. HHS, Washington, 1979—, Bklyn. Councilman-at-Large, 1979-82, Peer Rev. for Social Workers, N.Y.C., 1980—. Contbr. articles to profl. jours. Bd. dirs., exec. sec. Bklyn. Haitian Ralph Good Shepherd, 1981—; bd. dirs., pres., chmn. fundraising William Hodson Cmty. Ctr., Bronx, N.Y., 1989—; bd. dirs., trustee program com. United Bronx Parents, Inc., 1990—. Recipient award of courage Samuel J. Tilden High Sch., Bklyn., 1958; grantee Angel Guardian Home, 1969, Adelphi U., 1979, others. Mem. Nat. Assn. Social Workers, Nat. Assn. for Health Svcs. Execs., Assn. for Black Bus. and Profl. Women. Home: 25 Lefferts Ave Brooklyn NY 11225-3905 Office: Audrey Cohen Coll 345 Hudson St New York NY 10014-4502

CONYERS, GAYLE UTSEY, real estate mortgage owner; b. Jacksonville, Fla., Nov. 13, 1936; d. George Emmett and Hazel (Tyler) Utsey; divorced; children: Harrison Edward III, William Emmett. BA in Fashion Merchandising, Fla. State U., 1958. Advt. mgr. Davison's, Augusta, Ga., 1958-59; with advt. dept. Sears, Roebuck & Co., 1959-60, mgr. sportswear/swimwear dept., 1960-63; officer mortgage loans George E. Utsey Sr., Jacksonville, 1963-84, owner, mgr., 1984—. Leader prayer Concerned Women for America; mem. Rep. Nat. Com., Washington, 1986—; mem. exec. com. Rep. Party, Jacksonville, 1987—; exec. com. Christian Coalition, Jacksonville. Avocations: pro-family, pro-Am. ch. activities. Office: 3575 St Johns Ave Jacksonville FL 32205-8494

CONYERS, JEAN LOUISE, city official; b. Memphis, Nov. 10, 1932; d. Marshall Daniel and Jeffie (Ledbetter) Farris; m. James E. Conyers, June 4, 1956 (div.); children: Judith, James Jr., Jennifer. BA, LeMoyne Coll., 1956; MBA, Atlanta U., 1967. Exec. sec. Dept. Zoology, Wash. State U., Pullman, 1958-62, Sch. Bus., Atlanta U., 1965-68; dep. dir., planner Community Action Agy, Terre Haute, Ind., 1968-78, exec. dir., 1978-79; sr. assoc. exec. United Way of Genesee/Lapeer, Flint, Mich., 1980-82; pres., chief exec. officer Conyers & Assocs., Flint, 1982-86, Met. C. of C., Flint, 1986—, Ultimate Learning Systems, Inc., Flint, 1990—; program coord. Greater Flint OIC, 1983-85. Bd. dirs. Urban Coalition, Flint, 1988—, Dort-Oak-Pk. Neighborhood Ho., Flint, 1982—. Recipient Cmty. Svc. award Negro Bus. and Profl. Women, Terre Haute, 1977, Supportive Svcs. award Top Ladies of Distinction, Flint, 1989, Black Caucus Found. of Mich.'s Cmty. Svc. award, 1994, Nat. Negro Bus. and Profl. Women's Club Sojourner Truth award, 1994; named Woman of Distinction for contbns. to minority bus. U. Mich., Flint, Mott Coll., Mayor of Flint, Mich. legis., Mich. Dept. of Labor, 1992; enshrined Zeta Phi Beta Hall of Fame, Flint, 1988. Mem. Kiwanis, Zonta Club of Flint II, Alpha Kappa Alpha (Outstanding Grad. Soror of Great Lakes Region 1992). Office: Met C of C Inc 3306 Flushing Rd Flint MI 48504-4370

COOGAN-SHAFER, MICHELE ANN, elementary school educator; b. Auburn, N.Y., Mar. 13, 1954; d. Howard John and Nancy Jane (Charles) Coogan; m. Robert James Shafer, July 2, 1988; children: Alexander Merritt Coogan Shafer, Claire Rebecca Coogan Shafer. BA in Psychology, William Smith Coll., Geneva, N.Y., 1976; MS in Edn., SUNY, Cortland, 1980. Counselor/instr. Camp Columbus, Auburn, N.Y., 1969-76; elem. tchr. Holland Patent (N.Y.) Schs., 1988-89, Auburn (N.Y.), 1976-88, 89—. Mem. program devel. com. Nat. Women's Edn. and Cultural Ctr., Seneca Falls, N.Y., 1993—; mem. exec. com. Very Spl. Arts Festival, Syracuse, N.Y., 1980-83; bd. dirs. Early Childhood Ctr., 1994; mem. Blue Ribbon com. Seward Sch., 1994-95; mem. Owasco Parent Tchrs., 1976-85, Seward PTO, 1985—, Mothers' March of Dimes, Camillus, N.Y., 1990-95, Diabetes Assn., Camillus, 1992-95, Heart Assn., Camillus, 1993-95, East Hill PTA, 1994—, Friends of Burnett Park Zoo, Syracuse, N.Y., 1993-95. N.Y. State Regents scholar, 1972. Mem. Auburn Tchrs. Assn., N.Y. State United Tchrs., NOW, Hai Timai Sr. Honor Soc. at William Smith Coll. Office: Seward Sch Metcalf Dr Auburn NY 13021

COOK, ANDA SUNA, civil rights advocate; b. Riga, Latvia, Mar. 15, 1935; came to U.S., 1952.; d. Janis Suna and Erna Alexandra (Kletnieks) Sirmais; m. William E. Cook, May 27, 1961; children: Lisa Inara Hamilton, Inta Marie Mitterbach, John William. Student, Augustana Coll., Sioux Falls, S.D., 1954-55, Cleve. State U., 1970-85; MS, Case Western Res. U., 1989. Lic. real estate agt. With Cuyahoga Plan of Ohio, Inc., Cleve., 1976-91, dir. resource devel., 1988-91; exec. dir. Living in Cleve. Ctr., 1992—; v.p. regional div. U.S. Orgn. Internat. Trade, Inc., Cleve., 1989—; price analyst U.S. Steel Corp., Cleve., 1955-62; pres. ASC Cons.-Orgn. Devel., Cleve., 1988; presenter World Latvian Sci. Congress, Riga, 1991. Writer 60 Years of Leage of Women Voters, 1980; writer, prodr. Vol. Affirmative Mktg. Agreement in Action, 1989. Bd. mem. Dept. Human Svcs., Cuayhoga County, 1984-93, Citizens League, 1989—; trustee Friends of Cleve. Met. Housing Authority, Cleve., 1986-92; mem. bd. Cudell Sr. Adv. Coun., 1980-85; mem. Cuyahoga Cmty. Coll. Adv. Bd., 1980—; bd. trustees Citizens League, Cleve., 1989—; chair Young Audiences Vols., 1972-75; legis. chair Cleve. PTA, 1972-73; pres. PTA, Louisa May Alcott Elem. Sch., Cleve., 1971-72; pres. LWV, Cleve., 1975-77. Recipient Dedicated Svc. award The Cuyahoga Plan, Cleve., 1985, Cleve. Leadership award United Way, 1976, Cleve. Area Bd. Realtors Fair Housing award, 1993. Mem. Am. Soc. Tng. and Devel. Democrat. Lutheran. Home: 9801 Lake Ave Cleveland OH 44102-1230 Office: US Orgn Internat Trade Inc 9801 Lake Ave 4d Cleveland OH 44102

COOK, ANGELA DENISE, information systems director; b. Chgo., Oct. 31, 1963; d. Mary Grey; m. Joseph Clinton Cook, Jan. 1, 1989; 1 child, Meaghan Mary. BS in Computer Sci., Northeastern U., Chgo., 1984; MBA, Northwestern U., Evanston, Ill., 1986. Quality assurance mgr. Quality Assurance Inst., Orlando, Fla., 1985—; guest speaker Harold Washington Womens Affairs com., Chgo., 1987. Counselor Rape Victim Adv., Chgo., 1984-88; bd. dirs. Rape Trauma Victim Assistance, Chgo., 1989; adv. at large Chgo. Com. on Homeless, 1988. Democrat. Office: World Access Svc Corp 6600 W Broad St Richmond VA 23230

COOK, ANITA LONNETTE, social worker; b. Monroe, La., July 7, 1956; d. Lonnie Jr. Cook and Ruall Joyce (Jordan) Cook Arrington. BS, So. U., 1979; MSW, U. So. Calif., 1981. Cert. sociala worker, Tex. Med. social worker Tex. Childrens' Hosp., Houston, 1988-90; child placement worker II Harris County Children's Protective Svcs., Houston, 1981-82, child placement worker III, 1982-88, supr., 1990-94; cons. DeFore Group, counseling to elderly, Houston, 1993. Mem. Alpha Delta Mu. Democrat. Roman Catholic. Home: 7522 Gulfbriar Pl Missouri City TX 77489 Office: Harris County Children's Protective Svcs 5100 Southwest Fwy Houston TX 77056

COOK, ANNIS JANE, wellness coordinator; b. Ingleside, Tex., July 12, 1946; d. Jose Lopez and Evangelina (Resendez) Peña; m. John Edward Cook Jr., Oct. 23, 1970; children: John Edward III, Marcus Wayne. AA in Teaching, St. Christopher Coll., 1967; postgrad., South Tex. Coll., 1968. Office mgr. White's Cen. Credit, Houston, 1976-78; adminstrv. sec. Meml. Med. Ctr., Corpus Christi, Tex., 1978-81; adminstr. asst. Tex. Coll. Osteo. Medicine, Corpus Christi, 1981-84; dept. sec. Humana Hosp., Corpus Christi, 1984-85; sales assoc. Goldwater's, Tuscon, 1986-87; unit sec.-staff Univ. Med. Ctr., Tuscon, 1986-88; sec.-coord. Old Tuscon Studios, 1988-90; account exec. Ariz. Stagecoach, Tucson, 1990; wellness coord. Home Depot, Tucson, 1990—; photographer Branded Wild, Tucson, 1989-91; extra Old Tucson Studios, 1989; communications counselor C.C. Osteo. Hosp., Corpus Christi, 1982-84; instr. Red Cross First Aid and CPR; com. mem. Cardio Vascular Task Force. Tchr. Confraternity Christian Doctrine, Ingleside, 1962-70; pres., sec. GI Forum, Corpus Christi, 1965-69; employee co-chair United Way, Tucson, 1990; mem. adv. coun. Internat. Biog. Ctr. Recipient Person of Yr. award Cath. Youth Orgn., 1968, Vol. award Osteo. Care Unit, 1984, 85, Red Cross Torch award, 1992; named one of 2,000 Most Notable Women in Am., 1993. Mem. NAFE, Am. Legion Aux. Democrat. Roman Catholic. Home: 11610 W Desert Wren Dr Tucson AZ 85743-9438 Office: Home Depot 4755 N Oracle Rd Tucson AZ 85705-1641

COOK, BETH MARIE, writer, poet, volunteer; b. Electra, Tex., Jan. 4, 1933; d. Charles Bolivar Allen and Ida Marie (Nelson) Burton; m. William H. Cook, May 30, 1955 (div. Nov. 1981); children: David M., Dianne M. Gleason. Student, Rockmont Coll., 1951-54; BA, Antioch U. West, 1981. County coord. office econ. opportunity Upper Arkansas Coun., Salida, Colo., 1974-76; dir. area agy. on aging Upper Arkansas Coun./Dept. Social Svcs., State of Colo., 1976-80; specialist community devel. Mountain Plains Congress Sr. Orgns., Denver, 1980-82; sr. adminstrv. asst. Digital Rsch. Inc., Monterey, Calif., 1983-85, asst. to pres., 1985-87, retail rep., 1987-88; co-owner, ptnr. Scotia Gallery, Monterey, 1983-86; COO MiniSoft, Inc., Phoenix, 1988-89; property mgr. Parklane Arms Apts., 1989-92; exec. asst. Ft. Collins (Colo.) Housing Authority, 1989-92, occupancy specialist, 1992-95; vol. Peace Corps, 1995—; hostess Sr. Sound-Off show, Sta. KVRH-AM/FM, Salida, 1978-80; cons. Devel. Assocs. Inc., Denver, 1982. Author: (poem) Jessie, 1989-90. Coord. crisis intervention line Chaffee County Cmty. Crisis Ctr., Salida, 1976-80; committeewoman Chafee County Dem. Ctrl. Com., Salida, 1979-80; speaker, program com. Colo. Gov.'s Conf. on Aging, Denver, 1980; docent Lincoln Ctr.; vol. food distbn. SHARE; mem. bd. dirs. Project Self-Sustaining. Recipient Human Devel. Svc. award HHS, 1980, Golden Poet award, 1989; named Woman of Yr. Chaffee County Bus. and Profl. Women's Club, 1978. Mem. NAFE, Am. Assn. Ret. Persons, Nat. Notary Assn., Nat. Mus. Women in Arts, World Soc. Poetry. Presbyterian.

COOK, BETTE JEAN, health facility business office manager; b. Bluefield, W.Va., Mar. 7, 1961; d. John William and Vera Louis (Wetzel) Cook; m. Stephen Bryan Divers, Sept. 8, 1984 (div. Nov. 1989); m. Donald William Currence, Aug. 17, 1991 (div. May, 1993). BS in Mktg. Mgmt., Va. Tech., 1983. Claims processor Blue Cross of South West Va., Roanoke, Va., 1984-85; telemarketer External Degree Svcs., Roanoke, Va., 1985; data entry clk. Va. Tech. U. Libr., Blacksburg, Va., 1985-86; ins. clk. GMAC, Fairfax, Va., 1986; office mgr. Domino's Pizza, Reston, Va., 1986-88; bus. mgr. Riley Bros., Inc., Charlottesville, Va., 1988-91, Heritage Hall Nursing Home, Charlottesville, Va., 1991—.

COOK, CATHERINE COGHLAN, lawyer; b. Chgo., Jan. 25, 1934; d. John Patrick and Catherine Marie (Lyons) Coghlan; m. Bruce A. Cook, Dec. 5, 1956 (div. 1982); children: Robert, Catherine, Cecilia. BA, Loyola U., Chgo., 1954, MA, 1960; JD, George Washington U., 1974; LLM, Georgetown U., 1975. Bar: Md. 1974, D.C. 1975, Ill. 1991. Instr., lectr. Loyola U., Chgo., 1960-67, George Washington U., Washington, 1968-71; trial atty. U.S. Consumer Product Safety Commn., Washington, 1975-83; asst. gen. counsel, dep. gen. counsel Dept. Energy, Washington, 1983-86; gen. counsel, spl. counsel Fed. Energy Regulatory Commn., Washington, 1986-91; gen. counsel U.S. Railroad Retirement Bd., Chgo., 1991—. Ford Found. fellow, 1974-75. Office: US Railroad Retirement Bd 844 N Rush St Chicago IL 60611

COOK, CATHY WELLES, state legislator; b. New London, Conn.. BA, Conn. Coll.; postgrad., U. R.I., U. Conn., U. Mass. Mem. Groton Bd. of Edn., 1983-91; chmn. adv. coun. State Dept. Mental Retardation, Region 6, 1984—; mem. Eastern Conn. Long Island Sound Commn., 1990-92, Conn. State Senate, Hartford, 1993—. Republican. Office: Conn State Senate State Capitol Hartford CT 06106 Address: 8 W Mystic Ave Mystic CT 06355-2329*

COOK, CYNTHIA ELLEN, advertising copywriter; b. Dallas, Apr. 21, 1961; d. Richard Joseph and Ada Belle (Gordie) C. BA, E. Tex. State U., 1983; attended, U. N. Tex. Sr. editor Dallas Mag., 1983-88; sr. copywriter Rapp Collins Worldwide, Dallas, 1988-92, Temerlin McClain, Dallas, 1992-94. Patron Dallas Mus. Art; mem. Dallas County Dem. Ctrl. Com., Dem. Nat. Com. Recipient Gold Echo award Direct Mktg. Assn., 1992. Mem. Women in Direct Mktg. Orthodox Christian. Home: 7151 Gaston Ave Apt 908 Dallas TX 75214-6105

COOK, DIERDRE RUTH GOORMAN, English language educator; b. Denver, Nov. 4, 1956; d. George Edward and Avis M. (Wilson) Goorman; m. Donald Robert Cook, Apr. 4, 1981; 1 child, Christen. BA in Theatre Arts, Colo. State U., 1980, postgrad. Cert. secondary tchr. Tchr. Centennial High Sch., Fort Collins, Colo., 1983-87; educator Poudre High Sch., Fort Collins, 1987—; curriculum devel. com. Poudre R-1 Sch. Dist., Ft. Collins, 1984—, instrnl. improvement com., 1985—, trainer positive power leadership, 1986-87, profl. devel. com., 1994—; comm. cons. Woodward Gov. Co., Ft. Collins, 1991, 92; evaluation visitation team North Ctrl. Evaluation, Greeley, Colo., 1991; dir. student activities Poudre H.S. Campaign worker Rep. Party, Littleton, Colo., 1980, Ft. Collins, 1984, 88; mem. Colo. Juvenile Coun., Ft. Collins, 1986, 88, loaned exec., 1987; bd. dirs. Youth Unltd., 1994—; mem. Leadership Ft. Collins; troop leader Girl Scouts U.S., 1991—. NEH scholar, 1992; named Disting. Tchr. 1993 Colo. Awards Coun.; recipient Tchr. Excellence award Poudre High Sch., 1992. Mem. ASCD, NEA, Colo. Edn. Assn., Poudre Edn. Assn. (rep. 1989, 90, 91), Nat. Speech Comm. Assn., Nat. Forensics League (degree for outstanding distinction 1992), Nat. PTO, Nat. Platform Soc., Kappa Kappa Gamma (pres. 1985-90). Home: 1600 Burlington Ct Fort Collins CO 80525 Office: Poudre R-1 Sch Dist 201 Impala Dr Fort Collins CO 80521

COOK, DORIS MARIE, accountant, educator; b. Fayetteville, Ark., June 11, 1924; d. Ira and Mettie Jewel (Dorman) C. BS in Bus. Adminstrn., U. Ark., 1946, MS, 1949; PhD, U. Tex., 1969. CPA, Okla., Ark. Jr. acct. Haskins & Sells, Tulsa, 1946-47; instr. acctg. U. Ark., Fayetteville, 1947-52, asst. prof., 1952-62, assoc. prof., 1962-69, prof., 1969-88, Univ. prof. and Nolan E. Williams lectr. in acctg., 1988—; mem. Ark. State Bd. Pub. Accountancy, 1987-92, treas., 1989-91, vice chmn. 1991-92; mem. Nat. Assn. State Bds. of Accountancy, 1987-92; appointed Nolan E. Williams lectureship in acctg., 1988—. Mem. rev. bd. Ark. Bus. Rev., Jour. Managerial Issues; contbr. articles to profl. jours. Mem. Ark. Bus. Assn. (editor newsletter 1982-85), Am. Acctg. Assn. (chair nat. membership 1982-83, chair Arthur Carter Scholarship com. 1984-85, chair membership Ark. 1985-87), Am. Inst. CPAs, Am. Women's Soc. CPAs, Ark. Soc. CPAs (v.p. 1975-76, pres. NW Ark. chpt. 1980-81, sec. Student Loan Found. 1981-84, treas. Student Loan Found. 1984-92, pres. Student Loan Found. 1992—, chair pub. rels. 1984-88, 93-95, Outstanding Acctg. Educator award 1991), Acad. Acctg. Historians (trustee 1985-87, mem. rev. bd. of Working Papers Series 1984-92, sec. 1992-95, pres.-elect 1995), Ark. Fedn. Bus. and Profl. Women's Clubs (treas. 1979-80), Mortar Bd., Beta Gamma Sigma, Beta Alpha Psi (editor nat. newsletter 1973-77, nat. pres. 1977-78), Phi Gamma Nu, Alpha Lambda Delta, Delta Kappa Gamma (sec. 1976-78, pres. 1978-80, treas. 1989—), Phi Kappa Phi. Club: Fayetteville Bus. and Profl. Women's (pres. 1973-74, 75-76, Woman of Yr. 1977). Home: 1115 N Leverett Ave Fayetteville AR 72703-1622 Office: U Ark Dept Acctg Fayetteville AR 72701

COOK, ELLEN PIEL, counseling psychology educator; b. Woodbury, N.J., Sept. 28, 1952; married; children. BA summa cum laude in Psychology and Social Work, U. Toledo, 1973; PhD in Counseling Psychology, U. Iowa, 1977. Asst. prof. counseling psychology U. Nebr.-Lincoln, 1977-78; from asst. prof. to prof. counseling U. Cin., 1978—, dir. counseling program, 1984-86, 94—; contract psychologist Mental Health Svcs. W., Cin., 1987-91. Author: Psychological Androgyny, 1985; editor: Women, Relationships, and Power: Implications for Counseling, 1993. Active numerous community projects related to counseling. Mem. ACA (mem. 3 editorial bds.), APA (2 editorial bds.), Phi Lambda Theta, Phi Kappa Phi. Democrat. Episcopalian. Office: U Cin Divsn Human Svcs 527 Tchrs Coll Cincinnati OH 45221-0002

COOK, FRANCES D., diplomat; b. Charleston, W.Va., Sept. 7, 1945; d. Nash and Vivian Cook. B.A., Mary Washington Coll. of U. Va., 1967; M.P.A., Harvard U., 1978. Certificats d'Etudes, Université d'Aix-Marseille (France), 1966. Commd. fgn. svc. officer Dept. State, 1967; spl. asst. to R.S. Shriver amb. to France, Paris, 1968-69; mem. U.S. Del. Paris Peace Talks on Viet-Nam, 1970-71; cultural affairs officer, consul Am. Consul Gen., Sydney, Australia, 1971-73; cultural affairs officer, first sec. Am. Embassy, Dakar, Senegal, 1973-75; personnel officer for Africa USIA, Washington, 1975-77; dir. office public affairs African Bur. Dept. State, Washington, 1978-80; amb. to Republic of Burundi Dept. State, Bujumbura, 1980-83; consul gen. Dept. State, Alexandria, Egypt, 1983-86; dep. asst. sec. of state Dept. State, Washington, 1986-87, dir. Office of West African Affairs, 1987-89; amb. to Cameroon Dept. State, Yaoundé, 1989-93; U.S. coord. for Sudan Dept. State, 1993; dep. asst. sec. of state Dept. of State, Washington, 1993—. Recipient various honor awards Dept. State. Mem. AAUW, Am. Fgn. Svc. Assn., Am. Polit. Sci. Assn., Coun. on Fgn. Rels., Washington Alumni Coun. Kennedy Sch. Harvard U., Harvard Club of N.Y.C., Army-Navy Club/Washington, Phi Beta Kappa (alumni). Office: Pol Mil Affairs Bur 2201 C St NW Washington DC 20520

COOK, JUANITA KIMBELL, library director, educator; b. Pine Bluff, Ark., Aug. 25, 1948; d. Andrew Jackson and Queen Esther (Day) Kimbell; m. Curtis Lee Cook, Nov. 25, 1970; children: Melanie LaJune, Reginald, Cheryl Nicole. BS, U. Ark., Pine Bluff, 1970; MLS, Ball State U., 1972. Reference libr. Colorado Coll./Penrose Pub., Colorado Springs, 1971, Longview Community Coll., Lee's Summit, Mo., 1973-77; dir. IMC, instr. U. Ark., Pine Bluff, 1977-80; libr. Russellville Pub. Schs., Russellville, Ark., 1981-85, Arkadelphia Pub. Schs., Arkadelphia, Ark., 1985-87; libr. dir. Learning Resources Ctr., So. Ark. U., Camden, 1987—, asst. prof., 1987-92, assoc. prof., 1992—. Pres. Ouachita-Calhoun County Literacy, Camden, 1988-89. Danforth Found. fellow, 1970, Nat. Black Studies Ins. fellow, 1989. Mem. ALA, Ark. Libr. Assn., Nat. Assn. Female Execs., Nat. Assn. Devel. Edn., Internat. Reading Assn., Zeta Phi Beta. Democrat. Apostolic. Office: So Ark U Tech Tech Sta Camden AR 71701

COOK, JUDITH ELIZABETH, artist, educator; b. Meriden, Conn., Apr. 3, 1956; d. George and Stasia Patricia (Rynaski) C.; m. Roger R. Bell, June 21, 1992. Student, Heatherly Sch. Art, London, 1977; BS, So. Conn. State U., 1978; MFA, Ariz. State U., 1987. Instr. Indian River Arts Ctr., Milford, Conn., 1978-81; tchr. Shelton (Conn.) Jr. High Sch., 1979-80, Stratford (Conn.) Pub. Schs., 1980-82; asst. advt. prodn. mgr. Soundings Publs., Essex, Conn., 1982-84; graphic prodn. artist Axia Corp., Phoenix, 1987; dir. Mendenhall Gallery Whittier (Calif.) Coll., 1987-88; instr. graphic design program Platt Coll., Cerritos, Calif., 1989-90, curriculum coord., faculty coord. graphic design program, 1991-92; mem. adj. faculty, teaching asst. Ariz. State U., Tempe, 1985, 86; vis. assoc. prof. Whittier Coll., 1987-88; mem. vis. faculty ceramic dept. Calif. State U., Long Beach, 1988-89; mem. adj. faculty interior and fashion design depts. Brooks Coll., Long Beach, 1988-94; mem. adj. faculty fine art and interior design depts. Chapman U., Palm Desert, Calif., 1991—; mem. adj. faculty fine art dept. Coll. of the Desert, Palm Desert, 1991-94, asst. prof. art, 1994—; presenter in field, 1980—; freelance graphic artist, 1981-90; archtl. restorer pvt. homes, 1980-90, mural painter, 1989. One-woman shows include System M Gallery, Long Beach, 1988, 89, Frostburg (Md.) State U., 1991; exhibited in group shows, 1980—, including Mill Gallery, Guilford, Conn., 1981, U. Tex., San Antonio, 1986, Ariz. State U., 1985, 87, 91, 92, Downey (Calif.) Mus., 1989, 94, Miles Mus., Portales, N.Mex., 1992, Edward Dean Mus., Cherry Valley, Calif., 1993, Signature Gallery, San Diego, 1993, 94, Med. Coll. Ga., Augusta, 1994, San Fedele Gallery, Milan, 1994, Centro Espositivo della Rocca Paolina, Perugia, Italy, 1995; represented in permanent collections So. Conn. State U., Ariz. State U. Nelson Fine Arts Mus. Study grantee Du Bois Found., 1985-87, travel grantee, 1986; profl. devel. grantee Coll. of the Desert, 1993. Mem. Nat. Coun. for Edn. in Ceramic Arts. Office: Coll of Desert Divsn Fine Art 43500 Monterey Ave Palm Desert CA 92260

COOK, LAURA PULA, lawyer; b. N.Y.C., Dec. 19, 1955; d. Lawrence Joseph and Elizabeth Theresa (Good) Pula; m. Thomas Anthony Cook, Feb. 6, 1988. BA in English, Stanford U., 1977; MS in Journalism, Columbia U., 1980, JD, 1981. Bar: N.Y. 1983, Fla. 1983, Calif. 1990. Assoc. atty. Paul & Thomson, Miami, Fla., 1982; atty. Thomson Zeder Bohrer Werth & Razook (formerly Paul & Thomson), Miami, 1983-88; consulting atty. Sun Networks, Inc., Tampa, Fla., 1989; counsel 20th Century Fox, L.A., 1990-91, sr. counsel, 1991-92, v.p., 1992-93, sr. v.p., 1993—; owner Cook's Café, Cedar Key, Fla., 1988-89. Rotary scholar Rotary Internat., 1982-83. Office: 20th Century Fox PO Box 900 Beverly Hills CA 90213

COOK, LEANN CECILIA, paralegal; b. Wheeling, W.Va., Oct. 14, 1950; d. Leo Elbin Cook and Phyllis Marie (Bargiel) Cook-Allen. Cert. in computers and computer programming, Contemporary Inst., Pitts., 1971; student, Ohio U., 1979-81; Paralegal Cert., Am. Inst. Paralegal Studies, Inc., North Canton, Ohio, 1986. Computer operator Riechart's Furniture Co., Wheeling, 1971-72, Wheeling Machine Products Co., 1972-74; data technician Belmont Tech. Coll., St. Clairsville, Ohio, 1974-76; adminstrv. asst. Belmont County Treas. Office, St. Clairsville, 1977-87; paralegal specialist Office of Dist. Counsel VA, Lexington, Ohio, 1987-88; fin. litigation agt. U.S. Atty.'s Office, Columbus, 1988-90; office mgr. Streski Reporting Svc., Martins Ferry, 1990; legal practice St. Clairsville, Ohio, 1990—; data processing instr. adult edn. Belmont Joint Vocat. Sch., St. Clairsville, 1974-79; seminar speaker Profl. Edn. Svcs., Inc., 1993—, others; cons. Paralegal Cons. Assn., N.Y.C., 1993—; mem. Akron region U.S. Postal Consumer Adv. Coun.; personal injury paralegal faculty mem. P.E.S.I., Eau Claire, Wis., 1993. Author compilation Personal Injury Paralegal manual, 1993. Mem. pub. rels. com., Tri-County Task Force for Sexual Abuse, St. Clairsville, 1985-86; mem. Women's Crisis Ctr., St. Clairsville, 1986, St. Clairsville's Bus. and Profl. Women, 1986-87; coord. fed. women's program So. Dist. Ohio, Columbus, 1989; vol. amb. Chinese Imperial Arts Program, Columbus, 1989. Mem. St. Clairsville Law Libr. Assn., Columbus Bar Assn., Ohio State Bar Assn. Independent. Orthodox. Home and Office: PO Box 156 Saint Clairsville OH 43950-0156

COOK, LISA ANN, small business owner; b. Santa Monica, Calif., May 9, 1962; d. Donald George and Bertha Sophia (Krueger) Oliphant; m. Daniel Cook, Nov. 1, 1986 (div.); children: Tyler Donald, Jasmin Danniel. Student, Rouge C.C., Grants Pass, Oreg., 1979-81. Park maintenance worker Josephine County Youth Program, Grants Pass, 1976; mgr. Black Forest Restaurant, Grants Pass, 1977-80; restaurant mgr. Drowsey Maggies, San Diego, 1980-81; mgr. Birkenstock San Diego, 1981-94; ptnr., owner Island Birkenstock, Coronado, Calif., 1993—; wholesale buyer Island Birkenstock; design cons. Zeeta Shoes, Napa, Calif., 1993. Office: Island Birkenstock 1350 Orange Ave Coronado CA 92118

COOK, MARY KIMBERLY, medical-surgical/telemetry nurse; b. Johnstown, Pa., Aug. 13, 1967; d. Donald Elliot and Antoinette Linda Murphy; m. Arthur Franklin Cook III, Feb. 15, 1992; children: Jennifer Marie, Dustin, Kimberly. BSN, Indiana U. Pa., 1989. Staff nurse med./surg. unit Lee Hosp., Johnstown, Pa., 1989—. Home: RD 1 Box 91 South Fork PA 15956 Office: Lee Hosp 320 Main St Johnstown PA 15902

COOK, MARY MARGARET, steamfitter; b. Royal Oak, Mich., Apr. 28, 1944; d. John Patrick and Agnes Hannah (Anderson) McMahon; m. Barney Albert Cahill, Aug. 19, 1967 (div. Apr. 1971); m. Frank Melvin Cook, Jan. 26, 1974. BA in Elem. Edn., Ariz. State U., 1971; cert. United Assn. instr., Mich. State U., 1990; Cert., Ariz. Community Coll. Cert. elem. tchr., Ohio, Ariz.; lic. mech. journeyman. Tchr. St. Agnes Elem. Sch., Phoenix, 1967-71, Bevis Elem. Sch., Cin., 1971-73; GED instr. Scottsdale, Ariz., 1975-78; steamfitter United Assn. Local 469, Phoenix, 1978—; instr. apprentices Rio Salado C.C., Phoenix, 1984-90; math. cons. Ariz. Dept. Edn., 1988-90; state dir. AFL-CIO Apprenticeship Awareness Program, 1990-92. Chair State Com. Emerging Careers for Women; mem. Apprenticeship Adv. Coun., 1990—, Gov.'s Commn. on Nontraditional Employment for Women; Ariz. dir. Project Nontraditional Assistance and Info. Link, 1992—. Mem. Ariz.

State U. Alumni Assn. (life), Internat. Tng. in Comm. Club (sec. 1988-89, pres. 1989-90, del. to coun. 1990-91, coun. v.p. 1992-93, coun. newsletter editor 1991-92, region newsletter editor 1994-95). Home: 15827 N 23rd Dr Phoenix AZ 85023-4136

COOK, NANCY W., state legislator; b. May 11, 1936. Ed. U. Del. Mem. Del. Senate from 15th Dist.; mem. Kent County Dem. Com. Democrat. Home: PO Box 127 Kenton DE 19955-0127 Office: Del State Senate Legislative Hall Dover DE 19901*

COOK, PAMELA ALCYON REBECCA, fundraiser; b. New Brunswick, N.J., Mar. 14, 1955; d. Richard Cairns and Winifred Louise (Imhof) C.; m. Paul Conrad Gietzel, May 12, 1979; 1 child, Kevin Cook Gietzel. BA in Polit. Sci., Duke U., 1977; postgrad., Australian Nat. U., Canberra, 1978; MA in Fgn. Affairs, U. Va., 1981. Pub. affairs asst. Hoover Instn., Stanford, Calif., 1981-83; campaign assoc. United Way of Santa Clara (Calif) County, 1983-85, campaign divsn. dir., 1984-85; dir. engring. fund Stanford (Calif.) U., 1985-87, dir. individual giving Sch. Engring., 1987-92; assoc. dean devel. Arts and Scis. U. Va., Charlottesville, 1992—. Interview panelist Hewlett-Packard Scholarship, Palo Alto, Calif., 1985—; vol. Big Bros./Big Sisters, Inc., Palo Alto, 1982-92; mem. alumni interview program Duke U., Durham, N.C., 1981—; pers. solicitation vol. Stanford U., 1992—; mem. Leadership Charlottesville, 1994. Fulbright scholar, Australian Edn. Found., 1977-78, Panhellenic scholar, Duke U., 1976. Mem. Pub. Rels. Soc. Am., Coun. for Advancement of Sci. and Edn., Fulbright Alumni Assn., Duke U. Alumni Assn., U. Va. Alumni Assn., Pi Sigma Alpha. Home: 1905 N Pantops Dr Charlottesville VA 22901 Office: U Va 419 Cabell Hall Charlottesville VA 22903

COOK, PEGGY JO, psychotherapist, consultant; b. Greenville, Miss., Jan. 2, 1931; d. Bertram R. Coffing and Mary Josephine (Rodgers) McCarthy; m. Jack Storey Cook, July 15, 1951 (div. 1969); children: Bill S., Paul K., Monte C., Carol Rose Doss. BS in Psychology, SUNY-Albany, 1979; MEd in Counseling, North Tex. State U., 1980, PhD in Counseling and Student Svcs., 1987. Co-owner, mgr. Elec. Contracting, Co., Ft. Worth, 1952-68; co-founder, dir. Family Counseling Ctr., Ctr. for Creative Living, Ft. Worth, 1968—, psychotherapist, co-dir., 1980—. Mem. Am. Counseling Assn., So. Assn. Counselor Edn. and Supervision, Tex. Counseling Assn., Greater Fort Worth Bd. Realtors. Avocations: grandchildren, antiques, skiing, landscaping. Office: 2401 Oakland Blvd # 100 Fort Worth TX 76103-3240

COOK, SHARON EVONNE, university official; b. Pocatello, Idaho, July 16, 1941; d. Willard Robert and Marian (Bartlett) Leisy; m. John Fred Cook, June 19, 1971 (div. Nov. 1980). BEd, No. Mont. Coll., 1970; M in Secondary Edn., U. Alaska, Juneau, 1980; EdD, U. San Francisco, 1987. Cert. secondary sch. tchr., Alaska. Loan officer 1st Nat. Bank, Havre, Mont., 1964-68; adminstrv. asst. Alaska State Legis., Juneau, 1970-71; tchr. Juneau Dist. High Sch., 1971-75; instr. Juneau Dist. Community Coll., 1975-79; assoc. prof. U. Alaska, Juneau, 1979-90, dean Sch. Bus. and Pub. Adminstrn., 1986-90; assoc. dean Coll. Tech., Boise (Idaho) State U., 1990—; editor in chief office tech. McGraw Hill Book Gregg Div., N.Y.C., 1983-84; mem. exec. bd. statewide assembly U. Region V Vocat. Assn., 1978-80, del. 1982. Treas. Alaska State Vocat. Assn., 1980-82, pres.-elect, 1986, pres., 1987; pres. U. Alaska Juneau Assembly, 1978-80, v.p., 1980-82. No. Mont. Coll. scholar, Havre, 1968-70; named Outstanding Tchr., U. Alaska, 1976. Republican. Home: 2551 S Swallowtail Ln Boise ID 83706-6130 Office: Boise State U Coll Tech Assoc Dean's Office 1910 University Dr Boise ID 83725-0001

COOK, STACEY ANN, accountant; b. Neptune, N.J., Aug. 24, 1964; d. J. Philip and Rosemary C. (Read) C. BS, Bucknell U., 1985. CPA, N.J. Staff acct. Mortenson, Fleming, Grizzetti & Boiko, Cranford, N.J., 1986; acct. Gentile, Weiner, Penta & Co., Oakhurst, N.J., 1986-88; sr. tax acct. Pinsker Goldberg & Co., Lakewood, N.J., 1989-93; supr. Levine, Mandelbaum, Neider Wohl, N.Y.C., 1993. Mem. AICPA, N.J. Soc. Cert. Pub. Accts. Home: 380G Joe Parker Rd Lakewood NJ 08701-3858 Office: Levine Mandelbaum Neider Wohl 230 Park Ave New York NY 10169-0004

COOK, SUSAN FARWELL, alumni relations director; b. Boston, Apr. 28, 1953; d. Benjamin and Beverly (Brooks) Conant; m. James Samuel Cook Jr., Aug. 17, 1985; children: Emily Farwell, David McKendree. AB, Colby Coll., 1975. Bank teller Boston 5 Cent Savs. Bank, 1975-76; asst. technician plan cost John Hancock Mut. Life Ins. Co., Boston, 1976-77, technician plan cost, 1977-78, sr. technician plan cost, 1978-79, asst. mgr. group pension plan cost, 1979-81; assoc. dir. alumni rels. Colby Coll., Waterville, Maine, 1981-86; dir. alumni rels. Colby Coll., Waterville, 1986—; co-dir. adv. bd. women's studies Colby Coll., 1987-89, adv. women's group, 1987-89. Bd. dirs., newsletter sec. Literacy Vols. Maine, Waterville, 1986-89, 91-92; bd. dirs. Congress Lake Assns., Yarmouth, Maine, 1988-92; treas. Pitcher Pond Improvement Assn., 1988—. Mem. AAUW (sec. Waterville br. 1989-91, pres. 1991-93, co-pres. 1993—), Coun. Advancement and Support of Edn., CASE Dist. I (exec. bd. dirs. 1994—). Home: 6 Pray Ave Waterville ME 04901 Office: Colby Coll Mayflower Hill Waterville ME 04901

COOK, SYBILLA AVERY, school library consultant; b. Buffalo, Aug. 20, 1930; d. Edward Carrington and Elizabeth (Boorum) Avery; m. John D. Cook, June 12, 1951; children: Harold John, Robert Sherman, Raymond Avery. BS, Northwestern U., 1951; MLS, Rosary Coll., River Forest, Ill., 1968; MA, U. Oreg., 1982. Cert. ednl. media tchr. and supr., Oreg., Ill. Tchr. Glenview (Ill.) Pub. Schs., 1951; librarian Deerfield (Ill.) Pub. Schs., 1968-69; media specialist Des Plaines (Ill.) Pub. Schs., 1969-76; librarian Dillard (Oreg.) Pub. Schs., 1976-78; libr. media specialist Glide (Oreg.) Pub. Schs., 1978-90; sch. libr. cons., Roseburg, Oreg., 1986—; adj. instr. Western Oreg. State Coll., Monmouth, 1988-93; mem. libr. info. skills com. Oreg. Dept. Edn., 1987. Author: Instructional Design for Libraries, 1986; (with Cheryl Page) Battles, and Bees, 1994; contbr. articles to profl. jours. Recipient Gandalf award Douglas County Libr. System, 1994. Mem. ALA, AAUW, Am. Assn. Sch. Librs., Authors Guild, Lan Douglas Regional Libr. Assn. (chmn. 1982-84), Oreg. Ednl. Media Assn. (exec. bd. 1987—, Tchr. of Yr. 1984), Soc. Children's Book Writers, Beta Phi Mu. Home and Office: 19 N River Dr Roseburg OR 97470-9473

COOK, VIRGILENE HEDWIG, secondary school educator; b. Kansas City, Mo., June 30, 1949; d. Virgil Anton and Hedwig Catherine (Groner) Bartels; m. Roger Dale Cook, Oct. 7, 1972; children: Brad Lee, Ryan Scott, Heather Ann. BS in Edn., Ctrl. Mo. State U., 1972. Tchr. Hume (Mo.) Elem. Sch., 1971-72, Montrose (Mo.) Elem. Sch., 1972-73, Adrian (Mo.) H.S., 1973-79; tchr. bus. and computers Lakeland H.S., Deepwater, Mo., 1980—. Mem., chmn. Parish Coun. Cath. Women, Clinton (Mo.) Vocat.-Tech. Adv. Coun.; lay min. Holy Rosary Cath. Ch.; project leader Clinton Cool Cats 4-H Club. Mem. Mo. Tchrs. Assn. (Outstanding Educator award 1993), Mo. Vocat. Assn. (del. bus. sect. 1983—), Lakeland Cmty. Tchrs. Assn. (past treas.), Clinton Bus. and Profl. Women's Club (chmn. various coms. 1988—), Beta Sigma Phi (treas. Omicron Psi chpt. 1992-94). Home: 506 David Dr Clinton MO 64735 Office: Lakeland HS Rt 1 Box 230 1 Deepwater MO 64740-9732

COOK, VIRGINIA INCAO, librarian; b. Bklyn., Aug. 23, 1937; d. Philip Peter and Anne Marie (Ruisi) Incao; m. Richard Alan Cook, Nov. 28, 1959; children: Julie Marie, Anne Alexandra, Peter Alan. BA, Mt. Holyoke Coll., 1959; MSLS, L.I. U., 1979. Asst. libr. North Shore Univ. Hosp., Manhasset, N.Y., 1978-80; head libr., dir. Winthrop Univ. Hosp./Hollis Health Scis. Libr., Mineola, N.Y., 1980—. Contbr. articles to profl. jours. Bd. dirs. Port Washington (N.Y.) Children's Ctr., 1985—. Mem. Med. Libr. Assn. (advt. chair N.Y./N.J. chpt. 1990-93), Spl. Libr. Assn., Med. Sci. Libr. L.I., Acad. Health Info. Profls. (disting. mem.). Office: Winthrop Univ Hosp 259 1st St Mineola NY 11501-3987

COOK, VIVIAN, state legislator; b. Rock Hill, S.C., May 23, 1937; d. McDonald Eaves and Eva Phillips; m. John Cook; 1 child, Reginald. Grad., DeFrans Bus. Inst. Mem. alcoholism and drug abuse, commerce, industry and econ. devel., corps., authorities and commns., housing, ins., majority steering coms. N.Y. State Assembly, Albany, 1991—; dist. leader, Queens County; founder Cmty. Edn. Resource Ctr.; chairwoman Queens County Dem. Com.; mem. Dem. Nat. Com., Queens County Exec. Com.; del. Dem. Nat. Conv., 1988, 92. Recipient Sojourner Truth award Nat. Assn. Negro Bus. and Profl. Women's Club, Inc., Sr. Citizens award 113th Precinct, Cmty. Svc. award 103 and 113th Precincts, Sutphin Blvd. Civic Assn. award, Cmty. Svc. award Citizens for Jenkins, 10-Yr. Cmty. Bd. Svc. award City of N.Y., Cmty. Svc. award Neighborhood Coun., Mother's Day award Springfield Gardens, Commn. Svc. & Leadership award NYS Martin Luther King, Jr. Inst., Polit. Action Com. award P.E.F., Little League award Rochdal Village. Mem. Allied Regular Dem. Club, Inc. (founder, exec.), South Ozone Park Women's Assn. (founder, chairperson bd. dirs.). Home: 14215 Rockaway Blvd S Ozone Park NY 11436-1420 Office: NY State Assembly State Capitol Albany NY 12224*

COOK, WILLIE CHUNN, elementary school educator; b. Uriah, Ala., Feb. 3, 1935; d. Thompson Ann and Minnie Lee (Jay) Chunn; m. Clifford Thomas Cook, Feb. 3, 1974; children: Wendelin Martin Smith, Melanie Martin. BS, Livingston U., 1956, MEd, 1972. Elem. tchr. Jefferson County Pub. Sch. System, Birmingham, Ala., 1956-58, Mobile County Pub. Sch. System, Mobile, Ala., 1958-60, Norfolk (Va.) City Pub. Sch. System, 1960-61, Mobile County Pub. Sch. System, 1961-66, Pinellas County Pub. Sch. System, Clearwater, Fla., 1966-73; mid. sch. sci. tchr. St. Bernard Pub. Sch. System, Chalmette, La., 1973-76; elem. tchr. Jefferson Parish Pub. Sch. System, Gretna, La., 1976—; mem. system textbook adoption com. Pinellas County pub. Sch. System, Clearwater, 1970, Jefferson Parish Pub. Sch. System, Gretna, 1978-79; coordinating tchr. Yearly Sch. Sci. Fairs, Pinellas County, Fla., 1969-72, Jefferson Parish, La., 1981-92, yearly extended class field trips, Jefferson Parish, 1984-92; sponsor Jefferson Parish Nat. Acad. Games teams, 1981-85; workshop presenter. Treas. Caddo Presbytery Cumberland Presbyn. Women, Marshall, Tex., 1982-83; chmn. Faith Ch. Cumberland Presbyn. Women, Kenner, La., 1980; mem. Christian edn. com. Faith Cumberland Presbyn. Ch., Metairie, La., 1988—; com. on polit. effectiveness Jefferson Fedn. Tchrs., coun. mem. 1987-89, chmn. Ednl. Issues Com. 1987-89, mem. Govs. Edn. Adv. Com. 1987-88, lobbyist in state legis., Jefferosn Parish, and Baton Rouge, 1985-88. Mem. Am. Fedn. Tchrs., La. Fedn. Tchrs., Jefferson Fedn. Tchrs., Nat. Sci. Tchrs. Assn., La. Sci. Tchrs. Assn. Democrat. Home: 25 Trinidad Dr Kenner LA 70065 Office: Chateau Estates Elem Sch 4121 Medoc Dr Kenner LA 70065

COOKE, ALTHEA CAROL, writer, educator; b. Cabarrus County, N.C., May 28, 1935; d. William Lew and Rexie (Fields) Phillips; m. Sidney B. Cooke, June 13, 1953; children: Nathan B., John N. BA cum laude, Meredith Coll., 1957; MFA, U. N.C., Greensboro, 1977. Art and English tchr. various secondary schs., Cabarrus City, N.C., 1957-67; adj. prof. U. N.C., Charlotte, 1988-92; former dir. art workshops for tchrs.; former judge art exhbns. Author: Through a Glass Darkly: The Story of Eleanor of Aquitaine, 1990. Bd. dirs. N.C. PTA, Raleigh, 1963, Am. Cancer Soc., Raleigh, N.C., 1973; chair Cabarrus County Leadership Conf. for Women. Renaissance Art scholar Friends of Vielles Maisons Française, 1990. Mem. Nat. Trust for Hist. Preservation, So. Garden History Soc. Home: Mill Hill Plantation Stirewalt Rd Concord NC 28027

COOKE, BETTE LOUISE, retired library director; b. Emporia, Kans., Oct. 26, 1929; d. Oscar Oliver and Ada Luella (Williams) C. Student, Grinnell (Iowa) Coll., 1947-49; BS in Edn., U. Mo., 1951; MA in Libr. Sci., Vanderbilt U., 1964; EdD, Ind. U., 1971. Tchr. pub. schs. Mo. & Ill., 1951-63; instr. in libr. sci. N.E. Mo. State U., Kirksville, 1964-66; asst. prof. libr. sci. Western Ill. U., Macomb, 1966-72; assoc. prof., chair dept. libr. sci. and instructional tech. Cen. Mo. State U., Warrenburg, 1972-80; prof. libr. sci., dir. libr. St. Mary of the Plains Coll., Dodge City, 1983—; cons. sch. librs., Ill. and Mo., 1971-79; judge S.W. Kans. Project Fair Project, Dodge City, 1987—; grant evaluator Nat. Endowment for the Humanites, 1979; chair Dodge City Libr. Consortium, Dodge City, 1985. Mem. Dodge City Friends of Pub. Libr., 1987—; bd. dirs. Homeowners Assn., Dodge City, 1989k—. Ind. U. scholar, 1971; NEH/ACRL grantee, 1987. Mem. ALA, Kans. Libr. Assn., Kans. Coll. and Rsch. Librs. (program com.), Kans. Pvt. Acad. Librs., AAUW. Republican. Presbyterian. Home: 916 Lakewood Dr Monett MO 65708

COOKE, CONSTANCE BLANDY, librarian; b. Woodbury, N.J., Mar. 7, 1935; d. John Chase and Josephine Spond (Black) Blandy; m. Len B. Cooke Jr., Jan. 7, 1978 (div. 1987). B.A., U. Pa., 1956; M.A., U. Denver, 1957. Adult cons. Onondaga Library System, Syracuse, N.Y., 1965-66; asst. dir. Mt. Vernon (N.Y.) Public Library, 1966-75; dep. dir. Queens Borough Public Library, Jamaica, N.Y., 1975-79; dir. Queens Borough Public Library, 1980-94; founder pres. Literacy Vols. Mt. Vernon, 1972-74. Trustee METRO, 1980-81, v.p., 1985-88, pres., 1988-91; mem. N.Y. State Libr. Svcs. and Constrn. Act Adv. Coun., 1982-88, chmn., 1986-87; bd. dirs. Queens Coun. on the Arts, 1988-94, v.p., 1989-93; bd. dirs. Queens Mus. of Art, 1988—, v.p., 1994—. Mem. ALA, N.Y. Libr. Assn., Queens C. of C. (dir. 1982—), Circumnavigators Club. Democrat. Episcopalian. Home: 20920 18th Ave Flushing NY 11360-1452

COOKE, EILEEN DELORES, retired librarian; b. Mpls., Dec. 7, 1928; d. Walter William and Mary Frances C. BSLS, Coll. St. Catherine, 1952; extension courses, U. Minn. Bookmobile libr. Mpls. Pub. Libr., 1952-57; br. asst. Queensborough Pub. Libr., 1957-58; br. asst., hosp. libr., pub. rels. specialist Mpls. Pub. Libr., 1958-63; asst. dir. Washington office ALA, 1964-68, asso. dir., 1968-69, dep. dir., 1969-72, dir., 1972-94, ret., 1994; lectr. U. Mich., Ann Arbor; mem. steering com. White Conf. on Libr. and Info. Svcs. Task Force. Contbr. articles to profl. jours. Mem. bd. visitors Sch. Libr. and Info. Sci., Cath. U. Mem. ALA, Minn. Libr. Assn., D.C. Libr. Assn., Joint Coun. Ednl. Telecom. (past pres.), Higher Edn. Group Washington, World Future Soc., Women's Nat. Book Assn., Home and Sch. Inst., Nat. Adv. Coun.

COOKE, GLORIA GRAYSON, trust fund director; b. Smithfield, Va., Sept. 6, 1939; d. Dennis Merry Jones and Edna Ward (Gwaltney) Nash; m. Lenard Lee Cooke, June 4, 1957; children: Kelly, Karla, Lenard, Jr. Student, U. Md., Tachi Kowa, Japan, 1959-61. Cert. antiqaurian book appraiser. Jr. appraiser Imperial Antiquities, Ltd., Tokyo, 1958-61; owner Millwood Rare Books, Crenshaw, Miss., 1962—, Historic Restorations, Crenshaw, Miss., 1982—; prin. Gloria Grayson Cooke, Crenshaw, Miss., 1983—. Mem. LWV, Nat. Trust for Hist. Preservation, Habitat for Humanity, Memphis Heritage, Brooks Mus. Art, Dixon Galleries, Memphis Pink Palace Mus., Friends of Miss. Libr., Tate County Hist. Soc., Am. Farm-Land Trust. Democrat. Methodist. Home: RR 1 Box 461A Crenshaw MS 38621-9762 Office: Askew House Crenshaw MS 38621

COOKE, JOAN ELLEN, healthcare executive, consultant; b. Phila., Sept. 2, 1953; d. Joseph Thomas and Lillian Josephine (Tjarks) Cooke. AS, Columbus (Ohio) State U., 1973; BS, Franklin U., 1980. Supr. State Health Planing and Devel. Agy. Ohio Dept. Health, 1978-80; account exec. Nationwide Health Care, 1980-82; with HealthAm. Corp., 1982-86; exec. dir. HealthAm. Corp., Columbus, Ohio, 1984-85; v.p. ops. Health Am. Corp., Columbus, Ohio, 1985-86; sr. v.p. Vol. Health Plan, Nashville, 1986-87; exec. v.p. Managed Care Products, Inc., Columbus, 1987-89; regional strategic health planner Humana, Inc., Miami, Fla., 1989-90; assoc. exec. dir. S.W. Fla. market Humana, Inc., 1990-91, assoc. exec. dir. South Fla. region, 1991—. Author: The Development of an Efficient Health Care System, Planning Guidance to State and local Health Planning Agencies, Strategic Five-Year Health Plan for the State of Florida. Mem. NAFE, Group Health Assn. Am., Smithsonian Assocs. Office: Humana Med Plan 3400 Lakeside Dr Bldg 2B Miramar FL 33027

COOKE, MARY A., hospice director; b. Hoboken, N.J., Sept. 22, 1944; d. John F. and Mary A. (Schmidt) C. RN, St. Joseph Sch. Nursing, Syracuse, N.Y., 1966; BS, Seton Hall U., South Orange, N.J., 1968; MA, NYU, 1972. Staff nurse St. Mary's Hosp., Hoboken, N.J., 1966, Holy Name Hosp., Teaneck, N.J., 1967-68, St. Barnabas Med. Ctr., Livingston, N.J., 1969; instr. Elizabeth (N.J.) Gen. Hosp., 1969-72, clin. nurse specialist, 1972-74; nursing care coordinator Cabrini Med. Ctr., N.Y.C., 1974-82; nursing dir. Cabrini Hospice, N.Y.C., 1982-83; dir. Cabrini Hospice, 1983—; ptnr., prog. dir. Ahmed, Gordon & Mancino, N.Y.C., 1981-93; adj. faculty Sch. Nursing, Columbia U., 1992—. Contbr. articles to profl. jours. Mem. Am. Nurses Assn., N.Y. State Nurses Assn., N.J. Nurses Assn. (v.p. 1971, bd. dirs. 1972-76), Sigma Theta Tau. Democrat. Roman Catholic. Home: 160 E 27th St Apt 9A New York NY 10016-9023 Office: Cabrini Hospice 227 E 19th St New York NY 10003-2600

COOKE, SARA MULLIN GRAFF, daycare provider, kindergarten teacher; b. Phila., Dec. 29, 1935; d. Charles Henry and Elizabeth (Mullin) Brandt Graff; m. Peter Fischer Cooke, June 29, 1963 (div. July, 1984); children: Anna Cooke Smith, Peter Fischer Jr., Frances Elizabeth, Sara Reynolds, Laina Koerting. AA, Bennett Coll., 1955; BE in Child Edn., Westchester State Tchrs. Coll., 1956. Asst. to tchr. 1st grade The Woodlyn Sch., 1956-58; tchr. Sara Bircher's Kindergarten, Germantown, Pa., 1958-62, Chestnut Hill (Pa.) Acad., 1962-63, Tarleton Sch., Devon, Pa., 1963-64; with F.C.I. Mktg. Co-ordinators Inc., N.Y.C., New Canaan, Conn., 1980-86; fundraiser Children's Hosp., Phila., 1989-92, pres. women's com., 1987-88; coord., master of ednl. ceremonies Phila. Soc. for Preservation Landmarks, 1991-93; coord. Elderhostel Program Landmarks Soc., 1992-93; private day caretaker Spl. Care, Inc., 1988—. Mem. bd. aux. Children's Hosp. Phila., 1970-76, mem. women's bd., 1977—, pres., 1987-88; mem. commonwealth bd. Med. Coll. Pa., 1984—, mem. Gimbel award com., 1994; alt. del. Rep. Nat. Conv., 1992. Mem. Pa. Assn. Hosp. Auxs. (health rep.) Nat. Soc. Colonial Dames (garden com. 1988—), Ch. Women's Assn. (past pres.), Alumnae Assn. Madeira Sch. (class sec., class agt.), Phila. Cricket Club, Jr. League Garden Club. Republican. Episcopalian. Home and Office: 3421 Warden Dr Philadelphia PA 19129

COOKE, SARAH BELLE, health care facility professional, farmer; b. Murfreesboro, Tenn., Sept. 14, 1910; d. Robert Jesse and Mattie (Neal) C. BS, Middle Tenn. State U., 1961. Cert. tchr., Tenn. Patient funds clk. VA Med. Ctr., Murfreesboro, 1943; voucher auditor VA Med. Supply Svc., Murfreesboro, 1945-46, purchasing agt., 1946-83, contracting officer, 1984-89; now ret. Pres. VA Fed. Employees Credit Union, Murfreesboro, 1965-86. Mem. AAUW (pres. Murfreesboro chpt. 1977-79), Tenn. Credit Union League (br. pres. 1973-79). Democrat. Mem. Church of Christ. Home: 5078 Sulphur Springs Rd Murfreesboro TN 37129-7206

COOKE, SUZANNE GAMSBY, middle school educator; b. North Hornell, N.Y., Aug. 22, 1945; d. Frank Nelson and Katherine Louise (Hildebrand) Gamsby; m. Larry D. Watson, Sept. 2, 1967 (div. 1974); m. Martin Wayne Cooke, June 23, 1984. BA, Maryville Coll., 1967; MS, U. Tenn., 1975; postgrad., State Tech. Inst. Tchr. Knox County Sch. Bd., Knoxville, Tenn., 1967—; attendee Gov.'s Acad. for Tchrs. of Writing, 1991. Recording sec. Knoxville Community Theatre, 1978-81. Recipient Meritorious Service award Knox County Juvenile C., 1982. Mem. Knox County Edn. Assn., East Tenn. Edn. Assn., Tenn. Edn. Assn., NEA, Tenn. Assn. Middle Schs., Nat. Council Tchrs. of English, E. Tenn. Assn. Tchrs of English. Baptist. Office: Halls Mid Sch 4317 Emory Rd NE Knoxville TN 37938-4349

COOKE, SUZETTE ALLEN, state representative; b. Bellingham, Wash., Aug. 27, 1949. BA, Western Wash. U., 1972. Recreation supr. City of Seattle, 1972-75; dir. Kent (Wash.) Parks and Recreation Dept. Sr. Activity Ctr., 1975-81; exec. dir. Kent C. of C., 1981-92; rep. 47th Dist. Washington State, 1993—; mem. ho. human svcs. com., appropriations com., health care com., mem. joint com. on pension policy, mem. family policy coun., mem. gov. coun. on sch.-to-work transition. Former ex-officio bd. mem. Wash. State Small Bus. Improvement Coun.; mem. Wash. Rsch. Coun., Valley Area Transp. Alliance, Fist Christian Ch. of Kent; former mem. King County Housing Rehab. Adv. Com., Valley Med. Ctr. Citizens Adv. Coun. Mem. Wash. C. of C. Execs. (past pres.), Assn. Wash. Bus. (former bd. and exec. com. mem.), Wash. State Sr. Ctr. Dirs. Assn. (founding organizer), Rotary Club Kent (adv. coun. mem.), King County Sexual Assault Resource Ctr., Growth and Prevention Theatre. Home: 25307 144th Ave SE Kent WA 98042 Office: 320 John L O'Brien Bldg Olympia WA 98504

COOKE, WALTA PIPPEN, automobile dealership owner; b. Shreveport, La., Oct. 18, 1940; d. Billy Burt and Eula (Heaton) P.; m. John William Cooke II, Dec. 20, 1958; children: Cheryl Cooke Williams, John William III. BA, Baylor U., 1963. Co-owner, sec.-treas. Pippen Motor Co., Carthage, 1972-80, owner, sec.-treas., 1980—; dir. Sabine River Authority Tex., 1993—; bd. dirs. Sabine River Authority Tex., 1993—, sec. pro tem, chmn. mgmt. and project devel. com., 1995—. Pianist for sanctuary choir Ctrl. Bapt. Ch., Carthage, 1986—, children's choirs. Mem. Carthage 32 Club, Carthage Book Club. Democrat. Home: 200 Timberlane Dr Carthage TX 75633-2231 Office: Pippen Motor Co 1300 W Panola St Carthage TX 75633-2346

COOKE, WANDA (COOKIE COOKE), hearing aid specialist; b. Lexington, Okla., June 26, 1943; divorced; children: Eugene, Mike. Student, Cameron U. Lic. hearing aid dealer, Okla.; cert. hearing instrument specialist, occupational hearing conservationist. Loan officer Lawton Tchrs. Fed. Credit Union, 1971-82; hearing aid specialist Beltone Hearing Aid Svc., Oklahoma City, 1982-91; owner C2 Hearing Cons., Lawton, 1991—, Lawton Hearing Aid Ctr. V.p. bd. dirs. Lawton Tchrs. Fed. Credit Union. Mem. LaSill Optimist Club (bd. dirs.). Office: 1603 W Gore Blvd Lawton OK 73501

COOK-MARLOWE, DEBORAH, soprano; b. Phila., July 6; m. Robert L. Kashoff, Dec. 12, 1964 (dec. Dec. 1964); 1 child, Jeffrey; m. Ronald M. Marlowe, Aug. 30, 1985. Studied voice with, Irene Williams; studied chazzanut with Max Wohlberg, prof. Max Wohlberg. Mem. ensemble Theatre am Goetheplatz, Bremen, Germany, 1972-76, Bayerische Staatsoper, Munich, Germany, 1979-81; freelance opera and concert artist Europe, Eng., Can., U.S., Sydney and Melbourne, Australia; created role of Rachel in We Come to the River, Royal Opera House, London; cantor Cons. Synagogues, Phila., 1989—; tchr. of voice Westtown (Pa.) Sch., 1990—. Editor (collection of songs) Twelve Songs by Amy Marcy Cheney Beach, 1994; performed for recs. role of Meyerboer's Dinorah, role of Ariadne, Strauss' Ariadne auf Naxos, role of Prascovia, Myerbeer's L'Etoile du Nord; radio recs. BBC, Zerbinetta, Le Bourgois Gentihomme/Ariadne auf Naxos, Belgium Radio & TV, Stuttgart, Hamburg, Hong Kong, Radio Bremen, Leipzig Radio. Mem. AGMA. Jewish. Home: 402-A West Ave Jenkintown PA 19046

COOL, KIM PATMORE, retail executive, needlework consultant; b. Cleve., Feb. 1, 1940; d. Herman Chester Earl and Eva (Geneau) Patmore; m. Kenneth Adams Cool Jr., Mar. 12, 1963; 1 child, Heidi Adams. BA in Econs., Sweet Briar Coll., 1962; postgrad., Case Western Reserve U., 1962-63. Test adminstr. Pradco, Cleve., 1962-63; pvt. needlework cons. Cleve., 1970-72; retail v.p., treas., custom designer And Sew On, Inc., Cleve., 1973-92, exec. v.p., treas., 1982-92; v.p. Shure Stiches Inc., 1991-92; owner Shure Stitches, Inc., Cleve., 1992-93, The Hare Necessities, Venice, Fla., Germany, 1994—, Hare Necessities Craft & Needlework Mfg., Venice, Fla.; lectr. bus. seminars Nat. Needlework Assn.; tchr. Wellesley Coll. Continuing Edn. Program, 1986; pub. Fredericktown Press, Md.; designer and mktg. assoc. Kappioe OriginalsLtd., 1988-93. Artist collector quality custom hand-painted canvases; co-author: How to Market Needlepoint-The Definitive Manual, 1988, Easy Macrame, 1990, Basic Macrame, 1990, Wearable Macrame, 1990, Playmate Dolls to Stitch, 1991, Pillows and Purses to Stitch, 1991, Needlepoint from Start to Finish, 1992, Pathway to Profit in the Needlework Industry, 1995. Rep. committeeman Cuyahoga County, Shaker Heights, Ohio, 1964-72. Regional Curling champion, 1987-88. Mem. Nat. Needlework Assn. (lectr. seminar on mktg. needlepoint, seminars on buying and merchandising, 1988—, charter assoc. retail), Embroiderers Guild of Cleve. (bd. dirs. 1980-82), Am. Profl. Needlework Retailers, S.E. Yarncrafters Guild (conductor merchandising seminars 1989—), Nat. Standards Coun. Am. Embroiderers, U.S. Figure Skating Assn. (nat. precision judge, sr. competition judge, gold test judge 1967—), Sweet Briar Coll. Alumnae Assn. (nat. bd. dirs., upper MW region, 1965-66, class sec. 1988-92), Cleve. Skating Club, Mayfield Country Club. Mem. United Ch. of Christ. Home and Office: The Hare Necessities 312 Shore Rd Venice FL 34285-3725

COOL, MARY L., elementary school educator; b. Buffalo, Dec. 7, 1954; d. Paul G. and Dorothy R. (O'Brien) Wailand; m. Ronald J. Cool, June 23, 1979; children: Logan Elizabeth, Colin Jeffery. BS in Elem. Edn. cum laude, SUNY, Fredonia, 1976. Cert. tchr., N.Y., Fla. Tchr. grade 1 Buffalo, N.Y., 1976-77; tchr. grade 5 Orange County, Orlando, Fla., 1979-85; tchr. grade 1, ESEA Title I head tchr. Manatee County, Myakka City, Fla., 1977-79; tchr. grade 5, media specialist Volusia County, Osteen, Fla., 1985-89; intermediate resource tchr. S.W. Volusia County, Fla., 1989-91; dist. elem. resource tchr., elem. tchr. specialist Volusia County Schs., Fla., 1991—; grade level chairperson, sci. chairperson, reading chairperson, facilitative leader, coop. learning trainer, tchr. coach, tch. edn. coach, Volusia County Schs., Fla.; ednl. cons. Scholastic, Sports Illus. for Kids. Mem. ASCD, AAUW, Nat. Coalition for Sex Equity in Edn., Nat. Staff Devel. Coun., Kappa Delta Pi. Home: 1566 Gregory Dr Deltona FL 32738-6159 Office: PO Box 2410 Daytona Beach FL 32115

COOLEY, CYNTHIA FURBER, artist; b. Mpls., July 17, 1931; d. John Roscoe and Jessie Anna (Vilendrer) Furber; m. William Warren Cooley; children: Warren, Robin. BA, Lawrence U., 1953; postgrad., Mpls. Coll. Art & Design, 1954, Boston Mus. Fine Arts Sch., 1957. Artist-in-residence Am. Wind Symphony, summer European tour, 1989. Watercolors and acrylics shown in numerous exhbns. in Pitts., Washington, Mpls., Palo Alto, Calif., Honolulu, Portland, Maine and elsewhere; solo shows include Bird in Hand Gallery, Pitts., 1972-94, Pitts. Ctr. for the Arts, 1989, Adams Gallery, Dunkirk, N.Y., 1989, Nat Acad. Scis., Washington, 1994; represented in more than 1200 collections, including State Mus. Pa., Libr. of Congress, Sec. of Smithsonian Instn., Pitts. History and Landmarks Found., IBM, Westinghouse, Consol. Coal. Sec., trustee Pitts. Ctr. for the Arts, 1990—. Named Artist of Yr. Pitts. Ctr. for the Arts, 1989; recipient G. Fitzgibbon award Greater Pitts. Com. for Women, 1993, also various awards for paintings. Mem. Associated Artists of Pitts. (bd. dirs. 1979-85, life mem.), Pitts. Soc. Artists (founding mem., sec. 1968-72), Pitts. Watercolor Soc. (bd. dirs., pres. 1976-85). Home and Studio: 1609 Power Run Road Pittsburgh PA 15238

COOLEY, HILARY ELIZABETH, business manager; b. Leesburg, Va., May 8, 1953; d. Thomas McIntyre and Helen Strong (Stringham) C. BA in Econs., U. Pitts., 1976; postgrad. in bus. adminstrn., Hood Coll., Frederick, Md., 1985-90. Mgr. Montgomery Ward, Frederick, 1976-80, merchandiser, 1980-82; asst. bus. mgr. Arundel Communications, Leesburg, 1982-84; bus. mgr. Loudoun Country Day Sch., Leesburg, 1984-85, bd. trustees, 1989-93, sec. bd. trustees, 1989-90, v.p., 1990-92; contr. Foxcroft Sch., Middleburg, Va., 1984-86; v.p., 1991-92; corr. Loudoun Times Mirror, Leesburg, 1985-87; estate mgr. Delta Farm Inc., Leesburg, 1988—. Area chmn. Keep Loudoun Beautiful, Middleburg, 1983-90, pres. bd. dirs., 1993—; pres. Waterford (Va.) Citizen's Assn., 1985-86, Waterford Players, 1986-88; bd. dirs. Waterford Found., Inc., 1992—, Loudoun Hist. Soc., Leesburg, 1987. Mem. Penn Hall Alumnae Ann. (pres. 1987-90). Democrat. Episcopalian. Home and Office: Delta Farm PO Box 234 Philomont VA 22131-0234

COOLEY, SHEILA LEANNE, psychologist, consultant; b. Oakland, Calif., July 25, 1956; d. Philips Theadore and Helen Ellene (Newbill) C. BA, St. Leo Coll., 1979; MS, U. So. Miss., 1986; PhD, Miss. State U., 1990. Lic. psychologist, Ky. Counselor Charter Counseling Ctr., Jackson, Miss., 1988-89; staff psychologist Rivendell Psychiat. Ctr., Bowling Green, Ky., 1989-90; program dir. MidSouth Hosp., Memphis, 1990-91; resource ctr. dir. Mid-South Resource Ctr., Ridgeland, Miss., 1991-92; partial hosp. dir. Pathways Partial Hospitalization, Ridgeland, 1991-92; edn. specialist, sr. position Miss. Dept. of Edn., Bur. Spl. Svcs., Jackson, 1993-94; psychologist Western State Hosp., Hopkinsville, Ky., 1994—. Campaign organizer for Dem. mayor, Jackson, 1992. Mem. APA, Miss. Psychol. Assn., Ky. Psychol. Assn., Phi Delta Kappa, Psi Chi, Theta Pi Sigma. Baptist. Home and Office: PO Box 2200 Hopkinsville KY 42241-2200

COOLEY, WENDY, judge, lawyer; b. Birmingham, Ala., Jan. 1, 1948. BS, Ea. Mich. U., 1968; MA, U. Mich., 1971; JD, U. Detroit, 1982. cert. spl. edn. tchr., Mich. Spl. edn. cons. Detroit Bd. Edn., 1971-80; assoc. Kirk & McCargo, Detroit, 1982-84; judge Mich. 36th Dist. Ct., Detroit, 1984—; host TV show Winning Ways; instr. Wayne County Community Coll., Detroit, 1979-84. Contbr. articles to various publs. Bd. dirs. U. Detroit, Wayne County Community, Wayne County Econ. Growth; speaker various ch. and community groups, Detroit area; radio hostess Sta. WMTG, Detroit; active Leadership Detroit, Second Ebeneezer Bapt. Ch.; mem. Mich. Martin L. King Holiday Commn.; apptd. to Mich. Correction Officer Tng. Coun., 1987. Mem. Mich. Dist. Judges Assn., Mich. State Bar Assn., Eastern Star, Delta Sigma Theta. Office: Mich 36th Dist Ct 421 Madison St Detroit MI 48226-2358

COOLIDGE, MARTHA, film director; b. New Haven, Aug. 17, 1946; m. Michael Backes. Ed. RISD, Columbia U. Dir. films: Valley Girl, 1983, The City Girl, 1983, Joy of Sex, 1984, Real Genius, 1985, Plain Clothes, 1988, Rambling Rose, 1991, Crazy in Love, 1991, Lost in Yonkers, 1993, Angie, 1994, Three Wishes, 1995; dir. TV shows and TV films Sledge Hammer pilot episode, 3 episodes The Twilight Zone, CBS miniseries The Winners, Roughhouse pilot episode, 1988, Trenchcoat in Paradise, 1989, Bare Essentials, 1991, Crazy in Love, 1992; dir. documentaries David: On and Off, 1972, More Than A School, 1973, Old Fashioned Woman, 1974, Not A Pretty Picture, 1976 (all winners Am. Film Festival awards). Office: care Beverly Magid Guttman Assoc 118 S Beverly Dr Ste 201 Beverly Hills CA 90212-3016

COOLIDGE, MARTHA HENDERSON, volunteer environmental and East Asian specialist; b. Cambridge, Mass., Jan. 26, 1925; d. Robert Graham and Lucy (Gregory) Henderson; m. Harold Jefferson Coolidge, May 26, 1972 (dec. Feb. 1985). Student, Smith Coll., 1942-43; BA, Radcliffe Coll., 1946; MA, Harvard U., 1956, postgrad., 1956-57, 58-60. Asst. sec. China Program Harvard U., Cambridge, Mass., 1948; adminstr. Fulbright Program Inst. Internat. Edn., N.Y.C., 1949-50, assoc. dir. GARIOA program, 1950-51; staff mem. Ctr. for Internat. Studies at MIT, Cambridge, 1953-54; exec. sec. The Japan Soc. of Boston, 1958-62; asst. to mng. dir., dir. film services Ednl. Devel. Inc., Watertown, Mass., 1963-65; program dir. for internat. exchanges Smithsonian Instn., Washington, 1965-66; edn. assoc. Cen. Atlantic Regional Edn. Labs., Washington, 1966-68; sr. assoc. for edn. The Conservation Found., Washington, 1968-70; ednl. assoc. Pub. Broadcasting Environ. Ctr., Washington, 1970-71; vol., bd. dirs. Coolidge Ctr. for Environ. Leadership, Cambridge, 1983-94, vice chmn., 1983-85; assoc. to prof. Harvard U., Cambridge, 1989-91, assoc. in rsch. Fairbank Ctr. East Asian Rsch., 1992—; mem. temp. staff student adaption study MIT, 1962-63; cons. social studies curriculum project Harvard Grad. Sch. Edn., Cambridge, 1964-65. Author: P.R.C. section, bibliography for John K. Fairbank, China: A New History, 1992, (with John King Fairbank and Richard J. Smith) H.B. Morse, Customs Commissioner and Historian of China, 1855-1934, 1995; contbg. author: Fairbank Remembered, 1992; author annotated bibliography, Prospects for Communist China, 1954; author articles in field. Bd. dirs. Lincoln Filene Ctr. for Citizenship and Pub. Affairs Tufts U., Medford, Mass.; affiliate Dudley House, Harvard U.; council mem. New Eng. Aquarium, Boston; active Quebec-Labrador Found. Corp., Ipswich, Mass. Grantee Yenching Inst., 1958-59, Radcliffe Coll., 1955-56; Fulbright scholar Tokyo U., 1957-58. Fellow Royal Soc. Arts (London); mem. Fragment Soc., Assn. Asian Studies, Internat. House of Japan, Women's Travel Club, Harvard Travellers' Club. Episcopalian. Home: 19 Brewster St Cambridge MA 02138-2203 also: Harvard U Fairbank Ctr for East Asian Rsch 1737 Cambridge St Cambridge MA 02138-3016

COOLIDGE, RITA, singer; b. Nashville, May 1, 1945; m. Kris Kristofferson, Aug. 19, 1973 (div. June 1980); 1 dau., Casey. Student, Fla. State U. Singer with Delaney & Bonnie Bramlett, Joe Cocker, Leon Russell, Kris Kristofferson, also soloist; film appearance: Pat Garrett and Billy the Kid, 1973, A Star is Born, 1980; recordings include Love Me Again (recipient Grammy awards), Greatest Hits, Love Sessions, 1992; performed: title song All Time High in Octopussy; first female video jockey on Video Hits One (cable TV); rec. artist appearing regularly on MTV Networks. Office: care Shocorp Internat Ltd 11684 Ventura Blvd 899 Studio City CA 91604

COOMBER, BARBARA J., association executive; b. Tonawanda, N.Y., Aug. 17, 1954; d. Ernest A. and Georgia L. (Long) C.; children: Wilson, Angela. BS, State Univ. Coll., Brockport, N.Y., 1976; MSW, SUNY, Buffalo, 1981. Cert. social worker, N.Y.: lic. ind. clin. social worker, Mass. Dir. social svcs. Hopevale, Inc., Hamburg, N.Y., 1982-84; team leader Hallgarth Inst., Bourne, Mass., 1984-85; program dir. Justice Resource Inst., Boston, 1985-89; dir. placement Boston Children's Svcs., 1989-94; exec. dir. YWCA No. R.I., Woonsocket, 1994—; psychotherapist Acadia Counseling Svcs., Boston, 1989-93. Leader Girl Scouts Am., Tonawanda, 1976-77; foster parent N.Y. State Divsn. Social Svcs., North Tonawanda, 1976-77; advocate Alliance Young Families, Boston, 1987-94; bd. dirs., pres. New England Consortium Families and Youth, Boston, 1988-92; bd. dirs. Gay and Lesbian Healthy Boston Coalition, 1993. Recipient Dedicated Svc. award Justice Rsch. Inst. Foster Parents, 1989. Mem. NASW, NOW, Open Door Soc. Democrat. Episcopalian. Office: YWCA No RI 514 Blackstone St Woonsocket RI 02895-1891

COOMES, LISA ANN, critical care nurse; b. Loma Linda, Calif., Nov. 21, 1966; d. Timothy Gerald and Peggy Jean (Thomas) C. ASN, Riverside Community Coll., 1988; BSN, U. Phoenix, San Bernardino, 1993. RN, Calif.; CEN; cert. mobile intensive care nurse, Calif. Staff nurse emergency rm. Riverside (Calif.) Community Hosp., 1988-92, shift coord. emergency rm., 1992-94; with critical care transport Goodhow Ambulance, Riverside, 1990-94; critical care nurse, transport mgr. Mercy/Medic-1, Caroline, Calif., 1994—; instr. pediatric advanced life support Riverside Cmty. Hosp., 1992—, instr. ACLS, 1992—; emergency relief nurse 1994 Northridge Earthquake, Calif. Mem. Emergency Nurses Assn. Home: 155 Chant St Perris CA 92571-4654 Office: Riverside Community Hosp 4445 Magnolia Ave Riverside CA 92501-4135

COON, CHARLI E., legislative staff member. BA, Ariz. State U., 1973; MA in Pub. Adminstrn., Sangamon State U., 1979; JD, Loyola U., 1991. Tchr. Rome (Ill.) Elem. Sch., 1974-76; legis. budget and rsch. analyst minority staff Ill. Ho. of Reps., 1978-84; exec. asst. to dir. fin. and adminstrn. Ill. Dept. Transp., 1985-86; chief legis. liaison Ill. Dept. Children and Family Svcs., 1987-88; law clk. Shea, Rogal and Assocs. Ltd., Westchester, Ill., 1989-92; minority counsel subcom. commerce, consumer and monetary affairs, 1992-93; minority counsel subcom. environ., energy and natural resources Ho. Govt. Ops. Com., 1993—. Office: Subcom Environ Energy & Nat Resources 2158 Rayburn House Office Bldg Washington DC 20515*

COON, PENNY K., administrator; b. Penn Yan, N.Y., May 21, 1959; d. Wilfred Orval and Marilyn Estelle (Wells) Knapp; m. Thomas Allen Gray, Aug. 30, 1980 (div. July 1990); m. David Charles Coon, May 23, 1992; 1 child, Rachel Mariah. BSW, Keuka Coll., 1980. Residence counselor Cath. Charities Residential Program, Penn Yan, N.Y., 1981-82, residence mgr., 1982-92, residential supr., 1992—; bd. dirs. Yates County (N.Y.) ARC, Penn Yan, 1993—, mem. human rights com., 1989—, mem. admissions/discharge com., 1989—; co-chmn. Keuka Lake Conf. Com., Rochester, N.Y., 1986—; mem. Yates County Devel. Disabilities Subcom., 1990. Recipient Direct Care award, N.Y. State Assn. Community Residence Adminstrs., 1985. Mem. DAR, Daughters Am. Colonists. Republican. Home: 2599 Knapp Rd Dundee NY 14837-9730 Office: Cath Charities Residential Program 110 Exchange St Geneva NY 14456-1804

COONEY, JOAN GANZ, broadcasting executive; b. Phoenix, Nov. 30, 1929; d. Sylvan C. and Pauline (Reardan) Ganz; m. Timothy J. Cooney, 1964 (div. 1975); m. Peter G. Peterson, 1980. BA, U. Ariz., 1951; hon. degrees, Boston Coll., 1970, Hofstra U., Oberlin Coll., Ohio Wesleyan U., 1971, Princeton U., 1973, Russell Sage Coll., 1974, U. Ariz., Harvard U., 1975, Allegheny Coll., 1976, Georgetown U., 1978, U. Notre Dame, 1982, Smith Coll., 1986, Brown U., 1987, Columbia U., 1991, NYU, 1991. Reporter Ariz. Republic, Phoenix, 1953-54; publicist NBC, 1954-55, U.S. Steel Hour, 1955-62; producer Sta. WNET, Channel 13; pub. affairs documentaries Sta. WNET, Channel 13, N.Y.C., 1962-67; TV cons. Carnegie Corp. N.Y., N.Y.C., 1967-68; exec. dir. Children's TV Workshop (producers Sesame Street, Electric Company, others), N.Y.C., 1968-70, pres., trustee, 1970-88, chmn., chief exec. officer, 1988-90, chmn. exec. com., 1990—; trustee Channel 13/Ednl. Broadcasting Corp.; dir. Xerox Corp., Johnson & Johnson, Chase Manhattan Corp., Chase Manhattan Bank N.A., Met. Life Ins. Co. Mem. Pres.'s Commn. on Marijuana and Drug Abuse, 1971-73, Nat. News Council, 1973-81, Council Fgn. Relations, 1974—, Pres.'s Commn. for Agenda for 80's, 1980-81, Adv. Com. for Trade Negotiations, 1978-80; mem. Gov.'s Commn. on Internat. Yr. of the Child, 1979, Carnegie Found. Nat. Panel on High Sch., 1980-82. Recipient numerous awards for Sesame Street and other TV programs including Nat. Sch. Pub. Relations Assn. Gold Key 1971; Disting. Service medal Columbia Tchrs. Coll., 1971; Soc. Family Man award, 1971; Nat. Inst. Social Scis. Gold medal, 1971; Frederick Douglass award N.Y. Urban League, 1972; Silver Satellite award Am. Women in Radio and TV; Woman of Yr. in Edn. award Ladies Home Jour., 1975; Woman of Decade award, 1979; NEA Friends of Edn. award; Kiwanis Decency award; NAEB Disting. Service award; 5th Women's Achiever award Girl Scouts U.S.A.; Stephen S. Wise award, 1981; Harris Found. award, 1982; Ednl. Achievement award AAUW, 1984; Disting. Service to Children award Nat. Assn. Elem. Sch. Prins., 1985; DeWitt Carter Reddick award Coll. Communications, U. Tex.-Austin, 1986; Emmy Lifetime Achievement award Acad. TV Arts and Scis., 1989; named to Hall of Fame Acad. TV Arts and Scis., 1989. Mem. NOW, Nat. Acad. TV Arts and Scis., Nat. Inst. Social Scis., Internat. Radio and TV Soc., Am. Women in Radio and TV. Office: Children's TV Workshop 1 Lincoln Plz New York NY 10023-7170

COONEY, LYNN FUTCH, lawyer; b. St. Petersburg, Fla., Apr. 22, 1961; d. M. Daniel Jr. and Florence Corrine (Coe) Futch; m. Stephen Cooney, Mar. 1, 1986. Student, Broward Community Coll., 1978-79; BS in Mktg. cum laude, Fla. State U., 1982, JD with honors, 1984. Bar: Fla. 1985, U.D. Dist. Ct. (so. dist.) Fla. 1985. Intern Broward County State's Atty., Ft. Lauderdale, Fla., 1984; with Pyszka, Kessler, Massey, Weldon, Catri, Holton, & Douberley, P.A., Ft. Lauderdale, 1985-89; assoc. Conrad, Scherer, James & Jenne, PA, Ft. Lauderdale, 1989—. Bd. dirs. Friends Ft. Lauderdale Librs., 1987—, Jr. League Ft. Lauderdale, 1988-93; mem. jud. selection, adminstrn. and tenure com. Fla. Bar, 1990-93, bd. govs. young lawyers divsn., 1993—. Mem. Broward County Bar Assn. (bd. dirs. 1990—, young lawyers sect., exec. com., sec.-treas. 1989-90, pres.-elect 1990-91, pres. 1991-92), Fed. Bar Assn. (Broward County chpt., exec. com. 1988-90, sec. 1990-91, pres.-elect 1991-92, pres. 1992-93), Broward Lawyers Care (adv. com.), Tower Club, Zeta Tau Alpha. Republican. Roman Catholic. Office: Conrad Scherer James & Jenne PA 633 S Federal Hwy Fort Lauderdale FL 33301-3132

COONEY, PATRICIA RUTH, civic worker; b. Englewood, N.J.; d. Charles Aloysius and Ruth Jeannette (Foster) McEwen; m. J. Gordon Cooney, June 8, 1957; 1 child, J. Gordon, Jr. Student, Fordham U., 1950-51; DHL honoris causa, Phila. Theol. Sem. St. Charles Boromeo, 1991. Blood bank chmn. Strafford Village Civic Assn., 1968-69, sec., 1970-71; vice chmn. Spl. Gifts Com. Cath. Charities Appeal of Archdiocese of Phila., 1980—, chmn., 1985. Mem. Coun. of Mgrs. Archdiocese of Phila., 1982-88, sec., exec. com., 1983-88; bd. dirs. Cath. Charities of Archdiocese of Phila., 1984—, sec., exec. com., 1988-90, v.p., exec. com., 1991—; bd. dirs. Village of Divine Providence, Phila., 1982—, sec., 1983-85, v.p. exec. com., 1990—; bd. dirs. St. Edmond's Home for Crippled Children, Phila., 1984—, v.p. exec. com., 1990—; bd. dirs. Don Guanella Village of Archdiocese of Phila., 1984—, v.p. exec. com., 1990— ; mem. Archdiocesan Adv. Com. on Renewal, 1991—; mem. Women's Com. Wills Eye Hosp., 1973—, mem.-at-large, 1st v.p.; mem. Women's Aux. St. Francis Country House, Darby, Pa., 1976—, treas., 1978-82; exec. com. United Way of Southeastern Pa., 1984-90, sec., 1986-88; bd. dirs. Chapel of Four Chaplains, 1984-89, Phila. Criminal Justice Task Force, 1989-90. Decorated Cross Pro Ecclesia et Pontifice, 1982. Republican. Home: 320 Gatcombe Ln Bryn Mawr PA 19010-3628

COONS, BARBARA LYNN, public relations executive, librarian; b. Peoria, Ill., June 1, 1948; d. Harold Leroy and Norma (Brauer) C. BA, Stephens Coll., Columbia, Mo., 1970; MA, U. N.C., 1972; MLS, Cath. U., 1982. Research asst.Am. Revolution Bicentennical Office Library of Congress, Washington, 1974-76, editorial asst., office of the Asst. Librarian, 1976-78; Ednl. Liaison Specialist Library of Congress, Washington, 1978-82; dir. research service Gray and Co., Washington, 1982-85, v.p., 1985-86; v.p., dir. research services Hill and Knowlton Pub. Affairs Worldwide, Washington, 1986-92, sr. v.p., 1992—; pres. Library of Congress Profl. Assn., 1982. Mem. Spl. Libraries Assn., Am. Library Assn., Stephens Coll. Alumnae Club of Greater Washington (pres. 1987). Lutheran. Home: 532 N West St Alexandria VA 22314-2159 Office: Hill & Knowlton Pub Affairs Worldwide 901 31st St NW Washington DC 20007

COONS-VAN DE KOOLWYK, GAYLE MARIE, marriage, family, child counselor; b. Ventura, Calif., May 14, 1949; d. Robert Elliot and Virginia Marie (Pumphrey) Smith; m. Larry Bryon Coons, July 23, 1968 (div. May 1974); m.Peter Vincent Van De Koolwyk, Aug. 15, 1981; children: Peter Vincent II, Daniel Sebastian. AA in Mental Health, Cañada Coll., Redwood City, Calif., 1973; BA in Psychology, San Francisco State U., 1974, MA in Psychology, 1976; grad. guidance and counseling program, Creative Learning Systems, 1978. Lic. marriage, family, child counselor. Mental health asst. VA Hosp., Menlo Park divsn., Palo Alto, Calif., 1973; lectr. Calif. State U., San Francisco, 1974-76; counselor Prelab of Mesa, Ariz., 1976-79; counselor Victor Residential Ctr., Redding, Calif., 1979-80, asst. program coord., 1980-82; children's advocate Shasta County Women's Refuge, Redding, 1983-85, insight group leader, coord., cons., 1983-91; pvt. practice therapist Palo Cedro, Calif., 1985—; cons. Victim Witness, Redding, 1985-94. Recipient Outstanding Svcs. Support award Shasta County Women's Refuge, Redding, 1989, Outstanding Victim Advocacy award Victim/Witness, Redding, 1991. Mem. ACA, Am. Assn. Marriage and Family Therapists, Calif. Assn. Marriage and Family Therapists. Democrat. Episcopalian. Home and Office: PO Box 117 Palo Cedro CA 96073

COOPER, CAMILLE SUTRO, lawyer; b. Belleville, N.J., May 23, 1946; d. David Paul and Lotte (Weil) C. AB, Smith Coll., 1968; MS, Boston U., 1971; JD, Bklyn. Law Sch., 1982. Bar: N.Y. 1983, U.S. Dist Ct. (so. dist.) N.Y. Assoc. S.N. Solomon, Esq., N.Y.C., 1980-83; asst. gen. counsel Swissre Holding (N.A.) Inc., N.Y.C., 1983—; bd. dirs. Switzerland Ins. Holding USA, Inc., Del., 1986-91, Switzerland Ins. Svcs. Inc., 1987-91. Mem. ABA, Assn. of Bar of City of N.Y. Office: Swissre Holding (NA) Inc 237 Park Ave New York NY 10017-3142

COOPER, CAROL DIANE, publishing company executive; b. Williamsport, Pa., Aug. 14, 1953; d. Ray Calvin and Norma Jane (Stiger) C. BA, Colgate U., 1975; cert. in pub., Radcliffe Coll., 1975; MA, Syracuse (N.Y.) U., 1977. Editorial and promotion asst. St. Martin's Press, N.Y.C., 1977-78, sales rep., 1978-79; dir. sales, v.p. Clearwater Pub. Co., Inc., N.Y.C., 1979-80, dir. mktg., 1980-81, v.p., 1980-83; exec. v.p. K.G. Saur Inc., N.Y.C., 1983-87; v.p., pub. R.R. Bowker Co., N.Y.C., 1987-90; v.p. internat. pub. ops. Bowker, Martindale Hubbell, N.Y.C., 1990-92; v.p. internat. pub. ops. Reed Reference Pub., New Providence, N.J., 1992—, also bd. dirs. Mem. ALA (com. microform standards rsch. and tech. standards div. 1986). Office: Reed Reference Pub 121 Chanlon Rd New Providence NJ 07974-1541*

COOPER, CAROLINE ANN, hospitality faculty dean; b. Gardner, Mass., Oct. 16, 1943; d. Frank D. and Florence M. (O'Neal) Toohey; m. Paul Geoffrey Cooper, Apr. 16, 1972; children: Geoffrey Paul, Heather Ann. BS, Russell Sage Coll., 1966; MBA, Bryant Coll., 1983. Adminstrv. dietitian Mass. Gen. Hosp., Boston, 1967-68; with rsch., devel., mktg. Mkt. Forge Co., Everett, Mass., 1968-71; food svc. administr. Jane Brown R.I. Hosp., Providence, 1971-74; self-employed pres., cons. pvt. practice, Attleboro, Mass.; from instr. to asst. prof. Johnson & Wales U., Providence, 1978-86, acad. coord., 1984-86, dept. chair HRI, Hospitality, Food Svc. mgmt. and tourism, 1986—; asst. dean Hospitality Coll., 1991-94, dean, 1995—. Vol. Parent Orgn. for Sch., 1978-91, Prin. Edn. Sch., 1991—, Pub. Sch. System, 1981-84, Community Sports Program, 1989—. Named Pacesetter Nat. Roundtable for Women, 1989. Mem. Am. Dietetic Assn., Am. Hotel Motel Assn. (trustee Ednl. Inst. 1990—, Outstanding Educator 1990), Am. Hotel and Motel Industry, Computer Application Food Svc. Edn. (pres. 1987-89), Internat. Coun. on Hotel Restaurant Inst. Edn. (bd. dirs., pres. N.E. chpt. 1991—, pres. 1994-95). Office: Johnson and Wales U Abbott Park Pl Providence RI 02903

COOPER, CHARLOTTE MCHENRY, educational diagnostician; b. Portsmouth, Va., Feb. 27, 1948; d. Charles Hoyt and Ethel Mae (Sumlar) McHenry; m. Stanley Wardell Cooper, Nov. 18,. 1972 (dec. Jan. 1992); children: Sean, Heather. BS, Norfolk State U., 1972; MEd, Northwe. State U., 1988. Cert. tchr., La. Tchr. spl. edn. Mt. Hermon Elem. Sch., Portsmouth, 1972-73; program coord. St. Louis High Sch., Okinawa, Japan, 1973-74; tchr. adult edn. U. Hawaii, Okinawa, 1974-75; tchr. Vernon Parish Sch., Deesville, La., 1975-79, spl. edn. tchr., 1984-88, ednl. diagnostician, 1988—; tchr. Dept. Def. Schs., Geilenkirchen, Germany, 1979-84; Recorder Comprehensive Systems Profl. Devel., 1990-94. Charter mem. Concerned Citizens Dist. II, Leesville, La., 1994. Named La. Spl. Edn. Tchr. Yr. State Dept. Edn., 1988. Mem. Coun. Exceptional Children, Nat. Assn. Educators (treas. local chpt.), Am. Bus. Women's Assn., Sigma Gamma Rho. Democrat. Baptist. Home: 493 Hwy 1211 New Llano LA 71461 Office: Vernon Parish Sch Bd 201 Belview Rd Leesville LA 71446

COOPER, D. MICHELLE, retail buyer; b. Balt., Jan. 14, 1952; d. George Milton and Thelma Elizabeth (Robinson) C.; 1 child, Randy Brent Jett Cooper. BS in Biology, Morgan State U., 1974, MBA in Mgmt., 1980. Analytical technician I Allied Corp., Balt., 1974-76, analytical technician II, 1976-83, prodn. supr., 1983-85; prodn. supr. Lever Bros. Co., Balt., 1985-89, sr. buyer, 1989—. Home: 3304 Wild Cherry Rd Baltimore MD 21244

COOPER, DANA LEA, counselor educator; b. New Orleans, June 4, 1964; d. Samuel Harry Cooper and Judy Ann (Bennett) Blake. BS in Psychology, Ea. Ky. U., 1987, MA in Indsl./Community Svcs. Counseling, 1989; PhD in Counselor Edn., Miss. State U., 1991. Lic. profl. counselor, Tex., Miss. Mental health assoc. V, dir. work therapy Bluegrass East Comprehensive Care Ctr., Lexington, Ky., 1987-89; grad. asst. career svcs. Miss. State U., 1989-90, grad. asst. dept. continuing edn., 1990, rsch. asst. dept. counselor edn., 1990-91; asst. prof. dept. counseling and human svcs. St. Mary's U., San Antonio, 1991—, program dir. dept. counseling and human svcs., 1992—; counselor Alamo Mental Health Group, 1993—; presenter in field. Contbr. articles to profl. jours. Mem. Am. Counseling Assn. Home: 8602 Cinnamon Creek # 1304 San Antonio TX 78240 Office: Saint Marys U One Camino Santa Maria San Antonio TX 78228-8527

COOPER, DANA SEBREN, lawyer; b. San Angelo, Tex., Mar. 3, 1962. BA, La. Tech. U., 1984; JD, Tulane U., 1987. Atty. Emmett, Cobb, Waits and Kessenich, 1987-88; counsel Senate Com. Energy and Natural Resources, 1989-92, counsel subcom. water and power, 1992—. Office: Subcom on Water & Power 306 Dirksen Senate Office Bldg Washington DC 20510*

COOPER, DONNA LYNNE, secondary education educator; b. Davenport, Iowa, Oct. 31, 1945; d. Frank B. and Gertrude M. (Sayles) Ambrose; m. James R. Cooper, Nov. 25, 1967; children: Daniel, Michael, Mollie. BS, Iowa State U., 1967, MS, 1972. Cert. tchr. Tchr. Grayslake (Ill.) Dist. 46, 1978-84; tchr. math. dept., mentor Mad River Local Sch. Dist., Dayton, Ohio, 1984—; cons. in field. Recipient Excellence in Teaching award Alliance for Edn., 1994. Mem. ASCD, MAA, OCTM, NCTM, Ohio Assn. for Supervision and Curriculum Devel., WSU Area Coun. Tchrs. Math. (pres. 1993—). Office: Stebbins HS 1900 Harshman Dayton OH 45424

COOPER, DORIS JEAN, market research executive; b. N.Y.C., Dec. 17, 1934; d. James N. and Georgina N. (Cassidy) Breslin; student Sch. of Commerce, N.Y. U., 1953-55, Hunter Coll., 1956-57; m. S. James Cooper, June 17, 1956; 1 son, David Austin. Asst. coding supr. Crossley S-D Surveys, N.Y.C., 1955-57; asst. field supr. Trendex, Inc., N.Y.C., 1957-59; coding dir. J. Walter Thompson Co., N.Y.C., 1960-63, Audits & Surveys, N.Y.C., 1964-65; pvt. practice cons., N.Y.C., 1965-73; pres. Cooper Svcs., Irvington, N.Y., 1973—; pres., chief exec. officer, computer tabulation and lang. manipulation Doris J. Cooper Assocs., Irvington, N.Y., 1989—; cons. market rsch. Mem. Am. Mktg. Assn. (N.Y. chpt.), Nat. Bus. Women Owners Assn., Am. Assn. Pub. Opinion Researchers (N.Y. chpt.), Acad. Health Svcs. Mktg., Hastings C. of C. Republican. Episcopalian. Office: Doris J Cooper Assocs Ltd 1 Bridge St Ste 3 Irvington NY 10533-1543

COOPER, DOROTHY SUMMERS, real estate agent; b. Lee County, Ala., Aug. 8, 1918; d. Carl and Mattie Will (Thompson) Summers; m. Arthur Wiggins Cooper, July 20, 1940; children: Arthur Wiggins Jr., Mary Cooper Kitchen, Robert Wayne, Donald Summers. BS, Auburn U., 1939. Tchr. Columbus (Ga.) Jr. High Sch., 1939-40; grad. asst. Auburn (Ala.) U., 1941-42; tchr. Lee County Head Start, 1965-70; real estate agt. Stan Weber Real Estate, New Orleans, 1972-80, Shamrock and James Grant Realty, Auburn, 1981-88; real estate exec. A&D Properties, Opelika, 1989—; lectr. Nat. Gallery Art, Washington, 1971-72; New Orleans Mus. Art, 1973-78. Treas.

Auburn United Meth. Women, 1987-89. Named Honor Roll Bus., Auburn C. of C., 1990. Mem. PEO, Home Econs. Club, Sangahatchee Country Club, Delta Kappa Gamma, Green Gardeners. Democrat. Methodist. Home: 2590 Windy Hill Pl Auburn AL 36830-6408

COOPER, ELAINE JANICE, physical therapist; b. Detroit, Apr. 26, 1937; d. Morris and Sally (Mack) Braverman; divorced; children: Jeffrey, Michael, Jonathan. BS, U. Mich., 1959; cert. in massage therapy. Supr. Rehab. Inst., Detroit, 1959-61; cons. Redford (Mich.) Community Hosp., 1963-73; cons. in field Detroit, 1970-78; asst. dir. William Beaumont Hosp., Royal Oak, Mich., 1979-81; pres., cons. Cooper & Assoc. Physical Therapy P.C., Farmington Hills, Mich., 1981—; cons. Drs. Sobel & Castle, Detroit, 1965-66. Mem. Am. Phys. Therapy Assn. (edn. com. 1969), Mich. Phys. Therapy Assn., Biofeedback Soc. Mich., Am. Massage Therapy Assn., Mich. Dance Assn., Mich. State C. of C. (health care com.), Brookfield Highlands Club (chmn. land devel., restrictions coms. 1979-85). Office: Cooper & Assocs Phys Therapy PC 31800 Northwestern Hwy Ste 110 Farmington MI 48334-1663

COOPER, GINNIE, library director; b. Worthington, Minn., 1945; d. Lawrence D. and Ione C.; 1 child, Daniel Jay. Student, Coll. St. Thomas, U. Wis., Parkside; BA, S.D. State U.; MA in Libr. Sci., U. Minn. Tchr. Flandreau (S.D.) Indian Sch., 1967-68, St. Paul Pub. Schs., 1968-69; br. libr. Wash. County Libr., Lake Elmo, Minn., 1970-71, asst. dir., 1971-75; assoc. adminstr., libr. U. Minn. Med. Sch., Mpls., 1975-77; dir. Kenosha (Wis.) Pub. Libr., 1977-81; county libr. Alameda County (Calif.) Libr., 1981-90; dir. librs. Multnomah County Libr., Portland, Oreg., 1990—. Chair County Mgr. Assn.; county adminstr. Mayor's Exec. Roundtable. Mem. ALA (mem. LAMA, PLA and RASD coms., elected to coun. 1987, 91, mem. legislation com. 1986-90, mem. orgn. com. 1990—), Calif. Libr. Assn. (pres. CIL, 1985, elected to coun. 1986, pres. Calif. County Librs. 1986), Oreg. Libr. Assn. Office: Multnomah County Libr 205 NE Russell St Portland OR 97212-3796

COOPER, ILENE LINDA, magazine editor, author; b. Chgo., Mar. 10, 1948; d. Morris and Lillian (Friedman) C.; m. Robert Seid, May 28, 1972. BJ, U. Mo., 1969; MLS, Rosary Coll., 1973. Head of children's svcs. Winnetka (Ill.) Libr. Dist., 1974-80; editor children's books Booklist Mag., ALA, Chgo., 1981—. Author: Susan B. Anthony, 1983, Choosing Sides, 1990 (Internat. Reading Assn.-Children's Book Coun. choice 1990), Mean Streak, 1991, (series) Frances in the Fourth Grade, 1991, numerous others. Mem. Soc. Midland Authors, Soc. Children's Book Writers, Children's Reading Roundtable. Jewish. Office: Booklist Mag 50 E Huron St Chicago IL 60611-2729

COOPER, JACQUELYN BARBER, librarian; b. Harrisburg, Pa., Jan. 7, 1940; d. John and Belinda (Weakley) Barber; m. Stephen T. Toy, Aug. 11, 1962 (div. 1972); 1 child, Deborah Lynne; m. Arthur Raymond Cooper, Jan. 10, 1987. BS magna cum laude, Susquehanna U., 1961; MLS, Kent State U., 1969. Tchr. music Tredyffrin-Eastern Schs., Berwyn, Pa., 1961-62; supr. music Alachua County Schs., Gainesville, Fla., 1962-66; reference libr. Providence (R.I.) Pub. Libr., 1969-73, br. libr., 1973-87, br. head, 1987—. Sec. Mt. Hope Day Care Ctr. Inc., Providence, 1985—; substitute organist Providence Presbyn. Ch., 1989—. Pa. State Edn. Assn. scholar, 1957; recipient SAT scholar award Sigma Alpha Iota, 1961. Mem. ALA, New Eng. Libr. Assn. (exec. bd. 1982-92), R.I. Libr. Assn. (chmn. intellectual freedom com. 1980-82, Libr. of Yr. award 1992), Providence Pub. Libr. Staff Assn. (pres. 1971-72, 86-87, treas. 1987-89), Coalition Libr. Advs. (treas. 1994—), Beta Phi Mu, Sigma Alpha Iota. Democrat. Presbyterian. Office: Rochambeau Br Libr 708 Hope St Providence RI 02906

COOPER, JANELLE LUNETTE, neurologist, educator; b. Ann Arbor, Mich., Dec. 11, 1955; d. Robert Marion and Madelyn (Leonard) C.; children: Lena Christine, Nicholas Dominic. BA in Chemistry, Reed Coll., 1978; MD, Vanderbilt U., 1986. Diplomate Nat. Bd. Med. Examiners; diplomate in neurology Am. Bd. Psychiatry and Neurology. Med. technologist Swedish Hosp. Med. Ctr., Seattle, 1978-80, U. Wash. Clin. Chemistry, Seattle, 1980-82, Vanderbilt U. Hosp., Nashville, 1983-84; intern medicine Vanderbilt U. Med. Ctr., Nashville, 1986-87, resident neurology, 1987-90; instr. neurology Med. Coll. Pa., Phila., 1990-91, asst. prof., clerkship dir., 1991—, mem. curriculum com., 1990-91, vis. asst. prof., 1991—; neurologist Greater Ann Arbor Neurology Assocs., 1991-93; dir. neurological svcs., med. dir. Industrial Rehab. Program St. Francis Hosp., Escanaba, Mich., 1993—; founder, dir. No. Neuroscis., Escanaba, 1993—; physician MCP Neurology Assocs., Phila., 1990-91; emergency rm. physician Tenn. Christian Med. Ctr., 1989-90. Contbr. articles to Annals of Ophthalmology, Ophthalmic Surgery. Vol. Rape & Sexual Abuse Ctr., Nashville, 1988-90; mem. adminstrv. bd. Edgehill United Meth. Ch., Nashville, 1989-90; editorial bd. mem. Nashville Women's Alliance, Nashville, 1989-90. Recipient Svc. award for outstanding contbns. Rape & Sexual Abuse Ctr., 1990. Mem. AMA (Physician's Recognition award 1989-92), NOW, Am. Acad. Neurology, Am. Med. Women's Assn. (del. nat. meeting 1990), Mich. State Med. Soc., N.Y. Acad. Scis. Methodist. Home: 519 South Eighth St Escanaba MI 49829 Office: Northern Neurosciences 3415 Ludington St Ste 201 Escanaba MI 49829

COOPER, JANIS CAMPBELL, public relations executive; b. Laurel, Miss., July 26, 1947; d. Clifton B. and Hilna Mae (Welch) Campbell; m. William R. Cooper, Sept. 18, 1971; 1 child, Emily Susanne. BS, U. So. Miss., 1969. Certified home economist. Staff home economist Maytag Co., Newton, Iowa, 1969-73, supr. home econs., 1973-81, mgr. consumer edn., 1981-86; mgr. corp. pub. affairs Maytag Corp., Newton, Iowa, 1986-87, asst. dir. corp. pub. affairs, 1987-88, corp. dir. pub. affairs, 1988-89, corp. v.p. pub. affairs, 1989—; trustee Maytag Corp. Found., Newton, 1990—. Chmn. trustee Newton Cmty.Ednl. Found., 1992-95. Mem. Assn. Family and Consumer Scis., Pub. Rels. Soc. Am., Home Economists in Bus. (nat. chmn. 1981-82, Disting. Svc. award 1986, Nat. Bus. Home Economist of Yr. 1991), Iowa Assn. Bus. and Industry (bd. dirs., mem. exec. com.), Assn. Home Appliance Mfrs. (treas. 1988-89, 1st vice chmn. 1989-90, chmn. 1990-92, chmn. Major Appliance Divsn. Bd. 1993-95), Maytag Mgmt. Club, Kiwanis Internat. Office: Maytag Corp 403 W 4th St N Newton IA 50208

COOPER, JEAN SARALEE, judge; b. Huntington, N.Y., Mar. 7, 1946; d. Ralph and Henrietta (Halbreich) C.; stepchildren: Mitzi Concklin Ugolini, John Todd Concklin. B.A., Sophie Newcomb Coll. of Tulane U., 1968; J.D., Emory U., 1970. Bar: La. 1970, Ga. 1970, U.S. Dist. Ct. (ea. dist.) La. 1970, U.S. Ct. Appeals (5th cir.) 1972, U.S. Ct. Appeals (2d cir.) 1976, U.S. Ct. Appeals (4th cir.) 1979, U.S. Ct. Appeals (fed. cir.) 1982, U.S. Supreme Ct. 1974. Trial atty. Office of Solicitor, U.S. Dept. Labor, Washington, 1970-73, spl. projects asst., 1973, sr. trial atty., 1973-77; adminstrv. judge Bd. Contract Appeals, HUD, Washington, 1977—, acting chmn. and chief judge, 1980-81, vice chmn., 1983—; cons., lectr. Contbr. articles to profl. jours. Recipient Moot Court award Tulane Law Sch., 1968. Fellow ABA (standing com. on jud. selection, tenure, and compensation 1992—, jud. adminstrn. divsn., chmn. edn. com. Nat. Conf. Adminstrv. Law Judges jud. adminstrn. divsn. 1993—, exec. com., mem. editl. bd. Judges Jour., vice-chair debarment and suspension com. pub. contracts sect. 1992—); mem. La. Bar Assn., Am. Law Inst., Am. Inns. of Ct. Found (trustee 1992—), Prettyman-Leventhal Am. Inn of Ct. (past pres., master of bench), Am. Judicature Soc., Inst. Jud. Adminstrn., Bd. Contract Appeals Judges Assn., Nat. Assn. Women Judges (chair adminstrv. judiciary com.), Fed. Bar Assn., Am. Inst. Wine and Food, Bds. of Contract Appeals Bar Assn., L'Academie de Cuisine (tchr.). Republican. Office: HUD Bd Contract Appeals 451 7th St SW Ste 2131 Washington DC 20410-0001

COOPER, JILL, psychotherapist; b. Denver. BA, Colo. State U., 1974; MA, Antioch U., 1983; PhD, Profl. Sch. Psychology, San Francisco, 1993. Lic. marriage/family counselor. Psycotherapist San Francisco, 1985—; adj. faculty Calif. Sch. Profl. Psychology, Alameda, New Coll. of Calif., San Francisco, 1994, Antioch U., San Francisco, 1985-89, U. Calif. San Francisco, 1986-88; presenter in field. Contbr. articles to profl. and popular jours. Mem. No. Calif. Inst. for Psychoanalytic Psychology. Office: 3972 24th St San Francisco CA 94114

COOPER, JOSEPHINE SMITH, trade association and public relations executive; b. Raleigh, N.C., Aug. 2, 1945; d. Joseph W. and Marie (Peele) S. BA in bus. and econs., Meredith Coll., Raleigh, 1967; MS in mgmt., Duke U., 1977. Program analyst Office of Air & Quality Planning and Standards EPA, Rsch., Triangle Park, N.C., 1968-78; environ. protection specialist Office of Rsch. and Devel., Washington, 1978-80; mem. profl. staff majority leader Howard H. Baker, Jr., U.S. Senate Com. on Environ. and Public Works, Washington, 1980-83; asst. adminstr. for external affairs EPA, Washington, 1983-85; asst. v.p. for environ. and health program Am. Paper Inst., Washington, 1985-86; sr. v.p. for policy Synthetic Organic Chem. Mfrs. Assn., Washington, 1986-88; sr. v.p., dir. environmental policy Hill & Knowlton, Inc., Washington, 1988-91; founder, dir. Capitoline Internat. Group, Ltd., Washington, 1991-92; v.p. environ. and regulatory affairs Am. Forest & Paper Assn., 1992—; treas. RTP Fed. Credit Union, 1969-72, pres., 1975; pres. Women's Coun. on Energy and Environ., 1986-88, Nat. Coun. on Clean Indoor Air, 1988—; mem. nat. adv. environ. health scis. coun. NIH, 1990-94; mem. trade and environ. policy adv. com. USTR, 1995—; mem. adv. com. EPA Clean Air Act, 1994—; mem .trade and environ. policy adv. com. USTR, 1994—; mem. corp. coun. Nat. Parks and Conservation Assn. Congl. fellow, 1979-80. Mem. Federally Employed Women (treas., pres. 1972-77), Women in Govt. Rels., Tenley Sport and Health Club. Mem. Disciples of Christ. Office: Am Forest & Paper Assn 1111 19th St NW # 800 Washington DC 20036

COOPER, KATHLEEN BELL, economist; b. Dallas, Feb. 3, 1945; d. Patrick Joseph and Ferne Elizabeth (McDougle) Bell; m. Ronald James Cooper, Feb. 6, 1965; children—Michael, Christopher. B.A. in Math. with honors, U. Tex., Arlington, 1970, M.A. in Econs, 1971; Ph.D. in Econs, U. Colo., 1980. Research asst. econs. dept. U. Tex., Arlington, 1970-71; corp. economist United Banks of Colo., Denver, 1971-79, chief economist, 1980-81; v.p., sr. fin. economist Security Pacific Nat. Bank, Los Angeles, 1981-83, 1st v.p., sr. economist, 1983-85, sr. v.p., economist, 1985-86, sr. v.p., chief economist, 1986-87, exec. v.p., chief economist, 1988-90; chief economist Exxon Corp., Irving, Tex., 1990—. Trustee Scripps Coll., Com. for Econ. Devel.; mem. Dallas Com. on Fgn. Rels., Internat. Women's Forum. Mem. Nat. Assn. Bus. Economists (past pres. Denver and L.A. chpts.; bd. dirs. 1975-78, pres. 1985-86), Nat. Bur. Econ. Rsch. (bd. dirs., exec. com.), Am. Bankers Assn. (econ. adv. com. 1979-81, 86—, chmn. 1989—), Am. Econ. Assn., Western Econ. Assn., Conf. Bus. Economists (tech. cons. to bus. coun.). Office: Exxon Corp 225 E John W Carpenter Fwy Irving TX 75062-2298

COOPER, LORIE ANN, psychologist; b. Greenville, S.C., Oct. 23, 1957; d. Francis Joseph and Jessie Pearl (Spoone) Boniface; m. Adrian Paul Cooper, Aug. 7, 1977 (wid. July 1990); children: Paul, Philip, Andrew. BS in Edn., So. Coll., Collegedale, Tenn., 1979; MA in Community Counseling, Andrews U., 1994. Missionary Gen. Conf. of Seventh-day Adventist, Washington, 1979-90, Cen. African Union, Bujumbura, Burundi, 1979-82, Adventist Univ. of Cen. Africa, Gisenyi, Rwanda, 1982-90; pvt. practice psychology Univ. Med. Ctr., Berrine Springs, Mich., 1994—. Recipient Sirrine scholarship, Greenville, 1975, Steele scholarship, Berrien Springs, Mich., 1992, 94, Weniger scholarship, 1994. Mem. AACD, APA, Psi Chi. Seventh-day Adventist. Office: Univ Med Ctr Berrien Springs MI 49103

COOPER, MARY CAMPBELL, information services executive; b. Meadville, Pa., Aug. 14, 1940; d. Paul F. and Margaret (Webb) Campbell; m. James Nicoll Cooper, June 8, 1963; children: Alix, Jenny. BA, Mt. Holyoke Coll., 1961; MLS, Simmons Coll., 1963; MEd, Harvard U., 1965. Cert. museum adminstrn. With Harvard U. Libr., Cambridge, Mass., 1961-63, Carleton U. Libr., Ottawa, Can., 1965-85; archive cons. U.S., Can., 1985-86; info. mgr. Haley & Aldrich Inc., Cambridge, 1986-88, Tsoi/Kobus & Assocs., Cambridge, 1988-90; pres., founder Cooper Info., Cambridge, 1990—; pres. Mass. Com. for Preservation of Archtl. Records, Boston, 1991—, past bd. dirs. Author: Records In Architectural Offices, 1992. Bd. dirs. Berkshire Hist. Soc., Pitts., Mass., Constrn. Specifications Inst., Boston. Travel grantee Nat. Hist. Pub. Records Commn., 1991. Mem. Spl. Librs. Assn., Am. Mus. Assn., Assn. Ind. Info. Profls., Assn. Moving Image Archivists, Assn. for Info. and Image Mgmt., Assn. Records Mgrs. and Adminstrs. (nat. com. 1991—), Constrn. Specification Inst. (bd. dirs. 1994—). Home and office: 5 Ellery Pl Cambridge MA 02138

COOPER, PATRICIA DAWKINS, foundation administrator; b. Houston, Feb. 5, 1944; d. Austin Eli and Sarah Lorraine (Rountree) Dawkins; children from previous marriage: Catherine Sloane, Sarah Riley, Patricia Daily. BA, Columbia Coll., 1965; grad. Williamsburg Devel. Inst., 1990. Appointments sec. to Congressman Tom Gettys, Washington, 1965; tchr. Lugoff (S.C.) Elem. Sch., 1967-68, Camden (S.C.) Elem. Sch., 1969-70; ombudsman State of S.C., 1970-73; asst. dir. Carolina Cup and Colonial Cup Internat. Steeplechase, Camden, 1973-87; adminstr. Camden Feed Co., 1973-87; office mgr. Camden Tng. Ctr., thoroughbreds, 1973-87; asst. sec. Mulberry Resources, Inc., 1980-82; sec.-treas. Equistar Products Co., 1980-87; mktg. dir. Holiday Inn of Lugoff-Camden, Holiday Inn of Sumter, S.C., 1987-88; dir. Devel. Bapt. Med. Ctr. Found., 1988-89; exec. v.p. S.C. State Mus. Found., Columbia, 1989—. Bd. dirs. Kershaw County Fine Arts Ctr., Columbia Devel. Corp.; sustaining mem. Camden Jr. Welfare League; mem. Inaugural Class, Leadership Kershaw County, 1986-87, participant Statewide Program, 1987-88; adv. com. Charleston Steeplechase; mem. Santee-Lynches Coun. Govts., 1987-88; bd. dirs. Kershaw County unit Am. Cancer Soc., 1980-90; chmn. bd. dirs. Kershaw unit Am. Heart Assn., 1984-86; bd. dirs. Palmetto Balloon Classic, 1983-86; mem. Bd. Appeals, City of Camden, 1985-87; vice chmn. Kershaw County Tourism Adv. Com., 1987-88; adminstrv. bd. Lyttleton St. United Meth. Ch., Camden, 1986-88; chmn. leadership com. Kershaw County, 1988-89; mem. Columbia Action Coun., 1988-90, Columbia Forum, 1988—; adv. com. S.C. Joint Legis. Com. on Cultural Affairs, 1989—; active Assembly on the Future of S.C., 1989; trustee S.C. bd. Leukemia Soc. of Am., 1987-91. Mem. Nat. Soc. Fundraising Execs. (mem. regional bd. 1993—), Am. Assn. Mus., Media Club of Columbia, Greater Kershaw County C. of C. (v.p. pub. affairs 1983-86, William F. Nettles award 1988), Thoroughbred Assn. S.C. (sec.-treas. 1986-88), Leadership S.C. Alumni (bd. dirs. 1988-93, pres. 1992-93), S.C. Exec. Inst., Future Group of Richland County (cultural resources chair 1994), Newcomen Soc. of the U.S., S.C. Bd. Dirs., Greater Columbia C. of C., Capital City Club, Sprindale Hall Club, Univ. Assocs. Club, Rotary (mem. bd. dirs. Columbia, 1993—). Methodist. Home: 2429 1/2 Terrace Way Columbia SC 29205 Office: SC State Mus Found PO Box 100107 Columbia SC 29202-3107

COOPER, PAULA, art dealer; b. Mass., Mar. 14, 1938. Student, Pierce Coll., Athens, Greece, Sorbonne, Paris, Goucher Coll. Asst. World House Galleries, N.Y.C., 1959-61; pvt. dealer, 1962-63; with Paula Johnson Gallery, N.Y.C., 1964-65; dir. Park Place Gallery, N.Y.C., 1965-67, Paula Cooper Gallery, N.Y.C., 1968—; bd. chair The Kitchen Ctr., N.Y.C., 1985—. Office: Paula Cooper Gallery 155 Wooster St New York NY 10012-3159

COOPER, RACHEL BREMER, accountant; b. Oak Pk., Ill., Dec. 21, 1950; d. James Louis and Betty Charlene (Barfield) B.; m. Terry Linn Cooper, Aug. 14, 1981. BS in Acctg., Murray State U., 1982. CPA, Tenn. Gen. bookkeeper The Paducah (Ky.) Sun, 1975-80; staff acct. Kraft Bros., Esstman, Patton, & Harrell, CPAs, Nashville, 1983; acquisition analyst Freeman Cos., Nashville; asst. controller Surg. Care Affiliates, Nashville, 1984-86; sr. staff acct. O'Neill & Co. CPAs, Nashville, 1986, EQUICOR, Nashville, 1987; acctg. mgr. Times Pub. Co., DBA The St. Petersburg (Fla.) Times, 1987-93; pres. Eco Solutions, Inc., St. Petersburg Beach, 1993—; pres., owner Lady Rachael Imports, Nashville, 1986-87. Officer Don Cesar Property Owners Corp., St. Petersburg Beach, 1988-90. Named to Dean's List Paducah Community Coll., 1978, 79, Murray State U., 1980-82. Mem. Tenn. Soc. CPAs, Fla. Inst. CPAs, AICPA. Republican. Home: 3616 Casablanca Ave Saint Petersburg Bch FL 33706-3904

COOPER, REBECCA, art dealer; b. Phila., July 11, 1957; d. Frank N. Cooper and Bernice Silverstein; m. Michael J. Waldman, June 27, 1982. BA NYU, MA, postgrad. Cert. appraiser. Owner Gallery Rebecca Cooper, Washington; pres. Rebecca Cooper Fine Art, N.Y.C., 1980s-90s; hon. chairperson N.Y. Women Bus. Owners Art Roundtable, 1981; lectr. Resources Coun., 1983, N.Y. Mayor's com. on interior design and furnishings, 1983; sec. bd. assocs. Am. Craft Mus., lectr. Collectors Circle; nat. patron Am. Fed. Art., Ind. Curators Inc. Patron, Mus. Modern Art; benefactor New Mus. Dirs. Forum, Whitney Mus. Mem. Am. Appraisers Assn. (exhbn. assoc.), Pvt. Art Dealers Assn., Nat. Arts Club, Guggenheim Mus. (internat. cir.).

COOPER, SANDRA LENORE, writer; b. Bklyn., July 9, 1934; d. Edward Emanuel Kleeman and Mollie Kleeman Hantman; m. Ralph Sherman Cooper, Jan. 30, 1956; children: Laurie Mara Pohl, Brett Edward. Grad., The Cooper Union, N.Y.C., 1954; BFA, U. Colo., 1955. Pres. Northwestern Assn. on Indian Affairs, Richland, Wash., 1967-72; asst. dir. Eight No. Indian Pueblos Coun., San Juan Pueblo, N.Mex., 1973-78; pres. Creative Ent., Long Beach, Calif., 1978—; cons. Taos (N.Mex.) Pueblo, 1994—. Author: Black Fire, 1980, Love Trap, 1982, Forbidden Passion, 1983; (CD-ROM) The Engineering Adventure, 1994, When I Grow Up, 1995, Help Wanted, 1995. Vice pres. Class, Inc., Phoenix, 1993—. Mem. SAG (chpt. v.p. 1972-75), Sci. Fiction/Fantasy Writers of Am., Apple Programmers and Devel. Assn., Mensa, Am. Indian Sci. and Engrng. Soc. Home: 76 Santa Ana Ave Long Beach CA 90803 Office: Creative Enterprises Ste 200 5354 E 2d St Long Beach CA 90803

COOPER, SHARON MARSHA, marketing, advertising executive; b. Chgo., Feb. 6, 1944; d. Ralph and Esther Lepack; m. Steven Jon Cooper; children: Robin Eve, Erik Scott. BA, Northeastern Ill. U., Chgo., 1974; MEd, Loyola U., Chgo., 1977. Adj. asst. prof. Chgo. Med. Sch., North Chicago, Ill., 1974-79; edn./media coordinator Humana Hosp., Aurora, Colo., 1980-82; v.p. Healthcare Mktg. Corp., Denver, 1982-84; pres. Sharon Cooper Assocs., Ltd., Englewood, Colo., 1984—; cons./speaker Jason Pharms., Balt., 1988—; cons. Am. Soc. Bariatric Physicians; lectr. in field; guest lectr. U. Denver, 1988—. Illustrator: A Manual of Radiographic Positioning, 1973; contbr. articles to profl. jours. Bd. dirs., v.p. The Barre Assn./Colo. Ballet, Denver, 1989—; bd. dirs. Am. Diabetes Assn., Denver, 1983—, Am. Cancer Soc., Denver, 1988—, Hospice of St. John, Denver, 1986-90. Named Co-Woman of the Yr., Lerner Newspapers, Chgo., 1973, Silver Microphone award, 1988, Golden Leaflet award, Colo. Hosp. Assn., 1981, 84. Mem. Am. Hosp. Assn., Assn. Healthcare Pub. Rels. and Mktg. (reg. rep. 1987—), Colo. Soc. Health Care Pub. Rels., Pub. Rels. Soc. Am., Zonta, Toastmasters (sec. 1972-84). Home: 8522 E Dry Creek Pl Englewood CO 80112-2701 Office: Sharon Cooper Assocs Ltd 9085 E Mineral Cir Ste 160 Englewood CO 80112-3418

COOPER, SIGNE SKOTT, retired nurse educator; b. Clinton County, Iowa, Jan. 29, 1921; d. Hans Edward and Clara Belle (Steen) Skott. BS, U. Wis., 1948; MEd, U. Minn., 1955. Head nurse U. Wis. Hosp., Madison, 1946-48; instr. U. Wis. Sch. Nursing, Madison, 1948-51, asst. prof., 1952-57, assoc. prof., 1957-62; prof., assoc. dean U. Wis. Sch. Nursing, 1948-83, prof. emeritus, 1983—; prof. U. Wis. Extension, 1955-83. Contbg. author: American Nursing: A Biographical Dictionary, Vol. 1, 1988, Vol. 2, 1992; contbr. articles to profl. jours. 1st Lt. U.S. Army Nurse Corps, 1943-46. Recipient NLN Linda Richards award, ANA Honorary Recognition award, Adult Edn. Assn. Pioneer award; named Fellow Am. Acad. Nursing. Mem. ANA, Am. Assn. for History Nursing, Wis. Nurses Assn. (pres.).

COOPER, SUSAN, artist; b. L.A., Apr. 25, 1947; d. Morris and Zelda (Lefkowitz) C.; m. Joseph C. Anderson, July 25, 1976 (div. 1990); children: Martha Cooper, David Gaylord; m. Richard A. Cohn, Jan. 25, 1992. BA in Art and Anthropology with honors, U. Calif., Berkeley, 1968, MA, 1970. Instr. Met. State Coll., Denver, 1987-89, U. Colo., Denver, 1990-91; bd. dirs. Ctr. for Idea Art, 1985-87; guest spkr. U. Denver, 1988, 89, No. Ky. U., 1979, Met. State Coll., 1989. One-woman shows include Foothills Art Ctr., Golden, Colo., 1995, Inkfish Gallery, Denver, 1993, 90, Galleria Expositum, Mexico City, 1992, Henri Gallery, Washington, 1989, Denver Art Mus., 1989, others; paintings represented in permanent collections at Denver Art Mus., City and County Bldg., Denver, Std. Oil of Ohio, Ea. N.Mex. State U., Sch. Am. Rsch., Santa Fe, N.Mex., St. Luke's Hosp., Denver, Denver Pub. Libr., Congress Park, Denver, City and County Bldg., Denver, 1993, others. Pres., dir. Rocky Mountain Women's Inst. U. Denver, 1977-87.

COOPER, SUSAN CAROL, environmental, safety and health professional; b. Milw., Dec. 25, 1939; d. Carroll Arthur and Edith Estelle (Hicks) Brooks; m. William Randall Cooper, June 20, 1964; children: Darin Benbrook, Carol Kimberly, Ryan Randall. BS in Biology, U. Wis., Milw., 1962; MS in Physiology, Wash. State U., 1966; PhD in Physiology, U. Idaho, 1972, MS in Geol. Engrng., Hydrology, 1990. EIT. Sr. lab. technician Dept. Vet. Pathology, Wash. State U., Pullman, 1965-68; postdoctoral assoc. dept. chemistry U. Idaho, Moscow, 1972-74, vis. prof. chemistry, 1974; instr. facilitator for gifted/talented Highland Sch. Dist., Craigmont, Idaho, 1975-76; program dir. YWCA, Lewiston, Idaho, 1977-78; support asst. Exxon Nuclear Idaho Corp., Idaho Falls, 1983; engr. Exxon Nuclear Idaho Corp. and Westinghouse Idaho Nuclear Co. Inc., Idaho Falls, 1983-84; environ. engr., sr. environ. engr. Westinghouse Idaho Nuclear Co. Inc., Idaho Falls, 1984-86, mgr. environ., safety and health, SIS Project, 1986-90; mem. Environ. Compliance Office Dept. Energy Idaho Ops. Westinghouse Idaho Nuclear Co. Inc., 1989; mgr. environ. compliance, environ. permits and programs, adv. engr. Waste Isolation divsn., Westinghouse Electric Co., Carlsbad, N.Mex., 1990-92; sr. project mgr., regulatory compliance specialist S.M. Stoller Corp., Albuquerque, 1992—; pres. Cooper Creations, Albuquerque, 1993—; instr. hazardous waste mgmt. N.Mex. State U., Carlsbad, 1991; instr. Clean Air Act, Sch. Environ. Excellence, Westinghouse/Dept. Energy, 1990-91; mem. speaker's bur. Idaho Nat. Engrng. Lab./Westinghouse Idaho Nuclear Co. Inc., 1988-90, Waste Isolation divsn. Westinghouse Electric Co., 1990-92; presenter profl. confs. Contbr. articles to profl. jours. Mem. presenting team Marriage Encounter, 1980-90; campaign group leader United Way, 1986-87, campaigner, 1985-86; mem., historian Mayor's Com. for Employment of Handicapped and Older Workers, Idaho Falls, 1985-86; singer Idaho Falls Opera Theater, 1983-85; lay preacher, lay reader, lay Eucharistic minister Episc. Ch., Idaho and N.Mex., 1984—; mem. choir St. John's Ch., Idaho Falls, 1983-85, Grace Episc. Ch., Carlsbad, 1990-92, Holy Trinity St. Francis Ch., Albuquerque, 1992—; del. Dem. Conv., Boise, Idaho, 1975. NSF fellow, 1963, NDEA fellow, 1963-65, NASA trainee, 1968-70, Nat. Assn. Geology Tchrs. scholar, 1980. Mem. Toastmasters (past pres, founder 2 corp. clubs, adminstrv. v.p., Competent Toastmaster, Able Toastmaster). Home: 3413 Dellwood Ct NE Albuquerque NM 87110 Office: The SM Stoller Corp Ste 209 1717 Louisiana Blvd NE Albuquerque NM 87110

COOPER, SUSAN LOUISE, government agency executive; b. Washington, Aug. 19, 1950; d. Chester L. and Orah P. C.; m. Thomas J. Duesterberg, July 30, 1979; 1 child, James. BA, Ind. U., 1972, PhD, 1980; MA, SUNY, Stony Brook, 1974. Prodn. asst. CBS News, Washington, 1979-80; curator Nat. Archives, Washington, 1981-85, sr. pub. affairs specialist, 1985-88, dep. dir. pub. affairs, 1988—, acting dir. pub. affairs, 1992-93. Prodr. video news release Personal Accounts, Pearl Harbor to VJ Day, 1991 (Gold Screen award 1992); editor newsletter Nat. Archives Calendar of Events, 1992 (Blue Pencil award 1993). Mem. Nat. Assn. Govt. Communicators, Pa. Ave. Quarter Assn. Office: Nat Archives 8th & Pennsylvannia Ave NW Washington DC 20408

COOPER, SYLVIA JANE, librarian; b. Columbia, Mo., June 10, 1936; d. George B. and Jessie Merle (Turner) Edmondson; m. Richard Grant, Jan. 31, 1970. BS, U. Mo., Columbia, 1958; MEd, U. Mo., 1962, M.A. in Libr. Sci., 1972. Vocat. home econ. tchr. Paris High Sch., Paris, Mo., 1958-61, Macon High Sch., Macon, Mo., 1962-67; student asst. libr. U. Mo. Libr., Columbia, Mo., 1967-69; reader service librarian St. Louis County Libr., 1969-70; librarian U.S.D.I. Fish Pesticide Research Lab., Columbia, Mo., 1970-71; libr. dir. Okla. Osteo. Hosp. (name change to Tulsa Regional Med. Ctr.), 1976—. Recipient Scholarship Mo. C. of C. Edn. Found., 1965. Mem. ALA, South Cen. Regional Group of Med. Libr. Assn., Hosp. Sect. of South Cen. Regional Group of Med. Libr. Assn. (chmn. 1989-90), Spl. Libr. Assn., Okla. Health Soc. Libr. Assn. (past pres.), Nat. Network of Librs. of Medicine (south central region bd. 1993-95), Med. Libr. Assn. Acad. Health Info. Profls. (disting. mem. 1990—), Sungate Garden Club, Beta Sigma Phi. Office: Tulsa Regional Med Ctr Libr H230 744 W 9th St Tulsa OK 74127-9096

COOPER, VIRGINIA RAILSBACK, educator; b. Pine Bluff, Ark., Mar. 1, 1950; d. Glenn Albert Jr. and Virginia Lee (Dabney) Railsback; m. Carl Frederic Cooper, Jr., Aug. 27, 1977; children: Carl Frederic III, Seth Bernard. BFA, Miss. U. for Women, 1972; MS, U. Ctrl. Ark., 1993. Cert. tchr., Ark. Owner, pres. Cooper Advt. & Design, Little Rock, 1978-85; tchr. art Little Rock Sch. Dist., 1988—; Odyssey of Mind coach Terry Elem. Sch., Little Rock, 1991, 92; boys' soccer coach Little Rock Ctrl. High Sch.,

1993—. Exhibited in group shows Miss. Arts Festival, 1972, S.E. Ark. Art Ctr., 1973. Bd. dirs. Terry Elem. Sch. PTA, 1992-93. Mem. U.S. Soccer Fedn. (lic. coach). Presbyterian. Home: 923 Beacon Hill Ct Little Rock AR 72211-2511

COOPER-AVRICK, ANITA BEVERLY, television stage manager; b. Ottawa, Ontario, Can.; d. Albert and Edith (Sobie) Cooper; m. Andrew Jay Avrick, Apr. 15, 1984; 1 child, Ashley Nicole. AA, L.A. Valley Coll., 1968; BS in Bus. Adminstrn., Calif. State U., Northridge, 1974; LLM, Southwestern Sch. Law, 1984. Field rep., contract adminstr. AFTRA, Hollywood, Calif., 1975-80; stage mgr. Dirs. Guild Am., L.A., 1980—; segment producer Nat. Leukemia Telethon Nat. Leukemia Broadcasting Coun., L.A., 1989, 90, 91. Stage mgr. (TV shows) Soap, 1980-81, Lewis & Clark, 1981-82, The People's Court, 1982-83, Filthy Rich, 1982-83, Reggie, 1983, Nine to Five, 1983-84, This Is Your Life, 1983-84, Mr. Belvedere, 1985-90, Kids Incorporated, 1986, Jay Leno Special, 1987, The Johnsons Are Home, 1989, Davis Rules, 1990-91, (TV pilots) Weekends, 1982, Sam, 1985 Charlie & Co., 1985, Real Life, 1988, Homeroom, 1989, Babes, 1990, Fresh Prince of Bel Air, 1991, The Brave New World of Charlie Hoover, 1991, Dudley, 1993, Herman's Head, 1993-94, The Office, 1994, Daddy's Girls, 1994, Blame It On Ernie, 1995; assoc. dir. (TV series) Mr. Belvedere, 1990. Mem. AFTRA, Dirs. Guild Am. (nat. bd. mem., chairperson Assoc. Dir.-Stage Mgr.-Prodn. Assoc. Coun., various other coms.).

COOPER-LEWTER, MARCIA JEAN, educator, administrative assistant; b. Petersburg, Va., Nov. 2, 1959; d. Andrew Ezekiel and Lillian (Bonner) Wyatt; m. Nicholas Charles Cooper-Lewter, Nov. 29, 1986. BS in Elem. Edn., Va. State U., Ettrick, 1984; MEd in Spl. Edn. Lic. minister, 1987; ordained to clergy, 1990. Tchr. Marion (Ind.) Community Schs., 1985-86, Inglewood (Calif.) Unified Schs., 1986-87; office mgr. C.R.A.V.E. Christ Counseling, Tustin, Calif., 1986—; asst. minister New Garden of Gethsemane B.C., L.A., 1987-90; assoc. minister New Hope Bapt. Ch., St. Paul, 1990—; assoc. pastor New Garden of Gethsemane B.C., L.A., 1990—; assoc. minister New Hope Bapt. Ch., 1990—; pres. C.R.A.V.E. Christ Singers, L.A., 1987-90; adminstr. asst. Eldorado Bank, Orange, Calif., 1988-90; tchr. fine arts Mpls. Sch. Dist., 1990—; with Wyatt, Cooper-Lewter Consulting, Shoreview, Minn., 1986—; advisor Am. Biog. Inst., N.C., 1990—. Mem. C.R.A.V.E. Christ Ministries (Relax in Christ, Affirm with Christ, Visualize Christ, Experience Christ); nominated to Pres.'s Commn., White House Fellowships, 1993. Mem. NAFE, Alpha Kappa Alpha.

COOPER-SERVAITES, PAMELA SUE, nursing administrator; b. Flint, Mich., July 8, 1941; d. Francis S. Jr. and Pauline A. (Ringle) Pierce; m. Kenneth Cooper, June 22, 1963 (div. Aug. 1968); children: Kenneth Jr., Robert; m. Jerome Servaites, Nov. 16, 1991; stepchildren: Mathew, Mara. RN, Miami Valley Hosp. Sch.Nursing, Dayton, Ohio, 1962; BS, St. Joseph's Coll., North Windham, Maine, 1981. Quality assurance nurse VA Med. Ctr., Dayton, 1981; dir. nursing Med. Pers. Pool, Dayton, 1982, Nurses Calling, Dayton, 1983-84, Nursing Systems, Dayton, 1985-86; dir. utilization rev. and quality assurance All Care, Inc., Dayton, 1987, Wright Choice Health Plan, Dayton, 1987; cons. long term care facilities Dayton, 1985—; dir. nursing Covenant House, Dayton, 1989-90, Stillwater Ctr., Dayton, 1990-93, Kettering (Ohio) Convalescent Ctr., 1993—, Villa Convalescent Ctr., Troy, Ohio; bd. dirs. Joint Vocat. Schs. Practical Nursing, Dayton, 1992—. Mem. Nat. Assn. Dirs. Nursing Adminstrn./Long Term Care, Ohio Assn. Dirs. Nursing Adminstrn./Long Term Care. Episcopalian.

COOVER, PAULA LOUISE HENRY See HENRY, PAULA LOUISE

COPE, JEANNETTE NAYLOR, human resources consultant; b. Corpus Christi, Tex., Feb. 9, 1956; d. Glen R. and Jeannine (Withington) N.; m. John R. Cope, May 22, 1993. BA in Psychology and Sociology, Trinity U., 1978. Asst. fin. dir. Jim Baker for Atty. Gen. Campaign, Houston, 1978; fin. dir. Rep. Party of Tex., Austin, 1979-81; regional Eagle rep. Rep. Nat. Com., Washington, 1981-83; devel. officer Nat. Endowment for the Arts, Washington, 1983-87; sr. project mgr. Internat. Skye Assocs., Washington, 1988; spl. asst. to Pres. of U.S. The White House, 1989-90, dep. asst. to Pres. of U.S., dep. dir. of presdl. pers., 1990-93; pres. J. Naylor Cope Co., Washington, 1994—; NEA liaison Pres.' Com. on Arts and Humanities, Washington, 1985-87; dir. Internat. Skye Advisor, Washington, 1988; bd. dirs. Bush/Quayle Alumni Assn., 1991—, Pa. Ave. Devel. Corp.; mem. Office Pers. Mgmt.'s Task Force on Exec. and Mgmt. Devel., Washington, 1990. Chmn. alumni admissions coun. Trinity U., Washington, 1986-87; bd. dirs. Coop. Urban Ministry Ctr., Washington, 1987-89, Pennsylvania Avenue Devel. Corp., 1993—; vestrywoman St. John's Episcopal Ch., Washington, 1990—, co-chmn. outreach com., 1991—, chmn. search com. for 14th rector; jr. warden St. John's Episcopal Ch., 1994—. Tex. Coun. of Ch. Related Colls. scholar, 1974. Mem. The Pres.' Club, The 1925 F St. Club (Washington), Columbia Country Club (Chevy Chase, Md.), Tex. State Soc. (chmn. membership com. 1981), Nat. Trust for Hist. Preservation, Smithsonian Instn., Am. Film Inst., Mcpl. Art Soc. (N.Y.C.), Tex. Breakfast Club (Washington), Blue Key (sec. 1976-78), Chi Beta Epsilon (v.p. San Antonio coun. 1976). Republican. Episcopalian. Office: J Naylor Cope Co PO Box 40069 Washington DC 20016

COPELAND, ANNE B., research scientist, biologist; b. Chgo., Mar. 8, 1939; d. Harry A. and Lottie Berman; m. Donald B. Copeland, Mar. 10, 1957 (div. Aug. 1973); children: Rochelle (dec.), Deeana, Heather, Wendy. AA in Med. Lab. Tech., Wm. Rainey Harper C.C., Palatine, Ill., 1977; BA in Bd. of Govs. Program, Northeastern Ill. U., 1981; postgrad., Keller Grad. Sch., 1992—. Cert. med. lab. technician. Med. lab. technician in microbiology N.W. Cmty. Hosp., Arlington Heights, Ill., 1977-87; lab. technician I in phycology Met. Sanitary Dist. of Greater Chgo., 1978-85, lab. technician II in microbiology, 1985-87; lab. mgr. Abbott Labs., North Chicago, 1987-91, R & D scientist in animal health products, 1991—, project mgr., 1992—; presenter Choices Program, Lake County, Ill., 1993—. Inventor automated testing sys. Pres. Prairie Woods Aubudon Soc., Arlington Heights, 1991, 92, Friends of Volo Bog, Ingleside, Ill., 1981-87; tutor Adult Literacy Program, Palatine and North Chgo., 1993—. Mem. Am. Soc. Microbiology, Am. Soc. Clin. Pathologists (cert.), Internat. Assn. Great Lakes Rsch., Internat. Diatom Soc., N.Am. Diatom Soc., Ill. Soc. for Microbiology, Phi Theta Kappa. Office: Abbott Labs D-32P 1401 Sheridan Rd Bldg A1 North Chicago IL 60064-1803

COPELAND, CAROLYN ABIGAIL, retired university dean; b. White Plains, N.Y., May 5, 1931; d. Robert Erford and Mary Terwilliger; B.A. (CEW scholar), U. Mich., 1973, M.A. (Rackham Grad. Student scholar), 1979, postgrad. 1992—; m. William E. Copeland, Aug. 16, 1964; children—Rob Cameron, Diana Elizabeth Bosworth. With dean's office Coll. Lit., Sci. and Arts, U. Mich., Ann Arbor, 1967-91, asst. dean, 1980-84, assoc. dean, 1984-91. Mem. Mortar Bd., Phi Beta Kappa (v.p. Alpha chpt. 1984-86, pres. Alpha chpt. 1986-88). Author: Tankas from the Koelz Collection, 1980; Walter Norman Koelz, A Biography, in progress. Research in Buddhist art history. Home: 520 Darwin Rd Pinckney MI 48169-8113 Office: U Mich Ann Arbor MI 48109

COPELAND, CHRISTINE SUSAN, therapist; b. Milw., Jan. 8, 1949; d. Walter Horace and Doris Esther (Becker) C. BA in Psychology, Valparaiso (Ind.) U., 1971; MS in Psychology, U. Wis., 1974. Psychologist Curative Workshop, Green Bay, Wis., 1974-77, No. Wis. Ctr. for Developmentally Disabled, Chippewa Falls, Wis., 1977-86; behavior therapist Midelfort Clinic, Eau Claire, Wis., 1986-93, Systems Counseling and Cons., Inc., Eau Claire, 1994—. Mem. APA (assoc.), Am. Assn. Mental Retardation, Assn. for Advancement of Behavior Therapy, Wis. Psychol. Assn., C.H.A.D.D., Beta Sigma Phi (officer Wis. chpt. 1977—, Woman of the Yr. 1979). Home: 17962 W Edgewater Dr Chippewa Falls WI 54729-8753 Office: Sys Counseling and Cons Inc 110 E Grand Ave Eau Claire WI 54701

COPELAND, DRUSILLA GAIL, human resources executive; b. Birmingham, Ala., Nov. 21, 1955; d. Maple Lee and Harriette Magnolia (Eberhart) C. Student, Jefferson State Jr. Coll., 1973-74; BS, Samford U., 1977; MEd, U. Utah, 1981. Registered organizational devel. profl.; cert. tchr., Utah. Tchr. Salt Lake Sch. Dist., Salt Lake City, 1977-82; edn. analyst, tng. cons. Control Data Medlab, Salt Lake City, 1982-87; tng. and interactive video project mgr. 3M Health Info. Systems, Salt Lake City, 1987-90; tng. coord. 3M Co., Bedford Park, Ill., 1990-92, human resources supr., 1992—. Contbr. articles to profl. jours. Mem. Orgn. Devel. Inst. (Chgo. chpt., chair authorship 1992—), DuPage Page Turners, Phi Delta Kappa. Home: 2226 Abbeywood Dr F Lisle IL 60532 Office: 6850 S Harlem Ave Summit Argo IL 60501

COPELAND, MARY ELLEN, nurse; b. Atlanta, Sept. 14, 1957; d. Harold William and Mary Liz (Jones) C. AA, Freed-Hardeman Coll., 1978; BS in Nursing, Harding U., 1981. RN. Staff RN St. Vincent Infirmary, Little Rock, 1982, Piedmont Hosp., Atlanta, 1982-87, Hoag Meml. Hosp., Newport Beach, Calif., 1987—; wellness coordinator Pepperdine U., Malibu, Calif., 1987—. Mem. AACN, NAFE, Am. Heart Assn., Am. Assn. Occupational Health Nurses, Nat. Wellness Assn., Sigma Theta Tau. Mem. Ch. Christ. Home: 30856 Agoura Rd # C-3 Agoura Hills CA 91301

COPELAND, SUZANNE JOHNSON, real estate executive; b. Chgo., Aug. 1; d. John Berger and Eleanor (Dreger) Johnson; m. John Robert Copeland, Aug. 1, 1971 (div. June 1976). Assoc. French Lang. and Culture, Richland Coll., Dallas, 1974; BFA, Ill. Wesleyan U., Bloomington, 1965. Commercial artist Barney Donley Studio, Inc., Chgo., 1966-69; art dir. Levines Dept. Store, Dallas, 1970-74; creative dir. Titche-Goettinger, Inc., Dallas, 1974-78; catering mgr. Dunfey Hotel, Dallas, 1978-82; regional dir. corp. sales Lakeway/World of Tennis Resort, Austin, Tex., 1982-84; real estate sales assoc. Henry S. Miller, Dallas, 1984-86; v.p. Exclusive Properties Internat., Inc., Dallas, 1986—; cons. North Tex. Commn., Dallas, 1988. Acquisitions editor: Unser, An American Family Portrait, 1988. Mem. The Rep. Forum, Dallas, 1983-94; vol. Stars for Children, Dallas, 1988, Soc. for Prevention of Cruelty to Animals, Dallas, 1973-92; charter mem. P.M. League Dallas Mus. Art. Mem. Nat. Assn. Realtors, Tex. Assn. Realtors, Greater Dallas Assn. Realtors (com. chmn., Summit award 1984, 85), North Tex. Arabian Horse Club (bd. dirs. 1975-76, Pres.'s award 1978), Dallas Zool. Soc., Humane Soc. Dallas County (v.p. 1973-74), Humane Soc. U.S./Gulf States Humane Edn. Assn. (bd. dirs. 1990-91), Am. Montessori Soc., Delta Phi Delta, Phi Theta Kappa. Lutheran. Office: Exclusive Properties 5025 Capitol Ave Dallas TX 75206-6934

COPELAND, TATIANA BRANDT, accountant, tax executive; b. Dresden, Germany; came to U.S., 1959, naturalized, 1967; d. Cyril Alexander and Maria (von Satin) Brandt; m. Gerret van Sweringen Copeland, May 12, 1979. BS summa cum laude, UCLA, 1964; MBA, U. Calif.-Berkeley, 1966. Sr. tax cons. Price Waterhouse & Co., Los Angeles, 1966-72; asst. tax mgr. Whittaker Corp., L.A., 1972-75; mgr. internat. dept. E. I. Du Pont de Nemours, Wilmington, Del., 1975-80; pres. Tebec Assocs. Ltd., Wilmington, 1980—; co-owner, chief fin. officer Bouchaine Vineyards, Inc., Napa, Calif.; owner The Wine & Spirit Co., Greenville, Del.; co-owner and v.p. Rokeby Realty Co., Wilmington. Bd. dirs. Del. Symphony, Grand Opera House, Nat. Symphony Orch., Washington; presdl. appointee Adv. Com. for Trade Negotiations, 1982-87. Mem. Am. Inst. CPAs, Del. Soc. CPAs, Am. Woman's Soc. CPA's, Am. Soc. Women Accts., Internat. Fiscal Assn., Rodney Square Club (dir.), Phi Beta Kappa. Home: 175 Brecks Ln Wilmington DE 19807-3008 Office: PO Box 3662 Wilmington DE 19807-0662

COPENHAVER, MARION LAMSON, state legislator; b. Andover, Vt., Sept. 26, 1925; d. Joseph Fenwick and Christine (Forbes) Lamson; m. John H. Copenhaver, June 30, 1946; children: John III, Margaret, Christine, Eric, Lisa. Student, U. Vt., 1945-46. Legislator State of N.H., Concord, ranking Dem. health & human svcs. com., 1973—, mem. adminstrv. rules com., 1982—, mem. health & human svcs. oversight, 1990—. Chair Grafton County Dems., 1986-91; assoc. supr. Grafton County Soil Conservation Dist., 1980—; mem. Hanover (N.H.) Dem. Town Com., 1992; mem.-at-large Dem. State Com., Concord, 1992; bd. dirs. Dartmouth Hitchcock Found., Hanover, 1991—; bd. incorporators Dartmouth Hitchcock Med. Ctr., Lebanon, N.H., 1984—; bd. dirs. Crafton County Cr. Citizens Coun., Inc. Named N.H. Legislator of Yr. N.H. Nurses Assn., 1989. Mem. NOW, Bus. and Profl. Women's Club (outstanding mem. 1990). Democrat. Unitarian. Home: 14 Woodcock Rd Etna NH 03750-4402

COPLEY, CYNTHIA SUE LOVE, insurance adjuster; b. Defiance, Ohio, Oct. 26, 1957; d. Thomas Lee and Pauline Ann (Brandt) Love, Jr.; m. James Earl Copley, Jr., Oct. 19, 1985. B.Criminal Justice, Ohio U., 1981, A. in Law Enforcement, 1979, A in Fire and Safety Tech., 1982. Cert. profl. ins. woman. With Spangler Candy Co., Bryan, Ohio, 1976-77; guard Juvenile Detention Ctr., Chillicothe, Ohio, 1978; security officer J.C. Penney Corp., Inc., Chillicothe, Ohio, 1979, Rink's Bargain City, Chillicothe, Ohio, 1979; with Rubbermaid Sales Corp., Chillicothe, Ohio, 1980; asst. dept. sec. and computer lab asst. Ohio U., Chillicothe, 1977-81; supr. collections and investigation Bur. of Support, Ross County, Chillicothe, 1981-82; asst. mgr. Tecumseh Claims Svc., Chillicothe, 1982—; owner Copley Adjusting, Chillicothe, 1982—. Poll worker Rep. Party, Chillicothe, 1983—. Mem. So. Ohio Claims Assn., Ohio Assn. Ind. Ins. Adjusters (secy./treas. 1994), Ohio Assn. of Mutual Ins. Co., Nat. Assn. Ins. Women, Scioto Valley Assn. of Ins. Women (auditor 1991, sec. 1989-90, Claims Woman of Yr. 1989-91), Nat. Soc. of Profl. Ins. Investigators. Lutheran. Home and Office: Tecumseh Claims Svc PO Box 15 Chillicothe OH 45601-0015

COPLEY, HELEN KINNEY, newspaper publisher; b. Cedar Rapids, Iowa, Nov. 28, 1922; d. Fred Everett and Margaret (Casey) Kinney; m. James S. Copley, Aug. 16, 1965 (dec.); 1 child, David Casey. Attended, Hunter Coll., N.Y.C., 1945. Assoc. The Copley Press, Inc., 1952—, chmn. exec. com., chmn. corp. dir., 1973—, chief exec. officer, sr. mgmt. bd., 1974—; chmn. bd. Copley News Svc., San Diego, 1973—; chmn. editorial bd. Union-Tribune Pub. Co., 1976—; pub. The San Diego Union-Tribune, 1973—; bd. dirs. Fox Valley Press., Inc. Chmn. bd., trustee James S. Copley Found., 1973—; life mem. Friends of Internat. Center, La Jolla, Mus. Contemporary Art, San Diego, San Diego Hall of Sci., Scripps Meml. Hosp. Aux., San Diego Opera Assn., Star of India Aux., Zool. Soc. San Diego; mem. La Jolla Town Coun. Inc., San Diego Soc. Natural History, YWCA, San Diego Symphony Assn.; life patroness Makua Aux.; hon. chmn., bd. dirs. Washington Crossing Found.; trustee, mem. audit and compensation com. Howard Hughes Med. Inst.; hon. chmn. San Diego Coun. Literacy. Mem. Inter-Am. Press Assn., Newspaper Assn. Am., Calif. Press Assn., Am. Press Inst., Calif. Newspaper Pubs. Assn., Calif. Press Inst., San Francisco Press Club, L.A. Press Club. Republican. Roman Catholic. Clubs: Aurora (Ill.) Country, Army and Navy (D.C.), Univ. Club San Diego, La Jolla Beach and Tennis, La Jolla Country. Office: Copley Press Inc 7776 Ivanhoe Ave La Jolla CA 92037-4520

COPPAGE, PATRICIA ANN, librarian; b. Crestline, Ohio, Mar. 1, 1948; d. Samuel E. Sr. and Sophia Rowena (Minter) Mack; m. Luther Bristol Coppage Jr., Feb. 28, 1967; 1 child, Luther B. III. BS, Mid. Tenn. State U., 1970, MEd, 1975; Learning Resources Endorsement, Tex. Woman's Univ., 1991. Tchr. Murfreesboro (Tenn.) City Schs., 1970-83, Hurst-Euless-Bedford Ind. Sch. Dist., Bedford, Tex., 1984-93; sch. libr. Grapevine-Colleyville Ind. Sch. Dist., Grapevine, Tex., 1993—. Mem. AAUW, NEA, Tex. State Tchrs. Assn., Tex. Libr. Assn. Baptist. Home: 6521 Highview Ter Watauga TX 76148-1762 Office: Colleyville Elem 5800 Colleyville Blvd Colleyville TX 76034-6052

COPPERSMITH, SUSAN NAN, physicist; b. Johnstown, Pa., Mar. 18, 1957; d. Wallace Louis and Bernice Barbara (Evans) C.; m. Robert Daniel Blank, Dec. 20, 1981. BS in Physics, MIT, 1978; postgrad., Cambridge U., 1979; MS in Physics, Cornell U., 1981, PhD in Physics, 1983. Rsch. assoc. Brookhaven Nat. Labs., 1983-85; postdoctoral mem. tech. staff AT&T Bell Labs., Murray Hill, N.J., 1985-86, mem. tech. staff, 1987-90, disting. mem. tech. staff, 1990—; vis. lectr. Princeton U., 1986-87; vis. professorship for women NSF, 1986-87; gen. mem. Aspen Ctr. for Physics, 1991—; chancellor's disting. lectr. U. Calif., Irvine, 1991. Trustee Aspen Ctr. for Physics, 1993—. Winston Churchill scholar, 1978-79, Bell Labs. GRPW fellow, 1979-83. Fellow Am. Phys. Soc. Home: 692 Greenwich St Apt 4 New York NY 10014 Office: AT&T Bell Labs 600 Mountain Ave Rm 1D-351 New Providence NJ 07974

COPPOLA, ELAINE MARIE, librarian; b. Dunkirk, N.Y., Aug. 5, 1947; d. Henry Stanley and Althea May (Gloor) Hruby; m. Joseph Arthur McCoy III, Sept. 27, 1969 (div. 1972); 1 child, Richard Henry; m. Joseph Angelo Coppola, Aug. 15, 1981. BA, St. Bonaventure U., 1969; MLS, Syracuse U., 1979, MS Sc, 1989. Asst. mgr. manpower planning and devel. Oneida (N.Y.) Ltd., 1972-74, asst. mgr. pub. rels., 1974-78; libr. SUNY Inst. Tech., Utica, 1979; catalog libr. E.S. Bird Libr., Syracuse U., 1979-89, social scis. ref. bibliographer, 1989—. Author: Political Science Annotations within the Supplement to the Guide to Reference Books, 1992. Mem. ALA, N.Y. Libr. Assn., Am. Soc. for Pub. Adminstrn., Acad. of Polit. Sci., Am. Polit. Sci. Assn., Assn. of Coll. and Rsch. Librs. (ea. N.Y. chpt. pres. 1992-93, v.p. 1991-92, sec. 1989-91), Beta Phi Mu. Home: 103 Kenny St Fayetteville NY 13066-1230 Office: ES Bird Libr Syracuse Univ Syracuse NY 13244-2010

COPPS, SHEILA MAUREEN, Canadian government official; b. Hamilton, Ont., Can., Nov. 27, 1952; d. Victor Kennedy and Geraldine (Guthro) C.; 1 child, Danelle Lauran Copps. BA in French, English with hons., U. Western Ont., London; postgrad., U. Rouen, France, McMaster U., Hamilton. Reporter Ottawa Citizen, 1974-76, Hamilton Spectator, 1977; asst. to Ont. Liberal leader Stuart Smith, Hamilton, 1977-81; mem. Legis. Assembly Ont., Toronto, 1981-84, House of Commons, Ottawa, 1984-94; apptd. dep. leader Liberal Party Can., Ottawa, Ont., 1990—; dep. prime min., min. environment Govt. of Can., Ottawa, 1993—. Author: Nobody's Baby, 1986. Liberal. Roman Catholic. Office: House of Commons Rm 509S, Ottawa, ON Canada K1A 0A6

COQUEREL, DARLENE MILBURN, academic administrator, investor, realtor; b. Pitts., Sept. 18, 1961; d. Frank Mitchell and Elizabeth Ann (Bosco) Milburn; m. Andre Messan Coquerel, Dec. 18, 1986; children: Kelly Christine, Leah Nicole. Student, Duquesne U., 1979-81, Massey Inst., 1993-94. Lic. realtor. Asst. mgr. Hardee's FFR, Pitts., 1981-83; br. mgr. Ency. Britannica, Buffalo and Atlanta, 1983-89; admissions rep. Nanny Inst./Beverly Hills, Atlanta, 1989-90; placement coord. Selectively Yours Nanny Agy., Atlanta, 1990-91; ptnr., dir. Nat. Nanny Network, Atlanta, 1991-92; admissions rep. Massey Inst., Atlanta, 1992-94; with RE/MAX Profls., Norcross, Ga., 1994—. Vol. Massey Inst. Mem. NAFE, Ga. Real Estate Investors Assn., Gwinnett Bd. Realtors. Home: 2339 Tapanzee Ln Lawrenceville GA 30244

CORASH, MICHELE B., lawyer; b. May 6, 1945. BA, Mt. Holyoke Coll., 1967; JD cum laude, NYU, 1970. Legal advisor to chmn. FTC, 1970-72; dep. gen. counsel U.S. Dept. Energy, 1979; gen. counsel EPA, 1979-81; ptnr. Morrison & Foerster, L.A. Bd. editors Toxics Law Reporter; bd. advisors Jour. Environ. Law and Corporate Practice; mem. nat. editl. adv. bd. Prop 65 News. Bd. dirs. Calif. Counsel on Environ. and Econ. Balance, 1991—; mem. blue ribbon commn. Calif. Environ. Protection Agy. Unified Environ. Statute; active V.P. Bush Regulatory Task Force, 1981. Mem. ABA (mem. standing com. on environ. 1988-91, chair com. environ. crimes 1990), Inter-Pacific Bar Assn. (mem. environ. law com.). Office: Morrison & Foerster 555 W 5th St Ste 3500 Los Angeles CA 90013-1024 also: 345 California St San Francisco CA 94104*

CORBAT, PATRICIA LESLIE, special education educator; b. Washington, Feb. 28; d. Kenneth Lee and Stella Mary (Brey) C.; m. Noah Hughes Palmer IV, Aug. 16, 1975 (div.). BA, Coll. William and Mary, Williamsburg, Va., 1975, MEd, 1981. cert. learning disabilities/diagnostic prescriptive tchr. Learning disabilities resource/spl. edn. educator Virginia Beach (Va.) City Pub. Schs., 1981—; sec. spl. edn. eligibility com. Virginia Beach City Schs., 1981-87, chmn. gifted and talented selection com., 1985-86. Del. Va. State Dem. Conv., Norfolk, 1984, Roanoke, 1992; lobbyist Va. Gen. Assembly, Richmond, 1985; mem. Virginia Beach City Dem. Com., 1985-86; bd. dirs. Art and Company, Virginia Beach Ctr. for the Arts, 1993—, sec., 1994—. Mem. Virginia Beach Reading Coun., Virginia Beach Ctr. for the Arts, Virginia Beach Edn. Assn. (rep. 1982-85, del. Va. state conv. 1983-84, city coun. contact person polit. action com. 1983-85). Office: Virginia Beach City Schs Mcpl Ctr 2512 George Mason Dr Virginia Beach VA 23456-3413

CORBETT, IDNA MARITZA, university program director; b. San Pedro Sula, Honduras, Oct. 26, 1960; arrived in U.S., 1986; d. Samuel and Adaljiza Julieta (Rivera) Castellon; m. Robert James Corbett, June 17, 1986. BA, Goshen Coll., 1980; MA, Mich. State U., 1983; EdD, Temple U., 1995. Cons. Mktg. Ctr., San Pedro Sula, Honduras, 1982; tchr. Summer Hill Sch., Tegucigalpa, Honduras, 1982-83; prof., dept. head U. Pedagógica Nat., Tegucigalpa, Honduras, 1982-86; guidance counselor Escuela Internat. Sampedrana, San Pedro Sula, Honduras, 1983-86; tchr. Westtown (Pa.) Sch., 1986-87; instr. Messiah Coll., Phila., 1987-89; counseling coord. Temple U., Phila., 1988-89, program dir., 1989-92; dir. tutorial svcs. West Chester (Pa.) U., 1992-94, dir. acad. programs and support svcs., 1994—; advisor El Milagro Latino Student Union, West Chester U., 1992—. Youth comm. coord. Ptnrs. of Am., San Pedro Sula, 1985-86; bd. dirs. Big Sisters Phila., 1991-94; advisor Hispanic Students Assn. Temple U., 1991-92; bd. dirs. Chester County Migrant Ministry. Mem. ASCD, ACA, Pa. Assn. Ednl. Opportunities Program (sec. 1990-92), Am. Coll. Pers. Assn., Am. Ednl. Rsch. Assn., Nat. Tutoring Assn. Methodist.

CORBETT, KAREN MARY, secondary educator; b. St. Louis, Jan. 28, 1955; d. James J. and Kathaleen C. (Mathews) C. BA magna cum laude, U. Mo., 1977, MEd summa cum laude, 1988. Prof. educator Marquette Sr. High Rockwood Sch. Dist., St. Louis, 1978—; tutor Loretto Ctr., St. Louis, 1979-88. Mem. Greater St. Louis Tchrs. Am., Nat. Coun. Tchr. English, Alpha Delta Kappa. Home: 4624 Ambsdale Ct Saint Louis MO 63128-2436

CORBETT, SHIRLEY TUGWELL, counselor; b. Farmville, N.C., Aug. 8, 1936; d. John Walter and Ida Dail (Parker) Tugwell; m. Francis Marion Corbett, Sept. 12, 1954; children: Sharon Norris, Johnny, Marcus. BS, Francis Marion U., Florence, S.C., 1978, MS, 1982. Tchr. Florence-Darlington Tech., Florence, 1978-82, 88-92, counselor, 1983-87, adminstrv. coord., 1992-94; counselor in pvt. practice Florence, 1994—; prevention specialist Circle Park Prevention. Mem., vice chair Florence County Coun., 1984-92; pres., chair Florence Rep. Party, 1986-88; pres. Palmetto Civitans, Florence, 1985-86; grad. Leadership S.C., 1993. Mem. Psi Chi, Pi Gamma Mu, Alpha Delta Gamma. Baptist. Home and Office: 3126 Canal Dr Florence SC 29505

CORBETT, SUZANNE ELAINE, food writer, film producer, marketing executive, food historian; b. St. Louis, Jan. 23, 1953; d. George Edward and Opal Laverne (Duncan) Traxel; m. James Joseph Corbett, Jr., July 17, 1970; 1 child, James J. III. BA, Webster U., 1994, MA in Media Comm., 1983, postgrad. media comm., 1992. Cert. culinary profl., Nat. Inst. Food Svc. Industry, 1984, Internat. Assn. Culinary Profls., 1988; cert. tchr. vocat. home econs., food svc., Mo. Tchr. Inst. Continuing Edn. St. Louis Community Coll., 1976—; tchr. community edn. Lindbergh Sch. Dist. Pub. Schs., St. Louis, 1983-89; confectioner/caterer Suzanne Corbett Seasonal Confections, St. Louis, 1977-84; test baker Fleishman's Yeast, St. Louis, 1983; food stylist St. Louis, 1980—; rsch. cons./food mktg. and rsch. food/product history Suzanne Corbett/Culinary Resources Inc., St. Louis, 1988-94; rsch. cons. PanCor Prodns., 1994—; food historian/folk lorist St. Louis County Parks and Recreation, Mo. Hist. Soc., 1978—, St. Louis Art Mus., 1988—, Colonial Dames Am., 1989—; food media trainer Internat. Assn. Culinary Profls., 1990; lectr. in field. Author: Cowpuncher's Provision, 1988, River Fare, 1990, Pharoh's Pheast-Food from the Nile, 1991, Tips from Missouri Win Country, 1993; food writer, cookbook editor St. Louis Bugle food editor, columnist, 1991—. Bd. dirs. St. Louis South sect. Am. Heart Assn. Recipient Folklife Greentree grant award Ralston Purina, 1989, grant award Commerce Bank, 1990, grant award Wetterau Foods, 1991. Mem. Women in Communications (bd. dirs. 1988—, Communication awards 1989, 90, 91, 92), Mo. Press Women (pres., Communication award 1989, Named Communicator of Yr., 1993), Women's Commerce Assn., St. Louis Regional Commerce and Growth Assn. (exec. com., event chmn. 1989-90), Victorian Soc. Am. (past pres. St. Louis chpt.), James Beard Found. (charter), Am. Inst. Wine and Food, Internat. Assn. Culinary Profls. (cert., culinary historian Boston and Ann Arbor, internat. conf. com. 1990), Assn. Ind. Video and Filmmakers, St. Louis Press Club (co-editor Courier, Pres.'s award, Press Club Charitable Fund pres. 1993—), Nat. Fedn. Press Women (Communication and Writing awards), Nat. Trust for Hist. Preservation, St. Louis Culinary Soc. (sec., bd. dirs.), Order of Eastern Star. Roman Catholic. Home and Office: 5850 Pebble Oak Dr Saint Louis MO 63128-1412

CORBIN, ROSEMARY MAC GOWAN, mayor; b. Santa Cruz, Calif., Apr. 3, 1940; d. Frederick Patrick and Lorena Maude (Parr) MacGowan; m. Douglas Tenny Corbin, Apr. 6, 1968; children: Jeffrey, Diana. BA, San

Francisco State U., 1961; MLS, U. Calif., Berkeley, 1966. Libr. Stanford (Calif.) U., 1966-68, Richmond (Calif.) Pub. Libr., 1968-69, Kaiser Found. Health Plan, Oakland, Calif., 1976-81, San Francisco Pub. Libr., 1981-82, U. Calif., Berkeley, 1982-83; mem. coun. City of Richmond, 1985-93, vice mayor, 1986-87, mayor, 1993—; mem. Solid Waste Mgmt. Authority, 1985—, Contra Costa Hazardous Materials Commn., Martinez, Calif., 1987—, San Francisco Bay Conservation and Devel. Commn., 1987—; chair League of Calif. Cities Environ. Affairs Com., 1994—; mem. energy and environ. com. U.S. Conf. Mayors and Nat. League of Cities, 1993—. Contbr. articles to profl. publs. Mem. Calif. Libr. Assn., Local Govt. Commn., League Calif. Cities, Nat. League Cities, LWV, NOW, Nat. Women's Polit. Caucus. Democrat. Home: 114 Crest Ave Richmond CA 94801-4031 Office: Richmond City Hall 2600 Barrett Ave Richmond CA 94804-1654

CORCORAN, CANDACE MARIE, auditor, accountant; b. Fairfax, Va., Jan. 7, 1972; d. Dennis Scott Corcoran and Ellis Edson (stepfather) and Alice (Foley) Meredith. BBA in Acctg. magna cum laude, James Madison U., Harrisonburg, Va., 1994. Adminstrv. asst., office mgr. Newsletters, Inc., Bethesda, Md., 1987-94; staff acct./intern First Md. Bancorp, Balt., 1993; auditor, acct. Arthur Andersen & Co. (LLP), Washington, 1994—; asst. treas. Newsletters, Inc., Bethesda, Md., 1991—. Mem. Beta Alpha Psi (head alumni com. 1992—), Beta Gamma Sigma, Golden Key.

CORCORAN, EILEEN LYNCH, special education educator emerita; b. Newark, Mar. 12, 1917. A.B. in English, Montclair (N.J.) State Coll., 1938, Litt.D. (hon.), 1976; M.S. in Elem. Edn, SUNY, Brockport, 1953; spl. edn. cert., U. Rochester, 1958; Ed.D., SUNY, Buffalo, 1970. High sch. tchr. spl. edn., 1957-65; coordinator spl. edn. Bd. Coop. Ednl. Services, 2d Supervisory Dist., Monroe County, N.Y., 1965-67; asst. prof. to asso. prof. D'Youville Coll., Buffalo, 1967-72; dir. spl. edn. D'Youville Coll., 1969-72; dir. edn. Children's Psychiat. Centre, N.Y. State Dept. Mental Hygiene, 1970-71; mem. faculty SUNY, Brockport, 1972-81; prof. curriculum and instrn. SUNY, 1977-81, prof. emeritus, 1981—; bd. visitors Monroe Devel. Center, Rochester; mem. adv. council Commn. on Quality of Care for Mentally Disabled, State of N.Y.; cons. in field. Author curriculum materials, articles. Bd. dirs. Home Owner's Assn., Sun City, Ariz., Sun City Ambs. Fellow Am. Assn. Mental Deficiency; mem. AAUW, AAUP, Coun. for Exceptional Children (pres. N.Y. State 1971, Disting. Svc. award), Assn. for Children with Learning Disabilities, Sun City 79ers Lioness Club (sec.), Delta Kappa Gamma, Union Hills Country Club. Address: 10007 Pineaire Dr Sun City AZ 85351

CORCORAN, SISTER JANET, healthcare administrator; b. Long Beach, Calif., Nov. 19, 1938; d. Martin Patrick and Lillian Florence C. AA, Compton (Calif.) C.C., 1970; BA, Calif. State U., Dominguez Hills, 1972, MA, 1980; postgrad., U. So. Calif., L.A., 1986-87. Cert. adult edn. tchr., Calif.; cert. through mgmt. effectiveness program. Educator St. Mary's Elem. Sch., Santa Maria, Calif., 1960-62, St. Francis Elem. Sch., Sacramento, 1962-67; social worker St. Francis med. Ctr., Lynwood, Calif., 1972-73, chaplain, 1973-79; educator Lynwood Adult Sch., 1975-77, Compton C.C., 1976-83; v.p. St. Franics Med. Ctr., Lynwood, 1979-84, Marian Med. Ctr., Santa Maria, 1984—. Author: Don't Be Caught Dead - Plan Ahead, 1977, Conversation With a Dying Friend, 1977. City commr. Parks and Recreation, Lynwood, 1970-84, Santa Maria, 1991—; adv. bd. County Drug/Alcohol Bd., Santa Barbara County, Calif., 1990-91; pres. Assn. Pastoral Care Dirs., L.A., 1979-82, bd. dirs., 1974-84, adv. bd. Marian Residence, Santa Maria, Calif., 1986-87; bd. dirs. Hosp. Home Health Care Agy., Torrance, Calif., 1980-84. Recipient Humanitarian award NAACP, SM/Lompoc, Calif., 1993, Commendation, City Coun. Santa Maria, 1984. Mem. Nat. Soc. Honor Soc., Santa Maria C. of C., Nat. Assn. Cath. Hosps., Soroptimist Internat. Roman Catholic. Office: Marian Med Ctr 1400 East Church St Santa Maria CA 93454

CORCORAN, MARY ALICE, medical/surgical nurse, educator; b. West Point Twp., Wis., Sept. 19, 1934; d. Roman P. and Agnes M. (Ryan) Boehmer; m. Edward J. Corcoran, Aug. 16, 1958; children: Patrick, Bridget (dec.). Diploma, St. Mary's Sch. Nursing, Milw., 1955; cert. pub. health nurse, Marquette U., 1957. RN, Wis.; cert. diabetes educator, 1986, 91. Nurse clinician IV U. Wis. Univ. Health Svc., Madison, 1967—. Mem. hypertension faculty Am. Heart Assn., 1978-94. Mem. Am. Diabetes Assn. (Wis. bd. dirs. 1984-91, Vol. of Yr. award 1988, Program Vol. of Yr. award 1994), Am. Assn. Diabetes Educators. Office: U Wis Health Svc 1552 University Ave Madison WI 53705-4084

CORDAHL, MARY ANNE, psychologist; b. Seattle, Wash., Apr. 14, 1942; m. Robert Vestevich, Aug. 18, 1962 (div. May 1979); children: Jeanne Marie, James Cordahl, Katherine Cordahl; m. Stephen John Kelly, Nov. 21, 1981. AB, U. Detroit, 1970; MS, San Diego State U., 1977; PhD, Calif. Sch. of Profl., Psychology, San Diego, 1980. Lic. psychologist, Md. Exec. dir. Columbia Psychol. Svcs., Ellicott City, Md., 1984—. Office: Columbia Psychol Svcs 5032 Dorsey Hall Dr Ellicott City MD 21042-7711

CORDELL, CYNDY BINDER, entrepreneur, technical writer; b. St. Louis, May 23, 1954; d. George Farrell and Mary Virginia (Loewe) Binder; m. John Stewart Cordell, Dec. 30, 1976; children: Jonathon, Christopher, Allison. BS cum laude, Western Mich. U., 1976; MBA, DePaul U., 1983. Med. technologist Boulder (Colo.) Meml. Hosp., 1977-78, Skokie (Ill.) Valley Hosp., 1978-79; tech. svcs. specialist, assoc. product mgr., product mgr. Travenol Labs., Deerfield, Ill., 1979-82; product mgr., internat. specialist Abbott Labs., Abbott Park, Ill., 1982-86; exec. v.p. Ledell, Inc., Vernon Hills, Ill., 1987—; adj. instr. W.R. Harper Coll., Palatine, Ill., 1986-88, mem. mktg. adv. bd., 1986-88. Comms. chair Assn. Parents and Tchrs., Lake Forest, Ill., 1988; mem. sch. bd. Dist 67, Lake Forest, 1993—. Mem. Am. Soc. Clin. Pathologists, Lake Forest Caucus. Republican. Roman Catholic. Home: 805 N Summit Ave Lake Forest IL 60045 Office: Ledell Inc 262 Hawthorn Commons Vernon Hills IL 60061

CORDER, BILLIE FARMER, clinical psychologist, artist; b. Dundee, Miss., Sept. 12, 1934; d. Lee Kennith and Jimmy Louise (Hawkins) Farmer; B.S., Memphis State U., 1957; M.A., Vanderbilt U., 1959; Ed.D., U. Ky., 1966; student Memphis Acad. Art, 1959, Sch. Design, N.C. State U., 1971-75; m. Robert Floyd Corder, July 11, 1961. Intern, U. Tenn. Sch. Medicine, Memphis, 1959; staff psychologist Eastern State Hosp., Lexington, Ky., 1960-65, Child Guidance Clinic, Lexington, 1965-67; asst. prof. psychology Inter-Am. U., P.R., 1967-68; dir. psychology adolescent day care Area Community Mental Health Center, Washington, 1968-70; dir. psychol. services Alcoholic Rehab. Center, Butner, N.C., 1970-71; co-dir. psychol. services in child psychiatry Dix Hosp., Raleigh, N.C., 1971—; mem. adv. bd. Raleigh Developmental Evaluation Clinic, 1976-80; adj. faculty psychology dept. N.C. State U., Raleigh, 1975—, U. N.C. Sch. Medicine, 1975—. Mem. Wake County Youth Adv. Bd., 1979-80; mem. adv. com. Raleigh Arts Commn., 1980-82; bd. dirs. Haven House for Children, 1980-85, Nazareth House for Children, 1980-85. Recipient best research award N.C. Dept. Mental Health, 1965, cert. of appreciation Washington Tchrs. Assn., 1969, Outstanding Youth Svcs. award Wake Coun., 1991; numerous awards for art, including Purchase award N.C. Mus. Art, 1976, awards N.C. Watercolor Soc., 1978, 79; numerous research grants. Mem. Am. Psychol. Assn., Southeastern Psychol. Assn., N.C. Psychol. Assn., Am. Assn. Psychiat. Services for Children (program chmn. 1976-77), Raleigh Artists Guild (pres.), Raleigh Fine Arts Soc., N.C. Art Soc., Women's Equity Action League. N.C. Women's Polit. Caucus, Durham Artists Guild, N.C. Watercolor Soc. (v.p.), Wake Visual Artists Assn. (pres.), AAUW. Democrat. Baptist. Contbr. articles to profl. jours.; dir. editorial bd. N.C. Jour. Mental Health, 1974—; adj. editorial rev. bd. Hosp. and Community Psychiatry, Quar. Jour. Studies on Alcohol, Raleigh Acad. Women, 1993. Office: Child Psychiatry Clinic Dix Hospital Raleigh NC 27611

CORDES, GAYLE ANN, executive; b. Alton, Ill., Apr. 27, 1956; d. LEster Marvin and Alma Bernice (Wood) Milligan; m. David Joseph Cordes, June 10, 1977 (div. June 1989); 1 child, Joseph Patrick. BA, Millikin U., 1977; MBA, Southern Ill. U., 1981. Field sales rep. Herff Jones Co., Indpls., 1977-80; sales mgr. Price Wagner Studios, St. Louis, 1980-81; br. mgr., area mgr., area v.p., sr. area v.p., regional v.p. Adia Svcs., Inc., Menlo Park, Calif., 1981-90; v.p. ops., v.p. corp. sales Interim Svcs., Inc., Ft. Lauderdale, Fla., 1990-94; sr. v.p. The Olsten Corp., Melville, N.Y., 1994—. Vol., speaker Aid to Victims of Domestic Assault, DelRay Beach, Fla., 1993—. Mem. AAUW, NAFE, Alpha Chi Omega. Independent. Methodist. Home: 2930 Banyan Boulevard Cir NW Boca Raton FL 33431-6335 Office: The Olsten Corp 255 E Brown St Ste 118 Birmingham MI 48009

CORDES, KATHLEEN, family physician; b. Granite Falls, Minn., May 11, 1956; d. Martin and Elvera (Ohlmann) C. BA in Biology, Concordia Coll., Moorhead, Minn., 1978; MD, Mayo Med. Sch., Rochester, Minn., 1984. Diplomate Am. Bd. Family Practice. Resident in family practice So. Ill. U., Springfield, 1984-87; cardiology fellow Prairie Cardiovascular Cons., Springfield, 1987; emergency rm. physician Abraham Lincoln Meml. Hosp., Lincoln, Ill., 1988-89; family practice physician Eugene, Oreg., 1989-93; pvt. practice Eugene, 1994—; med. dir. Planned Parenthood of Lane County, Eugene, 1989-94, Health Team, Eugene, 1992—; med. cons. Dept. Vocat. Rehab., State of Oreg., Eugene, 1989-91; lectr. in field; panel mem. Perinatal Substance Abuse Conf., Eugene, 1991. Author med. column: Getting Ready, 1991. Vol. physician White Bird Med. Clinic, Eugene, 1990; bd. dirs. Lane County Direction Svc., Eugene, 1991—, med. cons., 1992—. Mem. AMA, Lane County Med. Assn., Oreg. Med. Assn., Oreg. Acad. Family Physicians, Am. Med. Women's Assn., Am. Acad. Family Physicians. Office: Wild Rose Med Clinic Ste 110 400 Country Club Rd Eugene OR 97401

CORDES, KATHRYN, public relations executive. V.p. consumer mktg. group Daniel J. Edelman, Inc., 1988-89; v.p. fashion beauty group Rowland Worldwide, 1989-90; dir. pub. rels. Hanes Hosiery, N.Y.C., 1990—. Office: Hanes Hoisery 1675 Broadway New York NY 10019*

CORDES, LESLIE BLACK, legislative staff member; b. L.A., Apr. 7, 1963; m. William Cordes. BA in Polit. Econs., U. Calif., Berkeley; MS in Internat. Trade and Fin., Georgetown U., 1987. Project analyst Overseas Pvt. Investment Corp.; mem. profl. staff Senate Com. Energy and Natural Resources, 1987-91, mem. profl. staff Subcom. Renewable Energy, Energy Efficiency and Competitiveness, 1991—. Mem. Adv. Neighborhood Commn. Office: Subcommittee Renewable Energy Rm 212 Senate Hart Office Bldg Washington DC 20510*

CORDIER, M.J., human resources specialist; b. Sturgeon Bay, Wis., Feb. 21, 1945; d. James E. and Laura A. (Mallien) C.; m. James G. Saboda, May 29, 1965 (div. May 1975). BA in Mgmt., Nat.-Louis U. With Sears Mdse. Group, 1966-93; from mgr. human resource ctrs. to dir. internat. human resources Sears Mdse. Group, Chgo., 1993—; mgr. mgmt. devel. ctr. Sears Mdse. Group, Orlando, Fla., 1993—. Recipient YWCA Leadership award, 1990. Mem. ASTD, Soc. Human Resource Mgmt., Inst. Internat. Human Resources. Home: 1015 Kelly Creek Cir Oviedo FL 32765-5703 Office: Sears Merchandise Group 3111 E Colonial Dr Orlando FL 32803-5107

CORDINGLEY, MARY JEANETTE BOWLES (MRS. WILLIAM ANDREW CORDINGLEY), social worker, psychologist, artist, writer; b. Des Moines, Jan. 1, 1918; d. William David and Florence (Spurrier) Bowles; m. William Andrew Cordingley, Mar. 17, 1942; children: William Andrew, Thomas Kent, Constance Louise. Student, Stephens Coll., 1936; BA, Carleton Coll., 1939; postgrad. U. Denver, 1944-45; MA in Psychiat. Social Work, U. Minn., 1948; grad. art student, 1963; MA in Counseling Psychology Pepperdine U., 1985; Co-pub. Univ. News, 1939-40; with U.S.O. Travelers Aid Service, 1942-44; mem. Jr. League, Des Moines, 1943, bd. dirs., sec. Mpls., 1951-56; clinic psychiat. social worker U. Minn. Hosp., 1947-48; social worker community service project neuropediatrics U. Minn., 1964-65; med. dir. med. sch. svc. Mont. Deaconess Hosp., 1970-74; instigator, pres. Original Pioneer Prints Notepaper Co.; paintings in variety of galleries and traveling shows; exhibited in numerous one-man shows including Chas. Russell Gallery, Mont., Student Union U. Minn., Nat. Biennial League Am. Pen Women, 1968, 70, U. Mont., 1974, Mont. Traveling Exhibit, 1966-67, Mus. of the Rockies hist. show, 1976, Bergen Art Guild, 1976, 78, U.S. Traveling Show, 1987-89, Russell Auction, 1977, 91, Kessel Long Gallery, Scottsdale, 1991, Great Falls Pub. Libr. hist. art show oil exhibit 1992—; Ariz. terrain show, Mayo Clinic, Scottsdale, 1991—; illustrator: The Tobacco Route, Geol. Soc. Guide Book, 1992; Mon. Artist Exhibit-Gov.'s Mansion, 1990; graphic artist in metal etchings; therapist Mental Health Center, 1977-82. Organizer, Hazeltine Nat. Golf Club Womens Assn., 1962-64, I. & R. Ctr., 1967; pres. adv. bd. Mont. State U.; past mem. bd. dirs. United Way, mem. arts adv. bd. Sierra Nev. Coll.; former mem. Youth Guidance Home Bd. Recipient various awards. Mem. NASW, State Arts Coun., Scottsdale Jr. League (sustainers 1986—, art instr.), Am. Mus. Women in Arts. Co-author: Series on Mont. Instns.; author: Speaking with a Brush. Home: 7878 E Gainey Ranch Rd Unit 47 Scottsdale AZ 85258-1770

CORDON, GLENDA SUE, college dean; b. Harlingen, Tex., Mar. 2, 1943; d. Nolan Edgar and Helen Doris (Hays) Wilborn; m. Ray Lewis Cordon, Aug. 30, 1964; children: Matthew Chandler, Heather Joan. BS, U. Ill., 1965. Rsch. asst. Ill. Geol. Survey, Urbana, 1965-67; tchr. Arcola (Ill.) Jr. High Sch., 1967-69; geology text author O'Fallon (Ill.) High Sch., 1976-82; compliance officer St. Clair County Grants Dept., Belleville, Ill., 1983-87; dir. job tng. McKendree Coll., Lebanon, Ill., 1987-88, dean of admissions, 1988—. Co-author: (high sch. text) Geology Is, 1977. Bd. dirs. bootstrap program St. Clair County Housing Authority, 1991—. Mem. Nat. Assn. Coll. Admissions Counselors, Nat. Assn. Collegiate Registrars and Admissions Officers, Ill. Assn. Collegiate Registrars and Admissions Officers, Ill. Assn. Coll. Admissions Counselors,. Home: 402 S Augusta St O'Fallon IL 62269-2303 Office: McKendree Coll 701 College Rd Lebanon IL 62254-1299

CÓRDOVA, FRANCE ANNE-DOMINIC, astrophysics educator; b. Paris, Aug. 5, 1947; came to U.S., 1953; d. Frederick Ben Jr. and Joan Francis (McGuinness) C.; m. Christian John Foster, Jan. 4, 1985; children: Anne-Catherine Cordova Foster, Stephen Cordova Foster. BA in English with distinction, Stanford U., 1969; PhD in Physics, Calif. Inst. Tech., 1979. Staff scientist earth and space sci. div. Los Alamos Nat. Lab., 1979-89, dep. group leader space astronomy and astrophysics group, 1989; prof., head dept. astronomy and astrophysics Pa. State U., University Park, 1989-93; chief scientist NASA, Washington, 1993—; mem. Nat. Com. on Medal of Sci., 1991-94; mem. adv. com. for astron. scis. NSF, 1990-93, external adv. com. Particle Astrophysics Ctr., 1989-93; bd. dirs. Assn. Univs. for Rsch. in Astronomy, 1989-93; mem. Space Telescope Inst. Coun., 1990-93; mem. com. space astronomy and astrophysics Space Sci. Bd., 1987-90, internat. users com. Roentgen X-ray Obs., 1985-90, extreme ultraviolet explorer guest observer working group NASA, 1988-92, com. Space Sci. and Applications Group, NASA, 1991-93; mem. Hubble Telescope Adv. Camera Team, 1993; chair Hubble Fellow Selection Com., 1992. Author: The Women of Santo Domingo, 1969; guest editor Mademoiselle mag., 1969; editor: Multiwavelength Astrophysics, 1988, The Spectroscopic Survey Telescope, 1990; contbr. numerous articles, abstracts and revs. to Astrophysics Jour., Nature, Astrophysics and Space Scis., Advanced Space Rsch., Astron. Astrophysics, Mon. Nat. Royal Astron. Soc., chpts. to books. Named One of Am.'s 100 Brightest Scientists under 40, Sci. Digest, 1986; numerous grants NASA, 1979—, recipient group achievement award, NASA, 1991. Mem. Internat. Astron. Union (U.S. nat. com. 1990-93), Am. Astron. Soc. (v.p. 1993—, chair high energy astrophysics divsn. 1990, vice chair 1989), Sigma Xi. Office: NASA 300 E St SW Code AS Washington DC 20546

CORDOVA, MARIA ASUNCION, dentist; b. Punta Arenas, Magallanes, Chile, May 14, 1941; came to U.S., 1972; d. Miguel Cordova and Maria Asucion Requena; m. Carlos F. Salinas, July 27, 1963; children: Carlos M., Claudio A., Lola. DDS, U. Chile, Santiago, 1965; DMD, U. S.C., 1986. From instr. to assoc. prof. medicine U. Chile Dept. Physiology, Valparaiso, 1965-72; postdoctoral fellow Johns Hopkins U., Balt., 1972-75; from instr. to asst. prof. M.U. S.C. Dept. Physiology, Charleston, 1975-86; pvt. practice Charleston, 1987—; vis. scientist N.Y. Med. Coll., 1975. Contbr. articles to profl. jours. Program coord. Circulo Hispanic Charleston; coord. Amnesty Internat. U.S.A., Piccolo Spoleto, Neighborday, Charleston, S.C.; bd. dirs. Ptnrs. of Ams.; active NOW. Mem. Charleston Women's Network (pres. 1989-90). Roman Catholic. Office: 159 Wentworth St Charleston SC 29401-1731

CORE, MARY CAROLYN W. PARSONS, radiologic technologist; b. Valpariso, Fla., Dec. 8, 1949; d. Levi and Mary Etta (Elliott) Willey; m. Joel Kent Core, Aug. 3, 1979; 1 child, Candace W. Parsons. Student, Peninsula Gen. Hosp. Sch. Radiologic Tech., Salisbury, Md., 1969; student, U. Del., 1969-73, Del. Tech. Community Coll., 1973-79, St. Joseph's Coll., 1983-86; BSBA, St. Joseph's Coll., 1987; postgrad., U. Md., 1994—. Technologist Peninsula Gen. Hosp., Salisbury, 1967-72; tech. dir. edn. Sch. Radiologic Tech., Salisbury, 1973-75; technologist Johns Hopkins Hosp., Salisbury, 1972-73, Nanticoke Meml. Hosp., Seaford, Del., 1975-79; adminstrv. chief technologist, imaging depts. Shady Grove Adventist Hosp., Rockville, Md., 1979-81; dir. dept. radiol. scis. Anne Arundel Diagnostics, Inc., Rockville, 1981—; chief ops. officer Anne Arundel MRI (Magnetic Resonance Imaging, Annapolis, Md., 1981—; chief exec. officer Anne Arundel Diagnostics, Inc. and Anne Arundel MRI, Annapolis, Md., 1981—; v.p. corp. svcs. Anne Arundel Healthcare Systems, Inc. Mem. Cen. Md. coun. Girl Scouts U.S., Pres.'s award svc. team, 1989. Recipient twin awards YWCA, 1988. Mem. NAFE, Md. Soc. Radiologic Technologists (pres. 1980-81, sr. bd. mem. 1982-83, various awards including 1st Pl. Essay awards 1974, 76, 84, 87), Am. Hosp. Radiology Adminstrs. (v.p. 1984-85, chmn. by-laws com. 1984-85, statis. resources com. 1985-86), Am. Mgmt. Assn., Radiology Bus. Mgrs. Assn., Ea. Shore Dist. Radiologic Technologists (pres. 1976-78). Republican. Methodist. Home: 1907 Harcourt Ave Crofton MD 21114-2103 Office: 135 E 55th St New York NY 10022

CORELL, GINA LEIGH, political science educator; b. Roanoke, Va., Dec. 10, 1962; d. Gaylord Stafford and Betty Frances (Spangler) C. BA, U. Va., 1985; MA, La. State U., 1992, postgrad., 1992—. Provider svcs. rep. Blue Cross/Blue Shield, Richmond, Va., 1985-86; mgmt. assoc. Sovran Bank, NA (now named Nations Bank), Richmond, 1986-87, comml. accounts asst., 1987-88, comml. planning analyst, 1988-90; grad. asst. polit. sci. dept. La. State U., Baton Rouge, 1990—. Co-author: Term Limits: Public Choice, 1994; grad. editl. asst. Jour. Politics, 1991-92; contbr. papers to profl. confs. Mem. selection com. Jefferson Scholars Program, Richmond, 1985-90; team leader United Way, Richmond, 1987-90; researcher Dept. Environ. Quality, Baton Rouge, 1993; campaign vol. Wilder for Gov. Election Campaign, Richmond, 1988; active Va. Mus. of Fine Arts, 1985-90. Mem. Am. Polit. Sci. Assn., U. Va. Alumni Orgn., La. State U. Alumni Orgn., Metro C. of C. (group chmn. 1985-87). Democrat. Methodist. Office: La State U 240 Stubbs Hall Baton Rouge LA 70803

COREY, JO ANN, management analyst; b. Methuen, Mass., Jan. 26, 1965; d. Joseph Augustine and Marie Ellen (Dowe) C. BA, Calif. State U., Fullerton, 1987, MPA, 1989. Adminstrv. intern City of Brea, Calif., 1987-90; mgmt. aide City of Mission Viejo, Calif., 1990-92, mgmt. analyst, 1992—. Mem. Mcpl. Mgmt. Assts. So. Calif. (programming com. 1987—), Calif. Parks and Recreation Soc., Phi Alpha Theta. Democrat. Roman Catholic. Office: City of Mission Viejo 25909 Pala Mission Viejo CA 92691

COREY, KAY JANIS, business owner, designer, nurse; b. Detroit, Aug. 22, 1942; d. Alexander Michael Corey and Lillian Emiline (Stanley) Kilborn; divorced; children: Tonya Kay, William James, Jason Ronald. Student, C.S. Mott Community Coll., 1960-62, Mich. State U., 1962-64; AA, AS in Nursing, St. Petersburg Jr. Coll., 1978; student, U. South Fla., 1985-86. RN; cert. perioperative nurse; cert. varitypist. Mgr. display Lerner Shops, Flint, Mich., 1960-62; layout artist Abdulla Advt., Flint, 1966-67; varitypist, artist City Hall Print Shop, Flint, 1967-70; nurse Suncoast Hosp., Largo, Fla., 1976-78; nurse, coord. plastic surgery svc., perioperative staff nurse Largo Med. Ctr. Hosp., 1978-81, 84—; assoc. dir. nursing Roberts Home Health Svc., Pinellas Park, Fla., 1982-84; co-owner Sand Castle Resort, White Bay, Jost Van Dyke, Brit. Virgin Island, 1990—; designer, artist K.J. Originals clothing line, 1990—; insvc. edn. instr., dir. video edn., team leader oncology dept. Largo Med. Ctr. Hosp., 1980-81, now part-time nurse. Editor, illustrator: (book) Some Questions and Answers About Chemotherapy, 1981, Thoughts for Today, 1981; illustrator (cookbooks) Spices and Spoons, 1982, Yom Tov Essen n' Fressen, 1983; various brochures and catalogues; art work in permanent collection of C.S. Mott Jr. Coll., Flint, 1962; artist, designer of casual and hand painted clothing for children and adults. Historian Am. Businesswomen's Assn., Flint, 1968-73 (scholarship 1976); outreach chmn. Temple B'nai Israel, Clearwater, Fla., 1981-85; regional outreach coord. Union of Am. Hebrew Congregations, N.Y.C., 1983-85. Mem. Assn. of Oper. Rm. Nurses, Phi Theta Kappa. Republican. Jewish. Office: Sandcastle Ltd, White Bay, Jost Van Dyke British Virgin Islands also: 6501 Red Hook Plz Ste 201 Saint Thomas VI 00802-1305

CORINBLIT, NITA GREEN, artist educator; b. Detroit, Mar. 3, 1924; d. Leo and Gussie Green; m. Jack Corinblit, Mar. 9, 1944; children: Meryl Marshall, Barbara Graff, Nancy Montgomery. BFA, Art Inst. Chgo., 1949; MA, Calif. State U., 1971. Cert. art tchr., Calif. Art, history of art and English tchr. jr. and sr. H.S. L.A., 1963-85; arts and humanities cons. L.A. Unified Sch. Dist., 1982-86; methods tchg. crafts instr. Calif. State U., Northridge, 1969-71; humanities instr. Lee Coll. U. Judaism, L.A.; participant NEH project, Greensboro, N.C., summer 1982. Exhibited in group shows at Libr. of Congress, Washington, nat. and local exhbns. Witness U.S. House Ways and Means com., Am. Assn. Mus., Washington, 1980; docent L.A. Mus. Contemporary Art, 1987-92; docent coord. Platt Gallery, U. Judaism, L.A., 1990-94; mem. Women's Polit. Com., L.A., 1992-94. Grantee Calif. Coun. for the Humanities, NEH, 1986, Calif. Arts Coun., 1983-84, U.S. Arts for the Aging, 1980-81. Mem. Calif. Humanities Assn. (pres. 1986-87, newsletter editor 1988—, treas. 1978-85, Perlee award 1991), Art Educators L.A., L.A. Art Assn., L.A. Printmaking Soc. Home: 5854 Hillview Park Ave Van Nuys CA 91401

CORK, HOLLY A., state legislator; b. Savannah, Ga., Mar. 8, 1966; d. William Neville II and Helen (Holloman) C. BA, U. S.C., 1988. Legis. asst. to Rep. Arthur Ravenel Jr., 1988-89; mem. S.C. Ho. Reps., dist. 123, 1989-92, S.C. Senate, 1992—. Republican. Episcopalian. Home: 3 Rowboat Row Hilton Head Island SC 29928 Office: PO Box 142 Columbia SC 29202

CORK, LINDA KATHERINE, veterinary pathologist, educator; b. Texarkana, Tex., Dec. 14, 1936; d. Albert James and Martine Sessions (Buntyn) Collins; m. P.S. Cork Jr., Mar. 1955 (div. 1965); children: Robin E., Jerald W. BS, Tex. A&M U., 1969, DVM, 1970; PhD, Wash. State U., 1974. Diplomate Am. Coll. Vet. Pathologists. Fellow Wash. State U., Pullman, 1970-74; asst. prof. U. Ga., Athens, 1974-76; asst. prof. Johns Hopkins U., Balt., 1976-82, assoc. prof., 1982-88, assoc. dir. rsch. Alzheimer's Disease Rsch. Ctr., 1985-93, prof., 1988-93; prof., chmn. Dept. Comparative Medicine Stanford U., 1994—; coun. mem. NIH div. Rsch. Resources, Bethesda, Md., 1985-89; adv. bd. Registry Comparative Pathology, Bethesda. Grantee Nat. Inst. on Aging, 1985-89, Nat. Inst. Health, 1986-91, 86-93, 87-92. Mem. Inst. Medicine, Am. Assn. Neuropathologists (chmn. June 1988), Am. Assn. Pathology, U.S.-Can. Acad. Pathology. Methodist. Office: Stanford Med Ctr Dept Comparative Medicine Quad 7 Bldg 330 Stanford CA 94305-5410

CORKUM, BETTY JEAN, foundation adminstrator, former nurse, author; b. Leominster, Mass., Apr. 8, 1946; d. Stewart William Corkum and Evelyn Claire (Rivard) Mallorey; m. Joseph Guy Alonzo Le Blanc, July 1, 1967 (dec. Jan. 1980); children: Julie Elizabeth, Michelle Denise. BS, Boston Coll., 1971. Nurse, 1971-84, author, poet, 1985-94; humanitarian Corkum Found., Lancaster, Calif., 1990—. Author: Aura of Rain, 1987; poet included in Am. Anthology of Poets, 1990, 93. Co-authored brochure So. Ariz. Spina Bifida Assn., assisted charter, 1987. Recipient for meritorious work for students of Inglewood, Calif. Project Invest award Inglewood Sch. Dist., 1982. Democrat. Jewish. Home: 44303 Hardwood Ave Lancaster CA 93534

CORLESS, KELLY, oncology nurse; b. Teaneck, N.J., Nov. 14, 1961; d. Harry and Marie (Petrali) C. ADN, County Coll. of Morris, 1983. RN, N.J. Nurse Hosp. Ctr. at Orange, N.J., 1983—; cons. on policies for nursing documentation; v.p. health care systems Madison Bus. Forms, 1990—. Named Sales Profl. of Yr., Bus. Forms & Systems, 1989. Office: 16 Gloria Ln Fairfield NJ 07004-3306

CORLEY, FLORENCE FLEMING, history educator; b. Augusta, Ga., Jan. 6, 1933; d. William Cornelius and Sarah Virginia (Sibley) Fleming; m. James Weaver Corley, Jr., Dec. 29, 1955; children: Florence Hart Corley Johnson, James Weaver Corley III, Mary Anne Corley Herbert, Sarah Virginia Corley

Turman, William Thomas Corley. BA, Agnes Scott Coll., 1954; MA, Emory U., 1955; PhD, Ga. State U., 1985. Cert. tchr., T-5, Ga. Alumnae rep. Agnes Scott Coll., Decatur, Ga., 1955; history tchr. The Westminster Schs., Atlanta, 1968-88, The Walker Sch., Marietta, Ga., 1989; history instr. Kennesaw State Coll., Marietta, 1989-91, asst. prof. history, 1991—; U.S. history cons. The Coll. Bd., N.Y.C., 1978—; reader, table leader Ednl. Testing Svc., Princeton, N.J., 1975—. Assoc. editor: American Presbyterians, Phila., 1984—, Ga. Jour. of So. Legal History, Atlanta, 1989; editor: The Landmarker, 1978-79; author: Confederate City: Augusta, Georgia 1860-65, 1960, 74; contbr. articles to hist. jours.; compiler (slides/tape) Where Were the Women? 1979. Sixth grade and adult tchr. First Presbyn. Ch., Marietta, 1960—, elder, 1990—; active U.S. history contest DAR, Marietta, 1991—; cons. Girls Club of Cobb/Marietta, 1981. Woodrow Wilson fellow Emory U., 1954-55; recipient fellowship in women's history NEH, Stanford U., Palo Alto, Calif., 1978-79, scholarship in classical studies, Vergilian Soc., Cumae, Italy, 1982, scholarships in medieval Eng. and Eng. today, English Speaking Union, U.K., 1979, 80. Mem. Cobb Landmarks and Hist. Soc. (charter bd. dirs., co-pres. 1985-86, 87-88), Atlanta Hist. Soc., Civil War Round Table, Ga. Assn. Historians, Ga. Hist. Soc., So. Assn. Women Historians, So. Hist. Assn., So. Garden History Soc., Richmond County Hist. Assn., Presbyn. Hist. Soc., Phi Beta Kappa, Phi Alpha Theta. Democrat. Home: 285 Kennesaw Ave Marietta GA 30060 Office: Kennesaw State Coll PO Box 444 Marietta GA 30061

CORLEY, JEAN ARNETTE LEISTER, infosystems executive; b. Charleston, S.C., June 16, 1944; d. William Audley and Arnette (Mason) Leister; widowed; children: Arnette Elizabeth, Daniel Lee. BS, Med. Coll. Ga., 1970; MBA, M of Pub. Adminstrn., Southeastern U., 1980. Various positions health care orgns., Augusta, Ga., 1960-70; office mgr., counselor Info. Ctr. for Alcohol and Drug Abuse, Augusta, 1970-71; planner health care systems Nat. Med. Assn. Found., Washington, 1971-72; research assoc., systems analyst GEOMET, Inc., Gaithersburg, Md., 1972-74; dir. med. records Georgetown U. Hosp., Washington, 1974-80; dir. med. info. svcs. Lahey Clinic Med. Ctr., Burlington, Mass., 1980-84; nat. sales mgr. 3M Health Info. Systems, Boston and Atlanta, 1984-91; mktg. mgr. 3M Health Info. Systems, Salt Lake City, 1992—. Contbr. articles to profl. jours. Mem. adv. bd. various colls., 1973-92; active Habitat for Humanity, Leadership Utah. Mem. Am. Health Info. Mgmt. Assn. (program com. 1977-80, chmn. 1981-82, fed. health program adv. com. 1978-80, computerized health info. task force 1983-87, subcom. on edn. 1990-93, Workgroup on Electronic Data Interchange 1992-94), Computer-based Patient Record Inst., Women in Info. Processing, New Eng. Med. Records Conf. (exec. dir. 1984-88), LWV, Common Cause. Democrat. Presbyterian. Home: 545 N DeSoto St Salt Lake City UT 84103

CORLEY, JENNY LYND WERTHEIM, educator; b. Lincoln, Ill., June 18, 1937; d. Robert Glenn and Nancy Lynd (Hoblit) Wertheim; m. William Gene Corley, Aug. 9, 1959; children: Anne Lynd Corley Baum, Robert William, Scott Elson. BS in Music Edn., U. Ill., 1959, MS in Music Edn., 1961; postgrad., U. Ill., Loyola U., 1985—. Tchr. choral music Mahomet (Ill.)/Seymour K-12, 1959-61; supr. music Fairfax County (Va.), 1961-63; Tchr. music Highland Park (Ill.) 107, 1969, dir. gifted edn., 1969-70; tchr. music Glenview (Ill.) 34, 1981—; sec.-treas. Corley Agroleum Properties, 1993—. Dir. mid-Am. bd. ARC, Chgo., 1980-86. Recipient Heart of Gold United Way, 1992, Community Svc. award Ill. Park & Recreation Assn./Ill. Assn. Park Dists., 1994. Mem. Music Edn. Nat. Conf., North Shore Music Tchrs. Assn. (treas. 1987-90), Jr. League Chgo. (treas. 1978-81), Sigma Alpha Iota, Phi Delta Kappa (found. chmn. 1994-95). Presbyterian. Home: 744 Glenayre Dr Glenview IL 60025-4411 Office: Springman Sch 2701 Ctrl Rd Glenview IL 60025-4411

CORNBLEET, AILEEN GAIL HIRSCH, English language and social studies educator; b. Chgo., Nov. 8, 1946; d. Irving Carlton and Anne (Ditlov) Hirsch; m. David H. Cornbleet, Aug. 18, 1968; children: Jonathan M., Jocelyn F. BS summa cum laude, U. Wis., 1968; interpreter's degree in German/History, U. Heidelberg, Fed. Republic Germany, 1970; MA in Secondary Edn. summa cum laude, Boston U., 1972. Instr. Heidelberg Am. High Sch., 1968-75, Temple Sholom, Chgo., 1976-88; instr. ESL Oakton Community Coll., Skokie, Ill., 1986-87; supervising tchr. MA students, instr. philosophy and history edn., social studies methods instr. Nat. Coll. Edn., 1987-92; tchr. lit. Armstrong Sch., Chgo., 1993—. Sec. Orgn. Rehab. Tng., Lincolnwood, Ill., 1980; mem. Lincolnwood Sch. Bd. Dist. 74, 1982-87. Recipient Master Tchr. award Bd. Jewish Edn., 1986, Loyola U. 2001 award Tchrs. Applying Whole Lang., 1993, 3d place award McDonald's Ednl. Contest, 1992. Fellow ASCD; mem. Stock Market Club, Phi Alpha Theta, Pi Lambda Phi. Home: 6532 N Christiana Ave Lincolnwood IL 60645-3812

CORNELL, CAROL ELLEN, psychologist; b. Inverness, Fla., Feb. 9, 1959; d. Lionel Leroy and Dorothy Joyce (Dodson) C ; m. Mark Stephen Menemeier, May 8, 1993. BA, MA, Johns Hopkins U., 1980; MPhil, Yale U., 1987, PhD, 1992. Coord. behavioral rsch. & svcs. U. Fla. Preventive Cardiology Program, Gainesville, 1989-91; coord. behavioral programs Drachman Ctr. Health Promotion U. Ariz., Tucson, 1991-93; lectr. psychology U. Ariz., Tucson, 1991-93; asst. prof. U. Ala. at Birmingham, 1993—. Contbr. chpts. to books and articles to profl. jours. Allan Sheldon III Meml. fellow Yale U., 1987-88, Yale U. fellow, 1986-87, Nat. Inst. Mental Health fellow Health Psychology, 1984-86, Sterling prize fellow Yale U., 1984. Mem. Am. Psychol. Assn. (divsn. health psychology, Dissertation Rsch. award 1988), Soc. Behavioral Medicine (Citation Poster award 1992). Democrat. Baptist.

CORNELL, WENDY ANN, administrative assistant; b. L.A., Aug. 6, 1962; d. James Melvin and Ruth Ann (Murphy) C. A in Gen. Studies, No. Va. C.C., Alexandria, 1993; postgrad., George Mason U. Adminstrv. specialist U.S. Army, Ft. Jackson, S.C., 1988, Office of Sec. Def., Pers. Divsn., Pentagon, Washington, 1989; receptionist Immediate Office Sec. Def., Pentagon, Washington, 1989-92, personal sec., 1992-93, personal and confidential asst., 1993-94. Patron, contbr. Kennedy Ctr., Washington, 1994; vol. Alexandria Domestic Violence Program, 1994—. Republican. Ch. of Christ.

CORNETT, CYNTHIA COLE, counselor; b. Boston, Apr. 13, 1951; d. John Harry and Dorothy Drummond (Strout) Cole; divorced; children: John S., Benjamin C., Robin A. BA, Auburn U., 1973; MA, U. Ctrl. Fla., 1989. Cert. counselor, Fla. Program asst. dir. Parent Resource Ctr., Orlando, Fla., 1985-87, program dir., 1987-89; guidance counselor Orange County Pub. Schs., Orlando, Fla., 1989—. Mem. partnership ministry Christian Svc. Ctr., Orlando, Fal., 1982-83; sec. Gateway PTA, Orlando, 1989-93; mem. Boone Sch. Adv. Com., Orlando, 1993—. Recipient Appreciation for Svc. award Ctrl. Fla. Parent Fairs, 1987-89, Multilevel Counselor of Yr. Orange County Pub. Schs., 1993-94. Mem. ACA, Am. Sch. Counselors Assn., Orange County Counseling Assn., Classroom Tchrs. Assn. Republican. Episcopalian. Office: Gateway Sch for Exceptional Edn 4000 Silver Star Rd Orlando FL 32808-4634

CORNETT, LINDA TAVEN, information systems manager, consultant; b. Salem, Ohio, Sept. 26, 1948; d. Robert and Myrtle (Miracle) C. BS, Kent State U., 1971; MS, Troy State U., 1975; MA, Webster Coll., St. Louis, 1982, Webster Coll., 1987. Pers. mgr. U.S. Army, 1971-79; asst. prof. mil. sci. Westminster Coll., Fulton, Mo., 1979-83; coll. instr. Drury Coll., St. Roberts, Mo., 1984-85; pres., owner LTC Cons., St. Louis, 1980—; systems programmer analyst ISC, St. Louis, 1989-90, computer systems analyst, 1990-91, computer systems programmer, 1991-92; info. systems mgr. Arpercen, St. Louis, 1992—; owner Ritz on Grand, St. Louis, 1989-92. Mem. Connect Mo., St. Louis, 1994, Pro Choice, St. Louis, 1991; vol. Salvation Army, St. Louis, 1992. Maj. U.S. Army, 1971-84, USAR, 1984-91. Recipient Spl. Act awards U.S. Govt., 1991, 92, 93. Mem. Nat. Assn. Women Bus. Owners, Exec. Women, Ctr. for Applications of Psychol. Type. Home: 4242 Westminster Saint Louis MO 63108 Office: Arpercen 9700 Page Blvd Saint Louis MO 63132

CORNING, JOY COLE, state official; b. Bridgewater, Iowa, Sept. 7, 1932; d. Perry Aaron and Ethel Marie (Sullivan) Cole; m. Burton Eugene Corning, June 19, 1955; children: Carol, Claudia, Ann. BA, U. No. Iowa, 1954. Cert. elem. tchr., Iowa. Tchr. elem. sch. Greenfield (Iowa) Sch. Dist., 1951-53, Waterloo (Iowa) Community Sch. Dist., 1954-55; mem. Iowa Senate, Des Moines, 1984-90, asst. rep. leader, 1989-90; lt. gov. State of Iowa, Des Moines, 1991—; bd. dirs. Iowa Nat. Bankshares Corp. Pres. Cedar Falls (Iowa) Sch. Bd., 1975-83; state pres. Iowa Talented and Gifted, 1975-77; mem. adv. bd. Waterloo Comty. Playhouse, Cedar Arts Forum; bd. dirs. Iowa Housing Fin. Authority, Des Moines, 1981-84, Iowa Assn. Sch. Bds., Des Moines, 1983-84, Iowa Peace Inst., 1987-91; mem. Edn. Commn. of States, 1987-90, The Caring Found., 1989—. Named Citizen of Yr., Cedar Falls C. of C., 1984; recipient ITAG Disting. Svc. to Iowa's Gifted and Talented Students award, 1991, Pub. Svc. award Iowa Home Econs. Assn., 1994, Friend of Math. award Iowa Coun. Tchrs. of Math., 1995; recognized for Extraordinary Advocacy for Children of Iowa chpt. Nat. Com. for Prevention of Child Abuse. Mem. AAUW, LWV, PEO, Nat. Assn. for Gifted Children (mem. adv. bd. 1991—), Delta Kappa Gamma, Alpha Delta Kappa. Republican. Mem. United Ch. of Christ. Office: State Capitol Office Of Lt Gov Des Moines IA 50319

CORNISH, ELIZABETH TURVEREY, stockbroker; b. Ionia, N.Y., Dec. 31, 1919; d. Clifford Dwight and Mildred Althea (Spicer) T.; m. Louis Joseph Cornish, June 21, 1941 (div. June 1955); 1 child, Carol Cornish Reeves. BS, Cornell U., 1941. Lic. stockbroker N.Y. Stock Exch., Prin. Reg. Options Prin., Commodity prin., Insur. prin. Teletype operator, sec. to mgr. Carl M. Loeb Rhoades & Co., Ithaca, N.Y., 1955-65; reg. rep. Carl M. Loeb Rhoades & Co., Ithaca, 1962-75; branch mgr. Loeb, Rhoades & Co., Ithaca, 1975-82; registered rep. Shearson Loeb Rhoades, Shearson Am. Express, Ithaca, 1982-86, Hutton, Shearson, Ithaca, 1986-88, First Albany Corp., Ithaca, 1988-91; registered rep., br. office mgr. A.G. Edwards & Sons, Inc., Ithaca, 1991—; charter mem. Nuveen Adv. Coun., 1984, 85, 86; instr. stock market and various br. office jobs for coll. interns. Mem. Planning Com. Downtown Mall, Ithaca, N.Y., 1972-75; chmn. campaign United Way Tompkins County, Ithaca, 1983, dir., 1983-89; bd. dirs. Ithaca Neighborhood Housing, Leadership Tompkins, 1986-88; pres. Friends of Ithaca Coll., 1985-86. Mem. Downtown Bus. Women (pres. 1971-72), Tompkins County C. of C. (bd. dirs. 1974-77, 83-86, v.p. 1980-81, pres.-elect 1989, pres. 1990), Ithaca Yacht Club (bd. dirs. 1988-90). Republican. Episcopalian. Office: A G Edwards & Sons Inc 107 N Aurora St Ithaca NY 14850-4301

CORNISH, JEANNETTE CARTER, lawyer; b. Steelton, Pa., Sept. 17, 1946; d. Ellis Pollard and Anna Elizabeth (Stannard) C.; m. Harry L. Cornish; children: Lee Jason, Geoffrey Charles. BA, Howard U., 1968, JD, 1971. Bar: N.J. 1976, U.S. Dist. Ct. N.J. 1976. Atty. Newark-Essex Law Reform, 1971-72; technician EEOC, Newark, 1972-73; atty., asst. sec. Inmont Corp., N.Y.C., 1974-82; sr. atty., asst. sec. Inmont Corp., Clifton, N.J., 1982-85; sr. atty. BASF Corp., Clifton, 1986—; speaker on women in bus. Bd. dirs. YWCA, Paterson, N.J., 1977-80, Lenni-Lenape coun. Girl Scouts U.S., 1986-94. Mem. ABA (sec. intellectual property, mem. com. on minorities and women in the profession, gen. practice sect., corp. counsel com., diversity vice-chair), Nat. Bar Assn., Assn. Black Women Lawyers, Am. Corp. Counsel Assn., Internat. Trademark Assn. (mem. edtl. bd. The Trademark Reporter 1991-92, exec. commn. com. 1994—). Home: 614 11th Ave Paterson NJ 07514-1302 Office: BASF Corp 3000 Continental Dr N Mount Olive NJ 07828-1234

CORNWALL, DEBORAH JOYCE, consulting firm executive, management consultant; b. Wilmington, Del., Dec. 9, 1946; d. Samuel and Norma (Bram) Handloff; m. Barry Newland Cornwall, June 22, 1968; 1 child, Deborah Leigh. BA, Mount Holyoke, 1968; MBA, Boston U., 1975. Editor Houghton Mifflin Co., Boston, 1967-69; editor Harbridge House, Inc., Boston, 1969-73, cons., 1973-74, assoc., 1974-75, sr. assoc., 1975-77, prin., 1977-79, v.p., 1979-81, v.p., div. mgr., 1981-83, sr. v.p., div. mgr., 1983-90; mng. v.p. Korn/Ferry Organizational Cons., Boston, 1991—; mem. mid. mgmt. excellence com. City of Boston, 1986. Bd. dirs. Mass. divsn. Am. Cancer Soc., 1994—. Mem. Human Resources Planning Soc., Phi Beta Kappa, Beta Gamma Sigma. Office: Korn/Ferry Organizational Cons 75 Federal St Boston MA 02110-1904

CORNWELL, ILENE JONES, writer, editor; b. Spartanburg, S.C., Sept. 27, 1942; d. Thurmond G. and Elizabeth (Furber) Jones; m. James H. Cornwell, Mar. 2, 1963 (div. 1977); children: James David, Robert Grant. Student, U. Tenn., 1975, Tenn. State U., 1987-88, Cumberland U., 1990—; Nashville Travel Inst., 1991. Pub. info. officer Tenn. Hist. Commn., Nashville, 1974-78; publs. editor, pub. info. officer Vanderbilt U. Med. Ctr., Nashville, 1978-81; writer, editor, owner So. Resources Unlimited, Nashville, 1981-92; copy editor, editorial cartoonist West Nashville Digest, 1993-94; contbg. editor New South Archtl. Press, Richmond, Va., 1993; ptnr., editor Serviceberry Press, Memphis, 1993; adminstrv. asst. tchr. edn. and pew retention program Fisk U., Nashville, 1995—; speaker, panelist Women in Media Com., Saginaw State U., Mich., 1990; speaker, workshop leader Elderhostel, 1990, Austin Peay State U., 1990; speaker to 15 civic, hist. and environ. groups; part-time asst. to coord. cmty. edn. Cohn Adult Learning Ctr., Nashville, 1992-93. Author: Footsteps Along the Harpeth, 1970, 76, Travel Guide to the Natchez Trace Parkway, 1984; Natchez Trace Treasury and Travel Guide; Biographical Directory of the Tennessee General Assembly, (4 vols.) 1987, 88, 89, 90, Ruskin!, 1972; (with Jim Leeson) The Old Trace in Tennessee, 1972; (2 screenplays) Early Travels on the Natchez Trace, 1974, Natchez Trace: Pathway to Parkway, 1986 (nominated Nashville's Emmy 1988); editor various publs.; contbr. to publs. Charter mem. West Nashville Founders' Mus., Nashville, 1987, bd. dirs., 1989; chmn. Richland Creek Campaign, West Nashville Community Coun., 1989, 90; founder Bellevue-Harpeth Hist. Soc., 1970, 3-term pres.; program presenter Internat. Conf. on Pkwys., Riverways, and Greenways Asheville, N.C., 1989; chair Natchez Trace Adv. Com., Tenn., 1990—; state judge Voice of Democracy student essay and scholarship contest, VFW, 1992, Tenn. Dept. Edn., Pencil student essay contest, 1994, history essay Tenn. students Tenn. Hist. Commn., 1989-95, others; program co-chmn. Tenn. women's history com. Vanderbilt U. Women's Ctr., 1994-95. Recipient Vintage award Internat. Assn. Bus. Communicators, 1980, MacEachern award Am. Hosp. Assn., 1981, Pres. award Natchez Trace Pkwy. Assn., 1989, Outstanding Svc. and Leadership award West Nashville Cmty. Coun., 1989, Cert. of Merit, Unsung Am. Woman Essay competition Nat. Women's History Project, 1994; named Tenn. Outstanding Young Woman, 1975; Lawlor scholar Cumberland U., 1990-91. Mem. AAUW, Nat. League of Am. Pen Women (Nashville br., former pres., v.p., state conv. chairwoman), Tenn. Woman's Press and Authors Club (affiliate of Nat. Fedn. of Press Women, pres. 1978, former v.p. and chairwoman of state conv.), White Bridge Neighborhood Assn. (charter, bd. dirs.), Tenn. Environ. Coun., Am. Biog. Inst. Rsch. Assn. (selected assoc. and mem. adv. bd. 1990), Friends of Richland Creek (charter), Nat. Women's History Project, Nat. Mus. of Women in the Arts (charter), Tenn. Native Plant Soc. Home: 5632 Meadowcrest Ln Nashville TN 37209-4631

CORO, ALICIA CAMACHO, federal executive; b. Havana, Cuba, Mar. 28, 1937; came to U.S., 1964; d. Daniel and Alicia (Mignagaray) Camacho; m. Carlos J. Coro (dec.); children: Alicia, Carlos, Christina. BA in English and Edn., U. Havana, 1961; MEd, U. Md., 1972. Elem. sch. tchr. Havana, 1956-59; tchr., supr. Montgomery County Pub. Schs., Rockville, Md., 1966-71; edn. specialist HEW, Washington, 1971-75, staff asst. to sec., 1975-77, program analyst, br. chief, 1977-80; dir. Horace Mann Learn Ctr. Dept. Edn., Washington, 1981-85, dep. asst. sec. for civil rights, 1985-86, acting asst. sec. for civil rights, 1986—; bd. dirs. Montgomery Community TV, Rockville, 1984—. Council mem. United Way, Rockville, 1985—; mem., vol. activites com. Chevy Chase (Md.) Rep. Women's Club, 1980—, Hispanic Rep. Club Montgomery County, Bethesda, Md., 1981—; mem. Rep. Nat. Hispanic Assmebly, Washington, 1972—; advisor at large Spanish-Speaking Community Md., Inc. Recipient Outstanding Achievement award Nat. Assn. Cuban-Am. Women, Nat. Council Hispanic Women, Cuban Circle of Md., 1986. Mem. Am. Soc. for Tng. and Devel., Am. Assn. for Adult-Continuing Edn., Fed. Exec. Inst. Alumni Assn., Soc. Fed. Linguists, Tchrs. English to Speakers of Other Langs., Nat. Assn. Cuban Women (dir. at large), Nat. Council Hispanic Women (bd. dirs.). Roman Catholic. Club: Who's Who Internat. (Marina del Ray, Calif.). Home: 7401 Westlake Ter Apt 102 Bethesda MD 20817-6525 Office: Dept of Edn 400 Maryland Ave SW Washington DC 20202-0001*

CORONADO, HERLINDA, college dean; b. El Paso, Aug. 28, 1949; d. Raymond G. and Julia (Beltran) Martinez. BS, U. Tex., El Paso, 1971, MEd, 1976. Instr. El Paso C.C., 1972-78; learning specialist South Plains Coll., Lubbock, Tex., 1985-90, dean of instrn., 1991—, interim provost, 1992; mem. com. of practitioners Tex. Higher Edn. Coordinating Bd., Austin, 1991-93. Bd. dirs. Lubbock Area Coalition for Literacy, Lubbock, 1990-93. Title VII grantee, 1975-76. Mem. Nat. Assn. Devel. Edn., Tex. Assn. Coll. Tech. Educators (exec. com. 1990—), Tex. Jr. Coll. Tchrs. Assn. Office: South Plains Coll 1302 Main St Lubbock TX 79401-3224

CORPORA, NICOLE ELIZABETH, oncological nurse, researcher; b. Wilkinsburg, Pa., June 4, 1943; d. Nicholas and Elizabeth Agnes (Martinac) Kauric; m. Donald Souders (div.); children: Donald, Jr., Audrey L. Student, Warren County C.C., Washington, N.J., 1982-89; BS in Edn., Pa. State U., 1964; postgrad., Marywood Coll., 1985; ADN, Northampton C.C., Bethlehem, Pa., 1991. RN, Pa., N.J. Tchr. Easton (Pa.) Are High Sch., 1964-67; rsch. and adminstr. asst. Warren County C.C., 1984-85; tchr. Am. Bankers Assn., Easton and Phillipsburg, N.J., 1989; tng. instr. Chem. Bank of N.J., Morristown, 1986-89; residential program worker Regional Devel. Corp., Pottsville, Pa., 1985; receptionist Warren Med. Assocs., Phillipsburg, N.J., 1985-87; nursing asst. Care Ctr. of Lopatcong, Phillipsburg, N.J., 1988-89; nursing asst. St. Luke's Hosp., Bethlehem, 1989-91, RN, 1991—. Home: Y-15 Brakeley Gardens Phillipsburg NJ 08865

CORRADINI, DEEDEE, mayor. Student, Drew U., 1961-63; BS, U. Utah, 1965, MS, 1967. Adminstrv. asst. for public info. Utah State Office Rehab. Svcs., 1967-69; cons. Utah State Dept. Community Affairs, 1971-72; media dir., press sec. Wayne Owens for Congress Campaign, 1972; press sec. Rep. Wayne Owens, 1973-74; spl. asst. to N.Y. Congl. Rep. Richard Ottinger, 1975; asst. to pres., dir. community rels. Snowbird Corp., 1975-77; exec. v.p. Bonneville Assocs., Inc., Salt Lake City, 1977-80; pres. Bonneville Assocs., Inc., 1980-89, chmn., CEO, 1989-91; mayor Salt Lake City, 1992—; mem. urban con. policy com. U.S. Conf. on Mayors, mem. unfunded fed. mandates task force, mem. crime and violence task force, trustee exec. com.; mem. interngovtl. policy adv. com. U.S. Trade Rep.; mem. transp. and comm. com. Nat. League of Cities; chair Mayor's Gang Task Force. Bd. trustees Intermountain Health Care, 1980-92; bd. dirs., exec. com. Utah Symphony, 1983-92, vice chmn., 1985-88, chmn., 1988-92; dir. Utah chpt. Nat. Conf. Christians and Jews, Inc., 1988; bd. dirs. Salt Lake Olympic Bid Com., 1989—; chmn. image com. Utah Partnership for Edn. and Econ. Devel., 1989-92; co-chair United Way Success by 6 Program; pres. Shelter of the Homeless Com.; active Sundance Inst. Utah Com., 1990-92; disting. bd. fellow So. Utah U., 1991; active numerous other civic orgns. and coms. Mem. Salt Lake Area C. of C. (bd. govs. 1979-81, chmn. City/County/Govt. com. 1976-86). Office: Office of the Mayor City & County Bldg 451 S State St Rm 306 Salt Lake City UT 84111-3104

CORRELL, HELEN BUTTS, botanist, researcher; b. Providence, R.I., Apr. 24, 1907; d. George Lyman and Albertine Louise (Christiansen) B.; m. Donovan Stewart Correll (dec. 1983); children: Louise, Stewart, Selena, Charles; m. William Merton Carter, Oct. 10, 1992. AB, Brown U., 1928, AM, 1929; PhD, Duke U., 1934. Instr. Smith Coll., Northampton, Mass., 1929-31, Wellesley (Mass.) Coll., 1934-39; assoc. prof. U. Md., Towson, 1956; research assoc. Tex. Research Found., Renner, 1959-65, co-investigator aquatic plant research, 1966-71; collaborator, adjunct staff Fairchild Tropical Garden, Miami, Fla., 1973-93. Co-author: Aquatic and Wetland Plants of the Southwestern United States, 1972, 2d edit. 1975, Flora of the Bahama Archipelago, 1982; editor: Wright Botanical Jour., 1959-63; contbr. articles to profl. jours. Chmn. Libr. Bd., Richardson, Tex., 1965-70; bd. dirs. East Ridge Retirement Village, 1992-94. Recipient disting. alumna citation Brown U., 1983, Marjory Stoneman Douglas award Fla. Native Plant Soc., 1985, medal for Individual Achievement in Horticulture award Fla. Fedn. Garden Clubs, Inc, 1992. Mem. Soc. Women Geographers, Friends of Fairchild (v.p. 1986-87, pres. 1987-89), Altrusa (officer 1964-71), Phi Beta Kappa, Sigma Xi. Congregationalist. Home: 216 E Ridge Village Dr Miami FL 33157

CORRICK, ANN MARJORIE, communications executive; b. Grosse Pointe, Mich; d. John A. and Mary (Nickell) C. B.J., U. Tex., 1943. Reporter Transradio Press Service, Washington, 1943-51; producer Am. Forum of the Air, Youth Wants to Know, NBC, Washington, 1951-52; Washington corr. and broadcaster Sta. WDSU-TV, New Orleans, 1954-58; asst. chief Washington News Bur.; also reporter-broadcaster Westinghouse Broadcasting Co., Washington, 1958-66; USIA congl. liason officer Expo '67, Montreal, Can., 1967; info. officer USIA Fgn. Service, Saigon, Vietnam, 1968-70; dir. promotion and communication Corrick Internat., Santa Cruz, Calif., 1980—. Recipient Sylvania citation for producing and moderating TV film Dateline Washington for WDSU-TV, 1955, Theta Sigma Phi Nat. Headliner award, 1962. Mem. Radio-TV Corrs. Assn. (pres. 1961-62). Home and Office: 3050 Dover Dr Apt 56 Santa Cruz CA 95065-1948

CORRIGAN, HELEN GONZÁLEZ, cytologist; b. San Diego, Tex., Sept. 30, 1922; d. Rodrigo Simon and Eva Ruby (Corrigan) Gonzalez. BS, Our Lady of Lake, San Antonio, 1943. Tchr. San Diego High Sch., 1943-45; microbiologist Nix Hosp. Profl. Lab., San Antonio, 1952-59; med. technologist Tucson Med. Ctr., 1959-60; cytologist in charge Jackson-Todd Cancer Detection Ctr., San Antonio, 1961-64; cytologist in charge cytology sect. Pathology Lab. 4th and 5th U.S. Army Ref. Area Lab., Fort Sam Houston, Tex., 1964-78; instr. trouble shooters, quality control analyst cytology sect. Brooks Med. Ctr., Fort Sam Houston, 1978-81; owner Corrigan Enterprises, San Diego, 1981-91; cytologist Waco (Tex. Med. Lab. Svc., 1988-89, Nat. Health Lab., San Antonio, 1989-90, Internat. Cancer Screening Lab., San Antonio, 1990-91; head cytologist Dr. R. Garza & Assocs., Weslaco, Tex., 1992—. Adv. bd. mem. EEO, Ft. Sam Houston, 1972-74. Mem. NAFE, Am. Soc. Clin. Pathologists (assoc.), Greater San Antonio Women's C. of C. Republican. Roman Catholic. Home: 149 Perry Ct San Antonio TX 78209-6211

CORRIGAN, LYNDA DYANN, banker; b. Selmer, Tenn., Nov. 24, 1949; d. A. Sammuel and Eunice (Burks) Davis. BBA, Mid. Tenn. State U., 1978; MBA, U. Tenn., 1979; JD, Nashville Sch. Law, 1984. CPA, Tenn.; bar: Tenn. 1985. Sr. v.p. First Am. Corp., Nashville, 1980—; faculty Am. Inst. Banking, Nashville, 1982—; mem. Nat. Panel Consumer Arbitrators, Nashville, 1985-87. Pres. Buddies of Nashville, 1985, adv. bd., 1986—; treas. Mid.-East Tenn. Arthritis Found., Nashville, 1982-85, Floyd Cramer Celebrity Golf Tournament, Nashville, 1981-84; bd. dirs. Nashville, 1981-84; bd. dirs. Nashville Br. Arthritis Found., 1980-87. Named Instr. of Yr. Am. Inst. Banking, 1994; recipient Leadership award Mid.-East Tenn. Arthritis Found., 1985, Gold award Jr. Chamber, 1981. Mem. ABA (mem. tax com. 1987—), Nashville Bar Assn. (mem. tax com. 1986—, vice chmn. tax sect. 1989, chair tax sect. 1990), Tenn. Taxpayers and Mfrs. Assn. (mem. tax com. 1986—), Tenn. Soc. CPA's. Home: 806 Fountainhead Ct Brentwood TN 37027-5833

CORROTHERS, HELEN GLADYS, criminal justice official; b. Montrose, Ark., Mar. 19, 1937; d. Thomas and Christene (Farley) Curl; m. Edward Corrothers, Dec. 17, 1968 (div. Sept. 1983); 1 child, Michael Edward. AA in Liberal Arts magna cum laude, Ark. Bapt. Coll., 1955; BS in Bus. Adminstrn. Mgmt., Roosevelt U., 1965; grad. officer leadership sch., WAC Sch., 1965; grad, Inst. Criminal Justice, Exec. Ctr. Continuing Edn., U. Chgo., 1973; postgrad., Calif. Coast U., 1981—. Enlisted U.S. Army, 1956, advanced through grades to capt., 1969; chief mil. pers. U.S. Army, Ft. Meyer, Va., 1965-67; dir. for housing Giessen Support Ctr., Fed. Republic Germany, 1967-69; resigned, 1969; social interviewer Ark. Dept. Corrections, Grady, 1970-71; supt. women's unit Ark. Dept. Corrections, Pine Bluff, 1971-83; commr. U.S. Parole Commn., Burlingame, Calif., 1983-85, U.S. Sentencing Commn., Washington, 1985-91; fellow U.S. Dept. Justice, Washington, 1992—; instr. women & crime U. Md., College Park, 1994; instr. corrections U. Ark.-Pine Bluff, 1976-79; mem. bd. visitation Jefferson County Juvenile Ct., Pine Bluff, 1978-81; bd. dirs. Vols. in Cts., 1979-83, Vols. Am., 1985-94; mem. Am./Can. study team Mex. penal system Am. Correctional Assn., Islas Marias, Mex., 1981; mem. Am. Commn. Crimes and Law Enforcement, 1975-78; mem. U.S. Atty. Gen.'s Correctional Policy Study Team, 1987. Mem. Ark. Commn. on Status of Women, 1976-78; bd. dirs. Com. Against Spouse Abuse, 1982-83; mem. nat. adv. bd. dept. criminal justice Xavier U., Cin., 1993; bd. dirs. Bapt. Mission Found. of Md./Del., Columbia, Md., 1993—. Recipient Ark, Woman of Achievement award Ark. Press Women's Assn., 1980, Human Rels. award Ark. Edn. Assn., 1980, Outstanding Woman of Achievement award Sta. KATV-TV, Little Rock,

1981, Correctional Svc. award Vols. Am., 1984, William H. Hastie award Nat. Assn. Blacks in Criminal Justice, 1986, Outstanding Victim Advocacy award Nat. Victim Ctr., 1991, Appreciation cert. Dept. Justice Office for Victims of Crime, 1994; recipient testimonial for svc. to fed. judiciary Adminstrv. Office of Cts., 1991. Mem. NAFE, Am. Correctional Assn. (treas. 1980-86, v.p. 1986-88, pres.-elect 1988-90, pres. 1990-92, E.R. Cass Correctional Achievement award 1993), N.Am. Assn. Wardens and Supts., Ark. Law Enforcement Assn., Nat. Coun. on Crime and Delinquency, Am. Soc. Criminology, Ark. Sheriff's Assn. (hon.), Delta Sigma Theta (local sec. 1976-79, local parliamentarian 1983). Baptist. Office: Am Correctional Assn 8025 Laurel Lakes Ct Laurel MD 20707-5075

CORSAW, ARDITH, geriatrics nurse, administrator; b. Decatur, Ill., Sept. 10, 1950; d. Everette Eugene and Norma L. (Swarm) Kirkman; m. David Corsaw, Dec. 19, 1971; children: Adam, Tara, Karen. Diploma, Decatur Meml. Hosp., 1971. RN. Pvt. duty nursing, charge nurse med.-surg. unit Graham Hosp., Canton, Ill., 1972-82; nurse Hooper-Holmes Port-A-Medic, Peoria, Ill., 1982-83; office nurse family practice physician's office, Cuba, Ill., 1982-87; factory first-aid sta. relief nurse Caterpillar, Inc., Mapleton, Ill., 1986-88; nursing supr., insvc. dir. Heartland of Canton (Ill.), Health Care and Retirement Corp., 1988-91, DON, 1991-92; quality assurance coord., rehab. coord. Health Care and Retirement Corp., 1992; DON Sprucewood Health Care, 1992—; supr. nursing, clin. support br. chief ambulatory svcs. McDill AFB. Lt. col. Ill. Air N.G., 1971—. Mem. Assn. Air N.G. Nurses, Alliance Air N.G. Flight Surgeons, Assn. Mil. Surgeons U.S., N.G. Assn. U.S., N.G. Assn. Ill. Home: RR 1 Box 61 Smithfield IL 61477-9716

CORSETTE, CHRISTINE MARIE, sales executive; b. Syracuse, N.Y., June 12, 1966; d. David Leo and Marilyn Anne (Vail) C. BS in Biochemistry, Syracuse U., 1988. Rsch. assoc. Syracuse (N.Y.) U., 1988-90; product specialist New Brunswick Sci., Edison, N.J., 1990-91; product mgr. New Brunswick Sci., Edison, 1991-92; sales rep. New Brunswick Sci., San Francisco, 1992—. Vol. Tri-Valley Humane Soc. Mem. Soc. Indsl. Microbiologists, Am. Soc. Microbiologists. Home: 5010 Owens Dr #313 Pleasanton CA 94588 Office: New Brunswick Sci 44 Talmadge Rd Edison NJ 08818

CORSI, DEBORAH ERANDA, editor; b. McKeesport, Pa., May 6, 1953; d. Adolph J. and Francesca S. (D'Arliano) C.; m. William V. Jenkins, 1985. AAS, No. Va. C.C., 1980; BA, Marymount Coll., 1984; postgrad., Valparaiso U. Sec. Northwestern Mut. Life Ins. Co., Arlington, Va., 1971-72, adminstrv. asst., 1972-79; editorial asst. Smithsonian Mag., Washington, 1979-80; editorial and promotion asst. Smithsonian Instn. Press, 1981-83, editor, 1984-85; editor Jour. Alcohol Studies, 1986-87; freelance editor, 1987-88; editor Am. Bankers Assn., 1989-93; membership dir. Greater Valparaiso C. of C., 1993-94; v.p. mem. svcs., editor Chamber Networks, 1995—. Roman Catholic. Home: 1002 Woodcrest Ct Valparaiso IN 46383

CORTHELL, KIM, legislative staff director; b. Perth Amboy, N.J., Dec. 18, 1953. BA, Am. Univ., 1977. Aide to Rep. William S. Cohen Bangor, Maine, 1978-79; office mgr. for Sen. William S. Cohen Portland, Maine, 1979-80; profl. staff mem. Senate Govtl. Affairs Com., 1980-91, minority staff dir. subcom. oversight govt. mgmt., 1991-93; minority staff dir. subcom. juvenile justice Senate Judiciary Com., 1993—. Office: Subcom on Juvenile Justice 162 Dirksen Senate Office Bldg Washington DC 20510*

CORTICELLI, JUDITH ALICE PACCONE, human and clinical services administrator; b. N.Y.C., Jan. 5, 1945; d. Humbert Ernest and Rita Marie (Guaraldi) Paccone; m. Angelo Philip Corticelli, July 14, 1969; children: Paolo Alessandro, Pierangelo. MusB, Marymount Coll., 1967; BA, Herbert H. Lehman Coll., 1975; MSW, NYU, 1982; Cert. in Pub. Adminstrn., Pace U., 1986. Cert. social worker; lic. real estate salesperson. Tchr. grades 5-8, chair modern math. dept. Sacred Heart Villa Acad., Dobbs Ferry, N.Y., 1967-70; social caseworker family svcs. Westchester County Dept. Social Svcs., Port Chester, N.Y., 1976-78; sr. social caseworker child protection svcs. Westchester County Dept. Social Svcs., White Plains, 1978-80; program specialist day care Westchester County Dept. Social Svcs., White Plains, N.Y., 1980-84, program specialist adult svc., 1984-87, program adminstr. clinical svs. for youth, 1987—; adjustment svcs. coord. Westchester PINS (Persons in Need of Supervision), White Plains, 1989—; co-chair Yonkers adolescent pregnancy prevention svcs. Yonkers (N.Y.) Youth Bur., 1992—; coord. Westchester svcs. incarcerated youth Westchester County Youth Bur., 1994. V.p. Valhalla (N.Y.) Internat. Fund, 1985-91; community leader, adv. Com. Restoration Italian Valhalla Mid. Sch./High Sch., 1993; assoc. mem. Nat. Mus. Women Arts, 1994—; trustee North Castle Libr. Bd., 1988-91, sec.; treas., bd. dirs. Valhalla High Sch. PTO, 1988-91. Recipient Cert. of Appreciation, Youth for Understanding, 1990, NaCo award Nat. Assn. Counties, 1993. Mem. NASW (treas., bd. dirs. Westchester chpt. 1987-91), SIAMO (Golden Svc. award 1993), Nat. Orgn. Italian Am. Women. Office: Westchester County Youth Bur 150 Grand St White Plains NY 10601

CORTINEZ, VERONICA, language and literature educator; b. Santiago, Chile, Aug. 27, 1958; came to U.S. 1979; d. Carlos Cortinez and Matilde Romo. Licenciatura en Letras, U. Chile, 1979; MA, U. Ill., Champaign, Ill., 1981, Harvard U., 1983; PhD, Harvard U., 1990. Teaching asst. U. Chile, Santiago, 1977-79, U. Ill., Champaign, 1979-80; teaching fellow Harvard U., 1982-86, instr., 1986-89; asst. prof. colonial and contemporary Latin Am. lit. UCLA, 1989—; fgn. corres. Caras, Santiago, 1987—. Editorial bd. Mester/Dept. Spanish and Portuguese of UCLA, 1989—; editor Plaza mag., 1981-89, Harvard Rev., 1983-89; contbr. articles to profl. jours. Recipient Award for Teaching Excellence, Danforth Ctr., Harvard U., 1982, 83, 84, 85, 86; Teaching prize, Romance Lang. Dept., Harvard U., 1986; Whiting fellow. Mem. Cabot House, Phi Beta Phi. Office: UCLA Dept Spanish and Portuguese 5310 Rolfe Hall Los Angeles CA 90024

CORTRIGHT, HELEN RAE, banker; b. Madison, Ohio, July 27, 1963; d. Raymond Earl and Evelyn Helen (Friedrich) Wolf; m. Ricky Lee Cortright, Oct. 16, 1982; 1 child, Rebecca Chelsea. Grad. high sch., Jefferson, Ohio. Cashier Ben Franklin's Store, Jefferson, 1980-82; mem. factory staff Lake City Plating, Ashtabula, Ohio, 1982; cashier, cook Mr. Hero's, Jefferson, 1982-83; cashier Fashion Bug, Jefferson, 1983-84; asst. mgr. Cinema Ctrs., Ashtabula, 1985-88; branch ops. supr. Peoples Savs. Bank, Ashtabula, 1984—. Mem. Am. Bus. Women's Assn. (treas. 1989-90). Home: 5269 State Route 46 S Jefferson OH 44047 Office: Peoples Savs Bank 4200 Park Ave Ashtabula OH 44004-6857

CORTRIGHT, INGA ANN, accountant; b. Silver City, N.Mex., Sept. 30, 1949; d. Lester Richard and Claudia Marcella (Huckaby) Lee; m. Russell Joseph Cortright, June 25, 1987. BS in Acctg., Ariz. State U., 1976, MBA, 1978; postgrad., Walden U., 1991—. CPA, Ariz., Tex. Sole practice cert. pub. acctg. Ariz., 1981—; cons. in field. Mem. AICPA, Beta Alpha Psi. Republican. Episcopalian. Office: 9421 W Bell Rd Ste 108 Sun City AZ 85351-1361

CORTRIGHT, LOUISE VERA, retired medical technologist, small business owner; b. Buffalo, Apr. 22, 1938; d. Asa Lawrence and Mary Lois (Ward) C. BS with honors, Fairleigh Dickson U., 1960; postgrad., Rutgers U., 1965-67. Nationally registered med. technologist. Bacteriology supr. Middlesex Gen. Hosp., New Brunswick, N.J., 1963-64; hematology supr. Princeton Hosp., Princeton, N.J., 1964-65; teaching supr. Somerset Med. Ctr., Somerset, N.J., 1965-67; chief technologist Somerset Med. Ctr., 1966-79; owner, operator Aurora Kennel, Bridgewater, N.J., 1973-1992; cons. N.J. State Dept. of Health, Trenton, 1979-80. Treas., v.p. Bridgewater Twp. Bd. of Health, 1974, 1975; chmn. Regional Animal Shelter, 1978-81. Mem. Morris Hills Dog Training Club (founding mem. 1961), North Jersey Shetland Sheepdog Club (founding mem. 1965).

CORUM COOK, CAROLINE FERGUSON, finance company executive; b. Madisonville, Ky.; d. William Montgomery and Frances (Ferguson) C. BS, Am. U., 1987, SUNY, Albany, 1988; postgrad. in bus., George Mason U., 1988-90, JD, 1992. Dir. bookkeeping, fin. records Corum Farms, Madisonville, 1979—; fin. planner Waddell & Reed Fin. Svcs., Washington, 1987-88; asst. mut. funds adminstr. trust dept. Riggs Nat. Bank, Washington, 1987-88, spl. asst. to exec. v.p. trust, 1992; portfolio mgr., pres. Va. Capital & Trust Mgmt., 1992-94; cash mgmt. specialist for N.E. Tenn. First Tenn. Bank, Johnson City, 1994—; realtor, real estate investment adv., 1987—. Rep. alumnae admissions Sweet Briar Coll., 1987—; elected rep. Arlington Co. Dem. Com., 1989-92; 29th Jud. Dist. Ct. apptd. spl. advocate program bd. of dirs. and treas., 1992-94. Mem. Nat. Assn. Pub. Interest Law (local pres., nat. bd. dirs. 1988-91), Panhellenic Assn. Washington (pres. alumnae), Jr. League Washington, Kappa Alpha Theta (exec. bd. alumnae assn.).

CORWELL, ANN ELIZABETH, public relations executive; b. Battle Creek, Mich.; d. James Albert Corwell and Marion Elizabeth (Petersen) Shertzer. BA, Mich. State U., 1971, MBA, 1981; cert. fin., Wharton Sch., 1986. Sr. publicist City of Dearborn, Mich., 1972-76; sr. assoc. Gen. Motors Corp., Detroit, 1976-77; media coord. Gen. Motors Corp., N.Y.C., 1977; mgr. community rels. Gen. Motors Corp., Pontiac, Mich., 1977-81; mgr. internal communications Gen. Motors Corp., Pontiac, 1981-82; dir. pub. rels. Pillsbury Co., Mpls., 1982-85, Avon Products Inc., N.Y.C., 1985-87; exec. v.p. MECA Internat., Flat Rock, Mich., 1987—. Dir. Mich. State U. Nat. Alumni Bd. Mem. Pub. Rels. Soc. Am., Women In Communications, Oakland County C. of C. (dir. 1988-91), Dearborn C. of C. (dir. 1989-91).

CORWIN, JOYCE ELIZABETH STEDMAN, construction company executive; b. Chgo.; d. Cresswell Edward and Elizabeth Josephine (Kimbell) Stedman; m. William Corwin, May 1, 1965; children: Robert Edmund Newman, Jillanne Elizabeth McInnis. Pres. Am. Properties, Inc., Miami, Fla., 1966-72; v.p. Stedman Constrn. Co., Miami, 1971—; owner Joy-Win Horses, Gray lady ARC, 1969-70. Guidance worker Youth Hall, 1969-70; sponsor Para Med. Group of Coral Park High Sch., 1969-70; hostess, Rep. presdl. campaign, 1968; aide Rep. Nat. Conv., 1972. Mem. Dade County Med. Aux. (chmn. directory com. 1970), Marion County Med. Aux., Fla. Psychiat. Soc. Aux., Fla. Morgan Horse Assn., Fla. Thoroughbred Breeders Assn. Clubs: Coral Gables Jr. Women's (chmn. casework com.), Golden Hills Golf and Turf, Heritage, Royal Dames of Ocala. Home: Windrift Farm 8500 NW 120th St Reddick FL 32686-4513

CORWIN, VALERIE JOYCE, artist; b. Winnipeg, Man., Can., Nov. 23, 1953; came to U.S., 1978; d. Carl Bernard and Vera Elinor (Finley) Ott; m. Donald James Corwin, June 30, 1978; children: Jesse, Timothy, Sara, Adam. Student, U. Winnipeg, 1977, U. St. Thomas, Houston, 1979; BFA, U. Houston, 1987. Exhibited in group shows at Galveston (Tex.) Art League, 1988, Springfield (Mo.) Art Mus., 1989, 90, Cheekwood Mus. Art, Nashville, 1993, others. Recipient Cash award Springfield Art Mus., 1989. Mem. Tex. Fine Arts Assn., Tenn. Art League. Home: 6011 Foxborough Sq E Brentwood TN 37027-5701

CORWIN, VERA-ANNE VERSFELT, small business owner, consultant; b. Glen Ridge, NJ; d. Porter LaRoy and Vera Anna (Price) Versfelt; m. John M. Corwin, Apr. 9, 1955; children: Gail Elizabeth Corwin Bayne, Gregory John, Lynn B. Corwin Byers. BS, Upsala Coll., 1954; MEd, Wayne State U., 1972, PhD, 1977. Instr. Wayne (N.J.) Sch. Dist., 1954-55; engr., spec., analyst Chrysler Corp., Highland Park, Mich., 1955-56, 78-85; instr. Royal Oak (Mich.) Sch. Dist., 1968-78; sr. systems engr. Electronic Data Systems, Troy, Mich., 1985-87; pres. Unique Solutions, Inc., Royal Oak, 1987—; adj. prof. U. Mich., Dearborn, 1989, Wayne State U., 1989. Pres. Arlington Park Homeowners Assn., Royal Oak, 1984-85, road commr., 1984-90. Mem. Soc. Automotive Engrs. (trainer 1991—), Automotive Industry Action Group (chmn. design expts. subgroup 1988-94), Am. Soc. Quality Control (sr.), Soc. Mfg. Engrs. (sr., trainer 1987-91), Am. Statis. Assn. Office: Unique Solutions Inc PO Box 1711 Royal Oak MI 48068-1711

CORY, JUDITH A., make-up artist. films include: Hook, 1991, Schindler's List, 1993, Forrest Gump, 1994 (Acad. award nom., Best Make-up). *

COSBY, CATHERINE, bank executive, lawyer. JD, U. Fla. Assoc. Mahoney, Adams and Criser, Jacksonville, Fla., until 1983; with Barnett Banks, Jacksonville, 1983—, sr. counsel, corp. sec., 1992—. Office: Barnett Banks Inc 50 N Laura St Jacksonville FL 32202*

COSPER, ANDREA VERBIE, management consultant; b. Brookline, Mass.; d. Andrew Sotir and Verbie Eudell (Brown) Bregou; m. Anthony Joseph Leech, Aug. 21, 1971 (div. May 1985); m. William Madison Cosper III, Nov. 16, 1990. AA in Bus., Wentworth Jr. Coll., 1987; BS in Bus. Mgmt. summa cum laude, Tarkio Coll., 1988. Mgr. adminstrv. svcs. Mgmt. Recruiters, Bridgeton, Mo., 1972-82; br. mgr. Ballwin (Mo.) Bus. Ctrs., 1982-83; v.p., co-owner PSS, St. Charles, Mo., 1983-85; dir. Mgmt. Info. Svcs. Fitronetics, Inc., Kansas City, Mo., 1985-87; cons. A L Consulting, Lexington, Mo., 1983—; habilitation specialist Higginsville (Mo.) Habilitation Ctr., 1988-90, 93—, habilitation specialist II, 1993—; cons. Desco Med. Co., Milw., 1983—. Mem. St. Louis Tng. Club. Home: RR 1 Box 76 Lexington MO 64067-9708

COSTA, D. MARGARET, history and women's studies educator, consultant, researcher; b. Lismore, NSW, Australia, Dec. 8, 1940; came to U.S., 1965; d. Oliver Frederick and Hilda Madeleine (Fordham) Munday; m. Dale Paul Toohey, Dec. 19, 1962 (div. Oct. 1983); 1 child, Dean Peter Toohey; m. Joseph Louis Costa, Oct. 3, 1985; 1 child, Robyn Maree Gugenheim. BSc, U. Mass., 1970, MEd, 1972; PhD, Ohio State U., 1975. Tchr. various schs., NSW, 1960-65; instr. Ohio State U., Columbus, 1973-74; from asst. prof. to prof. Calif. State U., Long Beach, 1974-84, prof., dir. interdisciplinary studies, 1984—; pres., rschr., cons. Costa Rsch. & Mgmt., Huntington Beach, Calif., 1990—. Author, editor: Women and Sport, 1994; contbr. articles to profl. jours. Mem. N.Am. Soc. Sport History, Nat. Women's Studies Assn., Nat. Womens Polit. Caucus (Orange County chpt.), numerous others. Office: Costa Rsch & Mgmt 6372 Turnberry Circle Huntington Beach CA 92648

COSTA, DONNA MARIE, secondary education educator; b. Peabody, Mass., Dec. 5, 1955; d. Antonio Sariva Costa and Lulu Rose (Silva) Costa-Smith; m. Brian Michael Phelan, Oct. 27, 1972 (div. 1982); children: Dawne Marie Phelan, Brian Michael Phelan II. AS, N. Shore Community Coll., Beverly, Mass., 1982; BA, U. Mass. at Boston, 1986; MEd in Sch. Adminstrn., Salem (Mass.) State Coll., 1988; cert. advanced studies, Harvard U., 1991; EdD candidate, 1992—. Cert. acad. and occpl. tchr., Mass. Instr./dept. head Peabody Sch. Dept., 1981—; instr. North Shore C.C., Mass., 1994—; mem. Faculty Adv., Vocat. Adv., Electronics Adv., Ednl. Tech., Extended After Sch. Program bds., Peabody Sch. Dept., ednl. tech. com. Author, editor: 4 yr. electronics curriculum, 1990. Vol. ARC. Recipient Horace Mann grants, 1988, 89. Mem. ASCD, NAFE, Phi Delta Kappa (bd. dirs. Harvard chpt.). Roman Catholic. Home: 8 Munroe St Peabody MA 01960-4468

COSTA, KATHY, librarian; b. Montgomery, Minn., July 28, 1933; d. John Egan and Bozena Rose (McKeon) Grathwol; m. Alfredo Costa, Aug. 5, 1957 (div. 1973). BA, Coll. of St. Catherine, 1955; MLS, U. Ariz., 1975. Libr. St. Paul Pub. Libr., 1961-72, U. N.Mex., Albuquerque, 1973-74, 76-79, Gallup, 1975-76; children's coord. Santa Fe (N.Mex.) Pub. Libr., 1979-94; youth outreach libr., 1994—. Mem. Coun. on Internat. Rels., Santa Fe, 1979—, Colonial N. Mex. Hist. Found., Santa Fe, 1973—. Fulbright Travel grantee U.S. Govt., 1955-56; recipient French Govt. Teaching Assistantship, 1955-56. Mem. ALA, AAUW, N.Mex. Libr. Assn., N.Mex. Coalition for Literacy, Internat. Reading Assn. (Celebrate Literacy award 1987), Nat. Assn. for Perpetuation and Preservation of Storytelling. Roman Catholic. Office: Santa Fe Pub Libr 145 Washington Ave Santa Fe NM 87501

COSTA, MARY, soprano; b. Knoxville, Tenn.; student Los Angeles Conservatory of Music. Film voice of Sleeping Beauty by Walt Disney; appeared TV commls., 1955-57; debut Los Angeles Opera, 1958, in La Boheme, San Francisco Opera, 1959, as Violetta in La Traviata at Met. Opera, N.Y.C., 1964; appeared Glyndebourne Opera House, Royal Opera House Covent Garden, Teatro Nacional de San Carlos, Grand Theatre de Geneve, Vancouver, Lisbon, Kiev, Leningrad, Tbilisi, Boston, Cin., Hartford, Newark, Phila., San Antonio, Seattle; toured U.S. with Bernstein's Candide; appeared English prodn. Candide; revival Bernstein's Candide at John F. Kennedy Center for Performing Arts, 1971; tour Soviet Union, 1970; Bolshoi debut in La Traviatta, 1970; starring role motion picture The Great Waltz, 1972; appeared internat. recitals, orchs.; v.p. Hawaiian Fragrances, Honolulu, 1972. Vice pres. Calif. Inst. Arts. Named Woman of yr., Los Angeles, 1959; recipient DAR Honor medal, 1974, Tenn. Hall of Fame award, 1987, Women of Achievement award Northwood Inst., Palm Beach, Fla., 1991, Woman of Achievement award So. Birmingham Coll., 1993; Mary Costa Scholarship established at U. Tenn., 1979. Address: 3340 Kingston Pike Unit 1 Knoxville TN 37919-4674

COSTA, ROBIN LEUEEN, psychologist, counselor; b. Hackensack, N.J., Dec. 9, 1948; d. Frank G. and Hazel L. (Brown) C. BA, Colby Coll., 1970; MA in Clin. Psychology, Fairleigh Dickinson U., 1973; MBA, Fla. Atlantic U., 1984. Lic. mental health counselor, sch. psychologist, Fla.; nat. cert. sch. psychologist. Sch. psychologist Broward County Sch. Bd., Ft. Lauderdale, Fla., 1973-91; pres., chief exec. officer Silver Linings Fin. Care, Ft. Lauderdale, 1986—; pvt. practice Ft. Lauderdale, 1991—. Home: 3750 Galt Ocean Dr Fort Lauderdale FL 33308-7656

COSTANTINO, LORINE PROTZMAN, woodworking company executive; b. Chattanooga, Feb. 8, 1921; d. John Edgar and Rosa Jane (Ellis) McClelland; student U. Balt., U. Ill.; m. Conrad Protzman, 1937 (dec. 1958); children—Rosa Lorine, Charles Conrad, James Paul, Sharon Lee; m. 2d, Anthony A. Costantino, Feb. 27, 1960. With Conrad Protzman, Inc., Balt., 1954-94, pres., chief exec., 1958-94, ret. 1994; developer apprenticeship programs for woodworking industry. Mem. Archtl. Woodworking Inst. (dir.), Bldg. Congress and Exchange Balt., Am. Sub-Contractors Assn., Nat. Assn. Women Bus. Owners, Iota Lambda Sigma (hon. mem. Nu chpt.). Republican. Roman Catholic. Club: Hillendale Country.

COSTANZO, NANCI JOY, fine arts educator; b. New Britain, Conn., June 2, 1947; d. Edward Francis and Vivian Evelyn (Allen) Sarisley; m. Joseph Paul Costanzo, Apr. 10, 1974; 1 child, Ashley Allen Bailey. BA, Cen. Conn. State U., New Britain, 1973; MAE, R.I. Sch. Design, 1979. Assoc. prof. art Elms Coll., Chicopee, Mass., 1985—, also chair dept. visual arts; lectr. in field. Exhibited in shows at Western New Eng. Coll., 1977, Springfield Art League Show, 1978, Zone Gallery, 1981, Westfield State Coll., 1985, Valley Women Arts Show, 1980, 83, 85, 86, 87, 88, 89, New Britain Mus. Am. Art, 1987, 88, 89, 90, Borgia Gallery at Elms Coll., 1989, 90, 91, 92, Hampden Gallery at U. Mass., 1990, Sino-Am. Women's Conf., Beijing, People's Republic of China, 1990, numerous others; one woman shows include Thronja Art Gallery, 1979-80, Elms Coll., 1992; represented in pvt. collections in Mass., R.I., Wash., N.Y., Italy, corp. collections in R.I. and Conn.; contbr. articles to profl. jours.; lectr. Greece, Mex. and China. Recipient Outstanding Arts Educator in Mass. award Mass. Alliance for Arts Edn., 1985, New Britain Mus. Am. Art, 1987, 88; Nat. Endowment for Humanities grantee, 1987, 88; Faculty Devel. grantee, Beijing, 1989, 90. Mem. Nat. Art Edn. Assn., Valley Women Artists, Mass. Art Edn. Assn. (mem. coun. 1984-86, v.p. 1986-88), Nat. Mus. of Women in the Arts, Coll. Art Assn., Nat. Women's Studies Assn., Internat. Soc. for Edn. through Art, Women's Caucus for Art. Office: Elms Coll 291 Springfield St Chicopee MA 01013-2839

COSTELLESE, LINDA E. GRACE, banker; b. Providence, Mar. 22, 1950; d. Lawrence A. and Lucy R. (Fiore) Grace; m. Dennis P. Costellese, May 8, 1971. AS in Bus. Adminstrn., Bryant Coll., 1981; cert., Sch. Bank Mktg., Colo., 1982; BS in Organizational Behavior, Lesley Coll., 1985, MS in Applied Mgmt., 1988. Sec. R.I. Hosp. Trust Nat. Bank div. Bank of Boston, Providence, 1969-78, adminstrv. asst., 1978-80, br. adminstrv. officer, 1980-81, community mktg. officer, 1981-82, retail sales officer, 1982-84, asst. v.p. sales and telemarketing, 1984-85, v.p. sales and tng., 1985-87, regional mgr., 1986-87, 1st v.p., dept. mgr. retail brs., 1987-89, sr. v.p., dept. head retail banking, 1989-90, exec. v.p., dir. R.I. retail banking, 1990-94; dir. N.E. sales, svc. and telebanking devel. group Bank of Boston, Boston, 1994—; mem. regional bd. New Eng. Banking Inst., 1993-94. Vol. Spl. Olympics, Providence, United Way Southeastern R.I., Providence; mem. St. Frances de Sales Women's Guild, Save-the-Bay; grad. Leadership R.I., 1993; advisor City Yr.-Providence, 1993—. Named Woman of Yr., North Kingstown Bus. and Profl. Women's Assn., 1987. Mem. Internat. Inst. R.I. (bd. dirs.), R.I. Bankers Assn. (pres. 1993-94), New Eng. Bank Mktg. Assn. (bd. dirs. 1985-87, 91-92, sec. 1987-88, 1st v.p. 1988-89, pres. 1990-91), Bank Mktg. Assn. (schs. adv. coun.). Office: Bank of Boston 100 Federal St Boston MA 02106-2016

COSTEN, LINDA MURA, public relations executive. BA in English and Speech Comm., Boston Coll. Faculty mem. tchr. pub. rels. Boston Coll.; acct. exec. Ingalls, Quinn & Johnson Pub. Rels.; pub. rels., comm. mgr. BJ's Wholesale Club, 1989-91; media rels. cons. Blue Cross & Blue Shield Assn., 1991-92; pub. info. officer, dept. news and info. AMA, Chgo., 1992—. Office: Am Med Assn 515 N State St Chicago IL 60610*

COSTON, KAREN PATRICE, secondary educator; b. Mar. 3, 1944; d. Dean Walter and Sara Kathryn (Moran) C.; children: Laura, Matthew. BS in Fgn. Svc., Georgetown U., 1967; MA in Econs., U. So. Calif., 1970; teaching cert., Radford U., 1982; postgrad., Va. Poly. Inst. & State U., 1993—. Cert. tchr. social scis., math. Instr. econs. U. So. Calif., L.A., 1968-72, Va. Poly. Inst. and State U., Blacksburg, 1972-73; tchr. Radford (Va.) City Schs., 1982-85, Shawsville High/Mid. Sch., Shawsville, Va., 1985-90, Blacksburg (Va.) H.S., 1990—. Editor: Financial Intermediaries, 1972. James Madison Found. fellow, 1987, 92—, NEH summer seminar fellow SUNY, Binghamton, St. John's, 1989, 92; named Tchr. of Yr. Va. Dept. Edn., 1990. Mem. LWV (pubs. editor 1990—), Nat. Coun. Social Scis. Democrat. Home: 209 Miller St Christiansburg VA 24073-3613 Office: Blacksburg High Sch Blacksburg VA 24060

COTE, BONNIE JUNE, education program specialist, artist, writer; b. Long Beach, Calif., June 7, 1949; d. Orville E. and Marian J. (Elle) Kadrie; m. Cortez Delano Bradshaw, Nov. 1, 1975 (div. July 1979); 1 child, Rondih Bradshaw; m. Richard Ronald Cote, Dec. 20, 1981; children: Kala, Kejon. Grad., Chgo. State U., 1975; MS in Pub. Adminstrn., No. State U., Aberdeen, S.D., 1983. Cert. prin. and supt. Budget analyst Kraft Foods, Chgo.; art tchr. United Tribes Tech. Ctr. and Coll., Bismarck, N.D.; exec. dir. Jamestown (N.D.) Fine Art Mus.; manpower devel. specialist Div. Indians and Native Ams., U.S. Dept. Labor, Washington, 1988-91; edn. program specialist Office of Indian Edn., U.S. Dept. Edn., Washington, 1991—. Mem. Nat. Indian Edn. Assn. Baha'i Faith. Office: US Dept Edn Washington DC 20202

COTE, DENISE LOUISE, federal judge; b. St. Cloud, Minn., Oct. 13, 1946; d. Donald Edward and Dorothy (Garberson) C.; m. Howard F. Maltby, Dec. 24, 1987. BA, St. Mary's Coll., 1968; MA, Columbia U., 1969, JD, 1975. Bar: N.Y. 1976, U.S. Dist. Ct. (so. and ea. dist.) N.Y. 1976, U.S. Ct. Appeals (2d cir.) 1984. Law clk. to Hon. Jack B. Weinstein U.S. Dist. Ct. (ea. dist.) N.Y., 1975-76; assoc. Curtis Mallet-Prevost, N.Y.C., 1976-77; asst. U.S. Attys. Office, N.Y.C., 1977-85, dep. chief criminal divsn. so. dist., 1983-85, chief criminal divsn. so. dist., 1991-94; atty. Kaye Scholer Fierman Hays & Handler, N.Y.C., 1985-88, ptnr., 1988-91; judge U.S. Dist. Ct. (so. dist.) N.Y., 1994—. Mem. Assn. of Bar of City of N.Y. (mem. fed. cts. com.). Office: US Courthouse Foley Square Rm 3006 New York NY 10007*

COTÉ, KATHRYN MARIE, psychotherapist, stress management educator; b. Oceanside, Calif., May 31, 1953; d. Richard Alfred Kauth and Carole Maxine Brue Potter; m. Dennis Malcolm Coté, Dec. 23, 1983; children: Claire Marie, Simone Gloria, Jesse Patrick. BA, St. Norbert Coll., DePere, Wis., 1975; MSSW, U. Wis., 1977. Lic. clin. social worker; cert. clin. social worker. Psychiat. social worker Napa (Calif.) State Hosp., 1977-79, team leader, 1979-80; supr. adolescent clin. svcs. Solano County Mental Health, Vallejo, Calif., 1980-83; sect. head of residential svcs. for children and adolescents London Borough of Camden, 1983-84; mental health program mgr. Solano County Mental Health, Fairfield, Calif., 1985-87; clin. social worker, county liaison West Ctrl. Community Svc. Ctr., Montevideo, Minn., 1987-90; pvt. practice as psychotherapist and stress mgmt. educator Berlin, N.H., 1990—; profl. cons. North Bay Suicide Prevention and Stressline, Napa, 1985-87. Bd. dirs. Coos County Family Health, Berlin, 1990—. Recipient Cert. of Appreciation, Solano County Mental Health Adv. Bd., 1987. Democrat. Roman Catholic. Home: 211 Cates Hill Rd Berlin NH 03570-1552 Office: 177 Main St Berlin NH 03570

COTE, LOUISE ROSEANN, creative director, designer; b. Quincy, Mass., Sept. 16, 1959; d. John Anthony and Theresa Janet (Oriola) Burke; m. Robert Andrew Cote, Aug. 6, 1983. BA, Bridgewater State Coll., 1981. Advt. asst. Dunnington Super Drug, Brockton, Mass., 1978-81; forms and graphics designer Shawmut Bank of Boston, N.A., 1981-86; artist Allied-Signal Inc., East Providence, R.I., 1986-89; creative svcs. adminstr. aftermarket electronic divsn. AlliedSignal, Inc., East Providence, R.I., 1989-92; creative svcs. supr. automotive aftermarket AlliedSignal Inc., East Providence, R.I., 1992-94, computer graphics supr. automotive aftermarket, 1994-95. Mem. Women's Advt. Club R.I. Roman Catholic. Office: AlliedSignal Inc Automotive Aftermarket 105 Pawtucket Ave Rumford RI 02916-2422

COTHERN, BARBARA SHICK, real estate investor, state legislator; b. Okmulgee, Okla., Mar. 5, 1931; d. Roy and Irene Maude (Baldwin) Shick; m. George Albert Cothern, Mar. 21, 1954; children: Cynthia Lou, Deborah Sue, James Albert. BA in Human Resources, Seattle U., 1980, MBA, 1983. Owner Human Resource Svc., 1980-85; ptnr. Cothern Partnership, Seattle, 1985—; mem. Wash. Ho. of Reps., Olympia, 1992—. Crisis counselor, 1979—; pres. Northshore Sch. Bd., Bothell, Wash., 1990-91, bd. dirs., 1987—, legis. rep., 1989-91; mem. resolutions com. Wash. State Sch. Dis. Assn., 1989—; pres. Shoreline Sch. Bd., 1974-75; chair Northshore Legis. Coalition, 1989-91; mem. Snohomish County Com. for Improved Transp., 1992; numerous other civic activities. Mem. NOW, AAUW, LWV, Nat. Women's Polit. Caucus. Mem. Reorganized Ch. of Jesus Christ of Latter Day Saints. Home: 20006 4th Ave SE Bothell WA 98012-9659 Office: Wash State Ho of Reps 305 Jl Obrien Bldg Olympia WA 98504

COTHRAN, ANNE JENNETTE, advertising and marketing sales executive; b. Buffalo, Nov. 28, 1952; d. Raymond John and Thelma Lorraine C. BA in English, Gordon Coll., 1975; MBA in Specialization Mktg., U. Chgo., 1989. Mgr. 1776 House, Salem, Mass., 1974-75; dept. mgr. Goldblatt's Dept. Store, Chgo., 1975-77; sales rep. Sta. WWMM, Arlington Heights, Ill., 1977-79, Sta. WYEN, Des Plaines, Ill., 1979-81; coop. mgr. Southtown Economist Newspapers, Chgo., 1981-83, div. sales mgr., 1983-88; retail advt. mgr. Lansing (Mich.) State Jour., 1988-90; advt. & mktg. dir. Herald-Bulletin Newspapers, Anderson, Ind., 1990-92; mgr. Dealer Network Advt. Sys. Newspaper Assn. of Am., Chgo., 1993-94; pub. dir. Standard Rate and Data Svc., Chgo., 1994—. Bd. dirs. Cabrini Green Legal Aid Clinic, Chgo., 1981-83. Mem. U. Chgo. Women's Bus. Group (bd. dirs. chpt. devel., chair 1987), Am. Mktg. Assn. (exec.), Rotary (v.p. Anderson suburban chpt. 1992-93), Chgo. Ad Club, Am. Statistical Assn., Mktg. Rsch. Assn., U.S. Power Squadron. Office: Standard Rate and Data Svc 3400 Glenview Rd Wilmette IL 60091

COTHRAN, PHYLLIS L., personal care industry executive; b. Charlottesville, Va., Feb. 12, 1947; d. James T. and Mary C. BS in Acctg., Va. Commonwealth U.; student, U. Va. sch. bus., Northwestern U., London Sch. Econs. Sr. acct. Blue Cross/Blue Shield Va., Richmond, 1972-74, systems acct., then sr. fin. analyst, 1974-75, adminstrv. asst. to v.p. fin., 1975-77, mgr. fin. planning and mgmt., 1977-78, corp. contr., 1978-81, v.p. fin., 1981-85, sr. v.p. fin. CHI, 1985-88, sr. v.p. fin. and planning HMC, 1988, chief. fin. officer, treas. BCBSVA, 1989, exec. v.p. ops., 1989-90, exec. v.p., chief oper. officer, then pres., chief oper. officer, 1990—; mem. audit com. Blue Cross/Blue Shield Assn., Chgo., 1990. Mem. cost rev. coun. VA Health Svcs., Richmond, 1990-91, Spl. Adv. Commn. on Mandated Health Ins. Benefits, Richmond, 1991; bd. dirs. Metro Richmond Drug Coalition, 1991, Va. Pub. Safety Found., Sci. Mus. Va. Found., Richmond Forum, Weed & Seed of Richmond, Nat. Mus. Health and Med. Found. Recipient Star award Va. Commonwealth U., 1990, YWCA Outstanding Women award. Mem. Fin. Execs. Inst., Soc. Internat. Bus. Fellows, Metro Richmond C. of C. (bd. dirs. 1991). Office: Trigon Blue Cross/Blue Shield 2015 Staples Mill Rd Richmond VA 23230

COTLER, JOANNA, children's book editor, artist; b. N.Y.C., Nov. 25, 1954; d. Gordon Cotler and Vera Lightstone. BA, SUNY, Purchase, 1977. Asst. editor, assoc. editor, editor children's books Avon Books, N.Y.C., 1979-83; freelance editorial cons., artist, writer, N.Y.C., 1983-87; editor children's books Harper & Row, N.Y.C., 1987-88; sr. editor children's books HarperCollins Pubs., N.Y.C., 1988, editorial dir., 1989; v.p., assoc. pub., editor-in-chief HarperCollins Pubs., Children's Books Div., N.Y.C., 1990-94, v.p., editorial dir. Joanna Cotler Books, 1994—. Author, illustrator: (children's book) Sky Above, Earth Below, 1990. Office: HarperCollins Pubs 10 E 53rd St New York NY 10022-5244*

COTNEY, CAROL ANN, engineering researcher; b. Huntsville, Ala., July 23, 1957; d. John Walter Sr. and Helen Maxine (Bechtold) C. BS in Family Resource Mgmt., Auburn U., 1979; BSE in Mech. Engring., U. Ala., Huntsville, 1986, MSE in Solid Mechanics, 1995. Clk. Jack Eckerd Drug Co., Huntsville, 1979-83; engring. student trainee U.S. Army Missile Command RDEC, Redstone Arsenal, Ala., 1983-86; aerospace engr. U.S. Army Missile Command, RDEC, Redstone Arsenal, Ala., 1986-88; rsch. aerospace engr. U.S. Army Missile Command RDEC, Redstone Arsenal, Ala., 1988-93; sales rep. DCA Promotions, Inc., Huntsville, 1993; substitute tchr. Madison County Bd. Edn., Huntsville, 1993—; with Taco Bell Corp., Huntsville, Ala., 1994—; mem. structures and mech. behavior subcom. material and properties and characterization panel, 1987-88, mem. structural analysis panel, 1987-88, acting program chmn., 1987-88, mem. profl. devel. com. originator, 1988, mem. propulsion systems hazards subcom. cookoff hazard tech. panel, 1991—; U.S. Army rep., 1991-93; mem. cookoff workshop originator and planning com., 1991-92, mem. propulsion industry cookoff tech. long range planning com., 1991; mem. Joint Army Navy NASA Air Force Interagency Propulsion Com., 1986—; ind. rschr., Huntsville, Ala., 1993—. Contbr. articles on propulsion mechanics, propulsion design, structural design, insensitive munitions, and structural dynamics to profl. jours. Sr. high advisor and singles coord. Covenant Presbyn. Ch., Huntsville, 1980-83; chmn. bylaws com. Christian Singles Fellowship, Huntsville, 1984, v.p., pres., 1985-86; singles coord. Hope Presbyn. Ch., Huntsville, 1984-87, trustee, 1987-88; treas. United Meth. Women, Circle 9, Latham United Meth. Ch., Huntsville, 1991-92, mem. missions com., 1992, sec., 1992; tutor Seminole Svc. Ctr., Huntsville, 1991; mem. Friends of the Symphony, 1993—, mem. com. 1994—; mentor DOD Sci. and Engring. Apprentice Program, 1987-88; judge local, regional, state Ala. Sci. and Engring. Fair. Recipient U.S. Army Commendation 1988, 92. Mem. AIAA (sr. mem.), NAFE, ASME, U.S. Army Missile Command (facility rep. Ala.-Miss. sect. 1991-92, assoc. dir. edn. 1991-92, dir. career enhancement 1992, dir. telemetry newsletter 1992, region II co-dep. dir. precoll. outreach 1992-94, nat. engrs. week planning com. region II rep. 1993, nat. precoll. outreach com. 1993—, nat. tchr. enhancement subcom. 1993—). Home: 13909 Clovis Cir SW Huntsville AL 35803-2509

COTTEN, CATHERYN DEON, medical center international advisor; b. Erwin, N.C., Apr. 13, 1952; d. Ben Hur and Minnie Lee (Smith) C. BS in Anthropology, Duke U., 1975. Asst. internat. advisor Med. Ctr. Duke U., Durham, N.C., 1975-76; internat. advisor Med. Ctr. Duke U., Durham, 1976—. Contbr. chpt. to Advisors Manual of Federal Regulations Affecting Foreign Students and Scholars. Key vol. City of Durham, 1990-91; pres. Durham County Lit. Coun., 1992-94. Recipient Cert. Recognition So. Regional Coun. Black Am. Affairs, Atlanta, 1985. Mem. Nat. Assn. Fgn. Student Affairs: Assn. Internat. Educators (gov. regulations adv. com. 1985—, nat. chair 1991-94, chair Southeastern region 1989-90), Altrusa Club (pres. Durham chpt. 1987-89). Office: Duke U Med Ctr PO Box 3882 Durham NC 27710

COTTEN-HUSTON, ANNIE LAURA, psychologist, educator; b. Oxford, N.C., Nov. 18, 1923; d. Leonard F. and Laura Estelle (Spencer) Cotten; diploma Hardbarger Bus. Coll., 1944; AB, Duke U., 1945; MEd, U. Hartford, 1965; PhD, Union Grad. Sch., 1979; children: Hollis W., Rebecca Ann, Laura Cotten. Diplomate Am. Bd. Sexology. Asst. to pres. So. Meth. U., 1953; rsch. asst. Duke U., 1947-49; exec. sec. Ohio Wesleyan U., 1955-56, Conn. Coun. Chs., 1958-60; adj. prof. U. Hartford, 1976-78; clin. pastoral counselor Hartford Hosp., 1962-65; asst., then asso. dir. social svcs. Hartford Conf. Chs., 1965-67; teaching fellow U. N.C., 1970-71; adj. prof. U. Hartford, 1976-78; assoc. prof. Cen. Conn. State U., New Britain, 1967—; dir. elderhostel programs, Cen. Conn. State U., 1989—; organizer ctr. adult learners Cen. Conn. State U., 1991—; cons. Somers Correctional Ctr. (Conn.), 1980-81, instr./researcher, 1980-81; cons. Life Ins. Mktg. Rsch., 1981—; amb. to China, spring, 1986; presenter 3d Internat. Interdisciplinary Cong. on Women, 1987; vis. prof., scholar Duke U., 1989; vis. prof. Conn. Coll. New London, Conn., 1990; dir. Ctr. Adult Learners Cen. Conn. State U., 1991—; clin. faculty, supr. Am. Bd. Sexology, 1991, 94. Elder hostel dir. Cen. Conn. State U., 1987-93, organizer Elder Hostel Affiliate Network, 1991. Mem. AAUW, Am. Personnel and Guidance Assn., Am. Assn. Marriage and Family Therapists (cert.), Am. Psychol. Assn. (presenter conf. 1987), Nat. Coun. Family Rels., Am. Assn. Sex Educators, Counselors and Therapists (cert., presenter conf. 1993), Conn. Psychol. Assn., Conn. Council Chs. (dir.), Hartford Women's Network. Contbr. articles to profl. jours. Home: 193 Westland Ave West Hartford CT 06107-3057 Office: Ctrl Conn State U Dept Psychology New Britain CT 06050 also: St Joseph Coll West Hartford CT 06119

COTTER, SANDRA MILLER, lawyer; b. Lansing, Mich., May 9, 1962; d. William Anton and Delores Ann (Zamarron) Miller; m. Michael James Cotter, Oct. 27, 1990; 1 child, Maria Tanila. BS, Mich. State U., 1984; JD, U. Mich., 1989. Bar: Mich. 1989. Legis. asst. Mich. Ho. Reps., Lansing, 1984-86; teaching asst. U. Mich., Ann Arbor, 1987-89; assoc. Dykema Gossett, Lansing, 1989—; bd. dirs. Mfrs. Life Ins. Co. Am., Mfrs. Life Ins. Co. (U.S.A.). Commr. Natural Resources Mgmt. & Environ. Code Commn., Lansing, 1992-94. Mem. ABA, Mich. State Bar (mem. ins. law com., mem. Latin Am. bar). Republican. Roman Catholic. Office: Dykema Gossett 800 Michigan Nat Tower Lansing MI 48933

COTTER, SHARON SUE, financial manager, information systems specialist, consultant; b. Wichita, Kans., Nov. 14, 1949; d. Basil Clayton and Shirley Rose (Nichols) Carter; m. Byron Raphael Cotter, Aug. 23, 1969. BSN, U. Wis., 1972, MSN, 1977; MBA in Finance, SUNY, Buffalo, 1981. RN, Wis., N.Y.; Cert. of Fin.; registered stock broker. Staff nurse U. Wis., Madison, 1972-74; intensive care clin. specialist Mt. St. Mary's Hosp., Lewiston, N.Y., 1974-77; asst. prof. Nursing Niagara U., Niagara Falls, N.Y., 1977-78; jr. cost. acct. Westwood Pharm. Bristol Myers, Buffalo, 1982-83; supr. sales fin. Clairol Bristol Myers, N.Y.C., 1983-84; mgr. fin. analysis Nynex Mobile NYNEX Mobile Comms., Pearl River, N.Y., 1984-85; mgr. corp. fin. Nynex Mobile NYNEX Mobile Comms., Pearl River, 1985-86; fin. cons. (stock broker) Shearson Lehman Hutton, Midland Park, N.J., 1987-88; bus. unit acct., project mgr. Lever Indsl. Unilever, Runcorn, Eng., 1988-90; mgr. trade mktg. fin. Vandenberg Foods Unilever, N.Y.C., 1990-92. Mem. NAFE, Beta Gamma Sigma. Home: 450 Crest Dr Northvale NJ 07647 Office: Vision Assocs 44 South Broadway Ste 500 White Plains NY 10601

COTTINGHAM, JENNIFER JANE, city official; b. Salt Lake City, July 10, 1961; d. Miles Dixon and Ruth Eugenia (Skeen) Cottingham; m. Richard Frame Cavenaugh, July 23, 1983 (div. Apr. 1989); 1 child, John Douglas. BS in Civil Engring., So. Meth. U., 1984. Lic. profl. engr., Tex. Estimator Avery Mays Constrn., Dallas, 1981-83, project engr., 1984; owner, gen. contr. Dallas, 1985-89; asst. project mgr. Austin Comml., Dallas, 1989; ct. appointed receiver 14th Dist. Ct., State of Tex., Dallas, 1990-91; engr. asst. Dallas Water Utilities, 1990-91, project mgr., 1991—; dir. CBC Investors, L.P., Dallas. Goodwill ambassador City of Dallas Water Utilities, 1990-92, fin. strength com., 1991. Mem. CBC Investments (founding pres.), Dallas Symphony Orch. League, DAR (pres. jr. group 1989-92), Cotillion Book Club (founding mem.). Republican. Episcopalian. Office: Dallas Water Utilities 320 E Jefferson Blvd Dallas TX 75203

COTTINGHAM, MARY PATRICIA, vocational rehabilitation counselor; b. Seattle, May 9, 1930; d. Carl Frank and Frances Mary (Keon) Fox; m. Ken Cottingham, Sept. 15, 1951 (div. Sept. 1982); children: Cathy Ann, David Carl, Susan Mary, Keith Bryan, Patricia Frances. BA, U. Wash., 1974, MEd in Psychology, 1977. Diplomate Am. Bd. Vocat. Experts; cert. mental health counselor, Wash.; cert. vocat. rehab. counselor, cons. Counselor Mental Health North, Seattle, 1974-77; vocat. rehab. counselor Counseling Svcs. Northwest, Lynnwood, Wash., 1977-79; owner, cons. People Systems Inc., Seattle, 1979—. Bd. dirs. King County Mental Health Bd., Seattle, 1982-84; guardian ad litem King County Juvenile Ct., Seattle, 1981-84. Mem. AACD, Am. Mental Health Counselors Assn., Nat. Rehab. Assn., Pvt. Rehab. Orgns. Wash. (sec. 1986-89), Wash. Mental Health Counselors Assn. (sec. 1983-85). Home: 14727 42d Ave W Lynnwood WA 98037 Office: People Systems Inc 155 NE 100th Ste 406 Seattle WA 98125

COTTLE, SUZANNE LEE, critical care nurse; b. Ridgewood, N.J., Aug. 10, 1962; d. Donald Gerald and Grace (Vermeulen) Hein; 1 child, Lauren Kristen. ADN, Felician Coll., 1983, B in Biology, 1994. Cert. defibrillation, intra-aortic balloon pump CPR, critical care nursing. RN open heart recovery intensive care St. Josephs Hosp. and Med. Trauma Ctr., Paterson, N.J., 1983—, open heart intensive care preceptor, 1985—; part-time phlebotomist Ecolab Corp., Upper Saddle River, N.J., 1992-93; intern biochemistry in cancer rsch. U. Medicine and Dentistry, Newark, 1992; biology lab. asst., biology tutor Felician Coll., Lodi, N.J., 1993. Vol. Rep. County Hdqrs., Hackensack, N.J., 1993—; RN vol. ARC, Ridgewood, 1993—; mem. Wyckoff Reformed Ch., 1970—. Named Woman of Yr., Felician Coll., 1994, Scientist of Yr., 1995; Albert and Genevieve Baiard Meml. scholar, 1992, 93. Home: 178 Surrey Ct Ramsey NJ 07446

COTTRELL, JANET ANN, controller; b. Berea, Ohio, Dec. 2, 1943; d. Carmen and Hazel (French) Volpe; m. Melvin M. Cottrell, Mar. 2, 1963; children: Lori A., Gregory C. Student, Los Angeles State Coll., 1961-63. Lic. ins. agt., Calif. Loan processing Eastern Lenders, Covina, 1962-64; asst. bookkeeper Golden Rule Discount Stores, Rosemead, Calif., 1964-66; acctg. supr. Walter Carpet Mills, Industry, Calif., 1967-69; co-owner Motorcycle Specialties Co., Industry, 1969-78, Covina (Calif.) Kawasaki, 1978-84; v.p., contr. M.C. Specialties Inc., Covina, 1984—; v.p., controller Aviation Communications Inc., Covina, 1992—; active various coms. relating to promotion, safety and advancement of the recreational vehicle and auto industry, So. Calif., 1981—. Mem. com. Miss Covina Pageant, 1986—, presdl. task force, nat., 1982—, Rep. nat. com., 1986—. Mem. Covina C. of C., Calif. Motorcycle Dealers Assn., Nat. Auto Dealers Assn., Internat. Jet Ski Boating Assn. Republican. Office: Aviation Communications Inc 1025 W San Bernardino Rd Covina CA 91722-4106

COTTRELL, JEANNETTE ELIZABETH, retired librarian; b. Buffalo, Dec. 10, 1923; d. Benjamin Birch and Mary Jeannette (Ashdown) Milnes; m. William Barber Cottrell, Jan. 21, 1944 (dec.); children: Karen Jean, Susan Marie, William Milnes, Scott Barber, Stephen Ashdown. BA in Sociology, U. Tenn., 1970, MS, 1976; student, Alfred U., 1940-43. Cert. tchr. libr., Tenn. Nursery sch. tchr. Concord Meth. Ch., Knoxville, Tenn., 1964-65; libr. City Sch. System, Knoxville, Tenn., 1971-84, ret., 1984. Author: (with husband) An American Family in the 20th Century, 1987; recorder textbooks for the blind, 1983—. Libr. Concord United Meth. Ch., Knoxville, 1975—, curriculum chairperson spl. studies class, 1989—, program chairperson Suzanna Wesley cir., 1990—. Mem. AAUW, Phi Kappa Phi, Beta Phi Mu. Republican. Methodist. Home: 308 Camelot Ct Knoxville TN 37922-2076

COTTRELL, MARY-PATRICIA TROSS, banker; b. Seattle, Apr. 24, 1934; d. Alfred Carl and Alice-Grace (O'Neal) Tross; m. Richard Smith Cottrell, May 17, 1969. BBA, U. Wash., 1955. Systems service rep. IBM, Seattle, also Endicott, N.Y., 1955-58, customer edn. instr., Endicott, 1958-60, 62-65, edn. planning rep., San Jose, Calif. and Endicott, N.Y., 1960-62; cons. data processing, Stamford, Conn., 1965-66; asst. treas. Union Trust Co., Stamford, 1967-68, asst. v.p., 1969-76, v.p., 1976-78, v.p., head corp. services, 1978-83; v.p. corp. fin. svcs. Citytrust, Bridgeport, Conn., 1983-90, sr. v.p. cash mgmt. svcs., 1990-91; v.p. cash mgmt. Chase Manhattan Bank of Conn., N.A., 1991-92, Centerbank, New Haven, Conn., 1992—. Bd. dirs. Family and Children's Aid of Greater Norwalk, Conn., chmn. 1986-87, Gaylord Hosp., 1986-92, vice chmn. 1991, chmn. devel. com., 1992—, Bridgeport Housing Svcs., 1985-91, New Eng. Network, Inc., Bank Mktg. Assn., 1988-91. Mem. Electronic Funds Transfer Assn. (vice chmn., bd. dirs., chmn. bd. dirs. 1983-84), Fairfield County Bankers Assn. (dir., pres. 1984-85), Phi Beta Kappa, Beta Gamma Sigma. Republican. Roman Catholic. Club: Grad. Office: Centerbank 55 Church St New Haven CT 06510-3014

COTTRILL, MARY ELSIE, family nurse practitioner; b. Charleston, W. Va., Sept. 17, 1939; d. Orville Hugh and Nancy Isabell (Fletcher) C. Diploma, RN, Sch. of Nursing, Chesapeake and Ohio Hosp., Clifton Forge, Va., 1964; diploma in Christian Edn., Appalachian Bible Coll., Bradley, W. Va., 1961; diploma in Spanish, Rio Grande Bible Inst. Missionary Lang., Edinburg, Tex., 1966; family nurse practitioner, Med. Sch. Nursing, U. Miami, Fla. Nurses asst. Thomas Meml. Hosp., S. Charleston, W. Va., 1953-58; RN Emmett Meml. Hosp., Clifton Forge, Va., 1961-64, Thomas Meml. Hosp., 1964-65; med. missionary Harvesters Internat. Mission, McAllen, Texas, 1965-74; primary care nurse Jackson Meml. Hosp., Miami, Fla., 1972-75; family nurse practitioner Martin Luther King Clinic, Homestead, Fla., 1975—. Asst. scout master Boy Scouts of Am., Miami, 1983—; den leader Cub Scouts of Am., Miami, 1983—. Recipient Migrant Health Provider award Nat. Assn. of Community Health Ctrs., 1989. Mem. Fla. Nurses Assn. Baptist. Home: 25510 SW 124 Ave Princeton FL 33032

COUCHMAN, GLENNIS MARLENE, home economics educator; b. Larned, Kans., Dec. 16, 1935; d. Norman C. and Edna M. (Galliart) Unruh; children: Larry Harold, Garry Duane, Terry Lyn. BS, Kans. State U., 1957, MS, 1972; PhD, Okla. State U., 1986. High sch. tchr. Ottawa (Kans.) High Sch., 1957-58, Larned (Kans.) High Sch., 1958-62, 65-69, Clay Center (Kans.) High Sch., 1969-77; asst. prof. Southwestern Coll., Winfield, Kans., 1977-85; assoc. prof. Clemson (S.C.) U., 1986-89; prof. family and consumer econs. Okla. State U., Stillwater, 1989—. Mem. nat. adv. bd. High Sch. Fin. Planning Program, Denver, 1988-94. Mem. AAUW, Am. Home Econs. Assn. (nat. com. chair 1991-92, 93-94), Okla. Home Econs. Assn. (treas. 1992-94, pub. affairs award 1992), Am. Coun. Consumer Interests, Assn. Fin. Planning and Counseling Edn., Exch. Club, Epsilon Sigma Phi (Diversity award 1992), Delta Kappa Gamma (internat. scholarship 1985-86, v.p. programs). Presbyterian. Home: 1601 Celia Ln Stillwater OK 74074 Office: Okla State U 336 HES Stillwater OK 74078

COUGHLIN, CAROLINE MARY, library consultant, educator; b. Bronx, N.Y., Dec. 6, 1944; d. Daniel Anthony and Antoinette (Aponte) C.; m. William Martin Weinberg, Oct. 3, 1981; 1 child, Nora Harie Weinberg. BA, Mercy Coll., 1966; MLS, Emory U., 1967; PhD, Rutgers U., 1976. Reference libr. First Nat. City Bank, N.Y.C., 1967-68; instr. Emory U., Atlanta, 1968-71; teaching asst. Rutgers U., New Brunswick, N.J., 1971-74; children's libr. Phillipsburg (N.J.) Pub. Libr., 1972-73; asst. prof. libr. sci. Simmons Coll., Boston, 1974-78; asst. dir. libr. Drew U., Madison, N.J., 1978-86, dir., 1986-94, assoc. prof. bibliography and rsch., 1986-94; cons. to librs. Highland Park, N.J., 1974—; cons. to librs., 1974—; team membership for site visits Mid. State Assn., 1979—; dir. Assn. Ind. Colls. and Univs. N.J. Office Edn., 1987-92; bd. dirs. Ctr. for Rsch. Librs., Chgo., 1987-92; vis. faculty mem. Rutgers U., 1988, 90, 93—; vis. prof. Internat. Librl Sch. U. Coll. Wales, 1993. Co-author: Lyle's Administration of College Library, 1992; editor: Recurring Library Issues, 1978; also articles. Bd. dirs. Women's Project of N.J., 1984—; mem. Women's Polit. Action Caucus, N.J., 1985—. Mem. ALA (councillor 1977-81), Assn. Libr. and Info. Sci. Educators (various coms.), Archons of Calaphon, N.J. Libr. Assn. (pres. coll. and univs. librs. sect. 1974-75, disting. svc. award 1993, rsch. award 1993), Beta Phi Mu. Democrat. Home: 304 Grant Ave Highland Park NJ 08904-1828

COUGHLIN, MARGARET ANN, marketing communications executive; b. Muncie, Ind., Oct. 14, 1955; d. Thomas Francis and Mary Alice (Guffigan) C. BA, Skidmore Coll., 1977; MBA, Babson Coll., 1984. With Procter & Gamble, Cin., 1977-79; account exec. Hill Holiday Advt., Boston, 1979-81; account supr. HBM/WCRS Advt., Boston, 1982-84; sr. v.p. Ingalls Quinn & Johnson/BBDO, Boston, 1984-91; pres. Cone Coughlin Comms., Boston, 1991—; bd. dirs. Stuarts Dept. Stores. Bd. dirs. Boston Children's Svc. Assn., 1988-92, Faneuil Hall Trust. Mem. Women in Communications (pres. 1989-90), Ad Club Boston (bd. dirs.). Office: Cone Coughlin Communications 90 Canal St Boston MA 02114-2009

COULON, KRISTINA VATHY, small business owner; b. Rochester, N.Y., Dec. 31, 1966; d. Florian Thomas and Eugenie Francis (Barlow) V.; m. Mark Allen Coulen, Sept. 16, 1989; 1 child, Ross Allen. BS, Nicholls State U., 1988. Intern in sales and mdse. Johnson & Johnson, Inc., New Brunswick, 1986, 87, 88; with dept. sales Screen Prints Inc., Harahan, La., 1989-94; owner, pres. River Bend Prodns., Harahan, 1994—; distbr. AD Specialty Inst., Langhorne, Pa., 1994. Active women and co-ed baseball leagues Harahan Parents' Club, 1994. Republican. Roman Catholic. Home: 595 Gordon Ave New Orleans LA 70123 Office: River Bend Promotions Inc 595 Gordon Ave New Orleans LA 70123

COULSON, DONNA SACKETT, human resources specialist, gas industry executive; b. Bklyn., Nov. 26, 1947; d. Benjamin R. and Florence M. (Bender) Gurdison; m. Dec. 1988. A.A. with high honors, Brookdale Community Coll., 1975; B.A. with high honors, Douglass Coll., 1977; M.S., Rutgers U., 1981. Staff sec. Bell Telephone Labs., Holmdel, N.J., 1965-75; student intern employee devel. dept. Johnson & Johnson, Skillman, N.J., 1977; tng. and personnel cons. Prudential Property & Casualty Ins. Co., Holmdel, 1977-84, editor The Prudential, 1985-86, assoc. mgr. personnel policies 1986-87; mgr. Prudential Realty Group, 1988-91; pres. Donna Coulson & Assocs., Cons. & Tng. Svcs., Red Bank, N.J., 1991—; mgr. employee devel. N.J. Natural Gas Co., 1992—; cons. U.S. Army Res., 1981; instr. Brookdale Community Coll., Lincroft, N.J., 1978—; instr. Bloomfield Coll., 1992—; bd. dir. CPC Supported Employment Svcs., 1992—. Mem. Eastern Monmouth C. of C., N.J. Assn. Women Bus. Owners (v.p. mktg.), N.J. Utility Assn. (chair), Am. Gas Assn. (HR steering com., 1995—). Office: PO Box 1464 Wall NJ 07719-1464

COULSON, ELIZABETH ANNE, physical therapy educator; b. Hastings, Nebr., Sept. 8, 1954; d. Alexander and Marilyn (Marvel) Shafernich; m. William Coulson, Feb. 14, 1986. Student, Wellesley Coll., 1972-73; BS in Edn., U. Kans., 1976; cert. in phys. therapy, Northwestern U., Chgo., 1977; MBA, Keller Grad. Sch. Mgmt., 1985; postgrad., U. Ill., 1991. Lic. phys. therapist, Ill. Assoc. prof. dept. phys. therapy Chgo. Med. Sch., North Chicago, Ill.; chmn. dept. phys. therapy Chgo. Med. Sch., North Chicgo, Ill., 1993—, chief del., 1991-93. Contbr. articles to profl. jours. Trustee Northfield Twp., Ill., 1993—. Mem. APHA, Am. Phys. Therapy Assn., Ill. Phys. Therapy Assn. Home: 1701 Sequoia Trl Glenview IL 60025-2022

COULSON, ZOE ELIZABETH, consumer marketing executive; b. Sullivan, Ind., Sept. 22, 1932; d. Marion Allan and Mary Anne (Thompson) C. BS, Purdue U., 1954; AMP, Harvard Bus. Sch., 1983. Asst. dir. home econs. Am. Meat Inst., Chgo., 1954-57; account exec. J. Walter Thompson Co., Chgo., 1957-60; creative consumer dir. Leo Burnett Co., Chgo., 1960-64; mag. editor-in-chief Donnelley-Dun & Bradstreet, N.Y.C., 1964-68; food editor Good Housekeeping, N.Y.C., 1968-75, dir. G H Inst., 1975-81; corporate v.p. Campbell Soup Co., Camden, N.J., 1981-91; mktg. cons., 1991—; mem. bd. dirs. Rubbermaid Inc., 1982-95. Author: Good Housekeeping Cookbook, 1972, Good Housekeeping Illustrated Cookbook, 1981 Trustee Cooper Hosp./Univ. Med. Ctr., 1982-91; elder Old Pine Presbyn. Ch., 1992—. Named Disting. Alumni, Purdue U., 1971. Mem. Women's Econ. Bus. Alliance (bd. govs.), Food and Drug Law Inst. (food bd. dir. 1979-81), Harvard Bus. Sch. Club (v.p. budget 1994—), Kappa Alpha Theta House Corp. (pres. U. Pa. chpt. 1992—). Republican. Avocation: Meso-Am. archaeology. Home: PO Box 18-B 220 Locust St Philadelphia PA 19106

COULTER, CATHERINE, writer; married. BA, U. Tex.; MA, Boston Coll. With human resources N.Y.C., San Francisco. Author: The Rebel Bride, 1979, Lord Harry's Folly, 1980, Lord Deverill's Heir, 1980, The Generous Earl, 1981, Devil's Embrace, 1983, Sweet Surrender, 1984, Devil's Daughter, 1985, Chandra, 1985, Midnight Star, 1986, Wild Star, 1986, Midsummer Magic, 1987, Jade Star, 1987, Moonspun Magic, 1988, Calypso Magic, 1988, Night Shadow, 1989, Night Fire, 1989, An Intimate Deception, 1989, False Pretenses, 1989, Portrait of Indifference, 1989, Night Storm, 1990, Impulse, 1990, Fire Song, 1990, Earth Song, 1990, Secret Song, 1991, Season of the Sun, 1991, The Hillion Bride, 1992, Beyond Eden, 1992, The Heiress Bride, 1993, Lord of Hawk Fell Island, 1992, The Aristocrat, 1992, Aftershocks, 1992, Afterglow, 1993, The Wyndham Legacy, 1994, The Nightingale Legacy, 1994, Lord of Raven's Peak, 1994, Lord of Falcon Ridge, 1995. Recipient Romantic Times award for best historical romance author, 1989. Office: c/o Robert Gottlieb William Morris Agy 1350 Ave of the Americas New York NY 10019*

COULTER, ELIZABETH JACKSON, biostatistician, educator; b. Balt., Nov. 2, 1919; d. Waddie Pennington and Bessie (Gills) Jackson; m. Norman Arthur Coulter Jr., June 23, 1951; 1 child, Robert Jackson. A.B., Swarthmore Coll., 1941; A.M., Radcliffe Coll., 1946, Ph.D., 1948. Asst. dir. health study Bur. Labor Stats., San Juan, P.R., 1946; research asst. Milbank Meml. Fund, N.Y.C., 1948-51; economist Office Def. Prodn., 1951-52; research analyst Children's Bur.-HEW, 1952-53; from statistician to chief statistician Ohio Dept. Health, 1954-65; lectr. econs., then clin. asst. prof. preventive medicine Ohio State U., 1954-65; asst. clin. prof. biostats. U. Pitts. Sch. Pub. Health, 1958-62; assoc. prof. biostats. U. N.C., Chapel Hill, 1965-72, assoc. prof. econs., 1965-78, biostats. prof., 1972-90; adj. assoc. prof., hosp. adminstr. Duke U., 1972-79; assoc. dean undergrad. pub. health studies U. N.C., Chapel Hill, 1979-86, prof. biostats. emerita, 1990—. Contbr. articles to profl. jours. Mem. AAAS, AAUP, APHA (governing coun. 1970-72), Am. Econ. Assn., Am. Statis. Assn., Am. Acad. Polit. and Social Sci., Biometric Soc., Am. Evaluation Assn., Assn. for Health Svcs. Rsch., Sigma Xi, Delta Omega. Methodist. Home: 1825 North Lakeshore Dr Chapel Hill NC 27514-6734

COULTER, PATRICIA MARIE, paralegal; b. Washington, Sept. 5, 1965; d. John Kendall and Clare Mary (O'Connor) C. AAS summa cum laude, J. Sargeant Reynolds Coll., 1993; BA, William and Mary Coll., 1987. Officer mgr. Accu-Beta, Inc., Mechanicsville, Va., 1988-90; collections paralegal Williams, Mullen, Christian and Dobbins, Richmond, Va., 1990; litigation paralegal Williams, Mullen, Christian and Dabbis, Richmond, Va., 1990-91; paralegal Russell, Cantor, Arkema & Edmonds, P.C., Richmond, 1991—. Paralegal vol. Ctrl. Va. Legal Aid Soc., 1991—. Capt. USAR, 1987—. Mem. Richmond Assn. of Legal Assts. (sec. 1993—), Va. Assn. of Trial Lawyers, Nat. Assn. of Legal Assts., Assn. of Trial Lawyers of Am., Phi Theta Kappa. Democrat. Home: 1513 Split Oak Ln Apt B Richmond VA 23229-5220 Office: Cantor Arkema & Edmonds PC 823 Main St PO Box 561 Richmond VA 23204-0561

COULTON, MARTHA JEAN GLASSCOE (MRS. MARTIN J. COULTON), librarian; b. Dayton, Ohio; d. Lafayette Pierre and Gertrude Blanche (Miller) Glasscoe; m. Martin J. Coulton; children: Perry Jean, Martin John. student Dayton Art Inst., 1946-47. Dir., Milton (Ohio) Union Pub. Libr., 1968-89; libr. cons., Centerville, Ohio, 1989—. Named Outstanding Woman Jaycees, 1978-1979; recipient Spl. Recognition award Ohio Ho. Reps., 1989. Mem. ALA, Ohio Library Assn., Miami Valley Library Orgn. (sec. 1981, v.p. 1982, pres. 1983), Internat. Platform Assn., Puppeteers of Am., DAR, Union Internat. Marionnette, Amnesty Internat., Pub. Citizen Health. Home and Office: 6029 Buggywhip Ln Dayton OH 45459-2407

COUNARD, ELIZABETH ANN, accountant; b. West Bend, Wis., Dec. 11, 1954; d. Robert Lee Faber and Vernita C. (Tackes) Bayer; m. Lee Robert Stoffel, Aug. 27, 1976 (div. Nov. 1985); children: Nic Michael, Joel Simon; m. Jeffrey Ronald Counard, Sept. 14, 1991; 1 child, Emily Kathryn. A degree, Moraine Park Tech. Coll., West Bend, 1988; student, Marian Coll., Fond du Lac, Wis., 1988-93. Fin. acctg. mgr. Smith & Nephew Rolyan, Menomonee Falls, Wis., 1987—. Mem. adv. com. Moraine Park Tech. Coll., 1992-93; jr. dir. Wis. Sixth Dist. Jr. Woman's Club, Ripon, 1984-85; pres., treas. Kewaskum (Wis.) Jr. Woman's Club, 1977-85. Mem. NAFE, Inst. Mgmt. Accts. Republican. Roman Catholic.

COUNCIL, PAULINE CARTER, lawyer, social services administrator; b. Camilla, Ga., Apr. 26, 1950; d. Willie Frank D. Sr. and Bernice (Brown) Carter; m. James F. Council, Jr., Jan. 26, 1980; children: Dawn Nichole, Kimberly Michelle, Ashley Monique, James F., III. BA, Morris Brown Coll., 1972; JD, U. Fla., 1994. Asst. planner S.W. Ga. Area Planning and Devel. Commn., Camilla, 1972-73, rev. coordinator, 1973-74, sr. planner, 1974-75; area agy. on aging coordinator S. Ga. Area Planning and Devel. Commn., Valdosta, 1975-77, area agy. on aging dir., 1977-85; dir. Quitman/Brooks CDC, 1987-89; worker adjustment specialist, 1989-91; atty. pvt. practice, 1995—. Chmn. Foster Grandparents, Valdosta, 1982-85, Dist. 8. Social Svcs. Adv. Coun. Valdosta/Albany Area, 1985—; mem. Ga. Coalition of Black Women, Minority Affairs Com. Moody AFB, Valdosta, 1975-78, Nat. Congress Community Econ. Devel., Citizens For Better Valdosta/Lowndes County, Lowndes County Community Ptnrs. in Edn.; local rep. Martin Luther King, Jr. Ctr. for Non-Violent Social Change, Atlanta, 1984-85; Brownie troop leader Flint River Council Girl Scouts U.S.A., Valdosta, 1982; pres., tchr. Young People Willing Workers, Faith Tabernacle Ch., Valdosta. Ga.; chairperson Westside Neighborhood Assn., 1994—; chairperson LMS Adv. Com., 1994-95. Com. for Humanities grantee, 1977, 79; Ga. Dept. Human Resources grantee, 1977-85. Mem. Ga. Bar Assn., Lowndes County Bar Assn., Nat. Council on Aging, Nat. Assn. AAAs, Ga. Assn. AAAs. Democrat. Pentecostal. Home: RR 10 Box 413 2410 Patrick Pl Valdosta GA 31601-8916

COUNIHAN, DARLYN JOYCE, mathematics educator; b. Cumberland, Md., May 1, 1948; d. Joseph Paul and Clara Kathryn (Miller) C.; m. Mark W. Chambré, Jan. 20, 1979. AB, Hood Coll., 1970, MA, 1982; postgrad., U. Md., 1971-73. Tchr. math. Cabin John Jr. High Sch., Montgomery County, Md., 1970-75, coach girls volleyball team, 1975; math. resource tchr. Takoma Park (Md.) Jr. High Sch., 1975-77, Ridgeview Jr. High Sch., Gaithersburg, Md., 1977-81; math. tchr. Kennedy High Sch., Silver Spring, Md., 1982-84; magnet math. tchr. Takoma Park Intermediate Sch., 1984—, also math. team coach; mem. area 3 adv. coun. Montgomery County Pub. Schs., 1972-73; coach boys basketball team Montgomery County Recreation Assn., 197l; mem. Mathcounts Adv. Group, Md. Mathalon Com. Co-author geometry textbook. Recipient various acad. athletic award in high sch., coll., Presdl. award for Excellence in Sci. and Math. Teaching, 1990, Women in Edn. award, 1986, David W. Taylor award Sigma Xi, 1993, Albert Shanker award, 1993; NSF grantee, 1971-72, 90, 92. Mem. Am. Fedn. Tchrs., Montgomery County Math. Tchrs. Assn., Nat. Coun. Tchrs. Math., Capts. Cove Golf and Yacht Club, Lake Holiday County Club, VFW Aux., Phi Kappa Phi. Home: 13900 Zeigler Way Silver Spring MD 20904-1160 Office: Taokoma Park Mid Sch 7611 Piney Branch Rd Silver Spring MD 20910-5102

COUNSELMAN, ANNE, librarian; b. Silas, Ala., Oct. 5, 1940; d. Chester Arthur and Elva (Daniels) Martin; m. Terry J. Counselman; children: Daphne, Bruce, Phillip. BS, U. Montevallo, Ala., 1961; MA, U. Ala., Birmingham, 1979; EdS, U. Ala., Tuscaloosa, 1988. Tchr. Clarke County Bd. Edn., Grove Hill, Ala., 1966-69; libr. asst. Birmingham Pub. Libr., 1971-72, head bookmobile, 1972-73; project dir. Appalachian Adult Edn. Ctr., Birmingham, 1974-75; libr. Birmingham City Bd. Edn., 1975-76, Wallace State C.C., Selma, Ala., 1980-83, Marengo County Bd. Edn., Linden, Ala., 1984—; reader rsch. and rev. team Libr. Rsch. and Demonstration Div. Libr. Programs, Washington, 1974. Mem. Thomaston (Ala.) Planning and Zoning Bd., 1992, 93; active Thomaston Bapt. Ch. Linly Heflin scholar, 1958-61, scholar Columbus Sch. Speech Correction, 1960, Pacers scholar Program for Rural Svcs. and Rsch., 1987; fellow Coun. for Basic Edn., 1992. Mem. NEA, Am. Edn. Assn., Ala. Edn. Assn., Thomaston Study Club. Home: 101 Lake Cir Thomaston AL 36783-3577 Office: AL Johnson High Sch Coates Ave Thomaston AL 36783

COUNTS, MARY LOU, retired telephone company executive; b. Prescott, Ark., June 14, 1933; d. Claude L. and Katie Gertrude (Bagwell) Barker; m. Eugene Counts, June 21, 1950; children: Brenda Kay, Jeanne Lou. Operator Southwestern Bell, Dallas, 1951-52, Hot Springs, Ark., 1952-62; clk. Southwestern Bell, Hot Springs, 1962-80, supr., 1980-83; mgr. Southwestern Bell, Little Rock, 1983-88; ret., 1988; pres. Ark. Chpt. Telephone Pioneers, Little Rock, 1986-87; co-chmn. State Pioneer Assembly, Ft. Smith, Ark., 1988-89. Vol. Nat. Park Svc., Hot Springs, 1989; pres. Jones Parent Tchrs. Assn., Hot Springs, 1962-63; mem. Pub. Sch. Curriculum Study, 1963-64, Friends of the Fordyce, Hot Springs, 1989; co-chmn. State Pioneer Assembly, Hot Springs, 1989-91; active Virginia Clington Kelley Dem. Women's Club of Garland County, Salvation Army Women Aux. Named Mrs. Ark. Pioneer, 1987. Mem. Telephone Pioneers (life, rep. Ark. chpt. 1991-93, chairwoman state assembly 1994), Belles Extension Homemakers Club, Rock Gardeners Horticulture Club, Garland County Coun. Garden Clubs (sec. 1993-94), Grow and Show Garden Club. Democrat. Methodist. Home: 513 2nd St Hot Springs National Park AR 71913-3629

COUPEY, SUSAN MCGUIRE, pediatrics educator, researcher; b. Montreal, Que., Can., June 29, 1942; came to U.S., 1978; d. Clarence Herbert and Paulette (Lefevre) McGuire; m. Pierre M.L. Coupey, July 1964 (div. 1981); children: Marc M.R., Ariane S.; m. James R. English III, Nov. 23, 1988. BA, Queen's U., Kingston, Ont., Can., 1962; postgrad., McGill U., Montreal, 1962-63; MD, U. B.C., Vancouver, Can., 1975. Diplomate Am. Bd. Pediatrics. Devel. chemist Merck, Sharp & Dohme, Ltd., Montreal, 1963-64; rotating intern Montreal Gen. Hosp., 1975-76; resident in pediatrics Montreal Children's Hosp., 1976-78; fellow in adolescent medicine Montefiore Med. Ctr., Bronx, N.Y., 1978-79, attending pediatrician, 1980—; rsch. asst. Cancer Rsch. Ctr., U. B.C., 1967-72; instr., asst. prof. pediatrics Albert Einstein Coll. Medicine, Bronx, 1979-85, assoc. prof., 1985-93, prof., 1993—, assoc. dir. div. adolescent medicine, 1984—, mem. faculty senate, 1983-84, 88-90; attending pediatrician North Ctrl. Bronx Hosp., 1979—; cons. in adolescent medicine Flushing (N.Y.) Hosp. and Med. Ctr., 1982—; Maricopa-Pima vis. prof. U. Ariz., 1989; vis. prof. Children's Hosp. Ea. Ont., U. Ottawa and Ea. Can. chpt. Soc. for Adolescent Medicine, 1990; chmn. health svcs. adv. com. Children's Aid Soc., 1985—, bd. trustees, 1993—; mem. adv. bd. Office Substance Abuse Ministry, Archdiocese of N.Y., 1983-85. Assoc. editor Adolescent Medicine: State of the Art Revs., 1990—, Jour. Devel. & Behavioral Pediatrics, 1992—, Jour. Pediat. & Adolescent Gynecology, 1992—; contbr. articles to med. jours., also chpts. to books and monographs. Fellow Am. Acad. Pediatrics; mem. Soc. for Adolescent Medicine (nominations com. 1984-85, chmn. jour. adv. com. 1987—, program com. 1991-93, awards com. 1992—), Ambulatory Pediatric Assn., Soc. for Behavioral Pediatrics, N.Am. Soc. Pediat. and Adolescent Gynecology (bd. dirs. 1993—), Ea. Soc. Pediat. Rsch., Soc. Rsch. in Adolescence, Sex Info. and Edn. Coun. U.S., Am. Acad. Physicians & Patients, Albert Einstein Coll. Medicine Alumni Assn. (v.p. pediatrics 1983-84, pres. 1984-85). Office: Montefiore Med Ctr Albert Einstein Coll Medicine 111 E 210th St Bronx NY 10467-2490

COURIC, KATHERINE, broadcast journalist; b. Arlington, Va., 1957; m. Jay Monahan; 1 child, Elinor. Grad., with Am. Studies major, U. Va. Began career with reporting and producing jobs NBC affiliates, Miami, Washington; joined NBC Network News, 1989; former nat. corr. Today, NBC, Washington; co-anchor Today, NBC, 1991—; co-host Now with Tom Brokaw and Katie Couric, NBC, 1993-94. Address: NBC TV Today Show 30 Rockefeller Plz New York NY 10112-0001*

COURNOYEA, NELLIE J., Canadian government official; b. Aklavik, N.W.T., Canada, 1940; div.; 2 children: John, Maureen. Radio announcer, later regional mgr. CBC, Inuvik, N.W.T.; negotiator, Com. for Original People's Entitlement; mem. territorial legislature Yellowknife, 1984—; minister of renewable resources, and of culture and communications, 1983-85, minister various portfolios, from 1987, govt. leader, 1991—; now premier N.W.T. Yellowknife. Office: Premier, PO Box 1320, Yellowknife, NT Canada X1A 2L9*

COURSEY, JOY HAMMOND, critical care nurse; b. Oxford, Ala., July 14, 1963; d. Franklin D. Hammond and Gloria Hammond Myers; m. Michael T. Coursey, July 31, 1988. BSN, Med. Coll. Ga., 1985; postgrad., U. S.C., 1994—. Cert. critical care RN, Ga. Staff nurse trauma ICU Med. Coll. Ga., Augusta, Ga., 1985-92; asst. nurse mgr. cardiovascular ICU Richland Meml., Columbia, S.C., 1990—; staff nurse float pool Humana Hosp., Augusta, 1991-92. Mem. AACCN. Home: 19 Wheatstone Ct Columbia SC 29223-9029

COURSEY, YVETTE L., social worker, public administrator, consultant; b. Cin., July 15, 1941; d. Harry William and Martha Elizabeth (Moore) C. BA, Ctrl. State U., Wilberforce, Ohio, 1963; MSW, Atlanta U., 1965; DPA, Nova U., 1982. Clin. social worker VA Hosp., Indpls., 1965-68; psychiat. social worker VA Hosp., Chgo., 1968-70; personal svc. specialist VISTA/OEO, Chgo., 1970-71; state program dir. Action, Chgo., 1971-72; cmty. svcs. rep. Social & Rehab. Svcs., HEW, Chgo., 1972-74; chief program ops. Adminstrn. on Aging./Dept. Health & Human Svcs., Chgo., 1974-87; program supr. Alcohol, Drug Abuse and Mental Health Fla. Dept. Health and Rehab. Svcs., West Palm Beach, 1987-88; substance abuse coord. Palm Beach County, West Palm Beach, 1988-93; pres. COTOM Assocs., West Palm Beach, 1993—; chair Riviera Beach (Fla.) Drug Coalition, 1990-93; adj. prof. Palm Beach C.C., Lake Worth, Fla., 1990—; program chair, mem. regional adv. bd. Just Say No Regional Office, Coral Springs, Fla., 1991-94; mem., bd. dirs. Palm Beach Cmty. Action Program, West Palm Beach, 1988—, vice chair, 1988-91. Contbr. articles to Palm Beach Gazette, Black Bus. Directory. Allocations vol. United Way of Palm Beach County, 1992—; dep. registrar West Palm Beach voter registration, 1992. Named Profl. of Yr., Fla. Alcohol and Drug Abuse Assn., 1992, Cert. of Appreciation, Bd. County Commrs. Palm Beach County, 1992, Outstanding Contbn. award Cert. Addictions Program, Palm Beach County, 1994. Mem. Nat. Caucus and Ctr. on Black Aged (conf. chair Chgo. chpt., v.p. 1982-86, award 1986), Gen. Alumni Assn. Ctrl. State U. (bd. dirs., sec. 1988-91, award 1990), Kiwanis (chair edn. Singer Island Sunrise chpt. 1989-94), Delta Sigma Theta (fin. sec. 1991-95). Office: COTOM Assocs PO Box 3823 West Palm Beach FL 33402

COURSON, MARNA B. P., public relations executive; b. Waynesboro, Pa., Feb. 22, 1951; d. Eugene Perry and Charlotte Mae (Sherman) Roschli; m. Sydney E. Courson, May 24, 1982; 1 child, Sydney Alexandra. BA, Franklin and Marshall Coll., 1973; postgrad., U. Kans., Kansas City. Reporter Beach Haven Times/The Beacon, Manahawkin, N.J., 1973-74, Dailey Observer Newspaper, Toms River, N.J., 1974-76; communications mgr. Frick India Ltd., New Delhi, 1976-77; reporter, dictationist UPI, Washington, 1978-80; reporter UPI, Richmond, Va.; reporter, editor AP, Balt., 1980-84; communications coord. St. Luke's Hosp. Found., Kansas City, Mo., 1986-88; exec. v.p. pub. rels. Spaw and Assocs., Inc., Overland Park, Kans., 1988-89; exec. v.p. CCI Pub. Rels. & Mktg. Comm., Inc., Shawnee Mission, Kans., 1990-92, pres., 1992—. Active adv. bd. Wonderscope Children's Mus., Vol. Leadership Coun.; vol. bd. dirs. Ctr. for Mgmt. Assist. Recipient Prism award for fund raising, numerous awards and honors for reporting, 1973-80; also pub. rels. awards, 1988-93. Mem. Internat. Assn. Bus. Communicators, Pub. Rels. Soc. of Am. (Pres.'s award with GKC), Silicon Prairie Tech. Assn., C. of C. Home and Office: 5832 Grand Kansas City MO 64113

COURT, PATRICIA GRACE, law librarian; b. Valparaiso, Ind., Oct. 13, 1953; d. Edward William and Phyllis Jean (Mahorney) C. BA in French, Ind. U., 1975, MLS, 1976; JD, Hamline U., 1984. Libr. Clay County Pub. Libr., Brazil, Ind., 1977-78, U. Wis., Platteville, 1979-81; law libr. U. Mo., Kansas City, 1984-90, Cornell U. Law Sch., Ithaca, N.Y., 1990—; bd. dirs. Women's Studies Exec. Bd., Cornell U. Contbr. articles to profl. jours. Mem. ABA, Am. Assn. Law Librs., Assn. of Law Librs. of Upstate N.Y. Office: Cornell Law Libr Myron Taylor Hall Ithaca NY 14853

COURTER, JEANNE LYNN, materials scientist; b. Flushing, N.Y., May 7, 1953; d. Harry Melvin Jr. and Ruth Jane (Rieben) C. B in Engring. Sci., SUNY, Stony Brook, 1975; PhD in Materials Sci., MIT, 1981. Rsch. scientist Am. Cyanamid Co., Stamford, Conn., 1981-83, materials section projects mgr., 1983-90, quality asst. to divsn. dir., 1990-94; sr. prin. rsch. scientist Cytec Industries, Inc., Stamford, 1994—. Inventor epoxy resin compound; patentee in field (with others), 1978-86. Pres., bd. dirs. Stamford Cross Road Residences, Inc.; coord. Interfaith Hospitality Network. Mem. Am. Soc. for Quality Control, Am. Chem. Soc., N.Y. Soc. for Coatings and Tech., N.Am. Guild Change Ringers, Tau Beta Pi. Methodist. Office: Cytec Industries Inc PO Box 60 1937 W Main St Stamford CT 06904-0060

COURTNEY, CAROLYN ANN, school librarian; b. Plainview, Tex., Aug. 1, 1937; d. John Blanton and Geneva Louise (Stovall) Ross; m. Moyland Henry Courtney, Aug. 17, 1957; 1 child, Constance Elaine. BA summa cum laude, Wayland Bapt. Coll., 1969; MEd, W. Tex. State Coll., 1976; MLS, U. North Tex., 1990. Cert. elem., secondary, libr. tchr. 5th grade tchr. Hale Ctr. (Tex.) Ind. Sch. Dist., 1970-77, libr., 1977—. Mem. LWV (bd. mem. 1970-75), DAR (Good Citizen chair 1981-85), Tex. State Tchs. Assn. (life), Tex. Classroom Tchrs. Assn. (sec. 1983-85), Tex. Libr. Assn., Delta Kappa Gamma (rsch. chair 1975-77, publs. chair 1984-86, scholarship 1975). Methodist. Home: 209 S Floydada St Plainview TX 79072 Office: Hale Center Ind Sch Dist Drawer M Hale Center TX 79041

COURTNEY, CONSTANCE E., lawyer; b. Plainview, Tex., Nov. 29, 1960; d. M.H. and Carolyn Courtney. BS, U. Tex., 1982, JD, 1985. Bar: Tex., U.S. Dist. Ct. (we. and ea. dists.) Tex., Ark., U.S. Dist. Ct. (we. dist.) Okla., U.S. Ct. Appeals (5th cir.) Tex. Com. clk. Natural Resources Com., Tex. Ho. of Rep., 1979; legis. staff to hon. Buck Florence Tex. Ho. of Rep., 1980-82; law clk. to hon. Jerre Williams U.S. Ct. Appeals (5th cir.), 1985-86; atty. Thompson & Knight, Dallas, 1986-92, Brown McCarroll, Dallas, 1992-94, Hutcheson & Grundy, Dallas, 1994—. Contbr. articles to profl. jours. Moderator So. Meth. U. Sch. Law Environ. Career Seminar, 1989-95. Mem. ABA, State Bar Tex. (coll., chair outreach com. environ. sect., law sch. com. 1988-90). Office: Hutcheson & Grundy Ste 6200 901 Main St Dallas TX 75202

COURTNEY, MARY ELAINE, nursing director; b. Galliano, La., Sept. 11, 1942; d. Frank Lamar and Eva (Adams) Smith; m. Wayne Courtney, Apr. 10, 1973 (div. July 1993); children: Kim Millien, Leon Lamar. Assoc. degree, Nicholls State U., 1987; student, Healing Arts Ctr., Baton Rouge, 1994. Cert. substance abuse nurse. Head teller Canal Bank, Bangor, Maine, 1976; EMT Lafourche Ambulance, Galliano, 1978-82; staff nurse Thibodaux (La.) Gen., 1987-88, Our Lady of the Lake, Baton Rouge, 1988-90; dir. nursing, insvc. dir. Dixon Med. Ctr., Denham Springs, La., 1990—; CPR, 1st aid instr. Lafourche Parish, Galliano, 1978-82; nurse cons. in field. Author: (children's book) The Ragman, 1994. Disaster chmn. ARC, Lafourche Parish, 1983-84. Mem. NAFE, Am. Practitioners of Infection Control. Roman Catholic. Avocations: hot air ballooning, writing, gardening. Home: 27923 Gaylord Rd Walker LA 70785 Office: Dixon Med Ctr 8375 Florida Blvd Denham Springs LA 70726

COUSINS, BERNICE BRIGANDO, minister, educator, consultant; b. Flushing, N.Y., Nov. 2, 1937; d. August and Olympia (Tortora) Brigando; BFA in Interior Design, Pratt Inst., 1955, postgrad. 1959; postgrad. City U. N.Y., 1966; children—David Bruce, Jason Bruce. Asst. to dir., tchr., Mus. Modern Art, Dept. Edn., N.Y.C., 1963-72; tchr. N.Y.C. Bd. Edn., 1966-73; with Am. Map Corp., N.Y.C., 1975-84, dir cartographic services, dir. mktg. services, also dir., 1979-81; co-dir. CW Assocs., Flushing, N.Y., 1982—; mgr. ops. support svcs. Consol. Appraisal Co., Inc., N.Y.C., 1987—; tchr. Adminstrv. Dir. Actualism Ctr., N.Y.C., 1980—; bd. trustees Actualism, Calif., 1991—, sec., 1991—, chair bd. dirs., 1992—, chair creative devel., 1992—; lectr. in field. Curriculum Adv. Com., Pub. Sch. 85Q, 1976-77. Mem. NAFE, Assn. for Research and Enlightment, Women Bus. Owners N.Y., Am. Space Found., High Frontier Soc., Am. Fedn. Astrologers. Contbr. articles to profl. jours.; researcher, compiler, editor: Nutritive Value of Common Foods, 1978; researcher, editor: Art Work: Schick-Colorprint Anatomy Charts, 1976-84. Office: 41-19 23d Ave Astoria NY 11105

COUTURE, JOSIE BALABAN, foundation director, insurance executive; b. Chgo., Dec. 10, 1922; m. Louis Couture, May 20, 1945 (div. 1948); 1 child, Dan B. Student, Tobias Matthay Sch. Pianoforte, London, Eng., 1938-39; studied with, Tobias Matthay; student, Yale U., 1939-40, Manhattan Sch. Music, 1940-42. Debut concert pianist Civic Theatre Chgo. Opera House, 1941; concert pianist live performances, radio, TV, 1941-50; entertainer USO tours; stockbroker N.Y. Stock Exch., 1955-60; ins. agt., broker, cons. N.Y.C., 1956—; internat. pub. info. coord. Al-Anon Hdqs., N.Y.C., 1970-76; founder, pres. TOVA (The Other Victims of Alcoholism, Inc.), N.Y.C., 1976—; lectr., speaker in field. Editor: Domino Quar., 1977—; past mem. editorial adv. bd. Alcoholism Digest, Labour-Mgmt. Alcoholism Jour.; contbr. articles to profl. jours. Liaison rep. nat. adv. coun. Nat. Inst. on Alcohol Abuse and Alcoholism U.S. Dept. Health and Human Svcs., Washington, 1977—; testified at senate hearings Women and Alcoholism, 1976, Impact Alcohol and Drug Abuse on Family Life, 1977, Comprehensive Alcohol Abuse and Alcoholism Prevention, Treatment, and Rehab. Act Amendments, 1979. Recipient New Pioneer award Office Women and Alcoholism Nat. Coun. Alcoholism Inc. and Women's Inst. Am. Univ., 1977; recognized in Congl. Record for New Nat. Orgn. TOVA, 1976. Home: 100 W 57th St New York NY 10019-3327 Office: TOVA PO Box 1528 Radio City Sta New York NY 10101

COVALT, GENEVIEVE, corporate executive secretary; b. Cortland, Ohio, June 8, 1919; d. Charles Stuart and Edith Lavette (Wildman) Fee; m. Lynn S. Covalt, July 22, 1945. Student, Tex. State Coll. for Women, 1942. Exec. sec. to chmn. of the bd. Sanray Corp., Niles, Ohio, 1970—. Served with WAAC, U.S. Army, 1942-43. Recipient Silver Poet award World of Poetry, 1989; named Hon. Ky. Col. Mem. Hist. Soc., Am. First Day Cover Soc., Am. Bible Soc., Women in Mil. Svc. for Am. (charter), Am. Legion (chaplain).

COVARRUBIAS, PATRICIA OLIVIA, small business owner, consultant, author, communications educator, public speaker; b. Mexico, Mex., Sept. 17, 1951; came to U.S., 1959; d. Alfredo Izaguirre and Carmen (Baillet) C.; m. Robert Elvin Smith, Sept. 11, 1982. BA in French, Calif. State U., Sacramento, 1973, MA in French, 1978; student, Clown Camp, LaCrosse, Wis., 1992; postgrad., U. Wash. Tchr. d'anglais High Sch., Albi, France, 1973-74; instr. French Calif. State U., Sacramento, 1974-75; videotape editor Sta. KCRA-TV, Sacramento, 1977, news asst. assignment editor, 1978, news reporter, 1978-82; founder, exec. dir., instr. OCELOTL OCELOTL, Stockton, Calif., 1984—; guest speaker OCELOTL Speakers Bur., 1984—, Stockton Speakers Bur., 1985—; instr. lifelong learning program U. Pacific, Stockton, 1985—; instr. in community edn. San Joaquin Delta Coll., 1989—; cert. tutor Laubach Literacy Program, Stockton, 1984—. Author: Speaking Up with Style, 1985, Marketing Your Professional Self, 1986, Getting Good Press, 1988, The Speech Planner. . .Ten Steps to Successful Speaking, 1990; author video programs: Gear Up for Speaking English, 1987, Conversational English Made Easy, 1988, Make Presentations Work for You, 1993; columnist Clearly Speaking, 1990—; columnist for news jours.; contbr. articles to profl. jours. Child sponsor Feed the Children, Oklahoma City, 1986—; bd. dirs. San Joaquin County Arts Coun., Stockton, 1985-88, v.p., 1987; mem. Leadership Stockton, 1991-92. Mem. NAFE, Internat. Tng. in Communication (instr. 1985—, Florence Van Gilder award 1985), Stockton Women's Network, Lodi Writers Assn., Calif. Reading Assn., Pacific Delta Area Trainers, Greater Stockton C. of C. (liaison com. 1989—), Calif. State U. Alumni Assn. (bd. dirs. 1988—, pres. 1991-92, Rookie of Yr. 1988-89, Alumni Honors award 1991), Nat. Speakers Assn., Pi Delta Phi, Phi Kappa Phi. Home: 3144 Sea Gull Ln Stockton CA 95219-4603 Office: OCELOTL 917 K St Davis CA 95616-2102

COVILLION, JANE TANNER, data processing executive, educator; b. Syracuse, N.Y., Aug. 20, 1956; d. Francis Duane and Barbara Ann (Zimmerman) Tanner; m. David Allen Covillion, Apr. 18, 1980. AB, Cornell U., 1978; MS, SUNY, Oswego, 1982; postgrad., SUNY, Syracuse, 1983-86. Cert. elem. and math. tchr., N.Y. Math. tchr. 7th grade Ray Jr. High Sch., Baldwinsville, N.Y., 1978-79; math. tchr. 6th/7th grades Zogg Mid. Sch., Liverpool, N.Y., 1979-81; tchr. math. Liverpool High Sch., 1981-82; assoc. prof. Onondaga Community Coll., Syracuse, 1982—; tchr. math. Lafayette (N.Y.) High Sch., 1986. Co-author: Mathematics Teacher, 1978; author: Association of Math Teachers of New York State Journal, 1983-86; prodn. mgr. The AMATYC Rev.; text reviewer in field. Mem. First Presbyn. Ch., 1971—, Greater Syracuse Sci. Fair Planning Com., 1982—; sec. Onondaga Community Coll. Fedn. Tchrs., Syracuse, 1987—. N.Y. State Regents scholar, 1974, James L. Sears Found. scholar, 1974. Mem. AAUW, Nat. Coun. Tchrs. Math., Assn. Math. Tchrs. N.Y. State, Math. Assn. Am., Assn. for Women in Math., N.Y. State United Tchrs., Am. Fedn. Tchrs., Onondaga County Math. Tchrs., N.Y. State Assn. Two-Yr. Colls., N.Y. State Math. Assn. Two-Yr. Colls., Am. Math. Assn. Two-Yr. Colls., Delta Kappa Gamma (rec. sec. and pres. Beta Kappa chpt. N.Y.). Republican. Home: 4129 Reddeer Rd Liverpool NY 13090-1605 Office: Onondaga Community Coll Bus Adminstrn Dept Syracuse NY 13215

COVINGTON, ANN K., judge, lawyer; b. Fairmont, W.Va., Mar. 5, 1942; d. James R. and Elizabeth Ann (Hornor) Kettering; m. James E. Waddell, Aug. 17, 1963 (div. Aug. 1976); children: Mary Elizabeth Waddell, Paul Kettering Waddell; m. Joe E. Covington, May 14, 1977. B.A., Duke U., 1963; J.D., U. Mo., 1977. Bar: Mo. 1977, U.S. Dist. Ct. (we. dist.) Mo. 1977. Asst. atty. gen. State of Mo., Jefferson City, 1977-79; ptnr. Covington & Maier, Columbia, Mo., 1979-81, Butcher, Cline, Mallory & Covington, Columbia, Mo., 1981-87; justice Mo. Ct. Appeals (we. dist.), Kansas City, 1987-89; justice Mo. Supreme Ct., 1989-93, chief justice, 1993—; bd. dirs. Mid Mo. Legal Services Corp., Columbia, 1983-87; chmn. Juvenile Justice

Adv. Bd., Columbia, 1984-87. Bd. dirs. Ellis Fischel State Cancer Hosp., Columbia, 1982-83; chmn. Columbia Indsl. Revenue Bond Authority, 1984-87; trustee United Meth. Ch., Columbia, 1983-86. Recipient Citation of Merit, U. Mo. Law Sch., 1993, Faculty-Alumni award U. Mo., 1993; Coun. of State Govt. Toll fellow, 1988. Fellow Am. Bar Found.; mem. ABA (jud. adminstrv. divsn., mem. adv. com. on Evidence Rules, U.S. Cts.), Mo. Bar Assn., Boone County Bar Assn. (sec. 1981-82), Acad. Mo. Squires, Order of Coif (hon.), Mortar Bd. (hon.), Phi Alpha Delta, Kappa Kappa Gamma. Home: 1201 Torrey Pines Dr Columbia MO 65203-4825 Office: Mo Supreme Ct PO Box 150 Jefferson City MO 65102-0150

COVINGTON, B(ATHILD) JUNE, business owner, advocate; b. Butte, Mont., June 21, 1950; d. Joe Talmage Covington Sr. and Betty Lou (Jones) Tomlinson; m. Mark Halsey Stephens, Aug. 2, 1969 (div. 1982); children: Mark Halsey Jr., Kimm Covington Stephens; m. James Bradford Hams, Feb. 20, 1987 (div. 1994); 1 stepchild, Brent Keir Mulvaney. Student, So. Utah State U., 1968-69, Indian Valley Colls., 1981-83. Advt. asst. McPhail's, Inc., San Rafael, Calif., 1973-75; mgr. Clothes Factory, San Francisco, 1976; graphic designer Press Rm. Printing, Redding, Calif., 1977; co-owner Player's Choice Retail Store, Redding, 1978-80; with advt. and in-house display dept. Indian Valley Colls. Book Store, Novato, Calif., 1981-82; advt. mgr. part-time Heritage Homes Realty, Novato, 1983-87; interior design asst., graphic designer, project coord. Ruth Livingston Interior Design, Tiburon, Calif., 1983-85, 87; project mgr., spl. needs design div. head Potter & Co. Builders, Richmond, Calif., 1987-88; owner, prin. CDT Assocs., Novato, 1988—; dir. ops. Tilia, Inc., San Francisco, 1989-92; master's candidate advisor Acad. Art Coll., San Francisco, 1989—; pvt. practice cons. sexual abuse, No. Calif., 1982—; instr. tng. seminars on social issues, internt. bus. ops. and procedures at colls., univs. and pub. agys., No. Calif., 1982—; prin. Friends Affecting Cohesive Efforts for Intervention and Treatment, Novato, 1991—; pub. rels. for Voices Unheard, San Francisco, 1994; mem. Action Against Sexual Violence, San Francisco, 1993. Co-producer video documentary Victims of Incest: The Price They Pay, 1983, Surviving Incest: A Path to the Future, 1988; producer video pilot program Straight From the Lip, 1985, We are 68, 1988; producer, editor photo essay and exhibit FACE IT, 1991—; contbr. articles to profl. jours. Mem. maj. gifts com. Novato Human Needs Ctr., 1988; foster parent Marin County Social Svcs., San Rafael, 1983-84; pub. speaker Ind. and Parents United, Calif., 1982—; sponsor Sexual Abuse Survivors, Marin County, 1988-89; mem. exec. com., adv. bd. and edn. com. Sexual Assault Prevention Agy., No. Calif., 1991—; bd. dirs. Survivorship, 1993—; co-founder Healing Kidz, Inc., San Francisco, 1992, v.p. bd. dirs.; co-producer Kicked-Up, an internat. portfolio featuring at-risk and homeless youth. Coll. of Marin Found. scholar, 1983; Marin Community Colls. grantee, 1983, 88. Mem. Hospitality Industry Assn. (co-chair philanthropy com. San Francisco chpt. 1988-89, chair, fundraiser San Francisco chpt. 1988-89), Parents United of Marin County (chair interior design com. 1987-89, bd. dirs., v.p., chair edn. com. 1989—). Democrat. Home: PO Box 1206 Novato CA 94948 Office: Advocate/Consultant 2559 Mission St Ste 117 San Francisco CA 94110-2512 also: Kicked Up 3655 No 25th St Phoenix AZ 85029

COVINGTON, PATRICIA ANN, university administrator; b. Mt. Vernon, Ill., June 21, 1946; d. Charles J. and Lois Ellen (Combs) C.; m. Burl Vance Beene, Aug. 10, 1968 (div. 1981). BA, U. N.Mex., 1968; MS in Ed., So. Ill. U., 1974, PhD, 1981. Lab dir. Anasazi Origins Project, Albuquerque, 1969; tchr. pub. schs., Albuquerque, 1969-70; teaching asst. So. Ill. U., Carbondale, 1971-74, prof. art, asst. dir., 1974-88, asst. dir. in admissions and records, 1988—; bd. dirs. Artist of the Month for U.S. rep. Paul Simon, Washington, 1974-81, Am. Coun. on Edn., Nat. Com. for AARTS, 1994—; vis. curator Mitchell Mus., Mt. Vernon, 1977-83; judge Mitchell Mus., Dept. Conservation; panel mem. Ill. Arts coun., Chgo., 1982; faculty advisor European Bus. Seminar, London, 1983; edn. cons. Ill. Dept. Aging, Springfield, 1978-81, Apple Computer, Cupertino, Calif., 1982-83; mem. Adminstrv. Profl. Coun. So. Ill. U., 1989-92. Exhibited papercastings in nat. and internat. shows in Chgo., Fla., Calif., Tenn., N.Y. and others, 1974—; author: Diary of a Workshop, 1979, History of the School of Art at Southern Illinois University at Carbondale, 1981; reviewer Mayfield Pub., Random House, (with William C. Brown) Holt, Reinhart & Winston. Bd. dirs. Humanities Couns. John A. Logan Coll., Carterville, Ill., 1982-88; mem. Ill. Higher Edn. Art Assn., chmn. bd. dirs., 1978-88; mem. Post-Doctoral Acad., 1981—; sec. adminstrv. profl. coun., 1989-90; mem. Girl Scouts U.S., 1988—, del. 1992, 93. Grantee Kresge Found., 1978, Nat. Endowment for the Arts, 1977, 81, Ill. Dept. Higher Edn. HECA grantee, 1994, 95; named Outstanding Young Woman of Yr. for Ill., 1981, Woman of Distinction, Girl Scouts U.S. Fellow Ill. Ozarks Craft Guild (bd. dirs. 1976-83); mem. Am. Assn. Coll. Registrars and Admissions Officers, Ill. Assn. Coll. Registrars and Admissions Officers (chair so. dist., exec. com. 1992-93, nominating com. 1993-94), Am. Coun. on Edns. (com. mem.), Nat. Com. for Army Registry, Spinx (hon.), Phi Kappa Phi. Presbyterian. Home: 389 Lake Dr Murphysboro IL 62966 Office: So Ill U Admissions and Records Carbondale IL 62901

COVINGTON, STEPHANIE STEWART, psychotherapist, writer, educator; b. Whittier, Calif., Nov. 5, 1942; d. William and Bette (Robertson) C.; children: Richard, Kim. BA cum laude, U. So. Calif., 1963; MSW, Columbia U., 1970; PhD, Union Inst., 1982. Pvt. practice psychotherapy, co-dir. Inst. for Relational Devel., La Jolla, Calif., 1981—; instr. U. Calif., San Diego, 1981—, Calif. Sch. Profl. Psychology, San Diego, 1982-88, San Diego State U., 1982-84, Southwestern Sch. Behavioral Health Studies, 1982-84, Profl. Sch. Humanistic Psychology, San Diego, 1983-84, U.S. Internat. U., San Diego, 1983-84, UCLA, 1983-84, U. So. Calif., L.A., 1983-84, U. Utah, Salt Lake City, 1983-84; co-dir. Inst. Relational Devel.; cons. L.A. County Sch. Dist., N.C. Dept. Mental Health, others; designer women's treatment, cons. Betty Ford Ctr.; presenter at profl. meetings; lectr. in field; addiction cons. criminal justice sys. Author: Leaving the Enchanted Forest: The Path from Relationship Addiction to Intimacy, 1988, Awakening Your Sexuality: A Guide for Recovering Women and Their Partners, 1991, A Woman's Way Through the Twelve Steps, 1994; contbr. articles to profl. jours. Mem. NASW (diplomate), Am. Assn. Sex Educators, Counselors and Therapists, Am. Bd. Med. Psychotherapists (diplomate), Am. Bd. Sexology (diplomate), Am. Pub. Health Assn., Assn. Women in Psychology, Calif. Women's Commn. on Alcoholism (Achievement award), Ctr. for Study of the Person, Friends of Jung, Internat. Coun. on Alcoholism and Addictions (past chair women's com.), Kettil Brun Soc. (Finland), San Diego Soc. Sex Therapy and Edn., Soc. for Study of Addiction (Eng.). Office: 7946 Ivanhoe Ave # 201B La Jolla CA 92037

COWAL, SALLY GROOMS, diplomat; b. Oak Park, Ill., Aug. 24, 1944; d. James Joseph and Virginia Richmond (Colborn) Smerz; m. Thomas B. Grooms, Aug. 26, 1967 (div. Jan. 1979); m. Anthony Charles Cowal, Nov. 26, 1987; stepchildren: Gregory, J. Kirsten, Alexandra. BA, De Pauw U., 1966; MA, George Washington U., 1969. Fgn. svc. USIA and State Dept., Washington, 1966-71; spl. asst. USIS, New Delhi, 1971-73; dir. Centro Colombo Americano, Bogota, Colombia, 1973-78; cultural attache U.S. Embassy, Tel Aviv, 1978-82; dir. internat. youth exchange USIS, Washington, 1982-83; polit. counselor U.S. Mission-UN, N.Y., 1983-85; min.-counselor U.S. Embassy, Mexico City, 1985-89; dep. asst. sec. State Dept., Washington, 1989-91; amb. U.S. Embassy, Port of Spain, Trinidad and Tobago, 1991—. Mem. Coun. on Fgn. Rels., Phi Beta Kappa. Office: US Embassy, PO Box 752, Port of Spain Trinidad and Tobago Office: Dept of State Port-of-Spain Embassy Washington DC 20521-3410

COWAN, CAROLYN CANNON, retired early childhood education educator; b. Slocomb, Ala., Mar. 28, 1924; d. Warren Denson and Leila (Reese) Cannon; m. Clinard Hartwell Cowan, Sept. 6, 1944; children: Carol Cowan Allen, Patricia Cowan Thompson, Nancy Cowan Swanson. Student, Judson Coll., 1942-44; BA in Edn., U. S.C., Aiken, 1981. Tchr. South Aiken Presbyn. Kindergarten, Aiken, S.C., 1960-68; tchr. First Bapt. Ch. Kindergarten, Aiken, 1968-80, tchr., dir., 1980-92, ret., 1992; past dir. First Bapt. Ch. Kindergarten. Mem. DAR, Town and Country, Cereus Garden Club. Baptist. Home: 1314 Evans Rd Aiken SC 29803-5336

COWAN, DEBORAH ANN, chemical engineer; b. Sacramento, June 26, 1955; d. Donald Raymond and Genevieve Marie Wilson; m. Robert John Cowan, Apr. 15, 1978; children: Elizabeth Marie, Natalie Joy, Rebecca Rose, John Donald. BS in Chem. Engring., Calif. Inst. Tech., 1977. Registered profl. engr., Calif. Engr. C.F. Braun & Co., Alhambra, Calif., 1977-79, sr. engr., 1980-85; engr. Ralph M. Parsons, Pasadena, 1979-80; v.p. software Lost Voltigeur Enterprises, San Dimas, Calif., 1985—; mgmt. systems spl. sr. Gen. Dynamics, Pomona, Calif., 1986-90; sr. engr. Brown & Root Braun, Alhambra, 1990-92, prin. engr., 1992—; registered VAR, Ashton-Tate, Torrance, Calif., 1985—. Choir mem. LaVerne Heights Presbyn. Ch., Calif., 1984—. Mem. Am. Inst. Chem. Engrs. Republican.

COWCHOCK, FRANCES SUSAN, geneticist, endocrinologist; b. Lebanon, Pa., June 19, 1941; d. John Robert and Mae Elsie (Williams) Zengerle; m. Michael Justin Cowchock, July 1, 1969 (dec. 1977); m. Richard Byrd Stewart, May 24, 1978. B.S., Pa. State U., 1962; M.A., Temple U., 1966; M.D., Jefferson Med. Coll., 1968. Diplomate Am. Bd. Internal Medicine, Am. Bd. Med. Genetics. Intern, Meth. Hosp., Phila., 1968-69; resident Jefferson Med. Hosp., Phila., 1971-73; fellow Columbia Presbyn. Med. Ctr., N.Y.C., 1969-71; instr. medicine Jefferson Med. Coll., Phila., 1973-75, asst. prof. medicine, ob-gyn., 1975-81, assoc. prof., 1981-89, prof. medicine, ob-gyn., 1989—. Contbr. articles to profl. jours. Fellow ACP, Am. Coll. Med. Genetics; mem. Am. Soc. Human Genetics, Am. Fertility Soc., Am. Soc. Reproductive Immunology, Soc. Obstetric Medicine, Phila. Genetics Group, Phila. Endocrine Soc., Sigma Xi. Office: Jefferson Med Coll 1100 Walnut St Philadelphia PA 19107-5502

COWDIN, MARIA VITA, management consultant; b. Manila, May 17, 1961; came to U.S., 1976; d. Eldon Abad and Bituin Ongchangco Vita. BS in Engring., Calif. State U., Long Beach, 1982; MBA, Pepperdine U., 1989. Mfg. data analyst Datatape, Inc., Pasadena, Calif., 1982-84; indsl. engr. Whittaker Electronic Systems, Simi Valley, Calif., 1984-87; sr. cons. Deloitte & Touche, L.A., 1987-91; prin. Cowdin & Assocs., Simi Valley, 1991—. Sr. mem. Inst. Indsl. Engrs. (dir. elect electronics industry div. 1990, chairperson electronics industry task force 1991). Republican. Mem. Ch. of Christ. Home and Office: Cowdin & Assocs 737 Talbert Ave Simi Valley CA 93065-5142

COWELL, LISA JOHNSON, accountant; b. Port Clinton, Ohio, Aug. 24, 1956; d. Robert Eugene and Norma Jean (Bunning) Johnson; m. Donald Eugene Cowell, Feb. 21, 1981; 1 child, Ariana Leigh Johnson. B in Comml. Sci. summa cum laude, Tiffin U., 1977; AA in Applied Bus. with highest honors, Owens C.C., 1986, AAS, 1993. Interviewer Cooperative Extension Office, Oak Harbor, Ohio, 1973; sec., bookkeeper Oak Harbor High Sch., 1973; sec. Thierwechter Ins., Oak Harbor, 1973-74; teaching asst. Tiffin (Ohio) U., 1975-77; controller Royal Tool Inc., Northwood, Ohio, 1975—; pres. Lei J Inc., Genoa, Ohio, 1986—. Recipient English award AAUW, 1974. Mem. Tau Alpha Pi (pres. 1993-94, v.p. 1991-93). Republican. Office: Lei J Inc 1308 Superior St Genoa OH 43430-1318

COWGER, DIANE, optometrist; b. Orange, N.J., Mar. 14, 1953; d. William Henry and Anna Mae (Sexton) C.; m. Marc A. Hudson. OD, Pa. Coll. Optometry, 1991. Lic. optometrist. Pres. Blue Ridge Eye Assocs., Harrisonburg, Va., 1992—. Recipient Outstanding Achievement in Chemistry award Am. Chem. Soc., 1986. Mem. Am. Optometric Assn., Va. Optometric Assn., Shenandoah Valley Optometric Soc., Harrisonburg Entrepreneurs, Working Women's Forum, Lions Club Internat. Republican. Mem. Ch. of Brethren. Home: 455 Hartman Dr Harrisonburg VA 22801 Office: Blue Ridge Eye Assocs 1790-136 E Market St Harrisonburg VA 22801

COWGILL, MARY LU, psychologist; b. Newton, Kans., Nov. 20, 1932; d. George David and Marian Chase (Axtell) Hanna; m. F. Brooks Cowgill, Dec. 22, 1954; children: David B., Ann M. AB, Stanford U., 1954; MA, Tufts U., 1972. Lic. sch. psychologist, Mass. Psychologist Fernald Lang. Grant Study, Mass. Dept. Health, Waltham, 1972-75, Learning Disorders unit Mass. Gen. Hosp., Boston, 1976-80; cons. on women's psychol. issues Winchester, Mass., 1980—; lectr. in field; treas., v.p., founder Waterfield Investors, Winchester, 1980—. Contbr. articles to profl. jours. Author and book reviewer Winchester Pub. Libr., 1991—. Mem. Wellesley Ctr. for Women's Studies, APA, Colonial Dames of Am., Boston Com. on Fgn. Rels., Stanford Alumni Assn. Congregationalist Ch. Home and Office: 75 Lawson Rd Winchester MA 01890-3153

COWLES, MILLY, education educator; b. Ramer, Ala., May 29, 1932; d. Russell Fail and Sara (Mills) C. B.S., Troy State U., 1952; M.A., U. Ala., 1958, Ph.D. (grad. fellow), 1962. Tchr. pub. schs. Montgomery, Ala., 1952-59; asst., then assoc. prof. Grad. Sch. Edn. Rutgers U., 1962-66; assoc. prof. U. Ga., 1966-67; prof., dir. early childhood devel. and edn. Sch. Edn. U. S.C., Columbia, 1967-73; assoc. dean, prof. Sch. Edn. U. Ala., Birmingham, 1973-80; dean, prof. Sch. Edn. U. Ala., 1980-87, disting. prof. edn., 1987—; Dir. Williamsburg County Schs. Career Opportunity Program, 1970-73; cons. So. Edn. Found., Atlanta, Ga. Inst. Higher Edn. U. Ga., also numerous sch. systems throughout Northeast and South. Editor, contbg. author: Perspectives in the Education of Disadvantaged Children, 1967; co-author: Taming the Young Savage, Developmental Discipline; author: Quality Early Childhood Education in the South, 1991, Activities in Early Childhood Education, 1992; mem. editorial bd. Dimensions, 1987—, The Profl. Educator, 1986—. Bd. dirs. S.C. Assn. on Children Under Six, 1969-73. Recipient Outstanding Pub. Educator award Capstone Coll. Edn. Soc. U. Ala., 1977, Outstanding Alumna award Troy State U., 1984, Early Childhood Edn. Leadership award S.C. State Coll., 1992. Mem. AAAS, AAUP, ASCD (mem. coun. on early childhood edn. 1969—, dir. 1978-82), NCATE (bd. examiners 1990), Am. Ednl. Rsch. Assn., Soc. for Rsch. Child Devel., Nat. Council Tchrs. English, Internat. Reading Assn., Nat. Assn. for Edn. Young Children (tchr. edn. panel 1991—), Assn. for Childhood Devel. Internat., So. Assn. Children Under Six (bd. dirs. 1985-87, chmn. editorial bd. 1989-91, Outstanding Mem. award 1992), Ala. Assn. Young Children (pres. 1984-85), Ala. Assn. for Colls. for Tchr. Edn. (pres. 1986-88), Ala. Assn. Supervision and Curriculum Devel. (pres. 1985-86), N.Y. Acad. Scis., Kappa Delta Pi (chpt. treas. 1964-66), Delta Kappa Gamma. Home: 60 Spring Water Chase Newnan GA 30265-1809

COWLISHAW, MARY LOU, state legislator; b. Rockford, Ill., Feb. 20, 1932; d. Donald George and Mildred Corinne (Hayes) Miller; m. Wayne Arnold Cowlishaw, July 24, 1954; children: Beth Cowlishaw McDaniel, John, Paula Cowlishaw Rader. BS in Journalism, U. Ill., 1954. Mem. editorial staff Naperville (Ill.) Sun newspaper, 1977-83; mem. Ill. Ho. of Reps., Springfield, 1983—, chmn. elem. and secondary edn. com., mem. joint Ho.-Senate edn. reform oversight com., 1985—; mem. Ill. Task Force on Sch. Fin., 1990—; vice chmn. Ho. Rep. Campaign Com., 1990—; co-chair Ho. Rep. Policy Com., 1991—; chmn. edn. com. Nat. Conf. State Legislatures, 1993—; mem. Joint Com. Adminstrv. Rules, 1992—. Author: This Band's Been Here Quite a Spell, 1983. Mem. Naperville Dist. 203 Bd. Edn., 1972-83; co-chmn. Ill. Citizens Coun. on Sch. Problems, Springfield, 1985—. Recipient 1st pl. award Ill. Press Assn., 1981, commendation Naperville Jaycees, 1986, Golden Apple award Ill. Assn. Sch. Bds., 1988, 90, 92, 94, Outstanding Women Leaders of DuPage County award West Suburban YWCA, 1990; named Best Legislator, Ill. Citizens for Better Care, 1985, Woman of Yr., Naperville AAUW, 1987, Best Legislator, Ill. Assn. Fire Chiefs, 1994, Outstanding Edn. Advt., Indian Prairie Sch. Dist. 204, 1994, Legislator of Yr., Ill. Assn. Pk. Dists., 1995. Mem. Am. Legis. Exchange Council, Conf. Women Legislators, Nat. Fedn. Rep. Women, DAR, Naperville Rep. Women's Club (pres. 1994—). Methodist. Home: 924 Merrimac Cir Naperville IL 60540-7107 Office: 552 S Washington St #119 Naperville IL 60540

COX, AMY B., employee benefits professional; b. Norwalk, Conn., Feb. 7, 1954; d. Joseph Earl and Dorothy Joy (Hyatt) Cox. BA in Journalism, Duquesne U., 1975; MA in Human Resources, St. Frances Coll., Loretto, Pa., 1983. Personnel tech. Allegheny County Health Dept., Pitts., 1979-82; personnel specialist Kane Hosp., Pitts., 1982-83; mgr. compensation and benefits Presbyn. Univ. Hosp., Pitts., 1983-90, West Penn Hosp., Pitts., 1990—. Bd. dirs. Pitts. Profl. Women Golf Network. Mem. Am. Compensation Assn., Soc. Human Resource Mgmt. Office: West Penn Hosp 4800 Friendship Ave Pittsburgh PA 15224-1722

COX, ANNA LEE, retired administrative assistant; b. Knoxville, Tenn., Feb. 18, 1931; d. Carter Calloway and Fairy Belle (Byers) Bayless; m. William Smith Cox, Sept. 4, 1952; 1 child, Catherine Anne Cox Faust. Grad. high sch., Knoxville. Sec. Am. Mut. Liability Ins. Co., Knoxville, 1948-53; flight procedures clk. FAA, Atlanta, 1963-66; legal sec., paralegal U.S. Atty.'s Office for Dist. S.C., Greenville, 1972-79; sec. criminal investigation div. IRS, Knoxville, 1981-84; sec., adminstrv. asst. CIA, Knoxville, 1984-88; adminstrv. asst. U.S. Dept. Def., Knoxville, 1988-91, ret., 1991. Tutor Greenville Literacy Assn., 1977-79; founder, dir. NATO Womens Chrous, Izmir, Turkey, 1969-71; choir dir., pres. United Meth. Women, Stephenson Meml. United Meth. Ch., Greenville, 1972-79; bd. dirs. Fountainhead Conservatory Music, Knoxville, 1983-85, 92—, sec. of bd. dirs., 1994—; singer Knoxville Choral Soc., 1955-56, Atlanta Symphony Chorus, 1971, Greenville Civic Chorale, 1973-79; vol. Ch. and Knoxville Mus. Art, 1992—. Republican. Home: 6724 Arapahoe Ln Knoxville TN 37918-9515

COX, BARBARA CLAIRE, costume designer, educator; b. Lock Haven, Pa., Apr. 4, 1939; d. Albert Clair and June Anna (Hutchins) Schultz; m. Richard Joseph Cox, Aug. 28, 1960 (div. 1970). BA, SUNY, Albany, 1961; student, Brandeis U., 1961, Cornell U., 1961-68; MFA, Carnegie-Mellon U., 1970. Mem. faculty Stanford U., Palo Alto, Calif., 1970-73; costume dir. Utah Shakespearean Festival, Cedar City, Utah, 1970-81; costume designer Alley Theatre, Houston, 1973-76; mem. faculty dept. theatre arts Calif. State U., Long Beach, 1976-81; costume designer South Coast Repertory Theatre, Costa Mesa, Calif., 1978-82; mem. faculty dept. dance and drama U. North Tex., Denton, 1988—; costume designer Dallas Shakespeare, 1991; owner Barbara C. Cox Designs, 1978—. costume dir. Circle Theatre, Ft. Worth, 1989—. Bd. dirs. Denton Civic Ballet. Recipient Excellence in Costume Design award Los Angeles Drama Critics Circle, 1982, Costume Design awards Drama Logue, Los Angeles, 1982-88, LA Weekly, 1985-88. Mem. AAUP, U.S. Inst. Theatre Tech., Costume Soc. of Am., United Scenic Artists. Home: 65 The Retreat Corinth TX 76205 Office: Univ N Tex Dept Dance Drama Denton TX 76203

COX, BETTY, public relations executive; b. Balt., July 20, 1938. Attended, Towson State Coll., Johns Hopkins U., NYU. Dir. occupl. therapy, program devel. & pub. rels. Stella Maris Hospice, Betty Cox & Assocs.; PA dir. Am. Occupl. Therapy Assn., comms. dir., 1973-83; pres. Betty Cox Assocs., 1983—. Mem. Am. Soc. Assn. Execs., Pub. Rels. Soc. Am., Am. Women in Radio and TV, Am. Film Inst., Soc. Nat. Assn. Publs., Women in Comms., Inc. Office: Betty Cox Assocs 232 E University Pkwy Baltimore MD 21218*

COX, BRENDA GALE, statistician; b. Princeton, W.Va., May 16, 1948; d. Ernest Monroe and Mona Virginia (Dove) C. BA magna cum laude, Concord Coll., 1970; MS, Va. Polytechnic Inst. and State U., Blacksburg, 1974, PhD, 1977. With Rsch. Triangle (N.C.) Inst., 1977-93, sr. statistician, 1981-93, dept. mgr., 1985-90; rsch. fellow Nat. Agrl. Stats. Svc., 1990-92; sr. statistician Math. Policy Rsch., Inc., Princeton, N.J., 1993-94; sr. fellow, 1994—; adj. assoc. prof. N.C. State U., Raleigh, 1989-90; mem. adv. panel Doctorate Records Project, 1993—. Author: Methodological Issues for Health Care Surveys, 1986; editor: Business Survey Methods, 1995; assoc. editor Jour. Bus. & Econ. Stats., 1989—; contbr. articles to profl. jours. Mem. Am. Statis. Assn. (pres. N.C. chpt. 1984-85, coun. rep. 1985-86, dist. 5 gov. 1986-88, sec.-treas. survey rsch. methods sect. 1986-88, survey rsch. methods tutorial com. 1990-93, organizing com. chair for Internat. Conf. on Establishment Surveys, 1991—, mem. com. on energy 1994—), Internat. Biometrics Soc. (regional adv. bd. 1986-88), Am. Assn. for Pub. Opinion Rsch., Internat. Assn. for Survey Statisticians, Pi Mu Epsilon. Democrat. Baptist. Office: Mathematica Policy Rsch PO Box 2393 Princeton NJ 08543-2393

COX, CAROL ANN, gerontology nurse; b. Ottawa, Ill., Dec. 28, 1948; d. Denzel and Loretta E. (Walker) Chapman; 1 child from previous marriage, Jimmy L.; m. Robert N. Cox, Aug. 31, 1991. AS, Coll. of the Mainland, 1983; student, Ill. State U., 1968-69. RN, Tex., Ind., Ohio. Hospice home care nurse Reid Meml., Richmond, Ind.; asst. dir. nursing Heritage House, Richmond; dir. nursing Randolph Nursing Home, Winchester, Ind.; quality assurance rsch. care coord., medicare specialist Brethren Home, Greenville, Ohio; surveyor long term care Bur. Med. Svcs. State of Ohio; nurse orthopedic fl. Reid Hosp., Richmond, 1992-93; dir. nursing Heartland of Greenville, Ohio, 1993—. Mem. Phi Theta Kappa.

COX, CAROLYN GLEATON, music educator; b. Bennettsville, S.C., Jan. 1, 1933; d. Wallace Duncan and Ellyn Mayfield (Allen) Gleaton; m. Gilbert Henry Cox Jr. (dec.); children: Gilbert Henry III, Mae Ellyn (Macie) Templeton. BA, Wesleyan Coll., 1955; MusB, Converse Coll., 1957, MusM, 1970; postgrad., Fla. State U., 1985-86. Instr. music Brevard (N.C.) Coll., Pub. Schs. Spartanburg (S.C.), North Augusta (S.C.), Lexington (Ky.), 1970-73; chairperson dept. music U. S.C., Conway, 1973—. Ch. choir dir. and organist. Recipient Humanitarian award Brevard Coll., 1973, Student Devel. Divsn. award U. S.C., 1981, Artist of the Yr. award Horry Cultural Arts Coun., 1993. Mem. Am. Choral Dirs., Music Educators Nat. Conf. United Methodist. Home: 141 Glass Hill Dr Conway SC 29526-6708

COX, DEBORA RICHARDSON, army nurse officer; b. Bellafonte, Pa., Aug. 4, 1960; d. Arthur Johnston and Barbara Ann (Richardson) Bugh; m. George Emerson Cox III, June 24, 1989. BSN, Pa. State U., 1982; MSN, U. Md., 1995. cert. ICU , EMT, ACLS, advanced trauma life support. Clin. staff nurse, ICU Kenner Army Community Hosp., Ft. Lee, Va., 1982-84; clin. staff nurse, emergency Bayne Jones Army Community Hosp., Ft. Polk, La., 1984-86; USAR nurse counselor Detroit Recruiting Bn., Detroit, 1987-89; clin. staff nurse 324th Gen. Hosp. Unit, Perrine, Fla., 1989; USAR nurse counselor Miami Recruiting Bn., 1989-93; adminstrv. fellow Office of the Surgeon Gen./U.S. Army/Chief Army Nurse Corps, 1995; nurse Walter Reed Army Med. Ctr., 1995—. vol. EMT City Police Dept., 1985-86; instr. BCLS Am. Heart Assn., 1984-86, unit inservice coord. emergency rm. Bayne-Jones Army Community Hosp., 1984-87; co-chair. Operation Desert Shield, Desert Storm Support Group, 1991. Recipient Up and Comer's Award in Health Care South Florida Mag., 1992; named Outstanding Employee USAR Nurse Corps Vital Signs Mag., 1992. Mem. ANA, Am. Cancer Soc. Thousand Plus Club (bd. mem. 1992-93), Am. Assn. CCRN's, Women in Mil. Svc. Am. Meml. Found. (field rep. 1992—), The U.S. Com. for UNICEF (co-chair 1991-92), Assn. of USAR, Assn. of Mil. Surgeons of the U.S., Fla. Nurses Assn. (Mil. Nurses coun. bd. mem. and chair 1990-92, dist. 21 chpt com. 1991-92), Md. Nurses Assn., Pa. State Univ. Alumni Assn., Helping Abused, Neglected, Dependent Youth, Young Profl's. for Covenant House, Hospice Hundred (treas. 1990-91, sec. 1991-92, bd. mem. 1992-93), Sigma Theta Tau Internat. (scholar Pi chpt. 1994). Home: 8635 Hayshed Ln Columbia MD 21045

COX, DIXIE SMITH, office manager; b. Pontotoc, Miss., Mar. 1, 1953; d. William Edward and Evelyn Estelle (Hobson) Smith; m. Herbert Thomas Cox, Oct. 20, 1970; 1 child, Thomas Jason. AS cum laude, Jackson State C.C., 1977; BS cum laude, Bethel Coll., 1979. Accts. payable clk. ITT Telecomm., Milan, Tenn., 1972-76; bookkeeper, acct. light and water dept. City of Trenton, Tenn., 1977-80; office mgr. T.B. Wood's Sons Co., Trenton, 1980—. Mem. Dem. Women's Orgn., Trenton, 1993; pres. Peabody High Sch. PTO, Trenton, 1988; chair Class of '71 reunion Peabody High Sch., 1981, 91. Mem. Am. Prodn. and Inventory Soc. (cert. internal auditor Excell Program 1994). Home: 1259 N 45 Bypass Trenton TN 38382 Office: T B Wood's Sons Co 1230 Manufacturer's Row Trenton TN 38382

COX, HELEN KEM CARSTARPHEN, elementary school educator; b. Washington, May 26, 1922; d. Oney Kem and Blanche Agusta (Towson) Carstarphen; m. Butler Ralston Cox, Mar. 28, 1942 (dec. 1991). BA, George Washington U., 1941; MEd in Guidance and Counseling, North Tex. State U., 1968; student, Queens U., 1953, 54, East Tex. State U., 1970, 71. Cert. elem. and spl. edn. tchr., Tex.; cert. diagnostician and counselor, Tex. Elem. tchr. N.Y.C. Bd. Edn., 1954-61; spl. edn. tchr. Carrollton (Tex.)-Farmers Branch Ind. Sch. Dist., 1961-85; instr. GED preparation Brookhaven C.C., Farmers Branch, Tex., 1985—. Elder Covenant Presbyn. Ch. Carrollton, ordained Stephen min., 1993; cir. moderator Presbyn. Women. Mem. AAUW, PTA (life), DAR, Assn. Childhood Edn. Internat. (pres.), Scottish Socs., Daus. of Caledonia (pres.), Farmers Br. Women's Club, Toastmistresses (pres.), Pi Lambda Theta, Kappa Delta. Democrat. Presbyterian. Home: 1831 Spring Ave Carrollton TX 75006-6101

COX, KATHRYN CULLEN, laboratory executive; b. Sedalia, Mo., June 29, 1943; d. Bernard Joseph and Ann (Matthews) Cullen; m. Paul John Cox, Oct. 3, 1964 (div. Sept. 1980); children: Donna, Eric. Diploma, St. John's

Mercy Med. Ctr., 1964; BS, Coll. St. Francis, 1986. Staff RN Bapt. Med. Ctr., Kansas City, Mo., 1969-80, staff RN surgery, 1980-84; oper. rm. supr. Ctr. Eye Surgery, Kansas City, 1984-86; dir. nursing Hunkeler Eye Clinic, Kansas City, 1986-93; staff nurse Glendale (Calif.) Eye Med. Group, 1993-94; consumer affairs supr. Alcon Labs., Irvine, Calif., 1994—; cons. ophthalmology, 1988—. Mem. Am. Soc. Ophthalmic Registered Nurses (pres. local chpt. 1984-86), Assn. Oper. Rm. Nurses, Am. Soc. Cataract & Refractive Surgery. Home: 23592 Windsong Apt 10H Aliso Viejo CA 92656-1324 Office: Alcon Labs 15800 Alton Pky Irvine CA 92718-3818

COX, KAY LYNETTE, health careers occupation educator, development consultant; b. Great Bend, Kans., Aug. 24, 1939; d. Herbert L. and Donna Dorothy (De Vore) Priest; children—Dana Suzanne Pothier, Tod Matthew Stevens, Ryan Austin Cox. A.A. in Nursing, Mt. San Antonio Coll., Walnut, Calif., 1962; B.A. with distinction, U. Redlands, 1978, M.A. in Mgmt., 1986. R.N., Calif.; cert. in vocat. edn.; community coll. credential. Nurse, South Coast Med. Ctr., South Laguna, Calif., 1965-72; tng. coordinator Capistrano-Laguna Beach Regional Occupational Program, San Juan Capistrano, Calif., 1972—; cons. Calif. Dept. Edn., Sacramento, 1978—, tchr. health careers tchr. tng., 1983—, profl. devel. cons. for spl. projects and curriculum devel., 1985—; chmn. Calif. Health Careers Adv. Com., 1982—; legis. rep. Med. Assts. Alliance in Calif., 1984—. Author: Being a Health Unit Coordinator, 2d. edit., 1985 Pet Facilitated Therapy, 1985. Mem. Nat. Assn. Health Unit Coordinators (founding mem.; dir. edn. 1985—), Calif. Assn. Health Career Educators (chmn. med. assts. task force 1982—), Am. Vocat. Assn., Nat. Honor Soc. Avocations: animals; reading; collecting china and crystal. Office: Capistrano-Laguna Beach Regional Occupational Program 31522 El Camino Real San Juan Capistrano CA 92675

COX, MARGARET ALBERTA (PEGGY COX), city clerk; b. Grafton, W.Va., Aug. 6, 1936; d. William Richard and Jean Irene (Gallaher) Kraft; divorced; children: Krista Kay Cox Rogers, Brent Keith. Grad. high sch., Grafton, W.Va. Aide, tutor Taylor County Bd. Edn., Grafton, 1972-80; city clk. City of Grafton, 1986—. Mem. Disabled Am. Vets., Order of Eastern Star, Vets. Fgn. Wars Auxiliary, WW I Vets., B. & O Auxiliary. Republican. Presbyterian. Home: 201 Monroe St Grafton WV 26354 Office: City of Grafton 1 W Main St Grafton WV 26354

COX, MARGARET STEWART, photographer; b. Indpls., Jan. 9, 1948; d. Douglass Falconer and Margaret Geraldine (Gates) Stewart; m. Herbert Leo Cox Jr., Dec. 21, 1977 (dec. Nov. 1985); 1 child, Matthew Michael. Student, Butler U., 1965-67. Real estate agt. Don Asher & Assocs., Orlando, Fla., 1972-80; real estate agt., appraiser Mary P. Logvin Real Estate, Orlando, 1987-90; freelance photographer Orlando, 1990—. Exhibited photographs in group shows at Marie Selby Gardens, 1993, 94 (Merit awards), Orlando Artists Biennial Exhbn., 1992 (Merit award), Mt. Dora Ctr. for the Arts, 1994 (Merit award), others. Bd. dirs. Adult Literacy League, Inc., Orlando, 1987—, pres., 1994—; vice chair Orange County Devel. Adv. Bd., Orlando, 1991-94. Recipient Spl. Mission Recognition award United Meth. Women, 1985. Mem. High Country Art and Craft Guild (exhibitor Ashville, N.C.), Nat. Audubon Soc., Fla. Audubon Soc., Orange Audubon Soc. (bd. dirs. 1993—). Democrat. Office: 3912 Harbour Dr Orlando FL 32806

COX, MARJORIE MILHAM, marketing manager; b. Hamlet, N.C., June 11, 1960; d. Seth Thomas and Claudia Ann (Milham) C. BS in Psychology, Duke U., 1981; MBA in Mktg., Vanderbilt U., 1985. Adminstr. Stanley H. Kaplan Edn. Ctr., Nashville, 1984-85; asst. brand mgr. Procter & Gamble, Cin., 1985-87; assoc. product mgr. Planters Lifesavers divsn. RJR Nabisco, Winston-Salem, N.C., 1987-90; promotions mgr. Holly Farms divsn. Tyson Foods, Wilkesboro, N.C., 1990; product mgr. Oscar Mayer divsn. Philip Morris, Madison, Wis., 1990-92; mktg. mgr. Hanes Hosiery Div. of Sara Lee Corp., Winston-Salem, 1992-93; brand mgr. Brown & Williamson Tobacco Corp., Louisville, Ky., 1994—. Democrat. Episcopalian. Home: 7209 Dux Ridge Rd Louisville KY 40059-9376 Office: Brown & Williamson Tobacco PO Box 35090 Louisville KY 40232

COX, MARLEEN ANN, artist; b. Covington, Ky., Dec. 19, 1946; d. Stanley L. and Mildred H. (Lubbers) C.; children: Robert H. Reddert, Theresa Reddert Schmidt. Student, Art Acad. of Cin. Self-employed artist, 1980—; lectr. Wilmington Coll., 1994, Warren County Corrections Inst., 1994, Cin. Art Mus., 1993, Greater Cin. Consortium of Colls. and Univ., 1993; founder and dir. ArtisTree Studios, Women Artists Co-Op Gallery, Miamitown, Ohio, 1994—. Group shows include Exo Gallery, Cin., 1993, Crazy Ladies Ctr., Cinn., 1993, Frieda Dean Gallery, Chgo. Invitational Exhibit (1st place), 1993, Art on The Square, Cin., 1994, The Minumental Exhibition, 1994, Take My Hand Exhibition, 1994. Recipient Mary Coulter Clark award Foun. Grant, Cin., 1992-93, Bertha Langhorst award, 1993-94. Mem. Woman's Caucus for Art, Cin. Art Mus. Home: PO Box 245 Miamitown OH 45041

COX, OLIVE JOSEPHINE, social services professional; b. Trinidad, W.I., Mar. 19, 1918; came to U.S., 1923; d. Vernon and Lavinia Elaine (Mulzac) Kirton; m. John William Cox, Mar. 29, 1937 (wid. May 1989); children: Patricia Joan, Barbara Ann/. AA cum laude, N.Y. City C.C., Bklyn., 1974; BA magna cum laude, CUNY, 1976. Various positions N.Y. City Dept. Social Svcs., 1951-77, dir. facilitative svcs., 1977-79; asst. dir. Cen. Fla. C.C., Ocala, 1980-81; adminstrv. dir. Christian Med. Clinic, Ocala, 1981-86; substitute tchr. and tutor Marion County Sch. Bd., Ocala, 1986—. Bd. dirs. Marion County Home Health Agy., Ocala, 1981—, Marion County Pub. Sch. Found., Ocala, 1990-94, Sch. Adv. Coun., Ocala, 1992—; exec. bd. dirs. Marion County Dem. Club, 1992. Recipient Averell Harriman award Office of Gov., State of N.Y., 1958, Resolution, Marion County Commrs., Ocala, 1982. Mem. AAUW (legis. chair 1986-88, nominating com. Fla. divsn. 1986), Marion Assn. Retarded Citizens (pres. 1987, Silver Bowl 1987), Nat. Coun. Negro Women, Nat. Coun. Cath. Women. Office: Emerald Shores Elem Sch 404 Emerald Rd Ocala FL 34472-3002

COX, ROBYN TRACY, vocational and employability consultant; b. Buffalo, Mar. 13, 1947; d. William Roy and Roxanne (Riddell) Houston; m. Garry Lee Cox, June 2, 1968; children: Suzanne Cox Ambrosini, Jenifer M. BA in Math. Edn., Ariz. State U., 1968, MA in Counseling Edn., 1971. Cert. rehab. counselor; cert. case mgr. Supr., counselor Crawford Rehab. Svcs., San Jose, Calif., 1975-79; vocat. rehab. counselor Tassano, Davie & Cox, San Jose, 1979-91; dir. Regain ADA Cons. Svcs., Millbrae, Calif., 1991—; seminar speaker on Ams. with Disabilities Act; instr. Ins. Edn. Assn., 1987, 89-91; mem. rehab. adv. com. Calif. Dept. Workers' Compensation, 1990-93. Contbr. articles to profl. publs. Bd. dirs. Mission Hospice, San Mateo County, Calif., 1988—, San Diego State U. Inst. for Worker Health and Rehab., 1991—; pres., bd. dirs. San Mateo County Mental Health Assn., San Mateo, 1990—. Mdm. ACA, Nat. Rehab. Assn., Nat. Rehab. Counselors Assn., State Bar Calif. (assoc. workers' compensation sect.), Calif. Assn. Rehab. Profls. (pres. 1979, 90, sec. 1983, peer rev. com. 1986—, joint legis. com. 1990). Democrat. Presbyterian. Home and Office: 260 Alta Loma Millbrae CA 94030-2104

COX, SARA BETH, food scientist; b. Columbia, Mo., Mar. 7, 1966; d. Ronald Finnell and Carolyn Sue (Winkler) C. BS in Agrl., U. Mo., 1988. Student microbiologist Oscar Mayer, Columbia Foods, Columbia, Mo., 1987; quality assurance project worker Ralston Purina, Davenport, Iowa, 1988; assoc. quality assurance tecnologist ConAgra Frozen Foods, St. Louis, Mo., 1989-90, Omaha, Nebr., 1989-90; assoc. food technologist ConAgra Frozen Foods, Omaha, 1990, food technologist, 1990-91, sr. food technologist, 1991—. Mem. Inst. Food Technologist. Office: ConAgra Frozen Foods 6 Conagra Dr Omaha NE 68102

COX, SYLVIA JEAN, systems analyst; b. St. Louis, Tenn., Dec. 9, 1950; d. Olga Maxine (Hayes) Bergjans. AA in Music Edn., Freed-Hardeman Coll., 1971; BA in Music Edn., Harding Coll., 1974; AS in Data Processing, State Tech. Inst., 1984. Music tchr. Sparta (Ill.) Dist. #140, 1974-76, David Lipscomb High Sch., Nashville, Ill., 1976-77; clk., computer ops. Nat. Bedding and Furniture, Memphis, 1977-80; programmer, data processing mgr. Delta Foremost Chem., Memphis, 1980-84; sr. programmer analyst Schering-Plough, Memphis, 1984-88; sr. systems analyst Fed Ex Logistics Systems, Memphis, 1988—. Co-chairperson MidSouth Conv., Ann. Memphis Sci. Fiction Conv., 1992—; vol. for fundraisers WKNO-TV, Memphis; vol. docent Ramesses the Great Exhbn., Memphis, summer 1987. Mem. Memphis Sci. Fiction Assn. (treas. 1989-90), Star Fleet Internat., Star Fleet Memphis. Mem. Church of Christ. Office: Federal Express Corp 3715 S Perkins Ste 1 Memphis TN 38118

COX, TERI P., public relations executive. BA, U. Pitts.; MBA in Mktg., NYU. Info. dir. United Mental Health; prodr., host weekly PA radio program; pub. rels. dir. Atlanta Merchandise Mart; mktg. rsch., pub. rels. cons. Pfizer Inc., NYU Stern Sch. Bus.; acct. supr. Burson-Marsteller, Coleman & Pellet, 1991-92; mng. ptnr. Cox Comms. Ptnrs., 1993—. Mem. Pub. Rels. Soc. Am., Am. Mktg. Assn., Healthcare Businesswomen's Assn. Office: Cox Comms Ptnrs 2 Roseberry Ct Lawrenceville NJ 08648*

COX, VALENA ANN, educator; b. Dallas, Nov. 26, 1955; d. Zane and Anita (McCurdy) Bartel; m. Calvin Cox, Aug. 26, 1978; 1 child, Tammy. BBA, Sam Houston State U., 1978; postgrad., Baylor U., 1984. Cert. secondary tchr. Bus. tchr. Hillsboro (Tex.) Ind. Sch. Dist., 1984-88; instr. Stenograph Inst. of Tex., Abilene, 1989-91; med. staff coord. Humana Hosp., Abilene, 1991-93; tchr. bus., journalism, theatre arts Trent (Tex.) Ind. Schs. Dist., 1993—. Mem. PTO Wylie Ind. Sch. Dist., 1988—. Scholarship Hammond Found.; recipient L.W. Gray award Tex. Assn. of Bus. Mem. Beta Sigma Phi. Republican. Baptist. Home: 4 Greenthread St Abilene TX 79606-5418 Office: Trent Ind Sch Dist PO Box 105 Trent TX 79561-0105

COX, VANDE LEE, critical care nurse; b. Takoma, Md., June 21, 1954; d. Vego Larkin and Lanette Lucille (Cunningham) Gooch; m. Larry L. Cox, Sept. 30, 1977; children: Andrea, Nathenial. Diploma, Deaconess Hosp. Sch. Nursing, 1976; BSN, U. Evansville, Ind., 1980, MSN, 1989. RN, Ind.; CEN, CCRN; cert. PALS, ACLS, TNCC, BTLS, ACLS instr. Nurse emergency rm. Deaconess Hosp., Evansville; clin. instr. Deaconess Hosp. Sch. Nursing, Evansville; clin. instr. ICU and med./surg. unit U. Evansville; critical care nurse Welborn Hosp., Evansville, emergency rm. nurse; charge nurse Thunder on the Ohio; clin. instr. Ivy Tech., Evansville, 1992. Mem. Emergency Nurses Assn., Critical Care Nurses Assn., Sigma Theta Tau. Home: 3417 Koring Rd Evansville IN 47720-2612

COX JOHNSON, KATY, small business owner; b. Washington, Nov. 18, 1944; d. Alexander Melville and Anita Irene (Tilley) Cox; m. Robert Paul Johnson, Jr., June 22, 1968; children: Robert Paul III, William T., Jennifer Kathryn. AA, Emory U., 1964; BS in Edn., U. Ga., 1966, MS in Edn., 1967. Tchr. 5th grade Fairfax County Schs., Springfield, Va., 1967-69, Newton County Schs., Porterdale, Ga., 1979-82; chief exec. officer, owner Cox Sales & Svc., Inc., Atlanta, 1982—. Mem. AAUW (corr. sec. 1993—). Office: Cox Sales & Svc 3276 Marjan Dr Atlanta GA 30340

COX-PURSLEY, CAROL SUE See PURSLEY, CAROL COX

COY, PATRICIA ANN, special educational programs director, consultant; b. Beardstown, Ill., Apr. 2, 1952; d. Ben L. and Dorothy Lee (Hubbell) C. BS in Elem. and Spl. Edn., No. Ill. U., 1974; MS in Spl. Edn., Northeastern Ill. U., 1976, MA in Spl. Edn., 1978; MEd in Spl. Edn., Northeastern U., 1984; postgrad., No. Ill. U., 1988—. Cert. elem. and spl. edn. tchr.; cert. counselor. Mental health supr. Waukegan (Ill.) Devel. Ctr., 1974-77; ednl. therapist Grove Sch. and Residential Program, Lake Forest, Ill., 1977-78; dir. residential svcs. N.W. Suburban Aid for the Retarded, Park Ridge, Ill., 1978-83; exec. dir. The Learning Tree, Des Plaines, Ill., 1983—; dir. residential svcs. Augustanan Ctr. Luth. Social Svcs. of Ill., Chgo., 1984-86, dir. planning and evaluation, 1986-93, dir. community svc., 1993—; behavior advisor Habilitative Systems, Inc., Chgo., 1985-88; program coord. Human Resource Devel. Inst., Chgo., 1986-89; project dir. Support Svcs. Ill., Inc., Chgo., 1987-91; dir. Tran Steps Inc. Steps for Success for Adults with Learning Differences, 1991—. Contbr. articles to profl. jours. Mem. Coun. for Exceptional Children, Am. Assn. Mental Deficiency, Chgo. Assn. Behavioral Analysis, Behavior Analysis Soc. Ill., Assn. for Supervision and Curriculum Devel., Nat. Rehab. Assn., Coun. for Disability Rights, Assn. for Learning Disability, Profls. in Learning Disabilities, Cwens, Echoes, Mortar Bd., Kappa Delta Pi. Democrat. Mem. United Ch. of Christ. Home: 8936 N Parkside Ave Apt 118 Des Plaines IL 60016-5517 Office: Transteps 7144 N Harlem Ave Ste 344 Chicago IL 60631-1017

COYLE, MARIE BRIDGET, microbiology educator, laboratory director; b. Chgo., May 13, 1935; d. John and Bridget Veronica (Fitzpatrick) C. BA, Mundelein Coll., 1957; MS, St. Louis U., 1963; PhD, Kans. State U., 1965. Diplomate Am. Bd. Med. Microbiology. Sci. instr. Sch. Nursing Columbus Hosp., Chgo., 1957-59; research assoc. U. Chgo., 1967-70; instr. U. Ill., Chgo., 1970-71; asst. prof. microbiology U. Wash., Seattle, 1973-80, assoc. prof., 1980-94, prof., 1994—; assoc. dir. microbiology labs Univ. Hosp., Seattle, 1973-76; dir. microbiology labs Harborview Med. Ctr., Univ. Wash., 1976—; co-dir. Postdoc Training Clinic Microbiology, Univ. Wash., 1978—. Contbr. articles to profl. jours. Fellow Am. Acad. Microbiology; mem. Acad. Clin. Lab. Physicians and Scientists (sec.-treas. 1980-83, exec. com. 1985-90), Am. Soc. Microbiology (chmn. clin. microbiology divsn. 1984-85, bioMerieux Vitek Sonnenwirth Meml. award 1994), Kappa Gamma Pi. Office: Harborview Med Ctr 325 9th Ave Seattle WA 98104-2499

COYNE, ELIZABETH LOUX PINKNEY, former elementary school science educator; b. Alexandria, Va., Nov. 1, 1965; d. James Faulkner and Patricia Ann (Loux) Pinkney; m. Kevin Anthony Coyne, July 7, 1990. BA with distinction, U. Va., 1987, MEd, 1990, postgrad., 1994—. Cert. tchr. collegiate level, Va. Lab. technician U. Va. Neurosci. Lab., Charlottesville, Va., 1984-87; psychiat. technician Charter Hosp., Charlottesville, 1987-88; grad. asst. U. Va., Charlottesville, 1988-90; gifted resource tchr. Virginia Beach City Pub. Schs., 1990-92, tchr. coord. elem. gifted sci., 1992-94; Mem. Virginia Beach City Pub. Schs. Gifted Program Planning Coun., 1992-94; coach future problem solving, Salem Middle Sch., Virginia Beach, 1992-94. Bd. dirs., tng. officer Blue Ridge Mountain Rescue Group, Charlottesville, 1986-90. Recipient Curry Sch. scholarship, U. Va., 1989, Future Tchr. scholarship Met. Life Found., 1989; named Tchr. of Yr. Old Donation Ctr. Va. Beach, 1993. Mem. ASCD, NEA, Va. Edn. Assn., Nat. Assn. for Gifted Children, Va. Assn. for Edn. of the Gifted, Phi Delta Kappa, Psi Chi (Nat. Svc. award 1987). Episcopalian.

COYNE, LINDA, educational administrator; b. Aurora, Ill., Jan. 12, 1949; d. Frances Patrick and Suzanne (Ruddy) C.; m. William E. Deeb, June 13, 1981; children: Colin Deeb, Robbie Deeb. BA in English magna cum laude, Calif. State U., Hayward, 1975; MA in Ednl. Systems Mgmt., Chapman U., 1984. Cert. secondary English tchr., C.C. tchr., C.C. supr., lang. devel. specialist, adminstr., Calif. Tchr. English and ESL Gonzales (Calif.) Union H.S., 1977-86; coord. ind. study program Gonzales Union High Sch. Dist., Soledad, 1986-91, vice prin. alternative edn., 1991-92, prin. cmty. edn. ctr., 1992—; typing tchr. Gonzales Union H.S. Dist., 1978-79; tchr. ESL Hartnell Coll., 1979-89; instr. Chapman U., 1992-93; sr. trainer Trainers Inst., Calif. State Dept. Edn., 1992-94; co-owner We Care Software; trainer cons. Lang. Devel. Specialist Exam Insvcs.; presenter in field. Mem. ASCD, Calif. Assn. Tchrs. of English to Speakers of Other Langs., Calif. Assn. for Cooperation in Edn., Assn. Calif. Sch. Adminstrs., Learning Styles Network, Calif. Consortium for Adult Edn., Calif. Continuation Edn. Assn. Home: 234 San Benancio Salinas CA 93908 Office: Gonzales Union High Sch Dst 690 Main St Soledad CA 93960

COYNE, M(ARY) JEANNE, state supreme court justice; b. Mpls., Dec. 7, 1926; d. Vincent Mathias and Mae Lucille (Steinmetz) C. B.S. in Law, U. Minn., 1955, J.D., 1957. Bar: Minn. 1957, U.S. Dist. Ct. Minn. 1957, U.S. Ct. Appeals (8th cir.) 1958, U.S. Supreme Ct. 1964. Law clk. Minn. Supreme Ct., St. Paul, 1956-57; assoc. Meagher, Geer & Markham, Mpls., 1957-70, ptnr., 1970-82; assoc. justice Minn. Supreme Ct., St. Paul, 1982—; mem. Am. Arbitration Assn., 1967-82; mem. bd. conciliation Archdiocese St. Paul and Mpls., 1981-82; instr. U. Minn. Law Sch., Mpls., 1964-68; mem. Lawyers Profl. Responsibility Bd., St. Paul, 1982; chmn. adv. com. rules of civil appellate procedure Minn. Supreme Ct., St. Paul, 1982—, chair adv. com. rules of civil procedure, 1984—. Editor: Women Lawyers Jour., 1971-72. Mem. ABA, Minn. State Bar Assn., Nat. Assn. Women Lawyers, Nat. Assn. Women Judges, Minn. Women Lawyers Assn., U. Minn. Law Alumni Assn. Office: Minn Supreme Ct 245 Minn Judicial Ctr 25 Constitution Ave Saint Paul MN 55155-1500

COZ, MARY KATHLEEN, respiratory therapist; b. Ravenna, Ohio, Aug. 1, 1952; d. John and Kathleen (Bronson) C. A in Secretarial Sci., U. Akron, 1972, A in Respiratory therapy, 1979, BS, 1986, MS in Tech. Edn., 1990. Registered and lic. respiratory therapist. Sec. Kent (Ohio) Bd. Edn., 1970; exec. sec. Ernst & Ernst, Akron, Ohio, 1972-75; respiratory therapist Akron City Hosp., 1977—. Mem. Am. Assn. Respiratory Care, Ohio Soc. Respiratory Care, Nat. Bd. Respiratory Care. Roman Catholic. Home: 1236 Chelton Dr Kent OH 44240-3240 Office: Akron City Hosp 525 E Market St Akron OH 44304-1619

COZIN, RENEE MICHELLE, geriatrics nurse; b. New Bern, N.C., Jan. 7, 1959; d. William Paul and Cherie (Powell) C. BSN, Cath. U., 1982, MSN, 1989. Cert. gerontol. nurse. Nurse I Providence Hosp., Washington, 1982-83; charge nurse Jeanne Jugan Residence, Washington, 1983—; tutor nursing student Jeanne Jugan Residence, 1985—. Vol. Assisting Elderly, Washington, 1978-80, So Others May Eat, Washington, 1985—, Care Wear, Washington, 1989—, Mother Theresa's Sisters of Charity, Washington. Mem. Nat. Gerontol. Nursing Assn., VFW Aux., Order Ea. Star.

COZORT, AMBER LYNNE, nurse; b. West Plains, Mo., Jan. 4, 1963; d. Norris Bert and Chlora Ivene (Brickey) C. BSN, Rockhurst Coll. and Rsch. Coll. of Nursing, Kans. City, Mo., 1985. Psychiat. staff nurse Cox Med. Ctr. North, Springfield, Mo., 1985; psychiat. technician Park Cen. Hosp., Springfield, 1985-86; orthopedic staff nurse St. John's Regional Health Ctr., Springfield, 1986—. Mem. com. St. John's Med. Explorer Post 339, 1991-92, pres., 1990-91; mem. Greene County Rep. Party-TARGET; chair S.W. Mo. Nurses Recognition Dinner Com. Mem. Mo. Nurse Assn. (corr. sec., past bd. dirs. 4th dist. nominating com. mem. med.-surg. spl. interest group, region F regional dir. 1994-96, chmn. S.W. Mo. Nurses recognition dinner com.), Nat. Assn. Orthopedic Nurses, Rsch. Nursing Alumni Assn., Rsch. Coll. Nursing Alumni Assn., Rsch. Coll. Nursing Hon. Soc.

COZZOLINO, DOROTHY ARAMINI, law librarian; b. Flushing, N.Y., Jan. 9, 1938; d. William George and Anna Amelia (Brignole) Aramini; student U. Conn., 1955-58; m. Joseph M. Cozzolino, Nov. 30, 1957; children: Suzan, Alison, Matthew. BS in Geography, Trenton State Coll., 1973; MS, Drexel U., 1975. Asst. librarian U.S. Ct. Appeals (3d Cir.), Phila., 1975-79, chief librarian, 1979-88; cons., 1988; law librarian Libr. Mgmt. Svcs., 1991-94. Trustee, Morrisville (Pa.) Vis. Nurse Assn., 1972-75; fin. chairperson, treas. Morrisville Jr. Women's Club, 1970-74. Mem. Am. Assn. Law Libraries, Greater Phila. Law Library Assn. (treas. 1979-81, dir. 1978).

CRABB, BARBARA BRANDRIFF, federal judge; b. Green Bay, Wis., Mar. 17, 1939; d. Charles Edward and Mary (Forrest) Brandriff; m. Theodore E. Crabb, Jr., Aug. 29, 1959; children: Julia Forrest, Philip Elliott. A.B., U. Wis., 1960, J.D., 1962. Bar: Wis. 1963. Assoc. Roberts, Boardman, Suhr and Curry, Madison, Wis., 1962-64; legal rschr. Sch. Law, U. Wis., 1968-70, Am. Bar Assn., Madison, 1970-71; U.S. magistrate Madison, 1971-79; judge U.S. Dist. Ct. (we. dist.) Wis., Madison, 1979—, chief judge, 1980—; mem. Gov. Wis. Task Force Prison Reform, 1971-73. Membership chmn., v.p. Milw. LWV, 1966-68; mem. Milw. Jr. League, 1967-68. Mem. ABA, Nat. Assn. Women Judges, State Bar Wis., Dane County Bar Assn., U. Wis. Law Alumni Assn.(defender svcs. com. jud. conf.). Home: 741 Seneca Pl Madison WI 53711-2950 Office: US Dist Ct PO Box 591 120 N Henry St Madison WI 53701-0591*

CRABILL, BARBARA LYNN, mental health therapist, counselor; b. Dayton, Ohio, Jan. 7, 1963; d. Charles Russell and Lois Mae (Keney) Breisch; m. Matthew Alan Crabill, Sept. 6, 1980; 1 child, Christine Lynn Crabill. AAS, Sinclair C.C., 1984; BS, Wright State Univ., 1989, MS, 1991. Nat. cert. counselor, 1992; lic. profl. counselor, 1994. Crisis counselor South Community Mental Health Ctr., Kettering, Ohio, 1984; activites therapist Dayton (Ohio) Mental Health Ctr., 1984-85; outpatient counselor Mental Health Resource Corp., Xenia, Ohio, 1990-91; therapist South Community, Inc., Dayton, 1991—; staff devel. com. South Cmty., 1992, I.S.P. subcom., 1993. Mem. ACD, Am. Mental Health Counselors Assn., Phi Theta Kappa, Chi Sigma Iota. Republican. Roman Catholic. Office: South Community 2745 S Smithville Rd Dayton OH 45420-2600

CRABTREE, BEVERLY JUNE, college dean; b. Lincoln, Nebr., June 22, 1937; d. Wayne Uniack and Frances Margaret (Wibbels) Dees Dernier; m. Robert Jewell Crabtree, June 1, 1958; children: Gregory, Karen. BS in Edn., U. Mo., 1959, MEd, 1962; PhD, Iowa State U., 1965. Tchr. home econs. area pub. schs., Pierce City and Sarcoxie, Mo., 1959-61; mem. faculty home econs. Mich. State U., East Lansing, 1964-67; assoc. prof. U. Mo., Columbia, 1967-72, coord. home econs. edn., 1967-73, prof., 1972-73; assoc. dean home econs., dir. home econs. extension programs U. Mo., 1973-75; dean Coll. Home Econs. Okla. State U., Stillwater, 1975-87; dean Coll. Family and Consumer Scis. Iowa State U., Ames, 1987—; mem. faculty Family Impact Seminar Inst. Ednl. Leadership, George Washington U., 1976-82, Cath. U. Am., 1982-87; mem. nat. panel cons. for Vocat. Ednl. Pers. Devel., 1969-70; mem. nat. com. on future of coop. extension USDA and Nat. Assn. State Univs. and Land Grant Colls., 1982; mem. joint coun. on food and agrl. scis., 1987-91. Contbr. articles in field to profl. jours. Gen. Foods fellow, 1963-64; recipient Centennial Alumni award Coll. Home Econs. Iowa State U., 1971, Alumni Citation of Merit, Coll. Home Econs. U. Mo., 1976, Profl. Achievement award Iow State U., 1983. Mem. Am. Home Econs. Assn. (pres. 1977-78, chmn. adv. coun. Ctr. for Family 1982-83, mem. coun. profl. devel. 1980-83, a leader to commemorate 75th anniversary 1984, pres. found. 1987-88, chair Coun. for Certification 1991-92, Disting. Svc. award 1993), Okla. Home Econs. Assn. (Profl. Achievement award 1983), Nat. Assn. State Univs. and Land Grant Colls. (mem. commn. home econs. 1981-84), Assn. Tchr. Educators, Home Econs. Edn. Assn., Nat. Council of Adminstrs. of Home Econs., Am. Ednl. Research Assn., Am. Assn. Higher Edn., Nat. Assn. Tchr. Educators for Home Econs. (pres. 1969), Nat. Council on Family Relations, Mortar Bd., Golden Key, Omicron Nu, Phi Upsilon Omicron, Phi Delta Kappa, Omicron Delta Kappa, Pi Lambda Theta, Phi Kappa Phi, Gamma Sigma Delta. Methodist. Home: 3113 Rosewood Cir Ames IA 50014-4589 Office: Iowa State U Coll Family Consumer Scis MacKay Hall Ames IA 50011

CRABTREE, CATHERINE ANNE, physical therapy assistant; b. Kansas City, Mo., Aug. 20, 1961; d. Paul Bernard and MaryAnna Catherine (Clark) Boyd; m. Gary Wayne Crabtree, Mar. 2, 1985. Student, U. Mo., 1979-81; A in Phys. Therapy, Penn Valley C.C., Kansas City, 1983. Cert. phys. therapy asst. Phys. therapy asst. Liberty (Mo.) Hosp., 1983—; mem. skin integrity com. Liberty Hosp., 1993—, mem. products com., 1994. Mem. Pi Theta Kappa. Democrat. Roman Catholic. Home: 19414 NE 69 Hwy Liberty MO 64068 Office: Liberty Hosp 2525 Glenn Hendren Dr Liberty MO 64068

CRABTREE, DAVIDA FOY, minister; b. Waterbury, Conn., June 7, 1944; d. Alfred and Davida (Blakeslee) Foy; m. David T. Hindinger Jr., Aug. 28, 1982; stepchildren: Elizabeth Anne, D. Todd. BS, Marietta Coll., 1967; MDiv, Andover Newton Theol. Sch., 1972; D of Ministry, Hartford Sem., 1989. Ordained to ministry United Ch. of Christ, 1972. Founder, exec. dir. Prudence Crandall Ctr. for Women, New Britain, Conn., 1973-76; min., dir. Greater Hartford (Conn.) Campus Ministry, 1976-80; sr. min. Colchester (Conn.) Federated Ch., 1980-91; bd. dirs. Conn. Conf. United Ch. of Christ, Hartford, 1982-90; conf. min. So. Calif. Conf., United Ch. of Christ, Pasadena, 1991—; rsch. assoc. Harvard Div. Sch., Cambridge, Mass., 1975-76. Author: The Empowering Church, 1989 (named one of Top Ten Books of Yr. 1990); editorial advisor Alban Inst., 1990—. Bd. dirs. Hartford region YWCA, 1979-82; trustee Cragin Meml. Libr., Colchester, 1980-91, Hartford Sem.,1983-91; founder Youth Svcs. Bur., Colchester, 1984-89; pres. Creative Devel. for Colchester Inc., 1989-91; coun. Religious Leaders of L.A.,1991—; v.p. Hope in Youth Campaign, 1992—; trustee Sch. of Theology at Claremont, 1993—; dir. UCC Ins. Adv. bd., 1993—. Recipient Antoinette Brown award Gen. Synod, United Ch. of Christ, 1977, Conf. Preacher award Conn. Conf., United Ch. of Christ, 1982, Woman in Leadership award Hartford region YWCA, 1987; named one of Outstanding Conn. Women, UN Assn., 1987. Mem. Nat. Coun. Chs. (bd. dirs. 1969-81), Christians for Justice Action (exec. com. 1981-91).

CRAFT, MARY ANNE S., business executive, librarian; b. Lancaster, Pa., Aug. 11, 1939; d. Benjamin L. and Anne (Breneman) Snavely; m. James A. Craft, Sept. 25, 1965; children: Melanie, Kira. AB, Wellesley Coll., 1961;

MLS, U. Calif., Berkeley, 1965; cert. Libr. and Info. Sci., U. Pitts., 1975. Picture specialist libr. Libr. of Congress, Washington, 1961-65; registrar, libr. Univ. Art Mus. U. Calif., Berkeley, 1965-68; bus. ref. libr. Purdue U., West Lafayette, Ind., 1968-69; pres. Craft Enterprises Ltd., Pitts., 1982—; founder, pres. Forums Internat., Pitts., 1992—. sr. editor Corp. Artnews, 1984-93. Vol. program coord. art program Pitts. Pub. Schs., 1992—. Mem. Art Table, Friends of Art Wellesley Coll. Club, Beta Phi Mu. Office: Craft Enterprises Ltd 1717 Murray Ave # 27 Pittsburgh PA 15217

CRAFT, ROBBIE WRIGHT, artist; b. St. Louis, Feb. 22, 1951; d. Robert Edward and Irene (Tosch) Wright; m. Joseph Walter Epply III (div. 1978); 1 child, Joseph Walter IV; m. Raymond Wood Craft II, Feb. 14, 1987. Student, Casper Jr. Coll., 1969-71. Mgr. restaurant and bar Widow Browns, Crofton, Md., 1978-84; adminstrv. asst. U.S. Dept. Def., Andrews AFB, Md., 1974-75; illustrator, supr. U.S. Dept. Def., Cheyenne, Wyo., 1985-88, EEO counselor, 1987—, chief visual info., 1988—; ind. artist Maryland, Wyo., 1974—; ind. interior designer Wyo., 1985—. Mem. Internat. Platform Assn., United We Stand. Lutheran. Home: 7223 Tumbleweed Dr Cheyenne WY 82009-1014 Office: Visual Info Bldg 242 Cheyenne WY 82005

CRAFTON-MASTERSON, ADRIENNE, real estate executive, writer, poet; b. Providence, Mar. 6, 1926; d. John Harold and Adrienne (Fitzgerald) Crafton; m. Francis T. Masterson, May 31, 1947 (div. Jan. 1977); children: Mary Victoria Masterson Bush, Kathleen Joan, John Andrew, Barbara Lynn. Student, No. Va. Community Coll., 1971-74; A in Biblical Studies, Christ to World Bible Inst., Jacksonville, Fla., 1992; A in Pastoral Leadership, Calvary Bible Inst., Jacksonville, Fla., 1993. Mem. staff Senator T.F. Green of R.I., Washington, 1944-47, 54-60; with U.S. Senate Com. on Campaign Expenditures Senator T.F. Green of R.I., 1944-45; asst. chief clk. Ho. Govt. Ops. Com., 1948-49; clk. Ho. Campaign Expenditures Com., 1950; asst. appointment sec. Office of Pres., 1951-53; with Hubbard Realty, Alexandria, Va., 1962-67; owner, mgr. Adrienne C. Masterson Real Estate, Alexandria, 1968-82; pres. Adrienne Investment Real Estate (AIRE) Ltd., Alexandria, 1982-91; devel. staff writer Calvary Internat., Jacksonville, Fla., 1992-93; Adrienne Crafton-Masterson Real Estate, Winchester, Va., 1993-94; pres. Adrienne Crafton-Masterson Real Estate, Haymarket, Va., 1994—; owner, prin. broker Winchester, Hagmarket, Va., 1994—; pres. AIRE-Merkli developers, 1988-92; founder AIHRE USA, Inc., 1993—. Mem. adv. panel Fairfax County (Va.) Coun. on Arts, 1987-88; founder, pres. Mt. Vernon/Lee Cultural Ctr. Found., Inc., 1984-92; life patron, life dep. gov. Am. Biog. Inst.; vice chmn. Haymarket Hist. Commn., 1994—. Fellow Internat. Biog. Ctr. (dep. dir. gen.); mem. Internat. Orgn. Real Estate Appraisers (sr.), Nat. Assn. Realtors, No. Va. Assn. Realtors (chmn. comml. and indsl. com. 1981-82, cmty. revitalization com. 1983-84, pres. land comml. indsl. mems. 1985, v.p. land comml. indsl. mems. 1989), Greater Piedmont Area Assn. Realtors, Fairfax Affordable Housing Inc. (sec. 1990-91), Alexandria C. of C., Mt. Vernon/Lee C. of C., Winchester/Frederick County C. of C., Friends of Kennedy Ctr. (founder). Office: Haymarket Profl Ctr 6611 Jefferson St PO Box 499 Haymarket VA 22069-0499

CRAHAN, PAULINE COLTON, human resources executive; b. Malone, N.Y., Sept. 3, 1949; d. Wilbur A. and Lena M. (Moquin) Colton; m. Earle I. Crahan, May 23, 1970; children: Eric, Colleen. AA, Canton (N.Y.) Coll., 1969; BS, Barry U., 1987; 1993—. Employment coord. Martin Meml. Hosp., Stuart, Fla., 1982-86; dir. human resources Savannas Hosp., Port St. Lucie, Fla., 1986-88; v.p. human resources 1st Citizens Fed. Bank, Ft. Pierce, Fla., 1988-90; dir. human resources Charter Hosp., West Palm Beach, Fla., 1990-91; assoc. dir. human resources Martin Meml. Health Systems, Stuart, 1991-94, dir. human resources, 1994—; sec.-v.p. St Lucie County Pers. Assn., Ft. Pierce, 1986-90; sec., pres. Am. Bus. Women's Assn., Ft. Pierce, Fla., 1986-91. Mem. Human Resource Mgmt. Assn. of Martin County (v.p. 1992-93, pres.-elect 1993-94, 95, pres. 1994), Soc. Human Resource Mgmt. (cert. sr. profl.). Roman Catholic. Office: Martin Meml Health Systems PO Box 9010 Stuart FL 34995

CRAIG, AMELIA AUDREY, lawyer; b. San Rafael, Calif., Apr. 30, 1960; d. Stephen Wright Craig and Margaret May (Baker) Chrisman. Student, U. Calif., Berkeley, 1981, Univ. Coll., London, 1981-82; BA, Dartmouth Coll., 1982; JD, Stanford U., 1986. Bar: Md. 1987, D.C. 1988, Calif. 1989, U.S. Dist. Ct. Md. 1988, U.S. Dist. Ct. D.C. 1988, U.S. Dist. Ct. (no. dist.) Calif. 1989, U.S. Dist. Ct. (ea. dist.) Calif. 1991, U.S. Ct. Appeals (9th cir.) 1991, U.S. Dist. Ct. (ctrl. dist.) Calif. 1993. Rsch. asst. Ariz. State Legislature, Phoenix, 1979; intern reporter The Bull., Phila., 1980; spl. assignment reporter The Times, London, 1981; paralegal Esdaile, Barrett & Esdaile, Boston, 1982-83; reporter The Bus. Jour., San Jose, Calif., 1984; legal extern Amnesty Internat., Washington, 1985; assoc. Baker & Hostetler, Washington, 1986-88; assoc. in litigation Heller, Ehrman, White & McAuliffe, San Francisco, 1988-93; mng. atty. western regional office Lambda Legal Def. and Edn. Fund, L.A., 1993-94, mng. atty., 1995—; com. crime victims and corrections Calif. Bar, 1992-94, exec. com. on legal svcs., 1994—. Bd. dirs. Washington Area Assn. for Children of Alcoholism and Other Addictions, 1988; mem. Calif. Bar Commn. on Corrections, 1990-91; vol. San Francisco AIDS panel, 1990-92; bd. dirs. Dartmouth GALA, 1994—, Bay Area Career Women; mem. Glide Meml. United Meth. Ch. Mem. ABA, ACLU, Nat. Gay and Lesbian Lawyers Assn., Calif. Women Lawyers, Bar Assn. San Francisco (mem. com. on gay and lesbian issues 1993—), L.A. County Bar Assn. (sec. 1993—, mem. com. on sexual orientation bias 1993-94), Bay Area Lawyers for Individual Freedom (bd. dirs. 1993—, gay legal referral svc. co-chair bd. dirs. 1993—), Lawyers for Human Rights (bd. dirs. 1994, chair jud. com. 1994, mem. adv. com. HIV legal svcs. delivery project for Greater L.A. 1994—), Dartmouth Lawyers Assn., Amnesty Internat., Barristers Club San Francisco (vice chair criminal law com. 1992-93), Harvey Milk Lesbian and Gay Dem. Club. Office: Lambda Legal Def and Edn Fund 6030 Wilshire Blvd Ste 200 Los Angeles CA 90036

CRAIG, CAROL MILLS, marriage, family and child counselor; b. Berkeley, Calif., May 7, 1952. BA in Psychology with honors, U. Calif., Santa Cruz, 1974; MA in Counseling Psychology, John F. Kennedy U., 1980; doctoral student, Calif. Sch. Profl. Psychology, Berkeley, 1980-87, Columbia Pacific U., San Rafael, Calif., 1987—. Psychology intern Fed. Correction Inst., Pleasanton, Calif., 1979-81, Letterman Army Med. Ctr., San Francisco, 1980-82; psychology intern VA Mental Hygiene Clinic, Oakland, Calif., 1981-82, Martinez, Calif., 1982-83; instr. Martinez Adult Sch., 1983, Piedmont Adult Edn., Oakland, 1986; biofeedback and stress mgmt. cons. Oakland, 1986—; child counselor Buddies-A Nonprofit, Counseling Svc. for Persons in the Arts, Lafayette, Calif., 1993—; founder Chesley Sch., 1994; rsch. asst. Irvington Pubs., N.Y.C., 1979, Little, Brown and Co., Boston, 1983. Mem. Calif. Assn. Marriage and Family Therapists (clin.), Musicians Union Local 424, Calif. Scholarship Fedn. (life).

CRAIG, DELENE JONES, trucking company executive; b. Ripley, Tenn., Mar. 21, 1934; d. Elmer Eldredge and Willie Mae (Walker) Jones; m. Stewart L. Craig, Nov. 14, 1952; 1 child, Kathie Lynn Craig Cepparulo. Grad. high sch., Ripley. Bookkeeper J.M. Morris & Sons, Ripley, 1954-56; sec. 1st Bapt. Ch., Ripley, 1958-64; sec., office mgr. Tenn. 16th Jud. Dist., Ripley, 1966-78; sec.-treas. D & L Trucking, Inc., Ripley, 1973—; cons. Mary Kay. Mem. Ripley High Sch. Band Boosters. Mem. Nat. Fedn. Ind. Bus., U.S. C. of C., Ripley C. of C. (bd. mem.), Ripley-Lauderdale County Jr. Aux. (pres. 1988—), Rotary (bd. mem.). Home: 120 Thompson Dr Ripley TN 38063-1627 Office: D&L Trucking Inc 295 Cleveland Ripley TN 38063-9301

CRAIG, JEAN (JEAN CRAIG MCNEILLY), advertising executive; b. Cin., June 1, 1937; d. Carl George and Loretta Rose (Meis) Westerman; m. Christopher Kevin Craig, Dec. 28, 1960 (dec. Oct. 1977); children: Deirdre, Christopher, Erin, Maureen; m. Edward R. McNeilly, Nov. 25, 1983 (dec. Mar. 1988). BA, Benedictine Heights Coll., Tulsa, 1959. Copywriter The Lansdale Co., L.A., 1961-62, Guild, Bascom, Bonfigli, L.A., 1963-65; assoc. creative dir. Foote, Cone & Belding, L.A., 1965-77; pres., creative dir. Cunningham, Root & Craig, L.A., 1977-85; ptnr. Kresser/Craig, L.A., 1985—. Author: Between Hello and Goodbye, 1991. Vice pres., bd. dirs. The Wellness Community Nat. Recipient Clio award, 1985, 87, Athena award Newspaper Advt. Bur., 1983, 84, 85, 15 Internat. Broadcasting awards, 1965-88, Agy. of Yr. award Am. Advt. Fedn., 1984, London Film Festival award, 1985, 87, numerous others. Mem. L.A. Creative Club (founder, 1st pres. 1979-80, 81). Roman Catholic. Home: 17847 Porto Marina Pacific Palisades CA 90272 Office: Kresser-Craig 2501 Colorado Ave 2d Fl Santa Monica CA 90404

CRAIG, JOAN CARMEN, secondary school educator, drama teacher; b. Sacramento, Calif., July 13, 1932; d. Frank Hurtado and Enid Pearl (Hogan) Alcalde; m. Elmer Lee Craig, Aug. 14, 1955 (dec. Jan. 1981); children: Shelley, Wendy, Cathleen, Scott. BA, San Jose State U., 1954, gen. secondary cert., 1955; postgrad. studies, various univs., 1956—. Cert. tchr. (life), Calif. Drama tchr. Willow Glen High Sch. San Jose (Calif.) Unified Sch. Dist., 1955-58, Kennedy Jr. High Sch. Cupertino (Calif.) Sch. Dist., 1968—; cons. Cupertino Unified Sch. Dist., 1990-93; coord. program activiy Growth Leadership Ctr., Mountain View, Calif., 1993; presenter Computer Use in Edn., 1990-93. Author, coord.: Drama Curriculum, 1971-93, Musical Comedy Curriculum, 1985-93, (Golden Bell, Calif. 1992). Dir. Nat. Multiple Sclerosis Soc., Santa Clara County, 1983-86. Recipient Spl. Svc. award Nat. Multiple Sclerosis Soc., Santa Clara, Calif., 1986;. Hon. Membership award Nat. Jr. Honor Soc., 1990; named Tchr. of Year, Kennedy Jr. High, Cupertino Union Sch. Dist., 1993. Mem. PTA (hon. svc. 1992), AAUW, NEA, Calif. Tchrs. Assn., Cupertino Edn. Assn. (rep. 1982). Home: 8121 Hyannisport Dr Cupertino CA 95014 Office: Growth Leadership Ctr 1451 Grant Rd Ste 102 Mountain View CA 94040

CRAIG, JUDITH, bishop; b. Lexington, Mo., June 5, 1937; d. Raymond Luther and Edna Amelia (Forsha) C. BA, William Jewell Coll., 1959; MA in Christian Edn., Eden Theol. Sem., 1961; MDiv, Union Theol. Sem., 1968; DD, Baldwin Wallace Coll., 1981; DHL, Adrian Coll., 1985, Otterbein Coll., 1993. Youth dir. Bellefontaine United Meth. Ch., St. Louis, 1959-61; intern children's work Nat. Coun. of Chs. of Christ, N.Y.C., 1961-62; dir. Christian edn. 1st United Meth. Ch., Stamford, Ct., 1962-66; inst. adult basic edn. N.Y.C. Schs., 1967; dir. Christian edn. Epworth Euclid United Meth. Ch., Cleve., 1969-72, assoc. pastor, 1972-76; pastor Pleasant Hills United Meth. Ch., Middleburg Heights, Ohio, 1976-80; conf. council dir. East Ohio Conf. United Meth. Ch., Canton, 1980-84; bishop United Meth. Ch., Mich. area, 1984-92, West Ohio area, 1992—; mem. Nat. Task Force on Itinerancy, 1977-80; responder to World Coun. of Chs. (document on Baptism, Eucharist and Ministry 1975); gen. conf. del., 1980, 84; mem. United Meth. Publ. House Bd., 1992—; bd. dirs. U.S. Health Corp.; frequent lectr. and preacher; bd. trustees 27 institutions in West Ohio. Contbr. articles to ministry mags. Bd. dirs. YWCA, Middleburg Heights, 1976-80. Recipient Citation of Achievement William Jewell Coll., 1985. Office: 471 East Broad St Ste 1106 Columbus OH 43215

CRAIG, KARA LYNN, social service administrator; b. Portland, Oreg., Nov. 29, 1962; d. Raymond L. and Donna J. (Telford) Spencer. BA in Communication, Boise State U., 1985; MA in Psychology, Pepperdine U., 1990. Office mgr. Ustick Chiropractic Clinic, Boise, 1983-85; communications asst. First Interstate Bank of Idaho, Boise, 1985-87; dir. Golden Gate U., Irvine, Calif., 1988-91; adj. prof. Golden Gate U., Irvine, 1990-91; case mgr. Big Bros./Big Sisters of S.W. Idaho, Boise, 1992-94; exec. dir. Children's Home Soc. of Idaho, Boise, 1994—; adj. prof. Boise State U., 1992—. Pub. rels. com. Sounds of Music (community choir), Boise, 1987-88. Mem. APA, Psi Chi. Home: 7903 W Queen Ct Boise ID 83704-7100 Office: Children's Home Soc Idaho 740 Warms Springs Ave Boise ID 83712

CRAIG, KAREN LYNN, accountant; b. Detroit, Mar. 17, 1959; d. John and Corinne (Legel) C.; m. Robert A. Steshetz, May 3, 1986; 1 child, Kamden. A. in Commerce, Henry Ford Community Coll., 1980; BS in Bus. and Acctg., Wayne State U., 1982. CPA, Mich., Calif. Cost and staff acct. Wilson Dairy Co., Detroit, 1982-83, sr. acct., 1983-84, acting contr., 1984; staff acct. Coopers & Lybrand, Detroit, 1984-85, sr. acct., 1986-87, supr. acct., Newport Beach, Calif., 1987-89; asst. corp. contr. J.F. Shea Co., Inc., Walnut, Calif., 1989—. Mem. Mich. Assn. CPA's, Calif. Soc. CPA's. Avocations: music, photography, baseball. Office: JF Shea Co Inc PO Box 489 Walnut CA 91788-0489

CRAIG, MARGARET WILCOX, education association executive; b. Hackensack, N.J., Jan. 3, 1934; d. John A. and Ethel M. (Furry) Wilcox; m. Robert B. Craig, Oct. 29, 1966; children: John R., Scott W., Todd A., James W. BS, Ohio State U., 1956; MA, William Paterson Coll., Wayne, N.J., 1979. Tchr. Newark (Ohio) Pub. Schs., 1956-57, Dade Co. Pub. Schs., Fla., 1957-58; bus. sch. tchr. Ridgewood (N.J.) Secretarial Sch., 1958-60, co-owner, dir., 1960-67; adminstrn. asst. to pres. Bergen Community Coll., Paramus, N.J., 1967-68; pres. Ramapo Assn. Parents, Tchrs. and Students, Franklin Lakes, N.J., 1985-87, 89-92; tchr. Ramapo/Indian Hills Sch. Dist., 1992—; mem. sch. bd. Wyckoff Pub. Schs., N.J., 1980-90. Chmn. cub pack 198 Boy Scouts Am., Wyckoff, 1977-87; treas. Economy Shop, Wyckoff, 1982-90; v.p. Wyckoff Sch. Bd., 1985-87, pres., 1988-90. Named Woman of Yr. Wyckoff YMCA, 1988. Mem. Mensa, Pi Lambda Theta. Republican. Episcopalian. Home: 647 Wishing Well Rd Wyckoff NJ 07481-1311

CRAIG, NADINE KARAMARKOVICH, pharmaceutical executive; b. Sewickley, Pa., Aug. 18, 1951; d. Nicholas and Mildred (Torbica) Karamarkovich; m. Jeffrey Lynn Craig, Oct. 10, 1977; 1 child, Jacquelyn Leslie. Nursing diploma, U. Pitts., 1972. RN, Fla. Staff nurse St. Francis Hosp., Pitts., 1972-74, Orlando (Fla.) Regional Med. Ctr., 1974-75; dir. aftercare Seminole Community Mental Health Ctr., Altamonte Springs, Fla., 1975-76; sales rep. Searle Pharm., Orlando, 1976-85; sales tng. supr. Searle Pharm., Skokie, Ill., 1985-86; dist. sales mgr. Searle Pharm., New Orleans, 1986-91; prod. mgr. Searle Pharm., Skokie, Ill., 1991-92; assoc. dir. Sci. Mktg. Comm., 1992—; regional sales dir Searle Pharm., Irving, Tex., 1992—. Office: Ste 470 5215 N O'Connor Blvd Irving TX 75039

CRAIG, SANDRA KAY, sales executive; b. Willoughby, Ohio, Nov. 21, 1962; d. Charles Soloman and Lacey Marie (Webb) Eggers; m. Robert Joseph Craig, June 28, 1986 (div. Jan. 1993); 1 child, Misty Marie Mangus; m. Robert David Del Tiempo, Feb. 14, 1995. AAB cum laude, Shawnee State U., 1985; BBA summa cum laude, Ohio U., 1987. Territory mgr. ARA Cory, San Diego, 1988-89, sales mgr., 1989-90; sales rep. Rsch. Inst. Am., Menifee, Calif., 1990-92; regional sales mgr. Rsch. Inst. Am., Menifee, 1992—; cons. Video Ave., Paradise Pizza, Chillicothe, Ohio, 1987-88. Active Girl Scouts U.S., Menifee, 1988-92. Mem. NAFE, NOW, PTA, Phi Kappa Phi, Phi Theta Kappa. Democrat. Home: 30617 Bayport Ln Menifee CA 92584

CRAIN, FRANCES UTTERBACK, retired dietitian; b. Crawfordsville, Ind., Dec. 28, 1914; d. Chelsey Chalmers and Margaret Myrtle (Henderson) Utterback; m. James William Crain, Sept. 13, 1937 (div. July 1944); children: James Michael, Patrick Desmond. BA, U. Ill., 1935; postgrad., Purdue U., 1945-46. Registered dietitian. Dietetic intern Indpls. City Hosp., 1935-36, therapeutic dietitian, 1936-37; dietitian Home Lawn Mineral Springs, Martinsville, Ind., 1937-38; WPA project dietitian Ill. Soldiers & Sailors Children's Home, Normal, 1939; chief dietitian Providence Hosp., Kansas City, Kans., 1939-40, Alexian Bros. Hosp., St. Louis, 1940-41; dietitian Ill. State Dept. Pub. Welfare, Springfield, 1943-45; exec. dir. Memphis Dairy Coun., 1947-61; program cons. Nat. Dairy Coun., Chgo., 1961-68; dietitian War on Poverty Com., Memphis, 1968-69, Shelby County Hosp., Memphis, 1969-74, Shelby County Penal Farm, Memphis, 1969-80; chief dietitian Oakville Health Care Ctr., Memphis, 1974-80; dietitian feeding programs Salvation Army, 1982-93. Writer food feature column. Comml. Appeal, 1952-61; author: To Your Taste-Butter, 1957. Mem. speakers and path. coms. Memphis in May Internat. Festival, 1983, 84, 85. Named Career Women of Yr., Pilot Club of Memphis, 1955; recipient Spl. Svcs. award Salvation Army, 1983. Mem. Am. Dietetic Assn., Tenn. Dietetic Assn. (pres. 1951-52, outstanding dietitian 1977), Memphis Dist. Dietetic Assn. (pres. 1949-50, editor bull. 1958-59), Memphis Area Nutrition Coun. (pres. 1973-74), Shelby County Retirees Orgn. (pres. 1987-89). Democrat. Home: 255 N Avalon St Memphis TN 38112-5101

CRAIN, GAYLA CAMPBELL, lawyer; b. Cleburne, Tex., June 13, 1950; d. R. C. and Marilyn Ruth (McFadyen) Campbell; m. Howard Leo Crain, May 27, 1978; 1 child, Robert Leo. BA, Baylor U., 1972, JD, 1974. Bar: Tex. 1974, U.S. Dist. Ct. (no., ea., we. and so. dists.) Tex., U.S. Ct. Appeals (5th cir.) 1988. Asst. counsel Trailways, Inc., Dallas, 1975-79; counsel Schering Plough, Inc., Kenilworth, N.J., 1979-80, sr. counsel, 1980-81; assoc. Epstein Becker & Green, P.C., Ft. Worth, 1985-86; ptnr. Epstein Becker & Green, P.C., Dallas, 1986—. Contbg. Author: State by State Guide to Human Resources Law, 1990, 91. Trustee Dallas Bapt. U., 1989—. Office: Epstein Becker & Green PC 12750 Merit Dr Ste 1320 Dallas TX 75251-1283

CRAIN, GERTRUDE RAMSAY, publishing company executive; m. G.D. Crain Jr. (dec. Dec. 1973); children: Keith, Rance. D in Journalism (hon.), DePauw U., 1987; LHD (hon.), U. Detroit, 1988. Asst. treas. Crain Communications Inc., Chgo., 1942, sec., asst. treas., 1943-62, sec., treas., 1962-74, chmn. bd., 1974—; bd. dirs. Internat. Advt. Assn., Mag. Pubs. Am., Execs. Club of Chgo., The Nat. Press Found. of Wash., Advt. Coun. of N.Y. Trustee Lincoln Acad. of Ill., James Webb Young Scholarship U. of Ill.; founding mem. Com. of 200, 1982; bd. dirs. Mus. of Broadcast Comm. in Chgo., Northwestern Meml. Hosp. Corp.-Chgo., Mus. of Sci. and Industry. Named to Working Woman Hall of Fame, 1987; named Chicagoan of Yr. Boys and Girls Club of Chgo., 1987, One of Top 60 Women Bus. Owners Saavy Mag., 1987, One of Top 50 Businesswomen Mich. Womans Mag., 1987; recipient Magnificat medal Mundelein Coll., Chgo., 1988. Mem. Internat. Advt. Assn (bd. dirs.), Mag. Pubs. Am. (bd. dirs.), Nat. Press Found. Washington, Advt. Club N.Y., Execs. Club Chgo. Office: Crain Communications Inc 740 N Rush St Chicago IL 60611-2525*

CRAIN, SUSAN KATE, educational counselor; b. San Angelo, Tex., Mar. 10, 1951; d. William Edward Benedict and Ann Marie (Mikulenka) Kohutek; children: Kelli Angela, Kacy Burt. BA, Angelo State U., 1972, MA, 1977. Cert. tchr., Tex. English tchr. Divide Sch., Nolan, Tex., 1973-75, Blackwell (Tex.) Sch., 1975-77; spl. edn. tchr. Edison Jr. High Sch., San Angelo, 1977-82; English and govt. tchr. Ctrl. High Sch., San Angelo, 1982—, high sch. counselor, 1989—. V.p. Tex. A&M Mothers Club, 1994—; tour guide Ft. Concho Mus.; vol. 4-H Club; active Tex. Dem. Women, Austin, 1993—, Tom Green Dem. Women, San Angelo, 1993—. Recipient Disting. 4-H Leader award Tom Green County 4-H, 1991; named Best Docent, Ft. Concho Hist. Program, San Angelo, 1992. Mem. Tex. Counseling Assn. (senator 1992—, Emerging Leader 1994), Three Rivers Counseling Assn. (sec. 1993, legis. chair 1993—). Roman Catholic. Office: San Angelo Ctrl High Sch 100 Cottonwood San Angelo TX 76901

CRAMER, BETTY F., life insurance company executive; b. Indpls., Dec. 9, 1920; d. Frank E. and Ethelyn L. (Jackson) C. B.A., Butler U., 1943. Sec. to v.p. and treas. Indpls. Life Ins. Co., 1951-69, supr. bond and stock acctg., 1969-75, securities asst., 1975-81, sec.-treas., 1981-89, ret., 1989. Advisor Jr. Achievement, Indpls., 1959-60; campaign chmn. United Way, 1980. Mem. Nat. Assn. Corp. Treas., Life Ins. Women's Assn. Indpls. (past v.p., pres.). Republican. Roman Catholic. Home: 5158 N Central Ave Indianapolis IN 46205-1060

CRAMER, LAURA SCHWARZ, realtor; b. St. Louis, Aug. 13, 1925; d. Frederick William and Gertrude Margaret (Kipp) Schwarz; AB, Duke U., 1947; MA, Washington U., St. Louis, 1948; m. Robert R. Cramer, Oct. 29, 1949; children: Anne Randolph, Carol Parker, Laura Forster. Model, John Robert Powers Agy., N.Y.C., 1946; grad. asst. dept. psychology Washington U., St. Louis, 1947-48, instr., 1948-49; psychometrist Clayton (Mo.) pub. schs., 1961; dir. testing Columbia Sch., Rochester, N.Y., 1964-71; asst. registrar and counselor for women students St. John Fisher Coll., Rochester, N.Y., 1971-72, registrar, dean of women, 1972-76; sales exec. Sea Pines Real Estate Co., Hilton Head Island, S.C., 1976—; registered rep. Sea Pines Securities, 1983-88. Bd. dirs. Vol. Svc. Bur., St. Louis, 1960-61, Monroe County Hosp. Aux., 1974-76, St. Louis Cmty. Music Sch., 1959-61, Vol. Ctr., Hilton Head Island, 1992—; cmty. adv. bd. Hilton Head Hosp., 1995—; bd. dirs. St. Louis Inst., chmn., 1960; bd. visitors Hilton Head Prep. Sch, 1989-93; bd. dirs. Hilton Head Coll. Ctr., 1994—. Jesse M. Barr fellow, 1947-48; named Leading Sales Exec., 1981, 84, 86, 87, 88, Leading Listing Exec., 1982, 83, 85, 86, 87, 88, 89. Mem. Hilton Head Island Bd. Realtors (Million Dollar Club, life), Jr. League Savannah, Phi Beta Kappa, Sigma Xi. Home: 9 Brown Pelican Rd Hilton Head Island SC 29928-0091 Office: Sea Pines Plantation Co Hilton Head Island SC 29928

CRAMER, ROXANNE HERRICK, gifted and talented education educator; b. Albion, Mich., Apr. 24; d. Donald F. and Kathryn L. (Beery) Herrick; m. James Loveday Hofford, Jan. 29, 1955 (div.); children: William Herrick, Dana Webster, Paul Christopher; m. Harold Leslie Cramer, Apr. 20, 1967. Student, U. Mich., 1952-55; BA, U. Toledo, 1956; EdM, Harvard U., 1967; EdD, Va. Poly. Inst. and State U., 1990. Tchr. Wayland (Mass.) Pub. Schs., 1966-70, Fairfax County (Va.) Pub. Schs., 1970—; tchr./team leader Gifted and Talented program, 1975—; coordinating instr. Trinity Coll., Washington, 1978; nat. coord. gifted children programs Am. Mensa, Ltd., 1981-84. Editor newletter Va. Assn. for the Edn. of Gifted, 1989-90; contbr. articles to profl. jours. Mem. NEA, Nat. Assn. Gifted Children, Fairfax County Assn. for the Gifted, Coalition for Advancement Gifted Edn. (bd. dirs. 1982-84), World Coun. Gifted and Talented Children, Intertel Found., Inc. (bd. dirs. 1986—), chmn. Hollingworth award com. 1984—, Fairfax County Assn. Gifted, Nat. Assn. Gifted Children, Va. Edn. Assn., Fairfax Edn. Assn., Mensa, Harvard Club, Phi Delta Kappa. Home: 4300 Sideburn Rd Fairfax VA 22030-3507 Office: Louise Archer Gifted Ctr 324 Nutley St NW Vienna VA 22180-4285

CRAMP, LORI ANGELL, finance executive; b. Kansas City, Mo., Apr. 17, 1955; d. William Greenleaf and Arline (Mullaney) Angell; m. John Stitzer, Aug. 13, 1977; children: Jeffrey William, Chelsea Angell, Trevor John. BA, Franklin & Marshall Coll., 1977; MBA, Harvard U., 1979. Mgmt. cons. Coopers & Lybrand Co., Washington, 1979-80, supr. mgmt. cons., 1980-81; supr. internal cons. Marriott Corp., Washington, 1981-82, mgr. internal cons., 1982-83, mgr. corp. fin., 1983-85, dir. corp. fin., 1985-86, v.p. corp. fin., 1987-89; v.p. project fin., 1990-92; sr. v.p. corp. and project fin. Coded Communications Corp., Carlsbad, Calif., 1994. Treas. Churchill Sq. Homeowners Assn., Falls Church, Va., 1983; treas. Painted Rock PTA, 1993-94; mem. Painted Rock Sch. Site Coun., 1992-94, dist. rep. sch. site coun., 1993-94, mem. dist. math. adv. bd. 1994—. Mem. Phi Beta Kappa, Pi Gamma Mu.

CRANDALL, DIANE, art educator, designer, author; b. Erie, Pa., Mar. 28, 1959; d. Thomas and Jenet (Erickson) C. BFA, Edinboro U. of Pa., 1981; MFA in Graphic Design, Kent State, 1993. Graphic designer Silk Screen Unlimited, Erie, Pa., 1977-79; asst. art dir. Gwynn Advt., Erie, Pa., 1981-83; graphic designer Graphic Works, Erie, Pa., 1983-85; art dir. Jack O'Brien Advt., Erie, Pa., 1986-89; asst. prof. art Edinboro U. of Pa., Edinboro, Pa., 1989—; designer Diane Crandall Design, Erie, Pa., 1990—; author, publisher For-giving Press, Erie, Pa., 1994—; advisor Studio 118, Edinboro, Pa., 1992-94; lectr. on Healing from Violent Crimes, 1994—. Designer, author: Violent Crime: I Never Thought It Would Happen To Me, But It Did, 1994. Individual Career Enhancement grantee State System Higher Edn., 1990; recipient Strathmore Renewal Rainforest Design Competition award Strathmore Paper Co., 1992, Computer Art & Design award Print Mag., 1994. Mem. Nat. Orgn. Victims Assistance, Publishers Mktg. Assn., U. and Coll. Designers Assn., Erie Advt. Club. (sec. 1988-91), Jr. League of Erie.

CRANDALL, SONIA JANE, medical educator; b. Quincy, Ill., Sept. 2, 1952; d. Gerald Madison and Roselma Louise (Zeiger) Syrcle; m. Edward Young Crandall, June 28, 1975. Diploma, Michael Reese Med. Ctr., Chgo., 1974; BS, Western Ill. U., 1974; MED, U. Ill., 1980; PhD, U. Okla., 1989. Med. tech. U. Mo. Med. Ctr., Columbia, 1974-75; med. tech., clin. instr. St. Johns Hosp., Springfield, Ill., 1976-81; med. tech., supr. Okla. Teaching Hosp., 1982-85, tng. officer, 1985-87; Kellog fellow U. Okla., Norman, Okla., 1987-89; asst. prof., dir. faculty devel. and edn. resources, dept. family medicine U. Okla. Health Scis. Ctr., Oklahoma City, 1989-94; asst. prof., dept. family and community medicine Bowman Gray Sch. of Medicine, Wake Forest U., 1994—. Contbr. articles to prof jours. Named one of Outstanding Young Women in Am. Mem. Am. Edn. Rsch. Assn., Am. Assn. for Adult and Continuing Edn., Am. Soc. Clin. Pathology, Soc. Tchrs. Family Medicine, Alliance for Continuing Med. Edn., World Found. of Successful Women (charter), Phi Kappa Phi. Home: 3969 E Valley Ct Winston Salem NC 27106 Office: Dept Family & Cmty Medicine Bowman Gray Sch Medicine Wake Forest U Medical Center Blvd Winston Salem NC 27157

CRANE, FAYE, small business owner; b. Amery, Wis., Dec. 2, 1947; d. Vaemond Hall and Irene C. (L'Allier) C.; 1 child, Camille Mills Seifert. Grad. high sch., Milltown, Wis. Premiums statis. clk. State Farm Ins., St.

Paul, 1968-73; pension adminstrn. asst. Mut. Svc. Ins., St. Paul, 1973-78; dist. dir. Avon Products, Inc., Morton Grove, Ill., 1978-79; sales rep. Midwest Bus. Sys., Duluth, Minn., 1979-84, REM's Inc., Grand Rapids, Minn., 1984; pres. prodn. Presto Print, Grand Rapids, 1984—. Mem. No. Minn. Citizen's League, Grand Rapids, 1984—, Nat. Mus. Women in the Arts, 1988—; commr. City of Grand Rapids Planning Commn., 1990-94; bd. dirs. Grand Rapids Econ. Devel. Authority, 1994—. Mem. NAFE, Nat. Fedn. Bus. and Profl. Women (treas. nat. conv. 1992), Minn. Fedn. Bus. and Profl. Women (mem. promotion com. 1982-92, emblem chmn. 1982-83, found. chmn. 1983-84, exec. dir., chmn. 1984-85, editor 1987-90, v.p. 1992-93, pres. 1994-95), Grand Rapids Bus. and Profl. Women (pres. 1985-86). Home: PO Box 404 Grand Rapids MN 55744-0404 Office: Presto Print 3 Golf Course Rd Grand Rapids MN 55744-3525

CRANE, FRANCES HAWKINS, artist, educator; b. Johntown, Tex., July 8, 1928; d. Henry Cleo and Laura Elizabeth (Jenkins) Hawkins; ed. Del Mar Coll., 1948; studied under Frederic Taubes, N.Y.C.; m. Gene Calvin Crane, May 10, 1946; children—Cindie Crane Reynolds, Cheryl Crane Garcia. Exhbns. include Highland Mall Gallery, Austin, Tex., Prichard Gallery, Houston, Heath and Brown Gallery, Houston, Salado (Tex.) Gallery, Bellas Artes Gallery, Kerrville, Tex., Visions in Art, San Antonio, Tex., Jerry Smith Gallery, Alice, Tex., Corpus Christi Mus., M. and N. Originals, Corpus Christi; represented in permanent collections Corpus Christi Mus., Lyndon Baines Johnson Library. Recipient top awards local, state, nat., internat. shows. Mem. South Tex. Traditional Art Assn. (sec.-treas. Corpus Christi chpt. 1970-76), Nat. League Am. Pen Women, Internat. Platform Assn., Hill Country Arts Found., Internat. Soc. Artists. Home: 5058 Wingfoot Ln Corpus Christi TX 78413-2223 Studio: Apple Tree Ranch PO Box 987 Leakey TX 78873-0987

CRANE, GAIL, lobbyist, management consultant; b. Phila., July 19, 1943; d. E. Forrest and Ann J. (Vrabel) Crane; m. Edward J. Dennis, June 18, 1968 (div. 1976); 1 child, Alicia Ann. Student, U. S.C., Georgetown U. V.p. Med. Svc. Cons., Arlington, Va., 1978-81; cons. to dir. ACTION, Washington, 1981-82; dir. spl. projects Appalachian Regional Commn., Washington, 1982-84; cons. to dir. Women's Bur. U.S. Dept. Labor, Washington, 1985; cons. to adminstr. U.S. VA, Washington, 1985; chmn. The Strategy Corp., Phila., 1986-90; pres. Govt. Strategies, Inc., Phila., 1985-89; prin. The Crane Group, Phila., 1989—; affiliate The Hellem Co., Alexandria, 1993. Trustee Independence Hall Preservation Fund, Phila., 1993; bd. dirs. Network Arts, Phila., 1993; dir. Boys and Girls Clubs, Washington, 1993. Mem. Women in Def., Forum of Exec. Women, Capitol Hill Club, Vesper Club. Office: The Crane Group 345 S 18th St Philadelphia PA 19103 also: The Advocacy Group 1350 I St NW Washington DC 20005

CRANE, GLENDA PAULETTE, private school educator; b. Orlando, Fla., June 29, 1946; d. James Author and Elizabeth Lorine (Johnson) C. AA in Edn., Orlando Jr. Coll., 1966; BA in Elem. Edn., U. S. Fla., 1967; postgrad. So. Bapt. Theol. Sem., 1970; MEd, Rollins Coll., 1985. Tchr., Orange County Schs., Orlando, 1967-70, 79-80, Lake Highland Prep. Sch., Orlando, 1981—; tchr. Belle Glade (Fla.) Christian Sch., 1970-79, asst. prin., 1970-74, prin., 1975-79. State treas. Fla. Rainbow Girls., 1964. Mem. NEA, Fla. Edn. Assn., Fla. Council Tchrs. English, Orange County Tchrs. Assn., Assn. Supervision and Curriculum Devel., Internat. Reading Assn., Orange County Reading Council of Internat. Reading Assn., Fla. Reading Assn., Nat. Council for the Social Studies, Alumni Assn. U. South Fla., Alumni Assn. So. Bapt. Theol. Sem., Fla. Coun. Tchrs. of Math, Kappa Delta Pi. Democrat. Baptist. Clubs: Winter Park Pilot, Eastern Star, Winter Park Rainbow Girls. Home: 2406 S Bumby Ave Orlando FL 32806-5011 Office: 901 N Highland Ave Orlando FL 32803

CRANE, JULIA GORHAM, anthropology educator; b. Mt. Kisco, N.Y., Nov. 8, 1925; d. Joseph Harold and Alma Evelyn (Reynolds) Crane. Student, Katharine Gibbs Sch., 1943-45; BS cum laude, Columbia U., 1959, PhD in Anthropology, 1966. Research asst. to Dr. Margaret Mead Am. Museum of Natural History, N.Y.C., 1956-59; asst. in anthropology Columbia U., N.Y.C., 1959-61; asst. prof. anthropology U. N.C., Chapel Hill, 1967-72; assoc. prof. U. N.C., 1972-76, prof., 1976-90. Author: Educated to Emigrate, 1971; co-author (with Michael Angrosino): Field Projects in Anthropology: A Student Handbook, 1974, 2d edit., 1984, 3d edit., 1992, Japanese edit., 1994, Saba Silhouettes, 1987. Recipient Prince Bernhard Fund award, The Netherlands, 1970; grantee NIH, 1961-66, U. N.C., 1970, 75, 85, 86, Cultural Cooperative Orgn. of Netherlands Antilles, 1985; Tanner award for teaching excellence, 1986. Mem. So. Anthropol. Soc., Phi Beta Kappa. Office: U NC Dept Anthropology Alumni Bldg 004A Chapel Hill NC 27514

CRANE, KEENAN DURKIN, human resource consultant, therapist; b. Phila., Jan. 6, 1944. AA cum laude, Montgomery County Community Coll., 1975; BA in Psychology magna cum laude, Rosemont Coll., 1978; MS in Exptl. Psychology, Villanova U., 1980, MS in Counseling and Human Relations, 1981; PhD, Temple U., 1988. Cert. practitioner in psychodrama. Asst. psychodramatist Interim House, Mt. Airy, Pa., 1980-81, Horsham Clinic, Ambler, Pa., 1981-82; therapist Alliance for Creative Devel., Quakertown (Pa.) Hosp., and Landsdale, Pa., 1982-85; pvt. practice, individual and group therapy Villanova, Pa., 1985—; founding mem., bd. dirs., chairperson mgmt. cons. firm DHORS (Devel. of Human and Organizational Systems), Villanova; part-time prof. Temple U., Del. County Community Coll., 1984-88; adminstrv. asst. Ctr. for Intergenerational Learning, group leader Inst. on Aging, Temple U., 1988; cons. trainer group therapy, psychodrama Jefferson Med. Sch., Sacred Heart Hosp., Haverford, Pa., Del. Valley Soc. Group Psychotherapy, Drug and Rehab. Ctr., Seabrook (N.J.) House; spl. lectr. West Chester (Pa.) U., Widener U.; cons. in group dynamics Interim House. Mem. Assn. Counseling and Devel., Am. Assn. Group Psychotherapy (psychodrama and sociometry research com.), Eastern Psychol. Assn., Delta Epsilon Sigma, Kappa Delta Pi. Home and Office: DHORS 1208 N Spring Mill Rd Villanova PA 19085-2143

CRANE, PATRICIA SUE, probation services administrator, social worker; b. Rockway, N.Y., Jan. 17, 1948; d. Herbert Milton and Miriam (Rosenblum) Brager; m. Marvin J. Crane, May 2, 1971; 1 child, Elizabeth A. BA, U. Wis., 1969; MS in Criminal Justice with honors, Wayne State U., 1984. Cert. social worker. Dir. probation svcs. 52d dist. ct. 1st div. State of Mich., Walled Lake, 1979—. Jewish. Home: 5042 Meadowbrook Dr West Bloomfield MI 48322 Office: 52nd Dist Ct 1st Divsn 48150 Grand River Ave Novi MI 48374-1222

CRANE, REGINA ANN, technical writer; b. Pine Bluff, Ark., Jan. 13, 1961; d. Lois Lynell and Lois Virginia (Martin) C. BA in Profl. & Tech. Writing, U. Ark. at Little Rock, 1983. Researcher, writer Ark. Women's History Inst., Little Rock, 1984; tech. writer UNISYS Corp., Nat. Ctr. for Toxicological Rsch., Jefferson, Ark., 1984-87; tech. editor CAE Link Corp., Jacksonville, Ark., 1988-93; assoc. tng. analyst CAE Link Corp., Jacksonville, 1993—. Recipient Acad. Scholarship U. Ark. at Little Rock, 1979-80, Journalism Scholarship, 1982. Mem. U. Ark. at Little Rock Alumni Assn. Office: CAE Link Corp PO Box 1282 Jacksonville AR 72078-1282

CRANFORD, DONNA BETH, business manager, bookkeeper; b. Farmerville, La., Nov. 7, 1961; d. Perry Donald and Neta Beth (Shaw) Nyegaard; m. Ronnie Kim Cranford, Feb. 27, 1981; children: Kacey Don, Kallie Elise. Grad., North Ctrl. Vo-Tech., Farmerville, 1980. Cert. sch. bd. adminstrn., La. Bookkeeper, bus. mgr. Union Parish Sch. Bd., Farmerville, 1980—. Troop leader Girl Scouts USA, Farmerville, 1993-94. Mem. La. Assn. Sch. Bus. Ofcls. Democrat. Baptist. Office: Union Parish Sch Bd Marion Hwy PO Box 308 Farmerville LA 71241

CRANIN, MARILYN SUNNERS, landscape designer; b. N.Y.C., Aug. 1, 1932; d. William And Rebecca (Yates) Sunners; m. A. Norman Cranin, June 14, 1953; children: Jonathan Blake, Andrew Ross, Elizabeth S. BA, Beaver Coll., Glenside, Pa., 1954; student, Harvard U., 1981-82. Landscape designer N.Y. Bot. Gardens, N.Y.C., 1974-76; hort. therapist Beth Abraham Hosp., 1975-85, N.Y. Bot. Gardens, N.Y.C., 1976-78; master gardener Nassau County Coop Extension Service, N.Y.C., 1976-80; landscape designer London Landscape, Massapequa, N.Y., 1984—. Columnist South Shore Record, 1980-82. V.p., bd. dirs. 5 Towns Music and Art Found., Woodmere, N.Y., 1962—; trustee, dep. mayor Village Hewlett Bay Park, N.Y., 1974-84; pres. bd. trustees Hewlett-Woodmere Pub. Library, 1977—; trustee Nassau Library System, Uniondale, N.Y., 1980-86, Waldorf Sch., Garden City, N.Y., 1985—, Am. Chamber Ensemble, 1981—, Beaver Coll. Alumni Bd., 1979-86, Beaver Coll., 1987—, sec. bd. trustees. Recipient Silver award for excellence in design L.I. Nurseryman's Assn., 1992, Alumni of Yr. Golden Disc award for meritorious svc. Beaver Coll., 1994; named Woman of Yr. Woodmere Merchants Assn., 1994. Mem. Am. Hort. Soc., Nassau County Coop Extension Service, N.Y. State Assn. Libr. Bds., N.Y. Bot. Garden, Wave Hill Hort. Soc. Clubs: Woodmere Bay Yacht, The Woodmere.

CRANNEY, MARILYN KANREK, lawyer; b. Bklyn., June 18, 1949; d. Sidney Paul and Aurelia (Valice) Kanrek; m. John William Cranney, Jan. 1, 1970 (div. June 1975); 1 child, David Julian. BA, Brandeis U., 1970; MA in History, Brigham Young U., 1975; JD, U. Utah, 1979; LLM in Tax Law, NYU, 1984. Bar: N.Y. 1980, U.S. Dist. Ct. (so. and ea. dists.) N.Y. 1992. Assoc. Cravath Swaine & Moore, N.Y.C., 1979-81; 1st v.p., asst. gen. counsel Dean Witter InterCapital Inc., N.Y.C., 1981—. Mem. N.Y. County Lawyers Assn., Order of the Coif. Democrat. Jewish. Home: 1830 E 23d St Brooklyn NY 11229 Office: Dean Witter InterCapital Inc 2 World Trade Ctr New York NY 10048

CRASTNOPOL, MARGARET, psychologist, psychoanalyst; b. N.Y.C., Mar. 19, 1954; d. Philip and Madeleine (Lasko) C.; m. Charles Herbert Purcell, May 25, 1985; children: Evan, Zachary, Julia. BS, Tufts U., 1975; MA, U. Cin., 1977, PhD, 1980. Lic. psychologist, N.Y., Wash. Supr. psychotherapy W.A.White Inst., N.Y.C., 1990—; pvt. practice N.Y.C., 1981-92, Seattle, 1992—; clin. instr. psychiatry and behavioral scis. U. Wash., Seattle, 1994; co-founder and assoc. dir. N.W. Ctr. for Psychoanalysis, Seattle, 1994; clin. instr. dept. psychology U. Wash. Assoc. editor Contemporary Psychoanalysis, 1991—; contbg. editor Psychoanalytic Dialogues, 1994. Mem. APA (divsn. 35 and 39 1985—), Wash. State Psychol. Assn., N.W. Alliance for Psychoanalytic Study, Pacific N.W. Psychoanalytic Soc., Phi Beta Kappa. Jewish. Office: 515-28th Ave E Seattle WA 98112

CRAVEN, ROBERTA JILL, literature educator; b. White Plains, N.Y., Feb. 4, 1962; d. Robert James and Norma Eleanor (Page) C. BS in Math., U. N.C., 1984, postgrad., 1989—. Account systems engr. IBM Nat. Fed. Mktg., Bethesda, Md., 1984-86, account mktg. rep., 1986-89; telecomm. mktg. support rep. IBM, Research Triangle Park, N.C., 1990; instr. U. N.C., Chapel Hill, 1990—. T.J. Watson Nat. Merit scholar IBM, Armonk, N.Y., 1980, Hon. Regents scholar N.Y. Bd. Regents, 1980. Mem. MLA, Phi Beta Kappa, Phi Eta Sigma. Office: U NC Comparative Lit CB # 3150 Chapel Hill NC 27599-3150

CRAW, ELIZABETH HARRIET, retired art educator; b. Prosperity, Mo., Sept. 10, 1917; d. Clarence Leroy and Mabell Ruth (Harris) Bryant; children: Robert, Elizabeth. BS in Art Edn., Southwest Mo. State U., 1940; MFA, Drake U., 1972. Tchr. primary grades Jerico Springs (Mo.) Pub. Schs., 1937-39; tchr. mid. grades Humansville (Mo.) Pub. Schs., 1940-43; art tchr. Callanan Jr. High Ind. Sch. Dist., Des Moines, 1943-60; art tchr. grade sch. Community Sch. Dist., Ft. Dodge, Iowa, 1964-82; textile conservator Ft. Dodge, 1980—; coord. textile conservation workshops; lectr. in field. Exhibited watercolor paintings in several juried exhbns. Pres. Iowa Soc. Preservation Hist. Landmarks, 1979-83, editor newsletter, 1983—; chair Save Our Archtl. Resources, Ft. Dodge, 1989-91; docent Blanden Mus. Art, Ft. Dodge, 1990—. Mem. AAUW (cultural chair 1993), Iowa State Tchrs. Assn. (com. chair Salisbury Preservation 1976-88), Nat. Art Educators Assn. (rep. Iowa 1984—, chair nominating com. 1994), Art Educators Iowa (bd. dirs. 1985—, columnist newsletter 1986—, Outstanding Art Educator Iowa 1990, Disting. Svc. award 1994). Home: 1226 N 24th Pl Fort Dodge IA 50501

CRAWFORD, BETTY LEE, financial executive; b. Clarksburg, W.Va., May 16, 1925; d. William and Anna Marie (Wright) Wyatt; m. William D. Crawford, Feb. 27, 1942 (dec. 1980); children: Elizabeth Ann Bowman, Dorothea Crawford-Weaver, W. David II. Student, W.Va. U., 1969-71. Accounts payable bookkeeper Fountain and Grays Stores, Clarksburg, W.Va., 1950-55; sheriff's bookkeeper Harrison County Commn., Clarksburg, 1965-70; fin. sec. Harrison County Bd. Edn., Clarksburg, 1970-72, head fin. sec., 1972-79, dir. fin., 1979—, treas., 1980-87, supr. fin. dept., 1980-92; acctg. com. W.Va. State Bd. Edn., 1984-92; fin. cons. Active Clarksburg Hist. Soc., 1991; active United Hosp. Ctr. Aux., Clarksburg, 1958. Mem. DAR, W.Va. Assn. Sch. Bus. Ofcls. (region chairperson 1982), Nat. Assn. Sch. Bus. Ofcls., Cath. Daus. Am. (regent). Republican. Home: 317 Grand Ave Bridgeport WV 26330-1831 Office: Harrison County Bd Edn 408 S Water St Clarksburg WV 26301-3712

CRAWFORD, CAROL ANNE, marketing executive; b. San Francisco, Jan. 17, 1945; d. Kenneth H. and Marcella (Schloesser) C. B.A., San Jose State U., 1967; M.B.A. in Mktg., Golden Gate U., 1985. Food publicist J. Walter Thompson, San Francisco 1967-70; asst. mktg and sales promotion dir. Eastridge Shopping Ctr., San Jose, Calif., 1970-72; consumer info. specialist Carl Byoir & Assocs., San Francisco, 1972-78; account supr. Ketchum Pub. Relations, San Francisco, 1978-80; v.p., dir. pub. relations Grey Advt., San Francisco, 1980-82; dir. corp. communications S&O Cons., San Francisco, 1982-84; mgr. mktg. and pub. relations GTE Sprint, 1984-86; dir. pub. relations U.S. Sprint, 1986; prin. Crawford Communications, 1986—; instr. pub. relations Golden Gate U., 1987—; cons., lectr. in field, 1987—. Bd. mgrs. YMCA, Embarcadero, 1980-82. Mem. Pub. Relations Soc. Am. (past chpt. pres.), San Francisco Profl. Food Soc., Home Economists in Bus. (past chpt. chmn., past chmn. nat. pub. relations); Commonwealth Club. Office: Crawford Comms 423 Lansdale Ave San Francisco CA 94127-1616

CRAWFORD, CAROL L., opera company executive. Student, Julliard Sch., Mozarteum, Salzburg; PhD in music, Yale Univ. Assoc. condr. Memphis Symphony, Tenn.; condr. Memphis Youth Symphony, Tenn.; artistic dir. Tulsa Opera, Okla., 1993—; music dir. Houston Grand Opera's Tex. Opera Theater, San Francisco Opera's Western Opera Theater, Aslawn-Highland Festival, Charlottesville, Va.; assoc. music dir. Va. Opera. Condr.: (Tulsa Philharmonic) Madama Butterfly, 1991, Carmen, 1992; apprentice condr.: (documentary) Bernstein: Conductor, Teacher, Composer, 1984. Recipient first prize San Diego Opera Young American Opera Condrs. Competition, 1981. Office: Tulsa Opera Chapman Music Hall 1610 S Boulder Ave Tulsa OK 74119*

CRAWFORD, CAROL TALLMAN, government executive; b. Mt. Holly, N.J., Feb. 25, 1943; m. Ronald Crawford; children: Timothy, Jeffrey, Richard. BA, Mt. Holyoke Coll., 1965; JD magna cum laude, Washington Coll. Law, Am. U., 1978. Bar: Va. 1978, D.C. 1979. Legis. asst. to Senator Bob Packwood Washington, 1969-75; assoc. firm Collier, Shannon, Rill & Scott, Washington, 1979-81; exec. asst. to chmn. FTC, Washington, 1981-83, dir. bur. consumer protection, 1983-85; assoc. dir. Office of Mgmt. & Budget, Washington, 1985-89; asst. atty. gen. legis. affairs U.S. Dept. Justice, Washington, 1989-90; commr. U.S. Internat. Trade Commn., 1991—; sr. advisor Reagan-Bush Transition Team, 1981. Trustee Barry Goldwater Chair of Am. Instns., Ariz. State U., Phoenix, 1983—. Republican.

CRAWFORD, CHRISTINE ANN, lawyer; b. Washington, Aug. 3, 1951; d. Edward Thomas and Emma Jo (Sabo) C.; m. Robert N. Spinelli, Apr. 25, 1981. BA, U. Va., Fredericksburg, 1973; JD, Temple u., 1978. Bar: Pa., 1978, U.S. Dist. Ct. (ea. dist.) Pa., 1981, Ariz., 1982. Participant fin. mgmt. program Gen. Electric Co., Phila., 1973-75; asst. dist. atty. Phila. Dist. Atty.'s Office, 1978-82; assoc. corp. counsel Commodore Bus. Machines, Inc., West Chester, Pa., 1983-85; gen. counsel, sec. Henkels & McCoy, Inc., Blue Bell, Pa., 1986—. Republican. Roman Catholic. Office: Henkels & McCoy Inc 985 Jolly Rd Blue Bell PA 19422

CRAWFORD, CINDY, model; b. Dekalb, Ill., Feb. 20, 1966; d. Dan and Jennifer C.; m. Richard Gere, Dec. 12, 1991. Student, Northwestern U. Model for Victor Skrebneski, 1984-86; signed with Elite Modeling Agy., 1986; spokesperson Revlon, 1989—, JH Collectibles, Pepsi Cola, Kay Jewelers; host MTV's House of Style, 1989—. First featured on cover Vogue, 1986; exercise videos: Cindy Crawford's Shape Your Body Workout, 1992, The Next Challenge Workout, 1993. Office: Elite Model Management Corp 111 E 22d St 2d Fl New York NY 10010*

CRAWFORD, JEAN ANDRE, counselor; b. Chgo., Apr. 12, 1941; d. William Moses and Geneva Mae (Lacy) Jones; student Shimer Coll., 1959-60; BA, Carthage Coll., 1966; MEd, Loyola U., Chgo., 1971; postgrad. Nat. Coll. Edn., Evanston, Ill., 1971-77, Northwestern U., 1976-83; m. John N. Crawford, Jr., June 28, 1969; cert. sch. counselor Nat. Bd. Cert. Counselors, elem. edn., spl. edn. and pupil personnel services, Ill. Med. technologist, Chgo., 1960-62; primary and spl. edn. tchr. Chgo. Pub. Schs., 1966-71, counselor maladjusted children and their families, 1971-88; counselor juvenile first-offenders, 1968-88, post-secondary vocat. counselor, 1988-93; tchr., transition coord. Cook County Dept. Corrections Alternative High Sch., Chgo., 1993-94; clin. therapist St. Mary of Nazareth Hosp. Ctr., Chgo., 1994—. Vol. Sta. WTTW-TV; vol. counselor deaf children and their families; counselor post-secondary students; vol., mem. community devel. bd. New City YMCA, 1987-92. Mem. scholarship com. Chgo. Urban League. Mem. AACD, Ill. Assn. Counseling and Devel., Am. Sch. Counselors Assn., Ill. Sch. Counselors Assn., Ill. Vocat. Counselors Assn., Am. Mental Health Counselor Assn., Ill. Mental Health Counselor Assn., IIll. Assn. Advancement Black Ams. in Vocat. Edn., Coun. Exceptional Children, Coordinating Coun. Handicapped Children, Shimer Coll. Alumni Assn. (sec. 1982-84), Phi Delta Kappa. Home: 601 E 32nd St Chicago IL 60616-4054 Office: 2233 W Division St Chicago IL 60622

CRAWFORD, LINDA SIBERY, lawyer, educator; b. Ann Arbor, Mich., Apr. 27, 1947; d. Donald Eugene and Verla Lillian (Schenck) Sibery; m. Leland Allardice Crawford, Apr. 4, 1970; children: Christina, Lillian, Leland. Student, Keele U., 1969; BA, U. Mich., 1969; postgrad., SUNY, Potsdam, 1971; JD, U. Maine, 1977. Bar: Maine 1977, U.S. Dist. Ct. Maine 1982, U.S. Ct. Appeals (1st cir.) 1983. Tchr. Pub. Sch., Tupper Lake, N.Y., 1970-71; asst. dist. atty. State of Maine, Farmington, 1977-79; asst. atty. gen. State of Maine, Augusta, Maine, 1979—; pvt. legal and litigation cons. Hallowell, Maine, 1988—; legal advisor U. Maine, Farmington, 1975; legal counsel Fire Marshall's Office,, Maine, 1980-83, Warden Svc., Maine, 1981-83, Dept. Mental Health, 1983-89, litigation divsn., 1989—; teaching team trial advocacy Law Sch. Harvard U., Cambridge, Mass., 1987—, lectr. Sch. Medicine, 1991, 93; chmn. editorial bd. Mental & Phys. Disability Law Reporter, 1993-94. Mem. Natural Resources Coun., Maine, 1985-90; bd. dirs. Diocesan Human Rels. Coun., Maine, 1977-78, Arthritis Found., Maine, 1983-88; atty. expert commn. experts UN War Crime Investigation in the former Yugoslavia, 1994. Named one of Outstanding Young Women of Yr. Jaycees, 1981. Mem. ABA (com. on disability 1992—), Maine Bar Assn., Kennebec County Bar Assn., Assn. Trial Lawyers Am., Maine Trial Lawyers Assn., Nat. Assn. State Mental Health Attys. (treas. 1984-86, vice chmn. 1987-89, chmn. 1989-91). Home: 25 Winthrop St Hallowell ME 04347-1150 Office: State of Maine Dept of Atty Gen State St # 6 Augusta ME 04330-4508

CRAWFORD, MARY LOUISE PERRI, naval officer; b. Grand Haven, Mich.; d. Louis and Helen Marie (Buckley) Perri; m. Keith Eugene Crawford, Feb. 23, 1974 (dec. Oct. 1986); children: Matthew Perri, Michael Kirk. AA, Muskegon County Community Coll., 1969; BA, U. Mich., 1971. Commd. ensign U.S. Navy, 1972, advanced through grades to capt., 1993; pub. affairs officer Naval Air Sta., Key West, Fla., 1974-77, adminstrv., personnel officer Naval Air Res. Detachment, Patuxent River, Md., 1977-78, adminstrn. br. head Strike Aircraft Test Directorate, Naval Air Test Ctr., Patuxent River, 1978-80, ops. watch officer Command Ctr., Comdr.-in-Chief Naval Forces Europe Staff, London, 1980-84, officer-in-charge Personnel Support Activity Detachment, Patuxent River, 1984-86; engring. officer Chief Test and Evaluation Div., Strategic C3 Systems Directorate, Ctr. for Command, Control, and Communications, Def. Communications Agy., Washington, 1986-89; mgr. ultra high frequency Joint Satellite Communications Ctr., Joints Chiefs Staff, Pentagon, Washington, 1989-91; comdr. N.Y. Mil. Entrance Processing Sta., 1991. Mem. AAUW, Women's Overseas Svc. League, U. Mich. Alumni Assn. Roman Catholic. Avocations: painting, ballet. Office: NY Mil Entrance Processing Sta Fort Hamilton Bldg # 116 Brooklyn NY 11252

CRAWFORD, MURIEL LAURA, lawyer, author, educator; d. Mason Leland and Pauline Marie (DesIlets) Henderson; m. Barrett Matson Crawford, May 10, 1959; children: Laura Joanne, Janet Muriel, Barbara Elizabeth. Student, U. Calif., Berkeley, 1958-60, 67-69; B.A. with honors, U. Ill., 1973; J.D. with honors, Ill. Inst. Tech., 1977; cert. employee benefit specialist U. Pa., 1989. Bar: Ill. 1977, Calif. 1991, U.S. Dist. Ct. (no. dist.) Ill. 1977, U.S. Dist. Ct. (no. dist.) Calif. 1991, U.S. Ct. Appeals (7th cir.) 1977, U.S. Ct. Appeals (9th cir.) 1991; CLU; chartered fin. cons. Atty., Washington Nat. Ins. Co., Evanston, Ill., 1977-80, sr. atty., 1980-81, asst. counsel, 1982-83, asst. gen. counsel, 1984-87, assoc. gen. counsel, sec., 1987-89, cons. employee benefit specialist, 1989-91; assoc. Hancock, Rothert & Bunshoft, San Francisco, 1991-92. Author: (with Beadles) Law and the Life Insurance Contract, 1989, (sole author) 7th edit. 1994; co-author Legal Aspects of AIDS, 1990; contbr. articles to profl. jours. Recipient Am. Jurisprudence award Lawyer's Coop. Pub. Co., 1975, 2nd prize Internat. LeTourneau Student Med.-Legal Article contest, 1976, Bar and Gavel Soc. award Ill. Inst. Tech./Chgo.-Kent Student Bar Assn., 1977. Fellow Life Mgmt. Inst.; mem. Ill. Inst. Tech./Chgo.-Kent Alumni Assn. (bd. dir. 1983-89). Democrat. Congregationalist.

CRAWFORD, NATALIE WILSON, applied mathematician; b. Evansville, Ind., June 24, 1939; d. John Moore and Edna Dorothea (Huthsteiner) Wilson; BA in Math., U. Calif., Los Angeles, 1961, postgrad., 1964-67; m. Robert Charles Crawford, Mar. 1, 1969. Programmer analyst N.Am. Aviation Corp., El Segundo, Calif., 1961-64; mem. tech. staff Rand Corp., Santa Monica, Calif., 1964—, project leader, engring. tech., theater conflict and force employment programs, 1975—; dir. Theater Forces Program, 1988-90, Theater Force Employment Program, 1990-92, Force Structure and Force Modernization Program, 1992-93, Force Modernization and Employment Program, 1993—; mem. Air Force Sci. Adv. Bd., 1988—, vice chmn., 1990-91; cons., joint tech. coordinating group munition effectiveness. Named YWCA Woman of Yr., 1983. Mem. Am. Def. Preparedness Assn., USAF Assn., IEEE. Republican. Home: 20940 Big Rock Dr Malibu CA 90265-5316

CRAWFORD, PAMELA J., critical care nurse; b. Houma, La., Aug. 10, 1957; d. Arthur Butler and Norma Vivien (Crawford) C.; children: Stephanie Pamela Cobb, Michele Anne Cobb. Assoc. of Legal Tech., Cumberland County Coll., Vineland, N.J., 1977; BSN, U. Mary Hardin-Baylor, Belton, Tex., 1987. Med. ICU-CCU staff nurse Scott and White Hosp., Temple, Tex., 1987-88; neuro ICU staff nurse Brooke Army Med. Ctr., San Antonio, 1989-91; case mgr. transplants, vendor negotiator, regional contact Traveler's Inc. Co., San Antonio, 1991-92; dir. quality control Brit-tex Home Health Svcs., 1992-94; dir. profl. svcs. Service Master Home Health, Stafford, Tex., 94—. Home Health Svcs., 1992-94; dir. Prof. Svcs., Svc. Master Home Health, Houston, 1994—. 1st lt. USAR, 1988—.

CRAWFORD, SARAH CARTER (SALLY CRAWFORD), broadcast executive; b. Glen Ridge, N.J., Oct. 3, 1938; d. Raymond Hitchings and Katherine Latta (Gribbel) Carter; m. Joseph Paul Crawford III, Sept. 10, 1960 (dec. 1966). BA, Smith Coll., 1960. Media dir. Kampmann & Bright, Phila., 1961-64; sr. media buyer Foote, Cone & Belding, N.Y.C., 1964-69; assoc. media dir. Grey Advt., Los Angeles, 1969-75; account exec., research dir. Sta. KHJ-TV, Los Angeles, 1975-76; mgr. local sales Sta. KCOP-TV, Los Angeles, 1977-82; gen. sales mgr. Sta. KTVF-TV, Fairbanks, Alaska, 1982—; bd. dirs. Vista Travel, Fairbanks; mem. adv. com. Golden Valley Electric Corp., Fairbanks, 1984-86; mem. coun. UAF Tanana County Campus, 1989—, chair mktg. com. Chmn. Fairbanks Health and Social Svc. Commn., 1986—; vice chmn. Fairbanks North Star Borough Health and Social Svc. Commn., 1993—; pres. Fairbanks Meml. Hosp. Aux., 1988-90, creator trust fund, chmn. fin. com., 1990—; bd. dirs. Fairbanks Downtown Assn., 1984-87; mem. FBKS Health Ctr. Coalition; mem. search com. UAF Tanana Valley Campus dir.; bd. dirs. Interior Regional Health Corp.; mem. Tesoro (Alaska) Citizens Adv. Coun. Mem. Fairbanks Women's Softball Assn., Fairbanks Women's Hockey Assn.. Episcopalian. Home: 518 Juneau Ave Fairbanks AK 99701-3771 Office: Sta KTVF-TV 3528 International Way Fairbanks AK 99701-7382

CRAWFORD, SUSAN, library director, educator; b. Vancouver, B.C., Can.; d. James Y. and S. Young; m. James Weldon Crawford, July 5, 1955; 1 son, Robert James. B.A., U. B.C., 1948; M.A., U. Toronto, 1950, U. Chgo., 1954; Ph.D., U. Chgo., 1970. With bur. library and indexing service ADA, 1954-56; with office exec. v.p. AMA, Chgo., 1956-60; dir. div. library and archival services AMA, 1960-81; asso. prof. Sch. Library Sci., Columbia U., N.Y.C., 1972-75; prof., dir. Sch. Medicine Library and Biomed. Communications Ctr. Washington U., 1981-92; with dept. psychiat. U. Ill., Chgo., 1994—. Author over 130 books and sci. papers; mem. editorial bd. Med. Socioecon. Rsch. Sources, Index to Sci. Revs., Jour. Am. Soc. Info. Sci., Med. Libr. Assn. News, Health Librs. Rev. (London), Health and Info. Librs. (Budapest); assoc. editor Jour. Am. Soc. Info. Sci., 1979-82; editor Med. Info. Systems, 1988-90; editor-in-chief Bull. of Med. Libr. Assn., 1982-88, 91-92. Bd. regents Nat. Library Medicine, NIH, 1971-75; mem. bd. overseers for univ. libraries Tufts U., 1988-89. Janet Doe hon. lectr., 1983; recipient Disting. Alumni award U. Toronto, 1987, Grad. medal U. Toronto, 1989. Fellow AAAS, Med. Libr. Assn. (life, Eliot award 1976, chmn. com. on surveys and stats. 1966-75, publs. panel 1977-80, chmn. consulting editors panel, 1981-88, spl. award to editor of bull. 1988, Noyes award 1992, pres.'s award 1992); mem. ALA, Soc. Social Studies of Sci., Assn. Acad. Health Scis. Libr. Dirs., Am. Soc. Info. Sci. (chmn. med. info. systems 1987-88, Outstanding Specialty Group award 1988, 89), Am. Med. Informatics Assn., Acad. Health Info. Profls. (disting. mem.), Sigma Xi (chmn. coms.). Home: 2418 Lincoln St Evanston IL 60201-2151

CRAWFORD, SUSAN JEAN, federal judge, lawyer; b. Pitts., Apr. 22, 1947; d. William Elmer Jr. and Joan Ruth (Bielau) C.; m. Roger W. Higgins; 1 child, Kelley S. BA, Bucknell U., 1969; JD, New Eng. Sch. Law, 1977. Bar: Md. 1977, D.C. 1980, U.S. Supreme Ct. 1993, U.S. Ct. Mil. Appeals 1995. Tchr. history, coach Radnor (Pa.) H.S., 1969-74; assoc. Burnett & Eiswert, Oakland, Md., 1977-79; ptnr. Burnett, Eiswert and Crawford, Oakland, 1979-81; prin. dep. gen. counsel U.S. Dept. Army, Washington, 1981-83, gen. counsel, 1983-89; insp. gen. U.S. Dept. Def., Arlington, Va., 1989-91; judge U.S. Ct. Appeals for the Armed Forces, Washington, 1991—; asst. states atty. Garrett County, Md., 1978-79; instr. Garrett County C.C., 1979-81. Del. Md. Forestry Adv. Commn., Garrett County, 1978-81, Md. Commn. for Women, Garrett County, 1980-83; chair Rep. State Cen. Com., Garrett County, 1978-81; trustee Bucknell U., 1988—, New England Sch. Law, 1989—. Mem. ABA, Md. Bar Assn., D.C. Bar Assn., Edward Bennett Williams Am. Inn of Ct. Presbyterian. Office: US Ct Appeals Armed Forces 450 E St NW Washington DC 20442-0001

CRAWFORD, SUSAN W., computing services professional; b. Redlands, Calif., Apr. 26, 1954; d. Lloyd Albert and Helen Louise (Edgar) Watts; 1 child, Douglas. BS, U. Utah, 1976, MBA, 1979. Cert. mgmt. acct., prodn. and inventory mgmt., integrated resource mgmt. Prodn. control supr. Evans & Sutherland Computer Corp., Salt Lake City, 1977-79; fin. analyst E-Systems Inc., Salt Lake City, 1979-81; stragetic planning analyst Christensen, Inc., Salt Lake City, 1981-82; sr. cons., mgr. Price Waterhouse, Salt Lake City, 1982-84; tech. cons. Ask Computer Sys., Los Altos, Calif., 1984-85; sr. mgr., consulting Deloitte & Touche, San Jose, Calif., 1985-92; dir. computing svcs. The Clorox Co., Oakland, Calif., 1992—. Coach Fremont (Calif.) Babe Ruth Baseball, 1994. Mem. Am. Prodn. and Inventory Control Soc. (chpt. pres.), Inst. Mgmt. Accts. Office: The Clorox Co 1000 Broadway Oakland CA 94607

CRAWFORD, VICKY CHARLENE, perinatal clinical nurse specialist; b. Waynesville, N.C., Aug. 20, 1959; d. Jerry Harrell and Geneva Pauline (Parker) C. BSN, Med. U. of S.C., 1981; MS in Maternal/Infant Nursing, Clemson U., 1991. Cert. in inpatient obstet. nursing. Staff nurse II ob Greenville (S.C.) Gen. Hosp., 1981-83; staff nurse labor and delivery Lexington County Hosp., West Columbia, S.C., 1983-84; staff RN III high risk ob-gyn Greenville Meml. Hosp., 1984-85, ob-gyn. clinician, 1985-91, ob-gyn. clin. nurse specialist, 1991-94; perinatal clin. nurse specialist Greenville (S.C.) Perinatal Assocs., 1994—; counselor, program coord. Resolve Through Sharing; developer Mother-Baby Care Cross-Tng. Program, 1989; sponsor Compassion Internat. Contbr. articles to profl. jours. Mem. Assn. Women's Health, Obstetrics and Neonatal Nursing (conv. speaker), Am. Heart Assn., Sigma Theta Tau. Home: 347 Bishop Dr Easley SC 29640-2585

CRAYCRAFT, JO LYNN, protective services official; b. Pt. Hueneme, Calif., Apr. 21, 1952; d. Charles Joseph and Martha Louise (Bullerdick) C.; children: Kady Marie, Erin Sue. BS, Ball State U., 1975; MBA, St. Mary's Coll., 1980; JD, Santa Clara U., 1985. Bar: Calif. 1985. Police officer, detective City of Tempe, Ariz., 1975-80; police officer City of Los Altos, Calif., 1980-81; police officer, investigator San Jose, Calif., 1981-87; spl. agent FBI, L.A., 1987—. Editor Santa Clara Law Rev., 1985. Active St. Monica's Ch., Santa Monica, Calif., 1994. Mem. Calif. Bar Assn., Spl. Agt's. Assn. Office: FBI 11000 Wilshire Blvd Los Angeles CA 90024

CREANZA, ALICE LAVERNE, counselor; b. Chgo., May 18, 1924; d. Arthur Algot and Alice (Carlson) Engeson; m. Joseph Creanza, June 12, 1943 (dec. Feb. 1986); children: Carol Creanza Freeman, Kathleen, Adrienne Creanza Hanley, Philip. AA, Ctrl. YMCA Coll., Chgo., 1943; MA, Roosevelt U., 1961; M in Counseling, Ariz. State U., 1992. Cert. assoc. counselor, Ariz., nat. cert. counselor. Tchr. Sch. Dist. # 1, Glen Ellyn, Ill., 1961-84; counselor intern Empact-Interfaith Svcs., Tempe and Sun City, Ariz., 1992-93; pvt. practice Phoenix, 1993—. Mem. AAUW, ACA. Democrat. Home and Office: 10921 Saratoga Cir Sun City AZ 85351

CREASEY, BEVERLY ANN, theater critic; b. Boston, Sept. 12, 1946; d. Palmer L. and Ruth (Newton) DeWolfe; m. David E. Creasey, Apr. 8, 1972. AB, Boston U., 1968, MS, 1970; postgrad., U. R.I., 1972-73. Psychotherapist Tufts New Eng. Med. Ctr., Boston, 1970-72; actress Repertory Four of N.Y., 1970-78; dir., Boston Br. Oxford (Eng.) Intensive Sch., 1980-82; dir., bd. L'Ecole Piano & Ballet, Boston, 1982-85; mng. dir. Artists Prodn. Co., Boston, 1985-88; dir., producer Playwright's Platform, Boston, 1985—; syndicated reviewer Jour. Newspapers, Boston, 1988—; prof. theater Lesley Coll., Cambridge, Mass., 1989-90, Mt. Ida Coll., Newton, Mass., 1991-92; affiliate North House Harvard U., Cambridge, 1986—; co-founder, bd. New Play Cafe, Boston, 1988—; dir., founder Non-Traditional Casting File, Boston, 1988—. Author: (with others) One Act Plays for Acting Students, 1988; freelance writer, 1975—; contbr. revs. mag. Cinema Francais, 1989-90, Art Dynamo, Art News. Bd. dirs. Changing Images Coalition, Boston, 1988—; mem. ad hoc com. Friends of Brighton (Mass.) Libr., 1987—; mem. Greater Boston Physicians for Social Responsibility, 1986—, Rainbow Coalition, Boston, 1986—, Coalition for Freedom of Expression, 1990—. Named Libr. Supporter of Yr. Brighton Br. Libr., 1989; recipient Leadership award Consortium of Local Arts Orgns. of Mass., 1989. Mem. Dramatists' Guild, Boston Resident Theatre Alliance, Boston U. Alumi Assn., Coalition to End Animal Suffering, People for Ethical Treatment of Animals, Occasional Wits (bd. dirs. 1989—), Defenders of Wildlife (lectr., rehab. handler 1989—), Delta Phi Kappa. Office: Playwrights Platform 164 Brayton Rd Brighton MA 02135-3049

CREASMAN, VIRENA WELBORN (RENE CREASMAN), retired elementary and secondary school educator, genealogist, researcher; b. Lebanon, Nebr., Dec. 10, 1909; d. Lawrence Morgan and Auretta Iva (Daffer) Welborn; m. Sam Doran Creasman, May 8, 1929 (dec. Jan. 1982); children: Gary W., Lee-Ellen Creasman Matzke. AA, McCook Jr. Coll., 1928; B in Edn., U. Nebr., 1962; postgrad., Kearney State Coll., 1967, Creighton U., 1968. Cert. elem., secondary tchr. Tchr. Rural Sch. grades 1-8, Red Willow County, Nebr., 1928-29; elem. tchr. McCook (Nebr.) City Schs., 1949-67, tchr. jr. high reading, English, 1968-76; tchr. genealogy, rschr. McCook Coll. and Southwest Nebr. Genealogy Soc., 1976—; rschr. state and local genealogy confs., 1976—. Vol., mem. Nebr. Hist. Soc. and Mus., High Plains Hist. Soc. and Mus., 1980—. Recipient Plaque of Appreciation from High Plains Hist. Soc. and Mus., 1990, Cert. of Appreciation from Nebr. State Hist. Soc. and Mus., 1989, Genealogist of Yr. cert. Southwest Nebr. Genealogy Soc., 1984, Appreciation of Svc. award as thrift shop coord. Congl. Ch., 1984-90. Mem. AAUW (chpt. leader 1962—), DAR (chpt. regent and registrar 1976—), NOW, LWV, UN Assn. U.S.A., Sierra Club, Arbor Day Found., Humane Soc., Assn. Retired Tchrs. (local pres. 1976—, nat., state), Delta Kappa Gamma (publicity com.), Eastern Star, Daus. of the Nile, Shriners Auxilliary, Genealogy Socs. (nat., local, state, libr. local chpt.). Democrat. Home: # 8 Parkview Mc Cook NE 69001

CREDE, CAROL ANN JOHNSON, principal. BA, Immaculate Heart Coll., 1979; MEd, Loyola Marymount U., 1989, MA in Counseling, 1993. Cert. tchr., adminstrn. svcs., pupil personnel svcs. and counseling credential, Calif. Tchr. Visitation Sch., L.A., 1972-80, prin., 1980—; tchr. credentialing adv. bd. Loyola Marymount Univ., 1990-93; sch. adminstr. adv. bd. mem. Loyola Marymount Univ., 1993. Mem. AACD, ASCD, Am. Assn. Sch. Adminstrs., Nat. Assn. Elem. Sch. Prins., Nat. Coun. Tchrs. of Math., Nat. Cath. Edn. Assn., Am. Sch. Counselor Assn., Assn. Counselor Edn. and Supervision, Calif. Assn. Supervision and Curriculum Devel., Calif. Assn. Sch. Psychologists, Assn. Calif. Sch. Adminstrs., Westchester-L.A. C. of C. (edn. affairs com.). Office: Visitation Sch 8740 Emerson Ave Los Angeles CA 90045-3797

CREDE, HELEN LOUISE, college director community education; b. Clifton Forge, Va., July 5, 1937; d. Harrold Lester and Sybal Cox VanNetta; m. Herbert Allen Crede, Aug. 23, 1961; children: Catherine Diane, Amy Elizabeth. BA, Morris Harvey Coll., 1959; MA, Northwestern U., 1963. Receptionist Ill. Agrl. Assn., Bloomington, 1963-64; instr. pre-sch. Vermont St. Pre-sch., Quincy, Ill., 1972-73; instr., dir. pre-sch. Pre-Schs. in the Park, Springfield, Ill., 1974-80; from coord. women's program to cmty. edn. John Wood C.C., Quincy, 1980-90, dir. cmty. edn., 1990—. Bd. dirs. West Ctrl. Child Care Connection, Quincy Area Network Against Domestic Violence, pres. 1992. Mem. AAUW (v.p. 1985), YWCA, Nat. Assn. Cmty. Svcs. and Continuing Edn., United Meth. Women. Democrat. Office: John Wood C C 150 S 48th St Quincy IL 62301-9147

CREECH, SHARON, children's author. Author: Walk Two Moons, 1994 (John Newbery medal 1995). Office: care HarperCollins Children's Bks 10 E 53rd St New York NY 10022*

CREEDON, JANICE LEIGH, advertising executive; b. Chgo., Feb. 16, 1939; d. Edwin Charles and Helen Louise (Jesperson) Brown; m. Gaylord Creedon, July 8, 1961 (div. Nov. 1975). BA in Radio, TV, Mich. State U., 1961; student, UCLA, 1975-76. Traffic asst. D'Arcy Advt., Chgo., 1963-65; traffic mgr. J. Walter Thompson, Chgo., 1965-67; asst. producer J. Walter Thompson, N.Y.C., 1967-69, broadcast mgr., 1969-72, producer, 1972-80; dir. prodn. Dancer, Fitzgerald, Sample, Torrance, Calif., 1980-86; v.p., exec. producer Lintas Campbell-Ewald, L.A., 1986—, sr. v.p., 1989—. Recipient Gold Internat. Film award N.Y.C., 1984, 87, 88, Silver and Bronze awards, 1984, Mobius award U.S. Festival, 1987. Republican. Presbyterian. Office: Lintas Campbell-Ewald 11100 Santa Monica Blvd Los Angeles CA 90025-3381

CREEDON, MADELYN R., counsel; b. Indpls.; d. Richard O. and Marilyn H. (Raub) C.; m. James J. Bracco. Grad., U. Evansville, 1973; JD, St. Louis U., 1976. Bar: Mo. 1976, Ind. 1977, Va. 1977. Assoc. Falcone, Gary & Rosenfeld, 1977-80; trial atty. Dept. Energy, 1980-90; counsel Senate Com. Armed Svcs., 1990—. Office: Armed Svcs 228 Senate Russell Office Bldg Washington DC 20510*

CREEDON, MARY ALICE, insurance company executive; b. Niagara Falls, N.Y., Apr. 1, 1950; d. Daniel Francis and Anne Walle (Moynihan) C. BA, Coll. New Rochelle, 1972. Dir. divns. ins. Fed. Savs. and Loan Ins. Corp., Washington, 1984-86, dep. exec. dir., 1987-88, exec. dir., 1989; assoc. dir. FDIC, Washington, 1989-91; COO Farm Credit System Ins. Co., McLean, Va., 1991—. Mem. Women in Housing and Fin. Home: 4315 N 31st St Arlington VA 22207 Office: Farm Credit System Ins Corp 1501 Farm Credit Dr Mc Lean VA 22102

CREEKMORE, SUSAN CAROL, nurse practitioner; b. Richmond, Va., June 11, 1962; d. Lloyd Clarence and Annis Gwendolyn (Hall) C. BS, U. Va., 1984; MS, Med. Coll. Va., 1991. RN, Va.; cert. critical care nurse. Nurse Henrico Doctors' Hosp., Richmond, Va., 1985-92; nurse practitioner Med. Coll. Va., Richmond, 1992—. Spkr. Am. Heart Assn., Richmond, 1994. Mem. Am. Assn. Critical Care Nurses, Richmond Assn. Nurse Practitioners. Office: Med Coll Va Internal Medicine Richmond VA 23298

CREEKMORE, VERITY VEIRS, media specialist; b. Cin., May 13; d. Noble L. and Maxine (Wright) Veirs; m. Kenneth L. Creekmore, Nov. 23, 1961; 1 child, Kenneth L. Jr. BS in Edn. magna cum laude, S.C. State U., 1975; MLS, U. S.C., 1978. Cert. libr. media specialist, S.C. Media specialist John Ford High Sch., St. Matthews, S.C., 1976-77, St. John High Sch., Cameron, S.C., 1977-82, St. John Elem./Mid. Sch., Cameron, 1982-86, Sheridan Elem. Sch., Orangeburg, S.C., 1986—; directed libr. U. S.C., Columbia, 1993-94; rep. S.C. Sci. Hub. Trainer Laubach Literacy Program, Orangeburg, 1990—. Mem. NEA, ALA, S.C. Assn. Sch. Librs., Nat. Assn. Storytelling, So. Assn. Colls. and Schs. (evaluator), S.C. Edn. Assn. (dist. rep. 1991-93, IPD rep. 1993—), Hon. Order Ky. Cols., Order Ea. Star (treas. 1989—), Alpha Kappa Mu. Home: Rte 2 Box 127 Saint Matthews SC 29135 Office: Sheridan Elem Sch 139 Hillsboro St NE Orangeburg SC 29115

CREELMAN, MARJORIE BROER, psychologist; b. Toledo, Dec. 5, 1908; d. William F. and Ethel (Griffin) Broer; m. George Douglas Creelman, June 29, 1932 (div. Dec. 1958); children: Carleton Douglas, Stewart Elliott, Katherine George Skrobela. AB, Vassar Coll., 1931; MA, Columbia U., 1932; PhD, Western Res. U., 1954. Asst. psychologist N.Y. Psychiat. Inst., N.Y.C., 1932-33, Sunny Acres Sanitorium, Cleve., 1947-48; clin. asst. dept. psychology Case Western Res. U., Cleve., 1947-49, supr. field work, dir. practicum tng. program, 1949-54; asst. to dir. parent edn. program Children's Aid Soc., Cleve., 1952-53; ptnr., sr. assoc. Creelman Assocs., Cleve., 1954-58; pvt. practice psychology Cleve., 1954-61, Washington, 1964-69; research psychologist behavioral studies St. Elizabeth's Hosp., Washington, 1963-65, dir. psycho-physiology, clin. and behavioral studies, 1965-67; dir. psychol. services Alexandria Community Mental Health Ctr., 1967-69; mem. policy and planning com. Midwest Tng. Ctr. in Human Relations, 1954-60; prof. psychology Cleve. State U., 1969-76, prof. emeritus, 1976—; pvt. practice psychology, 1969—; mem. profl. staff Gestalt Inst. Cleve., 1969-81, hon. fellow, 1978—. Author: The Experimental Investigation of Meaning, 1965; editor: Ohio Psychologist, 1956-59; contbr. articles to profl. jours. Mem. Citizen's Adv. Bd. Case Western Res. U. Psychiat. Habilitation Ctr., 1979-81. Fellow Internat. Council Psychologists (sec. 1964-65), Am. Soc. Group Psychotherapy and Psychodrama, Ohio Psychol. Assn.; mem. Internat. Soc. Gen. Semantics (v.p. Cleve. chpt. 1950-61), Am. Acad. Psychotherapists (life, publs. com. directory editor 1963-67), Cleve. Acad. Cons. Psychologists (pres. 1957-58), Sigma Delta Epsilon, Psi Chi, Alpha Chi Omega. Club: Cleve. Skating.

CREENAN, KATHERINE HERAS, lawyer; b. Elizabeth, N.J., Oct. 7, 1945; d. Victor Joseph and Katherine Regina (Lederer) Petervary; m. Edward James Creenan; 1 child, David Heras. BA, Newark State Coll., 1968; JD, Rutgers U., 1984. Bar: N.J. 1984, U.S. Dist. Ct. N.J. 1984. Various teaching positions including, Union and Stanhope, N.J., 1968-81; law clk. to presiding judge Superior Ct. of N.J. Appellate Div., Newark, 1984-85; assoc. Lowenstein, Sandler, Kohl, Fisher & Boylan, Roseland, N.J., 1985-88, Kirsten, Simon, Friedman, Allen, Cherin & Linken, Newark, 1988-89, Whitman & Ranson, Newark, 1989-93, Whitman Breed Abbott & Morgan, Newark, 1993—. Mem. ABA, N.J. State Bar Assn., Union County Bar Assn., Essex County Bar Assn. Office: Whitman Breed Abbott Morgan 1 Gateway Ctr Newark NJ 07102

CREIGHTON, JOANNE VANISH, academic administrator; b. Marinette, Wis., Feb. 21, 1942; d. William J. and Bernice Vanish; m. Thomas F. Creighton, Nov. 9, 1968; 1 child, William. BA with honors, U. Wis., 1964; MA, Harvard U., 1965; PhD, U. Mich., 1969. From instr. to prof. English Wayne State U., Detroit, 1968-85, assoc. dean liberal arts, 1983-85; dean arts and scis., prof. English U. N.C., Greensboro, 1985-90; v.p. acad. affairs, provost, prof. English Wesleyan U., Middletown, Conn., 1990—; now pres. Wesleyan U. Author: William Faulkner's Craft of Revision, 1977, Joyce Carol Oates, 1979, Margaret Drabble, 1985, Joyce Carol Oates: Novels of the Middle Years, 1992. Grantee Am. Coun. Learned Socs. Mem. Phi Beta Kappa, Phi Kappa Phi. Home: 164 Mt Vernon St Middletown CT 06457-3215 Office: Wesleyan U Office of the Pres Middletown CT 06457*

CRENSHAW, MARILYN JEAN, mathematics educator; b. Stewartsville, Mo., Apr. 27, 1947; d. Gilbert Gale and Mildred Virginia (Thompson) Whiteman; m. James Tiffin Crenshaw, June 20, 1965; children: Amelia Gale, Tiffiny Lee. BA in Edn., U. Mo., Kansas City, 1969; MS, U. Mo., Rolla, 1973. Tchr. Lathrop (Mo.) Sch. Dist., 1969-73, Adult Basic Edn., St. Joseph, Mo., 1971-75; instr. N.W. Mo. C.C., St. Joseph, 1992—; mem. sch. bd. Lathrop Schs., 1986—, pres. 1990-92, 93—. NSF scholar, 1971-73. Mem. Merchants Assn. (pres. 1979-81). Home: 607 Ash St Lathrop MO 64465-9709 Office: NW Mo C C 4315 Pickett Rd Saint Joseph MO 64503-1635

CRENSHAW, PATRICIA SHRYACK, manufacturing executive, consultant; b. Kansas City, Mo., Oct. 7, 1941; d. George Randolf and Velma Irene (Carroll) Shryack; m. Paul Burton, Mar. 24, 1961 (div. 1971); m. Peter Frederick Schmidt, Jan. 21, 1989. Student, William Jewell Coll., 1959-60, S.W. Mo. State U., 1960-61; BEd, U. Mo., 1967; postgrad., Cen. Mo. State U., 1971-73. Cert. tchr. secondary edn. and history, Mo. Tchr. Lillis High Sch., Kansas City, 1967-69, Park Hill High Sch., Kansas City, 1969-73; terr. mgr. Hollister, Inc., Kansas City, 1973-75, field trainer, 1974-75; sales edn. mgr. Hollister, Inc., Chgo., 1975; dist. sales mgr. Detroit Mich., 1976-81; regional sales mgr. Chgo., 1981-84; dir. contract sales Chgo. Serta, Inc., 1984-86, nat. dir. contract sales div., 1987-89, v.p. nat. contract sales, 1989-90; area v.p. B G Industries, Northridge, Calif., 1990-91, v.p. sales, 1992—. Mem. women's com. Young Reps., Kansas City, 1962. Mem. NOW, NAFE, U.S. Golf Assn., Lake Barrington Shores (Ill.) Golf Club. Republican. Avocations: golfing, skiing, scuba diving, racquetball, reading, gardening. Office: 8550 Balboa Blvd Northridge CA 91325

CREQUE, LINDA ANN, Virgin Islands education commissioner; b. N.Y.C.; d. Noel and Enid Louise (Schloss) DePass; m. Leonard J. Creque, July 29, 1967; children: Leah Michelle, Michael Gregory. BS, CUNY-Queens, 1963, MS, 1969; PhD, U. Ill., 1986. Tchr. 2d grade Bd. Edn., N.Y.C., 1963, tchr. demonstrations, team tchr., 1964-65, master tchr., 1965-66; elem. tchr. P.S. 69, Jackson Hgts., N.Y., 1963-67; tchr. English Cath. U., Ponce, P.R., 1967; cmty. exch. elem. tchr. grades K-6 Ponce, 1966-67; tchr. 4th grade Dept. Edn., V.I., 1967-69, tchr. remedial reading, master tchr., 1968-69; program coord. Project HeadStart, V.I., 1969-73, coord. Inst. Developmental Studies, 1970-71, acting dir., 1972-73; prin. Thomas Jefferson Annex Primary Sch., St. Thomas, V.I., 1973-80, Joseph Sibilly Elem. Sch., St. Thomas, 1980-87; commr. edn. Dept. Edn., St. Thomas, 1987—; cons. Edn. Devel. Ctr., Mass. Nat. SSI Project, 1992—; part-time instr. adult basic edn., 1975, Coll. V.I., 1978; mem. exec. com., bd. overseers Regional Lab. Ednl. Improvement NE and Islands, Andover, Mass.; bd. dirs. V.I. Pub. TV; mem. exec. bd. Leadership in Edn. Adminstrv. Devel., V.I., 1989—; presenter, keynote spkr. confs. in field. Contbr. articles to profl. jours. Chair Tabor-Harmony Home Owners Assn., 1981-82; trustee U. V.I., 1989—; mem. V.I. Residential Task Force for Human Svcs., 1989—, V.I. Labor Coun.; bd. dirs. Nat. Urban Alliance for Effective Edn. Tchrs. Coll. Columbia U., N.Y.C., 1993—, Cultural Inst. V.I., 1989—; mem. cultural endowment bd., V.I., 1989—; mem. governing bd. East End Health Ctr., 1979-80; mem. Gov.'s Conf. Librs., 1978. Recipient award NASA, award St. Thomas-St. John Counselors Assn., 1988; grantee NSF, 1989-93, Carnegie Found., 1988-90, Comprehensive Employment and Training Act, 1977, V.I. Coun. on Arts Ceramics for Primary Children, 1974-78. Mem. LWV, St. Thomas Reading Coun., Nat. Assn. Tchrs. Math., Edn. Commn. of States (commr. 1987-93, steering com. 1988-92, internal audit com. 1988, policies priority com. 1991, exec. com. 1992, alt. steering com. 1991—), Coun. Chief of State Sch. Officers (chair extra jurisdictions com., bd. dirs., task force early childhood edn., ednl. equity com., restructuring edn. com.), Phi Kappa Phi, Kappa Delta Pi, Phi Delta Kappa. Office: Office of the Gov Edn Dept Kogens Glade Saint Thomas VI 00802

CRESPIN, LESLIE ANN, artist; b. Cleve., Sept. 30, 1947; d. Edwin Creaver and Eunice Jane (Pierce) Ulrich; m. Raimondo J. Vinella; children: Greg, Chris, Tony. Student, Cleve. Art Inst., U. Capetown (S. Africa), Hiram (Ohio) U. Instr. Taos (N.Mex.) Sch. Fine Art; works in permanent collections at Johnson Humrick House Mus., Ohio, Harwood Found., Mus. Taos Art, Midland Savs. and Loan, Denver, Monsanto Internat., N.Y.C., St. Louis, Carlsbad Fine Art Mus., Tubac Ctr. for the Arts, Rolm Corp., Dallas, Wichita Art Assn., Kans. Exhibits include Cleve. Mus. Art, Jewish Community Ctr., Cleve., Hiram U., U. Capetown, N.Mex. State U., Peyton Wright Gallery, Santa Fe, Roanoke (Va.) Fine Arts Mus., The New Gallery, Taos, 1981-84, Amarillo Art Ctr., 1983, Carlsbad Fine Arts Mus., 1984, Beachwood Mus., Ohio, 1985, Tubac Ctr. for Arts, Ariz., 1985, Erie (Pa.) Art Mus., 1986, Albuquerque Mus., 1991, 92, 93, 94, Harwood Found. Mus. Taos Art, 1987, Fenix Gallery, N.Mex., 1990-91, 92, 93, J. Richards Gallery, Englewood, N.J., 1990-91, 92, 93, Sharon Blautstein, N.J. and N.Y., 1990, 91, 92, 93, Fenix Gallery, 1990, 91, 92, 93, Lumina Gallery, 1994, Albuquerque Mus., 1993-94, Upper Edge Gallery, 1994; represented in permanent collections Harwood Found., Maytag, Wichita Art Assn., Kans., Monsanto Internat., Carlsbad Fine Art Mus., Tubac Ctr. for the Arts, Bernard Ewell ASA, Rolm Corp., Johnson Humrick House Mus., N. Pajarola Museum-strasse, Switzerland, Carson County Square House Mus. Recipient numerous purchase awards; Masterfield award, North Coast Collage Soc., 1985, Grumbacher award, Beachwood Mus., Ohio, 1986, Master Field award, KennedyCtr. Gallery, 1987. Mem. Soc. Artists in Multi-Media, North Coast Collage Soc., Soc. Exptl. Artists, Contemporary Art Soc. N.Mex., Taos Art Assn. Home and Office: PO Box 1569 Taos NM 87571

CRESS, CECILE COLLEEN, retired librarian; b. Colorado Springs, Colo., Feb. 26, 1914; d. John Leo and Elizabeth Veronica (Rouse) Haley; m. Arthur Henry Cress, May 8, 1937 (div. 1960); children: Ronnie Lou Kordick, Dan, Elaine. BA, Adams State Coll., 1936; MA in English, Colo. Coll., 1964; MLS, Denver U., 1970. 5th grade tchr. Westcliffe (Colo.) Elem., 1953-56; English tchr. Penrose (Colo.) High Sch., 1956-59; English-social studies tchr. Excelsior Jr. High, Sch. Dist. 70, Pueblo, Colo., 1959-64; libr. Pueblo County High, Sch. Dist. 70, Pueblo, 1964-80, Nat. Coll./Pueblo Br., 1980-91; cataloger in library Pueblo C.C., 1992—. Tutor adult literacy program South Cen. Bd. Coop. Svcs., 1991. Recipient Ace of Clubs award Am. Contract Bridge League, 1988, 89. Mem. AAUW, Pueblo Ret. Sch. Employees (v.p. 1990-92, pres. 1982-84, state bd. 1982-86), Colo. Libr. Assn., Unit 369 Am. Contract Bridge Assn., Irish Club Pueblo, Welsh Terrier Club Colo., Alpha Delta Kappa (Pueblo chpt., pres. 1976-78, state historian 1980-82, state bd. 1980-82, rec. sec. 1994—). Democrat. Roman Catholic. Home: 901 Jackson St Pueblo CO 81004-2425

CRESS, KATHLEEN O., bank executive, association executive; b. Erie, Pa., Sept. 26, 1943; d. Lloyd E. Olson and Marjorie A. Palmer; m. John Cress, Sept. 2, 1967; children: Hudson, Suzanne. BA, Marietta Coll., 1965; JD, Fordham U., 1969. Assoc. Cowen, Leibowitz & Latman, N.Y.C., 1969-71; sr. v.p., trust risk mgmt. compliance officer NationsBank, Charlotte, N.C., 1972—. Allocation bd. mem. United Way, Charlotte; pres. YWCA, Charlotte, 1978-79; nat. bd. dirs. YWCA of U.S.A., 1982-92; bd. dirs. Sarasota (Fla.) Community Found., 1988-91. Office: NationsBank Nationsbank Plz Charlotte NC 28255

CRESWELL, DOROTHY ANNE, computer consultant; b. Burlington, Iowa, Feb. 6, 1943; d. Robert Emerson and Agnes Imogene (Gardner) Mefford; m. John Lewis Creswell, Aug. 28, 1965. AA, Burlington C.C., 1963; BA in Math., U. Iowa, 1965; MS in Math., Western Ill. U., 1970; postgrad., Iowa State U., 1974—. Cert. netware engr. Computer programmer Mason & Hanger, Silas Mason Co., Inc., Burlington, 1965-74; systems programmer Contractor's Hotline, Ft. Dodge, Iowa, 1974; dir. data processing Iowa Cen. C.C., Ft. Dodge, 1975-80; systems programming mgr. Norand Corp., Cedar Rapids, Iowa, 1980-82; spl. svcs. mgr. Pioneer Hi-Bred Internat., Inc., Cedar Rapids, 1982-87; owner, pres. D.C. Cons., Inc., Ankeny, Iowa, 1987—; computers-in-edn. del. to China, People to People Internat., Kansas City, Mo., 1987. Contbr. articles, papers to profl. publs. Mem. Data Processing Mgmt. Assn. (bd. dirs. 1986-87, v.p. 1988, 91-93, pres. 1993-94), Adminstrv. Mgmt. Soc. (sec. 1985-86, v.p. 1986-90, Merit award 1987), Assn. Computing Machinery, Hawkeye Pers. Computer Users, DEC Users Group (v.p. Ea. Iowa chpt. 1981-82), Ind. Computer Cons. Assn. (mem. editorial bd. 1989—, chpt. pres.-at-large 1993—), Systems Operator Computer Cons. Forum Computer Svc. Democrat. Methodist. Office: DC Cons Inc PO Box 195 Ankeny IA 50021-0195

CREWS, DENISE LOUISE, civil engineer, sanitary engineer; b. Toledo, Feb. 2, 1959; d. Robert Charles and Ruth (Fork) Kunz; m. Stephen Craig Crews, June 20, 1981; children: Alexander Stephen, Eleanor Louise. BS in

Civil Engring., Ohio State U., 1981. Profl. engr., Ohio. Pretreatment coord. Ohio Environ. Protection Agy., Columbus, 1981-82, environ. engr., 1982-86; sanitary engr. Licking County, Newark, Ohio, 1986—. Mem. adv. bd. Child Care Connections, Newark, 1988—; active 4 County Solid Waste Dist., 1988—; mgr. Licking County Litter Prevention, 1989—; vol. Licking Pk. Dist., Granville, Ohio, 1989—. Recipient Johnny Clearwater award Ohio Water Pollution Fedn., 1976. Mem. Am. Water Works Assn., Orgn. Solid Waste (past sec., v.p. Ohio dist.), Water Control Fedn., Rural Water Assn. Office: Licking County 20 S 2d St Newark OH 43055

CRICHTON, KIMBERLY, lawyer; b. Fort Morgan, Colo., July 22, 1945; d. John Henderson and Zula (Miller) C.; m. John W. Roper, June 22, 1967 (div. 1973); 1 child, Ingrid Lyda. BA, Harvard U., 1967; diploma, Inst. Anthropology, Oxford U., Eng., 1968; JD, Loyola U., L.A., 1977. Bar: N.Y. 1978, Conn. 1978, Calif. 1981. Staff atty. to spl. counsel SEC, N.Y.C. and L.A., 1977-84; assoc. Rogers & Wells, L.A., 1984-87; v.p. legal dept. Citibank, N.Y.C., 1987-92; gen. counsel Citicorp Investment Svcs., N.Y.C., 1992—. Bd. dirs. Westside Food Bank, Santa Monica, Calif., 1984-87, Woman's Bldg., L.A., 1986-87; mem. exec. com. Am. Field Svc. Returnees, L.A., 1984-87. Mem. ABA, Assn. Bar City of N.Y., Calif. Bar Assn., Conn. Bar Assn. Office: Citicorp Investment Svcs 1 Court Sq Fl 24 Long Is City NY 11120-0001

CRIDER, JEAN MARIE, employee communications specialist; b. Arlington, Va., Jan. 27, 1963; d. William Alton and Irma Virginia (Kemp) C. BA in Journalism, Ind. U., 1985. Assoc. editor Potomac Elec. Power Co., Washington, 1985-87, supr. employee communications, 1987—. Mem. Suburban Md./Montgomery County High Tech. Coun. Comm. Com., 1990-92; mem. Suburban Md./Montgomery County Tech. Coun. Pub. Rels. Network Steering Com., 1993—. Recipient Silver award United Way Am., 1990, Honorable Mention, 1991. Mem. Internat. Assn. Bus. Communicators. Office: Potomac Elec Power Co Rm 501 1900 Pennsylvania Ave NW Washington DC 20068-0068

CRIDER, KAREN KOCH, lawyer; b. St. Louis, Mar. 12, 1945; d. Robert E. and Elva (Hart) Koch. BA, Wellsley Coll., 1967; MA, Columbia U., 1968; JD, Boston U., 1973. Bar: N.Y. 1974. Assoc. Sage, Gray, Todd & Sims, N.Y.C., 1973-75, Cowan, Leibowitz & Latman P.C., N.Y.C., 1975-76; counsel Columbia Pictures Industries Inc., N.Y.C., 1976-78; v.p., gen. counsel, sec. The McCall Pattern Co. and Halston Enterprises Inc., N.Y.C., 1978-83; asst. group counsel Gen. Mills Inc., N.Y.C., 1983-86; asst. U.S. counsel Brit. Airways Plc., N.Y.C., 1986-88, U.S. counsel, 1988-92; gen. counsel Stride Rite Corp., Cambridge, Mass., 1992—. Office: Stride Rite Corp 5 Cambridge Ctr Cambridge MA 02142-1493

CRIDER, LOUISE ELAINE, accountant; b. Butler, Pa., Nov. 14, 1959; d. Charles Krenn and Ethel Myrtle (Bachman) C. B.S. in Bus. Adminstrn., Robert Morris Coll., 1981; MBA Clarion U., 1993. Credit mgr. Reidbord Bros. Co., Pitts., 1982-85; plant acct. Penreco, Karns City, Pa., 1985-87; assoc. acct., Penreco, Karns City, 1987-93; acct. Last In First Out inventory valuation expert Pennzoil, 1993—. Youth advisor Summit United Presbyn. Ch. Youth Group, Butler, Pa., 1984, 85; active Woodlands Community Presbyn. Ch. Mem. Inst. Mgmt. Accts. (nat. dir. 1993—), FBLA-PBL Alumni Chpt. (treas.), Phi Beta Lambda. Avocations: traveling; reading; swimming; hiking. Home: 2301 S Millbend Dr Apt 1104 The Woodlands TX 77380-1756 Office: Pennzoil Products Co 700 Milam St Houston TX 77002-2800

CRIDER, MELINDA GRAY, artist; b. Hattiesburg, Miss., Aug. 6, 1951; d. Howard R. and Sylvia O'Kain Gray; m. Ronald R. Adams, Aug. 29, 1969 (div. 1972); 1 child, Shae Marcus; m. Claude J. Crider, Feb. 7, 1976; 1 child, Lindsay Jeanne-Catherine. Student, Atlanta Coll. Art, 1975-77, 83, 84, Callanwolde Fine Arts Ctr., Atlanta, 1978-81. Dir. Claybasket Coop., Alpharetta, Ga., 1981-83; owner, dir. Studio III, Roswell, Ga., 1985-87, Heaven Blue Rose Gallery, Roswell, 1989-91; owner, Crider Studio, Alpharetta, 1982—; curator art gallery, Roswell, 1990—; state rep. membership Individual Visual Artists Coalition. Exhibited in numerous group shows, 1976—, including Arts Festival Atlanta, 1986, Roswell (Ga.) Arts Alliance, 1987, Highland Gallery, Atlanta, 1987-93, Novus Gallery, 1989-93, Roswell Visual Arts Ctr., 1991, Reinhardt Coll. Gallery, Canton, Ga., 1991, 92, Quinlan Arts Ctr., Gainesville, Ga., 1991, Ga. Inst. Tech. Gallery, Atlanta, 1991, 92, Emory Gallery, 1989—, Heaven Blue Rose Gallery, 1991—, Perrin Ctr. for Arts, 1992—, Art South Gallery, 1993—, Albany Mus., 1994; represented in permanent pub. collections. Fine arts juror Congregation Etz Chaim Arts Festival; mem. host com. Carl Ratcliff Dance Co.; mem. visual arts orgns. selection panel Fulton County Arts Coun. Recipient sculpture award Roswell Arts Festival, 1983, merit award Creative Art Guild, Dalton, Ga., 1983. Mem. Roswell Arts Alliance (v.p. 1994). Home and Studio: 850 Liberty Grove Rd Alpharetta GA 30201

CRIDER, RUTH L., nursing administrator, public health; b. St. Genevieve County, Mo., Aug. 23, 1936; d. Glen Allen and Ruby Ethel (Holmes) McDowell; m. Joseph E. Crider, June 28, 1957; children: Joseph Allen, Cheryl Lynette, Michael Ervin. ADN, So. Mo. State U., 1987, BSN, 1991. RN, Mo. Nurse, adminstr. Oreg. County Health Dept.; registray Oreg., Mo. and Howell County. Mem. Mo. League for Nursing (assoc.), Mo. pub. health assn., Dau. of Am. Revolution.

CRIER, CATHERINE, television news correspondent. Former judge 162nd Dist. Ct. Tex.; anchor Cable News Network, until 1989; now corr. 20/20 News Mag. Office: 20/20 10th Fl 147 Columbus Ave New York NY 10023*

CRIGER, NANCY S., professional society administrator; b. Ypsilanti, Mich., Apr. 16, 1951; d. Douglas D. and Edith (Nicoll) Smith; children: Amanda L. Denomme, William G. Denomme, Jr. Student, Mich. State U., 1969-71; BS in Elem. Edn., Wayne State U., 1973. Asst. v.p. Nat. Bank of Detroit, 1978-87; asst. v.p. Comerica Bank, Detroit, 1987-88, v.p. employee benefits, 1988-91; v.p. and mgr. trust adminstrn. and ops. Comerica Bank-Tex., Dallas, 1991-92; v.p. adminstrn., exec. v.p. Vis. Nurs Assn. Tex., 1992-94; pres. Continuum Healthcare Mgmt., Inc., Plano, Tex., 1994—. Asst. treas. Jr. League of Detroit, 1985-86, treas., 1986-87; treas. women's assn. Detroit Symphony Orch., 1987-89. Mem. Jr. League of Dallas, Rotary, The 500, Inc., Dallas Women's Found., Dallas Mus. of Art, DMA-PM Group, Dallas Hist. Soc., Dallas Symphony Assn., Dallas Arboretum, Dallas Zool. Soc., Dallas County Heritage Soc., Dallas Coun., Chi Omega. Office: 1721 W Plano Pkwy Ste 207 Plano TX 75075

CRILE, SUSAN, artist; b. Cleve., Aug. 12, 1942; d. George Jr. and Jane (Halle) C.; m. Joseph S. Murphy, May 18, 1984. Student, NYU; BA, Bennington Coll., 1965. Mem. faculty Fordham U., N.Y.C., 1972-76, Princeton (N.J.) U., 1974-76, Sarah Lawrence Coll., Bronxville, N.Y., 1976-79, Sch. Visual Arts, N.Y.C., 1976-82, Barnard Coll., N.Y.C., 1983-86, Hunter Coll., N.Y.C., 1983—; travelling rep. to Hungary and Portugal with exhbn. Am. Paintings in the Eighties, Internat. Comm. Agy., Washington, 1981; resident-in-painting Am. Acad. in Rome, 1990. One-woman shows include Kornblee Gallery, N.Y.C., 1971, 72, 73, Fischbach Gallery, N.Y.C., 1974, 75, 77, Brooke Alexander Gallery, N.Y.C., 1975, Phillips Collection, Washington, 1975, New Gallery, Cleve., 1977, Ctr. Gallery Bucknell U., Lewisburg, Pa., 1978, Droll Kolbert Gallery, N.Y.C., 1978, 80, Ivory Kimpton Gallery, San Francisco, 1981, 84, 88, Van Straten Gallery, Chgo., 1983, Lincoln Ctr. Gallery, N.Y.C., 1983, Cleve. Ctr. for Contemporary Art, 1984, Nina Freudenheim Gallery, Buffalo, N.Y., 1980, 84, Graham Modern, N.Y.C., 1985, 87, 88, 90, Adams Middleton Gallery, Dallas, 1986, Gloria Luria, Bay Harbor Island, Fla., 1987, 88, 90, St. Louis Art Mus., 1994, The Blaffer Gallery- U. Houston, 1994, Univ. Art Mus. U. So. Calif. at Long Beach, 1994, Fed. Reserve Bd., Washington, 1995, Herbert Johnson Mus. Cornell U., Ithaca, N.Y., 1995, Middlebury (Vt.) Coll. Mus. Art, 1995; exhibited in group shows at Whitney Mus. Art, N.Y.C., 1972, 82, Indpls. Mus. Art, 1972, 74, Kent State U., 1972, Art Inst. Chgo., 1972, Corcoran Gallery Art, Washington, 1973, Va. Mus. Fine Arts, 1975, U.S.I.A., 1979, Grey Art Gallery, N.Y.C., 1979, 83, Janie C. Lee Gallery, Houston, 1979, Meml. Art Gallery, U. Rochester, 1980, Bklyn. Mus., 1980, 81, 83, Carnegie Inst., Pitts., 1981, Inst. Contemporary Art, 1981, Am. Acad. Arts and Letters, 1983, 94, Weatherspoon Gallery, Greensboro, N.C., 1984, Columbus (Ga.) Mus. Arts and Sci., 1985, Queens Mus., 1986, Portland (Maine) Mus. Art, 1986, Mus. Fine Arts, Boston, 1986, Cleve. Mus. Art, 1987, Mt. Holyoke Coll. Art Mus., South Hadley, Mass., 1987, Hudson River Mus., 1988, Bowdoin Coll. Mus. Art, Brunswick, Maine, 1992, Denver Art Mus., 1993, 94; poster commn.: Live from Lincoln Ctr., N.Y.C., 1980, Mostly Mozart, 1985, IBM Gallery Aci. & Art, N.Y.C., 1989, Nat. Gallery Art, Washington, 1989, Detroit Inst. Art, 1991, Nat. Mus. Women in the Arts, Washington, 1991, William Proctor Art Gallery, Bard Coll., Annandale-on-Hudson, N.Y., 1992, Bowdoin Coll. Mus. Art, Brunswick, Maine, 1992, Andre Emmerich Gallery, N.Y.C., 1992, Denver Art Mus., 1993, Cleve. Ctr. for Contemporary Art, 1993; represented in permanent collections Albright-Knox Art Gallery, Buffalo, Bklyn. Mus., Mus. Art Carnegie Inst., Pitts., Guggenheim Mus., N.Y.C., Hirshhorn Mus., Washington, Met. Mus. Art, N.Y.C., Phillips Collection, Washington, Cleve. Mus. Art, Libr. Congress, Washington, Denver Mus. Art. Trustee Bennington Coll., 1979-81; active Yaddo Corp., 1986—, bd. dirs., 1991—. Resident grantee Yaddo, 1970, 71, 74-75, 78, MacDowell Colony, 1972, grantee Ingram Merrill Found., 1972; fellow Nat. Endowment for Arts, 1982, 89. Home: 168 W 86th St New York NY 10024-4033

CRIMLISK, JANE THERESE, judicial secretary; b. Boston, Dec. 2, 1945; d. Herbert Leo and Grace Beatrice (McGilvray) C. AS, Aquinas Coll., Newton, Mass., 1968; BA in Sociology cum laude, Boston Coll., 1974; MS in Bus. Edn., Suffolk U., Boston, 1978; MEd in Rehab. Counseling, U. Mass., 1991. Tchr. religious edn., 1965-88, 93—; legal sec. Hale, Sanderson, Byrnes & Morton, Boston, 1968-69; sec. Boston Coll. Law Sch., Chestnut Hill, 1969-74, Life Resources, Inc., Boston, 1974-75; tchr. Archbishop Williams High Sch., Braintree, Mass., 1975-78; exec. sec. Cramer Electronics, Newton, Mass., 1978-79; jud. sec. Com. of Mass. Ct. Systems, Boston, 1979—; tchr. adult edn. Hickox, 1979-88, Aquinas Coll., Milton, 1989—. Vol. counselor Pregnancy Help, Brighton, Mass., 1988-89, 92, Arthur Clark for U.S. Congress campaign, Newton, 1980, Marian Walsh for State Senate campaign, 1992, 94, Mass. Citizens for Life. Mem. Boston Coll. Alumni Assn. (bd. dirs. 1982-84), Boston Coll. Evening Coll. Alumni Assn. (bd. dirs., past pres.), Aquinas Coll. Alumni Assn. Democrat. Roman Catholic. Home: 416 Belgrade Ave Apt 25 West Roxbury MA 02132 Office: Supreme Jud Ct 1300 New Courthouse Boston MA 02108

CRINKLAW, KATHERINE MARY, artist; b. Newman, Calif., Feb. 11, 1959; d. John Joseph and Dorothy Ann (Oliviera) Menezes; m. Jerry Frank Palermo, Sept. 21, 1981 (dec. 1984); children: Jason Palermo; m. Michael John Crinklaw, Feb. 22, 1986; children: Mark, Morgan. Grad. high sch., Gustine, Calif. Self-employed artist Calif., 1977—; vol. art instr. Bonita Elem. Sch., Crows Landing, Calif., 1990-93. Recipient Mayor's award Turlock (Calif.) Art League, 1993. Mem. Ctrl. Calif. Art League (mem. coun. 1991-93, honorable mention award 1992, 93). Republican. Roman Catholic.

CRISCUOLO, WENDY LAURA, lawyer, interior design consultant; b. N.Y.C., Dec. 17, 1949; d. Joseph Andrew and Betty Jane (Jackson) C.; m. John Howard Price, Jr., Sept. 5, 1970 (div. Apr. 1981); m. Ross J. Turner, July 23, 1988. BA with honors in Design, U. Calif., Berkeley, 1973; JD, U. San Francisco, 1982. Space planner GSA, San Francisco, 1973-79; sr. interior designer E. Lew & Assocs., San Francisco, 1979-80; design dir. Beier & Gunderson, Inc., Oakland, Calif., 1980-81; sr. interior designer Environ. Planning and Rsch., San Francisco, 1981-82; interior design cons. Hillsborough, Calif., 1982—; law clk. to Judge Spencer Williams U.S. Dist. Ct., San Francisco, 1983-84; atty. Ciros Investments, Rancho Santa Fe, Calif., 1984—. Author: (with others) Guide to the Laws of Charitable Giving, 3d rev. edit., 1983; staff mem. U. San Francisco Law Rev., 1983. Bd. dirs., v.p. and treas. Marin Citizens for Energy Planning, 1986-89; bd. dirs., pres. Calif. Ctr. for Wildlife, 1987-90; trustee Cayote Point Mus. for Environ. Edn., 1990-93. Mem. ABA, State Bar Calif. Republican. Episcopalian.

CRISMAN, MARY FRANCES BORDEN, librarian; b. Tacoma, Nov. 23, 1919; d. Lindon A. and Mary Cecelia (Donnelly) Borden; m. Fredric Lee Crisman, Apr. 12, 1975 (dec. Dec. 1975). BA in History, U. Wash., 1943, BA in Librarianship, 1944. Asst. br. librarian in charge work with children Mottet br. Tacoma Pub. Libr., 1944-45, br. librarian, 1945-49, br. librarian Moore br., 1950-55, asst. dir., 1955-70, dir., 1970-74, dir. emeritus, 1975—; corp. libr. Frank Russell Co., 1985—; chmn. Wash. Community Library Council, 1970-72. Hostess program Your Library and You, Sta. KTPS-TV, 1969-71. Mem. Highland Homeowners League, Tacoma, 1980—, incorporating dir. 1980, sec. and registered agt., 1980-82. Mem. ALA (chmn. mem. com. Wash. 1957-60, mem. nat. library week com. 1965, chmn. library adminstrn. div. nominating com. 1971, mem. ins. for libraries com. 1970-74, vice chmn. library adminstrn. div. personnel adminstrn. sect. 1972-73, chmn. 1973-74, mem. com. policy implementation 1973-74, mem. library orgn. and mgmt. sect. budgeting acctg. and costs com. 1974-75), Am. Library Trustee Assn. (legis. com. 1975-78, conf. program com. 1978-80, action devel. com. 1978-80), Pacific N.W. (trustee div. nominating com 1976-77), Wash. Library Assn. (exec. bd. 1957-59, state exec., dir. Nat. Library Week 1965, treas., exec. bd. 1969-71, 71-73), Urban Libraries Council (editorial sec. Newsletter 1972-73, exec. com. 1974-75), Ladies Aux. to United Transp. Union (past pres. Tacoma), Friends Tacoma Pub. Library (registered agt. 1975-83, sec. 1975-78, pres. 1978-80, bd. dirs. 1980-83), Smithsonian Assocs., Nat. Railway Hist. Soc., U. Wash. Alumni Assn., U. Wash. Sch. Librarianship Alumni Assn. Roman Catholic. Club: Quota (sec. 1957-58, 1st v.p. 1960-61, pres. 1961-62, treas. 1975-76, pres. 1979-80) (Tacoma). Home: 6501 N Burning Tree Ln Tacoma WA 98406-2108 Office: Frank Russell Co Russell Bldg 909 S A St Tacoma WA 98402-5120

CRISMOND, LINDA FRY, association executive; b. Burbank, Calif., Mar. 1, 1943; d. Billy Chapin and Lois (Harding) Fry; m. Donald Burleigh Crismond, 1965 (dec.). B.S., U. Calif.-Santa Barbara, 1964; M.L.S., U. Calif.-Berkeley, 1965. Cert. county libr., Calif., assn. exec. Reference librarian, EDP coordinator San Francisco Pub. Library, 1965-72, head acquisition, 1972-74; asst. univ. librarian U. So. Calif., Los Angeles, 1974-80; chief dep. county librarian Los Angeles County Pub. Library, Los Angeles, 1980-81; county librarian Los Angeles County Pub. Library, Downey, 1981-89; exec. dir ALA, Chgo., 1989-92; v.p. public rels. Profl. Media Svc. Corp., Chgo., 1992—; Western rep. quality control council Ohio Coll. Library Ctr., Columbus, 1977-80; mem. Am. Nat. Standards Inst., N.Y.C., 1978-80; bd. councillors U. So. Calif. Sch. Library and Info. Mgmt., 1980-83; adv. bd. mem. UCLA Library Sch., 1981-89; chmn. bd. dirs. Los Angeles County Pub. Library Found., 1982-85; mem. OCLC Users Coun., 1988-89; mem. exec. com. L.A. County Mgmt. Coun., 1986-88, pres., 1988. Author: Directory of San Francisco Bay Area, 1968, Against All Odds, 1994; editor: Urban Librs. Coun. Exch., 1994—. Bd. dirs. So. Meth. U. Libr., 1992—. Named Staff Mem. of Year San Francisco Pub. Library, 1968. Mem. ALA, Calif. Library Assn. (council 1980-82), Calif. County Librarians Assn. (pres. 1984), L.A. County Mgmt. Assn. (pres. 1988). Home: 1350 Riverside Ave Tarpin Springs FL 34689 Office: Profl Media Svc Corp 19122 Vermont Ave Gardenia CA 90248

CRISP, POLLY LENORE, psychologist; b. Atlanta, May 20, 1952; d. John Pershing and Dorotha Amelia (Hogan) C. BA, U. Tenn., 1976; MA, Mich. State U., 1981, PhD, 1984. Psychotherapist Arbours Ctr., London, 1983-85; clin. psychologist Kennebec Valley Mental Health Ctr., Augusta, Maine, 1987-90, Overlook Mental Health Ctr., Maryville, Tenn., 1990—. Contbr. articles to profl. publs. Mem. APA (membership com. div. clin. psychology 1990—), Brit. Psychol. Soc., Soc. Psychotherapy Rsch., N.Y. Acad. Scis., Phi Beta Kappa, Phi Kappa Phi, Alpha Lambda Delta. Office: Overlook Mental Health 219 Court St Maryville TN 37801-4908

CRISPI, MICHELE MARIE, lawyer; b. Neptune, N.J., Mar. 10, 1962; d. Michael and Mary (Vaccaro) C.; m. Lawrence J. Moloney. BS in Accountancy magna cum laude, Villanova U., 1984, JD, 1987, LLM in Taxation, 1989. Bar: N.J. 1988, U.S. Dist. Ct. N.J. 1988, D.C. 1989, U.S. Tax Ct. 1989. Assoc. Lampf, Lipkind, Prupis & Petigrow, West Orange, N.J., 1987-88, Lautman, Henderson & Wight, Manasquan, N.J., 1990—. Mem. ABA (bus. law, real property, probate and trust law, taxation sects.), N.J. State Bar Assn. (corp. and bus. law, real property, probate and trust law and taxation sects.), D.C. Bar Assn. (taxation sect.), Monmouth County Bar Assn., Phi Kappa Phi, Beta Gamma Sigma, Gamma Phi. Republican. Roman Catholic. Home: 32 Hunters Pointe Rd North Middletown NJ 07734-2290 Office: Lautman Henderson & Wight 52 Abe Voorhees Dr Manasquan NJ 08736-3545

CRISPIN, MILDRED SWIFT (MRS. FREDERICK EATON CRISPIN), civic worker, writer; b. Branson, Mo.; d. Albert Duane and Anna (Harlan) Swift; m. Herbert William Kochs, Dec. 1, 1928 (div. Mar. 1955); children: Susan Kochs Judevine (dec.), Herbert William Jr., Judith Ann (Mrs. Nelson Shaw); m. George Walter King Snyder, Oct. 6, 1962 (dec. 1969); m. Frederick Eaton Crispin, May 20, 1972. Student, Galloway Woman's Coll., 1922-24. Bd. dirs. Travelers Aid Soc., Chgo., 1936-68, nat. dir., 1948-71; founding mem. U.S.O., Chgo., 1944-65, nat. dir., 1951-57; bd. dirs. John Howard Assn., 1958-67, Community Fund Chgo., 1950-56, Welfare Coun. Met. Chgo., 1950-56; chmn. woman's div. Crusade of Mercy, Chgo., 1964. Mem. U.S. Women's Curling Assn. (co-founder 1947, pres. 1950, founder Indian Hill Women's Curling Club, Winnetka, Ill., 1945, chmn. 1945-46), DAR, Daus. Am. Colonists, Town and Country Arts Club (pres. 1957-58, Chgo., Woman's Athletic Club Chgo., Everglades Club (Palm Beach, Fla.), Venice (Fla.) Yacht Club, Coral Ridge Yacht Club (Ft. Lauderdale, Fla.). Republican. Methodist. Home: 560 N Casey Key Rd PO Box 1098 Osprey FL 34229-1098

CRIST, JOSEPHINE C. (JODY CRIST), paramedic; b. Seattle, Mar. 27, 1962; d. James Lawrence and Marie Ann (Mullally) C. AA, Shoreline C.C., Seattle, 1983; cert. emergency med. tech., North Seattle C.C., 1986. Cert. paramedic., CPR instr., basic life support instr. Emergency med. tech. Shepard Ambulance, Seattle, 1986-91, paramedic, 1991—. Paramedic disaster relief Seattle King County Disaster Team, 1994. Mem. Internat. Assn. Firefighters (paramedic), Nat. Registry Emergency Med. Techs. Home: PO Box 1022 241 S Rainier St Buckley WA 98321-1022 Office: King County Medic One 7064 S 220th St Bldg 9 Kent WA 98032-1910

CRIST, JUDITH, film and drama critic; b. N.Y.C., May 22, 1922; d. Solomon and Helen (Schoenberg) Klein; m. William B. Crist, July 3, 1947 (dec. Apr. 1993); 1 son, Steven Gordon. A.B., Hunter Coll., 1941; teaching fellow, State Coll. Wash., 1942-43; M.Sc. in Journalism, Columbia, 1945; DHL (hon.), SUNY, New Paltz, 1994. Civilian instr. 3081st Army AFB Unit, 1943-44; reporter N.Y. Herald Tribune, 1945-60, editor arts, 1960-63, assoc. theater critic, 1957-63, film critic, 1963-66; film, theater critic NBC-TV Today Show, 1963-73; film critic World Jour. Tribune, 1966-67; critic-at-large Ladies Home Jour., 1966-67; contbg. editor and film critic TV Guide, 1966-88; film critic N.Y. mag., 1968-75, The Washingtonian, 1970-72, Palm Springs Life, 1971-75; contbg. editor, film critic Saturday Rev., 1975-77, 80-84, N.Y. Post, 1977-78, MD/Mrs., 1977—, 50 Plus, 1978-83, L'Officiel/USA, 1979-80; arts critic Sta. WWOR-TV Channel 9 News, 1981-87; critical columnist for Coming Attractions, 1985-93; cons. editor Hollywood Mag., 1985-93; contbg. editor Columbia Mag., 1993—; instr. journalism Hunter Coll., 1947, Sarah Lawrence Coll., 1958-59; assoc. journalism Columbia Grad. Sch. Journalism, 1959-62, lectr. journalism, 1962-64, adj. prof., 1964—. Author: The Private Eye, The Cowboy and the Very Naked Girl, 1968, Judith Crist's TV Guide to the Movies, 1974, Take 22: Moviemakers on Moviemaking, 1984, rev. edit., 1991; contbr. articles to nat. mags. Trustee Anne O'Hare McCormick Scholarship Fund. Recipient Page One award N.Y. Newspaper Guild, 1955; George Polk award, 1961; N.Y. Newspaper Women's Club award, 1955, 59, 63, 65, 67; Edn. Writers Assn. award, 1952; Columbia Grad. Sch. Journalism Alumni award, 1961; named to 50th Anniversary Honors List, 1963; Centennial Pres.'s medal Hunter Coll., 1970; named to Hunter Alumni Hall of Fame, 1973. Mem. Columbia Journalism Alumni (pres. 1967-70), N.Y. Film Critics Circle, Nat. Soc. Film Critics., Sigma Tau Delta. Office: 180 Riverside Dr New York NY 10024-1052

CRIST, MARY JANE, fundraising executive; b. Hobbs, N.Mex., Sept. 19, 1946; d. Robert Elliott and Jane Elizabeth (Murray) Jackson; m. Warren Anderson Crist, Sept. 28, 1973. BS, U. Ariz., 1968; MS, Ind. U., 1969. Asst. fgn. student advisor U. Ariz., Tucson, 1969-71, asst. dean of students, 1971-79, asst. dir. admissions, 1979-85; v.p. pub. affairs Tempe (Ariz.) St. Luke's Hosp., 1985-89; exec. dir. St. Luke's Found., Phoenix, 1989—. Mem. Leadership Am., allocations panel Valley of the Sun United Way, Valley Leadership Phoenix, 1981—; bd. dirs. Cancer Resource Network, Tempe Ctr. for Habilitation, 1988—. Mem. Assn. for Healthcare Philanthropy, Nat. Soc. Fund Raising Execs., Ariz. Hosp. Assn. (govt. rels. coun.), Kappa Kappa Gamma (devel. com.). Republican. Presbyterian. Office: St Lukes Found 1800 E Van Buren St Phoenix AZ 85006-3702

CRISWELL, KIMBERLY ANN, public relations executive, dancer; b. L.A., Dec. 6, 1957; d. Robert Burton and Carolyn Joyce (Semko) C. BA with honors, U. Calif.-Santa Cruz, 1980; postgrad. Stanford U., 1993—. Instr., English Lang. Services, Oakland, Calif., 1980-81; freelance writer Verbum mag., San Diego, Gambit mag., New Orleans, 1981; instr. Tulane U., New Orleans, 1981; instr., editor Haitian-English Lang. Program, New Orleans, 1981-82; instr. Delgado Coll., New Orleans, 1982-83; instr., program coord. Vietnamese Youth Ctr., San Francisco, 1984; dancer Khadra Internat. Folk Ballet, San Francisco, 1984-89; dir. mktg. comm. Centram Systems West, Inc., Berkeley, Calif., 1984-87; comm. coord. Safeway Stores, Inc., Oakland, 1985; dir. corp. comm. TOPS, div. Sun Microsystems, Inc, 1987-88; pres. Criswell Comm., 1988—. Vol. coord. Friends of Haitians, 1981, editor, writer newsletter, 1981; dancer Komenka Ethnic Dance Ensemble, New Orleans, 1983; mem. Contemp. Art Ctr.'s Krewe of Clones, New Orleans, 1983, Americans for Nonsmokers Rights, Berkeley, 1985; active San Francisco Multimedia Developers Group, Artspan. Mem. NAFE, Internat. Assn. Bus. Communicators, Sci. Meets the Arts Soc. (founding), Dance Action, Bay Area Dance Coalition, Oakland Mus. Assn., Mus. Soc., Commonwealth Club. Democrat. Avocations: visual arts, travel, creative writing.

CRITCHLOW, SUSAN MELISSA, public relations executive, advertising and printing consultant; b. Gainesville, Fla., Dec. 24, 1950; d. James Carlton and Mildred Estelle (Pringle) Barley; m. Warren Hartzell Critchlow, Jr., Aug. 18, 1973, 1 child, Suzanne Michele. BA, U. South Fla., 1972, MA in Speech Communication with honors, 1973. Asst. dir. pub. relations Goodwill Industries of N. Fla., Inc., 1973-74; dir. pub. relations St. Luke's Hosp., Jacksonville, Fla., 1974; dir. informational services Greater Orange Park Community Hosp., Orange Park, Fla., 1974-82; pres. Susan Critchlow & Assocs., New Home Life Pub., Inc.; CEO, SC&A Pub. Co., Inc., Orange Park, 1976—. Mem. bd. dirs. Children's Haven. Named N.E. Fla. Bus. Communicator of Month, 1975, 78, Outstanding Young Woman of Am. Charter mem. pub. rels. adv. coun. Coll. Journalism and Communications U. Fla., 1978-81. Mem. Fla. Hosp. Assn. (bd. dirs. pub. rels. coun. 1976-78, Gold award 1975, Silver award 1976, 78), Jacksonville Hosp. Pub. Rels. Coun. (chmn. 1975-77), Fla. Pub. Rels. Assn. (Golden Image award 1975-86), Pub. Rels. Soc. Am., Nat. Assn. Builders, Fla. Home Builders Assn. (sold award 1991), N.E. Fla. Home Builders Assn. (sales and mktg. coun.), Jacksonville Advt. Fedn. (Addy award 1982-93). Republican. Episcopalian. Office: 179 Wells Rd Orange Park FL 32073-3057

CRITTENDEN, ANN, author, lecturer; b. Dallas, Sept. 1, 1937; d. Norman Wirt and Mary Nell (O'Banion) C.; m. Michael Ruby, Aug. 1974 (div. Oct. 1978); m. John B. Henry, Jan. 30, 1982; 1 child, James Crittenden Henry. BA, So. Meth. U., 1959, MA, 1962; M in Internat. Affairs, Columbia U., 1967, postgrad. studies in History, 1963-66. Lectr. So. Meth. U., Dallas, 1960-62, Rutgers U., New Brunswick, N.J., 1964-65; reporter Fortune Magazine, N.Y.C., 1967-71; fin. writer, assoc. editor Newsweek, N.Y.C., 1971-72; fgn. corr. Newsweek, Asia, S. Am., 1972-74; writer, reporter N.Y. Times, 1975-83; project dir. Aspen Inst., Washington, 1984-85; exec. dir. Fund for Investigative Reporting, Washington, 1987-88; author, lectr. Washington, 1988—. Author: Sanctuary, 1988 (N.Y. Times Notable Books of Yr. 1988), Killing the Sacred Cows, 1993. Mem. U.S. Com. on UNICEF. Recipient award Newspaperwomen's Club 1972, 75, Page 1 award Newspaper Guild, 1977, Champion Media award, World Hunger Media award, 1982, N.Y. Deadline Club award 1978. Mem. Coun. on Fgn. Rels., Am. Rivers (bd. dirs. 1993—), Internat. Ctr. for Rsch. on Women (bd. dirs. 1993—), Phi Beta Kappa. Home and Office: 3412 Lowell St NW Washington DC 20016

CRITTENDEN, KATHERINE LUCINA, nurse; b. Newport News, Va., Aug. 16, 1957; d. James Tyler III and Lucina Nan (Titlow) C. Diploma,

York Acad., 1975; student, Longwood Coll., 1975-78; Assocs., John Tyler C.C., 1984. RN, Va., Wis.; cert. ACLS, Am. Heart Assn., Trauma Nursing Care. Nurse Med. Coll. Va., Richmond, 1985-94, Rappahannock Gen. Hosp., Kilmarnock, Va., 1994—. Vol. nurse No. Neck Free Clinic, Lancaster, Va., 1994. Mem. Jamestown Soc., Va. Nurses Assn. Mem. Philippi Christian Ch. Home: Box 581 Deltaville VA 23043

CRITTENDEN, MARY LYNNE, science educator; b. Detroit, Oct. 27, 1951; d. William and Marie (Ryall) C. BS, Wayne State U., 1974; MS, U. Detroit, 1984. Tchr. sci. Detroit Bd. Edn., 1974-77, Highland Park (Mich.) C.C., 1980—; faculty researcher Air Force program Wright Patterson AFB, Dayton, Ohio, 1991; speaker Mich. Ednl. Occupational Assn., 1989, Liberal Arts Network Devel., Lansing, Mich., 1990. Author ednl. materials; contbr. to profl. publs. Mem. AAAS, Am. Chem. Soc. (outreach program 1992—), Civic Ctr. Optimist Club (bd. dirs. 1991—, coord. scis. 1990—), Mich. C.C. Biologists. Home: 15386 Alden St Detroit MI 48238-2104 Office: Highland Park C C Glendale at 3rd Highland Park MI 48203

CRITTENDEN, MARY RITA, clinical psychology educator; b. Binghamton, N.Y., Apr. 6, 1928; d. John Patrick and Anna Elizabeth (Griffin) Saxton; m. Rodney Whitman Crittenden, Aug. 6, 1955; children: John Whitman, Anne Catherine, Jean Patricia. BA, Cornell U., 1950; MA, Mills Coll., Oakland, Calif., 1952; PhD, Calif. Sch. Profl. Psychology, San Francisco, 1977. Cert. Nat. Sch. Psychologist; lic. clin. psychologist, ednl. psychologist, Calif. Psychologist numerous schs., N.Y., Calif., 1953-67; chief psychologist, clin. prof. dept. pediatrics U. Calif., San Francisco, 1977—; lectr. Coll. Notre Dame, Belmont, Calif., 1963-66; bd. dirs. mem. Great Adventures Through Edn., San Francisco, 1981-92. Author book chpts. in profl. jours.; contbg. editor Jour. Soc. Pediatric Psychology, 1974-80. Mem. bd. dirs. San Francisco Assn. for Gifted and Talented, 1972-81. Mills Coll. fellow, 1950-52; grantee U. Calif. San Francisco Acad. Senate, 1981. Mem. APA, NASP, Nat. Acad. Neuropsychology, Western Psychology Assn., Calif. Assn. Sch. Psychologists, Calif. Psychology Assn., Soc. Behavioral Pediatrics. Roman Catholic. Office: U Calif Dept Pediatrics A-203 Box 0314 400 Parnassus San Francisco CA 94143

CRITTENDEN, PEGGY JOYCE, communications executive; b. Hubbard, Tex., July 31, 1930; d. William Frank and Stella Arabella (Kay) Kidd; m. John Rousseau Crittenden, Jr., May 7, 1955 (dec. Oct. 1961); 1 child, John Max. Student, Baylor U., Navarro Jr. Coll., East Tex. State; BS with teaching cert., Sam Houston State U., 1961. Cert. profl. secondary tchr. News and sports editor Navasota (Tex.) Examiner Review, 1951-56; tchr. Navasota High Sch., 1961-64, 66-74, Freeport (Tex.) Jr. High Sch., 1964-66; dir. pub. info. College Station (Tex.) Ind. Sch. Dist., 1974-95; editor newsletter Keeping in Touch, 1995—; dir. high sch. journalism workshop Tex. A&M U., College Station. Mem. Tex. Sch. Pub. Rels. Assn. (numerous awards), Kappa Gamma (chair com.). Baptist. Home: 1803 Laura Ln College Station TX 77840 Office: College Station Ind Sch Dist 1812 Welsh College Station TX 77840

CRITTENDEN, SOPHIE MARIE, communications executive; b. Mansfield, Ohio, Apr. 14, 1926; d. Joseph S. and Mary Ellen (Hagerman) Wojcik; m. Robert Eugene Crittenden, Aug. 24, 1946 (dec. 1987); children: Robert J., Mark A., Christopher E., Laura Ann. Student, Coll. St. Francis, 1944-45, Ohio U., 1945-46, North Cen. Tech. Coll., 1976-78. Substitute tchr. Mansfield City Schs., 1956-62; lab. technician The Ohio Brass Co., Mansfield, 1962-68, draftsman, 1968, mgr. internal publs., 1969-78, mgr. advt., 1978-83, mgr. communications, 1983-88; cons. communications EFE N.Am., Inc., Mansfield, 1989-90; account coord. D & S Creative Advt., Inc., Mansfield, 1990—. Creator and shower of quilts. Com. chmn. United Way Campaign, Mansfield and Richland, Ohio, 1978; pub. relations chmn. Tribute to Women and Industry Project, Mansfield, 1986 (award 1985). Named Mrs. Mansfield Mrs. Am. Contest, 1961. Mem. Mktg. Club North Cen. Ohio (bd. dirs., sec. 1987-90), Altrusa (pres. 1976, internat. chmn. mktg. and pub. rels. 1991-93). Republican. Roman Catholic. Home: 84 Wildwood Dr Mansfield OH 44907-1621 Office: 140 Park Ave E Mansfield OH 44902-1830

CROASDALE, NORMA RUTH, city clerk; b. Vandalia, Ill., Sept. 3, 1938; d. Louis Edward and Agnes Catherine (Durbin) Grubaugh; m. Delbert Dewayne Cearlock May 20, 1955 (dec. Dec. 1978); children: David Luke, Dorothy Ann, Delbert Dewayne II; m. Frank Edmond Croasdale, Jan. 8, 1993. City clerk City of Vandalia, 1985—. Mem. Vandalia Bus. & Profl. Women (sec. 1985-86, pres. 1991-92), Vandalia Cameo Women's Club (treas. 1994—), Women of the Moose. Democrat. Roman Catholic. Office: City of Vandalia 219 S 5th St Vandalia IL 62471

CROCE, ANNE LALLY, nurse, commissioner; b. Staten Island, N.Y., Mar. 7, 1926; d. Austin and Anne (McStravick) Lally; m. James P. Croce Jr., June 9, 1951; children: Patricia L. Balcom, James Peter III, Kathleen Kampmann. Diploma, Bayonne Hosp. Sch. Nursing, 1949; postgrad., Polyclinic Med. Sch. and Hosp., 1950, Osaka (Japan) U., 1951. Sch. nurse Friends Acad., Long Island, N.Y.; pub. sch. nurse, day care nurse Roslyn Pub. Schs., L.I.; sch., camp nurse Doug Pierce/Price County Day Sch., L.I.; commr., ombudsman Town of North Hempstead, Manhasset, N.Y., 1989—; pub. educator on blood pressure, CPR, diet; featured on local TV and in local newspaper. Bd. dirs. Roslyn Little League (Women of the Year award), Community Mammography and Breast Cancer Screening, Local Emergencies Planning Com., SARA III Program, Community Plus Program for Srs., Free Flu Shots Program; liason Town North Hempstead Civic Assn., Martin Luther King Edn., L.I. Heart Coun. (Gold Madalion award). Recipient Women of the Year award Roslyn Rotary Club., Roslyn Kiwanis Club. Mem. N.A.A.C.P. Office: Town North Hempstead 220 Plandome Rd Manhasset NY 11030-2327

CROCE, ARLENE LOUISE, critic; b. Providence, May 5, 1934; d. Michael Daniel and Louise Natalie (Pensa) C. Student, Women's Coll., U. N.C., 1951-53; BA, Barnard Coll., 1955. Founder, editor Ballet Rev., 1965-78; dance critic New Yorker mag., 1973—; dance panelist Nat. Endowment for Arts, 1977-80. Author: The Fred Astaire & Ginger Rogers Book, 1972, Afterimages, 1977, Going to the Dance, 1982, Sight Lines, 1987. Recipient AAAL award 1979, award of Honor for Arts and Culture Mayor N.Y.C., 1979, Janeway prize Barnard Coll., 1955; Hodder fellow Princeton U., 1971; Guggenheim fellow, 1972, 86, NEH fellow 1992. Fellow AAAS. Office: New Yorker Mag 20 W 43rd St New York NY 10036-7400

CROCKER, JANE LOPES, library director; b. Mass., Sept. 19, 1946; d. Joseph Barros and Mary (Faria) Lopes; m. Lowell Steven Crocker, Feb. 14, 1976; children: Susan J., Jennifer L., Jacqueline M. BA in English, Bridgewater State Coll., 1968; MS in Libr. Sci., Simmons Coll., 1971. Cert. libr., Mass.; cert. secondary edn. tchr., Mass. Libr. New Bedford (Mass.) Pub. Libr., 1968-71; pub. svcs. libr. Simmons Coll. Libr., Boston, 1971-73; head libr. Boston City Hosp., 1973-76; libr. dir. Gloucester County Coll., Deptford, N.J., 1976—; pres. Libr. Network Rev. Bd., 1994—. Editor Bay State Libr., 1974-76; contbg. author: Reference and Information Service, 1978, N.J. Libraries, 1984, 89-90, 94. Recipient Ray Murray award N.J. Assn. Libr. Assts., 1991. Mem. ALA, N.J. Libr. Assn. (pres.-elect 1991-92, pres. 1992-93), South Jersey Regional Libr. Coop. (pres. 1988-90, Resolution of Appreciation award 1990, Pres.'s award 1993). Roman Catholic. Office: Gloucester County Coll Tanyard Rd RR 4 Box 203 Sewell NJ 08080

CROCKETT, NORMA DREIFKE, psychologist, medical psychotherapist; b. Apr. 25, 1916; m. James L. Crockett; children: David B. Menkes, Antonia Reed Schappert. BS in Spl. Edn., Washington U., St. Louis, 1938; MA in Clin. Psychology, La. State U., 1944; postgrad., Stanford U., 1956-57. Lic. psychologist, Calif.; cert. med. psychotherapist, sex educator. Speech therapist Ctrl. Inst. for Deaf, St. Louis, 1938-39; dir. Speech Ctr., New Orleans, 1940-44; counselor U. Calif., Berkeley, 1947-49, 53, 69; psychologist Calif. Dept. Mental Health, San Francisco, 1944-47; sr. counselor, psychologist Stanford U., Palo Alto, Calif., 1956-68; psychologist, dir. Growth Ctr. San Jose (Calif.) C.C., 1970-76; dir. Counselling and Consulting Ctr., Palo Alto, 1977-84; pvt. practice Tucson and Green Valley, Ariz., 1985—. Support group facilitator, vol. Tucson AIDS Project, 1985—; pres. Lupus Assn. So. Ariz., Tucson, 1985-86, Tucson Coun. Internat. Visitors, 1988-90. Mem. APA. Home: 1870 N Curva Pasto Green Valley AZ 85614-4145 Office: 1870 N Curva Pasto Green Valley AZ 85614-4145

CROCKETT, PHYLLIS DARLENE, communications executive; b. Chgo., July 14, 1950; d. Leo F. Crockett and Mae (Corbin) Williams; divorced; 1 child, Adina Darlene Gittens. BA, U. Ill., Chgo., 1972; MS in Journalism, Northwestern U., 1979. Free-lance reporter AP and UPI, Raleigh and Durham, N.C., 1978-80; news writer Sta. WTTG-TV, Washington, 1981-82; free-lance writer Pacific News Svc., San Francisco, 1984; producer, reporter, anchorperson Sta. WSOC, Charlotte, N.C., 1978-79, Stas. WFNC/WQSM, Fayetteville, N.C., 1979-80; exec. editor, talk show moderator Sheridan Broadcasting Network, Washington, 1980-81; reporter gen. assignments Nat. Pub. Radio, Washington, 1981-89, White House corr., 1989-91, sr. corr., 1991-94; pres. Crockett Chronicle Communications, Johannesburg, South Africa, 1994—; panelist CNN & Co., CNN's Internat. Corrs., CNN's Inside Politics, 1992—, CNN's Both Sides with Jesse Jackson, Am.'s Black Forum, Washington, 1980-83; analyst C-Span Cable TV Network, Black Entertainment TV, Washington and Sta. WHMM-TV, Washington, 1987—; correspondent Pacifica Standard Radio News Network, others; cons. Clark-Atlanta U., others, 1982-94; vis. instr. Fayetteville State U., 1980, Johnson C. Smith U., Charlotte, 1979; guest lectr. Howard U., U. D.C., Fairfax (Va.) Pub. Schs., 1980-94; media cons. South African Broadcasting Co., Radio 702, others. Contbg. author: Split Image: African-Americans in the Mass Media, 1990, 93; contbr. book reviews to N.Y. Times, 1988, 92, L.A. Times, 1989, Washington Post, 1994; publisher The Crockett Chronicle. John S. Knight fellow Stanford U., 1990-91; recipient NEA award, 1988, Robert F. Kennedy award, 1990. Mem. Nat. Assn. Black Journalists (Frederick Douglass award 1984), Washington Assn. Black Journalists (v.p. 1982), Sigma Delta Chi. Baptist. Office: care Squire Padgett 1835 K St NW Ste 900 Washington DC 20006 also: PO Box 3257 Parklands, Johannesburg 2121, South Africa

CROCKETT, SYLVIA CARR, college program director; b. Pineville, N.C., June 9, 1939; d. Wallace Odie Carr and Doris Ada (Beam) DePriest; m. Lewis James Johnson, Apr. 14, 1960 (div. Dec. 1968); children: James Scott, Thomas Neal; m. Charles Richard Crockett, Dec. 7, 1972; 1 child: Matthew Carr. BA, U. Ark., 1972. Tchr. Town & Country Sch., Adelphia, Md., 1959-60; tchr. kindergarten show KATV-Channel 7, Little Rock, 1960-62; tchr. Eureka Springs (Ark.) Elem. Sch., 1962-66; educator, program coord. Ark. Enterprises for the Blind, Little Rock, 1973-75; program coord. Pulaski Tech. Coll., North Little Rock, 1975—; cons., presenter True Colors personality profiles, Little Rock, 1993; seminar spkr. Com. on Women's Concerns, Little Rock, 1993; workshop presenter Am. Coll. Personnel Assn., Little Rock, 1993. Devel., cons. Youthbuild, 1993; liaison Women in Constrn., 1993; county coord. March of Dimes, Eureka Springs, 1963; treas., spkr. Women's Aglow, Little Rock, 1973. Mem. Nat. Displaced Homemaker Network (state rep.), AAUW, Am. Vocat. Assn., Am. Counseling Assn., Ark. Soc. Tng. Devel. (program coord. 1992). Democrat. Office: Career Devel Ctr Single Parent Program 2020 W 3rd St Ste 520 Little Rock AR 72205-4466

CROCKETT-BLASSINGAME, LINDA KATHLEEN, artist, illustrator; b. Slater, S.C., June 14, 1948; d. Robert Roy and Karrie Mae (Cobb) Crockett; m. Steven Robert Blassingame, Oct. 12, 1985. Student, Cleve. Inst. Art, 1966-67; studies with B. Fuchs, B. Peak & others, Illustrator's Workshop Studies, N.Y., 1978. Fashion designer Cleve., 1967-69; artist Am. Greetings, Cleve., 1968-71; creative coordinator/stylist CPS Industries, Franklin, Tenn., 1985-87; illustrator/owner Crickett Studio, Euclid, Ohio, 1971—, Twelvetrees Studio, Euclid, 1993—; cons. in field; lectr. in field. Illustrator: Bologna Children's Book Fair Anns., 1979, 80, 81, Communication Arts Art Ann., 1982, World Wildlife Fund, Greenpeace, (children's picture book) See the Ocean, 1994, nat. mags., motion picture posters, children's books, and many others; exhibited in group shows Master Eagle Gallery. Recipient Cooperstown Art Assn. Painting award, 1979, Cleve. Press Club award for Excellence in Illustration, 1981, spl. painting award Cleve. Mus. Art., 1982, painting awards Scarab Club, Detroit, 1980, 81, and others. Mem. Nat. Mus. Women in the Arts, Soc. Illustrators (Gold medals 1982, one-woman show 1983), New Orgn. Visual Arts, Soc. Children's Book Writers and Illustrators, Cleve. Mus. Art, Butler Inst. Art. Address: 23336 Williams Ave Euclid OH 44123-1525

CROFT, BARBARA YODER, medical educator; b. Port Chester, N.Y., Aug. 11, 1940; d. Paul Henry Yoder and Harriet French (Postle) McBride; m. Joseph Edward Croft, Dec. 15, 1977 (dec. 1988); m. Jerry Porter, Oct. 15, 1989. BS, Swarthmore Coll., 1962; MS, Johns Hopkins U., 1964, PhD, 1967. Sr. scientist Johnston Labs., Inc., Balt., 1967-68; programmer U. Va., Charlottesville, 1968, instr. dept. radiology, 1969-72, asst. prof. dept. radiology, 1972-87, assoc. prof. dept. radiology, 1987—; rsch. assoc. Oak Ridge (Tenn.) Associated Univs., 1972; vis. scholar U. N.Mex., Albuquerque, 1975. Co-author: Basics of Radiopharmacy, 1974; author: Single Photon Emission Computed Tomography, 1986. Fellow Am. Coll. Nuclear Physicians; mem. AAAS, AAUP, Am. Chem. Soc., Am. Coll. Radiology, Soc. Nuclear Medicine (pres. 1988-89). Democrat. Episcopalian. Office: U Va PO Box 170 Charlottesville VA 22908-0170

CROMBIE, PAMELA GASPARIN, import and export company executive; b. Springfield, Ill., Jan. 22, 1949; d. Stephen Lewis and Rita Imogene (Donaldson) Gasparin; m. Frank Czech, Dec. 26, 1970 (div. 1974); 1 child, Kimberly; m. John Moncrieff Crombie, Sept. 15, 1979; 1 child, Katherine. AA, Springfield (Ill.) Coll., 1969; BS, So. Ill. U., 1973; postgrad., U. Ill., 1976-79. Cert. appraiser, New Eng. Ins. investigator Equifax, Chgo., 1973-79; pres. Internat. Antiques, Chgo., 1980—; v.p. Moncrieff Enterprises, Chgo., 1989—; ptnr., owner Mid-Atlantic Properties, Chgo., 1991—; appraisals cons. Internat. Art and Antiques Ctr., Chgo., 1991—; antiques expert guest Oprah Winfrey Show, 1994. Co-chair, commr. Chgo. Spl. Svcs. Area # 8, 1989-92; election judge, 1994—. Mem. ACLU, Citizens Utility Bd., NOW, Greenpeace, Lakeview C. of C. Office: Internat Art & Antique Ctr 2300 W Diversey Ave Chicago IL 60647-2107

CROMER, MARY JOAN, community services director; b. Scottsbluff, Nebr., Aug. 21, 1932; d. Miltetus H. and Lillian V. (Yount) Ouderkirk; m. John Dale Cromer, June 19, 1953; children: Bradley Allen, Gregory D., Karen Kay Cromer Johnson. BS in Home Econ., Colo. State U., 1953; MSW, U. Nebr., Omaha, 1981. cert. social worker. High sch. instr. Mitchell (Nebr.) City Schs., 1953-56; substitute talk show host Sta. KSTF-TV, Scottsbluff, 1960-67; pre-sch. dir. Gering, Nebr., 1962-67; head start tchr. Panhandle Community Svcs., Gering, 1967-68, head start dir., 1968-73, dir. child and family devel. programs, 1973-81, exec. dir., 1981—; bd. dirs. Panhandle Mediation, Inc., YMCA; early childhood cons. Regions VII and VIII, Kansas City, Mo., 1970-78; evaluator and workshop presenter Office Child Devel. Health Human Svcs., Denver, 1970-78; early childhood adj. tchr. Western Nebr. C.C., Scottsbluff, 1980-90; social work adj. prof. Kearney (Nebr.) State Coll., 1986-87; with Scotts Bluff Co. Family Preservation Project, 1986—, pres. 1991-92; mem. Gov.'s Task Force on Homelessness. Adv. bd. Scottsbluff County Extension Svc., 1963-66; bd. dirs. United Way, Scottsbluff/Gering, 1985-90, Panhandle Substance Abuse Coun., Scottsbluff, 1985-90. Named Outstanding Nebr. 4-H alumnus Coop. Extension Svc., Lincoln, 1962, Lady of Yr., Beta Sigma Phi, Scottsbluff, 1981. Mem. Nat. Assn. Edn. Young Children, Assn. Nebr. Community Action Agys. (chair 1987, 89), Soroptimists Internat. (gov. Rocky Mt. region 1990-92), YMCA (bd. mem. 1990-93), C. of C. (health and human svc. subcom. 1991). Protestant. Home: 160750 Carter Canyon Rd Gering NE 69341-9530 Office: Panhandle Community Svcs 3350 10th St Gering NE 69341-1700

CROMWELL, ADELAIDE M., sociology educator; b. Washington, Nov. 27, 1919; d. John Wesley, Jr. and Yetta Elizabeth (Mavritte) C.; 1 son, Anthony C. Hill. AB, Smith Coll., 1940; MA, U. Pa., 1941; cert. social work, Bryn Mawr Coll., 1943; PhD, Radcliffe Coll., 1952; LHD (hon.), U. Southwestern Mass., 1972, George Washington U., 1989. Mem. faculty Hunter Coll., 1942-44, Smith Coll., 1945-46; mem. faculty Boston U., 1951-85, prof. sociology, 1971-85, dir. Afro-Am. studies, 1969-88, prof. emerita sociology, 1985—; mem. adv. com. vol. fgn. aid AID, 1964-80; mem. NEH, 1968-70; adv. com. corrections Commonwealth Mass., 1955-68; mem. commn. instns. higher edn., 1973-74; adv. com. to dir. IRS, 1970-71, to dir. census, 1972-75. Bd. dirs. Wheelock Coll., 1971—74, Nat. Ctr. Afro-Am. Artists, 1971-80, African Am. Scholars Coun., 1971—, Nat. Fellowship Fund, 1974-75, Mass. Hist. Commn., 1993; bd. dirs. Sci. and Tech. for Internat. Devel., 1984-86; mem. exec. com. Am. Soc. African Culture, 1967. Mem. AAAS, African Studies Assn. (bd. dir. 1966-68), Am. Acad. of Arts and Scis., Am. Sociol. Assn., Council on Fgn. Affairs (bd. fgn. scholarships 1980-84), Phi Beta Kappa. Home: 51 Addington Rd Brookline MA 02146-4519 Office: Boston U 138 Mountfort St Brookline MA 02146-4083

CROMWELL, FLORENCE STEVENS, occupational therapist; b. Lewistown, Pa., May 14, 1922; d. William Andrew and Florence (Stevens) C. BS in Edn., Miami U., Oxford, Ohio, 1943; BS in Occupational Therapy, Washington U., St. Louis, 1949; MA, U. So. Calif., 1952; cert. in health facility adminstrn., UCLA, 1978. Mem. staff, then supervising therapist Los Angeles County Gen. Hosp., 1949-53; occupational therapist Goodwill Industries, L.A., 1954-55; staff therapist Vis. Nurse Assn., Phila., 1955-56; rsch. therapist United Cerebral Palsy Assn., L.A., 1956-60; dir. occupational therapy Orthopaedic Hosp., L.A., 1961-67; coordinator occupational therapy Rsch. and Tng. Ctr. U. So. Calif., L.A., 1967-70, assoc. prof., 1970-76, acting chmn. dept. occupational therapy, 1973-76, mem. adv. bd. project SEARCH, Sch. Medicine, 1969-72; founding editor Occupational Therapy in Health Care jour., 1984-88, editor emerita, 1988—; assoc. dir. L.A. Job Corps Ctr., 1977-78, cons. in edn. and program devel., 1976—; free-lance editor, 1990—. Author: Manual for Basic Skills Assessment, 1960; also articles. Mem. scholarship com. Los Angeles March of Dimes, 1963-70; bd. dirs. Am. Occupational Therapy Found., 1965-69, v.p., 1966-69; bd. dirs. Nat. Health Council, 1975-78; mentor U. Tex. Class 1990 Occupational Therapy. Served to lt. (j.g.) WAVES, 1943-46. Recipient Disting. Alumni award Washington U., 1978, Disting. Lectr. Calif. Occupational Therapy Found., 1986. Fellow Am. Occupational Therapy Assn. (pres. 1967-73); mem. Inst. Medicine NAS (sr. 1989), So. Calif. Occupational Therapy Assn. (pres. 1950-51, 75-76), Coalition Ind. Health Professions (chmn. 1973-74), Assn. Schs. Allied Health Professions (dir. 1973-74), World Fedn. Occupational Therapists, Cwen, Mortar Bd., Kappa Delta Pi, Kappa Kappa Gamma.

CRONE, MARCIA ANN, judge; b. Dallas, Dec. 12, 1952; d. Dan Moody and Marian Louise (Stewart) Cain; m. W. Seth Crone, Jr., Aug. 30, 1986; children: Kimball Montclair, Kirby Armitage. BA summa cum laude, Univ. of Tex., Austin, 1973; JD summa cum laude, Univ. of Houston, 1978. Bar: Tex. 1979, D.C. 1982. With Andrews & Kurth, 1978-92; magistrate judge U.S. Dist. Ct. (Tex. so. dist.), 5th circuit, Houston, 1992—. Methodist. Office: Federal Bldg 515 Rusk Ave Rm 9010 Houston TX 77002*

CRONENWETT, PAMELA JANE, educational assessment specialist; b. Ypsilanti, Mich., Mar. 25, 1941; d. Richard Kieth and Rosemary Therese (Deto) McClure; m. William James Cronenwett, June 24, 1967; children: William Thomas, Melissa Jane. Student, Northwestern U., 1959-60, U. Mich., 1964-65; BS, Eastern Mich. U., 1960-66. Asst. bus. mgr. M. Marks Hair Stylist, Ann Arbor, Mich., 1963-69; payroll adminstr. St. Alphonese Ch., Dearborn, Mich., 1979-80; area program dir. YWCA of Western Wayne County, Inkster, Mich., 1980-85; assessment specialist Henry Ford C.C., Dearborn, 1991—. Mem. AAUW (pres. Dearborn br. 1989-91), Mich. Assn. Women in Edn., Delta Zeta (metro alumnae pres. 1978-81, Mich. alumnae dir. 1981-91, nat. dir. 1991-93, internat. treas. 1993—). Home: 25720 W Hills Dr Dearborn Heights MI 48125-1055 Office: Henry Ford CC 5101 Evergreen Rd Dearborn MI 48128-2407

CRONICK-LEONARD, ANNE BERTHA, retired psychiatrist; b. Kalamazoo, May 18, 1910; d. Menno John and Elizabeth (VanderTill) Bosma; m. Charles Herbert Cronick, Feb. 28, 1938 (div. 1948); children: Karen Anne, Charles Herbert; m. Alan Thomas Leonard, Oct. 12, 1957. BA, Calvin Coll., Grand Rapids, Mich., 1932; MD, U. Mich., 1936. Intern Women's Hosp., Cleve., 1936-37; resident City Hosp., Cleve., 1937-38; assoc. psychiatrist Fair Oaks Villa Sanitarium, Cuyahoga Falls, Ohio, 1938-39; resident in psychiatry Inst. of Pa. Hosp., Phila., 1939-40; pvt. practice, Grand Rapids, Mich., 1940-46; assoc. psychiatrist Child Guidance Clinic, Grand Rapids, 1946-48, dir., 1948-50, cons., 1950-52; cons. Child Guidance Clinic, Muskegon, Mich., 1952-57; pvt. practice, Muskegon, 1950-93, ret., 1993. Mem. adv. bd. Hackley Adult Mental Health Clinic, Muskegon, 1954-56; mem. Citizens Action Comn. for Edn., North Muskegon, Mich., 1959-60; mem., v.p. Nutritional Svcs. Older Ams., Muskegon, 1974-77. Mem. AMA, Am. Psychiat. Assn., Soc. for Study Multiple Personality and Dissociation, Mich. Med. Assn., Muskegon County Med. Soc. Methodist. Home: 302 3d St North Muskegon MI 49445

CRONIN, BONNIE KATHRYN LAMB, legislative staff executive; b. Mpls., Mar. 11, 1941; d. Edwin Rector and Maude Kathryn (MacPherson) Lamb; m. Barry Jay Cronin, Jan. 23, 1963 (div. Feb. 1972); 1 son, Philip Scott. B.A., U. Mo., 1963, B.S., 1964; M.S., Ill. State U., 1970. Copywriter Neds & Wardlow Advt., Columbia, Mo., 1962-64; tchr. Columbia Sch. System, 1964-68, Normal (Ill.) Sch. System, 1968-69; asst. gen. mgr. Sta. WGLT, Normal, 1969-70; dir. devel. Radio Sta. WBUR, Boston, 1970-71; program dir. Radio Sta. WBUR, 1971-75, gen. mgr., 1975-78; dir. public relations Joy of Movement Center, 1978-80; dep. scheduler Anderson for Pres., 1980; scheduler Spaulding for Gov., 1980-81; dir. scheduling John Kerry Campaign, 1982; dir. of scheduling Mass. Lt. Gov.'s Office, dir. ops., 1983-84; dep. campaign mgr. Kerry for Senate Com., 1984; dir. ops. Senator John Kerry, Washington, 1985-86; dir. constituency outreach Senator John Kerry, Boston, 1986-92; exec. asst. Senator John Kerry, 1992—. Mem. Nat. Pub. Radio (dir. 1974-77, chairperson devel. com.), Mass. Broadcasters Assn. (dir. 1973-78, chairperson scholarship com., pub. service com., adminstrv. oversight com.). Office: 10th Fl 1 Bowdoin Sq Fl 10 Boston MA 02114-2919

CRONIN, KATHLEEN ANNE, executive search consultant; b. Oak Park, Ill., Sept. 17, 1933; d. Brendan C. and Rose J. (Mangini) Powell; m. Richard Cronin, May 29, 1954; children: Anne, Patrick, Richard, Edward, John, Michael, Eileen. BA, DePaul U., 1977. Sec., credit asst. Hills Bros. Coffee, 1951-53; estimator Alpha Portland Cement, 1953-54; v.p. adminstrn. and rsch. Hodge-Cronin & Assos., Inc., Rosemont, Ill., 1977—; conflict resolution cons. Office Cath. Edn. Ar . Mem. Human Rels. Com., City of Des Plaines, 1971-72, St. Mary Pastoral Coun., 1984-88, chmn., 1986-88; pres. St. Mary Sch. Bd., Des Plaines, 1969-71; rsch. Ill. Ctr. Parapsychol. Rsch.; conciliator Archdiocese Chgo. Office Conciliation and Arbitration, 1970-74. Cert. CPR instr. Mem. Internat. Assn. Corp. and Profl. Recruiters, Internat. Ind. Cons. Home: 1450 Harding Ave Des Plaines IL 60016-4379 Office: Hodge Cronin & Assocs 9575 W Higgins Rd Des Plaines IL 60018-4915

CRONIN, PATTI ADRIENNE WRIGHT, state agency administrator; b. Chgo., May 25, 1943; d. Rodney Adrian and Dorothy Louise (Thiele) Wright; m. Kevin Brian Cronin, May 1, 1971; 1 child, Kevin. BA, Beloit (Wis.) Coll., 1965; JD with honors, U. Wis., 1983. Vol. Peace Corps, Turkey, 1965-67; recruiter Peace Corps, Washington, 1967-68; tchr. English Kamehameha III Sch., Lahaina, Hawaii, 1968-70, Evansville (Wis.) High Sch., 1972-77; tchr. math. and history Killian Sch., Hartford, Wis., 1977-78; tchr. English Kaiser High Sch., Honolulu, 1979-80; intern Wis. Ct. Appeals, Madison, 1983; exec. dir. waste facility siting bd. State of Wis., Madison, 1983—; founder, v.p., bd. dirs. Justice Ctr. Honolulu, 1979-82; sec., treas. Cronin Constrn. Co., Inc., Madison, 1986—. Editor: Internat. Law Jour., 1982. Bd. dirs. Neighborhood Bd., Honolulu, 1979-82; chmn. United Way, 1989—; active Parent Citizens Adv. Coun. Recipient Mayor's award of outstanding achievement, City of Honolulu, 1980. Mem. Soc. Profls. in Dispute Resolution, ABA, State Bar Wis. Office: Waste Facility Siting Bd 101 E Wilson St 5th Flr Madison WI 53703-3476

CRONIN-WOLKOV, LAUREN, lobbyist; b. Phila.; d. Joseph A. and Elizabeth (Murray) Cronin; m. Harvey B. Wolkov. BS, Duquesne U., 1971; MSW, Temple U., 1975. Social worker Youth Conservation Svcs. and Dept. Pub. Welfare, Phila., 1971-74; grad. asst. Temple U., Phila., 1974-75; exec. dir. The Ripon Soc., Washington, 1976-77; govt. and consumer affairs rep. U.S. League of Savs. and Loan Assn., Washington, 1977-81; dir. community and govt. rels. Kaiser Cement Corp., Oakland, Calif., 1981-86; exec. dir. L.A. Oncologic Inst. St. Vincent Med. Ctr., L.A., 1986-90; exec. dir. Calif. Children's Lobby, Children's Rsch. Inst. of Calif., Sacramento, 1990-93; prin. Wolkov & Assocs. pub. affairs firm, Sacramento, 1993—; exec. dir. Sacramento Regional Found., 1994—. Bd. dirs. Child and Family Inst., Sacramento, 1993—; vol. U. Calif.-Davis Child Protection Ctr., Sacramento, 1993—; vol. St. Francis Elem. Sch., Sacramento, 1994—; pres. Women in Housing and Fin., Washington, 1979. Roman Catholic.

CROOG, ROSLYN DEBORAH, computer systems analyst; b. New Haven, July 14, 1942; d. Herbert Bernard and Belle (Brown) Croog; children: Bradley Jordan, Katie Miriam. AS, Quinnipiac Coll., 1962; BS, Fla. Internat. U., 1982. Analyst, programmer DBA Systems, Inc., Melbourne, Fla., 1982-84; system mgr. DBA Systems, Inc., Fairfax, Va., 1984-86; mem. tech. staff MRJ, Inc., Fairfax, Va., 1986—. Office: MRJ Inc 10560 Arrowhead Dr Fairfax VA 22030

CROOKE, ROSANNE MUZYKA, pharmacologist; b. Pittsfield, Mass., Oct. 30, 1955; d. Myron Michael and Marian Geneva (Russell) Muzyka; m. Stanley T. Crooke, Sept. 5, 1986. BA, Williams Coll., 1978; PhD, U. Pa., 1986. Rsch. asst. endocrine sec. dept. medicine U. Pa., Phila., 1978-81; fellow Wistar Inst. Anatomy and Biology, Phila., 1986-89; sr. scientist ISIS Pharms., Carlsbad, Calif., 1989—. Contbr. articles to profl. jours. Mem. AAAS. Home: 3211 Piragua St Carlsbad CA 92009-7840 Office: ISIS Pharms 2280 Faraday Ave Carlsbad CA 92008-7208

CROOKER, DIANE KAY, accountant; b. Elmira, N.Y., Nov. 19, 1945; d. John Woodrow and Katharine Eloise (Saunders) Wilson; m. Dennis H. Canfield, mar. 25, 1963 (div. June 1970); children: Douglas Arthur, Dennis John; m. Walter E. Crooker, Apr. 17, 1988. AAS in Computer Sci., Elmira Coll., 1987, BS in Acctg. summa cum laude, 1992. Assembler Westinghouse Elec. Corp., Horseheads, N.Y., 1979-81, traceability coord., 1981-87; buyer Imaging & Sensing Tech. Corp., Horseheads, 1987-89, acct., 1989—. Bd. dirs. Spalding Found. for Injured Drivers, Owego, N.Y., 1988—. Recipient Scholastic Achievement award N.Y. State CPA Soc., 1992. Mem. Inst. Mgmt. Accts. (v.p. membership 1994), Alpha Sigma Lambda (sec. 1993-94, treas. 1994—).

CROOKS, DORENA MAY (DEE CROOKS), administrative assistant, social worker; b. Center Point, W.Va., Sept. 15, 1938; d. Paul Jefferson and Ruby Catherine (Lasure) Ashcraft; m. William H.D. Crooks, June 27, 1956 (div. Nov. 1975); children: Charles Jefferson, Kimberly May, Raechelle Dee. Grad., W.Va. State Police Acad., 1977; BA, Glenville State Coll., 1992. Lic. social worker, W.Va. Legal sec. Hickel, Wilson & Hill, Attys., Parkersburg, W.Va., 1963-65, Robert T. Goldenberg, Atty., Parkersburg, W.Va., 1965-68; exec. sec. W.Va. State Rd., Parkersburg, 1968-70; dep. sheriff, sec. Wood County Sheriff Dept., Parkersburg, 1973-79; legal sec. George W. Hill, Atty., Parkersburg, 1984-88; Vista vol. Wood County Sr. Citizens Assn., Parkersburg, 1990-91, adminstrv. asst., social worker, various positions, 1991—. Mem. NAFE. Office: Wood County Citizens Assn 925 Market St Parkersburg WV 26101-4736

CROOT, SANDRA MEIXEL, gallery owner, jewelry designer; b. Phila., Dec. 29, 1934; d. H. Bruce and Mildred Mae (Haig) Meixel; m. m. Jonathan Rowland, Oct. 3, 1959 (div.); m. Joseph Walling Croot, July 15, 1972; 1 stepchild, Becky Croot Weiss. BFA, Beaver Coll., 1957. Cert. tchr., N.J. Elem. art tchr. Moorestown (N.J.) Twp. Pub. Schs., 1961-64, Delanco (N.J.) Twp. Pub. Schs., 1964-66, Mine Hill (N.J.) Twp., 1966-68; instr. fine arts dept. Centenary Coll. for Women, Hackettstown, N.J., 1969-72; tchr. St. Mary's Sch., Annapolis, Md., 1974-77; jewelry and craft shop owner The Bird's Nest, Annapolis, 1977-82, Moon Shell Gallery, Annapolis, 1986—; shop owner Kites Up & Away, Annapolis, 1993—; art instr. Merchantville (N.J.) Music Conservatory, 1962-64; art show chairwoman Black River Play House, Chester, N.J., 1968-72; portfolio chairwoman, mem. Md. Fedn. Art, Annapolis, 1980-86. Home: 300 Cape St John Rd Annapolis MD 21401 Office: Moon Shell Gallery 8 Fleet St Annapolis MD 21401

CROPPER, REBECCA LYNN, radiological engineer, radioactive waste engineer; b. LaGrange, Ky., Nov. 8, 1957; d. Clyde Carter and Dorothy Jean (Neblett) C. BA in Physics, Hanover Coll., 1979; MS in Health Physics, Ga. Inst. Tech., 1982. Radiol. control and safety technician U.S. Ecology, Inc., Louisville, 1979-81; rsch. asst. Ga. Inst. Tech., Atlanta, 1981-82; radiol. engr. Bechtel Nat., Inc., Oak Ridge, 1982-85; supervising engr. Impell Corp., Lincolnshire, Ill., 1985-90; licensing dir. Chem-Nuclear Systems, Inc., Springfield, Ill., 1990-92; prin. mem. tech. staff Ralph M. Parsons Co., Cin., Ohio, 1992-93; program health and safety mgr. Parsons Engring. Scis., Inc., Denver, 1993—. Mem. ASTM, Health Physics Soc., Am. Nuclear Soc.

CROPPER, SUSAN PEGGY, veterinarian; b. N.Y.C., Feb. 11, 1941; d. Eli and Ruth (Rader) Abrahams; divorced; 1 child, Tracy Lynn. BS, Kans. State U., 1962, DVM, 1964. Assoc. veterinarian Asbury Park (N.J.) Animal Hosp., 1964-65; instr. in Vet. Sci. Kans. State U., Manhattan, 1965-66; owner, veterinarian Markle (Ind.) Vet. Clinic, 1966-71, Meisels Animal Hosp. Clinic, Elmwood Park, N.J., 1971-73, Ridgewood (N.J.) Animal Hosp., 1973-75, Cropper House Call Practice, Wyckoff, N.J., 1975—; editor Nat. Assn. Women Vets., 1966-68; mem. Audibon Soc. Mus. Natural History. Editor WJMA Jour., 1973; photographer: Best Diving Spots in Western Hemisphere, 1987. Leader Brownie troop Girl Scouts of Am., Glen Rock, N.J., 1976-77, Wyckoff, 1977-83; chair No. Jersey Tridents, Ridgefield, N.J., 1985-86. Mem. AVMA, Soc. Aquatic Vet. Medicine (treas.), No. N.J. Vet. Med. Assn. (pres. 1972-73), Met. Vet. Med. Assn., N.Y. Zool. Soc., Van Saun Zool. Soc., N.J.. Acad., Ski and Scuba Club of Westwood, North Jersey Tridents Club (Ridgefield, chair 1985-86). Office: 310 Newtown Rd Wyckoff NJ 07481-2608

CRORY, ELIZABETH L., state legislator; b. Gardner, Mass., Sept. 12, 1932; d. James Quaiel and Mary (Reilly) Lupien; m. Frederick E. Crory, Aug. 21, 1954; children: Thomas, David, Ellen, Ann, Edward, Stephen. A.B., U. Mass., 1954; M.A.L.S., Dartmouth Coll., 1975. Tchr., Amherst (Mass.) Schs., 1954, Lyme (N.H.) Schs., 1972-76; mem. N.H. Ho. of Reps., 1977-87, 92-93, 94-95, mem. commerce/consumer affairs com., 1977-87, 93—, mem. spl. com. on med. malpractice, 1984; exec. dir. Children's Ctr. of Upper Valley, 1986-90; bd. incorporators Mascoma Savs. Bank; bd. overseers Mary Hitchcock Meml. Hosp. Roman Catholic. Home: 40 Rip Rd Hanover NH 03755-1614

CROSBY, CHRISTINE MCFADDEN, intelligence analyst; b. New Orleans, July 18, 1954; d. Grafton Ridout and Elesa Evelyn (Konigsberg) McFadden; m. David Malcom Crosby, Jan. 2, 1981. AB in Classical Civilizations, Coll. of William and Mary, 1976; student, Loyola U., Rome, 1974-75; MS in Strategic Intelligence, Def. Intelligence Coll., Washington, 1987; Grad. Cert., Univ. of the South, 1991. Lang. technician Nat. Security Agy., Ft. Meade, Md., 1977-79, intelligence analyst intern, 1979-82, project mgr., 1985-86, fellow to Def. Intelligence Coll., 1986-87, sr. rep. to commerce dept., 1987-90, asst. sr. intelligence officer, 1990-91; biographic analyst CIA, Langley, Va., 1982-85; dir., strategic comml. counseling Internat. Trade Adminstrn./Dept. Commerce, Washington, 1991—. Nat. coord. Episcopal Engaged Encounter, 1993—, presenting team, 1983—; mem. Episcopal Cursillo of Va., 1977—. Recipient Gold Medal award Sec. Commerce, Washington, 1989. Democrat. Home: 2602 Davis Ave Alexandria VA 22302-2815

CROSBY, ELLEN LOUISE, counselor; b. Edenville, Mich., July 9, 1944; d. Donald Wellington and Gladys Leona (Fowler) Marsh; m. James A. Crosby, Mar. 15, 1964; children: Angela Louise, Andrew James, Allen Jackson, James Alvin, JoAnne Marie. BA, So. Coll., 1987; MEd, U. Tenn., Chattanooga, 1990. Cert. Nat. Bd. Cert. Counselors. Counselor Advent Youth Ranch, Calhoun, Tenn., 1989-92; dir., supr., founder Young Women's Prep. Home, Macon, Mo., 1992—; pres. Christian Family Learning Ctrs., Inc., McDonald, Tenn., 1992—. Mem. ACA, Am. Assn. Christian Counselors, Adventist-Laymen's Svcs. and Industires, Toastmasters Internat. (sec. 1992-94). Republican. Seventh-Day Adventist. Home: 6818 White Oak Cir McDonald TN 37353 Office: Christian Family Learning Ctrs Inc PO Box 2153 Collegedale TN 37315

CROSBY, JACQUELINE GARTON, newspaper editor, journalist; b. Jacksonville, Fla., May 13, 1961; d. James Ellis and Marianne (Garton) C.; m. Robert Edward Legge, Jr., Oct. 19, 1985. ABJ, U. Ga., 1983; MBA, U. Cen. Fla., 1987. Staff writer Macon Telegraph & News, Ga., 1983-84; copy editor Orlando Sentinel, Fla., 1984-85; dir. spl. projects Ivanhoe Communications, Inc., Orlando, Fla., 1987-89; producer spl. projects Sta. KSTP-TV, Mpls., 1989-94; asst. news editor Star Tribune Online, Mpls., 1994—. Recipient award for best sports story Ga. Press Assn., 1982; award for best series of yr. AP, 1985, Pulitzer prize, 1985. Mem. Quill. Democrat. Episcopalian. Home: 6217 Concord Ave Minneapolis MN 55424-1737 Office: Star Tribune Online 425 Portland Ave Minneapolis MN 55488

CROSBY, NANCY L., principal; b. Ogdensburg, N.Y., Jan. 8, 1940; d. John S. and Ella Mae Langtry; m. Francis Patrick Crosby, Nov. 1, 1935; children: Lori Ann, Daniel Patrick. BS, SUNY, Potsdam, 1961, MS, 1972; Adminstrv. Degree, St. Lawrence U., Canton, N.Y., 1986, Supt. Degree, 1987. Lic. elem., secondary, social studies tchr., adminstr. Elem. tchr. Enlarged Ogdensburg Pub. Schs., 1961-69; secondary social studies tchr. Morristown (N.Y.) Ctrl. Sch., 1969-93, elem. supr., 1985-92, bldg. prin., 1992—. Named Outstanding Adminstr., SUNY-Potsdam, 1992-93. Mem. Morristown Tchrs. Assn., N.Y. State Tchrs. Assn., High Sch. Prins. Assn., Elem. Sch. Prins. Assn. Home: PO Box 78 Morristown NY 13664 Office: Morristown Ctrl Sch Governor St Morristown NY 13664

CROSBY, SUSAN, state legislator, mental health services executive; b. Muncie, Ind., Oct. 16, 1945; d. Thomas and Patricia (Richards) Ray; m. Joseph E. Crosby, Jan. 19, 1968; children: Todd, Thomas. BA in Psychology, Purdue U., 1979. Asst. dir. ann. fund Depauw U., Greencastle, Ind.; exec. dir., chief exec. officer Associated Patient Svcs., Indpls.; mem. Ind. Ho. of Reps., Indpls., 1990—. Recipient Jefferson award, Jane award State of Ind. Active Nat. Com. Mental Health Needs in Rural Am.; mem. Select Adv. Com. for Pub. Welfare, Com. on Dirs. Mental Health. Recipient Outstanding Freshman Legislator award Ind. Broadcaster's Assn., 1991, Legislator of Yr. award Mental Health Assn. Ind., 1992. Mem. Nat. Mental Health Assn. (v.p. tng.), Nat. Alliance for Rsch. on Schizophrenia and Depression (bd. dirs.), Mental Health Assn. Ind. (past pres.). Democrat. Presbyterian. Home: Box 134 RR 1 Box 134 Roachdale IN 46172-9529 Office: State House Fl 3 Indianapolis IN 46204

CROSE, GERI CLARETTE, nursing program coordinator, nurse consultant; b. Cleve., June 5, 1949; d. Robert Oscar and Eliza Jane (McAllister) Goes; m. Thomas Allen Crose, Dec. 5, 1970 (div. Jan. 1983); children: John Michael, Amy Christine. AD, Tacoma C.C., 1982. RN, Mont., Wash; cert. critical care nurse, nephrology nurse, ACLS. Staff nurse St. Joseph's Hosp., Bellingham, Wash., 1968, Deaconess Hosp., Spokane, Wash., 1968-72; staff nurse surg. ICU Bexar County Hosp., San Antonio, 1973-75, staff nurse dialysis, 1975-78; staff nurse emergency rm. Lakewood Gen. Hosp., Tacoma, 1978-80; charge nurse Gen.Med. and Emergency Care, Tacoma, 1980-82; staff nurse ICU St. Joseph's Hosp., Tacoma, 1983-85; staff nurse spl. care unit Kalispell (Mont.) Regional Hosp., 1985-88; program coord. Glacier Regional Dialysis Ctr., Kalispell, 1988—; cons.-med. rev. N.W. Renal Network, Seattle, 1993—. Mem. Am. Nephrology Nurse Assn., Am. Critical Care Nurse Assn. Republican. Office: Glacier Regional Dialysis Ctr 66 Claremont St Kalispell MT 59901-3552

CROSHAL, KATHLEEN KLOTZ See HEARN, KATHLEEN K.

CROSS, BETTY FELT, small business owner; b. Newcastle, Ind., Jan. 8, 1920; d. Frank Ernest and Olive (Shock) Felt; m. Paris O. Cross, July 14, 1939 (div.); children: Ernest, Betty J., Robert D., Paris, Toni, Frank; m. John B. Gatlin, 1976. Owner, mgr. Salon D'Or, Indpls., 1956-74; owner Bejon, Madison, Ind., 1974-78, Brass & Things, Madison, 1978-93; pres. Felts Mfg., Inc., 1966—, Silver City USA I, Madison, 1981—, Black Angus, Inc, 1991—, Silver City Viedo, Inc., Clarksville, Tenn., 1992—, Job Rock I and II, Inc., 1994—. Mem. Nashville C. of C. Avocation: collecting dolls, gold and silver coins, art objects, gold antique jewelry, silver sterling. Office: 928 Gallatin Rd S Madison TN 37115

CROSS, CHARLOTTE LORD, social worker; b. Andalusia, Ala., Dec. 1, 1941; d. Roy Olice and Laura Emily (Smith) Lord; m. Jack Allen Cross, May 5, 1960; children: Jack Allen III, James Duane, Jeffrey Miles. BA in English, Auburn U., Montgomery, Ala., 1979, MS in Psychology, 1980, MS in Secondary Edn./English, 1993. Social worker dept. human resources State of Ala., Andalusia, 1980—; tchr. in English conversation to Nat. Cancer Inst. research scientists, Tokyo, 1965-66; adj. instr. psychology Lurleen B. Wallace State Jr. Coll, 1988-89, Troy State U., Fort Rucker, 1991. Recipient Dept. of Human Resources Commr.'s Merit award, 1989. Mem. Ala. Psychol. Assn. (assoc.), United Coun. on Welfare Fraud (cert. welfare fraud investigator), Ala. Coun. on Welfare Fraud. Baptist.

CROSS, CONSTANCE KIRBY, banker; b. Ocala, Fla., Sept. 20, 1944; d. Edward Thomas and Theo Willie (Vaughn) Kirby; m. Ralph Edgar Cross, Aug. 13, 1966; children: Sarah Catherine, Thomas Jeffrey. BA, Rollins Coll., 1966; MBA, So. Meth. U., 1982. Contr., data processor Rep. Bank Corp., Dallas, 1983-84, strategic planner, 1984-85; treas. analyst 1st Nat. Cin. Corp., 1985-86; treas. officer 1st Rep. Bank Corp., Dallas, 1986-88; v.p. Amresco, Dallas, 1988-92, Nations Bank, Dallas, 1992—. Leader Girl Scouts of Am., Richardson, Tex., 1975-80; crisis counselor 1st United Meth. Ch., Richardson, 1979; pres. bd. dirs. Creative Presch., Richardson, 1980. Mem. AAUW, So. Meth. MBA Assn. Home: 6414 Brook Lake Dr Dallas TX 75248

CROSS, DEBORAH ANN, beverage industry executive; b. Cleveland, Tenn., Apr. 2, 1957; d. Kenneth B. and Virginia Jewell (Prueitt) Sink; m. Mark Elliott Cross, Oct. 25, 1981. BS, U. Tenn., 1979, MBA, 1981. Mktg. analyst Coca-Cola USA, Atlanta, 1983-85, fin. analyst, 1985-88, exec. asst. sr. v.p. planning, 1988-90, planning mgr. environ. affairs, 1990-93, mgr. customer mktg., 1993—; bd. dirs. Coun. Plastic & Packaging in Environ., 1990—. Vice chmn. Ga. Govs. Recycling Mkt. Devel. Coun., 1990—; mem. Recycling Adv. Coun. Plastic Container Task Force, 1990-92; active Hands On Atlanta. Mem. Am. Mktg. Assn., The Futures Soc. Home: 2615A Paces Rdg NW Atlanta GA 30339-4027

CROSS, DEBORAH JO ANN, school psychologist; b. Muncie, Ind., Feb. 14, 1957; d. Jimmy Elz and Mary Jo Ann (Mills) C. BS in Psychology, Ball State U., 1979, MS in Psychometry, 1980, EdS in Sch. Psychology, 1981. Cert. sch. psychologist. Sch. psychologist Adams Wells Spl. Svcs., Bluffton, Ind., 1981-83, Porter County Spl. Edn., Valparaiso, Ind., 1983-87, Greater Lafayette Area Spl. Svcs., Lafayette, Ind., 1987—; co-facilitator Visually Impaired Parent Support Group, Lafayette, 1992—. Pres. Welcome Wagon, Lafayette, 1990-91; govt. counselor Hoosier Girl's State, Terre Haute, Ind., 1986—; active Am. Heart Assn. Mem. Nat. Assn. Sch. Psychologists, Ind. ASsn. Sch. Psychologists (com. mem. 1988—), Tippecanoe County Bd. dirs. (pres. 1992—, v.p. 1994—), Delta Kappa Gamma (v.p. 1988—). Presbyterian. Home: Apt 210 1200 Happy Hollow Rd West Lafayette IN 47906-2784 Office: Grtr Lafayette Area Spl Svc 2300 Cason St Lafayette IN 47904-2692

CROSS, DOLORES EVELYN, university administrator, educator; b. Newark, Aug. 29, 1938; d. Charles and Ozie (Johnson) Tucker; children: Thomas E., Jane E. BA in Elem. Edn., Seton Hall U., 1963; MS, Hofstra U. 1968; PhD in Higher Edn. Adminstrn., U. Mich. 1971; hon. doctorates Marymount Coll., Skidmore Coll., Hofstra U., Elmhurst Coll. Asst. prof. edn. Northwestern U., Evanston, Ill. 1971-74; assoc. prof. Claremont Grad. Sch., Calif., 1974-78; vice chancellor CUNY, 1978-81; prof. Brooklyn Coll., 1978—; pres. N.Y. State Higher Edn. Service Corp., Albany, 1981-88; assoc. provost, assoc. v.p. academic affairs U. Minn., Mpls., 1988-90; pres. Chgo. State U., 1990—; bd. dirs. Coll. Bd., Campus Compact, Assn. Black Women in Higher Edn., No. Trust Co.; sr. cons. South Africa's Historically Black Colls. Editor: Teaching in a Multicultural Society, 1978. Chair Ill. Campus Compact Cmty. Svc., mem. Gov.'s Planning and Policy Com. of Edn. Commn.; mem. gov. bd. Hispanic Assn. Colls. and Univs.; bd. dirs. Field Mus., Chgo. Urban League, Leadership for Quality Edn., Chgo. Area Fulbright Scholars Program. Mem. NAACP (life), Am. Edn. Research Assn., Am. Council on Edn. (bd. dirs.), Women Execs. in State Govt. (adv. bd.), Commercial Club (Chgo.). Avocations: running, hiking, bicycling, theater, writing. Office: Chgo State U Office of the President 95th St King Dr Chicago IL 60628

CROSS, DOROTHY ABIGAIL, retired librarian; b. Bangor, Mich., Sept. 9, 1924; d. John Laird and Alice Estelle (Wilcox) C.; B.A., Wayne State U., 1956; M.A. in Library Sci., U. Mich., 1957. Jr. librarian Detroit Public Library, 1957-59; adminstrv. librarian U.S. Army, Braconne, France, 1959-61, Poitiers, France, 1961-63; area library supr., 1963, asst. command librarian, Kaiserslautern, Germany, 1963-67, acquisitions librarian, Aschaffenburg, Germany, 1967, Munich, Germany, 1967-69, sr. staff library specialist, Munich, 1969-72, command librarian, Stuttgart, Germany, 1972-75, dep. staff librarian, Heidelberg, Germany, 1975-77; chief librarian 18th Airborne Corps and Ft. Bragg (N.C.), 1977-79; chief ADP sect. Pentagon Library, Washington, 1979-80, chief readers services br., 1980-83, dir., 1983-91. Mem. ALA, U. Mich. Alumni assn., Delta Omicron. Methodist. Home: 6511 Delia Dr Alexandria VA 22310-2609

CROSS, JOAN ELAINE, nurse, insurance company representative; b. Cin., June 22, 1945. Diploma in Nursing, Bethesda Hosp. Sch. Nursing, Cin., 1966. Cert. assoc. in risk mgmt. Ins. Inst. of Am. Staff nurse emergency dept. Jewish Hosp., Cin., 1966-70; nurse, team leader ICU, critical care unit Bethesda Hosp., Cin., 1970-73, critical care instr., 1978-82; staff nurse ICU Christ Hosp., Cin., 1973-78; sr. risk mgmt. rep., med. svcs. St. Paul Fire and Marine Ins. Co., Cin., 1982—. Mem. NAFE, ARC, Am. Soc. Healthcare Risk Mgrs., Ohio Soc. Healthcare Risk Mgrs., Ky. Soc. Healthcare Risk Mgrs. Office: St Paul Fire and Marine Ins Co 250 W Court St Cincinnati OH 45202-1054

CROSS, LYNDA LEE, nurse; b. L.A., June 18, 1943; d. Fredrick Lewis Heyle and Bonnie Verda (Fridell) Covey; m. Jim Carl Eckler, June 7, 1963 (div. Sept. 1972); children: Barry, Dennis, Shantel, Candace; m. Douglas William Cross, Apr. 10, 1981. Diploma, Paradise Valley Sch. Nursing, 1964; BSN, Sonoma State U., 1981. RN; cert. infusion therapist, 1987. Clin. coord. urology San Diego Urological Med. Group, 1965-71; relief head nurse nursery Grossmont Hosp., La Mesa, Calif., 1971-76; relief head nurse neonatal ICU Balboa Naval Hosp., San Diego, 1976-77; coord. IV therapy St. Helena Hosp. and Health Ctr., Deer Park, Calif., 1977-79; staff nurse, IV therapist Mass. Eye and Ear Infirmary, Boston, 1982-84; pres., owner, IV clinician I.V. Lifeline, Inc., Berkley, Mass., 1984—. Developer IV homecare module, 1984 (1st Nurse award), Coop. extended IV therapy in the physicians setting, 1993; copyrights include IV Therapy: A Better Alternative. Fellow New England Chpr. Intravenous Nurses Soc. (scholar chair 1985), Intravenous Nurses Soc. Home and Office: 610 Winchuck River Rd Brookings OR 97415-9603

CROSS, TRUDY LYNN, city auditor; b. Reno, Nev., Jan. 6, 1963; d. Lorin Dee and Elizabeth Ann Hansen; m. Ronald Walter Cross, Aug. 31, 1985; 1 child. BSBA in Acctg., U. Nev., 1985. CPA, Nev. Audit agt. State of Nev. Gaming Control Bd., Reno, 1985-91; dep. legis. auditor Nev. Legis. Counsel Bur., Carson City, 1991-95; internal auditor City of Reno, 1995—. Mem. adv. bd. Cath. Svcs. Appeal, Reno, 1993—. Mem. Phi Kappa Phi, Beta Gamma Sigma. Democrat. Roman Catholic. Home: 810 S University Park Loop Reno NV 89512

CROSSLAND, ANN ELIZABETH, psychotherapist; b. Cambridge, Ohio, Apr. 24, 1940; d. H. Stewart and Laura Geraldine (Geese) Hastings; m. Eugene Joseph Szmuc, Nov. 30, 1963 (dec. Oct. 1976); m. Richard Ray Crossland, Feb. 16, 1988; children: Rae Ann, Nancy, Carol. BS in Edn., Kent State U., 1965; MSEd in Counseling, U. Akron, 1981. Cert. in edn. of handicapped K-12, learning disabilities/behavior disorders K-12. Third grade tchr. Bertha Bradshaw Elem. Sch., Rootstown, Ohio, 1963-64; substitute tchr. Kent (Ohio) City Schs., 1967-84, Portage County Schs., Ravenna, Ohio, 1979-84; assoc. tchr. severely behaviorally handicapped Portage County Schs., Ravenna, 1984-88, H.S. tchr. severe behavior handicap, 1988-92; therapist Child & Adolescent Svc. Ctr., Canton, Ohio, 1992—. Bd. dirs., facilitator Oncology Support Group, Akron, 1977-81; bd. dirs., vol. trainer, counselor WomanShelter, Ravenna, 1980-87; organizer, group facilitator Portage County Cancer Group, Ravenna, 1982-83; mem. steering com. Portage County Adolescent Network, Ravenna, 1987-92. Mem. Am. Counselors Assn., Am. Mental Health Counselors Assn., Delta Kappa Gamma (Theta chpt.). Democrat. Unitarian Universalist. Office: Child & Adolescent Svc Ctr 1226 N Market St Canton OH 44714

CROSSLAND, SUE DELL, artist, registered nurse; b. Roff, Okla., Oct. 12, 1933; d. Enoch Thomas and Sadie Alice (Lynn) Clements; m. Thomas Blackwell Crossland, Nov. 23, 1952; children: Thomas Bruce, Sherrie, Richard. AAS, El Centro, 1974; degree in nursing care adminstrn., East Tex. State U., 1975; student, So. Meth. U., 1978, U. Tex., Dallas, 1979. RN, Tex. Artist Dallas, 1967, 91—; RN Presbyn. Hosp., Dallas, 1974-76, Med. City Hosp., Dallas, 1976-78. Represented in permanent collections Tex. Art Gallery, Dallas. Mem. Artist and Craftsman Assn., Internat. Assn. for Contemporary Art, Nat. Women in the Arts, Oil Painters of Am., Assn. Pour la Promotion Artistique France (Galerie Art Matignon award 1991), McKinney Art Assn., Okla. City Hall of Fame. Republican. Roman Catholic. Home: 11839 FM 2478 Celina TX 75009-9802

CROSSON-CRAWFORD, JUNE, journalist; b. Detroit, Jan. 30; d. Wilmer Edgerton and Dorris (Van Loon) Madison; m. John Bruno, June 21, 1947 (div. 1960); m. Richard Crosson, Dec. 16, 1965 (dec. 1987); children: Doreen Bailo, John Bruno; m. Thomas A. Crawford, Apr. 8, 1989. BS, U. Mich., 1978. Columnist River Rouge (Mich.) Herald, 1971-86; spl. writer, columnist Detroit News, 1971-87; pub. info. officer Henry Ford C.C., Dearborn, Mich., 1988-89; freelance writer Downriver Profile mag., Wyandotte, Mich., 1991-93; correspondent Mich. Detroit News, 1993—; instr. writing Jackson (Mich.) C.C., 1990, instr. video prodn., 1991. Author: Sacred Spaces, 1993; author weekly column West Whirl, Detroit News, 1978-86. Recipient Keep Am. Beautiful award State of Mich., 1978, U.S. Keep Am. Beautiful Commn., 1978, Outstanding Svc. award VWF Aux., Polish-Am. Festival, City of Wyandotte, Best Video Prodn. award MacLean Hunter Cablevision, 1993. Mem. Detroit Women Writers Club, U. Mich. Alumni Assn., Polit. Sci. Internship Alumni Assn., River Rouge Rotary. Home: 5916 Rickfield S Jackson MI 49201

CROSSWAIT, DONNA LYNN, psychological examiner, counselor; b. Ann Arbor, Mich., Apr. 15, 1947; d. Neil Robert and Olive Sophia Hannah (Johnson) Korzuck; m. Steven George Crosswait, Aug. 6, 1983; children: Brian Richard Layher, Bradley Neil Layher; stepchildren: Christina L. Miller, Catherine L., Cynthia L. Carpenter. BA, Mich. State U., 1969; MEd, East Tenn. State U., 1993. Lic. psychol. examiner. Asst. dir. of svc. Saline (Mich.) Area Social Svcs., 1978; social worker, activity dir. Evang. Home, Saline, 1979-85; social worker Asbury Ctr., Johnson City, Tenn., 1989-94; counselor, psychol. examiner Behavioral Cons., Johnson City, 1994—. Bd. dirs., sec. Saline Area Social Svcs.; mem., sec., lay dir. United Emmaus Comty., 1986—; v.p., mem. United Meth. Women, 1986-90; mem. Munsey Meml. United Meth. Ch.; mem. dist. Coun. on Ministries. Mem. Am. Counseling Assn., Assn. for Assessment in Counseling, Tenn. Conf. on Social Welfare, South Highlands Coun. Healthcare Social Workers, Phi Kappa Phi. Home: 4 Beechwood Cir Johnson City TN 37604-6302

CROTHERS, NELL VEATCH, association executive, social worker; b. Buchanan, Ga., Mar. 21, 1916; d. Jesse William and Julia Bell (Kinsey) Veatch; m. William Clawson Crothers, Aug. 24, 1938; children: William Clawson Jr., Nina Crothers Fogg, Carolyn Crothers Ho. AB, LaGrange Coll., 1932-36; student, U. Ga., 1934; postgrad., Young Harris Coll., 1936-37. Tchr. Young Harris (Ga.) Coll., 1936-38, YWCA, Cleve., 1938-40; pub. rels. Case Sch. Applied Sci., Cleve., 1938-40; statistician Crane Co., Atlanta, 1940-42; tchr. YWCA, Winston Salem, N.C., 1945-47; mgr., social worker ARC, Salem, Oreg., 1963-66; exec. dir. YWCA, Salem, 1966-73. Editor: (cookbook) Y's Cookin, 1956. Pres. YWCA, LaGrange, Ga., 1935-36; trustee, tchr. Presbyterian Ch., 1947—; vol. bd. dirs., pres. YWCA, Salem, 1948-66; drama dir. Community Theatre and Presbyn. Ch., Salem, 1950-60; bd. dirs. YWCA Nat. Bd., N.Y.C., 1958-64; campaign mgr. United Fund, Salem, 1958; com. mem. Coun. of Governments, Salem, Oreg., 1960, City of Salem, 1960-79; organizer Human Rights Comm., Salem, 1963; com. mem. Salem Art Assn, 1973-79, Mission Mill Mus., 1979-85. Recipient Salem Women of The Year award Salem Hosp. Aux., 1958, Disting. Svc. award Salem C. of C., 1973, Disting. Svc. award City of Salem, 1970, 76, 77. Mem. Salem Hand Weavers Guild (4 awards northwest weavers conf., 1979). Republican. Home: 5934 Skyline Rd S Salem OR 97306-9432

CROTTO, RACHEL, insurance claims representative; b. N.Y.C., Dec. 25, 1958; d. Sidney and Isabel (Erganoff) C. Grad. diploma, Diller & Quaile Sch. Music, 1976; paralegal cert., U. La Verne, 1992. Profl. chess player, 1978; asst. claims mgr., small claims ct. rep. Surety Co. of Pacific, Northridge, Calif., 1983—; mem. U.S. Chess Olympic Team, Haifa, Israel, 1976,

Switzerland, 1982, Thessaloniki, Greece, 1986, United Arab Emirates, 1986. Facilitator, mem. Gay and Lesbian Svc. Ctr. U.S. Women's Chess Champion, U.S. Chess Fedn., 1978, 79; recipient Silver medal U.S. Chess Olympic Team, 1984. Mem. NOW, Feminist Majority. Democrat.

CROTTY, TERI, education educator; b. South Bend, Ind., June 10, 1950; d. Grayson Michael and Alice Elizabeth (Schneider) C. BS in Elem. Edn., Ind. U., 1972, MS Counseling and Guidance, 1981, PhD in Ednl. Psychology, 1992. Lic. elem. and cert. middle sch. tchr. Tchr. Edwardsburg and Cass Dist., Mich., 1972-75; cost analyst Bendix Corp., South Bend, Ind., 1975-81; career counselor Ind. U., South Bend, 1981-83; asst. dir. bus. outplacement svc. Ind. U., Bloomington, 1983-86, assoc. dir., 1987; assoc. instr. Ind. U., South Bend, 1988-90; asst. prof. U. Wis., River Falls, 1990—; vis. prof. Ind. U., Bloomington, 1990, 91; presenter in field. Grantee 3M, 1991, U. Wis., 1991. Mem. ASCD, APA, Am. Ednl. Rsch. Assn. (divsn. K), Am. Assn. of Colls. for Tchr. Edn. Democrat. Office: U Wis River Falls Ames Teacher Ctr River Falls WI 54022

CROUCH, ALTHA MARIE, health educator, consultant; b. Belton, Tex., Aug. 23, 1933; d. Walter Loy and Nancy Elizabeth (Harrison) C. BS in Health, Phys. Edn. and Recreation, Sul Ross State U., 1966, MA in Health, Phys. Edn. and Recreation, 1967; EdD in Curriculum and Instrn., U. N.Mex., 1977; MA in Counseling Edn., Western N.Mex. U., 1992. Bookkeeper Midland (Tex.) Reporter Telegram, 1954-63; instr. physical edn. and health Our Lady of Peace Cath. Elem. Sch., Alpine, Tex., 1964-65; asst. prof., coord. Womens' Programs Wayland Baptist Coll., Palinview, Tex., 1966-71; vis. instr. Tex. Tech. U., Lubbock, 1971-72; teaching assoc., grad. rsch. asst. U. N.Mex., Alburquerque, 1972-75; asst. prof. health edn. and recreation U. N.Mex., Gallup, 1975-80; asst. prof., co-coord. health edn. program U. N.Mex., Alburquerque, 1980-83; coord. community edn., part-time tchr. U. N.Mex., Valencia, 1983-88; asst. prof., coord. health edn. program U. N.Mex., Gallup, 1988-93, assoc. prof., 1993—; v.p. Faculty Senate, U. N.Mex., Gallup, 1989, 90; exec. dir. Crouch and Assoc. Health Cons., Gallup, 1979—; presenter in field. Assoc. editor N.Mex. Jour. HPERD, 1993; contrb. articles to profl. jours. Bd. mem. Am. Lung Assn., Albuquerque, 1981-87, Am. Heart Assn., Valencia County, 1967-94, Nat. Inst. on Alcoholism, 1980-92, Optimist Club, Gallup, 1990—; cert. ARC, Albuquerque, 1967. Recipient Cert. of Appreciation Svc. award ARC, 1980, 1500 Hours Vol. Svc. in CPR and First Aid award, 1984, Ten Year Svc. Recognition award, 1987, Five Year Disting. Svc. award Wayland Bapt. Coll, 1971, Ella May Small award N.Mex. Sch. Health Assn., 1981, Disting. Svc. award Am. Sch. Health Assn., 1983, Six Yrs. Dist. Svc. Bd. Dirs. award Am. Lung Assn., 1987. Fellow Am. Sch. Health Assn. (internat. health coun. 1989—, rsch. coun. 1981—, budget and fin. com. 1983-85, sec. to study com. 1982, chair 2 coms. 1981-83, conducted surveys 1981, state constituents constitution and by-laws ad hoc com. chair 1981, acting chair resolutions com. 1981); mem. AAHPERD (Southwest dist. asst. registrar 1981, presenter 1981, 92-94, N.Mex. chpt. v.p. health sect. 1981-82, 92-94, tchr. accountability task force), Am. Assn. Counseling and Devel., Am. Assn. Advancement Health Edn., N.Mex. Assn. Counseling & Devel., Coalition for Indian Edn. Office: U N Mex 220 College Rd Gallup NM 87301

CROUCH, ANGELA BETTY, association management executive, political science researcher, librarian; b. Lancaster, Ky., Mar. 10, 1966; d. Edward Kenneth and Betty Louise (Hulett) C. BA, Georgetown (Ky.) Coll., 1988; MSLS, U. Ky., 1990. Clk. UPS, Lexington, Ky., 1988-91; grad. asst. U. Ky., Lexington, 1989-90; libr. Georgetown (Ky.) Coll., 1990-91; rsch. assoc. Coun. of State Govts., Lexington, 1991-94; mgr. programs The Spieler Group, Lexington, 1994—. Libr. coord. Southland Christian Ch., Lexington, 1991-94. Christian Ch. Office: The Spieler Group 167 W Main St Ste 600 Lexington KY 40507-1910

CROUCH, ARLINE PARKS, librarian; b. Corbin, Ky., Jan. 13, 1947; d. Elijah and Edna (Gibbs) Parks; m. Robert Louis Crouch, Aug. 25, 1968; children: Cara Lynn, Carlin Robert. BS, Cumberland Coll., 1967; MA, Union Coll., 1970; postgrad., U. Ky., 1973. Tchr. 3d grade Boone County Bd. of Edn., Florence, Ky., 1967-68, tchr. 2d grade, 1968-69, tchr. 3d grade, 1969-74, libr., 1975—; libr. Crescent Springs (Ky.) Bapt. Ch., 1987-90. Mem. exec. coun. Ky. Educators Pub. Affairs Coun., Florence, 1975-78. Mem. NEA, Ky. Edn. Assn., Boone County Edn. Assn. (treas. Florence chpt. 1975-78), Ky. Libr. Assn., Ky. Sch. Librs. Assn., Boone County Sch. Libr. Assn., Phi Delta Kappa. Democrat. Home: PO Box 47 Burlington KY 41005-0047

CROUCH, DIANNE KAY, secondary school guidance counselor; b. Campbellsville, Ky., Apr. 28, 1954; d. James Edgar and Imogene (Bailey) Gabbert; m. Thomas Frederick Crouch, June 6, 1987. BA, Campbellsville Coll., 1976; MS, U. Ky., 1984, EdS, 1991. Cert. tchr. English, psychology, counselor, secondary schs., Ky. Tchr. English Grayson County High Sch., Leitchfield, Ky., 1976-78, Jessamine County Jr. High Sch., Nicholasville, Ky., 1978-83, Jessamine County High Sch., Nicholasville, 1983-89, Tates Creek Jr. High Sch., Lexington, Ky., 1989-90; guidance counselor Tates Creek High Sch., Lexington, 1990—; mem. pub. rels. com. Tates Creek H.S.; mem. task force on grouping/tracking Fayette County; selected Inst. Women in Sch. Adminstrn. Ky. Fund raiser Am. Leukemia Assn., Nicholasville, 1990-92; active Calvary Bapt. Ch., Lexington, 1991—; active Fayette County Task Force on Grouping Trucking. Named Jessamine County Tchr. of Yr., Jessamine County Bd. Edn., Nicholasville, Ky., 1986-87, Outstanding Tchr. 5th Dist., Campbellsville Coll., 1988; sponsor of Jr. High newspaper Tates Creek Clarion named 1 of top 5 in U.S Nat. Jr. Beta Club. Mem. NEA, Ky. Edn. Assn., Fayette County Edn. Assn., Ky. Counseling Assn. (bd. dirs.), Ctrl. Ky. Assn. Counseling and Devel., Coll. Bds. Coll. Scholarship Svc. Assembly, Kappa Delta Pi. Home: 716 Keene Way Ct Nicholasville KY 40356

CROUCH, THELMA RAE, university administrator; b. Alva, Okla., Apr. 12, 1938; d. Denver Harmon and Mary Louise (Shreeve) McMurphy; m. Allen J. Crouch; children: Tony, Linda. BS in Edn., Northwestern Okla. State U., 1960, MEd in Guidance and Counseling, 1994. Sec. Wharton Funeral Chapel, Alva, 1975-77, Northwest Translaor, Inc., Alva, 1977-79; dir. alumni Northwestern Okla. State U., Alva, 1979-87, sec. career svcs., 1987-92, dir. career svcs., 1992—. Chmn., sec. Alva Centennial Commn., 1984-94; mem., officer Woods County Genealogists, Alva, 1975—. Mem. Am. Counseling Assn., Okla. Computerized Devel. Placement Assn., S.W. Placement Assn., Beta Sigma Phi. Christian Ch. Office: Northwestern Okla State U 709 Oklahoma Blvd Alva OK 73717

CROUSE, LINDSAY, actress; b. N.Y.C., May 12, 1948; d. Russel and Anna (Erskine) C. BA, Radcliffe Coll., 1970. Appearences include (films) Slapshot, Between-the-Lines, All the President's Men, Prince of the City, The Verdict, Daniel, Iceman, Places in the Heart (Acad. award nomination 1985), House of Games, Communion, Desperate Hours, Being Human, Bye Bye Love, Indian in the Cupboard, (TV movies) Out of Darkness, Parallel Lives, Final Appeal, Chantilly Lace, (TV series) Hill Street Blues, Murder She Wrote, Columbo, Law and Order, Lifestories, Civil Wars, L.A. Law, Traps. Recipient Obie award for Acting in Reunion, 1980, Theater World award for The Homecoming, 1992.

CROVITZ, ELAINE SANDRA, clinical psychologist; b. N.Y.C., Oct. 18, 1936; d. Sydney and Jennie (Papier) Kobrin; children—Gordon, Deborah, Sara Pi. B.A., Bklyn. Coll., 1956; M.A., Duke U., 1960, Ph.D., 1964. Instr. med. psychology, staff psychologist Duke U. Med. Center, Durham, N.C., 1963-64, assoc. med. psychology, supervising psychologist, 1964-67, asst. prof. med. psychology, 1967-75, assoc. prof., 1975—; bd. dirs. Maferr Found., Va.; vis. assoc. prof. N.C. Cen. U., Durham, 1976-79. Mem. Am. Psychol. Assn., Southeastern Psychol. Assn., N.C. Psychol. Assn., Assn. for Advancement Psychology, Internat. Council Psychologists, Internat. Assn. Applied Psychology, Nat. Register Health Service Providers Psychology, AAUW. Author: (with Elizabeth Buford) Courage Knows No Sex, 1978; author research papers; contbr. articles to profl. jours. Home: 419 Gentry Ln Hillsborough NC 27278-8811 Office: Duke U Med Ctr PO Box 3895 Durham NC 27710

CROW, CECILE MARIE, sales executive; b. Wichita Falls, Tex., Apr. 21, 1938; d. Edward Patrick and Frances Beatrice (Bruckner) Hopkins. BS in Psychology, North Tex. U., 1971, MS in Social Sci., 1972; postgrad., Columbia U., 1980. Tchr. Eastfield Coll., Dallas, 1972-73; rep. sales Am. Can Co., Dallas, 1973-75; exec. nat. accounts Am. Can Co., Miami, 1975-77; mgr. dist. sales Am. Can Co., Boston, 1977-78; mgr. foodservice mktg. develop. Am. Can Co., Greenwich, Conn., 1978-81; dir. sales devel. James River Corp., Norwalk, Conn., 1981-87; dir. nat. accounts James River Corp., Norwalk, 1987—. Grantee North Tex. U., 1971. Mem. Internat. Foodsvc. Mfrs. Assn. (bd. dirs.). Office: James River Corp 800 Conn Ave PO Box 6000 Norwalk CT 06850

CROW, ELIZABETH SMITH, publishing company executive; b. N.Y.C., 1946; d. Harrison Venture and Marlis (deGreve) Smith; m. Charles P. Crow, Mar. 2, 1974; children: Samuel Harrison, Rachel Venture, Sarah Gibson. BA, Mills Coll., 1968; postgrad., Brown U., 1969-70. Editorial asst. New Yorker mag., N.Y.C., 1968-69; editorial asst., exec. editor New York mag., N.Y.C., 1970-78; editor in chief Parents mag., N.Y.C., 1978-88; pres., editorial dir., CEO Gruner & Jahr USA Pub., 1988-93; editor-in-chief Mademoiselle Mag., N.Y.C., 1993—; free-lance book reviewer N.Y. Times Book Rev.; screener, judge Nat. Mag. Awards, 1984—. Mem. Media adv. coun March of Dimes; bd. advisors The Giraffe Project; trustee Mills Coll., 1986-91; bd. dirs. YWCA N.Y., Peabody awards; bd. dirs., exec. com. Met. Opera Guild. Recipient Nat. Mag. award for gen. excellence, 1988. Mem. Am. Soc. Mag. Editors (exec. bd. 1984-88), Mag. Pubs. Am. (bd. dirs. 1988—), Cosmopolitan Club, Century Assn. Democrat. Office: Mademoiselle Mag Condé Nast Publs 350 Madison Ave New York NY 10017*

CROW, LYNNE CAMPBELL SMITH, insurance company representative; b. Buffalo, Oct. 13, 1942; d. Stephen Smith and Jean Campbell (Ruggles) Hall; m. William David Crow II, Apr. 16, 1966 (div. Dec. 1989); children: William David III, Alexander Fairbairn, Margaret Campbell. BA, Sweet Briar (Va.) Coll., 1964; postgrad., Am. Coll., 1986. CLU; ChFC. Claims rep. Liberty Mut. Ins. Co., Bklyn. and N.Y.C., 1964-66; with McGraw-Hill Corp., N.Y.C., 1966-67; claims rep. Liberty Mut. Ins. Co., East Orange, N.J., 1967-68; sales assoc. Realty World/Allsopp Realtors, Millburn, N.J., 1981-82; field rep. Guardian Life Ins. Co., 1982—. Bd. dirs. Jr. League of the Oranges and Short Hills, Millburn, 1979-80, Millburn LWV, 1979-80; campaign chair, bus. chair, bd. dirs. United Way of Millburn/Short Hills, 1981-88, 90—, sec., 1990-91. Mem. Nat. Assn. Life Underwriters (Nat. Quality award 1988, 91, Nat. Health Achievement award 1988, 90, Nat. Sales Achievement award 1988, 90), Am. Soc. CLUs and ChFCs (bd. dirs. 1994—), N.J. State Assn. Life Underwriters (dir. region II 1993—), Newark Assn. Life Underwriters (past pres. 1993-94, bd. dirs. 1986-94, sec. 1987-88, treas. 1988-89, 3d v.p. 1989-90, 2d v.p. 1990, pres.-elect 1991-92, pres. 1992-93), Million Dollar Round Table (qualifying mem.), Knight of Round Table, Women's Life Underwriters Confedn., Jr. League Oranges and Short Hills, Internat. Platform Assn., Millburn Bus. and Profl. Women (bd. dirs. 1990-91), LWV, Assn. Health Ins. Agts., Nat. Assn. Security Dealers, Racquets Club Short Hills (bd. dirs. 1982-84), Chatham (Mass.) Beach and Tennis Club. Republican. Episcopalian. Home: 22 Winding Way Short Hills NJ 07078-2814 Office: 1150 Raritan Rd Cranford NJ 07016

CROW, SHERYL, singer/songwriter, musician; b. Kennett, Mo., 1963. Degree in classical piano, U. Mo., 1984. Backup singer Bad tour Michael Jackson, 1987; backup singer The End of the Innocence tour Don Henley, 1989; also backup singer George Harrison, Joe Cocker, Stevie Wonder, Rod Stewart; singer, songwriter Tuesday Night Music Club, 1992—. Albums include Tuesday Night Music Club, 1993; singles include Leaving Las Vegas, All I Wanna Do (Grammy awards for Record of Year and Female Pop Vocal, 1995), Strong Enough. Recipient Grammy award for Best New Artist, 1995. Address: care A&M Records 1416 N La Brea Ave Los Angeles CA 90028*

CROWDER, BARBARA LYNN, lawyer; b. Mattoon, Ill., Feb. 3, 1956; d. Robert Dale and Martha Elizabeth (Harrison) C.; m. Lawrence Owen Taliana, Apr. 17, 1982; children: Paul Joseph, Robert Lawrence, Benjamin Owen. BA, U. Ill., 1978, JD, 1981. Bar: Ill. 1981. Assoc. Louis E. Olivero, Peru, Ill., 1981-82; asst. state's atty. Madison County, Edwardsville, Ill., 1982-84; ptnr. Robbins & Crowder, Edwardsville, 1985-87, Robbins, Crowder & Bader, Edwardsville, 1987-88, Crowder & Taliana, 1988—. Co-editor ISBA Family Law Newsletter, 1993; contbr. articles to profl. jours. Chmn. City of Edwardsville Zoning Bd. Appeals, 1986-87; committee woman. Edwardsville Dem. Precinct 15, 1986—; mem. City of Edwardsville Planning Commn., 1985-87. Named Best Oral Advocate, Moot Ct. Bd., 1979, Outstanding Young Career Woman, Dist. XIV. ILL. Bus. and Profl. Women, 1986; recipient Alice Paul award Alton-Edwardsville NOW, 1987; named Outstanding Working Woman of Ill. Ill. Fed. of Bus. and Profl. Women, 1988-89; recipient Athena award Edwardsville/Glen Carbon C. of C., 1991. Fellow Am. Acad. Matrimonial Lawyers; mem. ABA, Ill. Bar Assn. (assoc. mem. family law sect. coun. 1990-93, mem. 1994-95, co-editor family law newsletter 1993), Ill. Fedn. Bus. and Profl. Women (parliamentarian dist XIV 1991-92), Women Lawyers Assn. Met. East (v.p. 1985, pres. 1986), So. Ill. Mediation Assn. (v.p. 1992) Edwardsville Bus. and Profl. Women's Club (pres. 1988-89, treas. 1989-90, Woman of Achievement award 1985, Jr. Svc. award 1987), U. Ill. Alumni Assn. (v.p. met.-east club 1994). Democrat. Home: 982 Surrey Dr Edwardsville IL 62025-3807 Office: Crowder & Taliana 216 N Main St Edwardsville IL 62025-1604

CROWDER, BONNIE WALTON, small business owner, composer; b. Lafayette, Tenn., Apr. 14, 1916; d. Edward Samuel Bailey and Nannie Elizabeth (Goad) Walton; m. Reggie Ray Crowder, Nov. 19, 1936; 1 child, Rita Faye. Grad., Nashville Beauty Coll. Owner, operator Bonnie's Beauty Salon, Tampa, Fla. Composer: A Man of Faith, 1988, This Miracle, 1988, (with Willard E. Walton) God Bless Our President, 1988, Awake, Arise America, 1989, Touching My Jesus, 1990, (with Willard E. Walton) Muscle Jerky Boogie, 1992. Mem. ch. choir, Tampa; mem. Bus. and Profl. Women's Chorus, 1960's and 70's, U. South Fla. Community Chorus, 1973-81. Mem. Beta Sigma Phi.

CROWDER, ELIZABETH See WADDINGTON, BETTE HOPE

CROWE-HAGANS, NATONIA, manufacturing executive, engineer; b. Chgo., Feb. 10, 1955; d. Benjamin Kermit and Natalie (Williams) Crowe; m. Louis Fisher (div.); children: Sean Crowe, Tamara Fisher; m. William Hagans. AA, Vets. Hosp., Chgo., 1977; BSEE, U. Ill., Chgo., 1983; MS in Mgmt., Maryville U., 1988. Intern Corning Glass Works, Bluffton, Ind., 1980, Corning (N.Y.) Glass Works, 1981-82; assoc. engr. McDonnell Douglas, St. Louis, 1983-84, engr., 1984-85, sr. engr., 1986-87, laser team leader, 1987-88; staff mgr. McDonnell Douglas, Huntington Beach, Calif., 1988-89; mgr. quick response ctr. Loral Electro-optical Sys., Pomona, Calif., 1989, mgr. mfg. svcs., 1989-91, mgr. material control svcs., 1991-92, program mgr., 1992-93; mgr. prodn. Loral Electro-optical Sys., Pomona, 1993-94; mgr. projects, mgr. mfg. engr. Rockwell Automation, Allen Bradley, Milw., 1994—. Mem. Womens Aux., Yorba Linda, Calif., 1989, Illiteracy Com., St. Louis, 1984, PTA, Corona, Calif., 1991. Mem. NAFE, Nat. Soc. Black Engrs. (co-founding mem. Gateway chpt. 1987-88, Svc. award 1988), Nat. Mgmt. Assn. (sec., com. mem., numerous awards 1990). Home: PO Box 21792 Milwaukee WI 53221

CROWELL, SHERRY DIEGEL, clinical psychologist; b. Colorado City, Tex., Oct. 19, 1951; d. Charles Ambrose and Jo Ellen (Elliot) Diegel; 1 child, Charles Michael. BA, Tex. Tech U., 1983, MA, 1985, PhD, 1992. Lic. psychologist, Tex. Sr. dir. Psychol. Clinic, Lubbock, Tex., 1987-89; psychometrist Med.-Surg. Neurology Clinic, Lubbock, 1987-89; assoc. clin. psychologist Big Spring (Tex.) State Hosp., 1987-89; psychology intern Austin (Tex.) State Hosp., 1989-90; pvt. practice psychotherapy Abilene, Tex., 1990-93; clin. psychologist Abilene Regional Mental Health Mental Retardation Ctr., 1991-93; pvt. practice psychology Abilene; part-time asst. prof. psychology McMurry U., 1994—; chair symposium Tex. Assn. on Mental Retardation, 1992; presenter in field. Contbr. rsch. articles to profl. publs. Mem. adv. bd. Big Country AIDS Support Group, Abilene, 1992—; mem. Lubbock AIDS Health Care Planning Group, Lubbock, 1987-89; founding mem., trustee West Tex. AIDS Found., Lubbock, 1986-89. Mem. APA, Tex. Psychol. Assn. (chair symposium 1987, 88, 92-93, Alexander award for Rsch. Excellence in Psychobiologic Field 1992). Home: 1217 Ross Ave Abilene TX 79605-4230 Office: 3301 N 3rd St Ste 113 Abilene TX 79603-7044

CROWLEY, CANDY ALT, news correspondent; b. Kalamazoo; d. Richard Casper and Nadine Lois (Webster) Alt; children: Richard Webster, Jonathan Milligan. AB, Randolph-Macon Women's Coll., 1970. Newsroom asst. Metromedia-WAshington-FM, Washington, 1972-73; nat. editor, reporter AP Radio, Washington, 1974; anchor, reporter Mut. Broadcasting, Washington, 1975-77; anchor, White House corr. AP, Washington, 1981-85; corr NBC News, Washington, 1986; White House/Capital Hill corr. CNN, Washington, 1987—. Office: CNN Wash Bur 820 1st St NE Washington DC 20002-4243

CROWLEY, CYNTHIA JOHNSON, secondary school educator; b. Summit, N.J., June 28, 1930; d. Theodore Eames and Frances Lysett (Wetmore) J.; m. Robert J. Crowley, Sept. 6, 1952 (dec.); children: David Cochrane II, Cynthia Wetmore. BA, U. Pa., 1952; MA, Fairleigh-Dickinson U., Rutherford, N.J. Cert. English tchr., N.J. Tchr. econs. and reading St. Mary's Sch., Peekskill, N.Y., 1952-53; tchr. humanities Henry Hudson Regional Sch., Highlands, N.J., 1969-92, coord. gifted program, 1983-92; prodr.-dir. CR-Video Svcs., P.A.; pres. Associated Ednl. Svcs.; active N.J. Curriculum Revision Project; adv. bd. mem. Women's Athletics U. Pa., N.J. Council U.S. Congressional Awards Program; ednl. cons.; cons., lectr. creative writing workshops. Prodr. TV Tutor Series for Home and Schs. Former mem. Atlantic Highlands (N.J.) Bd. Edn., also past pres.; mem. exec. com. Monmouth County Sch. Bds. Assn. Mem. ASCD, Nat. Coun. Tchrs. English, Nat. Acad. TV Arts and Scis. (N.Y. chpt.), Gifted Educators (exec. com. 1986—), Shore Consortium for Gifted and Talented, Monmouth County Sch. Bds. Assn. (mem. exec. com.), Alumni Pres.'s Coun. Ind. Secondary Schs. (life, past pres.), Phi Delta Kappa. Home: 125 E Mount Ave Atlantic Highlands NJ 07716-1549

CROWLEY, MARILYN, critical care nurse, educator; b. Geuda Springs, Kans., Sept. 29, 1935; d. Wyatt Julian and Mary Alice Swaim; m. Dale Crowley, June 7, 1958; 1 child, Debra Crowley Schrag. Diploma, William Newton Meml. Hosp., Winfield, Kans., 1956. Cert. critical care nurse, emergency nurse, emergency med. svcs. instr., ACLS, BLS, others. Coord. fire med. rescue svcs. Wichita Fire Dept., 1981-86; mobile intensive care nurse Winfield Ambulance Svc. William Newton Meml. Hosp., 1970-76, charge ICU and emergency dept., house supr., 1990-93, travel nurse emergency dept., trama ctr., critical care, 1993—, supr., head nurse, 1970-77; surg. and emergency nurse Snyder Clin. Assn., Winfield, 1957-70; travel nurse emergency dept. Trauma Ctr. St. Francis Regional Med. Ctr., Wichita, Kans., 1993—, Robert Wood Johnson Univ. Hosp., New Brunswick, N.J., Hendrick Med. Ctr., Abilene, Tex.; dir. emergency med. tech. program Southwestern Coll. of Kans., Winfield; night nurse, emergency room supr. Mount Desert Island Hosp., Bar Harbor, Maine, 1994; staff nurse ICU N.W. Miss. Med. Ctr., Clarksdale, 1994; night nursing and ER supr. Mt. Desert Island Hosp., Bar Harbor, Maine, 1994; staff nurse ICU N.W. Miss. Med. Ctr., Clarksdale, Miss., 1994—; adj. staff edn., tng. and exam. Kans. Bd. Emergency Med. Svcs., Topeka; instr. nursing continuing edn. St. Francis Regional Med. Ctr. Outreach Edn. Active Am. Heart Assn., Am. Cancer Soc. Recipient Spl. award Kans. Emergency Med. Technicians Assn., 1980, Wichita Fire Dept., 1985, 86, Winfield Area Emergency Med. Svcs., 1978, numerous others. Home: 1002 E 13th Ave Winfield KS 67156-4513

CROWN, NANCY ELIZABETH, lawyer; b. Bronx, N.Y., Mar. 27, 1955; d. Paul and Joanne Barbara (Newman) C.; children: Rebecca, Adam. BA, Barnard Coll., 1977, MA, 1978; MEd, Columbia U., 1983; JD cum laude, Nova Law Sch., 1992. Cert. tchr.; Bar: Fla. 1992. Tchr. Sachem Sch. Dist., Holbrook, N.Y., 1978-82; dir. mail order dept. Haber-Klein, Inc., Hicksville, N.Y., 1984-88; mgr. mdse., dir. ops. Sure Card Inc., Pompano Beach, Fla., 1988-89; legal intern Office U.S. Trustee/Dept. Justice, 1992; assoc. John T. Kinsey, P.A., Boca Raton, Fla., 1993—. Recipient West Pub. award for acad. achievement, 1992. Mem. ABA, Am. Inns. of the Ct., Fla. Bar Assn., Fla. Assn. Women Lawyers (v.p. programming), Phi Alapha Delta. Democrat. Jewish.

CROWSEY, CHERYL ANN, marketing professional; b. Houston, Oct. 27, 1959; d. Henry Riley Crowsey and Delores (Kelly) Carson. BBA magna cum laude, U. Tex., San Antonio, 1993. Mgr. Olan Mills Portrait Studio, San Antonio, 1977-78; svc. rep., backfill mgr. Southwestern Bell Telephone Co., San Antonio, 1978-84; program mgr. AT&T, Basking Ridge, N.J., 1984-93; team leader AT&T Internat. Account Ctr., San Antonio, 1993—. Sec. Celebrate Hist. Morristown, N.J., 1991; note writer for shut-ins, Laurel Heights Meth. Ch., San Antonio, 1992. Mem. Alpha Chi. Home: #506 12222 Blanco San Antonio TX 78216

CROWSON, GATHA ANN, training developer, speaker, author; b. Athens, Ala., May 6, 1938; d. Barnabas Valentine and Nancy Ruth (Legg) Romine; m. Carey Wayne Crowson; children: Timothy B., Tom, Sari Buchanan, Toney, Terrell. Student, North Ala. Coll. Commerce, Athens State Coll. Adminstrv. asst. Teledyne Brown Engrng., Huntsville, Ala., 1973-77; pres., cons. Crowson Prodns., Inc., Athens, 1989—; instr. continuing edn. dept. Athens State Coll., 1990—. Author: Gifts from God, 1989, My Christmas Wish, 1989, My Alma Mater, 1989, Tha Ol' Rocking Chair, 1990, Becoming Me--My Choice, 1992, Cleaning Out the Closet of Your Life, 1992, What's In My Cup, 1992, Flight to Freedom, 1992, Gifts from Gatha, 1992, Gifts From God, 1992, Growth from Within, 1992, Dynamics of the Dysfunctional Family, 1992, Training Americans Workforce, 1992; editor (mag.) Coloring My Wings, 1990—. Mem. Mayor's Drug-Free Community task force, Huntsville, 1990; chair sustaining com. YMCA, 1989-90; mem. area adv. coun. N. Ala. Parenting Edn. Ctr.; bd. dirs. Partnership for a Drug-Free Athens/Limestone County. Mem. ASTD (pres., train Am.'s workforce liaison), NAFE, Nat. Speakers Assn., Ala. Speakers Assn., Athens C. of C., Ala. Coun. on Family Relations, Profl. Women's Fellowship, Bus. and Profl. Women's Club. Republican. Home and Office: Rte 12 Box 58 Athens AL 35611

CROWTHER, DOROTHY ELEANOR, librarian; b. Havre de Grace, Md., Feb. 4, 1945; d, James Huey Jr. and Blanche Cecelia (JOhnson) Fall; m. David Alfred Crowther. BA, Lake Erie Coll., 1967; MEd, Westfield State Coll., 1976; postgrad, Nova U., 1992—. Cert. tchr. Mass, Va. Tchr. Big Spring (Tex.) Sch. System, 1968; substitute tchr. Dept. Defense Schs., Clark AFB, Philippines, 1969-70; tchr. Fayetteville (N.C.) Sch. System, 1971-72, Granby (Mass.) Pub. Schs., 1973-78; eligibility tech. State of Conn., Danbury, 1980-85; libr. Loudoun Country Day Sch., Leesburg, Va., 1990—; ednl. liaison Granby Pub. Schs., Granby Pub. Libr., 1973-78; libr. trustee Loudoun County Libr. System, 1990-94; lectr. Shenandoah U., Winchester, Va., 1994—. Contbr. articles to newspapers and jours. Vol. ARC, Ala, Ohio, Philippines, 1960-69, United Way, Conn., Va., 1984-86, Am. Cancer Soc., Va., 1988; pres. P.E.O. sisterhood, 1988-90. Named Hidden Heroine Girl Scouts Am., 1976. Mem. ALA, ASCD, Va. Libr. Assn., P.E.O. Presbyterian. Office: Loudoun Country Day Sch 237 Fairview St NW Leesburg VA 22075

CROXFORD, LYNNE LOUISE, social services administrator; b. Schenectady, N.Y., Nov. 9, 1947; d. Frederick William and Elizabeth Elger (Irish) C.; BA, Kalamazoo Coll., 1969; MPA, Wayne State U., 1975; m. Daniel Roderick Talhelm; 2 children, Alan Frederick, Thomas Arthur. Caseworker dept. social svc. County of Calhoun, Battle Creek, Mich., 1969-70; caseworker, supr. County of Oakland, Pontiac, Mich., 1970-76; program specialist Mich. Dept. Social Svcs., Lansing, 1976-78; exec. coord. for programming Mich. State Planning Coun. for Devel. Disabilities, 1978-79; staff coord. Gov. Com. on Unification of Pub. Mental Health System, Lansing, 1979-80; dir. dept. social svc. County of Ingham, Lansing, 1980-90; dir. fin. control Mich. Dept. Social Svcs., 1990-91, dir. office payment systems, 1991—; adv. Mich. Assn. Non-Profit Residential Facilities, 1976-78; incorporating dir. Mich. Pub. Mgmt. Inst., 1990. Trustee, Unitarian Universalist Ch. of Greater Lansing, 1979-82, v.p., 1980-82; bd. dirs. Coun. for Prevention Child Abuse and Neglect, 1980-83; mem. Lansing Tri-County Pvt. Industry Coun., 1980-90; chair Pvt. Industry Coun. Steering Com., 1987-90. Mem. ASPA (nat. coun. 1986-92, Mich. Pub. Svc. award, 1993), Am. Pub. Welfare Assn., Michigan County Social Svcs. Assn. Club: Zonta (charter Mich. Capitol area, v.p. 1991-92, pres. 1992-93). Recipient Disting. Alumnus award Wayne State U. Grad. Program in Pub. Adminstrn., 1988, Spl. Recognition award Mich. Pub. Mgmt. Inst., 1994. Contbr. in field. Home: 750 Pebblebrook Ln East Lansing MI 48823-2140 Office: 235 S Grand PO Box 30037 Lansing MI 48909-7537

CROYLE, BARBARA ANN, health care management executive; b. Knoxville, Tenn., Oct. 22, 1949; d. Charles Evans and Myrtle Elizabeth (Kellam) C. BA cum laude in Sociology, Coll. William and Mary, 1971; cert. corp. tax and securities law Inst. Paralegal Tng., 1971; JD, U. Colo., 1975; cert. program mgmt. devel. Colo. Women's Coll., 1980; MBA, U. Denver, 1983. Bar: Colo. 1976. Paralegal Holland & Hart, Denver, 1972-73; law clk. Colo. Ct. Appeals, Denver, summer 1976; assoc. firm Shaw Spangler & Roth, Denver, 1976-77; mgr. acquisitions/lands Petro-Lewis Corp., Denver, 1977-85; mgr. strategic planning Westinghouse, Transp. Div., 1985-87; mng. dir. Benefit Resource Mgmt. Group (subs. Blue Cross We. Pa.), 1987-92; COO and v.p. D.T. Watson Rehab. Hosp., 1992-93; adminstr. dir. St. Elizabeth Med. Ctr., Dayton, Ohio, 1994—; tchr. oil and gas law Colo. Paralegal Inst., 1978, 79; arbitrator Am. Arbitration Assn.; mediator; vol. Suicide Prevention Ctr. Mem. NAFE, ABA, Pa. Bar Assn., Allegheny County Bar Assn., Am. Coll. Healthcare Execs. (ethics com., assoc.). Home: 330 Jones St Dayton OH 45410 Office: St Elizabeth Med Ctr 601 Edwin C Moses Blvd Dayton OH 45408

CROZIER, LUCILLE BREEDING, civic worker; b. Springfield, Ill., June 7, 1907; m. Alfred Crozier (dec.); 2 children. AB, U. Pitts., 1934, MLitt, 1946. Contbr. articles to med. aux. publs. Pres. Pa. Med. Aux., 1956-57; parliamentarian AMA Med. Aux., 1970-71; trustee U. Pitts., 1971-77. Recipient medal of distinction U. Pitts., 1987. Mem. AAUW (pres. Pa. 1958-60), Disting. Daus. Pa. (pres. 1975-76, medal of distinction 1963), Coll. Club (pres. 1960-62), 20th Century Club (lecture chmn. 1985-87), Pi Kappa Delta. Home: 4601 5th Ave Apt 820 Pittsburgh PA 15213-1705

CROZIER, PRUDENCE SLITOR, economist; b. Boston, Oct. 27, 1940; d. Richard Eaton and Louise (Bean) S.; m. William Marshall Crozier, Jr., June 20, 1964; children: Matthew Eaton, Abigail Parsons, Patience Wells. BA with honors, Wellesley Coll., 1962; MA in Econs., Yale U., 1963; PhD in Econs., Harvard U., 1971. Research asst. Fed. Reserve Bank, Boston, 1963-64; teaching fellow-tutor Harvard U., Cambridge, Mass., 1966-69; instr. Wellesley Coll., Mass., 1969-70; sr. economist Data Resources Inc., Lexington, Mass., 1973-74; bd. dirs. Mass. Health and Ednl. Facilities Authority, 1985-93, Omega Fund, 1984-87, Boston Pub. Libr. Found., 1994—; mem. vis. com. Harvard Sch. Pub. Health, 1993—. Contbr. articles to profl. jours. Trustee Newton Wellesley Hosp., Mass., 1978-90; overseer Center Research on Women, Wellesley, 1982-83; trustee Wellesley Coll., 1980—. Mem. Am. Econ. Assn., Boston Econ. Club, Phi Beta Kappa. Home: Ridge Hill Farm Rd Wellesley MA 02181

CRUM, JANIS MARIE, political consultant; b. Media, Pa., Nov. 26, 1968; d. Roger Jesse and Denise Ella (Lattin) C. BA, Calif. State U., 1991; MA, San Diego State U., 1994. Political cons. The Campaign Group, San Diego, 1993—. Campus coord. Planned Parenthood Bd. Dirs., San Diego, 1992-93; legis. aide U.S. Rep. Karen Shepherd, Washington, 1992-93; issues coord., scheduling dir. Lynn Schenk for Congress, San Diego, 1992; mem. Nat. Women's Polit. Caucus, San Diego, 1992—, Dem. Leadership Coun., San Diego, 1994—; founder Choice Pol. Action Com., Calif. Mem. Phi Kappa Phi, Kappa Alpha Theta. Home: 7309 Eads Ave La Jolla CA 92037-5035

CRUM, LUANNE, financial analyst; b. Louisville, Aug. 11, 1962; d. Joseph Willard and Marjorie Alice (Dobbs) C. BA, Hanover Coll., 1984; MBA, Bellarmine Coll., 1988. Analyst First Nat. Bank, Louisville, 1988-92; fin. analyst, officer Nat. City Bank, Louisville, 1992—; cons. Hanover Connection, Hanover (Ind.) Coll., 1992. Active Tyler Park Neighborhood Assn., Louisville, 1992—, Habitat for Humanity, Louisville, 1992. Mem. Nat. Assn. Accts., Phi Mu (alumni assn. reference chmn. 1990—, chpt. advisor 1993). Republican. Home: 1413 Goddard Ave Louisville KY 40204 Office: Nat City Bank 101 S 5th St T 12-13 Louisville KY 40202

CRUMBAUGH, BONNIE SUTTER, elementary education educator; b. Bloomington, Ill., Mar. 8, 1955; d. Harold Eugene and Catherine Jean (Carnahan) S.; m. Steven Wendell Crumbaugh, July 14, 1979; children: John Steven, Daniel Edward, Susan Elizabeth. BS, U. Ill., 1977. Cert. elem. tchr., Ill. Tchr. Manlius (Ill.) Unified Sch. Dist., 1977-79, Farmer City (Ill.) Unified Sch. Dist., 1979-83, Blue Ridge Unified Sch. Dist., Farmer City, 1991—; coord. Dist. Presch. Screening, Farmer City, 1991—, Early Childhood Spl. Edn. tchrs.'s Exch., Cooperative, Ill., 1994. Co-author, editor: District Manual for Early Childhood Education Programs. Deacon, elder com. chair, 1st Presbyn. Ch., LeRoy, Ill., 1983. Mem. LeRoy Hist. Soc., LeRoy C. of C. (bd. dirs. 1992), East Ctrl. Ill. Assn. for Edn. Young Children, Coun. for Exceptional Children, DAR, Child Study Club (former officers). Republican. Presbyterian. Home: RR 1 Box 146 Le Roy IL 61752-9601 Office: Schneider Elem Sch 309 N John St Farmer City IL 61842-1209

CRUMBLEY, ESTHER HELEN KENDRICK, realtor, retired educator; b. Okeechobee, Fla., Oct. 3, 1928; d. James A. and Corrine (Burney) Kendrick; m. Chandler Jackson, Oct. 24, 1949; children: Pamela E., Chandler A., William J. BS in Math. Edn., Ga. So. Coll., 1966; M in Math., Jacksonville (Fla.) U., 1979. Cert. secondary edn. tchr., Ga. Secondary edn. tchr. Camden County Bd. Edn., St. Mary's, Ga., 1958-92, ret.; realtor Watson Realty, St. Mary's, 1985—; dept. chairperson Camden High Sch., St. Mary's, 1966-72; pres., sec., treas. Camden GMA, St. Mary's, 1976-78. Area contact person Max Cleand Sec. of State, Atlanta, 1982—; councilwoman City of St. Mary's, 1979-86, mayor pro tem, 1981-86. Named Star Tchr., 1972, Camden GMA, 1979-88. Mem. Camden Ga. Assn. Educators (pres. 1976, sec.-treas. 1977-78, star tchr. 1972), PAGE (biog. com. rep. 1984—, named outstanding 8th dist. bldg. rep.), Camden Gen. Mcpl. Assn. (pres., sec.-treas. 1979-88), fin. and budget coms.), Math. Assn., Internat. Platform Assn. Republican. Baptist. Home: RR 3 Box 810 Folkston GA 31537-9729

CRUMMEY, F(RANCES) CAROLYN, social psychologist, biostatistician; b. Summerville, S.C., May 15, 1949; d. Robert Lee and Mary Etta Crummey. Student, Princeton U., 1970; BA magna cum laude, Lincoln U., Pa., 1971; MA, MPh, PhD in Social Psychology, Columbia U., 1983, postgrad., 1989. Cert. statis. issues in testing. Rsch. assoc. Olivia Frost Rsch. Assocs., N.Y.C., 1975-82; cons. Office of Instnl. Rsch. Antioch U., N.Y.C., 1984-85; rsch. assoc. dept. psychiatry Harlem Hosp., N.Y.C., 1986-87, co-dir. dept. psychiatry, 1986-89, coordinating mgr. dept. psychiatry, 1989-90; mgr., biostatistician Addiction Rsch. Treatment Corp., Bklyn., 1990-93; researcher dept. Psychiatry Harlem Hosp., N.Y.C., 1993—. Contbr. articles to profl. jours. Lincoln U. scholar, 1967-71; NIMH trainee, 1971-75; recipient award of merit Columbia U., 1973; named to Outstanding Young Women in Am., 1978. Mem. NAFE, Am. Assn. Pub. Health, Phi Beta Kappa, Beta Kappa Chi, Phi Kappa Epsilon. Home: 710 W 173d St Apt 21 New York NY 10032 Office: Harlem Hosp Dept Psychiatry WP4 506 Lenox Ave New York NY 10035

CRUMP, AUDREY GYDA, employment adviser, human resources administrator; b. Detroit, Aug. 6, 1954; d. Henry Lee and Verna Dean (Funches) C. BS in Pers. Mgmt./Labor Rels., U. Md., 1980. Pers. asst. Nat. Coun. on Aging, 1973-80; acct. exec. Consumer Dental Care, 1982; recruiter Tech Search, Inc., 1984-85; pers. analyst Met. Washington Coun. of Govts., 1985-89; human resources rep. II Kaiser Permanente Health Plan, Rockville, Md., 1990—; pres. Working Knowledge, Riverdale, Md., 1990—. With USN, 1973-80. Mem. Internat. Pers. Mgmt. Assn. (publs. adv. bd. 1993—), Soc. for Human Resources Mgmt. Democrat. Home: 5904 E Pine Dr Riverdale MD 20737 Office: Kaiser Permanente 2101 E Jefferson St Rockville MD 20849

CRUMP, MILDRED C., educational consultant, braille instructor; b. Detroit, Nov. 3, 1938; d. Edgar and Mattie Lee (Johnson) Coleman; widowed Mar. 1993; children: Cecil Lawrence, Sheri Elaine. BS in Edn., Wayne State U., 1961. Braille tchr. Detroit (Mich.) Bd. Edn., 1960-65; edn. cons., braille tchr. N.J. Commn. for the Blind and Visually Impaired; adv. bd. Pre-Coll. Ctr., Rutgers U., Newark. Active Friends of Newark Symphony Hall, Friends of N.J. State Opera, Friends of Newark Mus., Bethany Bapt. Ch., Newark, Hispanic Women's Task Force N.J.; pres. bd. dirs. Habitat for Humanity Newark, Inc.; trustee Boys' and Girls' Clubs Newark, Inc., Newark Preservation and Landmarks Com.; bd. dirs. Improve Newark, Met. Ecumenical Ministry; charter bd. mem. N.J. Coalition of 100 Black Women, Inc.; Newark edn. coun. Drop Out Prevention Task Force; others. Recipient Disting. Svc. award City of Newark, 1991, Cert. appreciation United Way Hudson and West Essex, 1992, Cert. appreciation Montclair Lions Club, 1992, Humanitarian award World Gospel Musical Assn., 1993, Hero award Habitat for Humanity Newark Inc., 1993, Outstanding Citizen award Project 2000 Seton Hall U., 1993; named Hon. mem. Concerned Community Women of Jersey City, 1991, 10 Outstanding Women in the South Ward Donald Bradley Civic Assn., 1993, others. Mem. NAACP (life mem. Newark br.), LWV (Newark chpt.), People's Orgn. for Progress (First Annual Black Women's Achievement award 1992), Nat. Coun. Negro Women, Minority Women in Trade Unions, Nat. Rainbow Coalition, Delta Sigma Theta. Democrat. Baptist. Home: 88 Hansbury Ave Newark NJ 07112

CRUMRINE, V(ERONA) SUZANNE, business educator; b. Skiatook, Okla., Apr. 21, 1944; d. John Vernon and Katy Elizabeth (Luter) C. Bs in Bus. Edn., BS in Phys. Edn., Phillips U., 1966. Tchr., counselor Shonto (Ariz.) Boarding Sch. Bur. Indian Affairs, 1966-67; tchr., counselor, recreation dir. Dilkon (Ariz.) Sch. Bur. Indian Affairs, 1967-84; tchr. bus. Winslow (Ariz.) High Sch., 1984—, vocat. dir., dept. chair, 1993—. Tchr. Sunday Sch., jr. high sch. 1st Christian Ch. Winslow, 1980-94. Mem. Nat. Bus. Edn. Assn., Ariz. Bus. Edn. Assn. (editor 1993—), Ariz. Vocat. Assn., Winslow Edn. Assn. (Tchr. of Month 1993), Western Bus. Edn. Assn., Delta Kappa Gamma (treas. 1990-94, pres. 1994—). Republican. Home: 412 W Cherry Winslow AZ 86047

CRUNICAN, GRACE, federal agency administrator. BA in Polit. Sci. and Criminal Justice, Gonzaga U., 1977; MA, Willamette U., 1979. Presdl. mgmt. intern Office of the Sec., Dept. Transp.; profl. staff mem. Subcommittee on Transp., Senate Com. on Appropriations; dep. dir. transp. City of Portland, Oreg.; dir. Surface Transp. Policy Project; dep. adminstr. Dept. Transp., Washington, 1993—. Office: Dept Transp Fed Transit Adminstrn 400 7th St SW Washington DC 20590-0001

CRUTCHER, AMELIA SYMPSON, human resource consultant; b. Lexington, Ky., May 25, 1947; d. Gordon Hoover and Matilda (Denton) Sympson; m. J. Thomas Crutcher, Dec. 30, 1970; 1 child, Kathryn Sympson. BA, U. Ky., 1969. Adminstrv. support Ga. Inst. Tech., Atlanta, 1969-70; office mgr. Norrell Temporary Svcs., Atlanta, 1970-72; pers. interviewer U. Va., Charlottesville, 1972-75; profl. recruiter U. Cin., 1975-76, dir. employment, wage, salary, 1976-77; human resource cons. self-employed, Cin., 1977-78; owner Child Care Profls., Inc., Cin., 1986—; cons. Cin. Ctr. for Alcoholism, 1992, 93. Past chmn., adv. mem. ProKids, Cin., 1993—; vice chmn. Children Svcs. Commn. for Hamilton County, Cin., 1987—; mktg. chair, state vol. Venture conf., United Way, Cin., 1993; chmn. Ultimate Auction Ursuline Acad., 1994. Republican. Home: 5473 Salem Rd Cincinnati OH 45230-1329

CRUTCHFIELD, CAROLYN ANN, physical therapy educator; b. New Castle, Colo., Apr. 2, 1942; d. Leland Arnold and Josephine Kathyrn (Leppink) C. BA, Western State Coll., 1964; cert. phys. therapy, Duke U., 1965; MS in Anatomy, West Va. U., 1970, EdD, 1976. Lic. phys. therapist, Ga. Dir. Rockingham Crippled Children's Ctr., Harrisonburg, Va., 1967-68; staff therapist Woodrow Wilson Rehab. Ctr., Fisherville, Va., 1966-67, West Va. U. Hosp., Morgantown, Va., 1968-70; asst. prof., asst. dir. Dept. Phys. Therapy, West Va. Sch. Medicine, Morgantown, 1970-75, assoc. prof., dir., 1975-78, prof., acting chair, 1978-80; prof., dir. grad. studies Dept. Phys. Therapy, Ga. State U., Atlanta, 1980—; chair Am. Bd. Phys. Therapy Specialties, Alexandria, Va., 1978-90; sec. Soc. for Behavioral Kinesiology, 1977-79. Author: The Muscle Spindle, 1972, Reflexes in Motor Development, 1978, Patient at Home, 1970, 84, Reflex and Vestibular Aspects of Motor Control, Motor Learning, Motor Development, 1990, Peripheral Components of Motor Control, 1984, Motor Control and Motor Learning in Rehabilitation, 1993, others; contbr. numerous chpts. to book and articles to jours. Chair ushers North Decatur Presbyn. Ch., Decatur, Ga., 1990, co-treas., 1991—. Recipient Cert. of Merit award Am. Bd. Phys. Therapy Specialties, 1990. Mem. Am. Phys. Therapy Assn. (chair neurology sect. 1983-85, treas. 1989-91, pres. West Va. chpt. 1978-79, Baethke-Carlin Teaching award 1984, Lucy Blair Svc. award 1991), Assn. Clin. Electrophysiology. Home: 3127 W Roxboro Rd NE Atlanta GA 30324-2541

CRUVER, SUZANNE LEE, communications and fundraising consultant; b. Indpls., Mar. 24, 1942; d. William Edward and Margaret Rosetta (McArtor) Ozzard; m. Donald Richard Cruver, June 9, 1963 (div. Feb. 1989); children: Donald Scott, Kimberly Sue, Brian Richard. BA in English, Rutgers U., 1964; postgrad., Rice U., 1990—. Asst. dir. pub. rels. dept. Upsala Coll., East Orange, N.J., 1964-65; asst. planner, pub. editor N.J. Divsn. State & Regional Planning, Trenton, 1967-68; realtor Vonnie Cobb Realtors, Houston, 1979-81; owner Sugar Land Comm., 1980—; exec. v.p., mktg. mgr. Photoflight Aviation Corp., Sugar Land, Tex., 1982; exec. v.p., artist mgr. H. McMillan Orgn., Inc., Sugar Land, 1983-85; account exec. Mel Anderson Comm., Inc., Houston, 1986; exec. dir. Ft. Bend Arts Coun., Sugar Land, 1986-87; dir. resource devel., vol. svcs., pub. info. Richmond (Tex.) State Sch., Tex. Dept. Mental Health/Mental Retardation, 1987-93; dir. corp. and found. giving Meml. Found., Meml. Healthcare Sys., Houston, 1993-94; mem. adv. bd. Ft. Bend Regional Coun. on Alcoholism and Drug Abuse, Rosenburg, Tex., 1989—. Writer, editor: PATCH Handbook: A Parent to Parent Guide to Texas Children's Hospital, 1983, Ft. Bend mag., 1985-86. Pres. Ft. Bend Arts Coun., Ft. Bend County, Tex., 1987-89; founding dir. PATCH, Tex. Children's Hosp., Houston, 1982; mem. adv. bd. Challenger Ctr. of Ft. Bend. Mem. NAFE, Nat. Soc. Fundraising Execs., Women in Comm., Ft. Bend Profl. Women, Pub. Rels. Soc. Am., Houston World Trade Assn., Ft. Bend C. of C., Rosenberg/Rich C. of C., Leadership Tex. Alumni Assn., Exch. Club of Sugar Land. Republican. Presbyterian.

CRUZ, LINDA GELSINGER, cardiac data systems research specialist, clinical research scientist; b. Robesonia, Pa., Jan. 8, 1950; d. Clarence Daniel and Esther (Forry) G.; m. Paul C. Cruz, Aug. 27, 1994. A, Pa. Jr. Coll. of Med. Arts, 1969; student, Ea. Coll., St. Davids, Pa., 1969-70; BA in Social Studies and Biology, St. Joseph's U., Phila., 1975. Supr. cardivascular research lab. Lankenau Hosp., Phila., 1970-76; sales rep. Med. Monitors, Inc., Wyncote, Pa., 1976-77, Data Med., Inc., Wynnewood, Pa., 1977-81; systems specialist Cardiac Data Corp., Inc., Bloomfield, Conn., 1980-81; mktg. rep. Cardio Data Systems, Haddonfield, N.J., 1981-82, nat. sales mgr., 1982-86, sr. research specialist, 1987-88; sr. clin. scientist Wyeth-Ayerst Research, Radnor, Pa., 1988—. Singer Kol Simcha Choral, Phila., 1973-90, Sweet Adelines Barbershop chorus, 1974, Wayne Oratorio Soc., 1993—; vol. Hospice, individuals in career transition. Mem. NAFE, Am. Soc. Profl. and Exec. Women, Healthcare Bus. Women's Assn., Am. Mktg. Assn., Assocs. Clin. Pharmacy, Drug Info. Assn., Sigma Eta Chi. Republican. Office: Wyeth-Ayerst Rsch 145 King Of Prussia Rd Wayne PA 19087-4588

CRUZ, WILHELMINA MANGAHAS, nephrologist; b. Bulacan, Philippines, July 20, 1942; d. Rectorino Bernardo and Mercedes Correa (Mangahas) C.; A.A., U. Santo Tomas (Philippines), 1960, M.D., 1965; m. Antonio I. Lee, May 28, 1977; children: Richard Anthony, Alexander Victor. Intern, Meml. Hosp., Albany, N.Y., 1967-68; resident in internal medicine Coney Island Hosp., Bklyn., 1968-71; fellow in nephrology VA Hosp., Bronx, 1971-72, Downstate Med. Center, Bklyn., 1972-73; staff physician King's County Hosp. Center, Bklyn., 1973-76; coordinator in medicine Kingsbrook Jewish Med. Center, Bklyn., 1976—; assoc. medical dir. ICU, Doctor's Community Hosp., Lanham, Md., 1977—; clin. asst. prof. SUNY, Downstate Med. Center, Bklyn., 1977—. Diplomate Am. Bd. Internal Medicine, Am. Bd. Nephrology (spl. qualifications in critical care medicine). Mem. ACP, Med. and Chirurg. Soc. Md., Prince George's Med. Soc., Nat. Kidney Found., Internat. Soc. Nephrology, Am. Soc. Nephrology, Soc. Critical Care Medicine, Philippine Med. Assn. Washington. Roman Catholic. Office: 7700 Old Branch Ave Ste D205 Clinton MD 20735

CRUZAN, CLARAH CATHERINE, dietitian; b. Cushing, Okla., Mar. 17, 1913; d. Ulysses Grant and Mamie Amanda (Montgomery) C. BS, Okla. State U., 1941; MS, U. Iowa, 1942. Lic. dietitian, Okla., 1984. Instr. household sci. Okla. State U., Stillwater, 1942-43, instr. home econs. edn., 1947-49; cons. dietitian Rest Haven Nursing Home, Cushing, Okla., 1967-91. Sec. Cushing Sr. Citizen's Steering Coun., 1972-91; reporter Okla. Pioneer club, Cushing, 1973-85; judge Precinct Election Bd., 1989—. With U.S. Army, 1943-46, ETO. Mem. Am. Dietetic Assn., Am. Assn. Univ. Women (life, treas. 1970-72, pres. 1974-75), Okla. Heritage Assn., Omicron Nu, Phi Kappa Phi. Republican. Presbyterian. Club: Iris Garden (pres. 1971-73), Eastside Garden (reporter 1970-75) (Cushing). Home: RR 4 Box 2445 Cushing OK 74023-9123

CRUZAN, PATRICIA, elementary school educator; b. Jacksonville, Fla., Nov. 15, 1945; d. Clarence E. and Ruth Agnes (Wallace) Cannon; m. Charles E. Cruzan, Nov. 4, 1977; 1 child, Christopher. BS, Tift Coll., Forsyth, Ga., 1967; postgrad., Ga. State U., Atlanta, Mountain View Coll., Dallas. Cert. elem. tchr. P-8, early childhood P-5. Tchr. 3d grade Muscogee Bd. Edn., Columbus, Ga., 1967-69; tchr. high sch. music DeSoto (Tex.) Ind. Sch. Dist., 1971-72; tchr. 3d and 4th grades Fulton County Bd. Edn., Atlanta, 1972-79, tchr. 5th grade, 1979-80; tchr. 5th grade Clayton County Bd. Edn., Jonesboro, Ga., 1980-81; tchr. 3d grade Fulton County Bd. Edn., Atlanta, 1982-84, tchr. 1st, 2d, 3d grades, 1986-90, Chpt. I tchr., 1990—; numerous voice solos. Active 1st Bapt. Ch., Fayetteville, Ga. Mem. NEA, Nat. Coun. Tchrs. Math., Ga. Internat. Reading Assn., Ga. Edn. Assn., Internat. Soc. Poets. Home: 115 Clear Creek Ct Fayetteville GA 30214-4642

CRUZ-ROMO, GILDA, soprano; b. Guadalajara, Jalisco, Mexico; came to U.S., 1967; d. Feliciano and Maria del Rosario (Diaz) C.; m. Robert B. Romo, June 10, 1967. Grad., Colegio Nueva Galicia, Guadalajara, 1958; student, Nat. Conservatory of Music of Mexico, Mexico City, 1962-64. Tchr. voice U. Tex., Austin, 1990—; asst. prof., coach, voice tchr. U. Tex., Austin, 1990—. With, Nat. and Internat. Opera, Mexico City, 1962-67, toured, Australia, N.Z., S.Am., with, Dallas Civic Opera, 1966-68, N.Y.C. Opera, 1969-72, Lyric Opera Chgo., 1975, Met. Opera debut as Madama Butterfly, 1970, leading soprano, 1970—, appeared in U.S. and abroad including, Covent Garden, La Scala, Vienna State Opera, Rome Opera, Paris Opera, Florence Opera, Torino Opera, Verona Opera, Portugal, Buenos Aires, others, concert appearances in, U.S., Can., Mexico; U.S. rep., World-Wide Madama Butterfly Competition, Tokyo, 1970; La Scala rep. in: Aida, USSR, 1974; appeared on radio, TV; filmed and recorded: Aida, with Orange Festival, France, 1976; roles include Aida, Madama Butterfly, Suor Angelica, Tosca, Odabella in Attila; Manon Lescaut, Leonora in Il Trovatore; Norma; Maddelena in Andrea Chenier; Desdemona in Otello; Donna Anna in Don Giovanni; Santuzza in Cavalleria Rusticana; (title role) La Gioconda; Adriana Lecouvreur; Luisa Miller; Elisabetta in Don Carlo; Margherite in Faust; Venus in Tannhauser; Giorgetta in Il Tabarro; also roles in Macbeth, Turnadot, Norma, Medea. Winner Met. Opera Nat. Auditions, 1970; recipient Critics award Union Mexicana de Cronistas de Teatro y Musica, 1973, Minerva al Arte award, Mexico, 1991, Ninerva al Arte, Mexico, 1991; named Best Singer, 1976-77; season Cronistas de Santiago de Chile, 1976. Home: 1315 Lockhill Selma Rd San Antonio TX 78213-1915

CRUZ-STOESSEL, PATRICIA A., nursing educator; b. Feb. 16, 1944; d. Emilio J. and Florence A. (Davis) C.; divorced; children: Byron Jefferson Jr., Danielle Jefferson; m. Erwin M. Stoessel, May 26, 1989. AAS, Bronx Community Coll., 1976; BA, Lehman Coll., 1983. Cert. neonatal nurse. Staff nurse surgery Columbia Presbyn. Hosp., N.Y.C., 1976; staff nurse NICU Bronx Mcpl. Hosp., 1976-78, asst. head nurse NICU, 1978-84, supr. nurses surgery, 1984-85, clinician NICU, 1986-89, writer, coord. NICU program, 1989—; nursing instr. Bronx Meml. Hosp., 1989-92; pub. health nurse Vis. Nurse Svc., Bronx, 1985-86; infection ctrl. practitioner, 1992—; nursing edn. nurse instr., 1993—. Mem. NAACOG, N.Y. State Nurses Assn., Phi Kappa Phi, Phi Theta Kappa.

CRYER, GRETCHEN, playwright, lyricist, actress; b. Indpls., Oct. 17, 1935; d. Earl William and Louise Gerladine (Niven) Kiger; m. Donald David Cryer, June 7, 1958 (div. June 1970); children: Robin, Jon, Shelly. BA, DePauw U., 1957; MAT, Harvard U., 1960; ArtsD (hon.), Ea. Mich. U., 1986. Cert. tchr. Writer and lyricist N.Y.C., 1967—; founder, owner The Extended Family, N.Y.C., 1991—; founder, pres. The Extended Family. Writer, lyricist (with Nancy Ford) Off-Broadway and Broadway musicals Now Is the Time for All the Good Men, 1967, The Last Sweet Days of Isaac, 1970 (Obie award 1970), Shelter, 1973, Booth Is Back in Town, 1981, I'm Getting My Act Together and Taking it on the Road, 1978, Hang on to the Good Times, 1984; (with Doug Dyer and Peter Link) The Wedding of Iphigenia and Iphigenia in Concert, 1971; theater appearances in Little Me, 1962, 110 In The Shade, 1963, Now is the Time For All Good Men, 1967, I'm Getting My Act Together and Taking it on the Road, 1978, A Circle of Sounds, 1978, Blue Plate Special, 1983, To Whom It May Concern, 1985-86, Alterations, 1986; film appearances include Hiding Out, 1987; author, singer: (albums) Cryer and Ford, 1976, You Know My Music, 1977; author: (musical) Booth is Back in Town, 1981, Eleanor, 1984; playwright: The House That Goes On Forever, 1988. Recipient Ind. Arts award Gov. of Ind., 1982. Mem. Dramatists Guild (council), Actors Equity Assn., Screen Actors Guild. Democrat. Home and Office: 885 W End Ave New York NY 10025-3501*

CRYMES, MARY COOPER, secondary school educator; b. Abilene, Tex., Oct. 27, 1950; d. James Travis and Mary Francis (Chapple) Cooper; m. David Stuart Crymes, Dec. 25, 1970. BS, U. Tex., 1974. Tchr. govt. Midland (Tex.) Ind. Sch. Dist., 1974-80, Abilene (Tex.) Ind. Sch. Dist., 1980—. Author: (poem) Young America Sings, 1970; co-author: County Records Inventory, 1974. Recipient Teaching Excellence in Free Enterprise 1st prize award West Tex. C. of C., 1980, Martha Washington medal SAR, 1990; named Taft Sr. fellow Taft Inst., 1993. Mem. NEA, Tex. State Tchrs. Assn., Abilene Educators Assn., Nat. Coun. for Social Studies, Tex. Coun. for Social Studies, Abilene Coun. for Social Studies (pres. 1984-86), Daus. of Republic of Tex. (treas. 1990—), West Tex. Geneal. Soc. Office: Abilene High Sch 2800 N 6th St Abilene TX 79603

CSAPOSS, JEAN FOX, English and religion educator; b. N.Y.C., Mar. 13, 1931; d. John Edward and Elizabeth Marie (Lynch) Fox; m. James Csaposs, Apr. 25, 1981. BA, Manhattanville Coll., 1953, MA, 1971; MA, Columbia U., 1954. Tchr. English, history Acad. of the Holy Angels, Ft. Lee, N.J., 1954-57; asst. in pub. info. Manhattanville Coll., Purchase, N.Y., 1958-66, dir. pub. rels., 1966-69, dir. devel. svcs., 1969-72; editor, mgr. publs. AAUW, Washington, 1972-77; spl. asst. to asst. sec. for pub. affairs U.S. Dept. HHS, Washington, 1977-82; instr. English Bergen Community Coll., Paramus, N.J., 1985—. Editor, contbr. mag. and newspaper of AAUW (annual awards from Ednl. Press Assn., 1973-77). Bd. trustees Manhattanville Coll., Purchase, 1987-90; bd. dirs. Bergen County coun. Girl Scouts U.S., 1989—. Recipient Disting. Alumni award Manhattanville Coll., 1978. Mem. Nat. Coun. Tchrs. English, N.J. Coll. English Assn., Reading Reform Found., Heightened Independence and Progress (bd. dirs. 1988—, v.p. 1989—, pres. 1990—), Nat. Soc. Fund Raising Execs., Columbia U. Alumni Club Bergen-Passaic Counties (v.p. 1989-91, pres. 1991-93). Democrat. Roman Catholic. Home: 644 Wyoming Ave Maywood NJ 07607-1544 Office: Bergen Community Coll 400 Paramus Rd Paramus NJ 07652-1508

CSERNOVICZ, BARBARA ANN, personnel administrator; b. Chgo., Mar. 8, 1933; d. Clarence and Elsa (Jamison) Gump; m. Lajos Csernovicz, 1964 (div. 1981); children: Lynda, Michael. BA, MacMurray Coll., 1954; MSIR, Loyola U., 1983. Office mgr. Am. Arbitration Assn., Chgo., 1978-81; with personnel dept. City Colls., Chgo., 1981-82; with retirement office Loyola U., Chgo., 1982-83; personnel asst. David Berg, Chgo., 1983-84; asst. personnel mgr. Guernsey Dell Co., Chgo., 1984-85; personnel mgr. Service Plastics, Elk Grove Village, Ill., 1986—; mem. tripartite group to conduct labor rels. tng. U.S. State Dept. and Labor Dept., Guatemala, 1989. Mem. Friends of Lincoln Park, Chgo., 1986—; bd. dirs. Francis W. Parker Sch. Alumni, 1979—, Loyola U. Chgo. Alumni, 1988—. Mem. Indsl. Rels. Assn. (treas. 1986-87, pres. 1991-92), Taurino de Chgo. Club (newsletter editor 1984-87).

CUBBEDGE, FRANKIE HOLLEY, librarian; b. Graniteville, S.C., Jan. 20, 1937; s. Otis Raymond and Peggy (Parker) Holley; m. A.B. Cubbedge, mar. 4, 1962; children: Alan Barry, Melanie Lynn. BA, Winthrop U., 1959; MSLS, U. N.C., 1969. Libr. Beaufort (S.C.) Dist. 1, 1959-61, Savannah (Ga.) Pub. Sch. System, 1961-62, East Carolina Univ. Libr., Greenville, N.C., 1962-66; ESEA Inst. instr. East Caroline Univ., Greenville, N.C., summer 1968; libr. Sumter (S.C.) Sch. Dist. 17, 1966-69; field instr. Sch. Edn. U. S.C., Columbia, 1968, 70, 71, dean of libr., 1971—; tchr. Aiken County Sch. Dist., Aiken, S.C., 1971; adj. instr. Sch. Edn., U.S. C., 1969; mem. accreditation teams So. Assn. Colls. and Schs., Atlanta, 1985—; chair scholarship selection com. Gregg-Graniteville Found., Graniteville, S.C., 1973—; mem. S.C. State libr. Adv. Coun., Columbia, 1979-85. Bd. dirs. Aiken County Libr. Br., 1978—; mem. adv. coun. Aiken County Sch. Dist.,

1983—; vol. Aiken County Heart Bd., 1976-78. Women's History Work grantee S.C. Com. for the Humanities, Aiken, 1981-82; public documents collection grantee Dept. Energy, Aiken, 1985—; grantee Aiken Co. Legal Libr., 1984-91. Mem. ALA (councilor 1982-92), S.C. Libr. Assn., S.E. Libr. Assn., Cen. Savannah River Area Libr. Assn. (pres. 1976-78). Baptist. Home: 33 Donald Pearson Dr Graniteville SC 29829-9526 Office: Univ S C-Aiken 171 University Pky Aiken SC 29801-6309

CUBIN, BARBARA LYNN, congresswoman, former state legislator, public relations consultant; b. Salinas, Calif., Nov. 30; d. Russell G. and Barbara Lee (Howard) Sage; m. Frederick William Cubin, Aug. 1; children: William Russell, Frederick William III. BS in Chemistry, Creighton U., 1969. Chemist Wyo. Machinery Co., Casper, Wyo., 1973-75; mem. Wyo. Ho. Reps., 1987-92, Wyo. Senate, 1993-94; pres. Spectrum Promotions and Mgmt., Casper, 1993-94; congresswoman, Wyom. U.S. House Reps., Washington, D.C., 1995—; mem com. Nat. Coun. State Legislators, San Francisco, 1987—, Lexington, Ky., 1990—. Mem. steering com. Exptl. Program to Stimulate Competitive Research (EPSCOR); mem. Coun. of State Govts.; active Gov.'s Com. on Preventive Medicine, 1992; vice chmn. Cleer Bd. Energy Coun., Irving, Tex., 1993—; chmn. Wyo. Senate Rep. Conf., Casper, 1993—; mem. Wyo. Rep. Party Exec. Com., 1993. Toll fellow Coun. State Govts., 1990. Mem. Am. Legis. Exch. Coun., Rep. Women. Episcopalian. Office: US House Reps Office House Mem Washington DC 20515

CUBITT, DORIS EVANS, accountant; b. Somerset, Ky., Sept. 23, 1950; d. William Clifford, Sr. and Hester Mae (McGowan) Evans; m. Earl David Pilgrim, Jan. 23, 1969 (div. Nov. 1984); children: William Blair, Catherine Maureen; m. John Benjamin Cubitt, July 18, 1986. BS in Bus. Adminstrn., U. S.C., Spartanburg, 1993. CPA. Office mgr. Monty Kirby State Farm Ins., Spartanburg, 1979-83; agt. Life of Va. Ins., Spartanburg, 1983-84; svc. specialist Glen Melton State Farm Ins., Spartanburg, 1985-89; staff acct. Rita P. Vinson, CPA, Spartanburg, 1994-95; tax auditor Dept. Revenue State of S.C., Spartanburg, 1995—. Mem. Inst. Mgmt. Accts. Home: 1101 Springfield Rd Inman SC 29349

CUCCINIELLO, DAWN GRACE, educator; b. Bklyn., Aug. 11; d. Vito Jack and Evelyn Anita (Simonetti) C. BS in Edn., CUNY, 1969, MS in Edn., 1973, postgrad., 1975; 6th yr. cert. in adminstrn.-supervision, Wagner Coll., 1986. Cert. tchr., N.Y.; lic. asst. prin., prin., N.Y.C. Tchr., reading Bd. of Edn., Bklyn, 1969-70, tchr., social studies, 1970-72, tchr., 2d grade, 1972-84, tchr., 5th grade, 1984—; jr. high and high sch. tutor, SAT, GED program, 1990—; chmn. comprehensive svc. program, Bklyn., 1987-90; mem. sch. liaison Gifted and Talented Network, Bklyn., 1987-90; developed creative writing program for upper grade children. Bd. dirs. Staten Island Coun. Animal Welfare; writer, producer, choreographer children's plays, 1985—. Mem. ASCD, United Fedn. Tchr., Am. Fedn. Tchrs., UFT Italian-Am. Studies com., Sacred Heart League, Animal Welfare League, Humane Soc., Worldwide Wildlife Fedn., Bklyn. Lit. Club, Cat Lovers Am., Phi Delta Kappa. Democrat. Roman Catholic.

CUCCO, JUDITH ELENE, international marketing professional; b. Summit, N.J., Aug. 9, 1951; d. Louis John and Patricia T. (Procaccini) C. BS in Internat. Rels. and Spanish, Am. U., 1973; MBA, U. Md., 1983. Prof. English Universidad Nacional Autonoma de Mex., Mexico City, 1971-72; tchr. Spanish, ESL Montgomery (Md.) County Pub. Schs., 1973-81; acct. exec., industry cons. AT&T Comms., Parsippany, N.J., 1983-87; mgr. internat. mktg. support ctr. AT&T, Morristown, N.J., 1987-89; dir. market devel. internat. ops. divsn. AT&T, Caracas, Venezuela, 1989-91; mgr. global product line Sch. Bus. AT&T, Somerset, N.J., 1991-93; regional mgr. market mgmt. Latin Am., Network Wireless Systems Bus. Unit AT&T, Whippany, N.J., 1994—. Sponsor Child Reach, Warwick, R.I., 1984—; mem. Small Faith Community, Bridgewater, 1992—; vol. Interfaith Hospitality Network, Bridgewater, N.J., 1993—. Mem. HISPA, U. Md. Alumni Assn., Am. U. Alumni Assn. Home: 308 Greenfield Rd Bridgewater NJ 08807 Office: AT&T Network Wireless Svcs Bus Unit 67 Whippany Rd Whippany NJ 07981

CUDAK, GAIL LINDA, lawyer; b. Bellville, Ill., July 13, 1952; d. Robert Joseph and Margaret Lucille (Martin) C.; m. Thomas Edward Young, Sept. 15, 1979. BA, Kenyon Coll., 1974; JD, Case Western Res. U., 1977, MBA, 1991. Bar: Ohio 1977, U.S. Dist. Ct. (no. dist.) Ohio 1977, U.S. Ct. Appeals (6th cir.) 1977. Assoc. Foerst, Leidner, Dougherty & Kasdan, Cleve., 1977-79; staff atty. The B.F. Goodrich Co., Akron, Ohio, 1979-84; sr. corp. counsel The B.F. Goodrich Co., Independence, Ohio, 1985-89; divsn. counsel The B.F. Goodrich Co., Brecksville, Ohio, 1990—. Corp. fundraiser Great Lakes Theater Festival, 1990—, Ohio Found. Ind. Colls., 1993—. Mem. ABA, Ohio State Bar Assn., Cleve. Internat. Lawyers Group. Home: 12520 Edgewater Dr # 1405 Lakewood OH 44107 Office: The BF Goodrich Co 9911 Brecksville Rd Cleveland OH 44141

CUDDIHY, JUNE T., pediatric nurse; b. Buffalo, June 15, 1936; d. John R. Sr. and Monica A. (Donahue) Tuck; m. Robert V. Cuddihy, Aug. 24, 1957; children: Robert V., Timothy, Kathleen. BSN, D'Youville Coll., Buffalo, 1957; MA, Seton Hall U., 1972, MSN, 1979. Cert. primary care nurse practitioner. Pub. health nurse Monroe County, Rochester, N.Y.; health coord. Early Childhood Learning Ctrs. N.J., Morristown; asst. prof. Seton Hall U., South Orange, N.J., 1977-81, William Paterson Coll., Wayne, N.J., 1981-94; clin. assoc. Coll. Nursing Ohio State U., 1994—; cons. Berkeley BioMedical Group, Inc., 1991—; clin. assoc. coll. nursing Ohio State U., 1994—. Contbr. articles to profl. jours. Named Outstanding Grad. Student, Seton Hall U., 1979. Mem. ANA (vice chmn. bd. examiners for cmty. health nursing practice, chmn. sch. nurse practice subcom.), N.J. State Nurses Assn., Nat. Child Abuse Assn., Nat. Burn Victim Found., Pub. Health Assn., Sigma Theta Tau. Home: 8798 Killie Ct Dublin OH 43017

CUDDIHY, NANCY ANN, development engineer; b. Wyandotte, Mich., Dec. 15, 1963; d. Mike William and Roberta Marie (Kur) Danyo; m. Mark Anthony Cuddihy, Sept. 5, 1987; children: Patrick Timothy, Alexander Michael. B in Chem. Engring., U. Detroit, 1986; postgrad., U. Mich., 1988-90. Process engr.-paint Ford, Dearborn, Mich., 1986-88; materials engr. Alcoa Fujikura Ltd., Dearborn, 1988-90, test and materials engr., 1990-93, devel. engr., 1993—. Mem. Soc. Mfg. Engrs. Roman Catholic. Home: 32975 West Rd New Boston MI 48164 Office: Alcoa Fujikura Ltd 999 Republic Dr Allen Park MI 48101

CUENOD, MARGARET L., retired association executive; b. L.A., Jan. 3, 1914; d. André Henri and Lily Willis (Branch) C. BE, UCLA, 1935; M of Christian Edn., Union Theol. Sem., 1949. Cert. social worker, NASW. Activities sec. YWCA, San Pedro, Calif., 1937-40; older girls' sec. YWCA, Greenwich, Conn., 1940-43; exec. dir. YWCA, Kauai County, Hawaii, 1943-48, Spokane, Wash., 1958-61; asst. exec. dir. YWCA, Portland, Oreg., 1949-58; cons. western region nat. bd. dirs. YWCA U.S.A., San Francisco, 1961-71, L.A., 1971-78. Author: Budgeting Guide, 1975, Guide to Finance Administration, 1975, Guide to Financial Development, 1977, Guide to Capital Campaigns, 1978, YWCA Finance Manual: Roles and Relationships, 1978.

CUGLER, CAROL MARIE MILLER, mental health services professional; b. Elizabeth, N.J., Dec. 25, 1942; d. Wilhelm Johannes Rudolph and Frances Caroline (Blank) Miller; m. Harry Clarke Cugler, Jan. 12, 1974; 2 stepchildren. Accredited records technician, Am. Med. Record Assn. Sec. Chris Craft Corporation, Salisbury, Md., 1960-64, Civil Def. Adminstrn., Salisbury, 1964-66; med. records libr. Pine Bluff State Hosp., Salisbury, 1966-74; dir. records/stats./quality assurance Holly Ctr., Salisbury, 1974-93, adminstrv. officer, 1993—. Vol. statistician Ea. Shore Hall of Fame, 1986; vol., sec. bd. dirs. Humane Soc. Wicomico County, Salisbury, 1988—, capital campaign sec., 1990—. Recipient numerous Appreciation awards United Charities Campaign, Appreciation award Ea. Shore Hall of Fame, 1986, Vol. of Yr. award Humane Soc. Wicomico County, 1992. Mem. Delmarva Peninsula Golf Assn. (sec. to adminstrv. asst. 1984—). Republican. Methodist. Home: 402 E Chestnut St Delmar MD 21875

CULBERT, PATRICIA A., accountant; b. Waterbury, Conn., Sept. 12, 1942; d. Stephen William and Mary V. Culbert; m. Raymond Gelinas (div.); children: Raymond R., Lawrence E. AS in Mgmt., Mattatuck C.C., 1975; BS in Acctg., Ctrl. Conn. U., 1984; MS in Pub. Adminstrn., U. Hartford, 1989; EdD in Higher Edn., Nova U., 1994. Acct. Lublin Law Offices, East Hartford, Conn., 1980-83; internal auditor Home Bank & Trust Co., Meriden, Conn., 1983-84; acct. Anquillare, Saas & Lipnicki, CPA, West Haven, Conn., 1984-86, Conn. Dept. Edn., Hartford, 1986-87, Conn. Office Policy and Mgmt., Hartford, 1987-89; mem. faculty Teikyo Post U., Waterbury, 1989—; acct., rschr. Conn. Dept. Transp., Newington, 1987—; mem. tech. adv. com., libr. advisor Conn. Dept. Transp., Newington, 1994. Active 1995 Spl. Olympics, New Haven, 1994—. Mem. AAUW, Women in Transp. (program com. 1994, lectr. 1994), A & R Employee Union (Outstanding Mem. award 1990-94). Office: Conn Dept Transp PO Box 317546 Newington CT 06131

CULBERTSON, CHERYL ANN, home health nurse, medical-surgical nurse; b. Dodge City, Kans., Oct. 7, 1943; d. John Lee and Enafae Georgina (Stark) Shipman; divorced; 1 child, Jennetta Marle Culbertson. Grad., Anchorage C.C., 1963. LPN, Alaska, Ariz. Charge nurse Alaska Psychiat. Hosp., Anchorage, 1963-68; floor nurse Valley Hosp., Las Vegas, 1972, pvt. duty nurse, 1972-77; nurse, instr. Red Cross, Kodiak, Alaska, 1977-80; pvt. duty nurse Kenai, Alaska, 1980-90; nurse Flagstaff (Ariz.) Med. Facility, 1991; home health nurse Home Works, Flagstaff, 1991—. Pres. Am. Cancer Soc., Kodiak, 1978; instr. ARC, Kodiak, 1975-90; leader 4-H, Kenai, 1984-87; den leader, coach Cub Scouts, Kenai, 1984-87. Recipient Outstanding Svc. award Cancer Soc., 1978. Mormon. Home: 721 N Main St Cottonwood AZ 86326

CULBERTSON, JANET LYNN, artist; b. Greensburg, Pa., Mar. 15, 1932; d. Joseph F. and Helen C. (Moore) Culbertson; m. Douglas I. Kaften, Sept. 30, 1964. BFA, Carnegie Inst. Tech., 1953; MA, NYU, 1963. Instr. art Pace Coll., N.Y.C., 1964-68, Pratt Art Inst., Bklyn., 1973; assoc. prof. Southampton Coll., 1976; drawing instr. Parrish Art Mus., 1979. Exhibited one-woman shows 20th Century West Gallery, N.Y.C., 1967, Molly Barnes Gallery, L.A., 1970, Midtown Gallery, Atlanta, 1971, Lerner-Misrachi Gallery, N.Y.C., 1971, Lerner-Heller Gallery, N.Y.C., 1973, 75, 77, Tower Gallery, Southampton, N.Y., 1976, Benson Gallery, Bridgehampton, N.Y., 1978, 81, 89, Interart Gallery, N.Y.C., 1979, Harriman Coll., N.Y., 1980, Nardin Gallery, N.Y.C., 1981, Aronson Gallery, Atlanta, 1982, Harrisburg State Mus. Pa., 1988, Women Artists Series Rutgers U., N.J., 1988, Carnegie Mellon U., Pitts., 1991, Acme Art Co., Columbus, Ohio, 1992, Islip (N.Y.) Mus., 1992; two-women shows Women's Art Ctr., San Francisco, 1975; four-women show Heckscher Mus., Huntington, N.Y., 1980; group exhbns. include Carnegie Mus., Pitts., 1953, ann. drawing Bucknell U., 1966-68, Palos Verdes (Calif.) Mus., 1970, 16th ann. all Calif. purchase L.A. Art Assn., 1969-70, nat. drawing ann. San Francisco Mus., 1970, Princeton Gallery Fine Arts, 1972, drawing show Fleisher Meml., Phila., 1974, Am. Acad. Arts and Letters, N.Y.C., 1975, Kingpitcher Gallery, Pitts, 1976, West Broadway Galley, N.Y.C., 1976, Bronx Mus., 1976, Guild Hall, East Hampton, N.Y., 1976, 79, 82, 89, (invitational) 94 (Abstract award 1979, Mixed Media award 1992), Orgn. Ind. Artists, N.Y.C., 1978, Parrish Mus., Southampton, N.Y. Meml. Art Gallery, Rochester N.Y., 1979, Western Carolina U., Cullowhee, Phoenix Mus, Tucson Mus., 1980, The Arsenal, N.Y.C., 1981, 50 nat. women artists Edison Coll. Art Gallery, Ft. Myers, Fla., 1982, Norton Art Gallery, W. Palm Beach, Fla., 1985-86, Easthampton (N.Y.) Ctr. Contemporary Arts, 1988, Newport (R.I.) Art Mus., 1988, 91, Trabia Macafee Gallery, N.Y.C., 1988, Vered Gallery, Easthampton, 1989, 90, 92, New Narrative, Hillwood Mus., Brookville, N.Y., 1990, Islip Art Mus., N.Y., 1990, Ucross Wyo. (invitational), 1990, Women's Caucus for Art, Dallas, 1990, Wash., 1991, Benton Gallery, Southampton, N.Y., 1991, 92, 93, Ark. Arts Ctr. (invitational), Little Rock, 1991, Arlene Bujese Gallery, East Hampton, N.Y., 1994, Hillwood Art Mus., L.I. U., Brookville, N.Y., 1994, Hamilton Coll., Clinton, N.Y., 1995, Stony Brook (N.Y.) U., 1995, others; Babcock Gallery traveling exhibit, 1993-94; contbr. collage to Attica Book, 1972; contbr. articles to profl. jours., prodr. and contbr. Heresies #13 mag. Creative Artists Pub. Service grantee, 1979. Recipient Shirk Meml. award for oil painting Nat. Assn. Women Artists, Inc., 1993, first place award Notorious L.I. exhibit Hillwood Art Mus., Brookville, N.Y., 1994; fellow Ossabaw Found., 1981, Dorland, 1983, Ucross Found., 1989, Blue Mt. Found., 1991, 94, VCCA Ctr. Found., 1992. Home: PO Box 455 Heights Shelter Island NY 11965

CULBERTSON, JUDI C., writer, social worker; b. Norfolk, Va., Mar. 1, 1941; d. Hubert Roe and Charlotte Eleanor (Hess) Chaffee; m. Paul Culbertson, June 23, 1962 (div. Feb. 1971); 1 child, Andrew William; m. Thomas Randall, June 22, 1974. BA, Wheaton Coll., 1962; postgrad., Vt. Coll. Editorial asst. Eternity Mag., 1962-64; various teaching positions; sr. caseworker Suffolk County Dept. Social Svcs., Ronkonkoma, N.Y., 1970—. Author: Games Christians Play, 1967, Little White Book on Race, 1970, Permanent Parisians, 1985, Permanent New Yorkers, 1987 (named One of 25 Best Rsch. Books of 1988, N.Y. Pub. Libr., 1988), Permanent Californians, 1988, Permanent Londoners, 1991; also articles. Mem. AAUW, Nat. Writers Union. Democrat. Home: 211 Hawthorne St Port Jefferson NY 11777-1608

CULLEN, ALISON CATHERINE, environmental health science educator; b. Melrose, Mass., Mar. 17, 1962; d. Seamus Francis and Elizabeth Margaret (Zsakovits) C. SB in Civil Engring., MIT, 1984; MS in Environ. Health, Harvard U., 1989, ScD in Environ. Health Sci., 1992. Environ. engr. U.S. EPA, Boston, 1984-86, Gradient Corp., Cambridge, Mass., 1986-88; rsch. assoc. Harvard Sch. Pub. Health, Boston, 1992-93, asst. prof., 1993—; ind. environ. cons., Cambridge, 1987—; mem. young investigator program Czech and Slovakia, NAS, 1993-94; rep. Harvard Sch. Pub. Health, Harvard Environ. Network, 1990-91; mem. Cambridge Recycling, 1990-91. Author: Yard Waste Composting, 1989. Recipient Fellowships U.S. HHS, 1987-89, U.S. EPA, 1988, Switzer Found., 1989-91. Mem. Assn. Women in Sci., Air and Waste Mgmt. Assn., Soc. Risk Analysis (mem. nominating com. 1987—), Am. Chem. Soc., Assn. MIT Alumnae. Office: Harvard Sch Pub Health Ctr for Risk Analysis 718 Huntington Ave Boston MA 02115-6021

CULLEN, KATHRYN MARIE, information technology executive; b. Chgo., Oct. 10, 1946; d. Philip Francis and Kathryn M. (Giroux) C.; m. Roy L. Dolgos, June 28, 1968 (div. 1978); m. Thomas M. McDonald, Oct. 11, 1980. BA in Math., St. Xavier U., 1968; MS in Computer Sci., Rensselaer Poly. Inst., 1972; MBA in Finance, U. Chgo., 1979. CPA, Ill. Programmer, analyst Pratt & Whitney, Hartford, Conn., 1968-70; asst. registrar Ctrl. Conn. State U., New Britain, 1970-72; project mgr. Montgomery Ward, Chgo., 1973-79; ptnr., cons. Grant Thornton, Chgo. and N.Y.C., 1979-87, Peat Marwick Main, N.Y.C., 1987-88, McKinsey & Co., N.Y.C., 1988-92; v.p. info. tech. Dun & Bradstreet, Princeton, N.J., 1992—; bd. dirs. Epode, Inc., N.Y.C. Contbr. articles to profl. jours. Bd. dirs. Ms. Found. for Women, N.Y.C., 1986-90; pres. 542 Holding Corp., N.Y.C., 1986—. Mem. AICPA, Am. Prodn. and Inventory Control Soc., Health Care Bus. Women's Assn. Office: Dun & Bradstreet Healthcare 34 Chambers St Princeton NJ 08542-3708

CULLEN, MARY LYNNE, artist; b. Camden, N.J., Nov. 2, 1962; d. Philip Anthony and Elizabeth (Townsend) Chiusano; m. James Francis Cullen; 1 child, Lynne Marie. BFA magna cum laude, U. Pa., 1993; postgrad., Pa. Acad. Fine Arts, 1993—; student, Santa Reparata Arts Studio, Florence, Italy, 1990. Cert. Pa. Acad. Fine Arts. Artistic cons., adminstr. Chiusano, Inc., Marlton, N.J., 1985—; shop asst. graphics dept. Pa. Acad. Fine Arts, Phila., 1991-93; co-founder Definity Group Artist Co-op, Camden, N.J., 1987-89; co-founder, curator, exhibitor Final State Printmaker's Co-op, Phila., 1991—. Exhibited works in numerous shows. Recipient Edna Pennypacker Stauffer Meml. prize, 1991, spl. notice Traditional Media Print prize, 1990, John R. Conner Meml. prize in printmaking, 1991, Morris Blackburn Print prize, 1991. Fellow Pa. Acad. Fine Arts; mem. Phila. Print Club (prize 1990), Plastic Club Phila. (award 1992). Home and Office: 305 Blueberry Ct Marlton NJ 08053

CULLEN, RUTH ENCK, reading specialist, elementary education educator; b. Freeport, N.Y., Mar. 13, 1937; d. Frederick Harold and Grace Bell (Morrow) Enck; m. Thomas J. Cullen, Aug. 22, 1959; children: Randall R., Lauren Cullen Radick, Amy A. BS, Trenton State U., 1959; MA, Montclair State U., 1966; PhD, Fordham U., 1977. Cert. elem. edn., reading tchr., reading specialist, pupil pers. svcs., adminstr., supr., N.J. Tchr. Bergenfield (N.J.) Pub. Schs., 1959-61, Tenafly (N.J.) Pub. Schs., 1961-63; reading specialist Westwood (N.J.) Regional Schs., 1967—; researcher, conf. Rockaway Twp. (N.J.) Schs., 1978; sepaker N.Y. Reading Assn., 1980, N.J. Edn. Assn., Atlantic City, 1979, Fordham U., Lincoln Ctr., 1976, Montclair State Coll., 1974; instr. summer spl. edn. program Westwood Regional Schs., summers, 1980—, childhood early excellence in reading program pilot, 1994-95. Mem. Assessment com. Westwood Reg. Schs., 1992-94. Mem. ASCD, NEA (editorial adv. com. 1980), Internat. Reading Assn., N.J. Edn. Assn., Kappa Delta Pi, Phi Delta Kappa. Home: 12 Shadow Rd Upper Saddle River NJ 07458 Office: Westwood Regional Schs School St Westwood NJ 07675

CULLEY, JUNE ELIZABETH, clinical reviewer, quality improvement specialist; b. Valley Station, Ky., July 22, 1933; d. Wilbur W. and Elizabeth Piper (Dodge) C. Diploma, Ky. Bapt. Hosp., Louisville, 1954; BSN, Case Western Res. U., 1963; MPH, Johns Hopkins U., 1970, ScD, 1981. Dir. nursing State Tb Commn., Louisville; dir. nursing svcs. Louisville/Jefferson County Dept. Pub. Health; dir. nursing, long-term care svcs. City Health Dept., Balt.; quality mgmt. analyst VA Med. Ctr., Ft. Howard, Md. Mem. AAUW, VA Nat. Nurses Rsch. Coun., VA Regional Nurses Rsch. Com., Sigma Theta Tau, Delta Omega (nat. award).

CULLINAN, MARY KAY THERESE, religious educator, musician; b. Plainfield, N.J., Jan. 16, 1961; d. Francis Joseph and Annamae Leona (Hauser) Isele; m. Patrick Alexander, Jan. 11, 1991; children: Joseph, Marie Noelle. BA, Georgian Court Coll., Lakewood, N.J., 1983; MA, Seton Hall U., 1987; doct. cnad., Fordham U., 1994. Cert. edn., N.J. Pvt. piano tchr. Lakewood, 1979-83; organist, choir dir. St. Joseph Ch., North Plainfield, N.J., 1983-88; dir. religious edn. St. Joseph Ch., North Plainfield, 1983-87; Diocesan dir. religious edn. Diocese of Metuchen, Perth Amboy, N.J., 1987—; organist Queenship of Mary Roman Cath. Ch., Plainsboro, N.J., 1990—; mentor Seton Hall U., South Orange, N.J., 1991-93. Rep. coun. Cath. Ch., 1993, 94. Mem. Am. Guild Organists, Nat. Cath. Edn. Assn., Nat. Conf. Catechetical Leadership (rep. coun. 1993). Roman Catholic.

CULLINGFORD, HATICE SADAN, chemical engineer; b. Konya, Turkey, June 10, 1945; came to U.S., 1966; d. Ahmet and Emine (Kadayifcioglu) Harmanci. Student, Mid. East Tech. U., 1962-66; BS in Chem. Engring. with high honors, N.C. State U., 1969, Engring. Honors Cert., 1969, PhD, 1974. Registered profl. engr., Tex.; cert. mgr. Statis. clk. Rsch. Triangle Inst., 1966; reactor engr. AEC, Washington, 1973-75; spl. asst. ERDA, Washington, 1975; mech. engr. U.S. Dept. Energy, Washington, 1975-78; staff mem. Los Alamos (N.Mex.) Nat. Lab., 1978-82; sci. cons. Houston, 1982-84; environ. control and life support systems test bed mgr. Johnson Space Ctr., NASA, Houston, 1984-85, sr. project engr. advanced tech. dept., 1985-86, sr. staff engr. divsn. solar system exploration, 1986-88, asst. divsn. advanced devel., 1988-90; sr. system engr. Exploration Programs Office NASA, Houston, 1990-92; engring. and mgmt. cons. Houston, 1992—; founder Peace U., 1993; mem. internal adv. com. Ctr. for Nonlinear Studies Los Alamos Nat. Lab., 1981; organizer tech. workshops, sessions at soc. meetings; lectr. in field; docent Mus. Fine Arts, Houston. Editor, author tech. reports; contbr. articles to profl. jours.; patentee in field. Mem. curriculum rev. com. U. N.Mex., Los Alamos, 1980. Recipient Woman's badge Tau Beta Pi, 1968, ERDA Spl. Achievement award, 1976, Inventor award Los Alamos Nat. Lab., 1982, Group Achievement award NASA Johnson Space Ctr., 1987, Outstanding Performance award NASA Johnson Space Ctr., 1987, 89, Superior Performance award NASA Johnson Space Ctr., 1987, 89, Cert. of Recognition for Inventions, NASA, 1988, 89, 90, 92, 93. Mem. AIAA (organizer, 1st chmn. human support com. Houston chpt. 1988—), Am. Nuclear Soc. (sec.-treas. fusion energy div. 1982-84, vice chmn. South Tex. sect. 1984-86, mem. local sects. com. 1986-88), Am. Inst. Chem. Engrs. (organizer, 1st chmn. No. N.Mex. club 1980-81, chmn. low-pressure processes and tech. 1981-89), Am. Chem. Soc., Soc. for Risk Analysis (organizer, sec. Lone Star chpt. 1986-88, chmn. soc. publicity 1990—), No. N.Mex. Chem. Engrs. Club, Engrs. Coun. Houston (councilor, sec. energy com.), Sierra Club, Houston Orienteering Club, Phi Kappa Phi, Pi Mu Epsilon.

CULP, MARGARET GERALYN, tax administrator; b. Saratoga Springs, N.Y., Sept. 29, 1954; d. William J. and Mary Frances (Collins) Hickey; m. Weldon Herbert Culp, July 22, 1979; children: Melanie Sue, Sarah Elizabeth. BS in Acctg. summa cum laude, Ithaca Coll., 1976. CPA 1978. Asst., staff acct. Peat, Marwick, Mitchell & Co., Syracuse, N.Y., 1976-78, sr. acct., 1978-79, supervising sr. auditor, 1979-80; sr. mgr., auditor Peat, Marwick, Mitchell & Co., Albany, N.Y., 1980-83; sr. tax mgr. Peat, Marwick, Mitchell & Co., Providence, R.I., 1983-86; tax mgr. Sansiveri, Ryan & Sullivan, Westerly, R.I., 1986-87, Urbach, Kahn & Werlin, Glens Falls, N.Y., 1988, KPMG Peat Marwick, Albany, 1988-90, Farm Family Ins. Cos., Glenmont, N.Y., 1990—. Mem. AICPA, N.Y. Soc. CPAs. Office: Farm Family Ins Cos PO Box 656 Albany NY 12201-0656

CULP, MILDRED LOUISE, corporate executive; b. Ft. Monroe, Va., Jan. 13, 1949; d. William W. and Winifred (Stilwell) C. BA in English, Knox Coll., 1971; AM in religion and literature, U. Chgo., 1974, PhD The Com. on History of Culture, 1976. Mem. faculty, adminstr. Coll., 1976-81; dir. Exec. Résumés, Seattle, 1981—; pres. Exec. Directions Internat., Inc., Seattle, 1985—; mem. MBA mgmt. skills adv. com. U. Wash. Sch. Bus. Adminstrn., 1993; speaker in field; writer Singer Media Corp., 1991—; featured on TV and radio; presenter WorkWise Report, Sta. KIRO, 1991—. Author: Be Work Wise: Retooling Your Work for the 21st Century; columnist Seattle Daily Jour. Commerce, 1982-88; writer Singer Media Corp., 1991—, WorkWise column, 1994—; featured on TV and radio; contbr. articles and book revs. to profl. jours.; presenter WorkWise Report, KIRO Radio, 1991—, WorkWise registered, 1992. Admissions counselor U. Chgo., 1981—; mem. Nat. Alliance Mentally Ill, 1984—, bd. dirs., 1987, mem. adv. bd., 1988; mem. A.M.I. Hamilton County, 1984—; founding mem. People Against Telephone Terrorism and Harassment, 1990; hon. army recruiter. Recipient Alumni Achievement award Knox Coll., 1990 and 8 other awards; named Hon. Army Recruiter. Mem. Nat. Assn. Radio Talk Show Hosts, U. Chgo. Puget Sound Alumni Club (bd. dirs. 1982-86), Knox Coll. Alumni Network. Office: Exec Directions Internat Inc 3313 39th Ave W Seattle WA 98199-2530

CULPEPPER, WANDA HUSKEY, elementary school educator; b. Sevier County, Tenn., Jan. 4, 1933; d. Charles Aaron and Cora Alice (McCarter) Huskey; m. Terry Don Culpepper, Feb. 28, 1959; children: Teresa Katherine Vigil, Terrell H. BS in Elem. Edn. magna cum laude, U. Tenn., 1959; MEd in Early Childhood Edn., Ga. State U., 1974. Lic. tchr., Ga. Tchr. Sevier County Sch. System, Sevierville, Tenn., 1958-59, Atlanta Pub. Schs., 1960-61, 63—, Ware County Schs., Waycross, Ga., 1961-63; supr. student tchrs. various colls. and univs., Atlanta; evaluator new tchrs. West Metro Ctr., Atlanta. Mem. Ga. Gov.'s Conf. on Edn., Marietta, 1991, Smoky Mountain Hist. Soc., PTA; vol. USO Holiday Travelers Benefits, Hartsfield Airport. Named Capitol View Elem. Tchr. of Yr., 1992-93. Mem. NEA, AAUW, Ga. Assn. Educators, Atlanta Assn. Educators, Am. Bus. Women's Assn. (Woman of Yr. 1985), Ga. Assn. Tchr. Educators (exec. bd., chair com.), Beta Sigma Phi, Kappa Kappa Iota (pres. 1992-93, named Disting. Educator of Yr. Ga. 1988, co-chair nat. conv. 1994), Delta Kappa Gamma. Baptist. Home: 4404 Briarcliff Rd NE Atlanta GA 30345

CULTON, SARAH ALEXANDER, psychologist, writer; b. Burwell, Nebr., Nov. 12, 1927; d. James Claude and Frances Ann (Evans) Alexander;m. Verlen Ross Culton, June 19, 1949; children: James Verlen, Sarah Ann. BA in Edn., Ea. Wash. U., 1953, MA in Edn., 1956; EdD in Psychology, U. Idaho, 1966. Tchr. pub. schs. Kennewick, Northport, Wash., Potlatch, Idaho, 1946-56; prof. Lewis-Clark U. of Idaho, Lewiston, 1956-59, North Idaho Jr. Coll., Coeur d'Alene, 1961-66; sch. psychologist Sch. Dist. 81, Spokane, Wash., 1966-67; prof. psychology Spokane Falls Community Coll., 1967-88; author Colville, Wash., 1988—; sch. psychologist, sch. counselor vol. Northport Schs., 1989-92; presenter convs. in field. Author: Psychology of Stress and Nutrition, 1991. Doctoral fellow Wash. State U., 1959, U. Idaho, 1964; recipient Faculty Achievement award Burlington No. Found., 1988. Fellow Am. Inst. Stress; mem. NEA, APA, Intenat. Coun. Psychologists, Internat. Stress Mgmt. Assn. (editor newsletter), Nat. Stroke Assn., Western Psychol. Assn., Am. Counseling Assn. (writer invitation 1992), Alpha Delta Kappa. Home and Office: 717 Prouty Corner Loop Rd Colville WA 99114-9208

CULVERWELL, ROSEMARY JEAN, principal, elementary education educator; b. Chgo., Jan. 15, 1934; d. August John and Marie Josephine (Westermeyer) Flashing; m. Paul Jerome Culverwell, Apr. 26, 1958; children: Joanne, Mary Frances, Janet, Nancy, Amy. BEd, Chgo. State U., 1955, MEd in Libr. Sci., 1958; postgrad., DePaul U., 1973. Cert. supr., tchr. Tchr. Otis Sch., Chgo., 1955-59; tchr., libr. Yates Sch., Chgo., 1960-61, Nash Sch., Chgo., 1962-63, Boys Chgo. Parental, 1969-72, Edgebrook and Reilly Schs., Chgo., 1965-67; counselor, libr. Reilly Sch., Chgo., 1968, tchr., libr., asst. prin., 1973, prin., 1974—. Pres. Infant Jesus Guild, Park Ridge, Ill., 1969-70; troop leader Girl Scouts U.S., Park Ridge, 1967-69; sec. Home Sch. Assn., Park Ridge, 1969, v.p. spl. projects, 1970; mem. Ill. Svc. Ctr. Six Governing Bd., 1994. Recipient Outstanding Prin. award Citizens Schs. Com., Chgo., 1987, For Character award, 1984-85, Whitman award for Excellence in Edn. Mgmt., 1990, Local Sch. Coun. award Ill. Bell Ameritech, 1991, Ill. Disting. Educator award Milken Family Found. Nat. Educators, 1991. Mem. AAUW, LWV (chmn. speakers bur. 1969), Delta Kappa Gamma, Phi Delta Kappa. Home: 1929 S Ashland Ave Park Ridge IL 60068-5460 Office: FW Reilly Sch 3650 W School St Chicago IL 60618-5358

CUMING, PAMELA JANE, marketing consultant, author; b. Denver, Oct. 13, 1944; d. John Gerald and Rosemary (Miller) C.; m. Terrence C. Shea, June 18, 1966 (div. 1973); m. William I. Bechard, June 23, 1974 (dec. July 1979); m. David Druetzer Gregory, Dec. 9, 1989; children: Monica Cuming, Melissa Cotter. BA, Smith Coll., 1966. Ins. underwriter Chubb & Son, N.Y.C., 1966-69; orgn. devel. specialist Am. Express, N.Y.C., 1969-71; orgn. devel. cons. Ednl. Systems & Designs, Westport, Conn., 1971-73; v.p. Dialectics Inc., Stamford, Conn., 1973-79; pres. Dialectics Inc., Stamford and Encinitas, Calif., 1979-93; sr. mng. dir., dir. mktg. Bear, Stearns & Co., Inc., N.Y.C., 1993—; developer computerized expert systems. Author: The Power Handbook, 1982, Turf and Other Corporate Power Plays, 1987; contbr. articles to profl. jours. Office: Bear Stearns & Co Inc 245 Park Ave New York NY 10167-0001

CUMMERTON, JOAN MARIE, social work educator; b. Batavia, N.Y., Jan. 11, 1931; d. John J. and Loretta E. (Geissler) C. BS in Social Sci., Carnegie Mellon U., 1953; MS in Social Adminstrn., Case-Western Reserve U., 1956; D in Social Work, Washington U., St. Louis, 1970. Cert. Acad. Cert. Social Workers. Group worker Ferry Rd. Playground, Phila., 1953-54; dist. dir. Girl Scouts, St. Louis, 1956-58, field staff supr., 1958-60; asst. prof. U. Iowa, Iowa City, 1963-70; assoc. prof. San Francisco State U., 1970-80, prof. social work edn., 1980—; cons. Family Svc. Assn., Des Moines, 1966-67, Women, Inc., San Francisco, 1988-89. Mem. NASW, Coun. on Social Work Edn., Women in Psychology, Nat. Women's Studies Assn. Office: San Francisco State U 1600 Holloway Ave San Francisco CA 94132-1722

CUMMING, JANICE DOROTHY, clinical psychologist; b. Berkeley, Calif., Nov. 20, 1953; d. Gordon Robertson and Helen (Stanford) Cumming; 1 child, Shauna Cumming Keddy. BA, U. Calif., Davis, 1975; MA, Calif. State U., Sacramento, 1980; PhD, Calif. Sch. Profl. Psychology, Berkeley, 1985. Lic. psychologist, Calif. Counselor and instr. Serendipity Diagnostic/Treatment, Citrus Hts., Calif., 1978-79; reg. psychologist asst. John Gibbins, PhD, Castro Valley, Calif., 1984-87, Enrico Jones, PhD, Berkeley, Calif., 1985-86; asst. rsch. specialist U. Calif., Berkeley, 1985-90; clin. cons. Family Guidance, Children's Hosp., Oakland, Calif., 1987-90; clin. supr. psychiat. svcs. Children's Hosp., San Francisco, 1987-90; pvt. practice psychology Castro Valley, 1987-90, San Francisco, 1987-90, Oakland, Calif., 1990—; mem. rschr. San Francisco Psychotherapy Rsch. Group, 1987—, instr., 1991, conf. chair, 1992-93; conv. chair Calif. State Psychol. Assn., Sacramento, 1985, 86; asst. clin. prof. U. Calif., San Francisco, 1992—. Mem. APA, Calif. Psychol. Assn. (continuing edn. com. chair 1986, co-chair 1987), Psychologists for Social Responsibility (bd. dirs. 1984-87, chair 1987-89), Soc. for Psychotherapy Rsch., No. Calif. Soc. for Psychoanalytic Psychology, Alameda County Psychol. Assn., Phi Beta Kappa. Office: 5835 College Ave Ste C Oakland CA 94618-1585

CUMMINGS, ANA GUERRERO, lawyer; b. Mexico, Jan. 13, 1941; d. Geronimo S. and Rebecca (Reta) Guerrero; m. Jerry P. Cummings, Oct. 25, 1975. B.B.A., U. Tex., 1963; J.D., U. Houston, 1978. Acct. Am. Airco, Houston, 1963-66; revenue agt. IRS, Houston, 1966-74, appeals officer, 1974-80, atty. IRS Dist. Counsel, Houston, 1980-88, spl. litigation asst., 1988-91; judge U.S. Adminstrv. Law OHA/SSA, 1991-92; chief hearing judge Office Adminstrv. Law, 1992—. Nat. bd. dirs. YWCA, 1968-72; chmn. local parish council, 1981-83; exec. v.p. Met. Orgn., Houston, 1982—; mem. Diocesan Bd. Edn., 1994—. Named Fed. Employee of Yr., 1981; recipient Spl. Merit award, 1983, 85, 86, 87, Outstanding Hispanic Leader award Ywca, 1986. Roman Catholic. Home: 1844 Harvard Houston TX 77008 Office: Office Hearings and Appeals 6800 W Loop S Ste 300 Bellaire TX 77401

CUMMINGS, CONSTANCE, actress; b. Seattle; d. Dallas Vernon and Kate Logan (Cummings) Halverstadt; m. Benn Wolfe Levy, 1933; children: Jonathan, Jemima. Chmn. Young People's Theatre Panel; mem. Arts Council, 1963-69. Broadway debut Treasure Girl, 1928; London debut Sour Grapes, Repertory Players, 1934; film debut Movie Crazy, 1932; appeared on radio, TV, films, theatre; joined Nat. Theatre Co., 1971; appeared in London stage prodns.: Madame Bovary, 1937; Romeo and Juliet, 1939, Saint Joan, 1939, The Petrified Forest, 1942, Return to Tyass, 1950, Lysistrata, 1957, The Rape of the Belt, 1957, Who's Afraid of Virginia Woolf?, 1964, Justice is a Woman, 1966, Fallen Angel, 1967, Nat. Theatre Co., A Long Day's Journey Into Night, 1972, The Cherry Orchard, 1973, The Circle, 1975, Mrs. Warren's Profession, Vienna, 1976, Wings, U.S., 1978, London, 1979 (Tony award 1979), Hay Fever, 1980, The Golden Age, 1981, The Chalk Garden, N.Y.C., 1982, The Glass Menagerie, N.Y.C., London, 1984, The Glass Menagerie, 1985, (one woman show) Fanny Kemble, 1986, Crown Matrimonial, 1987, Téte a Téte, Mass., 1989, The Chalk Garden, London, 1992, others; performed in Claudel-Honnegar oratorio St. Joan at the Stake, Albert Hall, London, 1949, Peter and the Wolf, Albert Hall, 1955, Wings on Am. pub. TV; dir. Royal Ct. Theatre. Recipient Obie award, 1979, Drama Desk award, 1979; decorated Comdr. Brit. Empire. Mem. Brit. Actors Equity (mem. council), Royal Soc. for Encouragement of Arts and Commerce. Mem. Labour Party. Club: Chelsea Arts.

CUMMINGS, ERIKA HELGA, financial planner; b. Offenbach, Germany; came to U.S., 1978; d. Erwin and Edith (Trunski) Maier; m. Robert H. Cummings, Dec. 1970; 1 child, Marisa Anne. BSBA, Calif. State U., Bakersfield; M in Internat. Mgmt., Am. Grad. Sch. Internat. Mgmt., Glendale, Ariz., 1983. CFP. Inflight supr. TWA, Paris; internat. ops. mgr. Cooper LaserSonics, Santa Clara, Calif.; bus. cons. Suncoast Bus. Industries, Sarasota, Fla., 1989—; personal fin. planner IDS Fin. Svcs., Sarasota. Mem. NAFE, Toastmasters, Beta Gamma Sigma. Office: IDS Fin Svcs 2 N Tamiami Trail Ste 700 Sarasota FL 34236-5570

CUMMINGS, FRANCES MCARTHUR, state official, retired educational administrator. BS in Bus. Edn., Livingstone Coll.; MS in Bus. and Office, N.C. Ctrl. U.; cert. vocat. dir., U. N.C. Cert. mgr. Classroom tchr. Robeson County Schs., 1961-65, Lumberton City Schs., 1965-87; assoc. exec. dir. NCAE, 1987-89; asst. dir. vocat. edn., 1989-93, ret., 1993; dist. 87 rep. N.C. Ho. of Reps., 1993—; bd. dirs. Lumber River Pvt. Industry Coun.; fellow N.C. Inst. of Polit. Leadership. Mem. Gov.'s Task Force on Pub. Sch. Adminstrs., Gov.'s Coun. on Phys. Fitness and Health; chairwoman Task Force on Women and Minority Panel; bd. dirs. Robeson County Pvt. Industry, N.C. Equity; mem. Robeson County Black Caucus; cons. Named Outstanding Young Educator Lumberton City Schs., 1970; recipient Recognition of Leadership and Svc. Livingston Coll., Robeson County Black Caucus, Women of Yr. award 1993, Par-Excellence award N.C. Gen. Bapt. Conv., Raleigh, Outstanding Leadership award S.E. region Assn. of Classroom Tchrs., Disting. Svcs. award N.C. Coun. of Sickle Cell Syndrome, 1993, numerous others. Named Outstanding Young Educator Lumberton City Schs., 1970; recipient Recognition of Leadership and Svc. Livingston Coll., Robeson County Black Caucus, Women of Yr. award 1993, Par-Excellence award N.C. Gen. Bapt. Conv., Raleigh, Outstanding Leadership award S.E. region Assn. of Classroom Tchrs., Disting. Svcs. award N.C. Coun. of Sickle Cell Syndrome, 1993, A Legislator's award, NCAE, numerous others. Republican. Home: PO Box 983 1708 Maryland St Lumberton NC 28359 Office: Legis Bldg Rm 2211 Raleigh NC 27601-1096

CUMMINGS, HARRIET ELEANOR, lawyer; b. Winslow, Ariz., June 1, 1960; d. Samuel Rowland and Dorothy (Davis) C. BA in Humanistic Studies, Johns Hopkins U., 1982; JD, U. Calif., Davis, 1987. Bar: Calif. 1988, Nev. 1990. Atty. Legal Svcs. No. Calif., Sacramento, 1987-88; legal rsch. and writing instr. Mc George Sch. Law, U. of the Pacific, Sacramento, 1988-89; jud. law clk. to Hon. Charles E. Springer Nev. Supreme Ct., Carson City, 1989-90, staff atty., 1990—, mem. bench, bar and media com., 1992; CLE lectr. State Bar Nev., Carson City, Las Vegas, 1993. Author: (with others) Covering the Courts in Nevada, 1992, Effective Advocacy Before the Supreme Court of Nevada, 1993. Mem. cabinet No. Nev. chpt., United Way, Carson City, 1993—. Mem. ABA, Nev. Bar Assn., Calif. Bar Assn. Democrat. Office: Nev Supreme Ct Capitol Complex Carson City NV 89710

CUMMINGS, JOAN E., health facility administrator. BA, Trinity Coll., 1964; MD, Loyola U., 1968. Diplomate Am. Bd. Internal Medicine, Geriatric Medicine. Med. internship St. Vincent Hosp., Worcester, Mass., 1968-69; med. residency Hines VA Hosp., Hines, Ill., 1969-71; sr. residency Nephrology Hines VA Hosp., 1971-72, ambulatory care svc. chief gen. med. section, 1971-84, med. dir., hosp. based home care, 1972-87, chief, intermediate care svc., 1984-87, assoc. chief of staff, extended care and geriatrics, 1987-90, med. dir., extended care center, 1987-90, dir., 1990—; asst. prof. Clinical Medicine U. Ill., 1976-82; asst. prof. Clinical Medicine Loyola U., 1983-91, assoc. prof. Clinical Medicine, 1991—; mem. ad hoc com. on primary care U. Ill., 1980-82, coll. edn. policy com. U. Ill., 1980-82, State Ill. Emergency Med. Svc. Coun., 1981-83, Comprehensive Health Ins. Plan Bd. State Ill., 1990—, Med. Licensing Bd. State Ill., 1992—, exec. com. Chgo. Fed. Exec. Bd. State Ill., 1992—; program dir. Loyola/Hines Geriatric Fellowship Program, 1987-90. Contbr. to profl. mags. and jour. Recipient Disting. Svc. award Abraham Lincoln Sch. Med. Univ. Ill., 1979, 81, Leadership award VA, 1980, Certificate of Appreciation award VA, 1980, Laureate award Am. Coll. Physicians, 1990. Fellow Am. Coll. Physicians; mem. AMA (Ill. delagation 1985—, vice speaker ho. delagates 1987-89), Chgo. Med. Soc. (pres. Hines-Loyola Branch 1982-83), Ill. State Med. Soc. (trustee 1984—, chmn. com. on Ill. med., 1988—, speaker ho delegates 1989-91, exec. com., 1989-91, policy com., 1989—), Am. Coll. Physicians (councilor Ill. chpt. 1984—), Chgo. Geriatric Soc., Am. Geriatric Soc. Office: Edward Hines Jr VA Hosp PO Box 5000 5th Ave & Roosevelt Rd Hines IL 60141-5000

CUMMINGS, JOSEPHINE ANNA, writer; b. Gainesville, Fla., July 12, 1949; d. Robert Jay and Marcella Dee (Mount) Cummings. A.B.J./Design cum laude, U. Ga., Athens, 1971. Copywriter William Cook, Jacksonville, Fla., 1971-73; creative dir. Leo Burnett, Chgo., 1973-76; sr. v.p., group creative dir. D. D. B. Needham, Chgo., 1976-84; sr. v.p., creative dir. Saatchi-Saatchi, N.Y.C., 1984; sr. v.p., sr. creative dir. Ted Bates, N.Y.C., 1984; exec. v.p., chief creative officer Tracy-Locke, Dallas, 1985-87; exec. v.p., exec. creative dir. Bozell, Chgo, 1989; exec. v.p., creative dir. Y&R, N.Y.C., 1990-92; pres. The Joey Co., N.Y.C., 1992—. Author: (play) Azaleas, 1988, (short story collection) Crimes of Passion, 1988, (childrens' book) The Hospital is a Funny Place, 1988, (short film) Night Magic, 1989. Named as creator One of Hundred Best TV Commls. Advt. Age, 1978-79, one of Advt. 100 Best Advt. Age, 1986, one of People to Watch Fortune mag., 1986, Ad Age one of Best and Brightest, N.Y. Mem. Amelia Earhard, Ninety Niners Club, N.Y. Women in Film. Office: The Joey Co 133 W 19th St 5th Fl New York NY 10011

CUMMINGS, LUCILLE MAUD, geriatrics, psychiatric mental health nurse; d. Adrian and Mabel Fuller; m. Elbert Cummings, Mar. 31, 1956. Diploma in nursing, Middlewood Hosp., Shefield, Yorkshire, Eng., 1960; BS in Gerontology cum laude, Mercy Coll., Dobbs Ferry, N.Y., 1981; MS in Gerontology, Coll. of New Rochelle, 1983. RN, Fla. Staff nurse med. psychiat. unit Montefiore Hosp. Med. Ctr., Bronx, N.Y., 1969-71, clin. nurse, 1971-72, coord. patient care, 1972-85; staff nurse gerontology unit Bronx VA Med. Ctr., 1985-86; staff nurse med.-surg. units Humana Mobile Nurse Inc., Louisville, 1986-88; traveling nurse ORMC, Orlando, Fla., 1989; staff nurse Flagler Hosp., St. Augustine, Fla., 1989-90. Mem. Am. Assn. Ret. Persons.

CUMMINGS, MAXINE GIBSON, elementary school educator; b. Tupelo, Miss., Oct. 7, 1940; d. T. Ruben and Maggie (Ruff) Gibson; m. Willie B. Cummings, Aug. 15, 1964; 1 child, Stanley. BS, Barber-Scotia Coll., Concord, N.C., 1962; MA, Northeastern Ill. U., Chgo., 1974. Cert. tchr., N.C., Ill. Tchr. Walter Reed Elem. Sch., Chgo., 1963-75, reading tchr., 1975-82, social studies tchr., 1982-85; reading resource tchr. Arna Bontemps Sch., Chgo., 1985-91, ESEA lab. tchr., 1991—; counselor Westside YWCA, Chgo., 1963-68; chmn. reading com. Bontemps Sch., 1986-92, chmn. activity com., 1992-93. Contbr. articles to profl. jours. Mem. Vol. Edna White Century Garden; sec. S.W. Morgan Parkk Civic Assn., Chgo., 1990-92; block rep. Neighborhood Watch Program, Chgo., 1989-90; trustee Morgan Park Presbyn. Ch., peace and justice com. Grantee Chgo.-Incentive, 1987, NEH, 1984, Northeastern Ill. U., 1980. Mem. Minority Students of Chgo. Area (recruiter), Barber-Scotia Alumni Club (sec. 1989-92), Pi Lambda Theta. Home: 11116 S Longwood Dr Chicago IL 60643-4043 Office: Bontemps Elem Sch 1241 W 58th St Chicago IL 60636-1994

CUMMINGS, PENELOPE DIRRIG, special education educator; b. Akron, Ohio, Sept. 16, 1944; d. Raymond Joseph and Pearl Penelope (Pantages) Dirrig; m. Ray Cummings, Jn. 21, 1967; children: Michael R., James E. BA in English, U. Akron, 1966; MS in Spl. Edn., U. Kans., 1992. Tchr. English Akron Pub. Schs., 1966-69; tutor learning disabled Delaware (Ohio) Pub. Schs., 1980-82; tutor homebound Trumbull (Conn.) Pub. Schs., 1982-87; tutor homebound, student support svcs. program Olathe (Kans.) Pub. Schs., 1987-91; tchr. English and learning disabled Penn Valley C.C., Kansas City, Mo., 1988-91; tchr. learning disabled Kansas City (Kans.) Pub. Schs., 1991—. Editor sorority mag. The Compass, 1976-78. Pres., sec. Officer's Wives' Club, Rickenbacher AFB, Columbus, Ohio, 1973-74; active Mortar Bd., Akron, 1965-66, PTA, 1976—. Scholar United Steelworkers Am., 1962-66, U. Akron, 1962-66, Theta Phi Alpha, 1992. Mem. NEA, Coun. of Learning Disabilities (v.p. 1992-93, pres. 1994—), Rosedale PTSA (v.p. 1994—), Kappa Delta Pi, Phi Sigma Alpha. Democrat. Roman Catholic. Home: 11014 W 126th Ter Overland Park KS 66213-2152

CUMMINGS, SALLY PAHNKE, critical care nurse, educator; b. Savannah, Ga., June 19, 1954; d. Robert Carl and Maggie Belle (Blackburn) Pahnke; m. P. Howard Cummings, Aug. 14, 1976; children: Amanda Grace, Joshua Daniel. BSN, U. N.C., Greensboro, 1976; MSN, East Carolina U., 1980; EdD, Clemson U., 1980. Staff nurse Pitt County Meml. Hosp., Greenville, N.C.; asst. prof. Sch. Nursing East Carolina U., Greenville, N.C., 1981-85; asst. prof. Troy (Ala.) State U., 1985-87, Clemson (S.C.) U., 1987-92, U. N.C., Wilmington, 1992—. Contbr. articles to profl. jours. Bd. dirs. Girls, Inc., Girl Scouts. Salvation Army Nurses fellow. Mem. AACN, Sigma Theta Tau.

CUMMINGS, SPANGLER (MELINDA JOHNSON), art dealer, artist; b. L.A., Dec. 27, 1936; d. Clyde Lewis and Lena Glyde (Spangler) Cummings; m. Richard Johnson, Nov. 25, 1955; children: Edward, Jeanne, Lisa. BA, Chatham Coll., Pitts., 1978; postgrad., Carnegie-Mellon U., Pitts., 1979-80. Founding pres., dir. Artists in Action, Pitts., 1981-82; founder, owner, operator Spangler Cummings Galleries, Columbus, Ohio, 1985-87, 93—. Mem. exec. bd. Three Rivers Art Festival Pitts., 1980; docent Columbus Mus. Art, 1985-87; docent Mus. Contemporary Art, L.A., 1989, mem. curator's coun., 1990-94. Finalist Internat. Soc. Artists, N.Y.C., 1979. Mem. So. Calif. Cmy. Artist (pres. 1972-73); mem. Internat. Soc. Artists (charter), Am. Watercolor Soc. (assoc.), Pitts. Soc. Artists (bd. dirs. 1980-81), Columbus Art League (bd. dirs. 1983-85), Screen Actors' Guild. Home: 11926 White Water Ln Malibu CA 90265-9724 Office: 641 N High St # 106 Columbus OH 43215

CUMMINGS, VIRGINIA J(EANNE), former real estate company executive; b. Greenwood, S.C., June 24, 1923; d. Samuel Barksdale and Alma Virginia (Davis) Jones; m. John W. Cummings, Nov. 7, 1938; children: John W., Martha Jean Wells. Student, U. Miami; PhD (hon.), Colo. State Christian Coll., 1973. Sec. Pine Crest Pvt. Sch., Ft. Lauderdale, Fla., 1956-59; real estate broker Am. Realty, Ft. Lauderdale, 1959-62; pres., founder Cummings Realty Inc., Ft. Lauderdale, 1962-85, chmn. bd. dirs., 1985—; v.p. Magic Carpet Travel, Ft. Lauderdale, 1975-89; pres. Women's Coun. Ft. Lauderdale Bd. Realtors, 1961; freelance writer. Feature writer Fla. Living Mag., 1969-74; contbr. articles to profl. jours. Mem. Nat. Bd. Realtors, Ft. Lauderdale Area Bd. realtors, DAR. Democrat. Home: 4300 N Ocean Blvd Apt 19A-B Fort Lauderdale FL 33308

CUMMINGS-AYOUB, VALERIE ANNE, health services professional, nurse; b. Milton, Mass., Aug. 8, 1958; d. Donald Lawrence and Irene (Budricki) Cummings; m. Raymond A. Ayoub, Aug. 28, 1993. BSN, Duke U., 1981, BS in Child Psychology, 1981. RN, Md., Va., D.C. Critical care nurse Children's Hosp., Nat. Med. Ctr., Washington, 1981-87; pvt. duty nurse The Ind. Group, Mitchellville, Md., 1989-91; clin. care coord. Coordinating Ctr. for Home Care, Millersville, Md., 1984-87; br. mgr. Kimberly Quality Care, Falls Church, Va., 1987-88; dir., owner Unique Nurses, Inc., Elkridge, Md., 1991—; cons. Rosebud Orgn., Alexandria, Va., 1987-88; guest spkr. Nat. Symposium on High Tech. Home Care, Balt., 1984, 85, 86. Contbr. articles to profl. jours. Mem. AAUW, NAFE, Duke U. Alumni Assn. Roman Catholic. Home: 3026 Barden Oaks Ct Oakton VA 22124 Office: Unique Nurses Inc PO Box 424 Vienna VA 22124

CUMMINS, EVELYN FREEMAN, retired social agency administrator; b. Beatrice, Nebr., Mar. 24, 1904; d. John Allen and Irene (Townsend) Freeman; m. Paul Otto Cummins, Oct. 8, 1927 (dec. Sept. 1943); 1 child, Beverly Anne (Mrs. Cummins Spangler). Student Nebr. Wesleyan, 1920-23; BA, U. Nebr., 1928; postgrad. U. Chgo., 1934-36, 41; MS, Columbia U., 1946. Tchr. rural Gage County, Nebr., 1921-22, Wilber, Nebr., 1923-25, Lincoln, Nebr., 1925-27; sch. social worker Lincoln, 1930-36; supr. Fla. Dept. Pub. Welfare, Orlando, 1936-42, dist. dir., 1942-45; dir. Nebr. Gov.'s Com. to Study Services to Blind, Lincoln, 1946-47; field rep. Fla. Dept. Pub. Welfare, Jacksonville, 1948-51, appeals officer, 1950-51; exec. dir. Community Coun. Oklahoma City Area, 1952-61; exec. dir. spl. projects Chgo. Community Fund, 1962-63; exec. dir. Family Svc. Assn. La Porte County (Ind.), 1964-89, ret., 1989; lectr. social problems Purdue North Cen.; participant rsch. seminar Non-Profits and Taxation NYU, 1988-89; field supr. Valparaiso U., Loyola U., Jane Addams Sch. Social Work, Chgo. Del. Area II Adv. Coun. on Aging, 1976-80; mem. housing com. Mayor of Michigan City (Ind.), 1973; pres. Community Svc. Coun. Michigan City, 1966-68; chmn. residential campaign United Way Michigan City, 1966-68. Diplomate Conf. Advancement Pvt. Practice in Social Work. Recipient Older Hoosier of Yr., 1989. Mem. DAR, AAUW, NASW, Acad. Cert. Social Workers, Coun. Social Work Edn. Assn., Ind. Coun. Family Svc. Assn., Ind. Home Service Agys. Assn., Ind. Conf. on Social Concerns, Internat. Platform Assn., Nat. Network Social Work Mgrs., Inc., Women in Mgmt., Michigan City C. of C., LaPorte County Coun. on Aging (pres. 1978). Democrat. Methodist. Home: 1317 Washington St Michigan City IN 46360-4230

CUMMINS, NANCYELLEN HECKEROTH, electronics engineer; b. Long Beach, Calif., May 22, 1948; d. George and Ruth May (Anderson) Heckeroth; m. Weldon Jay, Sept. 15, 1987; stepchildren: Tracy Lynn, John Scott, Darren Elliott. Student avionics, USMC, Memphis, 1966-67. Tech. publ. engr. Missile and Space divsn. Lockheed Corp., Sunnyvale, Calif., 1973-76, engring. instr., 1977; test engr. Gen. Dynamics, Pomona, Calif., 1980-83; quality assurance test engr. Interstate Electronics Co., Anaheim, Calif., 1983-84; quality engr., certification engr. Rockwell Internat., Anaheim, 1985-86; sr. quality assurance programmer Point 4 Data, Tustin, Calif., 1986-87; software quality assurance specialist Lawrence Livermore Nat. Lab., Yucca Mountain Project, Livermore, Calif., 1987-89, software quality mgr., 1989-90; sr. constrn. insp. EG&G Rocky Flats, Inc., Golden, Colo., 1990, sr. quality assurance engr., 1991, engr. IV software quality assurance, 1991-92, instr., developer environ. law and compliance, 1992—; customer engr. IBM Gen. Sys., Orange, Calif., 1979; electronics engr. Exhibits divsn. LDS Ch., Salt Lake City, 1978; electronic repair specialist Weber State Coll., 1977-78. Author: Package Area Test Set, 6 vols., 1975, Software Quality Assurance Plan, 1989. Vol., instr. San Fernando (Calif.) Search and Rescue Team, 1967-70; instr. emergency preparedness and survival, Clairmont, Calif., 1982-84, Modesto, Calif., 1989; mem. Lawrence Livermore Nat. Lab. Employees Emergency Vols., 1987-90, EG&G Rocky Flats Bldg. Emergency Support Team, 1990—. Mem. NAFE, NRA, Nat. Muzzle Loading Rifle Assn., Am. Soc. Quality Control, Job's Daus. (majority mem.). Republican. Mem. LDS Ch. Home: PO Box 414 Dubois WY 82513 Office: CRI PO Box 414 Dubois WY 82513-0414

CUNNANE, PATRICIA S., medical facility administrator; b. Clinton, Iowa, Sept. 7, 1946; d. Cyril J. and Corinne Spain; m. Edward J. Cunnane, June 19, 1971. AA, Mt. St. Clare Coll., Clinton, Iowa, 1966. Mgr. Eye Med. Clinic of Santa Clara Valley, San Jose, Calif. Mem. Med. Adminstrs. Calif. Polit. Action Com., San Francisco, 1987. Mem. Med. Group Mgmt. Assn., Am. Coll. Med. Group Adminstrs. (nominee), Nat. Notary Assn., NAFE, Exec. Women Internat. (v.p. 1986-87, pres. 1987—), Profl. Secs. Internat. (sec. 1979-80), Am. Soc. Ophthalmic Adminstrs., Women Health Care Execs., Healthcare Human Resource Mgmt. Assn. Calif. Roman Catholic. Home: 232 Tolin Ct San Jose CA 95139-1445 Office: Eye Med Clinic of Santa Clara Valley 220 Meridian Ave San Jose CA 95126-2903

CUNNINGHAM, GLORIA SWORD, librarian; b. Bath, Pa., June 28, 1929; d. Roy and Hilda (Brown) S; children: Rebekah Ann (dec.), Timothy David. BS, Trenton (N.J.) State Coll., 1974, MEd, 1984. Cert. tchr., libr., reading specialist. 4th and 6th grade tchr., now libr. Mansfield Twp. Elem. Sch. Dist., Port Murray, N.J., 1974—; Russian exch. tchr. Hands Across the Water, 1992. Mem. NEA, Internat. Reading Assn., Am. Libr. Assn., N.J. Edn. Assn., Manfield Twp. Edn. Assn., Delta Kappa Gamma, Kappa Delta Pi. Home: 52 Kinter St Clinton NJ 08809

CUNNINGHAM, JACQUELINE LEMMÉ, psychologist, educator; b. Biddeford, Maine, Apr. 22, 1941; d. S. James and Alice (Fréchette) Lemmé; m. Seymour Cunningham II, Dec. 16, 1960 (dec. 1987); children: Macklin Todd, Danielle, Alyssa. BA in Psychology, U. Maine, Orono, 1963; MS in Psychology, U. South Ala., 1983; PhD, U. Tex., 1994. Tchr. Mobile (Ala.) Pub. Schs., 1976-81; clinician Devereux Found., Devon, Pa., 1988-89; fellow devel. disabilities Harvard Med. Sch., Cambridge, Mass., 1990; prof. U. S.D., Vermillion, 1994—; cons. in field. Contbr. articles to profl. jours. Mem. Am. Psychol. Assn., Internat. Neuropsychol. Soc., Soc. History Behavioral Scis., Phi Kappa Phi.

CUNNINGHAM, JEAN WOODEN, state legislator, lawyer, educator; b. Hampton, Va., June 28, 1946; d. Roger Omly and Norville (King) Wooden; m. John Henry Cunningham, Jr., Sept. 9, 1967 (dec. Nov. 13, 1984); children: Brooke, Justin, Bradford. BA, Va. State U., 1968; JD, Howard U., 1974. Bar: Mich. 1975, Va. 1978. Tchr., Prince George County, Va., 1968; tech. writer IBM, Poughkeepsie, N.Y., 1968-71; intern Exec. Office of Pres., Washington, summer 1972; dir. arbitration Reynolds Metals Co., Richmond, Va., 1977-78, 81—, Ford Motor Co., Detroit, 1974-77; ptnr. Chambliss, Cunningham, Hughes and Macbeth, Richmond, 1979-81; prof. Va. Commonwealth U., Richmond, 1978-81; mem. Va. Ho. of Dels., 1986—. Mem. Va. State Bd. Social Services, 1982-86, Richmond Renaissance, 1982—, Indsl. Devel. Authority Richmond, 1980-84; bd. visitors Va. State U., 1984-86. Mem. Va. Bar Assn. (mem. exec. com. 1995—), Va. Assn. Black Women Attys. (sec.-treas. 1980-82, v.p. 1982-84), Old Dominion Bar Assn. (sec.-treas. 1979-83), Nat. Alumni Assn. Va. State U. (pres. 1981-89), Delta Sigma Theta. Democrat. Baptist. Club: Links. Home: 2607 E Grace St Richmond VA 23223-7351

CUNNINGHAM, KAREN LEE, marketing professional; b. St. Louis, Sept. 23, 1949; d. Everett R. and Madelyn Marie (Restivo) Saddler; m. David G. Cunningham, May 4, 1970 (div. 1974). Attended, Ind. State U., 1967-69, Butler U., 1975. Cmty. affairs rep. Am. Fletcher Nat. Bank, Indpls., 1969-80; owner Corporate Art Cons., Indpls., 1980-83; dir. pub. rels. and spl. evens L.S. Ayres & Co., Indpls., 1983-85; dir. pub. rels. and promotions Drum Corps Internat., Lombard, Ill., 1986; dir. bus. devel. Schmidt Assocs. Archs. Inc., Indpls., 1987-90; dir. mktg., bus. devel. and pub. rels. Eden Design Assocs, Inc., Carmel, Ind., 1990—. V.p. bd. dirs. Cathedral Arts, Inc., Indpls., 1978-86; mem. adv. coun. Humana Hosp., Indpls., 1983-85; mem. steering com. Eiteljorg Mus., Indpls., 1988-89; city govt. liaison Arts Coun. Indpls., 1989; mem. numerous coms. Meth. Hosp. Task Core, Indpls., 1987—, 500 Festival Assocs., Indpls., 1989—; bd. dirs. Ind. State Mus., Indpls., 1990—; mem. adv. bd. Ind. State U., Terre Haute, 1994—;. Mem. Pub. Rels. Soc. Am., Ind. Soc. Pub. Rels. Profls., Internat. Facility Mgmt.

Assn. (bd. dirs., Affiliate Member of Yr. 1993), Soc. Mktg. Profl. Svcs. (bd. dirs.), Network Women in Bus. (bd. dirs. 1978-82, Networker of Yr. 1984). Home: 8516 Hague Rd Indianapolis IN 46256 Office: Eden Design Assocs Inc 111 Congressional Blvd Ste 120 Carmel IN 46032

CUNNINGHAM, PATRICIA, lawyer; b. Phila., Jan. 3, 1959; d. Harry Joseph and Myrtle Bertha (Oeschlen) C.; widow; 1 child, Robert J. Moore. A in Criminal Justice, Temple U., 1979, BS in Criminal Justice, 1983; JD, Widener U., 1989. Bar: Pa. Jud. clk. Ct. Common Pleas, City of Phila., 1989-94; assoc. Charles S. Lieberman, P.C., Phila., 1994—. Active Internat. Visitors Coun., Phila., 1989—. Mem. Phila. Bar Assn. Home: 235 Montrose St Philadelphia PA 19147 Office: Charles S Lieberman PC 260 S Broad St Ste 1130 Philadelphia PA 19102

CUNNINGHAM, SALLY SCHLECHTER, association director; b. Allentown, Pa., July 9, 1952; d. Edward William and Elizabeth Lawton (Hummel) Schlechter; divorced; 1 child, Elizabeth Ann. Associates degree, Lehigh Jr. Coll., 1972. Asst. to exec. dir. Nat. Assn. Police Athletic League, Warwick, R.I., 1983-88; dir. mktg. and mem. svcs. Nat. Assn. Police Athletic League, North Palm Beach, Fla., 1988—. Editor Nat. Police Athletic League Update; dir. video Police Athletic League; creator Police Athletic League Hall of Fame calendar, promotional material. Mem. NAFE, NRA (com.), PGA (pres., bd. dirs. Palm Beach Gardens, Fla. chpt.), Am. Soc. Assn. Execs., Fla. Soc. Assn. Execs., Nat. Crime Prevention Coun. (rep.), Homeowners Assn., Gen. Fedn. Women's Clubs (nat. chmn. 1984-88), Rep. Club (Palm Beach Gardens). Lutheran. Office: Nat Assn Police Athletic League 200 Castlewood Dr Ste 400 West Palm Beach FL 33408

CUNNINGHAME, DONNA HOLT, trust company executive; b. Sunnyside, Wash., Sept. 6, 1939; d. Roy Emerson and Genevieve Gilberta (Gwynne) Holt; m. Ferguson Todd Cunninghame, June 3, 1967; children: Christina Gwynne, Todd Samuel. BBA in Acctg., U. Mo., 1974; MGA, U. Md., 1992. CPA, Mo. With KPMG Peat Marwick, Kansas City, Mo., 1975-78; dir. fin. Kansas City Area Transp. Authority, 1978-81; v.p. fin. Isis Foods, Kansas City, 1981-82; asst. treas. Higher Edn. Mgmt. and Resources Found., Overland Park, Kans., 1982-85; CFO, assoc. vice chancellor U. Md., Adelphi, 1985-93; CFO Resolution Trust Corp., Washington, 1993—. Mem. fin. com. Episcopal Diocese West Mo., Kansas City, 1984-85; bd. dirs. Assn. Clay County Dems., 1980-85; bd. dirs., treas. Clay County Indsl. Devel. Authority, 1980-85; bd. dirs., v.p. Northland Youth-Adult Project Com., North Kansas City, 1978-85, German Orphan Home, Upper Marlboro, Md., 1987—. Home: 1116 Windmill Ln Silver Spring MD 20905-6040 Office: Resolution Trust Corp 801 17th St NW Rm 1108 Washington DC 20434*

CUPRILL, MARIA, legislative staff director; b. Siales, P.R., Oct. 8, 1939. BA, Bklyn. Coll., 1962. Dir. programs Williamsburg Cmty. Corp., 1968; program dir. Cmty. Devel. Agy., N.Y.C., 1969-70; legis. aide, 1971-74, adminstrv. asst. to Rep. Major Owens, 1982-87; staff dir. subcom. select edn. and civil rights Ho. Edn. and Labor Com., 1987—. Office: Subcom on Select Edn & Civil Rights 518 O'Neill House Office Bldg Washington DC 20515*

CURIE, EVE, writer, lecturer; b. Paris, Dec. 6, 1904; d. Pierre (Nobel prize winner for work in radium 1903) and Marie (Sklodowska) (Nobel prize winner in radio-active substances, 1903, in chemistry 1911) Curie; m. Henry Richardson Labouisse, Nov. 1954 (dec. 1987). B.S., Ph.B., Sevigne Coll.; D.H.L. (hon.), Mills Coll., 1939, Russell Sage Coll., 1941; Litt.D. (hon.), U. Rochester, 1941; Hartwick Coll., 1983. Took up study of music and gave first concert as pianist, Paris, 1925; later concerts in France and Belgium; mus. critic for Candide (weekly jour.) for several years; also wrote articles on motion pictures and the theater; made first visit to U.S. with mother, 1921; on 2d visit lectured in 10 U.S. cities (speaks English, French and Polish), 1939; witnessed fall of France, 1940, went to London to work for cause of Free France; came to U.S., 1941, lectured on war in France and Eng.; because of pro-ally activities deprived of French citizenship by Vichy Govt., 1941. Served in Europe with Fighting French as officer in Women's div. of army; one of pubs. Paris Presse (daily), resigned to return to ind. writing, 1949. Spl. adviser Sec. Gen., NATO, 1952-54. Decorated Chevalier Legion of Honor (France), 1939; Polonia Restituta (Poland), 1939; Croix de Guerre (France), 1944. Author: Madame Curie (selection of Lit. Guild, Jr. Guild, Book-of-the-Month Club, Scientific Book of the month; Nat. book award for non-fiction), 1937; Journey Among Warriors (Lit. Guild Selection), 1943. Home: 1 Sutton Pl S New York NY 10022-2471

CURKENDALL, BRENDA IRENE, financial planner, business owner; b. Mesa, Ariz., Dec. 20, 1954; d. Arthur Blatt and Dorothy June Goodnight; m. James Patrick Monagle (div.); m. Christopher Lee Curkendall; children: Robert, Chad, Jeremy, Sean. Student, Edison Jr. Coll., 1971-72; BA in History, Fla. State U., 1976; postgrad., Coll. for Fin. Planning, 1992. CFP; registered investment advisor. Realtor Harold A. Allen Co. Realtors, Tacoma, 1983; salesperson Computerland, Bellevue, Wash., 1983-84; systems analyst Boeing Computer Svcs., Seattle, 1985; stock broker Shearson Lehman Bros., Tacoma, 1985-87; fin. planner Curkendall Fin. Programs, Inc., Puyallup, Wash., 1988—; instr. Pierce Coll., Tacoma. Contbr. articles to profl. jours. Capt. U.S. Army, 1976-82, Korea. Mem. Apt. Assn. Pierce County (pres. 1988), Ft. Hood Flying Club (pres. 1980). Office: 12012 98th Ave E Ste B Puyallup WA 98373-5027

CURLE, ROBIN LEA, computer software industry executive; b. Denver, Feb. 23, 1950; d. Fred Warren and Claudia Jean (Harding) C.; m. Lucien Ray Reed, Feb. 23, 1981 (div. Oct. 1984). BS, U. Ky., 1972. Systems analyst 1st Nat. BAnk, Lexington, Ky., 1972-73, SW BancShares, Houston, 1973-77; sales rep. Software Internat., Houston, 1977-80; dist. mgr. Uccell, Dallas, 1980-82; v.p. Info. Sci., Atlanta, 1982-83; v.p. sales TesserAct, San Francisco, 1983-86, Foothill Rsch., San Francisco, 1986-89; pres., founder Curle Cons. Group, San Francisco, 1987-89; mgr. strategic mktg. MCC, Austin, Tex., 1989-90; founder, exec. v.p. Evolutionary Tech., Inc., Austin, 1991—. Mem. U. Ky. Alumni Assn., Delta Gamma (pres. 1969). Republican. Home: 709 Hidatas Cv Austin TX 78748-2422

CURLEY, CLARE MARY, municipal bond analyst; b. Glen Cove, N.Y., May 25, 1961; d. Arthur James and Mary Elizabeth (Gavin) C. Student, Dartmouth Coll., 1982; BA, Wheaton Coll., Norton, Mass., 1983; MBA, Columbia U., 1990. Assoc. Fin. Guaranty Ins. Co., N.Y.C., 1983-87; sr. analyst Mcpl. Bond Investors Assurance Corp., Armonk, N.Y., 1987-89; asst. v.p. Capital Reinsurance Mgmt. Corp., N.Y.C., 1989—. Active St. Bartholomew's Community Club, N.Y.C. Mem. Mcpl. Analyst's Group of N.Y., Women's Mcpl. Bond Club of N.Y., Fin. Women's Assn., The Nature Conservancy, Wheaton Coll. Alumnae Assn. (bd. dirs., dir.-at-large 1983-86). Office: Capital Reinsurance Mgmt Corp 787 7th Ave New York NY 10019-6018

CURLEY, SARAH SHARER, federal bankruptcy judge; b. Oak Park, Ill.; d. Robert F. Sharer and Marian Elizabeth (White) Fitzgerald; m. Roger D. Curley; 1 child. BA, Mount Holyoke Coll., 1971; JD cum laude, N.Y. Law Sch., 1977. Bar: N.Y. 1978, Wis. 1983, Ariz. 1986, U.S. Dist. Ct. (so., ea. dists.) N.Y., U.S. Dist. Ct. Ariz., U.S. Ct. Appeals (2nd cir.). Law clk. U.S. Dist. Ct., N.Y.C., 1977; atty. Fogelson, Fogelson & Collins, N.Y.C., 1978, Otterbourg, Steindler, Houston & Rosen, N.Y.C., 1979-82; asst. counsel First Wisconsin Corp., Milw., 1982-86; atty. Ayers & Graham, Phoenix, 1986; U.S. bankruptcy judge Dist. of Ariz., Phoenix, 1986—. Contbr. articles to profl. jours.; exec. editor: Bankruptcy Bar Bulletin, 1978. Fellow Ariz. Bar Found., Nat. Assn. Women Judges; mem. Nat. Conf. Bankruptcy Judges, Ariz. State Bar, Maricopa County Bar Assn., Ariz. Women's Lawyers Assn., State Bar of Wis., Am. Bar Assn., Soroptimists, Mount Holyoke Club (v.p.). Office: US Bankruptcy Ct 230 N 1st Ave Ste 5208 Phoenix AZ 85025-0095*

CURLL, NANCY L., nurse anesthetist; b. Norristown, Pa., Apr. 28, 1955; d. Walter B. and Beatrice K. Curll. Diploma in nursing, Montgomery Hosp., Norristown, 1975; BSN, Gwynedd Mercy Coll., 1982; MSN, U. N.C., Greensboro, 1992; postgrad., N.C. Bapt. Hosp., 1992. Cert. registered nurse anesthetist. Staff nurse ICU Montgomery Hosp., 1975-82, staff nurse recovery room, 1982-83; commd. ensign USN, 1983, advanced through grades to lt.cmdr., 1994; staff nurse ICU U.S. Naval Hosp., Bethesda, Md., 1983-87; staff nurse nursery and ICU U.S. Naval Hosp., Guam, 1987-90; student nurse anesthetist N.C. Bapt. Hosp., Winston Salem, 1990-92; nurse anesthetist Naval Hosp., Orlando, Fla., 1992—. Decorated Navy Achievement medal; named one of Outstanding Young Women Am., 1985. Mem. Am. Assn. Nurse Anesthetists, Fla. Assn. Nurse Anesthetists (edn. com., pub. rels. com.), Assn. Mil. Surgeons U.S. (life), Navy Nurse Corps Assn., Order Ea. Star, Sigma Theta Tau.

CURME, ANN MARIE, lawyer; b. Sioux City, Iowa, Jan. 22, 1952; d. Lloyd Alden and Rosemary Connors Doescher; m. Ronald Lee Curme, June 7, 1975 (div.); children: Patrick, Daniel, Erin. BA, St. Mary's Coll., 1974; MSW, U. Ill., 1978; JD, Northwestern U., 1986. Assoc. Oppenheimer Wolff & Donnelly, Mpls., 1986-91; asst. gen. counsel Control Data Corp., Mpls., 1991-92; mng. counsel Ceridian Corp., Mpls., 1992-94, assoc. gen. counsel, dir. human resources, 1994—; adj. prof. William Mitchell Coll. Law, St. Paul, 1992—. Guardian ad Litem Hennpin County, Mpls.; parish coun. dir. Immaculate Heart of Mary, Minnetonka, Minn., also religious edn. tchr.; coach Odyssey of Mind, Hopkins, Minn. Office: Ceridian Corp 8100 34th Ave S Minneapolis MN 55425-1640

CURNS, EILEEN BOHAN, counselor, author; b. Chgo., May 22, 1927; d. Alvin Joseph and Lorraine Bohan; m. John R. Curns, July 1, 1950 (div. 1975); children: James Richard, Barbara Curns Obrokta. BA in Sociology, DePaul U., Chgo.; MEd in Psychology and Edn., Loyola U., Chgo.; postgrad. in health edn., U. Wis. Cert. Gestalt therapist. Prin. ACCORD, Vernon Hills, Ill.; cons. in health care cost containment, stress researcher, designer and implementer tng. progs., negotiator in field. Recipient Golden Deeds award Exchange Club, 1965, commendation Queen Mary Vets. Hosp., Montreal, 1975. Mem. Am. Bd. Med. Psychotherapists (cert.), Nat. Wellness Assn., Internat. Human Learning Resource Network. Home: 825 Waterview Cir Vernon Hills IL 60061-2550 Office: Accord PO Box 393 Deerfield IL 60015-0393

CUROL, HELEN RUTH, librarian, English language educator; b. Grayson, La., May 30, 1944; d. Alfred John and Ethel Lea (McDaniel) Broussard; m. Kenneth Arthur Curol, June 25, 1967 (div. 1988); children: Edward, Bryan. BA, McNeese State U., 1966; postgrad., L.I. U., 1969-70; MLS, La. State U., 1987. Tchr., libr. Cameron Parish Schs., Grand Lake, La., 1966-67; media specialist Brentwood (N.Y.) Sch. Dist., 1967-69; sch. libr. Patchogue (N.Y.) High Sch., 1969-70; reference libr., mgr. circulation dept. McNeese State U., Lake Charles, La., 1976—; test adminstr. Edn. Testing Svc., Princeton, N.J., 1987—; rschr. Boise Cascade, DeRidder, La., 1987-88, Vidtron, Dallas, 1990-92; asst. prof. McNeese U., 1989—; cons. Community Housing Resource Bd., Lake Charles, 1988-93, Boyce Internat. Engrs., Houston, 1988-89, La. Pub. Broadcasting, Baton Rouge, 1989; reference cons. Calcasieu Parish Pub. Libr., 1990—; rschr. Nat. Archives, Washington, 1989; presenter South Ctrl. Women's Assn. Conf. at Tulane U., 1994. Sr. arbitrator Better Bus. Bur., Lake Charles, 1986—; local facilitator La. Com. for Fiscal Reform, Lake Charles, 1988; state bd. dirs. PTA, Baton Rouge, 1981-83, LWV of La., Baton Rouge, 1983-85; chair budget panel com. United Way of S.W. La., Lake Charles, 1992-94; judge L.A. region IV Social Studies Fair, 1979-89; program spkr. HUD Region IV Tng. Conf., El Paso, 1992; bd. dirs. United Way of S.W. La., 1994—. Named Citizen of the Day, Sta. KLOU, 1978; grantee La. Endowment for Humanities, 1987, La. Div. of Arts, 1989, Fair Housing Initiative Program, 1990, HUD, 1992, La. Ctr. Women & Govt. of Nicholls State U., 1993. Mem. ALA (sec. coun. 1988-90, chair coun. 1990-91), AAUW (chair intellectual freedom com. 1988-89), La. Libr. Assn. (reference group chair 1988-90), La. Assn. Coll. & Rsch. Librs. (chair 1995—), McNeese U. Alumni Assn., S.W. La. C. of C. (legis. com. 1992), Krewe du Feteurs (Mardi Gras Ct. duchess 1992), Beta Sigma Phi (pres. Lake Charles chpt. 1983-84), Beta Phi Mu. Democrat. Lutheran. Office: McNeese State U Libr PO Box 91445 Lake Charles LA 70609

CURRAN, DOROTHY ELIZABETH, marketing professional, entrepreneur; b. Englewood, N.J., Mar. 9, 1952; d. J. Joseph and Eileen Elizabeth (Concannon) C.; m. Bernard Pierre Roesch, July 2, 1977; children: Jean-Philippe, Eleonore, Anne-Claire. BA with honors, Wellesley Coll., 1974. Mktg. rep. Cambridge (Mass.) Computer Assocs., 1974-75; mgr. documentation and tng. United Computing Systems, Wellesley, Mass., 1975-77; assoc. dir. circulation Macmillan Profl. Mags., Stamford, Conn., 1977-79; dir. circulation Criminal Justice Publs., N.Y.C., 1979-81, Prime Time Mag., N.Y.C., 1981; sr. v.p., cons. The Saugatuck Group, Westport, Conn., 1981-85; pres., co-owner Mission: A Cons. Group, Westport, 1985—, Mission: Inc., Westport, 1989—; speaker Entrepreneurs Club Yale U., New Haven, 1986; moderator grad. program direct mktg. NYU, 1987; panelist Direct Mktg. Assn. of Conn., 1993, Westport Pub. Schs. Supts. Forum, 1993. Contbr. articles to profl. jours. Co-chmn. ann. benefit scholarship fund Fairfield Villages (Conn.) Wellesley Coll. Club, v.p., 1985-89; host family Au Pair in Am./Am. Inst. Fgn. Study, Greenwich, Conn., 1986-91; mem. Fairfield Country Day Sch. Parents' Assn., 1986—, co-pres., 1991-92; mem. headmaster search com. Fairfield Country Day Sch., 1991-92; mem. Westport Young Woman's League, 1988-93, Green Farms Acad. Parents Assn., 1988-91, Long Lots PTA, 1991—, Coleytown Mid. PTA, 1993—. Mem. Women's Direct Response Group (moderator 1987), Info. Industry Assn., Direct Mktg. Assn. of Conn., Wellesley Coll. Alumnae Assn. (class sec. 1974-79, editor class record book 1989, 94). Democrat. Roman Catholic.

CURRAN, EMILY KATHERINE, museum director; b. Boston, Mar. 27, 1960; d. George Morton and Gloria Rose (Martino) C.; m. John Vincent Callahan, Oct. 8, 1989. AB in Fine Arts, Bard Coll., 1982; MS in Mus. Leadership, Bank Street Coll., 1992. Sr. developer The Children's Mus., Boston, 1982-88; dir. edn. The Old South Meeting House, Boston, 1988-92, exec. dir., 1992—; vis. community artist Great George's Project, Liverpool, Eng., 1983. Author: Science Sensations, 1989. Bd. dirs. Freedom Trail Found., Boston, 1992—. Mus. edn. fellow Bank Street Coll., 1989-91. Mem. Am. Assn. Mus., Am. Assn. State and Local History, New Eng. Mus. Assn., Boston Mus. Educators' Roundtable (chair steering com. 1989-91). Office: Old South Meeting House 310 Washington St Boston MA 02108

CURRENCE, GLENNDA KAY, elementary education educator; b. Davenport, Iowa, Feb. 4, 1954; d. Glenn Elston and Ethel Lucille (Watts) C. BME, Augustana Coll., 1976; M in Counseling, We. Ill. U., 1989. Tchr. elem. vocal music Clinton (Iowa) Cmty. Sch. Dist., 1976-77, Davenport (Iowa) Cmty. Sch. Dist., 1977—. Organist, pianist Faith United Meth.Ch., Davenport, 1968-77. Mem. NEA, ACA, Am. Sch. Counselors Assn., Internat. Assn. for Addictions and Offender Counselors, Iowa Music Educators Assn. Methodist. Home: 2032 N Ohio Ave Davenport IA 52804-2838 Office: Davenport Cmty Schs 1001 N Harrison St Davenport IA 52803-5099

CURREY, PATRICIA LOU, bank executive, trust officer; b. Youngstown, Ohio, May 20, 1954; d. Robert George and Betty Lou (Stiver) Alm; m. John Douglas Potter, June 21, 1975 (div. Feb. 1987); m. John Raymond Currey III, Aug. 17, 1991. BSBA, Miami U., 1976; MS in Gen. Adminstrn., U. Md., 1989. Cert. employee benefit specialist, 1994. Profit sharing analyst Booke & Co., Winston-Salem, N.C., 1977-78; indsl. engring. tech. Cons. and Designers, Inc., Winston-Salem, N.C., 1978-79; allocations unit supr. Wachovia Bank & Trust Co., Winston-Salem, 1979-80, asst. v.p. employee benefit plans dept., 1980-82, 84-85; v.p., group head, employee benefit trust group Nations Bank Trust, Balt., 1985-90, v.p., new bus. devel. personal trust unit, 1991—; evening lectr. asset mgmt. Anne Aryndel C.C., 1994. Mem. Hunt Meadow Homeowners Assn., Annapolis, Md., 1990-91. Mem. Internat. Found. Employee Benefit Plans (moderator round table mtg. 1991), Meml. Hosp. Easton (planned gifts com.), Salisbury State U. (planned gifts com.), Historic Annapolis Found. Republican. Office: Nations Bank Trust 36 N Washington St Easton MD 21601-3126

CURRIE, BARBARA FLYNN, state legislator; b. LaCrosse, Wis., May 3, 1940; d. Frank T. and Elsie R. (Gobel) Flynn; AB cum laude, U. Chgo., 1968, AM, 1973; m. David P. Currie, Dec. 29, 1959; children: Stephen Francis, Margaret Rose. Asst. study dir. Nat. Opinion Rsch. Ctr., Chgo., 1973-77; part time instr. polit. sci. DePaul U., Chgo., 1973-74; mem. Ill. Ho. of Reps., 1979—, chmn. House Dem. Study Group, 1981-83, asst. majority leader. Mem. adv. bd. Harriet Harris YWCA; v.p. Chgo. LWV, 1965-69; mem. ACLU, Hyde Park-Kenwood Community Conf., Ind. Voters of Ill.-Ind. Precinct Orgn., Hyde Park Coop. Soc., Ams. for Dem. Action. Named Best Legislator, Ind. Voters of Ill., 1980, 82, 84, 86, 88, 90, 92, 94, Best Legislator, Ill. Credit Union League, Outstanding Legislator, Ill. Hosp. Assn., 1987; recipient Ethel Parker award 1982, 86, 88, 90, 94, Leon Despres award, 1991, Ill. Environ. Coun. award, Ill. Community Action Agys. award, Ill. Women's Polit. Caucus Lottie Holman O'Neill award, Susan B. Anthony award, honor award Nat. Trust Historic Preservation; awards Welfare Rights Coalition of Orgns., Ill. Pub. Action Coun., Chgo. Heart Assn.; named Legislator of Yr., Ill. Nurses Assn., 1984, Nat. Assn. Social Workers, 1984, Ill. Women's Substance Abuse Coalition, 1984; recipient BEST BETS award Nat. Ctr. Policy Alternatives, 1988, Svc. award Nat. Ctr. For Freedom of Info. Studies, 1989, Beautiful Person award Chgo. Urban League, 1989, Friend of Labor award Ill. AFL-CIO, 1990, Ill. Maternal and Child Health Coalition award, 1990, Ill. Hunger Coalition award, 1991, Cert. of Appreciation SEIU Local 880, 1989, March of Dimes, 1988, Chgo. Tchrs. Union, Ill. Hosp. Assn., Ptnr. Vision award Families' and Children's AIDS Network. Mem. ACLU (bd. dirs. Ill.), DAV, Ill. Conf. Women Legislators, Nat. Order Women Legislators, Delta Kappa Gamma. Contbr. article to publ. Office: Ill Gen Assembly 300 State House Springfield IL 62704-1757

CURRIE, CONSTANCE MERSHON, marketing consultant; b. Missoula, Mont., June 22, 1950; d. Alan Clark Van Horn and Saralee (Neumann) Visscher; m. R. Hector Currie, Aug. 14, 1986. BA in Art with highest hons., Mont. State U., 1977; MFA in Painting, U. Cin., 1981, MA in Arts Adminstrn., 1988; grad., Tsukuba Daigaku, Ibariki, Japan, 1977-78. Bus. mgr. Fort Peck Summer Theatre, Glasgow, Mont., 1983; asst. telemarketing mgr. Cin. Symphony Orchestra, 1984, telemarketing mgr., 1985; mem. coord. Cin. Mus. of Natural History, 1986-88; mktg. cons. Currie Consulting, Cin., 1988—; lectr., art Raymond Walters Coll./U. Cin., 1988—. Exhbns. include SUNY, Binghamton, 1983, Tangeman Gallery/U. Cin., 1981, Miami U., 1981, No. Rockies Regional Exhbn./Sheridan (Wyo.) Coll., 1981, Bell Art Competition, Cin., 1981 (Purchase award. 1981), Willmington Coll., 1979, Mont. State U., 1976, 77 (Printmaking Purchase award 1976, 77), Yellowstone Ehbn., Billings, Mont., 1977 (Printmaking Purchase award 1977), others. Trustee Good Harvest Cooperative, Middletown, Conn., 1974-75, Methuen & Gertrude Currie Found., 1986—; bd. dirs. Bozeman (Mont.) Film Festival, 1982-83; vol. Cin. Chamber Orchestra, 1985-87, Cin. Mus. Natural History, 1988-90. Mem. Beta Gamma Sigma, Tau Pi Phi, Phi Kappa Phi. Office: Currie Consulting 504 Mcalpin Ave Cincinnati OH 45220-1534

CURRIE, LARA MEHR, publishing executive; b. Chandler, Ariz., Apr. 27, 1958; d. Richard Lawrence Mehr and Gladys (Fraser) Mainwaring; m. John V. Currie, Feb. 3, 1990. BSBA, George Mason U., 1981. Dir. asst. publs. and activities Arlington (Va.) C. of C., 1981-84, dir. comms., 1984; asst. dir. mktg. Am. Trucking Assns., Alexandria, Va., 1984-85, dir. mktg., 1985-89; v.p., ops. mgr. Currie Assocs., Lake George, N.Y., 1989—; adminstr. Vessel Operators Hazardous Materials Assn., Elizabeth, N.J., 1993—; mem. Hazardous Materials Adv. Coun., 1989—. Editor, pub.: Comply Quick Hazardous Material Transportation, 1991, Comply Quick International Maritime Dangerous Goods Code, 1993, Driver's Guide to Hazardous Material, 1994, Employees Handbook to Hazardous Material, 1994, (tng. program) International Maritime Dangerous Goods Code Training Program, 1993. Mem. N.Y. State Motor Truck Assn.

CURRIE, MADELINE ASHBURN, business administration educator; b. Rankin, Tex., Sept. 28, 1922; d. Herman and Ivan G. Vinson; BS, Tex. Woman's U., 1962; MA, Calif. State U., 1967; EdD, UCLA, 1974; m. Gail G. Currie; children: Robb Ashburn, Mark Ashburn, Michael Ashburn. Tchr., Edgewood High Sch., West Covina, Calif., 1962-69 ; instr. Rio Hondo Coll., Whittier, Calif., 1968-69; prof., grad. dir. Coll. Bus. Adminstrn., Calif. State Poly. U., Pomona, 1969-88, prof. emerita, 1988—. Recipient award Alpha Lambda Delta, Prof. Emerita award 1988, Exceptional Merit award, Meritorious Service awards Calif. State Poly. U., 1984. Mem. Grad. Sch. Edn., UCLA. Mem. Calif. Bus. Edn. Assn. (Recognition award), Tex. Woman's U. Alumnae Assn., Women in Mgmt., Rotary Internat. (Upland club, bd. mem.) Delta Pi Epsilon, Pi Lambda Theta, Delta Kappa Gamma, Delta Mu Delta. Home: 9749 Coca St Alta Loma CA 91737-2919

CURRIER, SUSAN ANNE, computer software company executive; b. Melbourne, Victoria, Australia, Nov. 20, 1949; d. David Eric and Irene Hazel (Baker) Bruce-Smith; m. Kenneth Palmer Currier, Feb. 16, 1974. Student, Melbourne U., 1967-70. Fashion model Eileen Ford Model Agy., N.Y.C., 1971-74, Wilhelmina Models, N.Y.C., 1974-82; owner Softsync Inc., N.Y.C., 1981-93; pres. Expert Software, Coral Gables, Fla., 1981—. Home: 201 Crandon Blvd Apt 509 Key Biscayne FL 33149-1520 Office: Expert Software Exec Tower 800 Douglas Entrance Miami FL 33134-3160

CURRIN, MARGARET PERSON, law educator; b. Oxford, N.C., June 17, 1950. AB, Meredith Coll., 1972; JD, Campbell U., 1979; attended, Georgetown U., 1980. Bar: N.C. 1979, U.S. Dist. Ct. (ea. dist.) N.C. 1982, U.S. Ct. Appeals (4th cir.) 1980, U.S. Supreme Ct. 1982. Legis. asst.to U.S. Senator John Tower, 1979-81; asst. dean, asst. prof. Sch. Law Campbell U., Buies Creek, N.C., 1981-88, prof. law, 1993-94, adj. prof. law, 1994—; U.S. atty. U.S. Dist. Ct. Ea. Dist. N.C., Raleigh, 1988—; gen. counsel N.C. Rep. Party, 1981-83; mem. Wake County Bd. Elections, 1983-87, chmn., 1985-87. Mem. Phi Kappa Phi. Office: Currin Law Firm PO Box 269 333 Fayetteville St Mall Raleigh NC 27602-0269 also: Currin Law Firm 20 S 5th Ave Wilmington NC 28401*

CURRY, ANN, broadcast journalist; b. Agana, Guam, Nov. 19, 1956; d. Robert Paul Hiroe (Nagase) C.; m. Brian Wilson Ross, Oct. 21, 1987; 1 child, Mckenzie Curry. Student, U. Oreg. Journalism Sch., 1974-78. Reporter Sta. KTVL-TV, Medford, Oreg., 1978-81; reporter, weekend anchor Sta. KGW-TV, Portland, Oreg., 1981-84; reporter Sta. KCBS-TV, L.A., 1984-90; corr., anchor NBC News at Sunrise NBC News, N.Y.C., 1990—. Recipient Golden Mike award RTNA, 1986, 87, 89, Cert. Excellence award AP, 1987, 88, Cert. Excellence award Greater L.A. Press Club, 1987, Superior Reporting award NAACP, 1989, Emmy award Acad. TV Arts and Scis., 1987, 89, Emmy nominations, 1985, 86, 87, 88. Office: NBC News 30 Rockefeller Plz # 315 W New York NY 10112*

CURRY, BEATRIZ REYNA, school system administrator; b. Monterrey, Nuevo Leon, Mex., June 20, 1950; came to U.S., 1955; d. Manuel Rangel and Tomasa (Ruiz) Reyna; m. Bruce deVelle Curry, Apr. 30, 1978; children: Juan-Manuel, Jessica Aylea. BA, Our Lady of the Lake U., 1973; MEd, Pan Am. U., 1981; PhD, U. Tex., 1989. Cert. adminstr., supt., secondary English tchr. Tchr. reading, ESL, and Spanish grades 7-9 Los Angeles County Uniform Sch. Dist., L.A., 1973-76; tchr. reading grades 9-12 Austin (Tex.) Ind. Sch. Dist., 1976-77, supr. Emergency Secondary Edn. Act reading program, 1978; cons. Prescription Learning Corp., McAllen, Tex., 1980-81; supr., insvc. dir., curriculum dir. La Joya (Tex.) Ind. Sch. Dist., 1979-80, 81-87; cons. Tex. Edn. Agy., Austin, 1987-88, Tex. Assn. Sch. Adminstrs., Austin, 1988-90; asst. supt. for spec. edn. Ysleta Ind. Sch. Dist., El Paso, Tex., 1990-92; supt. San Elizario (Tex.) Ind. Sch. Dist., 1992—. Author: (booklet) Getting Rid of the Test Taking Blues, 1983. Mem. Student Exchange Program City of San Antonio, 1972; bd. mgrs. Bi County Spl. Edn. Coop., El Paso, 1992-94; bd. dirs. Mothers-Daughters Program, El Paso, 1990-94; chair local spiritual assembly Bahá'í Faith El Paso, 1992—. Minnie Stevens Piper Found. scholar, 1969-73; Danforth Forum fellow Danforth Found., 1993-94. Mem. ASCD, Tex. Assn. Sch. Adminstrs., Regional Adv. Coun. (legis. liaison 1993—). Home: 18 Cumberland Cir El Paso TX 79903 Office: San Elizario Ind Sch Dist PO Box 920 San Elizario TX 79849

CURRY, CORINNE, music publishing executive, mezzo soprano; b. Brookline, Mass., July 21, 1933; d. Carleton Henry and Lucile Margaret (Taggart) C.; m. Harold Farberman, June 22, 1958; children: Thea, Lewis. BS, New Eng. Conservatory, 1958; postgrad., NYU, 1985. Pres., co-founder Cortelu Pub. Co., Germantown, N.Y., 1981—. Mezzo soprano with maj. operas, orchs. throughout world, including N.Y., Chgo., San Francisco, Brussels, Mexico City, Israel and others; appeared with Boston Pops conducted by Arthur Fiedler; recordings include works of Charles Ives on Boston Records, Mahler 4th Symphony with London Symphony on MMG Records. Exec. dir. Children's Blood Found., N.Y.C., 1985-93; v.p., bd. dirs. Hudson Opera House; trustee Columbia Meml. Hosp. Found. Office: Cortelu Publishing 516 Church Ave Germantown NY 12526-5955

CURRY, KATHLEEN, psychotherapist, minister; b. Jacksonville, Fla., Mar. 1, 1951; d. Arl and Katherine (Reardon) C.; m. Wallace Woodrow Hartsook, Jr., May 14, 1977 (div. Nov. 1992); children: Stacey Arlyn, Erin Ruth. BA in Sociology, U. Ctrl. Fla., 1973; MS in Counseling Psychology, Frostburg State U., 1988. Cert. hypnotherapist, Am. Bd. Hypnotherapy. Counselor Shenandoah U., Winchester, Va., 1987-89; pres. Letting Go., Inc., Ashburn, Va., 1990—; spkr. various orgns., 1992—. Recipient Dale Carnegie Effective Speaking Course Highest Achievement award, 1990. Mem. Am. Counseling Assn., Nat. Spkrs. Assn., Toastmasters Internat. (v.p. edn.). Office: Letting Go Inc PO Box 392 Ashburn VA 22011

CURRY, KATHLEEN BRIDGET, retired librarian; b. Parnell, Iowa, May 19, 1931; d. John Michael and Ellen Theresa (Clear) C. BS in Libr. Sci., Marycrest Coll., 1953. Head libr. Moline (Ill.) Sr. High Sch., 1953-90; part-time libr. Moline Pub. Hosp. Sch. Nursing, 1957-66; mem. sch. nursing libr. St. Anthony's Hosp., Rock Island, Ill., 1955; hist. librarian Rock Island Hist. Libr., Moline, 1956-59; libr. Black Hawk Coll., Moline, 1958-59. Exec. bd. Miss Iowa Pageant, Davenport, Iowa, 1987—; bd. dirs. Miss Black Hawk Valley Pageant, Moline, 1986—, Quad City Arts Coun., Davenport, 1990; guild mem. Quad City Symphony Orch., Davenport, 1972—. Recipient Disting. Svc. award Marycrest Coll., 1987, Disting. Svc. award Moline High Sch. PTA, 1983. Mem. Ill. Edn. Assn., NEA, Ill. Sch. Libr. Assn., AAUW, Moline Edn. Assn., Iowa Libr. Assn., Zonta Internat., Delta Kappa Gamma. Democrat. Roman Catholic. Home: 1851 18th Ave Moline IL 61265

CURRY, MARY ANN KEMPER, engineering and business consultant; b. Spring Grove, Pa.; d. Ralph Leroy and Mabel Ann (Moul) Kemper; m. Thomas F. Curry, July 2, 1949; children: Bostick, Thomas Lee, Ruth Ann, David, Laurie, Clinton. BA in Edn., Pa. State U., 1948; postgrad. in acctg. and fin., Syracuse U. Sch. Bus., 1963-65. Secondary sch. tchr. Mechanicsburg, Pa., 1948-50; sec., treas. CML, Inc., Syracuse, N.Y., 1963-65; libr. asst. Va. Poly. Inst. and State U., Reston, Va., 1973-74; adminstrv. asst. to v.p. Applied Rsch. Lab. div. of M/S, Inc., Vienna, Va., 1974-75; mgr., acct. coll. textbook store Va. Tech., U. Va., Va. Commonwealth U., Falls Church, 1976-92; ret. U. Va., Va. Commonwealth U., Va. Tech., Falls Church, Va., 1992; sec., treas. C-Systems, Inc., Oakton, Va., 1975—, v.p., gen. mgr., 1993—; No. Va. coord. Gt. Books Program. Mem. AAUW (charter, past pres. McLean br., chmn. fed. legis. program 1976-78, fellow 1971, 85), DAR, LWV, Bus. and Profl. Women's Club, Nat. Assn. Coll. Stores, Va. Coll. Stores Assn. (sec., scholarship chair, mem. nominating com., mem. exec. bd.), Daus. Am. Colonists), Pi Lambda Theta (life), Phi Delta Kappa (charter, past rec. sec., historian, chmn. wards com., Chpt. Mem. of Yr. award 1986, Svc. Key 1990), Delta Zeta (life). Office: C-Systems Inc PO Box 310 Oakton VA 22124-0310

CURRY, PATRICIA SNYDER, writer; b. Ft. Myers, Fla., Sept. 3, 1960. BS in Journalism, U. Fla., 1980. Editl. asst. Miami Herald, Ft. Lauderdale, 1981-84, 84-85; staff writer Boca Raton (Fla.) News, 1984-85, Sun-Tattler, Hollywood, Fla., 1986; pres. Words & Pictures Communications, Inc., Plantation, Fla., 1987—. Chmn. Habitat for Humanity, Broward, 1993-94, 94-95; com. mem. Am. Cancer Soc., Ft. Lauderdale, 1991; mem. Leadership Broward, 1993-94; bd. dirs. Leadership Broward Found.; class pres. Leadership Broward XII. Mem. Fla. Freelance Writers, Women in Comm. (bd. dirs. Atlantic-Fla. chpt.). Republican. mem. Christian ch. Office: Words & Pictures Comm Inc 5462 SW 1st St Fort Lauderdale FL 33317

CURRY, SUSAN, psychologist, researcher; b. Springfield, Mass., Jan. 8, 1954; m. Clifford R. Curry, Nov. 21, 1984; 1 child, Sarah Elizabeth. BA in Psychology magna cum laude, U. Mass., 1976; MA, U. N.H., 1979, PhD, 1981. Postdoctoral rsch. assoc. U. Wash., 1981-84; staff scientist Fred Hutchinson Cancer Rsch. Ctr., 1984-86; asst. scientific investigator ctr. for health studies Group Health Cooperative Puget Sound, Seattle, 1986-91, assoc. sci. investigator, 1991-94, sci. investigator, 1994—; asst. prof. dept. health svcs. U. Wash., 1987-91, assoc. prof., 1991—, adj. asst. prof. dept. psychology, 1985-91, adj. assoc. prof., 1991—, rsch. affiliate Alcoholism and Drug Abuse Inst., 1987—; grant reviewer Dutch Cancer Soc., 1992, 93, Nat. Heart, Lung & Blood Inst., 1992-93, Nat. Cancer Inst., 1991, 92; speaker in field. Assoc. editor Health Psychology; mem. editorial bd. Cancer Epidemiology, Psychology of Addictive Behaviors; editorial reviewer: Addictive Behaviors, Behavioral Assessment, Jour. Addictive Behaviors, Jour. Personality and Social Psychology, Jour. Studies on Alcohol, Abnormal Psychology, Health Psychology, Health Edn. Rsch., Jour. Cons. and Clin. Psychology, European Jour. Pub. Health; contbr. articles to profl. jours. Bd. dirs. Seacoast Task Force on Family Violence, Portsmouth, N.H., 1979-81. Mem. Am. Psychol. Assn., Assn. for Advancement Behavior Therapy, Soc. Psychologists in Addictive Behaviors, Soc. Behavioral Medicine (publs. com.), Am. Pub. Health Assn. Office: Group Health Coop Ctr for Health Studies 1730 Minor Ave Ste 1600 Seattle WA 98101-1404

CURRY, TONI GRIFFIN, counseling center executive, consultant; b. Langdale, Ala., June 23, 1938; d. Robert Alton and Elsie (Dodson) Griffin; m. Ronald William Curry, June 13, 1959 (div. 1972); children—Christopher, Catherine, Angela. B.A., Ga. State U., 1962; M.S.W., U. Ga., 1981. Lic. clin. therapist; cert. addictions counselor. Tchr. DeKalb County Bd. Edn., Atlanta, 1962-63; counselor Charter Peachford Hosp., Atlanta, 1974-79; dir. aftercare, 1976-79; dir. aftercare and occupational services Ridgeview Inst., Atlanta, 1979-82; owner, dir., adminstr., counselor Toni Curry and Assocs., Inc., Atlanta, 1982—; founder, bd. dirs. Anchor Hosp., 1985—; cons., lectr. to numerous cos. and orgns.; mem. adv. bd. Peachford Hosp., Atlanta, 1982-87, Rockdale House, Conyers, Ga., 1981—, Outpatient Addictions Clinics Am., 1983-85; bd. dirs. Employee Assistance Programs Inst.; lectr. local, nat. and internat. confs. Cloud's House, Wilshire, Eng., 1986; founder Internat. Recovery Ctr., Cannes, France, 1990; seminars on addiction in Italy and Switzerland; pres., mem. exec. bd. Ga. Employee Assistance Programs Forum, Atlanta, 1981-86; appointed to Gov.'s Advisory Council on Mental Health, Mental Retardation and Substance Abuse, 1984, Commn. on Drug Awareness and Prevention, 1986; chairperson Driving under Influence of Alcohol Assessment Task Force; adv. bd. Hawthorne House; presenter European Conf. Drugs and Alcohol, Edinburgh, Scotland. Mem. Nat. Assn. Social Workers, Ga. Addiction Counselors Assn. (dir. 1982-86), Ga. Citizens Council Alcoholism, Employee Assistance Programs Assn., Assn. Behavioral Therapists, Nat. Assn. Alcoholism and Drug Abuse Counselors, Mems. Guild of High Mus. Art, Kappa Alpha Theta. Home: 7245 Chattahoochee Bluff Dr Atlanta GA 30350-1071 Office: 1150 Lake Hearn Dr Ste 120 Atlanta GA 30342 also: 5775 Peachtree-Dunwoody Rd NE Atlanta GA 30342

CURT, DENISE MORRIS, artist, limner, photographer; b. New Haven, Nov. 15, 1936; d. Bertrand and Anna Geraldine (Fiak) Rocheleau; m. John Morris, Oct. 4, 1954 (div. 1970); children: Tyler John, Cynthia Leigh Morris Bell; m. Albert A. Curt, 1973 (div. 1981). Student of Louis Crescenti, Orange, Conn., 1950-52; student, Whitney Sch. Art, New Haven, 1950, Luchetti Sch. Art, New Haven, 1951, Paier Sch. Art, Hamden, Conn., 1951. Dir. Meet The Artists and Artisans, Milford, Conn., 1962—; interior designer State of Conn., Hartford, 1972-75. One-woman shows Gull Gallery, Provincetown, Mass., Chapelle Jean Cocteau, Villefranche Sur Mer, France, Garfield Galleries, Orange, Conn., Yale U., Stratford Gallery, Stevenson (Md.) Galleries, also others; represented in numerous pvt. and pub. collections throughout world. Lectr. to numerous civic orgns.; mem. Vis. Artists in Schs., 1970—; commr. Conn. Commn. on Arts, 1974-79; photography chmn. Milford Fine Arts Coun., New Haven Arts Coun.; bd. dirs. Milford Hosp. Aux. Recipient award Mystic Art Festival, 1969, Sterling House Art Show, 1985, Glastonbury Art Guild, 1988. Mem. Guilford Art League (bd. dirs. 1975-80), Nat. Soc. Am. Pen Women (category painting), Conn. Classic Arts, Milford Hist. Soc., Yale U. Gallery, Met. Mus. Art. Republican. Congregationalist. Home and Studio: 41 Green St Milford CT 06460

CURTIN, JANE THERESE, actress, writer; b. Cambridge, Mass., Sept. 6, 1947; d. John Joseph and Mary Constance (Farrell) C.; m. Patrick F. Lynch, Apr. 31, 1975. A.A., Elizabeth Seton Jr. Coll., 1967; student, Northeastern U., 1967-68. Appeared in plays The Proposition, Cambridge and N.Y.C., 1968-72, Last of the Red Hot Lovers touring co., 1973; Broadway debut in Candida, 1981; author, actress Off-Broadway mus. rev. Pretzels, 1974-75; star TV series NBC Saturday Night Live, 1975-79, Kate & Allie, 1984-88, Working It Out, 1990; appeared in films including Mr. Mike's Mondo Video, 1979, How to Beat the High Cost of Living, 1980, O.C. and Stiggs, 1987, Coneheads, 1993; TV films include Divorce Wars-A Love Story, 1982, Suspicion, 1988, Maybe Baby, 1988, Common Ground, 1990. Recipient Emmy nomination, 1977; Emmy awards for outstanding actress in comedy series, 1984, 85. Mem. Screen Actors Guild, Actors Equity, AFTRA. Office: CAA 9830 Wilshire Blvd Beverly Hills CA 90212*

CURTIN, LEAH LOUISE, editor, author, nurse, ethician, consultant; b. Chgo., Mar. 8, 1942; d. Jean Wilson and Veronica Eloise (Dunst) Sutter; m. Peter Joseph Curtin, Apr. 15, 1966 (div. May 1990); children: Peter James, Rose Mary, Christopher Charles, Joseph Wilson. Diploma in nursing, Good Samaritan Hosp. Sch. Nursing, Cin., 1965; BS in Community Health Planning, U. Cin., 1976, MS in Health Planning and Adminstrn., 1977; MA in Philosophy, Athenaeum of Ohio, 1977; DSc (hon.), SUNY, Utica, 1990. RN, Ohio. Staff nurse Vets. Hosp., Cin., 1965-66, Vis. Nurses' Assn., Cin., 1966-67; instr. No. Ky. U., Highland Heights, 1974-76; asst. prof. Coll. Mt. St. Joseph-On-The-Ohio, Cin., 1976-80; editor Nursing Mgmt. Springhouse Corp., Phila., 1979—; ptnr. Metier Cons., Cin., 1990—; adj. faculty U. Cin., 1984—; organizational cons. Franciscan Sisters of Poor Health System, N.Y.C., 1987—; cons. on nursing ethics Nurse Corps, USAF, Washington, 1991—. Author: Nursing Ethics: Theories and Pragmatics, 1982 (Am. Jour. Nursing Book of Yr. award 1982), DRGS: The Reorganization of Health, 1984, Curtin Calls, 1986, Cornerstones of Healthcare in the '90s, 1991; contbr. articles to profl. jours. Recipient Disting. Nurse award Virginia Mason Med. Ctr., 1986, recognition Med. Coll. Ohio, 1988, Mary Hammer Greenwood award Ohio Nurses Assn., 1990, Outstanding Svc. award Franciscan Sisters of Poor Health System, 1991; Am. Acad. Nursing fellow, 1983. Mem. ANA, Am. Nurses Assn., Internat. Acad. Nursing Editors, Nat. League for Nursing, Am. Acad. Polit. and Social Scis., Hastings Ctr., Sigma Theta Tau. Home: 5932 Rapid Run Rd Cincinnati OH 45233-4852 Office: Nursing Mgmt 672 Neeb Rd Cincinnati OH 45233

CURTIN, PHYLLIS, music educator, former dean, operatic singer; b. Clarksburg, W.Va.; d. E. Vernon and Betty R. (Robinson) Smith; m. Eugene Cook, May 6, 1956 (dec.); 1 child, Claudia Madeleine. BA, Wellesley Coll., 1943. Prof. Yale Sch. Music, New Haven, 1974-83; master Branford Coll. Yale U., New Haven, 1979-83; dean Sch. Arts, prof. music Boston U., 1983-91, prof. music, 1983—, dean emerita, prof. music, 1991—; artist-in-residence Tanglewood Music Ctr., Tanglewood, Lenox, Mass., 1965—; former mem. Nat. Coun. on the Arts; named Amb. for the Arts; tchr. master classes U.S., Can., Beijing, Moscow. Made recital debut Town Hall, N.Y.C., 1950, opera debut, N.Y.C. Opera in U.S. premiere of The Trial, 1953, recitals throughout, U.S. and fgn. countries; soprano soloist leading symphony orchestras; performer, tchr., Aspen Mus. Festival, 1953-57, appeared as Cressida in, Walton's Troilus and Cressida in, N.Y. premiere, 1955; title role in Floyd's: Susannah, world premiere, Tallahassee, 1955; title role in: Darius Milhaud's Medea, U.S. premiere, Brandeis U., 1955; world premiere Floyd's opera Wuthering Heights, 1958; leading soprano: Vienna Staatsoper, 1960, 61; debut as Fiordiligi in Cosi Fan Tutte, Met. Opera Co., 1961; debut, La Scala Opera, Milan, 1962; U.S. premiere Benjamin Britten's War Requiem, 1963; world premiere of Darius Milhaud's opera La Mére Coupable, Geneva, 1966; U.S. premiere Dimitri Shostakovitch's Symphony No. 14, with, Phila. Orch., 1971. Home: 20 Chapel St Apt 801C Brookline MA 02146-5458 Office: Boston Univ Sch for the Arts 855 Commonwealth Ave Boston MA 02215-1303

CURTIS, ALVA MARSH, artist; b. N.Y.C., June 15, 1911; d. Charles Johan and Elizabeth (Hagstrom) Berg; m. Terrill Belknap Marsh, Nov. 3, 1932; children: Owen Thayer, Charles Ames, Ronald Belknap; m. Russell G. Curtis, Aug. 11, 1979; children: Russell G. Jr., William E. Student Art Students League, N.Y.C., 1928-29, Grand Central Art Sch., 1934-36, N.Y. Sch. Fine Arts, 1930-31, Nat. Acad., N.Y.C., 1934-35, Columbia U., 1943-44, Yale U., 1969-70. Ptnr., art dir. Terrill Belknap Marsh, Assocs., N.Y.C., 1934-69; lectr. in field. One-woman shows: Scranton Meml. Libr., Madison, Conn., 1969, Phippsburg (Maine) Libr., 1964, Town and County Club, Hartford, Conn., 1976, Conn. Bank & Trust Co., Madison, 1977, 1st Fed. Savs. & Loan, Madison, 1977; group shows include: The Mariner's Mus., Newport News, Va., Va. Salmagundi Club, N.Y.C., Smithsonian Instn., Washington, 1964, 66, Internat. Maritime Art Award Show (Sculpture award), 1981, Nat. League Am. Pen Women Art Show (Sculpture award), Atlanta, 1982, Arnold Gallery, Newport, R.I., 1984, Copley Gallery, Boston, 1986, Candlewood Gallery (Sculpture award 1986), New Milford, Conn., 1986, Lyme Acad. Fine Arts, Lyme, Conn.; represented in permanent collections: Swedish Club, Chgo., Conn. Bank & Trust Co., Windsor, Phippsburg Libr., Essex Meadows Retirement Cmty., Essex, Conn., also pvt. collections. Mem. Am. Soc. Marine Artists, New Eng. Sculpture Assn., Nat. League Am. Pen Women (pres. 1978—, Greenwich br. 1958), Conn. Soc. Sculptors, Soc. Conn. Sculptors, Garden Club of Madison (life mem.). Republican. Episcopalian. Clubs: Lyme Art Assn., Madison Winter, Garden Club of Madison (life mem.). Home: 319 Essex Mdws Essex CT 06426-1525

CURTIS, BETTY ANN, community association administrator; b. Evergreen Park, Ill., Nov. 6, 1941; d. Leonard and Elizabeth (Kleinmark) Reno; divorced; 1 child, Timothy Albert. Grad. high sch., Oak Lawn, Ill. Coord. vols. Grand Island (Nebr.) Interfaith Task Force, 1980-81; exec. coord. Grand Island Area Clean Community System, 1981—; mgr. Juvenile Alternative Sentencing/Diversion Program, Grand Island, 1986—. Active Local Emergency Planning Com., Grand Island, 1992—; co-chair Hazardous Waste Subcom., 1993—. Recipient Cert., Nebr. State Judiciary Chief Justice, 1987, City of Grand Island, 1993, Keep Nebr. Beautiful, 1993. Mem. Sertoma. Office: Grand Island Area Clean Community System 205 N Wheeler Ave Grand Island NE 68801-5961

CURTIS, CATHY L., counselor; b. L.A., June 13, 1948; d. Norman A. and Catherine L. (Young) Bing; m. Michael A. Curtis, May 4, 1971; children: Andrew M., Nicole A. BS, U. So. Calif., L.A., 1970, MS, 1971; MS, Emporia State U., 1991; PhD, Kans. State U., 1993. Nat. cert. counselor; cert. tchr. elem. K-9, secondary history and social scis., 7-12, Calif.; cert. counselor edn., Kans., K-12, Kans.; lic. profl. counselor. Tchr. Redwood Intermediate Sch., Thousand Oaks, Calif., 1971-77, Internat. Sch. of Islamabad, Pakistan, 1977-80, Am. Internat. Sch. of Dusseldorf, Germany, 1980-82, Saudi Arabian Internat. Sch., Riyadh, 1982-84, Escola Am. de Rio de Janeiro, Brazil, 1989-90; grad. tchng. asst. Kansas State U., Manhattan, 1991-93; instr. Emporia (Kans.) State U., 1992-93; asst. prof. Stephen F. Austin State U., Nacogdoches, Tex., 1993—; coord. sch. counseling program Stephen F. Austin State U., Nacogdoches, 1993—; pres. faculty concerns com. Am. Sch. in Japan, Tokyo, 1987-88; presenter conf. in field. Presenter: (workshop) Pregnant Teenagers: A Reality in Rural Schools, 1992. Recipient H.J. Waters scholarship Emporia State U., 1990. Mem. ACA, Nat. Bd. Cert. Counselors, Tex. Assn. for Counselor Edn. and Supervision (bd. dirs. 1994—), Tex. Counseling Assn., Pineywoods Counseling Assn., Chi Sigma Iota, Phi Delta Kappa. Office: Stephen F Austin State U PO Box 13019 SFA Station Nacagdoches TX 75962-3019

CURTIS, FRANCINE MARCO, nurse; b. Can., Nov. 15, 1948; m. William M. Curtis, May 20, 1977. ADN, L.A. City Coll., 1971; BS in Health Sci., Calif. State U., 1985; MN, UCLA, 1992. Cert. infection control practitioner. House supr. Valley Park Med. Ctr., Canoga Park, Calif., 1984-85; infection control coord. Midway Hosp., L.A., 1985; utilization mgmt. coord. Hosp. of Good Samaritan, L.A., 1985-86; quality rev. nurse St. Vincent Med. Ctr., L.A., 1986-88; nurse epidemiologist UCLA Med. Ctr., 1989-90, 93—, staff nurse med.-surg., 1990-93; 1993—. Mem. ANA (cert. med.-surg. 1991—), APIC, Calif. Nurses Assn., Sigma Theta Tau (Gamma Tau chpt. 1992). Office: 10833 Le Conte Ave Los Angeles CA 90095

CURTIS, JAMIE LEE, actress; b. L.A., Nov. 22, 1958; d. Tony Curtis and Janet Leigh; m. Christopher Guest; 1 child. Student, U. of the Pacific. Actress: (films) Halloween, 1978, The Fog, 1980, Prom Night, 1980, Terror Train, 1980, Halloween II, 1981, Road Games, 1981, Love Letters, 1983, Trading Places, 1983, Grandview USA, 1984, Adventures of Buckaroo Banzai, 1984, Perfect, 1985, Amazing Grace and Chuck, 1987, Un Homme Amoreux, 1987, Dominick and Eugene, 1988, A Fish Called Wanda, 1988, Blue Steel, 1990, Queens Logic, 1991, My Girl, 1991, Forever Young, 1992, Mother's Boys, 1994, My Girl 2, 1994, True Lies, 1994 (Golden Globe award Best Actress - Musical or Comedy); (TV pilots) Callahan, She's in the Army Now, 1981, Tall Tales, (TV series) Operation Petticoat, 1977-78, Anything but Love, 1990-93, (TV movies) Death of a Centerfold: The Dorothy Stratten Story, 1981, Money on the Side, 1982. As Summers Die, 1982; author: When I Was Little, 1993. Office: care CAA 9830 Wilshire Blvd Beverly Hills CA 90212-1825*

CURTIS, KAREN EVON, health administrator; b. Gary, Ind., July 20, 1951; d. Eugene Floyd and Doris Jean (Pruitt) C.; m. Matthew A. Greene, Sept. 2, 1977 (div. 1985); children: Amanda Mae Greene, Monica Evon Greene. BBA, U. North Tex., 1991. Bus. cons. Tex. Cmty. Justice, Denton, Tex., Am. Med., Inc., Dallas; cmty. liaison Healthy Start, Lake Station, Ind., now ctr. dir. Bd. dirs. Econ. Devel. Mission, Lake Station, 1992-94, YMCA, Portage, Ind., 1994—. Mem. Am. Bus. Women's Assn., Lake Station C. of C. (bd. dirs.). Office: Healthy Start Lake Station Site 2580 Central Ave Lake Station IN 46405

CURTIS, KARLA LAUREN, customer support supervisor; b. West Point, N.Y., Nov. 3, 1956; d. Fred. D. and Margaret Erika (Buckmann) Spinks; m. David Jefferson Ashmore, Feb. 19, 1977 (div. Dec., 1978); 1 child, Erika Margaret Augusta; m. Robert Lynn Curtis, Nov. 10, 1991. BA, Ind. U.-Purdue U. at Indpls., 1982; MS, Ind. U., 1986. Mgr. Eastside Chiropractic Clinic, Indpls., 1978-80; English tutor univ. div. Ind. U.-Purdue U. at Indpls., 1980-82, composition instr. English dept., 1982-83, tech. writer computing services, 1983-84; tech. writer Ind. U. Adminstrv. Computing, 1984-87; computer tng. coordinator Melvin Simon and Assocs., Inc., Indpls., 1987-88, customer support administrator, 1988-90, MIS account rep., 1990-91; supr. Melvin Simon and Assocs., Indpls., 1991—; ptnr. KREL Labs, 1991—. Contbr. articles, book revs., poems to various publs.; editor: Lit. Jour., Genesis, All-Am. Mag., Am. Collegiate Press Assn., 1983. Mem. Soc. Tech. Communication (Cert. of Achievement 1985), Sigma Delta Chi, Pi Lambda Theta. Democrat. Disciples of Christ. Office: Melvin Simon & Assocs Inc 2 W Washington St Indianapolis IN 46204-3402

CURTIS, LORETTA O'ELLEN, construction executive; b. Washington, Pa., Apr. 5, 1937; d. Monroe and Mildred (Carr) Bogan; m. Joseph H. Dudley (div. Oct. 1964); children: Ronald S., Joseph T., Mildred M.; m. Wayne J. Curtis. AS, Franklin U., 1983, BS, 1989; Grad., Columbus Leadership Program, 1991. With Bur. Employment Svcs., Columbus, Ohio, 1962-87, examiner, equal employment opportunity officer, 1983-87, ret., 1987; v.p. Aries Constrn., Inc., Columbus, 1988-91, pres., 1991—; mediator small claims divsn. Franklin County; tour leader GLAMER; chmn. Sch. of Ushering ICUA, Columbus. Mem. Interdenominational Ch. Ushers Assn. Columbus. Recipient Plaque ICUA of Dayton, 1989, ICUA of Columbus, 1991. Mem. NAFE, Nat. Assn. Parliamentarians, Nat. United Ch. Ushers Assn., Ohio Assn. Colored Women (treas. 1990-94), Ohio Assn. Parliamentarians (pres. 1989-90), ICUA of Columbus (pres. 1977-84), Mayme Moore Club (pres. 1990-93, cert. 1989). Home: 2257 Century Dr Columbus OH 43211-1919 Office: Aries Constrn Inc 983 E Main St # 7014 Columbus OH 43205-2342

CURTIS, MARY ELLEN (MARY CURTIS HOROWITZ), publishing company executive; b. Paragould, Ark., Oct. 24, 1946; d. Lloyd E. and Jean (Cain) C.; m. Irving Louis Horowitz, Oct. 30, 1979. AB cum laude, Washington U., St. Louis, 1968. Editorial dir. Transaction Pubs., New Brunswick, N.J., 1968-74, exec. v.p., 1987—, chmn. bd. dirs., 1994—; editor in chief Praeger Pubs. subs. CBS Ednl. Pub., N.Y.C., 1974-79; v.p., pub. periodicals John Wiley and Sons, N.Y.C., 1979-87; v.p. Scripta Techica subs. John Wiley and Sons, Washington, 1984-86; chair adv. com. Serials Industry Systems, 1985-88; dir. Transaction Pubs. (U.K.) Ltd.; mem. mktg. com. Coun. Biology Editors, 1989—; lectr. in field. Contbr. articles to profl. jours. Mem. Soc. Scholarly Pubs. (bd. dirs. 1984-88), Assn. Am. Pubs. (Freedom to Read com.). Jewish.

CURTIS, MICHAELA SCHMITT, emergency and maternal/fetal nurse, educator; b. Bludenz, Austria, Oct. 28, 1963; came to U.S., 1964; d. Frank Henry and Maria (Mayer) Schmitt; m. Alex K. Curtis; children: Christina, Bradley, Matthew, Jonathan. AAS, Fayetteville Tech. Inst., 1987; postgrad., Hawaii Pacific U., 1991. RN, N.C., Hawaii, Tex.; cert. health, safety and nursing instr. ARC. Maternal-fetal nurse Sierra Med. Ctr., El Paso, 1987-88; medical-surg. nurse Berlin MEDDAC, 1988-90; nursing coord. ARC, 1988-90; nursing chmn. ARC, Hickam AFB, Hawaii, 1990-93; emergency room nurse 15th Med. Group, Hickam AFB, Hawaii, 1990-92; staff ob-gyn. Kaiser Med. Ctr., 1992-93; birthing instr., ob-gyn. patient counselor, BLS, first aide; tchr. Frei Universitat Berlin, 1988-90. Author: (booklet) Better Birthing, 1990. Active Spl. Parents Info. Network, Honolulu, 1991—, Hawaii Blood Bank, ARC. Named Vol. of Yr., ARC, Berlin, 1989. Mem. Am. Cancer Soc., Am. Soc. Labor Assts., Am. Hosp. Assn., Hawaii Nurses Union. Roman Catholic. Home: 1003 Cypress Pointe Demopolis AL 36732

CURTISS, CAROL PERRY, registered nurse, consultant; b. Worcester, Mass., Dec. 9, 1946; d. Joseph Anthony and Marjorie Ruth (Riedle) Perry; m. Jack Daniel Curtiss, Feb. 8, 1970; children: Paul Daniel, Jennifer Perry. Diploma in nursing, Mass. Gen. Hosp. Sch. Nursing, Boston, 1967; BS, Am. Internat. Coll., Springfield, Mass., 1978; MSN, Yale U., 1981. Cert. oncology nurse, Oncology Nursing Cert. Corp. Staff nurse Franklin Med. Ctr., Greenfield, Mass., 1970, insvc. supr., 1970-71; staff nurse Greenfield Ob-Gyn. Assocs., 1972-74, Greenfield Vis. Nurses, 1974-75; instr. Slim Living Program YMCA, Greenfield, 1977-78; instr. nursing Greenfield C.C., 1978; asst. prof. nursing Elms Coll., Chicopee, Mass., 1981-84; oncology program mgr. Franklin Med. Ctr, Greenfield, 1986-93; cancer care cons. Greenfield, 1981—; mem. faculty Greenfield C.C., 1985-87; vis. lectr., clin. instr. Fitchburg (Mass.) State Coll., 1985-86; vis. lectr. Elms Coll., Chicopee, Mass., 1984-85; mem. adj. faculty SUNY, 1987-90, U. Mass., Amherst, 1989—; mem. U.S. com. Internat. Union Against Cancer, NRC, 1992—, mem. nursing project, 1992—; peer reviewer Agy. for Health Care Policy and Rsch., Cancer-Related Pain Guidelines, HHS, 1993; presenter numerous instns., various U.S. and fgn. locations, 1981—. Guest editor Oncology Nurses Forum, 1993; contbr. articles to profl. jours. Bd. dirs. Franklin County, Am. Cancer Soc., Greenfield, 1979—, mem. nurse and social work scholarship com., 1988—, nursing com. liaison, 1990—; mem. steering com. Mass. Cancer Pain Initiative, 1988-90, liaison, 1990—. Mem. Oncology Nursing Soc. (mem. numerous sub coms. 1987—, bd. dirs. 1991, pres.-elect 1991-92, corp. adv. bd. 1991-93, Oncology Nursing Press pres. 1992-94, co-chair conf. on pain 1994, pres. 1993-94), Internat. Union Against Cancer (U.S. com. 1992—, nursing project 1992—), Sigma Theta Tau. Home and Office: Cancer Care Cons 73 James St Greenfield MA 01301

CURTISS, HELEN HUBER, food scientist; b. Orange, N.J., Apr. 18, 1954; d. Harold John and Helen Marie (MacNeal) Huber; m. Scott Jay Curtiss, Oct. 29, 1983. BS in Nutrition & Food Sci., Va. Polytech & State U., 1976; MS in Nutrition & Food Sci., U. Tenn., 1979. Food scientist Nestle, New Milford, Conn., 1979-82; Food scientist Pepsi, Valhalla, N.Y., 1982-89, prin. flavor specialist, 1989—. Office: Pepsi 100 Stevens Ave Vahalla NY 10595

CURZON, SUSAN CAROL, library administrator; b. Poole, Eng., Dec. 11, 1947; came to U.S., 1952.; d. Kenneth Nigel and Terry Marguerite (Morris) C. AB, U. Calif., Riverside, 1970; MLS, U. Wash., 1972; PhD, U. So. Calif., 1983. Spl. libr. Kennecott Exploration, San Diego, 1972-73; various positions L.A. County Pub. Libr., 1973-89; dir. libr. Glendale (Calif.) Pub. Libr., 1989-92; dean univ. libr. Calif. State U., Northridge, 1992—, vice provost info. & tech. resources, 1993—, dean univ. libr., 1993—; cons. Grantsmanship Ctr., L.A., 1981-83; vis. lectr. Grad. Sch. Libr. and Info Sci. UCLA, 1986—. Author: Managing Change. Librarian of the Year, Library Journal, 1993. Mem. ALA, Calif. Libr. Assn. Democrat. Office: Calif State U Libr Office of Dean 18111 Nordhoff St Northridge CA 91330-8326

CUSACK, JOAN, actress; b. N.Y.C., Oct. 12, 1962; d. Richard and Nancy C. Student, U. Wis. Stage appearances include Road, 1988, Brilliant Traces, 1989, Cymbeline, 1989; TV appearances include (series) Saturday Night Live (regular 1985-86 season), (movies) The Mother, 1994; film appearances include My Bodyguard, 1990, Sixteen Candles, 1984, The Allnighter, 1987, Broadcast News, 1987, Married to the Mob, 1988, Working Girl, 1988 (Acad. award nominee best supporting actress 1989), Say Anything, 1989, Men Don't Leave, 1989, My Blue Heaven, 1990, The Cabinet of Dr. Ramirez, 1991, Hero, 1992, Toys, 1992, Addams Family

Values, 1993, Corrina, Corrina, 1994, Nine Months, 1995. Office: Care Tracy Jacobs ICM 8942 Wilshire Blvd Beverly Hills CA 90211*

CUSIMANO, ADELINE MARY, educational administrator; b. Jamestown, N.Y., Apr. 18, 1939; d. Joseph and Rose (Bivona) Miletti; m. John Leo Cusimano, Sept. 24, 1960; children: Judith Ann Cusimano Pancio, John Anthony Cusimano. BS, Elmira Coll., 1961, MS, 1976. Cert. reading specialist, N.Y. Tchr. Horseheads (N.Y.) Sch. Dist., 1961-62; diagnostician, clinician Horseheads, 1962-76; reading specialist Elmira Heights Schs., N.Y., 1976-78; dir. Achievement Ctr., Horseheads, 1978—; presenter ednl. N.Y. St. Reading Conf., Kiamesha Lake, N.Y., 1982, Bd. Coop. Ednl. Svcs. Tchrs. Tng., Horseheads, 1978-80; researcher learning disabilities, Horseheads, 1962—. Author: Achieve Visual Memory Teaching Material, 4 Vols., 1980. Mem. pub. affairs edn. home life Chemung Valley Jr. Women's Club, 1968-78, 1st v.p., 1971-72; asst. treas. Horseheads Women's Club, 1983-85. Recipient Outstanding Jr. Women's Club award, 1975. Mem. Nat. Assn. Learning Disabilities, N.Y. State Head Injury Assn., Chemung Valley Reading Assn., Horseheads Women's Club (asst. treas. 1983, corr. sec. 1990-91). Republican. Roman Catholic. Office: Achievement Ctr 10 Ridge Rd Horseheads NY 14845

CUSIMANO, CHERYLL ANN, nursing administrator; b. New Orleans, Oct. 5, 1946; d. Raymond M. and Bernadette R. (Rich) Schroeder; m. Richard C. Cusimano, Aug. 27, 1967; children: Richard C. Jr., Beth Ann, Mark Allen. Diploma, Mercy Hosp. Sch. Nursing, New Orleans, 1967; cert. vocat. tchr., La. State U., 1979; student, U. New Orleans. RN, La.; cert. in ACLS, med. surg. nursing ANCC. Various nursing positions, 1967-76; asst. head nurse pediatric unit East Jefferson Hosp., 1976-77; instr. allied health field Jefferson Parish Vocat.-Tech. Sch., 1977-79; instr. med.-surg. nursing Charity Hosp., New Orleans, 1979-80; dir. operating room Marion County Gen. Hosp., Columbia, Miss., 1981; night house supr. Children's Hosp., New Orleans, 1984; asst. supr. progressive care unit Northshore Regional Med. Ctr., Slidell, La., 1985-87; pediatric staff nurse pediatric unit Touro Infirmary, New Orleans, 1982-85, charge nurse med.-surg. unit, 1987-91; nursing supr. Touro Infirmary Ctr. Chronic Pain, Rehab., New Orleans, 1992-94, program coord., 1994—. Mem. nursing com. East Jefferson chpt. ARC; ; former vol. classroom asst. Roudolph Matas Elem. Sch.; former mem. adv. bd. Project Head Start; guest speaker Am. Cancer Soc.; bd. dirs. Northshore Hospice, 1986-87, Charity Hosp. Sch. Surg. Tech., 1980. Nursing scholar Am. Legion. Mem. Am. Soc. Pain Mgmt. Nurses. Office: Touro Infirmary Chronic Pain Unit 1401 Foucher St New Orleans LA 70115

CUSTER, BARBARA ANN, lawyer; b. Mineola, N.Y., Mar. 2, 1945; d. Merton Davis and Virginia Mary (Estabrook) C. B.A., Trinity Coll., 1966; J.D., Southwestern U., 1977. Bar: Calif. 1977, U.S. Dist. Ct. (cen. dist.) Calif. 1978, U.S. Ct. Appeals (D.C. cir) 1979. Adminstrv. asst. United Calif. Bank, N.Y.C., 1968-70; asst. to exec. dir. Am. Council for the Arts in Edn., N.Y.C., 1971-74; asst. to reference librarian Southwestern U., Los Angeles, 1975-78; atty. network anti-trust project Columbia Pictures, Burbank, Calif., 1979; sole practice, Los Angeles, 1980; atty. Orion Pictures Corp., Los Angeles, 1981—, now v.p. bus. and legal affairs. Home: 8220 Waring Ave West Hollywood CA 90046-6813 Office: Orion Pictures Corp 1888 Century Park E Los Angeles CA 90067-2501*

CUSUMANO, JOANN DESIMONE, retail manager; b. Bklyn., Feb. 5, 1936; d. Joseph and Lee A. (Giardelli) DeSimone; m. Charles L. Cusumano, Aug. 16, 1958; children: David, Barbara, Jeanne, Mark. BS, Marymount Coll., 1957. Chemist Rockefeller Inst., N.Y.C., 1957-59, NIH, Washington, 1959-62; artist, potter JoAnn's Ceramics, Gainesville, Fla., 1968-79; bus. mgr. Chas. Cusumano, M.D., PA, Gainesville, 1979—; retail mgr. Four Seasons, Gainesville, 1983—. Contbr. articles to art publs. Bd. trustees Hippodrome Theater, Gainesville, 1972-80, Mus. Natural History, Gainesville, 1982-85; docent U. Fla. Mus. Natural History, Gainesville, 1979-85, 93—; active Alachua County Med. Aux. Roman Catholic. Home: 7128 NW 14th Ave Gainesville FL 32605

CUTHBERT, BILLIE-JO LAPRADE, accountant; b. Massena, N.Y., Dec. 7, 1970; d. Arthur William and Sharon Ann (Gemmill) LaPrade; m. Steven Gene Cuthbert, June 27, 1992. AAS in Acctg., SUNY, Canton, 1991; BS in Acctg., Clarkson U., 1993. Svc. desk supr. Jamesway Corp., Massena, N.Y., 1987-92; staff acct. KPMG Peak Marwick LLP, Albany, N.Y., 1993—. Mem. N.Y. Soc. CPAs, Inst. Mgmt. Accts. Democrat. Roman Catholic. Home: 15 Latham Village Ln # 9 Latham NY 12110 Office: KPMG Peat Marwick 74 N Pearl St Albany NY 12207

CUTLER, DEBORAH EILEEN, federal agency administrator; b. Camden, N.J., Mar. 21, 1956; d. Howard Taylor Cutler and M. Lois (Coble) Sherman. BA, U. Tenn., 1978. Editorial clk., asst. Office Sci. and Tech. Info. U.S. Dept. Energy, Oak Ridge, Tenn., 1980-81, computer operator, 1981-82, programmer, 1982-87, chief programming devel., 1988-90, analyst computer systems, 1990-91, analyst internat. activities, 1991-93, mgr. internat. activities, 1993—. Reader, monitor Recording for the Blind, Oak Ridge, 1991—. Mem. Oak Ridge Fed. Employees Assn. (pres. 1988-89), Federally Employed Women (v.p. 1985—), Toastmasters Internat. (pres., v.p. 1986—), USTA. Home: 105 Outer Dr Oak Ridge TN 37830

CUTLER, LAUREL, advertising agency executive; b. N.Y.C., Dec. 8, 1926; d. A. Smith and Dorothy (Glaser) C.; m. Stanley Bernstein, July 3, 1952 (div. 1983); children—Jon Cutler, Amy Sarah, Seth Perry. B.A., Wellesley Coll., 1946. Reporter Washington Post, 1946-48; copywriter J. Walter Thompson, N.Y.C., 1947-50; copy chief Wesley Assocs., 1950-56; v.p. Fletcher, Richard, Calkins & Holden, N.Y.C., 1956-63; sr. v.p., creative dir. McCann Erickson, N.Y.C., 1963-72; sr. v.p. Leber Katz Ptnrs., N.Y.C., 1972-80, exec. v.p., dir. mktg. planning, 1980-84, vice chmn., 1984—; vice chmn. FCB/Leber Katz Ptnrs., N.Y.C., 1986—; v.p. consumer affairs Chrysler Corp., Highland Park, Mich., 1988-91; global dir. mktg. and planning Foote Cone & Belding Comms., Chgo., 1991—; spkr. to orgns. including Assn. Nat. Advertisers, Am. Mktg. Assn., Produce Mktg. Assn., Grocery Mfrs. Am., Conf. Bd.; bd. dirs. True North Comms., Inc., Hannaford Bros. Co., Quaker State Corp. Recipient Matrix award Women in Communications, 1985, Achievement award Wellesley Alumni Assn., 1990; named Ladies Home Jour. One of Am.'s Fifty Most Powerful Women, 1990. Mem. Fashion Group (bd. dirs.), N.Y.C. Partnership, Com. of 200, Cosmopolitan Club. Home: 15 W 53rd St New York NY 10019-5410 also: 14 John St Sag Harbor NY 11963-2620 Office: Foote Cone & Belding Comms 767 5th Ave New York NY 10153-0001

CUTLER, LORRAINE MASTERS, interior designer, facilities manager; b. Indpls., Oct. 19, 1943; d. James Mark and Dorothy Aileen (DeLawter) Masters; m. Albert B. Cutler III, June 3, 1965 (div.); children: Valina Dawn, Anthony Bret. BFA, Ariz. State U., 1974, BA, 1974; MA, U. Phoenix, 1989. Intern Walsh Bros., Phoenix, 1973, jr. designer, 1973-74, staff designer, 1978-80; dir. interior design Dick & Fritsche Design Group, Phoenix, 1980-84; dir. interior design and space planning HNC Inc., Phoenix, 1984-87; mgr. advanced facilities planning PCS, Inc., Scottsdale, Ariz., 1987-89; cons. Cons. Mgmt. Systems, 1989—; asst. prof. interior design and facility mgmt. Ariz. State U., Tempe, 1991—. Participant Interior Design Efforts for Ariz. Legis., Phoenix, 1986-87; bd. dirs. Southwest Builds, 1985-88, chmn. fin. com., 1987-88. Recipient Presdl. Citation Am. Soc. Interior Designers, 1984. Mem. Internat. Interior Design Assn. (profl., acad. liaison 1991-93, pres. 1985-87, v.p. programs 1983-85, sec. 1981-83, Cert. Appreciation 1981), Internat. Facility Mgmt. Assn. (profl., treas.). Home: 4034 E Yowy St Phoenix AZ 85044-1527 Office: Ariz State U Coll Architecture and Environ Design Tempe AZ 85287-2105

CUTLER, RUTH ELLEN LEMON, publisher, writer; b. York, Nebr., Feb. 26, 1928; d. Harry Oliver and Ruby Elizabeth (Hartgrave) Lemon; m. Harold Max Cutler, Nov. 17, 1944 (div. 1971); children: Sheryl, Hal M., Pamela. Student Latter-day Saints Bus. Coll., 1946. Sec., photostat operator IRS, Salt Lake City, 1951-54; sec. Purdue U. Sch. Civil Engring., West Lafayette, Ind. and engring. firms, 1954-59; sec. to the fin. commn. State of Utah., 1959-60; exec. sec. Rico Argentine Mining Co., Salt Lake City and Rico, Colo., 1960-63; exec., legal sec. Manpower, Inc., Salt Lake City, 1959-71; owner, operator Mountain View Motel and Country Club Motel, Salt Lake City, 1963-64; exec. sec., adminstrv. asst. to clin. psychologist in pvt. practice, Salt Lake City, 1964-70; legal sec., head office staff Watkins & Faber, attys., Salt Lake City, 1971-73; adminstrv. sec. F-15 Radar div. Hughes Aircraft Co., El Segundo, Calif., 1973—; dir., v.p., sec. Cutler Enterprises, Inc., Salt Lake City, 1963-71; founder, pres., pub., bd. dirs. Gallant House Inc., Sandy, Utah, 1983—. Active various community drives; Rep. del. Utah, 1967-69, 90-92, 92—. Mem. League Utah Writers.

CUTLER, WINNIFRED BERG, biologist; b. Phila., Oct. 13, 1944; d. Adolph and Eleanor Berg; m. Stephen William Cutler, Dec. 18, 1962 (div. 1982); children: Jodie Elizabeth, Evan Karl; m. Thomas E. Quay, May. 13, 1989. PhD in Biology, U. Pa., Phila., 1979; BSc. in Psychology cum laude, Ursinus Coll., Collegeville, Pa. Post doctoral fellow in behavioral endocrinology Stanford U., 1980; asst. prof. biology Beaver Coll., Glenside, Pa., 1982-83; rsch. assoc. Gynecology Dept. U. Pa. Hosp., 1981-84; co-founder, sci. dir. Woman's Wellness Program U. Pa. Hosp., Phila., 1984-86; dir., pres. Athena Inst. for Women's Wellness Rsch., Haverford, Pa., 1986—; founder Stanford Menopause Study, Calif., 1980-81; co-discoverer of human pheromones, 1986. Author: Hysterectomy: Before and After, 1988, Love Cycles: The Science of Intimacy, 1991; co-author: Menopause: A Guide for Women and the Men Who Love Them, 1983, rev. edit., 1992, The Medical Management of Menopause, 1984, Searching for Courtship: The Smart Woman's Guide to Finding a Good Husband, 1993; inventor Athena Pheromone 10:13 cosmetic fragrance additive. Mem. Outreach Coun. Bryn Mawr Presbyterian Ch., Pa., 1984-90. Named Bus. Women of the Year in the U.S. Nat. Assn. of Women Bus. Owners, 1992. Mem. Internat. Soc. for Study of Time, Internat. Acad. Sex Rsch., Am. Fertility Soc., Conf. on Reproductive Behavior, Human Biology Coun. Republican. Presbyterian.

CUTRIGHT, FRANCES LARSON, marriage and family therapist; b. Visalia, Calif., July 11, 1935; d. Francis Oscar and Faye (Sawyer) Larson; m. Forest F. Cutright, June 30, 1962 (div. 1982); children: Melinda, Forest F. BA, U. Calif., Berkeley, 1958, MA, 1982; PhD, Profl. Sch. Psychol. Studies, San Diego, 1986. Lic. marriage and family therapist, Calif. Group therapist in alcohol and drug dependence program VA Hosp., La Jolla, Calif., 1982-85; mem. staff Psychotherapy Inst. of San Diego, 1982-87; co-founder, v.p. Ctr. for Healing Group, San Diego, 1987-92; women's group therapist San Diego, 1991—, psychotherapist in pvt. practice, 1992—; instr. drugs and alcohol U. Calif., San Diego, 1988—; adj. faculty The Union Inst., San Diego, 1984—. Contbr. articles to mags. Educator, trainer San Diego AIDS Project, 1989-91, Oasis, Serenity House Counselling Staffs, Escondido, Calif., 1987-89; developer, trainer adolescent and family groups Fellowship House, 1987-89. Mem. Am. Assn. Marriage and Family Therapists (clin. mem.), Calif. Assn. Marriage and Therapy Therapists (clin. mem.), San Diego Assn. Marriage and Family Therapists (clin. mem.), Nat. Assn. for Children of Alcoholics, Am. Orthopsychiatric Assn. (clin. mem.), Am. Group Psychotherapy (clin. mem.). Office: 5230 Carroll Canyon Rd Ste 220 San Diego CA 92121-1780

CUTTING, MARY DOROTHEA, audio and audio-visual communications company executive; b. N.Y.C., Feb. 20, 1943; d. Elliotte Robinson and Mary Dorothea (Clarke) Little; m. James H. B. Cutting, July 18, 1964; children—Gwendolyn Louise, Laura Elizabeth. Student Whitman Coll., 1960-62; B.A. in English Lit., U. Wash., 1964. Tchr. English, Severna Park High Sch., Md., 1965-66; remedial reading substitute tchr. St. Patrick's Day Sch., Washington, 1976-77; v.p. mktg. The Cutting Corp., Washington, 1978—; bd. dirs. Potomac Talking Book Svcs, Inc., 1990—; bd. dir. Editor children's cassettes: Fisher-Price Toys Spellbinder Series, 1983 (Consumer Com. of Ams. for Democratic Action award for being one of nation's 6 best toys for under $5 1983). Vol. chmn., bd. dirs. Washington Assn. for TV and Children, 1977. Mem. Internat. Assn. Bus. Communicators, Jr. League Washington (bd. dirs. 1977). Republican. Episcopalian. Office: 4940 Hampden Ln Ste 300 Bethesda MD 20814-2945

CYGANOWSKI, MELANIE L., bankruptcy judge; b. Chgo., June 8, 1952; d. Daniel F. and Sophia A. (Kolozenski) C.; m. Kenneth L. LeBrun, July 22, 1989. AB in anthropology, Grinnell Coll., 1974; postgrad. in urban devel., Cornell U., 1975, JD magna cum laude, 1979. Coord. program planning, planner, cons. dept. community devel. and human resources City of Buffalo, N.Y., 1974-78; dir. individual referral program Broadway-Filmore Area Coun., Inc., Buffalo, 1978-79; summer assoc. Hodgson, Russ, Andrews, Wood & Goodyear, Buffalo, 1980; law clerk to Hon. Charles L. Brieant U.S. Dist. Ct. (so. dist.) N.Y., 1981-82; litigation assoc. Sullivan & Cromwell, N.Y.C., 1982-89; sr. atty. Milbank, Tweed, Hadley & McCloy, 1989-93; judge U.S. Bankruptcy Ct. (ea. dist.) N.Y., Happauge, 1993—; Bar: N.Y. 1982, U.S. Supreme Ct., U.S. Ct. Appeals (2nd. cir.), U.S. Dist. Ct. (so., ea. and we. dists.) N.Y. Contbr. articles to legal jours. Mem. ABA, Fed. Bar Coun., N.Y. State Bar Assn. Roman Catholic. Office: US Bankruptcy Ct Rm 105 601 Veteran's Memorial Hwy Hauppauge NY 11788*

CYTRAUS, ALDONA ONA, university official, auditor; b. Hanau, Federal Republic of Germany, Dec. 16, 1947. BFA, U. Cin., 1970, MBA, 1978. CPA, Ohio. Art tchr., chmn. art dept. Seton High Sch., Cin., 1970-76; audit supr. Coopers & Lybrand, Cin. and Cleve., 1979-85; mgr. forecasting and data devel. Blue Cross/Blue Shield Ohio, Cleve., 1985-89; dir. internal audit Case Western Res. U., Cleve., 1989—; sec., treas. Triatic Enterprises, Euclid, Ohio, 1986-93, Real Intelligence Co., Euclid, 1994—; mem. exec. com. Assn. Home Care Agys., Cin., 1982-84. Mem. fin. planning com. ARC, Cin., 1983. Mem. AICPA, Ohio Soc. CPAs (chmn. mems. in industry com. 1988-91), Womens Law Fund (treas., mem. bd. trustees). Home: 60 Lake Edge Dr Cleveland OH 44123-1128

CZAJKOWSKI-BARRETT, KAREN ANGELA, human resources management executive; b. Bklyn., Sept. 13, 1957; d. Frank Henry and Cecilia (Artowicz) Czajkowski; div. Mar. 1992; children: Jennifer Marie, Michael Joseph. BSBA, Fairfield U., 1979; MBA, Sacred Heart U., 1984. Office systems analyst Union Trust Co., Stamford, Conn., 1979-80, sr. office systems analyst, 1980-81; ops. analyst Homequity, Inc., Wilton, 1981-82, project leader human rels. dept., 1982-85, organization devel. cons., 1985-87; tng. and devel. cons. People's Bank, Bridgeport, Conn., 1987-90; mgr. human resource planning and devel. Pitney Bowes Mgmt. Svcs., Stamford, 1990-93, dir. human resources planning and devel., 1993—; adj. instr. Sacred Heart U., Bridgeport, 1987. Sec. Cub Scouts Adv. Com., 1991-92; regional bd. mem. Conn. Fedn. Cath. Sch. Parents, 1993-94; treas. St. Theresa Sch.-Home Sch. Assn., 1994—. Recipient award Nash Engring., 1979; named Bus. Advisor of Yr., INROADS/Fairfield-Westchester Counties, Inc., 1993. Mem. ASTD, Am. Mgmt. Assn. Home: 28 Wendover Rd Trumbull CT 06611-1530 Office: Pitney Bowes Mgmt Svcs World Headquarters 33 # 03 Stamford CT 06926

CZARNECKI, SELINA MICHELLE SNYDER, sales and marketing executive, artist; b. Trenton, N.J., Aug. 16, 1961; d. Thomas Donald and Theresa (Dulick) Snyder; m. Robert E. Czarnecki, Mar. 16, 1985. AA in Fine Arts with distinction, Mercer County Community Coll., 1981; student, Md. Inst. Coll. Art; BA in Art and Art Edn., Trenton State Coll. Asst. banquet mgr. Cedar Garden, Trenton, 1978-85; office mgr. JC Tire Co., Trenton, 1984-85; English and history tchr. Mercer County Community Coll., Trenton, 1979-81; sales exec. Aspen Data Graphics, Newtown, Pa., 1986-90; dir. mktg. and sales Mktg. Industries, Mount Prospect, Ill., 1990-92; dir. nat. mktg. and sales. Transnational, Boston, 1992-94; dir. nat. mktg. and sales Quad/Graphics, N.Y.C., 1994—. Vol. arts and crafts YWCA, Trenton, 1980. Grantee Md. Inst. Coll. Art, 1981. Mem. Phila. Direct Mktg. Assn., Direct Mktg. Club. N.Y., Women's Direct Response Group, Humane Soc. of U.S., Save the Manatee, People for Ethcial Treatment Animals. Office: Quad/Graphics NYC Sales Office 540 Madison Ave New York NY 10022

CZARNEZKI, MARY ELAINE, media specialist; b. Milw., June 3, 1952; d. Gerald J. and Eleanor H. (Lietz) C. BS, U. Wis., Milw., 1973; MA, U. Wis., Madison, 1975; postgrad., U. Pitts., 1982. Cert. instructional library media specialist. Librarian for kindergarten through 8th grade Columbus (Wis.) Pub. Schs., 1976-90; media specialist Edgerton Elem. sch., Hales Corners, Wis., 1990—. Mem. ALA, Am. Assn. Sch. Librarians (mem. pub. awareness com.), Wis. Libr. Assn., Wis. Assn. Sch. Librs., Milw. Met. Sch. Libr. Assn., Columbia County Libr. Assn. (past pres.), Beta Phi Mu, Kappa Delta Pi. Home: 9446 W Allerton Ave Milwaukee WI 53228-2732

CZELUSNIAK, JUDITH ANN, public relations executive; b. N.Y.C., Apr. 4, 1957; d. Stanislaw F. and Helen T. (Perzanowski) C. Student, Hunter Coll., 1975-78. V.p. acct. supr. Hill and Knowlton, Inc., N.Y.C., 1982-87; dir. pub. rels. for eastern U.S. Security Pacific Corp., N.Y.C., 1987-89; v.p. Hill and Knowlton, Inc., N.Y.C., 1989-91; v.p., dir. corp. comm. Morgen-Walke Assocs., N.Y.C., 1991-93; prin. The Dilenschneider Group, N.Y.C., 1993-94; v.p., dir. pub. rels. AGCO Corp., Atlanta, 1994—. Office: AGCO Corp 4830 River Green Pkwy Duluth GA 30136

CZERNIK, JOANNE, elementary and secondary education educator; b. Phila., Apr. 12, 1948; d. Chester Joseph and Bertha (Los). BS, East Stroudsburg U., 1970; MEd, U. Del., 1974; PhD in Psychology of Reading, Temple U., 1989. Middle sch. humanities tchr. Capital Sch. Dist., Dover, Del., 1970-77; reading instr. and supr. Temple U. Reading Clinic Lab. Sch., Phila., 1977-88; reading specialist Delmar (Del.) Sch. Dist., 1988—; pvt. tutor, Jenkintown, Pa., 1977-88; cons. adult literacy Del. Tech. and C.C., Georgetown, 1992—; presenter workshops in field. Author, editor jour. articles in field. Mem. ASCD, Diamond State Reading Assn., Internat. Reading Assn. (chair clinic visits), Coun. for Exceptional Children, Phila. Coun. Internat. Reading Assn. (pres. 1984-89, 94—, Svc. award 1988), Sussex County Orgn. Reading Excellence (officer 1988—). Office: Delmar Sch Dist 8th And Jewel St Delmar DE 19940

CZERWIEC, IRENE THERESA, gifted education educator; b. Holyoke, Mass., Dec. 1, 1948; d. Stanley John and Pauline Martha (Zerek) Matuszek; m. Stanley Joseph Czerwiec, Jan. 24, 1970; children: Keith John, Daniel Paul. BS, U. Mass., 1969, MEd, 1987, EdD, 1992. Cert. secondary math. tchr., Mass. Math., physics tchr. Holyoke Cath. High Sch., 1969-71; substitute tchr. Chicopee (Mass.) Pub. Schs., 1979-85; gifted tchr. Bellamy Mid. Sch., Chicopee, 1985-90, math., gifted tchr., 1990-92, tchr. computer, gifted, 1992—; coach Future Problem Solving Program, Chicopee, 1985—; evaluator State of Mass., 1986—, cons., 1988—; presenter NSTA nat. conv., Boston, 1992, Mass. Future Problem Solving Conf., Harvard U., 1994, World Future Soc. Conf., Cambridge, Mass., 1994; participant current students/future scientists and engrs. workshop, Smith Coll., 1993. Coord. looking forward program Chicopee Centennial, 1990. Recipient Merit award Chicopee Coun. Parents and Tchrs., 1990, cert. of recognition for excellence in coaching a team Internat. Future Problem Solving Conf., Ann Arbor, Mich., 1987, 88, Ednl. Leaders in Math., 1987, 88, Cert. of Merit Mass. Bar Assn., 1988, 89; SpaceMet fellow NSF, 1990-91. Mem. NEA, AAUW, ASCD, World Future Soc., Nat. Space Soc., Coun. Exceptional Children, Mass. Tchrs. Assn., Hampden County Tchrs. Assn., Chicopee Edn. Assn. Roman Catholic. Home: 4 Plainville Cir South Hadley MA 01075-2664 Office: Bellamy Mid Sch 314 Pendleton Ave Chicopee MA 01020-2199

CZIN, FELICIA TEDESCHI, English language and literature educator, small business owner; b. Vallata, Avellino, Italy, Jan. 20, 1950; came to U.S., 1958; d. Pasquale Aurelio and Maria (Branca) Tedeschi; m. Peter Czin, Oct. 19, 1972; children: Jonathan, Michael. BA, Douglass Coll., Rutgers U., 1972; MA, NYU, 1978, ABD, 1981, postgrad. Assoc. producer RAI Corp. Italian TV, N.Y.C., 1973-77; teaching asst. dept. Italian NYU, 1977-79, adj. instr. dept. English, 1979-81; asst. prof. Vassar Coll., Poughkeepsie, N.Y., 1981-84; co-owner Czin Opticians, Teaneck, N.J., 1984—; coordinator Symposium on Italian Poetry, N.Y.C., 1978. Editor Out of London Press, N.Y.C., 1977-82, dir. pub. relations, 1977-82; editor jour. Yale Italian Studies, 1979-82; translator for jours. Home: 3 Horizon Rd Apt G1 Fort Lee NJ 07024-6703 Office: 491 Cedar Ln Teaneck NJ 07666-1710

CZUSZAK, JANIS MARIE, former credit company official, researcher; b. Greensburg, Pa., Aug. 3, 1956; d. Charles Clyde and Olga (Plica) C. BS, Indiana U. of Pa., 1978; MBA, U. Pitts., 1985, PhD studies, 1987—. Supervising sr. acct., computer audit specialist KPMG Peat Marwick, Pitts., 1979-81; fin. analyst Westinghouse Credit Corp., Pitts., 1981-83, staff analyst, 1983-84, fin. and computer auditor, 1984-86, real estate financing rep., 1986-88, assoc. investment mgr., 1988-91, investment mgr., 1991-93; fin. analyst Mellon Bank, Pitts., 1993—. Mem. Greater Pitts. Commn. for Women, 1989—. Mem. Nat. Comml. Fin. Assn., NAFE. Office: Mellon Bank 1 Mellon Bank Ctr Pittsburgh PA 15258-0001

D'ABATE, JANINA MONICA, library administrator; b. Providence, June 20, 1921; d. John Lawrence and Marya Ann (Swiatlowski) Barlowski; m. John D'Abate, Apr. 10, 1943; children: Marya Ann, John G., Janina V. BA, Brown U., 1943; MLS, U. R.I., 1977. Br. libr. Cranston (R.I.) Pub. Libr., 1966-70; dir. North Scituate (R.I.) Pub. Libr., 1974—; mem. steering com. Gov. Conf. on Libr. and Info. Sci., 1977-79. Pres. bd. trustees Mohr Meml. Libr., Johnston, R.I., 1964-69; bd. dirs. R.I. Philharm., chmn. children's concert com., 1976-78; bd. dirs. Nickerson House, Providence, 1947—, sec., 1952-72; bd. dirs. Camp Fire Inc. R.I., 1980—, sec., 1980-86, pres., 1987; pres. First Unitarian Alliance, 1993—. Mem. R.I. Libr. Assn., Beta Phi Mu. Home: 28 Reservoir Ave Johnston RI 02919-2900 Office: Greenville Rd North Scituate RI 02857

DABBS, JEANNE MCCLUER KERNODLE, retired public relations executive; b. Corsicana, Tex., 1922; d. Robert and Anne (Forrest) McCluer; m. John David Kernodle, June 27, 1942 (div. 1968); 1 child, Elizabeth Kernodle Cabell; m. Jack Autrey Dabbs, Feb. 14, 1981 (dec. 1993). BS in Sociology, Tex. Woman's U., 1970. Supr., writer pub. rels. St. Paul's Hosp., Dallas, 1974-76; dir., v.p. mktg. svcs. Fidelity Union Life Ins. Co., Dallas, 1976-81, ret., 1981. Author poetry book and greeting cards. Mem. comm. com. Mental Health Assn., Austin, Tex., 1991—; pres. aux. Seton Med. Ctr., Austin, 1985-86; mem. Dallas Civic Chorus, Austin Choral Union. Recipient Editorial medal Freedoms Found. Valley Forge, 1973, Eddy award Internat. Assn. Bus. Communicators, 1974, 76, 79, Matrix award Women in Comm., Inc., 1975, Best of Show award Life Ins. Advts. Assn., 1980, Sr. Vol. award Retirees Coordinating Bd., 1989. Mem. Tex. Women's U. Alumnae Assn. (pres. Capital Area chpt. 1987-89), Tuesday Book Club Austin (pres. 1986), Austin Poetry Soc. Methodist. Home: 2301 Lawnmont # 11 Austin TX 78756

DABBS, LISA J. GORDON, chiropractor; b. Springfield, Mass., Dec. 28, 1956; d. Efrem A. Gordon and Marion (Cohen) Rosen; m. Vaughan Martin Underhill Dabbs, Apr. 24, 1988. BA, Washington U., St. Louis, 1978; D of Chiropractic, Logan Coll. Chiropractic, 1987. Chiropractic cert. spinal trauma. Assoc. dr. chiropractic 1st Chiropractic Care Ctrs., Toronto, Ont., Can., 1988-89; dr. chiropractic Dabbs Chiropractic Wellness Ctr., Columbia, Md., 1989—; instr. clin. scis. Traditional Acupuncture Inst., Columbia, 1990—. Mem. Am. Chiropractic Assn. Office: Dabbs Chiropractic Wellness Ctr 6955 Oakland Mills Rd Columbia MD 21045

D'ABRUZZI, LISA NANCY, production planner; b. Paterson, N.J., Nov. 19, 1959; d. John James and Edith Karola (Doose) D'A. BA in Psychology, Montclair State Coll., 1987. Credit clk. Reitman Industries, West Caldwell, N.J., 1978-79; sr. acctg. clk. L'Oreal, Clark, N.J., 1979-87; prodn. planner Franco Mfg., Metuchen, N.J., 1987—. Roman Catholic. Home: 408-6 Cranbury Rd East Brunswick NJ 08816 Office: Franco Mfg 555 Prospect St Metuchen NJ 08840

DACEY, CAROLE ANN, investment company executive; b. Newark, N.J., Dec. 19, 1963; d. Thomas Dennis and Dolores Jean (Celentano) D. BS in Mktg., Internat. Bus., Ithaca Coll., 1986. Fin. analyst Eastman Kodak, Rochester, N.Y., 1986-89; fin. cons. Merrill Lynch, Rochester, N.Y., 1989-94; assoc. v.p. Essex Co., Rochester, 1994—. Mem. NAFE, Rochester Women's Coun., Rochester Women's Network. Home: 165 N Water St # 305 Rochester NY 14604 Office: Essex 100 Corporate Woods Rochester NY 14623

DACEY, EILEEN M., lawyer; b. N.Y.C., Dec. 15, 1948; d. Gabriel A. and Mary (Breen) D.; m. Kinchen C. Bizzell, Jan. 1, 1984. B.A. in Sociology, SUNY-Stony Brook, 1970; J.D., St. John's U., 1975. Assoc. Mendes & Mount, N.Y.C., 1976-80, jr. ptnr., 1980-88; ptnr. Adams, Duque & Hazeltine, N.Y.C., 1988-94; ptnr. Morrison Mahoney & Miller, N.Y.C., 1994—. Sec. Woodbury Hist. Soc.; mem. Vol. Lawyers for the Arts. Mem. ABA (chair subcom. fed. regulation of ins. co. investment sect.), N.Y. State Bar Assn., Assn. of Bar of City of N.Y. (com. profl. discipline class of 1996), Practicing Law Inst. (ins. law adv. bd.). Republican. Home: 71 Park Ave

New York NY 10016 also: 19 Maple Rd Central Valley NY 10917 Office: Morrison Mahoney & Miller 100 Maiden Ln New York NY 10038-4892

DACLOUSH, BARBARA JANE, bank examiner; b. Glendive, Mont., Dec. 22, 1955; d. William Charles and Marilyn Mae (Newman) Woolever; m. Nick Joseph Dacloush, May 30, 1981. BS, U. Wis., LaCrosse, 1979. CPA, Min. Tutor econs. and computer sci. U. Wis., LaCrosse, 1976-78; bookkeeper, night auditor, desk clerk Ramada Inn, LaCrosse, 1977-79; bank examiner Fed. Deposit Ins. Corp., Fargo, N.D., 1979-80, Billings, Mont., 1980, Rochester, Minn., 1981—. Mem. AICPA, Inst. Mgmt. Accts. Lutheran.

DADDIO, JO-ANN ROSE, marketing executive; b. New Haven, Sept. 21, 1959; d. Alphonse Henry and Lucille Louise (Gambardella) D. BSN, U. Conn., 1981; MSIA (MBA), Carnegie Mellon U., Pitts., 1988. Staff nurse Georgetown U. Med. Ctr., Washington, 1981-86; fin. controller Citibank N.A., Securities Svcs., N.Y.C., 1988-89, internal cons., 1990-91; mktg. communications staff Citibank N.A. Securities Svcs., N.Y.C., 1991-93; mktg. dir. Citicorp Dealing Resources, N.Y.C., 1993—. Active Kips Bay Boys and Girls Club, N.Y.C., 1990—, St. Bartholomew's Community Club, N.Y.C., 1990-94; jr. com. Play Schs. Assn., 1991—. Conn. State scholar, 1977-81. Mem. Fin. Comm. Soc. (bd. dirs. 1994—), Fin. Women's Assn. (advt. dir. newsletter 1991-92), Am. Mktg. Assn., Internat. Assn. Bus. Communicators, Sigma Theta Tau. Roman Catholic. Office: 1 Court Sq 11th Fl New York NY 10043

DADE, JOANN, critical care nurse, small business owner; b. Dewitt, Ark., June 27, 1948; d. Roosevelt and Ersylene (Ledbetter) Shorter; m. Paul Dade; children: Marvin, Marcus. ADN, U. Ark., 1980. RN, Ga.; cert. critical care nurse; cert. BLS instr./trainer, ACLS provider. Staff nurse Bapt. Med. Ctr., Little Rock, 1968-78; plant nurse Timex Corp., Little Rock, 1978-80; staff nurse Cen. Ark. Home Health Agy., Little Rock, 1980-86, VA Med. Ctr., Atlanta, 1986—; pres. Dade Enterprise, Decatur, Ga., 1994—. Mem. There is Hope-Ministries, Decatur, Ga., 1992, Arthritis Found., Atlanta, 1992, Dekalb County Concerned Citizens, Decatur, 1991—. Recipient Outstanding Nurse award Ga. Hosp. Assn., 1993. Mem. ANA (cert. med.-surg.), ACA, Ga. Nursing Assn. Pentecostal. Home: 2621 Rain Water Ct Decatur GA 30034

DADLEY, ARLENE JEANNE, sleep therapist; b. Cleve., Sept. 13, 1941; d. Bernard and Bernice Anne (Selleck) Davis; m. Charles George Dadley, Sept. 15, 1967 (div. Oct. 1977); children: Anitra, Charles. BA in Bus., Ursuline Coll., 1980; postgrad., Case Western Res. U., 1983-85, Stanford U., 1988. Registered polysomnographic technologist. Jr. fund acct. Am. Univ., Washington, 1967-70; v.p. Shenandoah Stables, Inc., Front Royal, Va., 1970-75; editor, publisher Trojan Horse Newspaper, Front Royal, 1972-74; biol. rsch. asst. Case Western Res. U., Cleve., 1976-87, gastroent. rsch. assoc., 1984, sleep rsch. assoc., 1985-87; chief clin. sleep technologist Metrohealth Med. Ctr., Cleve., 1987-92; tchr./trainer Metrohealth Med. Ctr., 1987—; judge regional and state sci. fairs., 1984-86. Exhbited in group shows at Cleve. Mus. Art, 1965 (1st prize graphics award), Butler Inst. Art, 1966, Corcoran Gallery Art, Washington, 1967, Internat. Traveling Am. Artists Exhibit, Cleve., 1965-66; contbr. articles to profl. jours., 1983, 85-87. Co-chairperson Ohio-Chgo. Art Project, Cleve., 1981; cons., resource person LWV, Cleve., 1977-79; pres., state rep. NOW, Cleve., 1976-78. Pell grantee, 1976-80, Ohio Instnl. grantee, 1976-80; scholar Case Western Rex. U., 1976-80, Yale U., 1982, Respironics, Inc., 1988; recipient presdl. lit. achievement citation League of Am. Pen Women, 1974, citation ARC, 1991. Mem. AAAS, Assn. Bus. and Profl. Women, Assn. Polysomnographic Technologists. Home: PO Box 894 Columbia Station OH 44028-0894 Office: Metrohealth Med Ctr 3395 Scranton Rd 100 Metro Health Dr Cleveland OH 44109

DAEHNICK, CLAIRE, tax collector; b. Yonkers, N.Y., Jan. 31, 1935; d. Alexander Campbell and Emilie Monica (Huber) Fullerton; m. Wilfried Daehnick, Jan. 30, 1960; children: Christian, Michael, Karen. BA, Washington U., 1957; MPA, U. Pitts., 1987. Lic. real estate salesperson, Pa. Sch. dir. Bd. Sch. Dirs. Hampton Twp., Allison Park, Pa., 1983-87; dir. rsch. Coalition to Improve Mgmt. in State and Local Govt., Pitts., 1988-93; tax collector Hampton Twp. and Hampton Sch. Dist., Allison Park, 1993—. Vice chair to chair Hampton Twp. Rep. Com., Allison Park, 1992-93; den mother cub scouts Boy Scouts Am., 1970-73. Recipient Gloria Fitzgibbons award U. Pitts., 1988. Mem. AAUW (pres., program v.p. 1975-79), Am. Soc. for Pub. Adminstrn. (bd. dirs. 1993—), U. Pitts. Women's Assn. (pres., sec. 1980-82), The Twentieth Century Club.

DAESCHNER, JUDITH ADELE, elementary educator; b. Lindsborg, Kans., Aug. 20, 1937; d. Adel Mauritz and Bernice Irene (Heline) Peterson; m. Roger Lee Daeschner, Dec. 28, 1958 (div. Mar. 1981); children: Roger Todd, Troy David, Timothy Mark. BA in Elem. Edn., Southwestern Coll., 1959; M in Edn. Curriculum and Instrn., Washburn U., 1982. 2d grade tchr. Mulvane (Kans.) Elem. Sch., 1959-61, Munson Elem. Sch., Mulvane, 1965-66; 4th grade tchr. Cen. Elem. Sch., Goodland, Kans., 1966-69; spl. reading tchr. Canton (Kans.) Elem. Sch., 1969-70; 6th grade tchr. Pauline South Elem. Sch., Topeka, 1974-87, Wanamaker Elem. Sch., Topeka, 1989—; Kans. project mgr. bicentennial commn. Ctr. for Civic Edn., Topeka, 1990—; tchr. Sylvan Learning Ctr., Topeka, 1989—. Coun. mem. First Luth. Ch., Topeka, 1993; merit badge counselor Boy Scout Am., Topeka, 1990—. Recipient We The People Spl. Work award Bicentennial Commn., Kans., 1991. Mem. NEA, Kans. NEA, Auburn Washburn NEA (pres. 1983-84, sec. 1978-80, negotiator 1992-93), Profl. Devel. Coun., Phi Kappa Delta. Democrat, Evangelical Lutheran. Home: 5513 SW 18th Ter Topeka KS 66604-3618

DAFFRON, MARTHA, retired education educator; b. Fairburn, Ga., Apr. 10, 1919; d. William D. and Sarah Jane (Cochran) Duggan; children: Patricia Ruth Daffron Kelly, Doris Vesta Daffron Dodson, Billy Wayne. B in Edn., Miss. State U., 1963, MEd, 1966, PhD, 1971. Lang. arts cons. Office of Dr. Joe Owens, Lincolnton, Ga., 1971-72; lab. asst. Midlands Tech., Columbia, S.C., 1975-76, speed reading tchr., 1976-78; prof. Morris Coll., Sumter, S.C., 1972-91, ret.; rschr. in field; presenter at various reading confs. Contbr. articles to profl. jours. Mem. Internat. Reading Assn., NEA, S.C. Edn. Assn., SEAOPP, SCCSP, Delta Kappa Gamma, Phi Kappa Phi, Kappa Delta Pi. Home: 2328 E Pass Rd Gulfport MS 39507-3807

DAFFRON, MARYELLEN, librarian; b. Richmond, Va., Nov. 12, 1946; d. William Charles and Ellen (Ahern) D. BA, Coll. Mt. St. Joseph on Ohio, Cin., 1968; MLS, Drexel U., 1970. Libr. Richmond Pub. Libr., 1969-73, FMC, Washington, 1973-93; with U.S. Immigration and Naturalization Svc. Office of Gen. Counsel, Washington, 1993—. Vol. No. Va. Hotline, Arlington, 1974-79. City of Richmond fellow, 1968. Mem. Law Libr. Soc. Washington, Beta Phi Mu. Roman Catholic. Office: US Immigration Naturalization Svc Office Gen Counsel 425 I St NW Rm 6100 Washington DC 20536

DAGGETT, BEVERLY CLARK, state legislator; b. Florence, S.C., Sept. 9, 1945; d. John and Beth Clark; m. Thomas A. Daggett, May 8, 1971; children: John, Page, Paul. BS in Biology, Hillsdale Coll., 1967. Mem. Maine Ho. of Reps., Augusta, 1987—. Coun. State Govts. Toll fellow, 1990. Democrat. Home: 10 Pine St Augusta ME 04330-5340

DAGGETT, LUANN MILLER, nursing educator; b. Woodbury, N.J., Apr. 1, 1952; d. Lawrence Raymond and Alice Thelma (Bleakley) Miller; m. Robert Broughton Daggett, Feb. 20, 1977; children: Diane, Robert. Diploma, Thomas Jefferson U., 1973; BSN, U. San Francisco, 1980; MSN, U. Calif., San Francisco, 1988. Cert. BLS, ACLS. Staff nurse Thomas Jefferson U. Hosp., Phila., 1973-75; nurse corps officer Balboa Naval Hosp, San Diego, 1975-78; clin. specialist U. Calif. San Diego Med. Ctr., 1989-90; nursing instr. Palomar Coll., San Marcos, Calif., 1990-92; program coord., instr. U. So. MIss. Sch. of Nursing, Meridian, 1993—. Mem. AACN, Am. Cancer Soc., Miss. Nurses Assn., Lauderdale County Coalition, Sigma Theta Tau (sec. 1990-92), Alpha Sigma Nu. Home: 5004 Hillside Dr Meridian MS 39305 Office: U So Miss 1000 Hwy 19 N Meridian MS 39307-5799

D'AGNESE, HELEN JEAN, artist; b. N.Y.C.; d. Leonardo and Rose (Redavid) De Santis; m. John J. D'Agnese, Oct. 29, 1942; children: John, Linda, Diane, Michele, Helen, Gina, Paul. Student CUNY, 1940-42; student Atlanta Coll. Art, 1972-76. One-man shows: Maude Sullivan Gallery, El Paso, 1964, John Wanamaker Gallery, Phila., 1966, U. N.Mex., 1967, Karo Manducci Gallery, San Francisco, 1968, Tuskegee Inst. Carver Mus., 1968, Lord & Taylor Gallery, N.Y.C., 1969, Harmon Gallery, Naples, Fla., 1970, Fountainbleau, Miami, 1970, Reflections Gallery, Atlanta, 1972, Williams Gallery, Atlanta, 1973, Atlanta Coll. of Art, 1976-80, Americana Gallery, Mineola, Tex., 1977, E. M. Howard Gallery, Amelia Island, Fla., 1978, Haitian Primitives Gallery, 1981, Highland Gallery, Atlanta, 1987, others; donated painting to Fernandiana Beach High Sch., 1991; group shows: Musseo des Artes, Juárez, México, 1968, Benedictine Art Show, N.Y.C., 1967, Southeast Contemporary Art Show, Atlanta, 1968, Atlanta U., 1969, Red Piano Gallery, Hilton Head, S.C., Terrace Gallery, Atlanta, Ann. Bible Heritage Art Exhibit, Marietta, Ga., 1976, Nat. Judaic Theme Exhbn., Atlanta, 1976, Crystal Britton Gallery, Atlanta, Odyssey Collection Gallery, Mich., 1988, Artist Gallery, Atlanta, 1991, Pompono Beach, Fla., Ft. Lauderdale, 1992; represented in permanent collections: Carter Pres. Ctr., Atlanta, Juarez (Mexico) Art Mus., Vatican Mus., Rome, Nassau (Fla.) County Pub. Library. Judge art show Mt. Loretto Acad., El Paso, 1967; commd. sculptor of Bob Marley in Limestone, 1985; art demonstration and lectr. Margaret Harris Sch., Atlanta, 1970; artist-in-residence Montessori Sch., Atlanta, 1978-79. Recipient Gold medal Accademia Italia delle Arti, Italy, 1979, Calvatone, 1982, Golden Flame award, 1986; 1st place sculpture award Tybee Island Art Festival, 1982, Golden Flame award Parliamento U.S.A., 1987, Golden Palette award Academia Europea, 1986, 87, Gold medal Internat. Parliament for the Arts, 1982. Mem. Nat. Mus. of Women in the Arts (chartered), Arts Alliance Amelia Island. Home: 3240 S Fletcher Ave Apt 557 Fernandina Beach FL 32034-4321 Office: D'Agnese Studio & Fine Art Gallery 14 1/2 N 4th St Fernandina Beach FL 32034-4124

DAHL, ARLENE, actress, author, designer, cosmetic executive; b. Mpls., Aug. 11, 1928; d. Rudolph and Idelle (Swan) D.; m. Marc A. Rosen; children: Lorenzo Lamas, Carole Christine Holmes, Stephen Andreas Schaum. Student, U. Minn., 1943-44, Mpls. Inst. Art, 1945, Minn. Coll. Music, 1944, Minn. Bus. Coll., 1944. Pres. Arlene Dahl Enterprises, 1952-67; v.p. Kenyon & Eckhart, 1967-72; pres. Woman's World divsn. Kenyon & Eckhart Advt. Agy., 1967-72; nat. beauty and health advisor Sears Roebuck Co., 1970-75; internat. dir. Sales and Mktg. Execs. Internat., 1972-75; fashion dir. O.M.A., 1975-78; pres. Dahlia Parfums, Inc., 1975-80, Dahlia Prodns., Inc., 1978-81, Dahlmark Prodns., 1981—, Scandia Cosmetics, Ltd., 1978-80; pres., chmn. Lasting Beauty Ltd., 1986—. Author: Always Ask a Man, 1965, 12 Beautyscope books, 1968, rev. edit., 1978, Arlene Dahl's Secrets of Hair Care, 1970, Arlene Dahl's Secrets of Skin Care, 1972, Beyond Beauty, 1980, Arlene Dahl's Lovescopes, 1983, Arlene Dahl's 1991 Astro Forecast, Arlene Dahl's 1992 Astrological Forecast, Arlene Dahl's 1993 Astrological Forecast, Arlene Dahl's 1994 Astrological Forecast, Arlene Dahl's 1995 Astrological Forecast; actress: (Broadway plays) including Mr. Strauss Goes to Boston, Questionable Ladies, Cyrano de Bergerac, Applause (Tony award musical), (films) including (debut) My Wild Irish Rose, The Bride Goes Wild, Reign of Terror, A Southern Yankee, Ambush, The Outriders, Three Little Words, Watch the Birdie, Scene of the Crime, Inside Straight, No Questions Asked, Desert Legion, Slightly Scarlet, Sangaree, Caribbean Gold, Jamaica Run, Diamond Queen, Here Come the Girls, Bengal Brigade, Kisses for My President, Woman's World, Journey to the Center of the Earth, Wicked as They Come, She Played with Fire, Les Poneyettes, Du Blé Enliases, The Land Raiders, The Way to Kathmandu, Fortune Is a Woman, The Big Bank Roll, Who Killed Maxwell Thorn?, Midnight Warrior, 1991, (TV shows) Lux Video Theatre, 1952-53, guest starring appearances on The Love Boat, Fantasy Island, Love American Style, One Life to Live, 1981-84, Night of 100 Stars, 1983, Happy Birthday Hollywood, 1987; hostess (TV series): Pepsi-Cola Theatre, 1954, Opening Night, 1958, Arlene Dahl's Beauty Spot, 1966, Arlene Dahl's Starscope, 1979-80, Arlene Dahl's Lovescope, 1980-82; played throughout U.S. in One Touch of Venus, The Camel Bell, Blithe Spirit, Liliom, The King and I, Roman Candle, I Married an Angel, Bell, Book and Candle, Applause, Marriage Go Round, Pal Joey, A Little Night Music, Forty Carats, Life with Father, Murder Among Friends, Dear Liar; nightclub acts Flamingo Hotel, Las Vegas, Latin Quarter, N.Y.C.; internat. syndicated beauty columnist Chgo. Tribune/N.Y. News Syndicate, 1950-70, Arlene Dahl's Lucky Stars Column, Globe Communications, 1988-90, Arlene Dahl's Astroscope Mag., 1991, 92, 93, 94, 95; designer sleepwear for A.N. Saab & Co., 1952-57, In Vogue with Arlene Dahl (Vogue Patterns), 1980-85, Arlene Dahl Pvt. Collection Jewelry, 1989—. Hon. life mem. Father Flannagan's Boys Town; internat. chair Pearl Buck Found.; bd. dirs. Hollywood Mus. Recipient 10 Laurel awards Box Office mag., Hollywood Walk of Fame Star, Coup de Chapeau Deaville Film Festival award, 1982, 92; named Best Coiffed, Heads of Fame awards, 1967-72, 80, Woman of the Yr., Advt. Club of N.Y.C., 1969, Mother of the Yr., 1982, Lifetime Achievement award WorldFest, 1994. Mem. NATAS (trustee), Acad. TV Arts and Scis. (bd. govs.), Motion Picture Arts and Scis. (N.Y. spl. events), Author's Guild, Commanderie des Bontemps du Medoc et Graves, Internat. Platform Assn., Nat. Trust for Hist. Preservation, Sierra Club, Vesterheim Norwegian/Am. Found., Film Soc., Smithsonian Assocs., UNIFEM. Office: Dahlmark Prodns PO Box 116 Sparkill NY 10976-0116

DAHL, BREN BENNINGTON, screenwriter; b. Gary, Ind., Nov. 15, 1954; d. Paul Wayland and Shirley Ann (Havard) Bennington; m. Curtis Ray Dahl; children: Austin Brooks, Darren Curtis. Student Principia Coll., Elsah, Ill., 1972-74, Sch. of Art Inst. of Chgo., 1983; BA in English with honors, U. Hawaii, 1977. Tchr. English, Peace Corps, Mbuji-Mayi, Zaire, 1977-79, Asahi Cultural Ctr., Osaka, Japan, 1981-82, Osaka Inst. Fgn. Trade, Osaka, 1981-82, Kansai U. of Fgn. Studies, Osaka, 1980-82, Matsushita Electric, Osaka, 1982; pres., owner Video Enterprises, North Palm Beach, Fla., 1983-87; producer's asst. Casady Entertainment, Hollywood, Calif., 1989-91. Mem. Palm Beach Opera Chorus, 1984-85. Fred Waring Scholar, 1972. Mem. Exec. Women of Palm Beaches, Fla. Motion Picture and TV Assn., Am. Film Inst., No. Palm Beach County C. of C. (co-chmn. spl. events 1985-86), Better Bus. Bur. Scriptwriters Network, Tourette Syndrome Assn.. Republican. Avocation: song recording, singing, gourmet cooking, running.

DAHL, LAUREL JEAN, human services administrator; b. Chgo.; d. James Edward and Gladys Uarda (Boquist) Findlay; m. Philip Nels Dahl, Aug. 29, 1970; children: Eric Nels, John Philip. BA, Trinity Coll., 1970; MS in Human Svcs., Nat. Louis U., 1992. Tchr. Grove Sch., Lake Forest, Ill., 1971, Little Bear Child Care Ctr., Waukegan, Ill., 1975-77; sec. to dir. Strang Funeral Home, Antioch, Ill., 1981-87; comptroller, office mgr. Village of Antioch, 1987-92; prevention specialist Lake County Dept. of Health: Mental Health Div., 1992; community coord. Fighting Back Project of Lake County, Round Lake, Ill., 1992-94; prevention adminstr. No. Ill.Coun. on Alcoholism and Substance Abuse, Lake, 1994—; adj. faculty Nat. Louis U., 1994—. Mem. Antioch Community High Sch. Bd. Edn., 1987—, pres., 1991—, sec. 1989-91; mem. Antioch Community High Sch. Drug Task Force, MADD; past pres. PTO; mem. adv. bd. WAY: bd. dirs. COURAGE. Mem. Alliance Against Intoxicated Motorists, Ill. Student Assistance Profls., Ill. Sch. Bd. Assn. Home: PO Box 613 Antioch IL 60002

DAHL, MARILYN GAIL, psychotherapist, nurse; b. Louisville, Dec. 6, 1946; d. James Blair and Dorothy Emma (McDermott) Swartzwelder; m. Charles Dalton Weaver, Dec. 30, 1967 (div. Apr. 1969); m. Donald Allan Dahl, Sept. 18, 1985. BSN, U. Ky., 1968; MEd in Clin. Counseling, The Citadel, 1987. Lic. profl. counselor. Instr. med.-surgical nursing Sch. Nursing Ky. Bapt. Hosp., Louisville, 1973-79; child psychiat. nurse Norton's Children's Hosp., Louisville, 1980-81; asst. prof., psychiat. nurse Sch. Nursing, U. Louisville, 1981-82; primary therapist/child psychiat. nurse Children's Treatment Service, Louisville, 1982-83; instr. psychiat. nursing Sch. Nursing Bellarmine Coll., Louisville, 1983-84; adult and geritric therapist Seven Counties Services, Louisville, 1984; psychiat. nurse So. Pines Hosp., Charleston, S.C., 1985-86; rev. specialist S.C. Peer Rev. Orgn., Charleston, 1986-87; psychotherapist Ctr. for Change, Charleston, 1987-88; pvt. practice North Charleston, 1988-94; home health field supr. Condell Home Health Agy., Libertyville, Ill., 1994—; hospice nurse Hospice of Charleston, Inc., 1991-92; pub. health nurse Trident Home Halth Svcs., 1992; mental health profl. Charleston/Dorchester Mental Health Ctr., 1993. Vol. Hospice of Louisville, Inc., 1978-85; mem. steering com. Highlands Adult Day Ctr., Louisville, 1984-85; bd. dirs. Ashley River Fire Dept., Charleston, 1986-90, chair, 1989-90; mem. ladies aux. Ashley River Fire Dept., 1985-94; mem. test rose panel Jackson & Perkins, 1989-91. Named to Honorable Order Ky. Cols., Commonwealth of Ky., 1977. Mem. ACA, Am. Assn. for Mental Health Counselors. Home: 2117 Edgewood Rd Waukegan IL 60087 Office: Condell Med Ctr Home Health Care 755 Milwaukee Ave Ste 292 Libertyville IL 60048

DAHLEN, PENNY L., counselor; b. Denver, Sept. 5, 1962. BA, The Coll. of Idaho, 1984; MEd, Colo. State U., 1989; EdD, Idaho State U., 1994. Counselor Colo. State U., Fort Collins, 1987-89; asst. dir. of career svcs. Mont. State U., Bozeman, 1989-92; teaching asst. Idaho State U., Pocatello, 1992—; supr., cons. Idaho State U. Counseling and Testing Ctr., Pocatello, 1992—; asst. prof. counselor edn. Idaho State U., Pocatello, 1994—; nat. grad. student com. chair Assn. of Counselor Edn. and Supervision, 1993—. Recipient Fgn. Student Career Opportunities grant Assn. for Fgn. Student Svcs., Ogden, Utah, 1991. Home: 515 Brown Ave Alamosa CO 81101-2308

DAHLL, INGER MARGARET, magazine production executive, graphic artist; b. New Rochelle, N.Y., Aug. 16, 1961; d. Hans Herlof and Dorothy Ann (Ayers) D. BA in Theatre, Elmira Coll.; postgrad., SUNY. Subscription mgr. Futura Publ. Co., Mt. Kisco, N.Y., 1983-87, prodn. mgr., advt. coord., 1987-89; mktg. mgr. Dental Lab. Publs., East Norwalk, Conn., 1989-90; freelance graphic artist, 1990—; advt. coord., prodn. mgr., graphic artist Knowledge Industry Publs., White Plains, N.Y., 1990—. Mem. Am. Bus. Press, Alpha Psi Omega. Office: Knowledge Industry Publs 701 Westchester AVe White Plains NY 10604

DAHN, DEBRA JANE, securities trader, options trader; b. Cleve., Oct. 24, 1956; d. Howard Frederick and Edythe Betty (Zeuch) D.; m. Stephen Craig Rufe, Oct. 16, 1982 (div. Sept. 1987). Student, Wells Coll., Aurora, N.Y., 1974-76; BA in Spanish, Ohio Wesleyan U., 1979. Tennis instr. Rawlings Heights (Md.) Racquet Club, 1979-80; tennis instr. pro shop Vander Meer Tennis Ctr., Hilton Head, S.C., 1980-81, Pinehurst (N.C.) Tennis Club, 1981; equity sales asst. McDonald & Co. Securities, Cleve., 1982-85, options trader, 1985-86, trader, sr. registered options prin., 1986—, mem. options tng. staff, 1986—, mem. com. options proposals, 1990—. Mem. Cleve. Security Traders Assn. (bd. dirs. 1989-91, treas. 1990-91, v.p. 1991-92, pres. 1992-93), Phi Beta Kappa, Phi Sigma Iota. Home: 6776 E Wallings Rd Brecksville OH 44141-1022 Office: McDonald & Co Securities 800 Superior Ave Ste 2100 Cleveland OH 44114-2601

DAIGLE, CANDACE JEAN, municipal services provider; b. Gilmanton, N.H., Jan. 25, 1953; d. Alfred Ephrem and Melba Jean (Clifford) LaRoche; m. Raymond Michael Daigle, Aug. 4, 1973. Student, N.H. Tech. Coll., 1994—. Adminstrv. sec. Laconia (N.H.) Fire Dept., 1971-86; adminstrv. clk. Laconia Zoning Bd. of Adjustment, 1984-92, Laconia Airport Authority, 1984-92; planning adminstr. Gilmanton (N.H.) Planning Bd., 1985—; proprietor Acad. Village Bus. Svc., Gilmanton, 1987—; co-owner R.M. Daigle Constrn. Co., Gilmanton, 1975—; town auditor Town of Gilmanton, 1987-88, property mgmt. cons., 1989-93, interim dep. town clk./tax collector, 1993; method and systems cons. Belmont (N.H.) Planning Bd., 1991—; zoning cons. Belmont Zoning Bd. of Adjustment, 1993—. Mem. Am. Legion Aux., Gilmanton, 1958—; supr. Gilmanton Voter Checklist, 1988—; trustee Gilmanton Cemeteries, 1990—; sec., treas. Gilmanton 4th of July Assn., 1990—. Recipient Honorable Mention, N.H. Office of State Planning, 1994. Mem. N.H. Planners Assn., Granite State Designers & Installers. Republican. Roman Catholic. Home: PO Box 56, State Rte 107 Gilmanton NH 03237 Office: Acad Village Bus Svc PO Box 56, State Rte 107 Gilmanton NH 03237

DAIL, HILDA LEE, psychotherapist; b. Franklin Springs, Ga., Aug. 23, 1920; d. Ransom Harvey and Mattie (Gray) Lee; m. Francis Roderick Dail, Dec. 27, 1941; children: Janice Sylvia, Roderick Lee. BA, Piedmont Coll., 1941; PhD, The Union Inst., 1979. Cert. expressive therapist. Tchr. pub. schs. N.C., Tenn. and Ga., 1939-54; assoc. sec. Bd. of Missions, Methodist Ch., New York, 1954-60; dir. pub. rels. and tchr. Leonard Theol. Coll., Jabalpur, India, 1960-64; editor lit. Bd. of Missions, United Meth. Ch., N.Y.C.; exec. dir. Int. Found. Ewha Women's Univ., Seoul, Republic of Korea, 1970-71; dir. devel. Ch. Women United., 1971-73; dir. resources cen. nat. bd. YWCA, 1973-75; pres. Hilda Lee Dail & Assoc. Internat., N.Y.C., 1975-83, Myrtle Beach, S.C., 1983—; mem. adj. faculty Coastal Carolina U., Conway, 1981-95, Webster U., Myrtle Beach, 1981—; bd. dirs. Enablement Inc., Boston, 1975-89, Assn. Coop. Agys. Asian Women's Coll., 1971-85; founder, pres. Internat. Ctr. for Creativity and Consciousness, 1989—; mem. Horry County Human Rels. Coun., 1994—. Author: Decision and Destiny, 1957, Encounters Extraordinary, 1969, Let's Try a Workshop With Teen Women, 1974, The Lotus and the Pool, 1983, How to Create Your Own Career, 1989. Dir. Citizens Against Spouse Abuse, Myrtle Beach, 1982-88, pres. Gotham Bus. and Prof. Women's Club, N.Y., 1978, dir. Green Chimney Sch., N.Y., 1978-83, v.p., Zonta Internat., N.Y., 1976-84. Fellow Nat. Expressive Therapy Assn. (speaker 1983-89); mem. ASTD (bd. dirs. 1972-89), Mental Health Assn. (bd. dirs., pres. 1988-89). Democrat. United Methodist. Home and Office: Briarcliffe Acres 154 Pine Tree Ln Myrtle Beach SC 29572

DAILEY, CHRISTIE LYNN, historical society administrator; b. Ames, Iowa, Dec. 21, 1953; d. William Mallery and Laura (Christensen) D. BA, Mich. State U., 1976; MA, Iowa State U., 1982; postgrad., U. Iowa, 1986-87. Curatorial asst., registrar Brunnier Gallery and Mus., Ames, 1976-78; teaching asst. history dept. Iowa State U., Ames, 1978-80; editor The Annals of Iowa Iowa State Hist. Dept., Des Moines, 1980-83; dir. publs. Iowa State Hist. Dept., Iowa City, 1983-86; dir. publs. and edn. bur. State Hist. Soc. Iowa, Iowa City, 1986-93, dir. Iowa City Ctr., 1993—; cons. Wildrows Oral History Project, Adel, Iowa, 1982, Shelby County Hist. Soc., Harlan, Iowa, 1983, Coalition for Children's and Family Svcs., Des Moines, 1987; cons. skills weekend tng. team Sch. Social Work, U. Iowa, 1985-89; presenter in field. Contbr. articles and stories to profl. jours. Counselor Listening Ear, East Lansing, Mich., 1973-75, Open Line, Ames, 1978-80, Community Telephone Counseling, Des Moines, 1981-83; bd. dirs. Iowa chpt. Victorian Soc. Am., 1980-83; house staff Domestic Violence Project, Iowa City, 1984—. Office: State Hist Soc Iowa 402 Iowa Ave Iowa City IA 52240

DAILEY, COLEEN HALL, lawyer; b. East Liverpool, Ohio, Aug. 10, 1955; d. David Lawrence and Deloris Mae (Rosensteel) Hall; m. Donald W. Dailey Jr., Aug. 16, 1980; children: Erin Elizabeth, Daniel Lester. Student, Wittenberg U., 1973-75; BA, Youngstown State U., 1977; JD, U. Cin., 1980. Bar: Ohio 1981, U.S. Dist. Ct. (no. dist.) Ohio 1981. Sr. library assoc. Marx Law Library, Cin., 1979-80; law clk. Kapp Law Office, East Liverpool, 1979, 1980-81, assoc., 1981-85; sole practice East Liverpool, 1985—; spl. counsel Atty. Gen. Ohio, 1985-92. Pres. Columbiana County (Ohio) Young Dems., 1985-87; bd. dirs. Big Bros. Big Sisters Columbiana County, Inc., Lisbon, Ohio, 1984-87, Planned Parenthood Mahoning Valley, Inc., 1993—; trustee Ohio Women Inc.; active Columbiana County Progress Coun., Inc. Mem. ABA, Ohio Bar Assn. (Ohio Supreme Ct. Joint Task Force on Gender Fairness), Columbiana County Bar Assn., Assn. Trial Lawyers Am., Ohio Trial Lawyers Assn., Ohio Fedn. Bus. and Profl. Women (rec. sec. 1991-92), East Liverpool Bus. and Profl. Women's Assn. Democrat. Lutheran. Office: PO Box 2519 16687 Saint Clair Ave Ste 103 East Liverpool OH 43920-9401

DAILEY, IRENE ELEANOR, hospital volunteer services professional; b. Pitts., May 13, 1952; d. Russell Ford and Betty (Andra) D. BS in Secondary Edn., Slippery Rock U., 1974. Personnel cons. Liken Svcs., Inc., Pitts., 1974-76; asst. to regional campaign coord. John Heinz for Senate Com., Pitts., 1976; staff asst. community rels. H. John Heinz III H. John Heinz, U.S. Senate, Pitts., 1977-82; asst. dir. community and vol. svcs. Forbes Regional Health Ctr., Monroeville, Pa., 1983-88; dir. vol. svcs. Sewickley (Pa.) Valley Hosp., 1988—. Mem. Women's Polit. Caucus, Pitts., 1980, Minority Bus. Devel. Com., Pitts., 1982; bd. trainer United Way, Pitts., 1988—. Mem. NAFE, Soc. Dirs. Vol. Svcs. (legis. chair Pitts. unit 1984-85, membership chair 1990-92, state v.p. 1992-93), Zonta Three Rivers Pitts. East (bd. dirs. 1984-85, v.p. 1986-88, pres. 1988-89, del. to internat. conv. 1988), Alpha Sigma Alpha. Republican. Roman Catholic. Home: 1512 Cooper Ave Pittsburgh PA 15212-1835 Office: Sewickley Valley Hosp Blackburn Rd Sewickley PA 15143-8386

DAILEY, JANET, novelist; b. Storm Lake, Iowa, May 21, 1944; d. Boyd and Louise Haradon; m. William Dailey; 2 stepchildren. Student pub. schs., Independence, Iowa. Sec. Nebr., Iowa, 1963-74. Author: No Quarter Asked, 1976, After the Storm, 1976, Boss Man From Ogallala, 1976, Savage Land, 1976, Land of Enchantment, 1976, Fire and Ice, 1976, The Homeplace, 1976, Dangerous Masquerade, 1977, Night of the Cotillion, 1977, Valley of the Vapors, 1977, Fiesta San Antonio, 1977, Show Me, 1977, Bluegrass King, 1977, A Lyon's Share, 1977, The Widow and the Wastrel, 1977, Giant of Mesabi, 1978, The Ivory Cane, 1978, The Indy Man, 1978, Darling Jenny, 1978, Reilly's Woman, 1978, To Tell the Truth, 1978, Sonora Sundown, 1978, Big Sky Country, 1978, Something Extra, 1978, Master Fiddler, 1978, Beware of the Stranger, 1978, The Matchmakers, 1978, For Bitter or Worse, 1979, Green Mountain Man, 1979, Six White Horses, 1979, Summer Mahogany, 1979, Touch the Wind, 1979, Strange Bedfellow, 1979, Low Country Liars, 1979, Sweet Promise, 1979, For Mike's Sake, 1979, Sentimental Journey, 1979, A Land Called Deseret, 1979, The Bride of the Delta Queen, 1979, Tidewater Lover, 1979, Lord of the High Lonesome, 1980, Kona Winds, 1980, The Boston Man, 1980, The Rogue, 1980, Bed of Grass, 1980, The Thawing of Mara, 1980, The Mating Season, 1980, Southern Nights, 1980, Ride the Thunder, 1980, Enemy in Camp, 1980, Difficult Decision, 1980, Heart of Stone, 1980, One of the Boys, 1980, Wild and Wonderful, 1981, A Tradition of Pride, 1981, The Traveling Kind, 1981, The Hostage Bride, 1981, Dakota Dreamin', 1981, For the Love of God, 1981, Night Way, 1981, This Calder Sky, 1981, Lancaster Men, 1981, Terms of Surrender, 1982, With a Little Luck, 1982, Wildcatter's Woman, 1982, Northern Magic, 1982, That Carolina Summer, 1982, This Calder Range, 1982, Foxfire Light, 1982, The Second Time, 1982, Mistletoe and Holly, 1982, Stands a Calder Man, 1983, Separate Cabins, 1983, Western Man, 1983, Calder Born, Calder Bred, 1983, Best Way to Lose, 1983, Leftover Love, 1984, Silver Wings, Santiago Blue, 1984, The Pride of Hannah Wade, 1985, The Glory Game, 1985, The Great Alone, 1986, Heiress, 1987, Rivals, 1989, Masquerade, 1990, Aspen Gold, 1991, Tangled Vines, 1992, Riding High, 1994, The Proud and The Free, 1994. Recipient Golden Heart award Romance Writers Am., 1981, Romantic Times Contemporary award, 1983. *

DAILEY, VICTORIA ANN, economist, policy analyst; b. San Antonio, Aug. 30, 1945; d. John Thomas and Helen (Bass) D. BA, Swarthmore Coll., 1967; PhD, U. Va., 1973. Economist FTC, Washington, 1972-79, U.S. Dept. Transp., Washington, 1979—. Brookings Econ. Rsch. fellow Brookings Instn., 1971-72. Office: US Dept Transp 400 7th St SW Washington DC 20590-0001

DAILY, ELLEN WILMOTH MATTHEWS, technical writer, training analyst; b. Marfa, Tex., Aug. 13, 1949; d. Lynn Henry Sr. and Wilmoth Hamilton (Cox) Matthews; m. John Scott Daily Sr., Mar. 21, 1970; children: John Scott Jr., Kristen Michelle. BS in Physics, U. Tex., El Paso, 1971; postgrad., George Mason U., Fairfax, Va., 1980. House dir., activity counselor Southwestern Children's Home, El Paso, Tex., 1965-68; analyst Schellenger Research Found. Labs, El Paso, 1968-70; computer operator, supr. keypunch El Paso Nat. Bank, 1970-73; supr., progam analyst El Paso Sand Products, 1973-74; tech. rep. Xerox Corp., Jackson, Miss., 1975-77; product tech. specialist Xerox Corp., Jackson, 1977-79; tech. trainer Xerox Corp., Leesburg, Va., 1979-82; sr. tech. writer, tng. analyst Xerox Corp., Lewisville, Tex., 1982-94; group rep. Xerox Corp., various cities, 1975-90; co-owner Triple "D" Enterprises, 1994—; owner Daily Delight Cattery, Chantilly, Va. and Carrollton, Tex., 1979-89; co-owner J & M Answering Svc., Dallas, 1983-84. Co-author: (electronic Bible verse) Verse of the Day, 1987-92. Team and divsn. mgr. Chantilly Youth Assn., 1980-82; bd. dirs., swim team dir. Brookfield Swim Club, Chantilly, 1980-82; vol. Metrocrest Svc. Ctr., Carrollton, 1986-89; elder Nor'Kirk Presbyn. Ch., Carrollton, 1989-91; founding mem. United We Stand Am., 1993—; vol. Catherine the Great, 1992. Mem. Internat. Platform Assn., U. Tex. El Paso Cannoneers Club (sec.-treas. 1967-71), Xerox Bowling League (pres. 1988-89), Sigma Pi Sigma, Kappa Delta (social svc. dir. 1969-70). Home: 3701 Grassmere Dr Carrollton TX 75007-2616 Office: DDD Enterprises 3701 Grassmere Dr Carrollton TX 75007-2616

DAILY, FAY KENOYER, botany educator; b. Indpls., Feb. 17, 1911; d. Fredrick and Camellia Thea (Neal) Kenoyer; A.B., Butler U., 1935, M.S., 1952; m. William Allen Daily, June 24, 1937. Lab. technician Eli Lilly & Co., Indpls., 1935-37, Abbott Labs., North Chicago, Ill., 1939, William S. Merrell & Co., Ohio, 1940-41; lubrication chemist Indpls. Propellor div. Curtiss-Wright Corp., 1945; lectr. botany Butler U., Indpls., 1947-49, instr. immunology and microbiology, 1957-58, lectr. microbiology, 1962-63, mem. herbarium staff, 1949-87, curator cryptogamic herbarium, 1987—. Grantee Ind. Acad. Sci., 1961-62. Mem. Am. Inst. Biol. Sci., Bot. Soc. Am., Phycol. Soc. Am., Internat. Phycol. Soc., Ind. Acad. Sci., Torrey Bot. Club, Sigma Xi, Phi Kappa Phi, Sigma Delta Epsilon. Republican. Methodist. Co-author book on sci. history. Contbr. articles on fossil and extant charophytes (algae) to profl. jours. Home: 5884 Compton St Indianapolis IN 46220-2653

DAILY, GRETCHEN CARA, ecologist, environmental policy analyst; b. Washington, Oct. 19, 1964; d. Charles Dennis and Suzanne Rachel (Schubert) D. BS, Stanford U., 1986, MS, 1987, PhD, 1992. Ctr. for Conservation Biology/Nature Conservancy fellow Stanford (Calif.) U., 1988-92; Winslow/Heinz postdoctoral fellow U. Calif., Berkeley, 1992—; sci. advisor IPAT Prodns. (film), Stanford, 1993—. Contbr. over 35 articles to profl. jours. Recipient Frances Lou Kallman award Stanford U., 1992, Pew scholar in conservation and environ., Pew Found., 1994. Mem. Rocky Mtn. Biol. Lab. Office: Univ Calif Energy and Resources Group 100 Bldg T-4 Berkeley CA 94720

DAJANI, VIRGINIA, arts administrator; b. Chgo., Jan. 19, 1936; d. Philip Linden Boddy and Lillian (McArdle) O'Brien; m. Majed Dajani (div. 1968); children: Magda, Tarek, Najeeb, Nadia. Student, Loyola U., Chgo., 1953-55, Am. U., Cairo, 1961, Am. U., Beirut, 1963-67; postgrad., Harvard U., 1980-81. News editor Archtl. Forum mag., N.Y.C., 1968-72, Architecture Plus mag., N.Y.C., 1972-74; asst. George Nelson, Architect, N.Y.C., 1975-76; editor The Livable City, quar. of Mcpl. Art Soc., N.Y.C., 1976-89; dir. spl. projects Mcpl. Art Soc., N.Y.C., 1977-89; exec. dir. Am. Acad. Arts and Letters, N.Y.C., 1990—; dir. archtl. competition Mcpl. Art Soc., N.Y.C., 1985, 87; competition advisor Bronx Mus. Arts, N.Y.C., 1989, Mcpl. Art Soc., N.Y.C., 1991—; lectr. Harvard U. Grad. Sch. Design, 1980-87. Author: Juror's Guide to Lower Manhattan, 1984, rev. edits., 1985, 87, 90; contbr. articles to profl. archtl. jours. Recipient Citation for editing design mus. catalogue Am. Inst. Graphic Artists, 1975, award for editing The Livable City, AIA, 1982; Loeb fellow Harvard U., 1980-81. Mem. Century Assn. Office: Am Acad Arts and Letters 633 W 155th St New York NY 10032-7501*

DAJANY, INNAM, academic administrator; b. American Fork, Utah, Oct. 9, 1951; d. Fuad Wafa and Doris Dean (Ault) Dajany; m. Nadia Jomanna Fenton (div.). BS, SUNY, Cortland, 1973; MEd, U. Idaho, 1985. Cert. elem. and secondary English tchr., Idaho, Wyo., N.Y. Tchr. Converse County Sch. Dist., Douglas, Wyo., 1973-75; newspaper reporter Casper (Wyo.) Star Tribune, 1974-76; rsch. asst. edn. dept. U. Idaho, Moscow, 1978-81, asst. dir. Early Childhood Learning Ctr., 1980-84, dir. Early Childhood Learning Ctr., 1984-90, cons., coord. Early Childhood Inst., 1989-91; mktg. and sales dir. Golden Arrow Hotel, Lake Placid, N.Y., 1990-92; continuing edn. asst. SUNY, Clinton C. C., 1992—; coord. Riverview Acad., 1993—; cons. Gov.'s Commn. Children and Youth, Boise, Idaho, 1988-90, child devel. specialist region II coun., 1986-90; conf. coord. U.S. Agy. Internat. Devel., 1988-90; independent grant writer, 1993—; ind. real estate agent, patent writer, invention marketer; speaker in field. Author: Building Your Child's Self Esteem During Home Reading, 1985, (booklet) You, Your Child, and Reading, 1986, (brochure) Help Arrest Child Abuse, 1982. Tchr., project coord. North Country Women at Work, 1993—; advisor child care licensing laws City of Moscow, advisor HUD grant; coord. Parents in Action, Moscow, 1989, 90; co-pres. Moscow Swim Team, 1989, 90; leader Bluebirds, Moscow; active N.W. Found. grant, Ford Found. grant with KAID-TV. Mem. Nat. Assn. for Edn. Young Children (state pres. 1989-90, conf. chair 1985-87, leadership trainer and presenter 1981—), Internat. Reading Assn. (state pres. 1987-88, nat. com. literacy devel. 1987-89, nat. com. reading and arts 1985-87, leadership trainer and presenter 1981—), Phi Delta Kappa, Kappa Delta Phi. Home: PO Box 277 Crown Point NY 12928 Office: Noteco Inc PO Box 533 Crown Point NY 12928

DAKIN, CHRISTINE WHITNEY, dancer, educator; b. New Haven, Aug. 25, 1949; d. James Irving, Jr. and Jean Evelyn (Coulter) Crump; m. Robert Ford Dakin, June 21, 1969 (div. Sept. 1982); m. Stephen J. Mauer, Aug. 1, 1985. Student, U. Mich., 1967-71. Performer, teacher Ann Arbor Dance Theater, Mich., 1965-71; tchr. Ann Arbor Pub. Schs., 1967-70, Lincoln Ctr. Inst., N.Y.C., 1978, Guanajuato U., Mex., 1982; vis. artist USIA Vladivastock, Vladivastok, Russia, 1992; tchr. Ballet Nacional de Mex., 1993—; vis. artist Ballet Contemporaneo, Buenos Aires, 1993; prin. dancer Martha Graham Dance Co., N.Y.C., 1976—; dancer, rehearsal dir. Pearl Lang. Dance Co., 1974-76, Kazuko Hirabayashi Dance Co., 1974-76; faculty Martha Graham Sch., 1972—, Julliard Sch., 1992—, Alvin Alley Am. Dance Ctr., 1989—. Appeared in: It's Hard to Be a Jew, 1972, The Dybuk, 1975; appeared (with Martha Graham Dance Co.) Covent Garden, London, 1976, Met. Opera, 1980, Sta. WNET Dance in Am. Series, 1979; Young Artist in Performance at The White House, Sta. WNET, 1982, (with Rudolph Nureyev) Paris Opera, Berlin Opera, 1984, N.Y. State Theater, 1985; NHK Film, Japan, 1990, Paris Opera Film, 1991, (documentary film) Les Printemps du Sacre, 1993. Scholar Am. Dance Festival, 1969; recipient award Dance Mag., 1994. Mem. Am. Guild Mus. Artists (life, bd. govs.). Office: Martha Graham Dance Co 316 E 63rd St New York NY 10021-7702

DAKOFSKY, LADONNA JUNG, radiation oncologist, educator; b. N.Y.C., Oct. 30, 1960; d. George S. and Kay (Han) Chung. BA magna cum laude, Columbia U., N.Y.C., 1982; MD, NYU, 1987. Bd. cert. radiation oncologist. Rsch. asst. dept. neurology UCLA, 1980-81, Harvard U., Boston, 1982; tchr. chemistry St. Ann's Sch., Brooklyn Heights, N.Y., 1982-83; resident in internal medicine Lenox Hill Hosp., N.Y.C., 1987-88; resident in radiation oncology Hosp. of U. Pa., Phila., 1988-91; instr. in radiation oncology New Eng. Med. Ctr., Boston, 1991-92; attending physician Norwalk (Conn.) Hosp., 1992—; clin. asst. prof. radiation oncology Yale U., 1994—. Mem. jr. com. Boys Club N.Y.; sponsor Mus. City of N.Y.; mem. com. Vocat. Found., N.Y.C.; mem. Jr. League of Stanford-Norwalk. Marine Biol. Lab. scholar, 1981. Mem. AMA, Assn. Therapeutic Radiology and Oncology, Fairfield County Med. Assn., New Eng. Cancer Soc., Met. Breast Cancer Group. Presbyterian. Office: Norwalk Hosp Radiation Medicine Norwalk CT 06856

DALE, BRENDA STEPHENS, educator; b. Hickory, N.C., Sept. 24, 1942; d. John Doyle and Bertha (Barger) Stephens; m. James Darrell Dale, June 13, 1964; children: Ginger Leigh Rizoti, Jami Lynne. BS in English, Appalachian State U., 1964, MA in Reading Edn., 1977; cert. edn. academically gifted, Lenoir Rhyne, Hickory, N.C., 1982. High. sch. tchr. Moore County Schs., Carthage, N.C., 1964; high sch. tchr. Asheboro (N.C.) City Schs., 1964-65; 8th grade tchr. Davidson County Schs., Thomasville, N.C., 1967-68; reading specialist Randolph County Schs., Trinity, N.C., 1970-72; reading specialist Wilkes N.C. Schs., Wilkesboro, 1972-82, tchr. acad. gifted, 1982—; part-time tchr. Davidson County Community Coll., Lexington, N.C., 1965-68, Wilkes Community Coll., Wilkesboro, 1982-87, adult literary tutor. Edn. chmn., bd. dirs. Am. Cancer Soc., North Wilkesboro, N.C., 1985-90; mem. Wilkes Regional Med. Ctr. Aux., 1992—, YMCA. Tchr. scholar fellow N.C. Ctr. for Advancement of Teaching, Western Carolina U., 1990; recipient C. B. Eller Teaching award C.B. Eller Found., 1991. Mem. AAUW (charter, fundraiser 1977-78, bd. dirs., chmn. edn. found. 1992—), NEA, N.C. Assn. Educators, Internat. Reading Assn. (sec. 1985-86), Internat. Platform Assn., Mary Hemphill Svc. Group, Lynnwoode Recreation Club, Alpha Delta Kappa. Methodist. Home: 187 Laurel Mountain Rd North Wilkesboro NC 28659-4617 Office: Wilkes County Schs Main St Wilkesboro NC 28697

DALE, CATHY JOE, vocalist; b. Mobile, Ala., May 26, 1963; d. Vernon Winfred and Mary Joe (Bramlett) D.; m. Michael Wayne Hancock, Aug. 21, 1981; 1 child, Michael Dale. Student, Valdosta (Ga.) Tech., 1982-83. Vocalist The Blues, Valdosta, 1975-80, Knight Riders, Quitman, Ga., 1981-82, Second Look, Valdosta, 1982-83; vocalist, musician SHILO Band Inc., Valdosta, 1984—; recording artist Broadland Internat. Records, Nashville, 1991—; owner The Country Palace, Vald, Ga., 1992—; vocal coaching Valdosta Music, 1979-80; dancer, Ga., Ala., S.C., 1967-70. Songwriter, vocalist (recordings) Colors, 1991, Treatin' Me Bad, 1991, Lookin' Back, 1992, (albums) I Believe in Me, 1994, (singles) Living in a World of Make Believe, 1993, Lie to Me, 1993, Somebody Else, 1994. Mem. Broadcast Music Inc., Musician Union, Country Music Assn. Baptist.

DALE, CHARLENE BOOTHE, international health administrator; b. Washington, June 10, 1942; d. John Edward and Frances Elizabeth (Jett) Boothe; children: Cynthia Lee, Anthony John, Jennifer Elizabeth. AA with high honors, Howard Community Coll., 1977; BA magna cum laude, U. Md., 1979. Asst. dir. univ. rels., alumni dir. U. Md., Catonsville, 1977-81; assoc. dir. univ. rels. and devel. U. Md., College Park, 1982-83; sr. devel. officer Internat. Ctr. Diarrhoeal Disease Rsch., Dhaka, Bangladesh, 1984-86; exec. v.p. Child Health Found. (formerly Internat. Child Health Found.), Columbia, Md., 1985—; cons. to organize symposium oral rehydration therapy Nat. Coun. Internat. Health, Washington, 1987; organizer internat. symposium on food-based oral rehydration therapy Aga Khan U., Pakistan, 1989; organizer consensus conf. cereal-based oral rehydration therapy, Columbia, Md., 1993. Author: (tng. manual) Prevention and Treatment of Childhood Diarrhea with Oral Rehydration Therapy, Nutrition and Breastfeeding, 1992; editor procs. Oral Rehydration Therapy Symposia, 1987, 89, 93, 94; editor Child Health News, 1993—; contbr. articles to profl. jours. Pub. affairs chmn. United Way, Washington Capital Area, Prince Georges County, 1981-83; v.p. Waterfowl Assn.; pres. Windstream Assn., 1988-89; v.p. Waterfowl Terrace Assn., 1994—; mem. pub. rels. com. Md., Del. Cable TV Assn., Balt., 1981-83. Mem. APHA (internat. maternal-child health com.), AAUW, Nat. Coun. Internat. Health Assn., U. Md. Balt. County Alumni Assn. (bd. dirs. 1979-83), Women's Internat. Pub. Health Network. Democrat. Club: Columbia Assn. Athletic (Md.) (capt. women's traveling racquetball team 1979-83). Home: Ste 325 10630 Little Patuxent Pky Columbia MD 21044-2465 Office: Child Health Found 10630 Little Patuxent Pkwy Columbia MD 21044-0205

DALE, JUDY RIES, religious organization administrator; b. Memphis, Dec. 13, 1944; d. James Lorigan and Julia Marie (Schwinn) Ries; m. Eddie Melvin Ashmore, July 12, 1969 (div. Dec. 1983). BA, Rhodes Coll., 1966; M in Religious Edn., So. Bapt. Theol. Sem., 1969, Grad. Specialist in Religious Edn., 1969. Cert. tchr. educable mentally handicapped, secondary English, adminstrn. and supervision in spl. edn. EMH tchr., curriculum writer, tchr. trainer Jefferson County Bd. Edn., Louisville, 1969-88, ednl. cons., 1988-90; dist. coord. Gt. Lakes dist. Universal Fellowship Met. Community Chs., Louisville, 1990—; lectr. Jefferson C.C., Louisville, 1987-93, U. Louisville, 1976-77, 87-90; mem. faculty Samaritan Coll., 1992—; mem. program adv. com. Internat. Conf. Spl. Edn., Beijing, 1987-88. Editor, writer: (handbook) Handbook for Beginning Teachers, 1989, A Manual of Instructional Strategies, 1985; author: (kit) Math Activities Cards, 1978. Bd. sec. Com. of Ten, Inc., Louisville, 1987-91; active Greater Louisville Human Rights Commn., 1985-90, Ky. Civil Liberties Union, 1986—; v.p. GLUE, 1988-92, pres., 1992-94; mem. Universal Fellowship of Met. Cmty. Chs., programs and budget divsn., mem. gen. coun., 1990—, active Women's Secretariat steering com.; mem. membership com. Cmty. Health Trust, 1991-94; trustee Samaritan Coll., 1992—. Recipient Honorable Order of Ky. Cols., 1976; named Outstanding Elem. Tchr. Am., 1975. Mem. AAUW, NOW, Coun. Exceptional Children (keynote speaker 1984-88, internat. pres. 1986-87, exec. com. 1984-88, bd. govs. 1981-88), Ky. Coun. Exceptional Children (bd. dirs. 1976-90, Mem. of Yr. 1987), Internat. Platform Assn., Women's Alliance, Phi Delta Kappa. Democrat. Home and Office: 1300 Ambridge Dr Louisville KY 40207-2410

D'ALENE, ALIXANDRIA FRANCES, management consultant; b. Buffalo, Oct. 21, 1951; d. Fern (Hill) D'A.; B.A., Canisius Coll., Buffalo, 1973, M.S., 1975, M.B.A., 1980. Tchr., Buffalo public schs., 1973-76; pers. cons. Sanford Rose Assos., Williamsville, N.Y., 1976-78; mgr. benefits adminstrn. Svc. Systems Corp., Clarence, N.Y., 1978-80; mgr. employee rels. Del Monte Corp., Walnut Creek, Calif., 1980-82; human resource mgmt. cons. H.R.S., Inc., Winston-Salem, N.C., 1982-87; corp. pers. specialist Advance Stores Co., Inc., Roanoke, Va., 1987-88; pers. dir. Alfred (N.Y.) U., 1988—; adj. prof. bus., 1988-90; human resources mgr. Lord Corp., Shelton, Conn., 1990—. Mem. Assn. Pers. Adminstrs., Indsl. Pers. Soc., Coll. and U. Pers. Assn., Phi Alpha Theta. Episcopalian.

D'ALESSIO, JACQUELINE ANN, English language educator; b. Morristown, N.J., Jan. 26, 1943; d. Clifford Corbet and Helen Ann (Chrenko) Compton; m. Harold F. D'Alessio, Oct. 28, 1967. BA English, Coll. New Rochelle, 1964; MA English, Seton Hall U., 1969. Tchr. Bridgewater (N.J.)-Raritan Regional Sch. Dist., 1964—; advisor, student coun., dramatics Hillside Sch., Bridgewater, N.J., 1966—. Chmn. pub. rels. Mt. St. Mary Devel. Office, 1985—; bd. dirs. N.J. Lit. Hall of Fame, 1990-94, N.J. Legis. Agenda for Women, Inc., 1993—; sec. Women's Agenda of N.J. Named Outstanding Elem. Tchr. U.S., 1971; Recipient Gov. Tchr. Recognition, N.J. Dept. Edn., Trenton, 1989. Mem. AAUW (N.J. pres. 1990-94, program v.p. 1988-90, rep. Women's Agenda 1989-94). Roman Catholic. Home: 30 Putnam St Somerville NJ 08876-2737

D'ALESSIO, NATALIE MARINO, artist; b. Elizabeth, N.J., July 4, 1951; d. John T. and Stefana (Sarullo) Marino; m. Anthony Paul D'Alessio, Aug. 28, 1968; 1 child, Stephanie Elsbeth. BA, NYU, 1969; postgrad., New Sch., N.Y.C., 1969-72; cert., N.J. Ctr. Visual Arts, 1977. One woman shows include Exxon Corp., Linden, N.J., 1985, Florence Gallery, Dallas, 1985, ART Insights, N.Y., 1994, Rosalyn Sailors, Phila., 1993; exhibited in group shows at N.J. State Mus., 1979, Bergen Community Mus., Paramus, N.J., 1980, Nat. Art Club, N.Y.C., 1981, Phila. Port of History Mus., 1984, Lincoln Ctr., N.Y.C., 1983, Cork Art Gallery, N.Y.C., 1983, numerous others; represented in permanent collections Rosalyn Sailor Gallery and Mus. Fine Art, Margate, N.J., Phila., Tom Weiner's Art Insights, N.Y.C., Marino Galleries Inc., Milburn, N.J.; contbr. illustrations to books; author: (screenplay) The Successor, 1989; illustrator: Art Lovers Cookbook, 1975; host cablecast series Art Forum; prodr., dir. video & TV programs. Vol. cons. N.J. Ctr. for Visual Arts, Summit, 1989; trustee TV 36, Communities on Cable, Summit, 1989; judge for sr. citizen art shows, Newark, 1989. Recipient Bee Co. award Pastel Soc. Am., 1981, European Banner of Arts, Accademia d'Europa, 1984, award-artists grant Union County Div. of Art and Cultural Affairs; N.J. state Coun. for Arts grantee Union County Cultural Commn., 1985-86, Lugwig Vogelstein Found. grantee, 1989. Fellow Artists Equity, Women's Caucus for Art, Riker Hill Art Park (exec. com.); mem. N.J. Ctr. Visual Art (award 1979). Home: PO Box 225 Springfield NJ 07081-0225

DALEY, BARBARA SABIN, clinical psychologist; b. Washington, Sept. 19, 1949; d. Hilbert Speich and Katherine (Keet) Sabin; m. Paul Patrick Daley, May 24, 1980; 1 child, Patrick Sabin. BS, Duke U., 1972; MSN, Yale U., 1975; PsyD, Mass. Sch. Profl. Psychology, 1992. Lic. psychologist, health svc. provider, Mass. Staff nurse Durham (N.C.) County Mental Health Ctr., 1972-73; coord. after-care svcs. Emerson Hosp., Concord, Mass., 1975-77; clin. specialist in mental health Harvard Cmty. Health Plan, Cambridge, Mass., 1977-88; coord. pediatric behavioral medicine Cambridge Hosp., 1994—; pvt. pracitce child assessment and treatment; clin. fellow in psychiatry Harvard U. Med. Sch., Cambridge, 1990-93, clin. instr., 1993—. Mem. APA, Mass. Psychol. Assn., Assn. for Advancement of Behavioral Therapies. Home: 9 Crofton Rd Waban MA 02168-1931 Office: Cambridge Hosp Cambridge St Cambridge MA 02139

DALEY, PAMELA, lawyer; b. Springfield, Mass., Oct. 1, 1952; d. Edward Murray and Elizabeth Bloom Daley. AB summa cum laude in Romance Langs. and Lit., Princeton U., 1974; JD, U. Pa., 1979. Bar: Pa. 1979, N.Y. 1991. Lectr. partnership taxation law U. Pa., Phila., 1982-89; assoc. tax sect. Morgan, Lewis & Bockius, Phila., 1979-86, ptnr., 1986-89; tax counsel GE, Fairfield, Conn., 1989-91, v.p., sr. counsel for transactions, 1991—; bd. outside advisors Va. Tax Review Assn., 1982—; speaker in field. Editor-in-chief U. Pa. Law Review; contbr. articles to profl. jours. Trustee MacDuffie Sch., Springfield, 1986-92; bd. govs. Pa. Economy League, 1986-89. Teaching fellow Salzberg Seminar on Am. Law and Legal Instns., 1986; named to Acad. Women Achievers YWCA, 1992. Mem. Am. Corp. Counsel Assn., Order Coif, Phi Beta Kappa. Office: GE 3135 Easton Tpk W3A Fairfield CT 06431

DALEY, ROSIE, cook, writer; b. South Seaville, N.J.; d. Fred and Joan Daley; 1 child, Marley. Chef's helper Cal-a-Vie, Vista, Calif., 1989-90, head cook, 1990-91; personal cook to Oprah Winfrey Chgo., 1991—. Author: (with Oprah Winfrey) In the Kitchen with Rosie: Oprah's Favorite Recipes, 1994. Office: care Harpo Prodns 110 N Carpenter St Chicago IL 60607-2101

DALEY, RUTH MARGARET, advertising agency administrator; b. Buffalo, Apr. 12, 1950; d. Russell Short and Emma Pleasant (Wear) Garrick; m. Jeffrey George Vanghel (dec. 1988); m. Patrick L. Daley. Student, Villa Maria Coll., Buffalo. Sec. McKesson & Robbins Drug Co., Cheektowaga, N.Y., 1972-78; sales rep. Nasco Inc., Springfield, Tenn., 1978-80; telemktg. sales rep. L.M. Berry & Co., Amherst, N.Y., 1980-81, mgr. telemktg. sales unit, 1981-83, mgr. telemktg. sales dept., 1984-90; mgmt. cons. Ameritech, Troy, Mich., 1990-92; mgr. tng. White Directory Pubs., Buffalo, 1992—; grad. asst. Dale Carnegie Inst., Buffalo, 1985. Mem. Nat. Assn. Female Execs. Home: 66 Parktrail Ln Buffalo NY 14227-2545 Office: The Talking Phone Book 1945 Sheridan Dr Buffalo NY 14223

DALIA, VESTA MAYO, artist; b. Atlanta, Aug. 14, 1932; d. Frank and Winnifred (Layton) Mayo; m. William Barber Macke, May 30, 1952 (div. 1971); children: William Barber Jr., Michael Mayo, Vesta Melissa, Mary Sue Macke Mullen; m. Joseph William Dalia, Aug. 31, 1973 (dec. 1990); stepchildren: Joseph W. Jr., Jeffrey Meade, Denise Marie Dalia Cooper, Nancy Dalia Cook. Student, U. Ga. Part owner Mayo Chem. Cos., other chem. cos., Smyrna and Dalton, Ga., chem. cos., Chattanooga; tchr. art Cen. Piedmont Coll., Charlotte, N.C. Exhibited art in shows in Charlotte and Atlanta. Mem. Nat. Tole and Decorative Painters (past pres. Dogwood chpt., recipient Golden Palet award 1990), Atlanta Better Films (v.p.), Weinman Mineral Mus., The One Hundred Club, Brookfield West Women's Club, Brookfield West Garden Club, West Fulton Owls Club, Frog Club. Republican. Methodist. Home: 11635 Mountain Laurel Dr Roswell GA 30075-1393

DALIS, IRENE, mezzo-soprano, opera company administrator, music educator; b. San Jose, Calif., Oct. 8, 1925; d. Peter Nicholas and Mamie Rose (Boitano) D.; m. George Loinaz, July 16, 1957; 1 child, Alida Mercedes. AB, San Jose State Coll., 1946; MA in Teaching, Columbia U., 1947; MMus (hon.), MS (hon.), San Jose State Coll., 1957; studied voice with, Edyth Walker, N.Y.C., 1947-50, Paul Althouse, 1950-51, Dr. Otto Mueller, Milan, Italy, 1952-72; MusD (hon.), Santa Clara U., 1987. Prin. artist Berlin Opera, 1955-65, Met. Opera, N.Y.C., 1957-77, San Francisco Opera, 1958-73, Hamburg (Fed. Republic Germany) Staatsoper, 1966-71; prof. music San Jose State U., Calif., 1977—; founder, gen. dir. Opera San Jose, 1984—; dir. Met. Opera Nat. Auditions, San Jose dist., 1980-88. Operatic debut as dramatic mezzo-soprano Oldenburgisches Staatstheater, 1953, Berlin Staedtische Opera, 1955; debut Met. Opera, N.Y.C., 1957, 1st Am.-born singer, Kundry Bayreuth Festival, 1961, opened, Bayreuth Festival, Parsifal, 1963; commemorative Wagner 150th Birth Anniversary; opened 1963 Met. Opera Season in Aida; premiered: Dello Joio's Blood Moon, 1961, Henderson's Medea, 1972; rec. artist Parsifal, 1964 (Grand Prix du Disque award); contbg. editor Opera Quarterly, 1983. Recipient Fulbright award for study in Italy, 1951, Woman of Achievement award Commn. on Status of Women, 1983, Pres.'s award Nat. Italian Am. Found., 1985, award of merit People of San Francisco, 1985, San Jose Renaissance award for sustained and outstanding artistic contbn., 1987, Medal of Achievement Acad. Vocal Arts, 1988; named Honored Citizen City of San Jose, 1986; inducted into Calif. Pub. Edn. Hall of Fame, 1985, others. Mem. Beethoven Soc. (mem. adv. bd. 1985—), San Jose Arts Round Table, San Jose Opera Guild, Am. Soc. Univ. Women, Arts Edn. Week Consortium, Phi Kappa Phi, Mu Phi Epsilon. Office: Opera San Jose 2149 Paragon Dr San Jose CA 95131-1312

DALITZKY, MARTHA OKUN, interior designer; b. Springfield, Mass., Aug. 6, 1932; d. Morris and Esther (Chase) Okun; m. Milton Dalitzky, July 4, 1955; children: Scott David, Nancy Beth. BS, U. Mass., 1954. Pres. Studio East, East Longmeadow, Mass., 1963—; chmn. DataPix Pub. Inc., Raleigh, N.C., 1989-90. Designer Solo Showhouse, Am. Cancer Soc.,

Longmeadow, Mass., 1983; designs shown in various mags. Recipient 1st Prize for Residential Kitchen, DuPont Corian, 1989. Mem. Am. Soc. Interior Designers. Office: Studio East Inc 15 Benton Dr East Longmeadow MA 01028-3153

DALLAPIAZZA, PATRICIA ANN, office manager; b. Canonsburg, Pa., Jan. 13, 1950; children: Michelle Lynn, Kevin Alan. Student, Community Coll. Allegheny, 1987-91. Cert. med. mgr. Liaison clk. Duquesne Light Co., Pitts., 1968-75; asst. mgr. Pa. Liquor Control Bd., McDonald, 1980-83; med. mgr. Marion M. Vujevich, M.D., Pitts., 1988—. Vol. Am. Heart Assn., North Versailles, Pa., 1993-94. Mem. Profl. Assn. Health Care Office Mgrs., Croatian Fraternal Union Poice, PATA, Phi Theta Kappa. Republican. Presbyterian. Office: Marion M Vujevich MD 1050 Bower Hill Rd Ste 305 Pittsburgh PA 15243-1870

DALLAS, NOELLE MARIE, financial analyst; b. Louisville, Sept. 24, 1959; d. Glenn Hoyle and Micheline Alice (Boudrias) Madison; m. Stephen Stavros Dallas Jr., Nov. 4, 1989; children: Dominique Marie, Stephen Stavros III. Student, Benjamin Franklin U., 1978-80; BS in Biology, George Mason U., 1984, postgrad, 1988; postgrad, Montgomery Coll., 1986-88. Mgr. Holly Enterprises, Alexandria, Va., 1975-81; gov. rels. intern TRW, Rosslyn, Va., 1984-85; med. asst. Cardiology and Internal Medicine, P.A., Chevy Chase, Md., 1985-86; sr. cons. Ernst & Young, Washington, 1986-90; sr. fin. analyst Community Energy Alternatives, Ridgewood, N.J., 1990—. Mem. NAFE, Coun. Econ. Priorities, Nat. Resources Defense Coun., N.J. Environ. Group, Friends of the Earth, Bound Brook Land Preservation Soc., Chi Omega Alumni Assn. Roman Catholic. Home: 511 Buttonwood Dr Downingtown PA 19335-4121 Office: Community Energy Alternatives 1200 E Ridgewood Ave Ridgewood NJ 07450-3915

DALLMANN-SCHAPER, MARY LOUISE, banker; b. Duluth, Minn., July 4, 1951; d. Norbert Henry and Lahja Mildred (Mykra) D. BA in Bus. Adminstrn., U. Minn., 1974; M in Mgmt. Adminstrn., Met. State U., 1987. With Norwest Info. Svcs., Inc., 1971-85; tech. contingency planner First Bank Sys., Inc., Mpls., 1985-87, tech. support supr., 1987-88, client mgr. human resource info. sys., 1988-89, sr. ops. project leader/officer, 1989-91, sr. project mgr., officer, 1991-92, MIS mgr., officer, 1992-93, sr. project mgr., asst. v.p., 1993—. Mem. NAFE, Data Processing Mgmt. Assn., Minn. Women's Network. Home: 1500 76th Ct Brooklyn Park MN 55444-2462 Office: First Bank Sys Inc 601 2nd Ave S Mpls MN 55402-4302

DALPINO, IDA JANE, educator; b. Newhall, Calif., Oct. 20, 1936; d. Bernhardt Arthur and Wahneta May (Blyler) Melby; m. Gilbert Augustus, June 14, 1963 (div. 1976); 1 child, Nicolette Jane. BA, Calif. State U., Chico, 1960; postgrad., Sacramento State, 1961-65, Sonoma State, 1970-71; MA, U. San Francisco, 1978. Cert. community counselor, learning handicapped, community coll. instr., exceptional children, pupil pers. specialist, secondary tchr., resource specialist. Tchr. Chico High Sch., 1959-60; counselor Mira Loma High Sch., Sacramento, 1960-66; tchr. ESL Phoenix Ind. High Sch., 1968-69; resource specialist Yuba City (Calif.) High Sch., 1971—; English tchr. Rough Rock Demonstration Sch., summers, 1975, 76. Office sec. Job's Daus., North Bend, Oreg., 1953—; active Environ. Def. Fund, Centerville Hist. Assn., Chico, 1991—. Mem. NEA, Calif. Tchrs. Assn., Calif. State Alumni Assn., Sigma Kappa Alumni. Democrat. Mem. Science of the Mind Church. Home: 4676 Cable Bridge Dr Chico CA 95926 Office: Yuba City Unified Sch Dist 850 B St Yuba City CA 95991

DALRYMPLE, MARGARET FISHER, university press editor, writer; b. Calgary, Alta., Can.; d. Anton and Marie (Rusnak) Fisher. PhD, U. Wash., 1972. Instr. history La. State U., Baton Rouge, 1970-72; copy editor La. State U. Press, 1978-82, sr. editor, 1982-89, editor in chief, 1989-94, asst. dir., 1994-95; editor in chief U. Nev. Press, Reno, 1995—; lectr. history U. Paris I, 1972-73; translator, rschr., editor, Baton Rouge, 1975-89. Author essays; editor: The Merchant of Manchac: The Letterbooks of John Fitzpatrick, 1978. Office: U Nev Press Reno NV 89557-0076

DAL SANTO, DIANE, judge; b. East Chicago, Ind., Sept. 20, 1949; d. John Quentin Dal Santo and Helen (Koval) D.; m. Fred O'Cheskey, June 29, 1985. BA, U. N. Mex., 1971; cert. Inst. Internat. and Comparative Law, Guadalajara, Mex., 1978; JD, U. San Diego, 1980. Bar: N.Mex. 1980, U.S. Dist. Ct. N.Mex. 1980. Ct. planner Met. Criminal Justice Coordinating Coun., Albuquerque, 1973-75; planning coord. Dist. Atty.'s Office, Albuquerque, 1975-76, exec. asst. to dist. atty., 1976-77, asst dist. atty. for violent crimes, 1980-82; chief dep. city atty. City of Albuquerque, 1983; assoc. firm T.B. Keleher & Assocs., 1983-84; judge Met. Ct., 1985-89, chief judge, 1988-89; judge Dist. Ct., 1989—; mem. faculty Nat. Jud. Coll., 1990—. Bd. dirs. Nat. Coun. Alcoholism, 1984, S.W. Ballet Co., Albuquerque, 1982-83; mem. Mayor's Task Force on Alcoholism and Crime, N.Mex. Coun. Crime and Delinquency, 1987—, bd. dirs., 1992, Mayor's Task Force Domestic Violence, 1987—; pres. bench, bar, media com., 1992, rules of evidence com. Supreme Ct., 1993. U. San Diego scholar, 1978-79; recipient Women on the Move award YWCA, 1989, Disting. Woman award U.N.Mex. Alumni Assn., 1994; named Woman of Yr. award Duke City Bus. and Profl. Women, 1985. Mem. ABA, LWV, AAUW, Am. Judicature Soc., N.Mex. Women's Found., N.Mex. Bar Assn., N.Mex. Women's Bar Assn. (bd. dirs. 1991-92), Albuquerque Bar Assn., Josephson Inst. Ethics, Nat. Assn. Women Judges, Greater Albuquerque C. of C. (steering com. 1989), N.Mex. Magistrate Judges Assn. (v.p. 1985-89), Dist. Judges Assn. (pres. 1994—), Inns Ct. (master bencher) Democrat. Office: Dist Ct 415 Tijeras Ave NW Albuquerque NM 87102

DALTON, CLAUDETTE ELLIS HARLOE, anesthesiologist, educator, university official; b. Roanoke, Va., Jan. 18, 1947; d. John Pinckney and Dorothy Anne (Ellis) Harloe; m. Henry Tucker Dalton, May 17, 1973 (div. 1979); 1 child, Gordon Tucker. BA, Sweet Briar Coll., 1969; MD, U. Va., 1974. Resident in anesthesiology U. N.C., Chapel Hill, 1974-77; med. edn. Lenoir County Meml Hosp./East Carolina U., Kinston, N.C., 1978-80; med. edn. in intensive care Presbyn Hosp., Charlotte, N.C., 1981-82; practice anesthesiology Charlotte Eye, Ear, Nose and Throat Hosp., 1982-85, Medivision of Charlotte and Orthopedic Hosp. of Charlotte, 1985-89; asst. dean alumni affairs, 1989-92; asst. dean med. edn. U. Va. Health Scis. Ctr., Charlottesville, 1992—, cmty. preceptor coord., 1992-94; dir. Office of Cmty. Based Med. Edn., 1994—; bd. dirs. Kinston Bd. Health, 1979-81. Author developer patient edn. materials for illiterate patients, 1979—, emergency med. svc. tng. program, 1981. Bd. dirs. Charlottesville Family Svcs., Family Svcs. Albemarle County, 1992-93, Coun. on Aging, Lenoir County C.C., Am. Cancer Soc.; exec. dir. Cmty. Involvement Coun. Lenoir County, Kinston, 1979; county coord. Internat. Yr. of Child, Kinston, 1979; mem. women's task force U. Va. Med. Sch.; also others. Recipient Gov.'s award State of N.C., 1980, cert. of merit for svc. to children N.C. Dept. Human Resources, Outstanding Teaching award U. Va. Sch. Medicine, 1993; named Commencement speaker U. Va. Sch. Medicine Graduation, 1993. Mem. Va. Med. Soc. (editor med. news Va. Med. Quar., mem. legis. com.), Albemarle County Med. Soc. (sec. treas. 1995—), Mecklenberg County Med. Soc. (chmn. com. on tel-med. sys.), Va. Soc. Anesthesiology, U. Va. Sch. Medicine Alumni Assn. (assoc. bd. dirs. 1989-92), Greencroft Club. Office: U Va Med Sch PO Box 325 Charlottesville VA 22902-0325

DALTON, JENNIFER FAYE, accountant; b. Maryville, Tenn., May 1, 1959; d. James Theodore Teffeteller and Melody (Potts) Allison; m. Robert Byron Dalton, Dec. 15, 1979. Student, U. Tenn., 1977-79, Coastal Carolina Community Coll., 1980-81, 84-86; BS in Mgmt., Golden Gate U., Camp Lejeune, N.C., 1982. Bookkeeper, with accounts payable dept. McMar Too, Inc., Jacksonville, N.C., 1980-83; acctg. technician City of Jacksonville, 1983-89; acctg. mgr., corp. sec. treas. Bankers Mortgage Corp., Louisville, 1989-92; sr. acct., payroll officer City of Louisville, 1992—. Alcoa Found. scholar, 1977. Mem. Am. Payroll Assn., Payroll Profls. Kentuckiana, Amateur Radio Transmitting Soc., Inst. Mgmt. Accts., Gamma Beta Phi. Republican. Baptist. Home: 827 Markham Ln Louisville KY 40207-4444

DALTON, MARGARET ANNE, lawyer; b. Pitts., Dec. 6, 1951; d. Thomas John and Mary Olive (Paul) D.; m. Oliver E. Martin, Dec. 26, 1987. BA in Polit. Sci., NYU, 1973; JD, Fordham U., 1977. Bar: N.Y. 1978, U.S. Dist. Ct. (so. and ea. dists.) N.Y. 1979, Pa. 1987, Fla. 1990. Assoc. Mendes & Mount, N.Y.C., 1979-80; atty. news div. ABC, N.Y.C., 1980-85; TV news producer ABC Network, N.Y.C., 1985-86; sr. atty. Radio City Music Hall Prodns., Inc., N.Y.C., 1986-87; pvt. practice Stroudsburg, Pa., 1987-91; asst. county att., asst. port authority atty. Lee County, Ft. Myers, Fla., 1991-94; pvt. practice Ft. Myers, 1994—; family law mediator Fla., 1994—; asst. dist. atty. Monroe County, Pa., 1989-90; spl. hearing master 20th Jud. Cir., Fla., 1991—; adj. prof. Edison C.C., Ft. Myers, Fla., Barry U., Ft. Myers. Recipient Clio award Internat. Clio Award Com., 1978. Mem. Pa. Bar Assn., Fla. Bar Assn., N.Y. Bar Assn., Lee County Bar Assn. Roman Catholic. Office: 2316 Clifford St Fort Myers FL 33901

DALTON, PHYLLIS IRENE, library consultant; b. Marietta, Kans., Sept. 25, 1909; d. Benjamin Reuben and Pearl (Travelute) Bull; m. Jack Mason Dalton, Feb. 13, 1950. BS, U. Nebr., 1931, MA, 1941; MA, U. Denver, 1942. Tchr. city schs., Marysville, Kans., 1931-40; reference libr. Lincoln Pub. Libr., Nebr.; libr. U. Nebr., Lincoln, 1941-48; libr. Calif. State Libr., Sacramento, 1948-57, asst. state libr., 1957-72; pvt. libr. cons., Scottsdale, Ariz., 1972—. Author: Library Services to the Deaf and Hearing Impaired Individuals, 1985, 91 (Pres.' Com. Employment of Handicapped award 1985); contbr. chpt., articles, reports to books and publs. in field. Mem. exec. bd. So. Nev. Hist. Soc., Las Vegas, 1983-84; mem. So. Nev. Com. on Employment of Handicapped, 1980-89, chairperson, 1988-89; mem. adv. com. Nat. Orgn. on Disability, 1982-94; mem., sec. resident coun. Forum Pueblo Norte Retirement Village, 1990-91, pres. resident coun., 1991-94; bd. dirs. Friends of So. Nev. Libraries; trustee Univ. Library Soc., U. Nev.-Las Vegas; mem. Allied Arts Council, Pres.' Com. on Employment of People with Disabilities, mem. emeritus 1989—, Ariz. Gov.'s Com. on Employment of People with Disabilities, 1990—, Scottsdale Mayor's Com. on Employment of People with Disabilities, 1990—, Scottsdale Pub. Libr. Ams. With Disabilities Com., 1994—. Recipient Libraria Sodalitas, U. So. Calif., 1972, Alumni Achievement award U. Denver, 1977, Alumni Achievement award U. Nebr., Lincoln, 1983; named Mover and Shaker Scottsdale Mag., 1994. Mem. LWV, ALA (councilor 1963-64, exceptional svc. award 1981, award com. O.C.L.C. Humphreys Forest Press award 1994), Am. Assn. U. Women, Assn. State Librs. (pres. 1964-65), Calif. Libr. Assn. (pres. 1969), Nev. Libr. Assn. (hon.), Internat. Fedn. Libr. Assns. and Instns. (chair working group on libr. svc. to prisons, mem. standing com. Sect. Librs. Serving Disadvantaged Persons 1981-94), Nat. League Am. Pen Women (Las Vegas chpt. 1988-94, mem. com. on qualifications for Letters membership 1994—, parliamentarian Scottsdale chpt. 1989-94, v.p. 1992-94), Am. Correctional Assn. (libr. svcs. instns. com. 1994—), Pilot Internat. (mem.-at-large). Republican. Presbyterian. Home: 7090 E Mescal St Apt 261 Scottsdale AZ 85254-6125

DALY, CHERYL, broadcast executive; b. Providence, Apr. 20, 1947; d. Francis Patrick and Mary Ann (Wallis) D.; m. Arthur James Generas, July 18, 1970; 1 child, Caroline. BA, Douglass Coll., 1969; postgrad., Rutgers U., 1975-78. Account exec. Phil Dean Assocs., N.Y.C., 1969-72; dir. pub. rels. Kirkland Coll., Clinton, N.Y., 1972-75; mgr. press svcs. CBS Radio, N.Y.C., 1976-80; assoc. dir. internal comm. CBS, Inc., N.Y.C., 1980-81, dir. corp. info., 1981-83; v.p. pub. rels. Group W Satellite Comm., N.Y.C., 1984—; examiner Westinghouse Quality Awards, Pitts., 1990. Recipient Best Co. Communication award Cable TV Bus., 1986, mktg. award Westinghouse Broadcasting Co., 1991. Mem. Cable TV Pub. Affairs Assn. (bd. dirs. 1985-87), Media Mommies (co-founder 1987). Democrat. Roman Catholic. Home: 1 W 67th St New York NY 10023-6200 Office: Group W Satellite Comm 685 3rd Ave New York NY 10017-4099

DALY, JANET MORGAN, home furnishings marketing consultant, editor; b. White Plains, N.Y., Jan. 14, 1937; d. William George and Laura Elizabeth (Josten) Russell; m. Hugh Thomas Morgan Jr., June 27, 1959 (div. Oct. 1976); 1 child, Hugh Thomas; m. Alan Frederic Daly, Oct. 4, 1985. Student, Washington Sq. Coll., N.Y.C., 1954-55. Ops. mgr. WISH-TV, Indpls., 1967-68; freelance writer various trade books and periodicals, 1969-72; assoc. pub. Earnshaw's Rev. and Small World, N.Y.C., 1972-75; sr. editor Men's Wear mag., N.Y.C., 1975-79, Chain Store Age, N.Y.C., 1979-80, HFD and Home Fashions Textiles, N.Y.C., 1980-84; v.p. Dan River Co., N.Y.C., 1984, Gear, Inc., N.Y.C., 1985; editor Floor Covering Weekly, Garden City, N.Y., 1985-94, Home Furnishings At Retail, 1994—; editor, pub. Floor Covering Weekly, Garden City, N.Y., 1992-94; pres. A Daly Co., North Chatham, Mass., 1994—; tchr. Parsons Buying Interior Furnishings, N.Y.C., 1986-87. Editor U.S.A. Rugs Internat., 1994—. Vol. fin. com. ARC, Westchester County, N.Y., 1988-94. Mem. Internat. Furnishings and Design Assn. (pres. N.Y. chpt. 1986, mem. career day com. 1987-90, program v.p. 1991, membership v.p. 1992). Home: 26 Rowland Dr North Chatham MA 02650-0407 Office: A Daly Co PO Box 407 North Chatham MA 02650-0407

DALY, JANETTE M., state agency administrator; b. Elizabeth, N.J., Sept. 10, 1950; d. Edwin and Helen Elizabeth (Stoll) Vandewater; m. Robert Paul Daly, July 17, 1976; children: Colleen Elizabeth, Amilynne Mara. BA in Sociology cum laude, Rutgers U., 1976; MPA, Rutgers U., Newark, 1995. Cert. pub. mgr., N.J. Unemployment clk., benefits determination aide, claims examiner, investigator unemployment ins. State of N.J. Dept. Labor, Trenton, 1974-81, sr. claims examiner, asst. supr., sect. mgr. disability ins. divsn., 1982—. Author: (booklets) The History of Temporary Disability Insurance, 1989, Historical Highlights-Disability Insurance, 1989. Leader Girl Scouts U.S., Florence, N.J., 1987-88; dir. religious instrn. Our Lady Perpetual Help, Oley, Pa.; fundraiser Life Ctr. Acad., Florence, N.J., 1991—. Recipient Outstanding Achievement award Divsn. Temporary Disability Ins., 1994. Fellow Cert. Pub. Mgr.'s Soc.; mem. Am. Soc. Pub. Mgrs., Internat. Assn. Personnel in Employment Security, Fedn. Christian Ministries. Office: Divsn Temp Disability Ins Labor Bldg John Fitch Plz Trenton NJ 08625

DALY, JOE ANN GODOWN, publishing company executive; b. Galveston, Tex., Aug. 7, 1924; d. Elmer and Jessie Fee (Beck) Godown; m. William Jerome Daly, Jr., Jan. 25, 1958 (dec.). BA in Journalism, U. Okla., 1945, BA in Piano, 1952. Asst. editor house organ Southwestern Bell Telephone, St. Louis, 1945-47; sec. to city mgr. Okla. Daily News, Oklahoma City, 1947-49; pvt. piano tchr. Alva, Okla., 1952-54; sec. to editor Prentice-Hall, Inc., N.Y.C., 1954-55, asst. to children's book editor, 1955-58; asst. editor children's books Dodd, Mead & Co., N.Y.C., 1963, dir. children's books, 1965-88, asst. v.p., assoc. pub. children's books, 1986-88; editorial dir. Cobblehill Books affiliate Dutton Children's Books, N.Y.C., 1988—; mem. Children's Book Council, N.Y.C., 1963, treas., 1969; mem. CBC/LA Com., N.Y.C., 1980, CBC/Prelude Com., N.Y.C., 1983. Active Bklyn. Heights Assn., 1976—; friend Carnegie Hall, N.Y. Philharm.; mem. Met. Opera Guild, Mus. Modern Art, Mus. Natural History. Mem. Phi Beta Kappa, Sigma Delta Chi, Theta Sigma Phi, Mu Phi Epsilon. Democrat. Methodist. Home: 80 Cranberry St Brooklyn NY 11201-1784 Office: Penguin USA 375 Hudson St New York NY 10014-3658

DALY, MARY, college administrator; b. Erie, Pa., Dec. 29, 1943; d. Damian John and Letitia (Lawson) D. BS, Mercyhurst Coll., 1966; MA, Fairfield U., 1987. Dir. found. rsch. Mercyhurst Coll., Erie, 1966-67, dir. pub. rels., 1967-78, dir. publs., 1978-80, dir. spl. events and presdl. functions, 1980—, asst. dir. devel., 1972-80, asst. to the pres. for external affairs, 1980-89, sr. asst. to the pres., 1989-91, v.p. pub. rels., 1991—; comm. cons. Sisters of Mercy of Erie County, Erie, 1970—; polit. cons. Rep. Joseph Giles, Erie, 1980-90, Mayor Joyce Savocchio, Erie, 1986, 92. Creative dir. for publs. Bd. dirs. Gannondale, Erie, 1990-92, Internat. Inst., Erie, 1988-90, Zonta Club Erie, 1980-83, March of Dimes, Erie, 1981-82, Muscular Dystrophy, Erie, 1981-82, Florence Crittendon Home, Erie, 1983-87; mem. pub. rels. com. Libr. 21-Erie County Libr.; mem. merchandising, pub. rels., mktg. com. Greater Erie Bicentennial; active Leadership Erie; mem., bd. dirs. N.W. Pa. Miss Am. Pageant. Fulbright scholar for summer study in Egypt, 1977. Mem. Coun. for Advancement and Support of Edn. (Silver Medal Recognition awards 1986), Pub. Rels. Soc. Am., Am. Coun. on Edn. (regional rep.), Nat. Identification Program for Advancement of Women in Higher Edn., Erie Ad Club (past pres., George Mead Disting. Career award 1984), Lake View Country Club, Sales and Mktg. Execs., Coun. on Pa. Coll. Pub. Rels. Execs. Democrat. Roman Catholic. Home: 1142 W 33rd St Erie PA 16508-2432 Office: Mercyhurst Coll Glenwood Hills 501 E 38th St Erie PA 16546-0001

DALY, MIRIAM SHAMER, retired family physician; b. Balt., Jan. 26, 1925; d. Maurice Emory and Bertha (Tapman) Shamer; m. Harold L. Daly, Jr., June 28, 1948 (dec. July 2, 1989); children: John, Martha, Thomas, David. AB, Goucher Coll., 1946; MD, U. Md., 1950. Diplomate Am. Bd. Family Practice. Intern Luth. Hosp. of Md., Balt., 1950-51, resident, 1951-52; clinic physician Balt. City Health Dept., Md. State Health Dept., 1952-55; practicing physician Balt., 1952-55; physician pvt. practice Albion, Mich., 1955-93; ret., 1993. Leader, camp counsellor Girl Scouts, South Ctrl. Mich., 1955—, pres. Irish Hills Coun., 1993—, bd. dirs., 1990—; bd. dirs. Albion Ambulance Svc., 1989—, ARC Calhoun County chpt., 1993—, Great Lakes Region Blood Svcs., ARC, 1994—. Recipient Girl Scouts Thanks badge Irish Hills Girls Scouts Coun., 1983, Second Girl Scouts badge, 1993. Mem. AMA, Mich. State Med. Soc., Calhoun County Med. Soc., Am. Acad. Family Practice, Mich. Acad. Family Practice, S.W. Mich. Perinatal Assn., AAUW.

DALY, TYNE, actress; b. Madison, Wis., 1947; d. James Daly and Hope Newell; m. Georg Stanford Brown (div.); children: Alyxandra, Kathryne, Alisabeth. Student, Brandeis U., Am. Music and Dramatic Acad. Performed at Am. Shakespeare Festival, Stratford, Conn.; appeared on Broadway in Gypsy, 1990, 91 revivals, The Seagull, 1992; films include Angel Unchained, 1970, The Enforcer, 1976, The Entertainer, 1976, Speed Trap, 1977, Telefon, 1977, Zoot Suit, 1982, The Aviator, 1985, Movers and Shakers, 1985; made TV debut in series The Virginian; guest appearances in various TV series, starring role in Cagney & Lacey, 1982-88 (Emmy awards 1982, 83, 84, 88); TV films include In Search of America, 1971, A Howling in the Woods, 1971, Heat of Anger, 1972, The Man Who Could Talk to Kids, 1973, Larry, 1974, Intimate Strangers, 1977, Better Late Than Never, 1979, The Women's Room, 1980, A Matter of Life and Death, 1981, The Great Gilly Hopkins, 1981, Your Place or Mine, 1983, Kids Like These, 1987, Stuck With Each Other, 1989, The Last to Go, 1990, Face of a Stranger, 1991, On the Town, 1993, Scattered Dreams, 1994, Christy, 1994, Colombo: Bird in the Hand, 1994, Columbo: Undercover, 1994, The Forget-Me-Not Murders, 1994. Recipient Tony award for Mama Rose role in Gypsy, 1990. Address: The Blake Agy 415 N Cander Dr Ste 121 Beverly Hills CA 90210*

DALY-GAWENDA, DEBRA, health facility administrator, nursing educator; b. Chgo., Aug. 30, 1956; m. Tom Gawenda; children: Christopher, Haley, Zachary. Diploma, Michael Reese Hosp. Sch. Nsg., 1978; AA in Liberal Arts, Richard J. Daley Coll., 1982; BSN, Rush U., 1983; MS, U. Ill., Chgo., 1984. RN, Ill. Staff nurse emergency room Rush Med. Ctr., Chgo., Mercy Hosp. and Med. Ctr., Chgo.; instr. Rush. U., Chgo.; unit leader health svcs. Rush-Presbyn.-St. Luke's Med. Ctr., Chgo., dir. health svcs.; asst. prof. Rush U., Chgo.; lectr. in field. Contbr. articles to profl. publs. Mem. NAFE, Nat. Wellness Inst., Am. Assn. Occupational Health Nurses, Ill. Hosp. Assn. Occupational Health Nurses (past v.p.), Ill. Coun. Nurse Mgrs., Sigma Theta Tau (mem. nominating com.). Home: 8438 Buckingham Ct Willow Springs IL 60480-1144

DALZELL, GRACE ROSALIE, medical asoociation administrator; b. Mexico City, Dec. 2, 1936; came to U.S., 1941; d. Robert M. Dalzell and Anita Fernandez Dalzell Daniel, H. Morgan Daniel (stepfather); m. Joseph J. Matz, Apr. 11, 1955 (div. 1973); children: Anna Matz Bennett, Elizabeth G., Amelia Matz Reed, Adrienne Matz Carter, Eva E.; m. Emmet O. Whitaker, Jr., Nov. 7, 1974; 1 stepchild, John L. Whitaker. Student, Tex. Tech. U., 1960, Del Mar Coll., Corpus Christi, Tex., 1961, San Antonio Coll., 1975, St. Mary's U., 1976. Office mgr. Law Office Carl R. Crites, San Antonio, 1973-75; adminstr. U. Tex. Health Sci. Ctr., San Antonio, 1975-85; mgr. and adminstr. S. Tex. Orthopaedic & Spinal Surgery Assocs., San Antonio, 1986—, Ray Vista, Inc., San Antonio, 1987-94, Med Ptnrs., Birmingham, 1994—. Author poetry. Participant office edn. prog. Clark High Sch., San Antonio, 1980—; rep. United Way Fund Dr., San Antonio, 1979-81, co-rep., 1985; mem. Valley St. light com. City of Leon, 1977-78; vol. San Antonio Crisis Intervention Telephone Ctr., 1975-76. Recipient Recognition award Clark High Sch., 1988-89, Recognition cert. San Antonio Crisis Intervention Ctr., 1976. Mem. San Antonio Med. Mgrs., Tex. Soc. Med. Assts., Am. Inst. Profl. Bookkeepers, Tex. Med. Group Mgmt. Assn., HMC Mgrs. Task Force, Med. Group Mgmt. Assn., Voice for Animals, Profl. Assn. Health Care Office Mgrs., People for Ethical Treatment of Animals, Women's Humane Soc. Home: 6910 N Forest Crest St San Antonio TX 78240-3312 Office: 9150 Huebner Rd Ste 350 San Antonio TX 78240-1551

DALZELL, HELEN DEXTER, human resources professional; b. Cin., Jan. 13, 1941; d. Morris W. and Helen (Taylor) Dexter; m. Robert C. Dalzell, Sept. 16, 1978; 1 child, Elizabeth Louise. Student, Vassar Coll., 1959-62; BS, U. Miami, 1963; cert. in fin. planning, Coll. Fin. Planning, 1985. Mgmt. trainee Macy's, N.Y.C., 1963-64; adminstrv. asst. Tina Leser Internat., Bombay, India, 1964; asst. buyer Frederick Atkins, N.Y.C., 1964-65; counselor, mgr. Snelling & Snelling, N.Y.C., 1965-68; v.p., cons. Barnest & Boswell, N.Y.C., 1968-73; founder, pres. Taylor Assoc., N.Y.C., 1973-79; fin. planner IDS-Am. Express, Clearwater, Fla., 1984-87; pres., founder Taylor Assoc. Pers., Clearwater, Fla., 1987—. Tutor Pinellas County Schs., Clearwater, 1990-92; bd. dirs. Girls Clubs Pinellas County, Clearwater, 1983-92; mem. strategic planning Oak Grove Sch., Clearwater, 1991. Mem. Fla. Assn. Pers. Cons., Fine Arts Soc. (life), Clearwater C. of C., Clearwater Yacht Club, Rotary (Belleair chpt.). Republican. Presbyterian. Home: 1983 Belleair Rd Clearwater FL 34624 Office: Taylor Assoc Pers Cons 612 E Druid Rd Clearwater FL 34616

DALZELL, JEANNE ALEXANDER, publisher; b. New Haven, Nov. 3, 1929; d. John Morrell and Winnifred (Keeler) Alexander; m. David Rudolf Dalzell, Jr., Feb. 9, 1952 (div. Apr. 1972); children: David Paul, Jeffrey Alexander; m. James Kibler Chapman, Aug. 26, 1977 (div. Apr. 1989). Student, U. Wis., Janesville, 1968-70, Rockford (Ill.) Coll., 1971-72, Beloit (Wis.) Coll., 1974. Dir. Wright Art Mus., Beloit Coll., 1970-75, ARC, Pittsfield, Mass., 1975-77; pub. Berkshire Homebuyers Guide, Lenox, Mass., 1982-90. Exhibited in juried shows Madison Art Ctr., 1970, Beloit and vicinity, 1970, 73, Rockford and vicinity, 1972, Pittsfield, 1976, 77, also several invitational exhbns.; work represented in several pvt. collections; represented by Earthwork Gallery, Rockton, Ill.; judge Ill. Profl. Art Show, 1975. Former mem. Jr. League, Pittsfield, Mass.; organizer Berkshire Hist. Soc.; former mem. bd. Cmty. Music Sch., Berkshire Mus., Berkshire Art Ctr., Pittsfield. Recipient Achievement in Art award, 1st pl. Two D Design, U. Wis., 1969; Nat. Endowment for Arts grantee 1972, 75; curatorship program Asian Mus., San Francisco, 1975. Mem. Am. Assn. Mus., Berkshire Art Assn. Home and Office: PO Box 997 Osprey FL 34229

D'AMATO, EVA MARIA, emergency room and critical care nurse; b. Huntington, N.Y., Aug. 30, 1959; d. Anthony and Rita (Leslie) Medile; m. Salvatore Frank D'Amato, Mar. 2, 1985; children: Jessica, Salvatore Anthony. BS in Nursing, NYU, 1976; postgrad. Cert. Nurse Practitioner, MSN, SUNY, Stony Brook, 1991—. Cert. BCLS, ACLS; ARC; cert. in chemo therapy, N.Y., LPN, RN, N.Y. From candy striper to LPN Middle Island (N.Y.) Nursing Home, 1974-80; staff nurse Maimonides Med. Ctr., Bklyn., 1980-82; critical care nurse Univ. Hosp., Stony Brook, N.Y., 1982-83; hemodyalisis and intensive care nurse Sloan Kettering Meml. Hosp., N.Y.C., 1983-84; emergency room nurse Meth. Hosp., Bklyn., 1984-86; charge nurse drug dependent unit VA Med. Ctr., Bklyn., 1986-88; emergency room nurse Southside Hosp., Bayshore, N.Y., 1988-93; AIDS counselor Apple Drug Rehab. Therapeutic Cmty., 1993—; adj. nurse The Care Group, Melville, N.Y., 1990—; substance abuse and AIDS nurse. Recipient Regent's scholarsip, State of N.Y., 1976, Academic scholarship, NYU, 1976. Roman Catholic. Home: 425 Bellmore Ave Islip Terrace NY 11752-2901

D'AMATO, JEAN MARIE, classics educator; b. Boston, July 20, 1945; d. Hector Loreto and Frances Lydia (Trotta) D'A.; m. Fleming A. Thomas, Mar. 12, 1989. AB, Tufts U., 1967; MA, Middlebury Coll., 1969; PhD, Johns Hopkins U., 1975. Teaching asst. Intercollegiate Ctr. for Classical Studies, Rome, 1973-74; lectr. Williams Coll., 1975-76; asst. prof. classics U. So. Calif., 1976-81; humanities adminstr. NEH, Washington, 1984-88; prof. in charge, dir. Intercollegiate Ctr. for Classical Studies Northwestern State U., Natchitoches, La., 1981-82; assoc. prof. La. Scholars' Coll. Northwestern State U., Natchitoches, 1988—; humanities adminstr. NEH, 1984-87; dir. Vergilian Soc. Am. Rome and Cumae, summer 1978; co-dir. U. So. Calif., summer 1979, summer session in Rome Northwestern U., 1992, 94; cofounder Classica Americana. Author: A New Fragment of Eustathius of Matera, Mediaeval Studies, Vol. 46, 1984; contbr. articles to profl. jours.

Rsch. grantee NEH, 1990, Am. Philos. Assn., 1991; recipient Mildred Hart Bailey Rsch. award Northwestern State U. Fellow Am. Philos. Soc.; mem. AAUW (dissertation fellow 1972), Am. Philol. Assn., La. Classical Assn. (pres. 1991-92). Home: 332 Henry Ave Natchitoches LA 71457-5834 Office: La Scholars' Coll Northwestern State U Natchitoches LA 71457

DAMATO, KATHRYN LEATHEM, dental hygienist; b. Troy, N.Y., Nov. 30, 1948; d. James J. and Margurite (Judge) Leathem; m. Kenneth James Damato, May 7, 1977; children: Meaghan Leathem Damato, Kaitlyn Leathem Damato; 1 stepchild, Kenneth J. Damato. AS, Hudson Valley C.C.; BS, U. Bridgeport, 1972; MS, So. Conn. State U., 1976. Registered dental hygienist. Clin. dental hygienist pvt. practice, New Haven, Conn., 1975-85; instr. dept. dental hygiene U. Conn. Sch. Dental Medicine and Tunxis Coll., Farmington, Conn., 1985-89, asst. prof., 1989—; course leader for clin. component of dental hygiene curriculum, 1989—, dir. clin. affairs, 1992—. Co-editor: Clinical Dental Hygiene Handbook. Adviser Student Am. Dental Hygienist Assn., Conn., 1985-90; cons. infection control and task force AIDS, 1988—. Grantee AIDS Found. participation in Grant Edn., 1991, 92. Mem. AAUP, Am. Dental Hygienist Assn., Sigma Phi Alpha. Roman Catholic. Home: 1280 Durham Rd Wallingford CT 06492-2667 Office: U Conn Sch Dental Medicine Dept Dental Hygiene Mail Code 2105 Farmington CT 06509 also: Tunxis Coll RR 6 # 177 Woodbridge CT 06525

D'AMBRUOSO, LORRAINE PASZKEICZ, secondary school educator; b. New Haven, Oct. 8, 1942; d. Anthony Vito and Louise E. (Bellucci) D'A. BA, Santa Clara U., 1965, teaching credential, 1966; cert. pedagogique, Alliance Francaise, Paris, 1975. Tchr. French Mt. Pleasant High Sch., San Jose, Calif., 1966—; fgn. lang. coord. E. Side High Sch. Dist., San Jose, 1985—; cons. fgn. lang. edn., Calif., 1985—; mem. Calif. Fgn. Lang. Project, Stanford, 1991—; mem. Bay Area Fgn. Lang. Project, Stanford, 1993—. Recipient scholarship Alliance Francaise, Paris, 1975, Rockefeller fellowship, 1985, Fullbright fellowship, 1986, Franco Am. fellowship, 1991, NEH fellowship, 1993. Mem. Am. Assn. Tchrs. of French (v.p. 1987-90, pres. 1990-92), Fgn. Lang. Assn. of Santa Clara County (pres., Svc. award 1987, Outstanding Tchr. 1989), Calif. Fgn. Lang. Tchrs. Assn. (v.p. 1990-92, pres. 1992-94, Outstanding Tchr. 1990). Office: East Stide Union High Sch Dist 1750 S White Rd San Jose CA 95127

DAME GREENE, SUSAN, non profit fundraiser; b. Syracuse, N.Y., Feb. 17, 1948; d. Harold Paul and Margaret Mary (Poznanski) Dame; m. John J. Demlein, June 12, 1970 (div. Mar. 1982); children: Christopher John Demlein, Jessica Margaret Demlein. BA, Ithaca Coll., 1969; MLS, U. R.I., 1977. Trust officer First Bank, New Haven, 1980-83; trust new bus. officer R.I. Hosp. Trust Nat. Bank, Providence, 1983-84; v.p., mgr. trust dept. Old Colony/Newport Nat. Bank, Providence, 1984-86; v.p., dr. trust v.p. 1st Nat. Bank Litchfield, Conn., 1987-89; sr. cons./trust and planned giving Investment Futures, Litchfield, 1989-92; assoc. dir. planned giving St. Jude Children's Rsch. Hosp., Memphis, 1992; dir. major and planned gifts Childreach, Warwick, R.I., 1992-94; sr. assoc. dir. gift planning ARC Nat. Hdqs., Washington, 1994—; cons. in field, 1985—. Bd. dirs. Women's Devel. Corp., Providence, 1983-87, Hospice Care of R.I., 1985-89, Susan B. Anthony Project, Torrington, Conn., 1989-90; fin. advisor to numerous nonprofit orgns, including Women's Health, New Haven, YWCA, Groton, Dorcas Pl., Providence; bd. mem. Litchfield County Women's Network, 1987-92, chair several coms.; founding incorporator Planned Giving Coun. of Memphis, 1992; dir. Project Hometown Am., United Way of Providence, 1986. Named Outstanding Vol. of Yr., United of S.E. Conn., 1987. Mem. Planned Giving Coun. R.I. (pres. 1993-94, founding incorporator), Planned Giving Group of New Eng., Nat. Com. on Planned Giving (del., local pres.), Planned Giving Coun. Memphis (nat. del. 1992-93), Planned Giving Study Group of Washington, Women in Devel. Unitarian Universalist. Home: Apt B 702 505 N Roosevelt Blvd Falls Church VA 22044

DAMES, JOAN FOSTER (MRS. URBAN L. DAMES), magazine editor, columnist; b. New Orleans, Sept. 29, 1934; d. Albert Steere and Lucia (Valdes) Foster; m. Urban Louis Dames, Feb. 10, 1959 (dec.); children: Alice Dames Whittaker, Lucia Ann Dames Byrns, Cecilia Dames Scherer, Madeline Sophie. Student, St. Louis U., 1953-56. Seismograph rec. librarian St. Louis U., 1954-55; feature writer St. Louis Globe Democrat, 1955-59; feature writer St. Louis Post-Dispatch, 1966-68, women's editor, 1968-79; editor Everyday mag., 1972-79, features editor, 1973-79, features dir., 1975-78, travel editor, 1979-91, columnist, 1979—; sr. feature writer St. Louis Post-Dispatch, 1991—; mem. pres.'s adv. coun. St. Louis U. High Sch., 1979-82; adv. Full Achievement, St. Louis U., 1982-84; v.p. St. Louis Bridal Bur., 1959—; bd. dirs. Southside Day Nursery, 1983-84; mem. pres. adv. coun. St. Louis area Girl Scouts Am., 1992-94. Radio personality: sta. KMOX-CBS, 1969-71; Author: Prelude, 1956. Bd. dirs. White House Retreat League Inc., 1993—. Recipient Mo. Press Women's Quest award, 1993, Media award, Mental Health Assn. St. Louis, 1993. Mem. Soc. Am. Social Scribes (bd. dirs. 1969-72), DAR (vice regent Ft. San Carlos chpt. 1992—). Home: 7149 Lindell Blvd Saint Louis MO 63130-4404 Office: 900 N Tucker Blvd Saint Louis MO 63101-1069

DAMICO, DEBRA LYNN, college administrator, English educator; b. Passaic, N.J., Apr. 15, 1956; d. Nicholas Biagio and Eleanore Lorraine (Hugle) D. BA, Montclair State Coll., 1978, MA, 1989; MA, 1989. Cert. tchr., N.J, reading specialist. Tchr. St. Francis Sch., Hackensack, N.J., 1978-79, Saddle Brook (N.J.) High Sch., 1979-80, St. Dominic Acad., Jersey City, 1980-84; adult basic edn./gen. edn devel. and ESL instr. Adult Learning Ctr. Montclair (N.J.) State Coll., 1974—; internat. student advisor Manhattan Coll., Bronx, N.Y., 1984—, ESL instr., 1986—; instr. Writing Inst. Adult Edn. Resource Ctr., Jersey City State Coll., 1987—; Outstanding Internat. Student advisor, 1989—. Mem. Dist. Wide Curriculum Council, Lodi, N.J., 1977-78; ch. cantor and musician. Nat. Assn. for Foreign Student Affairs grantee, 1985-86; named Outstanding Young Woman Am., 1986. Mem. Nat. Assn. Tchrs. of English as a Fgn. Lang., N.Y. Tchrs. of ESL, Nat. Assn. Fgn. Student Affairs-Assn. of Internat. Educators, Metro-Internat., Am. Assn. Tchrs. French, YMCA Internat. Student Svc., Kappa Delta Pi, Pi Delta Phi. Democrat. Roman Catholic. Office: Manhattan Coll 4513 Manhattan College Pky Bronx NY 10471-4004

D'AMICO, HILDA RUTH, pathologist; b. Santiago, Chile, Aug. 1, 1947; came to U.S., 1976; d. Orlando Martiniano and Hilda Ines (Scharpe) Pezoa; m. Jose Manuel D'Amico, Sept. 4, 1973; 1 child, Sebastian. BS, Liceo Santiago, 1964; MD, U. Chile, Santiago, 1973. Academic-in-tng. U. Chile, 1973-76, pathologist, 1976; resident pathology St. Joseph's Hosp., Phoenix, 1977-81; fellow hematopathology Meml. Hosp., Long Beach, Calif., 1981-83, U. Irvine, Orange, Calif., 1981-83; pathologist Colmery O'Neil VA Med. Ctr., Topeka, 1983—. Roman Catholic. Home: 3131 SW Arrowhead Rd Topeka KS 66614-4163 Office: Colmery O'Neil VA Med Ctr 2200 Gage Blvd Topeka KS 66622

D'AMICO, MARY BARBARA, nurse; b. Hope, Kans., Dec. 19, 1940; d. James Vincent Mullin and Rosyln Beverly (Page) McFarland; m. Vincent Mario D'Amico, Aug. 26, 1967; children: Michael Anthony, Matthew Morris. BS, Grove City Coll., 1962; MS in Nursing, N.Y. Med. Coll. Grad. Sch., 1966, MS in Neurol. Nursing, 1969. Sci. tchr. Peace Corps, Sierra Leone, West Africa, 1962-63; rsch. asst. Metabolic Rsch. Ctr./Highland Hosp., Oakland, Calif., 1963-64; med.-surgical nurse Georgetown U. Hosp./Mt. Sinai Hosp., Washington and N.Y.C., 1966-67; clin. instr. N.Y. Med. Coll. Grad. Sch. of Nursing, 1967-68; clin. specialist in neurosurg. Met. Hosp., N.Y.C., 1969-73; instr. Grad. Sch. of Nursing/Pace U., Pleasantville, N.Y., 1973-74, 76-77; adminstrv. asst. Wise Svcs., 1994; quality assurance com. Newborn Resources, Inc., 1993—. Editor/author: (procedure book) Metropolitan Hospital Nursing Procedures, 1971. Bd. dirs., sec. United Way of Greater White Plains, N.Y., 1988-91; pres. Elmsford (N.Y.) Beautification Com., 1989-94; bd. dirs. Westchester Tchr. Ctr., Hartsdale, N.Y., 1988-91; pres. Greenburgh Ctrl. Sch. Dist. #7, PTA, Hartsdale, 1991-93; assoc. dir. Westchester County PTA, 1994-95. Mem. Leinhard Sch. of Nursing Alumni Assn., N.Y. State Nurses Assn., N.Y. Acad. Sci., N.Y. Zool. Soc. Home and Office: 14 Crescent Dr S Elmsford NY 10523-2802

D'AMICO, MARY ELLEN LAWSON, account executive; b. Hawkinsville, Ga., Aug. 15, 1964; d. William Carlton and Lavada (Scarborough) Lawson; m. Joseph Allen D'Amico, Feb. 29, 1992. ABA, Middle Ga. Coll., 1984; BBA in Fin., U. Ga., 1987; MBA, Mercer U., 1993. Corp. sec.-treas. So. Cotton Co., Cochran, Ga., 1980-94; budget analyst Legis. Budget Office, Atlanta, 1987-88; realtor Coldwell Banker, Atlanta, 1988-94; risk mgr. Ga. State Govt., Atlanta, 1990-91; pres. Atlanta Internat., Inc., 1991—; internat. account exec. Scanwell Freight Express, 1994—. Sec. Young Dems. of DeKalb County, Decatur, Ga., 1990; mem. Jr. League of DeKalb County, Atlanta, 1992; county coord. County Coord. for Gov., 1982-86; nat. com. woman Young Dems. of Ga., 1991-92; vol. Internat. Reguge Com. Mem. NAFE, Women in Internat. Trade, Atlanta C. of C., Artemis Club (charter). Baptist. Office: Atlanta Internat Inc 2480 Briarcliff Rd NE # 304 Atlanta GA 30329-3034

DAMON, CINDY IRENE, nurse; b. Rochester, Minn., Sept. 1, 1958; d. Raymond Louis and Corrine Ida (Clark) Hinze; m. Darrel James Damon, July 5, 1986; children: Deanna, Jared, Deidre. Grad., St. Mary's Sch., Rochester, 1978; BS, U. Wis., Milw., 1992. LPN, Ill.; RN, Ill. Nursing asst. Ostrander (Minn.) Care Ctr., 1975-76, Madonna Towers, Rochester, 1976-77; nurse St. Marys Hosp., Rochester, 1981-86; asst. to dispatcher Elk River Concrete Co., Shakopee, Minn., 1980-81; nurse Rochester Meth. Hosp., 1981-86, Victory Meml. Hosp., Waukegan, Ill., 1986—. Mem. Golden Key Honor Soc., Sigma Theta Tau. Methodist.

DAMON, GENE See **GRIER, BARBARA G.**

D'AMORE, HALLIE, make-up artist. TV movies include: This Child is Mine, 1985, A Smoky Mountain Christmas, 1986, The Outside Woman, 1989, Gypsy, 1993; films include: Back to School, 1986, 52 Pick-Up, 1986, Steel Magnolias, 1989, Dick Tracy, 1990, The Indian Runner, 1991, Defending Your Life, 1991, Doc Hollywood, 1991, Bugsy, 1991, Unlawful Entry, 1992, Toys, 1992, Straight Talk, 1992, Josh and S.A.M., 1993, Fatal Instinct, 1993, Forrest Gump, 1994 (Acad. award nom., Best Make-up). *

DAMSBO, ANN MARIE, psychologist; b. Cortland, N.Y., July 7, 1931; d. Jorgen Einer and Agatha Irene (Schenck) D. B.S., San Diego State Coll., 1952; M.A., U.S. Internat. U., 1974, Ph.D., 1975. Diplomate Am. Acad. Pain Mgmt. Commd. 2d lt. U.S. Army, 1952, advanced through grades to capt., 1957; staff therapist Letterman Army Hosp., San Francisco, 1953-54, 56-58, 61-62, Ft. Devers, Ft. Devens, Mass., 1955-56, Walter Reed Army Hosp., Washington, 1958-59, Tripler Army Hosp., Hawaii, 1959-61, Ft. Benning, Ga., 1962-64; chief therapist U.S. Army Hosp., Ft. McPherson, Ga., 1964-67; ret. U.S. Army, 1967; med. missionary So. Presbyterian Ch., Taiwan, 1968-70; psychology intern So. Naval Hosp., San Diego, 1975; predoctoral intern Naval Regional Med. Ctr., San Diego, 1975-76, postdoctoral intern, 1975-76, chief, founder pain clinic, 1977-86; chief pain clinic, 1977-86; adj. tchr. U. Calif. Med. Sch., San Diego; lectr., U.S., Can., Eng., France, Australia; cons. forensic hypnosis to law enforcement agys.; approved cons. in hypnosis. Contbr. articles to profl. publs., chpt. to book. Tchr. Sunday sch. United Meth. Ch., 1945—; Rep. Nat. Candidate Trust Presdl. adv. com., platform planning commn. at-large-del. Fellow Am. Soc. Clin. Hypnosis (psychology mem. at large, exec. bd. 1989-90); mem. San Diego Soc. Clin. Hypnosis (pres. 1980), Am. Phys. Therapy Assn., Calif. Soc. Clin. and Hypnosis (bd. govs.), Am. Soc. Clin. Hypnosis Edn. Rsch. Found. (trustee 1992-94), AAUW, Internat. Platform Assn., Am. Soc. Clin. Hypnosis (exec. bd.) Ret. Officers Am., Retired officers Assn. (rep. presdl. task force, pres. adv. com.), Toastmasters (local pres.), Job's Daus. Republican. Home and Office: 1062 W 5th Ave Escondido CA 92025-3802

DAMSEY, JOAN, medical management consultant; b. Jamestown, N.Y., Sept. 12, 1931; d. Frederick Vincent and Sara (Caccamise) Landy; m. Lloyd Damsey, June 12, 1955 (dec. Oct. 1985); children: Eve, Laurie, Lloyd Jr., J. Landy. BA, Coll. St. Elizabeth, 1953; MA, Cath. U. Am., 1961. Founder, bd. dirs. First Nat. Bank Fla. Keys, Marathon, 1974-83; pres. Damsey & Assocs. Ltd., Portsmouth, Va., 1980—; dir. practice mgmt. Eastern Va. Med. Sch., Norfolk, 1982—; founder Resource Bank, Virginia Beach, Va. Author: Joan Damsey Mgmt. Semicars, 1986, (book) Increasing Referrals, 1993; mem. editorial adv. bd. Physicians Fin. News; contbr. chpts. to books and articles to mgmt. jours. Vice chmn. Dem. State Com., Fla., 1964-68; del. Dem. Nat. Conv., Atlantic City, 1964; bd. dirs., vice chmn. St. Mary's Infant Home. Fellow Am. Coll. Med. Group Adminstrs. (bd. dirs., devel. chmn. 1991—); mem. Med. Group Mgmt. Assn. (bd. dirs.), Tidewater Med. Group Mgmt. Assn., Soc. Med.-Dental Cons., Va. Med. Group Mgmt. Assn., Med. Soc. Va. (edn. com.), Chesapeake Bay Found. (chmn. bd. dirs. 1991—). Roman Catholic.

DANA, JERILYN, ballet company administrator; b. Portland, Maine, Aug. 16, 1949; d. Mark and Eleanore (Colvin) Doucette. Dancer Boston Ballet Co., 1967-74, Chgo. Lyric Opera, 1969-70; dancer Les Grands Ballets Canadiens, Montreal, 1975-86, prin. dancer; exec. asst. to artistic dir. Boston Ballet, 1987—. Scholar Ford Found., 1963, 64. Office: Boston Ballet 19 Clarendon St Boston MA 02116-6100

DANAHER, MALLORY MILLETT (MALLORY JONES), actress, photographer, writer, poet; b. St. Paul, 1939; d. James Albert and Helen Rose (Feely) Millett m. Thomas C. Danaher, Mar. 1985; 1 child by previous marriage, Kristen Vigard. BA, U. Minn. Chief fin. officer Sheets & Co., N.Y.C. Active with N.Y. Theatre 1971-90; mem. original cos. of Annie and The Best Little Whorehouse in Texas, 1977; appeared in stage roles in Dodsworth, Berkshire Theatre Festival, Hedda Gabler, Kennedy's Children (dir. Olympia Dukakis), Edward Albee's Everything in the Garden (dir. Shelley Winters), House of Blue Leaves by John Guare, Berkshire Theatre Festival, Tornado, Lincoln Ctr. Libr. Theatre, Stella, Nat. Horn Theatre, N.Y.C., Cocteau's one-character play The Human Voice at Deutsches-Haus, NYU, Full Moon and High Tide (dir. Shelley Winters); off-Broadway prodn. Loose Connections, Judith Anderson Theatre; also (TV series) Love of Life, CBS-TV, Another World, NBC, Hunter, Thirtysomething, Superior Ct., Divorce Ct., The Judge, (NBC Movie of the Week) Eischied: Only the Pretty Girls Die, (motion picture) Tootsie, Columbia Pictures, Hell Hath No Fury with Barbara Eden, New Line Cinema: Alone in the Dark; exhibitor of photography: Third Eye Gallery, N.Y.C., 1974—, Modernage Discovery Gallery, N.Y.C., 1976-79, Gallery of St. Clement's, N.Y.C., 1979; performer own poetry; author: Fatherless Child; co-producer, subject of film Three Lives; contbr. poetry to mags. Mem. The Actors' Studio. Mem. The Creative Coalition. Mem. Nat. Assn. TV Programming Execs., Women in Theatre, St. James Club, Nat. Assn. for Self-Employed, Am. Women's Econ. Devel., The Friars Club.

DANBURG, DEBRA, state legislator; b. Houston, Sept. 25, 1951; d. Stanley and Barbara Jean (Walker) D. BA, U. Houston, 1974, JD, 1979. Asst. dir., lobbyist Texans for ERA, 1974-75; atty. pvt. practice, Houston, 1979—; mem. Tex. Ho. of Reps., 1981—, house com. on state affairs, 1991—, chmn. house coms. on elections, 1991—; mem. Appropriations Com.; chair Budget & Oversight for Cultural and Hist. Resources Com., Appropriations Subcom. on AIDS; mem. Appropriations Subcom. on the State Employee Classification System; Speaker's appointments Tex. Adv. Commn. on Intergov. Rels. and Tex. Health & Human Svcs. Coord. Coun., 1992; del. Dem. Nat. Convention, 1984; mayoral appointee City of Houston's Mcpl. Arts Commn., 1991—; hon. bd. dirs. S.W. region Am. Jewish Congress; mem. Leadership Am., Tex. coun. Family Violence; ex-officio dir. San Jacinto River Assn., 1992; speaker's appointments Elections Adv. Com., State Artist Com., Select Com. on Rules; mem. faculty in residence, new leadership program Ctr. Am. Women in Politics, Rutgers, 1994; mem. 3rd Conf. Jewish Parliamentarians in Israel, 1993; speaker Jewish Women's Leadership Conf. in Israel, 1994. Named Outstanding feminist Now, 1975, best legislator Houston mag., 1981, Vol. of Yr. KS/AIDS Found., 1984, Outstanding Houston Profl. Woman by Fedn. of Houston Profl. Women, 1988, Tex. Recreation and Park Soc. Legislator of Yr., 1987, Friend of Psychology, Tex. Psychology Assn., 1992, Alumnae of Yr., U. Houston Coll. Social Scis., 1993; recipient Spl. Presdl. award Houston Apt. Assn., 1985, Environ. Def. award Sierra Club, 1987, Outstanding Legislator award Tex. Assn. of Symphony Orchs., 1990, Good Brick award Greater Houston Preservation Alliance, 1990, Mary Polk award Tex. Coun. Family Violence, Unsung Heroine award The Women's Advocacy Project, 1991, Women's Suffrage award Houston Area Women's Ctr., 1991. Mem. Harris County Criminal Lawyers Assn. (bd. dirs. 1982-83), Nat. Trust Hist. Preservation (hon.), Sierra Club. Office: Tex Ho Reps PO Box 2910 Austin TX 78768-2910

DANCY, VERONICA ANN, utilities company representive; b. Martinsville, Va., June 24, 1945; d. John and Sarah Hazel Robertson; m. John Oliver Brooks, Mar. 31, 1963 (div.); children: John Eugene, Anthony Burdette; m. James Elbert Dancy. A in Criminal Justice, Mattatuck Community Coll., 1992; B in Human Svcs., Springfield Coll., 1993; postgrad., LaSalle U., 1994—. Customer svc. rep. Northeast Utilities Co., Waterbury, Conn., now sr. bus. office rep.; sr. bus. rep. Yankee Gas Co.; pres. JARVAM, Inc.; land owner and developer. Active various Waterbury, Conn. civic orgns. including hospitality com. Zion Bapt. Ch., NOW, Inc., NAACP, v.p. Willing Workers; mem. Mayor's Task Force, Waterburn; chairwoman Scovill Home Assn.; tutor Grandville Acad. Recipient Women In Leadership award for community involvement YWCA, 1988. Mem. Hospitality Club. Home: 233 Wood St Waterbury CT 06704-3722

DANCYGER, RUTH, art historian; b. Cleve., Nov. 11, 1918; d. Henry and Nellie (Friedman) Steuer; married, Dec. 21, 1939; widowed, July 1968; children: Polly Sherard, Emily Edelstein. Student, Goucher Coll., 1936-38; BA, Case Western Res. U., 1942; MA, John Carroll U., 1966. Art historian John Carroll U., Cleve., 1987-93; art historian Cleve. Artists Found., 1986—, also bd. dirs.; art historian Cleve. Artists Now, 1993—. Author monographs in field. Bd. dirs. Temple Mus., 1984—; mem. mayor's com. Adopt-A-Sculpture, 1993, women's coun. Cleve. Mus. Art, 1994, Cleve. Ctr. for Contemporary Art, 1985—; docent Coun. of Cleve. Ctr. for Contemporary Art, 1989—. Ohio Bell Telephone Co. grantee, 1987. Mem. Cleve. Soc. for Contemporary Art (program and travel planner 1989—), Cleve. Print Club. Home: 2632 S Green Rd Cleveland OH 44122-1536

DANDOY, MAXIMA ANTONIO, education educator emeritus; b. Santa Maria, Ilocos, Sur., Philippines; came to U.S., 1949, naturalized, 1951; d. Manuel and Isidra (Mendoza) Antonio. Teaching cert., Philippine Normal Coll., 1938; A.B., Nat. Tchrs. Coll., Manila, 1947; M.A., Arellano U., Manila, 1949; Ed.D. (John M. Switzer scholar, Newhouse Found. scholar), Stanford U., 1951, postgrad. (Calif. Fedn. Bus. and Profl. Women's Club scholar), 1952. Tchr. elem. sch. Philippines, 1927-37; lab. sch. tchr. Philippine Normal Coll., Manila, 1938-49; instr. Arellano U., Manila, 1947-49; lab. sch. prin. U. of East, Manila, 1953-54; assoc. prof. U. of East, 1952-55; prof. edn. Calif. State U., Fresno, 1956-82, prof. edn. emeritus, 1982—; curriculum writer, gen. office supr. Manila Dept. Edn., 1944-45; Mem. com. for the selection social studies textbooks for state adoption Calif., 1970-71; vis. prof. UCLA, 1956; Floro Crisologo Meml. lectr. U. No. Philippines, 1977. Author: Teaching Competencies, A Workbook and Log, 1985. Mem. Friends of the Stanford (Calif.) U. Sch. Edn., 1993, Sch. of Edn. and Human Devel. Alumni and Friends, Calif. State U., Fresno, 1992-93; mem. Calif. Gov.'s Conf. on Traffic Safety, 1962, Calif. Gov.'s Conf. Delinquency Prevention, 1963. Named Disting. Woman of Year, Fresno Bus. and Profl. Women's Club, 1957, Woman of Achievement, 1973, Outstanding Filipino, 1982; recipient Higher Edn. and Internat. Understanding award Philippine Normal Coll. Alumni Assn., 1986. Mem. Nat. Council Social Studies (chmn. sec. internat. understanding, nat. conv. 1966), Calif. Fedn. Bus. and Profl. Women's Clubs (state chmn. scholarships 1961-63, treas. Fresno), Calif. Tchrs. Assn., AAUW (liaison Calif. State U. Fresno 1970-71), Orgn. Filipino-Am. Educators Fresno (pres. 1977-92, life pres.), Filipino-Am. Women's Club (adv. 1969-74), Internat. Platform Assn., Phi Delta Kappa, Pi Lambda Theta, Kappa Delta Pi (counselor 1972-79, nat. com. attendance and credentials 1975, nat. com. regional confs. 1966). Home: 1419 W Bullard Ave Fresno CA 93711-2324 Office: Calif State U Fresno CA 93740

D'ANDREA, DEBORAH DAWN, nurse consultant, critical care nurse; b. Chgo.. ADN, Prairie State Coll., Chgo. Heights, Ill., 1970; BA in psychology, Lewis U., 1980, BSN, 1984. RN, Ill., Fla. Staff nurse post anesthesia recovery-surg. ICU Cook County Hosp., Chgo., 1970-72; staff nurse surg. ICU U. Chgo. Hosp. and Clinic, 1972-75, dir. utilization review dept., 1975-79; cons. profl. review orgn. utilization review Chgo. Found. Med. Care, 1979-81; staff nurse psychiat. adolescent Chgo. Lake Shore Hosp., 1981-82; staff nurse psychiat. adolescent and adult Charter Barclay Hosp., 1982-84; utilization review quality assurance nurse Grant Hosp., Chgo., 1982-84, educator staff devel., 1983-84; staff nurse trauma ctr. Cook County Hosp., 1984-86; staff nurse emergency trauma Louis A. Weiss Hosp., Chgo., 1986-88; utilization review coord. Charter Barclay Hosp., 1986-90; prin. Deborah D. D'Andrea & Assoc., 1989—; legal nurse cons. Jeffrey M. Goldberg & Assoc., Chgo., 1991; owner Med. Legal Cons. Assoc., Chgo., 1992—. Recipient Internat. Woman of Yr., 1992-93. Mem. AACN, NAFE, ATLA, Am. Assn. Legal Nurse Cons. (bd. dirs. 1994), Am. Assn. Post Anesthesia Nurses, Nat. Nurses Bus. Assn., Emergency Nurses Assn. Home: 716 W Briar Pl Chicago IL 60657-4515 Office: Med Legal Consulting Assoc 716 W Briar Pl Ste 3 Chicago IL 60657-4515

DANFORD, ARDATH ANNE, retired librarian; b. Lima, Ohio, Feb. 11, 1930; d. Howard Gorby and Grace Rose (Klug) D. B.A., Fla. State U., 1951, M.A., 1952. Head tech. services Lima Pub. Library, 1956-60; librarian Way Pub. Library, Perrysburg, Ohio, 1960-70; asst. dir. Toledo-Lucas County Pub. Library, 1971-77, dir., 1977-85, ret., 1985. Author: The Perrysburg Story, 1966, Perrysburg Revisited, 1992. Bd. dirs. Toledo Cmty. Found., Hist. Perrysburg Inc., Libr. Legacy Found., Way Libr. Found., Sisters of Mercy No. Health Found.; mem. adv. bd. St. Charles Hosp. Recipient Toledo Headliner award Women in Communication, 1978, Boss of Yr. award PerRoMa chpt. Am. Bus. Women's Assn., 1978. Mem. ALA, Ohio Libr. Assn. (Librarian of Yr. 1985, Hall of Fame 1993), Toledo Club, Perrysburg Garden Club, Zonta (pres. Toledo club 1975-76). Methodist. Home: 1075 Cherry St Perrysburg OH 43551-1615

DANG, KATHERINE, school administrator; b. San Francisco, Nov. 17, 1948; d. Ling Dor and Lei (Chin) D. BA in History, U. Calif., Berkeley, 1970. Tchr. Am. Heritage Christian Sch., Hayward, Calif., 1970-77, asst. adminstr., 1977-79; co-founder, adminstrv. dir. Chinese Christian Schs., San Leandro, Calif., 1979—; cons. Cornerstone Christian Coop Sch., Gilroy, Calif., 1993-94. Contbr. articles to profl. jours. Mem. adv. bd. Am. Christian History Inst., 1990—; bd. dirs. Pilgrim Inst., 1994. Republican. Office: Chinese Christian Schs 750 Fargo Ave San Leandro CA 94579

D'ANGELO, BEVERLY, actress; b. Columbus, Ohio, Nov. 15, 1954. cartoonist Hanna-Barbera Studios, Hollywood, Calif., former singer with Rompin' Ronnie Hawkins. Actress: (feature films) The Sentinel, 1977, Annie Hall, 1977, First Love, 1977, Every Which Way but Loose, 1978, Hair, 1979, Coal Miner's Daughter, 1980, Honky Tonk Freeway, 1981, Paternity, 1981, National Lampoon's Vacation, 1983, Finders Keepers, 1984, National Lampoon's European Vacation, 1985, Big Trouble, 1986, Maid to Order, 1987, In the Mood, 1987, Aria, 1988, Trading Hearts, 1988, High Spirits, 1988, National Lampoon's Christmas Vacation, 1989, Daddy's Dying...Who's Got The Will?, 1990, Pacific Heights, 1990, The Miracle, 1991, The Pope Must Die, 1991, Man Trouble, 1992, Lonely Hearts, 1992; (stage prodns.) Rockabye Hamlet, Hey, Marilyn, The Zinger, Simpatico; (TV movies) A Streetcar Named Desire, 1984, Doubletake, 1985, Hands of a Stranger, 1987, Trial: The Price of Passion, 1992, A Child Lost Forever, 1992, Judgement Day: The John List Story, 1993. Recipient CMA award 1981, Golden Globe award, 1981, Golden Reed award, 1981, Emmy award Nomination, 1985. Office: William Morris Agy 151 El Camino Beverly Hills CA 90212*

DANIEL, BARBARA ANN, secondary education educator; b. LaCrosse, Wis., Mar. 22, 1938; d. Rudolph J. and Dorothy M. (Farnham) Beranek; m. David Daniel; children: Raychelle, Clarence, Bernadette, Brenda. BS in Edn. cum laude, Midwestern U., Wichita Falls, Tex., 1967; postgrad., U. Alaska, Fairbanks, Anchorage, Juneau, U. Alaska, Bethel. Cert. tchr., Alaska. Primary tchr. Bur. Indian Affairs, Nunapitchuk and Tuntutuliak, Alaska, 1967-70; tchr. English lang. devel. and ESL grades 5-12, site career counselor Lower Kuskokwim Sch. Dist., Tuntutuliak, 1981—; mem. lang. arts curriculum revision task force Lower Kuskokwim Sch. Dist.; mem. state bd. Academic Pentathlon, Alaska; acad. decathlon, pentathlon coach. Rsch. video recording of elders in Alaskan village. Mem. NEA, Lower Kuskokwin Edn. Assn., Nat. Coun. Tchrs. English, Alaska Coun. Tchrs. English. Home: 25 West Circle PO Box Wtl Tuntutuliak AK 99680-9998

DANIEL, BETH, professional golfer; b. Charleston, S.C., Oct. 14, 1956; d. Robert and Lucia D. Grad., Furman U., 1978. Profl. golfer Ladies Profl. Golf Assn. tour, 1979—; Winner U.S. Amateur Title, 1975, 77; youngest mem. S.C. Hall of Fame, 1979. Recipient 1st pl. awards: Patty Berg Classic, 1979, World Ladies, Japan, 1979, World Series Women's Golf, 1980, 81, Columbia Savs. Classic, 1980, 82, Patty Berg Classic, 1980, Golden Lights, 1980, J.C. Penney Classic, 1981, 90 (with Davis Love III), Lady Citurs, 1981, Bent Tree Classic, 1982, Sun City Classic, 1982, Birmingham Classic, 1982, J & B Putting Championship, 1982, 85, WUI Classic, 1982, McDonald's Kids Classic, 1983, Kyocera Inamori Classic, 1985, Rail Charity Classic, 1989, 90, Konica San Jose Classic, 1989, Greater Washington Open, 1989, Safeco Classic, 1989, LPGA Championship, 1990, Orix Hawaiian Open, 1990, Kemper Open, 1990, Centel Classic, 1990, Northgate Classic, McDonald's Championship, Phar Mor Classic, 1990, 91; Mazda Series winner, 1982; named Rookie of Yr., Ladies Profl. Golf Assn., 1979, Player of Yr., 1980, Golfer of Yr. Seagrams Seven Crown Royal, 1981. Office: care Pros Inc PO Box 673 Richmond VA 23206-0673

DANIEL, CATHERINE, accountant; b. Shamokin, Pa., Mar. 25, 1957; d. William Martin and Patricia (Bartholomew) Jaworski; m. David Andrew Daniel, Feb. 17, 1979; 1 child, Kelly Lynn. AA in Bus. Adminstrn., Harrisburg (Pa.) Area C.C., 1990; BS in Acctg., Pa. State U., 1992. Asst. acct. LWV, Harrisburg, 1990-92; acct. KPMG Peat Marwick, Harrisburg, 1992-94, Commonwealth Pa., Harrisburg, 1994—. Mem. Inst. Mgmt. Accts. (dir. roster book 1991-92, dir. employment 1992-94). Democrat. Roman Catholic.

DANIEL, CATHY BROOKS, tutor, educational consultant; b. Nashville, Sept. 1, 1946; d. Conway William and Alliene Marie (Gilliam) B.; m. James Newton Daniel Jr., Dec. 29, 1967 (div. July 1988; children: Laura Marie, James Newton III. Student, Memphis State U., 1964-66; BS, George Peabody Coll., 1968, MA, 1971. Cert. elem. tchr., special edn. tchr., learning disabilities and behavior disorders. Tchr. Fairview (Tenn.) Elem. Sch., 1968-69; special edn. tchr. Ross Elem. Sch., Nashville, 1969-70, Rosebank Elem. Sch., Nashville, 1970-71, Graymar Elem. Sch., Nashville, 1971-73, Norman Binkley Elem. Sch., Nashville, 1973-74; cons. edn1. and family counseling, ednl. testing Franklin, Tenn., 1976—. Methodist. Home and Office: 2203 Springdale Dr Franklin TN 37064-4962

DANIEL, CHRISTINE STEWART, lawyer; b. Anaheim, Calif., Dec. 16, 1963; d. Richard and Mary Ellen (Stewart) D. BA, Mills Coll., 1986; JD, U. Calif., Davis, 1989. Assoc. Hardin Cook et al., Oakland, Calif., 1989-92; dep. city atty. City of Berkeley, Calif., 1992—. Tutor adult literacy Berkeley Reads, 1993—; driver Project Open Hand, San Francisco, 1993—. Mem. ABA, State Bar Calif., Alumnae Assn. Mills Coll. (v.p. 1991—). Office: City of Berkeley 4th Fl 2180 Milvia St Fl 4 Berkeley CA 94704-1100

DANIEL, ELEANOR SAUER, economist, real estate executive; b. N.Y.C., Feb. 8, 1917; d. Charles Peter and Elsie Edna (Dommer) Sauer; m. John Carl Daniel, Dec. 31, 1952; children: Victoria Ann, Charles Timothy. BA magna cum laude (Bardwell fellow), Mt. Holyoke Coll., 1936; MA (Perkins fellow), Columbia U., 1937. Economist, U.S. Steel Co., N.Y.C., 1938; lectr. econs. Bklyn. Coll., 1939-40; with Mut. Life Ins. Co. N.Y., N.Y.C., 1940-74, asst. v.p., 1972-74, sr. econ. adviser, 1972-74; economist Fed. Home Loan Bank, N.Y.C., 1974-75; v.p., dir. Daniel Realty Cos., N.Y.C., 1975—; pres. Midtown Daniel, 1986—; former dir., chmn. fin. com. Atlantic City Electric Co.; past chmn. fin. com. Atlantic Energy, Inc.; former mem. bd. mgrs. U.S. Savs. Bank Newark; mem. Pres's. Task Force Fed. Credit Programs, 1968-69; mem. N.J. Gov's. Econ. Recovery Com., 1975-76; mem. econ. adv. bd. U.S. Sec. Commerce, 1971-73; mem. bus. research adv. council U.S. Bur. Labor Statistics, 1966-86. Author: (with J.J. O'Leary and S.F. Foster) Our National Debt and Our Savings; correspondent, author, mem. Am. editorial bd., The London Economist, 1946-52; contbr. articles to profl. jours. Former trustee Blue Shield of N.J., trustee fellow Mt. Holyoke Coll., also past vice chmn., mem. fin. com., trustee; active Nat. Rep. Com. Mem. Am. Econ. Assn., Am. Fin. Assn. (past dir.), N.J. Health Think Tank, Phi Beta Kappa. Home and Office: 34 North Dr East Brunswick NJ 08816-1122

DANIEL, ILENE CHARLES, retired science educator, researcher; b. N.Y.C., Aug. 19, 1944; d. Stanley Branford and Viola (Jones) Donawa; m. Franklyn David Daniel, Apr. 11, 1974; children: Victor T., Amen K. BA, CUNY, 1966; postgrad., Howard U., 1966-67, 69-71; EdM, Temple U., 1991; postgrad., Drexel U., 1990-92. Cert. biology and chemistry instructional I tchr., Pa. Jr. bacteriologist Bellvue Hosp., N.Y.C., 1967; lab. asst. N.Y.C. Rsch. Inst., 1967; biology tchr. St. Martin's Girls' High Sch., Port-of-Spain, Trinidad, 1978; gen. sci. tchr. Trinidad and Tobago Ministry Edn. and Culture, Port-of-Spain, Trinidad, 1978-85; substitute tchr. N.Y.C. Bd. Edn., Bklyn., 1986-87; substitute tchr. Phila. Sch. Dist., 1988, sci. tchr., 1988-94; student tchr. Camden (N.J.) City Pub. Schs., 1988; sci. fair coord. William Penn High Sch., 1991-93. Poet Nat. Libr. Poetry, other lit. and sci. works. Mem. World Wildlife Fund, Nat. Alliance Sr. Citizens, Am. Mus. Natural History, Nat. Wildlife Fedn. Recipient Sci. Honors diploma SUNY, Albany, 1962, Phi Beta Kappa scholarship, 1962, Howard U. Internal Medicine fellowship, 1967. Mem. AAAS, NSTA, N.Y. Acad. Scis., Smithsonian Air and Space, Smithsonian Assocs., Phila. Fedn. Tchrs., Nat. Audubon Soc. Adventist. Office: D J Pub Co 3820 N Marshall St Philadelphia PA 19140

DANIEL, JUDITH PALOTAY, lawyer; b. Tab, Somogy, Hungary, Sept. 24, 1942; came to the U.S., 1964; d. Theodore and Priscilla (Kovach) Palotay; m. Aron Daniel, Oct. 21, 1968 (div. 1973). BS, Sacred Heart U., 1975; MS, Nazareth Coll., 1978; JD, U. West L.A., 1988. Bar: Calif. 1988. Social worker Internat. Inst., Bridgeport, Conn., 1975-82; paralegal Asherson & Klein, Beverly Hills, Calif., 1982-88; lawyer Asherson & Klein, Beverly Hills, 1988-90, Nishiyama, Mukai, et al, L.A., 1990—. Mem. Trial Lawyers Assn., State Bar Calif., L.A. County Bar Assn. Democrat. Roman Catholic. Home: 100 S Doheny Dr Apt 607 Los Angeles CA 90048-2930 Office: Nishiyama Mukai 3435 Wilshire Blvd Ste 1800 Los Angeles CA 90010-2004

DANIEL, MARILYN S., lawyer; b. Tulsa, Okla., July 30, 1940; d. Basil M. and Kathryne (Shannon) Stewart; m. John A. Daniel, June 15, 1962; 1 child, John S. BA, Rhodes Coll., 1962; JD, U. Ky. Coll. of Law, 1976. Bar: Ky. Sec. math. tchr. Ky., N.J., 1962-71; legal clerk U.S. Dist. Judge, Lexington, Ky., 1977; asst. U.S. atty. U.S. Dept. Justice, Lexington, 1978-81; gen. counsel Mason & Hanger-Silas Mason Co., Inc., Lexington, 1982—, v.p. adminstrn., 1992—; dir. Mason Techs. Inc., 1988—, The Mason Co., Lexington, 1990—, Ky. Bar Assn. for Women, 1991-93. Mem. Fayette County Bd. Edn., 1985-88; trustee Transylvania Presbytery, 1985—; elder Maxwell St. Presbyn. Ch., 1993—. Recipient Women of Achievement award YWCA, 1993. Mem. ABA, KBA (CLE chair annual convention 1992), Fayette County Bar Assn. (Henry T. Duncan award 1994), Lexington Bar Assn. Office: Mason & Hanger-Silas Mason Co 2355 Harrodsburg Rd Lexington KY 40504

DANIEL, SUZANNE, media specialist; b. Plymouth, Mich., Nov. 25, 1936; d. Leslie Irvine and Margaret (Sheffler) D. BS in Edn., Miami U., Oxford, Ohio, 1958; MA in Edn., Eastern Mich. U., 1965; MS in LS, Wayne State U., 1970. Tchr. Rockford (Ohio) Sch., 1958-59, Garden City (Mich.) Pub. Sch., 1959-64, Southfield (Mich.) Pub. Sch., 1964-65; tchr., libr. Nankin Mills Sch. Dist., Westland, Mich., 1965-69; media specialist Livonia (Mich.) Pub. Schs., 1969—. Author: Big House on the Hill, 1980; editor: The Ryder Family, 1981. Chmn. Livonia Hist. Commn., 1974—; mem. Livonia Historic Preservation, 1978—. Named Vol. of Yr., City of Livonia, 1977, 1st Citizen, Livonia C. of C., 1989; recipient award of merit State Hist. Soc., 1981, Heritage award Livonia Hist. Soc., 1982, Salute to Women award Livonia AAUW, 1986. Mem. Livonia Hist. Soc., Alpha Delta Kappa (pres. Tau chpt.). Home: 11322 Melrose St Livonia MI 48150-2847

DANIEL-DREYFUS, SUSAN B. RUSSE, civic worker; b. St. Louis, May 30, 1940; d. Frederick William and Suzanne (Mackay) Russe; m. Don B. Faerber, Nov. 27, 1962 (div. Nov. 1968); 1 child, Suzanne Mackay; m. Marc Andre Daniel-Dreyfus, Aug. 9, 1969; 1 child, Cable Dunster. Student, Smith Coll., 1958-60, Corcoran Sch. Fine Arts, 1960-61, Washington U., St. Louis, 1961-62; MEd, Cambridge Coll., 1991. Mng. ptnr. Comm., Inc., 1980-82; asst. dir. Harvard Bus. Sch. Fund, Cambridge, 1982-86; pres. SCR Assocs. Corp., Cambridge, 1986—; mem. bd. advisors Odysseum, Inc.; bd. dirs. Future Mgmt. Systems. Mem. St. Louis-St. Louis County White House Conf. on Edn., 1966-68; mem. Mo. 1st Gov.'s Conf. on Edn., 1966, 2d Conf., 1968; bd. dirs. Tunbridge Sch., 1973-78, St. Louis Smith Coll.; hon. bd. dirs. New Music Circle; mem. woman's bd. dirs. Washington U., New Music Circle, 1963-67; mem. woman's bd. Mo. Hist. Soc.; bd. dirs. Non-Partisan Ct. Plan for Mo., Young Audiences Inc., 1967-69; bd. dirs. Childrens Art Bazaar, 1968-70; founder St. Louis Opera Theater; chmn. Art. Mus. Bond Issue election St. Louis, 1966; jr. bd. dirs. St. Louis Symphony, 1966-68, Opportunities Indsl. Center, Boston; legis. chmn. bd. dirs. Boston LWV, 1969-72; mem. coun., bd. dirs. Jr. League Boston, 1970-72, 74-76, v.p. Bd. of Family Counseling Services-Region West, Boston, 1979—; pres. Family Counseling Bd., Brookline, Mass.; trustee Chestnut Hill Sch., Boston, Brookline Friendly Soc.; mem. steering com. ann. fund Boston Children's Hosp. Med. Center, 1980-84; v.p. Nat. Friends Bd., Joslin Diabetes Found., 1980-83; mem. corp. bd. Joslin Diabetes Ctr.; v.p. bd. dirs. Boston Ctr. Internat. Visitors, 1979-82; Boston bd. dirs. Mass. Soc. Prevention of Cruelty to Children, 1980-84; exec. v.p. Ctr. for Middle East Bus., 1978-82; pres. bd. Brookline Community Fund, 1984—; overseer Old Sturbridge Village, 1987—. Mem. Colonial Dames, Soc. Art Historians. Clubs: Women's City (dir., Boston); Vincent (dir.). Home: 120 Middlesex Rd Chestnut Hill MA 02167-1800

DANIELE, JOAN O'DONNELL, clinical psychologist; b. Queens, N.Y., May 6, 1958; d. James and Joan (Cullen) O'Donnell; m. Richard James Daniele, May 19, 1991. BA in Dance, Hunter Coll., 1979, MS in Dance Therapy, 1983; MA in Sch. Psychology, Adelphi U., 1987, PhD in Clin. Psychology, 1989; postgrad., Psychoanalytic Inst Postgrad. Ctr. Mental Health, 1989-93. Lic. psychologist, N.Y.; cert. psychoanalyst. Dance therapist Bellevue Hosp., N.Y.C., 1982-85; sch. psychologist N.Y. Bd. Edn., Bklyn., 1987-90; psychology intern Postgrad. Ctr. for Mental Health, N.Y.C., 1988-89, asst. coord. substance abuse unit, staff therapist, 1989-91, supr., instr., psychology intern, 1991—; with Psychoanalytic Inst. Postgrad. Ctr. for Mental Health, N.Y.C., 1989-93; pvt. practice psychology N.Y.C., 1991—; assoc. clin. prof. Adelphi U., N.Y.C., 1993—; assoc. clin. prof. Adelphi U., 1993—. Pres. Staten Island (N.Y.) Clearwater Friends, 1976-78. Hunter Coll. Dance Co. scholar, 1978. Mem. Postgrad. Psychoanalytic Soc. (assoc.). Democrat. Roman Catholic. Office: 250 W 90th St Apt 6I New York NY 10024-1123

DANIELS, ARLENE KAPLAN, sociology educator; b. N.Y.C., Dec. 10, 1930; d. Jacob and Elizabeth (Rathstein) Kaplan; m. Richard Rene Daniels, June 9, 1956. B.A. with honors in English, U. Calif., Berkeley, 1952; M.A. in Sociology, 1954, Ph.D. in Sociology, 1960. Instr. dept. speech U. Calif., Berkeley, 1959-61; rsch. assoc. Mental Rsch. Inst., Palo Alto, Calif., 1961-66; assoc. prof. sociology San Francisco State Coll., 1966-70; chief Center for Study Women in Soc., Inst. Sci. Analysis, San Francisco, 1970-80; mem. faculty Northwestern U., Evanston, Ill., 1975-95; prof. dept. sociology Northwestern U., 1975-95, dir. Women's Studies, 1992-94; cons. NIMH, 1971-73, NEH, 1975-80, Nat. Inst. Edn., 1978-82. Editor: (with Rachel Kahn-Hut) Academics on the Line, 1970; co-editor: (with Gaye Tuchman and James Benét) Hearth and Home: Images of Women in the Mass Media, 1978, (with James Benét) Education: Straightjacket or Opportunity?, 1979, (with Rachel Kahn-Hut and Richard Colvard) Women and Work, 1982, (with Alice Cook and Val Lorwin) Women and Trade Unions in Eleven Industrialized Countries, (with Teresa Odendahl and Elizabeth Boris) Working in Foundations, 1985, Invisible Careers, 1988, (with Alice Cook and Val Lorwin) The Most Difficult Revolution: Women in the Trade Union Movement, 1992; editor: Jour. Social Problems, 1974-78; assoc. editor: Contemporary Sociology, 1980-82, Symbolic Interaction, 1979-84, Am. Sociol. Rev., 1987-90. Trustee Bus. and Profl. Women's Rsch. Found. Bd., 1980-85, Women's Equity Action League Legal and Ednl. Def. Fund, 1979-81; mem. Chgo. Rsch. Assoc. Bd., 1981-87. Recipient Social Sci. Rsch. Council Faculty Rsch. award, 1970-71; Ford Found. Faculty fellow, 1975-76; grantee Nat. Inst. Edn., 1978-79, 1979-80, NSF, 1974-75, NIMH, 1973-74. Mem. Inst. Medicine NAS, Sociologists Women in Soc. (pres. 1975-76), Am. Sociology Assn. (coun. 1979-81, chmn. occupations and orgns. 1987, chmn. pubs. com. 1985-87, sec. 1992-95), Soc. Study Social Problems (v.p. 1981-82, pres. 1987), Soc. Study Symbolic Inter-Action. Office: Northwestern U Dept Sociology 1810 Chicago Ave Evanston IL 60208-1330

DANIELS, BARBARA JOAN LUCAS, small business owner; b. McKeesport, Pa., Sept. 28, 1957; d. Bernard John and Betty Ellen (Zeile) Lucas; m. James Dean Daniels, Feb. 28, 1981; children: Trevor Lucas, Derek Dalton. Teaching lic., Pitts. Beauty Acad., 1976. Land agt. Geophys. Svc., Inc., Midland, Tex., 1980-82; office mgr. Irrigation Dist. # 1 Ward County, Barstow, Tex., 1982-84; owner, mgr., pres. Tredek, Inc./Stride Rite Shoes, Midland, Tex., 1989—. Mem. 1st Bapt. Ch., Barstow, 1981—. Mem. Greentree C. of C., Rep. Women's Club. Republican. Office: Tredek Inc/ Stride Rite Shoes 4511 N Midkiff El Midland TX 79705

DANIELS, CINDY LOU, space agency executive; b. Moline, Ill., Sept. 24, 1959; d. Ronald McCrae and Mary Lou (McLaughlin) Guthrie; m. Charles Burton Daniels, June 19, 1982. Student, Augustana Coll., Rock Island, Ill., 1977-78; BS cum laude, No. Mich. U., 1981. Field engr. Ford Aerospace, Houston, 1982-83; engr. flight ops. McDonnell Douglas Corp., Houston, 1983-85; electronics engr. Johnson Space Ctr. NASA, Houston, 1985-89; project mgr. multiple program control ctr. NASA, 1989-90; project mgr. NASA, Houston, 1989-91, mission control ctr. upgrade project mgr., 1990-91; mgr. program control office NASA, 1991-93; mgr. ground facilities Space Sta. Program Office NASA, Houston, 1993-94; engrng. and ops. mgmt., space sta. program NASA Hdqrs., Washington, 1994—; dynamics contr. NASA Johnson Space Ctr., 1982-83; payload data engr. NASA, 1983-84, earth radiation budget satellite joint ops. integration plan mgr., 1984; mem. payload assist module team NASA-McDonnell Douglas Corp., 1984-85. Home: 2700 Earls Ct Vienna VA 22181 Office: NASA Hdqrs Code ML 300 E St SW Washington DC 20546

DANIELS, DEBORAH VAN HOOSE, elementary education professional; b. Nov. 4, 1952; m. Brad Daniels; 1 child, Russell Cass Dean. BA degrees, Morehead State U., 1975, 92, MA in Comms., 1976. Cert. child care provider, Ky.; cert. gifted edn. tchr., Rank I secondary edn. tchr., Ky. Dir. speech and theatre Rowan County High Sch., Morehead, Ky., 1975-77; dir. pub. rels. Johnson County Schs., 1980-86, coord. gifted and talented edn., 1984-86; dir. speech and theatre Johnson Cen. High Sch., 1978-91, tchr., 1986-91; dir. speech and drama Porter Elem. Sch., Hager Hill, Ky., 1991—; dir. Day Care and School-Age Child Care Ctr., 1992—, Porter Elem. Family Resource Ctr., Hager Hill, 1991—; profl. devel. facilitator for secondary edn. on integrated curriculum (coord. through KEDC and the Morehead Regional Svc. Ctr.); guest speaker, workshop trainer for Family Resource Ctrs., 1992—; speech instr. for Prestonsburg C.C., 1980-81, others. Chair Johnson County Water Dist.; Johnson County Election Commr.; mem. JOBS Adv. Coun., Johnson County Day Care Coun., Johnson County Visions Coun.; sec. Johnson County Rep. Party. Dir. Porter Family Resource Ctr. which was recognized as Orgn. of the Yr., Ky. Assn. for Sch. Health, 1993, other awards; Named to Outstanding Young Women of Am., 1976; numerous pageant titles including Miss Tristate Burley Tobacco, 1973, Miss Ky. Apple Queen, 1971 and Miss Apple Queen USA (runner-up), 1971. Mem. Interagy. Task Force on Family Resource Ctrs., Ky. Coalition of School-Age Child Care, Ky. Assn. Comm. Arts (past v.p.), Ky. Ednl. Speech and Drama Assn. 9bd. dirs.), others. Office: Porter Elem Family Resource Ctr Box 780 Hager Hill KY 41222

DANIELS, DIANA M., lawyer; b. Dillon, Mont.. BA, Cornell U., 1971; JD, Harvard U., 1974; M of City Planning, MIT, 1974; diploma, U. Edinburgh, Scotland, 1976. Bar: N.Y. 1975, U.S. Dist. Ct. (ea. and so. dists.) N.Y. 1975, U.S. Ct. Appeals (2d cir.) 1975, D.C. 1978, U.S. Supreme Ct. 1988. Assoc. Cravath, Swaine & Moore, N.Y.C., 1975-78; asst. counsel Washington Post newspaper, 1978-79; gen. counsel Washington Post Co., 1988-89, v.p., gen. counsel, 1989-91, v.p., gen. counsel, sec., 1991—; v.p., counsel Newsweek, N.Y.C., 1979-85, v.p., gen. counsel, 1985-88. Office: Washington Post Co 1150 15th St NW Washington DC 20071-0002

DANIELS, ELIZABETH ADAMS, English language educator; b. Westport, Conn., May 8, 1920; d. Thomas Davies and Minnie Mae (Sherwood) Adams; m. John L. Daniels, Mar. 21, 1942; children: John L., Eleanor B. (dec.), Sherwood A., Ann S. A.B., Vassar Coll., 1941; A.M., U. Mich., 1942; Ph.D., N.Y. U., 1954. From instr. to prof. English Vassar Coll., Poughkeepsie, N.Y., 1948-85; dean freshmen Vassar Coll., 1955-58, dean studies, 1965-73, chmn. dept. English, 1974-76, 81-84, acting dean faculty, 1976-78, chmn. self-study, 1978-80, Vassar historian, 1985—. Author: Jessie White Mario, Risorgimento Revolutionary, 1972, Main to Mudd, Bridges to the World, 1994; also articles. Bd. dirs. Young Morse Hist. Site. Recipient Grad. award Alumnae Assn. N.Y. U., 1954; Vassar fellow, 1941; Nat. Endowment Humanities summer stipend, 1981. Mem. MLA, AAUP, N.E. Victorian Soc., Phi Beta Kappa. Democrat. Club: Poughkeepsie Tennis. Home: 129 College Ave Poughkeepsie NY 12603-2804 Office: Vassar Coll PO Box 74 Poughkeepsie NY 12601

DANIELS, FAITH, newscaster; b. Pitts., 1957; d. Steven and Mary Skowronski; m. Dean Daniels, 1981; children: Andrew, Alyx Rae, Aidan Rose. Host A Closer Look with Faith Daniels NBC, 1991-93; news anchor Today Show NBC, 1990-92; with Dateline NBC, 1993—. Mem. Nat. Coun. Adoption. Roman Catholic. Office: NBC News 30 Rockefeller Plz New York NY 10112-0001

DANIELS, HEATHER SUE, pediatrician; b. Corvallis, Oreg., June 6, 1949; d. Anson Henry and Yvonne (Hollenbeck) Smith; m. Terry Hale Daniels, May 1, 1982; 1 child, Christa Willamette. BS in Pharmacy, Oreg. State U., 1972; MD, Oreg. Health Scis. U., 1976. Commd. 2d lt. U.S. Army, 1976, advanced through grades to maj., 1981, resigned, 1986; resident Madigan Army Med. Ctr., Tacoma, 1976-79; staff physician Irwin Army Hosp., Ft. Riley, Kans., 1979-82; fellow Madigan Army Med. Ctr., Tacoma, 1982-84, staff physician, 1984-86; pediatrician Union Avenue Pediatrics, Tacoma, 1986—; developmental pediatrician, Tacoma, 1986—. Contbr. articles to profl. jours. Dir. Christian edn., tchr. Sunday sch. East Side Christian Ch., Tacoma, 1986—. Fellow Am. Acad. Pediatrics; mem. North Pacific Pediatric Soc., Christian Med. Soc. Office: Union Avenue Pediatrics 1530 S Union # 1 Tacoma WA 98405

DANIELS, IRISH C., principal; b. Miami, Fla.; children: Irisha, Jessica. BS, Fla. A&M U., 1964, MEd, 1974; postgrad., Fla. State U., 1978. cert. adminstrn., supervision, early childhood, elem. edn., reading gifted edn., health. Tchr. Gadsden County Sch. Bd., Quincy, Fla.; tchr. Leon County Sch. Bd., Tallahassee, asst. prin.; grade level chmn.; sch. SACS chmn.; originator, coord. vocat. incentive program Hartsfield Sch., 1988-90; establisher, coord. Help Ctr. for grades 3-5, 1991; organizer, coord. Parent Tutorial Program, 1993-94. Named Disting. Black Educator from Hartsfield, 1991, Disting. Educator of Minorities, 1992. Mem. Asst. Prins. Facilitator or Sch. Improvement (chair), Phi Delta Kappa, Kappa Delta Pi. Home: 2605 Vence Dr Tallahassee FL 32312-3239

DANIELS, LYDIA M., health care administrator; b. Louisville, Dec. 21, 1932; d. Effort and Gladys T. (Turner) Williams; student Calif. State U., Hayward, 1967, 69-72; BA, Golden Gate U., 1992, MS, 1993; cert. Samuel Merritt Hosp. Sch. Med. Record Adminstrs., 1959; student Cen. State Coll., Ohio, 1950-52; children by previous marriage: Danny Winston, Jeffrey Bruce, Anthony Wayne. Sec. chemistry dept. Cen. State Coll., Wilberforce, Ohio, 1950-52; co-dir. Indian Workcamp, Pala Indian Reservation, Pala, Calif., 1956-58; clk.-typist Camarillo (Calif.) State Hosp., 1956-58; student med. record adminstr. Samuel Merritt Hosp., Oakland, Calif., 1958-59, asst. med. record adminstr., 1962-63, asst. chief med. record adminstr., 1965, chief med. record adminstr., 1965-72; med. record adminstr. Albany (Calif.) Hosp., 1964-65; asst. med. record adminstr. Children's Hosp., San Francisco, 1960; co-dir. interns in community svc. Am. Friends Svc. Com., San Francisco, 1960-61; med. record adminstr. Pacific Hosp., Oakland, Calif., 1963-64; med. record cons. Tahoe Forest Hosp., Truckee, Calif., 1969-73; chief med. record adminstr. Highland Gen. Hosp., Oakland, 1972-74; dir. med. record svcs. U. Calif. San Francisco Hosps. and Clinics, 1975-82; mgr. patient appointments, reception and registration Kaiser-Permanente Med. Ctr., 1982-88; dir. ambulatory adminstrv. svcs., 1988-94, asst. dir. human resources, 1994—; adj. prof. mgmt., office automation Golden Gate U., 1978—; pres. Daniels Consultation Svcs., 1988—. Leader Girl Scouts Am. Oakland area council, 1960-62; sunday sch. tchr. Soc. of Friends, Berkeley, Calif., 1961-63, mem. edn. com., 1965-68; mem. policy and adv. bd. Far West Lab. Demonstration Sch., Oakland, 1973-75. Recipient Mgmt. Fellowship award U. Calif., San Francisco, 1979-80. Mem. Am. Med. Record Assn., Calif. Med. Record Assn. (editorial bd. 1976-77, pres. 1974-75), East Bay Med. Record Assn. (chmn. edn. com. 1971-72, pres. 1969-70), Assn. Systems Mgmt., Am. Mgmt. Assn., San Francisco Med. Records Assn. (pres.-elect 1982-83, pres. 1983-84), Am. Assn. Tng. and Devel. (Golden Gate chpt., v.p. prof. devel. 1994—). Author: Health Record Documentation: A Look at Cost, 1981; Inservice Training as a Tool in Managing the Changing Environment in the Medical Record Department, 1983; the Budget as a Management Tool, 1983. Issues editor Topics in Health Record Management, Parts I and II, 1983. Home: 545 Pierce St Apt 1105 Albany CA 94706-1048 Office: Kaiser-Permanente Med Ctr 280 W Macarthur Blvd Piedmont CA 94611-5642

DANIELS, NORMA, state legislator; m. Robert M. Daniels. Mem. state senate from dist. 31 State of Kans. Democrat. Office: PO Box 128 Valley Center KS 67147 also: State Senate State Capitol Topeka KS 66612*

DANIELS, SUSAN, academic administrator, educator; b. Chgo., Sept. 10, 1958; d. Dominic and Evelyn (Hobuss) Daniels; 1 child, Devin McGhee. BA in English, Barat Coll., Lake Forest, Ill., 1980; MA, Northeastern Ill. U., Chgo., 1990; PhD, U. Wis., 1994. Elem. tchr. of gifted Eldorado Sch. for Gifted, Orange, Calif., 1984-86; gifted/talented coord. Near North Montessori, Chgo., 1986-90, jr. high sch. English tchr.; adminstr. talented and gifted outreach program U. Wis. Extension, Madison, 1990-93; ednl. adminstr./enrichment program coord. McFarland (Wis.) Community Schs., 1993—; mem. faculty dept. ednl. psychology U. Wis., Madison, 1994—. Researcher in field; contbr. articles to profl. jours. Fellow NEH, 1988, Ill. Bd. Edn., 1988, 89. Mem. ASCD, Nat. Assn. for Gifted Children, Phi Delta Kappa.

DANIELS-DAMRON, WANDA LOUISE, artist; b. Huntington, W.Va., Jan. 1, 1942; d. Thomas Herbert and Wanda Elizabeth (Spence) D.; m. David Osborne Gebhardt, Aug. 18, 1958 (div. Mar. 1986); children: Terry David, Richard Edward, Paul Fred; m. Johnny Edwin Damron, Mar. 25, 1993; stepchildren: Mark Duane, Steven Kent. Student, Ohio U., 1992—. Tchr. Cabell County Vocat. Ctr., Huntington, W.Va., 1973-78. Group shows include W.Va. State Capitol Exhibit, Charleston, Art in Ritter Park, Huntington, W.Va., art exhbns. Ashland, Ky., Gallipolis, Ohio; works in pvt. collections. V.p. Tri-State Artist Guild, Huntington, 1970; tchr. Grace Gospel Ch., Huntington, 1975; counselor Grace Gospel Bible Camp, Huntington, 1975. Regional Higher Edn. scholar Ohio U.,1 992. Republican. Baptist.

DANIELSON, MARY LYNN, business manager; b. New Orleans, Oct. 16, 1962; d. William J. Jr. and Margaret (Kuehn) D. BS, Clemson U., 1985; MBA, The Citadel, 1990. Contract adminstr. Life Cycle Engring., Charleston, S.C., 1986-87; product mgr. Ingredient Specialties, Mt. Pleasant, S.C., 1987-88; benefits mgr. Roper Hosp., Charleston, 1988-90; bus. mgr. Rehab. Ctrs. of Charleston, 1990—. Mem. S.C. Med. Group Mgmt. Assn. Office: Rehab Ctrs of Charleston 1483 Tobias Gadson Blvd Ste 209 Charleston SC 29407-4796

DANILOVA, ALEXANDRA, ballet dancer, choreographer; b. Peterhof, Russia, Nov. 20, 1903; came to U.S., 1934; d. Dionis and Claudia (Gotovtzeva) D. Ed., Theatrical Sch. Petrograd. Mem. faculty Sch. Am. Ballet; adjudicator Southeastern Ballet Conf., 1960. Mem. Russian State Ballet, Maryinsky Theater, 1922-24, soloist Diaghileff Ballet, 1925, ballerina, 1929, Montecarlo Opera House, 1930-31; star: Oswald Stoll's prodn. Waltzes from Vienna, Alhambra Theatre, London, 1932; ballerina: Oswald Stoll's prodn. Col. de Basil's Ballet Russe, 1933-38; prima ballerina: Oswald Stoll's prodn. Ballet Russe de Monte Carlo, 1938-51; currently head own co. touring various countries, lecture tours, U.S., Europe; guest star: various ballets including Royal Ballet Covent Garden, 1946; star: various ballets including Song of Norway, 1944; Broadway musical Oh Captain, 1958; choreographer Broadway musical, Met. Opera Co.; staged: (with George Balanchine for) Broadway musical Coppelia, N.Y.C. Ballet, 1974, and Los Angeles Ballet, 1980; works for Nijinsky Festival Germany, 1975, for Md. Ballet, 1975; biography: Choura, 1986 (Della Torre Bueno prize 1987). Recipient Capezio Dance award, 1958, Dance mag. award, 1984, Kennedy Ctr. Honors award, 1989, Handel medal, 1989. Greek Orthodox. Address: 100 W 57th St New York NY 10019-3327*

DANILOW, DEBORAH MARIE, rancher, musician, bondsman; b. Mineral Wells, Tex., Dec. 9, 1947; d. Stanton Byron and Irval Leona (Vanhoosier) D.; m. William Paul Cook Jr., June 1965 (div. Oct. 1967); m. Chance Gentry, Oct. 1971 (div. May 1974); m. Ellis Elmer Aldridge, Dec. 3, 1977 (div. Nov. 1984); children: Chandra Desiree, Anthony Ellis; m. Carl Graham Quisenberry, Feb. 7, 1992. Student, Brantley Draughon Bus. Coll., Ft. Worth, 1965-66, Tex. Christian U., 1965-67, U. Ariz., 1967-69. Asst. to pres. Hollywood Video Ctr., L.A., 1969-72; producer Western Inst. TV, L.A., 1972-77; owner Chanelde Ranch, Weatherford, Tex., 1977-84; band musician Bonnie Raitt, Malibu, Calif., 1984, Mick Fleetwood, Malibu, 1984; lead musician Jazz Talk, Ft. Worth, 1985—; owner Brazos Valley Ranch Inc., Seymour, Tex., 1987—, AAA Bail Bonds, Seymour, 1990—. Composer numerous pub. songs, 1969—. Active Sheriffs Assn. Tex., Seymour, 1991—, North Tex. Taxpayers League, Wichita Falls, Tex., 1991—, Tex. State Notary Bd., Austin, 1990—. Mem. NAFE, NRA, Okla. Game Breeders Assn., United Game Breeders Assn., Tex. Game Breeders Assn., Tex. Limousin Assn., Tex. Southwestern Cattle Raisers Assn., Tex. Cattlewomen's Assn., Am. Quarter Horse Assn. (life), Dallas-Ft. Worth Profl. Musicians Assn., Ft. Worth Jazz Soc. (sec. 1987-89), N.Am. Limousin Found. (life), Australian Shepherd Club Am., Internat. Platform Assn., Marchigiana Cattle Assn. (life), N.Am. Fishing Club. Baptist. Office: Brazos Valley Ranch Inc 111 S Main Seymour TX 76380

DANIS, DIANE, rehabilitation nurse. BSN, Cath. U. Am., 1965. RN, Va.; cert. ins. rehab. specialist, rehab. RN, rehab. counselor, case mgr. Pub. health nurse Dept. Human Resources, Arlington County, Va., 1969-70; asst. coord. The Planning Coun., Woodbridge, Va., 1981-84; from case mgr. to dist. mgr. CorVel Corp., Fairfax, Va., 1984—; conductor seminars in field; lectr. in field. Lt. (j.g.) Nurse Corps, USN, 1965-68. Mem. Nat. Assn. Rehab. Profls. in Pvt. Sector (Nurse of the Yr. 1988), Assn. of Rehab. Nurses, Va. Head Injury Found., Sigma Theta Tau. Home: 9944 Portsmouth Rd Manassas VA 22110 Office: CorVel Ste 420 11350 Random Hills Rd Fairfax VA 22030

DANITZ, MARILYNN PATRICIA, choreographer; b. Buffalo. BS in Chemistry, Le Moyne Coll.; MS in Chem. Engring., Columbia U. Artistic dir. High Frequency Wavelengths/Danitz Dances, 1976—; assoc. prof. Tainan Cheng Chuan Coll., Taiwan, 1984; profl. dancer Ballet Mcpl. Strasbourg, France, Ballet Mcpl. Geneva, Switzerland; choreography commns. performances include The 11th Internat. Ballet Comp. Varna, Bulgaria, 1983, Tbilisi Ballet Co., USSR, Nat. Ballet of Colombia, Nat. Inst. Arts, Taiwan, Nanatsudera Theatre, Nagoya, Japan, The Shanghai Ballet and Shanghai Jiaotong U., Nat. Cheng Kung Dance Group, Taiwan, others internationally; master choreography workshops include Chinese Cultural U., Taipei, Taiwan, Okuda Studio, Nagoya, Japan, Ballet Philippines, Manila, New South Wales Coll. Dance, Sydney, Australia, The Ballet Sch., Bogota, Colombia, others internationally; video prodn. Real Art Ways Nat. Residency, funded by NEA, 1990; video art collaboration with Allen Ginsberg Internat. Conf. on Dance and Tech., 1993. presentations include Naropa Inst. 20th Anniversary Celebration, 1994; TV prodns. of works include Nat. Broadcasting, Venezuela, Nat. Broadcasting, Colombia, Pub. Broadcasting, Albany, N.Y.C., Mpls.; works performed by Nat. Ballet with the Nat. Philharm. Orch. of Colombia Gala Performance, 1984; co. tours include China, Japan, Taiwan, Europe, Hawaii; contbr. articles to Jour. Colloidal Chemistry, Jour. Clin. Pathology, others; video work in permanent collection Lincoln Ctr. Dance Collection. Recipient Gold medal, scholarships Conservatoire de Geneve, N.Y. State Regents award, one of 3 Outstanding Dance-Theater Works of 1986 award Dance Brew-ATV Cable Manhattan; NIH Fellow; N.Y. State Regents scholar, Le Moyne Coll. Chemistry scholar, others; chosen for Bessie Schonberg Lab. for Experienced Choreographers, Dance Theater Workshop; video work represented in permanent dance collection Lincoln Ctr. Mem. Dance Theater Workshop, Am. Dance Guild (exec. com., editor Am. Dance, bd. dirs., nat. conf. planning com.). Address: 560 Riverside Dr Apt 2E New York NY 10027-3203 also: PO Box 216 Sand Lake NY 12153-0216 also: 3200 Holly Rd Apt 2 Virginia Bch VA 23451-2926

DANKO, PATRICIA ST. JOHN, visual artist, writer, educator; b. Orange, Tex., Aug. 7, 1944; d. George Milton and Rebecca Alice (McCoppin) Solomon; m. Jim Danko, Aug. 19, 1973 (dec. 1983). BA, Dominican Coll., Houston, 1965; postgrad. U. Ibero-Americana, Mexico, 1965, Mich. State U., 1965, Mus. Fine Arts Sch., Houston, 1972; BFA, U. Houston, 1979, MEd in Second Lang. Edn., 1992. Teaching asst. Mich. State U., East Lansing, 1965; vol. Peace Corps, Chile, 1965-68; silkscreen apprentice, printer Atelier Zárate, Buenos Aires, 1969; tchr. high sch. Orange Ind. Sch. Dist. (Tex.), 1971, Houston Ind. Sch. Dist., 1973; instr. English, English Lang. Svcs., Houston, 1973-75; instr. English, Spanish, Inlingua Lang. Schs., 1976; instr. Art League Houston, 1978-81; performance art writer Houston Art Scene, 1979-84, editor, 1981-84, mng. editor, 1982-83, exec. editor, 1983-84; acting Tex. editor New Art Examiner, 1985-86; contbg. editor Tex. New Art Examiner, 1986-88; curriculum writer Houston Ind. Sch. Dist., 1990-91; ind. art hist. researcher, writer; freelance writer; visual artist, pub. collections: Nat. Mus. Women in Arts, Washington, Libr. and Rsch. Archives, Washington, N.Y. Feminist Art Inst., Equinox Theatre, Houston, Chomo Uri Collective, U. Mass., Memphis-Brooks Mus. Art, Several Dancers Core Sch., Atlanta, McGlothlin Ins. Agy., Houston, Cameron Petroleum Co., Houston, Emdyne, Inc. Designer numerous art therapeutic programs for children; designer and mask-maker numerous artistic and theatrical performances; exhbns. of artistic work to numerous museums and cultural instns. throughout U.S. and Mex.; designer, writer Bilingual Sci. Curriculum Houston Zoo, 1994. Jesse H. Jones Found. scholar, 1961-65; recipient Presdl. Commendation by Pres. Johnson for Service to U.S. and Chile, 1968; named Outstanding Young Woman of Am., OYWA Press, Chgo., 1970; Sum Arts grantee for sculpture The Matriarch as Phoenix, 1981; Shell Found. grantee for performance of Thanatopsis, 1983, grantee Ruth Chevon Found., Inc., 1987, Change, Inc., N.Y.C., 1987, Adolph and Esther Gottlieb Found., 1988; Lamar Found. grantee, 1989; Impact II Developer grantee, 1990-91; Bus. Com. for Ednl. Excellence grantee, 1991-92, 94—; Title VII Edn. Project grantee U. Houston, 1991-92; Bus. Com. for Ednl. Excellence grantee, 1994—; endowed chair to design and implement program for immigrant and refugee children, I Have a Dream Found., 1991—. Mem. Artists Equity Assn., Contemporary Arts Mus. (Houston). Represented by Thomas V. Robinson Galleries. Roman Catholic. Address: 2112 Dunlavy St Houston TX 77006-1704

DANKWORTH, MARGARET ANNE, management consultant; b. Bellaire, Ohio, July 22, 1920; d. Charles Henry and Annie Harvey (Parks) D. BA, Ohio Wesleyan U., 1942; MA, NYU, 1949; postgrad., Mich. State U., 1960. Cert. assn. mgr. Bus. mgr. Nat. Recreation Assn., N.Y.C., 1948-50; dist. rep. Nat. Recreation Assn., Toledo, Ohio, 1950-58; asst. exec. dir. Am. Inst. of Pk. Execs., Ogle Bay Park, W.Va., 1958-66; advt. mgr., pub. rels. dir. Nat. Recreation and Pks. Assn., Washington, 1966-71; exec. dir. Am. Assn. Zool. Pks. and Aquariums, Wheeling, W.Va., 1958-75; cons. Am. Inst. for Leisure, Wheeling, W.Va., 1985—; owner Historic Morristown, Ohio, 1975—; founder Nat. Sch. for Zool. Adminstrn., 1975—; bd. dirs. Buckeye Savs. Bank. Editor Parks and Recreation Mag., 1964-66; founder, editor AAZPA Newsletter, 1966-75. Bd. dirs. St. Clairsville Pub. Libr., 1988—. Lt. USNR, 1943-46, ret., 1980. Mem. Historic Morristown Pres. Assn. (sr. bd. 1988—), Questers Nat. Trail (bd. dirs.), Ohio Historic Soc., Nat. Trust for Historic Preservation, Tues. Night Club, Delta Gamma (pres. 1988-92). Republican. Methodist. Home: 145 Crisswill Rd Saint Clairsville OH 43950-1415 Office: Historic Morristown PO Box 335 Saint Clairsville OH 43950-0335

DANNA, JO J., publisher, author, anthropologist; b. N.Y.C.; d. Lucy (Macaluso) D.; m. David Pender (div. 1961). BA, Hunter Coll., 1948; MA, Columbia U., 1964, PhD, 1974. Elem. sch. tchr. N.Y.C. Bd. Edn., 1956-65; advisor to founder, asst. to dir. Villaggio Del Superdotato, Sicily, Italy, 1967-70; asst. prof. anthropology Baldwin Wallace Coll., Berea, Ohio, 1971-73, No. Ill. U., 1974; dir., writer ethnic studies curriculum edn. dept. NYU, Albany, 1975-76; asst. prof. La Trobe U., Melbourne, Australia, 1976-79; author, 1982—; pub. Palomino Press, N.Y.C., 1983—; founder Network Ind. Pubs. Greater N.Y.; mem. Inst. of Immigration and Ethnic Studies, La Trobe U., Melbourne, Australia, 1978. Contbr. articles to profl. jours. Mem. Good Neighbour Coun. of Melbourne, Australia, 1977. Mem. Pubs. Mktg. Assn., Com. Sml. Mag. Editors and Pubs., MENSA, N.Y. Acad. Scis. Home and Office: 86-07 144th St Briarwood NY 11435

DANNER, BLYTHE KATHARINE (MRS. BRUCE W. PALTROW), actress; b. Phila., 1944; d. Harry Earl and Katharine D.; m. Bruce W. Paltrow, Dec. 14, 1969; children: Gwyneth Kate, Jake, Laura. B.A. in Drama, Bard Coll., 1965, D.F.A. (hon.), 1981; L.H.D. (hon.), Hobart-Smith Coll., 1981. Appeared as Laura in Glass Menagerie, 1965; repertory at Theatre Co. Boston, The Knack, and 7 new Am. Plays, 1965-66; appeared as Helena in repertory Midsummer Night's Dream, Trinity Sq. Playhouse, R.I.; appeared as Irena in repertory Three Sisters, Trinity Sq. Playhouse, R.I., 1967; with Lincoln Ctr. Repertory Co. in Summertree, 1968, Cyrano de Bergerac, 1968, Elise in the Miser, 1969 (Theatre World award); appeared on Broadway as Jill Tanner in Butterflies Are Free (Tony award 1971); also appeared in Major Barbara, 1971, Twelfth Night, 1972, The Seagull, 1974, Ring Around The Moon, 1975, Betrayal, 1980 (Tony nomination), Blithe Spirit, 1987, A Streetcar Named Desire, 1988; TV appearances include To Confuse the Angel (with Lee J. Cobb), George M. (with Joel Grey), 1970, Doctor Cook's Garden (with Bing Crosby), To Be Young, Gifted and Black, 1971, F. Scott Fitzgerald and 'The Last of the Belles', 1974, The Seagull, 1975, Eccentricities of a Nightingale, 1976, The Scarecrow, Adam's Rib; TV movies include Dr Cook's Garden, 1971, F. Scott Fitzgerald and "The Last of the Belles", 1974, Sidekicks, 1974, A Love Affair: Eleanor and Lou Gehrig, 1978, Are You in the House Alone?, 1978, Roots: The Next Generations, 1979, Inside the Third Reich, 1982, In Defense of Kids, 1983, Helen Keller-The Miracle Continues, 1984, Guilty Conscience, 1985, A Streetcar Named Desire, 1988, Tattinger's, 1988, Judgment, 1990, Never Forget, 1991, Cruel Doubt, 1992, Getting Up and Going Home, 1992; motion picture appearances include 1776, 1972, To Kill a Clown, 1972, Lovin' Molly, 1974, Hearts of the West, 1975, Futureworld, 1976, The Great Santini, 1980, Too Far to Go, 1982, Man, Woman, And Child, 1983, Brighton Beach Memoirs, 1986, Another Woman, 1988, Mr. and Mrs. Bridge, 1990, Alice, 1990, The Prince of Tides, 1991, Husbands and Wives, 1992. Recipient Theatre World award, 1969; Best Actress award Vevey Film Festival, Switzerland, 1982. *

DANNER, PATSY ANN (MRS. C. M. MEYER), congresswoman; b. Louisville, Ky., Jan. 13, 1934; d. Henry J. and Catherine M. (Shaheen) Berrer; m. Lavon Danner, Feb. 12, 1951 (div.); children: Stephen, Stephanie, Shane, Shavonne.; m. C.M. Meyer, Dec. 30, 1982. Student, Hannibal-LaGrange Coll., 1952; B.A. in Polit. Sci. cum laude, N.E. Mo. State U., 1972. Dist. asst. to Congressman Jerry Litton, Kansas City, Mo., 1973-76; fed. co-chmn. Ozarks Regional Commn., Washington, 1977-81; mem. Mo. State Senate, 1983-1992, 103rd Congress from 6th Mo. dist., 1993—. Roman Catholic. Home: 6 Nantucket Ct Smithville MO 64089-9605 Office: US House of Representatives Office of House Members Washington DC 20515

DANNER, SHARON KAY, women's advocate; b. Des Moines, Dec. 1, 1946; d. David Thomas and Audrey Maureen (Wilson) Harter; m. Marlin Dwight Danner, Aug. 21, 1965 (div. 1984); children: Gregory Allan, Aaron Matthew, Jason Andrew. AA summa cum laude, Lakewood Comm. Coll., White Bear Lake, Minn., 1987; BA in Psychology/Lit. summa cum laude, Concordia Coll., St. Paul, 1990; MA in Psychology summa cum laude, St. Mary's Coll., Mpls., 1993. Bookkeeper Cherokee State Bank, St. Paul, 1965-67, teller, 1967-68; legal adv. St. Paul Intervention Project, 1989-91; women's adv. Women's Advs., St. Paul, 1991; group facilitator Women's Support Group, St. Paul, 1989-91; researcher, presenter in field. Exhibitor (paintings) New Acad., St. Paul, 1990. Urgent action coord. Amnesty Internat., St. Paul, 1989, 90; active troop #31 Boy Scouts Am., Roseville, Minn., 1990—. Recipient Edward A. Lange Writing award for Poetry, 1989. Mem. APA, Phi Beta Kappa, Sigma Tau Delta. Lutheran. Home: 637 Skillman Ave W Saint Paul MN 55113-6443

D'ANNIBALLE, PRISCILLA LUCILLE, contracting company executive; b. Martins Ferry, Ohio, Oct. 28, 1950; d. James Louis and Smyrna Isabell (Prieto) D'A; m. Terrence E. Holdren. BE, U. Toledo, 1973. Credit mgr. Kabat Distbg. Co., Toledo, 1973-80; comml. ops. officer Ohio Citizens Bank, Toledo, 1980-81, credit officer, 1981-82, mktg. officer, 1982-83, mortgage banking officer, 1983-85; owner, pres. D'Ann Enterprises, Inc. dba Paul Davis Systems, Holland, Ohio, 1985—; pres. district V Paul Davis Systems, Toledo, 1992—, mem. nat. exec. com., 1992—, treas. nat. exec. com., 1994-95; chmn. arbitration com. Paul Davis Systems, 1991. Mem. fund drive United Way, Toledo, 1982, Jr. Achievement, Toledo, 1983; bd. dirs. Voluntary Action Ctr., Toledo, 1981-82. Mem. Nat. Assn. Credit Mgmt. (bd. dirs. 1981-87, bd. dirs. Ednl. Forum 1976-82, pres. 1980, Credit Person of Yr. award 1982, Credit Exec. of Yr. award 1987), Holland-Springfield C. of C. (exec. bd. dirs., v.p. 1991-92, pres. 1993), Paul Davis Systems Franchisee Assn. (pres. 1991). Roman Catholic. Home: 704 Oak Park Dr Toledo OH 43617-2024 Office: D'Ann Enterprises Inc 1049 S Mccord Rd Holland OH 43528-9596

DANOFF-KRAUS, PAMELA SUE, shopping center development executive; b. Gallup, N.Mex., Aug. 29, 1946; d. Isadore Harry and Armida Catherine (Ceccardi) Danoff; m. Milo Joseph Warner III, Dec. 28, 1968 (div. 1974); m. Robert Warren Kraus, Nov. 30, 1985; 1 child, Jillian Amaris. BA, U. N.Mex., 1968. Lic. in real estate, Calif. Real estate rep. Kaiser Aetna, Newport Beach, Calif., 1975-76; leasing agt. Alexander Haagen Co., Rolling Hills, Calif., 1976-77; dir. leasing Warren Kellogg & Assocs., Newport Beach, 1977-81, Center Devel. Co., Newport Beach, 1981-84; exec. v.p., ptnr. The Von Der Ahe Co., Newport Beach, 1984-86; ptnr. Marketplace Properties, Tustin, Calif., 1986-92; lectr. in field; panelist various convs., univs.; conductor seminars in field. Contbr. articles to profl. jours. Sponsor Californians Working Together to End Hunger and Homelessness, Los Angeles, 1988; mem. Orange County Performing Arts Ctr., 1983-85. Mem. Internat. Coun. Shopping Ctrs. (program chmn. 1987-89, small ctr. devel. com., state dir. pub. rels. and community affairs for Calif., 1989-92, chair pub. rels. and community svc. Western div. 1992—), Calif. Bus. Properties Assn., Calif. Redevel. Assn., Women in Retail Real Estate, Chi Omega. Republican. Roman Catholic. Home: 10182 Brier Ln Santa Ana CA 92705-1531 Office: Danoff Kraus Enterprises 10182 Brier Ln Santa Ana CA 92705-1531

D'ANTONIO, CYNTHIA MARIA, sales executive; b. Chgo., Sept. 12, 1956; d. Michael Patrick and Joan Marie (Funk) D'A. BS in Natural Resource Devel., Mich. State U., 1979. Chemist Aqualab, Streamwood, Ill., 1980-83; R&D specialist Seaquist Closures, Crystal Lake, Ill., 1983-87; internat. sales & mktg. exec. Seaquist-Valois Australia, Sydney, 1987-93; internat. sales exec. Pfeiffer Inc., Princeton, N.J., 1993—; speaker in field. Contbr. articles and photos to profl. jours. Mem. Nat. Assn. Female Execs., Plastic Inst. Australia. Republican. Roman Catholic. Home: 10123 Taylor Ct Lawrenceville NJ 08648-5319

DANTSUKA, TRACY GAIL, police officer; b. Honolulu, Sept. 27, 1959; d. George Y. and Mildred (Dolfo) D. Chef Halekulani Hotel, Honolulu, 1978-81; met. police officer Honolulu Police Dept., 1982—. Author: (poetry books) Young Poets of America, 1977, America Sings, 1977; composer/lyricist: Keala, 1977. Mem. Police Activities League (first female field dir. 1993—). Home: 1506 Bernice St Honolulu HI 96817-2703

DANZANSKY, JOAN COX, child and family advocate and consultant, riding therapist; b. Phila., Mar. 1, 1941; d. Joseph Winston Cox Jr. and Edna Lee Gilchrist; m. Stephen Ira Danzansky, Apr. 29, 1967; children: Michael Winston, Katharine Cox. BA in Sociology and Psychology, Mt. Holyoke Coll., 1963. Founder, exec. dir. Family Stress Svcs. D.C. and D.C. chp. Nat. Com. Prevention Child Abuse, Washington, 1975-88; cons. on child abuse and neglect to pvt. agys. Washington, 1986—; instr. Nat. Ctr. for Therapeutic Riding, Washington, 1990—; instr. and program adminstr. Nat. Ctr. for Therapeutic Riding, Washington, 1994—; mem. faculty family crisis intervention program Met. Police Dept., 1979-88; mem. Task Force Exploited Children Met. Washington Coun. Govts., 1984-85; mem. Fed. Region III Task Force Child Abuse and Neglect, HHS, Phila., 1985-86; chmn. Washington Mayor's Adv. Com. Child Abuse and Neglect, 1986-93. Chmn. alumnae honors rsch. com. Mt. Holyoke Coll., South Hadley, Mass., 1988-91, 93—; bd. dirs. Child Health Ctr., Children's Hosp., Washington, 1977; mem. sustainer adv. rsch. group Internat. Assn. Jr. Leagues, N.Y.C., 1988-91; elephant interpreter Nat. Zoo, Washington, 1989—; mem. cmty. adv. com. Friends Nat. Zoo, 1989-91; mem. parents activities com. Nat. Cathedral Sch., Washington, 1989-91. Mem. alumnae honors rsch. com. Mt. Holyoke Coll., South Hadley, Mass., 1989-91, chmn., 1993—; bd. dirs. child Health Ctr., Children's Hosp., Washington, 1977—; mem. sustainer adv. rsch. group Internat. Assn. Jr. Leagues, N.Y.C., 1988-91; elephant interpreter Nat. Zoo, Washington, 1989—; mem. cmty. adv. com. Friends Nat. Zoo, 1989-91; mem. parents activities com. Nat. Cathedral Sch., Washington, 1989-91. Recipient Marian Chace award D.C. Mental Health Assn., 1978, Regional Dir.'s Disting. Vol. award HHS, 1982, Outstanding Community Svc. award Psychiat. Inst. Found., 1983, Washingtonian of Yr. award Washingtonian mag., 1985, Sesquicentennial award Mt. Holyoke Coll., 1987, Outstanding Svc. Recognition Resolution, Coun. of D.C., 1989. Mem. Am. Assn. for Protecting Children, Am. Profl. Soc. on Abuse Children, N.Am. Riding for Handicapped Assn., Am. Assn. Suicidology (vice chmn. local arrangements com. 1987-88), Elephant Mgrs. Assn. Episcopalian. Home: 3609 Edmunds St NW Washington DC 20007-1434 Office: Nat Ctr Therapeutic Riding 5110 Glover Rd NW Washington DC 20015

DANZIG, SARAH PALFREY, retired advertising agency executive, writer; b. Sharon, Mass., Sept. 18, 1912; d. John Gorham and Methyl (Oakes) Palfrey; m. Jerome A. Danzig, Apr. 27, 1951; children—Diana, Jerome Palfrey. Grad., Winsor Sch., 1930; spl. studies, Radcliffe Coll. Advt. cons. World Tennis mag., 1967-91; sports editor NBC-TV Home program, 1956-57; sports commr. N.Y.C., 1966—; exec. com. Nat. Tennis Found. and Hall of Fame Inc. Author: Winning Tennis and How to Play It, 1946, Tennis for Anyone, 1966, rev. paperback, 1972, 80, also articles. Chmn. spl. events Child Study Assn. Am., 1963-67; chmn. ann. benefit Vis. Nurse Service, N.Y.C., 1961-63; mem. spl. events com. People to People Sports Com., 1962-64, Eastern Tennis Patrons, 1962-67; Trustee Community Service Soc. N.Y., 1966-76. Won U.S. Women's Nat. Singles titles 1941, 45; recipient Svc. Bowl award USTA, 1981; elected Mass. Greatest Woman Athlete, Helms Hall of Fame, 1963, inducted into the Internat. Tennis Hall of Fame, 1963, Ea/ Tennis Assn. Hall of Fame, 1988, into New Eng. Law Tennis Assn. Hall of Fame, 1990; named Outstanding Mother, 1985. Mem. Lawn Tennis Writers Assn. Am., Internat. Lawn Tennis Club U.S.A. (hon., emeritus 1994), Internat. Tennis Hall of Fame (hon.). Clubs: 7th Regiment Tennis (hon.), Jr. League, Town Tennis (hon.); Longwood Cricket (Chestnut Hill, Mass.) (hon.); West Side Tennis (hon.). Home: 993 Park Ave New York NY 10028-0809

DANZIG, SHEILA RING, marketing and direct mail executive; b. N.Y.C., Mar. 18, 1948; d. David and Yetta Ring; m. William Harold Danzig, Aug. 11, 1968; children: David Scott, Gregory Charles. BS, CUNY, 1968. Tchr. N.Y.C. Bd. Edn., 1968-71; treas. Nat. Success Mktg. Inc., Sunrise, Fla., 1969—; pres. Innovative Comm. Market Cons., Plantation, Fla., 1984-87; cons. Crush Softball Team, Hollywood, Fla., 1986-87, The Eye Ctr., Sunrise, 1986-87, Bus. Expo., Plantation, 1987. Author: You Deserve to be Rich, 1972, A Free Press, 1990, A Better Medical Practice, 1986; author, pub.: Turn Your Computer Into A Money Machine, 1994; contbr. articles to profl. jours. Coord. Day Out program Mills Boys' Shelter, Ft. Lauderdale, Fla., 1985, 87, Put Seat Belts on Sch. Buses program Broward County Sch. Bd., 1986; vol. Miami Children's Hosp.; campaign dir. Help the Handicapped Keep Their Parking Spots, 1987. Mem. Mail Order Bus. Bd., Am. Med. Writers Assn., Plantation Bus. and Profl. Women's Assn., MADD, Speechcrafters. Office: Nat Success Mktg 2574 N University Dr Fort Lauderdale FL 33322-3045

DANZIGER, GERTRUDE SEELIG, metal fabricating executive; b. Chgo., Oct. 24, 1919; d. Isidor and Clara (Fuchs) Seelig; widowed; children: Robert, James. Student, Northwestern U., U. Wis. Treas. Homak Mfg. Co., Inc., Chgo., 1966-79; pres. Homak Mfg. Co., Inc., 1979—. Patentee in field.

DANZIGER, PAULA, author; b. U.S., 1944. Tchr. jr. high sch. Author: The Cat Ate My Gymsuit, 1974 (N.J. Inst. of Tech. award 1976, Mass. Children's Book award Edn. Dept. of Salem State Coll. 1979, Nene award Hawaii Assn. of School Librs. and Hawaii Libr. Assn. 1980, Children's Choice award Internat. Reading Assn. and Children's Book Coun. 1980), The Pistachio Prescription, 1978 (Children's Book of Yr. citation Child Study Assn. 1978, Mass. Children's Book award Edn. Dept. of Salem State Coll. 1979, Children's Choice award Internat. Reading Assn. and Children's Book Coun. 1979, Nene award Hawaii Assn. of School Librs. and Hawaii Libr. Assn. 1980, Ariz. Young Reader award 1983), Can You Sue Your Parents for Malpractice?, 1979 (Children's Choice award Internat. Reading Assn. and Children's Book Coun. 1980, N.J. Inst. of Tech. award 1980, Land of Enchantment award N. Mex. Libr. Assn. 1982), There's a Bat in Bunk Five, 1980 (Children's Choice award Internat. Reading Assn. and Children's Book Coun. 1981, CRABbery award Prince George's County Meml. Librs. 1982, Young Reader's medal 1984), The Divorce Express, 1982 (Children's Choice award Internat. Reading Assn. and Children's Book Coun. 1983, Parents' Choice award for lit. Parents' Choice Found. 1982, Woodward Park School Annual Book award 1983, S.C. Young Adult Book award S.C. Assn. of School Librs. 1985), It's an Aardvark-Eat-Turtle World, 1985 (Parents' Choice award for lit. Parents' Choice Found. 1985, Children's Book of Yr. citation Child Study Assn. 1985), This Place Has No Atmosphere, 1986, Remember Me to Harold Square, 1987, Everyone Else's Parents Said Yes, 1989, Make Like a Tree and Leave, 1990, Not for a Billion Gazillion Dollars, 1992, Earth to Matthew, 1992, Thames Doesn't Rhyme with James, 1994, Amber Brown Is Not a Crayon, 1994, You Can't Eat Your Chicken Pox, Amber Brown, 1995. Address: care G.P. Putnam's Sons The Putnam & Grosset Group 200 Madison Ave New York NY 10016*

DANZIS, ROSE MARIE, emeritus college president; b. Adrian, Pa.; d. Paul A. and Josephine (Bugala) Manger; m. James Gordon Channing, Jan. 24, 1954 (dec. 1973); children—Rose Marie Channing Buhrman, Lorraine Channing Genieczko; m. Sidney Danzis, June 1, 1986. Diploma, Jersey City Hosp. Sch. Nursing, 1949; B.S., N.Y. U., 1954; M.A., Columbia U., 1961, M.Ed., 1971, Ed.D., 1973. Staff nurse, asst. supr. Public Health Nursing Service, Jersey City, 1949-55; dir. health and recreation, clin. coordinator, asso. dir. nursing edn. Charles E. Gregory Sch. Nursing, Perth Amboy (N.J.) Gen. Hosp., 1958-66; chmn. dept. nurse edn., dir. health techs., dean div. health techs. Middlesex County Coll., Edison, N.J., 1966-78; pres. Middlesex County Coll., 1978-86; Mem. Middlesex County Comprehensive Health Planning Council, 1973-75, N.Y. Com. Regents External Degree in Nursing, 1972-80, Council on Continuing Edn. for Allied Health Personnel, N.J.; Regional Med. Program, 1968-71; chmn. N.J. Health Professions Edn. Adv. Council, N.J. Dept. Higher Edn., 1979-82, chmn. nursing subcom., 1975-78; mem. health careers com. J.F. Kennedy Hosp., 1972-75; chmn. Middlesex County Coll. Assembly, 1975-77; mem. Pres.'s Adv. Com. Sch. Allied Health, Coll. Medicine and Dentistry of N.J., 1976-79; commr. Middle States Assn. of Colls. and Schs.; chmn. Commn. High Edn., 1984-85; mem. liaison com. Am. Assn. Community and Jr. Colls. and Nat. League for Nursing, 1978-82; chmn. acad. affairs com. N.J. Council of Community Coll., pres., 1978-82; trustee Nat. Bank of N.J., 1979-81; exec. com. Acad. Pres.'s, Am. Assn. Community and Jr. Colls.; also exec. com. Internat./Intercultural Consortium. Contbr. articles to profl. jours. Recipient Torch of Liberty award Anti-Defamation League, 1981, Disting. Service award U. Medicine and Dentistry of N.J. Sch. Health Related Professions, 1983; named to Hall of Fame, Perth Amboy High Sch., 1985. Mem. Council of County Coll. Presidents, Am. Nurses Assn., Nat. League for Nursing, Am. Soc. Allied Health Professions, Am. Council on Edn., Am. Assn. Community and Jr. Colls. (bd. dirs. 1984-86), Coll. Consortium for Internat. Studies., Jersey City Sch. Nursing Alumni Assn., N.Y. U. Alumni Assn., Tchrs. Coll., Columbia Alumni Assn., Kappa Delta Pi. Home: 32 Troy Dr Short Hills NJ 07078-1334 Office: Middlesex County Coll Edison NJ 08817

DARBY, JOANNE TYNDALE (JAYE DARBY), arts and humanities educator; b. Tucson, Sept. 22, 1948; d. Robert Porter Smith and Joanne Inloes Snow-Smith; stepchildren: Margaret Loutrel, David Michael. BA, U. Ariz., 1972, MEd, U. Calif., L.A., 1986, postgrad. Cert. secondary tchr., gifted and talented tchr., Calif. Tchr. English, chmn. dept. Las Virgenes Unified Sch. Dist., Calabasas, Calif., 1979-82; tchr. English and gifted and talented edn. Las Virgenes Unified Sch.Dist., Calabasas, Calif., 1983-84; lang. arts/social studies and drama tchr. Las Virgenes Unified Sch. Dist., Calabasas, Calif., 1991-92; tchr. English and gifted and talented edn. Beverly Hills (Calif.) Unified Sch. Dist., 1982-83, 84-89, English and drama tchr., 1994; tchr., cons. Calif. Lit. Project, San Diego, 1985-87; cons., free lance editor L.A., 1977—; dir. Shakespeare edn. and festivals project Folger Libr., Washington, 1990-91; field work supr. tchr. edn. lab. Grad. Sch. Edn. and Info. Studies, UCLA, 1992—; cons. arts and edn., L.A., 1991—. Contbr. articles to profl. publs. Mem. Am. Alliance for Theatre and Edn., Am. Ednl. Rsch. Assn., Nat. Coun. Tchrs. English, Phi Beta Kappa, Phi Beta Phi, Alpha Lambda Delta. Home: 972 Hilgard Ave Apt 310 Los Angeles CA 90024-3066

D'ARCANGELO, MARCIA DIANE, educational media producer; b. Meadville, Pa., May 16, 1945; d. Terrence Benjamin and Eileene Marie (Judy) Darcangelo; m. Thomas Brown Andrews V, Sept. 16, 1989. BS in Chemistry, Grove City Coll., 1967. Info. specialist Eastman Kodak Co., Rochester, N.Y., 1967-68; singer/dancer Kids Next Door-Young Ams. Orgn. (Katand Prodns.), L.A., 1968-69, Stand Up and Cheer TV Show, The Johnny Mann Singers, L.A., 1970-74; singer, dancer, actor John Brown's Body AEA Nat. Tour, Fitzgerald Prodns., L.A., 1975-76; singer, dancer The Perry Como Show-Roncom Prodns., 1977-82; med. news journalist Physicians Radio Network, N.Y.C., 1983-84; prodn. asst., prodn. coord. ASCD, Alexandria, Va., 1985-86, producer, sr. producer, 1987-88, mgr. media prodns., 1989—; cons. Holbrook & Kellogg, Falls Church, Va., 1990, Developmental Studies Ctr., San Ramon, Calif., 1991, Soc. for Preservation of Social Security and Medicare, Washington, 1991. Composer 4 mus. pieces (words and music); co-author 20 tng. manuals; author/co-author 41 video-based tchr. tng. programs, articles. Recipient award of merit VFW, 1971, Jack Kennedy Alumni Achievement award Grove City Coll. Alumni Assn., 1984, Clarion award Women in Comm., 1991, 6 Cine Golden Eagle awards Coun. on Internat. Nontheatrical Events, 1991, 92, 93, Silver Apple award Nat. Ednl. Film and Video Festival, 1991, 93, Bronze Apple award, 1993, Silver Screen award and Cert. for Creative Excellence U.S. Internat. Film and Video Festival, 1993, Disting. Achievement award and Best of Category film Ednl. Press Assn., 1994. Mem. SAG, AFTRA, NAFE, AAUW, ASCD, ASTD, Am. Guild Variety Artists, Actors Equity Assn., Nat. Staff Devel. Coun., Internat. TV Assn., Internat. Interactive Comm. Soc., Women in Film and Video Internat.

DARDECK, KATHRYN LEE, psychologist; b. Oceanside, N.Y., Mar. 29, 1951; d. Philip A. and Shirley Ruth (Hahn) D. BS in Edn., Boston U., 1973; MEd in Psycholinguistics and Reading, U. Mass., 1979, EdD in Counseling Psychology, 1985. Lic. psychologist, health svc. provider, reading specialist, Mass. Tchr. Lewis (N.Y.)-Wadhams Sch., 1973-76; internship coord. U. Mass., Amherst, 1976-84; asst. dean students Amherst Coll., 1984-85; psychologist Brightside Outpatient Mental Health Clinic, West Springfield, Mass., 1985-86, Kaiser Permanente, Northampton, Mass., 1987—; instr. Greenfield (Mass.) Community Coll., 1986-88; cons. Chicopee's (Mass.) 7 Cath. Elem. Schs., 1986-87. Mem. APA, NOW, Mass. Psychol. Assn. Home: PO Box 36 Hatfield MA 01038-0036 Office: NE Permanente Med Group 70 Main St Northampton MA 01060-1466

DARDEN-SIMPSON, BARBARA L., library director; b. Cleve., Apr. 6, 1947; d. Curley and Cora (Chambliss) Brown; children: Michelle, Crystal, Twilla. BS, Ohio State U., 1967; MS in Ednl. Media, Kent. State U. (Ohio), 1971, MLS, 1971. Adminstrv. supr. Cleve. pub. schs., 1968-72; libr. Cuyahoga Community Coll., Cleve., 1972-75, coord., 1975-77, interim dir., 1977-78, asst. dean, 1978-80, dir., 1980-84; dir. libr. Kean Coll., Union, N.J., 1984—; cons. Dembsy Assocs., Boston, 1967-81; editorial cons. Max Pub. Co., N.Y.C., 1967-81; cons. reader U.S. Office Edn., Washington, 1979-80; editorial cons. Jossey-Bass Pub. Co., 1979. Cons. editor Probe, 1975, Sch. Media Ctr., 1968, Booklist, 1969; contbr. articles to profl. jours. Bd. dirs. N.J. Adv. Bd. on the Status of Women, 1988, Africana Studies, 1988, N.J. State Libr. Adv. Bd., 1987; chairperson N.J. Acad. Libr. Network, N.J. Ednl. Activities Task Force Libr. Com. Recipient Phillips award Kent State U., 1970. Mem. ALA, Higher Edn. Reps., N.J. Acad. Libr. Network (chmn. 1987), Council N.J. Coll. Librs. (pres. 1987—), N.J. Libr. Assn., Oral History Soc., N.J. Hist. Soc., Jr. League (Cleve. vice chmn. 1981, 83), Concerned Parents Club (pres. 1984), Women's City Club. Avocations: music, reading. Office: Kean Coll Libr Morris Ave Union NJ 07083-7117

DARGUSCH, TANYA MARIA, athletic trainer; b. Madison Heights, Mich., June 21, 1964; d. Edward and Bonnie Lee (Neff) Katschanow; m. James William Dargusch, July 6, 1991; 1 child, Katrina Tatiana. BS, Ctrl. Mich. U., 1986. Registered athletic trainer, N.J.; cert. athletic trainer. Indsl. athletic trainer Walbro Corp., Cass City, Mich., 1986-87; athletic trainer Life Care Inst., Glassboro, N.J., 1987-88; head athletic trainer Wash. Twp. High Sch., Sewell, N.J., 1988—; athletic trainer U.S. Team Handball Fedn. Women's Team, France Internat. Invitational Tournament, 1992, mem. med. adv. bd., 1994, North-South All Star High Sch. Footbal Game, N.J., 1991—, N.J. State Women's H.S. Swimming Champsionship, Trenton, 1991-92. CPR/first aid instr., Vol. Disaster Relief, 1992—, ARC, Woodbury, N.J., 1985—; vol. Am. Heart Assn. mem. Nat. Athletic Trainers Assn. (cert.) Athletic Trainers Soc. N.J. (exec. bd. dirs. So. rep. 1992-94, chmn. ad hoc com. 1994—), Ea. Athletic Trainers Assn., Sigma Sigma Sigma. Evangelical Presbyterian. Home: 2008 Tanglewood Ct Sewell NJ 08080-3519 Office: Wash Twp High Sch 529 Hurffville Crosskeys Rd Sewell NJ 08080-2746

DARIOS, BOBBI ALICE, administrative assistant; b. Jersey City, N.J., Feb. 23, 1949; d. Robert Samuel and Betty Alice (Patterson) Civitts; m. Joseph William Darios, Aug. 4, 1981; children: Lesley Marie, Jill Christine. Student, Coll. Eastern Utah, 1982-83, Garrett Commun. Coll., McHenry, Md., 1985-86, Belmont Tech. Coll., 1991—. Clk. Huntington Nat. Bank, Columbus, Ohio, 1967-69; adminstrv. sec. Madison House, Morgnatown, W.Va., 1985-86; accounts payable Newark (Ohio) Health Care/McMillen Village, 1988-89, W.Va. Dept. of Health, Hopemont, 1989-90; office mgr., adminstrv. asst. Carriage Inn, Cadiz, Ohio, 1991—; notary pub. State of Ohio, Cadiz, 1992—. Troop leader Girl Scouts U.S., Huntington, 1982; asst. instr. Catholic Community Christian Living, Morgantown, W.Va., 1984; mem. task force Ohio Valley Hosp., Steubenville, Ohio, 1990; sec. nat. coun. Catholic women, Diocese of Steubenville, Ohio, 1992; mem. Catholic womens coun. Sacred Heart Parish, Hopedale, 1990—; treas. Hopemont Hosp. Employee Coun., 1989-90. Democrat. Roman Catholic. Office: Carriage Inn 259 Jamison Ave Cadiz OH 43907-1125

DARISH, BERNICE STEIMAN, realtor; b. Everett, Mass., July 25, 1928; d. Samuel and Lena (Taple) Steiman; m. Joseph Darish, Oct. 27, 1951 (dec. Apr. 1989); children: Lee Raymond, Jay Lawrence, Neil Phillip, Susan Beth. Student, Boston Dispensary, 1948-49, Boston Evening Clinic, 1949-50, Northeastern U. Med. technologist Dr. Albert S. Lappin, Hyde Park, Mss., 1951-53, Dr. H. Archer Berman, Chelsea, Mass., 1953-56; office mgr. Torf Funeral Svc., Chelsea, 1982-90; realtor DeLuca Real Estate, Medford, Mass., 1990—; leader workshops. Mem., chair Malden (Mass.) Sch. Com., 1979. Mem. Internat. Tng. in Comm. (coun. sec., coun. 3d v.p.), Malden Cultural Coun. (chair 1990—), Mass. Cultural Coun. (vice chair). Democrat. Home: 63 Maple St Malden MA 02148-3828

DARKES, ETHEL MAY, lay church worker; b. Lebanon, Pa., Apr. 24, 1912; d. Harry Stonewall and Emma Jane (Swope) Hower; m. Clarence George Darkes, June 20, 1937; 1 child, Anetta Jane. BA cum laude, Lebanon Valley Coll., Annville, Pa., 1931; MEd, Temple U., 1955. Cert. tchr., Pa. Tchr. Drumore Twp. High Sch., Chestnut Level, Pa., 1931-32; tchr. Lebanon High Sch., 1939-55, counselor, 1955-64; counselor Kennard-Dale High Sch., Fawn Grove, Pa., 1964-77; ret. Author of the Washington Letter "Union Signal," Woman's Christian Temperance Union Mag., 1991—. Pres. Cleona-Lebanon Woman's Christian Temperance Union, 1941; mem. Pa. Women's Christian Temperance Union, pres., 1978-83, Woman's Christian Temperance Union. Mem. AAUW (pres. 1982-86), Am. Assn. Ret. Persons (pres. 1987-89, com. coord.), Woman's Club of Lebanon (treas. 1986-90), Delta Kappa Gamma (pres. 1970-72). Democrat. Methodist.

DARKOVICH, SHARON MARIE, nurse; b. Ft. Wayne, Ind., Dec. 10, 1949; d. Gerald Antone LaCanne and Ida Eileen (Bowman) LaCanne Cutler; m. Robert Eliot Ness, July 17, 1971 (dec. Aug. 1976); m. Paul Darkovich, Jan. 23, 1981 (div. May 1994); 1 child, Amy Elizabeth. BS in Nursing, Case Western Res. U., 1973, BA in Psychology, 1978; cert. in advanced bioethics, Cleve. State U., 1990, MA in Philosophy & Bioethics, 1994. RN, Ohio. Staff nurse Univ. Hosps., Cleve., 1973, asst. head nurse, 1973-76; quality assurance coord. St. Luke's Med. Ctr., Cleve., 1976-83, 84—, dir. nursing, 1983-84. cons. to long-term care facilities, 1986-92, pressure ulcer dressing devel. B.F. Goodrich Co., 1988-92; cons. to long term care facilities, 1989-93, cons. to ambulatory faculty for JCAHO Accreditation, 1994; lectr. U. Akron, Northeast Ohio U. Coll. Medicine. Mem. Am. Nurses Assn., Greater Cleve. Nurses Assn. (mem. dist. coun. on practice, 1982-84), Sigma Theta Tau. Avocations: reading, needlework, sewing, camping.

DARLING, CHERYL MACLEOD, health facility administrator, researcher; b. Detroit, Feb. 23, 1949; d. Norman Duncan and Elsie Ruth (Howland) MacLeod; m. Jeffery F. Hunter, Jan. 1, 1976 (div. 1982); m. Richard W. Darling, Dec. 31, 1986; 1 stepchild, Erin Marie. AA, U. S.C., 1979; BS, No. Ill. U., 1982, MS, 1984. Medic, clin. diagnostician U.S. Army, 1972-80; grad. rsch. asst. Sch. Allied Health Profls. No. Ill. U., DeKalb, 1982-84; planning aide Comprehensive Health Planning N.W. Ill., Rockford, 1982-83, health planner, cons., 1982-85; dir. community health edn. and safety svc. Dane County Chpt. ARC, Madison, Wis., 1985-88; coord. rsch., adminstrn. Ctr. for Clin. Ethics Luth. Gen. Hosp., Park Ridge, Ill., 1988-94, clin. rsch. assoc., 1994—; rsch. interviewer Ctr. for Clin. Med. Ethics U. Chgo., 1990. Bd. dirs. Vet's House, Madison, 1986-88; profl. vol. bereavement team, counselor Rainbow Hospice, Park Ridge, 1989, mem. quality assurance com., 1990—, mem. profl. adv. bd., 1991—; mem. planning com. Chgo. Women's AIDS Project, 1989-90. Mem. Soc. for Health and Human Values, Applied Rsch. Ethics Nat. Assn., Kennedy Inst. Ethics, Profl. Responsibility in Medicine and Rsch., Soc. Clin. Rsch. Assocs. (communications com.), Soc. Bioethics Consultation. Mem. Unity Ch. Home: 1264 Cedar Ave Elgin IL 60120-2205 Office: Luth Gen Hosp Div Hematology/Oncology 1775 Dempster St Park Ridge IL 60068-1143

DARLING, DIANNE IRENE, quality assurance professional; b. Bangor, Maine, June 19, 1942; d. David Irving and Irene Eleanor (Getchell) Mosbacher; m. Barry Louis Darling (div. 1975); children: Thomas Edward, Timothy James. Student, U. Maine, 1966-69, Russell Sage Coll., 1980-82. Cytotechnologist supr. Ea. Maine Med. Ctr., Bangor, 1965-77; cytology supr. N.Y. State Dept. Health, Albany, 1977-84, cytology clin. lab. cons., 1984-92; anatomic pathology quality assurance profl. MetPath/Corning, Teterboro, N.J., 1992—; mem. cytology tech. evaluation panel Health Care Financing Assn., Balt., 1992. Mem. Maine Soc. Cytology (founder, incorporator 1974, pres. 1974-77), Am. Soc. Cytology, Internat. Acad. Cytology, Upper N.Y. State Cytology Soc. (liaison rep. 1978, bd. dirs. 1982-84), Am. Soc. Clin. Pathologists, Am. Contract Bridge League (life master). Democrat. Roman Catholic. Home: 2114 Rankin Rd Niskayuna NY 12309-4237 Office: MetPath/Corning One Malcolm Ave Teterboro NJ 07608

DARLING, SHANNON FERGUSON, special education educator; b. Spokane, Wash., Feb. 25, 1968; d. Carl Frederick Jr. and Roberta Ernestine (Phelps) Ferguson; m. Paul Garner Darling, Jan. 9, 1988. BA in Elem. and Spl. Edn., La. State U., Shreveport, 1991. Cert. tchr., spl. edn. tchr., La., respite caregiver for handicapped foster children. Tchr. autistic spl. edn. Meadowview Elem. Sch., Bossier City, La., 1991—; mem. spl. edn. com. to devel. spl. edn. alternative program curriculum Boosier Parish, 1994—, mem. spl. edn. adv. coun., 1994—, sec., 1994—. Vol. Com. for Spl. Arts Festival and Sports Day, 1993-94; vol. tutor Bossier Parish, 1992—, spl. edn. adv. coun. mem., sec., 1994—; vol. Alternate Family Care Foster Svcs., 1985—, Caddo-Bossier Assn. Retarded Citizens, 1980-85; active Meadowview PTA, 1991—. Grantee Optimist Club, summer 1992, 93, Isle of Capri Casino, summer 1994. Mem. Coun. for Exceptional Children (Spl. Edn. Tchr. of Yr. 1994), Autism Soc. (North La. state chpt. 1991—, rep. to bd. dirs. meetings 1994—, sec. 1994—). Methodist. Home: 1275 Moran St Haughton LA 71037 Office: Meadowview Elem Sch 4315 Shed Rd Bossier City LA 71111

DARLINGTON, JUDITH MABEL, clinical social worker, Christian counselor; b. Deckerville, Mich., Nov. 29, 1942; d. Wallace and Mabel Lillian (Rich) Cole; m. Clare Robert Darlington, Dec. 15, 1962; children: Debra Lynn, Dawn Elizabeth. BA, Mich. State U., 1962; MSW, U. Mich., 1983. Tchr. Limestone (Maine) Presque Isle Schs., 1963-64; substitute tchr. Crestwood Sch. Dist., Dearborn Heights, Mich., 1971-74; monitor, tchr. Renewing Life Ministries, Annandale, Va., 1976-82; clin. social worker Westland (Mich.) Counseling Svc., 1983-84; family therapist, counselor Family Svc. of Detroit and Wayne County, Wyandotte, Mich., 1984-86; specialist substance abuse Plymouth (Mich.) Family Svc., 1986-87; exec. dir. Christian Conciliation Svc. of S.E. Mich., Detroit, 1987-90; pvt. practice clin. social worker/family therapist Livonia, Mich., 1990—; speaker in field. Mem. NASW (cert.) Christian Women's Club (chmn. Livonia chpt. 1981—), Inst. for Christian Conciliation, Kappa Delta Pi. Presbyterian. Home: 7911 Debora Dr Brighton MI 48116-9462 Office: 15195 Farmington Rd Livonia MI 48154-5412 also: 324 Main St Brighton MI 48116

DARNALL, ROBERTA MORROW, academic administrator; b. Kemmerer, Wyo., May 18, 1949; d. C. Dale and Eugenia Stayner (Christmas) Morrow; m. Leslie A. Darnall, Sept. 3, 1977; children: Kimberly Gene, Leslie Nicole. BS, U. Wyo., Laramie, 1972. Tariff sec., ins. adminstr. Wyo. Trucking Assn., Casper, 1973-75; asst. clerical supr. Wyo. Legislature, Cheyenne, 1972-77; congl. campaign press aide, 1974; pub. relations dir. in Casper, Wyo. Republican Central Com., 1976-77; asst. dir. alumni relations U. Wyo., 1977-81, dir. of alumni, 1981—; bd. dir. Ivinson Meml. Hosp. Found. Mem. Higher Edn. Assn. Rockies, Am. Soc. Assn. Execs., Laramie C. of C. (edn. com.), PEO (former courtesy com., officer), Zonta Internat. Republican. Episcopalian. Home: 15 Snowy View Laramie WY 82070-5358 Office: PO Box 3137 Laramie WY 82071-3137

DA ROZA, VICTORIA CECILIA, human resources administrator; b. East Orange, N.J., Aug. 30, 1945; d. Victor and Cynthia Helen (Krupa) Hawkins; m. Thomas Howard Kaminski, Aug. 28, 1971 (div. 1977); 1 child, Sarah Hawkins; m. Robert Anthony da Roza, Nov. 25, 1983. BA, U. Mich., 1967; MA, U. Mo., 1968. Contract compliance mgr. City of San Diego, 1972-75; v.p. personnel Bank of Calif., San Francisco, 1975-77; with human resources Lawrence Livermore (Calif.) Nat. Lab., 1978-86; pvt. cons. Victoria Kaminski-da Roza & Assocs., 1986—; lectr. in field; videotape workshop program on mid-career planning used by IEEE. Contbr. numerous articles to profl. jours. Mem. social policy com. City of Livermore, 1982. Mem. Am. Soc. Tng. and Devel., Western Gerontol. Soc. (planning com. Older Worker Track 1983), Gerontol. Soc. Am. Home and Office: 385 Borica Dr Danville CA 94526-5457

DARR, CAROL C., lawyer; b. Apr. 24, 1951; d. Patt Marks and Justine (DeCorse) Darr; m. Albert Louis May III Dec. 19, 1992. BA, Memphis State U., 1973, JD, 1976; postgrad., Christ's Coll., Cambridge U., 1985-87. Bar: Tenn. 1977, D.C. 1981. Atty. Fed. Election Commn., 1976-77; asst. counsel U.S. Senate Com. on Rules & Adminstrn., 1977-79; dep. gen counsel Carter/Mondale Presidential Com., 1979-81; in house counsel Dem. Nat. Com., 1981-82; assoc. Skadden, Arps, Slate, Meagher & Flom, 1983-85; chief counsel Dukakis/Bentsen Com., Inc., 1987-91; gen. counsel Dem. Nat. Com., 1991-92; with Clinton/Gore Transition Com., 1992-93; actg. gen. counsel, dep. gen. counsel U.S. Dept. Commerce, 1993-94; assoc. Adminstrn. Nat. Telecom. and Info. Agy., Office Internat. Affairs, 1994—. Author: Political Parties, Presidential Campaigns, and National Party Conventions, 1992; Contributions and Expenditures by National, State, and Local Party Conventions, 1990; Active Corporate Participation, 1993; Candidates and Parties 1982, Registration and Reporting, 1981. Recipient Memphis State U. Outstanding Young Alumnus award 1982. Mem. ABA, Fed. Bar Assn. (chair. com. on political campaigns and election laws 1983-85. Office: Department of Commerce General Counsel Rm 4720 14th & Constitution Ave NW Washington DC 20230*

DARROW, JILL E(LLEN), lawyer; b. N.Y.C., Jan. 6, 1954; d. Milton and Elaine (Sklarin) D.; m. Michael V.P. Marks, May 14, 1987. AB in English, Barnard Coll., 1975; JD, U. Pa., 1978; LLM in Tax Law, NYU, 1983. Bar: Pa. 1978, N.Y. 1979, U.S. Tax Ct. 1982. Assoc. Shearman & Sterling, N.Y.C., 1978-79; assoc. Rosenman & Colin, N.Y.C., 1979-86, ptnr., 1987—; lectr. Sch. Continuing Legal Edn. NYU, 1986-88. Mem. N.Y. State Bar Assn., Pa. Bar Assn., Phi Beta Kappa. Home: 860 Fifth Ave New York NY 10021-5856 Office: Rosenman & Colin 575 Madison Ave New York NY 10022-2511

DARROW, KATHERINE PRAGER, lawyer, publishing executive; b. Chgo., Dec. 26, 1943; d. Frank D. and Herta Prager; m. Peter H. Darrow, June 29, 1968; children: Alexander, Jessica, James. AB, U. Chgo., 1965; JD, Columbia U., 1969. Bar: N.Y. 1970. Assoc. N.Y. Times Co., N.Y.C., 1968, staff atty., 1970-71, 73-76, asst. gen. atty., 1976-80, gen. atty., 1980-81, gen. counsel, from 1981, v.p., from 1988, now v.p. broadcasting, info. svcs. and corp. devel.; assoc. Gottesman, Evans & Van Merkeanstein, 1971-73. Trustee U. Chgo., from 1982. Mem. ABA, Am. Newspaper Pubs. Assn. (mem. press/bar rels. com.), ABA/Am. Newspaper Pubs. Assn. Joint Task Force, Assn. of Bar of City of N.Y. Office: NY Times Co 229 W 43rd St New York NY 10036-3913*

DARROW, KATHLEEN MICHELLE, psychologist; b. New Brunswick, N.J., Jan. 6, 1949; d. James E. and Margaret M. McKenzie; 1 child, Lara Felicia Darrow. BA, Rutgers U., 1985; MSEd, Bucknell U., 1987. Cert. sch. psychologist. Programmer Salant Corp., N.Y.C., 1980-82; sch. psychologist Midd-West Sch. Dist., Middleburg, Pa., 1987—; therapist Susquehanna Valley Cmty. Care, Lewisburg, Pa., 1988—; cons. team mem. Snyder County Children's Clinic, Middleburg, 1987—. Bd. dirs. battered women's shelter Susquehanna Valley Women in Transition, Lewisburg; exec. com. Parents Anonymous, Snyder and Union Counties, Pa. Mem. APA (assoc.), NOW (state and nat. liaison Snyder, Union and Northumberland counties), Nat. Assn. Sch. Psychologists. Democrat. Presbyterian. Home: 1204 Washington Ave Lewisburg PA 17837-1776 Office: Midd-West Sch Dist 568 E Main St Middleburg PA 17842-1218

DART, JUDITH C(ANDELOR) LALKA, lawyer; b. Phila., Dec. 14, 1947; d. Samuel and Helen Margaret (DiVito) Candelor; m. Thomas J. Dart; children: Carolyn, Susan. BS, Drexel U., 1968; MS, Carnegie Mellon U., 1970; JD magna cum laude, Wayne State U., 1973. Bar: Mich. 1973. Assoc. Dickinson, Wright, Moon Van Dusen & Freeman, Detroit, 1973-81, ptnr., 1981-85; gen. counsel, sr. v.p., corp. sec. Comerica Inc., Detroit, 1985-92, gen. counsel, exec. v.p., corp. sec., 1992—. Mem. conf. bd. Coun. on Gen. Counsels; dir. Detroit Club, 1992—; trustee Detroit Bar Found., 1985-93. Fellow ABA (co-chairperson subcoms. secured trans., com. on Uniform Comml. Code, 1987-91), Mich. Bar. Assn., Detroit Bar Assn., Detroit Bar Found. (trustee 1985—, treas. 1985-87), Am. Coll. Comml. Fin. Lawyers, Am. Corp. Counsel Assn. (bd. dirs. Mich. chpt. 1985-88), Detroit Clearing House Assn. (sec.-treas. 1992), Coun. Gen. Counsels (conf. bd.). Office: Comerica Inc Comerica Tower Detroit Ctr 500 Woodward Ave Detroit MI 48226-3407

DARTING, EDITH ANNE, pharmaceutical company coordinator; b. Hillsboro, Kans., Jan. 1, 1945; d. Sammuel E. and Carrie (Swehla) Jewett; m. John Ronald Darting, Aug. 11, 1979; children: Theresa Michelle, Lloyd L., Hope Marie. Grad., Emporia State Tchrs. Coll., 1963-65. Materials insp. Sterling Drug Inc., McPherson, Kans., 1977-78, auditor, 1978-82, coordinator, 1982-94; coord. Sanofi Winthrop, McPherson, 1994—. Mem. NAFE, Am. Soc. Quality Control. Republican. Methodist. Home: 320 N Birch St Hillsboro KS 67063-1135 Office: Sanofi Winthrop Pharm Inc PO Box 1048 Mc Pherson KS 67460-1048

DARVAROVA, ELMIRA, violinist, concertmaster; came to U.S., 1986; MusB, State Conservatory, Sofia, Bulgaria, 1977, MusM, 1979; certificate, Guildhall Sch. Music, London, 1982; artist's diploma, Ind. U., 1987. Concertmaster Plovdiv (Bulgaria) Philharm. Orch., 1979-86, Owensboro (Ky.) Symphony Orch., 1986-88, Evansville (Ind.) Philharm., 1987-88; artistic dir., concertmaster Evansville Chamber Orch., 1987-88; assoc. instr. violin Ind. U. Sch. Music, Bloomington, 1986-88; acting concertmaster Rochester (N.Y.) Philharm., 1988; vis. lectr. Ind. U. Sch. Mus., 1988; guest concertmaster Columbus Symphony Orch., Columbus, Ohio; concermaster Met. Opera Orch., N.Y.C., 1989—, Chgo. Grant Park Symphony, 1990—; founding mem. New World Trio, 1991. Performer recitals and concerts throughout world. Recipient 1st medal internat. competition, Barcelona, Spain, 1979, hon. diploma, prize Tchaikovsky competition, Moscow, 1982, silver medal Viotti internat. competition, Vercelli, Italy, 1984, 3d prize internat. competition, Sion, Switzerland, 1985. Office: Met Opera Orch Lincoln Ctr New York NY 10023

DASPIT, JACQUELINE MARIE, lawyer; b. New Orleans, Sept. 7, 1964; d. Lee Driscoll and Janet Marie (Labiche) D. BS in Biochemistry, U. Ariz., Tucson, 1986; JD, Tulane U., 1991. Registered patent atty. Jud. extern clk. U.S. Dist. Ct. (ea., we. dists.) La., U.S. Ct. Appeals, New Orleans, 1990-91; assoc. atty. DeRussy, Bezou & Matthews, New Orleans, 1991—. Vol. Big Bros./Big Sisters, New Orleans, 1992—. Mem. ABA, La. Bar Assn., Young Leadership Coun., New Orleans Bar Assn., Chi Omega Alumni Assn. New Orleans. Roman Catholic. Office: DeRussy Bezou & Matthews 830 Union St Ste 300 New Orleans LA 70112

DAS-YOUNG, LEENA RANI, clinical pharmacist, consultant; b. St. Louis, June 22, 1961; d. Kshitish Chandra and Joyce Marie (Heimos) Das; m. Richard Keith Young, Mar. 28, 1987; children: Cameron Malcolm Young, Nicole Alexis Young. BS in Pharmacy, Purdue U., 1985, PharmD, 1986. Registered pharmacist, Ind., Fla., cons. pharmacist, Fla. Clin. pharmacist Meml. Hosp., South Bend, Ind., 1987-88; clin. specialist infectious diseases S.W. Fla. Regional Med. Ctr., Ft. Myers, 1988-90; clin. coord. Naples (Fla.) Community Hosp., 1990-92; dir. clin. pharmacology and rsch. Assocs. in Rsch., Ft. Myers, 1992-93; product mgr.-tech. Miles, Inc., West Haven, Conn., 1994—; clin. asst. prof. Southeastern Coll. Pharmacy, Miami, Fla., 1991—; mktg. cons. Miles, Inc., 1993—; mem. Orlando Region Pharmacy Adv. Bd., 1992—; active Infectious Disease Specialty Group, 1989—; mem. Sun Health Clin. Adv. Coun., 1991-92. Author, editor drug use evaluation Gulfcoast Planning Faculty, 1992; author clin. study Am. Jour. Medicine, 1993. Active speakers bur. Am. Cancer Soc., West Lafayette, Ind., 1984. Recipient Lillian and R.B. Stewart scholarship award Purdue U., 1981, Lillian and R.B. Stewart award for mus. excellence, 1982-83; Pharmacist Achievement award Merck Sharpe & Dohme, 1993. Mem. Am. Soc. Hosp. Pharmacists (author clin. svc. program 1989), Fla. Soc. Hosp. Pharamcists (chmn. clin. affairs 1991-92, comm. coun. 1992-93; editor Clin. Digest 1990-92, jour. 1992-93, Electronic Bull. Bd. 1993, Pres.' award 1993), Soc. Gulf Soc. Hosp. Pharmacists (pres. 1992), Am. Pharm. Assn. (student pres. 1984-85), Am. Coll. Clin. Pharmacy, Am. Soc. Microbiology, S.W. Fla. Assn. Clin. Microbiology and Infectious Disease (clin. advisor 1988—), Assocs. Clin. Pharmacology, Phi Delta Chi. Office: Miles Inc 400 Morgan Ln West Haven CT 06516-4140

DAUBENAS, JEAN DOROTHY TENBRINCK, librarian; b. N.Y.C.; d. Eduard J.A. and Margaret Dorothy (Schaffner) Tenbrinck; m. Joseph Anthony Daubenas, May 29, 1965. AB, Barnard Coll., 1962; grad. Am. Acad. Dramatic Arts, 1963; MA, N.Y. U., 1965; MLS, U. Ariz., 1972; PhD, U. Utah, 1986. Tchr., Beth Jacob Tchrs. Sem. Am., Bronx, 1965-66; caseworker, Dept. Social Services, N.Y.C., 1966-67; actress Boothbay (Maine) Playhouse, others, 1967-70; reference librarian Ariz. State U., Tempe, 1972-75; asst. librarian, asst. prof. library sci. Avila Coll., Kansas City, Mo., 1979-83; assoc. prof./librarian St. John's U., Jamaica, N.Y., 1983—; grad. asst. U. Utah, 1976-77. N.Y. State Regents scholar, 1958-62, U. Ariz. scholar, 1971-72. Mem. ALA, Actors Equity Assn., AAUP, Theatre Libr. Assn., Assn. Theatre in Higher Edn., Beta Phi Mu, Phi Kappa Phi. Roman Catholic. Office: St Johns U Library 8000 Utopia Pky Jamaica NY 11439

DAUGHERTY, KENDRA LEA, lawyer; b. Cin., July 11, 1956; d. Clifford Brooks and Viola (Mills) D. BA, U. Cin., 1978, JD, 1982. Bar: Ohio 1982, U.S. Dist. Ct. (fed. dist., so. dist., we. dist.) Ohio. Pvt. practice Cin., 1982—; part-time asst. pub. defender Clermont County Pub. Defender's Office, Batavia, Ohio, 1987—; former adj. prof. bus. law U. Cin.; former adj. prof. real estate law Cin. Tech. Coll. Mem. ABA (former mem. awards of achievement com., young lawyers divsn.), Ohio State Bar Assn. (former chair young lawyers bd. govs., dist. 1 rep. to coun. of dels.), Cin. Bar Assn. (mem. jud. ratings com., mem. continuing edn. bd., subcom. chair ethics and profl. responsibility com., bd. trustees 1987-88, former chmn. young lawyers sect.), Clermont County Bar Assn. (sec.-treas.), Greater Cin. Criminal Def. Lawyers Assn. (bd. trustees), Greater Cin. Women Lawyers Assn. (co-chair programming), Ohio Assn. Criminal Def. Lawyers Assn., Ohio Women Lawyers Assn., Phi Alpha Delta (dist. justice). Democrat. Methodist. Home: 3846 Field Ln Cincinnati OH 45255 Office: 4529 Aicholtz Rd Cincinnati OH 45255

DAUGHERTY, LINDA HAGAMAN, private school executive; b. Denver, Jan. 25, 1940; d. Charles B. and Agnes May (Wall) Hagaman; m. Thomas Daniel Daugherty, Nov. 20, 1965; children: Patrick, Christina Marie. BS in Bus., U. Colo., 1961; postgrad., Tulane U., 1963-64, U. St. Thomas, 1990-91.

Sr. systems analyst Lockheed Electronics NASA, Houston, 1966-73; sr. systems cons. TRW Systems Internat., Caracas, Venezuela, 1973-74; sy. systems cons. TRW Systems, L.A., 1974-75; sr. systems analyst Intercomp, Houston, 1979-80; cons. Daugherty Fin. Svcs., Inc., Katy, Tex., 1980-82, pres., 1979-91; mng. ptnr. Motivated Child Learning Ctrs., Katy, 1976—; pres. Williamsburg Country Day Sch., Katy, 1983—. Nottingham Country Day Sch., Katy, 1977—. Pres. Mason Creek Women Reps. Club, Katy, 1980; treas. Nottingham Country Civic Club, Katy, 1979; mem. adv. bd. Nottingham Country Club, 1982-85; co-founder Friends of Archaeology U. St. Thomas, pres., 1991-93; mem. Epiphany Ch. Social Works Commn.; asst. curator Archaeology Gallery, U. St. Thomas. Mem. Houston Archeology Soc., Tex. Archeology Soc., Archaeology Inst. of Am. Roman Catholic. Office: Nottingham Country Day Sch 20303 Kingsland Blvd Katy TX 77450

DAUGHERTY, RUTH ALICE, religious association consultant; b. Shenandoah, Va., Feb. 21, 1931; d. Lee Earl and Lena Alice (Heishman) Sheaffer; m. Robert Mowery Daugherty, July 11, 1953; children: Carole Ruth, Steven Robert, Beth Anne Daugherty Carr. AA, Shenandoah Jr. Coll., 1950; BA, Lebanon Valley Coll., 1952; HHD (hon.), Albright Coll., 1982, Shenandoah U., 1986. English and history tchr. Bruce H.S., Westernport, Md., 1952-53, Trotwood (Ohio) H.S., 1953-55; officer United Meth. Women, Pa., 1956-72; nat. pres. United Meth. Women, 1980-84; nat. chair ministry study United Meth. Ch., 1984-92; nat. v.p. United Meth. Comm. Commn., 1984-88; v.p. United Bd. for Christian Higher Edn. in Asia, N.Y.C., 1984-87; cons. Mission Pers. Resources Bd. of Global Ministries, N.Y.C., 1990—. Author: (booklet) United Methodist Women in Mission, 1994. Trustee Lebanon Valley Coll., Annville, Pa., 1971-89; chair pers. com., chair mus. com. Scarritt-Bennett Ctr., Nashville, 1991—; chair policy program com., chair directions for '90s, United Bd. for Christian Higher Edn. in Asia, 1990—; trustee East Pa. Conf. United Meth. Ch., Valley Forge, Pa., 1992—. Recipient Alumni award Lebanon Valley Coll., 1979. Home: 892 Justin Ln West Chester PA 19382

DAUGHTREY, MARTHA CRAIG, federal judge; b. Covington, Ky., July 21, 1942; d. Spence E. Kerkow and Martha E. (Craig) Piatt; m. Larry G. Daughtrey, Dec. 28, 1962; 1 child, Carran. BA, Vanderbilt U., 1964, JD, 1968. Bar: Tenn. 1968. Pvt. practice Nashville, 1968, asst. U.S. atty., 1968-69, asst. dist. atty., 1969-72; asst. prof. law Vanderbilt U., Nashville, 1972-75; judge Tenn. Ct. Appeals, Nashville, 1975-90; assoc. justice Tenn. Supreme Ct., Nashville, 1990-93; circuit judge U.S. Ct. Appeals (6th cir.), Nashville, 1993—; lectr. law Vanderbilt Law Sch., Nashville, 1975-82, adj. prof., 1988-90; mem. faculty NYU Appellate Judges Seminar, N.Y.C., 1977-90, 94—. Contbr. articles to profl. jours. Pres. Women Judges Fund for Justice, 1984-85, 1986-87; active various civic orgns. Recipient Athena award Nat. Athena Program, 1991. Fellow ABA (chair appellate judges conf. 1985-86, chair jud. adminstrv. divsn. 1989-90, ho. dels. 1988-91, standing com. on continuing edn. of the bar 1992-94, commn. on women in the profession 1994—), Tenn. Bar Assn., Nashville Bar Assn. (bd. dirs. 1988-90); mem. Am. Judicature Soc. (bd. dirs. 1988-92), Nat. Assn. Women Judges (pres. 1985-86), Lawyers Assn. for Women (Nashville pres. 1986-87). Office: US Ct Appeals 304 Customs House 701 Broadway Nashville TN 37203

DAUGHTRY, DIANE MORTON, educator; b. Memphis, Feb. 10, 1958; d. W. C. and Joan (Mitchell) Morton; m. James Samuel Daughtry, Aug. 11, 1979; children: Samantha, Joey, Matthew. BS in Edn., Miss. State U., 1980. Diversified occupations coord. Alcorn County Schs., Corinth, Miss., 1980-83; adminstrv. asst. West St. Mary C. of C., Franklin, La., 1986-87; mktg. asst. Edgewood Mall, McComb, Miss., 1987-88; diversified occupations coord. McComb Sch. Dist., 1988—; advisor McComb Vocat. Ctr., 1988—. Mem. Distributive Edn. Clubs of Am., Miss. Assn. Mktg. Educators (bd. dirs. 1994-95), Miss. Assn. of Coop. Edn. Tchrs. (bd. dirs. 1994-95), Miss. Assn. of Vocat. Educators, Am. Vocat. Assn. Baptist. Office: McComb Vocat Ctr 1003 Virginia Ave McComb MS 39648

DAUSER, KIMBERLY ANN, physician assistant; b. Detroit, Nov. 20, 1947; d. George Leonard and Jeanne (Austin) Wilkie; m. Steven Kent Dauser, Nov. 10, 1983; 1 child, Aaron Thomas. AA, Pensacola Jr. Coll., 1971; BS in Medicine, physician's asst. cert. in medicine, U. Ala., Birmingham, 1976; cert. in mgmt., Am. Mgmt. Assn., 1989; postgrad., U. West Fla. Cert. physician's asst. Asst. mgr. Christo's, Gulf Breeze, Fla., 1966-67; teller, bookkeeper loan dept. Bank Gulf Breeze, 1967-72; med. tech. aide USN Hosp., Pensacola, 1972, physician's asst., 1972-73; physician's asst. John Kingsley, MD, Pensacola, 1976, Mountain Comprehensive Health Corp., Whitesburg, Ky., 1976-78; physician's asst. N.W. Fla. Nephrology, Pensacola, 1978, med. adminstr., 1984—; asst. adminstr. Nephrology Ctr. of Pensacola, Fla., 1987-89, med. adminstr., 1989-90, v.p. med. affairs Nephrology Ctr. of Pensacola, 1990-91; physician's asst. N.W. Fla. Artificial Kidney Ctr., Pensacola, 1980-87; med. adminstr. Nephrology Ctr. Pensacola, Nephrology Ctr. Crestview, 1991—. Fellow Am. Acad. Physician's Assts. (del. nat. mtg. 1979), Nat. Commn. on Cert. Physician's Assts., Fla. Acad. Physician's Assts. (mem. jud. com. 1979-80), Natural Wildlife Assn. Republican. Roman Catholic. Office: NW Fla Nephrology 1717 N E St Ste 403 Pensacola FL 32501-6334

DAUTH, FRANCES KUTCHER, journalist, newspaper editor; b. St. Louis, Aug. 20, 1941; d. David Jacob Kutcher and Dorothy Marie (Baugh) Hedges; m. Jerry Donald Dauth, July 5, 1964 (div. Dec. 1980). BA, U. Colo., 1963; cert. mgmt. program, Smith Coll., 1989. Staff writer Alameda (Calif.) Times Star, 1966-67, Contra Costa Times, Walnut Creek, Calif., 1968-69, Oakland (Calif.) Tribune, 1969-77; project editor San Francisco Examiner, 1977-82; asst. city editor Phila. Inquirer, 1982, dep. N.J. editor, 1983, suburban editor, 1984-85, city editor, 1985-89, nat. editor, 1989-91, fgn. editor, 1991-94, assoc. mng. editor, 1994—. Home: PO Box 12951 Philadelphia PA 19108-0951 Office: Phila Inquirer 400 N Broad St Philadelphia PA 19130-4099

DAVENPORT, DEBRA BRITTAIN, business owner, career counselor; b. Chgo., Sept. 18, 1957; d. Joseph Frank and Verna Mary (Kuebler) Hospy. BA, Loyola Marymount U., 1977, MA, 1981. Lic. career counselor, Ariz.; cert. EMT. Dir. corp. comm. Maxicare Health Plans, L.A., 1983-85; prin. Davenport Mktg. Mgmt., L.A. and Austin, Tex., 1985-91; owner Debra Davenport Assocs. (Career Mgmt.), 1991—, Desert Creative Group, Scottsdale, Ariz., 1991—. Author features in Scottsdale Mag., 1993—, Today's Ariz. Woman, 1993, Ariz. Republic, 1993; creator card game Career Shuffle, 1991. Health care com. Conejo Valley Chamber, Thousand Oaks, 1988. Fellowships Loyola Marymount U., 1980-81. Mem. ACA, Am. Assn. Mus., Shemer Art Ctr. and Mus. (chair publicity and mktg. coms., edn. com. 1994—), Scottsdale C. of C., Ariz. Career Devel. Assn. (bd. dirs. 1994). Office: Debra Davenport Assocs/Desert Creative Group PO Box 4233 6619 N Scottsdale Rd Scottsdale AZ 85261-4223

DAVENPORT, DONA LEE, telecommunications consultant; b. Toledo, May 17, 1931; d. Juston Burns and Opal Thelma (Raines) D. B.A., tchrs.'s cert., U. Mich., 1953; summer postgrad., U. N.C., 1957, N.C. State U., 1958, Queens Coll., 1969. Tchr. Grosse Pointe, Mich., 1953-54, Jr. High Sch., Charlotte, 1955-58; radio-TV coordinator Charlotte Sch. System, 1958-60; co-founder, tchr. Am. Assn. U. Women Spl. Sch. for Academically Talented Children, Charlotte, 1960; radio-TV dir. Charlotte-Mecklenburg Schs., 1960-62; founding mgr. Sta. WTVI, Charlotte, 1962-72, gen. mgr., 1972-77; exec. dir. Sta. WTVI, Inc., Charlotte, 1977-79; telecommunications mgmt. cons. Atlantic Research Corp., 1979—; Chmn. FCC Instructional TV Fixed Service Com. for N.C., 1968-71; Bd. dirs. Pub. Broadcasting Service, 1972-79. Chmn. media libr. and tape ministry Myers Park Bapt. Ch., 1989—, mem. bd. edn., 1989—, mem. sr. minister seach com., 1992-94, deacon 1994—; vol. Belk Heart Ctr., Presbyn. Hosp., 1989—. Named Charlotte's Outstanding Career Woman in Communications, Central Charlotte Assn., 1967; recipient Broadcast Preceptor award Broadcast Industry Conf, 1969; Regent's scholar U. Mich., 1949-53. Mem. So. Ednl. Communications Assn. (dir. 1968-78, treas. 1973-74, vice chmn. 1977-78), Nat. Assn. Ednl. Broadcasters, Am. Women in Radio and TV (named First Woman Public TV Sta. Mgr. 1980), N.C. Adminstrv. Women in Edn., Am. Assn. U. Women, Delta Kappa Gamma, Alpha Xi Delta. Clubs: Business and Professional Women's (Charlotte); Charlotte-Mecklenburg Republican Women's. Home and Office: 1510 Exeter Rd Charlotte NC 28211-2233

DAVENPORT, JANET LEE, real estate saleswomen, small business owner; b. Napa, Calif., Dec. 10, 1938; d. George Perry and Stella Dolores (Ramalho) Gomez; m. Bingo George Wesner, Aug. 4, 1957 (July 1978); children: Bing George, Diane Estelle; m. Marvin Eugene Davenport, Jan. 13, 1979. Student, U. Calif., Davis, 1956-57, Nat. Jud. Coll., 1975-79. Co-owner, operator Bar JB Ranch, Benicia, Calif., 1960-71, Lovelock, Nev., 1971-78; owner, mgr. Wesner Bookkeeping Svc., Lovelock, 1973-78; chief tribal judge Ct. Indian Offenses, Lovelock, 1975-79; justice of peace, coroner County of Pershing, Lovelock, 1975-79; paralegal, legal sec. Samuel S. Wardle, Carson City, Nev., 1979; dep. ct. adminstr. Reno Mcpl. Ct., Reno, 1979-81; co-owner horse farm Reno, 1979—, freelance real estate investor, 1979—; real estate saleswoman Merrill Lynch Realtors, Sparks, Nev., 1981-82; realtor, farm and ranch div. mgr. Copple and Assocs., Realtors, Sparks, 1982-91; real estate saleswoman Vail and Assocs. Realty, Reno, Nev., 1991—; co-owner, operator Lovelock (Nev.) Merc. Co., 1988—; sec. Nev. Judges Assn., 1977-78. Dir. Pershing County Drug and Alcohol Abuse Council, Lovelock, 1976-78. Mem. Reno/Sparks Bd. Realtors, Nat. Assn. Realtors, Nev. Assn. Realtors, Am. Quarter Horse Assn. Republican. Roman Catholic. Home: 4805 Sinelio Dr Reno NV 89502-9510 Office: Vail and Assocs Realty 1700 S Virginia St Reno NV 89502-2811

DAVENPORT, MARSHA LYNN, pediatrician, educator; b. Louisville, July 13, 1955; d. Roy Dae and Cherry Joan (Cook) Davenport. AB, Harvard U., 01977; MD, U. Ky., 1982. Diplomate Am. Bd. Pediatrics. Resident in pediatrics U. N.C., Chapel Hill, 1982-85, fellow pediatric endocrinology, 1985-88, asst. prof. pediatrics, 1988—. Recipient awards NIH, 1988, 91, Mallincroft Found., 1993. Mem. Am. Fedn. Clin. Rsch., Soc. Pediatric Rsch., Endocrine Soc., Lawson Wilkins Pediatric Endocrine Soc. Democrat. Presbyn. Office: U NC CB #7220 509 Burnett-Womack Chapel Hill NC 27599

DAVENPORT, PAMELA BEAVER, rancher, small business owner; b. Big Spring, Tex., Nov. 18, 1948; d. Frank Jones and Doris Glynn (Wills) Beaver; m. Robert Sampson Davenport, Feb. 2, 1982; 1 child, Danielle. BS in Mktg. and Textiles, Tex. Tech U., 1969, MS, 1970; cert. in spinal orthotics, Northwestern U., 1976. Adminstrv. asst. Tex-Togs, Inc., El Paso, 1971-75; dir. edn. Camp Internat., Jackson, Mich., 1975-79; realtor Tom Carpenter, Realtor, San Angelo, Tex., 1979-83; retailer Davenport Barber & Beauty, San Angelo, 1985—; rancher Gail, Tex., 1970—. Copntbr. articles to profl. jours. Vice chmn. adv. bd. San Angelo Recreation Dept., 1987-88; chmn. adv. bd. Recreation Dept., River Stage, 1990; chmn. Tom Green County Adult Literacy Coun., 1989-90; publicity chmn. San Angelo Cultural Affairs Coun., 1986; treas. San Angelo Commun. Hosp. Aux., 1980-82; publicity chmn. Christmas at Old Fort Concho, 1986; mem. Leadership San Angelo. Mem. AAUW (cultural chmn. Tex. bd. 1988-89, pres. 1986-88, chmn. conv. 1984-86). Methodist. Home: 3234 Palo Duro Dr San Angelo TX 76904-7330

DAVICK, KYM MARIE, interior designer; b. Oregon, Ohio, Nov. 29, 1957; d. Charles James and Norma Jean (Hughes) Ulrich; m. Keith Jeffrey Davick, Feb. 6, 1976. Student, Toledo U., 1977. Cert. in basic counseling skills, Colo. Interior designer Homestead House, Littleton, Colo., 1985-86; owner, interior designer KD! Design, Highlands Ranch, Colo., 1986—; art cons. Art Boutique Gallery, Cherry Creek, Colo., 1991. Recipient Award of Merit for best interior design Home Bldrs. Assn. Met. Denver, 1988. Mem. Internat. Soc. Interior Designers (provisional), NAFE. Home and Office: 8471 S Timberwood St Highlnds Rnch CO 80126-2000

DAVID, BARBARA MARIE, medical, surgical nurse; b. Wisconsin Rapids, Wis., Mar. 3, 1935; d. Stanley Spencer and Olga Agatha (Bissig) Stark; m. Russell Paul David, Jan. 19, 1957; children: Dennis James, John Paul. Diploma, St. Joseph's Hosp. Sch. Nursing, Marshfield, Wis., 1956. Cert. med./surg. nurse, clin. nurse 3. Asst. to dir. nursing rsch. St. Joseph's Hosp., head nurse, ICU, staff nurse. Mem. ANA, Wis. Nurses Assn. (treas. dist. 18), Acad. Med.-Surg. Nurses. Home: 2007 S Maple Ave Marshfield WI 54449-4957

DAVID, ELIZABETH ADELINE, typesetter, writer; b. New Bedford, Mass., Mar. 21, 1957; d. Thomas Nacle Maroon and Octavia Jean (Peters) D. AA, Bristol C.C., 1978. Account exec. Help Wanted Advt., Boston, 1978-82; freelance typesetter, writer Boston, 1982—; recruitment advt. supr. Wang Labs., Lowell, Mass., 1982-83. Author: Gad's Trip to Park, 1981, Zebra Who Lost Stripes, 1983, Shep, Joe and Malunkus Harry, 1984, A Child with Wings, 1986, Reluctant Activist, 1991; editor, author The Legacy mag., 1984-93. Fundraiser Boston Women's Fund, 1993. Mem. NOW (membership chair local chpt., mem. state coun. 1990-91), Women's Statewide Legis. Alliance (organizing bd. dirs. 1993). Office: You Aint Seen Nothin Yet PO Box 766 Fairhaven MA 02719-0700

DAVID, JACQUELINE, educator; b. N.Y.C.; d. Jack and Ossie Belle (Pierce) D.; BA, Fordham U., 1974; MA, Columbia U., 1977; postgrad. Baruch Coll., 1979-85. Reading instr. Seton Hall U., South Orange, N.J., summer 1978; group tchr. Leggett Day Care Ctr., N.Y.C., 1975-76; basic skills improvement tchr. Lincoln Elem. Sch., East Orange, N.J., 1977-86; tchr. reading, staff developer Pub. Sch. 208, N.Y.C., 1986—; founder, dir. Garden of Knowledge Tutorial Svcs.; condr. in-service workshops for tchrs./parents. Co-editor: Listen to the Children, 1985. Recipient 5-yr. service award, 1983. Mem. Phi Delta Kappa. Baptist. Office: PS 208 21 W 111th St New York NY 10026-4396

DAVID, MARTHA LENA HUFFAKER, real estate agent, former educator; b. Susie, Ky., Feb. 7, 1925; d. Andrew Michael and Nora Marie (Cook) Huffaker; m. William Edward David, June 24, 1952 (div. Jan. 1986); children: Edward Garry, William Andrew, Carolyn Ann, Robert Cook. AB in Music magna cum laude, Georgetown (Ky.) Coll., 1947; postgrad., Vanderbilt U., 1957-58; Spanish cert., Lang. Sch., Costa Rica, 1959; MEd, U. Ga., 1972. Elem. tchr. Wayne County Bd. Edn., Spann, Ky., 1944-45; music tchr. Mason County, Mayslick, Ky., 1947-49, Hikes Grade Sch., Buechel, Ky., 1949-53; English and Spanish tchr. Jefferson (Ga.) High Sch., 1961-63; music and English tchr. Athens (Ga.) Acad., 1967-71; music tchr. Barrow County Bd. Edn., Winder, Ga., 1971-88; real estate agt. South Best Realty, Athens, 1986—; data collector Regional Ednl. Svcs. Agy., Athens and Winder, 19176-78; tchr. music Union Theol. Sem., Buenos Aires, 1957-60. Author: (poems) Parcels of Love, 1980; composer (music plays) The B.B.'s, The Missing Tune, A Dream Come True, The Stars Who Creep Out of Orbit, 1976-86. Active cultural affairs orgns., Athens, 1962—; entertainer nursing homes and civic orgns., Athens, 1962; chmn. cancer drives, heart fund drive United Way, March of Dimes, Athens, 1962—; elder, pianist Christian Ch. Winner regional piano competition Ky. Philharm. Orch., 1946; nominated Tchrs. Hall of Fame, Barrow County, 1981. Mem. Ret. Tchrs. Assn., Writer's Group, Ga. Music Tchrs., Nat. Music Tchrs. Assn., Athens Music Tchrs. Assn. (pres. recital chmn.), Ga. World Orgn. China Painters, Athens Area Porcelain Artists, Women's Mus. Arts (assoc.), Women's Mus. Art (Washington), Touchdown Club, Band Boosters, Alpha Delta Kappa, Delta Omicron (life, scholar 1944). Republican. Mem. Christian Ch. Home: 105 Nassau Ln Athens GA 30607

DAVIDOVICH, LOLITA, actress; b. Ont., Can., 1961. Actress (films) Class, 1983, Adventures in Babysitting, 1987, The Big Town, 1987, Blaze, 1989, The Object of Beauty, 1991, JFK, 1991, The Inner Circle, 1991, Raising Cain, 1992, Leap of Faith, 1992, Boiling Point, 1993, Intersection, 1994, Cobb, 1994 (TV) Two Fathers' Justice, 1985, Uncut Gem, 1990, Prison Stories: Women on the Inside, HBO, 1991 (ACE award nomination best actress in a movie or mini-series 1991), Keep the Change, 1992. Office: Internat Creative Mgmt 8942 Wilshire Blvd Beverly Hills CA 90211*

DAVIDSON, ANNE STOWELL, lawyer; b. Rye, N.Y., Feb. 24, 1949; d. Robert Harold and Anne (Breeding) Davidson. B.A. magna cum laude, Smith Coll., 1971; J.D. cum laude, George Washington U., 1974. Bar: D.C. 1975, U.S. Dist. Ct. D.C. 1975, U.S. Ct. Appeals (D.C. cir.) 1975, U.S. Supreme Ct. 1980. Asst. gen. counsel FDA, Rockville, Md., 1974-78; counsel Abbott Labs., North Chicago, Ill., 1978-79; counsel U.S. Pharm. Ops. Schering-Plough Corp., Kenilworth, N.J., 1979-83; sr. counsel Sandoz Pharms. Corp., Inc., East Hanover, N.J., 1983-86, v.p., assoc. gen. counsel, 1987—. Trustee, N.J. Pops Orch. Recipient Dawes Prize Smith Coll., 1971. Mem. ABA, Pharm. Mfrs. Assn., Food and Drug Law Inst., Non-prescription Drug Mfrs. Assn. (govt. affairs com.). Republican. Presbyterian. Club: Smith Coll. (pres. 1981-82). Contbr. articles to profl. jours. Office: Sandoz Pharms Corp 59 State Route 10 East Hanover NJ 07936-1011

DAVIDSON, BETTY LOU, real estate agent; b. Minot, N.D., Nov. 21, 1945; d. Roy Wilson and Julia Marie (Glaholt) Hartman; m. Richard A. Davidson, Jan. 4, 1964; children: Deborah Kay Dirks, Richard A. Jr. Diploma, Aaker's Bus. Coll., Grand Forks, N.D., 1980; grad., Realtors Inst., 1984. cert. residential specialist; cert. profl. stds. procedures, N.D. Real estate broker Greenberg Realty, Grand Forks, 1994—; career cons. Career Day, Distributive Edn. Clubs Am., U. N.D., 1984. Author: Sunnyside Terrace Neighborhood Directory, 1989. Recipient Rookie of Yr. award Gallery of Homes, Mpls., 1984. Mem. Residential Sales Coun., Grand Forks Bd. Realtors (mem. greivance com. 1992-94, program com. chairperson 1984-85), N.D. Bd. Realtors (mem. program com.), Grand Forks Country Club. Lutheran. Home: 2396 27th Ave S # 116 Grand Forks ND 58201 Office: Greenberg Realty 2850 24th Ave S # 201 Grand Forks ND 58201

DAVIDSON, CATHY NOTARI, English language educator, writer; b. Chgo., June 21, 1949; d. Paul Celestino Notari and Leona (Behnke) Ripes; m. Arnold E. Davidson ; 1 child, Charles Russell. BA, Elmhurst Coll., 1970; MA, SUNY, Binghamton, 1973, PhD, 1974; postdoctoral study, U. Chgo., 1975-76; LHD (hon.), Elmhurst Coll., 1989. Instr. St. Bonaventure U., Olean, N.Y., 1974-75; from asst. to full prof. Mich. State U., East Lansing, 1976-89; prof. dept. English Duke U., Durham, N.C., 1989—; vis. prof. Kobe (Japan) Coll., 1980-81, 87-88, Princeton U., 1988-89. Author: The Experimental Fictions of Ambrose Bierce, 1984, Revolution and the Word: The Rise of the Novel in America, 1986, Thirty-Six Views of Mt. Fuji: On Finding Myself in Japan, 1993; editor: The Book of Love: Writers and Their Love Letters, 1992, The Oxford Companion to Women's Writing in the United States, 1994; co-editor: The Lost Tradition: Mothers and Daughters in Literature, 1980, The Art of Margaret Atwood, 1982; editor: Reading in America: Literature and Social History, 1989, Charlotte Temple, 1986, The Coquette, 1986; assoc. editor Am. Lit., 1990-91, editor, 1991—; also over 50 articles. Woodrow Wilson fellow, 1970, Woodrow Wilson Dissertation fellowship, 1972, Irving J. Lee Meml. award, 1973, Newberry Libr. Scholar-in-Residence award, 1976, Mich. State Disting. Tchr.-Scholar award, 1979, Mich. State Disting. Faculty award, 1987, Kate B. and Hall James Peterson fellowship, hon. mem. Am. Antiquarian Soc., Worcester, Mass., 1984, Am. Coun. of Learned Socs. grant-in-aid, N.Y., 1986, John Simon Guggenheim Meml. fellowship, N.Y., 1986. Mem. ALA (exec. com. div. on late 19th century Am. lit. 1981-86, div. on early Am. lit. 1987—; mem. del. assembly 1980-86), Fulbright Sr. fellow, Australia, 1994, Bellagio Ctr. Rockefeller fellow, 1993. Mem. Am. Studies Assn. (pres. 1993). Office: Duke Univ Dept English 6697 College Station Durham NC 27708

DAVIDSON, EDITH YOUNG, school counselor; b. Hudson, N.Y., Oct. 15, 1940; d. Edward H. and Marie (Frick) Young; m. Dan Lee Davidson, Sept. 15, 1962; children: Gaelyn, Meridan. BS in Edn., Pa. State U., 1962; MEd, Boston U., 1979, cert. Advanced Grad. Study, Boston U., 1980. Tchr., Middletown Pub. schs., R.I., 1962-66; tchr. NIH program, Montgomery County Pub. Schs., Md., 1968-69; tchr. pre-sch., kindergarten, Va., 1971-75; substitute tchr./tchr. Dept. Def. Schs., Europe, 1976-78; counselor Anne Arundel County pub. schs., Annapolis, Md., 1980-82; part-time registrar Anne Arundel Community Coll., Arnold, Md., 1980-81; counselor Needham Pub. Schs. (Mass.), 1984-85, Old Orchard Beach (Maine) pub. schs., 1986-88, Portland, Maine, publ schs., 1988—, P.R.O. Assocs., 1990—. Bd. dirs., Kennebec Coun. Girl Scouts U.S.A., leader, 1975-77, 79-81, 87—, troop advisor, 1981-82, chmn. svc. unit, Wellesley, Mass., 1983-85, chmn. property com., 1992-94; PTA vol. coord., 1979-80; v.p. Bates Band Boosters, 1979-80. Mem. NEA, Am. Assn. Counseling Assn., So. Maine Counselors Assn. (pres.), Am. Sch. Counselors Assn., Maine Tchrs. Assn., Portland Tchrs. Assn., Phi Delta Kappa, Pi Beta Phi. Home: 26 Ocean View Rd Cape Eliz ME 04107-1344

DAVIDSON, FLORENCE HICKMAN, clinical psychologist, education consultant; b. Merion Station, Pa., Apr. 2, 1928; d. Alfred Marriner and Marjory Letitia (Bunting) Hickman; m. William D. Davidson, Aug. 31, 1949 (div. 1968); children: Christopher, John, Peter, Ben, Bernard, Miriam; m. Leonard Kreidermacher, Jan. 1, 1983. BA, Duke U., 1950; MEd, St. Cloud State U., 1965; EdD, Harvard U., 1974. Lic. psychologist, Mass. Rsch. assoc. Ctr. for Moral Devel., Harvard U., 1974-76; pvt. practice clin. psychology Falmouth, Mass., 1976—; co-founder Mass. Sch. Profl. Psychology; exec. dir. Mass. Psychol. Ctr., Boston, 1972-78. Author: (with Miriam Davidson) Changing Childhood Prejudice: The Caring Work of the Schools, 1994. Bd. dirs. Cambridge (Mass.) Friends Sch. Bunting Inst. fellow Radcliffe Coll., 1970-72; Milton fellow Harvard U., 1974-76. Democrat. Quaker. Home and Office: 457 Elm Rd Falmouth MA 02540

DAVIDSON, GRACE EVELYN, nursing educator, retired administrator; b. Wabash, Ind., Aug. 2, 1920; d. William Alexander and Jennie Lavinia (Baker) Davidson. Diploma, Columbia Presbyn. Sch. Nursing, 1942; BS, U. Minn., 1948; MA in Teaching, Columbia U., 1954, postgrad. 1961, 63-64. Instr. Sch. Nursing, Columbia U., N.Y.C., 1948-51; assoc. prof. Skidmore Coll., Saratoga Springs, N.Y., 1954-66; asst. adminstr., dir. nursing Univ. Hosp., NYU Med. Ctr., 1966-79, assoc. prof., 1977-79, prof. 1979—; cons. nursing svc. adminstrn., N.Y.C., 1980-88. Contbr. articles to profl. jours. Served to Maj. Army Nurse Corps, 1943-46, World War II, 51-53, Korea, Res., 53-60, Ret. Recipient Alumni Fedn. medal Columbia U., 1981, Plaque for leadership in nursing NYU Med. Ctr., 1983; Grace Davidson award established in her honor NYU, 1991. Mem. Nursing Edn. Alumnae Assn. Tchrs. Coll. Columbia U. (achievement award 1977), Am. Nurses Assn., Nat. League Nursing, Columbia U.-Presbyn. Hosp. Sch. Nursing Alumnae Assn. (pres. 1970-76, edn. bd. 1985-93, bd. dirs. 1993—, Disting. Alumnae award 1981), Fedn. Alumni Assn. Columbia U., Ret. Officers Assn., Ret. Army Nurse Corps., The Woman's Club of Dumont. Republican. Presbyterian. Home: 67 Chestnut St Dumont NJ 07628-3214

DAVIDSON, JANET ELAINE, business manager; b. Springfield, Mo., June 10, 1960; d. Marion Charles and Peggy June (Russell) D. BS in Secondary Edn., U. Ark., 1982; MBA, Sam Houston State U., 1991. Tchr., coach Amarillo (Tex.) Ind. Sch. Dist., 1982-84, Itasca (Tex.) Ind. Sch. Dist., 1984-85; tchr. math. Conroe (Tex.) Ind. Sch. Dist., 1985-91; bus. mgr. Amherst Family Practice, P.C., Winchester, Va., 1992—. Referee Va. High Sch. League, 1993, umpire, 1993; umpire nat. softball tournament Amateur Softball Assn., Midland, Tex., 1984. Am. Bus. Women's Assn. scholar, 1991. Mem. Winchester Med. Office Mgrs. Assn., Kappa Delta Pi. Office: Amherst Family Practice PC 522 Amherst St Winchester VA 22601-3802

DAVIDSON, JEAN DAIL, psychologist; b. Greenville, N.C., May 31, 1930; d. Frank Clifton and Pauline (Fornes) Dail; m. Elmer Hayes Davidson, Sept. 14, 1957; children: Brenda Joy, David Franklin. BA magna cum laude (Nat. Meth. Scholar), Greensboro Coll., 1957; MS (rsch. grantee), Pa. State U., 1963, PhD cand. (Gen. Foods fellow), 1964-65. Cert. psychol. assoc., N.C. Sch. psychometrist Greensboro (N.C.) Pub. Schs., 1958-60; instr. Tex. Technol. U., Lubbock, 1965-66; dir. New World Sch., Oklahoma City, 1966-71; dir. psychol. svcs. Southeastern Mental Health Ctr., Wilmington, N.C., 1971-74; dir. children's outpatient svcs. Edgecombe-Nash Mental Health Ctr., Rocky Mt., N.C., 1974-80; sr. psychologist Franklin County Family Counseling & Mental Health Ctr., Louisburg, N.C., 1980-87; founder, dir., pres. Little People Ednl. Day Care, Chapel Hill, N.C., 1987—; part-time instr. Nash County Tech. Inst., Rocky Mt., 1977-79, Cen. Carolina Community Coll., Silver City, 1988-91, infant/pre-sch. lab sch. steering com. mem., 1991-92. Mem. Com. Early Childhood Degree programs State Dept. Edn., Okla., 1969-70; bd. dirs Heald Start program New Hanover County, Inc., Wilmington, N.C., 1972-74; mem. Pub. Pvt. Ptnrship. Day Care Task Force, Chapel Hill, N.C., 1989-92. Fellow Vanderbilt U., 1957, Gen. Foods Co. fellow Pa. State U., 1963-65, Early Childhood Leadership Devel. Program fellow U. N.C., Chapel Hill., 1994. Mem. Nat. Assn. for Edn. Young Children, N.C. Assn. for Edn. Young Children, N.C. Day Care Assn., Omicron Nu. Methodist. Home: 59 Dogwood Acres Dr Chapel Hill NC 27516-3111 Office: Little People Ednl Day Care 1740 Smith Level Rd Chapel Hill NC 27516-3249

DAVIDSON, JEANNIE, costume designer; b. San Francisco, Mar. 21, 1938; d. Willis H. and Dorothy J. (Starks) Rich; children from previous marriage: David L. Schultz, Mark P. Schultz, Seana Davidson, Michael Davidson; m. Bryan N. St. Germain, June 14, 1980. BA, Stanford (Calif.) U., 1961, postgrad., 1965-68. Resident costume designer Oreg. Shakespearean Festival, Ashland, 1969-91; freelance designer, 1991—; owner Ravenna Fabric Studio, Inc., Medford, Oreg. Designer over 150 prodns. including all 37 of Shakespeare's plays. Recipient numerous awards for excellence in costume design. Mem. U.S. Inst. for Theatre Tech., Phi Beta Kappa.

DAVIDSON, JOAN GATHER, psychologist; b. Long Branch, N.J., Jan. 26, 1934; d. Ralph Paul and Hilde (Bresser) Gather; m. Harry Gene Davidson, Sept. 14, 1957; children: Guy, Marc, Kelly. BA, Shorter Coll., 1956; BA cum laude, U. South Fla., 1982; MS, Fla. Inst. Tech., 1986, PsyD, 1987. Lic. psychologist, Fla., RN, Ga. Clin. instr. Ga. Bapt. Sch. Nursing, Atlanta, 1956-59; dir. nurses Aidmore Hosp., Atlanta, 1959-60; dir. insvc. edn., asst. dir. nurses Bayfront Med. Ctr., St. Petersburg, Fla., 1960; instr. St. Petersburg Jr. Coll., 1971-76; pvt. practice St. Petersburg-Clearwater, 1987—. Mem. Am. Psychol. Assn., Fla. Psychol. Assn., Nat. Register Health Svc. Providers in Psychology, Assn. for Advancement Psychology, Am. Assn. Christian Counselors, Psi Chi, Phi Kappa Phi. Republican. Baptist. Home: 11600 87th Ave Largo FL 34642-3613 Office: Ste 105 25400 US 19 N Clearwater FL 34623

DAVIDSON, JOSEPHINE F., newspaper editor; b. El Paso, Tex.; d. Leon Amson and Estelle Therese (Lyon) Rosenfield; m.Herbert Marc Davidson, Jr., Dec. 27, 1947; children: Marc Leon, Julia Rose. BA in Polit. Sci., UCLA, 1943; D of Journalism (hon.), Stetson U., 1994. Reporter Ventura Star Free Press, Calif., 1943-45; reporter News-Journal, Daytona Beach, Fla., sch. editor, food editor, Sunday editor, asst. editor, 1945-85, co-editor, 1985, editor, 1986—; v.p. News-Journal Corp., Daytona Beach, Fla., 1985—; mem. jud. nominating commn. for Fla. Supreme Ct., 1994-98; first woman editor UCLA Daily Bruin, 1943. Chmn. Volusia County Student Bicentennial Park, 1974-76; bd. dirs. Fla. Endowment for the Humanities, Tampa, 1984-88, Ctrl. Fla. Cultural Endeavors, Daytona Beach, 1976—, Seaside Music Theater, Daytona Beach, 1978—, Civic League, Tiger Bay Club; program chmn. Volusia County Women's Network. Recipient J. Saxton Lloyd award for cmty. svcs. Civic League, 1995; honoree Daytona Beach C.C. Found., 1992, Tippen and Josephine Field Davidson Endowment for Arts. Mem. Am. Soc. Newspaper Editors. Office: News-Journal Corp 901 Sixth St Daytona Beach FL 32117

DAVIDSON, JOY ELAINE, mezzo-soprano; b. Ft. Collins, Colo., Aug. 18, 1940; d. Clarence Wayne and Jessie Ellen (Bogue) Ferguson; m. Robert Scott Davidson, Aug. 9, 1959; children: Lisa Beth, Robert Scott II, Jeremy Fergus, Bonnie Kathleen, Jordan Christian. B.A., Occidental Coll., Los Angeles, 1959; postgrad., Fla. State U., 1961-64. dir. vocal/opera dept. New World Sch. of Arts Coll./Conservatory Divsn., Miami, Fla. 1992—. Debut 1965 with Miami Opera; has performed with Met. Opera, opera cos. throughout U.S. and Can., La Scala, Vienna State Opera, Bayerische State Opera, Lyons (France) Opera, Welsh Opera, Florence (Italy) Opera, Torino (Italy) Opera. (recipient Gold medal Internat. Competition Young Opera Singers, Sofia, Bulgaria 1969), Rio de Janeiro; performed with numerous orchs. including N.Y. Philharm., Los Angeles Philharm., Boston Orch., Pitts. Orch., Columbus (Ohio) Orch.; rec. artist. Named Outstanding Miami Artist at Orange Bowl. Mem. PEO, United Meth. Women, Sigma Alpha Iota, Zeta Tau Zeta. Methodist. Home: 5751 SW 74th Ave Miami FL 33143-1735 Office: Sardos Artist Mgmt Corp 180 W End Ave New York NY 10023-4902 also: Vocal Opera Dept New World Sch Coll Conservatory Divsn 300 NE 2nd Ave Miami FL 33132-2204

DAVIDSON, JULI, writer, entrepreneur; b. Houston, Aug. 23, 1960; d. Martin J. Davidson and Ruth Marder. Diploma, Park Sch., Brooklandville, Md., 1978; Cert., Richmond Coll., Surrey, Eng., 1978; student, Austin Coll., U. N.Mex, others, 1978-84. Cert. med. terminology and transcription, 1981. Pres. mail order co. Surrenderings, Inc., Albuquerque, 1989-93; owner, artist Juli Davidson Studio Gallery, Albuquerque, 1987-89; freelance writer, editor, photographer Albuquerque, 1985-86; pres., paper artist, writer SI: A Paperworks Gallery, Sante Fe, 1993; exec. adminstr. Albuquerque Art Bus. Assn., 1989; bd. sec. Albuquerque United Artists, 1988. Contbr. to various publs. and is subject of various art revs.; writer, pub. mail-order publs., 1995—. Recipient 2d and 3d place photography awards Churches in N.Mex. Exhibit, 4th place Colorfest Human Interest Category, Colo. Mem. Garden Writers Assn. Am. (award for handmade booklet on dividing and multiplying potted plants), N.Mex. Organic Growers and Assocs., Comedy Writers Assn. Studio: PO Box 21669-ww Albuquerque NM 87154-1669

DAVIDSON, KAREN SUE, computer software designer; b. Chgo., July 24, 1950; d. Woodrow Wilson and Velma Louise (Dickinson) D. BS in Comm., U. Ill., 1972; MBA, De Paul U., 1977. News producer Sta. WIND, Westinghouse Broadcasting Co., Chgo., 1973-75; mktg. rep. div. data processing IBM, Chgo., 1977-80, process industry specialist, 1980; industry applications specialist IBM, White Plains, N.Y., 1981-83; sr. sales rep. Wang Labs., Chgo., 1983-84; ptnr. KDA-K Davidson & Assocs., Centralia, Ill., 1984—; pres. KDA Software Inc., Centralia, 1988-92; instr. Belleville (Ill.) Area Coll., 1992; vis. lectr. So. Ill. U., Carbondale, 1994; mem. rev. bd. State of Ill. Pvt. Enterprise. Author/designer software programs; contbr. articles to profl. pubs. State of Ill. Small Bus. Adv. Bd., Internat. Trade/Export Rep., 1990-93; WordPerfect cert. resource instr. WordPerfect Corp., 1991—. Named Outstanding Working Woman of Ill. Fedn. Bus. & Profl. Women's Clubs, 1990, Word Perfect Cert. Resource, Word Perfect Corp. Mem. Soc. Profl. Journalists, Ind. Computer Cons. Assn., Ill. Software Assn., Chgo. High Tech. Assn. Assn. St. Louis Info. Systems Trainers (v.p. 1988), Centralia Cultural Soc., Inventors' Assn. St. Louis, Greater Centralia C. of C. (bd. dirs. 1990-93, good will amb. 1990), Rotary, Zeta Tau Alpha. Presbyterian. Office: KDA Software Inc PO Box 1163 315 E 3d St Centralia IL 62801

DAVIDSON, LINDA SALE, elementary school counselor; b. Richmond, Va., July 22, 1950; d. David Nathaniel Sale and Aline Rosamond (McAnally) Melton; m. Matthew Oliver Davidson, Dec. 18, 1971; 1 child, Christian Matthew. AS, Germanna C.C., Locust Grove, Va., 1977; BA, Mary Washington Coll., 1979; MEd, Va. Commonwealth U., 1990. Postgrad. profl. cert. Sec. Va. Power Co., Richmond, 1968-71, La. Gas and Electric Co., Louisville, 1972; sec., dept. psychiatry U. Louisville, 1972-74; sec. Culpeper (Va.) Mental Health Clinic, 1975-76; substitute tchr. various sch. systems, Va., 1982-84; tchr. Hanover County Schs., Ashland, Va., 1983-84; admissions coord. Presbyn. Sch. Christian Edn., Richmond, 1985-89; elem. counselor Goochland (Va.) County Schs., 1989—; founding mem. Goochland Child Abuse Prevention Team, 1991—. Sunday sch. tchr. Glan Allen (Va.) Bapt. Ch., 1991—; co-presenter parenting groups Powhatan Correctional Ctr., State Farm, Va., 1993—; vol. Am. Cancer Soc., Glen Allen. Mem. Am. Counseling Assn., Va. Counseling Assn., Am. Sch. Counselor Assn., Va. Sch. Counselor Assn., Richmond Area Counselors Assn., Assn. for Play Therapy. Home: 10630 Meadowbrook Rd Glen Allen VA 23060

DAVIDSON, MELODY KAY, critical care nurse, educator; b. Carson City, Mich., Nov. 8, 1952; d. Donald Jay and Joan Estelle (Schweitzer) D. Vocat. nurse, Vocat. Nursing Sch. of So. Calif., L.A., 1971; ADN, U. State N.Y., Albany, 1981; BSN, Calif. Lutheran U., 1986; M in Nursing, U. Calif., L.A., 1988. CCRN. Staff nurse St Joseph Hosp., Orange, Calif., 1971-81, U. Calif. Med. Ctr., L.A., 1981, Valley Presbyterian Hosp., Van Nuys, Calif., 1981-88; clin. nurse specialist St. Joseph Med. Ctr., Burbank, Calif., 1988-89; clin. instr. Northridge (Calif.) Hosp. Med. Ctr., 1989-92; assoc. clin. prof. U. Calif., L.A., 1989—; clin. edn. specialist Hosp. of the Good Samaritan, L.A., 1992-93; clin. nurse specialist Doctors Med. Ctr., Modesto, Calif., 1993—. Mem. AACN San Fernando Valley Chpt. (v.p. elect 1988-89, v.p. 1989-90, pres. elect 1992-93), Calif. Nurses Assn. Region 3 (treas. 1985-86, mem.-at-large 1984-85). Home: 1304 Edwin Ct Modesto CA 95355 Office: Doctors Med Ctr 1441 Florida Ave Modesto CA 95356

DAVIDSON, NANCY ELAINE, county official; b. Ritzville, Wash., Dec. 5, 1946; d. Alfred and Ruby (Wahl) Sackmann; m. James A. Davidson, June 27, 1970; children: Jon Eric, Jeanette Marie. AA, Big Bend Community Coll., Moses Lake, Wash., 1967; BA, Cen. Wash. U., 1969. Cert. mcpl. clk. Recreation supr. City of Moses Lake, 1969-70; auto-tutorial ctr. coord. Big Bend Community Coll., Moses Lake, 1970-72; ch. sec. Bethany Presbyn. Ch., Grandview, Wash., 1978-80; city clk. City of Grandview, Wash., 1980-85; asst. county treas. Yakima (Wash.) County, 1985-91, county treas., 1991—. Pres. Ft. Simcoe coun. Boy Scouts Am., Yakima, 1990-93; mem. City Coun., Grandview, 1976-80. Mem. YWCA, Elected Women of Wash., Govt. Fin. Officers Assn., Wash. Assn. County Treas., Yakima Rep. Women's Club, Women's Rep. Club, Horizon Club. Presbyterian. Home: PO Box 56 Grandview WA 98930-0056 Office: Yakima County Treas Office PO Box 1408 Tacoma WA 98407

DAVIDSON, NOREEN HANNA, financial services company executive; b. Hartford, Conn., Sept. 13, 1950; d. Morris A. and Allene Sullivan (Gotis) Bezzini; m. Herbert L. Davidson, May 27, 1983 (div. 1991); 1 child, Stephanie Wells. BA, Stephens Coll., 1972. Senate intern U.S. Senator Thomas Dodd, Washington, 1970; legis. aide Mo. State Senate, Jefferson City, 1972; liaison econ. stabilization and White House Exec. Office of Pres., Washington, 1972-74; senate staff U.S. Senator Jacob Javitts, Washington, 1974; dir. legislation Nat. Assn. Plumbing, Heating and Cooling Contractors, Washington, 1975-77, Am. Aviation Found., Washington, 1977-81; mgr. nat. sales Nat. Standards, Bethesda, Md., 1981-84; v.p. Great Lakes Investment, Reston, Va., 1984-91; dir., v.p., br. mgr. Meyers, Pollack, Robbins, Inc., McLean, 1991—; mem. adv. bd. Heritage Fin. Corp., McLean, 1988-90. Author, editor Fixed Income newsletter Fin. Mgmt. Group, 1990, 91, Legislative News newsletter Nat. Assn. Plumbing, Heating and Cooling Contractors, 1976. Mem. exec. staff Presdl. Inaugural for Reagan, Washington, 1984, mem. staff, 1980, Presdl. Inaugural for Nixon, Washington, 1972; mem. PTA. Recipient Cert. of Appreciation, Presdl. Inaugural Com., 1984. Mem. Nat. Assn. Security Dealers (cert. series 7, 63, 24), Hunt Club Assn. (fin. advisor), Stephens Coll. Alumni, Hunt Club Girls Club (pres. 1988-89), Rotary Internat. Republican. Roman Catholic. Office: Meyers Pollock Robbins Inc 8280 Greensboro Dr # 100 Mc Lean VA 22102-3807

DAVIDSON, NORMA LEWIS, concert violinist, composer, music educator, psychologist; b. Provo, Utah, Oct. 12, 1929; d. Arthur and Mary (Mortimer) Lewis; m. William James Davidson, Dec. 29, 1949; children: Kevin James, Nathanael Arthur. Artist's diploma, Juilliard Sch., N.Y.C., 1950; BS, North Tex. State U., 1962, MS, 1965, MusM, 1970. Prof. violin and chamber music Mannes Coll. Music, N.Y.C., 1950-54; prof., artist-in-residence Tex. Womans U., Denton, 1961—; vis. prof. North Tex. State U., Denton, 1968-69; violinist Dallas Symphony Orch., 1955; violinist, soloist Utah Symphony, Salt Lake City, 1945-55, Ft. Worth Symphony Orch., 1955; assoc. concertmaster Graz (Austria) Symphony, 1993—; soloist movie documentary, Eng., 1987. Numerous concert tours in U.S., Europe, Asia, Mex., Can., 1945—; composer numerous works for voice, violin, viola, string quartet, and chamber music; contbr. articles to profl. jours. Recipient cert. of merit Federated Music Clubs, 1978, 1st prize for composition, 1984; 1st prize for composition Tex. Composers Guild, 1980; rsch. grantee Tex. Womans U., 1979. Mem. APA (assoc.), Am. String Tchrs. Assn., Phi Kappa Phi (internat. rep. for arts, pres. Tex. Womans U. chpt. 1991-93), Sigma Alpha Iota (arts assoc. 1980—), Phi Kappa Phi (nat. rep. for arts 1989-91, editorial bd. Nat. Forum 1994—). Office: Tex Womans U Dept Performing Arts Denton TX 76204

DAVIDSON, RONDA DARLENE, special education educator; b. San Bernardino, Calif., Nov. 15, 1961; d. Ronald Wayne and Wavel Darlene (Warstler) Yeager; m. Robert Price Davidson, Dec. 17, 1983; children: William Price, Joy Darlene. BS in Edn., Pittsburg (Kans.) State U., 1983, MS in Edn., 1985. Lic. tchr. learning disabled, mentally handicapped, behavioral disordered, elem. edn. Paraprofl. learning disabled/behavioral disordered Unified Sch. Dist. 250, Pittsburg, 1984-85; tchr. elem. learning disabled/educable mentally handicapped Wheaton (Mo.) R-III Schs., 1985-88; tchr. elem. educable mentally handicapped Steelville (Mo.) R-III Schs., 1988-91; tchr. elem. learning disabled/educable mentally handicapped/ North Wood R-IV, Salem, Mo., 1991—. Sec. Bapt. Young Women, Steelville, Mo., 1989-91. Mem. Learning Disabilities Assn., Mo. State Tchrs. Assn., Community Tchr. Assn. Republican. Home: 711 E Jack St Salem MO 65560-1833 Office: North Wood R-IV Sch Dist RR 4 Box 424 Salem MO 65560-9221

DAVIDSON, SHIRLEY A., construction company executive; b. Port Angeles, Wash., July 16, 1932; d. Ralph Clare and Ann Louise (Bobell) Ferguson; m. Gordon William Davidson, Dec. 26, 1970; children: Tracy Anne, Christopher Allen. Student, Northridge Coll., 1950, 51. Supv. records dept. Blue Cross of So. Calif., L.A., 1950, 55; bookkeeper, receptionist River Bend Sand & Gravel, Salem, Oreg., 1969-71; with acctg. dept. Stayton (Oreg.) Canning Co., 1971-79; v.p. Davidson Logging, Mill City, Oreg., 1979-89; pres. Sir Inc. of Oreg., Lyons, Oreg., 1991—. Mem. Associated Oreg. Loggers, Women Contrn. Owners & Execs. Republican. Office: Sir Inc of Oreg PO Box 115 Lyons OR 97358

DAVIDSON, SUZANNE MOURON, lawyer; b. Oxford, Miss., Aug. 5, 1963; d. Bertrand D. Jr. and Barbara Jean (Baca) Mouron; m. Garrison H. Davidson III, Dec. 12, 1987; 1 child, Jane Harrington. AB in English Lit., U. Calif., 1985, JD, 1988. Assoc. Peterson, Ross, L.A., 1988-89; asst. litigation counsel Ticor Title Ins., Rosemead, Calif., 1989-91; corp. counsel Forest Lawn, Glendale, Calif., 1991-94. Chair nat. area rush info. Chi Omega, 1988-95, adult edn. San Marino Community Ch., 1994-95; mem. Jr. League, Pasadena, Calif., 1989—. Mem. Calif. State Bar Assn., L.A. County Bar Assn., Pasadena Athletic Club, Salt Air Club. Presbyn. Office: Forest Lawn Company Legal Dept 1712 S Glendale Ave Glendale CA 91205

DAVIES, ALMA (ALMA ROSITA), producer, playwright, lyricist, composer, designer, sculptor; b. Bloemfontein, South Africa; came to U.S., 1949; d. Walter David and Elizabeth (Van der Kar) D.; m. Lee Kaye, Dec. 9, 1956 (dec. 1967); children: Elena-Beth Kaye, Walter Ian Kaye; m. Edwin William Williams, June 22, 1985. Tchr., choreographer Spanish dance ballet Sch. Dance Arts, Carnegie Hall, N.Y.C., 1944-55. Toured with Manhattan Opera Co. in Desert Song, 1946; soloist Dances of Spain, Am. Mus. Natural History, N.Y.C., 1947, Jose Greco Dance Co., Washington, 1954; soloist, choreographer Jacobs Pillow Dance Festival, Mass., 1948, Am. Youth Ballet, N.Y.C., 1951, Radio City Music Hall, N.Y.C., 1953; guest artist, soloist, choreographer Syracuse (N.Y.) Philharm. Orch., 1950; soloist, dancer, actress Voice of Firestone NBC-TV, N.Y.C., 1953; guest artist Simmons Cruise Concert-S.S. Olympia, Caribbean Seas, 1954-55; exhbns. for sculpted 3-D pictures include Schumacher Fabrics, N.Y.C., Warner Bros., others; puppeteer Rose Rivero Charity Showcase, N.Y.C., 1974-80; jewelry designer, 1966-74; author, composer, dir., prodr. musicals: Princessa, 1963, Moon Holiday, 1983, Little Lord, 1985, Dorinmore, 1986, Little Lord Fauntleroy, 1995. Mem. ASCAP, Dramatists Guild, The Drama League, Comml. Theatre Inst. Office: Alma Davies Prodns 1756 Broadway New York NY 10019-3207

DAVIES, DEBBIE THERESA, artist, gallery owner; b. Port of Spain, Trinidad and Tobago, July 19, 1966; came to U.S., 1974.; d. Anthony Winston Roosevelt and Judy Leonine (Joseph) D.; m. Thomas Brunelli, May 16, 1991 (div.). Student, Poly. U., Bklyn., 1985. Civil engring. technician E & K Engrs., N.Y.C., 1986-87; banquet sales agt. Sign of the Dove, N.Y.C., 1987-89; photographer's agt. Marc Cohen Photo, N.Y.C., 1989-92; illustrator's agt. Warshaw Blumenthal, N.Y.C., 1992; account exec. RC Comms., N.Y.C., 1992-94; owner Ad Finem Gallery, Bklyn., 1992—; mgr., designer, publicist The Noose, N.Y.C., 1994—; publicist Bklyn. Waterfront Artists Coalition, 1994. Democrat. Home and Office: Ad Finem Gallery 47 State St Brooklyn NY 11201

DAVIES, JANE B(ADGER) (MRS. LYN DAVIES), architectural historian; b. Amboy, Ill., Sept. 9, 1913; d. Henry Harold and Clara May (Heermans) Badger; m. Lyn Davies, July 18, 1942 (dec. 1994). BA, Wellesley Coll., 1935; MA, Columbia U., 1942, BLS with high honors, 1944; postgrad., U. Mich., 1936, U. Wis., 1937, 38. Tchr. Monticello Prep. Sch., Godfrey, Ill., 1935-37, Kent Sch. Girls, Denver, 1937-41; reference libr. Columbia Univ. Librs., 1944-50, rare book cataloger, 1951-77; cons. Nat. Trust for Hist. Preservation, 1965, 87-88, 91-94, Smithsonian Inst., 1967, Greensboro (N.C.) Preservation Soc., 1967-70, Historic Green Springs, 1970-73, 82, Llewellyn Park Hist. Dist., 1982-84, Hist. Hudson Valley, 1986-89, Met. Mus. Art, N.Y.C., 1988-92; guest curator, author catalog A.J. Davis and Am. Classicism, Fed. Hall Mus., N.Y.C., 1989; lectr. on Am. archtl. history. Author: intro. Houston Mus. Fine Arts: The Gothic Revival Style in America, 1830-1870, 1976; intro. Alexander Jackson Davis: Rural Residences (1837), 1980; contbr. to Prophet with Honor, A.J. Downing, 1989, Alexander Jackson Davis, American Architect, 1992; editorial asst. Jour. Soc. Archtl. Historians, 1964-65; contbr. articles on Am. archtl. history to mags., jours., symposiums and reference books. Am. Coun. Learned Socs. grantee, 1970, Am. Philos. Soc. grantee, 1970-71; NEH fellow, 1978. Mem. Soc. Archtl. Historians (sec.-treas. N.Y. chpt. 1959-67), Victorian Soc. Am. (adv. com. 1966-76), Nat. Trust Historic Preservation, Friends of Lyndhurst, N.Y. Hist. Soc., Preservation League N.Y. State, Greensboro Preservation Soc. (hon.), Phi Beta Kappa, Beta Phi Mu. Presbyterian. Home: 549 W 123rd St New York NY 10027-5026

DAVIES, LEAH GEESLIN, educational consultant; b. Cincinnati, Mar. 26, 1940; d. Albert Herald and Margaret Marie (Freeh) Geeslin; m. William Donald Davies, June 8, 1962; children: Matthew Donald, Joy Deanna Davies Hallett. BA, Transylvania U., 1962; MEd, Auburn (Ala.) U., 1977. Cert. sch. counselor K-12; cert. psychometrist Rank 1, Ala. Asst. teenage program dir. YWCA, Columbus, Ohio, 1962-63; tchr. Linmoor Jr. High Sch., Columbus, 1963-64; sch. counselor Lee Acad., Auburn, 1977-78; instr. family and child devel. dept. Auburn U., 1978-82; coord. consultation, edn. and prevention East Ala. Mental Health-Mental Retardation Ctr., Opelika, 1982—; speaker in field. Author: Kelly Bear Feelings, 1987, Kelly Bear Behavior, 1988, Kelly Bear Health, 1989, Kelly Bear Activities, 1992, Kelly Bear Drug Awareness, 1993, Drug Abuse Prevention Program Leader Guide, 1990; contbr. articles to profl. jours. Mem. ACA, Nat. Assn. for Edn. of Young Children, Assn. for Childhood Edn. Internat., Am. Sch. Counselors Assn., Nat. Head Start Assn., Phi Kappa Phi. Home: 4295 County Road 12 Lafayette AL 36862

DAVIES, MARTHA HILL, dance educator; b. East Palestine, Ohio. Studied with Martha Graham; BS, Tchrs. Coll., Columbia U.; MA, NYU; LHD (hon.), Adelphi U., Towson State U., 1981; DFA (hon.), Mt. Holyoke Coll., The Juilliard Sch., 1987; LittD (hon.), Bennington Coll. Dancer Martha Graham Dance Co., N.Y.C.; mem. faculty U. Oreg., Lincoln Sch. Tchrs. Coll.; dir. of dance NYU, N.Y.C., 1930-51; chmn., dance and choreographer Bennington Coll., 1932-51; dir. Bennington Sch. of Dance, 1934-39, Bennington Sch. of Arts, 1940-42; founding dir. Am. Dance Festival, 1948-65; founding chairperson dance dept. Juillard Sch., N.Y.C., 1951—, dir. dance divsn., 1951-85, artistic dir. emeritus, 1985—; bd. dirs. Choreographic Conf., U. NSW, U. Victoria, Australia, 1975-76. Recipient Presdl. citation NYU, 1982, Disting. Svc. award Dance Notation Bur., 1984, Mayor's Honor for Arts and Culture award City of N.Y., 1984, Disting. Svc. medal Tchrs. Coll., Columbia U., 1986, Ernie award Dance USA, 1994. Office: The Julliard Sch Dept Dance 60 Lincoln Ctr New York NY 10023-6588*

DAVILA, ELISA, Spanish language, literature educator; b. Libano, Tolima, Colombia, May 29, 1944; came to U.S., 1974; d. Rafael Antonio Davila and Amalia Parra; m. Bruce Roger Smith, Oct. 17, 1973 (div. 1981). BA, U. Pedagogica Nat., Bogota, Colombia, 1966; MA, U. Pacific, 1972; PhD, U. Calif., Santa Barbara, 1983. Asst. prof. U. Valle, Cali, Colombia, 1968-73; researcher Inst. Colombiano de Pedagogia, Bogota, 1973-73; assoc. U. Calif., Santa Barbara, 1974-78, 78-80; instr. W. Tex. State U., Canyon, Tex., 1978-80, Def. Lang. Inst., Calif., 1981-82; visiting lectr. U. Calif., Santa Cruz, 1982—; assoc. prof. SUNY, New Paltz, 1990—, chair fgn. langs., 1990-94, dir. Latin Am. studies, 1991—; reader, evaluator N.J. Dept. Higher Edn., Princeton, 1987-89; reader Ednl. Testing Svc., Princeton, 1987-89; acad. dir. Spanish Immersion Inst., Bd. Edn. and Office Mental Health, N.Y.C. and Albany, 1987-90. The Heloise Brainer scholar, 1964, LASPAU scholar, 1968. Mem. MLA, Am. Assn. Tchr. Spanish & Portuguese, Assn. Para la Ensenanza del Espanol, Latin-Am. Studies Assn. Avocations: creative writing, poetry. Home: 551 Mountain View Ave Old Hurley NY 12443

DAVILA, NORMA, developmental psychologist and program evaluator; b. Rio Piedras, P.R., Dec. 17, 1962; d. Fernando and Ana (Maldonado) D. BA in Psychology, Yale U., 1985; MA in Behavioral Sci., U. Chgo., 1988, PhD in Psychology, 1991. Asst. edn. coord. Head Start, New Haven, 1984-85; rsch. asst. Disengagement of Talent Project, Chgo., 1985-86, Chgo. Stress Project, 1986-87; project coord. Chgo. Stree Project, 1987; sr. pro-analyst Rsch. Pros, Chgo., 1988-89; instr. dept. psychology St. Xavier Coll., Chgo., 1988-89, 90, Roosevelt U., Chgo., 1990-91; asst. prof. dept. psychology U. P.R., Rio Piedras, 1991—; dir. evaluation PR-SSI Project, Rio Piedras, 1993—; career counselor and career devel. instr. Women Employed, Chgo., 1991. Recipient Trustee's Fellowship U. Chgo., 1985-86, Minority Grad. Incentive Program Fellowship, State of Ill., 1986-89, Dissertation of Yr. Fellowship, Dorothy Danforth Compton Found., 1990-91. Mem. APA, Psychol. Assn. of P.R., Am. Ednl. Rsch. Assn., Am. Evaluators Assn. Office: Dept Psychology U Puerto Rico Rio Piedras PR

DAVION, ETHEL JOHNSON, educator, administrator, curriculum specialist; b. Raleigh, N.C., July 21, 1948; d. John Arthur and Ethel Mae (Morgan) Johnson; m. Joel Davion, Aug. 6, 1988, 1 child, Laura Christal. BA, Livingstone Coll., 1971; MA, Glassboro (N.J.) State U., 1983. Cert. tchr., prin., supr., N.J. Sr. English tchr. Camden (N.J.) Bd. Edn., 1977-81; tchr. of English Westfield (N.J.) Bd. Edn., 1982-85, Union County Regional Dist. 1, Berkeley Heights, N.J., 1981-82, Hillside (N.J.) Bd. Edn., 1985-87; supr. English, lang. arts Irvington (N.J.) Bd. Edn., 1987-92; vice prin. Frank H. Morrell H.S., Irvington, N.J., 1992—; writer, researcher Collegiate Rsch. Systems, Camden, 1976-77; participant profl. devel. programs Harvard U., 1989, Notre Dame U., 1990. Author: A Tutorial Approach to Teaching English, 1983, Teachers' Resource Manual, 1987; contbr. articles to jours. Bd. dirs., sec. Emmanuel Tabernacle, Linden, N.J., 1988. Recipient Resolution Town Coun. Irvington, 1992. Fellow N.J. Edn. Assn., Nat. Coun. Tchrs. English; mem. Linden Scholarship Guild (sec. 1985—), Assn. for Supervision and Curriculum Devel., Prin. and Suprs. Assn., Irvington Adminstrs. Assn. (sec., treas.), Internat. Platform Assn., Good Samaritans Club, Obsidian Civic Club (Westfield, historian 1985—). Democrat. Pentecostal.

DAVIS, ALPHA, programmer, stock broker; b. Taichung, Taiwan, Republic of China, Nov. 17, 1961. B of Engring. Sci., U. Louisville, 1988, M of Computer Engring., 1989. IBM Dialog Mgr. Tag Lang. compiler IBM Corp., Cary, N.C., 1989-90; IBM SAA delivery mgr. IBM Corp., Cary, 1990, 91-92; with Dublin, Ireland, 1990-91; mem. IMS data base recovery control utility group IBM Corp., San Jose, 1992—; account exec. Barbara Securities Inc., Santa Clara, Calif., 1993—. Fin. advisor High Sch. Jr. Achievement Program. Mem. NAFE. Home: 789 Golden Creek Ter San Jose CA 95111-2688 Office: Baraban Securities Inc 2620 Augustine Dr Ste 280 Santa Clara CA 95054-2917

DAVIS, ANNA JANE RIPLEY, elementary education educator; b. Uhrichsville, Ohio, Sept. 7, 1931; d. Emmet Frank and Lillie Hazel (Kinsey) Ripley; m. H. Joe Davis, Mar. 16, 1951; children: Alan Joe, Kendal Jay. Assoc., Asbury Coll., 1953; BS, Kent State U., 1962, MEd, 1978, postgrad., 1980-94; student, Richmond Coll., London U., St. Andrews U., Dundee U., Cambridge U., U. Paris, Rome, U. Amsterdam. Cert. tchr., Ohio. Tchr. Kenston Schs., Chagrin Falls, Ohio, 1953-55, 58-62, Firestone's Rubber Plantation, Harbel, Liberia, West Africa, 1962-64, Newbury (Ohio) Schs., 1964-65, Orange Schs., Pepper Pike, Ohio, 1965-93; chaperone, counselor Am. Inst. for Fgn. Study, summers 1968-80. Active Chagrin Falls and Pepper Pike PTA, Am. Field Svc., Chagrin Falls, Pepper Pike Garfield Meml. United Meth. Ch., mem. edn. commn., Geauga Co. Personal Growth Com. for Workshops; book project vol. Geauga Co. Library for Amish Schs. Mem. NEA, ASCD, Ohio Edn. Assn., N.E. Ohio Tchr. Assn., Orange Tchrs. Assn.

DAVIS, ANNE JOE, nurse, educator; b. Greensboro, N.C., Dec. 5, 1931; d. Joel Joseph and Anne Lee (Goulsby) D. BS, Emory U., 1955, DSc (hon.), 1986; MS, Boston U., 1956; PhD, U. Calif., Berkeley, 1968. Clin. psychiat. nurse McLean Hosp., Boston, 1955-56, Bedford (Mass.) VA Hosp., 1956-57; lectr. U. Calif., San Francisco, 1958-61, prof., 1968-94; lectr. Ministry of Health, Israel, 1962; postdoctoral fellow Harvard U., Cambridge, Mass., 1977; cons. Nat. Nursing Ctr., Beijing, 1990-93; prof. Sun Yat Sen Med. U., Guangzhou, China, 1988-94. Author: Ethical Dilemas and Nursing Practice, 1978; editorial bd.: Nursing Ethics, London, 1994—; contbr. articles to profl. jours. Bd. dirs. Hospice By the Bay, San Francisco, 1990-94; local, nat. and internat. speaker on health care ethics, 1979—; fellow Hastings Ctr., 1978—, v.p., 1990-91. Rsch. grantee Inst. Nursing Rsch., Washington, 1992-95, Pacific Rim Rsch. Program, Berkeley, Calif., 1992-94. Mem. Am. Nursing Assn. (chmn. ethics coms. 1980-82, First Human Rights award 1986). Democrat. Home: 158 Funston Ave San Francisco CA 94118

DAVIS, BARBARA JEAN SIEMENS, service company executive; b. Louisville, Nov. 12, 1931; d. Gustav Adolph Siemens and Alberta Jeanette (McAdams) Simon; m. Donald Elmore Davis, Aug. 4, 1950; children—Dale Montgomery, Gale Sue Davis Beaty. Mktg. and personnel mgr. Kelly Services, Louisville, 1962-65; tchr. asst. TV English, Jefferson County Schs., Louisville, 1960-70; wedding and floral designer Wedding Ring, Louisville, 1971-73; owner, designer Nook Flowers and Gifts, Memphis, 1973-75; cons. pub. relations Dixie Rents, Memphis, 1975-79; div. mgr. pres. Party Concepts, Inc., Memphis, 1980-88; pres. Siemens-Davis Assoc., Cordova, Tenn., 1989-91; cons. Leon Loard, 1992; ficilitator/trainer Motivational Concepts Internat. 1993; pres., CEO, Siemens-Davis Assoc., 1993—. Author: Wedding Workshop Brides Work Book, 1984., Wedding Party Consultants Certification Program, 1984. Mem. Sales and Mktg. Execs., Am. Rental Assn. (mem. party council 1985-88), Nat. Assn. Wedding Cons. (pres. 1983-87); NAFE(dir. Memphis Network, mem. Internat. Platform Assn.). Republican. Presbyterian. Home: 105 Mckenzie Rd Selma AL 36701-6846

DAVIS, BARBARA JUDY, social worker; b. Lewisburg, W.Va., Apr. 27, 1955; d. Harris Wilson and Dorthea Pearl (Baker) Judy; m. Robin John Otis, May 10, 1980 (div. Nov. 1987); 1 child, Tamara; m. Ancel Barbour Davis Jr., Mar. 4, 1989; 1 child, Shannon. BA, U. Va., 1980, MEd, 1993. Cert. counselor. Social worker Charlottesville (Va.) Dept. of Social Svc., 1988—, benefits specialist, 1988-91; psychiatric technician U. Va. Med. Ctr., Charlottesville, 1990-91. Mem. adv. bd. Region X Cmty. Svc. Mental Retardation Divsn., Charlottesville, 1989—; founding mem. planning com. Disability Awareness Day, Charlottesville, 1992—, chair fund raising, 1993. Mem. ACA, Internat. Assn. Addiction and Offender Counselors, Nat. Bd. Cert. Counselors, Va. Counseling Assn., Va. Alliance Social Work Practitioners, Chi Sigma Iota. Office: Charlottesville Dept Social Svcs 120 7th St NE Charlottesville VA 22902

DAVIS, BARBARA LANGFORD, financial planner; b. Newberry, S.C., Jan. 2, 1957; d. Ella Mae (Harp) Langford; m. G. Bernard Davis, Aug. 8, 1981; children: Bryant Mckenzie, Brandan Langford. BA in Sociology, Newberry Coll., 1979. CFP. Customer svc. mgr. Riegel Textile Co., Johnston, S.C., 1979-80; knitwear dept. mgr. Riegel Textile Co., Johnston, 1980-82; fin. advisor Am. Express Fin. Advisors Inc., Columbia, S.C., 1981-95, Columbia, 1995—. Officer Sertoma Internat.-Landmark, Columbia, S.C., 1988-93; mem. Nat. Coun. Negro Women, 1990-94; bd. dirs. Family Shelter, Columbia Forum, Leadership Columbia. Mem. Newberry Coll. Lettermen's Club, Newberry Coll. Indian Club (bd. dirs.), Inst. CFPs, S.C. Soc. Inst. CFPs, Greater Columbia C. of C. (bd. dirs.), Am. Bus. Women's Assn. Home: 2 Cardigan Ct Columbia SC 29210-6112 Office: Am Express Fin Advisors Inc Ste 650 140 Stoneridge Dr Columbia SC 29210-8200

DAVIS, BARBARA LYNN, mental health therapist, consultant; b. Bend, Oreg., July 25, 1957; d. John Edwin and Betty Jean (Becker) D. AA, Minn. Bible Coll., 1977, BA, 1979; MA, Purdue U., Hammond, Ind., 1983. Lic. probation officer Jud. Conf. Ind.; cert. counselor. Probation officer juvenile div. Lake Superior Ct., Gary, Ind., 1984-85; crisis counselor The Crisis Ctr., Inc., Gary, 1985-86; sexual assault therapist YMCA Met. Chgo., Olympia Fields, Ill., 1986-88, dir. women's svcs., 1988-90; pvt. practice Orland Park, Ill., 1988—; mental health therapist III, Proviso Family Svcs., Westchester, Ill., 1990-91; cons. Harbor House Domestic Violence, Kankakee, Ill., 1991—, Mut. Ground Domestic Violence Shelter, 1993—; presenter profl. tng. seminars Ill. Coalition Against Sexual Assault, Springfield, 1990, 91, Kankakee County Coalition Against Domestic Violence, 1989, 91. Contbg. author: Child Sexual Abuse, 1990; contbr. articles to newsletters and periodical. Mem. help ministry coun. Deer Creek Christian Ch., Univeristy Park, Ill., 1990—. Recipient beautification award Village of Park Forest, Ill., 1989. Mem. AACD, AAUW (rec. sec. 1986-87, pres. 1987-88). Office: 64 Orland Square Dr Ste 212 Orland Park IL 60462

DAVIS, BARBARA M(AE), librarian; b. Cranston, R.I., Dec. 23, 1926; d. Harrie S. and Marguerite M. (Cameron) D.; SB in Chemistry, Brown U., 1948; MS in Library Sci., Simmons Coll., 1956. Asst. research librarian research and devel. dept. Cabot Corp., Cambridge, Mass., 1948-57, research librarian, 1957-61, research librarian Billerica (Mass.) Research Center, 1961-68, head tech. info. services, 1968-81, mgr. tech. info. center, 1981-87. Dir. Cabot Boston Credit Union, 1956-59, 61-64, 72-78, clk., 1961-64, 72-77, v.p., 1977-78. Vol., Lexington Coun. on Aging, 1990—, Lexington Hist. Soc., 1991—; chmn. research com. Greater Boston Young Rep. Club, 1959-61; treas. Women's Rep. Club Lexington, 1988—; committeeperson Lexington Republican Town Com., 1993—. Mem. Am. Chem. Soc. (sec. div. chem. lit. 1961-65), Spl. Libraries Assn. (chmn. Boston chpt. 1965-66, chmn. chemistry div. 1971-72), Simmons Coll. Library Sch. Alumni (v.p. 1965-66). Home: 37 Drummer Boy Way Lexington MA 02173-1200

DAVIS, BETTY BYRD HARRINGTON, entrepreneur; b. Longview, Tex., July 11, 1936; d. William Henry Byrd and Minnie Lee Tidwell; 1 child, Randy Lee Harrington. AA, Cedar Valley DCCCD, Dallas, 1988. Adminstrv. asst. Conf. Coun. on Ministries United Meth. Ch., Dallas, 1983-86; pres., actress, model, entertainer Kathy King Entertainment Agy., DeSoto, Tex., 1956—; pres. Gateway to Success/Resume Writing and Career Counseling, DeSoto, Tex., 1987—. Author: The Dallas Dazzler. Mem. AFTRA, AGVA, DeSoto C. of C., Greater Dallas C. of C. Republican. Baptist. Home and Office: 1338 E Parkerville Rd De Soto TX 75115-6421

DAVIS, BETTYE JEAN, academic administrator, state official; b. Homer, La., May 17, 1938; d. Dan and Rosylind (Daniel) Ivory; m. Troy J. Davis, Jan. 21, 1959; children: Anthony Benard, Sonja Davis Wade. Cert. nursing, St. Anthony's, 1961; BSW, Grambling State U., 1971; postgrad., U. Alaska, 1972. Psychiat. nurse Alaska Psychiat. Inst., 1967-70; asst. dir. San Bernardino (Calif.) YWCA, 1971-72; child care specialist DFYS Anchorage, 1975-80, soc. worker, 1980-82, foster care coordinator, 1982-87; dir. Alaska Black Leadership Edn. Program, 1979-82; exec. dir. Anchorage Sch. Bd., 1982-89; mem. Alaska Legislature, 1990—; chair Children's Caucus Alaska Legis., 1992—. Pres. Anchorage Sch. Bd., 1986-87; bd. dirs. Blacks in Govt., 1980-82, March of Dimes, 1983-85, Anchorage chpt. YWCA, 1989-90, Winning with Stronger Edn. Com., 1991, Alaska 2000, Anchorage Ctr. for Families, 1992—, active Anchorage chpt. of NAACP, bd. dirs. 1978-82. Toll fellow Henry Toll Fellowship Program, 1992; named Woman of Yr., Alaska Colored Women's Club, 1981, Child Care Worker of Yr., Alaska Foster Parent Assn., 1983, Social Worker of Yr., Nat. Foster Parents Assn., 1983, Outstanding Bd. Mem, Assn. Alaska Sch. Bds., 1990,; recipient Outstanding Achievement in Edn. award Alaska Colored Women's Club, 1985, Outstanding Women in Edn. award Zeta Phi Beta, 1985, Boardsmanship award Assn. Alaska Sch. Bds., 1989, Woman of Achievement award YWCA, 1991, Outstanding Leadership award Calif. Assembly, 1992. Mem. LWV, Nat. Sch. Bd. Assn., Nat. Caucus of Black Sch. Bd. Mems. (bd. dirs. 1986-87), Alaska Black Caucus (chair 1984—), Alaska Women's Polit. Caucus, Alaska Black Leadership Conf. (pres. 1976-80), Alaska Women Lobby (treas.), Nat. Caucus of Black State Legis. (chair region 12, 1994—), Women Legislators Lobby, Women's Action for New Directions, North to Future Bus. and Profl. Women (pres. 1978-79, 83), Delta Sigma Theta (Alaska chpt. pres. 1978-80). Democrat. Baptist. Club: North to Future Bus. and Profl. Women (past pres.). Home: 2240 Foxhall Dr Anchorage AK 99504-3350

DAVIS, CAROL LYN, research consultant, office assistant; b. West Palm Beach, Fla., Oct. 22, 1953; d. Robert Lee and Barbara Jean (Collett) D. BFA, Tex. Christian U., Ft. Worth, 1975, MA in Am. Studies, 1977. R & D product line designer Am. Handicrafts/Merribee Needlearts, Ft. Worth, 1977-81; ceramics/china sales cons. Dillard's, Ft. Worth, 1981-82, dept. mgr., 1981; dept. mgr. Stripling-Cox, Ft. Worth, 1982-83; freelance ceramic and string art designer, 1982-83; with phase III, IV, V hist. sites inventory of Tarrant County for Hist. Preservation Coun. for Tarrant County (Tex.) and Page, Anderson & Turnbull, Inc., San Francisco, 1983-86; rep. Tarrant County Greater Ft. Worth Housing Starts, Texas Update, Inc., 1987-94, M/PF Rsch., Inc., Dallas, 1989-94; summer sales clk. Trail Ridge subdivision Perry Homes, Inc., Ft. Worth, 1994—; Mem. mgmt. adv. panel Chem. Week, 1981; alternative precinct election judge Dem. Party, 1994. Author Pamphlets in field. Mem. Ft. Worth Opera Assn., Royal Over-Seas League. Democrat. Episcopalian. Home: 7800 Garza Ave Fort Worth TX 76116-7717

DAVIS, CAROLYNE KAHLE, health care consultant; b. Penn Yan, N.Y., Jan. 31, 1932; d. Paul Frederick Kahle and Alice Edgerton (Kahle) Cargill; m. Ott Howard Davis, June 28, 1953; 1 son, Richard Ott. BS in Nursing, Johns Hopkins U., 1954; MS in Nursing, Syracuse U., 1965, PhD in Higher Edn. Adminstrn., 1972; LittD (hon.), Georgetown U., 1982; DSc (hon.), U. Evansville, 1982, U. Medicine & Dentistry N.J., 1984; LLD (hon.), Adelphi U., 1985; LHD (hon.), Med. U. S.C., 1986; DSc (hon.), Eastern Mich. U., 1989; DHL (hon.), Med. Coll. of N.Y., 1992. Chmn. baccalaureate nursing program Syracuse U., 1969-73; dean sch. nursing U. Mich., Ann Arbor, 1973-75, prof. nursing and edn., 1973-81, assoc. v.p. acad. affairs, 1975-81; adminstr. Health Care Fin. Adminstrn. HHS, Washington, 1981-85; cons. Ernst & Whinney, Washington, 1985-89, Ernst & Young, Washington, 1989—; bd. dirs. Pharm. Mktg. Svcs., Inc., Scottsdale, Ariz., Beckman Inst., Irvine, Calif., Prudential Ins. Co. of Am., Newark, Merck, Rahway, N.J., Sci. Applications Internat. Corp., San Diego. Mem. editorial bd. Nursing Economics, Pitman, N.J.; contbr. more than 100 articles to profl. jours. Bd. dirs. ARC, 1988-94, Nat. Mus. Health and Medicine; assoc. trustee U. Pa. Med. Ctr., Phila., 1987—; bd. dirs., vice chmn. bd. trustees Nat. Rehab. Hosp., 1993—; mem. health adv. com. GAO, 1990—. Recipient Disting. Alumnus award Johns Hopkins U., 1981, Alumni award Syracuse U. Sch. Edn., 1983, Alumni award U. Mich., 1984, Spl. Recognition award Assn. Am. Med. Colls., 1986; named one of the Top Young Leaders in Am. Acad. Mag., 1978. Mem. NSF (elected to Inst. Medicine 1991), Nat. League for Nursing (bd. dirs. 1979-81, chmn. Community Health Accreditation Program 1987-92, Presdl. award 1993). Sigma Theta Tau, Phi Delta Kappa. Republican. Office: Ernst & Young 1225 Connecticut Ave NW Washington DC 20036

DAVIS, CHRISTINE NOELLE, lawn maintenance and equipment sales company executive; b. Nancy, France, Dec. 24, 1955; came to U.S., 1957, naturalized, 1974; d. Frederick and Marguerite (Marchal) Stelmach; m. Robert O. Davis, Mar. 24, 1978 (div. 1982); 1 child, Brian Andrew. B.S., Park Coll., 1977. Membership coordinator Kansas City C. of C., Kans., 1977-78; research dept. mgr. J.E. Stowers & Co., Kansas City, Mo., 1978-79; office services mgr. Watson, Ess, Marshall & Enggas, 1979-81; office services mgr., purchasing buyer Alfa-Laval, Inc., 1981-85; purchasing buyer, office services mgr. Ball Enterprises, Parkville, Mo., 1985—. Republican. Roman Catholic. Avocations: interior decorating; tennis; landscaping. Home: 7705 NW 79th Pl Kansas City MO 64152-2184 Office: Ball Enterprises RR 27 Kansas City MO 64152-9827

DAVIS, CLARICE MCDONALD, lawyer; b. New Orleans, Jan. 20, 1941; d. James A. and Helen J. (Ross) McDonald. BA, U. Tex., 1962, MA, 1964; JD, So. Meth. U., 1968. Bar: Tex. 1969, U.S. Dist. Ct. (no. dist.) Tex. 1970, U.S. Ct. Appeals (5th cir.) 1971, U.S. Supreme Ct. 1973. Law clk. to presiding justice U.S. Ct. Appeals (5th cir.), Dallas, 1969-71; from assoc. to ptnr. Akin, Gump, Strauss, Hauer & Feld, Dallas, 1971—; comments editor Southwestern Law Jour., 1967-68; instr. Southern Methodist Univ. Sch. of Law, 1968-69. Bd. visitors So. Meth. U., Dallas, 1979-82, v.p. Law Sch. Alumni Adv. Coun., 1992, pres. 1993-94. Home: 6317 Churchill Way Dallas TX 75230-1807 Office: Akin Gump Strauss Hauer & Feld 1700 Pacific Ave Ste 4100 Dallas TX 75201-4618

DAVIS, DAISY SIDNEY, history educator; b. Bay City, Tex., Nov. 7, 1944; d. Alex. C. and Alice M. (Edison) Sidney; m. John Dee Davis, Apr. 17, 1968; children: Anaca Michelle, Lowell Kent. BS, Bishop Coll., 1966; MS, East Tex. State U., 1971; MEd, Prairie View A&M, 1980. Cert. profl. lifetime secondary tchr., Tex.; mid-mgmt. adminstr. Tchr., Dallas pub. schs., 1966—; instr. Am. History El Centro Coll., 1991—. Coord. Get Out the Vote campaign, Dallas, 1972, 80, 84, 88, 92. Recipient Outstanding Tchr. award Dallas pub. schs., 1980, Jack Lowe award for ednl. excellence, 1982; Free Enterprise scholar So. Meth. U., 1987; Constl. fellow U. Dallas, 1988; named to Hall of Fame, Holmes Acad., 1979. Mem. NEA, Tex. State Tchrs. Assn., Classroom Tchrs. Dallas (faculty rep. 1971-77), Dallas County History Tchrs., Afro-Am. Daus. Republic of Tex. (founder), Zeta Phi Beta. Democrat. Baptist. Club: Jack & Jill, (Dallas) (rec. sec., v.p., chair Beautillion Ball). Home: 1302 Mill Stream Dr Dallas TX 75232-4604 Office: 9339 S Polk St Dallas TX 75232-5525

DAVIS, DEBORAH CAROL SMITH, pediatrics nurse, obstetrical nurse researcher; b. Birmingham, Ala., Nov. 16, 1951; d. Charles D. Jr. and Polly Anna (Ashley) Smith; m. Phillip Glen Davis, Feb. 9, 1973; children: Peter, Bethany, J. Simon, P. Michael. AS, Gadsden (Ala.) State Jr. Coll., 1972; diploma in nursing, Holy Name of Jesus Hosp., Gadsden, 1979; BSN, Jacksonville State U., 1980; MSN, U. Ala., Birmingham, 1990. RN, Ala.; cert. in ob-gyn. and neonatal nursing specialties; cert. childbirth educator. Dental asst., hygienist Dr. David Goodwin, Gadsden, 1971-76; staff RN Bapt. Meml. Hosp., Gadsden, 1979-80, Gadsden Clinic for Women, 1980-84, Bapt. Med. Ctr.-Cherokee, Centre, Ala., 1988; perinatal clinician Jacksonville (Ala.) State U., 1988, perinatal coord., 1988-91, instr., 1990-91; staff RN U. Ala. Hosp., Birmingham, 1990-91; RN, researcher U. Ala., Birmingham, 1991—; rsch. asst. Dr. Portia Foster, Gadsden, 1989, Dr. Bonnie Thornhill, Gadsden, 1989, Dr. Patricia Goodman, Gadsden, 1989, Jacksonville State U., 1991; cons. lactation, 1987—. Cons. health svcs. J.W. Stewart Head Start Child Devel. Ctr., Gadsden, 1989-90; presenter Cahaba Coun. Girl Scouts, Gadsden, 1990, 92. Recipient NLN Lamplighter award Ala. League, 1990. Mem. ANA, AWHONN (chpt. coord. 1990-93), Ala. State Nurses Assn., Ala. Perinatal Ptnrs., Nat. Perinatal Assn., Internat. Lactation Cons. Assn., Childbirth Edn. Assn. (v.p. 1985—, instr. 1979—), Internat. Childbirth Edn. Assn. (rep. 1985—), Am. Heart Assn., Alliance of Cmty. Health Orgns. Inc., Sigma Theta Tau. Home: 3554 U S Hwy 411 North Gadsden AL 35901 Office: U Ala Univ Obstetrics 1500 6th Ave S Birmingham AL 35233

DAVIS, DEBORAH CECILIA, auditor; b. Mt. Pleasant, Mich., Aug. 7, 1952; d. Arthur Francis Schaefer and Ninamae Ellen (Confer) Reber. BBA summa cum laude, Western Mich. U., 1974. CPA. Acct. Phoenix Optical, Bay City, Mich., 1968-70; analyst 2nd Nat. Bank, Saginaw, Mich., 1970-72; CPA Deloitte & Touche, Saginaw, Mich., 1975-77; cost acct. AC Sparkplug div. GM, Flint, Mich., 1977-78; corp. auditor GMC, Detroit, 1980; sr. statistician Detroit Diesel Allison div. GM, 1980-83; sr. budget, forecast analyst Cen. Foundry divsn. GM, Saginaw, 1983-91; fin. dir. City of Bay City, Mich., 1991-94; corp. contract supplier auditor GM, 1994—. Office: City Hall 301 Washington Bay City MI 48708

DAVIS, DENISE DIANE, psychology educator; b. Muskegon, Mich., Jan. 16, 1956; m. Charles R. Sharbel, Aug. 4, 1984; children: Charles D., Daniel D. BS, Fla. State U., 1977; PhD, U. S.C., 1982. Lic. health svc. provider in psychology, Tenn. Clin. psychologist Ind. U. Sch. Medicine, Indpls., 1982-88, asst. prof. psychiatry, 1983-88; asst. prof. psychiatry Mood Disorders Clinic Vanderbilt U., Nashville, 1988-94, asst. prof., dir. grad. studies in clin. psychology, 1992—, dir. Cognitive Therapy Ctr., 1995—. Co-author: Cognitive Therapy of Personality Disorders, 1990; archives editor Behavior Therapist, 1989-92; assoc. editor Cognitive and Behavioral Practice, 1993-94, editor, 1995—. Rsch. fellow NIMH, 1980; fellowship scholar Ctr. for Cognitive Therapy, U. Pa., 1984. Mem. APA, Assn. for Advancement of Behavioral Therapy, Internat. Assn. for Cognitive Therapy, Tenn. Psychol. Assn. (grass roots coord. 1988-91), Phi Beta Kappa. Office: Ctr Cognitive Therapy 340 21st Ave N Nashville TN 37203

DAVIS, DENISE WHITLOCK (DENISE LUCILLE WHITLOCK), accountant, financial analyst; b. Marietta, Ga., July 5, 1959; d. J. Winston and Martha Josephine (Phillips) Whitlock. BS in Bus. Adminstrn., Auburn U., 1981. CPA, Ga. Audit profl. KPMG Peat Marwick, Dallas, 1982-85; with exec. office KPMG Peat Marwick, N.Y., 1985-86; audit mgr. KPMG Peat Marwick, Atlanta, 1986-87; fin. analyst Columbian Chem. Co. div. Phelps Dodge Corp., Atlanta, 1987-90; asst. v.p. acctg. policy C&S/Sovran Corp., Atlanta, 1990-91, v.p. acctg. policy, 1991-92; controller CryoLife, Inc., Marietta, 1992-94; sr. analyst N.W. Airlines, Inc., Atlanta, 1994—. Treas., chmn. fundraising Atlanta Symphony Assn., 1987-89; bd. dirs., treas. Morningside Terrace Condominium Assn., Atlanta, 1987-90. Mem. AICPA (editorial advisor 1990—), Ga. Soc. CPAs (continuing profl. edn. com. 1990—, bd. dirs. 1994—), Auburn U. Alumni Assn., Atlanta Lawn Tennis Club, Delta Gamma.

DAVIS, DIANNE EUNICE, marketing and environmental design consultant; b. N.Y.C., Sept. 15, 1934; d. Samuel Lawrence and Marion (Morgan) DeJur Ellenberg; children: Hal Scott, S. Lawrence. BS, NYU, 1955; MA, Columbia U., 1959, PhD, 1963. Instr. adult divsn. Bd. Edn., N.Y.C., 1954-63; food editor Woman's Home Companion, N.Y.C., 1954-63; adj. prof. Finch Coll., N.Y.C., 1963-68; v.p. Transworld Industries, N.Y.C. and Geneva, 1966-74; adj. prof., designer, coord. Ctr. Foodsvc. Mgmt. Women Foodsvc. Inst., NYU, N.Y.C., 1975-82; sr. assoc. Food Sci. Assocs., N.Y.C., 1980-90; pres., dir. Hospitality Healthcare Designs Internat. TEAM Assocs., N.Y.C., 1979—; co-founder, pres. Internat. Coun. for Caring Cmtys., Inc., N.Y.C., 1993—; coord. food industry Washington com. Pres. Reagan's Initiative Nat. Convs. for Women's Bus. Ownership, 1982-83; developed hospitality quotient evaluation prcess, 1986; mem. adv. bd. Sch. Food, Hotel and Tourism Mgmt., Rochester Inst. Tech., 1984-86; mem. adv. bd. Sch. Hotel and Restaurant Mgmt., U. Denver, 1985-87. Author: (with Albert Bush-Brown) Hospitable Design for Healthcare and Senior Communities, 1992. Mem. exec. com. The Town Hall, 1986—; bd. dirs. Symphony of UN, 1991—, Rusk Inst. of Rehab., 1990—; bd. trustees NYU Med. Ctr., 1993—; active Comm. Coordination Com. for the UN, 1992—; World Fedn. for Mental Health, UN rep. NGO Com. for Aging and NGO Com. for Shelter and Human Settlements, 1993—. Mem. AAUW, Nat. Assn. for Sr. Living Industries, Internat. Foodsvc. Execs. Assn. (v.p. N.Y. chpt. 1985—, internat. ednl. chmn., Ea. regional conf. program chmn. 1986—, Svc. citation 1979), Roundtable for Women in Foodsvc. (founding pres. 1983), Royal Soc. Health (U.K.), Nat. Restaurant Assn., Am. Hotel and Motel Assn., World Fedn. Mental Health (UN rep. 1993—, mem. NGO com. for aging, shelter and human settlements), Internat. Study and Rsch. Inst., Soc. Internat. Devel., Coun. Hotel, Restaurant and Instnl. Edn., Woman's Econ. Roundtable, Am. Mgmt. Assn., Fgn. Affairs Assn., World Future Soc., Atrium Club. Office: 24 Central Park S New York NY 10019

DAVIS, DIANNE LOUISE, marketing professional; b. Fresno, Calif., Mar. 1, 1940; d. Edwin L. and Adeline (Irvin) Gribble; m. John R. Jansen, June 11, 1960 (dec. 1966); children: Anthony, Julia; m. Edward Kent Davis, May 13, 1967 (div. 1977); 1 child, Edward Kent Jr. AA cum laude, Colo. Woman's Coll., 1957; student, Minot State Coll., 1968, Ottawa State U., 1987—. Cert. real estate broker, Mo., Kans; cert. resdl. specialist. Co-ptnr. Key Realty, Warrensburg, Mo., 1973-77; residential broker, assoc. DeLozier Realty, Warrensburg, 1977-78; owner, broker Old Drum Realty, Warrensburg, 1978-81; comml. broker, assoc. Varnum-Armstrong-Deeter, Overland Pk., Kans., 1981-82; residential broker, assoc. Kroh Bros. Realty, Overland Pk., 1982-83, Re/Max-Overland Pk., 1983-87, J. D. Reece Real Estate, Overland Pk., 1987-89; dir. mktg. Riss Lake Realty, Parkville, Mo., 1989-92; broker-salesperson JC Nichols Real Estate, 1992-93, The Prudential Summerson-Burrows, Realtors, Overland Park, Kans., 1993—. Mem. Friends of Art Nelson Art Gallery, Kansas City, 1989-90, Friends of the Zoo, Kansas City, 1989-90. Mem. nat. Assn. Home Bldrs. (mem. Inst. Res. Mktg. designation), Met. Kansas City Home Bldrs. Assn. (sales and mktg. coun. 1989-92), Met. Kansas City Bd. Realtors (profl. standards com. 1990-92, chmn., 1992), Johnson County Bd. Realtors, Nat. Assn. Realtors (state del. 1991-92). Republican. Episcopal. Office: Prudential Summerson-Burrow Summerson-Burrows Realtors 8101 College Blvd Ste 100 Overland Park KS 66210

DAVIS, DONNIE MARIE, medical, surgical and geriatrics nurse; b. Crossett, Ark., Oct. 6, 1963; d. Ella Frances Walker. Diploma, Crowley's Ridge Vocat.-Tech., Forrest City, Ark., 1990; CAAS, East Ark. Community Coll., Forrest City, 1992. LPN, Ark. Staff nurse Bapt. Meml. Hosp., North Little Rock, Ark., 1991—, Des Arc (Ark.) Convalescent Ctr., 1993, Stuttgart Regional Med. Ctr., 1993-94, St. Joseph's Nursing Home, 1993—; presenter Black history/AIDS seminar, Brinkley High Sch., 1992—. Dietary advisor Brinkley (Ark.) Health Fair, 1991. Mem. Am. Legion Aux. (chmn. Girls State 1990-94). Democrat. Methodist. Home: 509 E Waco St Brinkley AR 72021-3026

DAVIS, DORINNE SUE TAYLOR LOVAS, audiologist; b. East Orange, N.J., Mar. 29, 1949; d. William Henry and Evelyn Doris (Thorp) Taylor; BA, Montclair State Coll., 1971, MA, 1973; m. Warren B. Davis, Jr., Aug. 10, 1985; children: Larissa Louise, Peter Alexander. Ednl. audiologist Kinnelon (N.J.) Bd. Edn., 1972-94, Inst. for Career Advancement, Inc., 1980-82, Dover Gen. Hosp., 1984-86; pres. Hear You Are, Inc., 1987—; kindergarten tchr. Kinnelon (N.J.) Bd. Edn., 1994—; adj. prof. Kean Coll., Union, N.J., 1993—; tchr. kindergarten Kinnelon Bd. Edn., 1994—. Cert. tchr. of hearing impaired, speech correctionist, tchr. speech and drama N.J. Dept. Edn.; supr. nursery sch. endorsement. Mem. NEA, Internat. Orgn. Educators Hearing Impaired, Am. Speech and Hearing Assn. (cert. of clin. competence in audiology), Am. Acad. Audiology, Alexander Graham Bell Assn., N.J. Speech and Hearing Assn., Morris County Speech and Hearing Assn., N.J. Edn. Assn., Morris County Edn. Assn., Kinnelon Edn. Assn., Self Help for the Hard of Hearing, Ednl. Audiology Assn. (past pres.). Methodist. Home: 4 Musconetcong Ave Stanhope NJ 07874-2936 Office: Stonybrook Sch Boonton Ave Kinnelon NJ 07405 also: Hear You Are Inc 4 Musconetcong Ave Stanhope NJ 07874-2936

DAVIS, DOROTHY SALISBURY, author; b. Chgo., Apr. 26, 1916; d. Alfred Joseph and Margaret Jane (Greer) Salisbury; m. Harry Davis, Apr. 25, 1946 (dec.). AB, Barat Coll., Lake Forest, Ill., 1938. Mystery and hist. novelist, short story writer. Author: A Gentle Murderer, 1951, A Town of Masks, 1952, Men of No Property, 1956, Death of an Old Sinner, 1957, A Gentleman Called, 1958, The Evening of the Good Samaritan, 1961, Black Sheep, White Lamb, 1963, The Pale Betrayer, 1965, Enemy and Brother, 1967, God Speed The Night, 1968, Where the Dark Streets Go, 1969, Shock Wave, 1972, The Little Brothers, 1973, A Death in the Life, 1976, Scarlet Night, 1980, A Lullaby of Murder, 1984, Tales for a Stormy Night, 1985, The Habit of Fear, 1987. Recipient Life Achievement award Bouchereon, 1989. Mem. Authors Guild, Mystery Writers of Am. (former pres., recipient Grand Master award 1985). Home: Palisades NY 10964

DAVIS, EILEEN THERESA BROCK, marriage and family therapist, clinical counselor; b. Medina, Ohio, Sept. 11, 1947; d. Raymond Joseph and Eileen Theresa (Kearney) Brock; m. Gregory Douglas Davis, June 29, 1968; children: Gregory Douglas Jr., Sarah Joyce, Bernadette Eileen, Jeremy Franklin, Joseph Frederick. BS in Edn., Kent State U., 1968; MS in Edn., U. Akron, 1989. Lic. profl. clin. counselor, Ohio. Elem. tchr. Madison Local Schs., North Madison, Ohio, 1968-69; tchr. adult basic edn. Medina County Schs., Medina, 1974-76; tchr., math. specialist Brunswick (Ohio) City Schs., 1975-78; fin. budget counselor Medina Coop. Ext., 1977-81; asst. mgr. Rawiga Country Club, Wadsworth, Ohio, 1981-84; office mgr. 4-B Wood, Wood's End Designs, Seville, Ohio, 1984-88; rsch. asst. to grad. dean edn. U. Akron, Ohio, 1988-89; coord. home-based therapy Cath. Social Svcs., Medina, 1989-93, psychotherapist, marriage and family therapist, 1989-94, coord. rsch. libr., 1990-94; outpatient therapist Akron Child Guidance Ctr., 1994—; program organizer Medina Inst., 1991-93; workshop presenter Stark County Family Svcs., Canton, Ohio, 1993; cons. Wayne-Ashland (Ohio) Family Svcs., 1994. Mem. ACA, Am. Assn. Marriage and Family Therapy (clin.), Nat. Coun. Family Rels., Ohio Asssn. Marriage and Family Therapy (polit. action com. 1992), Chi Sigma Iota (sec. 1988—, President's award 1990, fellow 1991). Roman Catholic. Home: 89 Edgerton Rd Akron OH 44303-1177 Office: Akron Child Guidance Ctr 312 Locust St Akron OH 44302

DAVIS, ELEANOR LAURIA, biology educator, volunteer, lecturer; b. Pitts., Aug. 29, 1923; d. Anthony Francis and Antonia Jennie (Bove) Lauria; m. Earle Richard Davis, May 7, 1946; children: Susan Davis Hickerson, Janice Davis Johnston, Lisa Davis Kulp, Elena Davis Smoulder, Amy Davis Gordon, Kent Earle, Eric J. BS, U. Pitts., 1944, M Letters in Biology, 1950. Grad. teaching asst. in physiology dept. biology U. Pitts., 1944-46; instr. in biology Pa. Coll. for Women (now Chatham Coll.), Pitts., 1946-53; libr. Carnegie Libr., Pitts., 1947-50. Co-author: Lab. Manual for Biology, 1948; contbr. editorials to profl. newsletter. Pres. St. Joseph's Hosp. Aux., Pitts., 1977-78, Allegheny County Med. Soc. Aux., 1981-83; mem. Coun. on Govt. Rels. and Pa. Med. Polit. Action Com., Harrisburg, 1987—, Pa. Atty. Gens. Task Force Drugs, 1989-90, Pa. Task Force on Aging, 1988-90, Pa. Task

Force on AIDS, 1988-90, Pa. Task Force on the Impaired Physician, 1988-90; com. woman Dem. Party O'Hara Twp., 1983—, chmn., 1990-95; by-laws com. Allegheny County Dems., 1986-88; bd. dirs. Parental Stress Ctr., 1977-94, Bright Beginnings, 1979-94, Am. Cancer Soc. Aux., 1984-86, Vocat. Rehab. Ctr., 1986-88, Injury Prevention Works; bd. dirs., mem. program devel. and pub. rels. coms. Self Help Group Network, 1989; chmn. pub. rels. program com. Rx Coun., 1993—; mem. S.W. region Pa. Assn. Hosp. Auxs., 1990—; pub. policy chmn. Alzheimers Disease and Related Disorders, 1987-94; mem. parish coun. St. Scholastica Ch., 1988-90, Grass Roots Intelligence Team, South Hills Health System, 1989—, adv. bd. by-laws com. Allegheny County Safe Kids Coalition, 1990—; elected del. AMA Aux. Conv., 1979-93; mem. smoke detector task force Allegheny County Health Dept., 1993—, mem. task force scald and burn prevention; mem. task force on health care reform Pa. Med. Soc. Alliance, 1993—. Recipient honor scholarship U. Pitts., 1941-44, Benjamin Rush award Allegheny County Med. Soc., 1987, Person of Yr. award South Hills Health System and Found., Pitts., 1989. Mem. AAUW (Women's Agenda), Nat. Inst. Adult Day Care (standards com.), Nat. Coun. Aging (task force for day care standards 1989-90), Allegheny County Fedn. of Women's Clubs (RX coun. bd. dirs. 1986—), Stanton Heights Garden Club (pres. 1974—), Piccadilly Herb Club (pres. 1994), Hosp. Assn. Pa. (grass roots intelligence team), Pa. Assn. Hosp. Auxs. (bd. dirs. S.W. region 1990—, legislation chmn. 1992-94, health chmn. 1993—), Pa. Med. Soc. (legis. key contact), Pa. Med. Soc. Alliance (PAMPAC rep. western dist. 1991-95, by laws com. 1990—, pres. 1988-89, 92-93, Past Pres.'s Gavel Club 1992-93), Allegheny County Med. Soc. (legis. com. 1989—), Health Advocacy for Women (mem. pub. policy com. 1995—), Theta Phi Alpha, Nu Sigma Nu. Home: 109 Woodshire Rd Pittsburgh PA 15215-1713

DAVIS, ELISE MILLER (MRS. LEO M. DAVIS), author; b. Corsicana, Tex., Oct. 12, 1915; d. Moses Myre and Rachelle (Daniels) Miller; student U. Tex., 1930-31; m. Jay Albert Davis, June 27, 1937 (dec. June 1973); 1 dau., Rayna Miller (Mrs. Michael Edwin Loeb); m. 2d, Leo M. Davis, Aug. 23, 1974. Freelance writer, 1945—; merchandiser and dir. Jay Davis, Inc., Amarillo, Tex., 1956-73; instr. mag. writing U. Tex., Dallas, 1978; lectr. creative writing Baylor U., Waco, Tex., 1980, 81, 83. Mem. Am. Soc. Journalists and Authors (bd. dirs. 1985-91). Author: The Answer Is God: The Personal Story of Dale Evans and Roy Rogers, 1955; articles to periodicals including Reader's Digest, Woman's Day, Nation's Business, others. Home: 7838 Caruth Ct Dallas TX 75225-8123

DAVIS, ELIZABETH HAWK, English language educator; b. Ft. Smith, Ark., Sept. 6, 1945; d. Arthur Carlton and Lolitta (Poe) Hawk; m. Leo Carson Davis, Aug. 31, 1968. BA, U. Ark., 1967, BM, 1967, MA, 1969; EdD, East Tex. State U., 1989. Classroom tchr. Springdale (Ark.) Pub. Schs., 1967-68; lectr. U. Md., Heidelberg, Fed. Republic Germany, 1978-79; from instr. to asst. prof. performing arts So. Ark. U., Magnolia, 1981-92, assoc. prof., 1992—, chair English and fgn. langs. dept., 1993—, interim dean Sch. Liberal and Performing Arts, 1993. Contbr. articles to profl. jours. Organist First Presbyn. Ch., Magnolia, 1984—. Mem. MLA, Nat. Coun. of Tchrs. of English, Ark. Tchrs. of Coll. English, Ark. Philol. Assn., Phi Beta Kappa. Office: So Ark U PO Box 1356 Magnolia AR 71753

DAVIS, EMMA-JO LEVEY, retired government executive, publishing executive; b. Greensboro, N.C., June 5, 1932; d. Harry Nelson and Alma (Snellen) Levey; m. Andrew Jackson Davis Jr., July 3, 1957 (div. July 1977); children: Anne Stone, Kelsie Lee. Student, Mary Washington Coll., 1949-51; AB, U. N.C., 1953; MEd, Coll. William and Mary, 1969. Tchr. local pub. schs., Gloucester, Va., 1959-61; editor U.S. Army, Ft. Eustis, Va., 1961-63, historian, 1963-67, curator Transp. Mus., 1967-80; chief curator U.S. Army, Washington, 1980-91. Author: History of the U.S. Army Transportation Corps, 1967, History of the U.S. Army Transportation School, 1967. Mem. Am. Assn. Mus., Am. Assn. State and Local History, Nat. Geneal. Soc., Mensa. Episcopalian. Home: 1202 Conway Dr # 202 Williamsburg VA 23185 Office: 117 Colony Sq Williamsburg VA 23185

DAVIS, EVELYN Y., editor, writer, publisher, investor; b. The Netherlands, Aug. 16; d. Herman H. and Marian (Witteboom) DeJong; m. William Henry Davis, 1957 (div. 1958); m. Marvin Knudsen, 1969 (div. 1970); m. Walter O. Froh Jr., 1991 (div. 1994). Student, Western Md. Coll., George Washington U., N.Y. Inst. Fin. Editor, pub., Highlights and Lowlights, 1964—. Trustee Evelyn Y. Davis Found., 1989—; mem. adv. bd. George Washington U. Med. Ctr. Fellow JFK Ctr. for Performing Arts. Mem. Luther Rice Soc. (life), Capitol Hill Club (life), Smithsonian Benefactors Cir., Andrew Carnegie Soc. (life). Republican. Episcopalian. Home: Watergate East 2510 Virginia Ave NW Washington DC 20037-1904 Office: Highlights and Lowlights Watergate Office Bldg 2600 Virginia Ave NW Ste 215 Washington DC 20037-1905

DAVIS, FLORENCE ANN, lawyer; b. Pitts., Feb. 22, 1955; d. Richard Davis and Charlotte (Saul) McGhee; m. Kevin J. O'Brien, May 28, 1978; children: Rebecca Davis, Sarah Davis. AB, Wellesley U., 1976; JD, NYU, 1979. Bar: N.Y. 1980, U.S. Dist. Ct. (ea. and so. dists.) N.Y., N.Y. Ct. Appeals (2d cir.), U.S. Tax Ct., U.S. Supreme Ct. Assoc. atty. Sullivan & Cromwell, N.Y.C., 1979-86; litigation counsel Morgan Stanley & Co., N.Y.C., 1986-88, v.p., 1988-90, dir. compliance, 1989—, prin., 1990—. Root-Tilden scholar NYU Law Sch., 1976-79. Mem. Securities Industry Assn. (v.p. edn. Compliance and Legal div. 1992, exec. com. Compliance and Legal div. 1990-92). Office: Stanley Morgan Co Inc 1251 Ave of the Americas New York NY 10020*

DAVIS, FRANCES KAY, lawyer; b. Phila., Apr. 1, 1952; d. Francis Kaye and Ida May (Lamplugh) D. BA, Mount Holyoke Coll., 1974; MA, Duke U., 1976; JD, Villanova U., 1983-86. Legal asst. Cozen, Begier & O'Connor, Phila., 1982-83; summer assoc. Montgomery, McCracken, Walker & Roads, Phila., 1985, assoc., 1986-89; assoc. Cozen & O'Connor, 1989—; gen. ptnr. April Racing Stables, Steel Fist Video Co., 1994—. Contbr. articles to profl. jours. Served to capt. USAF, 1977-82. Mem. ATLA (Trial Advocacy award Phila. chpt. 1986), Phila. Bar Assn., N.J. Bar Assn., Welsh Soc. Phila. (bd. stewards 1990-93, scholar 1984-85, chmn. scholarship com. 1990-92, counselor 1992-94, chmn. women's com. 1992-94).

DAVIS, GAY RUTH, psychotherapist, social welfare educator, consultant; b. Bellingham, Wash., Sept. 19, 1935; d. Lee Laverne Wickersham and Altha (Lund) Wickersham Knight; m. Paul Cushing Davis, Dec. 20, 1956; children: Jeffrey Richards, Jennifer Lynn. Student, Brigham Young U., 1953-55; BA summa cum laude, Western Wash. U., 1976; MSW, U. Wash., 1978, PhD, 1985. Diplomate in clin. social work, Qualified clin. social worker NASW; mem. Nat. Register Clin. Social Workers. Dir. social services dept. Sound Health Assn., Tacoma, 1977-78; social work profl. Harborview Med. Ctr., Seattle, 1979-81; lectr. social work U. Wash., Seattle, 1984-85; pvt. practice cons. social work and psychotherapy Seattle, 1985—. Contbr. articles to profl. jours. Grantee Wash. Dept. Health and Human Services, 1981-82. Mem. NASW, Wash. Assn. Social Workers, Wash. Profl. Soc. on Abuse of Children, Am. Profl. Soc. on Abuse of Children, Gerontol. Soc. Am. Democrat. Mormon.

DAVIS, GEENA (VIRGINIA DAVIS), actress; b. Wareham, Mass., Jan. 21, 1957; m. Richard Emmolo, 1981 (div. 1983); m. Jeff Goldblum, 1987 (div. 1990); m. Renny Harlin, 1993. BFA, Boston U., 1979; attended, New England Coll., Henniker, N.H. Founder Genial Pictures; mem. My. Washington (N.H.) Repertory Theatre Co. Motion picture appearances include Tootsie, 1982, Fletch, 1985, Transylvania 6-5000, 1985, The Fly, 1986, Beetlejuice, 1988, The Accidental Tourist, 1988 (Academy award Best Supporting Actress, 1989), Earth Girls Are Easy, 1989, Quick Change, 1990, Thelma and Louise, 1991 (Acad. award nominee Best Actress 1991, British Acad Film and TV Arts award Best Actress in leading role 1991, Golden Globe award nominee Best Actress 1991), A League of Their Own, 1992, Hero, 1992, Angie, 1994, Speechless, 1994; TV series: Buffalo Bill, 1983-84, Sara, 1985; appeared in TV film Secret Weapons, 1985, episodes series Family Ties, 1984. Address: care CAA 9830 Wilshire Blvd Beverly Hills CA 90212*

DAVIS, GERALDINE SAMPSON, special education educator; b. Tacoma, Wash., Aug. 18, 1919; d. Philip and Merta M. (Thomas) Sampson; m. John Allen Davis, Nov. 26 1942 (div. 1971); children: Denise, Karin, Glen (dec.), Grant (dec.), Page, Gail (dec.). BS with distinction, U. Minn., 1941; MEd, San Francisco State U., 1971. Cert. tchr., Calif., cert. adminstr., Calif. Art and English instr. White Bear Lake (Minn.) Jr. and Sr. High Sch., 1941-43; Am. club mobile operator ARC, Eng. and Europe, 1944-45; exec. dir. Lincoln County chpt. ARC, Newport, Oreg., 1947-48; substitute tchr. Santa Cruz (Calif.) County Dept. Edn., 1964-67; learning disabled instr. Live Oak Dist. Schs., Santa Cruz, 1967-89; peer tutor developer Live Oak Schs., 1970-73, reading program mgr., 1973-76; evaluation team mem. County of Santa Cruz, 1980-84. Exhibited paintings in numerous galleries shows including Los Gatos Art Cooperative, 1961-65, Santa Cruz Art Festival, 1962, San Juan Bautista Art Fair, 1963, Santa Cruz County Fair, 1965; paintings represented in several pvt. collections. Chpt. sec. March of Dimes, Lincoln County, 1949-51, Santa Cruz County; vol. tutor Vols. of Santa Cruz, 1978-83; fundraiser Boulder Creek (Calif.) Schs., 1963; scenic and prop designer Santa Cruz County Schs., 1964, Boulder Creek Theater Group, 1965. Mem. Calif. Assn. Nuerol. Handicapped Children (chair 1964-66, scholarships 1968-71), Women's Dem. Club, AAUW (com. chair for women's issues 1990—), Reproductive Rights Network, Santa Cruz Reading Assn. (sec. 1980, rep. Asilomar reading conf. bd. 1981-82, Chpt. and Internat. Reading Assns. award 1985), Calif. Ret. Tchrs. Assn. (nominating com. 1985—), Assn. Ret. Persons, Sr. Citizens Santa Cruz County, Pub. Citizens, Pub. Broadcasting Network, Conservation of Am, Amnesty, Delta Phi Delta (life, pres. Mpls. chpt. 1939-41), Pi Lambda Theta (life). Home: 319 35th Ave Santa Cruz CA 95062-5514

DAVIS, HELEN GORDON, former state senator; b. N.Y.C., Dec. 25; m. Gene Davis; children: Stephanie, Karen, Gordon. BA, Bklyn. Coll.; postgrad., U. South Fla., 1967-70. Tchr., High Sch. Commerce, N.Y.C., Hillsborough High Sch., Tampa, Fla.; grad. asst. U. South Fla., 1968; mem. Fla. Ho. of Reps., 1974-88, state senator, 1988-92; mem. Fla. Supreme Ct. Commn. on Gender Bias in the Cts., 1988-90; mem. Fla. Supreme Ct. Commn. on Mediation and Arbitration, 1987—. chmn. senate appropriations subcom. human svcs., mem. rules com., internat. trade and econ. devel. com., health and rehab. svcs. com. Jud. chmn. Local Govt. Study Commn. Hillsborough County (Fla.), 1964; mem. Tampa Commn. on Juvenile Delinquency, 1966-69, Mayor's Citizens Adv. Com., 1966-69, Quality Edn. Commn., 1966-68, Gov.'s Citizen Com. for Ct. Reform, 1972, Hillsborough County Planning Commn., 1973-74; mem. Gov.'s Commn. on Jud. Reform, 1976; mem. employment com. Commn. Community Relations, 1966-69; by-laws chmn. Arts Coun. Tampa, 1971-74; 1st v.p. Tampa Symphony Guild, 1974; bd. dirs. U. South Fla. Found., 1968-74, Stop Rape, 1973-74; founder Ctr. for Women, Tampa, 1978; past pres. PTA; active adv. commn. Nat. Child Care Action Campaign, Nat. Ctr. for Crime and Delinquency. Recipient U. South Fla. Young Democrats Humanitarian award, 1974, Diana award NOW, 1975, Woman of Achievement in Arts award Tampa, 1975, Tampa Human Rels. award, 1976, Hannah G. Solomon Citizen of Yr. award, 1980, St. Petersburg Times/Fla. Civil Liberties award, 1980, Friend of Edn. award, 1981, Fla. Alliance for Responsible Parenting award, 1981, Humanitarian award Judeo-Christian Clinic, 1984, Fla. Network of Runaway Youth award, 1985, Ctr. for Women Leader-advocate Friend award, 1985, Nat. Assn. Juvenile Ct. Judges Appreciation award 1986, Legis. Leadership appreciation Centre for Women, 1986, Children's Crisis Ctr. Leadership award, 1987, AAUW leadership award, 1987, Hillsborough County Halfway House appreciation, 1988, Martin Luther King award City of Tampa, 1988, Nat. Fedn. Dem. Women appreciation, 1989, Dept. Legal Affairs appreciation, 1990, Superwoman award Mus. Sci. and Industry, 1990, Nat. Childcare Merit award Nat. Assn. Sch. Psychologist, 1992, Am. Judicature award Am. Judicature Assn., 1993; named. Fla. Motion Picture and TV Outstanding Legislator, 1990, others. Mem. LWV (pres. Hillsborough County 1966-69, lobbyist, Fla. adminstrn. of justice chmn. 1969-74), Temple Guild Sisterhood (past pres.), Am. Arbitration Assn. Home: 45 Adalia Ave Tampa FL 33606-3301

DAVIS, HOLLY RAE, accountant; b. Newport, Vt., Dec. 25, 1965; d. Wendell Leigh and Nancy Rae (Dean) Herman; m. Todd Owen Davis, Oct. 27, 1990; 1 child, Jason Todd. B in Acctg., Bentley Coll., 1988. Assoc. cost acct. Data Gen. Corp., Southboro, Mass., 1988-89, cost acct., 1989-91; cost acct. Novametrix Med. Sys., Wallingford, Conn., 1991-93, cost acctg. mgr., 1993—. Mem. Inst. Mgmt. Accts. (sec. 1993-94, pub. rels. 1994—). Office: Novametrix Med Sys Inc 1 Barnes Indsl Park Wallingford CT 06492

DAVIS, IRMA NELL, alcohol/drug abuse services professional; b. Birmingham, Ala., Dec. 26, 1930; d. David and Millie (Allen) Washington; m. Robert David, Apr. 15, 1950; four children. Student, Youngstown State U. Cert. prevention specialist, Ohio. Door women Linton Funeral, Youngstown, Ohio, 1959-63; comml. cleaner and caterer Mahoning Bank & Met. Bank, Youngstown, 1964-78; dir. Needle's Eye, Youngstown, 1977—. Pres. South High Boosters, Youngstown. Recipient Good Samaritan award Cmty. of A.A., 1984, Paul Harris fellow award Rotary Found., 1987, award Iota Phi Lambda Sorority, Inc., 1987, Elizabeth Powell Civic award, 1988, Civic award Black Nurses Assn. Mahoning and Trumbull County, 1989, Cmty Svc. award Nat. Assn. Negro Bus. and Profl. Women Club, Inc., 1983, Cmty. Svc. awards Black Knight Police Assn., 1982, South Side Coalition for Better Cmty. Inc., 1983; named Alcohol Adminstr. of Yr., 1987. Mem. NAACP, Masons, B'nai B'rith, KC. Home: 1045 Parkwood St Youngstown OH 44502

DAVIS, JACQUELINE ANN, therapist; b. Chgo., Sept. 2, 1964; d. Edward L. and Lura L. (Migawa) D.; m. Jeffrey M. Waller, May 13, 1987 (div. 1990). AA, Thornton C.C., South Holland, Ill., 1985; BA in Psychology, Gov. State U., 1988, MA in Counseling, 1992. Tchg. asst. Pace H.S., Blue Island, Ill., 1987-89; vocat. instr. Tinley Park (Ill.) Mental Health Ctr., 1989-92; women's counselor South Suburban Family Shelter, Hazel Crest, Ill., 1991—; sr. therapist Tri-City C. Mental Health Ctr., East Chicago, Ill., 1992—.

DAVIS, JAN, small business owner, artisan, former secondary school educator; b. Corpus Christi, Tex., June 29, 1943; d. Reuben T. and Ruby (Englert) Pattillo; AA, Del Mar Coll., 1963; BA, U. Houston, 1965; teaching cert. S.W. Tex. State U., 1971; cert. prof. catechist, spiritual dir.; MA St. Mary's U., 1992; children: William A., Wade. Tchr., Edna (Tex.) Jr. High Sch., 1966-67, counselor, 1967-68; tchr. Pleasanton (Tex.) High Sch., 1972-85; mem. supt.'s com. Pleasanton Pub. Schs., 1975-77, 78-79; chmn. social studies dept., 1976-85; owner Crystal Rose Enterprises, 1988—. Leader 4-H, 1978-89, 4-H youth coord. County of Atascosa, Tex., 1986-89. Recipient Meritorious Svc. award Vol. Leaders Assn. Tex., Mem. Tex. Classroom Tchrs. Assn. (Tchr. of Year 1979), Pleasanton Classroom Tchrs. Assn., Nat. Speakers Assn., South Tex. Profl. Speakers Assn., Lay Preaching Guild, 4-H Vol. Leaders Assn. (pres. Dist. 13 1987-88), Pleasanton Jr. Woman's Club (1st v.p. 1976, pres. 1977), A&M Women's Club of Atascosa County (pres. 1978-80), Toastmasters. Roman Catholic.

DAVIS, JANE STRAUSS, business owner; b. Chgo., July 3, 1944; d. Joseph Loeb and Leanore (Purvin) Strauss; m. Muller Davis, Dec. 28, 1963; children: Melissa Davis Smith, Muller Jr., Joseph. BA with honors in Am. Culture, Northwestern U., 1980, postgrad. studies in Am. History, 1980-81. With residential sales Kenneth Friend Realty, Winnetka, Ill., 1971-74, J.H. Kahn Realty, Glencoe, Ill., 1974-77; v.p. personal trust dept. Harris Trust & Savs. Bank, Chgo., 1983-89; v.p. Bankers Trust Co. Pvt. Bank, Chgo., 1989-90; founder Jane Davis Connections, Chgo., 1991—, Connections Next Step, 1993—; Young Chgo. Authors, 1992—; dir. United Charities of Chgo. Mem. Women's bd. Rush-Presbyn.-St. Luke's Med. Ctr., Chgo., 1978—; co-chmn. med. rsch. campaign Michael Reese Med. Ctr., Chgo., 1982; mem. costume com. Chgo. Hist. Soc., 1980-90; mem. campaign for great tchrs. Northwestern U., Evanston, Ill., 1988-90, vis. com., 1989—; mem. Chgo. Symphony Orch. Woman's Assn., 1990—; mem. Children's Meml. Hosp. Med. Rsch. Inst. coun., 1991—, Coun. of One Hundred, Northwestern U., The Chgo. Bd., Roosevelt U., Chgo., 1994—; chair 50th anniversary day celebration Roosevelt U., 1995.

DAVIS, JOAN, general contractor, tax preparer; b. Anderson, Ind., Nov. 24, 1947; d. Harold Brewer and Alice Marie (Doll) Hall; m. L.R. Collier Sr., May 19, 1967 (div. 1980); children: Missy JoAn Collier Basham, L.R. Jr.; m. Timothy G. Davis, Oct. 10, 1982; stepchildren: Geraldine Marie, Eugene Francis. Grad. high sch., Riverside, Calif. Sec. Svc. Electric, Inc., Riverside, 1966-68; pres. Power Electric, Inc., Norco, Calif., 1972-76; office mgr. Cutter Electric, Inc., Rialto, Calif., 1976-77; exec. asst., controller, corp. sec. Home & Country, Inc., Riverside, 1977—; owner, tax preparer Davis Bus. Svc., Riverside, 1978—. Mem. Rubidoux Falcon Football Boosters (sec. publicity com. Riverside chpt. 1983-88). Republican. Home: 6981 Pacheco Ct Riverside CA 92509-6326 Office: Home & Country Inc 7265 Jurupa Ave Riverside CA 92504-1011

DAVIS, JOANNE FATSE, lawyer; b. Bridgeport, Conn., June 8, 1956; m. Thomas J. Davis, Jr.; 1 child, Thomas Gregory Milia Davis. BS, Boston U., 1977; JD, U. Bridgeport, 1982. Bar: Conn. 1982, N.Y. 1983. Motions law clk. U.S. Ct. Appeals (2d cir.), N.Y.C., 1982-83; assoc. Debevoise & Plimpton, N.Y.C., 1983-89; sr. corp. counsel Uniroyal Chem. Co., Middlebury, Conn., 1989—; bd. dirs. Legal Ctr. Conn. Nonprofit Orgns. Inc. Mem. Conn. Bar Assn. Soc. Farsarotul (officer). Eastern Orthodox. Office: Uniroyal Chem Co Inc Benson Rd Middlebury CT 06749

DAVIS, JOLENE BRYANT, magazine publishing executive; b. Lehigh, Iowa, Dec. 11, 1942; d. Joseph Albert and Joyce (Olson) Bryant; m. Richard Alan Alper, Feb. 12, 1967 (dec. July 1975); m. Steven Andrew Davis, Apr. 16, 1979; children: Bryant David, Suzanne Joyce. BA, U. Iowa, 1964; MA, Calif. State U., San Jose, 1972. Registered dietitian, Ind. Home economist The Oregonian, newspaper, Portland, 1965-67; dietitian Ind. U. Sch. Medicine, Indpls., 1973-74; clin. dietitian U. Calif. Hosps. and Clins., San Francisco, 1974-75, chief clin. dietitian, 1975-78, chief rsch. dietitian Clin. Study Ctr., 1979-83; pub., chief exec. officer Our Kids mag. Branford Pub., Inc., San Antonio, 1984—, v.p., 1988—, also bd. dirs.; sports nutritionist San Antonio Spurs, 1993—; sec., bd. govs. Parenting Publs. Am., San Antonio, 1988-89. Mem. San Antonio Conservation Soc., 1985—; bd. dirs. Jewish Family Svc. Assn., San Antonio, 1986-88, Family Resource Ctr., San Antonio; chmn. cultural arts PTA, San Antonio, 1988—. Mem. Women in Communications (editor Best Mag. Column and Mag. award of Merit 1988, 90), Am. Dietetic Assn., Soc. Nutrition Edn., San Antonio Dist. Dietetic Assn., Soc. Profl. Journalists, Pi Beta Phi. Home: 178 Country Ln San Antonio TX 78209-2228 Office: Branford Pub Inc 8400 Blanco Rd Ste 201 San Antonio TX 78216-3055

DAVIS, JOSEPHINE DUNBAR, university president; b. Waycross, Ga., Dec. 18, 1942; d. Simon Otis and Josephine Elizabeth (Bellamy) Dunbar; m. Gordon Nathaniel Davis, Aug. 28, 1965; children: Josette, Monique, Rodney. BA in Math. magna cum laude, Spelman Coll., Atlanta, 1964; MS in Math., Notre Dame U., South Bend, Ind., 1970; EdD in Math., Rutgers U., 1973. Tchr. math. high sch. Dougherty County Sch. System, Albany, Ga., 1960-66; tchr. math. Albany State Coll., 1970-78, 85-89, dean Grad. Sch., 1978-84, 85-89; acad. v.p. St. Cloud (Minn.) State U., 1989-91, acting pres., 1990; pres. York Coll., Jamaica, N.Y., 1991—; cons. math Nat. Sci. Found., Air Force Studies Bd. Author: Basic Mathematics: A Prelude to College Algebra, 1975, Coloring the Halls of Ivy, 1994; co-author: Problem Solving Activities, 1980; contbg. author: The Mathematics Education of Black High School Students, 1989. pres. Albany chpt. The Links, Inc.; organizer Albany Beautillion Presentation, Albany chpt. Jack and Jill, Inc.; pres. Flint River Girl Scout Coun., Albany; bd. dirs. Greater Jamaica Devel. Corp., Queens Coun. on Arts, Jamaica Arts Ctr. Named Outstanding Educator in Southwest Ga., State Ga., 1983, Woman of Yr., Albany Citizens Group, 1987; recipient Presdl. award Flint River Girl Scout coun., Albany, 1984; Merrill travel and study abroad fellow, 1965; fellow NSF, 1970, Ednl. Devel. Profl. Act, 1971; Kellogg Found. Group VIII fellow, 1987-90. Mem. Am. Assn. Higher Edn. (treas. black caucus 1994—, chairperson woman's caucus), Am. Assn. State Colls. and U.S. (internat. com.). Baptist. Office: York Coll Office of the President 94-20 Guy R Brewer Blvd Jamaica NY 11451-0001

DAVIS, JOY LEE, English language educator; b. N.Y.C., Apr. 3, 1931; d. William Henry and Genevieve (Rhein) Belknap; m. Peter John King, Aug. 26, 1955 (div. Feb. 1985); children: William Belknap King, Russell Stuart King; m. John Bradford Davis, Jr., July 5, 1986. AB, Wellesley Coll., 1952, AM, 1953; PhD, Rutgers U., 1968; postgrad., Oxford (Eng.) U., 1978. Tchr. English Dana Hall Sch. for Girls, Wellesley, Mass., 1953-54; instr. English U. Mo., Columbia, 1954-55, Boston U., 1955-56; tchr. English Brookline (Mass.) High Sch., Spartanburg (S.C.) High Sch., 1956-60; prof. English Ohio Wesleyan U., Delaware, 1966-71, Hamline U., St. Paul, 1972-74, U. Minn., Mpls., 1974-77, Coll. St. Thomas, St. Paul, 1977-88; lectr., dir. Joy Davis Seminars, St. Paul, 1988—; prof. MA in Liberal Studies Program, Hamline U., 1993—. Pub. poetry in New World Writing and Crisp Pine Anthology, lit. criticism in Midwest Quar., 1993. Bd. trustees Ramsey County Arts and Sci. Coun., St. Paul, 1974-80. Wellesley Coll. scholar, 1952. Mem. AAUW (dd. dirs., chair ednl. equity com. 1991, Svc. awrd St. Paul br. 1983), Midwest MLA, Mpls. Inst. Fine Arts, Minn. Club (bd. dirs. 1982-88), New Century Club (bd. dirs., spl. subjects chmn.) Schubert Club (bd. dirs., chmn. mus. com.), Wellesley Coll. Club (regional campaign com.), Delta Kappa Gamma. Republican. Presbyterian. Home and Office: 4312 Pond View Dr Saint Paul MN 55110-4155

DAVIS, JULIA MAE, claims specialist; b. Ft. Lauderdale, Fla., Jan. 28, 1962; d. James Hildery and Carrie Bell (Abrams) D.; 1 child, Victoria Jean. BBA, Bethune-Cookman Coll., 1984. Lic. all lines claim adjuster. Accounts payable clerk Broward Fed. Bank, Ft. Lauderdale, 1985-86; sr. claim rep. State Farm Ins. Co, Wilton Manors, Fla., 1985—. Mem. State Farm Activities Assn. Home: 3009 NW 8th St Fort Lauderdale FL 33311-6607

DAVIS, JULIA MCBROOM, college dean, speech pathology and audiology educator; b. Alexandria, La., Sept. 29, 1930; d. Guy Clarence and Addie (McElroy) McBroom; m. Cecil Ponder Davis, Aug. 25, 1951 (div. 1981); children: Mark Holden, Paul Houston, Anne Hamilton; m. David G. Reynolds, Aug. 26, 1987. BA, Northwestern State U., Natchitoches, La., 1951; MS, U. So. Miss., 1965, PhD, 1966. Cert. in clin. competence in audiology. Asst. prof. U. So. Miss., Hattiesburg, 1966-69, assoc., 1969-71; assoc. prof. Southwestern State U., Hammond, 1971; faculty U. Iowa, Iowa City, 1971-87; prof., chmn. dept. speech pathology and audiology U. Iowa, 1980-85, assoc. dean Coll. Liberal Arts, 1985-87, dir. Speech and Hearing Ctr., 1979-80; dean Coll. Social and Behavioral Scis. U. South Fla., Tampa, 1987-90, assoc. provost, 1990-91; dean Coll. Liberal Arts, U. Minn., Mpls., 1991—. Author: (with Edward J. Hardick) Rehabilitative Audiology for Children and Adults, 1981; editor: Our Forgotten Children, 1977; assoc. editor Jour. Speech Hearing Research, 1975-77, Jour. Speech Hearing Disorders, 1982-83. Fellow Am. Speech-Hearing-Lang. Assn. (chmn. program com. 1980-81), Iowa Speech and Hearing Assn. (v.p.-liaison 1972-73, honors 1985); mem. Acad. Rehabilitative Audiology (pres. 1979-80), Iowa Conf. for Hearing Impaired (pres. 1975-76), Sigma Xi. Democrat. Methodist. Office: U Minn Coll Liberal Arts 215 Johnston Hall 101 Pleasant St SE Minneapolis MN 55455-0432

DAVIS, JUNE LEAH, psychologist; b. Craigsville, W.Va., Nov. 10, 1922; d. Ernest Layton and Bessie May (Bostic) Taylor; m. Charles William Heasley, Jan. 16, 1943 (div. 1961); children: Denasse Ann Heasley Dugan, Wanda Lori Heasley Schwartz; m. Theodore R. Davis, Nov. 20, 1971. BA, Glenville (W.Va.) State Coll., 1962; MA, Ohio State U., 1967. Cert. psychologist, Ohio. Tchr. Nicholas County Bd. Edn., Summersville, W.Va., 1943-46, 1958-60; tchr. Columbus (Ohio) Bd. Edn., 1962-70, sch. psychologist, 1970—. Active First Baptist Ch., Columbus, 1975—. Mem. Sch. Psychologists Ctrl. Ohio (pres.; Best Practice award 1987), Ohio Sch. Psychologists Assn., Ctrl. Ohio Psychologists Assn. (Hueslman award for outstanding svc. 1989). Democrat. Home and Office: 432 S Weyant Ave Columbus OH 43213-2262

DAVIS, KAREN ANN, psychologist; b. N.Y.C., Sept. 15, 1939; d. Stanley S. and Claire (Whitman) Davis; 1 child, Gregory Davis Johansen. BS, CCNY, 1960, MS, 1965; PhD, Fordham U., 1978. Psychodiagnostitian Roosevelt Hosp., N.Y.C., 1965; sch. psychologist Merrick-Belmore N.Y., 1965-66; psychologist Floyd Patterson House, N.Y.C., 1966-67; instr. in edn., tchr. grad. and undergrad. psychology Adelphi U., Garden City, N.Y., 1967-73, acting coord. grad. & undergrad. edn., 1973; pvt. practice individual, group & couple psychotherapy N.Y.C., 1974—; pres. Davis Devel. Programs, 1990—; pres. Davis Devel. Programs, 1990—. Mem. APA, Internat. Coun. Psychology. Office: 201 E 28th St New York NY 10016

DAVIS, KAREN PADGETT, fund executive; b. Blackwell, Okla., Nov. 14, 1942; d. Walter Dwight and Thelma Louise (Kohler) Padgett; 1 child, Kelly Denise. BA, Rice U., 1965, PhD, 1969. Asst. prof. econs. Rice U., 1969-70; econ. policy fellow Social Security Adminstrn. Brookings Instn., Washington, 1970-71, rsch. assoc., 1971-74, sr. fellow, 1974-77; dep. asst. sec. for planning and evaluation, health HEW, Washington, 1977-80; adminstr. health resources adminstrn. USPHS, Washington, 1980-81; prof. Johns Hopkins U., Balt., 1981-92; chmn., 1983-92; exec. v.p. Commonwealth Fund, N.Y.C., 1992-94, pres., 1995—; bd. dirs. Somatrix Therapy Corp.; mem. Physician Payment Rev. Commn., 1986-94; dir. Commonwealth Health Fund Commn. on Elderly People Living Alone, 1985-91; vis. lectr. Harvard U., 1974-75. Author: National Health Insurance: Benefits, Costs and Consequences, 1975, Health and the War on Poverty, 1978, Medicare Policy: New Directions for Health and Long-Term Care, 1986, Health Care Cost Containment, 1990. Mem. Inst. Medicine, Am. Econs. Assn., Phi Beta Kappa. Democrat. Methodist. Home: 176 E 77th St New York NY 10021 Office: The Commonwealth Fund The Harkness House 1 E 75th St New York NY 10021

DAVIS, KAREN SUE, hospital nursing supervisor; b. Owensboro, Ky., June 5, 1950; d. Robert J. and Mona F. (Urlaub) D. Diploma, Deaconess Sch. Nursing, 1971. Cert. pediatrics advanced life support. Charge nurse pediatrics Owensboro Davies County Hosp., 1971-89, clin. supr. pediatrics 11-7 shift, 1989—. Republican. Lutheran. Home: RR 1 Hwy 70 Evanston IN 47531

DAVIS, KATHERINE LYON, transportation executive, state administrator; b. Boston, June 24, 1956; d. Richard Harold and Joy (Hallum) Winer; m. John Marshall Davis, Feb. 22, 1992; 1 child, Madeline Felton. BS, MIT, 1978; MBA, Harvard U., 1982. Engr. Cambridge (Mass.) Collaborative, 1978-80; mfg. mgr. Cummins Engine Co., Columbus, Ind., 1982-87, bus. dir., 1987-89; dep. commr. Ind. Dept. Transp., Indpls., 1989—. Mem. Transp. Rsch. Bd., 1990-93, Intelligent Vehicle Hwy. Systems, 1991-93. Recipient commendation Dept. Transp., Fed. Hwy. Adminstrn., 1991. Democrat. Home: 621 E 9th St Indianapolis IN 46202 Office: Ind Dept Transp 100 N Senate N 755 Indianapolis IN 46204

DAVIS, KATHLEEN A., lobbyist; b. Phila., Mar. 15, 1958; d. William D. and Laura M. (Colalongo) Badger; m. Mark J. Davis, Sept. 4, 1982; 1 child, Craig Mark. BA, Rowan Coll., 1981. Legis. aide Senator Raymond Zane, Woodbury, N.J., 1981-84; supr. govtl. affairs South Jersey Gas Co., Folsom, N.J., 1984-91; asst. to Gov. Jim Florio, Trenton, N.J., 1991-92; dir. govtl. affairs N.J.-Am. Water Co., Haddon Heights, 1992—. Com. chairperson Archway Programs, Atco, N.J., 1994; state chair Employer Legis. Com., 1992—. Mem. Nat. Assn. Water Cos. (mem. govt. affairs com.), N.J. Utilities Assn. (chair, legis. affairs com. 1994—), C. of C. So. N.J. (chair state affairs com. 1994—), N.J. Bus. and Industry Assn. (mem. govt. affairs com.). Office: NJ-American Water Co 500 Grove St Haddon Heights NJ 08035

DAVIS, KATHRYN WARD, fundraising executive; b. Florence, S.C., Oct. 11, 1949; d. Richard Dixon Ward and Kathryn (McFarland) Duncan; m. Michael R. Bumgardner, Feb. 16, 1974 (div. Nov. 1982); children: Carolyn E., Christopher G.; m. David Addison Davis, May 28, 1983. BA in English, U. N.C., 1971. Dir. devel. WFAE Radio, U. N.C., Charlotte, 1980-82, WUNC Radio, U. N.C., Chapel Hill, 1982-84, U. N.C. Hosps. Med. Found., Chapel Hill, 1984-87, St. Joseph Med. Found., Balt., 1987-88; exec. dir. MCG Found., Mt. Clemens, Mich., 1989—; fundraising coun. Macomb County Lit. Coun., Mt. Clemens, 1991. Tutor Macomb County Reading Ptnrs., 1992; cons. Jr. Achievement, Detroit, 1991. Named Disting Svc. Toastmasters, Chapel Hill, 1986. Mem. Nat. Soc. Fundraising Execs. (chmn. women in devel. com. 1993), Mich. Assn. Hosp. Devel. (pres. 1990-92), Assn. Healthcare Philanthropy (cert., region IV dir. 1994—), Sterling Hts. Kiwanis (bd. dirs. 1994—), Women's Econ. Club. Republican. Episcopalian. Office: MCG Found 1000 Harrington Blvd Mount Clemens MI 48043

DAVIS, KIM MCALISTER, real estate sales executive; b. Woodruff, S.C., Dec. 30, 1958; d. James Calhoun and Nancy (Caldwell) McAlister; m. Robert James Godfrey (div.); 1 child, Lindsey Paige; m. Don Brigham Davis, 1988. BA in Elem. Edn., U. S.C., 1982, MBA, 1983—. Cert. tchr., S.C.; lic. real estate, Fla. Adminstrv. asst. Dr. G.R. Shanbhag and Assocs., Woodruff, 1977-78; sales rep. Reimer's Dept. Store, Woodruff, 1978-80; tchr. Spartanburg County Sch. Dist., Woodruff, 1981-82; pres., owner Godfrey Carpets, Inc., Woodruff, 1983-88; pharm. sales rep. Parke-Davis Pharm. Co., Ponte Vedra Beach, Fla., 1989-90. Mem. decorating com. 1st Bapt. Ch., Woodruff, 1984-87; chmn. bd. dirs. Small Towns Program, Woodruff, 1987—; Rep. candidate for Spartanburg County Coun., 1987; mem. S.C. Rep. Com.; sustaining mem. S.C. Rep. Party; chmn. Nat. Bus. Women's Week, 1984; bd. dirs., pres. 1991-93, Ponte Vedra-Palm Valley Elem. Sch. Parent Tchr. Student Orgn.; sustaining mem. Fla. Rep. Party; bd. dirs. St. Johns Pub. Edn. Found., St. Johns County Edn. Found.; mem. human resources strategic planning com. St. Johns County Pub. Schs.; Rep. candidate St. Johns County Sch. Bd., 1994. Named Young Careerist of the Yr., Nat. Bus. and Profl. Women, 1984. Mem. NAFE, Nat. Fedn. Ind. Bus., Greater Woodruff Area C. of C. (pub. spkr., bd. dirs. 1985-87, pres. 1986), Bus. and Profl. Women (v.p. 1985), Woodruff Jr. Women's Club, Ponte Vedra Assn. Realtors, Disting. Million Dollar Club, St. JOhn's County C. of C. (Ponte Vedra coun.). Home: 6018 Bridgewater Cr Ponte Vedra Beach FL 32082 Office: 270 Solana Rd Ponte Vedra Beach FL 32082

DAVIS, KITTY O'ROURKE, elections administrator; b. Cumberland, Md., July 8, 1948; d. James Joseph and Esther (Broderick) O'Rourke; m. Philip Stephen Davis; 1 child, Melissa Ann. AD in Fin., Allegany C.C., Cumberland, 1990, AD in Bus. Adminstrn., 1992. Wirth Liberty Bank of Md., Cumberland, 1971-85; registrar Bd. Suprs. of Elections for Allegany County, Cumberland, 1985-91, elections adminstr., 1991—; mem. Md. Task Force Studying Implementation of Motor/Voter Legislation. Mem. Md. Assn. Election Ofcls. (bd. dirs. 1993—). Home: 410 Crestview Dr Frostburg MD 21532-1100 Office: Bd Suprs of Elections 701 Kelly Rd Ste 100 Cumberland MD 21502-3401

DAVIS, LAURA ARLENE, foundation administrator; b. Battle Creek, Mich., Apr. 14, 1935; d. Paul Bennett and Daisy E. (Coston) Borgard; m. John R. Davis, Aug. 7, 1955; children: Scott Judson, Cynthia Ann Davis Welker. BS, Cen. Mich. U., 1986. Sec., Mich. Loan Co., Battle Creek, 1952-56; legal sec. Ryan, Sullivan & Hamilton, Battle Creek, 1957-64; exec. sec. W.K. Kellogg Found., Battle Creek, 1965-76, adminstrn./program asst., 1976, fellowship dir., 1977, asst. v.p. adminstrn., asst. corp. sec., 1978-84; v.p. corp. affairs, corp. sec., 1984—. Pres. bd. dirs. Charitable Union, Battle Creek, 1983-85; mem. allocations panel United Way of Battle Creek, 1983, v.p. community rels., 1990-91, 1st v.p., 1994, pres. of bd. 1995—; bd. dirs. Battle Creek Gas Co., 1988—, Riding for the Handicapped Cheff Ctr., 1991—, sec., 1992—; trustee Binder Park Zoo; mem. adv. coun. Argubright Bus. Coll., 1989-90; mem. Visionquest 5000, 1989; mem. selection com. Community Leadership Acad.; bd. dirs. Coun. Mich. Founds., 1994—; mem. membership com. Recipient Athena award C. of C., Community Svc. award J.C. Penney. Mem. Adminstrv. Mgmt. Soc. (pres. chpt. 1982-83), Am. Mgmt. Assn., Battle Creek C. of C. Home: 124 Heather Hills Dr Battle Creek MI 49017-8307 Office: W K Kellogg Found One Michigan Ave E Battle Creek MI 49017

DAVIS, LAURIE IRENE (WILKINS), title company executive; b. Alliance, Nebr., June 25, 1958; d. Ervin Theodore and Fairy Ina (Roberts) Wilkins; m. Robert Allen Davis, Sept. 13, 1986; children: Daniel Allen-Ervin, Jessica LaFair. Grad. in comml. real estate, Comml. Coll., 1987. Lic. real estate agt., escrow officer. Closer, escrow officer Commerce Title, Dallas, 1986-87; escrow officer, mgr. Commonwealth Title, Dallas, 1987-91, Lawyers Title, Dallas, 1992-93; escrow officer Chicago Title, Dallas, 1991-92; escrow officer, mgr., ptnr. Fidelity Title, Dallas, 1992, Hytken & Ruschman, P.C., Safeco Title, Dallas, 1994—. Mem. Greater Dallas Bd. Realtors, Womens Assn. Realtors. Republican. Methodist. Home: Rt 4, Box 90 Mc Kinney TX 75070 Office: Safeco Title 5944 Luther Ln # 700 Dallas TX 75225

DAVIS, LINDA JACOBS, public affairs development professional; b. Miami, July 10, 1955; d. Martin Jacque and Doris Harriet (Stucker) Jacobs; m. John Joseph Mantos, Jan. 1, 1984 (dec. 1988); m. Perry Davis, June 4, 1989; children: Aaron, Jacob. Student, U. South Fla., 1977. Mgr., cons. Werner Erhard & Assocs., San Francisco, 1978-82, program leader, 1979-90; asst. exec. dir. The Breakthrough Found., San Francisco, 1982-88; owner Mantagaris Galleries, San Francisco, 1988-92; dir. mktg. devel. Marin Child Care Coun., San Rafael, Calif., 1992-94; dir. devel. and pub. affairs Planned Parenthood of Marin, Sonoma and Menodcino, Calif., 1994—; ptnr. Women's Initiative for Leadership Devel., 1994—; profl. fund-raiser. Vol. The Hunger Project, Fla., 1977-78; bd. dirs. Marin Child Care Coun.; appointed commr. Marin Commn. on Women, 1994—. Recipient Outstanding Young Women Am. Mem. NOW (pres. local chpt.), Marin Women's Coalition. Democrat. Jewish. Home: 75 Milland Dr Mill Valley CA 94941-4910 Office: Planned Parenthood 2 H St San Rafael CA 94901

DAVIS, LORETTA, association executive; b. Champaign, Ill., Nov. 12, 1935; d. Raymond Scott and Margarit (Smith) Minor; m. Arthur Davis; children: Arthur, Deborah, Sarah. BS in Human Svcs., Empire State Coll.; postgrad., Northeastern U., Boston, U. Ill. Dir. women's activities YWCA, Rochester, N.Y., 1975-76; dir. admissions coll. of edn. Northeastern U., Boston, 1976-79, assoc. program dir. continuing edn., 1979-80; sr. pers. tng. technician, dept. pers. adminstrn. Commonwealth of Mass., Boston, 1981-82, dir. exec. search, dept. pers. adminstrn., 1988-89, dir. bur. recruitment and referral, dept. pers. adminstrn., 1989-90; facilitator staff devel. Carney Hosp., Boston, 1982-83, dir. human rels., 1983-88; exec. dir. YWCA, Cambridge, Mass., 1990—. Bd. dirs. Project Joy, Cambridge, 1992—, Community Change, Boston, 1994—, Women's Statewide Legis. Network, Boston, 1994—. Recipient Disting. Leadership award United Negro Coll. Fund, Boston, 1980, 81, 83. Mem. Links, Inc. (chair spl. events Middlesex chpt.), Alpha Kappa Alpha. Office: YWCA of Cambridge 7 Temple St Cambridge MA 02139-2496

DAVIS, LYNN ETHERIDGE, political scientist, government official; b. Miami, Fla., Sept. 6, 1943; d. Earl DeWitt and Louise (Featherston) Etheridge. BA, Duke U., 1965; MA, Columbia U., 1967, PhD, 1971. Lectr. Miles Coll., Birmingham, Ala., 1966-67; asst. prof. polit. sci. Bernard Coll., Columbia U., N.Y.C., 1970-74; rsch. assoc. Internat. Inst. for Strategic Studies, London, 1973; program analysis staff Nat. Security Council, 1974; asst. prof., lectr. dept. polit. sci. Columbia U., 1974-76; prof., staff mem. Senate Select Com. on Intelligence, 1975-76; dep. asst. sec. of def. for policy plans and nat. security affairs Office of the Under Sec. for Policy, Dept. Def., Washington, 1977-79, asst. dep. under sec. for policy planning, 1979-81; rsch. Internat. Inst. Strategic Studies, London, 1981-82; prof. national security affairs National War Coll., Washington, 1982-85; dir. studies Internat. Inst. Strategic Studies, London, 1985-87; hon. sr. rsch. fellow, dept. war studies Kings Coll., London, 1988-90; rsch. fellow John Hopkins Fgn. Policy Inst, Paul H. Nitze Sch. Advanced Internat. Studies, 1988-91; v.p. army rsch. divsn., dir. Arroyo Ctr. RAND, Santa Monica, Calif, 1991-93; under sec. for internat. security affairs Dept. State, Washington, 1993—. Author: The Cold War Begins, Soviet American Conflict Over Eastern Europe, 1974. Woodrow Wilson fellow, 1965-66, 69-70, 81-82; Columbia U. fellow, 1965-66, 68-69; recipient David D. Lloyd prize Harry S. Truman Library, 1976. Mem. Coun. on Fgn. Rels., Phi Beta Kappa. Home: 827 S Lee St, Alexandria England SW3 Office: Dept State Under Sec Arms Control/Intl Security 2201 C St NW Rm 7208 Washington DC 20520

DAVIS, LYNN HAMBRIGHT, educator; b. Gaffney, S.C., Aug. 7, 1950; d. Samuel Anderson and Elizabeth (Nolen) Hambright; m. Ronnie Dale Davis, Aug. 10, 1969; children: Marty, Jennifer. BS in Home Econs. Edn., Winthrop Coll., 1972, MS in Home Econs. Edn., 1982. Cert. secondary home econs. edn. tchr., N.C., S.C. Tchr. Crest Sr. High, Shelby, N.C., 1975-76; dietitian Cleveland Meml. Hosp., Shelby, 1977-78; tchr. food svc. Cherokee Tech. Ctr., Gaffney, 1978—; chairperson Staff Devel. Com. and Culinary Arts Craft Coun., Gaffney, 1978—; advisor Future Homemakers Am., Gaffney, 1978—. Mem. Am. Vocat. Assn. (policy com. region II 1992-95), S.C. Vocat. Assn. (v.p. 1991-92), Nat. Assn. Vocat. Home Econs. Tchrs., S.C. Assn. Vocat. Home Econs. Tchrs. (pres. 1991-92, advisor 1992-93), Am. Home Econs. Assn., S.C. Home Econs. Assn. (sec. food svc. adminstrn. com. 1991-92, Tchr. of Yr. award 1993), Home Econs. Edn. Assn. Democrat. Baptist. Home: 2100 Albert Blanton Rd Shelby NC 28152 Office: Cherokee Tech Ctr 3206 Cherokee Ave Gaffney SC 29340

DAVIS, LYNN KAREN, health facility administrator; b. New Haven, Conn., Jan. 11, 1951; d. Benny and Loretta (Haroskiewicz) D. BSN, Boston U., 1972, MSN, 1977. Cert. nursing adminstr. ANA. Staff nurse to charge nurse to head nurse to asst. dir. nursing Boston City Hosp., 1973-82; nursing dir. Charlton Meml. Hosp., Fall River, Mass. Pres. Fall River chpt. Big Brothers/Big Sisters. Mem. Mass. Orgn. Nurse Execs., S.E. Mass. Orgn. Nurse Execs. (past pres.). Home: 35 Pilgrim Village Rd Taunton MA 02780 Office: Charlton Meml Hosp 363 Highland Ave Fall River MA 02720

DAVIS, MARGARET BRYAN, paleoecology researcher, educator; b. Boston, Oct. 23, 1931. AB, Radcliffe Coll., 1953; PhD in Biology, Harvard U., 1957. NSF fellow dept. biology Harvard U., Cambridge, Mass., 1957-58, dept. geosci. Calif. Inst. Tech., Pasadena, 1959-60; research fellow dept. zoology Yale U., New Haven, 1960-61, prof. biology, 1973-76; research assoc. dept. botany U. Mich., Ann Arbor, 1961-64, assoc. research biologist Great Lakes Research div., 1964-70, research biologist, assoc. prof. dept. zoology, 1966-70, research biologist, prof. zoology, 1970-73; head dept. ecology and behavioral biology U. Minn., Mpls., 1976-81, prof. dept. ecology, evolution and behavior, 1976-82, Regents prof. ecology, 1982—; vis. prof. Quaternary Research Ctr., U. Wash., 1973; vis. investigator environ. studies program U. Calif., Santa Barbara, 1981-82; mem. adv. panel for ecology NSF, 1976-79, mem. sci. adv. com. for biology, behavior and social scis., 1989-91, mem. adv. panel for geol. record of global change, 1991-92; mem. planetary biology com. NRC, 1981-82, mem. global change com., 1987-90, mem. screening com. in plant scis., internat. exch. of persons com. 1972-75, mem. sci. and tech. edn. com., 1984-86; vis. rsch. scientist scholarly exch. com. NAS/Nat. Rsch. Coun., People's Republic of China; mem. U.S. nat. com. Internat. Union Quaternary Rsch., 1966-74. Mem. editorial bd. Quaternary Research, 1969-82, Trends in Ecology and Evolution, 1986-92. Recipient Sci. Achievement award Sci. Mus. Minn., 1988, Alumnae Recognition award Radcliffe Coll., 1988, Nevada medal, 1993. Fellow AAAS, Am. Acad. Arts and Scis, Geol. Soc. Am.; mem. NAS (nominations com. 1988), Ecol. Soc. Am. (pres. 1987-88, Eminent Ecologist award 1993)), Am. Quaternary Assn. (councillor 1969-70, 72-76, pres. 1978-80), Internat. Assn. Vegetation Sci., Internat. Assn. for Great Lakes Research (bd. dirs. 1970-73), Nature Conservancy (bd. dirs. Minn. chpt. 1979-85), Brit. Ecol. Soc. (hon.), Phi Beta Kappa, Sigma Xi. Office: U Minn Dept Ecology 100 Ecology Bldg 1987 Upper Buford Cir Saint Paul MN 55108-1051

DAVIS, MARILYN JEAN, dean; b. Leominster, Mass., July 12, 1938; d. Arthur and Clara (Capra) D'Errico; 1 child, Michele Elaine. BS, U. Tenn., 1979; MA, Fisk U., 1981. Instr. psychology and sociology Vol. State C.C., Gallatin, Tenn., 1981-85, Columbia State C.C., Franklin, Tenn., 1985—; academic dean O'More Coll. of Design, Franklin, 1993—; fin. mgmt. pvt. practice Nashville, 1970—. Producer three slide presentations on Aging with Audio titles, 1981. Mem. Am. Gerontol. Soc., Nat. Coun. on Aging, So. Gerontol. Soc. Republican. Presbyterian. Office: O'More Coll of Design 423 S Margin St Franklin TN 37064-2816

DAVIS, MARILYNN A., housing agency administrator; b. Little Rock, Oct. 30, 1952; d. James Edwards and Erma Lee (Glasco) D. BA in Econs., Smith Coll., 1973; MA in Econs., U. Mich., 1976, Washington U., St. Louis, 1980; MBA, Harvard U., 1982. Sr. credit analyst State Street Bank, Boston, 198l; fin. staff analyst GM, Detroit, 1982-83; sr. fin. analyst GM, N.Y.C., 1984, asst. to group v.p. and chief economist, 1984-86; dir., fin. analyst Am. Express Co., N.Y.C., 1986-87, v.p. risk financing, 1987-92; dep. gen. mgr. finance N.Y.C. Housing Authority, 1992-93; asst. sec. for adminstrn. U.S. Dept. HUD, Washington, 1993—. Trustee Studio Mus. in Harlem, N.Y.C.; chmn. com. on residence, bd. counselors Smith Coll.; bd. dirs. Queensboro Soc. for Prevention Cruelty to Children; mem. mgmt. assistance com. Greater N.Y. Fund-United Way. Named One of 100 Top Black Bus. and Profl. Women, Dollars & Sense, 1988; recipient Black Achiever's award YMCA, N.Y.C., 1989. Office: NYC Housing Authority 451 7th St SW Washington DC 20410-0001

DAVIS, MARTHA ALGENITA SCOTT, lawyer; b. Houston, Oct. 1, 1950; d. C.B. Scott and Althea (Lewis) Scott Renfro; m. John Whittaker Davis, III, Aug. 21, 1976; children: Marthea, John IV. BBA, Howard U., 1971, JD, 1974. Bar: Tex. 1974, U.S. Dist. Ct. (so. dist.) Tex. 1975, U.S. Ct. Appeals (5th cir.) 1976, U.S. Supreme Ct. 1980. Tax atty. Shell Oil Co., Houston, 1974-79; counsel Port of Houston Authority, 1979-89; v.p., community affairs officer Tex. Commerce Bancshares, 1989—; ptnr. Burney, Edwards, Hall, Hartsfield & Scott, Houston, 1975-78; bd. dirs. Unity Nat. Bank. Bd. dirs. Houston Citizens Chamber, 1980-90, Neighborhood Ednl. Ctr., Houston, 1983-87, Peoples' Workshop to Performing Arts; coordinator Operation Big Vote, Washington, 1984-85; mem. planning commn. City of Houston, 1987-91; founding chair Houston Downtown Mgmt. Corp., 1991-92; with Natural Parliamentarian Links, Inc., 1994—. Recipient Achievement award Greek Council, Houston, 1973; Houston's Most Influential Black Women award Black Experience Mag., Five Young Outstanding Houstonians award Houston Jr. C. of C., 1989; named one of Houston Ten Women of Distinction, Chrones and Colitis Found. and The Houston Press, 1993, one of Women on the Move, Houston Post, 1994. Mem. Nat. Bar Assn. (pres. 1990-91, sec. 1983-88, chmn. voter edn./registration com. 1985-86, pres. award 1993, 94), Black Women Lawyers Assn. (vice chair 1983-84, profl. achievement award 1984), Houston Lawyers Assn. (bd. dirs. 1977-78, 85-89, pres. 1988-89). Baptist. Club: Links (Houston) (we. area fin. sec. 1982-83). Office: Tex Commerce Bancshares MS 26 TCBE 45 PO Box 2558 # 45 Houston TX 77252

DAVIS, MARY DUESTERBERG (MIMI DAVIS), librarian, publisher; b. Houston, June 27, 1934; d. Leonard A. Duesterberg and Lillian Palmire (Walter) Van Pelt; m. James Watson Davis, June 3, 1953 (dec.); children: James Watson Jr., John Van Pelt (dec.), Mary Lynn, Kenneth Walter (dec.). BS in Psychology, U. Houston, 1980; postgrad., Rice U., 1981-82; M in Theol. Studies, So. Meth. U., 1986; MS, U. North Tex., 1990. Lay adv. bd. mem. Southern Meth. U., Dallas, 1985-86; reference libr. Southern Meth. U., Bridwell Theol. Libr., Dallas, 1986-89, Plano Pub. Libr. System, Tex., 1989-93; assoc. dir. Waco-McLennan County Library, 1993—; owner All Things Press Pub. Co.; Sunday sch. tchr. 1st Meth. Ch., Houston, 1980-83, retreat leader, 1980—, summer faculty Perkins Sch. Theogy, So. Meth. U., Dallas, 1988—. Mem. ALA, Tex. Libr. Assn. Home: 2905 Lake Shore Dr # 208 Waco TX 76708

DAVIS, MARY HELEN, psychiatrist, psychoanalyst, educator; b. Kingsville, Tex., Dec. 2, 1949; d. Garnett Stant and Emogene (Campbell) D.; m. Timothy Krenke, Oct. 3, 1992. BA, U. Tex., 1970; MD, U. Tex., Galveston, 1975. Cert. Nat. Bd. Med. Examiners, Am. Bd. Psychiatry and Neurology, Child and Adolescent Psychiatry. Intern, then resident in psychiatry SUNY, Buffalo, 1975-78; fellow in child psychiatry U. Cin., 1978-80; tng. in adult and child psychoanalysis Inst. for Psychoanalysis, Chgo., 1982-92; asst. prof. Med. Coll. Wis., Milw., 1980-89, clin. assoc. prof., 1989-93; med. dir. adolescent treatment unit Milw. Psychiat. Hosp., 1981-86, Schroeder Child Ctr., 1986-89; pvt. practice, 1989-93; med. dir. Devereux-Victoria (Tex.) Psych. Residential Treatment Ctr., 1993—; cons. Milw. Mental Health Cons., 1980-93, Children's Svc. Soc., Milw., 1982-93. Bd. dirs. Next Generation Theatre, Milw., 1988-90, Next Act Theatre, Milw., 1990-92. Mem. Am. Psychiat. Assn., Am. Soc. Adolescent Psychiatry, Am. Med. Women's Assn., Assn. for Child Psychoanalysis. Baptist.

DAVIS, MARY JEAN, artist, educator; b. Shreveport, La., Dec. 13, 1958; d. Adolph Neal and Janet L. (Pratt) Chalupnik; m. Brice Jay Davis, Aug. 23, 1980; 1 child, Andrew Milton. BA, La. Tech. U., 1980. Tchr. art Hallsville (Tex.) Pub. Schs., 1981—; math tutor Learning Found., Longview, Tex., 1982-85; mus. artist/tchr. Longview Art Mus., 1986—. Group exhibitions include Route 66 Revisited, Gallup, N. Ill., 1990, Longview Art Mus., 1990, Longview Art Gallery, 1990, Tex. Fine Arts (Citation award 1985), Lamar U. Artist/Tchr. Exhbn., 1990, World Trade Ctr., New Orleans, 1991, East Tex. Fine Arts (Citation award 1991, 93, Best of Show 1991). Vol. Jr. League of Longview, 1991—; elder St. Andrew Presbyn. Ch., 1993—; bd. dirs. Longview Art Mus., 1992-94. Mem. East Tex. Fine Arts Assn., Upper Level Artist Coop.

DAVIS, MARY JOYCE, transportation administrator; b. Marshall, Tex., Dec. 10, 1942; d. Henry Clay and Annie Bell (Williams) McGlothin; m. Don Albert Davis, Apr. 12, 1963; children: Dianna, Caryn. BSN, Prairie View A&M Coll., 1963; MSN, U. Colo., 1975, PhD in Ednl. Psychol. Studies, 1983. RN, Colo. Staff and head nurse VA Hosp., Waco, Tex., 1963-70; instr. nursing McClennan C.C., Waco, 1970-73, Arapahoe C.C., Littleton, Colo., 1974-76; dir. health occupations C.C. of Denver, 1976-82; dean instrn. C.C. of Aurora, Colo., 1982-84; acad. affairs officer Colo. Commn. on Higher Edn., Denver, 1984-85; dir. adminstrn. Regional Transp. Dist., Denver, 1985—; cons. Western Interstate Commn. Higher Edn., Boulder, Colo., 1975-78, C.C. of Aurora, 1993; cons., evaluator North Ctrl. Assn. Colls. and Schs., Chgo., 1980-84; cons., presenter Nat. Wellness Conf., Stevens Point, Wis., 1992-94. Contbr. articles to profl. jours. Mentor exec. intern program Denver Pub. Schs., 1977—; bd. dirs. Adult Learning Source, Denver, 1985—, Am. Cancer Soc., Denver, 1989—. Recipient Outstanding Achievement award Prairie View A&M U. Alumni Assn., 1988, Outstanding Svc. award C.C. of Aurora, 1991. Mem. Am. Pub. Transit Assn. (chmn. women in transit 1993-95), Conf. Minority Transp. Ofcls. (Disting. Svc. award 1992), Nat. Wellness Inst. Mem. African Methodist Episcopal Ch. Avocations: designing jewelry, writing. Office: Regional Transp Dist PO Box 46530 Denver CO 80201-6530

DAVIS, MARY LOU, secondary education educator; b. Lansford, Pa., Aug. 25, 1943; d. Lester Earl and Susan (Depuy) Snyder; m. David Hugh Davis, June 29, 1968; children: Scott David, Sean Geoffrey. BA in Math., Susquehanna U., 1965; MEd in Math., West Chester Coll., 1969. Cert. tchr. N.Y., Pa. Math. tchr. Marple Newton Sch. Dist., Broomall, Pa., 1965-68, Arlington Ctrl.Sch. Dist., Poughkeepsie, N.Y., 1968-73, 77-79; math. tchr. Spackenkill Union Free Sch. Dist., Poughkeepsie, 1979—, dept. chmn., 1988-91; adj. math. tchr. Dutchess Community Coll., Poughkeepsie, 1973-77, Marist Coll., Poughkeepsie, 1983, 1992-93. Sustainer Jr. League of Poughkeepsie, 1979—; v.p. Arlington Sch. Bd., Poughkeepsie, 1988-94; budget com., past program chmn. Dutchess County Sch. Bd., Poughkeepsie, 1988-94. Recipient Vision award IBM-Semiconductor Rsch. Corp. Competitiveness Found. Edn. Alliance, 1991. Mem. AAUW (pub. rels. com. 1995), ASCD, Nat. Coun. Tchrs. of Math., N.Y. State Tchrs. Union (alternate retirement rep.), Assn. Math. Tchrs. of N.Y. State, Dutchess County Math. Tchrs. Assn., Advocacy for Gifted and Talented Edn. in N.Y. State, Dutchess-Ulster-Sullivan-Orange Math. League (pres. 1984—), Mid Hudson Alumnae Panhellenic, Habitat for Humanity. Republican. Methodist. Home: 369 Andrews Rd Lagrangeville NY 12540 Office: Spackenkill High Sch 112 Spackenkill Rd Poughkeepsie NY 12603-5099

DAVIS, MARY SUE, office assistant; b. Columbia, S.C., Nov. 22, 1965; d. Richard Cleo and Celestia Ann (Walker) Joyner; m. Charles William Davis, June 10, 1989. BBA cum laude, Columbia (S.C.) Coll., 1988. With Kelly Temporary Svcs., Columbia, 1988; receptionist, bookkeeper Arms Bus. Svc., Columbia, 1988-89; receptionist Constan, Inc., Columbia, 1989, payroll clk., 1989-90; receptionist, bookkeeper Basic Electric Co., Inc., Indian Trail, N.C., 1990-91; payroll clk., accounts payable clk. Superior Constrn. Corp., Matthews, N.C., 1991-92, accounts payable clk., 1992; jr. acct. Charles W. Davis, CPA, Matthews, 1992-93; with Kelly Temporary Svcs., Charlotte, N.C., 1993; office asst. III U. N.C., Charlotte, 1993—, office IV adult health nursing dept. Coll. Nursing, 1994—. Mem. Order Purple Seal. Office: U NC Coll Nursing Charlotte NC 28223

DAVIS, MATTIE BELLE EDWARDS, retired county judge; b. Ellabell, Ga., Feb. 28, 1910; d. Frank Pierce and Eddie (Morgan) Edwards; m. Troy Carson Davis, June 6, 1937 (dec. Aug. 1948); stepchildren: Jane (Mrs. Robert Gordon Potter), Betsy (Mrs. James W. Clark, Jr.). Student law in law office. Bar: Fla. 1936, U.S. Supreme Ct. 1950. Legal sec., 1927-36; practice with husband in Miami, 1936-48, pvt. practice, 1948-59; judge Met. Ct. County of Dade, Fla., 1959-72, judge County Ct., 1973-80, sr. judge County Ct., 1981—; mem. exec. com. Women's Conf. Nat. Safety Coun., 1960-80, chmn., 1968-70; bd. dirs. Nat. Safety Coun., 1972-80, v.p. women, 1973-80; mem. Fla. Gov.'s Hwy. Safety Com., 1970-81, Nat. Hwy. Safety Adv. Com., 1967-71; mem. registrants adv. bd. SSS, World War II. Pres. Dade County Tb Assn., 1960-62; exec. com. Fla. Tb and Respiratory Disease Assn., 1960-66; pres. Haven Sch. Mentally Retarded, 1958-60, sec., 1960-69; Trustee Andrew Coll., Cuthbert, Ga., 1960-81. Recipient Disting. Svc. to Safety award Nat. Safety Coun., 1988; first woman 50 yr. awardee Fellows of

Am. Bar Found., 1987. Mem. Nat. Assn. Women Lawyers (treas. 1961-62, corr. sec. 1962-63, v.p. 1963-64, pres. 1965-66, Appreciation award 1989), Fla. Assn. Women Lawyers (pres. 1957-58), ABA (ho. of dels. 1967-75, 77-81, resolutions com. 1973-75, com. on constitution and by laws 1980-86), Dade County Bar Assn., Fla. Bar, Internat. Fedn. Women Lawyers, Nat. Assn. Women Judges (founder, life mem.), Miami Bus. and Profl. Women's Club (pres. 1952-54), Nat. Fedn. Bus. and Profl. Women's Clubs (dir. dist. Fla. 1956-57), Kappa Beta Pi. Democrat. Methodist (supt. Sunday sch. 1948-54, chmn. ofcl. bd. 1957-60, trustee 1952-67, adminstrv. bd. 1968-90). Club: Zonta Internat. Home: 402 Como Ave Coral Gables FL 33146-3508

DAVIS, MONIQUE D. (DEON DAVIS), state legislator; b. Chgo., Aug. 19, 1936; d. James and Constance (Dutton) McKay; divorced; children: Robert Jr., Monique C. Conway. BS in Edn., Chgo. State U., 1967, MS in Guidance and Counseling, 1976. Tchr. Chgo. Bd. Edn., 1967-86, coordinator, 1986—; mem. Ill. Ho. of Reps. from 27th dist., 1987—, vice chmn. elem. and secondary edn. com. Mem. legis. com. Chgo. Area Alliance Black Sch. Edn., 1982-84, Independent Voters of Ill.-Independent Precinct Orgns., Chgo., 1982-83; coordinator 21st ward, Citizens for Mayor Washington, 1985, 87. Recipient GRIT award Roseland Womens Orgn., 1987; named a Tchr. Who Makes a Difference PTA, 1978, 85. Mem. Chgo. Area Tchrs. Alliance (chmn.), Christian Bd. Edn. (bd. dirs. 1978-82), Phi Delta Kappa. Mem. United Ch. of Christ. Office: Ill Ho of Reps State Capitol Springfield IL 62706*

DAVIS, NAOMI ANN, women's health nurse; b. Mt. Vernon, Ohio, Apr. 26, 1964; d. Harold Perry and Naomi Lysbeth (Houpt) D. AAS, Cen. Ohio Tech. Coll., Newark, 1984. Cert. neonatal resuscitation, clin. excellence program achievement. Staff nurse med.-surg. Riverside Hosp., Columbus, Ohio, 1984-85; telemetry nurse intermediate care St. Ann's Hosp., Westerville, Ohio, 1986-88, staff nurse labor and delivery room, 1988—. Office: St Ann's Hosp 500 S Cleveland Ave Westerville OH 43081-8998

DAVIS, PAMELA LOUISE, librarian, media specialist; b. DeQueen, Ark., Mar. 22, 1955; d. Denney Ferris and Marjorie Joy (Youngblood) Carpenter; m. Danny D. Davis, Dec. 14, 1980; children: Katherine, Daniel. BS in Edn., Henderson State U., 1977; Cert. Libr. Sci., So. Ark. U., 1979. Cert. bus. edn. tchr. Tchr. bus., libr. Fouke (Ark.) H.S., 1977-81; tchr. bus. Bish Mathis Inst., Longview, Tex., 1984-88, dir. edn., 1988-91; libr. New Diana Ind. Sch. Dist., Diana, Tex., 1991—. Leader Girl Scouts, 1987-91. Named Outstanding Leader by Girl Scouts, 1990. Mem. Tex. Libr. Assn. Home: Tchr's Hill PO Box 258 Diana TX 75640-0258 Office: New Diana Ind Sch Dist Junction Hwy 259 & Hwy 154 PO Box 26 Diana TX 75640-0026

DAVIS, PATRICIA MAHONEY, software engineer; b. Pitts., Dec. 26, 1957; d. John Francis and Lillian Rosemary (Peck) Mahoney; m. Larry Allen Davis, Dec. 1, 1989; 1 child, Mark Benjamin Mahoney. BS, Towson State U., 1980; postgrad., U. Md., 1980-83, Johns Hopkins U., 1993—. Computer programmer FBI, Washington, 1984-88; software engr. Quality Systems, Inc., Tysons Corner, Va., 1988-89; sr. software engr. Martin Marietta Corp., Washington, 1989-94; sr. software analyst E-Systems, 1994—. Vol. Big Bros. and Big Sisters, Balt., 1982. Recipient Md. State Senatorial scholarship, 1981. Mem. Assn. for Computing Machinery, Nat. Student Speech and Hearing Assn., Omicron Delta Kappa (Student Leader of Yr. 1981). Republican. Roman Catholic. Home: 9610 Sparrow Ct Ellicott City MD 21042-1773

DAVIS, REGINA CATHERINE (GINA DAVIS), advocate; b. Miami, Apr. 7, 1951; d. Leonard William and Elizabeth (Sirback) Bartish; m. James P. Davis, Jr., Feb. 1, 1974 (div. 1984); 1 child, Jesse Lee. Student, U. Md., 1993—. V.p. Davis Prodns., N.Y.C., 1974-84; exec. recruiter Cornell Comp Corp., N.Y.C., 1984-90; recruitment cons. Washington, 1990-91; v.p. MainFrame Applications, Inc., Washington, 1991-92; pres. Assn. Rape & Assault Prevention, Silver Spring, Md., 1993—. Active PTA, N.Y.C., 1976-83; vol. Beth Israel Hosp., N.Y.C., 1976; den leader Cub Scouts Am., N.Y.C., 1979-83; steering com. Md. Commn. Women Legis. Agenda, 1994. Mem. Women's Leadership Conf. Va. Democrat. Office: Assn Rape & Assault Prevention PO Box 3307 Silver Spring MD 20918

DAVIS, REGINA EVANS, insurance representative; b. Quitman, Miss., Oct. 16, 1961; d. Billy Ray and Kaye Frances (Odom) Evans; m. Timothy Gerald Davis, May 20, 1990. AA, Meridian Jr. Coll., 1981. Sr. comml. lines specialist USF&G Co., Meridian, Miss., 1982-90; ins. rep. Farm Bur. Ins., Picayune, Miss., 1990, State Farm Ins., Picayune, 1991, FRP&G Ins., Meridian, 1992, J.A. Terral Agy., Inc., Quitman, Miss., 1993—; sec. Ins. Women Meridian, Miss., 1989. Sec. Picayune (Miss.) Jaycees, 1990, Project Clarke Bd. Dirs., Quitman, 1993-94; vol. coord. Project Clarke, Quitman, 1993-94. Recipient Jaycees Presdl. award Picayune (Miss.) Jaycees, 1990; named Most Outstanding New Jaycee, Picayune (Miss.) Jaycees, 1990. Home: 134 County Rd 1511 Quitman MS 39355 Office: J A Terral Agy Inc 119 Main St Quitman MS 39355

DAVIS, ROSE LEE, real estate broker, real estate appraiser; b. Hempstead, N.Y., Jan. 28, 1944; d. William H. and Willie Mae (Stone) D. AAS, Fashion Inst. Tech., N.Y.C., 1967; BBA, Bernard M. Baruch Coll., N.Y.C., 1979. Asst. br. mgr. Chase Manhattan Bank, N.Y.C., 1979-86; sales M.E. Thomas Realty, St. Albans, N.Y., 1986-87; office mgr. St. Albans Village Realty, 1987-88; pres. Davis & Assocs. Realty, Jamaica, N.Y., 1988—; distbr. Rexall Showcase Internat., Ft. Lauderdale, Fla. Mem. Friends of L.I.'s Heritage. Mem. NRA (cert. instr.), AAUW, NAFE, Columbia Soc. Real Estate Appraisers , Nat. Assn. Real Estate Appraisers (cert.), Baruch Coll. Alumni Assn., N.Y. Assn. Realty Mgrs., Nassau-Suffolk Horsemen's Assn., Fortune 500 Bus. and Profl. Women's Club (1st v.p. 1983-85), Cresthaven Ski Club, Pathfinders Rifle and Pistol Club (bus. mgr. 1991-92), Hollis Mills Hunting and Pistol Club (rec. sec. 1988-91). Democrat. Methodist. Home: 88-35 164 St Jamaica NY 11432

DAVIS, RUTH A., ambassador; b. Phoenix, May 28, 1943. BA, Spelman Coll., 1966; MSW, U. Calif., Berkeley, 1968. Consular officer Kinshasa, Zaire, 1969-71, Nairobi, Kenya, 1971-73, Tokyo, 1973-76, Naples, Italy, 1976-80; spl. asst. internat. affairs Mayor of Washington, 1980-82; sr. watch officer ops. ctr. Dept. State, 1982-84, chief tng. and liaison, bur. pers., 1984-86; consul gen. Barcelona, Spain, 1987-91; amb. to Benin, 1992—; mem. sr. seminar Fgn. Svc. Inst., 1992. Office: US Consulate Benin, Rue Coporal Bernard Anani, BP 2012 Cotonou Benin*

DAVIS, RUTH C., pharmacy educator; b. Wilkes-Barre, Pa., Oct. 27, 1943; d. Morris David Davis and Helen Jane Gillis. BS, Phila. Coll. Pharmacy and Sci., 1967. Cert. pharmacist, Pa., Md. Mgr. pharmacist Fairview Pharmacy, Etters, Pa.; mgr., pharmacist Neighborcare Pharmacy, Balt.; dir. ambulatory svcs. Rombro Health Svcs., Balt.; tchr., pharmacist Boothwyn Pharmacy, Phila.; pharm. cons. Nat. Rx Svcs. of Pa. Republican. Baptist. Home and Office: 75 Lion Dr Hanover PA 17331-3847

DAVIS, SARA LEA, pharmacist; b. Knoxville, Tenn., Aug. 1, 1951; d. Horace William and Margaret Jewel (Hill) D. BS in Liberal Arts, U. Tenn., 1973; BS in Pharmacy, U. Tenn., Memphis, 1976, PharmD, 1977. Asst. mgr. Pharmaco Nuclear, Inc., Chgo., 1977-79; nuclear pharmacist Kansas City, Mo., 1979, Bapt. Meml. Hosp., Memphis, 1979-83; asst. mgr. Syncor, Inc., Washington, 1983-84; staff pharmacist Rite Aid Corp., Knoxville, 1984-87, pharmacist-in-charge, 1987—; rep. 3d High Country Nuclear Medicine Conf., Vail, Colo., 1983; mem. adv. bd. V.I.P. Home Nursing & Rehab., Knoxville, 1985-86. Active Leconte Exec. Women's Coun. Mem. Am. Pharm. Assn., Acad. Pharm. Sci. (sect. nuclear pharmacy), Soc. Nuclear Medicine, Memphis Bus. and Profl. Women's Assn. (bd. dirs. 1982-83), Club Leconte, U. Tenn. Century Club, Mortar Bd., Phi Beta Kappa, Phi Kappa Phi, Rho Chi, Alpha Lambda Delta. Baptist. Office: Rite Aid Pharmacy 508-B E Tri-County Blvd Oliver Springs TN 37840-1436

DAVIS, SHARLA JANE, court official; b. Sacramento, Oct. 24, 1963; d. Eddie Wayne and Lillie Louise (Little) Hash; m. David Russell Davis, Nov. 22, 1986. Student, Shasta Coll., 1982-83, 87-90. Legal sec. David L. Morrow, Redding, Calif., 1982-86, John A. Sandquist, Esq., Redding, Eureka, Calif., 1990-91; legal sec., ct. clk. to U.S. magistrate U.S. Dist. Ct. for Ea. Dist. Calif., Redding, 1990—; legal sec., office mgr. Law Offices of Traverse & Karjola, Eureka, 1991—. Mem. NAFE, Elks. Republican. Mem. Christian and Missionary Alliance Ch. Office: US Magistrate J Ross Carter 1736 Tehama St Redding CA 96001

DAVIS, SHERIE KAY, special education educator; b. Cin., Dec. 2, 1956; d. Earl Myron and and Irene (Alexander) Huffman; m. Dana Allen, June 18, 1985; 1 child, Lauren Nicole. BS in Edn. and Home Econs., U. Cin., 1979, MEd in Spl. Edn., 1980. Tchr. mid. sch. developmentally handicapped Ross Local Sch. Dist., Hamilton, Ohio, 1980-85, substitute tchr., 1985-87; substitute tchr. Three Rivers Local Sch. Dist., Cleve., 1985-87; tchr. high sch. developmentally handicapped New Miami Local Schs., Hamilton, 1987-92; tchr. to developementally handicapped Talawanda City Schs., 1992—; facilitator leadership conf. New Miami Care Team, Hamilton, 1989—; presenter Coun. for Exceptional Children-State Conv., Dayton, Ohio, 1990; coach varsity volleyball, jr. varsity basketball. Coach Three Rivers Knothole Baseball Assn., Cleve., 1991—. Recipient Quality Initiatives award Southwestern Ohio Spl. Edn. Regional Resource Ctr., Ohio, 1988. Mem. Coun. for Exceptional Children. Home: 608 N Miami Ave Cleves OH 45002 Office: Talawanda High Sch 101 W Chestnut St Oxford OH 45056

DAVIS, SHERYL ELIZABETH, printing company executive; b. Raleigh, N.C., Sept. 21, 1953; d. Barrie Spilman and Judy Rose (Robertson) D.; m. Rickey Staley Rogers, July 2, 1977 (div. Feb. 1988); children: Brook Elizabeth Rogers, Stacie Lynne Rogers. Student, N.C. State U., Charlotte, 1971-73, U. N.C., Charlotte, 1973-74. Proofreader Am. Check Co., Charlotte, 1974-75; estimator, prodn. planner Theo Davis Sons, Zebulon, N.C., 1975—, pres., 1993—, CEO; bd. dirs. Printing Industries of the Carolinas, Charlotte, 1988-92. Bd. dirs. N.C. State U. Sch. Design Found., Raleigh, 1993-94, Triangle chpt. ARC, 1994-95; grad. Leadership Raleigh 10, 1995. Mem. Rotary Club (sec. 1992-94, pres.-elect 1993-94, pres. 1994-95). Republican. Office: Theo Davis Sons Hwy 97 West PO Box 277 Zebulon NC 27597

DAVIS, SHIRLEY HARRIET, social worker, editor; b. Brookline, Mass., June 27, 1922; d. Jacob and Matilda (Goldberg) Freedman; m. Edward H. Davis, Nov. 11, 1943; children: Anita Maureen Davis Winn, Lawrence Paul. AB, Calvin Coolidge Coll., 1944; postgrad., Simmons Sch. of Social Work, 1944-45. Social worker Travelers Aid of N.Y., N.Y.C., 1944-48; dir. Community Svc. Workshop of Woodmere (N.Y.) Acad., 1966-70; v.p. for program and membership West End Aux. Peninsula Hosp. Ctr., Edgemere, N.Y., 1973-80; dir. Family Practice Playroom Coll. Medicine, Downstate Med. Ctr., Bklyn., 1977-83; officer mgr. Edward H. Davis, M.D., Loxahatchee, Fla., 1983-93; dir. publicity and pub. rels. Fla. Atlantic Region of Hadassah, 1994—; med. office mgr. Editor: Hadassah of Wellington Fla., 1990-93. V.p. membership Hadassah of Wellington, 1992-94, bulletin bus. mgr.; dir. publicity and pub. rels., bd. dirs., staff worker thrift shop Fla. Atlantic Region of Hadassah, 1994—. Republican. Jewish. Home: 13604 Firewood Ct West Palm Beach FL 33414-8522 Office: Edward H Davis MD 13005 Southern Blvd # 143 Loxahatchee FL 33470

DAVIS, SHIRLEY SMITH, parole officer; b. Clinton, N.C., July 24, 1953; d. W.D. and Mary (Smith) Smith; m. William M. Davis Jr.; children: Alice, Stephen. BA, N.C. Cen. U., Durham, 1986, MS, 1991. Parole officer N.C. Dept. Correction, Charlotte, 1987—. State dir. Internat. Residential and Community Alternative, 1988—; v.p. Help Ever Loving Parent, 1989—. Recipient Gov.'s award State of N.C., 1983; named Chief Marshall Chancellor Installation, U. N.C., Charlotte, 1990. Mem. Am. Correctional Assn., So. Criminal Justice Assn. (Best Grad. Student 1988), N.C. Assn. Residential and Community Alternatives. Republican. Mem. Ch. of God. Home: 301 Queens Rd Charlotte NC 28204-3255

DAVIS, SUSAN, serials librarian; b. Salamanca, N.Y.; d. Allen Stewart and Sylvia Edna (Smith) D.; m. Richard P. Bartl, Oct. 11, 1986. BA, State U. Coll. at Geneseo, 1978; M in Library Scis., Sch. of Library and Info. Sci., 1979. Head serials dept. Ill. Inst. Tech., Chgo., 1980-84; head serial records State U. of N.Y. at Buffalo, 1984-88, head periodicals, 1988—; mem. adv. bd. Dawson Subscription Svcs., Mt. Morris, Ill., 1986—. Mem. ALA, North. Am. Serials Interest Group (treas. 1985-89, sec. 1992—), NOTIS Serials Interest Group (co-chair 1992—), N.Y. Libr. Assn. Office: SUNY Lockwood Library Bldg Buffalo NY 14260

DAVIS, SUSAN ANN, contractor analyst; b. San Antonio, Tex., Dec. 18, 1951; d. Farrell Jackson and Margaret Ann (Schouweiler) Mock; m. Joseph Michael Davis, Dec. 21, 1974; children: Joseph Michael II, Jennifer Ann. BS in Bus. Mktg., Abilene Christian Coll., 1974. Clerk-typist U.S. Navy, Silver Spring, Md., 1985-86; quality technician VITRO Corp., Rockville, Md., 1986-94; analyst Techmatics, Inc, Arlington, Va., 1994—. vol. family support 352d Civil Affairs Command U.S. Army Reserve (named vol. of the yr. 1992), 1991—. Mem. Ch. of Christ. Office: Techmatics Inc 2231 Crystal Dr Ste 1000 Arlington VA 22202

DAVIS, SUSAN GLORIA, sales representative, consultant; b. St. Louis, Oct. 5, 1957; d. Victor Henry and Vivian Norma (Stille) D. BS, Maryville U., 1982; MBA, Oklahoma City U., 1983. Mktg. coord. HBE Bank Facilities, St. Louis, 1979-82; sales rep. NCR Corp., St. Louis, 1983-85; sr. sales rep. UNISYS, St. Louis, 1985-88; account exec. Gould Electronics, St. Louis, 1988-89; sales rep. Tandem Computers, St. Louis, 1989-94, Pacific Access Computers, St. Louis, 1994—. Mem. NAFE, AAUW. Republican. Congregationalist.

DAVIS, SUSAN LYNN, public relations executive; b. Brooklyn, N.Y., Nov. 29, 1947; d. Morton J. and Eunice Patricia (bailey) D.; 1 child. BA, Finch Coll., 1969; MA, George Wash. U., 1979. Dir. public relations Girls Clubs of Am., N.Y., 1978-81; pres. Susan Davis Pub. Relations, N.Y., 1982-90; dir. comm. YWCA of City of N.Y., 1991—. Contbr. article to Mag. Pres. Eye and Ear Theatre, 1980-90; mem. Pres. Comm. on the Arts and Humanities, Wash. 1983-90. Mem. Pub. Relations Soc. of Am., Alexander Julian Found. (advisor 1986--). Office: YWCA of the City of NY 610 Lexington Ave New York NY 10022

DAVIS, SUSAN SCHAEFER, anthropologist, consultant; b. Mpls., Mar. 1, 1943; d. Philip Alois and June Marie (Briseño) Schaefer; m. Douglas Allen Davis, Jan. 4, 1969; 1 child, Laila. BA, U. Minn., 1965; MA, U. Mich., 1970, PhD, 1978. Vol. Peace Corps, Morocco, 1965-67; asst. prof. anthropology Trenton State Coll., 1974-84; postdoctoral fellow Harvard U., Cambridge, Mass., 1981-83; ind. scholar, cons. World Bank, USAID, Peace Corps, 1984—; adj. prof. anthropology Rutgers Coll., 1973-74; vis. scholar Douglass Coll., 1986; vis. assoc prof. Haverford Coll., 1989; mem. Mid. East Panel, Internat. Dev. Exec. Com. Am. Friend Svc. Com., Phila., 1992—. Author: Patience and Power: Women's Lives in a Moroccan Village, 1983; co-author: Adolescence in a Moroccan Town, 1989; ethnographer: (videotape) Threads of Time: Wedding Textiles in Fez, Morocco, 1995; contbr. articles to books and profl. jours. Bd. dirs. Friends of Morocco, 1990—; mem. Arab-Am. Anti-Discrimination Com., Washington, 1985—, Emily's List, Washington, 1992—. Fellow U. Mich., 1967-70; Fulbright scholar U. Mich., 1970, Moroccan-Am. Commn., 1989-90. Mem. Assn. for Mid. East Women's Studies (pres. 1991-93), Am. Anthropol. Assn., Mid. East Studies Assn., Nat. Assn. Practicing Anthropologists, Assn. for Women in Devel., Coalition for Women in Devel., Phi Beta Kappa.

DAVIS, SUZANNE GOULD, temporary employment service executive; b. N.Y.C., Apr. 22, 1947; d. Lawrence Robert and Diana (Klotz) Gould; 2 children. Diploma in French Civilization Studies with honors, Sorbonne U., Paris, 1967; BA in French magna cum laude, Tufts U., 1968; MA in ESL Edn., Columbia U., 1975, MLS, 1984. Prodn. asst. James Garrett and Ptnrs., N.Y.C., 1969-70; adminstrv. asst. Alvin Toffler, N.Y.C., 1970-71; dir. mktg. Econ. Models Ltd., London, 1971; mgr. John Player Info. Bur., London, 1972-73; mgr. mktg. Berkey Film Processing, N.Y.C., 1974-75; freelance editor, translator N.Y.C., 1975-82; gen. mgr. Rosemary Scott Temps. Inc., N.Y.C., 1983-86; pres. Suzanne Davis Temps. Inc., N.Y.C., 1986—. Editor-translator: La Méthode Orange: Teacher's Manual, 1977. Mem. Arts and Bus. Coun., N.Y.C., 1984-86, Common Cents N.Y., 1991—. Mem. NAFE, Nat. Assn. Women Bus. Owners, Spl. Librs. Assn., N.Y. Assn. Temp. Svcs. (bd.dirs. 1986-87, co-chmn. program com.), Murray Hill Bus. and Profl. Women's Orgn. (scholar com. 1985, chair, Young Careerist award 1986-90), Gotham Bus. and Profl. Women's Orgn., Beta Phi Mu. Office: Suzanne Davis Temps Inc 20 E 46th St Ste 302 New York NY 10017-2417

DAVIS, SUZY, information center owner; b. Duncan, Okla., July 19, 1936; d. Elmer Arvin and Reba Dorril (Johnson) Gilstrap; m. Francis Jerome Dillard, Jan. 22, 1955 (div. May 1975); children: Jeri S., Lawrance A., Joe P., Marie E.; m. William Thomas Davis, Dec. 20, 1984 (dec.). Grad. high sch., Newman, Calif., 1954. Guest lectr. Calif. State U., Long Beach, 1986, 89; model Calif. State U., Riverside, 1988, San Bernardino, 1988—; model Cmty. Coll., San Bernardino, 1988—, Robert E. Wood Watercolor Workshop, Palm Springs, Calif., 1990, U. Nev., Las Vegas, 1993, Cheyenne C.C., North Las Vegas, 1993, Las Vegas Art Mus. Studio, 1994—; owner, operator Nudist Info. Ctr., North Las Vegas, Nev., 1984-92; bd. dirs. Beachfront USA, Moreno Valley; bd. dirs. Beachfront USA, Moreno Valley. Bd. dirs. Callen-Davis Meml. Fund, Moreno Valley, Calif., 1988—, Western Sunbathing Assn., Studio City, Calif., 1989-92; active adopt-a-hwy. Western Sunbathing Assn., Victorville, Calif., 1990-92, Earth Week (city clean-up), Daggett, 1990. Named as part of Family of Yr., Western Sunbathing Assn., 1986, for Membership Increase by Percentage, Am. Sunbathing Assn., 1986, Woman of the Yr., Am. Sunbathing Assn., 1992; recipient Glen Eden award Am. Sunbathing Assn., 1986. Mem. Am. Sunbathing Assn. (life), Western Sunbathing Assn. (life).

DAVIS, TAMMIE LYNETTE, music educator, director; b. Kingsport, Tenn., Jan. 17, 1961; d. James T. and Gertrude (Bridges) D. BS in Music Edn., Tenn. Technol. U., 1983; MEd in Ednl. Leadership, East Tenn. State U., 1992. Cert. tchr., Tenn. Chorus and orchestra director John Sevier Mid. Sch., Kingsport, 1983—; chmn. dept. fine arts John Sevier Mid. Sch., 1987, 91-93, chmn. adv. bd., 1991-93; participant Music Educators Nat. Conf., 1981—, Tenn. Arts Acad., 1993. Violist Kingsport Symphony Orch., 1979-89, 92—, bd. dirs., 1987-89; mem. (hammered dulcimer folk group) Wire Kwire, Kingsport, 1986—. Designated Career Ladder Tchr. II, State of Tenn., 1992; named one of Outstanding Music Educators, Gov.'s Sch. for Arts, Tenn., 1990. Mem. NEA, ASCD, Tenn. Edn. Assn., Nat. Sch. Orch. Assn., Am. Choral Dirs. Assn., Am. String Tchrs. Assn., East Tenn. Vocal Assn., East Tenn. Sch. Band and Orch. Assn. (orch. chmn. 1992-94), Kingsport Edn. Assn. (treas. 1992-94, pres.-elect 1994—), Nat. Assn. for Preservation and Perpetuation of Storytelling, Tenn. Assn. for Preservation and Perpetuation of Storytelling, Bays Mountain Dulcimer Soc. (pres. 1988-90). Home: 2021 Pendragon Rd Kingsport TN 37660 Office: John Sevier Mid Sch 1200 Wateree St Kingsport TN 37660

DAVIS, VIRGINIA MARIE, financial analyst, consultant; b. Chgo., Mar. 17, 1947; d. Robert Frank and Verne J. (Van Cata) Davis; divorced; children: Jack R. R. Barnette, Christopher D. M. Barnette, David T. J. Neuburger. Student Moorpark Coll., Calif., 1984-86. Ins. lic., Calif.; ordained to ministry Temple of Light, 1977. Sales mgr. Grand Plaza Hotel, Rosemont, Ill., 1975-77; pastor, founder God's House, Evanston, Ill., 1977-80; athletics bus. mgr. Pepperdine U., Malibu, Calif., 1980-82, budget and planning analyst, 1984-87; mktg. rep. GNA, Long Beach, Calif., 1987—; field underwriter N.Y. Life Ins. and Annuity Corp. Cons., Calif., 1984-87; founder budget control assistance co. My Manager, 1986; mgmt. cons. Checkbook, Thousand Oaks, Calif., 1984—; dir., founder Ins.. Seminars, Ventury County, Calif., 1984-85; cons. Farmers Ins., Simi Valley, Calif., 1985-86; dir., lectr. Alternative Med. Treatment, 1977-78. Author: Herbology, 1976. Com. chairperson Ventura council Boy Scouts Am., 1982-84; pres., founder Pepperdine Hiker's Club, 1985-86; affirmative action adv. com. Pepperdine U., 1985-87, sec., 1987, officer, 1986-87. Recipient Vol. of Yr. award Boy Scouts Am. Troop 799, 1982-84; State of Ill. scholar, 1965; Swedish Covenant Hosp., 1965. Mem. Nat. Assn. Life Underwriters. Republican. Club: Toastmasters (Malibu, Calif.)(adminstv. v.p. 1987). Lodge: Zonta (asst. treas. and budget chairperson local club 1984). Avocations: cross country hiking; herbology; geology.

DAVIS, WANDA ROSE, lawyer; b. Lampasas, Tex., Oct. 4, 1937; d. Ellis DeWitt and Julia Doris (Rose) Cockrell; m. Richard Andrew Fulcher, May 9, 1959 (div. 1969); 1 child, Greg Ellis; m. Edwin Leon Davis, Jan. 14, 1973 (div. 1985). BBA, U. Tex., 1959, JD, 1971. Bar: Tex. 1971, Colo. 1981, U.S. Dist. Ct. (no. dist.) Tex. 1972, U.S. Dist. Ct. Colo. 1981, U.S. Ct. Appeals (10th cir. 1981, U.S. Supreme Ct. 1976. Atty. Atlantic Richfield Co., Dallas, 1971; assoc. firm Crocker & Murphy, Dallas, 1971-72; prin. Wanda Davis, Atty. at Law, Dallas, 1972-73; ptnr. firm Davis & Davis Inc., Dallas, 1973-75; atty. adviser HUD, Dallas, 1974-75, Air Force Acctg. and Fin. Ctr., Denver, 1976-92; co-chmn. regional Profl. Devel. Inst., Am. Soc. Mil. Comptrollers, Colorado Springs, Colo., 1982; chmn. Lowry AFB Noontime Edn. Program, Exercise Program, Denver, 1977-83; mem. speakers bur. Colo. Women's Bar, 1995—, Lowry AFB, 1981-83; mem. fed. ct. liaison com. U.S. Dist. Ct. Colo., 1983; mem. Leaders of the Fed. Bar Assn. People to People Del. to China, USSR and Finland, 1986. Contbr. numerous articles to profl. jours. Bd. dirs. Pres.'s Coun. Met. Denver, 1981-83; mem. Lowry AFB Alcohol Abuse Exec. Com., 1981-84. Recipient Spl. Achievement award USAF, 1978; Upward Mobility award Fed. Profl. and Adminstrv. Women, Denver, 1979, Internat. Humanitarian award CARE, 1994. Mem. Fed. Bar Assn. (pres. Colo. 1982-83, mem. nat. coun. 1984—, Earl W. Kintner Disting. Svc. award 1983, 1st v.p. 10th cir. 1986—, Internat. Humanitarian award CARE, 1994), Colo. Trial Lawyers Assn., Bus. and Profl. Women's Club (dist. IV East dir. 1983-84, Colo. pres. 1988-89), Am. Soc. Mil. Comptrollers (pres. 1984-85), Denver South Met. Bus. and Profl. Women's Club (pres. 1982-83), Denver Silver Spruce Am. Bus. Women's Assn. (pres. 1981-82; Woman of Yr. award 1982), Colo. Jud. Inst., Colo. Concerned Lawyers, Profl. Mgrs. Assn., Fed. Women's Program (v.p. Denver 1980), Colo. Woman News Community adv. bd., 1988—, Dallas Bar Assn., Tex. Bar Assn., Denver Bar Assn., Altrusa, Zonta, Denver Nancy Langhorn Federally Employed Women. (pres. 1979-80). Christian.

DAVIS, YOLETTE MARIE TOUSSAINT, critical care, flight, orthopedic and surgical nurse; b. Port-au-Prince, Haiti, May 8, 1956; d. Edner Casimir and Ursule (Lamour) Toussaint; children: Jacques Edner, Noelle Lorraine. BSN, Incarnate Word Coll., San Antonio, 1985; cert. flight nurse, Sch. Aerospace Medicine, San Antonio, 1988; cert. in basic critical care, U. Tex., San Antonio, 1989; cert. in battlefield nursing, Sch. Aerospace Medicine, San Antonio, 1989; postgrad., Incarnate Word Coll. RN, N.Y., Calif., Ohio, Fla., Tex.; cert. ACLS. Staff nurse pediatrics unit Humana Hosp. San Antonio; staff-charge nurse surg. ICU, Humana Hosp. Met., San Antonio; pvt. practice nurse San Antonio; staff nurse Wilford Hall Med. Ctr.; enlisted as capt. USAF, 1991; asst. DON, Avalon Pl. Mem. NAFE, Nat. Assn. Orthopedic Nursing, Women in Bus. Home: 5380 Medical Dr Apt 101 San Antonio TX 78240-1949

DAVIS, YVONNE D., public administrator; b. Orange, N.J., Sept. 21, 1947; d. William J. and Alice-Ruth Patterson; m. Royce Davis; children: Shannon K., Sarah K. BA in Spanish, Montclair State Coll., Upper Montclair, N.J., 1975; cert. pub. mgmt., Kean Coll., Union, N.J., 1982; cert. equal employment, Rutgers U., 1984. Bilingual family svc. worker Essex County Div. Welfare, Dept. Citizen Svcs., Newark, 1971-78, family svc. supr., 1978-81, adminstrv. analyst, 1981-83, prin. personnel technician, 1983-86; personnel mgr., supr. prin. personnel technician Essex County Dept. Citizen Svcs., Newark, N.J., 1984—; adminstrv. deputy dir. of Welfare Dept. of Citizen Svcs. Div. of Welfare, Newark, N.J., 1992-93; dir. Essex County Dept. Citizen Svcs., 1994—. Mem. exec. bd. Essex County Minority Employees Assn., Newark, 1984-85; mem. employment coun. Tng., Inc., Newark; mem. Essex County Adv. Bd. on Status of Women; mem. Coordinating Coun. for Social Svcs., Essex County, N.J.; mem. Essex County Ins. Commn.; active Epilepsy Found. Am., Trenton. Recipient Excellence in Personnel Mgmt. award Essex County Minority Employees Assn., 1986, Excellence in Spanish award Nat. Assn. Tchrs. Spanish, 1964, 65, Excellence in French award Nat. Assn. Tchrs. French, 1965, Recognition award United Way, 1984-88; cert. of appreciation U.S. Dept. Treas., 1984, tng. cert. N.J. Div. Civil Rights, 1988. Mem. NAFE, Am. Mgmt. Assn., Am. Assn. Affirmative Action, Nat. Assn. Pub. Sector Equal Opportunity Officers, Mcpl. Career Women Newark Inc. Democrat. Baptist. Office: Essex County Dept Citizen Svcs Directors Office 18 Rector St 9th Fl Newark NJ 07102

DAVIS-CARTEY, CATHERINE BERNICE, bank executive; b. N.Y.C., Jan. 14, 1954; d. Edward James Doyle Davis and Adele Helen (Dixon) Cartey. BA, Simmons Coll., 1975; EdM, Harvard U., 1978. Program cons.

United Community Svcs. Met., Detroit; comml. credit analyst Nat. Bank Detroit Comml. Lending Div., 1980-82; dir. comml. devel. Detroit Econ. Growth Corp., 1982-93; v.p. Mich. Nat. Bank, Bloomfield Hills, 1993—; pres. CDC Consulting, Southfield, Mich., 1985—. Author: Neighborhood Economic Development Strategies, 1989. Mem. exec. com. Joy of Jesus; mem. fin. planning United Way Southeastern Mich., mem. allocations com.; dir. pers. com. Women's Econ. Club, Detroit; chmn., life mem. Comml. Real Estate Women, Troy, Mich., 1990—, Bus. Role Model/Detroit Pub. Schs., 1987-93; mem. exec. com. Ctrl. Bus. Dist. Assn. Mem. Harvard Club Eastern Mich. Office: Mich Nat Bank 1533 N Woodward Ave Bloomfield Hills MI 48304

DAVIS-DURANT, ERLYNNE, social work educator; b. Cleve., Oct. 16, 1925; d. Earle Vernon and Margaret Ruth (Sanders) Poindexter; m. Charles E. Davis Sr. (dec.); 1 child, Charles E. Jr.; m. John H. Durant. AB, Oberlin Coll., 1947; MS in Social Adminstrn., Western Res. U., 1950. Case worker Cuyahoga County Welfare Dept., Cleve., 1947-48, Family Svc. Assn., Cleve., 1950-54; supr. Cuyahoga County Welfare Dept., Cleve., 1956-63; assoc. prof. Sch. Applied Social Scis. Case Western Res. U., Cleve., 1963-87, assoc. prof. emerita Mandel Sch. Applied Social Scis., 1987—; cons., staff devel. trainer, continuing edn. instr., speaker in field, 1957-95. Bd. trustees Project Friendship, Cleve., 1986-91, pres., 1987, Youth Visions, 1991—; bd. dirs. Met. YWCA, Cleve., 1987-92; vol. Ret. Srs. Vol. Program, Cleve., 1989—; mem. St. James African Meth. Episc. Ch. (Disting. Svc. award 1983); mem. adv. coun. Coun. Ret. Srs. Vol. Program, Greater Cleve., 1991-94; assoc. Aldersgate United Meth. Ch.; active Fairhill Cmty. Coun. Fairhill Ctr. for Aging, 1993—; vol. Speakers Bur. & Intergenerational Resource Ctr. Recipient 20h Anniversary Founders Recognition, Ctr. for Human Svcs., Cleve., 1990, Living Legend award Murtis Taylor Multi-Svc. Ctr., Cleve., 1990, Disting. Alumni award Sch. Applied Social Scis. Case Western Res. U., 1987, African Meth. Episcopal Ch. Women of Distinction award Women's Missionary Soc. African Meth. Episcopal Ch., 1983. Mem. NAACP, Alpha Kappa Alpha (Achievement award Alpha Omega chpt. 1963, 74).

DAVIS-IMHOF, NANCY LOUISE, elementary school educator; b. Stamford, Conn., Feb. 17, 1940; d. Ernest A. and Margaret (Carlson) Davis; m. William A. Imhof, Nov. 17, 1962 (div. Dec. 1989); children: Samuel, Jacqueline, Susan. BA, Barnard Coll., 1962; MEd, George Mason U., 1975. Cert. tchr., Va. Tchr. Arlington (Va.) Pub. Schs., 1975—; freelance photographer. Mem. family life edn. com., Arlington Pub. Schs., 1990-91; mem. ad hoc com. on future of T.J. Community Ctr., 1991; mem. vestry St. Georges Episcopal Ch., Arlington, 1987-90. Arlington Sch. System grantee, 1988-89. Mem. NEA, Va. Edn. Assn., Arlington Edn. Assn. (sch. rep. 1989, 90). Democrat. Home: 894 N Ohio St Arlington VA 22205-1530 Office: Page Traditional Sch 1401 N Lincoln St Arlington VA 22201-4915

DAVIS-JEROME, EILEEN GEORGE, principal; b. N.Y.C., Nov. 10, 1946; d. Rennie and Flora May (Compton) George; m. Bruce Davis, Aug. 8, 1970 (div. 1978); m. Frantz Jerome, Sept. 7, 1982; 1 child, Thais Davis. BFA, Pratt Inst., 1968; MA, CUNY, 1971, PD, 1990. Lic. ednl. adminstr., prin., instrn. specialist, N.Y. Tchr. fine arts Herbert Lehman High Sch., Bronx, N.Y., 1971-75; tchr. English/fine arts Jr. High Sch. 131, Bronx, 1975-76; tchr. English Jr. High Sch. 22, Bronx, 1976-79; tchr. fine arts Andrew Jackson High Sch., Cambria Heights, N.Y., 1979-83, coord. art dept., 1986-92; admissions counselor Fashion Inst. Tech., SUNY, N.Y.C., 1983-85; coord. Queensborough Coll. Project Prize, Bayside, N.Y., 1991-92; project dir. Andrew Jackson Magnet High Sch., Cambria Heights, N.Y., 1993—, project dir. humanities and the arts, 1994—; ednl. adminstr. Queens High Sch. Office, N.Y.C. Pub. High Schs., Corona, N.Y., 1993-94; prin. humanities and the arts Magnet H.S., Cambria Heights, N.Y., 1994—; coord. internat. studies Friends of Jackson High Sch., Cambria Heights, 1986-93, equal opportunity coord., 1989-92; exam asst. N.Y. C. Bd. Edn., Bd. Examiners, Bklyn., 1983-87; curriculum/career cons. Fashion Inst., SUNY, Detroit, Washington, Phila., 1983-86. Curriculum writer N.Y. State Project ot Implement Career Edn., 1975, N.Y. State Futuring, 1984; proposal writer Magnet Sch. Funding, 1993; author: Resource Book, 1989. Mem., speaker Cambria Heights Civic Assn., 1983; mem. N.Y. Urban League, N.Y.C.; vol. Mayor's Vol. Action/Alpha Sr. Cr., Cambria Heights, 1984; vol. Black Spectrum Theatre Co., 1983-86. Recipient Recognition award Black Spectrum Theatre Co., 1983, Speakers award N.Y.C. Bd. Edn. Open Doors, 1983-84, Black Exec. Exch. Program Nat. Urban League, N.Y.C., 1984, Developer Grant award Impact II Grant, N.Y.C., 1989; named Educator of Yr. NAACP/ACT-50, N.Y.C., 1992. Mem. ASCD, N.Y. State Art Tchrs. Assn., N.Y.C. Art Tchrs. Assn. (v.p., sec. 1983-85, cert. 1983-86), Cultural Heritage Alliance (assoc., Recognition award 1986), Delta Sigma Theta (chair arts and letters 1991—, Golden Life award 1991), Phi Delta Kappa (Disting. Cert. 1994). Democrat. Episcopalian. Office: Magnet High Sch Humanities and the Arts 207-01 116th Ave Cambria Heights NY 11411

DAVISON, LILLIAN L., plastics manufacturing company executive; b. Laurence, Pa., Jan. 1, 1937; d. Moncton Hunter and Betsy (Malloy) Gunther; m. Robert Sexton Davison, June 26, 1958. B.S., CCNY, 1963; postgrad Baruch Sch. Bus., 1965. Asst. to pres. Publisher's Arm, N.Y.C., 1970-71; coordinator mktg. research MEI, N.Y.C., 1971-74; corporate strategic planner Gen. Electric Co., Fairfield, Conn., 1974-75; pres. McCordi Corp., Mamroneck, N.Y., 1978-80; chief exec. officer Resource Retrieval, Inc., N.Y.C., 1981—; pres. Environ. Control Mgmt., Inc., N.Y.C., 1985-87; chief exec. officer Advanced Materials of Del., Inc., New Castle, Del., 1984—, Micropropagation Del., Inc., 1994—. Mem. Am. Soc. Horticulutral Sci., Soc. for Invitro Biology, Assn. Objectivist Businessman, Inst. Objectivist Studies, N.Y. Acad. Scis. Avocations: Cross country skiing; hatha yoga; swimming; gourmet cooking; oenology. Home: 320 E 58th St New York NY 10022-2220

DAVISON, VICTORIA DILLON, real estate executive; b. Ada, Okla., Jan. 11, 1949; d. Wiliam Jackson Jr. and Helen Lucille (Cate) Dillon; m. Charles Alton Jewett, July 7, 1973 (div.); m. Denver Norris Davison, May 31 1985; stepchildren: Shaun, Malia, Denver II. BFA, Tulane U., 1970. Exec. sec. ITT Corp., Washington, 1970-71; adminstrv. asst. Berens Associated, Washington, 1972-73; real estate trainee Equitable Life Assurance Soc. Comml. Real Estate, Washington, 1974-75, real estate analyst, sr. appraiser, 1976-82; v.p. Am. Security Corp., Washington, 1983-85; exec. v.p. Ada Shopping Ctr., Inc., 1985—; pres. Victoria Properties, Ltd., Ada, 1989—; bd. dirs. W.J. Dillon Co., Inc., Ada, Ada Shopping Ctr. Inc. Jr. warden and vestry St. Luke's Episcopal Ch., Ada, 1990-91. Mem. Ada Area C. of C. (bd. dirs. 1990, co-chmn. area retail 1990-92), Appraisal Inst. (MAI), Edn. for Ministry (award 1992), Ada Music Club, Tanti, Leadership Ada. Republican. Home: 825 W Kings Rd Ada OK 74820-8045 Office: Victoria Properties Ltd 902 Arlington Ctr Ste 196 Ada OK 74820-9999

DAW, LENORE E., elementary school educator, librarian; b. Pitts.; d. James E. Owens and Lillian E. Gregory; m. Matthew L. Daw, July 27, 1947 (dec.); children: Andrea, Matthew Jr., Alan. BA, Calif. State U., 1968; MA, U. San Francisco, 1977; postgrad., Pacific Coll., 1979, Columbia Pacific U., 1990—. Cert. tchr., libr., adminstr., Calif. Elem. tchr. 3d and 4th grades Alvina Sch. Dist., Caruthers, Calif.; elem. libr., secondary libr./career edn. coord. Fresno (Calif.) Unified Sch. Dist., dist. libr. K-12, ret.; libr. media specialist Balderas Elem. Sch.; instrnl. materials evaluation panelist Calif. State Dept. Edn. Min. of music, soloist Second Bapt. Ch. Recipient G.W. Hayden award Second Bapt. Ch., 1990, Gold Apple award United Black Men Fresno, 1990, cert. of recognition Calif. Legis. Assembly, 1990, cert. of honor City of Fresno, 1990. Mem. ASCD, Assn. Calif. Sch. Adminstr., ALA, Am. Assn. Sch. Librs., Calif. Reading Assn., Reading Initiative Coordinating Coun., Internat. Reading Assn., NEA, Fresno Boys and Girls Club (exec. bd.), Calif. Media and Libr. Assn., Alpha Kappa Alpha (Mildred L. Robinson Alumna Basileus award 1975, Outstanding Svc. award Iota Omicron Omega chpt. 1990), Phi Delta Kappa, Iota Phi Lambda.

DAWBER, PAM, actress; b. Detroit; d. Gene and Thelma D.; m. Mark Harmon, Mar. 21, 1987; 2 children. Ed., Oakland Community Coll. Worked as model and appeared in commls.; appearances include (TV series) ABC-TV's Mork and Mindy, 1978-82, CBS-TV My Sister Sam, 1986-88, (TV movies) The Girl the Gold Watch and Everything, Remembrance of Love, NBC, 1982, Last of the Great Survivors, 1983, Through Naked Eyes, 1983, This Wife for Hire, 1985, Wild Horses, 1985, American Geisha, 1986, Quiet Victory: The Charlie Wedemeyer Story, 1988, Do You Know the Muffin Man?, 1989, Face of Fear, 1990, The Man Who Had Three Wives, 1993, Web of Deception, 1994, A Child's Cry For Help, 1994, (films) The Wedding, Stay Tuned; (Broadway play) My Fair Lady; Joe Papp's L.A. prodn. Pirates of Penzance, L.A. prodn., Love Letters, 1991. Nat. spokeswoman Big Bros., Big Sisters of Am. Office: care Mimi Weber 9738 Arby Dr Beverly Hills CA 90210-1203

DAWDY, FAYE MARIE CATANIA, photographer, lecturer; b. San Mateo, Calif., Sept. 15, 1954; d. Frank Benjamin and Melba Rita (Arata) Catania; m. John Thomas Dawdy, May 5, 1974; children: Tracy Marie, John Franco. AA, Coll. of San Mateo, 1979; student, San Francisco State U., 1979—. With Proctor & Gamble Distbg. Co., San Mateo, 1973-78; ptnr. Dawdy Photography, Millbrae, Calif., 1978—; dir., sec.-treas. Millbrae Stamp Co., 1980—; instr. Winona Sch. Profl. Photography, Mt. Prospect, Ill.; lectr. to high schs., various clubs, photography convs. including Goteborg, Sweden, Idaho, Oreg., Colo., Tex., Ill., Fla., Mo., Kans., Nev., Iowa, N.J. Contbr. articles to profl. jours. Area chmn. Millbrae Am. Heart Assn. Ann. Fund Dr., 1977-82; mem. fund raising and nutrition coms. San Mateo County chpt. Am. Heart Assn., 1980-88; co-chmn. Miss Millbrae Pageant, 1981, Queen Isabella Columbus Day Festival, 1981; judge arts and crafts exhbns. Millbrae Art and Wine Festival; judge photography competition Marin County Fair Photography Exhibit; vol. photographer Rotoplast, La Serena, Chile, 1994; mem. sister city com. City of Millbrae; trustee Golden Gate Sch. Profl. Photographers, 1985-90. Recipient awards No. Calif. Coun. Camera Clubs, 1979, 81, Mktg. Contest award Mktg. Today mag., 1988. Mem. Profl. Photographers Am. (photog. craftsman degree), Profl. Photographers Greater Bay Area, Profl. Photographers No. Calif., Profl. Photographers Calif., Wedding Photographers Assn., NAFE, Millbrae C. of C. (sec. women's div. 1979, bd. dirs. 1991), Millbrae Art Assn. (pres. 1979-80), Portola Camera Club (nature chmn. 1978—), Millbrae Hist. Assn., Friends Millbrae Libr., Italian Cath. Fedn., Calif. Women in Profl. Photography, Fedn. Ind. Bus., St. Dunstan Women's Club, Soroptimist (sec. 1981-82). Democrat. Roman Catholic. Office: 449 Broadway Millbrae CA 94030-1905

DAWKINS, BARBARA ELAINE, secondary school educator; b. Willimantic, Conn., Feb. 21, 1938; d. Stanley Potter and Gladys Mae (Buskard) Lamberton; m. James Elbert Dawkins, Aug. 7, 1965. BA in Math., U. Del., 1960; postgrad. studies, Brown U., 1963-64. Math. tchr. Bloomfield (N.J.) Pub. Schs., 1960-63; math. tchr. Dept. of Defense, Crailsheim, Germany, 1964-66, Nurenberg, Germany, 1966-67; math. tchr. Freehold (N.J.) High Sch., 1967-68, Lakes High Sch., Tacoma, Wash., 1973-74, Empire Sch., Duncan, Okla., 1977—. Recipient scholarship Brown U. Nat. Sci. Found. Acad., 1963-64. Mem. NEA, AAUW (treas. Lawton chpt. 1984-85, 88-90), Okla. Edn. Assn., Empire Edn. Assn. (Tchr. of Yr. 1982), Nat. Coun. Tchrs. Math., Okla. Coun. Tchrs. Math. Republican. Presbyterian. Avocations: needlework, knitting, golf, reading, bowling. Home: 2329 NE Village Dr Lawton OK 73507-2346 Office: Empire Sch RR 1 Box 155 Duncan OK 73533-9713

DAWKINS, DIANTHA DEE, librarian; b. McCamey, Tex., Oct. 6, 1942; d. Kirby Walls and Lucille (Watson) D. BA U. Tex., 1966, MLS, 1971. Cert. sch. librarian. Asst. librarian Lee High Sch., Midland, Tex., 1966-70; asst. librarian, media coord. Midland High Sch., 1970-73; librarian Austin Freshman Sch., Midland, 1973-79; librarian, media coord. Lee Freshman High, 1979—; lead librarian Midland ISD, 1994—. Editor Communication Report, 1980-81. Bd. dirs. Meml. Christian Ch., Midland, 1980-82, sec. bd., 1982. Treas. Lee Freshman PTA, 1985-86, mailing chmn., 1986-93, life mem.; mem. MISD Communications Com., 1988—, Ednl. Improvement Coun., 1991—. Mem. ALA, Tex. Library Assn. (life; coms. 1981-89, 91-94, 95—, coun. 1984-86 dist. chmn. elect 1985-86, chmn. 1986-87), Am. Assn. Sch. Librarians (affiliate assembly 1979, 82), Tex. Assn. Sch. Librarians (chmn. 1979-80, coun. 1978-86, dist. workshop coord. 1989—), Tex. Classroom Tchrs. Assn., Midland Classroom Tchrs. (dir. 1976-84, 86-88, pres. 1979-80), Tex. State Tchrs. Assn. (life; dir. ex-officio 1979-80), Grad. Sch. Library and Info. Sci. U. Tex. (life), U. Tex. Ex-Students (life), Freedom to Read Found., Tex. Hist. Assn., Delta Kappa Gamma., Epsilon Eta (first v.p. 1988-90, pres. 1990-92). Mem. Disciples of Christ Ch. Home: PO Box 80459 Midland TX 79708-0459 Office: Lee Freshman Sch Libr 1400 E Oak Ave Midland TX 79705-6899

DAWKINS, MARVA PHYLLIS, psychologist; b. Jacksonville, Fla., Apr. 12, 1948; d. Ralph and Altamese (Padgett) D.; student U. Freiburg, Germany, 1969-70; BS, Stetson U., 1971; MS, Fla. State U., 1972, PhD, 1975. Rsch. asst. Fla. State U., Tallahassee, 1970-72; clin. intern, psychology dept. Presby.-St. Luke's Med. Ctr. and mental health dept. Mile Square Health Ctr., Chgo., 1973-74; staff psychologist, dir. aftercare treatment program, mental health dept. Mile Square Health Ctr., Chgo., 1974-75, staff psychologist, coordinator devel. disabilities program, 1976-79; asst. prof. psychology U. North Fla., Jacksonville, 1975-76, Rush U.-Presbyn. St. Luke's Med. Ctr., Chgo., 1976—; pvt. practice clin. psychology, 1977—; exec. dir. Inst. for Community Mental Health, 1979—; cons. safety evaluation program Isaac Ray Ctr., 1986-91; dir. Ctr. for Applied Psychology and Forensic Studies, 1991—; psychology cons. Disability Policy Br. Social Security Adminstrn., Chgo, 1980—. Registered psychologist, Ill. Mem. Am. Psychol. Assn., Assn. Black Psychologists.

DAWLESS, MARIBETH STANGEL, nurse; b. Bridgeport, Conn., Dec. 27, 1964; d. John Edward and Carolyn Theresa (Mancine) Stangel; m. William Gillette Dawless, Oct. 5, 1990; 1 child, Kendra Lynne. BSN, So. Conn. State U., 1986. Cert. pediatric nurse, ANA. Staff nurse pediatrics Yale New Haven (Conn.) Hosp., 1985-90; tchr. pediatric unit R.I. Hosp., Providence, 1990-91; nurse clinician Critical Care Am., Warwick, R.I., 1991-94, Caremark, Warwick, R.I., 1994—. Mem. Assn. Pediatric Oncology Nurses, Sigma Theta Tau. Roman Catholic. Home: 54 Donald Potter Rd West Greenwich RI 02817-2263 Office: Caremark 20 Altieri Way Warwick RI 02886

DAWN, DEBORAH, dancer; b. Blytheville, Ark.. Dancer N.C. Dance Theater, 1978-83, The Joffrey Ballet, N.Y.C., 1983—. Office: The Joffrey Ballet 130 W 56th St New York NY 10019-3818*

DAWSON, CAROL GENE, former commissioner, writer, consultant; b. Indpls., Sept. 8, 1937; d. Ernest Eugene (dec.) and Hilda Lou (Carroll) D.; m. Robert Edmund Bauman, Nov. 19, 1960 (div. 1982); children: Edward Carroll, Eugenie Marie, Victoria Anne, James Shields; m. Franklin Dean Smith, Aug. 2, 1986. BA, Dunbarton Coll., Washington, 1959, Cath. U., Washington, 1960; MA in Internat. Transactions, George Mason U., 1994. Staff asst. Senator Kenneth B. Keating, Washington, 1959; exec. asst. Americans for Constl. Action, Washington, 1959; exec. sec. Youth for Nixon Lodge, Washington, 1959-60; legis. asst. Rep. Donald C. Bruce, Washington, 1961-63; dep. dir., pub. info. Goldwater for Pres. Campaign and Rep. Nat. Com., Washington, 1963-64; editor, assoc. editor The New Guard Mag., Washington, 1965-66; dir. info. Am. Conservative Union, Washington, 1966-67; publs. and news analyst White House, Washington, from 1969; staff reporter Easton (Md.) Star-Democrat, 1971-72; freelance writer Easton, 1972-77; real estate salesperson Latham Realtors, Easton, 1977-80; sr. staff asst. presdl. transition U.S. Office of Personnel Mgmt., Washington, 1980-81; dep. press sec. U.S. Dept. Energy, Washington, 1981-82, dep. spl. asst. to sec., 1982-84; commr. U.S. Consumer Product Safety Commn., Washington, 1984-93; editor Cath. Currents newsletter, Washington, 1969-70. Bd. visitors Inst. Polit. Journalism, Georgetown U., 1985-89; mem. Nat. Policy Forum, Coun. on Free Individuals in a Free Soc., 1994—; bd. dirs. Consumer Alert, 1994; active past polit. activities. Recipient Award of Merit Young Americans for Freedom, 1970. Mem. Exec. Women in Govt., The Charter 100, Reagan Appointees Alumni, The Fairfax Hunt Club (bd. govs. 1989-91). Roman Catholic. Home and office: PO Box 2 Morattico VA 22523-0002

DAWSON, DAWN PAIGE, publisher; b. Paradise, Calif., Nov. 10, 1956; d. Wayne Paul and Donna Jean (Peckham) D.; m. Justin Keith Anderson, Mar. 12, 1989; 1 child, Christopher Wayne Dawson Anderson. AB, Occidental Coll., 1979. Editorial asst. Salem Press Inc., Pasadena, Calif., 1979-80, copy editor, 1980-81, sr. editor, 1982-83, mr. editor, 1984-87, v.p. editing and prodn., 1987—. Mem. Customer's Guild West. Mem. Soc. Scholarly Pub., Nat. Assn. Female Execs. Office: Salem Press Inc 131 N El Molino Ave Ste 350 Pasadena CA 91101

DAWSON, JOANNE B., telemarketing service agency executive-consultant; b. Chgo., Apr. 11, 1950; d. Joseph Thomas and Marcella Anna (Laska) Bastuga; m. Edward John Dawson, Aug. 15, 1971. BA, Ill. Benedictine, 1972. Communication svcs. mgr. Tech. Pub. Co., Barrington, Ill., 1982-84, telemktg. mgr., 1984-86; telemktg. mgr. CAhners Pub. Co., Des Plaines, Ill., 1986-88; pres. JBD Enterprises, Inc., Wauconda, Ill., 1988—. Mem. Am. Telemktg. Assn. (Midwest chpt., v.p. 1989, pres. 1990-91), Telemktg. Mgmt. Assn. (sec. 1986, pres. 1987-88). Office: JBD Enterprises Inc 611 Lake Shore Blvd Wauconda IL 60084-1525

DAWSON, MARY RUTH, curator; b. Highland Park, Mich., Feb. 27, 1931; d. John Elson and Olga Josephine (Down) D. B.S., Mich. State Coll., 1952; postgrad., U. Edinburgh, 1952-53; Ph.D., U. Kans., 1957. Instr. zoology Smith Coll., 1958-61; asst. program dir. NSF, Washington, 1961-62; mem. staff Carnegie Mus., Pitts., 1962—, curator, 1971—, chmn. earth sci. div., 1973—, acting dir., 1982-83; adj. prof. earth scis. U. Pitts., 1971-85, prof., 1985—. Recipient Arnold Guyot award Nat. Geog. Soc., 1981, Woman in Sci. award Chatham Coll., 1983; named Disting. Dau. Pa., 1987; Fulbright scholar, 1952-53; fellow AAUW, 1958-59; research grantee NSF, 1961-62, 65—. Fellow Geol. Soc. Am., Arctic Inst. N.Am.; mem. Soc. Vertebrate Paleontology (v.p. 1972-73, pres. 1973-74), Paleontol. Soc., Paläontologische Gesellschaft, Bernese Mountain Dog Club Am., Am. Soc. Mammalogists, Phi Beta Kappa. Office: Carnegie Mus 4400 Forbes Ave Pittsburgh PA 15213-4007

DAWSON, MURIEL AMANDA, legislator; b. Ft. Lauderdale, Fla., July 18, 1956; d. Clifford and Altemease (Laws) Hardy; divorced; children: Shatereas (Tibby), Colongie, Ashley. Degree in social work, Fla. Agrl. and Mech. U., 1980. Legis. asst. Fla. Ho. of Reps., Ft. Lauderdale, 1988-92, state legislator Dist. 93, 1992—. Chairperson Fla. Commn. Minority Health, 1993—; bd. dirs. Broward County Urban League, Ft. Lauderdale, 1994—, Friends of Children, Youth and Families, Ft. Lauderdale, 1993; mem. NAACP, Ft. Lauderdale, 1989—. Recipient Trailblazer award Young Dems., 1993, Margaret Roach Leadership award Broward County Urban League, 1993, Hon. McKnight Achiever award, 1993, award Sickle Cell Anemia Found., 1993, 94. Mem. Bus. and Profl. Women, Optimists, Kiwanis, Order of Eastern Star. Democrat. Baptist. Office: Fla Legis 612 N Andrews Ave Fort Lauderdale FL 33311-7436

DAWSON, STELLA HOPE, journalist; b. Ft. Belvoir, Va., Jan. 18, 1954; d. Montagu Ellis Hawkins and Grace Mary (Birchwood) D.; life ptnr. Mary L. Klein. BA in Politics with honors, U. Durham, Eng., 1976; MA in Journalism, Am. U., 1982. Reporter Sta. WAGE, Loudoun Cable News, Leesburg, Va., 1982-83, Sta. WFVA-FM, Fredericksburg, Va., 1984, Sta. WAMU-FM, Washington, 1982-84, No. Va. Sun, Arlington, 1984-85; freelance bus. reporter Washington Post, 1985-86; state reporter AP, Washington and Providence, 1986-87; econ. reporter Reuters, Chgo., 1987-89; econ. corr. Reuters, Washington, 1989-94, Reuters Fin. TV, Washington, 1994—. Contbr. articles to Off Our Backs, women's news jour. Sec. Wise Up Econ. Revitalization Inc., Washington, 1991-94. Recipient award for best ann. feature story UPI, 1983, award for best spot news, 1983. Mem. Newspaper Guild N.Y. (shop steward 1988—), Nat. Journalism Scholastic Soc. Home: 1811 Varnum St NW Washington DC 20011 Office: Reuters Am. Inc 1333 H St NW Washington DC 20005-4707

DAWSON, SUZANNE STOCKUS, lawyer; b. Chgo., Dec. 29, 1941; d. John Charles and Josephine (Zolpe) Stockus; m. Daniel P. Dawson Sr., Sept. 1, 1962; children: Daniel P. Jr., John Charles, Michael Sean. BA, Marquette U., 1963; JD cum laude, Loyola U., Chgo., 1965. Bar: Ill. 1965, U.S. Dist. Ct. (no. dist.) Ill. 1965. Assoc. Kirkland & Ellis, Chgo., 1965-71, ptnr., 1971-82; ptnr. Arnstein & Lehr, Chgo., 1982-89, Foley & Lardner, Chgo., 1989-94. Mem. various coms. United Way Chgo.; corp. adv. bd. Sec. State of Ill., 1973; past mem. bd. advisors Loyola of Chgo. Law Sch.; trustee Lawrence Hall Youth Svcs., Chgo., 1983—, pres., 1991-93, chair 1993—; mem. adv. bd. Cath. Charities Chgo., 1985—; mem. exec. com., bd. governance Notre Dame High Sch., Niles, Ill., 1990—. Recipient Founder's Day award Loyola U., 1980, St. Thomas More award Loyola of Chgo. Law Sch., 1983. Mem. ABA, Ill. Bar Assn., Chgo. Bar Assn. Roman Catholic. Home: 2113 Valley Lo Ln Glenview IL 60025-1724

DAWSON, VIRGINIA SUE, newspaper editor; b. Concordia, Kans., June 6, 1940; d. John Edward and Wilma Aileen (Thompson) Morgan; m. Neil S. Dawson, Nov. 28, 1964; children: Shelley Diane Dawson Sedwick, Lori Ann, Christy Lynn. BS in Home Econs. and Journalism, Kans. State U., 1962. Publs. editor Ohio State U. Coop. Extension Svc., Columbus, 1962-64; home editor Ohio Farmer mag., Columbus, 1964-78; food editor Columbus Dispatch, 1978—. Recipient Commn. award Ohio Poultry Assn., 1980. Mem. Am. Assn. Family and Consumer Scis. (cert. home economist), Assn. Food Journalists, Home Economists in Bus. (past pres. Columbus chpt.), Ohio Newspaper Women's Assn. (several writing and newspaper design awards 1985-94). Office: Columbus Dispatch 34 S 3d St Columbus OH 43215

DAY, ANN, state legislator; b. EL Paso, Tex.. Former tchr., counselor; mem. Ariz. Senate. Republican. Home: Box 64276 Tucson AZ 85726 Office: Arizona State Senate State House Phoenix AZ 85007*

DAY, ANN ELIZABETH, artist, educator; b. Valetta, Malta, June 1, 1927; came to U.S., 1940; d. John Dwight and Joyce Elizabeth (Marett) Harvey; m. George Frederick Day, Oct. 23, 1948 (div. Oct. 1979); children: Georgianna Day Ludcke, John F., David S.; m. Donald Monturean Mintz, Dec. 30, 1980. BA, Mt. Holyoke Coll., 1948. Asst. to dir. advanced studies Nat. Ctr. Atmospheric Rsch., Boulder, Colo., 1962-67; edn. dir. Waterloo (Iowa) Recreation and Arts Ctr., 1967-76; curator edn. svcs. Utah Mus. Fine Arts, Salt Lake City, 1976-80; lectr. art history YMHA of No. N.J., Wayne, 1982—; freelance artist Ringwood, N.J., 1982—; represented by Nathans Gallery, West Paterson, N.J., Oasis Gallery, Savannah, Ga., Wilson Galleries, Nantucket, Mass.; vice chair, panelist Fed. State Ptnrship., NEA, Washington, 1972-77; mem. exec. com. Nat. Assn. Community Arts Agys., Washington, 1975-77. Author of poems; represented in collections in U.S. and abroad including Phillips Gallery, Salt Lake City. Recipient Silver medal Utah Watercolor Soc., Salt Lake City, 1976, Lake Mohawk Club award Sussex County Art Assn., Sparta, N.J., 1992, 93. Mem. Nat. Watercolor Soc., N.J. Watercolor Soc. (Heimrod award 1991), Phi Beta Kappa. Democrat. Home and office: 117 Cedar Rd Ringwood NJ 07456-1800

DAY, ANNE W., nurse; b. Cin., July 9, 1926; d. Pinkney McGill and Anna Pearl (Glendenning) White; m. Raymond Eric Parker, Mar. 6, 1948 (div. 1969); children: Douglas McGill, Stephanie Morse. Diploma, Christ Hosp. Sch. Nursing, Cin., 1947. RN, Ohio; cert. chem. dependency nurse Consol. Assn. Nurses in Substance Abuse. Staff nurse to asst. head nurse Holmes div. U. Cin., 1948-84; nursing supr. Villa Hope Extended Care Facility, Cin., 1970-72; staff nurse Hillenbrand Nursing Home, Cin., 1980-82, Emerson A. North Hosp., Cin., 1982—. Vol. Group Against Smoke Pollution, Cin., 1989—; donor Zoo, Cin., 1989—, Voters for Choice, Ohio, 1989—, Ams. for Non-Smokers Rights, Calif., 1989—, Action on Smoking or Health, 1989—, Stop Teenage Addiction to Tobacco; tutor for adult literacy. Mem. DAR (life). Episcopalian.

DAY, BILLIE ANN, secondary education educator; b. Wichita, Kans., Feb. 26, 1939; d. William Alvin and Velma Frances (Grieder) D. BA, Southwestern Coll., 1960; MA, Howard U., 1969; PhD, NYU, 1986. Cert. tchr., Kans., D.C. Tchr. Francis L. Cardozo High Sch., Washington, 1969-81, Benjamin Banneker High Sch., Washington, 1981—; cons. in field. Contbr. articles to profl. jours. Chairperson of bd. World Hunger Edn. Svc., Washington, 1990. Recipient Roselle Lecture award for Creative Communication in the Social Studies, 1986, Am. Women of Today award, 1991, YFU Internat. Edn. award, 1992; named Cafritz fellow, 1991, Woodrow Wilson fellow, 1993; Fulbright scholar, 1986, 93. Mem. Returned Peace Corps Vols. of Washington (pres. 1991—), Nat. Coun. for Social Studies (mem. nat. bd. 1980-83), Middle States Coun. for Social Studies (pres. 1980-82), D.C. Coun.

for Social Studies (pres. 1976-77). Office: Benjamin Banneker High Sch 800 Euclid St NW Washington DC 20001

DAY, JANICE ELDREDGE, cosmetic company executive; b. New Bedford, Mass., Sept. 26, 1919; d. Wendell Tripp and Lucy Forbush (Houghton) Eldredge; m. Frank Perrett, Apr. 22, 1949; 1 child, Janna. BA in English, Middlebury Coll., 1941, LittD (hon.), 1990. Publicity writer A.H. Handley, Boston, 1941-42; sec. media Ladies Home Jour., Boston, 1942-45, McCann, Erickson, N.Y.C., 1945; sec. Cambridge U. Press, MacMillan Co., N.Y.C., 1945-46; exec. sec. Fort Monroe, Va., 1946-47, Stone & Webster Engring., 1947-49; mgr. sales Collier Co., San Francisco, 1947-48; unit mgr. Stanley Home Products, L.A., 1949-51; dist. sales mgr. Beauty Creators Cosmetics, L.A., 1951-56; co-founder, v.p. sales and mktg. Jafra Cosmetics, Inc., Malibu, Calif., 1956-76, chmn. bd., 1976-87, pres. Jan and Frank Day Scholarship Fund, 1978. Recipient Alumni Achievement award Middlebury Coll., 1983. Mem. Direct Selling Assn. (dir.), DAR. Republican. Episcopalian. Office: Jafra Cosmetics Inc Westlake Village CA 91361

DAY, JENNIE D., state legislator; b. Madera, Pa., Dec. 13, 1921; m. Marvin Day. Ed. Temple U. City councilwoman, Coventry, R.I., 1978-84; realtor; mem. R.I. Senate, 1985—. Mem. Coventry Hist. Soc. Democrat. Roman Catholic. Office: R I Senate House State House Providence RI 02903 Other: 19 Beechwood St Coventry RI 02816-4334*

DAY, LUCILLE ELIZABETH, laboratory administrator, educator, author; b. Oakland, Calif., Dec. 5, 1947; d. Richard Allen and Evelyn Marietta (Hazard) Lang; m. Frank Lawrence Day, Nov. 6, 1965; 1 child, Liana Sherrine; m. 2nd, Theodore Herman Fleischman, June 23, 1974; 1 child, Tamarind Channah. AB, U. Calif., Berkeley, 1971, MA, 1973, PhD, 1979. Teaching asst. U. Calif., Berkeley, 1971-72, 75-76, research asst., 1975, 77-78; tchr. sci. Magic Mountain Sch., Berkeley, 1977; specialist math. and sci. Novato (Calif.) Unified Sch. Dist., 1979-81; instr. sci. Project Bridge, Laney Coll., Oakland, Calif., 1984-86; sci. writer and mgr. precollege edn. programs, Lawrence Berkeley (Calif.) Lab., 1986-90, life scis. staff coord., 1990-92; mgr. Hall of Health, Berkeley, Calif., 1992—. Author numerous poems, articles and book reviews; author: (with Joan Skolnick and Carol Langbort) How to Encourage Girls in Math and Science: Strategies for Parents and Educators, 1982; Self-Portrait with Hand Microscope (poetry collection), 1982. NSF Grad. fellow, 1972-75; recipient Joseph Henry Jackson award in lit. San Francisco Found., 1982. Mem. AAAS, No. Calif. Sci. Writers Assn., Nat. Assn. Sci. Writers, Math/Sci. Network, Phi Beta Kappa, Iota Sigma Pi. Home: 1057 Walker Ave Oakland CA 94610-1511 Office: Hall of Health 2230 Shattuck Ave Berkeley CA 94704

DAY, MARY, artistic director, ballet company executive; b. Washington; trained by Lisa Gardinier. Co-founder Washington Sch. of Ballet, 1944—; founder Washington Ballet, 1976—. Office: Washington Ballet 3515 Wisconsin Ave NW Washington DC 20016-3085*

DAY, MARY DEAN, federal agency administrator; b. Selma, Ala., May 12, 1952; d. Willie and Nona Nora (Williams) Day; m. Frankie Murry Jenkins, July 14, 1973 (div. 1988); children: Jarrod Demetrius, Alexander Rashid; m. Ollie Ross Jones, June 11, 1988. AA, Olive Harvey Coll., 1973; BS, Roosevelt U., 1978. Tech. sec. US EPA, Chgo., 1975-88; housing program asst. U.S. Dept. Housing & Urban Devel., Nashville, 1988—. Dir. New Alpha Self Devel. Cmty. Ctr., New Alpha P.B. Ch., Chgo., 1983-87; sgt.-at-arms AFGE Local 3980, Nashville, 1994—; coord. Nat. Labor Mgmt. Partnership Coun., Nashville, 1994—. Named Outstanding Vol., Cmty. Econ. Devel. Assn., 1982. Mem. NAFE, Mid. Tenn. Fed. Exec. Assn. (Fed. Employee of Yr. 1992), Nashville Urban League. Home: PO Box 6145 Madison TN 37116 Office: U.S. Dept Housing & Urban Devel 251 Cumberland Bend Dr Ste 200 Nashville TN 37228

DAY, MARY JANE THOMAS, cartographer; b. Connors, New Brunswick, Can., Oct. 12, 1927; d. Angus and Delina (Michaud) Thomas; m. Howard M. Day, July 1, 1949; children: Laurie Anne Day Greene, Angus Howard. BS in Geography, U. Md., 1974, BS in Bus. & Mgmt., 1977. Meteorol. aide Hangar 8 Eastern Airlines, N.Y.C., 1946-47, U.S. Weather Bur., Washington, 1948-50; cartographic aide U.S. Navy Hydrographic Office, Suitland, Md., 1950-57, cartographer, 1957-62; cartographer U.S. Navy Oceanographic Office, Suitland, 1962-72, Def. Mapping Agy., Suitland/Brookmont, 1972-93; cartographer USNS Harkness, 1978, Indonesian Naval Personnel, Jakarta, Indonesia, 1981-82. Compiled, wrote and published: The Descendants of John Thomas of Connors, N.B., 1988. Mem. Nat. Aeronautic Assn., Am. Soc. Photogrammetry & Remote Sensing. Club: Andrews Officers (Md.). Home: 3532 28th Pky Temple Hills MD 20748-2922

DAY, MARY LOUISE, volunteer; b. LaGrange, Ill., May 22, 1917; d. Kenneth Farwell Burgess and Louise Frances Todd; m. J. Edward Day, July 2, 1941; children: Geraldine Day Zurn, Mary Louise Day Himmelfarb, James E. Jr. (dec.). AB, Vassar Coll., 1939. bd. dirs. YWCA, Washington, 1962-80, chmn. internat. fair, 1966, 82; active YWCA World Svc. Coun.; mem. adv. bd. The Hospitality Info. Svc., Washington, 1964—, chmn., 1969-71; chmn. women's bd. Am. Heart Assn., Washington, 1981-83; mem. Smithsonian Women's Com., Washington, 1982—. Democrat. Methodist. Home: 5804 Brookside Dr Bethesda MD 20815

DAY, MARYLOUISE MULDOON (MRS. RICHARD DAYTON DAY), appraiser; b. St. Louis; d. Joseph A. and Dorothy (Lang) Muldoon; A.B., Washington U., St. Louis, 1940; postgrad. Air U., 1958, George Washington U., 1963-64; grad. Real Estate Inst. Md., 1972; m. Richard Dayton Day, Aug. 15, 1959. Intelligence specialist U.S. Air Force, Washington, 1947-60; program officer, spl. asst. to dir. project devel. VISTA, OEO, 1965-67; with Joint Intelligence Bur., London, Eng., 1953; appraiser, cons. on antiques, fine arts, 1969—; pres. Agts. For Sales Ltd., 1974—, Marylouise M. Day, Inc., 1978—. Recipient citation U.S. Air Force, 1960. Fellow Inc. Soc. Valuers and Auctioneers (London), Am. Soc. Appraisers (chpt. 1st v.p. 1977-78, pres. 1978-79, chmn. fine arts forum 1976-78, gov. Region 3 1980-82, internat. sec. 1982-84, treas. edn1. found. 1986-91); mem. Appraisers Assn. Am., Irish Georgian Soc., Winterthur Guild, Assn. Former Intelligence Officers, Decorative Arts Trust, Delta Gamma. Club: Kenwood Golf and Country (Washington). Home: 4928 Sentinel Dr Bethesda MD 20816-3591

DAY, SUSAN ELAINE, social scientist; b. Cin., May 2, 1961; d. David Elwood and Emma Kathryn (Peyton) D. BA in Psychology, U. Ky., 1989; MPA, U. Ctrl. Fla., 1991, postgrad., 1991—. Waitress Columbia Restaurant, St. Augustine, Fla., 1984-85; mgr., shoeshine girl Classic Shoe Shine Co., Orlando, Fla., 1985-86; salesperson Rollins Security Systems, Orlando, 1986-87; real estate salesman First Continental Corp., Kissimmee, Fla., 1987-89; researcher U. Ctrl. Fla., Orlando, 1989-91; self-employed researcher Orlando, summer 1991; instr. Fla. Atlantic U., Boca Raton, 1991-94, researcher, 1993—; cons. Info Express, Boca Raton, 1993—; mem. faculty U. Ctrl. Fla., Orlando, 1994—. Vol. sidewalker Horses and the Handicapped, Broward County, Fla., 1993, Ft. Lauderdale Br. NAACP Criminal Justice Bd. Mem. AAUW, Phi Kappa Phi, Pi Alpha Alpha. Home: 1700 Woodbury Rd Apt 1608 Orlando FL 32828

DAYANIM, TRUDY BANKS, realtor; b. Portsmouth, Va., Apr. 13, 1941; d. William Alger and Lottie (Abidan) Banks; m. Behrooz Dayanim; children: Behnam, Behzad, Shoshana. BS, Old Dominion U., 1963. Lic. realtor, Va. Tchr. Norfolk (Va.) Pub. Schs., 1963-67, Portsmouth (Va.) Pub. Schs., 1967-68; dir. presch. Gomley Chesed Congregation, Portsmouth, 1970-80; raltor GSH Real Estate, Chesapeake, Va., 1985—. Pres. Hatton Point Civic League, Portsmouth Acad. of Med. Aux., 1972-73. Mem. Portsmouth/Chesapeake Bd. Realtors. Home: 3720 Shoreline Dr Portsmouth VA 23703-4036

DAYHARSH, VIRGINIA FIENGO, educator; b. New Haven, Dec. 2, 1942; d. Edward Arthur and Rose (Giaquinto) Fiengo; m. George R. Dayharsh, Dec. 31, 1966 (div. Nov. 1983); children: Regina Lynn, Jennifer Allison. BA, Coll. of New Rochelle, N.Y., 1964; MA, So. Conn. State U., 1974, cert. advanced study, 1985. Cert. social studies tchr., Conn. Tchr. Troup Jr. High Sch., New Haven, 1964-65, East Haven (Conn.) Jr. High Sch., 1965-69; tchr., dept. chairperson Lauralton Hall, Milford, Conn., 1979-81; tchr. Nathan Hale Ray High Sch., East Haddam, Conn., 1981-85, Naugatuck (Conn.) High Sch., 1985—. Mem. Rep. Town Com., East Haven, 1968-72, Library Bd., East Haven, 1968-81, Bd. of Edn., East Haven, 1986-87. Mem. NEA, Conn. Coun. Social Studies, Conn. Edn. Assn., Naugatuck Tchrs.' League, Conn. Social Studies Coun., Coun. Cath. Women, New Eng. Assn. Schs. and Colls. (evaluation com. 1990, 91, 93, 94), Vietnam Vets. of Am. (assoc.). Home: 578 Thompson Ave East Haven CT 06512-2935

DAYS, RITA DENISE, state legislator; b. Minden, La., Oct. 16, 1950; d. Marion and Juliette (Mitchell) Heard; m. Frank S. Days, June 17, 1972; children: Elliott Charles, Natalie Rechelle, Evelyn Jeanine. BMus, Lincoln U., 1972. Tchr. Webster Parish Sch. Bd., Minden, La., 1972; clk. typist Urban League of St. Louis, 1973-74, asst. dir. pub. info., 1974, placement interviewer, 1974-76; office supr. Burroughs Corp., St. Louis, 1976-80; sec., admissions counselor Jewish Coll. of Nursing, St. Louis, 1989-93; mem. Mo. Ho. of Reps., St. Louis, 1993—; vice chair elections com. Mo. Ho. of Reps., St. Louis, treas. Mo. Legis. Black Caucus, sec. Women's Caucus, mem. Supreme Ct. Task Force on Children and Families. Mem. sch. bd. Normandy Sch. Dist., St. Louis, 1987—; active Ptnrs. for Kids, 1993—, New Sunny Mount Bapt. Ch. Mem. Alpha Kappa Alpha. Democrat. Office: Mo Ho of Reps State Capitol Jefferson City MO 65101

DAYTON, MARY LEE, association volunteer; b. Marshall, Mo., May 12, 1925; d. Arnold and Braddie Lowe; m. Wallace C. Dayton, Oct. 15, 1948; children: Sally, Ellen, Katherine, Elizabeth. BA in Child Study, Vassar Coll., 1946. Tchr. kindergarten Northrop Collegiate Sch., Mpls., 1946-48. Troop leader Girls Scouts of Am., 1955-58; chair YWCA Capital Campaign, 1973-79; co-chair major gifts Minn. Women's Fund, 1983-87, mem. capital campaign steering com.; mem. pastoral nominating com., Westminister Presbyn. Ch., Mpls.; trustee Breck Sch., Mpls., Macalester Coll., chmn. bd. dirs., 1989-92; trustee Vassar Coll., bd. dirs. 1980-81; past chmn. bd. trustees YWCA, Mpls., pres. bd. dirs. 1970-74; nat. bd. dirs. YWCA, chair World Svc. Coun.; chmn. bd. dirs. Ripley Meml. Found. 1968-70, Planned Parenthood of Minn., 1980-82. Recipient Woman of Yr. award Mpls. YWCA, 1974, Leader Lunch award YWCA, 1984, Vol. Svc. award Channel 11, 1985, vol. Fundraiser of Yr. award Minn. chpt. of Nat. Soc. of Fund Raising Execs., Ambassador award YWCA of the U.S.A., 1993. Home: 510 Ferndale Rd W Wayzata MN 55391-9626

DEAGON, JANET BURTON, employee relations coordinator; b. Birmingham, Apr. 29, 1960; d. Daniell Taylor and Hannah Louise (Sanders) Burton; m. Arthur Lloyd Deagon, Dec. 19, 1981; children: Tyler Kent, Brian Daniell. BS in Social Welfare, U. Ala., 1982. Lic. social worker, Ala. Social worker St. Martins in the Pines, Birmingham, 1982-83; classification specialist for social svcs. West Jefferson Correctional Facility, Oak Grove, Ala., 1983-85; customer svc. rep. Blue Cross and Blue Shield of Ala., Birmingham, 1985, employee rels. specialist, 1985-89, employee rels. coord., 1989—. Pres. Bapt. Young Women, Vestavia Hills, Ala., 1987, Loch Haven Neighborhood Club, Hoover, Ala., 1984; mem. Vestavia Hills Bapt. Ch., 1968—, mem. handbell choir, 1985—. Mem. Pers. Assn. Birmingham (v.p. mem. 1992, sec. 1990, bd. dirs. 1989, 91), Soc. Human Resource Mgmt., Leadership Devel. Assn. (bd. dirs. 1990-92, chmn. bd. dirs. 1991-92, sec. 1988-89), Nat. Mgmt. Assn. Home: 2331 Deerwood Rd Birmingham AL 35216 Office: Blue Cross/Blue Shield 450 Riverchase Pkwy East Birmingham AL 35298

DEAL, LUISA, management consultant, trainer, speaker; b. Naples, Italy, July 15, 1943; came to U.S., 1948; d. Elaine (DeMarino) Bonomo; children: Pamela, Mark, Paula. AA, Muskegon Community Coll., Mich., 1967; BA, Saginaw Valley State U., 1969; MA, Cen. Mich. U., 1973; Ednl. Specialist, Mich. State U., 1982. Tchr. Saginaw (Mich.) Twp. Community Schs., 1969-72, reading cons., 1972-77, reading specialist, 1977-86; mgmt. devel. trainer Automobile Club of Mich., Dearborn, 1986; assoc. mgr. ops. Gen. Physics Corp., Troy, Mich., 1987; tng. analyst Ball Systems Engring., San Diego, 1988; pres. Tng. Support Network, La Jolla, Calif., 1989—. Mem. oral history com. San Diego Mus. Contemporary Art, La Jolla, 1989; active Nine-Nines Internat., Detroit and San Diego, 1988—. Mem. ASTD (Detroit chpt. bd. dirs. 1987-88; San Diego chpt. EFO 1989-90, sec. 1990-91), Am. Soc. for Quality Control, Nat. Spkrs. Assn., Deming User Group. Office: Training Support Network PO Box 207 La Jolla CA 92038-0207

DEAL, LYNN EATON HOFFMANN, interior designer; b. Atlantic City, N.J., Nov. 7, 1953; d. Ralph Eaton and Helen P. Hoffmann; m. James A. Deal, Sept. 19, 1981. Diploma in environ. and interior design, U. Calif., Irvine, 1989. Prin. Lynn Deal and Assocs., Newport Beach, Calif., 1982—; mem. adv. bd. U. Calif., Irvine, 1984—. Author: Brunshwis Style, 1995. Chmn. Philharm. Showcase House, 1992. Mem. Am. Soc. Interior Designers (recipient Chpt. award 1991, Pres.'s award 1992, author introductory video Orange County chpt.), Internat. Furnishings and Design Assn., Interior Educators Coun., Internat. Platform Assn. Republican. Episcopalian. Home: 218 Via Palermo Newport Beach CA 92663-5502

DEAL, THERRY NASH, college dean; b. Iredell County, N.C., Apr. 21, 1935; d. Stephen W. and Betty (Sherrill) Nash; m. J.B. Deal, July 10, 1954 (dec. 1990); children: Melaney Dawne, J. Bradley. BS in Home Econs., U. N.C., 1957, MS, 1961, PhD, 1965; postgrad., Harvard U., 1964, 87. Instr. pub. schs. Iredell County, N.C., 1959-61; instr. U. N.C., Greensboro, 1961-65; prof. U. Ga., Athens, 1965-72; dept. chair Ga. Coll., Milledgeville, 1972-82, dir. continuing edn. and pub. svcs., 1982-84, dean continuing edn. and pub. svcs., 1984—; bd. dirs. Pvt. Industry Coun., Baldwin Co., 1985—; vis. prof. China, 1993. Author numerous poems; contbr. articles to profl. jours. Mem. Am. Home Econs. Assn., Nat. Coun. Adminstrs. of Home Econs., Nat. Assn. Edn. of Young Children, Milledgeville/Baldwin County C. of C., DAR. Democrat. Methodist. Office: Ga Coll Clark St Milledgeville GA 31061

DEALY, RUTH FRISCH, artist; b. Boston, May 3, 1947; d. David Henry and Rose Nona (Epstein) Frisch; m. James Bond Dealy III, Sept. 23, 1967; children: Molly Katherine, Emma Miranda Ruby. BFA, R.I. Sch. Design, 1971, MFA, 1973. Founding pres. Loft Horizons, Ltd., Providence, 1974-80; bd. dirs. Gallery One, Providence, 1981—; founding v.p. Regent Pl. Ptnrs., Ltd., Providence, 1992—, also bd. dirs.; bd. dirs. Asszo; vis. critic Brown U., Providence, 1985, 93, vis. lectr., 1988; guest critic R.I. Sch. Design, Providence, 1988—, mem. faculty, 1988—; vis. lectr. U. So. Maine, Portland, 1994. Solo shows include Bayard Gallery, N.Y.C., 1980, Wriston Art Ctr., Appleton, Wis., 1993, Arden Gallery, Boston, 1993. Tchr. Ch. House Settlement, Providence, 1969-70; founding mem. Hartford-Perry Storefrond Sch., Providence, 1970-71; commr. Mayor's Office, Providence, 1975; organizer Artist Against AIDS, Providence, 1988; panelist Conn. Com. on the Arts, Hartford, 1991; judge Wickfort (R.I.) Art Group, 1993, Providence Art Club, 1993, Warwick (R.I.) Art Mus., 1994; juror Scholastic Art Awards, nat., 1994. R.I. State Coun. on Arts fellow, 1986-87, grante, 1974, 75, 90-=91; New Eng. Found. on Arts fellow, 1994—. Mem. AS220 (adv. bd. 1992—, com. capital campaign), Art Advs. R.I. Democrat. Jewish. Office: Regent Plc Ptnrs Ltd 101 Regent Ave Providence RI 02908

DEAN, BARBARA POPE, agent for humanities scholar; b. Hillsdale, Mich., Aug. 27, 1942; d. Raymond Warren and Mary Alice (Powers) Pope; m. William Charles Dean, Aug. 3, 1963; children: Scott William, Stephen Charles. BA, Alma Coll., 1964; postgrad., Mich. State U., 1966-67. Primary tchr. East Lansing (Mich.) Pub. Schs., 1964-67; dir. Pilot Project on Volumtarism Colo. Rep. party, Denver, 1982-83; exec. dir. Ft. Collins (Colo.) Arts/Humanities Coun., 1983-86; arts. devel. dir. Rapid City (S.D.) Arts Coun., 1988-90; agt., scheduler SRW Assocs., Grand Haven, Mich., 1991—. Writer, editor Caucus Courier, supplement to Colo. Statesman. Mem. White House Commn. on Presdl. Scholars, Washington, 1989-92; precinct del. Ottawa County Rep. Com., 1992—; mem. Stille for Ho. of Reps. Campaign, Grand Haven, 1992—; pres. Ottawa County ARC, 1993—, Tri Cities Chautauqua, 1992—; co-chair program Friends West Shore Symphony, 1993—; regional coord. Working Ptnrs. Project Rep. Nat. Com., Washington, 1985-87; mem. physician recruitment com. North Ottawa Cmty. Hosp., 1994—; bd. dirs. Rapid City YMCA, Rapid City Concert Assn., Mus. Alliance. Mem. AAUW (bd. dirs.). Home: 16117 Vandenberg Dr Grand Haven MI 49417 Office: SRW Assocs PO Box 851 Grand Haven MI 49417

DEAN, CARROL C., retired social worker, association executive; b. Bradgate, Iowa, Apr. 20, 1915; d. Leigh Halford and Amy (Tilton) D. BS in Home Econs., Iowa State Tchrs. Coll., 1935-39; MSW, U. Minn., 1953-55. Girls work sec. YWCA, Mason City, Iowa, 1939-42; program dir. USO, YWCA, Alexandria, La., 1942-44, USO, YMCA, Temple, Tex., 1945-46, Army-Navy, YMCA, Shanghai, China, 1946-47; dir. teenagers YWCA, Cinn., 1947-53; exec. dir. YWCA, Lincoln, Nebr., 1955-58; mct. assoc. exec. dir. YWCA, Cleve., 1958-65; exec. dir. YWCA, Rochester, N.Y., 1965-73, St. Louis, 1973-76; dir. ctrl. region nat. bd. YWCA of U.S.A., Chgo., 1976-78; exec. field svcs. nat. bd. YWCA of U.S.A., N.Y.C., 1978-80; mem. state welfare com. Nebr. Welfare Dept., Lincoln, 1957-58; lectr. U. nebr. Sch. Social Work, 1957. Contbr. articles to mags. Mem. exec. com. NASW, Lincoln, Nebr., 1956-58; bd. dirs. Campus Ministries, Cleve., St. Louis, 1959-76; pres., mem. Altrusa Internat., Cleve., 1959-65, Rochester, N.Y., 1965-73, St. Louis, 1973-76; chair dist. fund raising United Way, Cleve., 1960-63; exec. dir. Meridian Hospice, Chgo., 1980-82; bd. dir. Ill. State Hospice, Chgo., 1981-82. Recipient Brotherhood award NCCJ, Cin. 1951. Mem. PEO (rec. sec. 1990—). Democrat. Home: 650 Carla Way La Jolla CA 92037

DEAN, DEAREST (LORENE GLOSUP), songwriter; b. Volin, S.D., Oct. 4, 1911; d. John Henry and Bessie Marie Donnelly Peterson; m. Eddie Dean, Sept. 11, 1931; children: Donna Lee Knorr, Edgar Glosup II. Grad. high sch., Yankton, S.D. Bd. dirs. Acad. Country Music, Hollywood, 1960-62. Composer songs including: One Has My Name, 1948, The Lonely Hours, 1970, 1501 Miles of Heaven, 1970, Walk Beside Me, 1980. Sec. ARC, Burbank, Calif., 1943. Mem. ASCAP. Republican. Roman Catholic. Avocation: golf.

DEAN, DIANE D., youth service agency executive, management consultant; b. Detroit, Aug. 26, 1949; d. Edward Lesley and Ada V. (Spann) D. Student, Mich. State U., 1966-68; BS, N.C. Argl. and Tech. State U., 1971; MS, Ind. U., 1973; postgrad., Stanford U. Summer Inst., 1981, UCLA, 1982-83; cert. in non-profit mgmt., Case Western Res. U., 1991. Area coord. U. Miami, Coral Gables, 1973-75; dir. housing Occidental Coll., L.A., 1975-78; asst. dir. admissions asst. and sch. rels. U. So. Calif., L.A., 1978-80; from asst. dir. to assoc. dir. admissions, dir. ops. LEAD program UCLA, 1980-85; dir. incentive grants and scholarship programs Nat. Action Coun. Minorities in Engring., N.Y.C., 1985-90; mgmt. cons. Girl Scouts of the U.S.A., N.Y.C., 1990—; appointed rep. Grad. Mgmt. Admissions Coun., Santa Monica, Calif., 1981-85. Author and editor: Directory of Minority Pers. Associated with Admissions, 1979-85. Named to J & B Winners Circle, Paddington Corp., N.Y.C., 1984. Mem. NAACP, Nat. Assn. Student Pers. Adminstrn. (regional co-chair 1985), Corporate Women's Network, Assn. Coll. and Univ. Housing Officers (chair, regional membership com.), Assn. Girl Scout Exec. Staff (bd. dirs.), N.Y. Women's Agenda, N.Y. Coalition of 100 Black Women, Trans Africa, Black Women's Forum, Girl Scouts U.S.A. (life), Schomberg Soc. for Preservation of Black Culture, Urban League, UCLA Alumni Assn. (life), N.C. Agrl. and Tech. State U. Alumni Assn., Alpha Kappa Alpha (v.p. 1969-71). Office: Girl Scouts USA 420 5th Ave New York NY 10018-2729

DEAN, JEAN BEVERLY, artist; b. South Paris, Maine, Aug. 23, 1928; d. Henry Dyer and Doris Filena (Judd) Small; m. Samuel Lester Dean. AS, Becker Coll., Worcester, Mass., 1948; AA, Edison Coll., Ft. Myers, Fla., 1980. Artist Ft. Myers, 1963—. One person shows include Edison C.C. Gallery, Ft. Myers, Fla., Joan Ling Gallery, Gainesville, Fla., Berry Coll., Mt. Berry, Ga., Gallery 10, Asheville, N.C., Cape Coral (Fla.) Arts Studio, Barbara B. Mann Performing Arts Hall, Ft. Myers, 1992, Sanibel (Fla.) Gallery, 1993, Barrier Islands Group for the Arts, Sanibel, Fla., 1994, Gallery Mido, Belleview, Mido Resort, Belleair, Fla.; exhibited in group shows at S.E. Painting and Sculpture Exhbn., Jacksonville, Fla., Soc. of Four Arts, Palm Beach, Fla., Southeastern Ctr. for Contemporary Art, Winston-Salem, N.C., LeMoyne Fine Arts, Tallahassee, Clocktower Gallery, N.Y.C., AIR Gallery, San Francisco, Fla. Ctr. for Contemporary Art, Ybor City, Park Shore Gallery, Naples, Fla., 1991, S.W. Fla. Internat. Airport, 1991, 95, Ctr. Art Show, St. Petersburg, Fla., 1991, Lee County Alliance of the Arts, Ft. Myers, 1991, Ridge Juried Art Show, Winter Haven, Fla., 1992, Fla. Artists Group, Sarasota, 1992, Women's Caucus for Art, Sarasota, 1993, Polk Mus., Lakeland, Fla., 1993, Barrier Island Group for the Arts, Sanibel, Fla., 1994, Daytona Mus., Fla., 1994, Women's Caucus Art Nat. Show, San Antonio, 1995; represented in permanent collections U.S. Embassy, Madrid, Edison Coll., First Fed. Savs. and Loan, Ft. Myers and Naples, Fla., NCNB Bank, Tampa, Fla., HealthPark, Ft. Myers, Clara Barton House, Washington, D.C., Hirshhorn Collection. Mem. Lee County Alliance for the Arts, 1994; chair invitational com. Barrier Island Group for the Arts, Sanibel, Fla., 1994. Recipient more than 100 awards. Mem. Nat. Mus. Women in the Arts (charter mem.), Maine Coast Artists, Women's Caucus for Art, Fla. Artists Group. Democrat. Unitarian. Home: 17643 Captiva Island Ln Fort Myers FL 33908

DEAN, LYDIA MARGARET CARTER (MRS. HALSEY ALBERT DEAN), nutrition coordinator, author, consultant; b. Bedford, Va., July 11, 1919; d. Christopher C. and Hettie (Gross) Carter; m. Halsey Albert Dean; children: Halsey Albert Jr., John Carter, Lydia Margerae. Grad., Averett Coll.; BS, Madison Coll., 1941; MS, Va. Poly. Inst. and State U., 1951; postgrad., U. Va., Mich. State U.; PhD, DNSc, UCLA, 1985. Cert. nutrition specialist Am. Coll. Bd. Nutrition. Dietetic intern, clin. dietitian St. Vincent de Paul Hosp., Norfolk, Va., 1942; sr. physicist U.S. Naval Op. Base, Norfolk, 1943-45; clin. dietitian Roanoke Meml. Hosps., 1946-51; assoc. prof. Va. Poly. Inst. and State U., 1946-53; community nutritionist Roanoke, Va., 1953-60; dir. dept. nutrition and dietetics Southwestern Va. Med. Ctr., Roanoke, 1960-67; food and nutrition cons. Nat. Hdqs. ARC, Washington, 1967—; staff and vol. Nat. Hdqs. ARC, 1973—; nutrition scientist, cons. Dept. Army, Washington, 1973—, Dept. Agr., 1973—; pres. Dean Assocs.; cons., assoc. dir. Am. Dietetic Assn., 1975—; coord. new degree program U. Hawaii, 1974-75; dir., nutrition coord. pub. health HHS, Washington, 1973—; mem. task force White House Conf. Food and Nutrition, 1969—; chmn. fed. com. Interagy. Com. on Nutrition Edn., 1970-71; tech. rep. to AID and State Dept.; chmn. Crusade for Nutrition Edn., Washington, 1970—; participant, cons. Nat. Nutrition Policy Conf., 1974. Author: (with Virginia McMasters) Community Emergency Feeding, 1972, Help My Child How to Eat Right, 1963, rev. edit., 1978, The Complete Gourmet Nutrition Cookbook: The Joy of Eating Well and Right, 1978, rev. edit., 1982, The Stress Foodbook, 1980; contbr. articles to profl. jours. Trustee World U., 1987—; apptd. rsch. bd. advisors Am. Biog. Inst., 1990. Named Women's Inner Cir. of Achievement N.Am., 1990. Fellow APHA, Internat. Inst. Comty. Svc.; mem. AAUS (Hall of Fame 1992), Am. Dietetic Assn., Bus. and Profl. Women's Club (cons. 1970—, pres. 1981-82), Am. Home Econs. Assn. (rep. and treas. joint congl. com.), Inst. Food Technologists (blue ribbon spkr. 1972). Home: 7816 Birnam Wood Dr Mc Lean VA 22102-2709

DEAN, SHERRY, news reporter, producer; b. New York, July 31, 1959. BA, NYU, 1980. Copyperson N.Y. Daily News, N.Y.C., 1980-81; newswriter, prodr., reporter WPIX-TV, N.Y.C., 1981-88; prodr., reporter Good Day New York Fox-TV, N.Y.C., 1988-89; freelance newswriter WCBS-TV, WNBC-TV, N.Y.C., 1989; reporter, prodr. entertainment news CNN, N.Y.C., 1990—. Home: 465 E 85th St Apt GB-8 New York NY 10028 Office: CNN Showbiz Today 5 Penn Plz 20th Fl New York NY 10001

DEANE, DEBBE, journalist, editor, consultant; b. Coatesville, Pa., July 30, 1950; d. George Edward and Dorothea Alice (Martin) Mays; widowed; children: Theo, Vonisha, Lorise, Voniece. AA in Psychology, Mesa Coll., 1989; BA Psychology, San Diego State U., 1993. News dir. Sta. KLDR, Denver, 1976-78; host, reporter Sta. KMGH-TV, Denver, 1978-81; news anchor, editor Sta. KHOW, Denver, 1978-79; news & pub. affairs dir. Sta. KLZ, Denver, 1979-80, Sta. KCBQ, San Diego, 1980-82; news anchor Sta. KOGO, San Diego, 1983-84; news anchor, reporter Sta. KCST-TV, San Diego, 1984-87; dir. comm. Omni Corp., San Diego, 1987—; news anchor Sta. KFI, L.A., 1990-91; media liaison United Negro Coll. Fund, San Diego, 1990-92; dir. comm. United Chs. of Christ, San Diego, 1989-92; cons. San Diego Assn. Black Journalists, 1985-92, San Diego Coalition Black Journalists, 1985-92. Campaign fin. analyst San Diego County Registrar of Voters, San Diego, 1990; cons. San Diego County Office Disaster Preparedness, 1990-91, Nu Way Youth Ctr. & Neighborhood House, Inc., San Diego, 1991-92; counselor Project STARRT, San Diego, 1991-92. Recipient San

Diego Black Achievement award Urban League, 1989, Best News Show & Spot News award San Diego Press Club, 1985, Golden Mike award So. Calif. Broadcast Assn., L.A., 1986; named one of Top 25 Businesswomen Essence Mag., 1978, Outstanding Humanitarian Worldvision, 1993, Outstanding Humanities Alumna Mesa Coll., 1993. Mem. AFTRA, APA, Am. Women in Radio & TV, Women in Comm., Black Students Sci. Orgn. (sec. 1989-91), Africana Psychol. Soc. (media coord. 1990-92), Psi Chi. Democrat. Home: 1335 S Woodman St # 3 Paradise Hills CA 92139

DEANE, SALLY JAN, health services administrator, consultant; b. Downey, Calif., Sept. 24, 1948; d. Virgil Eldred and Pearl Jan (Kettell) D. BA, Whittier Coll., 1970; MEd, Boston U., 1971, MPH, 1988. Mgr. community health Peter Bent Brigham Hosp., Boston, 1974-76; coord. WIC program Martha Eliot Health Ctr., 1976-78; dir. S.W. Boston WIC program Shattuck Hosp. Corp., 1978-80; exec. dir. Fenway Community Health Ctr., 1980-84; exec. asst. commr. Boston Dept. Health & Hosps., 1984-86; assoc. dir. spl. projects Health Policy Inst. Boston U., 1986-87; dir. ambulatory reimbursement Mass. Medicaid, 1987-88; assoc. Cambridge (Mass.) Mgmt. Group, 1989; ptnr. Integrated Health Strategies Inc., Cambridge, Mass., 1990—; asst. prof. Pub. Health Boston U., 1994—; cons. Mass. Dept. Pub. Health, Boston, 1978-80, Citicorp Corp. Hdqrs., N.Y.C., 1986. Mem. Mayor's Task Force on AIDS, Boston, 1983-86; v.p. Trustees Charitable Donations, Boston, 1984-88. Mem. Mass. Pub. Health Assn., Am. Pub. Health Assn., Women in Health Care Mgmt. Presbyterian. Home: 115 University Rd Brookline MA 02146-4545 Office: Integrated Health Strategies Inc 675 Massachusetts Ave Cambridge MA 02139-3309

DEANEHAN, REGINA M., federal commissioner; b. Easton, Pa.; d. Charles F. Sr. and Bertha C. (Back) Renz. BS, Georgian Ct. Coll., 1964; student, Loyola Coll., 1967-70; MPA, Syracuse U., 1987. Revenue agent IRS, Balt., 1967-75, br. chief, 1975-77; exec. asst. to asst. regional commr. IRS, Phila., 1977-80, asst. regional commr., 1980-86; asst. dist. dir. IRS, Hartford, Conn., 1987-88; dir. planning divsn., dep. asst. commr. planning, fin. and rsch. IRS, 1988-89, asst. commr. planning and rsch., 1989-90; asst. commr. IRS, Washington, 1990—. Office: Internal Rev Svcs 950 L'Enfant Plz SW Rm 4401 Washington DC 20024*

DE ANGELIS, DEBORAH ANN AYARS, university athletics official; b. San Diego, July 2, 1948; d. Charles Orvil and Janet Isabel (Glithero) Ayars; m. David C. De Angelis, Sept. 29, 1984. B.A., U. Calif.-Santa Barbara, 1970, Certificate in Social Services, 1972; M.S., U. Mass., 1979. Eligibility worker County Welfare Dept., Santa Barbara, Calif., 1970-73; women's crew coach, U. Mass., 1978-79, Northeastern U., Boston, 1979-83, bus. mgr. women's athletics, 1983-87, asst. dir. bus., 1987-89; mgr. athletics bus. Calif. State U., Northridge, 1989-93, assoc. dir., 1993—; com. mem. Women's Olympic Rowing Com., 1976-84; life trustee Nat. Rowing Found., 1984; life mem. selection com. Rowing Found. Hall of Fame, 1984—, bd. dirs., 1994—; rowing mgr. Women's Olympic Team, 1976, 80; head mgr. U.S. Olympic Festival, Syracuse, N.Y., 1981, coach, Indpls., 1982, Colorado Springs, Colo., 1983; mem. alcohol and drug awareness com. Northeastern U., 1983. Mem. Nat. Women's Rowing Assn. (pres. 1976-80, Woman of Yr. award 1983), Fedn. Sociétés d'Aviron (women's commn. 1978—, U.S. del. to ann. congress 1978, 80-88), U.S. Rowing Assn. (del. 1988, bd. dirs. 1975-80, 85—, co-chmn. internat. div., co-chmn. events div. 1985-86, chmn. internat. div. 1986-88, women's v.p. 1985-88, mem. exec. com. 1985-89, exec. v.p. 1988-89), Calif. State U. Northridge Intercollegiate Athletics Oversight Adv. Bd., Tri C. of C. July 4th Spectacular Com. Club: ZLAC Rowing. Home: 430 Jeremiah Dr Simi Valley CA 93065-1672

DEANGELIS, MARGARET SCALZA, publishing executive; b. Jersey City, May 27, 1936; d. Louis Patrick and Josephine M. (Cleary) Scalza; m. David Jenkins, Sept. 30, 1951 (div. 1962); children: Alison Brittain, Cynthia Higgins, Ann Marie; m. Henry DeAngelis, Aug. 28, 1977; children: Valerie, Brenda DeAngelis Falato, Louise DeAngelis Brine, Henry Jr. Owner Towne House Restaurant, Hackettstown, N.J., 1963-65; pres. Kinsley Assocs., Inc., Florham Park, N.J., 1966—, Kinsley Publs., Inc., Florham Park, 1972—; pub. purchasing guides, sch. directories, N.J., N.Y., Calif., Ill. Co-chmn. Northwestern N.J. divsn. U.S. Postal Customer Coun., 1978—. Mem. Nat. Assn. Sch. Bus. Ofcls., Morris County Bd. Realtors, Nat. Assn. Female Execs., Hackettstown Trade Assn. (sec.-treas., bd. dirs. 1963). Republican. Roman Catholic. Home: 20 E Madison Ave Florham Park NJ 07932-2634 Office: 8 Ridge Rd Hackettstown NJ 07840-4602

DEANGELIS, SUSAN PENNY, human resources professional; b. N.Y.C., Nov. 20, 1950; s. Milton Abraham and Anne Pearl (Fleischer) Zwilling; m. Ivo DeAngelis, July 25, 1971 (div. Feb. 1982); m. Benjamin H. Pfeffer, May 17, 1985. BA cum laude, Bklyn. Coll., 1971. Spl. projects coordinator, customer service rep. N.Y. Property Ins. Underwriting Assocs., N.Y.C., 1971-72; office mgr. Pyramid Personnel Agy., N.Y.C., 1972-73; v.p. human resources Feature Enterprises Inc., N.Y.C., 1973-92; cons. JWJ Enterprises, Inc., N.Y.C., 1984-85; dir. pers. Hebrew Immigrant Aid Soc. Inc., N.Y.C., 1992—; mem. bus. adv. com. RUSK Inst. of Rehab., 1993—. N.Y. State Bd. Regents scholar, 1967. Mem. N.Y. Assn. New Ams. (chairperson pvt. sector adv. com. 1985-93), Pers. Assn. of Non-Profit Orgns. (mem. exec. com. 1993—), U.S. Power Squadrons (lt. comdr.). Avocations: photography, calligraphy, painting, boating. Home: 2258 E 27th St Brooklyn NY 11229-5030 Office: Hebrew Immigrant Aid Soc Inc 333 7th Ave New York NY 10001

DEANS, JANICE P., librarian, media specialist, consultant; b. Daytona Beach, Fla., July 17, 1958; d. William Frederick Peshek and Patricia Anne (Woolley) Parrish. AA, Daytona Beach Community Coll., 1977; B in Liberal Studies, U. Cen. Fla., 1982, EdM in Media, 1987. Library asst. City Island Pub. Library, Daytona Beach, 1978-79, U. Cen. Fla., Daytona Beach, 1981-83; head media specialist St. Brendan Sch., Ormond Beach, Fla., 1983, Father Lopez High Sch., Daytona Beach, 1983-89; media specialist, TV prodn. tchr. Taylor High Sch., Pierson, Fla., 1989-92; dept. head media svcs. Deland High Sch. Media Ctr., Deland, Fla., 1992—. Recipient Apostolic Devel. Fund award Oblates of St. Francis de Sales, 1985, 86, Volusia County Leatha Garrison award, 1990; Tchr. Opportunities for Projects in Schs. grantee, 1989, Futures grantee, 1990-91, 1992-93. Mem. Volusia Assn. for Media in Edn., Fla. Assn. for Media in Edn. Democrat. Home: 323 Daytona Ave Daytona Beach FL 32117-3719 Office: Deland High Sch Media Center 800 N Hill Ave Deland FL 32724

DEANS, SUSAN CHRISTINE, newspaper editor; b. Chgo., Apr. 3, 1948; d. Russell Henry Schlaufman and Olive Claire Dahl; m. William O. Foss, June 22, 1968 (div. 1973); 1 child, Jeffrey W.; m. Malcolm A. Deans, Dec. 13, 1975. BA in English, Knox Coll., 1970; MA in Journalism, U. Colo., 1975. Pub. info. officer Carl Sandburg Coll., Galesburg, Ill., 1970-71; various part-time positions, 1971-77; from reporter to asst. mng. editor The Daily Camera, Boulder, Colo., 1977-87; mng. editor The Sun News, Myrtle Beach, S.C., 1987-90, editor, v.p., 1990—. Mem. steering com. Grass Roots Initiative for Planning and Progress, Myrtle Beach, S.C., 1992-93, Coastal Communities for Excellence, Myrtle Beach, 1992-93; active Harry County Human Rels. Coun., Myrtle Beach, 1990-92. Mem. Am. Soc. Newspaper Editors, Nat. Fedn. Press Women, AP Mng. Editors (bd. dirs. 1991—), S.C. AP News Coun. (bd. dirs. 1992—), Investigative Reporters & Editors, Myrtle Beach Rotary Club (bd. dirs. 1993—). Home: 5519 Springs Ave Myrtle Beach SC 29577-2313 Office: The Sun News PO Box 406 914 Frontage Rd E Myrtle Beach SC 29577-6700

DEARBORN, LAURA, advertising agency executive. Former sr. v.p. Dancer Fitzgerald & Sample (now Saatchi & Saatchi), San Francisco; now exec. v.p. Saatchi & Saatchi, San Francisco. Office: Saatchi & Saatchi 1010 Battery St San Francisco CA 94111-1202

DEARBORN, MAUREEN MARKT, speech and language clinician; b. Brockton, Mass., Jan. 19, 1948; d. Francis Joseph and Marjorie Agnes (White) M.; m. James Clement Bovin, Nov. 6, 1970 (div. June 1973); m. David C. Dearborn, Jan. 14, 1989. BA in Speech Pathology and Audiology, U. Mass., 1970; MA in Ednl. Psychology, Am. Internat. Coll., Springfield, Mass. Speech and lang. clinician Holyoke (Mass.) Pub. Schs., 1970—. Chmn. Holyoke Cancer Crusade, 1985; voter registration chmn. Holyoke Dem. Com., 1987; chmn. deaconesses 2d Congl. Ch. Holyoke. Mem. Hampden County Tchrs. Assn. (pres. 1981, 87, sec. 1982, v.p. 1984-86, treas. 1988—), Holyoke Tchrs. Assn. (treas. 1989, DAR historian), Am. Speech, Hearing and Langs. Assn. (continuing edn. adv. bd. 1988-91, congl. action contact continuing edn. adv. bd. 1988-90), Mass. Tchrs. Assn., Mass. Speech, Hearing and Langs. Assn., New England Hist. and Geneal. Soc., Friends of the Lib. Coun. (treas. 1992—), Mass. Genealogical Soc., Assn. for Gravestone Studies, DAR (historian Eunice Day 1984), Wrentham Hist Soc., Dorchester Hist. Soc. Home: 257 W Franklin St Holyoke MA 01040-2210 Office: Holyoke Pub Schs 57 Suffolk St Holyoke MA 01040-4458

DEARDORFF, ELEANOR FREEDMAN, public relations executive; b. Chgo., Mar. 1, 1962; d. Jerome Kenneth and Carol Ann (Rosenburg) Freedman; m. Craig Stephen Deardorff, Apr. 13, 1991; 1 child, Peter. BA in Eng. Lit. cum laude, Wheaton Coll., 1983. Account exec. Edelman Pub. Rels., N.Y.C., 1985-86, The Equity Group, N.Y.C., 1986; sr. account exec. Ecom Cons., N.Y.C., 1986-87; v.p. Edelman Pub. Rels., N.Y.C., 1987-91; pres. Deardorff Pub. Rels., Princeton, N.J., 1991—; cons. Gillespie Pub. Rels., 1994—. Mem. Wheaton Club. Office: Deardorff Pub Rels 308 Gallup Rd Princeton NJ 08540

DEARE, JENNIFER LAURIE, marketing professional; b. N.Y.C., Jan. 2, 1952; d. Bruce L. and Maxine L. (Schachter) Schneider; m. Jeffrey Cahn. Student, New Eng. Coll., Arundel, Eng.; BA in Fine Arts, Montclair State. Account executive Al Carlisle & Assocs., N.Y.C., 1979-81; account supr. The Hanley Partnership, N.Y.C., 1981-83; v.p. Walter Coddington Assoc., N.Y.C., 1983-87; pres. Deare Mktg., Inc., N.Y.C., 1987—. Fund raiser ARC, N.Y.C., 1988; bd. dirs. N.Y. Exploring div. Boy Scouts Am. Mem. Promotion Mktg. Assn. Am., Women's Direct Response Group. Office: Deare Mktg Inc 149 Fifth Ave New York City NY 10010

DEARMOND, BERNADETTE NAUGHTON, physician; b. Phila., Apr. 7, 1944; d. James Joseph and Emelia (Cundro) Naughton; m. Stephen J. De Armond, Apr. 6, 1968; children: Daniel, Jennifer. AB, Immcaulta Coll., 1966; MD, Med. Coll. Pa., 1970; MPH, U. Calif., Berkeley, 1983. Diplomate Am. Bd. Pediatricians. From intern to resident Med. Coll. Phila., 1970-72; physician St. Christopher's Hosp., Phila.; Physician pvt. practice, Half Moon Bay, Calif., 1975-78, Family Health Found., Alvislo, Calif., 1978-81, Loyola Pediatrics, Los Altos, Calif., 1981-83; assoc. pub. health officer Santa Clara County Health Dept., San Jose, Calif., 1983-87; assoc. med. dir. Syntex Labs., Palo Alto, Calif., 1987-88; dept. head Syntex Rsch., Palo Alto, Calif., 1988-90, group dir., 1990-92; v.p. med. affairs Syntex Labs., Palo Alto, Calif., 1992—. Contbr. articles to profl. jours. Home: 3571 Bryant St Palo Alto CA 94306 Office: Syntex Labs Inc 3401 Hillview Palo Alto CA 94303

DE ARTEAGA-MORGAN, IVETTE, school administrator; b. Santurce, P.R., Aug. 28, 1931; d. Julio Carlos and Irma (Ortiz) de Arteaga; m. Robert H. Morgan, June 13, 1959; children: Robert, Joseph, Elizabeth, Michael. BA in Liberal Arts, Polit. Sci., Spanish and Edn., Coll. Mt. St. Vincent, 1954; MA, Hofstra U., 1957; postgrad., Hunter Coll., 1959, Fla. Atlantic U., 1970; DA in Higher Edn. and Reading, U. Miami, 1976. Cert. elem. tchr., adminstrn. and supervision, reading clinician, lang. tchr., vis. tchr./social worker. Elem. tchr. 3rd, 5th and 6th grades Merrick (N.Y.) Schs., 1954-57; caseworker Cath. Foster Care Svcs., N.Y.C., 1957-58; adminstr. Lennox Hill Settlement House, N.Y.C., 1958-60; elem. tchr. disadvantaged students Roseville (Mich.) Sch. Bd., 1960-61; instr. modern lang. dept. U. Wis., Eau Claire, 1966-68; vis. tchr., social worker inner-city blacks and hispanics Miami, Fla., 1968-70; coord. Spanish Curriculum Devel. Ctr., Miami, 1970-73; assoc. prof. edn., chairperson edn., supr. student teaching Biscayne Coll., Miami, 1975-78; project mgr. Bilingual Alternative for Secondary Edn., Miami, 1978-82; asst. prin. Citrus Grove Mid. Sch., Miami, 1982-84, McMillan Mid. Sch., Miami, 1984-86; coord. Dept. Community Participation, Miami, 1986-88, Project Stay in Sch., Miami, 1988-89; asst. prin. Palmetto Adult and Community Edn. Ctr., Miami, 1989—; adj. prof. edn. Fla. Internat. U., 1976—; cons. Lau Desegration Ctr., Miami, 1973-89, Key West Sch. (Fla.) Bd., 1976-86, Pub. Sch. 25, Bronx, N.Y., 1970, Miccosukee (Fla.) Adult Edn., 1978, Del. Sch. Bd., numerous others; coord. Bilingual Tng. Classroom Tchrs., Hartford, Conn., Reading Bilingual Classroom, New Haven, Bilingual Curriculum, Phila.; field reader U.S. Dept. Edn., U.S. HHS; presenter, proposal writer in field; chair bd. dirs. League United Latin Am. Citizens Nat. Ednl. Svc. Ctr., Inc. Fla. Contbr. articles to profl. jours. Vol. social worker Cath. Welfare, 1961-66; bd. dirs. Coalition of Hispanic Mental Health and Human Svcs. Orgn., Fla. Cares, La Raza Fla., treas., Dade County's Youth and Family Devel., 1981—; mem. Community Rels. Bd., 1983—, Dem. Exec. Com., Fla., 1988—; past treas. Orgn. P.R. Dems., Fla., 1985; past sec. Coalition Hispanic Women, Fla., 1982; mem. adv. bd. South Fla. Employment and Tng. Consortium; vice chair Gov.'s Commn. Hispanic Affairs, 1984-89; active Women's Polit. Caucus. Recipient Cert. of Merit, Yeshiva U., Dept. Human Resources award Office Neighborhood Svc. Ctrs.; St. Vincent Coll. scholar, 1950-54, N.Y. State scholar, 1959, U. Miami fellow, 1973-77, W.K. Kellogg Found. fellow, 1980, 81. Mem. AAUW, ASCD, ASPIRA (v.p. personnel 1981-87), ASPIRA Fla. (founder, chair 1980—), Nat. Assn. Tchrs. English Speakers Other Langs., Nat. Mental Health Assn., Nat. Assn. for Bilingual Edn. (presentor nat. confs.), Nat. Assn. Latino Elected and Apptd. Ofcls. (founding mem.), Nat. Assn. Tchrs. English, Nat. Conf. Puerto Rican Women (nat. 1st v.p., founder, pres. Miami chpt., Educator of Yr. 1980), Fla. Tchrs. English to Speakers Other Langs. (minority com.), Bilingual Assn. Fla. (sec. 1978, v.p. 1980), Fla. Fgn. Lang. Assn., Am. Coun. on Learning Disabilities, Am. Pers. and Guidance Assn., Fla. Pers. and Guidance Assn. (bd. dirs.), Fla. Assn. for Supervision and Curriculum Devel., Internat. Reading Assn., Fla. Coun. Reading Assn., Bilingual Multicultural Consortium (bd. dirs.), Dade County Sch. Adminstrs. Assn. (legis. com.), Nat. P.R. Coalition, Inc. (bd. dirs.), Am. Hispanic Educators Assn. Dade, Miami Hispanic Club (sec. 1985-87, scholarship chair), Phi Delta Kappa, Epsilon Tau Lambda. Roman Catholic. Home: 6675 SW 55 Ln South Miami FL 33155 Office: Miami Palmetto Adult and Community Edn Ctr 7460 SW 118th St Miami FL 33156

DEATON, GWENDILYN JEANETTE, secondary education educator, gifted/talented; b. Camden, Ark., Jan. 10, 1950; d. Jewell Hollis and Frances Delno (Riggs) Stough; m. Charles Edward Deaton, Dec. 21, 1968; children: Tanya Lynette Deaton Ruble, Christie Rachelle, Micah Jeffrey. BS in Edn., Ark. State U., 1974; MS in Edn., U. Ark., 1988. Tchr. Carthage (Ark.) Sch., 1974-75; tchr. Delight (Ark.) Sch., 1975—, gifted/talented coord., 1986—, ACT program planner, 1992—; acad. coach Delight (Ark.) Sch., 1987—, counselor for students, 1990—. Leader 4-H, Delight, 1984-94. Named Tchr. of Yr., C. of C., Delight, 1994. Mem. Ark. Assn. for Gifted and Talented Edn., 4-H Alumni. Baptist.

DEBAKEY, LOIS, science communications educator, writer, lecturer, editor, scholar; b. Lake Charles, La.; d. S. M. and Raheeja (Zorba) DeBakey. BA in Math., Tulane U., 1949, MA in Lit. and Linguistics, 1959, PhD in Lit. and Linguistics, 1963. Asst. prof. English Tulane U., 1963-64; asst. prof. sci. communication Tulane U. Med. Sch., 1963-65, assoc. prof. sci. communication, 1965-67, prof. sci. comm., 1967-68, lectr., 1968-80, adj. prof., 1981-92; prof. sci. comm. Baylor Coll. Medicine, Houston, 1968—; mem. biomed. libr. rev. com. Nat. Libr. Medicine, Bethesda, Md., 1973-77, bd. regents, 1981-86, cons., 1986—, co-chmn. permanent paper task force, 1987—, lit. selection tech. rev. com., 1988-93, chmn., 1992-93, outreach planning panel, 1988-89; dir. courses in med. comm. ACS and other orgns.; exec. coun. Commn. on Colls. So Assn. Colls and Schs., 1975-80; mem. nat. adv. coun. U. So. Calif. Ctr. Continuing Med. Edn., 1981—, steering com. Plain English Forum, 1984, founding bd. dirs. Friends Nat. Libr. Medicine, 1985—, chmn. med. media award of excellence com. FNLM, 1992-95, adv. com. Soc. for Preservation English Lang. Literature., 1986—, Nat. Adv. Bd. John Muir Med. Film Festival, 1990-92, The Internat. Health and Med. Film Festival, Acad. of Judges, 1992-93; mem. adv. coun. U. Tex. at Austin Sch. Nursing Found., 1993—; cons. legal writing com. ABA, 1983—; former cons. Nat. Assn. Standard Med. Vocabulary; pioneered instruction in sci. communication in med. schs. Sr. author: The Scientific Journal: Editorial Policies and Practices, 1976; co-author: Medicine: Preserving the Passion, 1987; mem editorial bd.: Tulane Studies in English, 1966-68, Cardiovascular Research Center Bull., 1971-83, Health Communications and Informatics, 1975-80, Forum on Medicine, 1977-80, Grants Mag, 1978-81, Internat. Jour. Cardiology, 1981-86, Excerpta Medica's Core Jours. in Cardiology, 1981—, Health Comm. and Biopsychosocial Health, 1981-82, Internat. Angiology, 1985—, Jour. AMA, 1988—; mem. usage panel: Am. Heritage Dictionary, 1980—; cons. Webster's Medical Desk Dictionary, 1986; contbd. articles on biomed. communication and sci. writing, literacy, also other subjects to profl. jours., books, encys., and pub. press. Active Found. for Advanced Edn. in Sci., 1977—. Recipient Disting. Svc. award Am. Med. Writers Assn., 1970, Bausch & Lomb Sci. award, 1st John P. McGovern award Med. Libr. Assn., 1983, Outstanding Alumnae award Newcomb Coll., 1994. Fellow Am. Coll. Med. Informatics, Royal Soc. for the Encouragement of Arts Manufactures and Commerce; mem. Internat. Soc. Gen. Semantics, Med. Libr. Assn. (hon.), Coun. Biology Editors (dir. 1973-77, chmn. com. on editorial policy 1971-75), Coun. Basic Edn. (spl. commn. writing 1977-79), Assn. Tchrs. Tech. Writing, Dictionary Soc. N.Am., Nat. Assn. Sci. Writers, Soc. for Health and Human Values, Com. of Thousand for Better Health Regulations, Golden Key Nat. Hon. Soc. (hon.), Phi Beta Kappa (Outstanding alumna award Newcome Coll. 1994). Office: Baylor Coll Medicine One Baylor Plz Houston TX 77030

DEBAKEY, SELMA, science communication educator, writer, editor, lecturer; b. Lake Charles, La.. BA, Newcomb Coll., Tulane U., New Orleans, postgrad. Dir. dept. med. communication Ochsner Clinic and Alton Ochsner Med. Found., New Orleans, 1942-68; prof. sci. communication Baylor Coll. Medicine, Houston, 1968—; editor Cardiovascular Research Ctr. Bull., 1970-84; mem. panel judges Internat. Health and Med. Film Festival, 1992. Author: (with A Segaloff and K. Meyer) Current Concepts in Breast Cancer, 1967; former editor Ochsner Clinic Reports, Selected Writings from the Ochsner Clinic; contbr. numerous articles and chpts. to sci. jours. Mem. AAAS, Soc. Tech. Communication, Assn. Tchrs. Tech. Writing, Am. Med. Writers Assn. (past bd. dirs.; publ., nominating, fellowship, constn., bylaws, awards, and edn. coms.), Council Biol. Editors (past mem. trn. in sci. writing com.), Soc. Health and Human Values, Modern Med. Monograph Awards Com., Nat. Assn. Standard Med. Vocabulary (former cons.). Office: Baylor Coll Medicine 1 Baylor Plz Houston TX 77030-3498

DE BARBIERI, MARY ANN, nonprofit management consultant; b. Winston-Salem, N.C., May 1, 1945; d. Robert Carroll and Annie Louise (Neal) Hutcherson; m. Alfredo Emanuelle De B.; children: Maria Luisa, Riccardo Roberto. BA in Theatre Arts, Mary Washington Coll., 1967; student, Herbert Berghof Studio, 1967-69. With J. Walter Thompson, N.Y.C., 1967-68; asst. to producer Norman Twain Prodns., N.Y.C., 1968-69, Contemporary Theatre Co., N.Y.C., 1971-74; co. mgr. Folger Theatre Group, Washington, 1974-77, bus. mgr., 1977-80; mng. dir. Shakespeare Theatre at the Folger, Washington, 1980-90; performing arts cons. Alexandria, Va., 1990-92; dir. The Found. Ctr., Washington, 1992-94; pres. De Barbieri and Assocs., 1994—; adj. prof. arts mgmt. grad. program Am. U., 1994—; treas. League of Washington Theatres, 1983-86. Bd. dirs. Washington Area Lawyers for Arts, 1984—, Cultural Alliance Greater Washington, 1986—; chair Performing Arts Coun., Alexandria, Va., 1981-84; chair Alexandria Commn. for Arts, 1984-88, theatre commr., 1984—; contbr. to study of downtown stages for new theatre in Washington, 1985; v.p., bd. dirs. Cultrual Alliance Greater Washginton, 1990—; mem. panel Va. Commn. for the Arts, 1990—. Recipient Outstanding Svc. to Theatre Community award League of Washington Theatres, 1990. Home and office: 3812 Ft Worth Ave Alexandria VA 22304-1709

DEBARDELEBEN, MARIAN ZALIS, industrial librarian; b. New Brunswick, N.J., Sept. 30, 1946; d. Albert Anthony and Anita (Karch) Zalis; m. John F. DeBardeleben (div.). BA in Spanish and Eng. Lit., U. N.H., 1968; MS in Info. Sci., SUNY, Albany, 1969. Asst. libr. Philip Morris USA, Research Ctr., Richmond, 1969-73; assoc. libr. Philip Morris USA, Researh Ctr., Richmond, 1973-74; info. analyst, tech. writer Philip Morris USA, Research Ctr., Richmond, 1974-78, research scientist, 1978-85, assoc. sr. scientist, info. ctr. leader, 1985-91, assoc. sr. scientist, project leader strategic information, 1991-93, sect. leader, info. svcs. devel. and support, 1993—; cons. Bus. Govt. Editor: Dictionary of Tobacco Terminology, 1978, 2d edit., 1986. Mem. Spl. Librs. Assn., Am. Chem. Soc., Soc. Competitive Intelligence Profls. Home: 2106 Rocky Point Pky Richmond VA 23233-3625 Office: Philip Morris Rsch Ctr 4201 Commerce Rd Richmond VA 23234-2269

DE BATRES, REGINA PRADO, artist; b. Guatemela City, Guatemala, Aug. 14, 1943; d. Martin and Marta (Cobos) Prado Velez; m. Luis Arturo Batres Santolino, Jan. 7, 1967; children: Isabel, Arturo, Regina, Martin. B in Sci. and Letters, Colegio Monte María, Guatemala City, 1960; student, Nat. Sch. Art, Guatemala City, 1985-89. With acctg. Inst. Guatemala-Americano, Guatemala City, 1961-65; tchr. English Guatemala City, 1961-63, tchr. art., 1981-85; Guatemalan rep. VI Biennial Latin Am. Art, Mexico City, 1990; judge art Alianza Francesa, Guatemala, 1992; mem. panel women Guatemalan art U. San Carlos, Guatemala, 1993. One woman shows include Guatemalan Am. Inst., 1964, Ixchel Mus. Indian Dress, Guatemala, 1987, 89, Nat. Mus. Modern Art, 1991; group exhibitions include Biblioteca Nacional, Guatemala, 1985, El Tunel Gallery, Guatemala, 1985, 86, 87, 88, 89, 90, Expo-Guatel, 1985, Centro Cultural Universitario, Guatemala, 1988, Reencuentro por el Arte, Guatemala, 1989, Hispanic Culture Inst., 1989. Mem. Nat. Mus. Women Arts. Roman Catholic. Office: 444 Brickell Ave Ste 51-187 Miami FL 33131-2403

DEBENEDICTIS, JOANNE, elementary school educator; b. Jersey City, Nov. 26, 1949; m. Anthony DeBenedictis, Nov. 16, 1973; children: Nicole, Joseph. BA in Early Childhood Edn., Jersey City State Coll., 1974, MA Reading Specialist, 1993. Cert. elem. and early childhood tchr., cert. K-12, N.J. Tchr. Jersey City Head Start Program, 1974-75; tchr. Our Lady of Victories Sch., Jersey City, 1983—, tchr. 2nd grade, 1991—. Mem. ASCD, Internat. Reading Assn., N.J. Reading Assn., Nat. Coun. Tchrs. English, Cath. Tchrs. Sodality, Hudson Reading Coun., Alpha Upsilon Alpha (pres.). Roman Catholic. Home: 42 Williams Ave Jersey City NJ 07304

DEBERRY, FREDERICKA JOAN, library paraprofessional; b. Houston, Nov. 28, 1940; d. Rudolph Louis and Louise Alvina (Dabelgott) Richter; m. James Ellis DeBerry, Dec. 23, 1961 (dec. July 1992); children: Jennifer, James, Geoffrey. Student, Austin Coll., 1958-61, Pan Am. U., 1971-72. Cert. libr. paraprofl., Tex. Libr. paraprofl. Clear Creek Ind. Sch. Dist., Houston, 1977—. Co-author: The Richland Community, 1990; contbr. articles to profl. jours. Mem. Round Top Area Hist. Soc., German Free Sch. Guild. Mem. UDC, German-Am. Partnership Program (sponsor), German-Texan Heritage Soc. (bd. dirs., sec. 1988—, publicity chair 1987-92), Houston-Leipzig Sister City Assn., Clayton Libr. Friends (1st v.p. 1991-92), Winedale Hist. Soc., Round Top Hist. Soc. Presbyterian. Home: 1023 Kemberton Dr Houston TX 77062-2717

DEBIAGI, ANNA LILLIAN, retired educator; b. N.Y.C., July 21, 1930; d. Giovanni-Battista and Michelina (Caramanna) Pollara; m. Giovanni DeBiagi, Nov. 19, 1955; children: Gianni Deo, Maria-Michelina Cologera. BA, CUNY, 1952; MA, Columbia U., 1957; postgrad., L.I. U., 1977. Tchr. Massapequa (N.Y.) Pub. Schs., 1953-87. Tchr. Ch. St. John the Bapt., Bronx, 1952-54, supt. 1954-56; instr. CPR, Am. Heart Assn., 1976-78; tchr. rep. PTA. Mem. AAUW (chmn. 1964-65, pres. 1977-79, chmn. 1981—, Commendation award 1982, Eleanor Roosevelt Found. name grant 1990), Am. Italian Hist. Soc., Hist. Soc. Massapequas, Massapequa Fedn. Ret. Tchrs., Lang. Club. Home: 80 Avoca Ave Massapequa Park NY 11762-3019

DEBLASIO, DONNA MARIE, history museum curator; b. Youngstown, Ohio, Dec. 11, 1953; d. Alessio and Clotilda Mary (DiLullo) DeB.; m. Brian Roland Corbin, July 25, 1992. BA in History magna cum laude, Youngstown State U., 1974, MA in History, 1976; PhD in History, Kent State U., 1980. Grad. asst. Youngstown (Ohio) State U., 1974-76; tchg. fellow Kent (Ohio) State U., 1976-80; oral history field resident Ind. U., Bloomington, Ind., 1980-82; mus. mgr. Ohio Hist. Soc., Youngstown, 1985-94; history curator Ohio Hist. Soc., Columbus, Ohio, 1994—; part-time history instr. Youngstown State U., 1982-85. Sec. bd. dirs. Youngstown Area Arts Coun., 1993—; mem. labor studies adv. bd. Youngstown State U., 1991—; active Diocesan Commn. on Role of Women in Ch. and Soc., Youngstown, 1993—. Mem. Am. Assn. State and Local History, Ohio Acad. History, Oral History Assn., Oral History in Ohio (treas.), Rotary Club of Youngstown. Roman Catholic. Home: 30 Vermont Ave Youngstown OH 44512 Office: Ohio Hist Soc 1982 Velma Ave Columbus OH 43211

DEBOLD, CYNTHIA ANN, sculptor; b. Lexington, Ky., June 12, 1950; d. Louis Bryan and Consuelo (Lopez) Skaggs; m. William Frank Debold, Nov. 16, 1974 (div. July 1989); children: James Patrick, Casey Louis. AA, Orange Coast Coll., 1971, Art Ctr. Coll. of Design, 1973. instr. in field. Exhibited in numerous nat. juried art shows. Mem. Internat. Sculpture Ctr., Tex. Soc. Sculptors (chmn. Sculpfest 1993, pres. 1993-95), Tex. Sculpture Assn., Tex. Fine Arts Assn., Austin Visual Arts Assn., Austin C. of C. (bus. com. for the arts 1993—). Studio: 1117 W 5th # D Austin TX 78703

DE BONA, EVE, artist, foundation administrator; b. L.A., Nov. 10, 1941; d. Joseph Claiborne and Evelyn Mae (Lewis) De B.; m. James Bancroft Gore (div.); children: Leslie Selene, Ariel Fiona; m. John Stillman Duryea, June 5, 1976. BFA, San José State U., MA, 1983. Exec. dir., founder Helias Found. Art & Human Rights, Palo Alto, Calif., 1985—; guest lectr. Stanford U. Law Sch., Stanford U. Luth. Ctr., U. Calif. at Davis, San José State U., San José Bilingual Consortium, U. Nev. Sch. of Medicine, John F. Kennedy U., others, 1981—; artist/poet in residence Calif. Schs., San Quentin State Prison; organizer, curator travelling art exhbns. with human rights theme Georgetown U., U. Calif. at Berkeley, Stanford U., Utah State U., Ohio State U., Redding (Calif.) Mus. & Art Ctr., U. Ala., So. Oreg. State U., others, 1983-93. Bd. dirs. Palo Alto (Calif.) Chinese Sch., 1980-82; mem. Amnesty Internat., Palo Alto, 1977-85. Recipient 5th Place award Am. Artist, 1985; grantee Calif. Arts Coun., 1985-89. Democrat. Office: Helias Found Art & Human Rights 405 Lincoln Ave Palo Alto CA 94301

DE BRUN, SHAUNA DOYLE, investment banker; b. Boston, June 3, 1956; d. John Justin and Marie Therese (Carey) Doyle; m. Seamus Christopher de Brun, July 24, 1982; children: Brendan Joseph, Kieran Christopher. Student U. Salzburg, 1974-75; BA, Mt. Holyoke Coll., 1978; postgrad. Harvard U., 1981-82; M in Internat. Fin. Columbia U., 1984. Cert. fin. analyst. Assoc., Salomon Brothers, N.Y.C., 1978; research assoc. Kennedy Sch. Govt., Cambridge, Mass., 1979-80; faculty assoc. Harvard Bus. Sch., 1980-81; fgn. expert Beijing Normal U., Peoples Republic China, 1981-82; assoc. dir. N.Y. Capital Resources, N.Y.C., 1984-85; ptnr. Eppler & Co., Denver, 1985-87, pres., Teaneck, N.J., 1987-88; v.p. fin. Patten Corp., Stamford, Vt., 1988-91; pres. Serfimex USA, Inc., 1991-92; vice-chmn. bd. dirs., pres, CEO Texel S.A. de C.V., 1992—. Columbia U. Internat. fellow, 1982; Sarah Williston scholar Mt. Holyoke Coll., 1975. Mem. N.Y. Soc. Security Analysts, Am. C. of C. (treas., dir.), Phi Beta Kappa. Club: Harvard. Avocations: piano, horseback riding. Office: Texel S.A. de C.V., 346 Lamartine, Mexico City Mexico

DEBS, BARBARA KNOWLES, academic administrator; b. Eastham, Mass., Dec. 24, 1931; d. Stanley F. and Arline (Eugley) Knowles; m. Richard A. Debs, July 19, 1958; children: Elizabeth, Nicholas. BA, Vassar Coll., 1953; postgrad., Radcliffe Coll., 1956-58; PhD, Harvard U., 1967; LLD, N.Y. Law Sch., 1979; LHD, Manhattanville Coll., 1985. Instr. art Vassar Coll., 1955-56; freelance translation editor Ency. of World Art divsn. McGraw-Hill Pub., N.Y.C., 1959-62; asst. prof. art history Manhattanville Coll., Purchase, N.Y., 1968-73, assoc. prof., 1973-77, prof., 1977-86, pres., 1975-85; trustee, chmn. collections com. N.Y. Hist. Soc., 1985-87, pres., CEO, 1988-92; cons. area non-profit orgns. pvt. practice, Greenwich, Conn., 1992—. Contbr. articles on Renaissance and contemporary art to profl. publs. Mem. N.Y. Council Humanities, 1978-85; mem. Westchester Med. Ctr. Hosp. Implementation Bd., 1978-84; mem. Westchester County Bd. Ethics, 1979-84; trustee N.Y. Law Sch., 1979-89; trustee Geraldine R. Dodge Found., 1985—; bd. dirs. Internat. Found. for Art Rsch., 1985-92; trustee Com. Econ. Devel., 1985—; mem. Coun. Fgn. Rels., 1983—; mem. Commn. Ind. Colls. and Univs. of N.Y., 1977-79; mem. com. on higher edn., adv. council to Dems. N.Y. State Senate, 1979-85. AAUW Nat. fellow and Ann Radcliffe fellow, 1958-59; Am. Council Learned Socs. grantee, 1973; Fulbright fellow Scuola Normale, Pisa, Italy, 1953, U. Rome, 1954. Mem. Am. Coun. on Edn. (chmn. commn. acad. affairs 1977-79), Young Audiences (nat. dir. 1977-80), Hundred Club of Westchester (bd. dirs.), Renaissance Soc. of Am., Coll. Art Assn., Phi Beta Kappa. Club: Cosmopolitan, Century Assn.

DEBUONO, BARBARA ANN, state official, physician; b. N.Y.C., Apr. 13, 1955; d. Richard Francis and Catherine (Brutto) DeB.; m. David Lavington Farren, June 1, 1980; children: Adam, Douglas. BS, U. Rochester, 1976, MD, 1980; MPH, Harvard U., 1984. Diplomate Am. Bd. Internal Medicine, Nat. Bd. Med. Examiners. Intern in internal medicine New Eng. Deaconess Hosp., Boston, 1980-81, jr. med. resident, 1981-82, sr. med. resident, 1982-83; clin. fellow Brown U., Providence, 1984-86, clin. instr. dept. medicine, 1987-90, clin. asst. prof. medicine, 1990—; med. epidemiologist R.I. Dept. Health, Providence, 1986, state epidemiologist, med. dir. Office Disease Control, 1986-91; dir. dept. health State of R.I., 1991—; lectr. in field. Contbr. articles to profl. jours. Robert Wood Johnson Found. Ednl. scholar U. Rochester Sch. Med., 1976-80; recipient James L. Tulis Disting. Study Lectureship award New Eng. Deaconess Hosp., 1992; named Women of Yr. by Bus. and Profl. Women's Club Providence, 1989, Person of Yr. by The Women's Youth League R.I., 1990, Woman of Yr. by R.I. Fedn. Bus. and Profl. Women's Clubs, 1991. Fellow Am. Coll. Physicians (mem. CDC cancer project adv. panel 1992—); mem. AMA, APHA, Am. Soc. Microbiology, Assn. State and Territorial Health Officials (mem. HIV com. 1989—, mem. breast and cervical cancer com. 1991—, mem. immunizations task force 1991—), Coun. State and Territorial Epidemiologists (mem. HIV com. 1989-91, mem. exec. com. 1991), Infectious Disease Soc. Am., Providence Med. Assn., R.I. Med. Soc. (mem. AIDS exec. com. 1988—), R.I. Med. Women's Assn. (R.I. Women Physician of Yr. 1988), R.I. Environ. Health Assn., Hosp. Assn. R.I. (mem. AIDS task force 1988—), Am. Coll. Physicians (mem. R.I. chpt., mem. exec. coun.), Women Execs. in Govt. Office: RI Health Dept 3 Capitol Hill Rm 401 Providence RI 02908-5097*

DEBUS, ELEANOR VIOLA, retired business management company executive; b. Buffalo, May 19, 1920; d. Arthur Adam and Viola Charlotte (Pohl) D.; student Chown Bus. Sch., 1939. Sec., Buffalo Wire Works, 1939-45; home talent producer Empire Producing Co., Kansas City, Mo., sec. Owens Corning Fiberglass, Buffalo; public relations and publicity Niagara Falls Theatre, Ont., Can.; pub. rels. dir. Woman's Internat. Bowling Congress, Columbus, Ohio, 1957-59; publicist, sec. Ice Capades, Hollywood, Calif., 1961-63; sec. to contr. Rexall Drug Co., L.A., 1963-67; bus. mgmt. acct. Samuel Berke & Co., Beverly Hills, Calif., 1967-75; Gadbois Mgmt. Co., Beverly Hills, 1975-76; sec., treas. Sasha Corp., L.A., 1976-92; former bus. mgr. Dean Martin. Mem. Am. Film Inst. Republican. Lodge: Order Ea. Star. Contbr. articles to various mags.

DE CARLO, MICHELLE LYNN, insurance company official; b. Denver, Nov. 3, 1962; d. Matthew John and Patricia Ann (Phelan) De C. BS in Bus., U. Colo., 1986; cert. in gen. ins., Ins. Inst. Am., 1992. Loan officer Margaretten Mfg. Co., Denver, 1986-87; claims specialist State Farm Ins. Co., Denver, 1988—. Mem. Dante Soc., Therisians. Roman Catholic. Home: 3751 W 101st Ave Westminster CO 80030

DE CHAMPLAIN, VERA CHOPAK, artist, painter; b. Kulmbach, Germany, Jan. 26, 1928; Am. citizen; d. Nathaniel and Selma (Stiefel) Florsheim; m. Albert Chopak de Champlain, 1948. Student, Art Students League, N.Y.C., 1950-60; spl. studies with Edwin Dickinson, 1962-64. Art dir., tchr. Emanuel Ctr., N.Y.C., 1967—. One person show Consulate Fed. Republic of Germany, N.Y.C., 1986, Fusco Gallery, N.Y.C., 1969-70, B. Altman Gallery, N.Y.C., 1982; exhibited group shows including Munich, Fed. Republic of Germany, 1966, Rudolph Gallery, Woodstock, N.Y., 1967, Artists Equity Gallery, N.Y.C., 1970-77, Lever House, N.Y.C., 1974, 80, 85, 88; Avery Fisher Hall-Cork Gallery, N.Y.C., 1970, 82, 83, 84, 87, 89, Fontainebleau Gallery, N.Y.C., 1972, 73, 74, NYU, 1978, Met. Mus., 1979, Muriel Karasik Gallery, Westhampton Beach, N.Y., 1980, Lever House, N.Y.C., 1990, Broome St. Gallery, N.Y.C., 1991, 92, 93, 94, 95, Avery Fisher Hall-Cork Gallery, N.Y.C., 1994; represented in permanent collections Butler Inst. Am. Art, Youngstown, Ohio, Ga. Mus. Art, Athens, Slater Mus., Norwich, Conn., Webster Coll., St. Louis, Evansville Mus. Arts and Sci. (Ind.), Smithsonian Instn., Archives Am. Art, Washington, Jacob Javits Fed. Bldg., N.Y., Permanent Mission of The Netherlands to UN; traveling exhbn. in U.S, 1988-89. Recipient award in portrait painting, Hainesfalls, N.Y., 1965, First Prize-World award, Acad. Italia, Parma, 1985, 87; subject of TV interview, 1984; presented to Queen Elizabeth of England, 1991. Fellow Royal Soc. Arts (London); mem. Artists Equity Assn. N.Y., Arts Students League (life), Nat. Soc. Arts and Letters (art chmn. 1969—), Kappa Pi (life). Clubs: Woman Pays, Liederkranz City of N.Y. (trustee 1979—). Home: 230 Riverside Dr New York NY 10025-6172

DECHARY, JENET LYNN, broadcaster, freelance writer, researcher; b. Plaquemine, La., Feb. 14, 1946; d. Paul Luke and Mary Poynter (Schwing) D.; divorced; 1 child, Paul Joseph. BA, U. Southwestern La., 1968. Script asst. Sta. WRC-TV, Washington, 1969-71, mem. on-air promotion staff, 1971-72, license coord., 1972-74, reports analyst, 1980-86, analyst, standards coord., 1986-88, adminstr. reports and broadcast standards, 1988-91, broadcast standards mgr., 1991—; mem. comml. standards staff Stas. WRC-TV, WKYS-FM, WRC-AM, Washington, 1974-80. Author: (play) Souvenirs, 1984; author essays and feature articles. Mem. The Writer's Ctr., Washington Ind. Writers.

DECHERNEY, DEANNA SAVER, interior designer; b. Phila., Mar. 5, 1943; d. Martin and Bessie (Pitkoff) Saver; m. Alan Hersh DeCherney, June 26, 1965; children: Peter, Alexander, Nicholas. B.F.A., U. of Arts, 1966. Designer, Paul Planert Design Assocs., Pitts., 1967-68; assoc. designer Temple U., 1969-72; dir. interiors P.A.E., Tokyo, Japan, 1972-74; pres. The Nat. Design Service, Woodbridge, Conn., 1981-91, Weston, Mass., 1991—; instr. Paier Coll. Art, 1975-91, chmn. interior design dept., 1989-91; instr. Post Coll., 1987-89; mem. adv. bd. New England Sch. Art & Design, Boston, 1993—; mem. devel. bd. Boston Archtl. Ctr., 1993; bd. trustees New England Sch. Art and Design, 1995. Editorial dir. Design Times Mag., 1994—. Chmn. Vassar Coll. Parents & Friends Devel. Com., 1992; bd. dirs. Chamber Orch. of New Eng. 1975-88, The Neighborhood Music Sch., 1979-85; Bd. of Fider Vis., 1991—. Mem. Am. Soc. Interior Designers (pres. Conn. chpt. 1983, 84, 87 88, v.p. N.E. regional 1989-91), Interior Design Educator Council, Conn. Acad. Arts and Scis. Address: 54 Hillcrest Rd Weston MA 02193-2021

DECICCO, ANNE LOMMEL, association executive; b. N.Y.C., Sept. 27, 1950; d. Richard Arthur and Nancy (Robertson) Lommel; children: Geoffrey Lommel DeCicco, Melanie Paige DeCicco, Benjamin Bruce Hydo, Wynne Meredith Hydo. Cert. assn. exec., meeting profl.; European Cert. Assn. Mgmt. V.p. N.J. Hosp. Assn., Princeton, 1981-84, v.p. corp. and strategic planning, 1984; corp. v.p. Ctr. Health Affairs Inc., 1985-93; pres. Aral Sea Found., 1994; pres., CEO N.J. Health Inc., 1994—; bd. dirs. Somerset (N.J.) Med. Ctr., Somerset HealthCare Enterprises, Am. Soc. Assn. Execs., Carelift Internat. Home: 22 Franklin Dr Plainsboro NJ 08536 Office: NJ Health Inc 1065 Rte 22 W Bridgewater NJ 08807

DECKER, CAROL ARNE, magazine publishing consultant; b. Rochelle, Ill., Apr. 3, 1946; d. Irvin Norman Arne and Edna (Olsen) Stein; m. Charles Levitt Decker, Feb. 17, 1979; children: Katharine Elizabeth. BA, So. Ill. U., 1969. Advt. sales rep. Travel Agent mag., N.Y.C., 1971-74, Business Week mag., N.Y.C., 1974-80, Reader's Digest Publs., N.Y.C., 1980-82; assoc. pub. The Atlantic Monthly, N.Y.C., 1982-84; pub. Personal Investor, N.Y.C., 1984-86, Lear's Mag., 1992-93; pub. cons. C.A. Decker & Assocs., N.Y.C., 1986-94. Home and Office: 236 Nyac Ave Pelham NY 10803-3505

DECKER, CHRISTINE MARIE, nurse, administrator; b. Morristown, N.J., Feb. 4, 1947; d. George and Jenneke (Van Dyken) Laufenberg; m. James J. Decker, Oct. 5, 1968; children: James, Johanna. BSN, Villanova U., 1968; postgrad., Rider Coll., 1984—. RN, N.J., Pa. Supr. residential and profl. svcs. State of N.J., Skillman, 1981-82; mgr. quality assurance Managed Care System, Mt. Holly, N.J., 1987-88; program dir. health care accreditation programs N.J. Hosp. Assn., Princeton, 1982-87; asst. v.p. corp. quality assessment U.S. Healthcare, Blue Bell, Pa., 1988—. Mem. Nat. Assn. Healthcare Quality, N.J. Assn. Quality Assurance Profls. (sec. bd. dirs.). Home: 6 Charred Oak Ln Hightstown NJ 08520-1804

DECKER, JOSEPHINE I., clinic administrator; b. Barling, Ark., May 24, 1933; d. Ralph and Ada A. (Claborn) Snider; BS in Health Mgmt., Kennedy Western U., 1986, MS in Bus. Adminstrn., 1987; m. William Arlen Decker, Feb. 4, 1952; 1 son, Peter A. With Southwestern Bell Telephone Co., Ft. Smith, Ark., 1951-52; with Holt Krock Clinic, Ft. Smith, 1952—, bus. adminstr., 1970—. Bd. dirs. Sparks Credit Union, Adv. Council Northside and Southside high schs., Ft. Smith, Ft. Smith Girls Shelter, Ft. Smith Credit Bur. Mem. Credit Women Internat., Soc. Cert. Consumer Credit Execs. Office: Holt Krock Clinic 1500 Dodson Ave Fort Smith AR 72901-5193

DECKER, JUDITH ELAINE, land development company executive; b. Derry, N.H., Nov. 2, 1940; d. Clayton Kent and Ariel Almina (Palmer) Gillis; m. Marshall Norman Decker, Nov. 2, 1965 (div. 1994); children: Timothy, Jennifer, Amy, James, Wesley. Diploma, McIntosh Bus. Sch., 1958-59; BS magna cum laude, Franklin Pierce Coll., 1986. Treas. N.H. Electric, Inc., Salem, 1974-77; treas. J.E.D. Assocs., Inc., Danville, N.H., 1978-86, pres., chief exec. officer, 1986—; bd. dirs. J.E.D. Assocs., Inc., Danville, MarDec, Inc., Salem, Shalles Corp., Salem. Chmn. Thompson for Gov., Salem, 1970, Heart Fund, Salem, 1969, 70, 71; troop leader Girl Scouts of Am., Salem, 1969-72. Mem. Nat. Assn. Female Execs., Greater Haverhill C. of C., Nat. Assn. Self Employed. Republican. Home: 37 Chandler Dr Atkinson NH 03811 Office: J E D Assocs Inc PO Box 690 East Hampstead NH 03826

DECKERT, MYRNA JEAN, executive director; b. McPherson, Kans., Nov. 4, 1936; d. Francis J. and Grace (Killion) George; m. Ray A. Deckert, Sept. 29, 1957; children: Rachelle, Kimberly, Charles, Michael. AA, Coll. of Sequoias, 1956; BBA, U. Beverly Hills, 1983, MBA, 1984. Youth dir. Asbury Meth. Ch ., El Paso, Tex., 1960-63; teen program dir. YWCA, El Paso, 1963-69, assoc. exec. dir., 1969-70, exec. dir., 1970—. Exec. forum, pres., 1991-92; bd. dirs. Tex. Commerce Bank, El Paso; chmn. Tex. State Title XX DayCare Providers, 1987-89; commr. Housing Authority City of El Paso, 1989-92; trustee Columbia Med. Ctr. East Bd., Tex. Tech. Med. Found. Bd.; mem. blue ribbon policy com. Tex. Health and Human Svcs. Commn.; trustee Dues/High Tower Found.; chair Leadership EP, 1994-95; mem. UTEP Bus. Adv. Coun.; mem. Project Change-El Paso; trustee Unite El Paso. Recipient Hannah Soloman Community Svc. award Nat. Coun. Jewish Women, Sertoma Club award Svc. to Mankind, 1974, Cmty. Svc. award League United L.Am. Citizens, 1980, Humanitarian award, 1994, Vol. Svc. award Vol. Bur., 1984, Merit award Adalante Mujer, 1986, Social Svc. award KVIA/Sunturians, 1986, Excellence award Nat. Assn. YWCA Execs., 1990, Racial Justice award YWCA of the U.S.A., 1991; named Woman of Yr., AAUW, 1975, Dir. of Yr., United Way El Paso County, 1985, First Lady of El Paso, Beta Sigma Phi, 1991, One of 10 Most Influential Women, El Paso Times, 1995; inducted to El Paso Women's Hall of Fame, 1990. Mem. Coun. of Agy. Execs., UTEP Profl. Network, Rotary (Club of El Paso, 1990-93, v.p.). Methodist. Home: 4276 Canterbury Dr El Paso TX 79902-1352

DECOSTER, ANNE STRINGER, artist; b. St. Paul, June 6, 1933; d. Philip and Anne (Driscoll) Stringer; m. Earl Adelbert Samson, Feb. 4, 1956 (div. Sept. 1971), Earl Adelbert III, Edward S., Anne D., Robert K.; m. Steven Cole DeCoster, Aug. 22, 1976. AB in Painting and Drawing, Middlebury Coll., 1955; postgrad., Inst. Allende, San Miguel de Allende, Mex., 1974; MFA in Painting and Drawing, U. Minn., 1984. Instr. painting Art Ctr. Minn., Minnetonka, 1984-85; vis. artist Macalester Coll., St. Paul, 1986; lectr. St. Olaf Coll., Northfield, Minn., 1987; workshop condr. in field. Author, illustrator: Draw Me an Elephant, 1967, Lines, Spines, and Porcupines, 1969; illustrator: Forum Feasts Cookbook, 1970; one-woman shows include Katherine Nash Gallery, U. Minn., 1983, Thomson Gallery, Mpls., 1987, Concordia Coll., 1988, St. Benedict's Coll., St. Joseph, Minn., 1988, Suzanne Kohn Gallery, Mpls., 1989, 90, Groveland Galalery, Mpls., 1992, 94; group shows include Minn. Mus. Art, St. Paul, 1984, Pindar Gallery, N.Y.C., 1986; represented in corp. and numerous pvt. collections. Congregationalist. Home: 252 Maiden Ln Apt 2 Saint Paul MN 55102-1770

DE COSTER, BARBARA LOU, technical services librarian; b. Salt Lake City, Dec. 22, 1932; d. Frederic K. and Lucille (Campbell) Gray; m. Xie Bing Can, 1994; children from previous marriage: Don T. Jr., Carol Ann, Catherine Alvarez. BA, U. Wash., 1965, MLS, 1967; PhD, U. Tex., 1984. Tech. processes libr. Bellevue (Wash.) Community Coll., 1967—; cons. ECNU, Hua Dong Shifan Daxue, Shanghai, People's Republic China, summers, 1987, 88, 90, vis. prof., 1992-93; cons. Nat. Libr. China, Beijing, summers 1987, 90, U. Wash., Seattle, 1967. Subject indexer (book) Texas in Children's Books, 1986. Chair Polit. Action Com. Bellevue Community Coll. Assn. Higher Edn., Bellevue Community Coll., 1987-90. Grad. fellow U. Tex., 1982-83; scholar U. Tex., 1981-82, MIT, 1950. Mem. ALA, OnLine AudioVisual Catalogers (news editor 1985-92), Cmty. Coll. Librs. and Media Specialists (pres. 1985-87), Western Libr. Network-Wash. Users Group (chair 1989-91), Factoria Med. Ctr. Coun. Group Health Cooperate (chair 1989-91), Bellevue Cmty. Coll. Assn. Higher Edn. (pres./pres.-elect 1990-92). Home: 6343 NE 156th St Bothell WA 98011-4373 Office: Bellevue Community Coll Libr Media Ctr 3000 Landerholm Cir SE Bellevue WA 98007-6484

DECOSTER, TONI MARI, retail executive; b. Lewiston, Maine, Apr. 21, 1954; d. Gordon Elwood and Helen Mae (Waterhouse) DeC.; m. Wayne Terry Wentworth (div.); children: Sara Renee, Samuel Wayne. Grad. high sch., Fairfield, Calif. Dist. mgr. Foxmoor, Tampa, Fla., 1976-84; v.p. Petries, Seacucus, N.J., 1984-85; regional mgr., dir. real estate Carroll Reed, Portland, Maine, 1985-87; dist. mgr. Talbots, San Francisco, 1987-88, Bass Shoes, San Francisco, 1988-90, Dress Barn, Stamford, Calif., 1990-92; dir. store ops. and constrn. Ashley Stewart, N.Y.C., 1992—. Home: 158 Longfellow Ave Fairfield CT 06432-4715 Office: Ashley Steward Ltd 14th Fl 213 W 35th St New York NY 10001

DECOTIS, DEBORAH ANNE, investment banker; b. Salem, Mass., Nov. 13, 1952; d. John and Marie (Mahoney) DeC.; m. Nicholas B. Zoullas, Aug. 15, 1987. BA, Smith Coll., 1974; MBA, Stanford U., 1978. Analyst, Morgan Stanley & Co., Inc., N.Y.C., 1974-76, assoc., 1978-81, v.p., London, 1982-84, prin., N.Y.C., 1985-89, mng. dir., 1990—. Trustee Morgan Stanley Found. Miller scholar Stanford U., 1978. Home: 211 Central Park W New York NY 10024-6020 Office: Morgan Stanley & Co Inc 1251 Ave Of The Americas New York NY 10020-1001

DECRESCENZO, JAME MELISSE, insurance company executive; b. Midland, Tex., June 19, 1955; d. James Edward and Hari Jean (Jackson) Hanks; m. Michael Harry DeCrescenzo; children: Alexander, Andrew. BA, U. Md., Spain, 1975; BSN, Tex. Women's U., 1980; MA magna cum laude, U. Tex., 1984. RN. Dir. spl. accounts Dey Labs., Dallas, 1978-80; salesman SMI, Dallas, 1980-83; ind. oil and gas investor Dallas, 1983-88; with Am. Gen. Ins. Co., 1988; dir. devel. Travelers Ins. Co., Richardson, Tex., 1990-94; dir. provider devel. Found. Health, A Tex. Health Plan, Dallas, 1994—. Republican. Roman Catholic.

DECROSTA, SUSAN ELYSE, graphic artist; b. Cambridge, Mass., Aug. 28, 1956; d. Joseph Mario and Gertrude Ermelinda (Galligani) DeC. BFA, Mass. Coll. Art, 1980. certified art tchr., supr. Graphic artist Nixdorf Computer Corp., Burlington, Mass., 1981-86; lead artist, illustrator Raytheon Co., Andover, Mass., 1986—; illustrator, designer Raytheon Co., Burlington, Mass., 1994—; lead artist, illustrator Rivers, Trainor, Doyle, Providence, 1987; freelance graphic artist, 1980—; guest speaker to design and illustration students Northeastern U., 1992. Vol. AIDS Action Com., Boston. Recipient Excellence award Soc. Tech. Communications & Art Direction, 1986. Mem. Arlington Ctr. Arts, Mass. Art Alumni Assn., Creative Club Boston, The Boston Computer Soc. Office: Raytheon Co 350 Lowell St Andover MA 01810-4400

DECROW, KAREN, lawyer, author, lecturer; b. Chgo., Dec. 18, 1937; d. Samuel Meyer and Juliette (Abt) Lipschultz; m. Alexander Allen Kolben, 1960 (div. 1965); m. Roger DeCrow, 1965 (div. 1972, dec. 1989). BS, Northwestern U., 1959; JD, Syracuse U., 1972; DHL (hon.), SUNY, Oswego, 1994. Bar: N.Y., U.S. Dist. Ct. (no. dist.) N.Y. Resorts editor Golf Digest mag., Evanston, Ill., 1959-60; editor Am. Soc. Planning Ofcls., Chgo., 1960-61; writer Ctr. for Study Liberal Edn. for Adults., Chgo., 1961-64; editor Holt, Rinehart, Winston, Inc., N.Y.C., 1965; textbook editor L.W. Singer, Syracuse, N.Y., 1965-66; writer Ea. Regional Inst. for Edn., Syracuse, 1967-69, Pub. Broadcasting System, 1977; tchr. women and law, 1972-74; nat. bd. mem. NOW, 1968-77, nat. pres., 1974-77, also nat. politics task force chair; cons. affirmative action; lectr. topics including law, gender, internat. feminism to corps., polit. groups, colls. and univs., U.S., Can., Mex., Finland, China, Greece, former USSR; nat. coord. Women's Strike for Equality, 1970; N.Y. State del. Internat. Women's Yr., 1977; originator Schs. for Candidates; mem. bd. advisors Women's Inst.; participant DeCrow-Schlafly ERA Debates, from 1975; co-founder World Woman Watch, 1988; gender issues advisor Nat. Congress for Men; mem. Task Force on Gender Bias. Author: (with Roger DeCrow) University Adult Education: A Selected Bibliography, 1967, American Council on Education, 1967, The Young Woman's Guide to Liberation, 1971, Sexist Justice, 1974, First Women's State of the Union Message, 1977, (with Robert Seidenberg) Women Who Marry Houses: Panic and Protest in Agoraphobia, 1983, Turkish edit., 1988, 2d Turkish edit., 1989, United States of America vs. Sex: How the Meese Commission Lied About Pornography, 1988, (with Jack Kammer) Good Will Toward Men: Women Talk Candidly About the Balance of Power Between the Sexes, 1994; editor: The Pregnant Teenager (Howard Osofsky), 1968, Corporate Wives, Corporate Casualties (Robert Seidenberg), 1973; contbr. articles to USA Today, N.Y. Times, L.A. Times, Nat. Law Jour., Women Boston Globe, Vogue, Mademoiselle, Ingenue, Newsday, Chgo. Sun Times, Penthouse, Washington Post, L.A. Times Mag., Policy Review, Miami Herald, Internat. Herald Tribune, Social Problems, Houston Chronicle, Pitts. Press, Nat. NOW Times, Syracuse U. Mag., San Francisco Chronicle, Civil Rights Quar., Women Lawyers Jour., other newspapers, mags.; columnist: Syracuse New Times; recording: Opening Up Marriage, 1980. Hon. trustee Elizabeth Cady Stanton Found.; life mem. Art Inst. Chgo.; mem. coun. overseers Maripost Edn. and Rsch. Found.; mem. adv. panel Nat. Coun. Children's Rights; active Hon. Com. to Save Alice Paul's Birthplace, Syracuse Friends of Chamber Music; Liberal candidate for Mayor of Syracuse, 1969. Recipient Profl. Recognition award for best newspaper column Syracuse Press Club, 1990. Address: 7599 Brown Gulf Rd Jamesville NY 13078-9636

DECTER, BETTY EVA, artist; b. Birmingham, Ala., Apr. 22, 1927; d. Kara Miracle; m. William Fenske, May 14, 1943 (div.); children: William Jr., Karalee; m. Gerald A. Decter, July 9, 1961; 1 stepchild, Tom. Freelance fashion model, 1950s; designer, stylist Decter Mannikin Co., Inc., 1962-92; v.p. Bellagio Arabians, 1985—. One-woman shows at Roger Morrison Gallery, L.A., 1985, Brand Libr. Art Gallery, Glendale, Calif., 1988, Riverside County Mus./Edward-Dean Mus., 1989, Sam Francis Gallery, Crossroads Sch. for Arts and Scis., Santa Monica, Calif., 1992, Thinking Eye Gallery, L.A., 1986, 87, Absolute Gallery, L.A., 1986, Warner Ctr. Gallery, 1987, Otis Art Inst. of Parsons Sch. Design, 1988, J.C. Cooper Gallery, 1988, Mus. Without Walls, Bemus Point, N.Y., 1992; contbr. articles to profl. jours. and encys. Founding mem., co-chair Save the Santa Monica Mountains Com., 1970; founding mem., chair No on Nowell Com., 1973-74; mem. L.A. City Atty.'s Com. on Polit. Reform, 1973-74; founding mem., chair Com. for Enforcement of Campaign Laws, 1974-78; founding mem. bd. William O. Douglas Outdoor Classroom, 1980-90; helped establish Nat. Urban Park in Santa Monica Mountains, 1978-80; active local politics, 1969—; mem. The Group, 1984-93; mem. adv. bd. Woman's Bldg., L.A., 1988. Recipient award Assocs. of Brand Libr., 1991, Bronze award Calif. Discovery Awards, 1994. Studio: 5412 W Washington Blvd Los Angeles CA 90016

DEDE, BONNIE AILEEN, librarian, educator; b. Racine, Wis., Mar. 21, 1942; d. Edward Charles and Gracebelle Roeber; m. Metin Dede, Sept. 24, 1966; children: Suzan A., Ercan M. BA, U. Mich., 1963, MA, 1966, AM in LS, 1968; cert., U. Ill., 1970. Various positions U. Mich. Libr., Ann Arbor, 1967-88, head spl. formats cataloging, 1988—, adj. lectr. Sch. Info. and Libr. Studies, 1989—; mem. part-time faculty libr. and info. sci. program Wayne State U., Detroit, 1993—; cons. Gale Rsch., Detroit, 1993; reviewer Am. Reference Books Ann., 1992—. Mem. editl. bd. MC, Jour. Acad. Media Librarianship, 1992—. Grantee Title II-B, U.S. Office Edn., 1970, faculty-libr. coop. rsch. grantee Coun. on Libr. Resources, 1986-88, access grantee NEH, 1990-93. Mem. ALA, Alpha Lambda Delta, Beta Phi Mu (pres. Mu chpt. 1991—). Office: U Mich 100 Hatcher Libr-North Ann Arbor MI 48109-1205

DEDLOW, (EDNA) ROSELLEN, pediatrics nurse practitioner; b. West Palm Beach, Fla., July 24, 1958; d. Robert Eugene and Mary Margaret (Danner) D. AS in Nursing, Indian River Community Coll., 1978, AA,

1989; BSN, U. Fla., 1990, MSN Child Health, Pediatric Primary Care, 1992. RN, Fla.; cert. ARNP, BLS, pediatric ALS, Am. Heart Assn. Staff nurse Martin Meml. Hosp., Stuart, Fla., 1978-85; office nurse to pvt. practice pediatrician Stuart, 1986; nursing fellow Pediatric Pulmonary Ctr. U. Fla. Coll. Medicine, Gainesville, 1991-92; pediatric nurse practitioner/clin. nurse specialist Multihandicapped Splty. Clinics, U. Fla., Gainesville, 1992—; summer camp nurse Muscular Dystrophy Assn., Palm Beach, Fla., 1979-81, Am. Lung Assn., State of Fla., 1982, 84, 90, 92, 94; crisis care/foster care provider Div. Youth Svcs., Martin County Health and Rehab. Svcs., Fla., 1981-83. Mem. ANA (cert. pediatric nurse practitioner), Am. Acad. Nurse Practitioners, Fla. Nurses Assn., Nat. Assn. Pediatric Nurses and Practitioners, Spina Bifida Assn. Am., Fla. Cleft Palate/Craniofacial Assn., Sigma Theta Tau, Phi Kappa Phi, Phi Theta Kappa. Office: U Fla Coll Medicine Dept Pediatrics PO Box 100296 Gainesville FL 32610

DEDO, ANDREA KATSINAS, gifted/talented education educator; b. St. Louis, Nov. 3, 1947; d. Andrew Christ and Mary Margaret (Tsichlis) Katsinas; m. Thomas Marko Dedo, July 29, 1979; children: Alexis Kristine, Eleni Christine. BS in Edn., S.E. Mo. State U., 1969; MA in Edn., U. Mo., 1979; postgrad. in gifted edn., Maryville Coll., 1993. Cert. gifted/talented educator, Mo. Elem. tchr., third grade Maplewood-Richmond Heights Sch. Dist., St. Louis, 1969-89, gifted educator, first through sixth grades, 1989—. Mem. Kappa Delta Pi (pres. 1990-93), Delta Kappa Gamma (pres. 1986-88). Republican. Greek Orthodox. Home: 7066 Whitworth Ct Saint Louis MO 63123 Office: MRH High Sch 7539 Manchester Saint Louis MO 63117

DEDO, DOROTHY JUNELL TURNER, company executive, civic worker; b. Norway, Mich., Oct. 17, 1920; d. Raymond and Esther Elvira (Junell) Turner; m. Lewis Joseph Dedo, Dec. 24, 1945; children: Craig Turner, Drew Jonathan. Student, U. So. Calif., 1939-40; AB with honors, U. Mich., 1942; postgrad., U. N.D., 1942, Marquette U., 1942-43. Cert. tchr., Wis. Safety person Kearney & Trecker Corp., Milw., 1942-43; supr. Town of Shelby, La Crosse, Wis., 1973-77, clk., 1977-81, chmn., 1981-85; pres. Turner Lands, Inc., Milw., 1985—; supr. County of LaCrosse, 1990-94. Contbr. numerous articles to La Crosse Tribune. Producer, dir. actor La Crosse Children's Theater, 1959-65; sales mgr., actor LaCrosse Community Theatre, 1965-69; sec. Western Wis. Health Planning Orgn., 1964-68; chmn. Christian edn., mem. coun. English Luth. Ch., 1969-72; nominations chmn. bd. advisors Viterbo Coll., 1971-92; bd. dirs. Luth Hosp. Found., 1978-90, Winding Rivers Libr. System, 1990—, v.p., 1994—; sec. Wis. Towns Assn., 1973-85; v.p. LaCrosse Area Devel. Corp., 1981-85; mem. LaCrosse Area Planning Com., 1981-85; pres. LaCrosse County Rep. Women., 1976-78. Lt. comdr. USNR, 1943-55. Recipient Dionysos award in bus. La Crosse Community Theatre, 1965, Women of Yr. award La Crosse Bus. and Profl. Women, 1982, Tribute to Outstanding Woman award YWCA, La Crosse, 1983. Mem. AAUW (pres. LaCrosse 1974-76, Wis., 1981-83, named grant honoree 1977), AARP, Viterbo Coll. Pres.'s Club, Heritage Club, LaCrosse Country Club, Pearl Investment Club (pres. 1988-91), Earthwatch, Alpha Kappa Delta, Alpha Lambda Delta, Alpha Chi Omega. Home: 5870 W Cedar Rd La Crosse WI 54601

DEE, ROSITA HAO, neurologist; b. Manila, Oct. 12, 1948; d. Liong Sing and Hue Eng (Hao) Dy. BS, U. Santo Tomas, Manila, 1968, MD, 1972. Resident in neurology Med. Coll. Va., Richmond, 1976-78, fellow in neurophysiology, 1978-80; clin. instr. Howard U. Hosp., Washington, 1980-82; assoc. ptnr. Richard Restak, M.D., Washington, 1982-84; pvt. practice Silver Spring, Md., 1984—; profl. cons. Ciba/Geigy Pharm., 1986; mem. patient advisory com. Washington Adventist Hosp., Takome Park, Md., 1989, quality assurance com., 1993, staff campaign Com., 1994. Campaign worker Bd. of Edn., State of Md., 1994. Mem. Am. Acad. Neurology, Am. Soc. Law, Medicine and Ethics, Chinese-Am. Med. Soc. (v.p. 1994), Nat. Fedn. Small Bus. Office: RH Dee MD and Assocs 8830 Cameron Ct Ste 207 Silver Spring MD 20910

DEE, RUBY (RUBY DEE DAVIS), actress, writer, director; b. Cleve.; d. Marshall Edward and Emma (Benson) Wallace; m. Ossie Davis, Dec. 9, 1948; children: Nora, Guy, Hasna. BA, Hunter Coll., 1945; ArtsD (hon.), Fairfield U.; BA (hon. doctorate), Iona Coll., Va. State U.; apprentice, Am. Negro Theatre, 1941-44; LHD (hon.), SUNY, Old Westbury, 1990; DFA, Spelman Coll., 1991. Ind. actress, writer, dir., 1945—. Author: (poetry) Glowchild, 1972, (musical) Take It from the Top, (collected poetry, humor, short stories) My One Good Nerve; adaptor: (African folk tales) Two Ways to Count to Ten, The Tower to Heaven, (play) Books With Legs, 1993; contbr. column N.Y. Amsterdam News; co-writer (film) Uptight; dir., adaptor (stage prodn.) Zora is my Name!, 1983; stage appearances include Jeb, 1946, Raisin in the Sun, 1959, Purlie Victorious, 1961, The Imaginary Invalid, 1971, Wedding Band, 1972 (Drama Desk award 1972), Boesman and Lena, 1970 (Obie award 1971), Anna Lucasta, Taming of the Shrew, Checkmates, 1988, The Glass Menagerie, 1989; actress: (films) Gone are the Days, The Jackie Robinson Story, Take a Giant Step, St. Louis Blues, A Raisin in the Sun, Purlie Victorious, To Be Young, Gifted and Black, Buck and the Preacher, Countdown at Kusini, Cat People, 1982, Do the Right Thing, 1989 (NAACP Image award as best actress 1989), Jungle Fever, 1991; numerous TV appearances including It's Good to be Alive, 1974, Today Is Ours, 1974, The Defenders, Police Woman, Peyton Place, (TV films) To Be Young, Gifted and Black, All God's Children, The Nurses, Roots: The Next Generation, I Know Why the Caged Bird Sings, Wedding Band, It's Good to Be Alive, Decoration Day (Emmy award for Supporting Actress in a Miniseries or Special 1991), The Atlanta Child Murders, (TV spl. with Ossie Davis) Martin Luther King: The Dream and the Drum, The Winds of Change, Windmill of the Gods, TV miniseries Stephen King's The Stand, 1994; co-producer: (TV spl.) Today is Ours, The Ernest Green Story, 1993, (radio show) Ossie Davis and Ruby Dee Story Hour, 1974-78, (TV series) With Ossie and Ruby, 1981, (home videotape) Hands Upon The Heart, 1991, Middle Ages, 1992, Hands Upon The Heart II, 1993; rec. artist poems and stories. Recipient Martin Luther King Jr. award Operation PUSH, 1972, Drama Desk award, 1974, (with Ossie Davis) Frederick Douglass award N.Y. Urban League, 1970, (with Ossie Davis) NAACP Image award Hall of Fame, Master Innovator For Film award Sony, 1991. Mem. NAACP, CORE, Student Non-Violent Coordinating Com., SCLC. Address: The Artists Agy 10000 Santa Monica Blvd Los Angeles CA 90067-7007

DEEB, ANN MARIE, purchasing manager; b. Meadville, Pa., Feb. 10, 1929; d. Nigab and Emilene (Ezor) D.; 1 child, Virginia Jane. BA, Allegheny Coll., 1951. Cert. purchasing mgr. Order clk. Mameco Internat. (formerly named Master Mechs. Co.), Cleve., 1956-68, supr. customer rels., 1968-69; office mgr. Isonetics, Cleve., 1969-73; asst. purchasing agt. Electro-Gen. Plastics, Cleve., 1973-76, purchasing agt., 1976-90; purchasing mgr. Plastivax, Inc., Mentor, 1990-94; ret. Mem. Nat. Assn. Purchasing Mgmt., Purchasing Mgmt. Assn. Cleve. Roman Catholic. Home: 10405 Lake Ave Cleveland OH 44102

DEEHR, MARY ELAINE ELIZABETH, art educator; b. Sheboygan, Wis., Aug. 7, 1956; d. Martin Henry and Marcy Elaine (Brady) Thompson; m. Dennis Lee Deehr, Mar. 11, 1978 (div. 1989); children: Christopher Lee, Benjamin Edward, Adam Anthony. AA, W. Wis., Sheboygan, 1977; BA, Silver Lake Coll., 1994. Activity coord. R.C.S. Inc., Sheboygan; art asst. Ad-ONE Advt., Sheboygan; art and craft instr. Sheboygan Recreation Dept. Contbr. poetry to Days of Future Past, Vol. II, 1992, Best Poets of 1992, 1992, Golden Poets of 1989, 1989-90. Sec. Sheboygan Assn. for Severely Handicapped Adults, 1982—. Mem. Wis. Art Edn. Assn. Roman Catholic.

DEEKENS, ELIZABETH TUPMAN, writer; b. Washington, Aug. 25, 1926; d. William Spencer Tupman and Isabelle McNeil Roberts; m. William Carter Deekens, July 30, 1955 (dec. 1988); children: Arthur Carter, Christine Deekens Old, Catherine Deekens Ward. Student, George Washington U., 1945-49. parish sec. All Souls Episcopal Ch., Washington, 1951-52; Washington corres. The Living Ch., Mpls., 1951-52; woman's editor Episcopal Churchnews, Richmond, Va., 1952-57; mem. Episcopal Churchwomen Bd., Diocese of Va., Richmond, 1968; mem. Bishop's Liturgical Commn., Diocese of Va., 1975; newsletter editor Vestry, Ch. of Epiphany, Richmond, 1974-82; editor, layreader St. Martin's Ch., Richmond, 1983—. Contbr. articles to mags. including Seventeen, Good Housekeeping, features to various newspapers. Mem. publicity staff First Mills Godwin Gubernatorial Campaign, 1965; v.p. corp. comms. Va. Hosp. Assn., 1968-88. Recipient numerous state and nat. writing awards. Fellow Am. Soc. Hosp. Mktg. and Pub. Rels.; mem. Va. Hosp. Mktg. and Pub. Rels. (a founder, bd. dirs. 1969-88, treas. 1975-85), Richmond Pub. Rels. Assn. (pres. 1983-84), Va. Press Women Internat.), Order of St. Luke the Physician (sec.-treas. 1989-91). Republican. Home: 9711 Royerton Dr Richmond VA 23228-1217

DEEL, FRANCES QUINN, librarian; b. Pottsville, Pa., Mar. 9, 1939; d. Charles Joseph and Carrie Miriam (Ketner) Q.; m. Ronald Eugene Deel, Feb. 5, 1983. B.S., Millersville State Coll., 1960; M.L.S., Rutgers U., 1964; M.P.A., U. West Fla., 1981. Post librarian U.S. Army Armor (Desert Tng. Ctr.), Ft. Irwin, Calif., 1964-66; staff librarian Mil. Dist. of Washington, 1966-67; supervisory librarian 1st Logistical Command, APO San Francisco, 1967-68; tech. process specialist Naval Edn. and Tng. Supervisory Command, Washington, 1968-77, Pensacola, Fla., 1968-77; chief tech. library USAF Armament Lab., Eglin AFB, Fla., 1977-81; dir. command libraries Air Force Systems Command (Andrews AFB), Washington, 1981-92; mem. exec. adv. council Fed. Library and Info. Network, Washington, 1983-86; libr. Air Force Dist. of Washington(Bolling AFB), Washington, 1992-94; dir. Navy Dept. Libr., Washington, 1994—. Mem. ALA (dir.-at-large armed forces libraries sect. Chgo. 1983-86), Spl. Libraries Assn., D.C. Library Assn. Roman Catholic. Home: 9225 Forest Haven Dr Alexandria VA 22309-3216 Office: Navy Dept Libr Bldg 44 Washington Navy Yard Washington DC 20374-5060

DEEN, ALLISON MILLETT, realtor; b. Mineola, N.Y., Apr. 26, 1945; d. Daniel Caldwell and Mary (Allison) Millett; m. David Lewis Deen, Jan. 29, 1977; stepchildren: David Scott, Deborah Lynn. Student, Garrison Forest Sch., 1959-63; AA, Bennett Jr. Coll., 1965; BA, Columbia U., 1971. Lic. realtor. Eligibility worker Vt. Dept. Social Welfare, Brattleboro, 1972-74; field rep. Vt. Dept. Health, Springfield, 1974-87; real estate salesperson Homestead Realty, Brattleboro, 1988-89, Granger Real Estate, Newfane, Vt., 1990—; bd. dirs. Consumer Controlled Cmty. Child Care, Bellows Falls, Vt., 1980-86; mem. county com. Windham County Dem. Party, Brattleboro, 1973-93; justice of the peace Town of Westminster, Vt., 1991—; state committeewoman Vt. Dem. Party, Burlington. Mem. S.E. Vt. Bd. Realtors (mem. grievance com. 1992—, bd. dirs. 1993—). Episcopalian. Home: RFD 3 Box 800 Putney VT 05346

DEEN, EDITH ALDERMAN, author; b. Weatherford, Tex., Feb. 28, 1905; d. James Harris and Sara (Scheuber) Alderman; m. Edgar Deen, Dec. 30, 1945 (dec.). Student, Tex. U., 1922-23, Columbia U., 1926; student, Tex. Christian U., 1923-24, LittD, 1972; BA, Tex. Woman's U., 1953, LittD, 1959, MA, 1960; LittD (hon.), Pepperdine U., 1987. Woman's editor, daily columnist Ft. Worth Evening Press, 1924-54. Mem. Fort Worth City Council, 1965-67; mem. bd. regents Tex. Woman's Univ., 1951-63. Author: All of the Women of the Bible, 1955, Great Women of the Christian Faith, 1959, Family Living in the Bible, 1963, The Bibl's Legacy for Womanhood, 1970, All the Bible's Men of Hope, 1974, Wisdom from Women in the Bible, 1978. Named Exec. Woman of Year, Zonta Club, 1983; recipient First Lady award Altrusa Club, 1949, Disting. Sr. Citizen award Women's City Club, 1974, medal of honor Mary Isham Keith chpt. Nat. Soc. Am. Revolution, 1987. Mem. Tex. Inst. Letters, Women in Communications (Headliner award 1963). Home and Office: 6500 W Vickery Blvd Fort Worth TX 76116-9109

DEER, ADA E., federal agency official, social worker, educator; b. Menominee Indian Reservation, Wis., Aug. 7, 1935; d. Joe and Constance (Wood) D. BA in Social Work, U. Wis., 1957, LDH (hon.), 1974; MSW, Columbia U., 1961; postgrad., U. N.Mex., 1971, U. Wis., 1971-72; D in Pub. Svc. (hon.), Northland Coll., 1974. Group worker Protestant Coun. N.Y., N.Y.C. Youth Bd., 1958-60; program dir. Edward F. Waite Neighborhood House, Mpls., 1961-64; community svc. coord. bur. Indian affairs Dept. of Interior, Mpls., 1964-67; coord. Indian affairs Tng. Ctr. Cmty. Programs U. Minn., Mpls., 1967-68; trainer Project Peace Pipe Peace Corps., Arecibo, P.R., 1968; sch. social worker Mpls. Pub. Schs., 1968-69; dir. Upward Bound U. Wis., Stevens Point, 1969-70, dir. Program Recognizing Individual Determination through Edn., 1970-71; v.p., lobbyist Nat. Com. Save Menominee People and Forest, Inc., Washington and State of Wis., 1972-73; chair Menominee Restoration Com., Wis., 1974-76; sr. lectr. Sch. Social Work, Am. Indians Studies Program U. Wis., Madison, 1977—; asst. sec. Bur. Indian Affairs U.S. Dept. Interior, Washington, 1993—; legis. liaison Native Am. Rights Fund, Washington, 1979-81; cons., trainer Nat. Women's Edn. Fund, Washington, 1979-85; founding mem. Am. Indian Scholarships, Inc., Albuquerque, 1973-85; apptd. Joint Commn. on Mental Health of Children, Inc., Washington, 1967-68, Youth for Understanding, Wis., 1985-90; mem. adv. panel Office Technology Assessment, Washington, 1984-86; mem. Nat. Indian Adv. Com., Washington, 1989-91, Milw., 1990—, numerous other coms.; spkr. in field. Vice chair Nat. Mondale/Ferraro Presdl. Campaign, Washington, 1984; del.-at-large Dem. Nat. Conv., San Francisco, 1984; mem. spl. com. minority presence Girls Scouts U.S.A., N.Y.C., 1975-77, mem., 1969-75; bd. dirs. Planned Parenthood, Mpls., 1965-66, Indian Cmty. Sch., Milw., 1989—, Native Am. Rights Fund, Boulder, 1984-90, chmn., 1989-90, chair nat. support com., 1990—; mem. bd. improving health Native Ams. Robert Wood Johnson Found., Princeton, N.J., 1988—; bd. dirs. Quincentenary Com. Smithsonian Instn., Washington, 1989—, Hunt Commn. Dem. Nat. Com., Washington, 1981-82, Ind. Sector, Washington, 1980-84, Rural Am., Washington, 1978-85, Ams. for Indian Oppty., 1970-83; apptd. Pres. Commn. White House Fellowships, 1977-83; active Common Cause, Washington, 1974-78, Wis. Women's Coun., Madison, 1983-84, Camp Miniwanca, Stony Lake, Mich., 1953-57, Coun. Founds., Washington, 1977-83, Madison Urban League; Dem. candidate Wis. Sec. State, 1982. Recipient White Buffalo Coun. Achievement award, 1974, Politzer award Ethical Culture Soc., 1975, Wonder Woman Found. award, 1982, Indian Coun. Fire Achievement award, 1984, Nat. Disting. Achievement award Am. Indian Resources Inst., 1991; named Woman of Yr. by Girl Scouts Am., 1982; honoree Nat. Women's History Month Poster, 1987, Heroine Calendar Nat. Women's Studies Assn., 1987; Harvard U. fellow, 1977-78, Delta Gamma Found. Meml. fellow, 1960, John Hay Whitney Found. Meml. fellow, 1960; Menominee Tribal scholar, 1953-55. Mem. ACLU, NOW, Nat. Women's Polit. Caucus, Nat. Congress Am. Indians, Nat. Assn. Social Workers (pres. Wis. chpt. 1988-90, nat. com. women's issues 1988-90, decision making task force 1988-90, minorities com. 1977-81), Assn. Am. Indians and Alaska Native Social Workers (pres. Wis. 1978-80), Common Cause, Nature Conservancy. Office: Indian Affairs 1849 C St NW Washington DC 20240

DEES, SANDRA KAY MARTIN, psychologist, research consultant; b. Omaha, Apr. 18, 1944; d. Leslie B. and Ruth Lillian (May) Martin; m. Doyce B. Dees; BA magna cum laude, Tex. Christian U., 1965, MA, 1972, PhD, 1989. Adminstrv. asst./rsch. coord. Hosp. Improvement Project, Wichita Falls (Tex.) State Hosp., 1968-69; caseworker adoptions Edna Gladney Home, Ft. Worth, Tex., 1970-71; psychologist Mexia (Tex.) State Sch., 1971-72; sch. psychologist Ft. Worth Ind. Sch. Dist., 1971-78, program evaluator, 1978-86; pvt. counselor, 1986-88; assoc. rsch. scientist Tex. Christian U., 1989—; mem. adj. faculty, 1991-92, grad. faculty, 1994—; bd. dirs Because We Care, Ft. Worth, 1988-94, Hill Sch., 1994—. Dallas TCU Women's Club creative writing scholar, 1962-64, Virginia Alpha scholar, 1963; NASA research asst., 1965-67; USPHS trainee, 1967-68; cert. Am. Montessori Soc., 1977. Mem. APA, Am. Edn. Rsch. Assn., Mental Health Assn., Mortar Bd., Mensa, Alpha Chi, Phi Alpha Theta, Psi Chi, Phi Delta Kappa. Contbr. articles to profl. pubis. Home: 29 Bounty Rd W Fort Worth TX 76132-1003 Office: Tex Christian U Dept Psychology Fort Worth TX 76129

DEETHS, LENORE CLAIR, retired secondary education educator; b. Omaha, Oct. 27, 1940; d. Edward James and Bess Helen (Sabatka) Baburek; m. Harry Jeffrey Deeths, June 15, 1963; children: Lisa Marie, Matthew Jeoffrey, Maria Lenore. BA in English, Coll. St. Mary, Omaha, 1962. Tchr. English Holy Name High Sch., Omaha, 1962-64, Berlitz Lang. Sch., Tokyo, 1969-72; substitute tchr. Tachikawa (Japan) USAF High Sch., 1969-72; chair Coll. St. Mary Alumnae Assn., Omaha, 1979-80, chmn. breakfast series, 1990-92. Editor: (newsletter) Pulse Beat, 1965-69; author/producer (TV show) Health Topics, 1985-91. Chaired Officers' Wives Scholarship Com., 1971; br. chmn. Am. Assn. of Univ. Women Quality of Life Study, 1976-78; chaired fundraiser St. Joseph Hosp. and Creighton Med. Sch., 1979; publicity chmn. Emergency Pregnancy Svc. Omaha, 1980-85. Mem. AAUW (pres. 1991-92, 1st v.p. 1981-83, 3d v.p. 1983-84, br. chmn. 1978-80, br. del. chmn. nat. conv. 1991, br. del. chmn. Nat. Centennial Conv. 1981), Omaha Symphony Guild, Omaha Cmty. Playhouse Guild, Met. Omaha Med. Alliance (Merit award 1991, bd. dirs. 1989-91, pub. rels. com. 1985-90, pres. 1993-94, advisor 1994—), Nebr. Med. Assn. Alliance (bd. dirs. 1994—, parliamentarian 1994—), Friends of Children's Hosp., Girls Inc. (vice chair career devel. 1992-93, chair 1993-94). Home: 6729 Davenport St Omaha NE 68132-2737

DEFAZIO, LYNETTE STEVENS, dancer, choreographer, educator, chiropractor, author; b. Berkeley, Calif., Sept. 29; d. Honore and Mabel J. (Estavan) Stevens; children: J.H. Panganiban, Joanna Pang. student U. Calif., Berkeley, 1950-55, San Francisco State Coll., 1950-51; D. Chiropractic, Life-West Chiropractic Coll., San Lorenzo, Calif., 1983, cert. Techniques of Teaching U. Calif., 1985, BA in Humanities, New Coll. Calif., 1986; Lic. Chiropracter, Mich. Diplomate Nat. Sci. Bd.; eminence in dance edn., Calif. Community Colls. dance specialist, standard services, childrens ctrs. credentials Calif. Dept. Edn., 1986. Contract child dancer Monogram Movie Studio, Hollywood, Calif., 1938-40; dance instr. San Francisco Ballet, 1953-64; performer San Francisco Opera Ring, 1960-67; performer, choreographer Oakland (Calif.) Civic Light Opera, 1963-70; dir. Ballet Arts Studio, Oakland, Calif., 1960; teaching specialist Oakland Unified Sch. Dist., 1965-80; fgn. exchange dance dir. Academie de Danses-Salle Pleyel, Paris, France, 1966; instr. Peralta Community Coll. Dist., Oakland, 1971—, chmn. dance dept., 1985—; cons., instr. extension courses UCLA, Dirs. and Suprs. Assn., Pittsburg Unified Sch. Dist., 1971-73, Tulare (Calif.) Sch. Dist., 1971-73; researcher Ednl. Testing Services, HEW, Berkeley, 1974; resident choreographer San Francisco Childrens Opera, 1970—, Oakland Civic Theater; ballet mistress Dimensions Dance Theater, Oakland, 1977-80; cons. Gianchetta Sch. Dance, San Francisco, Robicheau Boston Ballet, TV series Patchwork Family, CBS, N.Y.C.; choreographer Ravel's Valses Nobles et Sentimentales, 1976. Recipient Foremost Women of 20th Century, 1985, Merit award San Francisco Children's Opera, 1985, 90. Author: Basic Music Outlines for Dance Classes, 1960, rev., 1968, Teaching Techniques and Choreography for Advanced Dancers, 1965, Basic Music Outlines for Dance Classes, 1965, Goals and Objectives in Improving Physical Capabilities, 1970, A Teacher's Guide for Ballet Techniques, 1970, Principle Procedures in Basic Curriculum, 1974, Objectives and Standards of Performance for Physical Development, 1975, Techniques of the Ballet School, 1970, rev., 1974, The Opera Ballets: A Choreographic Manual Vols. I-V, 1986. Assoc. music arranger Le Ballet du Cirque, 1964; assoc. composer, lyricist The Ballet of Mother Goose, 1968; choreographer: Valses Nobles Et Sentimentales (Ravel), Transitions (Kashevaroff), 1991, The New Wizard of Oz, 1991, San Francisco Children's Opera (Gingold); Canon in D for Strings and Continuo (Pachelbel), 1979; appeared in Flower Drum Song, 1993, Gigi, 1994. Mem. Calif. State Teacher Assn., Bay Area Chiropractic Research Soc., Profl. Dance Teacher Assn. Home and Office: 4923 Harbord Dr Oakland CA 94618-2506

DEFELICE, LINDA, librarian, educator; b. Phila., Dec. 29, 1952; d. Armando James and Ruth Elizabeth (Baur) DeF. BS, Shippensburg U., 1973; MA, Glassboro State Coll., 1980; cert. advanced study, Drexel U., 1987. Libr. Highland Regional High Sch., Blackwood, N.J., 1973-81; mktg. rep. Xerox Corp., Mt. Laurel, N.J., 1981; dir. media ctr. Pitman (N.J.) High Sch., 1981-82; assoc. prof. libr./media svcs. Gloucester County Coll., Sewell, N.J., 1982—; adj. prof. dept. comms. Gloucester County Coll., 1991—; mem. N.J. State Reference and Info. Svcs., 1990; cons. Deptford (N.J.) High Sch., 1988-89. Editor: (booklet) South Jersey Regional Library Cooperative Reference Guidelines, 1991; asst. editor Transformations: The N.J. Project jour., 1990-92. Bd. dirs. Allegro Soc., Sewell, 1991—; coord. Gloucester County Coll. United Way Campaign, Sewell, 1983. Ednl. Media Assn. N.J. scholar, 1978. Mem. ALA, N.J. Libr. Assn. (mem. scholarship com. 1983-92, chair 1992, reference sect. treas. 1987-88). Office: Gloucester County Coll Libr 1400 Tanyard Rd Sewell NJ 08080

DEFELICE, SOFIA, real estate broker, owner; b. Naples, Italy, Aug. 20, 1945; d. Antonio and Anna (Gambardella) DeFelice; children: Timothy J. Noreika, Steven P. Noreika. Student, Greater Hartford Community Coll., 1970-71; real estate sales lic., U. Conn., 1980, diploma in real estate appraisal, 1985; diploma in real estate finance, 1988. Lic. real estate broker Conn., 1989, Fla., 1993. Hostess Holiday Season Restaurant, Waterbury, Conn., 1974-79; owner Sofia Tops Plus, Woodbury, Conn., 1979-84; realtor RE/MAX Properties Unltd., Southbury, Conn., 1984-88; owner Action Realty, Watertown, Conn., 1988-93, DeFelice Art Gallery, 1992—; community sales mgr. Davis Homes, 1993; land developer, Watertown, 1987; dir. Multiple Listing Svc. Greater Waterbury, Inc., 1990—. Den mother Boy Scouts Am., Bethlehem, Conn., 1980-83; vol. Bethlehem Elem. Sch., 1980-85; fund raiser Little League Baseball, Bethlehem, 1983-85, United Way, 1989; sponsor Miss Greater Watertown, 1989; dir. Multiple Listing Svc. of Greater Waterbury, Inc., 1990—. Mem. Waterbury Bd. Realtors, Nat. Assn. Realtors, Conn. Assn. Realtors, Multiple Listing Svc., RE/MAX Hundred Percent Club, RE/MAX Internat. Referral Network, N.C. Assn. Realtors, Wilmington Bd. Realtors, Sons of Italy. Republican. Roman Catholic. Home: 501B 4th St Carolina Beach NC 28428 Office: PO Box 1044 Carolina Beach NC 28428

DE FERRARI, GABRIELLA, curator, writer; b. Tacna, Peru, June 3, 1941; came to U.S., 1959, naturalized, 1964; d. Armando and Delia De Ferrari; children: Nathaniel, Gabriella, Jeppson. BA, St. Louis U., 1962; MS, Tufts U., 1965; MA, Harvard U., 1981. Dir. Inst. Contemporary Art, Boston, 1975-77; acting curator Busch Reisinger Mus., Harvard U., Cambridge, Mass., 1978-79; asst. dir. for curatorial affairs and program Fogg Art Mus., 1979-82; cons. editor Mirabella mag. Author: A Cloud on Sand, 1990, Gringa Latina A Woman of Two Worlds, 1995. Office: 10 Jay St New York NY 10013-2819

DEFIBAUGH, GINGER DIANN, secondary education educator; b. Brookville, Pa., Jan. 27, 1953; d. William Arlington and Norma Jean (Simpson) D. BS in Edn., Slippery Rock State U., 1974. Cert. secondary English tchr., Tex., Pa. Reading tchr. Jack Yates Sr. H.S., Houston, 1975-76; English tchr. Woodson Jr. H.S., Houston, 1976-80, H.S. for Engring. Professions, Houston, 1980—; judge U. Interscholastic League, Houston, 1980—; sponsor Jr. Engring. Tech. Soc., Houston, 1992—. Co-author: (curriculum guide) Sexual Harrassment, 1994. Mem. Sunset Heights Civic Club, Houston, 1985—, Houstonians on Watch, Houston, 1993—; com. mem. Art Car Ball, Houston, 1993—. Democrat. Methodist. Office: High Sch For Engring Professions 119 E 39th St Houston TX 77018

DEFLEUR, LOIS B., university president, sociology educator; b. Aurora, Ill., June 25, 1936; d. Ralph Edward and Isabel Anna (Cornils) Begitske; m. Melvin L. DeFleur (div.). AB, Blackburn Coll., 1958; MA, Ind. U., 1961; PhD in Sociology, U. Ill., 1965. Asst. prof. sociology Transylvania Coll., Lexington, Ky., 1963-67; assoc. prof. Wash. State U., Pullman, 1967-74, prof., 1975-86, dean Coll. Liberal Arts, 1981-86; provost U. Mo., Columbia, 1986-90; pres. Binghamton U., SUNY, 1990—; disting. vis. prof. U.S. Air Force Acad., 1976-77; vis. prof. U. Chgo., 1980-81. Author: Delinquency in Argentina, 1965; (with others) Sociology: Human Society, 3d edit. 1981, 4th edit., 1984, The Integration of Women into All Male Air Force Units, 1982, The Edward R. Murrow Heritage: A Challenge for the Future, 1986; contbr. articles to profl. jours. Mem. Wash. State Bd. on Correctional Stds. and Edn., 1974-77, State of N.Y. Edn. Dept. Curriculum and Assessment Coun., 1991—, Trilateral Task for N.Am. Ednl. Collaboration, USIA, 1993—. Recipient Disting. Alumni award Blackburn Coll., 1991; grantee NIMH, 1969-79, NSF, 1972-75, Air Force Office, 1978-81. Mem. Am. Sociol. Assn. (publs. com. 1979-82, nominations com. 1984-86, coun. mem. 1987-90), Pacific Sociol. Assn. (pres. 1980-82), Inter-Univ. Seminar on Armed Forces and Soc., Coun. Colls. of Arts and Scis. (bd. dirs. 1982-84, pres. 1985-87), Aircraft Owners and Pilots Assn., Internat. Comanche Soc., Nat. Assn. State U. and Land-grant Colls. (exec. com. 1990-93, chair coun. of pres. 1994-95, chair-elect 1995-96), Am. Coun. Edn. (bd. dirs. 1994—), Consortium Social Sci. Assns. (bd. dirs. 1993—). Office: Binghamton U Office of Pres PO Box 6000 Binghamton NY 13902-6000

DEFLORIO, MARY LUCY, physician, psychiatrist; b. Chgo.; d. Anthony Ralph and Bernice (B. Bounell) D. m. Robert Y. Shapiro, Dec. 27, 1986. BA with distinction, U. Wis.; MD, MPH, U. Ill., Chgo., 1984; cert. writing program, Columbia U., 1988-91. Cert. emergency med. technician.

Adjudicator Fed. Disability Program, Ill. and Mass.; vocat. counselor U. Ill., Chgo.; resident internal medicine Mercy Hosp., Chgo., 1984-85; med. examiner Dept. Pub. Aid State of Ill., Chgo., 1985-87; resident psychiatrist St. Vincent's Hosp., N.Y.C., 1987-90; fellow cons. liaison psychiatry Meml. Sloan Kettering/Cornell Med. Ctr., N.Y.C., 1991-93; chief fellow Meml. Sloan Kettering, N.Y.C., 1992-93; attending physician Div. Psychiatry/Dept. Neurology Meml. Sloan Kettering and Cornell Med. Coll., N.Y.C., 1993—. Recipient Med. Econs. Writing award, 1987; James scholar U. Ill., Gen. Assembly scholar. Mem. AMA (Nutritional scholar 1983-84), Am. Women's Assn., Mass. Assn. Examiners (membership chmn.), Nat. Rehab. Assn., Assn. Acad. Psychiat. (Mead-Johnson fellow 1990), Am. Psychiat. Assn. (Br. Rsch. award 1990), Am. Psychiat. Arts Assn. (black and white photography and poetry award 1993). Roman Catholic. Home: 605 W 113th St Apt 21 New York NY 10025-7951 Office: Meml Sloan Kettering 1275 York Ave Rm 767C New York NY 10021-6007

DE FRANCISCO, DARLENE SUZANNE, collector, paralegal; b. Corry, Pa., Sept. 29, 1959; d. Russell James and Donna Belle (Nelson) H.; m. Morgan Dale Young, Feb. 24, 1979 (div. July 1983); 1 child, Andrea Marie; m. Michael Anthony De Francisco, July 22, 1989. Student, Jamestown Bus. Coll., 1977-78; A in Acctng., Cert. in Banking, Jamestown C.C., 1984; student, Empire State Coll., 1984-86. Teller trainer Marine Midland Bank, Jamestown, N.Y., 1979-84; paralegal James E. Westman, Esq., Jamestown, 1984-89; pres. Collection Svcs. Western N.Y., Sinclairville, N.Y., 1989—. Ward chair City Rep. Com., Jamestown, 1985-89. Named One of Outstanding Young Career Woman Bus. and Profl. Women's Club, Jamestown, 1986. Mem. NAFE, Ronald Reagan Presdl. Found. Republican. Roman Catholic. Office: Collection Svcs WNY PO Box 534 Sinclairville NY 14782-0534

DEGENERES, ELLEN, comedian, actress. TV appearances include: Duet, 1988-89, Open House, 1989, Laurie Hill, 1992, Ellen, 1994—; films include Coneheads, 1993. Office: UTA Inc 9560 Wilshire Blvd 5th Fl Beverly Hills CA 90212*

DE GETTE, DIANA LOUISE, lawyer, state legislator; b. Tachikawa, Japan, July 29, 1957; came to U.S., 1957; d. Richard Louis and Patricia Anne (Rose) De G.; m. Lino Sigismondo Lipinsky de Orlov, Sept. 15, 1984; children: Raphaela Anne, Francesca Louise. BA magna cum laude, The Colo. Coll., 1979; JD, NYU, 1982. Bar: Colo. 1982, U.S. Dist. Ct. Colo. 1982, U.S. Ct. Appeals (10th cir.) 1984, U.S. Supreme Ct. 1989. Dep. state pub. defender Colo. State Pub. Defender, Denver, 1982-84; assoc. Coghill & Goodspeed, P.C., Denver, 1984-86; sole practice Denver, 1986-93; of counsel McDermott, Hansen & Reilly, Denver, 1993—; mem. Colo. Ho. of Reps., 1992—; asst. minority leader, 1995—, mem. judiciary legal svcs., legis. coun. coms.; asst. minority leader Colo. Ho. Reps., 1995—; mem. judiciary legal svcs. com., legis. coun. Colo. Ho. Reps. Editor: (mag.) Trial Talk, 1989-92. Mem. Mayor's Mgmt. Rev. Com., Denver, 1983-84; resolutions chair Denver Dem. Party, 1986; bd. dirs. Root-Tilden Program, NYU Sch. Law, N.Y.C., 1986-92; bd. trustees, alumni trustee Colo. Coll., Colorado Springs, 1988-94. Recipient Root-Tilden scholar NYU Sch. Law, N.Y.C., 1979, Vanderbilt medal, 1982. Mem. Colo. Bar Assn. (bd. govs. 1989-91), Colo. Trial Lawyers Assn. (bd. dirs., exec. com. 1986-92), Colo. Women's Bar Assn., Denver Bar Assn., Phi Beta Kappa, Pi Gamma Mu. Office: McDermott Hansen & Reilly 1890 Gaylord St Denver CO 80206-1211

DEGNITZ, DOROTHY ELSIE, nursing administrator; b. Wis., Aug. 13, 1936; d. Fredrick William and Elsie Emily (Lawrenz) D. BSN, Northwestern U., 1959; cert., Frontier Sch. of Nursing, 1968; diploma in nursing edn., Armidale (Australia) Coll., 1981; MA in Social Sci., Azusa (Calif.) Pacific U., 1986. Instr. in psychiat. nursing Sch. of Nursing Evanston (Ill.) Hosp., 1960-66; missionary nurse tchr. Bd. for Mission Svcs., St. Louis, 1966-67, 68-70, Papua New Guinea, 1971-87; nursing supr. infirmary and nights Bethesda Luth. Home and Svcs., Watertown, Wis., 1987-94, part-time staff nurse, 1994—. Mem. Nat. League for Nursing, Wis. Nurse's Assn. (membership com.), APHA. Home: 1202 S 9th St Watertown WI 53094-6604

DE GOFF, VICTORIA JOAN, lawyer; b. San Francisco, Mar. 2, 1945; d. Sidney Francis and Jean Frances (Alexander) De G.; m. Peter D. Coppelman, May 2, 1971 (div. Dec. 1978); m. Richard Sherman, June 16, 1980. BA in Math. with great distinction, U. Calif., Berkeley, 1967, JD, 1972. Bar: Calif. 1972, U.S. Dist. Ct. (no. dist.) Calif. 1972, U.S. Ct. Appeals 1972, U.S. Supreme Ct. 1989. Rsch. atty. Calif. Ct. Appeal, San Francisco, 1972-73; Reginald Heber Smith Found. fellow San Francisco Neighborhood Legal Assistance Found., 1973-74; assoc. Field, De Goff, Huppert & McGowan, San Francisco, 1974-77; pvt. practice Berkeley, Calif., 1977-80; ptnr. De Goff and Sherman, Berkeley, 1980—; lectr. continuing edn. of bar, Calif., 1987, 90-92, U. Calif. Boalt Hall Sch. Law, Berkeley, 1981-85, dir. appellate advocacy, 1992; cons. California Civil Practice: Procedure, Bancroft Whitney, 1992. Author: (with others) Matthew Bender's Treatise on California Torts, 1985. Apptd. to adv. com. Calif. Jud. Coun. on Implementing Proposition 32, 1984-85; mem. adv. bd. Hastings Coll. Trial and Appellate Adv., 1984-91; expert 20/20 vision project, commn. on future cts. Jud. Coun. Calif., 1993, apptd. to appellate standing adv. com., 1993.; bd. dirs. Calif. Supreme Ct. Hist. Soc., State Bar Calif. Appellate Law Consulting Group. Fellow Woodrow Wilson Found., 1967-68. Mem. Am. Acad. Appellate Lawyers, Calif. Trial Lawyers Assn. (bd. govs. 1980-88, amicus-curiae com. 1981-87, editor-in-chief assn. mag. 1980-81, Presdl. Award of Merit 1980, 81), Calif. Acad. Appellate Lawyers (sec.-treas. 1989-90, 2d v.p. 1990-91, 1st v.p. 1991-92, pres. 1992-93), Am. Acad. Appellate Lawyers, Edward J. McFetridge Am. Inn. of Cts. (counsellor 1990-91, edn. chmn. 1991-92, social chmn. 1992-93, v.p. 1993-94, pres. 1994-95), Boalt Hall Sch. Law U. Calif. Alumni Assn. (bd. dirs. 1989-92), Order of Coif. Jewish. Office: 1916 Los Angeles Ave Berkeley CA 94707-2496

DEGOLIER, DANIELLE BEDFORD WILSON, political activist; b. Valhalla, N.Y., Dec. 6, 1947; d. Daniel Livingston and Lucy Ann (Collestano) Wilson; m. David Frederick DeGolier, Apr. 8, 1967 (div. 1984); children: Andrea Lynn, Jeffrey David; m. Charles Edward LaGreca, Feb. 14, 1986 (div. May 1993). AA in Liberal Arts Human and Social Scis., Niagara County C.C., 1991. Founder, pres. Citizens Against Pollution, Niagara County, 1980-82; founder, facilitator Love Addicts Anonymous, Niagara Falls, N.Y., 1982-88. Author: (children's book) A Lap for Leonard, 1977; columnist The Niagara Gazette, 1975-76, Nat. Women's Polit. Caucus, 1978. Founder, pres. Citizens Against Pollution, 1980-81; lobbyist for state/fed. stalkers act., Niagara Falls, 1991-93. Mem. NOW (pres. Niagara County chpt. 1993-94), Peoples Animal Lovers Soc. (founder, pub. rels. dir. 1975-76), Animal Birth Control Soc. Western N.Y. (pres. Niagara County chpt., publicity dir. 1994—).

DEGONIA, MARY ELISE, government community relations executive, publisher; b. St. Louis, Sept. 23, 1954; d. Joseph Milton and Janice Doris (Walls) DeG. Student, Riverside Community Coll., 1971-73, Calif. State U., 1973-76. Dir., youth svcs. Los Padrinos, San Bernardino, Calif., 1975-78; chief, planning and evaluation Mayor's Office of Employment and Tng., San Bernardino, 1978-79; program mgr., v.p. Mondale Task Force on Youth, Washington, 1979-80; sr. policy analyst Nat. Youth Work Alliance, Washington, 1979-81; v.p. govt. rels. Youth Employment, Washington, 1981-88; pres. Capitol Perspectives, Washington, 1988—; pub. Capitol Perspectives Update; dir. pub. policy and legislation Nat. Youth Employment Ctr., N.Y.C., 1979-89; founding mem. Nat. Assn. for Community Base Orgn., Washington, 1979-83. Co-author: State Coordination Guide, 1987, Food for Thought, 1988, Stalking the Large Green Grant, 1979, Fund Diversification Guide, 1988. Founding chmn. Calif. Child, Youth and Family Coalition, Sacramento, 1976-78; nat. bd. dirs. Wider Opportunities for Women. Recipient Outstanding Performance award, U.S. Dept. Labor, Washington, 1980, Disting. Achievement award, U.S. Basics, Alexandria, Va., 1988. Mem. Nat. Youth Employment Coalition, State Issues Forum (exec. mem., bd. dirs.), Nat. Job. Tng. Partnership. Home: 1915 17th St NW # 100 Washington DC 20009-6202 Office: Capitol Perspectives 1915 17th St NW # 200 Washington DC 20009-6202

DE GRAZIA, LORETTA THERESA, oil company executive; b. Boston, May 17, 1955; d. Gaetano T.P. and Nancy R. (Serino) De G. A in Mgmt./Mktg. magna cum laude, Newbury Coll., 1986. V.p. mktg. and sales Grimes Oil Co., Boston, 1977-85; pres. East Coast Petroleum, Boston, 1985—. Fellow NAFE, New Eng. Women Bus. Owners, Nat. Assn. Women in Constrn., Greater Boston Women's Network; mem. Women's Bus. Enterprise Alliance, Boston Women's Network. Office: East Coast Petroleum Corp 320 Adams St Dorchester MA 02122-1234

DEGUIRE, KATHRYN SILBER, psychologist; b. Mankato, Minn., Nov. 16, 1932; d. Ernest Albert and Anna (John) Silber; m. John Diaz, Aug. 22, 1981; 1 child, Lise Kathryn. MusB, Eastman Sch. Music U. Rochester, 1954; postgrad. Akademie für Musik und Darstellende Kunst, Vienna, 1954-55, Upsala Coll., 1966-69; MA, Fordham U., 1971, PhD, 1974. Pianist, organist, instr. piano, 1955-66; clin. asst. psychologist Meml. Sloan Kettering Cancer Center, N.Y.C., 1974-83; pvt. practice, N.Y.C., 1976-88, Fairfield, N.J., 1976-94, Morristown, N.J., 1988—, Blairstown, N.J., 1994—; lectr. Upsala Coll., East Orange, N.J., 1971-72, 78-81. Fulbright scholar, Vienna, 1954-55; USPHS grantee, 1969-71. Mem. APA, N.J. Psychol. Assn., Soc. Psychologists in Pvt. Practice (pres. 1986). Rec. artist: Orion. Home and Office: 55A Primrose Rd Blairstown NJ 07825

DEGUIRE, MARGARET ANN, nurse; b. Detroit, June 7, 1950; d. Gerard John and Althea Wenona (Orrill) DeG. AA, Riverside City Coll., 1973; AS, SUNY, Albany, 1981; postgrad., 1991—. RN; lic. vocational nurse; cert. advanced cardiac life support. Nurse Dr. Stamper, Riverside, Calif., 1973-75; team leader Knollwood Community Hosp., Riverside, Calif., 1975-77; nurse, critical care Riverside Community Hosp., 1977-78; staff nurse Kaiser Hosp., Fontana, Calif., 1978-81, 81-82, nurse, critical care, relief unit leader, 1982-86, treadmill nurse, 1986—. Mem. AACN, Am. Coll. Sport Medicine(exercise technologist), Internat. Dance Excercise Assn. (cert. fitness instr.), Am. Coun. Exercise (cert. aerobics instr.), Loma Linda Lopers. Home: 8809 Bennett Ave Fontana CA 92335-8648 Office: SCPMG 9961 Sierra Ave Fontana CA 92335-6720

DE HAAN-PULS, JOYCE ELAINE, sales account representative; b. Grand Rapids, Mich., Dec. 22, 1941; d. Harry Herman and Dorothy Elaine (Kikstra) DeHaan; student Calvin Coll., 1960-61; BS with honors, Grand Valley State Colls., 1978; postgrad. U. Sarajevo, Yugoslavia, 1978, Grad. Inst., Siedman Grad. Coll., 1979—; M in Speech Communications Wayne State U., 1986 ; children: Bruce Todd, Daniel Lane, Cristy-Ann Sara Elizabeth Puls. Owner, operator Joyce Elaine's Beauty Parlor, Grandville, Mich., 1960-64; asst. assessor City of Hudsonville, Mich., 1978; dir. displaced homemaker program Women's Resource Ctr., Grand Rapids, 1979-81; visual products rep. 3M Corp., Grand Rapids, 1982-85, sr. account rep., Detroit, 1985-89, regional sales mgr. S.E. Mich., 1989-93; v.p. mktg. TransContinental Traders, Ltd., Detroit, 1993—; mem. Ottawa County (Mich.) CETA Adv. Bd. Bd. dirs. Downtown Day Care Ctr., Grand Rapids, 1972. Recipient Cert. of Appreciation Bishop of Saigon, Vietnam, 1969; Top Sales rep. 3M/US, 1983, VIP, 1983, 84, 85, 86, 87, 88, 89; Phillip Morris scholar, 1975. Mem. Preservation Wayne, Detroit Internat. Vis. Coun. Mem. NAFE, Internat. Visitors Coun., Nat. Assn. Fgn. Students, Grand Rapids Coun. on World Affairs, Am. Soc. Pub. Adminstrn, Hist. Indian Village Assn. Republican. Home: 1060 Parker St Detroit MI 48214-2613 Office: Transcontinental Traders Ltd 1060 Parker St Ste 100 Detroit MI 48214-2613

DEHAVEN, NORMA JEANNE, municipal official and treasurer; b. Colorado Springs, Colo., Oct. 13, 1958; d. Burt W. DeHaven, July 29, 1983; children: John Parker, Spencer Paul, Jacob Craig. BSBA, Colo. State U., 1980. Cert. pub. mgr. and mcpl. treas., Wis. Office mgr. Van Creech Millwork, Manitou Springs, Colo., 1978-80; acct. LP Creech Acctg., Colorado Springs, 1980-83; office mgr. Kitchens by Custom Craftsman, Madison, Wis., 1983-85; fin. asst. dir. New Age Healing & Psychotherapy Clinic, Madison, Wis., 1983-85; bus. mgr., dep. treas. Town of Madison, Wis., 1987—, pers. dir., affirmative action and equal opportunity officer, 1987-93. artist watercolors and portraits. Mem. Wis. Cert. Pub. Mgrs. (charter, treas., bd. dirs. 1993—), Mcpl. Treas. Assn. Wis., Govt. Fin. Officers Assn. Office: Town of Madison 2120 Fish Hatchery Rd Madison WI 53713-1289

DEHN, LETHA ARLENE See FIGGINS, LETHA ARLENE

DEHOUSKE, ELLEN JANE, early childhood education educator, consultant; b. Cleve., Aug. 17, 1945; d. Joseph and Elsie (Eberling) D. BS in Edn., Duquesne U., 1967, MS in Edn., 1973; postgrad., California U. Pa., 1973; PhD, U. Pitts., 1981. High sch. English tchr. Boyle High Sch., Homestead, Pa., 1968-72; spl. edn. tchr. Allegheny Intermediate Unit, Pitts., 1972-79; grad. asst. U. Pitts., 1979-81; mental health cons. Psychiat. Assn. for Consultation and Therapy, Pitts., 1981-82; head tchr., pre-sch. tchr., play therapist Arsenal Family and Children's Ctr., Pitts., 1982-85; spl. edn. tchr. Highland Sch., Pitts., 1988; prof. early childhood edn. Carlow Coll., Pitts., 1988—; creative writing cons. Arts and Spl. Edn. Project, Harrisburg, Pa., 1980-90; ind. child devel. cons., Pitts., 1979-81; mem. Task Force on Family Resources, Pitts., 1991-92; mem. steering com. Alliance for Early Childhood Edn., Harrisburg, 1991-93. Contbr. articles to profl. jours. Mem. Assn. for Childhood Edn. Internat., Nat. Assn. for Edn. Young Children, Coun. for Exceptional Children, Pitts. Assn. for Edn. Young Children (v.p. 1992—), Coun. for Early Childhood Edn. (child advocate), Phi Delta Kappa. Home: 710 Copeland St. Unit 12 Pittsburgh PA 15232 Office: Carlow Coll Edn Divsn 3333 5th Ave Pittsburgh PA 15213-3165

DE HOYOS, DEBORA M., lawyer; b. Monticello, N.Y., Aug. 10, 1953; d. Luis and Marion (Kinney) de H.; m. Walter C. Carlson, June 20, 1981; children: Amanda, Greta, Linnea. BA, Wellesley Coll., 1975; JD, Harvard U., 1978. Bar: Ill. 1978, U.S. Dist. Ct. (no. dist.) Ill. 1980. Assoc. Mayer, Brown & Platt, Chgo., 1978-84, ptnr., 1985-91, mng. ptnr., 1991—; bd. dirs. Am. Paging, Inc., Evanston Hosp. Corp., Providence St. Mel. Sch. Contbr. chpt. to Securitization of Financial Assets, 1991. Chmn. strategic issues com. Econ. Devel. Commn., Chgo., 1992. Mem. Chgo. Coun. Lawyers. Office: Mayer Brown & Platt 190 S La Salle St Chicago IL 60603-3410

DEIDAN, CECILIA THERESA, neuropsychologist; b. N.Y.C., Oct. 24, 1964. BA Biology, Spanish, Psychology, St. Louis U., 1985; MEd in Counseling Psychology, U. Mo., 1987, PhD in Counseling Psychology, 1992. Lic. psychologist, Fla., sch. psychol. examiner, Mo. Counselor, detoxification asst. McCambridge Ctr. for Women, Columbia, Mo., 1986-88; shc. psychol. examiner Columbia Pub. Schs., 1988-90; geriatric neuropsychology postdoctoral fellow U. Miami Sch. Med., 1992-93; pvt. practice Pembroke Pines, Fla., 1993—; adj. prof. Fla. Internat. U., Miami, 1993—. Mem. ACA, NAN, APA, Kappa Delta Pi, Psi Chi, Sigma Delta Pi, Alpha Sigma Nu, Beta Beta Beta.

DEIOTTE, MARGARET WILLIAMS TUKEY, non-profit consultant, grants writer; b. Lafayette, Ind., Mar. 6, 1952; d. Ronald B. and Elizabeth A. (Williams) Tukey; m. Charles E. Deiotte, Sept. 11, 1971; children: Raymond, Karl, Ronald. Student, U. Wash., 1969-72, 77-79. V.p., treas. Logical Systems, Inc., Colorado Springs, 1982-86; v.p. CEDSYS, Inc., Colorado Springs, 1987-92; pres. Penrose Enrichment Program Found., Colorado Springs, Colo., 1988-89; free lance tech. and grant proposal writer, 1990-94; dir. Rexall Showcase Internat., 1994—; conf. coord. Colo. Assn. Ptnrs. in Edn., 1994; presenter seminar Pikes Peace Pace Conf., 1991, 92. Mem. adv. bd. gifted and talented Sch. Dist. 11, 1989—, mem. grant writing team; pres. Penrose Elem. PTA, 1989-91; 1st v.p. El Paso Coun. PTA, 1990-91, treas., 1991-92; mem. grants commn. Colo. State PTA, 1990-91; coach Odyssey of the Mind, 1990, 91-92; bd. dirs. YMCA Youth Leadership Inst., 1990-92, 92—; mem. dist. accountability com. Sch. Dist. 38, 1993-94; bd. dirs. Sch. Dist. 38 Found., 1994—; accountability chmn. Lewis-Palmer Mid. Sch. Mem. NAFE. Home and Office: 16955 Vollmer Rd Colorado Springs CO 80908-1622

DEISSLER, MARY A., foundation executive; b. Oneanta, N.Y., Dec. 30, 1955; d. George W. and Carol (Zorda) Baker; m. James N. Deissler, Nov. 24, 1987; children: Benjamin, Eliza. BA, U. Mass., 1978; MBA, Babson Coll., 1982. Fin. analyst Digital Equipment Corporation, Maynard, Mass., 1978-82; devel. dir. Handel & Haydn Soc., Boston, 1984-89, gen. mgr., 1984-89, exec. dir., 1990—; pres., bd. dirs. Studebaker Movement Theatre Co., Boston, 1986-88. Bd. dirs. Early Music Am., N.Y.C., 1989—, v.p., 1991—, pres., 1994; bd. dirs. Babson Coll., 1990-94, Chorus Am., 1991—, v.p., 1992; mem. adv. bd. Arts/Boston, 1994—, assoc. bd. dirs.; bd. dirs. Boston Ptnrs. in Edn. Mem. Am. Symphony Orch. League. Office: Handel & Haydn Soc 300 Massachusetts Ave Boston MA 02115-4544

DEITZ, PAULA, magazine editor; b. Trenton, N.J., Apr. 26, 1938; d. David and Rosalie (Nathanson) D.; m. (George) Frederick Morgan, Nov. 30, 1969. BA, Smith Coll., 1959; MA, Columbia U., 1969. Asst. editor Bollingen series Bollingen Found., N.Y.C., 1962-67; assoc. editor The Hudson Rev., N.Y.C., 1967-75, co-editor, 1975—; rsch. asst. Pakistan Mission to UN, N.Y.C., 1961; lectr. Columbia U., N.Y.C., 1962. Contbr. articles on art, architecture, landscape design to newspapers and mags. bd. counselors Smith Coll., 1992—. Mem. Cosmopolitan Club. Office: The Hudson Rev 684 Park Ave New York NY 10021-5043

DEITZ, SUSAN ROSE, newspaper advice columnist; b. Far Rockaway, N.Y., Mar. 21, 1934; d. Emanuel and Florence Jean (Goodstein) Davis; m. Morris J. Mandelker, Nov. 29, 1975; 1 son, Scott Richard; m. Richard Alan Deitz, Dec. 22, 1958 (dec. 1967). Student Smith Coll., Barnard Coll., N.Y.C., Art Students League, N.Y.C., Stella Adler Theater Studio. Syndicated advice columnist L.A. Times Syndicate, 1975—; mem. faculty New Sch., N.Y.C., 1977-79; radio personality, 1979; columnist Prodigy Svcs., White Plains, N.Y., 1987-93; speaker satellite conf. NAFE, 1990. Author: (novel) Valency Girl, 1976, Single File, 1989, paperback edit., 1990. Mem. Women in Communications (Outstanding Mem. award 1984), Authors Guild, Overseas Press Club (elect), Smith Coll. Club.

DEKALB, DONETTE LYNN, quality assurance professional; b. Granville, N.Y., Dec. 12, 1963; d. Donald Wayne and Sharon Louise (Aldous) DeK. BS in Bus., SUNY, Plattsburgh, 1986. Computer support McDonnell Douglas Helicopter Co., Mesa, Ariz., 1986-87; internat. salesperson Jensen Tools, Phoenix, 1987; mktg. developer Dir. Safety, Phoenix, 1987-88; with computer support TRW/MEAD, San Diego, 1988-89, quality engr., 1989-92; configuration mgmt. cons. Hughes-JVC, Carlsbad, Calif., 1993; quality assurance mgr. Trade Svc. Corp., LaJolla, Calif., 1994—. Mem. San Diego Quality Coun., ISO 9000 Users Group. Home: 14385 El Vestido St San Diego CA 92129 Office: Trade Svc Corp 10996 Torreyana Rd San Diego CA 92121

DE KANTER, ELLEN ANN, English language professional, educator; b. Spokane, Wash., Mar. 10, 1926; d. George L. and Alison P. (Christy) Tharp; m. Scipio de Kanter, Feb. 2, 1949 (dec.); children: Scipio, Georgette, Robert, Adriana. BA, Mexico City Coll.-U. of Ams., 1947; MEd, U. Houston, 1972, MA in Spanish, 1974, EdD, 1979. Dir. bilingual edn., prof. U. St. Thomas, Houston, dir. bilingual edn., 1979—. Contbr. articles to profl. jours. Title VII grantee, 1986-89, 88-91, 89-92, 92-93, 92-95, 94-97. Mem. Nat. Assn. Bilingual Edn. (chmn. 1989 conf., program chair 1993 conf.), Houston Area Assn. Bilingual Edn. (pres. 1987-88), Inst. Hispanic Culture (bd. dirs. 1989-90). Home: 3015 Meadowview Dr Missouri City TX 77459-3308 Office: U St Thomas 3800 Montrose Blvd Houston TX 77006-4626

DEKAY, BARBARA ANN, social worker; b. Louisville, Mar. 29, 1955; d. William Richard and Mildred Anita (Chapin) DeK.; div. 1989; 1 child, Jonathan Richard; m. Jonathon P. Hubbert, 1994. BA, U. Louisville, 1976, MSSW, 1979. Lic. clin. social worker, Ky. Residential aide Lynwood Treatment Ctr., Louisville, 1976-77; house mgr. Phoenix House Louisville Dept. Human Svcs., 1977-79; Ohio County coord. Green River Comprehensive Care Ctr., Owensboro, Ky., 1980-82; psychiat. social worker VA Med. Ctr., North Chicago, Ill., 1982; psychiat. social worker VA Med. Ctr., Louisville, 1982-83, 84-86, med.-surg. social worker, 1983-84, outpatient therapist, 1986-93, outpatient coord. post-traumatic stress disorder unit, 1993-94; asst. dir. emergency psychiatry svc., dept. psychiatry and behavioral scis., sch. medicine U. Louisville, 1994—; cons., therapist Naval Ordnance Sta., Louisville, 1989-93; cons. U.S. Post Office, Louisville, 1990. Mem. Nat. Assn. Social Workers. Republican. Methodist. Home: 10409 Cady Cove Ct Louisville KY 40223 Office: U Louisville Hosp Emergency Psychiatry Svcs 520 S Jackson St Louisville KY 40292

DEKKER, HARRIETT GROMB, psychologist; b. Bklyn., Mar. 1, 1942; d. Jack and Rachel (Bershinsky) Gromb; m. Marcel Dekker, July 22, 1967; children: Russell, David, Jacqueline. BA, Queens Coll., 1964; MA, NYU, 1967; postgrad. in spl. edn., Coll. of New Rochelle, 1974; cert. in handwriting, New Sch. for Social Rsch., 1988. Cert. elem. tchr. Tchr. grades 5 and 6 Pub. Sch. 152, Woodside, N.Y., 1964-64; tchr. grade 3 Flower Hill Sch., Huntington, N.Y., 1965-67; tchr. lang. arts Hallen Ctr. Maximum Edn., White Plains, N.Y., 1974-76; pvt. practice Greenwich, Conn., 1976-78; counselor, coord., dir. Support Svcs.-Aid for Retarded, Stamford, Conn., 1978-84; dir. Profl. Insight, Inc., Greenwich, Conn., 1985—. Bd. dirs. Gateway Communities, Inc., Greenwich, 1988—. Mem. Am. Psychol. Assn. (assoc.), Am. Soc. Profl. Graphologists, Nat. Graphological Soc. Home: 41 Londonderry Dr Greenwich CT 06830-3508 Office: Profl Insight Inc PO Box 7854 Greenwich CT 06836-7854

DE KONINCK, JESSICA GORTON, lawyer; b. N.Y.C., Apr. 14, 1953; d. David Joseph Gorton and Rosaline (Shevach) Diamant; m. Paul M. de Koninck, June 22, 1975; children: Isabel Hope and Henry Louis. BA magna cum laude, Brandeis U., 1975; JD, Boston U., 1978. Bar: Mass. 1978, U.S. Dist. Ct. Mass. 1979, U.S. Ct. Appeals (1st cir.) 1979, N.J. 1980, U.S. Dist. Ct. N.J. 1980, U.S. Ct. Appeals (3d cir.) 1983. With Greater Boston Legal Svcs., 1977-78, O'Connell & Macarelli, Lynn, Mass., 1978, de Koninck & Munsen, Boston, 1979-81; sect. chief govtl. affairs Essex County Counsel's Office, Newark, N.J., 1981-86; with Vogel, Chait, Schwartz & Collins, Morristown, N.J., 1987, Hyman & de Koninck, Montclair, N.J., 1988—. Councilwoman Montclair Twp. Coun., 1992—; appt. mem. State N.J. Consortium Consumer Edn., 1991—; mem. Montclair environ. adv. com., 1989-92, sec. 1990-91, vice-chair 1992; mem., guest spkr. Preservation N.J., 1990; trustee Jewish Edn. Assn. Metrowest, 1991—; exec. bd. dirs. B'nai Keshet/Montclair Jewish Ctr., 1989-92; mem. Consumers League N.J. Recipient mayor's award for disting. svc., Paterson, N.J., 1990; named one of 50 Women You Should Know, Montclair/West Essex YWCA, 1994. Mem. N.J. State Bar Assn. (local govt. law sect., real property, probate and trust law sect., land use law secct., environ. law sect., election law com.), Essex County Bar Assn. (cert. appreciation 1990, community dispute resolution panel), Women's Law Alumnae Orgn. Boston U. (pres. 1980), Essex County Women Lawyers Assn., N.J. Assn. Elected Women Officials. Office: 101 Park St Montclair NJ 07042-5948

DELABARRE POWERS, NANCY MAY, quality improvement administrator; b. Fargo, N.D., Aug. 17, 1941; d. Marvin Stanley Ness and Lila Mae (Mohagen) Weldon; m. Delbert Melvin DelaBarre, Apr. 1, 1961 (div. 1967); children: Garret Scott, Eric Allen; m. William Rhodes Powers, Feb. 28, 1988. Student, U. N.D., 1959-60, U. Nev., 1977, 83, 84. Cert. examiner 1993 U.S. Senate Productivity Awards. Legal sec. B.L. Spears, Atty., San Bernardino, Calif., 1967; asst. to pres. A & B Enterprises, Yucaipa, Calif., 1967-72; escrow agt., adminstrv. asst. Title Ins. and Trust, San Bernardino, 1972-75; customer svc. rep. Lewis Homes of Nev., Las Vegas, 1975-77; mgmt. analyst, asst. right of way agt. City of Las Vegas, 1977-84; dir. emergency mgmt., handicap compliance coord., mgmt. analyst, grant adminstr., registered lobbyist City of North Las Vegas, 1984-93, sr. mgmt. analyst, 1991-94, quality improvement administrator, 1995—; mentor U. Nev.-Las Vegas Women's Ctr. Mentoring Program, 1993-94. Mem. So. Nev. Women's Polit. Caucus, Clark County, 1988-89, chmn., 1991-92, state sec., 1993-94. Recipient Valley of Heros award Clark County Boys & Girls Club, 1988, Cert. of Appreciation ARC, 1986. Mem. Am. Soc. for Quality Control, Am. Pub. Works Assn. (exec. bd. 1986, sec.-treas. 1987-88, vice chair 1988-89, chair 1989-90, bd. dirs. Nev. chpt. 1991-93, Disting. Mem. of Yr. 1992, v.p. 1992-93, pres.-elect 1993-94, pres. 1994-95), Nat. C. of C. Emergency Mgrs. Office: City of North Las Vegas 2200 Civic Center Dr North Las Vegas NV 89030-6307

DE LAGUNA, FREDERICA, anthropology educator emeritus, consultant; b. Ann Arbor, Mich., Oct. 3, 1906; d. Theodore and Grace Mead (Andrus) de L. A.B., Bryn Mawr Coll., 1927; Ph.D., Columbia U., 1933; L.H.D. (hon.), U. Alaska, 1982. Asst., field dir. U. Pa. Mus., Phila., 1931-35; lectr. anthropology Bryn Mawr (Pa.) Coll., 1938-41, asst. prof., 1941-42, 46-49, assoc. prof., 1949-55, prof. anthropology, 1955-75, prof. emeritus, 1975—; vis. lectr. or vis. prof. U. Pa., U. Calif.-Berkeley, Bryn Mawr Coll. Author:

The Thousand March: Adventures of an American Boy with Garibaldi, 1930, The Archaeology of Cook Inlet, Alaska, 1934, reprinted, 1975, The Arrow Points to Murder, 1937, Fog on the Mountain, 1938, (with Kaj Birket-Smith) The Eyak Indians of the Copper River Delta, Alaska, 1938, Prehistory of Northern America as Seen from the Yukon, 1947, Chugach Prehistory: The Archaeology of Prince William Sound, 1956, reprinted 1967, The Story of a Tlingit Community, 1960, (with others) The Archeology of the Yakutat Bay Area, Alaska, 1964, Under Mount Saint Elias, 3 vols., 1972, Voyage to Greenland: A Personal Initiation into Anthropology, 1977, Tales from the Dena, 1995; editor: Selected Papers from the American Anthropologist, 1888-1920, 1960, reprinted 1976, The Tlingit Indians (George Thornton Emmons), 1991. Recipient Lindback award for Disting. Teaching, Bryn Mawr Coll., 1975, Rochester Mus. award and fellowship, 1941, numerous fellowships including: Columbia U., 1930-31, NRC, 1936-37, Rockefeller Found., 1945-46, Wenner-Gren Found., 1949-50, Social Sci. Research Council, 1962-63; grantee Am. Philos. Soc., Arctic Inst. of N.Am., Bryn Mawr Coll., NEH, NSF, U. Pa. Mus., Wenner-Gren Found. for Anthrop. Rsch. Fellow AAAS, Am. Anthrop. Assn. (pres.-elect, pres. 1965-67, Disting. Svc. award 1986), Arctic Inst. N.Am. (hon. life); mem. NAS, Soc. for Am. Archaeology (1st v.p. 1949-50, 50th Ann. award 1986), No. Studies Assn. (internat. secretariat, hon. pres. 1991—), Phila. Anthropology Soc. (pres. 1939-40), Alaska Anthrop. Assn. (hon. life, award for lifetime contbn. to Alaskan anthropology 1993), Homer (Alaska) Natural History Soc. (hon. life, Silver Trowel award). Democrat. Home and Office: Apt 510 830 Montgomery Ave Bryn Mawr PA 19010

DELAHANTY, REBECCA ANN, school system administrator; b. South Bend, Ind., Oct. 18, 1941; d. Raymond F. and Ann Marie (Batsleer) Paczesny; m. Edward Delahanty, June 22, 1963; children: David, Debbie. BA, Coll. of St. Catherine, Minn., 1977; MA, Coll. St. Thomas, Minn., 1983; PhD, Ga. State U., 1994. Cert. in adminstrn. and supervision, Ga. Initiator, tchr. gifted kindergarten Dist. 284 Sch., Wayzata, Minn., 1977-83; gifted kindergarten coord. St. Barts Sch., Wayzata, 1983-85; prin. Dabbs Loomis Sch., Dunwoody, Ga., 1987-91; asst. to supt. Buford (Ga.) City Schs., 1993—; mem. staff devel. adv. coun. Ga. Contbr. article to profl. publ. Mem. AAUW, ASCD, Am. Ednl. Rsch. Assn., Nat. Assn. Gifted Children, Minn. Coun. Gifted and Talented, Phi Delta Kappa, Omicron Gamma.

DELAMAR, LINDA M., primary care nurse, educator; b. N.Y.C., Sept. 21, 1954; d. Rudy J. and Olga DeLamar. BSN, U. Md., Balt., 1981; MSN, Widener U., 1990; postgrad. nursing anesthesia, Nazareth Hosp., Phila., 1992-94. CEN, CCRN; cert. flight nurse, ACLS instr., ATLS, PALS. Flight nurse, instr. USAFR, McGuire AFB, N.J.; flight nurse West Jersey Health Systems, Camden, N.J.; clin. nurse specialist, emergency dept. Cooper Hosp. Med. Ctr., Camden, 1992-94. Mem. Critical Incident Stress Debriefing Team. With U.S. Army, 1972-75, capt. USAFR, 1983—. Mem. AACN, Emergency Nurses Assn., Nat. Flight Nurses Assn., Am. Trauma Soc., U. Md. Alumni Assn., AANA, Sigma Theta Tau.

DELANEY, BETH MARIE PENNE, electrical engineer; b. Austin, Minn., Sept. 20, 1965; d. Robert S. and Una Mae (Astrup) Penne; m. Kurt Allan Delaney, June 10, 1989. BSEE, N.D. State U., 1988. Component engr. Hewlett Packard Co., Loveland, Colo., 1988—; ednl. ptnr. Bridges/ Hewlett Packard, Loveland, 1992—. Youth advisor Mt. View Presbyn. Experiencing Excitement and Religion, Loveland, 1990—. Mem. Tau Beta Pi, Eta Kappa Nu. Office: Hewlett Packard 815 SW 14th St Loveland CO 80537

DELANEY, ELEANOR CECILIA COUGHLIN, educator; b. Elizabeth, N.J.; d. John C. and Eleanor C. (Fadde) Coughlin; B.S., Sch. Edn. Rutgers U., 1930, M.A., 1939; Ph.D., Columbia U., 1954; 1 son, John. Tchr. public schs., Elizabeth, N.J., 1927; prin. Woodrow Wilson Sch., Elizabeth, 1941-55; prof. Grad. Sch. Edn., Rutgers U., New Brunswick, N.J., 1955-87, prof. emeritus, 1987—, chmn. dept. ednl. adminstrn. and supervision, 1974—; vis. prof. William and Mary Coll., U. Mex., Columbia U.; ednl. cons. sch. systems, N.J., N.Y., Va., 1950—; con. U.S. Dept. State, Health and Edn., coordinator Intern-Am. Affairs. Mem. Elizabeth Charter Commn., 1960-61; chmn. Mayor's Adv. Commn. on Urban Devel., 1962-64, Elizabeth Human Relations Commn., 1968-75; mem. Elizabeth Bd. Edn., 1972-79, pres., 1973-76; mem. exec. bd. Union County chpt. ARC; mem. exec. bd. Vis. Nurse and Health Assn., 1977—; pres., 1981-85. Mem. AAUW, Nat., N.J. edn. assns., Dept. Elem. Sch. Prins., AAUP, AAAS, Am. Ednl. Research Assn., Kappa Delta Pi (counelor 1970-87, Nat. Honor Key), Pi Lambda Theta, Phi Delta Kappa. Author: Spanish Gold, Lands of Middle America, Our Friends in South America, Science-Life Series, Book 4; Persistent Problems in Education. Contbr. articles to profl. mags. Home: 19220 SW 88th Ct Miami FL 33157-8933

DELANEY, JEAN MARIE, art educator; b. Jersey City, Nov. 14, 1931; d. John Francis and Genevieve Mary (Boulton) Reilly; m. Donald Kendall Delaney, Dec. 29, 1956; 1 child, Laura Marie. BA in Art Edn., Fairmont (W.Va.) State U., 1954; MA in Clin. Psychology, Loyola Coll., Balt., 1979; PhD in Art Edn., U. Wis., Milw., 1992. Cert. art tchr., prin., supr., Md. Tchr. English and social studies Reedurban Sch., Stark County, Ohio, 1954-56; art tchr. Perry Hall High Sch., Stark County, 1956-57, Margaret Brent High Sch., St. Mary's County, Md., 1957-59, Middle River Mid. Sch., Baltimore County, Md., 1959-62; home and hosp. tchr. Harford County (Md.) Bd. Edn., 1968-78; lectr. art appreciation U. Md. Extension, Harford County, 1971-76; art educator Baltimore County Bd. Edn., 1979-93; assoc. prof. art edn. S.W. Mo. State U., Springfield, 1993—; cons. Salisbury (Md.) State Coll., 1987; adj. prof. art edn. Md. Inst. Coll. Art, Balt., 1988-89; cons. bd. examiners and art edn. text devel. com. ETS, Princeton, N.J., 1988-92. Author: Art Image, 6th Grade Unites, 1988; editor: Art Scholarships, 1988; editor videotape Ernest Goldstein: Art Criticism, 1987; author, editor curriculum guide. Recipient Youth Art Month award of excellence Art and Craft Materials Inst., 1989, grant to coordinate Crayola Dreammakers program for Ctrl. Region U.S. and Can., 1994-96. Mem. NEA, Nat. Art Edn. Assn. (Eastern Region Art Educator award 1989, Nat. Secondary Art Educator award 1990), Md. Art Assn. (state coun. 1985—, v.p. arts advocacy 1988-89, pres.-elect 1992—, Md. Art Educator of Yr. 1988), Internat. Soc. for Edn. Through Art. Home: 634 S National # 402 Springfield MO 65804 Office: Southwest Missouri State U 901 S National Springfield MO 65804

DELANEY, LISA ANN, electrical engineer; b. Massapequa, N.Y., Apr. 6, 1965; d. John Richard and Lorraine (Thiell) D. BSEE, Fla. Inst. Tech., 1987; postgrad. in bus. adminstrn., U. Ctrl. Fla., 1995—. EIT, Fla. Sr. hardware engr. Grumman Tech. Svcs. Kennedy Space Ctr., Orlando, Fla., 1987—. Mem. IEEE, Nat. Mgmt. Assn., Soc. Women Engrs. Home: 7667 N Wickham Rd # 914 Melbourne FL 32940 Office: Grumman Tech Svcs GTS-646 Kennedy Space Ctr Orlando FL 32899

DELANEY, NANCY JO, statistician, consultant; b. Buffalo, N.Y., Sept. 15, 1941; d. Howard Joseph and Josephine Laura (Garguiolo) Klein; m. Thomas James Delaney; 1 child, Kathleen Grace Delaney. BS in Math., SUNY, 1962, MS in Math., 1963; MS in Stats., Rensselaer Poly. Inst., 1975, PhD in Stats., 1979. Math. tchr. various high schs. and jr. coll., Albany, Schenectady, N.Y., 1966-74; data analyst Space Astronomy Lab., Albany, 1974-76; asst. prof. Union Coll. Inst. Adminstrn. and Mgmt., Schenectady, 1978-82, Northeastern U. Coll. Bus., Boston, 1982-88; statis. advisor Mobil Solar Energy Corp., Billerica, Mass., 1988-92; asst. prof. Suffolk U., Sch. Mgmt., Boston, 1993—; cons. Gen. Foods Inc., Tarrytown, N.Y., 1978, Sterling Drugs, Albany, 1981, Bard Cardiosurgery, Billerica, 1985-86, Design Tech., Billerica, 1993. Contbr. articles to profl. jours. Mem. Am. Soc. for Quality Control, Ops. Rsch. Soc. Am., Am. Statis. Assn. (Boston chpt., program chmn. 1984-85, treas. 1986—), Epsilon Delta Sigma. Office: Suffolk U 8 Ashburton Pl Boston MA 02108-2701

DELANO, MARY LOUISE, photographer, small business owner; b. Tampa, Fla., Dec. 31, 1953; d. Carl Robert and Beatrice A. (Lees) Heise; m. James W. Delano, July 14, 1973 (div. Aug. 1982); children: Alicia Ann, Sarah Elizabeth. Grad., Rhode Island Sch. Photography, 1989, Our Lady of Good Coun. Acad., 1973. EMT Stamford Ambulance Corp., Stamford, Conn., 1978-83, Bridgeport Ambulance Svc., Bridgeport, Conn., 1981-83; prin. Doc's Hot Dogs, Providence, R.I., 1985-87; prin., photographer Delano Portraits, Smithfield, R.I., 1989-91; photographer Rainville Studios, Whitersville, Mass., 1988-91; prin., photographer Delano Portraits, Warwick, R.I., 1991—. Recipient Court of Honor award Profl. Photographers Assn. Rhode Island, 1989, 90, 95, Judges award, 1989, 90. 95., Kodak Gallery award 1995, Hallmark award, 1995, People's Choice award, 1995. Mem. Profl. Photographers Assn. R.I. (bd. dirs. 1991—, props chmn. 1991, 92, newsletter editor 1993-94), Profl. Photographers Assn. New England (chair 1995), Profl. Photographers Assn. Am. Roman Catholic. Home: 94 Sunnyside Dr Warwick RI 02889-4409 Office: Delano Portraits 94 Sunnyside Dr Warwick RI 02889-4409

DELANY, DANA, actress; b. N.Y.C., Mar. 13, 1956. Student, Wesleyan U. Appeared in TV series Love of Life, 1979-80, As the World Turns, 1981, Magnum PI, 1986-88, Sweet Surrender, 1987, China Beach, 1988-91 (Emmy award for best actress in a drama series 1989, 92), in TV films Threesome, 1984, Liberty, 1986, A Winner Never Quits, 1986, A Promise to Keep, 1990, The Enemy Within, 1994, Choices of the Heart: The Margaret Sanger Story, 1995, (miniseries) Wild Palms, 1993; in films The Fan, 1981, Almost You, 1984, Where the River Runs Black, 1986, Masquerade, 1988, Patty Hearst, 1988, Moon over Parador, 1988, Housesitter, 1992, Light Sleeper, 1992, Tombstone, 1993, Exit to Eden, 1994; on Broadway in Translations, 1995. Office: Internat Creative Mgmt 8942 Wilshire Blvd Beverly Hills CA 90211*

DELAPA, JUDITH ANNE, business owner; b. Bad Axe, Mich., Feb. 1, 1938; d. John Vincent and Ellen Agatha (Peters) McCormick; m. James Patrick DeLapa, Jan. 10, 1959; children: Joseph Anthony, James P. II, John M., Gina M. BS, Mich. State U., 1959, MA, 1985. Tchr. various schs., Mich., 1959-64; co-founder Saluto Foods Corp., Benton Harbor, Mich., 1963-76; founder Earthtone Interiors, St. Joseph, Mich., 1977-82, High Impact Mktg. Svcs., Grand Rapids, Mich., 1987—; mktg. cons., writer various clients, nationwide. Author: High-Impact Business Strategies, 1989; pub. (newsletter) High-Impact Communication Line. Bd. dirs. Leadership Grand Rapids. Judith A. DeLapa Perennial Garden named in her honor Michigan State U. Office: High Impact Mktg Svcs 2505 East Paris Rd SE Grand Rapids MI 49546

DELAVAN, JOANNE, communications executive; b. Atlanta, Sept. 4, 1953; d. William David and Joan Rae (Reaves) DeL.; 1 child, Erin Chandler Williams. BA summa cum laude, Agnes Scott Coll., 1975; postgrad., Emory U., 1975-80, Harvard U., 1976-80. Dir. pub. rels. Life Office Mgmt. Assn., Atlanta, 1980-84; dir. comm. VideoStar Connections, Atlanta, 1984-85; gen. mgr. pub. rels., speechwriter to pres. BellSouth Telecom., Atlanta, 1985-89; gen. mgr. pub. rels. BellSouth Cellular Corp., Atlanta, 1989-93; sr. comm. specialist Atlanta Com. for Olympic Games, 1993-94; dir. corporate comm. Randstad U.S.A., Atlanta, 1994—; speechwriter to former chief of staff The White House, for Ga. gubernatorial candidate, 1980-82; Breck Girl, Shulton USA, N.Y.C., 1987-88; nat. TV spokesperson, 1989-90; author more than 350 speeches delivered by polit. and bus. leaders, 1980—. Author more than 150 articles in nat. publs.; Olympic editor Delta Sky mag. Dir. Hardy Gregory for Supreme Ct. Campaign, Ga., 1983. Recipient Phoenix award Pub. Rels. Soc. Am., 1986, Silver Flame award Internat. Assn. Bus. Communicators, 1992, other awards; Stukes scholar Agnes Scott Coll., 1974-75; Emory U. fellow, 1975-80; Danforth honoree, 1974, Fulbright honoree, 1980.

DELBALZO, GAIL, general counsel; b. N.Y.C.; d. William and Alice (Boye) Millar; m. Vincent Del Balzo, Sept. 17, 1988; children: Joseph Vincent, Jeanne Francis. Student, SUNY, Oswego, 1973-75; BA, SUNY, Buffalo, 1977, JD, 1980. Bar: N.Y. 1981, D.C. 1981. Counsel U.S. Senate Com. Budget, 1981-82, sr. counsel, 1983-84; asst. U.S. Senate parliamentarian, 1984-88; assoc. gen. counsel Congl. Budget Office, Washington, 1989-92, gen. counsel, 1992—. Office: Congressional Budget Office Ford House Bldg Rm 408 Washington DC 20515*

DEL DUCA, RITA, educator; b. N.Y.C., Apr. 1, 1933; d. Joseph and Ermelinda (Buonaguro) Ferraro; m. Joseph Anthony Del Duca, Oct. 29, 1955; children: Lynn, Susan, Paul, Andrea. BA, CUNY, 1955. Elem. tchr. Yonkers (N.Y.) Pub. Schs., 1955-57; tchr. kindergarten Sacred Heart Sch., Yonkers, 1962-64; tchr. piano, Scarsdale, N.Y., 1973-79; asst. office mgr. Foot Clinic, Hartsdale, N.Y., 1977-85; tchr. ESL, Linguarama Exec. Sch., White Plains, N.Y., 1985-89; ESL tutor, Scarsdale, 1989—. Dist. leader Greenburgh (N.Y.) Rep. Com., 1991-92. Home and Office: 6 Paradise Dr Scarsdale NY 10583-1522

DELEE, NINA C., massage therapist, middle school educator; b. El Paso, Tex., Mar. 1, 1953; d. Salvador E. and Celia María (Campos) Chávez; m. John Scott DeLee III. BA in Mus., U. North Tex., 1975, BA in Spanish, 1976; MA, U. Dallas, 1980. Tchr. Dallas Ind. Sch. Dist., 1976-92; sales rep. Houghton Mifflin Pub. Co., Dallas, 1992-93; massage therapist Spa at the Crescent, Dallas, 1993—; owner, massage therapist Body Links, Dallas, 1994—; head trainer NLP Learning Sys. Corp., Dallas, 1990—. Life mem. W.H. Gaston Mid. Sch. PTA, Dallas, 1987—, mem. exec. bd., 1984-86, cosponsor student coun., 1986-92, coord. conflict resolution, 1990-92. Fellow Am. Massage Therapy Assn. Home: 2621 Brushwood Ln Mesquite TX 75150 Office: Body Links 12900 Preston Rd Ste 543 Dallas TX 75230

DELEO, CHRISTINE ELLEN, learning disabilities specialist; b. Quincy, Mass., May 13, 1952; d. Louis Philip and Ruth Edith (Kelly) Barker; m. Frederick Michael DeLeo, Aug. 26, 1976; children: Tara Kelly, Anna Kathryn. BS, Bridgewater State Coll., 1978. Cert. elem., spl. edn. and childbirth educator. Childbirth educator Charlton Meml. Hosp., Fall River, Mass., 1984, Childbirth Edn. Assn. Greater New Bedford, Dartmouth, Mass., 1983-88, Boston Assn. for Childbirth Edn., Newtonville, Mass., 1983-88; tchr. Dartmouth (Mass.) Pub. Schs., 1992-94. Mem. Nat. Tchrs. Assn., Mass. Tchrs. Assn., Dartmouth Sch. Music Assn., Siddha Yoga Dham Assn. Found. Democrat. Home: 26 Oliver St North Dartmouth MA 02747-3725

DE LEON, LIDIA MARIA, magazine editor; b. Havana, Cuba, Sept. 10, 1957; d. Leon J. and Lydia (Diaz Cruz) de L. B.A. in Communications cum laude, U. Miami, Coral Gables, Fla., 1979. Staff writer Miami Herald, Fla., 1978-79; editorial asst. Halsey Pub. Co., Miami, 1980-81, assoc. editor, 1981, editor, 1981—, editor Delta Sky mag., 1983—. Mem. Fla. Mag. Assn., Am. Soc. Mag. Editors, Am. Assn. Travel Editors, Jockey Club (Miami), Golden Key, Sigma Delta Chi. Democrat. Roman Catholic. Office: Halsey Pub Co 600 Corporate Dr Fort Lauderdale FL 33334-3637

DELESIO, ALICE BURCH, retired elementary education educator; b. Lyons, N.Y., Mar. 31, 1924; d. Charles Hulsaver and Elnora Carrie (Matthews) Burch; m. Dominic Anthony DeLesio, July 4, 1964. BS in Edn. cum laude, Buffalo State Tchrs. Coll., 1945; MA in English Edn., Syracuse U., 1954. Cert. tchr. grades 1-8, jr. h.s. Tchr. United Meth. and Vacation Bible Sch., Clyde, N.Y., 1944-45; tchr. 4th grade Silver Springs, N.Y., 1945-46; tchr. jr. h.s. Clyde-Savannah Sch., Clyde and Savannah, N.Y., 1946-71; election inspector Town of Galen, Clyde, 1974-77; judge, mem. honors selection com. Nat. Women's Hall of Fame, Seneca Falls, N.Y., 1993; sec. Mission Work Area, Clyde, 1980-94. Historian Village of Clyde and Town of Galen, 1974-77; co-organizer The Galen Hist. Soc., Clyde and Town of Galen, 1975-76; Sun. sch. tchr. Clyde United Meth. Ch., 1946-64. Mem. N.Y. State Ret. Tchrs. Assn. (friendly svc. chair ctrl. Western zone 1972-94, v.p. 1970-74, state historian 1982-94, Cert. Recognition), Wayne County Ret. Tchrs. Assn. (friendly svc. chair 1973-94, historian 1990-94), Clyde C. of C. (Achievement award 1979), Yorker Club (organizer, sponsor 1964-70), Delta Kappa Gamma (pres. 1974-76), Kappa Delta Pi, Clyde Rebekah Lodge (sec. # 478 1980-94, Decoration of Chivalry 1972). Democrat. Home: 94 Galen St Clyde NY 14433

DELEVORYAS, LILLIAN GRACE, artist; b. Chicopee Falls, Mass., Jan. 3, 1932; d. Basil John and Sophie Joanna (Dulchinos) D.; m. Samuel Rutenberg, June 19, 1953 (div. Feb. 1972); m. Robin Amis, Apr. 1, 1972; 1 child: Nicholas Emanuel. BFA, Cooper Union U., 1956. Dir. Weatherall Workshops, Coleford, Gloucester, U.K., 1972-79; designer greeting cards Elgin Ct., Gloucester, U.K., 1980-93; designer CR Gibson Co., Norwalk, Conn., 1993—; dir. Praxis Rsch. Inst., Newbury, Mass., 1989-93; textile designer Designers Guild, London, 1980-83; tapestry designer Rowan's Yarns, London, 1988-92. One-woman shows include Richmond (Calif.) Art Ctr., Sabersky Gallery, L.A., N.Y. SIX Gallery, N.Y.C., Robert Schoelkopf Gallery, N.Y.C., Royal Athena Gallery, N.Y.C., Wandsworth 401 1/2 Gallery, London, Brown's Living, London, Liberty's of London, Gloucester (Eng.) Mus. Art and Gallery, Eng., Lincolnshire Arts Ctr., Packhorse Gallery, Bath, Eng., Windjammer Gallery, Salcombe, Devon, Eng., Ernest Cook Gallery, Cirencester, Eng., Ebury Gallery, London, Stroud Festival, Gloucester, Gallery 10, London, Copernican Connection, Beverley, East York, Eng., Edinburgh (Scotland) Festival, The Gallery, Cardiff, Wales, Eng., Amerika-Haus, Munich, Germany, Kunsthandlung Hanfstaengl, Munich, Designers Guild, Paris, Ina Broerse Gallery, Laren, Holland, Coach House Gallery, Channel Islands, Churchill Gallery, Newburyport, Mass., Mus. of Art, San Francisco, DeYoung Mus., San Francisco, Victoria and Albert Mus., London, Royal Coll. Art, London, Brit. Genius, London, Brit. Crafts Ctr., London, Design Ctr., London, Rooksmore Gallery, Bath, Bath Arts Festival, Beaux Arts Gallery, Bath, Camden Art Ctr., London, Royal West Eng. Acad., Bristol, Eng., Royal Acad., London, Print 86, The Barbican, London, Royal Inst. Painters in Watercolors, London, Elaine Benson Gallery, L.I., N.Y., Australian Galleries, Collingwood, Victoria, Australia, The Copley Soc., Boston, Galerie Paul Vallotton, Lausanne, Switerland; pub. collections include Victoria and Albert Mus., U.K., Our Lady of Ransom Ch., Essex., U.K., Internat. Atomic Energy Commn., Vienna, Sisters of Mercy Convent, Essex, Guildford Coun. Chambers, U.K., Nat. Gallery of Art, Victoria, Australia, Teple Newsham House, Leeds, U.K. Recipient Louis Comfort Tiffany award, 1965, N.Y. Art Dir.'s Assn. Gold award, 1977, Hunting Group art prize, Mall Galleries, London, 1986. Office: Crinan 1 Kingston Ln Dartmout Devon MA 01951

DELIN, SYLVIA KAUFMAN, lawyer; b. Detroit, Nov. 10, 1945; d. Ira G. and Lillian (Farbman) Kaufman; m. Robert B. Smith, June 13, 1971 (div.); children: David, Mark, Barbara; m. Lewis I. Delin; 1 child, Philip. Student, U. Sheffield, Eng., 1965-66; BA, U. Mich., 1967; JD, Loyola U., Chgo., 1973. Bar: Ill. 1973, U.S. Dist. Ct. (no. dist.) Ill. 1980, U.S. Ct. Appeals (7th cir.) 1981, U.S. Supreme Ct. 1982, Mich. 1986, U.S. Ct. Appeals (6th cir.) 1989. Pvt. practice, Flossmoor, Ill., 1975-86, Southfield, Mich., 1986—. Author: Two Against One, 1964; Out of the Slums, 1968. Active Nat. Coun. Jewish Women. Mem. ABA, Mich. Bar Assn., Oakland County Bar Assn. Republican. Jewish. Home: 5622 Hobnail Cir West Bloomfield MI 48322-1629 Office: 2525 S Telegraph Rd Ste 306 Bloomfield Hills MI 48302-0289

DELL, MARY LYNN, psychiatrist, minister; b. Valley Forge, Pa., Sept. 12, 1959; d. Wayne Russell and Jane Ann (Barrett) D. BS, Milligan Coll., 1981; MD, Ind. U., Indpls., 1985; M in Theol. Studies, Emory U., 1993, ThM, 1995. Diplomate Am. Bd. Psychiatry and Neurology, Am. Bd. Gen. Psychiatry, Am. Bd. Child and Adolescent Psychiatry; ordained to ministry Christian Ch. Disciples of Christ. Resident in psychiatry Ind. U. Med. Ctr., Indpls., 1986-89; fellow in child psychiatry Emory U. Affiliated Hosps., Atlanta, 1989-91, attending psychiatrist summer treatment program for attention deficit disorders, 1991, attending psychiatrist Emory Hosp. Addictions Unit, 1991-92, attending psychiatrist Emory Hosp. Bone Marrow Transplant Team, 1992, assoc. med. dir. Emory U. Clergy Care, 1991—; asst. prof. psychiatry and pediatrics Emory U. Sch. of Medicine, 1991—; staff psychiatrist Grady Meml. Hosp., Atlanta, 1991—; med. dir., med. psychiatry unit Egleston Children's Hosp., Atlanta, 1993—; psychiat. cons. United Meth. Ch. Bd. Global Missions, N.Y.C., 1992—, Ga. Assn. Pastoral Care, Atlanta, 1993—; examiner Am. Bd. Psychiatry and Neurology-Child Psychiatry Examinations, Chgo., 1993—. Author: Handbook of Child and Adolescent Psychiatry, 1992, Psychiatric Disorders in Children and Adolescents, 1993; contbr. articles to profl. jours. Bd. mem., organist Speedway Christian Ch., Indpls., 1981-89; asst. organist Peachtree Christian Ch., Atlanta, 1989—; organist Holy Spirit Cath. Ch., Atlanta, 1994—. Recipient Janet M. Glasgow Meml. Achievement citation Am. Med. Women's Assn., 1985. Mem. AMA, Am. Psychiat. Assn., Am. Acad. Child and Adolescent Psychiatry, Assn. Women Psychiatrists, Soc. Pastoral Theology, Acad. Psychosomatic Medicine, Alpha Omega Alpha. Mem. Christian Ch. (Disciples of Christ). Home: 103 Fowler Ct Decatur GA 30030 Office: Egleston Childrens Hosp 1405 Clifton Rd NE Atlanta GA 30322

DELLAS, MARIE C., retired psychology educator and consultant; b. Buffalo; d. Theodore Andrew and Katherine (Callos) D. BS cum laude, State U. Coll., Buffalo, 1945; MEd, U. Buffalo, 1967; PhD, SUNY, Buffalo, 1970. Asst. editor Urban Edn. Jour., Buffalo, 1966-67; rsch. asst. SUNY, Buffalo, 1967-69; asst. prof. psychology Ea. Mich. U., Ypsilanti, 1969-73, assoc. prof., 1973-79, prof., 1979-93; mem. adv. bd. Inst. Study Children and Families, 1983-93. Author: Dellas Identity Status Inventory, 1979, 81, Creative Thinking Applied to Problem Solving Manual, 1993; contbr. articles to profl. jours.; mem. bd. editors Midwestern Ednl. Researcher, 1980-87, Urban Edn. Jour., 1977-94. Recipient Josephine N. Keal award Women's Commn., 1980, 85, 86; Grad. Rsch. grantee Ea. Mich. U., 1980-84. Mem. APA, Am. Ednl. Rsch. Assn., Nat. Assn. Gifted Children, Midwestern Ednl. Rsch. Assn., Midwestern Psychol. Assn., Mich. Acad. Gifted, Pi Lambda Theta.

DELNICK, MARTHA JOYCE, elementary education educator; b. Muncie, Ind., July 17, 1939; d. Doyt Randall and Susan (Straley) Whiteman; m. Jerry Spencer, July 6, 1962 (div. 1967); children: Jay Dee, Todd Alan. BA, Ball State U., 1970, MA, 1975; postgrad., Mich. State U., U. Mich. Cert. tchr., Mich. Tchr. Bennett Elem. Sch., Marion, Ind., 1965-67; tchr. elem. sch. Grand Rapids (Mich.) Pub. Schs., 1970-77, reading cons., 1977-87, tchr. compensatory edn., 1987—; Stocking Acad. Summer Success Acad., 1994; presenter Compensatory Edn. Parent Orgn., Grand Rapids, 1980-89, Jefferson Sch. Family Math. Program, Grand Rapids, 1992; mem. Mich. Math. Insvc. Project K-2, 1991-92, 3-6, 1992-93; math. svc. trainer Compensatory Edn. Tchrs. and Paraprofls., 1991-93. Author curriculum materials. Mem. NEA, Mich. Edn. Assn., Grand Rapids Edn. Assn. (rep. 1985-90, sch. bd. contact 1986-88), Mich. Reading Assn., Mich. Coun. Tchrs. Math. Mem. United Ch. of Christ. Office: Grand Rapids Pub Schs 1331 Franklin SE PO Box 117 Grand Rapids MI 49501-0117

DE LONG, KATHARINE, retired secondary education educator; b. Germantown, Pa., Aug. 31, 1927; d. Melvin Clinton and Katherine Frances (Brunner) Barr; m. Alfred Alvin De Long, June 21, 1947; children: Renée, Claudia, Jane. AA, Mesa Jr. Coll., Grand Junction, Colo., 1962; BA, Western State Coll., Gunnison, Colo., 1964; MA, Colo. State U., 1972. Camp dir. Kannah Creek Girl Scout Camp, 1960-64; tchr. Mesa County Valley Sch. Dist. #51, Grand Junction, 1964-84, dept. chmn., 1970-79; ret., 1984; tour coord., escort Mesa Travel, 1990—; substitute instr. Mesa State Coll., 1986-90; student council sponsor Mesa County Valley Sch., 1976-80; mem. bd. dirs. Am. Red Cross. Bd. dirs. Chipeta Girl Scout Coun., Grand Junction, 1960-66; pct. committeewoman Mesa County Dem. Party; mem., vice-chmn. Profl. Rights and Responsibilities Commn. for Dist. #51 Schs., Grand Junction, 1978-84; trustee Western Colo. Ctr. for the Arts, Grand Junction, 1987-88; mem. Mesa County Hist. Soc. Mem. AAUW (pres. local chpt. 1979-81, chmn. state cultural interest), AARP (Colo. legis. com. area I, asst. state dir. transp. task force, dist. dir. dist. 1, del. to nat. conv., 1994, dir. state convention, 1991), Pub. Employers Retirement Assn. (legis. adv. com. 1990-91), Colo. ret. Sch. Employees Assn., Phi Theta Kappa. Congregationalist.

DE LONG, SHIRLEY DOBBINS (D. RADLEY-REGAN), designer, author, artist; b. Guilford County, N.C.; B.S. in Math., U. N.C., 1964; postgrad. U. Mich. 1966-69, 75-76; m. Bruce E. de Long, Dec. 1967 (dec. Jan. 1969). Corp. exec. de Long & Assocs. Realtors, Radley Run, Inc., deAnne Designs, Ltd., Antiquity Designs, Ltd., Olde Jamestowne Art Gallery. Mem. Internat. Platform Assn., Art Guild Assn. Author: Wentworth Place; Return to Wentworth Place. Home and Office: PO Box 243 Jamestown NC 27282-0243

DELONY, PATTY LITTON, management consultant; b. Nashville, Oct. 12, 1948; d. Chase and Jane (Chadwell) D.;. BA in Econs., Duke U., 1970; MBA in Fin., Ga. State U., 1976; postgrad., Harvard U., 1985. Chartered fin. analyst. V.p., economist C&S Nat. Bank, Atlanta, 1970-79; v.p. investor relations Sara Lee Corp., Chgo., 1979-85, v.p. planning and devel., 1985-87; cons. Delony Assocs., Chgo., 1987—. Treas. Three Arts Club Chgo., 1983—. Recipient Woman Who Make A Difference award Minorities and Women in Bus. mag., 1986. Mem. Inst. Chartered Fin. Analysts, Econ. Club Chgo., Inst. Women's Studies. Republican. Presbyterian. Home and Office: 20 E Cedar St Chicago IL 60611-1149

DELOOZE, LORI LEILANI, space systems engineer; b. Ft. Carson, Colo., Mar. 21, 1962; d. Charles Ward and Loretta Eleanor (Pruss) Strang; m. Jason Lee DeLooze, Jan. 8, 1986; children: Christine Elizabeth, Garrett James. BA in Chemistry, U. Colo., 1985; MBA in Sci., Tech. and Innovation, George Washington U., 1989; MS in Computer Sci., Naval Postgrad. Sch., 1991. Commd. USN, 1985, advanced through grades to lt.; adminstrv. asst. Naval Mil. Pers. Command, Arlington, Va., 1985-87; head policy support ctr. Office Civilian Pers. Mgmt., Alexandria, Va., 1987-90; TENCAP project officer Naval Space Command, Dahlgren, Va., 1991-94; enlisted programs officer Navy Recruiting, Columbus, Ohio, 1994—. Decorated Armed Forces Def. medal. Mem. NAFE, AIAA, Armed Forces Comm. and Electronics Assn. Home: 253 Brownsfell Dr Columbus OH 43235 Office: 200 N High St Columbus OH 43215

DEL PAPA, FRANKIE SUE, state attorney general; b. 1949. BA, U. Nev.; JD, George Washington U., 1974. Bar: Nev. 1974. Staff asst. U.S. Senator Alan Bible, Washington, 1971-74; assoc. Law Office of Leslie B. Grey, Reno, Nev., 1975-78; legis. asst. to U.S. Senator Howard Cannon, Washington, 1978-79; ptnr. Thornton & Del Papa, 1979-84; pvt. practice Reno, 1984-87; sec. of state State of Nev., Carson City, 1987-91; atty. gen. State of Nev., 1991—. Mem. Sierra Arts Found. (bd. dirs.), Trust for Pub. Land (adv. com.), Nev. Women's Fund. Democrat. Office: Office of Atty Gen Capitol Complex 198 S Carson St Carson City NV 89710

DELPH, DONNA JEAN (MAROC), education educator, consultant, university administrator; b. Hammond, Ind., Mar. 7, 1931; d. Edward Joseph and Beatrice Catherine (Ethier) Maroc; m. Billy Keith Delph, May 30, 1953 (div. 1967); 1 child, James Eric. BS, Ball State U., 1953, MA, 1963, EdD, 1970. Cert. in ednl. adminstrn./supervision, reading specialist, Ind.; cert. elem. sch. tchr., Ind., Calif. Elem. tchr. Long Beach (Calif.) Community Schs., 1953-54; elem. tchr., reading specialist, asst. dir. elem. edn. Hammond Pub. Schs., 1954-70; prof. edn. Purdue U. Calumet, Hammond, 1970-84, 88-90, prof. emeritus, 1990—, head dept. edn., dir. tchr. edn., 1984-88; cons. pub. schs., Highland, Ind., 1970-88, Gary, Ind., 1983-88, East Chicago, Ind., 1987-88, Hammond, 1970-88; speaker/workshop presenter numerous profl. orgns., Hammond, 1964—; mem. exec. coun. Nat. Coun. Accreditation Tchr. Edn., 1991—. Author: (with others) Individualized Reading, 1967; contbr. articles, monographs to profl. jours. Bd. dirs. Bethany Child Care and Devel. Ctr., Hammond, 1972-77. Recipient Outstanding Teaching award Purdue U. Calumet, 1981. Mem. Assn. Tchr. Educators, Assn. for Supervision and Curriculum Devel. (rev. coun. 1987-91, bd. dirs. 1974-85), Internat. Reading Assn., Ind. Reading Profs. (pres. 1985-86), Pi Lambda Theta. Office: Purdue Univ Calumet Dept Education Hammond IN 46323

DEL SESTO, JANICE MANCINI, opera company executive. Gen. dir. Boston Lyric Opera Co., Boston, Mass. Office: Boston Lric Opera Co Emerson Majestic Theatre 114 State St Boston MA 02109-2402*

DE LUCA, ANDREA (HELEN SIGLAIN), psychoanalyst; b. Bklyn., Apr. 4, 1950; d. Wilbur Louis and Helen (Hansen) Siglain; m. June 1, 1973; children: Helena, Antoinette. BS in Edn., Wagner Coll., 1972; MSW, Fordham U., 1979; cert. sch. adminstrn., Coll. of S.I., 1993. Diplomate Cert. Bd. Clin. Social Workers; cert. psychotherapist, psychoanalyst, N.Y.; lic. N-6 tchr., spl. edn. grade advisor, sch. social worker, sch. supr., adminstr., N.Y.; lic. marriage counselor, N.J. Dir. spl. edn. svcs. Am. Inst. for Creative Living, S.I., N.Y., 1976—, co-exec. dir., 1976—; bd. dirs. clin. svcs. Internat. Sch. for Mental Health Practitioners, S.I., N.Y., 1980—; cons. S.I. Community TV. Named Tchr. of Yr. McKee Vocat. and Tech. High Sch., 1991. Fellow N.Y. State Soc. Clin. Social Work Psychotherapists; mem. ACA, ASCD, Am. Assn. Marriage and Family Therapists, Am. Group Psychotherapy Assn., Assn. for Specialists in Group Work, Phi Delta Kappa. Office: 2295 Victory Blvd Staten Island NY 10314-6625

DE LUCA, KATHY ANN, owner pet care facility; b. Pitts., May 7, 1947; d. James Thomas Krug and Gloria (Henn) Heilman; m. Hugo B. De Luca, Feb. 22, 1964; 1 child, Tiffany. Grad. h.s., Pitts.; student pet care, Pa. State Extension Course, 1972. Clothing sales rep. So. Hills Village, Pitts., 1964-65; owner, opeator De Luca's Canine Country Club, McMurray, Pa., 1965—; cons. on care of pets, tchr. for grooming pets and tng. pets De Luca's Canine Country Club, McMurray, 1980—. Coord. Pet Week, Washington County, 1990-94, Litter Control WAshington County, Pa., 1993-94. Mem. Tri-State Profl. Groomers Assn. (sec. 1987, bd. dirs. 1990, seminar coord.), Greater Pitts. Cage Bird Assn. (breeder, exhibitor), Soc. Parrot Breeders and Exhibitors (exhibitor), Washington County Humane Soc. Republican. Office: De Luca's Canine Country Club 196 S Spring Valley Rd Mc Murray PA 15317-2822

DELUCIA, THERESE MARIE, maternal/child health nurse; b. Cleve., Nov. 28, 1965; d. Jeffrey Alan and Judith Sharon (Dowd) Wade; m. Michael Angelo DeLucia Jr., June 9, 1990; children: Michael Angelo III, Rachel Marie, Regina Michelle. BSN, U. Akron, 1988; MSN, Kent State U., 1992. Cert. Inpatient Obstetrics. Staff nurse post partum Akron City Hosp., 1988-90, staff nurse nursery, 1990-92, per diem staff nurse postpartum and nursery; mem. faculty Children's Hosp. Med. Ctr. of Akron, instr. pediatric nursing. Mem. Sigma Theta Tau.

DE LUNG, JANE SOLBERGER, independent sector executive; b. Anniston, Ala., July 9, 1944; d. Samuel and Margaret Polk (Oldham) S.; m. Harry Leonard De Lung, Apr. 23, 1965 (div. 1972). BA in History, Emory U., 1966; MA in Urban Planning, Roosevelt U., Chgo., 1972. Exec. asst. Cook County Legal Assistance, Chgo., 1967-69; asst. dir. family planning Am. Coll. Ob-Gyn, Chgo., 1969-71; v.p. Ill. Family Planning Coun., Chgo., 1971-80; asst. commr. Chgo. Dept. Pub. Health, 1981-82; pres. Pub. Solutions, Princeton, N.J., 1982-88, Population Resource Ctr., N.Y.C., 1988—. Bd. dirs. Princeton Area Cmty. Planning 1983-85, Planned Parenthood Mercer County, Trenton, N.J., 1986—, UN Assn., U.S.A.; mem. adv. bd. dept. sociology Princeton U. 1981—. Mem. APHA, Nat. Family Planning and Reproductive Health (bd. dirs. 1975-81), Population Assn. Am. Democrat. Episcopalian. Office: Population Resource Ctr 15 Roszel Rd Princeton NJ 08540-6205

DEMAIRE, JUDITH M., federal agency administrator; b. Detroit, Aug. 4, 1947; d. Teophiel A. and Helen K. (Laethem) DeM. BA, Wayne State U., 1969. Specialist manpower devel. Dept. Labor, Washington, 1970-74; various analyst positions Fed. Energy Adminstrn., Washington, 1974-78; dir. scheduling, staffing, adminstrn. econ. registration adminstrn. Dept. Energy, Washington, 1978-79, dir. divsn. resource mgmt., 1979-82, acting dir. resource mgmt. office inspector gen., 1982-83, chief mgmt. and budget, 1983-87, dir. adminstrn. budget and disclosure, 1987-88, exec. dir., 1988-92, asst. inspector gen. policy, planning and mgmt., 1992—. Mem. Assn. Govt. Accts., Exec. Women in Govt. Office: Dept Energy Office Inspector Gen 1000 Indendence Ave SW Washington DC 20585

D'EMANUELE, MARY ANN, consulting company executive; b. Lawrence, Mass., June 21, 1934; d. Michael and Ann (Catanese) D'E. BA, Merrimack Coll., 1956. Chief ops. Alexander Proudfoot Co., Chgo., 1972-82; account exec. Inst. Mgmt. Resources, Westlake Village, Calif., 1982-85; v.p. ops. The Princeton (N.J.) Group, 1985-88; asst. bus. group mgr. Sci. Mgmt. Corp., Basking Ridge, N.J., 1988-90; pvt. practice D'Emanuele Inc, 1990—. Mem. NAFE, Am. Mgmt. Assn.

DE MAR, LEODA MILLER, fabric and wallcovering designer; b. N.Y.C., May 26, 1929; d. Benjamin and Malvina (Altman) Miller; m. Robert Mathis de Mar, Dec. 30, 1955 (div. Jan. 1985); children: Victoria, Miller Mathis, Charles David. Diploma, Parson's Sch. of Design, N.Y.C., 1946-49; postgrad., Parson's Sch. of Design, Eng., France, Italy, 1949, NYU, 1950-53. Designer Joseph B. Platt, Indsl. Design, N.Y.C., 1950-53; instr. textiles Parson's Sch. Design, N.Y.C., 1953-55; freelance designer various companies, N.Y.C., 1956-62; designer Leoda de Mar, Inc., N.Y.C., 1962-74; designer, advt. cons. Woodson Wallpapers, N.Y.C., 1975-85, Richard E. Thibaut, Inc., Irvington, N.J., 1985—. Designer 1st wallpaper collection Pippin Papers, N.Y.C., 1954, 1st wallpaper collection Woodson Wallpapers, 1955, own collections Richard E. Thibaut, Inc., 1985—, fabric and wallcovering designs featured in various popular mags.; contbr. articles to mags. Recipient Creativity award Art Direction mag., 1981. Home and Office: 350 Riversville Rd Greenwich CT 06831-3255

DEMARCO, ANNEMARIE BRIDGEMAN, telecommunications company manager; b. Long Beach, N.Y., July 27, 1960; d. Benet Eugene and Rosemarie Anne (Marchione) Bridgeman; m. James Thomas DeMarco, Feb. 22, 1987. BS, Cornell U., 1982. Writer Am. Re-Ins. Co., N.Y.C., 1983-85; systems analyst AT&T, East Brunswick, N.J., 1986-87, project mgr., 1987-89; product mgr. AT&T, Bridgewater, N.J., 1989-90; billing mgr. AT&T, Basking Ridge, N.J., 1990-92; comm. mgr. AT&T, Warren, N.J., 1992—; mktg. mgr. AT&T, Bridgewater, N.J., 1993-94; new bus. devel. coach AT&T Growth Svcs., Bridgewater, 1995—; freelance writer, speaker, 1991—; presenter philanthropic, mgmt. and career devel. workshops, 1991-95; participant AT&T Insight Program, 1993, leadership advisor, 1995. Mng. editor: (newsletter) BSM Today, 1991 (HARP award), BAISline (3 Effie awards 1994); author: (textbooks) Assessing and Improving Not for Profit Performance, 1991, First Step Career Development Workbook, 1991; columnist Westfield (N.J.) Leader newspaper. Ch. sch. dir. Cornell Cath. Ch., Ithaca, N.Y., 1981-82; capt./campaign AT&T United Way 1991-92, Somerset/Basking Ridge/East Brunswick, 1991; facilitator AT&T Adopt an Angel Program, Bridgewater, 1989; cons. trainer Good Counsel, Hoboken, N.J., 1990-92, bd. dirs., 1992-93, Support Ctr. of N.J., Newark, 1990, chairperson; mem. Westfield Rep. Women's Club, 1991. Recipient Comm. award United Way, 1992; named Alt. finalist for Ideal Am. Couple Contest, Family Circle Mag./Am. Greeting Cards, N.Y.C., 1989, Young Career Woman of Westfield, Bus. and Profl. Women's Club, 1990. Mem. Cornell Alumni Assn. (alumni admissions amb. 1990-93), Cornell Alumni Assn. no. N.J. Roman Catholic. Home: 354 W Dudley Ave Westfield NJ 07090-4021

DEMARCO, GINA, accountant; b. Marysville, Ohio, Nov. 12, 1971; d. Francis S. and Sally J. (Bartock) DeM. BA in Bus. and Econs., U. Pitts., 1993, cert. acctg., 1994. Auditor, acct. Coopers & Lybrand, Phila., 1994—. Mem. U. Pitts. Acctg. Assn., Golden Key Honor Soc., Omicron Delta Upsilon, Kappa Kappa Gamma (scholarship chair, asst. treas.), Beta Gamma Sigma. Roman Catholic. Home: 4800 Bulltown Rd Murrysville PA 15668 Office: Coopers & Lybrand 2400 Eleven Penn Center Philadelphia PA 19103

DEMARCO, KATHLEEN ANN, communications and marketing agent, consultant; b. New Brunswick, N.J., Apr. 5, 1949; d. Edward Anthony and Patricia Loretta (McCarron) DeM. BA, Fontbonne Coll., 1971; MA, U. Ga., 1978. TV editor coop. ext. svc. U. Ga., Athens, 1978-82; TV specialist coop. ext. svc. U. Md., College Park, 1982-87; comm. cons. Washington, 1987-89, Atlanta, 1989-92; mktg./comm. agent Cornell Coop. Ext. of Suffolk County, Riverhead, N.Y., 1992—; freelance reporter Washington bur. Cable News Network, 1988, American Women in Radio and TV, 1983-88; mem. connection day com. L.I. (N.Y.) Coalition Fair Broadcasting, 1992-95. Prodr., co-host (TV program) Backyard Gardener, 1980-81, (satellite program) Farm Bill Teleconference from College Park; co-prodr., host (TV program) L.I. Consumer Line, 1993-94. Mem. com. Fall Festival 1994, L.I., 1993-94; mem. group study exch. team to Ibaraki and Togichi prefectures, Japan, Rotary Internat., 1994. Named Pioneer winner Agrl. Comm. Edn., 1986. Mem. Epsilon Sigma Phi. Office: Cornell Coop Ext 246 Griffing Ave Riverhead NY 11901

DEMARINIS, NANCY A., state legislator, educator; b. Glen Ridge, N.J., Sept. 11, 1930; d. Edmund Theodore and Sara Antoinette (Rosewater) Nesbitt; m. James Robertson, Feb. 14, 1948 (div. 1976); children: Margaret, Elizabeth, Theodore, Carl; m. Anthony R. Demarinis, Mar. 9, 1979. AS, Mohegan C.C., Norwalk Conn., 1973; BS, U. Conn., 1975; MS, So. Conn. State U., 1981. Cert. guidance counselor. Tchr. Groton (Conn.) Pub. Schs., 1975-78, guidance counselor, 1978—; pvt. practice psychotherpist Groton, 1981-87; mem. Conn. Ho. Reps., Hartford, 1992—. Vol., bd. dirs., mem. various commns. United Way Women's Ctr., 1975—; town counselor, Groton, 1987-89. Address: 86 School St Groton CT 06340 Office: Conn Ho of Reps Legis Office Bldg Hartford CT 06106

DE MARNEFFE, BARBARA ROWE, volunteer; b. Boston, June 2, 1929; d. H.S. Payson and Florence Van Arnhem (Cassard) Rowe; m. James Hopkins, Oct. 9, 1954 (div. 1969); m. Francis de Marneffe; stepchildren: Peter, Daphne, Colette. BA, Vassar Coll., 1952; postgrad., Boston U., 1959. Tchr. Chapin Sch., N.Y.C., 1952-54; adminstrv. asst. to dean Sch. of Indsl. Mgmt. MIT, Cambridge, Mass., 1959-60; asst. pub. rels. dir. Peter Bent Brigham Hosp., Boston, 1960-61, pub. rels. dir., 1961-63; pub. rels. cons. Diabetes Found. and Joslin Clinic, Boston, 1963-64; pub. rels. dir. McLean Hosp., Belmont, Mass., 1964-68; pres. de Marneffe Selections, Cambridge, 1978-90. Contbr. articles to profl. jours. Trustee Archives of Am. Art of the Smithsonian Inst., Washington, D.C., 1983—; com. mem. Ellis Meml. Settlement House Antiques Show, 1968-89; bd. dirs. Friends of McLean Hosp., Belmont, Mass., 1967-89; officer, bd. dirs. Family Counseling Svc. of Cambridge, 1969-78; Mass. Rep. State Committeewoman, 1977-80; exec. sec. Cambridge Rep. City Com., 1956-57; pub. rels. dir. Peabody for Congress Campaign, Newton, Mass., 1968; bd. dirs. Nat. Com. on the Treatment of Intractable Pain, Washington D.C., 1980—; trustee Peterborough Players, N.H., 1983-89; docent N.C. Mus. of Art, Raleigh, 1992-93; mem. program com. Poe Ctr. for Health Edn., Raleigh, 1992-93. Mem. Jewelers of Am., Inc., Cambridge C. of C. (pub. affairs dir. 1975-78), Vassar Club (pres. Boston chpt. 1989). Home: 126 Coolidge Hill Cambridge MA 02138

DE MARR, MARY JEAN, English language educator; b. Champaign, Ill., Sept. 20, 1932; d. William Fleming and Laura Alice (Shauman) Bailey. B.A., Lawrence Coll., 1954; M.A., U. Ill., 1957, Ph.D., 1963; postgrad., Universitaet Tuebingen, 1954-55, Moscow State U., 1961-62. Asst. prof. English Willamette U., 1964-65; asst. prof. English Ind. State U., 1965-70, asso. prof., 1970-75, prof., 1975—. Co-author: Adolescent Female Portraits in the American Novel, 1961-81: An Annotated Bibliography, 1983, The Adolescent in The American Novel Since 1960, 1986; Am. editor: Annual Bibliography of English Language and Literature, 1979-90. Recipient Fulbright assistantship, 1954-55. Mem. MLA, Modern Humanities Research Assn., AAUP, Nat. Council Tchrs. English, ACLU, Phi Beta Kappa, Phi Kappa Phi. Home: 594 Woodbine Terre Haute IN 47803-1760 Office: Ind State U Dept English Terre Haute IN 47809

DEMAR-SALAD, GERALDINE, real estate sales and development executive, management consultant; b. Schenectady, N.Y., June 19, 1929; d. Matthew Peter and Mary Theresa (Sullivan) Relihan; m. Neil Joseph Demar, Aug. 5, 1950 (dec.); 1 child, Maureen Ann Demar-Hall; m. Bernard Salad, June 27, 1987; stepchildren: Andrew, Jane Salad-Bingham. BS, SUNY, Albany, 1979; MS, Russell Sage Coll., 1982. Cert. real estate broker, appraiser, cons.; cert. residential specialist. Real estate sales, 1964-69; dir. Mcpl. Leased Housing Program, Schenectady, 1969-71; pres. Geraldine M. Demar Realty & Devel., Schenectady, 1971—; pres Demar-Salad & Assocs., Mgmt. Consultants, Schenectady, 1988—; panel mem. Housing for Elderly, Housing for Low Income Families, Housing and Devel. Capitol Dist Region, N.Y. Active Fla. West Coast Symphony League, Fla. Ballet Ambassadors, Selby (Fla.) Bot. Gardens League, Friends of Schenectady Mus., League Schenectady Symphony Orch., Saratoga (N.Y.) Performing Arts Ctr.; mem. Gov.'s Panel for Housing for the Elderly and Low Income Families in N.Y. State; mem. Com. for Housing and Devel. for the Capitol Dist. Region of N.Y. State. Mem. AAUW, Nat. Assn. Realtors (grad. realtors inst. 1973, cert. residential specialist 1980), Soc. Real Estate Appraisers, N.Y. State Assn. Realtors, N.Y. State Assn. Real Estate Appraisers, Grad. Realtors' Inst., Nat. Trust for Historic Preservation, Schenectady Bd. Realtors, Albany Inst. History and Art, New Coll. Libr. Assn., Nat. Mus. Racing, Mohawk Golf and Country Club, Country Club Sarasota. Unitarian. Home: 1365-C30 Van Antwerp Rd Schenectady NY 12309-4441 Winter: 4021 Via Mirada Sarasota FL 34238

DE MASSA, JESSIE G., media specialist. BJ, Temple U.; MLS, San Jose State U., 1967; postgrad., U. Okla., U. So. Calif. Tchr. Palo Alto (Calif.) Unified Sch. Dist., 1966; librarian Antelope Valley Joint Union High Sch. Dist., Lancaster, Calif., 1966-68, ABC Unified Sch. Dist., Artesia, Calif., 1968-72; dist. librarian Tehachapi (Calif.) Unified Sch. Dist., 1972-81; also media specialist, free lance writer, 1981—. Contbr. articles to profl. jours. Mem. Statue of Liberty Ellis Island Found., Inc.; charter supporter U.S. Holocaust Meml. Mus., Washington; supporting mem. U.S. Holocaust Meml. Coun., Washington. Fellow Internat. Biog. Assn.; mem. Calif. Media and Libr. Educators Assn., Calif Assn. Sch. Librs. (exec. coun.) AAUW (bull. editor chpt., assoc. editor state bull., chmn. publicity, 1955-68), Nat. Mus. Women in Arts. (charter), Hon. Fellows John F. Kennedy Libr. (founding mem.), Women's Roundtable of Orange County, Nat. Writer's Club. Home: 9951 Garrett Cir Huntington Beach CA 92646-3604

DEMATTEO, GLORIA JEAN, insurance saleswoman; b. Perth Amboy, N.J., May 23, 1943; d. John J. and Helena (Elias) Kancz; m. Ronald D. DeMatteo, Feb. 20, 1965 (div. Nov. 1987); children: Douglas J., Keith G. Student, Berkeley Sch., 1961. Exec. sec. Rhodia Inc., New Brunswick, N.J., 1961-65; real estate saleswomen Mid-Jersey Realty, East Brunswick, N.J., 1974-79; pntr. Realty World Garden of Homes, East Brunswick, 1979-81; spl. agt. Prudential Ins. Co. Am., Iselin, N.J., 1981—. V.p. Belcourt Condo Assn., North Brunswick, N.J., 1987-88. Mem. Nat. Assn. Life Underwriters (nat. sales achievement award 1988, nat. quality award 1987, 92), Prudential Leaders Club. Home: 1144 Schmidt Ln New Brunswick NJ 08902-1362 Office: Prudential Ins Co Sutton Metro Park 33 Wood Ave S Iselin NJ 08830

DEMAY, HELEN LOUISE, nursing services administrator; b. Pitts., July 9, 1927; d. Patrick F. and Ellen (Kennedy) Duffy; m. John A. DeMay, Sept. 2, 1950; children: John A. III, Patrick J., Ann L., Mary Ellen, Theresa, Michael, Elizabeth, Stephen, Paul, David, Maureen. Nursing diploma, Braddock Gen. Hosp., 1948; postgrad., Cook County Hosp., 1949. Staff nurse Homestead (Pa.) Hosp., 1948; asst. head nurse Children Hosp., U. Pitts., 1949-52; staff nurse Kane Hosp., Pitts., 1978; activity dir. Jefferson Hills Nursing Home, Pitts., 1979-82; founder, officer Concerned Care Inc., Pitts., 1983-92; ret., 1992. Bd. dirs. St. Germaine Roman Cath. 1st Parish Coun., Bethel Park, Pa.; founding mem. Sch. House Arts Ctr., Bethel Park; bd. dirs., sec. St. Germaine Harbor, Bethel Park, 1990—; mem. Allegheny County Bd. Assistance, 1981-87; bd. advisor Allegheny County Single Parent Program, Pitts., 1984—. Mem. S.W. Pa. RN Club. Republican. Home: 7166 Keith Rd Bethel Park PA 15102-3741

DEMAY, SUSAN ANN, ceramic artist; b. Newark, N.Y., Apr. 6, 1952; d. Stanley Ray and Dorothy Mae (DeWispelaere) DeM.; m. Albert Douglas Wilbert, 1981; 1 child, Amanda DeMay Wilbert. BA, Eckerd Coll., 1977; MS, Vanderbilt U., 1979; MA, Tenn. Tech. U., 1989. Cert. tchr. Fine arts lectr. Vanderbilt U., Nashville, 1979-81, 86—; guest tchr., asst. La Maison Artisanale de Rochehaut, Belgium, 1981; mem. adj. faculty Mid. Tenn. State U., Murfreesboro, 1990; instr. Appalachian Ctr. for Crafts, Smithville, Tenn., 1986-92; owner Creek Ferry Pottery, Smithville, 1983—; cons. Mid-South Ceramic Supply, Nashville, 1993-94. Author: Glazing Guidelines, 1993, rev. edit., 1994. Recipient scholarship Foothills Crafts Guild, Pi Beta Phi; grantee Belgian Ministry of French Culture, 1981, Vanderbilt U., 1990. Mem. AAUW, AAUP, Am. Crafts Coun., Mus. Womens Art, Tenn. Assn. Craft Artists. Home: 801 S Mountain St Smithville TN 37166-2131

DEMELLO, BEVERLEE SUE, public relations professional; b. Augusta, Ga., Mar. 21, 1958; d. Ralph W. and Shirley M. (Sloan) Byrnes; m. Duane T. DeMello, Dec. 17, 1983. BA in Journalism and English, Baylor U., 1980; M in Drama, U. North Tex., 1985; MPA, Fla. State U., 1990. Staff writer The Meth. Hosp., Houston, 1980-81; sr. writer Tenneco, Inc., Houston, 1981-83; sr. coord. Otis Engring. - Halliburton, Dallas, 1983-85; mktg. specialist TalTran/City of Tallahassee, 1985-87; pub. info. office Fla. Pub. Svc. Commn., Tallahassee, 1987-91; community liaison officer City of Tallahassee, 1991; pub. info. dir. Fla. Pub. Svc. Commn., Tallahassee, 1991—; sub-com. chair pub. info., Nat. Assn. Regulatory Utility Commrs., Washington, 1993—; featured columnist Tallahassee Dem., 1991-92. Author: (plays) Tallahassee Community College, 1992, Country Playhouse, 1984. Vice-pres. Coun. of Neighborhood Assns., Tallahassee, 1991—; vice-chair Solid Waste Citizens Adv. Com., Leon County, Fla., 1992—. Recipient awards for plays Riverside Artsfest Playwrights, Ga., 1993, St. Lucie Community Theatre Playwright's Festival, Fla., 1993. Mem. Am. Soc. Pub. Adminstrn., Dramatists Guild. Democrat. Baptist. Home: 4074 Cottage Wood Trl Tallahassee FL 32311-4156 Office: Fla Pub Svc Commn 101 E Gaines St Tallahassee FL 32399-6501

DEMENTIS, KATHARINE HOPKINS, interior designer; b. Indpls., Dec. 20, 1922; d. Stephen Francis and Margaret Bell (Yeager) Hopkins; m. Gilbert X. Dementis, Feb. 1, 1953; children: Mary Margaret Dementis O'Dwyer, Stephen Ezra Hall. Student, John Herron Art Sch., 1941-44; BS, U. Wis., 1971. Interior designer L.S. Ayres and Co., Indpls., 1945-51; pres. Ariz. Questers, Phila., 1991-93. Mem. DAR, Lakes Club, Union Hills Country Club, Passport Club. Republican. Presbyterian. Home: 12830 Castlebar Dr Sun City West AZ 85375-3270 Office: Questers 210 S Quince St Philadelphia PA 19107-5534

DEMEREE, GLORIA See LENNOX, GLORIA

DEMERS, JUDY LEE, state legislator, university dean; b. Grand Forks, N.D., June 27, 1944; d. Robert L. and V. Margaret (Harming) Prosser; m. Donald E. DeMers, Oct. 3, 1964 (div. Oct. 1971); 1 child, Robert M.; m. Joseph M. Murphy, Mar. 5, 1977 (div. Oct. 1983). BS in Nursing, U. N.D., 1966; MEd, U. Wash., 1973, postgrad., 1973-76. Pub. health nurse Govt. D.C., 1966-68, Combined Nursing Service, Mpls., 1968-69; instr. pub. health nursing U. N.D., Grand Forks, 1969-71, assoc. dir. Medex program, 1970-72, dir., family nurse practitioner program, 1977-82, assoc. dir. rural health, 1982-85, dir. undergrad. med. edn., 1982-83, assoc. dean, 1983—; rsch. assoc. U. Wash., Seattle, 1973-76; mem. N.D. Ho. of Reps., 1982-92; mem. N.D. Senate, 1992—; cons. Health Manpower Devel. Staff, Honolulu, 1975-81, Assn. Physician Asst. Programs, Washington, 1979-82; site visitor, cons. AMA-Com. Allied Health Edn. Accreditation, Chgo., 1979-81. Author: Educating New Health Practitioners, 1976; mem. editorial bd.: P.A. Jour., 1976-78; contbr. articles to profl. jours. Sec., bd. dirs. Valley Family Planning and Edn. Ctr., Grand Forks, N.D., 1982—; exec. com., bd. dirs. Agassiz Health Systems Agy., Grand Forks, 1982-86; mem. N.D. State Daycare Adv. Com., 1983-93, Mayor's Adv. Com. on Police Policy, Grand Forks, 1983-85, N.D. State Foster Care Adv. Com., 1985-87, N.D. State Hypertension Adv. Com., 1983-85, Gov.'s Com. on DUI and Traffic Safety, 1985-91, Statewide Adv. Com. on AIDS, 1985-90; bd. dirs. Casey Found. Families First Initiative, 1988—; adv. com. Ruth Meiers Adolescent Ctr., Grand Forks, 1988—; mem. Commn. on Future Structure of VA Health Care, 1990-91; bd. dirs. Quad County Community Action Agy, 1991—; mem. Resource and Referral Bd. of Dirs., 1990—; mem. N.D. Health Task Force, 1992—. Recipient Alpha Lambda Delta award, 1963, Pub. Citizen of Yr. award N.D. chpt. Nat. Assn. Social Workers, 1986, Golden Grain award N.D. Dietitics Assn., 1988, Person of Yr. award U. N.D. Law Women Caucus, 1990, Legislator of Yr. award Northern Valley Labor Coun., 1990, N.D. Martin Luther King Jr. award, 1990, Legislator of Yr. award N.D. Mental Health Assn., 1993; U. Wash. regional med. program service fellow, 1972-73; Toll fellow, 1989, U. Wash. Kellogg Allied Health fellow, 1972. Mem. AAUW, NOW, ACLU, LWV, Am. Nurses Assn., N.D. Nurses Assn. (mem. cabinet on edn. and practice 1982-86, Nurse of Yr. 1983), Am. Pub. Health Assn., Am. Ednl. Research Assn., N.D. Pub. Health Assn., N.D. Mental Health Assn., The ARC (Assn. for Retarded Citizens), Pi Lambda Theta, Sigma Theta Tau. Democrat. Home: 1826 Lewis Blvd Grand Forks ND 58203-1642 Office: U ND Sch Medicine 501 N Columbia Rd Grand Forks ND 58203-2817

DEMERS, SUSAN VICTORIA BATTAGLINO, lawyer; b. N.Y.C., Jan. 29, 1953; d. Vincent Louis and Christine Susan Battaglino. BA, NYU, 1974, JD, 1977. Bar: N.Y.; U.S. Dist. Ct. (so. and ea. dists.) N.Y., U.S. Ct. Appeals, U.S. Supreme Ct. Assoc. Law Office of Emily Jane Goodman, N.Y.C., 1977-78; dir. matrimonial unit, staff atty. Legal Aid Soc./Bronx Neighborhood Office, Bronx, N.Y., 1978-82; dep. bur. chief, asst. dist. atty. Office of Dist. Atty., Queens County, N.Y., 1982-83; assoc. commr. and dep. gen. counsel N.Y. State Dept. Social Svcs., Bklyn., 1984-88, dep. commr., gen. counsel, 1988—; presenter at confs. on child support, family law and welfare law, 1979—. Mem. Am. Assn. Public Welfare Attys. (exec. com. 1990—). Democrat. Office: 40 N Pearl St Albany NY 12207-2702

DEMERSE, LEE ANNE, office administrator; b. Saranac Lake, N.Y., June 19, 1954; d. Richard Patrick and Marilyn Marion (Miller) DeM.; m. Loren A. Weaver, May 18, 1986. BA, St. Lawrence U., 1976. Assoc. dir. Nairobi program St. Lawrence U., Canton, N.Y., 1976-81; with Z. Boskovic Air

Charter Co., Nairobi, Kenya, 1981-86, John M. Anderson, Atty., LaPorte, Ind., 1986-88; office mgr., acct. Veterinary Equine, Constantine, Mich., 1986—. Mem. Constantine Garden Club, Midwest Dressage Assn. Home and Office: 63111 Peck Academy Rd Constantine MI 49042

DEMETREE, FRANCES MARY, real estate professional, educator; b. Jacksonville, Fla., Nov. 11, 1943; d. Jack Abraham and Mary Pia (Sandroni) D.; children: Amy Elizabeth, Karen Elise, Gregory John. BA, Barry U., 1965; MEd, Rollins Coll., 1970. Tchr. Orange County Sch. Bd., Orlando, Fla., 1965-69; guidance counselor Orange County Sch. Bd., Orlando, 1969-71, counselor emotionally disturbed children, 1971-73; real estate instr. ERA Svcs., Orlando, 1981; entrepreneur Demetree Sch. of Real Estate, Orlando, 1981-89, Century 21 Sch. Real Estate, Jacksonville, 1987-91; dir. Real Estate Inst. U. Cen. Fla., 1991—; resource cons. Demetree Sch. Securities, Orlando, 1987-89, Severely Emotionally Disturbed Network, 1990-91; dir. Real Estate Inst., U. Cen. Fla., 1991, Real Estate Inst., 1991—. Exec. v.p. Bert Rodgers Schs. of Real Estate, 1987-93; exec. bd. dirs. We Care Teen Hotline, 1987-91, rec. sec., 1988-91; pres. Demetree Schs., Inc., 1992-95; mem. task force Fla. Real Estate Commn., 1992-93. Mem. Real Estate Educators Assn. (state sec. 1987—) Orlando Area Bd. Realtors, Mid-Fla. Home Builders, Real Estate Educators Assn., We Care Women (bd. dirs. 1992-94), Mental Health Assn. (bd. dirs. 1990-92). Democrat. Roman Catholic. Office: Real Estate Investments 8809 El Prado Ave Orlando FL 32825-8303

DEMETREON, DAIBOUNE ELAYNE, minister; b. Brunswick, Maine, Aug. 5, 1945; d. James Demetreon and Grace Lewis; m. James Allison Devine, Mar. 3, 1986; children from previous marriage: William Anthony Decker, James Steven Decker. Degree, Unity Sch. Practical Christianity & Ordination, 1975; postgrad., Rio Salado Coll., 1992; BA in Psychology, Ottawa U., 1994. Ordained minister Unity Ch., 1975; cert. practitioner Neuro-Linguistic Program; cert. pscyhotherapist. Sr. minister Unity of Ann Arbor, Mich., 1975-77, Unity of Boulder, Colo., 1977-78, Unity of Colorado Springs, 1980-86, Unity of Scottsdale, Ariz., 1989—; chmn. World of One Fellowship, Colorado Springs, 1986—, pastoral counselor, Scottsdale, 1989—; adv. bd. dirs. Boulder (Colo.) Psychiat. Inst., 1977-78; campus minister U. Mich., Ypsilanti, 1975-77; conductor workshops chaplains program U.S. Army, Ft. Carson. Author, narrator audio tape Transformations, 1985; host talk show God and You, 1983; contbr. articles to profl. publs. Chem. dependency counselor St. Luke's Hosp., 1993—. Office: World of One Fellowship 8556 E Via De Risa Scottsdale AZ 85258-3931

DE METZ, DELLA CHRISTINE, executive, writer, social worker; b. Elkhart, Ind., Jan. 14, 1959; 1 child, Nathan Allen. Student, Purdue U., 1977-78, Ivy Tech. Vocat. Coll., 1994—. Retail sales Pepsico Franchise, Elkhart, Ind., 1980; bus. mgmt. McGrory Corp., Elkhart, Ind., 1990-91, bus. fin., 1990-91; entrepreneur DC & Co., Elkhart, Ind., 1990—. Author of poems. Vol. Homeless Shelter, Elkhart, 1993, Greenpeace, The Wilderness Soc., Washington, 1993, World Wildlife Fund, Sierra Club, Washington, 1993. Recipient Silver Poet award, The World of Poetry, Calif., 1990. Mem. Am. Mgmt. Assn. (assoc. mem. 1993), Nat. Wildlife Fedn., Internat. Soc. Poets, Nat. Linb. Poetry. Office: DC & Co PO Box 296 Union MI 49130

DEMILLION, JULIANNE, health and fitness specialist and personal trainer, rehabilitation consultant; b. Monessen, Pa., Dec. 20, 1955; d. William Vincent and Enise Mary (Tocci) DeM. BA, BS, U. Pitts., 1977; cert. massage therapist Phoenix Therapeutic Massage Coll., 1985. Mgr. program devel. Exclusively Women Spas, Scottsdale, 1977-81; pvt. exercise therapist, Scottsdale, 1981-83; ; cons. City of Phoenix, 1981-88; cons., pvt. personal trainer, Scottsdale, 1983—; instr. advanced techniques Phoenix Therapeutic Massage Coll., 1986-90. Mem. NAFE, Am. Massage Therapy Assn. (State Meritorious award 1989), Ariz. Massage Therapy Assn. (sec.-treas. 1986-90, Svc. award 1991), Internat. Dance and Exercise Assn., Circulo-Systems Ltd., Am. Coll. Sports Medicine.

DEMITCHELL, TERRI ANN, law educator; b. San Diego, Apr. 10, 1953; d. William Edward and Rose Annette (Carreras) Wheeler; m. Todd Allan DeMitchell, Aug. 14, 1982. AB in English with honors, San Diego State U., 1975; JD, U. San Diego, 1984; MA in Edn., U. Calif., Davis, 1990; doctoral study, Harvard U., 1989—. Bar: Calif. 1985, U.S. Dist. Ct. (so. dist.) Calif. 1985; cert. elem. tchr., Calif. Tchr. Fallbrook (Calif.) Union Elem. Sch. Dist., 1976-86; administrv. asst. gen. counsel San Diego Unified Sch. Dist., 1984; assoc. Biddle and Hamilton, Sacramento, 1986-88; instr. U. N.H., 1990—; teaching asst. U. Calif., Davis, 1987. Author: The California Teacher and the Law, 1985, The Law in Relation to Teacher, Out of School Behavior. Mem. ABA, Calif. Bar Assn., Sacramento County Bar Assn., Women Lawyers Sacramento Assn., Internat. Reading Assn., Nat. Orgn. Legal Problems in Edn., Pi Lambda Theta.

DEMONT, MARGO ANN, gerontologist; b. Plymouth, Ind., Sept. 10, 1949; d. Donald W. and Bertha Elizabeth (Cormican) Taviner; m. D. Eugene DeMont, Jan. 22, 1967; children: Gwen Ellen, Brandan Lynn. BS in Edn., Ind. U., 1973, MS in Edn., 1977, MS in Counseling, 1980; PhD, Purdue U., 1986. Clin. social worker; gerontol. counselor. Elem. tchr. Argos (Ind.) Sch. Corp., 1973-75; dir. admissions and fin. adi Ancilla Coll., Donaldson, Ind., 1979-83, dir. student svcs., 1983-86; unit dir. psychology Greenleaf Health Systems, Mishawaka, Ind., 1986-87; postdoctoral fellow U. Notre Dame, Ind., 1987-88; dir. sr. svcs. Meml. Hosp., South Bend, Ind., 1988—; cons. Meml. Hosp., South Bend, 1988—, therapy/counseling, 1991—; presenter teleconf. Am. Hosp. Assn., 1990; expert witness, Ind. Superior Ct., 1988. Reviewer articles for Gerontology and Geriatrics Edn., 1988. Diversity facilitator South Bend Sch. Corp., 1993; community facilitator United Way of St. Joseph County, South Bend, 1993. Pneumonia Pnockout grantee Area 2 Agy. on Aging, South Bend, 1993; recipient Best Practices nomination Brookdale Ctr. on Aging, N.Y.C., 1993, postdoctoral fellowship NIMH, Washington, 1987, Disting. Edn. Alumni award Ind. U., 1981. Mem. No. Ind. Arthritis Found. (bd. dirs. 1993—), No. Ind. Alzheimer's Assn. (bd. dirs. 1987—), Ind. Assn. Adult Devel. and Aging (bd. dirs. 1988-92), Am. Soc. on Aging (conf. planning coms. 1992-93), Ind. Counseling Assn. (conf. program chair 1988). Methodist. Home: 10620 Del Lo Me Ln Plymouth IN 46563-8602 Office: Memorial Hospital 615 N Michigan St South Bend IN 46601-1087

DEMONTE, CYNTHIA MARIA, management consultant; b. N.Y.C., May 23, 1956; d. Joseph James and Ammeda Ellan (Heiss) DeM.; m. Abraham Figueroa, Mar. 8, 1991. BA, NYU, 1978. Sr. dir. mktg. Tandem Computers, N.Y.C., Cupertino, Calif., 1978-82; assoc. Hambro Internat. Venture Fund, N.Y.C., 1982-84; sr. assoc. corp. fin. dept. Gruntal & Co., N.Y.C., 1984-88; pres. Cynthia DeMonte & Assocs., N.Y.C., 1988—. Mem. Astoria (N.Y.) Civic Assn., 1989—, Dinkin's Com., 1990—. Mem. NAFE, Nat. Assn. Profl. Organizers, Am. Women's Econ. Devel. Corp., Ctr. for Entrepreneurial Devel., Women in Music. Home: 138 Tatum Dr Middletown NJ 07748 Office: DeMonte Assocs 271 Madison Ave Rm 908 New York NY 10016-1092

DEMONTE, SISTER MARIA, Dominican sister, pastoral associate; b. Martins Creek, Pa.; d. Antonio and Giovina (Coccia) DeM. BA cum laude, St. Rose Coll., 1972; M.T.A. Cert., Cath. U., 1971; MA in Pastoral Ministry, St. Joseph Coll., 1980; MDiv, Immaculate Conception Sem., 1992. Cert. adolescent depression and suicide counseling, spiritual direction. Religion tchr. Walton, Altamont, Deposit, Delhi and Bainbridge, N.Y., 1960-75; asst. dir. Religious Edn. Diocesan Office, 1978-80; sec. program dir. Consultation Ctr.-Diocese, Albany, N.Y., 1984-90; bd. dirs. Administrv. Rev. Bd., Albany, 1991—; del. Congregation St. Catherine de'Ricci, Media, Pa., 1978—; instr. Our Lady of Angels Sem., Glemont, N.Y., 1988; dir. religious edn., pastoral assoc. Latham, N.Y., 1987—; religion tchr. Loudonville, N.Y., 1979-81; conductor directed retreats for clergy and religious Miami, Fla. 1994—; catechetical cons. Wm. Sadlier Co., Latham, 1989—; coord. Formation for Laity, Latham, 1987—; candidate dir. Congregation of St. Catherine de'Ricci, Media, 1980-86, gen. coun. 1986-90; v.p. Still Point house of Prayer, 1988-89; chairperson Congregation Centennial Celebration, Elkins Park, Pa., 1980; RCIA dir., parish, 1993, spiritual dir., retreat coord., 1995—. Author: (text) Look at Life, 1980, The Creed: We Look, We Hope, We Have Faith in God, 1994; lectr. The Role of the Deaconess: A Future Ministry?. Counselor Billy Graham Crusade, Capital Dist., N.Y., 1990; dir. Inner City Food Pantry, Latham, Albany, 1987; coord. World Hunger, Latham, 1986, 88, Drug Program, North Colonie, N.Y., 1985. Recipient

Maria de LaCruz award Diocesan Religious Edn., 1989, Mary Reed Newland award, 1988, Alumni award Easton Cath. High Sch., 1991; the Sister Maria DeMonte Religious Edn. Ctr. was dedicated in her honor, Aug. 15, 1991. Mem. Diocesan Coun. Sisters, Diocesan Religious Edn. Office (spl. asst. 1976-80), North Colonie Ambulance, Formation for Ministry (instr. 1981—), Religious Edn. Diocese (instr. 1976—). Home: 500 Watervliet Shaker Rd Latham NY 12110-4618 Office: Our Lady Assumption Ch 498 Watervliet Shaker Rd Latham NY 12110-4696

DE MORNAY, REBECCA, actress; b. Santa Rosa, Calif., Aug. 29, 1962; m. Bruce Wagner, Dec., 1989 (div.). Student, Lee Strasberg Theatre Inst., Los Angeles; also studied with Kristin Linklater. Apprentice with Francis Coppola's Zoetrope Studio, 1981. Actress: (films) Risky Business, 1983, Testament, 1983, The Slugger's Wife, 1985, The Trip to Bountiful, 1985, Runaway Train, 1985, Beauty and the Beast, 1986, And God Created Woman, 1987, Feds, 1988, Dealers, 1989, Backdraft, 1991, The Hand That Rocks the Cradle, 1992, Guilty As Sin, 1993, The Three Musketeers, 1993; (plays) Born Yesterday, 1988, Marat/Sade, 1990; (TV) The Murders in the Rue Morgue, 1986, By Dawn's Early Light, 1990, An Inconvenient Woman, 1992, Blind Side, 1993, Getting Out, 94.

DEMOTT, MARGARET ANN, educator; b. Lynwood, Calif., June 5, 1953; d. Stephen William and Dolores Ann (McCarthy) DeM. BA in Spanish, Immaculate Heart Coll., L.A., 1980; MA in TESOL (Teaching English to Speakers of Other Languages), Monterey Inst. Internat. Studies, 1983. Cert. English and ESL tchr., Calif. Tchr. English and ESL Laloma Jr. High Sch. Modesto (Calif.) City Schs., 1983-85, 86-93, Gonzales (Calif.) Union High Sch. Dist., 1985-86; tchr. ESL Modesto Jr. Coll., 1989-94; tchr. English and ESL, group leader ESL program Peter Johansen H.S., Modesto, Calif., 1993—; essay corrector Ednl. Testing Svc., Berkeley, Calif., summers 1987, 88; Calif. Lit. participant, summer, 1993. Curriculum writer ESL, Modesto City Schs., spring 1989. Vol. Stanislaus Wildlife Care Ctr., Ceres, Calif., 1987—. Nominated to participate in Calif. Tchr. of Yr. program, La Loma Jr. High, 1993, 94. Mem. Calif. Assn. Tchrs. of English to Speakers of Other Langs. Office: Peter Johansen High Sch 641 Norseman Dr Modesto CA 95357

DEMPSEY, ANN LOUISE, laboratory manager; b. Dixon, Ill., Feb. 19, 1952; d. Joseph Lawrence and Ethelle Caroline (Bates) D.; children: Daniel, Amanda. AS, Sauk Valley Jr. Coll.; student, Cambridge, Mass., 1994—. Staff tech., sonographer KSB Hosp., Dixon; staff sonographer Luth. Hosp., LaCrosse, Wis.; supr. ultrasound Beverly, Mass.; mgr. Boston U. Med. Ctr.; tchr. Middlesex C.C., Bedford, Mass.; ultrasound cons., Boston. Contbr. articles to profl. jours. Mem. Soc. of Diagnostic Ultrasound, Am. Soc. of Echo, Back Bay Echo Club (asst. dir.), Earthwatch, Mass. Teaching Assn. Democrat. Roman Catholic. Home: 290 Quarry St #816 Quincy MA 02169 Office: Boston U Med Ctr 88 E Newton St Boston MA

DEMPSEY, BARBARA MATTHEA, medical/surgical and critical care nurse; b. The Netherlands, July 27, 1943; d. Petrus Antonius and Hendrika Petronella (Kemp) Petersen; m. James D. Dempsey, June 13, 1981; children: Jennifer, Daniel. AA, Santa Monica (Calif.) Coll., 1970; cert. lactation educator, UCLA, 1982. Staff nurse med./surg. Santa Monica Hosp., 1967-72; surg. intensive care nurse VA Wadsworth Hosp., L.A., 1973-77; staff nurse med./surg. Community Hosp., Santa Rosa, Calif., 1988-90; staff nurse Redwood Nurses Registry, Santa Rosa, 1990-93, Norrell Healthcare, Santa Rosa, Calif., 1990-93; charge nurse Creekside Convalescent Hosp., 1994; nurse Bloodbank of the Redwoods, Santa Rosa, Calif., 1994—. Office: 2324 Bethards Dr Santa Rosa CA 95405

DEMPSEY, DENISE PAIGE, librarian; b. Roxboro, N.C., June 4, 1959; d. Joseph Page and Evelyntyne (Humphrey) D. BA, U. N.C., 1981; MLS summa cum laude, N.C. Ctrl. U., Durham, 1983. Disability determination specialist trainee State of N.C. Dept. Human Resources, Raleigh, 1983-84; grad. asst. Libr. of Congress, Washington, 1984, sci. reference libr., 1984—. Grad. Profl. Opportunities fellow N.C. Ctrl. U., 1981-83; recipient Meritorious Svc. award Libr. of Congress, 1987. Office: Libr of Congress 10 1st St SE Washington DC 20540

DEMPSEY, JACQUELINE LEE, special education director; b. Pitts., Jan. 4, 1951; d. Alexander and Catherine (Rankin) D. BS, Edinboro (Pa.) State Coll., 1972, MEd, 1974; PhD, U. Pitts., 1983. Tchr. Allegheny Intermediate Unit, Pitts., 1975-77, master tchr., 1977-78, instructional advisor, 1978-81, project dir., 1981-86, program administr., 1985-86; exec. dir. The Early Learning Inst., Pitts., 1986—; guest field reviewer Exceptional Children, 1989—. Chair Pa. Early Intervention Interagy. Coord. Com., 1992-93; mem. Gov.'s Comm. on Children and Families, 1992-93. Mem. Coun. for Exceptional Children, Early Intervention Providers Assn. Pa. (vice chair 1986-88), Pitts. Area Coun. Adminstrv. Women in Edn. (pres. 1985-86), Phi Delta Kappa. Office: The Early Learning Inst 2500 Baldwick Rd Ste 200 Pittsburgh PA 15205-4144

DEMPSEY, KAREN GOODWIN, underwriter; b. Nashville, June 9, 1957; d. Leo Martin and Mary Sue (Turner) Goodwin; m. Gary Douglas Dempsey, Dec. 11, 1976 (div. 1984); children: Alison Kaye, Kyle Brandon. Grad. high sch., Antioch, Tenn., 1975. Lic. property and casualty agent, Ariz., Fla., Ga., Iowa, Kans., S.C., S.D., Tenn., Tex., Va., Wis. Acctg./cash balancing clerk ComData, Nashville, 1983-84; underwriting asst. Am. Internat. Group, Nashville, 1984-85; adminstrv./underwriting asst. Podiatry Ins. Co. Am., Nashville, 1985-86, asst. underwriter, 1986-87, casualty underwriter, 1987-88; underwriting supr. Podiatry Ins. Co. Am., Brentwood, Tenn., 1988-89, risk mgmt. rep., 1989-91, mgr. underwriting, 1991-93, v.p. underwriting, officer, 1993—. Sec. bd. dirs. Cole Dixie Youth Baseball League, 1987; active Alive Hospice, Nashville, 1991—. Mem. Nat. Assn. Ins. Women. Methodist. Office: Podiatry Ins Co Am Brentwood TN 37027

DEMPSEY, SUSAN MARGARET, financial services company executive; b. Kalamazoo, Dec. 14, 1961; d. Joseph K. and Nancy N. (Tarpinian) Andonian; m. Barton N. Dempsey, Sept. 5,1 992. BBA, Western Mich. U., 1983; MBA, U. Houston, 1989. CPA, Mich. Bank teller Am. Nat. Bank (now Old Kent Bank), Portage, Mich., 1978-80; teller II Svc. Ctrs. Corp., Portage, 1980-83; sr. auditor Ernst & Young, Kalamazoo and Houston, 1983-86; acctg. mgr. Am. Capital Cos., Houston, 1986-89; audit supr. Kellogg Co., Battle Creek, Mich., 1989-92, mgr. customer fin. svcs., 1992-94, fin. bus prtnr. mktg. budget, 1992—. Treas. Safe Place, Battle Creek, 1994, asst. treas., 1993; big sister Kids Connection, Kalamazoo, 1990-91. Western Mich. U. acad. scholar, 1979-83, Kalamazoo Accts. Assn. scholar, 1982-83, Crowe, Chizeck & Co. scholar, 1981-82. Mem. AICPAs, Mich. Assn. CPAs, MBA Assn. of U. Houston, Beta Gamma Sigma, Beta Alpha Psi. Home: 106 Carriage Hill Dr Battle Creek MI 49017 Office: Kellogg Co One Kellogg Sq Battle Creek MI 49016

DEMUELLER, LUCIA, investment consultant; b. Manizales, Caldas, Colombia, Aug. 14, 1937; came to U.S., 1960; d. Ricardo Aristizabal and Soledad Villegas; m. Harold Charles Mueller, Feb. 26, 1966; children: Christine and Anne Marie (twins). Degree in journalism, U. Caldas, 1960; degree in bus. and fin., NYU, 1965; cert. in gerontology, Marymount Manhattan Coll., 1991. Editor Young Women's Mag., Bogota, Colombia, 1959-60; asst. export mgr. M & T Chems Inc., N.Y.C., 1963-66; mgr. banker acceptances Mitsui & Co., N.Y., N.Y.C., 1970-73; acct. exec. Conn. Mutual, N.Y.C., 1976-83; assoc. Cowan Agy., Mass. Fin., N.Y.C., 1983-86; investment cons. Chem. Investment Svcs., N.Y.C., 1993-94; internat. bus. cons., 1994—. Contbr. articles to profl. publs. Mgr. disaster assistance ctr. Fed. Emergency Mgmt., N.Y., 1985, 91. Mem. Nat. Def. Exec. Res. (mgr. various disaster sites), Latin Am. Progressive Group (pres. 1990—, founder). Home: 355 E 72d St New York NY 10021

DENE, LINDA JO, financial executive; b. L.A., Apr. 26, 1948; d. Hyman Chaim and Ruth (Goldstein) Bergman; m. Richard Eugene Dene, Feb. 16, 1967; children: Ronald, Anthony, Angela. Cost control specialist South Bend (Ind.) Range Co., 1972-75; accounts payable specialist Thrifty Drug Co., West Los Angeles, Calif., 1975-76; cost acct. Sun Litho, Inc., Sepulveda, Calif., 1976-77; lead cost acct. Products Rsch. & Chem., Glendale, Calif., 1977-84; acctg. mgr. PhotoSonics, Inc., Burbank, Calif., 1984—; CFO Instrumentation Mktg. Corp., Burbank, 1988—. Mem. NAFE. Republican.

Jewish. Office: Instrumentation Mktg Corp 820 S Mariposa St Burbank CA 91506-3108

DE NECOCHEA, NICOLE DIANNE, international trade policy advisor; b. Santa Barbara, Calif., Aug. 17, 1966; d. Fernando and Dianne (Whitington) de N. MPhil in Latin Am. Studies, Oxford U., Eng., 1992; BA in History and Lit., Harvard Coll., 1988. Vis. rschr. Inst. Torcvato Di Tella, Buenos Aires, 1990-91; policy analyst Ctr. for Policy Alternatives/Econ. Devel. Program, Washington, 1993; policy advisor for internat. trade U.S. Dept. of Commerce, Washington, 1994—. Liaison officer St. Antony's Coll. Oxford U., Washington, 1993—, trustee, 1994—. English-Speaking Union fellow, San Francisco, 1989-92, Rotary Internat. Found. fellow, 1990. Office: US Dept Commerce Office of the Secretary 14th and Constitution Washington DC 20230

DENEGRE-RUMBIN, MARILYN LOUISE, management consultant, health care administrator; b. New Haven, Oct. 19, 1954; d. Anthony Francis and Rose Mary (Curello) Denegre; m. Lawrence Rumbin, May 5, 1978 (div. 1983); 1 child, Marina Lee Rumbin; m. Douglas Shields, 1986 (div. 1992); 1 child, Stephan Bjorn Shields. BS in Edn., SCSC, 1979; AA in Legal Adminstrn. summa cum laude, U. Bridgeport, 1992, BS in Legal Adminstrn./Bus. Adminstrn. magna cum laude, 1993, MBA, 1994. Unit mgr. pediatric ICU, medicine and oncology Yale New Haven Hosp., 1974-84; office mgr. Dental Assocs., Newtown, Conn., 1984-86, New Haven Med. Group, 1986-88; pvt. practice as mgmt. cons. Milford, Conn., 1984—; ops. mgr. Southbury (Conn.) Med. Group, 1988-91; asst. Bridgeport Fgn. Trade Inst., 1993-94; mgmt. cons. Remington Corp., Bridgeport, 1993-94; dir. sr. healthcare cons. Hosp./Practice Mgmt., 1994. Supporter unwed mothers Pro-Life, Milford, 1988-94; organizer Sister-City Project, Milford, 1989-94. Rsch. grantee FDA, 1992. Mem. AAUW, NAFE, Nat. Assn. Credit Mgrs., Nat. Assn. Tng. & Devel., Healthcare Fin. Mgmt. Assn., Med. Group Mgmt. Assn., New Haven Paralegal Assn., Women Entrepreneur Inst., Fairfield Paralegal Assn., Beta Gamma Sigma, Phi Beta Gamma. Roman Catholic. Home: 9535 Sparrow Pl Mason OH 45040 Office: UASI Townview Bus Ctr 352 Gest St Cincinnati OH 45203

DENES, AGNES C., environmental artist; b. Budapest, Hungary, 1931. Student, CCNY, New Sch. Social Research, Columbia U., 1964-66; DFA, Ripon Coll., 1994. lectr. NYU, 1971, CUNY, 1972, 76Oberlin (Ohio) Coll., 1973, N.Y. Inst. Tech., N.Y.C., 1973, Corcoran Sch. Art, Washington, 1973, 74, U. Mass. Amherst, 1974, Ohio Wesleyan U., Delaware, 1974, Pratt Inst., N.Y.C., 1974, 76, 81, Ohio State U., Columbus, 1974, Moore Coll. Art, Phila., 1974, San Francisco Art Inst., 1975, 76, Kensington Arts Assn., Toronto, 1975, U. Calif., Berkeley, 1976, 90, U. Akron, Ohio, 1976, San Jose (Calif.) State U., 1976, Pratt Inst., N.Y.C., 1976, Newport Harbor Art Mus., Newport Bch., Calif., 1976, 81, Rutgers U., New Brunswick, N.J., 1976, Temple U., Phila., 1977, Art Gallery, Toronto, 1977, UCLA, 1978, Birmingham Poly. Inst., Eng., 1978, Rochester (N.Y.) Inst. Tech., 1979, St. Laurence U., Canton, N.Y., 1980, 82, Hunter Coll., N.Y.C., 1980, 81, MIT, Cambridge, Mass., 1980, Skidmore Coll., Saratoga Springs, N.Y., 1980, Wabash Coll., Crawfordsville, Ind., 1983, Miami (Fla.)-Dade C.C., 1984, Harvard U., Cambridge, Mass., 1984, Cooper Union Advancement Sci. and Art, N.Y.C., 1985, U. Hawaii, Honolulu, 1985, 1993, U. Genoa, Italy, 1986, Nat. Inst. Fine Arts, Guadalajara, Mex., 1986, U.N.D, Grand Forks, 1989, Architects House, Moscow, 1990, Fla. State U., Tallahassee, 1991, Royal Acad., Stockholm, 1992, Fine Arts Acad., Helsinki, Finland, 1992, Cornell U., Ithaca, N.Y., 1993, SUNY Albany, 1993; vis. critic sch. archtecture U. Pa., 1991; tchr. art Sch. Visual Arts, N.Y.C., 1974-79, San Francisco Art Inst., 1975, Skowhegan (Maine) Sch. Painting and Sculpture, 1979, Universita degli Studi di Genoa, Italy, 1986, Hartford (Conn.) Art Sch., 1988; speaker at numerous global confs. One-person shows include Columbia U., N.Y.C., 1965, Ruth White Gallery, N.Y.C., 1968, A.I.R. Gallery, N.Y.C., 1972, Ohio State U., Columbus, 1974, Corcoran Gallery Art, Washington, 1974, Stefanotty Gallery, N.Y.C., 1975, U. Akron, Ohio, 1976, Newport Harbor Art Mus., Newport Beach, Calif., 1976, Rutgers U., 1976, 112 Green St. Gallery, N.Y.C., 1977, Temple U., 1977, Centre Culturel Americain, Paris, 1977, Franklin Furnace, N.Y.C., 1978, Ikon Gallery, Birmingham, Eng., 1978, Amerika Haus, Berlin, 1978, Studio d'Arte Cannaviello, Milan, 1979, Inst. Contemporary Art, London, 1979, Gallerie Aronowitsch, Stockholm, 1980, Galleriet, Lund, Sweden, 1980, Elise Meyer Gallery, N.Y.C., 1980, 81, MIT, 1980, Kunsthalle, Nurnberg, Germany, 1982, No. Ill. U. Art Gallery, Chgo., 1985, U. Hawaii Art Gallery, 1985, Ricardo Barreto Arte Contemporaneo, Guadalajara, Mex., 1986, Arts Club Chgo., 1990, Anselmo Alvarez Galeria de Arte, Madrid, Spain, 1990, Cornell U., Ithaca, N.Y., 1992, Wynn Kramarsky, N.Y.C., 1994; group exhbns. include Hundred Acres Gallery, N.Y.C., 1970, Nat. Acad. Galleries, N.Y.C., 1970, 80, Dwan Gallery, N.Y.C., 1970, Jewish Mus., N.Y.C., 1970, Finch Coll. (N.Y.) Mus., 1971, Whitney Mus. Art, N.Y.C., 1971, 73, 76, Mus. Modern Art, Buenos Aires, 1971, Mus. Fine Arts, Santiago, Chile, 1971, Inst. Contemporary Art, Lima, Peru, 1971, NYU, 1972, Albion Coll. Mich., 1972, N.Y. Cultural Ctr., N.Y.C., 1972, 73, Kent State U., 1972, Oberlin Coll. 1972, N.Y. Inst. Tech., N.Y.C., 1972, Bklyn. Mus., 1972, 76, 80, Kunsthaus, Hamburg, Germany, 1972, Pace Coll., 1973, 78, Mus. Modern Art, 1973, 77, Kunstverein, Berlin, 1973, Inst. Arts, Valencia, Calif., 1973, Wadsworth Atheneum, Hartford, Conn., 1973, Kunsthalle, Cologne, 1974, Indpls. Mus., Ofart, Ind., 1974, San Francisco Mus. Art, 1974, Stadtisches Mus., Leverkusen, Germany, 1975, Grey Art Gallery N.Y.U., 1975, Inst. Contemporary Art, U. Pa., Phila., 1975, Michael C. Rockefeller Arts Ctr., Fredonia, N.Y., 1976, Arts Gallery, New South Wales, Sydney, Australia, 1976, Mus. Natural Hist., N.Y.C., 1977, Documenta VI, Kassel, Germany, 1977, Cleve. State U., 1977, Venice Biennale, Italy, 1978, 80, Yale U. Art Gallery, New Haven, 1978, Leo Castelli Gallery, N.Y.C., 1978, Rose Esman Gallery, N.Y.C., 1978, 79, Nat. Gallery, Wellington, Australia, 1978, Mus. Contemporary Arts, Brisbane, Australia, 1978, Seibu Art Mus., Tokyo, 1979, Gallerie AIX, Stockholm, 1979, Ackland Art Mus., Chapel Hill, N.C., 1979, Kunstmuseum, Berne, Switzerland, 1979, Mus. Ludwig, Cologne, 1979, Gulbenkian Found., Lisbon, Portugal, 1979, Museo Espanol de Arte Contemporaneo, Madrid, 1979, Tel Aviv Mus., 1979, Vienna Mus. des 20 Jahrhunderts, Austria, 1979, New Mus., N.Y.C., 1980, Albright Coll., Reading, Pa., 1980, 81, Wright State U., Dayton, Ohio, 1980, U. Pa., 1980, Kunstforeninger Mus., Copenhagen, 1980, Biblioteca Nacional, Madrid, 1980, Musee Nat. d'art Moderne, Paris, 1980, Museo de Arte Contemporanea, Brazil, 1980, Rutgers U., 1981, 86, Hofstra U., N.Y.C., 1981, 92, Aldrich Mus. Contemporary Art, Ridgefield, Conn., 1981, Palais des Beaux Arts, Brussels, 1981, U. Colo. Art Galleries, Boulder, 1981, Toledo (Ohio) Mus. Art, 1981, Galerie Nacional de Arte Moderna, Lisbon, 1981, New Gallery Contemporary Art, Cleve., 1981, Galleriet, Lund, Sweden, 1982, Nat. Acad. Design, N.Y.C., 1982, Va. Commonwealth U., Richmond, 1982, John Michael Kohler Art Ctr., Sheboygan, Wis., 1982, San Francisco Mus. Modern Art, 1983, Osaka U. Arts, Japan, 1983, Tacoma (Wash.) Art Mus., 1983, Nat. Mus. Art, Smithsonian Inst., Washington, 1984, 85, San Antonio Mus. Assn., 1984, Dayton (Ohio) Art Inst., 1984, Rhona Hoffman Gallery, Chgo., 1984, Germans van Eck Gallery, N.Y.C., 1984, Bard Coll., N.Y., 1984, 90, Ronald Feldman Fine Arts, N.Y.C., 1984, Am. Inst. Arts & Letters, 1985, 86, Moderna Museet, Stockholm, 1985, Rosemont (Pa.) Coll., 1985, Bass Mus. Art, Miami Bch., Fla., 1985, Winnipeg (Can.) Art Gallery, 1985, Anchorage (Alaska) Hist. & Fine Arts Mus., 1985, U. Minn., Duluth, 1985, Stamford (Conn.) Mus., 1985, Nurnburg, Kunsthalle, Germany, 1986, Print Club, Phila., 1986, Museo de Artes Moderno La Tertulia, Cali, Colombia, 1986, Santa Maria di Castello, Genoa, Italy, 1986, Ethnographic Mus., Belgrade, Yugoslavia, 1986, Nat. Acad. Design, N.Y.C., 1987, Circulo de Bellas Artes, Madrid, 1987, Kolnischer Kunstverein, Cologne, 1987, Goteborgs Kontsmuseum, Sweden, 1987, Sonya Henie-Neils Onstad Found., Hovikodden, Norway, 1987, Minn. Mus. Art, St. Paul, 1987, Kjarvalsstadir, Reykjavik, Iceland, 1987, Circulo de Bellas Artes, Madrid, 1987, Museu de Arte, Sao Paulo, Brazil, 1987, Cin. Art Mus., 1989, Denver Art Mus., 1989, 91, Pa. Acad. Fine Arts, Phila., 1989, L.I. U., Brookville, N.Y., 1989, Brandeis U., Waltham, Mass., 1991, Mus. Contemporary Art, Helsinki, Finland, 1992, The Mus. Tampere, Finland, 1992, Art Gallery, Hamilton, Can., 1992, Expo '92, Moguer, Spain, 1992, Laumeier Sculpture Park & Gallery, St. Louis, 1993, Dallas Mus. Nat. Hist., 1993, Epad, La Défense, Paris, 1993; commns. and installations include Artpark, Lewiston, N.Y., 1977, 79, Container Corp. Am., Chgo., 1979, Manhattan Pub. Art Fund, N.Y.C., 1982, Dept. Cultural Affairs, Genoa, Italy, 1986, First Nat. Bank Chgo, N.Y.C., 1986-87, Am.-Scandinavian Found, Sweden, 1988-89, NSW Masterplan City of Berkeley, Calif., 1988-91, City of Chgo. Pub. Art Program, 1990-91, Internat. Ctr. Preservation Wild Animals, Columbus, Ohio, 1990-93, "Tree

Mountain," Ylojarvi, Finland, 1992—; author: Paradox and Essence, 1976, Sculptures of the Mind, 1976, Isometric Systems in Isotropic Space: Map Projections, 1979, Book of Dust -- The Beginning and the End of Time and Thereafter, 1989. Creative Artists Pub. Svc. grantee N.Y. State Coun. Arts, 1972, 74, 80, Visual Arts Program grantee, N.Y. State Coun. Arts, 1979, 84, The Thord-Gray Meml. Fund, Rsch. and Devel. grantee Am.-Scandinavian Found., 1987, Herbert F. Johnson Mus. Art Purchase prize Richard A. Florscheim Art Fund, 1992; Individual Artists fellow NEA, 1974, 75, 81, 89, Collaboration in Art, Sci. and Tech. fellow Syracuse U., 1977, Deutscher Akademischer Austausdienst fellow Berlin, 1978, Rsch. fellow Ctr. Advanced Visual Studies, MIT, 1980, Studio for Creative Inquiry, Carnegie-Mellon U., 1993—; recipient Nat. Drawing Competition Purchase prize Rutgers U., 1974, Internat. Women's Yr. award Internat. Women's Art Festival, 1975-76, Berthe Von Moschzisker prize Print Club, 1980, The Ann and Donald McPhail award Print Club, 1982, Hassam and Speicher Fund Purchase award Am. Acad. Arts & Letters, 1985, The Eugene McDermott Achievement award MIT Coun. for Arts, 1990, Young Lawyers Pub. Art award Chgo. Bar Assn., 1992. Address: 595 Broadway New York NY 10012-3222*

DENES, MICHEL JANET, physical therapist, consultant in rehabilitation; b. Detroit, Apr. 29, 1950; d. Seymore Bernard and Clarine (Stierer) Swartz; m. George Denes, Jan. 22, 1984; 1 child, Zachary Todd. BS in Phys. Therapy, U. Mich., 1972. cert. in phys. therapy; cert. in neuro-devel. treatment in adult hemiplegia. Staff phys. therapist Sinai Hosp. of Detroit, 1972-77, supr., phys. therapist, 1977-78, chief phys. therapy supr., 1979-88; phys. therapist Rehab. Physicians, P.C., Birmingham, Mich., 1989; phys. therapy cons. closed head injury program Annie's House, Inc., Birmingham, 1989—; adj. instr. Wayne State U. Coll. Allied Health Professions, Detroit, 1982-90; lectr. in field. Mem. Am. Phys. Therapy Assn., Neurodevel. Treatment Assn., Am. Acad. Oral Medicine. Office: Annies House Inc 2100 E Maple Rd Ste 300 Birmingham MI 48009

DENGLER, PATRICIA LEE, home care executive; b. Harrisburg, Pa., Aug. 29, 1948; d. Ralph James Dengler and Betty May (Tobias) Dengler-Fisher. BA in Psychology, Mary Washington Coll. of the U. Va., 1970; MA in Psychology, Temple U., 1972. Career counselor, asst. dir. Temple U., Phila., 1970-75, dir. career planning and placement, 1975-80; dir. personnel and administrn. Coopers & Lybrand, Phila., 1980-89; pres., CEO VIP Companion Care, Gibbsboro, N.J., 1989—. Pres. Lakeview Commons South Condominium Assn.; bd. dirs. Camden County YMCA, 1988-90; coord. Explorer Troop Scouting, 1987-89. Recipient Outstanding Achievement in Bus. award Greater Phila. YMCA, 1983. Mem. Am. Coun. on Aging, Gerontological Soc. of Am., Better Bus. Bureau, Voorhees Bus. Assn., Am. Soc. Women Accts. (assoc. honorary mem 1984-89), Down Town Club (dir. 1986—). Democrat. Office: VIP Companion Care Ste 100 189 Lakeview Commons So Gibbsboro NJ 08026

DENHAM, CAROLINE VIRGINIA, retired college official; b. Detroit, June 22, 1937; d. Athel Fredric Denham and Emma Virginia (Franck) Kuhns. B.Mus., U. S.C., 1973. Sec. Shawnee Press, Inc., Delaware Water Gap, Pa., 1958-61, editorial asst., 1961-68; clk. typist U. S.C., Columbia, 1969-72, rsch. asst., 1972-76, dir. instnl. rsch., 1976-93; ret., 1994; libr. Columbia Philharm. Orch., 1970-82, pers. mgr., 1972-82; pers. mgr. S.C. Philharmonic Orch. Assn., Columbia, 1982—. Mem. S.C. State Employees Assn., S.C. Assn. for Instl. Rsch. (treas. 1987-91, pres. 1992-93), Assn. for Instl. Rsch., So. Assn. Instl. Rsch., Pi Kappa Lambda, Delta Omicron.

DENHAM, PATRICIA EILEEN KELLER, law librarian; b. Columbus, Ohio, Mar. 1, 1952; d. William Waite and Eileen Catherine (Miller) Keller; m. Richard Whitley Denham, Oct. 10, 1981 (div. Mar. 1986); 1 child, Michael Richard. BS, Findlay Coll., 1974; MSLS, U. Ky., 1978. Acquisitions libr. Supreme Ct. Ohio Law Libr., Columbus, 1974-76; acquisitions libr. Robert S. Marx Law Libr., U. Cin., 1978-88, head preservation and archives, 1988—; libr. Rendigs, Fry, Kiely & Dennis, Cin., 1979-85. Editor Tech. Svcs. Law Libr., 1990-94. Mem. AAUW, NOW, AAUP, Assn. Women Faculty, Am. Assn. Law Librs. (travel grantee 1984), Ohio Regional Assn. Law Librs. Republican. Episcopalian. Office: U Cin Location 142 Robert S Marx Law Libr Cincinnati OH 45221-0142

DENIOUS, SHARON MARIE, publisher; b. Rulo, Nebr., Jan. 27, 1941; d. Thomas Wayne and Alma (Murphy) Fee; m. Jon Parks Denious, June 17, 1963; children: Timothy Scot, Elizabeth Denious Cessna. Grad. high sch. Operator N.W. Pipeline co., Ignacio, Colo., 1975-90; pub. Silverton (Colo.) Standard & Miner, 1990—. Mem. Colo. Press Assn., Nat. Newspaper Assn. Office: Silverton Standard & Miner 1257 Greene St Silverton CO 81433

DENISON, SUSAN S., television executive; b. Waterbury, Conn., Apr. 12, 1946; d. David and Ruth (Lichter) Signal; m. Grant Denison (div.). BA in Psychology cum laude, Conn. Coll., 1969; MA in Psychology, U. Rochester, 1971; MBA, Harvard U., 1973. V.p. mktg. Showtime Network Inc., N.Y.C., 1979-84; sr. v.p. mktg. Revlon, N.Y.C., 1984-89; gen. mgr., exec. v.p. Showtime Satellite Network, N.Y.C., 1990—. Bd. dirs. Arts & Bus. Coun., N.Y.C., 1989—. Mem. Phi Beta Kappa. Home: Apt 40 340 W 55th St New York NY 10019-3766 Office: Showtime Networks Inc 1633 Broadway 37th Fl New York NY 10019-6708*

DENKO, JOANNE D., psychiatrist, writer; b. Kalamazoo, Mich., Mar. 29, 1927; d. John S. and Marian Mildred (Boers) Decker; m. Charles Wasil Denko, June 17, 1950; children: Christopher Charles, Nicholas Charles, Timothey Charles. BA summa cum laude, Hope Coll., 1947; MD, Johns Hopkins U., 1951; MS in Psychiatry, U. Mich., 1963. Lic. psychiatrist Md., Ill, Mich., Ohio. Pvt. practice Columbus, Ohio, 1961-68; staff psychiatrist Fairview Gen. Hosp., Cleve., 1968—; pvt. practice Rocky River, Ohio, 1968—; cons. Juvenile Diagnostic Ctr., Columbus, 1967-68, VA Hosp., Cleve., 1968-72, Community Mental Health Ctrs., Greater Cleve., 1974-80; clin. instr. Case Western Res. U., Cleve., 1981-83. Author: Through the Keyhole at Gifted Men and Women, 1977, (monograph) The Psychiatric Aspects of Hypoparathyroidism, 1962; contbr. articles to profl. jours.; author poetry, 1960—. Mem. AAAS (reviewer children's books), Cleve. Astron. Soc. (bd. dirs. 1984-86), Mensa Soc. (Cleve. area br. pres. 1986-87), Great Books Discussion Group (Rocky River, chmn. 1985-92). Russian Orthodox. Home and Office: 21160 Avalon Dr Cleveland OH 44116-1120

DENNEY, LUCINDA ANN, relocation services executive; b. Akron, Aug. 7, 1938; d. Charles Andrew and Madora Heinretta (Frederick) Shetter; m. Jon E. Denney; children: Mary, Jon, Andrew. BA cum laude, Ohio Wesleyan U., 1960. Cons. Cleve., 1978—; co-dir. corp. relocation Hackett & Arnold, Inc., Cleve., 1991—. Mem. adv. coun. to pub. rels. com. Mus. Arts Assn.; exec. com. Cleve. Orch., jr. com. 1968-84; mem. adv. com. Rock'n Roll Hall of Fame, Cleve., 1986—, Shaker Heights (Ohio) Citizens League, Cleve. Opera Coun., Shaker Heights Youth Ctr., 1982—, also v.p.; trustee Boy Scouts Am., 1984—, Jr. League Cleve., 1968-84, Big Bros./Big Sisters of Greater Cleve., 1968-84, St. Luke's Hosp. Jr. Bd., 1968-84, St. Luke's Hosp. Assn., 1988—; mem. Leadership Cleve., 1981-93, pres. 1993-94. Named one of 1977 Most Interesting Persons, Cleve. Mag.; recipient Outstanding Pace Setter award Directory of Greater Cleve.'s Enterprising Women, 1985, Disting. alumni award Cuyahoga Falls H.S., 1988. Mem. 20th Century Club, Mortar Bd., Alpha Theta Pi, Kappa Alpha Theta. Republican. Methodist.

DENNIES, SANDRA LEE, city official; b. Buffalo, Dec. 26, 1951; d. Norman John and Shirley Edith (Dils) D.; m. Robert Francis Gilbane, Sept. 21, 1974 (div. Apr. 1987); children: Brandon Michael, Gianpatrick. AS in Dental Hygiene, U. Bridgeport, Conn., 1972, BS in Dental Hygiene Edn., 1973; MS in Health Scis., So. Conn. State U., 1979. Dental hygienist various orgns., New Haven, 1972-73, Leonard B. Zaslow, DDS, Westport, Conn., 1973-81; lectr. U. Bridgeport, 1973-76; planner City of Bridgeport, 1977-79, planning asst., 1979-81; grants dir. City of Stamford, Conn., 1981—; sec. Com. on Emergency Med. Disaster Planning, Bridgeport, 1978-79; dir., dep. dir. Stamford Coliseum Authority, 1982-91; dep. dir. Stamford Film Commn., 1986-88. Editor, chief: Hy-Light Jour., 1973-76. Mem. Stamford Youth Planning and Adv. Bd., 1981-91, Stamford Youth Svc. Bur., 1991—, United Way Corp., Stamford, 1986-93; pres., sec. Alcohol and Drug Abuse Coun., 1987-92; mem. bd. Christian outreach North Stamford Congl. Ch., 1988-92; mem. Coun. Chs. and Synagogues Assembly, Stamford, 1989; pres. Stamford Mcpl. Supervisory Employees Union, 1991—. Democrat. Home: 171 Shadow Ridge Rd Stamford CT 06905-1813 Office: City of Stamford PO Box 2152 888 Washington Blvd Stamford CT 06904-2152

DENNING, MELINDA SUE, nurse; b. Hillsboro, Ill., Aug. 26, 1962; d. Richard Lee and Lila Marie (Crigler) Chaplin; m. David Lewis Denning, Aug. 1, 1981. BSN, Kaskaskia Coll., 1985. RN. Staff nurse, RN Sunnydale Acres Care Ctr., Vandalia, Ill., 1985-87, care plan nurse, RN, 1987-88; ADON Cherrywood Health Care Ctr., Vandalia, Ill., 1988-89; staff nurse, RN Van Dyke Convalescent Ctr., Effingham, Ill., 1989-91; DON Cherrywood Health Care Ctr., Vandalia, 1992-93; nurse Don Olivewood Health Care Ctr., Shelbyville, Ill., 1993—; CNA instr. Kaskaskia Coll., Centralia, Ill., 1990-91, rehab. nursing instr., 1990-91; CPR instr. Am. Heart Assn., Vandalia, 1991—. Methodist. Home: RR 1 Box 308 Vandalia IL 62471 Office: Olivewood Health Care Ctr 2116 S Third & Dacey Dr Shelbyville IL 62565

DENNIS, GAIL, government official; b. Phila., Nov. 26, 1943; d. Albert Eugene and Ruth Kathryn (Gruber) D. BA in Art History and Theory, George Washington U., 1966. Documents methods specialist, mgmt. analyst U.S. Govt. Printing Office, Washington, 1966-72; mgmt. analyst I and dir., mgmt. systems and review office Fed. City Coll., Washington, 1972-74; mgmt. analyst, lead mgmt. analyst standard and optional forms mgt. program GSA Info. Resources Mgmt. Svc., Washington, 1974—. Mem. Nat. Assn. for Miniature Enthusiasts, Smithsonian Inst., Friends Torpedo Factory, Washington Performing Arts Soc., Nat. Mus. for Women in Arts, Gourmet Group. Episcopalian. Office: Gsa Irms Kmr Washington DC 20405

DENNIS, HELEN MARION, gerontologist, educator; b. Lansdale, Pa., Aug. 27, 1940; d. Eric and Hedy (Gruenberg) Gutman; m. Lloyd B. Dennis, Dec. 1, 1963; children: Lauren, Susan. BA, Pa. State U., 1962; MA, Calif. State U., Long Beach, 1976. Asst. coordinator data analysis George Washington U., Washington, 1965-69; project dir., research assoc., lctr. Andrus Gerontology Ctr. U. So. Calif., Los Angeles, 1976—; project dir. The Conf. Bd., N.Y.C., 1988-90. Mem. exec. bd., trustee Temple Menorah, Redondo Beach, Calif., 1981-85, pres. 1991-95; mem. exec. bd. Los Angeles Council Careers Older Americans, 1985—; mem. adv. bd. Project Reinvest, Coro Found., Los Angeles, 1985; pres. Career Encores, 1991-93. Mem. Internat. Soc. Pre-Retirement Planners (nat. pres. 1986-87, pres. So. Calif. chpt. 1983-85), Am. Soc. Aging, Gerontol. Soc. Am. Home: 347 Via El Chico Redondo Beach CA 90277-6757 Office: U So Calif Andrus Gerontology Ctr Los Angeles CA 90089

DENNIS, KAREN MARIE, plastic surgeon; b. Cleve., Dec. 23, 1948; d. Chester and Adele (Wesley) Denwicz; m. Miles Auslander, June 21, 1974; 1 child, Kristin. BS, Ohio State U., 1971, MD, 1974. Diplomate Am. Bd. Plastic Surgery, Am. Bd. Otolaryngology. Intern Kaiser Permanente, L.A., 1974-75; resident in otolaryngology Roosevelt Hosp., N.Y.C., 1976-79; resident in plastic surgery Ohio State Univ. Hosps., Columbus, 1979-81; pvt. practice Beverly Hills, Calif., 1981—. Mem. Am. Soc. Reconstructive and Plastic Surgeons, Calif. County Med. Assn., L.A. County med. Assn., L.A. Soc. Plastic Srugeons (sec. 1993-94), Phi Beta Kappa. Office: 433 N Camden Dr Beverly Hills CA 90210

DENNIS, MARY JULIA, sanitarian; b. Ohio, Nov. 11, 1959; d. Wallace Eugene and Marian Ruth (Fahey) D.; 1 child, Julia Anne. BS in Edn., Bowling Green State U., 1990. Registered sanitarian; cert. tchr., Ohio. Tchr. Bowling Green (Ohio) City Schs., 1990-91; sanitarian Wood County Health Dept., Bowling Green, 1991—; mem. Local Emergency Planning Com., Bowling Green, 1992—; mem. work safety com. OSHA, Bowling Green, 1994—. Mem. Am. Bus. Women's Assn., Ohio Environ. Health Assn. Home: 138 Georgia Ave Bowling Green OH 43402 Office: Wood County Health Dept 1840 E Gypsy Lane Rd Bowling Green OH 43402

DENNIS, PAMELA SUE, accountant; b. Portland, Ind., Aug. 30, 1953; d. Willard Leroy and Marilyn Jean (Platt) Smith; m. Stanley Eugene Dennis, Sept. 8, 1973; 1 child, Shane Alan. BS, Ball State U., 1975; BBA magna cum laude, West Tex. A&M U., 1988. CPA, Tex. Cashier Marsh Supermarket, Portland, Ind., 1973-77; office mgr. Tom Thumb Page, Plano, Tex., 1977-85; acct. Mesa, Amarillo, Tex., 1989-90, H.V. Robertson & Co., CPAs, Amarillo, Tex., 1990-93; fin. officer City of Sachse, Tex., 1994—. Recipient scholarship Arthur Young, 1987, Hoosier scholarship, 1972-74. Mem. AICPA, Tex. Soc. CPAs, Dallas Soc. CPAs, Govt. Fin. Officers Assn. Home: 413 Woodhollow Dr Wylie TX 75098-3854

DENNIS, (MARY) RUTH, retired librarian; b. Bloomfield, Iowa, July 16, 1907; d. Claude Charles and Nora Jane (Townsend) Atwood; m. Donald A. Dennis, Sept. 11, 1932 (div. Dec. 1955); children: Larry, Mary Jo Bousek. Student, Ottumwa Heights Jr. Coll., Ottumwa, Iowa, 1927-28; cert. in libr. sci., USDA Grad. Sch., 1964. Libr. asst. Ottumwa Pub. Libr., 1929-31; agt. Met. Life Ins. Co., Marshalltown, Iowa, 1943-45; continuity writer Sta. KFJB, Marshalltown, 1953-56; housemother Signa Alpha Epsilon, Iowa City, 1956-57; libr. asst. U. Iowa, Iowa City, 1957-59; cataloging asst. U.S. Bur. Census, Andrews AFB, Md.; reference libr. U.S. Weather Bur. Libr., Washington, 1959-64; asst. libr. USDA, Peoria, Ill., 1964-66; libr. Herbert Hoover Presdl. Libr., Branch, Iowa, 1966-72; ret., 1972. Author: Homes of the Hoovers, 1986, The Wit and Wisdom of Herbert Hoover, 1995. Bd. dirs. Cedar County chpt. Am. Cancer Soc., Tipton, Iowa, 1987—; past pres. West Branch Heritage; v.p. Friends Eniow Pub. Libr., West Branch. Mem. Herbert Hoover Presdl. Libr. Assn., Questers (historian Red Cedar chpt., past pres.), Order Ea. Star (worthy matron, 1971, 81). Republican. Mem. Christian Ch. (Disciples of Christ). Home: 330 1/2 W Main St West Branch IA 52358

DENNISON, RAMONA POLLAN, special education educator; b. Floydada, Tex., Jan. 19, 1938; d. William C. and Anne M. (Tivis) Pollan; m. Bob Dennison, Oct. 12, 1956; 1 child, Tajquah. BS, MEd, E. Cen. U., 1972, cert. in psychometry, 1974, lic. in profl. counseling, 1975. Lic. psychometrist, profl. counselor. Tchr. Konawa (Okla.) Pub. Sch., 1972—. Mem. NEA, Okla. Edn. Assn., Okla. Assn. Children of Learning Disabilities, Konana Edn. Assn., Lic. Profl. Counselor Assn., Nat. Assn. Children Learning Disabilities, E. Cen. Alumni Assn., Tanti Study Club, Oak Hills Country Club, Delta Kappa Gamma, Phi Delta Kappa. Democrat. Baptist. Home: RR 4 Box 568 Ada OK 74820-9443

DENNISTON, MARJORIE MCGEORGE, educator; b. Coraopolis, Pa., Mar. 21, 1913; d. Chauncey Kirk and Elsie (George) McGeorge; m. Delbert Dicks Denniston, Dec. 25, 1942 (dec. 1973); 1 child, Robert Bruce. Student, Ohio U., 1931-33; BA, Westminster Coll., 1936; postgrad., U. Kans., 1959, Western Ill. U., 1962, 64. Elem. tchr. county schs. West Pittsburg, Pa., 1936-42, New Castle Sch. System, Pa., 1942, 51-78. Vol. aid Pa. Assn. Retarded Children, Jameson Hosp., Law County Home, 1984—; trustee, elder Presbyn. Ch., New Castle, 1986-92, v.p. Ch. Women United, 1990-94. Named First Lady of New Castle, 1989, Outstanding Woman of Yr. for Community Svc. Jr. Woman's Club, 1990. Mem. AAUW, LWV (sec. New Castle chpt. 1986—), Coll. Club (parliamentarian), Woman's Club (parliamentarian Lawrence County fedn. 1984—, sec. 1986-88), Woman's Club of New Castle (parliamentarian 1990-94), Fedn. Jrs. (v.p. 1994—), Pa. Assn. State Retirees (v.p. local chpt. 1994—), Delta Kappa Gamma. Republican. Home: 331 Laurel Blvd New Castle PA 16101-2523

DENNY, JUDITH ANN, lawyer; b. Lamar, Mo., Sept. 18, 1946; d. Lee Livingston and Genevieve Adelpha (Falke) D.; m. Thomas M. Lenard, May 29, 1976; children: Julia Lee, Michael William. BA, La. Tech. U., 1968; JD, George Washington U., 1972. Bar: D.C. 1973. Asst. spl. prosecutor Watergate Spl. Prosecution Force, Washington, 1973-75; pros. atty. U.S. Dept. Justice, Washington, 1975-78; dir. div. compliance U.S. Office Edn. HEW, Washington, 1978-80; acting asst. insp. gen. for investigations U.S. Dept. Edn., Washington, 1980; dep. dir. policy and compliance, office of revenue sharing U.S. Dept. Treasury, Washington, 1980-83, counselor to gen. counsel, 1983-89; insp. gen. ACTION, Washington, 1989-94; cons. Fed. Quality Inst., 1994—. Mem. D.C. Bar Assn. Home: 3214 Porter St NW Washington DC 20008-3211 Office: 1100 Vermont Ave NW Washington DC 20525-0001

DENNY, MARILYN ANN, advertising executive; b. Catskill, N.Y., May 3, 1947; d. Clyde Elmer and Cecelia (Perry) Alberti; m. Ronald F. Denny, June 1, 1968; children: Margie A. Hawkins, Matthew S., Michael F., Jacqueline C. Diploma, W.A.J. Ctrl. Sch., 1965; grad., Hartford Airline Sch., 1965. Clk.-typist CIA, Washington, 1966-68; acctg. sec. Brockway Glass Co., Zanesville, Ohio, 1968-74; br. mgr., sales exec. advt. and distbn. Dispatch Consumer Svcs., Inc., Zanesville, 1980—. Mem. Nat. Mgmt. Assn., Mid-East Ohio Women Entrepreneurs. Methodist. Office: Dispatch Consumer Svcs Inc 3561 Newark Rd Zanesville OH 43701

DENNY, MARY CRAVER, state legislator, rancher; b. Houston, July 9, 1948; d. Kenneth and Lois (Skiles) Craver; m. Henry William Denny, Jan. 26, 1969 (div. Aug. 1990); 1 child, Bryan William. Student, U. Tex., 1966-70; BS in Elem. Edn. magna cum laude, U. North Tex., 1973. Cert. tchr., Tex. Owner, mgr. Craver Ranch, Aubrey, Tex., 1973—; mem. Tex. Ho. of Reps., Austin, 1993—. Vol. Tex. Rep. Com., 1964—; chmn. Denton County Rep. Com., Denton, Tex., 1983-91; bd. dirs. Tex. Com. for Humanities, 1990, YMCA, Denton, 1985—, Tex. Fedn. Rep. Women, 1988-92, 94-96; life mem. president's coun. U. North Tex., Denton, 1974—, chmn., 1983; del. state and nat. Rep. convs., 1972—; mem. Denton Benefit League, 1976—, Denton Arts Coun., 1986—; member numerous other civic orgns. Named Outstanding Rep. Vol., Denton County Rep. Com., 1985, One of 10 Outstanding Rep. Women, Tex. Fedn. Rep. Women, 1991, Outstanding Alumna in Edn., U. North Tex. Coll. Edn., 1993. Mem. Am. Legis. Exch. Coun., Nat. Conf. State Legislatures, Ariel Club, Delta Zeta. Episcopalian. Address: RR 2 Box 271 Aubrey TX 76227-8732 Office: PO Box 2910 Austin TX 78768-2910 also: 416 W University Dr Ste 200 Denton TX 76201-1842

DENNY, WANDA JEAN, research director; b. Nashville, Nov. 12, 1946; d. John W. and Mildred B. (Wilkerson) D. BA in Sociology, Baker U., 1969; postgrad., George Washington U., 1985, U. Tenn., 1977-78. Program assoc. Urban Obs., Nashville, 1969-71; tchr., rsch. assoc. U.S. Peace Corps, Liberia, 1971-73; infection control practitioner Internat. Clin. Labs., Inc., Nashville, 1974-80; pharm. sales rep. Bristol Labs., Syracuse, N.Y., 1980-82; computer libr. mktg., planning and analysis MCI, Washington, 1982-85; program mgr. Kormos, Harris and Assocs., Nashville, 1987—. Author: Paris Sizzle, 1993; editor, publisher: Changing Reality, 1994—. Mem. 1st Ch. Unity. Home: 905 Mountain Valley Dr Nashville TN 37209 Office: Footwear Market Insights Ste 302 28 White Bridge Rd Nashville TN 37205

DENO, FERNANDE ELIZABETH, critical care nurse; b. Phila., Nov. 6, 1958; d. Francis E. Sr. and Elizabeth A. (Ayres) Boggs; m. D. Curtis Deno, June 7, 1980. AS, Hahnemann U., 1979; BSN, Holy Names Coll., 1987; MS, U. Calif., San Francisco, 1990. Staff nurse Hahnemann Hosp., Phila., 1979-80; asst. head nurse, preceptor Albany (N.Y.) Med. Ctr. Hosp., 1980-84; charge nurse, relief supr. Dr.'s Hosp., Pinole, Calif., 1984-91; cardiopulmonary clin. nurse specialist Vis. Nurses Assocs. No. Calif., Emeryville, 1991-92; critical care staff nurse Brookside Hosp., San Pablo, Calif., 1991-92; on call staff nurseICU/ER Fort Bend Hosp., Missouri City, Tex., 1992—; unit edn. coord. RN CCU Hermann Hosp., Houston, 1993—; lectr. Calif. State U., Hayward, 1990, Holy Names Coll., Oakland, Calif., 1991; critical care educator Fairmont Hosp., San Leandro, Calif., 1990-91, clin. instr. U. San Francisco, 1991. Mem. ANA, AACN, Emergency Nurses Assn., Holy Names Coll. Nursing Alumni Assn. (chpt. pres. 1991-92), Sigma Theta Tau. Home: 3118 Clyburn Ct Missouri City TX 77459-4805 Office: Hermann Hosp CCU Fannin St Houston TX 77004

DENOVIO, SUSAN WILLIAMS, marketing communications executive; b. Phila., Feb. 9, 1948; d. William Clinton and Catherine Irene (Currie) Williams; m. Carl James DeNovio, Aug. 9, 1969 (div. 1982); 1 child, Nicole Marie. BA Journalism, Rider Coll., 1969. Coordinator publications Ocean County Coll., Toms River, N.J., 1969-72; pub. info. officer Burlington County Coll., Pemberton, N.J., 1972-73, asst. to pres. for pub. info., 1973-75; freelance copywriter Yardley, Pa., 1978-80; mng. editor Ad World, Inc., Levittown, Pa., 1980-83; founder, pres. Catalyst Communications, Inc., Newtown, Pa., 1983-88, Vista Communications Inc., Holland, Pa., 1988—; mktg. cons. Mercer County Small Bus. Devel. Ctr., Trenton, N.J., 1983-84; instr. continuing edn. Bucks County Community Coll., Newtown, 1985-87. Editor, contbg. author: Bucks' Fortune, 1983. Bd. dirs. YMCA of Bucks County, Langhorne, Pa., 1984-90, rec. sec., 1984-86; instr. YWCA Women's Ctr., 1989. Recipient Outstanding Service award Bd. Trustees Burlington County Coll., 1975; cert. of Recognition Bucks County Community Coll., 1985; Addy award Phila. Club Advt. Women, 1985, Neographics Silver award Greater Del. Valley Graphic Arts Assn., 1986. Mem. Inst. Mgmt. Cons. (sec.-treas. 1993-94), Pi Delta Epsilon. Republican. Roman Catholic. Office: Vista Communications Inc 3209 Stockton Pl Southampton PA 18966-2918

DENSEN-GERBER, JUDIANNE, psychiatrist, lawyer, educator; b. N.Y.C., Nov. 13, 1934; d. Gustave A. and Beatrice D.; m. Michael M. Baden, June 14, 1958; children: Trissa Austin, Judson Michael, Lindsey Robert, Sarah Densen. A.B. cum laude, Bryn Mawr Coll., 1956; JD, Columbia U., 1959; MD, NYU, 1963. Bar: N.Y. 1961. Rotating intern French Hosp., N.Y.C., 1963-64; resident psychiatry Bellevue Hosp., N.Y.C., 1964-65, Met. Hosp., N.Y.C., 1965-67; mem. core staff Addiction Services Agy., N.Y.C., 1966-67; founder Odyssey House (psychiat. residence for rehab. narcotics addicts), N.Y.C., Mich., Maine, N.H., Utah, La., Australia, N.Z., 1967, clin. dir., 1967-69, exec. dir., 1967-74, pres. bd., 1974-82; pres., founder, chief exec. officer Odyssey Inst. Am., 1974-82; pres. Odyssey Inst. Australia, 1977-86, Odyssey Inst. Internat., Inc., 1978—; chairwoman Odyssey Inst. Corp. Conn., 1974—; attending physician Gracie Sq. Hosp., N.Y.C., 1982-93; attending physician Park City Hosp., Bridgeport, Conn., 1985—, mem. ethics com., 1988-93; attending physician Bridgeport Hosp., 1985—, mem. bd. ethics, 1993—; attending physician Northwest Gen. Hosp., Detroit, 1985-86; active staff St. Vincent's Hosp., Bridgeport, 1987—; courtesy staff Norwalk Hosp., 1993—; assoc. vis. prof. law U. Utah Law Sch., 1973-75; adj. prof. law N.Y. Law Sch., 1973-76; chairperson plenary session drug abuse Am. Acad. Forensic Scis., 1972, sec. psychiatry sect., 1973, chmn. sect., 1974—; founder, 1973, since pres. Inst. Women's Wrongs; founder, since pres. Odyssey Inst. (health care for socially disadvantaged), 1974—; bd. dirs. Simpson St. Devel. Assn., An Extraordinary Event (One to One for Mental Retardation), Bridge House; mem. Nat. Adv. Commn. Criminal Justice Standards and Goals, 1971-74, Pres.'s Commn. on White House Fellows, 1972-76; mem. drug experience adv. com. HEW, 1973-76; v.p. psychiat. sect. Internat. Forensic Medicine Conf., Budapest, 1967; pres. N.Y. Council Alcoholism, 1978—; co-chair com. on reproductive rights vs. best interest of the child Mich. State Senate, 1984-86; trustee Nat. Forensic Ctr., Princeton, N.J., 1985—, keynote speaker nat. conf., 1988, lectr., 1988; speaker Conf. for Multiple Personality Disorder, Chgo., 1985—; cons. to Mich. State Legislature to draft legislation on The Best Interests of the Child vs. the New Reproductive Techs., 1986; amicus curiae brief in Mary Beth Whitehead appeal Surrogate Mothering, 1987; sr. non-govt. psychiatrist L'Ambiance Plaza disaster, Bridgeport, 1987; guest lectr. narcotics addiction NYU Sch. Medicine, also Sch. Law.; in field dir. Daitch Shopwell, Inc.; cons. substance abuse device Insight Inc., Flint, Mich., 1987-88; guest speaker Cornell U., 1989, Internat. Hypnosis Soc. of Yale, 1989, Cumberland Law Sch., 1989, Sacred Heart U., 1994; founder, CEO, pres. The Family Maintenance Health Orgn., LLC. Author: (with Trissa Austin Baden) Drugs, Sex, Parents and You, 1972, We Mainline Dreams, The Odyssey House Story, 1973, Walk in My Shoes, 1976; (with David Sandberg) The Role of Child Abuse in Delinquency and Juvenile Court Decision-Making, 1984, Chronic Acting-Out Students and Child Abuse: A Handbook for Intervention, 1986, Shortened Forms: A Manual for Teachers On; (with John Dugan) Issues in Law and Psychiatry, 1988; contbr. articles to profl. jours.; editor: Jour. Corrective and Social Psychiatry, 1975; co-developer, co-inventor virocidal surface cleaner against AIDS, 1988. Mem. N.Y.C. Crime Control Commn., 1975-79, Gov.'s Task Force on Crime Control, Albany, N.Y., 1977-79, N.Y. State Crime Control Planning Bd., 1975-79; del. White House Conf. on Youth, 1971; bd. dirs. Nat. Coalition for Children's Justice, 1975—, Am. Soc. for Prevention of Cruelty to Children, 1979—, Mary E. Walker Found., 1978; psychiat. cons. Good Shepherd Home for Girls, 1989-90. Recipient Woman of Achievement award AAUW, 1970; Myrtle Wreath award Hadassah, 1970; B'nai B'rith Woman of Greatness award, 1971; Otty award for service to N.Y.C. Our Town1977; named Dame of White Cross Australia, Dame of Malta, Ky. Col., N.Y. State Hon. Fire Chief. Fellow Am. Coll. Legal Medicine (Congl. cert. merit 1990); mem. AMA, N.Y. State, N.Y. County Med. Socs., Soc. Med. Jurisprudence, Therapeutic Communities of Am. (founding mem., 1st v.p. 1975—), Am. Acad. Psychiatry and Law (mem. AIDS ad hoc com 1988—), Am. Psychiat. Assn., Women's Forum N.Y. (founding mem.), Nat. Women's Forum, Internat. Women's Forum, Internat. Soc. Multiple Personality and Dissociative States, Conn. Med. Assn., Am. Orthopsychiat. Assn., ABA, N.Y. State Bar Assn., N.Y. County Women's Bar Assn., N.Y. Assn. Vol. Agys. Narcotics Addiction and Substance Abuse (dir. 1968—), Am. Psychiat. Assn., N.Y. Med. Assn., Post Traumatic Stress Syndrome Soc., Fairfield County Med. Soc. (physicians health subcom. 1986-92). Republican. Unitarian. Club: Women's City (N.Y.C.). Office: Odyssey Inst Internat 5 Hedley Farms Rd Westport CT 06880

DENSLOW, DEBORAH PIERSON, educator; b. Phila., May 2, 1947; d. Merrill Tracy Jr. and Margaret (Aiman) D.; m. James Tracy Grey III, Nov. 24, 1972 (div. Dec. 1980); 1 child, Sarah Elizabeth. BS, Gwynedd Mercy Coll., 1971. Tchr. Willingboro (N.J.) Bd. Edn., 1971—; union rep. Burlington County Edn. Assn., Willingboro, 1981-82; mem. task force for reoganization Morrisville Sch. Dist., 1991-92. Committeewoman 1st ward Morrisville (Pa.) Rep. Com., 1986—; mem. Borough Coun., Morrisville, 1988—, pres. 1992-94, rep. candidate, 1986; borough chmn. Am. Cancer Soc., 1986-87; sec. bd. dirs. Morrisville Free Libr., 1988-90, bd. dirs. 1988—; mem. Morrisville Mcpl. Authority, chmn. 1994—. Mem. NEA, N.J. Edn. Assn., Willingboro Edn. Assn. (union rep. 1981-82, alt. union rep. 1988-89), Parents without Ptnrs. (bd. dirs. Mercer County chpt. 1981-82, sec. 1982-84), Bucks County Boroughs Assn. (bd. dirs. 1989—, v.p. 1990-92, pres. 1992-93). Presbyterian. Home: 1206 Ohio Ave Morrisville PA 19067-2417

DENSMORE, ANN, speech pathologist, audiologist, writer; b. L.A., Nov. 24, 1941; d. Ray B. and Margaret M. (Walsh) D.; children: Kristin Ann, Jennifer Ann. BS cum laude, UCLA, 1963; MA in Communicative Disorders, Calif. State U., 1975; student Cape Cod Conservatory of Arts, 1977-79, Harvard U. graphics-architecture program, 1980—; EdM in Human Devel. and Psychology, Harvard U., 1991; postgrad. Clark U., Worcester, Mass. Lic. speech pathologist and audiologist. Tchr., Santa Monica (Calif.) Unified Sch. Dist., 1973-74; speech pathologist Kennedy Child Study Center, 1975-76, Framingham (Mass.) Pub. Schs., 1979, Weston (Mass.) Schs., 1993—, Eliot-Pearson Children's Sch., Tufts U., Medford, Mass., 1993—; audiologist VA Hosp. Sepulveda, Calif., 1976-77, New Eng. Rehab. Hosp., Woburn, Mass., 1978; audiology cons. Wellesley (Mass.) Public Schs., 1979; speech pathologist and audiologist The Learning Center for Deaf Children, Framingham, 1978-80; dir. ann. fund Babson Coll., 1981-83; asst. dir. devel. Lakey Clinic Med. Ctr., 1984-86; assoc. dir. corp. devel. Harvard Med. Sch., 1986—; rsch. asst. Presch. Learning Lab., Harvard U., 1989, Judge Baker Children's Ctr., 1991-93; pvt. practice, Lexington, Mass., 1993—; freelance photographer, 1979—; career counselor corp. execs. Mackenna/Jandl Assoc., Inc., 1983—; v.p. U.S. sales Boston Corp.. Exhibited photographs Copley Soc. of Boston, 1979-80. Contbr. articles to Boston Globe, 1986—. Mem. Am. Speech and Hearing Assn. (cert. clin. competence, speech pathologist-audiologist), Copley Soc. of Boston. Episcopalian. Office: 1628 Mass Ave Lexington MA 02173

DENT, CATHERINE GALE, secondary education educator; b. Salem, Mo., Apr. 20, 1953; d. James Ferguson and Virgina Gale (Martin) Dent; m. Robert David Wells, Aug. 30, 1980 (div. Aug. 1990); m. Michael E. Schafer, Apr. 8, 1992; stepchildren: Heather Schafer, Cole Schafer. Student, U. Mo., 1971-74, 91—, Longview Commun. Coll., Lee's Summit, Mo., 1975, S.W. Bapt. U., Bolivar, Mo., 1985. Lic. funeral dir.; cert. secondary tchr., Mo. Feature writer, reporter Dent County Headliner, 1972-74; acctg. clk. Assn. of Unity Chs., Unity Village, Mo., 1974-77; graphic artist The Salem News, 1979; adminstrv. asst. Ozark Lead Co.-Kennecott Corp., Sweetwater, Mo., 1979-82; ch. organist United Meth. Ch., Salem, 1977—; music tchr. Salem, 1983—; substitute tchr. Salem R-80 Sch. Dist., 1991—. Bd. dirs. Salem Arts Coun., 1984—; mgr. Salem Community Jazz Band, 1985—; accompanist Salem Community Choir, 1984—, Salem R-80 Sch. Sys. Music Dept., 1990—; dir. Temple Carillons Handbell Choir, Salem, 1985-94. Recipient Children's award Cosmopolitan Club; named to Outstanding Young Women in Am., 1985. Mem. Salem Computer Club, Dent County Hist. Soc., Order Ea. Star, Salem Rebekah Lodge, Fraternal Order of Eagles Ladies Aux., Internat. Order Rainbow for Girls (Grand Cross of Color 1968), Sorosis Club (pres. 1992-93), Cosmopolitan Club (sec. 1994—). Democrat. Methodist. Home: 1200 W Center St Salem MO 65560-2736

DENT, ENID-MARY, art studio owner, muralist, furniture designer; b. Howarth, Eng., Sept. 22, 1950; d. Charles Richard and Kathleen (Rattigan) D. MA, St. Martins, London U., 1975. Art dir. Geary Moore Page, London, 1976-79; asst. dir. TV prodn. Reel to Reel, London, 1979-81; co-owner Dent & MacLeod, London, 1981-86; owner Decorative Art Studio, N.Y.C., 1986—. Home and Office: 612 W 144 St Ste A8 New York NY 10031

DENT, LEANNA GAIL, art educator; b. Manhattan, Kans., Oct. 21, 1949; d. William Charles and Maxine Madeline (Kackley) Payne; m. Stephen Alan Dent, Aug. 4, 1973; children: Laura Michelle, Jeffery Aaron. BS in Edn., U. Houston, 1973; postgrad., U. Tex., 1975-76; MS in Edn., Okla. State U., 1988. Cert. elementary and secondary art tchr., Okla., Tex. Tchr. art Popham Elem. Sch., Del Valle, Tex., 1973-77; graphic artist Conoco, Inc., Ponca City, Okla., 1987-88; tchr. art Garfiled Elem. Sch., Ponca City, Okla., 1988-91, Reed Elem. Sch., Houston, 1991-92, Copeland Elem. Sch., Houston, 1992-94, Campbell Jr. High Sch., Houston, 1994—; cons. and specialist in field. Author: Using Synectics to Enhance the Evaluation of Works of Art, 1988. Vol. 1st Luth. Day Sch., Ponca City, 1977-91, Ponca City Inds. Sch. Dist., 1987-91; work com. Cy-Fair Ind. Sch. Dist., Houston, 1991-94. Acad. and Mem. scholar Okla. State U., 1986-88. Mem. Nat. Art Edn., Tex. Art Edn. Assn. (judges commendation 1993), Assn. Tex. Profl. Educators, Houston Art Edn. Assn. (v.p. 1992-93, pres.-elect 1993—), Phi Delta Kappa, Phi Kappa Phi. Republican. Lutheran. Office: Campbell Jr High Sch 11415 Bobcat Rd Houston TX 77065-4441

DENT, SHARON PIERCE, transportation executive; b. Leachville, Ark., Jan. 24, 1948; d. Thomas Ralph and Margaret Evelyn (Scott) Pierce; m. Ronald R. Dent, Mar. 7, 1969; 1 child, Rachel. BA in Polit. Sci., Ark. State U., 1970; MPA, Memphis State U., 1973; postgrad., Northeastern, 1982. Intern, planning asst., assoc. planner, sr. planner Memphis Shelby County Planning Commn., 1972-78; asst. to adminstr., deputy dir. City of Phoeniz Pub. Transit Dept., 1978-90; exec. dir. Hillsborough Area Regional Transit Authority, Tampa, Fla., 1990; founding mem., pres. Phoenix chpt. Women's Transp. Seminar, 1985-90. Citizen advisor The Samaritans, Phoenix, 1988-90; chmn. ways and means Soroptimist, Phoenix, 1982-90; mem. LWV, Tampa, 1990-93. Mem. Am. Pub. Transit Assn. (bd. dirs. 1990-93), Southwest Transit Assn. (v.p. 1989-90, bd. dirs. 1986-90), Am. Planning Assn. (pres. West Tenn. chpt. 1977). Home: 420 S Royal Poinciana Dr Tampa FL 33609-3636 Office: Hillsborough Area Regional Transit 4305 E 21st Ave Tampa FL 33605-2311

DENTE, MARCIA ANN, accountant; b. Paterson, N.J., Nov. 3, 1944; d. Harry Edward and Gilda Margaret (Striano) D. BFA, William Paterson Coll., 1967; BA in Acctg., Fairleigh Dickenson U., 1978. Libr. exhibit artist Free Pub. Libr., Paterson, 1970-76; staff artist Epoch Universal Pub., Toronto, Ont., Can., 1980-84, Harp, Mississauga, Ont., 1984-86; sr. acct. Dept. Pub. Works, Paterson, 1986—. Author: Break-A-Leg, 1982; layout artist for books: Handbook of Musical Terms, 1981, Banners, Buttons and Songs, 1984. Recipient 1st Pl. Photo award Eastman/Kodak, 1989. Democrat. Roman Catholic. Home: 454 Kearney St Paterson NJ 07522 Office: Dept Pub Works 800 Broadway Paterson NJ 07514

DENTON, BETTY, lawyer, state representative; b. Waco, Tex., Aug. 19, 1946; m. Lane Denton; 1 child, Deeann Denton. BA, Baylor U., MA, JD, 1980. Bar: Tex. 1977, U.S. Dist. Ct. (we. dist.), U.S. Ct. Appeals (5th cir.); cert. family law, litigation and personal injury. Pvt. practice Waco, 1977—; state rep. State of Tex., 1977—; chair house jud. com., 1991—. Active Family Abuse Ctr., Parent Tchr. Assn., League of Women Voters, Tex. Dem. Women, McLennan County Women Elected Officials. Baptist. Home: 600 Columbus Ste C Waco TX 76701-1248 Office: Denton Law Office 600 Columbus Ste C Waco TX 76701-2134

DENTON, JANE GAIL, medical/surgical/intensive care, pediatric nurse; b. Jacksonville, Ark., June 20, 1962; d. Hubert Dewan and Flora Ann (Heard) Treat; m. Thomas Ray Tallas, Feb. 16, 1985 (div. 1990); 1 child, Amber Renee; m. John R. Denton, Mar. 15, 1994. BSN, West Tex. State U., 1984. BLS, ACLS, NRC, PALS. Staff nurse surg. ICU Clovis (N.Mex.) High Plains Hosp., 1984-85, 87-89; dir. nurses, vol. nurse ARC, Sembach Air Base, Germany, 1985-87; staff nurse USAF, Cannon AFB, N.Mex., 1989-92; asst. charge nurse Multi Svc. Unit, Sheppard AFB, Tex., 1992-93, nurse mgr., 1993; nurse mgr. Pediatric Clinic, Sheppard AFB, Tex., 1993-94; nurse mgr. maternal child flight Sheppard AFB, 1994—. Capt. USAF, 1989—. Fellow Nat. League Nursing; mem. Sigma Theta Tau. Democrat. Home: 38 Surrey Dr Iowa Park TX 76367 Office: Sheppard AFB 396 The Med Group Wichita Falls TX 76311

DENTON, JUDY ANN, special education educator; b. Lake Village, Ark., Nov. 8, 1954; d. John William and June Ietta (Coleman) Mashburn; m. David Kirk Horton, May 17, 1974 (div. May 1982); children: Sandra Jean, Joshua David; m. William Carroll Denton, June 15, 1990. BSE, Ark. State U., 1976; postgrad., U. Ark., 1977-89. Cert. secondary and spl. edn. tchr. Spl. edn. tchr. St. Charles (Ark.) Sch., 1976-77; 7th grade English tchr. DeWitt (Ark.) Sch., 1978-80, learning disabled tchr., 1980-84; spl. edn. tchr. England (Ark.) Sch., 1984-85, Lonoke (Ark.) Sch., 1985-91; libr. Des Arc (Ark.) Sch., 1991-92, spl. edn. tchr., 1992—; fed. coord. Des Arc (Ark.) Sch., 1992—, tchr. cons., 1992—; mem. Ark. state textbook com. Dept. Edn., Little Rock, 1993. Mem. Ark. Assn. Children with Learning Disabilities. Democrat. Baptist. Home: RR 2 Box 153 E Des Arc AR 72040-9510 Office: Des Arc High Sch RR 1 Box A Des Arc AR 72040-9801

DENZAU, DOROTHY HARRIET, insurance adjuster; b. Washington County, Va., Nov. 26, 1939; d. Clarence Henry and Lillian Hazel (Wolfe) Dye; m. Richard Charles Denzau, June 25, 1978. Degree in Secretarial, Washington County Tech., Abingdon, Va., 1959. Sec. Va. Dept. of Edn., Abingdon, 1959-60; med. transcriptionist Johnston Meml. Hosp., Abingdon, 1960-64; ins. clk. U.S. Fidelity and Guaranty Ins. Co., Abingdon, 1964-80; ins. adjuster U.S. Fidelity and Guaranty Ins. Co., Abingdon and Bristol, Tenn., 1980—. Mem. Southwest Va. Claims Assn. (treas. 1987-89, Ins. Adjuster of Yr. 1992), Ins. Women Southwest Va. (v.p. 1992). Penetecostal. Home: 22197 Guilford Dr Abingdon VA 24210-1843 Office: U S F&G Ins Co 100 5th St Bristol TN 37620-5920

DE PADRO, ANNE MICHELLE, banker, accountant, trust tax officer; b. Fort Lauderdale, Fla., Sept. 7, 1963; d. Michael Anthony and Anne Carroll (Tetaz) De P. BS in Bus. Adminstrn., Auburn U., 1986; postgrad Acctg., U. Ala., Birmingham, 1987-88. Trust tax acct. AmSouth Bancorp., Birmingham, Ala., 1989-91; trust tax officer SunBank/South Fla., Fort Lauderdale, 1991—. Mem. Broward Friends of Miami City Ballet, 1993—, Camerata, 1993—, Hospice Hundred, Jr. Alliance for Bonnett House; bd. dirs. Young Profls. for Covenant House, 1993—, Jr. League of Fort Lauderdale, 1993—, Jr. Philharmonic Guild; loaned exec. United Way; mem. Hospice Hundred, Bonnet House Jr. Alliance; bd. dirs. Jr. Philharmonic Guild, 1992—; mem. com. Festival of the Trees, Easter Lily Ball, Promenade in the Park. Mem. Inst. of Mgmt. Accts. (bd. dirs.). Office: SunBank South Fla NA 501 E Las Olas Blvd Fort Lauderdale FL 33308

DEPAOLI, GERI M., artist, art historian; b. June 8, 1941; m. Alexander DePaoli, July 4, 1961; children: Alexander Mark, Michael Alexander. BA, U. Md., 1974, MA, 1978; student, U. Calif., Davis, 1965-68. Art history educator, artist, curator slides and photos Nat. Mus., Bangkok, Thailand, 1968-71; art prof. Montgomery Coll., Rockville, Md., 1978-82; cons. oriental slide and photo collection Princeton U., 1983-84; lectr. Princeton Sch. Visual Arts, 1986-90; curator The Mus. Art, Ft. Lauderdale, Fla., 1986; dir. Coun. for Creative Projects, N.Y.C., 1989-91; faculty artworks Princeton Sch. Visual Arts, 1984-91; exec. dir. EducArt Projects Inc., Davis, Calif., 1991—; cons. in field. Author ednl. program Images of Power, also video prodr.; editor/co-curator Exhbn. Catalog, Transcending Abstraction, 1986; reviewer ArtMatters Newspaper, Phila., 1987-90; author/curator The Transparent Thread: Asian Philosophy in Recent Am. Art 1950-1990; contbr. author to Art of Calif. Mag.; one-person shows include E.W. Gallery, Bethesda, Md., 1978, Upstairs gallery, Kingston, N.J., 1982, Gallery at The Purple Barge, N.Y.C., 1984, The Art Gallery, Kingston, N.J., 1985, Back Door Gallery, Princeton, 1986, Campion Gallery of Art, 1987 Princeton, 1986, AT&T Corp. Gallery, Princeton, 1989, Rider Coll. Gallery, Lawrenceville, N.J., 1990; also numerous group shows. Councilor Nat. Abortion Rights Action League, 1989—. Recipient award for excellence in pub., Office of Pres. of U.S., 1969. Fellow Soc. for Arts Religion and Contemporary Culture; mem. Assn. Ind. Historians of Art (v.p. 1988—), Coll. Art Assn., Princeton Rsch. Forum, Nat. Coalition of Ind. Scholars, Sierra Club, Greenpeace. Buddhist. Office: EducArt Projects Inc PO Box 267 Davis CA 95617-0267

DE PASSE, SUZANNE, record company executive; m. Paul Le Mat. Student, Manhattan Community Coll. Former talent coordinator Cheetah Disco, N.Y.C.; creative asst. to pres. Motown Prodns., Los Angeles, 1968-81, pres., from 1981; now c.e.o. de Passe Entertainment, L.A. Acts signed and developed for Motown include The Commodores, The Jackson Five, Frankie Valli and the Four Seasons, Lionel Richie, Thelma Houston, Billy Preston, Teena Marie, Rick James, Stephanie Mills; co-author screenplay for film Lady Sings the Blues (Acad. award nomination); exec. producer: (TV miniseries) Lonesome Dove, (TV series) Motown on Showtime, Nightlife starring David Brenner, Motown Revue starring Smokey Robinson, Motown Returns to the Apollo (Emmy award, NAACP Image award), (TV spl.) Motown 25: Yesterday, Today, Forever (Emmy award, NAACP Image award); writer: (TV spls.) Happy Endings, Jackson 5 Goin' Back to Indiana, Diana; creative cons: Git on Broadway-Diana Ross & The Supremes & Temptations, TCB-Diana Ross & The Supremes & Temptations. Office: de Passe Entertainment 5750 Wilshire Blvd Ste 610 Los Angeles CA 90036*

DEPAUL, CAROL STONE, lawyer; b. Detroit, Nov. 17, 1956; d. Joshua James and Eunice (Schneider) Stone; m. Andrew Vincent DePaul, May 26, 1986; children: Michael, Nathan. BA, Mt. Holyoke Coll., 1978; JD, Washington U., St. Louis, 1981. Assoc. Isham, Lincoln & Beale, Chgo., 1981-83; corporate atty. Bally Entertainment Corp., Chgo., 1983—. Office: Bally Entertainment Corp 8700 W Bryn Mawr Ave Chicago IL 60631

DEPAUW, DARCY GAIL, nurse; b. Lake Forest, Ill., Nov. 26, 1951; d. Ronald Robert and Barbara (Thorup) Johnson; m. Donald Alfonse DePauw, Dec. 15, 1973; children: Courtney Lynn, Stacy Dianne. BS, U. Dubuque, 1974; cert. sch. nurse, Nat.-Louis U., 1990; postgrad., St. Xavier U., 1994—. RN, Ill. Staff nurse Delnor-Cmty. Hosp., St. Charles, Ill., 1974-90; nurse Unified Sch. Dist. U-46, Elgin, Ill., 1990—. Presdl. scholar U. Dubuque, 1969-71. Mem. AAUW (com. mem., Gift Recipient 1986), Ill. Assn. Sch. Nurses. Home: 1305 S 12th St Saint Charles IL 60174 Office: Unified Sch Dist 46 355 E Chicago St Elgin IL 60120

DEPEW, MARIE KATHRYN, retired secondary educator; b. Sterling, Colo., Dec. 1, 1928; d. Amos Carl and Dorothy Emelyn (Whiteley) Mehl; m. Emil Carlton DePew, Aug. 30, 1952 (dec. 1973). BA, U. Colo., 1950, MA, 1953. Post grad. Harvard U., Cambridge, Mass., 1962; tchr. Jefferson County Pub. Schs., Arvada, 1953-73; mgr. Colo. Accountability Program, Denver, 1973-83; sr. cons. Colo. Dept. Edn., Denver, 1973-85, ret., 1985. Author: (pamphlet) History of Hammil, Georgetown, Colorado, 1967; contbr. articles to profl. jours. Chmn. Colo. State Accountability Com., Denver, 1971-75. Fellow IDEA Programs, 1976-77, 79-81. Mem. Colo. Hist. Assn., Jefferson County Edn. Assn. (pres. 1963-64), Colo. Edn. Assn. (bd. dirs. 1965-70), Ky. Colonels (hon. mem.), Phi Beta Kappa. Republican. Methodist. Home: 920 Pennsylvania St Denver CO 80203-3157

DE PLANQUE, E. GAIL, physicist; b. Orange, N.J., Jan. 15, 1945; d. Martin William and Edna (Gilroy) de P. AB, Immaculata Coll., 1967; MS, N.J. Inst. Tech., 1973; PhD, NYU, 1983. Physicist U.S. AEC, U.S. Dept. Energy, N.Y.C., 1967-82; dep. dir. environ. measurement lab. U.S. Dept. Energy, N.Y.C., 1982-87, dir. environ. measurement lab., 1987—; adj. prof. NYU, N.Y.C., 1986—; pres. Pacific Nuclear Coun., 1989—; mem. engring. sci. dept. adv. com., bd. trustees N.J. Inst. Tech., Newark, 1985—. Contbr. articles to profl. jours. Fellow Am. Nuclear Soc. (bd. dirs. 1977-80, 84-91, v.p. 1987-88, pres. 1988-89), Health Physics Soc., AAAS, Am. Phys. Soc., Assn. for Women in Sci. (v.p. N.Y. met. sect. 1980-82). Office: Environ Measurements Lab 376 Hudson St New York NY 10014-3621*

DEPONTE, LINDA MAE, credit director; b. Wareham, Mass., Mar. 24, 1949; d. William and Kathleen Rose (Santiago) DeP. AA in Liberal Arts, Cape Cod C.C., Hyannis, Mass., 1971; BA in English, U. Mass., Amherst, 1973; MBA, U. Bridgeport, 1986; postgrad., Dartmouth Coll., 1990-92. Asst. credit mgr. UST, Inc., Greenwich, Conn., 1976-79; customer svc. mgr. Hilti, Stamford, Conn., 1979-80; asst. credit mgr. paper divsn. Champion Internat., Stamford, 1980-83, treasury analyst, 1983-85, mktg. analyst, 1985-86, credit mgr. pub. papers divsn., 1986-89, dir. credit nationwide papers divsn., 1989—. Bd. dirs. Shelter for Homeless, Stamford, 1987. Mem. Nat. Assn. Credit Mgrs., U.S. Golf Assn. Home: 660 Penfield Rd Fairfield CT 06430 Office: Champion Internat Nationwide Papers One Champion Plz Stamford CT 06921

DEPUE, SUSAN EASTERLING, insurance sales agent; b. Hattiesburg, Miss., Mar. 7, 1948; d. Henry Vernon Lowery and Cleo Velma (Gandy) White; m. David Fred Deese, Sept. 1, 1968 (div.); children: David Kevin Deese, Bryan Win Deese; m. Roy Lee DePue, Feb. 12, 1994. BS in Math., Trevecca Coll., 1970. CLU, ChFC. Tchr. math Raines H.S., Jacksonville, Fla., 1970-72; tchr. Advanced Learning Ctr. Christian Heritage Acad., Jacksonville, 1978-79; bookkeeper Music City Tire, Nashville, 1979-81; sales agent Mutual Benefit Life, Nashville, 1981-86; owner, sales agent Benefit Brokers (formerly Easterling & Assocs.), Nashville, 1986—. Mem. Am. Soc. CLU (pres. 1994—, Huebner Sch. chair 1990-94), Mid. Tenn. Assn. Health Underwriters (pres. 1992-93, Presdl. award 1993), Nashville Assn. Life Underwriters. Home: 70 Ravenwood Hills Cir Nashville TN 37215 Office: Benefit Brokers 955 Woodland St Nashville TN 37206

DEPUY, BRENDA JANE, personnel specialist; b. St. Louis, Nov. 25, 1946; d. Harry and Elsie Irene (Bilyeu) Anderson; m. Roger Dean King, Apr. 3, 1965 (div. 1978); children: Carol Ann Kinder, Christina King. Student, Drury Coll., U. Mo., Cen. Tex. Coll. Supr. mil. pers. Spl. Dept. of the Army, Ft. Leonard Wood, Mo., 1975-78; supervisory staffing specialist, affirmative employment Spl. Dept. of the Army, Ft. Lee, Va., 1978-91; DMA staffing policy, employment planning, affirmative action policy reductions-in-force/incentives Def. Agy., 1991-93; head employment/classification NSA, Naples, Italy, 1993—; guest instr. handicapped program mgr. course U.S. Dept. of Army, Washington, 1987; mem. U.S. Dept. of Army Mobilization Task Force, Ft. Monroe, Va., 1989; guest speaker EEO Conf., TRADOC. Contbr. article to profl. jour. Mem. Internat. Pers. Mgmt. Assn., Order of Rosicrucians. Home and Office: NSA Human Resource Office PSC 810 Box 29 FPO AE 09619

DERAMUS, BETTY JEAN, columnist; b. Tuscaloosa, Ala., Mar. 29, 1941; s. Jim Louis and Lucille (Richardson) DeR. B.A., Wayne State U., 1963, M.A., 1977. Reporter, copy editor Mich. Chronicle, Detroit, 1963-67; writer Detroit Bd. Edn., 1967-71; reporter Detroit Free Press, 1972-75, instr. English Wayne State U., 1976-78; editorial writer, columnist, from 1978; now columnist Detroit News. Contbr. Essence mag., N.Y.C., 1982—; author: The Constant Search, 1969; contbr. anthologies Sturdy Black Bridges, 1979, The Third Coast, 1982. Recipient 1st prize commentary Edn. Writers Assn., 1981; Ernie Pyle award spl. citation Scripps-Howard Found., 1981; Best Editorial Series award Overseas Press Club Am., 1982; finalist Pulitzer Prize for Commentary, 1993; Gen. Excellence award ASCAP, 1983. Mem. Nat. Conf. Editorial Writers, Nat. Assn. Black Journalists (2d v.p. 1982). Home: PO Box 1825 Detroit MI 48231-1825 Office: Detroit News 615 W Lafayette Blvd Detroit MI 48226-3124*

DERBY, CHERYL ANN, insurance company executive; b. Paterson, N.J., Jan. 19, 1946; d. Elles Mayo and Sarah Emma (Steele) D. BA, Elmira Coll., 1967; MBA, NYU, 1982. Tchr. Ramsey (N.J.) High Sch., 1967-70; contbns. analyst Met. Life Ins. Co., N.Y.C., 1970-83, fin. writer investments dept., 1983-93, asst. sec., 1994—. Bd. trustees United Meth. Ch. of Waldwick, N.J., v.p., 1989-91, pres., 1992-93. Fellow Life Mgmt. Inst. (bd. dirs. Greater N.Y. chpt. 1984-91, pres. 1986, edn. coun. 1990-93), Life Mgmt. Inst. Edn. Coun. (nat. adminstrv. com. chmn. 1990-92, mktg. subcom. 1985-93), Nat. Orchestral Assn. (bd. dirs. 1990-92); mem. Elmira Coll. Alumni Club N.J. (exec. bd. 1982-87). Methodist. Office: Met Life 1 Madison Ave New York NY 10010

DERCHIN, DARY BRET INGHAM, writer; b. Camden, N.J., Sept. 15, 1941; d. Charles and Dorothy Roberta (Ingham) Lambiase; m. Michael Wayne Derchin, Dec. 29, 1970; children: Taylor-Leigh, Danielle Lacey. BA, Montclair State Coll., 1962; postgrad., NYU, 1965, New Sch., 1966. Tchr. Randolph, N.J., 1962-64; rsch. asst. NYU, N.Y.C., 1965-67, Bolivian Peace Corps Project, N.Y.C., 1966; co-head rsch. Derchin Enterprises, N.Y.C., 1970-75. Author: Real Talk, 1992; playwright Blue No More; contbr. articles to the N.Y. Times, Harper's and book the Big Picture, others; talk show host Sta. WALE, 1995; spkr., guest talk shows. Mem. New Dramatists, Lincoln Ctr. Film Soc., Am. Film Inst., Friends of Poets and Writers, Univ. Club, Nat. Art Club (lit. com., film com.), Joseph Kesselring Playwright award com.). Home: Laurel Cove PO Box 200 Fair Haven NJ 07704-0200

DE RIVAS, CARMELA FODERARO, psychiatrist, hospital administrator; b. Cortale, Italy, Nov. 25, 1920; came to U.S., 1935, naturalized, 1942; d. Salvatore and Mary (Vaiti) Foderaro; m. Aureliano Rivas, Oct. 30, 1948; children: Carmen, Norma, Sandra, David. Student, U. Pa., 1940-42; M.D., Women's Med. Coll. Pa., 1946. Diplomate: Am. Bd. Psychiatry and Neurology. Intern women's Med. Coll. Pa. Hosp., 1946; gen. practice Phila., 1947-49, Tex., 1947-49; mem. staff Norristown (Pa.) State Hosp., 1949—, supt., 1963-70, dir. family planning, 1979-87, clin. dir. spl. assignments, 1979-82; assoc. psychiatry U. Pa., 1963-75; psychiatrist Penn Found. Mental Health, Sellersville, Pa., 1970-72; dir. intake coping svcs. Ctrl. Montgomery Mental Helath/Mental Retardation Ctr., Norristown, Pa., 1972-77, med. dir., 1977-82, psychiatrist, 1987—; cons., surveyor Health Care Fin. Adminstrn., 1980-82; dir. program evaluation Norristown State Hosp., 1979-82, med. dir., 1982-87. Named to Hall of Fame S. Phila. H.S., 1968; recipient citation Women's Med. Coll. Pa., 1968, Amita achievement award, 1976, achievement award Grad. Club Phila., 1976; named Woman of Yr. Pa. Fedn. Bus. and Profl. Women, 1979. Fellow Am. Psychiat. Assn., Pa. Psychiat. Soc. (rep. assembly of dist. brs. 1979-88)); mem. AMA, Phila. Psychiat. Soc. (councilor), Montgomery County Med. Soc. (bd. dirs., past pres.), Pa. Med. Soc. (chmn. adv. com. to aux. 1981-88, mem. ho. of dels., mem. commn. on med. edn. 1991-94, mem. com. on continuing med. edn. 1994—). Home: 700 Joseph Dr Wayne PA 19087-1021

DERJUE, RITA, artist, educator; b. Warwick, R.I., July 12, 1934; d. Gustav Herman Heinrich and Lisette Anna (Gossler) Derjue; m. Carle C. Zimmerman, Jan. 30, 1960; children: Andrew Erik, Heidi Anna. BFA, R.I. Sch. Design, 1956; MA, Cornell U., 1962; postgrad., Akademie den Bildenden Kunste, Munich, Germany, 1956-57. Artist self-employed, Denver, 1963—; featured, tchr. White River Inst., Beaver Creek, Colo., 1994—; artist, mentor tchr. Arapahoe C.C., Littleton, Colo., 1964—; workshop leader, painter Truro (Mass.) Ctr. for Arts, 1970—; workshop tchr. Acapulco (Mex.) Arts Workshop, 1988—; cons. Littleton Fine Arts Guild, 1965-75; founder L'Aasemblage, Englewood, 1976-86; theater stage designer Friends of Libr./Mus., Littleton, 1988. Exhibited in solo shows at Edgar Britton Gallery, Denver, 1980, Ohio State U., Newark, 1989, Art of Denver Gallery, 1985, Gov.'s Mansion, Colo., 1986, Panache Gallery, Denver, 1988-93; group shows include Colo. Gallery of Arts, 1987, 89, U. Colo., Colorado Springs, 1988, Colo. History Mus., Denver, 1990, 92, 94; represented in collections at R.I. Hist. Soc., Littleton Hosp., Women's Bank, Denver, Cornell U.; subject of newspaper and mag. articles. Bd. dirs. Littleton Hist. Mus., 1972-82, Town Hall Art Ctr., Littleton, 1986-90; mem. adv. bd. Colo. Gallery of the Arts, Littleton, 1986-91, South Suburban Park Dist., Arapahoe County, Colo., 1994. Recipient numerous awards for art. Mem. Denver Art Mus., Colo. Watercolor Soc. (pres. bd. dirs. 1986). Home: 2539 W Ridge Ct Littleton CO 80120-3029

DERKSEN, CHARLOTTE RUTH MEYNINK, librarian; b. Newberg, Oreg., Mar. 15, 1944; d. John Philip and Wanda Marie (Rohrbough) Meynink; m. Roy Arthur Derksen, Dec. 27, 1966; children: Kathryn Marie Lesedi, Elizabeth Charlotte. BS in Geology, Wheaton (Ill.) Coll., 1966; MA in Geology, U. Oreg., 1968, MLS, 1973. Faculty and librarian Moeding Coll., Ootse Botswana, 1968-70, head history dept., 1970-71; tchr. Jackson Pub. High Sch. (Minn.), 1975-77; sci. librarian U. Wis., Oshkosh, 1977-80; librarian and bibliographer Stanford (Calif.) U., 1980—, acting chief scis., 1985-86, head Sci. and Engring. Librs., 1992—. Contb. author: Union List of Geologic Field Trip Guidebooks of North America, contbr. articles to profl. publs. Mem. ALA (rep. 1983-85), Spl. Library Assn., Western Assn. Map Librarians, Geosci. Info. Soc. (rep. 1985), Cartographic Users Adv. Council (chair 1988-90). Republican. Lutheran. Home: 128 Mission Dr Palo Alto CA 94303-2753 Office: Stanford U Branner Earth Scis Library Stanford CA 94305

DERN, LAURA, actress; b. Santa Monica, Calif., Feb. 10, 1967; d. Bruce Dern and Diane Ladd. Student, Lee Strasberg Inst., Royal Acad. Dramatic Art, London. Appeared in films Alice Doesn't Live Here Anymore, 1975, Foxes, 1980, Ladies and Gentlemen, The Fabulous Stains, 1982, Teachers, 1984, Mask, 1985, Smooth Talk, 1985, Blue Velvet, 1986, Haunted Summer, 1988, Fat Man & Little Boy, 1989, Wild At Heart, 1990, Rambling Rose, 1991 (Acad. award nomination for best actress, Golden Globe nomination for best actress in a drama), Jurassic Park, 1993, A Perfect World, 1993; TV appearances Afterburn, 1992 (Golden Globe award for best actress in TV movie or mini series), Fallen Angels (Murder, Obliquely), 1993 (Emmy nomination, Best Actress - Drama, 1994); stage appearances include The Palace of Amateurs (N.Y.), 1988, Brooklyn Laundry (L.A.); dir. The Gift. Office: Wolf Kasteler PR 1033 Gayley Ave Ste 208 Los Angeles CA 90024

DE ROECK, L. MILLIE, educational administrator; b. Puerto Rico, Dec. 14, 1950; came to U.S., 1950; d. Basilio Perez-Lugo and Carmen Mary (Hernandez); m. Luke De Roeck, 1978 (div. 1983). BA, Northeastern Ill. U., 1973; MA, Roosevelt U., 1976. Counselor Roberto Clemente H.S., Chgo., 1973-78, acting asst. prin., 1978-86; guidance counselor evening program and adult H.S. program summer sch. City-Wide Colls., Chgo., 1988-91; counselor Lane Tech. H.S., Chgo., 1986-91, summer program mgr., 1987, 88, 89, spl. edn. case mgr., 1989-91; acting asst. prin. Ellis Middle Sch., Elgin, Ill., 1992; dean of students Elgin H.S., 1991-94, Hinsdale (Ill.) Ctrl. H.S., 1994—; mem. North Central Evaluations com. Chgo. Sch. System, 1978-86, mem. peer counseling implementation com., 1987, mem. sch. improvement com., 1990. mem. Adminstr. Educator Supr. Assn., Ill. Prin. Assn.

DEROO, SALLY A., biology and geology educator. BS, Eastern Mich. U., 1958; MS, U. Mich., 1961; student, Wayne State U., 1962-64. Cert. elem. tchr., middle level, all subjects K-8; cert. high sch. level environ. scis., social studies, English, econs. 9-12; cert. tchr. mentally handicapped and emotionally impaired K-12. Asst. prof. sci. Ea. Mich. U., Ypsilanti, 1958-63, asst. prof. biology and geology, 1968—, cons., 1958-89; tchr. special edn., cons. Ea. Mich. U., 1989-91; tchr. sci. and geology Plymouth-Canton Cmty. Schs., 1963—; cons. curriculum Ctrl. Mich. U., 1989-90; instr. dept. tchr. edn. Mich. State U., 1994—; advisor Salem H.S., 1990—; mem. satellite conf. Tchrs. Making a Difference, 1990; mem. support team Sci. Teaching Edn. STEP adv. bd. Madonna Coll., Livonia, Mich.; guest lectr., tchr. Concordia Coll., Ann Arbor, Mich., 1990-92; mem. math. and sci. challenge grant design com. Wayne County, 1991; adv. bd. SEMSplus Mich. Envirothon; project coord. sci. curriculum support guides Mich. Dept. Edn., 1989-90, mem. Mich. curriculum frameworks joint steering com., 1992-94, mem. writing panel high sch. proficiency exam, 1993, mem. adv. com. high sch. sci. proficiency test, 1993-94; project chairperson Project Cattail, Teachers and Students Making an Environmental Difference, 1992—; project dir. Great Lakes-Thunderbay Great Lakes Basin Work Shop, Alpena, Mich., 1993; presenter in field. Author: (newsletter) Fledgeling, 1990—, (teaching manuals) Exploring Our Environment; contbr. articles to sci. mags.; writer, dir. 26-week sci. TV series Explore with Me; sci. editor Ann Arbor Pubs., 1968-86; elem. publ. editor Mich. Sci. Tchrs. Active Rouge River Restoration, 1988—, Friends of Mattaei Bot. Gardens Ann. Flower Show; established Model Adopt-a-Stream Project for Rough River Water Shed, 1994. Recipient Outstanding Educator award Mich. Jaycees, 1963, Best of West Edn. award, 1984, Outstanding Svc. Recognition award Mich. Assn. Mid. Sch. Educators, 1989, 90, gov.'s citation State of Mich., 1990, 91, Tchr. of Yr. Program award IBM, 1990, Can Doers award Mich. Tech. Coun., 1993; named Outstanding Sci. Educator, Metro Detroit Sci. Tchrs. Assn., 1994. Mem. NEA, NSTA (presenter regional and nat. confs.), Mich. Sci. Tchrs. Assn. (dir.-at-large), Nat. Mid. Level Sci. Tchrs. Assn. (state dir.), Nat. Resource Def. Coun., Mich. Assn. Sci. Suprs., Mich. Edn. Assn., Sci. Curriculum Devel. Assn. (mid. sch. goal-based curriculum), Wayne County Task Force (intermediate sch. dist. writing team 1989), Mich. Sci. Discovery (bd. dirs.), Mich. Alliance for Outdoor Edn., Internat. Joint Commn. (Great Lakes), Phi Delta Kappa (editor newsletter U. Mich. chpt.).

DE ROSE, SANDRA MICHELE, psychotherapist, educator, supervisor, administrator; b. Beacon, N.Y.; d. Michael Joseph Borrell and Mabel Adelaide Edic Sloane; m. James Joseph De Rose, June 28, 1964 (div. 1977); 1 child, Stacey Marie. Diploma in nursing, St. Luke's Hosp., 1964; BA in Child and Community Psychology, Albertus Magnus Coll., 1983; MS in Counseling Psychology with honors, Century U., 1986, PhD in Counseling Psychology with honors, 1987. Gen. duty float nurse St. Luke's Hosp., Newburgh, N.Y., 1964-65; supr. nurses Craig House Hosp., Beacon, N.Y., 1965-70; staff devel., team dir., divsn. outpatient treatment svc. Conn. Mental Health Ctr., New Haven, 1970-94; dir. edn., 1994—; clin. instr. Sch. Nursing Yale U., New Haven, 1979-84, clin. instr. dept. psychiatry, 1989—; dir. edn. outpatient divsn. Conn. Mental Health Ctr., New Haven and Norwich, Conn., 1994—; pvt. practice, New Haven, 1976—, Norwich, Conn., 1994—. Mem. ANA (cert.), Conn. Nurses Assn., Conn. Soc. Psychoanalytic Psychologists, Conn. Soc. Nurse Psychotherapists, Assn. for Advancement Philosophy and Psychiatry, Sigma Theta Tau, Delta Mu, Alpha Sigma Lambda. Office: Conn Mental Health Ctr 34 Park St New Haven CT 06519-1187 also: 210 Prospect St New Haven CT 06519 also: 200 W Town St Norwich CT 06360

DEROSSETT, LINDA KAREN, artist; b. Petoskey, Mich., Sept. 12, 1953; d. Ivan Waldo and Margarete (Kramer) Dunning; m. Calvin Derossett, Jr., Dec. 19, 1970; children: Lisa Marie, Justin Christopher. BFA cum laude, Austin Peay State U., 1993. Owner, artist Smoky Mountain Woodcrafts, Clarksville, Tenn., 1986-89; recruiter adult edn. Montgomery County Bd. Edn., Clarksville, 1989-90; owner, artist Smoky Mountain Studios, Clarksville, 1993—. Exhibited in group shows including Austin Peay State Univ., Clarksville, 1994, U. Ky., Lexington, 1994, Trans. Fin. Bank, Clarksville, 1994, Vaanguard Gallery, Nashville, 1994; photography included in Photographer's Forum Mags. Annual, 1994. Vol. adult edn. Montgomery County Bd. Edn., Clarksville, 1989; panel guest adult edn. forum participatory planning com., Clarksville, 1989, Leadership Clarksville, 1990; guest speaker adult edn. Sta. WCTZ, Clarksville, 1989, 90;. Recipient GED Nat. award Am. Coun. on Edn., 1989, cert. merit Am. Assn. Adult and Continuing Edn., 1990. Mem. Mid. Cumberland Arts League, Visual Artists Alliance Nashville. Office: Smoky Mountain Studios PO Box 3764 Clarksville TN 37043-3764

DERRICKSON, DENISE ANN, social studies educator; b. Seaford, Del., Sept. 20, 1956; d. William Hudson and Patricia Ann (Adkins) D. BS, James Madison U., 1978; MEd in Counseling and Human Devel., George Mason U., 1990, MEd in Curriculum & Instrn., 1994. Social studies instr. Brentsville Dist. High Sch., Nokesville, Va., 1978-91; Woodbridge (Va.) Sr. High Sch., 1991—; faculty liaison Parent-Tchr. Action Coun., 1990-91; prin.'s adv. coun., 1994-96. Vol. Childrens Hosp., Washington, 1983-86, Action in the Community through Svc., Inc.-Helpline, Manassas, Va., 1988-92. Recipient Cert. Appreciation Prince William County Sch. Bd., 1989, Outstanding Educator award Va. Govs. Sch., 1990. Mem. NEA, Am. Assn. Curriculum Devel., Nat. Soc. for Study of Edn., Va. Edn. Assn., Va. Counselors Assn., Prince William Edn. Assn., Kappa Delta Phi, Phi Delta Kappa. Office: Woodbridge Sr High Sch 3001 Old Bridge Rd Lakeridge VA 22192-3221

DERRICKSON, SHIRLEY JEAN BALDWIN, elementary school educator; b. Balt., Aug. 7, 1943; d. James Francis and Dorothy Elizabeth (Jubb) Baldwin; m. Ernest Hughes Derrickson, Aug. 19, 1978. BA, Knox Coll., 1965; MEd, Goucher Coll., 1969; postgrad., Towson State U., 1970-77. Cert. profl. status elem. tchr., Del. Tchr. Howard Park Elem. Sch., Balt., 1969-70, Lida Lee Tall Learning Resource Ctr., Towson (Md.) State U., 1970-83, Selbyville (Del.) Middle Sch., 1983-84, East Millsboro (Del.) Elem. Sch., 1984—. Foreign affairs chmn. Dagsboro (Del.) Century Club, 1990—, sec., 1986-88; sec. Dagsboro Rep. Club, 1986-88; active Friends of Prince George's Chapel, 1994—. Recipient Washington Regional scholarship, 1961-64. Mem. NEA, Del. State Edn. Assn., Indian River Edn. Assn., PTO. Republican. Methodist. Office: East Millsboro Elem Sch 500 E State St Millsboro DE 19966-1199

DERRYCK, VIVIAN LOWERY, non-profit organization executive; b. Cleve., Jan. 30, 1945; d. Collins Henry Lowery and Mildred Olivia (Lovejoy) Jackson; m. Dennis Anthony Derryck, Sept. 14, 1968 (div. 1986); children: David Pollard, Amanda Jahdne; m. Robert Joel Berg, June 24, 1989; stepdaughter Belinda Z. BA, Chatham Coll., Pitts., 1967; postgrad., Columbia U., 1967-69, MIA, 1990. African curriculum specialist, multicultural heritage tchr. African and Hispanic History and Culture Program N.Y.C., 1969-70; asst. dir. African-Am. Studies Program N.Y.C. C.C., Bklyn., 1970-71; project dir. Edn. Devel. Ctr., Cambridge, Mass., 1972-73; sr. rschr., instr. social scis. Univ. Liberia, 1974-77; rsch. assoc. U.S. House Reps., Washington, 1978; cons. Carnegie Corp., N.Y.C., 1979, U.S. Agy. Internat. Devel. Office Women in Devel., Washington, 1978-79; sr. assoc. V.P.'s Task Force Youth Employment, Washington, 1979; dir. U.S. Secretariat World Conf. UN Decade Women, Washington, 1979-80; dep. asst. sec. Equal Employment Opportunity, Civil Rights U.S. Dept. State, Washington, 1980-82; exec. v.p., dir. internat. divsn. Nat. Coun. Negro Women, Washington, 1982-84; cons. U.S. Agy. Internat. Devel., Washington, 1984-85; v.p. programs Nat. Dem. Inst. Internat. Affairs, Washington, 1984-88; v.p. Meridian House Internat., exec. dir. Washington Internat. Ctr., 1988-89; pres. African-Am. Inst., N.Y.C., 1989—; bd. dirs. African Ctr. Devel. and Strategic Studies, Ibeju-Ode, Nigeria, Meridian Internat. Ctr.; sec. bd., exec. com. InterAction, Washington, 1990—; v.p., bd. dirs. Internat. Devel. Conf., Washington, 1983-89, mem., 1983—; mem. adv. com. on voluntary fgn. aid U.S. AID. Author: Yoruba Blue; Yoruba Brown, 1973; contbr. articles to profl. jours. Bd. dirs. TransAfrica (D.C. chpt.), 1983-89, Overseas Edn. Fund Internat., 1981-91, Assn. Women in Devel., 1983-85, UN Assn., 1987-90, Emergency Appeal South African Families, 1986-89. Named Woman of Yr. Freetown, Sierra Leone, 1990. Mem. Coun. Fgn. Rels., African Studies Assn. (Bretton Woods com.), Nat. Coun. Negro Women (life), Assn. Women in Devel. Democrat. Presbyterian. Office: African-Am Inst 833 United Nations Plaza New York NY 10017

DERSH, RHODA E., management consultant, business executive; b. Phila., Sept. 10, 1934; civ; d. Maurice S. and Kay (Wiener) Eisman; m. Jerome Dersh, Dec. 23, 1956; children: Debra Lori, Jeffrey Jonathan. BA, U. Pa., 1955; MA, Tufts U., 1956; MBA, Manhattan Coll., 1980. Interpreter Consul of Chile, 1954-57; various teaching and staff positions Albright Coll., Mt. Holyoke Coll., Amherst Coll., Marple Newtown Sch., 1957-58; pres., chief exec. officer Profl. Practice Mgmt. Assocs., Reading, 1976—, Pace Inst., Reading, 1981—, Pace Mgmt., Inc., 1983—; 1984-90; mem. regional adv. bd. Hamilton Bank, 1991—; mem., bd. dirs. Ctr. City Devel. Corp., 1992—. Author: The School Budget is Your Business, 1976, Business Management for Professional Offices, 1977, The School Budget: It's Your Money, It's Your Business, 1979, Improving Public School Management Practices, 1979, Part-Time Professional and Managerial Personnel: The Employers View, 1979; contbr. articles to profl. jours. Bd. dirs. Pa. State Bd. Pvt. Lic. Schs., 1987-93; cons. dir. pub. sch. budget study project City of Reading, 1967-78, chmn. comprehensive community plan task force, 1973-75; chmn. pub. svc. cons. project 1980-90; panel chmn. budget allocations United Way, 1974-76; del. White House Conf. on Children Youth, 1970; co-founder World Affairs Coun., Reading and Berks County, 1963-65; chmn. Berks County Com. for Children Youth, 1968-72; commr. Trial Ct. Nominating Commn. of Berks County (Pa.), 1982-84; bd. dirs. United Way of Berks County, 1984-89; chmn. programs Leadership Berks, 1986-87; bd. dirs. Reading Ctr. City Devel. Corp., Berks Bus.-Edn. Coalition Corp., 1991—. Recipient Trendsetter award YWCA, 1985. Mem. AAUW (ednl. found. grant.), LWV, Pa. Assn. Pvt. Sch. Bus. Adminstrs. (bd. dirs. 1985-89), Berks County C. of C. (bd. dirs. 1983-86, chmn. edn. com. 1983-85), Am. Acad. Ind. Cons. (pres. 1978-80), Reading and Berks C. of C (Entrepreneur of Yr. 1985), Rotary (bd. dirs. Reading, Pa., chpt. 1989-90). Office: 606 Court St Reading PA 19601-3542

DERUBERTIS, PATRICIA SANDRA, software company executive; b. Bayonne, N.J., July 10, 1950; d. George Joseph and Veronica (Lukaszewich) Uhl; m. Michael DeRubertis, 1986. BS, U. Md., 1972. Account rep. GE, San Francisco, 1975-77; tech. rep. Computer Scis. Corp., San Francisco, 1977-78; cons., pres. Uhl Assocs., Tiburon, Calif., 1978-81; cons. mgr. Ross Systems, Palo Alto, Calif., 1981-83; COO, exec. v.p. Distributed Planning Systems, Calabasas, Calif., 1983-92; pres. DeRubertis & Assocs., Thousand Oaks, Calif., 1992-94; v.p. IDC Fin. Pub., Hartland, Wis., 1994; pres. DeRubertis Software Sys., Inc., 1995—. Author: Rose Gardening By Color, 1994. Troop leader San Francisco council Girl Scouts U.S., 1974; participant Women On Water, Marina Del Rey, Calif., 1983. Mem. NAFE, Delta Delta Delta. Democrat.

DERVIN, BRENDA LOUISE, communications educator; b. Beverly, Mass., Nov. 20, 1938; d. Ermina Diluiso; adopted d. John Jordan and Marjorie (Sullivan) D. BS, Cornell U., 1960; MA, Mich. State U., 1968, PhD, 1972. Pub. info. asst. Am. Home Econ. Assn., Washington, 1960-62; pub. info. specialist Ctr. Consumer Affairs, U. Wis., Milw., 1962-65; instr., rsch. and teaching asst. dept. communications Mich. State U., E. Lansing, 1965-70; asst. prof., Sch. Info. Transfer Syracuse (N.Y.) U., 1970-72; asst. to assoc. prof. U. Wash., Seattle, 1972-85; prof. dept. communication Ohio State U., Columbus, 1985—. Co-author: The Mass Media Behavior of the Urban Poor, 1980; editor: Rethinking Communication, 1989; editor jour. Progress in Communication Sci., 1981-92; contbr. numerous articles to profl. publs. Grantee U.S. Office Edn., 1974-76, Calif. State Libr., 1974-84, Nat. Cancer Inst., 1984. Fellow Internat. Communication Assn. (pres. 1986-87); mem. Internat. Assn. Mass Communications Rsch. (governing coun. 1988—). Home: 4269 Kenridge Dr Columbus OH 43220-4157 Office: Ohio State U Dept Communications 154 N Oval Mall Columbus OH 43210-1330

DE SÁ E SILVA, ELIZABETH ANNE, educator; b. Edmonds, Wash., Mar. 17, 1931; d. Sven Yngve and Anna Laura Elizabeth (Dahlin) Erlandson; m. Claudio de Sá e Silva, Sept. 12, 1955 (div. July 1977); children: Lydia, Marco, Nelson. BA, U. Oreg., 1953; postgrad., Columbia U., 1954-56, Calif. State U., Fresno, 1990, U. No. Iowa, 1993; MEd, Mont. State U., 1978. Cert. tchr., Oreg., Mont. Med. sec., 1947-49; sec. Merced (Calif.) Sch. Dist., 1950-51; sec., asst. Simon and Schuster, Inc., N.Y.C., 1954-56; tchr. Casa Roosevelt-União Cultural, São Paulo, Brazil, 1957-59, Coquille (Oreg.) Sch. Dist., 1978—; tchr. piano, 1967-78; instr. Spanish, Southwestern Oreg. C.C., Coos Bay, 1991-94. Chmn. publicity Music in Our Schs. Month, Oreg. Dist. VII, 1980-85; sec. Newcomers' Club, Bozeman, Mont., 1971. Quincentennial fellow U. Minn. and Found. José Ortega y Gasset, Madrid, 1991. Mem. AAUW (sec., scholarship chmn.), Nat. Trust Hist. Preservation, Am. Coun. on Teaching Fgn. Langs., Am. Assn. Tchrs. Spanish and Portuguese, Nat. Coun. Tchrs. English, Music Educators Nat. Conf., Oreg. Music Educators Assn., Oreg. Coun. Tchrs. English, Confedn. Oreg. Fgn. Lang. Tchrs., VoiceCare Network. Republican. Home: 3486 Spruce St North Bend OR 97459-1130 Office: Coquille Sch Dist 140 E 10th St Coquille OR 97423-1370

DESAI, ANITA, writer; b. Mussoorie, India, June 24, 1937; d. D.N. and Toni (Nime) Mazumdar; m. Ashvin Desai, Dec. 13, 1958; children: Rahul, Tani, Arjun, Kiran. BA, Delhi U., 1957. Author: Cry, the Peacock, 1963, Voices in the City, 1965, Bye-Bye Blackbird, 1968, The Peacock Garden, 1974, Where Shall We Go this Summer?, 1975, Cat on a Houseboat, 1976, Fire on the Mountain, 1977, Games at Twilight and Other Stories, 1978, Clear Light of Day, 1980, The Village by the Sea, 1982, In Custody, 1985, Baumgartner's Bombay, 1989. Recipient Winifred Holtby prize Royal Soc. Lit., 1978, Shaitya Acad. award, 1979, Guardian award for children's book, 1982, Literary Lion award N.Y. Pub. Libr., 1993. Office: Mass Inst of Tech Dept of Writing 77 Massachusetts Ave Cambridge MA 02139-4307*

DESAI, VEENA BALVAMTRAI, obstetrician/gynecologist, educator; b. Karvan, Gujarat, India, Oct. 5, 1931; came to U.S., 1973; d. Balvantrai P. and Mahiben (Vashi) Desai; m. Vinay D. Gandevia, Sept. 19, 1994. MBBS, Seth G.S. Med. Coll., Bombay, 1957, MD, 1961. Jr. resident Bombay U., 1957-59; home officer gyn. Chalmer's Hosp., Edinburgh, Scotland, 1962-63; registrar ob-gyn. Neath (U.K.) Gen. Hosp., 1962-63, Scunthorpe (U.K.) Gen. Hosp., 1963-64; chief resident ob-gyn. St. John (Can.) Gen. Hosp., 1973-74; attending ob-gyn. Portsmouth (N.H.) Hosp., 1975-84; assoc. prof. Boston U., 1985-86; sr. staff ob-gyn. Santa Clara (Calif.) Valley Med. Ctr., 1986-87; mem. sr. staff ob-gyn. West Anaheim (Calif.) Med. Ctr., 1988-94, chief dept. ob-gyn., 1991-93, vice chmn. med. staff, 1994—; assoc. clin. prof. ob-gyn. U. Calif., Irvine, 1990; pres. Desai Med. Corp., Anaheim, 1989—. Chmn.'s advisor Nat. Security Coun.; charter mem. Presdl. Task Force; mem. Rep. Party Inner Cir., 1984-94. Decorated Medal of Freedom by U.S. Senate, 1994, Order of Liberty by U.S. Congress, 1993, Presdl. Medal of Merit by Pres. Reagan, 1982; recipient Spl. Congl. Adv. Bd. award, 1984. Fellow ACS, Internat. Coll. Surgeons, Am. Coll. Ob-gyn., Royal Coll. Ob-gyn.; mem. Buema Park Rotary (pres. 1994, chair internat. svc. 1992-93). Home: 5502 Burlingame Ave Buena Park CA 90621 Office: Desai Med Corp 3010 W Orange Ave Ste 110 Anaheim CA 92804

DESAI, VISHAKHA N., gallery director, society administrator; b. Ahemedabad, Gujarat, India, May 1, 1949; came to U.S., 1966; m. Robert B. Oxnam, 1993. BA, Bombay U., Elphinstone Coll., 1970; MA in History of Art, U. Mich., 1975, PhD in History of Art, 1984. With edn. div. Bklyn. Mus., N.Y.C., 1972-74; head exhibit resource Mus. sect. edn. dept. Fine Arts, Boston, 1977-80; acting dir. edn. dept. Mus. Fine Arts, Boston, 1980-81, coord. acad. program, 1981-88, asst. curator, 1981-90; dir. The Asia Soc. Galleries, N.Y.C., 1990—; v.p. The Asia Soc., 1993—; adj. asst. prof. Boston U., 1982-87; assoc. prof. U. Mass., Boston, 1986-90; bd. dirs. Am. Com. South/S.E. Asian Art; reviewer Bunting Inst., Radcliffe Coll., Boston, 1990—; bd. dirs. Art Table, N.Y.C., 1991-94. Contbr. articles to profl. jours. Pres. Mass. Found. for Humanities, 1989-91. Outstanding Teaching fellow U. Mich., 1977, Am. Inst. of Indian Studies fellow, 1978; grantee, Nat. Endowment for the Arts, NEM, 1979—, Mus. Sabbaticatal grantee Nat. Endowment for the Arts, 1982. Mem. Coll. Art Assn., Am. Assn. of Mus. Dirs. Office: The Asia Soc Galleries 725 Park Ave New York NY 10021-5025

DESCHAINE, BARBARA RALPH, real estate broker; b. Syracuse, N.Y., Feb. 16, 1930; d. George John and Dora Belle (Manchester) Ralph; children by previous marriage: Olav Bernt Kollevoll, Kristan George Kollevoll, Eric John Kollevoll; m. Bernard Richard Deschaine, May 23, 1981. BA, St. Lawrence U., 1952; postgrad. Pa. State U., 1969-72; grad. Pa. Realtors Inst., 1973; student Realtors Nat. Mktg. Inst., 1974-75. Salesman Brose Realty, Easton, Pa., 1967-72, assoc. broker/mgr., 1973, broker, owner, 1974-85; broker, mgr. John W. Monaghan Corp. Realtors, 1985-91; assoc. broker The Prudential/Paul Ford Realtors, Easton, 1991—; mem. Pa. Real Estate Polit. Edn. Com. Bd. dirs. Easton Area C. of C., 1973-79, v.p. organizational improvement, 1975-76, v.p. econ. devel., 1976-77, pres., 1977-78; mem. Greater Easton Corp. Strategy Group, 1977-78; mem. Northampton County Revenue Appeals Bd., 1982—; trustee Easton area YWCA, 1984-91; bd. dirs. State Theatre for the Arts, 1994—. Mem. NAFE, Nat. Assn. Realtors, Pa. Assn. Realtors, Bethlehem Bd. Realtors, Eastern Northampton County Bd. Realtors (bd. dirs. 1973-87, sec. 1977, v.p. 1980-81, Realtor of Yr. 1978), Ea. Northampton County Multiple Listing Svc. (bd. dirs. 1987-91), Realtors Nat. Mktg. Inst., Homes for Living Network (state chmn. 1980), Sales & Mktg. Execs. (bd. dirs. Easton area chpt. 1976-91; Disting. Sales award 1982), Phi Beta Kappa. Republican. Presbyterian. Home: 330 Paxinosa Rd W Easton PA 18042-1322 Office: 126 Bushkill St Easton PA 18042-1842

DESCHNER, JANE WAGGONER, collage artist, public relations consultant; b. Bellefont, Pa., Feb. 9, 1948; d. George Ruble and Helen Louise (Talbert) Waggoner; m. William Henry Deschner, July 26, 1969 (div. Dec. 1987); children: John William, Elisabeth Anne. BA in Geography, U. Kans., 1969; BA in Art, Mont. State U., Billings, 1987. Economist Mid-Am. Regional Coun., Kansas City, Mo., 1970-73; ptnr., owner Castle Art Gallery, Billings, Mont., 1982-88; asst. dir. client svcs. Mont. Inst. of Arts Found., Billings, 1988-89; account exec., artist, writer Exclamation Point Advt., Billings, 1989-94; artist Billings, 1981—, cons. pub. rels./graphic design, 1994—; pers. rep. Fred. J. Urbaska Investments, Billings. Exhibited in group shows at Toucan Gallery, Billings, Sutton West Gallery, Missoula, Mont., Missoula Mus. of the Arts, Mont. State U., Billings, Holter Mus. Art, Helena, Mont., Broken Diamond Gallery, Billings, U. Mont., Missoula. Bd. dirs. Billings Mental Health Assn., 1988-92, v.p., 1989, 90; gallery dir., bd. dirs. The Women's Ctr., St. Vincent Hosp. and Health Ctr., Billings, 1991—; mem. Youth Ct. Conf. Com. 13th Jud. Dist. Mont., Billings, 1992—. Recipient 1st pl. award in non-comml. art Billings Advt. and Mktg. Assn., 1992, 93. Mem. Nat. Mus. of Women in Art, Paris Gibson Sq., Yellowstone Print Club (bd. dirs., pres. acquisitions chair), Yellowstone Art Ctr. (Auction Artist 1989—). Unitarian. Studio: 2606 Poly Dr Billings MT 59102

DESELM, MARY ELIZABETH (BEE DESELM), county official; b. Columbus, Ohio, June 1, 1925; d. Lincoln Henry and Inez (Fultz) Hersee; m. Henry Rawie De Selm, June 11, 1948; children—Diane DeSelm Overcast, Richard Lowell. B.S. in Nursing, Ohio State U., 1946, B.S. in Edn., 1948. Violinist Columbus Ohio Symphony, 1943-46; head nurse obstetrics Ohio State U. Hosp., Columbus, 1948-49; tchr. obstetrical nursing White Cross Hosp., Columbus, 1949-52; violinist Knoxville Symphony Orch., 1956-65; religious edn. dir. Tenn. Valley Unitarian Ch., Knoxville, 1965-75; squire County of Knox, Tenn., 1976-80, commr., 1980—. Pres., fin. chmn. LWV, Knoxville, 1960—; mem. Met. Planning Commn., Knox County, Tenn., 1976-80; mem. adv. com. Knoxville Women's Ctr., 1978-90, bd. dir. 1990—; mem., sec. Hist. Zoning Commn., Knox County, 1980-86; mem. adv. com. Knoxville Job Corps, 1980-86, Agape (Alcoholic Women), Knoxville, 1981-86; pres. Tenn. Valley Unitarian Ch., 1985-87. Recipient Annie Selwyn award Knoxville Women's Ctr., 1985. Mem. Tenn. County Commrs. Assn., County Services Assn. (bd. dirs. 1986-90), Nat. Assn. Counties (fin. and taxation steering com. 1987-92). Republican. Club: Music Study (sec. 1975-76). Avocations: music; swimming; walking. Home: 424 Hillvale Turn W Knoxville TN 37919-6623 Office: City County Bldg 400 W Main Ave Knoxville TN 37902-2405

DESFORGES, JANE FAY, medical educator, physician; b. Melrose, Mass., Dec. 18, 1921; d. Joseph Henry and Alice (Maher) Fay; m. Gerard Desforges, Sept. 11, 1948; children—Gerard Joseph, Jane Alice. BA cum laude (Durant scholar), Wellesley Coll., 1942; MD cum laude, Tufts U., 1945; ScD (hon.), Holy Cross Coll., 1990. Diplomate: Am. Bd. Internal Medicine, Am. Bd. Hematology. Intern in pathology Mt. Auburn Hosp., Cambridge, Mass., 1945-46; intern in medicine Boston City Hosp., 1946-47, resident in medicine, then chief resident, 1948-50; USPHS research fellow in hematology Salt Lake Gen. Hosp., Salt Lake City, 1946-47; research fellow in hematology hosp. Thorndike Lab., 1950-52; physician-in-charge RH lab., 1952-53; mem. faculty Tufts U. Med. Sch., 1952—, prof. medicine, from 1972, disting. prof., from 1992, prof. emerita, 1994; asst. dir. Tufts Med. Svc., Boston City Hosp., 1952-67; assoc. dir. Tufts Med. Svc., 1967-68; acting dir., physician in charge, 1968-73; dir. Tufts Med. Svc., 1968-69, assoc. dir. Tufts hematology lab., 1954-67, asst. dir. hosp. labs., 1958-67, acting dir. labs., 1967-68; sr. physician in hematology, rsch. assoc. blood rsch. lab. New Eng. Med. Ctr. Hosp., Boston, 1973—; attending physician VA Hosp., Jamaica Plain; cons. in hematology to various area hosps., 1955-72. Assoc. editor New Eng. Jour. Medicine, 1960-93; mem. editl. bd. Blood, 1976-79; contbr. numerous articles to med. jours. Bd. dirs. Med. Found., Inc., 1976-82; trustee Boston Med. Library, 1977-81; chmn. automation in med. lab. scis. rev. com. Nat. Inst. Gen. Med. Scis., 1974-76; mem. subcom. on hematology Am. Bd. Internal Medicine, 1976-82, bd. dirs., 1980-88, exec. com., 1984-88; chmn. blood diseases and resources adv. com. Nat. Heart, Lung and Blood Inst., 1978-81. Recipient Disting. Alumna award Wellesley Coll., 1981; NIH fellow, grantee, 1955-88. Mem. ACP (Master 1983, Disting. Tchr. award, 1987, chmn. med. knowledge self assessment program IX 1989-92), Am. Fedn. Clin. Rsch., Am. Soc. Clin. Pathology, Am. Soc. Hematology (exec. com. 1974-78, adv. bd. 1980-82, v.p. 1982-83, pres. 1984-85), Internat. Soc. Hematology, Mass. Med. Assn., N.Y. Acad. Scis., Am. Assn. Physicians, Inst. Medicine, Phi Beta Kappa, Alpha Omega Alpha. Home: 49 Lake Ave Melrose MA 02176-2701 Office: New England Med Ctr 750 Washington St Boston MA 02111-1526

DESHANNON, YOLANDA (YOLANDA DARNELL), videomaker, filmmaker, writer; b. L.A., May 23, 1960; d. Charles and Hortense (Decatur) Washington. Student, U. So. Calif., L.A., 1978-83, 85-86, UCLA, 1984-86.

Pres. First Choice Entertainment, Lynwood, Calif., 1989—. Prodr., writer: (young adult soap) Almost There, 1989-93; prodr., writer, dir.: (film) Until Tomorrow Comes, 1992. Democrat. Office: First Choice Entertainment PO Box 54502 Phoenix AZ 85078-4502

DE SHERBININ, BETTY VARVARA, writer; b. Vancouver, B.C., July 30, 1917; came to the U.S., 1917; d. Andrew Granville and Elizabeth (Tamblyn) de S. Ed., abroad. Various positions including sec., treas. and dir. Roger Williams Tech. and Econ. Svcs., Princeton, N.J., 1951-83; ret., 1983. Author: Wind on the Pampas, 1941, Bindweed, 1942, By Bread Alone, 1945, The Challenged Land, 1946, The River Plate Republics, 1947, The Monkey Puzzle, 1951. Mem. Inst. Mgmt. Accts., Am. Pen Assn., Soroptimist Internat. Ams. Episcopalian. Home: 86 Olden Ln Princeton NJ 08540-4942

DE SILVA, DEEMATHIE WILHELMINA, university administrator, educator; b. Galle, Sri Lanka, Apr. 27, 1939; came to U.S. 1977; d. Peter and Wilhelmina (Silva) Dantanarayana; m. Dharma de Silva, Apr. 11, 1962; children: Harshini, Mahinda, Duminda, Lathika. Grad., Govt. Tchrs. Coll., Colombo, Sri Lanka; MA, Stanford U., 1964; PhD, Columbia Pacific U., 1988. Cert. tchr., Kans. Testing coordinator women's equity program Wichita State U., 1977-78, research assoc. coll. bus., 1979-81, lectr. biology, 1980, instr. anthropology, 1982-83, dir. and grant writer student support svcs., 1985—; pres. Transcultural Mktg. Comm., Wichita, 1995—; dir. operation success, Wichita (Kans.) State Univ., 1985—. Co-author tutor handbook; author: Mosquito, 1968, A Teacher's Guide for Effective Science Education, 1975; dir., scriptwriter tutor video tapes, 1981; prodr. video Tutoring Strategies, 1995. Mem. exec. bd. dirs., membership co-chair Global Learning Ctr., Wichita, 1991. Fulbright scholar, 1963-64, NSF fellow, 1964, AAUW fellow, 1975-76, Nat. Sci. Council Sri Lanka grantee, 1977. Mem. Mo.-Kans.-Nebr. Assn., Internat. Soc. for Intercultural Edn. and Rsch., Mid-Am. Assn. Ednl. Opportunity Program Pers. (exec. bd. dirs., archivist), World Trade Coun. Wichita (exec. bd. dirs.), Sri Lanka Assn. for Advancement Sci., Ind. Scholars Asia (bd. dirs. S.E. region 1985-95). Home: 4453 Mission Wichita KS 67226 Office: Operation Success Student Support Svcs Box 81 1845 N Fairmount Campus Wichita KS 67260-0081

DESIMONE, ANGELA ROSE, controller, financial consultant; b. Boston, Sept. 19, 1947; d. Henry John and Rose Marie (Boschetto) DeS. Student, Bentley Coll., 1965-67. Acct. Raytheon Corp., Waltham, Mass., 1968-71; bookkeeper Fgn. Auto, Watertown, Mass., 1971-75; office mgr., bookkeeper Waltham Racquet Club, 1975-77; pvt. practice bookkeeping, fin. cons., Boston, 1977-94; contr., office mgr., corp. clk. C-Q Constrn. Corp., Watertown, 1979-93; pres., treas. Cousins Contracting, Watertown, 1992—. Treas. Al Anon, Belmont, Mass., 1981-83; big sister Friend to Friend Orgn., Watertown, 1985-86. Office: C-Q Constrn Corp 541 Pleasant St Watertown MA 02172

DESIMONE, DIANE MARIE, marketing professional; b. Mishawaka, Ind., Dec. 28, 1949; d. John Dixon and Helen Theresa B. Garrett; m. John Paul DeSimone, June 13, 1970. BS in Econs., Purdue U., 1971; MBA, U. Notre Dame, 1975. With Garrett's Restaurant, Mishawaka, Ind., 1965-75; mktg. asst. 1st Nat. Bank, Elkhart, Ind., 1971-73; systems mgr. Tower Fed. Savs. & Loan, South Bend, Ind., 1975-77; mktg. rep. IBM, South Bend and Dallas, Ind., 1977-83; mktg. cons. Williamson & York, Dallas, 1983; product mkgt. mgr. Computer Automation, Richardson, Tex., 1983-84; asst. v.p. bus. devel. No. Telecom., Richardson, Tex., 1984—; presenter in field. Contbr. articles to profl. jours. Del. People to People Citizen Ambassadrs, Seattle, 1992. Mem. IEEE (chmn. internat. com. 1989, 94). Home: 165 Springfield Bend Argyle TX 76226 Office: No Telecom 2221 Lakeside Blvd Richardson TX 75082-4357

DESISTO, ELIZABETH AGNES, medical records specialist; b. Medford, Mass., May 15, 1954; d. John Anthony and Josephine Loretta (Passero) DeS. AS cum laude, Mass. Bay Community Coll., 1974; BS magna cum laude, Northeastern U., 1979. Sr. med. record technician Children's Hosp. Med. Ctr., Boston, 1974-76; asst. dir. med. records dept. Glover Meml. Hosp., Needham, Mass., 1980-82; asst. dir. med. records dept. McLean Hosp., Belmont, Mass., 1982-83, acting dir. med. records dept., 1983-84, dir. med. records dept., 1984-91; dir. med. records dept. New Eng. Meml. Hosp., Stoneham, Mass., 1991—. Vol. Big Sister Assn. Greater Boston, 1985-87, Greater Boston Walk for Hunger, 1983-94, nat. and local congl. campaigns; bd. dirs. New Eng. Meml. Hosp. Aux., 1992-95. Mem. Am. Health Info. Mgmt. Assn. (registered records adminstr., mental health record sect., bd. dirs. 1987-90, chmn. 1988-90), Mass. Health Info. Mgmt. Assn. (bd. dirs. 1985-94, sec. 1989-90). Democrat. Roman Catholic. Home: 723 Fellsway W Medford MA 02155-1205 Office: New England Meml Hosp 5 Woodland Rd Stoneham MA 02180-1706

DESJARLAIS, ERIKA ELSE, retired management analyst; b. Hamburg, Germany, Oct. 28, 1934; came to U.S., 1959; d. Friedrich Heinrich Paul Franz and Else Anna (Klussman) Fehrke; m. Leo Raymond Desjarlais, 1956 (dec. 1956); 1 child, Raymond Marcel; m. Richard Alexis Poirier, 1959 (div. 1985); 1 child, Denise Simone. AS, Monterey Peninsula Coll., 1975; BA, Antioch U., 1980; postgrad., Donsbach U., 1982. Peace Officer Standards and Tng. Certificate, Calif., 1973. Office asst. A. Rienaecker, Goslar, Fed. Republic Germany, 1952-53, J. Wenig, Oker, Fed. Republic Germany, 1953; clk. Konsumgenossenschaft "Nordharz", Goslar, 1953-55; clk. typist 2d Can. Inf. Brigade, Soest, Fed. Republic Germany, 1956; purchasing clk. U.S. Army Quartermaster Market Ctr., Frankfurt, Fed. Republic Germany, 1957-58; sec./translator V Corps Hdqrs., Frankfurt, 1958-59; accounts maintenance clk. USAF So. Command, Panama Canal Zone, 1968-69; sec. U.S. Army Combat Devel. Experimentation Ctr., Ft. Ord, Calif., 1970-83; correctional officer Sheriff's Office, Salinas, Calif., 1974-75; mgmt. analyst Texcom Experimentation Ctr., Ft. Ord, Calif., 1983-89, 7th Infantry Div. (Light) and Fort Ord Base Closure and Realignment Team, Ft. Ord, Calif., 1989-92. Mem. Fed. Women's Program Adv. Com., Ft. Ord, Calif., 1975-88; mem. Adv. Governing Bd., Rape Crisis Ctr., Monterey, 1980-83; commr. Commn. on Status of Women, Monterey County, 1986-88, Affirmative Action Commn., 1986-88; adv. Women Against Domestic Violence, 1980-81, Monterey Rape Crisis Ctr., 1980-82; active YWCA, Tucson Jazz Soc. Nominated One of the Ten Most Outstanding Women on the Monterey Peninsula, 1988.,. Mem. NAFE, AARP, Nat. Assn. Ret. Fed. Employees (pub. rels. officer), Am. Soc. Mil. Comptrs., Internat. Tng. in Comm. Inst., Am. Nutrition Cons. Assn. Libertarian. Evangelical-Lutheran. Club: Monterey Bay Hot Jazz Soc. (publicity chairwoman 1978, corres. sec. 1977). Home: 102A S Paseo Quinta Green Valley AZ 85614-2743

DE SMET, LORRAINE MAY, artist; b. Passaic, N.J., May 5, 1928; d. Peter John and Mary (Lovas) Prevelige; m. Louis John de Smet, May 17, 1952; children: Mary Lizabeth, Jean Marie, Carolyn, Allise Marie. Student, Berkeley Sch., 1945, Art Students League, 1979-82. One woman show Pen and Brush Club, 1984 (Solo Show award). Bd. dirs. Art Ctr. of N.J., 1993—. Recipient 1st prize Livingston (N.J.) Art Assn., 1987, 88, Art Ctr. N.J., 1994, and numerous other awards. Mem. U.S. Coast Guard Artists, Am. Artists Profl. League, Pen and Brush Club of N.Y. (bd. dirs. 1985-92, v.p. 1989-92, dir. brush divsn. 1987-89, membership dir. 1990-92, co-chair brush sect. 1994—), Art Ctr. of N.J. (bd. dirs. 1993—), Somerset Art Assn., West Essex Art Assn. (bd. dirs. 1992—), Art Students League of N.Y. (life), Millburn-Short Hills Art Assn. Home: 33 Campbell Rd Fairfield NJ 07004-1735

DESMOND, JANE CAROL, American studies educator, choreographer, dancer; b. Providence, Aug. 5, 1951; d. Alton Harold and Dorothy Ann (Garfield) D. BA, Brown U., 1973; MFA, Sarah Lawrence Coll., 1975; MPhil, Yale U., 1991, PhD, 1993. Asst. prof. theatre Cornell U., Ithaca, N.Y., 1975-80; artist-in-residence in dance Duke U., Durham, N.C., 1982-93; assoc. prof. Am. studies and women's studies U. Iowa, Iowa City, 1993—. Co-prodr. film: Chuck Davis: Dancing Through West Africa, 1987 (Cine Golden Eagle 1987); contbr. articles to profl. jours. Mary Duke Biddle Found. grantee, 1985, N.Y. State Coun. for the Arts grantee, 1980. Mem. Am. Studies Assn., Soc. for Cinema Studies, Congress on Rsch. in Dance (exec. bd. 1993—). Office: Univ of Iowa Am Studies Program Iowa City IA 52246

DE SOLA, ISABELLA MIRIAM, lawyer, poet. JD, Columbia U., 1982. Bar: N.Y. 1984, U.S. Dist. Ct. (so. dist., ea. dist.) N.Y. 1984. Law clk. to Hon. Irving R. Kaufman U.S. Ct. Appeals (2nd cir.), 1983-84; pvt. practice N.Y.C., 1984—; former fashion model; tchr. women's self-defense. Contbr. (anthologies) Something For Everyone, Poetic Voices of America, Sunrise, Sunset, American Poetry Annual, Visions, American Poetry Anthology, Of Diamonds and Rust, Vol. 2, Another Place in Time. Sec.-treas. Beyond Shelter Coalition for Permanent Housing, N.Y.C., 1989-91. Harlan Fiske Stone Scholar Columbia U., Harold P. Seligson scholarships in N.Y. Civil Practice, Bankruptcy Law, Securities Law, N.Y. Real Estate Practice, Immigration Law, Practising Law Inst., 1989. Mem. ABA (litigation, tort and ins. practice, family law, bus. law, antitrust law, criminal justice, natural resources, energy and environmental law, internat. law, law practice mgmt., and gen. practice sects.), Assn. Trial Lawyers Am. (membership com.; comml. litigation and ins. sects.), N.Y. State Bar Assn. (trial lawyers, comml. and fed. litigation, ins., negligence and compensation law, family law, bus. law, antitrust law, law office econs. and mgmt., gen. practice sects.), N.Y. State Trial Lawyers Assn., N.Y. County Lawyers' Assn. (apptd. to com. family ct. and child welfare), Assn. of Bar of City of N.Y., Columbia Law Sch. Assn. (life), Columbia Law Women's Assn., Trial Practice Inst., Pub. Interest Law Students Assn., Profl. Karate League, Pi Upsilon Delta Honor Soc.

DESORMIER-CARTWRIGHT, ANNÉ MARIA, lawyer; b. Lincoln, R.I., July 16, 1959; d. Lawrence Gerard Sr. and Gilda Josephine (Grossi) D.; m. Gary Robert Cartwright. BA with high honors, Pa. State U., 1981; JD, Boston U., 1984. Bar: Fla. Assoc. DeSantis, Cook & Gaskill, PA, North Palm Beach, Fla., 1984-87, Levine & Frank, P.A. and predecessor, North Palm Beach, 1987-88, Lewis, Vegosen, Rosenbach and Fitzgerald, PA, West Palm Beach, Fla., 1988—. Instr. volleyball, coach Centre County Park, State College, 1978-80; bd. dirs. Seagull Industries for the Disabled Inc., 1994—. Recipient President's award Tropical Dist., 1987-88. Mem. ABA, ATLA, Fla. Bar Assn., Palm Beach County Bar Assn. (chmn. sports com. 1985-87), Fla. Assn. Women Attys., Civitan (charter, pres. North County 1987-88, bd. dirs. 1988-94, softball instr. West Palm Beach 1986-88). Republican. Roman Catholic. Home: 241 Old Meadow Way West Palm Beach FL 33418-3734 Office: Lewis Vegosen Rosenbach 500 S Australian Ave Fl 10 West Palm Beach FL 33401-6237

DESOUZA, JOAN MELANIE, psychologist; b. Bombay, Sept. 17, 1956; came to U.S., 1987; d. Anthony Julius and Natalia Marie (Alvares) deS.; m. John Alec Krzewinski, Sept. 7, 1990. BA in Psychology with honors, U. Bombay, 1976; BS in Guidance and Counseling, Wayne State U., 1984, MA in Psychology, 1986, PhD in Ednl. Psychology, 1991. Lic. psychologist, Mich.; cert. sch. psychologist. Grad. asst. Wayne State U., Detroit, 1984-85; editor, mem. part-time faculty Inst. Gerontology, Detroit, 1985-87; extern St. Joseph Mercy Hosp., Pontiac, Mich., 1986; psychologist Huron Valley Mens' Facility, Ypsilanti, Mich., 1987—; cons. Arab-Am. cmty., Detroit, 1988, Ctr. Behavior and Medicine, 1994—. Co-author: (handbook) Medicare Survey Project: Effectiveness of DRG's, 1987; editor (newsletter) Info. on Aging, 1985-87. Intern Parents and Children Together, Detroit, 1984; activist for Laotian community and immigrants Internat. Inst., Detroit, 1983; asst. soup kitchen Mother Theresa's order, Detroit. Grad. profl. scholar Wayne State U., 1985, Rumble fellow, 1986-87, 87-88; parenting skills grantee for low-functioning child abusers Mich. Dept. Edn., Lansing, 1989-90. Mem. APA, Mich. Psychol. Assn., Mich. Assn. Sch. Psychologists, Pi Lambda Theta (Detroit chpt.). Roman Catholic. Home: 203 Russell St Saline MI 48176 Office: Huron Valley Mens Facility 3201 Bemis Ypsilanti MI 48197

DESPAIN, BECKY ANN, dental educator; b. Oklahoma City, July 14, 1948; children: Brian Thomas, Meredith Lynn. BS in Dental Hygiene, Baylor U., 1970; MEd, Cen. State U., Okla., 1982. Registered dental hygienist. Pvt. practice clin. dental hygienist Oklahoma City, 1970-73; instr. Coll. Dentistry, Okla. U. Health Scis. Ctr., Oklahoma City, 1973-82, asst. prof., 1982-85, acting chair dept. dental hygiene, 1984-85, clin. dental hygienist faculty practice, 1977-85; assoc. prof., dir. Caruth Sch. Dental Hygiene Baylor Coll. Dentistry, Dallas, 1985-93, assoc. prof. dept. pub. health scis., 1993—; clin. instr. Rose Jr. Coll., Midwest City, Okla., 1972; mem. affiliate staff Okla. Children's Meml. Hosp., Oklahoma City, 1977-85; clin. dental hygienist North Tex. Periodontal and Implant Assn., Richardson, 1988-91; mem. test constrn. com. Nat. Bd. Dental Hygiene, ADA, Chgo., 1987-91, dental hygiene cons. Commn. on Dental Accreditation, 1989—; investigator grants and contracts HHS, NIH. Editorial rev. bd.: Jour. Dental Hygiene, Chgo., 1982—; contbr. abstracts and articles to profl. jours. Speaker Sch. Vols. Program, Oklahoma City Pub. Schs., 1976-85; project dir. Oral Healthlink: Dallas/Ft. Worth Coalition for Oral Health 2000; bd. dirs. Dallas chpt. ACLU of North Tex. Recipient small grant award Rsch. Coun., OUHSC, Oklahoma City, 1985, Dental Hygiene Rsch. grant Oral-B Labs., Redwood City, Calif., 1985. Mem. Am. Assn. Dental Schs., Am. Assn. Dental Rsch., Am. Dental Hygienists Assn. (del. 1980-84), Tex. Dental Hygienists Assn., Tex. Dental Hygiene Dirs. Assn. (sec. 1990-92), Dallas Dental Hygienists Soc. (v.p. 1994), Dallas Women's Found., The Women's Ctr. of Dallas (chair health care task force, bd. dirs. 1994—), Sigma Phi Alpha, Kappa Delta Pi. Office: Baylor Coll Dentistry PO Box 660677 Dallas TX 75266

DES RIOUX, DEENA VICTORIA COTY, artist, graphics designer; b. Cambridge, Mass., Dec. 7, 1941; d. Sam and Sophina G. (Cohen) Coty; m. Philippe Roger Armand des Rioux de Messimy, Aug. 29, 1964. Student R.I. Sch. Design, 1959-62, Brown U., 1960-62, Sorbonne, Paris, 1961, 63-64. Package designer, illustrator, pvt. tchr., free-lance artist, Boston, 1962-63, 64-70; guest lectr. Mass. Coll. Art, Boston, 1975, Harvard Grad. Sch. Design, Lesley Coll., Cambridge, Mass., 1976, 77, UN Photography Soc., N.Y.C., 1993; juror Heritage Plantation Mus., Cape Cod, Mass., 1977; exhbns. coordinator Women Exhibiting in Boston, Inc., 1973-75; founder, dir. 7 at Large (artists collective), Boston, 1975-78; exhbns. coordinator Assn. Artist-Run Galleries, N.Y.C., 1980-82, pub. relations dir., 1983-84. Solo exhbns.: Psychoanalytic Inst., Boston, 1974, Ward-Nasse Gallery, N.Y.C., 1978, Maison Française of Columbia U., N.Y.C., 1992, R.I. Sch. Design, Providence, 1993-94, U. Wyo. Art Mus., Laramie, 1994 ; participant exhbns. including: Ward-Nasse Gallery, 1975-84, Helander Gallery, Palm Beach, Fla., 1984-86, Gallery Hirondelle, N.Y.C., 1985-87, Mokotoff Gallery, N.Y.C., 1986, Grace Harkin Gallery, N.Y.C., 1989, Ea. Wash. U. USA Mus. Tour, 1994—; represented in permanent collections Ind. U. Art Mus., Internat. Print Triennale, Krakow, Poland, Boise (Idaho) State U., Mus. Art/RISD, Laguna Gloria Art Mus., Austin, Tex., Alexandria (La.) Mus. Art, Universal Graphic Mus., Cairo, Egypt, Downey (Calif.) Mus. Art; coordinator, exhibitor Art Inst. Boston, 1975 (grant), Mus. Sci., Boston 1977-78 (grant); exhibit cons. spl. exhibit Mus. City of N.Y., 1983-84; guest exhibitor Danvers Art and Hist. Soc., Attleboro Mus., Mass., Nashua Arts and Sci. Ctr., (N.H.); competitive exhbns. include: 62d Newport Annual Nat., 1973, 45th Annual New Eng. Painting, Jordan Marsh, Boston, 1974, Past/Post/Future, Robert Atkins, N.Y.C, 1985, Photo-Derived, Joel-Peter Witkin, Ind. U., 1989, At The Edge II, Wendy Weitman, Laguna Gloria Art Mus., Austin, Tex., 1990, La Sierra U., Riverside, Calif., 1991, Seattle Ctr. Internat., 1991, Warwick Mus. Invitational, R.I., 1991, Hill Country Arts Found. Nat., Ingram, Tex., 1991, Boise State U., Sun Valley Ctr. for the Arts, Idaho, 1991, ADOGI Barcelona, Tour, Cadaqués, and Cities of Japan Tour 1991-92, Juniper Gallery, Napa, Calif., 1991-92, Internat. Print Triennale, Krakow, Poland/Nuremberg, Germany, 1991-92, City Without Walls Gallery, Invitation, Newark, 1992, L.A. Printmaking Soc. 12th Nat. Exhbn., Palos Verdes Art Ctr., Calif., 1993, The Boston Printmakers 44th N.Am. Exhbn., Boston (Mass.) U. Gallery, 1993, Lubbock (Tex.) Fine Arts Ctr., Illuminance '93, Alexandria (La.) Mus. Art 12th Ann. Sept. Exhbn., 1993, Soc. for Am. Graphic Artists 65th Nat. Print Exhbn., N.Y.C., 1993, Fine Arts Ctr./Giza, Egypt, 1st Egyptian Internat. Print Trienniale, Cairo, 1994, Fla. Ctr. Contemporary Art, Tampa, 1994—, Eastern Washington U., 1994—, Rhode Island Sch. of Design Mus. Art, 1993-94, One West Art Ctr., Ft. Collins, Colo., 1994. Scholar R.I. Sch. Design, 1959-61; named one of New York Outstanding Artists, Ethel Scull, N.Y.C., 1983; travel citation Mid-Am. Arts Alliance, 1990-92, recipient Juror/Roberta Waddell award Soc. Am. Graphic Artist, N.Y.C., 1993, Grantee Duggal Color Projects, Inc., N.Y., 1992; guest speaker UN Photography Soc., N.Y., 1993. Mem. Boston Visual Artists Union (coordinator 1973-75), Art & Sci. Collaborations, Cambridge Art Assn. (juror 1973-74), R.I. Sch. Design N.Y. Alumni Chpt., Art and Sci. Collaborations Inc. Democrat. Jewish. Avocations: psychology, yoga, jewelry design. Home and Studio: 251 W 19th St New York NY 10011

DESROCHES, DIANE BLANCHE, English educator, writer, director, actor, editor; b. Webster, Mass., Nov. 17, 1947; d. Victor Joseph and Rose Blanche Blouin; m. Roger John DesRoches, Aug. 27, 1966 (div. Apr. 16, 1974); 1 child, Bill. AA with high honors in French, Mesa Coll., 1976; BA in English magna cum laude, San Diego State U., 1979, MA, 1981. Cert. lang. arts, lit. and ABE:ESL instr., Calif. community colls. ESL instr. Coll. of English Lang., San Diego, 1982—; ESL instr. Kearny Ctr. San Diego Community Coll. Dist., 1982—. Author: (short story) Something Special, 1979, Cinderella of the 80s, 1980; (software) Basic Map Reading Skills, 1981; writer (video) The College of English Language, 1989, numerous recipes, word search puzzles, variety puzzles and ednl. puzzles., 1980—; writer, dir. (video) The Challenge Is Ours, 1989; co-writer (multimedia show) Holiday Sky Show, 1988, (screen adaptation) The Wind From the Sun, 1989; contbr. articles to mags.; contbr. (reading comprehension series) Comprehension Plus, 1982, (student assessment system) CASAS, 1982; editorial cons. (multimedia shows) Dimensions, 1987, Cycles, 1987, Star Tracks, 1988, Thundering Water, 1988, Flying Blue Marble, 1988, Night on Dream Mountain, 1988, Mars, 1988, From Here to Infinity, 1989, To Worlds Beyond, 1989, Stars Over China, 1989, Eclipse!, 1991; translator: ABC of Ecology, 1982; actor (photoplay) And the Winner Is...?, 1982, (film) Killer Tomatoes Eat France, 1991, Tainted Blood, 1993. Recipient Gregg award Gregg Inst., 1965; fellow State of Calif., 1979; DB Williams scholar San Diego State U., 1979. Mem. Am. Fedn. Tchrs., Am. Film Inst., Phi Kappa Phi, Psi Chi, Pi Delta Phi. Democrat. Roman Catholic.

DESS, LISA MARIE, orthopedics nurse; b. Mansfield, Ohio, Sept. 8, 1965; d. Charles Bernard and Angeline Louise (Cioppa) D. BSN, Pa. State U., 1987. RN, Pa., Ohio; cert. in cardiac critical care nursing, ACLS. Nurses' aide Overlook Med. Clinic, New Wilmington, Pa., 1986; clin. nurse I orthopedics unit St. Elizabeth Hosp Med. Ctr., Youngstown, Ohio, 1987-91, clin. nurse I progressive cardiac care unit, 1991—. Mem. Nat. League Nursing, Pa. State U. Alumni Assn. Home: 24 E Oakwood Way New Castle PA 16105-1206

DESSASO, DEBORAH ANN, social welfare organization specialist, communication specialist; b. Washington, Feb. 6, 1952; d. Coleman and Virginia Beatrice (Taylor) D. AS in Bus. Adminstrn., Southeastern U., 1986, BSBA, 1988; postgrad. U. D.C., 1993—. Clk.-stenographer FTC, Washington, 1969-70; sec. NEA, Washington, 1970-72; sec. AARP, Washington, 1972-79, assoc. adminstrv. specialist, 1979-80, adminstrv. specialist, 1979-89, legis. specialist, 1989—; founding mem., sec. Andrus Fed. Credit Union, 1980. Mem. NAFE. Mem. Worldwide Ch. of God. Home: 3052 Stanton Rd SE Washington DC 20020-7883 Office: 601 E St NW Washington DC 20049-0001

DESSAUER, CARIN, journalist; b. Pottstown, Pa., Dec. 31, 1963; d. Ralph and Margot (Abrams) D.; m. Marc Richard Engel, May 29, 1988. BA cum laude, Bucknell U., 1985; postgrad., George Washington U., 1987. Reporter The Polit. Report, Washington, 1986-87; off-air reporter ABC News Polit. Unit, Washington, 1988; assoc. editor Congl. Quarterly's Politics in Am., Washington, 1989; contbg. editor Campaigns and Elections mag., Washington, 1989-91; head Washington polit. unit Cable News Network, 1990-91; assoc. polit. dir. CNN, Washington, 1991-95, dep. pol. dir., 1995—. Co-author: (monograph) Running to Win, 1988. Mem. recruiting com. for sports challenge Cystic Fibrosis of Washington, 1990; mem. devel. com. New Endeavors by Women, Washington; vol. Make a Wish Found., Doing Something, Washington. Mem. USA Bus. and Profl. Women's Network, Phi Beta Kappa. Office: CNN 820 1st St NE Washington DC 20002-4205

DESSYLAS, ANN ATSAVES, human resources and office management executive; b. Bklyn., Jan. 28, 1927; d. Charles and Agnes (Cocoros) Atsaves; m. George Dessylas, Dec. 28, 1969. BA, Bklyn. Coll., 1957; MA, NYU, 1961, MBA, 1977. Exec. asst. W.R. Grace & Co., N.Y.C., 1950-70; asst. sec. St. Joe Minerals Corp., N.Y.C., 1970-81, asst. v.p., 1981-85; cons. Cyprus Minerals, Denver, 1985-91; pres. AAD Enterprises, Forest Hills, N.Y., 1992—; dir. Continental Owners Corp. Home and Office: 70-20 108th St Ste 8-P Forest Hills NY 11375

DESTAFFANY, SANDRA RUSSELL, childbirth educator, author; b. Billings, Mont., Mar. 15, 1957; d. Alexander Emmett and Cleora Jean (Saunders) Russell; m. Joe Lee DeStaffany, Oct. 13, 1979; children: Naomi Jo, Andrea Renee, James Russell. BS, Mont. State U., 1979. cert. childbirth educator. Childbirth educator Conrad (Mont.) Childbirth Edn. Assn., 1983—; U.S. we. dir. Inter Childbirth Edn. Assn., Mpls., 1990-92, pres. elect 1992-94, pres. 1994—. Contbr. numerous articles to profl. jours. Home: 200 Homestead Rd Conrad MT 59425

D'ESTE, MARY ERNESTINE, health administration executive; b. Chgo., Apr. 1, 1941; d. Ernest Gregory and Mary (Turcich) D'E. Student, Mundelein Coll., 1958-61. Sec. MMM, Bedford Park, Ill., 1961-69, Michael Reese Med. Ctr., Chgo., 1969-73; adminstrv. asst. Thomas Jefferson U., Phila., 1973-85, divisional adminstr., 1985-86; adminstr. dept. cardiothoracic surgery Hahnemann U., Phila., 1986—; v.p. CTS Cardiac & Thoracic Surgeons PC, Phila., 1986—. V.p. archtl. review com. GTV Homeowners Assn., Marlton, N.J., 1979-85. Mem. Med. Group Mgmt. Assn., Am. Assn. Notaries, NAFE. Roman Catholic. Office: Hahnemann U Hosp Broad and Vine MS 111 Philadelphia PA 19102-1192

DESVIGNES SCHILLING, MICHELE K., city public policy planner, researcher; b. Chgo., Oct. 25, 1963; d. Robert and Gwendolyn Desvignes. BA, U. Chgo., 1987. City planner Dept. Pub. Works, City of Chgo., 1988-91; asst. dir. city-wide infrastructure mgmt. sys. Office of Budget and Mgmt. City of Chgo., 1991-94, coord. spl. projects Dept. of Bldgs., 1994—. Precinct capt. 4th Ward, Chgo., 1992—; mentor U. Chgo. Coord. Coun. for Minority Affairs, 1989—; mem. Chgo.-Accra com., Sister Cities Internat., 1993; bd. dirs. Three Arts Club, 1993—. Mem. Am. Soc. Pub. Adminstrs., Nat. Forum Black Pub. Adminstrs. Office: City of Chicago Dept Bldgs 121 N La Salle St Rm 900 Chicago IL 60602-1208

DE TABOAS, HILDA RIVERA, occupational health nurse; b. Coamo, P.R., Dec. 19, 1919; d. Dàmaso and Ramona (Zayas) Rivera; m. Julio Oscar Taboas; children: Julio Oscar, Alberto Jose, Carlos E. Cert., Bishop Willinger Sch. Nursing, 1941, Presbyn. Hosp., 1962, Met. Hosp., 1969, Coutinuos Edn., 1980. RN., P.R. RN U.S. Vet. Hosp., San Juan, P.R.; coronary care nurse Presbyn. Hosp., San Juan, P.R.; pvt. nurse Directory Nurses, San Juan, P.R.; first aid nurse Airport Internat. Islavarda, San Juan, P.R. Contbr. articles to profl. jours. Mem. Colegio Profesionales de Enfarmaria de P.R. Home: Purus 1687 Rp Hts Rio Piedras PR 00926

DETER, LENA LOUISE, community health nurse, rehabilitation nurse,; b. Worcester, Mass., Mar. 8, 1952; d. Edgar Stephen and Anita Beatrice (Deschenes) Despin; m. Harry J. Deter Jr., July 31, 1971; children: Jonathan Christopher, Stephanie Lynne. Diploma, St. Vincent Sch. Nursing, Worcester, 1973; A in Liberal Arts, Quinsigamond Community Coll., Worcester, 1992; BS in Health Edn., Worcester State Coll., 1994; postgrad., Boston U., 1994—. Charge nurse pediatrics Henry Heywood Meml. Hosp., Gardner, Mass., 1973-74; head nurse med.-surg. Doctor's Hosp., Worcester, 1975-76; asst. dir. nursing Leewood Geriatric Facility, Annandale, Va., 1977; day supr. People's Ch. Nursing Home, Worcester, 1978; floater Hubbard Regional Hosp., Webster, Mass., 1978-79; IV therapist The Meml. Hosp., Worcester, 1979-80; charge nurse telemetry, radiation oncology St. Vincent Hosp., Worcester, 1980-83; primary nurse Milford-Whitinsville Regional Hosp., Milford, Mass., 1983-84; meal site mgr., adult foster care nurse then outreach coord. TriValley Elder Svcs., Southbridge, Mass., 1986-91; assoc. nurse Fairlawn Rehab. Hosp., Worcester, 1990-92; cmty. health nurse Cert. Nursing Svcs., Worcester, 1992-95; residential mgr. Com. to End Elder Homelessness, Boston, 1995—; clin. instr. Quinsigamond C.C., 1991; instr., coord. ARC, Worcester, 1992-94. Mem. pub. edn. com. Am. Cancer Soc., 1986-94, co-chmn. com., 1991-94. Recipient Lifesaver of Yr. award Am. Cancer Soc., 1991. Mem. Am. Cancer Soc. (pub. edn. com. 1986-94, co-chair pub. edn. com. 1991—, cert. CHES 1994, Lifesaver of Yr. award 1991). Home: 17 Brook St Whitinsville MA 01588-2301

DETERDING, DIANA MARGARET, equine advertising agency executive; b. Akron, Nov. 9, 1949; d. Frank Charles and Margaret Audrey (Penzenik)

LaSalle; m. William Joseph Sanders, Mar. 25, 1972 (div. 1979); children: Aaron Michael, Phillip Andrew; m. Richard Lee Deterding, Apr. 4, 1981. AA, U. Akron, 1972. Sec. U. Akron, 1969-72; office mgr. Buckeye Fence Co., Akron, 1979-84; designer/writer Dymar Agy., Akron, 1980-83; pres. Dymar Agy., Inc., Gurnee, Ill., 1984—; cons. Smithsonian Nat. Mus. Natural History, Washington, 1989-91. Contbr. articles to profl. jours. Bd. dirs. No. Ill. Coun. for Alcoholism and Substance Abuse, 1994—, adminstrv. v.p. women's bd., 1994. Recipient Design award HOW Mag., 1990; named Woman of the Yr. Wadsworth Jaycee Women, 1979, 83; named to Ohio Jaycee Women Hall of Fame, 1981. Mem. U.S. Equine Mktg. Assn. (pres. chmn. bd. 1989-90), Women's Bus. Exch. (pres. 1988-89), Horse Coun. of Ill. (bd. dirs. 1991-94), Am. Horse Pubs., Am. Horse Coun. Republican. Lutheran. Office: Dymar Agy Inc 1300 Skokie Hwy #102 Gurnee IL 60031

DETERMAN, SARA-ANN, lawyer; b. Palmerton, Pa., Aug. 17, 1938; d. Albert H. and Evelyn (Tucker) Heimbach; m. Dean W. Determan, July 28, 1957 (div. Nov. 1981); children: Dann, David; m. Gary Sellers, May 21, 1988. Student, Conn. Coll., 1956-57, Stanford U., 1958; AB, U. Del., 1960; LLB, George Washington U., 1967. Bar: U.S. Dist. Ct. D.C. 1968. Law clk. to sr. judge U.S. Ct. Appeals (D.C. cir.), Edgerton, 1967-68; assoc. Hogan & Hartson, Washington, 1968-75, ptnr., 1975—; trustee Lawyers Com. for Civil Rights Under Law, Washington, 1982-94, co-chmn., 1994—. Bd. dirs. Mex.-Am. Legal Def. and Ednl. Fund, 1983-88, Women's Legal Def. Fund, 1980—. Fellow Am. Bar Found.; mem. ABA (chmn. individual rights sect. 1985-86, commr. legal programs for elderly 1983-89, com. on delivery of legal svcs. 1989-93, mem. consortium on legal svcs.), ACLU (bd. dirs. 1975-92), D.C. Bar (pres. 1990-91). Democrat. Unitarian. Office: Hogan & Hartson Columbia Square 555 13th St Washington DC 20004-1109

DETERT-MORIARTY, JUDITH ANNE, graphic artist, civic worker; b. Portage, Wis., July 10, 1952; d. Duane Harlan and Ann Jane (Devine) Detert; m. Patrick Edward Moriarty, July 22, 1978; children: Colin Edward, Eleanor Grace, Dylan Joseph. Student U. Wis.-Madison, 1970-73; BA, U. Wis.-Green Bay, 1991. Cert. in no-fault grievance mediation, Minn. Legis. sec., messenger State of Wis. Assembly, Madison, 1972, 74-76; casualty-property div. clk. Capitol Indemnity Corp., Madison, 1976-77; sec./credit clk. comml. credit div. Affiliated Bank of Madison, 1977-78; word processor consumer protection div. Wis. Dept. Agr., Madison, 1978; graphics arts composing specialist Moraine Park Tech. Inst., Fond du Lac, Wis., 1978-79; free-lance artist Picas, Pictures and Promotion (formerly Detert Graphics), 1978-90; prodn. asst. West Bend News, 1980-83; devel. assoc. Riveredge Nature Ctr., Inc., Newburg, Wis., 1983-84; exec. dir. Voluntary Action Ctr. of Washington County, West Bend, 1984-86; devel. cons. West Bend Hospice Program, 1985; instr. community svcs. Austin (Minn.) Community Coll., 1988; art and promotional publs. dir. Michael G. & Co., Albert Lea, Minn., 1988-89; corp. art dir. Newco, Inc., Janesville, Wis., 1989-91; owner, artist ProArt Plus, 1991—; bd. dirs. Health Net Janesville, Inc., 1993. Vol. activities include Austin Pub. Schs. Omnibus Program polit. cartooning instr. Dane County vol. Udall for Pres., 1976; student vol. McCarthy for Pres., U. Wis., Madison, 1968, coord. student residences McGovern for Pres., 1972; Washington County campaign coord. Nat. Unity Campaign for John Anderson for Pres., 1980; Washington County ward coord. Earl for Gov., 1982; Washington County campaign chmn. Peg Lautenschlager for Wis. state senate, Washington County ward coord. Mondale/Ferraro, 1984; vol. coord. Rock County Dukakis for Pres., 1988; campaign chair Lew Mittness for Wis. State Assembly, 1990; vol. Rock County Clinton For Pres.; sec., newsletter editor Dem. Party of Manitowoc County, Wis., 1986, Rock County, 1988—; local chair Women's Polit. Caucus, 1987-88; publicity coord. Wis. Intellectual Freedom Coalition, 1981; founding exec. bd. dirs., newsletter editor Moral Alternatives, Catholics for a Free Choice Wis. community contact, 1990-92; v.p., 1990-92, newsletter editor Rock County Voice for Choice, 1990-94; bd. dirs., v.p. Wis. Pro-Choice Conf., 1981-82; pres., founder People of Washington County United for Choice, 1981-83; mem. Rock County Citizens for Peace; bd. pres. Planned Parenthood of Washington County, 1984-85, newsletter editor, mem. coms., 1980-85; bd. mem. Montessori Children's House, West Bend, 1983-85, newsletter editor, com. chmn.; artist LWV Washington County, 1984-86; newsletter editor, artist Friends of Battered Women, West Bend, 1983-86; apptd. to Austin Human Rights Commn, 1987-88, Janesville Historic Commn., 1991-94, sec., 1992-94; fundraiser Victims Crisis Ctr., 1987; v.p., comm. officer Rock County Dem. Party, 1988—; cartooning instr., contbg. artist Janesville Pub. Schs., 1989-93, contbr. articles to profl. jours.; Mower County Dem. precinct chair, affirmative action officer, county sec. Dem. Party, 1988; artist LWV Rock County; vol. contbd. artist Janesville Concert Assn., Spolight on Kids Theatre, 1995—. Recipient award of Excellence Bd. Report Graphic Artists, 1994, 95. Mem. ACLU, NAFE, NOW (newsletter editor Dane County 1977-78, Wis. state 1994—, coord. Wis. state reproductive rights task force 1982-84, coord. reproductive rights task force North Suburban Chpt., 1981-84, Minn. pub. rels. coord., 1987-88, Rock County chpt.), Nat. Assn. Desktop Pubs., Wis. Women Entrepreneurs, Graphic Artists Guild, Design-Print Info. Source, Janesville Area C. of C. (steering com. for Celebrate Janesville 1992, 93, 94). Quaker. Avocations: reading, hand spinning and knitting, world wide correspondence, antiques, gardening. Office: ProArt Plus 23 S Atwood Ave Janesville WI 53545-4003

DETMAR-PINES, GINA LOUISE, business strategy and policy educator; b. S.I., N.Y., May 3, 1949; d. Joseph and Grace Vivian (Brown) Sargente; m. Michael B. Pines, Sept. 11, 1988. BS in Edn., Wagner Coll., 1971, MS, 1972; MA in Urban Affairs and Policy Analysis, New Sch. for Social Rsch., 1987; postgrad., CUNY, 1987—. Cert. adminstr. and supr., sch. dist. adminstr. Tchr. pub. schs. N.Y.C., 1971-82; coord. spl. projects, pub. affairs N.Y.C. Bd. Edn., 1982, spl. asst. to exec. dir. pupil svcs., 1983, asst. to chancellor, 1983-84, dir. Tchr. Summer Bus. Industry Program, 1984-93; prof. pub. adminstrn. and mgmt. John Jay Coll. Criminal Justice CUNY, 1992-93; vis. prof. Hartford Grad. Ctr., 1993—; liaison for the Tech. Industry Program, N.Y.C. Partnership, 1985-93. Mem. com. to re-elect Borough pres. Lamberti, S.I., 1985-86; com. mem. Hartford Symphony 50th Anniversary Gala, 1993; chair Greater Hartford Eastern Seals Rehab. Ctr., Crystal Ball, 1994, trustee, 1994—; trustee Greater Hartford Easter Seals Rehab. Ctr.; bd. dirs. Hartford Symphony. Mayor's scholar City of N.Y., 1984—. Mem. ASPA, Fgn. Lang. Instrs. Assn., U.S. Seaplane Pilot's Assn., Internat. Orgn. for Lic. Women Pilots, Chinese-Am Soc., Am. Mgmt. Assn., Acad. Mgmt., Strategic Mgmt. Soc., Ea. Acad. Mgmt., Cambridge Flying Group Club. Episcopalian. Office: Hartford Grad Ctr 275 Windsor St Hartford CT 06120

DE TORNYAY, RHEBA, nurse, university dean emeritus, educator; b. Petaluma, Calif., Apr. 17, 1926; d. Bernard and Ella Fradkin; m. Rudy de Tornyay, June 4, 1954. Student, U. Calif., Berkeley, 1944-46; diploma, Mt. Zion Hosp. Sch. Nursing, 1949; A.B., San Francisco State U., 1951, M.A., 1954; Ed.D., Stanford U., 1967; Sc.D. (hon.), Ill. Wesleyan U., 1974; LHD (hon.), U. Portland, 1974, Georgetown U., 1994. Mem. faculty San Francisco State U., 1957-67, prof. nursing, 1966-67, chmn. dept., 1959-67; assoc. prof. U. Calif. Sch. Nursing, San Francisco, 1968-71; prof. U. Calif. Sch. Nursing, 1971; dean, prof. Sch. Nursing UCLA, 1971-75; dean emeritus, prof. U. Wash., Seattle, 1986—. Author: Strategies for Teaching Nursing, 1971, 3rd edit., 1987, Japanese transl., 1974, Spanish edit., 1986. Trustee Robert Wood Johnson Found. Mem. ANA, Am. Acad. Nursing (charter fellow, pres. 1973-75), Inst. Medicine (governing coun. 1979-81), Nat. League for Nursing. Office: U Wash Sch Nursing SM-24 Seattle WA 98195

DE TORRES, LILIAM INES, ESL educator; b. Havana, Cuba, Dec. 20, 1963; came to U.S., 1965; d. Luis Ernesto and Ana Maria (de la Prida) de T. AS, Union C.C., Cranford, N.J., 1983; BA in Elem. Edn., Kean Coll., 1986, MA in Instrn. & Curriculum, 1990. Cert. elem. tchr., Spanish, ESL. Substitute tchr. Hillside (N.J.) Bd. Edn., 1984-87, tchrs. aide, 1987, EST tchr., 1987—; substitute tchr., 1984-87; adj. prof. Union C.C., Elizabeth, N.J., 1992-94. Chairperson Juvenile Conf. Com., Hillside, 1989. Mem. Hillside Edn. Assn. (bldg rep. 1988-90). Republican. Baptist.

DETRANA, MARY ANN, author, lecturer, consultant; b. Hannibal, Mo., June 24, 1941; d. James Vincent and Martha Taylor (Jenkins) McAllister; m. George Frank DeTrana, Nov. 23, 1963; children: John Andrew, Paul Alexander, Alexander George. BA, Rosary Coll., 1963; MA, U. Durham, Eng., 1991. Rsch. analyst Ill. Dept. Labor, Chgo., 1963-64; tchr. Alverno High Sch., Chgo., 1964-65; writer, lectr. Richmond, Va., 1980—; cons. St. Vladimir's Orthodox Theol. Sem., Crestwood, N.Y., 1987—; participant Internat. Orthodox Women's Consultation, Ch. and Culture, Crete, 1990; coord. Nat. Support Group for Wives of Orthodox Clergy, 1983—. Author various theol. literary works; book rev. editor The Orthodox Ch. Newspaper, Syosset, N.Y., 1976-86; contbr. articles and revs. to profl. jours. Dir. music St. Cyprian Orthodox Ch., Richmond, 1974—; tutor English Ridge Elem. Sch., Richmond, 1983-88. Recipient Disting. Svc. to Children and Youth award Va. Congress Parents and Tchrs., Richmond, 1988. Mem. Ecumenical Soc. Blessed Virgin Mary (corr. sec. 1980-84, recording sec. 1984-88, v.p. 1988-92, pres. 1992—. Mem. Ea. Orthodox Ch.

DETTMAN, LAUREL ALYSSA, industrial engineer; b. Kewaunee, Wis., July 9, 1966; d. Richard Walter Dettman and Gloria Lorraine (Swanson) Burkett. BS in Indsl. Engring., U. Wis., 1989; MBA, De Paul U., 1994. Instr. engr. Admiral Tool and Mfg. Co., Chgo., 1989-93; stds. and analysis mgr. Caterair Internat., Chgo., 1993-94; tech. cons. AT&T Istel, Chgo., 1994—. Mem. Inst. Indsl. Engrs. Office: AT&T Istel 1600 Golf Rd Rolling Meadows IL 60008

DETWILER, SUSAN MARGARET, information brokerage executive; b. Bklyn., Dec. 8, 1953; d. Marshall and Anna (Dembrofsky) Pallas; m. Mark Fredrick Detwiler, Mar. 13, 1977; children: John Marshall, Elizabeth Ann. BS, SUNY, Albany, 1974; MBA, U. Mich., 1976. Market analyst Am. V. Mueller, Niles, Ill., 1976-80; mgr. market rsch. Zimmer Inc., Warsaw, Ind., 1980-85; pres. S.M. Detwiler & Assocs., Inc., Ft. Wayne, Ind., 1985—. Editor: The Detwiler Directory of Medical Market Sources. Mem. Med. Surg. Market Rsch. Group, Assn. Ind. Info. Profls. (past v.p.), Regulatory Affairs Profls. Soc. Assn., Am. Hosp. Assn. Democrat. Office: PO Box 15308 Fort Wayne IN 46885-5308

DEUCHLER, SUZANNE LOUISE, state legislator; b. Chgo., July 21, 1929; m. Walter E. Deuchler Jr.; children: Mark, Maryll. BA, U. Ill. Mem. Ill. Ho. of Reps., Springfield, 1980—. Mem. Aurora reg. adv. com., Ill. Dept. Children and Family Svcs., 1976, citizens adv. bd., Aurora U., 1981; bd. dirs. Copley Meml. Hosp., 1982. Mem. AAUW, Altrusa, Bus. and Profl. Women. Republican. Office: Ill Ho of Reps State Capitol Springfield IL 62706*

DEUEL, M. CAROLYN, arts administrator, piano and organ teacher; b. Casper, Wyo., Jan. 23, 1952; d. Arch Waldron and Janis Kathryn (Henderson) D. MusB cum laude, U. No. Colo., 1974; MA, U. Iowa, 1976. Cert. permanent piano and organ tchr. MTNA. Pvt. piano and organ tchr. Casper, 1976—; exec. dir. Arts Coordinating Reps. (ARTCORE), Casper, 1986—; project dir. Overland Stage Co. Sch. Tours, Casper, 1978—. Dir. music, organist 1st Presbyn. Ch., Casper, 1976-87; organist Our Saviour's Luth. Ch., Casper, 1988—; dir. Festival Choir & Orch., Casper, 1979-86, 89—, Jubilate Ringers handbell choir, 1981-87, Phoenix Ringers, 1987—; chair Casper Performing Arts Coalition, 1990—; percussionist Wyo. Symphony Orch., 1976—, Casper Mcpl. Band, 1976—; singer Casper Civic Chorale, 1976—, Wyo. State Choir, 1978—; past pres. Casper Fine Arts Club. Named Musician of Yr. Bus. & Profl. Women, Casper, 1982; recipient Gov.'s Art award 1992. Mem. AAUW (readers group 1976—), Wyo. Music Tchrs. Assn. (state pres. 1990-92), Casper Music Tchrs. Assn. (treas. 1978—), PEO Sisterhood (past pres. chpt. Y). Republican. Methodist. Home: 1824 Lynwood Pl Casper WY 82604-3319 Office: ARTCORE Inc PO Box 874 Casper WY 82602-0874

DEURR, CHRISTINE B. SIMPSON, bank executive; b. Akron, Ohio, Oct. 3, 1952; d. John Glass Stewart Simpson and Martha B. (Jobe) Jackson; m. Robert L. Deurr, June 7, 1975 (div. Sept. 1994). BA, Calif. State U., San Bernardino, 1986, MBA, 1988; cert. in personal fin. planning, U. Calif., Riverside, 1993. Asst. v.p., comml. loan officer Security Pacific Nat. Bank, Riverside, 1975-88; v.p., comml. loan officer De Anza Nat. Bank, Riverside, 1988—. Mem. corp. com. Mar. Dimes, Riverside, 1993—, walk site chairperson, 1994—. Mem. Greater Riverside C. of C. (pres. Hunter Park divsn. 1994—, bd. dirs.). Office: De Anza Nat Bank 1650 Spruce Ste 100 Riverside CA 92507

DEUSS, JEAN, librarian; b. Chgo.; d. Edward Louis and Harriet (Goodwin) D. B.A., U. Wis., 1944; M.S., Sch. Library Service, Columbia U., 1959. Cataloger library N.Y.C. Council Fgn. Relations, 1959-61; head cataloger research library Fed. Res. Bank N.Y., N.Y.C., 1961-68; asst. chief librarian Fed. Bank N.Y., N.Y.C., 1969-70, chief librarian, 1970-85. Author: Banking in the U.S.: An Annotated Bibliography, 1990; editor: Banking and Fin. Collections, Spl. Collections, vol. 2, No. 3, 1983. Mem. U. Wis. Found., 1977—, bd. dirs., 1983—; bd. dirs. Abingdon Square Painters, 1990—. Mem. Spl. Libraries Assn. (assoc. treas. 1967-70, pres. N.Y. chpt. 1971-72, bd. dirs. 1972-76). Episcopalian. Home: 260 W 12th St New York NY 10014-1912

DEUTSCH, FLORENCE ELAYNE GOODILL, nursing and health care consultant; b. San Diego, Aug. 1, 1923; d. George Ehrlich and Beatrice Marie (Urick) Goodill; m. Edward Thomas Deutsch, June 27, 1953 (dec.); 1 son, George Edward. Student, San Diego State Coll., 1942-43; B.S.N., Villa Maria Coll., 1948; diploma in nursing Evanston Hosp., Northwestern U., 1947; M.Ed., Edinboro U., 1961. Staff nurse St. Vincent Hosp., Erie, Pa., 1947; clin. instr.-supr. Hamot Med. Ctr., Erie, 1948-58, dir. edn., 1958-62, dir. Sch. Nursing, 1962-66, asst. adminstr., dir. Sch. Nursing, 1969-73; exec. dir. Florence Crittenton Home, Erie, 1966-69; asst. adminstr., dir. nursing Capitol Hill Hosp., Washington, 1974-79; assoc. adminstr. profl. services Millcreek Community Hosp., 1980-82; v.p. nursing East Liverpool City Hosp. (Ohio), 1982-87; lectr., cons. on nursing and nursing law, 1988-89; lectr. Gannon U., Erie, Pa. Editor newsletter U.S. Brig Niagara, 1991-93. Past bd. dirs. Columbiana County Cancer Soc.; bd. dirs. Sarah A. Reed Retirement Ctr., Erie, 1991—, treas. 1992-95. Served with USNR, 1948-53. Recipient Vol. of the Year award U.S. Brig Niagara, 1993, Named Most Outstanding Nurse Erie County, 1969, Disting. Nursing Alumna Villa Maria Coll. Gannon U., 1989, Disting. Alumnus Gannon U., 1991. Mem. Nat. League Nursing, Am. Orgn. Nurse Execs., Svc. Corps Of Ret. Execs. (vice-chmn. Erie chpt. 1988-90), Sigma Theta Tau, Delta Kappa Gamma. Republican. Presbyterian. Editor: Penn League News, 1968-70; contbr. articles to profl. jours. Address: 3207 Georgian Ct Erie PA 16506

DEUTSCH, JUDITH, clergywoman; b. N.Y.C., Apr. 18, 1929; d. Charles Shepard and Sadie (Freedman) Greene; m. Marshall E. Deutsch, June 27, 1947; children: Pamina Margret, Ethan Amadeus, Freeman Sarastro. BA, Hunter Coll., 1950; MA, New Sch. Social Rsch., 1965, Boston Coll., 1980. Ordained to ministry Unitarian-Universalist Ch., 1981. Dir. Hexiad, Cambridge, Mass., 1979-80; intern First Parish, Framingham, Mass., 1981; assoc. minister Unitarian-Universalist Soc., Hartford, Conn., 1982-85; interim minister First Parish Petersham, Mass., 1985-87, First Parish Sharon, Mass., 1988-90, Unitarian Universalist Ch., Worcester, Mass., 1990-91; minister Unitarian-Universalist Ch., Rockland, Mass., 1987-88, First Parish Medfield, Mass., 1991—; bd. dirs. Internat. League Religious Socialism, Stockholm, 1989—; chair religion and socialism commn. Dem. Socialists Am., 1989—; chmn. Religious Coalition for Abortion Rights, Boston, 1987-90; acting exec. com. pres. James Luther Admas Found., Newton, Mass., 1989-91; former sr. co-chair Collegium, now chair ethics sect. Producer, interviewer TV program Religous Issues in The News; author curriuclum materials; contbr. articles to profl. publs. Co-chair Citizens for Kennedy and Johnson, Morris County, N.J., 1960; mem. Sudbury (Mass.) Dem. Town Com., 1985—; del. Mass. Dem. Conv., 1990, 94; lobbyist Coalition for Choice, Boston, 1988-92; mem. Medfield Alcohol and Other Drug Action Com. Mem. Unitarian Universalist Ministers Assn., Liberal Religious Education Dirs. Assn., Mass. Bay Ministers Assn. Home: 41 Concord Rd Sudbury MA 01776-2328 Office: First Parish Medfield 26 North St Medfield MA 02052-2314

DEUTSCH, MELODEE J., maternal/newborn nurse; b. Allentown, Pa., Apr. 23, 1949; d. William H. and Jean L. (Conrad) Wagner; m. Gary A. Deutsch, July 18, 1970; children: Christy Anne, Bryan Conrad. BS, Temple U., 1971; MS, U. Hawaii, 1982, MPH, 1982. Instr. in nursing U. Hawaii, Honolulu, 1976-83; supr. neonatal ICU-NSY Kaiser Med. Ctr., Honolulu, 1985-87; asst. prof. nursing Hawaii Loa Coll., Kaneohe, 1983-85; clin. nurse specialist Kaiser Med. Ctr., Honolulu, 1987-92, asst. dir. nursing, 1992—. Mem. ANA (cert. perinatal nursing), NAACOG (sect. chair Hawaii, named Nurse of Yr. 1991, Nurse Mgr. of Yr. 1986), Hawaii Nurses Assn. (creative writing award 1980-81, Nurse of Yr. 1989), Am. Orgn. Nurse Execs. (Nurse of Yr. Hawaii sect. 1993), Sigma Theta Tau. Home: 46-304 Kahuhipa St Kaneohe HI 96744-3514

DEUTZ, NATALIE RUBINSTEIN, actress, consultant; b. Plymouth, Mass., Sept. 26; d. Louis and Lillian Rubinstein; student Simmons Coll., 1937, Modern Sch. Applied Art, 1938-40; m. Nov. 29, 1947 (dec.). Fashion buyer Wm. Filene's Sons Co., Boston, 1940-47; asst. to corp. pres. Columbia Textiles, Inc., N.Y.C., 1956-68; dir. John Robert Powers Sch., N.Y.C., 1968-72; v.p., nat. dir. fashion merchandising, dir. advt. workshop Barbizon Internat., Inc., N.Y.C., 1972-83; cons., 1983—. Mem. Nat. Acad. TV Arts and Scis., Screen Actors Guild, AFTRA.

DEVANEY, CYNTHIA ANN, real estate broker, educator; b. Gary, Ind., Feb. 6, 1947; d. Charles Barnard and Irene Mae (Nelson) Burner; m. Harold Verne DeVaney, Nov. 23, 1974 (dec. 1981). BS, Ball State U., 1970, MS, 1972; postgrad., Ind. U. and Purdue U., 1974-76. Cert. real estate broker, Ind. Real estate broker Century 21 McColly Realtors, Merrillville, Ind., 1979-86; real estate broker Better Homes and Gardens McColly Realtors, Merrillville, 1986—, with Pres.' Coun.; tchr. Merkley Elem. Sch., Highland, Ind., 1969—. Active Schubert Theater Guild, Chgo. Mem. N.W. Ind. Bd. Realtors (Million Dollar Club), Nat. Bd. Realtors, Jr. Ind Hist. Soc., Innsbrook Country Club, Match Point Tennis Club. Democrat. Methodist. Home: 607 E 78th Pl Merrillville IN 46410 Office: McColly Better Homes & Gardens 9143 Indianapolis Blvd Hammond IN 46322-2504

DEVANY SERIO, CATHERINE, clinical psychologist; b. N.Y.C., July 27, 1964; d. Edward Heath and Mary Langley (Peebles) Devany; m. Vincent Joseph Serio, III, May 2, 1992. BA in Am. Studies magna cum laude, U. Tex., 1987; MS in Clin. Psychology, Va. Commonwealth U., 1990, PhD in Clin. Psychology, 1993. Rsch. assoc. Dept. Mental Health, Mental Retardation and Substance Abuse, Richmond, 1988-90; extern in family therapy Family Therapy Practice Ctr., Washington, 1993-94; postdoctoral fellow dept. phys. medicine and rehab. Med. Coll. Va., Richmond, 1993-94; clin. dir. Community Rehab. Svcs., Richmond, 1994—; invited lectr. in field. Contbr. articles to profl. jours. Rehab. Psychology fellow Nat. Inst. Disability and Rehab. Rsch., 1990-92; recipient Young Investigator award Nat. Head Injury Found., 1993. Mem. APA (divsn. family psychology). Office: Community Rehab Svcs 4128 Innslake Dr Glen Allen VA 23060-0542

DEVARIS, JEANNETTE MARY, psychologist; b. Burbank, Calif., Jan. 7, 1947; d. Nicholas Propper Klein and Elizabeth (Von Lichtenberg) Schaeffer; m. Robert Lee Blake, May 20, 1967 (div. 1979); 1 child: Brendon; m. Panayotis Eric DeVaris, Dec. 5, 1988. BA, Adelphi U., 1968; MA, Fairleigh Dickinson U., 1977; PhD, Seton Hall U., 1987. Lic. psychologist, N.J. Caseworker N.Y.C. Welfare Dept., 1968-72; alcohol and drug rehab. counselor U.S. Army, Ft. Monmouth, N.J., 1972-76; psychol. intern N.J. State Intern Program, Trenton, 1977-78; psychologist Greystone Psychiat. Hosp., Greystone Park, N.J., 1979; sr. psychologist R. Hall Community Mental Health Ctr., Bridgewater, N.J., 1979-90; pvt. practice South Orange and Somerset, N.J., 1988—; tng. supr. Grad. Sch. Applied and Profl. Psychology; adj. prof. Seton Hall U.; sponsor and participant in Cable TV program. Contbr. articles to profl. jours. Mem. APA, Nat. Register Health Svc. Providers, N.J. Psychol. Assn. (interprofl. rels. com.), Soc. Psychologists in Pvt. Practice (bd. dirs., speakers bur. com.). Office: 15 Cedar Grove Ln Somerset NJ 08873-1377

DE VARONA, ESPERANZA BRAVO, librarian; b. Sancti Spiritu, Las Villas, Cuba, Sept. 29, 1929; came to U.S., 1965; d. Rómulo Segundo and Armantina (Lopez-Callejas) Bravo; m. Frank J. de Varona, July 9, 1950; children: Beatriz, Frankie, Essie. Degree, U. Havana, Cuba, 1951; MLS, Fla. State U., 1981; diploma, Gen. Svc. Adminstrn. Archives, Washington, 1982. Sch. libr. Colegio Santo Domingo, Dominican Republic, 1961-63; prof. history of art Escuela Miramar Santo Domingo, 1963-65; libr. Our Lady of Lourdes Acad., Miami, Fla., 1965-67; libr., archivist Richter Libr., U. Miami, Coral Gables, Fla., 1981—; mem. Fla. State Hist. Records Adv. Bd., Tallahassee, 1987—; mem. Seminar on Acquisition of Latin Am. Libr. Materials. Author: Cuban Exile Periodicals at the University of Miami Library, 1987, Posters of the Cuban Diaspora: a Bibliography, 1993; contbr. articles to profl. publs. Recipient Juan J. Remos award Cruzada Educativa Cubana, 1986, El Personaje de la Semana award El Nuevo Herald Newapaper, 1989. Mem. ALA, Soc. Am. Archivists, Soc. Fla. Archivists (pres. 1987-88), Acad. Cert. Archivists, Fla. Libr. Assn., Dade County Libr. Assn., Colegio Nacional de Bibliotecarios Cubanos en le Exilio (sec. 1987-89), Big-Five Club, Beta Phi Mu. Roman Catholic. Home: 2824 SW 92nd Ct Miami FL 33165-3130 Office: U Miami Richter Libr 1300 Memorial Dr Coral Gables FL 33124

DEVAUD, JUDITH ANNE See HALVORSON, JUDITH ANNE

DEVAUGHN, LEAH MARION, clinical nurse manager; b. Chgo., May 1, 1953; d. James Leander and Katherine Louise (Thomas) Clardy; m. Ralph Alfred DeVaughn Jr., Dec. 22, 1973; children: Damone Todd, Dana Adrianne. BSN, Loyola U., Chgo., 1975. RN, Ill. RN St. Francis Hosp., Colorado Springs, Colo., 1975-76, Mercy Hosp. Med. Ctr., Chgo., 1976-80, Rush Presbyn. Hosp., Chgo., 1980-83; clin. nurse mgr. Midwestern Regional Med. Ctr., Zion, Ill., 1983—. Recipient Women of Achievement award Lake County YWCA, 1989, 92. Mem. NAFE, Intravenous Nurses Soc., Oncology Nursing Soc., Chgo. Chpt. Oncology Nursing Soc., Ill Coun. Nurse Middle Mgrs. Home: 1781 Wausau Ln Gurnee IL 60031-1784 Office: Midwestern Regional Med Ctr 2501 Emmaus Ave Zion IL 60099-2555

DEVEAUX, DAWN DELLA, adult education regional specialist; b. Washington, Mar. 10, 1962; d. William Philips and Patricia Ann (Morris) DeV.; m. Clarence Daren Thomas, July 27, 1987; 1 child, Ryanne Patricia. BS, Howard U., 1984; MS, Austin Peay State U., 1987. Adj. prof., instr. Austin Peay State U., Clarksville, Tenn., 1987-89; grad. asst. Memphis State U., 1989; test examiner Amry Edn. Ctr., Ft. Polk, La., 1990—; adj. prof. Northwestern State U., Ft. Polk, 1991—. Contbr. articles to profl. jour. Mem. Drop-Out Prevention Coun., Petersburg, Va. Mem. AAUW, Assn. Black Women in Higher Edn. (bd. dirs. 1991—, officer). Democrat. Methodist. Home: 19513 Temple Ave Colonial Heights VA 23834-5666

DEVENDITTIS, GLORIA-CORTINA, executive secretary; b. New London, Conn., Sept. 11, 1941; d. Antonio and Clementina Marie (Silva) Cortina; m. Paul James Devendittis, Oct. 21, 1961; children: Louie Paul, Monte Anthony. Student, U. Conn., 1959-60, U. Hartford, 1960. Notary public. Legal sec. Gruskin and Gruskin, New London, 1957-59; sec. receptionist Sponsored Rsch. Acctg. U. Mich., Ann Arbor, 1961-63; floor sec. U. Rochester (N.Y.) Med. Ctr., 1963-65; ophthalmic med. asst. to Chief of Ophthalmology Jericho, N.Y., 1977-78; asst. to office mgr., bookkeeper Real Estate Mgmt., Jericho, N.Y., 1978-79; mgr. Non-Traditional Jobs for Women, Mineola, N.Y., 1979-80; office mgr., asst. to pres. Quality Tree Svc. Inc., Roslyn Heights, N.Y., 1980-91; adminstrv. asst. to pres. Capitol Warehouse Corp., Farmingdale, N.Y., 1991-92; exec. sec. to dir. mktg.Ueksler Instruments Corp., Freeport, N.Y., 1993—. Author: Mama's Kitchen Goes to College, 1988; original recipes published in Potpourri of Cooking and Who's Cooking What in America, 1994. Treas. Duncan Estates Civic Assn.; active Women's Info. Exchange, Greenpeace, N.Y. Pub. Interest Rsch. Group, Neighbor to Neighbor, The Arts Council at Freeport, New Community Cinema; convener and officer South Nassau NOW, 1980-82. Mem. Nat. Mus. of Women in Arts, L.I. Country Music Assn., Lusitano Soccer Club. Democrat. Home: 16 Primrose Ln Hempstead NY 11550-4623

DEVENEY, SUSAN ELAINE, lawyer, state legislator; b. Sept. 14, 1958. JD, Suffolk Law Sch., 1986. With sales and mktg. AT&T, Boston, 1981-88; atty. Wallick & Paolino, Providence, 1988-90; ptnr. Deveney & Hagopian, Cranston, R.I., 1990—; mem. R.I. Ho. of Reps., 1992—; commr. Commn. on Jud. Tenure and Discipline, Providence, 1992—, Select Commn. to Study Airport Devel., 1993; bd. dirs. Warwick (R.I.) Econ. Devel. Corp. Officer Edgewood Waterfront Preservation Soc., Cranston, 1994—. Republican. Home: 75 Bartlett Ave Cranston RI 02905 Office: Deveney & Hagopian 900 Reservoir Ave Providence RI 02910

DEVENNY, LILLIAN NICKELL, trophy company executive; b. Chesapeake, Ohio; d. Hayes Basil and Alice Irene (Noble) Nickell; m. John Paul DeVenny Jr., Dec. 31, 1955; children: Carrie DeVenny Paganini (dec.), John Hayes. Student, Covington Bus. Sch., 1954-55, Norfolk Coll., 1980-81. Office mgr., bookkeeper Nickell Electric Co., Covington, Va., 1950-55; exec. Nickell Electric Co., 1960-62; sec. 5th Naval Dist. Hdqtrs., Norfolk, Va., 1955-58, Profl. Realty, Va. Beach, 1971; pub. relations corp. sec. Hobby Industries, Va. Beach, 1973-74; owner, mgr., instr., sec.-treas. Deste Corp. t/a Hobby Assoc., Va. Beach, 1974—; singer, actress Tidewater Dinner Theater, Norfolk, part-time, 1971-75; involved numerous continuing edn. units. Writer coloumn on Va. travel, 1978-79; editor news letter, 1972-73. Founding mem., chmn. bd. dirs. Va. Opposing Drunk Driving, 1981—, state v.p., 1981-86, state pres., 1986—; mem. adv. bd. Va. Commn. on Alcohol Safety, 1987-91; participant Va. Assembly on Future of Va.'s Cts., U. Va., Commn. Pub. Svc., 1989; mem. spl. White House briefing on ways to combat tragedy of drunk driving, 1989; mem. Va. Civilian-Mil. Cmty. Safety Com., 1988; mem. Va. Alcohol Safety Action Program Commn., 1991—; co-chmn. Va. Coalition Against Drunk Driving, 1989—; contbr. passage Omnibus Alcohol Safety Act, Va. Gen. Assembly, 1994. Recipient Community Svc. award J.C. Penney Co., 1985, Hometown Hero, Sta. WVEC-TV, 1986. Mem. Internat. Ceramic Assn. (accredited ceramic artist, tchr.), Va. Ceramists Assn., Antique Auto Club Am., Modern Woodmen Am. (regional sec. 1954), Beta Sigma Phi (mem.-at-large). Episcopalian. Office: Deste Corp t/a Hobby Assocs 5004 Cleveland St Virginia Beach VA 23462-2504

DEVEREAUX, SHARON MURPHY, research scientist; b. Ridgewood, N.J., Nov. 13, 1956; d. Hugh George and Patricia Kathleen (Gilmore) Murphy; m. Patrick John Devereaux, Sept. 16, 1978; children: Jaime Erin, Allison Caye, Peter Hugh. Student, U. Durham, Eng., 1976; BS in Biology, Mundelein Coll., 1977. Apprentice pharmacist, mgr. M & H Pharmacists, Inc., Skokie, Ill., 1976-83; quality control trainer Abbott Labs., Abbott Park, Ill., 1982-83, assoc. rsch. scientist, 1983-84, rsch. scientist, 1984, quality coord., 1985, R & D project mgr., 1986-90, product mgr., 1991-92, project mgr., 1992, regulatory scientist, 1993—. Co-inventor in field. Cmty. rep. Au Pair Programme U.S.A., Gurnee, Ill., 1990—; vol. fundraiser Children's Home and Aid Soc. of Ill., Chgo., 1990—. Mem. Abbott Parent Network (pres. 1992, newsletter editor 1991), Am. Assn. Clin. Chemistry, Am. Assn. Blood Banks. Home: 4937 Carriage Dr Gurnee IL 60031-1925 Office: Abbott Labs 1 Abbott Park Rd Abbott Park IL 60064-3500

DEVERS, GAIL, track and field athlete. Student, UCLA. Gold medalist, 100m Track and Field Barcelona Olympic Games, 1992. Address: US Olympic Committee 1750 E Boulder St Colorado Springs CO 80909*

DEVIGNE, KAREN COOKE, amateur athletics executive; b. Phila., July 31, 1943; d. Paul and Matilda (Rich) Cooke; m. Jules Lloyd Devigne, June 26, 1965; children: Jules Paul, Denise Paige, Paul Michael. AA, Centenary Coll., Hackettstown, 1963; student, Northwestern U., 1963-65; BA, Ramapo Coll., Mahwah, 1976; MA, Emory U., Atlanta, 1989. Founder, owner GYMSET, Marietta, Ga., 1981—. Cons. Girls Club Am. Marietta, 1989; vol. Cobb County Gymnastic Ctr., Marietta, 1976-81, Atlanta Lawn Tennis Assn., Marietta, 1976—, Ga. Youth Soccer Assn., Atlanta, 1976—; fundraiser Scottish Rite Children's Hosp., Atlanta, 1989—. Recipient recognition awards from various youth groups, Atlanta, 1976—; named Nominee Woman of Yr. ABC News, Atlanta, 1984. Mem. U.S. Gymnastic Fedn, U.S. Assn. Ind. Gymnastic Clubs, Amateur Athletic Union, Ga. Gymnastic Coaches Assoc. Home: 3701 Clubland Dr Marietta GA 30068-4006 Office: GYMSET 4957 Lower Roswell Rd Marietta GA 30068-4337

DEVINE, KATHERINE, publisher, environmental consultant; b. Denver, Oct. 15, 1951. BS, Rutgers U., 1973, MS, 1980; postgrad., U. Md., 1981-82. Lab. technician Princeton (N.J.) U., 1974-76; econ. and regulatory affairs analyst, program mgr. U.S. EPA, Washington, 1979-81, 82-89, cons., 1989—; exec. dir. Applied BioTreatment Assn., Washington, 1990-91; pres. DEVO Enterprises, Inc., Washington, 1990—; chair adv. bd. Applied Bioremediation '93 Conf., 1993. Author: N.J. Agricultural Experiment Station of Rutgers Uniersity, 1980, Bioremediation Case Studies: An Analysis of Vendor Supplied Data, 1992, Bioremediation Case Studies: Abstracts, 1992; co-author: Biomediation: Field Experiences, 1994, Bioremediation, 1994; founder, pub., editor (mag.) Biotreatment News, 1990—; pub. The Gold Book; contbr. articles to profl. jours., chpts. to books. Mem. Women's Coun. on Energy and the Environment, 1991-93. Recipient numerous fed. govt. and non- govt. awards. Mem. NAFE, Am. Chem. Soc., Met. Washington Environ. Profls., Futures for Children, Alpha Zeta. Office: DEVO Enterprises Inc 1003 K St NW Ste 501 Washington DC 20001-4425

DEVINE, NANCY, postmaster; b. Hyannis, Mass., Feb. 8, 1949; d. Joseph Peter and Rose (Almeida) Cabral; m. Michael G. Devine, Mar. 20, 1971 (div. 1975); 1 child, Paul. Student, U. Mass., 1967-70. Postal clk. U.S. Postal Svc., Centerville, Mass., 1977-80; postmaster U.S. Postal Svc., West Hyannisport, Mass., 1980—; Affirmative Action planner U.S. Postal Svc., Brockton, Mass., 1979-80, prin. rep./exec. bd., Providence, 1993. Painter in acrylics. Art and Humanities grantee Barnstable Arts Coun., Mass. Art Coun., Nat. Endowment for the Arts. Mem. Cape Cod Art Assn., Smithsonian Instn. Home: PO Box 361 West Hyannisport MA 02672-0361

DEVINE, SHARON JEAN, lawyer; b. Milw., Feb. 27, 1948; d. George John Devine and Ethel May (Langworthy) Devine Chase; m. Curtiss Coughlin; children: Devin Curtiss, Katharine Langworthy. BS in Linguistics magna cum laude, Georgetown U., 1970; JD, Boston U., 1975. Bar: Ohio, Colo. Staff atty. FTC, Cleve., 1975-79; asst. regional dir., Denver, 1979-82; atty. Mountain Bell, Denver, 1982-84, US West Direct, 1984-85; assoc. gen. counsel U.S. West Direct, 1985-87, Landmark Pub. Co., Denver, 1987-88; antitrust counsel US West, Denver, 1988-91, corp. counsel, 1991; dir. Denver Consortium, 1982-83, Ctr. for Applied Prevention, Boulder, Colo., 1982-90; dir. Legal Aid Found. of Colo., 1990—, Suzuki Assn. of Colo., 1990-94. Active mem. Jr. League, Denver, 1980-87. Contbr. article to law rev. Mem. Colo. Bar Assn., Denver Bar Assn., Colo. Women's Bar Assn. Home: 2360 Dartmouth Ave Boulder CO 80303-5262 Office: US West 1801 California St Ste 5100 Denver CO 80202-2651

DEVITO, TERESA MARIE, artist; b. Bangoli del Tigino, Italy, June 11, 1920; came to U.S., 1924, naturalized, 1926; d. Bartolomeo and Santo Donatello Cimaglia; m. Americao DeVito; children: Richard (dec.), Sandra Ann DeVito King. BA inEdn., Fairmont State Coll., 1960; MA, W.Va. U., 1964; postgrad., Wagner Coll., 1968; D (hon.), Minsitry Fgn. Affairs of Malta. Tchr. East Fairmont (W.Va.) High Sch., 1960-68, Miller Jr. High Sch., Rivesville, W.Va., 1969-70; instr. art Fairview H.S., 1970-86, Barrockville H.S., Farmington H.S. One-woman shows include Lynn Katler Gallery, N.y.C., 1975; exhibited at group shows at Morgantown Art Assn. Exhbn., 1960; commd. work includes paintings on cloth at Immaculate Conception Ch., Fairmont, Fairmont Bowling Ctr., 1988, Disney World. Recipient Internat. Statue of Victory, Einstein Peace Medal, Rhodeodendron Festival award, Honoris Causea, Internat. Found., 1987. Mem. AAUW, NEA, Nat. Art Edn. Assn., Tole Painters Am., W.Va. Art Assn., W.Va. Artist and Craftsman Guild, Artists Equity, League Ind. Artists (past v.p.), Village Garden Club, Cath. Daus. Am. Roman Catholic. Home: 417 Newton St Fairmont WV 26554

DEVITT, PAMELA KRUSE, legislative staff member; b. Washington, May 31, 1964. BA, Wheaton Coll., 1986. Staff asst. Ho. subcom. Edn. and Labor, 1986-87; legis. asst. to Rep. Marge Roukema, 1987-89, legis. asst. to Sen. James Jeffords, 1989-92; minority staff dir. subcom. edn., arts and humanities Senate Labor and Human Resources, 1993—. Office: Subcom on Edn Arts & Humanities 727 Hart Senate Office Bldg Washington DC 20510*

DEVITT-GRASSO, PAULINE VIRGINIA, civic volunteer, nurse; b. Salem, Mass., May 13, 1930; d. John M. and Mary Elizabeth (Cologey) Devitt; m. Frank Anthony Grasso, Oct. 26, 1968; 1 stepson, Christopher Anthony. BSN, Boston Coll., 1952; student, Boston U., 1954-55, Boston State Tchrs. Coll., 1953-54. RN. Staff nurse J.P. Kennedy Jr. Meml. Hosp., Brighton, Mass., 1952-53; head nurse, day supr. J.P. Kennedy Jr. Meml. Hosp., Brighton, 1953-54, day supr., 1955, clin. instr., 1955-58, adminstrv. asst., 1968, dir. nursing edn., 1958-68; vis. instr. Boston Coll., Mass. State Coll., Meml. Hosp. Sch. Nursing, Newton, Mass. Meml. Hosp. Sch. Nursing, 1955-68, CUA S of N, 1990; bd. dirs. Behavioral Health Svcs. Inc. Pres. Project H.O.P.E., Manhattan Beach, Calif., 1982; pres. adv. coun. Meals on Wheels, Salvation Army, 1989, 90, 91, bd. dirs. Redondo Beach, 1992—, sec. bd. dirs., 1994; cons. Manhattan Beach Housing Found., 1986—, Manhattan Beach Case Mgr., 1982—; mem. adv. coun. South Bay Sr. Svcs., Torrance, Calif., 1986—, pres., 1994; sr. advocate City of Manhattan Beach, 1982; bd. dirs. Ret. Sr. Vol. Program, Torrance, 1986-90, Behavioral Health Svcs., 1992—; neighborhood chair Girl Scouts U.S.; mem. Beach City Coun. on Aging, 1983-91; mem. Salvation Army Ladies Aux.; mem. adv. bd. Salvation Army Corps, Redondo Beach. Recipient Cert. of Appreciation, County of L.A., 1988, Vol. of the Yr. award City of Manhattan Beach, 1988, Award of Honor County of L.A., 1989, State of Calif. Senate Rules Com. Resolution Commendation, 1988; named Outstanding Vol. Cath. Daus. of Am., 1986, Vol. of Yr. City Manhattan Beach, 1986-87; Rose and Scroll award Manhattan Beach C. of C., 1989, Art Michel Meml. Community Svc. award Manhattan Beach Rotary Club, 1989, Cert. of Appreciation KC's Queen of Martyers Coun., 1989, Redondo Beach Lila Bell award Salvation Army, 1989, others, Manhattan Beach Vol. Appreciation award, 1982, 83, 84, 85, 86, 88, 90, 91, 92, 93, cert. South Bay Centinela Credit Union, 1990; nominated for Pres's. Vol. Action award Project H.O.P.E., 1987. Mem. AARP, Am. Martyrs Altar Soc. (pres. 1983, coun. mem.-at-large 1992), Cath. U. Am. Nat. Alumni Assn. (hon.), Cath. U. Am. Sch. Nursing Alumni Assn. (hon.), Boston Coll. Alumni Assn., Manhattan Beach Sr. Citizens Club (pres. 1985-86, 88-89), Lions (Citizen of Yr. award Manhattan Beach club 1986), DAV (comdr.'s club 1990, 91, 92), Equestrian Order of Holy Sepulchre of Jerusalem. Democrat. Roman Catholic. Home: 329 3rd St Manhattan Beach CA 90266-6410

DEVIVO, ANGE, former small business owner; b. Bay Shore, N.Y., Oct. 20, 1925; d. Romeo Zanetti and Karolina (Hodapp) King; m. John Michael DeVivo, Dec. 30, 1950; 1 child, Michael. Student, Washington Sch. for Secs., N.Y.C., 1945-46. Sec. Am. Airlines, N.Y.C., 1946-51; exec. sec. W.C. Holzhauer, N.Y.C., 1951-52; dist. sales mgr. Emmons Jewelers, Inc., Bound Brook, N.J., 1952-53; adminstrv. sec. Mercy Hosp., Charlotte, N.C., 1973-81; pres. Secs., Plus, Convs., Plus, Charlotte, 1983-91; prin. Ange DeVivo & Assocs., Inc., Charlotte, 1991-92; assoc. prof. U. Ala., Birmingham. Editor: The North Carolina Republican Woman, 1994, 2nd edit., 1995. Mem. Human Svcs. Coun., Charlotte, 1984-88; mem. Emergency Med. Svc. Adv. Coun., Charlotte, 1981-92, chmn., 1988-90; mem. Charlotte Women's Polit. Caucus, 1972—; pres. Mecklenburg Evening Rep. Women's Club, Charlotte, 1970—, pres., 1973-74, 93-94; mem. citizens adv. com. Conv. and Visitors Bur., 1986-90; coord. Women's Equality Day celebration Mecklenburg County Women's Commn., 1990, 91, coord., 1991, fin. chmn., 1991, 93-94, co-chmn., 1993-94, mem. adv. bd., 1993—, vice chair, 1995. Recipient Order of Long Leaf Pine award Gov. of N.C., 1974, Entrepreneur of Yr. award Women Bus. Owners, 1987; honoree N.C. Fedn. Rep. Women, 1987; nominee for Cmty. Svc. award, 1994. Mem. Women's Roundtable. Roman Catholic.

DEVLIN, JEAN THERESA, educator, storyteller; b. Jamaica, N.Y., Apr. 14, 1947; d. Edward Philip and Frances Margaret (Tillman) Creagh; children: Michael, Bernadette, Patrick. BA magna cum laude, Queens Coll., 1972, postgrad., 1994—; MA, St. John's U., Jamaica, 1987; PhD, So. Ill. U., 1991. Substitute tchr. Diocese of Bklyn., 1969-75; tchr. St. Gregory's Sch., Bellerose, N.Y., 1975-82; dist. mgr. Creative Expressions, Robesonia, Pa., 1980-83; asst. to dean, adj. instr. workshop supr. Spl. Univ. Program St. John's U., Jamaica, 1983-87, asst. prof. dept. English, 1992; asst. dean St. John's Coll. Liberal Arts, St. Johns U., 1993—; owner Tara's Tees and Golden Hands Embroidery, 1984-87; from grad. asst. to doctoral fellow English dept. So. Ill. U., Carbondale, 1987-89, storytelling tchr. Continuing Edn., 1992; adj. asst. prof. St. John's U., Jamaica, 1992--; cons. Family Lit. Project; supr. workshops Popular Culture, 1991—, Children's Lit. Assn., 1990-92, Midwest Popular Culture, 1991, Wyo. Centennial, 1990; presenter poetry readings, dramatic interpretation, storytelling, including Internat. Rsch. Soc. in Children's Lit., Paris, 1991, Nat. Coun. Tchrs. English Conf., 1992, Ill. Assn. Tchrs. of English, 1990, 91, 92, South Atlantic MLA, 1992, Mid Atlantic Popular/Am. Culture, 1993; speaker Speak Easy Workshop, 1981; showcased Nat. Congress Storytelling, Children's Reading Roundtable, 1990; world-wide storyteller, 1991—. Author: Gabby Diego, 1992, repub. 1994; contbr. articles to profl. jours. and children's mags.; actress (videotape and audiocassette) Peter Kagan and the Wind, 1990, 91, played at White House, 1992, Sta. WKTS, 1992-94; performed as storyteller on 5 continents, 1991—. Den leader Boy Scouts Am., Bayside, N.Y., 1975-80; troop leader Girl Scouts U.S.A., Flushing, N.Y., 1976-78; vol. Elderwise Day Care, Carbondale, Ill., 1992, Alice Wright Day Care Ctr., Carbondale, 1989-92, ABC Quilts (A Pediatric AIDS group), 1991—; mem. The Stage Co., Cill Cais Players. Honored for outstanding svc. Boy Scouts Am., 1978; recipient Outstanding Cmty. Svc. award, named Most Admired Woman of the Decade Sta. WPSD-TV, 1991, Internat. Women of Yr., 1993; grantee So. Ill. Art Coun., 1992. Mem. MLA, ALA, ASCD, AAUW, Am. Assn. U. Profs., Nat. Coun. Tchrs. English, Nat. Assn. Preservation and Perpetuation of Storytelling, Ill. Assn. Tchrs. English, Children's Lit. Assn., Coun. Colls. Arts and Scis., Found. for Children's Books, Internat. Platform Assn., Mid-Atlantic Popular Culture Assn., Popular Culture Assn., Am. Humor Assn., Conf. on Coll. Composition and Communication, Ladies Ancient Order Hibernians (chpt . founder, pres. 1984-85), Beatrix Potter Soc., Skull & Circle Honor Soc. (St. John's Univ.), Alpha Sigma Lambda, Sigma Tau Delta, Phi Delta Kappa, others. Home: 14965 45th Ave Flushing NY 11355-1710

DEVOE, MARLENE RUTH, psychology educator; b. Chgo., Dec. 13, 1942; d. John Joseph Persik and Marjorie Lucille (Hoffman) Glazier; m. James Peter DeVoe, Mar. 3, 1962 (div. 1985); children: Deborah Marie, Kathie Lynn. BS in Psychology and Health Scis., Grand Valley State U., 1982; MA in Psychology, Wayne State U., 1988, PhD in Psychology, 1990. Grad. rsch. asst. Lafayette Clinic, Detroit, 1983-84, Wayne State U., Detroit, 1985-89; rsch. scientist Phila. Geriatric Ctr., 1989-92; asst. prof. St. Cloud State (Minn.) U., 1992—; adj. asst. prof. Drexel U., Phila., 1990-92; instr. C.C. of Phila., 1990-92, Temple U., Phila., 1991, Ea. Mich. U., Ypsilanti, 1989, Mercy Coll., Detroit, 1986-89; ad hoc reviewer Psychology and Aging, 1990-91. Author: (with others) Annual Review of Gerontology and Geriatrics, 1991; contbr. articles to profl. jours. Dir. Q-7 New Venture Grant, State Univ. System of Minn., 1993—. Fellow NIMH, 1987-88, 90-92, Wayne State U., 1984-85; grantee Alzheimer's Assn., 1992-94. Mem. APA, Gerontol. Soc. Am., Women's Internat. League for Peace and Freedom, Phi Kappa Phi. Office: St Cloud State U Dept Psychology Waite Ave S # 102 Saint Cloud MN 56301-7302

DE VONTINE, JULIE ELISABETH (THE MARCHIONESS DE ROE DEVON), systems analyst, consultant; b. Edmund, Wis., Jan. 7, 1934; d. Clyde Elroy and Matilda Evangeline Knapp; m. Roe (Don Davis) Devon Gerringer-Busenbark, Sept. 30, 1968 (dec. Dec. 1972); student Madison Bus. Coll., 1952, San Francisco State Coll., 1953-54, Vivian Rich Sch. Fashion Design, 1955, Dale Carnegie Sch., 1956, Arthur Murray Dance Studio, 1956, Biscayne Acad. Music, 1957, L.A. City Coll., 1960-62, Santa Monica (Calif.) Jr. Coll., 1963; JD U. Calif., San Francisco, 1973; postgrad. Wharton Sch., U. Pa., 1977, London Art Coll., 1979; Ph.D., 1979; attended Goethe Inst., 1985. Bar: Calif., 1965. Actress, Actors Workshop San Francisco, 1959, 65, Theatre of Arts Beverly Hills (Calif.), 1963, also radio; cons, and systems analyst for banks and pub. accounting agys.; artist, poet, singer, songwriter, playwright, dress designer. Pres., tchr. Environ Improvement, Originals by Elizabeth; atty. Dometrik's, JIT-MAP, San Francisco, 1973—; steering com. explorations in worship, ordained min. 1978. Author: The Cardinal, 1947, Explorations in Worship, 1965, The Magic of Scents, 1967, New Highways, 1967, The Grace of Romance, 1968, Happening - Impact-Mald, 1971, Seven Day Rainbow, 1972, Zachary's Adversaries, 1974, Fifteen from Wisconsin, 1977, Bart's White Elephant, 1978, Skid Row Minister, 1978, Points in Time, 1979, Special Appointment-A Clown in Town, 1979, Happenings, 1980, Candles, 1980, Votes from the Closet, 1984, Wait for Me, 1984, The Stairway, 1984, The River is a Rock, 1985, Happenings Revisited, 1986, Comparative Religion in the United States, 1986, Lumber in the Skies, 1986, The Fifth Season, 1987, Summer Thoughts, 1987, Crimes of the Heart, 1987, Toast Thoughts, 1988, The Contrast of Russian Literature Through the Eyes of Russian Authors, 1988, A Thousand Points of Light, 1989, The Face in the Mirror, 1989, Voices on the Hill, 1991, It's Tough to Get a Matched Set, 1991, Equality, 1991, Miss Geranium Speaks, 1991, Forest Voices, 1991, Golden Threads, 1991, Castles in the Air, 1991, The Cave, 1991, Angels, 1991, Real, 1991, An Appeal to Reason, 1992, We Knew, 1992, Like It Is, 1992, Politicians Anonymous, 1993, Wheels Within Wheels, 1994. Mem. Assn. of Trial Lawyers of Am. Address: 1500 W El Camino Ave # 382 Sacramento CA 95833-1921

DEVORE, JUDITH T., executive recruiter; b. Detroit, Sept. 13, 1959; d. Thomas E. and Lillian A. (Appenzeller) DeV. BGS, Oakland U., Rochester, Mich., 1988. Sr. human resources rep. CIS Corp., Bloomfield Hills, Mich.; personnel staff asst. Campbell-Ewald Co., Advt., Warren, Mich.; recruiting specialist Kelly Assisted Living, Troy, Mich. Mem. NAFE, Soc. Human Resource Mgmt. Home: 12342 Canterbury Dr Warren MI 48093-1842

DEVORE, KIMBERLY K., sales executive; b. Louisville., June 19, 1947; d. Wendell O. and Shirley F. DeV.; student, Xavier U., 1972-76; AA, Coll. Mt. St. Joseph, 1979. Patient registration supr. St. Francis Hosp., Cin., 1974-76; cons., bus. mgr. Family Health Care Found., Cin., 1976-77; exec. dir. Hospice of Cin., Inc., 1977-80; pres. Micro Med, 1979-86; v.p. Sycamore Profl. Assn., 1979-86; ptnr. Enchanted House, 1979-86, sec., 1979-80, treas. 1980-83; dist. sales rep. Control-O-Fax, 1986, br. sales mgr., 1987, nat. dealer devel. rep., 1987—, computer specialist, 1987, nat. computer field sales trainer, 1987-90; pres. U.S. Exec. Leasing and U.S. Med. Leasing, Inc., 1991—, Accu Svcs., Inc., 1993—, U.S. Med. Mgmt., Inc., 1994—; pres. Saddle Creek Homeowners Assn., Inc., 1992-94, Roswell Citizen's Police Acad., Inc., 1994—; mem. North Fulton Civic League, Inc., 1993—; bd. dirs. Nat. Hospice Orgn., 1979-82, chmn. long-term planning com., fin. com., ann. meeting com., 1979-82, sec., 1980-81. treas., 1981-82; bd. dirs. Hospice of Miami Valley, Inc., 1982-86, also chmn. pers. com., by-laws com. Mem. Greater Cin. Soc. Fund Raisers, Better Housing League; Mem. service and rehab. com. Hamilton County Unit, Am. Cancer Soc., 1977-78; chair road com. Saddle Creek Homeowners Assn., 1991-92. Mem. Ohio Hospice Assn. (co-founder, state chmn., pres., 1978-83), Nat. League for Nursing, Ohio Hosp. Assn., Nat. Fedn. Bus. and Profl. Women's Clubs, Ohio Fedn. Bus. and Profl. Women's Clubs, Cin. Bus. and Profl. Women's Clubs (pres. 1973-75).

DE VRIES, JUDITH, computer scientist; b. Jackson Heights, N.Y., Mar. 25, 1943; d. James Leroy and Adelaide Louise (Paddenburg) Harvey; m. Chris Gregory de Vries, 1972 (div.); 1 child, Matthew Thomas. BA in Math., Marymount Manhattan Coll., 1965; MA in Math., Hunter Coll., 1970. Cert. info. systems auditor, cert. internal auditor. Programmer/analyst Shell Oil Co., N.Y.C., 1966-70; systems analyst Fed. Res. Bank of N.Y., N.Y.C., 1970-75, tech. dir./specialist, 1975-77; sr. EDP auditor Chubb & Son, Inc., Short Hills, N.J., 1977-81, project mgr., 1981-83; dir.systems devel. Ideal Mut. Ins. Co., N.Y.C., 1983-84; mem. adv. staff Computer Scis. Corp., Piscataway, N.J., 1984-86; dir. MIS auditing NBC, N.Y.C., 1986-88; mem. tech. staff Bellcore, Piscataway, 1988—. Editor Women's Info. Network Newsletter, 1992-95; editor, prodn. mgr. Women's History Calendar, 1992—. Vol. Telephone Pioneers Am., Piscataway, 1988—, Community Foodbank of N.J., Hillside, 1992—. NSF grad. trainee in math. CUNY, 1965-66. Office: Bellcore 3 Corporate Pl Piscataway NJ 08854

DE VRIES, MARGARET GARRITSEN, economist; b. Detroit, Feb. 11, 1922; d. John Edward and Margaret Florence (Ruggles) Garritsen; m. Barend A. de Vries, Apr. 5, 1952; children: Christine, Barton. B.A. in Econs. with honors, U. Mich., 1943; Ph.D. in Econs., MIT, 1946. With IMF, Washington, 1946-87, sr. economist, 1949-52, asst. chief multiple currency pratices div., 1953-57, chief Far Eastern Div., 1957-59, econ. cons., 1963-73, historian, 1973-87; professorial lectr. econs. George Washington U., 1946-49, 58-63. Author: The International Monetary Fund, 1966-71, The System Under Stress, 2 vols., 1977, The International Monetary Fund, 1972-78, Cooperation on Trial, 3 vols., 1985, The IMF in a Changing World, 1945-85, transl. into Chinese, 1986, Balance of Payments, Adjustment: The IMF Experience, 1945-86, transl. into Chinese, 1989, (with I.S. Friedman) Foreign Economic Policy of the United States in the Postwar, 1947, (with J.K. Horsefield) The International Monetary Fund, 1945-65, Twenty Years of International Monetary Cooperation, 3 vols., 1969; contbr. articles to profl. jours. Recipient Disting. Alumni award U. Mich., 1980, Cert. of Appreciation George Washington U., 1987, Outstanding Washington Woman Economist award, 1987; AAUW scholar, 1939-42; U. Mich. Univ. scholar, 1942; MIT fellow, 1943-46; Ford Found. grantee, 1959-62. Mem. Am. Econ. Assn., U. Mich. Alumni Assn., MIT Alumnae Assn., Phi Beta Kappa, Phi Kappa Phi. Mem. United Church of Christ. Home: 10018 Woodhill Rd Bethesda MD 20817-1218

DE VRIES, ROBBIE RAY PARSONS, author, illustrator, international consultant; b. Idabel, Okla., Sept. 11, 1929; d. General Forrest Sr. and Jessie Demma (Burch-Oldham) Parsons; m. Douwe de Vries, Apr. 2, 1953; children: Jessica Joan de Vries Kij, Peter Douwe. BS in Bus. Adminstrn. and Journalism, Okla. State U., 1952; postgrad., U. Houston, 1987, 88, Rice U., 1988, 89. Sec. to mgr. drafting and survey Shell Oil Co., Houston, 1952-53; sub. tchr. Spring Br. Ind. Sch. Dist., Houston, 1989-92; pres., owner Robbie P. de Vries Interests, Houston, 1983—, author, illustrator, pub., 1989—; mem. governing bd. Oilfield Systems, Inc., Houston, 1981—; bd. dirs. Friends of Okla. State U. Libr., Stillwater; mem. Friends of U. Houston Libr., 1981—; bd. dirs., cons. Ctr. for Internat. Trade, Okla. State U., Stillwater, 1990—; invited guest Peoples Republic of China/U.S. State Dept., China, 1992. Columnist Conroe, Tex. Daily Courier, 1988-89; editor Idabel Warrior newspaper (Gold medal), 1947, Houston Symphony League newspaper, 1974-75; author, illustrator, pub.: A Cultural Exchange: American and Chinese Weddings, 1993. Vol cultural and internat. areas, New Orleans, 1960-69, Houston, 1969—; bd. dirs. New Orleans C. of C., 1964-69; bd. dirs. Houston Symphony Soc. and League, 1972—, Inst. Internat. Edn., Houston, 1969—; home host internat. youth exch./The Netherlands, 1978; grand jury mem. Harris County Tex., 1986-87; patron Jr. League, Houston, 1970—; docent Mus. Fine Arts, Houston, 1974—; mem., yearbook cover designer Tuesday Music Club, Houston, 1975—; mem. Forum Club Houston, 1980—; co-chmn. Houston-Baku, Azerbaijan, USSR Sister City, 1979-89; bd. dirs. Boy Scouts, Houston, 1985—; bd. dirs., chair Internat. Conf. YWCA, Houston, 1986-87; mem. magic cir. Rep. Women of Houston, 1989—; mem. donor Baylor Med. Sch. Devel., 1990—. Recipient Ann. Fund Silver Tray award Houston Symphony League, 1972, Miss Ima Hogg Orchid award Houston Symphony Soc., 1975, Gen. Maurice Hirsch Leaf and Letter award Symphony Soc., 1980, 81, 82, Tex. Mother of Yr., Alpha Delta Pi, 1982, Mayor's award Baku, Azerbaijan USSR, 1979, 83, 87, 89, U.S. State Dept. pin, 1986, 10-Yr. Leadership award Mayor of Baku, 1988, U. Houston Ball Merit/Honor, 1991, Merit award Boy Scouts of Am., 1993, 10-Yr. Svc. award, 1995; named Acting First Lady of Houston for goodwill trip to Baku, Azerbaijan, USSR, by Mayor of Houston Jim McConn, 1979, Hon. Dep. Sheriff, Harris County Sheriff Johnny Klevenhagen, 1986, feature Honor Villages mag., 1994. Mem. AAUW (past pres.), Tex. Fine Arts Assn., Inspirational Writers, Houston Coun. Writers, Nat. Women's Hall of Fame, Étoffe Littéraire (founder, Founder's award 1985), Tex.-Netherlands Bus. Assn., Mu Kappa Tau. Republican. Presbyterian. Avocations: classical music, international entertaining, travel, interior decorating, reading. Home and Office: Robbie P de Vries Interests 802 Piney Point Rd Houston TX 77024-2725

DEWALL, KAREN MARIE, marketing consultant; b. Phoenix, May 31, 1943; d. Merle C. and Agnes M. (Larson) Feller; m. Charles E. DeWall, Sept. 3, 1963 (div. Feb. 1988); 1 child, Leslie Karen. A.A., Phoenix Coll., 1969. Media buyer Wade Advt., Sacramento, 1964-66; media dir., Harwood Advt., Phoenix, 1967-71; co-owner, account exec. DeWall & Assocs. Advt. Co., 1971-87; dir. advt. Auto Media, Inc./Automotive Investment Group, Phoenix, 1987-93; owner Karen & Co. Advt., Phoenix, 1993—. Bd. dirs. Bosom Buddies-Breast Cancer Orgn., Sunday on Ctrl. Festivals; sustaining mem. Jr. League of Phoenix; mem. Heritage Sq. Commn., City of Phoenix. Named Ad-2 Advt. Person of Yr., Phoenix, 1984. Mem. Am. Women in Radio and TV (achievement award 1986), Phoenix Union Alumni Assn. Republican. Club: Phoenix Country. Home: 10847 N 11th St Phoenix AZ 85020-5836 Office: Karen & Co Advt 10847 N 11th St Phoenix AZ 85020-5836

DE WAN-CARLSON, ANNA THERESA, artist; b. Syracuse, N.Y., Dec. 29, 1949; d. William Martin and Sarah Theresa (Kirchhof) De Wan; m. David G. Carlson, Aug. 8, 1971 (div. 1981); 1 child, Adam Edward. Student, Syracuse U., 1967, 68, 87; AAS in Design and Illustration,

Art Inst. Pitts., 1971. Dir. 12rms-4 Gallery, Syracuse, N.Y., 1992-94; artistic dir. N.Y.C. Art Open, 1995—. Selected exhibits include The Space Group of Korea 6th Internat. Miniature Print Biennial, Seoul, Arts Ctr. of the Grand Prairie 5th Nat. Miniature Annual Art Exhibit, Stuttgart, Ark., Cooperstown Nat. Juried Art Exhibit, Cooperstown, N.Y., Munson-Williams-Proctor Inst. Artists of Cen. N.y. Annual Juried Exhibit, Utica, N.Y., San Bernadino County Mus., Redlands, Calif., Chapman Art Ctr. Gallery, Arena Internat. Art Exhibit, Binghamton, Print Club Albany, Print Club Rochester, Womanart Gallery, N.Y.C., Keane Mason Gallery, St. David's Invitational Celebration of Arts, Dewitt, N.Y., Sussex House Gallery, London, Cayuga C.C., Auburn, N.Y., Wilson Art Gallery, LeMoyne Coll., Syracuse, N.Y., Everson Mus. Art, Syracuse, Payne Hall, Mohawk Valley C.C., Utica, N.Y., Art Assn. Harrisburg (Pa.), Fingerlakes Exhbn. Meml. Art Gallery U. Rochester (N.Y.), Art Assn. Harrisburg, Pa., Pyramid Arts Ctr., Rochester, 12rms-4 Gallery, others; represented in collections Print Club of Albany, Onondaga Savs. Bank, Carrier Corp., Syracuse Savs. Bank, Dey Bros., Maria Regina Coll., Onondaga Hist. Assn., others. Fundraiser March of Dimes, Jordan, N.Y., 1978-79; gallery fundraiser Everson Mus., S.W. Community Ctr., Vera House, Hospice Ctrl. N.Y., Onondaga County Pub. Libr., 1992—. Recipient 1st Prize Graphics award Allentown Festival Arts, Syracuse Arts and Crafts Festival, 2nd Prize award Art Ctr. of Grand Prairie, 2nd and 3rd prizes Syracuse Printmakers Ann. Mems. Exhibit, Merit award Ctrl. N.Y. Art Open Juried Exhibit, Best Shot Feature award Popular Photography mag., Best Graphics award Keane Mason Gallery. Mem. Print Club of Albany, Print Club Rochester, Print Club Phila., Everson Mus., Syracuse (N.Y.) Printmakers (pres. 1981, bd. dirs., collection curator, exhibits curator, publicist 1989-91). Home: 145 Avon Rd Syracuse NY 13206-3036

DEWBERRY, BETTY BAUMAN, retired law librarian; b. Dallas, Jan. 18, 1930; d. William Allen Bauman and Julia Ella (Owen) Hurt; m. James A. Dewberry Jr., Mar. 22, 1952 (div. Apr. 1976); children: Mary Julienne, Jennifer Camille, Robert Bruce. BA, U. Tex., 1951; MLS, Tex. Women's U., 1982. Asst. librarian Johnson & Swanson, Dallas, 1979-85; dir. librs. Johnson & Gibbs, Dallas, 1985-94; retired, 1994. Mem. Am. Assn. Law Libraries, Dallas Assn. Law Librarians, Women's Nat. Book Assn., Lakeside Browning Club, Zeta Tau Alpha. Democrat. Methodist.

DEWBERRY, JUDY ANN, administrative supervisor; b. Landstuhl, Germany, Sept. 2, 1958; came to the U.S., 1959; d. Roy Lee and Dorothy Elizabeth (Barnes) Turner; m. Curtis Dale Dewberry, July 28, 1978; 1 child Amy Renee. BS in Mgmt., U. West Fla., 1984. Cert. compensation profl. Sec. Gulf Power Co., Pensacola, Fla., 1981-84, compensation analyst, 1984-89; compensation analyst So. Nuclear Ops. Co., Birmingham, Ala., 1989-91, EEO analyst, 1991-92, tng. coord., 1993, sr. human resources analyst, 1994, adminstrv. supr., 1994—. Mem. Nat. Mgmt. Assn. Office: So Nuclear Operating Co JM Farley Nuclear Plant Po Drawer 470 Ashford AL 36312

DEWEY, ANNE ELIZABETH MARIE, lawyer; b. Balt., Mar. 16, 1951; d. George Daniel and Elizabeth Patricia (Mohan) D.; children: Brendan M., Andrew P., Meghan E. BA, Mich. State U., 1972; JD, U. Chgo., 1975; grad., Stonier Grad. Sch. Banking, East Brunswick, N.J., 1983. Bar: D.C. 1976. Legal clk. and atty. FTC, Washington, 1975-78; atty. enforcement div. Comptr. of Currency, Washington, 1978-81, sr. atty. office legis. counsel, 1981-83; sr. atty. dist. office Comptr. of Currency, Dallas, 1983-86; sr. atty. legal adv. services div. Comptr. of Currency, Washington, 1986; assoc. gen. counsel corp. and adminstrv. law Farm Credit Adminstrn., Mc Lean, Va., 1986-87, gen. counsel, 1987-91; spl. counsel Farm Credit Adminstrn., McLean, Va., 1991-92; FDIC counsel, closed bank litigation and policy sect., 1993-94; gen. counsel Office of Fed. Housing Enterprise Oversight, HUD, 1994—. Mem. ABA (bus. law sect., mem. banking law com.), Fed. Bar Assn. (bd. dirs. D.C. chpt. 1988-91), D.C. Bar Assn., Women in Housing and Fin. (bd. dirs. 1982-83, gen. counsel 1991-93), Women's Bar Assn. Roman Catholic. Home: 833 Fontaine St Alexandria VA 22302-3610

DEWITT, EULA, accountant; b. Conway, S.C., Feb. 5, 1948; d. Joseph and Ethel Maude (Parmley) D.; m. John Ramos; children: Andre Carter, John Ramos III, David Carter. BS in Acctg., CUNY, 1981; cert., Bethlehem Missionary Bible Inst., 1990. Jr. acct. Kenneth Laventhol, CPA Firm, N.Y., 1981; agent IRS, N.Y., 1981—, staff pub. speakers bur., 1985—, instr. for revenue agents, 1986—. Author newsletter; contbr. numerous articles to profl. jours. tutor York Coll. CUNY, Jamaica, 1991-94; guest speaker Hunter Coll. 6th Annual Conv., N.Y., 1991, Exploring Divsn. Greater N.Y., 1991, Catholic Charities Archdioces, N.Y., 1991. Mem. Inst. Mgmt. Accts. (mem. bd. dirs. 1982—, v.p. profl. edn. 1994-95), Bethlehem Missionary Ch. (sunday sch. tchr. 1979-94), Toastmaster's 21 Club (v.p., past pres.). Office: IRS 110 W 44 St New York NY 10163

DEWITT, JANE CLAIRE, health facility administrator; b. Champaign, Ill., Sept. 3, 1965; d. Walter G. and Carol Lee (Hulett) DeW. BA, Lafayette Coll., 1987; MBA, U. Ill., 1991. Sales rep. Am. Frozen Foods, Stratford, Conn., 1987-89; gen. mgr. ops. Amigaz, Inc., Warminster, Pa., 1991-93; adminstr. Cat Hosp. Phila., 1994—. Mem. NOW.

DE WITT, JANICE M., lawyer; b. Madison, Wis.. BS in Acctg., Edgewood Coll., 1984; JD, Marquette U., 1987. Office: 139 S Sixth St West Bend WI 53095

DEWITT, KAREN LEE (KELLY DEWITT), computer information consultant; b. San Francisco, Apr. 13, 1963; d. Martin Johann and Dixie Lee (Mayhak) Whitted; m. Abel M.V. Garcia, Dec. 1, 1984 (div. Aug. 1986); m. Robert Martin DeWitt, Jan. 1, 1990. Student, Mills Coll., Oakland, Calif., 1981-82. Mgr. Video Outlet, Pitts., 1983-84; asst. mgr. ECX Computers, Walnut Creek, Calif., 1984-90; accounts payable mgr. Byte & Floppy Computers, San Diego, 1990—; owner MicroByte, Concord, Calif., 1988-90, Pvt. Res. Products (now Berkshire Publishing), Lakeside, Calif., 1990—; cons. Svcs. Aiding Ind. Living, Concord, 1985-90, U.S. Submarine Vets. of W.W. II, Vallejo, Calif., 1985-90. Sponsor Save the Children, Mali, Africa, World Wildlife Fund, 1988, 91, Planned Parenthood, San Diego Zoo Soc. Mem. NAFE, Humane Soc. of U.S., Am. Inst. Profl. Bookkeepers.

DEWITT, KATHERINE LOUISE, bank executive; b. Cleve., Mar. 25, 1948; d. DeMarquis Dale and Leonora Louise Wyatt; 1 child, Christina. V.p. Govt. Services S.L., Bethesda, Md., 1969-80, Md. Nat. Bank, Balt., 1980-86; chief exec. officer, pres. Republic Fed. Savs. Bank, Rockville, Md., 1987-88; pres., chief exec. officer Concord Savs. Bank, FSB, 1988-89; pres. Dewitt & Assocs., 1989-91; asst. dir. Resolution Trust Corp., 1991-92; bus. devel. mgr. Herndon, Va., 1992—; bd. dirs. exec. com. Nat. Savs. Loan League, Washington, 1974-80; chmn. standing com. Md. Savs. Loan League, Balt., 1972-79. Trustee Newport Schs. Wheaton, Md., 1984-89; bd. dirs. Bethesda Chevy Chase C. of C., 1976-80; commr., v.p., pres., Montgomery County Commn. Women, Rockville, 1976-79; mem. steering com. womens' council Dem. Nat. Com., Washington, 1976-82. Mem. Women in Housing and Fin., Network, Nat. Assn. Bank Women, Women Advt. and Mtkg. Assn., Nat. Forum Exec. Women (chmn. bd. dirs. 1974-80). Democrat. Unitarian.

DE WITT, MARY CAROL PARISE, financial consultant; b. Syracuse, May 8, 1961; m. Bruce J. De Witt, Oct. 21, 1983; 1 child, Michelle E. BA, U. Rochester, 1983. Dir. info. systems & security commdr. oceanographic sytems U.S. Navy, Norfolk, Va., 1986-89; test dir. joint tactical command, control, comm. agy. U.S. Navy, Ft. Monmouth, N.J., 1989-90; facilites mgr. Naval Air Tech. Tng. Ctr. U.S. Navy, Lakehurst, N.J., 1990-91; fin. cons. Merrill Lynch, Wall, N.J., 1991—. Brownies co-leader Girl Scouts USA, Monmouth County, N.J., 1993-94; fundraiser Leukemia Soc., Rochester, 1980, March of Dimes, Monmouth County, 1993; bd. dirs. Monmouth-Ocean Devel. Coun., 1992—; sec., trustee Edn. Found., 1993—. Recipient joint svc. achievement medal Def. Info. Systems Agy., Washington, 1991, nat. def. svc. medal Sec. Def., Washington, 1991. Mem. Navy League of U.S., Data Processing Mgmt. Assn. Home: 1906 S Wanamassa Dr Ocean NJ 07712-4618

DEWITT, MARY THERESE, private investigator; b. Chgo., Aug. 25, 1948; d. Robert Baldwin and Helen (Rossman) DeW.; m. Geoffrey M. Tait, Aug. 1, 1988. AA, Coll. of DuPage, 1968; BA in Edn., U. Wis., Whitewater, 1969; postgrad., U. North Tex., 1992-93, U. Tex., Arlington, 1993—. With customer relations dept. John M. Smyth Furniture, Oak Brook, Ill., 1968-71, Wiggs Furniture, Bloomfield Hills, Mich., 1971; dir. pub. relations Hotel de las Hadas, Manzanillo, Mex., 1972; dir. promotion Ramco-Gershenson, Southfield, Mich., 1973-75; dir. mktg. Homart Devel. Co., Florence, Ky., 1975-76, Melvin Simon & Assocs., Inc., Hurst, Tex., 1976-79; pres. Mary DeWitt Co., Ft. Worth, 1979-85; v.p. mktg. Southmark Comml. Mgmt., Dallas, 1986-87; prin. DeWitt Group and subs. Cat's-Eye Intelligence Svc., Dallas and Ft. Worth, 1988—; cons. logistics and documentation one team Internat. Group for Hist. Aircraft Recovery, The Phoenix Group South Pacific, 1989. Founder, co-dir. Svc. to Elist Resident Vols. in Euless, Tarrant County, Tex., 1989-91. Recipient award of excellence Jones Report, 1978. Mem. Internat. Council Shopping Ctrs., Pub. Relations Soc. Am. Episcopalian. Home: 1905 Cripple Creek Dr Euless TX 76039-2204

DE WITT-MORETTE, CÉCILE, physicist; b. Paris, Dec. 21, 1922; came to U.S., 1948; d. André and Marie Louise (Ravaudet) Morette; m. Bryce S. DeWitt, Apr. 26, 1951; children—Nicolette, Jan, Chris, Abigail. B.S., U. Caen, 1943; Ph.D., U. Paris, 1947. With Centre Nat. de la Recherche Sci., 1944-65, Maitre de Confs. prof., 1965-88; mem. Inst. Advanced Studies in Dublin, 1946-47, Copenhagen, 1947-48, Princeton, 1948-50; lectr. U. Calif. at Berkeley, 1952-55, U. N.C., Chapel Hill, 1956-71; prof. U. Tex., 1972-93, Jane and Roland Blumberg Centennial prof. physics, 1993—; founder, dir. Ecole d'ete de Physique Theorique, Les Houches, France, 1951-72. Author: Particules Elementaires, 1951, (with Y. Choquet-Bruhat and M. Dillard-Bleick) Analysis, Manifolds and Physics, 1977, rev. edit., 1982, (with A. Maheshwari, B. Nelson) Path Integration in Non Relativistic Quantum Mechanics, 1979, (with Y. Choquet Bruhat) Analysis, Manifolds and Physics, Part II, 92 Applications, 1989, also articles. Decorated chevalier Ordre Nat. du Mérite, chevalier Ordre des Palmes Académiques; Rask-Oersted fellow, 1947-48, Prix des Sciences Physiques et Mathematiques (Comite du Rayonnement Français, 1992). Fellow Am. Phys. Soc.; mem. Internat. Astron. Union, European Phys. Soc. Home: 2411 Vista Ln Austin TX 78703-2343 Office: U Tex Dept Physics Austin TX 78712

DEWITT-ROGERS, JOHARI MARILYN, community college administrator; b. Montgomery, Ala., Jan. 28, 1950; d. Rufus Birchard and Mary Lease (Borders) DeWitt; m. Paul Sabu Rogers, Dec. 21, 1976; children: Malachi Omari, Kofi Ayinde. BS, Howard U., Washington, 1971, MEd, 1973; postgrad., U. So. Calif., 1980-83. Abstractor APA, Washington, 1971-72; media technician San Diego Unified Schs., 1974-75; media coord. L.A. Regional Family Planning, 1975-79; asst. producer KABC TV News, 1979-80; dir. audio visual svcs. U. So. Calif. Dental Sch., 1979-81; dir. media Pasadena (Calif.) City Coll., 1987—; cons. City of Pasadena, 1991-92. Author: (play) All That Glitters, 1989. Sec. Linda Vista PTA, 1991, v.p., 1992; pres. Sch. Site Coun., 1992, 93, 94. Recipient Paragon award Nat. Coun. Mktg. and Pub. Rels., New Orleans, 1990, Pro award Calif. Assn. C.C., 1990. Mem. Am. Assn. Women in Colls. and Jr. Colls. (chpt. pres. 1992-93), Assn. Calif. Community Coll. Adminstrs. (mentor program 1992), Dirs. Ednl. Tech. in Calif. Higher Edn., Delta Sigma Theta. African Methodist Episcopal. Office: Pasadena City Coll 1570 E Colorado Blvd Pasadena CA 91106-2041

DE WREEDE, CLARICE EVANS, retired special education educator; b. East St. Louis, Ill., July 12, 1928; d. Cecil Field and Clara Helen (Kindsvater) Evans; m. Harry Richard Schoen, June 21, 1947 (div. 1964); children: Richard Evans, Sara Diane, William Francis; m. John De Wreede, Mar. 29, 1967 (dec. 1986). BA cum laude, Mich. State U., 1964; postgrad., U. Mich., 1966-67, Santa Clara U., 1973. Tchr. Grand Rapids (Mich.) Sch. Dist., 1963-67; tchr. counselor for physically handicapped Kent County Edn. Dist., Grand Rapids, 1967-71; tchr. of deaf Union Sch. Dist., San Jose, Calif., 1971-88; home-tchr. of deaf East Side Union High Sch. Dist., San Jose, 1991. Mem. DAR (John Mitchell chpt. Anchorage), Daus. of Am. Colonists (Ala. chpt.), Am. Hist. Soc. of Germans from Russia (Golden Gate chpt. sec. 1990—), Calif. Assn for Tchrs. of Hearing-Impaired, Internat. Assn. Cancer Victors and Friends (nat. bd. govs. 1990—), South Bay Scottish Soc. Genealogy (chmn. 1991—), Santa Clara County Hist. and Geneal. Soc. (cons. in libr. genealogy room, chmn. family newsletter 1980—), Daus. of 1812 (David Farragut chpt. Santa Clara County, Calif.). Democrat. Lutheran. Home: 1336 Star Bush Ln San Jose CA 95118-3543

DEXHEIMER, KATHRYN ELAINE, adult day care and health promotion executive; b. Independence, Mo., July 30, 1948; d. Elmer Earl and Mary Louise (Pratt) Fye; m. Gregory R. Dexheimer, Mar. 2, 1970; 1 child, Deborah Diane. Diploma, Independence Sanitarium and, Hosp. Sch. Nursing, 1970; BSN, Graceland Coll., 1987; MSN, U. Mo., Kansas City, 1989. RN, Mo., Kans.; cert. BLS. Staff nurse VA Med. Ctr., Kansas City, Mo., 1970-72, St. Luke's Hosp., Kansas City, 1975-77; instr. Kansas City (Mo.) Bd. Edn., 1977-78, Independence (Mo.) Bd. Edn., 1978-82; nurse coord. adult day care Independence (Mo.) Sanitarium and Hosp., 1982-84; rsch. cons. ANA, Kansas City, 1989; adj. faculty Webster Univ., Kansas City, 1990; nursing instr. Avila Coll., Kansas City, 1990-94; health promotion mgr. Clinicare, Kansas City, 1994—; adj. faculty Avila Coll., 1994—. Mem. Mo. Nurses' Assn., Midwest Nursing Rsch. Soc., RLDS Profl. Nurses' Assn., Sigma Theta Tau (Beta Lambda chpt. community counselor 1992, Lambda Phi chpt. sec. 1992), Phi Kappa Phi. Office: Wellness/Assisted Living Svcs of Health Midwest 3908 Washington Kansas City MO 64111

DEXHEIMER, MARION LOUISE (MARION LOUISE HINES), retired educator; b. Chgo., Dec. 31, 1920; d. Herbert Waldo and Helen (Gartside) Hines; m. Fred J. Dexheimer, Sept. 28, 1947; children: Gary Frederick, Helen Louise, William Henry. BS in Spanish, U. Ill., 1943; BS in Comml. Sci., Boston U., 1947; MS in Teaching, U. Wis., Whitewater, 1975. Sec. Fed. Civil Svc. AFB, Orlando, Fla., 1948, USDA, Madison, Wis., 1949; tchr. Spanish jr. and sr. high sch. Jefferson, Wis., 1963-65; tchr. Spanish and typing sr. high sch. Ft. Atkinson, Wis., 1965-80; ret., 1980. Treas. Women's Fellowship Congl. Ch., 1990—; mem. bd. trustees, bd. deaconesses Union Congl. Ch., Tavares, Fla.; participant hosp. aux. Waterman Med. Ctr. Lt. (j.g.) USNR, 1944-46. Mem. AAUW (past treas. Ft. Akinson br., past membership v.p., past v.p. programs, past treas. Lake County br., spl. recognition award 1989), Lake Country Waves (publicity chmn. 1989—), Lake Frances Estates Residents Assn. (bd. dirs., activities dir. 1986—). Home: 1437 Apache Cir Tavares FL 32778-2519

DEXTER, DEIRDRE O'NEIL ELIZABETH, lawyer; b. Stillwater, Okla., Apr. 15, 1956; d. Robert N. and Paula E. (Robinson) Maddox; m. Terry E. Dexter, May 14, 1977; children: Daniel M. II, David Maddox. Student, Okla. State U., 1974-77; BS cum laude, Phillips U., 1981; JD with highest honors, U. Okla., 1984. Bar: Okla., U.S. Dist. Ct. (no. and ea. dists.) Okla. 1985, U.S. Dist. Ct. (we. dist.) Okla. 1987, U.S. Ct. Appeals (10th cir.) 1987; grad. Nat. Inst. Trial Advocacy Advanced Trial seminar, 1990. Jud. intern Supreme Ct. Okla., Oklahoma City, summer 1983; assoc. Conner & Winters, Tulsa, 1984-90, ptnr., 1991, shareholder, 1991—. Article editor Okla. U. Law Rev., 1982-84. U. Okla. scholar, 1983. Mem. ABA, Okla. Bar Assn. (advising atty. state champion H.S. mock trial team competition 1992), Tulsa County Bar Assn., Order of Barristers, Order of Coif, Am. Inns of Ct. (barrister Robert D. Hudson chpt. 1990-93), Delta Theta Phi. Republican. Episcopalian. Office: Conner & Winters 2400 First National Tower 15 E 5th St Tulsa OK 74103

DEXTER, SHEILA SHERIE, paralegal; b. Orlando, Fla., Sept. 17, 1962; d. James William and Dahna Lou (Dexter) Taylor; m. Robert Williams Dexter, Oct. 18, 1980. AS with honors, Daytona Beach (Fla.) C.C., 1985; postgrad., U. N.C., 1992—. Cert. legal asst. Legal sec. Stanley J. Solomon, P.A., Daytona Beach, Fla., 1980-85; paralegal Bronstetter & Winesett, P.A., Ft. Myers, Fla., 1985-87, Perry, Patrick, Farmer & Michaux, P.A., Charlotte, N.C., 1989—. Mem. Nat. Assn. Legal Assts., Metrolina Paralegal Assn. Democrat. Office: Perry Patrick Farmer & Michaux PA 227 W Trade St # 2200 Charlotte NC 28202

DEYOUNG, BILLIE SCHAEFER, medical clinic administrator; b. Shreveport, La., Dec. 3, 1936; d. William Henry and Catherine (Russell) Schaefer; widowed; children: Dennis Ray, Denette DeYoung Johnson. Student, La. State U., Shreveport, 1972. Cert. adminstrv. med. asst. Career registry sec. La. State U. Med. Ctr., Shreveport, 1956-60; adminstr. The Diagnostic Clinic, Shreveport, 1961—; clin. instr. La. Tech. U., Ruston, 1981—. Mem. Caddo-Bossier Med. Assts. (pres. 1964), Am. Assn. Med. Assts., La. State Assn. Med. Assts., Shreveport C. of C. Office: The Diagnostic Clinic 925 Olive St Shreveport LA 71104-2103

DE ZAGON, BARONESS MONIQUE S., lawyer; b. Brussels, Belgium, Feb. 4, 1944; came to U.S., 1973; d. Jules C. and Marie (Goux) de Vos; m. Baron Istvan Szentkereszty de Zagon, Apr. 20, 1965; children: Zita, Paul-Andre. B in Philosophy and Lit., Cath. U. of Louvain, Belgium, 1964, JD cum laude, 1967; LLM in Corp. Law, NYU, 1978. Bar: N.Y., 1979. Law advisor Ministry of Pub. Health and Family, Belgium, 1967-70, Ministry of Social Security, Belgium, 1970-73; asst. counsel, asst. v.p. European Am. Bank, N.Y.C., 1978-84; assoc. Windels, Marx, Davies & Ives, N.Y.C., 1984-86; assoc., ptnr. Dechert, Price & Rhoades, N.Y.C., 1986-89; ptnr. Kelley, Drye & Warren, N.Y.C., 1989-94, Baker & McKenzie, N.Y.C., 1994—. Mem. ABA, Belgium C. of C. (dir.). Roman Catholic. Home: 260 Warwick Ave South Orange NJ 07079 Office: Baker & McKenzie 805 Third Ave New York NY 10022

DHESSE, AMBER LYNN, accounting manager; b. Peru, Ill., May 22, 1965; d. John Curtis and Cheryl Ann (Bartolucci) Stowe; m. Paul Arthur Dhesse, June 10, 1989; children: Desiree Alexis, Gabriella Jade. A in Acctg., Ill. Valley C.C., 1986; BS, Ill. State U., 1988. Cost acctg. and accounts payable mgr. BWD Automotive Corp., Ottawa, Ill., 1988—; mem. culture shift com. BWD Automotive Corp., Ottawa, 1993—, mem. bill of material structure com., 1993—, mem. diaphragm spring quality team, 1993—, mem. mfg. systems team, 1993—, chair cost reduction com., 1993—. Bd. dirs. Honeypot Nursery Sch., 1993—. Mem. Inst. Mgmt. Accts. Roman Catholic. Office: BWD Automotive Corp 1111 McKinley Rd Ottawa IL 61350

DIAL, ELEANORE MAXWELL, foreign language educator; b. Norwich, Conn., Feb. 21, 1929; d. Joseph Walter and Irene (Beetham) Maxwell; BA, U. Bridgeport (Conn.), 1951; MA in Spanish, Mexico City Coll., 1955; PhD, U. Mo., 1968; m. John E. Dial, Aug. 27, 1959. Mem. faculty U. Wisc.-Milw., 1968-75, Ind. State U., Terre Haute, 1975-78, Bowling Green (Ohio) State U., 1978-79; asst. prof. dept. fgn. langs. and lits. Iowa State U., Ames, 1979-85, assoc. prof. 1985—; cons. pub. co.; participant workshops; del. 1st World Congress Women Journalists and Writers, Mex., 1975, also mem. edn. commn. NDEA grantee, 1967; Center Latin Am. grantee, 1972; Nat. Endowment Humanities summer seminar UCLA, 1981, U. Calif.-Santa Barbara, 1984; active Gov's. Commn. on Fgn. Langs. and Internat. Studies, 1988—. Mem. Am. Assn. Tchrs. Spanish and Portuguese, Midwest MLA, MLA, N. Central Council Latin Americanists, Midwest Assn. Latin Am. Studies, Clermont County Geneal. Soc., Ohio Geneal. Soc., Caribbean Studies Assn., Phi Beta Delta, Phi Sigma Iota, Sigma Delta Pi. Contbr. articles and revs. to scholarly jours. Home: 119 9th St Ames IA 50010-6343 Office: Iowa State U Ames IA 50011

DIAMANT, ANITA, literary agent; b. N.Y.C., Jan. 15; d. Sidney J. and Lea (Lyons) D.; m. Harold Berke, Dec. 22, 1945 (dec. 1972); 1 child, Allyson. B.S., NYU. Former mem. editor bd. Forum mag., N.Y.C., McCall's mag., N.Y.C.; reporter Macy Newspapers, N.Y.; now prin. Anita Diamant Lit. Agy., N.Y.C.; lectr. at writers' confs. throughout U.S.; adj. prof. Journalism, L.I. Univ., 1967. Contbr. articles to McCall's Mag., Writer, Women's News, others. Mem. Women in Communications (past pres. N.Y. chpt.), Nat. Assn. Newspaper Women, Soc. Author's Reps., Overseas Press of Am. (pres. 1981-86, Meritorious Service award 1970), Williams Club. Office: 310 Madison Ave New York NY 10017-6006

DIAMOND, CHERYL BETH, psychiatrist; b. N.Y.C., May 13, 1943; d. Paul and Zosia (Seitz) D. BA, Swarthmore Coll., 1963; MD, Med. Coll. Pa., 1972. Diplomate Am. Bd. Psychiatry and Neurology; cert. Am. Psychoanalytical Assn. Asst. counsel instr. N.Y. Psychoanalytic Inst.; asst. clin. prof. psychiatry Cornell U. Med. Ctr.; clin. lectr. psychiatry U. Ariz. Med. Ctr.; course instr. Ariz. divsn. So. Calif. Psychiatric Inst.; pvt. practice Tucson. Office: 2500 N Tucson Blvd Ste 136 Tucson AZ 85718

DIAMOND, DEBORAH BEROSET, writer; b. Flint, Mich., Feb. 1, 1960; d. John Edward and Martha Jean (Hastings) Beroset; m. Michael Alan Diamond, May 29, 1988; children: Tova Beroset, Simone Beroset. B Journalism, U. Mo., 1987. Staff writer Gulf News, Dubai, United Arab Emirates, 1980-81; freelance writer Dubai, 1981-83; intern Ladies' Home Jour., N.Y.C., 1986; freelance writer Columbia, Mo., 1986—; instr. journalism Westminster Coll., Fulton, Mo., 1988, U. Mo., Columbia, 1993. Editor, Vet. Med. Rev. mag., Columbia, 1987-90; contbg. editor Ladies' Home Jour., N.Y.C., 1994—; contbr. articles to various publs. Mem. Am. Soc. Journalists and Authors, Investigative Reporters and Editors, Internat. Platform Assn., Soc. Profl. Journalists. Democrat. Jewish. Home and Office: 1740 River Bluff Ct Columbia MO 65203-1561

DIAMOND, ELAYNE FERN, interior designer, small business owner; b. Newark, July 1, 1945; d. Charles Ronald and Louise Pearl (Fern) Newman; m. Stanley Diamond, Nov. 20, 1965; children: Garrett L., Robin Fern. Student, N.Y. Sch. Interior Design, 1963-67. Pres. Elayne Diamond Interiors, Union, N.J., 1964—; owner, pres. Novelty Express, Union, Springfield, Totowa, N.J., 1975-80, Personalitees, Beach Haven, N.J., 1978-84, Put Togethers, Surf City, N.J., 1979-81, Designer's View Inc., Greenbrook, N.J., 1988—; cons. in field; designer, owner Yellow Brick Rd., Inc., Springfield, Beach Haven, 1975-79; cons. to constrn. cos., window mfgs., N.J., 1969—; distbr. Energy Controls, Springfield, 1985-86; pres. Advantage Point, Woodbridge, N.J., 1990. Publisher, editor Trade Secrets Interior Design Directory; contbr. designs to trade and comml. mags., various home tours, newspaper articles, 1964—. Fund raiser Ctr. Sch. for the Learning Disabled, N.J., Am. Cancer Soc., others. Mem. Allied Bd. Trade.

DIAMOND, IRENE, foundation administrator; b. Pitts., May 7, 1910; d. Horace and Leah (Grekin) Levine; m. Aaron Diamond, 1942 (dec.); 1 child, Jean. Ed., Pitts. Pub. Schs.; LHD (hon.), City Coll., CUNY, 1989, The Juilliard Sch., 1992; LLD (hon.), Queens Coll., CUNY, 1990, New Sch. Social Rsch., N.Y.C., 1994. Asst. editor story div. Warner Bros., Hollywood, Calif., 1934-35, editor, 1937-40; supr. dept. lit. Leland Hayward, Hollywood, 1935-37; editor story and talent div. Samuel Goldwyn-MGM, Hollywood and N.Y.C., 1940-41; editor story div., head talent div. Hal Wallis-Paramount Pictures, Hollywood and N.Y.C., 1941-70; pres., bd. dirs. Aaron Diamond Found., Inc., N.Y.C., 1986—. Bd. dirs. Aaron Diamond AIDS Rsch. Ctr., 1989—. Recipient Pres.'s medal Bank St. Coll., 1989, Liberty award Lambda Legal Def. and Edn. Fund, 1990, Disting. Community Svc. award United Hosp. Fund, 1990, medal Correctional Assn. of N.Y./Osborne Assn., 1990. Mem. Film Soc. of Lincoln Ctr., Sundance Inst., Young Concert Artists, Fund for Free Expression. Office: Aaron Diamond Found Inc 1270 Ave of Americas Ste 2624 New York NY 10020-1700

DIAMOND, KAREN STEIN, fundraiser, consultant; b. Miami Beach, Fla., May 29, 1943; d. Donald Marvin and Mildred Frances (Shenkan) Stein; m. David M. Diamond, June 28, 1964; children: Sara Moore Diamond-Patterson, Samuel David. BA, Vassar Coll., 1964. Coord. membership Hunter Mus. Art, Chattanooga, 1978-84; dir. membership Chattanooga Regional History Mus., 1987-89; exec. dir. Friends Chickamauga, Chattanooga Nat. Mil. Park, 1989-91; assoc. dir. athletics U. Tenn., Chattanooga, 1991-94; coord. The Stadium Campaign, Chattanooga, 1994—. Editor: Hunter Mus. Bulletin, 1970-74; author, prodr.: (play) Our Constitution: Perfect and Changing, 1987; editor: Signed with Their Honor, 1990. Pres. Hunter Mus. Art, Chattanooga, 1976-78, Chattanooga Regional History Mus., 1986-88, Friends of the Park, Chattanooga, 1990-92, treas., 1992—; grad. Leadership Chattanooga, 1985; bd. dirs. Chattanooga Neighborhood Enterprise, 1987-94, Chattanooga Basketball Found., 1991—; sec. Ochs meml. Temple, Chattanooga, 1991-93; trustee Baylor Sch., Chattanooga, 1992—. Mem. NAFE, Nat. Soc. Fundraising Execs. Jewish. Home: 208 Fairy Trl Lookout Mountain TN 37350

DIAMOND, MARIAN CLEEVES, anatomy educator; b. Glendale, Calif., Nov. 11, 1926; d. Montague and Rosa Marian (Wamphler) Cleeves; m. Richard M. Diamond, Dec. 20, 1950 (div.); m. Arnold B. Scheibel, Sept. 14, 1982; children: Catherine, Richard, Jeffrey, Ann. AB, U. Calif., Berkeley, 1948, MA, 1949, PhD, 1953. With Harvard U., Cambridge, 1952-54, Cornell U., Ithaca, N.Y., 1954-58, U. Calif., San Francisco, 1954-58; prof. anatomy U. Calif., Berkeley, 1962—; asst. dean U. Calif., Berkeley, 1967-70, assoc. dean, 1970-73, dir. The Lawrence Hall of Sci., 1990—; vis. scholar Australian Nat. U., 1978, Fudan U., Shanghai, People's Republic China, 1985, U. Nairobi (Kenya), 1988. Author: Enriching Heredity, 1989; coauthor: The Human Brain Coloring, 1985; editor: Contraceptive Hormones Estrogen and Human Welfare, 1978; contbr. articles to profl. jours. V.p.

County Women Dems., Ithaca, 1957; bd. dirs. Unitarian Ch., Berkeley, 1969. Recipient Calif. Gifted award, 1989, C.A.S.E. Calif. Prof. of Yr. award, Nat. Gold medalist, 1990, Woman of Yr. award Zonta Internat., 1991, U. medal La. Univerisdad Del Zulia, Maricaibo, Venezuela, 1992; grantee NSF, 1960-72, NIH, 1960's-70's; fellow Calif. Acad. Scis., 1991. Fellow AAAS; mem. AAUW (fellowship chair 1970—), Am. Assn. Anatomists, Soc. Neurosci., Philos. Soc. Washington, The Faculty Club (Berkeley) (v.p. 1979-85, 90—). Club: The Faculty (Berkeley) (v.p. 1979-85, 90—). Home: 2583 Virginia St Berkeley CA 94709-1108 Office: U Calif Dept Integrative Biology 345 Mulford Hall Berkeley CA 94720 also: U Calif Office of Dir Lawrence Hall Sci Berkeley CA 94720

DIAMOND, MARY ELIZABETH BALDWIN (MARY E.B. DIAMOND), artist; b. Detroit, Sept. 2, 1951; d. Harold Barber and Evelyn (Glenn) Weaver; m. David Baldwin III, June 24, 1972 (div. Nov. 1982); 1 child, David Damar; m. Robert Proctor Diamond, Oct. 6, 1986; 1 child, Angelique Krista. Freelance artist, cartoonist, photographer Phase II Mag., Detroit, 1981-85; artist Montague Art Galleries Inc., Locust Valley, N.Y., 1989-95; guest speaker Jimmy Ernst Artists Alliance, East Hampton, N.Y., 1991, Southampton (N.Y.) Intermediate Sch., 1994; judge Parrish Art Mus., Southampton, 1993; mem. awards panel N.Y. Coun. on the Arts, 1993—. Exhbns. include: Landscape Today: East End Views Guild Hall Mus., East Hampton, N.Y., 1994, 39th Ann. L.I. Artists Juried Exhbn., Heckscher Mus., Huntington, N.Y., 1994, Landscape Observed, Landscape Transformed, Islip Art Mus., East Islip, N.Y., 1992, Nat. League Am. Pen Women, 12th Juried Exhibit, Vanderbilt Mus., Centerport, N.Y., 1992, Art Assn. Harrisburg (Pa.) 66th Ann. Exhibit, 1994, Galerie Segahier, Vienna, Austria, 1990. Grantee N.Y. Found. for the Arts, 1994. Mem. Am. Soc. Portrait Artists, East End Arts Coun., Allied Artists of Am., Southampton Artists Assn. (organized life drawing workshop 1989-94, v.p. 1991, pres. 1992), The Onyx Group (founder, treas., pres. 1992-94). Home and Studio: 83 North Side Dr Sag Harbor NY 11963

DIAMOND, SUSAN ZEE, management consultant; b. Okla., Aug. 20, 1949; d. Louis Edward and Henrietta (Wood) D.; m. Allan T. Devitt, July 27, 1974. AB (Nat. Merit scholar, GRTS scholar), U. Chgo., 1970; MBA, DePaul U., 1979; Cert. office automation profl. Dir. study guide prodn. Am. Sch. Co., Chgo., 1972-75; publs. supr. Allied Van Lines, Broadview, Ill., 1975-78, sr. account svcs. rep., 1978-79; pres. Diamond Assocs. Ltd., Melrose Park, Ill., 1978—; condr. seminars Am. Mgmt. Assn. Author: How to Talk More Effectively, 1972, Preparing Administrative Manuals, 1981, How to Manage Administrative Operations, 1981, How to be an Effective Secretary in the Modern Office, 1982, Records Management: A Practical Guide, 1983, 2nd edit., 1991; co-author: Finance Without Fear, 1983; editor Mobility Trends, 1975-78; contbr. numerous articles to profl. jours. Mem. Inst. Mgmt. Accts., Assn. Records Mgrs. and Adminstrs., Internat. Records Mgmt. Coun., Assn. Info. and Image Mgmt., Office Automation Soc. Internat., Adventuresses of Sherlock Holmes, Delta Mu Delta. Office: 2851 Pearl Ave Melrose Park IL 60164-1421

DIAMONDSTEIN, ANDRA BETH, neonatal nurse practitioner; b. Newport News, Va., Oct. 31, 1963; d. Leonard Myron and Abby Lou (Stahl) D. BSN, Georgetown U., 1985; MSN, Old Dominion U., 1993. RN; cert. neonatal nurse practitioner, Va. Staff nurse Children's Hosp. Kings Daughters, Norfolk, Va., 1985-87, Charter Colonial Inst., Newport News, 1987-89, Virginia Beach Gen. Hosp., 1989—; neonatal nurse practitioner Riverside Hosp., Newport News, 1994—; instr. neonatal advanced life support Am. Acad. Pediatrics, Virginia Beach, 1991—; coord. Perinatal Continuing Edn. Program, Virginia Beach, 1993—. Mem. Nat. Assn. Neonatal Nurses, Sigma Theta Tau. Office: Riverside Regional Med Ctr 500 J Clyde Morris Blvd Newport News VA 23606

DIAMONSTEIN-SPIELVOGEL, BARBARALEE, writer, television interviewer/ producer; b. N.Y.C.; d. Rubin Robert and Sally H. Simmons; m. Alan A. Diamonstein, July 22, 1956; m. Carl Spielvogel, Oct. 27, 1981. BA, BC, MA, doctorate, NYU, 1963. Staff asst. The White House, 1963-66; dir. dept. cultural affairs City of New York, 1966-67; dir. of Forums McCall Corp., 1967-69; editor spl. supplements, columnist Harper's Bazaar, 1969-71; spl. project dir., guest editor Art News, 1971-93; columnist Ladies Home Jour., 1979-84; contbr. to Saturday Rev., Vogue, Ms., Partisan Rev., N.Y. Times, Condé Nast, Traveller, others; mem. faculty Hunter Coll., CUNY, 1974-76, New Sch., 1976-84, Duke U. (Inst. Policy Scis.), 1978; arts cons. Sunday Morning CBS-TV, 1978-82; curator Buildings Reborn, Collaborations, Visions and Images, Remaking America, The Landmarks of N.Y. I and II (nat. travelling museum exhbns.), 1978—. TV interviewer, producer: About the Arts, WNYC-TV, 1975-79, ABC-TV Arts, 1980-86, A&E Network, 1980-88; videotape exhibitions Leo Castelli Gallery, 1978, 84, 88, 94; author: Open Secrets: 94 Women in Touch With Our Time, 1972, The World of Art, 1902-77, 75 Years of Art News, 1977, Buildings Reborn: New Uses, Old Places, 1978, Inside New York's Art World, 1979, American Architecture Now, 1980, Collaboration: Artists and Architects, 1981, Visions and Images: American Photographers on Photography, 1981, Interior Design: The New Freedom, 1982, Handmade in America, 1983, Fashion: The Inside Story, 1985, American Architecture Now, 1985, Remaking America, 1986, The Landmarks of New York, 1988, 18 Wonders of the New York World, 1992, The Landmarks of New York: Vol. II, 1993, Inside the Art World: Conversations with Barbaralee Diamonstein, 1994; editor: Our 200 Years: Tradition and Renewal, 1975, MoMA at 50, 1980. Commr. N.Y.C. Landmarks Preservation Commn., 1972-87, N.Y.C. Cultural Commn., 1975-86, N.Y.C. Arts Commn., 1991-94; bd. dirs. Mcpl. Art Soc., 1973-83, Am. Council Arts, 1982-89, N.Y.C. Bicentennial Commn., 1973-77, Bklyn. Acad. Music, 1969-74, N.Y. Landmarks Conservancy, 1973—, vice chmn., 1983-87; bd. advisors Film Anthology Archives, 1969—; mem. vis. com. Met. Mus. Art., 1982—, Fresh Air Fund, 1983—, Big Apple Circus, 1989-92; chmn. N.Y. Landmarks Preservation Found., 1987—; mem. Pres.' council Rockefeller U., 1987—; bd. visitors Pub. Policy Inst. Duke U., 1987-93; mem. U.S. Nat. Commn. on the Holocaust, 1987-93, PEN Am. Ctr., 1990—; bd. dirs. Corcoran Gallery Art, Washington, 1992—; trustee N.Y. Hist. Soc., 1993—, Ctrl. Pk. Conservancy, 1993—. Home: 720 Park Ave New York NY 10021-4954

DIANGE, VICTORIA DIANE, educational administrator; b. Bremerhaven, Germany, Sept. 22, 1956; d. Arthur Lee and Esther Marie (Barney) Stephens; 1 child, Theodore Z. BS in Elem. Edn. magna cum laude, Towson State U., 1978; M Adminstrn. and Supervision, Bowie State U., 1992. Cert. tchr., Md. Tchr. Calvert County Pub. Schs., Prince Frederick, Md., 1978-89, supr. staff devel., Tchr. Ctr., student tchrs., media svcs., 1989—; cons. coop. learning strategies, adult learners, team-building strategies, 1990—; adv. com. Bowie (Md.) State U., 1990-91. Bd. dirs. St. Mary's Elem. Sch., sec., 1990—. Mem. Calvert Assn. Suprs. and Adminstrs. (pres.-elect), Calvert County Pub. Sch. Ctrl. Office Social Com. (chairperson), So. Md. Tri-County Staff Devel. Consortium. Roman Catholic. Office: Calvert County Pub Schs 1305 Dares Beach Rd Prince Frederick MD 20678

DIAZ, DONNA GAIL, public service official; b. Glasgow, Ky., Sept. 20, 1946; d. Claude Elvert and Bessie Ovalene (Bernard) Beck; m. Kenton Wayne Hopper, Feb. 23, 1962 (div. Apr. 1982); children: Jennifer, Heather, Holly, Laura; m. Ronilo Dionisius Diaz, Oct. 9, 1993; stepchildren: Christopher, Michael, Carolyn, Ronald. AA, Lindsey Wilson Coll., Columbia, Ky., 1980; BS, Western Ky. U., 1981, MPS, 1982. Cert. econ. devel. fin. profl. (EBFP). Community devel. specialist Lake Cumberland Area Devel. Dist., Russell Springs, Ky., 1982-86, asst. dir., 1986-91, dir. community/ econ. devel., 1991—. Pres. Russell County Arts Coun., 1986—; mem. Ky. Indsl. Devel. Coun., 1982—, Russell County Band Boosters, 1976—. Recipient Hometown Pride award Bank of Jamestown, Ky., 1990. Mem. Ky. C. of C. (cert. cities evaluation team), Russell County C. of C. Democrat. Christian Ch. Office: Lake Cumberland Devel Dist PO Box 1570 Russell Springs KY 42642

DÍAZ, ELENA R., community health nurse; b. Aubuquerque; d. María E. Lopez. BSN, U. Ariz., 1975. RNC, Ariz.; cert. community health nursing. Community health nurse Pima County Health Dept., Tucson, 1975—; mem. minority recruitment and retention community task force Coll. Nursing U. Ariz. Tucson. Recipient St. Cyril's Clair Dunn/Judith Lovchik award Peace and Justice Com., 1987, La Esperanza award, 1987. Mem. APHA, Am. Assn. Hispanic Nurses, Am. Heart Assn., Nat. Coalition Hispanic Health and Human Svcs. Orgns., Tucson Assn. Hispanic Nurses.

DIAZ, MARGARET ROSE, neonatal intensive care; b. Bridgeport, Conn., Apr. 7, 1962; d. William Davis and Margaret (Vizi) Hindie; m. Luis Manuel Diaz, Sept. 6, 1986; children: Valen Rose, Kellen William, Deven Michael, Brennen David. Student, U. Conn., 1980-83; nursing diploma, Bridgeport Hosp. Sch. Nursing, 1985; BSN, Fairleigh Dickinson U., 1988; postgrad., Columbia U., 1991—. Cert. neonatal ICU nursing, NAACOG; RN, N.Y., Conn. RN neonatal ICU Columbia-Presbyn. Med. Ctr., N.Y.C., 1985—; regional instr. Neonatal Resuscitation Program, N.Y.C., 1991—; item writer certification exam. in Neonatal ICU Nursing, Chgo., 1992—, lectr. in field. Contbr. articles to profl. jour. Mem. ANA, N.Y. State Nurses Assn., Nat. Assn. Neonatal Nurses, Sigma Theta Tau. Roman Catholic. Home: 38 Chestnut Tree Hill Rd Oxford CT 06478 Office: Columbia-Presbyn Med Ctr Babies Hosp 12 North ICU 622 W 168th St New York NY 10032

DIAZ, ORFELINA ROSA, podiatrist; b. Marianau, Cuba, Dec. 22, 1962; came to the U.S., 1968; d. Roberto Clemente and Adelfa Orlanda (Alonso) Diaz; m. Joseph Patrick Boylan, Apr. 10, 1987. AA in Biology, Key West Community Coll., 1982; BA in Biology, U. South Fla., 1984; DPM, N.Y. Coll. Podiatric Medicine, 1988. Pvt. practice Union City, N.J., 1989-91; staff mem. St. Mary Hosp., Hoboken, N.J., 1990-91. Mem. N.J. Podiatric Med. Soc., Phi Theta Kappa. Office: 2008 Kennedy Blvd Union City NJ 07087-2028

DIAZ, SHARON, education administrator; b. Bakersfield, Calif., July 29, 1946; d. Karl C. and Mildred (Lunn) Clark; m. Luis F. Diaz, Oct. 19, 1968; children: Daniel, David. BS, San Jose State U., 1969; MS, U. Calif., San Francisco, 1973. Nurse Kaiser Found. Hosp., Redwood City, Calif., 1973-77; lectr. San Jose (Calif.) State Coll., 1969-70; nurse San Mateo (Calif.) County, 1970-71; instr. St. Francis Meml. Hosp. Sch. Nursing, San Francisco, Calif., 1971-72, asst. dir., 1973-78; dir. Samuel Merritt Hosp. Sch. Nursing, Oakland, Calif., 1978-84; founding pres. Samuel Merritt Coll., Oakland, 1984—; v.p. East Bay Area Health Edn. Ctr., Oakland, 1980-87; mem. adv. com. Calif. Acad. partnership Program, 1990; mem. nat. adv. com. Nursing Outcomes Project. Bd. dirs., head Royce Sch., 1990—; bd. dirs. Ladies Home Soc., 1992—. Mem. Nat. League for Nursing, Am. Assn. of Pres. Ind. Colls. and Univs., Sigma Theta Tau. Office: Samuel Merrritt Coll Office of Pres 370 Hawthorne Ave Oakland CA 94609-3108

DÍAZ DE GONZALEZ, ANA MARÍA, psychologist, educator; b. San Juan, P.R., July 26, 1943; d. Esteban Díaz-González and Petra (Guadalupe) De Díz; m. Jorge Gonzalez Monclova, Jan. 7, 1968; children: Ana Teresa, Jorge, Julio Esteban. BS, U. P.R., Río Piedros, 1965, MEd, 1973; MS, Caribbean Ctr. Advanced Study, San Juan, 1982, PhD, 1983. Lic. psychologist, P.R. Home economist U. P.R., Fajordo and San Juan, 1965-82; specialist in human devel. and gerontology U. P.R., San Juan, 1983—. Mem. APA, Assn. Economists Hogor (pres. 1965-92, Disting. Svc. award 1973), Assn. Specialists SEA (pres. 1982-93), Assn. Psychology P.R., Epsilon Sigma Phi (sec. 1970—), Gamma Sigma Delta. Roman Catholic. Home: 1325 Calle 23 San Juan PR 00924-5249 Office: U PR Svc Extension Agr Terrenos Estacion Exptl Río Piedras PR 00928

DIBARI, JANET ANN, community health nurse; b. Southampton, N.Y., Aug. 12, 1959; d. Harry E. Jr. and Anna May (Huson) Nugent; m. Nicholas R. DiBari Jr., Sept. 14, 1985; children: Christina Ann, Nicholas Ralph III. AAS in Nursing, Suffolk Community Coll., Selden, N.Y., 1979. RN. N.Y. Pvt. duty nurse Southampton, N.Y.; office nurse Hamptons Gynecology and Obstetrics, P.C., Southampton; coll. nurse Suffolk Community Coll.-East, Riverhead, N.Y. Contbg. writer For Your Health. Recipient Excellence in Practical Nursing award, 1977. Mem. Suffolk County Assn. Nurses. Home: 11 Gleason Dr East Quogue NY 11946

DIBATTISTE, CAROL A., assistant U.S. attorney, lawyer; b. Phila., Dec. 28, 1951; d. Peter Martin DiBattiste and Hilda Yolanda (Battilana) Mignogna. BA, LaSalle U., 1976; JD, Temple U., 1981; LLM, Columbia U., 1986. Bar: Pa. 1982, N.Y. 1989, D.C. 1989, Fla. 1990, U.S. Ct. Mil. Appeals 1982, U.S. Supreme Ct. 1985. Commd. 2d lt. USAF, 1976, advanced through grades to maj., 1987, retired, 1991; acad. instr. USAF, Maxwell AFB, Ala., 1986-89; chief recruiting atty. Office of Judge Advocate Gen. USAF, Washington, 1989-91; asst. U.S. atty. So. Dist. Fla., Miami, 1991—; dir. Exec. Office for U.S. Attys., Washington. Editor: The Reporter, 1986-87; mem. editorial bd. Air Force Law Rev., 1984, 85, 87; contbr. articles to profl. jours. Mem. ABA (chmn. standing com. on mil. law 1989-91), Pa. Bar Assn., Fed. Bar Assn. (Young Fed. Lawyer award 1985), Nat. Dist. Atty.'s Assn., Nat. Inst. for Trial Advocacy, USAF Assn., Phi Alpha Delta. Democrat. Roman Catholic. Home: 2451 Brickell Ave # 9S Miami FL 33129-2423 Office: Main Justice Bldg 10th St & Constitution Ave NW Washington DC 20530*

DIBENEDETTO, DEBORAH V., healthcare executive, occupational health nurse; b. N.Y.C.. BSN, Hunter Coll., 1976; MBA in Mgmt., Manhattan Coll., 1991. Cert. occupational health nurse. Rehab. specialist Internat. Rehab. Assn., Woodbury, N.Y., 1979-81; rehab. clinician Francis Schervier Home and Hosp., Bronx, N.Y., 1981-82; nurse employee health Am. Bank Note Co., Bronx, 1983-84; corp. mgr. occupational health North Am. Philips Corp., N.Y.C., 1984-89; med. adminstr. N.Y.C. Transit Authority, N.Y.C., 1989-92; dir. The Rockefeller Group, N.Y.C., 1992—. Author: OEM Occupational Health and Safety Manual; mem. editorial bd. OEM Health Info. Report, Boston; contbr. articles to profl. jours. Recipient N.Y. Schering Corp. Achievement award, 1988. Mem. APHA, ANA, Am. Assn. Occupational Health Nursing (dir.), N.Y. State Assn. Occupational Health Nurses (pres.), Greater N.Y. Assn. Occupational Health Nurses.

DIBIETZ, ERICA MARGRETHE, cultural psychologist; b. N.Y.C., Nov. 2, 1935; d. August and Elizabeth (Hutka) DiBietz; B.A., Columbia U., 1955; M.S.W. (John F. Kennedy fellow), U. Md., 1976, PhD in Human Devel., 1993; children—Regina Antunes, Lisette Antunes, Alexander Antunes. Asst. to sec. for trust and estate law Trust div. N.Y. State Bankers Assn., N.Y.C., 1956-59; tchr. child life, counselor Johns Hopkins Hosp., Balt., 1973-74, mem. women's bd., 1966—; med. social worker John F. Kennedy Inst. Habilitation of Children, Balt., 1974-75; dir. spl. programs Md. Dept. Health and Mental Hygiene, Springfield Hosp. Center, Sykesville, Md., 1977-85, co-founder, Family support group in state hosp., 1979-82, dir. spl. population programs, chmn. staff devel. com., 1978-79, spl. asst. to asst. secretariat, 1985—, mem. patient adv. coms. Md. Atty. Gen.'s Office, 1979-83; mem. continuing edn. com. U. Md., 1978-80; coordinator human rights adv. com. Springfield Hosp., chmn. unit for deaf psychiat. patients steering com., Health and Mental Hygiene, 1983-92; spl. asst. to the secretariat Mental Health, Devel. Disabilities, Drug and Alcohol Prevention Adminstrn.; chief divsn. for dual diagnosis Mental Hygiene Adminstrn.; dir. South Kachemak, Inc. Alcoholism Program, Seldovia, Alaska; pvt. practice Alaska; cons. dual diagnoses. Mem. women's com. Balt. Symphony Orch., 1965-69; founder Dulaney Symphony Soc., 1968; del. public edn. nominating conv. Baltimore County Bd. Edn., 1977-78. HEW grantee, 1974; Mem. Nat. Alliance for Mentally Ill. (edn. and curriculum com.). Episcopalian. Author works in field. Home: PO Box 263 Seldovia AK 99663

DIBLE, ROSE HARPE MCFEE, special education educator; b. Phoenix, Apr. 28, 1927; d. Ambrose Jefferson and Laurel Mabel (Harpe) McFee; m. James Henry Dible, June 23, 1951 (div. Jan. 1965); 1 child, Michael James. BA in Speech Edn., Ariz. State U., Tempe, 1949; MA in Speech and Drama, U. So. Calif., L.A., 1950; fellow, Calif. State U., Fullerton, 1967. Cert. secondary tchr., spl. edn. tchr. English and drama tchr. Lynwood (Calif.) Sr. High Sch., 1950-51, Montebello (Calif.) Sr. High Sch., 1952-58; tchr. English and Social Studies Pioneer High Sch., Whittier, Calif., 1964-65; spl. edn. tchr. Bell Gardens (Calif.) High Sch., 1967-85, spl. edn. cons., 1985-90. Mem. DAR, Daus. Am. Colonists, Whittier Christian Woman Assn., La Habra Womans Club, Eastern Star Lodge, Kappa Delts, Phi Delta Gamma. Republican. Presbyterian. Home: 1201 Russell St La Habra CA 90631-2530 Office: Montebello Unified Sch Dist 123 Montebello Blvd Montebello CA 90640

DI CARLO, SUSAN MARIE, speech and language pathologist; b. Buffalo, Oct. 12, 1955; d. Carmen Anthony and Clara (Serio) De C.; children: Daniel Russell McDonald, Matthew Brian McDonald. BA, SUNY, 1976, MA, 1979. Cert. lang. and speech pathologist; lic. in N.Y. State. Clin. intern SUNY, Buffalo, 1976-78, VA Med. Ctr., Buffalo, 1978-79; speech, lang. pathologist Healthwood Health Care Ctr., Williamsville, N.Y., 1979-81, pvt. practice, 1980-85; sr. speech, lang. pathologist People, Svcs. to the Developmentally Disabled, Inc., Buffalo, 1985-87; speech, lang. pathologist Assn. Retarded Citizens-Childrens Svcs., Geneseo, N.Y., 1987-88, Continuing Devel. Svcs., Inc., Fairport, N.Y., 1988-89, Specialized Rehab. Svcs., Victor, N.Y., 1989-90; speech. lang. pathologist, cons. pvt. practice, Buffalo, 1990—; cons. in field. Mem. Internat. Assn. Laryngectomies, Am. Speech, Lang., HEaring Assn., N.Y. State Head Injury Assn., Speech and HEaring Assn. Western N.Y., Alexander Graham Bell Assn., Computer Disabilities Resource Ctr. Home: 140 Harrogate Square Williamsville NY 14221

DICARLO, SUSANNE HELEN, financial analyst; b. Greensburg, Pa., Nov. 24, 1956; d. Wayne Larry and Clara Emogene (Weaver) Gower; m. John Joseph DiCarlo, June 21, 1980; children: Sarah Rose, Kristen Marie. BS in Acctg., Va. Poly. Inst. and State U., 1978. Auditor U.S. Army Audit Agy., Ft. Monroe, Va., 1978-79; acct. technician Fleet Combat Tng. Ctr., Virginia Beach, Va., 1980-82, supervisory auditor, 1982-83; fin. analyst Comml. Activity Mgmt. Team, Norfolk, Va., 1983—; fed. women's program mgr. Fleet Combat Tng. Ctr., 1980-83. Creator newsletter Fed. Women's Program Manager, 1980-83. Mem. Am. Soc. Mil. Comptrollers. Club: Seaside Mountaineers (Va. Beach) (treas. 1986-88). Home: 4013 Dillaway Ct Virginia Beach VA 23456-1257

DICHTER, TOBEY GORDON, public relations executive; b. Phila., Apr. 16, 1944; d. Abraham David and Meelya (Slobodkin) Gordon; m. Mark S. Dichter; children: Aliza Beth, Melissa Eve. BS, Temple U., 1965, M in Indsl. Psychology, 1968. Assoc. editor Harvard U. Grad. Sch. of Edn., Cambridge, Mass., 1968-69; co-editor, co-prodr. SKF News, SmithKline & French, Phila., 1969-72, sr. employee comm. educator, 1972-74, educator corp. pubs., 1974-77, sr. comm. specialist, 1977-81, mgr. corp. TV and comm. programs, 1981-87; mgr. corp. comm. SmithKline Beecham, Phila., 1987-89; dir. comm. and pub. affairs SmithKline Beecham Clin. Labs., King of Prussia, Pa., 1989-93; v.p., dir. comm./pub. affairs SmithKline Beecham Clin. Labs., Collegeville, Pa., 1993—. Dir. bd. trustees The Children's Hosp. Phila., 1990—; mem. adv. bd. West Phila. Collaborative Program for Child Health, Phila.; dir. 21st Century League, Phila. Recipient Sarah award Women in Comm., 1978, Emmy award Nat. Acad. Film & TV, 1983, Chgo. Film Festival award. Mem. Am. Assn. Clin. Chemistry, Am. Clin. Lab. Assn. (comm. and legis. coms.), Internat. Assn. Bus. Communicators (Gold Quill award), Coun. Comm. Mgmt. Office: SmithKline Beecham Clin Labs 1201 S Collegeville Rd Collegeville PA 19426

DICICCO, MARGARET C., lawyer; b. Bklyn., Mar. 22, 1961; d. Vincent Richard and Margaret Josephine (Ciullo) DiC.; m. James Louis O'Rourke, Sept. 18, 1994. BA in Polit. Sci., Bklyn. Coll., CUNY, 1983; JD, U. Bridgeport, 1987. Bar: N.Y. 1989, Conn. 1994, U.S. Dist. Ct. (so. dist.) N.Y. 1989, U.S. Dist. Ct. (ea. dist.) N.Y. 1990. Assoc. Ginsberg & Caesar, N.Y.C., 1988-89, Abrams & Martin P.C., N.Y.C., 1989-93, Chesney, Murphy & Moran, Westbury, N.Y., 1993-94, Law Offices of James L. O'Rourke, 1994—. Mem. ABA. Roman Catholic. Home: 236 Breakers Ln Stratford CT 06497

DICK, AURORA CLAUDETTE, insurance company executive; b. Manhattan, N.Y., Apr. 7, 1946; d. Emanuel Sr. and Josephine (Galanti) Palmieri; m. Douglas E. Tandberg, Oct. 17, 1965 (div. 1975); m. Frank Raymond Dick III, Sept. 4, 1984. CLU, chartered fin. cons.; cert. fin. planner; registered prin. Nat. Assn. Securities Dealers. Bank officer Garden State Nat. Bank, Hackensack, N.J., 1963-73; sales rep., gen. mgr., exec. N.Y. Life Ins. Co., N.Y.C., 1973-83; mng. dir. The Acacia Group, Washington, 1983—. Mem. Salvation Army Women's Aux., Washington, 1988—. Fellow Am. Soc. CLU, ChFC, Gen. Agts. Mgrs. Assn., D.C. Life Underwriters Assn., Capital Speakers Club (former bd. dirs.). Home: 15201 Baughman Dr Silver Spring MD 20906-1200 Office: The Acacia Group 6411 Ivy Ln Ste 300 Greenbelt MD 20770-1405

DICK, CAROL LYNNE, psychology educator; b. Ann Arbor, Mich., Oct. 26, 1942; d. C. H. and Lois M. (Wubbena) D. Student, Albion Coll., 1960-62; BA, U. Mich., 1965, MA in Edn., 1970. Rsch. asst. dept. psychology U. Mich., 1966-70; rsch. asst. High/Scope Ednl. Rsch. Found., Ypsilanti, Mich., 1971-72; counselor Cath. Social Svc., Ann Arbor, Mich., 1972-75; communications specialist Ann Arbor (Mich.) Schs., 1975-76; religious coord. U. Mich., Ann Arbor, 1976-77; office asst. U. Mich. Continuing Edn., Ann Arbor, 1977-78; bookkeeper Money Mgrs., Inc. (Debt Aid, Inc.), Ann Arbor, 1978-82; instr. psychology Holyoke (Mass.) Community Coll., 1985—; interviewer psychology dept. U. Mass., Amherst, 1992; mem. support staff Nat. Evaluation Systems, Amherst, 1992-94. Author: (poetry book) Transcendent Ways of God, 1976, (short book) Henry's Mother, 1990. Vol. Project Progress, Friends of the Earth and Ecology Ctr., Ann Arbor, 1976-82; forum coord. Unitarian Ch., Ann Arbor, 1978-79; vol. bd. dirs. LWV, Ann Arbor, 1978-82; active Action for Children's TV, Telecomm. Rsch. and Action Ctr., Coalition for Responsible Genetic Rsch., 1978-82; v.p. Lay Acad. Ecumenical Studies, Amherst, 1990-91, others.

DICK, PATRICIA A., counselor; b. Indpls., Mar. 31, 1929; d. Harold D. and Mary R. (Crockett) Barton; m. Richard D. Dick, Sr., June 21, 1947; children: G. Daniel, Richard D. Jr., Lynda S., Kevin D., Deborah D. AA, Wm. Rainey Harper Coll., Palatine, Ill., 1976; BA, Mundelein Coll., Chgo., 1978; MA, Northeastern Ill. U., Chgo., 1984; postgrad., Alfred Adler Inst., Chgo. Cert. sr. addiction counselor, clin. hypnotherapist; nat. cert. counselor. Counselor in pvt. practice Barrington, Ill., 1979—. Contbr. articles on alcoholism to local papers. Mem. Am. Mental Health Counselor Assn., Nat. Assn. Alcoholism and Drug Counseling, Nat. Assn. for Adult Children of Alcoholics, Am. Assn. for Counseling and Devel., Nat. Guild of Hypnotists, Internat. Assn. Marriage and Family Counseling. Roman Catholic. Office: 28662 W Northwest Hwy Barrington IL 60010-5928

DICK, SUSAN MARIE, English language educator; b. Battle Creek, Mich., Nov. 6, 1940; d. James Allen and Mildred Marie (Thomas) D. BA with honors, Western Mich. U., 1963; MA, Northwestern U., 1964, PhD, 1967. Prof. dept. English Queen's U., Kingston, Ont., 1967—. Editor: Virginia Woolf: Holograph of to the Lighthouse, 1982, Complete Shorter Fiction of V. Woolf, 1989, To the Lighthouse, 1992; author: Virginia Woolf, 1989; mem. editorial com.: Virginia Woolf, 1989—. Fellow Royal Soc. Can. Home: 177 Churchill Crescent, Kingston, ON Canada M7L 4N3 Office: Queens Univ, Dept English, Kingston, ON Canada K7L 3N6

DICKENS, DORIS LEE, psychiatrist; b. Roxboro, N.C., Oct. 12; d. Lee Edward and Delma Ernestine (Hester) D.; BS magna cum laude, Va. Union U., 1960; MD, Howard U., 1966; m. Austin LeCount Fickling, Oct. 15, 1975. Diplomate Nat. Bd. Med. Examiners. Intern, St. Elizabeth's Hosp., Washington, 1966-67, resident, 1967-70; staff psychiatrist, dir. Mental Health Program for Deaf, St. Elizabeth's Hosp., Washington, 1970-87; clin. prof. Howard U. Coll. Medicine, 1982—. Co-founder Nat. Health Care Found. for Deaf (named now Deaf Reach); med. officer Region 4 Community Mental Health Ctr., Washington, Commn. on Mental Health, 1987— . Recipient Dorothea Lynde Dix award, 1980. Mem. Am. Psychiat. Assn. (achievement awards bd. 1988-89), Washington Psychiat. Soc., St. Elizabeth's Med. Soc. (mem. exec. com. 1993—), Alpha Kappa Mu, Beta Kappa Chi. Author: How and When Psychiatry Can Help You, 1972; You and Your Doctor; contbg. author: Hearing and Hearing Impairment, 1979, Counseling Deaf People, Research and Practice. Home: 12308 Surrey Circle Dr Fort Washington MD 20744-6244

DICKERSON, CLAIRE MOORE, lawyer, educator; b. Boston, Apr. 1, 1950; d. Roger Cleveland and Ines Idelette (Roullet) Moore; m. Thomas Pasquali Dickerson, May 22, 1976; children: Caroline Anne, Susannah Moore. AB, Wellesley Coll., 1971; JD, Columbia U., 1974; LLM in Taxation, NYU, 1981. Bar: N.Y. 1975, U.S. Dist. Ct. (ea. and so. dists.) N.Y. 1975, U.S. Ct. Appeals (2d cir.) 1975, U.S. Supreme Ct. 1980. Assoc. Coudert Brothers, N.Y.C., 1974-82, ptnr., 1983-86; ptnr. Schnader, Harrison, Segal & Lewis, N.Y.C., 1987-88, of counsel, 1988—; assoc. prof. law St. John's

U., Jamaica, N.Y., 1986-88, prof., 1989—. Author: Partnership Law Adviser; contbr. articles to profl. jours. Trustee Rye (N.Y.) Presbyn. Nursery Sch., 1988-90. Mem. ABA, Assn. of Bar of City of N.Y., Union Internat. des Avocats, Shenorock Club. Democrat. Office: St John's U Sch Law Grand Central and Utopia Pkys Jamaica NY 11439

DICKERSON, CYNTHIA ROWE, marketing firm executive, consultant; b. Cin., Apr. 14, 1956; d. Richard Emmett and Frances Jeanette (Ellwanger) Rowe; m. Mark Alan Dickerson, Oct. 24, 1981; children: Shannon Gayle, Meredith Lynne. BSBA, U. So. Calif., 1979. Mgmt. asst. Computer Scis. Corp., Pasadena, Calif., 1974-78; rsch. asst. Dailey & Assocs., L.A., 1978-79; account exec. Young & Rubicam, L.A., 1979-81, Rowley & Linder Advt., Wichita, Kans., 1981-82, Chiat/Day Inc. Advt., San Francisco, 1983-85; product mgr. Sun-Diamond Growers of Calif., Pleasanton, 1985-88; mktg. cons. San Francisco, 1988-90; sr. bus. mgr. Del Monte Foods, San Francisco, 1990-93; dir. mktg. Yorkshire Dried Fruit & Nuts, INc., San Francisco, 1993-94, Potlatch Corp., 1995—. Named Outstanding Youth Women of Am., Jr. C. of C., 1985. Mem. Am. Rose Soc., Heritage Rose Group. Republican.

DICKERSON, MARTHA ANN, health facility administrator; b. Iowa City, Feb. 2, 1953; d. Wilbur R., Jr. and Phyllis (Schroeder) D. Diploma, Mass. Gen. Hosp. Sch. Nursing, Boston, 1975; BS, Iowa State U., 1978; MS, Rush U., 1983, postgrad. Head nurse, adminstrv. ednl. svcs. coord. Michael Reese Hosp. Med. Ctr., Chgo., 1978-87; clin. health edn. supr., corp. mgr., staff devel. Michael Reese Health Plan, Chgo., 1987-90; clin. svcs. mgr., nat. dir. nursing Buddy Systems, Inc., Chgo., 1990-92; corp. dir. clin. rsch. and spl. projects Cardiac Alliance, Inc., Chgo., 1992-95; mgr. cardiac care unit VNA of Chgo., 1995—; rsch. in field. Contbr. articles to profl. jours. Mem. AACN, Am. Soc. Health Edn. and Tng., Intravenous Nurses Soc., Am. Soc. Parenteral and Enteral Nutrition, Am. Heart Assn. (Chgo. divsn., chair CPR targeted activity groip 1992—, nat. CPR faculty 1992-95), Ill. Nurses Assn., Ill. League Nursing (pres. 1988-89), Sigma Theta Tau (eligibility com., by-laws com., rec. sec.). Home: 1522 W Thorndale Chicago IL 60660

DICKERSON, NANCY (WHITEHEAD), free lance television producer, news correspondent; b. Milw.; d. Frederick R. and Florence (Conners) Hanschman; m. Claude Wyatt Dickerson, 1962 (div. 1983); children: Elizabeth, Ann, Jane, Michael, John; m. John C. Whitehead, Feb. 25, 1989. Student, Clarke Coll., Dubuque, Iowa, 1945-46; BS in Edn., U. Wis., 1948; HHD (hon.), Am. Internat. Coll., Springfield, Mass.; ArtsD (hon.), Pine Manor Coll., 1988. Sch. tchr. Milw.; staff asst. Senate Fgn. Relations Com., Washington; producer CBS News, 1956-60; 1st woman news corr. for CBS News, 1960-63; news corr. NBC, 1963-70; news analyst Inside Washington (syndicated nationally for TV stas.), 1971—; producer spl. syndicated TV programs, pres. Dickerson Co., 1971—; polit. commentator Newsweek Broadcasting Service; founder, exec. producer Television Corp. Am., 1980—; reporter Pres. Kennedy's funeral, Republican and Democratic convs., Civil Rights March on Washington, Kennedy, Johnson and Nixon inaugurations; represented Pub. Broadcasting Corp. (on all-network Conversation with Pres. Nixon), 1970; lectr.; commentator Fox TV News, 1986-91. Author: Among Those Present, 1976. Bd. trustees Covenant House, N.Y.C., Hosp. for Spl. Surgery, N.Y.C., Fgn. Policy Assn.; bd. dirs. N.Y. Pub. Libr., White House Endowment Fund, Nat. Fund U.S. Botanic Garden; mem. women's com. Cen. Park Conservancy. Recipient Collegian award LaSalle Coll., Phila; Spirit of Achievement award Albert Einstein Coll., Yeshiva U.; Sigma Delta Chi award Boston U.; Pioneer award New Eng. Women's Press Assn.; Assoc. fellow Pierson Coll., Yale, 1972—; Peabody award for 1982 TV program on Watergate; Silver Gavel award for 1982 TV program on Watergate ABA. Mem. Radio-TV News Analysts, Washington Press Club (past v.p.), The Century Club (N.Y.C.).

DICKEY, ELLEN MAE, accountant; b. Omaha, Jan. 10, 1960; d. Dale Eugene and Mary Josephine (Swaney) Schmitz; 1 child, Jacquelyn Ann Wright; m. Mark Douglas Dickey, Oct. 24, 1992; 1 child, John Eugene. BS in Bus.-Acctg., Wright State U., 1982; M in Accountancy, U. Okla., 1989. CPA, Okla., Nebr.; cert. mgmt. acct. Staff acct. Ernst & Whinney, Okla. City, 1982-84; shareholder Brooks Wright & Co., Okla. City, 1984-89; sr. acct. Price Waterhouse, Okla. City, 1989-91, tax mgr., 1991—. Mem. AICPAs, Am. Soc. Women Accts. (trustee ednl. found. 1991-94, grad. fellow 1991, pres., sec., treas.), Inst. Mgmt. Accts. (v.p.). Republican. Methodist. Office: Price Waterhouse 15 N Robinson Ste 400 Oklahoma City OK 73102

DICKEY, JOAN DIANE, freelance indexer; b. San Francisco, Mar. 1, 1938; d. Mario John and Mable Ann (Niehaus) Poli; 1 child, Renee Joy Dickey-Johnson-Pedalino. BS in Human Rels., U. San Francisco, 1985; postgrad., Stanford U., 1990, USDA Grad. Sch., 1991-92. Office adminstr. dept. pathology St. Joseph's Hosp., San Francisco, 1957-59, 62-64; office adminstr. med. dir.'s office Laguna Honda Hosp., San Francisco, 1964-72; office adminstr. chief juvenile probation office City and County of San Francisco, 1972-75, office adminstr. mayor's budget office, 1975-78; corp. sec., database developer Eureka Mgmt. Corp., San Francisco, 1978-85; fin. controller Graphisoft Computer, South San Francisco, 1989-91; freelance indexer, 1991—; text editor, graphic artist for computer hardware documentation Mary Kantor Tech. Pubs., Half Moon Bay, Calif., 1989—; database developer for OMNIS 3 applications, 1983—; computer cons., trainer, word processing bus. owner, 1984—. Contbr. articles to profl. jours. Mem. Am. Soc. Indexers (chpt. rep. to conf. 1993), Half Moon Bay C. of C., Peninsula Lisa Users Group (chmn. 1983-85), Mid-Day Mac Users Group (chmn. 1986-87), Toastmasters Internat. Republican. Lutheran. Office: PO Box 133 Moss Beach CA 94038

DICKEY, JULIA EDWARDS, aviation consultant; b. Sioux Falls, S.D., Mar. 6, 1940; d. John Keith and Henrietta Barbara (Zerell) Edwards; m. Joseph E. Dickey, June 18, 1959; children: Joseph E., John Edwards. student DePauw U., 1958-59; AB, Ind. U., 1962, MLS, 1967, postgrad., 1967. Asst. acquisitions libr. Ind. U. Regional Campus Librs., 1965-67; head tech. svcs. Bartholomew County Libr., Columbus, Ind., 1967-74; dir. reference svcs. Southeastern Ind. Area Library Svc. Authority, Columbus, 1974-78, exec. dir., 1978-80; pres. Jedco Enterprises, 1981—; legis. strategy chmn. Ind. Library Coop. Devel., 1975; dir. Ind. Libr. Trustees Assn. Governance Project, 1982. Mem. Columbus exec. bd. Mayor's Task Force on Status of Women, 1973-76; del. Ind. Sch. Nominating Assembly, 1973-75, 75-77; bd. dirs. Human Svcs. Inc. (Bartholomew, Brown and Jackson Counties community action program), 1975-79, sec., 1975, v.p., 1979, pres., 1976-78; mem. adv. coun. Ind./Nat. Network Study, 1977-78; adv. coun. Salvation Army Local, 1984-88; bd. dirs. Columbus Women's Ctr.; precinct coord. Vols. For Bayh, 1974; sheriff Columbus 1st precinct, 1975, clk., 1976-77, insp., 1978, judge, 1980-83; treas. Hayes for State Rep. Com., 1978, 82—. Named Outstanding Young Woman Am., 1973. Mem. ALA, Ind. Library Assn. (dist. chmn. 1972-73, chmn. library edn. div. 1980-81, ad hoc com. on legis. effectiveness, 1982, various coms.), Library Assts. and Technicians Round Table (chmn. 1968-69), Tech. Services Round Table (chmn. 1971-72, sec. library planning com. 1969-72), AAUW (pres. 1973-75), Bartholomew County Library Staff Assn. (pres. 1975-76), Exptl. Aircraft Assn. (charter pres. chpt. 729, Inc. 1981, advisor 1982, sec. 1984-85, treas., 1990—; Ind. EAA Council (pres. 1982-88, advisor 1988—, internat. EAA conv. antique/classic mgmt. team 1988—), Internat. Expt. Aircraft Assn. (Major Achievement award 1983, Antique Airplane Assn., First Tuesday, Psi Iota Xi (thrift shop steering 1985-94, v.p. thrift shop chmn. 1986-87, Mem. of Yr. 1988-89, pres. elect 1991-92, pres. 1992-93, advisor 1993-94, mem. state assn. project com. 1992-93, constn./by-laws com. 1993-94), Zonta Club (newsletter editor Tel-Zon 1981-89, recording sec. 1984-85, treas. 1990-93, v.p. 1993-94). Home and Office: 55 Oakey Ave Lawrenceburg IN 47025-1538

DICKEY, PATRICE JANE, public relations executive, sales educator; b. Evanston, Ill., Sept. 24, 1955; d. Joseph Merrel and Mary Elizabeth (Mauntel) D. BA in Journalism and English, U. N.C., 1977. Regional program adminstr. Am. Mgmt. Assn., Atlanta, 1977-79; cons Donor Resources divsn. ARC, Atlanta, 1979-80; tng. specialist Dale Carnegie Inst., Atlanta, 1980-83; dir. corp. sales and pub. rels. Downtown & Lenox Athletic Clubs, Atlanta, 1983-84; dir. spl. events Atlanta C. of C., 1984-85; account exec. Tom Deardorff Assocs., Atlanta, 1985-87; account supr. Anderson, Eilers & Blumberg, Atlanta, 1987-89; owner, pres. PD Comm., Atlanta, 1989—; instr. sales course Dale Carnegie Inst., 1986—. Contbr. articles to profl. publs. Mem. ASTD, U. N.C. Alumni Assn., Union Concerned Scientists, Peace Action, GARAL, Planned Parenthood, Ga. Conservancy, NARAL, Journalism Alumni and Friends Assn., Soc. Profl. Journalists, Kiwanis (1st female pres. N.W. Atlanta chpt. 1991-92, Disting. Pres. award, Outstanding Kiwanian, 1991. 92), Internat. Assn. Bus. Communicators, Kappa Kappa Gamma. Presbyterian.

DICKINSON, ANN, fundraiser; b. Topeka, Sept. 12, 1961; d. Jacob Alan II and Ruth (Curd) D.; m. Michael James Mahoney, May 29, 1993. AB in History, Grinnell Coll., 1983; postgrad., McGill U., Montreal, Quebec, Can., 1985. Analyst, corp. fin. dept. E.F. Hutton & Co., Inc., N.Y.C., 1983-85; pres., owner The Dark Side, N.Y.C., 1985-87; asst. dir. individual giving Meml. Sloan-Kettering Cancer Ctr., N.Y.C., 1987-88, dir. spl. gifts, 1988-91; assoc. dir. devel. Sch. Humanities and Scis. Stanford (Calif.) U., 1991—; devel. asst. regional office Brandeis U., N.Y.C., 1987. Vol. interviewer Grinnell Coll., N.Y.C., San Francisco, 1983—; vol. Tom Huening for Congress, Palo Alto, Calif., 1992; active Hist. Topeka Assn., Friends of Filoli, Woodside, Calif. Mem. Nat. Soc. Fund Raising Execs., Jr. League San Francisco, Hist. Topeka Assn., Friends of Filoli (Woodside, Calif.). Republican. Episcopalian. Office: Stanford U Bldg One Stanford CA 94305

DICKINSON, ELEANOR CREEKMORE, artist, educator; b. Knoxville, Tenn., Feb. 7, 1931; d. Robert Elmond and Evelyn Louise (Van Gilder) C.; m. Ben Wade Oakes Dickinson, June 12, 1952; children: Mark Wade, Katherine Van Gilder, Peter Somers. BA, U. Tenn., 1952; postgrad., San Francisco Art Inst., 1961-63, Académie de la Grande Chaumière, Paris, 1971; M.F.A., Calif. Coll. Arts and Crafts, 1982, Golden Gate U., 1984. Escrow officer Security Nat. Bank, Santa Monica, Calif., 1953-54; mem. faculty Calif. Coll. Arts and Crafts, Oakland, Calif., 1971—, assoc. prof. art, 1974-84, prof., 1984—, dir. galleries, 1976-86; artist-in-residence U. Tenn., 1969, Ark. State U., 1993; lectr. in field. Co-author, illustrator: Revival, 1974, That Old Time Religion, 1975; also museum catalogs; illustrator The Complete Fruit Cookbook, 1972, Human Sexuality: A Search for Understanding, 1984, Days Journey, 1985, Commissions: University of San Francisco, 1990-92; one-person exhbns. include Corcoran Gallery Art, Washington, 1970, 74, San Francisco Mus. Modern Art, 1965, 68, Fine Arts Mus. San Francisco, 1969, 75, U. Tenn., Michael Himovitz Gallery, Sacramento, Calif., 1993; touring exhbn.: Smithsonian Inst., 1975-81, Oakland Mus., 1979, Interart Ctr., N.Y., 1980, Tenn. State Mus., 1981-82, Galeria de Arte y Libros, Monterrey, Mexico, 1978, Hatley Martin Gallery, San Francisco, 1986, 89, Gallery 10, Washington, 1989, Himovitz Gallery, Sacramento, 1988, 89, 91, 93, Diverse Works, Houston, 1990, Ewing Gallery, U. Tenn., 1991, G.T.U. Gallery, U. Calif., Berkeley, 1991, Coun. Creative Projects, Mus. Contemporary Religious Art, St. Louis, 1994; represented in permanent collections Nat. Collection Fine Arts, Corcoran Gallery Art, Library of Congress, Smithsonian Instn., San Francisco Mus. Modern Art, Butler Inst. Art, Oakland Mus., Santa Barbara Mus.; prodr. (TV program) The Art of the Matter—Professional Practices in Fine Arts, 1986—. Bd. dirs. Calif. Confedn. of the Arts, 1983-88; bd. dirs., v.p. Calif. Lawyers for the Arts, 1986—; mem. coun. bd. San Francisco Art Inst., 1966-91, trustee, 1964-67; sec., bd. dirs. YWCA, 1955-62; treas., bd. Westminster Ctr., 1955-59; bd. dirs. Children's Theater Assn., 1958-60, 93-94, Internat. Child Art Ctr., 1958-68. Recipient Disting. Alumni award San Francisco Art Inst., 1983, Master Drawing award Nat. Soc. Arts and Letters, 1983, cert. Recognition El Consejo Mundial de Artistas Plasticos 2d Internat. Conf., 1993, Pres.'s award Nat. Womens Caucus for Art, 1995; grantee Zellerbach Family Fund, 1975, NEH, 1978, 80, 82-85, Thomas F. Stanley Found., 1985, Bay Area Video Coalition, 1988-92, PAS Graphics, 1988, San Francisco Community TV Corp., 1990, Skaggs Found., 1991. Mem. Coalition of Women's Art Orgns. (dir., v.p. 1978-80), Coll. Art Assn., AAUP, Calif. Confederation of Arts (bd. dirs. 1983-89), Calif. Lawyers for Arts (v.p. 1986—), San Francisco Art Assn. (sec., dir. 1964-67), NOW, Artists Equity Assn. (nat. v.p., dir. 1978-92), Arts Advocates, Women's Caucus for Art (nat. Affirmative Action officer 1978-80). Democrat. Episcopalian. Office: Calif Coll Arts and Crafts 5212 Broadway Oakland CA 94618-1426

DICKINSON, JANE W., social services administrator; b. Kalamazoo, Sept. 27, 1919; d. Charles Herman and Rachel (Whaler) Wagner; student Hollins Coll., 1938-39; B.A., Duke U., 1941; M.Ed., Goucher Coll., 1965; m. E.F. Sherwood Dickinson, Oct. 23, 1943; children: Diane Jane Gray Clem, Carolyn Dickinson Vane. Exec. sec. Petroleum Industry Com., Balt., 1941-43; exec. sec. Sherwood Feed Mills Inc., Balt., 1943-79. Mem. exec. com. Children's Aid Md., 1960-61; mem. bd. women's aux. Balt. Symphony Orch., 1958-60; dist. chmn. Balt. Cancer Drive, 1958; dist. chmn. Balt. Mental Health Drive, 1957; co-chmn. Balt. United Appeal, 1968; bd. mgrs. Pickersgill Retirement Home. Mem. Alpha Delta Phi, Three Arts Club (Balt., sec. 1958-60, bd. govs. 1960-64, 67-70, pres. 1970-72), Women's Club of Roland Park (bd. govs. 1960-64, 86-88, 92-94), Cliff Dwellers Garden Club. Republican. Episcopalian. Home: 1708 Killington Rd Baltimore MD 21204-1807

DICKINSON, JANET MAE WEBSTER, relocation consulting executive; b. Cleve., Oct. 2, 1929; d. Richard and Gizella (Keplinger) Fisher; m. Rodney Earl Dickinson, June 18, 1965 (div. 1976); 1 child, Kimberly Cae. Grad., Larson Coll. for Women, New Haven; student, Portland State Coll. Lic. broker, Oreg. Pub. rels./promotion dir. KPTV-Channel 27, Portland, Oreg., 1951-54; exec. dir. Exposition-Recreation Commn., Portland, 1954-58; v.p. Art Lutz & Co., Realtors, Portland, 1975-79, Lutz Relocation Mgmt., Portland, 1977-79; corp. relocation mgr. Ga. Pacific Corp., Portland, 1979-82; pres., broker Ga. Pacific Fin. Co., Portland, 1980-82; pres., chief exec. officer The Dickinson Cons. Group, Portland, 1982—; pres. Wheatherstone Press, Lake Oswego, Oreg., 1983—, The Relocation Ctr., Portland, 1984—; cons. in field; lectr. in field; conductor workshops/seminars in field. Author: The Complete Guide to Family Relocation, The International Move, Building Your Dream House, Obtaining the Highest Price for Your Home, Have a Successful Garage Sale, Moving with Children, My Moving Coloring Book, The Group Move, Counseling the Transferee, Games to Play in the Car, Portland (Oreg.) Facts Book, Welcome to the United States, many others; contbr. articles to profl. jours. Mem. Pres.'s Com. to Employ Physically Handicapped, Oreg. Prison Assn.; established Women's Aux. for Waverly Baby Home; bd. dirs. Columbia River coun. Girl Scouts U.S.A., Salvation Army; active various polit. orgns.; chmn. ways and means com. Oreg. Symphony Soc., Portland Art Mus., Assistance League, Portland Jr. Symphony, March of Dimes, others. Mem. Employee Relocation Coun., City Club, Multnomah Athletic Club, Tualatin Valley Econ. Devel. Assn. (dir. 1988—). Republican. Episcopalian. Home: 20 Wheatherstone Lake Oswego OR 97035-1916 Office: The Dickinson Cons Group Lincoln Ctr 10250 SW Greenburg Rd Ste 125 Portland OR 97223-5460

DICKMAN, CAROLYN BUTCHER, science educator; b. Sarasota, Fla., Dec. 15, 1948; d. John Mack and Janet (Rivers) B.; m. J. Frederick Dickman, Mar. 18, 1972; children: Stephen, Deborah, Andrew, Caroline. AA with honors, St. Petersburg Jr. Coll., Clearwater, Fla., 1971; BA, U. South Fla., 1976, MA, 1981, PhD, 1991. Tchr. chemistry Land O' Lakes (Fla.) High Sch., 1978-82; assoc. contract prof. St. Leo Coll., Tampa, 1984-92; dir. tchr. tng. evaluation Stanley H. Kaplan Ednl. Ctr., Tampa, Fla., 1985-92; mem. adj. faculty U. South Fla., Tampa, 1991; asst. prof. sci. Radford (Va.) U., 1992—. Referee Jour. Women and Minorities in Sci. and Tech., 1993—; contbr. articles to sci. publs. Radford U. grantee, 1993, Dwight D. Eisenhower grantee, 1994. Mem. Nat. Sci. Tchrs. Assn., Nat. Coun. Tchrs. of Math. (jour. referee 1993—), Nat. Assn. for Rsch. in Sci. Teaching, Am. Ednl. Rsch. Assn., Assn. for Edn. of Tchrs. in Sci., Nat. Mid. Sch. Assn. Office: Radford Univ PO Box 6959 Radford VA 24142-6959

DICKSON, EVA MAE, credit bureau executive; b. Clarion, Iowa, Jan. 16, 1922; d. James and Ivah Blanche (Breckenridge) D. Grad. Interstate Bus. Coll., Klamath Falls, Oreg., 1943. Reporter, Mchts. Credit Service, Klamath Falls, 1941; credit dept. Montgomery Ward, Klamath Falls, 1941-42; bookkeeper Heilbronner Fuel Co., Klamath Falls, 1942; stenographer City of Klamath Falls, 1943, bookkeeper, office mgr., 1943-52; owner, operator All Star Bus. Service, Klamath Falls, 1953-58, Ace Mimeo Service, Klamath Falls, 1958-73; mgr. Mchts. Credit Service, 1973-87; customer service rep. CBI/Credit N.W., 1987-91. Bd. dirs. United Way, Klamath Falls, 1980—; sec. Klamath Community Concert Assn., 1956—; treas., memls. chmn. Klamath County chpt. Am. Cancer Soc., 1956—; bd. dirs., treas. Hope in Crisis; mem. Klamath County Centennial Com., 1982, Unification for Progress Joint Planning Com., 1985; mem. nursing adv. com. Oreg. Inst. Tech., 1982—; mem. Klamath Employment Tng. Adv. Com., 1983-86; bd. dirs., sec., treas. Klamath Consumer Council; sec. Unified City for Progress Task Force, 1983-84, Snowflake Winter Festival, 1984—; sec. First Presbyn. Ch., 1992—. Recipient Bronze Leadership award Assoc. Credit Burs., Inc., 1976. Mem. Daughters of Am. Colonists (past regent local chpt.), Consumer Credit Assn. Oreg. (pres. 1984-85), Credit Profl. Internat. (treas. dist. 10 1984-85, 2d v.p. dist. 10 1987-88, 1st v.p. 1988-89, pres. 1989-90, internat. bull. chmn. 1990-91, 92—), Assoc. Credit Bur. Pacific N.W. (pres. 1981-82), Assoc. Credit Bur. Oreg. (pres. 1978-80), Klamath Basin Credit Women-Internat. (pres. 1976-78), Soc. Cert. Consumer Credit Exec., Internat. Consumer Credit Assn., Klamath County C. of C. (pres. 1979, ambs. com. 1980—, Nat. Fedn. Bus. and Profl. Women's Club (chmn. nat. fin. com. 1983-84, nat. fin. com. 1982-83), Oreg. Fedn. Bus. and Profl. Women's Club (state pres. 1971-72), Klamath Falls Bus. and Profl. Women's Club (pres. 1966-67, 76-77). Republican. Presbyterian. Club: Quota (pres. 1958-59, dist. gov. 1969-70). Avocations: painting, traveling.

DICKSON, SUZANNE ELIZABETH (SUE DICKSON), educational administrator; b. Dallas, Jan. 21, 1931; d. DeForest Zeller and Fay (Schmitz) Rathbone; m. Robert E. Dickson, Dec. 29, 1954 (div. 1984); children: Dianne Dickson Fix, Robert Jr., Franklin D. BS in Edn., James Madison U., 1952. Cert. tchr., N.J. Tchr. Arlington (Va.) Pub. Schs., 1952-56, Merrydowns Sch., Annandale, Va., 1962-64, Fairfax (Va.) Christian Sch., 1964-66, Mahwah (N.J.) Pub. Schs., 1966-83; cons. Edn. program/TV/CBN, Virginia Beach, Va., 1983-86; author/cons. Kelwynn Effective Schs. Group, 1986-89; pres. Internat. Learning Systems, Inc., Chesapeake, Va., 1988—; workshop provider to schs., 1972—. Author reading/lang. arts program: Sing, Spell, Read and Write, 1972-92, social studies program: Songs of America's Freedoms, 1987, Songs that Teach: U.S. Presidents, 1986, 91, Winning: The Race to Independent Reading Ability, 1989; author play: Pathway to Liberty, 1968, Musical Math Facts, 1992. Recipient George Washington Tchr's. Medal Freedom Found., Valley Forge, 1968. Mem. Internat. Reading Assn. (pres. North Jersey coun. 1979-80), Soc. Women Educators (past treas., past v.p.), Delta Kappa Gamma (chpt. pres. 1979-81). Office: Internat Learning Systems Inc 1000 112th Cir N Ste 100 Saint Petersburg FL 33716

DICKSON, VIVIAN FRANCO, biomedical research consultant; b. Phila., June 2, 1937; d. Joseph Patrick and Vivian (Lange) Franco; m. James F. Dickson, III, Dec. 23, 1977. BA, U. Del., 1958; postgrad., Jefferson Med. Coll., 1959. Cert. med. technologist Am. Soc. Clin. Pathologists. Med. technologist NIH, Bethesa, Md., 1959-67, adminstr., 1968-74, 78-88; health policy analyst Office of Asst. Sec. Health, Dept. Health and Human Svcs., Washington, 1975-77; cons. in health care policy Mass., 1988—; cons. Hospice for Visiting Nurse Assn., Cape Cod, Mass., 1988—; mem. hospice profl. adv. com. Vis. Nurse Assn., Cape Cod, Mass., 1991—. Office: PO Box 343 Provincetown MA 02657-0343

DICKSTEIN, CYNTHIA DIANE, international professional exchange specialist; b. Binghamton, N.Y., June 28, 1946; d. Simon and Marcella D. BA, Syracuse U., 1968; MA, Calif. State U., L.A., 1973. Peripatologist Braille Inst. Am., L.A., 1974-77, Perkins Sch. for the Blind, Boston, 1978, Mass. Assn. for the Blind, Boston, 1981-84; developer exch. programs Orgn. Internat. Profl. Exchs., Inc., Boston, 1980—, pres., 1981—; adminstr. dept. of ophthalmology Mass. Eye and Ear Infirmary Harvard Med. Sch., Boston, 1981-89; dir. Russian program New Eng. Soc. Newspaper Editors, Boston, 1984—. Contbr. articles to Boston Globe, various profl. publs. Developer program Citizen Exch. Coun., Boston, 1979-80, field advisor, 1980—.

DICKSTEIN, RUTH HARRIET, reference librarian; b. Bayonne, N.J., May 9, 1941; d. Howard and Anne (Kliman) Jacobs; m. Stephen Samuel Dickstein, Aug. 4, 1963; children: Wendy Lynn, Jonathan Seth. BA, U. Mich., 1962, MS, 1964; MLS, U. Ariz., 1977. Tchr. Hackensack (N.J.) High Sch., 1962-63; libr. skills librarian U. Ariz. Main Libr., Tucson, 1977-79, reference librarian, 1979—. Co-author: Women in LC's Terms, 1988, Women in International Studies, 1987, Minority American Women, 1991, An Index to Women's Studies Anthologies: Research Across the Disciplines, 1980-84, 1994. Recipient Faculty Achievement award Alumni Assn. U. Ariz., Tucson, 1984. Mem. Assn. for Women Faculty (pres. 1990-91), Assn. Coll. and Rsch. Librs.-ALA (sec. women's studies sect. 1989-91), Ariz. State Libr. Assn., Nat. Women's Assn., Phi Beta Kappa. Office: U Ariz Main Library Tucson AZ 85721

DICLAUDIO, JANET ALBERTA, health information administrator; b. Monroeville, Pa., June 17, 1940; d. Frank and Pearl Alberta (Wolfgang) DiC. Cert. in Med. Rsch. Libr. Sci., Luth Med. Ctr., 1962; BA, Thiel Coll., 1975; MS, SUNY, Buffalo, 1978. Registered record adminstr. Dir. med. records Bashline Hosp., Grove City, Pa., 1962, St. Clair Meml. Hosp., Pitts., 1963-73; asst. prof. Ill. State U., Normal, 1976-81; corp. dir. med. records Buffalo Gen. Hosp., 1981-85; dir. med. records Candler Hosp., Savannah, Ga., 1985—; med. record cons. White Cliff Nursing Home, Greenville, Pa., 1973-75; mgmt. cons. Gifford W. Lorenz MD, Savannah, 1992-94. Contbr. articles to periodicals. Bd. dirs. Mid-Ill. Areawide Health Planning Corp., Normal, 1979-81. Mem. Am. Health Info. Mgmt. Assn., Ga. Health Info. Mgmt. Assn. Office: Candler Hosp 5353 Reynolds St Savannah GA 31405

DICOSIMO, PATRICIA SHIELDS, art educator; b. Hartford, Conn., June 27, 1946; d. Richard Nichols and Rose Aimee (Roy) Shields; m. Joseph Anthony DiCosimo, Apr. 18, 1970. BFA in Art Edn./Printmaking, U. Hartford, 1969; MS in Edn./Art, Ctrl. Conn. State Coll., 1972; postgrad., Rochester Inst. Tech., 1986, 87. Cert. tchr., Conn. Tchr. art Simsbury (Conn.) High Sch., 1969—; tchr. Farmington Valley Art Ctr., Avon, Conn., 1989—; supr. Nat. Art Honors Soc., Simsbury, 1989—; mem. Conn. regional adv. bd. Scholastic Art Awards, 1991, 93, Conn. Scholastic Art Awards Com., 1989—, prin.'s faculty adv. com., 1969—; guest lectr. secondary methods in art edn. Ctrl. Conn. State U.; presenter jewelry workshop. One-woman shows include Farmington Woods, 1972, Ellsworth Gallery Simsbury, 1974, Annhurst Coll., 1976, Canaan Nat. Bank, 1991, Terryville Pub. Libr., 1994; represented in group shows at Ctrl. Conn. State Coll., 1969-72 (Best in Show award 1972), Bristol Chrysanthemum Festival Art Show, 1973-84 (Non-objective award 1973, Graphic award 1975, Mixed Media award 1977, Tracy Driscoll Co. Inc. award 1981, Plymouth Spring award 1983, Dick Blick award 1984), Hartford Ins. Co. Art Educators Exhibit, 1990, Simsbury Libr. Gallery Art Educators Exhibit, 1991, 92, 93, Henry James Meml. Gallery, 1992, Riverview Gallery, 1993. Sec. Greater Bristol (Conn.) Condo Alliance, 1990—; mem. Family Life & Marriage Enrichment, New Britain, Conn., 1970-77. Patricia Shields DiCosimo Day proclaimed by Town of Simsbury, 1993; recipient Book award Hartford Art Sch., 1969. Mem. NEA, Nat. Art Edn. Assn., Conn. Art Edn. Assn. (high sch. rep. 1983-85, sec. 1985—, Conn. Art Educator 1993, presenter Fall Conf. 1992, 93, 94), Conn. Edn. Assn., Conn. Craftsman, Farmington Art Guild (tchr. 1992, 93, 94). Independent. Roman Catholic. Home: 19 Hampton Ct Bristol CT 06010-4738 Office: Simsbury High Sch 34 Farms Village Rd Simsbury CT 06070

DIDIO, MILDRED CATHERINE, lawyer; b. Huntington, N.Y., Oct. 5, 1964; d. Daniel Francis and Lucy Rosalie D. BA magna cum laude, U. Conn., 1986, JD, 1989. Bar: Conn. 1989, N.Y. 1990, Mass. 1990, U.S. Dist. Ct. Conn., U.S. Dist. Ct. (so. and ea. dists.) N.Y. Legal intern Law Offices of Samuel L. Schraeger, Storrs, Conn., spring 1985; prison interviewer Conn. Civil Liberties Union, Hartford, November 1986; criminal investigator U. Conn. Criminal Investigator Program, Hartford, 1986-88; law clk. Trowbridge, Ide, Courtney & Mansfield, P.C., Hartford, 1986-87; summer assoc., law clk. Sorokin, Sorokin, Gross, Hyde & Williams, P.C., Hartford, 1988-89; law clk. to Hon. John J. Daly Conn. Appellate Ct., Hartford, 1989-90; assoc. Hebb & Gitlin, Hartford, 1990-92; pvt. practice N.Y.C., 1993—; prodn. editor, Am. coord. Woman and Earth Global Eco-Network, Woman and Earth mag., N.Y.C., 1992—; counsel, account rep. ATI Title Agy., Bohemia, N.Y., 1993-94, Boundary Title Svcs., Inc., Mineola, N.Y., 1994—. Contbr. articles to profl. jours. Liaison mem. State of Conn. Gender Bias Task Force; vol. tutor Ned Coll Revitalization Corps, Hartford, 1984-85; mem. Harford Chorale, bd. govs., mem. at large, 1992-94. Named one of Internat. Women of Year, 1992-93. Mem. ABA (internat. law com. Young Lawyers Divsn. 1993—), Conn. Bar Assn. (head of Task Force on Women and Minorities Young Lawyers Sect. 1993—, co-chair Pub. Svc. Projects Com.

1992-93), Nat. Assn. Women Lawyers, Bar Assn. City of N.Y. Home and Office: 467 Central Park W Ste 7F New York NY 10025-4023

DIDION, JOAN, author; b. Sacramento, Calif., Dec. 5, 1934; d. Frank Reese and Eduene (Jerrett) D.; m. John Gregory Dunne, Jan. 30, 1964; 1 child, Quintana Roo. BA, U. Calif., Berkeley, 1956. Assoc. feature editor Vogue mag., 1956-63; former columnist Saturday Evening Post, Life, Esquire; now contbr. The N.Y. Rev. of Books, The New Yorker. Novels include Run River, 1963, Play It As It Lays, 1970, A Book of Common Prayer, 1977, Democracy, 1984; books of essays: Slouching Towards Bethlehem, 1968, The White Album, 1979, After Henry, 1992; nonfiction Salvador, 1983, Miami, 1987; co-author: (with John Gregory Dunne) screenplays for films The Panic in Needle Park, 1971, Play It As It Lays, 1972, A Star Is Born, 1976, True Confessions, 1981. Recipient 1st prize Vogue's Prix de Paris, 1956, Morton Dauwen Zabel prize AAAL, 1978. Mem. Am. Acad. Arts and Letters, Am. Acad. Arts and Scis., Coun. Fgn. Rels. Office: care Janklow & Nesbit 598 Madison Ave New York NY 10022-1614

DIE, ANN MARIE HAYES, college administrator, psychologist, educator; b. Baytown, Tex., Aug. 15, 1944; d. Robert L. and Dorothy Ann (Cooke) Hayes; m. Jerome Glynn Die, June 5, 1971; 1 child, Meredith Anne. BS with highest honors, Lamar U., 1966; MEd, U. Houston, 1969; PhD, Tex. A&M U., 1977. Lic. psychologist. Asst. prof. dept. psychology Lamar U., Beaumont, Tex., 1977-82, assoc. prof., dir. Psychol. Clinic, 1982-86, dir. grad. programs in psychology, 1981-86, Regents prof. psychology, 1986, pres. faculty senate, 1985-86; pvt. practice clin. psychology Beaumont, 1979-87; prof. Tulane U., New Orleans, 1988-92, dean Newcomb Coll., 1988-92, assoc. provost, 1991-92; pres., prof. psychology Hendrix Coll., Conway, Ark., 1992—; adminstr. adolescent residential unit Mental Health/Mental Retardation of S.E. Tex., 1979-80; cons. in field; coordinating bd. Tex. Coll. and Univ. System Internship, 1986; bd. dirs. Nat. Merit Scholarship Corp., 1993—. Contbr. articles to profl. jours. Active community adv. com. Beaumont State Ctr. Human Devel., 1981-88, Mental Health/Mental Retardation S.E. Tex., 1981-87; participant Nat. Identification Program for Women, Am. Coun. on Edn., 1985, govtl. rels. commn., 1993—, chair, 1995; chair exec. com. coun. Am. Coun. on Edn. Fellows, 1993—; bd. dirs. Beaumont Civic Opera, Lamar U. and Tulane U. Wesley Found. Bds., Acxiom Corp., 1993—; bd. govs. Isidore Newman Sch., 1991-92; trustee Robert Morris Coll., 1990— chair edn. com., 1990-95, chair pers. com., 1995—; univ. senate United Meth. Ch., 1993—. Am. Coun. Edn. fellow Coll. William and Mary, 1986-87; recipient Regents Merit award, 1979, Coll. Health and Behavioral Sci. Merit award, 1982; named one of Women in Ark., Ark. Bus., 1995. Mem. APA, Southwestern Psychol. Assn., Family Svcs. Assn. (bd. dirs. 1988-89), Tex. Psychol. Assn. (dir. divsn. acad. psychologists 1986), S.E. Tex. Psychol. Assn. (treas. 1978-79, 79-80, pres. 1983), Nat. Coun. Family Rels., Mental Health Assn. Jefferson County, Nat. Register Health Svc. Providers in Psychology, Nat. Assn. Ind. Colls. and Univs. (bd. dirs. 1993—, vice chair 1995—), Nat. Identification Program for Women Higher Edn. Adminstrs. (coord. La.). Home: 1256 Winfield St Conway AR 72032-2741 Office: Hendrix Coll 1601 Harkrider St Conway AR 72032-3001

DIEBOLT, JUDY, newspaper editor; b. Atchison, Kans., Oct. 6, 1948; d. George Edward and Mary Lou (Hill) D.; m. John C. Aldrich, Oct. 25, 1985. BSJ, U. Kans., 1970. Reporter Detroit Free Press, 1970-80, columnist, 1980-82, asst. city editor, 1982-85; reporter Detroit News, 1986-88, asst city editor, 1988-89, suburban editor, 1989-91; mng. editor Burlington (Vt.) Free Press, 1991-94; city editor Detroit News, 1994—. Recipient Pub. Svc. award AP, 1978. Mem. AP Mng. Editors, Detroit Press Club (bd. govs., 1990-91), Univ. Club Detroit. Roman Catholic. Office: The Detroit News 321 W Lafayette Blvd Detroit MI 48226

DIEDERICH, ANNE MARIE, college president; b. Cleve., Apr. 8, 1943. BA in English, Ursuline Coll. for Women, 1966; MA in Ednl. Adminstrn., John Carroll U., 1975; PhD in Edn. Policy and Leadership, Ohio State U., 1988. Joined Order St. Ursula, Roman Cath. Ch., 1961. Tchr. Villa Angela Acad., Cleve., 1966-70, asst. prin., 1971-76, prin., 1976-82; tchr. Beaumont Sch. for Girls, 1982-84; pres. Ursuline Coll., Pepper Pike, Ohio, 1986—. Mem. Leadership Cleve. '89. Dan H. Eikenberry scholar Ohio State U., 1985; William R. and Marie A. Flesher fellow Ohio State U., 1986. Mem. Phi Kappa Phi. Office: Ursuline Coll Office of Pres 2550 Lander Rd Cleveland OH 44124

DIEDERICHS, JANET WOOD, public relations executive; b. Libertyville, Ill.; d. J. Howard and Ruth (Hendrickson) Wood; m. John Kustings Diederichs, 1953. BA, Wellesley Coll., 1950; Sales agt. Pan Am. Airways, Chgo., 1951-52; regional mgr. pub. relations Braniff Internat., Chgo., 1953-69; pres. Janet Diederichs & Assocs., Inc., pub. relations cons., Chgo., 1970—; lectr. Harvard U.; mem. exec. com. World Trade Conf., 1983, 84. Com. mem. Nat. Trust for Historic Preservation, 1975-79, Marshall Scholars (Brit. Govt.), 1975-79; trustee Northwestern Meml. Hosp., 1985—, Fourth Presbyn. Ch., mem. bd. dirs. 1990-93; bd. dirs., mem. exec. com. Chgo. Conv. and Visitors Bur. 1978-87; bd. dirs. Internat. House, U. Chgo., 1978-84, Com. of 200, 1982—, Latino Inst., 1986-89, Chgo. Network, 1987—; com. mem. Art Inst. Chgo., 1980-83; mem. exec. com. Vatican Art Council Chgo., 1981-83; pres. Jr. League Chgo., 1968-69. Mem. Chgo. Assn. Commerce and Industry (bd. dirs. 1982-89, exec. com. 1985-88), Internat. Women's Forum, Pub. Relations Soc. Am., Pub. Relations Exch. Internat., Publicity Club Chgo., Chgo. Network, Econ. Club, Woman's Athletic Club of Chgo., Comml. Club of Chgo., The Casino Club (Chgo.), The River Club (N.Y.), The Exec. Svc. Corps. (mem. adv. com.). Office: Janet Diederichs & Assocs 333 N Michigan Ave Chicago IL 60601-3901

DIEHL, BARBARA ROHRMAYER, lawyer, educator; b. West Chester, Pa., June 4, 1945; d. Francis Peter and Mabel Emma (Anderson) Rohrmayer; m. David Waring Diehl, Aug. 28, 1965; children: David, Nathaniel, Deborah. AB, Bryn Mawr Coll., 1967; JD, Pace U., 1981. Bar: N.Y. 1982, Fla. 1982, Calif. 1983. Tchr. Ossining (N.Y.) H.S., 1967-68; instr. The Kings Coll., Briarcliff Manor, N.Y., 1968-81; pvt. practice law Yorktown Hgts., N.Y.; instr. Nyack (N.Y.) Coll., 1992—. Pres. Sch. Bd. Yorktown Hgts., mem., 1976—; gen. counsel, dir. planned giving programs Am. Bible Soc., 1994—. Mem. ABA, N.Y. State Bar Assn., Christian Legal Soc. Office: 2074 Crompond Rd Yorktown Heights NY 10598 also: 1865 Broadway New York NY 10023

DIEHL, DOLORES, communication arts director; b. Salina, Kans., Dec. 28, 1927; d. William Augustus and Martha (Frank) D. Student pub. schs., Kans., 1941-45. Bus. rep. Southwestern Bell Telephone Co., St. Louis and Kansas City, Mo., 1948-49, Mountain States Telephone Co., Denver, 1949-50; edn. coord. pub. rels. Pacific Telephone/AT&T, L.A. and San Diego, 1950-83; cons. Bus. Magnet High Sch., L.A. Unified Sch. Dist., 1977-79; pres. First Calif. Acad. Decathlon, 1979; owner Community Connection, 1983—; mgr., dir. DelMar Media Arts, Burbank, Calif., 1985-89; mgr. Susan Blu workshops Blupka Prodns., L.A., 1989—; dir. animation and commls. voiceover workshops Elaine Craig Voicecasting, Hollywood, Calif., 1989—; freelance performer, voiceover L.A., 1990—; mgr. Sounds Great Film Looping Workshops, L.A., 1992—; owner Voiceover Connection, 1994—; v.p. pub. rels. San Diego Inst. Creativity, 1965-67; mem. exec. com. San Diego's 200th Anniversary Celebration, 1967. Recipient Dedication to Edn. award Industry Edn. Coun., Calif., 1964. Mem. L.A. Area C. of C. (bd. dirs. women's coun.), Calif. Magnet Sch. Consortium of Cities (chairperson), Industry Edn. Coun. Calif., L.A. and San Diego (past pres.), Bus. and Profl. Women's Club, Delta Kappa Gamma (hon.). Republican. Methodist. Home and Office: 691 Irolo St Apt 212 Los Angeles CA 90005-4107

DIEKMANN, NANCY KASSAK, stage producer; b. Elizabeth, N.J., Oct. 22, 1952; d. Michael John and Eleanor Ruth (Wilson) Kassak; m. Mark Stefan Diekmann, Sept. 2, 1984; 1 child, Michael Kassak. BA, Clark U., 1974. Mng. dir. New Eng. Repertory Theatre, Worcester, Mass., 1973-79; adminstrv. dir. Theatre Communications Group, N.Y.C., 1979-84; mng. dir. N.Y. Theatre Workshop, N.Y.C., 1984—; chmn. theatre panel N.Y. State Coun. Arts, 1989-92; pres. N.Y. chpt. Assn. Non-Profit Theatre Cos., 1990—. Recipient OBIE award Village Voice, 1991. Office: NY Theatre Workshop 220 W 42nd St Fl 18 New York NY 10036-7211

DIENSTAG, ELEANOR FOA, corporate communications consultant; b. Naples, Italy; d. Bruno Garibaldi and Lisa (Haimann) Foa; m. Jerome Dienstag (div. 1978); children: Joshua Foa, Jesse Paul. BA, Smith Coll., Northampton, Mass. Asst. editor Random House/Harper & Row, N.Y.C.; editor/writer Monocle Mag., N.Y.C.; book pub. columnist and reviewer N.Y. Herald Tribune, N.Y.C.; cultural columnist Genesee Valley Newspapers, Rochester, N.Y.; sr. writer/mgr. mgmt. comms. Am. Express, N.Y.C., 1978-83; pvt. practice as corp. communications cons., freelance journalist N.Y.C., 1983—; lit. resident Yaddo Y., 1980, Virginia Ctr. for Creative Arts, 1990, 91; lectr. in field. Author: Whither Thou Goest, 1976, In Good Company: 125 Years at the Heinz Table, 1994; contbr. articles, essays, feature stories to profl. jours., including N.Y. Times, Harper's, Psychology Today, Travel and Leisure, The New Republic, McCall's, Frequent Flyer; columnist New Choices Mag. Recipient Award of Merit for Speechwriting, N.Y. chpt. Internat. Assn. Bus. Comm., 1981, 82, Award of Merit, "Backgrounder" Am. Express mgmt. newsletter, 1981, Outstanding Mem. award Women in Comm., 1984. Mem. Am. Soc. Journalists and Authors, Nat. Writer's Union. Home and Office: Eleanor Foa Assocs 435 E 79th St New York NY 10021-1034

DIERCKS, EILEEN KAY, educational media coordinator; b. Lima, Ohio, Oct. 31, 1944; d. Robert Wehner and Florence (Huckemeyer) McCarty; m. Dwight Richard Diercks, Dec. 27, 1969; children: Roger, David, Laura. BSEd, Bluffton Coll., 1962-66; MS, U. Ill., 1968. Tchr. elem. grades Kettering City Schs. (Ohio), 1966-67; children's libr. St. Charles County, St. Charles, Mo., 1968-69; libr. Rantoul (Ill.) High Sch., 1970-71; elem. tchr. Elmhurst (Ill.) Sch. Dist., 1971-72; media coordinator Plainfield (Ill.) Sch. Dist., 1980—; evaluator Rebecca Caudill Young Readers' Book Award, 1990—. Founder, treas. FISH orgn., Plainfield, 1975-78; pres. Ch. Women United, 1974; sec. Plainfield Community TV Access League, 1987-89; treas. Plainfield Congl. Ch., 1983-88; bd. dirs. Cub Scouts, 1983-86; leader Girl Scouts U.S., Plainfield, 1985—; active Bolingbrook (Ill.) Community Chorus, 1986-90. Mo. State Libr. scholar, 1967, Naperville chpt. Valparaiso Univ. Guild, treas., 1993—. Mem. ALA, NEA, Ill. Edn. Assn., Plainfield Assn. Tchrs., Ill. Sch. Libr. Media Assn. (membership chmn. 1992-93), Plainfield Athletic Club (sec. 1984-86), Rotary (Plainfield chpt. 1992—), Delta Kappa Gamma (Beta Rho, treas. 1993—), Pi Delta, Beta Phi Mu. Home: 13440 S Rivercrest Dr Plainfield IL 60544-8979 Office: Plainfield Sch Dist # 202 611 W Ft Beggs Dr Plainfield IL 60544

DIERSCHKE, BINNIE CHARLOTTE, real estate broker; b. San Angelo, Tex., July 26, 1943; d. Wilburn Charles and Evelyn Marie (Schroeder) Jeschke; m. Kenneth William Dierschke, May 7, 1966; children: Kenneth William, Patrick Michael, Kara Annemarie. BS in Edn., S.W. Tex. State U., San Marcos, 1965. Cert. residential specialist; grad. Realtors Inst. Real estate broker Tom Carpenter, Realtor, San Angelo, 1975—. Mem. pastoral coun. Holy Angels Ch., 1990-93, sec., 1991-92, v.p., 1992-93. Named Family of Yr., Holy Angels Cath. Ch., San Angelo, 1990. Mem. San Angelo Assn. Realtors (pres. 1989, Realtor of Yr. 1987), Tex. Assn. Realtors (state dir. 1994—, mem. profl. standards com. 1994—), Tex. A&M Mothers Club (treas. San Angelo chpt. 1989-91, pres. 1991-93). Roman Catholic. Office: Tom Carpenter Realtor 2902 W Beauregard Ave San Angelo TX 76901-3639

DIESTELKAMP, DAWN LEA, systems analyst; b. Fresno, Calif., Apr. 23, 1954; d. Don and Joy LaVaughn (Davis) Diestelkamp. BS in Microbiology, Calif. State U.-Fresno, 1976, MS in Pub. Adminstrn., 1983, postgrad., 1994—, cert. in tng. design & mgmt., 1992. Lic. clin. lab. technologist, Calif.; cert. clin. lab. dir. Clin. lab. technologist Valley Med. Ctr., Fresno, 1977-82, info. systems coord., 1983-84, quality control coord. Valley Med. Ctr., Fresno, 1984-90, systems & procedures analyst, 1990-91; systems & procedures analyst Mcpl. Ct. Consol. Fresno Jud. Dist., 1991—; instr. Fresno City Coll. Tng. Inst., 1993—; cons., instr. in field. Mem. ASTD (dir. info.), Assn. Mcpl. Ct. Clks. Calif. (edn. and tng. com.), Fresno Women's Network (scholarship com. asst. chair, newsletter reporter), Computer Systems User's Network Fresno County (chair), Fresno Met. Mus. Soc. Democrat. Office: 1100 Van Ness Ave Rm 200 Fresno CA 93721-2012

DIETER, ALICE HUNT, journalist; b. Denver, Apr. 16, 1928; d. Thomas Addison and Alice (McCullough) Hunt; BA cum laude in English Lang., U. Colo., 1949; m. Leslie Louis Dieter, Sept. 10, 1948; children: Alice Dieter Crowley-Mize, Philip Leslie, Paul Wesley. Columnist, reporter, feature writer Intermountain Observer, Boise, Idaho, 1962-72, asst. editor, 1965-72, also TV news reporter Sta. KBOI, and news librarian, 1966-73; stringer Newsweek mag., 1970-73; editorial assoc. corp. communications Boise Cascade Corp., 1973-83; ret., 1983; weekly editorial columnist Idaho Daily Statesman, 1977-85. Chair, Idaho Assn. Humanities, 1972-78; bd. dirs. Idaho Farm Workers Svcs., Inc., 1963-69, pres., 1965-69; bd. dirs. "Friends of Four" (pub. TV sta. KAID), 1988-92; mem. Boise Com. Fgn. Rels.s, 1975—; mem. Idaho Gov.'s Commn. on Excellence in Edn., 1983; mem. Idaho Selection Com. for Rhodes Scholars, 1983-84; pres. Boise LWV, 1957-59; Idaho rep. UNICEF, 1963-65; mem. Boise Valley World Affairs Assn., 1956-65; mem. Boise City Park Bd., 1964-79; co-chair Idaho Johnson for Pres., 1964, Citizens for Andrus for Gov., 1966; del. Women's Conf., Houston, 1978; active YWCA, St. Michael's Episc. Parish, Boise Philharm., Friends of Boise Library, Idaho Hist. Soc.; press advisor Episc. Bishop Idaho, 1991—; bd. dirs. Paradise Point Conf. Ctr., 1991—. Recipient Idaho Press awards for feature writing and news photography, 1967, for gen. interest column, 1983. Mem. Idaho Press Club (bd. dirs.), Phi Beta Kappa. Home: 1563 E Holly St Boise ID 83712-8355

DIETRICH, LOUISE MEDER, principal; b. Coaldale, Pa., Mar. 5, 1946; d. Frederick George and Eva (Albert) Meder; m. Ronald E. Dietrich, July 22, 1967 (div. Nov. 1983); children: Laurie L., Kristen H. BS in Edn., Mansfield U., 1967; MEd, Kutztown U., 1972; MS in Sch. Leadership, Marywood Coll., Scranton, Pa., 1993. Cert. secondary counselor, Pa.; cert. elem. and secondary prin., Pa. Tchr. home econs. Blue Mountain (Pa.) Sch. Dist., 1967-69; substitute tchr. area schs., Pa., 1969-73; counselor Mahanoy Area Sch. Dist., Mahanoy City, Pa., 1973-94, intermediate school principal, 1994—. Republican. Lutheran. Home: 14 Clay St Tamaqua PA 18252-1302 Office: Mahanoy Area Sch Dist 400 E South St Mahanoy City PA 17948-2946

DIETRICH, MARTHA JANE (MARTHA JANE SHULTZ), genealogist; b. Brazil, Ind., Aug. 19, 1916; d. Charles Russell and Florence Delilah (McIntire) Shultz; grad. Ind. State U.; m. E(arl) Donald Dietrich, June 17, 1939; children: Florence Ann Dietrich Harris, Jean Carol Dietrich Litterst, Charles Donald. Clk., CSC, Washington, 1937-43; personnel officer Armed Forces Med. Library, Washington, 1948-54; personnel staffing specialist Navy Dept., Washington, 1954-70, ret., 1970; profl. freelance genealogist, College Park, Md., 1973-88. Cert. Am. lineage specialist; authorized Bd. Cert. of Genealogists, Washington; Author: The Whitenack Family From New Jersey to Kentucky, 1972, Charles Russell Shultz 1876-1959, 1992, Family Reminiscenses, 1992. Mem. Ky. Hist. Soc. (life), Ind. Hist. Soc., Clay County (Ind.) Geneal. Soc. (life), Somerset County (Pa.) Geneal. Soc. (life), Geneal. Soc. Pa., DAR, Nat. Officers Club (bd. dirs. Eastern region 1988-90), DAR, (state registrar 1973-76, state vice regent 1976-79), Md. DAR (state regent 1979-82, hon. state regent 1982—), Md. State DAR Officers Club, Daus. Am. Colonists (state chmn. 1977-79), Daus. Colonial Wars, UDC (2d v.p. gen. 1988-90), Daus. of 1812, Sons and Daus. of Pilgrims (lt. gov. Md. br. 1980-82, 88-90), Magna Charta Dames, Order Crown of Charlemagne (registrar gen. 1983-86, hon. registrar gen. life 1986), Soc. Ind. Pioneers (life), Order Ky. Cols., Dames of Court of Honor, Clan MacIntyre Assn. (genealogist 1978-84), Daus. Barons of Runnymede, Colonial Dames XVII Century (state pres. D.C. state soc. 1975-77, acting registrar gen. 1974-75, registrar gen. 1975-79, service awards 1977, 78), Soc. Ky. Pioneers, Colonial Daus. Seventeenth Century, Flagon and Trencher (life), Hereditary Order Descendants Twin Territories (life), Palatines to Am., Philippe du Trieux Descendants Assn., Point Lookout Prisoner of War Descendants Assn., Md. Soc. So. Dames (state sec. 1990-92), Kappa Kappa, Kappa Kappa Kappa (Ind.). Episcopalian. Home and Office: 4616 Guilford Rd College Park MD 20740-3732

DIETRICH, RENÉE LONG, educational foundation executive; b. Emerald, Pa., Oct. 10, 1937; d. Emmett A. and Arlene I. (Fenstermaker) Long; m. Bruce L. Dietrich, Nov. 25, 1959; children: Dodson, Katie. BS, Kutztown (Pa.) U., 1959; MLS, Rutgers U., 1966. Cert. fund raising exec., ednl. specialist. Tchr. history Reading (Pa.) Pub. Schs., 1959-65, libr., 1965-69; coord. coop. ed. Reading (Pa.) Area Community Coll., 1978-81, program adminstr. title III grant, 1982-92, coord. community and legis. rels., 1983-91, dir. institutional advancement, 1991—; exec. dir. Foundation for Reading Area Community Coll., 1986—; cons. Pa. Power and Light Co., Allentown, 1981—; U.S. Office of Edn., Washington, 1990—. Editor Reading Area Community Coll. newsletter, 1983—; contbr. articles to profl. jours. Bd. dirs. Kutztown U. Found., 1981-90; chmn. bd. trustees Kutztown U., 1976-81; mem. Berk's County Commn. for Women, 1993—; mem. LWV; host-moderator (TV talk show) LWV Presents...; mem. program com. Berks Cmty. TV, Reading, 1989—. Recipient Disting. Alumni award, Kutztown U., 1981. Mem. Coll.-Univ. Pub. Rels. Assn. Pa., Nat. Soc. Fundraising Execs., Delta Kappa Gamma (hon. edn. soc.). Mem. United Ch. of Christ. Home: 1546 Dauphin Ave Reading PA 19610-2118 Office: Reading Area C C 10 S 2d St Box 1706 Reading PA 19603

DIETRICH, SUZANNE CLAIRE, instructional designer; b. Granite City, Ill.; d. Charles Daniel and Evelyn Blanche (Waters) D.; B.S. in Speech, Northwestern U., 1958; M.S. in Pub. Communication, Boston U., 1967; postgrad. So. Ill. U., 1973-83. Intern, prodn. staff Sta. WGBH-TV, Boston, 1958-59, asst. dir., 1962-64, asst. dir. program Invitation to Art, 1958; cons. producer dir. dept. instructional TV radio Ill. Office Supt. Pub. Instruction, Springfield, 1969-70; dir. program prodn. and distbn., 1970-72; instr. faculty call staff, speech dept. Sch. Fine Arts So. Ill. U., Edwardsville, 1972-73, grad. asst. for doctoral program office of dean Sch. Edn., 1975-78; research asst. Ill. public telecommunications study for Ill. Public Broadcasting Council, 1979-80; cons. and research in communications, 1980—; exec. producer, dir. TV programs Con-Con Countdown, 1970, The Flag Speaks, 1971. Mem. sch. bd. St. Mary's Cath. Sch., Edwardsville, 1991-92; mem. cable TV adv. com. City of Edwardsville, 1994—; bd. dirs. Goshen Preservation Alliance, Edwardsville, 1992-94. Roman Catholic. Home: 1011 Minnesota St Edwardsville IL 62025-1424

DIETZ, DEBORAH JEAN, paralegal; b. Honolulu, Apr. 26, 1958; d. John James Edwin and Josephine Y.M. (Chun) D. AA in Liberal Arts, Windward Community Coll., 1978; BA in Psychology, U. Hawaii, 1980. Substitute presch. tchr. Emmanuel's Presch. & Day Care, Kailua, Hawaii, 1981; supr. Cades Schutte Fleming & Wright, Honolulu, 1981-83, paralegal asst., 1983-85, corp. paralegal, 1985—; spl. asst. sec. C T Corp. System, Honolulu, 1983—; bus. owner Pins 'N Things, 1992—. Sponsor Christian Childrens Fund, Inc., Va., 1985; active People for Ethical Treatment of Animals, Washington, 1986, Greenpeace, Washington, 1985. Republican. Roman Catholic. Office: Cades Schutte Fleming Wrigh 1000 Bishop St Fl 15 Honolulu HI 96813-4212

DIETZ, JANIS CAMILLE, sales executive; b. Washington, May 26, 1950; d. Albert and Joan Mildred (MacMullen) Weinstein; m. John William Dietz, Apr. 10, 1981. BA, U. R.I., 1971; MBA, Calif. Poly. U., Pomona, 1984; postgrad. Claremont McKenna Coll., 1991—. Customer svc. trainer People's Bank, Providence, 1974-76; salesman, food broker Bradshaw Co., L.A., 1976-78; salesman Johnson & Johnson, L.A., 1978-79, GE Co., L.A., 1979-82; regional sales mgr. Leviton Co., L.A., 1982-85; nat. sales mgr. Jensen Gen. div. Nortek Co., L.A., 1985-86; retail sales mgr. Norris div. Masco, L.A., 1986-88; nat. sales mgr. Thermador Waste King div. Masco, L.A., 1988-91; nat. accts. mgr. Universal Flooring div. Masco, 1991-92; western regional mgr. Peerless Faucet div. Masco, 1992-95; performance devel. cons., Delta Faucet, div. Masco, 1995—; sales trainer, Upland, Calif., 1985—; instr. Calif. Poly. U., 1988—; lectr. Whittier Coll., 1994. Dir. pub. rels. Jr. Achievement, Providence, 1975-76; bd. trustees Nat. Multiple Sclerosis Soc., So. Calif. chpt. Recipient Sector Svc. award GE Co., Fairfield, Conn., 1980, Outstanding Achievement award, 1988. Mem. NAFE, Sales Profls. L.A. (v.p. 1984-86), Toastmasters (adminstrv. v.p. 1985). Unitarian. Avocations: sewing, running.

DIETZ, JENNIE LEE, nutritionist; b. Pt. Arthur, Tex., Apr. 28, 1942; d. Jesse Cleveland and Mary Elizabeth (Loughridge) D.; m. Leighton Baugh Brown, Jan. 25, 1964 (div. June 1983); children: Anthony Leighton, Jesse Baugh Brown; m. Eldon Whitworth, Aug. 8, 1992. BS in Home Econs. with honors, U. Tex., 1964; dietetic traineeship, Fairfax Hosp., 1975; MS in Nutrition and Foods, Va. Poly. Inst. & State U., 1979. Registered dietitian; lic. dietitian, Tex. Clin. dietitian Arnot Ogden Meml. Hosp., Elmira, N.Y., 1972-73; cons. nutritionist Oak Springs of Warrenton (Va.) Nursing Home, 1976-81; renal nutritionist Warrenton Dialysis Ctr., 1980-86; cons. nutritionist Primavera Drug Rehab. Ctr., Warrenton, 1986; renal nutritionist BMA Dialysis Ctrs., Washington and Va., 1978-86; chief dietitian Rappahannock Westminster-Canterbury, Irvington, Va., 1986-88, Mary Washington Hosp., Fredericksburg, Va., 1988, HCA North Hills Med. Ctr., North Richland Hills, Tex., 1989-91; nutritionist surveyor Tex. Dept. Humn Svcs., Arlington, 1991—; organizer, chair, mem. Coun. Renal Nutrition, Washington, 1979-86. Mem. task force on women Nat. Capitol Presbytery, Washington, 1974-79; foster mother fgn. exch. student Open Door, Irvington, 1987; vol. ARC, Naval Hosp., Yokosuka, Japan, 1965-66. Mem. NOW, Am. Dietetic Assn., Tex. Dietetic Assn. Unitarian Universalist. Home: 3416 Ruth Rd Fort Worth TX 76118-5846 Office: Tex Dept Human Svcs Long Term Care Regulatory 2561 Matlock Rd Arlington TX 76015

DIETZ, MARGARET JANE, retired public information official, tutor; b. Omaha, Apr. 15, 1924; d. Lawrence Louis and Jeanette Amalia (Meile) Neumann; m. Richard Henry Dietz, May 30, 1949 (dec. July 1971); children: Henry Louis, Frederick Richard, Susan Margaret, John Lawrence (dec.). BA, U. Nebr., 1946; MS, Columbia U., 1949. Wire editor Kearney (Nebr.) Daily Hub, 1946-47; state society editor Omaha World-Herald, 1947-48; library aide Akron (Ohio) Pub. Library, 1963-66, publicity and display dir., 1966-74, editor Owlet, 1966-74; pub. info. officer Northeastern Ohio Univs. Coll. Medicine, Rootstown, 1974-85, dir. Office of Comm., 1985-87, ret. 1987; writer Ravenna (Ohio) Record-Courier, 1988-92; cons. Kent (Ohio) State U. Sch. Music, 1988-91. Mem. culture and entertainment com. Goals for Greater Akron, 1976; pres. bd. Weathervane Community Playhouse, Akron, 1982-85, sec. to the bd., 1988-93, trustee, 1991-93, historian, 1993—, chair 60th anniversary season, 1994—; trustee Family Svcs. Summit County, Ohio, 1980-84, dist. trustee, 1994—, Am. Heart Assn., Akron dist., 1986-91, Mobile Meals Found., Akron, 1988-91; v.p. Friends of Akron-Summit County Pub. Libr., 1988-94, pres., 1994—; student tutor LEARN Literacy Coun., 1988-94, trustee 1988—. Author: Akron's Library: Commemorating Twenty Five Years on Main Street. Recipient Trustee award Weathervane Community Playhouse, 1985, Family Svcs. Bernard W. Frazier award, 1994. Mem. Women in Comm., LWV (edn. found. 1989-92, newsletter editor Akron 1957-60), College Club, Press Club, Akron Women's City Club. Home: 887 Canyon Trl Akron OH 44303-2401

DIETZ, VIDA LEE, utility company executive; b. Brawley, Calif., July 2, 1952. BSBA, U. Nev., 1975. Spl. asst. Sierra Pacific Co., Reno, 1976-78, asst. analyst, 1978-79, adminstr. extension agreement, 1979-83, adminstr. speaker's bur. and sch. programs, 1983-85, rep. community info., 1985-87; dir. spl. events, adminstr. charitable foundation Sierra Pacific Power Co., Reno, 1988—. Bd. dirs., 1st v.p. Sierra Nev. coun. Girl Scouts U.S., Reno, 1984-90, mem. nominating com., 1991-93; chmn. pub. rels. com. Jr. League Reno, 1986, chmn. ways and means, trustee, 1990-91, 93-94; chmn. meetings and events com. United Way No. Nev., 1987, mem. pub. rels and spl. events com., 1988—; mem. individual sessions com. Nev. Gov.'s Conf. Women, 1989; mem. Sierra Arts Found., Nev. Women's Fund Scholarship Selection Com., 1989; bd. dirs. Western Nev. Clean Communities, 1990—, Nev. Women's Fund, 1992—; vol. pub. TV Sta. KNPB. Mem. AAUW (program v.p. 1986), Reno Women in Advt. (ednl. chmn. 1986), Western Indsl. Nev., Reno-Sparks C. of C. (ednl. com. 1986-87), Leadership Reno Alumni Assn. (bd. dirs. 1995—), U. Nev. Coll. Bus. Alumni Assn. (bd. dirs., treas. 1989-90, pres.-elect 1993-94, Outstanding Alumnus award 1994), U. Nev. Reno Alumni Assn. (treas. 1992-93, pres. 1994), Meetings Profls. Internat. Office: Sierra Pacific Power Co 6100 Neil Rd BO Box 10100 Reno NV 89520

DIFABIO, CAROL ANNA, psychotherapist; b. Newark, Aug. 6, 1955; d. Rosario and Antoinette Sarah (Palermo) Nicosia; m. Dante Michael DiFabio, Oct. 13, 1979; 1 child, Nicholas. AB, Youngstown State U., 1977, MS, 1979. Lic. prof. clin. counselor. Psychotherapist Cath. Community League, Lisbon, Ohio, 1980-81, Child and Adolescent Svc. Ctr., Canton, Ohio, 1981-88; psych. asst. Robert Lesowitz, M.D., Inc., Canton, 1987—.

Mem. Am. Counseling Assn., Nat. Bd. Cert. Counselors. Roman Catholic. Office: Robert Lesowitz MD Inc 304 15th St NE Canton OH 44714-2523

DIFFLEY, JUDY HIGH, educator; b. Monticello, Ark., Apr. 19, 1947; d. Horace Eugene and Barbara Lucille (Allison) High; m. Gary Gene Diffley, Dec. 23, 1978. BS in Bus. and Office Edn., N.E. La. U., 1968, MBA in Bus. Adminstrn., 1970; PhD in Bus. Edn., U. Okla., 1982; postgrad., Zhejiang Normal U., Jinhua, China, summer 1992. Cert. profl. sec. Grad. teaching asst. N.E. La. U., Monroe, 1968-70; asst. prof. S.W. Mo. State U., Springfield, 1970-80; grad. teaching asst. U. Okla., Norman, 1976-77; prof., chair office legal and tech. dept. Washburn U., Topeka, Kans., 1982—; cons. and speaker Colmery-O'Neil VA Med. Ctr., Topeka, 1991—, The Menninger Found., Topeka, 1985; lectr. in field. Mem. Everywoman's Resource Ctr., Topeka, 1985—. Washburn U. rsch. grantee, 1992. Mem. Nat. Assn. Bus. Tchr Edn., Profl. Secs. Internat. (sec.), Adminstrv. Mgmt. Soc. (v.p. programs 1989-90), Nat. Bus. Edn. Assn., Kans. Bus. Edn. Assn., Alpha Lambda Delta, Delta Pi Epsilon, Phi Delta Kappa, Phi Kappa Phi, N.E. La. U. Alumni Club. Democrat. Baptist. Office: Washburn Univ 1700 College Topeka KS 66621-1110

DI FRANCO, LORETTA ELIZABETH, lyric coloratura soprano; b. Bklyn., Oct. 28, 1942; d. Philip Carl and Lavinia (Russo) Di F.; m. Anthony Martin Pinto, June 15, 1968; 1 dau. Student, Hunter Coll., Julliard Sch. Music. Mem. chorus Met. Opera Assn., N.Y.C.; now soloist N.Y. Met. Opera, debut in Pique Dame, 1965; performances in Paris, also summer concerts, Lewisohn Stadium, 1966; mem. various choruses, festivals and concert series, including Empire State Music Festival, Mozart Opera Festival, Chautauqua, N.Y., 1964; also performed on radio and TV. (Recipient 1st prize Met. Opera Nat. Auditions 1965). Stuart and Irene Chambers award, 1965; Kathryn Turney Long scholar, 1965-66; Martha Baird-Rockefeller Fund for Music grantee, 1964. Mem. Am. Guild Mus. Artists. Office: care Met Opera Assn Inc Lincoln Ctr New York NY 10023*

DIGGS, LINDA STASER, training and development administrator, instructional designer, speaker, writer; b. San Francisco, Nov. 10, 1955; d. Glenndon Staser and Josephine Marie (Katen) Smith. AA, Coll. of San Mateo (Calif.), 1976; BS, U. San Francisco, 1989. Cert. internat. hospitality mgr. Dept. motor vehicles specialist The CTA Credit Union, Burlingame, Calif., 1976-79; asst. product adminstr. Itel Corp., San Francisco, 1979-81; adminstrv. asst. Main Hurdman, KMG, San Francisco, 1981-83; asst. mgr. Met. Club, San Francisco, 1983-88; mgr. tng. The CIT Group, Livingston, N.J., 1990—. Recipient scholarships Lions, Brisbane, Calif., 1973, Masons, San Francisco, 1984. Mem. ASTD (v.p. profl. devel. No. N.J. 1993-94, bd. dirs. 1993-94), U. San Francisco (newsletter pub. N.Y. Chpt. Alumni 1990-92), Federated Women's Club of Brisbane (pres. 1987-88), Gen. Fedn. Women's Clubs (aide to dist. pres. Golden Gate dist. 1987-88). Roman Catholic. Home: 44 Center Grove Rd E5 Randolph NJ 07869 Office: The CIT Group 650 CIT Dr Ste 2110 Livingston NJ 07039

DIGIAMARINO, MARIAN ELEANOR, realty administrator; b. Camden, N.J., July 23, 1947; d. James and Concetta (Biancosino) DiG. BS in Mgmt., Rutgers U., 1978. Clk. stenographer transp. div. Dept. of Navy, Phila., 1965-70, sec., 1970-73, realty asst. Profl. Devel. Ctr.. program, 1973-75, realty specialist, 1975-81, supervisory realty specialist, head acquisition and ingrant sect., 1981-85, supervisory realty specialist, mgr. ops. br., 1985—; instr. USNR, Phila., 1983, 88. Contbr. articles to profl. jours. Mem. AAUW, Soc. Am. Mil. Engrs., Nat. Assn. Female Execs., Phi Chi Theta (pres. Del. Valley chpt. 1984-86, nat. councillor 1984, nat. fundraising com., pres. and corr. sec. (Alpha Omega chpt. 1976-78). Office: Dept Navy No Div Naval Facilities Engring Command Real Estate Div 10 Indsl Hwy Mail Stop # 82 Lester PA 19113-2090

DIGIOVANNI, ELEANOR ELMA, scaffold installation company executive; b. Long Island City, N.Y., May 14, 1944; d. Charles and Josephine (Laureni) DiG. Student Queensboro Coll. Collector Atlas/Re/Sun Ins. Co., N.Y.C., 1965-69; instr. Oak Manor Equitation, Weyers Cave, Va., 1970-76; dispatcher, salesperson Safway Steel Products, Long Island City, N.Y., 1977-83; ops. mgr. York Scaffold, Long Island City, 1983—; ptnr. E-Z Scholarship Data Svc., 1992—. Mem. Mus. Natural History, Nat. Assn. Female Execs., Women in Constrn., Internat. Platform Assn. Democrat. Roman Catholic. Avocations: reading, horseback riding, needlepoint. Home: 14-34 30th Rd Astoria NY 11102

DIKE, MARGARET HOPCRAFT, retired education administrator; b. Prescott, Ariz., July 15, 1921; d. Walter Irving and Margaret Jennie (Lindsay) Hopcraft; m. Sheldon Holland Dike, Nov. 28, 1941 (div. 1971); children: Lawrence, Walter, Robert, Martin, Martha. BA, U. N.Mex., 1941, MA, 1975. Draftsman U. Calif., Los Alamos, N.Mex., 1943-45; coord. Albuquerque Pub. Schs., 1972-85; chmn. pub. adv. com. U. N.Mex., Albuquerque, 1973-74, chmn. search com. regional v.p., 1975. Co-editor: Bicentennial '76 - Albuquerque, 1977; editor booklet New Mexico Arts Resources Survey, 1957, rsch. papers in field. Trustee Albuquerque Mus., 1969-81; chmn. Albuquerque R.R. Centennial, 1979-80, Keep Albuquerque Beautiful Schs., 1984—; pres. Albuquerque Sister Cities Found., 1985-87, Albuquerque Hist. Soc., 1971-78, N.Mex. Assn. for Cmty. Edn. Devel., 1980-82; life mem. N.Mex. PTA, pres., 1977-79, 92-95; sec. Edn. Forum N.Mex., 1988-89. Recipient Lobo award U. N.Mex., 1968, Gov.'s award for outstanding N.Mex. women, Commn. on Status of Women, 1986, 90. Mem. AAUW (pres. N.Mex. 1989-93), Exec. Women Internat. (treas. 1983-85), Mortar Bd. (pres. alumni chpt. 1988-90), Phi Delta Kappa, Phi Kappa Phi, Phi Alpha Theta. Methodist.

DILEONE, CARMEL MONTANO, dental hygienist; b. New Haven, Aug. 24, 1926; d. Nicholas and Martha (Ercolano) M.; m. Eugene Francis Dileone, Jan. 28, 1948; children: Gina, Richard. Dental Hygienist, Temple U., 1945; AA, Albertus Magnus Coll., 1980; BS, U. Bridgeport, 1983; MS, So. Conn. State U., 1985. Registered dental hygienist. Dental hygiene practitioner George M. Montano, DDS, New Haven, 1946-50; George V. Montano, DDS, 1959—; dental hygiene practitioner Francis R. Mullen, DDS, West Haven, 1950-55; dental hygiene practioner Herbert Saunders, DDS, Orange, Conn., 1958-63; instr. Huntington Inst., North Haven, Conn., 1983; adj. assoc. prof. U. Bridgeport (Conn.), Fones Sch. Dental Hygiene, 1985—; adj. lectr. U. New Haven, 1994—. Mem. APHA, Am. Soc. Dentistry for Children, Am. Dental Hygienist Assn., Conn. Dental Hygienists Assn. (treas. 1986-88, v.p. 1988-89, pres.-elect 1989-90, pres. 1991, Mabel C. McCarthy award 1983, Pres.'s award 1994). Roman Catholic. Home: 348 Racebrook Rd Orange CT 06477-3109 Office: George V Montano DDS 436 Whalley Ave New Haven CT 06511-3032

DILKS, SATTARIA S., mental health nurse, therapist; b. Iola, Kans., Oct. 12, 1955; d. Paul J. and Janice E. (McHenry) Smith; m. Lawrence S. Dilks, Feb. 24, 1990; children: Jason Kaine Alexander, Cameron Gray Alexander, Russell Morris Alexander, Michelle Elizabeth Dilks. BSN, West Tex. State U., 1978; MA in Psychology, McNeese State U., 1988. Cert. psychiat./mental health nurse; lic. profl. counselor, La. Mental health technician Killgore Children's Psychiat. Hosp., Amarillo, Tex.; nurse mgr. psychiat. unit St. Patrick Hosp., Lake Charles, La.; DON, clin. coord. Charter Hosp. of Lake Charles, adolescent svcs. program adminstr.; pvt. practice mental health counseling and consultation. Pres. adv. bd. Lake Charles Mental Health Ctr., 1990; active Girl Scouts U.S. Mem. La. Counseling Assn., La. Mental Health Counseling Assn., Sigma Theta Tau. Home: 2416 N Constance Ln Lake Charles LA 70605-2340 Office: 121 Williamsburg St Lake Charles LA 70605-5719

DILL, MARY ALYSON, information services executive; b. Aug. 30, 1951; d. William Allen and Marjorie Dill. BS, Edinboro (Pa.) State U., 1973; MS in Instl. Communications, Shippensburg U., 1979; MLS, Case Western Res U., 1982. Libr. elem. and secondary schs. Bd. Coop. Ednl. Svcs., Stamford, N.Y., 1973-76; media specialist West Point (N.Y.) Elem. Sch. U.S. Mil. Acad., 1976-81; records analyst Standard Oil of Ohio, Cleve., 1981-83, info. analyst, 1983-87; tech. writer Presearch, Aiken, S.C., 1987-88; tech. writer Info Pro Tech. (formerly Maxwell Online, Inc.), McLean, Va., 1988-89, database design analyst, 1989-92; head pub. info. svcs. Aspen Systems Corp., Rockville, Md., 1992—, HUD Libr. Home: 2156 Evans Ct Apt 202 Falls Church VA 22043-2131

DILLARD, ANNIE, author; b. Pitts., Apr. 30, 1945; d. Frank and Pam (Lambert) Doak; m. R.H.W. Dillard, 1965 (div.); m. Gary Clevidence, 1980 (div.); 1 child, Cody Rose; stepchildren: Carin, Shelly; m. Robert D. Richardson, Jr., 1988. B.A., Hollins Coll., 1967, M.A., 1968. Columnist The Living Wilderness, Wilderness Soc., 1973-75; contbg. editor Harper's Mag., N.Y.C., 1974-81, 83-85; scholar-in-residence Western Wash. U., Bellingham, 1975-78; disting. vis. prof. Wesleyan U., 1979-83, adj. prof., 1983—, writer-in-residence, 1987—, bd. dirs. Writers Conf., 1984—, chmn., 1991—; Phi Beta Kappa orator Harvard-Radcliffe U., 1983; mem. U.S. writers del. UCLA US.-Chinese Writers Conf., 1982; mem. U.S. cultural del. to China, 1982; bd. dirs. The New Press; mem. usage panel Am. Heritage Dictionary; bd. dirs. Key West Writers Conf. Author: Tickets for a Prayer Wheel, 1974, Pilgrim at Tinker Creek, 1974 (Pulitzer prize for gen. non-fiction 1975), Holy the Firm, 1978, Living by Fiction, 1982, Teaching a Stone To Talk, 1982, Encounters with Chinese Writers, 1984, An American Childhood, 1987 (Nat. Book Critics Circle award nomination 1987), The Writing Life, 1989 (English-speaking union Amb. Book award 1990), The Living, 1992, The Annie Dillard Reader, 1994, Mornings Like This, 1995; editor: (with Robert Atwan) Best Essays, 1988. Mem. Nat. Com. on U.S.-China Rels., 1982—, Cath. Commn. Intellectual and Cultural Affairs; bd. dirs. Milton Ctr., Authors League Fund. Recipient N.Y. Presswomen's award for excellence, 1975, Wash. Gov.'s award for contbn. to lit., 1978, Appalachian Gold medallion U. Charleston, 1989, Found. award St. Botolph's Club, 1989, History Maker award Hist. Soc. Western Pa., 1993, Milton Ctr. prize, 1994, Campion award Am. Mag., 1994; grantee NEA, 1980-81, Guggenheim Found., 1985-86. Mem. NAACP, Soc. Am. Historians, Poetry Soc. Am., Authors Guild, Nat. Citizens for Pub. Librs., Century Assn., Phi Beta Kappa. Democrat. Address: care Timothy Seldes Russell & Volkening 50 W 29th St New York NY 10001-4205*

DILLARD, BEVERLY LEIGH, publishing company executive, educator; b. Stuart, Va., Mar. 29, 1951; d. Henry Langston and Barbara Ann (Wilkinson) D. AA, Averett Coll., Danville, Va., 1971, BS, 1973; MIS, Va. Commonwealth U., 1992. Cert. tchr. Educator Patrick County Pub. Schs., Stuart, Va., 1973—; desktop pub./owner Desktop Pub. Svcs., Stuart, 1991—. Author: (booklet) From the Heart . . . Through the Lens, 1979. AIDS awareness grantee Dept. Edn., Richmond, 1991. Mem. NEA, Nat. Assn. Desktop Pubs., Va. Edn. Assn. Home and Office: RR 2 Box 217 Stuart VA 24171-9519

DILLARD, MARILYN DIANNE, property manager; b. Norfolk, Va., July 7, 1940; d. Thomas Ortman and Sally Ruth (Wallerich) D.; m. James Conner Coons, Nov. 6, 1965 (div. June 1988); 1 child, Adrienne Alexandra Coons (dec.). Studied with Russian prima ballerina, Alexandra Danilova, 1940's; student with honors at entrance, UCLA, 1958-59; BA in Bus. Adminstrn. with honors, U. Wash., 1962. Modeling-print work Harry Conover, N.Y.C., 1945; ballet instr. Ivan Novikoff Sch. Russian Ballet, 1955; model Elizabeth Leonard Agy., Seattle, 1955-68; mem. fashion bd., retail worker Frederick & Nelson, Seattle, 1962; retail worker I. Magnin & Co., Seattle, 1963-64; property mgr. Seattle, 1961—; antique and interior designer John J. Cunningham Antiques, Seattle, 1968-73; owner, interior designer Marilyn Dianne Dillard Interiors, 1973—; mem. rsch. bd. advisors Am. Biog. Inst., Inc., 1990—. Author: (poetry) Flutterby, 1951, Spring Flowers, 1951; contbr., asst. chmn. (with Jr. League of Seattle) Seattle Classic Cookbook, 1980-83. Charter mem., pres. Children's Med. Ctr., Maude Fox Guild, Seattle, 1965—, Jr. Women's Symphony Assn., 1967-73, Va. Mason Med. Ctr. Soc., 1990—, Nat. Mus. of the Am. Indian, Smithsonian Instn., Washington, 1992; mem. Seattle Jr. Club, 1962-65; bd. dirs. Patrons N.W. Civic, Cultural and Charitable Orgns. (chmn. various coms.), Seattle, 1976—, prodn. chmn., 1977-78, 84-85, auction party chmn., 1983-84, exec. com., 1984-85, chmn. bd. vols., 1990-91, adv. coun., 1991—; mem. U. Wash. Arboretum Found. Unit, 1966-73, pres., 1969; bd. dirs. Coun. for Prevention Child Abuse and Neglect, Seattle, 1974-75; v.p., mem. various coms. Seattle Children's Theatre, 1984-90, asst. in lighting main stage plays, 1987-93, mem. adv. coun., 1993—; asst. in lighting main stage plays Bathhouse Theatre, 1987-90; adv. bd. N.W. Asian Am. Theatre, 1987—, Co-Motion Dance Co., 1991—; organizer teen groups Episcopal Ch. of the Epiphany, 1965-67; provisional class pres. Jr. League Seattle, 1971-72, next to new shop asst. chmn., 1972-73, bd. dirs. admissions chmn., 1976-77, exec. v.p., exec. com., bd. dirs., 1978-79, sustaining mem., 1984—; charter mem. Jr. Women's Symphony Assn., 1967-73; mem. Seattle Art Mus., 1975-90, Landmark, 1990—, Corp. Coun. for the Arts, 1991—; founding dir. Adrienne Coons Meml. Fund, 1985, v.p., 1985-92, pres. 1992—; mem. steering com. Heart Ball Am. Heart Assn., 1986, 87, auction chmn., 1986; mem. steering com. Bellevue Sch. Dist. Children's Theatre, 1983-85, pub. rels. chair, 1984, asst. stage mgr., 1985. Named Miss Greater Seattle, 1964. Mem. AFTRA, Am. Biographical Inst., U. Wash. Alumnae Assn. (life), Pacific N.W. Ballet Assn. (charter), Progressive Animal Welfare Soc., Associated Women (student coun. U. Wash. 1962), Profl. Rodeo Cowboys Assn. (assoc.), Seattle Tennis Club. Republican. Episcopalian. Home and Office: 2053 Minor Ave E Seattle WA 98102-3513

DILLARD, TERESA MARY, school counselor; b. Columbus, Ga., May 12, 1956; d. Francis Joseph and Sadayo (Takabayashi) Luther; m. David Howard Dillard, July 22, 1978; children: Christine Marie, Justin David. BA, U. Md., 1977, MEd, 1981. Cert. guidance counselor, social studies tchr., modern fgn. lang. tchr., Mass., N.C. Asst. to supr. Bur. Govtl. Rsch., U. Md., College Park, 1977-78; tchr. high sch. Montgomery County Pub. Schs., Rockville, Md., 1978-80; substitute tchr. Anne Arundel Pub. Schs., Annapolis, Md., 1981, Bourne County Pub. Schs., Cape Cod, Mass., 1982-84; guidance counselor Camden County Pub. Schs., Camden, N.C., 1989—; counselor, advisor U. Md. Relief Ctr., College Park, 1977, tutor Japanese lang., 1977, vol. substitute instr. Japanese lang. dept., 1977; cons. WCNC Radio Talk Show, Elizabeth City, N.C., 1991; program developer Grandy Primary Sch., Camden, N.C., 1989—. Designer, creator children's clothing. Religious edn. tchr. Ft. Meade (Md.) Chapel Ctr., 1978, St. Bernadette Ch., Severn, Md., 1979-80; religious edn. tchr. Otis Chapel, Otis Air Nat. Guard Base, Mass., 1982-83, coord., dir. religious edn. program, 1983-84; bd. mem. Holy Family Religious Edn. Program, Elizabeth City, N.C., 1989-91, tchr., 1989-91; asst. music ministry Holy Family Ch., Elizabeth City, 1991—. Mem. ACA, Am. Sch. Counselors Assn., U. Md. Alumni Assn., Phi Beta Kappa, Phi Kappa Phi, Alpha Kappa Delta. Roman Catholic.

DILLEY, BARBARA JEAN, college administrator, choreographer, educator; b. Chgo., Mar. 13, 1938; d. Robert Vernon and Jean Phyllis (Fairweather) D.; m. Lewis Lloyd, May 1961 (div.); 1 child, Benjamin Lloyd; m. Brent Bondurant, Mar. 1977 (div.); 1 child, Owen Bondurant. BA, Mt. Holyoke Coll., 1960. Dancer Merce Cunningham Dance Co., N.Y.C., 1963-68; ind. dancer, choreographer N.Y.C. and Boulder, Colo., 1966-82; dancer Yvonne Rainer Co., N.Y.C., 1967-70; dancer, choreographer The Grand Union, N.Y.C., 1970-76; dir., faculty mem. dance program Naropa Inst., Boulder, 1974-84; condr. pvt. workshops Toronto, Ont., Can., Montreal, Que., Can., Halifax, N.S., Can., The Netherlands, Eng., Switzerland, Germany, 1978—; vis. faculty European Dance Devel. Ctr., Arnheim, The Netherlands, 1993-94; artistic dir. Crystal Dance, Boulder, 1978-81; mem. vis. faculty NYU, Radcliffe Coll., Cornell U., U. Colo., George Washington U., others; dir. dance symposium, 1981; adjudicator S.W. divsn. Am. Coll. Dance Festival, Loretto Heights, Colo., 1986. Mem. grants selection panel Colo. Coun. of Arts and Humanities, 1981, mem. panel on policy devel. for individual grants, 1983. NEA Choreographic fellow, 1974, 76, 81; Boulder City Arts Coun. grantee, 1981. Democrat. Buddhist. Office: Naropa Inst 2130 Arpahoe Ave Boulder CO 80302-5915

DILLEY, DEBORAH KAY, sales and marketing executive; b. Paynesville, Minn., Sept. 20, 1952; d. Walter Lowell and Rosemary Ann (Thielen) D.; m. Ken Rosenberg, June 11, 1988; 1 stepson: Jason Rosenberg. BA, Coll. St. Benedict, 1974. Customer svc. rep. Blue Cross/Blue Shield of Minn., Mpls., 1974-75; sales rep. Equitable Life, Pasadena, Calif., 1975-79, dist. mgr., 1979-82; bus. devel. officer Wells Fargo Bank, San Francisco, 1982-84; v.p. First Interstate Bank, San Francisco, 1984-88; v.p., mgr. instl. trust and investments First Interstate Bank, L.A., 1988-92, mem. investment policy com., 1988-92, mem. mktg. coun., 1988-92; mng. dir. Bankers Trust, N.Y.C., 1992—; mem. seminar com. Western Pension and Benefits Conf., L.A., 1990. Bd. dirs. The ERAs Ctr., Inc., L.A., 1991-92; mem. constituent rels. com. The H.E.L.P. Group, Sherman Oaks, Calif., 1991-92. Mem. Assn. Investment Mgmt. Sales Profls., Calif. Treas. Assn., Western Pension and Benefits Conf., Women in Fin. Office: Bankers Trust 280 Park Ave New York NY 10017-1216

DILLEY, LAURA LYNN, pediatrics nurse; b. Castle AFB, Calif., May 18, 1953; d. Carl John and Jeanne Violet (Koski) Schra; m. Roger Wayne Davidson, June 14, 1976 (div. June 1982); 1 child, Sara Elizabeth; m. Robert P. Dilley, June 12, 1983; 1 child, Michelle Colleen. BSN, Wright State U., 1976; MA in Human Resource Mgmt., Pepperdine U., 1979; MSN in Nursing Care of Children, Case Western Res. U., 1992. Cert. pediatric nurse practitioner. Enlisted U.S. Army Nurse Corps, 1977; advanced through grades to lt. col. U.S. Army Nurse Corps, Fort Ord, Calif., 1977-78; clin. head nurse Tripler Army Med. Ctr., Honolulu, 1989-90; nurse practitioner U.S. Army Aeromed. Ctr., Ft. Rucker, Ala., 1992—. Mem. Nat. Assn. Pediat. Nurse Assocs. and Practitioners, Sigma Theta Tau. Office: US Army Aeromedical Ctr Pediatric Clinic Fort Rucker AL 36362

DILLINGHAM, MARJORIE CARTER, foreign language educator; b. Bicknell, Ind., Aug. 20, 1915; m. William Pyrle Dillingham, (dec. 1981); children: William Pyrle (dec.), Robert Carter, Sharon Dillingham Martin. PhD in Spanish (Delta Kappa Gamma scholar and fellow), Fla. State U., 1970. High sch. tchr. Fla.; former instr. St. George's Sch., Havana; former mem. faculty Panama Canal Zone Coll., Fla. State U., Duke U., Univ. Ga.; dir. traveling Spanish conversation classes abroad, U.S. rep. (with husband) Hemispheric Conf. on Taxation, Rosario, Argentina. Named to Putnam County Hall of Fame, 1986. Mem. Am. Assn. Tchrs. Spanish and Portuguese (past pres. Fla. chpt.), Fla. Edn. Assn. (past pres. fgn. lang. div.), La Sociedad Honoraria Hispanica (past nat. pres.), Fgn. Lang. Tchrs. Leon County, Fla. (pres.), Delta Kappa Gamma (pres.), Phi Kappa Phi, Sigma Delta Pi, Beta Pi Theta, Kappa Delta Pi, Alpha Omicron Pi, Delta Kappa Gamma. Home: 2109 Trescott Dr Tallahassee FL 32312-3331

DILLINGOFSKI, MARY SUE, marketing executive; b. Madison, Wis., Dec. 27, 1944; d. Albert F. and Camille M. (Blott) D. BA, Lawrence U., 1967; MS, U. Wis., 1970, PhD, 1980. Tchr. English, Madison Pub. Schs. (Wis.), 1967-70; tchr. reading Niles Pub. Schs. (Ill.), 1971-72, Kamehameha Schs., Honolulu, 1972-77; lectr. U. Wis., Madison, 1977-80; cons. Scott, Foresman & Co., Glenview, Ill., 1980-81, mktg. mgr., 1981-86; dir. mktg. Films Inc., Chgo., 1986-87; pres. Dillingofski and Assocs., 1987—; cons. diagnostician Univ. Hosp. Learning Disability Clinic, Madison, Wis., 1977-80; ednl. cons. Kalihi Palama Adult Edn. Ctr., Honolulu, 1973-75. Author: Nonprint Media and Reading, 1979; Sociolinguistics and Reading (W.S. Gray Rsch. award 1980), 1978; also articles in profl. jours. Active Apollo Chorus, Chgo., 1983-85, Friends of Sta. WHA, Madison, 1978-80, Ripon Sch. Bd., 1994—; mem. Art Deco Soc. Chgo., Bus. Vols. for Arts; mem. econ. devel com. Chgo. Commn. on Women, 1988-89; mem. steering com. Triton Coll. Bus. Women's Conf., 1988-89; mem. Ripon (Wis.) Revitalization Corp., 1989-91, mktg. chair, 1989-91, v.p., 1990-91 (Gov.'s award Outstanding Image Campaign Wis. Main Str. program, 1990, Outstanding Vol. of Yr. Govs. award 1990, Govs. award, 1991, hon. bd. dirs.; mem. Fond du Lac County Econ. Devel. Corp, 1990. Mem. Internat. Reading Assn. (com. chmn. 1979-81), Wis. Reading Assn. (membership com. 1978-80), North Shore Reading Assn., Women in Mgmt., Am. Mktg. Assn., Nat. Assn. Women Bus. Owners (publicity com. 1987-88, pub. affairs com. 1988-89), Ripon Kiwanis (bd. dirs. 1993—), Ripon LWV, Ripon C. of C. (bd. dirs. 1993—, pres. 1995). Home and Office: 527 Fairview Ave Ripon WI 54971-1614

DILLMAN, KRISTIN WICKER, educator, musician; b. Ft. Dodge, Iowa, Nov. 7, 1953; d. Winford Lee and Helen Caroline (Brown) Egli; m. Kirk Michael Wicker, Jan. 1, 1982 (dec. June 1982); m. David D. Dillman, Apr. 13, 1990; 1 child, Alek Joseph (adopted). AA, Iowa Cen. Coll., 1974; B in Music Edn., Morningside Coll., 1976; M in Mus., U. S.D., 1983. Cert. tchr., Iowa. Tchr. instrumental music Garrigan Affiliated Schs., Algona, Iowa, 1976-77, Sioux City (Iowa) Community Schs., 1977—. Asst. prin. bassist Sioux City Symphony, 1974-93, prin. bassist, 1993—; freelance bassist, Sioux City, 1976—. Named Tchr. of Yr. Sioux City Community Schs., 1988-89. Mem. NEA, Iowa Edn. Assn., Sioux city Edn. Assn., Iowa Bandmasters Assn., Sioux City Musicians Assn., Zeta Sigma, Mu Phi Epsilon. Republican. Lutheran. Office: Woodrow Wilson Mid Sch 1010 Iowa St Sioux City IA 51105-1711

DILLON, PATRICIA ANNE, state legislator; b. Flushing, N.Y., July 9, 1948; d. Raymond Walter and Patricia Marie (Kuhlmann) D.; m. John Schley Hughes, July 5, 1977; 1 child, Patrick John. BA, Marymount U., 1970; MA, Ohio State U., 1974. Researcher Yale Sch. Medicine, New Haven, Conn., 1974-77; dir., founder New Haven Project Battered Women, 1977-80; devel. adminstr. City of Norwalk (Conn.), 1980-82; state legislator State of Conn., Hartford, 1984—; chmn. pub. health com. State of COnn., Hartford, 1990—; chmn. appropriations subcom. health and hosps. State of Conn., Hartford, 1992—, dep. majority leader, 1992—; adj. prof. Albertus Magnus Coll., New Haven, 1982-83; bd. dirs. Alcohol Svcs. Ctrl. Conn., New Haven, VA Hosp. Westhaven. Contbr. articles on family violence, health, taxation, solid waste and Irish issues to various publs. Ward chmn. Dem. Town Com., New Haven, 1976-86; alderwoman New Haven Bd. Alderman, 1979-85. Recipient Susan B. Anthony award Conn. NOW, 1987, Advocacy award Conn. Commn. Children, Hartford, 1991, Leadership award United Way Conn., Hartford, 1991. Mem. Nat. Acad. State Health Policy, Irish Am. Community Ctr. Roman Catholic. Home: 68 W Rock Ave New Haven CT 06515-2221 Office: Capitol Ave Hartford CT 06106

DIMAIO, VIRGINIA SUE, gallery owner; b. Houston, July 6, 1921; d. Jesse Lee and Gabriella Sue (Norris) Chambers; AB, U. Redlands, 1943; student U. So. Calif., 1943-45, Scripps Coll., 1943, Pomona Coll., 1945; m. James V. DiMaio, 1955 (div. 1968); children: Victoria, James V. Owner, dir. Galeria Capistrano, San Juan Capistrano and Santa Fe, N.Mex., 1979—; founder Mus. Women in Arts, Washington; cons., appraiser Southwestern and Am. Indian Handcrafts; lectr. Calif. State U., Long Beach; established ann. Helen Hardin Meml. scholarship for woman artist grad. Inst. Am. Indian Art, Santa Fe, also ann. Helen Hardin award for outstanding artist at Indian Market, S.W. Assn. on Indian Affairs, Santa Fe; bd. dirs. Mus. of Man, San Diego, 1989; mem. Intertribal Coun. U. Calif., Irvine, 1990; founder Inst. Am. Indian Art, Santa Fe, 1993, bd. dirs., 1992—. Author: (forward to Mus. of Man exhibit catalogue) Paths Beyond Tradition. Recipient Bronze Plaque Recognition award Navajo Tribal Mus., 1977. Mem. Inst. Am. Indian Art (founder, bd. dirs.), Indian Arts and Crafts Assn., S.W. Assn. Indian Affairs, Heard Mus., San Juan Capistano C. of C. Republican. Roman Catholic. Office: 31892 Camino Capistrano San Juan Capistrano CA 92675-3216

DI MARCO, BARBARANNE YANUS, special education educator multiple handicapped; b. Jersey City, Nov. 16, 1946; d. Stanley Joseph and Anne Barbara (Dalack) Yanus; m. Charles Benjamin DiMarco, Mar. 15, 1986; 1 child, Charles Garrett. BA in Music Edn., Trenton State Coll., 1968; MA in Spl. Edn., Kean Coll., 1971, elem. edn. cert., 1974, adminstrv. cert., 1976. Cert. elem., music, adminstrn., spl. edn., N.J. Vocal music educator Roselle (N.J.) Bd. Edn., 1968-69, tchr. trainable mentally retarded, 1969-76, tchr. multiple handicapped, 1976—; color guard instr. Roselle Bd. Edn., 1973-88, elem. tutor, 1976-92, adminstrv. asst. to supt., 1980-85; program dir., sec., Expanded Dimensions in Gifted Edn., Westfield, N.J., 1978—. Vestryperson St. Luke's Ch., Roselle, 1989-91. Recipient Govs. Tchr. Recognition award, Gov. Florio, N.J., Trenton, 1992-93. Mem. NEA, N.J. Edn. Assn., Roselle Edn. Assn., N.J. Assn. for Retarded Children, Eastern Star (25-yr award 1991), Delta Omicron. Republican. Episcopalian. Home: 13 Gentore Ct Edison NJ 08820-1029 Office: Dr Charles C Polk Sch 1100 Warren St Roselle NJ 07203-2736

DIMARGIO, TONI, counselor; b. Youngstown, Ohio, Jan. 27, 1950; d. Nick Anthony and Martha Louise (Paige) DiM.; 1 child, Thomas Giblin. BSBA, Youngstown State U., 1988, MSEd, 1992. Lic. social worker, Ohio. Mem. asst. alumni assn. U. Calif., Berkeley, 1972-73, prodn. coord./editor alumni assn., 1973-74, adminstrv. asst. alumni assn., 1974-75; sec. Western Res. Care System, Youngstown, 1977-92; counselor Comprehensive Psychiatry Specialists, Boardman, Ohio, 1992-93, Churchill Counseling Svcs., Youngstown, 1993—. Mem. Ohio Counseling Assn., Chi Sigma Iota. Office: Churchill Counseling Svcs 310 Churchill Hubbard Rd Youngstown OH 44505-1371

DI MARIA, VALERIE THERESA, public relations executive; b. Bronx, N.Y., Apr. 5, 1957; d. Victor Joseph and Vivian Roslyn (D'Amico) Di

Maria. BA in Journalism, NYU, 1978. Asst. dir. U.S. Div. Sidonie S. Ltd., N.Y.C., 1978-79; acct. supr. The Rowland Co., N.Y.C., 1979-82, Ketchum Pub. Rels., N.Y.C., 1982-83; pub. rels. dir. Charles of the Ritz Group Ltd., N.Y.C., 1983-84; sr. v.p. Porter/Novelli Pub. Rels., N.Y.C., 1984-89; mng. dir. GCI Group, N.Y.C., 1989—. Mem. Pub. Rels. Soc. Am. (Silver Anvil award 1986), The Fashion Group, Am. Film Inst., Women Execs. in Pub. Rels. (bd. dirs.), Women in Comms., Advt. Women of N.Y., Women's Sports Found., Phi Beta Kappa. Office: GCI Group 777 3rd Ave New York NY 10017

DIMASI, LINDA GRACE, epidemiologist; b. Trenton, N.J., Feb. 7, 1949; d. Nick and Pearl LaVerne (White) D. BS in Biology, Alderson-Broaddus Coll., 1970; MPA, Rutgers U., 1992. Cert. pub. mgr. Field rep. N.J. State Dept. of Health, Trenton, 1971-85, epidemiologist, 1985—. Contbr. articles to profl. jours. Mem. ASPA, APHA, Phi Alpha Alpha.

DIMATTEO, RHONDA LYNN, speech-language pathologist, audiologist; b. Easton, Pa., Sept. 12, 1955; d. Michael John and Betty Lenora (O'Brien) DiM. Assoc. in Gen. Edn., Northampton County Area Community Coll., 1981; BS, Trenton State Coll., 1983; MA, Hahnemann U., 1985. Cert. clin. competence in speech-lang. pathology and audiology. Lead tchr. The Nursery Sch. of Easton, Inc., 1974-83; speech-lang. pathologist, audiologist Warren Hills Regional Bd. Edn., Washington, N.J., 1985—, child study team mem., 1985—; speech-lang. pathologist, audiologist, lang. devel. tchr. Mountainview Youth Correctional Facility, Annandale, N.J., 1990—, theater instr., child study team mem., 1990—; dir. speech and hearing screening ARC, Easton, 1982—; coach cross-country and track Warren Hills Regional Bd. Edn., Washington, N.J., 1987—. Author several poems; actress several theatre co.'s. Operation Search screening dir. ARC Hearing Screenings, Easton, 1982—; trainer dogs Northampton County Soc. for The Prevention of Cruelty to Animals, Easton, 1970—; mem. hearing ear dog program New Eng. Assistance Dog Svcs., West Boylston, Mass., 1985—; mem. adoption svc. Northampton County SPCA, Easton, 1970—. Recipient Proudly We Hail cmty. award Easton, Pa., 1993. Mem. ASHA (cert., Project Enhance media campaign recruiter 1989), NEA (profl.), Pa. Speech-Lang.-Hearing Assn. (profl.), N.J. Speech-Lang.-Hearing Assn. (profl.), N.J. Edn. Assn. (prof.), N.J. Interscholastic Coaching Assn. (profl.), Nat. Coun. Tchrs. English (profl.), Nat. Student Speech-Lang.-Hearing Assn., Comm. Workers Am. (profl.), Warren County Edn. Assn., Warren Hills Edn. Assn., The Drama League. Lutheran. Home and Office: 803 Cattell St Easton PA 18042-1524

DI MAURO, CATHERINE GORNEY, insurance agent; b. Wilmington, Del., Mar. 14, 1950; d. Leo Michael and Wanda Catherine (Yedliczka) Gorney; m. Michael J. Di Mauro Sr.; children: Michael Jr., Christopher, Edward, Allison. Student, U. Del., 1989-94. Teller, head teller Bank of Del., Wilmington, 1977-87; cons. Chase Manhattan Bank, Wilmington, 1987-88; regional ops. staff Am. Internat. Ins. Co., Wilmington, 1988-89; assoc. ins. agt. R. A. Finney Nationwide Ins., Wilmington, 1989—. Tax assesor Town of Bellefonte, Wilmington, 1993-95; mem. pub. rels. Brandywine Hundred Fire Co. Ladies Aux., Wilmington, 1978-94. Mem. Ins. Women No. Del. (bd. dirs. 1992-94, ways and means chmn. 1992—, co-chair 1994—, info. dir. 1993—, legis. com. 1993-94). Home: 900 Elizabeth Ave Wilmington DE 19809 Office: RA Finney Nationwide Ins PO Box 9737 Wilmington DE 19809

DIMAURO, NANCY MARION, nursing administrator; b. N.Y.C., July 18, 1951; d. James F. and Antoinette (Grimaldi) DiM. BS in Nursing, L.I. U., Bklyn., 1973; MA, NYU, N.Y.C., 1982. Cert. in continuing edn. and staff devel., ANCC, BLS instr., trainer, Am. Heart Assn. Sr. staff nurse, charge nurse N.Y. Hosp., N.Y.C., 1973-81; dir. staff devel. Victory Meml. Hosp., Bklyn., 1981-86; acting asst. dir., instr. nursing edn. Beth Israel Med. Ctr., N.Y.C., 1986-89; dir. continuing edn. Am. Jour. Nursing Co., N.Y.C., 1989—; bd. dirs. Nurses House. Recipient Cert. of Appreciation for Svc., ARC, 1984-85. Mem. ANA (coun. on continuing edn., cert. ANCC credentialing ctr. test devel. com. 1993—), Met. Continuing Edn. Assn., N.Y. State Nurses Assn., Sigma Theta Tau (treas. Upsilon chpt. 1989-93, Pres.' award Upsilon chpt. 1992, publicity com., eligibiity com. 1994).

DIMINO, SYLVIA THERESA, elementary and secondary educator; b. N.Y.C., June 6, 1955; d. John Anthony and Elena (Berardesca) D. BA, St. John's U., 1977; MPA, NYU, 1980, MA in Elem. and Secondary Edn., 1982, cert. advance studies in ednl. adminstrn., 1986, cert. in advanced studies in mgmt., 1992. Cert. elem. and secondary tchr., sch. adminstr., in mgmt. practices, social studies, math., N.Y. Traffic coord. Creamer Inc., N.Y.C., 1977-79; tchr. St. Patrick's Sch., N.Y.C., 1979-82; tchr. IS 131, Manhattan, N.Y.C., 1984-90, adminstr., coord., 1985-90, asst. prin., 1990—;, 1985-90. Named to 2000 Most Notable Women. Mem. NAFE, AAUW, Nat. Orgn. Women in Adminstrn., Bus. Cir. N.Y., Nat. Coun. Adminstrv. Women in Edn., Nat. Orgn. Italian-Am. Women (mentoring dir.). Roman Catholic. Office: IS 131 Manhattan 100 Hester St New York NY 10002-5293

DIMMICK, CAROLYN REABER, federal judge; b. Seattle, Oct. 24, 1929; d. Maurice C. and Margaret T. (Taylor) Reaber; m. Cyrus Allen Dimmick, Sept. 10, 1955; children: Taylor, Dana. BA, U. Wash., 1951, JD, 1963; LLD, Gonzaga U., 1982, CUNY, 1987. Bar: Wash. Asst. atty. gen. State of Wash., Seattle, 1953-55; pros. atty. King County, Wash., 1955-59, 60-62; sole practice Seattle, 1959-60, 62-65; judge N.E. Dist. Ct. Wash., 1965-75, King County Superior Ct., 1976-80; justice Wash. Supreme Ct., 1981-85; judge U.S. Dist. Ct. (we. dist.) Wash., Seattle, 1985-94, chief judge, 1994—; chmn. Jud. Resources Com., 1991—, active, 1987—. Recipient Matrix Table award, 1981, World Plan Execs. Council award, 1981, others. Mem. ABA, Am. Judges Assn. (gov.), Nat. Assn. Women Judges, World Assn. Judges, Wash. Bar Assn., Am. Judicature Soc., Order of Coif (Wash. chpt.), Wash. Athletic Club, Wingpoint Golf and Country Club, Harbor Club. Office: US Dist Ct 911 US Courthouse 1010 5th Ave Seattle WA 98104-1130

DIMMITT, CORNELIA, psychologist, educator; b. Boston, Mar. 16, 1938; d. Harrison and Martha Fredericka (Read) D.; m. (div.); children: Colin Barclay Church, Jeffrey Harrison Church. BA, Harvard U., 1958; MA, Columbia U., 1966; PhD, Syracuse U., 1970; diplomate, C. G. Jung Inst., Zurich, Switzerland, 1985. Asst. prof. Am. U., Washington, 1970-71; from asst. to assoc. prof. (with tenure) Georgetown U., Washington, 1971-82; pvt. practice Boston, 1985—; Mem. admissions com. Coll. Arts and Scis., Georgetown U., Washington, 1974-76, mem. rank and tenure com., 1977-78; dir. admissions com. C. G. Jung Inst., Boston, 1986-89, pres. tng. bd., 1989-91; pres. NESJA, 1993—. Author: Classical Hindu Mythology, 1978. NEH fellow, 1979-80. Mem. Am. Oriental Soc., New England Soc. Jungian Analysts, Assn. Grads. in Analytical Psychology (Switzerland), Internat. Assn. for Analytical Psychology. Home and Office: 4 Otis Pl Boston MA 02108-1036

DIMOND, ROBERTA RALSTON, psychology and sociology educator; b. Bakersfield, Calif., Mar. 25, 1940; d. Robert Leroy Vickers and Gail Anderson (Tritch) Ralston; m. James Davis, June 18, 1963 (div. 1970); 1 child, Jamie Amundsen Davis; m. Frederick Henry Dimond, Oct. 20, 1970; children: Frederick Ralston, Robert Vickers (div. 1991). BA in History and English, Stanford U., 1962, MAT in Edn., 1963; MS, U. Pa., 1970, EdD, 1973. Cert. secondary educator, ednl. specialist, counselor, coll. personnel adminstr. Thcr. Kamehameha Sch., Honolulu, 1965-67; asst. to dean of women U. Pa., Phila., 1969-70; asst. prof. Temple U., Ambler, Pa., 1970-87, Montgomery County Coll., Blue Bell, Pa., 1975-80; prof. psychology, speech, sociology Del. Valley Coll., Doylestown, Pa., 1987—; cons. ETS, Princeton, N.J., 1989—; speaker in field; lectr. on sexual responsibilities in the 90s and assertive affirmative action topics; researcher on athletics and aging females syngerism. Author: Gender & RAcial Bias by Vocational Counselors, 1973. Bd. dirs. Concerned Citizens of Upper Dublin, Maple Glen, Pa., 1980-91, Arrowhead Assn., Ambler, Pa., 1990-91. Fellow Newhouse Found., 1960-63; grantee APA, 1969-70. Mem. AAUP, APA, U.S. Tennis Assn., Middle States Tennis Assn., MADD, Phila. Tennis Patrons, Phila. Tennis Assn. (v.p.). Democrat. Episcopalian. Home: 236 Amherst Dr Doylestown PA 18901-2381 Office: Delaware Valley Coll Rte 202 Doylestown PA 18901

D'IMPERIO, CONNIE BOLING, franchising specialist; b. Columbus, Ohio, July 18, 1946; d. Leonard Delbert Boling and Elizabeth (D'Imperio) Zoll; m. James J. Cort, July 26, 1975 (div. May 1980); children: Brandon Cort D'Imperio, Ernest David Lockhart, Michael James Lockhart. Cert. hearing aid specialist, Kent State U., 1974. Cert. hearing and speech audiologist, Ohio. Sales dir. DuraSeal, Columbus, Ohio, 1981-85; franchise dir. Peppermint Fudge, Oklahoma City, 1985-86, Caribbean Clear, Leesville, S.C., 1986-87; pres., CEO Franchise Profiles, Inc., Orange Park, Fla., 1975—, Color Your Carpet, Inc., Orange Park, 1990—, Comprehensive Franchising, Inc., Orange Park, 1989—; owner, mgr. Franchise Axis, Orange Park, 1985—; pres. Omniworks!, Orange Park, 1989—; dir. devel. Franchise Registration Svc., Washington, 1991—; franchise exporter Western Foods Project, Beijing, 1991—; panelist Gulf Coop. Coun. Mem. States Franchise Seminar, Manama, Bahrain, 1992—. Author: Franchising: The Newest Security Blanket, 1985, Master Franchising: A Global Approach, 1990, Franchising 101. Mem. NAFE, Am. Assn. Textile Chemists and Colorists, Nat. Cert. Franchise Execs., Fla. Franchise Assn., Fla. Coalition for Responsible Franchising, Minority Bus. Devel. Group. Office: Franchise Profiles Inc 2465 Ridgecrest Ave Orange Park FL 32065-6235

DI MUCCIO, MARY JO, retired librarian; b. Hanford, Calif., June 16, 1930; d. Vincent and Theresa (Yovino) DiMuccio. B.A., Immaculate Heart Coll., 1953, M.A., 1960; Ph.D., U.S. Internat. U., 1970. Tchr. parochial schs. Los Angeles, 1949-54, San Francisco, 1954-58; tchr. Govt. of Can., Victoria, B.C., 1959-60; asst. librarian Immaculate Heart Coll. Library, Los Angeles, 1960-62; head librarian Immaculate Heart Coll. Library, 1962-72; adminstrv. librarian City of Sunnyvale, Calif., 1972-88; ret., 1988; part-time instr. Foothill C.C., 1977—. Exec. bd., past pres. Sunnyvale Community Services. Mem. ALA, ICF (past pres.), Spl. Libr. Assn., Cath. Libr. Assn. (past pres.), Calif. Libr. Assn., Sunnyvale Bus. and Profl. Women, Peninsula Dist. Bus. and Profl. Women (past pres.). Home: 736 Muir Dr Mountain View CA 94041-2509

DINCAUZE, DENA FERRAN, archaeologist, educator; b. Boston, Mar. 26, 1934; d. Archibald H. and Dora (Buckman) Ferran; BA magna cum laude, Barnard Coll., 1956; diploma in prehistoric archaeology (Fulbright scholar 1956-57), Cambridge U., 1957; PhD, Harvard U., 1967; children:Eric Jean, Jacqueline Marie. Research fellow New Eng. archaeology Peabody Mus., Harvard U., 1967-69, asst. curator N.Am. archaeology, 1970-72; lectr. anthropology Harvard U., 1968-69; asst. prof. SUNY Coll., Buffalo, 1972-73; mem. faculty U. Mass., Amherst, 1973—, assoc. prof. anthropology, 1978-85, prof. anthropology, 1985—, New Eng. prehistory and paleo-environ., archeol. resource mgmt.; disting. lectr. U. Mass., 1989; vis. fellow Cambridge U., 1986-87; mem. vis. com. Peabody Mus. of Harvard U., 1975-81; mem. vis. com., adv. bd. R.S. Peabody Mus., Andover, 1992—; mem. Mass. Hist. Commn., 1978-89. grantee NSF, NHCF, NPS, Mass. Hist. Commn.; recipient Chancellors's medal, 1989. Fellow Am. Anthrop. Assn., AAAS; mem. Am. Soc. Conservation Archaeology (exec. bd. 1977-79), Soc. Am. Archaeology (chmn. com. public archaeology 1978-80, pres.-elect 1985-87, pres. 1987-89), Am. Quaternary Assn., Soc. Profl. Archaeologists (pres.-elect 1983-84, pres. 1984-85), Archtl. Inst. of Am. (com. on am. archaeology 1978-83), Phi Beta Kappa, Sigma Xi. Author papers, monographs in field; contbg. editor Rev. Archaeology, 1980—; assoc. editor N.Am. Archaeologist, 1977-80, Man in the Northeast, 1971-92; editor Am. Antiquity, 1981-84; mem. adv. bd. for archaeology Current Anthropology, 1991-92; mem. editorial bd. Cambridge Manuals in Archaeology, 1990—. Office: U Mass Dept Anthropology Amherst MA 01003

DINGLE, MARGARET CONCETTA SPARGO, retired elementary reading director; b. New Haven, Conn., Apr. 2, 1918; d. Frank Curtlin and Clara (Eck) Spargo; m. Frederick Marvin Dingle, Sr., Aug. 23, 1941; children: Patricia, Frederick Jr., Marcia, Louise. EdB, New Haven State Tchr's. Coll., 1940; MS, So. Conn. State U., 1964. Elem. tchr. Clinton (Conn.) Grammar Sch., 1940-41, Ridge Rd. Sch., North Haven, Conn., 1949-50, Prince St. Sch., New Haven, 1950-55, Alice Peck Sch., Hamden, Conn., 1956-69; reading cons. elem. schs., Hamden, 1969-73; dir. reading grades kindergarten-12 Hamden, 1973-82. Author: (curriculum guide) Individualized Reading Program, 1975-80; contbr. Instructor mag., 1971. Literacy vol. and vol. tutor in cmty. Recipient Recognition of Svc. Plaque Internat. Reading Assn., 1972; federal grantee, 1976-79. Mem. Conn. Assn. Reading Rsch. (rsch. chairperson), Ret. Tchrs. Conn., Nutmeg Reading Coun. (charter mem., 1st pres.), Assoc. Reading Coun. Conn., Internat. Reading Assn., Delta Kappa Soc. Internat., Phi Delta Kappa. Republican. Mem. Congregational Ch. Home: Mill Pond Ln Apt 25A Durham CT 06422

DINGLE, SUSAN, library science educator; b. Kankakee, Ill., Aug. 31, 1950; d. Harold Eugene and Julia Martha (Condon) Dingle; m. Gerald Howard Cliff, June 30, 1975 (div. Feb. 1984). AB, U. Ill., 1972, MS, 1975, postgrad., 1981—. Sessional reference librarian U. Alberta, Edmonton, Can., 1975-76; pub. services librarian Grant MacEwan Community Coll., Edmonton, 1976-77; librarian Alberta Alcoholism & Drug Abuse Commn., Edmonton, 1977-81; assoc. editor Grad. Sch. Library and Info Sci. U. Ill., Urbana, 1981-86, fellow, 1986-87; asst. prof. dept. L.S. Clarion U., Pa., 1987-92; instr. Sch. Libr. and Informational Sci. U. Mo., Columbia, 1992—. contbr. articles to profl. jours. Mem. ALA, LWV, Am. Soc. for Info Sci. (chair local arrangements 1979), Spl. Libraries Assn., U. Ill. Alumni Assn. (life), Beta Phi Mu. Democrat. Mem. Soc. of Friends. Office: U Mo Sch Libr & Infor Scis 104 Stewart Hall Columbia MO 65211

DINICU, CAROLINA VARGA (MOROCCO), dancer, choreographer, educator; b. Mar. 2, 1940; d. Samuel and RoseLee (Varga) D.; divorced. BA, Bklyn. Coll., 1958. Solo performer Mideastern and N. African dance various internat. cities, 1960—; solo and group performer Ballet Espagnol Ximenez-Vargas U.S., 1960-61; dance ethnologist, Morocco and Casbah Dance Experience Dance Co., 1963—; dance tchr. Amas Repertory Theater, N.Y.C., 1970-77; tchr. Mideastern dance SUNY-Purchase, N.Y.C., 1975-78; lectr., performer Mus. of Natural History, N.Y.C., 1972—; performer N.Y.C. Dept. Cultural Affairs, 1972—; dir./tchr. Morocco/Casbah Dance Acad., N.Y.C., 1976—; seminar master tchr. various internat. cities, 1975—; dir., choreographer, founder Morocco and the Casbah Dance Experience, N.Y.C., 1977—. Contbr. articles to profl. jours. Tchr. Eng. as 2nd Lang., N.Y. Assn. for New Americans, N.Y.C., 1979; dir. Russian Lang. Program, Ctr. for Fgn. Study, N.Y.C., Moscow, 1977-79; group leader Russian Lang., Am. Inst. for Fgn. Study, N.Y.C., USSR, 1975-77. Named to Mideastern Dancer Hall of Fame, Am. Assn. Mideastern Dance, N.Y.C., 1992; recipient Community Svc. grant N.Y.C. Dept. Cultural Affairs, 1986, 87, Arts Exposure grant, 1983-84, Summer Program grant, 1979, Workshop grant, 1985-87; recipient Creative Artists Pub. Svc. award N.Y. State Coun. on the Arts, N.Y.C., 1972, 81. Mem. Actors Equity Assn., Am. Fedn. TV and Radio Artists, Am. Guild of Musical Artists, Am. Guild Variety Artists, Screen Actors Guild, Mensa. Office: 320 W 15th St New York NY 10011

DINKINS, CAROL EGGERT, lawyer; b. Corpus Christi, Tex., Nov. 9, 1945; d. Edgar H. Jr. and Evelyn S. (Scheel) Eggert; children: Anne, Amy. BS, U. Tex., 1968; JD, U. Houston, 1971. Bar: Tex. 1971. Prin. assoc. Tex. Law Inst. Coastal and Marine Resources, Coll. Law U. Houston, Tex., 1971-73; assoc., ptnr. Vinson & Elkins, Houston, 1973-81, 83-84, 85—, mem. mgmt. com., 1991—; asst. atty. gen. environ. and natural resources Dept. Justice, 1981-83, U.S. dep. atty. gen., 1984-85; chmn. President's Task Force on Legal Equity for Women, 1981-83; mem. Hawaiian Native Study Commn., 1981-83; dir. Nat. Consumer Coop. Banks Bd., 1981; bd. dirs. Oryx Energy Co. Dallas. Author articles in field. Chmn. Tex. Gov.'s Flood Control Action Group, 1980-81; bd. dirs. Oryx Energy Co. of Dallas, U. Houston Law Ctr. Found., 1985-89, Environ. and Energy Study Inst., Houston Mus. of Natural Sci., Tex. Nature Conservancy, 1985—. Mem. ABA (ho. of dels., past chmn. urgan, state and local govt. sect.), FBA (bd. dirs. Houston chpt. 1986), State Bar Tex., Houston Bar Assn., Tex. Water Conservation Assn., Houston Law Rev. Assn. (bd. dirs. 1978). Republican. Lutheran. Office: Vinson & Elkins 3300 First City Tower 1001 Fannin Houston TX 77002

DINOWITZ, DEBRA, lawyer; b. Bklyn., Oct. 16, 1955; d. Sidney A. and Gloria (Spring) D. BA in Art History magna cum laude, Hofstra U., 1976, JD with distinction, 1979. Bar: U.S. Dist. Ct. (so. dist.) N.Y. 1980. Assoc. Cahill, Gordon & Reindel, N.Y.C., 1979-82, Colton, Weissberg et al, N.Y.C., 1982-83; v.p., gen. counsel Chemical Bank (formerly Mfrs. Hanover Corp.), N.Y.C., 1983—; vis. prof. Hofstra U. Sch. Law, Hempstead, N.Y., 1983. Mem. ABA, Phi Beta Kappa.

DIPASQUA, LUCY ANN, restaurant franchise executive; b. Norwalk, Conn., Feb. 12, 1927; d. Dominick Felix and Eva Renzulli Nardi; m. Peter M. Dipasqua, Oct. 4, 1947; (div. 1986); children: Gayle, Michael, Donna, Curtis, Lynn, Peter Jr. Sec. HCA, Norwalk, 1945--; sec., treas. Lucy Dipasqua, Inc., Maitland, Fla., 1977-86; pres. Dipasqua Enterprises, Maitland, 1986--; v.p. The Teaste of Ctrl. Fla.'s Best; pres. Perkit's Devel. Co. of Ctrl. Fla.; bd. dirs. ITT Tech. Inst., Mid Fla. Tech., Webber Coll. Mem. Franchise Advt. Fund (bd. dirs. 1981—, recipient Plaque), Fla. Restaurant Assn. (bd. dirs. 1986—, chmn. edn. com. 1989, sec. Chpt. 4, 1989, pres. elect 1990, pres. 1991, pres. elect 1992, pres. 1993—, chmn. 1994). Roman Catholic. Home: 411 Melanie Way Maitland FL 32751-3136 Office: Dipasqua Enterprises Inc 167 Lookout Pl Maitland FL 32751-8420

DIPERSIO, DEBORAH ANN, radiologist; b. Livorno, Tuscany, Italy, June 4, 1959; d. Romeo and Anita (Barchiesi) Di P.; m. William Joseph Birmingham, July 4, 1992. B in Engring. Scis., Johns Hopkins U., 1981; MS, PhD in Engring., Duke U., 1986; MD, Bowman Gray Sch Medicine, 1990. Resident in radiology U. Fla., Gainesville, 1990-94; fellow in neuroradiology Bowman Gray Sch. Medicine Wake Forest U., Winston-Salem, N.C., 1994-96. Composer: (piano) Album I, 1986, Album II, 1990, Album III, 1993. NIH Fellow, 1982-86; scholar Bowman Gray Sch. Medicine, 1986-90. Mem. Tau Beta Pi.

DIPIETRO, MELANIE, lawyer; b. Greensburg, Pa., Oct. 29, 1944; d. Joseph and Jessie (Detoro) DiP. BA cum laude, Seton Hill Coll., 1969; MA, Occidental Coll., 1971; JD, Duquesne U., 1975; cert., Harvard U., 1985; JCL summa cum laude, U. St. Thomas, Rome, 1987. Joined Sisters of Charity of Seton Hill, Roman Cath. Ch., 1962. Bar: Pa. 1975, U.S. Dist. Ct. (we. dist.) Pa. 1975, U.S. Supreme Ct. 1980, Mo. 1991. Tchr. Diocese of Pitts., 1965-69, Elizabeth Seton Sch., Pitts., 1971-74; assoc. gen. counsel Diocese of Pitts., 1975-81; assoc. Mansmann, Cindrich & Titus, Pitts., 1981-87, ptnr., 1987-91; ptnr. Buchanan, Ingersoll, Pitts., 1991—; lectr. bus. law Seton Hill Coll., Greensburg, 1978-79; lectr. adminstrv. agy. law grad. sch. bus. Duquesne U., Pitts., 1979-80, developmentally disabled law U. Pitts., 1979-81; cons. SSM Healthcare System Inc., St. Louis, 1986-87, bd. dirs. pub. policy, 1987-93. Author: (monograph) Congregational Sponsorship, 1985; co-author: Legal Bulletin, 1991, Hospital Contracts Manual, 1992, The Search for Identity: Canonical Sponsorship of Catholic Healthcare, 1993; contbr. articles to profl. jours. Vol. Elderly Law Project Neighborhood Legal Svcs., 1976-80. Coro Found. grantee, 1970-71; recipient West Pub. award, 1975, Cardinal Cooke award Nat. Assn. Cath. Chaplains, 1984; named one of Outstanding Young Women Am., 1975, 77. Mem. ABA, Allegheny County Bar Assn. (religious and charitable orgns. com., pub. svc. com., mental health com.). Democrat. Office: Buchanan Ingersoll 600 Grant St Fl 57 Pittsburgh PA 15219

DIPPO, JEANETTE FAYE, health educator, registered nurse; b. Miami, Fla., Sept. 15, 1943; d. Llewellyn and Marie Elizabeth (Wanser) Potter; m. Walter Allen Dippo, June 27, 1964; children: Julie Lynn, Kimberly Michelle. RN, St. Luke's Hosp., Newburgh, N.Y., 1964; BS in Health Edn., SUNY, Cortland, 1967, MS in Health Edn., 1969. Cert. tchr., N.Y. RN Cortland Meml. Hosp., 1964-66; health educator Cortland City Schs., 1966-73; health and drug edn. coord. Cortland-Madison Bd. Coop. Ednl. Svcs., 1973-75; health edn. and wellness coord. Cortland City Schs., 1975—; workshop conf. presenter various drug and health edn. confs., 1974—; cons., turnkey trainer N.Y. State Dept. Edn., Albany, 1968-92; coop. master tchr. SUNY, Cortland, 1968—, Ithaca (N.Y.) Coll., 1968—; mentor tchr. Cortland Jr./Sr. H.S., 1989—; freedom from smoking clinic coord. Am. Lung Assn., Cortland, 1990—; cons. feature TV segment on family dynamics course CBS 30 Minutes, 1978-79; grant co-dir. Healthy Me project Met. Life Found., SUNY, Cortland, 1988-89. Editor: (newsletter) Instrnl. Resource Ctr., 1973-75; mem. editl. bd. Catalyst, 1979-81. Sun. sch. and confirmation tchr. First United Meth. Ch., Cortland, 1986—; original founder's com., mem. Seven Valleys Coun. on Alcohol and Substance Abuse, Cortland, 1987—; mem. Tri-County Tobacco Prevention Coalition, Tompkins, Cortland and Cayuga Counties, 1993—. Recipient commendation award Cortland County Legislature, 1989; Project Empathy grantee Zero Adolescent Pregnancy (ZAP), 1992; grantee Project Think It Over, 1995. Mem. NEA, Am. Sch. Health Assn., Cortland United Tchrs., N.Y. State United Tchrs., N.Y. State Fedn. Profl. Health Educators (life, regional chmn. 1974-75, pres. 1976, Outstanding Sch. Health Educator 1979, Past Pres. award 1990), Delta Kappa Gamma (internat. Beta chpt. 1991—). Republican. Methodist. Home: RR 1 Mc Graw NY 13101-9801 Office: Cortland City Schs 8 Valley View Dr Cortland NY 13045-3264

DI PRIMA, STEPHANIE MARIE, educational administrator; b. Chgo., Aug. 29, 1952; d. Joseph and Ann Marie (Albate) Di P. BA in English, Rosary Coll., 1974; MEd in Adminstrn. and Supervision, Loyola U., Chgo., 1979. Tchr. St. Vincent Ferrer Sch., River Forest, Ill., 1974-78; prin. Our Lady of Hope Sch., Rosemont, Ill., 1978-81, Sacred Heart Sch., Winnetka, Ill., 1981-84, St. Monica Sch., Chgo., 1984-91, St. Martha Sch., Morton Grove, Ill., 1991—; instr. Rosary Coll., River Forest, Ill. Mem. NAESP, ASCD, Nat. Cath. Ednl. Assn., Ill. Prins. Assn., Ill. Assn. Supervision and Curriculum Devel., Women in Mgmt., Archdiocesan Prins. Coalition for Arts. Office: St Martha Sch 8535 Georgiana Ave Morton Grove IL 60053-2909

DIRADDO, DEBORA JEAN, speech pathologist; b. Phila., May 24, 1966; d. Joseph and Gevena (Francis) DiR. BS in Communication Disorders, Marywood Coll., 1988; MA in Speech and Hearing Scis., Ohio U., 1990. Lic. speech pathologist, Del., Pa. Extern Magee Rehab. Hosp., Phila., 1989-90, Bryn Mawr Rehab. Hosp., Malvern, Pa., 1990; clin. fellow Med. Ctr. of Del., Wilmington, 1990-91; clin. supr. Magee Rehab. Hosp., Phila., 1991—; presenter profl. groups. Contbr. articles to profl. convs. Mem. Am. Speech and Hearing Assn., Pa. Speech and Hearing Assn., N.J. Speech and Hearing Assn., Del. Speech and Hearing Assn., Southeastern Speech and Hearing Assn. (exec. coun.). Roman Catholic. Home: 32 Fairmount Dr Glassboro NJ 08028-1326 Office: Magee Rehab Hosp Philadelphia PA

DISALVO, KATHY KUHL, computer programmer, analyst; b. Olney, Ill., Oct. 26, 1956; d. John Joseph and Jeanette Catherine (Ochs) Kuhl; m. Michael Anthony DiSalvo, Aug. 31, 1985 (div. Dec. 1988). BS in Bus., Ea. Ill. U., 1977. Systems programmer, systems analyst, programmer/analyst Western Ill. U., Macomb, 1980-85; cons. Mattoon, Ill., 1985-86; programmer analyst St. Lucie County Sch. Bd., Ft. Pierce, Fla., 1986-88; rsch. programmer U. Ill., Urbana, 1989—. Mem. NAFE. Home: 1619 Sangamon Dr Champaign IL 61821-4936

DISANDRO, DEBORAH JEAN, columnist; b. Chgo., June 20, 1959; d. Jack Raymond Dempsey and Jean Ann (Rose) Podgornik; m. Anthony Gerald DiSandro, May 20; children: Marcus James, Lauren Michelle. BA in Communications, Columbia Coll., 1983. TV prodn. asst. Fred A. Niles, Chgo., 1983-84; sales asst. John Blair & Assocs., Chgo., 1984-86; with advt. dept. Teleview Cable 5, Urbana, Ill., 1985-86; TV promotion asst. Sta. WCIA-TV, Champaign, Ill., 1987-88; self-syndicated newspaper columnist, freelance writer various cities, 1988—; adult edn. instr. various colls., Waukesha, Wis. and northwest Ill., 1992-94; speaker in field. Active Pauline Haas Friends of Libr., Sussex, Wis., 1991-93. Mem. Nat. Soc. Newspaper Columnists. Home and Office: 1168 Sagebrush Cary IL 60013

DISBENNET, LINDA K., accountant; b. Lancaster, Ohio, Nov. 7, 1953; d. Eugene Vincent and Norma Jean (Seifert) Kilbarger; m. H. Keith Disbennet, Oct. 26, 1974; 1 child, Loree Jean. AA, Ohio U., 1974, BBA, 1980. CPA, Ohio. Sec. The Midland Mutual Life Ins. Co., Columbus, Ohio, 1974-78; acctg. technician Groner, Boyle & Quillin CPAs, Columbus, 1982-83; acct. Scheffler Scherer CPA Group, Lancaster, 1983—. Grad. leadership tomorrow program Lancaster-Fairfield County C. of C., Lancaster, 1991; chairperson comml. divsn. United Way Fairfield County, Lancaster, 1994; chairperson acctg. Fairfield Career Ctr., 1992—, mem. tech. adv. com., 1987. Mem. AICPA, Ohio Soc. CPAs, Inst. Mgmt. Accts. (bd. dirs. Zane Trace Ohio chpt. 1985—), Lancaster Rotary (bd. dirs. 1994—). Office: Scheffler Scherer CPA Group Inc 110 E Main St Lancaster OH 43130

DISBROW, LYNN MARIE, communications educator; b. Chgo., Sept. 2, 1961; d. Ervin John and Patricia Ann (Grabarek) Lodyga; m. Michael Ray Disbrow, July 14, 1984; children: Matthew Ray, Nicole Marie. BA, Ind. U.,

South Bend, 1982; MA with distinction, Emerson Coll., Boston, 1986; PhD, Wayne State U., Detroit, 1989. High sch. program mgr. Jr. Achievement of Michiana, Inc., South Bend, 1982-84; account exec. AM The WNDU Stas., South Bend, 1984; instr. Emerson Coll., Boston, 1985-86; instr. Wayne State U., Detroit, 1986-87, grad. teaching asst., 1987; lectr. Ind. U., South Bend, 1988; lectr. I Sinclair C.C., Dayton, Ohio, 1989-90, asst. prof., 1993—; asst. prof. comm. U. Dayton, 1990-92. Author conv. papers Mass. Comm. Assn., 1985, Speech Comm. Assn., 1986-91, 94, Ctrl. State Comm. Assn., 1989, 91, 92, 94, 95, others; mem. editorial bd. Ohio Speech Jour., 1993, N.D. Jour. Speech and Theatre, 1992. Rumble fellow, 1986-87. Mem. Speech Comm. Assn., Ctrl. States Comm. Assn., Speech Comm. Assn. Ohio (exec. bd. 1995). Republican. Roman Catholic.

DISERENS, HELEN BARNETT, research chemist; b. Huntington, W.Va., Feb. 16, 1919; d. Arthur Leroy and Leah (Gilmore) Barnett; m. Robert Carver Diserens, Jr., Apr. 5, 1947 (dec. July 1989); children: Deborah Fairbanks, Robert Carver III. BS in Chemistry, U. Mich., 1941. Coll. bd. editor Mademoiselle Mag., N.Y.C., 1940; with pub. rels. mktg. dept. Elizabeth Arden, N.Y.C., 1941-42; analytical rschr. Hoffman LaRoche, Nutley, N.J., 1942-43; head new product R & D Bristol Myers Co., Hillside, N.J., 1943-50; bus. mgr. Rippowam Cisqua Sch., Bedford, N.Y., 1962-92; prin. Moneyminder Svc., Mt. Kisco, N.Y., 1981—; chmn. bus. affairs com. Nat. Assn. Ind. Schs., Boston, 1978-81, N.Y. State Assn. Ind. Schs., Albany, 1980; mem. fin. com. Rippowam Cisqua Sch., 1993—. Inventor Ban Deodorant, 1948; co-prodr. (book) Accounting for Independent Schools, 1977; contbr. articles to profl. jours. Trustee Dublin (N.H.) Sch., 1974-87; bd. dirs. Adoption Svc. West, White Plains, N.Y., 1953-63, Mt. Kisco Community Concerts, 1970-73; mem. adv. com. St. Matthews Ch., 1993—. Republican. Episcopalian. Home: 111 Tripp St Mount Kisco NY 10549

DISMUKES, CAROL JAEHNE, county official; b. Giddings, Tex., July 17, 1938; d. Herbert Emil and Ruby (Alexander) Jaehne; m. Harold Charles Schumann, Feb. 7, 1959 (div. May 1970); children: Timothy, Michael, Keith, Gregory; m. Milton Brown Dismukes, Mar. 19, 1971. Student Tex. Lutheran Coll., 1958. Dep. Lee County Clk., Giddings, Tex., 1970-74, chief dep., 1975-77; accounts receivable clk. Invader Inc., Giddings, 1977-79; prodn. sec. Humble Exploration, Giddings, 1979-80; county clk. Lee County, Giddings, 1980—. Mem., Dime Box Ind. Sch. Dist. Trustees, Tex., 1972-80, pres., 1977-80; v.p. St. Johns Lutheran Ch. Council, 1982-84; chmn. Dime Box Homecoming and Mini-Marathon, 1978—; chmn. scholar com. Lee Co. Jr. Livestock Show, 1982—; sec. St. John's Luth. Ch., 1986, treas., 1987-89; chmn. St. John's Luth. Ch., 1991-93. Mem. County and Dist. Clks Assn. Tex. Democrat. Avocations: reading; sewing. Office: Lee County Clk PO Box 419 Giddings TX 78942-0419

DISMUKES, VALENA GRACE BROUSSARD, physical education educator; b. St. Louis, Feb. 22, 1938; d. Clobert Bernard and Mary Henrietta (Jones) Broussard; m. Martin Ramon Dismukes, June 26, 1965; 1 child, Michael Ramon. AA in Edn., Harris Tchrs. Coll., 1956; BS in Phys. Edn., Washington U., St. Louis, 1958; MA in Phys. Edn., Calif. State U., L.A., 1972; BA in TV and Film, Calif. State U., Northridge, 1981. Cert. phys. edn. tchr., standard svcs. supr. Phys. edn. tchr., coach St. Louis Pub. Schs., 1958-60; phys. edn. tchr., coach L.A. Unified Sch. Dist., 1960-84, health and sci. tchr., mentor tchr., 1984-93; coord. gifted and talented program 32d St./U.So. Calif. Magnet Sch.; adminstrv. asst. Ednl. Consortium of Ctrl. L.A., Calif., 1993—; owner, bus. cons. Grace Enterprises, 1994—; coord. Chpt. I, 1989-93, coord. gifted and talented program, 1993-95; mem. sch. based mgmt. team, 1990-93. Editor parent newsletter, 1975-80; photographs exhibited in one-woman shows include The Olympic Spirit, 1984, L.A.-The Ethnic Place, 1986; contbr. articles to profl. jours. Mem. adv. com. Visual Comm., L.A., 1980; bd. dirs. NACHES Found., Inc., L.A., 1985-86; mem. Cmty. Consortium, L.A., 1986-87; mem. adv. com. L.A. Edn. Partnership, 1986-87; mem. adv. bd. Expo Sports Club, L.A., 1994. Marine Educators fellow, 1992; photography grantee L.A. Olympic Organizing Com., 1984, Teaching grantee L.A. Edn. Partnership, 1987-89; recipient Honor award L.A.-Calif. Assn. Health, Phys. Edn. and Recreation, 1971. Mem. ACLU, NAACP, Am. Fedn. Tchrs., United Tchrs. of L.A., Am. Home Bus. Assn., Urban League, Sierra Club. Home: 3800 Stocker St # 1 Los Angeles CA 90008 Office: 32d St/USC Magnet Sch 822 W 32d St Los Angeles CA 90007

DISNEY, ANTHEA, editor; b. Dunstable, Eng., Oct. 13, 1946; came to U.S., 1973; d. Alfred Leslie and Elsie (Wale) Disney; m. Peter Robert Howe, Jan. 28, 1984. Ed., Queen's Coll., Eng. Fgn. corr. London Daily Mail, N.Y.C., 1973-75; features editor London Daily Mail, London, 1975-77; bur. chief London Daily Mail, N.Y.C., 1977-79; columnist London Daily Express, N.Y.C., 1979-84; former dep. mng. editor N.Y. Daily News, N.Y.C., 1984-87; editor Sunday Daily News, 1984-87, U.S. Mag., 1987-88; editor-in-chief Self mag., 1988-89; mag. developer Murdoch Mags., 1989-90; exec. producer Fox TV's A Current Affair, 1990-91; editor-in-chief TV Guide mag., N.Y.C., 1991—; editorial dir. Murdoch Mags., 1994—. Office: TV Guide 1211 Ave of Americas 4th Fl New York NY 10036-8701

DISSETTE, ALYCE MARIE, television and multimedia producer, nonprofit foundation executive; b. Flint, Mich., Mar. 16, 1952; d. Leland Richard and Carol A.R. (Scott) D. Student, Genesee Coll., 1970-72, U. Mich., Flint, 1972-73, U. Wis., 1975-76. Personal asst. Gilbert V. Helmsly Jr., Madison, Wis., 1975-78; adminstrv. asst. Presentations, Met. Opera, N.Y.C., 1977-79; co. mgr. Ballet Hispanico N.Y., N.Y.C., 1980-81; exec. dir. Oberlin Dance Co., San Francisco, 1983-86; producer, exec. dir. David Gordon/Pick Up Co., N.Y.C., 1986-89; founder 501C3 Inc., N.Y.C., 1994—; project co-dir. A Study of Choreographers, NEA, Washington, 1989-91; dir. computer art competition New Voices, New Visions, 1994. Prodr. (dance-theater) David Gordon's U.S., 1987-89; exec. prodr. (PBS series) Alive TV/Alive from Off-Center, 1991-93; project work for Bklyn. Acad. Music, Performance Space 122, Pepsico Summerfun, MTV (Music TV Cable Ace award, 1994). Office: 501C3 Inc care Sci Am 415 Madison Ave New York NY 10017

DISTEFANO, RITA-ANNE ANTONIA, occupational therapist; b. Boston, Nov. 21, 1964; d. Salvatore and Angela Santa (Sciucco) DiS. BS, Boston U., 1986; cert. in advanced profl. studies, Tufts U., 1990; Cert. in Drug/Alcohol Counseling, Middlesex C.C., 1993. Lic. occupational therapist, Mass., ultracare rehab./clin. supr. Occupational therapist Vets. Affairs, Bedford, Mass., 1987-94; occupational therapist substance abuse dept. Choate Hosp., Woburn, Mass., 1988-89; occupational therapist Acton (Mass.) Pub. Health Nursing Svcs., 1994—; HIV prevention counselor, 1991-94; substance abuse specialist, 1988-94. Mem. Mass. Assn. Occupational Therapy (univ. liaison 1984-86, mem. chair 1987-88, exec. bd. dirs. 1987-90, treas. 1988-90), Am. Occupational Therapy Assn., Sons of Italy (treas. Medford chpt. 1988—). Roman Catholic.

DITOMASO, NANCY KAY, organization management educator; b. Canton, Ohio, Aug. 29, 1946; d. Americo DiTomaso and Betty Jo (Ash) DiTomaso Claugus; m. Thomas Ross Schink, Oct. 18. 1980; children: Jessica Barbara, Alisa Elizabeth. BA in Sociology, Ohio State U., 1969; MS in Sociology, U. Wis., 1971, PhD in Sociology, 1977. Asst. prof. Northwestern U., Evanston, Ill., 1976-82, NYU, N.Y.C., 1982-83; asst. prof. Rutgers U., Newark, N.J., 1983-85, assoc. prof., 1985-93, prof. orgn. mgmt., 1993—, chair. Co-author: Coordinating Human Services, 1975; co-author and co-editor: Ensuring Minority Success in Corporate Management, 1988; chair editorial and pub. com. Soc. for Study of Social Problems, 1983-84; contbr. articles to profl. jours. Trustee, coun., coord. adult edn. United Ch. of Rogers Park, Chgo., 1976-80; mem. spl. concerns subcom. Ill. Employment and Tng. Coun., Springfield, 1979-81. Grantee U.S. Dept. of Labor, Washington, 1979-80, Rockefeller Found., 1980-82, Ctr. for Innovation Mgmt. Studies, 1990, Alfred P. Sloan Found., 1993-95. Mem. Am. Sociol. Assn. (coun. 1986-88, divsn. chair 1990-91), Soc. for Advancement Sociol. Econs. (v.p. 1992-93, pres. 1994-95), Acad. Mgmtm. (divsn. steering com. 1990-91). Democrat. Home: 143 S Martine Ave Fanwood NJ 07023 Office: Rutgers U 180 U Ave Newark NJ 07102

DITTMAN, DEBORAH RUTH, real estate broker; b. Sacramento, Apr. 15, 1932; d. Charles Harwood and Ruth (Potter) Kinsley; m. John Alvin Cardoza, Sept. 1950 (div. 1964); children: Harold Cardoza, Nancy Jongeward, John Allan Cardoza, Gregory Cardoza, Janice Boswell; m. Edgar Marshall Dittman, Jan. 22, 1967 (dec. Jan. 6 1982); m. Philip George Vrieling, July 7, 1990. Student Humprey's Coll., Stockton, Calif., 1966; grad. real estate sales Anthony Schs., 1978; cert. in real estate San Joaquin Delta Coll., 1977. Lic. real estate broker, Calif., 1978, real estate sales assoc., 1974-78; cert. residential specialist. Sec. Calif. Dept. Water Resources, Patterson and Tracy, 1966-72; hostess Welcome Wagon, Tracy, 1973-74; assoc. realtor Reeve Assocs., Tracy, 1975-80; broker Allied Brokers, Tracy, 1980-83; ptnr. real estate Putt, Fallavena, Willbanks & Dittman, Tracy, 1983—; mem. adv. bd. Tracy Fed. Bank(formerly Tracy Savings & Loan), 1989—, Women's Coun. Realtors, 1990—. Mem. Residential Sales Coun., 1989, Women's Coun. Realtors, 1990. Mem. Tracy Bd. Realtors (pres. 1981, 85, dir. 1976, 77, 80-83, 85-86), Calif. Assn. Realtors (dir. 1980-81, 85), Cert. Real Estate Specialists (v.p. no. Calif. chpt. 1990, pres. 1991), Nat. Assn. Realtors, Tracy Assn. Realtors, So. Alameda Assn. Realtors, Tracy C. of C. (bd. dirs. 1988-90). Presbyterian. Home: 12134 Midway Dr Tracy CA 95376-9113 Office: 1045 Tracy Blvd Tracy CA 95376-3726

DITTMER, SHARON JUANITA, prison nurse; b. Litchfield, Ill., Sept. 16, 1941; d. Norman William and Vera Christine (Jackson) Sumpter; m. James Jerry Dittmer, Mar. 22, 1963; children: James William, Jerry Alan. Diploma, Meml. Hosp. Sch. of Nursing, Springfield, Ill., 1962. RN, Ill, Ky., Ind. Psychiat. staff Madison (Ind.) State Hosp., 1963-64, Norton's Infirmary, Louisville, 1964-68; clinic supr. Louisville Meml. Hosp., 1968-70; obstetrics staff Harrison County Hosp., Corydon, Ind., 1973-75; house supr. Frazier Rehab. Ctr., Louisville, 1979-85; prison nurse Ind. Dept. Corrections, Tell City, 1991—; mem. state quality assurance com. Ind. Dept. Corrections, Indpls., 1991-92. Chairperson community svcs. com. Am. Heart Assn., Crawford County, Ind., 1977-79. Recipient Key to City of Louisville, Mayor, 1969, State Disting. Program award, Am. Heart Assn., Ind. 1973. Mem. Ind. Correctional Nurses Assn. (state rep. 1991-92). Home: RR 1 Box 282 Marengo IN 47140-9745

DITTRICH, VALERIE MONICA, investment consultant; b. Riverside, N.J., June 11, 1955; d. Francis George and Anne (Rohaly) D. BS in Commerce, Rider Coll., 1977; MBA, Drexel U., 1994. Registered investment advisor; lic. ins. agt., N.J., Pa. Investment adminstr. N.J. Nat. Bank, Trenton, 1977-80; instnl. sales asst. Merrill Lynch Govt. Securities, Phila., 1980-81; account exec. Paine Webber Inc., Phila., 1981-85, Smith Barney Harris & Upham, Phila., 1985-92; sales assoc. Prudential Securities, Inc., Jenkintown, Pa., 1992-94; investment cons. Samuel A. Ramirez & Co., Inc., N.Y.C., 1995—. Mem. Omicron Delta Kappa (alumna chpt.). Republican. Roman Catholic. Home: 195 Greenwood Ave Riverside NJ 08075-4223 Office: Samuel A Ramirez & Co Inc 61 Broadway New York NY 10006

DIVILA, JOYCE MARIE, counselor; b. Chgo., Nov. 2, 1942; d. Alex F. and Mary J. (Zdon) Zabinski; m. Franklin Bruce Divila, Jan. 9, 1965; children: Jill Suzanne, Martin Jay. BS, U. Ill., 1969; MA, Roosevelt U., 1972. Cert. elem. sch. tchr., sch. counselor, alcohol and other drug counselor, mediator, Ill. Tchr. Sch. Dists. 122 and 111, Oak Lawn, Burbank, Ill., 1964-78; home/hosp. tutor Sch. Dist. 144 & 152-1/2, Markham, Hazel Crest, Ill., 1979-87; court caseworker dept. social svc. Cir. Ct. Cook County, Markham, 1987-94; mediator, conciliator domestic rels. divsn. Cir. Ct. Cook County, Chgo., 1994—; coord., tchr. gifted Sch. Dist. 152-1/2, 1984-87; mem. tng. com. social svc. dept. Cir. Ct. Cook County, 1991-93; trainer various profl. orgns.; cons., counselor local chs., Chgo., 1994; trainer Chgo. Marriage Encounter. Active domestic violence and other emerging issues com. Marriage and Family Counseling Svc. Mem. Mediation Coun. Ill., Assn. Family and Conciliation Cts., Ill. Alcohol and Other Drug Addictions Profl. Cert. Assn., Homewood-Flossmoor Parents Assn., Homewood-Flossmoor Chpt. I Parents Orgn. (chmn. adv. bd. 1993), Homewood-Flossmoor Organized Parents United Support Orch. Orgn., AAUW (3d v.p. , chair publicity), LWV (chair hospitality Hazel Crest chpt.), Roosevelt U. Alumni Orgn., NAFE. Roman Catholic. Office: Marriage Family Counseling 32 W Randolph Ste 1050 Chicago IL 60601

DIXON, ARMENDIA PIERCE, school program administrator; b. Laurel, Miss., July 15, 1937; d. L.E. and Denothras (Pickens) Pierce; m. Harrison D. Dixon Jr., Aug. 28, 1971; 1 child, Harrison D. III. BS in Edn., Jackson (Miss.) State U., 1960; postgrad., No. Ill. State U., 1965-66; MEd, Edinboro (Pa.) U., 1978; PhD, Kent State U., 1994, Kent State U., 1994. Cert. English and secondary edn., Miss. Tchr. English, libr. Laurel City Schs., 1962-67; tchr. English, dir. summer pre-sch. Erie (Pa.) Pub. Schs., 1967-72; tchr. English, drama, journalism, forensic coach Crawford Cen. Schs., Meadville, Pa., 1972-85, asst. prin., facilitator sch. improvement coun., 1985-89, coord. successful student partnership, 1988—; prin. Meadville Area Sr. High; exec. dir. Meadville Latch-Key Program, 1985—; coord. Urban Tchrs. Project, Kent State U., adj. asst. prof., 1989—, dir. Prospective Tchrs. Program for Phi Delta Kappa; charter mem. Results chpt., Kent State U., 1990; dir. high sch. edn. Sch. dist. City of Erie, 1993—; dir. of high sch. edn., The Sch. Dist. of the City of Erie, Pa., 1993—. Fundraiser Cystic Fibrosis Found., Pitts., 1976. 79, 81, Sickle Cell Anemia, Erie, 1978-83; pres. Martin Luther King Jr. Scholarship Fund, Inc., 1979-89. Mem. NAACP (pres. Meadville chpt. 1984—), Nat. Assn. Secondary Sch. Prins., Pa. Assn. Secondary Sch. Prins., Order Eastern Star (worthy matron), Navy Mothers, Rainbow lll, Burres, Phi Delta Kappa, Alpha Kappa Alpha. Methodist. Home: 716 Jefferson St Meadville PA 16335-2205 Office: Crawford Ctrl Schs 847 N Main St Meadville PA 16335-2655

DIXON, IRMA MUSE, state commissioner, former state legislator, social worker; b. New Orleans, July 18, 1952; d. Joseph Sr. and Irma (White) Muse; m. Reuben Dixon, June 26, 1976. BA, So. U. of New Orleans, 1976; MSW, Tulane U., 1979; postgrad., Harvard U., 1985. Dir. community devel. New Orleans, 1980, bur. chief mgmt. svcs. Office of Employment and Tng., 1981-82, dir. dept. recreation, 1982-84; undersec. Dept. Culture, Recreation and Tourism Baton Rouge, 1984-86; dir. dept. property mgmt. New Orleans, 1987-88; state rep. Ho. of Reps., New Orleans, 1988-93; commr. La. Pub. Svc. Commn. Dist. III, 1993—; cons. Audubon Inst. Aquarium, New Orleans, 1985. Recipient Legislator of Yr. Alliance for Good Govt., 1988, Outstanding Svc. award City of New Orleans-Mayor's Office, 1988, Leadership award Earhart-Tulane Corridor Assn., 1989, Legis. Women's award La. Conf. Elected Women, 1989, Presidential award Nat. Caucus State Legislators, 1989. Mem. Am. Planning Soc., Am. Soc. Pub. Adminstrs., Nat. Orgn. Black Elected Legis. Women, Nat. Black Caucus State Legislators, Nat. Conf. State Legislators (bd. dirs.), Ind. Fee Appraisers, Young Leadership Coun., Harvard Club of La. Democrat. Baptist. Office: Fl 2D 650 S Pierce St New Orleans LA 70119-6838

DIXON, JEANE, writer, lecturer, realtor, columnist; b. Medford, Wis., Jan. 5, 1918; d. Gerhart and Emma (von Graffe) Pinckert; m. James L. Dixon, 1939. Founder, chmn. bd. Children to Children Inc., 1964—; pres. James L. Dixon & Co., Realtors, Washington. Author: My Life and Prophecies, 1969, Reincarnation and Prayers to Live By, 1970, The Call to Glory, 1972, Yesterday, Today and Forever, 1976, Jeane Dixon's Astrological Cookbook, 1976, Horoscopes for Dogs (Pets and Their Planets), 1979, The Riddle of Powderworks Road, 1980; syndicated columnist: Horoscope and Predictions, Universal Press Syndicate., featured in Star Mag.; exponent of extrasensory perception (subject of book A Gift of Prophecy), 1988. Chmn. Christmas Seal campaign, Washington, 1968; hon. chairperson, hostess Mystic Ball Cystic Fibrosis Found., 1990-94; pres. exec. adv. coun. United Cerebral Palsy of Washington and No. Va., 1992; mem. disting. citizen adv. bd., 1994. Recipient Loreto Internat. award Loreto Shrine, Italy, 1969; Internat. L'Enfant award Holy Family Adoption League, 1969; named Woman of Year Internat. Orphans, 1968; knight Internat. Order of St. Martin, Vienna; award Md. chpt. Cystic Fibrosis Found., hon. chairperson/hostess Mystic Carnival, 1992; St. John of Jerusalem Internat. Humanitarian Christian Chivalry award; knighted Dame of Humanity; Imperial Byzantine Order of St. Constantine the Great of St. George; Fall Gal award Nat. Saints and Sinners Conv.; Unsung Heroine award Ladies aux. VFW; Golden Lady Humanitarian award AMITA Internat.; Internat. Nostradamus award Internat. Platform Assn.; Leif Erikson Humanitarian award Sons of Norway; First Anglo hon. Navajo princess, 1968; Disting. Am. award (first female) Sales & Mktg. Execs. Met. Washington D.C., 1989; Rep. Senatorial medal of freedom, 1994, Am. Police Hall of Fame. Mem. ASCAP, Nat. League Am. Pen. Women, Internat. Platform Assn. Club: Internat. (Washington). Office: James L Dixon & Co 1765 N St NW Washington DC 20036-2802*

DIXON, JO-ANN CONTE, management consultant; b. Orange, N.J., Aug. 5, 1942; d. Rocco Louis and Antoinette (DeRosa) Conte; m. Michael Eugene Dixon, July 26, 1964; children: Christopher Michael, Peter Eugene. Student, Paterson State Coll., 1960-63; AA, Thomas A. Edison Coll., 1976, BA, 1978. Tchr. St. Raphael's Sch., Livingston, N.J., 1963-68; owner Orgn. Unltd., Glen Ridge, N.J., 1972-76; market rsch. analyst Harkness & Assoc., San Francisco, 1976-78; adminstr. corp. tng. dept. Rapidata, Inc., Fairfield, N.J., 1978-80, mgr. corp. tng. dept., 1980-81; pres., prin. cons. Q, Inc., Essex Fells, N.J., 1980—; pres. MatchPlay Internat., Inc. 1992—; bd. trustees Mt. St. Dominic Acad., 1989—; bd. dirs. alumni rels. N.J. Inst. Tech., Newark 1981-83, West Essex Community Health Svcs., devel. chair, 1988—, pres. 1993—; dir. mgmt. devel. Rutgers U. Grad. Sch. Mgmt., 1983-84; bd. dir. alumni affairs/devel. officer Seton Hall Law Sch., Newark, 1984-85; chmn. bd. trustees Nat. Inst. for Orgnl. and Mgmt. Rsch., Essex Fells, N.J., 1987-92. Chmn. bd., sec. Passaic River Coalition, Basking Ridge, N.J., 1976-83, vice chmn. bd., 1983-88, regional coord., 1971-76; chmn. mayor's com. on environ., Glen Ridge, 1974-75; mem. N.J. Gov.'s Task Force for Passaic River, 1976-78; mem., pres. Home and Sch. Bd., Glen Ridge, 1978-79; mem. Nat. Trust Hist. Preservation scholar, 1977; citation Borough of Glen Ridge, 1975; Kiwanis award for excellence in citizen involvement, 1974, Charles T. Morgan award for excellence in tng. and devel, 1989. Mem. Am. Soc. Tng. and Devel. (v.p. communications, profl. excellence award 1980), LWV, Knights of Malta-Order St. John of Jerusalem (Dame of Malta 1986), Glen Ridge Hist. Soc. (founder), West Essex C. of C. (bd. dirs. 1988-89, v.p. 1990-91, pres. 1991-92), Kiwanis (bd. dirs. 1990-93, N.J. Found. bd. trustees 1990-92). Home: 97 Lane Ave West Caldwell NJ 07006-7426 Office: 6 Bucker Farm Rd Roseland NJ 07068

DIXON, KATIE LOOSLE, county official; b. Clarkston, Utah, Oct. 10, 1925; d. Reuben O. and Sylvia (Griffiths) Loosle; divorced; children: Jerry, Michael, Keven Todd, Darcy. BS, Utah State U., 1945; LDH, Salt Lake C.C., 1993. Recorder Salt Lake County, Salt Lake City, 1975-94; trainer, facilitator workshops and seminars; mem. panel to evaluate U.S. std. lics. and certs. Nat. Ctr. Stats., USPHS, 1984-85; mem. State of Utah adv. bd. Nat. Hist. Publs. and Records Commn., 1979-91, chmn. local govt. records task force, 1983-84. Contbr. articles to profl. publs. Bd. dirs., mem. strategic planning com. Leadership Am., Fairfax, Va., 1991—; mem. Concord Coalition Adv. Bd., 1993—; mem. alumni recognition adv. com. Utah State U., 1991; nat. adv. bd. U. Utah Children's Dance Theater, Salt Lake City, 1990-91; adv. bd. Utah Women's Arts Project, Salt Lake City, 1989—; mem. Salt Lake C.C. Devel. Bd., Salt Lake City, 1989-91; chmn. Utah Columbus Quincentenary Commn., 1988-92; mem. celebrity roast com. Am. Lung Assn. of Utah, 1988; bd. dirs. Women's Fedn. Utah Reps., 1968-69; active Salt Lake County Rep. Party, 1960-89, Utah State Rep. Party, 1966-84; campaign co-mgr. Sherman P. Lloyd Congl. campaigns, 1964, 66, 68, 70; mem. adv. bd. Utah Citizens for Arts, 1981-89, Utah Assn. Retarded Citizens, 1982-89; mem. Utah com. Fifty States Project on Discrimination Against Women in the Law, 1982-83; mem. art adv. bd. Salt Lake County, 1982, mem. bicentennial community com. on U.S. Constitution, 1986-87; mem. funding study com. Utah State Bd. Edn., 1984; mem. adv. com. Utah Women's Conf., 1984—; chmn. child care task force Salt Lake County, 1985; mem. dean's adv. coun. Coll. Bus. Utah State U., Logan, 1986-89; chair membership com., chair govt. com. Utah Women's Forum, Salt Lake City, 1987; bd. dirs. Utah Opera Guild, Salt Lake City, 1987-94, Westminster Coll. Found., Salt Lake City, 1987-89; mem. adv. bd. U. Utah Grad. Sch. Social Work, 1987-93, vice chair, 1989, chair, 1990-93; mem. policy coun. on strengthening the family Nat. Policy Form, Washington, 1994. Katie Dixon scholar, 1993, scholar Nat. Dem. and Rep. Coms., 1986; recipient Cert. of Honor, Soroptimist Internat. of Salt Lake, 1990, Alumnus of Yr. award Utah State U., 1978, Disting. Svc. award Utah Tech. Coll., 1979, Susa Young Gates award Utah Women's Polit. Caucus, 1980; named Hon. Chmn. Ann. Banquet, NAACP, 1977. Mem. ASPA (chmn. state conf. 1977), Nat. Assn. Counties (bd. dirs. 1980-81, 83-5, 87—, mem. various coms., mem. NACoNet 1992-93, chmn. bd. event 1991, Salt Lake County com. for ann. conf. 1991), Nat. Assn. County Recorders and Clks. (bd. dirs. 1976-78, 79—, sec./treas. 1979-80, chmn. convention com. 1976-77, v.p. 1982-83, pres. 1983-84, mem. various coms.), Women Ofcls. of Nat. Assn. Counties (v.p. 1979-80, pres. 1980-81), Inst. for Land Info. (1st v.p. 1986, 87, pres. 1988-90), Utah Women's Internat. Connection, Internat. Women's Forum, Utah Assn. Counties (bd. dirs. 1976-77), Salt Lake Area C. of C. (civic responsibility com. 1987, state legis. action com. 1987—, WIBCO program planning com. 1987), Utah Key Rep. Club (bd. dirs. 1985—), Pi Alpha Alpha. Mem. LDS Ch. Home: 3781 Lois Ln Salt Lake City UT 84124 Office: Salt Lake County Recorder 2001 S State N # 1600 Salt Lake City UT 84190-1150

DIXON, KELLY A., investment banker; b. Chgo., June 3, 1963; d. William Nathan and Mary Berneice (Duncan) D. BS in Fin., U. Pa., 1985; MBA, U. Chgo., 1989. Sr. credit analyst Mfrs. Hanover, N.Y.C. and Chgo., 1985-87; brand asst. Procter & Gamble, Cin., 1989-91; asst. v.p. 1st Chgo. (Ill.) Capital Markets, 1992—. Recipient Dollars and Sense award Dollars and Sense Mag., Chgo., 1991. Mem. Nat. Black MBA Assn., Alpha Kappa Alpha.

DIXON, LINDA, child, adolescent and adult therapist; b. Bronx, June 2, 1962; d. Joseph and Francine Marilyn (Rega) Incoronato; m. Charles Richard Dixon, Aug. 17, 1987; children: Joseph Anthony, Danielle Marie. AA, Dutchess C.C., Poughkeepsie, N.Y., 1979; BS, BA magna cum laude, Brockport Coll./SUNY, 1982; MA, Marist Coll., Poughkeepsie, 1986; postgrad., Fordham U., 1985. Lic. mental health counselor extern, Fla. Behavioral edn. counselor Nutri-System Weight Loss Ctr., Fishkill, N.Y., 1983-85; nutrition/fitness cons. IBM/Mariott Corp., Poughkeepsie, 1985-86; psychol. specialist Eckerd Youth Developmental Found., Okeechobee, Fla., 1986-87; counseling cons. Child Protection Team/Children's Spl. Edn. Needs Team, Okeechobee, Fla., 1987-89; day treatment dir. West County Mental Health Ctr., Belle Glade, Fla., 1988-90; counseling cons. Counseling and Behavioral Assocs., Port St. Lucie, Fla., 1990-93; staff trainer/counseling cons. Calvary Assembly of God, Port St. Lucie, Fla., 1990-91; exec. dir. Network for Christian Counselors, Port St. Lucie, Fla., 1992—; EMT, Alamo Ambulance, Poughkeepsie, 1983-85; grad. asst. Office of Health Svcs., Psychology, Marist Coll., Poughkeepsie, 1984-86; cmty. rep. Sandypines Hosp., Tequesta, Fla., 1989-91; cons. Samaritan House for Boys, Stuart, Fla., 1993-94. Contbr. articles to profl. jours. Bd. dirs. Crisis Pregnancy Svcs., Port St. Lucie, 1992-93; vol. worker Heart Assn. Dutchess County, Poughkeepsie, 1980-81, March of Dimes, 1978-79, Muscular Dystrophy, 1978-79; mem. Congl. Campaign Com./Dutchess County Youth Adv. Com. to Legis, 1980-82. Day Treatment for adolescents Children's Svcs. Coun. grantee, 1988. Mem. Fla. Soc. Psychotherapists, Am. Assn. Christian Counselors, Am. Counseling Assn., Am. Mental Health Counselor Assn., Fla. Sheriff's Assn. Democrat. Office: Network for Christian Couns 8450 S Federal Hwy Port Saint Lucie FL 34952-3306

DIXON, MARGUERITE ANDERSON, retired nursing educator; b. Pitts., May 18, 1930; d. William Orlando and Ida Mary (Taylor) Anderson; m. Relyea M. Dixon, June 15, 1952 (dec.); children: Marguerite Elise Dixon-Roper, Relyea Paul. BSN, U. Ill., Chgo., 1959; BA, Andrews U., Berrien Springs, Mich., 1952; MSN, U. Ill., Chgo., 1971, PhD, 1982. RN, Ill. Rsch. asst. coll. dentistry U. Ill.; adminstrv. nurse I, II & III U. Ill. Hosp., asst. dir. nursing; asst. prof., coord. grad. program psychiat. nursing U. Ill., Chgo., 1985-90; acting dean Chgo. State U., 1990-93. Contbr. articles to profl. jours. Mem. Mayor's Task Force on Women's Health, Chgo., 1993-94. Mem. ANA, Ill. Nurses Assn., Sigma Theta Tau.

DIXON, ROSINA BERRY, physician, pharmaceutical development consultant; b. Columbus, Ohio, Dec. 3, 1942; d. Loren C. and Florence H. (Bateson) Berry; m. Richard W. Dixon, July 4, 1970; children: Erica H., Douglas R., Andrew D. BA in Chemistry, Radcliffe Coll., 1964; MD, Columbia U., 1968. Diplomate Am. Bd. Internal Medicine. From sr. assoc. to exec. dir. Ciba-Geigy, Summit, N.J., 1972-81; med. dir. Schering Labs., Kenilworth, N.J., 1981-84; v.p. Med. Market Spltys., Boonton, N.J., 1985-86; cons. pharm. devel. Bernardsville, N.J., 1986—; bd. dirs. Enzon, Inc., Piscataway, N.J., Church & Dwight Co., Inc., Princeton, N.J.; instr. medicine Coll. Phys. and Surg., Columbia U., 1972—; preceptor in family practice Overlook Hosp., Summit, 1979—; mem. adv. bd. Daytop at Mendham, N.J., 1991—; trustee Bonnie Brae, N.J., 1992. Mem. Am. Coll. Clin. Pharmacology, Am. Soc. Clin. Pharmacology and Therapeutics, Nat.

Assn. Corp. Dirs. Episcopalian. Home and Office: 43 Old Wood Rd Bernardsville NJ 07924

DIXON, SHIRLEY JUANITA, restaurant owner; b. Canton, N.C., June 29, 1935; d. Willard Luther and Bessie Eugenia (Scroggs) Clark; m. Clinton Matthew Dixon, Jan. 3, 1953; children: Elizabeth Swanger, Hugh Monroe III, Cynthia Owen, Sharon Fouts. BS, Wayne State U., 1956; postgrad., Mary Baldwin Coll., 1958, U. N.C., 1977. Acct. Standard Oil Co., Detroit, 1955-57; asst. dining room mgr. Statler Hilton, Detroit, 1958-60; bookkeeper Osborne Lumber Co., Canton, N.C., 1960-61; bus. owner, pres. Dixon's Restaurant, Canton, 1961—; judge N.C. Assn. Distributive Edn. Assn., state and dist., 1982—; owner Halbert's Family Heritage Ctr., Canton. Past Pres. Haywood County Assn. Retarded Citizens Bd., 1985-94, past v.p., chmn. bd. dirs.; bd. commrs. Haywood Vocats. Opportunities, 1985-94, treas. bd. dirs.; Haywood Sr. Leadership Council; dist. dir. 11th Congl. Dist. Dem. Women, 1982-85; state Teen-Dem. advisor State Dem. party, 1985-90; del. 1988 Dem. Nat. Conv., Atlanta; alderwoman Town of Canton, N.C.; vice-chair Gov.'s. Adv. Coun. on Aging, State N.C., 1982-89; 1st v.p. crime prevention Community Watch Bd., State N.C., 1985, 86; mem. Criminal Justice Bd., N.C. Assembly on Women and the Economy; chair Western N.C. Epilepsy Assn., Haywood County N.C. Mus. History, 1987—; co-chair Haywood County Commn. on the Bi-Centennial of Constn., 1987-92; Haywood County Econ. Strategy Commn.; v.p., bd. dirs. Haywood County Retirement Coun., Region A Coun. on Aging; bd. dirs. Haywood County Sr. Housing, C.B.C. United Way (mem. chair); chair bd. Canton Sr. Citizen's Ctr.; mem. Haywood County Ease Retirement Com.; pres., chairwoman bd. Haywood County Assn. Retarded Citizens; pres. N.C. coun. Alzheimer's Disease and Related Disorders Assn.; bd. dirs. Canton Recreation Dept., Western N.C. Alzheimer's Disease and Related Disorders Assn., 1987-91, v.p., C.B; bd. dirs. Haywood Literary Coun., Haywood Sr. Leadership Coun., W.N.C. Econ. Devel. Com., United Way, 1991—, drive chmn.; mem. legis. subcom. Alzheimer's-State of N.C.; bd. dirs. N.C. Conf. for Social Svcs., 1987-91; v.p. bd. Western N.C. Alzheimer's Assn., 1987-91; pres. State Coun. on Alzheimer's; apptd. mem. Legis. Study Com. on Alzheimer's; apptd. mem. State of N.C. Adv. Bd. on Community Care and Health; mem. Habitat for Humanity Haywood County; bd. chair Pigeon Valley Optimist Club; apptd. by Senate Western N.C. Econ. Devel. Commn.; appointee Haywood County Econ. Devel. Commn., Canton Hist. Commn. Recipient Outstanding Svc. award Crime Prevention from Gov., 1982, Gov.'s Spl. Vol. award, 1983, Outstanding Svc. award N.C. Community Watch Assn., 1984, Community Svc. award to Handicapped, 1983-84, Outstanding Svc. award ARC, 1988; named Employer of Yr. for Hiring Handicapped N.C. Assn. for Retarded Citizens, 1985, Community Person of Yr. Kiwanis Club, 1991; Rec. Outstanding award Haywood Co. Sr. Games, 1992. Mem. AAUW, NAFE, NOW, Women's Polit. Caucus, Internat. Platform Assn., Women's Forum N.C., Nat. Bd. Alzheimers Assn. (regional del.), Canton Bus. and Profl. Assn. (pres. 1974-79, Woman of Yr. 1984), Altrusa (Women of Yr. in N.C. 1989). Democrat. Episcopalian. Home: 104 Skyland Ter Canton NC 28716-3718 Office: Dixons Restaurant 30 N Main St Canton NC 28716-3805

DIXON-BALSIGER, NANCY MARIE, publisher, actress, television production assistant; b. Ogden, Utah, May 9, 1958; d. Clarence Alfred and Dorothy Elaine (Rasmussen) Dixon; m. David Wayne Balsiger, Oct. 12, 1991. Student, Weber State Coll., 1977-79; flight attendant tng., Frontier Airlines, 1979; student, Jones Real Estate Coll., 1983, Mike Jones' Sch. Real Estate, 1990. Lic. ins. agt. Office asst., jr. loan processor Admiral Fin. Svcs., Mission Viejo, Calif., 1986-87; title rep. Commerce Title Co., Santa Ana, Calif., 1987; escrow rep. Burrow Escrow Co., Irvine, Calif., 1987-88; rep. to div. mortgage loans Am. Family Mortgage Credit Union Svcs., Orange, Calif., 1988-89; title rep. Southland Title Ins., Santa Ana, Calif., 1989-90; ins. agt. Primerica, Irvine, Calif., 1990-91; co-founder, pub. Christian Singles Connection Mag., Ogden, Utah, 1991-93; exec. dir. Christian Datemate Connection, Ogden, 1991-93; loan officer Freedom Mortgage, Salt Lake City, 1993-94; regional dir. LifeWorks, San Diego, 1993—; sec. Christian Singles Connection, Inc., Costa Mesa, 1992-94; actress cmty. theatre and TV commls. Prodn. asst. CBS TV network spl. Ancient Secrets of the Bible, The Incredible Discovery of Noah's Ark, Ancient Secrets of the Bible II, Ancient Mysteries of the World, (video) Ancient Secrets of the Bible Collectors Series. Mem. fundraising com. Living Well Med. Clinic, Santa Ana, Calif., 1988-89, Ogden Newcomers, 1993-94; bd. dirs. Nat. Citizens Action Network, Costa Mesa, 1991—. Mem. Irvine Bd. Realtors (affiliates com. 1987-91, Home Restoration-Handicapped award 1987, 1st Pl. award golf tournament 1989), Singles Press Assn., Toastmasters (dir. membership 1989-90). Republican.

DIXSON, J. B., communications executive, columnist; b. Norwich, N.Y., Oct. 19, 1941; d. William Joseph and Ann Wanda (Teale) Barrett; BS, Syracuse U., 1963; postgrad. in bus. adminstrn. Wayne State U., 1979-81; MA, Central Mich. U., 1984. Public relations editorial asst. Am. Mus. Natural History, N.Y.C., 1963-64; writer/producer Norman, Navan, Moore & Baird Advt., Grand Rapids, Mich., 1964-67; prin. J.B. Dixson Comm. Cons., Detroit, 1967-74; dir. Public Info. Services div. Mich. Employment Security Commn., Detroit, 1974-82; news relations mgr. Burroughs Corp., 1982-83, dir. creative services, 1983-85, dir. pub. relations, 1985-86; prin. Dixson Comm., Detroit, 1986-93, Durocher Dixson Werba, Inc., Detroit, 1994—; lectr., speaker in field at colls., univs., community orgns. Columnist Detroit News. Mem. Detroit Mayor's Transition Com. of 100, 1972; mem. bd. mgmt. Detroit YWCA, 1974; chmn. Detroit Women's Equality Day Com., 1975; bd. dirs., founding mem. Feminist Fed. Credit Union, Detroit, 1976; centennial chair Indian Village Assn., 1993-95; founding mem. Mich. Women's Campaign Fund, 1980; active Mich. Task Force on Sexual Harassment in Workplace, Mich. Women's Com. of 100, Mich. Women's Polit. Caucus, Mich. Women's Found. Named Outstanding Sr. Woman in Radio and TV, Syracuse U., 1963; recipient Five Watch award Am. Women in Radio and TV, Mich., 1969, cert. of recognition Detroit City Council, 1976, Feminist of Yr. award NOW, 1977, City of Detroit Human Rights Commn., 1988, Design in Mich. award Mich. Council of Arts/Gov. William G. Milliken, 1977, Achievement award U.S. Dept. Labor, 1979, Spirit of Detroit award Detroit City Council, 1980, PR Casebook, 1983, PR News case study, 1986; subject of Mich. Senate Resolution 412, 1979. Recipient Nat. Sch. Pub. Rels. Assn. award, 1992, Mich. Hosp. Pub. Rels. Assn. Pinnacle award, 1987. Fellow Public Relations Soc. Am. (accredited, pres. chpt. 1983-84, Dist. award and citation 1984, 86, 87, 93), Internat. Assn. Bus. Communicators (Silver Quill award chpt., 1987, 88, 91, 93, dist., 1987, Renaissance award, 1988, 91, Mercury award, 1987), Nat. Assn. Govt. Communicators (Blue Pencil award 1977, Gold Screen award 1980), Econ. Club Detroit, Clubs: Thames Yacht, Maple Grove Gun, Detroit Press. Author: Guidelines for Non-Sexist Verbal and Written Communication, 1976; Sexual Harassment on The Job, 1979; The TV Interview: Good News or Bad?, 1981. Office: Durocher Dixson Werba 400 Renaissance Ctr Ste 2250 Detroit MI 48243

DJALATTA, LORETTA JEAN, securities company executive, real estate broker; b. Columbus, Ohio, June 16, 1943; d. Charles Edward and Vivian Edwards (Burton) Rose; m. James Peterson, Dec. 3, 1957 (div. 1963); children: James, Carlos, Shelley Foster, George Carr. Student, Long Beach (Calif.) City Coll., 1976-79. Real estate agt. Century-21 A Marketplace, Long Beach, 1985-86, Wagner-Jacobson Brokerage, L.A., 1986-87, Exclusive Realtors, L.A., 1987-89; real estate broker Long Beach, 1989—; registered rep. NAP Fin. Corp., Santa Ana, Calif., 1989-91, registered prin., 1991—; arbitrator Better Bus. Bur., Cypress, Calif., 1989—; mem. State Panel Consumer Arbitrators, Nat. Panel Consumer Arbitrators. chief exec. officer Youth Devel. Agy., Long Beach. Mem. Long Beach Area C. of C. Office: Aragon Fin Svcs Ste 204 555 Pointe Dr Bldg 3 # 204 Brea CA 92621

DOANE, CARA GRADY, dermatologist; b. Flint, Mich., July 31, 1938; d. Paul Jackson and Mary Ella (Decker) G.; m. Conn Burdette Doane, June 13, 1959; children: Grady Connor, Autum Elizabeth, Kathleen Devin. Student, Flint C.C., U. Mich.; MD, U. Mich., 1962. Intern U. Mich., Ann Arbor, 1962-68, resident in dermatology, 1968-69; pvt. practice Ypsilanti, Mich., 1969—. Office: 1715 Washtenaw St Ypsilanti MI 48197

DOANE, FAYE HICKS, mathematics educator; b. Perry, Ga., Aug. 24, 1944; d. Carlton Turner and Billie (Robinette) Hicks; m. Robert E. Doane, June 13, 1981; 1 child, Jeremiah Robert. BS, Auburn U., 1966; MEd, U. Ga., 1972, EdS, 1976. Cert. specialist/adminstrn and supervision. Tchr. math. Muscogee County Bd. Edn., Columbus, Ga., 1966-70, Glynn County Bd. Edn., Brunswick, Ga., 1970-71; tchr. math. Houston County Bd. Edn., Perry, Ga., 1972-80, math. coord., 1980—. Mem. Nat. Coun. Tchrs. Math., Profl. Assn. Ga. Educators (dist. dir. 1983-84), Ga. Suprs. Math. (sec. 1992-94), Ga. Coun. Tchrs. Math. (treas. 1993—), Delta Kappa Gamma, Phi Delta Kappa. Office: Houston County Bd Edn 1211 Washington St Perry GA 31069-2555

DOBB, BARBARA JEANE, state legislator, accountant; b. Hancock, Mich., Aug. 21, 1949; d. John Albert and Vivian Louise (Carpenter) Dobb. B in Acctg., Walsh Coll., 1978, MS in Taxation, 1984. Acct. Gerald B. Sallan & Co., Southfield, Mich., 1978-84; acct., pres. Barbara J. Dobb, CPA, P.C., West Bloomfield, Mich., 1984—; bd. dirs. N. Pointe Ins. Co., Southfield. Planning commr. Commerce Twp., Mich., 1989—; mem. Mich. Ho. of Reps., 1990—. Recipient Spl. Tribute, Richard D. Fessler, 1989. Mem. AICPAs, Mich. Assn. CPAs, Walsh Coll. Alumni Assn., Lakes Area C. of C. (treas. Walled Lake, Mich. chpt. 1985-86, pres. elect 1986-87, pres. 1987-88, pres. 1989—, Outstanding Citizen of Yr. award 1989). Republican. Presbyterian. Office: Ste 310 6960 Orchard Lake Rd West Bloomfield MI 48322-4527 also: Mich State Senate State Capitol Lansing MI 48909*

DOBBIE, DOROTHY, Canadian legislator; b. Jan. 5, 1945; d. Glenn Dobbie, 1964; children: Lori, Shauna. Founder Assn. Publs. Ltd.; mem. from Winnipeg South Ho. of Commons, 1988-93. Pres. Winnipeg (Man., Can.) Conv. and Visitors Bur. Named Outstanding Bus. Citizen of Yr., Man. C. of C., 1983, YMCA Woman of Yr., 1987. Mem. Winnipeg C. of C. (1st woman pres.). Mem. Progressive Conservative Party. Office: House of Commons, Parliament Bldgs, 70 Jewett Bay, Winnipeg, ON Canada R3R 2N7

DOBBINS, DOLORES PAULINE, educator, counselor; b. Saltville, Va., Aug. 1, 1943; d. William Ellis and Pauline Goldie (McNew) Farris; m. Ernest Freddrick Dobbins, Aug. 14, 1965; children: Michelle, Christopher. BA, Evangel Coll., 1965; MS, East Tenn. State U., 1971; Specialist Degree in Edn., U. So. Miss., 1979; EdD, Auburn U., 1989. Lic. profl. counselor; cert. sch. counselor, Miss. Tchr. Springfield (Mo.) Schs., 1965-66, Bristol (Va.) Schs., 1966-68; sch. counselor Greene County Schs., Leakesville, Miss., 1968-93; adj. prof. U. So. Miss., Hattiesburg, 1990—. Mem. Ladies Variety Club, Leakesville, !972—. Mem. NEA, Am. Counseling Assn., Nat. Bd. Cert. Counselors, Miss. Assn. Educators, Am. Sch. Counselors Assn., Greene County Edn. Assn., Fine Belt Counselors Assn., Phi Kappa Phi. Home: PO Box 579 Leakesville MS 39451-0579

DOBBS, SUSAN ELIZABETH, elementary education educator; b. El Paso, Tex., Dec. 20, 1962; d. George Anthony and Mary Lou (Tiller) McBride; m. Larry Edward Dobbs, Sept. 4, 1992; children: Hansel, Meredith, Ethan. BS in Edn, North Tex. State U, 1987; MEd, U. North Tex., 1993. Cert. elem. tchr., Tex. Tchr. 2nd grade Mesquite (Tex.) Ind. Sch. Dist., 1987-88; tchr. 3rd grade Dallas DIocese, 1988—; tchr. ESL, El Centro Jr. Coll., Dallas, 1988-91, Eastfield Jr. Coll., Mesquite, 1988-91; instr. cheerleading, 1991-93. Grantee U. North Tex., 1991-93. Mem. Alpha Chi Omega, Phi Kappa Phi. Methodist. Home: 708 Robin Rockwall TX 75087

DOBBS, VERNA ROYSTER, educational administrator; b. Shelby, Miss., Feb. 14, 1945; d. Roscoe and Johnnie Mae (Gamble) Royster. BA, LeMoyne Coll., 1966; MEd, Memphis State U., 1972. Tchr. Memphis City Schs., 1967-78, guidance counselor, 1978-84, 88-93, adminstr., 1993—; counselor evaluator Tenn. Dept. of Edn., Nashville, 1984-88. Editor West Tenn. Counseling Assn. Newsletter, 1991-92, Tenn. Counseling Assn. Newsletter, 1991-92; contbn. author: Living Smart, 1990-91; contbr. articles to profl. jours. Mem. Tenn. Sch. Counselors Assn. (pres.-elect 1992), Alpha Kappa Alpha. Home: PO Box 280216 Memphis TN 38168-0216 Office: Hamilton Middle Sch 1478 Wilson Memphis TN 38106

DOBEL, KATHRYN ELIZABETH, lawyer; b. San Francisco, Mar. 10, 1948; d. Max and Vaida (Corbett) Hoffman; m. Mark W. Dobel, Aug. 5, 1967 (div. 1973); children: Danielle, Lisa and Gabrielle Dobel; m. David M. Weitzman, June 27, 1978; children: Gwendolyn Weitzman, Laura Weitzman. Student, U. Santa Clara; BA, Calif. State U., San Francisco, 1975; JD, U. San Francisco, 1978. Bar: Calif. 1979. Atty. Law Office of Kathryn E. Dobel, Berkeley, Calif., 1979—. Mem. Calif. Bar Assn., Alameda County Bar Assn. Office: Law Office of Kathryn Dobel 2026 Delaware St Berkeley CA 94709-2122

DOBELIS, INGE NACHMAN, editor; b. Würzburg, Germany, Nov. 16, 1933; came to U.S., 1938, naturalized, 1951; d. Rudolf Hugo and Resi (Hamburger) Nachman; B.A. in English, U. Ga., 1956; m. Miervaldis C. Dobelis, May 4, 1969; 1 son, Arthur N. Editorial positions Buttenheim Publs. and Crowell-Collier, 1956-64; copy editor Gen. Book div. Readers Digest, N.Y.C., 1965-72, asso. editor, 1973-79, sr. editor, 1979-85, sr. staff editor, 1985—. Exec. bd., officer Murray Hill Democratic Club, 1968-74; exec. bd. Community Bd. No. 6, N.Y.C., 1973-78, sec., 1976, chmn. health and hosps. com., 1974-78; trustee, officer Brotherhood Synagogue, 1983—, pres. 1993—; mem. N.Y. Dem. County Com., 1967-74. Mem. Phi Beta Kappa. Assoc. editor: Reader's Digest Family Encyclopedia of American History, 1975; Reader's Digest Family Health Guide and Medical Encyclopedia, 1976; Reader's Digest Illustrated Guide to Gardening, 1978; editor: Readers Digest Family Legal Guide, 1981; Quick and Thrifty Cooking, 1984; Magic and Medicine of Plants, 1986; Great Recipes for Good Health, 1988; America: Land of Beauty and Splendor, 1992, Legal Problem Solver, 1994. Club: Nat. Arts (N.Y.C.). Home: 201 E 17th St New York NY 10003-3607 Office: Reader's Digest Gen Books 260 Madison Ave New York NY 10016-2401

DOBIS, JOAN PAULINE, elementary education educator; b. S.I., N.Y., Sept. 11, 1944; d. Victor Raymond and Rosanna Elizabeth (Dandignac) Mazza; m. Robert Joseph Dobis, Dec. 21, 1968. BA in History, Notre Dame Coll., S.I., 1966; MS in Advanced Secondary Edn. and Social Studies, Wagner Coll., 1968; profl. diploma in ednl. adminstrn. supervision, Fordham U., 1979, postgrad. Cert. adminstr. and supr. K-12, social studies and math. tchr. K-12, elem., intermediate and jr. high sch. asst. prin., elem., intermediate and junior high sch. prin., N.Y. Tchr. Prall Intermediate Sch., Staten Island, 1966—, administv. asst., 1977-82. Mem. S.I. Hist. Soc., 1968-78, Friends of Down's Syndrome Found., S.I., 1978—, Sister Helen Flynn Scholarship Com., S.I., 1981—, Friends Seaview Hosp. and Home, S.I., 1984—, Friends S.I. Coll., 1979—. Scholar N.Y. State Bd. Regents, 1962, Can. Consulate St. Lawrence U., 1987, Internat. Brotherhood Teamsters U. Calif., 1988, Nat. Geographic Soc. Geography Edn. Program SUNY, Binghamton, 1989; recipient St. John's U. Pietas medal, 1991; Impact II grantee N.Y.C. Bd. Edn., 1992; named Tchr. of Yr. Fordham U., 1993. Mem. ASCD, Nat. Coun. Social Studies, N.Y. State Coun. Social Studies, N.Y.C. Coun. Social Studies, S.I. Coun. Social Studies, United Fedn. Tchrs., Am. Fedn. Tchrs., N.Y. State Hist. Soc., Notre Dame Coll. Alumnae Assn. (regent 1978-80, pres. 1982-84), St. John's U. Alumni Fedn. (del. 1980-88, sec. exec. bd. 1988-90, chmn. bd. 1990-94), Phi Delta Kappa (co-founder S.I. chpt., pres. 1985-87, other offices, Tchr. of Yr. award Fordham U. 1993, named Disting. Kappan 1994). Republican. Roman Catholic. Home: 174 Bertha Pl Staten Island NY 10301-3807 Office: Prall Intermediate Sch 11 Clove Lake Pl Staten Island NY 10310-2798

DOBRIANSKY, PAULA JON, business and communications executive; b. Alexandria, Va., Sept. 14, 1955; d. Lev Eugene and Julia Kusy D. BS summa cum laude, Sch. Fgn. Service, Georgetown U., 1977; MA, Harvard U., 1980, PhD, 1991. Adminstrv. aide Dept. Army, Washington, 1973-76; staff asst. Am. embassy, Rome, 1976; rsch. asst. joint econ. com. U.S. Congress, Washington, 1977-78; NATO analyst Bur. Intelligence and Rsch., Dept. State, Washington, 1979; staff mem. NSC, White House, Washington, 1980-83, dep. dir. European and Soviet affairs, 1983-84, dir. European and Soviet affairs, 1984-87; dep. asst. sec. of state for Human Rights and Humanitarian Affairs, 1987-90; dep. head U.S. Del. to Conf. on Security and Cooperation in Europe, Copenhagen, 1990; assoc. dir. for policy and programs U.S. Info. Agy., 1990-93; co-chair internat. TV coun. Corp. Pub. Broadcasting, 1993-94; sr. internat. affairs and trade advisor Hunton and Williams, Washington, 1994—. Host Freedom's Challenge, Nat. Empowerment Television, 1994—. Bd. dirs. Am Com. for Aid to Poland, 1994—, Congl. Human Rights Found., 1994—, Western NIS Enterprise Fund, 1994—, Am. Com. for Aid to Poland, 1994—; bd. vis. George Mason U., 1994—. Fulbright-Hays scholar, 1978; Rotary Found. fellow, 1979, Ford Found. fellow, 1980, adj. fellow, Hudson Inst., 1993—; named one of ten Most Outstanding Young Women in Am., 1982, one of ten Outstanding Working Women of 1990, Ethnic Woman of Yr., 1990; recipient Georgetown U. Alumni Achievement award, 1986, State Dept. Superior Honor award, 1990. Mem. Internat. Inst. Strategic Studies, Coun. Fgn. Rels., Am. Polit. Sci. Assn., Fulbright Assn., Phi Beta Kappa, Phi Alpha Theta, Pi Sigma Alpha, U.S. Environ. Tng. Inst. (bd. adv. 1992-93), Harvard Club (bd. dirs. 1982-85), Nat. Endowment for Democracy (bd. dirs. 1993—, vice chmn. 1995—), Am. Coun. of Young Polit. Leaders (trustee 1993—), University Club (Washington). Office: Hunton & Williams Ste 9000 2000 Pennsylvania Ave NW Washington DC 20006-1877

DOBRONSKI, AGNES MARIE, state legislator; b. Detroit, Apr. 21, 1925; d. Clarence Robert and Agnes Frieda (Franz) Dobronski; m. James Z. Cichocki, June 27, 1987; stepchildren: Thomas, Jerry. BS, Detroit Coll. Bus., 1970; MA, Eastern Mich. U., 1975. Bus. mgr. Dearborn (Mich.) Pub. Schs., 1943-80; exec. dir. Retirement Coord. Coun., Lansing, Mich., 1980-85; mem. Mich. Ho. of Reps., 1987-88, 91—. Trustee Dearborn Bd. Edn., Henry Ford Community Coll., 1980-86. Recipient Disting. Alumna award Detroit Coll. Bus., 1974, Disting. Citizen award Henry Ford Cmty. Coll., 1987, Disting. Alumni award Henry Ford Cmty. Coll., 1989; named Sch. Adminstr. of Yr. Dearborn PTA Council, 1978. Democrat. Lutheran. Home: PO Box 1948 Dearborn MI 48121-1948 Office: House of Reps State Capitol Lansing MI 48909-7514*

DOBRYNSKI, ROXANNE HOWALD, company executive; b. St. Louis, Feb. 1, 1947; d. Kenneth Williams and Dixie Doine (Kimberlin) Howald; m. Peter Vincent Dobrynski, Sept. 21, 1968 (div. 1981); children: Douglas, Amy; m. James F. Sherry, June 2, 1992. BA, U. Mo., 1968. Analyst Ctrl. Intelligence Agy., Langley, Va., 1968-72; tech. photographer, analyst U.S. Dept. State, Seoul, Korea, 1975-78; from mktg. and sales adminstrn. to N.E. sales mgr. Federal Leasing, Inc., Vienna, Va., 1978-85; gen. mgr. Computer Consoles, Inc., Rochester, N.Y., 1985-89; pres. Fed. Schedules, Inc., Herndon, 1989—; COO EnStar Internat., Herndon, Va., 1993—. Contbg. mem. Am. Conservative Union, Washington, 1993. Republican. Lutheran. Office: Federal Schedules Inc 790 Station St Ste 3000 Herndon VA 22070-4606

DOBS, ADRIAN SANDRA, endocrinologist, educator; b. June 27, 1954; m. Martin Auster; children: Nina Auster, Becky Auster, Harry Auster, Paul Auster. BS in Human Nutrition and Food Scis., Cornell U., 1973; MD, Albany Med. Coll., 1978; MHS in Cardiovascular Epidemiology, Johns Hopkins U., 1990. Diplomate Nat. Bd. Med. Examiners, Am. Bd. Internal Medicine, Am. Bd. Endocrinology and Metabolism. Resident in internal medicine Montefiore Hosp. Med. Ctr./Albert Einstein Coll. Medicine, Bronx, N.Y., 1978-81, chief resident, 1981-82; instr. medicine, physicians asst. program CCNY, N.Y.C., 1981-82; endocrinology fellow Johns Hopkins U., Balt., 1982-84, instr. divsn. endocrinology and metabolism, 1984-87, asst. prof. medicine, 1987-93, assoc. prof. medicine, 1993—; mem. study sect., adv. com. Nat. Inst. Aging, 1992, NIH, 1993, 94; lectr. in field. Reviewer Am. Jour. Clin. Nutrition, Am. Jour. Medicine, Diabetes Care, Jour. AMA, Jour. Clin. Endocrinology and Metabolism, New Eng. Jour. Medicine; contbr. articles, abstracts to profl. jours., chpts. to books. Recipient Rsch. award Women Physicians Stetler Found., 1986-87; scholar Leopold Schepp Found., 1975, Vanderbilt U., 1976, Carnegie-Mellon Found., 1984-85, Robert Glassner Found. Diabetes Rsch., 1985-86; grantee Merck, Inc., 1991-93, TheraTech, Inc., 1991-94, NIH, 1992-93, 92—, Diabetes Rsch. and Edn. Found., 1992-93, Johns Hopkins Out-patient Clin. Rsch. Ctr., 1992-93. Mem. ACP, Am. Coll. Nutrition, Am. Diabetes Assn. (award Md. chpt. 1986-87), Am. Fedn. Clin. Rsch. (Johns Hopkins rep. 1990—, sch. coun. 1990—), Am. Heart Assn. (epidemiology coun. 1985, grantee 1990-94), Endocrine Soc. Home: 3510 Anton Farms Rd Baltimore MD 21208 Office: Johns Hopkins Hosp 906B Blalock Bldg 600 N Wolfe St Baltimore MD 21287-4904

DOBSON, ANDREA CAROLE, secondary school educator; b. Spokane, Wash., Sept. 25, 1956; d. Carl Elvin and Neysa Carole (Johnson) D. AA, Spokane Falls C.C., 1977; BA in Edn., Ea. Wash. U., 1979; EdM, Wash. State U., 1990. Cert. tchr. K-12, Wash. Tchr. history Grand Coulee (Wash.) Dam Dist., 1979-81, Lind (Wash.) Sch. Dist., 1981-85; tchr. sci. and history Granger (Wash.) Sch. Dist., 1986-87; tchr. sci. Sunnyside (Wash.) Sch. Dist., 1985-94; homebase coord., food drive coord., drug and alcohol awareness coord. Harrison Mid. Sch. Sunnyside, volleyball coach, 1979—; tchr. history, Reardan, Wash., volleyball, basketball, track and tennis coach. Dir. Evergreen Girls State, Ellensburg, Wash., 1994—, counselor planning com., 1980—. Mem. Wash. Edn. Assn., Nat. Fed. High Sch. Coaches, Sci. Tchrs. Wash., wash. Coaches Assn., Am. Legion Aux. (dir. Evergreen Girls State 1994—, exec. com. 1981—), NAFE. Lutheran. Office: Reardan Sch Dist Box 225 Reardan WA 99029

DOBSON, BRIDGET MCCOLL HURSLEY, television executive and writer; b. Milw., Sept. 1, 1938; d. Franklin McColl and Doris (Berger) Hursley; m. Jerome John Dobson, June 16, 1961; children: Mary McColl, Andrew Carmichael. BA, Stanford U., 1960, MA, 1964; CBA, Harvard U., 1961. Assoc. writer General Hospital ABC-TV, 1965-73, head writer General Hospital, 1973-75; producer Friendly Road Sta. KIXE-TV, Redding, Calif., 1972; head writer Guiding Light CBS-TV, 1975-80, head writer As the World Turns, 1980-83; creator, co-owner Santa Barbara NBC-TV, 1983—, head writer Santa Barbara, 1983-86, 91, exec. producer Santa Barbara, 1986-87, 91, creative prodn. exec. Santa Barbara, 1990-91; pres. Dobson Global Entertainment, L.A., 1994—. Author, co-lyricist: Slings and Eros, 1993; prodr. Confessions of a Nightingale, 1994. Recipient Emmy award, 1988. Mem. Nat. Acad. TV Arts and Scis. (com. on substance abuse 1986-88), Writers Guild Am. (award for Guiding Light 1977, for Santa Barbara 1991), Am. Film Inst. (mem. TV com. 1986-88). Office: 3490 Piedmont Rd NW Ste 1206 Atlanta GA 30305

DOBSON, CASSANDRA ELAINE, nursing educator, consultant; b. Jamaica, N.Y., Mar. 2, 1960; d. Joseph Wallace and Phyllis M. Hall; m. Christopher St. Albans Dobson, Mar. 27, 1987; children: Crystol, Christian. Diploma, Flushing Sch. Nursing, 1987; BSN, Lehman Coll., 1990, MSN, 1992. RN, N.Y.; cert. BLS, AHA, Med. Surgical Nurse. LPN Flushing Hosp. and Med. Ctr., Flushing, N.Y., 1982-83; RN staff Flushing Hosp. and Med. Ctr., Flushing, 1985-87, Westchester Sq. Hosp., Bronx, N.Y., 1988-89; unit preceptor Westchester Sq., Bronx, N.Y., 1989-90; sr. preceptor Westchester Sq., Bronx, 1990-91, clin. instr., 1990-91; clin. instr. North Ctrl. Bronx, Bronx, 1991—; cons. North Ctrl. Bronx Hosp., 1991—. Mem. ANA, N.Y. Surgical Nurse Assn., Am. Black Nurses Assn., Internat. Assn. Sickle Cell Nurses and Physician Assts., Sigma Theta Tau. Baptist. Home: 10714 Watson Pl Jamaica NY 11433-2511 Office: North Ctrl Bronx 3424 Kossuth Ave Bronx NY 10467-2410

DOBSON, CATHY, avant-garde wildlife artist, poet; b. N.Y.C., June 9, 1954; d. Robert T. and Virginia (Sutton) Bluhm; m. Mark Dobson, Feb. 12, 1979; children: Matthew, Michael. Student, Art Students League, N.Y.C., 1973-74, Parsons Sch. Design, 1974-75; apprentice, Elizabeth Pecchioli, N.Y.C., 1960-62. Gallery owner Rainbows Unltd., N.Y.C., 1974-75; clothing designer N.Y.C., 1973-75; playground artist PlayLofts, Melbourne, Fla., 1982-86; fine artist Fat Saturn Inc., Satellite Beach, Fla., 1985—. Author: Universe Trilogy, 1984-92; co-author: (songs-words) Fat Saturn Collection, 1978-93. Recipient Via Dei Serragli award Centro Studi e Scambi Culturali, Florence, 1975; Diploma alla Pittrice, Centro Artistico Regionale Pittore a Scultori, Italy, 1975; 4th place Viareggio (Italy) Collezione, 1976, 3d place Associasione Amici Dell'Arte-Prato, Italy, 1977. Mem. Nat. Mus. Women in the Arts (assoc.), Knickerbocker Artists, Salmagundi Club (N.Y.C.), Allied Artists Am. (assoc.), Nat. Arts Club (N.Y.C.), Artists Forum of Brevard Art Ctr. and Mus., Brevard Cultural Alliance. Democrat. Home and Office: Fat Saturn Inc 148 Berkeley St Satellite Beach FL 32937

DOBYNS, BETH MCCURDY, clergy member; b. Hot Springs, Ark., July 7, 1952; d. Melvin Jr. and Wilma Lou (Prichard) McC.; m. Bruce Warren Dobyns, Aug. 18, 1979; Leslie Ann, Nicole Kristine. BS in Med. Tech., Tex. Christian U., Ft. Worth, 1974, MDiv, 1979; DMin, St. Paul Sch. Theology, Kansas City, Mo., 1995. Ordained minister, Christian Ch., 1979. Med.

technologist Palo Pinto Gen. Hosp., Mineral Wells, Tex., 1974-76, Johnson County Hosp., Cleburne, Tex., 1976-77, Med. Plaza Hosp., Ft. Worth, 1977-79; assoc. minister 1st Christian Ch., Cedar Rapids, Iowa, 1979-81; co-minister Forest Ave and Univ. Christian Chs., Buffalo, N.Y., 1981-83, 1st christian Ch., Perry, Iowa, 1983-93; assoc. regional minister interim Christian Ch. in the Upper Midwest, Des Moines, 1993—. Trustee Dallas County Hosp., Perry, Iowa, 1985-91. Mem. Assn. Christian Ch. Educators. Democrat.

DOCKTOR-SMITH, MARY ANN, employee benefits consultant; b. Indpls., Jan. 26, 1957; d. Leo Edward and Geraldine Marie (Staudt) Docktor; m. Randolph Davis Smith, July 11, 1981. Student, Loyola U., Chgo., 1988—. Cert. Qualified Pension Adminstr. Asst. dir. pension adminstrn. Indpls. Life, 1976-78; pres. Pen-Ad, Inc., Chgo., 1978-82; mgr. Aetna Life Ins. Co., Chgo., 1982-83; pres. Creative Pensions, Inc., Chgo., 1982-84, EBI Employee Benefits, Inc., Chgo., 1984—, The Flag Docktor Inc., Chgo., 1993—; treas. Adv. Flag Co., Inc., Chgo., 1983—. Co-author: The Only Tax-shelter You'll Ever Need, 1991; column author: Gene Balliett Report, 1984—; contbr. articles to profl. jour. Vol. adult reading tutor Literacy Chgo.; donor Ayn Rand Inst., Marina Del Rey, Calif., 1990—; mem. chmn.'s coun. Rep. Nat. Com. Acad. scholar Otto Lehman Found., Chgo., 1991-94. Mem. Am. Soc. Pension Actuaries, N.Am. Vexillogical Assn. (chmn. pub. rels. com., corr. sec. 1993—), Chgo. Coun. Fgn. Rels., Golden Key, Alpha Sigma Nu, Alpha Sigma Lamda, Pi Sigma Alpha. Republican. Office: EBI Employee Benefits Inc 4949 W Diversey Ave Chicago IL 60639-1705

DODD, DARLENE MAE, nurse, air force officer; b. Dowagiac, Mich., Oct. 11, 1935; d. Charles B. and Lila H. D.; diploma in nursing Borgess Hosp. Sch. Nursing, Kalamazoo, 1957; grad. U.S. Air Force Flight Nurse Course, 1959, U.S. Air Force Squadron Officers Sch., 1963, Air Command and Staff Coll., 1973; BS in Psychology and Gen. Studies, So. Oreg. State Coll., 1987, postgrad., 1987; Commd. 2d lt. U.S. Air Force, 1959, advanced through grades to lt. col., 1975; staff nurse, Randolph AFB, Tex., 1959-60, Ladd AFB, Alaska, 1960-62, Selfridge AFB, Mich., 1962-63; Cam Rahn Bay Air Base, Vietnam, 1966-67, Seymour Johnson AFB, N.C., 1967-69, Air Force Acad., 1971-72; flight nurse 22d Aeromed. Evacuation, Tex., 1963-66; chief nurse Danang AFB, Vietnam, 1967; flight nurse Yokotu AFB, Japan, 1969-71; clin. coordinator ob/gyn and flight nurse, Elmendorf AFB, Alaska, 1973-76; clin. nurse coordinator obstetrics-gynecology and pediatric services USAF Med. Center, Keesler AFB, Miss., 1976-79, ret., 1979. Decorated Bronze Star, Meritorious Service medal, Air Force Commendation medal (3). Mem. Soc. of Ret. Air Force Nurses, DAV, Ret. Officers Assn., Vietnam Vets. Am., VFW, Uniformed Services Disabled Retirees, Air Force Assn., Psy Chi, Phi Kappa Phi. Club: Women of Moose. Home: 712 1st St Phoenix OR 97535-9787

DODD, SARA MAE PALMER, executive assistant; b. Cin.; d. Charles Austen and Ruth Halsey (Miller) Palmer; m. Edward Dodd, Mar. 31, 1953 (dec.); children: J. Edward, Diane Dodd Peterson. BA, Hiram Coll., 1949; postgrad., Rutgers U., 1968. Exec. dir. Camp Fire Girls, Inc., Indpls., 1949-53; regional field advisor Camp Fire Girls, Inc., N.Y.C., 1973; substitute tchr. Piscataway (N.J.) Sch. Dist., 1974-79; asst. to pres. Ctr. for Profl. Advancement, East Brunswick, N.J., 1979-89. Active LWV, Piscataway, N.J., 1957-87, pres., fin. chmn., newsletter editor, 1957-87, v.p., 1985-87, leadership com., 1987-89; adv. Piscataway Twp. Sr. Citizen Adv. Commn.; vol. tutor in ESL program Literacy Vols. of Am. Mem. Honor Roll of Women, Piscataway. Methodist.

DODD, SYLVIA BLISS, special education educator; b. Ft. Worth, July 21, 1939; d. William Solomon and Sylvia Bliss (Means) Fisher; m. Melvin Joe Dodd, Sept. 4, 1959 (div. 1967); children: Lisa Dawn, Marcus Jay, Chadwick Scott. BA, Tex. Wesleyan Coll., Ft. Worth, 1960; MEd, Tex. Christian U., Ft. Worth, 1976. Tchr. Castleberry Ind. Sch. Dist., Ft. Worth, 1960-62; tchr. Hurst-Euless-Bedford (Tex.) Ind. Sch. Dist., 1967-69, dir. spl. edn., 1969-94; instr. Tex. Wesleyan Coll., Ft. Worth, 1978, 94-95, Tex. Christian U., Ft. Worth, 1980. Bd. dirs. Mental Health Assn., Ft. Worth, 1983-88, 91-94, March of Dimes, Mid Cities, Tex., 1990, United Cmty. Ctrs., Ft. Worth, 1989-94, pres., 1994; bd. dirs. So. Meth. U. Campus Ministry, 1992-94; adminstrv. bd. 1st United Meth. Ch., Ft. Worth, 1990-93; lay leader West Ft. Worth Dist. United Meth. Ch., 1992-94. Named Conf. Chairperson of Yr. Nat. Health and Welfare Ministries, 1981; recipient Outstanding Woman award Tex. Wesleyan U., 1991, Disting. Educator award, 1991. Mem. ASCD, Mental Health Assn. (pres. 1979-80), Nat. Coun. Exceptional Children, Nat. Coun. Adminstrs. Spl. Edn., Tex. Coun. Adminstrs. Spl. Edn. (Hall of Honor award 1991, pres. 1975-76), Assn. Tex. Profl. Educators. Democrat. Methodist. Home and Office: 829 Timberhill Dr Hurst TX 76053-4240

DODDS, BRENDA KAY, nurse; b. Wheeling, W.Va., July 14, 1961; d. Ray Charles and Kathryn June (Ries) D. BS, Graceland Coll., 1983; A in Child Devel., 1990. RN. Staff nurse Resthaven Retirement Home, Independence, Mo., 1983-84; staff nurse telemetry unit Independence Regional Health Ctr., 1983—; camp nurse Mo-Kan Salvation Army Camp, Kansas City, Mo., 1984; dental asst. Ronald E. Jennings, DDS P.C., Independence, 1985-87; med. resource informant Noland Child Devel. Ctr., Independence Pub. Sch. Dist., 1988—, head tchr., 1990—, morning supr., 1993—. Vol. ARC, Independence, 1983—, Voluntary Action Ctr., 1987—; vocalist Independence Messiah/Festival Choir, 1983—; musician Independence Symphony Band, 1988—. Mem. Nat. Assn. for Edn. Young Children, Mo. Nurses Assn., Profl. Nurses Assn., Mensa.

DODDS, CLAUDETTE LA VONN, radio executive and consultant; b. Lenapah, Okla., Sept. 2, 1947; d. Willie Lee and Dora (Harrell) Davis; m. Donald Howard Dodds, Jan. 14, 1965 (div. June 1982); children: Clarence Adam, Donyielle Alana, Erin Michelle. AAS with honors, Kennedy-King Coll., 1984; BA, U. Ill., Chgo., 1989. Newscaster, newswriter Sta. WKKC-FM, Chgo., 1983-84, news dir., 1984-85, program and music dir., 1985, sta. mgr., 1985-87; research asst. Vernon Jarrett Chgo. Sun Times, 1988-89; exec. asst. to pres. Sta. WVON, Chgo., 1989; asst. sta. mgr. Sta. WYCA-FM, Crawford Broadcasting Co., Chgo., Hammond, Ind., 1989-90; mem. adv. com. Coll. Broadcasting, 1985-87; cons. Chgo. Nite Life, 1985-87, Hayes & Co., 1986—, Morning Show/Danny Jack Sta. KWEZ, Monroe, La., 1986—, Sta. WKKC-FM, Future Records, 1988—; music rschr. Let's Dance, Chgo., 1986-88; broadcast asst. Sta. WVON, Chgo., 1989, exec. bd. Young People's Network Sta. WKKC-FM, 1988—, Youth on the Move, 1994, facilitator YPN workshops, 1994. Producer: (TV special) Messiah, 1985, Youth on the Move, 1994; producer, writer (radio and TV specials) Dr. Martin Luther King, 1985-86; producer, hostess (radio specials) Englewood Parade, 1986, Bud Billiken Parade, 1986; mag. music reporter, 1987; editor current affairs newsletter, 1992. Mem. Dem. Student task Force, Chgo., 1984, Student Disciplinary Bd., Chgo., 1986; coord. Concerned Studens for Broadcasting Equipment, 1984; mem. Task Force for AIDS Prevention, 1993—, cons. AIDS task force, mem. program evaluation com., 1994—; vol. Darrell Stingley Youth Found., 1994. Recipient Alumni Recognition award Kennedy-King Coll., 1993. Home and Office: 305 W 69th St Chicago IL 60621-3720

DODERER, MINNETTE FRERICHS, state legislator; b. Holland, Iowa, May 16, 1923; d. John A. and Sophie S. Frerichs; BA, U. Iowa, 1948; m. Fred H. Doderer, Aug. 5, 1944 (dec. 1991); children: Dennis, Kay Lynn. Mem. Iowa Ho. of Reps. 1964-69, 80—, minority whip, 1967-68, chairperson ways and means com., 1983-88, chair commerce com., 1989-90, chair small bus., econ. devel. and trade com., 1991-92; mem. Iowa Senate, 1970-79, pres. pro tem, 1975-76; vis. prof. Stephens Coll., Iowa State Coll. (both 1979); vice-chairwoman Iowa Interstate Cooperation Commn., 1965-66; Vice-chairwoman Democratic Party Johnson County, 1957-60; vice chairperson com. on budget and taxation Nat. Conf. State Legislator's; mem. Dem. Nat. Com., 1968-70, Dem. Nat. Policy Council Elected Ofcls., 1973-76; chairwoman Iowa del. Internat. Women's Yr. Del. bd. fellows Iowa Sch. Religion. Recipient Disting. Service award Iowa Edn. Assn., 1969, Wilson award Commn. on Status of Women, 1989; named to Iowa Women's Hall of Fame, 1978. Mem. LWV, Pioneer Lawmakers (pres. 1993—), Delta Kappa Gamma (hon.). Democrat. Methodist.

DODGE, STEPHANIE LEE, vocational rehabilitation counselor; b. Phoenix, July 8, 1957; d. Robert Hollister and Mary Josephine (Dearstyne) D. BS, U. No. Colo., 1979; MS, Calif. State U., Sacramento, 1984. Fed. govt. cert. Vocat. rehab. counselor Pioneer Rehab., Elk Grove, Calif., 1982-86, Lisa Suhonos Rehab., Sacramento, 1986-91, Profl. Rehab. Svcs., Sacramento, 1991-94, Dodge & McElroy, Sacramento, 1994—. Mem. Calif. Assn. Rehab. Profls.

DODOHARA, JEAN NOTON, music educator; b. Monroe, Wis., Feb. 21, 1934; d. Albert Henry and Eunice Elizabeth (Edgerton) Noton; BA, Monmouth (Ill.) Coll., 1955; MS, U. Ill., 1975, adminstrv. cert., 1980, EdD, 1985; m. Laurence G. Landers, June 7, 1955 (div.); children: Theodore Scott, Thomas Warren, Philip John; m. Edward R. Harris, Nov. 27, 1981 (dec.); stepchildren: Adrianne, Erica; m. Takashi Dodohara, Aug. 7, 1988; 1 stepchild, Eve D. Dodohara. Tchr. music schs. in Ill. and Fla., 1955-76; tchr. ch. music for children, 1957-72; tchr. music Dist. 54, Schaumburg, Ill., 1976-93; teaching asst. U. Ill., 1979. Named Outstanding Young Woman of Yr., Jaycee Wives, St. Charles, Mo., 1968; charter mem. Nat. Mus. Women in Arts. Mem. NEA (life), AAUW, Music Educators Nat. Conf. (life), Ill. Music Educators Assn., Alliance for Arts Edn., U. Ill. Alumni Assn. (life), Mortar Bd., Mensa, Delta Kappa Pi. Mem. United Ch. of Christ. Home: 1068 Hampshire Ln Elgin IL 60120-4905

DODSON, CLAUDIA LANE, program supervisor; b. Washington, Aug. 31, 1941; d. Claude James and Edna Vera (Lane) D. BS in Phys. Edn., Westhampton Coll., 1963; MS in Phys. Edn., U. Tenn., 1965. Cert. tchr., Va. Tchr., coach Meadowbrook H.S., Chesterfield, Va., 1963-64, 65-71; grad. asst. U. Tenn., Knoxville, 1964-65; program supr. Va. H.S. League, Charlottesville, Va., 1971—; chmn. USOC Women's Basketball Com., Colorado Springs, Colo., 1976-80; mem. Nat. Basketball Rules Com., Elgin, Ill. and Kansas City, 1976-81; mem. U. Richmond (Va.) Athletic Coun., 1982-85; officials observer Atlantic Coast Conf., Greensboro, N.C., 1989—; spkr. in field. Mem. AAHPERD, Va. Assn. Health, Phys. Edn., Recreation and Dance, Nat. Interscholastic Athletic Adminstrs. Assn. (cert. adminstr.), Women's Basketball Coaches' Assn., Westhampton Coll. Alumnae Assn. (chpt. pres. 1977-79), Delta Kappa Gamma (Rho chpt., pres. 1982-84), Phi Delta Kappa (treas. 1986—). Presbyterian. Home: 2540 Cedar Ridge Ln Charlottesville VA 22901 Office: Va High Sch League 1642 State Farm Blvd Charlottesville VA 22901

DOE, BARBARA STEWART, museum administrator; b. Chgo., Aug. 9, 1950; d. William Bethel and Doris (Charn) D. BA, U. Colo., 1972; MA, Sangamon State U., 1975. Dir. Wilderness Study Project, Springfield, Ill., 1973-75, Environ. Ctr., Boulder, Colo., 1976-79; natural resource specialist U.S. Bur. Reclamation, Denver, 1977-78; rsch. assoc. Nat. Conf. State Legislatures, Denver, 1979-80; asst. to transp. dir. City of Boulder, 1980-81, project mgr., 1981-85, parking coord., 1985-90, open space planner, 1991-92; interpretive park naturalist Jefferson County, Golden, Colo., 1992, adminstr. Nature Ctr., 1993—; vice chmn. Boulder County Energy Adv. Com., Boulder, 1987; bd. mem. County Bd. Rev., Boulder, 1984-86, Historic Boulder, 1991-92. Bd. mem. Colo. Open Space Coun., Denver, 1979-80; mem. Leadership Boulder C. of C., 1986. Named Young Career Woman Colo. Bus. and Profl. Women's Fedn., Denver, 1981; recipient Innovation award Denver Coun. Govts., 1985. Mem. Nat. Assn. Interpretation, Denver Botanic Gardens, Denver Mus. Natural History, Boulder Bus. and Profl. Women (treas. 1983-84, v.p. 1987-88, pres. 1989-90, winner speech contest 1985), Sierra Club (bd. mem. Sangamon Valley Group 1973-75). Office: Lookout Mountain Nature Ctr 910 Colorow Rd Golden CO 80401-9510

DOEHR, RUTH NADINE, home economics educator; b. Kingsford, Mich., Nov. 1, 1932; d. Helmuth Herbert and Olga Amanda (Olsen) D.; m. Ray Orentas, July 26, 1957 (div. 1960). BS, Mich. State U., 1961, MA, 1964. Job coord. Lansing (Mich.) Sch. Dist., 1964-68, tchr. sex edn., 1968-69; tchr. personality devel. No. Mich. U., 1969-70; tchr. Engadine (Mich.) Pub. Sch., 1970-72; lectr., supr. student tchrs. Northern Mich. U., Marquette, 1977-78; substitute tchr. Dickinson-Iron Intermediate Sch. Dist., Kingsford, 1988—. Editor: (newsletter) Lansing Ednl. Achievement Programs, 1964-68. Office vol. Crystal Lake Sr. Ctr., Iron Mountain, Mich., 1981-84; election insp. Breitung Twp., East Kingsford, Mich., 1972—; gift shop vol. Dickinson Meml. Hosp., Iron Mountain, 1984—, lifeline program participant, 1984-89, mem. exec. bd. women's league, 1984—, knitting chmn., 1984—. Mem. AAUW. Democrat. Lutheran. Avocations: reading, writing. Home: 229 Hyland St Iron Mountain MI 49801-4904

DOELL, JEAN MARTHA, small business owner, Spanish educator; b. Kewaunee, Wis., Oct. 17, 1946; d. Leo Albert and Virginia Emma (Ollmann) Krohn; m. Arlie Edmund Doell, May 2, 1970; children: Patrick, Timothy. BA, U. Wis., 1968; postgrad., Carleton U., Ottawa, Can., 1968-69. Cert. tchr., Wis. Spanish tchr. Green Bay (Wis.) Pub. Schs., 1970-76; office mgr., corp. officer Krohn Dairy Products, Luxemburg, Wis., 1976—; Spanish tchr. Kewaunee (Wis.) High Sch., 1991—. Sec. Kewaunee Area Scholarships, Inc., 1991—; bd. dirs., past pres. Bay Area chpt. Am. Diabetes Assn., Green Bay, 1984—, bd. dirs., exec. com. Wis. affiliate, Milw., 1985-91; choir dir., organist St. Paul Luth. Ch., Luxemburg, Wis., 1970—. Recipient Fundraising award Am. Diabetes Assn., 1985; named Kewaunee County Outstanding Woman, Kewaunee Jaycees, 1987, Vol. of Yr., Am. Diabetes Assn., 1991. Mem. NEA, Wis. Assn. Fgn. Lang. Tchrs., Wis. Edn. Assn., Wis. Ind. Bus., Kewaunee and U.S. C. of C. Republican. Home: N2989 State Hwy 163 Luxemburg WI 54217

DOEPKE, KATHERINE LOUISE GULDBERG, choral director, former music educator; b. Suttons Bay, Mich., Dec. 18, 1921; d. Gottfred Johannes and Aasta Agnethe (Kalstad) Guldberg; m. Henry August Doepke, Aug. 13, 1944; children: Karen Sernett, Chris, Bruce, Barbara Potuck. BS, U. Minn., 1944, MA, 1967, postgrad. Tchr. music Mpls. Pub. Schs., 1963-83; choral dir. Trinity First Luth. Ch., Mpls., 1953-92; cons./mentor Mpls. Pub. Schs., 1984-87; organizer, producer 3 jr. high sch. honors choirs Am. Choral Dirs. Assn., 1986, 88, 89. Editor monograph; author curriculum materials; composer children's musicals for sch. and ch., 1966—; contbr. articles to profl. jours. Vol. Courage Ctr., Mpls., 1983-86, Food at Your Door, 1984-88; dir. Gray Aires Chorus, Mpls. 1986-95, Thursday Musical, 1984—. Named composer in residence Mpls. Pub. Schs., 1985. Mem. AAUW (chair coms.), Am. Choral Dirs. Assn. (state sec.-treas., historian), Music Educators Nat. Conf. (clinician 1976, 78, 80), Mu Phi Epsilon (internat. pres. 1992-95). Lutheran. Home: 2212 Mary Hills Dr Minneapolis MN 55422-4252

DOHANIAN, PHYLLIS, cultural organization administrator; b. Cambridge, Mass., June 22, 1951; d. Armen and Rachel (Koumrian) D. BA in History and Math., U. Mass., 1973; MS in Adminstrn., U. Pa., 1974. Acad. counselor Sch. Mgmt. Boston U., 1974-77; exec. asst. to pres. BonTon Rug Cleaners, Inc., Watertown, Mass., 1977-84; head vol. svcs. Mus. of Sci., Boston, 1984-88, dir. pub. svcs., 1986-88, dir. ann. support and ops., 1988-89; exec. dir. French Libr. and Cultural Ctr., Boston, 1989—. Exec. com. Mus. Fine Arts Coun., Boston, 1981-93; overseer, vol. Boston Symphony Orch., 1986—; chmn. overseer Boston Ballet, 1991. Mem. The Boston Club, Chevalier Dans L'Ordre Des Arts et des Lettres of France, Mortar Bd. Inc. (nat. v.p. 1978-80). Home: 36 Elizabeth Rd Belmont MA 02178-3821

DOHANICH, LAUREL ANNE, accountant; b. Bethpage, N.Y., Feb. 16, 1959; d. John Joseph and Evelyn (Johnston) O'Keeffe; m. Stephen Leo Dohanich, Jan. 16, 1982; children: Keryn Michelle, Christopher Adam, Joshua Stephen. BS in Acctg., SUNY, Binghamton, 1981. Cert. of mgmt. acct. Cost acct. IBM, Owego, N.Y., 1981-83, gen. acct., 1983-85, mgr. payroll, employee disbursements, 1985-88, mgr. intracompany acctg., 1988, fin. info. ctr., 1989-92; govt. practices acct. IBM, Bethesda, Md., 1993—. Patentee in field. Mem. Inst. Mgmt. Accts. (treas. 1992).

DOHERTY, SISTER BARBARA (ANN DOHERTY), academic administrator; b. Chgo., Dec. 2, 1931; d. Martin James and Margaret Eleanor (Noe) D. Student, Rosary Coll., 1949-51; BA in Latin, English and History, St. Mary-of-the-Woods Coll., 1953; MA in Theology, St. Mary's Coll., 1963; PhD in Theology, Fordham U., 1979; LittD (hon.), Ind. State U., 1990. Enter order of the Sisters of Providence. Tchr. Jr. and Sr. High Schs., Ind. and Ill., 1953-63; asst. prof. religion St. Mary-of-the-Woods Coll., Ind., 1963-67, 71-75, pres., 1984—; provincial supr. Chgo. Province of Sisters of Providence, 1975-83; summer faculty NCAIS-KCRCHE, Delhi, India, 1970. Author: I Am What I Do: Contemplation and Human Experience, 1981, Make Yourself an Ark: Beyond the Memorized Responses of Our Corporate Adolescence, 1984; editor: Providence: God's Face Towards the World, 1984; contbr. articles to New Cath. Ency. Vol. XVII, 1982, Dictionary of Catholic Spirituality, 1993. Pres. Leadership Terre Haute, Ind., 1985-86; bd. regents Ind. Acad., 1987—; bd. dirs. 8th Day Cen. for Justice, Chgo., 1978-83, Family Svcs., Swope Art Mus., Terre Haute, Ind., 1988—. Arthur J. Schmidt Found. grantee, 1967-71. Mem. Women's Coll. Coalition (nat. bd. dirs. 1984-90), Assn. Colls. Ind., Ind. Colls. and Univs. of Ind. (exec. bd.), Assn. Am. Colls. (chair Ind. Conf. Higher Edn. 1992-93), Leadership Conf. of Women Religious of USA (program chairperson nat. assembly 1982-83, chair Neylan commn. 1993—). Democrat. Roman Catholic. Home and Office: Office of the President Saint Mary Of The Woods IN 47876

DOHERTY, DONNA KATHRYN, editor; b. New Haven, Oct. 15, 1948; d. Donald Thomas and Kathryn Marie (Jones) D. BA in English and Journalism, Northeastern U., 1971; postgrad., Syracuse U., 1972. Paralegal Wiggin & Dana, New Haven, 1973-75; staff writer sports sect. The New Haven Register, 1975-79; asst. editor Tennis Mag., Trumbull, Conn., 1979-80, assoc. editor, 1980-86, sr. editor, 1986-88, mng. editor, 1988-90, editor, 1990—. Mem. U.S. Tennis Writers' Assn., Am. Soc. Mag. Editors, Assn. Women in Sports Media, Pine Orchard Yacht and Country Club. Office: Tennis Mag 5520 Park Ave Trumbull CT 06611-3426

DOHERTY, EVELYN MARIE, data processing consultant; b. Phila., Sept. 26, 1941; d. James Robert and Virginia (Checkley) D. Diploma, RCA Tech. Inst., Cherry Hill, N.J., 1968. Freelance data processing programmer N.J., 1978-81; data processing cons. N.J., 1981—; cons. collection agy., brokerage, banking, med., edn., transp., pub., food wholesaleing, utility systems, mfg.; reseller of PC's and software; lectr. data processing Camden County (N.J.) Coll. Contbr. articles in field. Chairwoman Collingswood (N.J.) Dems., 1968; founder Babe Didrikson Collingswood Softball Team for Women; organizer Erlton South Town Watch (pub. cmty. notebook). Mem. Data Processing Mgmt. Assn. (chmn., mem. ednl. com., bd. dirs. N.J. chpt. 1980—). Roman Catholic. Office: PO Box 3780 Cherry Hill NJ 08034-0584

DOHERTY, KAREN ANN, corporate executive; b. Elizabeth, N.J., July 6, 1952; d. Eugene Nason Godfrey and Helen L. (Andersen) D.; m. Jonathan Kent Tillinghast, June 17, 1972 (div. Oct. 1978). Account exec. The John O'Donnell Co., N.Y., 1979-80; nat. conservation rep. Sierra Club, N.Y., 1980-81; mgr. membership programs Am. Mgmt. Assn., N.Y., 1981—. Mem. Women's Econ. Roundtable, Trinity Coll. Alumnae Assn. (bd. dirs. Com. N.Y.C. group 1979-82), Direct Mktg. Assn., Internat. Coun., Women in Need (corp. adv. coun.). Democrat. Roman Catholic. Home: 138 71st St Apt F1 Brooklyn NY 11209-1141 Office: Am Mgmt Assn 135 W 50th St New York NY 10020-1201

DOHERTY, REBECCA FEENEY, federal judge; b. Ft. Worth, June 3, 1952; d. Charles Edwin Feeney and Annabelle (Knight) Smith; divorced; 1 child, George Jason. BA, Northwestern State U., 1973, MA, 1975; JD, La. State U., 1981. Bar: La. 1981, U.S. Dist. Ct. (mid., ea. and we. dists.) La. 1981, U.S. Ct. Appeals (5th cir.) 1981, U.S. Dist. Ct. (so. dist.) Tex. 1986, U.S. Dist. Ct. (ea. dist.) Tex. 1989. Assoc. Onebane, Donohoe, Bernard, Torian, Diaz, McNamara & Abell, Lafayette, La., 1981-84, ptnr., 1985-91; U.S. dist. ct. judge We. Dist. La., Lafayette, 1991—; adj. instr. Northwestern State U., Natchitoches, La., 1975; co-dir. secondary level gifted and talented program Webster Parish, La., 1978. Contbr. articles to profl. jours.; mem. La. Law Rev., 1980, 81. Recipient Am. Jurisprudence award Lawyers Coop. Pub. Co., 1980, Career Achievement award 1991; inducted into La. State U. Law Ctr. Hall of Fame, 1987. Mem. ABA, La. Bar Assn., La. Assn. Def. Counsel, La. Assn. Trial Lawyers, Acadian Assn. Women Attys., Order of Coif. Office: US Dist Ct 705 Jefferson St Ste 153 Lafayette LA 70501-6936*

DOHERTY, SHANNEN, actress; b. Memphis, Apr. 12, 1971; d. Tom and Rosa D.; m. Ashley Hamilton, 1993 (div. 1994). TV series: Little House: A New Beginning, 1982-83, Our House, 1986-88, Beverly Hills, 90210, 1990-94; TV movies: The Other Lover, 1985, Robert Kennedy and His Times, 1985, Obsessed, 1992, Rebel Highway: Jailbreakers, Showtime, 1994, A Burning Passion: The Margaret Mitchell Story, 1994; films: Night Shift, 1982, (voice) The Secret of Nimh, 1982, Girls Just Want to Have Fun, 1985, Heathers, 1989, Blindfold: Acts of Obsession, 1993. Baptist. Office: c/o Fox Broadcasting Co PO Box 900 Beverly Hills CA 90213*

DOHMEN, MARY HOLGATE, retired educator; b. Gary, Ind., July 28, 1918; d. Clarence Gibson and Margaret Alexander (Kinnear) Holgate; m. Frederick Hoeger Dohmen, June 27, 1964; children: William Francis, Robert Charles. BS, Milw. State Tchrs. Coll., 1940; M of Philosophy, U. Wis., 1945. Cert. tchr., Wis. Tchr. primary grades Baraboo (Wis.) Pub. Schs., 1940-43, Whitefish Bay (Wis.) Pub. Schs., 1943-64. Contbr. articles, story, poems to various pubs. Bd. dirs. Homestead H.S. chpt. Am. Field Svc., Mequon, Wis., 1970-80; mem. Milw. Aux. VNA, 1975—, 2d v.p., 1983-85, Milw. Pub. Mus. Enrichment Club, 1975—, Boys and Girls Club of Greater Milw., 1986—; vol. Reading is Fun program, 1987—, Milw. Symphony Orch. League, 1960—, Ptnrs. in Conservation, World Wildlife Fund, Washington, 1991—, Milw. Art Mus. Garden Club, 1979—, com. chmn., 1981-86; mem. Chancellor's Soc. U. Wis.-Milw., 1991—; travel lectr. various orgns., 1980—. Mem. AAUW, Milw. Coll. Endowment Assn. (v.p. 1987-90, pres. 1991-93), Woman's Club Wis., Alpha Phi (pres. Milw. alumnae 1962-64), Pi Lambda Theta (pres. Milw. alumnae 1962-64), Delta Kappa Gamma. Republican. Presbyterian. Home: 3903 W Mequon Rd Mequon WI 53092-2727

DOHRENWEND, SANDRA BLACKMAN MASTERMAN, superintendent; b. New London, Conn., Oct. 22, 1935; d. Frank Arlington and Dorothy Irene (Danforth) Blackman; m. Robert Masterman, June 22, 1958 (dec. 1976); children: Todd, Drew; m. James Wilckes Dohrenwend, July 1, 1979. BS, Cen. Conn. State U., 1957; MA, Columbia U., 1980. Cert. tchr., prin., supt. Tchr. various schs., Southbury and Fair Lawn, Conn.-N.J., 1957-59, Glen Rock (N.J.) Pub. Schs., 1963-80; coord. physicians insvc. tng. Am. Acad. Pediatrics, Evanston, Ill., 1980-82; prin. Ray Graham Asn. for the Handicapped, Lombard, Ill., 1982-85; dir. edn. Ray Graham Asn. for the Handicapped, Lombard, 1985-86; prin. Morris Sch. Dist., Morristown, N.J., 1986-89; supt. of schs. Denville (N.J.) Twp. Schs., 1990—; mem., v.p. bd. edn. Wheaton (Ill.) Pub. Schs., 1983-86; mem. bd. edn. Dupage County Spl. Svcs. Bd., Lombard, 1985-86. Mem. Legis. Ednl. Network DuPage, Ill., 1984-86; mem., sec. bd. trustees Denville (N.J.) Libr., 1990—; mem. Vanguard, Morris County United Way; exec. bd. dirs. Challenge Unltd., Morristown; mem. DuPage County Mental Health Bd., LWV. Named Outstanding Women Leader in Edn., DuPage YWCA, Lombard, 1986. Mem. ASCD, Am. Assn. Sch. Adminstrs., N.E. Coalition of Ednl. Leaders, Morris County Assn. Sch. Adminstrs., Ill. Large Dist. Schs. (exec. bd.), N.J. Assn. Sch. Adminstrs. (curriculum com.). Presbyterian. Office: Denville Twp Schs 501 Openaki Rd Denville NJ 07834

DOI, DOROTHY MITSUE, educator, consultant; b. Honolulu, Feb. 21, 1934; d. Tokuju Yano and Hisayo Kashiwabara; children: Ken Kenichi, Claire Emiko, Garret Seitoku. BS in Edn., Phillips U., Enid, Okla., 1956; postgrad., UCLA, 1958, U. Hawaii, Honolulu, 1966-67, 72-74, Chaminade Coll. Honolulu, 1972-74, 77, LaVerne (Calif.) Coll., 1970-71. Cert. tchr., Hawaii. Tchr. L.A. City Schs., 1957-58, Hawaii, 1956-57, 65, 70-71; account exec. Catering, ind. contractor, Honolulu; skin care, health and beauty cons. Honolulu, travel agt., ind. contractor; pres. Triple C Svcs., Honolulu, 1983—; researcher Manoa ethnic studies program U. Hawaii; account exec., cons. Royal Banquet, 1988-89; writer, researcher, editor, mng. editor Bulldogrowl. Active Kamuki Y-Teens, 1947-52; fund-raising co-chair Kaimuki High Sch., Hui O'Hauolani Y-Teens Jesters Ball, 1952; mem. World Wildlife Fund, 1991—, Hawaii Theatre Ctr., 1990—. Mem. NAFE, Nature Conservancy Local, National, Hawaii Fukuoka Kenjin Kai (gen. chairperson 35th anniversary and award ceremony, com. chair editor commemorative booklet, sec. 1988-91, 2nd v.p. 1992-93, 1st v.p. 1993-94, 94—), Smithsonian Instn., Kaimuki High Sch. Alumni Assn. (charter, bd. dirs., 1988—, pub. rels. chairperson 1988-90), Okla. Sooners Club (Hon. Citizen of Okla. 1985), Japanese Cultural Ctr. of Hawaii (hon. lifetime charter), Future Tchrs. of Am. (treas. 1955-56), United Japanese Soc. of Hawaii (sec. 1991-92, 92-93, 93-94, youth com. chair 1992-93, 93-94, 94—, gen. chair 1st Annual Youth Com. Picnic 1994, co-chair fundraising com. 1992-93, mc New Year luncheon 1993, 2nd v.p. 1994—), Internat. Platform Assn. Home: 2431 Yvonne Pl Honolulu HI 96816-3431

DOI, LOIS, psychiatric social worker; b. Honolulu, Oct. 24, 1951; d. James Masato and Thelma Kimiko Miyamoto; m. Brian Doi, May 26, 1972; children: Michael, Lorian. BS, U. Hawaii, 1974, MSW, 1978. Lic. clin. social worker, Calif. Psychiat. social worker, child specialist Desert Community Mental Health Ctr., Indio, Calif., 1979-92, coordinator children's day treatment program, 1982-91; pvt. practice psychiat. social worker 1-2-1 Counseling, Palm Springs, Calif., 1992—; psychiat. social worker, adult case mgr. Desert Community Mental Health Ctr., Palm Springs, Calif., 1992-93; expert examiner, Bd. of Behavioral Sci. Examiners, 1987—. Vol. advisor Community Recreation Ctr. Youth Group, Hawaii, 1967-69; vol. interviewer ARC Food Stamp Program, Hawaii, 1973; vol. asst. YWCA Programs Young Mothers and Teens, Hawaii, 1973; vol. group leader YWCA Juvenile Delinquent Program, Hawaii, 1973; placement counselor Vols. In Service to Am., L.A., 1975; VISTA counselor L.A. Urban League, 1975-76. Mem. Nat. Assn. Social Workers. Office: 1-2-1 Counseling 400 S Farrell Dr Ste B116 Palm Springs CA 92262-7964

DOIG, BEVERLY IRENE, systems specialist; b. Bozeman, Mont., Oct. 21, 1936; d. James Stuart Doig and Elsie Florence (Andes) Doig Townsend. AA, Graceland Coll., 1956; BA, U. Kans., 1958; MS, U. Wis., 1970; cert. in Interior Design, UCLA, 1993. Aerodynamic technician II Ames Labs.-NACA, Moffett Field, Calif., 1957; real time systems specialist Dept. of Army, White Sands Missile Range, N.Mex., 1958-66; large systems specialist computing ctr. U. Wis., Madison, 1966-70; sr. systems analyst Burroughs, Ltd., Canberra, Australia, 1970-72; systems specialist Tech. Info. Office Burroughs Corp., Detroit, 1973-78; sr. systems specialist Burroughs Gmbh, Munich, 1978-79, Burroughs AB, Stockholm, 1979-80; networking cons. Midland Bank, Ltd., Sheffield, Eng., 1980-83; networking specialist Burroughs Corp. (now UNISYS), Mission Viejo, Calif., 1983—; teaching asst. Canberra (Australia) Coll., 1972; tchr. Wayne State U. Ext., Detroit, 1976-77; freelance interior designer, 1992—. Vol. youth groups and camps Reorganized LDS Ch., N.Mex., Wis., Australia, Mich., Calif., Germany, U.K.; inner youth worker, Detroit. Scholar Mitchell Math., 1956-58, Watkins Residential, 1956-58. Mem. Assn. Computing Machinery (local chpt. chmn. membership 1969), Lambda Delta Sigma. Republican. Office: UNISYS 25725 Jeronimo Rd Mission Viejo CA 92691-2792

DOKOUDOVSKY, NINA LUDMILA, dance educator; b. N.Y.C., Nov. 7, 1947; d. Vladimir Dokoudovsky and Nina Rigmor (Ström) Stroganova; m. Antoni Francis Zalewski. Student, Ballet Arts Carnegie Hall, 1954-78, Profl. Children's Sch., N.Y.C., 1959-66, Am. Acad. Dramatic Arts, 1960-62, Am. Ballet Theater Sch., 1968-70, N.Y. Conservatory of Dance, 1978-81. Faculty Ballet Arts Carnegie Hall, N.Y.C., 1964-70; tchr. dance Dokoudovsky Sch. of Classical Ballet, Englewood, N.J., 1964-70; head adminstr. Acad. Fine Arts Music and Dance, 1974-81; faculty Washington U., St. Louis, 1983-86; co-dir. Ballet Ctr. of St. Louis, 1984—; co-assoc. artistic dir. St. Louis Ballet (formerly Mo. Concert Ballet), 1981-84, co-artistic dir., 1984—; dir. Ballet Arts Lecture Demo Co., 1967-68; dancer, soloist with Ballet Arts Workshop, 1966-68, Marvin Gordon's Ballet Concepts, 1968, Empire State Ballet, 1969, Internat. Dance Competition, Varna, Bulgaria, 1970, Buffalo Ballet, 1970-72, Am. Classical Ballet, 1972, Wolf Trapp Co., 1972, L.I. Ballet Co., 1973, Festival Ballet of N.J., 1975-77, St. Louis Ballet (formerly Mo. Concert Ballet), 1982—; coach Am. dancers Internat. Dance Competition, Moscow, 1982. Choreographer: (ballets) Dance of the Hours, 1965, While the Cat's Away, 1966, Tchaikovsky Violin Concerto, 1967, In the Park, 1968, The Nyad, 1968, Adam Pas De Deux, 1969, Adam Pas de Cinq, 1974, 83, 86, 89, Weber Piano Concerto (complete), 1986-88, 93, Nutcracker, 1980, 81—, La Fille Mal Gardee, 1980, Une Petite Comedie, 1984, (staged ballets) Swan Lake, 1967, 69, 79, 80, 92, Les Sylphide, 1974, 79, 82, 84, 87, 93, Raymonda, 1972, Don Quixote, 1972, 84, 88, Sleeping Beauty, 1976, 79, 84, 91, 92, 94, La Bayadere 1989, 91, Bronislava Nijinska's Les Biches in collaboration with Irina Nijinska St. Louis Ballet, 1989, 90, Tulsa Ballet Theatre, 1990, Paris Opera Ballet, 1991, Cinderella, 1995. Office: Ballet Ctr of St Louis 10 Kimler Dr Maryland Heights MO 63043-3703 also: St Louis Ballet Co PO Box 2101 Saint Louis MO 63158-0101

DOLAK, ANNA ELIZABETH, lawyer; b. Ft. Monmouth, N.J., Apr. 18, 1957; d. George Albert and Charlotte Elizabeth (Robertson) D.; m. David Mark Wiener, Jan. 8, 1986. BA, Pa. State U., 1978; JD, Duquesne U., 1981. Bar: Pa. 1981, U.S. Dist. Ct. (we. dist.) Pa. 1981, Tex. 1987, U.S. Dist. Ct. (no. dist.) Tex. 1987. Assoc. counsel Brooks & Ewalt, P.C., Pitts., 1981-82; gen. counsel, sr. v.p. Stockton Savs. Assn., Dallas, 1987-88, Commodore Savs. Assn., Dallas, 1988; gen. counsel, exec. v.p. Bluebonnet Savs. Bank, F.S.B., Dallas, 1988—. Contbr. chpt. in book. Capt. U.S. Army, 1982-86, Korea. Mem. Tex. Bar Assn., Dallas Bar Assn., Am. Corp. Counsel Assn., Am. Mgmt. Assn., Price Waterhouse Gen. Counsel Forum, Rotary Club of Dallas (chmn. recognition com., chmn. elect Salvation Army com.). Republican. Lutheran. Office: Bluebonnet Savs Bank FSB 3100 Monticello Ave Dallas TX 75205-3431

DOLAN, CATHERINE ELLEN, financial executive; b. N.Y.C., June 26, 1942; d. Thomas Michael and Margaret Mary (O'Neill) D.; B.A. cum laude, Newton Coll. of Sacred Heart, 1964; postgrad. Emporia State U., 1989—. Statis. analyst Drexel, Harriman, Ripley, Inc., N.Y.C., 1966-68; mgr. Statis. Dept., Laird, Inc., N.Y.C., 1968-70; asst. treas. Old Lyme Corp., N.Y.C., 1970-78, treas., 1979-84; treas. Tru-Die, Inc., Franklin Park, Ill., 1976-84; asst. treas. Fabco-Air, Inc., 1981-84, Moore-Handley, Inc., 1982-84; v.p. Lyon & Stubbs, Inc., 1984-88; with reference and tech. svcs. staff Vail (Colo.) Pub. Libr., 1988—. Mem. U.S. C. of C., Fin. Women's Assn., Women's Econ. Roundtable. Home: 1975 Placid Dr Vail CO 81657-4330

DOLAN, DOROTHY ROSE, painter, sculptor, educator; b. Boston, Oct. 6, 1912; d. Joseph and Angela (Sinisgalli) Padula; m. Charles F. Dolan, 1940; 4 children. BSE, Mass. Coll. Art, 1933; MA, Boston Coll., 1965, postgrad. Formerly art tchr. Boston Pub. Schs.; ret. Painter, sculptor; creator signs and posters for Sea Haven condominiums. Bd. dirs., landscape designer, overseer Sea Haven Gardens, Pompano Beach, Fla. Mem. Phi Beta Kappa Gamma. Home: 2731 NE 14th St Pompano Beach FL 33062

DOLAN, JAN CLARK, state legislator; b. Akron, Ohio, Jan. 15, 1927; d. Herbert Spencer and Jean Risk (Morton) Clark; m. Walter John Dolan, Apr. 22, 1950 (dec. July 1986); children: Mark Raymond, Scott Spencer, Gary Clark, Todd Alvin. BA, U. Akron, 1949. Home svc. rep. East Ohio Gas Co., Akron, 1949-50; dietitian Akron City Hosp., 1950-51; tchr. Brecksville (Ohio) Sch. Dist., 1962-66; adminstr. Orchard Hills Adult Day Ctr., West Bloomfield, Mich., 1978-83; mem. Farmington Hills (Mich.) City Coun., 1975-88, Mich. Ho. of Reps., Lansing, 1989—. Mayor City of Farmington Hills, 1978, 85; elder Presbyn. Ch. Republican. Home: 22587 Gill Rd Farmington Hills MI 48335-4037 Office: Mich Ho of Reps State Capitol Bldg Lansing MI 48909

DOLAN, KATHRYN JANE, anthropologist; b. Milw., Nov. 11, 1947; d. Charles Victor and Jane Louise (Wagner) D. BA in Anthropology, U. Wis., 1970; MA in Anthropology, U. Tex., 1974, PhD in Anthropology, 1980. Rsch. assoc. Ctr. Orgnl. Rsch. Tex. Christian U., Ft. Worth, 1981-84; asst. prof. Tex. Coll. Osteopathic Medicine, Ft. Worth, 1984-89; children's project dir. Mental Health Assn., Ft. Worth, 1989-92; human svcs. needs assessment coord. United Way Tarrant County, Ft. Worth, 1992-93; adminstrv. assoc. Fedn. State Med. Bds., Ft. Worth, 1993—; community resource coord., group facilitator Tex. Dept. Human Svcs., 1990. Mem. Tarrant County Sexual Abuse adv. com., Ft. Worth, 1984-91; sec., treas. North Ctrl. Tex. Regional Network for Children, Tarrant County, 1987-91; vol., docent Kimbell Art Mus., 1987—. Mem. Am. Anthrop. Assn. Office: Fedn State Med Bds 6000 Western Pl Ste 707 Fort Worth TX 76107

DOLAN, LOUISE ANN, physicist; b. Wilmington, Del., Apr. 5, 1950. BA, Wellesley Coll., 1971; PhD in Physics, MIT, 1976. Jr. fellow in physics Harvard U., 1976-79; asst. prof. physics Rockefeller U., N.Y.C., 1979-82, assoc. prof., 1983-90, lab. head, 1990; prof. physics U. N.C., Chapel Hill, 1990—. John Simon Guggenheim fellow, 1988. Fellow Am. Phys. Soc. (Maria Goeppert-Mayer award 1987). Office: U NC Dept Physics Chapel Hill NC 27599-3255

DOLAN, M. CRISTINA, multimedia and interactive television executive, researcher; b. N.Y.C., Feb. 16, 1961; d. John and Cristina (Penalver) D. BEE, Manhattan Coll., 1983, M of Computer Sci. Engring., 1984; MS in Media Arts and Scis., MIT, 1994. Acct. systems engr. IBM, N.Y.C., 1984-88, lead devel. mktg. rep., 1988-91, multimedia cons., 1991-94; dir. multimedia and interactive television I-Cube, Cambridge, Mass., 1994—; co-chmn. activities MIT, Cambridge, 1993-94, joint adv. coun., 1992-93, athletics bd. dirs. Mem. IEEE (program chmn. 1988-90, edn. chmn. 1988-90), U.S. Bobsled and Skeleton Assn. (team mem. 1990-92). Home: Univ Park at MIT 129 Franklin St # 418 Cambridge MA 02139 Office: I-Cube Ctrl Plz 675 Massachusetts Ave Cambridge MA 02139

DOLAN, MARYANNE MCLORN, small business owner, writer, educator, lecturer; b. N.Y.C., July 14, 1924; d. Frederick Joseph and Kathryn Cecilia (Carroll) McLorn; m. John Francis Dolan, Oct. 6, 1951 (dec.); children: John Carroll, James Francis McLorn, William Brennan. B.A., San Francisco State U., 1978, M.A., 1981. Tchr. classes and seminars in antiques and collectibles U. Calif., Berkeley, Davis, Santa Cruz, Coll. of Marin, Kentfield, Calif., Mills Coll., Oakland, St. Mary's Coll., Moraga, 1969-90, Solano C.C., 1990—; tch. writing Dolan Sch., 1969-90; owner antique shop, Benicia, Calif., 1970—; lectr. Nat. Assn. Jewelry Appraisers Symposium, Tucson; lectr. Vintage Fashion Expo., Oakland, Coll. for Appraisers, Placentia, Calif. Author: Vintage Clothing, 1880-1960, 1983, Collecting Rhinestone Jewelry, 1984, Old Lace and Linens, 1989, Commonsense Collecting, 1991, 300 Years of American Sterling Silver Flatware, 1992; weekly columnist The Collector, 1979-88; contbr. articles to profl. jours. Mem. AAUW, Antique Appraisal Assn. Am. Inc., Costume Soc. Am., New Eng. Appraisers Assn., Questers, Women's Nat. Book Assn. Inc., Nat. Assn. Jewelry Appraisers, Internat. Soc. Appraisers (lectr. ann. meeting), Internat. Platform Assn. Republican. Roman Catholic. Home: 138 Belle Ave Pleasant Hill CA 94523-4640 Office: 191 W J St Benicia CA 94510-3143

DOLAN, REGINA TOUSIGNANT, psychologist; b. Mpls., Jan. 26, 1963; d. Ronald Vincent Dolan and Mary Jane Tousignant-Dolan. BA, U. VA., 1985; MA, Cath. U. Am., 1988, PhD, 1992. Rsch. psychologist NIMH, Rockville, Md., 1988-91; clin. psychology intern VA Hosp., Washington, 1990-91; staff clinician Lab. Sch. of Washington, 1991-94; clin. psychologist READS Inc., Middleboro, Mass., 1994—. Contbr. articles to profl. publs., chpt. to book. Recipient Thelma Hunt award D.C. Psychol. Assn., 1989, Outstanding Dissertation award Met. Psychiat. Clinic, 1990. Mem. APA (Sci. Directorate award 1991), Raven Soc.-U. Va. Home: 1167 Boylston St # 23 Boston MA 02215

DOLAND, JUDY ANN, retired financial rating company associate; b. Duluth, Minn., June 29, 1940; d. Burnham Oscar and Mary Katherine (Sederholm) D. Student, Mt. San Antonio Jr. Coll., Walnut, Calif., 1960. Subs. ledger acct. Pacific Intermountain Express, L.A., 1963-64; various positions Dun & Bradstreet, L.A., 1958-63, 64-80, state sales guide rep., 1980-83; payroll cashier Dun & Bradstreet, Monterey Park, Calif., 1983-85; exec. sec. Dun & Bradstreet, Long Beach, Calif., 1985-90; exec. sec. L.A. zone Dun & Bradstreet, Van Nuys, Calif., 1990-92; exec. sec. Woodland Hills dist. Dun & Bradstreet, Woodland Hills, Calif., 1992-93, ret., 1993.

DOLCE, DONNA MARIE, association executive; b. Fredonia, N.Y., July 12, 1951; d. Rocco William and C. Mary Joy Dolce. BA in Phys. Edn., Bethany Coll., 1973; MEd in Phys. Edn., U. Pitts., 1976. Tchr. Orchard Park (N.Y.) Sch., 1979; program/property mgr. Chautauqua Area coun. Girl Scouts U.S., Fredonia, 1979-86; dir. program Del-Raritan coun. Girl Scouts U.S., East Brunswick, N.J., 1986-89; orgn. and mgmt. specialist Girl Scouts U.S., N.Y.C., 1989-93; assn. network specialist YWCA U.S.A., N.Y.C., 1993—. Mem. Am. Camping Assn. (pres. upstate N.Y. sect. 1985-87). Office: YWCA USA 726 Broadway New York NY 10003

DOLE, ELIZABETH HANFORD, charitable organization administrator, former secretary of labor, former secretary of transportation; b. Salisbury, N.C., July 29, 1936; d. John Van and Mary Ella (Cathey) Hanford; m. Robert Joseph Dole (U.S. Senator from Kans.), Dec. 6, 1975. B.A. with honors in Polit. Sci., Duke, 1958; postgrad., Oxford (Eng.) U., summer 1959; M.A. in Edn., Harvard U., 1960, J.D., 1965. Bar: D.C. 1966. Staff asst. to asst. sec. for edn. HEW, Washington, 1966-67; practiced law Washington, 1967-68; assoc. dir. legis. affairs, then exec. dir. Pres.'s Com. for Consumer Interests, Washington, 1968-71; dep. dir. Office Consumer Affairs The White House, Washington, 1971-73; commr. FTC, Washington, 1973-79; chmn. Voters for Reagan-Bush, 1980; dir. Human Services Group, Office of Exec. Br. Mgmt., Office of Pres.-Elect, 1980; asst. to Pres. for pub. liaison, 1981-83; sec. U.S. Dept. Transp., 1983-87; with Robert Dole Presdl. Campaign, 1987-88; participant 1988 Presdl. and Congl. campaigns; sec. U.S. Dept. Labor, 1989-90; pres. American Red Cross, 1991—; mem. nominating com. Am. Stock Exchange, 1972, N.C. Consumer Council, 1972. Trustee Duke U., 1974-88; mem. coun. Harvard Law Sch. Assocs., vis. com. Harvard Sch. Pub. Health, 1992—; bd. overseers Harvard U., 1989. Recipient Arthur S. Flemming award U.S. Govt., 1972, Humanitarian award Nat. Commn. Against Drunk Driving, 1988, Disting. Alumni award Duke U., 1988, N.C. award, 1991, Lifetime Achievement award (Breaking the Glass Ceiling) Women Execs. in State Govt., 1993, North Carolinian of the Yr. award N.C. Press Assn., 1993, Radcliffe medal, 1993, Leadership award LWV, 1994; named one of Am.'s 200 Young Leaders, Time mag., 1974, one of World's 10 Most Admired Women, Gallup Poll, 1988; selected for Safety and Health Hall of Fame Internat., 1993. Mem. Phi Beta Kappa, Pi Lambda Theta, Pi Sigma Alpha. Office: ARC care Roy Clason External Comm 431 18th St NW Washington DC 20006-5310

DOLE, KAREN FAYE, librarian; b. Eldora, Iowa, Feb. 14, 1951; d. Richard Joseph and Norma Lucinda (Schelling) D. BA in Spanish, U. No. Iowa, 1973, MLS, 1977. Cert. secondary tchr., Iowa. Substitute tchr. Cedar Rapids (Iowa) Schs., 1973-74; media sec. Taylor Elem. Sch., Cedar Rapids, 1974-76; libr. B-G-M High Sch., Bklyn., 1977-80, North Iowa C.C., Mason City, 1980—; pres. North Iowa Libr. Coop., Mason City, 1991-92. Mem. Iowa Libr. Assn., Pilot Club (pres.-elect 1994—), Delta Kappa Gamma (sec. Xi chpt. 1984-86, v.p. 1990-92, pres. 1992-94). Democrat. Roman Catholic. Home: 1413 10th St SW Mason City IA 50401 Office: North Iowa Community Coll 500 College Dr Mason City IA 50401

DOLE, WANDA VICTORIA, librarian; b. Melrose Park, Ill., Sept. 10, 1942; d. Malburn Sanford and Victoria Bernice (Berner) D.; m. David Richards Helmstadter, May 7, 1966 (div.). BA magna cum laude, Lawrence U., Appleton, Wis., 1964; MA in Classics, Tufts U., 1965; MS, U. Ill., 1975. Asst. editor Scott, Foresman & Co., Glenview, Ill., 1967-68; arch. librarian U. Ky., Lexington, 1976-78; humanities bibliographer U. Ill., Chgo., 1978-80; asst. dir. collection devel. U. Miami, Coral Gables, Fla., 1980-82; reg. sales mgr. Blackwell N. Am./B.H. Blackwell Ltd., Lake Oswego, Oreg., 1982-86; head librarian Pa. State U., Abington, 1986-91; asst. dir. collections and pub. svcs. SUNY, Stony Brook, 1991—; mem. curriculum adv. com. So. Conn. State U. Sch. Library Sci., New Haven, 1983-85; mem. Ill.-Princeton Expedition to Morgantina, Sicily, 1970. Contbr. articles to profl. jours. Mem. ALA, Art Librs. Soc. N.Am. Episcopalian. Home: 26 Pembrook Dr Stony Brook NY 11790-2636 Office: SUNY Main Libr Stony Brook NY 11794

DOLEN, LENISE, elder care consultant; b. N.Y.C., July 15, 1937; d. George and Sue (Schneider) Schachner; m. Michael Dolen, July 4, 1960; children: Stacey B. Dolen, Eric G. Dolen. BA, Hunter Coll., 1959, MS, 1962; MPh, CUNY, 1979, PhD, 1980. Lic. psychologist, N.Y. Tchr., group counselor N.Y. City Bd. Edn., 1959-63; tchr. N.Y. City Pub. Schs., 1967-69; tchr., group counselor N.Y. City Pub. Sch. System, 1969-71; co-chmn. doctoral rsch. group, 1973-74; rsch. assoc., cons. Ctr. for Gerontol. Studies, Grad. Ctr., CUNY, 1978-81; rsch. assoc. Lefkowith, Inc., 1978-81; pvt. practice in psychotherapy, 1981-82, 82—; coord. Office of Mental Health Harlem Valley Regional Psychogeriatric Ctr. of N.Y. State, Wingdale, 1981-82; pres. Dolen Cons. Systems, Chappaqua, N.Y., 1982—; asst. prof. gerontology Grad. Sch. of Health Scis., N.Y. Med. Coll.; adj. faculty Hunter Coll., 1978; speaker in field. guest reviewer Rsch. on Aging: A Quarterly of Social Gerontology; contbr. numerous articles to profl. jours. Bd. dirs. Legal Awareness of Westchester, Vis. Nuse Svcs. in Westchester; past pres. No. Westchester Geriatric Com., bd. dirs. hon. chmn.; adv. coun. Westchester County Office for the Aging. Mem. APA, Am. Soc. on Aging, Nat. Assn. of Pvt. Geriatric Care Mgrs. (founder, v.p.), Alzheimer's Assn. (v.p.), Nat. Coun. on Aging, Am. Parkinson's Disease Assn., Assn. of Employee Assistance Profls., Internat. Soc. Retirement Planners, Am. Soc. on Aging. Office: Dolen Cons Systems 290 Quaker Rd Chappaqua NY 10514

DOLITZKY, SARAH MARGARET, artist, illustrator; b. Queens, N.Y., July 7, 1951; d. Meyer and Ida (Dolitzky) Horowitz; m. Harvey Schneider, Apr., 1972 (div. 1981); children: Benjamin, Abraham. BA, SUNY, Buffalo, 1972; Cert. of Art, Md. Coll. Art and Design, 1973-75. Artist Saul's Litho Co., Washington, 1974-75. Illustrator: NAACP/Lowell chpt. fundraising brochure, 1987-89, Mosaic Mag., 1989, Mass. Dept. of Health and Hosps. Lead Poison Prevention brochure, 1992, Waiting for Jerusalem, 1993; works represented at Gallery Revel, N.Y.C., 1986—, EV Gallery, N.Y.C., 1987-88, DeHavilland Gallery, Boston, 1991-92, Starving Artist Gallery, Boston, 1992-93; pvt. shows include Tower I Gallery, New Haven, 1975, Mack Bldg., Lowell, 1983, Boston Govt. Ctr., 1986, Black Genesis, 1985, Boston Jewish Cmty. Ctr., 1986;. Md. Coll. Art and Design scholar, 1974-75. Mem. Boston Visual Artists Union, Artists for Survival, Phi Beta Kappa. Democrat. Jewish.

DOLL, LYNNE MARIE, public relations agency executive; b. Glendale, Calif., Aug. 27, 1961; d. George William and Carol Ann (Kennedy) D.; m. David Jay Lans, Oct. 11, 1986. BA in Journalism, Calif. State U., Northridge, 1983. Freelance writer Austin Pub. Rels. Systems, Glendale, 1978-82; asst. account exec. Berkhemer & Kline, L.A., 1982-83; exec. v.p., ptnr. Rogers & Assocs., L.A., 1983—; exec. dir. Suzuki Automotive Found. for Life, Brea, Calif., 1986-91; mem. strategic planning com. Gateway to Indian Am. Corp. for Am. Indian Devel., San Francisco, 1988-90. Pub. rels. cons., Rape Treatment Ctr., L.A., 1986—. Mem. Ad Club L.A. (bd. dirs., pres. 1994-95), Pub. Rels. Soc. Am., So. Calif. Assn. Philanthropy, Coun. on Founds., Internat. Motor Press Assn. Democrat. Office: Rogers & Assocs 1875 Century Park E Ste 300 Los Angeles CA 90067-2504

DOLL, PATRICIA MARIE, marketing and public relations consultant; b. Bryn Mawr, Pa., Apr. 13, 1960; d. Otello Louis (dec.) and Eleanor Caroline (De Pasquale) De Grandis; m. John Russell Doll, Oct. 5, 1985. BS in Speech Communications, Millersville (Pa.) U., 1982. Lic. radio operator. Advt. asst. ELMCO Merchandising, Wayne, Pa., 1983-85; freelance writer, 1984-90; dir. communications Rouse & Assocs., Malvern, Pa., 1987-90; pres. Publicity Works Award-Winning Comms., Bowmansville, Pa., 1990—; part time broadcaster, writer, promoter Sta. WNAR Radio, Sta. WLAN Radio, Sta. WGAL-TV8, 1982-85. Contbr. articles to local newspapers and trade mags.; producer TV documentary, 1982. Mem. Women's Bus. Com. of Berks County, other chambers, trade, local orgns. Recipient awards for work. Mem. Pub. Rels. Soc. of Am., Chester County C. of C., Chester County Devel. Coun., Am. Heart Asns., Berks County C. of C. Roman Catholic.

DOLLENMAYER, JUDITH BRISTOL, communications consultant; b. Knoxville, Tenn., Nov. 27, 1941; d. Raymond J. and K. Ruth (Bristol) D. AB, Harvard U., 1963; MS, Syracuse U., 1974. Gordon traveling fellow Harvard U., Asia and Africa, 1963-64; editor Doubleday & Co., N.Y.C., 1964-69; instr. polit. sci. Syracuse (N.Y.) U., 1970-73; chief of staff to Rep. Elizabeth Holtzman U.S. Congress, 1975-77; sr. assoc. Ednl. Testing Svc., Washington, 1978-82; dir. Dollenmayer Comms., Washington, 1983—; bd. dirs. coun. social work edn. Nat. Commn. on Accreditation, 1985-90. Editor: Personal Justice Denied: Japanese-American Internment in World War II, 1983 (scholarly seires) The Anchor Bible, 1966-69; bd. dirs. mag. Who Cares, 1993—. Bd. dirs. Internat. Student House, Washington, 1990-93; pres. Georgetown Reservoir Assn., Washington, 1993-94. Recipient 1st pl. writing awards L.A. Times, 1960; German Marshall Fund travel grantee, 1988; poetry fellow Jenny M. Moore Found., 1993-94. Mem. Women's Fgn. Policy Group, Washington Ind. Writers, Harvard Club of Washington (bd. dirs. 1991-93, v.p. 1994—), Maxwell Alumni Assn. D.C. (pres. 1979-80), Radcliffe Alumnae Assn. (sec. class of 1963 1993—). Office: Dollenmayer Comms S 802 1666 K St NW Washington DC 20006

DOMAN, MARGARET HORN, civic official, consultant; b. Portland, Oreg., July 28, 1946; d. Richard Carl and Dorothy May (Teepe) Horn; m. Steve Hamilton Doman, July 12, 1969; children: Jennifer, Kristina, Kathryn. BA, Willamette U., 1968; postgrad., U. Wash., 1968-69, 72. Cert. tchr. Tchr. jr. high Bellevue (Wash.) Sch. Dist., 1969-70, subs. tchr., 1990-91; tchr. jr. high University City (Mo.) Sch. Dist., 1970-71; employment counselor employment security dept. State of Wash., Seattle, 1971; planning commn. mem. City of Redmond, Wash., 1980-83, chmn., 1982-83; city coun. mem. City of Redmond, 1983-91, pres., 1990-91; exec. dir. Eastside Human Svcs. Coun., Redmond, Wash., 1992; employment specialist Wash. State Dept. Employment Security, 1993; cons. land use planning & govt. process Redmond, 1993—; Redmond rep. Puget Sound. Coun. of Govt., Seattle, 1984-91, vice chmn., 1988, 90, chmn. transp., 1986-88, exec. bd., 1987, mem. standing com. on transp., 1986-91; bd. dirs., pres. Eastside Human Svcs. Coun., Bellevue, 1983-91, pres., 1990. Bd. dirs. Redmond YMCA, 1985-86; mem. state exec. com. Nat. History Day, Olympia, Wash., 1986; vol. Bellevue Sch. Dist., 1977—; bd. dirs. Eastside br. Camp Fire, Bellevue, 1992-94. Mem. Redmond C. of C. (land use and transp. com. 1994—). Republican. Unitarian. Home: 2104 180th Ct NE Redmond WA 98052-6032

DOMBROWSKI, ANNE WESSELING, microbiologist, researcher; b. Cin., Jan. 26, 1948; d. Robert John and Margaret Mary (Bell) Wesseling; m. Allan Wayne Dombrowski, Apr. 17, 1982; children: Amy, Alicia. BA summa cum laude, Xavier U., 1970; MS, U. Cin., 1972, PhD, 1974. Fellow Scripps Clinic & Rsch. Found., La Jolla, Calif., 1974-76; sr. rsch. microbiologist Merck & Co., Inc., Rahway, N.J., 1976-87, rsch. fellow, 1987—. Patentee in field; contbt. articles to profl. jours. Mem. AAAS, Soc. Indsl. Microbiology (sec. 1982-85), Am. Soc. Microbiology, Soc. Gen. Microbiology, Mycol. Soc. Home: 51 Landsdowne Rd East Brunswick NJ 08816-4156 Office: Merck & Co Inc PO Box 2000 Rahway NJ 07065-0900

DOMEYER, SUSAN COLLINS, artist; b. Chgo., July 7, 1955; d. David Merrill and Monica (Buergler) Collins; m. Dean Andrew Domeyer, Oct. 26, 1991; 1 child, Cole Collins. BA, Northland Coll., 1977. Artist Romano Studio, Chgo., 1977-79, Fla. Keys Souvenier Co., Marathon, 1979-81, Prime Graphics, New Orleans, 1981-82. Illustrator: The Door Into Shadow, 1983; illustrator books and mags. TSR Publs., 1982—, Bluejay, Del Ray, Baen Books, 1982—; illustrator paingin The Forrest Ghost, 1982; one woman show includes Valloti Rep., Media, Pa., 1987, M.A. Doran Gallery, Tulsa, 1989-93, Gleason Fine Art, Boothbay Harbor, Maine, 1991. Recipient Best in Show award World Sci. Fiction Conv., 1982. Home: PO Box 412 West Southport ME 04576

DOMIAN, JUDITH LEA, marketing professional; b. St. Louis, Aug. 5, 1948; d. Robert Held and Pauline Louise (Hayo) Sihnhold; divorced; children: Thomas Brian, Matthew Alan. BS in Bus. Edn., Ctrl. Mo. State U., Warrensburg, 1970, MS in Edn., 1971. Sales cons. Jeffco Travel, Arnold, Mo., 1988—; mktg. coord. Fox C-6 Sch. Dist., Arnold, 1971—; sales cons. Field Studies of N.Y., N.Y.C., 1985—; mem. bd. dirs. Mo. DECA, 1990—, pres., 1993. Author textbook/workbook Display. Vol. Salvation Army, St. Louis, 1989, U.S. Olympic Com., St. Louis, 1993. Recipient Mktg. Educator of Yr. award State of Mo., 1988. Mem. RA of NEA, Mo. Vocat. Assn. (Sec.), Sales Mktg. Assn. (bd. dirs.), Arnold C. of C., Mktg. Edn. Assn. Home: 1166 Summit Meadows Dr Fenton MO 63026-3846

DOMINGO, CHRIS, interpreter for the Deaf; b. Balt., Nov. 27, 1951; d. Walter Edward and Sylvia (Domingo) Pocock. BA in Psychology/Theater, U. R.I., 1979; Am. sign lang., interpreter tng., Vista Coll., 1986; grad. interpreter tng. program, Ohlone Coll., 1987; MA in Women Studies, San Francisco State U., 1995. Cert. Calif. Assn. Deaf, 1991. Interpreter, tutor, braillist, reader, scribe San Francisco State U., Ohlone Coll., others, Calif., 1982—. Author: (poetry chapbooks) A Dime a Dozen, Some Very Free Verses, Notes from the Madhouse, The Hen and the Wolf, (book chpt.) Femicide: The Politics of Woman Killing, 1992; editor: (newsletter) Memory and Rage, 1990-92; contbr. poetry and articles to feminist and anti-war pubs.; dir. Lavender Abalone Presents: A Live Women's Poetry Sensation, 1980; prodr. Mime, Movement, Magic, 1985. Founder, coord. Berkeley Clearinghouse on Femicide, 1989—; phone counselor R.I. Rape Crisis Ctr., 1978-79, Bay Area Women Against Rape, 1979-80; info. coord. Women Against Femicide, 1980-81; interpreter World Games for the Deaf, 1985. Named one of 10 Outstanding Berkeley Women, Commn. on Status of

Women, 1991. Mem. No. Calif. Registry of Interpreters for Deaf. Office: Berkeley Clearinghouse PO Box 12342 Berkeley CA 94701-3342

DOMINGO, ESTRELLA TINA, fashion designer, consultant, paralegal; b. Bacarra, The Philippines, Sept. 26, 1965; came to U.S., 1969; d. Jaime Madrid and Estrella (Taganas) D. AA in Fashion Design, Brooks Coll., Long Beach, Calif., 1986; BA in Psychology, San Francisco State U., 1989; postgrad. Sawyer Coll., 1994. Cert. paralegal. Sales assoc. J.C. Penney Co., Salinas, Calif., 1984; clk.-typist VA Med. Ctr., Palo Alto, Calif., 1987, sec. to chief anesthesiology svc., 1988-89; clk.-typist VA Med. Ctr., Menlo Park, Calif., 1987-88; paralegal Wegner & Peterson, San Jose, Calif., 1992-93; adminstrv. asst. Western Digital, 1993; adminstrv. asst., v.p., sec., gen. counsel Robert Half Internat., Inc., Menlo Park, Calif., 1993—. Mem. rsch. adv. bd., editorial bd., dep. gov. ABI, adv. coun. IBC. Recipient Commemorative Medal of Honor, N.C. & Women of the Yr. award, 1991, Spl. Contbn. award VA Med. ctr., 1987, Superior Performance award, 1989; scholar Calif. Scholarship Assn., 1984. Mem. NAFE (hon. advisor, dep. gov. ABIRA & Women's Inner Circle of Achievement, The World Found. Successful Women, fellowship), Smithsonian Assocs., Calif. Honor Soc. Roman Catholic. Office: Robert Half Internat Inc Ste 200 2884 Sand Hill Rd Menlo Park CA 94025

DOMINGUEZ, MIRIAM KAY, technical sales specialist; b. Corpus Christi, Sept. 1, 1956; d. Howard Otto and Wilbern Terry (Hamblin) Kinsey; m. Joe Dominguez Jr., Nov. 8, 1984 (div. June 1990); 1 child, Christopher Cody. BMusicEdn summa cum laude, Tex. A&M U., Corpus Christi, 1978. Music tchr. Tuloso Midway Elem. Sch., Corpus Christi, 1978-79; comms. cons. Southwestern Bell, Houston, 1980-81; account exec. Southwestern Bell/AT&T, Houston, 1982-91; tech. sales specialist AT&T, Houston, 1991—. Chair staff-parish rels. Cokesbury United Meth. Ch., Houston, 1993, pres. chancel choir, 1990-93; cubmaster Pack 1032 Boy Scouts of America, 1994—. Mem. Am. Bus. Women's Assn. (pres. Houston City Lights chpt. 1990-91, Woman of Yr. 1990), Houston Fedn. Profl. Bus. Women (Woman of Excellence 1992). Office: AT&T 5 E Greenway Plz Houston TX 77046-0501

DOMM, ALICE, lawyer; b. Phila., May 22, 1954; d. William Donald and Alice Frances (Day) D.; m. Richard Coles Grubb, Sept. 26, 1987; children: Stephanie Elizabeth, Samuel William. BA, Gettysburg Coll., 1976, JD, Rutgers U., 1981. Bar: N.J. 1981, Pa. 1981. Assoc. prof. Glassboro (N.J.) Coll., 1980-81; atty., juvenile sect. chief Office Pub. Defender, New Brunswick, N.J., 1982-92; sr. trial atty. Office of Pub. Defender, Belvidere, N.J., 1992-93, Trenton, N.J., 1993—. Bd. dirs. Police Athletic League, New Brunswick, 1982-85; mem. Middlesex County Youth Services Commn., New Brunswick; steering com. treas. Middlesex County Women Lawyers Com.; mem. Gov.'s Council on Child Abuse and Neglect, Middlesex County, Gov.'s com. childrens Services Planning Juvenile Justice Subcom.; mem. Middlesex County Commn. Child Abuse and Missing Children, Criminal Justice Planning Com. Middlesex County. Mem. ABA, N.J. Bar Assn., Middlesex County Bar Assn. (trustee), Middlesex County Women's Bar Assn. (steering com., treas.), Assn. Criminal Def. Lawyers N.J. Office: Office Pub Defender 210 S Broad St Trenton NJ 08608

DOMMEL, DARLENE HURST, writer; b. Charles City, Iowa, July 11, 1940; d. Roy and Elsie (Hopkes) Hurst; B.S. with high distinction, U. Minn., 1963; m. James H. Dommel, Oct. 15, 1961; children: Diann, Christine, David. MS, 1965, grad. exec. program Grad. Sch. Bus. Administrn., 1972; postgrad. So. Meth. U., 1976-77. Pub. health nurse Combined Nursing Service, Mpls., 1963-64; contbr. articles on pottery to various collectors and antiques mags., 1967—; organizer, exhibitor of art pottery display touring fin. instns. in upper midwest, 1976—; lectr. and cons. health care, antiques, journalism; health care specialist Health Services Research Center, St. Louis Park Med. Center, 1978-79; instr. Augsburg Coll., 1979-81. Mem. Minn. Adv. Task Force on Epilepsy, 1981-83, State Council for Handicapped, 1982-84, Dept. Pub. Welfare Adv. Council on Mental Retardation and Phys. Disabilities, 1982-84; mem. profl. adv. bd. Epilepsy Found. Minn., 1984—. Mem. Mpls. Inst. Arts. USPHS trainee, 1964-65; Sigma Theta Tau scholar, 1962-63; Martha Ripley scholar, 1961-62: U. Minn. Sch. Nursing Found. scholar, 1962. Mem. U. Minn. Alumni Assn., Nat. Writers Club, Nat. League for Nursing (regional assembly constituent leagues for nursing. exec. com. 1985-87), Minn. League for Nursing (pres. 1983-85). Gethsemane Luth. Ch. Women, Am. Art Pottery Collectors Assn., Sigma Theta Tau, Delta Delta Delta. Lutheran. Home: 510 Westwood Dr N Minneapolis MN 55422-5266

DONA, NOREEN, lawyer; b. Webster, Mass., June 17, 1961; d. George William and Mary Phil (Viley) D. BS, Quinnipiac Coll., Hamden, Conn., 1983; JD, Southwestern Sch. Law, L.A., 1990. Sr. tax acct. Far West Savs. & Loan Assn., Newport Beach, Calif., 1985-87; tax specialist KPMG Peat Marwick, Long Beach, Calif., 1990-92; pvt. practice Huntington Beach, Calif., 1992—; vol. atty. L.A. County Bar AIDS Project, L.A. and Orange County, 1993—, Pub. Law Ctr., Santa Ana, Calif., 1993—; mediator Cmty. Svc. Programs, Inc., Irvine, Calif., 1992—. Lit. vol. Lit. Vols. Am., Huntington Beach, Calif., 1992—. Mem. ABA, So. Calif. Mediation Assn., L.A. County Bar Assn., Orange County Bar Assn. (chair summons 1993—). Office: 19913 Beach Blvd Ste 110 Huntington Beach CA 92648-3703

DONAHOE-FILLMORE, BETSY KAY, physical therapist; b. Urbana, Ohio, Sept. 8, 1966; d. William A. and Doris E. (Robison) D. BS in Allied Health summa cum laude, Ohio State U., 1988; MS in Phys. Therapy, U. Indpls., 1992. Phys. therapist Children's Hosp. Med. Ctr., Cin., 1988—; assoc. prof. phys. therapy Andrews U., Dayton, Ohio, 1994—. Mem. Am. Phys. Therapy Assn. (dist. chair Ohio chpt. S.W. dist. 1992—), pediatric cert. specialist 1993, state rep. 1993—), Cin. Alumnae Panhellenic (corr. sec. 1993—), Phi Mu (alumnae pres. 1992-93). Home: 992 Walnut Ct Mason OH 45040-2011 Office: Children's Hosp 3333 Burnet Ave Cincinnati OH 45229-3026

DONAHUE, AGNES H., federal agency administrator; b. Ocean Springs, Miss., Nov. 21, 1945; d. Henry Y. and Valletta A. (Baker) D. DDS with honors, Meharry Med. Coll., 1975; MScD, Boston U., 1977; MPH with honors, U. Calif., Berkeley, 1980. Asst. prof. med. ctr. U. Miss., 1977-80; staff fellow NIH, 1980-82, sr. staff fellow, 1982-84, PHS grants assoc., 1984-85, health scientist adminstr., 1985-88; exec. sec. Dept. HHS, Washington, 1988-90, exec. dir. pub. health svc. coord. com. women, 1990-91, dir. Office Women's Health, USPHS, 1991—. Recipient Disting. Alumni award Goldman Sch. Dentistry, Boston U., 1992. Mem. Am. Assn. Dental Rsch., Nat. Dental Assn., Internat. Coalition Women Physicians, Internat. Assn. Dental Rsch. Office: US Pub Health Svc Dept of Health & Human Svcs 200 Independence Ave SW Rm 730-B Washington DC 20201*

DONAHUE, BARBARA LYNN SEAN, television producer; b. Trenton, N.J., Feb. 14, 1956; d. Donald Paul and Elizabeth (Anderson) D.; m. Charles R. Boyce II, Aug. 20, 1983; 1 child, Terrence Donahue Boyce. BA, U. Vt., 1978. Sports coord. ABC Sports, 1984-86. Producer: Badminton Horse Trials, 1988, The Hampton Classic Show Jumping, 1988, Mercedes Grand Prix of Dallas-Show Jumping, 1988, Thomas Hearns v. Iran Barkley Championship Fight, 1988, 1987 World Water Skiing Championships, 1988, U.S. Synchronized Swimming Fedn. Indsl., 1988, Seoul Olympic Profiles, 1988, World Alpine Ski Championships, 1989, Knievel Legend Continues: Can Son Avenge Evel's Crash?, 1989, Chgo. Internat. Dog Show, 1989, World Super Heavywright Weightlifting Championships, 1989, U.S. Women's Open Indsl., 1987, 89, 90, Olympic Sports Festival, 1987, Sunday Showcast: Jackie Robinson, 1987, The Game of the Century: Nebr. vs. Oklahoma 1971 recap, 1987, Beauty and Soul, 1986, Volvo World Cup Show Jumping, 1986, Wide World of Sports Moments, 1985, Lake Tahoe Tennis Festival, 1985, Superbikers Motocross, 1985, N.Y.C. Mini-Marathon, 1985, UCLA Invitational Track and Field Meet, 1985, United Airlines In-Flight Movies, 1985, Sarajevo Winter Olympics, 1984, L.A. Summer Olympics, 1984, Grand Prix of Monaco, 1984, U.S. vs. The World in Amateur Boxing, 1983, Battle of the Network Stars, 1983, History of the U.S. Open Golf Championship, 1982, NCAA Football, 1982; various programs ESPN, RTE, USGA, NBC, 1989-93, numerous others; co-author Dandelions, A study in Vermont traditions. Mem. Jr. League Greenwich, 1985—; adv. bd. Greenwich Community, 1986-88. Recipient Unity award Internat. Spl. Olympics, 1983, Christopher award, 1983, Sports Emmy awards Games of the XXIII Olympiad, 1984-85, ABC's Wide World of Sports, 1986, 25th Anniversary Special, 1986, Commendation award Am. Assn. State and Local History, 1989. Mem. Nat. Horse Show Assn., Dir. Guild Am., Am. Horse Show Assn., U.S. Combined Tng. Assn., U.S. Dressage Fedn., U.S. Equestrian Team Gold Medal Club, The Field Club. Office: Grand Prix Prodns 35 Mead Ave Cos Cob CT 06807

DONAHUE, ELINOR, actress; b. Tacoma, Apr. 19, 1937; d. Thomas William and Doris Genevieve (Gelbaugh) D.; m. Harry Stephen Ackerman, Apr. 21, 1961 (dec. Feb. 1991); children: Brian Patrick, Peter Kyran, James Jay, Christopher Asher; m. Louis G. Genevrino, Feb. 29, 1992. AA, UCLA. Began show bus. career singing on Sta. KMO-Radio, Tacoma, 1939; with song and dance act Bert Levy Vaudeville Circuit, 1944-46; appeared in films Tenth Ave. Angel, Mr. Big, Unfinished Dance, Three Daring Daughters, Girls Town, Love is Better Than Ever, Going Beserk, 1983, Pretty Woman, 1990, Freddy's Dead, 1991, on TV series Father Knows Best, 1954-63, Andy Griffith Show, 1960-61, Many Happy Returns, 1964-65, Odd Couple, 1972-74, Mulligan's Stew, 1977, Please Stand By, 1978-79, Drs. Private Lives, New Adventures of Beans Baxter, 1987-88, Get a Life, 1990-92; numerous guest roles on TV including No Margin For Error on Police Story, 1978, Newhart, Golden Girls, 1989-91; television movies include In Name Only, 1969, Gidget Gets Married, 1972, Mulligan's Stew, 1977, Doctor's Private Lives, 1978, Condominium, 1980, High School U.S.A, 1983. Former 2d v.p. Share, Inc. (charitable orgn. for mentally retarded and developmentally disabled). *

DONAHUE, LAURA KENT, state senator; b. Quincy, Ill., Apr. 22, 1949; d. Laurence S. and Mary Lou (McFarland) Kent; m. Michael A. Donahue, July 16, 1983. B.S., Stephens Coll., 1971. Mem. Ill. State Senate, Quincy, 1981—. Mem. Lincoln Club of Adams County, Ill. Fedn. Republican Women. Mem. P.E.O. Lodge: Altrusa. Office: Ill State Senate State Capitol Springfield IL 62706*

DONAHUE, MARY ROSENBERG, psychologist; b. N.Y.C., Dec. 20, 1932; d. Lester and Ethel (Hyman) Rosenberg; children: Laurie, Rachel. BA, Adelphi U., 1954; MA, N.Y. U., 1958; PhD, St. John U., 1968. Tchr. Elmont, N.Y., 1954-57, sch. psychologist, 1957-63; cons. psychologist NIMH, 1964-65; sch. psychologist Mamaroneck, N.Y., 1966-67; pvt. practice psychology Bethesda, Md., 1971—; pres. Automated Psychol. Svcs.; bd. dirs. SPIFE, comprehensive testing svc.; expert witness local jurisdictions regarding domestic issues, womens issues, abuse, 1974—; speaker on custody evaluations and expert witness considerations. Co-author: On Your Own, 1993. NIMH grantee, 1962-63, 64-65. Mem. Am. Psychol. Assn., Md. Psychol. Assn., D.C. Psychol. Assn., Am. Orthopsychiat. Assn., Assn. Pvt. Practitioners, Nat. Assn. Women Bus. Owners. Home: 12017 Edgepark Ct Rockville MD 20854-2138 Office: 5902 Hubbard Dr Rockville MD 20852-4823

DONAHUE, PATRICIA TOOTHAKER, retired social worker, administrator; b. Alamo, Tex., Sept. 6, 1922; d. Henry Tull and Minnie Elizabeth (Scott) Toothaker; m. Hayden Hackney Donahue, Feb. 22, 1947; children: Erin Kathleen, Kerry Shannon, Patricia Marie. BA, U. Okla., 1977, MSW, 1978. Lic. social worker with specialty in clin. social work, Okla. Clin. social worker Cen. Okla. Community Mental Health Ctr., Norman, 1979-91; participant VII World Congress Mental Health, Vienna, Austria, 1983; adj. asst. prof. U. Okla. Sch. Social Work, Norman, 1989—. Vol. counselor Woman's Resource Ctr., Norman, 1978-79; active Cleve. County Aging Svcs. Adv. Coun., 1988-91, pres., 1991. Mem. Nat. Alliance for Mentally Ill, Cleve. County Mental Health Assn., Cleve. County Med. Aux. (pres. 1970-71), Reviewers Club Norman (pres. 1970). Democrat. Methodist. Home: 1109 Westbrooke Ter Norman OK 73072-6308

DONAHUE, SHIRLEY OHNSTAD, elementary education educator; b. Darlington, Wis., Aug. 29, 1937; d. Joseph and Edna L. (Peterson) Ohnstad; m. John V. Donahue, Aug. 20, 1960; children: Roger K., Jeffrey J. BS, U. Wis., Platteville, 1959; MS, No. Ill. U., 1978. Cert. tchr., Ill. Tchr. Freeport (Ill.) Sch. Sys., 1959-62, Belvidere (Ill.) Sch. Sys., 1962-64, Pecatonica (Ill.) Sch. Sys., 1964-66, Orangeville (Ill.) Sch. Sys., 1966-67, Rock Falls (Ill.) Sch. Sys., 1967-93; ret. Rock Falls (Ill.) Sch. System, 1993. Co-author gifted student curriculum materials. Mem. liturgical com. St. Mary's Ch., Sterling, Ill., 1980-84, aux. min., 1980-94; mem., pres. Friends of Sterling Pub. Libr., v.p., 1990-93; bd. dirs. YWCA, sec. bd. dirs., 1994-95; mem. Cmty. Gen. Hosp. Med. Aux., 1993—, co-chair sr. health ins. program, 1994—. Recipient Western Ill. Master Tchr. award, 1991. Mem. Rock Falls Elem. Edn. Assn. (chmn. polit. action com. for edn. 1985-87), Ill. Edn. Assn., NEA, AAUW, Sterling Democratic Women. Roman Catholic. Home: 303 W 12th St Sterling IL 61081-2201

DONALD, AIDA DIPACE, publishing executive; b. Bklyn., Apr. 19, 1930; d. Victor E. and Bessie DiPace; m. David Herbert Donald; 1 child, Bruce Randall. AB cum laude, Barnard Coll., 1952; MA, Columbia U., 1953; PhD, U. Rochester, 1961. Instr. history dept. Columbia U., N.Y.C., 1955-56; editor Mass. Hist. Soc., Boston, 1960-64, Johns Hopkins U. Press, Balt., 1972-73; social sci. editor Harvard U. Press, Cambridge, Mass., 1973-79, exec. editor, 1979-89, editor in chief, 1989—, asst. dir., 1991. Editor: John F. Kennedy and the New Frontier, 1966, (with David Herbert Donald) Charles Frances Adams Diary, 2 vols., 1965. Columbia U. Dibblee fellow, 1952-53, U. Rochester fellow, 1953-55, 56-57, Oxford U. Fulbright fellow, 1959-60. Fellow AAUW; mem. Am. Hist. Assn., Orgn. Am. Historians, Polit. Sci. Assn. Am. Office: Harvard Univ Press 79 Garden St Cambridge MA 02138-1499

DONALD, BERNICE B., judge; b. Miss., Sept. 17, 1951; d. Perry and Willie Bell (Hall) Bowie; m. W. L. Donald, Oct. 9, 1973. BA in Sociology, Memphis State Univ., 1974, JD, 1979; student, Nat. Judicial Coll., 1983, 84. Bar: Tenn. 1979, U.S. Fed. Ct. 1979, U.S. Supreme Ct. 1989. Clk. South Central Bell Telephone Co., 1971-75, mgr., 1975-80; staff atty. Memphis Area Legal Svcs., 1980, Shelby County Public Defenders Office, 1980-82; judge Gen. Sessions Criminal Ct. of Shelby County, Tenn., 1982-88; bankruptcy judge U.S. Bankruptcy Ct. (we. dist.) Tenn., Memphis, 1988—; faculty mem. Fed. Judicial Ctr., 1991—, Nat. Judicial Coll., 1992—; adj. prof. Cecil C. Humphreys Sch. of Law. Recipient Cmty. Svcs. award Nat. Conf. on Christians and Jews, 1986, Martin Luther King Cmty. Svc. award, Young Careerist award State of Tenn. Raleigh Bureau of Profl. Women; named Citizen of Yr. Excelsior Chpt. of Eastern Star, Woman of Yr. Pentecostal Ch. of God in Christ. Mem. Nat. Assn. of Women Judges (pres. 1990-91), Am. Judges Assn., Nat. Ctr. for State Cts., Am. Bar Assn., Nat. Bar Assn., Tenn. Bar Assn., Memphis County Bar Assn., Shelby County Bar Assn., Am. Trial Lawyers Assn., Assn. of Women Attys. (pres. 1991, bd. dirs.), Nat. Conf. of Bankruptcy Judges (bd. dirs. 1993), Nat. Conf. of Women's Bar Assn. (bd. mem.), Nat. Conf. of Spl. Ct. Judges (sec.), Leadership Memphis (pres. 1987, bd. dirs.), Internat. Women's Forum. Office: US Dist Ct 969 Madison Ave Rm 625 Memphis TN 38103*

DONALDSON, DARCY MILLER, publishing executive; b. Glen Ridge, N.J., June 17, 1953; d. Paul Richardson and Susan (Alling) Miller; m. James R. Donaldson III, Feb. 6, 1988 (div.); 1 child, Zoe Alling. Co-founder, assoc. pub. Mus. Mag., N.Y.C., 1979-83; pub. Crop Protection Chemicals Reference, N.Y.C., 1983-85; assoc. pub. Chief Exec. Mag., N.Y.C., 1986-87, pub., 1987-89, exec. v.p., 1989—. Mem. ASCAP, Advt. Women of N.Y. Democrat. Episcopalian. Office: Chief Exec Mag 733 3d Ave New York NY 10017

DONALDSON, LORETTA MARIE, librarian; b. Butler, Pa., Jan. 2, 1943; d. Harry Vernon and Anna Agnes (Lehnerd) Kidd; m. Raymond Benjamin Snyder Jr., June 6, 1964 (dec. Dec. 1985); children: Kenneth Scott Snyder, Timothy Patrick Snyder; m. Wilbert James Donaldson, Jr., Oct. 31, 1992. BS in Edn., Clarion U., 1964; MA in English, Slippery Rock (Pa.) U., 1989. Cert. tchr., Pa. Libr. Keystone Oaks High Sch., Dormont, Pa., 1964-66, Butler (Pa.) Area Sr. High Sch., 1966-67, Butler County Community Coll., 1967-68; substitute tchr. Butler Area Sch. Dist., 1971-83; English tchr. Moniteau Jr./Sr. High Sch., West Sunbury, Pa., 1983-89, libr., 1989—; English instr. Butler County Community Coll., 1988—; advisor Moniteau chpt. Nat. Honor Soc., West Sunbury, 1988—; libr. specialist Mid. States Evaluation Com., Punxsutawney, Pa., 1987. Editor (newsletter) The Good News, 1987-93. With pub. rels. LWV, Butler, 1989—; personnel mgr. Butler County Symphony, 1994—. Grantee NEH, Ind. U. of Pa., 1986. Mem. NEA, AAUW (Butler chpt. pres. 1990-92, v.p. 1988-90, treas. 1992—), Moniteau Edn. Assn. (negotiation team mem. 1989), Pa. State Edn. Assn. Republican. Methodist. Home: 104 Wild Wood Dr Butler PA 16001-3906 Office: Moniteau Jr/Sr High Sch 1810 W Sunbury Rd West Sunbury PA 16061-9609

DONALDSON, MARCIA CHANDLER, marketing communications consultant; b. Cooperstown, N.Y., May 12, 1944; d. Kenneth Miller and Alice Eleanor (Johnson) D. BA, Hartwick Coll., 1967. Advt. & sales Mutual Benefit Life Ins., Newark, N.J., 1967-72; mktg. comm. Digital Equipment COrp., Merrimack, N.H., 1972-87; founder, pres. The Write Source, Inc., Hollis, N.H., 1988—; mem. bd. dirs. Home Health & Hospice, Nashua, N.H., 1992—, Gr. Nashua Coun. on Alcoholism, 1987—. Recipient Bronze award Boston Art Dirs. Club, 1990. Republican. Office: The Write Source Inc POB 733 Hollis NH 03049

DONALDSON, RUTH LOUISE, construction executive; b. Maryville, Mo., Nov. 16, 1909; d. Charles Adolph and Elva Bessie (McClurg) Jensen; m. John Clayton Donaldson, Jan. 3, 1931; children: Jacqueline, Elvalee, Patricia. BS in Edn., N.W. Mo. State U., 1930, AB, 1935. Prin. Hazen (Ark.) Jr. High Sch., 1930-31; engr., draftsman Sunflower Ordnance Plant, Eudora, Kans., 1941-43; elec. engr. Kaiser Shipyard, El Cerrito, Calif., 1943-45; tchr. Warwick High Sch., Providence, 1945-46; gen. contractor design and constrn. pub. utilities Donaldson Engrng. and Constrn. Co., Maryville, Mo., 1946—; county engr. Gentry County, Albany, Mo., 1950-52, asst. county engr., 1952-70. Bd. dirs. St. Francis Hosp., Maryville, 1974-88. Mem. AAUW. Democrat. Presbyterian. Home and Office: RR 1 Maryville MO 64468-9801

DONALDSON, VIRGINIA LEE, librarian; b. Leavenworth, Kans., Feb. 24, 1950; d. Leo Otto and Lorene Marie (Koebrich) Schrick; m. Wayne Lee Donaldson, Sept. 1, 1979; children: Rebecca Lee, Matthew Lee; stepchildren: Michael Lee, Jennifer Elizabeth. BA, Morningside Coll., 1972; MA in Librarianship, U. Denver, 1977. Cert. tchr., Kans. Clk. Western Hills Area Ednl. Agy., Sioux City, Iowa, 1972; librarian Washington Elem. Sch., Atchison, Kans., 1972-82; instr. Benedictine Coll., Atchison, Kans., 1973-74; librarian Atchison High Sch., 1982—. Leader Girl Scouts U.S.A., Atchison, 1986-90; Kans. Scholars' Bowl coach, 1989—. Mem. NEA, Kans. Assn. Sch. Librarians, Am. Assn. Univ. Women, Beta Phi Mu. Democrat. Roman Catholic. Home: 712 Fletcher Ave Atchison KS 66002-3144 Office: Atchison High Sch 1500 Riley St Atchison KS 66002-1599

DONATH, THERESE, artist, author; b. Hammond, Ind.; m. Jefferson Richardson Scoville, 1986; student Monticello Coll., 1946-47; BFA, St. Joseph's Coll., 1975; additional study Oxbow Summer Sch. Painting, Immaculate Heart Coll., Hollywood, Calif., Penland, N.C., Haystack, Maine; radio/TV personality, 1978-92. Interviewer, producer Viewpoint, Sta. WLNR-FM, Lansing, Ill., 1963-64; reporter, columnist N.W. Ind. Sentinel, 1965; freelance writer Monterey Peninsula Herald, 1981-85; contbg. author Monterey Life mag. 1981-85; asst. dir. Michael Karolyi Meml. Found., Vence, France, 1979; one-woman shows include: Ill. Inst. Tech., Chgo., 1971; group shows include: Palos Verdes (Calif.) Mus., 1974, L.A. Inst. Contemporary Art, 1978, Mus. Contemporary Art, Chgo., 1975, Calif. State U., Fullerton, 1973, No. Ill. U., DeKalb, 1971, Bellevue (Wash.) Mus. Art, 1986-87; represented in permanent collections including Kennedy Gallery, N.Y.C., also pvt. collections; creative cons. Aslan Tours and Travel, 1983-85; instr., lectr. Penland, N.C., 1970, Haystack Mountain Sch., Deer Isle, Maine, 1974, Sheffield Poly., Eng., 1978. Bd. dirs., sec. Mental Health Soc. Greater Chgo., 1963-64; exec. dir. Lansing (Ill.) Mental Health Soc., 1963-64. Recipient awards No. Ind. Art Mus., 1966, 70, 71, 73; grantee Ragdale Found., Lake Forest, Ill., 1982. Represented in The Mirror Book, 1978; author: Screams and Laughter, 1992; author, illustrator: Before I Die, A Creative Legacy, 1989; contbr. articles to profl. jours., newspapers; illustrator: Run Computer Run, 1983.

DONCASTER, HILARY LOUISE, nurse; b. Fitchburg, Mass., Dec. 9, 1960; d. Donald Dempsey and Janet Maryann (McKay) D. BS in Nursing, Fitchburg State Coll., 1982; postgrad computer programming, Cen. N.E. Coll., 1988-89; postgrad. in Mgmt. Info. Systems, Nichols Coll., 1990—. RN, Mass. Staff nurse neurosurgery USAF Med. Ctr., Lackland AFB, Tex., 1983-86; ambulatory surg. specialist Katy (Tex.) Community Hosp., 1986; community nurse Worcester (Mass.) VNA, 1986; nurse reviewer Mass. Peer Rev. Orgn., Waltham, 1986-89; utilization rev. coord., assoc. fin. analyst/DI Fin. Report Paul Revere Ins. Co., Worcester, Mass., 1989—. Capt. USAF, 1983-86. Decorate Air Force Commendation medal. Mem. NAFE, Air Force Assn., Health Ins. Assocs., Loma Level I, Fitchburg State Coll. Alumni Assn. Democrat. Roman Catholic. Home: 15 Duncannon Ave Apt 4 Worcester MA 01604-5107

DONEGAN, PATRICIA MORRIS, librarian; b. Balt., May 17, 1953; d. Richard James and Lois Ray (Parnell) Morris; m. Craig Donegan, Apr. 28, 1979; children: Sherman, Richard. BA, U. Md., 1975, MLS, 1978; MS in Health Professions, S.W. Tex. State U., 1986. Ref. asst. U. Md., College Park, 1977-79; ref. libr. Mt. Vernon Coll., Washington, 1979-80, The Am. Univ., Washington, 1980-81; pub. svcs. libr. San Antonio Coll., 1981—. Mem. ALA, AAUP, Assn. Coll. Rsch. Librs., Tex. Libr. Assn., Tex. Jr. Coll. Tchrs. Assn. Democrat. Episcopalian. Home: 133 E Elmview Pl San Antonio TX 78209-3805 Office: San Antonio Coll 1300 San Pedro Ave San Antonio TX 78212-4299

DONELSON, ANGIE FIELDS CANTRELL MERRITT, real estate executive; b. Hermitage, Tenn., Dec. 2, 1914; d. Dempsey Weaver and Nora (Johnson) Cantrell; student public and pvt. schs., Hermitage, Nashville; m. Gilbert Stroud Merritt, Dec. 15, 1934 (dec.); 1 son, Gilbert Stroud; m. 2d, John Donelson, Jr., VII, Apr. 23, 1966 (dec.); step-children: John, Agnes Donelson Williams (dec.), William Stockley. Pres., So. Woodenware Co., Nashville, 1955-61, So. Properties, Co., Hermitage, 1961—. Chmn. comml. flower exhibits Tenn. State Fair, 1951; committeewoman and v.p. Davidson County Agrl. Soil and Conservation Community Com., 1959-60; bd. mem. Nashville Symphony Assn., 1961-64, regional council mem., 1977-79; chmn. bd. Nashville Presbyn. Neighborhood Settlement House; elder Presbyn. Ch., 1989-92; founding bd. mem. Davidson County Cancer Soc.; bd. mem. Nashville Vis. Nurse Service; dist. chmn., speakers bur. Am. Red Cross. Proclaimed First Lady Donelson-Hermitage Community, 1986. Mem. Vanderbilt U. Aid, Peabody Coll. Aid, Tenn. Hist. Soc., Descs. of Ft. Nashboro Pioneers (bd. dirs. 1984-87), English Speaking Union. Clubs: Ladies Hermitage Assn. (dir. 1949-89), DAR, (chpt. regent 1941), Tenn. Pres.' Trust, Lebanon Rd. Garden Club (pres. 1947), Horticulture Soc. Davidson County (v.p. 1949). Clubs: Ravenwood Country, Centennial, Belle Meade. Contbr. to books and mags. on history of Tenn. Home and Office: Stone Hall 1014 Stones River Rd Hermitage TN 37076-2030

DONEY, JUDITH KAREN, minister, consultant, educator; b. Winston-Salem, N.C., Aug. 24, 1942; d. Parks Harvey and Dorothy (Hanna) Vanderlip; m. Malcolm Edwards Doney, Sept. 30, 1981 (div. Apr. 1992). Student, U. N.C., 1965-66, Vennard Coll., 1970-71, U. So. Miss., 1976, Phillips Coll., 1981-82. Audit clk. Consol. Credit Corp., Charlotte, N.C., 1963-64; operating rm. technician Mercy Hosp., Charlotte, 1965-66; operating and emergency rms. technician St. Dominics Hosp., Jackson, Miss., 1975-76; acute care technician U. Miss. Med. Ctr., Jackson, 1981; co-founder, sec.-treas., bd. dirs. New Beginnings Ministries, Inc., Jackson, 1983—; asst. to comptr. and computer sys. mgr. Dust Free, Inc., Royse City, Tex., 1989—. Author: Biomedical Techniques for Post Head Trauma Victims, 1985. Campaign mgr. U.S. Senatorial candidate Mahaska County, Iowa; mem. disaster team, instr. ARC, Jackson, 1980-81. Mem. Christian Coalition. Republican. Address: PO Box 776 Dallas TX 75221-0776

DONICHT, CANDIS RENEE, school superintendent; b. San Francisco, Apr. 1, 1950; d. John C. Duarte and Gloria F. (Dakin) Jones; m. Terrell L. Donicht, Mar. 26, 1986; 1 child, Brian J. Welch. BA in Elem. Edn., Idaho State U., 1980, MA in Ednl. Adminstrn., 1984, EdS in Ednl. Adminstrn., 1988; EdD, U. Idaho, 1990. Cert. tchr., prin., supt. Tchr. Challis (Idaho) Schs., 1980-85, Boise (Idaho) Schs., 1985-86; prin. Snake River Schs., Blackfoot, Idaho, 1986-89, asst. supt., 1989-91; supt. Salmon (Idaho) Schs., 1991—; ednl. cons., 1992—. Mem. ASCD, Idaho Assn. of Sch. Adminstrn.,

Idaho Sch. Supt.'s Assn., Rotary Internat. (sgt. 1992-93), C. of C. (bd. dirs. 1993-96).

DONIGER, WENDY, history of religions educator; b. N.Y.C., Nov. 20, 1940; d. Lester L. and Rita (Roth) Doniger; m. Dennis M. O'Flaherty, Mar. 31, 1964; 1 child, Michael Lester O'Flaherty. BA summa cum laude, Radcliffe Coll., 1962; PhD, Harvard U., 1968. Lectr. Sch. Oriental and African Studies U. London, 1968-75; vis. lectr. U. Calif., Berkeley, 1975-77; prof. history of religions Div. Sch., dept. South Asian langs., com. on social thought U. Chgo., 1978-85, Mircea Eliade prof., 1986—. Author: (under name of Wendy Doniger O'Flaherty) Asceticism and Eroticism in the Mythology of Siva, 1973, Hindu Myths, 1975, The Origins of Evil in Hindu Mythology, 1976, Women, Androgynes and Other Mythical Beasts, 1980, The Rig Veda: An Anthology, 1981, Karma and Rebirth in Classical Indian Traditions, 1980, Dreams, Illusion and Other Realities, 1984, Other Peoples' Myths, 1988, (under name of Wendy Doniger), The Laws of Manu, 1991, Mythologies, 1991, Purana Perennis, 1993; editor Jour. Am. Acad. Religion, 1977-80, History of Religions, 1979—; mem. bd. editors Ency. Britannica, 1987—, Daedalus, 1990—. Recipient Lucy Allen Paton prize, 1961, Phi Beta Kappa prize, 1962; Jonathan Fay Fund scholar, 1962, Am. Inst. Indian Studies fellow, 1963-64, NEH summer stipend, 1980, Guggenheim fellow, 1980-81. Fellow Soc. for the Arts, Religion and Culture, Am. Acad. Arts and Scis.; mem. Am. Acad. Religion (pres. 1984), Am. Soc. for Study Religion, Am. Oriental Soc., Assn. Asian Studies, Phi Beta Kappa. Home: 1319 E 55th St Chicago IL 60615-5301 Office: U Chgo Div Sch 1025 E 58th St Chicago IL 60637-1509

DONISTHORPE, CHRISTINE ANN, state senator; b. Christina, Mont., May 31, 1932; d. Lambert A. and Ludmilla (Hruska) Benes; m. Oscar Lloyd Donisthorpe, 1951; children—Paul, Karen, Bruce, Brian. Student U. Mont., 1951-53, San Juan Coll., N.Mex. Real Estate Sch., 1958-70. Pres. Bd. of Edn., Bloomfield, N.Mex., 1975-81; mem. N.Mex. State Senate, 1979—, mem. edn. com., 1979, fin. com., 1980, edn. study com., 1981; mem. Bd. Realtors San Juan County, 1978-81. Adv. bd. Salvation Army, 1970-75; active C. of C. Recipient U.S. Soil and Water Conservation award, 1967; Hon. State Future Farmers Adv. award, 1975. Mem. N.Mex. Hay Growers Assn. Republican. Methodist. Office: NM Senate House State Capitol New Mexico State Capitol NM 87503*

DONLEY, ROSEMARY, university official. Diploma in Nursing, Pitts. Hosp., 1961; BSN summa cum laude, St. Louis U., 1963; M in Nursing Edn., U. Pitts., 1965; postgrad. tng. in psychiatry, U. Pitts., Columbia U., 1967-69; PhD, U. Pitts., 1972; postgrad., Harvard U., 1986; LittD (hon.), Felician Coll., 1981, Villanova U., 1985; LLD (hon.), Loyola U., Chgo., 1988; HHD (hon.), Madonna Coll., 1988; Dr. Pub. Svc. (hon.), R.I. Coll., 1988, La Roche Coll., 1989. Staff nurse St. Mary's Hosp., St. Louis, 1961-63; instr. Pitts. Hosp. Sch. Nursing, 1963-71; cons. Vis. Nurses Assn. Allegheny County, Pitts., 1972; from instr. to assoc. prof. Sch. Nursing U. Pitts., 1971-79; dean and assoc. prof. Sch. Nursing Cath. U. Am., Washington, 1979-86, exec. v.p., 1986—; bd. dirs. Ea. Mercy Health Care System, Forbes Health Care System, Nursing Econs. Found.; cons. in field; advisor internat. programs, lectr. various colls. and univs. Contbr. articles to profl. jours.; mem. editorial bd. Ednl. Record, 1985—, Jour. Contemporary Health Law and Policy, 1985—. Bd. dirs. Seton Hill Coll., 1991. Recipient Hon. Recognition award Pa. League for Nursing, 1978, Alumni Merit award St. Louis U., 1980, Woman of Yr. award Pres.'s Commn. on Women, Cath. U. Am., 1984, McGrady award, Cath. Youth Assn. of Pitts. Inc., 1987, Medal of Distinction. U. Pitts., 1987; fellow Robert Wood Johnson Found. and Inst. Medicine, Nat. Acad. Sci., 1977-78. Fellow Am. Acad. Nursing; mem. Inst. Medicine, Nat. League for Nursing (pres. 1987-89), Sigma Theta Tau (sr. editor Image Jour. Nursing, nat. 1st v.p. 1971-74, nat. pres. 1975-81). Home: 7004 Riggs Rd Hyattsville MD 20783-2933 Office: Cath U Am Office of Exec VP Washington DC 20064

DONN, EVVA MEYER, principal, educator; b. Mpls., Feb. 24, 1941; d. Norman Bourghard and Adris Esther (Crawford) Meyer; m. Alan Henry Donn, Sept. 6, 1966 (div. 1990); children: Brynna Yvette, Andrew Alan. BA, Principia Coll., 1963; MAT, Conn. Coll., 1973. Tchr. Fitch Jr. High Sch., Groton, Conn., 1979-82; state sch. tchr. Niantic (Conn.) Correctional Inst., 1987-91; prin. N.E. Coorectional/Bklyn. Correctional, Storrs, Conn., 1991-93, Gates Correctional Inst./Radgowski Correctional, Niantic, Conn., 1993-94, York Correctional Inst., 1995—; adj. instr. Mohegan C.C., Norwich, Conn., 1984—. Lt. USN, 1963-68, London. Mem. ASCD, Conn. Edn. Assn., Correctional Edn. Assn., Mystic Art Assn., Phi Delta Kappa. Office: Gates Correctional Inst 131 N Bridebrook Rd Niantic CT 06357-1026

DONNELLY, ANN, clinical psychologist; b. Barcelona, Spain, Jan. 29, 1955; d. Julio Ramon and Alicia Ana Tello; m. J. Donnelly, Feb. 7, 1987 (div. 1990). BA in Psychology, U. Barcelona, Spain, 1977, MA in Clin. Psychology, 1980; MA in Social Psychology, UCLA, 1984, PhD in Personality Psychology, 1987. Lic. psychologist, Calif., 1989, clin. psychologist, Guam, 1992. Mental health psychologist Dept. Mental Health, L.A., 1987-89; clin. psychologist Chief Adminstrv. Office, L.A., 1989-90, Camarillo (Calif.) State Hosp., 1990-91, Guam Dept. Mental Health, 1992-93, Guam Dept. Corrections, 1993—; pvt. practice clin. psychology, 1993—; established treatment program for sexual offenders Dept. Corrections, Guam, 1993. Fulbright fellow, 1981-83. Mem. APA, Guam Psychol. Assn., Guam Assn. Ind. Marriage and Family Therapists, Guam Assn. Clin. Psychologists (treas. 1994), UCLA Alumni Assn., Rotary Club of Guam (fellow). Office: Guam Dept Corrections PO Box 3236 Agana GU 96910

DONNELLY, BARBARA SCHETTLER, medical technologist; b. Sweetwater, Tenn., Dec. 2, 1933; d. Clarence G. and Irene Elizabeth (Brown) Schettler; A.A., Tenn. Wesleyan Coll., 1952; B.S., U. Tenn., 1954; cert. med. tech., Erlanger Hosp. Sch. Med. Tech., 1954; postgrad. So. Meth. U., 1980-81; children—Linda Ann, Richard Michael. Med. technologist Erlanger Hosp., Chattanooga, 1953-57, St. Luke's Episcopal Hosp., Tex. Med. Ctr., Houston, 1957-58, 1962; engring. R &D SCI Systems Inc., Huntsville, Ala., 1974-76; cons. hematology systems Abbott Labs., Dallas, 1976-77, hematology specialist, Dallas, Irving, Tex., 1977-81, tech. specialist microbiology systems, Irving, 1981-83, coord. tech. svc. clin. chemistry systems, 1983-84, coord. customer tng. clin. chemistry systems, 1984-87, supr. clin. chemistry tech. svcs., 1987-88, supr. clin. chemistry customer support ctr., 1988-93, supr. clin. chemistry and x-systems customer support ctr., 1993—. Mem. Am. Soc. Clin. Pathologists (cert. med. technologist), Am. Soc. Microbiology, Nat. Assn. Female Execs., U. Tenn. Alumni Assn., Chi Omega. Contbr. articles on cytology to profl. jours. Republican. Methodist. Home: 204 Greenbriar Ln Bedford TX 76021-2006 Office: 1921 Hurd Dr Irving TX 75038-4313

DONNELLY, LYNNE CAROL, writer; b. Cin., Oct. 18, 1955; d. Francis Moreland and Marion Elizabeth (Yunkes) D.; m. Ronald John Donovan, Feb. 14, 1981; children: Marina Rose Donnelly Donovan, Keaton John Donnelly Donovan. BA in Linguistics summa cum laude, U. Cin., 1977. Editor Alaska Pub. Broadcasting, Anchorage, 1981-82; adj. faculty mem. Alaska Pacific U., Anchorage, 1982-85; columnist Anchorage Daily News, 1985-87; columnist, corr. Portsmouth (N.H.) Press, 1987-90; free-lance writer, editor Anchorage, Rollinsford, N.H. and Durham, N.H., 1982—. Editor Learning in Prime Time TV Guide mag., 1981-82; author over 170 articles on family, health, life styles. Bd. dirs. Tudor Community Sch., Anchorage, 1984-85. Mem. Phi Beta Kappa. Home and Office: 10 Carriage Way Durham NH 03824-4500

DONNELLY, SHEILA RENEE, educational administrator; b. Valentine, Nebr., Mar. 2, 1962; d. Louie E. and Valda Joyce (Norberg) DeSmet; m. Anthony James Donnelly, June 15, 1984; children: Jake, Jason, Jared. BS in Acctg., Mankato (Minn.) State Coll., 1984. Acct. Williams & Co., CPA's, Sioux City, Iowa, 1984-86; bus. mgr. Elk Point (S.D.) Sch. Dist. 61-3, 1986-90, Vermillion (S.D.) Sch. Dist. 13-1, 1990—; guest instr. grad. mgmt. class U. S.D., 1990—. Mem. S.D. Assn. Sch. Bus. Ofcls. (bd. dirs. 1992—), Sch. Adminstrs. of S.D. (chmn. audit and mgmt. com. 1992-93), Area II Bus. Ofcls. (sec. 1988-89, pres. 1989-90), Quota Club for Hearing Impaired. Office: Vermillion Sch Dist 13-1 17 Prospect St Vermillion SD 57069-2107

DONNELLY, TRUDY A., nurse anesthetist; b. Topeka, Kans., July 19, 1953; d. Edward Patrick and Helen Ann (Cavanaugh) D.; 1 child; Alexander Patrick. BSN, Washburn U., 1977; MSN, La. State U., 1982; cert., Xavier U., 1984. RN, Kans., Mo., Tex., La.; cert. RN anesthetist. RN Touro Infirmary, New Orleans, 1977-80, So. Bapt. Hosp., New Orleans, 1980-84; cert. RN anesthetist Lakeside Hosp., Morgan City, La., 1984-85, Metairie (La.) Anesthesia Assn., 1985-86, Anesthesiology Chartered, Kansas City, Kans., 1986-90, Physicians Associated, Overland Park, Kans., 1990—. Mem. Am. Assn. Nurse Anesthetists, Kans. Assn. Nurse Anesthetists, Jr. League Kansas City Mo. Roman Catholic. Home: 8067 Hall St Lenexa KS 66219-1872 Office: 10550 Quirira Rd Overland Park KS 66215

D'ONOFRIO, MARY ANN, medical transcription company executive; b. Detroit, Jan. 24, 1933; d. Charles Henry and Cecilia Rose (Levan) Clifford; m. Dominic Armando D'Onofrio, Apr. 19, 1958; children: Margaret Clement, Anthony, Elizabeth, Maria Spurgeon. BA, Marygrove Coll., 1954; MLS, U. Mich., 1955. Cert. med. transcriptionist. Reader's advisor Detroit Pub. Libr., 1955-58; cataloger Willow Run (Mich.) Pub. Libr., 1959-61, St. Thomas Grade and High Sch., Ann Arbor, Mich., 1968-72; med. record analyst Chelsea (Mich.) Community Hosp., 1972-79; pres. Meditranscript Svc., Ann Arbor, 1979-81; asst. office mgr. Dr. Maxfield, D.O., Tucson, 1981-82; quality assurance analyst, utilization rev. Tucson (Ariz.) Gen. Hosp., 1983-86; exec. asst. Dr. McEldoon M.D., Tucson, 1986-88; pres. Meditranscript Svc., Tucson, 1986-88; co-owner Med-Comm Assocs., Tucson, 1989—; co-owner, assoc. designer EMA of Tucson custom apparel and jewelry design co. Co-author: Psychiatric Words & Phrases, 1990; contbr. articles to profl. jours; co-developer Cross-Search. Block leader Infantile Paralysis Assn., Ann Arbor, 1975-80, Easter Seal Assn., Tucson, 1983-86, Am. Heart Assn., 1994; capt. Tucson chpt. Am. Cancer Soc., 1992. Mem. NAFE, Am. Assn. for Med. Transcription (parliamentarian Sonora Desert chpt. 1984-86, 90-93, 95—, compiler/editor AAMT Annotated Bibliography, 1981, named disting. mem. 1984, treas. Sonora Desert chpt. 1987, jour. communist 1982-86), Ednl. Honor Soc., Pi Lambda Theta (life).

DONOGHUE, MILDRED RANSDORF, education educator; b. Cleve.; d. James and Caroline (Sychra) Ransdorf; m. Charles K. Donoghue (dec. 1982); children: Kathleen, James. Ed.D., UCLA, 1962; J.D., Western State U., 1979. Asst. prof. edn. Calif. State U.-Fullerton, 1962-66, assoc. prof., 1966-71; prof. Calif. State U., Fullerton, 1971—. Author: Foreign Languages and the Schools, 1967, Foreign Languages and the Elementary School Child, 1968, The Child and the English Language Arts, 1971, 75, 79, 85, 90; co-author: Second Languages in Primary Education, 1979; contbr. articles to profl. jours. and Ednl. Resources Info. Ctr. U.S. Dept. Edn. Mem. AAUP, AAUW, Nat. Coun. Tchrs. English, Am. Dialect Soc., Am. Ednl. Rsch. Assn., Nat. Soc. for Study of Edn., Am. Assn. Tchrs. Spanish and Portuguese, Tchrs. of English to Speakers of Other Langs., Advocates for Lang. Learning, S.W. Conf. on Lang. Teaching, Internat. Reading Assn., Nat. Assn. Edn. Young Children, Orange County Med. Assn. Women's Aux., Authors Guild, Assn. for Childhood Edn. Internat., Phi Beta Kappa, Phi Kappa Phi, Pi Lambda Theta, Alpha Upsilon Alpha. Office: Calif State U Dept Elem Edn Fullerton CA 92634

DONOHOE, THERESA MARIE, nurse; b. Columbus, Ohio, July 19, 1959; d. John Charles and Lela Margret (Euman) Golden; m. Michael Dominic Donohoe, Mar. 19, 1983; children: Michael, Kaitlyn, Patrick. ADN, Columbus State C.C., 1980; BSN, Franklin U., Columbus, 1991. RN, Ohio; cert. med.-surg. nurse ANCC. Nurse Northland Terrace, Columbus, 1978-82; nurse Doctors Hosp., Columbus, 1982—, clinician IV, 1992—. Contbr. to nursing newsletter. Active community cleanup, Columbus, 1982—; sch. bd. rep. Holy Name Sch., Columbus, 1991-93. Recipient Founders award Doctors Hosp., 1990. Mem. Acad. Med.-Surg. Nurses. Roman Catholic. Office: Doctors Hosp 1087 Dennison Ave Columbus OH 43201-3496

DONOHUE, EDITH M., career development specialist, consultant; b. Balt., Nov. 10, 1938; d. Edward Anthony and Beatrice (Jones) McParland; m. Salvatore R. Donohue, Aug. 23, 1960; children: Kathleen, Deborah. BA, Coll. Notre Dame, Balt., 1960; MS, Johns Hopkins U., 1981, CASE, 1985, PhD in Human Resources, 1990. Dir. pub. relations Coll. Notre Dame, Balt., 1970-71, asst. dir. continuing edn., 1978-81, dir. continuing edn., 1981-86; coord. program bus. and industry Catonsville C.C., Baltimore County, Md., 1986-88; mgr. tng. and devel. Sheppard Pratt Hosp., Balt., 1988-90; assoc. prof. Barry U., advisor grad. program, 1993—; adj. faculty Loyola Coll. Grad. Studies Program, Barry U., Fla. Inst. Tech., Indian River C.C. Co-author: Communicate Like a Manager, 1989; co-editor, contbg. author career devel. workshop manual, 1985; contbr. articles to profl. jours. Pres. Cathedral Sch. Parents Assn., 1972-74; asst. treas., treas. Md. Gen. Hosp. Aux., 1975-78; dir. Homeland Assn., 1978-81; regional rep., leader Girl Scouts Cen. Md., 1975-76; dir. sect. Exec. Women's Network, Balt., 1983-85; adv. bd. Mayor's Com. on Aging, 1981-86; dir. Md. Assn. Higher Edn., 1985-88; vol. trainer United Way Martin County, co-chair campaign, 1994—; mem. steering com. Chautaugua South. Recipient Mayor's Citation, City of Balt. Council, 1985. Mem. Am. Assn. Tng. and Devel (bd. dirs.), Am. Counseling Assn., AAUW (dir., v.p. 1980-83), Soc. Human Resources Mgmt., Martin County Personnel Mgt. Assn. (edn. chmn. 1991—), Martin County C. of C. (edn. com. 1991—), Friends of Lyric (bd. dirs., chmn., strategic planning), Chi Sigma Iota (pres.), Phi Delta Kappa. Republican. Roman Catholic. Avocations: tennis, performing arts, reading, wellness. Home: Ste 3103 144 NE Edgewater Dr Stuart FL 34996 Office: Barry U 590 NW Peacock Blvd #5 Port Saint Lucie FL 34986

DONOHUE, PATRICIA CAROL, university dean; b. St. Louis, Jan. 11, 1946; d. Carroll and Juanita D.; m. James H. Stevens, Jr., Aug. 27, 1966 (div. Mar. 1984); children: James H. III, Carol Janet. AB, Duke U., 1966; MA, U. Mo., 1974, PhD, 1982. Tchr. math, secondary schs. Balt., St. Louis and Shawnee Mission, Kans., 1966-71; lectr. U. Mo., Kansas City, 1975-76, rsch. asst. affirmative action, 1976-79, coord. affirmative action, 1979-82, instl. rsch. assoc., 1982-84, acting dir. affirmative action and acad. pers., 1984; dir. instl. rsch. Lakeland C.C., 1984-86; asst. dean acad. affairs, math., engring. and tech. Harrisburg Area C.C., 1986-89, dean sch. bus., engring., and tech., 1989—; dean Lebanon campus Pa. Coun. on Vocat. Edn., 1989-93, v.p. cmty. devel. and external affairs, 1993; vice chancellor edn. St. Louis C.C., 1993—; chair Pa. Occupational Deans, 1988-93. Bd. dirs., v.p. Am. Cancer Soc. Jackson County, 1975-84; mem. adv. coun. Ben Franklin Partnership, 1988-93; leader Hemlock coun. Girl Scouts U.S.A., bd, dirs. 1986-93; bd. dirs. PTA, 1975-77, Cmty. Lebanon Assocs.; mem. steering com. New Baldwin Corridor Coalition, 1991-93, chair edn. task force, 1992-93. Recipient Outstanding Service and Achievement award U. Mo. Kansas City, 1976; Jack C. Coffey grantee, 1978; named Outstanding Woman AAUW, 1989, one of Outstanding Leaders Nat. Inst. Leadership Devel., 1986, Exec. Leadership Inst., 1990. Mem. ASCD, Nat. Coun. Tchrs. Math., Mat. Assn. Am., Am. Vocat. Assn., Nat. Coun. on Occupational Edn. (chair diversity task force, 1991, chair job tng. 2000 task force, 1992, bd. dirs. 1992—), v.p. programs 1992-93, v.p. membership 1993-94, pres.-elect. 1994—), Am. Assn. Women in Community and Jr. Colls. (Pa. state coord. 1988, dir. region 3 1989-91)), Soc. Mfg. Engrs. (chmn.-elect 1988, chmn. 1989-90), Women's Equity Project, Nat. Assn. Student Pers. Adminstrs., Women's Network, Assn. Inst. Research, Phi Delta Kappa, (pres. 1975, Read fellow 1989), Phi Kappa Phi, Pi Lambda Theta, Delta Gamma (past v.p., del. nat. conv. 1988, pres., 1989-91), Cream Rose Outstanding Service award 1970). Home: 6235 Washington Ave Saint Louis MO 63130-4847 Office: St Louis C C 300 S Broadway Saint Louis MO 63102

DONOHUE, THERESE BRADY, artistic director, choreographer, designer; b. Washington, Jan. 13, 1937; d. John Bernard and Mary Catherine (Rupert) B.; m. Joseph W. Donohue Jr., June 13, 1959 (div. 1987); children: Sharon Marie, Maura Cathleen (dec.), Sheila Patricia. BA, Coll. of Notre Dame Md., 1958. Cert. tchr. ballet Royal Acad. Dance London. Advt. artist Kronstadt Advt. Agy., Washington, 1958; instr. art The Maret Sch., Washington, 1958-60, Princeton (N.J.) U., 1967-71; artist dir. Amherst (Mass.) Ballet Theatre Co., 1977—; founder, dir. Amherst Ballet Centre, 1971—; co-dir., founder Pioneer Valley Ballet, Northampton, Mass., 1972-77; dancer, tchr. Princeton Ballet, 1962-71; animal masks Charleston (S.C.) Ballet, 1985—; choreographer Roanoke (Va.) Ballet Theatre, 1983; chairperson N.E. Region Craft Choreography Conf., Amherst, 1979; artist/choreographer Nat. Gallery Art, 1986, 88, Guggenheim, 1986, Nat. Mus. Am. Art, 1989, Hirshhorn Mus. & Sculpture Garden, 1993. Choreographer (ballets for children) Peter & the Wolf, 1973, One Thousand Cranes, 1974, Punch & Judy, 1975, Amherst Poets, 1977, Uncle Wiggily & the Duck Pond, 1979, (Springfield Symphony) History of Dance, 1983, (Project Opera) Hansel & Gretel, 1983, Sea Study (included in Aberdeen Internat. Youth Festival in Scotland), 1994. Mem. Amherst Arts Coun., 1983-89. Mem. Amherst Club. Home: 17 Juniper Ln Amherst MA 01002-1227 Office: Amherst Ballet Centre 29 Strong St Amherst MA 01002-1890

DONOR, MARY ELIZABETH, library director; b. Bklyn., May 21, 1938; d. Wayne Matthew and Elizabeth Marie (Brunner) Ikola; m. Albert Edward Donor, Dec. 4, 1936; children: Albert, Brian, Alyson. AA, Nassau Community Coll., 1970; BA, L.I. U., 1972; MS in Libr. Sci., Palmer Sch. Libr. & Info. Sci., 1973; MBA, Dowling Coll., 1991. Cert. pub. librarian, N.Y. Young adult svcs. librarian Jericho Pub. Libr., Jericho, N.Y., 1973-80; sch. librarian West Hempstead Sr. High Sch., West Hempstead, N.Y., 1980-84; librarian Hempstead Pub. Libr., Hempstead, N.Y., 1985; libr. dir. Floral Park Pub. Libr., Floral Park, N.Y., 1985-87, Jericho Pub. Libr., 1988—. Mem. ALA (product and svcs. mktg. com.), Nassau County Libr. Assn. (sec. 1978-80, bd. dirs. 1983-84, 87-88, chair legis. com., pres. 1992), N.Y. Libr. Assn., L.I. Coalition Against Censorship, L.I. Libr. Resources Coun. (legis. com., chair 1994), Pub. Libr. Dirs. Assn. of N.Y. State (v.p., pres.-elect 1992), Nassau County Libr. Dirs. (exec. bd.), Automated Libr. Info. Svcs. Corp. (exec. bd. 1994), Zonta Club L.I. Office: Jericho Pub Library 1 Merry Ln Jericho NY 11753-1792

DONOVAN, CAROL ANN, state legislator; b. Lynn, Mass., June 5, 1937; d. John Barrows and Virginia Mary (Pearce) D. AB, Regis Coll., Weston, Mass., 1959, MA, 1980. Tchr. home econs. Woburn (Mass.) Sch. System, 1959-74, spl. edn. tchr., 1974-84, spl. edn. liaison, 1984-90; mem. Mass. Ho. of Reps., Boston, 1990—, vice chair Bills in 3d reading, mem. ways and means; polit. cons. Mass. Tchrs. Assn., Boston, 1985-89. Mem. Mass. Caucus of Women Legislators, 1991—; mem. Nat. Women's Polit. Caucus, 1989—; bd. dirs. Winchester (Mass.) Hosp., 1992—; bd. dirs. Ctrl. Middlesex Assn. Retarded Citizens, Woburn, 1984—, also past pres.; sec. Woburn Dem. City Com., 1984—. Recipient Elder Advocacy award Minuteman Home Care, Burlington, Mass., 1993, Disting. Citizen award ARC Mass., Waltham, 1993, Legislator of Yr. award Mass. Disabilities Coun. and ARC, 1994. Mem. Women's Legis. Lobby, Woburn Middlesex Lions Club. Roman Catholic. Office: State House Rm 167 Boston MA 02133

DONOVAN, DEBORAH A., process engineer; b. Newport, R.I., Oct. 30, 1966; d. Lawrence F. and Suzanne M. (Fitzgerald) Sullivan; m. Patrick J. Donovan, May 25, 1991. BSChemE, Northeastern U., 1989; MBA, Calif. State U., 1993. Process engr. Tex. Instruments, Attleboro, Mass., 1989-90; process engr. Ashland Chem., L.A., 1990-94, asst. to mfg. mgr., 1994—. Mem. Phi Delta Gamma (sec. 1994), Phi Kappa Phi, Beta Gamma Sigma. Home: 218 Sanbridge Cir Worthington OH 43085 Office: Ashland Chem 5200 Blazer Meml Pky Los Angeles CA 42017

DONOVAN, DEBORAH CAROLYN, chemical company executive, lawyer, educator, mediator; b. Binghamton, N.Y., Jan. 10, 1951; d. Robert Frances and M. Carolyn (Hamilton) D.; m. Thomas Cushing; children: Rachael, Sierra Belle Donovan Cushing. BA, SUNY, Buffalo; M of Pub. Adminstrn. in Fin. Mgmt., Temple U., 1975; JD, U. Del., 1978. Bar: Del., Tenn. Rep. Phila. Ct. Common Pleas, 1972-74; asst. supt. Newark (Del.) Sch. Dist., 1974; dist. rep. Congressman Pierre S. du Pont, Washington, 1974-77; spl. asst. to Del. Gov. du Pont Dover, 1977; exec. dir. Ingergovtl. Task Force, Wilmington, Del., 1977-79; dep. atty. gen. Office Atty. Gen., Wilmington, 1979; atty., area mgr., dir. state govt. affairs The Du Pont Co., Wilmington and Nashville, 1979-89, mgr. pub. affairs, product publicity, 1989-91; mgr. environ. and external affairs The Du Pont Co., Diablo, Calif., 1991—; prin. No Contest, Inc.; instr. U. Del., Newark, 1979-80; sec.-treas. Fla. Chem. Industry Council, Tallahassee, Tenn. Bus. Roundtable, Nashville; adj. prof. Massey Graduate Sch. Bus. Bd. dirs. Tenn. Assn. Planned Parenthood, Nashville Planned Parenthood; sec. bd. dirs. YMCA of Del., 1979-83. Mem. Tenn. Bar Assn., Nashville Bar Assn., Tenn. chpt. Am. Corp. Counsel Assn., Del. Bar Assn., Del. Assn. Pub. Adminstrn. (pres. 1979-80). Unitarian-Universalist. Home and Office: PO Box 677 1515 Avenida Nueve Diablo CA 94528

DONOVAN, HELEN W., newspaper editor. Exec. editor Boston Globe. Office: Globe Newspapers Co 135 Morrissey Blvd Boston MA 02107*

DONOVAN, LOWAVA DENISE, data processing administrator; b. Galesburg, Ill., Mar. 27, 1958; d. Richard Eugene and Lowava Jeanine (Squire) Corbin; m. James Dean Rutledge, June 17, 1977 (div. May 1981); 1 child, Tiffany Michelle; m. Neal Edwin Donovan, July 9, 1983. Computer operator cert., Carl Sandburg Coll., 1977, student, 1976-86; student, IBM Edn., Chgo., 1979-87. Keypunch operator Fin. Industry Systems, Galesburg, Ill., 1977-79; computer operator Solution Assocs., Peoria, Ill., 1979-80; programmer, data processing mgr. May Co., Galesburg, 1980-81; programmer Kirkendall Gen. Offices, Galesburg, 1981-82; programmer, data processing mgr. Munson Transp., Monmouth, Ill., 1982-85, programmer/analyst, dir. data processing, 1985-87, dir. mgmt. info. systems, 1987-89; ind. contract programmer analyst Oklahoma City, Okla., 1989-92; product line mgr. Innovative Computing Corp., 1992-94; sr. programmer analyst, dir. info. resources Freymiller Trucking, Inc., Oklahoma City, 1994—. Mem. Ch. of God. Home: 11204 NW 113th Yukon OK 73099

DONOVAN, MARGARET, consultant, investigator; b. Yankton, S.D., Jan. 1, 1950; d. Robert Bauerle and Norma Louise (Miller) D. BA in Psychology, Loretto Heights Coll., Denver, 1973; MS in Counseling and Pers., Drake U., 1986. Cert. substance abuse counselor II, Iowa. Svc. worker II div. youth svcs. State of Colo., Denver, 1976; youth svc. worker Woodbury County Juvenile Ct., Sioux City, Iowa; mental health, substance abuse advocate Woodbury County Ct., Sioux City, 1983-85; dir. chem. dependency treatment ctr. Winnebago Indian Reservation, 1984; residential dir. Intersect. United Advanced Planning Ctr., Des Moines, 1986-87; pvt. practice tng. and devel. Donovan & Assocs., Des Moines, 1987—; instr. devel. edn. Briar Cliff Coll., 1989-90; hospitalization adv. Woodbury County; coord. alcohol and edn. and disabled student svcs. Iowa State U., Ames, 1987-89; chair steering com. Univ. Without Walls, 1971; apptd. by gov. to State Vocat. Adv. Coun., 1993-94; owner mediation counseling and child custody investigation svc. Donovan Cons. and Rehab.-Expert Testimony, 1991—. Asst. editor: T'Akra, 1972-73; poet, author, 1970—. Mem. edn. com. Interfaith Resources, Sioux City, 1982-83. Mem. ACA, NOW. Home and Office: PO Box 12076 Des Moines IA 50312-9402

DONOVAN, MARIE PHILLIPS, television executive; b. Detroit; m. Tom Donovan; children: Kathleen Marie, Kevin Thomas. Student, Wayne U. Profl. actress Actors Equity Assn., N.Y.C., AFTRA, N.Y.C.; bus. mgr. Dirs. Service Inc., N.Y.C., exec. v.p., treas. Mem. NAFE, Young Men's Philanthropic League, Am. Contract Bridge League (life master), Am. Bridge Tchr.'s Assn. (accredited tchr.), Cavendish Club.

DONOVAN, MEG, federal official; b. Rockville Centre, N.Y., Feb. 6, 1951; d. Daniel J. and Arline M. (Brassil) D.; m. Stephen C. Duffy, Sept. 21, 1974; 3 children. Student, Emmanuel Coll., 1968-72. Legis. asst. Mass. State Legislature, Boston, 1972-74; adminstrv. asst. Nat. Conf. Soviet Jewry, Washington, 1975-76; mem. profl. staff Commn. Security and Cooperation in Europe U.S. Congress, 1976-84; staff cons. Ho. Com. Fgn. Affairs, 1985-93; sr. policy advisor Dept. State, Washington, 1993—; mem. Dept. State transition team Clinton-Gore Transition, 1992-93. Office: Dept of State 2201 C St NW Rm 7261 Washington DC 20520*

DOODY, AGNES G., communications educator, management and communication consultant; b. New Haven; d. Daniel M. and Carrie Mae (Goodrich) D.; m. Arthur D. Jeffrey, Dec. 22, 1962 (dec. Sept. 1985); children: Andrew N., Jill; m. Ellis H. Maris, Jr., June 28, 1991. BA, Emerson Coll., 1952; MA, Pa. State U., 1954, PhD, 1961; cert. program on negotiation, Harvard U. Prof. communications U. R.I., Kingston, 1958—; pres. Arthur Assocs.; bd. dirs., co-chairperson PierBank, Narragansett, R.I., 1994. Mem. Soc. Profls. in Dispute Resolution, Internat. Communication Assn., Speech Communication Assn., Ea. Communication Assn. (pres. 1967-68), Rotary (newsletter editor Wakefield 1989-90). Home: One Post Rd Wakefield RI 02879-7503

DOODY, BARBARA PETTETT, computer specialist; b. Cin., Sept. 18, 1938; d. Philip Wayne and Virginia Bird (Handley) P.; 1 child, Daniel Frederick Reasor Jr. Attended Sinclair Coll., Tulane U., 1973-74. Owner, mgr. Honeysuckle Pet Shop, Tipp City, Ohio, 1970-76; office mgr. Doody & Doody, CPAs, New Orleans, 1976-77; computer ops. mgr. Doody & Doody, CPAs, 1979—; office mgr. San Diego Yacht Club, 1977-79; owner Hope Chest Linens, Ltd., 1994—. Mem. DAR, UDC, Jamestown Soc., Magna Charta, So. Dames, Colonial Dames of 17th Century, Nat. Soc. Daus. of 1812, Daus. Am. Colonists, Dames Ct. Honor, Colonial Order of the Crown, Societe Huguenot Nouvelle-Orleans, Huguenot Soc. Manakin, Soc. Knights of the Garter, Americans of Royal Descent, Plantaget Soc. Republican. Lutheran. Home: 36 Cypress Rd Covington LA 70433-4306 Office: 2525 Lakeway III 3838 N Causeway Blvd Metairie LA 70002-1767

DOOLEY, ANN ELIZABETH, freelance writers cooperative executive, editor; b. Mpls., Feb. 19, 1952; d. Merlyn James and Susan Marie (Hinze) Dooley; m. John M. Dodge, May 8, 1983; children: Christopher Dooley Dodge, Kathryn Dooley Dodge. BA in Journalism, U. Wis., 1974. Freelance journalist, 1974-75; photo editor C.W. Communications, Newton, Mass., 1975-77, writer, photographer, 1977-79; editor Computerworld O A, Framingham, Mass., 1979-83; editorial dir. Computerworld Focus, Framingham, 1983-92; pres. freelance writers coop. Dooley & Assocs., West Newbury, Mass., 1992—; speaker, chmn. mem. editorial adv. bd. various computer confs. Mem. Pub. Relations Soc. Am., Women in Communications (sec. 1982-84). Democrat. Home and Office: 1 Olde Parish Way West Newbury MA 01985

DOOLEY, JO ANN CATHERINE, publishing company executive; b. Cin., Nov. 24, 1930; d. Joseph Frank and Margaret Mary (Flynn) D. Ed. U. Cin., 1966. Clk. Castellini Co., Cin., 1949-52; IBM operator Kroger Co., Cin., 1952; asst. acct. Gardner Publs., Inc., Cin., 1953-67, treas., sec., 1967—, dir., 1983—, v.p. fin., 1986—, also trustee employees profit sharing trust, trustee retirement trust. Mem. Am. Soc. Women Accts. (advt. mgr. Woman CPA 1979-81, nat. pres. 1982-83, exec. com., achievement award). Roman Catholic. Office: 6600 Clough Pike Cincinnati OH 45244-4028

DOOLEY, SUE ANN, information systems specialist; b. Brockton, Mass.; d. Joseph Henry and May Isabelle (Card) Jessop; 1 child, Erika. BSBA, Northeastern U., Boston, 1993. Programmer, analyst Arthur D. Little Systems, Burlington, Mass., 1979-80, Wang Labs., Lowell, Mass., 1980-82; sr. programmer analyst Wang Labs., 1982-83, prin. programmer, analyst, 1983-84, project mgr., 1984-87, sr. project mgr., 1987-90, info. mgmt. cons., 1990—; sr. project mgr. Home: 139 North End Blvd Salisbury MA 01952 Office: Wang Labs 1 Industrial Ave Lowell MA 01851-5106

DOONE, MICHELE MARIE, chiropractor; b. Oak Park, Ill., Oct. 3, 1942; d. Robert Emmett and Tana Josephine (Alioto) D. Cert., Valley Coll. of Med. and Dental Careers, 1962; student, L.A. Valley Coll., 1960-63, Dallas County Community Coll., 1983-84; D in Chiropractic summa cum laude, Parker Coll. of Chiropractic, 1986. Lic. chiropractic, Calif., Tex.; cert. Nat. Bd. Chiropractic Examiners, impairment rater; diplomate Am. Acad. Pain Mgmt.; bd. eligible chiropractic orthopedist. Med. asst. William Orlando M.D., Edwin Crost, M.D., 1962-65; nursing supr., chief radiologic technologist Vanowen Med. Group, North Hollywood, Calif., 1965-76; radiologic technologist/purchasing agt. Lanier-Brown Clinic, Dallas, 1976-83; faculty mem./ chief radiologic technologist Parker Coll. of Chiropractic, Irving, Tex., 1983-85; exam and X-Ray doctor Margolies Chiropractic Ctr., Richardson, Tex., 1986; clinic staff doctor, assoc. prof. Parker Coll. of Chiropractic, Irving, Tex., 1986-87; doctor/ mgr. contractor Accident Ctrs. of Am., Garland, Tex., 1987; clinic dir. Back Pain Chiropractic, Carrollton, Tex., 1988-91; assoc. in group practice Mullican Chiropractic Ctr., Addison, Tex., 1991—; adviser health-related matters Inner Devel. Inst., Dallas, 1977—; seminar com. Back Pain Chiropractic, Inc., Metairie, La., 1989-91, clinic dir., 1988-91. Mem. Tex. Chiropractic Assn. (radiology com. chmn. 1990-94, practice protocols and parameters com. 1992-94), Metroplex Neurospinal Diagnostic Med. and Surg. Group (med. adv. com. 1989—), Parker Chiropractic Rsch. Found., Parker Coll. Alumni Assn. (bd. dirs. 1988-90, 93-94, Dr. of Yr. 1990), Pi Tau Delta. Home: 4837 Cedar Springs Rd Apt 216 Dallas TX 75219-1280 Office: Mullican Chiropractic Ctr 4021 Beltline Rd Ste 201 Addison TX 75244

DOORY, ANN MARIE, lawyer, legislator; b. Yonkers, N.Y., Aug. 19, 1954; d. Gerard R. and Patricia M. Lowe; m. Robert Leonard Doory Jr., Sept. 29, 1979; children: Brian Robert, Elizabeth Lowe. BA in Polit. Sci., Towson State U., 1976; JD, U. Balt., 1979. Bar: Md. Counsel to majority leader Md. State Senate, 1981; vol., arbitrator Better Bus. Bur., 1984-86; chm. bd. York Woodbourne Action Area and York Rd. Planning Com. Md. Ho. of Dels., 1982—, zoning chairperson Homeland Assn., 1984-86, v.p. Homeland Assn., 1987—. Mem. Dem. State Cen. Com. 43d Legis. Dist., Baltimore City, 1982—, 3d Dist. Cittizens for Good Govt., Baltimore City, issues and legis. com., Mayors Drug Abuse Adv. Council, Baltimore City, 1983-86. Mem. Women's Bar Assn., Md. Bar Assn. Democrat. Roman Catholic. Home: 112 Taplow Rd Baltimore MD 21212-3312 Office: Md Ho of Reps State Capitol Annapolis MD 21401*

DOPSON, ELIZABETH SCHULTZ, health system executive; b. Ancon, Panama, Jan. 8, 1951; d. Robert U. and Virginia (Richard) Schultz. BS, U. Southwestern La., 1975; postgrad., La. State U., 1981-82. Registered record administr. Dir. med. records, quality assurance, utilization rev. E.K. Long Hosp., Baton Rouge, 1975-81; dir. med. records Humana-Ft. Walton, Fla., 1984-86, Bay Med. Ctr., Panama City, Fla., 1986-88, HCA/L.W. Blake Hosp., Bradenton, Fla., 1988-91; cons., health info. mgmt. Ernst and Young, Tampa, Fla., 1991-92; corp. dir. health info. mgmt. Cmty. Health Sys., Seminole, Fla., 1992—; cons. HMO of Baton Rouge, 1978-80; nursing home cons. Greenwell Springs Hosp., 1976-81. With US Womens Army Corp., 1969-71. Mem. Am. Health Info. Mgmt. Assn., Am. Health Info. Clin. Coding Soc., Fla. Med. Record Assn., North Panhandle Fla. Assn. (v.p. 1986). Roman Catholic. Office: Cmty Health Sys 9423 Seminole Blvd Seminole FL 34642

DOPSON, VALERIE ANN, pharmacist; b. Balt., July 7, 1962; d. John Robert and Joan Ann (Almony) D. BS in Chemistry, Salisbury (Md.) U., 1985; BS in Pharmacy, U. Md., Balt., 1990. Chemist IGI Biotech., Columbia, Md., 1985-86; pharmacist Rite Aid Corp., Eldersburg, Md., 1990—. Mem. Md. Pharm. Assn. Republican. Methodist. Home: 6157-D Timdan Ct Eldersburg MD 21784 Office: Rite Aid Corp Georgetown Blvd Eldersburg MD 21784

DORA, JOAN TERESA, municipal clerk; b. Jersey City, Jan. 7, 1935; d. Samuel Francis and Helen Elizabeth (Curry) Kaminsky; m. Ewald Dora, Feb. 6, 1960; children: Deborah Ann, Walter John. Student County Coll. Morris-Randolph, N.J., 1970-73, Rutgers U., 1978—. Cert. mcpl. clk., N.J. Bookkeeper, office mgr. Lake Hopatcong Water Corp., High Ridge Water Co./High Ridge Sewer Co., N.J., 1970-77; acct. Lieberman & Co., Netcong, N.J., 1977-78; mcpl. clk. Borough of Hopatcong, N.J., 1978—. Trustee, corp. sec. U.S. Land & Utilities, N.Y.C., 1973-77; chairperson Hopatcong Woman's Club Community Improvement Program, 1982-90, Hopatcong Constnl. Bicentennial Com., 1987-92; mem. bd. edn. Vocat. Sch. County Sussex, 1990-94. Recipient Merit award Rotary Club, 1982, Citizenship award, Rotary Club, 1985. Mem. Hopatcong C. of C. (pres. 1982-84), N.J. Fedn. Bus. and Profl. Women (asst. treas. 1982-83), Mcpl. Clks. Assn. N.J. (resolution chairperson 1991—), Sussex County Mcpl. Clks. Assn. (pres. 1981-82), Mcpl. Clks. Assn., Internat. Inst. Mcpl. Clks., Hopatcong Econ. Devel. Comm. Clubs: Hopatcong Women's (chmn. public rels. 1990-92, 2nd v.p. 1992-94, comm. chair 1994—), N.W. Morris Bus. and Profl. Women's (pres. 1982-83), Deborah Hosp. Found. (1st v.p. 1982-83). Avocations: walking, golf, yogi exercise, travel. Home: PO Box 112 Hopatcong NJ 07843-0112 Office: Borough Hopatcong Mcpl Bldg River Styx Rd Hopatcong NJ 07843

DORADO, MARIANNE GAERTNER, lawyer; b. Neptune, N.J., May 18, 1956; d. Wolfgang Wilhelm and Marianne L. (Weber) Gaertner; m. Richard Manuel Dorado, Oct. 1, 1982; children: Marianne Christine, Kathleen Gina. BA, Yale U., 1978; JD, U. Mich., 1981. Bar: N.Y. 1982, U.S. Supreme Ct. 1993. Assoc. Shearman & Sterling, N.Y.C., 1981-91; ptnr. Robinson Brockett & Parnass, N.Y.C., 1991-92, Eaton & Van Winkle, N.Y.C., 1992—; bd. dirs. W.W. Gaertner Research Inc., Norwalk, Conn. Contbr. articles to profl. jours. Extern office legal advisor U.S. Dept. State, Washington, 1980. Republican. Roman Catholic. Office: Eaton & Van Winkle 600 3rd Ave New York NY 10016-1901

DORAN, MYRNA MARIE, media educator; b. Thief River Falls, Minn., Dec. 23, 1943; d. John Edward and Ruby Lenore (Hall) D. BS, Concordia Coll., 1965; MA, U. Minn., 1972. Libr. Centennial Schs., Circle Pines, Minn., 1965-68, libr. coord., 1968-70; libr. Osseo (Minn.) Area Schs., 1970-83; exec. dir. Osseo Fedn. Tchrs., Brooklyn Park, Minn., 1983-88; media generalist Osseo Area Schs., 1988—; chair bd. dirs. Tchr. Fed. Credit Union, Golden Valley, Minn. Contbr. articles to local union publs. Registrar clk. Minn. Ctrl. Labor Union Coun., Mpls., 1982—; vice chair DFL Precinct, St. Anthony Village, Minn., 1989—. Mem. AASL, Minn. Ednl. Media Orgn., Minn. Fedn. Tchrs. (legis. com. 1980—, treas. 1983—), Osseo Fedn. Tchrs. (pres., sec., v.p. 1976-83), Delta Kappa Gamma (com. chair 1989—). Home: 4002 Foss Rd Saint Anthony MN 55421-4542 Office: Osseo Area Schs Maple Grove Jr High Sch 7000 Hemlock Ln N Maple Grove MN 55369-5572

DORAY, ANDREA WESLEY, advertising copy administrator, writer; b. Monte Vista, Colo., Oct. 4, 1956; d. Dant Bell and Rosemary Ann (Kassap) D. BA, U. No. Colo., 1977, postgrad., 1994—. Cert. post secondary tchr. Asst. advt. mgr. San Luis Valley Publ. Co., Monte Vista, 1977-78; mktg. dir. Stuart Scott & Assocs. (formerly Philip Winn & Assocs.), Colorado Springs, Colo., 1978-80; sr. v.p. Heisley Design & Advt., Colorado Springs, Colo., 1980-85; pres., creative dir. Doray Doray, Monument, Colo., 1985—; account svcs. dir. Praco Ltd., Advt., Colorado Springs, 1987-88; dir. corp. community rels. Current, Inc., Colorado Springs, 1988-90; creative writer greeting cards, children's books, 1990-93; copy mgr. Cheeks Advt., 1993—; artist in residence The Childrens Mus., Colorado Springs, Colo.; part-time instr. Pikes Peak C.C., Colorado Springs, 1983-86, 92, 95, mem. mktg. adv. coun., 1985-93, chair, 1994-95, chair mktg. mgmt. com.; guest lectr. Colo. Mountain Coll., 1982-84, U. So. Colo., 1983, Pikes Peake C.C., 1983-87, U. Colo., Colorado Springs, 1988—. Author: The Other Fish, 1976, Oil Painting Lessons, 1986, Coming to Terms, 1986, Roger Douglas, 1987, Sunshine and the Very First Christmas, 1991, The Wonderful Birthday Star, 1991, Too-Late Tiffany and the Little Shepherd, 1991, If Only It Would Snow, 1992, The Year There Could Be No Christmas, 1992, Boris Bear Remembers His Manners, 1992, The Day Daisy Found Christmas, 1992, Friends, 1993, What Do We Want for Christmas, 1994; editor: Current Impressions, 1988-90; contbg. editor Colorado Springs Bus. Mag., 1984-86; creative writer World Cycling Fedn. Championships, 1986; speaker in field. Chmn. Colorado Springs Local Advt. Rev. Program, 1985; chmn., mem. exec. com. advt. and pub. rels. task force U.S. Olympic Hall of Fame, 1986; mem. State Legis. Alert and Action Coalition, 1985-87; mem. project bus. cons. Jr. Achievement, Colorado Springs, 1985-87; trustee Citizen's Goals Colorado Springs, 1988-89; speaker Nat. Coun. Community Rels., Orlando, Fla., 1988; grad. Leadership 2000, 1988; commencement speaker Yuma (Colo.) High Sch., 1987; social styles trainer Producing Results with Others; mem. adv. bd. El Paso County Ptnrs. Program, 1995. Named One of Colorado Springs Leading Women, Colorado Springs Gazette Telegraph, 1984, One of Women of 90s, 1989; Outstanding Young Alumna, U. No. Colo., 1987. Mem. Am. Advt. Fedn. (chmn. dist. 12 legis. com. 1985-87, pub. rels. com. 1986, Silver medal award 1986), Pikes Peak Advt. Fedn. (pres. 1984-86, Advt. Person of Yr. award), Colorado Springs C. of C. (advt. roundtable, spkr. small bus. coun. 1986—, comm. task force 1989-90, spkr. woman in bus. conf.), U. No. Colo. Alumni Assn. (bd. mem.). Office: Current Inc PO Box 2559 Colorado Springs CO 80901-2559

DORCSJAK, PAULA SCOTT, mental health nurse; b. L.A., June 24, 1945; d. Thomas Lynch and Constance L. (Greer) Booth; m. Charles Dorcsjak, June 6, 1989; children: Charles, Donald, John Borsellino. Assoc. Diploma Nursing, Coll. of the Mainland, Texas City, Tex., 1985. RN, Tex.; cert. psychiat. nurse. Float pool nurse U. Tex. Med. Br., Galveston, 1985-89; charge nurse neurology UTMB, Galveston; nurse Bay Wood Hosp., Clear Lake, Tex.; contract nurse Alternative's Inc., Webster, Tex.; investigator and surveyor long term care State of Tex., Houston, 1993—. Home: 1413 Lake Rd La Marque TX 77568-5272

DORDEK, JEAN IRENE, pre-school director, psychotherapist, education consultant; b. Berkeley, Calif., May 14, 1947; d. John Joseph and Nellie Irene (Miller) Zingsheim; m. Harvey Joel Dordek, Aug. 25, 1973; children: Jennifer, Heather, Joshua, Corey. BLS, St. Edwards U., 1987; MEd, S.W. Tex. State U., 1991. Tchr. Farm Ednl. Rsch. Ctr., Summertown, Tenn., 1976-83; asst. tchr. Austin (Tex.) Waldorf Sch., 1983-86; owner, dir. Starbright Pre-school, Austin, 1986—; therapist Day Glo MHMR, Austin, 1993-94; edn. cons. Austin, 1994—. Active Parent Action, 1993—. Recipient Excellence in Early Childhood Edn. award Austin Child Care Coun., 1994. Mem. ACA, Nat. Assn. Edn. Young Child, Austin Assn. Edn. Young Child (Creative Excellence award 1991), Kappa Delta Pi, Psi Chi. Office: Starbright Preschool 3900 Valley View Rd Austin TX 78704

DORE, BONNY ELLEN, film and television production company executive; b. Cleve., Aug. 16, 1947; d. Reber Hutson and Ellen Elizabeth (McNamara) Barnes; m. Sanford Astor, May 22, 1987. BA, U. Mich., 1969, MA, 1975. Cert. tchr., Mich. Dir., tchr. Plymouth (Mich.) Community Schs., 1969-72; gen. mgr. Sta. WSDP-FM, Plymouth, 1970-72; prodn. supr. pub. TV N.Y. State Dept. Edn., 1972-74; producer TV series Hot Fudge Sta. WXYZ-TV, Detroit, 1974-75; mgr. children's programs ABC TV Network, L.A., 1975, dir. children's programs, 1975-76, dir. prime time variety programs, 1976-77; dir. devel. Hanna-Barbera, L.A., 1977; v.p. devel. and prodn. Krofft Entertainment, L.A., 1977-81, Centerpoint Prodn., L.A., 1981-82; pres., owner in assn. with Orion TV The Greif-Dore Co., L.A., 1983-87, Bonny Dore Prodns. Inc., L.A., 1988—; mem. Caucus of Writers, Producers and Dirs., 1989—; Marsh speaker Pres. Fund for Pres. Weekend U. Mich., 1989. Producer TV series The Krofft Superstar Hour, ABC, 1978 (2 Emmy awards 1979), comedy series The 1/2 Hour Comedy Hour (starring Arsenio Hall and Victoria Jackson), ABC, 1983-84, mini-series Sins (starring Joan Collins), CBS, 1986, comedy series First Impressions, CBS, 1987-88, mini-series Glory! Glory! (starring Ellen Greene, Richard Thomas and James Whitmore; 2 Ace cable awards), HBO, 1988-89, NBC movie Reason for Living, The Jill Ireland Story, 1990-91, ABC movie Captive!, 1991, The Sinking of the Rainbow Warrior, 1993, numerous others. Mem. fundraising com. U. Mich., 1990—; assoc. mem. Nat. Trust for Hist. Preservation, 1988—. Named Outstanding Young Tchr. of Yr., Cen. States Speech Assn., 1973; Cert. of Appreciation, Gov. of Mich., 1985, City of Beverly Hills, Calif., 1985, Coun. on Social Work Edn., 1990; recipient Action for Children's TV award, 1975, Gold medal Best TV Mini-series, Best TV Screenplay Silver medal Houston Internat. Film Festival, 1990, Best. TV Actress award, 1990, Best TV Supporting Actor, 1990, Best Music, 1990, Winner Best Mini Series Houston Film Festival, 1990. Mem. NATAS, Am. Film Inst. (corr. sec.), Women in Film (v.p. 1978-81, pres. 1980-81), Women in Film Found. (trustee 1981—, exec. prodr. The Signature Series, co-chair 1994—), Nat. Cable TV Assn., Beverly Hills C. of C. (cons. 1985), Exec. Roundtable L.A. (trustee 1987—), Hollywood Radio and TV Soc., Acad. TV Arts and Scis. (mem. caucus of writers, prodrs., dirs. 1991—, co-chair caucus writers, prodrs. and dir.). Office: Bonny Dore Prodns Inc 9454 Wilshire Blvd PH Beverly Hills CA 90212

DOREMUS, KATHLEEN LA BOMBARD, geriatrics nurse, infection control nurse; b. Rochester, N.Y., Oct. 30, 1955; d. Leonard Adrian and Virginia June (Matejcek) La Bombard; m. Wyatt David Doremus, July 30, 1977; children: Joshua, Benjamin, Virginia. BSN, D'Youville Coll., Buffalo, 1977; postgrad., St. John Fisher Coll., Rochester. RN, N.Y. Staff nurse pediatrics Genessee Hosp., Rochester, 1977-81; staff nurse Hill Haven Nursing Home, Rochester, 1982-84, Western Temporaries, Rochester, 1982-90; staff devel. coord. Penfield (N.Y.) Nursing Home, 1986-90, Wesley-on-East, Rochester, 1990—. EMT Ontario (N.Y.) Vol. Emergency Squad, 1988—; instr. CPR and first aid Rochester chpt. ARC, Wayne County, 1989—; instr. B.S.E. Am. Cancer Soc., Rochester, 1992; leader, cubmaster Boy Scouts Am., 1991-93, Girl Scouts U.S., 1991—. Mem. Regional Staff Devel. Coords., Rochester Area Assn. Homes and Svcs. for Aging, Inc. (nurse asst. adv. com. 1990-93). Democrat. Office: Wesley-on-East 8 N Goodman St Rochester NY 14607

DORENKAMP, ANGELA GLORIA, English language educator; b. St. Louis, Sept. 11, 1929; d. Leo S. and Rose Marie (Gualdoni) Donati; m. John Henry Dorenkamp, July 21, 1956; children: Erica Ann, John Henry III, Thomas More, Monica Clare. BA summa cum laude, Webster Coll., 1950; MA, St. Louis U., 1956; PhD, U. Conn., 1974. Instr. Webster Coll., Webster Groves, Mo., 1955-57; prof. Assumption Coll., Worcester, Mass., 1974—; cons. Worcester Pub. Schs., 1972, 73, 77, SUNY, Binghamton, N.Y., 1980, 84, St. Mary's (Ind.) Coll., 1982. Editor: Images of Women, 1985, 2nd edit., 1995; contbr. articles to profl. jours. Chmn. Mass. Found. Humanities, Amherst, 1979-81; dir. Worcester Pub. Libr., 1991—; trustee Quinsigamond Cmty. Coll., Worcester, 1981-82; bd. dirs. Gov.'s Commn. on Status of Women, Boston, 1977-79. Recipient Sears award for Excellence in Teaching, 1990. Mem. Nat. Coun. Tchrs. English, Modern Lang. Assn., Coll. English Assn. (pres. 1986-87, Disting. Svc. award 1993), Conf. on Coll. Composition Communication, Phi Beta Kappa. Roman Catholic. Home: 13 Pointe Rok Dr Worcester MA 01604 Office: Assumption Coll 500 Salisbury St Worcester MA 01615

DORFMAN, ANDREA RANDALL, journalist; b. N.Y.C., Sept. 18, 1959; d. Irvin Sherrod Dorfman and Jane Randall. BS, Yale U., 1981. Prodn. editor Acad. Press, N.Y.C., 1981-82; asst. editor, assoc. editor to sr. writer Sci. Digest mag., N.Y.C., 1982-85; reporter to asst. editor, dept. head Time mag., N.Y.C., 1985—. Mem. Nat. Assn. Sci. Writers, Soc. Environ. Journalists, Yale Club. Office: Time Mag 1271 Ave Of The Americas New York NY 10020-1300

DORLAND, BYRL BROWN, civic worker; b. Greenwich, Utah, Apr. 25, 1915; d. David Alma and Ethel Myrle (Peterson) Brown; m. Jack Albert Dorland, June 11, 1944; children: Lynn Elise Dorland Trost, Lee Allison. Cert. AA, Snow Jr. Coll., Ephraim, Utah, 1936; teaching cert. Brigham Young U., 1937; BS, Utah State Coll., Logan, 1940; grad.Family Inst. Vassar Coll., Poughkeepsie, N.Y., 1978; John Robert Powers Sch. Profl. Women, N.Y.C., 1980. Sch. tchr., Utah, 1937-39, 40-42; restored Washington Irving's graveplot in Sleepy Hollow Cemetery, North Tarrytown, N.Y. (named Nat. Hist. Landmark 1972); nat. dir. Washington Irving Graveplot Restoration Program, 1968—, designer landmark plaque for grave; mem. Nat. Coun. State Garden Clubs,1959—; pres. Potpourri Garden Club, Westchester, N.Y., 1966—; nat. chmn. for graveplot programs Washington Irving Bicentennial, 1983-84; dir. Dorland Family Graveyard Restoration, N.J. Hist. Landmark, 1983—. Recipient Disting. Alumni award for Community Svc. Snow Coll., 1989; Recipient May Duff Walters trophy Nat. Coun. State Garden Clubs, 1974; nat. trophy Nat. Historic Landmark Com., 1974; citation Keep Am. Beautiful, 1974. Mem. Nat. Trust for Historic Preservation (Pres.'s award 1977), Nat. Historic Soc. Am., Gen. Soc. Mayflower Desc., Internat. Washington Irving Soc. (founder, pres. 1981—), Nat. Assn. for Gravestone Studies (hon.), Herb Soc. Am., DAR. Home and Office: 10 Castle Heights Ave Tarrytown NY 10591-3702

DORMAN, HATTIE LAWRENCE, management consultant, trainer, former government agency official; b. Cleve., July 22, 1932; d. J. Lyman and Claire A. (Lenoir) Lawrence; m. James L. Dorman, May 16, 1959; children—Lydia, Lynda, James Lawrence. Student Fenn Coll. (Cleve. State U.), part time 1950-58, D.C. Tchrs. Coll., 1960-64, Dept. Agr. Grad. Sch., 1968-69; BA, Howard U., 1987. Clk., tax specialist, mgmt. analyst, supr., staff advisor IRS, Washington, 1954-79; spl. asst. to dep. asst. sec. adminstrn. Dept. Treasury, Washington, 1978-79; dep. dir. Interagency Com. on Women's Bus. Enterprise, SBA; Task Force on EEO, Dept. Treasury 1978-79; mem. Pres.'s Task Force on Women Bus. Owners, 1979, now ret.; assoc. prof. continuing edn. U. D.C.; guest lectr. continuing edn. Howard U.; chief of staff for Dep. Dir. Presdl. Transition Team, 1992-93; bd. dirs. Wider Opportunities for Women, 1992-94; trainer and spkr. in field. Sec. Linton Hall Guild, 1978-80; chmn. trainer, cons., leader Girl Scout Service Unit, 1971-92; ofcl. observer Nat. Women's Conf., Houston, 1977; bd. dirs. YWCA, 1957-62; mem. planning com. Black Women's Summit, 1981; mem. Vestry Register, St. Paul's Episcopal Ch., 1981-86, Jr. Warden 1992-94. Recipient spl. achievement award Commr. IRS, 1978, thanks badge Girl Scout Nation's Capital, 1977, recognition cert. for work in Christian edn. St. Paul's Episcopal Ch., 1976, Mary McLeod Bethune Centennial award Nat. Council Negro Women, 1975, other awards and certs. of appreciation. Mem. ASTD, Am. Soc. Public Adminstrs., Fed. Exec. Inst. Alumni Assn., Assn. Psychol. Type Inc., Howard U. Alumni Assn. Club: Delta Sigma Theta. Journalist Neighbor's Inc., 1969-71.

DORMAN, MERRE THIGPEN, educational facility administrator; b. Bainbridge, Ga., Dec. 13, 1944; d. Harry Marvin and Mildred Catherine (Morris) Thigpen; (div.); children: Beth, Nancy , Merrie. BA in Sociology, Valdosta State Coll., 1966; MEd in Spl. Edn., U. So. Miss., 1976; EdS in Spl. Edn., MIss. State U., 1977, EdD in Ednl. Adminstrn., 1987. Cert. tchr., ednl. adminstr., Miss., Tex. Elem. and spl. edn. tchr. Pub. Schs. in N.Mex. and Tex., 1966-73; spl. edn. tchr., adminstr. Ellisville (Miss.) State Schs., 1973-74; acad. counselor Columbia (Miss.) Tng. Sch., 1974; spl. edn. curriculum specialist Miss. State U., Miss. State, 1974-75; media ctr. dir. spl. edn. dept. U. So. MIss., Hattiesburg, 1975-76; dir. spl. edn. Ohtibpeha County Sch. Dist., Starkville, Miss., 1977-85; dir. adult community edn. Starkville Sch. Dist., 1985-93; ICF-MR facility adminstr. fha Health Svcs., Inc., Statesville, N.C., 1993—. Mem. AAUW (bd. dirs. Miss. div. 1989-92), bd. dirs., v.p. programs Starkville br. 1989-90 Woman of Achievement, Miss. div. 1992), Miss. Assn. of Adult Community Edn., (pres. 1992-93), Kiwanis Internat (v.p., pres. Starkville Daybreak Br. 1990-92, meritorious award 1993). Methodist. Home: 606 B4 Foxcroft Ter Statesville NC 28677

DORN, MARIAN MARGARET, educator, sports management administrator; b. North Chicago, Ill., Sept. 25, 1931; d. John and Marian (Petkovsek) Jelovsek; m. Eugene G. Dorn, Aug. 2, 1952 (div. 1975); 1 child, Bradford Jay. B.S., U. Ill., 1953; M.S., U. So. Calif., 1961. Tchr., North Chicago Community High Sch., 1954-56; tchr., advisor activities, high sch., Pico-Rivera, Calif., 1956-62; tchr., coach Calif. High Sch., Whittier, 1962-65; prof. phys. edn., chmn. dept., coach, asst. chmn. div. women's athletic dir. Cypress (Calif.) Coll., 1966—; men's, women's golf coach; mgr. Billie Jean King Tennis Ctr., Long Beach, Calif., 1982-86; founder King-Dorn Golf Schs., Long Beach, 1984; pres. So. Calif. Athletic Conf., 1981; curriculum cons. Calif. Dept. Edn., 1989-92. Recipient cert. of merit Cypress Elem. Sch. Dist., 1976; Outstanding Service award Cypress Coll., 1986. Mem. Calif. (v.p. So. dist.), San Gabriel Valley (pres.) assns. health, phys. edn. and recreation, So. Calif. Community Coll. Athletic Council (sec., dir. pub. relations), NEA, Calif. Tchrs. Assn., AAHPERD, Ladies Profl. Golf Assn. Republican. Conglist. Author: Bowling Manual, 1974. Office: 9200 Valley View St Cypress CA 90630-5805

DORN, VIRGINIA ALICE, art gallery director; b. Mpls., June 22, 1916; d. Raymond Edwin and Ruth Virginia (Nylander) Henneman; m. John Emil Dorn, Feb. 22, 1937 (dec. Sept. 1971); children: John Robert, Michael Raymond. BS, U. Minn., 1937. Mgr. med. lab. Orinda, Calif., 1955-61; instr. art Orinda Civic Ctr., 1980-81; mgr., tchr. San Francisco Women Artists Gallery, 1984—. One woman shows include Lucien LaBaudt Gallery, San Francisco, 1975, St. Paul's Towers, Oakland, Calif., 1976, Contemporary Arts, Berkeley, Calif., 1977, 80, Trinity Gallery, Berkeley, 1982, Valley Arts Gallery, Walnut Creek, Calif., 1982, Univ. Club, San Francisco, 1983, Holy Names Coll. Gallery, Oakland, 1987, Wellness Cmty. Gallery, Walnut Creek, 1991, Vincent's Ear Gallery, Orinda, Calif., 1994, also many juried and invitational shows in Calif. Mem. San Francisco Women Artists (bd. dirs., fund raiser, mgr., instr., coord.), Oakland Art Assn., Valley Art Assn., Ctr. for the Visual Arts. Home: 95 Evergreen Dr Orinda CA 94563-3114

DORNBERGER-DAVIS, SHERRIE, geriatrics nurse, nursing administrator; b. Woodbury, N.J., June 30, 1956; d. Adam John And Edith Laura (Serfass) Dornberger; 1 child, Lauren Ashley. AAS, Gloucester County Coll., 1976. Dir. nursing Pitman (N.J.) Manor, 1984-94; clin. instr. Gloucester County Vocational, Sewell, N.J., 1993—; exec. dir. N.J. Nursing Students, Mullica Hill, N.J., 1981-93. Mem. editorial bd. Geratric Nursing, The Director, Long Term Care Abstracts jour; co-editor The N.J. Dir.,

1990—. Mem. ANA, N.J. State Nurses Assn., N.J. Assn. Dir. Nursing Adminstrs. (pres. 1994—, Dir. of Nurses for the Yr. award 1993, Newsletter for the Yr. award 1992), Nat. Assn. Dirs. Nursing Adminstrn. (v.p. 1994—, Dir. of Nurses for the Yr. award 1993), Long Term Care (bd. dirs., v.p.), N.J. League Nursing, N.J. Pub. Health Assn. (bd. dirs.). Home: 326 Ewan Rd Mullica Hill NJ 08062 Office: Pitman Manor 535 N Oak Ave Pitman NJ 08071

DORNEMAN, PENNY LEE HARDING, buyer; b. Greensburg, Pa., May 10, 1957; d. William R. Jr. and Amelia (Strief) Harding; m. Stephen H. Dorneman, Dec. 29, 1979. BSBA summa cum laude, Northeastern U., 1988; MBA with honors, Simmons Coll., 1991. Head buyer Boston Mus. Sci., 1982-88; purchasing agt BKM, Inc., Charlestown, Mass., 1988-90; dir. learning products WGBH Learningsmith, Cambridge, Mass., 1991—. Mem. Boston Mus. Sci., Sigma Epsilon Rho. Office: Learningsmith Inc 10 Fawcett St Cambridge MA 02138

DORNER, BARBARA EMILIA, elementary school educator; b. Bronx, N.Y., Jan. 6, 1945; d. Helmut H. and Pierina E. (Gillio) D. BS, SUNY, New Paltz, 1967; MA, Hofstra U., 1971; AS in Bus. Adminstrn., Nassau Community Coll., 1979; postgrad., Adelphi U., 1988. Cert. fin. planner. Tchr. Merrick (N.Y.) Union Free Sch. Dist., 1967—. Vol. Internat. Games for Disabled, 1984; bd. dirs. 280 Guy Lombardo Owners' Assn., 1986-87. Mem. AAUW, Am. Fedn. Tchrs., N.T. State United Tchrs., Merrick Faculty Assn. (sec. exec. bd. 1968-69, exec. bd. 1968-78, 79-82, 91—, treas. 1991—), Phi Theta Kappa. Home: 280 Guy Lombardo Ave Freeport NY 11520-4955 Office: Lakeside Sch Merrick Rd Merrick NY 11566

DORNER, VIRGINIA MARY, travel agency executive; b. Milw., Mar. 18, 1939; d. John Henry and Ruth Hope (Nowatney) Wynhoff; m. John Robert Dorner, Apr. 30, 1960 (div.); children: Michael John, Denise Marie, Scott Patrick. Student, U. Wis., 1957-59, Milw. Inst. Tech., 1961, Jefferson C.C., Watertown, N.Y., 1973-76; student entrepreneurial program diploma, U. Tex., San Antonio, 1987; grad., SABRE computer key coordinator program, 1988. Chmn. N.Y. Bd. Assessment Rev., Watertown, N.Y., 1976-79; sales rep. Rosow & Kline, San Antonio, 1980; travel cons. Gelco Travel Svcs., San Antonio, 1981-84, mgr., 1984-85; pres. Travel Focus, Inc., San Antonio, 1985—. Past chmn. Good Neighbor Program, San Antonio; bd. dirs., pres. PTA; sec. Mt. Laurel Service and Tax Study Com.; mem. Total Living Complex; mem. State Legis. Task Force., U. Tex. San Antonio Entrepreneurial Leadership Program, 1987-88; mem. golf bd. tournament com. Children's Transplants of Tex., San Antonio, 1989—; customer adv. com. USPO, San Antonio, 1993-94; mem. Besar Hugs Aux. of Assistance League of San Antonio, chmn. pub. rels. com.; marshall Tex. Open Golf Tournament. Mem. Women's Bus. Owners, North San Antonio C. of C. (mem. sports com., mem. Diplomats, mem. urban affairs com., tourism com.), Greater San Antonio C. of C. (tax equity com.), Exec. Women's Golf Assn., San Antonio Leads Exchange (past pres.), Export Assistance Com., Buy SA Task Force, Bons Vivant, World Affairs Coun., Los Amigos Club. Republican. Home: 3422 Wellsprings Dr San Antonio TX 78230-2512 Office: Travel Focus Inc 613 NW Loop 410 Ste 350 San Antonio TX 78216

DORNER-ANDELORA, SHARON AGNES HADDON, educator; b. Morristown, N.J., Nov. 3, 1943; d. William P. and Eleanor (Dygert) Haddon: BA in Bus. Edn., Montclair State Coll., 1965, MA in Bus. Edn., 1970, MA in Guidance and Counseling, 1978; EdD in Vocat.-Tech. Edn., Adminstrn. and Supervision, Rutgers U., 1982; m. Robert Andelora, Feb. 17, 1985: children: Wendy, Meridith. Tchr., Morris Knolls High Sch., 1965-70; tchr. Katherine Gibbs Sec. Sch., Montclair, N.J., 1973-74; tchr. Leonia (N.J.) High Sch., 1974-75; tchr. bus. Woodcliff Sch., Woodcliff Lake, N.J., 1976—, adminstrv. intern to supt., 1980-82; computer tech. cons., 1992—; tchr. adult sch. Sussex Vocat. Sch., County Coll. Morris, Randolph, N.J. Judge, Election Bd., Montclair, 1972-82. Author: Southwestern Pub. Co., 1992—. Mem. ASCD, Am. Vocat. Assn., Am. Vocat. Research Assn., N.J. Vocat. Assn., NEA, N.J. Edn. Assn., Bergen County Edn. Assn., Woodcliff Lake Edn. Assn. (sec. 1976-84, treas. 1991—), N.J. Bus. Edn. Assn. (coeditor Observer 1988-90, historian/photographer 1990-92, sec. 1992-94, 1st v.p. 1994—), Internat. Soc. Bus. Edn., Nat. Bus. Edn. Assn., Ea. Bus. Edn. Assn., Consumers League (dir. 1979-85), N.J. Coll. Ednl. Leaders (v.p. 1985-89, treas. 1983-84, Northeastern regional rep. 1982-83, chairperson membership com. 1989-93), Northeast Coalition Ednl. Leaders, N.J. Assn. Ednl. Tech., N.J. Macintosh Users' Group, Delta Pi Epsilon (pres. Beta Phi chpt. 1979-80, v.p. 1978-79, sec. 1976-78, newsletter editor 1974-76, 89—, nat. com. 1980-84, nat. council rep. 1981-88, nat. historian 1987-89, chmn. nat. com. 1982-84), Sigma Kappa (nat. alumnae province officer 1977-81, nat. alumnae dist. dir. 1981-87, Nat. Colby award 1994), Phi Delta Kappa (pres. 1980-82 treas. 1975-79, 82-84, council del. 1977-80, 84-86, research rep. 1986-88, found. rep. 1988—), Omicron Tau Theta (pres. Delta chpt. 1987-88, v.p. 1986-87, nat. parliamentarian 1986-88). Lodges: Daus. of Nile, N.J. Eastern Star, Women of the Moose. Mem. adv. bd. Today's Sec., 1981-82. Home: 28 College Ave Montclair NJ 07043-1604 Office: 134 Woodcliff Ave Westwood NJ 07675-8245

DORON, MARY ELLEN, steel rule diemaker-executive; b. Pikesville, Ky., Dec. 5, 1946; d. Frank Day Marrs and Draxie Marie (Newsome) McKay; m. Robert Dale Doron, Oct. 18, 1969; 1 child, Christine. Office mgr. Steel Rule Die Co., Detroit, 1965-80; sales profl., estimator Advance Die Cutting, Warren, Mich., 1980-81; pres. Metro Trim Die & Rubber, Detroit, 1981—. Office: Metro Trim Die & Rubber Inc 6340 E Nevada St Detroit MI 48234-2825

DOROSHOW, ROBIN WINKLER, pediatric cardiologist, pediatric educator; b. L.A., Mar. 28, 1948; d. Bernard and Miriam Fanny (Heller) Winkler; m. James Halpern Doroshow, July 9, 1978; 1 child, Deborah Blythe. AB in Biology, Brown U., 1969, M in Med. Scis., 1971; MD, Harvard U., 1973. Diplomate Am. Bd. Pediat., Am. Bd. Pediat. Cardiology. Intern, resident in pediat. U. Colo. Affiliated Hosps., Denver, 1973-75, fellow in pediat. cardiology, 1975-77; rsch. fellow in pediat. cardiology Children's Hosp., Boston, 1977-78; pediat. cardiologist Harbor-UCLA Med. Ctr., Torrance, Calif., 1986—; assoc. prof. pediat. UCLA Sch. Medicine, L.A., 1986-94, prof. pediat., 1994—. Bd. dirs. Temple Shaarei Torah, Arcadia, Calif., 1991-94. Mem. Am. Coll. Cardiology, Am. Acad. Pediat. (mem.-at-large Dist. IX chpt. 2 L.A. 1984-87, chair bioethics com. 1988—, chpt. sec. 1992-94, chpt. treas. 1994—), Am. Heart Assn. Office: Harbor/UCLA Med Ctr-Peds 1124 W Carson St N-4 Torrance CA 90502

DORR, STEPHANIE TILDEN, psychologist; b. Orlando, Fla., Sept. 21, 1950; d. Luther Willis Tilden II and Lillian Murfee (Grace) Owen; m. Darwin Dorr, May 21, 1986. AA, El Camino Coll., 1975; BA, U. N.C., 1985; MA, Western Carolina U., 1991. Registered psychologist, Kans. Cons. psychologist Sylva (N.C.) Psychol. Assocs., 1991-92; staff psychologist Park Ridge Hosp., Naples, N.C., 1992, Blue Ridge Ctr., Asheville, N.C., 1991-93; pvt. practice psychology Asheville, 1991-93; project mgr. Sedgwick County Dept. Mental Health, Wichita, Kans., 1993—; presenter in field. Contbr. articles to profl. pubs. Mem. Interagy. Coun., Wichita, 1994, Mental Health Coalition, Wichita, 1993; mem. tng. adv. group Children's Case Mgmt., Topeka, 1994. Mem. APA, Internat. Rorschach and Projective Techniques Soc., Soc. for Personality Assessment, Soc. for Psychologists in Mgmt., Psychoanalytic Study Group (sec. 1989-93, award 1993), Western N.C. Psychol. Assn. (mem.-at-large 1985-93, pres.-elect 1993), Psi Chi, Pi Gamma Mu. Episcopalian. Office: Sedgwick County Dept Mental Health 7701 E Kellogg Ste 300 Wichita KS 67207

DORROH, GALE SMITH, financial executive; b. Grenada, Miss., Mar. 4, 1950; m. Curtis Wayne Dorroh, Dec. 19, 1970; children: Adrianne, Audrey. BME, U. Miss., 1971. Mktg. clk. Sunburst, Grenada, Miss., 1991-92, sales and svc. quality officer, 1992—. Ch. Dir. of Music Grenada Presbyn. Ch., 1970—; chairperson Berta B. Fine Arts Coun., Grenada; pres. Jr. Aux. Mem. Am. Soc. Quality Control, Am. Soc. Tng. and Devel. Office: Sunburst 2000 Gateway Grenada MS 38901

DORROS, KAREN GAIL, psychologist; b. N.Y.C., Feb. 16, 1948; d. William and Nettie (Feuer) D.; m. Alex Bekker, Aug. 17, 1986; children: Andrew, Tatiana, William. BA, Conn. Coll., 1969; MA, NYU, 1971; PhD, New Sch. Social Rsch., 1976. Rsch. asst. NYU Med. Ctr., 1969-71, Rockefeller U., N.Y.C., 1972-74, Harlem Hosp./New Sch., N.Y.C., 1974; postdoctoral fellow Columbia U. Sch. Pub. Health, N.Y.C., 1978-80; psychologist Queens Hosp., N.Y.C., 1980-82; co-dir. A Starting Place, Inc., Pearl River, N.Y., 1979—. Office: A Starting Place Inc 664 Orangeburg Rd Pearl River NY 10965

DORSA, CAROLINE, pharmaceuticals executive. Treas. Merck & Co., White House Station, N.J. Office: Merck & Co Inc 1 Merck Dr White House Station NJ 08889*

DORSETT, PATRICIA JEAN POOLE, educator, consultant; b. New Castle, Ind., May 26, 1935; d. George Meredith and Margaret (Bryan) Poole; m. Carroll Edwin Cleek, Jan. 8, 1954 (div. 1976); children: Cynthia Anne Cleek, Patricia Jill Cleek, Deborah Susan Cleek, David Carroll Cleek; m. John Ford Dorsett, Feb. 11, 1978. BS in Edn. cum laude, Ga. State U., 1982, MS in English Edn., 1986. Cert. tchr., Ga. Pres. Direct Systems Corp., Orchard Park, N.Y., 1969-72; coordinator reservations and travel Ciba-Geigy Corp., Greensboro, N.C., 1975-78; pvt. practice travel cons. Conyers, Ga., 1979-81; cons. property mgmt. and bus. P&J Assocs., Conyers, 1980—; sec.-treas. Dorsett & Hightower (formerly P&J Assocs.), Conyers, 1979—; tchr. language arts Cousins Mid. Sch., Covington, Ga., 1983-93, staff devel. chair, 1987-89; part-time English instr. DeKalb C.C., Rockdale County, Ga., 1993—. Editor: (newsletter) St. Mark's Caller, 1964-69, The Voter, 1982-87, Direct Systems Corp. Mail Order Catalog, 1969-72. Pres. Coop. Nursery Sch., Orchard Park, 1961-62; leader 4-H Club, Orchard park, 1964-74; active Atlanta Post-polio Assn., 1990—. Mem. LWV (1st pres. Rockdale County chpt. 1982-83, fin. chmn. 1984-85, sec. 1986-87, adminstrv. v.p. 1987-89, chmn. natural resources 1987-89, bd. dirs. Ga., 1987-89, Outstanding Svc. award 1986), Nat. Fedn. Women's Club (chmn. scholarship fund 1974-75). Episcopalian. Home: 2090 Lost Forest Ln SW Conyers GA 30207-6173 Office: Dorsett & Hightower 954 Main St NE Conyers GA 30207

DORSEY, CYNTHIA MARGOT, psychologist, sleep researcher; b. White Plains, N.Y., Nov. 17, 1959; d. George Kenneth and Margie (Dennler) D.; m. Scott Edward Lukas, July 25, 1992; stepchildren: Lily, Robin. BA, Wesleyan U., Middletown, Conn., 1981; PhD in Clin. Psychology, Northwestern U., 1989. Lic. psychologist, Mass.; diplomate Am. Bd. Sleep Medicine. Intern McLean Hosp., Belmont, Mass., 1988-89, clin. fellow psychology, 1989, adminstr., 1989-90, asst. dir., 1990—, assoc. psychologist, 1993—; instr. psychology Harvard Med. Sch., Boston, 1989—; cons. Ctr. Sleep Diagnostics, Newton, Mass., 1993—; internat. conf. speaker. Contbr. chpts. to books, numerous articles and abstracts to profl. jours. Vol. speaker to local elderly community, Mass., 1990—. Walter Dill Scott fellow, 1987; NIH grantee, 1993-95; recipient teaching fellowship Northwestern U., Evanston, Ill., 1985-87, travel fellowship award Northwestern U., 1988. Fellow Am. Sleep Disorders Assn. (chair publs. com. 1993—); mem. APA, European Sleep Rsch. Soc., Sleep Rsch. Soc. Office: McLean Hosp Sleep Disorders Ctr 115 Mill St Belmont MA 02178-1048

DORSEY, DOLORES FLORENCE, business executive, corporate treasurer; b. Buffalo, May 26, 1928; d. William G. and Florence R. D. B.S., Coll. St. Elizabeth, 1950. With Aerojet-Gen. Corp., 1953—; asst. to treas. Aerojet-Gen. Corp., El Monte, Calif., 1972-74; asst. treas. Aerojet-Gen. Corp., 1974-79, treas., 1979—. Mem. Cash Mgmt. Group San Diego (past pres.), Nat. Assn. Corp. Treas., Fin. Execs. Inst. (v.p.). Republican. Roman Catholic. Office: 10300 N Torrey Pines Rd La Jolla CA 92037-1020

DORSEY, DONNA BAGLEY, insurance agent; b. Macon, Ga., May 26, 1952; d. Clarence Henry and Sybil Audrey (Phillips) Bagley; m. David M. Lewis, June 14, 1969 (div. May 1979); children: Scott D., Jeffrey A.; m. J. Larry Dorsey, July 1, 1980. Grad. high sch., Macon, Ga. Cert. ins. counselor; cert. profl. ins. woman. Rating clk. Bibb Underwriters Ins., Macon, 1977-80; book-keeper Wilson Typewriter, Macon, 1980-85; customer svc. rep. Ga. Ins. Agy., Macon, 1985; agt., customer svc. rep. Johnson and Johnson Ins., Inc., Macon, 1985—. Recipient Outstanding Customer Svc. Rep. Ga. award Ind. Ins. Agts. Ga., 1993; Ruth Dupree Meml. scholar, 1987. Mem. Profl. Ins. Agts. Ga. (bd. dirs. 1990-93, Eagle award 1989), Young Profl. Coun. Ga. (chmn. 1991-92), Ins. Women Macon (treas. 1991-92, v.p. 1992-93, pres.-elect 1993-94, pres. 1994-95, Macon Ins. Woman of the Yr. 1994, Ga. Ins. Woman of Yr. 1994). Office: Johnson and Johnson Ins Inc 420 Rogers Ave Macon GA 31204-2617

DORSEY, HATTIE, community economic development executive; b. Teachey, N.C., May 31, 1939; d. Edward Henry and Gladys (Alderman) Dorsey; m. James F. Harlow, Nov. 1, 1979 (div.); m. Kenneth Samuel Hudson, Nov. 3, 1990 (div.); 1 child, Victoria Michelle Dorsey. Student, Clark Coll., 1957-61. Exec. dir. Stanford Mid-Peninsula Urban Coalition, Stanford, Calif., 1979-81; program officer Edna McConnell Clark Found., Calif., 1982-84; v.p. Atlanta Econ. Devel. Corp., 1985-91; pres. Atlanta Neighborhood Devel. Partnership, Inc., Atlanta, 1991—; cons. Spartanburg (N.C.) Devel. Coun., 1991, Econ. Devel. Alternatives, Washington, 1984. V.p. Young Dems., Washington, 1965-66; founding pres., organizer Metro Atlanta Coalition 100 Black Women, Atlanta, 1986-91; v.p. Nat. Coalition 100 Black Women, N.Y.C., 1987-92, pres., 1995—; dir. Nat. Assn. Housing Ptnr. Mem. Spelman Coll. Corp. Roundtable. Democrat. Methodist. Office: Atlanta Neighborhood Devel Partnership 57 Forsyth St NW Ste 1250 Atlanta GA 30303-2210

DORSEY, JANEEN L., fine arts and animation executive; b. Evergreen Park, Ill., May 29, 1962. BFA, St. Xavier U., 1989. Ops. mgr. Circle Fine Art Corp., City of Industry, Calif., 1989-92; CEO Dorsey Internat., Rancho Cucamonga, Calif., 1992-93; exec. dir. DIC Entertainment and Capital Cities/ABC, Inc., Burbank, Calif., 1993—; estate invetory contr. Format Films, Tarzana, Calif., 1993—; promoter Calif. Youth Theatre, L.A., 1993—. Mem. ASIFA, Women in Animation, Animation Art Guild. Office: DIC Entertainment 4247 Dixie Canyon Ave Ste 201 Sherman Oaks CA 91423

DORSEY, LUCIA IANNONE, university art gallery administrator; b. Buffalo, Nov. 23, 1959; d. Albert J. and Jean M. (Adams) Iannone; m. James Mark Dorsey, Aug. 3, 1985; 1 child, James Albert. BA in Art History, Wesleyan U., 1980. Curatorial asst. printroom Yale U. Art Gallery, New Haven, Conn., 1980-82; coord. Arthur Ross Gallery U. Pa., Phila., 1984—. Sec. West Phila. Ptnrs. for Arts, 1992-93; active Amnesty Internat., Phila., 1988-92. Democrat. Roman Catholic.

DORSEY, MONICA ANNE, dietitian; b. Pasadena, Calif., Aug. 18, 1960; d. Harold Lloyd and Gloria Dolores (Swanson) Macomber; m. George Anthony Dorsey, May 30, 1986 (div. Sept. 1992); 1 child, Brittany Anne. Student, Mills Coll., 1978-80; BS cum laude, U. Conn., 1983. Registered dietitian. Clin. dietitian Marriott Corp., Washington, 1983-84; food svc. mgr. Marriott Corp., Virginia Beach, 1984-86; food svc. dir. Marriott Corp., Balt., 1987-88; oncology nutrition supr. Johns Hopkins U., Balt., 1988-89; cons. dietitian Beverly Enterprises, Balt., 1989-91; corp. menu coord. Beverly Enterprises, Ft. Smith, Ark., 1991—; cons. dietitian, Virginia Beach, 1985-86. Author: (pamphlet) Campus Weekend Cooking Simplified, 1983; contbr. Beverly Enterprises Diet Manual, 1993. Recipient Spkr.'s award Eli Lilly, Inc., 1985. Mem. Am. Dietetic Assn., Va. Dietetic Assn., Tidewater Dist. Dietetic Assn. (treas. 1985-86), Md. Dietetic Assn. (job referral coord. 1987-89), Ark. Dietetic Assn., Ark. Cons. Dietitians (Ark. Health Care Assn. health care facilities liaison 1992—, chair-elect 1994—). Roman Catholic. Office: Beverly Enterprises 5111 Rogers Ave Ste 40-a Fort Smith AR 72919-3700

DORSEY, RHODA MARY, retired academic administrator; b. Boston, Sept. 9, 1927; d. Thomas Francis and Hedwig (Hoge) D. BA magna cum laude, Smith Coll., 1949, LLD, 1979; BA, Cambridge (Eng.) U., 1951, MA, 1954; PhD, U. Minn., 1956; LLD (hon.), Nazareth Coll. Rochester, 1970; DHL (hon.), Mount St. Mary's Coll., 1976, Mount Vernon Coll., 1979, Coll. St. Catherine, 1983, Johns Hopkins U., 1986, Towson State U., 1987. Mem. faculty Goucher Coll., Balt., Md., 1954-94; prof. history Goucher Coll., 1965-68, dean, v.p., 1968-73, acting pres., 1973-74; pres. Goucher Coll., Balt., 1974-94, pres. emeritus, 1994—; lectr. history Loyola Coll., Balt., 1958-62, Johns Hopkins U., Balt., 1960-61; bd. dirs. Bell Atlantic-Md., First Nat. Bank Md. Bd. dirs. Friends of Cambridge U., 1978—, sec., 1989-93; bd. dirs. Gen. German Aged Peoples Home, Balt., 1984—, Greater Balt. Med. Ctr., 1990—, Balt. City Life Mus., 1993—, Hist. Hampton, Inc., 1992—, Leadership Balt. County, 1993—, Md. Healthcorp, 1993—, Balt. County Community Found., 1993—; mem. selection com. Gov.'s Medal of Excellence, 1992—; mem. Gov.'s Commn. on Sch. Funding, 1993, Md. Humanities Coun., 1994—, Balt. County Landmarks Preservation Commn., 1994—, Md. Econ. Growth Task Force, 1994; trustee Loyola, Notre Dame Libr., Balt., 1994—; chair Gov.'s Commn. Svc., 1994—. Named Outstanding Woman Mgr. of 1984 U. Balt. Women's Program in Mgmt. and WMAR-TV, Woman of Yr. Balt. County Commn. for Women, 1993; recipient Outstanding Achievement award U. Minn. Alumni Assn., 1984, Andrew White medal Loyola Coll., Balt., 1985; named in peer survey as one of 100 Most Effective Coll. and Univ. Pres. in U.S., Chronicle of Higher Edn., 1986. Mem. Md. Ind. Coll. and Univ. Assn. (chmn. 1985-89, vice chmn. 1993-94), Internat. Women's Forum, Smith Club, Hamilton St. Club (Balt.), Cosmopolitan Club (N.Y.C.).

DORSEY, VIRGINIA LEE, software engineer; b. Tulare, Calif., Nov. 27, 1937; d. John B. and Florence Ethyl (Hall) D.; children: Thor A. Leonard, Sterling A. Leonard. BS, Calif. State U., Dominguez Hills, 1974. Staff engr. Martin Marietta, Orlando, Fla., 1976-79; engr. Xerox, El Segundo, Calif., 1979; sr. engr. Honeywell, Tampa, 1980-81; engr. Martin Marietta, Orlando, 1981; sr. engr. Singer-Link, Columbia, Md., 1981-86, Honeywell, Herndon, Va., 1986-89; engring. cons. Westinghouse, Monroeville, Pa., 1989-92; software engr. Kurt J. Lesker Co., Clairton, Pa., 1993—. Mem. IEEE. Office: Kurt J Lesker Co 1515 Worthington Ave Clairton PA 15025-2700

DORSEY-PETERSON, JEANINE, public health administrator; b. Pitts., July 25, 1951; d. Cornelius H. and Clara M. (Walker) Dorsey; m. William F. Peterson, Nov. 6, 1976; 1 child, Kendra Rose. BA, Mich. State U., 1973; MPA, Pa. State U., 1978. Case worker St. Francis Hosp., Pitts., 1973-74; program analyst Gov. Coun. on Drug and Alcohol Abuse, Harrisburg, Pa., 1974-78, dir. divsn. planning, 1978-80; dir. divsn. intervention Office Drug and Alcohol Programs Dept. Health, Harrisburg, 1980-82, dir. Bur. Program Svcs., 1982-87, dep. sec., 1987-93, dep. sec. Office Health Promotion, Disease and Substance Abuse, 1993—; adj. prof. Lincoln (Pa.) U., 1983-84; med./legal adv. com. Pa. Atty. Gen., 1991-94; cons. CSAP, Washington, 1992, NYU, P.R., 1992, U.S. V.I., 1992, Hawaii, 1993, Birch and Davis, New Orleans, 1994, George Washington U., Tampa, Fla., 1994; active Nat. Adv. Coun. Health Human Svcs. CSAT, 1993—. Active Jack & Jill in Am., 1993—. Mem. Nat. Assn. State Alcohol and Drug Abuse Dirs. (bd. dirs. 1993—), Alpha Kappa Alpha. Home: 114 Curvin Dr Harrisburg PA 17112 Office: Pa Dept Health Rm 809 Health & Welfare Bldg PO Box 90, 7th & Forster Sts Harrisburg PA 17108

DORTON, LOUISE, library director; b. Oklahoma City, Mar. 6, 1936; d. Charles William Blatt and Beula O. (Williams) Nelson; m. Jack M. Dorton, Sept. 30, 1956 (div. 1985); children: Brenda, Kenneth, Janet, Dana. BA, Douglass Coll., 1973; MLS, Rutgers U., 1974. Dir. Pemberton (N.J.) Community Libr., 1974-79, Johnson City (Tenn.) Pub. Libr., 1979-89; br. dir. Chattanooga Libr.-Northgate, 1989-90; owner, mgr. Spoken Word Book Shop, Knoxville, Tenn., 1990-93; dir. Darlington County Libr., Darlington, S.C., 1991—. Mem. North Johnson City Bus. Club, 1985-89; bd. dirs. Johnson City Girls' Club, 1986-89, pres., 1987-88. Grantee N.J. State Libr., 1975, 76, 77, N.J. Labor Dept., 1976, Tenn. State Libr., 1986, 87, U.S. Dept. Edn., 1987. Mem. AAUW (pres. 1984-85), C. of C. (Leadership 2000 1986-87). Office: Darlington County Libr 204 N Main St Darlington SC 29532-3106

DORWARD, JUDITH A., food company executive; b. Hazleton, Pa., Apr. 16, 1941; d. Eugene Joseph and Dorothy Cecelia (Shields) McNertney; m. Douglas Dean Owens, Apr. 15, 1961 (div. 1968); children: Kevin Patrick, Kelly Shawn; m. Clifford Neal Dorward, July 4, 1969 (div. 1974). AA, Lehigh County Community Coll., 1979; BA, Muhlenberg Coll., 1984; grad. in statis. process control, Process Mgmt. Inst., Inc., Mpls., 1986. Customer svc. clk. Pa. Power & Light Co., Allentown, 1959-61; mgr. Merle Norman Cosmetic Studios, Allentown and Bethlehem, Pa., 1968-70; adminstrv. clk. Pillsbury Co., East Greenville, Pa., 1970-85; ops. prodn. mgr. Pillsbury Co., East Greenville, 1985-87, mgr. distbn. and prodn. control, 1987-93, chair labor rels. com., 1987-91, customer svc., vender liaison mgr., 1993-94; Pillsbury customer svc. rep. Americold Corp., Fogelsville, Pa., 1994—. Former voting machine operator Lehigh County, Slatington, Pa.; held various offices Gen. Fedn. of Women's Clubs. Mem. Exec. Women Internat. (dir. publs. 1991, dir. membership 1992-93, v.p., pres.-elect 1994, pres. 1995), Phi Beta Kappa. Democrat. Roman Catholic. Home: 2830 Linden St 3C Bethlehem PA 18017-3962 Office: Americold Corp 651 Mill Rd Fogelsville PA 18051

DORWART, BONNIE BRICE, internist, rheumatologist, educator; b. Petersburg, Va., Jan. 27, 1942; d. Gratien Bertrand and Myrtle Elizabeth (Houser) Brice; m. William Villee Dorwart, Jr., June 22, 1963; children: William Bertrand, Brice Burdan, Michael Walter. AB, Bryn Mawr Coll., 1964; MD, Temple U., 1968. Diplomate Am. Bd. Med. Examiners, Am. Bd. Internal Medicine, Am. Bd. Rheumatology. Intern, then resident in internal medicine Lankenau Hosp., Jefferson Med. Coll., Phila., 1968-72; instr. medicine Hosp. of U. Pa., Phila., 1972-74; fellow rheumatology U. Pa. Sch. Medicine, Phila., 1974; instr. medicine Jefferson Med. Coll., 1974-76, asst. prof., 1976-81, assoc. prof., 1981—; assoc. investigator div. rsch. Lankenau Hosp., 1978-88, chief arthritis clinic, 1982-86, chief connective tissue disorders, 1982—; assoc. dir. Greater Delaware Valley Arthritis Control Program, 1975; mem. Gov.'s adv. bd. on Systemic Lupus Erythematosus, Phila., 1981-88. Contbr. articles to med. jours., chpts. to books. Med. career advisor, active cells workshop Merion (Pa.) Elem. Sch., 1984—; fund raiser Arthritis Found., Am. Cancer Soc., Phila., 1974—; mem. resources com. Bryn Mawr Coll., 1985—. Named Physician of Yr., 32 Carat Club, Phila., 1986; Janet M. Glasgow scholar Temple U. Sch. Medicine, 1968. Fellow ACP; mem. AMA, Am. Coll. Rheumatology, Phila. Rheumatism Soc. (pres. 1981-82), Pa. Med. Soc., Philadelphia County Med. Soc. Lutheran. Home and Office: 124 Maple Ave Bala Cynwyd PA 19004-3031

DOTO, IRENE LOUISE, statistician; b. Wilmington, Del., May 7, 1922; d. Antonio and Teresa (Tabasso) D. BA, U. Pa., 1943; MA, Temple U., 1948, Columbia U., 1954. Engring. asst. RCA-Victor, 1943-44; research asst. U. Pa., 1944; actuarial clk. Penn Mut. Life Ins. Co., 1944-46; instr. math. Temple U., 1946-53; commd. lt. sgt. health services officer USPHS, 1954, advanced through grades to capt., 1963; statistician Communicable Disease Ctr., Atlanta, 1954-55, Kansas City, Kans., 1955-67; chief statis. and publ. services, ecol. investigations program Ctr. for Disease Control, Kansas City, 1967-73, chief statis. services, div. hepatitis and viral enteritis, Phoenix, 1973-83; statis. cons., 1984—; mem. adj. faculty Phoenix Ctr., Ottawa U., 1982—. Mem. Am. Statis. Assn., Biometrics Soc., Am. Pub. Health Assn., Ariz. Pub. Health Assn., Ariz. Council Engring. and Sci. Assn. (officer 1982-90, pres. 1988-89), Primate Found. Ariz. (mem. animal care and use com. 1986—), Bus. and Profl. Women's Club Phoenix, Sigma Xi, Pi Mu Epsilon. Office: PO Box 22197 Phoenix AZ 85028-0197

DOTSON, LINDA SUE, entertainment agent and manager; b. Richmond, Ky., Jan. 4, 1951; d. Mason and Ida Helen (Adams) Edington; m. Sheb F. Wooley, Dec. 30, 1985; 1 child, Shauna Michelle Dotson. AS in Nursing, U. Ky., 1978; BA in Nursing, U. Tenn., 1980. RN., Ky., Tenn. Talent buyer U.S. Govt.-Germany, Babenhausen, Fed. Republic of Germany, 1968-70; head writer Stars and Stripes, U.S. Govt., Frankfurt, Fed. Republic of Germany, 1969-70; die test, extruder Parker Hanifen, Berea, Ky., 1972-75; staff, head nurse Bapt. Hosp., Nashville, 1978-83; owner Pub. Relations/Talent Agy., Nashville, 1979—; co-owner Dotson-Wooley Entertainment Group (Film), Nashville, 1982—, Channel-Cordial Music Cos. (Pubs.), Nashville, 1982—; chief executive officer, owner Lito Internat. Inc. (Export/Import), Nashville, 1988—. Composer numerous songs; author: Elbows, 1979; assoc. TV Series, To Nashville, 1982, Cable TV show, Fandango, 1984. Named Top Ten Women in Entertainment, Performance Mag., 1988, finalist CBS Records/Am. Song Festival, 1982. Mem. ASCAP, Am. Fedn. Musicians, AFTRA, Internat. Country Music Buyers Assn., Nashville Assn. Talent Dirs. Office: Cir Rider Talent & Mgmt 123 Walton Ferry Rd 2nd Fl Hendersonville TN 37075

DOTY, AMY ELIZABETH, chemical engineer; b. Alliance, Ohio, Nov. 30, 1964; d. Henry Kurt and Jennie Gilda (Chille) Schmitt; m. Stuart Franklin Doty, Sept. 9, 1989; 1 child, Kyle Edward. BS in Chem. Engring., Ohio

State U., 1988. Quality control chemist PPG Industries, Gurnee, Ill., 1989-90, rsch. and devel. chemist, 1990-92, sr. process engr., 1992—.

DOTY, DELLA CORRINE, organization administrator; b. Marshalltown, Iowa, Apr. 12, 1945; d. Edwin Francis and Della Edna (Keller) Mack; BSBA in Acctg., Drake U., 1967; m. Philip Edward Doty, Dec. 23, 1967; children: Sarah Corrine, Anne Elizabeth. CPA, Colo. Audit staff Alexander Grant & Co., CPAs, Denver, 1967-71; controller Valley View Hosp. and Med. Ctr., Denver, 1971-75; rate rev. specialist Colo. Hosp. Assn., Denver, 1975-79; dir. Colo. Medicare Group Appeal Program, Littleton, Colo., 1979-91; assoc. dir. Communications Inst., 1992-94; lectr. in field. Dir., asst. treas. YWCA of Metro Denver, 1972-74; bd. dirs. Colo. Heart Assn., 1974-82; dir. Families First, Inc., 1987-89, chmn., bd. dirs., 1988-89; trustee Colo. Children's Chorale, 1988-94, chmn., 1992-94; mem. Jr. League of Denver, 1979—, v.p. mktg., 1985-86; sec. Littleton Pub. Schs. Bldg. Authority, 1983-86; active various charitable orgns.; v.p. fin. and housing Alpha Phi Internat., 1974-78, trustee, 1980-86; dir., treas. Alpha Phi Found., 1978-86. Recipient Founders Merit award Healthcare Fin. Mgmt. Assn., 1976, 83, Outstanding Vol. award Jr. League of Denver, 1984, Systainer Cmty. Svc. award, 1994. Mem. Alpha Phi (Ursa Major award 1980). Republican. Baptist. Contbr. articles to profl. jours. Address: 5981 S Coventry Ln W Littleton CO 80123

DOTY, PAMELA ANN, pharmacist; b. Ukiah, Calif., July 11, 1944; d. Ben and Mary Ellen (Morgan) Bruno; m. Richard G. Doty, July 23, 1966 (div. Mar. 1986); children: Michele Lynn, Brian Richard. BS in Pharmacy, U. of Pacific, 1967. Staff pharmacist Thrifty Drug Store, Sacramento, 1967-71; vacation relief pharmacist Thrifty Drug Store, Stockton, Calif., 1972-82, head pharmacist, dist. pharmacy trainee, 1982-94; pharmacy mgr., dist. pharmacy trainee Thrift-Payless, Stockton, 1994—. Mem. Lambda Kappa Sigma (Miss Personality 1966, alumnae pres. 1976-80, co-chmn. ann. convention 1966). Home: 4135 Boulder Creek Cir Stockton CA 95219 Office: Thrifty Cos 7932 N El Dorado Stockton CA 95210

DOUBLEDEE, DEANNA GAIL, software engineer, consultant; b. Akron, Ohio, July 29, 1958; d. John Wesley and Elizabeth (Nellis) Doubledee; m. Philip Henry Simons, Jan. 1, 1986. BSc in Computer Sci., Ohio State U., 1981; MSc in Software Engring., Nat. U., Inglewood, Calif., 1988. Cons. Ohio State U., Columbus, 1980-81; engr. Ocean Systems div. Gould, Inc., Cleve., 1981-82, Aircraft div. Northrop Corp., Hawthorne, Calif., 1982-83; tech. staff SEDD, TRW, Inc., Redondo Beach, Calif., 1983-85; staff engr. MEAD, TRW, Inc., Redondo Beach, Calif., 1985-88, subproject mgr., 1988-89; project engr. SDD, TRW, Inc., Redondo Beach, Calif., 1989-91; CEO, pres. Innovatice Concepts Continuum, Redondo Beach, Calif., 1993—; dir. software engring. TWI Engring., Inglewood, Calif., 1991-92; cons. Micrbelieve, Inc., Torrance, Calif., 1990-91; sr. computer scientist IIT Rsch. Inst., 1993-94; cons. JAPA Sys. Engring.; judge state sci. fair Ohio Acad. Sci., Columbus, 1988; active Orange County Venture forum, 1992, MIT Enterprise forum, Chgo., 1992-93. Chmn. bd. dirs. Fedn. of Presch. and Community Edn. Svcs. (Headstart), Carson, Calif., 1988-90, bd. dirs., 1990-91. Recipient award for outstanding vol. svc. Fedn. of Presch. and Community Edn. Ctrs., 1987; Exemplar Ohio Acad. Sci., 1987, 89, 90. Mem. IEEE, ACM, IEEE Computer Soc., Soc. Women Engrs. (awards chair 1987), Am. Astron. Soc.

DOUCETTE, MARY-ALYCE, computer company executive; b. Pitts., Feb. 12, 1924; d. Andrew George and Alice Jane (Sloan) Newland; m. Adrian Robert Doucette, Feb. 6, 1945 (dec. June 1983); children: David Robert, Regis Robert. BS cum laude, U. Pitts., 1945. Mgr. Newland Bros., Millvale, Pa., 1946-53; gen. mgr. Newland-Ludlo, Pitts., 1953-72; mgmt. cons. D3 Software, Garden City, N.Y., 1972-80, sec., corp. officer, 1980—. Fin. sec. Cerebral Palsy Assn., Garden City, Helen Keller Svcs. for Blind, Garden City; mem. Winthrop-U. Hosp. Aux., Mercy League, Friends of Adelphi Univ. Libr., Friends of Hist. St. George Ch. of Hempstead, N.Y., Adv. Coun. for Continuing Edn., Garden City Sch. Dist., 1988—. Mem. AAUW, L.I. Panhellenic, Univ. Club, Nassau County Hist. Soc. (life), Garden City Hist. Soc., Community Club Garden City-Hempstead, Woman's Club Garden City, Alpha Delta Pi, Pi Lambda Theta. Home: 146 Washington Ave Garden City NY 11530-3013 Office: D3 Software PO Box 8051 Garden City NY 11530-8051

DOUGAN, DEBORAH RAE, neuropsychology professional; b. Urbana, Ill., Jan. 22, 1952; d. Francis William and Barbara Belle (Ash) D. BA in Psychology, U. Ill., 1973; MA in Counseling, Gov.'s State U., 1978; PhD in Neuropsychology, Oreg. State U., 1982. Lic. psychol. assoc., Tex. Staff therapist Ozark Community Mental Health, Joplin, Mo., 1982-85; neuropsychol. cons. Tex. Commn. for the Blind, Austin, 1985-87; psychol. assoc. Warm Springs Rehab. Hosp., Gonzales, Tex., 1987-88, Rehab. Hosp. South Tex., Corpus Christi, 1988-89; psychosocial dir. New Medico Rehab. Ctr., Lindale, Tex., 1989-90; clin. coord. Rainbow Rehab. Ctrs., Ft. Worth, 1991-93; neuropsychology profl. Cypress Creek Rehab. Ctr., Houston, 1993—; predoctoral intern State Hosp., Vinita, Okla., 1981-82. Mem. APA, Tex. Head Injury Assn. (North Ctrl. chpt. bd. dirs., survivors coun. liaison 1991-93, survivors group leader Corpus Christi head injury chpt. 1988-89, Tyler (Tex.) head injury chpt., 1989-90, survivors group leader Ft. Worth head injury chpt., 1991-93, bd. dirs. Houston chpt., sec. 1993—), Toastmasters Internat. Home: 36 N Circlewood Glen The Woodlands TX 77381

DOUGHERTY, ANN R., association executive; b. Cambridge, Ohio, Feb. 26, 1937; d. John William and Freda Elois (Booth) Rigby; m. Neal Robert Dougherty; children: Benjamin, Jeanine. BS in Edn., Muskingum Coll., 1960. Elem. tchr. Marion (Ohio) Bd. of Edn., 1960-63; program dir. YMCA, Dayton, Ohio, 1963-66; exec. dir. World Affairs Coun., Dayton, 1966-70; youth dir. Mid-Peninsula YWCA, Palo Alto, Calif., 1970-71; field dir. Glendale-Crescenta Campfire, Calif., 1972-79; exec. dir. San Gabriel Valley YWCA, West Covina, Calif., 1979—; mem. So. Calif. Coun. Pres. and Execs., 1979-94; asst. chair United Way Coun. of Execs., Arcadia, Calif., 1992-93, chair, 1993-94. Mem. Lions (bd. dirs. West Covina club 1988-91). Methodist. Office: San Gabriel Valley YWCA 961 S Glendora Ave West Covina CA 91790-4205

DOUGHERTY, BARBARA LEE, artist, writer; b. L.A., Apr. 25, 1949; d. Cliff and Muriel Tamarra (Rubin) Beck; m. Michael R. Dougherty, Feb. 10, 1970; children: Jessie, Luke, Elvi. BS in Fine Art, N.Y. State Coll., 1975. Staff writer South Coast Community Newspapers, Santa Barbara, Calif., 1988-90; contbg. editor Art Calendar, Upper Fairmont, Md., 1991-93; dir. mktg. Art Calendar, Frenchtown, Md., 1993—; instr. art programs, 1975—; mem. City Adv. Bd. on Art, Santa Barbara, 1979-89, chmn., 1991-94; producer KCTV, Santa Barbara, 1990-94; CEO Harvest Am. Publs., 1992-93. Author, artist: In Search of a Sunflower, 1992, Harvest California, 1990; prodr. 4 videos on art, 1990—; contbr. articles in Mktg. Art, 1991—. Fundraiser Boys and Girls Club of Am., Carpinteria, Calif., 1977—. Recipient Best of Show award Hosp. Aux., Boulder, Nev., 1991, 1st place award Death Valley 49ers Club, 1989, 2d place award, 1990. Democrat. Roman Catholic. Home and Office: Dougherty Studios PO Box 170 Upper Fairmount MD 21867

DOUGHERTY, CHARLENE, legislative staff member; b. Great Falls, Mont., Nov. 13, 1941; d. Arthur Holland and Marjorie (Rustad) Weinland; married Alfred F. Dougherty Jr., Feb. 8, 1964 (div. 1979). BA in Polit. Sci., George Washington U., 1963, MA in Polit. Sci., 1970. Program officer Office of Emergency Preparedness now FEMA, Washington, 1970-73; dir. comm. Environ. Defense Fund., Washington, 1974-76, legis. dir., 1977-79; asst. Washington rep. Tenn. Valley Authority, Washington, 1979-80; dir. environ. liaison divsn. Dept. Energy, Washington, 1980-81; dir. legis. Nat. Audubon Soc., Washington, 1981-87; profl. staff Nat. Resources Com., U.S. Ho. Representatives, Washington, 1987—. Recipient Conservation award Chevron, 1987. Home: 5023 V St NW Washington DC 20007 Office: 1328 Longworth House Office Bldg Washington DC 20515

DOUGHERTY, CHARLOTTE ANNE, financial planner, insurance and securities representative; b. Canton, Ohio, Nov. 9, 1947; d. Myron Martin and Wilma Rose Brown; m. John Edwin Dougherty, Jr., Feb. 14, 1976; 1 child, John Edwin. BA, Miami U., Oxford, Ohio, 1969; postgrad. Kent State U. (Ohio), 1971-73. Cert. fin. planner. Social worker Summit County Welfare, Akron, Ohio, 1971-73; research coordinator Tufts U., Medford, Mass., 1973-74; corp. recruiter Lincoln Nat. Sales Corp., Ft. Wayne, Ind., 1976-79; registered rep. Lincoln Nat. Life, Cin., 1980—, LNC Equity Sales Corp., Cin., 1989—. Contbr. articles to profl. jours. Mem. Inst. Cert. Fin. Planners, Internat. Assn. Fin. Planners (v.p. Cin. chpt. 1990—), Internat. Assn. for Fin. Planning (pres.-elect Cin. chpt. 1991, pres. 1992-93), Nat. Assn. Life Underwriters, Cin. Assn. Life Underwriters. Office: Oxford Fin Group 8044 Montgomery Rd Ste 400W Cincinnati OH 45236

DOUGHERTY, COLLEEN SUE, substance abuse counselor; b. Norristown, Pa., Dec. 11, 1968; d. William Francis Dougherty and Susan Darline (Wanner) Wilds. BA in Psychology, U. N.C., Wilmington, 1990; MS in Counselor Edn., West Chester (Pa.) U., 1991. Cert. alcohol and drug edn. traffic school instr., N.C. Peer advisor Alternatives-Drug and Alcohol Prevention Ctr., Wilmington, N.C., 1989-90; adminstrv. asst. Wild Flowers Quality Wholesale, Linwood, Pa., 1990-91; grad. asst. PRIDE Drug and Alcohol Resource Ctr., West Chester, Pa., 1990-91; drug and alcohol intervention specialist Shalom, Inc., Phila., 1992; substance abuse counselor Wayne County Mental Health, Goldsboro, N.C., 1992, Wilson (N.C.)-Greene Substance Abuse Counseling Ctr., 1992—; notary pub. Wilson County, 1993—. Pres. Keywanettes, Wilson, 1986. Recipient Grad. assistantship West Chester U., 1990; named one of Outstanding Young Women of Am., 1991. Mem. Am. Counseling Assn., Internat. Assn. Addictions and Offender Counselors, Alpha Delt Pi Sorority. Republican. Methodist. Home: 2623 Joel Ln N Wilson NC 27896-6931 Office: Wilson-Greene Substance Abuse Counseling Ctr 208 N Goldsboro St Wilson NC 27893

DOUGHERTY, JANET KAY, ambulatory surgery/recovery room nurse; b. Belleville, Ill., Dec. 2, 1959; d. James Ralph and Frances (Baer) Mueller; m. David G. Dougherty, Apr. 23, 1988. Diploma, St. Luke's Hosp., 1980; BSN, Elmhurst Coll., 1986; MSN in Nursing Adminstrn., Loyola U., 1991. RN, Ill., Mo. Staff nurse St. Elizabeth's Hosp., Belleville, 1980-81; staff nurse gen. surg. Rush-Presbyn.-St. Luke's Med. Ctr., Chgo., 1981-85, asst. head nurse gen. surgery, 1985-87, staff nurse ambulatory surgery, 1987-89, asst. head nurse ambulatory surgery, 1989-91, asst. unit leader ambulatory/recovery rm., 1991-93; unit dir. ambulatory/recovery rm., 1993—. Mem. Am. Acad. Ambulatory Care Nurses, Nat. Assn. Orthopedic Nursing, Sigma Theta Tau. Home: 104 S Cornell Ave Villa Park IL 60181 Office: Rush Presbyn St Lukes Ctr 1650 W Harrison Chicago IL 60612

DOUGHERTY, JUNE EILEEN, librarian; b. Union City, N.J., Mar. 27, 1929; d. Robert John and Jane Veronica (Smith) Beyrer; B.A. in Edn., Peterson State Coll., 1967; postgrad. Rutgers U. Sch. Library Sci., 1959-69; m. Donald E. Dougherty, Dec. 2, 1946; 1 son, Glen Allan. With A. B. Dumont, Paterson, N.J., 1950-54; sch. librarian St. Paul's Elementary Sch., Prospect Park, N.J., 1957—; dir. North Haledon (N.J.) Free Pub. Library, 1957—; sec.-treas. Dougherty & Dougherty, Inc., North Haledon, 1968—. Den mother Boy Scouts Am., 1954-57; mem. Gov. N.J.'s Tercentenary Com., 1962-64. Mem. Am., N.J., N. Haledon library assns., Cath. Library Assn., N.J. Libraries Roundtable, Bergen-Passaic Library Club, Friends N. Haledon Library. Roman Catholic. Club: St. Paul's Social. Home: 155 Westervelt Ave Haledon NJ 07508-3074 Office: 129 Overlook Ave North Haledon NJ 07508

DOUGHERTY, MOLLY IRELAND, organization executive; b. Austin, Tex., Oct. 3, 1949; d. John Chrysostom and Mary Ireland (Graves) D. Student, Stanford U., 1968-71, Grad. Theol. Union, Berkeley, 1976; BA, Antioch U., 1980. Tchr., fundraiser Oakland Community Sch., Calif., 1973-77; assoc. producer, asst. editor film Nicaragua: These Same Hands, Palo Alto, Calif., 1980; free-lance journalist, translator, Nicaragua, 1981; assoc. producer, film: Short Circuit: Inside the Death Squads; exec. dir. Vecinos A Tex. Inter-Am. Initiative, Austin, Tex., 1984—; cons. Magee & Magee Assocs., 1991—. Spanish lang. tutor St. Stephen's Episcopal Sch., Austin, 1988-89. Bd. dirs. Nat. Immigration Refugee and Citizenship Forum, Washington, 1985-88; speaker, fund-raiser Salvadoran Assn. for Rural Health, 1986—; lectr. St. Stephen's Episcopal Sch., 1989. Home: 1100 Claire Ave Austin TX 78703-2502 Office: Vecinos A Tex Inter-Am Initiative PO Box 4562 Austin TX 78765-4562

DOUGHERTY, URSEL THIELBEULE, communications, marketing executive; b. Rotenburg, W. Ger., July 30, 1942; naturalized U.S. citizen, 1965; d. Hugo and Margarete (Marquardt) Thielbeule; m. Erich A. Eichhorn, Jan. 3, 1979. BA summa cum laude in Polit. Sci., Cleve. State U., 1971; MA in Polit. Sci., U. Wis., 1972; MBA in Fin., Case Western Res., 1982. Journalist maj. daily, women's mag., Germany, 1962-66; assoc. editor Farm Chems., 1967; publs. mgr. Trabon Systems, 1967-68; rsch. analyst Legis. Coun., State of Wis., 1972; pub. rels. adminstr. to mgr. pub. info. Eaton Corp., Cleve., 1972-84; dir. pub. affairs Freightliner/Mercedes-Benz Truck Co., Portland, Oreg., 1984-87, v.p. chmn.'s office Daimler Benz N.A. Holding Co., Inc., Washington, 1987-90; v.p. bus. devel., corp. affairs Penske Corp., Cleve.; v.p. investor rels. Detroit Diesel Corp.; cons. small bus. Trustee, Lake Erie coun. Girl Scouts U.S., 1975-82, Sr. Citizen Resources, 1978-81; amb. Jr. Achievement, 1979; steering com. YWCA Career Women of Achievement, 1981; adv. bd. Women's Career Networking, 1980-84; trustee, chmn. fin. com. Young Audience Greater Cleve., 1982-84. Mem. Nat. Investor Rels. Inst., Pub. Rels. Soc. Am., Nat. Press Club. Home: 1510 Crest Rd Cleveland OH 44121-1722 Office: 13400 W Outer Dr Detroit MI 48239-1309

DOUGHTEN, MARY KATHERINE (MOLLY DOUGHTEN), retired secondary education educator; b. Belvidere, Ill., Apr. 26, 1923; d. Edwin Albert and Theora Teresa (Tefft) Loop; m. Philip Tedford Doughten, Oct. 15, 1947; children: Deborah Doughten Hellriegel, Susan Doughten Myers, Ann Doughten Fichenscher, Philip Tedford Jr., David, Sarah Doughten Wiggins. BA, DePauw U., 1945; MS, Western Res. U., 1947. Social worker Children's Svcs., Cleve., 1947, San Antonio, 1948-49; tchr. English Indian Valley High Schs., Gradenhutten, Ohio, 1962-66; tchr. English and sociology New Philadelphia (Ohio) High Sch., 1966-86. Bd. dirs. Tuscarawas Valley (Ohio) Guidance Ctr., 1950-62, Cmty. Mental Health Care, Inc., formerly Mental Health Svcs. Cmty. Profl. Svcs., 1974-82, 84-92, pres., 1979-81, Alcohol, Drug and Mental Health Svcs. Bd., formerly Cmty. Mental Health Alcohol and Drug Svcs., Tuscarawas-Carroll County, 1992—, Tuscarawas County Juvenile Judges Rev. Bd., 1984—, Tuscarawas County United Way, 1960-67, ARC, PTA, 1955-58, coun. pres., 1960-62, mental health chmn. state bd., 1963-65, libr. chmn., 1966-68, Mobile Meals, 1986—, Dem. Women, 1986—, Hospice, 1987—, State C.C. Bd., 1965-68; founder, bd. dirs. Ohio Cmty. Mental Health Svcs., Columbus, 1970-80s; founding com. Kent State U. Tuscarawas campus, 1960s; bd. dirs. Tuscarawas County U. Found., 1994—. Recipient Mental Health award Community and Profl. Svcs., 1978; Martha Holden Jennings scholar, 1975-76. Mem. AAUW (sec. 1962), Ohio Ret. Tchrs. (sec. 1987-89), New Philadelphia Edn. Assn., Friends of Libr., Chestnut Soc. (bd. dirs. 1987-91), Tuscarawas County Med. Aux. (pres. 1959-60, stae bd. 1960-64), Union Hosp. Aux. (bd. dirs. 1986—, editor 1986—), DAR, Coll. Club (scholarship chair 1989-91), Union Country Club, Atwood Yacht Club, Lady Elks, Mortar Board, Phi Beta Kappa, Alpha Chi Omega, Theta Sigma Phi. Democrat. Presbyterian. Home: 204 Gooding Ave NW New Philadelphia OH 44663

DOUGLAS, CAROLYN TEMPLE, librarian, audio-visual media director; b. L.A., Sept. 9, 1934; d. Clyde Hanson and Ruby Viola (Moon) Temple; m. Robert R. Douglas (dec.), June 8, 56; children: David, Deborah. BA in English, U. So. Calif., 1955, MA in English, 1956, MSLS, 1967. Tchr. L.A. Unified Schs., 1956-66, media libr., 1967-69; libr. Beverly Hills High Sch., Calif., 1969-72, head libr., 1972-89; media libr. Mt. St. Mary's Coll., L.A., 1989—. Mem. ALA, Beta Phi Mu (pres., 1977-78). Home: 1783 Mandeville Canyon Rd Los Angeles CA 90049-2525 Office: Mt St Marys Coll 12001 Chalon Rd Los Angeles CA 90049

DOUGLAS, DEBRA ANN, critical care, oncological nurse; b. Woonsocket, R.I., Jan. 30, 1955; d. John H. III and Alice (LeBeau) D. Diploma, St. Joseph's Hosp. Sch. Nsg., 1976; BSN, R.I. Coll., 1984; MSN, Anna Maria Coll., 1990. RN, R.I., Mass., N.H.; cert. in nursing adminstrn. Cardiac testing nurse Cardiac Testing Ctr., Woonsocket, 1979-81; nurse mgr. ICU-CCU Woonsocket Hosp., 1981-86, assoc. dir. nursing, 1986-88; dir. critical care, spl. projects, budget Landmark Med. Ctr., Woonsocket, 1988-95, asst. v.p. patient care svcs., 1995—. Mem. AACCN, Am. Heart Assn. (instr. BLS, ACLS, cert. of appreciation 1987).

DOUGLAS, DIANE MIRIAM, museum director; b. Harrisburg, Pa., Mar. 25, 1957; d. David C. and Anna (Barron) D.; m. Steve I. Perlmutter, Jan. 23, 1983; 1 child, David Simon. BA, Brown U., 1979; MA, U. Del., 1982. Oral history editor Former Members of Congress, Washington, 1979-80; assoc. curator exhibitions John Michael Kohler Arts Ctr., Sheboygan, Wis., 1982-83; dir. arts ctr. Lill Street Gallery, Chgo., 1984-88; exec. dir. David Adler Cultural Ctr., Libertyville, Ill., 1988-91; dir., chief curator Bellevue (Wash.) Art Mus., 1992—; program chair, exec. bd. nat. Coun. for Edn. in Ceramic Arts, Bandon, Oreg., 1990-93; nat. adv. bd. Friends of Fiber Art, 1992; artists adv. com. Pilchuck Glass Sch., 1993—. Office: Bellevue Art Mus 301 Bellevue Sq Bellevue WA 98004-5000

DOUGLAS, EILEEN, news broadcaster; b. Syracuse, N.Y., Sept. 17, 1946; d. Marvin and Shirley (Nadel) Bernstein; m. Jeffrey Stewart Zients, Dec. 17, 1967 (wid. Nov. 1975); 1 child, Rachel Susan; m. Stanley Israel, Aug. 24, 1985. BA with honors, Syracuse U., 1968. Reporter Sta. WNYS-TV, Syracuse, 1967-68, Herald Jour., Syracuse, 1969-70, Sta. WAKY Radio, Louisville, 1970; reporter, anchorman Sta. WKLO Radio, Louisville, 1970-74, news dir., 1974-76; producer, co-host show NOW Sta. WHAS-TV CBS, Louisville, 1974-75; writer, editor Sta. WINS Radio, N.Y.C., 1976-83, anchorwoman, reporter, 1983—; on-air corr. ABC-TV News Lifetime Mag., N.Y.C., 1993-94; ptnr. Douglas/Steinman Prodns., N.Y.C., 1994—. Author: New York Inflation Fighter's Guide, 1983, Rachel and the Upside Down Heart, 1990; creator Lets Make a Dream, 1985-90. Mem. AFTRA, Writers Guild Am. Jewish. Office: Lifetime Mag Kaufman Astoria Studios 34-12 36th St Astoria NY 11106

DOUGLAS, J(ANE) YELLOWLEES, English educator; b. Detroit, June 25, 1962; d. Sylvester Kernicky and Irene Hutton Scott. BA in English., U. Mich., 1982, MA in English, 1983; PhD, NYU, 1992. Teaching asst. U. Mich., Ann Arbor, 1982-83; media cons., 1984-91; adj. prof. NYU, N.Y.C., 1985-88; lectr. Am. Coll. in London, 1990-91; adj. prof. English NYU, 1991-92; rsch. fellow Brunel U., London, 1992-93; asst. prof. Lehman Coll., CUNY, 1993—. Contbr. articles to profl. jours. Recipient Hopwood award U. Mich., 1984. Mem. MLA, Nat. Coun. Tchrs. English, Brit. Computers and Writing Assn.

DOUGLAS, JOAN DELAHANTY, psychologist, educator; b. Brockport, N.Y., Sept. 21, 1934; d. John and Katherine (Kelly) Delahanty; m. Robert M. Douglas, Jan. 26, 1957 (div. 1978); children: Robert, Christina, James. BS, Cornell U., 1956; PhD, SUNY, Albany, 1974. Lic. clin. psychologist, sch. psychologist. Instr. Skidmore Coll., Saratoga Springs, N.Y., 1969—, prof., chair psychology, 1989—; pvt. practice Ballston Lake, N.Y., 1980—. Author: (chpt.) Women's Studies and the Curriculum, 1983; contbr. articles to profl. jours. Recipient Profl. Devel. award NSF, 1978. Mem. APA, Ea. Psychol. Assn., Assn. for Women in Psychology. Democrat. Home: 222 East Ave Saratoga Springs NY 12866

DOUGLAS, MARIAN ELIZABETH, writer, researcher; b. Washington, 1951; d. Joseph F. Sr. and Edna (Nichols) D.; 1 child, Suriya. BA in Comm. Studies, Pa. State U., 1978; postgrad., U. Minn., 1986-91. News writer Fox News Svc., Washington, 1991-92; press sec., aide on Haiti Rep. Major Owens, Washington, 1992-93; mem. OAS/UN Human Rights Mission in Haiti, Port-au-Prince, 1993-95; mem. OAS Electoral Observer Team, Peru, 1995. Pub. Minn. Women's Press, 1989-91, St. Paul Pioneer Press, 1991. Grad. fellow U. Minn., 1986. Mem. Nat. Assn. Black Journalists (scholar 1986), Washington Assn. Black Journalists (v.p. 1992-93), Native Am. Journalists Assn. (assoc.), Washington Ind. Writers, Nat. Women's Polit. Caucus, Capitol Hill Women's Polit. Caucus (founding chair women of color task force 1993-94). Democrat. Episcopalian. Home: 1108 46th St SE Washington DC 20019

DOUGLAS, MARION JOAN, labor negotiator; b. Jersey City, May 29, 1940; d. Walter Stanley and Sophie Frances (Zysk) Binaski; children: Jane Dee, Alex Jay. BA, Mich. State U., 1962; MSW, Sacramento State Coll., 1971; MPA, Calif. State U.-Sacramento, 1981. Owner, mgr. Linkletter-Totten Dance Studios, Sacramento, 1962-68, Young World of Discovery, Sacramento, 1965-68; welfare worker Sacramento County, 1964-67, welfare supr., 1968-72, child welfare supr., 1972-75, sr. personnel analyst, 1976-78, personnel program mgr., 1978-81, labor relations rep., 1981-89; cons. State Dept. Health, Sacramento, 1975-76; cons. in field. Author/editor: (newsletter) Thursday's Child, 1972-74. Presiding officer Community Resource Orgn., Fair Oaks, Calif., 1970-72; exec. bd. Foster Parent's Assn., Sacramento, 1972-75; organizer Foster Care Sch. Dist. liaison programs, 1973-75; active Am. Lung Assn., 1983-87, 93-94; rep. Calif. Welfare Dirs. Assn., 1975-76; county staff advisor Joint Powers Authority, Sacramento, 1978-81; mem. Mgmt. Devel. Com., Sacramento, 1979-80; vol., auctioneer sta. KVIE Pub. TV, Sacramento, 1970-84, 88-90; adv. bd. Job and Info. Resource Ctr., 1976-77; spl. adv. task force coordinator Sacramento Employment and Tng. Adv. Council, 1980-81; vol. leader Am. Lung Assn., Sacramento, 1983-86, 94—, Calif. Dept. Social Welfare ednl. stipend, 1967-68, County of Sacramento ednl. stipend, 1969-70. Recipient Achievement award Nat. Assn. Counties, 1981. Mem. Mgmt. Women's Forum, Indsl. Relations Assn. No. Calif., Indsl. Relations Research Assn., Nat. Assn. Female Execs., Mensa. Republican. Avocations: real estate, nutrition. Home: 7812 Palmyra Dr Fair Oaks CA 95628-3423

DOUGLAS, PATRICIA JEANNE, systems designer; b. Coats, Kans., Sept. 27, 1939; d. Curtis Claire and Pearl L. (Haney) D.; div.; children: Tricia Jeanne, Robert Charles, Jr. Student, Willamette U., 1958-59; BA, U. Ariz., 1961, MEd, 1973; PhD, Colo. State U., 1988; postgrad., Columbia U. Cert. tchr., Ariz., Colo. Tchr. Amphitheater Sch. Dist., Tucson, 1962-83; corp. trainer IBM, Boulder, Colo., 1983-86, systems analyst Internat. Purchasing and Distbn. Ctr., 1987-88, rsch. statistician, 1988-89, instnl. system designer, 1989—; asst. expense acct. analyst Colo. State U., Ft. Collins, 1986-87, rsch. assoc., 1988-89; project mgr. cert. and testing IBM, 1988—; chair industry task force IEEE/ACM, 1994—. Mem. tchr. workshops LDS Ch., Boulder, 1988; mem. Substance Prevention Project, Boulder, 1988; election judge Boulder County, 1988; vol. in schs., Wappingers Falls, N.Y., 1991. IBM grantee, 1988. Mem. Inter-Am. Orgn. for Higher Edn., Internat. Coun. for Distance Edn., Consortium-Distance Edn. Network Orgn. U.S., Phi Delta Kappa, Omicron Tau Theta. Office: 500 Columbus Ave Thornwood NY 10594-1900

DOUGLAS, ROXANNE GRACE, secondary school educator; b. Orange, N.J., Dec. 17, 1951; d. Joseph Samuel and Mary (Ferro) Battista; m. Richard Joseph Douglas, June 26, 1982; 1 child, Regina Grace. BA cum laude, Montclair State Coll., 1973; student, Sorbonne U., Paris. Cert. French, social studies and elem. sch. tchr., N.J. Tchr. social studies West Orange (N.J.) Bd. Edn., 1973-74, Orange (N.J.) Bd. Edn., 1974-75; substitute tchr. various schs. N.J., 1975-76; supplemental tchr. Irvington (N.J.) Bd. Edn., 1976-80, tchr. govtl. programs, 1980—; advisor 7th dist. NJSFWC-JM State Bd., 1991-93. Mem. Montclair Hist. Soc., West Caldwell Hist. Soc., membership chmn., Montclair Mus., Newark Mus., Rahway Hist. Soc.; chmn. children's com. First Night, West Essex, 1994; troop leader Daisy Girl Scouts; vol. Family and Children's Svcs. North Essex, United Way. Recipient Creative Writing awards NJSFWC-JM, Citizenship award Am. Legion. Mem. Victorian Soc., N.J. Edn. Assn., Nat. French Hon. Soc., Nat. Edn. Hon. Soc., Jr. Women's Club of West Essex (co-pres., liaison internat affairs chmn., pub. affairs chmn.), Coll. Club Orange-Short Hills, West Essex Women's Club (liaison to jr. woman's club, chmn. internat. affairs and pub. affairs dept. first night com. mem., pres. 1994—, parent adv. coun.- bd. edn.). Roman Catholic.

DOUGLAS, SUSAN, data processing specialist, consultant; b. Chgo., Oct. 29, 1946; d. Lawrence and Phoebe Fern (Sibbald) D.; m. John D. Hauenstein, Dec. 21, 1972 (div. June 1975). BA, U. Iowa, 1972; postgrad., U. Wis., Whitewater, 1985, U. Wis., 1991—. Project coordinator Westinghouse Learning Corp., Iowa City, Iowa, 1967-75; echocardiology technician Chgo. Osteo. Hosp., 1975-78; systems programer, analyst Household Fin. Corp., Prospect Heights, Ill., 1978-81; applications analyst Burdick Corp., Milton, Wis., 1981-84; cons. Edgerton, Wis., 1984—. Mem. Data Processing Mgmt. Assn. Episcopalian. Home and Office: 8203 N State Road 184 Edgerton WI 53534-8887

DOUGLAS, VIVIAN LEE, musician, storyteller; b. Gainesville, Fla., Oct. 29, 1962; d. Gavin Lee and Ruth H. Douglas. Student, Baylor U., 1981-84; B of Music Performance, St. Louis Conservatory Music, 1986; M of Music Performance, Cleve. Inst. Music, 1988. Cert. early childhood edn. Tchr. Briar Patch Childrens Ctr., Austin, Tex., 1981-85; substitute player Ashland, Wooster, Mansfield Symphonies, Ohio, 1986-93; dir. presch. program, tchr. Stella Marris Child Ctr., St. Louis, 1986; horn player, mem. orch. Am. Wind Symphony, Cleve. Philharm., Waco Symphony, San Angelo Symphony, Spoleto Festival Orch., S.C. and Italy, 1982-90; asst. dir., tchr. Heights Edu-Care Ctr., Cleveland Heights, Ohio, 1987—; owner, performer Miss Vivi-Storyteller, Cleve., 1993—; founder, mem. Melody Brass Horn Duet, Cleve., 1989—; mem. Heritage Brass Quintet, Cleve., 1987—. Sunday sch. tchr., Vacation Bible Sch. tchr. Bethel Bapt. Ch., Cleveland Heights, 1990-94, dir. children's choir, 1991, chair, mem. music and worship com., 1992-93. Mem. Internat. Jugglers Assn., Western Res. Assn. for Preservation of Storytelling, Pi Kappa Lambda, Gamma Beta Phi. Office: Miss Vivi Storytelling Melody Brass Horn Duet 2020 Rossmoor Rd Cleveland Heights OH 44118

DOUGLASS, ENID HART, educational program director; b. L.A., Oct. 23, 1926; d. Frank Roland and Enid Yandell (Lewis) Hart; m. Malcolm P. Douglass, Aug. 28, 1948; children: Malcolm Paul Jr., John Aubrey, Susan Enid. BA, Pomona Coll., 1948; MA, Claremont (Calif.) Grad. Sch., 1959. Research asst. World Book Ency., Palo Alto, Calif., 1953-54; exec. sec., asst. dir. oral history program Claremont Grad. Sch., 1963-71, dir. oral history program, 1971—, history lectr., 1977—; mem. Calif. Heritage Preservation Commn., 1977-85, chmn. 1983-85. Contbr. articles to hist. jours. Mayor pro tem City of Claremont, 1980-82, Mayor, 1982-86; mem. planning and rsch. adv. coun. State of Calif., mem. city coun., Claremont, 1978-86; founder Claremont Heritage, Inc., 1977-80, bd. dirs., 1986—; bd. dirs. Pilgrim Pla., Claremont; founder steering com., founding bd. Claremont Community Found., 1989—, pres., 1990-94. Mem. Oral History Assn. (pres. 1979-80), Southwest Oral History Assn. (founding steering com. 1981, J.V. Mink award 1984), Nat. Council Pub. History, LWV (bd. dirs. 1957-59, Outstanding Svc. to Community award, 1986). Democrat. Home: 1195 N Berkeley Ave Claremont CA 91711-3842 Office: Claremont Grad Sch Oral History Program 1027 N Dartmouth Ave Claremont CA 91711-5908

DOUGLASS, KAREN DENISE, commercial director, film; b. Shawnee, Okla.; d. Carl Warner and Virginia Rose (Morgan) D. Student, U. Nev., 1975-78, UCLA, 1981, 82, 87. Asst. to dir. Alexander Singer, L.A., 1981-83; dir. Stargazer Prodn., L.A., 1982-84; coord. Post Plus, Inc., L.A., 1984-85; asst. to agt. William Morris Agy., Beverly Hills, Calif., 1988-89; asst. to exec. prodr. Andrew Solt Prodn., L.A., 1989-90; asst. segment prodr. Goodwill Games, Seattle, 1990; asst. to Bette Midler, Beverly Hills, 1991—; bd. trustees Spaceport Mus. and Sci. Ctr., Lompoc., Calif., 1985-89. Republican. Presbyterian. Home and Office: 5010 Cahuenga Blvd # 112 North Hollywood CA 91601-4751

DOUMLELE, RUTH HAILEY, communications company executive, broadcast accounting consultant; b. Charlotte County, Va., Nov. 6, 1925; d. Clarrie Robert Hailey and Virginia Susan (Slaughter) Ferguson; m. John Antony Doumlele, May 8, 1943; children: John Antony, Suzanne Denise Doumlele Owen. Cert. in commerce, U. Richmond, 1968; BA, Mary Baldwin Coll., 1982. Sta. acct. WLEE-Radio, Richmond, Va., 1965-67, bus. mgr., 1967-73; area bus. mgr. Nationwide Communications Inc., Richmond, 1973-75; corp. bus. mgr., Neighborhood Communications Corp., Inc., Richmond, 1978-86, asst. v.p., 1981-86; owner Broadcast Acctg. Cons., Midlothian, Va., 1986—; treas., dir. Guests of Honor, Ltd., Richmond, 1984-89; sec., Inner Light, Inc., 1984—. Contbr. articles to profl. jours.; mem. editorial rev. bd. The Woman C.P.A., 1980—. Mem. Am. Soc. Women Accts. (chpt. pres. 1974-76, contbg. editor The Coord. 1990, Chgo., Woman of Achievement award 1991), Broadcast Fin. Mgmt. Assn., Nat. League Am. Pen Women (br. pres. 1984-86), Am. Fedn. Astrologers, Va. Assn. Amateur Athletic Union (records chmn. 1959-62), Women's Club of Powhatan, Selective Svc. System Local Bd. Episcopalian. Avocations: salt water fishing, Civil War history, travel, astrology. Home and Office: 2510 Chastain Ln Midlothian VA 23113-9400

DOUSE, GWEN, elementary school educator; b. Phila.; d. Bernard and Yetta Richman; children: Jason, Jeffrey, Jennifer. BS with highest distinction, Pa. State U., 1975; MEd, Beaver Coll., 1983. Cert. reading specialist. Reading specialist Upper Dublin Sch. Dist., Fort Washington, Pa., 1977-79, Montgomery County Intermediate Unit, Springfield, Pa., 1979-80; reading coord. Silver Springs-Martin Luther Sch., Plymouth Meeting, Pa., 1980-88; chpt. 1 reading specialist Wissahickon Sch. Dist., Ambler, Pa., 1988—; mem. dist. lang. arts com., social studies rev. com., instrnl. support team, profl. develop. coun., co-editor of staff newsletter, Wisshickon Sch. Dist, facilitated staff devel. session for techrs. in reading langs. arts, 1993. Vol. Youth Svc. Program; chairperson book fair, 1992. Mem. ASCD, AAUW, Internat. Reading Assn. Home: 1605 Claudia Way North Wales PA 19454

DOUSKEY, THERESA KATHRYN, health facility administrator; b. New Haven, Conn., Nov. 30, 1938; d. Stanley Anthony and Wadia (Mekdeci) D. RN, Grace New Haven Sch. Nursing, 1959; BS in Nursing, So. Conn. State U., 1962; MPA in Health Care, U. New Haven, 1979. Various positions Yale New Haven Hosp., 1959-80; asst. dir. nursing Meriden (Conn.) Wallingford Hosp., 1980-81; nurse Regional Visiting Nurse Agy., North Haven, Conn., 1983-87; home care coord. Milford (Conn.) Hosp., 1990-93; case mgr., nurse Community Care, Inc., New Haven, 1988-90, 93—, nurse case mgr., 1993—. Mem. Am. Nurses Assn., Conn. Nurses Assn. (nominating com. 1972-74), Conn. Assn. Continuity of Care, Sigma Theta Tau. Republican. Home: 412 Narrow Ln Orange CT 06477

DOUTHITT, SHIRLEY ANN, insurance agent; b. Mexia, Tex., Feb. 21, 1947; d. Othello Young and Hazel Lorene (Corley) Thompson; m. A. Dwane Douthitt, Nov. 24, 1966; 1 child, Steven Dwane. Student, Leonard's Tng Sch., Houston, 1979; student Tex. local recording agts. licensing course, Austin, Tex., 1980; student farmers ins. group tng. program, Austin, 1980; student life underwriters trng course, Tyler, Tex., 1987. Lic. ins. agt. Sec. Lindsey & Newsom Ins. Adjusters, Palestine, Tex., 1965-73, J. Herrington Ins. Agy., Palestine, 1973-76, Ramsey Ins. Agy., Palestine, 1976-79; agt. Farmers Ins. Group, Palestine, 1979—. Recipient Bus. Woman of Yr. Palestine Profl. Bus. Women, 1983. Mem. NAFE, Women's Club. Office: Shirley Douthitt Ins Agy 101 7th St PO Box 7000 Palestine TX 75802

DOUVAN, ELIZABETH, social psychologist, educator; b. South Bend, Ind., Nov. 3, 1926; d. John and Janet F. (Powers) Malcolm; m. Eugene Victor Douvan, Dec. 27, 1947; children—Thomas Alexander, Catherine Des Ormiers. A.B., Vassar Coll., 1946; M.A., U. Mich., 1948, Ph.D., 1951. Study dir. Survey Research Center, U. Mich., Ann Arbor, 1950-58; lectr. dept. psychology Survey Research Center, U. Mich., 1951-61, asso. prof., 1961-65, Kellog prof. psychology, 1965—; also program dir. Inst. for Social Research, 1970—; assoc. dir. Inst. for Social Rsch., 1994—; dir. residential coll. U. Mich., 1985-88; cons. NIMH, NSF, various founds.; mem. Ann Arbor Bd. Health, 1972-76. Author: The Adolescent Experience, 1966, Feminine Personality and Conflict, 1970, The Inner American, 1981, Mental Health in America, 1981; contbr. articles to profl. jours. Recipient various grants. Mem. AAAS, APA (pres. div. 35, 1970-71), Am. Psychol. Soc., Assn. for Women in Psychology, Nat. Women's Studies Assn. Democrat. Office: U Mich Dept Psychology 580 Union Dr Ann Arbor MI 48109-1346

DOVALE, FERN LOUISE, civil engineer; b. Ft. Leavenworth, Kans., May 11, 1956; d. Riel Stanton and Beatrice Marie (Mayor) Crandall; m. Antonio Joseph DoVale Jr., Oct. 17, 1981. BSCE, MIT, 1978; MSCE, Columbia U., 1982. Registered profl. engr., N.J. Assoc. engr. M.W. Kellogg Co., Hackensack, N.J., 1978-80; engr. Nuclear Power Svcs., Inc., Secaucus, N.J., 1980-83, sr. engr., 1983-85, lead engr., 1985-86, project engr., 1986-88; project mgr. NPS Technologies Group, Inc., Secaucus, 1988-89; engring. mgr. NPS Technologies Group, Inc., Elmwood Park, N.J., 1989-92, Integrated Engring. Software, Inc., Englewood Cliffs, N.J., 1992—. Author, editor computer manuals. Mem. ASCE, ASME, NSPE, Am. Nuclear Soc. (exec. com. No. N.J. sect. 1986-89), MIT Alumni Club No. N.J. (bd. dirs. 1979—, membership v.p. 1982-84, 89-92, program v.p. 1984-85, 92-94, pres. 1985-86, 94—), MIT Ednl. Coun. Home: PO Box 865 Oakland NJ 07436-0865 Office: Integrated Engring Software Inc 560 Sylvan Ave Englewood Cliffs NJ 07632-3104

DOVE, RITA FRANCES, English language educator, writer; b. Akron, Ohio, Aug. 28, 1952; d. Ray A. and Elvira E. (Hord) D.; m. Fred Viebahn, Mar. 23, 1979; 1 child, Aviva Chantal Tamu Dove-Viebahn. BA summa cum laude, Miami U., Oxford, Ohio, 1973; postgrad., Universität Tübingen, Fed. Republic Germany, 1974-75; MFA, U. Iowa, 1977; LLD (hon.), Miami U., Oxford, Ohio, 1988, Knox Coll., 1989, Tuskegee U., 1994, U. Miami, Fla., 1994, Washington U., St. Louis, 1994, Case Western Res. U., 1994, Akron U., 1994, Ariz. State U., 1995, Boston Coll., 1995, Dartmouth Coll., 1995. Asst. prof. English Ariz. State U., Tempe, 1981-84, assoc. prof., 1984-87, prof., 1987-89; prof. U. Va., Charlottesville, 1989-93, Commonwealth prof. English, 1993—; U.S. poet laureate/cons. in poetry Libr. of Congress, Washington, 1993-95; writer-in-residence Tuskegee (Ala.) Inst., 1982; lit. panelist Nat. Endowment for Arts, Washington, 1984-86, chmn. poetry grants panel, 1985; judge Walt Whitman award Acad. Am. Poets, 1990, Pulitzer prize in poetry, 1991, Ruth Lilly prize 1991, Nat. Book award in poetry 1991, Anisfield-Wolf Book awards, 1992—. Author: (poetry) The Yellow House on the Corner, 1980, Museum, 1983, Thomas and Beulah, 1986 (Pulitzer prize 1987), Grace Notes, 1989 (Ohioana award 1990), Selected Poems, 1993 (Ohioana award 1994), Lady Freedom Among Us, 1994, Mother Love, 1995, (verse drama) The Darker Face of the Earth, 1994, (novel) Through the Ivory Gate, 1992 (Va. Coll. Stores Book award 1993), (short stories) Fifth Sunday, 1985 (Callaloo award 1986), (essays) The Poet's World, 1995; mem. editorial bd. Nat. Forum, 1984—, Iris, 1989—; mem. adv. bd. Ploughshares, 1992—, N.C. Writers Network, 1992—, (mag. of Libr. of Congress) Civilization, 1994—; assoc. editor Callaloo, 1986—; adv. and contbg. editor Gettysburg Rev., 1987—, TriQuar., 1988—, Ga. Review, 1994—. Commr. The Schomburg Ctr. for Rsch. in Black Culture, N.Y. Pub. Libr., 1987—; mem. Renaissance Forum Folger Shakespeare Libr., 1993—, Coun. of Scholars Libr. of Congress, 1994—; mem. nat. launch com. AmeriCorps, 1994. Presdl. scholar, 1970, Nat. Achievement scholar, 1970-73; Fulbright/Hays fellow, 1974-75, rsch. fellow U. Iowa, 1975, teaching/writing fellow U. Iowa, 1976-77, Guggenheim Found. fellow, 1983-84, Mellon sr. fellow Nat. Humanities Ctr., 1988-89, fellow Ctr. for Advanced Studies, U. Va., 1989-92; grantee NEA, 1978, 89; recipient Lavan Younger Poet award Acad. Am. Poets, 1986, GE Found. award, 1987, Bellagio (Italy) residency Rockefeller Found., 1988, Ohio Gov.'s award 1988, Literary Lion citation N.Y. Pub. Libr., 1991, Women of Yr. award Glamour Mag., 1993, NAACP Great Am. Artist award, 1993, Golden Plate award Am. Acad. Achievement, 1994, Disting. Achievement medal Miami U. Alumni Assn., 1994, Renaissance Forum award for leadership in the literary arts Folger Shakespeare Libr., 1994, Carl Sandburg award Internat. Platform Assn., 1994; inducted Ohio Women's Hall of Fame, 1991; named Phi Beta Kappa poet Harvard U., 1993. Mem. PEN, Poetry Soc. Am., Associated Writing Programs (bd. dirs. 1985-88, pres. 1986-87), Am. Acad. Achievement (mem. golden plate awards coun. 1994—), Phi Beta Kappa (senator 1994—), Phi Kappa Phi. Office: U Va Dept English Charlottesville VA 22903

DOVER, TERESA HOLBROOK, banker; b. Franklin, N.C., Oct. 24, 1957; d. Donald Fred and Ruby Lee (Gragg) Holbrook; 1 child, Jana Marie. BA, Piedmont Coll., 1985. Teller Bank of Toccoa (Ga.), 1979-84; staff acct. Huth & Bellamy, Toccoa, 1984-86; asst. v.p. Habersham Bank, Cornelia, Ga., 1986—. Mem. Piedmont Coll. Alumni Assn. (treas. 1990-94). Baptist. Home: RR 2 Box 608-21 Mount Airy GA 30563-9693 Office: Habersham Bank PO Box 1980 Cornelia GA 30531

DOVRING, KARIN ELSA INGEBORG, author, poet, playwright, communication analyst; b. Stenstorp, Sweden, Dec. 5, 1919; came to U.S., 1953, naturalized, 1968; m. Folke Dovring, May 30, 1943. Grad., Coll. Commerce, Gothenburg, Sweden, 1936; MA, Lund (Sweden) U., 1943, PhD, 1951; Phil. Licentiate, Gothenburg U., 1947. Journalist several Swedish daily newspapers and weekly mags., 1940-60; tchr. Swedish colls.; rsch. assoc. of Harold Lasswell Yale U., New Haven, 1953-78; fgn. corr. Swedish newspapers, Italy, Switzerland, France and Germany, 1956-60; freelance writer, journalist, 1960—; represented by Joseph Nicoletti Hollywood, Calif., 1994—; vis. prof. Internat. U., The Vatican, Rome, 1958-60, Gottingen (W.Ger.) U., 1962; lectr. U.S. Army, Peace Corps, numerous univs. including Yale U., U. Wis., McGill U., U. Iowa, U. Warsaw, Poland; rsch. assoc. U. Ill., Urbana, 1968-69; invited contbr. Social Sci. Rsch. Coun., 1988; featured speaker Ann. Conf. Law and Policy, Yale U. Law Sch., 1992, 93; interviewee radio and TV programs; writer Ill. Alliance to Prevent Nuclear War, radio, theater; Hollywood songwriter; plays for TV movies. Author: Songs of Zion, 1951, Land Reform as a Propaganda Theme, 3d edit. 1965, Road of Propaganda, 1959, Optional Society, 1972, Frontiers of Communication, 1975, (short stories) No Parking This Side of Heaven, 1982, Harold D. Lasswell: His Communication with a Future, 1987, 2d edit., 1988, Forked Tongue? Body-Snatched English in Political Communications, 1989, (novel) Heart in Escrow, 1990, (poems) Faces in a Mirror, 1995; contbr. numerous articles to mags. Recipient Swedish Nat. award for short stories Bonniers Pub. House Stockholm, 1951; lit. awards Internat. Acad. Leonardo da Vinci, Rome, 1982-83. Mem. NOW, Société Jean Jacques Rousseau of Geneva (hon. life), Inst. Freedom of Press (life asso.), Internat. Biog. Centre (Cambridge, England) (hon., adv. coun.). Democrat. Address: 613 W Vermont Ave Urbana IL 61801-4824 Office: care Creative Network Nicoletti Music Co PO Box 2818 Newport Beach CA 92659

DOW, LESLIE WRIGHT, communications company executive, photographer, writer; b. N.Y.C., Apr. 28, 1938; d. Charles Leslie Kerr and Margaret Scott (MacArthur) Wright; m. William Arthur Dow, 1987; 1 child, John M. Haywood. AA, Colby-Sawyer Coll., 1957; cert., Katharine Gibbs Sch., 1958. Prodn. asst. Time Inc., N.Y.C., 1958-60; exec. asst. Jefferson-Standard Broadcasting Co., Charlotte, N.C., 1960-68, G.B. Wilkins Inc., Charlotte, 1981-82; pres., pub. relations cons. Wright Comm., Inc., Charlotte, 1982—. Contbr. photography to mags. and profl. jours.; contbr. articles to mags. Bd. dirs. Charlotte Symphony Women's Assn., 1964-71, Charlotte Symphony Orch., 1965; mem. Aux. of the Mint Mus., Charlotte, 1965—. Mem. NAFE, Am. Soc. Interior Designers (dir. pub. rels. Carolinas chpt. 1984-88), Am. Bus. Women's Assn., Am. Soc. Mag. Photographers, Profl. Photographers N.C., Profl. Photographers Am. Home and Office: 3721 Pelham Ln Charlotte NC 28211-3723

DOW, MARY ALEXIS, financial executive; b. South Amboy, N.J., Feb. 19, 1949; d. Alexander and Elizabeth Anne (Reilly) Pawlowski; m. Russell Alfred Dow, June 19, 1971. BS with honors, U. R.I., 1971. CPA, Oreg. Staff acct. Deloitte & Touche, Boston, 1971-74; sr. acct. Price Waterhouse, Portland, Oreg., 1974-77, mgr., 1977-81, sr. mgr., 1981-84; CFO Copeland Lumber Yards Inc., Portland, 1984-86; ind. cons. in field, 1986-94; auditor Metro, Portland, 1995—; bd. dirs. Longview Fibre Co. Bd. dirs., past treas. Oreg. Mus. Sci. and Industry; past chmn. bd., mem. exec. com. Oreg. Trails chpt. N.W. Regional Blood Svcs. ARC; pres. Portland chpt. Fin. Execs. Inst. Mem. AICPA, Am. Woman's Soc. CPAs, Oreg. Soc. CPAs (bd. dirs. ednl. found.), Fin. Execs. Inst. Roman Catholic. Clubs: City (bd. govs.), Multnomah Athletic. Contbr. articles to profl. publs. Office: Office of Auditor Metro 600 NE Grand Ave Portland OR 97232

DOW, RUBY ELAINE, nurse; b. Princeton, Ill., Oct. 27, 1950; d. A. Wayne and Gladys M. (Swanson) Mohr; m. William L. Dow, Dec. 29, 1973; children: Daniel, Michael, Anthony. BSN, Ill. Wesleyan U., 1972. RN; lic. pub. health nurse. Staff nurse Luther Hosp., Eau Claire, Wis., 1972-74; staff nurse Marquette County Pub. Health, Montello, Wis., 1974-78, dir., 1978-94. Home: PO Box 484 Mauston WI 53948

DOWBEN, CARLA LURIE, lawyer, educator; b. Chgo., Jan. 22, 1932; d. Harold H. and Gertrude (Geitner) Lurie; m. Robert Dowben, June 20, 1950; children: Peter Arnold, Jonathan Stuart, Susan Laurie. AB, U. Chgo., 1950; JD, Temple U., 1955; cert., Brandeis U., 1968. Bar: Ill. 1957, Mass. 1963, Tex. 1974, U.S. Supreme Ct., 1974. Assoc. Conrad and Verges, Chgo., 1957-62; exec. officer MIT, Cambridge, Mass., 1963-64; legal planner, Mass. Health Planning Project, Boston, 1964-69; assoc. prof. Life Scis. Inst., Brown U., Providence, 1970-72; asst. prof. health law U. Tex. Health Sci. Ctr., Dallas, 1973-78, assoc. prof., 1978-93; ptnr. Choate & Lilly, Dallas, 1989-92; head health law section Looper, Reed, Mark and McGraw, 1992—; adj. assoc. prof. health law U. Tex., 1993—; cons. to bd. dirs. Mental Health Assn., 1958-86, Ft. Worth Assn. Retarded Citizens, 1980-90, Advocacy, Inc., 1981-85; bd. dirs. Nova Health Systems, 1975—. Contbr. articles to profl. jours.; active in drafting health and mental health legis., agy. regulations in several states and locat govts. Mem. vis. com. sch. law Temple U., 1992—. Mem. ABA, Tex. Bar Assn., Dallas Bar Assn., Nat. Health Lawyers Assn., Hastings Inst. Ethics, Tex. Family Planning Assn. Soc. of Friends. Home: 14 Loring Ave Providence RI 02906 Office: Looper Reed Mark & McGraw 1601 Elm St 4300 Thanksgiving Tower Dallas TX 75201

DOWCETT-GREGORY, KAREN MARIE, family nurse practitioner; b. Winchester, Mass., May 29, 1960; d. John Philip and Eileen Patricia (O'Brien) D. LPN, Youville Hosp. Sch. Nursing, Cambridge, Mass., 1981; BSN, U. Lowell, 1987; MSN, U. Mass., Lowell, 1992. Cert. clin. emergency nurse, clin. nurse specialist, family nurse practitioner. Staff LPN Mass. Gen. Hosp., Boston, 1981-87; staff nurse pediatrics Boston City Hosp., 1987-90, staff nurse emergency dept., 1990-93, clin. nurse specialist, 1993-94; family nurse practitioner Orchard Park Health Ctr., Roxbury, Mass., 1992-94, Teen Health Clinic, Salem, Mass., 1994—; peer support Met. Boston Critical Incident Debriefing Team, Boston, 1992—. Mem. Am. Heart Assn., Emergency Nursing Assn., Mass. Pub. Health Assn., U. Mass. at Lowell Alumni Assn., Appalacian Mountain Club. Roman Catholic. Office: Boston City Hosp 818 Harrison Ave Boston MA 02118

DOWD, JANICE LEE, foreign language educator; b. N.Y.C., Jan. 6, 1948; d. Edward H. and Mary A. (Vanek) D. BA, Marietta (Ohio) Coll., 1969; MA, Columbia U., 1971, MEd, 1979, EdD, 1984. Cons. tchr. Teaneck (N.J.) Bd. Edn., 1970—; adj. asst. prof. Queens Coll., CUNY, 1984-94, Columbia U., N.Y.C., spring 1988, 93—; asst. prof. MA TESOL program in China, Changsha, 1986, Shanghai, 1987; SAT program adminstr. Teaneck High Sch., 1978-83, yearbook sponsor, 1975-79, newspaper sponsor, 1984-92, co-chair Global/Multicultural Mgmt. Team, 1992—. Contbr. articles to profl. jours. Mem. program com. PEO, Teaneck, 1966—. Fellow Rockefeller Found., 1988. Mem. Am. Assn. Tchrs. of French, Tchrs. English to Speakers Other Langs., N.Y. State Tchrs. English to Speakers Other Langs., N.J. Tchrs. English to Speakers Other Langs., Am. Assn. Applied Linguists, Am. Coun. Tchrs. Fgn. Langs., Fgn. Lang. Educators N.J., Second Lang. Acquisition Circle N.Y., Nat. Assn. of Dept. Heads and Suprs. of Fgn. Langs. Home: 56 Boulevard New Milford NJ 07646-1602 Office: Teaneck High Sch 100 Elizabeth Ave Teaneck NJ 07666-4798

DOWDELL, RUTH E., retired association executive; b. Trenton, N.J., Dec. 9, 1927; d. Marc Pritchard and Emily (Buckman) D. BA, Colo. Coll., 1950; MEd, Boston U., 1962. Cert. assn. exec. Dist. dir. Camp Fire Girls, Boston, 1957-62; exec. dir. Camp Fire Girls, Quincy, Mass., 1962-65; mem. field staff Nat. Camp Fire Girls, N.Y.C., 1966-76; conv. and confs. exec., nat. bd. dirs. YWCA U.S.A., N.Y.C., 1977-86; ret., 1986. Sec bd. govs. Rossmoor Cmty. Assn., Jamesburg, N.J., 1990-91, mem. golf. mgmt. com., 1993—, mem. govt. rels. com., 1993-94; bd. dirs., pres. Mut. One, Rossmoor, Jamesburg, 1988-91. Mem. Rossmoor Croquet Club (bd. dirs., pres. 1990-92, mem. edn. and competition com. 1993-94).

DOWDY, DOROTHY WILLIAMS, political science educator; b. Limon, Colo., June 11, 1939; d. Thomas Edwin and Rachel Mae (Henry) Williams; m. Thomas William Dowdy, Feb. 28, 1963; children: Jessica, Laura, Thomas. AA, George Washington U., 1958; BA, George Washington U., 1961; MA in Polit. Sci., Tulane U., 1965. Cert. secondary educator in social studies and history, Va. Analyst CIA, Washington, 1961-62; govt. tchr. Fairfax (Va.) County Pub. Schs., 1964-69, 83-93; co-owner, mgr. Buckingham Springs Stables, Fairfax Station, Va., 1973-94; advanced placement U.S. govt. polit. scientist Chantilly (Va.) High Sch., 1987—; coach Nat. Acad. Decathlon, Chantilly, 1989-90, "It's Academic Team", Chantilly, 1985-93; del. Russian-Am. Joint Conf. on Edn., Moscow, 1994. Pres. Fairfax Lawyers Wives, 1976; co-founder Fairfax 4-H Therapeutic Riding Program, 1978; pres. Burke (Va.) Elem. Sch. PTA, 1982-84; mem. Fairfax Com. of 100, 1988-90, St. Georges United Meth. Ch., 1984-93. Named Tchr. of Yr., Chantilly High Sch., 1989, Tchr.-Leader, People to People Soviet Union Friendship Caravan, 1989; recipient Disting. Svc. award Fairfax 4-H Ext. Svc., 1988. Mem. Topical Symposia Nat. Def. U. Methodist. Office: Chantilly High Sch 4201 Stringfellow Rd Chantilly VA 22021-2600

DOWLING, AUDREY KAY, gifted/talented education educator; b. Jamestown, N.Y., Oct. 11, 1952; d. Edmund F. and Audrey (Owen) Kay; m. Donald Douglas Dowling, Jr., Apr. 14, 1973; children: Forrest Blake, Joseph Campbell. BS, SUNY, New Paltz, 1974; MS in Edn., SUNY, Fredonia, 1990. Cert. tchr. art and elem. edn., N.Y. Tchr. art Warwick (N.Y.) Cen. Sch., 1974-79; edn. coord. Access to the Arts, Westfield, N.Y., 1980; tchr. art Bemus Point (N.Y.) Cen. Sch., 1985-86; gallery owner, artist Portage Hill Gallery, Westfield, N.Y., 1980—; tchr. gifted and talented edn. Erie II, Chautauqua, Catt. BOCES, Orchard Park, N.Y., 1986—; cons. various state and internat. confs. in field; juror Chautauqua Crafts Alliance, Mayville, N.Y., 1982-92; artist-in-residence various places, 1977—. Artist in clay and fiber work; numerous one-woman shows. Co-founder Chautauqua Crafts Alliance, 1980, bd. dirs., 1980-90; mem. Chautauqua Arts Coun., mem. regrant program, 1982-83, projects pool grant, 1987, individual artist's grant, 1988. Mem. AAUW, Assn. for Gifted and Talented Edn., Gifted Edn. Tng. Svc. Network, Audubon Soc. Democrat. Universalist/Unitarian. Home: 6439 S Portage Rd Westfield NY 14787

DOWLING, LONA BUCHANAN, nurse; b. Washington, Feb. 7, 1950; d. Aaron Ernie and Louise Katherine (Willis) Buchanan; m. Frankie Lee Dowling, Sept. 18, 1976; children: David Lee, Allison Lynn. Diploma in nursing Washington Hosp. Ctr., 1971. Staff nurse Prince George Gen. Hosp., Cheverly, Md., 1971-72, asst. head nurse emergency room, 1972-74, head nurse, 1974-75; asst. head nurse emergency room Doctors Hosp., Lanham, Md., 1975-79; staff nurse Ashland Dist. Hosp., Kans., 1979-81; community health nurse, county sch. nurse Comanche County, Coldwater, Kans., 1981-90; staff nurse oper. rm. internship program U. Utah, Salt Lake City, 1990—, asst. nurse mgr. gen. surgery, 1991-94, staff nurse oper. rm., 1994—; coord., instr. Laparoscopic Cholecystectomy Course for Nurses, 1991-92, Advanced Laparoscopic Course, 1993. Organizer 1st SADD chpt. in Southwest Kans., 1984; ednl. chmn. Comanche County Cancer Soc., 1984—; ednl. co-chmn. South Central Coalition for Health Services, Kans., 1983-84; CPR instr. ARC, Wichita, Kans., 1982—; bd. dirs. Iroquois Ctr. Human Devel. Mem. Kans. Pub. Health Assn., Kans. Assn. Local Health Depts., Bus. and Profl. Women's Club (corr. sec. 1983). Republican. Clubs: Twin Hills Extension Homemaker Unit, Mothers Advancement Protection. Avocations: photography, needlework, horses, entertaining, fishing. Home: 1930 Bonneview Dr Bountiful UT 84010-4116

DOWLING, REGINA NELL, nurse; b. Cumberland, Md., Sept. 30, 1930; d. Ralph Westly and Edna Naomi (Davis) Ferguson; m. Robert James Dowling, Sept. 29, 1956; children: Charles James Dowling, Karen Regina Tavenner. RN, Meml. Hosp. Sch. Nursing, Cumberland, Md., 1952. RN, Md. Staff nurse Meml. Hosp., Cumberland, 1952-54, head nurse, 1954-58, staff nurse, 1958-62; apheresis head nurse NIH, Bethesda, Md., 1963-81, apheresis supr., 1981-90, ret., 1990; leader discussion groups, symposia and workshops on apheresis. Co-author: (chpt.) Client Care During Hemapheresis; presenter in field. Pres. Trinity United Meth. Women, Germantown, Md., 1986-89, 92-93; mem. Md. chpt. 4-H All Star, Friendship Star Quilters Club, 1991-93. Recipient Recognition and Spl. Achievement award U.S. Dept. Health and Human Svcs., NIH, Bethesda, 1986; Regina Nell Dowling Apheresis Clinic named in her honor NIH. Mem. Am. Soc. for Apheresis (hon., bd. dirs. 1982-83), Soc. for Hemapheresis (bd. dirs. 1978-80). Home: 1 Flagstone Ct Germantown MD 20874-2231

DOWN, MELINDA MAGUIRE, clinical psychologist, researcher; b. Dallas, June 8, 1964. BS in Psychol., Duke U., 1987; PhD in Clin. Psychol., U. Tex., 1993. Testing tech. Dallas Psychiat. Assocs., 1987-88; clin. psychol. intern U. Tex. Southwestern Med. Ctr. Terrell State Hosp., 1989-90, Juvenile Detention Ctr., Dallas, 1990, Parkland Psychiat. Emergency Room, Dallas, 1989-91, U. Rehab. Clinic, Dallas, 1990-91, So. Methodist U., Dallas, 1991-92; rsch. intern Mental Health Clin. Rsch. Ctr., Dallas, 1990-93; clin. psychol. intern Southwest Adult Clinic, Dallas, 1989-92; clin. supr. ADAPT Behavioral Healthcare, Dallas, 1992—. Contbr. articles to profl. jours., chpts. to books. mem. bd. dirs. Turtle Creek Manor, Dallas, 1986-93, mem. adv. bd., 1994—; group facilitator AIDS Support, 1993—. mem. APA, Tex. Psychol. Assn., Dallas Psychol. Assn.

DOWNEY, DEOBORAH ANN, systems specialist; b. Xenia, Ohio, July 22, 1958; d. Nathan Vernon and Patricia Jaunita (Ward) D. Assoc. in Applied

Sci., Sinclair C.C., 1981, student, 1986-91; BA, Capital U., 1994. Jr. programmer, project mgr. Cole-Layer-Trumble Co., Dayton, Ohio, 1981-82; sr. programmer, analyst, project leader Systems Architects Inc., Dayton, 1982-84, Systems and Applied Sci. Corp. (now Computer Sci. Corp.), Dayton, 1984; analyst Unisys, Dayton, 1984-87; systems programmer Computer Sci. Corp., Fairborn, Ohio, 1987—; cons. computer software M&S Garage/Body Shop, Beavercreek, Ohio, 1986-87. Mem. NAFE, Am. Motorcyclist Assn., Sinclair Community Coll. Alumni Assn., Cherokee Nation Okla., Cherokee Nat. Hist. Soc., Beavercreek COPP. Democrat. Mem. United Ch. of Christ.

DOWNEY, SCHEHERAZADE SHULA, academic administrator; b. Heidelberg, Germany, Aug. 19, 1952; came to U.S., 1954; d. Howard William and Dorothy Elizabeth (Mulliken) Rossow; m. John Harold Shula, Jan. 15, 1971 (div. Jan. 1976); m. Michael John Downey, July 29, 1989; 1 child, Joshua John. AA, Morgan C.C., 1979; BA magna cum laude, U. Denver, 1981, postgrad., 1988-90. Libr. asst. Morgan C.C., Ft. Morgan, Colo., 1977-79; rsch. asst. dept. anthropology U. Denver, 1979-80, project coord. dept. anthropology, 1980-81, graduation evaluator registrar, 1981-85, functional coord. registration, 1985-89, dir. univ. registrations, 1989—; counselor U. Denver, 1986-92. Contbr. poetry to anthols. Advocate hotline Rape Awareness/Assistance Program, Denver, 1992—; advisor Rape Awareness Counseling Edn., U. Denver, 1991—. Mem. Am. Assn. Collegiate Registrars and Admissions Officers (Best State Regional Profl. Activity award 1991), Colo. Collegiate Registrars Assn., Colo. Orgn. for Victims Assistance, Rocky Mountain Assn. of Collegiate Registrars and Admissions Officers (com. mem. 1991—, Best State award 1991), Com. for Women on Campus (chair 1992—), Phi Beta Kappa (membership com. 1992, 93).

DOWNIE, PAMELA, career counselor; b. Chester, Calif., Dec. 1, 1954; d. William John and June (De La Mont) D. BA, Widener U., 1980; MS, Villanova U., 1985; postgrad., U. So. Calif. Counselor Del. County C.C., Media, Pa., trainer, educator; counselor, educator New Beginnings, Media; teaching asst. U. So. Calif., 1989-91, instr. practicum, 1991, psychol. intern., 1991-94; staff psychologist U. San Diego, 1994—. Mem. APA (student), NAFE, AACD, Am. Mental Health Coun. Assn., Assn. for Multicultural Counseling, Pa. Counselors Assn., Assn. for Specialists in Group Work, Assn. for Coun. Edn. and Supervision. Home: PO Box 660582 Arcadia CA 91066-0582 Office: Student Counseling Svcs U San Diego Linda Vista Ave San Diego CA 92110

DOWNING, CHRISTINE ROSENBLATT, religious studies educator; b. Leipzig, Germany, Mar. 21, 1931; came to U.S., 1935; d. Edgar Fritz and Herta (Fischer) Rosenblatt; m. George Downing, June 9, 1951, (div. Jan. 1978); children: Peter, Eric, Scott, Christopher, Sandra; m. River Malcolm, Sept. 2, 1984. BA, Swarthmore Coll., 1948; PhD, Drew U., 1966; MA, U.S. Internat. U., 1982. From instr. to assoc. prof. religion Rutgers U., New Brunswick, N.J., 1963-75; prof., chmn. dept. religious studies San Diego State U., 1974-92; mem. core faculty Calif. Sch. Profl. Psychology, San Diego, 1974-90. Author: The Goddess, 1981, Journey Through Menopause, 1987, Psyche's Sisters, 1988, Myths and Mysteries fo Same Sex Love Continuum, 1989; co-author: Face to Face to Face, 1975, Women's Mysteries, 1992, Gods in Our Midst, 1993; editor: Mirrors of the Self (Tarcher), 1991; contbr. articles to profl. jours. Fellow NEH, 1982-83. Fellow Soc. Values in Higher Edn. (bd. dirs. 1966-81); mem. AAUP, Am. Acad. Religion (pres. 1973-74). Office: San Diego State U Dept Religious Studies San Diego CA 92182

DOWNING, CYNTHIA HURST, therapist, addiction and abuse specialist; b. Fort Wayne, Ind., Sept. 10, 1942; d. James Dickson Hurst and Bernadette (Dygert) Lawyer; m. James S. Downing, Sept. 9, 1961 (div. 1979); children: David, Elizabeth, Jeffrey. BA in Psychology, Ursuline Coll., 1980; MA in Human Svcs., John Carroll U., 1982; PhD, Saybrook Inst., 1991. Lic. profl. counselor, Ohio; cert. alcoholism counselor, cert. relapse prevention specialist; nat. cert. addiction counselor level II. Counselor United Meth. Alcohol and Chem. Counseling, Berea, Ohio, 1980-82; clin. dir. Earthrise Recovery Svcs., Inc., Chagrin Falls, Ohio, 1982—; clin. dir. chem. dependency Brentwood Hosp., Cleve., 1985; coord. case study, instr. Ctr. Applied Scis. Corp. Nat. Relapse Prevention Cert. Sch., Chgo., 1988—. Author: Triad: The Evolution of Treatment for Chemical Dependency, 1989; mem. editorial adv. bd. Behavioral Health Mgmt. mag., 1991—; contbr. articles to profl. jours. Mem. Nat. Assn. Alcoholism and Drug Abuse Counselors, Nat. Assn. Relapse Prevention Specialists (charter), Assn. Humanistic Psychology, Internat. Soc. for the Study of Dissociation. Office: Earthrise Recovery Svcs Inc 25 W Summit St Chagrin Falls OH 44022-2724

DOWNING, DANIELLE SANTANDER, brokerage house executive; b. N.Y.C., Sept. 17; d. Vincent and Pilar (Santander) D. Student, Taiwan Nat. U., Taiwan, 1984-85; BA, Princeton U., 1987; MBA, The Warton Sch., Phila., 1992; MA, The Lauder Inst., Phila., 1992. Terr. asst. Mfrs. Hanover, N.Y.C., 1987-88; dir. and advisor to bd. dir. Moscow Commodity Exchange, Moscow, Russia, 1990-91; pres. MOSGRAIN, Moscow, Russia, 1991; dir. Kouri Capital Group, Greenwich, Conn., 1992; ind. cons. KPMG, Moscow, Russia, 1993; dir. C.A. & Co. Russian Brokerage House, Moscow, Russia, 1994—. Author: (with others) Guide to World Equity Markets: Chapter on Russia, 1991, 92, 93, 94. Princeton U. Rsch. grantee 1986; recipient Chinese Speech Competition prize Taiwan Rotary Club 1986. Home: 1060 Park Ave Apt 2E New York NY 10128 Office: CA & Co Russian Brokerage House, Olkhovskaya Street No 22, 107066 Moscow Russia

DOWNING, DIANE VIRGINIA, public health nurse; b. Cin., Dec. 18, 1948; d. Edward Patrick and Virginia Agnes (Heis) D. BSN, U. Va., 1971, MSN, 1981; cert. psychiatric nurse clin. specialist, San Francisco Army Med. Ctr., 1972. RN, Va., N.Y. Commd. lt. Nurse Corps U.S. Army, 1967; lt. col. USAR, 1975; chief nurse 343d Combat Support Hosp., Ft. Hamilton, N.Y., 1992—; sudden infant death syndrome project coord. Ind. State Bd. Health, Indpls., 1981-85, dir. local health stds., 1985-87, dir. maternal and child health div., 1987-90; asst. commr. nursing and quality assurance N.Y.C. Dept. Health, 1990-92; dir. policy rsch. Pub. Health Found., Washington, 1992-93; nurse mgr. Arlington County Health Svcs. Divsn., Dept. Human Svcs., Arlington, Va., 1993—. Vol. Big Sisters-Little Sisters, Indpls., 1982-89. Lt. col. USAR, 1988. Mem. APHA (governing coun. representing pub. health nursing sect. 1992-95), ANA, Pub. Health Assn. N.Y.C., Ind. Pub. Health Assn. (treas. 1987, v.p. 1988, pres. 1989), Nat. Sudden Infant Death Syndrome Found. (chair Greater Indpls. chpt. 1983-85, Outstanding Contbn. award 1986). Office: Arlington County Health Svc Dept Human Svcs 1800 N Edison St Arlington VA 22207

DOWNING, JOAN FORMAN, editor; b. Mpls., Nov. 16, 1934; d. W. Chandler and Marie A. (Forster) Forman; children: Timothy Alan, Julie Marie Downing Giesen, Christopher Alan. BA, U. Wis., 1956. Editorial asst. Sci. Research Assocs., Chgo., 1960-61; asst. editor Sci. Research Assocs., 1961-63, Childrens Press, Chgo., 1963-66; assoc. editor Childrens Press, 1966-68, mng. editor, 1968-78, editor-in-chief, 1978-81, sr. editor, 1981—; dir. Chgo. Book Clinic, 1973-75, publicity chmn., 1973-74. Author: (with Eugene Baker) Workers Long Ago, 1968, Baseball Is Our Game, 1982, Junior CB Picture Dictionary, 1978; project editor: 15 vol. Young People's Story of Our Heritage, 1966 (Graphic Arts Council of Chgo. award), 20 vol. People of Destiny (Chgo. Book Clinic award 1967-68), 20 vol. Enchantment of South and Central America, 1968-70, 36 vol. Open Door Books, 1968, 42 vol. Enchantment of Africa, 1972-78, Hobbies for Everyone: Collecting Toy Trains, 1979 (Graphic Arts award Printing Industries Am.), (multi-vol.) World at War, 1980-87, (52 vol.) America the Beautiful, 1987-91, (52 vol.) From Sea to Shining Sea, 1991-95. Election judge, Cook County (Ill.), 1974—. Mem. Authors Guild, Authors League Am., Alpha Phi. Democrat. Home: 2414 Brown Ave Evanston IL 60201-2526 Office: 5440 N Cumberland Ave Chicago IL 60656-1452

DOWNING, MARGARET MARY, newspaper editor; b. Altoona, Pa., June 3, 1952; d. Irvine William and Iva Ann (Regan) D.; m. Gary Beaver; children: Ian Downing-Beaver, Timothy Downing-Beaver, Abby Downing-Beaver. BA magna cum laude, Tex. Christian U., 1974. Reporting intern Corpus Christi Caller Times, 1973; reporter, bur. chief Beaumont Enterprise & Jour. (Tex.), 1974-76, Dallas Times Herald, 1976-80; from reporter, asst. city editor, asst. bus. and met. editor to mng. editor Houston Post, 1980-93; mng. editor Jackson (Miss.) Clarion-Ledger, 1993—; jurist Pulitzer Prize Awards 1992, 93; bd. dirs. News Media Credit Union, 1993, Santa's Helpers, 1992-93; respite foster parent vol. Harris County Children's Protective Svcs., 1993; mem. PTA Madison Sta. Elem., 1993—. Mem. AP Mng. Editor's Assn., YMCA (runners club 1994, activities adv bd. 1994), Soc. Profl. Journalists, Press Club of Houston (pres. 1984, bd. dirs. 1982-85), Quota Club, Leadership Jackson. Episcopalian. Home: 114 Windsor Hills Dr Madison MS 39110-8563 Office: The Clarion Ledger 311 E Pearl St Jackson MS 39201-3407

DOWNS, FLORELLA MCINTYRE, civic worker, pilot; b. Selmer, Tenn., Sept. 19, 1921; d. Edward N. and Ella Pearle (Byrd) McIntyre; m. James Harold Downs, May 27, 1946; children: Linda Downs Ulner, William Edward, James Patrick. BA, LaVerne U., 1969. Flight instr., comml. pilot FAA, Memphis, 1945-46; pilot flight examiner CAA, 1946; owner, mgr. Basic Tutoring Svc., Ventura, Calif., 1982-86; civil air patrol pilot, 1956-57. Pres. Naval Officer;s Wives, Patuxent River, Md., 1957; active charitable orgns., Md., Italy, Ventura, Calif., 1946—; vol. Children's Home Soc., Ventura, 1962-70. Ferry pilot WASP, USAF, 1943-44, 1st lt. USAFR, 1952-56. Mem. AAUW (area rep. community issues VTA 1980-82), Women's Air Force Svc. Pilots, Toastmistress (pres. Ventura 1982-83). Democrat. Home: 751 Montgomery Pl Ventura CA 93004-2169

DOWNS, JEANETTE LEE, counselor; b. Detroit, Jan. 31, 1946; d. Bernard LaVerne and Paulina Grace (Howard) McLane; m. Edward Gerald Downs, Oct. 23, 1943 (dec. Aug. 30, 1993); children: Michael Garen, Jonathan Edward. BA, Olivet Nazarene U., 1968; MS, U. Kans., 1981. Cert. secondary tchr., marriage enrichment leader. Tchr. English Carmen Sch. Dist., Flint, Mich., 1968-72; instr. English Olivet Nazarene U., Kankakee, Ill., 1973-75; rschr. Risk Birth Registry, Shawnee, Kans., 1976-79; tchr. English Shawnee Mission (Kans.) Sch. Dist., 1981-86; counselor Assocs. in Family Care, Olathe, Kans., 1986-90; counselor, dir. MidAm. Nazarene Coll., Olathe, Kans., 1990—; chairperson Career Offices of Small Coll., Kans. City, Mo., 1992. Contbr. articles to profl. jours. Mem. APA, Kans. Career Counselors, Coll. Placement Counsel. Republican. Nazarene. Office: Mid America Nazarene Coll 2030 E College Way Olathe KS 66062-1899

DOWNS, KATHLEEN ANNE, healthcare operations director; b. Toledo, Sept. 20, 1951; d. Keith Landis and Cecelia Josephine (Wood) Babcock; m. Michael Brian Thomas, July 17, 1971 (dec. Oct. 1973); m. David Michael Downs, Aug. 8, 1981. Student, San Diego Mesa Coll., 1968-70; BS, Union Inst., 1989. Cert. med. staff coordinator. Sec. Travelodge Internat., Inc., El Cajon, Calif., 1970-73; intermediate stenographer City of El Cajon, 1973-77; adminstrv. asst. MacLellan & Assocs., El Cajon, 1977-78; sr. sec. WESTEC Services, Inc., San Diego, 1978; adminstrv. sec. El Cajon Valley Hosp., 1978-80; asst. med. staff Grossmont Dist. Hosp., La Mesa, Calif., 1980-83, coordinator med. staff, 1983-87, mgr., 1987-94; mgr. med. staff Sharp Meml. Hosp., San Diego, 1994; dir. med. staff svcs. Sharp HealthCare, San Diego, 1994—; tchr. The Vogel Inst., San Diego, 1986; mem. med. staff svcs. adv. com. San Diego Community Dist.; adj. faculty Union Inst., 1991—, Chemeketa Community Coll., 1991—. Mem. Nat. Assn. Med. Staff Svcs. (edn. coun. 1989-93, chmn. 1991-93, mem. editl. bd. Over View 1993—, lectr., speaker), Calif. Assn. Med. Staff Svcs. (treas. San Diego chpt. 1984-86, pres. 1986-87). Office: Sharp Healthcare Crowder Grove 7901 Frost St San Diego CA 92123

DOWNS, MELANIE, minister; b. Denver, Oct. 8, 1957; d. Harmon Jay Jr. and Maryann (Hambrick) D.; m. Fredric David Rosa, May 31, 1986; children: Mark, Katherine. BA summa cum laude, Met. State Coll., 1979; MDiv, Iliff Sch. Theology, 1984. Chaplain Hendrix Coll., Conway, Ark., 1982-83; assoc. min. Grace Meth. Ch., Denver, 1984-86; min. Eagle (Colo.)-Gypsum Meth. Ch., 1986-89; sr. min. Trinity Meth. Ch., Colorado Springs, Colo., 1989—. Mem. bd. ordained ministry United Meth. Ch. Named Outstanding Recent Grad., Iliff Sch. Theology, 1990. Mem. Acad. for Preaching, Joint Rev. Com., Garden of the Gods Rotary Club. Democrat. Office: Trinity United Meth Ch 701 N 20th St Colorado Springs CO 80904-2799

DOYLE, ALISON LOUISE, lawyer; b. Buffalo, N.Y., Nov. 10, 1955; d. Albert W. and Sylvia K. (Keeler) D. Student, Stockholms Univ., Sweden, 1975-76; BA in Internat. Rels., U. Pa., 1977; JD, Georgetown U., 1983, MS in Fgn. Svc., 1983. Contract specialist U.S. Naval Air Sys. Command, Arlington, Va., 1977-79; assoc. McKenna & Cuneo, Washington, 1983—. Contbr. articles to profl. jours. Mem. ABA (vice chair pub. contracts sect. ethics and conflicts of interes com. 1992—, vice chair pub. contracts sect. state and local procurement divsn. 1992-94), Nat. Contract Mgmt. Assn. (com. chair D.C. chpt. 1986-89), D.C. Bar Assn., U. Pa. Alumni Club of D.C. (secondary schs. com. 1989—). Office: McKenna & Cuneo 1575 I St NW Washington DC 20005-1105

DOYLE, CONSTANCE TALCOTT JOHNSTON, physician, educator; b. Mansfield, Ohio, July 8, 1945; d. Frederick Lyman IV and Nancy Jean Bushnell (Johnston) Talcott; m. Alan Jerome Demsky, June 13, 1976; children: Ian Frederick Demsky, Zachary Adam Demsky. BS, Ohio U., 1967; MD, Ohio State U., 1971. Diplomate Am. Bd. Emergency Medicine. Intern Riverside Hosp., Columbus, Ohio, 1971-72; resident in internal medicine Hurley Hosp., U. Mich., Flint, 1972-74; emergency physician Oakwood Hosp., Dearborn, Mich., 1974-76, Jackson County (Mich.) Emergency Svcs., 1975—; cons. Region II EMS, 1978-79, disaster cons., co-chmn. emergency med. svcs. disaster com., 1983—; survival flight physician helicopter rescue svc. U. Mich., 1983-91; course dir. advanced cardiac life support and chmn. advanced life support com. W.A. Foote Meml. Hosp., Jackson, 1979—; clin. instr. emergency svcs., dept. surgery U. Mich., 1981—; instr. Jackson County Emergency Med. Technician refresher courses, Jackson Community Coll. Contbg. author: Clinical Approach to Poisoning and Toxicology, 1983, 89, May's Textbook of Emergency Medicine, 1991, Schwartz Principles and Practice of Emergency Medicine, 1992, Reisdorff Pediatric Emergency Medicine, 1993; contbr. articles to profl. jours. Fellow Am. Coll. Emergency Physicians (pres. Mich. disaster com. 1987-88, bd. dir. Mich. 1979-88, chmn. Mich. disaster com. 1979-85, mem. nat. disaster med. svcs. com. 1983-85, chmn., 1987-88, cons. disaster mgmt. course Fed. Emergency Mgmt. Agy., 1982, treas. 1984-85, emergency med. svcs. com. 1985, pres. 1986-87, councillor 1986-87), Nat. Am. Coll. Emergency Physicians (vice chair sect. of disaster med. svcs. 1990-92, nat. disaster subcom. 1989-90, chair subsection psychological rehab svcs., disaster med. svcs. 1992-94, task force on hazardous materials 1993—, steering com. sect. disaster medicine 1994—); mem. ACP, Am. Med. Women's Assn., Am. Assn. Women Emergency Physicians, Mich. Assn. Emergency Med. Technicians (bd. dirs. 1979-80), Mich. State Med. Soc., Jackson County Med. Soc., Sierra Club. Jewish. Home: 1665 Lansdowne Rd Ann Arbor MI 48105-1052 Office: WA Foote Hosp Emergency Dept Jackson MI 49201

DOYLE, ELIZABETH ANN, developmental engineer; b. Lawrence, Mass.. BS, U. Lowell, 1990. Mfg. engr. Cooper Industries, Brighton, Mass., 1990, devel. engr., 1991, mgr. R & D, 1992, mgr. R & D and quality assurance, 1993—. Bd. dirs., sec. Merrimack Valley Food Bank, Lowell, 1992—. Mem. Soc. Automotive Engrs., Soc. Mfg. Engrs. Office: Wagner Brake Co 145 N Beacon St Brighton MA 02135

DOYLE, GILLIAN, actress; b. Maidenhead, Berkshire, Eng.; came to U.S., 1977; d. John Joseph and Joan (Walker) D. BA in Theatre magna cum laude, Am. U., Washington, 1981. Appeared in (off Broadway mus.) Ernest in Love, N.Y.C., 1980, (plays) No Exit, Washington, 1985, Fefu and Her Friends, 1985, The Winters Tale, 1987, A Christmas Carol, 1987, Erpingham Camp, 1989, Turn of the Screw, 1989, Season's Greetings, 1986, Terra Nova, 1987, Mountain, 1990, Old Favorites, 1991, What the Butler Saw, 1993, Fawlty Towers, 1994, (film) Chances Are, 1989, Born Yesterday, 1993, North, 1993, Decade of Love, 1994, (television) Ancient Prophecies III, 1995, (music video) Johnny Sportcoat and the Casuals, 1987, (comml.) United Way, 1988. Mem. SAG, AFTRA, Actors Equity Assn., Phi Kappa Phi. Democrat. Roman Catholic.

DOYLE, IRENE ELIZABETH, electronic sales executive, nurse; b. West Point, Iowa, Oct. 5, 1920; d. Joseph Deidrich and Mary Adelaide (Groene) Schulte; m. William Joseph Doyle, Feb. 3, 1956. RN, Mercy Hosp., 1941. Courier nurse Santa Fe R.R., Chgo., 1947-50; indsl. nurse Montgomery Ward, Chgo., 1950-54; rep. Hornblower & Weeks, Chgo., 1954-56; v.p. William J. Doyle Co., Chgo., 1956-80, Ormond Beach, Fla., 1980-88. Served with M.C., U.S. Army, 1942-46. Mem. Electronic Reps. Assn. Republican. Roman Catholic. Club: Oceanside Country (Ormond Beach).

DOYLE, JENNIFER, surgical educator, scholar; b. Milw., Aug. 23, 1952; d. Sylvester Edward and Ethel Anna (Axmann) D. BA, Mt. Mary Coll., 1974; MA, U. Wis., 1979; postgrad., Brown U., 1979-84. Grad. teaching asst. U. Wis., Milw., 1977-79; fellow Brown U., Providence, 1979-80, grad. teaching asst., 1981-84; adj. instr. Bryant Coll., Smithfield, R.I., 1985; adj. instr. history R.I. Coll., Providence, 1986-90; residency coord. dept. family medicine Brown U., Providence, 1986-87, edn. coord. dept. surgery, 1987-90; assoc. surgery Harvard Med. Sch., Boston, 1990-92, lectr. in surgery, 1992—; asst. dir. surg. edn. Deaconess Hosp., Boston, 1990—. Dem. committeeman, Wauwatosa, Wis., 1976-78; mem. Big Sisters of R.I., Providence, 1980-88; co-organizer Providence Freeze Coalition, 1982. Recipient Charles Edison Meml. fellowship, 1974, Lucetta Bissell Meml. fellowship, 1978, univ. fellowship Brown U., 1979, Wayland Collegium fellowship Brown U., 1988. Mem. Am. Ednl. Rsch. Assn., Assn. Am. Med. Colls., Assn. Surg. Edn., Assn. Program Dirs. in Surgery (assoc.), Assn. of Women Surgeons (assoc.), Assn. for Study of Med. Edn. (U.K.), Generalists in Med. Edn., Am. Evaluation Assn., AAUW. Home: 219 Willow St West Roxbury MA 02132-1326 Office: Deaconess Harvard Surg Svc 110 Francis St Ste 3B Boston MA 02215-5501

DOYLE, JOELLEN MARY, special education educator; b. N.Y.C., Jan. 19, 1951; d. Daniel Francis and Florence (Ward) D. BA, Wilson Coll., Chambersburg, Pa., 1972; MS in Edn.-Spl. Edn., Coll. New Rochelle (N.Y.), 1974, MS in Edn.-Gifted Edn., 1990; profl. diploma in adminstrn./supervision, Fordham U., N.Y.C., 1984; postgrad., Columbia U. Itinerant tchr. B.O.C.E.S., Port Chester, N.Y., 1974-76; spl. needs tchr., team leader Brookfield (Conn.) Pub. Schs., 1976-81; spl. edn. tchr. Hendrick Hudson Sch. Dist., Montrose, N.Y., 1981-82; spl. edn. tchr., coord. gifted and talented, curriculum coun. mem. Tuckahoe Pub. Schs., Estchester, N.Y., 1982—; coord. sch./coll./bus. partnership, Coll. New Rochelle/IBM, 1990—; grad. asst. Coll. New Rochelle, 1974-75, rsch. asst., 1990; policy bd. Tchrs. Ctr.; mem. steering com., program chair, local coord. BEPT; bd. dirs. Tuckahoe After Sch. Care Program, chair scholarship com. Saturday Morning Math and Sci. Program. Bd. sec. Fordham U. Sch. of Edn. Alumni Assn.(achievement award, 1995). Recipient Recognition Svc. award Tuckahoe PTA, 1990, 91, Alumni Achievement award Fordham U.; nominated for Phoebe Appearson Hearst award and 1993 Tchr. of Yr.; grantee ACES, CEC Found., Meet the Composer Found. Mem. Tuckahoe Tchrs. Assn. (sec., bd. trustees, Tchr. of Yr. 1993), Coun. Exceptional Children (pres.), Conn. Assn. Children with Disabilities (bd. dirs., sec., Hall of Fame award 1982), Bldg. Compact Team, Westchester Assn. Children with Disabilities, Assn. Women Adminstr. in Westchester, Assn. Edn. Gifted Underachieving Students, Kappa Delta Pi. Office: Tuckahoe Pub Schs 2 Siwanoy Blvd Tuckahoe NY 10707-3799

DOYLE, JOYCE ANN, lawyer; b. Youngstown, Ohio, Aug. 13, 1937; d. Norbert Harry Doyle and Corinne (Johnson) McCoy. BA, Youngstown U., 1960; MSW, Cath. U., 1964; JD, Fordham U., 1972. Bar: N.Y. 1973, D.C. 1987, U.S. Supreme Ct., 1991. Assoc. Fogarty, McLaughlin & Semel, N.Y.C., 1973-76; asst. gen. counsel Belco Petroleum Corp., N.Y.C., 1976-85; commr. Fed. Mine Safety and Health Rev. Commn., Washington, 1985—. Mem. D.C. Bar Assn., Women's Bar Assn. D.C. Home: 1514 17th St NW # 6022 Washington DC 20036 Office: Fed Mine Safety & Health Rev Commn Fl 6 1730 K St NW Washington DC 20006-3867

DOYLE, JOYCE ANN, speech language pathologist, consultant; b. Pitts., Jan. 13, 1954; d. William Earle and Patricia (Buckley) Gloeckl; div.; 1 child, Cameron. BS, U. Pitts., 1977, MA, 1981. Cert. clin. competence. Speech pathologist Easter Seal Soc., Pitts., 1981-83; coord. dept. audiology and comm. disorders Children's Hosp. Pitts., 1983—; cons. Western Psychiat. Inst. and Clinic, Pitts., 1987—. Mem. Am. Speech and Hearing Assn., Nat. Head Injury Found., Southwestern Pa. Speech and Hearing Assn., Orton Dyslexia Soc. Democrat. Office: Childrens Hosp Pitts One Children's Pl Pittsburgh PA 15213

DOYLE, JUDITH STOVALL, real estate executive; b. Dothan, Ala., Apr. 19, 1940; d. E.H. and Justine (Knowles) Stovall; m. John P. Doyle Jr., Aug. 22, 1964; children: John Patrick III, Michael D., Julie A. Boedicker. BS, Miss. State Coll. for Women, 1961. Tchr. math., jr. high sch., Gulfport, Miss., 1961-62; asst. dir. dept. pub. rels. SUNY-Buffalo, 1962-64; tchr. math., jr. high schs., Alexandria, Va., 1964-65, Auburn, N.Y., 1970-71; realtor, assoc. Mosher Real Estate, Auburn, 1972-80, Doyle Real Estate, 1991—; owner real estate property, apt. units, Auburn, Boca Raton, Fla. Active, past pres. Mercy Aux., Auburn; chairperson Owasco Bd. Assessment Rev., N.Y., 1976—; v.p. Sacred Heart Parish Council, Auburn, 1985-89; bd. dirs. Unity House, Auburn, 1985-87. Democrat. Roman Catholic. Lodge: Ancient Order Hibernians (charter mem. Ladies Aux. 2).

DOYLE, MARGARET MCCAFFREY, employee benefits consultant; b. Plainfield, N.J., Dec. 3, 1961; d. Thomas Bernard and Joan Violet (Kelly) D. BA, Trinity Coll., 1983. Intern Securities and Exch. Commn./Enforcement Divs., Va., 1983; trust adminstr. 1st Nat. Bank of Cin., 1984-85; trust specialist Bank of Boston, 1985-86; cons., mgr. Coopers & Lybrand, Boston, 1986-88; cons., sr. mgr. employee benefits Deloitte & Touche, Parsippany, N.J., 1988-94; cons. Towers Perrin, Saddle Brook, N.J. and N.Y.C., 1994—. Vol. George Bush for Pres., 1980, Congressman George McEwen, Senator Paula Hawkins, 1981-82; puppeteer The Kids on the Block Program, Inc., N.Y. Cares; vol. Manhattan Spl. Olympics,. Mem. N.Y. Employee Benefits Group, Jr. League. Republican. Roman Catholic. Office: Towers Perrin Plaza Two Park 80 West Saddle Brook NJ 07663

DOYLE, MARJORIE ELLEN SMITH, controller; b. Oakland, Calif., May 5, 1953; d. Hugh Edward and Carol Lucille (Parker) Smith; children: Tyler Edward, Spencer Mills. Student, U. of the Pacific, 1971-74; BA in Liberal Studies, San Jose State U., 1975; MBA, Santa Clara U., 1994. Acctg. clk. Levin Metals Corp., San Jose, 1974-75, office mgr., 1975-78; acctg. supr. Micro Metallics Corp., San Jose, 1978-86, asst. contr., 1986-89, contr., 1989—. Bd. mem. Van Meter Elem. Sch. Home and Sch. Club, Los Gatos, Calif., 1992—. Mem. Inst. Mgmt. Accts., Am. Compensation Assn., Am. Fin. Assn., Alpha Chi Omega Alumni chpt. Gamma Iota Gamma. Democrat. Episcopalian. Office: Micro Metallics Corp 1695 Monterey Hwy San Jose CA 95112-6191

DOYLE, SALLY A., controller; b. Somerville, N.J., Jan. 19, 1956; d. Edward L. and Sarah M. (Wenrich) Padrazas. BA in Bus., Coll. of St. Elizabeth, Convent Station, N.J., 1989. CPA, Ga.; cert. mgmt. acct. Payroll clk. Ethicon, Somerville, 1974-78, asst. supr. payroll, 1978-81, payroll supr., 1981-86; payroll supr. J & J Advanced Materials Co., New Brunswick, N.J., 1986-89; gen. acctg. supr. J & J Advanced Materials Co., New Brunswick, 1989-90; sr. acct. J & J Advanced Materials Co., Gainesville, Ga., 1990-92, plant acctg. mgr., 1992-94; regional plant controller J & J Advanced Materials Co., Benson, N.C., 1994-95; regional contr. Chicopee, Inc., Benson, 1995—. Mem. AICPA, Inst. Mgmt. Accts. Office: Chicopee Inc PO Box 308 Benson NC 27504

DOYLE, SUZANNE, advertising executive. Pres., bd. dirs. Club Cars Inc., Livonia, Mich. Office: Club Cars Inc 38705 Seven Mile Rd Livonia MI 48152*

DOZIER, DONA SUE, airline executive; b. Jan. 4, 1962. BS, Purdue U., 1983. Reservations supr. Britt Airways Inc., Bloomington, Ill., 1983-86; gen. mgr. Britt Airways d.b.a. Continental Express, various locations, 1986-89; regional tng. mgr. Continental Express Airlines, Houston, 1989-92; dir. customer svc. and tng. Lone Star Airlines, Ft. Worth, Tex., 1992—. Bd. dirs. Looking to the Future Ramp Conf., 1991—. Mem. ASCD, NAFE, Am. Soc. Tgn. and Devel., Assn. Quality and Performance, Nat. Soc. Participation and Instrn., Soc. Accelerated Learning and Tchg. Office: Lone Star Airlines 131 E Exchange Ave #222 Fort Worth TX 76106

DOZIER, JOYCE K., sociology educator; b. East Liverpool, Ohio, Mar. 27, 1948; d. Joseph Edward and Helen (Danver) Armstrong; 1 child, Andrea

Katherine Dozier. BBA, Augusta Coll., 1982; MA, Kent State U., 1984, postgrad. Tchg. fellow Kent (Ohio) State U., 1985-89; asst. prof. Wilmington (Ohio) Coll., 1991—; adj. prof. Wright State U., Dayton, Ohio, U. Dayton, Miami Univ., Oxford, Ohio, Ind. Univ., Richmond, 1989-91, Wilmington (Del.) Coll., 1993—; convener Racial Understanding Group, Wilmington, 1991-92; adv. Women of Color, 1993. Bd. dirs. Clinton County Coalition for Prevention of Family Violence, Wilmington, 1991—; instr. Dayton Area AIDS Found., 1993; advisor Clinton County Victim Witness Assistance Program, 1994—; active ACLU. Mem. Am. Correctional Assn., So. Poverty Law Ctr., Soc. for Women in Sociology, Ohio Correctional and Ct. Svcs. Assn. Office: Wilmington Coll Ludovic St Wilmington OH 45177

DOZIER, LINDA GAIL, communications executive; b. Ellensburg, Wash., Jan. 2, 1941; d. Clarence Eugene and Hazel (Thurlow) Anderson; m. Tom J. Dozier, May 8, 1978; children by previous marriage: Colinda M. Cole, Susan T. Cole. BA, U. Wash., 1963; MA, U. So. Calif., 1990. News reporter Yakima (Wash.) Daily Republic, 1963-64; various mgmt. positions Western Airlines, L.A., 1964-78, dir. pub. rels., 1978-87; account supr. Berkhemer Kline Golin/Harris, L.A., 1987-89; mgr. fin. comm. ARCO, L.A., 1989—; bd. dirs. L.A. chpt. Nat. Investor Rels. Inst., ARCO Plaza Fed. Credit Union. Chairperson TV Adv. Bd., City of Torrance, Calif., 1993-94. Mem. Aviation Space Writers, Western Fed. Credit Union (dir. 1983-93), Aero Club So. Calif. (dir., v.p.). Office: ARCO 515 S Flower St Los Angeles CA 90071-2201

DOZIER, NANCY POPE, customer service administrator; b. Phila., May 24, 1955; d. Oliver Rothchild and Beatrice Nellie (Wooding) Pope; m. Henry Washington Dozier, Jr., Oct. 8, 1988; 1 child, Lindsay Marie. BA, Morgan State U., 1977. Personal lines underwriter Md. Casualty Co., Balt., 1978-83; claims supr. Selective Ins. Co., Hunt Valley, Md., 1983-88; customer svc. supr. ITT Hartford-Personal Ins. Ctr., Charlotte, N.C., 1988—; mem. ins. program adv. com. Ctrl. Piedmont C.C., Charlotte, 1990-91. Mem. exec. bd. St. Mark's Child Devel. Ctr., Charlotte, 1992—. Mem. Charlotte Assn. Ins. Women (chmn. cmty. svcs. 1988—), Alpha Kappa Alpha. Home: 6540 Wickville Dr Charlotte NC 28215

DRAAYER, SHARI LYNN, sociologist; b. Clorinda, Iowa, Dec. 11, 1948; d. Gerald and Barbara (McGregor) Draayer; children (adopted): Ryan, Randy, Rodney, Gregory, Halle. BA cum laude, Eastern Coll., St. Davids, Pa., 1987; MA in Sociology summa cum laude, Temple U., 1989, postgrad. Hotline counselor, trainer Aware Shelter & Emergency Counseling Ctr., Inc., Jackson, Mich., 1978-83; adminstrv. assoc. Foote Hosp., Jackson, 1982-83; counselor, night mgr. Laurel House, Montgomery County, Pa., 1984-87; teaching asst. Temple U., Phila., 1987—; rsch. intern Women's Ctr. Montgomery County, Norristown, Pa., 1988-89; lectr. in Sociology Chestnut Hill Coll., Phila., 1988—; intern clin. and forensic sociology Walden Counseling and Therapy Ctr., Bryn Mawr, Pa., 1989; clin. sociologist, dir. McGregor Counseling and Therapy Assocs., Norristown, 1981-94; foster care social worker and parent trainer Luth. Children and Family Svcs., Upper Darby, Pa., 1993—; adj. prof. Eastern Coll., Pa., 1991—; specialized foster parent adoption and foster care agys., Utah, Mich., Pa. Mem. Am. Sociol. Assn., Sociol. Practice Assn., Eastern Sociol. Assn. Office: Luth Children/Family Svc 45 Garrett Rd Upper Darby PA 19082-2302

DRACHMAN, SALLY SPAID, educational foundation administrator; b. Washington, July 3, 1931; d. William and Estelle (Abbott) Spaid; m. Harold D. Adamson, Aug. 23, 1952 (div. 1972); children: David, Douglas, Daniel; m. Roy P. Drachman, Mar. 16, 1978. BS, U. Ariz., 1951, MEd, 1974, PhD in Adminstrn., 1983. Tchr. Vine Grove (Ky.) High Sch., 1952-54; co-counselor Student Counseling Bur. U. Ariz., Tucson, 1973, in-svc. trainer Student Housing, 1978-84, project dir. Student Housing, 1974-84; devel. officer U. Ariz. Found., Tucson, 1983-84, exec. dir. Pres.'s Club, 1984-90, dir. devel. Ariz. Arthritis Ctr., 1986-90, dir. devel. Ariz. Astronomy, 1988-90, assoc. dir. major gifts, 1990—; chair Nat. Philanthropy Day Conf. and Banquet, Tucson, 1991. Contbr. articles to profl. jours. Bd. dirs. La Jolla (Calif.) Cancer Rsch. Ctr., 1989—, Div. Sch. of Pacific, Berkeley, Calif., 1989—, Tucson Symphony, 1983-91, pres., 1988-90; hon. chair Women on Move Banquet, Tucson, 1990; mem. Ariz. Women's Town Hall, Chandler, 1991, Ariz. Town Hall, Grand Canyon, 1991. Recipient Ann Eve Johnson award Jr. League Tucson, Inc., 1993; named to Order of Omega Greek Hall of Fame, U. Ariz., 1994. Mem. AAUW, Nat. Soc. Exec. Fundraisers (cert., bd. dirs. local chpt. 1989—, pres.-elect 1993, Fund Raising Exec. of the Yr. award 1993), Women Mgrs., Pi Delta Kappa, Pi Lambda Theta. Office: U Ariz Found 1111 N Cherry Ave Tucson AZ 85721-0001

DRACHNIK, CATHERINE MELDYN, art therapist, artist; b. Kansas City, Mo., June 7, 1924; d. Gerald Willis and Edith (Gray) Weston; m. Joseph Brennan Drachnik, Oct. 6, 1946; children: Denise Elaine, Kenneth John. BS, U. Md., 1945; MA, Calif. State U., Sacramento, 1975. Lic. family and child counselor; registered art therapist. Art therapist Vincent Hall Retirement Home, McLean, Va., Fairfax Mental Health Day Treatment Ctr., McLean, Arlington (Va.) Mental Health Day Treatment Ctr., 1971-72, Hope for Retarded, San Jose, Calif., Sequoia Hosp., Redwood City, Calif., 1972-73; supervising tchr. adult edn. Sacramento Soc. Blind, 1975-77; ptnr. Sacramento Div. Mediation Svcs., 1981-82; instr. Calif. State U., Sacramento, 1975-82, 92-93, Coll. Notre Dame, Belmont, Calif., 1975—; art therapist, mental health counselor Psych West Counseling Ctr. (formerly Eskaton Am. River Mental Health Clinic), Carmichael, Calif., 1975-93; instr. U. Utah, Salt Lake City, 1988-92; lectr. in field. One woman shows throughout Calif., East Coast and abroad; group juried shows in Calif. and Orient. Active various charitable orgns. Mem. Art Therapy Assn. (hon. life, pres. 1987-89), No. Calif. Art Therapy Assn. (hon. life), Calif. Coalition Rehab. Therapists, Nat. Art Edn. Assn., Am. Assn. Marriage and Family Therapists, Kappa Kappa Gamma Alumnae Assn. (pres. Sacramento Valley chpt. 1991-92), Alpha Psi Omega, Omicron Nu. Republican. Home and Office: 4124 American River Dr Sacramento CA 95864-6025

DRAGO-SEVERSON, ELEANOR ELIZABETH, middle school and secondary education educator; b. N.Y.C., Nov. 25, 1961; d. Rosario Philip and Betty Louise (Brisgal) Drago; m. David Irving Severson, Dec. 30, 1989. BA summa cum laude, L.I. U., 1986; EdM, Harvard U., 1989, postgrad., 1991—. Cert. biology, chemistry tchr., N.Y. Math. tchr. Palm Beach (Fla.) Acad., 1986-87; high sch. math. tchr., basketball coach Hackley Sch., Tarrytown, N.Y., 1988-89; biology tchr., dir. human devel. Palm Beach Day Sch., 1990-91, dir. human devel., 1992; tchg. fellow Harvard U., Cambridge, Mass., 1993—; co-dir. J.V. Mara C.Y.O. Sports Camp, Putnam Valley, N.Y., summer 1987. Mem. colloquilium com. Harvard U., Cambridge, Mass., 1991, 92, now chmn.; mentor to incoming grad. students, 1992-95. Joseph Klingenstein fellow, 1987, teaching fellow 1994—; named Doctoral fellow, 1994. Mem. ASCD, AAUW, APA, AERA, Phi Eta. Home: 39 Kirkland St Ste 403 Cambridge MA 02138

DRAKE, DIANE MARIE, English language educator; b. Webster, S.D., Apr. 3, 1950; d. Earl and Berniece (Schmidt) D. BA in English, Augustana Coll., Sioux Falls, S.D., 1972; MA in English, S.D. State U., 1976, MIddlebury Coll. Breadloaf Sch, 1985; PhD in English, U. N.D., 1992. English/Spanish instr. Irene (S.D.) Schs., 1972-74; grad. teaching asst. in English S.D. State U., Brookings, 1974-76; jr. h.s. English, Spanish tchr. Hopkins (Minn.) Pub. Schs., 1972-82; sr. h.s. English, Spanish tchr. Sauk Ctr. (MInn.) Pub. Schs., 1977-82; English instr. Northland C.C., Thief River Falls, Minn., 1982—; grad. teaching asst. U. N.D., Grand Forks, 1990-91; mem. articulation coun. for composition Minn. Higher Edn. Merger Commn., 1992-94. Editor: (book) Coya Come Home, 1989; presenter dramatic monologue Drama Presentation Lydia Maria Guild, 1990-94. Women's Studies Essay Contest award, U. N.D., 1990. Mem. Northland C.C. Faculty Assn. (local chpt. pres. 1988-90), Modern Lang. Assn., Nat. Coun. Tchrs. of English, Women in Higher Edn., Western Lit. Assn. Home: 919 Labree Ave N Thief Rvr Fls MN 56701-1636 Office: Northland CC English Dept Thief Rvr Fls MN 56701

DRAKE, ELISABETH MERTZ, chemical engineer; b. N.Y.C., Dec. 20, 1936; d. John and Ruth (Johnson) Mertz; m. Alvin William Drake, July 31, 1957 (div. 1984); 1 child, Alan Lee. S.B. in Chem. Engring., MIT, 1958, Sc.D. in Chem. Engring., 1966. Registered profl. engr., Mass. Staff engr. Arthur D. Little Inc., Cambridge, Mass., 1958-64, sr. staff, 1966-76, mgr. risk analysis, 1977-82, v.p. tech. risk mgmt., 1980-82, 86-89, cons., 1990-94; assoc. dir. new tech. MIT Energy Lab., 1990—; acting dir., 1994—, MIT Energy Lab., 1994—; lectr. U. Calif., Berkeley, 1971; vis. prof. MIT, Cambridge, 1973-74; chmn. chem. engring. dept. Northeastern U., Boston, 1982-86; corp. mgr. MIT, 1981-86; mem. tech. pipeline safety stds. com. U.S. Dept. Transp., 1980-85; mem. mng. bd. Ctr. for Chem. Process Safety, 1988-90; vice chair com. on rev. and evaluation on army chem. stockpile disposal program NRC, 1993—. Contbr. articles to profl. jours.; inventor fractionation method and apparatus, 1972. Fellow AIChE (bd. dirs. 1987-90); mem. AAAS, NAE, Am. Chem. Soc., Sigma Xi. Home: 30F Inman St Cambridge MA 02139-2411

DRAKE, GRACE L., state senator; b. New London, Conn., May 25, 1926; d. Daniel Harvey and Marion Gertrude (Wiech) Driscoll; m. William Lee Drake (dec.), June 9, 1946; children—Sandra DeNobile Drake. With Am. Photographic Corp., N.Y.C., 1944-72; senator State of Ohio, Columbus, 1984—. Mem. Carmelite Guild of Cleve., 1973—, Tech. Leadership Coun., Leadership Cleve., Cleve. Music Sch. Settlement. Recipient Outstanding Woman award Nat. Fedn. Rep. Women, 1984; named Legislator of Yr. Nat. Rep. Legis's. Assn, 1988, Public Official of Yr Ohio chpt. Nat. Assn. Social Workers, 1989, Outstanding Legislator of Yr. Ohio Speech and Hearing Assn., 1989. Roman Catholic. Avocations: bridge, golf. Office: Ohio Senate State Capital Columbus OH 43215*

DRAKE, JANET MARIE, office and corporate risk manager; b. Mineola, N.Y., Nov. 9, 1952; d. Alexander and Antonio (Capone) Kolomick; m. John Thomas Drake, June 25, 1974 (div. 1985); children: Carrie Elizabeth, Alexander Kolomick. Grad. high sch., Port Jefferson, N.Y., 1970. Ins. lic. for property and casualty. Project clk. Stone & Webster Engring. Corp., Boston, 1974, sr. project clk., 1974-75; adminstrv. asst. Weiss & Assocs., Montreal, 1975-77; sec. Southworth Machinery, Inc., Hopkinton, Mass., 1985-87, asst. office mgr., 1987-88; office mgr. Southworth Machinery, Inc., Milford, Mass., 1988—; risk mgr. Southworth-Milton, Inc., Milford, 1991—; safety com. Southworth Machinery, Inc., 1988—. Treas. Califon (N.J.) PTA, 1984-85. Mem. Risk and Ins. Mgmt. Soc. Roman Catholic. Office: Southworth-Milton Inc 100 Quarry Dr Milford MA 01757-1729

DRAKE, JESSICA, dialect and speech coach; b. L.A., Apr. 25, 1956; d. Kenneth and Sylvie D. BA, Julliard Sch. Drama, 1981. Accent reduction/speech coach UCLA, 1988—; faculty, dialect coach L.A. City Coll., 1988-90; faculty, speech/dialect Am. Acad. Dramatic Art, Pasadena, Calif., 1986-88, Calif. inst. for Arts, Valencia, 1989-90. Dialect coach: (films) Don Juan de Marco and The Centerfold, 1995, Geronimo, 1994, I'll Do Anything, 1994, Forrest Gump, 1994, Ed Wood, 1994, What's Love Got To Do With It, 1993, Bram Stoker's Dracula, 1992, Ruby, 1992, Hot Shots, 1991, Indian Runner, 1991, Shattered, 1991, (TV shows) A Woman of Independent Means, 1995, A Streetcar Named Desire, 1995, Return to Lonesome Dove, 1993, Murder Between Friends, 1993, Brooklyn Bridge, 1991-93, An Inconvenient Woman, 1991, The Broken Chain, 1993; actress: (TV shows) A Woman of Independent Means, 1995, Return to Lonesome Dove, 1993, thirtysomething, 1989, Highway to Heaven, 1988, 87, Return of Dennis the Menace, 1987, others; extensive stage work in regional theatre. Recipient Edith Skinner Speech award Julliard Sch. Drama, N.Y.C., 1979. Office: c/o Diane Kamp PO Box 1185 Big Timber MT 59011-1185

DRAKE, MIRIAM ANNA, librarian, educator; b. Boston, Dec. 20, 1936; d. Max Frederick and Beatrice Celia (Mitchell) Engleman; m. John Warren Drake, Dec. 19, 1960 (div. Dec. 1985); 1 child, Robert Warren. BS, Simmons Coll., Boston, 1958, MLS, 1971; postgrad., Harvard U., 1959-60; LittD (hon.), Ind. U., 1994, LHD (hon.), 1994. Assoc. United Research, Cambridge, Mass., 1958-61; with mktg. services Kenyon & Eckhardt, Boston, 1963-65; cons. Boston, 1965-72; head research unit libraries Purdue U., West Lafayette, Ind., 1972-76, asst. dir. libraries, prof. library sci., 1976-84; dean, dir. libraries, prof. Ga. Inst. Tech., Atlanta, 1984—; trustee Online Computer Libr. Ctr., Inc., 1978-84, chair, 1980-83; trustee Corp. for Rsch. and Edn. Networking, 1991-94, U.S. Depository Libr. Coun., 1991-94. Author: User Fees: A Practical Perspective, 1981; co-author: (with James Matarazzo) Information for Management, 1994; mem. editl. bd. Coll. and Rsch. Librs. Jour., 1985-90, Librs. and Microcomputers Jour., 1983—, Sci. and Tech. Librs., 1989—, Database, 1989—; contbr. chpts. to books, articles to profl. jours. Recipient Alumni Achievement award Simmons Coll. Sch. Libr. and Info. Sci., 1985, Kent Meckler Media award U. Pitts., 1994. Mem. ALA (councilor at large 1985-89, Hugh Atkinson Meml. award 1992), Am. Mgmt. Assn., Am. Soc. Info. Sci., Spl. Librs. Assn. (pres.-elect 1992-93, pres. 1993-94, H.W. Wilson award 1983). Office: Ga Inst Tech Lib Info Ctr Atlanta GA 30332

DRAKE, NANCY BETH NUGENT, residential designer; b. Hackensack, N.J., Apr. 19, 1954; d. Fredrick George and Mildred Shirley (Grieder) Nugent; m. Gayland Duane, May 26, 1979; 1 child, Keaton Max. Student, Massey Jr. Coll., 1971, Vocat. Tech. Inst. Sarasota, 1972; studied pottery and ceramic design with Frank Colson, Sarasota, Fla., 1973; AA, Manatee C.C., 1982, postgrad., 1989; postgrad. in art history and design, U. So. Fla., 1982; cert. designer, Vocat. Tech. Inst. Sarasota, 1984; postgrad., Ringlin Sch. Art, 1990, Vocat. Tech. Inst. Sarasota, 1992, Eckerd Coll., 1993—. Registered real estate sales assoc. Asst. interior design dept. Richmond Constrn. Corp., Sarasota, 1972; draftsperson, sec. Winningham and Lively, Inc., Venice, Fla., 1975-76; asst. mgr., chef Le Petit Jardin Cafe, Venice, 1976-77, 78-79; sec., receptionist A.G. Edwards & Sons, Inc., Venice, 1977; ward clk. Venice Hosp., 1977-78; realtor assoc. Bradway, Moore & Assoc., Inc., Venice, 1979-80; grower Gorenflo Wholesale Nursery, Venice, 1980; draftperson surveying and civil engring. Brigham & Winningham, Inc., Venice, 1983-84; draftsperson archtl. and site devel. landscape design Vodicka, Toth & Assoc., Bradenton, Fla., 1984-85; owner, designer Frog Creek Studio, Venice and Palmetto, Fla., 1985—; residential designer, draftperson Robert Miller Homes, Murdock, Fla., 1993; salesperson Boatyard Ctr. Don Freedman Designs, Sarasota, 1992; mgr. Collectors Gallery, Venice, 1994-95; part-time salesperson Paradox, Sarasota. Illustrator: (book) Kiln Building With Space Age Materials, 1975; pottery exhibited at Paradox Gallery, Sarasota. Vol. Youth Coun. Sarasota County Commn., 1972, Drug Rehab. Ctr., Bradenton and Sarasota, 1971-72, Triangle Inn Restoration Project, Venice, 1992—, Venice Mainstreet Design Com., 1992, 93, 94. Recipient various art awards Sarasota County Art Assn., 1968-70. Mem. Fla. Residential Designers Assn. (bd. dirs. 1990-93, sec. 1993, Designer's Choice award 1990, Merit award 1990), Fla. Real Estate Commn. (sales assoc. 1979—). Home and Office: 1109 Groveland Ave Venice FL 34292

DRAKE, PATRICIA EVELYN, psychologist; b. Lewiston, Maine, Feb. 9, 1946; d. Lewis and Anita (Bilodeau) D.; m. Colin Matthew Fuller, May 13, 1973 (div. Aug. 1983); children: R. Matthew, Meaghan Merry. Diploma, St. Mary's Sch. Nursing, 1967; BS, U. Nev., 1985; MA, Calif. Sch. Profl. Psychology, 1987, PhD, 1989. RN. Nurse Maine Med. Ctr., Portland, 1967-73, U. Calif. Sacramento Med. Ctr., 1973-78, Ben Taub Hosp., Houston, 1978-79; psychology intern Shasta County Mental Health Ctr., Redding, Calif., 1988-89, clin. psychologist, 1989-91, tng. dir., chief psychology, 1991—; psychologist pvt. practice, Redding, Calif., 1991—. Mem. AAUW, APA, Calif. Psychol. Assn., Shasta County Psychol. Assn., Phi Kappa Phi. Democrat. Roman Catholic. Office: Shasta County Mental Health 2640 Breslauer Way Redding CA 96001 also: 2464 Old Eureka Way Reading CA 96001

DRAKE, SARAH FRANCES ASHFORD, electronic manufacturing company executive; b. Dallas, Jan. 31, 1943; d. Roger F. and Rosa M. (Hancock) Ashford; children: Sonja Mozelle Ayers, Monica Grace Harding. Student pub. schs., Odessa, Tex. Bookkeeper 1st State Bank, Odessa, 1963-64; pres. Magnum Mfg., Inc., Austin, 1974—. Recipient Outstanding Achievement for Entrepreneurship award Univ. YWCA, Austin, 1990; named Mfr. of Yr., Austin C. of C., 1990, Employer of Yr., Goodwill Industries Cen. Tex., 1990, Nat. Employer of Yr., Goodwill Industries of Am., 1991. Mem. Leadership Austin. Baptist. Office: Magnum Mfg Inc 1915 Kramer Ln Austin TX 78758-4009

DRAKE, SYLVIE (JURRAS DRAKE), theater critic; b. Alexandria, Egypt, Dec. 18, 1930; came to U.S., 1949, naturalized, 1952; d. Robert and Simonette (Barda) Franco; m. Kenneth K. Drake, Apr. 29, 1952 (div. Dec. 1972); children—Jessica, Robert I.; m. Ty Jurras, June 16, 1973. M. Theater Arts, Pasadena Playhouse, 1969. Free-lance TV writer, 1962-68; theater critic Canyon Crier, L.A., 1968-72; theater critic, columnist L.A. Times, 1971-91, theater critic, 1991-93, theatre critc emeritus, 1993—; lit. dir. Denver Ctr. Theatre Co., 1985; free lance travel writer, book reviewer, pres. L.A. Drama Critics Circle, 1979-81; mem. Pulitzer Prize Drama Jury, 1994; adv. bd. Nat. Arts Journalism Program. Dir. media rels. and publs. Denver Ctr. for the Performing Arts, 1994—; artistic assoc. for spl. projects Denver Ctr. Theatre Co., 1994—. Mem. Am. Theater Critics Assn. Office: Denver Ctr for Performing Arts 1245 Champa St Denver CO 80204-2104

DRAKOS, IRENE SASSO, chemist; b. Bklyn., Dec. 28, 1932; d. Peter John and Lillian (Abraham) Sasso; m. James Drakos; children: Diane Eugenia Drakos Jaeger, Melissa Ann Drakos Maurer. BA, Agnes Scott Coll., Decatur, Ga., 1954; MA, Central Mich. U., 1988. Chemist Pontiac div. GM, Pontiac, Mich., 1955-59; consumer chemist Texize Chems., Greenville, S.C., 1959-64; plant chemist Cryovac div. W.R. Grace Co., Simpsonville, S.C., 1965-66; sr. project specialist automotive ops. Rockwell Internat., Troy, Mich., 1966-90, chemistry lab. supr. automotive ops., 1990—. Mem. Am. Chem. Soc., Soc. Automotive Engrs., Soc. Plastic Engrs., Soc. Detroit Inst. Arts (founder), Detroit Rubber Group, Smithsonian Inst., Toastmasters (pres. 1984-85), Rockwell Women's Club (treas. 1983-84). Greek Orthodox. Office: Rockwell Internat 2135 W Maple Rd Troy MI 48084-7121

DRANT, SANDRA ELIZABETH, court reporter, educator; b. L.A., July 18, 1939; d. Archie Delbert and Clara Mae (Sether) DeLane; m. Richard David Drant, Sept. 5, 1959 (div. 1965), m. Feb. 3, 1966; children: Stacey Allada, Ryan David. AA, Cypress Coll., 1989; BA in English, Chapman U., 1992; postgrad. in Edn., Pepperdine U., 1992—. Cert. shorthand reporter, cert. reporting instr. Freelance reporter Long Beach, Calif., 1960-65; state hearing reporter Calif. Unemployment Ins. Appeals Bd., Long Beach, Workers' Compensation Appeals Bd., Bell Gardens, 1972-82; cert. reporting instr. Cerritos Coll., Norwalk, Calif., 1990—. Vol. chaperone Mammoth Mountain Ski Edn. Found., Mammoth Lakes, Calif., 1982-84; co-chair Grad-Night com. Mammoth High Sch., Mammoth Lakes, 1988; vol. archaeologist Cypress Coll., 1989—. Recipient Cert. of Recognition Calif. Legis. Assembly, 1993; named Parent of Yr., Mammoth Mountain Ski Edn. Found., 1983-84. Mem. AAUW, Nat. Ct. Reporters Assn., Calif. Ct. Reporters Assn., Faculty Assn. Calif. C.C.s, Pacific Coast Archaeol. Soc., Stanford Univ. Mothers Club (vol. contbr. 1988—). Home: 4109 Avenida Sevilla Cypress CA 90630-3413 Office: Cerritos Coll 11110 Alondra Blvd Norwalk CA 90650-6298

DRANTZ, VERONICA ELLEN, science educator and consultant; b. Chgo., Sept. 5, 1943; d. Albert William and Veronica Grace (Crowe) D. BS with high honors, U. Ill., Urbana, 1965, MS, 1969; PhD, De Paul U., Chgo., 1987. Biol. sci. forensic analytical chemist Chgo. Police Dept., Chgo., 1970-72, asst. head forensic analytical chemist, 1972-74; instr. Ravenswood Hosp. Sch. Anesthesia, Chgo., 1975—; instr. East-West Univ., Chgo., 1982-84, dir. biol. and phys. sciences, 1984—, asst. prof., 1987-88, assoc. prof., 1988-91, prof., 1991—, dir. electroneurodiagnostic technology program, 1988—; adj. prof. in MS of nursing DePaul U., Chgo., 1989—; speaker Ill. Assn. Nurse Anesthetists, 1978-80, Ill. Soc. ElectroneurodiagnosticTech., 1986-94, Am. Soc. Electroneurodiagnostic Tech., 1994—; sci. cons., speaker Chgo. Tchrs. Ctr., 1989; instr. Chgo. Heart Assn., 1989—. Co-author: Population Genetics A BSCS Self Instructional Prog., 1969. Recipient Rsch. assistantship NSF, U. Ill., 1965-66, Rsch. Fellowship NSF, U. Ill., 1966-70, Schmidt Acad. fellowship Schmidt Found., DePaul U., 1975-80, Cardiopulmonary Resuscitation award Chgo. Heart Assn., 1990. Mem. Phi Beta Kappa. Office: 4942 W School St Chicago IL 60641

DRAPER, MARY ELLEN LYTTON, writer; b. Staunton, Va., Nov. 30, 1940; m. David W. Draper, November 30, 1940; children: David W. Jr., Darryl L. BA, Coll. of William and Mary, Williamsburg, Va., 1962; MALS, Georgetown U., 1988, postgrad., 1989-91. Freelance writer; editor-in-chief Colonial Echo, Coll. William and Mary. Mem. NAFE, AAUW, Am. Orchid Soc., Nat. Capitol Orchid Soc., Hist. Staunton Found., Nat. Geographic Soc., Washington Opera Guild, Tamarack Civic Assn., Sierra Club, World Wildlife Fund, Nat. Audubon Soc., Soc. of the Alumni Coll. William and Mary (Met. Washington area), Pi Delta Epsilon, Chi Delta Phi, Psi Chi. Baptist. Home and Office: 1602 Northcrest Dr Silver Spring MD 20904-1459

DRAZIN, LISA, real estate and corporate investment banker, financial consultant; b. Washington, Nov. 26, 1953; d. Sidney and Bernice Ann (Jeweler) D. A.B. with honors, Wellesley Coll., 1976; M.B.A., George Washington U., 1980. Chartered Financial Analyst. Securities analyst Geico, Inc., Chevy Chase, Md., 1982; mng. prin. Jefferson Securities Ltd., Bethesda, Md., 1983; chmn., chief exec. officer Drazin & Co., Inc., Bethesda, 1983-89, Drazin Properties, Inc., Bethesda, 1985-89, Drazin Securities, Inc., Bethesda, 1985-88; chmn., chief exec. officer Woodmont Asset Mgmt., Inc., 1989—; affiliate Montgomery County Bd. Realtors; real estate investment banker Restructuring Fed. Deposit Ins. Corp. Founder, Ivy Connection, Washington, 1982; bd. dirs. Friends of Tel Aviv U., active planning com. Jewish Nat. Fund. Mem. Nat. Trust for Historic Preservation, UJA Fedn. of Greater Washington (young leadership divsn., Ruth Heritage Forum), Am. Friends Hebrew U., Nat. Kidney Found. Fellow Wexner Heritage Found., Assn. for Investment Mgmt. and Rsch.; mem. Nat. Assn. Realtors, Comml. Investment Real Estate Council, Realtors Nat. Mktg. Inst., Wash. Soc. Investment Analysts, Inc., Beta Gamma Sigma. Club: Wellesley (interns coordinator, recent grads. rep. 1981-84) (Washington), Ben Gurion. Office: Woodmont Asset Mgmt Inc 4600 East West Hwy Ste 300 Bethesda MD 20814-3415

DREES, ELAINE HNATH, artist and educator; b. Orange, N.J., Aug. 20, 1929; d. John Anthony and Helen Louise (Godlesky) Hnath; m. Thomas Clayton Drees, Feb. 9, 1952; children: Danette, Clayton, Barry, Nancy. A.Comml. Art, Parsons Sch. Design, N.Y.C. Colorist and designer Hesse Wallpaper, N.Y.C., 1950-51; designer Lanz Wallpaper, N.Y.C., 1951-52; gallery asst. Longpre Gallery, La Canada, Calif., 1976-78; pvt. art tchr. La Canada, Calif., 1985—; pres. Elly's Originals, La Canada, 1980—. One-woman shows include La Canada, Calif., 1984, Barbara's Gallery, Agoura, Calif., 1989; group shows include Hasenbein Gallery, Glendale, Calif., 1978, White's Gallery, Montrose, Calif., 1980, Graphic Showcase Gallery, Pas, Calif., 1985, Artistic Endeavors Gallery, Simi Valley, Calif., 1987, Mission West Gallery, South Pasadena, Calif., 1991; commns. include paintings for Alpha Therapeutic, Pasadena, 1980, Shannon Interiors, Pasadena, 1988-92; contbr. reproductions to Cal. Art Rev. 1989. Recipient Cert. of Honor, Centre Internat. D'Art Contemporain, Paris, 1984. Mem. Verdugo Hills Art Assn. (awards 1988-94). Republican. Roman Catholic. Home and Studio: 784 Saint Katherine Dr La Canada CA 91011-4119

DREHER, NANCY C., federal judge; b. 1942. BA, U. Wis., 1964, JD, 1967. Bar: Minn. 1967, U.S. Dist. Ct. Minn. 1969, U.S. Ct. Appeals (8th cir.) 1969, U.S. Supreme Ct. 1981. Law clk. to chief justice Calif. Supreme Ct., San Francisco, 1967-68; assoc. Leonard, Street & Deinard, 1968-72, ptnr., 1973-88; bankruptcy judge U.S. Dist. Ct., Mpls., 1988—. Recipient Pres. Award for Profl. Excellence, Minn. State Bar Assn., 1985. Office: US Dist Ct Towle Bldg 330 2nd Ave S Rm 600 Minneapolis MN 55401-2211*

DREHOFF, DIANE WYBLE, electrical engineer, total quality director; b. Amarillo, Tex., Oct. 11, 1950; d. James Stanley and Barbara Luella (Park) Wyble; m. John James Drehoff III, June 25, 1977; children: John, Brian, David. BSEE, Stanford U., 1972. Mktg. rep. Westinghouse, Jefferson City, Mo., 1972-74; sales engr. Westinghouse, Balt., 1974-75; Congl. fellow IEEE, Washington, 1976; govt. rep. Westinghouse, Washington, 1977-80; mktg. staff mgr. Westinghouse, Phila., 1980-81, regional mktg. mgr., 1981-82; regional mktg. mgr. Westinghouse, Orlando, Fla., 1982-84, projects mgr., 1986-89, sales staff mgr., 1989-91, total quality dir., 1991—. Contbr. tech. papers to profl. jours. Sun. sch. tchr. Community Alliance Ch., Orlando, 1989-93; participant Leadership Orlando C. of C., 1991-92. Recipient IEEE Congl. fellowship IEEE, 1976, Quality Achievement award Westinghouse, 1985, Corp. Controllers award Westinghouse, 1991. Mem. IEEE (spectrum editorial bd. 1980-81, Congl. fellows selection 1983, long-range planning com. 1989), Am. Soc. for Quality Control, IEEE/Power Engring. Soc. Office: Westinghouse Electric Corp The Quadrangle 4400 N Alafaya Trl Orlando FL 32826-2398

DREIZEN, ALISON M., lawyer; b. Bklyn., Sept. 14, 1952; d. Nathan Dreizen and Florence (Morgenstern) Barth. BA, Cornell U., 1974; JD, Harvard U., 1977. Assoc. White & Case, N.Y.C., 1977-85, ptnr., 1985-93; ptnr. White & Case, Moscow, 1993—. Mem. Bar Assn. City of N.Y. Office: White & Case 1155 Avenue Of The Americas New York NY 10036-2711

DRENNEN, EILEEN MOIRA, editor; b. Suffern, N.Y., May 27, 1956; d. D.A. and M. Eileen (Connolly) D.; m. Robert Wesley Townsend, Aug. 27, 1982. AA, Dutchess C.C., N.Y., 1978; BA in English, Fla. State U., 1983. Writer Fla. Flambeau, Tallahassee, 1980-84, editor, 1984-86; features editor Marietta (Ga.) Daily Jour., 1986-87; copy editor Atlanta Jour.-Constn., Atlanta, 1987-89, asst. arts editor, 1989-90, Leisure editor, 1990-93, Weekend Preview editor, asst. features editor, 1993—. AAUW scholar, 1978; recipient Hon. Mention award Fla. Press Club, 1982, Spotlight award Women in Comm., 1986. Home: 304 Georgia Ave SE Atlanta GA 30312 Office: Atlanta Jour-Constn Arts & Entertainment Desk 72 Marietta St NW Atlanta GA 30303

DRESBACH, MARY LOUISE, program administrator; b. St. Paul, Feb. 17, 1950; d. Ernest Joseph and Kathryn Marion (Lauer) Mathes; m. David Philip Dresbach, Nov. 29, 1980. BA, Coll. St. Catherine, 1972; postgrad., U. St. Thomas, 1979-80; MA, Coll. of St. Catherine, 1995. Teacher St. Paul Pub. Schs., 1974-78; program mgr. Minn. Higher Edn. Coord. Bd., St. Paul, 1978—. Mem. AAUW, Am. Bus. Women's Assn. (sec. 1979-80), Nat. Assn. Exec. Women, Mpls. Inst. Arts, Met. Mus. Art, Dakota County Leadership Initiative, Phi Beta Kappa, Pi Gamma Mu.

DRESCHER, DEBRA LYNN, nurse; b. Gary, Ind., Nov. 5, 1955; d. Robert H. Plews and Doris O. (Tuthill) Broomhead; m. Mark S. Drescher, Jan. 8, 1983; children: David Mark, Jennifer Lynn, Danielle Helen. ADN, Ind. U., Gary, 1982. Cert. med.-surg. nurse. Staff nurse Meth. Hosp., Merrillville, Ind., 1982—. Mem. Meth. Hosp. Order of Lucille. Home: 11040 Forest Ln Demotte IN 46310

DRESCHER, JUDITH ALTMAN, library director; b. Greensburg, Pa., July 6, 1946; d. Joseph Grier and Sarah Margaret (Hewitt) Altman; m. Robert A. Drescher, Aug. 10, 1968 (div. 1980); m. David G. Lindstrom, Jan. 10, 1981. AB, Grove City Coll., 1968; MLS, U. Pitts., 1971. Tchr. Hempfield Sch. Dist., Greensburg, 1968-71; children's libr. Cin. Pub. Libr., 1971-72; br. mgr. Cin. Pub. LIbrary, 1972-74; dir. Rolling Meadows (Ill.) Pub. Libr., 1974-79, Champaign (Ill.) Pub. Libr., 1979-85, Memphis/Shelby County Pub. Libr. and Info. Ctr., 1985—; cons. Providence Assocs., Dallas, 1986—; Tenn. del. White House Conf. on Librs. and Info. Svcs. Task Force, 1991, 92—; mem. Tenn. Sec. of State's Commn. on Tech. and Resource Sharing, 1991, 93, steering com. Tenn. Info. and Infrastructure, 1994—, nat. adv. panel for assessment of role of sch. and pub. librs. U.S. Dept. Edn., 1995—. Mem. Rhodes Coll. Commn. on 21st Century, Memphis, 1986-88, presdl. adv. com. Rhodes Coll., 1992—; mem. Leadership Memphis, 1987—, selection com., 1992—; mem Memphis Arts Coun., 1989—; bd. dirs. Literacy Coun., 1986-91, Memphis NCCJ, 1989-93, Memphis Grants Info. Ctr., 1992—, sec., 1993—; bd. dirs. Memphis Literacy Found., 1988-92, v.p., 1989-90; bd. dirs. Goals for Memphis, 1988-93, chair edn. com., 1989-91, chair nominating com., 1992; mem. exec. adv. bd. Children's Mus., 1988—, exec. adv. coun. U. Memphis, 1989—; mem. allocations subcom. United Way, 1989-91, allocations com. Memphis Arts Coun., 100 for the Arts, 1989-91, Libr. Self-study Com. U. Memphis; pres. adv. coun. Lemoyne Coll. Recipient Govt. Leader award U. Ill. YWCA, 1981; Communicator of Yr. award Pub. Rels. Soc. of Am., 1992. Mem. ALA (chmn. intellectual freedom com. 1986-87, coun. 1992—), Tenn. Libr. Assn., Memphis Libr. Coun., Pub. Libr. Assn. (v.p., pres. 1994-95), Rotary (bd. dirs. 1992-94, sec. 1993-94, chair membership devel. com. 1994—), Beta Phi Mu. Home: 1505 Vance Ave Memphis TN 38104-3810 Office: Memphis Shelby County Pub Libr & Info Ctr 1850 Peabody Ave Memphis TN 38104-4025

DRESKIN, JEANET STECKLER, painter, medical artist, educator; b. New Orleans, Sept. 29, 1921; d. William Steckler and Beate Bertha (Burgas) Steckler Gureasko; m. E. Arthur Dreskin, May 9, 1943; children: Richard Burgas, Stephen Charles, Jeanet Dreskin Haig, Rena Dreskin Schoenberg. BFA, Newcomb Coll., 1942; grad. cert. in med. art Johns Hopkins U., 1943; MFA, Clemson U., 1973; postgrad., Art Students League, N.Y.C., Art Inst. Chgo., 1946, Balt. Mus. Fine Art, 1943. Cert. med. illustrator. Staff artist Am. Mus. Natural History, N.Y.C., 1943-45, U. Chgo. Med. Sch., 1945-50; mem. faculty Mus. Sch. Art, Greenville, S.C., 1950-52, 62—, dir., 1968-75; adj. prof. art U. S.C. at Mus. Sch. Art, 1973—; mem. faculty Govs. Sch. for Arts, Greenville, 1980—; condr. workshops, lectr. in art edn., 1970-93; mem. arts adv. bd. S.C. State Mus., Columbia, 1984-90; workshop leader art dept. U. Ga., 1985; rep. by Fay Gold, Atlanta, Hampton III, Taylors, S.C., also by Art South Gallery, Washington. Group shows Butler Inst. Am. Art, Youngstown, Ohio, 1974, 83, Chataugua exhbn. Am. Art, N.Y., 1970, Nat. Mus. Illustrators, N.Y.C., 1986; represented in permanent collections Nat. Mus. Am. Art, Washington, S.C. State Art Collection, Columbia, Ga. Mus. Art, Athens, Greenville County Mus. Art, Guild Hall Mus., East Hampton, N.Y., Gibbes Mus., Charleston, S.C., Columbia Mus. Art, Tex. Fine Art Assn., Sunrise Valley Mus., Charleston, W.Va., Beaufort Mus., S.C., Kate Shipworth Mus. at U. Miss., McDonald Corp. Coll., Chgo., N.C. Nat. Bank Coll., Asheville (N.C.) Mus. Art, Fed. Res. Bank, Richmond, Va., C & S Collection, Columbia, S.C., U. Ala. Mus.; exhibited at Butler Inst. Am. Art, 1974, 83, Nat. Mus. of Ill., N.Y.C., 1986, Nat. Print and Drawing, Clemson U., 1987-89, 93, Mid.-Am. Arts Alliance, Emporia, Kans., 1989-91, 93, 94, Broome St. Gallery, N.Y.C, Am. Contemporary Artists, 1994, traveling invitational exhbns. of so. graphics, 1990—, numerous others; Contbr. med. drawings to various publs. Mem. community Found. Greenville, 1968-84, chmn. projects com., 1968-76; historian, hon. mem. Rose Ball, Greenville, 1972—; bd. dirs. Charity Ball, Greenville, 1971—. Recipient Kaplan award Nat. Assn. Painters in Casein, 1969, 71, Keenen award Am. Contemporary Exhbn., Palm Beach, Fla., 1970. Mem. Guild S.C. Artists (pres. 1970-71, bd. dirs. 1981-86, numerous awards 1965, 67, 68, 71, 73, 84), S.C. Watercolor Soc. (pres. 1983-84, bd. dirs. 1985—), So. Watercolor (So. Watercolor-Mabry award 1981, 85, 88, numerous other awards), So. Graphics Coun. (invitational exhibits 1975-77, 88, v.p. 81-83, treas. 1988—), Nat. Assn. Women Artists (S.C. membership chmn. 1970—), Nat. Assn. Med. Illustrators, Am. Contemporary Artist N.Y.C., Greenville Artists Guild (pres. 1956-58, 63, bd. dirs. 1954-83). Avocation: sailing. Home: 60 Lake Forest Dr Greenville SC 29609-5038 Office: Mus Sch Art 420 College St Greenville SC 29601-2017

DRESSEL, DIANE LISETTE, dancer, choreographer, electrical designer; b. Las Cruces, N.Mex., Apr. 24, 1955; d. Ralph William Dressel and Elizabeth Tupper (Taylor) Dressel Hoobler; m. Arthur Stephen Bazan, Mar. 24, 1977 (div. June 1982). BFA in Dance, U. N.Mex., 1990; assoc. computer aided draft and design, ITT Tech. Inst., 1992. Journeyman's lic. N.Mex. Apprentice electrician Internat. Brotherhood Elec. Workers Local 611, Albuquerque, 1979-82, journey person electrician, 1982—; relay technician apprentice Plains Electric Generation and Transmission Coop., Albuquerque, 1983-85; dancer Elizabeth Waters Dance Workshop, Inc., Albuquerque, 1985-89; dancer, choreographer Albuquerque, 1983—; dancer, choreographer Mary Wang Sch. of Dance Benefit Prodns., Grants, N.Mex., 1982—; pres. U. N.Mex. Dance Club, Albuquerque, 1988-89; dance tchr. Devel. Dance, Albuquerque, 1988-89; mem., choreographer N.Mex. Dance Coalition, Santa Fe, 1989, 91; mem., pres. student prodn. adv. bd. U. N.Mex. Choreographer, dancer Wolf Eyes, 1982, Stages, 1985, A Little Plumbing Problem, 1988, Butch Babes Don't Wear Bras, 1989, Cypher Breaks the Original Spell, 1990, When I Don't Feel Celebration, 1992, That's How I Know, 1994. Mem. Parkland Hills Neighborhood Assn., Albuquerque, 1988-92. Recipient Elizabeth Waters scholarship U. N. Mex., 1987-90, Disting. Undergrad. scholarship, 1990. Mem. NAFE, NOW, Golden Key Honor Soc., Tech. Vocat. Honor Soc., Phi Kappa Phi. Home: 500 Val Verde Dr SE Albuquerque NM 87108-3464

DRESSEL, IRENE EMMA RINGWALD, alcoholism and family therapist; b. Enderlin, N.D., Oct. 26, 1926; d. Albert William and Emma Anna Magdelena (Trapp) Ringwald; m. Clarence Irvin Dressel, Jr., Mar. 13, 1946 (div. Nov. 1972); 1 son, Keith Alan. Student pub. schs., Casselton, N.D. Cert. Master addiction counselor, N.D.; cert. chem. dependency counselor, Minn. Alcoholism counseling trainee Heartview Found., Mandan, N.D., 1974-75, family therapy intern, 1975-76, family counselor, 1976-77, supr. family mems. program, 1978; designer, supr. family program The Meadows, Wickenburg, Ariz., 1978-79; treatment programs cons., dir. consultation dept. Johnson Inst., Mpls., 1979-81; assoc. dir. chem. dependency unit Presbyn. Hosp., Oklahoma City, 1981-83; supr. adolescent counseling staff United Recovery Ctr., Grand Forks, N.D., 1983-85; dir. Irene Dressel Counseling, Grand Forks, 1985-89; program dir. the Dressel Ctr., Fargo, N.D., 1989-90, ret., 1990; cons. S.W. Inst. Alcohol Studies, Norman, Okla., Kans. Alcoholism Counselors Assn., Okla. Assn. Alcoholism and Drug Abuse; lectr. U. N.D., Grand Forks, N.D. Sch. Alcohol Studies. Mem. N.D. Alcoholism Counselors Assn., Nat. Alcoholism and Drug Addiction Counselors Assn., Am. Assn. Counseling and Devel., Democrat. Lutheran.

DRESSELHAUS, MILDRED SPIEWAK, physics and engineering educator; b. Bklyn., Nov. 11, 1930; d. Meyer and Ethel (Teichteil) Spiewak; m. Gene F. Dresselhaus, May 25, 1958; children: Marianne Dresselhaus Cooper, Carl Eric, Paul David, Eliot Michael. BA, Hunter Coll., 1951, DSc (hon.), 1982; Fulbright fellow, Cambridge (Eng.) U., 1951-52; MA, Radcliffe Coll., 1953; PhD in Physics, U. Chgo., 1958; D Engring. (hon.), Worcester Poly. Inst., 1976; DSc (hon.), Smith Coll., 1980, N.J. Inst. Tech., 1984; Doctorat Honoris Causa, U. Catholique de Louvain, 1988; DSc (hon.), Rutgers U., 1989, U. Conn., 1992, U. Mass., Boston, 1992, Princeton U., 1992; DEngring, Colo. Sch. of Mines, 1993; D (hon.), Technion, Israel Inst. Tech., Haifa, 1994; dr honoris causa, Johannes Kepler U., Linz, Austria, 1993. NSF postdoctoral fellow Cornell U., 1958-60; mem. staff Lincoln Lab., MIT, Lexington, 1960-67; prof. elec. engring. MIT, Cambridge, 1967—, assoc. dept. head elec. engring., 1972-74, prof. physics, 1983—, Inst. prof., 1985—, Abby Rockefeller Mauze chair, 1973-85, dir. Ctr. for Materials Sci. and Engring., 1977-83; vis. prof. dept. physics U. Campinas, Brazil, summer 1971, Technion, Israel Inst. Tech., Haifa, 1972, 90, Nihon and Aoyama Gakuin Univs., Tokyo, 1973, IVIC, Caracas, Venezuela, 1977; vis. prof. dept. elec. engring. U. Calif., Berkeley, 1985; Graffin lectr. Am. Carbon Soc., 1982; chmn. steering com. on evaluation panels Nat. Bur. Stds., 1978-83; mem. Energy Rsch. Adv. Bd., 1984-90; bd. dirs. Rogers Corp. Contbr. articles to profl. jours. Bd. govs. Argonne Nat. Lab., 1986-89; mem. governing bd. NRC, 1984-87, 89-90, 92—. Recipient Alumnae medal Radcliffe Coll., 1973, Killian Faculty Achievement award 1986-87, Nat. Medal of Sci., 1990; named to Hunter Coll. Hall of Fame, 1972. Fellow IEEE, AAAS (bd. dir. 1985-89), Am. Phys. Soc. (pres. 1984), Am. Acad. Arts. and Scis.; mem. Nat. Acad. Engring. (coun. 1981-87), Soc. Women Engrs. (Achievement award 1977), Nat. Acad. Scis. (coun. 1987-90, chmn. engring. sect. 1987-90, chmn. class III 1990-93, treas. 1992—), Brazilian Acad. Sci. (corr.), The Engring. Acad. Japan (fgn. assoc. 1993—). Office: MIT Rm 13-3005 Cambridge MA 02139

DRESSER, LINDA ANN, catering executive; b. San Diego, Jan. 31, 1948; d. Jesse Dale and Mary Ann D. Student, Southwestern Jr. Coll., George Brown Coll. Applied Art, 1980-82, Coleman Coll., 1991-92. Flight attendant Pacific S.W. Airlines, San Diego, 1968-70; sales rep. Sta. ABC-TV Channel 39, San Diego, 1973-75, Pennysaver Newspaper, Orange County, Calif., 1978-79, Tatung of Am., Long Beach, Calif., 1979-80; hospitality cons. Constellation Hotel, Toronto, Ont., Can., 1982-84; owner, operator Cruising Gourmet, San Diego, 1984—. Mem. Jr. League, Kona Kai Internat. Yacht Club (historian 1991, co-chmn. Am.'s Schooner Cup 1988-90). Republican. Office: Cruising Gourmet Ste 222 9842 Hibert St San Diego CA 92131

DRESSLER, BRENDA JOYCE, health educator, consultant, book and film reviewer; b. N.Y.C., Jan. 30, 1943; d. Herbert and Betty (Kirshner) Dressler; m. Irving Kaufman, Dec. 30, 1961 (div. Dec. 1979); 1 child, Joshua Ari. BA, CCNY, 1964; MA, CUNY, 1969; PhD, NYU, 1986. Cert. health edn. specialist. CHES educator sex and health N.Y.C. Bd. Edn., 1964-75, 1979—; educator sex and health Sex Info. and Edn. Coun. U.S., N.Y.C., 1985-86; cons. PTA and curriculum adv. com. Steinway Jr. High Sch., N.Y.C., 1985-87, Bayside High Sch., 1987-90; regional coord. and cons. on family living, Queens, 1990—; comprehensive health coord. high sch. HIV/AIDS Edn., Queens, 1991—; adj. instr. C.W. Post, N.Y. Inst. Tech., 1992—. Columnist: Women Mean Business; contbr. numerous articles to profl. jours.; curriculum writer HIV/AIDS Edn. K-6; writer instrnl. tng. design on HIV/AIDS. Mem. Am. Bd. Sexology, Soc. Phys. and Health Edn., Kappa Delta Pi. Home: 16241 Powells Cove Blvd Whitestone NY 11357-1449

DRESSMAN, LAURIE ATCHITY, nurse, research coordinator; b. Kansas City, Sept. 3, 1958; d. Frederick John and Myrza Marie (Aguillard) Atchity; m. Martin Joseph Dressman, Sept. 24, 1988; 1 child, Alexandrea Mezille. Diploma in Nursing, Rsch. Sch. Nursing, Kansas City, 1980; B. Liberal Arts, U. Mo., Kansas City, 1993. RN, Mo. Staff nurse med./surg. and ob/gyn. units St. Joseph Hosp., Kansas City, 1980-81; ambulatory care nurse ob/gyn. Truman Med. Ctr., Kansas City, 1981-85, staff nurse ob/gyn., 1985-87, clin. rsch. nurse ob/gyn., 1989-93; nurse paralegal Shughart, Thomson & Kilroy, P.C., Kansas City, 1987-88; study coord. in neurology Ctr. for Clin. Neurol. Studies, Kansas City, 1993—; owner, calligrapher/artist Calligraphy Etc., Kansas City, 1989—; lectr. in field; med./legal reviewer pvt. atty., Overland Park, Kans., 1991; lectr. Dept. Ob/Gyn., Truman Med. Ctr., U. Mo., 1990—; notary public State of Mo., 1987-92. Contbr. articles to profl. jours. U. Mo.-Kansas City scholar, 1985-88. Mrm. Rsch. Alumni Assn. (corres. sec. 1986), Golden Key. Democrat. Roman Catholic. Home: 6130 Oak St Kansas City MO 64113-2233

DREW, ELIZABETH, television commentator, journalist; b. Cin., Nov. 16, 1935; d. William J. and Estelle (Jacobs) Brenner; m. J. Patterson Drew, Apr. 11, 1964 (dec. 1970); m. David Webster, Sept. 26, 1981. B.A., Wellesley Coll., 1957; LHD, Hood Coll., 1976, Yale U., 1976, Trinity Coll., 1978, Reed Coll., 1979, Williams Coll., 1981, Georgetown U., 1981, George Washington U., 1994. Writer editor Congl. Quar., 1959-64; free lance writer, 1964-67; Washington editor Atlantic Monthly, 1967-73; host TV interview program Thirty Minutes With, 1971-73; commentator TV program Agronsky and Company, 1973—; commentator syndicated TV program Inside Washington, 1973-92; Washington corr. New Yorker Mag., 1973-92; commentator Monitor Radio, 1992—. Author: Washington Journal, 1975, American Journal, 1977, Senator, 1979, Portrait of an Election, 1981, Politics and Money, 1983, Campaign Journal, 1985, Election Journal, 1989, On the Edge: The Clinton Presidency, 1994; contbg. Washington Post; contbg. author various mags. and jours. Recipient award for excellence Soc. Mag. Writers, 1971, Wellesley Alumnae Achievement award, 1973, DuPont award, 1973, Mo. medal, 1979, Sidney Hillman award, 1983, Ambassador of Honor award Books Across the Sea, 1984, Literary Lion award N.Y. Pub. Library, 1985, Edward Weintal prize, 1988. Home: 3000 Woodland Dr NW Washington DC 20008-3543 Office: 815 15th St NW Rm 825 Washington DC 20005-2201

DREW, ELIZABETH HEINEMAN, publishing executive; b. Evanston, Ill., Aug. 26, 1940; d. Ben Harlow and Marion Elizabeth (Heineman) D. BA, U. Wis., 1961. With Doubleday & Co., Inc., N.Y.C., 1961-84, prodn. asst., 1961-63, personal asst. to editor in chief, 1963-66, adminstrv. asst. to editor in chief, 1963-69, editorial asst. to editor in chief, 1969-71, assoc. editor, 1971-74, editor, 1974-77, sr. editor, 1977-79, exec. editor, editorial dir., 1979-84; v.p., sr. editor William Morrow and Co., N.Y.C., 1984-92; v.p., pub. Lisa Drew Books/Macmillan Pub. Co., N.Y.C., 1993-94; v.p. pub. Lisa Drew Books/Charles Scribner's Sons, N.Y.C., 1994—; tchr. NYU Sch. Continuing Edn., 1981-82. Mem. PEN (N.Y. chpt.), Women's Media Group (treas. 1982-84, pres. 1985-86), Nat. Press Club (Washington), Assn. Am. Pubs. (internat. freedom to pub. com. 1978—, chmn. 1990-93, freedom to read com. 1988—, chmn. 1994—), Century Assn. (N.Y.), First City Club (Savannah, Ga.). Democrat. Episcopalian.

DREW, K, financial advisor, management consultant; b. Freeport, N.Y.; d. Harry P. and Kathleen (Isdal) Barton; m. Peter Pantazes; children: Karen, Donna. BA, U. Ga., 1960; postgrad., U. Ill., 1961. Dir. YWCA, Corpus Christi, Tex., 1969-72, Dwoskin Nat. Wallcovering Co., Atlanta, 1974-76; dep. asst. fin. presdl. campaign, 1976-77; dir. fin. Presdl. Inaugural, Washington, 1976; dep. adv. for small bus. SBA, Washington, 1977-80, asst. to adminstr., 1980-82; v.p. Alpha Systems, Inc., Washington and Athens, Greece, 1980-85; human resource cons. MBA Mgmt., Inc., McLean, Va., 1982-84; bus. cons. Drew Cons., McLean, 1984—; cons. assoc. Walling, June & Assocs., Old Town Alexandria, Va., 1986-89; fin. advisor The Family Extended, Washington, 1990—; fin. advisor SAKA, Inc., Merrifield, Va., 1991—, Warrenton, Va., 1991-92, DeLeo and Assocs., McLean, Va., 1991-92; fin. dir. Disting. Environments, Reston, Va., 1992—. State rep. poverty program and suicide prevention bds. Corpus Christi Bus. Coun., 1969-71; bd. dirs. YWCA, Washington, 1983-85; head speaker's bur. Fairfax Symphony, 1979-85, mem. exec. devel. com., 1979-86; mem. Mental Health Exec. Bd. dirs., Washington, 1983-88; deacon Nat. Presbyn. Ch., Washington, 1988-90; asst. to exec. dir. T. Monk Found., Jazz Sch., Duke U., 1987-89; event dir. Easter Seal Soc., 1990-91; mem. Youth for Tomorrow devel. com. Joe Gibbs Charities, Washington, 1990-92; presdl. campaign team captain Va. and Ga. Inaugural Com., 1993; Ga. Ball host, Washington, 1993; host Presdl. Inaugural Gala, Washington, 1993; mem. White House Advance Office of Pres., 1993—. Mem. Nat. League Am. Pen Women (v.p., pres. Washington Capital chpt. 1987-89, nat. bd. dirs. 1987-90, nat. roster chmn. 1989—), Bus. and Profl. Women Washington, Nat. Platform Assn., Alpha Gamma Delta. Office: Ste 1-121 8350 Greensboro Dr Mc Lean VA 22102-3533

DREW, KATHERINE FISCHER, history educator; b. Houston, Sept. 24, 1923; d. Herbert Herman and Martha (Holloway) Fischer; m. Ronald Farinton Drew, July 27, 1951. B.A., Rice Inst., 1944, M.A., 1945; Ph.D., Cornell U., 1950. Instr. history Rice U., 1946-48; asst. history Cornell U., 1948-50; mem. faculty Rice U., 1950—, prof. history, 1964—, Harris Masterson, Jr. prof. history, 1983-85, Lynette S. Autrey prof. history, 1985—, chmn. dept. history, 1970-80; editor Rice U. (Rice U. Studies), 1967-81, acting dean humanities and social scis., 1973. Author: The Burgundian Code, 1949, Studies in Lombard Institutions, 1956, The Lombard Laws, 1973, Law and Society in Early Medieval Europe, 1988, The Laws of the Salian Franks, 1991, also articles; editor: Perspective in Medieval History, 1963, The Barbarian Invasions, 1970; mem. bd. editors Am. Hist. Rev., 1982-85, Am. Hist. Assn. Guide to Hist. Lit., 1987—; contbr.: Life and Thought in the Middle Ages, 1967. Guggenheim fellow, 1959; Fulbright scholar, 1965; NEH Sr. fellow, 1974-75. Fellow Mediaeval Acad. Am. (coun. 1974-77, 2d v.p. to pres. 1985-87, del. to Am. Coun. Learned Socs. 1977-81); mem. Am. Hist. Assn. (coun. 1983-86), Am. Soc. Legal History, So. Hist. Assn. (vice chair, chair European sect. 1986-88, exec. com. 1989-91), Phi Beta Kappa. Home: 509 Buckingham Dr Houston TX 77024-5804 Office: Rice Univ Dept History 6100 South Main Houston TX 77251-1892

DREW, NANCY MCLAURIN SHANNON, counselor, consultant; b. Meridian, Miss., Apr. 29, 1934; d Julian Caldwell and Emma Katherine (Sanders) Shannon; m. Thomas Champion III, Feb. 11, 1956; children: Thomas Champion IV, Julian C. Shannon. BA, Furman U., 1956; MEd, N.C. State U., 1968. Cert. sch. counselor; cert. supr. curriculum and instrn., N.C. Rsch. asst. N.C. State U., Raleigh, 1957-59; tchr. English Raleigh City Schs., 1959-60; dir. guidance program Millbrook Sr. High/Wake County Schs., Raleigh, 1969-77; guidance chmn. Daniels Middle Sch./Wake County Schs., Raleigh, 1977-84, guidance info. specialist, 1984-85; guidance supr. Wake County Pub. Schs., Raleigh, 1985-88; coord. model dropout prevention program Wake County Pub. Sch./State Dept. Pub. Inst., Raleigh, 1985-88; counseling chmn. Garner Middle Sch., Raleigh, 1988—; presenter, cons. 1st and 2d Nat. Dropout Prevention Confs., Winston-Salem, N.C., 1986-87, Raleigh, 1986-88, N.C. Sch. Counselors Conf., Raleigh, 1986-88, Am. Pers. and Guidance Assn., 1976. Contbr. article to profl. jours. Vice chmn. bd. trustees Crossnore (N.C.) Sch., 1977—; sec., bd. dirs. Wake Teen Med. Svcs., Raleigh, 1978-88. Mem. AACD, NEA, DAR (area rep. speakers staff N.C. 1975-78, vice chmn. nat. DAR sch. com. 1986-89, chmn. state DAR sch. com. 1985-88, state editor DAR News, chpt. regent 1992-95, nat. house com. 1991-94, state officer 1988-91, N.C. Outstanding Jr. Mem. 1970), N.C. Edn. Assn., Am. Sch. Counselors Assn, N.C. Sch. Counselors Assn., Phi Delta Kappa, Delta Kappa Gamma (pres. chpt. 1985-88, state chmn. 1991-93, state mem. com. 1993-94). Democrat. Methodist. Home: 6000 Winthrop Dr Raleigh NC 27612-2142

DREW, SHARON LEE, caseworker; b. L.A., Aug. 11, 1946; d. Hal Bernard and Helen Elizabeth (Hammond) D.; children: Keith, Charmagne. BA, Calif. State U., Long Beach, 1983; postgrad., Calif. State U., Dominguez Hills, 1988—. Clerical support Compton (Calif.) Unified Sch. Dist., 1967-78; case worker L.A. County Dept. Pub. Social Svcs., 1978—. Den mother Boy Scouts Am., Compton, 1971-72; employee vol. Dominguez Sr. H.S., Comptn, 1972-73; project coord. Calif. Tomorrow's Parent Edn. Leadership Devel. Project, 1990; mem. L.A. Caregiver's Network, 1993—; vol. Calif. State Univ., Dominguez Hill's Older Adult Ctr., 1994. Recipient cert. Calif. Tomorrow-Parent Edn. Leadership Devel. Project, 1990. Mem. Am. Statis. Assn. (so. Calif. chpt.), Internat. Soc. for Exploratoin of Teaching Alternatives, Calif. Sociol. Assn. (1st gov. at large grad. student 1990-91), Dominguez Hills Gerontology Assn. (chairperson 1990-91), Sociology of Edn. Assn., Alpha Kappa Delta (Xi chpt. treas. 1992—). Home: 927 N Chester Ave Compton CA 90221-2105

DREWER, MARITA ANTOINETTE, reading teacher; b. Clinton, Iowa, Aug. 8, 1941; d. Robert Arnal and Marjorie Cecelia (Wendel) Gibson; m. Thomas Gene Drewer, Sept. 6, 1969; children: John Edward II, Carole Lynn. AA, Clinton Jr. Coll., 1961; BA in Edn., Libr. Sci., Northland Coll., Ashland, Wis., 1964; MRE, Eden Theol. Seminary, St. Louis, 1969; MSLS, Chgo. State U., 1990. 4th grade tchr. Shawano, Wis., 1964-66; libr. Winfield (Mo.) Sch. Dist., 1972-76; dir. day care Faith Salem, Jennings, Mo., 1979; tchr. third grade Jennings Sch. Dist., 1976-79; elem. libr. St. Louis Pub. Schs., 1979-81, Windsor Sch. Dist., Imperial, Mo., 1981-85; cons. Chpt. 1 K-W Curriculum Svc., Peotone, Ill., 1985-88; elem. libr. Peotone (Ill.) Dist. 207-4, 1985-90, Chpt. 1 reading tchr., 1990—. Named to Outstanding Young Women of Am., 1976. Mem. Ill. Reading Coun. Mem. United Ch. of Christ.

DREXLER, JOANNE LEE, art appraiser; b. Washington, Mar. 21, 1944; d. Elias J. and Beatrice Charlotte (Goldberg) D.; m. James R. Cohen, May 31, 1965; children: Terri I., Brett F. Student, Louvre, Paris, 1963-64; BA, Tufts U., 1965; Diamond and Pearl Cert., GIA, N.Y.C., 1974. Tchr. of French Stuyvesant High Sch., N.Y.C., 1965-66; decorator, art cons. Joanne Cohen Interiors, Mamaroneck, N.Y., 1967-69; assoc. prof. Hofstra U., L.I., N.Y., 1979-80; pres. Esquire Appraisals, N.Y.C. and Larchmont, N.Y., 1969—; numerous TV appearances including CNN, Sept. 1991; cons., lectr. in field; art judge various contests, art dealer. Organizer, curator N.S. in N.Y. art show Nat. Arts Club, 1993, African Am. art show Nat. Arts Club, 1994; weekly columnist Gannett chain newspapers, 1980-86. Mem. Am. Soc. Appraisers (sr., v.p. White Plains chpt. 1989, bd. dirs. 1987, pres. 1991—), Appraisers' Assn. Am. (cert.), Nat. Arts Club N.Y. (art show coord., curator N.C. in N.Y. show 1993, curator African-Am. art show 1994). Home: 10 Normandy Rd Larchmont NY 10538 Office: Esquire Appraisals Inc 45 East End Ave New York NY 10028-7953

DREXLER, MARY SANFORD, financial executive; b. Pontiac, Mich., Apr. 19, 1954; d. Arthur H. and Kathryn S. (Sherda) Sanford; m. Brian Day, 1975 (div. 1978); m. York Drexler, 1980. BS, Ea. Mich. U., Ypsilanti, 1976, MA, 1979; postgrad., Walsh Coll., Troy, Mich., 1983. CPA, Mich. Spl. edn. tchr. Oakland Schs., Pontiac, Mich., 1976-83; staff auditor Coopers & Lybrand, Det., 1983-84; sr. auditor Coopers & Lybrand, Det., Mich., 1984-86; asst. contr. Webasto Sunroofs Inc., Rochester Hills, 1986-88; contr. Inalfa Hollandia, Inc., Farmington Hills, Mich., 1988—, v.p. fin., 1992—; bd. dirs. Coun. for Exceptional Children, Oakland County 1976--83. Bd. Dirs. Neighborhood Civic Assn., Troy, 1986—. Mem. Inst. Mgmt. Accts., Oakland County, Mich. Assn. CPA Mich., Forest Lake Country Club. Office: Inalfa Hollandia Inc 26700 Haggerty Rd Farmington Hills MI 48331

DREXLER, NORA LEE, educator, writer, illustrator; b. Bellefonte, Pa., Nov. 17, 1947; d. Bengt Gerdis and Leanore Francis (Bates) Bjalme; m. Raymond George Drexler, June 27, 1970; 1 child, Michelle Ann. BA of Sci., Villa Maria Coll., 1969; MEd, Gannon U., 1974. Tchr. gifted and talented Millcreek Sch. Dist., Erie, Pa., 1969—; free-lance writer, illustrator, 1989—; pres. Drexler Assocs., Inc.; writer, dir., prodr. children's TV programming; author, illustrator nationwide drug and alcohol program grades K-8 SPARKS (Smart Pupils Act Responsibly to Keep Safe). Creator more than 500 cartoon characters; nat. and internat. workshops and presentations; computer tech., Pride World Conf., 1994. Mem. NEA, Pa. Edn. Assn., Millcreek Edn. Assn. Democrat. Roman Catholic. Home: 5639 Mill St Erie PA 16509-2923 Office: Drexler Assocs Inc PO Box 722 Erie PA 16512-0722

DREYFUSS, PATRICIA, chemist, researcher; b. Reading, Pa., Apr. 28, 1932; d. Edmund T. and Anna J. (Oberc) Gajewski; m. M. Peter Dreyfuss, Jan. 30, 1954; children: David Daniel, Simeon Karl. BS Chemistry, U. Rochester, 1954; PhD, U. Akron, 1964. Postdoctoral fellow U. Liverpool (Eng.), 1963-65; rsch. chemist B.F. Goodrich, Brecksville, Ohio, 1965-71; rsch. assoc. Case Western Res. U., Cleve., 1971-73, sr. rsch. assoc., 1973-74; rsch. assoc. Inst. Polymers Sci., U. Akron, Ohio, 1974-84; sr. rsch. scientist, rsch. prof. Mich. Molecular Inst., Midland, 1984-90; vis. rsch. fellow U. Bristol, 1972; cons. in field, 1974—; vis. prof. Polish Acad. Scis., Poland, 1974; adj. prof. Cen. Mich. U., Mt. Pleasant, Mich. Tech U., Houghton, 1986-92, Mich. Molecular Inst., Midland, 1990-92. Author: Poly (Tetrahydrofuran), 1982; contbr. over 85 articles to profl. jours.; co-author books. Flutist West Suburban Philharmonic Orch., Lakewood, Ohio, 1969-75, Midland (Mich.) Community Orch., 1990—; Explorer advisor Explorer post 2069 Boy Scouts Am., Akron, 1975-81; sec., bd. dirs. Adhesion Soc., 1976-88; treas. LWV, 1959-60; mem. ensemble Blessed Sacrament Ch., Midland; occasional flute soloist. Centennial scholar U. Rochester, 1950-54; Sohio fellow U. Akron, 1960, NSF Coop. Grad. fellow, 1961-63, Internat. fellow AAUW, 1964-65, NIH Spl. fellow, 1972-73. Mem. Am. Chem. Soc. (cen. region mtg. chmn. 1984-90, loc. sec. chmn., vice chmn., sec. and bd. dirs. Akron chpt. 1974-84, bd. dirs. Midland chpt. 1985-89, Outstanding Leadership Performance award 1981, Disting. Svc. award Akron chpt. 1985), AAUW (bd. dirs. Akron chpt.). Home: 3980 Old Pine Trl Midland MI 48642-8891

DRIES, ALICE EMERITA, horticulturist, educator; b. Danville, Ill., Dec. 16, 1920; d. Joseph and Theresa M. (Steger) Fazekas; widowed; 1 child, Joseph M. BS in Ornamental Horticulture, U. Ill., 1954, MS, 1965, postgrad., 1991—; attended, Hixson Sch. Design, Cleve., 1975, Boomer Sch. Design, Hawaii, 1982. Cert. in floral design, landscaping, interiorscaping, floral judging, botany, Rosarian and agriculture. Founder ornamental horticultural program Danville Area Community Coll., 1965, instr. ornamental horticulture, 1965-91; owner flower shop, profl. floral designer, judge Danville; designer, judge Danville; judge at various flower shows throughout U.S., 1970—; lectr., commentator program designer for garden clubs, tchrs. seminars, civic orgns., 1965—. Contbr. articles on floriculture to profl. jours. Recipient awards Ill. State Garden Club, 1990, Ill. Assn. Community Coll. 1972, Agriculture Instrs., 1980, Ill. Assn. Community Coll., 1966, Tchrs., Danville Area Community Coll., Holiday Workshop, 1991, Nat. Coun. of State Garden Clubs, 1990, Head Start, 1986-88, Men's Garden Club of Am., 1989. Mem. AAUW, Florist Profl. Orgn., Ill Assn. Agriculture Tchrs., Exec. Club, Roselawn Garden Club, Ill. State Garden Club, Rose Soc., Danville Women's Club, Toastmasters, Altar and Rosary Soc., Delta Kappa Gamma. Home: RR 1 Box 22214 Old Fort NC 28762-9766

DRIES, KATHLEEN MARIE, social worker; b. Beaver Dam, Wis., Feb. 21, 1946; d. Henry Frank and Eloise Marianne (Rake) D. BS in Sociology, No. Mich. U., 1969. Social worker Dept. Social Svcs., West Bend, Wis., 1969—; social work cons. Group Home Elderly, Slinger, Wis., 1972-75. Mem. Labor Assn. of Wis., Cath. Knights Ins. Soc. (bd. dirs. 1979-94), Alpha Xi Delta. Roman Catholic. Home: 601 Declark St Beaver Dam WI 53916-1309 Office: Dept Social Svcs 333 E Washington St Ste 3100 West Bend WI 53095-2585

DRISCOLL, CAROLYN JEAN, nurse, clinical coordinator; b. N.Y.C., June 12, 1962; d. Lawrence Allen and Mariann Patricia (McNamara) D. BSN, Coll. Mt. St. Vincent, 1984; MSN, U. Va., 1992. CCRN, Va. Staff nurse Bronx (N.Y.) VA Med. Ctr., 1984-86, NIH, Bethesda, Md., 1986-87; program rev. analyst Island Peer Rev. Orgn., Rego Park, N.Y., 1987-89; nurse SICU U. Va. Med. Ctr., Charlottesville, 1989-94, hepatology nurse coord., 1994—; clin. instr. Bronx (N.Y.) VA Med. Ctr., 1986; cons. Ernst & Young, N.Y.C., 1989. Mem. Am. Assn. Critical Care Nurses (historian 1990-92, membership chair 1992-93, pres-elect 1993-94, pres. 1994—), Internat. Transplant Nurses Soc. (charter mem., treas. 1994—). Roman Catholic. Home: 1213 Belleview Ave Charlottesville VA 22901 Office: U Va Health Scis Ctr Box 145 GI Divsn Charlottesville VA 22908

DRISCOLL, CONSTANCE FITZGERALD, educator, writer; b. Lawrence, Mass., Mar. 29, 1926; d. John James and Mary Anne (Leecock) Fitzgerald; AB, Radcliffe Coll., 1946; postgrad. Harvard U., U. Hartford (Conn.), U. Bridgeport (Conn.), Worcester (Mass.) State Coll.; m. Francis George Driscoll, Aug. 21, 1948; children: Frances Mary, Martha Anne, Sara Helene, Maribeth Lee. Secondary sch. tchr., North Andover, Mass., 1946-48; book reviewer N.Y.C. and Boston pubs., 1955-64; asst. conf. edn. dir. U. Hartford, 1964-68; lectr. Pace U., N.Y.C., 1973-74; edn. commentary Radio WVOX, New Rochelle, N.Y., 1974-75; asst. ednl. adv. Nat. Girl Scouts, 1972-74; pres., owner, dir. Open Corridor Schs. Cons., Inc., Bronxville, N.Y., 1972-84, pres., dir. Open Corridor Schs., Inc., Oxford, Mass., 1984—; creator in-svc. edn. programs pub. schs., Norwalk, Conn., 1983-88; assoc. Worcester State Coll. (Mass.) 1984-85, Fitchburg State Coll., 1986-87; dir. grad. edn. programs for tchrs. Anna Maria Coll., Paxton, Mass., 1990-94; assoc. grad. tchr. edn. courses Fitchburg State Coll., 1995—; tutor, cons. Worcester County sch. dists., 1989—; CEU mgr. for Conn. Dept. Edn. O.C.S., Inc., Conn., 1989—; dir. off-campus grad. credit tchr. edn. courses O.C.S., Mass., Conn., 1990—; bi-lingual instr. for Indian and Vietnamese students in grades 5-12, 1988-91; freelance writer newspapers and small jours., 1991—. Author curriculum materials; contbr. poetry to newspaper and small presses. Recipient Educator award Nat. Coun. ARC, Washington, 1985, Edn. award Nipmuc Am. Indian Coun., Webster, Mass, 1985. Home: 338 Main St Oxford MA 01540-1728 Office: PO Box 564 Oxford MA 01540

DRISCOLL, GENEVIEVE BOSSON (JEANNE BOSSON DRISCOLL), management and organization development consultant; b. Pitts., Mar. 26, 1937; d. George August and Emma Haling Bleichner; B.S. cum laude, Fla. State U., 1959; postgrad. program for specialists in orgn. devel. Nat. Tng. Labs., 1970. m. John Edwin Bosson, June 17, 1959; 1 son, Matthew Edwin; m. 2d Frederick Driscoll, Oct. 7, 1972; stepchildren—Jennifer Locke, Cynthia Hall, Molly Davis, Julie Ann. Planning asst. Center for Planning and Innovation, Dept. Edn. State of N.Y., 1967-71, planning cons. So. Tier Regional Office for Ednl. Planning, Elmira, N.Y., 1971-72; tng. dir. Neusteters, Inc., Denver, 1973-74; orgn. devel. specialist CONNECT, Inc., N.Y.C., 1975-77; cons. Robert H. Schaffer & Assos., Stamford, Conn., 1977-80; partner Driscoll Cons. Group, Williamstown, Mass., 1980—; sales tng. mgr. Sheaffer Eaton, Pittsfield, Mass., 1983, mgr. human resources and orgn. devel., 1983-88; dir. human resources Canyon Ranch, Berkshires, 1989—; cons. in field. Office: 24 Lee Ter Williamstown MA 01267-2039

DRISCOLL, JEANNE BAKER, art dealer; b. Pipestone, Minn.; d. John B. and Marie Helena (Kallemeyn) B.; m. John Paul Driscoll, Mar. 20, 1971; children: Emily Vida-Marie, Gillian Paula-Jean. BA, U. Minn., 1969; MEd, Pa. State U., 1973, PhD, 1978; bus. cert., U. Pa., 1980. Cert. counselor, career counselor. Admissions counselor U. Minn., Morris, 1969-71; career counselor Pa. State U., State Coll., 1971-75, counselor of edn. faculty, 1975-78; dir. placement and transfer Quinsigamond Community Coll., Worcester, Mass., 1979-80; dir. grad. programs Fitchburg (Mass.) State Coll., 1981-82, dir. career services, 1982-87; owner, v.p. Babcock Galleries, N.Y.C., 1987—; adj. grad. faculty Fitchburg State Coll., 1978-87. Author: Optimizing Women's Leadership Skills, 1974; contbr. articles to profl. jours. Pres. Mental Health Assn., Fitchburg, 1983; review bd. mem. United Way, Fitchburg, 1984-85; v.p. First Parish Ch., Fitchburg, 1985-86. Mem. Am. Assn. for Counseling and Devel. (career info. svc. reviewer 1983-88), Nat. Career Devel. Assn. (del. 1976, 77), New Eng. Assn. for Sch., Coll., and Univ. Staffing (treas. 1985-87), Mass. Pub. Coll. Career Planning and Placement Assn. (pres. 1985-86), Ea. Coll. Personnel Officers (presenter 1986). Office: Babcock Galleries 724 5th Ave New York NY 10019-4106

DRISCOLL, KIMBERLEE MARIE, lawyer; b. Binghamton, N.Y., July 17, 1961; d. Patrick Donald and Diane Cecile (Richmond) Lake; m. Matthew Victor Driscoll, Aug. 6, 1983; 1 child, John Patrick. BA, Colgate U., 1983; JD, Union U., 1986. Bar: N.Y. 1987, Mass. 1988. Asst. gen. counsel Oxbow Corp., Dedham, Mass., 1987-90; corp. counsel, sec. Putnam, Hayes & Bartlett, Inc., Cambridge, Mass., 1990-92; v.p., gen. counsel Merrill Internat. Ltd., Cambridge, 1992—. Mem. ABA (vice chair spl. com. internat. energy law 1993—), Am. Corp. Counsel Assn., Mass. Bar Assn., N.Y. Bar Assn. Home: 30 Curve St Bedford MA 01730 Office: Merrill Internat Ltd 20 University Rd Ste 510 Cambridge MA 02138

DRIVER, LOTTIE ELIZABETH, librarian; b. Newport News, Va., Dec. 6, 1918; d. James W. and Lottie (Williams) D. Student, Averett Coll., 1936-37; B.S., Mary Washington Coll. of U. Va., 1939; B.L.S., Coll. William and Mary, 1944. Band instr. Hampton (Va.) Sch. System, 1939-41; asst. librarian Newport News Pub. Library, 1941-47, librarian, 1947-69; asst. dir. Newport News Pub. Library System, 1969, dir., 1977-81; author book rev. column in Daily Press; library news reporter radio sta. WGH, 1959. Author articles for library supply house. Active United Fund. Recipient Community Service certificate Kiwanis Clubs Newport News, 1970; named Outstanding City Employee, 1970. Mem. ALA, Southeastern, Va. library assns., AAUW, P.E.O., DAR, Phi Theta Kappa, Alpha Phi Sigma. Baptist.

DRIVER, SHARON HUMPHREYS, marketing executive; b. Staten Island, N.Y., Jan. 5, 1949; d. William Edward and Gloria Patra (McCrave) Humphreys; m. William Weston Driver, Jr., June 3, 1972; children: Christopher John, Andrea Nicole. BA, Manhattanville Coll., Purchase, N.Y., 1970; MA, Coll. New Rochelle (N.Y.), 1973. Lic. tchr., N.Y. Tchr. Somers (N.Y.) Cen. Sch. Dist., 1970-76, Ossining (N.Y.) Village Recreation Dept., 1983-87; media coord./bookkeeper Equation Communications, White Plains, N.Y., 1986-89; media dir. Sims Freeman O'Brien, Elmsford, N.Y., 1989-90; project dir. Rsch. Advantage, Hawthorne, N.Y., 1990-92; pres. Quality Media Cons., Briarcliff, N.Y., 1990—; cons. Merson/Greener Assocs., Tarrytown, N.Y., 1992-94. Sec. tng. liason, Jr. League, Westchester-on-Hudson, 1982-88; sustainer, trainer-facilitator, Jr. League, Tarrytown, N.Y., 1988—; past pres. St. Teresa's Parish Coun., Briarcliff Manor, N.Y.; sec. bd. dirs. Ossining Open Door Health Clinic, 1985-89. Mem. Women in Communications, Sleepy Hollow Toastmasters (charter, sec. exec. com.). Roman Catholic. Home: 197 Macy Rd Briarcliff Manor NY 10510-1017

DROKE, EDNA FAYE, elementary school educator; b. Sylvester, Tex., Dec. 4, 1932; d. Ira Selle and Faye Emily (Seckinger) Tucker; m. Louis Albert Droke, June 2, 1951; children: Sherman Ray, Lyndon Allen, Lona Faye Droke Cheairs. BEd, Tarleton State U., Stephenville, Tex., 1983. Cert. ESL and 3d-8th lang. arts tchr., Tex. Tchr. ESL in 3d-8th grades Wingate (Tex.) Ind. Sch. Dist., 1983-86; tchr. 2d grade and ESL Collidge (Tex.) Ind. Sch. Dist., 1986-88; tchr. 4th grade and ESL Peaster (Tex.) Ind. Sch. Dist., 1988-89; tchr. Chpt. I in 1st-6th grades, ESL in K-12th grades Ranger (Tex.) Ind. Sch. Dist., 1989—. Mem. ASCD, Kappa Delta Pi, Alpha Chi. Baptist. Home: Box 44 Comanche TX 76442

DRONET, JUDY LYNN, elementary educator, librarian; b. Kaplan, La., Dec. 9, 1946; d. Percy Joseph and Zula Mae (Harrington) D. BA in Elem. Edn., McNeese State U., 1968, MEd, 1971. Cert. tchr., libr., adminstr., La. Tchr. Shady Grove High Sch., Rosedale, La., 1968-69, Lake Arthur (La.) Elem. Sch., 1969-86, 88-90, Lake Arthur High Sch., 1986-88, 91-92; libr. Henry Heights Elem. Sch., Lake Charles, La., 1992-93, Welsh Elem. Sch., 1993—; univ. supr. McNeese State U., Lake Charles, 1990-91, student tchr. supr.; dir. sch. musical prodns., Lake Arthur, 1976-85; judge sci. and social studies fairs, Lake Arthur, 1985-90, math fair, Jeff Davis Parish, 1993; presenter workshops. Coach girls' softball Lake Arthur Jaycees, 1974; mem. Jeff Davis Parish Arts Coun., Jennings, La., 1990—; mem., hostess Friends of Zigler Mus., Jennings, 1990—. Mem. La. Assn. Educators, Jeff Davis Parish Assn. Educators (rep.), Calcasieu Parish Assn. Educators, Calcasieu Reading Coun., Women's Libr. Club, Cath. Daus. Am. (sec., regent 1968-93, Dau. of Yr. 1979-80, 93-94), La. Songwriters' Assn. (sec.-treas.), A Block Off Broadway Theater Group, Delta Kappa Gamma (dist. dir., state chmn., state music rep.). Democrat. Roman Catholic. Home: PO Box 214 211 Pleasant Dr Lake Arthur LA 70549

DROST, MARIANNE, lawyer; b. Waterbury, Conn., Feb. 21, 1950; d. Albin Joseph and Henrietta Jean (Kremski) D. BA, Conn. Coll., 1972; JD, U. Conn., 1975. Bar: Conn. 1975. Assoc. Ritter, Tapper & Totten, Hartford, Conn., 1975-77; sr. atty. GTE Service Corp., Stamford, Conn., 1977-84, Chesebrough-Pond's Inc., Greenwich, Conn., 1984-85; corp. sec. GTE Corp., Stamford, 1985—; v.p., assoc. gen. counsel fin. GTE Svc. Corp., Stamford, 1991—. Tutor Lit. Vols., Stamford, 1985-90, bd. dirs. Lit. Vols. Am., 1988—. Mem. ABA, Am. Soc. Corp. Secs. (former pres., bd. dirs. Fairfield-Westchester chpt.). Office: GTE Corp 4 Union Park # 2 Norwalk CT 06850-3315

DROUKAS, ANN HANTIS, management executive; b. Boston, Aug. 27, 1923; d. Charles George and Paula (Kanaris) Hantis; m. Peter Droukas Jr., Sept. 28, 1941; children: P. Ronald, Paulette D., Roger C. Grad. high sch., Roxbury, Mass. With Droukas Cut Sole, Inc., Brockton, Mass., 1947—, pres., treas., 1985—; with DBA Drew Leather, Brockton, 1985-89; pres., treas. DBA Campello Tanning, Brockton, 1985—. Contbr. to translater textbooks from Spanish and Greek to English. Mem. adv. bd. Lincoln Trust; past adult participant Boy Scouts Am., Girl Scouts U.S.; active Two-Ten Nat. Found., Brockton Art Mus. 1st woman in U.S. to own and operate a cowhide tannery. Mem. Nat. Fedn. Ind. Bus., Assn. Industries Mass., Greek Ladies Philophotos Soc. (past. treas.), Brockton Hist. Soc., Nat. Trust for Historic Preservation, U.S. C. of C., New England Tanners Club, Shoe and Leather Club Cin., Rainbow Mothers Club, Order Ea. Star, Ten Times One Club (past pres.). Office: PO Box 4068 Brockton MA 02403-4068

DRUCKER, JACQUELIN F., lawyer, arbitrator, author; b. Celina, Ohio; d. Jack Burton and Dorothea (Eckenstein) Davis; m. John H. Drucker, Sept. 8, 1990. BA with distinction and honors, Ohio State U., 1977, JD with honors, 1981. Bar: Ohio 1981, N.Y. 1992, U.S. Supreme Ct. 1989. Legis. asst. Speaker of Ohio Ho. of Reps., Columbus, 1974-78; rsch. asst. United Auto Workers, Columbus, 1978-81; labor atty. Porter, Wright, Morris & Arthur, Columbus, 1981-84; gen. counsel Ohio Employment Rels. Bd., Columbus, 1984-86, exec. dir., 1986-88, vice chmn., 1988-90; pvt. practice law and labor arbitration, N.Y.C., 1990—; dir. labor mgmt. programs sch. indsl. and labor rels. Cornell U., 1994—; adj. prof. Cornell U., 1994—; cons. on collective bargaining Ohio Dept. Adminstrv. Svcs., Columbus, 1983-84; adj. prof. law Franklin U. Columbus, 1988-89; mem. panel of arbitrators Fed. Mediation and Conciliation Svc., Am. Arbitration Assn., N.Y. State Employment Rels. Bd.; mem. roster of neutrals N.Y.C. Office of Collective Bargaining; mem. panel V.I. Pub. Employment Rels. Bd., N.J. Pub. Employment Rels. Commn.; lectr., speaker in field. Author: Collective Bargaining Law in Ohio, 1993, 94, 95 supplements; contbg. editor Public Sector Law and Employment Law, 1994 supplement; contbr. numerous articles to profl. jours. Mem. ABA, Ohio State Bar Assn., Assn. of Bar of City of N.Y., N.Y. State Bar Assn. (labor and employment law sect., contbg. editor 1994 supplement), N.Y. County Lawyers Assn. (labor rels. com., sec.), Nassau County Bar Assn., Suffolk County Bar Assn., Indsl. Rels. Rsch. Assn. (N.Y. chpt.), Soc. Fed. Labor Rels. Profls. Jewish. Office: 432 E 58th St # 2 New York NY 10022-2331

DRUCKMAN, MARGARET SMITH, consultant, retail executive, administrator; b. Wilkes-Barre, Pa., May 9, 1937; d. Gibson Willard and Mary Louise (Schuster) Smith; m. Clayton Edward Hudnall, 1964 (div. 1976); children: Mary Margaret, Clayton John; m. Harvey Saul Druckman, 1981. BA, Coll. Misericordia, 1958; postgrad., U. Edinburgh, Scotland, 1960; MA, Marquette U., 1960; postgrad., U. Ill., 1962-64. Proposal writer Vanderbilt U., Nashville, 1967-70; tchr. N.W. Cath. High Sch., West Hartford, Conn., 1973-79; dir. communications U. Hartford, West Hartford, 1979-81, dir. found. rels., 1980-81, dir. capital support, 1981-85; dir. capital campaign U. Hartford, Springfield, Mass., 1985-86; pres. Windsor (Conn.) Findings, Inc., 1986-91; chief operating officer Golden Apple Jewelers, Windsor, 1986—; exec. dir. devel./alumni rels. U. of Hartford, 1988-91; cons. fund raising Druckman Assocs., Windsor, Conn., 1991—; dir. corp./found. resources U. Conn., Storrs, 1993—. Contbr. articles to mags. Mem. NAFE. Democrat. Roman Catholic. Office: Druckman Assocs 10 Sylvia Ln Windsor CT 06095-2337

DRUM, ALICE, college administrator; b. Gettysburg, Pa., June 22, 1935; d. David Wentz and Charlotte Rebecca (Kinzey) McDannell; m. D. Richard Guise, June 15, 1957 (div. Aug. 1975); children: Gregory, Brent, Richard, Robert, Clay; m. Ray Kenneth Drum, Mar. 2, 1979; 1 child, Trevor. BA magna cum laude, Wilson Coll., 1957; PhD, Am. U., 1976. Adj. prof. gen. studies Antioch U., Columbia, Md., 1976-78; adj. asst. prof. English Gettysburg (Pa.) Coll., 1977-80; lectr. in gen. studies Georgetown U., Washington, 1980-81; lectr. in gen. honors U. Md., College Park, 1980-83; asst. prof. English Hood Coll., Frederick, Md., 1981-85, coord. writing program, 1981-83, assoc. dean acad. affairs, 1983-85; dean of frehmen Franklin and Marshall Coll., Lancaster, Pa., 1985-88, v.p., 1988—; team mem. Mid. States Accreditation Assn., 1989-91; cons. in field. Contbr. chpts. to books, articles and book revs. to profl. jours. Chair Lancaster County DA Commn., Lancaster, 1990-91; mem. Lancaster County Commn. on Youth Violence, Lancaster, 1990-91. Mellon grantee, 1979, Davison Foreman fellow, 1975-76. Mem. MLA, N.E. MLA, Am. Assn. Higher Edn., Assn. Am. Colls., Eastern Assn. Coll. Deans (pres. 1988-89), Coll. English Assn., Phi Beta Kappa (pres. chpt. 1990-91), Phi Kappa Phi. Democrat. Episcopalian. Office: Franklin and Marshall Coll Lancaster PA 17604-3003

DRUM, JOAN MARIE MCFARLAND, federal agency administrator; b. Waseca, Minn., Mar. 31, 1932; d. Leo Joseph and Bergetthe (Anderson) McFarland; m. William Merritt Drum, June 13, 1954; children: Melissa, Eric. BA in Journalism, U. Minn., 1962; MEd, Coll. William and Mary, 1975, postgrad., 1984-85. Govt. ofcl. fgn. claims br. Social Security Adminstrn., Balt., 1962-64; freelance writer Polyndrum Publs., Newport News, Va., 1967-73; tchr. Newport News (Va.) Pub. Schs., 1975-79; writer, cons. Drum Enterprises, Williamsburg, Va., 1980-82; developer, trainer communicative skills U.S. Army Transp. Sch., Ft. Eustis, Va., 1982-86; govt. ofcl. test assistance div. U.S. Army Tng. Ctr., Ft. Eustis, 1986, course devel. coord. distributed tng. office, 1992; adj. faculty English dept. St. Leo Area Coll., Ft. Eustis, 1975-78; del. Communicative Skills Conf., Ft. Leavenworth, Kans., 1983; mem. Army Self-Devel. Test Task Force, 1991-92; lectr. in field. Author: Ghosts of Fort Monroe, 1972, Travel for Children in Tidewater, 1974, Galaxy of Ghosts, 1992; editor: army newsletter for families, 1968-73, Social Services Resource Reference, 1970; contbr. articles to profl. jours. Chmn. Girl Scouts U.S., Tokyo, 1964-66, Army Community Svc., Ft. Monroe, Va., 1967-68; chmn. publicity Hist. Home Tours, Ft. Monroe, 1971-73; chmn. adv. bd. James City County Social Svcs., 1989, chmn. adult svcs., 1989-90; mem. James City County Leadership Devel. Program Bd. Recipient numerous civic awards including North Shore Community Svc. award, Hialeah, Hawaii, 1966, Home Bur. Svc. award, 1975, Svc. award Girl Scouts U.S., Tokyo, 1965. Mem. Nat. Soc. for Performance Instrn. (v.p. adminstrn. Tidewater chpt.), Va. Writers Club, Kappa Delta Pi. Home: 9 Bray Wood Rd Williamsburg VA 23185-5504 Office: Individual Test Evaluation Directorate US Army Tng Ctr Newport News VA 23604

DRUMMOND, ANNETTE MARIE, computer consultant; b. Jamestown, N.D., July 25, 1952; d. William D. and Phyllis P. (Domek) D.; m. Andrew J. Pope, Sept. 15, 1979; children: Christopher J.D. Pope, Rachel E.D. Pope. BBA with honors, U. Wis., 1974, MS, 1976. Spl. projects analyst 1st Wis. Mortgage Co., Milw., 1974-75; programmer/analyst Cummins Engine Co., Columbus, Ind., 1976-77, managerial acct. specialist, 1977-79, mgr. compensation, 1979-80; ptnr. A & A Enterprises, Russell, Pa., 1979—; computer cons. A & A Enterprises, South Charleston, Ohio, 1981-86, Shared Resources, Columbus, Ohio, 1988-90; cons. Midland Mut. Ins. Co., Columbus, 1990-91; systems analyst Corry (Pa.)-Hiebert Corp., 1991-93; permit specialist Chautauque Co. Bus. Permit Ctr., Jamestown, N.Y., 1994—. Social chair Welcome Club Warren County, Warren, Pa., 1991-92, pres., 1992-93; fellowship chair St. Francis Episc. Ch., Youngsville, Pa., 1992—, asst. treas., 1994—; cub leader Boy Scouts Am., Russell, Pa., 1993—, asst. cubmaster, 1994—. Home and Office: A & A Enterprises RR 1 Box 1114 Russell PA 16345-9721

DRUMMOND, CAROL CRAMER, voice educator, singer, artist, writer; b. Indpls., Mar. 5, 1933; adopted d. Burr Ostin and L. Ruth Welch; m. Roscoe Drummond, 1978 (dec. 1983). Student, Butler U., 1951-53; studied with Todd Duncan, Rosa Ponselle,, John Bullock and Dr. Peter, Herman Adler. Original performer Starlite Musicals, Indpls., 1951; singer Am. Light Opera Co., Washington, Seagle Opera Colony, Schroon Lake, N.Y., 1963, 64; soloist 5th Ch. of Christ, Scientist, Washington, 1963-78; performer Concerts in Schs. Program, Washington Performing Arts Soc., 1967—; soloist with Luke AFB band ofcl. opening Boswell Meml. Hosp, Sun City, Ariz., 1970; painter, artist, 1980—; pvt. tchr. voice and speech Mt. Desert Island, Maine, 1987—; voice tchr. Mt. Desert Island High Sch., 1988—; soloist numerous oratorio socs., appearances with symphony orchs., including Nat. Symphony Orch., Fairfax (Va.) Symphony Orch., 1970, 71, Buffalo Philharm. Orch. Concerts in the Pk., Arlington Opera Co., Lake George Opera Co., Glen Falls, N.Y., Washington Opera; voiceover radio and TV commls., 1965-84, U.S. Govt.; host The Sounding Bd., Sta. WGTS-FM, Washington, 1972-78; dir. ensembles Summer Festival of Arts, S.W. Harbor, Maine, 1992—; dir. Amahl and the Night Visitors, 1992. Former columnist Animal Crackers; writer newspaper and mag. articles and stories; exhibited in art group shows; one-woman shows include Singing!, Smithsonian Instn., 1980, paintings, oils and acrylics at Maine Med. Ctr., Bangor, 1995. Bd. dirs. Washington Sch. Ballet, 1978; life bd. dirs. Internat. Soundex Reunion Registry, Carson City, Nev. Recipient 1st pl. women's divsn. Internat. Printers Ink Contest, 1951. Mem. Nat. League Am. Pen Women, Am. Art League, Nat. Press Club (Washington), Maine State Soc. (life), Kappa Kappa Gamma. Republican. Episcopalian. Home: Dream Come True PO Box 791 Clark Point Rd Southwest Harbor ME 04679 Office: 1350 Beverly Rd Ste 115-135 Mc Lean VA 22101

DRUMMOND, DOROTHY WEITZ, geography education consultant, educator, author; b. San Diego, Dec. 19, 1928; d. Frederick W. and Dora (Weidenhofer) Weitz; m. Robert R. Drummond, Sept. 5, 1953 (dec. June 1982); children: Kathleen, Gael, Martha. AB, Valparaiso U., 1949; MA, Northwestern U., 1951. Cert. tchr., Ind. Social studies tchr. Woodrow Wilson Jr. High Sch., Oxnard, Calif., 1949-50; editorial asst. Am. Geog. Soc., N.Y.C., 1951-53; substitute tchr. Vigo County Sch. Corp., Terre Haute, Ind., 1960-67; social studies tchr. Ind. State U. Lab. Sch., Terre Haute, 1963-64; geog. edn. cons., author, workshop presenter, Terre Haute, 1953—; adj. asst. prof. geography Saint Mary-of-the-Woods (Ind.) Coll., 1967—, Ind. State U., Terre Haute, 1990—; dir. project GEO, Ind. State U., 1992—; cons. McGraw-Hill, Scott-Foresman, Agy. for Instrnl. Tech., Hudson Inst. Author: The World Today, 3d edit., 1971, People on Earth, 3d edit., 1988, World Geography, 1989; contbr. numerous articles to profl. jours. Bd. dirs. Mental Health Assn. Wabash Valley, Terre Haute, 1984-93, Coun. on Domestic Abuse, Terre Huate, 1987-92, United Ministries Ctr., Terre Haute, 1991-94; organizer, leader ednl. tours to China, 1986, 88, Australia, 1993. Fulbright scholar, Burma, 1957-58; grantee Geography Educators Network Ind., 1988, 89, 90, 91, 92, 93, Ind. Commn. Higher Edn., 1990, 92, 94, NSF, 1993, U.S. Dept. Edn., 1992-95. Mem. Ind. Coun. Social Studies, Geography Educators Network Ind. (bd. dirs.), Nat. Coun. Geog. Edn. (pres. 1990), Nat. Coun. Social Studies, Nat. Sci. Tchrs. Assn., Nat. Sci. Suprs. Assn., Assn. Am. Geographers.

DRVAR, MARGARET ADAMS, vocational education educator; b. Morgantown, W.Va., Dec. 22, 1953; d. Lester Morris and Daun Collette (Benson) Adams; m. Marvin Lynn Drvar, July 29, 1978; children: Jacob Elias, Jared Nathaniel. BS in Family Resources, W.Va. U., 1977, MS in Family Resources, 1982. Cert. tchr., vocat. home economist tch. W.Va. Substitute tchr. Monongalia County Bd. Edn., Morgantown, 1983-86; tchr. vocat. home econs. Clay Battelle Jr.-Sr. High Sch., Blacksville, W.Va., 1986-89, 91-92, South Jr. High Sch., Morgantown, 1992—; instr. culinary arts Monongalia County Tech. Edn. Ctr., Morgantown, 1989-91; youth group adv. Future Homemakers of Am., 1986—. Advisor, Future Homemakers of Am., 1986—; v.p. United Meth. Women, Brookhaven, W.Va., 1985-92; sec. bd. trustees Brookhaven United Meth. Ch., 1989—; bd. dirs., sec. Morgantown AES Fed. Credit Union, 1989—; vol. 4-H leader Brookhaven Bulls 4-H Club, 1992—; mem. Monongalia County 4-H Leaders Assn. Mem. NEA, Am. Assn. Family and Consumer Scis. (cert.), W.Va. Edn. Assn., Monongalia County Edn. Assn., W.Va. Home Econs. Assn., Monongalia County Home Econs. Assn., Am. Vocat. Assn., W.Va. Vocat. Assn., Alpha Upsilon Omicron, Gamma Phi beta. Home: 3307 Darrah Ave Morgantown WV 26505 Office: Monongalia County Schs South Jr High Sch 500 E Parkway Dr Morgantown WV 26505-6839

DRY, MICHELLE RENEE, financial executive; b. Richwood, W.Va., Oct. 29, 1956; d. William Eugene Robinson and Beverly Joy (Sturm) Gail; m. Dan Raymond Cantrell, Dec. 24, 1978 (div. Mar. 1991); m. Fred L. Dry, June 18, 1994; children: Danica Rae, Jessica Nichole, Russell Drummond. Cert. TBA Tex. Sch. Trust Banking, ABA Nat. Trust Sch., FWI cert. leader tng. Sec. VA, Washington, 1975-76, Volpe, Boskey & Lyons,

Washington, 1976-77; mgr. Brass Monkey Lounge & Pkg. Store, Marathon, Fla., 1977-78; sec. UTMB Marine Biomed. Inst., Galveston, Tex., 1978-79, Smith & Herz, Galveston, 1979-80; adminstrv. asst. trust U.S. Nat., Galveston, 1981-82, asst. trust officer, 1982-84, trust officer, 1984-88, asst. v.p., trust officer, 1988-91; v.p., CFO Vista Tng. Group, Houston, 1991—. Mem. MADD, Houston, 1989-90, Ross Elem. PTA, League City, Tex., 1986-90, Bales Intermediate PTA, 1994—, Friendswood Jr. H.S. PTA, 1994—. Mem. NAFE, ASTD, Fin. Women Internat., Inc. (group v.p. 1986-87, group pres. 1987-88, edn. and tng. 1989-90, chair publicity/mktg. chair 1990-91, Tex. state coun. edn. and tng. chair 1991-92), Women's C. of C., Toastmaster's Internat. Office: Vista Tng Group 7007 Gulf Fwy Ste 234 Houston TX 77087-2540

DRYDEN, MARY ALINE CURRIE, counselor; b. Hattiesburg, Miss., Dec. 6, 1951; d. Edward James and Carol Marie (Praytor) Hickman; m. Stephen Ryan Dryden, Nov. 22, 1970; children: James Stephen, Christina Beverly. BS in Elem. Edn., U. So. Miss., 1975, MS in Counseling Psychology, 1992; cert., William Carey Coll., 1988. Cert. tchr. K-8, gifted K-12; cert. counselor. Sec. M.M. Roberts, Atty., Hattiesburg, 1968-70; teller, loan sec. First Fed. Savs. and Loan, Hattiesburg, 1971-73; kindergarten tchr. First Presbyn. Kindergarten, Hattiesburg, 1980-84; tchr. 2d grade Hattiesburg Pub. Sch., 1986-87; tchr. gifted (1-5) Forrest County Schs., Hattiesburg, 1987-90; counselor children's spl. edn. Pine Belt Mental Health, Hattiesburg, 1992-93; tchr. gifted 3d grader Petal (Miss.) City Schs., 1994—; cons. Parents and Educators of Gifted Students, Petal, 1994; tchr. cons. Miss. Geographic Alliance, 1994—. Contbr. articles to profl. jours. Vol., sec. Hattiesburg Jr. Aux., 1984-86; leader Girl Scouts Am., Hattiesburg, 1984-86. Mem. ACA, Miss. Psychol. Assn., Miss. Counseling Assn., Miss. Profl. Educators, U. So. Miss. Alumni, Kappa Delta Pi. Methodist. Home: 123 Dogwood Dr Hattiesburg MS 39402-3304

DRYDEN, MARY ELIZABETH, law librarian, writer, actress; b. Chgo., Oct. 18, 1952; d. James Heard and Hazel Anne (Potts) Rule; m. Ian Dryden, Nov. 22, 1975 (div. 1990); m. Stephen Quadros, Sept. 12, 1992. Student, U. London, 1969, Bath U., 1970; BA, Scripps Coll., 1971; postgrad. U. Edinburgh, 1971-74. Head librarian Hahn, Cazier & Leff, San Diego, 1980, Fredman, Silverberg & Lewis, San Diego, 1980-83, Riordan & McKinzie, L.A., 1983—; freelance photog. model, 1973—. Theatrical appearances include Antony and Cleopatra, McOwen Theatre, London, 1984, Table Manners, L.A., 1985, Julius Caesar, L.A., 1986, Witness for the Prosecution, L.A., 1987, Come and Go, L.A., 1988, The Actor's Nightmare, L.A., 1989, The Dresser, L.A., 1989, Absent Friends, Long Beach, Calif., 1990, Run For Your Wife!, Long Beach, 1991, The Hollow, Long Beach, 1992, Cock and Bull Story, Fountainhead Theatre, Hollywood, 1993, Towards Zero, Long Beach, 1993, Angel Street, L.A., 1994 (film) Private Collections, 1989, Eye Opener, 1992, A Situation, 1994, Porn Queens of the Seventies, 1994, also music videos and TV Commls.; book critic L.A. Times; contbr. articles to newspapers. Mem. ABA, Brit. Equity, So. Calif. Soc. Law Librs., Brit. Assn. Film and Television Arts, Mensa, Phi Beta Kappa. Avocations: photography, wine, architecture, fine art, languages. Office: Riordan & McKinzie 300 S Grand Ave Fl 29 Los Angeles CA 90071-3109

DRYLIE, CHRISTINE MARIE, lawyer; b. Jacksonville, Fla., Jan. 10, 1966; d. James Todd and Constance Marie (Wallis) D. BA summa cum laude, U. Colo., 1987; JD cum laude, U. Mich., 1990. Bar: Colo. 1990, Ill. 1991, U.S. Dist. Ct. Colo. 1991, U.S. Dist. Ct. (no. dist.) Ill. 1991, U.S. Dist. Ct. (ctrl. dist.) Ill. 1994, U.S. Ct. Appeals (10th cir.) 1991, U.S. Ct. Appeals (7th cir.) 1993, U.S. Supreme Ct. 1995. Clk. to chief judge Sherman G. Finesilver U.S. Dist. Ct. Colo., Denver, 1990-91; assoc. McDermott, Will & Emery, Chgo., 1991—; adminstr. Family Law Project, Ann Arbor, Mich., 1988-91; judge Julius H. Miner Moot Ct., Northwestern U. Sch. Law, 1993-95, Northwestern U. Sch. Law Negotiation Competition, 1992-94. Writer newspaper The Res Gestae, 1987-90; editor yearbook The Quadrangle, 1988-90; contbg. editor Jour. of Law Reform, 1988-90. Vol. Lincoln Park Homeless Shelter, Chgo., 1991-92, Chgo. Cares, 1993—. Recipient Negligence Sect. award Mich. Bar Assn., 1990; Carl B. Gussin Meml. prize U. Mich., 1991; scholar Elk's, 1983-84, faculty U. Colo., 1983-84; U. Colo. grantee, 1987. Mem. ABA, Colo. Bar Assn., Ill. Bar Assn., Denver Bar Assn. (vol. teen ct. 1991), Chgo. Bar Assn., Chgo. Coun. Laywers, Women Law Students Assn., U. Colo. Alumni Assn., U. Mich. Alumni Assn., Moot Ct., Mortar Bd., Phi Beta Kappa, Pi Sigma Alpha. Democrat. Presbyterian. Office: McDermott Will & Emery 227 W Monroe Chicago IL 60606-5096

DRYNAN, MARGARET ISOBEL, music teacher, retired consultant; b. Toronto, Ont., Can., Dec. 10, 1915; d. William James and Ellen (Rowney) Brown; MusB, U. Toronto, 1943; m. George Drynan, July 3, 1940; children: Judith, John, James. Mem. nat. exec. bd. Royal Can. Coll. after 1951, nat. 1st v.p., 1980-82, nat. pres., 1982-84; charter mem., pres. Oshawa Coun. for the Arts, Ont., Can., 1972-74; founder, dir. Canterbury Singers, Oshawa, 1952-69; music supr., cons. Durham Bd. Edn., 1960-81; bd. dirs. Oshawa Symphony, 1960-80, 1st v.p., 1984-86, pres., 1986—, percussionist. Dir. Oshawa Sr. Citizens Choir; adjudicator for piano and choral music Ontario Festivals. Recipient award Royal Conservatory Toronto, 1975, Lescarbot award Can. Govt., 1992, other awards; named Outstanding Women of Yr., YWCA, 1986. Fellow Royal Can. Coll. Organists (Honorary award 1976); mem. Fedn. Women Tchrs., Can. Fedn. Adjudicators, Registered Music Tchrs. (past pres.). Anglican. Clubs: Univ. Women's (past pres.); Heliconian of Toronto. Compositions include: Songs for Judith, Why do the bells?, Including Me, Missa Brevis in F, The Fate of Gilbert Gim, The Canada Goose (operetta), British Columbia, Rainy Day Song, Superjogger, Rollerskating, November, To Mary and Joseph, Prelude and Fugue in C minor for organ. Home: 589 Pinewood St, Oshawa, ON Canada L1G 2S2

DRYSDALE, ESTHER ANN, elementary school educator; b. Bessemer, Ala., Apr. 18, 1952; d. Robert Lee and Marion Roberta (Criss) Coker; m. James Duncan Drysdale IV, Mar. 12, 1974; children: James Robert, Jennifer Ann. BS, U. Montevallo, Ala., 1974; MA, U. Ala., 1982; postgrad., 1994—. Tchr. Thomas Acres Pvt. Sch., Bessemer, 1972-76; tchr. reading and math. C.F. Hard Elem. Sch., Bessemer, 1976-80, Jonesboro Elem. Sch., Bessemer, 1980—; mentor, persenter to faculty on elem. curriculum documents Ala. Dept. Edn., 1987-88; pilot reading tchr. for system on reading series adoption, 1988-89; curriculum writer. Mem. ASCD, NEA, Ala. Edn. Assn., Alpha Delta Kappa. Democrat. Baptist. Home: Southlake Estates 1001 Lake Shadows Dr 3269 Birmingham AL 35244 Office: Jonesboro Elem Sch 125 Owen Ave Bessemer AL 35020-7699

DRYSDALE, NANCY ALLENSWORTH, art dealer; b. Chgo., July 22, 1931; d. William Rolland and Frances Gertrude (Mason) Allensworth; m. Lloyd E. Hawkinson, Aug. 1, 1953 (dec. Apr. 1955); m. Robert C. McIntosh, Apr. 26, 1958 (div. 1969); 1 child, Amy Bennett; m. Douglas D. Drysdale, June 9, 1978. BS, Northwestern U., 1953. Owner, dir. Nancy Drysdale Gallery, Washington, 1977—, McIntosh/Drysdale Gallery, Washington and Houston, 1980-85. Chmn. bd. Cin. Cont. Art Ctr., 1974-75, pres., 1973-74. Named Woman of the Yr. Cin. Enquirer, 1968. Mem. Washington Art Dealers Assn. (v.p. 1991-93, pres. 1993—). Office: Nancy Drysdale Gallery 2103 O St NW Washington DC 20037

DUARTE, PATRICIA M., real estate and insurance broker; b. Truro, Mass., Feb. 23, 1938; d. Antone Jr. and Marjorie (Beckley) Duarte. Grad. high sch., Provincetown, Mass. Lic. ins. and real estate broker; constrn. supt. Sec. various ins. agys., Amherst, Mass., 1957-60; ins. and real estate agt. Duarte Ins. & Real Estate, Truro, 1960-66, owner, prin. agt., 1966-78; ins. risk mgr. J.L. Marshall & Sons, Inc., Pawtucket, R.I., 1979-92; owner, mgr. Patricia-Duarte Real Estate, Rockport, Maine, 1988—; restorer antique homes New Eng., Mass., 1979—. Mem., sec. Truro Planning Bd., 1965-72, chmn., 1974-78; mem. exec. com. Cape Cod Planning and Econ. Devel. Com., 1971-76; mem. Reelect Brawn for Senate Com., Camden, Maine, 1988; mem. Rockport Planning Bd., 1991-94, Rockport Comprehensive Plan Implementation Com., 1991-94; co-chmn. Rockport Capital Improvement Com., 1991—; bd. dirs. Cape Cod chpt. Am. Heart Assn., 1963-70; mem. Opera House Commn., 1992-94. Mem. Penobscot Bay Bd. Realtors, Profl. Ins. Agts. New Eng. (bd. dirs. 1974-76), Gen. Fedn. Women's Clubs (2nd v.p. Camden chpt. 1989). Republican. Roman Catholic. Home and Office: The Anchorage Saint Thomas VI 00802 also: 46 Pascal Ave Rockport ME 04856 also: 6600 Estate Nazareth # 55 Saint Thomas VI 00802

DUARTE, SUSANA, corporate relations executive; b. Mexico City; came to the U.S., 1984; BA, Ohio State U., 1991; grad. Campaign Mgmt. Coll. Caucus page State of Ohio Senate, Columbus, 1989, constituent aide, 1989-91; spl. asst. for polit. coalitions Rep. Nat. Com., Washington, 1991-92; exec. dir. Hispanic Internat. Trade Coun., Washington, 1992—; dir. public affairs/internat. affairs U.S. & Latin Am. Bus. Coun., Washington; mgr. corporate rels. Anheuser-Busch Corp., Woodland Hills, Calif. Bd. dirs. East L.A. YMCA, Bilingual Found. of Arts, L.A.; active in coalition building nationally for Bush/Quayle '92 campaign; prominent in statewide campaigns in Ohio. Recognized as one of 74 women changing Am. politics by Campaigns and Elections mag., 1993; recognized as one of top Hispanics in the Bush/Quayle campaign by Hispanic Business mag., 1992. Mem. D.C. Young Reps., Young Reps., Rep. Nat. Com., Rep. Hispanic Nat. Assembly. Roman Catholic. Home: 1415 Peg Pl # 302 Los Angeles CA 90035

DUBKE, MARIE EUNICE, accountant, educator, consultant; b. Buffalo, Jan. 30, 1930; d. Harold Ohm and Eunice G. (Flanders) D.; m. Gabriel P. Racz, June 16, 1962 (dec. Nov. 1988). BSBA in Acctg., SUNY, Buffalo, 1950, MBA in Acctg., 1955; PhD in Acctg., Mich. State U., 1961. CPA, Mich., Tenn. Staff acct. Deloitte Touche, Buffalo, 1950-52; instr. SUNY, Buffalo, 1952-55, Mich. State U., East Lansing, 1955-57; audit staff Deloitte Touche, Detroit, 1957-61; assoc. prof. Ctrl. Mich. U., Mt. Pleasant, 1961-67; prof. The Univ. of Memphis, 1967—; owner Fall Acctg. and Auditing Seminars, Memphis, 1991—. Contbr. articles to profl. jours. V.p., bd. dirs., mem. coms. United Way of Greater Memphis, 1970-82; bd. dirs. Opera Memphis, 1976-82, Cmty. Daycare and Comprehensive Social Svcs. Assn., Memphis, 1979-92; mem. com. on fiscal policies and procedures Dept. Human Resources, State of Tenn., 1979-81, 82, 84. Mem. AICPA (coms. 1973-89), Am. Soc. Women Accts. (A.T. Cross Woman of Achievement 1985, Ann. Disting. Svc. award 1986), Inst. Mgmt. Accts. (Harry Canon Disting. Svc. award 1981), Am. Women's Soc. CPAs (pres. 1968-69), Tenn. Soc. CPAs (coun. 1980-84, 86—, pres. Memphis chpt. 1994-95), Alpha Gamma Delta. Mem. Christian Ch. Home: 300 Vescovo Dr Memphis TN 38117 Office: U Memphis Sch Accountancy Memphis TN 38152

DUBLIN, ELVIE WILSON, clinical psychologist; b. Athens, Greece, May 18, 1937; d. Anthony I. and Rosa (Protecdicos) Nicolopoulos; m. John Wilson, Oct. 29, 1958 (div. 1967); children: David Wilson, Toni Wilson; m. James Dublin, Dec. 21, 1973 (div. 1978). BA, Ind. U., 1966, PhD, 1972. Cons. Hospitality House Nursing Home, Bedford, Ind., 1972-73; psychotherapist Choice, Inc., 1973-79, sec.-treas., 1973-79; pres. Studentworld, Inc., 1978-81; pvt. practice psychology, Bloomington, Ind., 1979—; Arabian horse breeder, founder, owner Tall Oaks Arabians, 1980-86, Dublin Racing Arabians, 1986—; bd. dirs. Midwestern Psychotherapy Inst., 1977. Trainee NSF, 1965-67, USPHS, 1967-70. Mem. Am. Psychol. Assn., Ind. Psychol. Assn., Assn. Advancement Psychology, Internat. Arabian Horse Assn., Arabian Horse Registry of Am. (assoc.), Arabian Racing Assn. Calif., Phi Beta Kappa. Clubs: Arabian Jockey, Ind. Arabian Horse. Home: 9401 E State Rd 46 Bloomington IN 47401-9243 Office: 4151 E 3rd St Bloomington IN 47401-5539

DUBOIS, NANCY Q., elementary school educator; b. St. Petersburg, Fla., June 6, 1960; d. Thomas Malcolm and Barbara Jean (Leitner) Quehl; m. Donald F. Dubois, Nov. 27, 1981; children: Jacquelyn Nicole, Justin Jared. BA, U. South Fla., Tampa, 1983; MEd, U. Fla., 1993. Cert. tchr., Fla., N.Mex., Tex. Tchr. St. Patricks Sch., Fayetteville, N.C., 1984-85, The Most Holy Name Sch., Gulfport, Fla., 1985-88, Kirtland Elem. Sch., Albuquerque, 1988-91; field advisor Coll. Edn., U. Fla., Gainesville, 1991-93; 4th grade tchr. Schulze Elem. Sch., San Antonio, 1993—. Mem. ASCD, Fla. Coun. Tchrs. of Math., Kappa Delta Pi. Republican. Roman Catholic.

DUBOUX, PATRICIA JANE, advertising agency and human resources executive; b. Chgo., Mar. 26, 1956; d. Carl Andrew and Rita Ann (Sullivan) Hulik; stepmother, Mercedes Elizabeth (Rusch) Hulik; m. Dennis Vincent DuBoux, May 17, 1986. BA in Advt., Mich. State U., 1978; MS in Indsl. Relations, Loyola U., Chgo., 1985. Media asst. Joint Commn. on Accreditation Health Care Orgns., Chgo., 1978-79, brochure asst., 1979-80, mktg. coord., 1980-81, recruitment/compensation coord., 1982-84, recruitment/employee relations mgr., 1984-86; human resources mgr. DDB Needham Worldwide, Chgo., 1986-87, dir. personnel adminstrn., 1987-89, dir. human resources, 1989-90, v.p., dir. human resources, 1990—. Mem. Human Resources Mgmt. Assn. Chgo., Soc. for Human Resource Mgmt. Home: 1025 Prairie Ave Park Ridge IL 60068-3939 Office: DDB Needham Worldwide 303 E Wacker Dr Chicago IL 60601-5212

DUBROW, MARSHA ANN, high technology company executive, composer; b. Newark, Dec. 27, 1948; d. Leo and Rose (Haberman) Dubrow; m. Daniel Leon Chaykin, Jan. 17, 1970 (div. 1985); 1 child, Alexander; m. David Lorin Rosenberg, July 3, 1988; 1 step-child, Oliver. BA cum laude, U. Pa., 1970; MA, NYU, 1975; MFA, Princeton U., 1977, postgrad., 1977-78, 81-82; postgrad., Tufts U., 1987, Am. Women's Econ. Devel. Corp. Inst., 1987-88, Leadership Am., 1988, Leadership N.J., 1990, Leadership Inst. for Workforce Devel., 1993. Prodn. coord. Children's TV Workshop, N.Y.C., 1970-73; instr. Princeton U., N.J., 1976-78; mgr. mktg. communications, ops., human resources AT&T/Techs., Inc., Morristown, N.J., 1978-80; dir. mktg. and ops. Acadia Communications, N.Y.C., 1980-83; dir. planning and mktg. Access Methods, Inc., N.Y.C., 1984-85; mng. dir. Marsha Dubrow Assocs., Upper Montclair, N.J., 1981—; pres., CEO Technolog, Inc., Upper Montclair, N.J., 1985—. Life mem. bus. and profl. group Nat. Coun. Jewish Women, Essex County, N.J., 1983—; mem. The Gathering, Whole Theater, Montclair, 1987-91, BMI Musical Theatre Workshop, N.Y.C., 1989-91; mentor U.S. Sml. Bus. Adminstrn., Office of Women Bus. Ownership, Washington, 1989—. Recipient Theodore Presser award U. Pa., 1970; fellow Tisch Sch. Arts, 1993-94; named William C. Langley fellow NYU, 1974, Princeton U. fellow, 1976-78, Josephine de Karman fellow Aerojet-Gen. Corp., 1981, Composer's fellow in Opera-Musical Theatre N.J. State Coun. Arts, 1990. Mem. NAFE, Internat. Women's Forum, Am. Women Entrepreneurs, Am. Mgmt. Assn., Dramatists Guild (assoc.), Leadership Am. Assn. (bd. dirs.), N.J. Bus. Higher Edn. Forum, N.J. Women's Forum (bd. dirs.), Dramatists Guild, Essex County Coll. Found. (bd. dirs.), Hadassah (life mem. Essex County chpt.). Home: 34 Marion Rd Montclair NJ 07043-1932 Office: Technolog Inc PO Box 913 51 Upper Montclair Plz Ste 2 Montclair NJ 07043-1340

DUBSON, JEAN CAROL, financial planner; b. N.Y.C., Oct. 26, 1932; d. Julius and Jeannette (Schad) Unger; m. Stanley Zwanger, Feb 2, 1955 (div. Mar., 1961); children: Lynn, Carol; m. Philip Dubson, June 27, 1975. BA, Bklyn. Coll., 1959; MS in Edn., CUNY, 1969; Cert. in Mgmt., Adelphi U., 1982. Cert. fin. planner, N.Y. Tchr. N.Y.C. Bd. of Edn., Bklyn., 1959-81; intern Blue Cross/Blue Shield, N.Y.C., 1981; ins. underwriter Mut. of N.Y., N.Y.C., 1982-84; registered rep. Life Planning/Global Capital, Garden City, N.Y., 1984-89, Commonwealth Equity Svcs., Newton, Mass., 1989—; pvt. practice fin. planning Fresh Meadows, N.Y., 1984—. Fin. columnist West Cunningham Pk. Civic Assn., Fresh Meadows, 1984—; vol. North Shore Univ. Hosp., Manhasset, N.Y., 1990—. Mem. Intl. Assn. Fin. Planning (bd. dirs. L.I. chpt. 1990—), Intl. Assn. Registered Fin. Planners (v.p. edn., bd. dirs. L.I. chpt 1990—). Home and Office: 73-18 192d St Fresh Meadows NY 11366

DUBUC, MARY ELLEN, educational administrator; b. N.Y.C. July 20, 1950; d. Patrick Joseph and Catherine (McKenna) Reynolds; BA cum laude (scholar), Marymount Manhattan Coll., 1972; MA, Columbia U., 1973; cert. advanced grad. studies R.I. Coll., 1985; m. Leo Dennis Dubuc Jr., Sept. 9, 1978; children: Brian Robert, Kimberly Ann. Spl. edn. tchr. Cardinal Cushing Sch., Hanover, Mass., 1973-76, Ferncliff Manor Sch., Yonkers, N.Y., 1976-77; program coordinator Bronx Devel. Services, 1977-78; dir. edn. R.I. Assn. Retarded, Woonsocket, 1978-84, spl. edn. cons., 1984-92; qualified med. retardation profl. Seacliff, Inc., Cumberland, R.I., 1988-91; tchr. BICO Collaborative Program, North Attleboro, Mass., 1989; acting exec. dir. Seacliff, Inc., 1991-93; dir. quality assurance Avatar, Inc., 1992; dir. specialized svcs. The ARC of No. R.I., Woonsocket, 1992—. Fed. trainee, 1971, 72. Mem. North Smithfield PTA, 1986—; ednl. evaluator No. R.I. Collaborative, 1992. Mem. Assn. Severely Handicapped, R.I. Assn. Retarded Citizens, NAFE, R.I. Assn. Adult and Continuing Edn. (v.p. pub. rels. 1986-89, corr. sec. 1991-93), Alpha Chi. Democrat. Roman Catholic. Office: The ARC of No RI 80 Fabien St Woonsocket RI 02895-6292

DUCHI, TONI JO, public relations professional; b. Kane, Pa., Nov. 24, 1952; d. Farry and Marjory June (Hayduk) D. BS, Pa. State U., 1988. Sec. IPM Corp., Ridgway, Pa., 1970-76, North Cen. Pa. Regional Planning/Devel. Commn., Ridgway, 1976-82; sec. Pa. State U., University Park, 1982-88, asst. to the dean for pub. rels. Coll. of Edn., 1988—. Editor: College of Edn. Alumni mag., 1988—. Vice-pres. bd. dirs. PAWS (Promotion of Animal Welfare and Safety), State College, Pa., 1986—. Recipient Gold medal in alumni programming, Coun. for Advancement and Support of Edn., Washington, 1993. Mem. Coun. of Pa. Pub. Rels. Profls., NAFE, Phi Delta Kappa (treas. 1992-94), Gamma Sigma Delta. Home: RR 2 Box 532 Port Matilda PA 16870-9617 Office: Pa State Univ 248 Chambers Bldg Univ Park PA 16802-3206

DUCKETT, JOAN, law librarian; b. Bklyn., Oct. 21, 1934; d. Stephen and Mary (Wehrum) Kearney; m. Richard Duckett, Aug. 25, 1956; children: Richard, David, Daniel, Deirdre. BA, Kean Coll., 1974; MLS, Rutgers U., 1977; JD, Suffolk U., 1983; postgrad., Oxford (Eng.) U., 1986. Bar: Mass. 1983, U.S. Ct. Appeals (fed. cir.) 1984. Media specialist Oak Knoll Sch., Summit, N.J., 1976-80; law clk. Dist. Atty. Suffolk County, Boston, 1982; vol. atty. Cambridgeport Problem Ctr., Cambridge, Mass., 1984-85; reference libr. Harvard Law Sch. Libr., Cambridge, 1982-84, coord. The New Eng. Law Libr. Consortium, 1984-87, head reference svcs., 1987—, profl. devel. com., chmn. Bryant fellowship award panel, 1987—. Contbr. articles to profl. jours. Protocol hostess L.A. Olympic Com., 1984. Fellow Mass. Bar Found.; mem. Mass. Bar Assn., Boston Bar Assn., Am. Assn. Law Librs., Law Librs. New Eng., Assn. Boston Law Librs., Alpha Sigma Lambda, Beta Phi Mu. Office: Harvard Law Sch Libr Langdell Hall Cambridge MA 02138

DUCKWORTH, ROSEMARY ELLEN, trust officer; b. Iowa City, Iowa, Apr. 12, 1949; d. Joseph Asa Hoyt and Mary Jane (Brobst) Vandermark; m. Louis O. Scott, Oct. 16, 1965 (div. Nov. 1968); children: Wayne L. Lawson, Jo Anna Jane Kollasch; m. David K. Duckworth, July 23, 1983 (div. Dec. 1994); 1 child, Mary Rose. Cert. in applied banking/consumer credit, Am. Inst. Banking, 1988; cert. in trust adminstrn., Cannon Fin. Inst., 1989, cert. trust ops. specialist, 1991; BBA, So. Calif. U., 1992. Teller Community Bank of Fla., St. Petersburg, 1973-75; bookkeeper Chevron Svc. Sta., St. Petersburg, 1975-77, Landmark Bank, St. Petersburg, 1977-80; teller First Nat. Bank of Ely, Nev., 1981, Nev. Bank and Trust, Ely, 1982; asst. v.p. and trust officer First Nat. Bank Farmington, N.Mex., 1983—; pres., founder Day Camp Southside, St. Petersburg, 1976-77. Planning chmn. terr. 5 ann. meeting ARC, Farmington, 1990-91, babysitting instr., 1990—, basic aid tng. instr., 1992, Project Read instr., 1994. Recipient Appreciation award ARC, 1991. Mem. Fin. Women Internat. (by-laws com. 1990-91, treas. 1993-94), Nat. Assn. Trust Ops. Specialists (bd. dirs. 1992), Am. Bus. Women's Assn. (v.p. 1991, pres. 1992, Appreciation award 1989, Woman of Yr. 1995). Republican. Baptist. Home: 218 N Court Ave #3 Farmington NM 87401-5721 Office: First Nat Bank Farmington PO Box 4540 Farmington NM 87499-4540

DUCKWORTH, TARA ANN, insurance company executive; b. Seattle, June 7, 1956; d. Leonard Douglas and Audrey Lee (Limbeck) Hill; m. Mark L. Duckworth, May 16, 1981; children: Harrison Lee III, Andrew James, Kathryn Anne. AAS, Highline Community Coll., Seattle, 1976. Acctg. clk. SAFECO Inc. Co., Seattle, programmer analyst, 1977-80, programming supr., 1980-85, info. systems supr., 1985-90; rate systems mgr. mut. funds SAFECO Credit, SAFECO Trust, PNMR, Seattle, 1990-94, sys. mgr., 1994—; mem. tech adv. com. for the computer info. svcs. program North Seattle Community Coll., 1984—, chairperson tech. adv. com., 1988-90. Mem. STar Lake Improvement Club, 1988-94, St. Lukes Luth. Ch., 1986—, fellowship com. Mem. NAFE, Nat. Assn. for Ins. Women, Soc. for State Filers, Nat. PTA. Office: SAFECO Ins Co SAFECO Plz Seattle WA 98185

DUCOTE, CHARLOTTE ANNE, allied health services administrator; b. Baton Rouge, Oct. 21, 1951; d. Gaston Camille and Edna Lora (Bossier) D. BA in Speech and Hearing Therapy, La. State U., 1972, PhD in Speech-Lang. Pathology, 1983; MA in Speech and Hearing Scis., Vanderbilt U., 1973. Cert. clin. competence in speech-lang. pathology; lic. speech-lang. pathology, La. Speech-lang. clinician Met. Schs. of Nashville and Davidson County, 1973-74; speech and hearing cons., acad. instr. dept. spl. edn. U. New Orleans, 1974-78; speech-lang. pathologist, coord. speech and hearing svc. dept. pediatrics and adult units Earl K. Long Meml. Hosp., Baton Rouge, 1978-81; head sect. speech-lang. pathology La. Rehab. Inst. of Charity Hosp., New Orleans, 1982-87; assoc. program dir. New Medico Rehab. Ctr. of La., Folsom, 1987; asst. prof. medicine rehab. medicine sect./dept. medicine La. State U. Sch. Medicine, 1986-87; program dir. New Medico Rehab. Ctr. La., Folsom, 1987-88; program dir. post-acute brain injury program Touro Rehab. Ctr., New Orleans, 1989-94; dir. div. communicative disorders Ochsner Med. Instns., New Orleans, 1994—; speech-lang. pathology cons. dept. pediatrics Ochsner Med. Ctr., 1978; instr. speech dept. La. State U., Baton Rouge, 1979, clin. supr. articulation disorders and cleft palate clinics, 1979, 81-82; speech-lang. pathologist Upjohn Home Health Care Svc. and Americare Home Health Svc., Baton Rouge, 1981-82; speech-lang. pathology cons. Greenwell Springs Hosp., Baton Rouge, 1981-82; mem. utilization review com. St. Tammany Parish Home Health Svcs., Covington, La., 1980, Am. Healthcare Svc., Baton Rouge, 1981-82; clinical supr. off-site clinical training program La. State U., 1983-86; program com. chair Gov's task force La. Conf. for Disabled Persons, 1986; mem. Hosp./Sch. Linkage Com., 1991—; mem. program com. Internat. Brain Injury Symposium, 1991; adj. instr. comm. disorders La. State U. Med. Ctr., 1992—. Contbr. articles and revs. to profl. publs. Active Coalition for Citizens with Disabilities. Phi Mu-Mary King Shepardson fellow, 1978. Mem. Am. Speech-Lang.-Hearing Assn. (clin. reviewer 1977-85, assoc. editor 1986-90), Nat. Head Injury Found., La. Speech and Hearing Assn. (mem. rehab. and med. agys. com. 1984—), La. Head Injury Found. (co-founder 1983, coord., pres. 1983-86, bd. dirs. 1986—, sec., bd. dirs. 1987-90, program co-chair ann. conf. 1990, 91, 92, pres. 1993-94, Profl. of Yr. award 1991), New Orleans Neuropathology Interest Group. Office: Ochsner Clinic 6-South 1514 Jefferson Hwy New Orleans LA 70121

DUCRAN, CLAUDETTE DELORIS, bank officer; b. Trinityville, St. Thomas, Jamaica, July 23, 1941; came to U.S., 1962; d. Wellesley Provan and Hilda Maude (Beckford) DuC. Student, Corcoran Sch. Art, Washington, 1967; cert. of diploma, USDA Grad. Sch., Washington, 1972; BBA, George Washington U., 1982. Adminstrv. asst. World Bank, Washington, 1964-75, fin. asst., 1975-85, ops. asst., 1985-88, disbursement asst., 1988—; mem. adv. com. Very Spl. Arts Kennedy Ctr., Washington, 1990-93, Hands Across Hemisphere Craft Ctr., Washington, 1991; founder, pres. Let's Learn by Reading, Jamaica, 1990—; bd. dirs. Universal Investment Bank Ltd., Kingston, Jamaica. Author: (booklet) Exhibitors Guidelines, 1989, 90. Bd. dirs. Craft Ctr., Washington, 1991—; panelist Career Week George Washington U., Washington, 1991, Women's Ctr., McLean, Va., 1991. Recipient 1st prize Writer's League, Washington, 1967, Internat. Order of Merit, 1994; named Internat. Woman of Yr., 1993-94. Mem. Profl. Bankers Assn., World Affairs Coun., Soc. for Internat. Devel., IMF-World Bank Caribbean Assn., The World Bank Art Soc. (v.p. 1986-88, pres. 1988-93), UN Assn./Nat. Capital Assn. Home: The Brighton 2123 California St NW # B-1 Washington DC 20008-1874 Office: World Bank 1818 H St NW Washington DC 20433

DUCY, PATRICIA CORNELIA, financial executive; b. Bklyn., July 17, 1945; d. Clement Ambrose and Ellen Catherine (O'Brien) D. Student, Ottumwa Heights Jr. Coll., 1963-64, George Washington U., 1967-69, No. Va. Community Coll., 1980-83, USDA Grad. Sch., Washington, 1983-84. Mgr. staffing audit dept. Arthur Andersen & Co., Washington, 1973-75; comptroller The Co. Inkwell, Arlington, Va., 1976-78; registrar Antioch Sch. Law, Washington, 1978-79; dir. fin. and adminstrn. SRA Corp., Arlington, Va., 1979-81; mem. staff com. govt.-univ. rels. NAS, Washington, 1981-83; dir. fin. and adminstrn. Advanced Systems Devel. Inc., Alexandria, Va., 1983-90; adminstrv. exec. Vanguard Svcs. Unltd., 1990-93; prin. Ancient City Estates & Liquidations, 1994—; cons. in field; treas. Vanguard Svcs., Inc., Arlington, 1989-90, also bd. dirs. Del. Citizen Amb. Program to China, 1988; vol. J.F. Kennedy Campaign, Bethesda, Md., 1960, Georgetown U. Hosp., Washington, 1960-63; sec. D.C. chpt. Am. Jr. Red Cross, 1962; prodn. coord. Am. Light Opera Co., Washington, 1964-67. Recipient 500-hour award Georgetown U. Hosp., 1961. Mem. Nat. Bus. and Profl. Women's Orgn., Am.

Soc. Pers. Adminstrs., Nat. Orgn. Victim Assistance, Ams. for Legal Reform. Democrat. Roman Catholic.

DUDACK, GAIL MARIE, brokerage house executive; b. Johnson City, N.Y., Aug. 17, 1948; d. John and Maria (Kostun) D.; m. Pasquale J. Colombo, Feb. 14, 1987; 1 child, James Ross Colombo. BA, Skidmore Coll., 1970; postgrad., NYU, 1971-72, N.Y. Inst. Fin., 1971-72. With Pershing div. Donaldson, Lufkin & Jenrette, Inc. and predecessor firm, N.Y.C., 1970-87, v.p., head tech. analysis, 1977-87; sr. v.p., market strategist S.G. Warburg & Co. Inc., N.Y.C., 1987-93; mng. dir., head U.S. Investment Strategy S.G. Warburg & Co., Inc., N.Y.C., 1993—; panelist Wall St. Week, PBS, 1975—; mem. bus. rsch. adv. coun. U.S. Dept. Labor, 1977-80; pres. DLJ, Inc., Fed. Credit Union, 1977-79; arbitrator Nat. Assn. Securities Dealers, 1976-80. Contbr. articles to profl. jours. Co-chmn. bus. dept. adv. coun. Skidmore Coll., 1978-79, fin. adv. to bd. trustees, 1982; bd. dirs. S.G. Warburg & Co. retirement plan. Mem. Assn. for Investment Mgmt. and Rsch., N.Y. Soc. Security Analysts (bd. dirs.) Market Technicians Assn. (treas. 1978-79, 79-80, v.p. 1982-83, sec. 1983-84, v.p., chair sem. 1984-85, pres. 1985-86, 86-87), Internat. Fedn. Tech. Analysts (founding mem., liaison Market Techs. Assn. 1987-89), Fin. Women's Assn., Am. Econs. Assn., Trends (v.p. 1990-92). Office: SG Warburg & Co Inc 787 7th Ave New York NY 10019-6018

DU DASH, KAREN SHREFFLER, community health nurse; b. Melrose Park, Ill., Mar. 15, 1947; d. Keith Donald and E. Ruth (Kraemer) Shreffler; m. Joseph F. Du Dash, Feb. 23, 1985; 1 child, Ryan Matthew. BS in Nursing, Northeast Mo. U., 1970. Staff nurse gastro-intensive ICU Hines (Ill.) VA Hosp., 1970; staff/charge nurse Story County Hosp., Nevada, Iowa, 1972-73; sch. nurse Lenox (Iowa) Community Sch. System, 1971-72; staff/charge nurse med.-surg. Mercy Hosp., Cedar Rapids, Iowa, 1973-85; Staff/charge nurse oncology med.-surg. Franklin Square Hosp., Balt., 1985-86; home health nurse Balt. County Health Dept., Balt., 1987—, Johns Hopkins Home Health, 1993—. Mem. Assn. for Home Care, Inc. (rep.), Northeast Mo. U. Alumni Assn.

DUDASH, LINDA CHRISTINE, insurance executive; b. Pitts.; d. Andrew Daniel and Lillian (Reynolds) D. BA in English, Point Park Coll., 1969. Tech. writer Am. Insts. for Rsch., Pitts., 1968-69; claim svc. rep. Reliance Ins. Co., Pitts., 1969-70, claim rep., 1970-71; claim mgr. Reliance Ins. Co., Jacksonville, Fla., 1971-73, Harrisburg, Pa., 1973-80, Chgo., 1980-86; H.O. sr. claim supr. Zurich Ins. Co., Schaumburg, Ill., 1986-88; asst. v.p., mgr. liability claims Zurich-Am. Ins., Schaumburg, Ill., 1988-91, asst. v.p., mgr. claims continuous improvement, 1991-92, v.p. dir. field ops., 1992—. Office: Zurich Ins Co Zurich Towers 1400 American Ln Schaumburg IL 60196-1056

DUDGEON, RUTH ARLENE, historian; b. Lansdale, Pa., Oct. 31, 1938; d. Abram Meyers and Pearl Erb (Sterner) Fluck; m. William O. Dudgeon, June 8, 1957 (div. Jan. 12, 1976); children: William Scott, Renee Lynne. BA, Anderson Coll., 1960; MA, Ball State U., 1966; PhD, George Washington U., 1975. Tchr. history and math Madison Heights High Sch., Anderson, Ind., 1961-66; instr. history Ball State U., Muncie, Ind., 1966-68; asst. to dir. rsch. UMW Health & Retirement Funds, Washington, 1975-77, mgr. invoice rev., 1977-78; vis. asst. prof. Howard U., Washington, 1981-82, W.Va. U., Morgantown, 1982-84; sr. historian History Assocs. Inc., Rockville, Md., 1984—, v.p. ops., 1987-91, exec. v.p., 1991—; hist. cons. U.S. Dept. Edn., Washington, 1980-81; dir. History Assocs. Inc., Rockville, 1988—. Contbr. articles and book revs. to profl. publs. Grad. Teaching fellow George Washington U., 1968-72, Young scholar Leningrad State U., 1978-79, Vis. scholar Kennan Inst. for Advanced Russian Studies, 1981. Mem. Am. Assn. for Advancement Slavic Studies, Am. Hist. Assn., Nat. Coun. for Pub. History, Soc. for History in Fed. Govt. Office: History Assocs Inc 5 Choke Cherry Rd Rockville MD 20850-4004

DUDICS-DEAN, SUSAN ELAINE, interior designer; b. Perth Amboy, N.J., Oct. 22, 1950; d. Theodore W. and Joyce M. (Ryals) D.; m. Rick Dean, Apr. 30, 1989; 1 child, Merissa Joyce. BS in Sociology, W.Va. U., 1972; postgrad. Rutgers U., 1975-78, U. Calif., Irvine, 1979-81, Can. Coll., 1981-89. Programmer Prudential Life, Newark, 1972-73; sr. systems analyst Johnson & Johnson, New Brunswick, N.J., 1973-78, Sperry Univac, Irvine, Calif., 1978-80; sr. systems analyst, project leader Robert A. McNeil, San Mateo, Calif., 1981-83; dist. design dir. TransDesigns, Woodstock, Ga., 1982-93. lectr. in the field of interior design, 1994—. Contbr. articles to profl. jours.; writer (newspaper column) Design Lines, 1993—; guest (TV shows) House Doctor, Marketplace Sta. KGO-TV. High sch. mentor Directions, San Francisco, 1985—. Mem. Women Entreprenuers (membership com., treas. 1983-87), Cen. N.J. Alumni Assn. Delta Gamma (assoc. sec., founder, pres.), San Francisco C. of C., Nat. Assn. of Profl. Saleswomen, Am. Soc. Interior Designers (allied mem. 1989-92), Women's Bus. Network, Delta Gamma. Recipient awards TransDesigns, Woodstock, Ga., 1984, 85, 86, 87, 89, 90, 91. Avocations: skiing, sewing, scuba diving, ballet, hand crafts.

DUDIS, LOUISE ANNE, artist; b. Gardner, Mass., Mar. 4, 1950; d. Roger George and Priscella Estelle (LaFlamme) D. BA, Conn. Coll., New London, 1972. Exhibited in shows at MMC Gallery, N.Y.C., 1990, Orgn. Ind. Artists, N.Y.C., 1991, 93, Sculpture Ctr., N.Y.C., 1992, Trenkmann Gallery, N.Y.C., 1992, Penine Hart Gallery, N.Y.C., 1993, Conn. Coll., 1994, Ben Shahn Galleries/William Patterson Coll., Wayne, N.J., 1993, others. Home: 9 E Broadway New York NY 10038-1072

DUDLEY, BARBARA, environmental association administrator. Dir. Nat. Lawyers Guild, 1983-87, Veatch Program, N.Y.C., 1987-93; exec. dir. Greenpeace U.S.A., D.C., 1993—. Office: Greenpeace USA 1436 U St NW Washington DC 20009-3997*

DUDLEY, ELIZABETH HYMER, retired security executive; b. Hibbing, Minn., Mar. 12, 1937; d. Howard Golden and Esther Juliette (Wanner) Hymer; m. Richard Walter Dudley, 1962. BA Brown U., 1959; postgrad. U. Calif., Berkeley. With AT&T Bell Labs., Murray Hill, N.J., 1959-89, systems programmer, personnel info., 1965-67, systems analyst, personnel info., 1967-71, sr. systems analyst, mgmt. info. and adminstrv. systems, 1971-77, applications systems coordinator mgmt. info. and adminstrv. systems, 1977-78, group supr. affirmative action compliance and reports, 1978-81, group supr. service ops. system support group, 1982-84, mgr. security, 1984-85, mgr. govt. security, 1986-89; ret., 1989. Bd. dirs. Boca Ballet Theatre Co., 1994—; treas. Fla. Atlantic U. Vol. League, 1993-94; chmn. sales Boca Ballet Guild, 1994, pres. 1994—. Mem. Humanitarian Society, Brown Nat. Alumni Sch. Program, Nat. Security Indsl. Assn., Women's Rights Assn. (treas. 1977, v.p. 1978), Am. Soc. Indsl. Security, Nat. Classification Mgmt. Soc., Brown Network, Royal Palm Improvement Assn. (bd. govs., chair. environ. inspection 1993-94, v.p., 1994, pres. 1994—, chair security, 1994), Freinds of the Boca Pops. Club: Pembroke Coll. of N.J. (publicity chmn. 1965-69, v.p. 1969-70).

DUDLEY, LAQUITA JOY, resource specialist, educational consultant; b. Amherst, Tex., May 26, 1932; d. James Henry and Mable Claire (Bostick) Dillingham; m. Harold Clay Dudley; children: Harold Scott, Janet Ellen. BA in History, Mills Coll., Oakland, Calif., 1953; MA in Spl. Edn., Chapman Coll., Monterey, Calif., 1980. Tchr. Salinas (Calif.) City Schs., 1954-64, tchr., 1972-82, resource specialist, 1982-91; assoc. Dudley & Assocs., Salinas, 1991—. Mem. AAUW, Calif. Sch. Leadership Acad., Monterey County Reading Assn., Calif. Reading Assn., Calif. Tchrs. Assn., NEA, Calif. Assn. Resource Spl., Monterey Bay Resource Spl. (pres. 1986-88), Monterey Mills Club (pres. 1962-63), Delta Kappa Gamma (pres. 1988-90), Salinas Elem. Tchrs. Coun. (rep., scholarship com. 1975-90). Democrat. Presbyterian. Office: 75 San Miguel Ave Salinas CA 93901-3059

DUER, ELLEN ANN DAGON, anesthesiologist; b. Balt., Feb. 3, 1936; d. Emmett Paul and Annie (Sollers) Dagon; m. Lyle Jordan Millan IV, Dec. 21, 1963; children: Lyle Jordan V, Elizabeth Lyle, Ann Sheridan Worthington.; m. T. Marshall Duer, Jr., Aug. 23, 1985. A.B., George Washington U., 1959; M.D., U. Md., 1964; postgrad., Johns Hopkins U., 1965-68. Intern Union Meml. Hosp., Balt., 1964-65; resident anesthesiology Johns Hopkins Hosp., Balt., 1965-68, fellow in surgery, 1965-68; practice medicine specializing in anesthesiology Balt., 1968—; faculty Church Home and Hosp., Balt., 1969—; attending staff Union Meml. Hosp., Church Home and Hosp., Frankling Sq. Hosp., Children's Hosp., James Lawrence Kernan Hosp., Balt., 1982-94; co-chief anesthesiology James Kernan Hosp., 1983-94, med. dir. out-patient surgery dept., 1987-94; mem. med. exec. com. Kernan Hosp., 1988-94; affiliate cons. emergency room Church Home and Hosp., Balt., 1969—, mem. med. audit and utilizaions com., 1970-72, mem. emergency and ambulatory care com., 1973-74, chief emergency dept., 1973-74; cons. anesthesiologist Md. State Penitentiary, 1971; fellow in critical care medicine Md. Inst. Emergency Medicine, 1975-76; mem. infection control com. U. Md. Hosp., 1975—; instr. anesthesiology U. Md. Sch. Medicine, 1975—; staff anesthesiologist Mercy Hosp., 1978—, audit com., 1979-80, 82; asst. prof. anesthegiology U. Md. Med. Sch., 1989—; mem. med. exec. com. Kernan Hosp., 1990—, v.p. 1990, chief of staff, 1992—; mem. Tappahannock Family Practice, 1994—; mem. Commonwealth of Va. Med. Bd. Mem. AMA, Am. Coll. Emergency Physicians, Met. Emergency Dept. Heads Am., Md. Soc. Anesthesiologists, Balt. County Med. Soc., Mid. Peninsula Med. Soc., No. Neck Med. Soc., Med. Soc. Va., Med. and Choir Faculty Med., Chiurgical Soc., Internat. Congress Anaesthesiologists, Internat. Anesthesia Rsch. Soc., Am. L'Hirondelle Club, Annapolis Yacht Club, Chesapeake Bay Yacht Racing Assn. Episcopalian. Address: Deep Creek Farm House Rt 3 Box 4634 Lancaster VA 22503

DUERIG, GILBERTE JILL, water quality engineer; b. Milw., Mar. 8, 1953; d. William R. and Germaine M. (Reback) Frey; m. Thomas W. Duerig, June 8, 1974; children: Kristin, Laura, Thomas J. BS in Fundamental Sci., Lehigh U., 1974; MSCE, U. Pitts., 1978. Registered civil engr., Calif.; cert. operator, grade 5, Calif., WA-1, Pa. Chemist Western Pa. Water Co., Pitts., 1975-77, water quality supr., 1977-79, dir. water quality, 1979-80; asst. engr. Alameda County Water Dist., Fremont, Calif., 1986-88, assoc. engr., 1988-89, divsn. engr., 1989-92, prodn. mgr., 1992—; bd. dirs. South Bay Engrs., Fremont; mem. Hazardous Waste Tech. Adv. Com., Alameda County, 1990-92; co-chair Watekeuse-Potable Reuse Subcom., San Diego, 1992-94. Mem. ASCE, Am. Chem. Soc., Am. Water Works Assn. Office: Alameda County Water Dist PO Box 5110 Fremont CA 94537

DUERME, ELIZA DOBLE, engineering manager; b. Quezon City, The Philippines, May 19, 1959; came to U.S., 1981; d. Joe A. and Ester (Doble) D. BS in Stats., U. of the Philippines, 1981; MS in Stats., Calif. State U., Hayward, 1983. Software engr. U.S. Sprint, Burlingame, Calif., 1981-88; sr. engr. Network Equipment Tech., Redwood City, Calif., 1988-90, prin. engr., 1990-92, mgr., 1992—. Pres. Philippine Internat. Aid, San Francisco, 1989—; mem. Amnesty Internat., San Mateo, Calif., 1988-90. Home: 1285 Montecito Ave # 43 Mountain View CA 94043

DUERR, DIANNE MARIE, physical education educator, professional sports medicine consultant; b. Buffalo, July 14, 1945; d. Robert John and Aileen Louise (Scherer) D. BS in Health and Phys. Edn., SUNY, Brockport, 1967; cert., SUNY, Oswego, 1982; postgrad., Canisius Coll., 1970-71. Cert. tchr., N.Y. Tchr. North Syracuse (N.Y.) Sch. Dist., 1967—; tchr. dept. orthopedic surgery SUNY Health Sci. Ctr. at Syracuse, 1982—; creator Inst. for Sports Medicine and Human Performance SUNY Health Sci. Ctr., Syracuse, 1988; coord. scholastic sports injury reporting system project SUNY, 1985—; mem. com. on scholastic sports-related injuries NIH Inst. Arthritis, Musculoskeletal and Skin Diseases, 1993—. Author: SSIRS Pilot Study Report, 1987, SSIRS Fall Study Report, 1988, SHASIRS Report, 1991; creator Scholastic Sports Injury Reporting System, 1985, Scholastic Head and Spine Injury Reporting System, 1989. Mem. com. on scholastic sports-related injuries NIH, Inst. Arthritis, Musculoskeletal and Skin Diseases, 1993—; co-chmn. sports medicine USA Amateur Athletic Union, Nat. Jr. Olympic Games, Syracuse, 1987; vol. sports medicine N.Y. State Sr. Games, 1990-94; active Girl Scouts U.S.A. Mem. AAHPERD (N.Y. State chpt. pres. exercise sci. and sports medicine sect.), Am. Coll. Sports Medicine, United Univ. Profs., Am. Fedn. Tchrs., N.Y. United Tchrs., North Syracuse Tchrs. Assn. Home: 418 Buffington Rd Syracuse NY 13224-2208 Office: SUNY Dept Orthopedic Surgery 550 Harrison Ctr Syracuse NY 13202-3054

DUFF, DORIS EILEEN (SHULL), critical care nurse; b. Va., Feb. 23, 1960; d. Harley Ray and Eloise (Whitmer) Shull; m. William DeLaney Duff, Feb. 1, 1992; 1 child, William D. II. BS in Gen. Sci., Radford (Va.) U., 1983; diploma in nursing, Roanoke (Va.) Meml. Hosps., 1985. RN, Va. Med.-surg. nurse Roanoke Meml. Hosp., 1985-87, nurse emergency-trauma dept., 1987—. Mem. Emergency Nurses Assn. (pres. Roanoke chpt. 1995), Roanoke Mem. Hosps. Sch. Nursing Alumni Assn. Office: Roanoke Meml Hosp Belleview at Jefferson Sts Roanoke VA 24033

DUFF, PATRICIA, foundation administrator; b. L.A., Apr. 12, 1954; d. Robert Orr and Mary Williamson; m. Ronald Perelman; 1 child, Caleigh Sophia Perelman. Student, Internat. Sch. Brussels, 1971, Barnard Coll.; BS in Internat. Econs., Georgetown U., 1976. Spl. asst. to chief counsel house select com. on assassinations U.S. Ho. of Reps., Washington, 1969; prodr., writer, researcher John McLaughlin Show-NBC Radio, Washington, 1979-80; asst. rsch. dir. Dem. Nat. Com., Washington, 1980; v.p. Patrick Caddell and Assocs., Washington, 1980-82, Squier, Eskew Assoc., 1982-84; advt. cons. Communications Co., Washington, 1982-83; celebrity coord. Mondale for Pres., L.A., 1984, Americans for Hart, L.A., 1984; ind. producer Columbia Pictures, Burbank, Calif.; pres. Revlon Found., 1995—; assoc. producer Dem. Nat. Conv., Atlanta, 1988; mem. nat. media adv. bd. Hart for Pres., L.A., 1988. Contbg. editor Vogue Mag., 1969; co-producer films Limit Up, 1989, documentary For Your Family's Sake, 1987. Mem. platform com. Dem. Nat. Conv., 1984, N.Y.C., 1992; mem. Hollywood Women's Polit. Com., 1986; mem. adv. bd. Children's Action Network; mem. bd. councilors Ascus sch. pub. policy and adminstrn. U. So. Calif.; founder, chair bd. dirs. Show Coalition, L.A., 1988-89; founder, bd. dirs. Edn. 1st, Calif., 1988; bd. visitors sch. fgn. svc. Georgetown U., 1988—; founder Am. Spirit Awards, 1992; active L.A. Colors United, City Kids, Summer of Svc., Nat. Svc., 1993, L.A. Commn. on Status of Women, 1994—; chair Gov.'s Task Force Teen Pregnancy, 1994-95; trustee Nat. Pub. Radio; bd. dirs. Planned Parenthood, L.A., 1988—, Citizen's Rsch. Found., 1988-90, Show Coalition/The Common Good, 1988—, Nat. Abortion Rights Action League, Washington, 1990, Women in Film Found., 1990—. Named one of Rising Young Stars L.A. Times, 1989; named Dem. of Yr. L.A. County, 1989; recipient Women We Love award for polit. activism Esquire Mag., 1990. Office: 38 E 63d St New York NY 10021

DUFFY, BETTY MINOR, art gallery owner, art appraiser; b. Ft. Smith, Ark., Dec. 13, 1920; d. Robert West and Wrenetta M. (Tanner) Minor; m. Douglas Monteith Duffy, July 3, 1945; children: Wrenetta Ward, Elizabeth Woodford. BA, Okla. State U., 1942; postgrad., U. Conn., 1944, Paris, 1947-49. Owner, operator Bethesda (Md.) Art Gallery, 1975—. Office: 7950 Norfolk Ave Bethesda MD 20814

DUFFY, CYNTHIA ANN, art educator; b. Providence, June 16, 1947; d. George and Margaret (Falcone) DiNunzio; m. William Charles Duffy, June 23, 1972; 1 child, Amanda. BS, R.I. Coll., 1969; MA in Tchg. in Fine Arts, Assumption Coll., Worcester, Mass., 1976; MLS, U. R.I., 1985. Cert. profl. life art tchr., R.I. Tchr. art Pawtucket (R.I.) Sch., 1969-73; instr. art Providence Coll., 1971-81; tchr. art East Greenwich (R.I.) Sch., 1979—; instr. art RISD, Providence and Barrington, 1986—, R.I. Coll., Providence, 1992—; organizer R.I. Scholastic Art Awards, 1989-92, chair exhibit wrapup, transition dir., 1992-93, mem. coms. 1988—. Bd. dirs. Scenic R.I., Warwick, 1993-94. Mem. NEA, Nat. Art Edn. Assn., R.I. Art Tchrs. Assn. (pres.-elect 1989-91, pres. 1991-93, programs com. 1993—, editor newsletter 1993—). Roman Catholic. Home: 5 Cold Spring Rd Barrington RI 02806

DUFFY, JUDITH F., public relations consultant, freelance writer; b. Chgo., July 18, 1942; d. Joseph Michael and Rita Mary (Sammons) Fay; m. Daniel Joseph Duffy, July 16, 1942; children: Timothy Sean, Patrick Joseph, Michael Fahey. BA cum laude, Duchesne Coll., 1964; postgrad., Georgetown U., 1965-66, U. Nebr., 1988—. Pres. Intermedia Assocs. Inc., Omaha, 1975—; dir. comm. Mostly Media & Pixel Image Tranformatte, Omaha, 1989-91; cons., dir. BASE, Inc., Omaha, 1989—; cons. Cottonwood Comm., Omaha, 1993—. Bd. dirs. Nebr. Alzheimers Assn., Omaha, 1990—, Duchesne Acad., 1980—, Gen. Crook House Bd., 1980—, Jr. League Omaha, 1980—, St. Joseph's Hosp., 1980—. Mem. Nebr. Women's Amateur Golf Assn., Omaha Women's Golf Assn., Kappa Gamma Pi, Omaha Country Club. Home: 615 Fairacres Rd Omaha NE 68132-1833 Office: Intermedia Assocs Inc 615 N 64th St Omaha NE 68132

DUFFY, LAUREL ANN, lawyer; b. Mpls., Dec. 17, 1946; d. John I. and Betty Harriet (Sommer) D. BS with distinction, U. Minn., 1972; MS, U. Nev., 1977; JD, U. Colo., 1988. Bar: Nev. 1988, U.S. Dist. Ct. Nev. 1988, U.S. Ct. Appeals (9th cir.) 1989. Tchr. learning disabilities St. Paul Pub. Schs., 1972-73; tchr. learning disabilities Gallup (N.Mex.) Pub. Schs., 1973-74, psychometrist, 1974-75; tchr. phys. handicapped Clark County Pub. Schs., Las Vegas, 1975-78, tchr. learning disabled, 1978-85; assoc. Galane, Tanksley, Rickdall & Ballif, Las Vegas, 1988-93, Combs & England, Las Vegas, 1993-94, Law Offices E. Leslie Combs, Jr., Las Vegas, 1994—. Author: Duffysigns-Sign Language, 1985. Recipient Legal Aid award U. Colo., 1987. Mem. ABA, Nev. State Bar Assn., Clark County Bar Assn., Nev. Trial Lawyers Assn., Assn. Trial Lawyers Am. (inadequate security litigation group), Nev. Am. Inn of Ct. Democrat. Office: 704 S 9th St Las Vegas NV 89101-7015

DUFFY, MARGARET MCLAUGHLIN, nephrology nurse, educator; b. N.Y.C., Feb. 5, 1939; d. Paul Anthony and Margaret Doris (Thorne) McLaughlin; children: William, Paul, Eileen. BSN, Villanova U., 1960; MA, Columbia U., 1966; EdD, U. S.C., 1989. Cert. nephrology nurse; cert. case mgr. Instr. nursing Salve Regina Coll., Newport, R.I., 1970-72; asst. prof. nursing Bristol C.C., Fall River, Mass., 1973-75, Grossmont C.C., El Cajon, Calif., 1976-77; assoc. prof. nursing Med. U. S.C., Charleston, 1978—, case mgr. renal transplant svc., 1990-94, clin. educator, 1994—. Contbr. articles to profl. jours. Lt. comdr. USN, 1960-69; lt. col. USAR, 1983—. Sandoz Pharms. clin. practice fellow, 1989; Amgen Ednl. scholar, 1990; U.S. Army 9A designation. Mem. ANA, Trident Nurses Assn. (pres.), Am. Nephrology Nurses Assn. (pre. Palmetto chpt., chair continuing edn.), Nat. Kidney Found. (chmn. resource devel. com.), Sigma Theta Tau. Home: 304 Stratford Dr Summerville SC 29485-8638

DUFFY, NANCY KEOGH, TV broadcast professional; b. Washington, Nov. 24, 1947; d. William Francis and Gertrude K. (Keogh) D.; divorced; children: Peter Patrick, Matthew Michael. Student, St. Mary of the Woods Coll.; AB, Marywood Coll., 1967. News reporter Sta. WHEN TV and Radio, Syracuse, N.Y., 1967-70; city press sec. City of Syracuse, 1970; news reporter Sta. WTVH, Syracuse, 1971-77; news anchorperson Sta. WIXT-TV, Syracuse, 1977—; talk show host Syracuse New Channels, 1986-87; talk show host, producer Community Connections, 1987-89; instr. Syracuse U. Producer t.v. series Duffy's People. Founder Syracuse St. Patrick's Parade, 1983, pres., organizer, 1983—; organizer Cooperstown 50th Ann. Baseball Hall of Fame Parade, 1989, opening ceremonies Empire State Games, 1990; co-organizer Save Our Syracuse Symphony, 1984—; bd. dirs. Syracuse Symphony, 1992-94, The Media Unit, 1977—; active Project Children, Syracuse, YMCA; telethon hostess Muscular Dystrophy Assn.; mem. Onondaga County Traffic Safety Bd., 1977-82, Le Moyne Coll. Pres. Assocs.; cons. Jr. League, J. Dist. 4 Nurses. Recipient Nat. Angel award Best Spl. Religion in Media, Post Standard Woman of Achievement award, First Downtown award for excellence 1986, Mayor's Achievement award 1985, Outstanding Communicator award WICI (Women in Comms.), Humanitarian award Project Children, 1993; named Woman of Achievement N.Y. State Fair, 1994. Mem. Am. Women in Radio and TV (nat. award 1973), Women in Communications, Syracuse Press Club (bd. dirs. 1987—, v.p. 1990, pres. 1991-92), Syracuse Rotary (pub. rels. 1989-92). Roman Catholic. Office: Sta WIXT-TV 5904 Bridge St East Syracuse NY 13057-2941

DUFFY, NICOLE, dancer; b. Charleston, S.C.. Student, Princeton U., 1984-85; scholarship student, The Joffrey Ballet Sch., 1985-87. Dancer Ballet de San Juan, P.R., 1981-84, Joffrey II Dancers, N.Y.C., 1987-89, Dennis Wayne Dancers, 1989, The Joffrey Ballet, N.Y.C., 1990—. Office: The Joffrey Ballet 130 W 56th St New York NY 10019-3818*

DUFFY, SALLY M., psychologist; b. Charleston, S.C., Mar. 16, 1953; d. Edward Baker and Mary Jane (Hutchins) D. BA, U. S.C., 1976; MS, Ea. Ky. U., 1979; PhD, U. Ky., 1989. Diplomate Am. Acad. Pain Mgmt. Psychologist, dir. Partial Hospitalization Program, Stanton, Ky., 1979-80; staff psychologist Frazier Rehab. Ctr., Louisville, 1981-84; psychologist Comprehensive Med. Rehab. Ctr., Lexington, Ky., 1987-89; postdoctoral fellow Med. U. S.C., Charleston, 1989; psychology svcs. coord. Carolinas Spine & Rehab. Ctr./HealthSouth, Charlotte, N.C., 1990-92; health psychologist The Rehab. Ctr., Charlotte, 1992—; adj. prof. psychology Georgetown Coll., 1988-89; lectr. in field. Contbr. articles to profl. jours. Mem. OneVoice Chorus, Charlotte, 1991—. NIMH traineeship, 1985-86, 86-87; Counseling Psychology Departmental merit fellow U. Ky., 1984-85. Mem. APA (div. 17 counseling psychology of women), Am. Bd. Med. Psychotherapists, Ky. Psychol. Assn., N.C. Psychol. Assn., Southeastern Psychol. Assn., Am. Pain Soc. Democrat. Office: The Rehab Ctr 2610 E 7th St Charlotte NC 28204-4375

DUGAN, LUAN M., accountant, payroll and timekeeping supervisor; b. Dimmitt, Tex., Dec. 9, 1952; d. Walter Johnnie and Nellie Beth (Connell) Martin; 1 child, Dani D'Ann. Grad., Amarillo Jr. Coll., 1986. Credit mgr. Castro County Credit Bur., Dimmitt, 1978-79; parts mgr. Case Power and Equipment, Dimmitt, 1979-82; bookkeeper Dimmitt Agri Industries, Inc., 1982; personnel dir. Deaf Smith Gen. Hosp., Hereford, Tex., 1983-84; payroll acct. Mason & Hanger-Silas Mason Co., Inc., Amarillo, Tex., 1984—; owner, pres. Dugan Mgmt., Amarillo, 1987-94. Vol. local sch.; spkr. in behalf of blood, bone marrow and organ donations. Mem. Toastmasters Internat. (Pantex Lunch Bunch chpt.). Methodist. Office: Mason Hanger Silas Mason Co PO Box 30020 Amarillo TX 79177-0001

DUGAN, M. DIANE, librarian; b. Phila., Oct. 27, 1955; d. Albert Joseph and Jean Marie (Cavanaugh) Dugan; m. Jeffrey Peter Meade, Sept. 11, 1981; 1 child, Sarah Elizabeth. BA cum laude, Chestnut Hill Coll., 1977; MLS, Drexel U., 1983. Corp. libr. Colonial Penn Group, Phila., 1981-84; asst. libr. mgr. Cigna Corp., Phila., 1984-89; sr. rsch. specialist Powell, Goldstein, Frazier & Murphy, Washington, 1989-90; libr. mgr. Right Assocs., Phila., 1990-93; rsch. libr. The Partnership Group Inc., Blue Bell, Pa., 1994—. Mem. Spl. Librs. Assn. (exec. bd. Phila. chpt. 1991—), Women's Ordination Conf. (Southeastern Pa. chpt.), Phila. Area Ref. Librs. Info. Exchange. Democrat. Roman Catholic. Office: The Partnership Group Inc 1400 Union Meeting Rd Blue Bell PA 19422

DUGAN, SHEILA MIRA, voice educator; b. St. Louis, Mar. 27, 1948; d. Max and Mildred (Dubinsky) Gale; divorced; 1 child, Kathryn Alexis. MusB in Voice Performance, So. Ill. U., 1970, MusM in Voice Performance, 1972; postgrad., St. Louis U., 1980, Fontbonne Coll., 1981. Mem. voice faculty So. Ill. U, Edwardsville, 1970-76; coord. vocal studies St. Louis Conservatory and Schs. for the Arts, 1976-82; pres., owner Sheila Dugan Voice and Speech Studio, St. Louis, 1982—; ofcl. voice coach Metro Theatre Co., St. Louis, 1984—, Stages St. Louis, 1992—. Mem. NAFE, Nat. Assn. Tchrs. of Singing, Maryland Heights C. of C. Home: 12425 Leigh Ln Maryland Heights MO 63043

DUGGAN, CAROL COOK, research director; b. Conway, S.C., May 25, 1946; d. Pierce Embree and Lillian Watkins (Eller) Cook; m. Kevin Duggan, Dec. 29, 1973. BA, Columbia Coll., 1968; MS, U. Ky., 1970. Reference asst. Richland County Pub. Libr., Columbia, S.C., 1968-69, asst. to dir., 1970, chief adult svcs., 1971-82; dir. Maris Rsch., Columbia, 1982—; lectr., mem. Friends of Richland County Pub. Libr., 1977—, Greater Columbia (S.C.) Literacy Council, 1973—; mem. worship com. Washington St. United Meth. Ch., Columbia, 1985-86, mem. staff-parish relations com., 1986-91, mem. history and archives com., 1988—, mem. adminstrv. bd., 1992—, chair staff-parish relations com., 1993; mem. exec. bd. United Meth. Women 1983—, treas. unit 7, 1989-91, pres. unit 7, 1992—. Recipient Sternheimer award, 1968. Mem. ALA (councilor 1980-82, chmn. state membership com. 1979-83), S.C. Libr. Assn. (sec. 1976, exec. bd. 1976, 78-82), S.C. Pub. Libr. Assn. (pres. 1980-81), Beta Phi Mu. Methodist. Club: PEO (pres. 1983-85, chmn. amendments and recommendations com. 1983-85, historian 1986-87, 90—, treas. State conv., 1987-88), Columbia Coll. Afternoon of S.C. Home: 2101 Woodmere Dr Columbia SC 29204-4341

DUGGAN, JANICE LYNNE, computer engineer consultant; b. Grosse Pointe, Mich., Feb. 23, 1958; d. Leonard L. and Helen J. (O'Neill) Baker; m. Robert James Duggan, May 22, 1993; 1 child, Sean Michael. B of Elec. and Computer Engring., U. Mich., 1980; M of Computer Engring., U. So. Calif., L.A., 1983. Computer engr. TRW Def. and Space Systems, Redondo Beach, Calif., 1980-84; sr. computer engr. Logicon Inc., San Diego, 1984-90; sr. prin. engr. Orincon Corp., San Diego, 1990-93; computer cons. Orlando, Fla., 1993—. Mem. IEEE.

DUGGAR, N(INA) PATRICIA, French language educator; b. Jackson, Miss., Nov. 28, 1941; d. Thomas Patrick and Nina Margaret (Witt) Reidy; m. Jan Warren Duggar, Sept. 1, 1962; children: David Charles, Patricia Grace Duggar King, Christopher O'Neil. BA, Fla. State U., 1962, MA in Edn., 1965; MA in French, La. State U., 1978, EdS, 1991. Cert. tchr. French, German and gifted/talented edn. Peace Corps tchr. English Hebret/Godaif Mid. Schs., Asmara, Ethiopia, 1962-64; tchr. French Indian River Jr. Coll., Ft. Pierce, Fla., 1966-67, S.E. La. U., Hammond, 1976; with libr. La. State U., Baton Rouge, 1977-78; tchr. East Baton Rouge Parish Scotlandville Sr. H.S., Baton Rouge, 1978-79; tchr. French Episcopal H.S., Baton Rouge, 1979-80; tchr. English orientation La. State U., Baton Rouge, 1981; tchr. French Robert E. Lee H. S., Baton Rouge, 1984-89; tchr. French and German McKinley Mid. Sch., Baton Rouge, 1989-90; chair French dept. gifted and talented Paul Breaux Mid. Sch., Lafayette, La., 1991—; realtor Century 21/Gold Star Mackey Co., Baton Rouge, 1980-84; presentations in La. and France. Coord. Am. Host, Baton Rouge, 1969-79; leader Girl Scouts Am., Baton Rouge, 1980-83; coord. info. booth River City Fest-for-All, Baton Rouge, 1985, 86, 87. Scholar French Cultural Svcs., 1973, 87, 94, MICEFA-TRIADE, 1989, NEH, 1991. Mem. MLA, Am. Coun. Teaching of Fgn. Langs., So. Conf. Lang. Teaching, La. Fgn. Lang. Tchrs. Assn. (pres. 1993-95), Am. Assn. Tchrs. French (state pres. 1992-94). Roman Catholic. Office: Paul Breaux Mid Sch 1400 S Orange St Lafayette LA 70501

DUHADAWAY, SANDRA LEE, accountant; b. Wilmington, Del., Nov. 25, 1948; d. Kenneth Lank and Doris Elizabeth (Elliott) Richardson; m. David Duhadaway, June 8, 1968; children: April, David. AS in Acctg. cum laude, Goldey Beacon Coll., Wilmington, Del., 1983. Computer programmer Elec. Hose & Rubber, Wilmington, 1966-68; pvt. practice acctg. Wilmington, 1971—.

DUILLO, ELAINE ISOBEL, illustrator; b. Bklyn., July 28, 1928; d. William Lewis and Gerda Irmgard (Niwell) Harwetel; m. John Duillo, Sept. 24, 1949; children; Melissa Jane Duillo Gallo, Bettina Jean Duillo Wright. Cert., Pratt Inst., Bklyn., 1949. Freelance illustrator hist. romance novels, 1959—; former lectr. Fashion Inst. Tech., N.Y.C., Suffolk C.C., L.I., N.Y., Syracuse U. One-woman show Soc. Illustrators; exhibited in numerous group shows throughout U.S., including Pratt Inst., Soc. Illustrators; represented in numerous pvt. collections in U.S. and abroad. Named Illustrator of Yr., Romantic Times mag., 1986. Mem. Soc. Illustrators (lectr.). Home and Studio: 146 Dartmouth Dr Hicksville NY 11801-3423

DUJACK, SUSAN MARION, lawyer; b. N.Y.C., Mar. 18, 1955; d. Raymond Leon and Inge (Wassermann) D.; m. Gary Lane Litovitz, Sept. 13, 1981; children: Erica, Matthew. BA with honors, Grinnell Coll., 1977; JD with honors, George Washington U., 1983. Bar: D.C. 1983, N.J. 1983. Lawyer O'Neill & Haase PC, Washington, 1983-87, Fed. Home Loan Mortgage Corp., McLean, Va., 1987—. Mem. D.C. Bar, N.J. Bar, Phi Beta Kappa, Order of the Coif. Office: Freddie Mae 8200 Jones Branch Dr McLean VA 22102

DUKAKIS, OLYMPIA, actress; b. Lowell, Mass., June 20, 1931; d. Constantine S. and Alexandra (Christos) D.; m. Louis Zorich; children: Christina, Peter, Stefan. BS, Boston U., 1952, MFA, 1957. Co-founder, artistic dir. Whole Theatre, Montclair, N.J., 1970-90; co-founder Charles Playhouse, Boston; master tchr. NYU, 1970-85. Appeared in over 125 prodns. for regional theatres, N.Y. Shakespeare Theatre, Circle Repertory Theatre, American Place Theatre and numerous Off-Broadway theatres; appearances on stage include King of America, Social Security; appearances in film include Lilith, 1964, Twice a Man, 1964, John and Mary, 1969, Made for Each Other, 1971, Death Wish, 1974, Rich Kids, 1979, The Wanderers, 1979, The Idolmaker, 1980, National Lampoon Goes to the Movies, 1982, Flanagan, 1985, Moonstruck, 1988 (Golden Globe, Academy Award Suppporting Actress), Working Girl, 1988, Steel Magnolias, 1988, Look Who's Talking, 1988, Dad, 1989, In the Spirit, 1990, Look Who's Talking II, 1990, Over the Hill, 1992, Look Who's Talking Now, 1993, The Cemetery Club, 1993, I Love Trouble, 1994, Digger, 1994, (TV movies) Nicky's World, 1974, The Neighborhood, 1982, The Last Act is a Solo, 1990 (Ace award), Lucky Day, 1991, Fire in the Dark, 1991, Sinatra: The Mini-Series, 1992, Armistead Maupin's Tales of the City, 1994, A Century of Women, 1994. Del. Dem. Nat. Convention, 1988. Recipient 2 Obie awards, Los Angeles Film Critics award, 1988. Mem. Actor's Equity Assn., Screen Actors Guild, Am. Fedn. TV and Radio Artists. Home: 222 Upper Mountain Ave Montclair NJ 07043-1016 Office: William Morris Agy 1350 Ave of the Americas 32d Fl New York NY 10019*

DUKE, ELLEN KAY, mortgage company professional, community activist; b. Indpls., June 7, 1952; d. Richard Thomas and Ruby Mae (Wright) D. Student Chapman Coll., Orange, Calif., 1972; BS in Pub. Affairs, Ind. U.-Bloomington, 1975; postgrad. Portland State U., 1980-81. Cert. Dale Carnegie Pub. Speaking Instr., 1987-93; News reporter, Salem Statesman, Corvallis, Oreg., 1976-78; com. adminstr. Oreg. State Legislature, Salem, 1979-80; pub. involvement coordinator Met. Regional Service Dist., Portland, 1981-82; account mgr. Thunder & Visions, Portland, 1982-83; project asst. Amdahl Corp., Sunnyvale, Calif., 1983-84; spl. project coordinator Computerland Corp., Hayward, Calif., 1984-89; prodr., lead facilitator Sage, Inc., Walnut Creek, Calif., 1989-92; loan broker Capital Trust Mortgage, Campbell, Calif., 1994—; pub. rels. dir. local YMCA. Co-author: (ednl. film) Communication Skills, 1975. Chairperson Corvallis Budget Commn., Oreg., 1978; commr. Hayward Library, Calif., 1985—, Alameda County Consumer Affairs, Oakland, 1985; rep. Nat. Democratic Conv., N.Y.C., 1982. Named Able Toastmaster Toastmasters Internat., 1981; grad. Leadership Oakland, 1991. Mem. NAFE, Pub. Rels. Soc. Am., Sierra Club (San Francisco). Office: Capital Trust Mortgage 155 E Campbell Ave # 101 Campbell CA 95008

DUKE, GAIL FRANCES, accountant; b. Nuremberg, Fed. Republic of Germany, Mar. 24, 1948; d. Walter O. and Helene B. (Postemsky) H.; m. Gary A. Duke, Aug. 27, 1967; children: Carrie L., Stacey Scott. Student, Stephen S. Austin State U., 1967-69, Lamar U., 1980-81. CPA, Tex. Staff acct. Spain, Ham & Co. P.C., Pasadena, Tex., 1973-81; staff acct. McGee, Wheeler & Co., Houston, 1981-85, tax supr., 1985-86, tax mgr., 1986-91; v.p., 1991—. Bd. dirs. Harris County Mcpl. Utility Dist. 119, Houston, 1984-88, re-elected, 1988—, pres., 1988—; chmn. Houston rels. chpt. IRS Com. Mem. AICPA's, Tex. Soc. CPA's (com. mem. Houston chpt., chmn. com. on rels. with IRS), Am. Woman's Soc. CPA's. Republican. Home: 6222 Elkwood Forest Dr Houston TX 77088-2420 Office: McGee Wheeler & Co Ste 400 2550 North Loop West Houston TX 77092-8734

DUKE, PATTY (ANNA MARIE DUKE), actress; b. N.Y.C., Dec. 14, 1946; d. John P. and Frances (McMahon) Duke; m. John Astin, 1973 (div. 1985); children: Sean, Mackenzie; m. Michael Pierce, March 15, 1986. Grad., Quintano's School for Young Profls. Pres. SAG, 1985-88, lectr. Am. Film Inst., 1988. TV appearances include Armstrong Circle Theatre, 1955, The SS Andrea Doria, The Prince and the Pauper, 1957, Wuthering Heights, 1958, U.S. Steel Hour, 1959, Meet Me in St. Louis, 1959, Swiss Family Robinson, 1958, The Power and the Glory, 1961, All's Fair, 1981-82; (series) The Brighter Day, 1957, Kitty Foyle, 1958, Patty Duke Show, 1963-66, It Takes Two, 1982-1983, Hail to the Chief, 1985, Karen's Song, 1987; (TV films) The Big Heist, 1957, My Sweet Charlie, 1970 (Emmy award 1970), Two on a Bench, If Tomorrow Comes, 1971, She Waits, Deadly Harvest, 1972, Nightmare, 1972, Look What's Happened to Rosemary's Baby, 1976, Fire!, 1976, Rosetti and Ryan: Men Who Love Women, Curse of the Black Widow, Killer on Board, The Storyteller, 1977, Having Babies III, Captain and the Kings, 1977 (Emmy award 1977), A Family Upside Down, 1978, Women in White, Hanging By A Thread, Before and After, The Miracle Worker, 1979 (Emmy award 1980), The Women's Room, Mom, The Wolfman and Me, The Babysitter, 1980, Violation of Sarah McDavid, Please, Don't Hit Me Mom, 1981, Something So Right 1982, September Gun, 1983, Best Kept Secrets, 1984, George Washington: The Forging of a Nation, 1984, A Time To Triumph, 1986, Fight for Life, 1987, Perry Mason: The Case of the Avenging Angel, Fatal Judgement, 1988, Everybody's Baby: The Rescue of Jessica McClure, Amityville: The Evil Escapes, 1989, Call Me Anna, 1990, Always Remember I Love You, 1990, Absolute Strangers, 1991, Last Wish, 1992, Grave Secrets: The Legacy of Hilltop Drive, 1992, A Killer Among Friends, 1992, A Family of Strangers, 1993, Cries From the Heart, 1994, One Woman's Courage, 1994; (theatre) The Miracle Worker, 1959-61, Isle of Children, 1962; motion picture appearances in I'll Cry Tomorrow, 1955, The Goddess, 1958, Happy Anniversary, The 4-D Man, 1959, The Miracle Worker, 1962 (Acad. award as best supporting actress 1962), Billie, 1965, Valley of the Dolls, 1967, Me, Natalie, 1969 (Golden Globe award as best actress 1970), The Swarm, 1978, Something Special, 1987, Prelude to a Kiss, 1992; co-author Surviving Sexual Assault, 1983, Call Me Anna, 1987, A Brilliant Madness: Living with Manic-Depressive Illness, 1992. Nat. corp. council Muscular Dystrophy Assns. Am. Recipient Emmy Awards, 1964, 69, 76, 79. Mem. AFTRA. Office: William Morris Agy 151 El Camino Beverly Hills CA 90212*

DUKE BIEDERMAN, SUSAN, fine arts lawyer, author; b. Chgo., Nov. 17, 1952; d. Boris and Alice (Schwimmer) D.; m. Daniel Alan Biederman, June 28, 1981; children: Robert, Brooke. AB in Mathematics and French, U. Calif., 1975; JD, U. Chgo., 1978. Bar: N.Y. Assoc. Stroock & Stroock & Lavan, N.Y., 1978-81, Greenbaum, Wolff & Ernst, N.Y., 1981-82; pvt. practice N.Y., 1982—; mem. exec. com., bd. dirs. Vo. Lawyers of the Arts, N.Y., 1988-94. Author: (legal treatise) Art Law, 1993; co-author: (legal treatise) Art Law, 1988, 1986 (Scribes award 1986). Mem. N.Y. State Bar Assn. (founding chmn. fine arts com. 1988-94), Bar of City of New York (mem. art law com. 1993—). Office: Susan Duke Biederman Esq 575 Madison Ave 10th Fl New York NY 10022

DUKERT, BETTY COLE, television producer; b. Muskogee, Okla., May 9, 1927; d. Irvan Dill and Ione (Bowman) Cole; m. Joseph M. Dukert, May 19, 1968. Student, Lindenwood Coll., St. Charles, Mo., 1945-46, Drury Coll., Springfield, Mo., 1946-47; B.J., U. Mo., 1949. With Sta. KICK, Springfield, Mo., 1949-50; adminstrv. asst. Juvenile Office, Green County, Mo., 1950-52; with Sta. WRC-TV-NBC, Washington, 1952-56; assoc. producer Meet the Press, NBC, Washington, 1956-75; producer Meet the Press, NBC, 1975—; sr. producer Meet the Press, NBC News, 1992—; mem. Robert F. Kennedy Journalism Awards Com., 1978-82. Trustee Drury Coll., Springfield, Mo., 1984—. Recipient Disting. Alumna award Drury Coll., 1975; Disting. Alumni award U. Mo., 1978; Ted Yates award Washington chpt. Nat. Acad. TV Arts and Scis., 1979; Pub. Rels. award for pub. svc. Am. Legion Nat. Comdrs., 1981, Internat. Disting. Svc. Journalism medal U. Mo. Sch. Journalism, 1993. Mem. Am. Women in Radio and TV, Am. News Women's Club, Radio/TV Corrs. Assn., Women's Forum Washington, Soc. Profl. Journalists (dir. 1983-84, inducted into Hall of Fame 1991), Silver Circle Broadcasting, Nat. Acad. TV Arts and Scis., Nat. Press Club. Office: NBC News 4001 Nebraska Ave NW Washington DC 20016-2733

DUKES, JOAN, state legislator; b. Tacoma, Wash., 1947; 3 children. BA, Evergreen State Coll. Mem. Oreg. State Senate, Dist. 1, 1987—. Democrat. Home: RR 2 Box 503 Astoria OR 97103-9617 Office: Oreg State Senate State Capitol S # 210 Salem OR 97310*

DUKES, REBECCA WEATHERS (BECKY DUKES), musician, singer, songwriter; b. Durham, N.C., Nov. 21, 1934; d. Elmer Dewey Weathers and Martha Rebecca (Kimbrough) Weathers-Hall; m. Charles Aubrey Dukes Jr., Dec. 20, 1955; children: Aurelia Ann, Charles Weathers, David Lloyd. BA, Duke U., 1956. Lic. elem. sch. tchr. Tchr. Durham City Schs., 1956-57; sec. USMC, Arlington, Va., 1957-58; tchr. Arlington County Schs., 1958-59; office mgr. Dukes and Kooken, Landover, Md., 1976; musical performer Washington and various locations, Va., Md., 1982—. Vocal student Todd Duncan; pianist, vocalist Back Alley Restaurant Lounge, 1982, also various hotels, lounges, 1982—; original program, A Life Cycle in Song, presented throughout mid-Atlantic states and Washington; full operatic solo recital, 1983; featured performer benefit for Nat. Symphony Orch.; frequent performer pvt. functions, athletic, civic, religious and cultural events including appearances at Capital Ctr., Cole Field House, George Washington U., Smith Ctr.; operatic solo concert with pianist Glenn Sales, 1985; benefit appearance U. Md. Concert Series, 1986, 87; holds copyrights for over 100 original songs including Between the Lovin' and the Leavin', Covers of My Mind, Gentle Thoughts (lead song Nat. Capitol Area Composers Series), Headin' Home Again, I Would Like to Be Reborn, Miss You, Tears, You Played a Part in My Life; songwriter, vocalist Alive, 1992, Rainbow, 1994; author: (poems) Pottery, Canyons and Connections, Let the Trees of the Forest Rustle with Praise; contbr. poems to A Question of Balance, 1992, Treasured Poems of America, 1993, Distinguished Poets of 1994. Pres. Nat. Capitol Law League, Washington, 1976-77; pres. women's group, deacon, elder Riverdale Presbyn. Ch., Hyattsville, Md., 1968-94, elder, 1994; chmn. event honoring wives of Supreme Ct. justices, 1981; mem. women's com. Nat. Symphony, 1980—; chmn. awards event Marian Anderson Internat. Vocal Arts Competition, 1991. Recipient Friend of Yr. award Md. Summer Inst. for Creative and Performing Arts, U. Md., 1986, award for Vol. Svcs., Duke U., 1992; named Hon. trustee Prince George's (Md.) Arts Coun., 1984—, one of Women of Outstanding Achievement, Prince George's County, 1994. Mem. ASCAP (Popular Music award 1994), Songwriter's Assn. Washington, William Preston Few Assn. of Duke U. (pres. couns., exec. bd. of ann. fund), Internat. Platform Assn., Pres.'s Club of U. Md., Univ. Club, Founders Club of Duke U. Republican. Home and Office: 7111 Pony Trail Ln Hyattsville MD 20782-1031

DULANY, ELIZABETH GJELSNESS, university press administrator; b. Charleston, S.C., Mar. 11, 1931; d. Rudolph Hjalmar and Ruth Elizabeth (Weaver) Gjelsness; m. Donelson Edwin Dulany, Mar. 19, 1955; 1 son, Christopher Daniel. BA, Bryn Mawr Coll., 1952. Editor R.R. Bowker Co., 1948-52; med. editor U. Mich. Hosp., Ann Arbor, 1953-54; editorial asst. E.P. Dutton & Co., N.Y.C., 1954-55; editorial asst. U. Ill. Press, Champaign, 1956-59, asst. to editor, 1959-60, asst. editor, 1960-67, assoc. editor, 1967-72, mng. editor, 1972-90, asst. dir., 1983-90, assoc. dir., 1990—. Democrat. Episcopalian. Home: 73 Greencroft Dr Champaign IL 61821-5112 Office: U Ill Press 1325 S Oak St Champaign IL 61820-6680

DULATT, LORRAINE EDWINA SIMON, special education educator, reading specialist; b. St. Louis, July 12, 1949; d. Richard Kenneth and Leora B. (Zoleman) Simon; m. Patrick Michael Dulatt, Aug. 4, 1972; children: Joseph William, Christopher Patrick, Edward Matthew. AA, Florissant (Mo.) Valley, 1969; BS in Elem. Edn., So. Ill. U., 1971, BS in Spl. Edn., 1971; MAT in Spl. Edn. and Reading, Webster U., Webster Groves, Mo., 1992. Cert. in K-12 learning disabilities, K-12 behavior disorders, K-12 educable mentally handicapped, K-12 trainable mentally handicapped, 1-8 elem., kindergarten, reading specialist, all Mo.; cert. 1-8 elem. edn., trainable mentally handicapped, Tex. Substitute tchr. Spl. Sch. Dist., Town & Country, Mo., 1970-71, tchr. mentally handicapped, 1971-72; tchr. multicategorical El Paso (Tex.) Ind. Schs., 1972-73; tchr. aide early childhood Spl. Sch. Dist., Town & Country, 1983-84, tchr. asst. behavior disorder, 1984-85, tchr. resource learning disabilities/behavioral disorders, 1985—. Religious coord. St. Agatha Parish. Mem. Coun. for Exceptional Children, Mo. State Tchrs. Assn., Internat. Soc. for tech. in Edn., Learning Disability Assn., Attention Deficit Disorder Assn., Regional Consortium for Edn. and Tech., Found. for Applied Rsch. in Edn., Internat. Reading Assn., Mo. State Coun. of Internat. Reading Assn., Lindawood-Bell Learning Processes Network, Orton Dyslexia Soc., Reading Reform Found., Alumni Assn. So. Ill. U. Edwardsville, Phi Theta Kappa. Roman Catholic. Home: 288 Portwind Pl Ballwin MO 63021-5058 Office: Spl Sch Dist 12110 Clayton Rd Saint Louis MO 63131-2516

DULEY, CHARLOTTE DUDLEY, vocational counselor; b. Lincoln, Nebr., Oct. 2, 1920; d. Millard Eugene and Inez Kathryn (Miller) Dudley; student U. Nebr., 1938-41; M.A. in Guidance Counseling, U. Idaho, 1977; B.S., Lewis and Clark State Coll., 1973; m. Phillip D. Duley, Mar. 28, 1942; (dec. Sept. 1984); children: Michael Dudley (dec.), Patricia Kaye; m. P. Fredrik Nordgaard, Sept.1, 1990. Tchr., Nebr. schs., 1951-56; with Dept. of Employment, Lewiston, Idaho, 1958-81, local office counselor handling fed. tng. programs, 1958-81; ind. job cons.; counselor; rep. Avon, Lewiston; part-time counselor, tester, 1981—. Pres., bd. dirs. Civic Arts, Inc., 1972-81; mem. women's svc. league Wash.-Idaho Symphony Orch., 1972—; bd. dirs. YWCA, 1980-88, treas., 1981-88; mem. adv. bd. Salvation Army, 1980—; dir. artist series Lewis and Clark State Coll., 1984-90. Recipient Altrusa Woman of Achievement award, 1984. Mem. Am., Idaho pers. guidance Assns., Idaho State Employees Assn., Internat. Assn. Employees in Employment Security, Am. Assn. Counseling & Devel., Idaho State Employment Counselors Assn. (pres. 1979-80), Stateline Guidance and Counseling Assn. (sec.-treas. 1964, 76-77), Lewiston Community Concert Assn. (bd. dirs., pres. 1980—), Greater Lewiston C. of C. (chmn. conv. and tourism com. 1984-87), Altrusa (bd. dirs.), Elks (pres. 1986-87, exec. bd. 1985-88, election bd. chmn. 1986-94, 1st v.p., 1993—). Baptist. Home: 1819 Ridgeway Dr Lewiston ID 83501-3890

DUMAS, CLAUDIA JEAN, lawyer; b. Kingston, N.Y., Aug. 2, 1959; d. Allan Mason and Virginia Nellie (Bell) D. AB, Wellesley Coll., 1981; JD cum laude, Cornell U., 1984. Bar: Mass. 1985, N.Y. 1987. Assoc. Peabody & Brown, Boston, 1984-86, Shearman & Sterling, N.Y.C., 1986-89, 93—; staff atty. IBM, Armonk, N.Y., 1989-93. Durant Scholar Wellesley Coll., 1981. Mem. ABA, Phi Beta Kappa. Office: Shearman & Sterling 599 Lexington Ave New York NY 10022-6069

DUMAS, LORI JEAN, physician assistant; b. Albany, N.Y., Apr. 19, 1957; d. Stephen Michael and Doris Claire (Dupree) D. BS, Trevecca Nazarene Coll., 1984. Physician asst. Albany Med. Coll., 1985, Albany Meml. Hosp., 1985-89; physician asst. Sunnyview Rehab. Hosp., Schenectady, N.Y., 1989—, spinal cord injury program dir., 1991—, clin. liaison, 1990—. Mem. Am. Paraplegic Soc., Nat. Spinal Cord Injury Assn. Office: Sunnyview Rehab Hosp 1270 Belmont Ave Schenectady NY 12308

DUMAS, RHETAUGH ETHELDRA GRAVES, nursing school dean; b. Natchez, Miss., Nov. 26, 1928; d. Rhetaugh Graves and Josephine (Clemmons) Graves Bell; m. A.W. Dumas, Jr., Dec. 25, 1950; 1 child, Adrienne. BS in Nursing, Dillard U., 1951; MS in Psychiat. Nursing, Yale U., 1961; PhD in Social Psychology, Union Grad. Sch., Union for Experimenting Colls. and Univs., Cinn., 1975; also various other courses; D Pub. Svc. (hon.), Simmons Coll., 1976, U. Cin., 1981; LHD (hon.), Yale U., 1989; LLD (hon.), Dillard U., 1990; LHD, U. San Diego, 1993. Instr. Dillard U., 1957-59, 61; research asst., instr. Sch. Nursing Yale U., 1962-65, from asst. prof. nursing to assoc. prof., 1965-72, chmn. dept. psychiat. nursing, 1972; dir. nursing Conn. Mental Health Ctr., Yale-New Haven Med. Ctr., 1966-72; chief psychiat. nursing edn. br. Div. Manpower and Tng. Programs, NIMH, Rockville, Md., 1972-76; dep. dir. Div. Manpower and Tng. Programs NIMH, 1976-79, dep. dir., 1979-81; dean U. Mich. Sch. Nursing, 1981-94; vice provost health affairs U. Mich., 1994—; dir. Group Rels. Confs. in Tavistock Model; cons., speaker, panelist in field; fellow Helen Hadley Hall, Yale U., 1972, Branford Coll., 1972; dir. Community Health Care Ctr. Plan, New Haven, 1969-72; mem. U.S. Assessment Team, cons. to Fed. Ministry Health, Nigeria, 1982; mem. adv. com. Health Policy Agenda for the Am. People, AMA, 1983-86; cons. NIH Task Force on Nursing Rsch., 1984; mem. Nat. Commn. on Unemployment and Mental Health, Nat. Mental Health Assn., 1984-85; mem. com. to plan maj. study of nat. long-term care policy Inst. Medicine, 1985; mem. adv. com. to dir. NIH, 1986-87; mem. Sec.'s Nat. Commn. on Future Structure of VA Health Care System, 1990-91. Author profl. monographs; contbr. articles to profl. publs.; mem. editorial bd. Community Mental Health Rev., 1977-79, Jour. Personality and Social Systems, 1978-81, Advances in Psychiat. Mental Health Nursing, 1981. Bd. dirs. Afro Am. Ctr., Yale U., 1968-72; mem. New Haven Bd. Edn., 1968-71, New Haven City Demonstrations Agy., 1968-70, Human Rels. Coun. New Haven, 1961-63, Nat. Neural Circuitry Database Com., Inst. Medicine, Nat. Acad. Scis.; mem. commn. on future structure of vets. health care U.S. Dept. Vets. Affairs, 1990. Named Disting. Alumna Dillard U., 1966; recipient various awards, including cert. Honor NAACP, 1970, Disting. Alumnae award Yale U. Sch. Nursing, 1976, award for outstanding achievement and service in field mental health D.C. chpt. Assn. Black Psychologists, 1980. Fellow A.K. Rice Inst., Am. Coll. Mental Health Adminstrs. (founding), Am. Acad. Nursing (charter, pres. 1987-89); mem. Inst. Medicine NAS, Am. Nurses Assn., Nat. Black Nurses Assn., Am. Assn. Colls. Nursing (govtl. affairs com. 1990-93), Am. Pub. Health Assn., NAACP, Sigma Theta Tau Internat. (mentor award 1989), Delta Sigma Theta. Office: U Mich Sch Nursing 400 N Ingalls St Bldg 1320 Ann Arbor MI 48109-2003

DUMAS, SARA LEE, psychologist; b. Boston, Apr. 21, 1949; d. Herbert Michael and Joyce (Chaban) Marcus; m. Steven Silber, June 21, 1968 (div. Feb. 1989); children: Rachel, Victoria, Adam; m. John R. Dumas, Apr. 26, 1991. BA, U. Tex., 1977; MS, Va. Poly. Inst., 1979, PhD, 1982. Lic. psychologist, Tex. Staff psychologist Southwestern State Hosp., Marion, Va., 1980-81; intern Austin (Tex.) State Hosp., 1981-82, cons. cmty. programs, 1982-84; counseling specialist Travis County Jail, Austin, 1982-83; pvt. practice clin. psychology Austin, 1983—; mental health cons. Head Start Program, Bastrop County, Tex., 1984-90, Ctr. for Battered Women, Austin, 1986—; cons. Nat. Multiple Sclerosis Soc., Austin, 1986-91. Vol. Capital Area Mental Health, Austin, 1983-85; del. Dem. Party State Conv., Ft. Worth, 1994, Travis County Dem. Conv., Austin, 1994. Home: 10601 Little Thicket Rd Austin TX 78736 Office: 3755 CapTX Hwy So Ste 180 Austin TX 78704

DUMITRESCU, DOMNITA, Spanish language educator, researcher; b. Bucharest, Romania; came to U.S., 1984; d. Ion and Angela (Barzotescu) D. Diploma, U. Bucharest, 1966; MA, U. So. Calif., L.A., 1987, PhD, 1990. Asst. prof. U. Bucharest, 1966-74, assoc. prof., 1974-84; asst. prof. Spanish, U. So. Calif., 1985-89; asst. prof. Calif. State U., L.A., 1990-94, prof., 1995—. Author: Gramatica Limbii Spaniole, 1976, Indreptar Pentru Traducerea Din Limba Romana in Limba Spaniola, 1980; translator from Spanish lit. to Romanian; contbr. articles to profl. jours. Fulbright scholar, 1993—. Mem. MLA, Am.-Romanian Acad. Arts and Scis., Am. Assn. Tchrs. Spanish, Linguistic Soc. Am., Internat. Assn. Pispanists, Assn. Linguistics and Philology L.Am., Am. Assn. Tchrs. Spanish and Purtuguese (past pres. So. Calif. chpt.). Office: Calif State U 5151 State University Dr Los Angeles CA 90032-4221

DUMLER, PATRICIA ANN, critical care nurse; b. San Antonio, Feb. 16, 1960; d. Raymond Lee and Ann Dell (Comer) Dumler; m. David Hastings Smith, Dec. 28, 1985. BSN, U. Md., Balt., 1983; student, James Madison U., Harrisonburg, Va., 1978-81. Staff nurse Bon Secours Hosp., Balt., Rockingham Meml. Hosp., Harrisonburg, Va.; clin. nurse II Homewood Hosp. Ctr., Balt.; clin. nurse Johns Hopkins Hosp., Balt.

DUMOULIN, DIANA CRISTAUDO, marketing professional; b. Washington, Jan. 5, 1939; d. Emanuel A. and Angela E. (Cogliano) Cristaudo; m. Philip DuMoulin, May 30, 1964; children: Joanmarie Patricia, John Philip. MA, U. Wis., 1967; BA, Rosary Coll., 1961. Project mgr. IDC Cons. Group, Framingham, Mass., 1982-84; sr. market analyst Cullinet, Inc., Westwood, Mass., 1984-86; prof. assoc. Ledgeway Group, Lexington, Mass., 1987-89; prin. Customer Mktg. Specialist, Brookline, Mass., 1989-93; pres. Customer Solutions Int., Phoenix, 1994—; adj. faculty Ulster Count Community Coll., Stone Ridge, N.Y., 1967-74, Mass. Bay Community Coll., Wellesley Hills, Mass., 1983; lectr. Boston Coll., Chestnut Hill, Mass., 1976. Contbr. articles to profl. jours. Pres. League Women Voters, Kingston, N.Y., 1973-74. Recipient Svc. to Young Adults award 70001 Career Assn., 1977; faculty fellow U. Wis., 1964-66. Mem. Am. Field Svc. Mgrs. Internat. (software support spl. interest group, chmn. minuteman chpt. 1991-92), New Eng. Women Bus. Owners, Boston Computer Soc. Home: 8441 N 1st Dr Phoenix AZ 85021 Office: Customer Solutions Internat 8441 N 1st Dr Phoenix AZ 85021

DUNAGAN, GWENDOLYN ANN, special education educator; b. Youngstown, Ohio, Sept. 27, 1941; d. Charles Jefferson and Emma Juanita (Alexander) Hicks; m. Willie Miles, 1966; 1 child, Byron Keith Miles; m. Kenneth Robert Dunagan, July 1, 1972. BS in Edn., Youngstown U., Ohio, 1963; postgrad., Ashland U., 1986-89. Cert. elem. tchr., Ohio, learning disabilities tchr., Ohio, tchr. to severe behavior disorder, Ohio. Elem. tchr. Youngstown Bd. Edn., 1963-67, 1968-72; adminstr., tchr. Free Kindergarten Assn., Youngstown, 1967-68; liaison home-sch. Alliance (Ohio) Bd. Edn., 1972-86, tchr. disadvantaged pupils, 1986-89, intervention tchr. learning disabilities,

1989-90, tchr. specific learning disabilities, 1990-94, tchr. spl. edn., 1994—; contestant, winner TV show Price is Right; group leader Youngstown Detention Ctr. Contbr. articles to profl. mags., area newspapers. Pres. Domestic Violence Shelter, Alliance, 1990-92, John Slimack Homeless Shelter, Alliance, 1989-93, v.p., 1993—; pres., founder Community Civic Com., Alliance, 1987—; treas. Altrusic Civic Club, Alliance, 1988-91; mem. choir Holy Temple Ch. God in Christ, Alliance, 1972—, mem. usher bd. dirs., fin. sec., sec. Sunday sch., 1989—; chairperson Alliance Area Desert Storm Celebration, 1991; mem. Family Counseling Ctr., Young Women's Christian Assn., Dr. King Birthday Celebration Com.; tchr. Prayer and Bible Band, 1990—; mem. adv. bd. Salvation Army, 1994—. Honored for community svc. Stark County Community Action Agy., 1990. Mem. Alliance Edn. Assn. (Dowling scholaarship com.), NAACP (2d v.p. 1990-93), McKinley Reading Assn., Quota Club, Alpha Kappa Alpha. Home: 1115 S Seneca Ave Alliance OH 44601-4068

DUNAWAY, CAROLYN BENNETT, sociology educator; b. Atlanta, Mar. 3, 1943; d. Clarence Rhodes and Gay (McKensie) Bennett; m. William Preston Dunaway, Aug. 26, 1967; 1 child, Robert Bennett Dunaway. BS, Auburn U., 1966, EdD, 1983; MA, U. Ala., Tuscaloosa, 1967. Instr. Jefferson State C.C., Birmingham, Ala., 1967-69; prof. Auburn U., Montgomery, Ala., 1970-71; prof. sociology and gerontology dept. Jacksonville (Ala.) State U., 1971—; student counselor Jacksonville State U., Ala., 1971—. Contbd. articles to profl. jours. Cons., trainer Calhoun County Hospice Anniston, Ala., 1983—; presenter Calhoun County Gerontology, Anniston, 1985—; officer Jacksonville Book Club, Ala., 1984; officer, tchr. St Luke's Episcopal Ch., Jacksonville, 1993. Recipient 100 Most Outstanding Women Alumna award Auburn U., 1991, U. Rsch. award Jacksonville State U., 1989. Mem. Ala. Miss. Sociological Assn. (v.p. 1975—), Sociology Club, Phi Kappa Phi, Kappa Delta Pi, Delta Delta Delta, Phi Delta Kappi. Democrat. Episcopalian. Home: 902 11th Street NE Jacksonville AL 36265-1230 Office: Jacksonville State U Sociology Dept Jacksonville AL 36265

DUNAWAY, (DOROTHY) FAYE, actress; b. Bascom, Fla., Jan. 14, 1941; d. John and Grace D.; m. Peter Wolf, Aug. 7, 1974 (div.); m. Terrence O'Neill; 1 son. Student, U. Fla., Boston U. Appearences include as original mem. Lincoln Ctr. Repertory Co., N.Y.C., off-Broadway in Hogan's Goat; also in (play) Curse of the Aching Heart, 1982; motion picture appearences include Bonnie in motion picture Bonnie and Clyde, 1967, Hurry Sundown, 1967, Puzzle of a Downfall Child, The Happening, 1967, The Thomas Crown Affair, 1968, A Place For Lovers, 1969, Little Big Man, 1970, Doc, 1971, La Maison Sous les Arbres, 1971, The Getaway, 1972, Oklahoma Crude, 1973, The Three Musketeers, 1973, Chinatown, 1974, The Towering Inferno, 1974, The Four Muscateers, 1975, Three Days of the Condor, 1975, Network, 1976 (Acad. award for Best Actress), The Voyage of the Damned, 1976, The Eyes of Laura Mars, 1978, The Champ, 1979, The First Deadly Sin, 1980, Mommie Dearest, 1981, The Wicked Lady, 1982, Ordeal by Innocence, 1985, Supergirl, 1984, Barfly, 1987, Burning Secret, 1988, La Partita, 1988, Midnight Crossing, 1988, The Gamble, 1989, In a Moonlit Night, 1989, Wait Until Spring, Bandini, 1989, The Handmaid's Tale, 1990, Three Weeks in Jerusalem, 1990, Scorchers, 1990, Arrowtooth Waltz, 1991, Double Edge, 1992, The Temp, 1993, Point of No Return, 1993, Even Cowgirls Get the Blues, 1994, Don Juan DeMarco, 1995, others; TV movies: After the Fall, 1974, The Disappearance of Aimee, 1976, Evita Peron, 1981, 13 at Dinner, 1985, Beverly Hills Madame, 1986, Casanova, 1987, Cold Sassy Tree, 1989, Silhouette, 1990 (co-exec. prodr.), Columbo: It's All in the Game (Emmy award for Guest Actress in Drama 1994), Mother Love, 1995, A Family Divided, 1995; TV miniseries: Ellis Island, 1984, Christopher Columbus, 1985; TV series: It Had To Be You, 1993. Recipient Most Promising Newcomer Award Brit. Film Acad., 1968. Address: c/o ICM 8942 Wilshire Blvd Beverly Hills CA 90211*

DUNAWAY, MARGARET ANN (MAGGIE DUNAWAY), consultant; b. Fresno, Calif., Feb. 10, 1943; d. Joseph John and Anna Frances (Dice) Cumero; children from previous marriage: Christian Anthony Freitag, Erika Lynn Bullard; m. Michael Earl Babcoke, Oct. 6, 1990; 1 stepchild, Jason Ethan Babcoke. Student, U. Calif., Davis, 1960-62, U. Calif., Berkeley, 1962-63. Supr. Gov's Office, Sacramento, 1969-72; office mgr. State Health and Welfare Agy., Sacramento, 1972-73; analyst regulations devel. Calif. State Depts. Health and Social Svcs., Sacramento, 1974-84, cons. adult and children's svcs., 1984-90, rep. adult svcs., 1984-90, with food drive com., 1987-88, rep. ind. living program com., 1989-90; community program specialist Calif. State Dept. Devel. Svcs., Sacramento, 1990—; project coord. SDSS study L.A. County Children's Svcs. Caseload, 1989-90. Active Southpark Homeowner's Assn., Sacramento, 1974-78; presenter Adult Svcs. Ann. Asilomar Conf., 1987. Office: Calif Dept Devel Svcs 1600 9th St Rm 340 Sacramento CA 95814

DUNBAR, HOLLY JEAN, communications and public relations administrator; b. Plainfield, N.J., May 15, 1960; d. Robert Kenneth and Marian (DuBets) D. BA, Rutgers U., 1982. Graphic designer Chubb & Son, Inc., Warren, N.J., 1983-86; freelance writer, 1984—; pub. rels. rep., archivist AT&T Bell Labs., Warren, 1987; self-employed graphic designer North Plainfield, N.J., 1987-88; direct response mktg. coord. U.S. and Can. Beneficial Mgmt. Corp. of Am., Peapack, N.J., 1988-94; comms. supr., editor Beneficial Mgmt. Corp., Peapack, N.J., 1994—; artist, graphic designer, editor St. Luke's Roman Cath. Ch., North Plainfield, N.J., 1987—; cons. Rutgers Coop. Extension Svc. 4-H Program, Bridgewater, N.J., 1990—; judge N.J. County 4-H Agts. Promotional Materials, 1991. Photographer: (survey) Tark Farm Site Monmouth Battlefield, 1982, Ellis Island Restoration, 1988-92; designer: Official Logo and Slogan of Somerset County, N.J., 1985 (Winning entry). Recipient Photography awards Cook Coll., New Brunswick, N.J., 1981, Chubb & Son, Inc., Warren, N.J., 1984, N.J. Agrl. Fair, 1994; STAR award nominee United Way of Somerset County, Bridgewater, N.J., 1992; cited for Distinctive Contbr. N.J. Culture and History Am. Studies Dept., Douglass Coll., New Brunswick, 1982. Mem. DAR (dep. rep. Nat. Soc to Vet. Affairs Vol. Svc., 1983-92, state chmn. Am. Heritage-Art N.J. Soc. 1989-92, state chmn. N.J. Jr. Mem. Centennial Project N.J. Soc. 1991-92, artist N.J. Soc. 1989—, nat. and N.J. state page 1983—, regent Elizabeth Snyder chpt. 1992-95, registrar, 1991-92, Continental Congress Thatcher award 1992, state chmn. DAR Mag. Advt. N.J. Soc. 1992-95, Ad Excellence award, 1993, 94, state corr. sec. N.J. soc. 1995—), Internat. Platform Assn., Internat. Assn. Bus. Communicators, Douglass Coll. Alumnae Assn., Somerset County 4-H Assn., Clan Dunbar. Home: 725 Ayres Ave North Plainfield NJ 07063-1607 Office: Beneficial Mgmt Corp 200 Beneficial Ctr Peapack NJ 07977

DUNBAR, MARY ASMUNDSON, communications executive, investor and public relations consultant; b. Sacramento, Calif., Feb. 6, 1942; d. Vigfus Samundur and Aline Mary (McGrath) Asmundson; m. Robert Copeland Dunbar, June 21, 1969; children: Geoffrey Townsend, William Asmundson. BA in English Lit., Smith Coll., 1964; MA in Communications, Stanford, 1967; MBA in Fin., Case Western Res. U., 1985. Cert. pub. rels. profl. Tchr. Peace Corps, Cameroun, Africa, 1964-66; writer, editor Ednl. Devel. Corp., Palo Alto, Calif., 1967-68, Addison-Wesley, Menlo Park, Calif., 1969-70; free lance writer, editor various, Cleve., 1970-85; account exec. Edward Howard & Co., Cleve., 1985-87; account exec. Dix & Eaton, Inc., Cleve., 1987—, v.p., 1992—. Author publs. in field (Arthur Page award 1990, IABC award 1987, Women in Communications award 1987). Trustee Cleve. Scholarship Program, 1993—, Cleve. Coun. World Affairs, 1994—; mem. mktg. com. Univ. Sch., Cleve., 1989—. Recipient scholarship Smith Coll., Northampton, Mass., 1960-64; fellowship Stanford Univ., Palo Alto, Calif., 1967. Mem. Smith Coll. Club Cleve., Pub. Rels. Soc. Am., Nat. Investor Rels. Inst. (sec. Cleve.-Akron chpt.), Cleve. Soc. Security Analysts, Cleve. Com. Fgn. Rels. Republican. Episcopalian. Home: 2880 Fairfax Rd Cleveland OH 44118-4014 Office: Dix & Eaton Inc 1801 E 9th St Ste 1300 Cleveland OH 44114

DUNBAR, MARY MELANIE, lawyer; b. Omaha, Mar. 13, 1963; d. Jean Francis and Mary Kathryn (Buckley) D. BS with distinction, U. Nebr., 1985; JD, U. Va., 1991. Staff asst., mem. profl. staff U.S. Senate Com. on Agr., Washington, 1985-88, counsel, 1993—; assoc. Akin, Gump, Strauss, Hauer & Feld, Washington, 1991-93. Scholar Food and Drug Law Inst., 1990-91. Democrat. Office: US Senate Com on Agr 328-A Russell Senate Office Bldg Washington DC 20510

DUNBAR, PATRICIA LYNN, new product development consultant; b. St. Louis, Feb. 11, 1953; d. William R. and Beryl Ione Noland (Ferrand) Dunbar; m. Michael R. Jeffrey, Oct. 2, 1950. BS, Northwestern U., 1973, MFA, 1975. With NBC-TV, Chgo., 1975-79; regional sales/mktg. mgr. HBO, Chgo., 1979-81; sr. product mgr. Bank of Am., San Francisco, 1981-82, v.p., 1982-84; interactive comm. svcs. prodr. and cons., 1984—; bd. dirs. Sci. and Tech. Enrichment Program, 1982—, pres., 1993-94. Mem. Women in Cable (1st pres. Chgo. chpt. 1981), Jr. League Seattle. Episcopalian. Patentee on child's chair, 1973.

DUNCAN, AUDREY WANZER, training manager; b. N.Y.C., Nov. 14, 1961; d. Arthur Phillip and Allie Dease (Ellerbe) W.; m. James Clydetiteous Duncan, Oct. 25, 1991. A in Bus., Florence Coll., 1982; postgrad., Limestone U. Customer rep. Citibank, N.Y.C., 1983-85; mgr. of tng. BCBS of S.C., Florence, 1985—. Mem. ASTD, Carolina Soc. for Tng. and Devel., NAFE. Office: BSBS SC Champus Div 100 Bldg 200 N Dozier Ave Florence SC 29501

DUNCAN, CONSTANCE CATHARINE, psychologist; b. Watertown, Wis., Nov. 2, 1948; d. Howard Burton and Mary Elizabeth (Fagan) Duncan; m. Allan Franklin Mirsky, July 4, 1986. BA, Northwestern U., 1970; AM, U. Ill., 1973, PhD, 1978. Sr. rsch. analyst Adolf Meyer Mental Health Ctr., Decatur, Ill., 1971-73; rsch. and teaching asst. Dept. Psychology, U. Ill., Champaign, 1974-78; postdoctoral fellow in neuroscis. Dept. Psychiat. and Behavioral Scis., Stanford U. Sch. Medicine, Palo Alto, 1978-81; rsch. psychologist VA Med. Ctr., Palo Alto, 1978-81; sr. staff fellow Lab. of Psychology & Psychopathology, NIMH, Bethesda, Md., 1981-88; chief unit on psychophysiology NIMH, Bethesda, Md., 1982-89, rsch. psychologist, 1988-89, rsch. specialist, 1989—; pvt. practice psychology Bethesda, Md., 1981—; adj. assoc. prof. Johns Hopkins Sch. Hygiene and Pub. Health, Balt., 1987—; rsch. asst. prof. to rsch. assoc. prof. Uniformed Svcs. U. of the Health Scis., Bethesda, 1993—. Assoc. editor Psychophysiology, 1987-91; cons. editor 15 sci. jours.; contbr. articles to profl. jours., chpts. to books. Found. assoc. Nat. Women's Econ. Alliance. Recipient Nat. Rsch. Svc. award, NIMH, 1978-81, Golden Anniversary Scholarship award, AAUW, 1974; USPHS fellow, 1970-74. Mem. APA (fellow 1992—), Soc. for Psychophysiol. Rsch. (dir. 1982-85, Disting. Sci. award for early career contbn. 1980, chmn. awards com. 1981-84, chmn. conv. com. 1983-87, chmn. program com. 1987, mem. Blue Ribbon panel on State of the Soc. in the Yr. 2000, 1990-93, chmn. enhancement com., 1992-93, chmn. early career award com. 1994—), Soc. for Rsch. in Psychopathology (dir. 1986-88, membership com. 1987-88), Soc. for Neurosci., Internat. Neuropsychol. Soc., Am. Psychopathol. Assn., Mortar Bd., Shi-Ai, Sigma Xi, Phi Kappa Phi, Alpha Lambda Delta, Pi Mu Epsilon, Phi Beta Kappa. Home: 6204 Perthshire Ct Bethesda MD 20817-3348 Office: NIMH Lab Psychology & Psychopathology Bldg 10 Rm 4C110 10 Center Dr MSC 1366 Bethesda MD 20892-1366

DUNCAN, DONNA FOWLER, secondary school educator; b. Greenville, S.C., July 15, 1957; d. James Robert Fowler and Betty (Worthy) Goodnough; children: William Jennings, Emily Jo. BS, Clemson U., 1979, MEd, 1991. Cert. tchr., S.C. Tchr. math. Wren Mid. Sch., Piedmont, S.C., 1979—; sch. rep. Supt. Tchr. Com., Piedmont, 1991-92, dist. pub. rels. com., 1991—; tchr. rep. Sch.-Wide Restructuring Com., Piedmont, 1991-92, rep. Dist.-wide Math. Curriculum Com., 1991-93, dist.-wide total quality edn. team, 1993. Mem. ASCD, S.C. Edn. Assn., S.C. Coun. Tchrs. Math., Alpha Delta Kappa. Baptist. Home: 288 Old Mill Rd #123 Mauldn SC 29662 Office: Wren Mid Sch 1010 Wren School Rd Piedmont SC 29673-8028

DUNCAN, ELIZABETH CHARLOTTE, marriage and family therapist, educational therapist, educator; b. L.A., Mar. 10, 1919; d. Frederick John de St. Vrain and Nellie Mae (Goucher) Schwankovsky; m. William McConnell Duncan, Oct. 12, 1941 (div. 1949); 1 child, Susan Elizabeth Duncan St. Vrain. BA, Calif. U., Long Beach, 1953; MA, UCLA, 1962; PhD, Internat. Coll., 1984. Cert. marriage and family therapist, Wash. Dir. gifted program Palos Verdes Sch. Dist., Calif., 1958-64; TV tchr., participant ednl. films L.A. County, 1961-64; dir. U. So. Calif. Presch., L.A., 1965-69, Abraham Maslow rsch. assoc., 1962-69; pvt. practice family counselor, Malibu and Ventura, Calif., Eastsound, Wash., 1979—, also, Seattle; pub. spkr., lectr. comm.; cons. in field; psychotherapist Mentor Program Eastsound, 1992; bd. dirs. Children's Program North Sound Regional Support Network, 1992; resident psychologist for film series Something Personal, 1987—; mem. Rsch. Inst. of Scripps Clinic, La Jolla, Calif.; charter mem. Inst. Behav. Med., Santa Barbara, Calif.; TV performer: (documentary) The Other Side, 1985. Creator: Persephone's Child, 1988; author: Do Hearts Really Break? 1990. Active Chryalis Ctr., L.A., 1984-86, Ventura County Mental Health Adv. Bd., Calif., 1985-86, United Way, L.A., 1985-92; mem. Menninger Found. San Juan County, Wash., 1992; adv. bd. North Sound Regional Support Network, 1992. Recipient Emmy award for best documentary Am. TV Arts and Scis., 1976, Child Adv. of Yr. Calif. Mental Health Adv. Bd., 1987. Mem. AACD (Disting. Svc. award 1990), Transpersonal Psychol. Assn., Calif. State Orgn. Gifted Edn. (sec. 1962-64), Internat. Platform Assn., Am. Assn. for Marriages and Family Therapy. Democrat. Avocations: swimming, plays, concerts, boating, political issues, especially women and child abuse. Address: Rte 1 Box 311 Eastsound WA 98246 Office: 410 Burnett Ave S Renton WA 98055

DUNCAN, FRANCES MURPHY, educator; b. Utica, N.Y., June 23, 1920; d. Edward Simon and Elizabeth Myers (Stack) Murphy; m. Lee C. Duncan, June 23, 1947 (div. June 1969); children: Lee C., Edward M., Paul H., Elizabeth B., Nancy R., Richard L. BA, Columbia U., 1942; MEd, Auburn U., 1963, EdD, 1969. Head sci. dept. Arnold Jr. High Sch., Columbus, Ga., 1960-63; tchr. physiology, Spanish, Jordan High Sch., Columbus, 1963-64; tchr. spl. edn. mentally retarded Muscogee County Sch. System, Columbus, 1964-65; instr. spl. edn. Auburn (Ala.) U., 1966-69; assoc. dir. Douglas Sch. for Learning Disabilities, Columbus, 1969-70; prof. edn. and spl. edn. Columbus Coll., 1970-85; ret., 1985; dir. Columbus Devel. Ctr. Past sec. exec. bd. Muscular Dystrophy Assn., 1968-70; 73-74; mem. Gov.'s Commn. on Disabled Georgians; past trustee Listening Eyes Sch. for Deaf; past mem. Mayor's Com. on Handicapped; mem. team for evaluation and placement of exceptional children Columbus Public Schs. Fellow Am. Assn. Mental Retardation; mem. AAUP, AAUW (pres. 1973-75, div. rec. sec. 1975—), Council Exceptional Children (legis. chmn. 1973-74), Psi Chi, Phi Delta Kappa. Roman Catholic. Home: 1811 Alta Vista Dr Columbus GA 31907-3210

DUNCAN, JOYCE LOUISE, real estate broker; b. Canton, Ohio, Jan. 11, 1946; d. William Clayton and Virginia Ruth (Wilgus) Sommers; m. Daniel Bruce Duncan, Mar. 3, 1989 (dec. 1990); children: David Michael Calhoun, Traci Lyn Calhoun. Student, U. Chattanooga, 1963-65, Mansfield Bus. Coll., Canton, Ohio, 1992-93; Assoc in Bus. Adminstrn., Mansfield Bus. Coll., Canton, Ohio, 1993. Cert. property mgr. Property mgr. Niebel Realty, North Canton, Ohio, 1981-85, Century 21 Americana Properties, St. Petersburg, Fla., 1987, Royal Estate Mgmt. Corp., Canton, 1989-90; broker, pres. Greystone Group, Inc., Canton, 1994; Ostendorf-Morris Co., Canton, 1993—. Mem. Women's Coun. Realtors (phone chmn. 1982, publicity chmn. 1983, treas. 1984, pres.-elect 1985, phone com. 1990), Canton/Massilon-St. Petersburg Bd. Realtors (program com. 1982-85, bldg. com. 1985, equal opportunity in housing com. 1990), Inst. Real Estate Mgmt., Nazir Caldron #27, Order Eastern Star (Delta chpt. #539). Home: 2748 Deer Pass Dr SW Canton OH 44706 Office: Ste 810 4450 Belden Village St Canton OH 44718

DUNCAN, MARGARET CAROLINE, physician; b. Salt Lake City, June 9, 1930; d. Donald and Margaret Aileen (Eberts) D.; m. N. Paul Arceneaux, Dec. 26, 1958; children—David Paul, Eleanor Anne, Stephen Louis, Andre. B.A., U. Tex., 1952, M.D., 1955. Intern Kings County Hosp., Seattle, 1955-56; resident in pediatrics John Sealy Hosp., Galveston, Tex., 1956-58; resident in neurology Charity Hosp., New Orleans, 1958-60; fellow child neurology Johns Hopkins Hosp., 1960-61; mem. faculty La. State U. Med. Center, New Orleans, 1961—; prof. neurology and pediatrics La. State U. Med. Center, 1973—. Chmn. La. Com. Epilepsy and Cerebral Palsy, 1976-79. Fellow Am. Acad. Neurology, Am. Acad. Pediatrics; mem. Child Neurology Soc., Profs. Child Neurology, Alpha Omega Alpha. Episcopalian. Office: 1542 Tulane Ave New Orleans LA 70112-2825

DUNCAN, MIM STOLTZFUS, counselor, consultant; b. Lancaster, Pa., Feb. 21, 1949; d. Samuel U. and Emma (Glick) Stoltzfus; m. William H. Duncan Jr., Dec. 7, 1973. BS in Elem. Edn., Millersville U., 1971; MA in Counseling Psychology, Lesley Coll., 1986. Tchr. Penn Manor Schs., Millersville, Pa., 1971-73, Palm Beach Co. Schs., West Palm Beach, Fla., 1973-74, Jefferson County Schs., Golden, Colo., 1975-90; sch.-home-community liaison Jefferson County Schs., Golden, 1990-92, guidance counselor, 1992—. Mem. ACA, NEA, Colo. Sch. Couns. Assn. Internat. Reading Assn., Phi Delta Kappa. Office: Evergreen Jr High Sch 2052 Hwy 74 Evergreen CO 80439

DUNCAN, NORA KATHRYN, lawyer; b. Chgo., Feb. 23, 1946; d. Robert Ferrie and Elise Grace (Walker) D. BA in Sociology, MacMurray Coll., 1968; JD, La. State U., 1973; LLM in Internat. and Comparative Law, George Washington U., 1979. Bar: La. 1973, U.S. Dist. Ct. (mid. dist.) La. 1974, U.S. Supreme Ct. 1978, D.C. 1979, U.S. Dist. Ct. (we. dist.) La. 1981, U.S. Ct. Appeals (5th and 11th cirs.) 1981. Staff atty. La. Dept. of Justice, Baton Rouge, 1973-76; contract counsel lands and natural resource La. Dept. of Justice, Washington, 1976-78; staff atty. La. Dept. of Justice, Shreveport, 1980; assoc. Cady & Thompson, Shreveport, 1981-82; ptnr. Cady, Thompson & Duncan, Shreveport, 1983; sole practice Shreveport, 1984-86, 87-88; ptnr. Walker, Tooke, Perlman & Lyons, Shreveport, 1986; atty. U.S. Immigration and Naturalization Service Dept. Justice, Oakdale, La., 1988-92, ret., 1992; instr., dir. paralegal studies program Draughon Bus. Coll., 1987. Atty., speech writer Gahagan for U.S. Senate, Augusta, 1978; bd. dirs. Better Bus. Bur., Shreveport, 1985-86. Paul Harris fellow Rotary Found., 1981. Mem. Toastmasters Internat. (area 11 gov. 1986-87, area 18 gov. 1994-95, pres. local chpt. 1986, 88, 94, named Gov. of Yr. 1987), Rotary. Republican.

DUNCAN, SANDY, actress; b. Henderson, Tex., Feb. 20, 1946; d. Mancil Ray and Sylvian Wynne (Scott) D.; m. Don Correia; children: Jeffrey, Michael. Studied dance at, Lon Morris Coll. Stage debut in The King and I at State Fair Music Hall, Dallas, 1958; N.Y. stage debut in The Music Man, 1965; stage appearances include The Boyfriend (Outer Critics Circle award, N.Y. Drama Desk award), Ceremony of Innocence, (Theater World award), Your Own Thing, The Music Box, Love Is a Time of Day, Peter Pan, My One and Only, 1984; starred in TV series Funny Face, 1971, The Sandy Duncan Show, 1972, Valerie's Family (title changed to The Hogan Family 1988), 1987-91; appeared in TV mini-series Roots, 1977; TV movies include My Boyfriend's Back, 1989, Miracle on I-880, 1993; other TV appearances include The Flip Wilson Show; film appearances include Million Dollar Duck, Star Spangled Girl, 1971, The Cat From Outer Space, 1978, (voice) Rock-a-Doodle, 1992, (voice) The Swan Princess, 1994; appeared in video Barney & Friends, 1988. Recipient Gold medal Photoplay, 1971, Golden Apple award, 1971. *

DUNCAN, SYLVIA LORENA, gifted education educator; b. Henderson, Tex., Dec. 19, 1949; d. William Presley and Sylvia Lorena (Cherry) Bumpass; m. Barry Patrick Duncan, Apr. 13, 1981. AA, Kilgore (Tex.) Jr. Coll., 1969; BS, North Tex. State U., 1971, MEd, 1975. Cert. tchr. generic spl. edn., elem., elem. English, tchr. mentally retarded, Tex. Spl. edn. tchr. Henderson Ind. Sch. Dist., 1971-72; spl. edn. tchr. Mesquite (Tex.) Ind. Sch. Dist., 1972-85, tchr. 2nd grade, 1985-88, tchr. of gifted/talented, 1988—; faculty rep. Mesquite Ind. Sch. Dist., 1974-76, vice chairperson admission, rev. and dismissal com., 1979-85, chairperson spl. edn. referral, 1990—. Contbr. editor (newspaper) News at 10, 1976. Zoo parent Dallas Zool. Soc.; sustaining mem. Dallas Mus. Art, Dallas Symphony Assn.; active Assn. Retarded Citizens, Dallas and Richardson, Tex. Mem. Tex. Assn. for Gifted and Talented, Mesquite Edn. Assn., Smithsonian Assocs., Nat. Mus. Women in Arts (charter). Office: Galloway Elem Sch 2329 Candleberry Dr Mesquite TX 75149-3010

DUNDON, MARGO ELAINE, museum director; b. Cleve., July 3, 1950; d. Elmer Edward and Ruth Ann (Dreger) Buckeye. BS in Communications cum laude, Ohio U., 1972; postgrad. in Mus. Studies, U. Okla, 1987. Mem. gen. staff Grout Mus. History and Sci., Waterloo, Iowa, 1974-75; coordinator edn. Grout Mus. History and Sci., Waterloo, 1976-78, co-dir., 1979-87, dir., 1988-90; exec. dir. Mus. Sci. and History, Jacksonville, Fla., 1990—. Chairperson Waterloo Hist. Preservation Commn., 1987-88; cultural com. Visitors and Conv. Bur., Waterloo, 1988-90, My Waterloo Days, 1982, 93; mem. Jacksonville Women's Network, Non-Profit Execs. Round Table; bd. dirs. Resource Plus, Waterloo-Cedar Falls, Iowa, 1986-88; mem. Jacksonville C. of C., 1990, mem. cmty. affairs and CJI bds.; bd. dirs. Girls Inc. of Jacksonville. Am. Law Inst.-ABA scholar, 1979, 86; recipient Mayor's Vol. Performance award, Waterloo, 1983, Vol. award Gov. of Iowa, 1990. Mem. Am. Assn. Mus. (site surveyor nat. assessment program 1982—, site examiner nat. accreditation commn. 1987-90, regional councilor 1988-90), Midwest Mus. Conf. (pres. 1988-90), S.E. Mus. Conf., Fla. Assn. Mus. (v.p. 1993—), Iowa Mus. Assn. (pres. 1984-86), Rotary, Quota Club (pres. 1982). Office: Mus Sci & History 1025 Museum Circle Jacksonville FL 32207

DUNEA, MARY MILLS, governor's aide; b. Des Moines; d. George Sturginne and Mary Brackett (Sweney) Mills; m. John Robert Barr (div. Oct. 1967); children: Mary Louise, John Mills; m. George Dunea; 1 child, Melanie Serena Alexandra Dunea. AB, Grinnell Coll., 1957. Pub. rels. dir. Cook County Hosp., chgo., 1968-70, Comprehensive State Health Planning Agy., chgo., 1970-73, Chgo. Tchrs. Union, 1975-77; book reviewer WGN Radio-Roy Leonard Show, Chgo., 1980-92; owner Walton Books, Inc., Chgo., 1978-84; asst. to the sec. Staff of Sec. of State Jim Edgar, Chgo., 1984-91; asst. to the gove. Staff of Gov. Jim Edgar, Chgo., 1991—; bd. dirs. Internat. Vis. Ctr., Chgo., English Speaking Union, Chgo.; Chgo. com. mem. Coun. on Fgn. Affairs, 1993—. Mem. campaign staff Dick Ogilve for Gov., Chgo., 1968, Jim Edgar for Gov., Chgo., 1990. Recipient award Ill. Ctr. for the Book, Chgo., 1990, Grand Decoration of Honor, The Republic of Austria, 1994. Fellow The Royal Soc. Arts; mem. Woman's Athletic Club, Cliff Dweller Club, Skyline Club, Carlton Club. Republican. Methodist. Home: 175 E Delaware Pl # 5907 Chicago IL 60611 Office: Office of Gov 100 West Randolph Chicago IL 60601

DUNGAN, GLORIA KRONBECK, critical care nurse; b. Little Falls, Minn., July 4, 1938; d. Hans Emil and Marie (Hahn) Kronbeck; divorced; 1 child, Kirk. Diploma, Abbott Hosp. Sch. Nursing, Mpls., 1958; BS in Nursing, U. Alaska, 1978. CCRN. Nurse at hosps. Mpls., Anchorage, 1958-63; staff nurse, charge nurse Narrabri (Australia) Hosp., 1963-64; night supr., staff nurse, charge nurse Providence Hosp., Anchorage, 1964-65; night supr., staff nurse Anchorage Community Hosp., 1966-67, Greater Juneau Borough Hosp., Juneau, Alask, 1968-69; asst. head nurse nights intensive care unit Providence Hosp., Anchorage, 1970-77; staff nurse Alaska Nurses Registry, Anchorage, 1977-78; from nurse mgr. to staff nurse intensive care unit Providence Hosp., Anchorage, 1978-83; staff nurse intensive care unit King Fahd Mil. Hosp., Jeddah, Saudi Arabia, 1983-84; staff nurse intensive care Providence Hosp., Anchorage, 1984-90; staff nurse critical care Am. Critical Care Svcs., Anchorage, 1990-92, Humana Hosp. Alaska, Anchorage, 1992, Alaska Native Med. Ctr., 1992—. Mem. Am. Assn. Critical Care Nurses (pres. Anchorage chpt. 1980-81, presenter ednl. programs), Sigma Theta Tau.

DUNGAN, MARTHA JAN, journalist, editor; b. DeQueen, Ark., Feb. 6, 1954; d. Joe L. and Sheilah Ione (Peek) D.; divorced; 1 child, Jennifer Marie. BS, East Tex. State U., 1976; postgrad. in nursing, Temple Jr. Coll. Reporter Paris (Tex.) News, 1976-78; mgr. Lamar Gardens Nursery and Landscape, Paris, 1978-80; asst. editor Lamar County Echo, Paris, 1981-83; exec. sec. Temple (Tex.) C. of C., 1984-85; exec. sec. Strasburger Enterprises, Temple, 1985-86, dir. advt., 1986; asst. editor lifestyle Temple Daily Telegram, 1986-87, editor lifestyle, 1987-93; nurse tech. II Scott & White Meml. Hosp., Temple, Tex.; owner A Touch of Glass by Jan. Mem. Azalee Marshall Cultural Activities Ctr., Temple. Mem. City Fedn. of Women's Club, Contemporaries. Methodist. Home: 1119 N 3rd St Temple TX 76501-1957

DUNHAM, BONNIE M., public relations professional; b. St. Joseph, Mo., Oct. 30, 1945; d. Roy J. and Viola M. (Hardin) Dunn; m. Jon W. Dunham, Sept. 5, 1964; 1 child, Gregory K. AA with hons., Johnson County C.C., Overland Park, Kans., 1976; BS in Journalism, U. Kans., 1980. Writer/editor Journal-World, Lawrence, Kans., 1981-89; comms. coord. Lawrence

Pub. Schs., 1989—; v.p. Lawrence Comms. Network, 1990-91; co-chmn. Building for Our Kids bond election com., Lawrence, 1990. Contbr. articles to profl. jours. Bd. dirs. United Way, Lawrence, 1994-97, divsn. leader, 1989-94, others. Recipient state awards in feature writing, Kans. Press Women, 1982-88, 1st pl. nat. award for series on health issues, Nat. Fedn. Press Women, 1986, media award Kans. State Nurses' Assn., 1987, ARC of Excellence Media award Kans. Assn. for Retarded Citizens, 1984, others; grantee Carl Knox Staff Devel. Grant, Lawrence, 1991. Mem. Nat. Sch. Pub. Rels. Assn. (Golden Achievement award 1991, awards of merit and excellence for publs. 1990, 92), Kans. Sch. Pub. Rels. Assn. (Excellence in Publs. awards 1989-91, 93-94), Phi Kappa Phi, Kappa Tau Alpha. Presbyterian. Office: Lawrence Pub Schs 3705 Clinton Pkwy Lawrence KS 66047

DUNHAM, CHRISTINE, dancer; b. Dallas. Studies with Myrtha Rosello; student, Sch. of Am. Ballet. Mem. Dallas Ballet; mem. Am. Ballet Theatre, 1985-87, soloist, 1987-89, prin. dancer, 1989—; Guest artist, Australian Ballet, 1991—. Lead dancer ballet Imperial, La Bayadere, Variation Six, Birthday Offering, Bouree Frantasque, Don Quixote (Kitire's Wedding), Fall River Legend, Giselle, Sleeping Beauty, Swan Lake, Firebird, Raymonda, Etudes; featured role in The Leaves are Fading, La Bayadere, Drink to Me Only With Thine Eyes, Les Sylphides; leading role in Nine Sinatra Song, Symphonie Conertante, Three Virgins and a Devil, Paquita, Manon; solo role in Paquita, Raymonda, Requiem, The Sleeping Beauty, Swan Lake. Scholar Sch. of Am. Ballet. Office: Am Ballet Theatre 890 Broadway New York NY 10003-1211*

DUNHAM, GAIL ANN, sales representative; b. Chgo., Apr. 9, 1944; d. August John Herbert and Loraine Clarice (Reitzke) Hagemann; m. Harold L. Green, Apr. 1, 1973 (div. Aug., 1975, dec. 1991); 1 child, Gretchen; m. Kenneth R. Dunham, Dec. 26, 1978. Student, No. Ill. U., 1963-64, Northwestern U., 1970-73. Sales rep. Am. Airlines, Cin., 1967—; supr. Naperville (Ill.) Twp., 1989-93. Bd. dirs. Indian Prarie Sch. Dist. 204, 1983-87, Copley/Rush Presbyn. St. Luke's Hosp., 1985-90; mem. Du Page County Health Coun.; past bd. dirs. Copley Meml. Hosp.; past Girl Scout co-leader; mem. City of Aurora 4th of July Parade board; dep. registrar for voter registration, Du Page County, 1982—; Rep. precinct com., 1982—; co-chair 1st and 2nd fundraisers Naperville Community Outreach program. Mem. LWV. Methodist. Home: 1454 Frenchman's Bend Rd Naperville IL 60564

DUNHAM, GLORIA, computer specialist; b. Lake Providence, La., Oct. 27, 1949; d. Elbert Augusta Armstrong and Annie (Scott) Reynolds; m. John Lee Dunham, Aug. 18, 1972 (div. 1978); 1 child, Natasha Deneen. Student, Cornell Coll., Mt. Vernon, Iowa, 1967-69; BA in English, Chgo. State U., 1973. Cert. tchr. secondary schs., Ill. Programmer analyst Commonwealth Edison, Chgo., 1973-74; sr. computer programmer Fed. Reserve Bank, Chgo., 1974-78; bus. analyst CNA Insur., Chgo., 1978-84; sr. software specialist Digital Equipment Corp., Rolling Meadows, Ill., 1984-85; prodn. support mgr. Time Inc., Chgo., 1985-88; computer specialist U.S. R.R. Retirement Bd., Chgo., 1988—. Mem. Bremen Community High Sch. Bd. Edn., Dist. 228, Midlothian, Ill., 1989—, strategic planning com., vice chmn. fin. com. 1990—, chmn. policy com., 1990-92, v.p., 1991—. Recipient plaque Bremen Bd. Edn., Midlothian, 1991. Home: 3313 Fountainbleu Dr Hazel Crest IL 60429-2248

DUNHAM, KATHERINE, choreographer, dancer, anthropologist; b. Glen Ellyn, Ill., June 22, 1909; d. Albert Millard and Fanny June D.; m. Jordis McCoo, 1931 (div.); m. John Thomas Pratt, July 10, 1941; 1 child, Marie Christine. BA in Anthropology, U. Chgo., 1936, MS; PhD, Northwestern U.; LhD (hon.), MacMurray Coll., 1972. Dir., tchr. of own schs. of dance, theatre and cultural arts Chgo., N.Y.C., Haiti, Stockholm and Paris, from 1931; profl. dancer, from 1934, choreographer for theatre, opera, motion pictures and TV; mem. Chgo. Opera Co., 1935-36; supv. Chgo. City Theatre Project on cultural studies, 1939; dance dir. Labor Stage, 1939-40; prodr., dir. Katherine Dunham Dance Co., from 1945; established dance sch. Port-au-Prince, Haiti, 1961; advisor to First World Festival on Negro Art U.S. Dept. State, 1966; artistic and tech. advisor to Pres. of Senegal, 1966-67; cultural counselor and dir. Performing Arts Tng. Ctr., So. Ill. U., East St. Louis, from 1967; prof. So. Ill. U., Edwardsville, from 1968. Choreographed works include: (concerts) Tropics, 1937, Schulhoff Tango, 1937, Madame Christoff, 1937, Primitive Rhythms, 1937, Biguine-Beguine, 1937, Florida Swamp Shimmy, 1937, Lotus Eaters, 1937, Haitian Suite, 1937, Peruvienne, 1938, Le Jazz Hot (Boogie-Woogie), 1938, Saludade da Brazil, 1938, Spanish Earth Suite, 1938, Island Songs, 1938, Mexican Rhumba, 1938, L'Ag'Ya, 1938, A Las Montanas, 1938, Bre'r Rabbit an' de Tah Baby, 1938, Bahiana, 1939, Cuidad Maravillosa, 1939, Concert Rhumba, 1939, Cumbancha, 1939, Plantation Dances, 1940, Babalu, 1941, Haitian Suite II, 1941, Honky-Tonk Train (added to Le Hot Jazz), 1941, Rites de Passage, 1941, Tropical Revue, 1943, Callaco, 1944, Choros Nos. 1-5, 1944, Flaming Youth 1927, 1944, Para Que Tu Veas, 1944, Havana 1910/1919, 1944, Carib Song, 1945, Bal Negre, 1946, Motivos, 1946, Haitian Roadside, 1946, Nostalgia (Ragtime), 1946, Batacada, 1947, Bolero, 1947, C'Est Lui, 1947, Rhumba Trio, 1947, Floor Exercises, 1947, La Valise, 1947, Octaroon Ball, 1947, Angelique, 1948, Blues Trio, 1948, Macumba, 1948, Missouri Waltz, 1948, Street Scene, 1948, Veracruzana, 1948, Adeus Terras, 1949, Afrique, 1949, Jazz in Five Movements, 1949, Brazilian Suite, 1950, Los Indios, 1950, Frevo, 1951, Rhumba Jive, 1951, Rhumba Suite, 1951, Spirituals, 1951, Caymmi, 1952, Ramona, 1952, La Blanchisseuse, 1952, Southland, 1952, Afrique du Nord, 1953, Samba, 1953, Cumbia, 1953, Dora, 1953, Honey in the Honeycomb, 1953, Incantation, 1953, Carnaval, 1955, Floy'd Guitar Blues, 1955, Jazz Finale, 1955, Just Wild About Harry, 1955, New Love, 1955, Banana Boat, 1957, Plating Rice, 1957, Sister Kate, 1957, Ti'Cocomaque, 1957, A Touch Of Innocence, 1959, Bamboche, 1962, Diamond Thief, 1962, Anabacoa, 1963; (theatre works) The Emperor Jones, 1939, Cabin in the Sky (co-choreographed with George Balanchine), 1940, Pins and Needles, 1940, Tropical Pinafore, 1939, Les Deux Anges, 1965; (film) Carnaval of Rhythum, 1939, Pardon My Sarong, 1942, Star Spangled Rhythum, 1942, Stormy Weather, 1943, Casbah, 1948, Boote e Risposta, 1950, Mambo, 1954, Green Mansions, 1958, The Bible, 1966; (opera) Aida, 1963; author: Katherine Dunham's Journey to Accompong, 1946, rev. edit., 1972, (autobiography) A Touch of Innocence, 1959, rev. edit., 1980, Island Possessed, 1969, Kasamance: A Fantasy, 1974; co-author (play) Ode to Taylor Jones, 1967-68; author of TV scripts, produced in Mexico, Australia, France, Eng. and Italy; contbr. short stories, somtimes under psedonym Kaye Dunn to mags.; consulting editor: Dance Scope. Pres. Dunham Fund for Rsch. and Devel. Cultural Arts, Inc.; founder Found. Study of Arts and Scis. of Vodun; v.p. Found. Devel. and Preservation Cultural Arts, Inc.; bd. dirs. Nat. Inst. Aging, Ill. Arts Coun.; mem. Ill. com. JFK Ctr. Alliance Arts Edn., Am. Coun. Arts in Edn., Arts World/Intercultural Com.; cons. Interamerican Inst. Ethnomusicology and Folklore, Caracas, Venezuela, NEH; mem. rev. com. OAS; mem. adv. bd. Modern Orgn. Dance Evolvement. Decorated Legion of Honor (Haiti), Merit Chevalier (Haiti), Cmdr. (Haiti), Grand Officer (Haiti); Julius Rosenfeld Travel fellow, 1936-37, Fulbright fellow State Dept. Internat. Edn.; Mather scholar Case Western Res. U., 1973; recipient Dance Mag. award, 1968, Eight Lively Arts award, 1969, Disting. Svc. award So. Ill. U., 1970, East St. Louis. Monitor award, 1970, Dance Divsn. Heritage award Am. Assn. Health, Physical Edn. and Recreation, 1972, Nat. Ctr. Afro-Am. Artists award, 1972, Black Merit Acad. award, 1972, Am. Dance Guild award, 1975, 6th Kennedy Ctr. Honors award, 1983, Profl. Achievement award U. Chgo., Samuel M. Scripps/Am. Dance Festival award, 1986, Nat. Medal Arts, 1989, Capezio Dance award, 1991; given key to city East St. Louis, Ill., 1968; named hon. citizen Port-au-Prince, Haiti, 1957. Mem. ASCAP, SAG, AEA, Am. Guild Variety Artists, Am. Guild Music Artists (bd. govs. 1943-49), Am. Fedn. Radio Artists, Writers Guild, Black Acad. Arts and Scis., Inst. Black World (bd. dirs.), Negro Actors Guild, Royal Anthrop. Soc., Lincoln Acad., Sigma Epsilon. Office: Katherine Dunham Mus 532 N 10th St East Saint Louis IL 62201-1946*

DUNHAM-CRAGG, MELISSA KAY, treasurer, health administrator; b. Chgo., Aug. 19, 1956; d. C. James Dunham and Monica (Kozasa) Mori; m. Thomas Leslie Cragg, May 5, 1984; children: Kathryn, Timothy. BA, Washington U., St. Louis, 1978, MBA, 1979. Analyst Comerica Bank, Detroit, 1979-81, lending officer, 1981-86, v.p., group mgr., 1986-88, first v.p., group mgr., 1988-92; treas., v.p. corp. fin. Detroit Med. Ctr., 1992—. Episcopalian. Home: 774 Westchester Rd Grosse Pointe MI 48230-1826 Office: Detroit Med Ctr 4201 Saint Antoine St Detroit MI 48201-2194

DUNKIS, PATRICIA B., principal. Prin. C.R. Streams Elem. Sch., Upper St. Clair, Pa. Recipient Elem. Sch. Recognition award U.S. Dept. Edn., 1989-90. Office: C R Streams Elem Sch 1560 Ashlawn Dr Upper Saint Clair PA 15241

DUNLAP, CONNIE, librarian; b. Lansing, Mich., Sept. 9, 1924; d. Frederick Arthur and Laura May (Robinson) Robson; m. Robert Bruce Dunlap, Aug. 9, 1947. A.B., U. Mich., 1946, A.M. in Library Sci, 1952. Head acquisitions dept., then head grad. library U. Mich. Library, 1961-75, dep. asso. dir., 1972-75; univ. librarian Duke U., 1975-80; cons., 1981—. Authors articles in field, chpts. in books. Forewoman Grand Jury U.S. Dist. Ct. 13th Dist. Mich., 1967-68; bd. dirs. U. Mich. Libr. Friends, 1993—. Recipient Disting. Alumnus award U. Mich. Sch Library Sci., 1977. Mem. ALA (council 1974-83, exec. bd. 1978-83, pres. resources and tech. services div. 1972-73), Assn. Coll. and Research Libraries (pres. 1976-77), Assn. Research Libraries (bd. dirs. 1976-80, pres. 1979-80), AAUP. Address: 1570 Westfield St Ann Arbor MI 48103

DUNLAP, CONNIE SUE ZIMMERMAN, real estate professional; b. Defiance, Ohio, Mar. 3, 1952; d. John Eldon and Loisann (May) Zimmerman; m. Joseph Richard Dunlap, Dec. 20, 1972; children: Brad, Todd, Eric. Student, MacMurray Coll., 1970-71, Ohio State U., 1973; BA, Wayne State U., 1989. Grad. Realtor Inst.; cert. residential specialist, 1991. Dental hygienist Dr. A. Lamar Byrd, San Diego, 1973-75; realtor, assoc. broker Champion & Baer, Inc., Grosse Pointe, Mich., 1986-95, Bolton-Johnston Assocs., Grosse Pointe Farms, Mich., 1995—; mem. Grosse Pointe Bd. Realtors, Macomb Bd. Realtors. Mem. Jr. League of Detroit., 1981—. Nat. Merit scholar Mature and Returning Women Wayne State U., Detroit, 1985-89. Mem. Phi Beta Kappa, Kappa Alpha Theta. Republican. Presbyterian. Home: 544 University Pl Grosse Pointe MI 48230-1640 Office: Bolton-Johnston Assocs 18332 Mack Ave Grosse Pointe Farms MI 48236

DUNLAP, ELAINE SMITH, English language educator, poet, critic; b. Denver, June 19, 1940; d. Henry Darrell and Ida Bobbie (Hershkowitz) Smith; m. Gregory John Dunlap, May 31, 1969; children: Oliver Quinn, Chandler Lauren. BA, U. Colo., 1964; MA, San Francisco State U., 1972; postgrad study of ancient Greek, U. Calif., Berkeley, 1988-92. Film editor, TV continuity coord. Sta. KBTV-KOA TV, Denver, 1965-66; English instr. Coll. of Marin, Ross, Calif., 1972-73; instr. in English City Coll. San Francisco, 1975; instr. in English and Humanities Diablo Valley Coll., Pleasant Hill, Calif., 1975—; mem. arts and lectr. com. Diablo Valley Coll., Pleasant Hill, 1977, 90—, fgn. study com., 1994—; instr. for humanities Diablo Valley Coll. and Am. Inst. Fgn. Students, London, 1987. Contbr. poetry tos literary mags., 1955—; drama, ballet and art critic, newspapers, 1986—. Bd. dirs. Contra Costa Ballet Found., Walnut Creek, Calif., 1989; camerata and vol. soc. Philharm. Baroque, San Francisco, 1989—; art commr. City of Walnut Creek, 1991-92. Cited for Outstanding Svc. Contra Costa Ballet Found., Walnut Creek, 1991. Mem. NOW, Am. Archeol. Soc., Inst. of Nautical Archaeology, Humanities West, Friends of Troy. Democrat. Office: Diablo Valley Coll Golf Club Rd Pleasant Hill CA 94523

DUNLAP, ELLEN S., library administrator; b. Nashville, Oct. 12, 1951; d. Arthur Wallace and Elizabeth (Majors) Smith; m. Arthur H. Dunlap, Jr., Dec. 27, 1972 (dec. 1977); m. Frank Armstrong, May 11, 1979; 1 child, Libbie Sarah. BA, U. Tex., Austin, 1972, MLS, 1974. Rsch. assoc. Humanities Rsch. Ctr. U. Tex., Austin, 1973-76, rsch. libr., 1976-83; exec. dir. Rosenbach Mus. and Library, Phila., 1983-92; dir. Conservation Ctr. for Art and Hist. Artifacts, Phila., 1985-92, Greater Phila. Cultural Alliance, 1985-92; mem. exec. com. Phila. Area Consortium Spl. Collections Librs., 1985-91; pres. Am. Antiquarian Soc., Worcester, Mass., 1992—; dir. Worcester (Mass.) Mcpl. Rsch. Bur., 1993—; chmn. archives manuscripts and spl. collections program com. Rsch. Librs. Group, Inc., Mountain View, Calif., 1989-91; dir. 18th Century Short Title Catalogue/N.Am., 1992—; corporator Alliance for Edn., Worcester, Mass., 1993—. Overseer Old Sturbridge Village, Mass., 1993—. Mem. Am. Antiquarian Soc., Colonial Soc. Mass., Grolier Club (N.Y.C.), Worcester Club. Office: Am Antiquarian Soc 185 Salisbury St Worcester MA 01609-1636

DUNLAP, VIRGINIA JO, lawyer; b. Sacramento, Oct. 7, 1961; d. Lyman Eugene and Virginia Ruth (Marsh) D. BA in Journalism, U. Nev., 1983; JD, U. Pacific, 1989. Bar: Calif. 1989, Nev. 1992. Sports publicist U. Nev., Reno, 1981-83, Boise (Idaho) State U., 1983-84; sports writer Mountain Dem., Placerville, Calif., 1984-85; atty. Diehl, Steinheimer, Riggio, Haydel & Mordaunt, Stockton, Calif., 1989-92, Porter Simon, Truckee, Calif., 1992—. Editor: (sch. newspaper) Dialogue, 1988; assoc. editor: Pacific Law Jour., 1988-89. Membership chair Truckee Rep. Women Fedn., 1994. Mem. State Bar Nev. (mem. Reno fee dispute panel 1994—), Nev. County Legal Assistance (bd. dirs., sec. 1993—). Office: Porter Simon 40200 Truckee Airport Rd Truckee CA 96161-3307

DUNLEAVY, MARY ANN, telecommunicaitons company representative; b. N.Y.C., July 30, 1956; d. Anthony and Mary Frances (Glennon) D.; m. Terence Spillane, June 20, 1993. BA in Communication Arts, Iona Coll., 1978; MBA in Mktg., Fordham U., 1989. Asst. buyer Abraham and Straus, Bklyn., 1979-80; rep. NYNEX, N.Y.C., 1981—. Contbr. articles to profl. jours. Vol. Central Park Conservancy, N.Y.C., 1991. Mem. Manhattan Soc., Columba Soc., Fordham U. Aluni Assn., Iona Coll. Alumni Assn., St. Batholomews Community Club. Office: N Y Telephone Co 111 Livinston St New York NY 10028

DUNLEAVY, ROSEMARY, ballet dancer; b. N.Y.C.; d. John Francis and Lucy (Wavrik) D. Grad., High Sch. Performing Arts, N.Y.C. Ballet dancer N.Y.C. Ballet, 1961-71, asst. ballet mistress, 1968-83, ballet mistress, 1983—. Performances include Balanchine's A Midsummer Night's Dream, Harlequinade, Don Quioxote, Jewels. Office: NYC Ballet Inc NY State Theater Lincoln Ctr Pla New York NY 10023*

DUNMEYER, SARAH LOUISE FISHER, health care consultant; b. Ft. Wayne, Ind., Apr. 13, 1935; d. Frederick Law and Jeanette Blose (Stults) Fisher; m. Herbert W. Dunmeyer, Sept. 9, 1967; children: Jodi, Lisa. BS, U. Mich., 1957; MS, Temple U., 1966; EdD, U. San Francisco, 1983. Lic. clin. lab. technologist, Calif. Instr. med. tech. U. Vt., Burlington, 1966-67; instr. med. tech. Northeastern U., Boston, 1967-68, instr. lab. asst. program, 1968-70; educator, coord. sch. med. tech. Children's Hosp., San Francisco, 1970-73; dir. continuing edn. program Pacific Presbyn. Med. Ctr., San Francisco, 1974-82; project mgr., cons. Peabody Mktg. Decisions, San Francisco, 1983-87; sr. rsch. assoc. Inst. for Health and Aging, U. Calif., San Francisco, 1986-89; external cons. Health Care Consulting Svcs., San Francisco, 1986-92; rsch. analyst student acad. svcs. U. Calif., San Francisco, 1991-94; seminar presenter Am. Assn. Blood Banks, San Francisco, 1976, Am. Soc. Clin. Pathologists, Miami Beach, Fla., 1977, Ann. Meeting of Am. Soc. Med. Technology, Atlanta, 1977; site surveyor Nat. Accrediting Agy. for Clin. Lab. Scis., Chgo., 1974-80. Contbr. articles to profl. jours. Vol. Buck Ctr. for Rsch. on Aging. Club: U. Mich. Alumni (San Francisco).

DUNN, BARBARA ANN, nursing administrator; b. Detroit, July 11, 1950; d. Michael Joseph and Mildred Mary (Meldrum) Dunn; m. James Edward Heileman, June 27, 1992; 1 child from previous marriage, Heather. Diploma in nursing, Providence Hsop., Southfield, Mich., 1972; BS in Health Svcs., U. Detroit, 1989; M of Health Svcs. Adminstrn., Cen. Mich. U., 1993. Staff nurse Holy Cross Hosp., Detroit, 1972-74; staff nurse phase II-ICU St. John Hosp., Detroit, 1974-76, staff nurse ICU, 1976-81, asst. clin. supr. ICU, 1981-85, clin. supr. SICU, 1985-88, mgr. same day surgery, 1988—; faculty critical care St. John Hosp., Detroit, 1982-88, mem. quality assurance nursing, 1982-86. Office: St John Hosp Same Day Surgery 22101 Moross Detroit MI 48236

DUNN, BERNICE MARIE, women's health nurse; b. Danforth, Maine, Oct. 11, 1934; d. Henry Augustus Harding and Leah Orale (Gould) Crossman; m. Scott Andrew Dunn, Oct. 19, 1957 (div. Mar. 1984); children: Audrey M. Nutter, E. Lee Dunn Shirland, Janet L. Dunn Doucette, John E. II. Diploma, EMMC Sch. of Nursing, Bangor, Maine, 1975. RN, Maine. Psychiat. aide to LPN, RN State of Maine, Bangor, 1953-76; aide, charge aide, charge LPN, med. nurse to supr. ob/gyn Ea. Maine Med. Ctr., Bangor, 1976—. Vol. March of Dimes; organist, pianist, choir dir., Sunday Sch. tchr., Faith Bible Ch., Olarnon, Maine, 1957-82. Mem. ANA, AWHONN (cert.), Maine State Nurses Assn., Nat. Assn. Am. Coll. of Ob/Gyn. Democrat. Baptist. Office: EMMC Ltd 489 State St Bangor ME 04401

DUNN, BONNIE BRILL, chemist; b. Bethesda, Md., Mar. 10, 1953; m. William H. Dunn, July 13, 1974; children: Daniel Brill, Vanessa Thompson. AA, Montgomery Coll., 1972; BS in Food Sci., U. Md., 1974, MS in Food Chemistry and Statistics, 1978, PhD in Food Chemistry, 1982. Rsch. asst. U. Md., College Park, 1976-79, teaching asst., 1977-80; researcher div. chemistry and physics U.S. FDA, Washington, 1979; statistian USDA, Beltsville, Md., 1980, researcher, 1980-82; radiochemist Positron Emission Tomography; head quality assurance NIH, Bethesda, 1984-93; rev. chemist FDA, Rockville, Md., 1993—; mem. adv. bd. on intramural woman scientists NIH. Contbr. numerous articles to profl. jours. Sec., v.p. PTA, 1988-94; mem. PTA Forest Knolls Elem., Montgomery County, 1988-94; exec. bd. dirs. PTA Ea. Mid. Sch. Montgomery County, Md., 1992-94; leader Girl Scouts U.S., 1988-91. Recipient performance award NIH, 1987-92, USPHS, 1993-94. Mem. AAAS, Am. Chem. Soc., Soc. Nuclear Medicine. Home: 18506 Viburnum Way Olney MD 20832 Office: FDA 5600 Fishers Ln HFD160 Rockville MD 20857

DUNN, BRIDGET BRYANS, business manager; b. Boulder, Colo., June 26, 1961; d. Richard Waldron and Carol Jean (Appelquist) Bryans; m. Scott A. Dunn, Apr. 23, 1988. Student, U. Colo., Boulder, 1979-81, U. Colo., Denver, 1982. Exec. asst. Mission Viejo Co., Highlands Ranch, Colo., 1985-87; exec. asst. to pres. Rifkin & Assocs., Denver, 1987-89; regional bus. mgr. Prime Sports Network, Denver, 1989—; COO, CFO Tri-R Constrn., Denver, 1988—. Mem. Nat. Assn. Minorities in Cable, Women in Cable, Cable TV Adminstrn. and Mktg. Soc. The Rocky Mountains (bd. dirs., treas. 1994—). Office: Prime Sports Network 44 Cook St Ste 600 Denver CO 80206

DUNN, DEBORAH DECHELLIS, trust administrator, assistant treasurer; b. Plainfield, N.J., Jan. 16, 1960; d. Anthony and Joan Dora (Brown) DeChellis; m. Paul Michael Dunn, May 13, 1989; children: Joseph Daniel, Brian Jacob. BS in Elem. Spl. Edn., U. Hartford, 1982. Spl. edn. tchr. Hartford (Conn.) Pub. Schs., 1982-83, East Hartford (Conn.) Pub. Schs., 1983-84; individual retirement account ops. supr. Conn. Nat. Bank, Hartford, 1984-87; individual retirement account adminstr. Glastonbury (Conn.) Bank & Trust, 1987, mgr. fin. mgmt. svc. ops., 1987-91; asst. treas., FMS adminstr. Glastonbury (Conn.) Bank & Trust Co., 1988—, investment rep., trust adminstr., asst. treas.; investment cons., 1994—; ind. edn. cons. Democrat. Methodist. Office: Mktg One Securities Inc care First Fidelity Bank 2500 Morris Ave Union NJ 07083

DUNN, GRACE VERONICA, retired executive secretary; b. Bklyn.; d. Richard William and Grace Veronica (Mason) D. BA, Our Lady of the Lake U., 1940; postgrad., Columbia U., 1958. Sec. Hunt Oil Co., Dallas, 1947-48, Standard Oil Co. (N.J.), N.Y.C., 1955-59, Pan Am. Health Orgn., Washington, 1964-76. Mem., Vol. Stephanie Roper Com., Upper Marlboro, Md., 1987-92, Friends of the Kennedy Ctr., Washington, 1991—; soprano soloist Holy Trinity Cath. Ch., Dallas, 1945-47, Ch. of the Incarnation Episcopal Ch., Dallas, 1945-47; soloist White House Christmas Tree, 1988. Grad. fellow Karl Schultz Found., 1940; pvt. scholar Elisabeth Schumann, N.Y.C., 1948-52. Roman Catholic.

DUNN, JENNIFER BLACKBURN, congresswoman; b. Seattle, Wash., July 29, 1941; d. John Charles and Helen (Gorton) Blackburn; div.; children: Bryant, Reagan. Student, U. Wash., 1960-62; BA, Stanford U., 1963. Former chmn. Rep. Party State of Wash.; now mem. 103rd Congress from 8th Wash. dist., Washington, D.C., 1993—. Del. Rep. Nat. Conv., 1980, 84, 88; presdl. apptd. adv. coun. Historic Preservation; presdl. apptd. adv. coun. volunteerism SBA. Mem. Gamma Phi Beta. Office: 1641 Longworth Hob Washington DC 20515

DUNN, JUDITH LOUISE, secondary school educator; b. L.A., Jan. 6, 1945; d. Arthur B. and Lillian M. (Eyrich) D. BA, U. Calif., Santa Barbara, 1966; MA Edn., Pepperdine U., 1978; postgrad., U. Calif., Santa Barbara, 1967. Cert. secondary tchr., adminstr., Calif; cert. lay speaker United Meth. Ch. English tchr. Santa Maria (Calif.) Joint Union High Sch. Dist., mentor tchr., chmn. dept. English, 1991-94; mem. adv. coun. Student Age Parenting and Infant Devel. Program; dist. tchr. rep. Impact II Adv. Coun.; dist. rep. Ctrl. Coast Literacy Coun. Assoc. lay leader Santa Barbara dist. Calif.-Pacific Annual Conf., 1986-89, United Meth. Ch., bd. Higher Edn. and Campus Ministry, 1982-90. Fellow South Coast Writing Project; Disseminator grantee, 1988, 89. 91. Mem. CTA, NEA, Nat. Coun. Tchrs. English, Local Faculty Assn. (profl. rels. chair 1986-88), Delta Kappa Gamma (immediate past pres. Eta Lambda chpt.). Office: Santa Maria High Sch 901 S Broadway Santa Maria CA 93454-6613

DUNN, LAURA-LEE MAE, artist and author; b. Prince Albert, Sask., Can., Jan. 15, 1959; naturalized, 1981; d. Raymond Gerald and Dorothy (Hersche) Andrews; m. David Anderson Dunn, July 1, 1989; 1 child, David Ray. M in Denturitry, The Internat. U., 1985; A in Massage Therapy, Reilly Sch. Massotherapy, 1987. Co-owner ArtForms, Princeton, Ind., 1992—; mem. art coun., co-chair Southwestern Ind. Artists Collaborative. Exhibited in group shows at Krannert Gallery, Evansville, 1991, Art Evansville, 1991, Ohio River Arts Festival, 1992, Evansville C. of C., 1993, Midstates Contemporary Gallery, Evansville, 1993, Brescia Coll., Owensboro, Ky., 1993, Owensboro Mus. Sci. and History, 1993, Custom Framing Gallery Showroom, Vincennes, Ind., 1993, Evansville Mus. Arts and Scis., 1993. Active Evansville Mus. Arts & Sci., Sta. WNIN Fundraising Auction, Evansville, Ind. Mem. Owensboro Art Guild, Evansville Art Guild, Southwestern Ind. Artists Collaborative (co-chair, mem. arts coun. southwestern Ind.). Roman Catholic.

DUNN, LINDA KAY, physician; b. Grand Rapids, Mich., Jan. 11, 1947; d. Roger John and Mary Kathryn (Bouwer) Kloote; m. Jeffrey Marc Dunn, June 3, 1972; children: David Alan, Kathryn Ann. AB in Chemistry, Hope Coll., 1968; MD, U. Mich., 1972. Diplomate Am. Bd. Ob-Gyn, Am. Bd. Maternal-Fetal Medicine, Am. Bd. Med. Genetics. Resident in Ob-Gyn. U. Mich., Ann Arbor, 1972-75, fellow in maternal-fetal medicine, 1975-77; hon. research registrar St. Mary's Hosp., London, 1977-78; dir. of perinatology Temple U. Sch. Medicine, Phila., 1978-79, assoc. prof. ob-gyn, 1991—; dir. subsect. on genetics Pa. Hosp., Phila., 1980-90; pres Medigen, Inc., Phila., 1987-90; dir. maternal-fetal medicine and genetics Abington (Pa.) Meml. Hosp., 1991—; med. dir. Comprehensive Maternal and Infant Svcs., Phila., 1987-90; pres. Abington Perinatal Assocs., P.C. Mem. alumni bd. govs. U. Mich. Med. Ctr. Fellow Am. Coll. of Ob-Gyn.; mem. AMA, Soc. of Perinatal Obstetricians, Am. Soc. Human Genetics, Am. Med. Women's Assn., Pa. State Med. Soc., Phila. Obstet. Soc., Norman Miller Gynecologic Soc. (pres.-elect). Mem. Soc. of Friends. Office: Ste 119 Medical Plz 1235 Old York Rd Abington PA 19001-3788

DUNN, MARGARET ANN, religious studies educator, administrator, minister; b. Marshall, Mich., Nov. 18, 1953; d. Lee Donald and Hazel Lucille (Boehmer) D. BS cum laude, Alma Coll., 1975; MDiv, Asbury Theol. Sem., 1983; MA, Ball State U., 1989; postgrad., U. Houston, 1991—. Lic. min. Ch. of God (Anderson, Ind.), 1989. Tchr. Lydia Patterson Inst., El Paso, Tex., 1976-79; campus affiliate InterVarsity Christian Fellowship, Richmond, Ky., 1980-81; teaching asst. Asbury Theol. Sem., Wilmore, Ky., 1981-83; tchr. Southwood Christian Acad., Indpls., 1984-85, Liberty Christian Sch., Anderson, 1985-86; libr. clk. Anderson Sch. Theology, 1986-88; prof. religious studies, registrar, dir. admissions Bay Ridge Christian Coll., Kendleton, Tex., 1988—, registrar, 1993—; vis. lectr. Asbury Theol. Sem., 1983; min.Christian edn. Rosenberg (Tex.) 1st Ch. God, 1991-92, coord. women in ministry-mission Ch. of God, Anderson, Ind., 1992-94; dir. student ministries Bay Ridge Christian Coll., 1992-93, 94—; team mem. Sunday Sch. TEAM Bd. of Christian Edn., Ch. of God, 1993—. Co-author: Framework of Our Faith, 1983. Chairperson South East Tex. Ministerial Assembly Christian Edn. Com. Mem. ASCD, Southwest Ednl. Rsch. Assn., NAFSA Assn. Internat. Educators, Gamma Delta Alpha, Omicron Delta Kappa. Office: PO Box 58 East Bernard TX 77435-0058

DUNN, MÁRIA BACH, writer, researcher, translator; b. Kleinbettange, Luxembourg, Feb. 6, 1910; came to U.S., 1946; naturalized, 1950.; d.

Dominique and Marie (Müller) Bach; m. James Taylor Dunn, Dec. 23, 1946. Student, Pensionnat Ste Anne Soeurs du Sacré Coeur, Hougaerde, Belgium. interpreter, translator, negotiator hist. documents, 1967-71; translator ednl. program Voice Am., N.Y. State Hist. Assn., Cooperstown, 1953; initiator, sponsor Bibliotheque Luxemburgiana, St. Thomas U., St. Paul, 1993. Contbg. editor: Luxembourg News Am., 1959—. Vol. Mary Imogene Bassett Hosp., Cooperstown, 1950-55; contbg. mem. Luxembourg Heritage Soc. Inc.; charter mem. U.S. Holocaust Mus. Recipient Nat. Medal of Merit, Luxembourg Govt., 1993, award of merit regional chpt. Nat. Red Cross Am., 1950, 52. Mem. NOW, ACLU. Democrat. Roman Catholic. Home: 7039 San Pedro # 907 San Antonio TX 78216-6241

DUNN, MARY BETH, law librarian; b. Mpls., June 21, 1949; d. Edward James and Elizabeth Antoinette (Malat) McConville; m. Paul William Dunn, Aug. 19, 1972; children: Nora Rose, Will Patrick, Hugh Michael, Eileen Elizabeth. BA, Coll. of St. Catherine, St. Paul, 1971; MLS, Syracuse U., 1977. Law libr. Supreme Ct. Libr., Syracuse, N.Y., 1978-91; ptnr. Law Libr. Cons., Syracuse, 1980—. Mem. Am. Assn. Law Librs. (coun. of cpt. pres. 1983-85, chmn. legal info. to pub. com. 1987-88, interlibr. comms. com. 1987-88), N.Y. State Unified Ct. Law Librs. Assn. (prs. 1986-87), Assn. Law Librs. Upstate N.Y. (bd. dirs. 1981-83, 85-86, pres. 1984-85), Ctrl. N.Y. Libr. Resources Coun. (bibliog. svcs. com. 1985-91), Assn. for Irish Culture. Roman Catholic.

DUNN, MARY JARRATT, public relations executive; b. Clifton Forge, Va., Oct. 29, 1942; d. Robert Bell and Mary Louise (Wood) J. B.A., Mary Baldwin Coll., Staunton, Va., 1964; cert. bus., Katharine Gibbs Sch., Boston, 1965. Staff asst. com. on agr. U.S. Ho. of Reps., 1975-81; asst. sec. food and consumer services Dept. Agr., 1981-85; v.p. Wampler & Assocs. Inc., Washington, 1985-86; pres. Jarratt & Assocs., Inc., Washington, 1986-90. Editor various legis. reports. Republican. Episcopalian. Home: The Pines 6 Farmington Dr Charlottesville VA 22901-3241

DUNN, MARY MAPLES, college president; b. Sturgeon Bay, Wis., Apr. 6, 1931; d. Frederic Arthur and Eva (Moore) Maples; m. Richard S. Dunn, Sept. 3, 1960; children—Rebecca Cofrin, Cecilia Elizabeth. BA, Coll. William and Mary, 1954, LHD (hon.), 1989; MA, Bryn Mawr Coll., 1956, PhD, 1959; LLD (hon.), Marietta Coll., 1987, Amherst Coll., 1987, Brown U., 1989; LittD (hon.), Lafayette Coll., 1988, Haverford Coll., 1991; LHD (hon.), Transylvania U., 1991. Mem. faculty Bryn Mawr Coll., 1958-85, prof. history, 1974-85; acting dean Undergrad. Coll. Bryn Mawr (Pa.) Coll., 1978-79, dean, 1980-85; pres. Smith Coll., Northampton, Mass., 1985—. Author: William Penn: Politics and Conscience, 1967; editor: Political Essay on the Kingdom of New Spain (Alexander von Humboldt), 1972, rev., 1988, (with Richard S. Dunn) Papers of William Penn, vols. I-IV, 1979-87. Trustee The Clarke Sch. for the Deaf, 1985, Acad. Mus., 1985, Hist. Deerfield, Inc., 1986—, Bingham Fund for Teaching Excellence at Transylvania U., 1987—, Baystate Med. Ctr., 1990—, John Carter Brown Libr., 1994—; dir. Bank of New England West, 1986. Recipient Lindbeck Found. award distinguished teaching, 1969; Fellow Inst. Advanced Study Princeton U., 1974. Mem. Berkshire Conf. Women Historians (pres. 1973-75), Coordinating Com. Women Hist. Profession (pres. 1975-77), Am. Hist. Assn., Inst. Early Am. History and Culture (chmn. adv. council 1977-80), Mass. Hist. Soc., Phi Beta Kappa. Office: Smith Coll Office of the President Northampton MA 01063

DUNN, MIGNON, mezzo-soprano; b. Memphis, June 17, 1931; d. Dudley and Nancy Christine (Lundee) D.; m. Kurt Klippstatter, July 1972. Studies with Karin Branzell; MusD (hon.), Southwestern Coll., 1975; studies with Armen Boyajian, studies with Mrs. Hardesty Johnson. Recorded with Heritage, Angel, Deutsche Grammophon, Serato, EMI; faculty Am. Inst. Mus. Studies, Graz, Austria, Music Club Am., N.C., Internat. Vocal Arts Inst., Fla., Israel, Manhattan Sch. Music, U. Ill., Urbana. Debut at Town Hall with Little Orch. Soc., 1954, debut in New Orleans as Carmen, 1955; debut at N.Y.C. Opera as Carmen, 1956; debut with Met. Opera in Boris Godunov, 1958, debut Arena diVerona, Italy, 1970, Covent Garden, Eng., 1973, Teatro Colon, 1964, Vienna, 1973, LaScala, Milan, 1986; appeared with maj. opera cos. throughout Europe, U.S., Can., Mex., and S.Am.,including, Paris Opera, Vienna State Opera, Hamburg State Opera, Berlin, Helsinki, Budapest, Monte Carlo, Arena d'Orange; numerous roles including Judith in Bartok's Bluebeard's Castle, Azucena in Verdi's Il Trovatore, Amneris in Aida, Dalila in Saint Saens's Samson et Dalila, Carmen in Bizet's Carmen, Kostelnicka in Janacek's Jenufa, Marina in Boris Godunov, Herodias in Strauss' Salome, Jerzi Baba in Janacek's Rusalka; also entire Wagnerian, Straussian and Verdian repertoire of mezzo-soprano roles; recitalist; soloist with major orchs. in Europe, U.S., Can., Mex.; appeared at Spoleto Festival, Charleston, S.C., 1987-88, Spoleto, Italy; recs. include Rigoletto, Mother of Us All, Salome, Verdi Requiem. Recipient Beethoven prize Memphis, Exptl. Opera Theatre Am. award, 1955, N.Y. Singing Tchrs. award 1984, Hall of Fame Vocal Arts Acad. award, Phila., 1986. *

DUNN, MIRIAM D., legislative research firm executive; b. Lawrence, Mass., Oct. 17, 1927; d. Henry F. and Emilie W. (White) Dearborn; m. Vincent de Paul Dunn, July 28, 1951 (div. Jan. 1981); children: Mark, Jonathan (dec.), Vincent Jr. Student, Antioch Coll., 1945-48; BA, U. N.H., 1950; postgrad., Smith Sch. Psychiat. Soc. Work, 1950-51. Sch. social worker Derry and Concord, N.H., 1963-68; legal adminstr., rschr. Maynard, Dunn & Phillips Law Firm, Concord, 1968-78; pres. Capitol Eye of N.H., Inc., Concord, 1982—; state rep. N.H. Ho. of Reps., Concord, 1988—; mem. adv. bd. N.H. Small Bus. Devel. Ctrs., 1984—; del. White House Conf. on Small Bus., Washington, 1986. Contbr. articles to newspapers. Del. Dem. Nat. Conv., Miami, Fla., 1972, N.Y.C., 1992. Mem. Bus. & Profl. Women, Paralegals Assn., Greater Concord C. of C. Democrat. Home: 77 Pleasant St Concord NH 03301 Office: Capitol Eye of NH Inc 77 Pleasant St Concord NH 03301 also: NH State Capitol Concord NH 03301

DUNN, PATRICIA ANN, school system administrator, English language educator; b. Englewood, N.J., Mar. 17, 1942; d. Thomas Joseph and Rosanna Valerie (Cummings) D.; m. James Edward Egan, 1963 (div. 1974); 1 child, Deirdre Tracy. BA in English Edn., William Paterson Coll., 1963, MA in Communication Arts, 1974; postgrad., Montclair (N.J.) State Coll., 1986—. Cert. tchr., N.J., N.Y.; cert. prin., supr., N.J. Tchr. English, Intermediate Sch. Dist. 218, Bklyn., 1965-66, tchr. English and humanities, 1966-67, co-chmn. dept. humanities, 1967-68; tchr. English Midland Park (N.J.) Schs., 1969-91, staff devel. coord., 1987—, dir. curriculum, instrn., staff devel., 1991—; coord. bus. workshops Women in Bus., 1983, Stress, 1983; dir. N.J. Staff Devel. Coun., 1991-94, pres.-elect., 1994. Editor N.J. Staff Devel. Coun. Newsletter, 1988-91; contbr. articles to profl. publs. Cofounder, coord. Ministry for Separated and Divorced Caths., Montclair, 1983-86. Mem. ASCD, N.J. Prins. and Suprs. Assn., Nat. Staff Devel. Coun., N.J. Staff Devel. Coun. (co-founder), Nat. Assn. Secondary Sch. Prins., Nat. Coun. Tchrs. English, Le Terrace Club (Nutley, N.J.). Democrat. Roman Catholic. Office: Midland Park High Sch 250 Prospect St Midland Park NJ 07432-1398

DUNN, PATRICIA DIXON, eye clinic administrator; b. Charlotte, N.C., Aug. 25, 1946; d. Leonard Neston Dixon and Ina Maude (Pickette) Moore; married; children: Frances Michelle, Patrick Earl. Diploma, Lenoir Community Coll., 1966. Nurse Craven County Hosp., New Bern, N.C., 1966-68; with Coastal Eye Clinic, New Bern, 1968—; bus. mgr. Coastal Eye Clinic, P.A., New Bern, 1985—. Mem. Am. Soc. Ophthalmic Adminstrn., NAFE. Home: 205 Spring Meadows Rd Vanceboro NC 28586-8435

DUNN, REBECCA DIANE, personnel specialist; b. Roanoke, Ala., May 8, 1948; d. Avery Moore and Iva Delle (Brewer) Cunningham; children: Elizabeth, Catherine. Student, Jacksonville (Ala.) State U., 1968; BS in Mgmt. of Human Resources, Faulkner U., Montgomery, Ala. Pvt. practice piano tchr. Alexander City, Ala., 1971-85; mfg. interviewer personnel Russell Corp., Alexander City, 1985-87; cons. Horizons for Learning Russell Corp., Alexander City, Ala., 1983-86; supr. clerical dept. and hourly employees Russell Corp., Alexander City, 1987-89; personnel mgr. Corporate Svcs., 1989-91, mgr. ednl. svcs., 1991—; corp. rep. Adult Basic Edn. Adv. Bd., Alexander City, 1986-92, v.p., 1992-93, pres., 1993-94; chmn. bus. edn. craft com. Area Vocat. Tng. Ctr., Alexander City, 1987-93, pres. adv. bd., 1994-95; chmn. edn. com. Russell Corp. Mem. Ala. Textile Mfrs. Assn. (chmn. edn. com.), Laubach Literacy Action. Baptist. Office: Russell Corp Lee St PO Box 272 Alexander City AL 35010

DUNNE, DIANE C., marketing executive; b. Milw.; d. Francis and Ruth Borman Cantine; 1 child, Dana Philip. BS, Marquette U., 1970; MBA, NYU, 1985. Mgr. advt. NBC, N.Y.C., 1975-77; dir. mktg. CBS, N.Y.C., 1977-80; dir. funding Bloomingdale's, N.Y.C., 1980—; dir. 750 Park Ave. Corp., N.Y.C., 1985—; dir. Women's Econ. Round Table, 1988—; v.p. events The Oxford U. Alumni Assn. N.Y., 1994—; v.p. events Oxford U. Alumni Assn. of N.Y., 1994—. Author: Guidelines to Advertising All News Radio, 1976, Guidelines for Catalogue Copywriters, 1985; asst. editor Am. Cancer Soc., Gourmet Guide for Busy People by Famous People, 1985, The Internat. Directory of Disting. Leadership; contbr. articles to profl. jours. Mem. Am. Cancer Soc., N.Y.C., 1980—; chair St. James Ch. Feed the Homeless com., N.Y.C., 1984—; mem. pastoral and community ministry com. St. James Altar Guild. Mem. Fashion Group (co-chair regional com.), Women's Econ. Roundtable (bd. dirs. 1988), NYU Exec. MBA Assn. Episcopalian. Avocations: opera, jogging, skiing, squash. Home: 750 Park Ave New York NY 10021-4252 Office: Bloomingdales 770 Lexington Ave New York NY 10021-8165

DUNNE, KATHERINE ANNE, lawyer; b. Jacksonville, Fla., Nov. 13, 1956; d. Frank Russell and Jeanne Therese (Stenach) D. AB, Dartmouth Coll., 1978; JD, U. Va., 1981. Law clk. to Hon. Robert Kelleher U.S. Dist. Ct. (cen. dist.) Calif., L.A., 1981-82; assoc. Kilpatrick & Cody, Atlanta, 1982-83, Morgan, Lewis & Bockius, Phila., 1983-86; atty. Bell Atlantic Corp., Phila., 1986-90; sr. atty. Bell Atlantic Network Svcs., Phila., 1990-93, gen. atty. mergers and acquisitions, 1994—.

DUNNING, FRANCES LOUISE, small business owner; b. Alma, Mich., Jan. 6, 1946; d. Fredrick William and Allyce Marie (LaLonde) Radke; m. Clarence Verness Roth, July 21, 1962 (div. 1974); children: Tammy, Penny, Kelly, Terry, Kanddy; m. Dallas Donald Dunning, Dec. 31, 1983; stepchildren: Irene, Chris, Bonnie, Ray. Cert. of completion, Lifetime Career Sch., 1984. Line worker A.C. Spark Plug, Flint, Mich., 1969-70; machine operator press Metal Fab G.M., Flint, 1976-78; welder Fisherbody G.M., Grand Blanc, Mich., 1979-83; owner, operator Ma & Pa's Junque, Millington, Mich., 1983-89; notary Otisville, Mich., 1989—; owner, operator Ma's Doll Shop, Otisville, 1989-90; cons. Children's Mus., Flint, 1989-90, Caro (Mich.) Doll Club, 1992. Author: Fisher Price Dolls, 1990, Chatty Cathy Doll Repair, 1991; contbr. articles to jours. Mem. 20 Lakes Tractor Club, Ma's Doll Club (pres. 1988-91). Lutheran. Office: Ma's Doll Shop 1226 Arbor Dr Lake MI 48632

DUNPHY, MAUREEN ANN, educator; b. Springfield, Mass., Feb. 25, 1949; d. Donald J. and Mary C. (Tabb) Milbier; m. Terrence Michael Dunphy, June 30, 1979. BS in Edn., Westfield State Coll., 1971, MEd, 1975, Cert. Advanced Grad. Study, 1988. Tchr. Thornton Burgess Intermediate Sch., Hampden, Mass., 1971-75; reading specialist, dept. head West Springfield Jr. High Sch., 1975—; acting asst. prin. W. Springfield Jr. High Sch., 1989; cons. Nat. Evaluations Systems, Amherst, Mass. Mem. Long Range Bldg. Needs Com., Westfield, 1986-87. Mem. Pioneer Valley Reading Council (pres. 1977-79), Mass. Reading Assn. (dir. 1977-81), W. Springfield Edn. Assn. (negotiations sec.), Mass. Tchrs. Assn., Hampden Co. Tchrs. Assn. Home: 282 Steiger Dr Westfield MA 01085-4934 Office: West Springfield Jr High Sch 115 Southworth St West Springfield MA 01089-2724

DUNSFORD, DEBORAH WILLIAMS, agricultural journalism educator; b. Sedalia, Mo., Dec. 17, 1956; d. Clyde Marion and Oleta Jean (Hoard) Williams; m. Bart Roberts Dunsford, May 24, 1980. BS in Agrl., Kans. State U., 1979; MA in English, Tex. A&M U., 1987, PhD, 1993. Asst. editor, reporter Ag Press Publ., Manhattan, Kans., 1978-80; editorial asst. High Plains Jour., Dodge City, Kans., 1980-82; adminstrv. clk., customer svc. rep. Gen. Tele. Co. the S.W., Bryan, Tex., 1982-85; asst. editor Tex. Real Estate Rsch. Ctr., College Station, 1985-86; instr. English, journalism Tex. A&M U., College Station, 1987-91; lectr. English, journalism Old Dominion U., Norfolk, Va., 1991; lectr. English, study skills Mt. St. Clair Coll., Clinton, Iowa, 1992-93; asst. editor, ext. N.C. State U., Raleigh, 1993-94; asst. prof. agrl. journalism Tex. A&M U., College Station, 1994—; instr. Wake Tech. C.C., Raleigh, 1993, Ctrl. Carolina C.C., Sanford, N.C., 1993, Clinton (Iowa) C.C., 1992-93, Blinn C.C., College Station, 1989-90; tech. writer Computer Data Systems, Inc., Norfolk, Va., 1991; comm. specialist, ext. Tex. A&M U., College Station, summers, 1986-91, grad. teaching asst., 1987, 89-90; freelance writer Fayetteville (N.C.) Observer-Times, 1993, Raleigh News & Observer, 1993. Contbr. articles to local newspapers. Vice-chair Clinton County Dem. Party, 1993; vol. campaign worker Brazos County, 1988; sec.-treas. Internat. Assn. Bus. Communicators, 1986-87, Brazos bravo com. 1987-88; Tex. A&M Conf. on lang. and lit. com. English Grad. Students Assn., 1989-90; dir. Bryan-College Station Jaycees, 1985-86. Recipient Brazos Bravo award Internat. Assn. Bus. Communicators, Bryan, 1986, Future Farmers Am. awards, Kans., 1974-75. Mem. MLA, Nat. Coun. Tchrs. English, Assn. for Edn. in Journalism and Mass Comm., Assn. for Advanced Composition, Eighteenth Century Soc., Gold Key Nat. Honor Soc. Democrat. Office: Tex A&M U Dept Journalism Reed Mcdonald Bldg College Station TX 77843

DUNTLEY, LINDA DAY, network executive; b. Corona, Calif., Aug. 5, 1955; d. Donald Elmes and Leah Doris (Staudte) Day; m. Mark Andrew Duntley Jr., June 1978 (div. Dec. 1986). BA, San Francisco U., 1980, MA, 1982. cert. tchr., Calif. Regional supervising mgr. Western Empire, Seattle, 1973-76; artist Wash., Calif., 1973—; model/talent/art judge Calif., 1978—; substitute tchr. Marin County Pub. Schs., Calif., 1980-82; doctor of dress, color doctor Profl. Image Color, 1982—; corp. instr. BFAS, 1983-88; TV speaker Public TV, Santa Barbara, Calif., 1990; documentary movie speaker Faces in the Fire, Santa Barbara, Calif., 1991; pres., network exec. Profl. Image Color, Santa Barbara, Calif., 1982—; juror Marin Soc. of Artists, Kent, Calif., 1979-82. Author: (book) Color of Dress as it Relates to First Impressions of Personality Traits, 1982. Mem. NAFE, Pi Lambda Theta. Home: PO Box 2422 Santa Barbara CA 93120 Office: 2015 State St Santa Barbara CA 93105

DUPEY, MICHELE MARY, communications specialist; b. Bronx, N.Y., Feb. 26, 1953; d. William B. and Sandra Nancy (Raia) D.; m. Daniel Michael Gieser, July 14, 1980 (div. May 1991). BA, Montclair State Coll., 1975; cert. in Copywriting, NYU, 1988. Sec. DDB Needham Worldwide Inc. Advt. (formerly Doyle Dane Bernbach Advt. Co.) N.Y.C., 1985-88; asst. comm. dir. Hudson County, N.J., 1988—. Creator ann. Hudson County women's history month program and named athletic program Womansport; In-house planning chair 150th anniversary celebration of Hudson County; freelance copywriter Jersey City, 1988—; ind. distbr. Km/Matol Botanical Internat. Comm. Gay Games IV, N.Y.C.; developer Hudson County Adv. Commn. on Women; with leadership N.J. Fellow, 1995. Contbr. articles to profl. publs. Mem. NOW (pres. local chpt. 1982-83, 84-86, chmn. fin. com. N.J. orgn. 1984-85, chmn. fund raising com. 1984-85, mem. N.J. state bd. 1982-86). Democrat. Episcopalian. Home: 206 Washington St Apt 3A Jersey City NJ 07302-4566

DUPLANT, MAX STEPHANIE, accountant; b. Port Arthur, Tex., June 10, 1956; d. Gerald and Pat (Sinclair) Oubre; m. John K. Duplant, May 14, 1977; children: Jason, Stephanie, Julien. BBA with honors, Lamar U., 1977. CPA, Tex. Staff acct. Bruce W. Jackson, CPA, Beaumont, Tex., 1978; ptnr. Charles E. Reed & Assocs. CPAs, Port Arthur, 1978-93; dir. fin. City of Groves, Tex., 1993—. Bd. dirs. Montessori Sch., Port Arthur, Tex., 1983-84, Am. Heart Assn., 1988—. Named S.E. Tex. CPA of the Year, 1989. Mem. AICPA, NAFE, Tex. Soc. CPAs (Young CPA of Yr. 1990, v.p. 1993-94), Southeast Tex. Soc. CPAs (pres. 1987-88), Bus. and Profl. Women's Assn. (pres. 1990-91, Young Career Woman award 1986). Office: City of Groves PO Box 846 Groves TX 77619

DUPLANTIER RHEA, BÉATRICE MARIE CHARLOTTE, international art consultant, interior decorator; b. Bayonne, France, Oct. 10, 1942; came to U.S., 1960; d. Jean Pierre Marie Ferdinand Duplantier and Odile Marie Mathilde (Guilhot) de Spens d'Estignols; m. Edward Jenkins Rhea, July 13, 1964 (div. Aug. 1989); children: Alexander, William (dec.), Jean-Edwin, Kenneth. BA in Langs., Ecole Supérieure Interprètes Traducteurs, Paris, 1964; BA in Russian, Ecole Nat. Langs. Orientales, Paris, 1971. Restorer old farms and manors, St.-Sever-sur-Adour, France, 1966-76, old apts., Paris, 1966-76; interpreter Ministry Fgn. Affairs, Paris, 1979-81; cons. art, entertainment Bread Oven Restaurants, Washington, 1982-86; cons., decorator various cities, 1986—; internat. art agt., cons. Four Winds Designs, Winter Park, Fla., 1986—; coord. cultural visits for tourists St.-Sever-sur-Adour, Landes, France, 1962-64; agt. internat. artists, 1986—; coord. art. and cultural visits for guests of French govt., Paris, 1979-81; exhbn. cons. Orlando (Fla.) Mus. Art, 1991; cons. exhibitions Boca Raton Hotel Club, 1990-95, Museum Montaut-en-Chalosse, France, 1991, 92, 93, 94, French Embassy, N.Y.C., 1992, Alliance Francaise, Miami, 1994. Mem. Friends of Olney Theatre, 1982-93, Allied Bd. Trade, 1989-93, Cornell Fine Art Mus., Maitland Art Mus., Nat. Mus. Women in the Arts, Enzian Theatre, Friends of Vielles Maisons Françaises, Musée de Montaut-en-Chalosse, Washington Design. Ctr., Design. Ctr. Ams., Atlanta Decorative Ctr. Am. Field Svc. scholar, 1960. Mem. Design Ctr. of the Ams., Washington Design Ctr., Minority Bus. Women Enterprise (cert. Orange County 1990, Orlando 1991), Friends Vieilles Maisons Francaises (coord. art confs., Atlanta, 1990), Winter Park C. of C., Greater Orlando C. of C., Hispanic C. of C. Roman Catholic. Home: 1645 N Park Ave Winter Park FL 32789-2436 Office: Four Winds Designs Internat Art 1645 N Park Ave Winter Park FL 32789-2436

DUPONT, BONNIE LEE, underwriting assistant; b. Merrill, Wis., Sept. 8, 1946; d. Earl E. and Jane A. (Powers) Smith; m. Donald W. Bellin, Jan. 16, 1965 (div. Aug. 5, 1992); children: Chad, Jeremy. Grad. high sch., Merrill, Wis., 1964. Registered assoc. in underwriting. Gen. liability specialist Wausau (Wis.) Ins. Co., 1967-85; underwriting asst. Church Mut. Ins. Co., Merrill, Wis., 1985—. Mem. Mid-Wis. Ins. Assoc. (pres. 1994-95). Home: 15385 Brandenburg Ave Merrill WI 54452-9167

DUPRAT, JO ANN, pediatric rehabilitation nurse, consultant; b. Vallejo, Calif., May 21, 1948; d. Albert John Chester Jr. and Dorothy Marie (Anderson) Smith; m. Dennis Albert Duprat, May 14, 1966; children: Dana Marie, Daniel Gordon. ASN, Contra Costa Coll., San Pablo, Calif., 1982; BS in Health and Human Svcs., Columbia Pacific U., San Rafael, Calif., 1991, MS in Health and Human Svcs., 1992, postgrad., 1994—. RN, Calif.; CRRN, cert. rehab. nursing, UR/QA/discharge planning/risk mgmt. Learning Tree Univ. Staff nurse, adolescent Children's Hosp., Oakland, Calif., 1982-83, staff nurse med./surg. pediatric, 1983-84, pediatric rehab. nurse specialist, 1984—; nursing supr. Adult Care Svcs., Walnut Creek, Calif., 1992-93; nurse cons. in pvt. practice, San Pablo, 1984—; nurse cons. Regional Ctr. of East Bay, Emeryville, Calif., 1985—; panel nurse Calif. Children's Svcs., Sacramento, 1985—. Author: Spina Bifida, Current Trends, 1991; Historical Perspectives and Attitudes Towards Women, Sexuality, Childbirth and Parenting, 1993. Supporting mem. San Pablo Little League, 1991-92. Mem. Spina Bifida of Calif., Assn. Rehab. Nurses, Children's Orthotics/Prosthetics Clinics, Nat. Neurofibramatosis Soc., Assn. for Syringomyelia, Alpha Gamma Sigma. Office: Children's Hosp 747 52nd St Oakland CA 94609

DUPRÉ, JUDITH, writer, consultant; b. Woonsocket, R.I., Oct. 3, 1956; d. Robert Edgar and Dolores (Albanese) D. BA in Art, Brown U., 1978, BA in English Lit., 1978; postgrad., Hunter Coll., 1985-90. Pres. Artlog Systems, N.Y.C., 1980-86; mktg. assoc. Olympia & York Co., N.Y.C., 1986-89; pres. Judith Dupré & Assocs., N.Y.C., 1989—; speaker, lectr. N.Y.C. Pub. Schs., 1992—; lectr. on Am. Indian culture, nationally, 1990—; mktg. cons. to several Native Am. orgns. Author: First Americans, 1992, 93, 94, The Mouse Bride, 1993; editor: Artlog Directory of Contemporary Art, 1982, The Heart of the Beast, 1994. NEH fellow, Newberry Libr., Chgo., 1991; N.Y. State Coun. on the Arts grantee, 1988. Office: 428 Greenwich St New York NY 10013-2004

DUPRE, JUDITH ANN NEIL, real estate agent, interior decorator; b. Houma, La., May 7, 1945; d. Herbert Joseph and Doris Mae (LeFouef) Neil; m. Michael Anthony Dupre, Jan. 7, 1962 (div. Aug. 1987); children: Arienne Danielle, Travis Lance. BA in Psychology, Southeast Okla. State U., 1982. Fin. mgr., supr. Gen. Fin. Loan Co., La., Colo., 1960-69; exec. sec. Progressive Bank & Trust Co., Houma, La., 1973-74; health coordinator Spring Cypress Cultural & Recreation Ctr., 1974-75; bus. mgr., buyer June Morris Boutique, Ardmore, Okla., 1978-79; actress, model David Payne Agy., Dallas, 1985—; real estate agt. Vonnie Cobb Inc. Realtors, Sugar Land, Tex., 1986-91, Raymond Jepta Daniel, Jr., 1991—; nat. mktg. asst. North American Mortgage Co. (subs. MONY Mut. N.Y.), Houston, 1987-88; mgr., care coord. Sanus N.Y. Life, Inc., 1988-89; mgr. PPO Am. Health Network, 1989—; dir. admissions and bus. devel. The Transitional Learning Community, Galveston, Tex., 1990-92; owner Paradigm Health Care, 1993—; exec. dir. Rehab. Svcs. Network, Inc.; workers compensation cons. ETHIX S.E.; owner, pres. Summit Internat. Cons., Charlotte, N.C., 1991—, Ams. With Disabilities Act, Charlotte, 1991, JD Enterprises Internat., Inc., 1994—. Active Strake Jesuit-Mothers' Club, Houston, 1985-87, St. Agnes Acad. Women's Club, Houston, 1985-87, Ft. Bend Republican Women, Sugar Land, 1985-86, Charlotte Philharm., 1994—, mem. CAST, 1994—; chmn. Texans War on Drugs, Sugar Land, 1985-86; bd. dirs. MUD (Dist. 6), Sugar Land, 1986-92. Mem. Cath. Daus. of the Americas, Nat. Assn. Realtors, Tex. Assn. Realtors, Bal Harbour Homeowners Assn., Assn. Profl. Mortgage Women, Lake Wylie Homeowners Assn., Sweetwater Ladies Golf Assn. Club, Sweetwater Country Club (Sugar Land), Assn. River Hills Country Club, Ladies Assn., Alpha Chi. Roman Catholic. Avocations: tennis, golf, fishing, boating, dancing. Home: 42 Fairway Ridge Lake Wylie SC 29710

DUPREE, MARSHA ANNE, academic administrator; b. Miami Beach, Fla., Oct. 19, 1951; d. James Thomas Taylor and Daisy Mae (Comer) Wallace; m. Kenneth Ray Dupree, Aug. 14, 1976; children: Kenneth R. II, Anita R., Marcus A. BA in Sociology, Calif. State U., Long Beach, 1973; MA in Counseling, U. Nev., 1994. Personnel asst. So. Calif. Air Pollution Control, L.A., 1976; tchr. gen. music Reno (Nev.) Jr. Acad., 1978-79; office mgr. Reno Seventh Day Adventist Ch., 1978-82; adminstrv. aid II, mgmt. asst. I Sch. of Home Econs. U. Nev., Reno, 1983-85, mgmt. asst. II Affirmative Action Office, 1985-87, mgmt. asst. III, 1987-88, outreach coord., 1988-90, admission and recruitment coord., 1990-94, acting dir. Affirmative Action Office, 1994-95; mentor Project Call/Community Action Leaders' Liasion, U. Nev., 1993—. Bd. dirs. No. Nev. Black Cultural Awareness Soc., Reno, 1989—, Reno Jr. Acad., 1990-94; mem. Nev. Women's Fund Allocation Com., Reno, 1993, Washoe-at-Risk Taskforce, Reno, 1993—; co-facilitator 12-Step Recovery Group Program, Sparks (Nev.) Seventh Day Adventist Ch., 1994—; mem. Nev.-Utah Conf. Seventh Day Adventist Assn. Bd., 1992—; mem. Heavenbound Prison Ministry, Carson City, Nev., 1989—, Reno-Sparks Interfaith Gospel Choir, 1977—. Named Outstanding Faculty Mem., Black Student Orgn., U. Nev., 1993. Mem. Am. Counseling Assn., Assn. for Multicultural Counseling and Devel., Nev. Assn. for Counseling and Devel., We. Assn. of Student Fin. Aid Adminstrs., UNS Alliance of Racial Minorities (pres. 1993-94, sec. 1985-88), Western Assn. Coll. Admission Counselors. Democrat. Home: 95 El Molino Dr Sparks NV 89436-9246 Office: U Nev 9th And Center St Reno NV 89557

DUPREE, SHERRY SHERROD, reference librarian, religion consultant; b. Raleigh, N.C., Nov. 25, 1946; d. Matthew Needham and Mary Elouise (Heartley) Sherrod; m. Herbert Clarence DuPree, Jan. 11, 1975; children: Amil, André, Andrew. BS, N.C. Cen. U., 1968, MA, 1969; MLS, U. Mich., 1974, Cert. ednl. specialist, 1978. Media specialist Ann Arbor (Mich.) Pub. Schs., 1970-77; assoc. ref. libr. U. Fla. Librs., Gainesville, 1977-83; ref. libr. Santa Fe C.C. Libr., Gainesville, 1983—; project dir. Inst. Black Culture U. Fla., Gainesville, 1982—; vis. prof. Ea. Mich. U., Ypsilanti, 1975; prof. edn. Bethune Cookman Coll., Daytona Beach, Fla., 1984-88. Author: Displays for Schools: All Avenue of Communication, 1976, rev. edit., 1979, Busy Bookworm: Good Conduct, 1980, Mini Course in Library Skills, 1983, Bible Lessons for Youth, 1987, What You Always Wanted to Know About the Card Catalog But Was Afraid to Ask, 1988, Biographical Dictionary of African American Holiness--Pentacostals: 1880-1990, 1989, African American Pentecostals: Sourcebook, 1992, Exposed! Federal Bureau of Investigation (FBI) Unclassified Reports on Churches and Church Leaders, 1993, African-American Good News (Gospel) Music, 1993. Chair Rosewood Massacre Forum. Recipient Gov.'s Achievement award State of Fla., 1986; rsch. grants Nat. Coun. Chs., 1983, Gatorade Found., 1987, 88, 90; travel grants NEH, 1983, So. Regional Edn. Bd., 1987, 88, 89, 90; grant-in-aid fellow Bd. Regents, State of Fla., 1980-81, Horace H. Rackham's Opportunity grant, 1975-76, OEG Libr. Sci. grant U. Mich., 1973-74, grad. fellow N.C. Cen. U., 1968-69. Mem. ALA, NAACP, Soc. Pentacostal Studies, Soc. Am. Archivists, Alachua Libr. League, Fla. Libr. Assn. (chiar religion caucus), Fla. Community Coll. Assn. Democrat. Mem. Ch. of God in Christ. Office: Santa Fe C C Libr Bldg P Rm 208 3000 NW 83d St Gainesville FL 32602

DUQUETTE, DIANE RHEA, library director; b. Springfield, Mass., Dec. 15, 1951; d. Gerard Lawrence and Helen Yvette (St. Marie) Morneau; m. Thomas Frederick Duquette Jr., Mar. 17, 1973. BS in Sociology, Springfield Coll., 1975; MLS, Simmons Coll., 1978. Libr. asst. Springfield City Libr., 1975-78; reference libr. U. Mass., Amherst, 1978-81; head libr. Hopkins Acad., Hadley, Mass., 1980; instr. Colo. Mountain Coll., Steamboat Springs, 1981-83; libr. dir. East Routt Libr. Dist., Steamboat Springs, 1981-84; agy. head Solono County Libr., Vallejo, Calif., 1984; dir. libr. svcs. Shasta County Libr., Redding, Calif., 1984-87; dir. librs. Kern County Libr., Bakersfield, Calif., 1987—; chmn. San Joaquin Valley Libr. System, 1988. Contbr. articles to profl. jours. Recipient John Cotton Dana Spl. Pub. Rels. award, H.W. Wilson and ALA, 1989. Mem. ALA, Calif. Libr. Assn. (mem. coun. 1987—), Calif. County Librs. Assn. (pres. 1990). Democrat. Roman Catholic. Home: PO Box 6595 Pine Mountain Club Frazier Park CA 93222 Office: Kern County Libr 701 Truxtun Ave Bakersfield CA 93301-4816

DURAN, KARIN JEANINE, librarian; b. Burbank, Calif., Aug. 31, 1948; d. Jose Antonio and Sophia (Cortez) D.; m. Richard Mark Nupoll, Sept. 5, 1971. AA, L.A. Pierce Coll., Woodland Hills, Calif., 1968; BA, Calif. State U., 1970; MLS, U. So. Calif., 1972, PhD, 1986. Libr. Calif. State U., Northridge, 1972—; lectr. Calif. State U., Northridge, 1977-84. Mem. Comision Feminil Nacional, San Fernando Valley, Calif., 1987—. Named Woman of Year Calif. Women Higher Edn., Northridge, 1989, Bicentennial Woman, L.A. Human Rels. Com., 1976. Mem. ALA, Nat. Assn. Chicano Studies, Calif. Libr. Assn., Calif. Acad. Rsch. Librs., Women's Coun. Calif. State U., Assn. Governing Bds., REFORMA, Computer Using Educators. Office: Calif State U Northridge Libr 18111 Nordhoff St Northridge CA 91330-0001

DURAND, SYDNIE MAE M., state legislator; b. Lafayette, La., Apr. 30, 1934; d. Sidney August and Hattie Ann (Belaire) Maraist; m. Alcee J. Durand, Oct. 16, 1955; 1 child, Alcee J. (Chip). Student, U. Southwestern La., 1952-55. Landman Sohio Pet, Lafayette, 1955-60; acct. Austral Oil, Lafayette, 1960-79; environ. coord. Mobil Oil, Lafayette, 1979-91; mem. La. Ho. of Reps., Baton Rouge, 1991—. Police juror St. Martin Parish Govt., 1980-92. Recipient Conservation award Woodman of the World, 1988, Bishop's medal Diocese of Lafayette, 1989. Mem. Nat. Assn. Counties, L.A. Policy Jury Assn. (exec. bd. 1982-92), Evangeline Econ. Bd. (v.p. 1985-92). Democrat. Roman Catholic. Address: PO Box 2674 Saint Martinville LA 70582-2500 Office: 1010 Marie St Saint Martinville LA 70582-6619 also: La Ho of Reps State Capitol Baton Rouge LA 70804*

DURBIN, MARGARET, legislative counsel, legislative staff director; b. Washington, Dec. 28, 1945. BA, Cath. U., 1967, JD, 1975. Legis. atty. Am. law divsn. Congl. Rsch. Svc., 1975-76; minority counsel Subcom. Consumer Protection and Fin., Subcom. Commerce, Transp. and Tourism Com. Energy and Commerce, 1977-84; counsel Am. Ins. Assn., 1984-85; assoc. gen. counsel Am. Coun. Life Ins., 1985-88; minority chief counsel, staff dir. Com. Energy and Commerce, 1988—. Office: Energy & Commerce 2322 Rayburn House Office Bldg Washington DC 20515*

DURBIN, (MARGARET) ROSAMOND, marketing executive; b. Shelbyville, Ind., Feb. 25, 1952; d. Willard Clyde and Irma Frances (Havens) Sandefur; m. Timothy Mark Durbin, Dec. 27, 1986. BA in English, Xavier U., 1974. Office mgr. Pryde, Inc., Cin., 1975-77; media mgr. Intermedia, Inc., Cin., 1977-80; media dir. Caldwell-Van Riper, Inc., Ft. Wayne, Ind., 1980-82; media supr. Jerrico/Abbott Advt., Lexington, Ky., 1982, Marsteller, Inc., Chgo., 1982-85; mgr. Midwest mktg. Pearle Vision Ctr., Chgo., 1985-86; v.p. Bonsib Inc. Mktg. Svcs., Indpls., 1986-94; pres. Durbin Mktg. Inc., 1994—; guest lectr. Ind. U.-Purdue U., Indpls. Pres. YWCA, Ft. Wayne, 1982; mem. local advt. rev. bd. Ctrl. Ind. BBB. Mem. Am. Mktg. Assn., Advt. Club Indpls., Nat. Wildlife Fedn., Xavier Alumni Assn. Republican. Roman Catholic.

DURBIN-VOSS, MARVIE LOU, computer programmer analyst; b. Denver, June 2, 1937; d. Lewis Amos and Marvie Grace (Owens) Durbin; m. Howard Dwight Saunders, June 10, 1960; m. Harvey Arthur Voss, Aug. 23, 1980; children: Steven Paul Saunders, Randall Scott Saunders. BA, Colo. State U., 1959, MA, 1966; Assocs. degree, Front Range Coll., 1979. Cert. tchr. secondary edn. Tchr. Twin Falls (Idaho) High Sch., 1959-60, St. John's Sch., San Juan, P.R., 1960-61, Du Valle High Sch., Prince George's County, Mo., 1962-63, Poudre High Sch., Ft. Collins, Colo., 1964-65; counselor Adams City Jr. High, Commerce City, Colo., 1966-79; sr. programmer analyst Nat. Jewish Rsch. Ctr., Denver, 1979—. Mem. Am. Contract Bridge League (treas. 1964—, Grand Life Master 1976). Home: 1603 Lincoln Ct Longmont CO 80501

DURDAHL, CAROL LAVAUN, psychiatric nurse; b. Crookston, Minn., Jan. 18, 1933; d. Elmer Oliver and Ovidia (Olson) Durdahl; m. Hans A. Dahl, May 22, 1956 (div. 1983); children: Hana Sorensen, Carla Pederson. RN, St. Lukes Hosp., Duluth, Minn., 1953; BA in Human Svcs., Met. State U., St. Paul, 1982. Staff nurse various hosps., Minn., 1953-59; human svcs. tech. Willmar (Minn.) State Hosp., 1970-74, supplemental tchr., 1974-83; staff nurse Rice Meml. Hosp., Willmar, 1983-86; utilization rev. various nursing homes, Willmar, 1985-86; tchr. Willmar Area Vocat. Tech. Inst., 1986; dir. nurses Glenmore Recovery Ctr., Crookston, Minn., 1986-88; shift supr. Golden Valley (Minn.) Health Ctr., 1988-92; with crisis dept. Hennepin County Med. Ctr., 1988—; managed care of psychiat. and substance abuse MCC Managed Behavioral Care, Mpls., 1992. Contbr. articles to profl. jours. Mem. AAUW, Bus. and Profl. Women, League Women Voters (pres. and state bd.), Federated Women, Does. Republican. Lutheran. Home: 6450 York Ave S Apt 403 Minneapolis MN 55435-2341 Office: Hennepin County Med Ctr 701 Park Ave Minneapolis MN 55415-1623

DURDEN, MARLA K., business owner, association executive; b. Houston, July 20, 1965. BA in Fine Arts, U. Tex., 1989. Owner Marla Durden Fine Comtemporary Jewelry, Austin, Tex., 1987-89; pres. Beso de Luna, Seattle, 1992—. Bd. dirs. YWCA of U.S.A., N.Y.C., 1991—, nat. student coun., 1985-88, pres. student coun., 1989, devel. edn. cons., 1989—; exec. com. World YWCA, Geneva, 1991—, resource team Waste Recycling and Resource Conservation Workshop, Crete, Greece, 1991, resource team UN Conf. Environment and Devel., Rio de Janeiro, 1992; spl. events and vols. coord. Nat. Abortion Rights Action League, Washington, 1990. Home: 816 E Prospect St Apt 1 Seattle WA 98102-4345

DUREGGER, KAREN MARIE, health facility administrator; b. Des Moines, Jan. 16, 1952; d. Francis William and Luella Marie (Smith) Moore; m. Michael Steven Duregger, Feb. 26, 1972; children: Chadwick Michael, Joshua William (dec.), Francis Steven. Secretarial diploma, Am. Inst. Bus., Des Moines, 1971; cert. health care adminstr., Des Moines Area Community Coll., 1985. Sec. Harry Rodine Co., Des Moines, 1970, Iowa State Assn. Secondary Sch. Prins., Des Moines, 1971-72; asst. adminstr. Hancock County Care Facility, Garner, 1973-74, adminstr., 1974-89; adminstr. Duncan Heights, Inc., Garner, 1989—, bd. dirs., recording sec., 1989—; mem., sec. Mental Health, Mental Retardation and Devel. Disabled Adv. Bd., Garner, 1983-93. Mem. Comty. Edn. Bd., Garner, 1989; mem. ch. choir, 1993—; music booster Garner-Hayfield Sch. Mem. County Care Facility Adminstrs. (dist. pres. 1985-87, treas. 1989-91), Human Svcs. Tng. Network, Tng. Planning Group Health Task Force. Republican. Lutheran. Home: 145 W Lyons St Garner IA 50438-1920 Office: 1465 Hwy 18 Garner IA 50438-9619

DUREN-POLSKI, CHAUNTEL, paralegal; b. Germany, Mar. 22, 1959; came to the U.S., 1961; d. Albert and Rose (Doerfler) Duren; m. Philip L. Polski, Mar. 10, 1984; children: Abe, Angelina, Stephanie, Andrea. Assoc. degree, Wades Mdse. Coll., Dallas, 1981; student, Normandale Coll., 1983. With Honeywell, Bloomington, 1981-84; pres. Duluth (Minn.) Bus. Svcs., 1989—. Editor: (directories) Antiques of Iowa, 1990, Women Pages, 1991. Office: Duluth Bus Svcs 3725 Grand Ave Duluth MN 55807

DURGIN, DIANE, lawyer; b. Albany, N.Y., May 17, 1946; d. Leslie P. and Shirley A. (Albright) D. BA, Wellesley Coll., 1970; JD magna cum laude, Boston Coll., 1974. Assoc. Shearman & Sterling, N.Y.C., 1974-83; corp. sec. Ga.-Pacific Corp., Atlanta, 1983-92, v.p. law, dep. gen. counsel, 1986-89, sr. v.p. law, gen. counsel, 1989-93; arbitrator, mediator Atlanta, 1993—; gen. counsel Atlanta Housing Authority, 1994—; bd. dirs. Am. Arbitration Assn. Bd. dirs. Atlanta Symphony Orch., 1991—, Met. Atlanta chpt. ARC, 1988-94; bd. dirs., mem. exec. com. Alliance Theatre Co., 1985—; mem. bd. sponsors Georgian Chamber Players, Inc., 1986-92. Mem. ABA, Am. Corp. Counsel Assn., N.Y. State Bar Assn., Ga. State Bar, Am. Law Inst., Nature Conservancy (bd. dirs. Ga. chpt. 1989—), Order of Coif, Ga. Exec. Women's Network, Commerce Club Atlanta.

DURHAM, BARBARA, state supreme court justice; b. 1942. BSBA, Georgetown U.; JD, Stanford U. Bar: Wash. 1968. Former judge Wash. Superior Ct., King County; judge Wash. Ct. Appeals; assoc. justice Wash. Supreme Ct., 1985—, chief justice, 1995—. Office: Wash Supreme Ct Temple of Justice PO Box 40929 Olympia WA 98504-0929

DURHAM, CHRISTINE MEADERS, state supreme court justice; b. L.A., Aug. 3, 1945; d. William Anderson and Louise (Christensen) Meaders; m. George Homer Durham II, Dec. 29, 1966; children: Jennifer, Meghan, Troy, Melinda, Isaac. A.B., Wellesley Coll., 1967; J.D., Duke U., 1971. Bar: N.C. 1971, Utah 1974. Sole practice law Durham, N.C., 1971-73; instr. legal medicine Duke U., Durham, 1971-73; adj. prof. law Brigham Young U., Provo, Utah, 1973-78; ptnr. Johnson, Durham & Moxley, Salt Lake City, 1974-78; judge Utah Dist. Ct., 1978-82; assoc. justice Utah Supreme Ct., 1982—. Pres. Women Judges Fund for Justice, 1987-88. Fellow Am. Bar Found.; mem. ABA (edn. com. appellate judges' conf.), Nat. Assn. Women Judges (pres. 1986-87), Utah Bar Assn., Am. Law Inst. (coun. mem.), Nat. Ctr. State Courts (bd. dirs.). Home: 1702 Yale Ave Salt Lake City UT 84108-1836 Office: Utah Supreme Ct 332 State Capitol Building Salt Lake City UT 84114-1202*

DURHAM, DEBORAH JEAN, retail assistant manager; b. New Castle, Ind., July 25, 1954; d. Eugene Clayton Crockett and Thelma Christine (Gregory) Crockett Hall; m. Keith Douglas Durham, Oct. 10, 1981 (div. Dec. 1993). Student, DePauw U., 1973-74, Grossmont Coll., La Mesa, Calif., 1974-76, Nova, Sterling, Va., 1993-94. Book-keeper K-Mart Enterprises, Spring Valley, Calif., 1976-77; asst. mgr. K-Mart Enterprises, Chula Vista, Calif., 1977-79, mgr., 1979-83; adminstrv. mgr. Price Co., Azusa and Pomona, Calif., 1983-85; merchandise mgr. Price Co., Pomona, 1985-87, asst. mgr., 1987-90; buyer Pice Co., Sterling, Va., 1991-92, mgr. gen. merchandise, 1993; asst. mgr. Price Club, Sterling, Va., 1994—. Res. officer San Diego Police Dept., 1976-79. Mem. Smithsonian Inst. (assoc.). Democrat. Home: 47685 Whirlpool Sq Sterling VA 20165 Office: Price Club 21398 Price-Cascades Plz Sterling VA 20164

DURHAM, JEANETTE RANDALL, artist, educator; b. Plainfield, N.J., June 17, 1945; d. F. Gilbert and Alice (Petricek) Randall; m. Ormonde G. Durham III, June 26, 1971; 1 child, O. Ethan. BA in Fine Arts, Montclair State Coll., 1967; postgrad., Art Students League, 1970-72, Westchester Art Workshop, 1980-81; MS in Edn., SUNY, Oneonta, 1991. Cert. art tchr. N.Y., N.J.; cert. reading tchr. N.Y. Art instr. Mohawk Valley Ctr. Arts, Little Falls, N.Y., 1983, Owen D. Young Cen. Sch., Van Hornesville, N.Y., 1987-92. One woman shows include Gallery 57, Cambridge (Mass.) Arts Coun., 1984, Gannett Gallery, SUNY Tech., Utica, N.Y., 1988, South Shore Arts, Little Falls, N.Y., 1991, Pleiades Gallery, N.Y.C., 1993, Mohawk Valley Ctr. for Arts, Little Falls, 1994; exhibited in group shows at 37th Art of N.E. U.S.A., Silvermine, New Canaan, Conn., 1986, WMHT Exhbn. N.Y. State Mus., Albany, 1988, 56th Ann. Nat. Exhbn. The Cooperstown Art Assn., 1991, 94, Coast to Coast Pleiades Gallery, N.Y.C., 1991, 56th Midyear Ann. Butler Inst. Am. Art, 1992, Albany Inst. History and Art, 1993, Arts Coun. Ctrl. N.Y., Utica, 1994. Named Best in Show, Mohawk Valley Ctr. Arts Invitational, 1983, People's Choice, N.Y. State Art Tchrs. Assn. Cen. Sect., 1990. Mem. Nat. Assn. Women Artists (elected artist mem., William Meyerowitz Meml. award 1991), Copley Soc. of Boston, N.Y. Artists Equity (elected artist mem.). Home: RR 1 Box 123 Jordanville NY 13361-9731

DURHAM, MARY ANN, pharmacist, pharmacy owner; b. Bryan, Tex., Feb. 19, 1948; d. Philip Charles and Mable (Young) Hamlin; m. Harry Mahlon Durham, Sept. 20, 1975; children: Muriel Michelle, Darcie Ann. Student, Our Lady of the Lake, San Antonio, 1966-68; BS in Pharmacy, U. Houston, 1971. Pharmacist City Drug, Angleton, 1971-75, Meth. Hosp., Houston, 1971-75; pharmacist, owner Del Oro Pharmacy, Houston, 1975—, One Fannin Pharmacy, Houston, 1994—. Active Citizen Commn. Human Rights, Austin, 1980—; chmn. bd. dirs. Perfect Schooling, Inc., Houston, 1989—. Named Young Businesswoman of Yr., Bus. Women Am., 1974. Mem. Feingold Assn., Oak Forest Homeowners (chair 1993-94). Scientologist.

DURHAM, SUSAN B., state legislator; b. Portsmouth, Va., Nov. 15; d. J.C.G. Wilson and Irene Leona Jones; m. Frank Conrad Durham, July 26, 1958; children: Kimberly, Alison, Elizabeth, George. Student, U. Hawaii, 1957-58, U. Mich., 1963. Mem. N.H. Ho. of Reps., Concord; mem. edn. com. N.H. Ho. of Reps., 1991-94. Walk leader Beaver Brook Conservation Land, Hollis, N.H., 1980—; nature educator Soc. for Protection of N.H. Forest, Concord, 1985-90; mem. Hollis Sch. Bd., 1980-86, v.p., 1984-86; mem. Hollis Planning Bd., 1986-90; trustee Beaver Brook Assn., v.p. 1988-90, pres. 1990-91. Mem. LWV (bd. dirs. Milford area 1978-80). Republican. Unitarian-Universalist. Office: Rep's Hall State Capitol N Main St Concord NH 03301

DURKOVIC, KRISTY LEE, lawyer; b. Ashtabula, Ohio, Nov. 7, 1958; d. Steven J. Durkovic and Doris Jane (Mullen) Havens. BS in Polit. Sci., U. Houston, 1988, JD, 1991. Bar: Tex. 1992, D.C. 1994. Pvt. practice Houston, 1992—. Mem. steering com. Kent Ellis for 315th Dist. Ct., Houston, 1993; vol. George Godwin for 174th Dist. Ct., Houston, 1992, Gary Block Election Campaign, Houston, 1992. Grantee Wittenberg U., 1977; George Record Found. scholar, 1977. Mem. Tex. Young Lawyers Assn. Republican. Office: 5118 Dunlop St Houston TX 77009

DURNING, LUCINDA JEANE, human resources director; b. Hartford, Conn., June 25, 1955; d. Richard Lincoln and Barbara Elaine (Spring) Donnelly; m. James Jay Durning, Sept. 26, 1992. BA in English, Skidmore Coll., 1977; MA in Psychology, Columbia U., 1991. Buyer Federated Dept. Stores, Bklyn., 1977-79, dir. tng., 1979-81; dir. human resource mgmt. Home Box Office, N.Y.C., 1981-86; dir., v.p. human resources Shearson Lehman, N.Y.C., 1986-89; dir. human resources Times Pub. Co., St. Petersburg, Fla., 1991—; bd. dirs. Trend Mags.; chmn. bd. Suncoast Mgmt. Inst., Fla., 1992-93; diversity trainer Newspaper Assn. Am., 1993; outdoor adventure facilitator Millenium, 1990. Bd. dirs. Juvenile Diabetes Found., Tampa Bay, Fla., 1992-93; Poynter fund trustee Poynter Inst. for Media Studies, Fla., 1992—. Mem. Am. Soc. for Tng. and Devel., Human Resources Planning Soc., Soc. for Human Resources Mgmt., St. Petersburg C. of C. (chmn. bd., health care reform com. 1993-94, participant Leadership St. Pete 1993-94, Recognition Plaque 1993). Office: Times Pub Co 490 1st Ave S Saint Petersburg FL 33731

DUROCHER, FRANCES ANTOINETTE, physician, educator; b. Woonsocket, R.I., Mar. 11, 1943; d. Armand D. and Teresa (Leverone) DuRocher. BA (with honors), Trinity coll., 1964; MS, Brown U., 1966; postgrad., Woman's Med. Coll., 1970. Med. resident Phila. VA Hosp. and Med. Coll. Pa., 1971-73; assoc. in internal med. Guthrie Clinic Ltd., Sayre, Pa., 1973-79, Annandale (Va.) Group Health Assocs., 1979-87; assoc. chair internal med. Annandale Group Health Assoc., 1986-87; pvt. practice, Fairfax, Va., 1987—; clin. asst. prof. med. and health svcs. George Washington U. Med. Sch., Washington, 1994—. Mem. AMA, Am. Med. Women's Assn. (exec. bd. br. I, 1985-91, pres. 1987-88), Med. Soc. Va., Am. Soc. Internal Medicine, Fairfax County Med. Soc. Office: 9926 Main St Fairfax VA 22031-3901

DUSANEK, LINDA SUE, housing association administrator; b. Ottumwa, Iowa, Oct. 24, 1942; d. Walter Carol and Mildred Mozelle (Gharrett) Edmund; m. Donald Allen Carlson, Dec. 30, 1962 (div. May 1980); children: Lisa, John, Jeffrey; m. Robert John Dusanek, June 28, 1987; children: Michelle, Christine, Kendra, Andrea, Jonathan. Student, Black Hawk Coll., 1981, Marycrest U., 1988; cert. property mgmt., Inst. Real Estate Mgmt., 1989. Cert. property mgr., housing quality inspector. Asst. exec. dir. Housing Authority City of Rock Island, Ill., 1974-91; dir. of adminstrn. Housing Authority City Ft. Pierce, Fla., 1991—. Charter mem. Rock Island Clean and Beautiful, 1980-91; grad. St. Lucie County Leadership Bd., 1993, 94; campaign supporter Friends of Senator Bob Graham, Fla., 1992; mem. exec. bd. Boys & Girls Club St. Lucie County. Mem. Nat. Assn. Housing and Redevel. Ofcls. (cert. pub. housing mgr. 1980), Adminstrn. Mgmt. Soc. (treas. Quad-Cities 1989-91), Bi-State Housing Assn. (pres., founder Iowa and Ill. chpts. 1987-91), No. Ill. Coun. Housing Assn. (sec.-treas. 1986-91), St. Lucie Pers. Assn. (sec. 1992, pres. 1994, 95, advisor program coord. com. 1993, advisor resident coun. 1993), Soc. Human Resource Mgmt. (mem. state coun. 1994, 95). Lutheran. Home: 4103 Smokey Pines Ct Fort Pierce FL 34951-3341 Office: Housing Authority Ft Pierce 707 N 7th St Fort Pierce FL 34950-3131

DUSHANE, PHYLLIS MILLER, nurse; b. Portland, Oreg., June 3, 1924; d. Joseph Anton and Josephine Florence (Eicholtz) Miller; m. Frank Maurice Jacobson, Mar. 13, 1945 (dec. 1975); children: Karl, Kathleen, Kraig, Kirk, Karen, Kent, Krista, Kandis, Kris, Karlyn; m. Donald McLelland DuShane, July 21, 1979 (dec. 1989); stepchildren: Diane DuShane Bishop, Donald III. BS in Biology, U. Oreg., 1948; BS in Nursing, Oreg. Health Scis. U., 1968. R.N., Oreg. Pub. health nurse Marion County Health Dept., Salem, Oreg., 1968-77; pediatric nurse practitioner Marion County Health Dept., Salem, 1977-91, Allergy Assocs., Eugene, Oreg., 1979-89; mem. allied profl. staff Sacred Heart Gen. Hosp., Eugene, 1979—. Named Oreg. Pediatric Nurse Practitioner of Yr., 1991. Mem. P.E.O., Oreg. Pediatric Nurse Practioners Assn. (v.p. Salem chpt. 1977-78), Am. Nurses Assn., Oreg. Nurses Assn., Nat. Assn. Pediatric Nurse Assocs. and Practitoners, Am. Acad. Nurse Practitioners, Nurse Practitioners Spl. Interest Group, Salem Med. Aux. (sec. 1968), Oreg. Republican Women, Delta Gamma Alumni (v.p. 1979), Rep. Rubicon Soc. Presbyterian. Home: 965 E 23rd Ave Eugene OR 97405-3074 Office: Clinic For Children & Young Adults 755 E 11th Ave Eugene OR 97401-3702 also: Oakway Pediatrics P C 465 Oakway Rd Eugene OR 97401-5622 also: Eugene Pediatric Assocs 1680 Chambers St Eugene OR 97402-3636

DUSTAN, HARRIET PEARSON, former physician, educator; b. Craftsbury, Vt., Sept. 16, 1920; d. William Lyon and Helen Gordon (Paterson) D. BS, U. Vt., 1942, MD, 1944, DSc (hon.), 1977; DSc (hon.), Med. Coll. Wis., 1986. Diplomate Am. Bd. Internal Medicine. Intern Mary Fletcher Hosp. U. Vt., Burlington, 1944-45; asst. resident medicine Royal Victoria Hosp., Montreal, Que., Can., 1945-46; asst. prof. Coll. Medicine U. Vt., 1946-48; rsch. fellow Cleve. Clinic, 1948-51, mem. staff rsch. dir., 1951-77, asst. dir., 1971-77; prof. medicine Sch. Medicine U. Ala., Birmingham, 1977-90; VA disting. physician Birmingham VA Med. Ctr., 1987-90; emeritus prof. medicine Sch. Medicine U. Ala., Birmingham, 1990—; mem. adv. coun. Nat. Heart, Blood, Lung Inst., Bethesda, Md., 1972-76; bd. regents Am. Coll. Physicians, Phila., 1979-84; mem. Am. Bd. Internal Medicine, Phila., 1973-79. Recipient Sci. Achievement award AMA, 1988. Fellow Am. Heart Assn. (pres. 1976-77, Lifetime Achievement award 1991); mem. Am. Coll. Physicians (master, John Phillips Meml. award 1994), Assn. Am. Physicians, Inst. Medicine. Home: 34 Lang Dr Essex Junction VT 05452

DUTCHER, JANICE JEAN PHILLIPS, oncologist; b. Bend, Oreg., Nov. 10, 1950; d. Charles Glen and MayBelle (Fluit) Phillips; m. John Dutcher, Sept. 8, 1971 (div. 1980). BA with honors, U. Utah, 1971; MD, U. Calif., Davis, 1975. Diplomate Am. Bd. Internal Medicine, Am. Bd. Med. Oncology. Intern Rush-Presbyn. St. Luke's Hosp., Chgo., 1975-76, resident, 1976-78; clin. assoc. Balt. Cancer Rsch., Nat. Cancer Inst., 1978-81, sr. investigator, 1981-82; asst. prof. U. Md., Balt., 1982; asst. prof. Albert Einstein Coll. Medicine, N.Y.C., 1983-86, assoc. prof., 1986-92, prof., 1992—; course co-dir. Advances in Cancer Treatment Rsch. Albert Einstein Coll. Medicine, Manhattan, 1984—; chmn. biol. response mod. com. ECOG, Madison, Wis., 1989—; mem. data safety com. Nat. Heart Lung Blood Inst., Bethesda, Md., 1990—; mem. biologic response modifier study sect. Nat. Cancer Inst., Bethesda, 1988, 90, 94; mem. NIH Consensus Panel on Early Melanoma, 1992. Editor: Handbook of Hematology/Oncology Emergencies, 1987, Modern Transfusion Therapy, 1990; sect. editor: Neoplastic Diseases of the Blood, 1995; mem. editl. bd. Jour. Immunotherapy; contbr. articles to Blood, Leukemia. Recipient Beecham award in Hematology So. Blood Club, 1983, Henry C. Moses Clin. Rsch. award Montefiore Med. Ctr., 1989, Outstanding Alumnus award U. Calif., Davis, 1989; named Outstanding Young Investigator Ea. Coop. Oncology Group, 1993; recipient numerous grants. Fellow ACP; mem. Am. Soc. Clin. Oncology (mem. program com. 1988), Am. Assn. Cancer Rsch., Am. Soc. Hematology, Soc. for Biol. Therapy, Phi Beta Kappa (Presdl. scholar 1968), Alpha Lambda Delta, Phi Kappa Phi, Alpha Omega Alpha. Office: Albert Einstein Coll Med 1825 Eastchester Rd Bronx NY 10461-2301

DUTIKOW, IRENE VLADIMIROVNA, librarian; b. Tallinn, Estonia, Estonia, Sept. 7, 1938; came to U.S., 1951; d. Vladimir A. and Ludmilla P. (Minjaev) Vekshin; m. Wsewolod M. Dutikow, July 26, 1959; children: Ekateriana, Larissa. BA, Hunter Coll., 1970; MLS, Queens Coll., 1975; MA, Hunter Coll., 1980. Cert. librarian, N.Y. Tech. asst. N.Y.C. Pub. Library, 1970-78, librarian, 1978-80; reference librarian, head librarian Radio Free Europe-Radio Liberty, Inc., N.Y.C., 1980-94; archivist Synod of Bishops, N.Y.C., 1994—. Author: K.I. Chukovsky, 1975, 2d edit., 1979; contbr. to profl. publs.; compiler scrapbooks on Greek and Brit. royal families. Mem. ALA, Am. Assn. Advancement of Slavic Studies, Spl. Library Assn., Congress Russian Ams. (pres. Flushing chpt. 1978-86), Slavic Heritage Council Am. (bd.dirs. 1979-85). Republican. Russian Orthodox. Home: 25-36 37th St Astoria NY 11103 Office: Synod of Bishops 75 E 93rd St New York NY 10128

DUTIL, JAYNE ANNE, librarian, computer programmer; b. Williston Park, N.Y., Apr. 29, 1947; d. John William and Margaret Marie (Neil) D. BA in English, St. John's U., Jamaica, N.Y., 1969, MLS, 1973; AAS in Data Processing magna cum laude, Nassau Community Coll., Garden City, N.Y., 1984. Cert. pub. libr. Sec. to actress/playwright June Havoc, Weston, Conn., 1969; asst. pers. mgr. Winston's Dept. Store, Hempstead, N.Y., 1969; head adult svcs. Uniondale (N.Y.) Pub. Libr., 1970-84; computer programmer Town of North Hempstead, Manhasset, N.Y., 1984-85; applications programmer The Conf. Bd., N.Y.C., 1985-89; head adult svcs. Elmont (N.Y.) Pub. Libr., 1989-93, dir., 1993-94; children's libr. Levittown (N.Y.) Pub. Libr., 1970; reference libr. Bryant Libr., Roslyn, N.Y., 1978-81, Shelter Rock Pub. Libr., Albertson, N.Y., 1984-90. Mem. ALA, N.Y. Libr. Assn., Nassau County Libr. Assn. Home: 143 Cushing Ave Williston Park NY 11596-1637

DUTTON, DIANA CHERYL, lawyer; b. Sherman, Tex., June 27, 1944; d. Roy G. and Monett (Smith) D.; m. Anthony R. Grindl, July 8, 1974; children: Christopher, Bellamy. BS, Georgetown U., 1967; JD, U. Tex., 1971. Bar: Tex. 1971. Regional counsel U.S. EPA, Dallas, 1975-79, dir. enforcement div., 1979-81; ptnr., coord. firm-wide environ. sect., mem. Dallas practice com. Akin, Gump, Strauss, Hauer & Feld, L.L.P., Dallas, 1981—. Mem. ABA, Tex. Bar Assn. (chmn. environ. and natural resources law sect. 1985-86), Dallas Bar Assn. (chmn. environ. law sect. 1984). Episcopalian. Office: Akin Gump Strauss Hauer & Feld LLP 1700 Pacific Ave Dallas TX 75201

DUTTON, SHARON GAIL, elementary school educator; b. Greenville, S.C., Jan. 5, 1947; d. Melvin Thornton and Bessie Mae (Whitmire) B. BS in Elem. Edn., E. Tenn. State U., 1969; MA in Early Childhood Edn., Western Carolina U., 1976, EdS in Early Childhood Edn., 1983. Cert. tchr. N.C. elem, secondary, sch. adminstrn., early childhood. Tchr. grade 4 Brevard (N.C.) Elem. Sch., 1970; tchr. grade 3 Rosman (N.C.) Elem. Sch., 1970, tchr. grade 2, 1970-72, tchr. reading, 1972-73, tchr. grades 2, 3, 1973-87, tchr. grade 4, 1987-89; tchr. Headstart Rosman Elem. Sch. 1971, summer sch., 1972; lead tchr. Teacher Corps Grade 2 Western Carolina U., Cullowhee, N.C., Rosman, 1974-76; clin. practicum and reading conf. Western Carolina

U., VA Ctr., Oteen, N.C., summer 1976. Organist, pianist, East Fork Bapt. Ch., Brevard, N.C. Mem. NEA, ASCD, Am. Fedn. Tchrs., N.C. Assn. Edn., Transylvania County Assn. Edn. Democrat. Home: PO Box 422 Rosman NC 28772-0422

DUTZ-KOHOUT, ELFRIEDE, former physician, educator; b. Vienna, Austria, June 23, 1926; came to U.S., 1974; d. Leopold and Valerie (Schiffer) Kohout; children: Peter, Micheal. MD, U. Vienna, 1952. Intern Miseri Cordia Hosp., Edmonton, Alta., Can., 1954-55; resident Nassau County Hosp., L.I., N.Y., 1956-58, Delafield Hosp., N.Y., 1958-59; fellow Columbia U., N.Y., 1959-60, Mt. Silai Hosp.; from asst. prof. to prof. clin. pathology Pahlavi U., Shiraz, Iran, 1960-76; prof. pathology Med. Coll. Va., Richmond, 1974-94. Grantee NIH, 1964, Med. Coll. Va., 1988. Fellow Royal Soc. Pathology, Am. Soc. Pathology, Am. Soc. Clin. Pathology, Am. Soc. Microbiology; mem. Soc. Clin. Pathology. Home: 111 N 28th St Richmond VA 23223-7325

DUVALL, BERNICE BETTUM, artist, exhibit coordinator; b. Washington, Mar. 17, 1948; d. William A. and Bergny (Farovig) Bettum; m. Donald Dunn Duvall, Oct. 5, 1968; children: Gregory Thomas, Peter Brian. Grad. high sch., Washington, 1966; art edn. pvt. study, 1970-74. Artist watercolor, acrylic, needlework design Chevy Chase, Md., 1972—; exhibit coord. Discovery Channel, Learning Channel, Discovery Comms., Inc., Bethesda, N.Y.C., 1993—; with pub. rels. and publicity Town Ctr. Gallery, Rockville, Md., 1986-89; banner designer St. Paul's Luth. Ch., Washington, 1985—. Exhbns. include Capricorn Gallery, Bethesda, Md., 1982, Westmoreland Mus. Art, Greensburg, Pa., 1982, 87, Hull Gallery, Washington, 1983, 85, Butler Inst. Am. Art, Youngstown, Ohio, 1983, DeLand (Fla.) Mus., 1984, Springfield (Mo.) Art Mus., 1988, Newberry Gallery, Pa., 1989, Broadway Gallery, Va., 1989, Watergate Gallery, Washington, 1990, Fine Art Mus. of South, Mobile, Ala., 1990, Images Internat. Gallery, Bethesda, 1991, 92, 93, So. Watercolor Soc., 1993, Charles Sumner Sch. Mus., Washington, 1994, Sugar & Frichtl Gallery, Kensington, Md., 1994, others; juried exhbns. include Internat. Artists in Watercolor, London, 1981; prin. works represented in many pub. and pvt. collections, including Montgomery County Contemporary Art Acquisitions, New England Life Ins. Co., Pelavin Assocs., Inc., Capricorn Gallery; contbr. articles to Am. Artist, Watercolor, The Artist mag. Vol. artist Nat. Zoo, Washington, 1985-91; art judge Art in Schs., Parks, Pub. Places, Montgomery County, Md., 1988-90; speaker various pub. schs., Montgomery County, 1988, 92. Recipient Award of High Commendation Internat. Artists in Water Colors, 1981, Arthur Alexander award So. Water Color Soc., 1981, Award of Merit Md. Fedn. Art, 1980, Liquitex award Adirondacks Am. Watercolorists, 1989, Bendann Gallery award Balt. Water Color Soc., 1990, Washington Water Color Assn. award, 1993. Mem. Pa. Watercolor Soc., Art League (bd. dirs. 1982-86), Washington Water Color Assn. (bd. dirs. 1986-87, award 1993), Town Ctr. Gallery (bd. dirs. 1986-89), Potomac Valley Watercolorists (bd. dirs. 1993—), Artists Equity, Arts Coun. Montgomery County, So. Watercolor Soc. (co-chmn. ann. juried exhibit 1993), Balt. Watercolor Soc., Strathmore Arts Found. Lutheran. Home and Studio: 3414 Taylor St Chevy Chase MD 20815

DU VALL, BRENKA LYNN, telemetry nurse; b. Douglas, Ga., Oct. 31, 1953; d. Freddie La Vare and Ruby Lee (Walsh) Du V. BS in Elem. Edn., U. Ga., 1975; BSN, Ga. Coll., 1989, postgrad., 1990—. Cert. BLS, ACLS. Tchr. Laurens County Schs., East Laurens, Ga., 1975-76; supr. small display advt. Greensheet Advt. Paper, Houston, 1976-78; sec. BMC Software, Mobil Oil Corp., Houston, 1978-86; nurse USAFR, Warner Robins, Ga., 1989-92; telemetry nurse Oconee Regional Med. Ctr., 1992—. With USAFR, 1989—. Whitehall scholar Whitehall Found., 1988-89; recipient Air Force Commendation medal. Mem. Nightingale Honor Soc., Sigma Theta Tau. Republican. Home: 123 Knight Cove SE 3425-M North David Hills Rd Decatur GA 30033

DUVALL, CATHLEEN ELAINE, elementary school educator, consultant; b. Port Hueneme, Calif., Apr. 19, 1954; d. Joseph Manuel and Mary Kathryn (Gerweck) Morris; m. Edward Mehl Duvall, Aug. 16, 1980; children: Nicolette Mareen, Rebecca Lauren. BS, Longwood Coll., 1976; MEd, Va. Commonwealth U., 1980; postgrad., U. St. Thomas, 1989-92. Cert. reading specialist, supr., early childhood tchr., gifted specialist, elem. tchr., writing project trainer, Tex. Classroom tchr. Chesterfield (Va.) County Pub. Schs., 1976-80; classroom tchr. Alief (Tex.) Ind. Sch. Dist., 1980-82, reading specialist, 1982-85, gifted specialist, 1985-86, social studies specialist, 1985-90; English lang. arts coord. Fort Bend Ind. Sch. Dist., Sugar Land, Tex., 1990—; instr. U. Houston/Victoria; cons. Port Nueces Groves Ind. Sch. Dist., LaMarque Ind. Sch. Dist., Alief Ind. Sch. Dist., Tex. Mem. Internat. Reading Assn., Tex. State Reading Assn., Greater Houston Area Reading Coun. (bd. mem. 1991—), Nat. Coun. Tchrs. English, Tex. Coun. Tchrs. English, West Houston Area Coun. Tchrs. English (bd. mem. 1991—, v.p. 1993—), Assn. Tex. Profl. Educators (pres. region IV 1990-93, Christa McAuliffe Teaching Excellence award 1988). Republican. Office: Fort Bend Ind Sch Dist 16431 Lexington Blvd Sugar Land TX 77479-2308

DUVALL, LORRAINE, recreation center owner; b. Hamilton, Ohio, Jan. 31, 1925; d. Saul and Martha Jane (Huff) Baker; m. Ray DuVall, June 12, 1951; children: Sharon DuVall Keese, Deborah D. Velchoff, Steve, Annette. BA, U. Cin., 1951; MA, Tex. A&I U., 1963; postgrad. Miami U., Oxford, Ohio, 1958, U. Toledo, 1959, U. Tex.-Austin, 1968. Elem. tchr. Larkmoor, Lorain, Ohio, 1956-60; tchr. math. Incarnate Word High Sch., Corpus Christi, 1964-70; owner, instr. Aerobic Fitness, Corpus Christi, 1973-93; owner, coach Corpus Christi Marlin Swim Team, 1972—; mgr. Corpus Christi Country Club Pool, 1973-88; pres., mgr. Club Estates Pool Chems., Corpus Christi, 1980-89, Club Estates Recreation, Corpus Christi, 1977—. Vol. psychiat. ward Meml. Hosp., Corpus Christi, 1966-70; bd. dirs. vol. YWCA, Corpus Christi, 1970-77; water safety trainer ARC, Corpus Christi, 1975-82; CPR instr. Am. Heart Assn., Corpus Christi, 1980-84; vol. children's choir dir. St. John Methodist Ch., Corpus Christi, 1966-78, Asbury United Meth. Ch., 1980-93. NSF grantee U. Tex.-Austin, 1968. Mem. Am. Swim Coaches Assn., Am. Harp Soc. Avocations: music, swimming, tennis, skiing, backpacking. Home: 6709 Pintail Dr Corpus Christi TX 78413-2337 Office: 4902 Snowgoose St Corpus Christi TX 78413

DUVALL, SHELLEY, actress; b. Houston, Tex., July 7, 1949; d. Robert Duvall and Bobby Crawford. Founder Amarillo Prodns. Actress: films (debut) Brewster McCloud, 1970, McCabe and Mrs. Miller, 1971, Thieves Like Us, 1974, Nashville, 1975, Buffalo Bill and the Indians, 1976, Three Women, 1977 (Cannes Film Festival Best Actress award), Annie Hall, 1977, Popeye, 1979, The Shining, 1980, Time Bandits, 1981, Roxanne, 1987, Suburgan Commando, 1991, (TV movies) Bernice Bobs Her Hair, 1977, Lily, 1986, (TV episode) Twilight Zone, 1986; exec. producer: Showtime pay TV series Faerie Tale Theatre, (Peabody award), Shelley Duvall's Bedtime Stories, Shelley Duvall's Tall Tales and Legends, The Strange Case of Dr. Jekyll and Mr. Hyde, Mrs. Piggle-Wiggle. Founder, Think Entertainment prodn. co., 1988. Mem. Nat. Acad. Cable Programming (bd. govs.). Office: c/o Think Entertainment 12725 Ventura Blvd Suite J Studio City CA 91604*

DUVALL-ITJEN, PHYLLIS, retail sales executive; b. Passaic, N.J., Oct. 13, 1951; d. August Richard and Joanne (Aquilina) D'Alessandro; m. Brian Alan Itjen, Apr. 1, 1979 (div.); 1 child, Shannon Alys. Office mgr. Servometer Corp., Cedar Grove, N.J., 1972-82; owner, mgr. Sweet Shoppe, Etc., Lyndhurst, N.J., 1979-82; adminstr.-pers. coord. Watson Machine Co., Paterson, N.J., 1982-88; pres. S.A.I. Personnel Svcs., West Paterson, N.J., 1988—, S.A.I. Expressions Unltd., Inc., West Paterson and Wayne, N.J., 1988—, Shannon Designs div. S.A.I. Expressions, 1991—. Sustaining mem. Rep. Nat Com.; human rights activist, West Paterson, N.J., 1988—. Fellow Am. Biog. Inst. (rsch. bd. advisors); mem. NAFE, Internat. Platform Assn., Am. Mgmt. Assn. Republican. Roman Catholic. Home: 220A Overmount Ave West Paterson NJ 07424-3247 Office: SAI Expressions Unltd PO Box 1233 Little Falls NJ 07424

DUVIVIER, KATHARINE KEYES, lawyer; b. Alton, Ill., Jan. 1, 1953; d. Edward Keyes and Marjorie (Attebery) DuV.; m. James Wesley Perl, Mar. 30, 1985; 2 children: Alice Katharine Perl, Emmett Edward Perl. BA in Geology and English cum laude, Williams Coll., 1975; JD, U. Denver, 1982. Bar: Colo. 1982, U.S. Dist. Ct. Colo. 1982, U.S. Ct. Appeals (10th cir.) 1982. Intern-curator Hudson River Mus., Yonkers, N.Y., 1975; geologist French Am. Metals Corp., Lakewood, Colo., 1976-79; assoc. Sherman & Howard, Denver, 1982-84, Arnold & Porter, Denver, 1984-87; atty. Office of City Atty., Denver, 1987-90; instr. sch. law Univ. Colo., 1990—. Contbr. articles to profl. jours. Mem. Denver Botanic Garden, 1981-88; vol. Outdoor Colo., Denver, 1985-87. Mem. ABA (vice chmn. subcom. 1985-91), Colo. Bar Assn., Boulder Bar Assn., Boulder Women's Bar Assn. (pres. 1991-93), Alliance Profl. Women (bd. dirs. 1985-90, pres. 1988-89), Work and Family Consortium (bd. dirs. 1988-90), St. Ives, William Coll. Alumni Assn. (co-pres. Colo. chpt. 1984-86), Phi Beta Kappa. Home: 4761 McKinley Dr Boulder CO 80303-1142 Office: U Colo Sch Law PO Box 401 Boulder CO 80303

DUVO, MECHELLE LOUISE, oil company executive, consultant; b. East Stroudsburg, Pa., Apr. 25, 1962; d. Nicholas and Arlene Birdie (Mack) D. AS, Lehigh County Community Coll., 1982. Rehab. counselor Phoenix Project, Bakersfield, Calif., 1982-84; nat. sales mgr. Olympia Advt., L.A., 1984-85; oil exploration cons. Cimmaron Mgmt., Nashville, 1985-86; exec. sec. Pueblo Resources Corp., Bowling Green, Ky., 1986-87; nat. oil cons. El Toro, Inc., Bowling Green, 1986-87; founder, pres. and CEO Majestic Mgmt. Corp., Albany, Ky., 1987—; nat. oil cons. Impact Oil, Inc., Bowling Green, 1987—; lease procurator El Toro, Inc., 1986-87, Impact Oil, Inc., 1987—. Fundraiser Am. Cancer Soc., L.A., 1984-85; vol. Humane Soc., Nashville, 1985-86, Humane Soc., Bowling Green, 1986—; counselor Salvation Army, Bakersfield, 1982-84. Mem. NAFE (exec. program), AAUW, Ky. Oil & Gas Assn. Home and Office: Majestic Mgmt Corp 1015 Tennessee Road Albany KY 42602-1065

DVORAK, JANE ANN, property management executive; b. Cin., Dec. 19, 1955; d. Ralph Harold and Mary Elizabeth (Rodenburg) Teke; m. Alan Eugene Dvorak, Mar. 19, 1977. BBA, Ohio U., 1977. Part-time emergency med. tech. Southeast Ohio Emergency Med. Services, Athens, Ohio, 1977-80; patient coordinator O'Bleness Hosp., Athens, 1977; loan officer Athens Credit Union, 1978-79; mgr. Athens Mall JMB Property Mgmt. Corp., 1980-87; v.p. Athens Marine & Tire Inc., 1987-91; gen. mgr. Univ. Mall Beerman Realty, Athens, 1990—; bd. dirs. Athens Pvt. Industry Coun., 1985-87. Pub. rels. coord. Athens County Emergency Mgmt. Svcs., 1985-94; exec. dir. Athens chpt. Big Bros./Big Sisters, 1989-92; mem. USCG Aux., 1990—, staff officer, 1992-93, flotilla comdr., 1994-95; mem. Athens County Crime Solvers Anonymous; mem. Program com. Am. Heart Assn., 1993-94. Mem. Internat. Coun. Shopping Ctrs., Athens C. of C. (bd. dirs. 1983-87), Athens Crime Solvers Anonymous, Phi Mu (house corp. v.p. 1984-87). Home: 14525 Kincade Rd Athens OH 45701-9444 Office: U Mall Mgmt 1002 E State St Athens OH 45701-2149

DVORNEK, LINDA SMITH, chemist; b. Stamford, Conn., Nov. 11, 1951; d. Thomas I. and Marguerite A. (Tiani) Smith; m. Jerome Dvornek, June 26, 1982; children: Jeffrey, Allison. BS, Sacred Heart U., Fairfield, Conn., 1973; MS, U. Bridgeport, 1986. Chemist R.T. Vanderbilt Co., Norwalk, Conn., 1973-79, sr. chemist, 1979-87, rsch. assoc., 1987-90, mgr. analytical dept., 1990-92, dir. analytical svcs., 1992—. Mem. ASTM, Am. Chem. Soc. (analytical divsn. local chpt.). Republican. Roman Catholic. Office: R T Vanderbilt Co 30 Winfield St Norwalk CT 06855-1316

DWORKIN, ELIZABETH, artist, educator; b. Rochester, N.Y., July 7, 1943; d. William Dworkin and Miriam (Loeb) Nemerow; m. Derek U. Huntington, May 24, 1981 (div. 1989); 1 child, Samuel. BFA, Cornell U., 1965. Instr. drawing Butera Sch. Art, Boston, 1971-73; instr. painting Windham Coll., Putney, Vt., 1973; instr. art Pine Manor Coll., Boston, 1979-80; instr. painting and drawing Mass. Coll. Art, Boston, 1973-74; lectr. visual arts, vis. artist Princeton (N.J.) U., 1991; mem. part-time faculty, vis. artist RISD, Providence, 1991-92; instr. painting, vis. artist U. Hartford, Conn., 1992; artist-in-residence St. Andrews Sch., Sewanee, Tenn., 1977, Ill. State U., Normal, 1983; vis. assoc. prof. art Bard Coll., Annandale-on-Hudson, N.Y., 1984-86; vis. artist U. Del., Newark, 1990, Brown U., Providence, 1993, Md. Coll. Inst. Art, Balt., 1993, Cooper Union, N.Y.C., 1994; juror Ohio Arts Coun., 1984, 90; vis. artist or lectr. Cornell U., Ithaca N.Y., Sch. Mus. Fine Arts, Boston, Kent (Ohio) State U., Provincetown (Mass.) Fine Arts Workshop, Wake Forest U., Stevens Coll., others. One-woman shows include Nielsen Gallery, Boston, 1976, 78, 80, 83, Rochester Meml. Art Gallery, 1980, Victoria Munroe Gallery, N.Y.C., 1984, 86, 87, 88, 91; exhibited in numerous group shows including Inst. Contemporary Art, Boston, 1970, Brockton (Mass.) Art Mus., 1976-81, Worcester Art Mus., 1978, Boston Mus. Fine Arts, 1982, Aldrich Mus. Contemporary Art, Ridgefield, Conn., 1986, Montclair (N.J.) Art Mus., 1989; represented in permanent collections DeCordova Mus., Rose Art Mus., also others. Recipient award Mass. Coun. on Arts, 1975, 80. Home and Studio: 125 Rivington St New York NY 10002

DWORSKY, CLARA WEINER, merchandise brokerage executive, lawyer; b. N.Y.C., Apr. 28, 1918; d. Charles and Rebecca (Becker) Weiner; m. Bernard Ezra Dworsky, Jan. 2, 1944; 1 child, Barbara G. Goodman. BS, St. John's U., N.Y.C., 1937, LLB, 1939, JD, 1968. Bar: N.Y. 1939, U.S. Dist. Ct. (ea. dist.) N.Y. 1942, U.S. Dist. Ct. (so. dist.) Tex. 1993. Pvt. practice, N.Y.C., 1939-51; assoc. Bessie Farberman, N.Y.C., 1942; clk., sec. U.S. Armed Forces, Camp Carson, Colo., Camp Claiborne, La., 1944-45; abstractor, dir. Realty Title, Rockville, Md., 1954-55; v.p. Kelley & Dworsky Inc., Houston, 1960—; appeals agt. Gasoline Rationing Apls. Bd., N.Y.C., 1942; bd. dir. Southlan Sales Assocs., Houston. Vol. ARC, N.Y.C.; vice chmn. War Bond pledge drive, Bklyn.; vol. Houston Legal Found., 1972-73; pres. Women's Aux. Washington Hebrew Acad., 1958-60, v.p. bd. trustees, 1959-60; co-founder, v.p. S. Tex. Hebrew Acad. (now Hebrew Acad.), Houston, 1970-75, hon. pres. women's div., 1973. Recipient Cert. award Treas. of U.S., 1943; Commendation Office of Chief Magistrate of City N.Y., 1948; Pietas medal St. Johns U., 1985. Mem. ABA (chmn. social security com., sr. lawyers div. 1989-93, chair subcom. 1993—, mem. sr. lawyers div. coun.), N.Y. State Bar Assn., Fed. Bar Assn. (vice-chair for programs, sr. lawyers divsn., 1994), Nat. Assn. Women Lawyers (chmn. organizer Juvenile Delinquency Clinic N.Y. 1948-51), St. Johns U. Alumni Assn. (coord. Houston chpt. 1983-86, pres. 1986), Delphians Past Pres.'s Club, Amit Women Club, Hadassah. Jewish. Home: 9726 Cliffwood Dr Houston TX 77096-4406

DWYER, CHRISTINE MARIE, marketing director; b. N.Y.C., Dec. 18, 1955; d. James Edward and Mary B. (Brannelly) D. BS, Cornell U., 1981. Lic. real estate assoc. Salesperson Gen. Drapery, N.Y.C., 1981-82; bus. mgr. K&R Music, Ithaca, N.Y., 1982-84; real estate sales Gallagher Real Estate, Ithaca, 1984-93; mktg. dir. Kendal Devel., West Chester, Pa., 1993—; mktg. and admissions dir. Kendal Corp., Oberlin, Ohio, 1993—. Mem. Cornell Real Estate Coun., Loraine C. of C. Home: 12900 Lake Ave # 1426 Lakewood OH 44107

DWYER, KELLY, writer, educator; b. Torrance, Calif., Feb. 28, 1964; d. Richard Stanley and Sharon Arlene (Speigler) D.; m. Louis A. Wenzlow, Jan. 5, 1991. BA, Oberlin Coll., 1987; MFA, U. Iowa, 1990. Teaching asst. U. Iowa, Iowa City, 1988-90; asst. prof. Oberlin (Ohio) Coll., 1994—. Author: The Tracks of Angels, 1994. Field mgr. Voting Power Action Com., Berkeley, Calif., 1984. James Michener/Paul Engle fellow Iowa Writers' Workshop, 1991-92. Democrat. Office: Rice Hall 14 Oberlin Coll Oberlin OH 44074

DWYER, LAURAINE T., ambulatory care administrator, rehabilitation nurse practitioner; b. Detroit, Feb. 29, 1948; d. Thomas Z. and Mary Alice (Parker) D. BSN, Ariz. State U., 1970, MS in Nursing, 1976. Cert. spinal cord injury nurse practitioner, rehab. nurse. Staff and charge nurse Good Samaritan Hosp., Phoenix, 1970-75; staff nurse in neurology VA Med. Ctr., Phoenix, 1976-77, spinal cord injury nurse practitioner, 1980-85; rehab. clin. nurse specialist, 1977-85; assoc. chief nursing svc. spinal cord injury unit and ambulatory care VA Med. Ctr., San Diego, 1985-91, assoc. chief nursing svcs., ambulatory care, 1991—. Mem. editorial adv. bd. Rehab. Mgmt., 1992-94. Named Nurse of Yr., Dist. 18 Ariz. Nurses Assn., 1982. Mem. Assn. Rehab. Nurses (pres. Ariz. chpt. 1979-81, treas. San Diego chpt. 1990-94), Am. Assn. Spinal Cord Injury Nurses (bd. dirs. 1991-94, chmn. editl. bd. 1988-94, co-editor SCI Nursing 1983-86, Disting. Svc. award 1994), Am. Acad. Ambulatory Care Nursing (sec. San Diego chpt. 1993—), Sigma Theta Tau. Home: 8719 Ginger Snap Ln San Diego CA 92129-3715

DWYER, MARGARET ANN, university administrator; b. Syracuse, N.Y.; d. Edward P. and Margaret M. (O'Donnell) D. AB, Le Moyne Coll., 1954; MEd, Boston Coll., 1956; PhD (hon.), Le Moyne Coll., 1994. Tchr. Kingsford Park Pub. Schs., Oswego, N.Y., 1955-56; med. sch. worker St. Joseph's Hosp., Syracuse, 1956-60; registrar Le Moyne Coll., Syracuse, 1960-62, dean of women, 1962-71, asst. acad. dean, 1971-73; exec. asst. to pres. Boston Coll., 1973-75, v.p., asst. to pres., 1975—; mem. consumer's adv. bd. Dey Bros. Dept. Store, 1966-70; bd. dirs., dir. Bay Bank Newton Waltham (now Bay Banks Inc.), 1976-91. Sec. adv. bd. St. Mary's Hosp., Syracuse, 1965-70; trustee Cath. Charities Archdiocese Boston, Le Moyne Coll., Syracuse, 1987-93; mem. United Way, Mass.; chmn. bd. dirs. Syracuse chpt. ARC. Mem. AAUW, Nat. Assn. for Women in Edn. Home: 40 Carver Rd Wellesley MA 02181-5304 Office: Boston College Chestnut Hill MA 02167

DWYER-DOBBIN, MARY ALICE, television network executive; b. St. Louis, Dec. 22, 1942; d. Paul Arthur and Mary Albertina (Goessling) Dwyer; m. Leon Dobbin, July 29, 1973. BA in Speech and Drama, Webster U., 1963; MFA in Theatre, Cath. U., 1967. Chmn. speech and drama dept. St. Joseph's Acad., St. Louis, 1963-65; stage mgr. Olney (Md.) Theatre, 1967; asst. to producer Bob Stewart Prodns., N.Y.C., 1968-70; producer Rankin/Bass Prodns., N.Y.C., 1970-73; mgr. daytime program, dir. children's program ABC, N.Y.C., 1974-77; dir. daytime and children's programs, v.p. children's program NBC, N.Y.C., 1977-81; v.p. programming Daytime cable network Hearst/ABC Video Svcs., N.Y.C., 1981-83; v.p. programming Lifetime cable network Hearst/ABC/Viacom Entertainment Svcs., N.Y.C., 1983-86; v.p. daytime programming east coast Capital Cities/ABC, Inc., N.Y.C., 1986-90; v.p. daytime programming ABC TV Network, N.Y.C., 1990-91; sr. v.p. daytime programming ABC-TV Network, N.Y.C., 1991-93; exec. v.p. ABC Daytime, N.Y.C., 1993—. Recipient Maggie award for TV documentaries Planned Parenthood Fedn. Am., 1982, Ace award for best mag. show, 1983, Clean Air Week award Am. Lung Assn., 1989. Mem. NATAS (bd. dirs. 1985-87), Nat. Cable TV Assn. (chmn. Ace awards com. 1983-84). Office: Capital Cities/ABC 77 W 66th St New York NY 10023-6201

DY-ANG, ANITA C., pediatrician; b. Cavite, The Philippines, Feb. 21, 1943; came to U.S., 1970; m. Raynundo Ang, May 1, 1977; children: Aileen Ang, Audrey Ang. MD, UERMMMC, Quezon City, Philippines, 1967. Diplomate Am. Bd. Pediatrics. Pediat. resident Tulane U. Charity Hosp. New Orleans, 1973; pvt. practice Warsaw, N.Y. Office: 78 N Main St Warsaw NY 14569-1329

DYAR, KATHRYN WILKIN, pediatrician; b. Colquitt, Ga., Feb. 20, 1945; d. Patrick McWhorter and Virginia (Wilkin) Dyar; m. James Ansley Patten, Jan. 1, 1985. BS in Biology, Emory U., Decatur, Ga., 1966; MD, Med. Coll. Ga., Augusta, 1970. Resident in pediatrics Eugene Talmadge Meml. Hosp., Augusta, Ga., 1970-72, Georgetown U. Hosp., Washington, 1972-73; pediatrician Children's Clinic, Tifton, Ga., 1973-74, Children & Youth Project, Norfolk, Va., 1974-83, 90—; dir. Children & Youth Project, Norfolk, 1990-94; pediatrician Hampton (Va.) Health Dept., 1983-90. Fellow Am. Acad. Pediatrics. Office: Children & Youth Project 606 W 29th St Norfolk VA 23508-3396

DYBELL, ELIZABETH ANNE SLEDDEN, clinical psychologist; b. Buffalo, Sept. 25, 1958; d. Richard Edward and Angela Brigid (Scimone) Sledden; m. David Joseph Dybell, Nov. 30, 1985. BA in Psychology summa cum laude, U. St. Thomas, Houston, 1980; PhD in Psychology, Tex. Tech. U., 1986. Lic. clinical psychologist, Tex. Rsch. asst. health sci. ctr. Tex. Tech. U., Lubbock, 1983-84, psychol. cons. health sci. ctr. neurology dept., 1982-84; psychology intern U. N.Mex. Med. Sch., Albuquerque, 1984-85; psychotherapist Katz & Assocs. P.C., Houston, 1985-88, Meyer Ctr. for Devel. Pediatrics Tex. Children's Hosp., Houston, 1988-92; pvt. practice Houston, 1990—. Author: (monograph) When Will Life Be Normal?, 1989; contbr. articles to numerous publs. choir mem. St. Thomas More Ch., Houston, 1974-87. Mem. Am. Psychol. Assn., Assn. for Care of Childrens Health, Nat. Ctr. Clin. Infant Programs, Soc. Pediatric Psychology, Southwestern Psychol. Assn., Tex. Psychol. Assn., Houston Psychol. Assn., Am. Psychol. Soc. (charter). Roman Catholic. Office: 6001 Savoy Dr Ste 208 Houston TX 77036-3322

DYCHE, KATHIE LOUISE, secondary school educator; b. Waynoka, Okla., Sept. 8, 1949; d. Loren Neil and Bessie Louise (Wait) Callaway; m. Steven Lee Dyche, July 5, 1969; children: Cherilyn Nettie, Bradley Callaway. BA in Edn. in Art, Northwestern Okla. State U., 1972; postgrad., Southwestern Okla. State U., 1975, 78, Phillips U., 1981, 83-85; MEd, U. Cen. Okla., 1993. Cert. art, Am. history and democracy tchr., Okla. Tchr. art Fairview (Okla.) Pub. Schs., 1973-81, cons., 1973-76; asst. to handicapped Glenwood Elem. Sch., Enid, Okla., 1982-83; reading and math. asst. Longfellow Jr. High Sch., Enid, 1983-84; tchr. art Emerson Jr. High Sch., Enid, 1984—; freelance artist Gaslight Theater, Okla. Small Bus. Devel. Ctr., also others; represented by Dean Lively Gallery, Edmond, Okla. Exhibited in group shows Amarillo (Tex.) Artists' Studio, 1975, Kallistos Invitational Show, 1986, Dean Lively Gallery, Edmond, Okla., Philbrook Mus. Art, Tulsa. Pres., v.p., sec., historian, reporter Gamma Mother's Club, Fairview, 1973-80; co-chmn. Fairview Show of Arts, 1979, 80; art vol. Glenlwood Elem. Sch., 1981-82; pres., historian, parlimentarian Delta Child Study Club, Enid, 1981-84. Recipient honor award Okla. Fall Arts Inst., 1992, 94; scholar Northwestern Okla. State U., 1968. Mem. NEA, Nat. Art Edn. Assn., Okla. Art Edn. Assn., Okla. Edn. Assn., Cardinal Key, Kappa Delta Pi, Delta Kappa Gamma Soc. Internat. (sec. 1986-88, scholar 1993, 2d v.p. 1994-96). Episcopalian. Office: Emerson Jr High Sch 700 W Elm Ave Enid OK 73701-3000

DYCKMAN, SUZANNE BARBARA, secretary, administrative assistant; b. DuBois, Pa., May 4, 1941; d. Earl E. Houck and Katherine M. Harris; children: Laura Kafka, Linda Kafka; m. Douglas G. Dyckman, May 4, 1994. Grad., DuBois Bus. Coll., 1961. Clk., receptionist Coca-Cola Bottling of N.Y., Inc., N.Y.C., 1961-62; actress various film and stage prodns., N.Y.C., 1964-85; girl friday League of Women Voters, N.Y.C., 1982-84; sec. Office Temporary, N.Y.C., 1984-85; adminstrv. sec. Philip Morris Cos., N.Y.C., 1985-88; adminstrv. ins. analyst Chase Manhattan Bank, N.Y.C., 1988-90. Leader, asst. dist. fin. coord. Girl Scouts Am., N.Y.C.; active role in ch. and community, 1968—; active Maison Internationale des Intellectuals, Rosicrucian U. Mem. Am. Mgmt. Assn., Am. Film Soc., Internat. Parliament for Safety and Peace, Soka Gakkai Internat. Democrat.

DYE, MERYL RENE, human resources director; b. Hutchinson, Kans., Apr. 29, 1954; d. Merle Gayford and Dorothy Mae (Teegardin) D.; m. Jimmy Riley Hodges, Nov. 26, 1971 (div. Apr. 1983); 1 child, Cassie Leigh Hodges. AA, Hutchinson (Kans.) C.C., 1978; B of Adminstrn. of Justice, Wichita State U., 1984, MPA, 1993. Adminstrv. sec. City of Hutchinson, 1979-80, human rels. staff aide, 1980-83, human rels. dir., 1983-90, human resources dir., 1990—. Vol. Reno County Rape Ctr., Hutchinson, 1975-79, First Call for Help, 1983-85, Sexual Assault/Domestic Violence Ctr., Hutchinson, 1984-88. Vol. award Kans. Gov. Hayden & First Lady, Topeka, Kans., 1990; recipient Cert. Appreciation for Crime Victim Assistance, U.S. Dept. Justice, Hutchinson, 1990. Mem. Soc. Human Resources Mgmt., Internat. Personnel Memgt., Kans. Human Rels. Assn. (pres. 1984-86, v.p. 1982-84), Rotary. Democrat. Methodist. Office: City of Hutchinson 125 E Ave B Hutchinson KS 67504-1567

DYE, NANCY SCHROM, academic administrator, history educator; b. Columbia, Mo., Mar. 11, 1947; d. Ned Stuart and Florence Andrea Elizabeth (Ahrens) Schrom; m. Griffith R. Dye, Aug. 21, 1972; children: Molly, Michael. AB, Vassar Coll., 1969; MA, U. Wis., 1971, PhD, 1974. Asst. prof. U. Ky., Lexington, 1974-80, assoc. prof., 1980-88, prof., 1988, assoc. dean arts and scis., 1984-88; dean faculty Vassar Coll., Poughkeepsie, N.Y., 1988-92; acting pres. Vassar Coll., 1992-94; pres. Oberlin Coll., Oberlin, Ohio, 1994—. Author: As Equals And As Sisters, 1981; contbr. articles to profl. jours. Mem. Coun. of Colls. of Arts and Scis. (bd. dirs. 1989—). Office: Oberlin Coll Office of the President Oberlin OH 44074

DYE, REBECCA FEEMSTER, legislative counsel; b. Charlotte, N.C., May 8, 1952. BA, U. N.C., 1974, JD, 1977. Spl. counsel Broughton (N.C.) Psychiat. Hosp., 1977-78; atty. project coord. Legal Svcs. N.C., 1978-79; atty. office of chief counsel USCG, 1979-83; law instr. USCG Acad., 1983-

85; atty. office of chief counsel Fed. Maritime Adminstrn., 1985-87; minority counsel Com. Merchant Marine & Fisheries, Washington, 1987—. Office: Com Merchant Marines & Fisheries 538 Ford House Office Bldg Washington DC 20515*

DYER, ARLENE THELMA, retail company owner; b. Chgo., Oct. 23, 1942; d. Samuel Leo Sr. and Thelma Arlene (Israel) Lewis; m. Don Engle Dyer, July 3, 1965 (div. 1970); 1 child, Artel Terren. Cert. in mgmt. effectiveness, U. So. Calif., 1987. Community resource rep. Calif. State Employment Devel. Dept., Los Angeles, 1975-76, spl. projects rep., 1976; employment services rep. Culver City, Calif., 1977; contract writer Los Angeles, 1976-80, employment program rep., 1980—; pres. Yabba and Co., Los Angeles, 1981-83; pres., designer, cons. Spiritual Ties Custom Neckwear, Los Angeles, 1985—; pres. Dyer Custom Shirts, Blouses and Suits, Beverly Hills, Calif., 1988—; founder self-evaluation seminar. Author: Who Are You and What Are You All About?, 1994; exhibited in fashion shows, Calif., 1984—. Vol. Big Sister Gwen Bolden Found., L.A., 1986; mem. Operation PUSH, Chgo., 1983, Mahogany Cowgirls & Co.; program chair Black Advs. in State Svc., 1987—; leader Girl Scouts U.S., L.A., 1982, L.A. Urban League. Mem. Nat. Alliance Homebased Businesswomen (v.p., program chair 1987), Nat. Assn. Female Execs., Calif. State Employees Assn., U. So. Calif. Alumni Assn., Los Angeles Urban League, Black Women's Forum, NAACP (Beverly Hills-Hollywood chpt.). Democrat. Club: 92d St Block.

DYER, CYNTHIA MYERS, library director; b. Camp Lejeune, N.C., June 26, 1955; d. Louis B. and Shirley Jean (Shimon) Myers; m. Grant E. Dyer, Nov. 24, 1984; children: Katherine Elizabeth, Sarah Caroline. BA, U. Iowa, 1977, MLS, 1978. Tech. svcs. librarian Simpson Coll., Indianola, Iowa, 1978-83, dir. library svcs., 1983—, assoc. prof., 1994—, mem. com. on status of women, mem. AIDS task force, 1993—; program co-chmn. Iowa Gov.'s Pre-White House Conf. on Librs., 1990-91; mem. Blue Ribbon Task Force on Librs., 1988; mem. adv. bd. Cen. Iowa Regional Libr., 1987-88. Contbr. articles to profl. jours. Com. chmn. Simpson Guild, Indianola, 1981-84; spkr. on AIDS, 1992—; chmn. various libr. adv. coms., 1986—, Women's History Month, 1990-91; tri-chmn. Campus Capital Campaign, 1990. Mem. ALA, Iowa Libr. Assn. (acad. and rsch. librs. conf. planner 1979, 82, 95, exec. bd. dirs. 1984-86, 88-90, pres. 1989, nominating com. 1991-93, strategic planning com. 1993), Iowa Libr. Assn. Found. (v.p. 1990-92, chmn. distbn. 1991-92, pres. 1993, 94), Iowa Pvt. Acad. Librs. (chmn. 1986, panelist 1993), Indianola Breakfast Club (bd. dirs. 1988-90), Rotary (spkr. for various groups), Phi Beta Kappa, Phi Beta Mu, Epsilon Sigma. Democrat. Office: Simpson Coll Dunn Libr # 508 Nc Indianola IA 50125

DYER, DORIS ANNE, nurse; b. Washington, Jan. 14, 1944; d. William Edward and Helen Gertrude (Smith) Swain; m. Robert Francis Dyer, Jr., June 27, 1970; children: Robert Francis, William Edward, Anne-Marie Helen Sallie, Scott Robertson McGavin. RN cum laude, Sibley Nursing Sch., Washington, 1964; BS, Am. U., 1966, MEd, 1969. Mem. staff emergency medicine dept. George Washington U. Hosp., 1960-69, emergency specialist protective svcs. clinic, 1967-70, adminstr. asst. to dir. clinic, 1970-78; nurse cons., 1987—. Author: Say Ah, 1971; also articles. Patron Sibley Meml. Hosp. Chapel, 1992. Trinity Coll. scholar, 1960; Lucy Webb Hayes scholar, 1964; recipient Martha Washington award Md. Soc. SAR, 1977, Community Leaders award, 1979, Washington medal, 1984, Disting. Women of Washington award 1987; decorated Comdr. Order of St. Lazarus, 1984, medal of Merit, 1989; created dame Order of Sovereign Mil. Order, 1980, dame comdr., 1992; named Dame Grand Officier, 1992. Mem. Am. Nurses Assn., D.C. Nurses Assns., Am. Acad. Ambulatory Nursing Adminstrs., Washington Med.-Surg. Soc. Aux. (pres.), Am. U. Grads. Assn., DAR, Washington Assembly, Washington Club, Annapolis Yacht Club, Kenwood Golf and Country Club. Address: 5608 Albia Rd Bethesda MD 20816

DYER, GERALDINE ANN (GERI DYER), artist, poet; b. Bklyn., Nov. 4, 1921; d. Edward and Chattie (Holmes) Bingham; m. Ralph Dyer, Oct. 1956. Student, N.Y. Phoenix Sch. Design, N.Y.C., 1946-48, Bklyn. Mus. Art Sch., 1959, Bklyn. Coll., 1939; pvt. studies in voice with Julia Gille, 1947-50; reader poetry Bklyn. Poetry Circle, Bklyn., Moroccan Star, Bklyn., 1994. Commd. U.S. Army, 1941, ret. exec. USCG, 1979. One-woman shows include Henry Hicks Gallery, N.Y.C., 1978-79, 81, Womanart Gallery, N.Y.C., 1980, Keane Mason Gallery, N.Y.C., 1981, Esta Robinson Gallery, N.Y.C., 1983, Bklyn. Heights Br. Libr., Bklyn., 1986-89, St. Mary Star of the Sea, Bklyn., 1993; exhibited at numerous group shows; represented in permanent collection Samuel Schulman Inst., Bklyn.; author: (poetry) Edge of Twilight, 1994, Echoes of Yesterday, 1994 (Editor's Choice award, Nat. Libr. Poetry, 1994). Recipient numerous awards including Art Horizons Internat. Art Competition, 1988, Alma E. Wright Meml. poetry award, 1989, 90, Critics award, 1991, 94, Editor's Choice award Libr. of Poetry, 1994; recipient ABI Gold Record Achievement award, 1994, Women of the Year Commemorative medal, 1994; named Internat. Woman of Yr., 1991-92. Mem. Poetry Soc. Am., Officers Club (Governors Island, N.Y.), Bklyn. Poetry Circle (v.p. 1990, 93, 1st prize Meml. Contest 1994). Avocation: writing poetry.

DYER, SUSAN KRISTINE, library administrator; b. Coos Bay, Oreg.; d. Stanley Keith and Betty Loray (Jameson) D.; m. Michael E. Gehringer. BA, U. Oreg., 1967, MLS, 1968; MBA, Golden Gate U., 1983. Libr. Morrison & Foerster, San Francisco, 1968-75, info. and gen. svcs. mgr., 1975-80; law libr., records mgr. Thelen, Marrin, Johnson & Bridges, San Francisco, 1980-83; libr. World Bank Sectoral Libr., Washington, 1984-89; ops. mgr. Faxon Co. Fed. Divsn., Herndon, Va., 1989-90, dir., 1990-92, nat. sales mgr. fed., 1992-94; fed. ops. mgr. EBSCO Industries, Springfield, Va., 1994—. Author: Manual of Procedures for Private Law Libraries Supplement, 1984. Bd. dirs. Miriam's Kitchen, Washington, 1986-88. Mem. ALA, Am. Assn. Law Librs. (editor Recruitment Checklist 1974, newsletter editor 1976-79, pres. Western Pacific chpt. 1977-79, exec. bd. 1979-82), Spl. Librs. Assn., D.C. Libr. Assn. Office: EBSCO Subscription Svcs 6800 Versar Ctr Ste 131 Springfield VA 22151

DYER-COLE, PAULINE, school psychologist, educator; b. Methuen, Mass., Aug. 20, 1935; d. E. Dewey and Rose Alma (Des Jardins) Dyer; m. Richard Grey, Aug. 1, 1964 (dec. 1977); children: Douglas Richard, Christopher Lachlan, Heather Judith; m. Malcolm A. Cole, July 23, 1983. BS in Edn. and Music, Lowell State Coll., 1957; MEd, Boston State Coll., 1961; EdD, Clark U., 1991. Lic. psychologist; cert. sch. and ednl. psychologist. Supr. music and art Merrimac and W. Newburg (Mass.) Pub. Schs., 1957-59; music editor textbooks Allyn & Bacon, Inc., Boston, 1959-64; prof. music West Pines Coll., Chester, N.H., 1969-72; sch. psychologist Nashoba Regional Sch. Dist., Bolton, Mass., 1979—; vis. lectr., then vis. prof. Framingham (Mass.) State Coll., 1980—; dir. psychol. testing Nashoba Regional Sch. Dist., Bolton, Mass., 1980—. Author: The Play Game Songbook, 1964. V.p., bd. dirs. Timberlane Devel. Ctr., Plaistow, N.H., 1970-73; founder Friends of Kimi Nichols Devel. Ctr., Plaistow, 1973; chmn. human svcs. St. Ann Parish, Southborough, Mass., 1974-77, active, 1973—; active The Regional Lab., Andover, Mass., 1993—. Frances L. Hyatt Sch. Psychology & Edn. fellow Clark U., 1977-79. Mem. NASP, Mass. Assn. Sch. Psychologists, Mass. Tchrs. Assn., CASE Sch. Psychologists Assn. Roman Catholic. Home: 50 Framingham Rd Southborough MA 01772 Office: Nashoba Regional Sch Dist 11 Green Rd Bolton MA 01740

DYER-DAWSON, DIANE FAYE, educational administrator; b. Chgo., Feb. 16, 1941; d. Coy F. and Geraldine C. (Hardie) Smith; m. Nelson F. Dyer, Mar. 11, 1961 (div. 1983); children: Ouida F., Nelson F. Jr., Deidre M.; m. Bernarr E. Dawson, Apr. 9, 1988. BEd, Chgo. State U., 1970; MEd, U. Ill., 1976; EdD, Loyola U., Chgo., 1991. Tchr. Luella Elem. Sch., Chgo., 1970-74; learning disabilities tchr. Betsy Ross Elem. Sch., Chgo., 1974-76; asst. prin. Cather Elem. Sch., Chgo., 1976-84; prin. Park Manor Elem. Sch., Chgo., 1984-92, Proviso East High Sch., Maywood, Ill., 1992—; trainer Ill. Bd. Edn., Chgo., 1988—, mentor, 1989—, assoc., 1991—; instr. grad. sch. Chgo. State U., 1991-92, Loyola U., Chgo., 1992—. Mem. selection com. Golden Apple Found., Chgo., 1988—; bd. dirs. Salem House, Chgo., 1991—; sec. coun. Salem Luth. Ch., Chgo., 1992—. Named Prin. of Excellence, Chgo. Pub. Schs., 1992; grantee Chgo. Pub. Schs., 1991, Ill. Bd. Edn., 1991. Mem. ASCD, IASCD, IHSA, Nat. Assn. Secondary Sch. Prins., Ill. Prins. Assn., Chgo. Prins. Assn. (assoc.), Samuel B. Stratton Edn. Assn., Nat. Alliance of Black Sch. Educators, Innovators Serving Deprived Children (pres. 1984-88), Alpha Kappa Alpha, Phi Delta Kappa. Democrat. Home: 2561 Lake Shore Dr Lynwood IL 60411-1384

DYER-RAFFLER, JOY ANN, special education diagnostician, educator; b. Stiltner, W.Va., Aug. 10, 1935; d. Ralph William and Hazel (Terry) Dyer; m. John William Raffler, Sr., Jan. 1, 1993; 1 child from a previous marriage, Keith Brian DeArmond. BA, U. N.C., 1969; MEd, U. Ariz., 1974, MEd in Spl. Edn., 1976. Cert. spl. edn.-learning disabilities, art edn., spl. edn.-emotionally handicapped. Art educator Tucson Unified Sch. Dist., Tucson, 1970-75, spl. edn. educator, 1975-89, spl. edn. diagnostician, 1989—. Den mother Cub Scouts Am., Raleigh, N.C., 1968-69. Recipient grant Tucson Unified Sch. Dist., 1977. Mem. NEA, Tucson Edn. Assn., Learning Disabilities Assn., Coun. Exceptional Children, Coun. Ednl. Diagnostic Svcs. Home: 4081 N Kolb Rd Tucson AZ 85715-6127 Office: AJO Svc Ctr 2201 W 44th St Tucson AZ 85713-4575

DYKEMAN, ALICE MARIE, public relations executive; b. Fremont, Nebr., May 18; d. Cecil Victor and Dorothy Lillian (Sillik) Jansen; divorced; children: David Clair, Cinda Cecille Dykeman Nordgren. Student, Nebr. Wesleyan U., 1949-50, So. Meth. U., 1960-70. Women's editor, feature writer Fremont (Nebr.) Guide and Tribune and Biloxi (Miss.) Daily Herald, 1950-55; adminstrv. asst. to v.p. sales promotion A. Harris & Co., Dallas, 1957-60; account exec. Contact Corp., Dallas, 1960-61; pub. relations dir. Meth. Hosp., Dallas, 1961-72; regional pub. info. officer Small Bus. Adminstrn., Dallas, 1972-74; owner Dykeman Assocs. Inc., Dallas, 1974—; adj. prof. U. Dallas Grad. Sch. Mgmt., Irving, Tex. 1972-78; guest lectr. numerous Univs., and seminars; mem. pub. relations com. Dallas/Ft. Worth Fed. Exec. Bd., 1973, mem. minority bus. oportunity com., 1974; mem. Gov.'s Council on Small Bus., Tex., 1980-81, 500, Inc., 1982-90; chmn. export council pub. affairs task force U.S. Dept. Commerce, 1980-83. Contbr. articles to health care and pub. relations jours. Mem. fgn. visitors com. Dallas Council on World Affairs, 1962—, North Tex. Commn., Dallas Pub. Health Bd., 1972-74, Dallas Urban Rehab. Standards Bd., 1981-83, Econ. Devel. Adv. Bd., City of Dallas, 1983-86; pres. Concerned Citizens for Cedar Springs, 1982—; bd. dirs. Oak Lawn Forum, 1983-92; mem. exec. com. Oak Lawn Com., 1983—. Recipient Matrix award Women in Communications, Dallas, 1968, 88. Fellow Pub. Relations Soc. Am. (chairperson southwest dist. 1971-72, bd. dirs. N. Tex. chpt. 1966-72, pres. 1969, assembly del. 1970-73, 91); mem. Internat. Pub. Relations Assn., Internat. Trade Assn. Dallas, North Dallas Fin. Forum, Nat. Assn. Women Bus. Owners, S.W. Venture Forum, 1985—, North Dallas C. of C. (bd. dirs. 1980-82), Greater Dallas Chamber, Dallas Rep. Club, Press Club Dallas (headliner 4 times, bd. dirs. 1981-83), others. United Methodist. Office: Dykeman Assocs Inc 4115 Rawlins St Dallas TX 75219-3661

DYKES, KATHRYN A., community health nurse, educator, administrator; b. Racine, Wis., Sept. 11, 1951; d. Frank R. and Stella Korzilius; m. Herman J. Dykes, Apr. 2, 1977; children: Kathryn, Stephanie, John. BS, Coll. St. Teresa, Winona, Minn., 1973; postgrad., U. Wis., Oshkosh. Cert. in infection control, CPR, BLS. Critical care staff nurse Milwaukee County Med. Complex, Milw.; case mgr./home health Vis. Nurse Assn., Milw.; staff., case mgmt. home health Vis. Nurses of Family Svc. Assn., Green Bay, Wis., staff devel. coord., dir. nursing. Recipient Presdl. award Community Svc., 1990; named Vol. of Yr. Brown County, Wis., 1990, Outstanding Vol. Wis. Crisis Ctr., 1989. Mem. Assn. for Practitioners in Infection Control, Transcultural Nurses Soc., Nat. Parish Nurses Assn., Health Ministries Assn. Office: Visiting Nurses 1550 Dousman St Green Bay WI 54303

DYKES, VIRGINIA CHANDLER, occupational therapist, educator; b. Evanston, Ill., Jan. 10, 1930; d. Daniel Guy and Helen (Schneider) Goodman; children: Ron Lee, Chuck Lee Chandler, James R. Jr. BA in Art and Psychology, So. Methodist U., 1951; postgrad. in occupational therapy Tex. Women's U., 1953. Occupational therapist Beverly Hills Sanitarium, Dallas, 1953-55; dir. occupational and recreational therapy Baylor U. Med. Ctr., Dallas, 1956-60, 68-89; pvt. practice, Dallas, 1989-92; dir. occupational and recreational therapy Fla. Hosp., Orlando, 1962-65; staff therapist Parkland Meml. Hosp., Dallas, 1965-68; cons. Arthritis Found., 1974-89, benefactor; Fanny B. Vanderkodi lectr. Tex. Women's U., 1993—. Mem. coordinating bd. allied health adv. com. Tex. Coll. and Univ. System, 1980-88; bd. dirs. Tex. Arthritis Found., chmn. patient svcs. com., 1985-89, exec. bd. sec.; sponsor Kimball Art Mus.; bd. dirs. Dallas Opera, also women's bd., CPA Wives, Theatre Ctr. Guild; women's bd. Dallas Arboretum; pres. Diana Dean Head Injury Guild, 1992-93. Named Tex. Occupational Therapist of Yr., 1985. Mem. Tex. Occupational Therapy Assn. (life mem. award), Am. Occupational Therapy Assn. (del. Fla. 1964, Tex. 1980-88), World Fedn. Occupational Therapists (participant 8th Internat. Congress, Hamburg, Germany, 1982, del. to 10th European Congress on Rheumatology, Moscow 1983), Chi Omega. Clubs: Boomerang (dir. 1971-88), Les Femmes du Monde, Pierian Lit. Club. Author: (manual) Lightcast II Splints, 1976; Adult Visual Perceptual Evaluation, 1981; contbr. articles to profl. jours. Home: 3203 Alderson St Dallas TX 75214-3059

DYKSTRA, EDIE M., manager, consultant; b. Gary, Ind., Nov. 9, 1954; d. Wayne H. and Edith P. (Christoff) D. BA in History, Ind. U., 1976; MPA in Urban, State, Fed. Gov. and Human Resources, Golden Gate U., 1986. Supr. internal acctg. KPMG Peat Marwick, San Francisco, 1980-87; asst. to dir. fin. City of Oakland, Calif., 1987; compensation and benefits analyst The Harper Group, San Francisco, 1987-89; mgr. internal svcs. The Wyatt Co., San Francisco, 1989-92, mgr. human resources, 1992-94, dir. human resources, 1994—. Vol. Raphael House Shelter for Homeless Families, San Francisco, 1988—, vol., crisis counselor Woman Inc., 1988—. Mem. ASTD, Soc. for Human Resource Mgmt., Bay Area Personnel Assn. (pres. 1990-91), Bay Area Orgnl. Devel. Network, No. Calif. Human Resource Coun. Democrat. Office: The Wyatt Co 345 California St San Francisco CA 94104-9999

DYKSTRA, LINDA PERRY, quality improvement professional, nursing administrator; b. Wareham, Mass., May 17, 1948; d. Albino Anthony and Ezaura Ann (Thomas) Perry. BSN, U. Va., 1972; MS, Boston Coll., 1976; postgrad., U. R.I., 1993—. RN, R.I. Staff nurse U. Va., Charlottesville, 1971-72; nursing instr., coord. Piedmont (Va.) Community Coll., Charlottesville, 1972-74; charge nurse Pondville (Mass.) Hosp., 1974-75; clin. nurse specialist Faulkner Hosp., Boston, 1976-79; dir. continuing edn. Morton Hosp., Taunton, Mass., 1979-81; asst. dir. project mgmt. R.I. Hosp., Providence, 1981-83, assoc. dir., 1983-92, assoc. dir., interim dir. nursing profl. devel., 1992—, clin. nurse specialist, 1993—; cons. nursing models Leonard Morse Hosp., Mass., 1987; cons. quality assurance South County Hosp., Wakefield, R.I., 1989-90, Copley Hosp., Morrisville, Vt., 1991, U. Mass. Med. Ctr., Worcester, Mass., 1992. Designer Professional Nursing Model, 1986, Work Redesign, 1993. Mem. ANA (cert. nursing adminstr. advanced, bd. mem. R.I. 1991—, congl. senate dist. coord. 1989—), Nat. Assn. Healthcare Quality Assurance Profls., Nat. Nurse Staff Devel. Orgn., R.I. State Nurses Assn. (chair legis. com. 1989—), Sigma Theta Tau. Office: RI Hosp 593 Eddy St Providence RI 02902

DYLAG, HELEN MARIE, healthcare administrator; b. Cleve., Oct. 14, 1950; d. Stanley John and Helen Agnes (Jarkiewicz) D. BSN, St. John Coll., Cleve., 1971; MS, Ohio State U., 1973. RN, Ohio. RN V.A. Adminstrn. Hosp., Brecksville, Ohio, 1971-72; clin. specialist, psychiat.-mental health nursing Marymount Hosp./Mental Health Ctr., Garfield Heights, Ohio, 1973-78, dir. consultation and edn. dept., 1978-84, dir. Ctr. for Health Styles, 1984-88; adminstrv. dir. Women's Healthcare Ctr./St. Luke's Hosp., Cleve., 1988-90; adminstrv. dir. dept. of psychiatry MetroHealth Med. Ctr., Cleve., 1990—. Contbg. author: Nursing of Families in Crisis, 1974, Distributive Nursing Practice: A Systems Approach to Community Health, 1977; producer and host "Health Styles" TV Talk Show, 1987-88; contbr. articles to profl. jours. Trustee The Stroke Assn. of Ohio, Cleve., 1990-91; mem. Women of Achievement com., Women's City Club, Cleve., 1989-91. Recipient award Greater Cleve. Hosp. Assn., 1981, Innovator award Am. Hosp. Assn./Ctr. for Health Promotion, 1985. Mem. Assn. Mental Health Adminstrs., Am. Coll. Healthcare Execs., Healthcare Adminstrs. Assn. of Northeast Ohio, Sigma Theta Tau. Home: 5709 Onaway Oval Cleveland OH 44130-1642 Office: Metro Health Med Ctr 2500 Metrohealth Dr Cleveland OH 44109-1900

DYNER, SHERYL A., programming and system administrator; b. Phila., Sept. 26, 1953; d. Benjamin Leonard and Elaine (Rudolph) D. BS in Biology, Pa. State U., 1975, M in Mgmt., 1991. Mng. editor Franklin Inst. Rsch. Ctr., Phila., 1975-81; analyst Shared Med. Systems, Malvern, Pa., 1981-83; mgr. Shared Med. Systems, Malvern, 1984—, cons. software engring., 1987—, cons. total quality mgmt., 1989—. Mng. editor: Gastroenterology Abstracts and Citation, 1975-80, Biological Effects of Non-Ionizing Elctromagnetic Radiation, 1979-81; editor (book): PHS 1979 Chemicals Tested for Carcinogenic Activity, 1979. Mem. archtl. com. Westover Crossing Townhome Assn., West Norriton, Pa., 1994; vol. United Way, Norristown, 1994. Mem. Am. Soc. Quality Control, Quality Assurance Inst. Office: Shared Med Systems 55 Valley Stream Pky Malvern PA 19355

DYONZAK, JANE V., psychologist, educator; b. St. Louis, Mar. 10, 1962; d. Anthony C. and Helen V. (Garwacki) D. BA, U. Mo., 1984; MA, So. Ill. U., 1987; PhD, Pa. State U., 1991. Lic. clin. psychologist. Instr. dept. psychology Rush-Presbyn.-St. Luke's Med. Ctr., Chgo., 1990-91, asst. prof., psychologist dept. psychology, 1991-93; lab. dir., asst. prof., psychologist Sleep Disorders Svc. and Rsch. Ctr., Rush-Presbyn.-St. Lukes, Chgo., 1993—; polysomnographer Ingalls Meml. Hosp., Harvey, Ill., 1990-92, clin. dir. Sleep Disorder Ctr., 1992—; lectr. and presenter in field. Contbr. chpt. to book and articles to profl. jours. Vol. psychologist local domestic violence shelter, Chgo., 1992—. Mem. APA, Soc. for Psychophysiol. Rsch., Associated Profl. Sleep Socs., Sigma Xi. Home: 11352 S Champlain Ave Chicago IL 60628-5122 Office: Rush Presbyn St Lukes Med Ctr 1653 W Congress Pky Chicago IL 60612-3809

DYRSTAD, JOANELL M., former lieutenant governor; b. St. James, Minn., Oct. 15, 1942; d. Arnold A. and Ruth (Berlin) Sletta; m. Marvin Dyrstad, 1965; children: Troy, Anika. BA, Gustavus Adolphus Coll., St. Peter, Minn., 1964; postgrad., Hamline U., 1988—. Mayor City of Red Wing, Minn., 1985-90; lt. gov. State of Minn., 1991-94; ptnr. Corner Drugstore, Red Wing, 1968—; v.p. League Minn. Cities, 1990-91, Minn. Mayors Assn., 1989-90. Trustee Gustavus Adolphus Coll., 1989—, U. Minn. Found., 1993—. Mem. AAUW (Citizen of yr. award 1985), League of Women Voters, Minn. Women Elected Ofcls. (chair nat. conf. lt. govs. 1993-94). Office: Office of the Lt Gov 130 State Capitol Saint Paul MN 55155-1002

DYSART, DIANA BARCELONA, school system administrator; b. New Orleans, Oct. 14, 1955; d. Anthony and Mildred (Schroeder) Barcelona; m. Daniel Lee Dysart, Aug. 12, 1978; children: Cori, Katie, Daniel J., Christopher. BA in Elem. Edn., U. Southwestern La., 1976; MEd in Supervision and Adminstrn., La. State U., 1977. Mem. St. Bernard Parish Sch. Bd., Chalmette, 1983—, v.p., 1985-88, pres., 1988—; with Nat. Sch. Bds. Assn., La. Sch. Bds. Assn. Chmn. Mothers March, March of Dimes, 1985-91, bd. dirs., 1985—; bd. dirs. Nunez Community Coll. Found., Chalmette, 1990-94, Am. Heart Assn., 1994; mem. Ednl. Excellence Com., Chalmette, La.; booth chmn. St. Mark Fair; active St. Bernard Beautification Com.; co-chair St. Bernard Cleanest Parish Com.; bd. dirs. Discovery Festival, YWCA. Mem. AAUW, Internat. Reading Assn., Just Between Friends Homemakers Assn., C. of C. (mem. exec. com.), KOC (women's aux.). Democrat. Roman Catholic. Office: St Bernard Sch Bd 67 E Chalmette Cir Chalmette LA 70043

DZIEWANOWSKA, ZOFIA ELIZABETH, neuropsychiatrist, pharmaceutical executive, physician; b. Warsaw, Poland, Nov. 17, 1939; came to U.S., 1972; d. Stanislaw Kazimierz Dziewanowski and Zofia Danuta (Mieczkowska) Rudowska; m. Krzysztof A. Kunert, Sept. 1, 1961 (div. 1971); 1 child, Martin. MD, U. Warsaw, 1963; PhD, Polish Acad. Sci., 1970. MD recert. U.K., 1972, U.S., 1973. Asst. prof. of psychiatry U. Warsaw Med. Sch., 1969-71; sr. house officer St. George's Hosp., U. London, 1971-72; assoc. dir. Merck Sharp & Dohme, Rahway, N.J., 1972-76; vis. assoc. physician Rockefeller U. Hosp., N.Y.C., 1975-76; adj. asst. prof. of psychiatry Cornell U. Med. Ctr., N.Y.C., 1978—; v.p., global med. dir. Hoffmann-La Roche, Inc., Nutley, N.J., 1976-94; sr. v.p. and dir. global med. affairs Genta Inc., San Diego, 1994—; lectr. in field. Contbr. articles to profl. publs. Bd. dirs. Royal Soc. of Medicine, U.K. Recipient TWIN Honoree award for Outstanding Women in Mgmt., Ridgewood (N.J.) YWCA, 1984. Mem. AMA, AAAS, Am. Soc. Pharmacology and Therapeutics, Am. Coll. Neuropsychopharmacology, N.Y. Acad. Sci., Pharm. Rsch. and Mfrs. Assn. of Am. (vice chmn. steering com. med. sect.), Drug Info. Assn. (Women of the Yr. award 1994, Most Admired Women of the Decade from Am. Biog. Inst. 1994), Alumni Coun. Cornell Med. Ctr., Am. Assn. Pharm. Physicians. Roman Catholic. Office: Genta Inc 3550 General Atomics Ct San Deigo CA 92121

EACHEMPATI, UMA RAMAGOPAL, obstetrician, gynecologist; b. Madras, India, Dec. 26, 1935; came to U.S. 1969; d. Narasimha Rao Kamaraju and Susila Radhakrishna; m. May 7, 1960; children: Aditya, Soumitra. BS, Madras U., 1954; dipl. obstetrics and gynecology, Bombay U., 1962; MD, Osmania U., Hyderabad, India, 1962. Diplomate Am. Bd. Obstetrics and Gynecology. Rotating internship Osmania Gen. Hosp., Hyderabad, 1959-60; tutor obstetrics and gynecology Osmania Med. Coll. and Govt. Maternity Hosp., Hyderabad, 1960-62, asst. prof. obstetrics and gynecology, 1962-65; asst. prof. obstetrics and gynecology Niloufer Hosp., Hyderabad, 1965-66; sr. lectr. in obstetrics and gynecology Post Grad. Inst. for Med. Edn. and Rsch., Chandigarh, India, 1966-68; internship in obstetrics and gynecology St. Louis U., 1969-70; resident in obstetrics and gynecology St. Louis U. Hosp., 1970-72; resident in pathology St. Mary's Hosp., St. Louis, 1973; resident in surgery St. Luke's Hosp., St. Louis, 1973; asst. clin. prof. St. Louis U., 1975—; fellow in gynecology Mass. Gen. Hosp., Boston, 1963-64. Fellow Royal Soc. Medicine, Internat. Med. Scis. Acad. (trustee), Am. Coll. Obstetrics and Gynecology; mem. Royal Coll. Obstetrics and Gynecology, N.Am. Soc. Pediat. Adolescent Gynecology, Am. Assn. Physicians from India, Am. Assn. Gynecol. Laparoscopists, AMA (Recognition awards 1987, 90, 93), St. Louis Med. Soc., St. Louis Gynecol. Soc., Am. Med. Women's Assn. Hindu. Home: 14499 Ladue Rd Chesterfield MO 63017 Office: 4150 Jeffco Blvd Arnold MO 63010

EADIE, CYNTHIA, advertising executive. B, Boston Coll., 1980. Exec. dir. Subway Franchise Advt. Fund, Milford, Conn., 1990—. Office: Subway Frnchise Advtg Fund 325 Bic Dr Milford CT 06460-3072*

EADS, M. ADELA, state legislator; b. Brooklyn, N.Y., Mar. 2, 1920. Ed. Sweet Briar Coll. Mem. Conn. Ho. of Reps., 1976-89; mem. Conn. Senate, from 1980; senate minority leader serving on legis. mgmt. com., exec. nominations com.; mem. adv. bd. New Milford Bank & Trust Co., Glenholm Devereux Sch.; mem. task force on minority farmers. Trustee Marvelwood Sch., Cornwall, Conn.; bd. dirs. Drugs Don't Work. Republican. Mem. Conn. Bd. Edn., 1972-76, Nat. Orgn. Women Legislators. Home: 160 Macedonia Rd Kent CT 06757-1306 Office: Conn State Senate State Capital Bldg Hartford CT 06106*

EAGAN, CLAIRE VERONICA, lawyer; b. Bronx, N.Y., Oct. 9, 1950; d. Joseph Thomas and Margaret (Lynch) E.; m. M. Stephen Barrett, Aug. 25, 1978 (div. 1984); m. Anthony J. Loretti, Jr., Feb. 13, 1988. Student, U. Fribourg, Switzerland, 1971-72; BA, Trinity Coll., Washington, 1972; postgrad., U. Paris, 1972-73; JD, Fordham U., 1976. Bar: N.Y. 1977, Okla. 1977, U.S. Dist. Ct. (no. dist.) Okla. 1977, U.S. Ct. Appeals (10th cir.) 1978, U.S. Dist. Ct. (we. dist.) Okla. 1981, U.S. Ct. Appeals (5th cir.) 1982, U.S. Dist. Ct. (ea. dist.) Okla. 1988, U.S. Ct. Appeals (Fed. cir.) 1990, U.S. Supreme Ct. Mem. Hall, Estill, Hardwick, Gable, Golden & Nelson, Tulsa, 1978—, shareholder, 1981—; also bd. dirs., exec. com. Editor Fordham Law Rev., 1975-76. Bd. dirs. Cath. Charities, Tulsa, 1983—, Cystic Fibrosis Found., Tulsa, 1982-84; mem. Jr. League Tulsa, Inc., 1983—; bd. dirs. Okla. Sinfonia, Tulsa, 1982-86; adj. settlement judge, Tulsa County, 1990—. Mem. Tulsa County Bar Assn., 10th Cir. Jud. Conf., Am. Inns of Ct. Republican. Roman Catholic. Office: Hall Estill Hardwick Gable Golden & Nelson 320 S Boston Ste 400 Tulsa OK 74103

EAGAN, KRISTA ANN, pharmacist; b. Pottsville, Pa., July 8, 1962; d. James Joseph and Gaye Diane (Anderson) E. BS in Pharmacy, Temple U., 1985. Registered pharmacist. Pharmacist People's Drug, Harrisburg, Pa., 1985-86; pharmacist, mgr. Amcare Health Svcs., Harrisburg, 1986—. Mem.

Pa. Pharm. Assn., Capital Area Pharm. Assn. Office: Amcare Health Svcs 6400 Flank Dr Ste 1000 Harrisburg PA 17112-2778

EAGAN, MARIE T. (RIA EAGAN), chiropractor; b. Rockville Ctr., N.Y., June 17, 1952; d. John F. and Mary (Ebner) E. BA, Goddard Coll., 1975; D in Chiropractic Medicine, N.Y. Chiropractic Coll., 1983. Pvt. practice chiropractic medicine N.Y.C., 1983—; chiropractic examiner N.Y. State Bd. Chiropractic, 1995. Bd. dirs. Chalice Found., L.A., 1986. Fellow N.Y. Chiropractic Assn., Am. Chiropractic Assn., Internat. Chiropractic Assn. Democrat.

EAGLES, CATHERINE CALDWELL, judge; b. Memphis, Aug. 30, 1958; d. Marvin Bounds and Dorothy Carolyn (Reddell) Caldwell; m. William A. Eagles, Aug. 27, 1983; children: John Ivey, Thad. BA, Southwestern U., Memphis, 1979; JD, George Washington U., 1982. Bar: Mo. 1982, Ark. 1983, N.C. 1984; cert. mediator, N.C. Law clk. to Hon. J. Smith Henley U.S. Ct. Appeals (8th cir.), Harrison, Ark., 1982-84; assoc. Smith Helms Mulliss & Moore, Greensboro, N.C., 1984-89, ptnr., 1989-93; judge Superior Ct., State of N.C., Greensboro, 1993—; arbitrator Am. Arbitration Assn., Charlotte, N.C., 1992-93. Office: Superior Ct Judges Chambers 201 S Eugene St Greensboro NC 27401-2319

EAGLY, ALICE HENDRICKSON, social psychology educator; b. L.A., Dec. 25, 1938; d. Harold Martin and Josara Alberta (Whyers) Hendrickson; m. Robert Victor Eagly, Sept. 8, 1962; children: Ingrid Victoria, Ursula Elizabeth. BA, Radcliffe Coll., 1960; MA, U. Mich., 1963, PhD, 1965. Asst. prof. Mich. State U., East Lansing, 1965-67; asst. to assoc. to full prof. U. Mass., Amherst, 1967-80; vis. asst. prof. U. Ill., Champaign, 1970-71; vis. assoc. prof. Harvard U., Cambridge, Mass., 1974-75; prof. social psychology Purdue U., West Lafayette, Ind., 1980-95, Northwestern U., Evanston, Ill., 1995—; MacEachern Meml. lectr. U. Alta., 1985; vis. prof. U. Tuebingen (Germany), 1991-92. Author: Sex Differences in Social Behavior: A Social Role Interpretation, 1987, (with Shelly Chaiken) The Psychology of Attitudes, 1993; cons. editor Jour. Personality and Social Psychology: Attitudes and Social Cognition, 1979—, mem. editorial bd., 1983—; cons. editor Psychology of Women Quar., 1978-86, also others; contbr. articles to profl. jours. Recipient Disting. Pub. award, Assn. for Women in Psychology, 1978, Gordon Allport Intergroup Rels. prize, Soc. Psychol. Study Social Issues, 1976; Nat. Merit scholar, 1956-60, Fulbright fellow, 1960-61, Woodrow Wilson fellow, 1961-62, NSF fellow, 1962-65; various rsch. grants. Mem. APA (citation as disting. leader for women in psychology com. on women in psychology), Soc. Personality and Social Psychology (pres. 1981), Donald Campbell award for disting. contbn. to social psychology 1994), Soc. for Exptl. Social Psychology (exec. com. 1973-76, 81-83), Midwestern Psychol. Assn., Phi Beta Kappa, Sigma Xi. Office: Northwestern U Dept Social Psychol Scis Evanston IL 60200

EAGON, CARRIE WILSON, former librarian; b. Chattanooga, Aug. 19, 1920; d. Sam D. and Carrie Belle (Robinson) Wilson; m. Bruce Eagon, June 27, 1943 (dec. Sept. 1967); 1 child, Rex W. BA, U. Tulsa, 1942; MLS, La. State U., 1950. Circulation asst. Tulsa Pub. Libr., 1942-43; libr. Douglas Aircraft, Tulsa, 1943-44; circulation libr. U. Tulsa, 1945-50; head libr. Jersey Prodn. Rsch., Tulsa, 1955-65, Esso Prodn. Rsch., Houston, 1965-70; libr. Esso Math & Systems, Florham Park, N.J., 1970-71, Esso Ea. Inc., Houston, 1971-82; ret., 1982—; John Cotton Dana lectr. Spl. Librs. Assn. U. Denver, 1969; rsch. cons. Prestige Mag. Co., Huntington, W.Va., 1987. Chmn. Svc. Corps Ret. Execs., Huntington, 1991-92; bd. dirs. YWCA, Huntington, pres. bd. dirs., 1994—. Mem. AAUW (pres. Huntington br. 1991-94, bd. dirs. 1994—), Am. Assn. Ret. Persons (W.Va. women's initiative spokesperson 1992—), Huntington Women's Club (dir. internat. travel 1991—, auditor 1994—). Republican. Presbyterian. Home: 1427 5th Street Rd Huntington WV 25701-4701

EAKIN, MARGARETTA MORGAN, lawyer; b. Ft. Smith, Ark., Aug. 27, 1941; d. Ariel Thomas and Oma (Thomas) Morgan; m. Harry D. Eakin, June 7, 1959; 1 dau., Margaretta E. B.A. with honors, U. Oreg., 1969, J.D., 1971. Bar: Oreg. 1971, U.S. Dist. Ct. Oreg. 1973, U.S. Ct. Appeals (9th cir.) 1977. Law clk. to chief justice Oreg. Supreme Ct., 1971-72; Reginald Heber Smith Law Reform fellow, 1972-73; house counsel Hyster Co., 1973-75; assoc. N. Robert Stoll, 1975-77; mem. firm Margaretta Eakin, P.C., Portland, Oreg., 1977—; tchr. bus. law Portland State U., 1979-80; speaker; mem. state bd. profl. responsibility Oreg. State Bar, 1979-82. Mem. bd. visitors U. Oreg. Sch. of Law, 1986-93, vice chair, 1989-91, chair, 1992-93; mem. ann. fund com. Oreg. Episc. Sch., 1981, chmn. subcom. country fair, 1981; sec. Parent Club Bd., St. Mary's Acad., 1987; mem. Oreg. State. Bar Com. on Uniform State Laws, 1989-93. Paul Patterson fellow. Mem. ABA, Assn. Trial Lawyers Am., Oreg. Trial Lawyers Assn., Oreg. Bar Assn., Multnomah County Bar Assn. (jud. selection com. 1992-94), 1000 Friends of Oreg., City Club. Office: 30th Fl Pacwest Ctr 1211 SW 5th Ave Portland OR 97204-3713

EALY, CARYL DIANE, writer, counselor, consultant; b. Sharon, Pa., June 17, 1947; d. Robert Glenn and Margaret Helen (Steele) E. BS in Speech, Slippery Rock (Pa.) U., 1969; MS in Comm., U. Pitts., 1972; PhD in Behavioral Sci., U. for Humanistic Studies, Del Mar, Calif., 1980. Coord. sr. edn. Pima C.C., Tucson, 1983-84, counselor, mem. faculty, 1988-92; mgr. mktg. rsch. Westin La Paloma, Tucson, 1985-88; vocat. counselor Regional Reemployment Ctr., Tucson, 1992—; counselor, cons., speaker Ealy & Assocs., Tucson, 1980—; cons., workshop leader for numerous pvt. and pub. orgns., Ariz., 1980—. Author: The Woman's Book of Creativity, 1994; coprodr. video Women's Creativity: Five Arizona Photographers, 1992. Recipient Video Prodn. award U. Ariz., 1992. Mem. Assn. Humanistic Psychology, Inst. Noetic Sci. Office: 5210 E Pima Ste 200 Tucson AZ 85712

EARHART, EILEEN MAGIE, retired home and family life educator; b. Hamilton, Ohio, Oct. 21, 1928; d. Andrew J. and Martha (Waldorf) Magie; m. Paul G. Earhart; children: Anthony G., Bruce P., Daniel T. B.S., Miami U., Oxford, Ohio, 1950; M.A. in Adminstrn. and Ednl. Services, Mich. State U., 1962, Ph.D. in Edn., 1969; H.H.D. (hon.), Miami U., Oxford, Ohio, 1980. Tchr. home econs. W. Alexandria (Ohio) Schs., 1950-51; elementary tchr. Waterford Twp. Schs., Pontiac, Mich., 1958-65; reading specialist Waterford Twp. Schs., 1965-67; prof., chmn. family and child ecology dept. Mich. State U., East Lansing, 1968-84; prof., head dept. home and family life Fla. State U., Tallahassee, 1984-89; ret., 1989. Author: Attention and Classification Training Curriculum; co-editor spl. issue of Family Relations, 1984; contbr. chpts. to profl. jours., books. Mem. adv. bd. Lansing Com. on Children's TV, Family/Sch./Community Partnership Project, Tallahassee; bd. dirs. Women's Resource Ctr., Grand Rapids, Mich., Wesley Found., 1989-95; mem. Mich. Gov.'s Task Force on Youth. Mem. Nat. Coun. on Family Rels. (pres. Assn. of Couns. 1987-88, bd. dirs. 1986-88, chair nat. meeting local arrangements 1992), Fla. Coun. on Family Rels. (pres. elect 1985-86, pres. 1986-87), Nat. Assn. Edn. Young Children, Assn. Childhood Edn. Internat., Am. Home Econs. Assn. (named an AHEA Leader at 75th Ann. of Assn. 1984), Internat. Fedn. Home Econs., Mich. Home Econs. Assn. (pres. 1980-82), Fla. Home Econs. Assn. (chmn. scholarship com. 1986-88, dist. chmn. 1990-91, chmn. nominating com. 1991-92, co-chair ann. meeting 1995), Ednl. Rsch. Assn., Phi Kappa Phi (pres. Fla. State U. chpt. 1988-89), Delta Kappa Gamma, Omicron Nu, others. Home: 4009 Brandon Hill Dr Tallahassee FL 32308-2653

EARLE, MARY MARGARET, marketing executive; b. Newberry, Mich., June 26, 1947; d. William Loren and Naida Theresa (Ward) E. Student, St. Mary's Coll., Notre Dame, Ind., 1965-67. Cert. employment cons. Receptionist Western Girl World, San Francisco, 1968-69; receptionist, sec. Advanced Memory Systems, Sunnyvale, Calif., 1969-71; career cons. Qualified Personnel, Madison, Wis., 1972-75; VIP asst. Summit Sports Arena Grand Open, Houston, 1975, S. Petroleum Gp/OTC, Houston, 1976, Astrodomain Assn., Houston, 1976-77; bus. mgr. Mobile Colo TV Prodn., Houston, 1977-80; broadcast bus. affairs dir. G.D.L. & W. Adv., Houston, 1980-90; broadcast talent cons. Willis, Tex., 1990-93; pvt. practice Marquette, Mich., 1993—, mktg. cons.,, 1994—; modeling judge Page Parks Sch. Modeling, Houston, 1988-91; cons. industry/union rels. AFTRA/SAG, Houston, 1985-92. Houston mem. Fashion Group, 1989-90; sec. Bluebell Estates Assn., Willis, 1991, pres. 1992; pub. rels. vol. Women's Ctr. seminars, Houston, 1984-85. Named Disting. Salesman of Yr. Sales and Mktg. Execs., Madison, 1973, 74. Mem. Adminstrv. Mgmt. Soc. (cons. ofcl. panel 1974), Pers. Adminstrs. Soc., Am. Assn. Advt. Agys. (so. broadcast policy com.). Home and Office: 612 County Rd 480 Marquette MI 49855

EARLE, SYLVIA ALICE, research biologist, oceanographer; b. Gibbstown, N.J., Aug. 30, 1935; d. Lewis Reade and Alice Freas (Richie) E. BS, Fla. State U., 1955; MA, Duke U., 1956, PhD, 1966, PhD (hon.), 1993; PhD (hon.), Monterey Inst. Internat. Studies, 1990, Ball State U., 1991, George Washington U., 1992; DSc (hon.), Duke Univ., 1993, Ripon Coll., 1994, U. Conn., 1994. Resident dir. Cape Haze Marine Lab., Sarasota, Fla., 1966-67; research scholar Radcliffe Inst., 1967-69; research fellow Farlow Herbarium, Harvard U., 1967-75, researcher, 1975—; research assoc. in botany Natural History Mus. Los Angeles County, 1970-75; research biologist, curator Calif. Acad. Scis., San Francisco, from 1976; research assoc. U. Calif., Berkeley, 1969-75; fellow in botany Natural History Mus., 1989—; chief scientist U.S. NOAA, Washington, 1990-92, advisor to the adminstr., 1992-93; founder, pres., CEO, bd. dirs. Deep Ocean Tech., Inc., Oakland, Calif., 1981-90; founder, pres., CEO Deep Ocean Engring., Oakland, 1982-90, bd. dirs., 1992—; bd. dir. Dresser Industries. Author: Exploring the Deep Frontier, 1980, Sea Change, 1995; editor: Scientific Results of the Tektite II Project, 1972-75; contbr. 90 articles to profl. jours. Trustee World Wildlife Fund U.S., 1976-82, mem. coun., 1984—; trustee World Wildlife Fund Internat., 1979-81, mem. coun., 1981—; trustee Charles A. Lindbergh Fund, pres., 1990—; trustee Ctr. Marine Conservation, 1992—, Perry Found., chmn., 1993—; mem. coun. Internat. Union for Conservation of Nature, 1979-81; corp. mem. Woods Hole Oceanographic Inst.; mem. Nat. Adv. Com. on Oceans and Atmosphere, 1980-94. Recipient Conservation Service award U.S. Dept. Interior, 1970, Boston Sea Rovers award, 1972, 79, Nogi award Underwater Soc. Am., 1976, Conservation service award Calif. Acad. Sci., 1979, Lowell Thomas award Explorer's Club, 1980, Order of Golden Ark Prince Netherlands, 1980, David B. Stone medal New Eng. Aquarium, 1989, Gold medalist Soc. of Women Geographers, medal Radcliffe Coll., 1990, Pacon Internat. award, 1992, Dirs. award Natural Resources Coun. Am., 1992; named Woman of Yr. L.A. Times, 1970, Scientist of Yr., Calif. Mus. Sci. and Industry, 1981. Fellow AAAS, Marine Tech. Soc., Calif. Acad. Scis., Explorers Club, Calif. Acad. Sci.; mem. Internat. Phycological Soc. (sec. 1974-80), Phycological Soc. Am., Am. Soc. Ichthyologists and Herpetologists, Am. Inst. Biol. Scis., Brit. Phycological Soc., Ecol. Soc. Am., Internat. Soc. Plant Taxonomists, Explorers Club (fellow, bd. dirs. 1989—, hon.). Home: 12812 Skyline Blvd Oakland CA 94619-3125 Office: Deep Ocean Engring 1431 Doolittle Dr San Leandro CA 94577-2225

EARLEY, KATHLEEN SANDERS, municipal management assistant; b. Ortonville, Minn., Jan. 14, 1946; d. Robert E. and Shirley C. (Stansfield) Sanders; m. Jack L. Earley; children: Michael, Ralph. BA in English, Carroll Coll., Waukesha, Wis., 1975; student, Wright State U., 1974-75, 78-79; postgrad., Ariz. State U., 1985, 90. In accounts receivable Pickett Industries, Inc., Santa Barbara, Calif., 1969-71; in customer svc. Vernay Labs. Inc., Yellow Springs, Ohio, 1972-76; contracts adminstr. Western Gear, Flight Systems, Jamestown, N.D., 1977-78; adminstrv. asst. City of Fairborn, Ohio, 1978-79; new student coord. DeVry Inst. Tech., Phoenix, 1979-80; adminstrv. asst. City of Mesa, Ariz., 1980-90; asst. to city mgr. City of Big Bear Lake, Calif., 1990-92; budget & mgmt. analyst Coconino County, Flagstaff, Ariz., 1992-94; pub. mgmt. cons. Cin., 1994—; mem. staff Big Bear Lake Film Commn., 1990-92. Editor: Earley Stop Smoking Plan, 1987, Earley Approach to Hatha Yoga, 1988, Earley's Customer Service, 1988; author: (poetry) Into the Night, 1967. Chair bd. dirs. Mesa Leadership Tng. and Devel. Alumni Assn., 1985; chair com. Mesa Community Coun., 1986. Mem. Internat. City/County Mgmt. Assn., League of Calif. Cities, Mcpl. Mgmt. Assts. So. Calif., Ariz. Mcpl. Mgmt. Assts. (sec. 1983), Calif. Assn. Pub. Info. Ofcls., Pub. Risk Mgmt. Assn., Gov. Fin. Officers Assn., Minn. Assn. Urban Mgmt. Assts., Mesa Red Tape Toastmasters (charter mem., adminstrv. v.p. 1987, pres. 1989, 1st Place Area Speech Contest 1990). Home and Office: 5714 Glengate Ln Cincinnati OH 45212

EARLY, SANDRA TERESA IVY, procurement technician supervisor; b. Phila., Oct. 8, 1954; d. Frederick Sr. and Loretta (Corbin) E. BS, Lincoln U., 1979. Adminstrv. asst. Black Music Assn., 1981-82; procurement technician I City of Phila., 1984-86, procurement technician II, 1986-93, procurement technician supr., 1993—. Treas. Faith Ensemble, Wharton Wesley United Meth. Ch., Phila., 1982—, sec. Pastor-Parish rels. com., 1990-93, treas., 1995—. Democrat. Office: City of Phila Rm 110 1401 JFK Blvd Philadelphia PA 19102

EARTHROWL, KATHLEEN JOAN, psychotherapist; b. Springfield, Mass., Dec. 27, 1939; d. Francis Henry and Ruth (Harris) E.; m. Seymour Meyer Syna, Apr. 21, 1960 (div. May 1964); children: Deborah Ruth, Joshua Emil; m. Robert Theodore Lardon, Mar. 22, 1986. BA, Bennington Coll., 1962; MA, Columbia U., 1967, profl. diploma, 1969; EdD, U. Mass., 1979. Lic. profl. counselor, marriage & family therapist. Tchr. N.Y.C. Pub. Schs., 1964-66, The Walden Sch., N.Y.C., 1966-69; asst. prof. No. Ill. U., Dekalb, 1969-74, State Coll., Fitchburg, Mass., 1974-78; asst. dir. program for aesthetic edn. U. Houston, 1979-81; therapist St. Joseph's Hosp., Houston, 1981-83; psychotherapist pvt. practice, Kingwood, Tex., 1984—; tchr. Kingwood Coll., 1987-90, The Jung Ctr., Houston, 1980-83. Mem. Am. Counselors Assn., Nat. Assn. Drug & Alcohol Counselors. Office: Counseling & Therapy Ctr 1 Kingwood Pl Ste 103 Kingwood TX 77339

EASLEY, CHRISTA BIRGIT, nurse, researcher; b. Berlin, Apr. 30, 1941; came to U.S., 1966; d. Albert and Marianne (Uhlmann) Baldauf; m. Loyd Allen Easley, Oct. 23, 1964 (widowed Dec. 1993). Degree in nursing, Pawlow Coll. of Nursing, Aue, Fed. Republic of Germany, 1959; BS, NYU, Albany, 1978; MBA, Cen. Mich. U., 1979; EDS, Ctrl. Mo. U., 1983; PhD, Kensington U., Glensdale, Calif., 1983. With placement sect. Sembach, A.B., Fed. Republic of Germany, 1972-73, suggestion program mgr., 1973-74; adminstrv. clk. Lajes Field, A.B., Terceira, Acores, Portugal, 1975-78, incentive awards and suggestion program mgr., 1978-79; intern Cen. Mo. State U., Warrensburg, 1980-81; instr. in bus. overseas campus Cen. Tex. Coll../Yokota, A.B., Japan, 1983; instr. Tokyo Ctr. for Lang. and Culture, 1981-83; tchr. dept. of def. Yokota Dept. of Def., Yokota AFB, Japan, 1981-84; tax examiner IRS, Austin, Tex., 1984-86; clin. rsch. coord. HealthQuest Rsch., Austin, 1987—. Treas. Am. Sch. System PTA, Acores, 1978-79; precinct chmn. Austin Rep. Com., 1988—. Mem. Assocs. of Clin. Pharmacology, Am. Assn. Translators, AAUW, Sigma Tau Delta. Methodist. Home: 12422 Deer Trak Austin TX 78727-5746 Office: HealthQuest Rsch 7200 N Mo Pac Expy Austin TX 78731-2560

EASLEY, JUNE ELLEN PRICE, genealogist; b. Chgo., June 7, 1924; d. Fred E. and Bernadette (Mailloux) Price; m. Raymond Dale Easley, Dec. 24, 1945. Student, McCormack Sch. Commerce, Englewood Jr. Coll., Chgo. Lic. genealogist Assn. Profl. Genealogists. Statis. clk. Arthur Andersen & Co., Chgo., 1968-74; corr. sec. ICG R.R., Chgo., 1974-86; self-employed genealogist-computers Arlington Heights, Ill., 1986-94, Mountain Home, Ark., 1994—. Contbr. religion articles to Daily Herald, 1991; editor romance stories, 1990—. Mem. DAR (auditor-treas. Chgo. chpt. 1981-82, rec. sec. Chgo. chpt. 1982-88), Daus. War of 1812 (curator 1990-93, newsletter Chgo.), Huguenot Soc., Nat. Soc. R.R. Bus. Women (newsletter editor 1991—), Northwest Suburban Coun. Genealogists (pres. 1988-90, corr. sec. 1990—). Republican. Methodist. Home and Office: 1601 Franklin Ave Mountain Home AR 72653-2041

EASLEY, LOYCE ANNA, painter; b. Weatherford, Okla., June 28, 1918; d. Thomas Webster and Anna Laura (Sanders) Rogers; m. Mack Easley, Nov. 17, 1939; children: June Elizabeth, Roger. BFA, U. Okla., 1943; postgrad., Art Students League, N.Y.C., 1947-49; 1977; postgrad., Santa Fe Inst. Fine Arts, 1985. Tchr. Pub. Sch., Okmulgee, Okla., 1946-47, Hobbs, N.Mex., 1947-49; tchr. painting N.Mex. Jr. Coll., Hobbs, 1965-80; tchr. Art Workshops in N.Mex., Okla., Wyoming. Numerous one-woman shows and group exhbns. in mus., univs. and galleries, including Gov.'s Gallery, Santa Fe, Selected Artists, N.Y.C., Roswell (N.Mex.) Mus., N.Mex. State U., Las Cruces, West Tex. Mus., Tex. Tech U., Lubbock; represented in permanent collections USAF Acad., Colorado Springs, Colo., Roswell Mus., Carlsbad (N.Mex.) Mus., Coll. Santa Fe, N.Mex. Supreme Ct, also other pvt. and pub. collections; featured in S.W. Art and Santa Fe mag., 1981, 82. Named Disting. Former Student, U. Okla. Art Sch., 1963; nominated for Gov.'s award in Art, N.Mex., 1988. Mem. N.Mex. Artists Equity (lifetime mem. 1963). Democrat. Presbyterian. Home: 10909 Country Club Dr NE Albuquerque NM 87111-6548

EASLEY, MARJORIE MAE, legal administrator; b. Fulton County, Ill., Mar. 6, 1935; d. Calvin Leo and Rita Jean (Henderson) Bainter; m. David L. Easley, Apr. 10, 1954 (dec. May 1992); children: James David, Joseph Leon, Julie Ann Easley Smick. Grad. high sch. Legal sec. Arthur D. Young, Atty., Lewistown, Ill., 1954-56, Martin M. Love, Atty., Lewistown, Ill., 1964-78; clk., recorder Fulton County, Lewistown, Ill., 1978-82; data processing cons. Fidlar Chambers Co., Moline, Ill., 1982-87; legal adminstr. Davis & Morgan Law Firm, Peoria, Ill., 1987-89, Husch & Eppenberger Law Firm, Peoria, Ill., 1989—. Mem. Ctrl. Ill. Legal Adminstrs. (treas. 1991-92), Nat. Inst. for Certifying Secs. (cert. profl. sec.). Republican. Presbyterian. Home: RR 4 Box 28 Lewistown IL 61542-9508 Office: Husch & Eppenberger Law Firm 101 SW Adams St # 800 Peoria IL 61602-1335

EASON, KATHLEEN S., management professional; b. Indpls., Feb. 27, 1954; d. C. A. and Marilynn E. (Mahin) Bowman; m. Richard C. Eason, Nov. 1, 1976 (Div. Nov. 1987); 1 child, Chris A. BA in Psychology, U. Tenn., 1984, MS in Bus. and Edn., 1989; postgrad., U. Okla. Adminstrv. clk. Dist. Office Social Security Adminstrn., Knoxville, Tenn.; gallery adminstrv. asst. Art & Architecture U. Tenn., Knoxville; rsch. asst. curriculum and instrn. U. Tenn., Knoxville; chief exec. officer, coord. World Future Soc. E. Tenn. 11 charter of/for 38 county seats, Knoxville, 1985-88; Notary Pub. Knox County, Tenn. Coord. voter registration, Knox County Adult Edn., Knoxville, 1986. Mem. NAFE, Internat. Mgmt. Assn., Am. Mgmt. Assn., Pi Lambda Theta.

EAST, CATHERINE SHIPE, retired government executive, consultant, writer; b. Barboursville, W.Va., May 15, 1916; d. U. G. and Bertha (Woody) Shipe; m. Charles D. East, July 2, 1937 (div. Aug. 1956); children: Mary Victoria, Elizabeth Rose. AB, Marshall U., 1943. Clk. to chief div. career svcs. U.S. Civil Svcs. Commn., Washington, 1939-63; exec. sec. presdl. adv. commn. on women Dept. Labor, Washington, 1963-75; dep. coord. Nat. Commn. on Observance Internat. Women's Yr. Dept. State, Washington, 1975-77; lobbyist Va. Women's Polit. Caucus, Arlington, 1977-79; coord. women's issues Anderson Campaign for Pres., Washington, 1979-80; coord. study on women's issues George Washington U., Washington, 1980-83; legis. dir. Nat. Women's Polit. Caucus, Washington, 1983-86; writer on women's movement Arlington, 1986—; lectr. in field. Author: (pamphlet) American Women, 1963-1983-2003, 1983; author annual reports to pres. of govt. adv. commns. Inducted into Nat. Women's Hall of Fame, Seneca Falls, N.Y., 1994. Mem. AAUW, ACLU, NOW, LWV, Nat. Fedn. Bus. and Profl. Women's Clubs, Nat. Abortion Rights Action League, Planned Parenthood. Mem. Unitarian Ch. Home: 5212 N 32d St Arlington VA 22207

EASTIN, DELAINE ANDREE, state legislator; b. San Diego, Aug. 20, 1947; d. Daniel Howard and Dorothy Barbara (Robert) Eastin; m. John Stuart Saunders, Sept. 17, 1972. BA in Polit. Sci., U. Calif., Davis, 1969; MA in Polit. Sci., U. Calif., Santa Barbara, 1971. Instr. Calif. Community Colls., various locations, 1971-79; acctg. mgr. Pacific Bell, San Francisco, 1979-84; corp. planner Pacific Telesis Group, San Francisco, 1984-86; assemblywoman Calif. State Legis., Sacramento, 1986—. Bd. dirs. CEWAER, Sacramento, 1988—; commr. Commn. on Status of Women, Sacramento, 1990—; mem. coun. City of Union City, Calif., 1980-86; chair Alameda County Libr. Commn., Hayward, Calif., 1981-86; planning commr. City of Union City, 1976-80; mem., pres. Alameda County Solid Waste Mgmt. Authority, Oakland, Calif., 1980-86. Named Outstanding Pub. Ofcl. Calif. Tchrs. Assn., 1988, Cert. of Appreciation Calif. Assn. for Edn. of Young Children, 1988-92, Legislator of the Yr. Calif. Media Libr. Educators, 1991, Calif. Sch. Bd. Assn., 1991, Ednl. Excellence award Calif. Assn. Counseling and Devel., 1992. Mem. Am. Bus. Women's Assn. (Outstanding Bus. Woman 1988), The Internat. Alliance (21st Century award 1990), World Affairs Coun., Commonwealth Club. Democrat. Home: 2140 Springwater Dr Fremont CA 94539-5956 Office: 3013 State Capital Sacramento CA 95814

EASTMAN, CAROLYN ANN, microbiology company executive; b. Potsdam, N.Y., Sept. 8, 1946; d. Frank Orvis and Irene (Rheaume) Eastman. BS in Biology, Nazareth Coll., 1968; AAS in Photography, Rochester Inst. Tech., 1976. Technician U. Rochester, N.Y., 1968-69; chemist Castle/Sybron, Rochester, 1969-79; owner, v.p. Sterilization Tech. Svcs., Rush, N.Y., 1979—; owner Fairfield Cosmetics, Rush, 1986—; ptnr. EFC Properties, 1983—; owner Microdispersions, Inc., 1988—, Medisperse L.P., 1988—; owner STS Ouotek Inc., 1991—, STS Particles Inc., 1991—, STS Biopolymers Inc., 1991. Contbr. articles to profl. jours.; patentee in field. Recipient various awards for photography, sculpture and painting. Mem. NOW, Assn. for Advancement of Med. Instrumentation, Sierra Club, Henrietta Art Club. Democrat. Roman Catholic. Home: 6 Genesee St Scottsville NY 14546-1310 Office: 7500 W Henrietta Rd Rush NY 14543-9790

EASTON, MICHELLE, foundation executive; b. Phila., Aug. 12, 1950; d. Glenn H. Jr. and Jeanne (Mulhall) Easton; m. Ron Robinson, Sept. 14, 1974; children: Ronald Jr., Daniel, Thomas. AA, BA, Briarcliff Coll., 1972; JD, Am. U., Washington, 1980. Bar: Va. 1981. Asst. to exec. dir. Young Ams. for Freedom, Sterling, Va., 1973-78; asst. to dir. pub. rels. Nat. Right to Work Com., Springfield, Va., 1978; legal asst. Nat. Right to Work Legal Def. Found., 1979; transition team mem. Office of Pres.-Elect, Equal Employment Opportunity Commn., Washington, 1980-81; atty. U.S. Dept. Justice, Washington, 1981; spl. asst. to gen. counsel U.S. Dept. Edn., Washington, 1981-83; pvt. vol. orgns. liaison officer, Africa Bur. Agy. for Internat. Devel., 1984; dir. Missing Children's Program Office of Juvenile Justice and Delinquency Prevention, U.S. Dept. Justice, 1985-87; dir. intergovtl. affairs U.S. Dept. Edn., Washington, 1987-88, dep. under sec. for intergovtl. and interagy. affairs, 1988-91; dir. Office Pvt. Edn., Washington, 1991-93; pres. Clare Boothe Luce Policy Inst., 1993—. Apptd. by Gov. Allen to Va. State Bd. Edn., Richmond, 1994—. Republican. Episcopalian.

EASTWOOD, SUSAN, medical scientific editor; b. Glens Falls, N.Y., Jan. 2, 1943; d. John J. and Della Eastwood; m. Raymond A. Berry. BA, U. Colo., 1964. Diplomate Bd. Editors in Life Scis. Adminstr. rsch. assoc. Depts. Psychol., Psychiat., Stanford (Calif.) U., 1965-68; prin., tchr. Colegio Capitan Correa, Arecibo, P.R., 1968-70; sr. editor dept. lab. medicine U. Calif., San Francisco, 1971-77, prin. analyst sci. publs. dept. neurol. surgery and Brain Tumor Rsch. Ctr., 1977—; cons. Medtronic Inc., Mpls., 1987—, March of Dimes Calif. Birth Defects Monitoring Program, Emeryville, Calif., 1988—. Collaborating editor: Current Neurosurgical Practice, 1984-91, Brain tumor biology and therapy, 1984; editor: Brain Tumors: A Guide, 1992; author: Guidelines on Research Data and Manuscripts, 1989. Recipient Pres. award Am. Med. Writers Assn., Bethesda, Md., 1989, Chancellors Outstanding Achievement award U. Calif., San Francisco, 1989, 94, Cert. of award Nat. Brain Tumor Found., 1992, Am. Soc. Journalists and Authors, 1992. Mem. European Assn. Sci. Editors, Internat. Fedn. Sci. Editors, Am. Med. Writers Assn., N.Y. Acad. Scis., Coun. of Biology Editors. Office: Neurosurgery Editorial Office 1360 9th Ave Ste 210 San Francisco CA 94122

EATHORNE, ROSEANNE M., geriatrics nurse; b. Lawrence, Mass., Oct. 23, 1942; d. Charles William Sr. and Bernadette (Ouellette) McHenry; m. Larry G. Eathorne, June 29, 1963; children: Kenneth, Brian, Michele, Kristina, William, Brenda, Marc, Alan, Marion, Patricia, Paul, Wayne, Eric. BS, Cen. Conn. State U., 1967; postgrad., Greater Hartford (Conn.) Community Coll., 1984-86, Manchester (Conn.) Community Coll., 1985; RN, SUNY, Albany, 1987. Cert. gerontological nurse. Nurse Riverside Health Care Ctr., East Hartford, Conn., 1981-86; nurse supr. Grafton County Home, Woodsville, N.H., 1986; staff nurse Cottage Hosp., Woodsville, 1987; nurse coord. Glencliff (N.H.) Home for the Elderly, 1988—. Mem. Nat. League for Nursing. Roman Catholic. Home: RFD 2 Box 240 French Pond Rd Woodsville NH 03785

EATON, AUDREY BARBARA, advertising executive; b. South Huntington, N.Y., Dec. 23, 1959; d. Warren William and Gladys (Petry) Umbach; m. Philip Alan Eaton, Oct. 27, 1984. BS, U. Fla., 1982. Graphic artist Fla. Sch. for the Deaf and Blind, St. Augustine, 1981-83; account exec. Fox and Fink, Inc., Tampa, Fla., 1982-83; media dir. Sawyer and Assocs. Agy.,

Sarasota, Fla., 1983-84; advt. exec., owner Creative Ink, Inc., Sarasota, 1984—. Active Big Bros./Big Sisters, Sarasota, 1986—; pub. rels. com. F.A.C.E. Charities, Sarasota, 1988—; bd. dirs. FAME Charities, Sarasota, 1985-86, Better Bus. Coun., Sarasota, 1988—, also pub. rels. chmn. Mem. Sarasota C. of C. (pub. rels. com. 1988—), SBV Advt. Fedn. (4th dist. ADDY award for Black and White Newspaper 1985-86), Soc. of Writers, Artists and Photographers, Profl. Advt. Frat. Office: Creative Ink Inc 1727 2nd St # 1 Sarasota FL 34236-8523

EATON, DORLA DEAN See KEMPER, DORLA DEAN

EATON, JANA SACKMAN, secondary school educator; b. Riverton, Wyo., Nov. 5, 1943; d. Kemper Eugene and Lois Barbara (Horn) Sackman; m. Leonard Middleton Eaton; children: Heather Grace, Brook Leonard. BA, Northwestern U., 1966; MEd, West Chester U., 1970. Cert. tchr. social studies, comm. Tchr. social studies Unionville (Pa.) H.S., 1969-73, 80—; cons. comm. West Chester, 1973-80. Mem. exec. com. Rape Crisis Coun., Chester County, Pa., 1973-74. Named Pa. State Tech. Tchr. of Yr., 1992. Mem. NOW (exec. com. 1970-74), AAUW, Unionville-Chadds Ford Edn. Assn. (pres. 1971-73, exec. com. 1992—), Delta Kappa Gamma. Home: 365 Firethorne Dr West Chester PA 19382 Office: Unionville H S 750 Unionville Rd Kennett Square PA 19348

EATON, JUDITH SHEILA, education council administrator; b. Trenton, N.J., June 6, 1942. BA in Philosophy, U. Mich., 1964, MA in History, 1966; PhD in Edn., Wayne State U., 1975. Claims investigator Mich. Civil Rights Commn., 1967-68; instr., asst. prof. natural sci. Wayne State U., Detroit, 1968-70; instr., asst. prof. history Orchard Ridge Campus Oakland C.C., 1970-74, admissions counselor Orchard Ridge Campus, 1974-75, dean adminstrv. svcs. Highland Lakes Campus, 1975-76; acad. v.p. Johnson County C.C., 1976-79; pres. C.C. of So. Nevada, 1979-83, C.C. of Phila., 1983-89; v.p. Am. Coun. on Edn., Washington, 1989-92; pres. Coun. for Aid to Edn., N.Y.C., 1992—; project com. mem. on Good Practice in Gen. Edn., 1988—; external adv. bd. Ctr. for Teaching Excellence, The Ohio State U., Columbus, 1991—; bd. dirs. Coun. for Aid to Edn., 1991—; adv. bd. mem. Corporate Philanthropy Report, 1992—; mem. Commn. on Govt. Rels., Am. Coun. on Edn., 1993—; bd. dirs. Allegheny Health, Edn. and Rsch. Found., 1993—. Editor: Women in Community Colleges, 1981, Colleges of Choice: The Enabling Impact of the Community College, 1988, Financing Nontraditional Students: A Seminar Report, 1992, Faculty and Transfer: Academic Partnerships At Work, 1992; author: The Unfinished Agenda: Higher Education and the 1980s, 1991, Strengthening Collegiate Education in Community Colleges, 1994; contbr. numerous articles to profl. jours. Mem. nat. adv. com. Black Higher Edn. and Black Colls. and Univs., 1979-82; mem. pres.'s adv. com. Assn. Cmty. Coll. Trustees, 1980-83; bd. dirs. Cmty. Coll. Polit. Action Com., 1987-89; presdl. com. on info. literacy ALA, 1987-89; nat. adv. bd. U. Mich. Cmty. Coll. Consortium, 1987—; bd. trustees Univ. of the Arts, 1988-91; mem. Pa. State Bd. Edn., 1987-94. Recipient Outstanding Young Women of Am. award, 1976, Thomas J. Peters Nat. Leadership award, 1989. Mem. Am. Coun. on Edn (chair, bd. dirs. 1988), Am. Assn. Cmty. and Jr. Colls. (chair, bd. dirs. 1984-85), League for the Humanities (chair, bd. dirs. 1980—), Pa. Assn. Colls. and Univs. (chair 1987-88), Pa. Commn. for Cmty. Colls. (chair 1986-87). Home: 110 E 57th St Apt 3F New York NY 10022-2601

EATON, KATHERINE GIRTON, retired library educator; b. St. Paul, Mar. 9, 1924; d. John Frances and Mary Ahleen (Peck) Girton; m. Burt Elliott Eaton, Oct. 18, 1947; children: John Girton, Marilee Eaton Warkentin, David Elliott. BA in Journalism, U. Minn., 1944; MS in Journalism, U. Oreg., 1952, MLS, 1968. Reporter Bakersfield Calif., 1945-46; women's editor Rochester (Minn.) Post Bulletin, 1946-47; legal sec. Broady Law Offices, St. Paul, 1949-51; editor Oreg. State System Higher Edn., Eugene, 1952-53; cons. Oreg. State Libr., Salem, 1968-70; head pub. affairs libr. U. Oreg., Eugene, 1970-85, assoc. prof. emerita, 1985—. Author and editor rsch. reports. Chmn. Lane County Mental Health Bd., Eugene, 1964-88, Lane County Libr. Bd., 1981-85, Eugene City Budget Com., 1988-92, Citizens for Lane County Librs., 1980—, Human Resources Planning Project, Lane County, 1986-89; founding bd. dirs. Passages, Lane County substance abuse residential program for offenders, 1990—; pres. Wilani coun. Camp Fire Inc., 1967-68, nat. bd. dirs., 1966-70, N.W. regional chmn. 1966-70; adv. bd. Oreg. State Mental Health, 1989—. Named Outstanding Young Woman, Eugene Jaycettes, 1956, Outstanding Women of Yr., Lane County Orgns., 1974; recipient Gulick, Seaton, Hiitina awards Camp Fire, Inc., 1959, 66, 71. Mem. AAUP (bd. dirs. U. Oreg. 1976-85, pres. 1977-78), ALA (coun. 1976-80), Oreg. Libr. Assn. (hon. life, pres. 1973-74), Nat. Coun. Planning Librs. (pres. 1978-79, 88-89), Pacific N.W. Libr. Assn. (editor. quar. 1985—), Assn. Oreg. Faculties (state bd. dirs. 1981-89, v.p. 1983-85), AAUW (pres. Oreg. 1975-77, pres. legal adv. fund 1981-85, nat. exec. v.p. 1981-85), LWV Oreg. (1st v.p. 1989-91, pres. 1991-93), LWV Lane County (pres. 1963-65), Oreg. Women's Rights Coalition (pres. 1994—). Democrat. Presbyterian.

EATON, NANCY RUTH LINTON, librarian, dean; b. Berkeley, Calif., May 2, 1943; d. Don Thomas and Lena Ruth (McClellan) Linton; m. Edward Arthur Eaton III, June 19, 1965 (div. 1980). AB, Stanford U., 1965; MLS, U. Tex., 1968, postgrad., 1969. Cataloger U. Tex. Library, Austin, 1968-71, head MARC unit, 1971-72, asst. to dir., 1972-74; automation librarian SUNY, Stony Brook, 1974-76; head tech. services Atlanta Pub. Library, 1976-82; dir. libraries U. Vt., Burlington, 1982-89; dean libr. svcs. Iowa State U., Ames, 1989—; bd. dirs. Ctr. for Rsch. Librs., 1988-92, chair, 1989-90; del. users' coun., mem. exec. com. Online Computer Libr. Ctr., Inc., Dublin, Ohio, 1980-82, 86-88, trustee, 1987—, chair bd. trustees 1992—; mgr. Nat. Agrl. Text Digitalizing Project, 1986-92; bd. dirs. New Eng. Libr. Network, 1987-89. Co-author: Optical Information Systems: Implementation Issues for Libraries, 1988.; co-editor: A Cataloging Sampler, 1971, Book Selection Policies in American Libraries, 1972; contbr. articles to profl. jours. U.S. Office of Edn. post-master's fellow, 1969; Dept. Edn. Title II-C grantee, 1985, 87, 88, Title II-D grantee, 1992-95. Mem. ALA, AAUW, Libr. and Info. Tech. Assn. (pres. 1984-85, bd. dirs. 1980-86), Assn. Rsch. Librs. (bd. dirs. 1994—), Iowa Libr. Assn. Democrat. Home: 3320 Kingman Rd Ames IA 50014 Office: Iowa State Univ 302 Park Ames IA 50011-2140

EATON, PAULINE, artist; b. Neptune, N.J., Mar. 20, 1935; d. Paul A. and Florence Elizabeth (Rogers) Friedrich; m. Charles Adams Eaton, June 15, 1957; children: Gregory, Eric, Paul, Joy. BA, Dickinson Coll., 1957; MA, Northwestern U., 1958. Lic. instr., Calif. Instr., Mira Costa Coll., Oceanside, Calif., 1980-82, Idyllwild Sch. Music and Arts, Calif., 1983—; juror, demonstrator numerous art socs. Recipient award Haywood (Calif.) Area Forum for the Arts, 1986. Exhibited one-woman shows Nat. Arts Club, N.Y.C., 1977, Designs Recycled Gallery, Fullerton, Calif., 1978, 80, 84, San Diego Art Inst., 1980, Spectrum Gallery, San Diego, 1981, San Diego Jung Ctr., 1983, Marin Civic Ctr. Gallery, 1984, R. Mondavi Winery, 1987; group shows include Am. Watercolor Soc., 1975, 77, Butler Inst. Am. Art, Youngstown, Ohio, 1977, 78, 79, 81, NAD, 1978, N.Mex. Arts and Crafts Fair, (Best in Show award) 1994, Corrales Bosque Gallery; represented in permanent collections including Butler Inst. Am. Art, St. Mary's Coll., Md., Mercy Hosp., San Diego, Sharp Hosp., San Diego, Redlands Hosp., Riverside, 1986; work featured in books: Watercolor, The Creative Experience, 1978, Creative Seascape Painting, 1980, Painting the Spirit in Nature, 1984, Exploring Painting (Gerald Brommer); author: Crawling to the Light, An Artist in Transition, 1987. Trustee San Diego Art Inst., 1977-78, San Diego Mus. Art, 1982-83. Recipient Best of Show award N.Mex. Arts and Crafts Fair, 1994. Mem. Nat. Watercolor Soc. (exhibited traveling shows 1978, 79, 83, 85), Rocky Mountain Watermedia Soc. (Golden award 1979, Mustard Seed award 1983), Nat. Soc. Painters in Acrylic and Casein (hon.), Watercolor West (Strathmore award 1979, Purchase award 1986), Soc. Experimental Artists (pres. 1989-92, Nautilus Merit award 1992), Marin Arts Guild (instr. 1984-87), San Diego Watercolor Soc. (pres. 1976-77, workshop dir. 1977-80), Artists Equity (v.p. San Diego 1979-81), San Diego Artists Guild (pres. 1982-83), N.Mex. Watercolor Soc. (Grumbacher award), Western Fedn. Watercolor Socs. (chmn. 1983, 3d prize 1982, Grumbacher Gold medal 1983), West Coast Watercolor Soc. (exhbns. chmn. 1983-86, pres. 1989-92), Eastbay Watercolor Soc. (v.p. 1988-90), Soc. Layerists in Multi-Media (bd. dirs. 1992—), Corrales Bosque Gallery (charter mem.). Democrat. Home: 68 Hop Tree Trl Corrales NM 87048-9613

EAVES, MARIA PERRY, realtor; b. Cluj, Romania; d. Nicholas Brudan and Ema (Filipescu) Perry; m. John Eaves, June 16, 1951; children: Bryan Perry, Susan Eaves Curry. BA, UCLA, 1945, MA, 1945; postgrad., Columbia U., 1947-51, U. London, 1953-54. Lic. realtor, Md., Va.; cert. environ inspector, rev. appraiser. Advt. and market analyst Foote, Cone & Belding, N.Y.C., 1948-49; media reaction analyst U.S. Dept. State, N.Y.C., 1950-53; dir. rsch. Free Europe Press, N.Y.C., 1955-56; info. officer, media reaction analyst USIA, Washington, 1956-58, rsch. cons., 1958-61; contractor market and pub. opinion cons. Market and Pub. Opinion Cons., Washington, 1969-72; realtor Colquitt Carruthers Inc., Bethesda, Md., 1972-81, Long & Foster Real Estate Inc., Potomac, Md. and McLean, Va., 1982—. One-woman paintings show at Nicosia, Cyprus; group shows include New Delhi (India), White Plains, N.Y., Bethesda, Md.; also pvt. collections. Vol. Gov. Nelson Rockefeller's Com. to Welcome UN Diplomats, N.Y.C., 1968, 69; mem. World Affairs Coun. Washington; Woodrow Wilson Info. Ctr. for Scholars, Washington; charter mem. Nat. Mus. Women in the Arts, Washington. Mem. NAFE, LWV, AAUW, Environ. Assessment Assn., Internat. Real Estate Inst. (registered), Nat. Assn. Realtors, Nat. Assn. Rev. Appraisers and Mortgage Underwriters, Md. Assn. Realtors, No. Va. Assn. Realtors, Women's Coun. Realtors, Montgomery County Assn. Realtors (life Sales award club). Democrat. Episcopalian. Home: 11312 Coral Gables Dr North Potomac MD 20878-3803 Office: Long & Foster Realtors 9812 Falls Rd Potomac MD 20854-3976

EAVES, SANDRA AUSTRA, social worker; b. Chgo., Aug. 30, 1960; d. Maris and Ilze (Kursulis) Muiznieks; m. Gerald Eaves, Oct. 7, 1989. BA, Northwestern U., 1982; MSW, Loyola U., Chgo., 1984. Social worker Chgo. Pub. Schs., 1982-83, Cook County Hosp., Chgo., 1983-84; pvt. practice Dr. Harry A. Croft & Assoc., PA, San Antonio, 1990—; social worker VA, San Antonio, 1984-91. Mem. NASW, Tex. Soc. fon Clin. Social Work, Coun. Nephrology Social Workers. Lutheran. Office: Dr Harry A Croft & Assoc 5430 Fredericksburg Rd Ste 510 San Antonio TX 78229-3539

EAVES-HERRERA, MARYRUTH, psychologist; b. Brawley, Calif., Mar. 1, 1958; d. Raymond Odell and Bernice Elenore (Knutson) Eaves; m. William Guillermo Herrera, Jan. 5, 1985. BA in Biology and Psychology, U. Calif., San Diego, 1982; MA in Psychology, U. Colo., Colorado Springs, 1987; PhD in Psychology, U. Colo., Boulder, 1991. Lic. psychologist, Colo. Rsch. asst. Salk Inst., La Jolla, Calif., 1980-84; emergency psychiat. svcs. worker Boulder County Mental Health Ctr., 1988-90; forensic psychologist Colo. Mental Health Inst., Inst. for Forensic Psychiatry, Pueblo, 1991-94; pvt. practice Affiliated Therapists of So. Colo., Inc., 1994—. Mem. APA, Am. Assn. Christian Counselors, Christian Assn. for Psychol. Studies, Guidians Internat. Aux. (chaplain 1992-94), Pueblo Bike 'n Dine Cycling Club (sec. 1994). Christian Ch. Home: 1088 S Lynx Dr Pueblo West CO 81007

EBBECKE, MICHELLE ANN, rental company executive; b. Wilkes Barre, Pa., Nov. 27, 1958; d. Theodore Lee and Cecelia Jean (Parr) Scott; m. Frederick William Ebbecke, Oct. 17, 1987; children: Frederick, Sandra, Victoria, Robert, Thomas, Candice, Michael Ann, Matthew. Grad. high sch., Middletown, N.Y. Clk., typsit Bd. Edn., Middletown, 1975-76; sec., co-owner Fred's Auto Clinic, Pasadena, Tex., 1980—; co-owner U-Haul Dealership, Pasadena, Tex., 1991—. Mem. NAt. Fedn. Ind. Bus., Tex. Notary Pub. Assn. (notary), Ind. Order Foresters. Republican. Roman Catholic. Office: Fred's Auto Clinic 2041 Allen Genoa Pasadena TX 77502

EBBEN, JOY MARIE, human factors/ergonomics psychologist; b. Stanley, Wis., Nov. 11, 1952; d. Delton Joseph and Marie Elizabeth (Benzschawel) Ebben. BA, U. Wis., Eau Claire, 1974, MS, 1977; MA, Calif. State U., Northridge, 1984; PhD, Claremont Coll., 1989. cert. profl. ergonomics. Sch. psychologist Tucson Pub. Schs., Tucson, 1977-80; human factors specialist Hughes Aircraft Co., Canoga Park and Fullerton, Calif., 1982-93; ind. cons. Alto Loma, Calif., 1986—; human factors and ergonomics specialist IAC Industries, Brea, Calif., 1993—. Mem. APA, Human Factors and Ergonomics Soc., Am. Soc. Safety Engrs.

EBBERTS, DIANE KATHRYN, state administrator; b. Oct. 25, 1952. BS, U. Md., 1974, MA, 1976; postgrad., Howard U., 1977-81. Tech. cons. Hallmark Films, Owings Mills, Md., 1982-83; staff psychologist Rosewood Ctr., Owings Mills, 1976-84, residential svcs. administr., 1984-85, asst. to the supt., 1985-87; exec. dir. state coordinating coun. Residential Placement of Handicapped Children, Balt., 1987-90; dir. Gov.'s Office for Individuals with Disabilities, Balt., 1991—. Scholar State Senatorial, Severn Towne Club, Margaret Boone Moss; recipient Danforth award for Leadership, 1970. Home: 8009 Silver Fox Dr Glen Burnie MD 21061

EBBING, ELIZABETH ANN, art educator; b. Zanesville, Ohio, Sept. 26, 1944; d. Lester Ray and Mary Elizabeth (Claudy) Stiers; m. Gary Michael Ebbing, Oct. 24, 1970; children: Michael Aaron, Nicholas Allan. BFA, Ohio U., 1967; MS in Edn., U. Dayton, 1992. Cert. art tchr., Ohio. Art instr. Sidney (Ohio) City Schs., 1966-67, Wooster (Ohio) City Schs., 1967-70, Wapakoneta (Ohio) City Schs., 1971—. Exhibited in group shows at Zanesville Art Inst., 1964, Wapakoneta Art Guild, 1972-74; actress Encore Theater, Lima, 1974; actress, dir. Wapakoneta Theatre Guild, 1971-75. Sec. Black Swamp Potters Guild, Lima, Ohio, 1976-77; office chmn. St. Jude Telethon, Lima, 1977—. Partnership grantee Apollo Career Ctr., 1991. Mem. AAUW, Wapakoneta Edn. Assn. (membership co-chair 1987), Western Ohio Art Edn. Assn. (connector 1992-94), Beta Sigma Phi (v.p. 1990-91). Lutheran. Home: 1382 Fetter Rd Lima OH 45801

EBERLE, HEIDI FRANCES, assets protection manager; b. Breckenridge, Minn., Dec. 3, 1963; d. Jerrold Wayne and Shirley Ann (O'Keefe) Scheiterlein; m. Timothy Warren Newbury, Feb. 13, 1984 (div.); 1 child, Alyssa Rae; m. Joel Alfons Eberle, May 21, 1994. BA, N.D. State U., 1991. Assets protection mgr. Target Stores, Coon Rapids, Minn., 1991—; com. mem. Diversity Task Force, Minn., 1992—. Com. mem. PTA, Plymouth, Minn., 1991—. Mem. NAFE. Democrat. Roman Catholic. Home: 13794 Orchid St Andover MN 55304 Office: Target Stores 8600 Spring Brook Dr Minneapolis MN 55433

EBERLEIN, DORIS JEAN, former association executive; b. Ann Arbor, Mich., Apr. 16, 1928; d. Ervin Fred and Alice Merritt (Farmer) Fulkerson; m. Arthur Lombard Eberlein, July 11, 1947; children: Thomas Lombard, Ann Mary, James Arthur, Jean Marie. BS in Edn., U. Wis., 1951. Adult program dir. YWCA, Wausau, Wis., 1951-52. Pres. vol. bd. Wausau Hosp., 1972-73, bd. dirs., 1973-81; founder, bd. dirs. Wausau Child Care, 1969-74. Mem. U.S. Women's Curling Assn. (pres. 1984-85), Wausau C. of C. (bd. dirs. 1980-83). Universalist.

EBERLE-MCCARTHY, KAREN, foreign language educator; b. Rockville Center, N.Y., Dec. 23, 1946; d. Walter and Olga (Sokol) Eberle; m. John McCarthy, Feb. 21, 1975. BA, Ohio Wesleyan U., 1968; MA, NYU, Madrid, 1969; PhD, SUNY, Albany, 1981. Instr. SUNY, New Paltz, 1969-73; adj. instr. SUNY, Albany, 1973-75, Siena Coll., Loudonville, N.Y., 1975-76; from instr. to prof. Mt. St. Mary Coll., Newburgh, N.Y., 1976—. Co-author: Pastoral Spanish, 1992. Fulbright scholar, 1979-80. Mem. MLA, NOW, Assn. Tchrs. Spanish and Portuguese, Instituto Internacional de Literatura, Hudson River Sloop Club. Office: Mt St Mary Coll Aquinas Hall Newburgh NY 12550

EBERLEY, HELEN-KAY, opera singer, classical record company executive, poet; b. Sterling, Ill., Aug. 3, 1947; d. William Elliott and P. (Conneely) E. MusB, Northwestern U., 1970, MusM, 1971. Chmn., pres. Eberley-Skowronski, Inc., Evanston, Ill., 1973-92; founder H.K.E. Enterprises, 1993—, pres., 1993—; artistic coord. Eberley-Skowronski, Inc., 1973-92; founder EB-SKO Prodns., 1976, tchrs., coach, 1976—; exec. dir., performance cons. E-S Mgmt., 1985-92; featured artist Honors Concert, Northwestern U., 1970, Master Class and guest lectr. various colls. and univs.; numerous TV and radio talk show appearances and interviews. Operatic debut in Peter Grimes, Lyric Opera, Chgo., 1974; starred in: Cosi Fan Tutte, Le Nozze Di Figaro, Dido and Aeneas, La Boheme, Faust, Tosca, La Traviata, Falstaff, Don Giovanni, Brigadoon, others; jazz appearances with Duke Ellington, also with Dave Brubeck; performing artist Oglebay Opera Inst., Wheeling, W.Va., 1968, WTTW TV/PBS, Chgo., 1968; solo star in: Continental Bank Concerts, 1981-89, United Airlines-Schubert, Schumann, Brahms, Mendelssohn, Fauré, Mozart, Duparc/Wolf, Supersta. WFMT Radio, Chgo., 1982—; featured artist with North Shore Concert Band, 1989; starring artist South Bend Symphony, 1990, Mo. symphony Soc., 1990, Milw. Symphony, 1990; producer-annotator Gentleman Gypsy, 1978, Skowronski: Strauss and Szymanowski, 1979, One Sonata Each: Franck and Szymanowski, 1982; starring artist-exec. producer Separate But Equal, 1976, All Brahms, 1977, Opera Lady, 1978, Eberley Sings Strauss, 1980, Helen-Kay Eberley: American Girl, 1983, Helen-Kay Eberley: Opera Lady II, 1984; performed Am. and Can. Nat. Anthems for Chgo. Cubs Baseball Team, 1977-83, Chgo. Bears Football, 1977; also star in numerous concert recital and symphony appearances, Europe, Can., U.S; author: Angel's Song, 1994, The Magdaleva Poems, 1995. Vol. Christian Indsl. League, Evanston Shelter for Battered Women, Rape Victim Advocate; mem. Mayor's founding com. Evanston Arts Coun., 1974-75; judge Ice-skating Competition, Wilmette (Ill.) Park Dist., 1985-88; fin. chmn. Chgo. Youth Orch., 1974-77, bd. dirs., 1973-77; bd. dirs. Ctr. for Voice, 1994—. Recipient Creative and Performing Arts award Ind. Jr. Miss. and South Bend Jr. Miss, 1965, Milton J. Cross award Met. Opera Guild, 1968; prize winner Met. Opera. Nat. Auditions, 1968; F.K. Weyerhauser scholar Met. Opera, 1967. Mem. People for Ethical Treatment of Animals, Am. Soc. for Prevention of Cruelty to Animals, Am. Guild Mus. Artists, Internat. Platform Assn., Whale Adoption Project, Amnesty Internat., Environ. Def. Fund, Doris Day Animal Found., Humane Soc., Greenpeace. Clubs: St. Mary's Acad. Alumnae Assn., Delta Gamma. Office: HKE Enterprises 1726 Sherman Ave Evanston IL 60201-3713

EBERSOLE, PATRICIA SUE, advertising executive, design educator; b. Poughkeepsie, N.Y., Nov. 6, 1952; d. Edward and Virginia Mae (Vanderof) E. AAS, Dutchess Community Coll., Poughkeepsie, 1974; student, Art Ctr. Coll. of Design, 1976-77; BS, SUNY, 1981; MA, Syracuse U., 1993. Graphic artist So. Dutchess News, Wappingers Falls, N.Y., 1974; asst. illustrator Jarvis Studio, Westwod, Calif., 1975-78; freelance illustrator Poughkeepsie, N.Y., 1978—; graphic dir. Ulster County Coun. for the Arts, Kingston, N.Y., 1979; art dir. Diversified Creative Svcs., Kingston, 1979; graphic designer Advertiser's Graphic Svcs., Poughkeepsie, 1981-82; pres. Ebersole Graphiks, Poughkeepsie, 1982—; adj. instr. Dutchess Community Coll., 1980-87. Recipient Recognition award IBM Corp., 1987, Cert. of Excellence Silver award Strathmore Graphics Gallery, 1988, 90, Desi award Graphi Design, 1984, 88, Excellence award Pritning Industries of Am., 1988, Activtities award Nat. Assn. for Campus Activtities, 1985, Gold and Silver awards HUAMA ECLAT, 1989, Nat. Calendar Bronze award 1991, Award of Excellent, Am. Econ. Devel. Coun., 1992, Notable Merit award FPG, 1992. Mem. Graphic Artists Guild N.Y., Greater So. Dutchess C. of C. Office: Ebersole Graphiks 9 High Ridge Rd Hopewell Junction NY 12533-5560

EBERT, ANN MARIE, pharmacist; b. San Francisco, Jan. 13, 1964; d. Charles H. and Inez D. (Lansing) Nutt; m. Steven C. Ebert, Aug. 27, 1994. PharmD, U. Minn., 1988. Pharmacy resident in pediat. St. Paul Children's Hosp., 1988-89; clin. pharmacy specialist-pediat. and perinatology Meriter Hosp., Madison, Wis., 1989—. Mem. Am. Soc. Hosp. Pharmacists, Am. Coll. Clin. Pharmacy, Wis. Soc. of Hosp. Pharmacists (chair program com.), Wis. Assn. Perinatal Care.

EBERT, BARBARA A., health facility administrator; b. LaCrosse, Wis.; d. Clyde and Virginia (Amundson) Pophal; children: Jaime Jonathan, David Michael. Diploma in nursing, Madison Gen. Hosp. Sch. Nursing, 1977; BS in Bus., Edgewood Coll., 1992; MBA, Cardinal Stritch Coll., 1995. RN, Wis. Supr. nursing U. Wis., Madison, 1977—; mem. adv. bd. Madison Area Tech. Coll. Mem. Assn. Oper. Room Nurses, Sigma Theta Tau. Office: 600 Highland Ave Madison WI 53792-3212

EBERT, PAMELA MARY, elementary education educator; b. Columbus, Ohio, Dec. 17, 1949; d. Wayne and Geraldine (Conaway) Wentz; m. Gary A. Ebert, Aug. 5, 1972; children: Carrie, Amanda, Brian. BS in Edn., Ashland U., 1972. Art tchr. K-6 St. Leo Sch., Cleve., 1972-73; art tchr. K-8 Rocky River (Ohio) Sch., 1973-78; music tchr. K-8 St. Christopher, Rocky River, 1979-90; music tchr. K-7 St. Bernadette, Westlake, Ohio, 1990—; leader recreation program Rocky River Recreation, 1974-80; tchr. Bay Crafts, Bay Village, 1975-76. Active Bay Jr. Women, Bay Village, 1976-83; leader Girl Scouts Am., Bay Village, 1980-85; pres. St. Raphael Guild, Bay Village, 1983—; sec. Welcome Wagon, Bay Village; group chair United Way, 1988—; mem. ways and means com. Westshone Pre-sch., 1985—. Mem. Home and Sch. Assn. (mem. ways and means com. 1983—, v.p.), Bay Soccer Club, Magnificent Mothers Club. Republican. Roman Catholic. Home: 153 Kensington Cir Bay Village OH 44140-1060

EBINGER, MARY RITZMAN, pastoral counselor; b. Reading, Pa., Nov. 23, 1929; d. Michael Erwin and Daisy Mae (Shaeffer) R.; m. Warren Ralph Ebinger, Aug. 11, 1951; children: Lee, Lori, Jonathan. BA, North Cen. Coll., Naperville, Ill., 1951; MS, Loyola Coll., Balt., 1981; grad. student, Wesley Theol. Sem., 1976, Cath. U., 1977. Cert. nat. counselor Dept. of Md. Health and Mental Hygiene, cert. nat. counselor Am. Assn. Pastoral Counselors. Elem. tchr. Naperville Washington Sch., 1952-54; dir. adult work Millian Ch., Rockville, Md., 1974-76; pastoral counselor Washington Pastoral Counselors, 1976-81; assoc. dir. Balt. Conf. Pastoral Care and Counseling, Wheaton, Md., 1990—; mem. adj. faculty psychology Frederick (Md.) C.C., 1982-87, Anne Arnold (Md.) C.C., 1988-90; pres. Wesley Guild Wesley Theol. Seminary, Washington, 1987-89; del. gen. conf. U. Meth. Ch., 1988, 92. Author: I Was Sick and You Visited Me, 1976, Does Anybody Care, 1978. Pres. Ch. Women United, Springfield, Ill., 1969-71; chmn. Episcopacy com. United Meth. Ch., Balt., 1988-90; del. gen. and jurisdictional conf. United Meth. Ch., 1988, 92. Recipient Disting. Alumnus award North Cen. Coll., 1990, Loyola Coll., 1991, Two Thousand Women of Achievement award Dartmouth Eng. Mus., 1969. Mem. Am. Assn. Counseling and Devel., Am. Assn. Pastoral Counseling (cert., Atlantic region chmn. theol. and social concerns 1988—). Home: 6 St Ives Dr Severna Park MD 21146-1430 Office: Balt Conf Pastoral Care and Counseling 5124 Greenwich Ave Baltimore MD 21229-2393

EBITZ, ELIZABETH KELLY, lawyer; b. LaPorte, Ind., June 9, 1950; d. Joseph Monahan and Ann Mary (Barrett) Kelly; m. David MacKinnon Ebitz, Jan. 23, 1971 (div. 1981). AB with honors, Smith Coll., 1972; JD cum laude, Boston U., 1975. Bar: Maine 1979, Mass 1975, U.S. Supreme Ct 1982, U.S. Dist. Ct. Mass. 1976, U.S. Dist. Ct. Maine 1979, U.S. Ct. Appeals (1st cir.) 1976. Law clk. Boston Legal Assistance Project, 1973-75; law clk., assoc. Law Offices of John J. Thornton, Boston, 1974-76; ptnr. Ebitz & Zurn, Northampton, Mass., 1976-79; assoc. Gross, Minsky, Mogul & Singal, Bangor, Maine, 1979-80; pres. Elizabeth Kelly Ebitz, P.A., Bangor, 1980-92; pres. Ebitz & Thornton, P.A., 1993—. Pres. Greater Bangor Rape Crisis Bd., 1983-85; bd. dirs. Greater Bangor Area Shelter, 1985-92, 93—, Maine Women's Lobby, 1986-89, No. Maine Bread for the World, 1987-90; bd. dirs. Am. Heart Assn., Maine, 1989—, chair-elect, 1991-93, chair, 1993—; mem. various peace, feminist and hunger orgns., Bangor, 1982—. Named Young Career Woman of Hampshire County, Nat. Bus. and Profl. Women, Northampton, 1979. Mem. ABA, Assn. Trial Lawyers Am., Sigma Xi. Democrat. Roman Catholic. Home: 111 Maple St Bangor ME 04401-4031 Office: 15 Columbia St PO Box 641 Bangor ME 04402

EBNER, DIANE MARIE, secondary education educator; b. Canton, Ohio, Dec. 17, 1954; d. Robert Joseph and Caroline Elizabeth (Vincent) Fallot; m. Mark Shannon Kelly, Sept. 4, 1977 (div. Nov. 1979); m. James Joseph Ebner Jr., Feb. 27, 1982. BA, Malone Coll., 1977; MA, U. Akron, 1986. Profl. tchg. cert. Tchr. Brown Local Schs., Malvern, Ohio, 1977—; drug-free grant coord. Brown Local Schs., Malvern, 1989-94, Teen Inst./Prevent and Neutralize Drugs/Alcohol advisor, 1989-94; power pen writing coach Malvern (Ohio) H.S., 1989-94. Sunday sch. tchr. Indian Run Christian Ch., East Canton, Ohio, 1976-94, children's ch. skit team, 1990-94. Mem. NEA, Ohio Edn. Assn., Malvern Edn. Assn. Republican. Office: Malvern High Sch 401 W Main St Malvern OH 44644-9482

ECHOLS, IVOR TATUM, educator, assistant dean; b. Oklahoma City, Dec. 28, 1919; d. Israel E. and Katie (Bingley) Tatum; AB, U. Kans., 1942; postgrad. (A.R.C. scholar) U. Nebr., 1945-46; MS in Social Work (Nat. Urban League fellow, Porter R. Lee fellow), Columbia, 1952, postgrad. (NIMH fellow), U. So. Calif., 1961-62, D.S.W., 1968; m. Kenneth Johnston,

Dec. 28, 1948 (div. June 1951); 1 child, Kalu Helene; m. 2d, Sylvester J. Echols, June 13, 1954 (div. 1976); 1 child, Kim Arnett. Tchr. social studies high sch., Holdenville, Okla., 1942-43, Geary, Okla., 1943-45; caseworker A.R.C., Chgo., 1946-47; resident group worker, Dosoris House for Teen-Age Girls, Community Svcs. Soc., N.Y.C., 1950-51; supr. group work Walnut Grove Ctr. Neighborhood Clubs, Oklahoma City, 1948-51; program dir. Camp Lookout YWCA, Denver, 1951; dir. program svcs. Presbyn. Neighborhood Svcs., Detroit, summer 1960, supr. group work Merrill-Palmer Inst., Detroit, 1951-70; asst. dir. Merrill-Palmer Camp, Dryden, Mich., 1951-59; prof. Sch. Social Work, U. Conn., West Hartford, 1970-89, also asst. dean; ret., 1989; del. Inter-Univ. Consortium of Social Devel., Hong Kong, 1980; chairperson Conn. adv. com. U.S. Commn. Civil Rights. Mem. Ad Hoc Com. Citizens Concerned with Equal Ednl. Opportunity, Detroit, 1964—; cons. to N.E.A. Conf. Family Camping Washington, 1959, ednl. film Scott Paper Co., Phila., 1963, 64; summer study skills project Presbyn. Ch. Bd. Nat. Missions, Knoxville, Tenn., 1965—; sec. United Neighborhood Ctrs. Am.; pres. Protestant Community Svcs., Detroit, 1969-70; trustee Conn. Energy Found., 1987-92; commr. Conn. Hist. Commn., 1986—. Recipient Educator Human Rights award UN Assn. , 1987, Sojourner Truth award Detroit chpt. Nat. Assn. Negro Bus. and Profl. Women, 1969, UN Assn. award for Edn. and Women's Rights, 1987, Maria R. Stewart Women's Rights award Conn. Women's Ednl. and Legal Found, 1991, Outstanding Women award U. Conn., 1991; named Conn. Social Worker of Year, 1979. Mem. Nat. Assn. Colored Women's Clubs (participant White House Conf. on Children and Youth 1960), A.M.E. Ministers Wives, Acad. Certified Social Workers, Delta Sigma Theta. Mem. A.M.E. Ch. Home: 51 Chestnut Dr Windsor CT 06095-1113 Office: U Conn 1800 Asylum Ave West Hartford CT 06117-2600

ECHOLS, MARY LOUISE BROWN, elementary school educator, secondary school educator; b. Milligan, Fla., Nov. 13, 1906; d. Edward Reese and Barbara Alabama Brown; m. Louie Samuel Echols Jr., June 18, 1932 (dec. Oct. 1984); 1 child, Louie Samuel III. AB, cert. in spoken English, Fla. State Coll. for Women, 1928; MEd, U. Fla., 1953, postgrad. Cert. elem. tchr., English tchr., biology tchr., sci. tchrs., Fla. (life); cert. jr. coll. instr. Tchr. Greenville (Fla.) High Sch., 1928-29, Madison (Fla.) High Sch., 1929-30, Dixie County High Sch., Cross City, Fla., 1930-37, 41-43, Gainesville (Fla.) High Sch., 1951-66; agronomist technician U. Fla., Gainesville, 1946; coord. lang. arts Alachua County Sch. Bd., Gainesville, 1966-67, reading specialist, 1967-68, 1969-71; reading coord., 1971-72; ret. Alachua County Sch. Bd., Gainesville, 1972; mem. leadership res. pool Bd. Pub. Instruction, Gainesville, 1969—; compiler curriculum guide lang. arts Alachua County Sch. Bd., Gainesville, 1966; mem. team teaching unit. Vol. hospice Light Up a Life, Gainesville, 1989-90; active Friends of Libr. Alachua County; contbr., active Matheson Hist. Ctr., Gainesville. Mem. AAUW (telephone com.), Alachua County Ret. Tchrs., Fla. Ret. Educators, Gainesville Woman's Club, Nat. Ret. Tchrs. Assn., Gainesville Garden Club (assoc.), Fla. State U. Emeritus Club, Phi Kappa Phi, Delta Kappa Gamma. Democrat. Methodist. Home: 710 NE 11th Ave Gainesville FL 32601

ECK, DOROTHY FRITZ, state senator; b. Sequim, Wash., Jan. 23, 1924; d. Ira Edward and Ida (Hokanson) Fritz; B.S. in Secondary Edn., Mont. State U., 1961, M.S. in Applied Sci., 1966; m. Hugo Eck, Dec. 16, 1942 (dec. Feb. 1988); children: Laurence, Diana. Mgr. property mgmt. bus., 1955—; conf. coord. Am. Agrl. Econs. Assn., 1967-68; state-local coord. Office of Gov. Mont., Helena, 1972-77; mem. Mont. State Senate, 1981—; mem. Mont. Environ. Quality Council, 1981-87. Bd. dirs. Methodist Youth Fellowship, 1960-64, Mont. Council for Effective Legislature, 1977-78, Rocky Mountain Environ. Council, 1982—; del., Western v.p. Mont. Constl. Conv., 1971-72; chmn. Gov.'s Task Force on Citizen Participation, 1976-77; mem. adv. com. No. Rockies Resource and Tng. Center (now No. Lights Inst.), 1979-81. Recipient Outstanding Alumna award Mont. State U., 1981, Centennial Equity award, 1989. Mem. LWV (state pres. 1967-70), Common Cause, Nat. Women's Polit. Caucus. Democrat. Office: State Senate State Capitol Helena MT 59620*

ECKARDT, GLADYS EVANGELINE (MRS. KARL PAUL KONRAD ECKARDT), librarian; b. Hartland, N.Y., Sept. 7, 1912; d. Isaac John and Flora Caroline (Hofmeister) Beach; student U. Buffalo, 1930-32; m. Karl Paul Konrad Eckardt, Oct. 19, 1940; 1 dau., Susan (Mrs. Edward Misiewicz). BA, U. Rochester, 1934; MLS, Rutgers State U., 1958. Dir. Wood-Ridge (N.J.) Pub. Library, 1956-59, Rutherford (N.J.) Pub. Library, 1959-85; ref. librarian, Jane Bancroft Cook Library, U. South Fla., Sarasota, 1986—. Trustee Wood-Ridge Pub. Libr., 1954-56. Mem. Am., N.J. (sec. 1964-65, chmn. N.J. insts. 1968), Bergen-Passaic (pres. 1964-66), N.Y. library assn., Pub. Rels. Coun., Bergen County Small Librs. (v.p. 1963), Rutgers U. Alumni Assn., Friends of Library. Club: Rutherford Women's Coll. Office: 7236 Pennsylvania Ave Sarasota FL 34243-1704

ECKELKAMP, CAROL KAY, county official; b. Washington, Mo., Sept. 27, 1944; d. Richard Lauchstaedt and Doris Helen (Pohlmann) Van Leer; m. James Anthony Eckelkamp, Sept. 12, 1964; children: James, Cindy, Christy, John, Carol Lea. Student, U. Mo., 1963, East Ctrl. Coll., 1991. Bookkeeper Fraser Shoe Co., Union, Mo., 1963-65; final insp. new homes Union; bookkeeper Great Plains Gas Co., Washington, 1987-91; pub. adminstr. Franklin County, Union, 1992—. Past sec. ch. bd. St. Mary's Ch., Moselle, Mo., 1992, 93; project leader 4-H, Union; sec. Parent Tchr., Union, Franklin County Dem. Ctrl. Com., 1993-94. Mem. Am. Legion Aux., Franklin County Dem. Club (chaplin 1993-94). Roman Catholic. Office: Franklin County Pub Adminstr PO Box 503 Union MO 63084

ECKELKAMP, MARYLYN, psychologist; b. Ottawa, Ont., Can., Feb. 20, 1946; came to U.S., 1960; d. Edward Joffre and Irene Ceclia (Madigan) Greenway; m. Vincent C.J. Eckelkamp, May 30, 1964; children: Lisa Ann, Vincent Edward. AA, Colo. Women's Coll., Denver, 1964; BA, U. So. Fla., 1974, MA, 1976. Nat. cert. sch. psychologist; lic. marriage and family therapist, Nev. Tchr. remedial Big Bend C.C., Afcent, The Netherlands, 1977-78; edn. counselor Civil Svc., Afcent, The Netherlands, 1978-80; psychologist Clark County Sch. Dist., Las Vegas, Nev., 1980—; intern in marriage and family therapy Family Cousneling Ctr., Las Vegas, 1988-90, HCA Montevista Hosp., Las Vegas, 1986-90, group leader eating disorders, 1987-89; pvt. practice marriage and family therapy, Las Vegas, 1991—. Parenting group leader schs. and chs., Las Vegas, 1980—. Mem. Am. Assn. Marriage and Family Therapists, Nat. Assn. Sch. Psychologists, Nev. Assn. Sch. Psychologists (pres. 1980—). Roman Catholic.

ECKER, SUSAN RUTH, mechanical engineer; b. Glen Cove, N.Y.; d. Adam and May Ecker. BSME, Lehigh U., 1984. Design engr. Leo A. Daly Co., Washington, 1985-88; staff engr. CUH2A, Princeton, N.J., 1988-90; sr. engr. Parsons Main, Inc., Boston, 1990—. Editorial adv. bd. Plumbing Engr. Mag., 1994—; contbr. articles to profl. publs. Mem. ASME, Am. Soc. Plumbing Engrs. Office: Parsons Main Inc Prudential Ctr Boston MA 02199

ECKERT, ANN MELISSA, insurance agent; b. Syracuse, N.Y., Mar. 4, 1948; d. Arthur Irving and Emily Ruth (Lavine) Goldman; m. Barton Mayer Eckert, Nov. 19, 1972 (div. Mar. 1981); 1 child, Andrew Evan. Student, Parsons Coll., 1966-67, Cazenovia Jr. Coll., 1967-68, Syracuse U., 1968. Accredited adviser of ins. Underwriter Liberty Mut. Ins. Co., Silver Spring, Md., 1968-70, H. Gabriel Murphy & Co., Inc., Washington, 1970-72, Bogley, Harting & Betts, Inc., Rockville, Md., 1972-75; exec. sec. Bechtel Corp., Rockville, 1975-76; account exec. Max Holtzman, Inc., Chevy Chase, Md., 1980-86; ops. mgr. Levy Assocs., Inc., Rockville, 1986-88; comml. mktg. mgr. Brendler Ins. Agy., Inc., Rockville, 1988—. Mem. Nat. Assn. Ins. Women, Ins. Agts. Assn. (pres.), Ins. Women Montgomery and Prince George's County, Vanguard-Hadassah Orgn. (steering com. 1993). Office: Brendler Ins Agy Inc 5515 Security Ln Ste 600 Rockville MD 20852-5003

ECKERT, GERALDINE GONZALES, language professional, educator, entrepreneur; b. N.Y.C., Aug. 5, 1948; d. Albert and Mercedes (Martinez) Gonzales; m. Robert Alan Eckert, Apr. 1, 1972; children: Lauren Elaine, Alison Elizabeth. BA, Ladycliff Coll., Highland Falls, N.Y., 1970; student, U. Valencia, Spain, 1968; MA, N.Y.U., 1971; student, Instituto de Cultura Hispanica, Madrid, 1970-71. Tchr. Spanish Clarkstown High Sch. N. (N.Y.), 1971-73, Rambam Torah Inst., Beverly Hills, Calif., 1973-75; translator City of Beverly Hills, 1976-83; edn. cons. Los Angeles County of Calif. Dept. Forestry, Capistrano Beach, 1982-84; lang. services and protocol Los Angeles Olympic Organizing Com., 1983-84; pension adminstr. Pension Architects, Inc., Los Angeles, 1984-87; instr. El Camino Coll., Torrance, Calif., 1987-88, Santa Monica (Calif.) Coll., 1975—; owner, pres. Bilingual Pension Cons., L.A., 1987-89; bd. dirs. Institute for Hispanic Cultural Studies, Los Angeles; spl. asst. to Internat. Olympic Com., Lausanne, Switzerland, 1983—. V.p. Notre Dame Acad. Assoc., West L. A., 1987—; mem. L.A. March of Dimes Ambassadors Group, 1987; co-founder, pres. Blind Cleaning Express, L.A., 1989—; bd. dirs. Inst. Hispanic Cultural Studies, L.A., 1984-89; spl. asst. to pres. Internat. Olympic Com. Lausanne, Switzerland, 1983—. Democrat. Roman Catholic. Clubs: Five Ring, Los Angeles, Friends of Sport, Amateur Athletic Found., Los Angeles. Office: 8885 Venice Blvd Ste 103 Los Angeles CA 90034-6387

ECKERT, OPAL EFFIE CALVERT, retired journalism educator; b. Bolckow, Mo., Mar. 19, 1905; d. Price Wallingford and Mary Jane (Pittsenbarger) Calvert; m. Thomas H. Eckert, June 19, 1929 (dec.). BS in Edn., Northwest Mo. State U., 1928, AB, 1944, MS in Edn., 1963. Instr. prin. Butler, Bolckow & Pickering, Mo., 1928-44; instr., dir. pub. Maryville (Mo.) High Sch., 1944-65; freelance writer, feature writer, columnist, reporter Maryville Daily Forum, St. Joseph, News-Press Gazette, Mo., 1955-93; dir. journalism workshops N.W. Mo. State U., Maryville, 1963-74; instr. English, journalism, chmn. Northwest Mo. State Univ., Maryville, 1965-74; cons. Project Communicate, Northwest, Mo., 1964-67. Author: Grassroot Reflections, vols. I and II, Nodaway County Pictorial History, 1994; co-editor: Tales of Nodaway County; contbr. articles to profl. jours. Delegate, U.S. White House Conf. Aging, Wash., 1981; sec., treas. Mo. Divsn. AAUW; founder, pres. Nodaway County Heritage Collection Com., 1982-92; disting. svc. honoree First Christian Ch., Maryville, 1993. Named U.S. Journalism Tchr. of Yr. Newspaper Fund, Inc., 1963, One of Two Mo. Outstanding Vols., 1981, Mo. Pioneer Educator, 1979, Disting. Mo. Woman AAUW-Mo. div., 1990. Mem. Mo. Assn. Tchrs. of English (pres., life mem.), Mo. Writers' Guild, Maryville C. of C. (Disting. Svc. award 1975). Democrat. Home: 610 W Halsey St # 5 Maryville MO 64468-2162

ECKHARDT, CAROLINE DAVIS, comparative literature educator; b. N.Y.C., Feb. 27, 1942; d. Joseph and Lilian (Lerner) Davis; m. Robert B. Eckhardt, Aug. 22, 1964; children—David, Naomi, Jonathan, Jennifer Ruth. BA, Drew U., 1963; MA, Ind. U., 1965; PhD, U. Mich., 1971. Lectr. U. Mich., Ann Arbor, 1971; asst. prof. Pa. State U., Univ. Park, 1971-76, assoc. prof., 1976-85, prof., 1985—, program head, grad. officer comparative lit. program, 1977-84, planning officer liberal arts, 1984-85, head dept. Comparative Lit., 1985—. Author: The Prophetia Merlini of Geoffrey of Monmouth, 1982; editor: Essays in the Numerical Criticism of Medieval Literature, 1980, Chaucer's General Prologue, 1990; co-editor Jour. Gen. Edn., 1974-87; mem. editorial bd. Comparative Literature Studies, 1987—; contbr. articles to profl. jours., books. Mem. MLA (exec. com. medieval comparative sect. 1980-86), Am. Comparative Lit. Assn. (adv. bd. 1986-89), Assn. Depts. and Programs Comparative Lit. (nat. sec. 1994—), Medieval Acad., New Chaucer Soc. Jewish. Office: Pa State Univ Comparative Lit Dept Univ Park PA 16802

ECKL, MARY EVELYN, process engineer; b. Florence, Ala., Apr. 24, 1969; d. Leonard Clarence and Rosalia Ruth (Hollman) E. BSChemE, U. Ala., 1992. Operator asst. Occidental Chem. Corp., Muscle Shoals, Ala., 1989-90, summer engr., 1990-93; process engr. Occidental Chem. Corp., Delaware City, Del., 1993—; mem. com. Environ. Symposium, Tuscaloosa, Ala., 1991-92. Editor Signatures, 1987. Evangelist, team leader Nat. Evang. Team, St. Paul, 1992-93; religious edn. tchr. Holy Family Ch., Newark, Del., 1993-94. Recipient scholarship U. Ala., 1987-88; named Girl of Yr., Am. Legion, 1987. Mem. AIChE (sec. Tuscaloosa chpt. 1989-92), Phi Eta Sigma, Alpha Lambda Delta. Roman Catholic. Office: Occidental Chem Corp River Rd Rt 9 Delaware City DE 19706

ECKLUND, CONSTANCE CRYER, French language educator; b. Chgo., Nov. 20, 1938; d. Gilbert and Electra (Papadopoulos) Cryer; m. Robert Lyons, June 18, 1966 (div. 1974); m. John E. Ecklund, Mar. 22, 1975. BA magna cum laude, Northwestern U., 1960; PhD, Yale U., 1965. Asst. prof. Ind. U., Bloomington, 1964-66; asst. prof. French Southern Conn. State U., New Haven, 1967-70, assoc. prof., 1970-76, prof., 1976—; speaker in field. Contbr. articles to profl. jours. Mem. AAUP, Am. Coun. Teaching Fgn. Langs., Am. Assn. Tchrs. French, Modern Lang. Assn., Phi Beta Kappa. Republican. Episcopalian. Home: 27 Cedar Rd Woodbridge CT 06525-1642

ECKMAN, DIANNE INGEBORG, critical care nurse; b. Pitts., Aug. 8, 1965; d. Mary M. Moloney Eckman. BS in Nursing, Carlow Coll., Pitts., 1987. Commd. 2d lt. U.S. Army, 1987, advanced through grades to capt., 1993; staff nurse orthopedic surgery Walter Reed Army Med. Ctr., Washington, 1987-90, staff nurse ICU, 1990-91, 92-95; staff nurse surg. ICU Johns Hopkins Hosp., Balt., 1991-92; staff nurse ICU DeWitt Mary Cmty. Hosp., Ft. Belvoir, Va., 1995—. Mem. Am. Assn. Critical Care Nurses, Sigma Theta Tau. Home: 2210 Montgomery Ave Woodbridge VA 22191 Office: DeWitt Army Cmty Hosp Fort Belvoir VA 22060-5901

ECKSTEIN, MARLENE R., vascular radiologist; b. Poughkeepsie, N.Y., Sept. 6, 1948; d. Marc and Lola (Charm) E.; A.B., Vassar Coll., 1970; M.D., Albert Einstein Coll. Medicine, 1973. Diplomate Nat. Bd. Med. Examiners; cert. Am. Bd. Radiology. Intern in medicine Yale-New Haven Med. Center, 1973-74, resident in diagnostic radiology, 1974-77; asst. radiologist, chief vascular radiology sect. South Nassau Communities Hosp., Oceanside, N.Y., 1977-78, asso. radiologist, chief vascular radiology sect., 1978-81, asst. dir. dept. radiology, chief vascular radiology sect., 1981-83; asst. prof. clin. radiology SUNY-Stony Brook Med. Sch., 1980-83; instr. radiology, Harvard Med. Sch., 1983-84, asst. prof., 1984—; asst. radiologist Mass. Gen. Hosp., 1983-87, assoc. radiologist, 1987—. Mem. exec. com. and hosp. chmn. United Jewish Appeal of Physicians and Dentists of Nassau County (N.Y.), 1981-83. Fellow Am. Coll. Angiology, Soc. Cardiovascular and Interventional Radiology; mem. Am. Coll. Radiology, Am. Inst. Ultrasound in Medicine, Mass. Radiol. Soc., Am. Assn. Women Radiologists, Am. Med. Women's Assn., AMA, Mass. Med. Soc., New Eng. Soc. Cardiovascular and Interventional Radiology (pres. 1985-86), Radiol. Soc. N.Am., Designer and developer line of vascular catheters. Avocations: writing poetry, exercising, video and electronic equipment, musical keyboard, computer. Home: 141 Fulton Ave Apt 312 Poughkeepsie NY 12603-2841 Office: Mass Gen Hosp Vascular Radiology Sect Boston MA 02114

ECONOMOU-PEASE, BESSIE CARASOULAS, city planner, consultant; b. N.Y.C., Sept. 29, 1933; d. Alexander Stelianos and Maria (Trilivas) Carasoulas; m. Constantine J. Economou, Sept. 10, 1955 (div. May 1966); m. Robert Barnard Pease, Oct. 1, 1976; children: Robert W., Richard B. BA, Barnard Coll., 1955; postgrad., Columbia U., 1955-57, MS in Urban Planning, 1960. Med. researcher Coll. Physicians and Surgeons Columbia U., N.Y.C., 1955-60; planning and renewal cons. Brown & Anthony, Engrs. Planners, N.Y.C., 1960-62; dir. research, edn. ACTION Inc., N.Y.C., 1962-66; exec. asst. to adminstr. N.Y.C. Housing and Devel. Admin., N.Y.C., 1966-69; dep. dir., exec. asst. N.Y. State Urban Devel. Corp., N.Y.C., 1969-73; exec. v.p. Nat. Housing Conf., Washington, 1973-76; prin. Bessie C. Economou Assocs., Pitts., 1976—; dir. ACTION Housing, Inc., Pitts., 1982-88, Nat. Housing Conf., Washington, 1973—, also exec. v.p. 1973-76, Health Systems Agy. Western Pa., Pitts., 1984-87; adj. prof. U. Pitts, 1986—; mem. adv. com. Bur. Census Housing, 1977-81. Mem. Am. Inst. Cert. Planners (cert.), Nat. Assn. Housing and Redevel. Officials, Lamda Alpha.

ECTON, DONNA R., business consultant; b. Kansas City, Mo., May 10, 1947; d. Allen Howard and Marguerite (Page) E.; m. Victor H. Maragni, June 16, 1986; children: Mark, Gregory. BA (Durant Scholar), Wellesley Coll., 1969; MBA, Harvard U., 1971. V.p. Chem. Bank, N.Y.C., 1972-79, Citibank, N.A., N.Y.C., 1979-81; pres. MBA Resources, Inc., N.Y.C., 1981-83; v.p. adminstrn., officer Campbell Soup Co., Camden, N.J., 1983-89; chmn. Triangle Mfg. Corp. subs. Campbell Soup Co., Raleigh, N.C., 1984-87; sr. v.p., officer Nutri/System, Inc., Willow Grove, Pa., 1989-91; pres., CEO Van Houten N.Am., Delavan, Wis., 1991-94, Andes Candies Inc., Delavan, 1991-94; bus. cons. Radnor, Pa., 1994—; bd. dirs. Barnes Group Inc., Bristol, Conn., Vencor, Inc., Louisville, Ky. H&R Block, Kansas City, Mo., PETsMART, Inc., Phoenix, Ariz.; commencement speaker Pa. State U., 1987. Bd. Overseers Harvard U., 1984-90; mem. Coun. Fgn. Rels., N.Y.C., 1987—; trustee Inst. for Advancement of Health, 1988-92. Named One of 80 Women to Watch in the 80's, Ms. mag., 1980, One of All Time Top 10 of Last Decade, Glamour mag., 1984, One of 50 Women to Watch, Bus. Week mag., 1987, One of 100 Women to Watch, Bus. Month mag., 1989; recipient Wellesley Alumnae Achievement award, 1987; Fred Sheldon Fund fellow, 1971-72. Mem. Harvard Bus. Sch. Assn. (pres. exec. council 1983-84), N.Y.C. Harvard Bus. Sch. Club (pres. 1979-80), Wellesley Coll. Nat. Alumnae Assn. (bd. dirs., 1st v.p.).

EDDISON, ELIZABETH BOLE, entrepreneur, information specialist; b. Bronxville, N.Y., June 3, 1928; d. Hamilton Biggar and Elizabeth Owsley (Boyle) Bole; m. John Corbin Eddison, Feb. 10, 1951 (dec. Jan. 1993); children: Jonathan B., Elizabeth O., Martha C. AB, Vassar Coll., 1948; MS, Simmons Coll., 1973. Pres., bd. dirs. Lahore (Pakistan)-Am. Sch., 1959-61; chmn. evaluation com. Karachi (Pakistan)-Am. Sch., 1961-63; treas. bd. dirs. La Paz Coop. Sch., Bolivia, 1963-65; v.p. Assn. Am. Fgn. Svc. Women; coord. social svcs. Urban Svc. Corps, Washington Pub. Schs., 1965-69; sec. bd. dirs. Colegio Nueva Granada, Bogota, Colombia, 1969-71; chmn., treas. Warner-Eddison Assocs., Inc., Cambridge, Mass., 1973-88, pres., 1981-88; chmn., v.p. Inmagic Inc., Woburn, Mass., 1984—; mem. steering com. State House Conf. on Small Bus., Mass., 1986-88; mem. bd. advisors Internat. Sch. Info. Mgmt., Irvine, Calif., 1984—; mem. adv. com. Engring. Info., Inc., N.Y.C., 1989-93; mem. computer applications com. Cary Meml. Libr., Lexington, Mass., 1986; mem. State Adv. Commn. on Librs., Boston, 1993—. Compiler: Words that Mean Business, 1981; contbr. articles to profl. jours. Mem. adv. com. on internat. and tech. devel. U.S. Dept. State, 1980-83; mem. small bus. com. Mass. Gov.'s Bus. Adv. Coun., 1985-89; co-chmn. Lexington Dem. Town Com., 1990-92; active Mass. Bd. Libr. Commrs., 1990-91; mem. bd. corporators Symmes Hosp., Arlington, Mass., 1992—; mem. Bd. Selectmen, Lexinton, 1993—. Recipient Alumni Achievement award Simmons Coll., 1986, Disclosure Achievement award Libr. Mgmt. Bus. and Fin. div. Spl. Librs. Assn., 1987. Mem. Am. Soc. Info. Scis., Info. Industry Assn. (chmn. emeriti com. 1983-88, small bus. forum 1986-89, entrepreneur award com. 1989-90, co-chmn. publs. com. 1984-87, Entrepreneur award 1989), Assoc. Info. Mgrs. (chmn. publs. com. 1984-86, bd. dirs. 1984-86, Knox award 1988), Spl. Librs. Assn. (chmn. program com. libr. mgmt. divsn. 1984-85, profl. devel. com. 1987-88, chmn.-elect 1988, chmn. 1989-90, bd. dirs. 1991-94, mem. consultation com. 1994—), Nat. Info. Stds. Orgn. (bd. dirs. 1994—), Beta Phi Mu. Democrat. Office: Inmagic Inc 800 W Cummings Park Woburn MA 01801-6357

EDDOWES, E(LIZABETH) ANNE, early childhood education specialist; b. Sandusky, Ohio, Nov. 23, 1931; d. Carl Emerson and Helen Ruth (Sutter) Evans; m. Edward Everett, June 17, 1956; children: Andrew Wayne, Scott Edward. BS, Ohio State U., Columbus, 1953; MEd, U. Mo., St. Louis, 1969; PhD, Ariz. State U., Tempe, 1977. Tchr. Sandusky (Ohio) Pub. Schs., 1954-56, Alachua County Pub. Schs., Gainesville, Fla., 1957-59; dir. Florissant (Mo.) Coop. Nursery Sch., 1967-70; instr. Florissant Valley Community Coll., Ferguson, Mo., 1970-73; grad. and faculty assoc. Ariz. State U., Tempe, 1974-78, coord. student teaching, 1979-84; child devel. assoc. rep. Coun. for Early Childhood Profl. Recognition, Washington, 1978—; asst. prof. U. Ala., Birmingham, 1985-91, assoc. prof., 1991—; validator Nat. Assn. Edn. Young Children, Washington, 1986—; cons. Southside Bapt. Child Devel. Ctr., Brookwood Forest Child Devel. Ctr., Mountain Brook, 1986-92. Contbr. articles to profl. jours. Pres., v.p. Family Resource Ctr., Tempe, 1977-79, children's ctr. bd. Desert Palm United Ch. of Christ, Tempe, 1978-84. Recipient Outstanding Svc. award Ariz. State U., 1984. Mem. Orgn. Mondiale pour Edn. Prescolaire, Ala. Assn. on Young Children (pres. 1989-90), Ala. Assn. Early Childhood Tchrs., Jefferson County Assn. Young Children, Phi Delta Kappa, Alpha Phi. Office: U Ala Dept Curriculum & Instrn University Sta Birmingham AL 35294

EDDY, CHRISTINE MARIE, hydrogeologist; b. Everett, Wash., Aug. 1, 1959; d. Paul Andrew and Ellen Marie (Hagglund) E.; m. James Martin Doesburg, Aug. 29, 1987; 1 child, Katherine Marie. BS in Geol. Sci., U. Wash., 1982; MS in Geology, No. Ill. U., 1989. Registered profl. geologist, Idaho. Geologist Rockwell Hanford Ops., Richland, Wash., 1982, Battelle Meml. Inst., Richland, 1983-85; hydrogeologist, groundwater modeling Argonne (Ill.) Nat. Lab., 1985-88; pres., environ. cons. Christine Eddy & Assocs., Kent, Wash., 1988—. Contbr. articles to profl. publs. Active numerous environ. orgns., humane soc. Mem. Nat. Wildlife Fedn., Nature Conservancy. Office: Christine Eddy & Assocs 26221 Marine View Dr S Kent WA 98032

EDDY, COLETTE ANN, aerial photography studio owner, photographer; b. Sept. 14, 1950; d. William F. and Jeanne (Valeski) Trump; m. Robert K. Eddy, Aug. 21, 1976 (div. Sept. 1992). AA, St. Petersburg (Fla.) Jr. Coll., 1970; BA, U. South Fla., 1973; MS, Nova U., 1988. Yacht caretaker The Sundowner, St. Petersburg, 1972-73; mgr. Aunt Hattie's Restaurant, St. Petersburg, 1973-79, Johnathan Jones, Inc., St. Petersburg, 1979-80; photographer, sales rep. Smith Aerial Photos, Tampa, Fla., 1980-87; owner, aerial photographer Aerial Innovations, Inc., Tampa, 1987—; owner Havanna Connection Inc., Carribean. Mem. Tampa Mus. Art. Mem. Profl. Photographers Am. (recipient 18 Merit awards), Fla. Profl. Photographers (12 Merit awards 1987-90), Profl. Aerial Photographers Assn., Tampa C. of C. Republican. Home: 198 Ceylon Ave Tampa FL 33606-4053 Office: Aerial Innovations Inc 1413 S Howard Ave Ste 206 Tampa FL 33606-3191

EDDY, ELSBETH MARIE, retired government official, statistician; b. Buffalo, Apr. 8, 1934; d. Willy and Wilhelmine (Hartman) Gnueg; m. Leonard John Eddy, Feb. 5, 1956; children: John, Bruce, Lisa. Student, schs. in Md., Va., N.C.; spl. courses, U.S. Dept. Agriculture Grad. Sch.; cert. in mgmt., Prince Georges Coll., 1976. With fgn. trade div. U.S. Bur. Census, Washington, 1967-90, chief metals and minerals, 1980-90. Recipient Cert. of Appreciation, USAF, 1973. Democrat. Home: 13000 Piscataway Dr Fort Washington MD 20744-6620

EDDY, JANET EWART, learning specialist; b. L.A., July 4, 1931; d. Park James and Pansy (Hutchinson) Ewart; m. James Arnold Eddy, June 15, 1953; children: Beryl Leigh (Mrs. Jon Cianci), James Arnold III, Park Ewart, Andrew Karl. BS cum laude, U. So. Calif., 1954, MS in Edn., 1978, PhD, 1991. Cert. reading specialist, Calif.; cert. learning disabilities specialist. Reading specialist Nat. Charity League-U. So. Calif. Sch., L.A., 1976-78, resource and curriculum coord., 1978-81, prin., 1981-84; learning specialist Learning Ctr. U. So. Calif., L.A., 1984-92, dir. dept. learning svcs./learning disabilities support svc., 1992—. Mem. Learning Disabilities Assn., Assn. Ednl. Therapists (profl. mem.), Internat. Reading Assn., Women in Mgmt. (treas.), Coll. Reading and Learning Assn. (conf. mgr. 1986), Phi Kappa Phi (v.p. alumni U. So. Calif. chpt. 1990—), Phi Delta Kappa, Pi Beta Phi (adv. bd. 1960-65, corp. bd. treas. 1974-75), Pi Lambda Theta. Office: U So Calif Dept Learning Svcs STU 301 Los Angeles CA 90089-0896

EDEL, KATHLEEN, realtor; b. Painesville, Ohio, Aug. 5, 1944; d. Frank Charles and Geraldine Audrey (Young) Jepson; divorced; 1 child, Robert John. Student, Willoughby Eastlake Sch. Practical Nursing, 1963. Lic. realtor, notary, practical nurse. Lic. practical nurse Lake County Hosp. East, Painesville, 1963-64; lic. practical nurse surgery Euclid (Ohio) Gen., 1964-66, Huron Rd. Hosp., Cleve., 1966-67, Lake County Hosp. West, Willoughby, Ohio, 1967-69, Hillcrest Hosp., Mayfield, Ohio, 1969-76; surg. asst. Dr. Renner, Mayfield, 1976-78; realtor Smythe Cramer Co., Lyndhurst, Ohio, 1984—; builder rep. Three-M-Homes, Mayfield Village, Ohio, 1986—. Recipient Silver award Nat. Assn. Home Builders, 1989-91; named to Presidents Sales Club Cleve. Area Bd. Realtors, 1988-91. Republican. Mem. Christian Ch. Home: 338 Longspur Rd Highland Heights OH 44143 Office: Smythe Cramer Co 5010 Mayfield Rd Lyndhurst OH 44124

EDELMAN, JUDITH HOCHBERG, architect; b. Bklyn., Sept. 16, 1923; d. Abraham and Frances (Israel) Hochberg; m. Harold Edelman, Dec. 26, 1947; children: Marc, Joshua. Student, Conn. Coll., 1940-41, NYU, 1941-42; BArch, Columbia U., 1946. Designer, drafter Huson Jackson, N.Y.C., 1948-58; Schermerhorn traveling fellow, 1950, pvt. practice architecture, 1958-60; ptnr. Edelman & Salzman, N.Y.C., 1960-79; partner Edelman Partnership (Architects), N.Y.C., 1979—; adj. prof. Sch. Architecture CUNY, 1972-76, vis. lectr. grad. program in environ. psychology, 1977, 77; vis. lectr. Washington U., St. Louis, 1974, U. Oreg., 1974, MIT, 1975, Pa. State U., 1977, Rensselaer Poly. Inst., 1977, Columbia U., 1979; First Claire Watson Forrest Meml. lectr. U. Oreg., U. Calif., Berkeley, U. So. Calif.,

1982. Major archtl. works include: Restoration of St. Mark's Ch. in the Bowery, N.Y.C., 1970-82, Two Bridges Urban Renewal Area Housing, 1970-86, Jennings Hall Sr. Citizens Housing, Bklyn., 1980, Goddard Riverside Elderly Housing and Community Ctr., N.Y.C., 1983, Columbus Green Apartments, N.Y.C., 1987, Chung Pak Bldg., N.Y.C., 1992. Recipient Bard 1st honor award City Club N.Y., 1969, Bard award of merit, 1975, 82, award for design excellence HUD, 1970, 1st prize Nat. Trust for Hist. Preservation, 1983, award of merit Mcpl. Art Soc. N.Y., 1983, Pub. Svc. award Settlement Housing Fund, 1983, Women of Vision award NOW, 1989, 1st prize for design excellence C. of C., Borough of Queens, N.Y., 1989, Best in Srs.' Housing award Nat. Assn. Home Builders, 1993. Fellow AIA, dir. N.Y. chpt., chmn. commn. on archtl. edn. 1971-73, chmn. nat. task force on women in architecture 1974-75, v.p. N.Y. chpt. 1975-77, chmn. ethics com. 1975-77, Residential design award 1969, Pioneer in Housing award 1990, N.Y. State Assn. Architects-AIA Honor award 1975); mem. Alliance of Women in Architecture (founding, mem. steering com. 1972-74), Architects for Social Responsibility (mem. exec. com. 1982-85), Columbia Archtl. Alumni Assn. (bd. dirs. 1968-71). Home: 13 Bank St New York NY 10014-5252 Office: Edelman Partnership 434 6th Ave 6th Fl New York NY 10011-8431

EDELMAN, MARIAN WRIGHT (MRS. PETER B. EDELMAN), lawyer; b. Bennettsville, S.C., June 6, 1939; d. Arthur J. and Maggie (Bowen) Wright; m. Peter B. Edelman, July 14, 1968; children: Joshua, Jonah, Ezra. Merrill scholar, Univs. Paris, Geneva, 1958-59; BA, Spelman Coll., 1960; LLB (J.H. Whitney fellow 1960-61), Yale U., 1963, LLD (hon.); LLD (hon.), Smith Coll., 1969, Lowell Tech. U., 1975, Williams Coll., 1978, Columbia U., U. Pa., Amherst Coll., St. Joseph's Coll., Hartford, Conn.; DHL (hon.), Lesley Coll., 1975, Trinity Coll., Washington, Russell Sage Coll., 1978, Syracuse U., Coll. New Rochelle, 1979, Swarthmore Coll., 1980, SUNY Old Westbury, Northeastern U., 1981, Bard Coll., 1982, U. Mass., 1983, Hunter Coll., U. So. Maine, SUNY, Albany, 1984, Columbia U., U. Pa., Yale U., 1985, Rutgers U., Bates Coll., Maryville Coll., Bank St., 1986, Claremont Grad Sch., Lincoln U., Georgetown U., Chgo. Theol. Coll., 1987, Wheaton Coll., Tulane U., Grinnell Coll. Brandeis U., Wheelock Coll., Dartmouth Coll., U. S.C., U. N.C., Grad. Ctr. CUNY, U. Wis. Milw., 1988, Interdenom. Theol. Ctr., Hofstra U., Tufts U., Borough Manhattan Community Coll., Wesleyan U., Calif. State U. L.A., Dillard U., U. Md., U. Miami, 1989, Howard U., Beloit Coll., Queens Coll., Am. U., New Sch. of Social Rsch., Coll. of Notre Dame, DePaul U., 1990, Beaver Coll., Fordham U., Simmons Coll., Hamline U., Clark U., Harvard U., Union Coll., 1991, Tuskegee U., Washington U. St. Louis, Hood Coll., Duke U., Mercy Coll., 1992, Princeton U., U. Ill., Calif. State U. San Francisco, Wittenberg (Ohio) Coll., Shaw U., So. Meth. U., 1993, Brown U., U. Balt., Ea. Conn. State U., U. Notre Dame, 1994. Bar: D.C., Miss., Mass. Staff atty. NAACP Legal Def. and Ednl. Fund, Inc., N.Y.C., 1963-64; dir. NAACP Legal Def. and Ednl. Fund, Inc., Jackson, Miss., 1964-68; Congl. and fed. liaison Poor People's Campaign, summer 1968; partner Washington Research Project of So. Center for Pub. Policy, 1968-73; dir. Harvard U. Center for Law and Edn., 1971-73; pres., founder Children's Def. Fund, 1973—. Author: The Measure of Our Success: A Letter To My Children and Yours, 1992, Families in Peril, 1987. Mem. exec. com. Student Non-Violent Coordinating Com., 1961-63; mem. adv. com. Martin Luther King Jr. Meml. Libr.; mem. adv. bd. Hampshire Coll.; mem. Presdl. Commn. on Missing in Action, 1977, Presdl. Commn. on Internat. Yr. of Child, 1979, Presdl. Commn. on Agenda for 80's, 1980; bd. dirs. NAACP Legal Def. and Ednl. Fund; trustee Spelman Coll., Carnegie Coun. on Children, 1972-77, Martin Luther King Jr. Meml. Ctr.; mem. Yale U. Corp., 1971-77, Aetna Found., Nat. Commn. on Children, 1989—; bd. dirs. Aetna Life Casualty Found., Citizens for Constitutional Concerns, US. com. UNICEF, Robin Hood Found., Aaron Diamond Found., Nat. Alliance Business, City Lights, Leadership Conf. Civil Rights, Skadden Fellowship Found., Parents as Tchrs. Nat. Ctr., Inc.; U.S. rep. UNICEF; active U.S. Olympic Com. Named one of Outstanding Young Women of Am., 1966; recipient Mademoiselle mag. award, 1965, Louise Waterman Wise award, 1970, Washington of Yr. award, 1979, Whitney M. Young award, 1979, Profl. of Yr. award Black Ent., 1979, Leadership award Nat. Women's Polit. Caucus, 1980, Black Womens Forum award, 1980, medal Columbia Tchrs. Coll., Barnard Coll., 1984, Eliot award Am. Pub. Health Assn., John W. Gardner Leadership award of Ind. Sector, Pub. Svc. Achievement award Common Cause, Compostela award Cathedral St. James, 1987, MacArthur prize fellow, 1985, Albert Schweitzer Humanitarian prize Johns Hopkins U., 1987. Philip Hauge Ahelson award AAAS, 1988, Hubert Humphrey Civil Rights award, AFL-CIO award, 1989, Radcliffe Coll. medal, 1989, Fordham Stein prize, 1989, Gandhi Peace award, 1990, M. Carey Thomas award, Robie award for humanitarianism, Essence award, numerous others; hon. fellow U. Pa. Law Sch. Hon. mem. Phi Beta Kappa. Address: Childrens Def Fund 25 E St NW Washington DC 20001

EDELMANN, CAROLYN FOOTE, author, poet, editor; b. Toledo, Ohio. Pvt. studies with Theodore Weiss, Galway Kinnell, Stanley Plumly, Princeton U. Author: (poetry) Gatherings, 1987; appearances include (TV) People are Talking, Phila., (radio) Pub. Radio, Manhattan. Recipient William Carlos Williams prize Paterson Pub. Libr., 1977, N.J. Poetry Monthly prize, 1978, Poets prize Delaware Valley, 1992. Mem. Acad. Am. Poets, Nat. League Am. Penwomen, Poetry Soc. Am., N.J. Penwomen, U.S. 1 Poet's Coop., Poets and Writers.

EDELSON, MARY BETH, artist, educator; b. East Chicago, Ind.; d. Albert Melvin and Mary Lou (Young) Johnson; children: Lynn Switzman, Nick. Student, Art Inst. Chgo., 1953-54; BA, DePauw U., 1955; MA, NYU, 1959; DFA (hon.), DePauw U., 1993. Instr. Corcoran Sch. Art, Washington, 1970-75; artist in residence U. Ill., Chgo., 1982, 88, U. Tenn., Knoxville, 1983, Ohio U., Columbus, 1984, Md. Inst. Art, Balt., 1985, Kansas City Art Inst., Mo., 1986, Cleve. Art Inst., 1991, U. Colo., 1993, Clemson U., 1994; lectr. at various art gatherings. Solo exhbn. Creative Time, N.Y.C., 1994; group exhbns. include Internat. Feministische Kunst, Stichting de Appel, Amsterdam, The Netherlands, 1980, Mendel Gallery, Mus. du Que., Phillips Gallery, Can., 1986-88, Queens (N.Y.) Mus., 1988, Corcoran Gallery Art, Washington, 1989, Mus. Modern Art, N.Y.C., 1988-89, Walker Art Ctr., Mpls., 1989, W.P.A., Washington, 1989, Dolan/Maxwell Gallery, N.Y.C., 1989, 90, Hillwood Mus., L.I., 1991, A.C. Project Room, N.Y.C., 1991—, Nicole Klagsburn Gallery, 1993, Phillippe Rizzo, Paris, 1992, P.P.O.W., N.Y.C., 1992, Fawbush Gallery, N.Y.C., 1992, Amy Lipton Gallery, N.Y.C., 1992, David Zwirner Gallery, N.Y.C., 1993, Turner/Krail Galleries, L.A., 1993, Momenta, N.Y.C., 1994; represented in permanent collections: Walker Art Ctr., Nat. Mus. Am. Art, Washington, Nat. Collection, Washington, Nat. Mus. Women in the Arts, Washington, Guggenheim Mus. Art, N.Y.C., Mus. Contemporary Art, Chgo., Gilford Coll., N.C., 1992, Cleveland Inst. Art., 1993, and others; subject of 15-yr. retrospective travelling to numerous art and ednl. instns. throughout U.S., 1988-91; author: Seven Cycles: Public Rituals, 1981, To Dance: Painting with Performance in Mind, 1985, Seven Sites, 1988-90, Shape Shifter: Seven Mediums, 1990; author/photographer: Firsthand, 1993; contbr. articles to profl. jours.; included numerous books. Recipient Visual Arts grant NEA, 1981, Creative Artists Pub. Svc. grant State of N.Y., 1982. Mem. Conf. Women in Visual Arts (founding mem.), Women's Action Coalition, Heresies Mag. Collective (founding mem.). Home: 110 Mercer St New York NY 10012-3865

EDELSON, ZELDA SARAH TOLL, editor; b. Phila., Oct. 18, 1929; d. Louis David and Rose (Eisenstein) Toll; m. Marshall Edelson, Dec. 27, 1952; children: Jonathan Toll, Rebecca Jo, David Jan. BA, U. Chgo., 1949, postgrad., 1949-52. Editor-writer Consol. Book Pubs., Chgo., 1953-56; social worker Balt. City Dept. Pub. Welfare, 1956-57; pub. relations writer Md. Dept. Employment Security, Balt., 1958-59; museum editor Yale Peabody Mus., New Haven, 1970-76, head publs., 1976—, editor mus.'s Discovery mag., 1983—; lectr. in sci. writing Yale U., 1983-84. Editor numerous publs. including: The Great Dinosaur Mural at Yale: The Age of Reptiles, 1990. U. Chgo. scholar, 1947-51. Mem Council Biology Editors, Soc. Scholarly Publishing, Am. Assn. Museums (awards of distinction 1985, 86, award of merit 1989), New Eng. Conf. Museums. Office: Yale Peabody Mus Natural History Publs Office PO Box 208118 170 Whitney Ave New Haven CT 06520-8118

EDELSTEIN, D. VERA, management consultant; b. Pavlodar, Kazakhstan, USSR, Feb. 5, 1952; came to U.S., 1965; d. Joseph and Gienia (Berman) E. BA, Bklyn. Coll., 1972; MS, NYU, 1977, MBA, 1984. Mem. tech. staff Bell Labs, Whippany, N.J., 1972-81; dept. chief Western Electric Co., Newark, 1981-84; dist. mgr. Bellcore, Piscataway, N.J., 1984-86; dir. sci. and tech. NYNEX, White Plains, N.Y., 1986-92; pres. VeraQual Assocs., Inc., N.Y.C., 1992-94; mng. cons. Electronic Data Systems Corp., Mgmt. Consulting Svcs., Plano, Tex., 1994—; mem. site visit team N.Y. State Sci. and Tech. Found., 1988, mem. rsch. and devel. grant proposal rev. panel, 1990—; publicity chair Iternat. Standards Orgn./Internat. Electrotech. Commn. subcom. 7 U.S. Tech. Adv. Group, 1989-93; panel chair software engring. edn. Ctr. Advanced Software Engring. Syracuse U., Minnowbrook, N.Y., 1990; program evaluator computer sci. accreditation commn. Computer Soc. of IEEE and ACM, 1990—; session chair Reliability Computer Sci., Internat. Conf., Charles U., Prague, Czechoslovakia, 1990, mem. program com., 1991; mem. tech. adv. bd. Single Internal Market Comm., 1992—. Contbr. articles to profl. jours. Mem. IEEE (sr., chairperson Software Engring. Standards Subcom. confs., chair IEEE Std. 1219-1992-Std. Software Maintenance 1988—, conf. chair software engring. stds. subcom. 1989-93, referee IEEE Transaction Engring. Mgmt. 1991—, Computer Soc. Cert. of Appreciation 1991, Computer Soc. Outstanding Contbn. award 1993), Internat. Stds. Orgn. (del., tech. expert software engring. internat. plenary session 1989-94, internat. convener integral software life cycle processes 1990—), Am. Soc. Quality Control, N.Y. Software Industry Assn. (bd. dirs., chair export com.), Soc. Women Engrs. (sr., moderator several sessions 1990 nat. conv.), Beta Gamma Delta. Home: 111 Mulberry St 65 Newark NJ 07102

EDELSTEIN, JOAN ERBACK, physical therapy educator; b. East Orange, N.J., Mar. 28, 1935; d. Frank William and Sadie Edith (Levine) Erback; m. Haskell Edelstein, Jan. 19, 1964; children: David, Benjamin. BS magna cum laude, NYU, 1956, MA, 1958. Lic. phys. therapist, N.Y. Chief phys. therapist children's div. Rusk Inst. (formerly Inst. Phys. Medicine & Rehab.), N.Y.C., 1956-59; instr. U. Wis., Madison, 1959-61; clin. asst., prof., sr. rsch. scientist NYU, N.Y.C., 1961-91; assoc. prof. clin. phys. therapy Columbia U., 1991—, dir. program in phys. therapy, 1992—; organizer and condr. seminars nationwide and worldwide. Author: Prosthetic & Orthotic Educational Aids, 1987; contbr. numerous articles to profl. jours.; mme. editorial bd. Jour. of the Assn. Children's Prosthetic-Orthotic Clinics, 1983—, Jour. Rehab. Rsch. & Devel., 1984—, Archives Phys. Medicine and Rehab., 1991—. Trustee N.Y. Youth Symphony, N.Y.C., 1986—, Lark Quartet, N.Y.C., 1989-94. Nat. Found. for Infantile Paralysis grantee, 1959. Fellow Internat. Soc. for Prosthetics and Orthotics (sec., treas. 1979-88, vice chmn. 1988-91); mem. Am. Phys. Therapy Assn., Am. Congress of Phys., Medicine and Rehab., N.Y. Acad. Scis., Acad. of Content Experts, Soc. Scholarly Publs., Nat. Flute Assn. (performance health com. 1991—). Home: 340 E 69th St New York NY 10021-5706 Office: Columbia St # 630 New York NY 10002

EDELSTEIN, TERI J., museum administrator, educator; b. Johnstown, Pa., June 23, 1951; d. Robert Morten and HuldaLois (Friedhoff) E. BA, U. Pa., 1972, MA, 1977, PhD, 1979; cert. NYU, 1984. Lectr., U. Guelph, Ont., Can., 1977-79; asst. dir. for acad. programs Yale Ctr. for Brit. Art, New Haven, 1979-83; dir. Mt. Holyoke Coll. Art Mus., South Hadley, Mass., 1983-90, dir. Skinner Mus., 1983-90, mem. faculty dept. art, 1983-90; dir. Smart Mus. Art, U. Chgo., 1990-92, sr. lectr. U. Chgo. dept. of art, 1990—; dep. dir. Art Inst. of Chgo., 1992—. Adv. bd. Sculpture Chgo. Penfield scholar U. Pa., 1975. Mem. Coll. Art Assn., Artable, Am. Assn. Museums, Am. Soc. 18th Century Studies, Walpole Soc. Office: Art Inst Chgo 111 S Michigan Ave Chicago IL 60603-6110

EDEN, F(LORENCE) BROWN, artist; b. Jericho Center, Vt., Oct. 10, 1916; d. Arthur Castle and Eva Merita (Lowery) Brown; m. Edwin Winfield Eden, Sept. 4, 1937; children: Donna Jean, Sandra Elizabeth, Kathy Lynn. Student, U. Fla. Extension, 1955-59, U. Mich., 1963. Art instr. Ann Arbor (Mich.) City Club, 1962-63; tchr., oil painting, printmaking Jacksonville (Fla.) Art Mus., 1963-68; profl. artist pvt. practice Jacksonville, 1962—. One-person shows include The Fox Galleries, Atlanta, 1986, The Donn Roll Galleries , Sarasota, 1987, 89, 90, 92, 93, Gallery Contemporanea, Jacksonville, 1988, Artist Assocs. Gallery, Atlanta, 1990, The Harmon Galleries of Am. Art, Sarasota, Fla., 1993, The Donn Roll Galleries, Sarasota, 1994; corp. collections include Fed. Res. Bank Atlanta, Bank Am., Coca-Cola Co., So. Bell, Sheraton Corp., AT&T, Trust Co. Ga., Shell Oil, Touche Ross, Cooper and Lybrand, Delta Airlines, 5th Dist. Ct. Appeals Bldg., Daytona Beach, Fla., 1982; group exhibits Ala. Nat. Watercolor Exhbn., Fla., Ga. Nat., Audubon Nat., Painters in Casein and Acrlics Nat., N.Y.C., Jacksonville Art Mus. Mem. Jacksonville Art Mus. Recipient First award Fla. Artist Group, 1971, 79, Fla. Artists, 1969, The Painting award Major Fla. Artists, 1979, numerous other 1st place awards. Mem. Nat. Mus. of Women in the Arts (charter mem.), Nat. Soc. Painters in Casein and Acrylics, Southern Watercolor Soc., Audubon Artists, Fla. Watercolor Soc., Ga. Watercolor Soc., Ala. Watercolor Soc., Jacksonville Coalition of Visual Artists. Home and Studio: 5375 Sanders Rd Jacksonville FL 32277

EDEN, MARGIE COHEN, public relations executive; b. Atlanta, May 22, 1948; d. Morris and Lil (Bloom) Cohen; divorced; children: Jason M., Brent M. BS in Edn., U. Ga., 1970. Tchr. elem. sch. DeKalb County, Atlanta, 1970-71; mgr. hotel tour and travel Exec. Park Hotel, Atlanta, 1971-73; acct. exec. Ketchum Pub. Rels., Atlanta, 1989-90, sr. acct. exec., 1990-94, v.p./spl. projects, 1994—. Campaign mgr. statewide PSC Citizens for Cathey Steinberg, Atlanta, 1987-88; polit. cons. Atlanta C. of C.-Edupac, 1993; mem. midtown leadership program Midtown Alliance, Atlanta, 1992, project chmn. First Night, 1993. Recipient Gold Quill award Internat. Assn. Bus. Communicators, 1991. Mem. Pub. Rels. Soc. Am. (Silver Anvil award 1990, 91, Phoenix award 1991—). Jewish. Office: Ketchum Pub Rels 999 Peachtree St NE Ste 1850 Atlanta GA 30309

EDEN-FETZER, DIANNE TONI, nurse, project coordinator; b. Washington, Mar. 1, 1946; d. Lawrence Antonio Laurenzi and Eleanor Charlotte (Sparrough) Watson; m. William Earle Eden, Aug. 5, 1967 (div. 1982); 1 child, Christopher Lance; m. John Thompson Fetzer, Sept. 2, 1987. AA in Nursing, SUNY, Farmingdale, 1978; BS in Nursing, Towson (Md.) State U., 1990. RN, N.Y., Md. Charge nurse dept. neurosurgery U. Md. Hosp., Balt., 1978-79, nurse clincian I, 1979-84, dept. nursing and neurology project coord. Nat. Stroke Data Bank, 1984-90, nursing edn. cons. dept. neurology and neurosurgery, 1984—, sr. ptnr. neuro critical care unit, 1990—. Fellow Stroke Coun. Am. Heart Assn.; mem. AACN, Sigma Theta Tau. Democrat. Roman Catholic. Home: 1303 Maywood Ave Ruxton MD 21204 Office: Univ Md Hosp 22 S Greene St Baltimore MD 21201-1544

EDGAR, MARILYN RUTH, counselor; b. Springfield, Mo., Oct. 2, 1948; d. Donald LaVerne Sr. and Ruth Elenor (McClellan) Wilson; m. Robert Stephen Edgar, June 23, 1979; stepchildren: Terri, John, Shawna. BA in Psychology, Calif. State U., Sacramento, 1983, MS in Counseling, 1987. Lic. marriage, family, and child counselor, Calif. Counselor Sacramento Life Ctr., 1983-91; marriage and family therapist New Horizons Counseling Ctr., Carmichael, Calif., 1987—, exec. dir., supr. intern counselors, 1993—. Guest profl. therapist Faith in Crisis Group, Sacramento; mem. Warehouse Ministries of Sacramento, 1978—. Mem. Calif. Assn. Marriage and Family Therapists (sec. Valley chpt. 1992—), Capital City Motorcycle Club (pub. rels. officer 1994). Republican. Office: New Horizons Counseling Ctr 3300 Walnut Ave Carmichael CA 95608-3240

EDGAR, RUTH R., educator, retired; b. Great Falls, S.C., Jan. 7, 1930; d. Robert Hamer and Clara Elizabeth (Ellenberg) Rogers. AA, Stephens Coll., Columbia, Mo., 1949; BS, So. Meth. U., 1951; MA, Appalachian State U., Boone, N.C., 1977; postgrad., Limestone Coll., Gaffney, S.C., 1971. Lic. real estate salesman, broker. Home economist Lone Star Gas Co., Dallas, 1951-53, So. Union Gas Co., Austin, Tex., 1953-56, Southwestern Pub. Svc. Co., Amarillo, Tex., 1956-57; with Peeler Real Estate, 1970-71, Burns High Sch., Lawndale, N.C., 1971-73, Cen. Cleveland Mid. Sch., Lawndale, 1973-77, Burns Jr. High Sch., Lawndale, 1977-88; resource tchr. South Cleveland Elem. Sch., Shelby, N.C., 1988-90, Elizabeth Elem. Sch., Shelby, 1990-94, Washington Elem. Sch., Waco, N.C., 1990-94; ret., 1994. Mem. supts. adv. coun., Cleveland County, 1971-75, Cleveland County Art Soc., 1972-73, Cen. United Meth. Ch. Mem. N.C. Assn. Educators, NEA. Home: 401 Forest Hill Dr Shelby NC 28150-5520

EDGEMON, CONNIE KAY, psychologist, administrator; b. Edinburg, Tex., Nov. 27, 1947; d. R. P. and Verna Lou (Graham) E.; 1 child, Alexander. Bachelor's degree, Pan Am. U., 1969; MA, Chapman U., 1975. Lic. psychol. assoc., marriage and family counselor, profl. counselor; cert. secondary sch. tchr., Tex., Calif. Tchr. Mercedes (Tex.) Ind. Sch. Dist., spring 1968, Corpus Christi (Tex.) Ind. Sch. Dist., 1969-70, Lemoore (Calif.) Unified Sch. Dist., 1971-74, Mission (Tex.) Ind. Sch. Dist., fall 1975; staff psychologist Big Spring (Tex.) State Hosp., 1976-86, psychologist, adminstr., 1986—; instr. Howard Coll., Big Spring, 1984-87. Active Am. Heart Assn., Big Spring, 1989—. Mem. Southwestern Psychol. Assn., Tex. Pub. Employees Assn. (past pres., past sec.), Beta Sigma Phi (Beta Sigma Phi Pledge of Yr. 1978, Beta Sigma Phi Girl of Yr. 1979, 85, 90, 93, Beta Sigma Phi of Yr. 1982). Office: Big Spring State Hosp PO Box 231 Big Spring TX 79721-0231

EDGREN, GRETCHEN GRONDAHL, magazine editor; b. Portland, Oreg., Mar. 17, 1931; d. Jack W. and Alice Belle (Wells) Grondahl; m. James McNeese, Oct. 22, 1955 (div. Nov. 1974); children: Amy, Terence James; m. Alvin H. Edgren, Dec. 14, 1984. BJ, U. Oreg., 1952. Staff writer The Oregonian, Portland, 1952-61; editor Sunday mag. The San Juan (P.R.) Star, 1963-65; inventory and info. specialist USAF and U.S. Army Recruiting Command, San Antonio and Chgo., 1965-67; assoc. editor VIP mag. (Playboy Clubs), Chgo., 1967-69, mng. editor, 1969-70; assoc. editor Playboy mag., Chgo., 1970-74, sr. editor, 1974-92, contbg. editor, 1992—. Author: The Playboy Book, 1994; editor: New Credit Rights for Women, 1976; contbr. articles to mags. Adv. bd. Old Oreg. Alumni mag., U. Oreg., Eugene, 1988—; pres. bd. dirs. Civic Arts Coun., Oak Park, Ill., 1976-84; bd. dirs. Village Players, Oak Park-River Forest (Ill.) Symphony Assn., Oak Park Concert Chorale, 1975-91; mem. Oak Park Cable TV commn., 1984-86. Mem. Confrerie des Vignerons de St. Vincent Mâcon (maitresse du chpt. 1988-92), Webfoot Soc. U. Oreg., Phi Beta Kappa, Delta Delta Delta. Episcopalian.

EDGREN, MARJORIE FRANCES, dermatologist; b. Whittier, Calif., July 29, 1926; d. Oscar Conrad and Florence L. (Wolin) E.; m. Joseph V. Brown, Feb. 2, 1951 (div. 1965); children: Cynthia Martin, Kathleen Brown, Susan Brown; m. Lowell J. Peck, 1966 (dec. 1991); children: Marcia C. Peck and Melicent C. Peck (twins). MD, State U. of Iowa, 1951; JD, Western State Coll. Law, 1980. Bar: Calif. 1981; Diplomate Am. Bd. Dermatology. Intern Orange County Hosp., Calif., 1951-52; with student health svcs. State U. Iowa, 1952-55; resident in dermatology Univ. Hosps., Iowa City, 1956-60; pvt. practice Anaheim, Calif., 1961-65; ptnr. Edgren & Peck Dermatology, Anaheim, Calif., 1965-91; pvt. practice Anaheim, 1991—. Dir. Hoko Temple Zen Ctr. Zen Buddhist. Office: 1110 W La Palma Ave # 2 Anaheim CA 92801

EDIC-CRAWFORD, DARLENE MARIE, AIDS nurse; b. Las Vegas, Aug. 18, 1967; d. Robert Franklin and Belinda Lee (Brunning) E.; m. Robin Patrick Crawford, Dec. 1, 1990. BSN, U. Fla., 1990; postgrad. in Nursing, U. Miami, 1991—. Clin. nurse II in-patient AIDS unit Jackson Meml. Hosp., Miami, 1990-92; unit mgr. sub-acute AIDS unit Human Resources Health Ctr., Miami, 1992—. Mem. ANA (congl. dist. coord. 1991—), Fla. Nurses Assn. (bd. trustees polit. action com. 1989—, pres. dist. #21 1993, editor newsletter 1991—), NLN, Fla. League for Nursing, Assn. Nurses in AIDS Care (mem. 1992 conf. planning com. 1991-92, nat. bylaws com. 1993—, treas. Miami chpt. 1993—). Republican. Office: Human Resources Health Ctr 2500 NW 22 Ave Miami FL 33142

EDIDIN, BARBARA KAY, artist; b. Chgo., Oct. 1, 1952; d. Bernard David and Ingeborg (Kupfer) E.; m. Michael Evan Lubin, Oct. 13, 1991. Student, Kansas City Art Inst., 1970-71, No. Ariz. U., 1973, Ariz. State U., 1978-79. ARt dir. Accent Fine Arts, Phoenix, 1981-89. One-woman shows and group exhibits include Mesa (Ariz.) Cultural Ctr., 1984, Tucson (Ariz.) Mus. Art, 1984, 86, Fountain Hills (Ariz.) Ctr. for Arts, 1984, Moons Gallery, Tempe, Ariz., 1985, Meml. Union Gallery, Redlands, Calif., 1987, San Bernardino County (Calif.) Mus., 1987, Leslie Levy Gallery, Scottsdale, Ariz., 1987, 88, 89, 90, 91, 92, 93, Uptown Gallery, N.Y.C., 1988, 89, 90, 91, 92, 93, 94, Somerstown Gallery, N.Y.C., 1990, Steven Scott Gallery, Balt., 1991, others. Mem. Colored Pencil Soc. Am. Home: 10401 N 22nd Pl Phoenix AZ 85028-3603

EDISON-SWIFT, SUSAN ELISE, editor; b. Stoughton, Wis., Apr. 4, 1954; d. Kermit and Norma E. (Huebner) Edison; m. Paul David Swift, Aug. 14, 1976; 1 child, Anne Cecile. BS, U. Wis., 1976; MEd, U. Wis., Oshkosh, 1978. Mng. editor Woman Today (Women of the Evang. Luth. Ch. in Am.), Chgo., 1988—; bd. dirs. Associated Ch. Press, Ada, Mich. N.Am. coord. young women's leadership program Luth. World Fedn. Office: Women of the Evang Luth Church in Am 8765 W Higgins Rd Chicago IL 60631-4101

EDMANDS, SUSAN BANKS, consulting company executive; b. New Rochelle, N.Y., Oct. 7, 1944; d. George Dixon and Marian (Lepied) Banks; children: Whatleigh Winthrop, Benjamin Bruce II. BS, Boston U., 1966; cert. in libr. sci., Northeastern U., Boston, 1974. Tchr. project head start Office Econ. Opportunity, Washington, 1966; English tchr. Wattana Sch., Bangkok, 1969-71; market researcher Pauline Rendell Assocs., Somerville, Mass., 1971-72; food info. specialist FIND/SVP Inc., N.Y.C., 1977-80; mgr. tech. and indsl. group Find/SVP, Inc., N.Y.C., 1980-90, dir. consulting svcs. divsn., 1990—. Mem. Soc. Chimie Industrielle (v.p. Am. sect.), Chem. Mktg. Rsch. Assn., Chemists Club (trustee). Home: 24 Deming Ln Stamford CT 06903-4729 Office: Find/SVP Inc 625 Avenue Of The Americas New York NY 10011-2034

EDMISTEN, LINDA HARRIS, historical preservation administrator; b. Fayetteville, Ark., Oct. 9; d. Robert Lee and Peggy Louise (Sellers) Harris; m. Rufus Lige Edmisten, Dec. 22, 1983. BFA, Ohio U., 1968. Preservation planner Raleigh (N.C.) City Planning Dept., 1973-86; cons. Raleigh, 1986-93; nat. regional coord. State Hist. Preservation Office, Raleigh, 1993—; bd. advisors Nat. Trust Hist. Preservation, Washington, 1992—; bd. dirs. Preservation Found. N.C., Raleigh. Author: (biography) J. W. York, 1987; editor: Early Raleigh Neighborhoods and Buildings, 1983. Pres. Wake County Soc. Prevention of Cruelty to Animals, Raleigh, 1989-93. Recipient Robert E. Stipe Profl. Achievement award Preservation Found., 1984. Democrat. Office: Dept Cultural Resources 109 E Jones St Raleigh NC 27601-2807

EDMISTON, MARILYN, clinical psychologist; b. Lewiston, Maine, Dec. 9, 1934; d. Lewis Walter and Anne Mary (Nezol) Burgess; m. John Laing Edmiston (div. May 1969); children: John Laing, Eric James. BA, Fla. Atlantic U., 1967, MA, 1969; PhD, U. Ga., 1973. Lic. ind. practice psychologist, Calif., Fla. Staff psychologist children and adolescent unit Cen. Ga. Regional Hosp., Milledgeville, 1973-74, chief psychologist, 1974-75; clin. psychologist South Fla. State Hosp., Pembroke Pines, 1976-77; state psychol. cons. Office Vocat. Rehab., Fla. Dept. Health and Rehab. Svcs., Tallahassee, 1977-83; sr. psychologist forensic svcs. Fla. State Hosp., Chattahoochee, 1983—, pres.-elect, pres. profl. clin. staff, 1990-94; expert witness Fla. cts., 1983—. Mem. APA, Capital Area Psychol. Assn. (pres. 1983-84), World Fedn. for Mental Health, Internat. Coun. Psychologists. Democrat. Home: 2161 Shangri-La Ln Tallahassee FL 32303-2360 Office: Fla State Hosp Forensic Svcs Chattahoochee FL 32324

EDMOND, VIVIAN PIRKLE, counselor; b. Atlanta, Mar. 13, 1941; d. John Herbert and Dorothy (Robbs) Pirkle; m. Richard Eugene Edmond, Oct. 16, 1965 (div.); children: Richard Todd, John Jacob. AA, Truett-McConnell, 1962; BA, Belmont Coll., 1964; MEd, U. So. Ala., 1988; Ednl. Specialist, West Ga. Coll., 1993. Cert. sch. counselor, Ga. Employment counselor Equal Opportunity Program, Wichita Falls, Tex., 1967-69; tchr. Mobile (Ala.) Christian Sch., 1977-88; counselor Forsyth County Sch., Cumming, Ga., 1988—. Author: (manual) Preparing Lessons to Use With Students and Staff, 1993. Hotline vol. Battered Women's Home, Cumming, 1989—; mem. Child Abuse Coun., Cumming, 1989—; family selection com. Habitat for Humanity, Cumming, 1993. Named Woman of Yr., Bus. and Profl. Woman's Club, 1993, Outstanding Young Woman of Am., 1967. Mem. Am. Counseling Assn., Am. Sch. Counselor Assn., Profl. Assn. Ga. Educators. Baptist. Home: 4710 Pilgrim Pt Cumming GA 30131 Office: North Forsyth Mid Sch 3645 Coal Mountain Dr Cumming GA 30130

EDMONDS, ANNE CAREY, librarian; b. Penang, Malaysia, Dec. 19, 1924; d. William John and Nell (Carey) E. Student, U. Reading, Eng., 1942-44; BA, Barnard Coll., 1948; MSLS, Columbia U., 1950; MA, Johns Hopkins U., 1959; postgrad., Western Res. U., 1960-61; LHD Mount Holyoke Coll., 1994. With War Damage Commn., London, Eng., 1944-46; children's asst. Enoch Pratt Free Libr., Balt., 1948-49; reference libr. Sch. Bus. Adminstrn., CCNY, 1950-51; reference libr., then asst. libr. readers' services Goucher Coll., Balt., 1951-60; exchange reference libr. European svcs. libr. BBC, London, 1955; instr. Sch. L.S., Syracuse U., summer 1960; libr. Douglass Coll., Rutgers U., New Brunswick, N.J., 1961-64, instr., summer 1962, fall 1963; libr. Mt. Holyoke Coll., 1964-94; vis. librarian U. North, Turfloop, South Africa, 1976-77; mem. libr. vis. com. Wheaton Coll., Norton, Mass., 1978-92; mem. local systems adv. group Online Computer Libr. Ctr., Inc., 1984-87, mem. adv. com. on coll. and univ. librs., 1988-89. Author: A Memory Book: Mount Holyoke College, 1837-1987, 1988, (with Gai Carpenter and others) Computing Strategies in Liberal Arts Colleges, 1992. Mem. South Hadley (Mass.) Bicentennial Com., 1975-76; mem. accreditation teams Middle States Assn. Colls. and Secondary Schs., 1963-94, New Eng. Assn. Schs. and Colls., 1986-94; bd. dirs. U.S. Book Exchange, 1973-76, 80-83; exec. com. New Eng. Libr. Info. Network, 1974-76, 79-85, chmn., 1982-84; mem. Adv. Commn. Historic Deerfield, 1975-81, 86-94. Mem. ALA, Am. Hist. Assn., Assn. Coll. Rsch. Libraries (pres. 1970-71, chmn. constn. and bylaws com. New Eng. chpt. 1975-76, pres. New Eng. chpt. 1983-84).*

EDMONDS, MARY PATRICIA, biological sciences educator; b. Racine, Wis., May 7, 1922; d. Millard Samuel and Sarah (Gibbons) E. BA, Milw.-Downer Coll., 1943; MA, Wellesley (Mass.) Coll., 1945; PhD, U. Pa., 1951; DSc (hon.), Lawrence U., 1983. Instr. Wellesley Coll., 1945-46; postdoctoral fellow U. Ill., Urbana, 1950-52, U. Wis., Madison, 1952-55; rsch. assoc. Montefiore Hosp., Pitts., 1955-65; asst. prof. U. Pitts., 1965-71, assoc. prof., 1971-76, prof., 1976—; mem. molecular biology study sect. NIH, Bethesda, Md., 1974-78. Contbr. articles to profl. jours. Recipient Woman of Yr. in Sci. award Chatham Coll., 1986; Rsch. Career Devel. award NIH, 1962-71, rsch. grantee, 1962-91. Mem. NAS, Am. Soc. Biol. Chemists, Am. Soc. for Cancer Rsch. Office: U Pitts Dept Biol Sci Pittsburgh PA 15260

EDMONDS, VELMA MCINNIS, nursing educator; b. N.Y.C., Feb. 17, 1940; d. Walter Lee and Eva Doris (Grant) McInnis; children: Stephen Clay, Michelle Louise. Diploma, Charity Hosp. Sch. Nursing, New Orleans, 1961; BSN, Med. Coll. Ga., 1968; MSN, U. Ala., Birmingham, 1980; postgrad. in doctoral nursing sci., La. State U., 1994—. Staff nurse Ochsner Found. Hosp., New Orleans, 1961-63, 1987—, clin. educator, 1987-89; staff nurse Suburban Hosp., Bethesda, Md., 1963-65; asst. DON svc., dir. staff devel. Providence Hosp., Mobile, Ala., 1967-70; staff nurse MICU U. So. Ala. Med. Ctr., Mobile, 1980-82, clin. nurse specialist, nutrition/metabolic support, 1982-84; instr., coord., BSN completion program Northwestern State Univ., Coll. Nursing, Natchitoches, La., 1984-86; head nurse So. Bapt. Hosp., New Orleans, 1986-87; asst. prof. sch. nursing med. ctr. La. State U., New Orleans, 1991—; clin. coord. Transitional Hosp. Corp., 1994—; mem. La. State Bd. Examiners in Dietetics and Nutrition. Recipient Excellence in Nursing group award Ochsner Fedn. Hosp., New Orleans, 1987, cert. Merit Tuberculosis Assn. Greater New Orleans, 1961. Mem. ANA, La. State Nurses' Assn. (dist. 7), Am. Soc. Parenteral and Enteral Nutrition, La. State Soc. Parenteral and Enteral Nutrition (program and edn. coms.), Assn. La. State Soc. Parenteral and Enteral Nutrition, Mobile Area Nonvolitional Nutrition Support Assn. (past pres.), Sigma Theta Tau.

EDMONDSON, ORELIA JOANNE, counselor/educator; b. Byron, Ga., Oct. 1, 1940; d. William Joseph and Frances Orelia (Herndon) Holt; m. Gerald Gelon Edmondson, Aug. 23, 1958; children: Sheree Dawn Edmondson Anderson, Gerald Gelon Edmondson, Jr. BS, Tift Coll., 1969; MEd, North Ga. Coll., 1980; EdS, Ga. State U., 1988, PhD, 1993. Cert. sch. counselor; cert. tchr. K-8. Tchr. music various, Ga., 1958-69; tchr. English Dudley Hughes Vocat. Sch., Macon, Ga., 1961-62; tchr. 4th and sixth grades Clisby Elem. Sch./Bibb County, Macon, 1969-70; tchr. sixth and second grades Pye Elem. Sch./Bibb County, Macon, 1970-72; migrant tchr. Lumpkin County Bd. Edn., Dahlonega, Ga., 1973-77; asst. coord. North Ga. Migrant Edn. Consortium, Canton, 1977-78, coord., 1978-80; tchr. fourth grade Lumpkin County Elem. Sch., Dahlonega, 1980-85; sch. counselor Lumpkin County Mid. Sch., Dahlonega, 1985—; cons., presenter nat. confs. on migrant edn., 1977-80, Ea. Stream Conf., 1977-80, Ga. Conf. on Migrant Edn., 1975-80; cons., presenter Internat. Reading Assn., 1979-80, Nat. Com. on Career Edn., 1977-80, Southeastern Confs. on At-Risk Students, 1990-94. Co-author: Career Education K-12, 1979; author: (musical drama) Celebrating the Chattahoochee Baptist Association's Sesquicentennial, 1976. Mem. Lumpkin County Youth Coun., Dahlonega, Ga., 1988-92; chair for Goal 2, Lumpkin 2000, Dahlonega, 1992-94. Named Tchr. of Yr. Ga. Dept. Edn./Migrant Edn., Atlanta, 1978, Coord. of Yr., 1980. Mem. Profl. Assn. Ga. Educators, Am. Counseling Assn., Ga. Sch. Counselor Assn., Am. Sch. Counselor Assn., Alpha Delta Kappa, Kappa Delta Pi, Chi Simga Iota. Baptist. Home: 1155 Cloudland Rd Dahlonega GA 30533-8819 Office: Lumpkin County Mid Sch 200 School Hill Rd NE Dahlonega GA 30533-1065

EDMONSON, AVA MCDANIEL, environmental geologist; b. Magnolia, Miss., Sept. 25, 1951; d. Dewitte Eugene and Geraldine (Eisworth) McDaniel; m. John Tinsley Edmonson, Feb. 13, 1977; children: Joshua, Benjamin, Jesse. BS in Geology, Millsaps Coll., Jackson, Miss., 1985. Environ. field tech. Environ. Engring., Inc., Norman, Okla., 1976-77; paralegal Howell Law Firm, Jackson, Miss., 1987-90; Right of Way clearance sect. chief Miss. Dept. Transp., Jackson, 1990—. Mem. Internat. Right of Way Assn. (environ. chmn. 1992-93). Office: Miss Dept Transp PO Box 1850 Jackson MS 39215

EDMONSON, JUDITH ANNE, cemetery manager; b. Burbank, Calif., Dec. 14, 1957; d. Donald James and Claire Mary (Loroña) Miller; m. Steven Alec Edmonson, Aug. 4, 1984. Grad., Coll. Marin, 1977. Adminstrv. asst. Congregation Emanu-El, San Francisco, 1977-87; gen. mgr. Home of Peace Cemetery, Colma, Calif., 1987—, Hills of Eternity Cemetery, Colma, 1993—; sec./treas. Associated Cemeteries of San Francisco, 1989—. mem. Interment Assn. Calif., Am. Cemetery Assn. Office: Home of Peace Cemetery 1299 El Camino Real Colma CA 94014-3238

EDMUNDS, JANE CLARA, communications consultant; b. Chgo., Mar. 16, 1922; d. John Carson and Clara (Kummerow) Carrigan; m. William T. Dean, Aug. 30, 1947 (div. 1953; dec. July 1984); 1 son, John Charles; Edmund S. Kopacz, Sept. 24, 1955 (div. 1973); children: Christine Ellen, Jan Carson. Student in math., Northwestern U. Chemist Mars Inc., Oak Park, Ill., 1942-47; with Cons. Engr. Mag., Maujer Pub. Co., St. Joseph, Mich., 1953-58, 69-74; sr. editor Cons. Engr. Mag. Tech. Pub. Co., Barrington, Ill., 1975-77, exec. editor, 1977-82, editorial dir., 1983-86; asst. editor women's pages rewrite desk News-Palladium, Benton Harbor, Mich., 1967-68; free lance journalist St. Joseph, 1959-68; communications cons. Schaumburg, Ill., 1987—. Chmn. Berrien County (Mich.) Nat. Found. March of Dimes, 1968; mem. campaign com. Rep. Party, 1954. Recipient award Bausch & Lomb, 1940, award Nat. Found. Service, 1969, Silver Hat award Constrn. Writers Assn., 1986, Chmn.'s award Profl. Engrs. in Pvt. Practice div. NSPE, 1987; grantee AID, 1979. Assoc. fellow Soc. Tech. Communication (chmn. St. Joseph chpt. 1972 Disting. Tech. Communication awards); mem. Am. Soc. Bus. Press Editors (past bd. mem.), Constrn. Writers Assn. (past dir.), Smithsonian Instn., Chgo. Art Inst. Assocs., Field Mus. Assocs. Republican. Episcopalian. Office: 1404 Hampton Ln Schaumburg IL 60193-2531

EDMUNDS, NANCY GARLOCK, federal judge; b. Detroit, July 10, 1947; d. Joseph and Phyllis (Sandelman) Garlock; m. William C. Edmunds, 1977; children: Ben, Nathan. BA cum laude, Cornell U., 1969; MA in Teaching, U. Chgo., 1971; JD summa cum laude, Wayne U., 1976. Bar: Mich. 1976. With Plymouth Canton Public Schools, 1971-73; law clk. Barris, Sott, Denn & Driker, 1973-75; law clk. to Hon. Ralph Freeman U.S. Dist. Ct. (ea. dist.) Mich., 1976-78; ptnr. litigation sect. Dykema Gossett, 1984-92, resident Oakland County, 1986-92; judge U.S. Dist. Ct. (ea. dist.) Mich., 1992—; trustee Hist. Soc. U.S. Dist Ct. (ea. dist.) Mich. Bd. trustees Temple Beth El; mem. bus. and profl. women's divsn., lawyers' divsn. Jewish Welfare Fedn./Allied Jewish Campaign; mem. Saginaw Valley State U. Bd. Control, 1991-92. Mem. ABA, Fed. Judges Assn., Nat. Assn. Women Judges, Federalist Soc., State Bar Mich. (chair U.S. cts. com. 1990-91). Office: US Courthouse 231 W Lafayette Blvd Rm 211 Detroit MI 48226*

EDMUNDS, SHEILA, art historian; b. N.Y.C., Apr. 7, 1929; d. Mortimer and Mary Beatrice (Clark) E. BA in Art and English, St. Mary-of-the-Woods Coll., 1950; MA in Art History, Columbia U., 1952, PhD in Art History, 1961. Elem. sch. tchr. Omaha Pub. Schs., 1952-53, art tchr., 1953-56; from instr. to asst. prof. Smith Coll., Northampton, Mass., 1961-65; from asst. prof. to prof. Wells Coll., Aurora, N.Y., 1965-89, prof. emeritus, 1989—, curator art collection, 1989-92. Editor (local monthly newspaper) The Cricket, 1990-94; contbr. articles to profl. jours. Pres., trustee Schweinfurth Meml. Art Ctr., Auburn, N.Y., 1989-95; mem. Cayuga County Cath. Sch. Bd., Auburn, 1992-94; chair Cmty. Preservation Panel, Aurora, 1993—. Founders fellow AAUW; grantee NEH, 1985, Italian Govt., 1958-59. Mem. Coll. Art Assn., Internat. Ctr. of Medieval Art, Early Book Soc. Home: PO Box 358 Aurora NY 13026-0358

EDSON, MARIAN LOUISE, communications executive; b. Sidney, Mont., Mar. 21, 1940; d. David Ira and Myrtle (Ewing) Drury; m. James Arthur Edson, Oct. 14, 1961; children: Nadine L. Mykins, Jeanine Clare Edson. Student, U. Wash., 1961-62; BS, Mont. State U., 1962; postgrad., SUNY, Binghamton, 1975-76. Cert. tchr. Mont., Wash., N.Y. Lead editor, flight data file Johnson Space Ctr., Houston, 1980-85, coordinator for payload reconfiguration data collection, 1985-86, supr. flight data file, 1986-87; lead technical editor Bell Aerospace/Textron, Buffalo, N.Y., 1987; prodn. mgr. ASYST Software Tech., Rochester, N.Y., 1987-88, publ. mgr., 1988-94; publ. mgr. Raymond Corp., Greene, N.Y., 1994—; project dir. Raymond Corp., Greene, N.Y., 1994—. Edn. com. Bay Area League Women Voters, Houston, 1984-85; assoc. Rochester Women's Network, 1987—; founding mem. Macedon (N.Y.) Reading Ctr., 1968—. Fellow Life Office Mgmt. Assn.; mem. AIAA, Soc. Tech. Communicators (pres.), Nat. Mgmt. Assn., Nat. Assn. Purchasing Mgrs., Women in Comm. Inc., Genesee Ornithol. Soc., Rochester Acad. Sci. Republican. Home: 4 Boulevard Pky Rochester NY 14612-5515

EDWARDS, ALISYN ARDEN, psychologist; b. Winfield, Kans., Nov. 8, 1960; d. Warren Dale and Vera Colleen (Edwards) A. BA, U. Kans., 1982; M Marriage and Family Therapy, Abilene Christian U., 1984. Registered psychologist. Psychotherapist Mental Health Ctr. East Cen. Kans., Emporia, 1988-90; psychologist Sedgwick County Dept. Mental Health, Wichita, Kans., 1990-92; psychotherapist MCC Behavioral Care, Wichita, 1992-93, R & L Counseling & Referral Svc., Wichita, 1993-94; psychologist El Dorado Correctional Ctr, Eldorado, 1994—; intra-familial sexual abuse treatment team Mental Health Ctr. East Cen. Kans., Emporia, 1988-90. Violinist Mid-Kans. Symphony Orch., Friends U. Community Symphony, 1991-92. Mem. Am. Assn. Marriage and Family Therapy (clin.), Kans. Assn. Marriage and Family Therapy. Office: El Dorado Correctional Facility PO Box 311 El Dorado KS 67042

EDWARDS, ANNETTE WINFREY, nurse; b. Richmond, Va., June 25, 1963; d. William Elisha and Addie Nell (Price) Winfrey; m. David Scott Edwards, Dec. 28, 1957. BSN, Oral Roberts U., 1985; MSN, Marymount U., 1988. Cert. ACLS instr., PALS instr. Clin. nurse in med./surg. area Malcolm Grow USAF Med. Ctr., Andrews AFB, Md., 1985-88; clin. nurse in emergency rm. Malcolm Grow USAF Med. Ctr., Andrews AFB, 1988-90; charge nurse in outpatient clinics 63D Med. Group, Norton AFB, Calif., 1990-93; nurse mgr. in pediatric clinic 722D Med. Group, March AFB, Calif., 1994—. Mem. Air Force Assn., Emergency Nurses Assn. (cert.), Sigma Theta Tau Internat. Soc. of Nursing. Republican. Baptist. Home: 28227 Cherokee Rose Dr Highland CA 92346 Office: USAF 722D Med Group SGHMC March AFB CA 92518

EDWARDS, CAROLYN MULLENAX, public relations executive; b. French Camp, Calif., Dec. 3, 1943; d. Charles Harold and Jessie Jewel (Frost) Mullenax; m. Helton Pressley (div.); m. Dennis D. Edwards, May 29, 1993. BFA, U. Tulsa, 1967; MEd, Ea. N.Mex. U., 1976. Artist Wessels Agy., Spokane, Wash., 1968-70; pub. rels. dir. Spokane (Wash.) Symphony Soc., 1970-72; advt. coord. Crescent Dept. Store, Spokane, 1972-73; art dir., copywriter Sta. KMTY Radio, Clovis, N.Mex., 1976; news editor Clovis News Jour., Clovis, 1976-77; promotion and art dir. Sta. KENW-TV, Portales, N.Mex., 1977-78; coord. alumni affairs and pubs. Ea. N.Mex. U., Portales, 1978-80; dir. pubs., TV and pub. info. Ea. N.Mex. U., Clovis, 1985-90; dir. mktg. & pub. info. Clovis Community Coll. (formerly Ea. N.Mex. U.-Clovis), 1990—; producer pub. affairs program Sta. KMCC-TV, Clovis, 1981-84; devel. and pub. info. dir. Mental Health Resources Inc., Portales, N.Mex., 1980-85. Bd. dirs. N.Mex. Outdoor Drama Assn., San Jon, 1986—, Univ. Symphony League, Clovis, 1984-88. Mem. N.Mex. Press Women (scholarship chair 1994—, comm. awards 1981-94), Nat. Fedn. Press Women (comm. awards 1984-93), Am. Women in Radio and TV, Clovis C. of C. (bd. dirs. 1984-89), Jr. League (Lubbock, Tex.), Coun. for Advancement and Support Edn. (sec.-editor dist. IV 1990-92, design award 1991), Nat. Coun. for Mktg. and Pub. Rels. (dist. IV award 1989, 90, 91), Altrusa Club. Republican. Episcopalian. Office: Clovis CC 417 Schepps Blvd Clovis NM 88101-8381

EDWARDS, DAWN ANN, marketing professional; b. Valley Forge, Pa., Jan. 13, 1956; d. George Francis and Severina (Bacer) E. BS, Syracuse U., 1978, MS, 1979. Account mgmt. staff asst. Ted Bates Worldwide, Inc., N.Y.C., 1980-83; asst. account exec. Backer & Spielvogel, Inc., N.Y.C., 1983-85; asst. product mgr. Am. Home Products Corp., N.Y.C., 1985-86, Carter-Wallace, Inc., N.Y.C., 1986-89; product mgr. L&F Products Inc. subs. Eastman Kodak, Montvale, N.J., 1989-91; bus. devel. mgr. Pfizer, Inc., N.Y.C., 1991-93; worldwide mktg. sr. product mgr. Oral-B Labs. divsn. The Gillette Co., Redwood City, Calif., 1993—. Mem. Healthcare Bus. Womens Assn., Am. Mktg. Assn., Soc. Childrens Book Writers and Illustrators, Syracuse U. Alumni Assn., Delta Gamma Alumnae. Home: 751 Laurel St Box 424 San Carlos CA 94070 Office: The Gillette Co Oral-B Labs divsn 1 Lagoon Dr Redwood City CA 94065-1562

EDWARDS, ESTHER G., museum administrator, former record, film and entertainment company executive; b. Oconee, Ga.; d. Berry and Bertha Ida (Fuller) Gordy; m. George H. Edwards, Apr. 12, 1951 (dec.); 1 son (by previous marriage), Robert Bullock. Ed., Howard U., Wayne State U. Sr. v.p., sec., dir. Motown Record Corp., Detroit, 1959-1988; sec., dir. Jobete Music Pub. Co., Inc., 1959—; sr. v.p., corporate sec. Motown Industries, Hollywood, Calif., 1973-88; founder, pres. Motown Hist. Mus., Detroit, 1988—; dir. Bank of the Commonwealth, 1972-79. Bd. dirs. Detroit Econ. Growth Corp.; exec. dir. Gordy Found., 1968—; chmn. Wayne County Democratic Women's Com., 1956; Mich. del.-at-large Dem. Nat. Conv., 1960; bd. dirs. Martin Luther King Center for Social Change; trustee Founders Soc. of Detroit Inst. Arts; mem. corp. Lawrence Tech. U., Southfield, Mich.; chmn. Motown Mus. Hist. Found., Detroit, 1985—; commr. Mich. Hist. Commn., 1989—. Mem. Greater Detroit C. of C. (treas., exec. bd. 1973-79), Met. Detroit Conv. and Visitors Bur. (v.p. exec. bd.), Econ. Club Detroit (dir.), African Am. Heritage Assn. (founder, chmn.), Alpha Kappa Alpha, Gamma Phi Delta. Office: Motown Hist Mus 2648 W Grand Blvd Detroit MI 48208-1237

EDWARDS, FLORENCE RENAÉ, medical laboratory administrator; b. Bklyn., Sept. 17, 1943; d. William and Addie Carolyn (Brown) Stephens; m. James Maurice Lemmons, Dec. 13, 1964 (div. Sept. 1970); children: James Jr., Lisa, Stephen; m. Ivory Gene Edwards, Feb. 4, 1976. BS in Chemistry, Bklyn. Coll., 1975; MS in Community Health, L.I. Coll., 1992. Histology technician N.Y. Hosp., N.Y.C., 1965-66; histology technician Kingsbrook Jewish Med. Ctr., Bklyn., 1967-80, supr. anatomic pathology, 1980-91, lab. adminstr., 1991—; mem. Elim Internat. Women's Health Com., Bklyn., 1993. Pres. Putnam 700 Jr. Block Assn., Bklyn., 1965-90. Recipient Award of Merit, Putnam Ave. Block Assn., 1991, Achievement awards Stuyvesant Heights Lions Club, 1993. Mem. Am. Soc. Clin. Pathologists (cert.), Nat. Soc. Histotech. (cert.), Clin. Lab. Mgmt. Assn., Order of Ea. Star (matron 1975-80). Democrat. Home: 753 Putnam Ave Brooklyn NY 11221

EDWARDS, GWEN ELIZABETH, superintendent; b. Harrisonburg, Va., Nov. 2, 1946; d. Alvin Gordon and Mary Elizabeth (Wonderley) E.; m. Bobby L. Lilly, Dec. 18, 1968 (div. Oct. 1988); children: Amy Beth Huddleston, Scot E. Lilly. BS in Elem. Edn., Va. Commonwealth U., 1979, MEd in Adminstrn. and Supervision, 1984, PhD in Urban Svcs., 1988. Tchr. Henrico County Pub. Schs., Richmond, Va., 1979-84, adminstrv. asst., 1984-86; asst. prin. King William (Va.) County Pub. Schs., 1986-87, dir. instruction and pers., 1987-89; prin. Rockingham County Pub. Schs., Harrisonburg, Va., 1989-91; asst. supt. for instruction Page County Pub. Schs., Luray, Va., 1991-93; asst. supt. for adminstrv. svc. Danville (Va.) City Pub. Schs., 1993—; facilities cons. Nelson County Pub. Schs., Lovingston, Va., 1986-87; edn. adv. com. Lord Fairfax C.C., Winchester, Va., 1992; chmn. prins. adv. com. Rockingham County Schs., Harrisonburg, Va., 1990; curriculum cons. Chesapeake Bay Found., Annapolis, Md., 1984. Contbr. articles to profl. jours. Mem. Port Rep. (Va.) Meth. Ch., 1954—; mem. Lord Fairfax Tech Prep, Winchester, 1992-93. Fellowship Va. Commonwealth U., 1986. Mem. ASCD, Riverview Rotary Club, Am. Assn. of Sch. Adminstrs., Danville Mus., Phi Delta Kappa, Phi Kappa Phi (scholarship 1986). Office: Danville City Pub Schs 313 Municipal Bldg Danville VA 24541

EDWARDS, IRENE ELIZABETH (LIBBY EDWARDS), dermatologist, educator, researcher; b. Winston-Salem, N.C., Mar. 17, 1950; d. Robert Dixon Edwards and Irene Octavia (Temple) Fisher; m. Clayton Samuel Owens, Apr. 19, 1985; 1 child, Sarah Tay. BS magna cum laude, Wake Forest U., 1972; MD, Bowman Gray Sch. Medicine, 1976; postgrad., N.C. Bapt. Hosp., 1979, U. Ariz., 1981, 84. Diplomate Nat. Bd. Med. Examiners, Am. Bd. Internal Medicine, Am. Bd. Pediatrics, Am. Bd. Dermatology. Intern N.C. Bapt. Hosp., Winston-Salem, 1976-78, resident in pediatrics, 1978-79; resident in internal medicine U. Ariz. Health Scis. Ctr., Tucson, 1979-81, resident in dermatology, 1982-84; instr. dermatology U. Ariz. Coll. Medicine, Tucson, 1984-85, asst. prof. dermatology, 1985-90; chief section dermatology Tucson VA Med. Ctr., 1984-90; chief dermatology Carolinas Med. Ctr., Charlotte, N.C., 1990—; clin. assoc. prof. dermatology Bowman Gray Sch. Medicine, Winston-Salem, 1993—, U. N.C., Chapel Hill, 1993—; nat. lectr. in field. Co-author: Genital Dermatology, 1994; contbr. chpts. to books, numerous articles to profl. jours. Reynolds scholar, 1969-72; recipient Lange Med. Publs. award, 1976. Fellow Am. Acad. Dermatology, Am. Acad. Pediatrics; mem. Soc. Pediatric Dermatology, Internat. Soc. Tropical Dermatology, Soc. Investigative Dermatology, Women's Dermatologic Soc., Internat. Soc. Study of Vulvar Disease, Charlotte Dermatological Soc., Phi Beta Kappa, Alpha Epsilon Delta. Home: 2409 Cuthbertson Rd Waxhaw NC 28173 Office: Carolinas Med Ctr 1000 Blythe Blvd Charlotte NC 28203

EDWARDS, JANE, computer consultant; b. St. Louis, May 21, 1953; d. William Clark and Rose (Szyrwiel) E.; m. Louis Samuel Zarfas, Sept. 18, 1976 (div. 1994); children: Katherine, Davis. BA in English and Journalism, N.Y.U., 1976. Freelance computer cons., Annandale, Va., 1989—. Author: Ventura 4.2: Beyond the Basics, 1993. Leader, trainer Girl Scouts Am. (Thanks award 1992). Mem. Ventura Pub. Users Group. Episcopalian. Home and Office: 3341 Monarch Ln Annandale VA 22003-1152

EDWARDS, JANE PETERSON, guidance counselor; b. Glasgow, Ky., Aug. 29, 1956; d. Robert Terry and Elizabeth Ann (Dooley) Peterson; m. Kenneth C. Edwards Jr., July 15, 1978; children: Katherine Barrett, Meghan Elizabeth. BS, U. Ky., 1978; MA, Western Ky. U., 1979, postgrad., 1987—. Tchr. Barren County H.S., Glasgow, Ky., 1984-91; counselor Barren River Area Alternative Sch., Glasgow, Ky., 1991-92, Caverna H.S., Horse Cave, Ky., 1992—; presenter Dropout Prevention Conf., Louisville, 1987, Region 2 Edn. Reform Act Sharing Conf., Elizabethtown and Bowling Green, Ky., 1992. Leader, judge local 4-H Clubs, Barren County, 1978—; mem. Ky. Young Farmers Assn., Glasgow, 1979—, Am. Pvt. Enterprise Planning Com., Barren and Hart Counties, 1987—. Recipient Cert. of Appreciation U.S. Army Recruiting Command, 1993, USAF Recruiting Svc., 1993, Cert. of Leadership Am. Pvt. Enterprise Program, 1987—. Mem. ASCD, DAR, Ky. Assn. Sch. Adminstrs., Ky. Sch. Counselors Assn., South Ctrl. Counseling Assn., Ky. Counselors Assn., Alpha Gamma Delta (scholarship advisor 1989—). Home: 460 Jack Turner Rd Cave City KY 42127 Office: Caverna HS 2276 S Dixie Hwy Horse Cave KY 42749

EDWARDS, JANE WEBB, controller; b. High Point, N.C., Feb. 8, 1944; d. Wesley O. and Dorothy Mae (Price) W.; m. Larry David Edwards, Aug. 6, 1966; children: Mary Ann, Larry David Jr. Attended, Marywood Coll., 1961-63; BS in Math., U. N.C., 1965. Computer programmer Burlington Industries, Mooresville, N.C., 1966-68; systems analyst Burlington Industries, Cramerton, N.C., 1968-71; programmer-analyst Carolina Computer Systems, Charlotte, N.C., 1971-72, American & Efird Mills, Mt. Holly, N.C., 1973-78; bookkeeper Turtle Creek Nursery, Huntersville, 1972-78; pres., gen. mgr. Turtle Creek Garden Ctr., Charlotte, N.C., 1978-88; controller, v.p. Turtle Creek Nursery, Davidson, N.C., 1988-94; mem. bd. dirs. N.C. Nurserymen's Assn., Knightdale, N.C., 1989-93; lt. gov. Am. Assn. Nurserymen, Washington, D.C., 1994-95. Author, prodr. 5min. radio PSA spots on nursery and plant care, 1984-90. Sec., v.p. PTA Huntersville Elem. Sch., N.C., 1976-79; chmn. ways & means com. PTA Alex Jr. High Sch., 1979-81; pres. finance, mem. parish coun. St. Therese Cath. Ch., Mooresville, N.C., 1984-85; chmn. Huntersville Park and Recreation Commn., 1975-77. Mem. Am. Assn. Nurserymen, So. Nursery Assn., N.C. Nurserymen's Assn., Internat. Plant Propagators Soc. Roman Catholic. Office: Turtle Creek Nursery Inc 12037 Mooresville Rd Davidson NC 28036

EDWARDS, JUDITH ELIZABETH, advertising executive; b. St. Louis, May 22, 1933; d. Archie Earl and Ivy Elizabeth (Jones) Hector; m. George N. LaMont Jr., Jan. 9, 1960 (div. Oct. 1965); m. Gary W. Edwards, Nov. 25, 1966; stepchildren: Michael Brent, David Reed Edwards. Grad. high sch., St. Louis, 1951; student, Brown's Bus. Coll., St. Louis. Exec. sec., asst. to chmn. Rep. Nat. Com., Washington, 1958-60; dep. to county clk. Vandervurgh County, Evansville, Ind., 1972-76; sec.-treas. Edwards Outdoor Advtg., Carmi, Ill., 1979—; mem. Evansville Health Planning Coun., 1974-76. Pres. White County Rep. Women's Club, Carmi, 1989—, White County Hosp. Aux. Named Ky. Col. Mem. Carmi Bus. and Profl. Women's Club, Carmi C. of C., Kiwanis, Order Ea. Star, Sigma Alpha. Methodist. Office: PO Box 250 Carmi IL 62821-0250

EDWARDS, KATHRYN INEZ, educational technology consultant; b. L.A., Aug. 26, 1947; d. Lloyd and Geraldine E. (Smith) Price; 1 child, Bryan. BA in English, Calif. State U., L.A., 1969, supervision credential, 1974, adminstrn. credential, 1975; MEd in Curriculum, UCLA, 1971; PhD, Claremont Grad. Sch., 1979. Tchr., L.A. Pub. Schs., 1969-78, adv. specially funded programs, 1978-80, advisor librs. and learning-resources program, 1980-81, instructional specialist, 1981-84; cons. instructional media L.A. County Office of Edn., Downey, Calif., 1984-90; coord. edn1. media and tech. Pomona (Calif.) Unified Sch. Dist., 1990-92; cons. edn. tech. Apple Computer, Inc., 1992—; cons. Walt Disney Prodns., Alfred Higgins Prodns., others. Author guides and curriculum kits. Appointed by assembly speaker Willie Brown to Calif. Ednl. Tech. Com., 1990-92, Calif. State Assembly Resolution from Gwen Moore, 1988, Edn. Coun. for Tech. in Learning, 1993; mem. spl. com. Cable Access Corp. Cowners, 1991-92. Recipient cert. commendation Senator Diane Watson, 1988; Mabel Wilson Richards scholar, 1968, Calif. Congress Parents and Tchrs. scholar, 1968; UCLA fellow, 1968; named Outstanding Woman of Yr. L.A. Sentinel, 1987. Mem. Nat. Assn. Minority Polit. Women, Internat. Reading Assn. (speaker nat. conv. 1988), L.A. Reading Assn. (pres.), Calif. Assn. Tchrs. of English (conf. del. 1982), Assn. Supervision and Curriculum Devel., Calif. Media and Libr. Educators Assn. (state conf. co-chair 1989, v.p. legal divsn. 1992—), Nat. Assn. Media Women (Media Woman of Yr. 1987), Alpha Kappa Alpha. Democrat. Roman Catholic. Avocations: reading, gardening, sewing. Office: Apple Computer Inc 600 Corporate Pt Ste 1200 Culver City CA 90230

EDWARDS, KIMBERLY, elementary educator; b. Norristown, Pa., Apr. 11, 1961; d. Freeman Lee and Bette Mae (Young) E. BA, Eastern Coll., 1984. Residential supr. Devereux Found., Devon, Pa., 1981-84, North East Mental Health Ctr., Phila., 1984-86; instr. for tellers Penn Savings Bank, Reading, Pa., 1986-88; 5th grade tchr. Reading Sch. Dist., 1988—. Mem. Reading Edn. Assn. (recipient We Honor Our Own award 1991). Democrat. Home: 1401 N 10th Stt Reading PA 19604 Office: Reading Sch Dist 400 N 10th St Reading PA 19604

EDWARDS, LORI MICHELLE, accountant; b. Kansas City, Mo., July 20, 1961; d. McGill and Erma Lee (Handy) E. BSBA, Rockhurst Coll., Kansas City, Mo., 1986. Staff auditor Coopers & Lybrand, Kansas City, 1986-88;

divisional acct. Olsten Kimberly Quality Care, Overland Park, Kans., 1988-94; acctg. mgr. The Lewer Agy., Kansas City, Mo., 1994—. Bd. dirs. Palestine OutReach Ctr., Kansas City, 1992-94. Mem. Gamma Phi Delta. (editor-in-chief 1991-92). Baptist. Home: 6211 E 108th Ter Kansas City MO 64134

EDWARDS, LYDIA JUSTIS, state official; b. Carter County, Ky., July 9, 1937; d. Chead and Velva (Kinney) Justice; m. Frank B. Edwards, 1968; children: Mark, Alexandra, Margot. Student, San Francisco State U. Began career as acct., then Idaho state rep., 1982-86; treas. State of Idaho, 1987—; legis. asst. to Gov. Hickel, Alaska, 1967; conf. planner Rep. Gov.'s Assn., 1970-73; mem. Rep. Nat. Commn., 1972, del. to nat. conv., 1980. Mem. Rep. Womens Fedn. Congregationalist. Office: State Treas Office PO Box 83720 Boise ID 83702-0091*

EDWARDS, MARGARET MCRAE, college administrator, lawyer; b. Wadesboro, N.C., July 2, 1931; d. Martin Alexander and Margaret Ashe (Redfearn) McRae; m. Sterling J. Edwards, June 30, 1953; children: Martin, Robert, Lee, Elizabeth. BA cum laude, Agnes Scott Coll., 1953; JD cum laude, Cumberland Law Sch., 1979. Bar: N.C. 1979, Ala. 1980, Fla. 1981. Asst. to alumnae dir. Mt. Vernon Coll., Washington, 1961-64; devel. staff S.E. Inst., Chapel Hill, N.C., 1973-75; law clk. U.S. Dist. Ct., Birmingham, 1979-80; atty. Carlton, Fields, Tampa, Fla., 1980-82; pvt. practice Birmingham, 1983-85; dir. planned giving Birmingham-So. Coll., 1985-90, assoc. v.p. for endowment and planned giving, 1991—; cons. Blackbaud Planned Giving Conf., Charleston, S.C., 1991—, Planned Giving, Philanthropic Action Coun., Tampa, 1980-82, Am. Philanthropy Group, Birmingham, 1983-88; prof. bus. law Samford U., Birmingham, 1984. Index editor: Manual for Complex Litigation, 1985. Bd. dirs. Girls Club, Birmingham, 1984-90, Ala. Planned Giving Coun., 1991-94, Ala. divsn. Am. Cancer Soc., co-chair major gifts, 1991—; speakers bur. Nat. Com. on Planned Giving. Recipient Achievement award in Planned Giving, Coun. for Achievement and Support of Edn., 1992, Will/Tax award Young Lawyers Assn., 1979, Estate Planning award Am. Jurisprudence, 1979. Mem. Am. Arbitration Assn. (arbitrator 1985—), Audubon Soc. (bd. dirs.), Agnes Scott Alumnae (pres. Birmingham 1967-69, Charleston, S.C. 1954-55). Presbyterian. Home: 4239 Chickamauga Rd Birmingham AL 35213-1811 Office: Birmingham-So Coll Arkadelphia Rd Birmingham AL 35254

EDWARDS, MARIE BABARE, psychologist; b. Tacoma; d. Nick and Mary (Mardesich) Babare; B.A., Stanford, 1948, M.A., 1949; m. Tilden Hampton Edwards (div.); 1 son, Tilden Hampton Edwards Jr. Counselor guidance center U. So. Calif., Los Angeles, 1950-52; project coordinator So. Calif. Soc. Mental Hygiene, 1952-54; pub. speaker Welfare Fedn. Los Angeles, 1953-57; field rep. Los Angeles County Assn. Mental Health, 1957-58; intern psychologist UCLA, 1958-60; pvt. practice, human rels. tng., counselor tng. Mem. Calif., Am., Western, Los Angeles psychol. assns., AAAS, So. Calif. Soc. Clin. Hypnosis, Internat. Platform Assn. Author: (with Eleanor Hoover) The Challenge of Being Single, 1974, paperback edit., 1975. Office: 6100 Buckingham Pky Culver City CA 90230-7237

EDWARDS, MARSHA EPPS, lawyer, educator; b. Covington, Tenn., June 11, 1951; d. Willie Artway and LaVerne (Epps) Edwards. BS, U. Tenn., Martin, 1974; JD, Howard U., 1983. Bar: D.C., Pa. Teaching asst. U. Tenn., Martin, 1974-76; tchr., dir. Martin Day Care Ctr., 1976-77; tchr. Tipton County Schs., Covington, Tenn., 1977-79; mentoring advocate Greater Washington Urban League, 1993—; atty. Scott & Yallery-Arthur, Washington, 1983—. Editor Sierra Leone Rev., 1991—; mem. editorial staff Howard Law Jour., 1981-83. Mem., vol. TransAfrica, Washington, 1985—; mem. D.C. steering com. Efficacy, Washington, 1989-91; gen. counsel The Rep, Inc., Washington, 1993—. Mem. Howard U. Law Alumni Assn. (com. chair 1983—), Delta Sigma Theta, Phi Delta Phi. Office: Scott & Yallery-Arthur 7603 Georgia Ave NW Ste 200 Washington DC 20012-1617

EDWARDS, MARY JANE, artist, educator; b. DuQuoin, Ill., May 12, 1946; d. Frank Robert Jr. and Marion Catherine (Downs) E. BA, U. Dallas, 1969; MA, No. Ill. U., 1971, MFA, 1972. mem. adv. com. Handmade in Am., 1994. Asst., then assoc. prof. Nazareth Coll., Rochester, N.Y., 1972-88; prof., head dept. art U. Wyo., Laramie, 1988—. Craftsman trustee Am. Craft Coun., N.Y.C., 1986-91, trustee emeritus, 1993; bd. dirs. Nat. Campaign for Freedom of Expression, Washington, 1992—; mem. nat. adv. bd. Handmade in Am., 1994—. Fellow Nat. Coun. on Edn. for Ceramic Arts (pres. 1986-92, publs. chair, editor 1982-86); mem. Coll. Art Assn., Wyo. Arts Coun., Nat. Assn. Arts Adminstrs. (bd. dirs., sec. 1991—). Democrat. Buddhist. Home: 1067 Empinado Dr Laramie WY 82070-5018 Office: U Wyo Dept Art Box 3138 Laramie WY 82071-3138

EDWARDS, MARY LOUISE, clergywoman, accountant; b. Schlater, Miss., Mar. 22, 1946; d. Eugene Wilson and Mary Eliza (Flowers) Wall; m. Alton Edwards, Dec. 31, 1971 (div. Dec. 1993); 1 child, Alton. BBA, Memphis State U., 1975; student, Memphis Theol. Sem., 1987. Ordained minister Christian Meth. Episcopal Ch., 1988. Pastor Johnson Chapel Christian Meth. Episcopal Ch., Memphis, 1988-91, Grady Chapel Christian Meth. Episcopal Ch., Memphis, 1991-92, Coleman Chapel Christian Meth. Episcopal Ch., Memphis, 1992—; agt. IRS, Memphis, 1977—; dir. of employment Nat. Assn. Accts., Memphis, 1981-82. Mem. Inst. Mgmt. Accts. Home: 4428 Pepper Tree Rd Memphis TN 38109

EDWARDS, MONA GILLIS, local government administrator; b. Newport News, Va.; d. Clarence M. and Elizabeth (Bell) Gillis; m. Emanuel C. Edwards; 2 children. BA, U. Va., 1979; JD, Washington and Lee U., 1983; postgrad., Inst. of Govt., U. N.C., 1993. Bar: Va. 1983. Atty. Edwards Law Offices, Roanoke, Va., 1984-87; claims dep. Va. Employment Commn., Roanoke, 1987-88; Gov.'s mgmt. intern Commonwealth of Va., Richmond, 1988-90; EEO/Affirmative Action compliance officer Va. Tech U., Blacksburg, 1990-91; spl. asst. adminstrv. programs City Mgrs. Office City of Greensboro, N.C., 1992—; mem. Mgmt. Roundtable, City of Greensboro, 1993. Mem., mem. program com. Leadership Greensboro, 1992—; chair, mem. bus. ptnrs. com. Summerfield (N.C.) Elem. Sch. PTA, 1993. Mem. Am. Soc. Pub. Adminstrs., Nat. Forum for Black Pub. Adminstrs., Jack and Jill of Am., Inc. (group leader 1992), Girl Scouts Am. (parent mem.). Office: City of Greensboro 301 W Washington Greensboro NC 27402-3136

EDWARDS, PHYLLIS MAE, accountant, graphologist; b. Wichita, Kans., June 25, 1921; d. William Noble and Nettie Mae (Riggs) Merry; m. Joseph Andrew Edwards, Sept. 19, 1945 (dec.); children: Joseph Noble (dec.), James Richard, Robert Andrew, Jacqueline Merry. Student, Bus. Preparatory Sch., Wichita, Kans., 1939; BA in Journalism, Wichita State U., 1944; grad. advanced graphologist, Sampson Inst. Graphology, 1967; cert. of proficiency, Tao Acupuncture, 1975; D of Graphology Sci., Rocky Mountain Graphology, 1978. Cert. profl. graphologist. Sec., bookkeeper Healy & Co., Wichita, 1939-42, Wichita State U., 1942-43; acct. Moberly & West, Pub. Accts., Wichita, 1943-45, McQuain, Edwards & Teffs, Oakland, Calif., 1952-55; acct., graphologist Rocky Mountain Graphology Sch., Denver, 1972-81; prin. Multi-Pro Svcs., Denver, 1976—; acct. Indsl. Hard Chrome Plating Co., Denver, 1957—; expert witness for all levels of ct., Colo., Wyo., 1976—; pub. and pvt. speaker Colo., Wyo., 1976—; sec., treas. Indsl. Hard Chrome Plating Co., Denver, 1990-94. Den mother Aurora (Colo.) Cub Scout Troop, 1956-59; asst. troop leader Girl Scouts U.S., Denver, 1960-64; charity fund raiser various churches, schs., and non-profit orgns., 1967—. Mem. AAUW (Denver br. treas. 1975-77, bull. editor 1980-81, 92-93, sec. 1986-88, roster/circulation editor, pres.-elect 1988-90, pres. 1990-92, chair interbr. coun. 1991-92), Am. Handwriting Analysts Found. (Rocky Mountain chpt.), Am. Assn. Handwriting Analysts, Coun. Graphological Socs., Rocky Mountain Graphology Assn. (treas. 1972-81), U. Denver Women's Libr. Assn. Home: 2986 S Fairfax St Denver CO 80222-6841 Office: Indsl Hard Chrome Plating 919 Santa Fe Dr Denver CO 80204-3936

EDWARDS, ROBIN MORSE, lawyer; b. Glens Falls, N.Y., Dec. 9, 1947; d. Daniel and Harriet Lois (Welpen) Morse; m. Richard Charles Edwards, Aug. 30, 1970; children: Michael Alan, Jonathan Philip. BA, Mt. Holyoke Coll., 1969; JD, U. Calif., Berkeley, 1972. Bar: Calif. 1972. Assoc. Donahue, Gallagher, Thomas & Woods, Oakland, Calif., 1972-77, ptnr., 1977-89; ptnr. Sonnenschein, Nath & Rosenthal, San Francisco, 1989—. Mem. ABA, Calif. Bar Assn., Alameda County Bar Assn. (bd. dirs. 1978-84, v.p. 1982, pres. 1983), Entrepreneurship Inst. East Bay (bd. dirs. 1985-89). Jewish. Office: Sonnenschein Nath & Rosenthal 685 Market St Ste 1000 Oakland CA 94105*

EDWARDS, SARAH ANNE, radio, cable television personality, clinical social worker; b. Tulsa, Jan. 7, 1943; d. Clyde Elton and Virginia Elizabeth Glandon; B.A. with distinction, U. Mo., Kansas City, 1965; M.S.W., U. Kans., 1974; m. Paul Robert Edwards, Apr. 24, 1965; 1 son, Jon Scott. Community rep. OEO, Kansas City Regional Office, 1966-68; social service/parent involvement specialist, program rev. and resource specialist Office Child Devel., HEW, Kansas City, Kans., 1968-73; dir. tng. social services dept., children's rehab. unit U. Affiliated Facility, U. Kans. Med. Ctr., Kansas City, 1975-76; co-dir. Cathexis Inst. S., Glendale, Calif., 1976-77; pvt. practice psychotherapy, tng. and cons. personal, interpersonal, organizational behavior, Sierra Madre, Calif, 1973-80; systems operator working from home CompuServe Info. Svc., 1983—; prodr., co-host radio show Working From Home on the Business Radio Network, 1988—; co-host cable show Working From Home Scripp's Howard Home and Garden Cable TV Network, 1995—. Columnist for Home Office Computing Mag., 1988—; co-author: How to Make Money with Your Personal Computer, 1984, The Paul and Sarah Edwards Complete Start Up Kit for a Home Business Computer, 1984, Working From Home, rev. edit. 1994, Making it on Your Own, 1994. Address: 2607 2nd St #3 Santa Monica CA 90405-4123

EDWARDS, SUSAN DAVIS, educational administrator, lawyer, accountant; b. Dayton, Ohio, Mar. 24, 1954; d. Robert George and Velma Pauline (Baker) Davis; m. Paul N. Edwards, Dec. 14, 1974 (div. Dec. 1993); children: Christopher Colin, Amanda Elise; m. Robert H. Colson, Feb. 1, 1994. BA, Ohio State U., 1974; JD, Cleve. State U., 1979. Bar: Ohio 1980, D.C. 1989; CPA, Ohio. Staff atty. Allen County Legal Aid, Lima, Ohio, 1980-83; lectr. acctg. Ohio State U., Columbus, 1983-86; with Prentice-Hall Pub., Washington, 1986-88; tax and ins. specialist Am. Chem. Soc., Washington, 1988-90; asst. prof. acctg. Daemen Coll., Amherst, N.Y., 1990-91, dir. Instnl. Advancement, 1991—. Bd. dirs. Town of Amherst Septquicentennial Com., 1993-94. Mem. AICPA.

EDWARDS, TARA ANNE, accountant; b. Denver, Aug. 13, 1971; d. David Charles and Susan Loree (Cowley) M. BSBA, U. Colo., 1994. Head lobby teller Equitable Bank, Littleton, Colo., 1989-94; staff acct. Price Waterhouse, Denver, 1994—. Vol. Spl. Olympics, Denver, 1989. Recipient Gold Key award Colo. Soc. of CPA's, 1994, Wasley award Fin. Execs. Inst., 1993, scholarship. Mem. Sigma Iota Epsilon (former treas. 1991), Beta Gamma Sigma, Golden Key. Home: 31-8328 Russet Ct Highlands Ranch CO 80126

EDWARDS, TINA LOUISE, cost accountant; b. Kingsport, Tenn., Oct. 20, 1966; d. Clifton Eugene and Alma Lee (Miller) E. BS in Acctg., Milligan Coll., 1991; postgrad. in bus. adminstrn., East Tenn. State U., 1993—. Acctg. clk. Mountain Empire Oil Co., Johnson City, Tenn., 1983-85; payroll clk. Watauga Apparel Corp., Johnson City, 1985; accounts payable clk. Baxter Healthcare, Johnson City, 1985-88, acctg. coord., 1988-90, staff acct., 1990-91, cost acct., 1991—. Mem. Inst. Mgmt. Accts. Republican. Baptist. Home: 1514 Stoneybrook Dr Johnson City TN 37601 Office: Baxter Healthcare 2301 Buffalo Rd Johnson City TN 37604

EDWARDS, VIRGINIA DAVIS, music educator, concert pianist; b. Syracuse, N.Y., Jan. 8, 1927; d. Leslie Martz and Elsie (Gannon) Davis; m. William B. Edwards, Jan. 12, 1954. BA magna cum laude, Marshall U., 1948; MusB, Cin. Conservatory of Music, 1950, MusM, 1950; postgrad., U. Chgo., 1950-56, U. Calif., Berkeley, 1963. Pianist, young artists series Conservatory of Music, Cin., 1949-50; piano instr. Conservatory of Music, Evanston, Ill., 1955-56; music instr. Harvard Sch. for Boys, Chgo., 1954-55; pianist Opera Studios of Dimitri Onofrei/Bianca Saroya, Chgo., 1957-61; piano instr. Community Music Ctr., San Francisco, 1962-63; v.p. Gold Rush Gun Shop, Benet Arms Co. Imports, San Francisco, 1963-68, Afton, Va., 1968—; pvt. practice Afton, Va., 1978—; instr. piano Mary Baldwin Coll., Staunton, Va., 1988—; Soloist Marshall U. Symphony Orch., 1948, Chgo. Pops Concert Orch., Duluth, Minn., 1961; recitalist Curtis Hall, Chgo., 1961, Legion of Honor, San Francisco, 1966, Sta. WRFK-FM, Richmond, Va., 1979; prodr., performer Presbyn. Hunger Program Series, 1984-87, St. John's Cath. Ch., Waynesboro, Va., 1985, Basic Meth. Ch., 1989, Augusta Hosp. Corp. Benefit, 1989; author: Conspiracy of 30 -- Their Misuse of Music From Aristotle to Onassis, 1994. Soloist Marshall U. Symphony Orch., 1948, Chgo. Pops Concert Orch., Duluth, Minn., 1961; recitalist Curtis Hall, Chgo., 1961, Legion of Honor, San Francisco, 1966, Sta. WRFK-FM, Richmond, Va., 1979; prodr., performer Presbyn. Hunger Program series, 1984-87, St. John's Cath. Ch., Waynesboro, Va., 1985, Basic Meth. Ch., 1989, Augusta Hosp. Corp. Benefit, 1989; author: Conspiracy of 30 -- Their Misuse of Music from Aristotle to Onassis, 1994. Mem. AAUW, DAR, Va. Museum Soc. Presbyterian. Home: PO Box 87 Waynesboro VA 22980-0066

EDWARDS-SUTTON, JILL LORRAINE, child and family services director; b. Pontiac, Mich., Sept. 28, 1961; d. Sonny Grey and Patricia Gretchen (Colling) Edwards; m. Jack Ayers Sutton, Sept. 18, 1993; stepchildren: Trevor, Shane, Tiffany. B in Human Environ. Studies, Ctrl. Mich. U., 1982, M in Community Agy. Counseling, 1989. Lic. profl. counselor, Mich. Asst. dir. Learn & Play Presch., Mt. Pleasant, Mich., 1982-84; field svcs. supr. Hoogerland Rehab. Ctrs., St. Louis, Mich., 1984-85; dir. early childhood edn. Shepherd (Mich.) Pub. Schs., 1985-89; dir. child and family svcs. Mid Mich. Community Action Agy., Clare, 1989—; adj. prof. Ctrl. Mich. U., Mt. Pleasant, 1989—. Chairperson Isabella County Child Protection Coun., 1991-93, Clare County Youth Coun., 1991-92, 94-95; edn. chair Gladwin County Child Abuse Coun., 1992-93. Mem. Am. Assn. Counseling and Devel., Mich. Assn. Counseling and Edn., Mich. Assn. Childrens Alliances, Nat. Assn. Edn. Young Children, Children's Def. Fund. Home: 8500 Chippewa Trl Mount Pleasant MI 48858-9489 Office: Mid Mich Cmty Action Agy 1141 N Mcewan St Clare MI 48617-1109

EDWIN, ELLEN OWENS, chief executive officer; b. Pensacola, Fla., Dec. 13, 1953; d. Ernest S. and Edna (Kell) Owens; m. James R. Edwin, Aug. 25, 1990; children: EJ, Emily, Jeremy. BS in Edn., Memphis State U., 1975; MA, U. West Fla., 1982. Instrnl. designer interactive media ManTech/Mathetics Divs., Alexandria, Va., 1985-88; design, asst. program mgr. Person-System Integration, Alexandria, Va., 1988-90; instr. U. Wyo., Laramie, 1990-91, rsch. asst., cons., 1991-92; chief exec. officer IntraTech Inc., Laramie, 1992—; contract negotiator, curriculum cons. in field. Contbr. articles to profl. jours. and chpt. to book. Trustee, pianist Trinity Bapt. Ch., Laramie, 1992. Mem. NAFE, Nat. Assn. Govt. Communicators, Internat. Visual Literacy Assn., Assn. for Ednl. Comm. and Technology, Am. Ednl. Rsch. Assn., Fed. Ednl. Technology Assn., Soc. for Advancement of Learning Technologies, No. Rocky Mtn. Rsch. Assn. Republican. Baptist.

EFFEL, LAURA, lawyer; b. Dallas, May 9, 1945; d. Louis E. and Fay (Lee) Ray; m. Marc J. Patterson, Sept. 19, 1992; 1 child, Stephen. BA, U. Calif., Berkeley, 1971; JD, U. Md., 1975. Bar: N.Y. 1976, U.S. Dist. Ct. (so. and ea. dists.) N.Y. 1976, U.S. Ct. Appeals (2d cir.) 1980, U.S. Supreme Ct. 1980, D.C. 1993. Assoc. Burns Jackson Miller Summit & Jacoby, N.Y.C., 1975-78, Pincus Munzer Bizar & D'Alessandro, N.Y.C., 1978-80; v.p., sr. assoc. counsel Chase Manhattan Bank, N.A., N.Y.C., 1980—. Mem. ABA (co chair com. on banking and comml. litigation litigation sect. 1992—), Am. Corp. Counsel Assn. (com. chair 1992—, pro bono svc. award 1989), Assn. of Bar of City of N.Y. (com. on lectures and continuing edn. 1991—). Office: Chase Manhattan Bank NA 1 Chase Manhattan Pla 29th New York NY 10081

EFTIMOFF, ANITA KENDALL, educational consultant; b. Granite City, Ill., May 3, 1927; d. David Harlow and Ollie Lorena (Galloway) Kendall; m. Vasil Eftimoff, June 14, 1959; 1 child, James Kendall. BA, Washington U., St. Louis, 1949; MA, So. Ill. U., Edwardsville, 1978, EdD, 1983. Cert. in multiple gen. edn., spl. edn., Ill. Spl. edn. instr. Community Unit 9, Granite City, 1968-83; ednl. cons. Efti Enterprises, Granite City, 1982—; program dir. At-Risk Presch. Grant, Granite City, 1986—; del. NDEA Conf. Ea. Mich. U., Ypsilanti, 1968, Gifted Edn. Conf. Ill. Office of Edn., Springfield, 1975-77; adminstrv. intern Ill. State Bd. Edn., Springfield, 1981. Editor: Symphony Youth Orch. Newsletter, 1991—, Symphony Vol. Key Notes Newsletter, 1991-93. Bd. dirs. Ill. Gov.'s Adv. Coun. on Women's Affairs, Springfield, Rape Crisis and Sexual Abuse Ctr., So. Ill. U., 1978-82, Family Resource Ctr.; chmn. adopt-a-friend St. Louis Ambs., 1982-84, co-chmn. Vets. Day, 1984-86; chmn. St. Louis Symphony Youth Orch., 1985—, St. Louis Symphony Young Artists Competitions, 1993—; mem. aux. St. Louis Children's Hosp., 1980; v.p. mus. activities St. Louis Symphony Vol. Assn.; bd. pres. Ill. Ctr. for Autism, 1993. At-risk presch. grantee Ill. Bd. Edn., 1986—. Mem. World Coun. for Gifted and Talented Children, Nat. Assn. for Gifted Children, Assn. for the Gifted, Ill. Council for the Gifted, Women's Assn. (bd. dirs. 1961—, pres. 1989-91), St. Louis Symphony Women's Assn., AAUW, Delta Kappa Gamma, Phi Delta Kappa. Lodges: Daus. of Nile, Rotary-Anns. Home: 2800 Michigan Ave Granite City IL 62040-3536 Office: At-Risk Presch Program 2300 W 25th St Granite City IL 62040-2025

EGAN, SISTER M. SYLVIA, hospital administrator; b. Oshkosh, Wis., Sept. 15, 1930; d. Edward James and Dorothy Loretta (Loewen) E. BS in Nursing, Marquette U., 1956; postgrad., Wayne State U., 1969; MSA, Notre Dame U., 1981; LLD (hon.), Kans. Newman Coll., 1987. Rn., Kans.; joined Congregation of Sisters of Sorrowful Mother, Roman Cath. Ch., 1949. Nurse Mercy Hosp. Sch. Nursing, Oshkosh, 1952-54, night supr., 1954-55; med. supr. Mercy Hosp., Oshkosh, 1956-57; instr. St. John's Hosp. Sch. Nursing, Tulsa, 1975-63; dir. St. Mary's Hosp. Sch. Practical Nursing, Roswell, N.Mex., 1963-65; dir. novices, Tulsa Province Sisters of Sorrowful Mother, 1965-69, provincial adminstr., 1970-78; pres. Franciscan Villa, Broken Arrow, Okla., 1978-79; pres., CEO St. Francis Regional Med. Ctr., Wichita, Kans., 1979—; del. renewal chpt. Sisters of Sorrowful Mother, Milw., 1967-68, 69, chmn. formation com., Tulsa Province, 1968, chpt. del. to Rome, 1970, 74, 78, internat. chmn. Centenary Com., Fed. Republic of Germany, 1980, internat. chpt. Brazil, 1992; bd. dirs. Union Nat. Bank; adj. prof. Health Adminstrn. and Geronotology, Wichita State U., 1988—; alternate del. Am. Hosp. Assn., 1988. Bd. dirs. ARC, 1981—, pres., 1991-93, Accent on Kids, Task Force for Kans. Econ. Devel., Cath. Charities, Wichita, Central States Cardiac Transplant Support Group, 1988-89, Gerard House Inc. (pres. 1988-90), United Way, 1987-89, Leadership 2000, Wichita, Sedgwick County Partnership for Econ. Growth, Wichita Downtown Adv. Com., 1989, Catholic Health Assn. Kans., Guadalupe Clinic, Kans. Hosp. Assn., Union Nat. Bank; adv. bd. YMCA, Wichita, adv. coun. YMCA, Wichita. Recipient Nursing Alumna award Marquette U., 1993. Fellow Am. Coll. Healthcare Execs.; mem. NCCJ (bd. dirs.), Am. Coll. Hosp. Adminstrs., Kans. Hosp. Assn. (bd. dirs. 1988), Cath. Health Assn. of Kans., Med. Edn. Assn., Kans. Forum for Women Healthcare Execs. (bd. dirs.), Kans. Community Svc. Orgn. (bd. dirs.), Kans. C. of C., Notre Dame Alumnae Assn., Rotary Club Witchita, Kans. Forum for Women Healthcare Execs., Sigma Theta Tau, Internat. Honor Soc. of Nursing, Epsilon Gamma. Republican. Home and Office: St Francis Regional Med Ctr 929 N Saint Francis St Wichita KS 67214-3882

EGAN, MARTHA AVALEEN, history educator, archivist; b. Kingsport, Tenn., Feb. 26, 1956; d. Jack E. and Opal (Pugh) E. BS in Comms., U. Tenn., 1978; MA in History, East Tenn. State U., 1986; postgrad., U. Ky., 1986-89, Milligan Coll., 1990. Cert. tchr., Tenn. News reporter, anchor WJCW-AM/WQUT-FM, Johnson City, Tenn., 1980-82; staff asst. 1st Dist. Office U.S. Senator Jim Sasser, Blountville, Tenn., 1982-84; instr. history East Tenn. State U., Johnson City, 1984-86; teaching asst. dept. history U. Ky., Lexington, 1986-89; teaching intern Dobyns-Bennett High Sch., Kingsport, Tenn., 1990; researcher history project Eastman Chem. Co., Kingsport, 1991; adj. faculty history Northeast State Tech. C.C., Blountville, 1992-93; archivist Kingsport Pub. Libr. and Archives, 1993—; adj. asst. prof. history King Coll., Bristol, Tenn., 1994—. Researcher: Eastman Chemical Company: Years of Glory, Times of Change, 1991. Vice chair Sullivan County Dem. Party, 1992-93; rec. sec. Sullivan County Dem. Women's Club, 1992, corr. sec., 1994—; mem. Kingsport Tomorrow Exploritorium Task Force; mem. Kingsport Symphony Chorus, sec.-treas., 1994—. Mem. Orgn. Am. Historians, Nat. Coun. Social Studies, Soc. Am. Archivists, Tenn. Archivists, Kingsport Music Club, Phi Alpha Theta, Pi Gamma Mu, Sigma Delta Chi. Episcopalian. Home: PO Box 481 Kingsport TN 37662-0481 Office: Kingsport Pub Libr/Archives 400 Broad St Kingsport TN 37660-4208

EGAN, PATRICIA, special education institute administrator, psychologist; b. N.Y.C., Feb. 7, 1956; d. John Joseph and Elizabeth (Davey) E. Therapist, tchr. May Inst. Inc., Chatham, Mass., 1979-82, supr., team coord., 1982-85; rsch. asst. Juniper Gardens Children's Project, Kans. City, Kans., 1985-86; teaching asst. U. Kans., Lawrence, 1986-87; psychology trainee Kans. Neurol. Inst., Topeka, 1986-87; therapist Assn. for Children with Learning Disabilities, L.I., N.Y., 1986; program dir. May Inst., Inc., 1987—; behavioral cons., Kans., Mass., 1985—; adj. prof. dept. edn. Fitchburg, Mass. State Coll., 1994—. Mem. Assn. for Behavior Analysis, Berkshire Assn. for Behavior Analysis and Therapy, Autism Soc. of Am., Assn. for Persons with Severe Handicaps. Democrat. Roman Catholic. Home: 67 Brook St Wollaston MA 02170 Office: The May Inst Inc 22 Blanchard Blvd Braintree MA 02184

EGAN, PATRICIA JANE, realtor; b. San Francisco, Aug. 7, 1951; d. James Egan; 1 child, Kathryn Michele. AB, U. Calif., Berkeley, 1978. Cert. fund raising exec. Grants officer The Mus. Modern Art, N.Y.C., 1979-81; assoc. devel. officer grants Whitney Mus. Am. Art, N.Y.C., 1981-84; assoc. dir. devel. Columbia Bus. Sch., Columbia U., N.Y.C., 1984-86; mgr. major gifts New York Bot. Garden, N.Y.C., 1987-88; dir. devel. N.Y.C. Partnership, 1989-91; dir. devel. Cal Performances U. Calif., Berkeley, 1991-92; realtor assoc. Prudential Zinn Assocs., Montclair, N.J., 1993—; cons. to various cultural and environ. orgns., N.Y., N.J., 1983—. Producer, program host including Terpsichore, KUSF-FM, 1978-79. Bd. dirs. Universala Esperanto Asocio/N.Y., 1980-83, Dance Perspectives FDN, N.Y.C., 1985—; trustee The Riverside Ch., N.Y.C., 1986-87. Recipient fellowship NEA, 1977. Mem. Esperanto League of N.Am., Jr. League of Montclair-Newark, Order of Ea. Star. Democrat. Office: PO Box 347 Montclair NJ 07042-0347

EGAN, ROBERTA ANN, illustrator; b. Mt. Kisco, N.Y., June 26, 1955; d. John Anthony and Florence Lillian (Collins) E. BFA with honors, Sch. Visual Arts, N.Y.C., 1978. Head designer Kukoff Mfg., N.Y.C., 1978-82; designer, illustrator Holt Mfg., N.Y.C., 1982-85; v.p. Demrae Devel. Co., White Plains, N.Y., 1987-92; freelance illustrator White Plains, 1985—. Mem. United We Stand Am., Dallas, 1993. Recipient Excellence in the Field of Graphic Communication, Master Eagle Family of Cos., N.Y.C., 1978. Home and Office: RR 2 Box 413 Red Hook NY 12571

EGAN, SHIRLEY ANNE, retired nursing educator; b. Haverill, Mass.; d. Rush B. and Beatrice (Bengle) Willard. Diploma, St. Joseph's Hosp. Sch. Nursing, Nashua, N.H., 1945; B.S. in Nursing Edn., Boston U., 1949, M.S., 1954. Instr. sci. Sturdy Meml. Hosp. Sch. Nursing, Attleboro, Mass., 1949-51; instr. sci. Peter Bent Brigham Hosp. Sch. Nursing, Boston, 1951-53, ednl. dir., 1953-55, assoc. dir. Sch. Nursing, 1955-59, med. surg. coord., 1971-73, assoc. dir. Sch. Nursing, 1973-79, dir., 1979-85; cons. North Country Hosp., 1985-86; infection control practitioner, 1986-87; contract instr. Natchitoches Area Tech. Inst., 1988-90, Sabine Valley Tech Inst., 1990-91; coord. quality assurance Evangeline Health Care Ctr., 1991-92, asst. dir. nursing, 1992-93; coord. quality assurance Evangeline Health Care Ctr., Natchitoches, La., 1994—; nurse edn. adviser AID (formerly ICA), Karachi, Pakistan, 1959-67; prin. Coll. Nursing, Karachi, 1959-67; dir. Vis. Nurse Service, Nashua, N.H., 1967-70; cons. nursing edn. Pakistan Ministry of Health, Labour and Social Welfare, 1959-67; adviser to editor Pakistan Nursing and Health Rev., 1959-67; exec. bd. Nat. Health Edn. Com., Pakistan; WHO short-term cons. U. W.I., Jamaica, 1970-71; mem. Greater Nashua Health Planning Council. Contbr. articles to profl. publs. Bd. dirs. Matthew Thornton health Ctr., Nashua, Nashua Child Care Ctr.; vol. ombudsman N.H. Council on Aging; mem. Nashua Service League. Served as 1st lt., Army Nurse Corps., 1945-47. Mem. Trained Nurses Assn. Pakistan, Nat. League for Nursing, Assn. for Preservation Hist. Natchitoches, St. Joseph's Sch. Nursing Alumnae Assn., Boston U. Alumnae Assn., Brit. Soc. Health Edn., Cath. Daus. Am. (vice regent ct. Bishop Malloy), Statis. Study Grads. Karachi Coll. Nursing, Sigma Theta Tau. Home: 729 Royal St Natchitoches LA 71457-5716

EGELSTON, ROBERTA RIETHMILLER, writer; b. Pitts., Nov. 20, 1946; d. Robert E. and Doris (Bauer) Riethmiller; m. David Michael Egelston, Oct. 10, 1975; 1 child, Brian David. BA in Bus. Adminstrn., Thiel Coll., 1968; MLS, U. Pitts., 1974. Bus. mgr. Pitts. Pastoral Inst., 1968-70; administrv. asst. Coun. Alcoholism and Drug Abuse, Lancaster, Pa., 1970-72; dir. career planning libr. U. Pitts., 1974-78; writer, 1978—; libr. Pitts. Inst. Mortuary Sci., 1991—, instr. bus. English, 1992—; part-time libr., part-time instr. bus. English, Pitts. Inst. Mortuary Sci., 1991—; instr. beginning genealogy, 1991—; book reviewer Coll. Placement Coun., Bethlehem, Pa., 1977-78; cons. State Affiliated Colls. and Univs., 1976; group leader Johns-Norris Assocs., Pitts., 1975-76. Author: Career Planning Materials, 1981, Credits and Careers for Adult Learners, 1985. Bd. dirs. Lauri Ann West Libr., Pitts., 1983-84; active PTA, 1985-88; mem. peace and justice com. Fox Chapel Presbyn. Ch., 1994—, deacon, 1995—. Mem. AAUW (bd. dirs. Fox Chapel Area br. 1980-91), Les Lauriers (sr. women's hon. at Thiel Coll.), Western Pa. Geneal. Soc. (libr. rsch. com. 1990-94, edn. com. 1992—), Beta Phi Mu.

EGEN, KRISTEN MARGARET, range conservationist; b. Rochester, Minn., Nov. 12, 1962; d. Robert Glen and Anna Barbara (Cornwell) E. BS in Range Ecology, Colo. State U., 1985. Range aide USFS, Yampa, Colo., 1983; reclamation technician Kaiser Coal Co., Raton, N.Mex., 1985-87; range conservationist USDA Soil Conservation Svc., Tucson, Ariz., 1988—; pres. So. Ariz. Fed. Women's Program Interagy. Coun., Tucson, 1994, sec., treas. 1992-94. Mem. Soc. Range Mgmt. (sec./treas. 1994, scholarship 1984-85). Democrat. Office: USDA Soil Conservation Svc Bldg 320 2000 E Allen Rd Tucson AZ 85719

EGER, MARILYN RAE, artist; b. Offett A.F.B., Nebr., Jan. 2, 1953; d. John W. and Joyce Faye (Carpenter) Shaver, stepmother Myrle I. MAsoner; m. Darrell W. Masoner, Feb. 28, 1971 (div. Sept. 1977); children: William Matthew, Melissa Rae; m. Gerard J. Eger, Jan. 30, 1982. BA, Calif. State U., Turlock, 1987. Cert. art tchr. 1990, Calif., lang. devel. specialist, 1993. Freelance artist oil painting Gibson Greetings Inc., Cin.; tchr. art, A.P. art, sculpture and ceramics Bear Creek High Sch., Stockton, Calif.; tchr. art privately. One-woman shows include Stockton Fine Arts Gallery, 1984-88, Accurate Art Gallery, Sacramento, 1989-90, Sharon Gile Gallery, Isleton, Calif., 1988-91, Le Galerie, Stockton, 1989-91, Masterpiece Gallery, Carmel, Calif., 1991—, Alan Short Gallery, Stockton, 1991; represented in permanent collections Gulf Oil Chemicals, Kaiser Permanent, Masterpiece Gallery; prints published in Mus. Edits. West. Bd. dirs. Lodi Art Ctr., 1988-91, chmn. 1989. Recipient Award of Excellence Unitarian Fall Art Festival, 1990, Award of Excellence in Oils, 1992, Ben Day Meml. award, 1993, Bank Stockton award and H.M. Haggin Mus., 1989, U.S. Nat. Collegiate Art Merit award, 1988, Lodi 31st Ann., 1st Oils, 1988, Award of Excellence in Pastel, Haggin Mus., 1992, 1st Oils and Don Morrell Meml. award CCAL Gallo Show, 1993, Art of Calif. Bronze Discovery award, 1993; Mellon grantee, 1994. Mem. C.A.E.A., Stockton Art League, Nat. League Am. Pen. Women, West Coast Pastel Soc., Calif. Art League, Ctrl. Calif. Art League. Republican. Methodist. Home: 1295 E Peltier Rd Acampo CA 95220-9652 Office: Gallery III Art Studio 104 N School St Ste 306 Lodi CA 95240-2120

EGGERS, JOAN FRANCES, dietitian; b. Iowa City, Mar. 11, 1934; d. Raymond Francis and Johanne Barbara (Kelsen) Dalbey; m. William Charles Eggers, Sept. 1, 1956; children: Michael, Deborah, Susanne, Steven. BS, U. Iowa, 1957. Registered dietitian; lic. dietitian, Kans. Clin. dietitian Iowa Meth. Med. Ctr., Des Moines, 1961-63; adminstrv. and clin. dietitian Iowa Luth. Hosp., Des Moines, 1963-65, Malcolm Bliss Mental Health Ctr., St. Louis, 1966-68; adminstrv. dietitian St. Louis State Hosp., 1968-70, Shawnee Mission (Kans.) Med. Ctr., 1982-85; cons. dietitian C.L. Gerwick & Assocs., Overland Park, Kans., 1975-82; chief dietitian Western Mo. Mental Health Ctr., Kansas City, 1985—. Mem. P.E.O., Am. Dietetic Assn., Am. Soc. Hosp. Food Svc. Adminstrs., Kans. Dietetic Assn., Kansas City Dietetic Assn., Mems. with Mgmt. Reponsibilities in Health Care Delivery Systems (DPG #41). Republican. Roman Catholic. Home: 10205 W 97th Ter Overland Park KS 66212 Office: Western Mo Mental Health Ctr 600 E 22d St Kansas City MO 64108

EGGLAND, ELLEN THOMAS, community health nurse, consultant; b. Canton, Ohio, Nov. 2, 1947; d. John Marron and Mary Mernabelle (Miller) Thomas; m. Gregory Hugh Eggland, Sept. 9, 1972; children: Karen, Ryan. BSN, Georgetown U., 1969; MN, Emory U., 1972. Staff nurse Cleve. Clinic Hosp., 1969-71; nurse clinician Univ. Hosps., Cleve., 1972-73; dir. nursing Med. Personnel Pool, Cleve., 1975-83; v.p. Healthcare Pers., Inc., Naples, Fla., 1984—; nursing cons., Ohio and Fla., 1983—; v.p. MedPad, Atlanta, 1991-93; mem. adv. bd. Springhouse (Pa.) Skillbuilder Series, 1991-92. Author: Nursing Documentation Resource Guide, 1993, Nursing Documentation: Charting, Reporting and Recording, 1994; contbg. author: Better Documentation, 1992, Managing the Nursing Shortage, 1989; Community and Home Health Care Plans, 1990; inventor computerized clin. record. Chmn. St. William Respect Life/Sr. Citizens, Naples, 1985-86; mem. health com. Naples C. of C., 1985-86; sec. Pelican Bay Incorporation Study Com., Naples, 1990-91; bd. dirs. Prevent A Care, Naples, 1986-87; bd. dirs., sec. Pelican Bay Found., Naples, 1993-96; bd. vis. Georgetown U. Sch. Nursing, 1993-96. Fed. grantee for edn. U.S. Govt., 1971; recipient Involved Mem. of Yr. award Greater Cleve. Nurses Assn., 1978. Mem. ANA, Fla. Nurses Assn., Nat. League Nursing, Leaders in Nursing, Nat. Assn. for Home Care, Greater Cleve. Hosp. Assn. (info. tech. and nursing com. 1991—), Sigma Theta Tau. Democrat. Roman Catholic. Office: Healthcare Personnel Inc # 407 2335 Tamiami Trail N Naples FL 33940

EGGLESTON, TWILA RUTH, counselor; b. St. Joseph, Mo., Apr. 21, 1944; d. Charles Washington Sr. and Leota Rebecca (Wells) Wilson; m. John D. Eggleston Jr., Oct. 29, 1965; children: John D. III, Nancy Elaine. BS in Elem. Edn., N.W. Mo. State U., 1968, M in Elem. Counseling, 1992. Tchr. grades 3-5 Fairport (Mo.) R-VI Sch., 1967-72; kindergarten tchr. Maysville (Mo.) R-I Sch., 1973-85, tchr. gifted edn., 1985-94; elem. counselor Maysville (Mo.) R.-I Sch., 1994—, golf coach, 1983-94. Mem. county com. DeKalb County Dem. Club; chair adminstrv. bd. Fairport United Meth. Ch. Mem. Gifted Assn. Mo.

EGINTON, MARGARET L., movement educator, dancer; b. Iowa City, June 9, 1955; d. William Leonard and Kay Ruth (Boehnke) E.; m. John Alden Howell, June 16, 1979 (div. 1985); 1 child, Robert Burr. BA, Sarah Lawrence Coll., 1977. Registered movement therapist. Prin. dancer Merce Cunningham Dance Co., N.Y.C., 1977-80, Stephen Petronio Co., N.Y.C., 1984-88, Bill Irwin & Friends, N.Y.C., 1988-90; artistic dir. Meg Eginton & Dances, N.Y.C., 1980-87; movement educator Yale U., New Haven, 1988, NYU, 1988-94, Practical Aesthetics Workshop, Burlington, Vt., 1994; theatre fellow U. Iowa, Iowa City, 1994—; movement coach Atlantic Theatre Co., N.Y.C., 1988-94. Mem. edtl. bd. Dance Ink, N.Y.C., 1988-89. With workshops with retarded adults Kennedy Ctr. Spl. Arts, N.Y.C., 1987; with workshops with homeless children Children's Aid Soc., N.Y.C., 1988. Young Profl. Artist fellow Am. Dance Festival, 1975, Iowa Arts fellow U. Iowa, 1994—; choreography grantee JCT Found., 1985; recipient N.Y. Dance and Performance award BESSIE Com., 1987. Mem. AFTRA, NAFE, SAG, AEA, Am. Guild Mus. Artists, Internal Somatic Movement Therapy and Edn. Assn. Democrat. Episcopalian. Home: 422 N Dubuque St Iowa City IA 52245 Office: U Iowa Theatre Arts Riverside Dr Iowa City IA 52244

EHLENFELDT, JAN ALEXIS, traditional herbalist, management consultant; b. Terre Haute, Ind., July 7, 1952; d. John Nelson and Phyllis Inez (White) Turnbloom; m. Earl J. Chidester, Jan. 18, 1971 (div. 1976) 1 child, John; m. Rollin Sakeeta, Apr. 29, 1989; children: Brendan Lorithian, Allayne Carson. AA in English, Contra Costa Coll., 1978. Tutor English and trigonometry Contra Costa Coll., San Pablo, Calif., 1976-78; sales rep., asst. mgr. Avon, Richmond, Calif., 1977-78; sales mgr. C-Shor Sales, San Leandro, Calif., 1978-80; exec. sec. C.N. Petsas, CPA, Richmond, 1980-81; mgr., designer Jan's Attic, Bamberg, Germany, 1982-85; writing team Jovialis, Austin, Tex., 1988-89; pres., chief exec. officer Arcane Attic Ltd., Colorado Springs, Colo., 1988—; owner Fairy Spirit, Colorado Springs, 1989—; herbal cons. North Star Gardens, Colorado Springs, 1990—; mng. dir. Pagan Merchant Coop., Colorado Springs, 1992—. Author: Cyclopedia Talislanta, Vol. 3, 1989, Cyclopedia Talislanta, Vol. 5, 1990. Organizer Fairy Spirit and Friends Metaphys. Faire, Colorado Springs. Mem. North Circle Circle (chairperson 1988—), Gaianauts. Office: PO Box 6708 Colorado Springs CO 80934-6708

EHLERS, ELEANOR MAY COLLIER (MRS. FREDERICK BURTON EHLERS), civic worker; b. Klamath Falls, Oreg., Apr. 23, 1920; d. Alfred Douglas and Ethel (Foster) Collier; BA, U. Oreg., 1941; secondary tchrs. credentials Stanford, 1942, master gardener cert. Oreg. State U., 1993; m. Frederick Burton Ehlers, June 26, 1943; children: Frederick Douglas, Charles Collier. Tchr., Salinas Union High Sch., 1942-43; piano tchr. pvt. lessons, Klamath Falls, 1958—. Mem. Child Guidance Adv. Coun., 1956-60; mem. adv. com. Boys and Girls Aid Soc., 1965-67; mem. Gov.'s Adv. Com. Arts and Humanities, 1966-67; bd. mem. PBS TV Sta. KSYS, 1988-92, Friends of Mus. U. Oreg., 1966-69, Arts in Oreg., 1966-68, Klamath County Colls. for Oreg.'s Future, 1968—; co-chmn. Friends of Collier Park, Collier Park Logging Mus., 1986-88, sec. 1988—; chpt. pres. Am. Field Svc., 1962-63; mem. Gov.'s Com. Governance of Community Colls., 1967; bd. dirs. Favell Mus. Western Art and Artifacts, 1971-80, Community Concert Assn., 1950—, pres., 1966-74; established Women's Guild at Merle West Med. Ctr., 1965, sec. bd. dirs, 1962-65, 76-90, bd. dirs., 1962—, mem. bldg. com. 1962-67, mem. planning com., chmn. edn. and rsch. com. hosp. bd., 1967—; pres., bd. dirs. Merle West Med. Ctr., 1990-92, vice chmn., 1992—. Named Woman of Month Klamath Herald News, 1965; named grant to Oreg. Endowed Fellowship Fund, AAUW, 1971; recipient greatest Svc. award Oreg. Tech. Inst., 1970-71, Internat. Woman of Achievement award Quota Club, 1981, U. Oreg. Pioneer award, 1981. Mem. AAUW (local pres. 1955-56), Oreg. Music Tchrs. Assn. (pres. Klamath Basin dist. 1979-81), P.E.O. (Oreg. dir. 1968-75, state pres. 1974-75, trustee internat. Continuing Edn. Fund 1977-83, chmn. 1981-83), Pi Beta Phi, Mu Phi Epsilon, Pi Lambda Theta. Presbyterian. Home: 1338 Pacific Terr Klamath Falls OR 97601

EHLERS, FLORENCE RAUSH (FLORA JUNE), actress; b. Bklyn., Mar. 20, 1925; d. Philip and Pauline (Ginsberg) Raush; m. Harold Ludlow Ehlers (div. Feb. 1979); children: Allen Richard, Phillis F. Ehlers-Hardie, Donna Lael Ehlers, Anita Diane Torres. AA in Theatre Arts, Fullerton Coll., 1978; AS, San Antonio Coll., 1978. Lic. psychiat. technician state devel. disabled hosps., 1976-89; judge acting and musical talent awards Placentia/Yorba Scholarship/Arts, 1973-75; participant poetry readings. Actress: Arsenic and Old Lace, 1986, Watch on the Rhine, 1985, Desert Song, Journey to the Day, 1983, Forty Carots, The Hot-L-Baltimore, 1982, (video) Living in Sin, 1992, The Odd Couple (female version), 1993, others; dir. (play) Done to Death, 1975; playwright, lyricist, melodic composer (mus.) Autumn Promise, 1990; appearances in tng. films and commls.; author numerous poems. Chairlady chor., music, arts for Orange County, Calif. State PTA, 1969-72; founder, dir., producer Yorba Linda (Calif.) Theatre Corp., 1975; founder Women's Chorus, Whittier, Calif., 1953-64, Note & Belles, Placentia Calif., 1964-75. Winner in Internat. Poetry Symposium for Peace, 1991; named Internat. Woman of Yr. Internat. Biog. Ctr., 1991-92. Fellow Am. Fedn. TV and Radio Artists; mem. Internat. Soc. Poets (life). Home: 1533 Merion Way # 26H Seal Beach CA 90740-4979

EHLERT, MARY ANNE, marketing and sales professional; b. Chgo., May 4, 1950; d. Roy Arthur and Helen (Bocieck) Wallace. AA, Harper Jr. Coll., Palatine, Ill., 1970; postgrad., Loyola U., Chgo., 1972. Programmer analyst A.C. Nielsen, Northbrook, Ill., 1971-75; application specialist banking Weiland Computer Group, Oakbrook, Ill., 1975-80; systems mgr. Deutsche Credit Corp., Deerfield, Ill., 1980-85; v.p. systems Heller Fin., Chgo., 1985-87, v.p. mktg. and planning, 1987-89; chief ops. officer Citicorp Distbn. Fin., Waukesha, Wis., 1989-91; pres. Ehlert Fin. Group, Bannockburn, Ill., 1991—; cons. in field. Bd. dirs. Clearbrook Ctr. for Handicapped, Lake County Soc. for Human Devel., SEDOL Found. Mem. Structured Techniques Assn. (bd. dirs., founder 1980-85), North Shore Network Women Entrepreneurs (v.p.), Chgo. Assn. Life Underwriters, Chgo. Assn. Retarded Citizens, Alliance for the Mentally Ill, Assn. for Retarded Citizens Ill, Inst. Cert. fin. Planners (bd. dirs.), Rotary. Office: Ehlert Fin Group Inc 2529 Waukegan Rd Bannockburn IL 60015

EHLINGER, JANET ANN DOWLING, elementary school educator; b. Des Moines, Mar. 1, 1955; d. Joseph Patrick and Sadie Agnes (Klein) Dowling; m. Steven Mark Ehlinger, July 22, 1989; children: Bridget Ann, Brian Mark. BS, Benedictine Coll., Atchison, Kans., 1977; MEd, U. St. Thomas, Houston, 1985. Cert. tchr., Tex. Tchr. English, sci. Our Lady Mt. Carmel, Houston, 1977-78; tchr. social studies, history, religion St. Michael's Sch., Houston, 1978-82; tchr. social studies, history Kinkaid Sch., Houston, 1982-90. Mem. Mus. Fine Arts, Houston, 1992, Children's Mus. of Houston, 1993-96; bd. dirs. St. Cyril of Alexandria Ladies Guild, Houston, 1992. Mem. Nat. Coun. Social Studies, Tex. State Hist. Assn., Kappa Delta Pi (rep.-at-large Pi Lambda chpt. 1985-86, sec. 1987-89). Home: 6111 Cheena Dr Houston TX 77096

EHRENBERG, DARLENE BREGMAN, psychoanalyst; b. N.Y.C., Aug. 15, 1942; d. Samuel and Pauline (Gellman) Bregman; m. Bernard Ehrenberg, Nov. 26, 1970; children: Jonathan, Erica. BA magna cum laude, CCNY, 1963; MS, Yale U., 1965; PhD , NYU, 1970; cert. William Alanson White Inst. Psychiatry, Psychoanalysis and Psychology, 1973 . Intern Montefere Hosp., 1966-67; pvt. practice psychoanalysis and psychotherapy, N.Y.C., 1969—; tng. and supervising analyst faculty William Alanson White Inst. Psychiatry, Psychoanalysis and Psychology, N.Y.C., 1977—; teaching faculty Chgo. Ctr. for Psychoanalysis, 1993—. supr. Inst. for Contemporary Psychotherapy, 1974-83; clin. instr. psychiatry Albert Einstein Coll. Medicine, 1968-69; conf. presenter. Author: The Intimate Edge: Extending the Reach of Psychoanalytic Interaction, 1992; editor: Contemporary Psychoanalysis, 1993-94, asst. editor, 1979-93; editorial bd., 1975-79, 94—; contbr. articles to profl. jours. Carnegie Teaching fellow CCNY, 1964, Harrison fellow Yale U., 1963, NIMH fellow NYU, 1964-66. Mem. Am. Psychol. Assn., William Alanson White Psychoanalytic Soc., Phi Beta Kappa. Home and Office: 11 E 68th St New York NY 10021-4955

EHRENBERG, SARA JEAN, psychologist; b. Chgo., June 24, 1948; d. Isadore Jack and Marilyn (Millman) E.; m. Jeffrey Kent Tulis, July 16, 1978; children: Elizabeth, Hanna. BA in Am. History, U. Calif., Santa Cruz, 1970; EdM, Harvard U., 1973; MA in Psychology, U. Chgo., 1978, PhD in Psychology, 1989. Lic. psychologist, Tex. Tchr. Moss Landing Sch., Watonsville, Calif., 1971-72; adminstrv. asst. Brookline (Mass.) Early Edn. Project, 1973-75; tchr. Franklin Sch., Lexington, Mass., 1973-74; exec. dir. Westminster Child Care Ctr., Charlottesville, Va., 1978-80; post-doctoral tgn. U. Tex., Austin, 1989-91; post-doctoral intern Austin (Tex.) Child Guidance Ctr., 1991-92; cert. psychologist Balcones Spl. Svcs. Coop., Austin, 1992-93; psychologist Lago Vista (Tex.) Ind. Sch. Dist., 1993—; clin. tng. Billings Hosp., U. Chgo., Ill., 1975-76; cons. Princeton (N.J.) Ednl. Resources, Inc., 1987, Psychol. Corp., San Antonio, 1989; pschoednl. examiner Learning Abilities Ctr., Austin, 1990-91. Del. Travis County Dem. Ctrl. Com., Austin, 1988, 92; v.p. Congregation Agudas Achim Religious Sch., 1989-90. Recipient NIMH Child Devel. fellowship U. Chgo., Ill., 1974-77. Mem. APA, Sch. Psychology Divsn. 16, Tex. Psychol. Assn., Tex. Assn. Marriage and Family Therapists. Democrat. Jewish. Office: Lago Vista Ind Sch Dist PO Box 4929 Lago Vista TX 78645

EHRESMAN, PAULA SUZETTE, information manager, researcher; b. Bloomington, Ill., Mar. 5, 1951; d. Earl Loyd and Betty Adiene (Diggle) E. BA, Western State Coll., 1974; MLS, Emporia State U., 1992; cert. in computer mgmt., U. Colo., 1993. Edn. specialist Dickson Mounds State Mus., Lewistown, Ill., 1978-80; med. asst. Western Neurol. Group, Denver, 1980-82; rsch. historian Roxborough State Pk., Littleton, Colo., 1982-83, Chatfield State Recreation Area, Littleton, Colo., 1983-86, Denver Botanic Gardens, Denver, 1984; rsch. specialist KRMA-TV, Denver, 1984-85; co-producer cablevision program Littleton Pub. Schs., 1985-86; edn. asst. internship Littleton Hist. Mus., 1986; rschr., info. mgmt. Internat. Broadcasting Network, Denver, 1986-93; photo libr. Rocky Mountain News, Denver, 1994—; cons. Chatfield State Recreation Area, Littleton, 1990-91; mem. Chatfield Hist. Restoration Subcom., Littleton, 1985—, chairperson, 1991—. Mem. Colo. Women's C. of C., Denver, 1990-93, Coun. of Homeowner's for a Planned Environment, Denver, 1985-90, pres., 1987-88, adv. coun. Arapahoe C.C., Littleton, 1988. Named one of Outstanding Young Women of Am., 1984. Mem. ALA, Spl. Libr. Assn. (bd. dirs. 1994—), Denver Art Mus.

EHRHARDT, MARGARET WRIGHT, retired librarian; b. Orangeburg, S.C., Sept. 17, 1918; d. Harry Alison and Florence Olive (Black) Wright; B.A., Duke U., 1939; B.A.L.S., Emory U., 1949; postgrad. Furman U., 1970, U. S.C., 1978, U. Pitts., 1978; m. Benedict Groseclose Ehrhardt, Oct. 27, 1951; 1 son, Benedict Glen. High sch. librarian, library supr. Orangeburg (S.C.) Public Schs., 1945-51; children's librarian Richland County (S.C.) Public Library, Columbia, 1952-58; asst. order librarian U. S.C., Columbia, 1960-64; order librarian Wofford Coll., 1964-65; library cons. S.C. Dept. Edn., Columbia, 1965-87. Mem. ALA, Southeastern Library Assn., S.C. Library Assn. (sec. 1971-72, pres. 1977), Delta Kappa Gamma. Lutheran. Editor: Media Services Newsletter, 1965-77, contbr. articles, revs. to S.C. Librarian, Media Center Messenger. Home: 227 Lawand Dr Columbia SC 29210-7557

EHRLICH, ANNETTE, psychologist, educator; b. N.Y.C., Mar. 23, 1931; d. Alexander and Henrietta (Frant) Goldhirsch; m. Daniel Ehrlich, June 1956 (div. 1963). BA, Bklyn. Coll., 1954; MA, CUNY, 1956; PhD, McGill U., Montreal, 1960. Rsch. assoc. Med. Sch., Northwestern U., Chgo., 1960-64; asst. prof. Bowling Green (Ohio) State U., 1966-69; from asst. prof. to assoc. prof. Calif. State U., L.A., 1969-75, prof., 1975—; cons. in rsch. design, L.A., 1982—. Contbr. articles to profl. jours. Columbia U. fellow, 1975-76; Rsch. grantee NIMH, 1969-73, The Grant Found. N.Y., 1973. Mem. Am. Soc. Primatologists, Internat. Primatological Soc. Office: Calif State U 5151 State Univ Dr Los Angeles CA 90032

EHRLICH, AVA, television executive producer; b. St. Louis, Aug. 14, 1950; d. Norman and Lillian (Gellman) Ehrlich; m. Barry K. Freedman, Mar. 31, 1979; children: Alexander Zev, Maxwell Samuel. BJ, Northwestern U., 1972, MJ, 1973; MA, Occidental Coll., 1976. Reporter, asst. mng. editor Lerner Newspapers, Chgo., 1974-75; reporter, news editor Sta. KMOX, St. Louis, 1976-79; producer Sta. WXYZ, Detroit, 1979-85; exec. producer Sta. KSDK-TV, St. Louis, 1985—; guest editor Mademoiselle mag., N.Y.C., 1971; freelance writer, coll. prof. Detroit, Chgo., St. Louis, 1987; adj. faculty mem. Washington U. Trustee CORO Found., St. Louis, 1976-77, 86—; bd. dirs. Nat. Kidney Found., St. Louis, 1987. Named Outstanding Woman in Broadcasting, Am. Women in Radio & TV, 1983, Journalism award Am. Chiropractic Assn., 1989, AP award Ill. UPI, 1989, Illuminator award AMC Cancer Rsch., 1994, Women in Comms. Nat. award, 1988, 6 local Emmy awards; CORO Found. fellow in pub. affairs, 1975-76. Mem. NATAS (com. mem. 1986—, 13 local Emmy awards 1986—), Women in Comms., Inc. (sec. 1978-79, Clarion award 1989, Best in Midwest Feature award 1989), Soc. Profl. Journalists. Democrat. Jewish. Home: 8002 Walinca Drve Saint Louis MO 63105 Office: Sta KSDK-TV 1000 Market St Saint Louis MO 63101-2011

EHRLICH, GERALDINE ELIZABETH, food service management consultant; b. Phila., Nov. 28, 1939; d. Joseph Vincent and Agnes Barbara (Campbell) McKenna; m. S. Paul Ehrlich, Jr., June 20, 1959; children: Susan Patricia, Paula Jeanne, Jill Marie. BS, Drexel Inst. Tech., 1957. Dietary mgmt. cons. HEW, Washington, 1967-68; nutrition cons., hypertension rsch. team U. Calif. Micronesia, 1970; regional sales dir. Marriott Corp., Bethesda, Md., 1976-78; dir. sales and profl. svcs. Coll. and Health Care div. Macke Co., Cheverly, Md., 1978, gen. mgr., 1978-79; v.p. ops., div., 1979-80, pres. Health Care div., 1980-81; regional v.p. Custom Mgmt. Corp., Alexandria, Va., 1981-83, v.p. mktg., 1983-87; v.p. mktg. and healthcare sales Morrison's Custom Mgmt., Mobile, Ala., 1987-88; v.p. sales ARA Svcs., Phila., 1988-93; v.p. bus. devel., ARAMARK, Phila., 1993—; cons. mktg. The Green House, Tokyo, 1987-88; chmn. bd. Mktg. Matrix, Falls Church, Va., 1984-88. Mem. Health Systems Agy. No. Va., 1976-77; chmn. Health Care Adv. Bd. Fairfax County Va., 1973-77; vice chmn. Fairfax County Community Action Com., 1973-77; treas. Fairfax County Dem. Com., 1969-73; trustee Fairfax Hosp., 1973-77; bd. dirs. Tennis Patrons, Washington, 1984-88, Phila. Singers, 1993—, Physicians for Peace, 1994—. Mem. AAUW, Internat. Women's Assn., Am. Mgmt. Assn., Nat. Assn. Female Execs., Soc. Mktg. Profls. Club: Internat. (Washington). Home: 6512 Lakeview Dr Falls Church VA 22041-1102 Office: ARA Svcs 1101 Market St Philadelphia PA 19107-2934

EHRLICH, MARGARET ISABELLA GORLEY, systems engineer, mathematics educator, consultant; b. Eatonton, Ga., Nov. 12, 1950; d. Frank Griffith and Edith Roy (Beall) Gorley; m. Jonathan Steven Ehrlich. BS in Math., U. Ga., 1972; MEd, Ga. State U., 1977, EdS, 1982, PhD, 1987; postgrad. Woodrow Wilson Coll. of Law, 1977-78. Cert. secondary tchr., Ga. Tchr. DeKalb County Bd. Edn., Decatur, Ga., 1972-83; chmn. dept. math. Columbia High Sch., Decatur, 1978-83; with product devel. Chalkboard Co., Atlanta, 1983-84; math instr. Ga. State U., Atlanta, 1983-92; pres. Testing and Tech. Svcs., Atlanta, 1983—; course specialist Ga. Pacific Co., Atlanta, 1984-86; systems engr. Lotus Devel. Corp., 1986-89; rsch. assoc. SUNY-Stony Brook, 1976; modeling instr. Barbizon Modeling Sch., Atlanta, 1991; instr. Ga. State Coll. for Kids, 1984-85; test-taking cons., hon. mem. Communication Workers of Am. Local 3204, Atlanta, 1985—. Author: (software user manual) Micro Maestro, 1983, Music Math, 1984, (test manual) The Telephone Company Test, 1991, AMI Pro Advanced Courseware, 1992, A Study Guide for the Sales and Service Representative Test, 1993; mem. editorial bd. CPA Computer Report, Atlanta, 1984-85. Active Atlanta Preservation Soc., 1985, Planned Parenthood; tchr. St. Phillips Ch. Sch., Atlanta, 1981-88; vol. Joel Chandler Harris Assn., Atlanta, 1984-87; mem. St. Phillips welcome com., 1988—, drug and alcohol counseling HOPE, 1988—; sponsor Fair Test 1991—, Ctr. Fair and Open Testing. Named STAR Tchr. DeKalb County Bd. Edn., 1979, 80, 81, Most Outstanding Tchr., Barbizon Schs. of Modeling, 1980, Colo. Outward Bound, 1985, Disting. Educator, Ga. State U., 1987. Mem. LWV, Math. Assn. Am., Nat. Coun. Tchrs. Math., Ga. Council Tchrs. Math., Math. Assn. Am., Assn. Women in Math. (del. to China Sci. and Tech. Exch., 1989-90), Am. Soc. Tng. and Devel. Greater Atlanta, DeKalb Personal Computer Instr. Assn. (pres. 1984), Aux. Med. Assn. Ga., Daus. of Confederacy, Atlanta Track Club, N.Y.C. Track Club. Democrat. Episcopalian. Avocations: piano, jogging, fashion modeling, skiing, bonsai. Home: 240 Cliff Overlook Atlanta GA 30350-2601 Office: PO Box 500173 Atlanta GA 31150-0173

EHRMAN, MADELINE ELIZABETH, government administrator; b. N.Y.C., July 4, 1942; d. Donald McKinley and Marie Madeleine (Brandeis) Ehrman. BA summa cum laude Brown U., 1964, MA, 1965; M of Philosophy, Yale U., 1967; PhD, The Union Inst., 1989. Sci. linguist U.S. Dept. State, Washington, 1969-73, regional lang. supr. U.S. Embassy, Bangkok, Thailand, 1973-75, lang. tng. supr. U.S. Dept. State, Washington, 1975-84, curriculum and tng. specialist, 1984-85, acting chmn. dept. Asian and African Langs., 1985, chmn. dept. Asian and African Langs., 1986-88, acting assoc. dean Sch. Lang. Studies, 1987-88, dir. rsch., evaluation and devel., 1989—. Author: The Meanings of the Modals in Present Day American English, 1966, Contemporary Cambodian, 1975, Indonesian Fast Course, 1982, Communicative Japanese Materials, 1984, Ants and Grasshoppers, Badgers and Butterflies: Qualitative and Quantitative Exploration of Adult Language Learning Styles and Strategies, 1989; mem. editorial bd. Jour. Psychol. Type, 1991—. Mem., ESOL/HILT Citizen's Adv. Council, Arlington County, Va., 1985-89; psychotherapist Meyer Treatment Ctr. Washington Sch. Psychiatry, 1989-94. Woodrow Wilson Found. fellow, 1964; NSF fellow, 1964-69; recipient Meritorious Honor award U.S. Dept. State, 1972, 83. Mem. Am. Psychol. Assn., Tchrs. of English to Speakers of Other Langs., Am. Assn. Asian Studies, Assn. for Psychol. Type, Am. Orthopsychiat. Soc., Phi Beta Kappa, Psi Chi. Avocations: reading, bicycling, gardening. Office: Fgn Svc Inst 4000 Arlington Blvd Arlington VA 22204-1500

EICHINGER, MARILYNNE H., museum administrator; m. Martin Eichinger; children: Ryan, Kara, Julia, Jessica, Talik. BA in Anthropology and Sociology magna cum laude, Boston U., 1965; MA, Mich. State U., 1971. With emergency and outpatient staff Ingham County Mental Health Ctr., 1972; founder, pres., exec. dir. Impression 5 Sci. and Art Mus., Lansing, Mich., 1973-85; pres. Oreg. Mus. Sci. and Industry, Portland, 1985—; bd. dirs. Portland Visitors Assn., 1994—; bd. dirs. Portland Visitors Assn., 1994—, NW Regional Edn. Labs., 1991—; instr. Lansing (Mich.) C.C., 1978; ptnr. Eyrie Studio, 1982-85; bd. dirs. Assn. Sci. Tech. Ctrs., 1980-84, 88-93; mem. adv. bd. Portland State U.; condr. numerous workshops in interactive exhibit design, adminstrn. and fund devel. for schs., orgns., profl. socs. Author: (with Jane Mack) Lexington Montessori School Survey, 1969, Manual on the Five Senses, 1974; pub. Mich. edit. Boing mag. Founder Cambridge Montessori Sch., 1964; bd. dirs. Lexington Montessori Sch.,

1969, Mid-Mich. South Health Sys. Agy., 1978-81, Cmty. Referral Ctr., 1981-85, Sta. WKAR-Radio, 1981-85; active Lansing "Riverfest" Lighted Boat Parade, 1980; mem. state Health Coordinating Coun., 1980-82; mem. pres.'s adv. coun. Portland State U., 1986—; mem. pres.' adv. bd. Portland State U., 1987-91. Recipient Diana Cert. Leadership, YWCA, 1976-77, Woman of Achievement award, 1991, Community Svc. award Portland State U., 1992. Mem. Am. Assn. Mus., Oreg. Mus. Assn., Assn. Sci. and Tech. Ctrs., Zonta Lodge (founder, bd. dirs. East Lansing club 1978), Internat. Women's Forum, Rotary Club Portland, City Club Portland, Portland C. of C. Office: Oreg Mus Sci and Industry 1945 SE Water Ave Portland OR 97214-3356

EICHMAN, CAROLINE, marketing professional; b. Melrose Park, Ill., Oct. 31, 1963; d. Martin Leonard and Despina (Calathes) E.; m. Howard Jay Cure, Sept. 1, 1991. BA, Rutgers Coll., 1985; MA, U. Chgo., 1987; PhD, NYU, 1993. Seasonal plan mgr. N.Y.C. Parks Dept., 1987-88; rsch. dir. Child Care Action Campaign, N.Y.C., 1989-93; market rsch. mgr. Warner Music Group, N.Y.C., 1993—; mem. adv. bd. study on cost and quality of child care provision U. Colo., N.Y.C., 1991-93. Contbr. articles to reports and profl. jours. Tutor N.Y.C.-Base Ch., 1988; vol. Friends of Ruth Messinger, N.Y.C., 1989-91. Urban Inst. grantee, 1992. Mem. N.Y. Women's Agenda (domestic violence com. 1993), Village Ind. Dems., Ind. Neighborhood Dems. Office: Warner Music Group Inc 75 Rockefeller Plz 30th Fl New York NY 10019

EICHNER, KAY MARIE, mental health nurse; b. Des Moines, Apr. 28, 1955; d. Earl C. and Rachel L. (Martens) E. BSN, Grand View Coll., 1979. Staff nurse U. Iowa Hosp., Iowa City, 1979-80; staff nurse, supr. nursery Oasis Day Care Ctr., Indianola, Iowa, 1985-86; staff nurse Iowa Meth. Med. Ctr., Des Moines, 1980-83, 87—; speaker on survivors of child sexual abuse. Mem. Nat. Nurses Soc. on Addictions. Republican. Mem. Christian Ch. Home: 6640 SE 5th St Apt 9 Des Moines IA 50315-6443 Office: Powell CDC Iowa Meth Med Ctr 1200 Pleasant St Des Moines IA 50309-1406

EIDE, LAURA VIEHMYER, human resources specialist; b. Balt., Oct. 3, 1955; d. Edward Earl and Barbara Lacy (Hough) V.; m. James E. Vaughn, July 3, 1982 (div. May 1992); 1 child, Edward Andrew; m. Peter J. Eide, May 21, 1994; stepchildren: Cheryl, Karalyn A., Merissa A. BA in Psychology, Edn. summa cum laude, U. Md., Balt., 1976. Sr. pers. analyst, asst. dir. Seminole County Govt., Sanford, Fla., 1978-81; dir. pers. Piezo Technology, Inc., Orlando, Fla., 1981-84; mgr. human resources, adminstr. Travelers/EBS, Inc., Maitland, Fla., 1984-90; dir. human resources Arnold Palmer Golf Mgmt. Co., Orlando, 1990-92; mgr. employment and employee rels. Am. Coun. Life Ins., Washington, 1992—. Cons. Christian Ex-Offenders Employment Svcs., Orlando, 1988-90. Mem. Soc. for Human Resource Mgmt. (bd. dirs. 1988-93), Human Resources Fla. (state dir. 1989-90, dist. dir. 1987), Ctrl. Fla. Pers. Assn. (chpt. pres. 1985-86, Ctrl. Fla. Pers. Exec. of Yr. 1987), Psi Chi, Phi Kappa Phi. Home: 10209 Camelford Ct Ellicott City MD 21042 Office: Am Council Life Insurance 1001 Pensylvania Ave NW Washington DC 20004

EIDSON, KATHLEEN O'NEAL, advertising account executive; b. New Rochelle, N.Y., May 19, 1962; d. Patrick William and Mary Sarah (Hosie) O'Neal; m. Mark A. Eidson. BA in Spanish with distinction, Trinity Coll., Washington, 1984. Cert. English tchr. to speakers of other langs. Mktg. rep. Rustin and Assoc., Inc., Tampa, Fla., 1984-85, mktg. mgr., 1985-87; retail advt. acct. exec. St. Petersburg Times, Clearwater, Fla., 1987-93, nat. advt. sr. acct. exec., 1993—; mem. Tampa Bay Internat. Trade Coun., 1984-89, Suncoast Export Coun., St. Petersburg, 1984-87, Internat. Vis.' Coun., Tampa, 1984-87; asst. English tchr. St. Louis U., Madrid, 1983. Mem. Jr. League of Tampa, 1992—. Recipient Modern Lang. award Trinity Coll., 1984. Mem. Suncoast Travel Industry Assn., Pacific Am. Tourism Assn. (Fla. chpt.), Propeller Club U.S. (Tampa chpt.), Women's Yacht Racing Assn. (v.p., chair race com. 1986-87), Davis Island Yacht Club, Trinity Coll. Alumnae Assn. (area coord., west coast of Fla. student recruiter 1985—). Roman Catholic. Home: 14802 N Florida Ave Tampa FL 33616 Office: St Petersburg Times 490 First Ave S Saint Petersburg FL 34701

EIERMANN-WEGENER, DARLENE MAE, paralegal; b. New Orleans, June 10, 1959; d. Wilbur Joseph and Dorothy M. (Walton-Palmer) Eiermann; m. Edmund T. Wegener, Jr., Apr. 26, 1991. Student, U. New Orleans, 1991—. Cert. paralegal. Adminstrv. asst. Jefferson Parish Coun., Gretna, La., 1980; sec. Robin Towing Corp., Harvey, La., 1980-83; legal sec. Oster & Wegener, APLC, New Orleans, 1983-86, paralegal, 1986—. Mem. Assn. Trial Lawyers of Am., New Orleans Paralegal Assn., La. State Paralegal Assn., Nat. Paralegal Assn.; Mensa, Beta Sigma Phi, others. Republican. Lutheran. Office: Oster & Wegener 1515 Poydras St Ste 2600 New Orleans LA 70112

EIGEL, MARCIA DUFFY, editor; b. Denver, July 15, 1936; d. Eugene and Margaret (Foley) Duffy; m. Edwin G. Eigel Jr., May 30, 1959; children: Edwin III, Mary. BA, Webster U., 1958. Reg. rep. N.Y. Stock Exch. Dir. continuing edn. Mo. Soc. CPAs, St. Louis, 1978-79; dir. mktg. Greater Bridgeport (Conn.) Transp. Dist., 1979-81; security analyst Tucker, Anthony & R. L. Day, Stamford, Conn., 1981-84; fin. editor Evaluation Assoc., Westport, Conn., 1984-85; editor, writer corp. hdqrs. GE, Fairfield, Conn., 1985-92; dir. comms. Girl Scouts USA of Hausatonic Coun., Bridgeport, Conn., 1994—; instr. in bus. writing So. Conn. State U., New Haven, 1986, U. Bridgeport, 1990. Writer, editor newsletter Customer Fin. Svcs. News, 1987-92, Woman Traveler, 1990—; contbr. articles to profl. jours. Bd. dirs. Friends McDonnell Planetarium, St. Louis, 1974-78, St. Louis U. Women's Club, 1975-79, YWCA, Bridgeport, 1980-83, Conf. Women, Bridgeport, 1981-83; founder, treas. St. Louis Free Lance Writers, 1977-79. Mem. NAFE. Home: 33 Pepperbush Ln Fairfield CT 06430-4036

EIGER, ELISA MUI, editor; b. Honolulu, May 3, 1963; d. Thomas Lawrence and Lois Wing-han (Thom) Mui; m. Martin Isaiah Eiger, June 21, 1987. BA in Biology, Wellesley Coll., 1985; MA in Sci. Edn., Columbia U., 1986. Cert. tchr. sci., N.J.; cert. tchr. biology, N.Y. Tchr. biology Rumson (N.J.)-Fair Haven Regional High Sch., 1986-87; assoc. editor Prentice-Hall, Inc., Englewood Cliffs, N.J., 1987-90, project editor, 1990-93, project leader, 1993—. Democrat. Jewish. Home: PO Box 743 Pine Brook NJ 07058-0743 Office: Prentice Hall Inc Sci Editl Dept 1 Lake St Upper Saddle River NJ 07458

EIKENBERRY, JILL, actress; b. New Haven, Jan. 21, 1947; m. Michael Tucker; 1 stepchild. Student, Yale U. Actress stage prodns. Saints, 1976, Uncommon Women and Others, 1977, Watch on the Rhine, 1980, Onward Victoria, 1980, Holiday, 1982, Porch, 1984, Fine Line, 1984, Life Under Water, 1985, feature film appearances include Between the Lines, 1977, An Unmarried Woman, 1977, The End of the World in Our Ususal Bed in a Night Full of Rain, 1978, Rich Kids, 1979, Butch and Sundance: The Early Days, 1979, Hide in Plain Sight, 1980, Arthur, 1981, Grace Quigley, 1985, The Manhattan Project, 1986; TV movie appearances include The Deadliest Season, 1977, Orphan Train, 1979, Swan Song, 1980, Sessions, 1983, Kane and Abel, 1985, Assault and Matrimony, 1987, Family Sins, 1987, A Stoning in Fulham County, 1988, My Boyfriend's Back, 1989, The Diane Martin Story, The Secret Life of Archie's Wife, 1990, An Inconvenient Woman, 1991, Living A Lie, 1991, Doc: The Dennis Littky Story, 1992, Chantilly Lace (cable) 1993; teleplay Uncommon Women and Others, 1978; regular (TV series) L.A. Law, 1986-94 (Emmy nomination, Supporting Actress - Drama Series, 1994). Office: care William Morris Agency 151 El Camino Beverly Hills CA 90212*

EILENBERGER, JILL C., psychotherapist; b. Binghamton, N.Y., Dec. 31, 1957; d. Edward Milton Milo and Patricia Wyoma (Bagby) E. BS, SUNY, Binghamton, 1984; MSW, U. N.C., 1986. Cert. clin. social worker, marital and family therapist. Willie M. Case mgr. Gaston Mental Health Ctr., Gastonia, N.C., 1986-87, child/youth therapist, 1987-88; adult/adolescent therapist Kaiser Permanente HMO Mental Health Unit, Charlotte, N.C., 1988-90; psychotherapist United Family Svcs., Charlotte, N.C., 1990-92, Carolina Psychol. Resource Ctr., Charlotte, N.C., 1990—; intern N.Y.S. Divsn. for Youth, 1983-84, Chapel Hill (N.C.) Headstart, 1984-85, Meml. Hosp. Alamance, County Psychiat. Unit, Burlington, N.C., 1985-86; vol. counselor Women's Health Counseling Ctr., Chapel Hill, 1984-85; helpline therapist Gaston Mental Health Ctr., Gastonia, 1986-88; cons. Charter Counseling Ctr., Concord, N.C., 1988-89, The Diet Ctr.- Arboretum, Charlotte, 1990-91; founder therapy group for women with eating disorders, 1988—; bd. mem. Eating Disorders Edn. Project, Community Health Ctr., Charlotte, 1990-92; field instr. U. S.C., Columbia, 1994—; presenter in field. Bd. mem. health ctr. com. YMCA, Charlotte, 1990-92. Mem. Am. Assn. Marital and Family Therapists (clin., v.p. Charlotte chpt. 1991, pres. 1992-93), Nat. Assn. Social Workers, Toastmasters Internat. (Charlotte chpt.). Democrat. Office: Carolina Psychol Resource Ctr 1801 E 5th St Ste 212 Charlotte NC 28204

EILERMAN, BETTY JEAN, marriage and family counselor; b. Phila., Nov. 1, 1942; d. Frank Irving and Elizabeth Marquerite (Lennon) Gunsauls; m. Jerome Louis Eilerman, Dec. 15, 1969. BA, Rosemont Coll., 1964; M.Rel.Ed., Loyola U., Chgo., 1970; PhD, Calif. Pacific U., 1980; MA, U. San Francisco, 1984. Lic. marriage and family therapist, Calif., Minn. Instr. Maria Goretti High Sch., Phila., 1964-66, Bishop McDevitt High Sch., Wyncote, Pa., 1966-68; assoc. editor George A. Pflaum Pub., Dayton, Ohio, 1968-69; instr. Acad. of Our Lady of Peace, San Diego, 1970, The Bishop's Schs., LaJolla, Calif., 1970-80; ptnr. Write Right!, LaJolla, 1979-81; counselor Ctr. Creative Consciousness, Santa Rosa, Calif., 1982; intern Clin. Cognitive Inst., Santa Rosa, 1982-83; counselor Cath. Community Svc., Santa Rosa, 1983-84; pvt. practice Santa Rosa, 1988-92, Fargo, N.D., 1988-92; bereavement counselor Home Hospice, Santa Rosa, 1983-85; hypnotherapist, Santa Rosa and Fargo, 1985—; co-facilitator Rebuilding: Divorce Workshops, Santa Rosa, 1986-88; co-dir. Reconnections, Santa Rosa, 1987-88, Counselor Employee Support Systems, Santa Rosa, 1987-88; founder Crossing, Fargo, 1988-92, Bridge House, Santa Rosa, 1993—. Pres. Profl. Women's Group, Phila., 1966=67, Newcomers Club, Santa Rosa, 1982; dir. Svc. League, LaJolla, 1970-80. Honoree Nat. Disting. Svc. Registry for Counseling and Devel., 1990. Mem. Am. Assn. Marriage & Family Therapy, Calif. Assn. Marriage & Family Therapy, Assn. Humanistic Psychology, Assn. Transpersonal Psychology, Am. Mental Health Counselors Assn., Am. Assn. Counseling and Devel., Am. Assn. Pastoral Counselors, Nat. Honor Soc., Delta Epsilon Sigma. Office: 1211 Pacific Ave Santa Rosa CA 95404-3401

EILTS, SUSANNE ELIZABETH, physician; b. Council Bluffs, Iowa, Oct. 12, 1955; d. Ervin Edwin and Mary Margaret (Leonard) E. BS, Nebr. Wesleyan U., 1976; MD, U. Iowa, 1980. Diplomate Am. Bd. Internal Medicine. Intern, resident U. Nebr. Med. Ctr., Omaha, 1980-83; pvt. practice, Omaha, 1983—; clin. instr. internal medicine U. Nebr., Omaha, 1983—; med. dir. Ambassador Nursing Home, Omaha, 1990-92; quality assurance reviewer Sunderbruch Corp. Nebr., Lincoln, 1990—; v.p. quality assurance Internal Med. Assocs., 1993—; chmn. dept. of medicine Clarkson Hosp., 1994—. Med. columnist Omaha World Herald, 1986-88. Mem. ACP, Am. Geriatric Soc., Nebr. Med. Assn. (alt. del. 1990-91, del. 1992, young physician com. 1989-93, com. health care reform 1993—, legis. com. 1993—), Am. Women's Med. Assn. Nebr. (sec. 1987), Nebr. Soc. Internal Medicine (bd. dirs. 1994—), Dundee-Meml. Park Neighborhood Assn., Beta Beta Beta, Phi Kappa Phi, Phi Lambda Upsilon. Office: Internal Medicine Assocs PC 4242 Farnam St Ste 650N Omaha NE 68131-2850

EINIGER, CAROL BLUM, foundation executive; b. Phila., Nov. 30, 1949; d. Bernard Michael and Bella (Karff) Blum; m. Roger William Einiger, Dec. 21, 1969; 1 child. BA, U. Pa., 1970; MBA, Columbia U., 1973. With Conde Nast Publs., N.Y.C., 1970-71, Goldman, Sachs & Co., N.Y.C., 1971-72; with 1st Boston Corp., N.Y.C., 1973-88, with corp. fin. dept., 1973-79, with capital markets dept., 1979-88, mng. dir., 1982-88, head short-term fin. dept., 1983-88, head capital markets dept., 1985-88; vis. prof., exec.-in-residence Columbia U. Bus. Sch., N.Y.C., 1988-89; mng. dir. Wasserstein Perella & Co. Inc., N.Y.C., 1989-92; v.p., chief fin. officer Edna McConnell Clark Found., N.Y.C., 1992—. Trustee Horace Mann Sch., 1988-94, U. Pa., 1989—; bd. overseers Columbia U. Bus. Sch., 1988—; investment com. Mus. Modern Art, 1994—; mem. steering com. Wall Street div. UJA Fedn., 1989-93. Office: Edna McConnell Clark Found 250 Park Ave New York NY 10177-0001

EINODER, CAMILLE ELIZABETH, secondary education educator; b. Chgo., June 15, 1937; d. Isadore and Elizabeth T. (Czerwinski) Popowski; student Fox Bus. Coll., 1954; BEd in Biology, Chgo. Tchrs. Coll., 1964; MA in Analytical Chemistry, Gov.'s State U., 1977; MA in Adminstrn. and Supervision, Roosevelt U., 1986; postgrad 1992—. m. Joseph X. Einoder, Aug. 5, 1978; children: Carl Frank, Mark Frank, Vivian Einoder, Joe Einoder, Tim Einoder, Sheila Einoder, Jude Einoder. Secretarial positions, Chgo., 1955-64; tchr. biology Chgo. Bd. Edn., 1964—, tchr. biology and agr., 1975-81, tchr. biology, agr. and chemistry, 1981—; human rels. coord. Morgan Park High Sch., Chgo., 1980—, tchr. biology Internat. Studies Sch., 1983—, mem. adv. bd., 1989—; career devel. cons. for agr. related curriculum. Bds. dirs., founding mem., author constn. Community Coun., 1970—; bd. dirs., edn. cons. Neighborhood Coun., 1974; rep. Chgo. Tchrs. Union, 1969. Mem. Phi Delta Kappa, Iota Sigma Pi. Home: 10637 S Claremont Ave Chicago IL 60643-3101 Office: 1744 W Pryor St Chicago IL 60643

EISELE, KAREN ELIZABETH, reporter; b. St. Louis, Jan. 29, 1965; d. Adolf and Anita E. BJ, U. Mo., 1987. Anchor/reporter KOMU-TV, NBC, Columbia, Mo., 1986-87; news reporter WTXL-TV, ABC, Tallahassee, Fla., 1987; morning anchor/health reporter KQTV-TV, ABC, St. Joseph, Mo., 1987-89; health/news reporter/anchor WMAZ-TV, CBS, Macon, Ga., 1989-93; health reporter WAGA-TV, CBS, Atlanta, 1993—. Author news series: Radon Gas, 1988, Water Shortage, 1989, Breast Cancer, 1991, Condition Critical: Healthcare Reform, 1992. Recipient award for best documentary in pub. affairs AP-Ga., 1989, 90. Mem. Atlanta Press Club. Office: WAGA-TV 1551 Briarcliff Rd NE Atlanta GA 30306-2274

EISENBERG, DOROTHY, federal judge; b. 1929. LLB, Bklyn. Law Sch., 1950. Bar: N.Y. 1951, U.S. Dist. Ct. (ea. and so. dists.) N.Y., U.S. Ct. Appeals (2nd cir.), U.S. Supreme Ct. Assoc. Otterbourg, Stiendler, Houston & Rosen, N.Y.C., 1950-51, Goldman, Horowitz & Cherno, Mineola, N.Y., 1970-80; pvt. practice Garden City, N.Y., 1981; ptnr. Shaw, Licitra, Eisenberg, Esernio & Schwartz, P.C., Garden City, 1981-89; bankruptcy judge U.S. Bankruptcy Ct. (ea. dist.) N.Y., 1989—; mem. Com. on Character and Fitness, Appellate divsn., 2nd Dept., 1983-89; panel trustee U.S. Dist. Ct. (ea. dist.) N.Y., 1975-89, U.S. Dist. Ct. (so. dist.) N.Y., 1979-89. Fellow Am. Bar Found.; mem. ABA, Bankruptcy Lawyers Bar Assn., Nassau County Bar Assn., N.Y. Women's Bar Assn., Theodore Roosevelt Am. Inn Ct. Office: U S Bankruptcy Ct 1635 Privado Rd Westbury NY 11590*

EISENBERG, EDIE BROWN, artist, graphic designer; b. N.Y.C., July 7, 1920; d. Louis and Helen Beatrice (Cohn) Kerpner; m. Dan Brown, Feb. 4, 1941 (dec. June 1944); 1 child, Jeffrey Peter Brown; m. Ben Eisenberg, Dec. 15, 1947 (dec. Jan. 1991); 1 child, John Louis Eisenberg. Student, The Cooper Union, 1938-39. Co-owner, artist Display by the Browns, Baldwin, N.Y., 1941-43; asst. art dir. Diorama Corp., N.Y.C., 1944-47, McArthur Advt., N.Y.C., 1947-52; prin. Tannar-Brown, N.Y.C., 1952-66; writer, co-dir., prodr. film The Egg and The Eye, Woodmere, N.Y., 1966-67; freelance designer Woodmere, 1967—. One-person shows include The Gathering, The Egg and The Eye, A Face, A Flower, Spectre, Portraits and Places, numerous exhibits. Vol. graphic designer logo Sch. Dist. 14, The Hewlett-Woodmere Pub. Libr., Sr. Ctr. Home and Studio: 48 Brower Ave Woodmere NY 11578

EISENBERG, KAREN SUE BYER, nurse; b. Bklyn., Mar. 11, 1954; d. Marvin and Florence (Beck) Byer; m. Howard Eisenberg, May 11, 1974; children: Carly Beth, Mariel Bryn. Diploma, L.I. Coll. Hosp. Sch. Nursing, 1973; BS in Nursing, L.I. U., 1976, M in Profl. Studies, 1977. Nurse recovery room and surg. intensive care unit Downstate Med. Ctr., Bklyn., 1973-75; utilization rev. analyst Bezallel Health Related Facility, Far Rockaway, N.Y., 1975-76; utilization rev. analyst, R.N. supr. Seagirt Health Related Facility, Far Rockaway, 1976; staff nurse neurosurg. and rehab. nursing Downstate Med. Ctr., Bklyn., 1978, nurse intensive care unit, 1978-79; asst. nursing dir. pathology, clin. rsch. assoc. Rsch. Found., Bklyn., 1979-90; instrl. support specialist pathology Health Sci. Ctr. SUNY, Bklyn., 1990-92; nurse practitioner pathology SUNY Rsch. Found., Bklyn., 1992—. Contbr. articles to profl. jours. Mem. Oncology Nursing Soc., Am. Nurses Assn., N.Y. State Nurses Assn., N.Y. Acad. Scis., L.I. Coll. Hosp. Alumnae Assn. Office: 450 Clarkson Ave Brooklyn NY 11203-2012

EISENBERG, MARILYN, former hotel executive, consultant; b. Chgo., Mar. 3, 1941; d. Frank and Rose (Kreisman) Spiegel; m. Jack Leo Eisenberg, Nov. 28, 1965; children: Erik, Amy Ilene. Exec. mgr. Knickerbocker Hotel, Chgo., 1966-70, Ambassador West Hotel, Chgo., 1976-85; tchr. hotel mgmt. City Coll. of Chgo., 1986-88. Co-founder, pres. Edn. Resource Ctr., Chgo., 1974-80; co-founder Chgo. Children's Mus., 1980, pres. 1983-86, bd. dirs., 1980—; vol. tchr. Nr. North High Sch., Chgo., 1983-90; bd. dirs. Hild Arts Ctr., Chgo., 1989—, vice-chmn., 1989—; bd. dirs. Body Politic Theatre, 1977-79, Personal PAC; bd. dirs. Residents for Emergency Shelter, 1995. Home: 3100 N Sheridan Rd Chicago IL 60657-4954

EISENBERG, ROBIN LEDGIN, religious education administrator; b. Passaic, N.J., Jan. 10, 1951; d. Morris and Ruth (Miller) Ledgin. BS, West Chester State U., 1973; M Edn., Kutztown State U., 1977. Adminstrv. asst. Keneseth Israel, Allentown, Pa., 1973-77; dir. edn. Cong. Schaarai Zedek, Tampa, Fla., 1977-79, Kehilath Israel, Pacific Palisades, Calif., 1979-80, Temple Beth El, Boca Raton, Fla., 1980—. Contbr. Learning Together, 1987. Chmn. edn. info., Planned Parenthood, Boca Raton Fla. 1989. Recipient Kamiker Camp award Nat. Assn. Temple Educators, Pres.'s award for adminstrn., 1990. Mem. Nat. Assn. Temple Educators (pres. 1990-92), Coalition Advancement of Jewish Edn. Home: 5692 Santiago Cir Boca Raton FL 33433-7297 Office: Temple Beth El 333 SW 4th Ave Boca Raton FL 33432-5798

EISENBERG, SONJA MIRIAM, artist; b. Berlin, June 10, 1926; came to U.S., 1938, naturalized, 1947; d. Adolf and Meta Cecilie (Bettauer) Weinberger; student Queens Coll., 1943-46, Middlebury Coll., 1945; NYU, 1952-54; BA, NYU, 1954; postgrad. Nat. Acad. Sch. Fine Arts, 1961; m. Jack Eisenberg, Mar. 31, 1946; children: Ralph, Lynn, Lauren. One-woman shows: Bodley Gallery, N.Y.C., 1970, 73, 75, 80, Galerie Art du Monde, Paris, 1973, Buyways Gallery, Sarasota, Fla., 1973, 74, 75, 78, Galerie de Sfinx, Amsterdam, Netherlands, 1974, Huntsville (Ala.) Mus. Art, 1974, Anglo-Am. Art Mus., Baton Rouge, 1974, Comara Gallery, Los Angeles, 1974, Palm Spring (Calif.) Desert Mus., 1975, Fordham U., N.Y.C., 1976, Omega Inst., New Lebanon, N.Y., 1979, Am. Mus., Hayden Planetarium, N.Y.C., 1980, Avila Graphics, Ltd., 1981, YWCA, N.Y.C., 1981, Cathedral of St. John the Divine, N.Y.C., 1983, 85, The Millbrook Gallery, N.Y., 1989, 94, Christopher Leonard Gallery, N.Y.C., 1993, Park Hotel, Vitznau, Switzerland, 1994; group shows include Mus. Fine Arts, St. Petersburg, Fla., 1973, Am. Watercolor Soc., 107th, 108th Exhbn., 1974, 75, Galerie Frederic Gollong, St. Paul de Vence, France, 1978, Betty Parson's Gallery, N.Y.C., 1981, Foster Harmon Galleries of Am. Art, Sarasota, Fla., 1988, Tokyo Met. Art Mus. 14th Internat. Art Friendship Exhbn., 1989, Galerie Herbert Leidel, Munich, Germany, 1991, Park Hotel, Vitznau, Switzerland, 1994, Burgenstock (Switzerland) Hotels, 1995; represented in permanent collections: Archives Am. Art, Smithsonian Inst., Jewish Mus., N.Y.C., Fordham U. Mus., N.Y.C., Palm Springs Desert Mus., Omega Inst., Cathedral of St. John the Divine; artist-in-residence Cathedral of St. John the Divine, N.Y.C.; designer WFUNA cachet for UN Water Power Conf., 1977, UN Internat. Yr. of Disabled Persons, 1981. Regent Cathedral of St. John the Divine, N.Y.C., 1990, commisioned painting to commemorate Crystal Night for Telecom Telefon Karte, Munich, 1993. Recipient gold medal for artistic merit Internat. Parliament for Safety and Peace, 1983, Palma D'Oro Europe, 1986. Mem. Accademia Italia delle Arti e del Lavoro (Gold medal 1981). Completed project Seeing the Gospel According to St. John (text and 41 paintings) for Cathedral of St. John, 1987; appointed art dir. Hermes Media B.V., Amsterdam, The Netherlands, 1992. Home and Office: 1020 Park Ave New York NY 10028-0913

EISENMAN, TRUDY FOX, dermatologist; b. Chgo., Oct. 14, 1940; d. Nathan Henry and Bernice (Greenberg) Fox; student U. Ill. at Navy Pier, Chgo., 1958-60; M.D., U. Ill., 1964; m. Theodore S. Eisenman, Aug. 19, 1962 (div. 1985); children: Lawrence, Robert. Rotating intern Milw. County Gen. Hosp., 1964-65, med. resident, 1965-66; resident in dermatology Northwestern U. Med. Sch., Chgo., 1970-73, instr., 1973—; practice medicine specializing in dermatology, Chgo., 1973—; attending dermatologist Louis A. Weiss Meml. Hosp., Chgo., 1973—. Diplomate Am. Bd. Dermatology. Fellow Am. Acad. Dermatology; mem. Chgo. Dermatol. Soc., Am. Med. Women's Assn., AMA, Chgo. Med. Soc., Alpha Omega Alpha. Home: 2526 Thornwood Ave Wilmette IL 60091-1377 Office: 4640 N Marine Dr Chicago IL 60640-5719

EISENMENGER, LINDA THATE, accountant; b. Fairmont, Minn., Oct. 4, 1956; d. Benjamin Rudolph and Emma Gertrude (Rose) Thate; m. Dale Richard Eisenmenger, Sept. 24, 1977; 1 child, Levi Benjamin. AA, Southwestern Tech. Coll., Jackson, Minn., 1977. Lic. pub. acct. Bookkeeper Fairmont Community Edn., 1973-75; bookkeeper, computer operator Gary Beckman, Acct., Fairmont, 1977-80; bookkeeper Fairmont Sch. Dist. 454, 1980; computer operator, acct. Pierce & Findley, CPAs, Fairmont, 1980, Steve Pierce, CPA, Fairmont, 1980-81; acct. in pvt. practice Fairmont, 1981-82; computer operator, acct. City of Fairmont, 1982-83; acct., office mgr. B. Krahmer Law Office, Ltd., Fairmont, 1983—. Dir. fin. St. John Vianney Cath. Ch., Fairmont, 1992—. Mem. Nat. Soc. Pub. Accts., Minn. Assn. Pub. Accts. (sec.-treas. 1989-91, 2d v.p. 1991-92, 1st v.p. 1992-93, pres. 1993-94), North Ctrl. Users Group (bd. dirs. 1989—), Fairmont Interlaken Golf Club, Fairmont Chain of Lakes Yacht Club. Republican. Roman Catholic. Office: Bruce Krahmer Law Office 115 W 1st St Ste 307 Fairmont MN 56031-1815

EISENSTADT, PAULINE DOREEN BAUMAN, investment company executive, state legislator; b. N.Y.C., Dec. 31, 1938; d. Morris and Anne (Lautenberg) Bauman; BA, U. Fla., 1960; MS (NSF grantee), U. Ariz., 1965; postgrad. U. N.Mex.; m. Melvin M. Eisenstadt, Nov. 20, 1960; children: Todd Alan, Keith Mark. Tchr., Ariz., 1961-65, P.R., 1972-73; adminstrv. asst. Inst. Social Research U. N.Mex., 1973-74; founder, 1st exec. dir. Energy Consumers N.Mex., 1977-81; dir., host TV program Consumer Viewpoint, 1980-82; host TV program N.Mex. Today and Tomorrow, 1992—; chmn. consumer affairs adv. com. Dept. Energy, 1979-80; v.p. tech. bd. Nat. Center Appropiate Tech., 1980—; pres. Eisenstadt Enterprises, investments, 1983—; mem. N.Mex. Ho. of Reps., 1985—, chairwoman majority caucus, chair rules com. N.Mex. House of Reps., 1987—, chair sub. com. on children and youth, 1987; mem. exec. com., vice chair pvt. coun. Nat. Conf. State Legislators, 1987; vice chmn. Sandoval County (N.Mex.) Democratic Party, 1981—; mem. N.Mex. Dem. State Central Com., 1981—; N.Mex. del. Dem. Nat. Platform Com., 1984, Dem. Nat. Conv., 1984; pres. Sandoval County Dem. Women's Assn., 1979-81; vice chmn. N. Mex. Dem. Platform Com., 1984—; mem. Sandoval County Redistricting Task Force, 1983-84; mem. Rio Rancho Ednl. Study Com., 1984—; mem. N.Mex. First. Named one of N.Mex.'s Outstanding Women, 1992. Mem. NEA, LWV, NOW. Author: Corrales, Portrait of a Changing Village, 1980. Mem. Kiwanis (1st woman mem. local club). Home: PO Box 658 Corrales NM 87048-0658

EISENSTEIN, ELIZABETH LEWISOHN, historian, educator; b. N.Y.C., Oct. 11, 1923; d. Sam A. and Margaret V. (Seligman) Lewisohn; m. Julian Calvert Eisenstein, May 30, 1948; children: Margaret, John (dec.), Edward. A.B., Vassar Coll., 1944; M.A., Radcliffe Coll., 1947, Ph.D., 1953; Litt. D. (hon.), Mt. Holyoke Coll., 1979. From lectr. to adj. prof history Am. U., Washington, 1959-74; Alice Freeman Palmer prof. history U. Mich., Ann Arbor, 1975-88, prof. emerita, 1988—; scholar-in-residence Rockefeller Found. Center, Bellagio, Italy, June 1977; mem. vis. com. dept. history Harvard U., 1975-81, vice-chmn., 1979-81; dir. Ecole des Hautes Etudes en Sciences Sociales, Paris, 1982; guest speaker, participant confs. and seminars; I. Beam vis. prof. U. Iowa, 1980; Mead-Swing lectr. Oberlin Coll., 1980; Stone lectr. U. Glasgow, 1984; Van Leer lectr. Van Leer Fedn., Jerusalem, 1984; Hanes lectr. U. N.C., Chapel Hill, 1985 first resident cons. Center for the Book, Library of Congress, Washington, 1979; mem. Coun. Scholars, 1980-88; pres.'s disting. visitor Vassar Coll., 1988; Pforzheimer lectr. N.Y. Pub. Libr., 1989, Lyell lectr. Bodleian Libr., Oxford, 1990, Merle Curti lectr. U. Wis., Madison, 1992; vis. fellow Wolfson Coll., Oxford, 1990. Author: The First Professional Revolutionist: F. M. Buonarroti, 1959, The Printing Press as an Agent of Change, 1979 , 2 vols. paperback edit., 1980 (Phi Beta Kappa Ralph Waldo Emerson prize 1980), The Printing Revolution in Early Modern Europe, 1983 (reissued as Canto Book, 1993), Grub Street Abroad,

1992; mem. editorial bd. Jour. Modern History, 1973-76, 83-86, Revs. in European History, 1973-86, Jour. Library History, 1979-82, Eighteenth Century Studies, 1981-84; contbr. articles to profl. jours., chpts. to books. Belle Skinner fellow Vassar Coll., NEH fellow, 1977, Guggenheim fellow, 1982, fellow Ctr. Advanced Studies in Behavioral Scis., 1982-83, 92-93, Humanities Rsch. Ctr. fellow Australian Nat. U., 1988. Fellow Am. Acad. Arts and Scis., Royal Hist. Soc.; mem. Soc. French Hist. Studies (v.p. 1970, mem. program com. 1974), Am. Soc. 18th Century Studies (nominating com. 1971), Soc. 16th Century Studies, Am. Hist. Assn. (com. on coms. 1970-72, chmn. Modern European sect. 1981, council 1982-85), Renaissance Soc. Am. (council 1973-76, pres. 1986), Am. Antiquarian Soc. (exec. com., adv. bd. 1984-87), Phi Beta Kappa. Office: U Mich Dept History Ann Arbor MI 48109

EISENZIMMER, BETTY WENNER, insurance agency executive; b. Twisp, Wash., July 25, 1939; d. Bren William and Julia Emogene (Salmon) Wenner; m. Erwin LeRoy Cook, June 19, 1955 (div. 1960); 1 child, Richard Jeffrey; m. Jerome Anthony Eisenzimmer, Feb. 18, 1966. Cert. in gen. ins. Ins. Inst. Am., 1981; cert. profl. ins. woman. Clk. typist MR Ins., Seattle, 1957-59; records clk. Assigned Risk Plan, Seattle, 1959-61; acct. asst. Robinson Jenner, Inc., Seattle, 1961-66; sec., acct. asst. Falkenberg & Co., Seattle, 1966-75, adminstrv. asst., 1975-77; ins. agt., corp. officer Service Ins. Inc., Seattle, 1975—; mem. adv. bd. Sch. Ins., Wash. State U. Coll. Bus., 1981-90. Asst. editor Today's Ins. Woman, 1980-81. Exec. bd. Wash. chpt. Cystic Fibrosis Found., 1978-86, pres., 1983-85. Recipient Disting. Svc. award, 1984; named Vol. of Yr. Wash. chpt., 1980; mem. Wash. State Centennial Speakers' Bur., 1987-89; mem. long range planning com. Cedar Cross United Meth. Ch., 1986-87, mem. worship com., 1988-91; community sponsor and vol. Wash. State Reformatory, 1992—. Mem. Ins. Women Puget Sound (pres. 1970-72, Ins. Woman of Yr. 1978, 81, Industry award 1984, Wash. State Communicate with confidence speakoff winner 1989, chmn. 1992 conf.), Ins. Women's Assn. Seattle (Ins. Woman of Yr. 1981), Nat. Assn. Ins. Women (nat. sec. 1976-77, regional dir. 1981-82, mem. exec. bd. 1976-77, 81-82, You Make the Difference award 1977, Regional IX Lace Speakoff winner 1983), Ind. Ins. Agts. and Brokers Wash. (edn. com. 1982-83), Ind. Ins. Agts. and Brokers King County (chmn. bylaws 1984-85), Profl. Ins. Agts. Wash. (edn. com. 1982-86, chmn. 1983-86), Wash. Ins. Council (mem. speakers bur. 1980—), Women Life Underwriters Conf. (nat. bd. dirs., region I dir. 1987-88), Acad. Prodr. Ins. Studies (fellow of acad.). Club: Toastmasters (dist. 2 sec. 1989-90, dist. 2 admin. lt. gov., 1990-91, mentor 1988-91, dist. 2 area Gov. of Yr, 1988, dist. 2 div. Gov. of Yr. 1989, dist. Gov. 1992-93, Disting. Toastmaster 1989, Gov.'s Trophy, 1990 and other awards and positions). Home: 8932 240th St SW Edmonds WA 98026-9020 Office: Svc Ins Inc 131 2nd Ave S Edmonds WA 98020-3554

EISLER, SUSAN KRAWETZ, advertising agency executive; b. N.Y.C., Aug. 18, 1946; d. Aaron and Bertha (Platt) Krawetz; m. Howard Irwin Eisler, June 8, 1980; 1 stepchild, Robin Joy, 1 adopted son, Joseph. BA, U. Pitts., 1967; MA, New Sch. for Social Rsch., 1971. Analyst, Marplan, Inc., N.Y.C., 1968-69; project dir. Market Facts, Inc., N.Y.C., 1969-70; assoc. rsch. mgr. Gen. Foods, Inc., White Plains, N.Y., 1970-75, product mgr., 1975-80; rsch. dir. Elizabeth Arden, N.Y.C., 1980-81; v.p., assoc. rsch. dir. Lintas: N.Y. (formerly SSC&B: Lintas Worldwide), N.Y.C., 1981-87, sr. v.p., assoc. research dir., 1987-92, exec. v.p., dir. strategic planning and rsch., 1992—. Named Woman of Yr. YWCA Acad. Women Achievers, 1989. Mem. Am. Mktg. Assn., Advt. Women N.Y., Advt. Rsch. Found. (copy rsch. coun.). Office: Lintas NY 1 Dag Hammarskjold Plz New York NY 10017-2279

EISNER, DIANA, pediatrician; b. Houston, May 7, 1951; d. Elmer and Edith (Dubow) E. BA in Biology cum laude, Brandeis U., 1973; MD, Southwestern Med. Sch., 1977. Diplomate Am. Bd. Pediatrics. Intern, resident Baylor Coll. Medicine, Houston, 1977-80; pvt. practice Houston, 1981—; chmn. dept. pediatrics Meml. N.W. Hosp., Houston, 1990. Recipient Commendation award Children's Protection Com. Tex. Children's Hosp., 1978, Physician's Recognition award AMA, 1983. Mem. Am. Acad. Pediatrics, Tex. Med. Assn., Tex. Pediatric Soc., Houston Pediatric Soc., Harris County Med. Soc. Office: 1740 W 27th St Ste 170 Houston TX 77008

EISNER, GAIL ANN, artist, educator; b. Detroit, Oct. 17, 1939; d. Rudolph and Florence (White) Leon; m. Marvin Michael Eisner, June 14, 1959 (dec. Feb. 1993); 1 child, Alan. Rsch. fellow, Art Inst. Chgo., Art Student League of N.Y.; BFA, Wayne State U. One-woman shows include OK Harris/David Klein Gallery, Birmingham, Mich., Sinclair Coll., LRC Gallery, Dayton, Ohio, U. Mich. Hosps., Ann Arbor; exhibited in group shows at Islip Art Mus., East Islip, N.Y., Columbia (Mo.) Coll., Tubac (Ariz.) Ctr. of the Arts, Ft. Wayne (Ind.) Mus. of Art, C.W. Post Coll., Brookville, N.Y., NAWA, Jacob K. Kavits Ctr., N.Y.C., Schoharie County Coun. of the Arts, Cobbleskill, N.Y., ARC Gallery, Chgo., McPherson (Kans.) Coll., Med. Coll. Ga., Augusta, Heckscher Mus. Art, Huntington, Nassau County Mus. Art, Roslyn, N.Y., Guild Hall, East Hampton, N.Y., Castle Gould, Sands Point, N.Y., Pastel Soc. Am., N.Y.C., Carrier Found., Belle Meade, N.J., Hill Country Arts Found., Ingram, Tex., Cunningham Meml. Art Gallery, Bakersfield, Calif., Henry Hicks Gallery, Bklyn. Hgts., U. N.D., Grand Forks, Nassau C.C., Garden City, N.Y., Trenton (N.J.) State Coll., Wenatchee Valley (W.Va.) Coll., Del Mar Coll., Corpus Christi, Tex., Minot(N.D.) State U., Ctrl. Mo. State U., McNeese State U., Lake Charles, La., Art Ctr., Mt. Clemens, Mich., Oakland C.C., Mich., Krasl Art Ctr., St. Joseph, Mich., Fontana Concert Soc., Kalamazoo, Mich., Art Ctr. Battle Creek, Mich., Ctrl. Mich. U., Mt. Pleasant, Birmingham (Mich.) Bloomfield Art Assn., Cmty. House, Birmingham, Sch. of Art Inst., Chgo., Cheekwood Mus. Art, Nashville, Grand Rapids (Mich.) Mus. Art, Flint (Mich.) Inst. Arts, Ariana Gallery, Royal Oak, Mich., Judith Paul Gallery, Medford, Oreg., The Art Collector, San Diego, Gwenda Jay Gallery, Chgo. Recipient Adriana Zahn award, Pastel Soc. Am., Heckscher Mus. award. Mem. Nat. Assn. Women Artists (Sara Winston Meml. award 1992), N.Y. Artist Equity Assn., Art Student League N.Y. (Sidney Dickinson Meml. award), Birmingham Bloomfield Art Assn. Office: Gail Eisner Studio 104 W Fourth # 303 Royal Oak MI 48067

EISNER, REBECCA SUZANNE, lawyer; b. Wheeling, W.Va., Aug. 27, 1962; d. Paul and Marilyn June (Muffeny) Redosh; m. Craig George Eisner, Dec. 29, 1988. BA, Ohio State U., 1984; JD, U. Mich., 1989. Assoc. Mayer, Brown & Platt, Chgo., 1989-92; assoc. group counsel, asst. v.p. Equifax, Inc., Atlanta, 1993—. Exec. vol. United Way of Metro Atlanta, 1994; vol. fund raiser Atlanta Women's Fund, 1994. Mem. ABA. Office: Equifax Inc 1600 Peachtree St NW Atlanta GA 30302

EIZENBERG, JULIE, architect. BArch, U. Melbourne, Australia, 1978; MArch II, UCLA, 1981. Lic. architect, Calif., reg. architect, Australia. Principal, architect Koning Eizenberg Architecture, Santa Monica, Calif., 1981—; instr. various courses UCLA, MIT, Harvard U.; lectr. in field; jury member P/A awards. Exhbns. incl. "House Rules" Wexner Ctr., 1994, "The Architect's Dream: Houses for the Next Millenium" The Contemporary Arts Ctr., 1993, "Angels & Franciscans" Gagosian Gallery, 1992, Santa Monica Mus. Art, 1993, "Broadening the Discourse" Calif. Women in Environmental Design, 1992, "Conceptional Drawings by Architects" Bannatyne Gallery, 1991, Exhbn. Koning Eizenberg Projects Grad. Sch. Architecture & Urban Planning UCLA, 1990; prin. works include Digital Domain Renovation and Screening Room, Santa Monica, Lightstorm Entertainment Office Renovation and Screening Room, Santa Monica, Gilmore Bank Addition and Remodel, L.A., 1548-1550 Studios, Santa Monica, (with RTA) Materials Rsch. Lab. at U. Calif., Santa Barbara, Ken Edwards Ctr. Community Svcs., Santa Monica, Sepulveda Recreation Ctr., L.A., PS # 1 Elem. Sch., Santa Monica, A.L.A. Sr. Svc. Ctr., West Hollywood, Vitalize Fairfax Project, L.A., Farmers Market, L.A. Additions (Westside Urban Forum prize 1991), Stage Deli, L.A., Simone Hotel, L.A. (Nat. Honor award AIA 1994), Boyd Hotel, L.A., Community Corp. Santa Monica Housing Projects, St. John's Hosp. Replacement Housing Program, Santa Monica, Liffman Ho., Santa Monica, (with Glenn Erikson) Electric Artblock, Venice (Beautification award L.A. Bus. Coun. 1993), 6th St. Condominiums, Santa Monica, Hollywood Duplex, Hollywood Hills (Record Houses Archtl. Record 1988), California Ave. Duplex, Santa Monica, Millen Apts., Santa Monica, Tarzana Ho. (Award of Merit L.A. chpt. AIA 1992, Sunset Western home Awards citation 1993-94), 909 Ho., Santa Monica (Award of Merit L.A. chpt. AIA 1991), 31st St. Ho., Santa Monica (Honor award AIACC 1994), others. Recipient 1st award Progressive Architecture, 1987; named one of Domino's Top 30 Architects, 1989. Mem. L.A. County Mus. Art, Westside Urban Forum, Urban Land Inst., Architects and Designers for Social Responsibility, Mus. Contemporary Art, The Nature Conservancy, Sierra Club. Office: Koning Eizenberg Architecture 1548 18th St Santa Monica CA 90404

EKANGER, LAURIE, state commissioner; b. Salt Lake City, Mar. 4, 1949; d. Bernard and Mary (Dearth) E.; m. William J. Shupe, Nov. 6, 1973; children: Ben, Robert. BA in English, U. Oreg., 1973. Various pos. Mont. State Employment & Tng. Divsn., Helena, 1975-80, dep. adminstr., 1980-82; adminstr. Mont. State Purchasing Divsn., Helena, 1982-85, Mont. State Personnel Divsn., Helena, 1985-93; labor commr. Mont. Dept. Labor & Ind., Helena, 1993—; council chair State Employee Group Benefits Coun., 1985-93; bd. dirs. Pub. Employee Retirement Bd., 1988. Home: 80 Pinecrest Clancy MT 59634 Office: Labor & Industry Dept 1315 E Lockey Helena MT 59624

EKMAN, PATRICIA, lawyer; b. Boston, Jan. 16, 1957; d. Robert and Charlotte (Grass) Schneider; m. Gerhson Ekman, Sept. 25, 1983. AB, Radcliffe Coll., 1978; JD, Stanford U., 1981. Bar: N.Y. 1982. Assoc. Seward & Kissel, N.Y.C., 1981-83, Thacher, Proffitt & Wood, N.Y.C., 1983-86; v.p., counsel, sec. finance Citicorp/Citibank NA, N.Y.C., 1986—. Mem. ABA. Democrat. Jewish. Clubs: Stanford (N.Y.), Stanford (N.J.). Home: 244 E 30th St # 1B New York NY 10016-8221 Office: Citicorp/Citibank 399 Park Ave New York NY 10043*

EKSTROM, KATINA BARTSOKAS, educator, artist; b. Springfield, Ill., Nov. 8, 1929; d. Tom A. and Elsie (Heinrich) Bartsokas; m. John Warren Ekstrom (div. Feb. 1978); children: John A., Kenneth M., Richard M., Timothy W., Christopher P. BFA, U. Ill., 1955, MAE, 1975. Tchr. art Urbana (Ill.) Jr. High Sch., 1974-89, Bronx (N.Y) Sch. Dist., 1990-91, Astoria (N.Y.) Jr. High Sch., 1991—; tchr. adult edn., 1975-80, Urbana Pk. dist., 1977-88; artist Colwell Collection catalog, Champaign, Ill., 1985; juror Chgo. Ann. Met. History Fair, 1985, Cen. Ill. Scholastics High Sch., Springfield, 1988-89, also others; Fulbright cultural exch. tchr., 1986. Exhibited in group show Champaign Arts and Humanities Assn., 1983-84, Swoope Gallery, Ind., Lincoln Ctr., N.Y.C., 1994, Abney Gallery, N.Y.C., 1995. Artist Peace Coalition Concerts, Champaign, 1985-86, U. Ill. Sinfonia, Champaign, 1986-88. Recipient Award of Merit 1994 Manhattan Arts Internat. Cover Art Competition, 2d pl. award in painting Ill. 28th Ann. Art Exhbn. Mem. Urbana Educators Assn. (Outstanding Educator award 1986), Ind. Artists Ill., U. Ill. Alumni Assn., Kappa Delta, Phi Delta Kappa. Home: 30 W 96th St # 2D New York NY 10025-6555

EKSTROM, RUTH BURT, psychologist; b. Bennington, Vt., July 2, 1931; d. Ralph Amos and Bertha Paisley (Lambert) Burt; m. Lincoln Ekstrom, Nov. 9, 1957. AB, Brown U., 1953; EdM, Boston U., 1956; EdD, Rutgers U., 1967; LLD (hon.) Brown U., 1988. Pub. sch. tchr., Beverly, Mass., 1953-57; sr. rsch. asst. Ednl. Testing Svc., 1957-64; vis. lectr. Rutgers U., 1958-60; dir. documentation svcs. Ednl. Testing Svc., Princeton, N.J., 1964-68, rsch. scientist, 1968-80, sr. rsch. scientist, 1980-91, prin. rsch. scientist, 1991—, acting dir. edn. policy rsch. divsn., 1992-94. Co-author: Education and American Youth: The Impact of the High School Experience, 1988; co-editor: Kit of Factor-Referenced Cognitive Tests, 1976; editor: Measurement, Technology and Individuality in Education, 1983; mem. editorial bd. Psychology of Women Quar., 1978-86, Jour. Counseling & Devel., 1982-85, Measurement & Evaluation in Counseling & Devel., 1989-91; contbr. articles to profl. jours. Mem. corp. (governing bd.) Brown U., 1972-88, trustee, 1972-77, fellow, 1977-88, sec. corp., 1982-88, joint com. on testing practices, 1994—, co-chair, 1994—. Fellow APA, AAAS, Am. Psychol. Soc.; mem. ACA (Rsch. award 1994), Am. Ednl. Rsch. Assn. (chmn. rsch. on women and edn. 1984-85), Assn. For Study of Higher Edn. (program com. 1993), Assn. for Assesment in Counseling (chair com. on test use 1991-93, exec. coun. 1992—), Nat. Coun. Measurement Edn. Home: 78 Westerly Rd Princeton NJ 08540-2621 Office: Ednl Testing Svc Princeton NJ 08541

ELAM, MERRILL L., architectural firm executive; b. Nashville, June 28, 1943. BArch, Ga. Inst. Tech., 1971; MBA, Ga. State U., 1983; postgrad., Harvard U., 1980. Intern Taylor and Collum Architects, 1967-69; architect, sr. assoc. Heery & Heery Architects & Engrs., Inc., 1969-81, architect, v.p., 1981-84; prin. Scogin, Elam and Bray Architects, Inc., Atlanta, 1984—; bd. dirs. Art Papers; vis. critic Miss. State U., 1984, Ga. Inst. Tech., 1985, 89, 90, Auburn U., 1986, Harvard U., 1987, 93, So. Calif. Inst. Architecture, 1990, Clemson U., 1990, Ohio State U., 1991; Harry S. Shure vis. prof. architecture U. Va., 1991; Caudill vis. lectr. architecture Rice U., 1992; Louis Henri Sullivan rsch. prof. architecture U. Ill., 1994; guest lectr. Tulane U., Carnegie-Mellon, Cooper Union, Boston Architecture Ctr., U. Tenn., Miss. State U., Auburn U., U. Fla., Pa. State U., Ariz. State U., U. Va., Princeton U., Va. Polytechnic Inst., Pensselaer Polytechnic Inst., numerous others. Prin. works include Martin Mountain House, Clayton Ga., Heer House, Charlotte, N.C., Roderique Residence, Stone Mountain, Ga., Chmar Residence, Atlanta, Carol Cobb Turner Br. Libr., Morrow, Ga., Gallery for the Bur. Cultural Affairs, Atlanta, Atlanta C. of C. Corp. Hdqrs., High Mus. at Ga.- Pacific Ctr., Atlanta, Tallahassee (Fla.) City Hall, Ga. Power Co. Corp. Hdqrs. Office Bldg., Atlanta, Shelby County Jail, Columbiana, Ala., Crestwood High Sch., Fulton County, Ga., Martin Luther King Jr. Mid. Sch., Atlanta, numerous others. Recipient Ga. Bus. Coun. for the Arts award, 1986, Outstanding Mus. award Gallery and Mus. Assn. Ga., 1986, Urban Design Commn. award of Excellence, High Mus. Ga.- Pacific Ctr., 1987, Buckhead Br. Libr., 1990, Record Houses award House Chmar, 1991. Mem. AIA (Atlanta chpt., adjudicator, corp., nat. com. design, chair membership com., book ctr. bd. dirs., past chairperson, past exec. com. mem., numerous awards), Ga. State Bd. Architects (past pres.), Architecture Soc. Atlanta (founder, past pres.), Women in Architecture. Office: Scogin Elam and Bray Architect 1819 Peachtree Rd NE Atlanta GA 30309-1848

ELBERRY, ZAINAB ABDELHALIEM, insurance company executive; b. Alexandria, Egypt, Sept. 30, 1948; came to U.S., 1973; d. Abelhaliem Elberry and Nazieha Ahmed (Ezzat) E.; m. Mohammed Nour Naciri, Aug. 7, 1975; 1 child, Nadeam El Shami. BA, Ain Shams U., Cairo, 1971; MA, Am. U., Cairo, 1975. Cataloger Vanderbilt Joint U. Librs., Nashville, 1976-77; sales rep. Equitable Life Assurance Soc., 1977-80; with Met. Life Ins., Nashville, 1980—, account rep., 1981—, mgr., 1984; mem. adv. bd. Parkview Surgery Ctr., 1983-84. Chmn. com., bd. dirs. Nashville Internat. Cultural Heritage, 1983—, also bd. dirs.; chmn. Internat. Women Nashville Fair, 1977-78; bd. dirs. YWCA, Coun. for Nat. Interest; fundraiser Peace Links, 1989, YMCA Internat. House, 1987-89, Nashville Animal Shelter, 1979, Nashville League Hearing Impaired, 1976-81; mem. adv. bd. Nashville celebration Internat. Yr. of Disabled Persons; pres. Internat. Women Nashville. Recipient Spl. Contbn. award U.S. Coun. Internat. Disabled Persons, 1981. Mem. Nat. Assn. Life Underwriters, Nat. Assn. Profl. Saleswomen (Recognition award 1986), Gen. Agy. Mgrs. Assn., UN Assn. (bd. dirs. Nashville chpt.), Altrusa Club. Islam. Home: 5600 B Kendall Dr Nashville TN 37209-4548

ELCANO, MARY S., general counsel. BA cum laude, Lynchburg Coll., 1971; JD, Cath. U., Washington, 1976; postgrad., Georgetown U. Litigation atty. Balt. Legal Aide Bur., 1976; staff atty. Office Solicitor Dept. Labor, 1979; gen. trial and appellate atty. Office Labor Law U.S. Postal Svc., 1982, exec. dir. Office EEO, 1984, regional dir. human resources N.E. region, 1987, sr. v.p., gen. counsel, 1992—. Office: US Postal Svc Gen Counsel 475 L'Enfant Plz SW Rm 6004 Washington DC 20260-1100*

ELDENBURG, MARY JO CORLISS, mathematics educator; b. Tacoma, Wash., Mar. 5, 1942; d. John Ronald and Mary Margaret (Slater) Corliss; m. Paul Garth Eldenburg, Aug. 31, 1963; 1 child, Anthony Corliss. BA with honors, Wash. State U., 1964; MS, SUNY, Buffalo, 1971. Cert. secondary math. tchr. Tchr. math. Colton (Wash.) High Sch., 1964-65, Bellevue (Wash.) Jr. High Sch., 1965-68, Issaquah (Wash.) Jr. High Sch., 1968-75, Issaquah High Sch., 1975-77; tchr. math., dept. chair Liberty High Sch., Issaquah, 1977—. Co-editor books: Cartesian Cartoons, 1980, Cartesian Cartoons, Holiday, 1990, Lil Gridders, 1977. Treas. Sch. Bd., Kirkland, Wash., 1987-90; pres. Bridle Trails/South Rose Hill Neighborhood Assn., Kirkland, 1987-93; precinct committee woman Issaquah Precinct, 1980-84. Mem. Issaquah Edn. Assn. (sec., negotiator 1969-75, 74-86), Wash. Edn. Assn. (dir. 1970-74), Math. Assn. Am., Oreg. State Coun. Tchrs. Math., Wash. State Coun. Tchrs. Math., Nat. Coun. Tchrs. Math., Phi Kappa Phi. Democrat. Roman Catholic. Office: Holy Names Acad 728 21st Ave E Seattle WA 98112

ELDER, KATHERINE KERNS, real estate development company executive; b. East Orange, N.J., June 12, 1943; d. Robert Delano and Katherine (Kerns) E.; m. Alver W. Napper, Jr., July 10, 1965 (div. July 1978). BA, Syracuse U., 1965. Pres. Katherine Napper Assocs., Albany, N.Y., 1968-73; regional mktg. dir. Homart Devel. Co., Chgo., 1973-78; pres. Retail Mktg. Cons. Inc., 1978-85; leasing agt. Kaplan Group, Boston, 1983-86; leasing dir. Kravco Co., Phila., 1986—. Home: 234 Goddard Blvd King Of Prussia PA 19406-2954

ELDERKIN, HELAINE GRACE, lawyer; b. New Rochelle, N.Y., Sept. 18, 1954; d. EllsworthJay and Madelyn A. (Roberts) E.; m. Stefan Shrier, Feb. 23, 1985. BA, Fla. Atlantic U., 1975; JD, George Mason U., 1985. Bar: Va. 1985, U.S. Ct. Appeals (4th cir.) 1985, U.S. Ct. Fed. Claims 1994. Aide Carter/Mondale Presdl. Campaign Com., Atlanta, 1976, Presdl. Transition Staff, Washington, 1976-77; spl. asst. Agy. Internat. Devel. U.S. Dept. State, Washington, 1977; spl. asst. U.S. Dept. Def., Washington, 1977-79; mem. tech. staff System Planning Corp., Arlington, Va., 1980-83; dir. corp. rsch. Analytics, Inc., McLean, Va., 1983-85; v.p., gen. counsel Analytics, Inc., Fairfax, Va., 1985-91; of counsel Feith and Zell, P.C., Washington, 1986-91; sr. counsel Computer Scis. Corp., 1991—; bd. dirs. Mil. Ops. Rsch. Soc., Alexandria (elected fellow 1990), Army Sci. Bd. Democrat. Home: 624A S Pitt St Alexandria VA 22314-4138 Office: Computer Scis Corp 3170 Fairview Park Dr Falls Church VA 22042-4501

ELDERS, (MINNIE) JOYCELYN, public health administrator, endocrinologist; b. Schaal, Ark., Aug. 13, 1933; d. Haller Jones; m. Oliver B. Elders, Feb. 14, 1960; children: Eric D., Kevin M. BA, Philander Smith Coll., 1952; MD, U. Ark. Med. Sch., 1960; MS, U. Ark., 1967. Pediatric intern Univ. Minn. Hosp., Mpls., 1960-61; pediatric resident Univ. Ark. Med. Cen., Little Rock, 1961-63, chief pediatric resident, 1963-64, pediatric rsch. fellow, 1964-67, asst. prof. of pediatrics, 1967-71, assoc. prof. of pediatrics, 1971-76, prof. of pediatrics, 1976-87; dir. Ark. Dept. of Health, Little Rock, 1987-93; surgeon gen. of U.S., 1993-94; Bd. dirs. Nat. Bank of Ark., North Little Rock, 1979-89. Editorial bd. Jour. Pediatrics, 1981—; contbr. articles on pediatrics to profl. jours. Bd. dirs. Northside YMCA, Little Rock, 1973—; vol. vols. in pub. schs., Little Rock, 1973—. 1st lt. U.S. Army, 1953. Recipient Worthen Bank's Ark. Profl. Woman of Distinction award, 1987; named one of 100 Women of Ark., 1980, Ark. Dem. Woman of Yr. statewide newspaper, 1988. Mem. So. Soc. Pediatrics (rsch. pres. 1979-80), Lawson Wilkins Endocrine Soc. (com. chair 1976), Ark. Sci. and Tech. Commn. (sec. 1975-89), Little Rock C. of C. (bd. dirs. 1980—), Endocrine Soc., Acad. Pediatrics, Am. Pediatric Soc. *

ELDREDGE, DEBRA CAMPBELL, lawyer; b. Kosciusko, Miss., June 15, 1955; d. Max C. and Nina Sue (Bell) Campbell; m. George Badge Eldredge, Oct. 4, 1975; children: George Badge Jr., Christopher Campbell. BS, U. Md., 1979; JD, La. State U., 1986. Bar: La. 1986, U.S.Dist. Ct. (we. and mid. dists.) La. 1987, U.S. Dist. Ct. (ea. dist.) ind. 1992, U.S. Ct. Appeals (5th cir.) 1987. Corp. atty. Marine Shale Processors, Inc., Amelia, La., 1987-90, dep. gen. counsel, 1990—; ptnr. Eldredge & Eldredge, Attys., Baton Rouge, 1987—. Mem. ABA, La. State Bar Assn., Baton Rouge Bar Assn., Baton Rouge Assn. Women Attys. Office: Eldredge & Eldredge Attys 8146 One Calais Ave Ste 101 Baton Rouge LA 70809

ELDREDGE-MARTIN, MARTHA PENNI, health care administrator; b. Boston, Apr. 7, 1948; d. Richard Thorne and Martha (Shaw) E.; m. Brooks Collins Martin; children: Andrew, Ashley. BA, U. Mass., 1972; MA, Middlebury Coll., 1975. Tchr. English Newton (Mass.) South High Sch., 1972-74; co-head tchr. Barclay Friends Sch., Towanda, Pa., 1974-76; coord. nonviolence & children project Friends Peace Com., Phila., 1976-78; human resources cons. pvt. practice, Ulster, Pa., 1979-82; dir. edn. Planned Parenthood So. Tier, Elmira, N.Y., 1982-86; assoc. dir. Planned Parenthood South Tier, Horseheads, N.Y., 1986—; adj. faculty Elmira Coll., 1986—. Bd. dirs. YMCA, Elmira, 1990—, pres., 1994—; bd. dirs. Mather Meml. Libr., Ulster, Pa., 1993—; mem. strategic planning com. Athens Area Sch. Dist., 1993—; founding mem. Abuse & Rape Crisis Ctr., Towanda, 1979-85; mem. Bradford County Choice Coalition, Wysox, Pa., 1989—. Mem. Religious Soc. of Friends. Democrat. Mem. Soc. of Friends. Office: Planned Parenthood So Tier 301 S Main St Horseheads PA 14845

ELDREDGE-THOMPSON, LINDA GAILE, psychologist; b. Lubbock, Tex., Apr. 3, 1959; d. Jerry Greever and Madge (Harshbarger) Eldredge; m. Paul Edward Thompson, May 26, 1979. BS, Howard Payne U., 1980; MA, Tex. Woman's U., 1981; EdD, Baylor U., 1989. Lic. psychologist, chem. dependency counselor, Tex.; cert. chem. dependency specialist; cert. tchr. hearing impaired, sch. counselor, spl. edn. sch. counselor, Tex.; lic. marriage and family therapist; cert. verbal self def. trainer; cert. eye movement desensitization and reprocessing. Tchr. hearing impaired Waco (Tex.) Ind. Sch. Dist., 1982-85, spl. edn. sch. counselor, cons. hearing impaired, 1986-87; doctoral teaching fellow Baylor U., Waco, 1985-87; dir. regional alcohol and drug abuse svcs. Heart of Tex. Coun. Govts., Waco, 1987; psychotherapist Clin. Psychology Assocs., Houston-Webster, Tex., 1989-91; psychologist Clin. Psychology Assocs., Houston-Webster, 1991-93; pvt. practice psychology Austin, 1993—; psychologist Tex. Sch. for the Deaf, Austin, 1993—. Mem. APA, Nat. Assn. Alcoholism and Drug Abuse Counselors, Am. Deafness and Rehab. Assn., Gentle Art of Verbal Self-Defense Trainers Network, Tex. Assn. Alcoholism and Drug Abuse Counselors (sec.-treas. Waco chpt. 1988-89). Office: 7719 Wood Hollow Ste 152 Austin TX 78731 also: Tex Sch for the Deaf 1102 S Congress Ave Austin TX 78764

ELENICH, PHYLLIS MARIE, school district administrator; b. Indpls., Jan. 8, 1934; d. Isaac W. and Martha W. (Lovell) Flanagan; m. Victor E. Birkle, Nov. 8, 1953 (dec. Oct. 1954); 1 child, Victor E.; m. John L. Elenich, Sept. 14, 1956; children: Adele Berry, Angela Stout, Amy Kunkle. BA, Ind. State U., Terre Haute, 1977, MLS, 1978. Cert. in English/edn., libr. sci. Legal asst. U.S. Govt., Indpls., 1951-53; teller Parke State Bank, Rockville, Ind., 1958-60; paraprofl. Turkey Run Schs., Marshall, Ind., 1963-73; media dir. North Vermilion Sch. Corp. R1, Cayuga, Ind., 1978—; dir. Stone Hills Area Libr. Svcs., Bloomington, Ind., 1978—, West Cen. Ind. Ednl. Svc. Ctr., Greencastle, 1980—; mem. Parke Adult Tutor Svc., Rockville, 1988—. Ind. State U. fellow, 1977. Mem. NEA, Ind. State Tchrs. Assn. (pres. 1979-80), Nat. Ret. Tchrs. Assn., Assn. for Ind. Media Educators, Sigma Tau Delta. Republican. Roman Catholic. Office: North Vermillion High Sch RR 1 Box 191 Cayuga IN 47928-9753

ELEUTERIUS, NANCY LEA, health administrator; b. Biloxi, Miss., Aug. 19, 1943; d. Leo and Mary (Cochran) E.; m. Nick Cefalu, Sept. 9, 1961 (div. Oct. 1975); children—Deborah, Cindy. Student Thomas Nelson Coll., 1972-73, U. Ind., 1975-76, Va. Wesleyan Coll., 1986-87. Dir. patient adminstrv. services Riverside Hosp., Newport News, Va., 1970-80; dir adminstrv. svcs. Sentara Norfolk (Va.) Gen. Hosp., Va., 1980-86; COO Sentara Health Systems, Norfolk, 1986-89; pres. Sentara Mental Health Mgmt., 1989—; workshop leader Ea. Va. Med. Sch., Norfolk, 1981. Contbr. articles to profl. jours. Bd. dirs. local unit Am. Cancer Soc., 1979-80, Jackson Field Homes, 1991-93, Virginia Beach Health Clinic, 1991-93, Cmty. Alliance Drug Rehab. and Edn., 1991—. Named Outstanding Dept. Head of Yr., Norfolk Gen. Hosp., 1983, recipient Dept. Head Leadership award, 1984. Mem. Nat. Assn. Hosp. Admitting Mgrs. (accredited; regional facilitator 1984, regional rep. to edn. com. 1983—), Tidewater Assn. Hosp. Admitting Mgrs. (pres., founder 1979, bd. dirs. 1979—, v.p. 1981—), Va. Hosp. Assn. (prin. speaker 1980), Am. Hosp. Assn., Norfolk Gen. Hosp. Vols. Roman Catholic. Avocations: music, theatre, sailing. Home: 2217 Sunvista Dr Virginia Beach VA 23455-1674 Office: Sentara Mental Health Mgmt 4417 Corporation Ln Ste 250 Virginia Beach VA 23462

ELEWSKI, BONI ELIZABETH, dermatologist, educator; b. Cleve., Aug. 7, 1953; d. John Stanley and Alberta (Gulish) E.; married. BA summa cum laude, Miami U., Oxford, Ohio, 1975; MD cum laude, Ohio State U., 1978. Intern U. N.C., Chapel Hill, 1978-79, resident, 1979-82; staff dermatologist Akron (Ohio) Clinic, 1982-88; assoc. prof. dermatology Univ. Hosps. of Cleve., Case Western Res. U., 1988—. Author chpts. to books; editor: Cutaneous Fungal Infections, 1992; contbr. articles to profl. jours. Fellow

Cleve. Dermatology Soc. (sec. bd. dirs., chair skin cancer screening program 1988—, pres. 1994), Am. Acad. Dermatology; mem. Am. Dermatol. Assn., Women's Dermatology Soc. (sec.-treas.). Roman Catholic. Home: PO Box 5475 Akron OH 44334-0475 Office: Univ Hosp 11100 Euclid Ave Cleveland OH 44106

ELFMAN, JULIA ANN YOUNGBLOOD, gifted/talented education educator; b. Little Rock, July 6, 1942; d. Julius Henry and Anna Marie (Crump) Youngblood; m. William Wayne Carlton, May 20, 1956 (div. July 1962); children: Teresa Lynn, Bradley Wayne; m. Bradley Sayre Elfman, Oct. 25, 1965 (div. Aug. 1974); 1 child, Douglas Sayre. BA in English, San Francisco State U., 1969, MA in Early Childhood Edn., 1976, Edn. Specialist, 1976; PhD in Devel. Psychology, U. Ga., 1978. Cert. tchr., Calif., La. Asst. prof., cognitive devel. specialist U. Ga., Athens, 1976-80; pres. Elfman Enterprises, Atlanta and Athens, 1978-84; gifted tchr. Gentilly Terrace, New Orleans Pub. Schs., 1984—; coord. mini coll. U. New Orleans, 1985—; cons. Savannah/Chatham County Schs., 1978-80; workshop presenter New Orleans Pub. Schs., 1984—; cons. Pocatello, Idaho, Lee County, Va., Gulfport, Miss., Pickens and Thomaston, Ga. Author: Piaget's Theory of Development, 1977, Parent and Child Together, 1978, Updating the Update, 1980. Keisai Koho Ctr. fellow Japanese Govt., Tokyo, San Francisco, 1987, Fulbright fellow U. New Orleans, Thailand, 1988. Mem. Jean Piaget Soc., Nat. Assn. Edn. Young Children, Am. Ednl. Rsch. Assn., UTNO Tchrs. Union, Phi Delta Kappa. Democrat. Methodist. Home: 4900 Arts St New Orleans LA 70122 Office: Gentilly Terrace 4720 Painters St New Orleans LA 70122

ELGAVISH, ADA, biochemist; b. Cluj, Romania, Jan. 23, 1946; came to U.S. 1979; d. David and Malca (Neuman) Simchas; m. Gabriel A. Elgavish, Dec. 28, 1968; children: Rotem, Eynav. BSc, Tel-Aviv U., 1969, MSc, 1972; PhD, Weizmann Inst. Sci., Rehovot, Israel, 1978. Postdoctoral vis. fellow NIH, Balt., 1979-81; instr. U. Ala. Sch. Medicine, Birmingham, 1981-82, rsch. assoc., 1982-84, rsch. asst. prof., 1984-89, asst. prof. comparative medicine, 1989-92, assoc. prof., 1992—; assoc. scientist Cystic Fibrosis Ctr., Birmingham, 1984-90. Grantee Cystic Fibrosis Found., 1986-90, Am. Lung Assn., 1987-92, NIH, 1989—. Mem. AAAS, Am. Physiol. Soc., N.Y. Acad. Sci., Ala. Acad. Sci., Soc. for Basic Urol. Rsch., Am. Thoracic Soc., Sigma Xi. Home: 1737 Valpar Dr Birmingham AL 35226-2343 Office: U Ala Sch Medicine Dept Comparative Medicine Birmingham AL 35294

ELIAS, PATRICIA JOAN MILLER, research psychologist; b. Wis., Sept. 14, 1929; d. Rollin Francis and Rosette Ellen (Ellsworth) Miller; m. Albert Elias, Oct. 16, 1954; children: Caprice Catherine. BA, U. Calif., Berkeley, 1951, MA, 1969, PhD, 1973. Dir. spl. projects Edn. Testing Service. Writer, artist. Area coordinator Am. Cancer Soc.; dir. Berkeley Mental Health fund raising. NIMH fellow. Mem. Am. Edn. Research Assn., Am. Psychol. Assn., Calif. Assn. Sch. Psychologists (chair legis. com.). Liberal Democrat. Home: 820 San Luis Rd Berkeley CA 94707-2053 Office: 1947 Center St Berkeley CA 94704-1105

ELIAS, ROSALIND, mezzo-soprano; b. Lowell, Mass., Mar. 13, 1931; d. Salem and Shelahuy Rose (Namy) E.; m. Zuhayr Moghrabi. Student, New Eng. Conservatory Music, Accademia di Santa Cecilia, Rome; studies with, Daniel Ferro, N.Y.C. Singer New Eng. Opera, 1948-52, Met. Opera, 1954—; artistic dir. Am. Lyric Theatre. Debut with Boris Goldowsky, Boston, 1948; appeared in numerous roles including Cherubino, Dorabella, Rosina, Hansel, Cenerentola, Carmen, Amneris and Azucena (Verdi), Charlotte and Giulietta (Massenet), Herodias, 1987; originated role of Erika in Vanessa (Samuel Barber) and Cleopatra in Antony and Cleopatra (Barber); also appeared with Scottish Opera, Vienna Staatsoper, Glynbourne Festival, many others; prodr. Carmen, Cin., 1988, Il Barbiere di Siviglia, Opera Pacific, Costa Mesa, Calif., 1989; recs. for RCA and Columbia records include La Gioconda, La Forza del Destno, Il Trovatore, Falstaff, Madama Butterfly, Rigoletto, Der fliegende Holländer. Mem. Sigma Alpha Iota. Office: Opera Pacific 3187 Red Hill Ave Ste 230 Costa Mesa CA 92626*

ELIASON, BONNIE MAE, county treasurer; b. Stanley, N.D., Jan. 10, 1947; d. Melvin Otis and Mabel Isabel (Borst) Howell; m. Murrey Allen Eliason, June 23, 1971; 1 child, Christal Medora. BA, Minot (N.D.) State Coll., 1970. Clk. N.D. Personal Property Tax Collector, Bismarck, summer 1965, Mountrail County Auditor, Stanley, 1970-74; dep. Mountrail County Treas., Stanley, 1974-77, treas., 1979—. Vice pres., mem. Am. Legion Aux., Stanley, 1980. Mem. Stanley Women's Bowling League (sec., treas. 1973-74, v.p. 1976-77, pres. 1977-78), Stanley Women's Bowling Assn. Presbyterian. Home: RR 1 Box 15 Stanley ND 58784-9713 Office: PO Box 69 Stanley ND 58784-0069

ELIASOPH, JOAN, radiologist, educator; b. N.Y.C.; d. Samuel and Martha (Coe) Freeman. A.B., Hunter Coll., 1946; M.D., NYU, 1949. Diplomate Am. Bd. Radiology. Intern Mt. Sinai Hosp., N.Y.C., 1949-50, resident in radiology, 1951-53; instr. Columbia U., N.Y.C., 1953-55; asst. attending radiologist Mt. Sinai Hosp., N.Y.C., 1955-70, attending radiologist, 1985-90; clin. asst. prof. Mt. Sinai Med. Sch., N.Y.C., 1970-77; assoc. prof. radiology U. So. Calif., Los Angeles, 1977-82, Columbia U., N.Y.C., 1982-85; assoc. prof. Mt. Sinai Med. Sch., N.Y.C., 1985-90, Dartmouth Med. Sch., Hanover, N.H., 1990-92; attending radiologist Dartmouth-Hitchcock Med. Ctr., 1990-92; prof. radiology Mt. Sinai Med. Ctr., N.Y.; cons. Silver Hill Found., Conn., 1965-77, Stamford Hosp., Conn., 1970-77. Contbr. articles to profl. jours. Mem. Friends of Ballona Wetlands, Los Angeles, 1977-82. Heineman Pathology fellow Mt. Sinai Hosp., 1950-51, Radiology fellow, 1955-56. Fellow Am. Coll. Radiology, Am. Coll. Gastroent.; mem. Am. Roentgen Ray Soc., Am. Gastroent. Soc., Radiol. Soc. N.Am., Soc. Gastroent. Radiologists, N.Y. Roentgen Soc., Assn. Univ. Radiologists. Avocations: the environment, birding, marine biology, Ukiyo and Japanese woodblock prints. Office: Kingsbridge Vets Adminstrv Med Ctr 130 W Kingsbridge Rd Bronx NY 10468

ELIEN, MONA MARIE, air transportation professional; b. Atwood, Kans., June 13, 1932; d. Lawrence Wallace Berry and Adele Rosina (Gulzow) Wright; m. R.J. Wright, Jan. 1952 (div. 1957); m. J.P. Kobus, Nov. 1968 (div. 1991); m. Robert Louis Tour, Oct. 3, 1992. BS, U. Ariz., 1961; grad., Swiss Mountain Climbing Inst., Rosenlaui, 1963; postgrad., No. Ariz. U., 1966-67, Ariz. State U., 1967-69, 86-87; MPA, Ariz. State U., 1981. Customer rels. rep. Ariz. Pub. Svc. Co., Casa Grande, Flagstaff, Ariz., 1961-67; owner/operator Mona's Clipping Svc., Phoenix, 1969-74; various positions City of Phoenix, 1974—; contract mgr. Phoenix CETA/PSE/PNP, 1978-81; planning and devel. asst. Phoenix Sky Harbor Internat. Airport, 1986—; staff asst. 1988 Citizens Bond Com. for Aviation, Phoenix, 1987-88. Compiler, editor: Aviation Acronyms and Abbreviations, 1987, 2d rev. edit., 1992; editor, writer (newsletter) Rapsheet, 1972-75; author profl. columns, 1961-67. Pres. state home econs. occupations adv. bd. Ariz. State U., 1983-84; mem. Phoenix City Mgr.'s Women's Issues Com., 1989-91; pres. elect Tri-City (Ariz.) Zonta Internat., 1964-65; vol. speaker's bur. Phoenix Cmty. Alliance and Prep. Acad. Partnership, 1992—; mem. exec. com. Svc. Fund Drive, Phoenix, 1984-86; mem. precinct com. Yuma County Dem. Com., 1958; mem. employee-of-yr. com. Phoenix Aviation Dept., 1993, co-chmn., 1994. Recipient recognition pub. svc. award Ariz. Dept. Econ. Security, 1975, Heart and Soul award Barry M. Goldwater Terminal 4, 1990, PHXcellence awards, 1993, 94, Art Hero award Phoenix Sky Harbor Internat. Airport, 1993; named one of outstanding young women of Am., 1966. Mem. ASPA (life; Phoenix chpt. awards banquet com. 1991, 92, nat. com. 1990-91), Am. Home Econs. Assn. (life), Ariz. Home Econs. Assn. (pres. no. region 1965-67), Sinagua Soc. Museum No. Ariz., Satisfied Frog Gold Mountain Club, Flagstaff C. of C. (chmn. Indian princesses, retail mchts. sect. 1965-67), So. Ariz. Hiking Club, Desert Bot. Gardens, Swinging Stars Square Dance Club, Delta Delta Delta. Republican. Lutheran. Home: 2201 E Palmaire Ave Phoenix AZ 85020-5633 Office: Phoenix Sky Harbor Internat Airport 3400 E Sky Harbor Blvd Phoenix AZ 85034-4403

ELION, GERTRUDE BELLE, research scientist, pharmacology educator; b. N.Y.C., Jan. 23, 1918; d. Robert and Bertha (Cohen) E. AB, Hunter Coll., 1937; MS, NYU, 1941; DSc (hon.), Hunter Coll., 1989; MS, NYU, 1941, DSc (hon.), 1989; DMS (hon.), Brown U., 1969; DSc (hon.), U. Mich., 1983, N.C. State U., 1989, Ohio State U., 1989, Poly. U., 1989, U. N.C., Chapel Hill, 1990, Russell Sage Coll., 1990, Duke U., 1991, MacMaster U., 1992, SUNY, Stony Brook, 1992, George Washington U., 1969, Columbia U., 1992, Washington Coll., 1993, U. South Fla., 1993, U. Wis., 1993, East Carolina U., 1993, Wake Forest U., 1994, Utah State U., 1994. Lab. asst. biochemistry N.Y. Hosp. Sch. Nursing, 1937; rsch. asst. in organic chemistry Denver Chem. Mfg. Co., N.Y.C., 1938-39; tchr. chemistry and physics N.Y.C. secondary schs., 1940-42; food analyst Quaker Maid Co., Bklyn., 1942-43; rsch. asst. in organic synthesis Johnson & Johnson, New Brunswick, N.J., 1943-44; biochemist Wellcome Rsch. Labs., Tuckahoe, N.Y., 1944-50; sr. rsch. chemist Wellcome Rsch. Labs., 1950-55, asst. to assoc. rsch. dir., 1955-62, asst. to the rsch. dir., 1963-66, head exptl. therapy, 1966-83, sci. emeritus, 1983—; adj. prof. pharmacology and exptl. medicine Duke U., 1970, rsch. prof. pharmacology, 1983—; adj. prof. pharmacology U. N.C., Chapel Hill, 1973; chmn. Gordon Conf. on Coenzymes and Metabolic Pathways, 1966; mem. bd. sci. counselors Nat. Cancer Inst., 1980-84; mem. coun. Am. Cancer Soc., 1983-86; mem. Nat. Cancer Adv. Bd., 1984-91. Contbr. articles to profl. jours.; patentee in field. Recipient Garvan medal, 1968, Pres.'s medal Hunter Coll., 1970, Medal of Honor Am. Cancer Soc., 1990; Disting. Chemist award N.C. Inst. Chemists, 1981, Judd award Meml. Sloan-Kettering Cancer Ctr., 1983, Bertner award M.D. Anderson Hosp., 1989, Third Century award Fedn. for Creative Am., 1990, Discoverers award Pharm. Mfg. Assn., 1990, City of Medicine award Durham, N.C., 1990; co-recipient Nobel prize in medicine, 1988, Nat. Medal of Sci. NSF, 1991; inductee Hunter Coll. Hall of Fame, 1973, Nat. Inventors Hall of Fame, 1991, Nat. Women's Hall of Fame, 1991, Engrng. and Sci. Hall of Fame, 1992; named Dame, Order of St. John of Jerusalem Ecumenical Found. (Knights of Malta) 1992. Fellow N.Y. Acad. Scis.; mem. AAAS, NAS (coun. 1994-97), Am. Chem. Soc., Am. Acad. Arts and Scis., Inst. of Medicine, Chem. Soc. London, Am. Soc. Biol. Chemists, Am. Assn. Cancer Rsch. (bd. dirs. 1981, 83, pres. 1983-84, Cain award 1984), Am. Soc. Hematology, Transplantation Soc., Am. Soc. Pharmacology and Exptl. Therapeutics. Home: 1 Banbury Ln Chapel Hill NC 27514-2504 Office: Burroughs Wellcome Co 3030 W Cornwallis Rd Research Triangle Park NC 27709

ELIOT, LUCY CARTER, artist; b. N.Y.C., May 8, 1913; d. Ellsworth and Lucy Carter (Byrd) E. B.A., Vassar Coll., 1935; postgrad., Art Students League, 1935-40. tchr. painting and drawing Red Cross Bronx Vets. Hosp., N.Y.C., 1950, 51. Exhibited one-woman shows, Rochester Meml. Art Gallery, 1946, Cazenovia Coll., 1942, 47, 62, Syracuse Mus. Fine Arts, 1947, Wells Coll., 1953, Ft. Schuyler Club, Utica, N.Y., 1971, Nat. Shows, Pa. Acad. Fine Arts, Phila., 1946, 48, 49, 50, 52, 54, Corcoran Biennial, Washington, 1947, 51, Va. Biennial, Richmond, 1948, NAD, N.Y.C., 1971, 78, 90, Butler Inst. Am. Art, 1965, 67, 69, 70, 72, 74, 81, Cooperstown Art Assn. ann. exhbn., 1978, 80, 90; represented in permanent collections: Rochester Meml. Art Gallery, Munson-Williams-Proctor Inst., also pvt. collections. Bd. dirs. Artists Tech. Research Inst., 1975-79. Recipient First prize Rochester Meml. Art Gallery, 1946, Purchase prize Munson-William-Proctor Inst., 1949, Painting of Industry award Silvermine Guild, 1957, 1st prize in oils Cooperstown Art Assn., 1978. Mem. Nat. Assn. Women Artists (Moore-Greenblatt Meml. award 1993), N.Y. Soc. Women Artists, N.Y. Artists Equity, Audubon Artists (bd. dirs. oil 1983-85, chmn. award 1986-88, Elaine and James Hewitt award 1991, Michael M. Engel Meml. award 1994), Am. Soc. Contemporary Artists, Pen and Brush Club N.Y.C. (Liquitex Art award spring oil exhbn. 1989, 90, Cecilia Cardman Meml. award 1991, Grumbacher Art award Pen and Brush 1993), Cazenovia Club, Cosmopolitan Club. Episcopalian. Home: Apt 11G 131 E 66th St New York NY 10021-6129 also: 70 Sullivan St Cazenovia NY 13035

ELKINS, LANA ANN, counselor; b. Wichita, Kans., Mar. 28, 1950; d. John Leslie and Arla Jean (Presley) Bear; m. Mark Christopher James, July 25, 1970 (div. Aug. 1979); children: Mark Christopher Jr., Matthew Todd; m. Bill Dale Elkins, Dec. 31, 1987. BS, U. Kans., 1972; MEd, U. Ark., 1985. Lic. profl. counselor, Ark. English tchr. Alma (Ark.) Schs., 1979-87; elem. sch. counselor Ft. Smith (Ark.) Schs., 1987-93; counselor Meth. Counseling Svcs., Ft. Smith, 1990—; youth dir. Faith United Meth. Ch., 1994—. Sec. bd. dirs. Suspected Child Abuse and Neglect (SCAN), Ft. Smith, 1989-92; mem. steering com. Belle's Bldg. Brigade Habitat, Ft. Smith, 1993—; chmn. Mash Bash, Ft. Smith, 1991, 93. Mem. Am. Counseling Assn., Ark. Counseling Assn., Nat. Bd. Cert. Counselors, Phi Kappa Delta. Democrat. Methodist. Home: 2200 Dundee Dr Fort Smith AR 72903-0933

ELKINS, LIZABETH JEAN, university administrator; b. Denton, Tex., Aug. 31, 1952; d. James Clay and Yolanda (Hernandez) E. AA, Tyler Jr. Coll., 1972; BA, Tex. Woman's U., 1974. Asst. to registrar Tex. Woman's U., Denton, 1974-77, asst. dir. admissions, 1977-82, asst. dir. rsch. and stats., 1982-91, coord. registration and admissions, 1985-86, dir. instnl. rsch. and stats., 1991—; mem. ad hoc com. Tex. Higher Edn. Coord. Bd., Austin, 1990, 92; mem. task force project State of Tex. Select Com. on Higher Edn., Austin, 1986; mem. exec. com. Lonestar User's Group, Austin, 1989-94; presenter in field; facilitator Roundtable on Enrollment Mgmt., 1991, Roundtable on Enrollment Forecasting, 1992; panelist Panel on Performance Measures/Funding, 1993. Vol. Tex. Woman's U. United Way, Denton, 1991-92. Mem. Am. Assn. Collegiate Registrars and Admissions Officers, Tex. Assn. Collegiate Registrars and Admissions Officers (chmn. task force 1992-94, chmn. data collection com. 1991-92), Soc. Coll. and Univ. Planners (program com. S.W. region 1990-91, program chair s.w. reg. 1993-94, reg. coun. 1993-94), Tex. Assn. Instnl. Rschrs. (program com. 1990—, exec. com. 1993—, treas. 1993—, reg. 3 rep. to data adv. com.), So. Assn. Collegiate Registrars and Admissions Officers, So. Assn. Instnl. Rschrs. (program planning com. 1993-94), North Tex. Coun. Area Registrars and Admissions Officers, Tex. Woman's U. Nat. Alumnae Assn. (v.p. Denton County chpt. 1981-82, pres. 1982-84). Home: 163 Osburn Rd Pilot Point TX 76258 Office: Tex Woman's U PO Box 22547 Denton TX 76204-0547

ELKINS, SHARON PATRICIA, nursing educator; b. Monticello, Ky., Jan. 30, 1948; d. James G. and Mary J. (Jones) Ragan; m. Garis Elkins Jr., June 18, 1966; children: Alicia Jael, John Garis, Amy Elizabeth. ASN, Ind. U., 1985, BSN, 1992. Nursing edn. coord. Henry County Meml. Hosp., New Castle, Ind., 1985—. Mem. Sigma Theta Tau. Home: 7679 E 100th N Hagerstown IN 47346

ELLEMAN, BARBARA, editor; b. Coloma, Wis., Oct. 20, 1934; d. Donald and Evelyn (Kissinger) Koplein; m. Don W. Elleman, Nov. 14, 1970. BS in Edn., Wis. State U., 1956; MA in Librarianship, U. Denver, 1964. Sch. libr. media specialist Port Washington (Wis.) High Sch., 1956-59, Homestead High Sch., Thiensville-Mequon, Wis., 1959-64; children's libr. Denver Pub. Libr., 1964-65; sch. libr. media specialist Cherry Creek Schs., Denver, 1965-70, Henry Clay Sch., Whitefish Bay, Wis., 1971-75; children's reviewer ALA, Chgo., 1975-82, children's editor, 1982-90, editor Book Links, 1990—; vis. lectr. U. Wis., 1974-75, 81-82, U. Ill., Circle Campus, 1983-85, Marquette U., 1989—; cons. H.W. Wilson Co., 1969-75; mem. Libr. Congress Adv. Com. on selection for children's books for blind and physically handicapped, 1980-88, Caldecott Calendar Com., 1986; judge The Am. Book Awards, 1982, Golden Kite, 1987, Boston Globe/Horn Book, 1990; mem. faculty Highlights for Children Writers Conf., 1985-90; mem. orgn. com. MidWest Conf. Soc. Children's Books Writers, 1974-76; chair Hans Christian Anderson Com., 1987-88; advisor Reading Rainbow, 1986—, Ind. R.E.A.P. project, 1987—; speaker in field. Author: Reading in a Media Age, 1975, 20th Century Children's Writers, 1979, rev. edit., 1984, What Else Can You Do With A Library Degree?, 1980, Popular Reading for Children, 1981, Popular Reading II, 1986, Children's Books of International Interest, 1984; contbr. articles to profl. jours. Publicity chair Internat. Bd. Books for Young People Congress, Williamsburg, Va., 1990. Mem. ALA, Soc. Children's Book Writers (mem. orgn. com. MidWest Conf. 1974-76), Internat. Bd. Books for Young People (U.S. assoc. editor Bookbird 1978-86, chair nominating com., 1985, bd. dirs. 1990-92), Children's Reading Round Table Chgo. (award 1987), Nat. Coun. Tchrs. English (bd. dirs. children's lit. assembly 1986-88, mem. editorial adv. bd. CLA bull. 1989-91, mem. using nonfiction in classroom com. 1990—), AAUW. Office: ALA 50 E Huron St Chicago IL 60611-2729

ELLENBERGER, DIANE MARIE, nurse, consultant; b. St. Louis, Oct. 5, 1946; d. Charles Ernst and Celeste Loraine (Neudecker) E.; R.N., Barnes Hosp., St. Louis, 1970; B.S. in Nursing St. Louis U., 1976; M.S. in Nursing, U. Colo., 1977. Staff nurse hosps., clin. nurse, St. Louis, 1973-76; nurse clinician, Sedalia, Mo., 1977-78; nurse clinician, educator Bothwell Hosp., Sedalia, 1977-78; clin. nurse specialist, coord. perinatal outreach edn. Cardinal Glennon Meml. Hosp. Children, St. Louis, 1978-80; instr. McKendree Coll., Lebanon, Ill., 1980; asst. prof. Maryville Coll., St. Louis, 1982-85; nurse cons. Carr, Korein, Tillery, Kunin, Montroy, & Glass, Attys. at Law, 1986—; owner, operator Diane Designs Needlepoint, St. Louis, 1981—. Served with Nurse Corps, USAF, 1970-72. Mem. Am. Nurses Assn., Nat. Perinatal Assn., Assn. Women's Health, Obstetric and Neonatal Nurses, Mo. Nurses Assn. (3d dist. sec. 1991-93, 1st v.p. 1993, pres. 1993—), Mo. Perinatal Assn. (v.p. 1980), Sigma Theta Tau. Mem. Divine Sci. Ch. Contbr. articles profl. jours. Office: 412 Missouri Ave East Saint Louis IL 62201

ELLENSOHN, KAROL KAYE, psychotherapist; b. Dubuque, Iowa, Sept. 14, 1942; d. Walter Alden and Winifred Mae (Putney) Roe; m. James Henry Mitchell, June 8, 1963 (div. 1984); 1 child, Jennifer Kaye; m. Edgar Ulrich Ellensohn, Sept. 27, 1989. AAS, RN, William Rainey Harper Coll., Palatine, Ill., 1977; BS, U. San Francisco, 1982; MS, U. La Verne, 1984; postgrad., Fielding Inst., Santa Barbara, Calif., 1984-86. RN, Calif., Ill.; MFCC; cert. community coll. tchr. Personnel dir. Mercy Hosp., Cedar Rapids, Iowa, 1963-64; personnel dir., exec. sec. to adminstr. Meml. Hosp., Colorado Springs, 1964-67; primary care and charge nurse oncology-hematology unit Evanston (Ill.) Hosp., 1977-78; adminstrv. asst. to interior designer Westlake Village, Calif., 1978-79; oncology nurse Vis. Nurses Assn., Ventura, Calif., 1979-81; contract therapist Caostal Radiation Oncology Med. Svcs., Inc., 1984—; art dealer, 1986—l contract chem. dependency therapy, 1983-84; pvt. practice as nurse therapist, Ventura County, Calif., 1979-83; quality assurance coord. Oxnard (Calif.) Community Hosp., 1982, acting dir. nurses, 1982; part-time clin. instr. in psychology and neurology Ventura Coll., 1981-82; cons. in quality assurance Simi Valley (Calif.) Community Hosp.; cons. Wellness Community, Westlake Village, 1988—, Palm Desert (Calif.) Art Assn., 1988—. Contbr. articles to local newspapers. Mem. lectr. staff Camarillo Women's Day.; vol., contbr. Bighorn Inst., Palm Desert, 1989—, AIDS Assistance Program, Palm Springs, 1993; contbr. McCallum Theatre for the Performing Arts, Palm Desert, 1993. Recipient award Danforth Found., 1956. Mem. AACD, Calif. Assn. Marriage and Family Therapists, Ill. Nurses Assn., ABA, Calif. Nurses Assn., So. Calif. Hospice Assn., Ventura County Hospice Assn. (lectr.), Ventura County Discharge Planners Assn., Nat. Assn. Quality Assurance Profls., Am. Cancer Soc. (vol. svc. and rehab. com., speaker's bur., facilitator coping with cancer therapy groups, co-facilitator understanding cancer course, bd. dirs., Midge Wilson award 1980, Order Golden Sword 1981, Outstanding Svc. 1983), Art Dealers Assn. Home: 55-801 Congressional La Quinta CA 92253

ELLERBEE, DIANE TURNER, elementary school educator; b. Gordon, Ga., Apr. 15, 1948; d. J.C. and Johnie (Pagett) Turner; m. Terrell Stanton Ellerbee, Dec. 20, 1969; 1 child, Amy Diane. AS, Kennesaw (Ga.) Jr. Coll., 1968; BS in Edn., West Ga. Coll., 1969, MEd, 1973. Tchr. Cobb County Bd. Edn., Marietta, Ga., 1969—; tchr. 7th grade sci. McEachern Jr. High Sch., Powder Springs, Ga., 1969-74; Title I edn. tchr. Big Shanty Elem. Sch., Kennesaw, 1975-77; tchr. 3rd grade Due West Elem. Sch., Marietta, 1977—. Active PTA, Powder Springs, 1969-92, Citizens Adv. Coun., Marietta, 1984-85; ch. leader First Meth. Ch., Powder Springs, 1966-89. NEA, Ga. Edn. Assn., Cobb County Edn. Assn., Ga. PTA (hon. life). Democrat. Office: Due West Elem Sch 3940 Due West Rd Marietta GA 30064

ELLERBEE, LINDA, broadcast journalist; b. Bryan, Tex., Aug. 15, 1944; children: Vanessa, Joshua. Ed., Vanderbilt U. Newscaster, disc jockey Sta. WVON, Chgo., 1964-67; program dir. Sta. KSJO, San Francisco, 1967-68; reporter Sta. KJNO and AP, Juneau, Alaska, 1969-72, Sta. KHOU-TV, Dallas, 1972-73, Sta. WCBS-TV, N.Y.C., 1973-76; Washington corr. NBC News, 1975-78; co-anchor Weekend, NBC News, NBC-TV, 1978-80; reporter NBC Nightly News, 1980-82; co-anchor NBC News Overnight, 1982-84; corr., reporter Today Show, NBC-TV; writer, anchor Our World, ABC-TV, 1986; founder, pres. Lucky Duck Prodns., N.Y.C., 1987—; commentator Cable News Network, 1989. Author: And So It Goes: Adventures in Television, 1986, Move On: Adventures in the Real World, 1991; exec. prod. (TV spls.) A Conversation with Magic (Cable ACE award 1992), It's Only Television (Peabody award 1992); exec. prod., writer, host (news/mag. program) Nick News (Columbia duPont award 1993, Parents' Choice Found. Gold TV award); writer, anchor Our World (Emmy for best writing 1986); weekly syndicated columnist King Features, New York. Office: Lucky Duck Prodns 96 Morton St 6th Fl New York NY 10014-3326*

ELLETT, CATHERINE ANN, postal service administrator; b. Omaha, Aug. 12, 1954; d. Joseph Thomas and Marion (Sullivan) Fitzpatrick; m. James Francis Ellett, Apr. 7, 1973 (dec. Feb. 1974); children: Dallas Dlouhy, Neil Dlouhy. Student, U. Nebr., Omaha, 1974-78. Clk. Mut. of Omaha, Omaha, 1972-74; letter carrier U.S. Postal Svc., Omaha, 1978-87, supr., 1983-87, mgr., 1987—. Roman Catholic. Office: US Postal Svc Ames Br 3030 Meredith Ave Omaha NE 68111-2334

ELLINGSON, JACQUELINE MEYERS, guidance counselor; b. Monroe, Wis., Jan. 28, 1946; d. Edward and Dora Lillie (Siegenthaler) Meyers; 1 child, Michael. BS, U. Wis.-Stout, Menomonie, 1968; MSEd, No. Ill. U., 1992. Tchr. home econs. Darlington (Wis.) Jr./Sr. High Sch., 1968-69; tchr. home econs. North Boone High Sch., Poplar Grove, Ill., 1969-92, guidance counselor, 1993—; adviser Future Community Leaders Am., Gifted Enrichment Mastery Studies. Recipient Outstanding Educator award Ill. Bd. Edn., 1988. Mem. NEA, ACA, Ill. Edn. Assn., North Boone Edn. Assn., Ill. Assn. of Coll. Adminstrv. Counselors, No. Ill. Counseling Assn. Home: 336 Biester Dr Belvidere IL 61008 Office: North Boone High Sch 17641 Poplar Grove Rd Poplar Grove IL 61065

ELLINGSON, KIM IRENE, marketing professional; b. Milw., Sept. 12, 1952; d. Bruce Peter and Margy Mae (Weber) Morrissey; m. Donald Gene Ellingson, June 9, 1973; children: Eric Joseph, Ashley Beth. BA, U. Wis., Milw., 1974. Fin. dir. Menominee (Mich.) County Community Mental Health, 1989-92, budget cons., 1992-93; mktg. dir. Stephenson Nat. Bank and Trust, Marinette, Wis., 1992—. Bd. dirs., v.p. Rainbow House Domestic Abuse Svcs., Inc., Marinette, 1993—; mem. Women's Adv. Coun. Mem. AAUW. Office: Stephenson Nat Bank & Trust 1820 Hall Ave Marinette WI 54143-1715

ELLINGSON, LYNN MARIE, flight attendant; b. Mpls., June 5, 1957; d. Marvin Leslie and Jeanette Amanda (Tollefson) E. Student, Oxford U., Eng., 1977-78; BA in English magna cum laude, St. Olaf Coll., 1979; postgrad., U. Minn., 1988, 94; MALS summa cum laude, Hamline U., 1993. Secondary tchr. Kodaikanal Internat. Sch., Tamil Nadu, India, 1979; freelance writer, photographer, 1979—; flight attendant N.W. Airlines, St. Paul, 1980—; writer, photographer, graphic designer corporate newsletter, 1989; guest speaker various chs. and schs. 1981—. Author, photographer travel articles Inflight Mag. 1985, 86, 87. Vol. pub. and correctional schs., 1976-79, Mother Teresa's Missionaries of Charity, Calcutta, India, Home for the Dying, 1981, 82; orphan escort Ams. for Internat. Aid, 1981, 92. Home: 13791 Heywood Ct Saint Paul MN 55124-9588 Office: NW Airlines MS 575 Mpls St Paul Airport Saint Paul MN 55111

ELLINGTON, MILDRED L., librarian; b. Marion, Ohio, June 7, 1921; d. Edward J. and Julia Ellen (Oiler) E. BA, Olivet Nazarene Coll., Kankakee, Ill., 1943; MA in French, Ohio State U., 1952; MA in English, Bowling Green (Ohio) U., 1964; MLS, Rosary Coll., River Forest, Ill., 1976. English and French tchr. Morral (Ohio) High Sch., 1944-49, Reddick (Ill.) High Sch., 1949-55; English tchr. Bremen Community High Sch., Midlothian, Ill., 1955-58, Bloom Twp. High Sch., Chicago Heights, Ill., 1958-60, Willowbrook High Sch., Villa Park, Ill., 1960-66; English tchr., then library dir. Addison (Ill.) Trail High Sch., 1966-82; reference librarian Maywood (Ill.) Pub. Library, 1982—. Sunday sch. supt. Elgin (Ill.) Ch. of the Nazarene, 1985-92. Mem. Ill. Library Assn. Democrat. Mem. Ch. of the Nazarene. Office: Maywood Pub Libr 121 S 5th Ave Maywood IL 60153-1307

ELLIOT, SHEILA HOLLIHAN, arts company executive; b. Phila., 1946; 1 child, Gilbert John. AB in Physics, Vassar Coll., 1967; MS in Mgmt. Sci., Fairleigh Dickinson U., 1979. Creative dir. Graphics for Industry Inc., Englewood, N.J., 1967-76, v.p. fin., 1976—; sr. bus. systems analyst Thomas J. Lipton Inc., 1978—. Producer (pub. svc. films) American Phenomenon, 1973, Historic Preservation, 1975, Daniel Chester French 1850-1931, 1976; (presentation film) Advertising Council, 1974; contbg. editor; Condensed

Computer Encyclopedia, 1968, The Artist's Magazine, 1986—; editor: Pastellagram, 1981—, Art & Artists (U.S.), 1983—; author: Introduction to Oil Pastels, 1987, Pastels and the Portrait, 1989, The Total Pastelist (series), Oil Pastel Techniqus, Vol. I, 1990. Active in the arts, pub. service, films and hist. preservation; rep. to Federated Art Assns., N.J., 1977. Recipient Gold award N.Y. Internat. Film and TV Festival, 1973, Bronze award, 1974, 75, Silver award, 1977. Mem. Pastel Soc. Am. (spl. advisor to bd. 1978, bd. dirs. 1978), Soc. Illustrators, Pen and Brush Inc. (chmn. publicity 1987), Oil Pastel Assn. (exec. dir. 1983—), Nat. Trust Hist. Preservation. Office: Graphics for Industry Inc PO Box 544 Tenafly NJ 07670-0544

ELLIOTT, BETTY F., telecommunications industry executive. Formerly pres. Ameritech Credit Corp., Schaumburg, Ill.; v.p., comptr. Ameritech, Chgo., 1991—. Office: Ameritech 30 S Wacker Dr Chicago IL 60606

ELLIOTT, CANDICE K., interior designer; b. Cedar Rapids, Iowa, Aug. 29, 1949; d. Charles H. and Eunice A. (Long) Goodrich; m. John William Jr. Elliott, Jan. 27, 1973; 1 child, Brandon Christian; 1 stepchild, John William III. BA, U. Iowa, 1971. Interior designer Dayton's, Mpls., 1971-76, Candice Interior Space Planning and Design, Guilford, Conn., 1981-87; owner, interior designer Sofa Works, King of Prussia, Pa., 1987-90; interior designer Jerrehians's Home Furnishings, West Chester, Pa., 1990-92; dir. sales and visual merchandising Sheffield Furniture, Malvern, Pa., 1992—. Bd. dirs. The Old Capitol Restoration Com., Iowa City, 1970-76; curator Guilford Keeping Soc., 1983-88; cons. Zion Episcopal Ch., North Branford, Conn., 1985-88. Mem. Am. Soc. Interior Designers (bd. dirs. Conn. chpt., profl. mem.). Republican. Home: 13 Windsor Ct Wayne PA 19087-5724

ELLIOTT, CORINNE ADELAIDE, retired copywriter; b. Chgo., Nov. 20, 1927; d. Bertram Otto and Lylia Arletta (Mansfield) Briscoe; m. William S. Elliott, June 18, 1947 (div. Nov. 1985); children: Patricia Frances, Christine Grace, Annie Lou. Cert., Famous Artists Schs., Conn., 1959; BA in English maxima cum laude, Carroll Coll., 1975. Advt. writer Sandy McPherson, Realtor, Helena, Mont., 1975-79; advt. copywriter KCAP Radio, Helena, 1979-83; Helena corr. Great Falls (Mont.) Tribune, 1981-83; radio copywriter Sta. KMTX-AM-FM, Helena, 1986-93; writer in field, 1994—; pres., owner The Funding Edge, Helena, 1991—, Elliott Impress Silk Screen Works, Whitefish, Mont., 1960-70, Lotus Light Designs, Helena, 1988—; contbr. Salem Press, Pasadena, Calif. One-person show at Mont. Hist. Soc., 1956-59, Deer Lodge, Mont., 1994; exhibited in group shows at Electrum Fine Arts Show (Merit award), Hockaday Art Gallery, Kalispell, Mont., Ball State U., Mont. Inst. Arts, 1992, Art Chateau, Butte, Mont., 1992, New Eng. Fine Arts Inst., Boston, 1993, Mont. Interpretations, Butte, 1994 (Honorable mention); works represented in permanent collections Cason Gallery, Helena, also Utick and Grosfled Collection, Helena; contbr. articles to mags. Leader 5-8th grades Girl Scouts U.S., Stanford, Mont., 1955-59; tchr. Happy Medium Art Group, Whitefish, 1959-68; violinist Waukegan Philharm., 1945-47, Billings Symphony, 1951-55; donated art works for benefit auctions to Hockaday Gallery, 1970, Kalispell, 1971, Mont. Food Bank, 1991, 92, 93, Aids Found., 1990, Helena Area Habitat for Humanity, 1993. Mem. Mont. Inst. Arts, Mont. Watercolor Soc. (bd. mem. 1983), Nat. Writers Club.

ELLIOTT, DOROTHY GALE, public library administrator; b. Waltham, Mass., Mar. 6, 1948; d. Robert Straight and Grace Moore (Mills) Sanborn; m. W. Mitchell Elliott, Oct. 10, 1970. BA, Wellesley Coll., 1970; MA, U. Mo., 1977. Exec. sec. Coun. for Pub. Schs., Boston, 1970-72; asst. Jerry Litton for Congress, North Kansas City, Mo., 1972; exec. sec. Stephens Coll., Columbia, Mo., 1972-74; coord. Univ. Without Walls, Stephens Coll., Columbia, Mo., 1975-76; pub. svcs. libr. St. Joseph Pub. Libr., Mo., 1977-78, dir., 1978-89, dir. River Bluffs Regional Libr., 1989—. Sec., Grand River Libr. Conf., 1982-84; bd. dirs. Mo. LibRs. Film Coop., 1980-83; sec./treas. Mo. Librs. Network Bd., 1984-85; pres. N.W. Mo. Library Network Bd., 1983-85; pres. adv. coun. Sch. Libr. and Info. Sci., U. Mo., Columbia, 1985-89; mem. libr. adv. com. Mo. Coordinating Bd. for Higher Edn., 1987-89, Gov.'s Adv. Coun. on Literacy, 1987-89, Project Literacy U.S. Task Force, 1986—; mem. exec. bd. Friends of St. Joseph Pub. Libr., 1982-90; active Mo. Gov.'s Conf. Com. on Libr. and Info. Svcs., 1987-90. Editor newsletter Jr. League St. Joseph, 1985-86. Bd. dirs. Mental Health Assn. St. Joseph, 1978-81; pres. bd. dirs. St. Joseph Area Literacy Coalition 1992; com. mem. United Way Greater St. Joseph, 1981—, com. Leadership St. Joseph; bd. dirs. Interfaith Community Services, 1982-85; mem. steering com. Lifelong Learning, St. Joseph, 1983—,judge cotillion for achievement, 1990-91; mem. St. Joseph Area Women's Career Network, 1983-87, Downtown St. Joseph, Inc., 1983-87. Wellesley scholar, 1969; recipient Literacy St. Joseph award, 1988; named YWCA Woman of Merit, 1994. Mem. ALA, Pub. Libr. Affiliates Network (pres. 1992-93), Mo. Libr. Assn. (sec. 1983-84, chmn. legis. com. 1986-87, v.p., pres.-elect 1987-88, pres. 1988-89), Mo. Pub. Libr. Dirs., Beta Phi Mu, Wellesley Club (Kansas City), Runcie Club (St. Joseph), St. Joseph Women's Press Club (v.p. 1989-90), St. Joseph Area C. of C. (entrepreneur's coun. 1992, govt. rels. com. 1993, arts fund drive 1993). Democrat. Disciples of Christ. Office: River Bluffs Regional Libr 927 Felix St Saint Joseph MO 64501-2706

ELLIOTT, INGER MCCABE, designer, textile company executive, consultant; b. Oslo, Feb. 23, 1933; came to U.S., 1941; naturalized, 1946; d. David and Lova (Katz) Abrahamsen; m. Osborn Elliott, Oct. 20, 1973; children by previous marriage: Kari McCabe, Alexander McCabe, Molly McCabe. AB in History with honors, Cornell U., 1954; postgrad., Harvard U., 1955; AM, Radcliffe Coll., 1957. Photographer Rapho-Guillumette, U.S. and fgn. countries, 1960-94; pres. China Seas, Inc., N.Y.C., 1972-90, Gifted Textile Collection to L.A. County Mus. Art, 1991—; cons. Sotheby's, Inc., 1992—; tchr. Newton (Mass.) Pub. Schs., 1955-56; mem. Coun. Fgn. Rels. Mem. East Asia vis. com. Harvard U. Jean Birdsall fellow Radcliffe Coll., 1957; trustee The Asia Soc.; recipient Roscoe awards, 1978, 79, 80, 82-88. Mem. Am. Soc. Mag. Photographers, Am. Women's Econ. Devel. Corp., Com. of 200, Nat. Home Fashions League, Cosmopolitan Club, Ellis Island Yacht Club (lt. comdr.), Phi Beta Kappa, Asia Soc. (trustee). Avocations: skiing, tennis. Author: Women Photographers, 1970, A Week in Amy's World, 1970, A Week in Henry's World, 1971, Batik: Fabled Cloth of Java, 1985, Exteriors, 1992; contbr. photographic essays to Esquire, Vogue, Life, Newsweek, N.Y. Times, Infinity, House & Garden. Home: 36 E 72nd St New York NY 10021-4247 Office: IME Ltd 157 E 72nd St New York NY 10021-4331

ELLIOTT, JACQUELINE MARIE, marketing professional; b. Indpls., Aug. 4, 1963; d. Paul William and Janet Marilyn Rose (Clouser) E. BS in Mktg., Ball State U., 1986. Retail intern L.S. Ayres & Co., Indpls., 1985-86; various mktg. and mgmt. positions RCI, Indpls., 1987—; mgr. mktg. cons. Jabot Productions, 1988-90; with creative entertainment Walt Disney World, 1992—; agrl. frequency coord. Nat. License, Indpls., 1981-87. Mem. Am. Mktg. Assn. (social com. 1982—), Lambda Chi Alpha (social com. 1982-86). Democrat. Roman Catholic. Home: 5343 Evanston Ave Indianapolis IN 46220-3444

ELLIOTT, JEAN ANN, library administrator; b. Martinsburg, W.Va., Jan. 18, 1933; d. Howard Hoffman and Dorothy Jean (Horn) E. AB in Edn., Shepherd Coll., Shepherdstown, W.Va., 1954; MS in Libr. Sci., Syracuse U., 1957; MS, Shippensburg (Pa.) U., 1974. Asst. libr. Fairmont (W.Va.) State Coll., 1957-60; reference asst. U. Pitts., 1960-61; acting libr. Shepherd Coll., 1961-62, coord. libr. sci., 1962—; compiler Jefferson County Hist. mag., 1990. Nat. treas. Palatines of Am., Columbus, Ohio, 1986-88. Mem. ALA, W.Va. Libr. Assn. (election chmn. 1988-90), W.Va. Edn. Media Assn., Va. Edn. Media Assn., Southeastern Libr. Assn. (continuing edn. com. 1991—), Jefferson County Hist. Soc., AAUW, Nat. Geneal. Soc., Nat. Soc. Daus. Am. Colonies (nat. libr. 1991-94), Nat. Soc. Daus. 1812 (nat. libr. 1994—), DAR (W.Va. treas. 1980-83, 86-89, 95—), W.Va. Soc. Daus. 1812 (state pres. 1991-94), Alpha Beta Alpha (nat. exec. sec. 1968-76). Presbyterian. Home: PO Box 239 Shepherdstown WV 25443-0239

ELLIOTT, JEANNE MARIE KORELTZ, transportation executive; b. Virginia, Minn., Mar. 9, 1943; d. John Andrew and Johanna Mae (Tehovnik) Koreltz; m. David Michael Elliott, Apr. 30, 1983. Student, Ariz. State U., 1967, U. So. Calif. Cert. aviation safety inspector. Tech. asst. Ariz. State U., Tempe, 1966-68; from supr. to mgr. inflight tng./in-svc. programs Northwest Airlines Inc. (formerly Republic Airlines, Hughes Airwest, Air West Inc.), Seattle, 1968—; air carrier cabin safety specialist Flight Standards Service, FAA, Washington, 1975-76; cons. Interaction Research Corp., Olympia, Wash., 1982—. Contbg. editor Cabin Crew Safety Bull., Flight Safety Found., 1978—. Recipient Annual Air Safety award Air Line Pilots Assn., Washington, 1971, Annual Safety award Ariz. Safety Council, Phoenix, 1972; first female to hold FAA cabin safety inspector's credential, 1976. Mem. Soc. Air Safety Investigators Internat., Survival and Flight Equipment Assn., Assn. Flight Attendants (tech. chmn. 1968-85), Soc. Automotive Engrs. (chmn. cabin safety provisions com. 1971—), Teamsters Local 2000 (chair nat. safety and health). Republican. Roman Catholic. Home: 16215 SE 31st St Bellevue WA 98008-5704 Office: NW Airlines Inc Inflight Svcs Dept Seattle-Tacoma Internat Airport Seattle WA 98158 also: IBT Minneapolis MN 55425

ELLIOTT, LEE ANN, federal official. BA, U. Ill.; cert., Northwestern U. Cert. assn. exec. Commr. Fed. Election Commn., Washington, 1981—, chmn. commn., 1984, 90; v.p. Bishop, Bryant amd Assocs., Inc., 1979-81; lectr., author and inventor in field. Bd. dirs., pres. Chgo. Area Pub. Affairs Group; bd. dirs. Kids Voting, USA. Mem. Am. Med. Polit. Action Com. (asst. dir. 1961-70, assoc. exec. dir. 1970-79), Am. Assn. Polit. Cons. (bd. dirs.), Nat. Assn. Mfrs. (award of excellence), U.S. C. of C. (pub. affairs com.). Office: Federal Election Commn 999 E St NW Washington DC 20463-0002

ELLIOTT, LEEANN, medical/surgical nurse; b. Bremen, Ind., June 13, 1964; d. Duwaine Jr. and Geraldine (Spencer) Elliott. BSN, Ball State U., 1986. RN, Ind., Mich. Staff nurse Lu Ann Nursing Home, Nappannee, Ind., Bremen Community Hosp.; commd. USAF, 1986; asst. charge nurse med./surg. Wolfsmith AFB, Mich., 1987-92; charge nurse Family Practice Unit Tinker AFB, Okla., 1992-93; asst. charge nurse multi svc. unit Tinker AFB Hosp., 1993—; ACLS instr., hosp. coord. Tinker AFB Hosp. Mem. Sigma Theta Tau.

ELLIOTT, LISA KARIN, small retail business owner; b. Ramsdorf, Germany, Sept. 28, 1943; came to U.S., 1978; d. Hans Weiss and Margret Kopp; m. Richard L. Elliott, Sept. 6, 1965 (div. 1978); children: Scott A., Stephanie A. Office mgr. Richard F. Cromwell Agy., Scharnhausen, Germany, 1976-78; tax acct., auditor Ray E. Cox, Tucson, 1979; med. clerk State of Ariz., Tucson, 1979-80; bookkeeper, bonding rep. Rowe Ins. Inc., Tucson, 1980-83; nurses aid Tucson, 1983-85; asst. acct., sec. Mort R. Saul, Tucson, 1978—; owner Rainbow Moods, Tucson. Office: Rainbow Moods Bookstore 3532 E Grant Rd Tucson AZ 85716

ELLIOTT, MELISSA JAN HANNA, elementary educator; b. Rock Hill, S.C., May 3, 1959; d. Herbert Alexander and Barbara Jane (Abernathy) Hanna; m. James Allen Elliott Sr., Apr. 18, 1981; children: Jan Hanna, James Allen Jr. BS in Elem. Edn., Winthrop Coll., 1980, MEd in Ednl. Media, 1990. Acctg. bookkeeper Rock Hill (S.C.) Nat. Bank, 1981-84; tchr. 5th grade Rock Hill Sch. Dist. #3, 1984-86, tchr. 1st grade, 1986-94, tchr. 4th grade, 1994—; sci. coord. Rock Hill Sch. Dist. # 3, 1988-89, computer coord., 1986-87, lit. recommendation com., 1991-94. Illustrator: (book) Getting a Grip on ADD, 1994. Vol. Rock Hill Jr. Welfare League, 1990—, Hope, Inc.; youth group leader 1st Assoc. Reformed Presbyn. Ch., also co-chmn. reception com. Mem. Porcelain Painters Club (sec. 1979-81), Richmond Dr. Booster Club (treas. 1992-93). Presbyterian. Home: 730 Summerwood Rd Rock Hill SC 29732-2004

ELLIOTT, PEGGY GORDON, university president; b. Matewan, W.Va., May 27, 1937; d. Herbert Hunt and Mary Ann (Renfro) Gordon; children from previous marriage: Scott Vandling III, Anne Gordon. B.A., Transylvania Coll., 1959; M.A., Northwestern U., 1964; Ed.D., Ind. U., 1975. Tchr. Horace Mann High Sch., Gary, Ind., 1959-64; instr. English Ind. U. N.W., Gary, 1965-69, lectr. Edn., 1973-74, asst. prof. edn., 1975-78, assoc. prof., 1978-80, supr. secondary student teaching, 1973-74, dir. student teaching, 1975-77, dir. Office Field Experiences, 1977-78, dir. profl. devel., 1978-80, spl. asst. to chancellor, 1981-83, asst. to chancellor, 1983-84, acting chancellor, 1983-84, chancellor, 1984-92; instr. English Am. Inst. Banking, Gary, 1969-70; pres. U. Akron, Ohio, 1992—; vis. prof. U. Ark., 1979-80, U. Alaska, 1982; bd. dirs. Lubrizol Corp., A. Schulman Corp., Akron Tomorrow, Ohio Aerospace Consortium, Ohio Super Computer Com.; holder VA Harrington disting. chair edn., 1994—. Author: (with C. Smith) Reading Activities for Middle and Secondary Schools: A Handbook for Teachers, 1979, Reading Instruction for Secondary Schools, 1986, How to Improve Your Scores on Reading Competency Tests, 1981, (with C. Smith and G. Ingersoll) Trends in Educational Materials: Traditionals and the New Technologies, 1983, The Urban Campus: Educating a New Majority for a New Century, 1994, also numerous articles. Bd. dirs. Meth. Hosp., N.W. Ind. Forum, N.W. Ind. Symphony, Boys Club N.W. Ind., Akron Symphony, NBD Bank, John S. Knight Conv. Ctr., Inventure Pl., Akron Roundtable, Cleve. Com. Higher Edn. Recipient Disting. Alumni award Northwestern U., VA Disting. Alumni award, 1994, numerous grants; Am. Council on Edn. fellow in acad. adminstrn. Ind. U., Bloomington, 1980-81. Mem. Assn. Tchr. Educators (nat. pres. 1984-85, Disting. Mem. 1990), Nat. Acad. Tchrs. Edn. (dir. 1983—), Ind. Assn. Tchr. Educators (past pres), North Cen. Assn. (commn. at large) Am. Assn. State Colls. and Univs. (bd. dirs.), Am. Coun. Edn. (bd. dirs.), Leadership Devel. Coun. ACE, Internat. Reading Assn., Phi Delta Kappa (Outstanding Young Educator award), Delta Kappa Gamma (Leadership/Mgmt. fellow 1980), Pi Lambda Theta, P.E.O., Chi Omega. Episcopalian. Home: 311 Ely Rd Akron OH 44313-4513 Office: U Akron Office of Pres Akron OH 44325-4702

ELLIOTT, ROXANNE SNELLING, consultant to independent schools; b. Ft. Eustis, Va., Aug. 17, 1954; d. William Rodman and Anne Louise (Kurtz) Snelling; m. Vincent James Elliott, Oct. 1, 1983; children: Brian William, Lauren Elizabeth. B.A., Denison U., 1976; M.B.A., Syracuse U., 1978. Internat. loan officer First Pa. Bank, Phila., 1978-82; ins. assoc. Ind. Sch. Mgmt., Wilmington, Del, 1982-83, dir. mgmt. insts., 1983-87, cons., exec. dir. consortium, 1984—, v.p., 1986-90, pres., 1990—. Republican. Episcopalian. Office: Ind Sch Mgmt 1316 N Union St Wilmington DE 19806-2534

ELLIOTT, SUSAN AUGUSTE, psychologist, psychotherapist, consultant; b. Mt. Shasta, Calif., Aug. 24, 1951; d. Cecil Edwin and Edith Ruth (Holland) E.; m. Richard Martinez, 1973 (div. 1975); 1 child, Lorin Wade Alder. AB, U. Calif., Berkeley, 1973; postgrad., Calif. State U., San Francisco, 1975-76, Towson (Md.) State U., 1984-85; MA, Goddard Coll., 1988. Lic. psychologist, Vt. Co-founder, crisis worker, fundraiser, project dir. Humboldt Women for Shelter and Umbrella Project, Arcata, Calif., 1976-81; devel. coord. House of Ruth, Balt., 1984; orgnl. cons., Balt., 1984-85; counselor Tri-County Youth Svcs., Charlotte Hall, Md., 1985-86; sexual assault clinician Walden Counseling Ctr., California, Md., 1986-87; coord., organizer SAFELINE, Chelsea, Vt., 1987-88; clinician Orange County Mental Health Svcs., Randolph, Vt., 1988-92; psychologist, psychotherapist, Montpelier & Barre, Vt., 1989-94; founding co-dir. Our House, Barre, Vt., 1989; conf. coord. Women and Therapy, Plainfield, Vt., 1988; supr., trainer Vt. Dept. Corrections, Vt. Dept. Mental Health, 1988-91, World Congress Mental Health, Washington, 1983. Contbg. author: Politics of the Heart, 1987; guest reviewer Women and Therapy, 1987; co-editor Vt. Psychologist, 1990. Lobbyist Md. Food Com., Balt., 1982. Recipient appreciation award Humboldt Easter Seal Soc., 1981, Svc. to Children and Families award Ct. Vt. Social Workers Assn., 1991; grantee Reader's Digest, 1976, Jenny McKean Moore Fund for Writers, 1984; Charlotte Newcombe scholar Towson State U., 1985. Mem. Internat. Soc. for Study Multiple Personality & Dissociation, Vt. Psychol. Assn., New England Soc. Clin. Hypnosis. Home and Office: RR # 3 Box 787 Middlesex VT 05602

ELLIOTT, SUSAN SPOEHRER, data processing executive; b. St. Louis, May 4, 1937; d. Charles Henry and Jane Elizabeth (Baur) Spoehrer; m. Howard Elliott Jr., Sept. 2, 1961; children: Kathryn Spoehrer Love, Elizabeth Gray. AB, Smith Coll., 1958. Systems engr. IBM, St. Louis, 1958-66; pres., founder Sys. Svc. Enterprises, Inc., St. Louis, 1966—; systems analyst Mo. State Dept. Edn., Jefferson City, Mo., 1967-70; systems coord. Boatmen's Nat. Bank, St. Louis, 1979-83; bd. dirs. Mo. Automobile Club, First Nat. Bank St. Louis, St. Louis Zoo; bd. dirs. St. Louis Regional Commerce and Growth Assn., sec. bd. dirs., 1990-94. Trustee, vice chmn. Mary Inst., St. Louis, 1976-89, Webster U., 1987—; commr., vice chmn. St. Louis Civil Svc. Commn., 1985-86, Mo. Lottery Commn., Jefferson City, 1985-87; mem. corp. partnership coun. St. Louis Sci. Ctr.; mem. pres.'s adv. coun. area coun. Girl Scouts U.S. Mem. Nat. Assn. Women Bus. Owners, Mo. Women's Forum. Republican. Presbyterian. Home: 46 Clermont Ln Saint Louis MO 63124-1351 Office: Sys Svc Enterprises Inc 795 Office Pky Ste 101 Saint Louis MO 63141-7166

ELLIOTT-BROWN, JUDITH ANN, audio engineer; b. N.Y.C., July 30, 1955; d. Joseph Paurel and Catherine B. (Collins) Rudensey; m. Randolph W. Brown, Mar. 25, 1981; 1 child, Kerry Brown. Diploma, Inst. Audio Rsch., N.Y.C., 1976. Night mgr. Studio Instrument Rentals, N.Y.C., 1976-79; asst. rec. engr. Sound Palace Studio, N.Y.C., 1979-80; installation technician Audio Techniques, N.Y.C., 1980; svc. technician Martin Audio Video Corp., N.Y.C., 1981-82; chief tech. engr. Skyline Studios, N.Y.C., 1982-84; owner Mixers & Fixers, Germantown, N.Y., 1984—. Mem. Audio Engrng. Soc. Office: Mixers & Fixers 89 Block Factory Rd Germantown NY 12526

ELLIOTT-MOSKWA, ELAINE SALLY, psychologist, researcher; b. St. Louis; d. Walter Leonard and Helen (Krelo) E.; m. Alexander Moskwa Jr.; 1 child, Katherine. BA in Psychology, U. Mo., 1973; MA in Psychology, San Diego State U., 1977; PhD in Psychology, U. Ill., 1980. Vis. rsch. assoc. Lab. Human Devel., Harvard U., Cambridge, Mass., 1980-81; lectr. dept. psychology Brandeis U., Waltham, Mass., 1981; fellow Ctr. for Cognitive Therapy, U. Pa., Phila., 1982-83; cons. Presbyn. U. Pa. Med. Ctr., Phila., 1984-85; pvt. practice Newton Centre, Mass., 1985-92; dir. Ctr. for Cognitive Therapy Greater Boston, Newton Centre, 1988-92; pvt. practice Princeton, N.J., 1992—; instr. Med. Sch. Harvard U., 1989—; asst. dir. tng., cognitive therapy and rsch. program Mass. Gen. Hosp., 1991-92, cons. depression rsch. program, 1992—. Author: chpt. Carmichael's Handbook of Child Psychology, 1983, Advances in Psychology, 1989. Nat. Inst. on Aging grantee Brandeis U., 1988. Mem. Am. Psychol. Assn., Assn. for Advancement Behavior Therapy. Office: 20 Nassau St Ste 232 Princeton NJ 08542-3727

ELLIOTT-WATSON, DORIS JEAN, psychiatric, mental health and gerontological nursing educator; b. Caney, Kans., Dec. 6, 1932; d. Alva Orr and Mary Amelia (Boyns) Elliott; children Marsha Jean Watson, Sherwood Elliott Watson. BE, U. Miami, Fla., 1952, MEd, 1954; EdD, Pacific Western U., 1982; BSN, U. Kans., 1985; AS in Psychology, Kansas City (Kans.) C.C., 1989; AA in Music, Kansas City C.C., 1994. RN, Kans., Mo.; cert. clin. specialist gerontology nurse, gerontology nurse generalist, psychiat.-mental health nurse, med.-surg. nurse, ANCC; cert. elem. to jr. coll. tchr., Kans., Mo.; lic. adult care home adminstr., Kans. Tchr. learning disabled, gifted, emotionally disturbed Shawnee Mission, Kans., 1961-76; instr. hospitalized psychiat. and med.-surg. children U. Kans. Med. Ctr., Kansas City, 1979-82; pvt. practice, gerontol. nursing educator Bonner Springs, Kans., 1985—; libr. U. Miami, 1952, Kans. U., 1978; nurse ARC, Kansas City, 1985—; nurse educator Am. Heart Assn., Kansas City, 1985—; program designer mainstreaming spl. needs children into regular classrooms, 1969; specialist geriatric sexuality nursing homes, 1986. Editor Park Stylus, Parkville, Mo., 1952; author, speaker Kansas City area, 1950—. Tutor/organizer Tutoring Vol. Orgn. for Innter City Children, 1965-68; sustaining mem. Rep. Nat. Com., Washington, 1978—, rep. Congl. Com., 1978—, Rep. Senatorial Com., 1978—; pres. Young Reps., Kansas City, 1960; patron, charter mem. Kaw Valley Cmty. Choir, 1990-92, mem. Kansas City Cmty. Choir, 1992—, Mid-Am. Nazarene Coll. Cmty. Choir, 1993—, Leavenworth Cmty. Carnegie Choir, 1994—. Recipient Coast to Coast 2810 miles award Am. Running and Fitness Assn., 1994; inducted Rep. Nat. Hall of Honor, Rep. Nat. Conv., 1992. Mem. ANA (coun. on gerontol. nurses), NEA (life, del. state conv. 1980, nat. conv. 1973), Kans. Nurses Assn., U. Kans. Alumni Assn., Bus. and Profl. Women, Order Ea. Star (Electra 1982, Martha 1994), Order Rainbow for Girls (worthy advisor 1950), Am. Volkssport Assn. (Tri-Athlete 1993, 94, 4500 Km Walking award 1994, 5500km, 1994, Sunflower State Games Athlete 1993, Sooner State Games Athlete award 1994, Mid-Am. Walking Marathon 1994), Tiblow Trailblazers Walking Club (pres. 1993—), Nat. Wildlife Fedn. (cert. backyard wildlife habitat, 1994), Kappa Delta Pi, Pi Delta Epsilon, Phi Theta Kappa, Alpha Kappa Delta, Phi Alpha Theta. Home and Office: 231 Sheidley Ave Bonner Springs KS 66012-1410

ELLIOTT-ZAHORIK, BONNIE, nurse administrator; b. Algona, Iowa. AAS, Coll. Lake County, Grayslake, Ill., 1979; student, U. Iowa; BS, Coll. St. Francis, Joliet, Ill., 1988; MSM, Nat. Louis U., Evanston, Ill., 1989. RN, Ill.; CCRN; cert. nurse adminstr.-advanced; cert. critical care preceptor and instr. Evening nursing dir. Victory Meml. Hosp., Waukegan, Ill., 1991—. Mem. AACN, Ill. Coun. Nurse Mgrs. (pres. elect Region 2B).

ELLIS, ANNE ELIZABETH, fundraiser; b. Orngestad, Aruba, Aug. 21, 1945; d. Thomas Albert and Anne Elizabeth (Belis) Wolfe; m. Earl Edward Ellis, Feb. 14, 1970. BS, La. State U., 1967. Fashion coord. Baton Rouge, 1962-67; textile researcher La. State U., Baton Rouge, 1965-67; buyer I.H. Rubensteins., Baton Rouge, 1967-68; fashion distbr. J.C. Penney, Inc., Arlington, Tex., 1969-70; asst. buyer J.C. Penney, Inc., Dallas, 1970-73; exec. dir. Nassau County Mus. Fine Art Assn., Roslyn, N.Y., 1985-88; speaker C.W. Post U., Greenvale, N.Y., 1988—; cons. in field. Chmn., editor: (cookbook) Specialities of the House, 1981-83. Bd. dirs., com. chmn. Congregational Ch., Manhasset, N.Y., 1975—; exec. vp., bd. dirs., com. chmn. Jr. League L.I., Roslyn, 1977—, Area I Coun. Jr. League Internat.; benefit gala chmn., com. chmn. Grenville Baker Boys & Girls Club, Locust Valley, N.Y., 1983-91; pres. bd., vice-chmn. community outreach, benefit gala chmn. Tilles Performing Art Ctr. L.I. U., Greenvale, N.Y., 1985—; bd. dirs., benefit co-chmn. Nassau County Family Assn. Svcs., Hempstead, 1988—; benefit vice-chmn. Glen Cove/North Shore Community Hosp., 1989-93; mem. exec. bd., exec. v.p., trustee WLIW, L.I. Pub. TV, 1990—; trustee Community Found. of Oyster Bay, 1991—; trustee Dowling Coll., Oakdale, N.Y., 1993; adv. bd. Westbury (N.Y.) Gardens, 1993—. Recipient Vol. of Yr. award Jr. League L.I., 1984, 85, Outstanding Vol. Svcs. and Commitment award County of Nassau, 1989, Juliette Low award Nassau County Girl Scouts, L.I., 1991, Disting. Leadership award, L.I., 1991, Outstanding Community Vol. award Jr. League of L.I., 1991-92. Mem. P.E.O. (pres. 1985-87), The Creek Inc., Meadowbrook Club Inc., Lost Tree Club, Kappa Kappa Gamma (alumna pres. 1971-72). Republican. Congregationalist.

ELLIS, BERNICE, financial planning company executive, investment advisor; b. Bklyn.; d. Samuel and Clara (Schrier) H.; m. Seymour Scott Ellis; children: Michele, Wayne. BA, Bklyn. Coll.; MS, Queens Coll., 1970. Cert. fin. planner, N.Y. 1987, elem. educator, N.Y.C. Elem. tchr. L.I. Sch. Dists., Merrick, N.Y.; tchr. reading N.Y.C. Bd. of Edn., Bklyn., 1972-73; coordinator Reading is Fundamental, Lawrence, N.Y., 1973-75; pres., founder N.Y. State Assn. for the Gifted and Talented, Valley Stream, N.Y., 1974-87; pres. Ellis Planning, Valley Stream, N.Y., 1984—; cons. Nassau County Bd. Coop. Ednl. Svcs., Westbury, N.Y., 1973-74; adminstrv. intern region II U.S. Office Edn., 1977-78; adj. asst. prof. Nassau Community Coll., Garden City, N.Y., 1975-91, adj. assoc. prof., 1991—; fin. commentator Money Talk radio program WHPC FM. Contbr. articles to profl. jours and fin. newsletters. Recipient Ednl. Professions Devel. Act fellow CUNY Inst. for Remediations Skills for Coll. Personnel, Queensborough Community Coll., 1970-73. Mem. AAUW (North Shore bd., chmn. Money Talk 1991—), Inst. for Cert. Fin. Planners, Inst. for Cert. Fin. Planners L.I. (bd. dirs.), Internat. Assn. Fin. Planners (legis. com. L.I. chpt. 1986-87), N.Y. State Reading Assn., Adj. Faculty Assn. Nassau Community Coll., Sales Exec. Club N.Y., L.I. C. of C. Office: Ellis Planning Inc 628 Golf Dr Valley Stream NY 11581-3550

ELLIS, BERNICE ALLRED, personnel executive; b. Lincoln, Ala., Mar. 15, 1932; d. Bernard Bobo and Lucille (Hogue) Allred; m. Marvin Leonard Ellis; 1 child, Jeffrey Craig. Student, Ala. A&M U., 1990, U. Ala., Huntsville, 1990, Gadsden State C.C., Ala., 1993. Personnel staffing specialist Bd. of U.S. Civil Svc. Examiners, Anniston, Ala., 1957-66; personnel mgmt. specialist Dept. of Army, Anniston, 1966-73; tech. svcs. officer Dept. of Army, 1973-74; personnel mgmt. specialist Dept. of Army, Redstone Arsenal, Ala., 1974-79; supervisory personnel mgmt. specialist U.S. Army Europe, Mannheim, Fed. Republic of Germany, 1979-83; tech. svcs. officer U.S. Army Europe, Darmstadt, Fed. Republic of Germany, 1983-86; supervisory personnel mgmt. specialist Dept. of Army, Fort Ritchie, Md., 1986-87; ret., 1987; tax preparer H&R Block, Gadsden, Ala., 1994, 95; tax preparer H&R Block, Gadsden, 1994-95. Vol. Huntsville Bot. Gardens, 1989-92; mem. local group Master Gardeners, Huntsville, 1990, Huntsville Wildflower Assn, 1990-92, State and Local Master Gardeners Assn., 1990-93. Mem. Huntsville Bot. Soc. (vol.), Ala. Master Gardeners Assn. (local and state vol.), Huntsville Wildflower Assn. Home: 82 Ty Pl Ohatchee AL 36271-9231

ELLIS, BRENDA LEE, mathematician, computer scientist, consultant, educator; b. Norfolk, Va., Jan. 4, 1965; d. Lester and Annie Mae (Leak) E. BS cum laude, Norfolk State U., 1987; postgrad., Old Dominion U., 1988-89, Cleve. State U., 1991, Hampton U., 1994. Computer clk. Naval Electronics Systems Engring. Ctr., Portsmouth, Va., 1986-88; rsch. asst. Old Dominion U., Norfolk, 1988-89; computer analyst Dept. Def., Ft. Meade, Md., 1989; mathematician NASA Lewis Rsch. Ctr., Cleve., 1989—; lab. dir., instrnl. support Norfolk State U., 1993—; tutor SAT Tutorial, Bethel H.S., 1994; panelist Sonia Kovalesky Math. Day, Cleve. State U., 1990-92; guest speaker Math. Counts Workshop, 1991; mentor Hampton U., 1994; tax preparer H&R Block, 1994. Usher Rock Ch., Virginia Beach, 1983-91, Mt. Calvary Bapt. Ch., Cleve., 1991; vol. Combined Fed. Campaign, Cleve., 1991, Norfolk Community Hosp., 1982; tutor, mentor, sci. fair coord. East Tech. High Sch., Cleve., 1991-92; meet dir. Lake Erie Indoor Track Field Championship, 1992. Recipient scholarships and fellowship, first place trophy North Coast Relays, 1991, 1992. Mem. IEEE, NAFE, Am. Bus. Women's Assn., Nat. Tech. Assn. (Hampton Roads chpt.), Assn. Computing Machinery (acting sec. 1986-87), Norfolk State U. Alumni (co-chair spl. projects com. 1993), Nat. Tech. Assn., Internat. Platform Assn., Over the Hill Track Club (v.p. 1991-92), Beta Kappa Chi. Baptist. Office: NASA Lewis Rsch Ctr 21000 Brookpark Rd Cleveland OH 44135

ELLIS, CAROLINE GRIFFIN, lawyer; b. Balt., July 26, 1962; d. Joseph Gardner and Carmen (Arellano) Griffin; m. Douglas Hassel Ellis, May 30, 1993. BA, Loyola Coll., 1984; JD, U. Md., Balt., 1987. Law clk. Hon. Elsbeth L. Bothe, Balt., 1987-88, Hon. Joseph C. Howard, Balt., 1988-90; assoc. Irwin, Kerr, Green, McDonald & Dexter, Balt., 1990-93, Gordon, Feinblatt, Rothman, Hoffburger & Hollander, Balt., 1993—. Counsel Jr. League Balt., 1994—. Mem. ABA, Md. State Bar Assn., Balt. City Bar Assn., Women's Bar Assn. Office: Gordon Feinblatt Rothman Hoffburger & Hollander 233 E Redwood St Baltimore MD 21202

ELLIS, CAROLLYN, religious organization administrator; b. McPherson, Kans., Aug. 25, 1938; d. Joseph Hugh Reid and Lola Jean (Fairbairn Reid) Robinson; m. Raymond Wendel Ellis, Aug. 22, 1960; children: Timothy Ray, Wendel Joseph, Annette Jean, Janette Ruth. Diploma, Greenville Coll.; postgrad., U. Mich., Nova U. Pres. Women's Ministries Internat., 1989—; exec. v.p. Tykestown U.S.A., 1992-93; regional v.p. Free Meth. Found., Indpls., 1993—. Home: 8531 W Chapel Pines Dr Indianapolis IN 46234 Office: Free Meth Ch of NA 770 N High Sch Rd Indianapolis IN 46214

ELLIS, CAROLYN TERRY, lawyer; b. N.Y.C., Apr. 20, 1949; d. Francis Martin and Sarah Baker (Ames) Ellis; m. H. Lake Wise, Feb. 27, 1982; children: Carolyn Campbell Wise, Burke Ames. BA, U. Chgo., 1971; JD, NYU, 1974. Bar: N.Y. 1975. Rsch. analyst Dept. Justice, N.Y.C., 1973-74; assoc. Lord, Day & Lord, N.Y.C., 1974-84, ptnr., 1984-86; ptnr. Coudert Bros., N.Y.C., 1986—; instr. Bklyn. Law Sch., 1980-82. Mem. ABA, N.Y. State Bar Assn., Assn. of Bar of City of N.Y. (antitrust and trade regulation com. 1989-92, internat. trade com. 1993—). Office: Coudert Bros 1114 Avenue of Americas New York NY 10036-7701

ELLIS, CYNTHIA ATKINSON, judge; b. Ft. Myers, Fla., Oct. 9, 1955; d. Thomas Harris and Alice (Martin) Atkinson; m. Gerald Francis Ellis, Dec. 29, 1975; children: Denise Nicole, Michelle Lauren. BA, U. Fla., 1976, JD, 1978. Bar: Fla. 1979, Collier County 1988. Asst. state's atty. State Atty's Office, Gainesville, Fla., 1978-86, Naples, Fla., 1986-89; county judge Collier County Courthouse, Naples, 1990—. Chairperson Naples Alliance for Children, 1990-92; bd.dirs. YMCA, Naples, 1991, Consumer Credit Svcs. of S.W. Fla., 1991-92; adv. coun. Collier County Extension, Naples, 1990-94. Recipient She Knows Where She's Going, Girls, Inc., 1991. Mem. Fla. Bar Assn., Collier County Bar Assn., Nat. Assn. of Women Judges, Fla. Ctr. for Children and Youth. Roman Catholic. Office: Collier County Courthouse Naples FL 33999

ELLIS, ELLEN WILKINS, government relations specialist; b. Oxford, Miss., Aug. 11, 1962; d. William Thomas and Martha Ann (Huddleston) Wilkins; m. Joseph John Ellis, Dec. 17, 1989; 1 child, Michael Alexander. AB cum laude, Mt. Holyoke Coll., 1984; MA, Ind. U., 1986; postgrad., Princeton U., 1987. Assoc. instr. Ind. U., Bloomington, 1984-86; dir. communications Mass. Rep. Party, Boston, 1987, Joe Malone for U.S. Senate, Boston, 1988; assoc. dir. govt. rels. Mass. Mut., Springfield, 1989, dir. govt. rels., 1990-94, asst. v.p., 1994—; Mem. Corp. Profl. Devel. Bd., Springfield, 1990. Vol. cons. pub. rels. Children's Mus., Holyoke, Mass., 1988-89; active Planned Parenthood League Mass., Boston, 1989-90, City Task Force on Violence Against Women, Springfield, 1994. Grad. fellow Princeton U., 1986-87. Mem. Pub. Affairs Coun. Episcopalian. Office: Mass Mut 1295 State St Springfield MA 01111-0001

ELLIS, EVA LILLIAN, artist; b. Seattle, June 4, 1920; d. Carl Martin and Hilda (Persson) Johnson; m. Everett Lincoln Ellis, May 1, 1943; children: Karin, Kristy, Hildy, Erik. BA, U. Wash., 1941; MA, U. Idaho, 1950; M in Painting (h.c.), U. delle Arti, 1983. Assoc. dir. art Best & Co., Seattle, 1943; dir. Am. Art Week, Idaho, 1949-55; mem. faculty dept. art U. Idaho, 1946-48; dir., tchr. Children's Art Oreg., 1966-71; mem. faculty aux. bd. U. Wash., Seattle, 1987—, faculty chair, 1988—; freelance artist, 1943-46; lectr. in art, New Zealand, 1971-73. Author: A Comparison of the Use of Color of Old and Modern Masters, 1950; works include: Profilo d'Artisti Contemporanei Premio Centauro D'Oro, 1982; exhbns. shows include Henry Gallery, U. Wash., 1941, Immanuel Gallery, N.Y.C., 1943-46, Rackham Gallery, U. Mich., 1956-64, Detroit Inst. Art, 1959, Kresge Gallery, 1959-64, Portland Art Mus., 1967, Corvallis Art Ctr., Oreg., 1966, U. Idaho, 1946-56, U. Canterbury, N.Z., 1979, Boise Mus., 1949-55, CSA, 1972, 79, small gallery, Sydney, Australia, 1971-73, Survey of New Zealand Art, 1979, Shoreline Mus., Seattle, 1981, N.Z. Embassy, London, 1979, Karlshamn Art Soc., Sweden, 1979, Italian Acad. Art, 1982, Palos Verdes (Calif.) Art Ctr., 1982, Swedish Embassy, 1982, Aigantighe Gallery, N.Z., 1983; represented in permanent collections U. Calif.-Berkeley, U. Wash., Calif. Forest Products Lab., 1991; portrait commns. U.S.A. and Japan; pvt. commns. Wash., Calif., N.Y., Engl., Sweden, 1986-92; guest appearances on NBC-TV, N.Y.C. Counselor Cancer Soc.; active Girl Scouts U.S., People to People Friendship Worldwide, 1943-90, Art in Embassies Abroad Program, U.S., 1980-90; elected to Acad. of Europe, 1980; mem. sister com. Christ Ch., New Zealand and Seattle, 1981-83; chair '41 Class Reunion U. Wash.; chmn. scholarship drive for fgn. students U. Wash., Seattle, 1992; mem. Painting Commns. U.S. and Japan. Recipient awards Acad. Art and Sci., 1958-66, Ann Arbor Women Painters, diploma with gold medal, Italian Acad. Art, 1980, hon. diploma fine art, 3 Nat. awards Nat. League Profl. Artists, N.Y.C.; World Culture prize, 1984; Internat. Peace award in Art, 1984; Internat. Art Promotion award, 1986, others. Fellow I.B.C. (Cambridge, Eng. chpt.); mem. Mich. Acad. Art and Sci., Nat. League Am. Pen Women, Nat. Mus. Women in Arts (charter mem.), Royal Overseas League (London), Fine Arts Soc. Idaho, Canterbury Soc. Art New Zealand, Copley Soc. Fine Arts (Boston), Inst. D'Arte Contemporanea Di Milano (Italy), Women's Caucus for Art, Nat. Slide Registry of Artists (New Zealand and Australia), Alpha Omicron Pi. (featured in nat. mag.), Scandinavian Club (pres. 1977—), Faculty Wives Club (pres. 1979). Address: 19614 24th Ave NW Seattle WA 98177-2402

ELLIS, LOUISA CARNS, social worker; b. Birmingham, Ala., Oct. 9, 1950; d. George Dameral and Barbara Anne (Savoie) Carns Jr.; m. Stephen Allen Ellis, Sept. 29, 1979 (div. 1986); 1 child, Julia Savoie. BA in Psychology, SE Mass. U. (now U. Mass. Dartmouth), 1987; MSW, Boston Coll., 1990. Emergency mental health clinician Goldberg Med. Assocs., Bridgewater, Mass., 1987-92; emergency mental health svcs. site mgr. Emergency Med. Svcs. Assocs., Bridgewater, Mass., 1992-93; emergency mental health clinician Ctr. Health and Devel., Brookline, Mass., 1993; juvenile ct. clinician Ctr. for Human Svcs., New Bedford, Mass., 1994—. Mem. Nat. Assn. Social Workers. Unitarian.

ELLIS, MARCELLA M., elementary education educator, nurse's aide; b. Deadwood, S.D., Feb. 14, 1946; d. Carson John and Vera Estella (Farber) Schroeder; m. Loren G. Larsen, June 5, 1966 (div. May 1974); children: Robb Nels, Will Joel, Jeff Troy; m. Kenneth B. Ellis, Jan. 10, 1976 (div. July 1992); 1 child, James Carson. Student, S.D. State U., 1964-67, Edgewood Coll. of Sacred Heart, 1968-69; BA, Chapman U., 1976. CNA. Registered cosmetologist Monroe St. Salon, Madison, Wis., 1967-68; reporter, typographer Valley Irrigator Newspaper, Newell, S.D., 1979-82, 84; owner, pres., typographer Quality Type, Inc., Orlando, Fla., 1983; mechs. adminstr. First Impressions & Greenes Printing, Ocala, Fla., 1985-90; customer svc. rep. Unicover Corp., Cheyenne, Wyo., 1990-91; with camera dept. Mail West Printing, Tucson, 1991; ednl. asst. Newell (S.D.) Sch., 1992—. Mem. Am. Assn. Psychiat. Technicians (Psychiat. Technician of Yr. 1994), Internat. Tng. Comm., Internat. Reading Assn. Home: PO Box 319 Newell SD 57760

ELLIS, MARY LOUISE HELGESON, insurance company executive; b. Albert Lea, Minn., May 29, 1943; d. Stanley Orville and Neoma Lois (Guthier) Helgeson; children: Christopher, Tracy; m. David Readinger, Nov. 5, 1994. BS in Pharmacy, U. Iowa, 1966; MA in Pub. Adminstrn., Iowa State U., 1982, postgrad., 1982-83. Faculty Duquesne U., Pitts., 1977; cons. in pharmacy, Colville, Wash., 1978-79; dir. pharmacy Mt. Carmel Hosp., Colville, 1978-79; clin. pharmacist Iowa Vets. Home, Marshalltown, Iowa, 1980-81; instr. Iowa Valley Community Coll., Marshalltown, 1981-83; dir. Iowa Dept. Substance Abuse, Des Moines, 1983-86; dir. State of Iowa Pub. Health, dir. Iowa Dept. Pub. Health, Des Moines, 1986-90; spl. cons. health affairs Blue Cross/Blue Shield of Iowa, 1990-91; v.p. Blue Cross/Blue Shield of Iowa and S.D., 1991—; chair Iowa Health Data Commn., Des Moines, 1986-90; bd. dirs. Health Policy Corp. Iowa, 1986-90; adj. asst. prof. U. Iowa, Iowa City, 1984—; comd. officer U.S. Food & Drug Adminstrn., 1989-90; mem. alumnae bd. dirs. U. Iowa Coll. of Pharmacy, 1989—; chair Nat. Commn. Accreditation of Ambulance Svcs., 1992—. Mem. Iowa State Bd. Health, 1981-83, v.p., 1982-83; mem. adv. council Iowa Valley Community Coll., 1983-85. Recipient Woman of Achievement award Des Moines YWCA, 1988. Mem. Iowa Pharmacists Assn., Am. Pub. Health Assn., Iowa Pub. Health Assn. (bd. dirs., Henry Albert award 1990), Alpha Xi Delta, Phi Kappa Phi, Pi Sigma Alpha. Republican. Home: 503 Hwy R57 Norwalk IA 50211 Office: Blue Cross and Blue Shield Iowa 636 Grand Ave Des Moines IA 50309-2502

ELLIS, SARAH AMES, clinical psychologist; b. St. Paul, Jan. 10, 1925; d. Charles Lesley and Linda (Baker) Ames; m. Francis Martin Ellis, Sept. 13, 1947 (dec. 1982); children: Carolyn Terry, Francis Lyman, Nathan Ames; m. Adam Yarmolinsky, Feb. 3, 1990. AB, Barnard Coll.; MSW, Columbia U.; MA in Psychology, New Sch. for Social Rsch., 1973; cert. in Psychoanalytic Psychotherapy and Psychoanalysis, Inst. Contemporary Psychotherapy, 1975; PhD in Clin. Psychology, New Sch. for Social Rsch., 1982. Lic. psychologist, N.Y., D.C. Counselor Women's Intensive Treatment Ward, 1964-66; psychiat. caseworker Mental Hygiene Clinic, 1966-69; psychiat. social worker family therapy unit Bellevue Psychiat. Hosp., N.Y.C., 1969-71; pvt. practice N.Y.C., 1972-90; staff therapist Inst. Contemporary Psychotherapy, N.Y.C., 1975-80, 86-90; psychology cons. Inst. Reconstructive Plastic Surgery-NYU Med. Ctr., N.Y.C., 1978-86; pvt. practice Washington, 1990—; staff psychotherapist D.C. Inst. for Mental Health, Washington, 1990-93; rsch. psychologist Project H.E.L.P., Gouverneur Hosp., N.Y.C., 1989-90; instr. NYU Med. Sch. With WAC, 1945-46. Mem. APA, Washington Psychologists for Study of Psychoanalysis (bd. dirs. 1993-94), D.C. Psychol. Assn. (com. mem. 1993—). Home and Office: 3700 33d Pl NW Washington DC 20008

ELLIS, SUSAN GOTTENBERG, psychologist; b. N.Y.C., Jan. 24, 1949; d. Sam and Sally (Hirschman) Gottenberg; B.S., Cornell U., 1970; M.A., Columbia U., 1971; M.A., Hofstra U., 1975, Ph.D., 1976; m. David Roy Ellis, July 23, 1972; children: Sharon Rachel, Dana Michelle. Instr. health edn. Nassau Community Coll., Garden City, N.Y., 1971-73; sch. psychologist public schs., Somerville, N.J., 1976-77; clin. psychologist Somerset County Community Mental Health Center, Somerville, 1976-77; sch. psychologist, Pinellas County, Fla., 1977-78; instr. St. Petersburg (Fla.) Jr. Coll., 1978; clin. psychologist, Largo, Fla., 1977—; cons. Fla. Dept. Health and Rehab. Services, Med. Center Hosp., Largo, Morton Plant Hosp., Clearwater, Fla., 1978-79, N.Y. State Regents scholar, 1966-71; adj. prof. Eckerd Coll. St. Petersburg, 1988. Author: Interpret Your Dreams, 1987, A Dream Primer, 1988, Make Sense of Your Dreams, 1988. Mem. Am. Psychol. Assn., Fla. Psychol. Assn., Pinellas Psychol. Assn. (treas. 1978, polit. action chmn. 1979), Kappa Delta Pi. Club: Cornell U. Suncoast (v.p. 1979-80). Office: 3233 E Bay Dr Ste 100 Largo FL 34641

ELLIS, WENDY ELIZABETH, former teacher; b. Shawnee Mission, Kans., Mar. 1, 1968; d. Richard Dwayne and Beverly Sue (Ferguson) Williams; m. Geoffrey Earl Ellis, July 17, 1993. BA in Elem. Edn., Wheaton (Ill.) Coll., 1990; MA in Human Svcs., Concordia U., River Forest, Ill., 1993. Cert. tchr., Ill. Tchr. Dist. 89, Maywood, Ill., 1990-92; presch. tchr. Tuesday's Child, Chgo., 1992-93; salesperson Crate and Barrel, Palo Alto, Calif., 1993-94; tchr. After-Sch. program El Carmelo Kids Corner, Palo Alto, 1994; dir. after sch. program Palo Verde Kid's Club, Palo Alto, 1994—. Mem. Am. Counseling Assn., Ill. Counseling Assn.

ELLISON, ELLEN WELLS, horticulturist; b. Lufkin, Tex., Mar. 20, 1934; d. Charles E. and Elsie (Bowen) Guinn; m. James R. Ellison, Sept. 7, 1952; children: Charles, Margaret, Pamela Jo. BS, Tex. Tech U., 1964; postgrad., Tex. A&M U., 1968-69. Cert. tchr. Tchr. Shallowater (Tex.) Ind. Sch. Dist., 1964-66, Aldine Ind. Sch. Dist., Houston, 1968, Brenham (Tex.) Ind. Sch. Dist., 1968-70; pres. Ellison's Nursery and Gardent Ctr., Brenham, Tex., 1972-78, Ellison's H. of Flowers and Gifts, Brenham, 1975-92, Ellison's Greenhouses, Inc., Brenham, 1990—; mem. chancellor's coun. Tex. A&M U., College Station, 1987—; adv. coun. Wharton (Tex.) Jr. Coll., 1983-85; horticulture adv. coun. Tex. State Tech. Inst., Waco, 1978-85. Pres. Brenham Ind. Sch. Dist., 1972-75; home tour chmn. Washington County Heritage Soc., Brenham, 1982; bd. dirs. First United Meth. Ch., Brenham, 1984-87; vol. Brenham State Sch., 1984—; mem. Leadership, Tex., 1990. Mem. Tex. State Florist Assn. (bd. dirs. 1980-82, edn. commn. 1985-90), Soc. of Am. Florists, Nat. Assn. for Women in Horticulture, Fortnightly Club, Allied Florist, Washington County C. of C. (agrl./nominating com. 1985—), Acad. Am. Floriculture. Office: Ellison's Greenhouses Inc 2107 E Stone St Brenham TX 77833-5131

ELLISON, KATHERINE RUFFNER WHITE, psychologist, educator; b. Charleston, W.Va., Jan. 17, 1941; d. Christian Streit and Katherine Ruffner (Hughey) White. BA, Agnes Scott Coll., 1962; PhD, CUNY, 1976. Prof. Montclair State Coll., Upper Montclair, N.J., 1977—; cons. various law enforcement agys., 1973—. Author: Psychology & Criminal Justice, 1981, Stress & The Police Officer, 1983; contbr. articles to profl. jours. Ruling elder Maywood (N.J.) Presbyn. Ch., 1987—. Mem. Am. Psychol. Assn. (sec.-treas. police psychology sect. 1977-93), Internat. Assn. Chiefs of Police, Phi Beta Kappa. Democrat. Office: Montclair State Coll Psychology Dept Upr Montclair NJ 07043

ELLISON, M. JEANETTE, human resources specialist; b. Lubbock, Tex., Nov. 26, 1948; d. Ervin John and Irene Anita (Heinrich) Ehler; m. Kenneth John Ellison, Feb. 16, 1974 (div. May 1993); children: Christy, Gary, Wendy, Carol, James. BBA, Tex. Tech. U., 1971. Loan officer Bank of Calif., San Francisco, 1971-74; dir. compensation and employee rels. Hughes Airwest, San Francisco, 1975-80; mgr. compensation and benefits Pacific Lumber Co., San Francisco, 1980-86; dir. compensation and benefits Harrah's Reno (Nev.), 1986-92; dir. human resources Harrah's Lake Tahoe (Nev.), 1990-91; v.p. human resources Harrah's Atlantic City, 1993—. Bd. dirs. Atlantic City Women's Ctr., 1993—, Child Care Resource Coun., Reno, 1991-93. Mem. Am. Compensation Assn., Soc. for Human Resources Mgmt. Democrat. Roman Catholic. Office: Harrahs Atlantic City 1725 Brigantine Blvd Atlantic City NJ 08401

ELLISON, PATRICIA LEE, lawyer; b. Elizabeth, N.J., Oct. 17, 1943; d. Harry C. and Leila D. Ellison. BA, Denison U., 1965; student, U. Paris, France, 1963-64; MA, U. Calif., Riverside, 1967; JD cum laude, U. San Diego, 1973. Bar: Calif. 1973, N.Y. 1983. Fin. analyst NASA, Greenbelt, Md., 1967-68; rsch. atty. Dist. Atty.'s Office, San Diego, 1973-74; assoc. atty. Butler Ruff & Harrigan, San Diego, 1974-75; ptnr. Ellison Eichten & Bell, San Diego, 1975-82; sole practice Kingston, N.Y., 1983—. Bd. dirs. Ulster County YWCA, Kingston, 1988-91, pres. bd. dirs., 1992; chairperson Dem. Com. Town of Shandaken, N.Y., 1993—. Recipient Internat. Acad. Trial Lawyers Advocacy award, 1973. Mem. NOW, Ulster County Bar Assn., N.Y.C. Human Ecology Action League, Catskill Women's Network, Alpha Chi Omega. Office: 93 St James St PO Box 1717 Kingston NY 12401-0717

ELLISON-ROSENKILDE, WENDY MAUREEN, psychologist, educator; b. Meadville, Pa., July 6, 1941; d. Allen Vincent and Anna Winifred (Hickman) Ellison; m. Roy N. Bidwell, May 28, 1982 (div.); m. Carl Edward Rosenkilde, May 24, 1992; step-children: Karen Louise Rosenkilde, Paul Eric Rosenkilde. AB in English, Allegheny Coll., 1962; MS in Neurol. Learning Disabilities, U. Pacific, 1974; MS, Calif. State U., 1984; PhD, U. So. Calif., 1983. Learning specialist South Bay Psychiatric Med. Clinic, Campbell, Calif., 1971-81; registered psychol. asst. Santa Clara County Mental Health, Pleasanton, Calif., 1981-84; intern in psychology Santa Clara County Mental Health, San Jose, Calif., 1982-83; psychologist Family Svc. East Bay, Livermore, Calif., 1985-86; psychologist child devel. ctr. Children's Hosp., San Francisco, 1985-86; affiliate staff psychologist CPC Walnut Creek (Calif.) Hosp., 1985—; pvt. practice Pleasanton, 1985—; affiliate staff psychologist Valleycare Hosp., Pleasanton, Calif., 1993—; part-time instr. child devel. Foothill Coll., Los Altos, Calif., 1976-77, Los Positas Coll., Livermore, Calif., 1984-92. Co-author: Student Guide for Teaching for Learning, 1981. Mem. APA, Calif. Psychol. Assn., Alameda County Psychol. Assn. (pres. 1989, pres-elect and chair program and nomination coms., chair info. and referral 1986), Soc. Personality Assessment, San Francisco Psychoanalytic Inst., Livermore Valley Tennis Club, Rorschach Internat., Kappa Kappa Gamma. Democrat. Presbyterian. Home: 2604 Crater Rd Livermore CA 94550 Office: 5674 Stoneridge Dr # 217 Pleasanton CA 94588-8537

ELLIS-VANT, KAREN MCGEE, elementary and special education educator, consultant; b. La Grande, Oreg., May 10, 1950; d. Ellis Eddington and Gladys Vera (Smith) McGee; m. Lynn F. Ellis, June 14, 1975 (div. Sept. 1983); children: Megan Marie, Matthew David; m. Jack Scott Vant, Sept. 6, 1986; children: Kathleen Erin, Kelli Christine (dec.). BA in Elem. Edn., Boise State U., 1972, MA in Spl. Edn., 1979; postgrad. studies in curriculum and instruction, U. Minn., 1985—. Tchr. learning disabilities resource room New Plymouth Joint Sch. Dist., 1972-73, Payette Joint Sch. Dist., 1973, diagnostician project SELECT, 1974-75; cons. tchr. in spl. edn. Boise Sch. Dist., 1975-90; tchr. 1-2 combination, 1990-91, team tchr. 1st grade, 1991—, chpt. 1 program cons., 1992—; mem. profl. Standards Commn., 1983-86. Bd. dirs. Hotline, Inc., 1979-82; mem. Idaho Coop. Manpower Commn., 1984-85. Recipient Disting. Young Woman of Yr. award Boise Jaycettes, 1982, Idaho Jaycettes, 1983; Coffman Alumni scholar U. Minn., 1985-86. Mem. NEA (mem. civil rights com. 1983-85, state contact for peace caucus 1981-85, del. assembly rep., 1981-85), NSTA, ASCD, Internat. Reading Assn., NCTE, Internat. Coop. Learning Assn., Idaho Edn. Assn. (bd. dirs. region VII 1981-85, pres. region VII 1981-82), Boise Edn. Assn. (v.p. 1981-82, 84-85, pres. 1982-83), Nat. Council Urban Edn. Assn., World Future Soc., Council for Exceptional Children (pres. chpt. 1978-79), Nat. Coun. Tchrs. English, Minn. Coun. for Social Studies, Calif. Assn. for Gifted, Assn. for Grad. Edn. Students, Phi Delta Kappa. Contbr. articles to profl. jours.; editor, author ednl. texts and communiques; conductor of workshops, leadership tng. coop. learning. and frameworks. Office: Boise Pub Schs Adminstrn Bldg 1207 W Fort St Boise ID 83702-5314

ELLMANN, SHEILA FRENKEL, investment company executive; b. Detroit, June 8, 1931; d. Joseph and Rose (Neback) Frenkel; BA in English, U. Mich., 1953; m. William M. Ellmann, Nov. 1, 1953; children: Douglas Stanley, Carol Elizabeth, Robert Lawrence. Dir. Advance Glove Mfg. Co., Detroit, 1954-78; v.p. Frome Investment Co., Detroit, 1980—. Mem. U. Mich. Alumni Assn., Nat. Trust Hist. Preservation. Home: 28000 Weymouth Ct Farmington Hills MI 48334-3267

ELLSTROM-CALDER, ANNETTE, clinical medicine educator; b. Duluth, Minn., Dec. 19, 1952; d. Raymond Charles Ellstrom and Ruth Elaine (Bloomquist) Larson; m. Jeffrey Ellstrom-Calder, July 30, 1982; children: Hannah, Ian. BA in Social Work, Psychology, Sociology, Concordia Coll., 1974; MSW, U. Wis., 1978. Group therapist N.D. State Indsl. Sch., 1973; social worker Fergus Falls (Minn.) State Hosp., 1974, Jackson County Dept. Social Services, Black River Falls, Wis., 1975-77; sr. clin. social worker U. Wis. Hosp., Madison, 1979-90, clin. instr. medicine, 1989—; cons. Medical Media Associates, Madison, Wis., 1990—, Med. Media Assocs., Madison, 1990—; cons. Waupun (Wis.) Meml. Hosp., 1979-84, Med. Media Assocs., Madison, 1990—; lectr. grad. sch. social work U. Wis., Madison, 1979-82, prin. investigator in rsch. U. Wis. Hosp., Madison, 1985—. Editor: A Guide to Patients and Families, 1984; mem. editl. bd. Advances in Renal Replacement Therapy; contbr. articles to profl. jours. Del. trustee, bd. dirs. Nat. Kidney Found., N.Y.C., 1983-91, chmn. bd. dirs., Milw., 1985-87, vice chmn., 1983-85, sec., 1982-83, chmn. patient svcs. com., 1981-82, bd. dirs., 1981—, chmn. nat. tng. and edn. com., mem. nat. patient svcs. com., N.Y.C., 1987-91, mem. pers. com., bd. dirs. Madison chpt., 1979-80; bd. dirs. Combined Health Appeal Wis., 1990—, sec., 1992—; mem. nat. rsch. com. Am. Assn. Spinal Cord Injury Psychologists and Social Workers, N.Y.C., 1988—. Recipient Health Advancement award Nat. Kidney Found. Wis., 1985, Vol. Yr. award Nat. Kidney Found. Wis., 1984, Vol. Service award Nat. Kidney Found. Wis., 1983, Nat. Nephrology Social Worker of Yr. Merit award Nat. Kidney Found. and Council of Nephrology Social Workers, 1987; hon. adoptee Winnebago Indian Tribe, 1978; named Outstanding Young Wisconsinite Wisc. Jaycees, 1988. Mem. Council Nephrology Social Workers (nat. v.p. 1984-86, nat. exec. com. 1984-86, Nat. Nephrology Social Worker Yr. award 1987), Nat. Assn. Social Workers, Pi Gamma Mu. Democrat. Office: U Wis Hosp 600 Highland Ave #H4/510 Madison WI 53792-0001

ELLSWORTH, CYNTHIA ANN, counseling administrator; b. Springfield, Ohio, Jan. 19, 1950; d. Donald Harry and Jeanne Marie (Glover) E. BE, Western Conn. State U., 1972; M in Spl. Edn., Ohio U., 1976; Postgrad., Ohio State U., 1985-86; MS in Counseling, U. Dayton, 1988. Tchr. LBD Fed. Hocking Schs., Stewart, Ohio, 1972-76; supr. EMR/LBD Vinton County Schs., McArthur, Ohio, 1976-77; tchr. Southwestern City Schs., Grove City, Ohio, 1977-88, sch. counselor, 1989—. Mem. ACA, Am. Sch. Counselors Assn., Phi Delta Kappa. Office: 194 Winfall Dr Gahanna OH 43230

ELLSWORTH, ELAINE HARVEY, marketing educator; b. Balt., June 29, 1950; d. Harold Edwin and Margaret Angela (Buckingham) Harvey; m. Gene Harlan Ellsworth, Aug. 13, 1977. AA, San Bernardino Valley Coll., 1988; BS in Liberal Studies, SUNY, 1992. Cert. bus. edn. instr. From sales assoc. to buyer Stewart & Co., Associated Dry Goods, Balt., 1968-75; dist. mgr. Parklane Inc., New Hyde Park, N.Y., 1975-80, regional mgr./west coast merchandiser, 1980-88; advt. sales cons. GTE Directories, Glendale, Calif., 1988; dist. mgr. Clothestime, Inc., Fremont, Calif., 1988-90; mktg. instr. Profl. Experience Tri-Valley Regional Occupational Program, Livermore, Calif., 1990—; mem. fashion merchandising adv. bd. Las Positas Coll. Vol. gala/fundraising Rubicon Children's Ctr., 1991—; friendly visitor Coordinated Assn. United Srs., 1991-93; active New-In-Town, Fremont, 1991-93; campaign activist Fremont Dem. Forum, 1992. Mem. NOW (demonstration co-coord. So. Alameda County chpt. 1992), Assn. Marketing Students (formerly DECA/Distributive Edn. Clubs Am., Calif. chpt., cert. advisor 1990—), Calif. Assn. Regional Occupational Programs, Calif. Bus. Edn. Assn., Calif. Mktg. Edn. Assn. (pres.-elect), Livermore C. of C. (mem. bus. and edn. com.). Methodist. Office: Tri-Valley Regional Occupational Program 2600 Kitty Hawk Rd Ste 117 Livermore CA 94550-9625

ELMAN, NAOMI GEIST, artist, producer; b. Chgo.; d. Harry and Rita (Goldstein) Geist; m. Murray Elman, May 29, 1946 (dec. Dec. 1965); 1 child, Margaret (Peggy) Gillespie. Student, Hamilton Inst. for Girls, Nat. Acad. of Design, Art Students League. Personal mgr. in performing arts, prodr. concerts in N.Y.C. and Hawaii, N.Y., Hawaii, 1968-80. One-woman show Churchill Gallery, 1962, Pen and Brush Club, 1986; exhibited in group shows. Vol. nurses aid pvt. and army hosps., ARC, 1939-44; v.p. N.Y. Diabetes Assn., 1955-58; mcpl. chmn. Dem. Club, Tenafly, N.J., 1958; Dem. com. woman, 1959-61; bd. dirs. Nat. Children's Cardiac Home, N.Y.C., 1940-49, Bergen County Dem. Club, 1958-60. Recipient Margareet Sussman award,

1985, Salamagundi award, 1987, Julia Lucille award, 1988. Mem. Internat. Platform Assn., Soc. Mil. Widows, Retired Officers Club (life), Disabled Am. Vets., Artists Equity. Democrat. Address: 500 E 77th St New York NY 10021

ELMER, LISA, respiratory therapist; b. Ogden, Utah, Oct. 7, 1963; d. George Hyrum and Joyce (Johns) E. A of Respiratory Therapy, Weber State Coll., 1987, B of Gerontology, 1988. Registered respiratory therapist, Utah. Respiratory technician Lakeview Hosp., Bountiful, Utah, 1984-87; respiratory therapist, sleep lab. coord. Brigham City (Utah) Comty. Hosp., 1987—, cardiopulmonary supr., 1994—. Mem. Am. Assn. Respiratory Care, Nat. Bd. Respiratory Care. Mormon. Office: Brigham City Cmty Hosp 950 South 500 West Brigham City UT 84302

ELMORE, PATRICIA BORGSMILLER, educational psychologist; b. Murphysboro, Ill., Nov. 19, 1943; c. Charles Edward and Lillian Resides (Stewart) Borgsmiller; m. Donald Eugene Elmore, Apr. 4, 1970; 1 child, Donald Eugene Jr. BA in Liberal Arts and Sci., So. Ill. U., 1965, ME, 1967, PhD, 1970. Instr. So. Ill. U., Carbondale, 1967-70, asst. prof., 1970-74, assoc. prof., 1974-80, prof. dept. ednl. psychology, 1980—; cons. various sch. dists. on Interpretation and Use of Standardized Achievement Test Results, Ill. Office of Edn.; validator for Title IV-C U.S. Office of Edn.. Mem. editorial bd. Jour. Applied Measurement in Edn., Measurement and Evaluation in Counseling and Devel.; editor: Significant Perspectives, 1984-91; past mem. editorial bd. Jour. Ednl. Psychology, Score; contbr. chpts. to books and articles to profl. jours. Bd. dirs. Friends of Morris Library, 1981—, pres., 1987-89, v.p., 1983-85; bd. dirs. St. Joseph Meml. Hosp., 1988-89; sec., St.Andrew Sch. Home and Sch. Assn., 1984-86; v.p. St. Andrew Sch. Bd. 1986-87, pres. 1987-88. Recipient numerous rsch. grants Ill. Office of Edn., So. Ill. U., Counseling and Human Devel. Found. Mem. AAUW, APA, Am. Counseling Assn. (rsch. award 1994), Am. Ednl. Rsch. Assn., Am. Statis. Assn., Nat. Coun. on Measurement in Edn., Assn. for Assessment in Counseling (treas. 1988-90, pres.-elect 1990-91, pres. 1991-92, past pres. 1992-93), Alpha Lambda Delta, Kappa Delta Pi, Phi Delta Kappa, Pi Mu Epsilon, Pi Lambda Theta.]. Home: 1640 Tina Dr PO Box 1090 Murphysboro IL 62966-1090 Office: So Ill U Dept Ednl Psychology and Spl Edn Carbondale IL 62901-4618

ELOFSON, NANCY MEYER, retired office equipment company executive; b. Glencoe, Ill., Jan. 27, 1923; d. Bernard Francis and Agnes (Ulbrich) Meyer; m. Carl L. Elofson, Nov. 27, 1946 (dec. Dec. 1991); 1 child, Peter Carl. BA, Western Coll., 1944; postgrad., SUNY, Jamestown, 1960-80. Sales corr. Scott, Foresman Pub., Chgo., 1944-46; sec., treas. Office Machines and Equipment Co., Jamestown, 1948-86; ret., 1986—. Mem. coun. camp com. Girl Scouts U.S.A., Jamestown, 1962-66, Girl Scout Alumnae Archives Com., 1992—; candidate Chautauqua County Legis., 1979; mem. choir 1st Congl. United Ch. of Christ, Jamestown, 1948—, moderator, 1978-79, mem. ch. coun., 1990—, chmn. 175th anniversary com., 1990-91, ch. growth com., long range planning com., 1993—; founder, pres. bd. dirs. Chautauqua Adult Day Care Ctrs., Inc., Jamestown, 1981-91; pres. bd. dirs. YWCA, Jamestown, 1983-85, trustee 1987—; mem. exec. bd./com. United Way, Jamestown, 1991—, allocations chmn., 1991—; active Chautauqua County Domestic Violence Guidance Team, 1994. Named Chautauqua County Caregiver of Yr., Chautauqua County Office of Aging, 1988, Vol. of Yr., United Way, 1992; recipient Caregiver's award N.Y. State Office of Aging, 1988, Women Making a Difference award Jamestown Post Jour., 1991. Mem. AAUW (sec. 1958), Women's Polit. Caucus, Jamestown Audubon Soc. Home: 81 Gordon St Jamestown NY 14701-1641

ELRICK, BILLY LEE, English language educator; b. Jackson, Miss., May 21, 1941; d. William Robert and Wesley James (Hall) Chambers; m. Donald Lee Elrick, June 29, 1965; children: Laura Katherine, John William. BA, Millsaps Coll., 1963; MA in Edn., U. Phoenix, 1992. Tchr. lang. arts North Arvada (Colo.) Jr. High, 1963-92, dept. chair, 1984-92; dean Wheat Ridge (Colo.) High Sch., 1993; tchr. English Arvada (Colo.) H.S., 1993-94, asst. prin., 1994—; mentor tchr. Jefferson Couty Schs.-North; workshop presenter in field. Mem. ASCD, Phi Delta Kappa, Delta Kappa Gamma (sec. 1990-94, 2d v.p. 1994—), Sigma Lambda, Kappa Delta Epsilon. Democrat. Methodist. Home: 10615 Irving Ct Westminster CO 80030 Office: Arvada High Sch 7951 W 65th Ave Arvada CO 80004

ELROD, LU, music educator, actress, author; b. Chattanooga, Tenn., Apr. 23, 1935; d. John C. Elrod and Helen Pauline (Kohn). MusB, Ga. State U., 1960; M in Music Edn., U. Ga., 1970, EdD, 1971; PhD, U. London, 1975. Prof. music, music coach U. Md., Balt., 1972-78, Calif. State U., L.A., 1978—; singer with Dallas (Tex.) Opera, 1957. Appeared in (movies) Major Pettigrew and Me, 1976, Seduction of Joe Tynan, 1977, Atlanta Child Murders, 1985, Children Don't Tell, 1986, For Love or Money, 1986, (TV) Lazarus Syndrome, 1980, Hill Street Blues, 1988, Superior Court, 1988, TV Bloopers, 1989, Beakman's World (Emmy award), Dream On, 1993, TV commercials. Recipient Leadership Devel. award Ford Found., 1967, Leadership Fellows award Ford Found., 1968; Tift Coll. voice scholar, 1953, Baylor U., 1956; Lu Elrod scholarship named at Calif. State U., L.A., 1989. Mem. AAUP, AFTRA, SAG, Am. Guild Variety Artists, Calif. Faculty Assn., Coll. Music Soc. Office: Calif State Univ 5151 State University Dr Los Angeles CA 90032-4221

ELROD, MARILYN A., legislative director; b. Indpls., Feb. 26, 1945; d. French M. and Burrlene (Holland) E. BA, Purdue U., 1967; postgrad., Am. U., 1967-69. Adminstrv. aide Rep. Allard K. Lowenstein, 1969-71; mem. legis. staff Rep. Ronald V. Dellums and Ho. Com. on D.C., 1971-83; mem. profl. staff Subcom. Mil. Installations and Facilities Ho. Armed Svcs. Com., 1983-89, mem. profl. staff Subcom. Rsch. and Devel., 1989-92; staff dir. Ho. Com. Armed Svcs., 1993—. Mem. Pi Sigma Alpha, Kappa Sigma Phi. Office: Armed Services Rm 2120 Rayburn House Office Bldg Washington DC 20515*

ELSBERRY, SUSAN DAVISE, computer-aided manufacturing engineer; b. Lincoln, Nebr., Oct. 27, 1953; d. Leo Herbert and Genevieve (Richards) Bischof; m. Terence Ray Elsberry, Aug. 9, 1986; 1 child, Colin Ray. BS, Brigham Young U., 1985, MS, 1992. Computer-aided mfg. engr. Northrop, Hawthorne, Calif., 1986-91; owner, tng. instr. mine safety Safety First, 1993—; ptnr. Elsberry Enterprises, 1994—; software trainer ExecuTrain, 1994—. Mem. Westec Adv. Com., 1987-90. named Whirlpool Corp. fellow, 1984-86. Fellow Inst. for Advancement of Engring.; mem. Soc. Mfg. Engrs. (officer chpt. 106 1993—). Democrat. Roman Catholic. Home: 1555 W Highsmith Dr Tucson AZ 85746-3308

ELSER, LOIS MARTIN, psychiatric and mental health nurse; b. Waynesboro, Pa., Oct. 26, 1932; d. Abram Paul and Sarah Catherine (Etter) Martin; m. Theodore Edwin Elser, Sept. 24, 1953 (div. Mar. 1978); children: Linda Sue, Jeanne Lynn, Theodore Jr. Diploma, Washington County Hosp. Sch. of Nursing, 1953; BA in Psychology, U. Balt., 1980; postgrad., Salisbury State U., 1984-86. RN; cert. psychiat. and mental health nurse. Various health positions, 1953-68; community health nurse Washington County Health Dept., Hagerstown, Md., 1968-70; community health nurse supr. Howard County Health Dept., Ellicott City, Md., 1970-73; community mental health nurse Anne Arundel County Health Dept., Annapolis, Md., 1973-77; community mental health nurse supr. Walter P. Carter Ctr., Balt., 1977-80; staff nurse psychiat. in-patient mental health unit Greater Laurel (Md.)-Beltsville Hosp., 1980-81; psychiat. nurse team leader day hosp. U.S. Pub. Health Hosp., Balt., 1981-82; head nurse Springfield Hosp. Ctr., Sykesville, Md., 1982-83, backup to nursing div. chief, 1983-84; nursing div. chief Ea. Shore Hosp. Ctr., Cambridge, Md., 1984-87; nursing supr. Great Oaks Ctr., Silver Spring, Md., 1987; community mental health nurse day treatment program Prince George's County Health Dept., Cheverly, Md., 1987-88, community mental health nurse outpatient clinic, 1988-93; ret., 1993. Home: 7355 Hickory Log Cir Columbia MD 21045

ELSON, JANE, social worker, life skills instructor; b. Bklyn., May 29, 1951; d. William Frank and Mary (Cannatella) Gaudino; m. Steven Richard Mauro, Dec. 12, 1970 (div. Mar. 1981); m. Barry Franklin Elson, Sept. 2, 1985; 1 child, Gregory Franklin. AS in Applied Sci., SUNY, Farmingdale, 1980; BA, Adelphi U., 1982, paralegal cert., 1983; M of Social Work, SUNY, Stony Brook, 1987; cert. in Adkins life skills, Columbia U., 1993. Cert., lic. social worker, N.Y. Sec. N.Y. Times, 1983-85; social worker intern North Shore Child and Family Guidance, Roslyn, N.Y., 1985-86, Price Counseling Ctr., Farmingdale, N.Y., 1986-87; social worker Olsten Health Care, Westbury, N.Y., 1992-93; case mgr., counselor Rsch. Found. SUNY, Farmingdale, 1993—. Mem. NASW, AAUW. Democrat. Roman Catholic. Home: 276 Wolf Hill Rd Melville NY 11747 Office: LI Ednl Opportunity Ctr SUNY at Farmingdale 1090A Suffolk Ave Brentwood NY 11717

ELSON, SARAH LEE, art historian; b. Valley Forge, Pa., Oct. 1, 1962; d. John Everett and Ione (Coker) Lee; m. Louis Goodman Elson, Aug. 26, 1989; 1 child, Isabel Coker Elson. BA, Princeton U., 1984; MA, Columbia U., 1990, MPhil in Art History, 1992. Prof. English Beijing Normal U., 1984-85; pub. affairs asst. Guggenheim Mus., N.Y.C., 1985-87; lectr. Met. Mus. Art, N.Y.C., 1990-92; freelance lectr. Nat. Gallery, London, 1994—; rschr. Tate Gallery, London, 1992-93; fellow The Frick Collection, N.Y.C., 1990—; rschr. Met. Mus., 1990-92. Author catalogs. Trustee Coker Coll., Hartsville, S.C., 1991—. Nat. Endowment for Arts fellow, 1988, Pres.'s fellow Columbia U., 1988-90, Luce Travel grantee, 1992. Mem. Woolnoth Soc. in the City of London, Jr. League of London. Democrat. Home: 27 Eaton Terr, London SW1W 8TP, England

ELSON, SUZANNE GOODMAN, community activist; b. Memphis, Oct. 17, 1937; d. Charles F. and Isabel (Ehrlich) Goodman; m. Edward Elliott Elson, Aug. 24, 1957; children: Charles Myer, Louis Goodman, Harry II. Student Randolph-Macon Women's Coll., Lynchburg, Va.; B.A., Agnes Scott Coll., 1959. Sec. Nat. Council Jewish Women, N.Y.C., 1977-79; pres., Nat. Mental Health Assn., 1980-82, pres., 1986-87; trustee, Randolph Macon Woman's Coll., 1986—, Atlanta Historical Soc., 1991—, Am. Federation of Arts, 1992—; chmn. Am. Craft Coun., 1989-92, honorary chmn., 1992—; bd. dirs. Rosalynn Carter Inst., Nat. Coun. Medicine Emory U., 1988—; bd. trustees Project Interconnections, Inc., Atlanta, 1989—, Va. Mus. of Fine Art., 1992—; bd. regents U. System of Ga., 1993—. Home: 65 Valley Rd NW Atlanta GA 30305

ELWELL, CELIA CANDACE, legal assistant; b. Ardmore, Okla., Oct. 12, 1954; d. James B. and Audra Eve (Wolleson) Baxter; m. Phillip B. Elwell, Aug. 11, 1973; 1 child, Christopher Brent. Cert. legal asst., U. Okla., 1986. Clk. Okla. Gas and Electric Co., Oklahoma City, 1973-82; legal sec. various law firms, Oklahoma City, 1982-84; legal asst. Robert Shoemaker, Esq., Oklahoma City, 1984-85; legal asst. to justice Supreme Ct. Okla., Oklahoma City, 1985-87; legal asst. Fellers, Snider, Blankenship, Bailey & Tippens, Oklahoma City, 1987-90, Linn & Helms, Oklahoma City, 1990; legal asst. office of mcpl. counselor City of Oklahoma City, 1990—; adj. instr. U. Okla., Norman, 1986—, adv. com. legal asst. dept. edn. coll. law; mem. approval commn. on-site evaluation team ABA, 1994; lectr. in field. Contbr. articles to profl. jours. Mem. Am. Assn. Paralegal Edn., Cen. Okla. Assn. Legal Assts. (2d v.p. 1989-90, sec. 1988), Nat. Fed. Paralegal Assns., Kans. Legal Assts. Soc. Methodist. Home: 1714 Barb Dr Norman OK 73071-3026 Office: Office Mcpl Counselor 309 Municipal Bldg 200 N Walker Ave Oklahoma City OK 73102-2247

ELY, BETTY JO, school system educational consultant; b. Oakland, Calif., June 28, 1947; d. Levi and Betty (Turner) E.; m. Joseph Dettling, July 15, 1967 (div.); 1 child, Aiyana A. BA, San Diego State U., 1969; postgrad., U. Calif.-San Diego, La Jolla, 1971-74, U. Hawaii, 1973; PhD in Clin. Psychology, Cambridge Grad. Sch. Psychology, L.A., 1991. Cert. tchr., learning handicapped tchr., spl. edn. tchr., Calif. Tchr. Carlsbad (Calif.) Unified Sch. Dist., 1970-74; resource specialist The Learning Ctr., Jackson, Wyo., 1977-78; dir. Carlsbad Montessori Sch., 1979-81; learning handicapped specialist Del Amo Hosp., Torrance, Calif., 1982-87; owner, dir. Ely Edn., San Pedro, Calif., 1983—; resource specialist Torrance Unified Sch. Dist., 1987-92, program specialist, 1992-94; program specialist, coord. spl. edn. Hawthorne Sch. Dist., 1994—; speaker, cons. in field; instr. U. Wyo., Laramie, 1978, Loyola Marymount U., L.A., 1985. Author: Interface, 1987; interviewee TV, radio and profl. publs. Mem. Nat. Abortion Rights Action League. Recipient PTA Hon. Svc. award, 1991. Mem. AAUW, So. Coast Bot. Garden Found., Sierra Club. Democrat. Office: Ely Edn 322 S Miraleste Dr Unit 179 San Pedro CA 90732-3037

ELY, JOANN DENICE, health science facility administrator; b. Bay City, Mich., Dec. 18, 1951; d. Phillip C. Maurer and Elsie (Etherington) McGowan. AS, Eas. Mich. U., 1979; BS in Pharmacy, Mercer U., 1982, PharmD, 1983. Registered Pharmacist, Ga., Fla. Pharmacy intern Drs. Meml. Hosp., Atlanta, 1979-82; pharmacist Egleston Hosp., Atlanta, 1982-84; clin. specialist Lee Meml. Hosp., Ft. Myers, Fla., 1984-90; asst. clin. prof. U. Fla., 1989-90; clin. mgr. Beyer Hosp., Ypsilanti, Mich., 1991—. Lectr. Arthritis Found., Ft. Myers, 1984—. Mem. Am. Soc. Hosp. Pharmacists, So. Gulf Soc. Hosp. Pharmacists (pres. 1988), Fla. Soc. Hosp. Pharmacists, Am. Soc. Parenteral and Enteral Nutrition, Phi Theta Kappa. Republican. Episcopalian. Home: 185 East Shore Dr Whitmore Lake MI 48189

ELY, MARICA MCCANN, interior designer; b. Pachuca, Mex., May 2, 1907 (parents Am. citizens); d. Warner and Mary Evans (Cook) McCann; m. Northcutt Ely, Dec. 2, 1931; children: Michael and Craig (twins), Parry Haines. B.A., U. Calif.-Berkeley, 1929; diploma Pratt Inst. of Art, N.Y.C., 1931. Free-lance interior designer, Washington and Redlands, Calif., 1931—; lectr. on flower arranging and fgn. travel, 1931—; prof. Sogetsu Ikebana Sch., Tokyo, 1972. Art editor (calendar) Nat. Capital Garden Club League, 1957-58. Pres. Kenwood Garden Club, Md.; bd. dirs. Nat. Libr. Blind, Washington; mem. adv. bd. George C. Marshall Home Preservation Fund, Inc. Leesburg, Va.; v.p. bd. dirs. Washington Hearing and Speech Soc., 1969; co-founder Delta Gamma Found. Pre-Sch. Blind Children, Order of Delta Gamma Rose. Finalist Nat. Silver Bowl Competition, Jackson-Perkins Co., 1966; garden shown on nat. tour Am. Hort. Soc., 1985. Mem. Calif. Arboretum Found., Redlands Hort. and Improvement Soc. (bd. dirs. 1982—), Redlands Panhellenic Soc., Redlands Country Club, Chevy Chase Club (D.C.), Delta Gamma.

ELY-RAPHEL, NANCY, diplomat; b. N.Y.C, Feb. 4, 1937; d. Thomas Clarkson and Margaret (Merritt) Halliday; widowed; children: John Duff Ely, Robert Duff Ely, Stephanie Joyce Raphel. AB, Syracuse U., 1957; JD, U. San Diego, 1968. Bar: Calif. 1968, U.S. Supreme Ct. 1976. Dep. city atty. City San Diego, 1969-70; asst. U.S. atty. So. Dist. Calif., 1970-71; assoc. Tyler, Cooper, Grant, Bowerman and Keefe, New Haven, 1971-72; from asst. to assoc. dean Sch. Law Boston U., 1972-75; atty.-advisor U.S. Dept. State, Washington, 1975-77; spl. atty. Boston Strike Force U.S. Dept. Justice, 1977-78; asst. legal advisor African Affairs U.S. Dept. State, Washington, 1978-87, asst. legal advisor Nuclear Affairs, 1988-89; dep. asst. Sec. of State Bur. Democracy, Human Rights and Labor Affairs, Washington, 1989-93; prin. dep. asst. Sec. of State Bureau Human Rights and Humanitarian Affairs, Washington, 1993—. Mem. Council on Fgn. Rels., 1988—, Obor Found., 1988—. Recipient Outstanding Alumni award U. San Diego Law Sch., 1979, Superior Honor award U.S. Dept. State, Washington, 1983, 84, Presdl. Meritorious Svc. award U.S. Govt., Washington, 1986, 94, Presdl. Disting. Svc. award, 1992. Home: 1304 30th St NW Washington DC 20007 Office: Dept of State Human Rights 2201 C Street NW Washington DC 20520

EMANUEL, GLORIA PAGE, counselor, social studies educator; b. Dallas, Apr. 5, 1947; d. Daniel and Leola (Green) Page; m. Lawrence Ray Emanuel, Oct. 2, 1971; children—Lawrence Ray, Jr., Kevin Lawrence. B.S., E. Tex. State U., 1970; student Paul Quinn Coll., 1966-67; M.Ed., Prairie View A & M U., 1975. Cert. tchr., profl. counselor, Tex. Tchr. social studies Waco High Sch., Tex., 1971-82; University Middle Sch., Waco, 1982—, chairperson social studies, block leader, 1985-92; assn. rep. UMS, 1985-93, Adopt-a-Sch. coord., 1992—; mem. Campus Action Com., 1985, Campus Adv. Coun., 1990-91, Supt. Adv. Coun. for Social Studies, 1991-92. Mem. Central Tex. Minister Wives, Waco-Temple Dist., 1971—, asst. sec. area II Waco-Temple Missionary Soc.; mem. sr. choir Wayman Chapel A.M.E. Ch., Temple, Tex., 1983—, tchr. Sunday sch., local supr. E.C.B. Lequey Missionary Soc.; historiographer Gloria Emanuel Unit, Temple, 1985—; mem. Anderson Chapel AME Ch., Killeen, Hamilton Maijang Missionary Soc.; active Parent Student Tchr. Assn. Mem. ASCD, NEA, Nat. Coun. for Social Studies Tchrs., Heart of Tex. Counselors Assn. (cert 1984), Waco Classroom Tchrs. (faculty rep. 1973-74), Tex. State Tchrs. Assn., Nat. Assn. Female Execs. (cert. 1984), Sigma Gamma Rho. Lodge: Order of Eastern Star. Avocations: photography; reading; travel. Home: 2024 King Cole Dr Waco TX 76705-2749

EMANUEL, YVONNE CAROL, government agency administrator; b. Burtonwood, U.K., Nov. 10, 1952; d. Richard Oneal and Ora Helen (Vaughn) E. BA in Modern Langs., Angelo State U., 1973; MPA, U. Okla., 1989. Cert. secondary tchr., Tex. Claims rep. Social Security Adminstrn., Tyler and San Angelo, Tex., 1973-77; ops. supr. Social Security Adminstrn., Ft. Worth, 1977-80; asst. dist. mgr. Social Security Adminstrn., Ardmore, Okla., 1980-87; pub. affairs officer Social Security Adminstrn., Dallas, 1987—. Author: Juneteenth, A Celebration of Freedom, 1994. Bd. dirs. Gloria Ainsworth Day Care Ctr., Ardmore, Okla., 1984-87, South Dallas Remembered, 1993-94; charter mem. Nat. Women of Achievement, Ft. Worth, 1984. Mem. NAFE, Nat. Assn. Negro Bus. and Profl. Women's Club (dist. corr. sec., pub. rels. dir. South Ctrl. dist. 1992—, Leadership award Tex. 1979).

EMBLETON, MARY ELLEN, economist, consultant; b. Seattle, July 9, 1959; d. Maurice Lease and Mary Isabell (Chesney) E. BS Polit. Economy of Natural Resources, U. Calif., Berkeley, 1982; MS in Applied Econs., Mont. State U., Bozeman, 1987. Rsch. assoc. Mont. State U., Bozeman, 1985-87, adj. instr. econs., 1987-89; rsch. assoc. Found. for Rsch. on Econs. and the Environment, Bozeman, 1989; assoc. Huckell/Weinman Assocs., Seattle, 1990—. Contbg. author: (guidebook) Water Quality Swales, 1991; contbg. editor, author: Economics and Mineral Planning, 1984; author: (leaflet) Does Montana Need a Dam Safety Program?, 1984. Mem. Assn. Environ. and Resource Econs., Seattle Assn. Women Econs., Seattle Econs. Club, Phi Beta Kappa. Office: Huckell/Weinman Assocs Inc 205 Lake St S Ste 202 Kirkland WA 98033-6457

EMCH-DÉRIAZ, ANTOINETTE SUZANNE, historian; b. Geneva, Nov. 9, 1935; came to U.S., 1964; d. Louis Georges and Renée Gabrielle (Bonnet) Dériaz; m. Gérard Gustav Emch, July 25, 1959; children: Florence Christiane, René-Didier Guillaume. PhD, U. Rochester, N.Y., 1984. Tech. asst. Am. Inst. of Physics, N.Y.C., 1968-70; vis. scholar U. Pa., Phila., 1981; rsch. assoc. U. Rochester, 1984; asst. prof. U. Miss., Oxford, 1985-92; mem. adj. faculty U. Fla., Gainesville, 1992—; vis. scholar U. Goettingen, Germany, 1985, Wellcome Inst., London, 1994. Author: 18th Century Concept of Health, 1984, Tissot: Physician of the Enlightenment, 1992, (chpt.) L'éveil Medical Vaudois, 1987, The Popularization of Medicine, 1992; contbr. articles to profl. jours. Mem. AAUW, Am. Hist. Assn., Am. Assn. for History Medicine, Am. Soc. 18th-Century Studies, So. Hist. Assn. Presbyterian. Office: U Fla Gainesville FL 32611

EMEK, SHARON HELENE, business insurance and risk management specialist; b. Bklyn., Oct. 23, 1945; d. Hyman Sampson and Cynthia Gertrude (Roth) Rabinowitz; children: Aleeza Judith, Joshua Michael, Elana Yael. B.A., CCNY, 1967; M.A., Bklyn. Coll., 1970; Ed.D., Rutgers U., 1977; cert. ins. counselor. Dir. preliminary program for small coll. Bklyn. Coll., 1969-71, 73-74; dir. Am. Ctr. Reading Skills, Tel Aviv, 1972; asst. prof. Brookdale Community Coll., Lincroft, N.J., 1975-77, Rutgers U., New Brunswick, N.J., 1977-82; pres. The Emek Group, Inc., N.Y.C., 1980—; speaker profl. meetings. Author: Answers For Managers, 1986; Dealing Successfully with Key Management Issues, 1986. Contbr. articles to profl. jours. Recipient Promising Research award Nat. Council Tchrs. of English, 1978. Mem. Profl. Ins. Agents Assn., Ind. Ins. Agents Assn. Avocations: writing; reading; jogging; tennis; travel. Office: The Emek Group Inc 111 John St New York NY 10038

EMERSON, ALICE FREY, political scientist, educator emerita; b. Durham, N.C., Oct. 26, 1931; d. Alexander Hamilton and Alice (Hubbard) Frey; divorced; children: Rebecca, Peter. AB, Vassar Coll., 1953; PhD, Bryn Mawr Coll., 1964; LLD (hon.), Wheaton Coll., 1986; DHL (hon.), Trinity Coll., 1992. Tchr., Newton (Mass.) High Sch., 1956-58; mem. faculty Bryn Mawr (Pa.) Coll., 1961-64; mem. faculty U. Pa., Phila., 1966-75, asst. prof. polit. sci., 1966-75, dean of women, 1966-69, dean of students, 1969-75; pres. Wheaton Coll., Norton, Mass., 1975-91, pres. emerita, 1991—; sr. fellow Andrew Mellon Found., N.Y.C., 1991—; bd. dirs. AES Corp., Bank of Boston Corp., First Nat. Bank Boston, Champion Internat. Paper, Eastman Kodak Co.; trustee Penn Mut. Life Ins. Co., 1977-92; adv. bd. HERS Mid-Am. Bd. dirs. Corp. for Pub. and Pvt. Ventures, World Resources Inst., Salzburg Seminar, Wolf Trap Found. for Performing Arts. Mem. Coun. on Fgn. Rels. Home: 353 E 72nd St # 10A New York NY 10021 Office: Andrew W Mellon Found 140 E 62d St New York NY 10021

EMERSON, ANDI (MRS. ANDI EMERSON WEEKS), sales and advertising executive; b. N.Y.C., Nov. 1, 1932; d. Willard Ingham and Ethel (Mole) E.; m. George G. Fawcett, Jr. (div.); children—Ann Emerson II, George Gifford III, Christopher Babcock; m. Kenneth E. Weeks (div.); 1 child, Electra Ingham. Student, Barnard Coll. Successively v.p. Eugene Stevens, Inc., N.Y.C.; pres., dir. Emerson Mktg. Agy., Inc., N.Y.C., 1960—; pres., dir. Mail Order Operating Co. Ltd., N.Y.C. and London, 1976-88, Ingham Hall, Ltd., 1977-83; chmn. bd. dirs. Sonal World Mktg. Ltd., N.Y.C. and Delhi, India, 1983-87; instr. NYU, 1960-65, 87—. Vol. children's ward Meml. Hosp., 1964-66, Hosp. for Spl. Surgery, 1967; mem. adv. com. African Students League, 1965-67; bd. dirs. Violet Oakley Meml. Found., Phila., 1964-81; founder, pres., chmn. John Caples Internat. Awards, 1977—; elected N.Y. State Del. to White House Conf. on Small Bus., 1986. Inducted into Silver Apple Hall of Fame, 1985. Mem. Nat. Assn. Women Bus. Owners, Direct Mktg. Assn. (Hall of Fame selection comn. 1989-91), Soc. Profl. Writers, Direct Mktg. Creative Guild (Andi Emerson award 1991, pres. 1975-81, bd. dirs. 1975-93), Direct Mktg. Club of N.Y. (treas. 1960-61). Home: 16 E 96th St New York NY 10128-0753 Office: Emerson Mktg Agy Inc 145 W 28th St Ste 1102 New York NY 10001

EMERSON, ANN PARKER, dietician, educator; b. Twin Lakes, Fla., Dec. 3, 1925; d. Charles Dendy and Gladys Agnes (Chalker) Parker; B.S., Fla. State U., 1947; M.S., U. Fla., 1968; m. Donald McGeachy Emerson, Sept. 22, 1950; children—Mary Ann, Donald McGeachy, Charles Parker, William John. Research dietitian U. Chgo., 1948-50; adminstrv. research dietitian U. Fla. Coll. Medicine, Gainesville, 1962-68, dir. dietetic edn., 1968-74, dir. dietetic internship program, 1968-75, dir. program in clin. and community dietetics, 1974-83; mem. Commn. on Dietetic Registration, 1974-77, Commn. on Accreditation, 1980-83. Pres., Gainesville chpt. Altrusa, Internat., 1977-78. VA Allied Health Manpower grantee, 1974-81; HEW Allied Health Manpower grantee, 1975-78, 78-81. Mem. Am., Fla. Dietetic Assns. Republican. Roman Catholic. Clubs: Jr. League, Altrusa.

EMERSON, ANNE DEVEREUX, university administrator; b. Boston, Oct. 6, 1946; d. Kendall and Margaret (Drew) E.; (div. 1980); children: Josephine, Hannah; m. Peter Alexander Altman, 1992. BA magna cum laude, Brown U., 1968; MA, Fletcher Sch. Law and Diplomacy, Tufts U., 1969; MBA, Boston U., 1990. Asst. to dir. Pathfinder Fund, Brookline, Mass., 1970-71; asst. to dir tech.adaptation project MIT, Cambridge, Mass., 1971-73; exec. asst. to v.p. adminstrn. Boston U., 1977-85, dir. adminstrn., program devel., 1985-88; exec. dir. Ctr. for Internat. Affairs Harvard U., Cambridge, 1988—; cons. State Legis. Leaders Found., Boston, 1984-87. Panelist NEH, 1987; bd. dirs. Integrated Foster Care, Cambridge, 1985-89; trustee Winsor Sch., 1989-91; bd. dirs. World Affairs Coun., Boston. Mem. Phi Beta Kappa. Home: 200 Pond St Jamaica Plain MA 02130-2723 Office: Harvard U Ctr for Internat Affairs 1737 Cambridge St Cambridge MA 02138-3016

EMERSON, SUSAN, oil company executive; b. Bryan, Tex., Nov. 2, 1947; d. Joseph Nathanialand Lorraine Parks; m. John S. Emerson, June 5, 1970 (div. 1984); children: John H., Christopher P.; m. Gerald W. Parker, May 4, 1985. Owner Emerson Ins. Agy., San Antonio, 1970-84, Emerson Oil Co., San Antonio, 1970—; bd. dirs. Washington Hosp. Ctr. Mem. Washington Hosp. Ctr. Women's Aux., 1988—; mem. D.C. Rep. Com., 1991—, alt. del. Rep. Nat. Conv., Washington, 1992, 4th ward committeewoman, 1992; commr. Adv. Neighborhood Commn., Washington, 1990—; 2d v.p. 4D Commn., Washington, 1990—; founder Boarder Baby Project, 1991—; Rep. candidate for D.C. del. to Congress, 1992. Recipient Sr. Adv. Silver Fox award Wash. Hosp. Women's Aux., 1989, Vol. award, 1990. Mem. LWV, D.C. Hosp. Assn. (trustee 1989), Am. Hosp. Assn. (D.C. del. 1990-92), Vis. Nurses Assn. (bioethic com. 1991—), League Rep. Women, Tex. Breakfast

Club. Lutheran. Address: USSAH 497 3700 N Capitol St NW Washington DC 20317-9998

EMERY, CECILIA RUTH, learning disability educator; b. Prague, Okla., Sept. 11, 1950; d. Francis Riley and Minnie (Sekera) E. AS, St. Gregory Coll., 1970; BEd, East Ctrl. State U., 1972, M i Learning Disabilities, 1976, M in Counseling Psychology, 1981. Cert. elem. tchr., learning disabilities tchr., emotional distrubance, sch. psychologist, sch. psychometrist. Elem. tchr. Prague (Okla.) Pub. Schs., 1972-75, learning disability tchr., 1975-78, 85—; sch. psychometrist State of Dept., Oklahoma City, 1978-79; ednl. coord. Boley (Okla.) Sch. for Boys, 1979-81, 81-83; psychol. asst. Dept. of Corrections, Boley, 1983-85. Mem. North Ctrl. Edn. Accrediation Team, 1990, 93. Mem. NEA, Okla. Edn. Assn., Learning Disability Assn. Home: RR 2 Box 129A Prague OK 74864-9537

EMERY, NANCY BETH, lawyer; b. Shawnee, Okla., July 9, 1952; d. Paul Dodd Finefrock and Kathryn Jo (Saling) Hutchens; m. Lee Monroe Emery, May 18, 1974. BA with highest honors, U. Okla., 1974; JD, Harvard U., 1977. Bar: Okla. 1977, D.C. 1981. Atty. advisor Office Gen. Counsel, U.S. Dept. Agri., Washington, 1977-79; legal adv. to Fed. Energy Regulatory Commr. Matthew Holden, Jr., Washington, 1979-81; assoc. firm Pierson, Ball & Dowd, and predecessor Sullivan & Beauregard, Washington, 1981-83, Paul Hastings, Janofsky & Walker, Washington, 1983-87, ptnr., 1987-93; ptnr. Sutherland, Asbill & Brennan, Washington, 1993—. Bd. dirs., sec. Park Place Condominium Assn., Inc., Washington, 1982-84; page Continental Congress, DAR, 1978-82, chpt. del. Continental Congress, 1981, 84. Mem. ABA (natural resources energy & environ. law sect., bd. editors Natural Resources & Environ.), Fed. Energy Bar Assn., Soc. Profl. Journalists, Mortar Bd., Phi Beta Kappa. Democrat. Office: Sutherland Asbill & Brennan 1275 Pennsylvania Ave NW Washington DC 20004-2404

EMERY, RITA DOROTHY, physical education educator; b. Berkeley, Calif., Sept. 21, 1939; d. Byron Elden and Charlotte Antoinette (Siwinski) E. AA, Contra Costa Coll., 1960; BA, Chico State Coll., 1963; MA, Wash. State U., 1977. Cert. tchr., Calif. Instr. phys. edn., coach Churchill County High Sch., Fallon, Nev., 1963-65; instr. phys. edn., coach, dept. chair Lower Lake (Calif.) High Sch., 1967-76; coach women's volleyball Contra Costa Coll., San Pablo, Calif., 1977; coach women's softball Oreg. State U., Corvallis, 1977-80; instr. phys. edn., coach, athletic dir. St. Leonard Sch., Fremont, Calif., 1985-89; instr. phys. edn. Campbell (Calif.) Unified Sch. Dist., 1989-90; elem. phys. edn. specialist, coach Vacaville (Calif.) Unified Sch. Dist., 1990-95; dir. jr. programming Club Sport of Pleasant, Calif., 1995—; intramural dir. Contra Costa Coll., 1957-60; coach, coord. recreation Holy Spirit Ch., Fremont, 1980-85; instr. youth sports Fremont Leisure Svcs., 1988-90, teen youth coord., 1988-93; girls basketball coach Wood High Sch., Vacaville, 1993-95. Speaker Alameda County chpt. Am. Heart Assn., 1983-90; vol. coach, officer, ofcl. Fremont Little League, 1983-86; vol. Hall of Health/Kids Safe Program, Berkeley, Calif., 1990—. Named Vol. of Yr. Am. Heart Assn., 1986, 88. Mem. AAHPERD (adv. com. for devel. of athletic tng. coun.), Calif. Assn. Health, Phys. Edn., Recreation and Dance. Office: Club Sport of Pleasant 7090 Johnson Dr Pleasanton CA 94588

EMERY, SUSAN WOODRUFF, investment trust official; b. Salt Lake City, Jan. 13, 1923; d. Russell Kimball and Margaret Anglin (McIntyre) Woodruff; m. Terrence John Osborn, May 30, 1959 (div. Dec. 1963); 1 child, John Russell; m. Stephen Earnest Emery, Apr. 7, 1972 (dec. Apr. 1977). BA, U. Utah, 1944. Cashier Merrill Lynch, Pierce, Fenner & Beane, Portland, 1946-51; personal sec. to parents, Portland, 1951-71; co-trustee R.K.-M.M. Woodruff Trust, Portland, 1971—. Vol. driver ARC, Portland, 35 yrs.; mem. Rep. Nat. Com., 1944—, Oreg. Rep. Com., 1944—. Mem. AAUW (life), U. Utah Alumni Assn. (life), Univ. Club, Alpha Delta Pi. Episcopalian. Home and Office: Garden Apt 10 255 SW Harrison St Portland OR 97201

EMERY, VIRGINIA OLGA BEATTIE, psychologist, researcher; b. Cleve., Apr. 9, 1938; d. Joseph P. and Antoinette Pauline (Misja) Kennick; m. Paul Hamilton Beattie Sr., 1960 (div. 1975); children: Tamsan Beattie Tharin, Paul Hamilton Beattie Jr.; m. Paul E. Emery, 1979. BA, U. Chgo., 1962, PhD, 1982; MA, Ind. U., 1973. Lic. psychologist, N.H., Ohio. Adj., clin. asst. prof. psychiatry Dartmouth Med. Sch., Lebanon, N.H., 1983-85; asst. prof. psychology Case Western Res. U., Cleve., 1986-89, asst. clin. prof. psychiatry, 1986-89; sr. faculty assoc. Ctr. on Aging and Health, 1986-89; clin. assoc. prof. psychiatry Dartmouth Med. Sch., Lebanon, N.H., 1989—; dir. Ctr. on Aging, Health and Soc., Concord and Hanover, N.H., 1989—; mem. com. human devel. NIMH, Adult Devel. & Aging Traineeship, U. Chgo., 1974-76; sub-project dir. Case Western Res. U. Sch. Medicine, 1986-90; sec. women's faculty assn. Case Western Res. U., 1987-89; cons. Vets. Affairs Med. Ctr., Manchester, N.H., 1989—; sub-project dir. NIMH Mental Health Clin. Rsch. Ctr. Grant, Case Western Res. U. Sch. Medicine, 1986-90; mem. Dartmouth Coll. and Dartmouth Med. Sch. Neurosci. Group, 1990—. Author: Language and Aging, 1985, Pseudodementia: A Theoretical and Empirical Discussion, 1988; editor: Dementia: Presentations, Differential Diagnosis, and Nosology, 1994; contbr. articles to profl. jours. Bd. dirs., pres. Frontiers of Knowledge Civic Trust, Concord, N.H., 1990—. Recipient Adult Devel. and Aging grant/traineeship NIH/NIMH, 1974-76, Rsch. prize Am. Aging Assn., 1983, Havighurst prize for aging rsch. U. Chgo., 1984; named Frontiers of Knowledge Atlee Zellers lectr., 1994; rsch. grantee Western Res. Coll., 1986-87, NIMH Mental Health Clin. rsch. grantee, 1986-89. Fellow N.H. Psychol. Assn. (bd. dirs. 1991-93, chair com. acad. rsch. interests 1992-94, sec. 1994—), Riggs Disting. Contbn. award 1991); mem. AAAS, APA (student rsch. award 1984), AAUW, Internat. Psychiat. Rsch. Soc., Internat. Psychogeriatric Assn., Gerontol. Soc. Am. (disting. creative contbn. award behavioral and social sci. sect. 1989), Boston Soc. Gerontol. Psychiatry, Acad. Psychosomatic Medicine, N.Y. Acad. Scis. Home: 15 Buckingham Dr Bow NH 03304-5207 Office: Dept Psychiatry Box HB 7750 Dartmouth Med Sch Lebanon NH 03756

EMMER, BARBARA LOUISE, librarian, consultant; b. Charleroi, Pa., Apr. 11, 1947; d. William John and Helen Martha (Radzik) E. BS in Edn., Clarion U. Pa., 1969, cert. advanced studies, 1989; MLS, U. Pitts., 1978. Libr. dir. Pa. State U., DuBois, 1984-89; libr. Ridgway (Pa.) Area Sch. Dist., 1969-84, Brockway (Pa.) Area Sch. Dist., 1989—; sec. Riverview Libr. Consortium, Shippenville, Pa., 1990-93; reviewer, cons. Choice 1985-89. Pres. Friends of the Libr., DuBois, 1989-91; mem. hosp. aux. DuBois Regional Med. Ctr., 1985—. Mem. AAUW (bd. dirs. 1979—, legis. chair 1990—, Woman of Yr. 1991), NEA, ALA (chair off-campus libr. svcs. 1988-89), Pa. State Edn. Assn., Pa. Sch. Librs. Assn., Brockway Area Edn. Assn. (sec. 1991-93), DuBois Area Coun. on the Arts, DuBois Hist. Soc. (print libr. and property com. 1994—), Delta Kappa Gamma Soc. Internat. Home: 526 1st St Du Bois PA 15801-3059 Office: Brockway Schs 100 Alexander St Brockway PA 15824-1097

EMMERICH, KAROL DENISE, former retail company executive, consultant; b. St. Louis, Nov. 21, 1948; d. George Robert and Dorothy (May) Van Houten; m. Richard James, Oct. 18, 1969; 1 son, James Andrew. B.A., Northwestern U., 1969; M.B.A., Stanford U., 1971. Nat. div. account officer Bank of Am., San Francisco, 1971-72; fin. analyst Dayton Hudson Corp., Mpls., 1972-73; sr. fin. analyst Dayton Hudson Corp., 1973-74, mgr. short term financing, 1974-76, asst. treas., 1976-79, treas., 1979—, v.p., 1980-93; exec. fellow U. St. Thomas Grad. Sch. Bus., 1993—; mem. corp. bd. Met. Fin. Corp., Piper Funds Inc., Hercules Funds, Slumberland. Mem. nat. adv. coun. Ctr. for Applied Christian Ethics, Wheaton Coll.; bd. dirs. Women's Opportunity Fund, Minn. Hemerocallis Soc. Mem. Minn. Women's Econ. Roundtable, Minn. Women's Forum, Internat. Women's Forum, Mpls. Club. Home: 7302 Claredon Dr Edina MN 55439-1722

EMMERT, ROBERTA RITA, health facility administrator; b. Buffalo, Aug. 28, 1953; d. Robert George and Rita Rose (Lambert) E. Diploma, St. Elizabeth Hosp. Sch. Nsg., 1974; BSN magna cum laude, SUNY, Utica, 1989; MS, Syracuse U., 1993, postgrad., 1993—. RN, N.Y., Calif. Charge nurse, staff nurse pediatrics and spl. care pediatric St Joseph Hosp. Health Ctr., Syracuse, N.Y., adminstrv. supr., nurse educator; instr. Am. Heart Assn. Mem. ANA (cert. pediat. nurse), NAFE, Am. Orgn. Nurse Execs., N.Y. State Nurses Assn., Soc. Pediat. Nurses, Sigma Theta Tau. Home: 4750 Woodard Way Apt 9K Liverpool NY 13088-4630

EMMONS, JOANNE, state senator; b. Big Rapids, Mich., Feb. 8, 1934; d. Ray J. and Emma M. (Von Glahn) Gregory; m. John Francis Emmons, June 9, 1956; children: Sarah, Dorothy. BS, Mich. State U., 1956; degree in pub. svc. (hon.), Ferris State U., 1992. Tchr. Mecosta (Mich.) High Sch., 1956-58; treas. Big Rapids Twp., 1976-86; state rep. State of Mich., Lansing, 1987-91, state senator, 1991—. Chair Mecosta County Rep. Com., 1976-80; vice chair 10th dist. Rep. Com., 1984-86; bd. dirs. Luth. Child and Family Svcs., 1990—. Named Nat. Rep. Legislator of Yr., Nat. Assn. State Legislators, 1993, Legislator of Yr., Mich. Twp. Assn., 1993. Mem. Am. Legion Aux., Mich. Farm Bur. (legis. com. 1970—), Omicron Delta Kappa. Home: 13904 Northland Dr Big Rapids MI 49307-9475 Office: Mich State Senate State Capitol Lansing MI 48909

EMPERADO, MERCEDES LOPEZ, librarian; b. Manila, Aug. 9, 1941; came to U.S., 1969; d. Evaristo Villasor and Marina (Gallardo) Lopez; m. Conrado Emperado, June 30, 1968; children: Joshua Caleb, Marita Eve. BS in Elem. Edn., Philippine Normal Coll., 1963; MLS, Cath. U. Am., 1974. Libr. math. and computation lab. Fed. Preparedness Agy., Washington, 1976-79; libr. Fed. Emergency Mgmt. Agy., Washington, 1979—. Mem. ALA, Spl. Librs. Assn. Baptist. Home: 6303 Elm Way Clinton MD 20735-3928 Office: Fed Emergency Mgmt Agy Libr 500 C St SW Washington DC 20472-0002

EMPSON, CHERYL DIANE, validation engineer; b. Wichita, Kans., Jan. 13, 1962; d. Charles Lee Empson and Luella Lorajean (Peterson) Eshelman. BS in Chem. Engring., U. Mo., 1984; MBA, Baker U., 1992. Mem. tech. svcs. staff Genentech, South San Francisco, Calif., 1984-86; rsch. asst. Sanoti Animal Health, Lenexa, Kans., 1989-90; process devel. engr. Pfizer Animal Health, Lee's Summit, Mo., 1990-93; sr. qualification validation specialist Triad Techs., Inc., New Castle, Del., 1993-94; validation specialist Warner-Lambert, Lititz, Pa., 1994—. Ct. appointed children's advocate, Jackson County, Kansas City, Mo., 1992. Monsanto fellow, Columbia, 1986; Mag. fellow U. Mo., Kansas City, 1988. Mem. Internat. Soc. Pharm. Engrs. Office: Warner-Lambert 400 W Lincoln Ave Lititz PA 17543

EMPSON, CYNTHIA SUE, state legislator, retail executive, nurse; b. Mpls., May 29, 1947; d. Charles and Mary Jane (Levernier) Wiersch; m. Charles Lee Empson, Oct. 8, 1970; children—Stacey Renee, Stepanie Lea. R.N., Mastin Sch. Nursing, Mobile, Ala., 1968. R.N. Charge nurse Research Hosp., Kansas Cit, Mo., 1968-70; nurse Raytown Clinic, Mo., 1970-72; mgr./buyer Mardee's Clothing Store, Independence, Kns., 1982-83, owner/buyer, 1983—; office nurse, Independence, 1972—; mem. Kans. Ho. of Reps. Mem. Riley PTA, Independence, 1974-82, pres., 1976-77; pres. PTA City Council, 1979-80; active Neewollah, Inc., Independence, 1975-82; chair comml. div. drive Community Chest, 1982, bd. dirs., 1984—; city chmn. Mental Health Fund Dr., 1979; mem. bd. Unified Sch. Dist. 446, 1983-84, pres., 1984—; bd. dirs. Tri County Spl. Edn. Coop., Independence, 1981—, v.p., 1982-83, pres., 1983—; mem. SEK Med. Aux., 1975—, pres., 1979-80; mem. SEK Lutherans Assn. Republican. Club: PEO (Independence). Avocations: tennis; reading. Home: PO Box 848 Independence KS 67301-0848 Office: Kans Ho of Reps State Capitol Topeka KS 66612*

ENCARNACION, ANA ALICIA, customs inspector; b. Christiansted, St. Croix, V.I., July 1, 1962; d. Luis and Saturnila (Encarnacion) E. BSBA, Barbera-Scotia Coll., 1984. Mgr. Computer Logistics, St. Croix, 1985-87; sr. insp. U.S. Customs, Miami, Fla., 1987—. Office: US Customs Svc 1500 Port Blvd Miami FL 33132

ENDERS, ELIZABETH MCGUIRE, artist; b. New London, Conn., Feb. 18, 1939; d. Francis Foran and Helen Cuseck (Connolly) McGuire; m. Anthony Talcott Enders, June 9, 1962; children: Charles Talcott, Alexandra Eustis, Camilla, Ostrom II. BA, Conn. Coll., 1962; MA, NYU, 1987. Trustee Artists Space, N.Y.C., 1986—, Conn. Coll., New London, 1988-93; assoc. dept. prints and illustrated books Mus. Modern Art, 1993, Lyman Allyn Art Mus., 1994. One woman shows include Paul Schuster Gallery, Cambridge, Mass., 1966, Ulysses Gallery, N.Y.C., 1992, 94, Lyman Allyn Art Mus., New London, Conn., 1994; exhibited in group shows at Boston Symphony Orch., 1982, NYU, 1983, Conn. Conn., 1988, Bronx Coun. on Arts, 1990-91, Addison Gallery Am. Art, 1993, Angel Art, L.A., 1993, Lyman Allyn Art Mus., New London, Conn., 1994-95, Southern Alleghenies Mus. Art, Loretto, Pa., 1994, Artists Space Multiple, 1995; traveling group show Artists Space, 1992, 94, Southeastern Ctr. Contemporary Art, Winston-Salem, N.C., 1993, Allentown (Pa.) Art Mus., 1994, Cleve. Ctr. Contemporary Art, 1994; represented in permanent collections at Addison Gallery of Am. Art, Andover, Mass., Graham Gund, Cambridge, Daimler Benz Holding Co., Lyman Allyn Art Mus. Mem. nat. fin. coun. Dem. Nat. Com., Washington, 1988—. Recipient Citation of Appreciation, Conn. Coll., 1990, medal, 1993. Mem. The Drawing Soc., The Bklyn. Mus., Williams Coll. Mus. of Art, Mus. Modern Art (assoc.), Williams Club. Democrat. Roman Catholic. Home: 530 E 86th St New York NY 10028-7535

ENDERS, PAMELA LYNN, clinical psychologist, educator; b. Milw., May 15, 1949; d. Ralph L. and Marian E. (Price) E.; m. Robert L. Weber, May 31, 1980. BA, U. Wis., Milw., 1976; MA, Temple U., 1979, PhD, 1981. Lic. psychologist, health svc. provider, Mass. Psychologist Spaulding Rehab. Hosp., Boston, 1980-83; psychology fellow Mass. Gen. Hosp., Boston, 1983-85, assoc. in psychology, 1985—, dir. Ctr. for Therapy and Study of Women, 1991-94; dir. assoc. clin. fellow program Boston Inst. for Psychotherapy, 1989-91; clin. instr. Harvard Med. Sch., Boston, 1985—. Chmn. joint com. on status of women Harvard Med. Sch., 1991-92. Mem. APA, Am. Group Psychotherapy Assn., Mass. Psychol. Assn., Northeastern Soc. for Group Psychotherapy. Office: 385 Broadway Cambridge MA 02139-1602

ENDLICH, LEATRICE ANN, therapist; b. Topeka, Aug. 27, 1928; d. Harry and Roselle (Dauer) E.; m. Howard L. Swartzman, June 27, 1950 (div. Aug. 1984); children: Susan Swartzman Freeman, Steven Swartzman, Julie Swartzman Krop. BA, Mills Coll., 1950; MSW, U. Kans., 1963. Social worker Jewish Family and Children's Services, Kansas City, Mo., 1968-73, dir. family life edn., 1973-77; pvt. practice clin. social work Prairie Village, 1977-78; teaching assoc. dept. child psychiatry U. Kans. Med. Ctr., Kansas City, 1978-84; day treatment therapist Gillis Ctr., Kansas City, 1984-86; pvt. practice, 1986-88; dir. client svcs. Good Samaritan Project, Kansas City, 1988-94, ret., 1994; past bd. dirs. Crittenden Ctr., Kansas City. Mem. adv. com. Kans. Behavioral Scis. Regulatory Bd., 1983; mem. Menorah Med. Ctr. Aux. (life), Kansas City, Friends of Art, Kansas City, Lyric Opera Guild, Kansas City, William Jewell Coll. Fine Arts Guild; trustee Conservatory Music, Kansas City, 1988-92; mem. adv. bd. Johnson County Nursing Ctr., 1988—; bd. dirs. Jewish Family and Children Svcs., 1988-92; mem. nat. com. HIV-AIDS, Union of Am. Hebrew Congregations, 1993—. Named Kans. Social Worker of Yr. Mokan Unit of Nat. Assn. Social Workers, 1992. Mem. Nat. Assn. Social Workers, Acad. Cert. Social Workers (cert.), Nat. Coun. Jewish Women (life mem. Mo. chpt.). Democrat. Home: 12239 Ash St Shawnee Mission KS 66209-3513

ENDRASKE, MARILYN JOANN, financial administrator; b. St. Charles, Mo., Feb. 24, 1947; d. Joseph Matthew and Rose Lea (Martinek) Podhorsky; m. Stanley Joseph Endraske, Feb. 24, 1968; children: Stanley J., Jeffrey L., Jaclyn R., Matthew B. BS, Lindenwood Coll., 1983. Lead key punch operator data entry dept. AT&T, St. Louis, 1970-77, assignment coord. data entry dept., 1977-80, computer equip. operator data entry dept., 1980-83, fin. analyst fin. dept., 1983, acct. forecaster fin. dept., 1983-84, acct. analyst billing dept., 1984-85, collection assoc., 1985-88; credit specialist AT&T, Atlanta, 1988-89, asst. mgr. accounts receivable, 1989—. Leader Girl Scouts of U.S., St. Louis, 1969-87, Atlanta, 1987-89; cons. Jr. Achievement, St. Louis, 1986-88; chairperson Hug-A-Bear program. Mem. NAFE, Female Exec. of N. Am., Nat. Assn. Credit Mgmt., Telephone Pioneers.

ENDRESS, PATRICIA KATHLEEN, physician; b. Detroit, Nov. 20, 1957; d. Richard Fredrick and Kathleen Charlotte (Riley) E.; m. Samuel James Congello, Oct. 8, 1988; 1 child, Joshua Patrick Congello. BA, Albion Coll., 1980; D of Osteopathy, Coll. Osteopathic Medicine, Kirksville, Mo., 1985. Diplomate Am. Bd. Osteopathic Family Practice. Intern Garden City (Mich.) Osteopathic Hosp., 1985-86; resident Cmty. Gen. Osteopathic Hosp., Harrisburg, Pa., 1986-87; staff physician Woodbourne Med. Group, Levitown, Pa., 1986-87, The Bryn (Pa.) Mawr Hosp., 1987-88; staff physician, med. dir. Marion Health Care Hosp., Fairmont, W.Va., 1988-91; staff physician Mercy Family Care, Sheffield, Iowa, 1991—, Dumont, Iowa, 1991—; med. dir. Sheffield Care Ctr., Sheffield, 1991—; staff physician Lake Mills, Iowa, 1994—. Mem. Am. Osteopaths Assn., Am. Coll. Osteopathic Family Practice, Iowa Osteopathic Assn. (sec.-treas. 1992—), Mason City Women's Club. Republican. Episcopalian. Home: 10 Bur Oak Ln Mason City IA 50401-1400

ENDSLEY, JANE R., nursing educator; b. Harrisburg, Ill., Oct. 14, 1942; d. Clifford B. Bond and Haroldene (Malone) Miller; d. William R. Endsley. Grad., Deaconess Hosp. Sch. Nursing, Evansville, Ind., 1963; student, So. Ill. U., 1968; BSN cum laude, U. Evansville, 1978. RN, Ind., Ill. Staff nurse Deaconess Hosp., 1963-64; psychiat. nurse med.-surg. emergency room and obstetrics Ferrell Hosp., Eldorado, Ill., 1964-68, DON, 1969-70; DON, Good Shepherd Nursing Home, Eldorado, 1971-72; instr. nursing Southeastern Ill. U., Harrisburg, 1973—; cons. parents too soon Egyptian Pub. Health Dept., Eldorado, 1985. Vice chmn. Pvt. Industry Coun., Harrisburg, 1983-91; precinct committeeperson Harrisburg Dem. Com., 1986-90; donor chmn. ARC, Harrisburg, 1970—; instr. CPR to civic orgns. and students, 1980-87. Mem. AAUW, Ill. Nurses Assn. (nominating com. 1975), Southeasterrn Ill. Coll. Edn. Assn. (pres. 1988-91), Faculty Wives and Women Southeastern Ill. Coll. (sec.-treas. 1974-75), Sigma Theta Tau. Home: PO Box 345 1075 Shawnee Hills Rd Harrisburg IL 62946-4943

ENG, CATHERINE, health care facility administrator, physician, medical educator; b. Hong Kong, May 20, 1950; came to U.S., 1953; d. Doi Kwong and Alice (Yee) E.; m. Daniel Charles Chan, Apr. 2, 1978; 1 child, Michael B. BA, Wellesley Coll., 1972; MD, Columbia U., 1976. Diplomate Am. Bd. Internal Medicine, Am. Bd. Gastroenterology; cert. added qualifications geriatrics. Intern in internal medicine Presbyterian Hosp./Columbia Presbyterian Med. Ctr., 1976-77, resident in internal medicine, 1977-79; fellow in gastroenterology/hepatology N.Y. Hosp./Cornell U. Med. Coll., 1979-81; instr. medicine Cornell U. Coll. Medicine, N.Y.C., 1980-81; staff physician On Lok Sr. Health Svcs., San Francisco, 1981-86, supervising physician, 1986-91, med. dir., 1992—; asst. clin. prof. dept. family and cmty. medicine U. Calif., San Francisco, 1986—, asst. clin. prof. dept. medicine, 1992—; primary care specialist Program of All-inclusive Care for the Elderly, San Francisco, 1987-94; asst. chief dept. medicine Chinese Hosp., San Francisco, 1993-94. Instr. BLS Am. Heart Assn., San Francisco, 1988-92; mem. nominating com. YWCA of Marin, San Francisco, San Mateo, 1991—; mem. mgmt. com. YWCA-Chinatown/North Beach, San Francisco, 1989—; bd. dirs. Chinatown Cmty. Children's Ctr., San Francisco, 1987-90. Durant scholar Wellesley Coll., 1972. Mem. ACP, Am. Geriatrics Soc., Am. Soc. Aging, Am. Gastroent. Assn., Calif. Med. Assn. (assoc.), San Francisco Med. Soc. (assoc.), Sigma Xi, Alpha Omega Alpha. Office: On Lok Sr Health Services 1333 Bush St San Francisco CA 94109

ENGEL, CHARLENE ALICIA, elementary education educator; b. Bellflower, Calif., May 31, 1955; d. Jacob and Frances Johanna (Ehlers) E. BA, Calvin Coll., 1977; cert., U. Wash., 1982. Tchr. Worthington (Minn.) Sch. Dist., 1977-78; tchr. pvt. sch. Sunnyside (Wash.) Sch. Dist., 1978-85, tchr. pub. sch., 1986—. Mem. ASCD, Internat. Reading Assn. (conf. mem. 1990, 92, 94), Delta Kappa Gamma. Home: 121 Olive Ave Sunnyside WA 98944 Office: Sunnyside Sch Dist 1700 E Lincoln Sunnyside WA 98944

ENGEL, EDITH SCHICK, writer, advocate; b. N.Y.C., Dec. 20, 1915; d. Johann and Ottilie (Gluck) Schick; m. Henry W. Engel; children: Judith Engel Wilson, Ginger Engel Benlifer. BA, Hunter Coll., 1936. Producer, editor, mgr. Info. Please, N.Y.C., 1938-53; mgr., copywriter, pub. rels. specialist Internat. Franchises Pro Hardware, Inc., Larchmont, N.Y., 1954-64; writer, editor, mgr. Ednl. Records, Mamaroneck, N.Y., 1966-68; writer, mgr. Creative Printing, White Plains, N.Y., 1968-71; advocate, activist for grandparents children's rights Scarsdale Family Counseling Svc., Inc., Scarsdale, N.Y., 1981—, Legis. Activists, Haslett, Mich., 1983—; cons. Scarsdale Family Counseling Svc., 1981—; cons. ABA, Washington, 1989. Editor: How To Cope With Learning Problems, 1981; compiler, editor: One God: Peoples of the Book, 1990; contbr., editorial advisor: Grandparenting in a Changing World, 1994. Support group leader Grandparents in Divided Families, Scarsdale, 1984—; activist, cons. Found. for Grandparenting, Cohasset, Mass., 1984—. Mem. Nat. Writers Union. Democrat. Jewish. Home: 10 Gerlach Pl Larchmont NY 10538

ENGEL, EMILY FLACHMEIER, school administrator; b. Columbus, Tex., Sept. 15, 1938; d. William August and Jeanette D. (Hastedt) F.; m. Lars N. Engel, Dec. 28, 1957; children: Jan Kristin, Karen Gale. BSEd, U. Tex., 1959, MEd, 1966. Cert. tchr., counselor, adminstr., N.Mex. Sch. counselor, guidance team leader Los Alamos (N.Mex.) Pub. Schs., 1967-85, coord., fed. projects, 1985-87; prin. Los Alamos Mid. Sch., 1987-89, Mountain Elem. Sch., Los Alamos, 1989—, 1989—; mem. bd. dirs. Family Strengths Network, 1994; presentor nat. confs. and convs. Bd. dirs. Los Alamos Family Coun., 1985-91, Family Strengths Network, 1994—, Self-Help, Inc., 1993—; mem. adv. com. Sci.-at-Home, 1994—. Mem. ASCD, NDEA (mem. counseling and guidance inst. U. Tex. Austin 1962-63), Nat. Assn. Elem. Sch. Prins., N.Mex. Assn. Elem. Sch. Prins. (pres.-elect 1992-93, pres. 1993-94), N.Mex. Assn. Sch. Adminstrs., Los Alamos Assn. Sch. Adminstrs. (pres. 1991-92), Delta Kappa Gamma (Rho chpt. sec.), Pi Lambda Theta. Methodist. Home: 192 Loma Del Escolar Los Alamos NM 87544-2525 Office: Mountain Elem Sch 2280 North Rd Los Alamos NM 87544-1726

ENGEL, LOIS ELEANOR, industrial engineer; b. Bethpage, N.Y., Jan. 6, 1961; d. Alfred Carl and Eleanor Gertrude (Schwenger) E. BS in Indsl. Engring., Hofstra U., 1982, MBA in Fin., 1987. Indsl. engring. clk. United Parcel Svc., Uniondale, N.Y., 1982; indsl. engr. GSSD div. Harris Corp., Syosset, N.Y., 1983-84; indsl. engr. ADEMCO, Syosset, 1984-89, supr. indsl. engring. and telecom., 1989-91; mgr. telecom. and indsl. engring. support ADI (Ademco Distbn. Inc.), Syosset, 1991—; adj. prof. N.Y. Poly. Inst., Farmingdale, N.Y., 1988-89. Mem. Inst. Indsl. Engrs. (sr., pres. chpt. 86, 1987-93, bd. dirs. 1993-95), Internat. Facility Mgmt. Assn. Home: 1 Soma Pl Farmingdale NY 11735 Office: ADI 275 Oak Dr Syosset NY 11791

ENGEL, MADELINE HELENA, sociology educator; b. N.Y.C., Feb. 11, 1941; d. William Francis and Adelaide Veronica (Boitano) E.; m. Thomas P. Moran, Apr. 18, 1970; 1 child, Magdalene. BA, Barnard Coll., 1961; MA, Fordham U., 1963, PhD, 1966. Research asst. Fordham U., Bronx, N.Y., 1962-70, research assoc., 1970-74; instr. dept. sociology Lehamn Coll., CUNY, Bronx, 1964-66, lectr., 1966-68, asst. prof., 1968-72, assoc. prof., 1972-92, chmn. dept., 1980-92, prof., 1992—, dir. grad. studies, 1993—; research assoc. CUNY Research Found., N.Y.C., 1985. Author: Inequality In America, 1971, The Drug Scene, 1974; co-author Minorities in American Society, Sleuths in Skirts, 1993; mem. editorial bd. Internat. Migration Rev., 1967-74; contbr. articles on sociology and women's studies to profl. jours. Mem. Bronx Borough Pres. Commn. on Homeless, 1986. Mem. Eastern Sociol. Soc., Am. Sociol. Soc., N.Y. State Sociol. Soc., Alpha Kappa Delta. Democrat. Roman Catholic. Office: Lehman Coll Dept Sociology and Social Work Bedford Park Blvd W Bronx NY 10468-1539

ENGEL, MARCY, lawyer; b. N.Y.C., Aug. 22, 1959. BA in Econs., U. Mich., 1980; JD, U. Pa., 1983. Bar: N.Y. 1984, U.S. Dist. Ct. (so. and ea. dists.) N.Y. 1984. Assoc. Sullivan & Cromwell, N.Y.C., 1983-87; counsel, v.p. Salomon Bros., Inc., N.Y.C., 1987—. Mem. N.Y. State Bar Assn., Assn. of Bar of City of N.Y. (com. on futures regulation), City Bar Assn. N.Y., Futures Law Assn. (law and compliance div.). Home: 70 Riverside Dr New York NY 10024-5714 Office: Salomon Bros Inc 1 New York Plz New York NY 10004*

ENGER, KATHLEEN MAY, preschool administrator; b. Colorado Springs, Aug. 26, 1944; d. John Edward and Olga Ceceil (Sommer) Kennedy; m. Filmore G. Enger, Nov. 15, 1971; children: Olga, Filmore, Gabriel, Gretchen. BS, RN, PHN summa cum laude, Cornell U., 1969. RN; cert. pub. health nurse. Dir. nursing Edgemeont Hosp., Hollywood, Calif., 1971-78; bd. dirs. Minn. Opera Bd., Mpls., 1979-85; CEO Children's Heart Fund, Mpls., 1985-90; CEO, pres. Kountry Kids Preschool., Edina, Minn., 1990—, Auntie Kay's (Children's Inn), Edina, 1982—; owner, dir. Cobble Hill Day, In-Home Toddler Day Care Program, 1993—; lectr. in field, Hennepin County, Minn., 1979—. Author: Policy and Procedure Manual for Childcare

Providers, 1990. Fundraiser Rep. Party, Mpls., 1990, Edina. Sunday sch. tchr. Edina Comm. Luth. Ch., 1991-92. Mem. Adult Children's Alliance, Edina Childcare Alliance, Women Investing Now (pres. 1980—), Nat. Assn. Nursing, Internat. Childcare Unit (founder 1980—). Home: 5301 Minnehaha Blvd Edina MN 55424-1406

ENGERRAND, DORIS DIESKOW, educator; b. Chgo., Aug. 7, 1925; d. William Jacob and Alma Willhelmina (Cords) Dieskow; B.S. in Bus. Adminstrn., N. Ga. Coll., 1958, B.S. in Elementary Edn., 1959; M. Bus. Edn., Ga. State U., 1966, Ph.D., 1970; m. Gabriel H. Engerrand, Oct. 26, 1946 (dec. June 1987); children: Steven, Kenneth, Jeannine. Tchr., dept. chmn. Lumpkin County High Sch., Dahlonega, Ga., 1960-63, 65-68; tchr., Gainesville, Ga., 1965; asst. prof. Troy (Ala.) State U., 1969-71; asst. prof. bus. Ga. Coll., Milledgeville, 1971-74, asso. prof., 1974-78, prof., 1978-90, chmn. dept. info. systems and comms., 1978-89, ret., 1990; cons. Named Outstanding Tchr. Lumpkin County Pub. Schs., 1963, 66; Outstanding Educator bus. faculty Ga. Coll., 1975, Exec. of Yr. award, 1983. Fellow Assn. for Bus. Communication (v.p. S.E. 1978-80, 81-84, 89-92, bd. dirs.), Nat., Ga. (Postsecondary Tchr. of Yr. award 10th dist. 1983, Postsecondary Tchr. of Yr. award 1984) bus. edn. assns., Am., Ga. (Educator of Yr. award 1984, Parker Liles award 1989) vocat. assns., Profl. Secs. Internat., Ninety-nines Internat. (chmn. N. Ga. chpt. 1975-76, named Pilot of Year N. Ga. chpt. 1973). Methodist. Contbr. articles on bus. edn. to profl. publs. Home: 1674 Pine Valley Rd Milledgeville GA 31061-2465 Office: Ga Coll Milledgeville GA 31061

ENGFER, SUSAN MARVEL, zoological park executive; b. Mpls., Dec. 6, 1943; d. Frederick Paul and Dorothy M. Engfer. BS, Albion Coll., 1965; MS, U. Wyo., 1968; postgrad., U. Calif., Santa Barbara, 1975-76; dipl., Sch. Profl. Mgmt. Devel. for Zoo and Aquarium Pers., 1981. Ranger, naturalist Grand Teton Nat. Park, Moose, Wyo., 1967; cancer rsch. technician U. Calif., Santa Barbara, 1967-68; zoo keeper Santa Barbara Zool. Gardens, 1968-70, edn. curator, 1970-72, asst. dir., 1972-88; pres., CEO Cheyenne Mountain Zool. Park, Colorado Springs, Colo., 1988—; cons. oiled bird rehab. Union Oil and Standard Oil Co., 1968-70; master plan cons. Moorpark (Calif.) Coll., 1986-88; instr., bd. regents Sch. Profl. Mgmt. Devel. Zoo and Aquarium Pers., Wheeling, W.V., 1984-87. Author: North American Regional Studbook, Asian Small-Clawed Otter (Aonyx cinerea), 1987—. Fellow Am. Assn. Zool. Pks. and Aquariums (profl., bd. dirs. 1987-90, mem. accreditation commn. 1990—, chmn. accreditation commn. 1994-95); mem. Internat. Union Dirs. Zool. Gardens, Internat. Union Conservation of Nature and Natural Resources (mem. otter specialist group), Soc. Conservation Biology, Colo. Women's Forum, Rotary. Office: Cheyenne Mountain Zool Pk 4250 Cheyenne Mntn Zoo Rd Colorado Springs CO 80906-5728

ENGHOLM, MARY KORSTAD MUELLER, art education consultant, author, educator; b. Seattle, May 7, 1918; d. Martin and Mary Emily (Green) Korstad; BE, UCLA, 1940; MEd, St. Lawrence U., 1949; postgrad. Syracuse U., 1950-52; m. Walter Weigel, Dec. 22, 1949 (dec.); 1 child, Erica Weigel-Langston; m. Paul G. Mueller, Nov. 9, 1968 (dec. 1976); m. Glenn S. Engholm, Aug. 6, 1982. Tchr. art Riverside (Calif.) City Schs., 1944-46; art supr. Canton (N.Y.) Sch. Dist., 1946-48; asst. prof. art SUNY, Potsdam, 1948-58; art supr. Watertown (N.Y.) City Sch. Dist., 1962-67; cons., lectr. U. Nebr., Lincoln, 1966; art supr. Bakersfield (Calif.) City Sch. Dist., 1967-78; instr. art, continuing edn. Calif. State U., Bakersfield, 1971-74, 76, adj. instr., lectr., 1982-83; free-lance art cons., Bakersfield, 1978-84. Trustee Kern County Arts Council, 1976-83, Bakersfield Sister City Com., 1978-83, H. Weil Child Guidance Clinic, 1980-83, Kern County Mus. Alliance, 1978-84; pres. Kern County chpt. Young Audiences of Am., 1980-81; pres. bd. dirs. H. Weil Meml. Child Guidance Clinic, 1981-83; community adv. Jr. League Bakersfield, 1980-83; pres. cen. coast Am. Scandinavians Assn., 1986-87; bd. dirs. Lori Brock Jr. Mus., 1975-78. Recipient Bienniel Nat. Colby award Sigma Kappa, 1990. Mem. AAUW, Nat. Art Edn. Assn., Monterey History & Art Assn. (trustee 1986-92), Monterey Civic Club (bd. dirs.), Nat. League Am. Pen Women, Inc., Greater Bakersfield C. of C. (Woman of Yr. 1983), Calif. Art Edn. Assn. (trustee 1979-82), Kern County Art Edn. Assn. (pres. 1982-83), Calif. Tchrs. Assn., Delta Kappa Gamma. Episcopalian. Author: (with Thomas and Wells) Elementary Art, 1967, Murals: Creating an Environment, 1979, One to Follow: A Tale of Two Women, 1990; contbr. articles to profl. jours.

ENGLAND, BARBARA LEE, communications executive; b. poplar Bluff, Mo., Oct. 20, 1943; d. Joseph Chester Allen and Daisy Ann (Adams) Heifner; children: Kenneth Wayde Howell, Sherri Rene Bolen, Michelle Linn Wingo; m. Gary Franklin England, Nov. 18, 1989. Grad. high sch., Poplar Bluff, Mo. Cert. real estate broker, Mo. Gen. mgr. Sta. KUGT, Jackson, Mo., 1984-94; office mgr., mktg. dir. Broadcast Cablevision Wireless Cable TV, Malden, Mo., 1994—. V.p. Women's Aglow, Cape Girardeau, Mo., 1988-89; mem. Mo. bd. Nat. Assn. Evangels; motivational speaker on women's issues. Mem. Am. Family Assn. (bd. advisors). Home: 501 Stokes Blvd Malden MO 63863 Office: BCW Malden MO 63863

ENGLAND, KATHLEEN JANE, lawyer; b. Boston, July 29, 1953; d. Frank W. and Kathleen E. (Van DenHouten) E. BA cum laude, Mich. State U., 1975; postgrad., U. Exeter, summer 1977; JD, Suffolk U., Boston, 1978. Bar: Mass. 1979, Nev. 1979, U.S. Dist. Ct. Nev. 1980, U.S. Ct. Appeals (9th cir.) 1980. Intern Middlesex Dist. Atty. Bur., Cambridge, Mass., 1978; law clk. Withington, Cross, Park & Groden, Boston, 1976-78; law clk. City of Las Vegas, Nev., 1978-79, dep. city atty., 1979-82; assoc. mem. Vargas & Bartlett, Las Vegas, 1982-89; ptnr. Combs & England, Las Vegas, 1989-93; pres. England & Assocs., Las Vegas, 1994—; bd. dirs., legal counsel Planned Parenthood So. Nev., Las Vegas; mem. Nev. Supreme Ct. Task Force on Gender Bias, 1987—; bd. dirs. Nat. Conf. Women's Bar Assn., 1992—. Contbr. articles to profl. jours. Bd. dirs. Nat. Kidney Found. of So. Nev., Las Vegas, 1983, U. Nev., Las Vegas Womens Ctr.; active Amnesty Internat., Campaign for Choice, 1990, Nev. Women's Lobby, chair Ethics Review Bd. City Las Vegas. Recipient Woman of Yr. award Desert Sands Bus. & Profl. Women's Club, 1993; named Disting. Woman of So. Nev., 1992, Woman of Achievement, Legal Women's Coun., C. of C., 1994. Mem. ABA, AAUW, So. Nev. Assn. Women Attys., Nev. Inn of Ct. (chmn. programs 1992—), State Bar Nev. (founder chair young lawyers sect.). Office: England & Assocs 704 S 9th St Las Vegas NV 89101

ENGLAND, LYNNE LIPTON, lawyer, speech pathologist, audiologist; b. Youngstown, Ohio, Apr. 11, 1949; d. Sanford Y. and Sally (Kentor) Lipton; m. Richard E. England, Mar. 5, 1977. BA, U. Mich., 1970; MA, Temple U., 1972; JD, Tulane U., 1981. Bar: Fla. 1982, U.S. Dist. Ct. (mid. dist.) Fla. 1982, U.S. Ct. Appeals (11th cir.) 1982; cert. clin. competence in speech pathology and audiology. Speech pathologist Rockland Children's Hosp., N.Y., 1972-74, Jefferson Parish Sch., Gretna, La., 1977-81; audiologist Rehab. Inst. Chgo., 1974-76; assoc. Trenam, Simmons, Kemker, Scharf, Barkin, Frye & O'Neill, Tampa, Fla., 1981-84; asst. U.S. atty. for Middle Dist. Fla. Tampa, 1984-87; asst. U.S. trustee, 1987-91; ptnr. Stearns, Weaver, Miller, Weissler, Alhadeff & Sitterson, P.A., 1991-94, Prevatt, England, Ambler, Klink & Snyder, Tampa, Fla., 1994—. Editor Fla. Bankruptcy Casenotes, 1983. Recipient clin. assistantship Temple U., 1972-74. Mem. Comml. Law League, Am. Speech and Hearing Assn., Tampa Bay Bankruptcy Bar Assn. (dir. 1990—), Am. Bankruptcy Inst., Assn. Trial Lawyers Am., Fla. Bar Assn., Hillsborough County Bar Assn., Fed. Bar Assn., Order of Coif. Jewish. Office: PO Box 2920 1 Tampa City Ctr Ste 2505 Tampa FL 33601-2920

ENGLE, BARBARA LOUISE, state legislator; b. Berne, Ind., Sept. 11, 1945; d. Luther and Maxine (Moser) E. B in English, Ball State U., 1967; MEd, St. Francis Coll., 1971. Tchr. North Adams Cmty. Schs., 1967—; mem. Ind. Ho. of Reps. Divsn. leader United Way, Adams County, Ind., 1989-94. Recipient Pacesetter award Ind. State Tchrs. Assn., 1985. Mem. Decatur Bus. and Profl. Women. Republican. Mem. Ch. of Christ. Home: 916 Waynesboro Ave Decatur IN 46733-2624 Office: Ind State Ho of Reps State Capital Indianapolis IN 46204

ENGLE, JANE, research nurse; b. L.A., June 15, 1942; d. John Dean and Florence (Updike) E. BA with honors, U. N.C., 1965; BSN, Cornell U., 1970; MS in Nursing, U. Ill., Chgo., 1974; MDiv magna cum laude, Wesley Theol. Sem., 1988. RN. Tchr., vol. trainer Peace Corps, Afganistan, 1965-68; pub. health nurse Tufts Delta Health Ctr., Mound Bayou, Miss., 1969; coord. pub. health nursing Ill. Community Clinic, Chgo., 1970-72; nursing cons. rsch. edn. Dept. Pub. Health, Chgo., 1974-78; rsch. nurse AIDS NIH, Bethesda, Md., 1989—; AIDS task force Interfaith Conf. Met. Washington, 1988-90. Author: Outcome Measures in Home Care, 1987. V.p. women's bd. Episcopal Ch., Washington, 1981-82; mem. bd. deacons Nat. Presbyn. Ch., Washington, 1982-86; mem. Mayor's Task Force on Standards, Washington, 1985-87. Wesley Theol. Sem. Biblocal scholar, 1988; named Person of Week Washington Times, 1992. Mem. ANA (pres. local chpt. 1976-78), Assn. Nurses in AIDS Care, Phi Beta Kappa, Sigma Theta Tau. Democrat. Home: 4831 Sedgwick St NW Washington DC 20016

ENGLE, JEANNETTE CRANFILL, medical technologist; b. Davie County, N.C., July 7, 1941; d. Gurney Nathaniel and Versie Emmaline (Reavis) Cranfill; m. William Sherman Engle (div. 1970); children: Phillip William, Lisa Kaye. Diploma, Dell Sch. Med. Tech., 1960; BA, U. N.C., Asheville, 1976; postgrad., Marshall U., 1991—. Instr. Dell Sch. Med. Tech., Asheville, 1960-67; rotating technologist Meml. Mission Hosp., Asheville, 1967-68, asst. supr. hematology, 1968-71; supr. Damon Subs. Pvt. Clinic Lab., Asheville, 1971-73; chemistry technologist VA Med. Ctr., Durham, N.C., 1973-74, 75-76, supr., 1974-75; asst. supr. microbiology VA Med. Ctr., Salem, Va., 1976-79; supr. rsch. Med. Svc. Lab., Salem, 1979-90; flow cytometrist VA Med. Ctr., Huntington, W.Va., 1990-92, cons. to clin. lab. flow cytometry dept., 1992—; reviewer Jour. Club, Roanoke-Salem, Va., 1980-90. Author: (poem) Reflections on a Comet, 1984; contbr. numerous articles and abstracts on med. tech. to profl. jours., 1982—. Mem. The Acting Co. Ensemble. Democrat. Episcopalian. Home: 4775 Green Valley Rd Huntington WV 25701-9793

ENGLEHART, JOAN ANNE, trade association executive; b. Susquehanna, Pa., Sept. 15, 1940; d. George Louis and Muriel Elois (Washburn) Wanatt; m. Dale John Englehart, Nov. 24, 1958. AAS, Broome Community Coll., 1981; BS in Cultural Studies, Empire State Coll., 1984; postgrad., SUNY, Binghamton, 1984; PhD in Bus. Adminstrn., Century U., 1994. Office mgr., coord. sales Bush Transformer Corp., Endicott (N.Y.), Boston, 1959-65; mgr., cons. Snelling & Snelling, Binghamton, Endicott, 1965-71; tchr., mgr. Can. Acad., Kobe, Japan, 1971-72; owner Typewriting, Endicott, 1980-85; exec. v.p. Tioga County C. of C., Owego, N.Y., 1985-87, pres., 1988—; exec. v.p. Chamber Found., 1987—. Mem. Broome C.C. Found., Binghamton, 1984-87; mem. scholarship com. Civic Club Binghamton, 1984-87; mem. Health Fair Adv. Bd., Broome and Tioga Counties, 1985-87; sec.-treas. Tioga County C. of C. Found., 1987—; chmn. sustaining membership com. Broome United Way, Binghamton, 1986-87; mem. planning process com. Broome-Delaware Tioga BOCES vocat. edn. coms. 1989, 92; bd. dirs NYPENN Health Systems Agy., 1989-91, Pvt. Industry Coun., Tioga County Rural Ministry, 1992—, chmn., 1993—; pres. Tioga County divsn. Am. Heart Assn., 1994—; active Tioga County Tourism Coun., 1994—, County Comprehensive Plan Econs. Com., 1994—. Recipient award Boy Scouts Am., 1979, Evening Student Assn., 1991, Friends Binghamton Libr., 1982, ATHENA award C. of C., 1986; named Woman of Achievement Broome County Status of Women Coun., 1978, Nat. Achievement award Nat. Assn. in C. of C., 1993. Mem. AAUW (life, pres. 1986-87), So. Tier World Commerce Assn. (bd. dirs. 1992—), Nat. Assn. Women in C. of C.'s (charter mem., Nat. Achievement award, 1993), Am. C. of C. Execs., N.Y. State C. of C. Execs. (bd. dirs. 1991), Zonta (pres. Tioga county area club 1985-89, mem. internat. bd. govs. dist. II 1982-84, Woman of Achievement 1985-88). Republican. Baptist. Home: 4 Lancaster Dr Endicott NY 13760-4320 Office: Tioga County C of C 188 Front St Owego NY 13827-1521

ENGLE-MCELYEA, MARSHA GAIL, pastor; b. Greenville, Tex., Sept. 11, 1964; d. Charles Stuart Jr. and Maxine Gail (Swanson) Engle; m. Michael Rowbottom, Aug. 1, 1987 (div. Sept. 1991); m. Ronald Thomas McElyea, Nov. 14, 1992; 1 child, Shawn. BA, Austin Coll., 1987; MDiv, Perkins Sch of Theology, 1991. Ordained elder United Meth. Ch., 1993, ordained deacon, 1989; cert. leader; cert. instr. Chaplain resident Meth. Med. Ctr., Dallas, 1985; guest preacher Austin Coll., 1986-87; chaplain intern Home Hospice of Grayson County, Sherman, Tex., 1987; dir. youth ministries First United Meth. Ch., Bonham, Tex., 1986-87; min. of youth Preston Hollow United Meth. Ch., Dallas, 1987-88, First United Meth. Ch., Paris, Tex., 1988-89; preacher orientation worship svcs. Perkins Sch. Theology, So. Meth. Univ., 1991; pastor various United Meth. Chs., 1969—, Richland United Meth. Ch., Richardson, Tex., 1992—; pvt. music instr., 1981-89; pianist Durham Bapt. Ch., Fairlie, Tex.; mem. acappella choir Austin Coll., 1984-85. Beekeeper Engle Apiaries, Wolfe City Tex., 1985-86. Mem. NAFE, Lions Internat. (pres. Celeste chpt. 1991-92), Zeta Chi Omega (v.p. 1986-87). Democrat. Office: Richland United Meth Ch 1701 N Jupiter Rd Richardson TX 75081-2146

ENGLES, LORETTA GRAHAM, physician, educator; b. Lebanon, Okla., June 3, 1926; d. Joseph Levi and Letha Evelyn (Null) Graham; m. Charles Franklin Jr., Lilly Lori, Eric David, Alex. BS, Okla. U., 1947, MD, 1951. Intern Okla. U. Hosps., Oklahoma City, 1951-52; gen. practice medicine Oklahoma City, 1952—; adj. prof. medicine Okla. Med. Sch., Oklahoma City, 1975—; chief of staff South Community Hosp. Family Practice, Oklahoma City, 1983-84. Mem. Oklahoma Med. Soc. (com. mem. 1986), Okla. Med. Women's Assn. (pres. 1985-86), S.W. Bus. and Profl. Women's Assn., Nat. Assn. Women bus. Owners, South Oklahoma city C. of C., Lucky 13 Investment Club. Home: 800 SW 36th St Oklahoma City OK 73109-2429 Office: 2416 S Harvey Ave Oklahoma City OK 73109-5932

ENGLISH, DIANE, television producer, writer, communications executive; b. Buffalo, NY, 1948; d. Richard and Anne English; m. Joel Shukovsky. Grad., Buffalo State Coll., 1970. Tchr. high sch. English Buffalo, 1970-71; with Theatre In Am. series Sta. WNET-TV, N.Y.C., assoc. dir. TV lab.; TV columnist Vogue Mag., N.Y.C., 1977-80; creator, prodr., writer Foley Sq. CBS, N.Y.C., 1985-86, exec. prodr., writer My Sister Sam, 1986-87; exec. prodr., creator, writer Murphy Brown Shukovsky English Entertainment, N.Y.C., 1988—, creator, exec. prodr. Love And War, 1992—; co-creator, exec. prodr. Double Rush, N.Y.C., 1995—; ptnr. Shukovsky English Entertainment. Co-author: (motion pictures-for-TV) The Lathe of Heaven, 1980 (Writers Guild award nomination), My Life as a Man, Classified Love. Recipient Outstanding Writing in a Comedy Series award Writers Guild, 1990, 92, Genie award Am. Womenin Radio and TV, 1990, Commrs.' award Nat. Commn. on Working Women, (3) Emmy awards, Peabody award 1991. Office: CBS Studio Ctr 4024 Radford Ave Studio City CA 91604

ENGLISH, EVA UBER, volunteer arts council executive; b. Neumarkt, Silesia, Germany, Apr. 20, 1925; came to U.S., 1954, naturalized, 1957; d. Konrad and Margarete (Reimann) Uber; m. Charles B. English, Oct. 3, 1954; children: Gwendolyn, Carolyn (dec.). Lab. asst. diploma, Fachschule Chemistry & Physics, 1943. Lab. asst. Bosch GmbH., Reichenbach, Silesia, 1944; with U.S. Mil. Govt., Wiesbaden, 1946-49; cons. edn. br. Am. Consulate, Frankfurt, West Germany, 1949-54; pres. Champaign County Mental Health Assn., Urbana, Ohio, 1967-69; mem. Logan-Champaign County Bd. Mental Health and Retardation, 1970-77, v.p., 1970-72; bd. dirs. Springfield (Ohio) Symphony Orch. Assn., 1968-80; founder, pres., vol. exec. dir. Champaign County Arts Coun., 1974-79, chmn. arts-in-schs. program, 1974-82, trustee, 1974-88. Co-honoree The Eva and Charles B. English Fine Arts Scholarship Endowment, Champaign County (Ohio) Arts Coun., 1988—. Home: Raiffeisenweg 7, 86923 Finning Germany

ENGLISH, JOAN PATRICIA, municipal official; b. Newark, N.J., Feb. 11, 1944; d. John Patrick Sr. and Mary Joan (McGrail) E. BA, U. W.Va., 1966; MPA, U. So. Calif., 1968. Community svc. officer State of N.J. Dept. Community Affairs, 1968-69; dep. dir. Hoboken (N.J.) Model Cities Agy., 1969-73; fin. mgmt. system project mgr. Office Mgmt. Svcs., Portland, Oreg., 1973-74; asst. pub. works adminstr. City of Portland, 1974-79, exec. asst. to mayor, 1980, dir. traffic mgmt. Office Transp., 1985-89, pub. works system mgr., 1989-90; mgmt. cons., interim mgr. Washington County Washington County Oreg. and Portland Bur. Transp., 1980-85; dir. transp. and pub. works City fo West Hollywood, Calif., 1990—. Mem. ASPA, Am. Pub. Works Assn., Internat. City Mgmt. Assn., League Calif. Cities (com. transp. and pub. works), Womens Transp. Seminar. Home: 999 N Doheny Dr West Hollywood CA 90069 Office: City of West Hollywood 8611 Santa Monica Blvd West Hollywood CA 90069

ENGLISH, KARAN, state representative; b. Berkeley, Calif., Mar. 23, 1939. Formerly Ariz. State Rep. and State Senator. Democrat. Office: US Ho of Reps Washington DC 20515

ENGLISH, KAREN ELAINE, educational program director; b. Dallas, Mar. 12, 1959; d. A. W. and Neta Joan (Moore) Jackson; m. Richard Paul English, Nov. 17, 1984; 1 child, Elizabeth Diana. BS, Tex. Woman's U., 1979, MEd, 1989. Instr. deaf edn. Corpus Christi (Tex.) Ind. Sch. Dist., 1979-80, Arlington (Tex.) Sch. Dist., 1980-92; asst. prin. Kennedale (Tex.) Ind. Sch. Dist., 1992-93, dir. spl. programs, 1993—; instr. sign lang. continuing edn. U. Tex., Arlington, 1991-92; ednl. asst. Fed. Correctional Inst., Ft. Worth, 1983. Mem. Leadership South Tarrant County, 1993; life mem. PTA, 1984—. Mem. Tex. Assn. Secondary Sch. Prins., Tex. Coun. Adminstrs. of Spl. Edn., Phi Delta Kappa. Office: Spl Programs Office 120 W Mansfield Hwy Kennedale TX 76060-2416

ENNS, CAROLYN ZERBE, psychologist; b. Yokohama, Japan, May 3, 1951; came to U.S., 1967; d. Benjamin and Esther Bertha (Reddig) Zerbe; m. Richard Bernard Enns, Apr. 1973; children: Larissa Esther, Jessica Anne. BA, Tabor Coll., 1972; MA, Calif. State U., 1977; PhD, U. Calif., 1987. Lic. psychologist, Iowa. Counseling coord. Fresno (Calif.) Pacific Coll., 1976-84; assoc. prof. Cornell Coll., Mt. Vernon, Iowa, 1987—; sr. staff psychologist U. Iowa, Iowa City, 1988—. Mem. APA (Barbara Kirk award 1987), ACA, Assn. Women in Psychology, Midwestern Psychol. Assn., Iowa Psychol. Assn. Office: Cornell Coll 600 1st St W Mount Vernon IA 52314-1098

ENOS, MINDY See PARSONS, MINDY

ENRIGHT, CYNTHIA LEE, illustrator; b. Denver, July 6, 1950; d. Darrel Lee and Iris Arlene (Flodquist) E. BA in Elem. Edn., U. No. Colo., 1972; student, Minn. Sch. Art and Design, Mpls., 1975-76. Tchr. 3d grade Littleton (Colo.) Sch. Dist., 1972-75; graphics artist Sta. KCNC TV, Denver, 1978-79; illustrator No Coast Graphics, Denver, 1979-87; editorial artist The Denver Post, 1987—. Illustrator (mag.) Sesame St., 1984, 95; illustrator, editor "Tiny Tales" The Denver Post, 1991-94. Recipient Print mag. Regional Design Ann. awards, 1984, 85, 87, Phoenix Art Mus. Biannual award, 1979. Mem. Mensa. Democrat. Home: 1210 Ivanhoe St Denver CO 80220-2640 Office: The Denver Post 1560 Broadway Denver CO 80202-5133

ENRIQUEZ, CAROLA RUPERT, museum director; b. Washington, Jan. 2, 1954; d. Jack Burns and Shirley Ann (Orcutt) Rupert; m. John Enriquez, Jr., Dec. 30, 1989. BA in history cum laude, Bryn Mawr Coll., 1976; MA, U. Del., 1978, cert. in mus. studies, 1978. Personnel mgmt. trainee Naval Material Command, Arlington, Va., 1972-76; teaching asst. dept. history, U. Del., Newark, 1976-77; asst. curator/exhibit specialist Hist. Soc. Del., Wilmington, 1977-78; dir. Macon County Mus. Complex, Decatur, Ill., 1978-81; dir. Kern County Mus., Bakersfield, Calif., 1981—; pres. Kern County Mus. Found., 1991—; advisor Kern County Heritage Commn., 1981-88; chmn. Historic Records Commn., 1981-88; sec.-treas. Arts Council of Kern, 1984-86, pres. 1986-88; county co-chmn. United Way, 1981, 82; chmn. steering com. Calif. State Bakersfield Co-op Program, 1982-83; mem. Community Adv. Bd. Calif. State Bakersfield, Anthrop. Soc., 1986-88; bd. dirs. Mgmt. Council, 1983-86, v.p., 1987, pres. 1988; bd. dirs. Calif. Council for Promotion of History, 1984-86, v.p., 1987-88. pres., 1988-90; mem. community adv. bd. Calif. State U.-Bakersfield Sociology Dept., 1986-88; mem. women's adv. com. Girl Scouts U.S., 1989-91; bd. dirs. Greater Bakersfield Conv. and Visitors Bur., 1993—; co-chair 34th St. Neighborhood Partnership, 1994—. Hagley fellow Eleutherian Mills-Hagley Found., 1977-78; Bryn Mawr alumnae regional scholar, 1972-76. Mem. Calif. Assn. Mus. (regional rep. 1991—, v.p. legis. affairs 1992—), Am. Assn. for State and Local History (chair awards com. Calif. chpt. 1990—), Exces. Assn. Kern County. Unitarian Universalist. Office: Kern County Museum 3801 Chester Ave Bakersfield CA 93301-1395

ENSIGN, RUTH SINGLEY, artist; b. Tokyo, Apr. 22, 1923; parents Am. citizens; d. Dewees Franklin and Ada (Schlichter) S.; m. John Edward Ensign, Sept. 13, 1947; children: Jacqueline, Martha, Stephen, Josephine. BS in Edn. with honors, BFA with honors, Temple U., 1946, MFA, 1947. adj. prof. Presbyn. Sch. Christian Edn., Richmond, 1967-70, Va. Commonwealth U., Richmond, 1987-88, Va. State U., Petersburg, 1988-89; artist in residence Henrico Pub. Schs., Highland Springs, Va., 1985-88. Numerous one-woman shows in Va., N.C., Fla.; group exhbns. include Phila. Print Club, Libr. Congress Print Exhbn., Smithsonian Inst., Va. Mus. Fine Arts, Women's Contemporary Art Winston-Salem, N.C., Hunterdon Nat. Print Anns., Clinton, N.J., Montgomery (Ala.) Mus. Fine Arts (purchase prizes) Mus. Fine Arts, Richmond, Traveling Exhbns., Valentine Mus., Richmond, Somerhill Gallery, Chapel Hill, N.C., Schoolhouse Gallery, Sanibel, Fla., Duck Blind Ltd., Kitty Hawk, N.C., others; represented in permanent collections including Philip Morris Corp., Federal Reserve Bank, NIH, Colonial Williamsburg Motor Lodge; author: (with husband) Camping Together as Christians, 1958, Make that Story Live, 1964; subject of film: Nature's Poet of Vision, 1989. Elder Presbyn. Ch. BLAI fellow Temple U., 1945. Mem. Richmond Artists Assn. (pres. 1966). Home: 1315 Whitby Rd Richmond VA 23227

ENSOR, PATRICIA LEE, librarian; b. Birmingham, Ala., July 28, 1959; d. William Lee Ensor and Sharon Patricia (Garrick) Tavari; m. Jeffrey Coleman Binyon, Dec. 17, 1983 (div. Jan. 1994); children: Leslie Patricia, Bryant Weigand. BA, U. Ala., Birmingham, 1979; MLS, U. Ala., Tuscaloosa, 1981. Libr. intern IBM Programming Lab., Santa Teresa, Calif., 1980; libr. asst. Health Scis. Libr. U. Ala., Tuscaloosa, 1980-81; reference libr. Calif. State U., Long Beach, 1981-83; coord. electronic info. svcs. Ind. State U., Terre Haute, 1984-92; head info. svcs. U. Houston, 1992—; cons. Applied Computing Devices, 1988, Rose-Hulman Inst. Tech., 1986-92; adj. faculty Ind. U. Author: CD-ROM Research Collections, CD-ROM Periodicals Index, CD-ROM Collection Development, CD-ROM for Library Users; editor Info. Stds. Quar., CD-ROM Libr. sect. Computers in Librs. Mem. ALA, Libr. and Info. Tech. Assn., Desktop Pub. Interest Group (chair 1993), Ind. Online Users Group (pres. 1986-87). Democrat. Home: 14222 Kimberley Ln # 452 Houston TX 77079 Office: U Houston Librs Houston TX 77209-2041

EPEL, LIDIA MARMUREK, dentist; b. Buenos Aires, Argentina, Sept. 30, 1941; came to U.S., 1966; d. Israel and Ita Rosa (Sonabend) Marmurek; children: Diana, Bryan. BS, Buenos Aires U., 1959, DDS, 1964. Lic. dentist, N.Y. Gen. practice dentistry Argentina, 1965-66, Long Beach, N.Y., 1967-70, Lynbrook, N.Y., 1970-73, Rockville Centre, N.Y., 1973—. Bd. dirs. Rosa Lee Young Childhood Ctr., Rockville Centre, 1982—, Rockville Ctr. Edn. Found., 1990—; mem. adv. com. on HIV/AIDS Bd. Edn. Rockville Ctr. Pub. Schs., 1994—; past. pres. Queens L.I. Women's Dental Study Group. Mem. ADA, Am. Assn. Gen. Dentistry, Fedn. Dentaire Internat., Nassau County Dental Soc. (bd. dirs., chair com. on pub. and profl. rels. 1990—, chairperson com. on health. 1989-92, chair membership com. 1993, treas. exec. com. 1993, sec. exec. com. 1994, v.p. 1995, membership task force 1994-95), Overseas Dentists Assn. (pres. N.Y. chpt. 1968-72), Dental Soc. of State of N.Y. (coun. for pub. and profl. rels. 1990—, chair children's dental health month campaign 1991), Hadassah Club (bd. dirs. Rockville Ctr. 1983-84, 92-93). Democrat. Jewish. Office: 165 N Village Ave Rockville Centre NY 11570-3701

EPHRON, NORA, writer; b. N.Y.C., May 19, 1941; d. Henry and Phoebe (Wolkind) E.; m. Dan Greenburg (div.); m. Carl Bernstein (div.); children: Jacob, Max; m. Nicholas Pileggi. BA, Wellesley Coll., 1962. Reporter N.Y. Post, 1963-68; free-lance writer, 1968—; contbg. editor, columnist Esquire mag., 1972-73, sr. editor, columnist, 1974-78; contbg. editor N.Y. mag., 1973-74. Author: Wallflower at the Orgy, 1970, Crazy Salad, 1975, Scribble Scribble, 1978, Heartburn, 1983, Nora Ephron Collected, 1991; screenwriter: (with Alice Arlen) Silkwood (nominated Acad. award for best original screenplay), 1983, Heartburn, 1986, Cookie, 1989, When Harry Met Sally (nominated Acad. award, BAFTA award for best screenplay), 1989, My Blue Heaven, 1990; dir., screenwriter (with Delia Ephron) This Is My Life, 1992, Mixed Nuts, 1994; co-screenwriter, dir. Sleepless in Seattle (nominated Acad. award for best original screenplay), 1993. Mem. Writers Guild Am., Authors Guild, Dirs. Guild of Am., Acad. Motion Picture Arts and Scis. Office: care Sam Cohn ICM 40 W 57th St New York NY 10019-4001

EPLER, PAMELA E. COAN, education educator, supervisor; b. Teaneck, N.J., Aug. 19, 1959; d. George Pruitt and Marjorie Elaine (Martin) C.; m. Tony K. Epler, May 2, 1994. AA, Brevard Coll., 1979; BA, U. N.C., Asheville, 1982; MEd in Adminstrn. and Supervision, George Mason U., 1988. Cert. secondary math. and history tchr., prin., adminstrn./supervision, Va. Tchr./supr./pub. rels. officer/drill team dir. Prince William County Schs., Woodbridge, Va., 1982-83, 85—; tchr. Aquinas Sch., Woodbridge, 1983-85; corp. ops. Nat. Technology, Arlington, Va., 1985; asst. prin. Prince William County Summer Sch., Dumphies, 1988. Lead Emergency Med. Technician O.W.L. Vol. Fire and Rescue, Woodbridge, 1988-92; charter mem. Community Task Force, Woodbridge, 1988—; mem. Prince William County Youth Assessment, Woodbridge, 1988, Woodbridge Community Choir, 1982-85, Prince William County Commn. on Women, 1990; vol. counselor for children's program Action Through Community Svc., 1983; usher St. Paul's Meth. Ch., Sunday sch. tchr., acolyte chairperson; started first women's history month ceremonies in Prince William County, 1982-85; started first All Night Grad. Party Prince William County Schs.; counselor Trauma Debriefing Team; tutorial and travel program coord. in field. Mem. AAUW (v.p. Woodbridge chpt. 1984-90), Emmaus, Ski Club of Washington (coord., bd. dirs.), Phi Alpha Theta. Home: 13009 Smoketown Rd Lakeridge VA 22192-3353 Office: Woodbridge Sr High Sch 3001 Old Bridge Rd Lakeridge VA 22192-3221

EPLETT, MARY DIANE, mathematics educator; b. Pitts., Aug. 25, 1947; d. Martyn Henry and Anna Marjorie (Kessler) Foss; m. Richard James Eplett, June 2, 1968; children: Steven Craig, Brian Keith. BS in Math., Carnegie-Mellon U., 1968; MA in Guidance and Counseling, No. Ariz. U., 1978; MAT in Math., U. West Fla., 1990. Actuarial trainee/programmer Gt. So. Life Ins. Co., Houston, 1968-70; rsch. asst. Ariz. Health Plan, Phoenix, 1970; math. tchr. Glendale (Ariz.) Unified High Sch. Dist., 1978-80, Kettering (Ohio) City Schs., 1981-82, North High Sch., Springfield, Ohio, 1982-85, Soesterberg Am. High Sch., The Netherlands, 1985-88; math./computer tchr. Niceville (Fla.) Sr. High Sch., 1989—; math. workshop leader Leadership Devel. and Enabling Change Project, 1992-94; speaker Fla. State math. confs. Okaloosa County, U. West Fla. Confs., 1991—. Recipient Presdl. Award for excellence in Math. Teaching, NSF, Washington, 1989; Fla. Bus. Partnership Challenge grantee State of Fla., 1991, Retrofit for Tech. grantee, 1993; Tandy Tech. scholar Tandy Corp., 1993. Mem. ASCD, NEA, Nat. Coun. Tchrs. Math., Fla. Coun. Tchrs. Math. (dist. I rep. 1994—), Fla. Presdl. Awardees Assn., Coun. Presdl. Awardees in Math., Okaloosa County Tchrs. Math. (rep. Nat. Coun. Tchrs. Math. 1992-93, grants chair 1990-91, pres. elect 1994, pres. 1995), Sch. Sci. and Math. Assn., Fla. Tchrs. Assn., Okaloosa County Edn. Assn., Phi Delta Kappa. Office: Niceville Sr High Sch 800 John Sims Pky E Niceville FL 32578-1210

EPPERSON, BARBARA, missionary; b. Neosho, Mo., Jan. 2, 1921; d. Clarence Raymond and Fay Marie (Duncan) E. BS, Okla. Bapt. U., 1952. Lifetime appointee Fgn. Mission Bd. So. Bapt. Conv., Richmond, Va., 1953-86; ret. Fgn. Mission Bd. So. Bapt. Conv., 1986. Author: Tales from IRE, 1957, Out of Shango's Shadow, 1967; editor-in-chief Bapt. Women's Missionary Union publs.; contbr. articles to mags. Pres. Ottawa County Rep. Women's Club, 1989-91, treas., 1992; state committeewoman Ottawa County, Okla., 1993—. Republican. Baptist. Home and Office: 2525 N Elm St Apt 19 Miami OK 74354-1420

EPPERSON, MARGARET FARRAR, civic worker; b. Hickman, Ky., Feb. 9, 1922; d. John Henry and Helen Margaret (Thompson) White; m. Liberty Weir Birmingham III, June 14, 1947 (dec. Feb. 1965); children: Margaret W., Elizabeth J., Richard L.; m. Ralph Cameron Epperson, Sept. 18, 1971. Student, Washington Sch. Art, 1940; BA magna cum laude, Judson Coll., Marion, Ala., 1945; postgrad., Lambuth Coll., Jackson, Tenn., 1964. Cert. secondary tchr., Ky. Tchr. biology and typing Robert L. Osborne High Sch., Marietta, Ga., 1945-46; tchr. typing Hickman High Sch., 1946-47; tchr. day care ctr. Southside Bapt. Ch., Jacksonville, Fla., 1972-73; sec. to min. of Edn. Jacksonville, Fla., 1973; file clk. Epperson Appraisers, Pensacola, Fla., 1986-87; formerly substitute tchr. various high schs. and jr. high schs., staff mem. Ridgecrest Bapt. Assembly, summer 1946, 1971. Exhibited in group shows, Jackson, Tenn., 1957, 58, West Tenn. Exec. Club, 1958-59. Pres. Alexander Sch. PTA, Jackson, 1959-60, devotional chmn., 1956-57, chmn. rm. mothers, 1957-58, 1st v.p., 1958-59; sec. Reelfoot Lake coun. Girl Scouts U.S.A., 1969-71, troop mother cookie chmn. 1958-65; PTA sec. Jackson, Tenn. High Sch., 1967-68, 70-71; PTA 1st v.p. Jackson, Tenn. Ctrl. Coun., 1960-61; mem. auxiliary assn. Jackson-Madison County Bar, 1960-65; vol. ARC, Jackson, 1955, Meml. Med. Hosp. Aux., Jacksonville, 1978-86, Am. Heart Assn., 1987-90, Sacred Heart Hosp. Aux., Pensacola, 1986—; life mem. Jacksonville Children's Hosp. Aux., 1974—; hostess designer show house Symphony Guild, 1979-80; dir. Women's Missionary Union, Bapt. Ch., 1976-78; sec. Newcomers Club Greater Pensacola Area, 1988-89, Bon Appetit Luncheon Group, 1986-87, sunshine chmn., 1987-88, sec., 1988-89, nom. com., 1993-94, scholarship com., 1993-94; publicity chmn. MacDowell Music Club, Jackson, 1954-55, program chmn. 1957-58, social chmn. 1959-60, parliamentarian 1961; com. mem. Jackson Comm. Concert Assn., 1958-64; mem. women's bd. Baptist Health Care Found., 1993—, mem. invitations and tickets com. for Style Show, 1993-94; active Friday Musicale of Jacksonville, Fla., 1979-86. Mem. AAUW (sec. 1988-90, 2d v.p. 1990-92, br. area rep. community problems Tenn 1970-71, chmn. Tenn. divsn. cultural interests 1969-70, Fla. chmn. interest groups 1977-78), DAR (treas. 1981-82, chmn. Am. Heritage 1989-91, chmn. mag. 1991-93), UDC (sec. Jacksonville chpt. 1979-81, historian Jacksonville chpt. 1981-83, sec. Pensacola chpt. 1989-90, corr. sec. Pensacola chpt. 1992-94, mem. com. chmn. 1993-94), Christian Women's Club (prayer chmn. 1991—, book chmn. 1987, 88, 92-94, hostesses asst. chmn. 1994—), Pensacola Fedn. Garden Clubs (pres. Poinciana Circle 1989-91, pres. Bells of Ireland Circle 1978-80, civic chmn., 1991, sec. Alderman Park Cir., Jacksonville 1980-82), Judson Coll. Alumnae Assn. of Pensacola (pres. 1993—), Friends of Libr., Tenn. Fedn. Garden Clubs (pres. Jackson jr. 1958-60, 60-70, chmn. exec. bd. 1970-71, chmn. flower show 1968).

EPPERSON, STELLA MARIE, artist; b. Oakland, Calif., Nov. 6, 1920; d. Walter Peter and Martha Josephine (Schmitt) Ross; m. John Cray Epperson, May 10, 1941; children: Therese, John, Peter. Student, Calif. Coll. Arts & Crafts, 1939, 40-41, 56, Art Inst., San Miguel d'Allende, Mex., 1972. Portrait artist Oakland Art Assn., 1956—, San Francisco Women Artists, 1962—, Marin Soc. Artists, Ross, Calif., 1971—; art docent Oakland Mus., 1969-71, mem. women's bd., 1971—, art chmn. fund raiser, 1971-89, art guild chmn., 1965-69. One-woman shows include Oakland Mus. Auction, 1993, Univ. Club, San Francisco, 1994. Recipient San Francisco Women Artists award, 1989, Oakland Art Assn. award, 1991, Marin Soc. Artists award, 1992. Mem. U. Calif. Berkeley Faculty Club, Orinda Country Club. Republican. Roman Catholic. Home: 31 Valley View Rd Orinda CA 94563

EPPLEY, FRANCES FIELDEN, educator, author; b. Knoxville, Tenn., July 18, 1921; d. Chester Earl and Beulah Magnolia (Wells) Fielden; m. Gordon Talmage Cougle, July 25, 1942; children:Russell Gordon Eppley, Carolyn Eppley Horseman; m. Fred Coan Eppley, Mar. 8, 1953; 1 child, Charlene Eppley Sellers. BA in English, Carson Newman Coll., 1942; M.A., Winthrop Coll., 1963. Tchr., East Corinth (Maine) Acad., 1942-43; tchr. pub. schs., Charlotte, N.C., 1950-53, 59-83, Greenville, S.C., 1954-56, Spartanburg, S.C., 1957-58; head start tchr., summers 1964-68. Mem. hist. com. N.C. Bapt. Conv., 1985-88. Alpha Delta Kappa grantee, 1970. Mem. NEA, N.C. Social Studies Conf., Writers Assn., Alpha Delta Kappa, Pi Kappa Delta, Alpha Psi Omega. Baptist. Author: First Baptist Church of Charlotte, North Carolina: Its Heritage, 1981, History of Flint Hill, 1983, The First Astrologer, 1983, Sammy's Song, 1984, No Show Dog, 1985, Sun Signs for Christians, 1985, Astrology and Prophecy, 1987, Our Heavenly Home, 1987, Men Like-, 1987, A Hammer in the Land, 1988, Aunt Lillian's Seafoam Candy, 1988, Women's Lib in the Bible, 1988, William Penn, 1988, Columbus Was a Christian, 1988, Horoscopes of the Presidents, 1988, Messiah, 1989, 93, The Signs of Your Life, 1994; (musical drama): The Place To Be, 1982, Praise in the West, 1987; (musical show): Songs of The People, 1983; (song): Katie, 1985, (cantata) How Come, Jesus?, Stubborn Stella and The Sitting Stone, 1990, Columbus: The Race Home, 1990, Religion and Astrology, 1991, Astrology and Prophecy, 1991, The Ghosts of Elmwood, 1992, Full Circle, 1992, Sonnet to Charlotte, 1992, How Children Learn, 1992, Your Child and Astrology, 1992, Use Astrology to Help Your Child, 1992, Christmas Magnus, 1993, Ah, Jericho!, 1993, The Parthenon, U.S.A., 1993, The Shepherds Fields, 1993, Another Spring and World War II, 1994, The Mystery of Laura K. Barnes, 1994, Contamination, 1994, First Landings, 1994, The Signs of Your Life, 1994, Teach the Children to Read, 1994; editor: Chester's Letters, 1994.

EPPS, HELEN CHARLOTTE, psychologist; b. Bklyn., Oct. 17, 1946; d. Gerald J. and Lillian J. (Joffe) E.; m. James Marvin Statman, Apr. 1, 1979 (div. Feb. 1984). BA, Conn. Coll., 1968; MA, U. Mich., 1971, PhD, 1976. Lic. clin. psychologist, Va., D.C. Trainer of vols. Ozone House, Ann Arbor, Mich., 1973-75; project dir. Edn. Systems Corp., Washington, 1976-78; mental health therapist III Mt. Vernon Ctr. Community Mental Health, Springfield, Va., 1978-81; clin. psychologist pvt. practice, Alexandria, Va., 1981-86, Arlington, Va., 1986—. Sec. Tenley & Cleveland Park Emergency Com., Washington, 1986—. Mem. APA, Am. Orthopsychiat. Assn. (program faculty 1985), Va. Psychol. Assn., Va. Acad. Clin. Psychologists, No. Va. Soc. Clin. Psychologists, D.C. Psychol. Assn. (mem.-at-latge 1994—, sec. bd. dirs. 1992-94). Jewish. Office: 4001 9th St N Apt 220 Arlington VA 22203-1900

EPPS, ROSELYN ELIZABETH PAYNE, pediatrician, educator; b. Little Rock, Dec. 11, 1930; d. William Kenneth and Mattie Elizabeth (Beverly) Payne; m. Charles Harry Epps, Jr., June 25, 1955; children: Charles Harry III, Kenneth Carter, Roselyn Elizabeth, Howard Robert. BS, Howard U., 1951, MD, 1955; MPH, Johns Hopkins U., 1973; MA, Am. U., 1981. Intern Freedmen's Hosp., Howard U., Washington, 1955-56, pediatric resident, 1956-59, chief resident, 1958-59; practice medicine specializing in pediatrics Washington, 1960; med. officer, pediatrics D.C. Dept. Pub. Health, Washington, 1961-64, dir. Clinic for Retarded Children, 1964-67, chief Infant and Pre-Sch. div., 1967-71, dir. children and youth project, 1970-71, dir. maternal and crippled children services, 1971-75; chief Bur. Clin. Services D.C. Dept. Human Services, Washington, 1975-80, acting commr. pub. health, 1980; instr., asst. research investigator Howard U. Coll. Medicine, Washington, 1960-61, prof. Dept. Pediatrics and Child Health, 1980—, chief div. child devel., 1985-89, dir. Child Devel. Ctr., 1985-89; rsch. assoc., vis. scientist smoking tobacco and cancer program, div. cancer prevention and control Nat. Cancer Inst. NIH, Washington, 1989-91; expert Nat. Cancer Inst. NIH, Pub. Health Applications Rsch. Branch, Bethesda, Md., 1991—; chmn. task force to prepare comprehensive child care plan for D.C. Dept. Human Services, 1973-74; mem. nat. task force on pediatric hypertension Heart, Lung and Blood Inst., NIH, 1975; chmn. rsch. grants rev. com. maternal and child health and crippled children's svcs. HEW, Rockville, Md., 1978-80; sec. Commn. Licensure to Practice Healing Arts, Washington, 1980; trustee med. svc. D.C. Blue Shield Plan Nat. Capital Area, 1980; chmn. sec.'s adv. com. on rights and responsibilities of women HEW, Washington, 1981; dir. high-risk young people's project Howard U. Hosp., 1981-85; Washington coord. Know Your Body Program Am. Health Found., N.Y.C., 1982-91; mem. bd. advs. Coll. Home Econs. Ohio State U., Columbus, Ohio, 1983-87; adv. com. Nat. Ctr. for Edn. in Maternal and Child Health Georgetown U., Washington, 1983-89; nat. steering com., subcom. chmn. Healthy Mothers, Healthy Babies Coalition, Washington, 1983-90, mem. nominating com., 1991; cons. sickle cell disease NIH, 1984-88, Govt. Liberia and World Bank, 1984, UN Fund for Population Activities, N.Y. and Caribbean, 1984, filmstrip Miriam Berg Varian/Parents Mag. Films, 1978; bd. dirs. Vis. Nurse Assn., Inc., Washington, 1983-89; pres. bd. dirs. Hosp. for Sick Children, Washington, 1986-90, bd. dirs., 1984-94; frequent guest lectr. Weekly columnist Your Child's Health, Afro-Am. Newspaper, Washington, 1960-63; contbr. articles syndicated column Nat. Newspaper Pubs. Assn., 1982, Nat. Newspaper Assn., 1986-87; co-author audiocassettes; exhibitor sci. program; contbr. over 70 articles to profl. jours. Trustee nat. bd. Palmer Meml. Inst., Sedalia, N.C., 1969-71, Ford's Theatre, Washington, 1973-79; U.S. trustee Children's Internat. Summer Villages, Casstown, Ohio, 1969-76, pres. 1974-75; bd. mgrs. YWCA of D.C., 1970-76, 77-83, vice chmn. 1975-76; v.p. Jack and Jill of Am., Inc., Washington, 1970-71; nat. bd. dirs. Ctr. Population Options, Washington, 1980-86, Alexander Graham Bell Assn. for Deaf, Washington, 1974-78; bd. dirs. Washington Performing Arts Soc., 1971-81, v.p. 1979-81, hon. dir. 1981—; nat. bd. dirs. Meridian House Internat., Washington, 1974-81, counselor, 1981—; bd. dirs. YWCA Nat. Capital Area, 1975-76, United Negro Coll. Fund D.C., 1981-85; nat. bd. dirs. Girls Inc. (formerly Girls Clubs Am., Inc.), N.Y.C., 1984—, asst. sec., 1986-88, sec., 1988-90, pres., 1990-92; bd. dirs. Nat. Assembly Vol. Health and Welfare Agys., 1985-90, exec. bd. 1986-90, sec., 1988-90; bd. dirs. Mut. of Am., 1992—. Recipient Leadership and Meritorious Service in Medicine award Palmer Meml. Inst., 1968, 14th Ann. Fed. Women's award CSC, Washington, 1974, Superior Performance award D.C. Govt., 1975, Meritorious Community Servicd Howard U. Sch. Social Work Alumni Assns. and vis. com., 1980, Cert. Commendation Mayor of D.C., 1981, Roselyn Payne Epps M.D. Recognition Resolution of 1983 Council D.C., 1983, Disting. Vol. Leadership award March of Dimes Birth Defects Found., 1984, Community Svc. award D.C. Hosp. Assn., 1990, Physician of Yr. award Women's Med. Assn. N.Y.C., 1990, 91; named Outstanding Vol. in Leadership category YWCA Nat. Capital Area, 1983; inducted into D.C. Women's Hall of Fame D.C. Commn. for Women, 1990; grantee Robert Wood Johnson Found., Princeton, N.J., 1982, div. maternal and child health HHS, Rockville, Md., 1986; honored Tribute Resolution of 1981 declaring Feb. 14 Dr. Roselyn Payne Epps Day, Council of D.C., 1981; recipient Ophelia Settle Egypt award Planned Parenthood of Met. Washington, 1991. Fellow Am. Acad. Pediatrics (alt. state chmn. D.C. 1973-75, exec. com. D.C. chpt. 1983—, pres. D.C. chpt. 1988-91, sec. community pediatrics sect. 1973-75, cert. appreciation 1979, mem. coun. of child and adolescent health, community and internat. health sect., charter mem., exec. com. 1992-94); mem. Acad. Medicine, AMA (alt. del. Nat. Med. Assn. 1983-85), Am. Med. Women's Assn. (chmn. pub. health com. 1973-75, pres. br. 1 1974-76, sec. 1988, v.p. 1989, pres-elect nat. 1990, pres. 1991, found. founding pres. 1992, bd. dirs. 1992—, chmn. nominating com. 1993, Physician of Yr. award 1991, Community Svc. award 1990, Elizabeth Blackwell award 1992), Med. Soc. D.C. (exec. bd. 1990, sec. 1990, pres.-elect 1991, pres. 1992, chair exec. bd. 1993, ann. Community Svc. award 1982), Am. Pediatric Soc., D.C. Hosp. Assn. (Community Svc. award 1990), Am. Pub. Health Assn. (action bd. 1977-79, joint policy com. 1978-79, gov. council 1978-81), Met. Washington Pub. Health Assn. (gov. council 1975-78, 81-83, ann. award 1981), Nat. Med. Assn. (chmn. pediatric sect. 1977-79, Ross Labs. award 1979, Outstanding Svcs. to Children during Internat. Yr. of Child award 1979, Meritorious Service Appreciation award 1979, W.M. Cobb co-lectr. 1985, mem. Coun. on Maternal and Child Health, 1974-92, chmn. 1979-89, Grace Marilyn James award for Disting svc. Pediatric sect. 1991, Achievement award 1993), Am. Hosp. Assn. (maternal and child health sect. governing coun. 1989, 1992-94, maternal and child health nominating com. 1991), Alpha Omega Alpha, Delta Omega, Alpha Kappa Alpha. Mem. United Ch. of Christ. Clubs: Pearls (pres. 1984-86), Carrousels (corr. sec. 1978-80), Links (pres. Met. chpt. 1986-89) (Washington), Cosmos. Lodge: Zonta. Home: 1775 N Portal Dr NW Washington DC 20012-1014 Office: Nat Cancer Inst NIH DCPC/CCSP/PHARB/EPN-241 6130 Executive Blvd MSC7333 Bethesda MD 20892-7333

EPPS, RUTH WILLIAMS, accounting educator, researcher; b. Richmond, Va., Jan. 28, 1948; d. W. Edward and Charlotte Margaret Williams; m. Thomas H. Epps Jr., Aug. 21, 1971; children: Thomas III, Thomalyn. BS in Chemistry, Virginia Union U., 1967; MS in Chemistry, U. Pitts., 1971; M in Acctg., Va. Commonwealth U., 1981, PhD in Acctg., 1987. CPA, Va. Math and sci. tchr. U.S. Peace Corps, West Africa, 1967-69; math tchr. Richmond (Va.) Pub. Schs., 1972-73; sci. tchr. St. John's Vianney Sem., Goochland County, Va., 1973-76; univ. instr. Va. Union U., Richmond, 1982-83; rsch. asst. Va. Commonwealth U., Richmond, 1983-86, asst. prof., 1987-92, assoc. prof., 1992—; tax preparer IRS, Richmond, 1990-93; cons. in field. Contbr. articles to profl. jours. Ch. sch. tchr. Ebenezer Bapt. Ch., Richmond, 1978—; chair audit com. Not-for-profit Orgn., Richmond, 1990-93; career ctr. vol. Manchester H.S., Midlothian, Va., 1992—. Grantee Va. Commonwealth U., 1990-93. Mem. AICPAs, Am. Acctg. Assn., Nat. Assn. Black Accts. (Outstanding Member 1993), Assn. Govt. Accts., Inst. Mgmt. Accts. (dir. manuscripts). Office: Va Commonwealth U 1015 Floyd Ave Richmond VA 23284-4000

EPSTEIN, BARBARA, editor; b. Boston, Aug. 30, 1929; d. H.W. and Helen (Diamond) Zimmerman; children: Jacob, Helen. B.A., Radcliffe Coll., 1949. Editor N.Y. Rev. Books, N.Y.C., 1963—. Office: NY Rev of Books 250 W 57th St New York NY 10102-0158

EPSTEIN, CYNTHIA FUCHS, sociology educator, writer. B.A. in Polit. Sci., Antioch Coll., 1955; postgrad., U. Chgo. Law Sch., 1955-56; M.A. in Sociology, New Sch. Social Research, 1960; Ph.D., Columbia U., 1968. Instr. anthropology Finch Coll., 1961-62; assoc. in sociology Columbia U., 1964-65, instr. Barnard Coll., 1965; instr. sociology Queens Coll., N.Y.C., 1966-67, asst. prof., 1968-70, assoc. prof., 1971-74, prof., 1974-84; prof. grad. ctr. CUNY, 1974, Disting. prof. Grad. Ctr., 1990; resident scholar Russell Sage Found., 1982-88; co-dir. Program in Sex Roles and Social Change Ctr. Social Scis., Columbia U., 1977-82, co-dir. NIMH tng. grant on sociology and econs. of women and work Grad. Ctr., disting. prof. Grad. Ctr., 1990—; vis. prof. Health Sci. Ctr., SUNY-Stony Brook, 1975; vis. scholar Stanford U., 1991; Phi Beta Kappa vis. scholar, 1991-92; cons., lectr. and speaker in field; mem. com. on women's employment and related social issues NRC-Nat. Acad. Scis., 1981-88; adv. com. on econ. role of women Pres.' Council Econ. Advisers, 1973-74. Author: Woman's Place: Options and Limits in Professional Careers, 1970, Women in Law, 1981, 2d edit., 1993, Deceptive Distinctions: Sex, Gender and the Social Order, 1988; editor: (with William J. Goode) The Other Half: Roads to Women's Equality, 1971; (with Rose Laub Coser) Access to Power: Cross-National Studies of Women and Elites, 1981; mem. editorial bds.: Signs, Women's Studies, Internat. Jour. Work and Occupations, Sociol. Focus, Women 1974, Dissent, Am. Jour. Sociology, CUNY Mag., Gender and Soc.; contbr. chpts. to books, articles to profl. jours. Trustee Antioch U., 1984—. Inst. Life Ins. grantee, 1974; Ford Found. grantee, 1975-77, Rsch. Found. grantee City of N.Y., 1974-76, 1990-93, Guggenheim Meml. Found. grantee, 1976-77, Ctr. Advanced Study in Behavioral Scis. grantee, 1977-78, Russell Sage Found. grantee, 1982-90; NIH fellow, 1963-66, MacDowell Colony fellow, 1973, 74, 77, 80, Guggenheim fellow, 1976-77, Ctr. Advanced Study in Behavioral Sci. fellow, 1977-78, Va. Ctr. Creative Arts fellow, fall 1984; award for contbn. to study of sex and gender ASAN, 1994. Mem. Eastern Sociol. Soc. (v.p. 1977-79, exec. council 1973-74, pres. 1983-84 I. Peter Gellman award), Am. Sociol. Assn. (council 1974-77, com. exec. office and budget, 1978-81, chmn. sect. on sociology of sex roles 1973-74), Social. Research Assn., AAAS, Internat. Sci. Commn. on Family. Office: CUNY Grad Ctr 33 W 42nd St New York NY 10036-8003

EPSTEIN, ELLEN SUE, outplacement, human resource consulting executive; b. N.Y.C., Dec. 30, 1948; d. Leonard Epstein and Suzanne (Le Win) Schneiderman. BA, U. Charleston, 1970; postgrad., Marshall U., 1973-74; MA, U. Cin., 1976. Cert. tchr. Tchr. Charleston (W.Va.) High Sch., 1971-73; audiologist Robert C. Kratz, MD, Newport, Ky., 1976-77; mkt. rsch. adminstr. Procter & Gamble Co., Cin., 1978-85; human resource specialist Xetron Corp., Cin., 1986-88; cons. Epstein & Assocs., Cin., 1988-89; v.p. Drake Beam Morin, Inc., Cin., 1989—; speaker, cons. Job Support Club, Cin. and Hamilton, 1990. Mem. North Avondale Community Assn., Cin., 1991, U. Cin. Alumni, 1991. Recipient Academic scholarship Marshall U., Huntington, W.Va., 1974, U. Cin., Ohio, 1974-76. Mem. ASPCA (pres. 1994-95), Tri State Human Resource Assn. (bd. mem. 1990-91), Internat. Assn. Outplacement Profls. (bd. mem. Cin. chpt.), Wildlife Assn., U. Charleston Alumni (contbg. mem. 1980—), U. Cin. Alumni Assn. Alpha Xi Delta. Jewish. Home: 9 Avon Fields Pl Cincinnati OH 45229 Office: Drake Beam Morin Inc 11590 Century Blvd Ste 114 Cincinnati OH 45246

EPSTEIN, JUDITH ANN, lawyer; b. L.A., Dec. 23, 1942; d. Gerald Elliot and Harriet (Hirsch) Rubens; m. Joseph I. Epstein, Oct. 4, 1964; children: Mark Douglas, Laura Ann. AB, U. Calif., Berkeley, 1964; MA, U. San Francisco, 1974, JD, 1977. Bar: Calif. 1978, U.S. Dist. Ct. (no. dist.) Calif 1978, U.S. Supreme Ct. 1983, U.S. Ct. Appeals (9th cir.) 1984. With social svcs. dept. Sutter County, Yuba City, Calif., 1964-66; bus. devel. assoc. Yuba County C. of C., Marysville, Calif., 1968-70; rsch. clk. Calif. Supreme Ct., San Fransisco, 1977; ptnr. Crosby, Heafey, Roach & May, Oakland, Calif., 1978-91; gen. counsel and sec. Valent USA Corp., 1991—; lectr. U. Calif. Grad. Sch. Journalism in Media Law, Berkeley, 1987-91; bd. dirs. Sierra Pacific Steel, Hayward, Calif. Bd. dirs., v.p. Oakland Ballet, 1980—. Recipient Pres.'s award Oakland Ballet, James Madison Freedom of Info. award Soc. Profl. Journalists, 1992. Mem. Calif. Women Lawyers Assn., Alameda Bar Assn., Berkeley Tennis Club. Office: Valent USA Corp Ste 600 1333 N California Blvd Walnut Creek CA

EPSTEIN, MARSHA ANN, public health administrator, physician; b. Chgo., Feb. 4, 1945; m. Syyed Tariq Mahmood, June 14, 1975; 1 child, Lee Rashad. BA, Reed Coll., 1966; MD, U. Calif., San Francisco, 1969; MPH, U. Calif., Berkeley, 1971. Diplomate Am. Bd. Preventive Medicine. Intern French Hosp., San Francisco, 1969-70; resident in preventive medicine Sch. Pub. Health, U. Calif., Berkeley, 1971-73; fellow in family planning dept. ob-gyn. UCLA, 1973-74; med. dir. Herself Health Clinic, L.A., 1974-79; pvt. adult gen. practitioner L.A., 1978-82; dist. health officer L.A. County Pub. Health, Inglewood, Calif., 1982—; part-time physician U. Calif. Student Health, Berkeley, 1970-73; co-med. dir. Monsenior Oscar Romero Free Clinic, L.A., 1992-93. Mem. APHA, Am. Coll. Physician Execs., Am. Med. Women's Assn., So. Calif. Pub. Health Assn., L.A. County Med. Women's Assn., L.A. County Sr. Women Mgrs. Democrat. Jewish. Office: Inglewood Health Dist 123 W Manchester Blvd Inglewood CA 90301

EPSTEIN, SANDRA GAIL, psychologist; b. Boston, July 19, 1939; d. Mischa and Frances (Greenfield) Schneiderman; 1 child, Suanne Charyl. AB, Boston U., 1962; MA, U. Conn., 1969, diploma, 1978, PhD, 1979. Sch. psychol. examiner various pub. schs., Conn., 1970-73, sch. psychologist, 1973—; staff psychologist Day Kimball Hosp. Mental Health Clinic, Putnam, Conn., 1971-74; psychologist Thompson (Conn.) Med. Ctr., 1973-80; staff psychiatry dept. Day Kimball Hosp., Putnam, 1983—; pvt. practice Woodstock, Conn., 1980-85, Putnam, 1983—, Farmington, 1985—; instr. Annhurst Coll., Woodstock, Conn., 1971-76; cons. N.E. Area Regional Ednl. Svc., Wauregan, Conn., 1978-79, Capitol Region Ednl. Coun., West Hartford, Conn., 1980—, Ctr. for Interpersonal Rels., Putnam, 1985-88, Hebrew Acad. Greater Hartford, Bloomfield, Conn., 1983-89, Conn. Bur. Rehab. Svcs., Norwich, 1992—. Mem. Am. Psychol. Assn., Internat. Soc. Hypnosis, Internat. Psychosomatics Inst., N.Y. Acad. Sci., Conn. Psychol. Assn., Am. Soc. Clin. Hypnosis, Am. Acad. Pain Mgmt., N.Y. Acad. Sci. Office: PO Box 207 Woodstock CT 06281-0207

EPSTEIN, WILMA GELLER, advertising agency executive; b. N.Y.C., Jan. 6, 1946; d. Jack R. and Dorothy (Brill) Geller; m. Jeffrey L. Epstein, Oct. 27, 1968; 1 child, Jill. Student, Bernard Baruch Sch. Bus., 1963-64, New Sch. for Social Rsch., 1964-65. Asst. planner Batten, Barton, Durstine & Osborne, N.Y.C., 1965-66; planner West Weir & Bartel, N.Y.C., 1966-68; planner Ogilvy & Mather, N.Y.C., 1968-76, asst. media dir., 1976-79, sr. v.p., assoc. media dir., 1979—, mem. oper. bd., 1986—; bd. dirs., chmn. Bus. Publs. Audit, N.Y.C., 1982-88. Bd. dirs. Jewish Guild for Blind, N.Y.C., 1974-79. Named Industry Media Allstar Mktg. & Media Decisions Mag., 1987. Office: Ogilvy & Mather Advt Worldwide Plz 309 W 49th St New York NY 10019*

EPSTEIN-SHEPHERD, BEE J., consultant, professional speaker; b. Tubingen, Fed. Republic Germany, July 14, 1937; came to U.S., 1940, naturalized, 1945; d. Paul and Milly (Stern) Singer; student Reed Coll., 1954-57; m. Leonard Epstein, June 14, 1959 (div. 1982); children: Bettina, Nicole, Seth; m. Frank Shepherd, 1991 (dec. 1992). BA, U. Calif., Berkeley, 1958; MA, Goddard Coll., 1976; PhD, Internat. Coll., 1982. Bus. instr. Monterey Peninsula Coll., 1975-85; owner, mgr. Bee Epstein Assos., cons. to mgmt., Carmel, Calif., 1977—; pres. Success Tours Inc., Carmel, 1981—; founder, prin. Monterey Profl. Speakers, 1982; instr. Monterey Peninsula Coll., Golden Gate U., U. Calif., Santa Cruz, Am. Inst. Banking, Inst. Ednl. Leadership, Calif. State Fire Acad. Monterey Peninsula Coll., U. Calif., Berkeley, Foothill Coll., U. Alaska. Author: How to Create Balance at Work, at Home, in Your Life, 1988, Stress First Aid for the Working Woman, 1991, Free Yourself From Diets, 1994; contbr. articles to newspapers and trade mags. Research grantee, 1976. Mem. NAFE, Nat. Speakers' Assn., Peninsula Profl. Women's Network. Democrat. Jewish. Office: PO Box 221383 Carmel CA 93922

ERB, DORETTA LOUISE BARKER, polymer applications scientist; b. Upper Darby, Pa., June 21, 1932; d. Ralph Merton and Pauline Kaufman (Isenberg) B.; m. Robert Allan Erb, June 27, 1953; children: Sylvia Ann, Susan Doretta, Carolyn Joy. BS in Pharmacy, Phila. Coll. Pharmacy and Sci., 1954. Registered pharmacist, Pa. Pharmacist Borland's Pharmacy,

Upland, Pa., 1954-65; assoc. scientist Franklin Rsch. Ctr., ATC div. Calspan Corp., Norristown, Pa., 1974-93; sole propr., pres. Siliclone Studio, Valley Forge, Pa., 1982—. Mem. Am. Anaplastology Assn., Sigma Xi (chpt. sec. 1990-93). Presbyterian. Home and Office: PO Box 86 Jug Hollow Rd Valley Forge PA 19481-0086

ERBACHER, KATHRYN ANNE, editor, art and design writer, marketing consultant; b. Kansas City, Mo., Dec. 11, 1947; d. Philip Joseph and Thelma Lillian (Hines) E. BS in English Edn., U. Kans., 1970; BA magna cum laude in Art, Metro State Coll., Denver, 1983. Reporter, Kansas City Star (Mo.), 1970-71; newswriter, publicist Washington U., St. Louis, 1972-76; copy editor Kansas City Star-Times (Mo.), 1976-79; corp. comm. mgr., editor Petro-Lewis Corp., Denver, 1979-82; assoc. Artours, Inc., Denver, 1983-84; assoc. editor arts and travel editor Denver Mag., 1984-86; owner Arts Internat., 1987—; internat. editor Gates Rubber Co., Denver, 1987-90; writer, fund raiser, mktg. cons. Creative dir. TV shorts for contemporary art collection Denver Art Mus., 1983. Bd. dirs. Metro State Coll. Alumni Assn., 1986-87, co-chair 1987 Metro State Coll. Alumni Awards Dinner, Denver; bd. govs. Metro State Coll. Found., 1986-87; mem. program com. Colo. Bus. Com. for the Arts, 1989-90; mem. pub. affairs com. Denver Ctr. for Performing Arts., 1989—; active Denver Art Mus. Alliance for Contemporary Art, 1984—. Recipient award for arts writing Denver Partnership, 1986, award for Artbeat column in Denver mag. Colo. MAC News, 1986, also award for spl. fashion sect. Dressing the Part; co-recipient award for Gates Rubber Co. Global Communications Bus./Profl. Advt. Assn., 1988. Mem. Denver Art Mus. (mem. design coun.), Museo de las Americas, Am. Assn. Museums. Avocations: visual art, theater, films, travel, Spanish language. Home: 819 Warren Landing Fort Collins CO 80525 Office: Arts Internat 819 Warren Landing Fort Collins CO 80525

ERBE, JANET SUE, medical/surgical, orthopedics and pediatrics nurse; b. Hamilton, Ohio, Aug. 25, 1952; d. Robert A. and Evon R. (Walls) Schlotterbeck; m. Gene Erbe. ADN, Miami U., Hamilton, 1972; BS summa cum laude, Coll. Mt. St. Joseph, 1989. Cert. in neonatal resuscitation, BLSC. With; asst. nurse mgr. Ft. Hamilton-Hughes Hosp., Hamilton, 1972—. Mem. ANA, ONA (legis. liason). Home: 916 Alberton Ave Hamilton OH 45013-2646 Office: 630 Eaton Ave Hamilton OH 45013-2767

ERBE, YVONNE MARY, music educator, marketing specialist; b. Wausau, Wis., Nov. 18, 1947; d. Rudolph Anton and Lucille Virginia (Andrew) Karlen; children: Daniel, Heather. B.Mus.Edn., U. Wis., Madison, 1969; postgrad. U. Wis.-Milw., MA in Guidance/Counseling Edn. Psychology, Eastern Ky. U., Richmond. Lic. music educator, Wis, Ky. Music-vocal tchr. Bayport Jr. High Sch., Greenbay, Wis., 1969-70; tchr. bassoon, oboe U. Wis.-Greenbay, 1969-70; jr. high choral dir. Kenosha Unified Schs., Wis., 1970-76; univ. supr.-edn. U. Wis.-Parkside, Kenosha, 1976-78; parent adv. com. mem. Northern Hills Sch. and Onalaska Mid. Sch., 1987-88; mktg. specialist Metro Prodns., La Crosse, Wis., 1984-85; tchr. music elem., jr. high sch., sr. high, LaCrosse, Wis., 1988-89, secondary high sch. choral dir., Lexington, Ky., 1989—. Parent vol. coord. Fauver Hill Sch., 1983-84; sec. exec. bd. Great River Festival of Arts, La Crosse, 1982-83, 1st v.p. exec. bd., chmn. adult choral workshop and performance, chmn. swing choir workshop, 1983-84, pres. bd. dirs., 1984-85; pres. La Crosse Area Newcomers Club, 1982-83; tchr. Confraternity of Christian Doctrine, 1985-88, bd. dirs. La Crosse Boy Choir, 1985-88, Lexington Children's Choir, 1994—; upward bound instr. Eastern Ky. U., 1994—. Mem. NEA, Am. Choral Dirs. Assn., Ky. Music Educators Assn., Ky. Edn. Assn., Phi Delta Kappa, Sigma Alpha Iota. Roman Catholic. Avocations: tennis, cross-country skiing, aerobic exercises, needlecrafts, gourmet cooking.

ERDEL, SALLY ELIZABETH, nurse; b. Peoria, Ill., Mar. 28, 1952; d. Robert William and Mary Maxine (Vick) Birky; m. Timothy Paul Erdel, Aug. 28, 1977; children: Sarah Beth, Rachel Elaine, Matthew Robert. AA summa cum laude, Ft. Wayne Bible Coll., 1972; grad. with highest honor, West Suburban Hosp. Sch. Nursing, Oak Park, Ill., 1975; BSN with high honor, U. Ill. Med. Ctr., Chgo., 1977, MS, 1980. Staff nurse West Suburban Hosp., 1975-77; teaching asst. U. Ill. Med. Ctr., 1980; staff nurse Highland Park (Ill.) Hosp., 1981-82; staff nurse Carle Found. Hosp., Urbana, Ill., 1982-87; mem. nursing faculty Bethel Coll., Mishawaka, Inc., 1994—; staff nurse St. Joseph's Hosp., Mishawaka, Ind., 1994—; seminar/workshop speaker, 1982—; clin. nurse specialist, 1985—; campus nurse, Jamaica Theol. Sem., Kingston, Jamaica, 1988-93, lectr. abnormal psychology, 1992-93; thesis sec. Caribbean Grad. Sch. Theology, Kingston, Jamaica, 1988-93; nursing cons. Devel. and Behavioral Evaluation Svcs., South Bend, Ind., 1994; team mem. Med. Group Mission, Liberia, 1975; vol. clinic nurse St. Andrew's Settlement, Kingston, 1991-93; missionary World Ptnrs., 1987-94. Mem. Oncology Nurses Soc., Cen. Ill. Oncology Nurses (co-editor newsletter 1983-87), Missionary Ch. Hist. Soc., Ill. Mennonite Hist. and Geneal. Soc. Home: 56111 Frances Ave Mishawaka IN 46545-7507 Office: Bethel Coll Divsn Nursing 1001 W McKinley Ave Mishawaka IN 46545

ERDEN, SYBIL ISOLDE, artist; b. N.Y.C., Nov. 30, 1950; d. Mark and Annelise (Stautner) E.; m. Philip M. Freund, July 7, 1970 (div. 1978); m. Jerry Buley, June 15, 1991. Student, Acad. of Art, San Francisco, 1970-71, San Francisco Art Inst., 1971-73, Ariz. State U., 1992-93. lectr. Calif. Coll. Arts and Crafts, 1978, Tempe Fine Art Ctr., 1985, Collins Gallery, San Francisco, 1986, Collage Art Appreciation Group, Colorado Springs, Colo., 1987, South Park Sch. Dist., Fairplay, Colo., 1987, Al Collins Sch. Graphic Design, 1989-90, Cerro Coso C.C., Calif., 1991, Chico State U., 1991; tchr. workshops City of Phoenix, 1991, Cerro Coso C.C., 1991, Phoenix Coll., 1992—, Cochise Coll., 1993; guest speaker 6th ann. Tempe Art Ctr. Seminar for Artists, 1993, Mesa C.C., 1994—, Gilbert/Chandler C.C., 1995. Shows include San Francisco Art Inst., 1973, The Bush Street Gallery, San Francisco, 1977, The Top Floor Gallery, San Francisco, 1979, I-Beam, San Francisco, 1980, Diablo Valley Coll., Walnut Creek, Calif., 1980, The Stable, San Francisco, 1982, Tempe Fine Arts Ctr., 1985, Collins Gallery, San Francisco, 1986, 89, 90—, Berkeley (Calif.) Art Ctr., 1986, The Cave, San Francisco, 1981, Alwun House, Phoenix, 1985, 87-93 (award 1989), Grand Canyon Coll., Phoenix, 1988, N.Mex. Jr. Coll., 1988, 90 (award 1990), San Francisco State U., 1988, Pa. State U., 1989, Ohio State U, 1989, Mendocino Art Ctr., 1990, Jewish Community Ctr., Denver, 1990, Cerro Coso Community Coll., Kern County, Calif., 1990-91, Chico State U., 1991, Sierra Arts Found., 1991, Ea. N.Mex. U., 1992, Shemer Art Ctr., Phoenix, 1991, Chico (Calif.) State U., 1992, Sierra Arts Found., Reno, Nev., 1992, Mars Artspace, 1993—; executed mural office of Dr. Peter Eckman, San Francisco, 1977, HandBall Express, San Francisco, 1981; archived by Smithsonian Mus. Archive Am. Art, Washington. Mem. Am. Surrealist Initiative, Ariz. Visionary Alternative (founder, dir. 1984-85, 87—), Movemiento Artiscico del Rio Salado Artspace (artist mem.). Democrat. Jewish.

ERDMAN, BARBARA, visual artist; b. N.Y.C., Jan. 30, 1936; d. Isidore and Julia (Burstein) E. Postgrad., Chinese Inst., 1959-60; BFA, Cornell U., 1956. Visual artist Santa Fe, 1977—; guest critic Studio Arte Centro Internat., Florence, Italy, 1986; guest lectr. Austin Coll. Sherman, Tex., 1986; mem. Oracle Conf. Polaroid Corp., nationwide, 1986-88. One-woman shows include Aspen Inst., Baca, Colo., 1981, Scottsdale (Ariz.) Ctr. for Arts, 1988, AAAS, Washington, 1994; exhibited in group shows, 1959—, including AAAS; represented in permanent collections N.Mex. Mus. Fine Arts, Santa Fe, IBM, N.Y.C.; author: New Mexico USA, 1985. Bd. dirs. N.Mex. Right to Choose, Santa Fe, 1981-87, Santa Fe Ctr. for Photography, 1983, pres. bd. 1985-89; mem. N.Mex. Mus. Found., Albuquerque Mus. Found. Mem. Art Student's League (life), Soc. for Photographic Edn. (guest lectr. 1987), Santa Fe Ctr. for Photography (pres., bd. dirs. 1984-89), Am. Coun. Arts. Home and Office: 1070 Calle Largo Santa Fe NM 87501-1090

ERDRICH, (KAREN) LOUISE, fiction writer, poet; b. Little Falls, Minn., June 7, 1954; d. Ralph Louis and Rita Joanne (Gourneau) E.; m. Michael Anthony Dorris, Oct. 10, 1981; children: Abel (dec.), Sava, Madeline, Persia, Pallas, Aza. BA, Dartmouth Coll., 1976; MA, Johns Hopkins U., 1979. Vis. poet, tchr. N.D. State Arts Council, 1977-78; tchr. writing Johns Hopkins U., Balt., 1978-79; communications dir., editor Circle-Boston Indian Council, 1979-80; textbook writer Charles Merrill Co., 1980. Author: (textbook) Imagination, 1981; (poems) Jacklight, 1984, Baptism of Desire, 1989; (novels) Love Medicine, 1984 (fgn. edits. in over 18 langs., numerous awards including Nat. Book Critics Cir. award 1984), expanded edit., 1993, The Beet Queen, 1986, Tracks, 1988, (with Michael Dorris) The Crown of Columbus, 1991, (with Dorris) Route 2, 1991, The Bingo Palace, 1994; contbr. short stories, essays and poems to popular mags., other publs. Johns Hopkins U. teaching fellow, 1979; Macdowell Colony fellow, 1980; Yaddo Colony fellow, 1981; vis. fellow Dartmouth Coll., 1981; Guggenheim fellow, 1985-86; recipient numerous awards for profl. excellence including Nelson Algren award, 1982, Pushcart prize, 1983, Nat. Mag. Fiction award, 1983, 87, First prize O. Henry awards, 1987. Mem. PEN (exec. bd. 1985-90), Authors Guild, Writers Guild, Am. Lit. Assn. Address: c/o Rambar and Curtis 19 W 45th St New York NY 10036

EREKSON, LAURIE IDA, school administrator; b. San Jose, Calif., Jan. 10, 1957; d. Harry and Geraldine Anne (Caliri) Copelan; m. Scott Erekson; children: Scott R., Nicholas J., Daniel R. BS in History with honors, Portland State U., 1982; MPA, Lewis & Clark Coll., 1993, cert. in ednl. adminstrn., 1993. Math. and sci. team leader, math. tchr. Parrish Mid. Sch.-Salem (Oreg.) Sch. Dist., 1984-91, math. counts coach, 1986-91; math. tchr. Mountain View Intermediate Sch.-Beaverton (Oreg.) Sch. Dist., 1983-84; sch. adminstr. Richmond Elem. Sch., 1993-94, Waldo Mid. Sch., 1994—; del. Oreg. Math. Leaders, 1990; com. mem. Mid. Sch. Improvement Process and implementation, Salem, 1990-94; mem. task force gifted and talented, 1994; trainer and presenter in field. Author: Mathematics Laboratory, 1985, The Seeds of Change: An Interdisciplinary Unit on the Cultural Encounter of 1492, 1992, Interdisciplinary Teaming: A Guide for Teachers and Principals, 1992, Interdisciplinary Teaming: The Centerpiece for Middle School Restructuring, 1993. Mem. Boys and Girls Aid Soc., Salem, 1991-94; planner, trainer, presenter Expanding Your Horizons Conf., 1987-95. Mem. ASCD, AAUW, N.W. Women in Adminstrn., Confedn. Oreg. Sch. Adminstrs., Oreg. Mid. Level Assn., Nat. Mid. Sch. Assn. Home: 5056 Cindy Pl SE Salem OR 97306

ERIACHO, BELINDA PEARL, environmental scientist; b. Ft. Defiance, Ariz., May 28, 1963; d. Tony Leopoldo Eriacho Sr. and Irene Rosalyn Lewis. BS, Ariz. State U., 1986; postgrad., U. N.Mex., 1988-89; MPH, U. Hawaii, 1990; postgrad., U. Mich., 1992, Ariz. State U., 1993—. Adminstrv. asst. health educator Maricopa County Health Svcs., Phoenix, 1986-87; health educator Navajo Nation Dept. Health, Window Rock, Ariz., 1987-88; tng. coord. Navajo Nation Family Planning Corp., Window Rock, Ariz., 1988-89; extern Navajo Area Indian Health Svc., Window Rock, Ariz., 1989-90, jr. health adminstrv. officer, 1990; sr. environ. sci. Ariz. Pub. Svc. Co., Phoenix, 1991—; speaker No. Ariz. U., Flagstaff, 1994; speaker math., engring., sci. achievement, Phoenix, 1992, Window Rock H.S., 1992, NTUA, Ft. Defense, Ariz., 1994—. Environ. cons. Navajo Tribal Utility Authority, 1993—; pre-med. intern Scottsdale Meml. Hosp., 1986; health assoc. Phoenix Indian Med. Ctr., 1985; Phys., Intellectual, Emotional and Spiritual vol. Ariz. State U. Health Svcs., Tempe, 1984-85; EMT asst. Navajo Emergency Med. Svcs., Ft. Defiance Indian Health, 1983; bd. dirs. Indian Comty. Health Inc., 1994. Recipient scholarship Navajo Nation, 1990, Nat. Action Coun. for Minorities in Engring., 1981-82; named one of Outstanding Young Women of Am., 1994-95. Mem. APHA, Am. Indian Sci. and Engring. Soc., Am. Indsl. Hygiene Assn., Ariz. Indsl. Hygiene Assn., Ariz. State U. Alumni, Ariz. State Native Am. Alumni Assn. (bd. dirs. 1988-89), Ariz. State U. Indian Grad. Assn., Environ. Auditing Roundtable, U. Hawaii Pub. Health Alumni Assn., Delta Omega. Office: Ariz Pub Svc Co PO Box 53999 Sta 9366 Phoenix AZ 85072-3999

ERICKSEN, BARBARA ELAINE, association executive; b. Kalamazoo, Mich., Mar. 23, 1953; d. Robert Einar and Grace May (Collins) E. BA in Humanities, U. Louisville, 1975, BA in Comm. cum laude, 1981. Coord. Sylvia Watson Reelection Campaign, Louisville, 1980; announcer, talk show host WINN, Louisville, 1980-81; mktg. rep. Bradford Nat. Corp., Fla., 1981-83; with sports dept. WINZ, Miami, Fla., 1983; mgr. photo/calligraphy Touch of Class, Ft. Lauderdale, 1983-85; photographer Weaver Photo Lab., Ft. Lauderdale, 1985-87; photographer, columnist South Fla. Rev., Ft. Lauderdale, 1986-88; community rels. coord. The Starting Pl., Hollywood, Fla., 1987-93; exec. dir. Sunrise (Fla.) C. of C., 1993—. Columnist Broward Informer Newspaper, 1994—. Bd. dirs. Channel 6 Neighbors Helping Neighbors, Miami, 1993—, Colee Hammock Home Owners Assn., Ft. Lauderdale, 1993—, Bus. Against Narcotics and Drugs, 1994—, Sunrise Econ. Devel. Bd., 1994, Broward County Commn. Substance Abuse, 1994—; co-chair small bus. campaign United Way of Broward County, 1994; mem. Children's Consortium County Report Card, 1993-94; active Am. Cancer Soc., 1993—; sec., newsletter editor, chair advt. com. Broward County Coun. Chambers, 1994-95. Recipient Presdl. award Ft. Lauderdale Jaycees, 1988-92, Broward County Govt. and United Way award of appreciation, Ft. Lauderdale, 1990-91, Suncoast Signature award Nat. Soc. Fundraising Execs., Fla., 1992, City of Ft. Lauderdale Community Appearance award Home and Garden, 1993, Plaque of Appreciation from bd. dirs. Sunrise C. of C., 1994, Best Group Project award Leadership Sunrise IV, 1994; named Ky. Col., 1987. Mem. NAFE, Fla. Soc. Assn. Execs., Broward County Coun. Chambers, AAUW, Ft. Lauderdale Jaycees (bd. dirs. 1988-93, Jaycee of Yr. and Outstanding Project of Yr. 1993), Women's History Coalition. Office: Sunrise C of C 10116 W Oakland Park Blvd Sunrise FL 33351-6963

ERICKSON, CORNELIA FLAHERTY, legislative researcher; b. Helena, Mont., Aug. 22, 1946; d. Neil Edward and Elizabeth Theresa (Coyle) Flaherty; m. James Sheridan Erickson, Nov. 24, 1981; 1 child, Joshua Wright. BA, Carroll Co., 1968; MA, U. Mont., 1985. Tchr. elem. sch. Hayward (Calif.) Unified Sch. Dist., 1968-76; historian, archivist Diocese of Helena (Mont.), 1979-86; researcher Mont. AFL-CIO, Helena, 1986; office mgr. Mont. Women's Lobby, Helena, 1986-87; legis. researcher Mont. Legis. Coun., Helena, 1987—. Author: Go With Haste Into the Mountains, 1984. Bd. dirs. United Way, Helena, 1985-87; mem. Helena Citizens Coun., 1983-87, Mont. Religious Legis. Coun., Helena, 1988-91. Mem. AAUW, Mont. Women's Lobby (treas. 1982-83). Roman Catholic. Home: 2201 5th Ave Helena MT 59601-4819 Office: Mont Legis Coun Rm 138 State Capitol Helena MT 59620

ERICKSON, DIANE LOUISE, art educator; b. Northfield, Minn., May 1, 1963; d. Glenn Orville and Maureen Cecelia (Hanks) E. BFA magna cum laude, Mankato State U., 1988; MFA, U. Mich., 1990. Instr. design Ea. Mich. U., Ypsilanti, 1991; instr. ceramics Ann Arbor (Mich.) Potter's Guild, 1992, Schoolcraft Coll., Livonia, Mich., 1992—; cons. studio renovation Schoolcraft Coll., Livonia, 1994—; instr. three dimensional design Henry Ford C. C., Dearborn, 1993—; instr. ceramics Interlochen (Mich.) Arts Camp, 1993; head dept. Elliott's Floral Interiors, Detroit, 1994—; instr. workshop Siena Heights Coll, Adrian, Mich., 1993. Recipient Clay Merit award Cedar Heights Clay Co., 1993. Mem. Nat. Coun. Edn. Ceramic Art, Mich. Potters Assn., Ann Arbor Art Assn. (coord. exhibit 1993), Detroit Artists Market. Home: 310 Burwood Ave Ann Arbor MI 48103 Office: Schoolcraft Coll 18600 Haggerty Rd Livonia MI 48152

ERICKSON, DONNA JEAN, interior decorator; b. Decatur, Ill., Apr. 27, 1947; d. Carl E. and Betty J. (Cross) Maxey; m. Gary L. Erickson, June 7, 1969; children: Jami Kathryn, Tara Ann. BA in Liberal Arts and Edn., Bradley U., 1969; MBA in Mktg., Rochester Inst. Tech., 1977; postgrad., Palomar Coll., 1989. Tchr. home econs. Spencerport (N.Y.) H.S., 1969-70; store mgr. Fabric Tree, Rochester, N.Y., 1970-73; interior decorator Designs By Donna, San Diego, 1985—. Chmn. Country Christmas Festival Cmty. Ch., Poway, Calif. 1992-94, mem. design furnishings com., 1993-94, pres. women's fellowship, 1987. Mem. Poway C. of C. (amb. 1991—, pres. 1992), LeTip-San Diego North-Networking (speaker chmn. 1988-89, membership chmn. 1990, social chmn. 1991-93), Soroptimist Internat. Poway, Delta Zeta (pres. North County alumnae 1994, co-chmn. flame fantasy Lamplighters So. Calif. 1993-94, Betsy Bradley Leach svc. award 1994). Office: Designs By Donna 354 Rancheros Dr Ste 107 San Marcos CA 92069

ERICKSON, LINDA RAE, educator; b. Huron, S.D., Aug. 17, 1948; d. Robert Emil and Esther (Schorzman) E. BS, U. Nebr., 1966; MA, U. No. Colo., Greeley, 1970; cert., U. Denver, 1990. Cert. elem. tchr., adminstr., prin. Spl. edn. resource tchr. Ignacio, Colo., 1983-85; elem. tchr. Woodland Park, Colo., 1985-86; tutor spl. edn. Am. Sch. London, 1987; elem. tchr. Borough of Brent, London, 1987, Internat. Sch. Hampstead, London, 1987-88; tchr. spl. edn. Carronhill Sch. for Handicapped, Stonehaven, Scotland, 1988-89; elem. tchr. Littleton (Colo.) Pub. Schs., 1970-83, 89—; enrichment program coord. Sandburg Sch., 1991-93; co-chair Alternative Authentic Assessment Com., 1991—, Sandburg Parent Adv. Com., 1993—; facilitator Littleton Pub. Schs., 1977-83, 90—; workshop presenter Nat. Coun. Tchrs. English, Nat. Coun. Social Studies, WNET-TV Sta. Active Fawcett Soc., London, 1987-89, NEA-Colo. Edn. Assn. Women's Caucus, 1979—. Woman of Yr. nominee Littleton Jaycees, 1982; fed. grantee Use of Group Paperbacks in the Elem. Classroom, 1978. Mem. NEA (women's leadership tng. cadre 1978-85), NOW, Colo. Edn. Assn., Littleton Edn. Assn. (bd. dirs., chair unit-bargaining team 1976-85), Internat. Reading Assn. (chair Pikes Peak 1986, Colo. coun. children's book award com. 1993—, workshop presenter), Colo. Assn. Sch. Execs., Alpha Delta Kappa, Phi Delta Kappa. Democrat. Lutheran. Home: 439 Saddlewood Cir Highlands Ranch CO 80126-2284 Office: Sandburg Elem Sch 6900 S Elizabeth St Littleton CO 80122-1829

ERICKSON, MARIANNA CUANY, family physician; b. Washington, Iowa, Apr. 12, 1954; d. Robin Louis and Carolyn Ella (Brewer) Cuany; m. Kenton Lloyd Erickson, July 5, 1980; children: Matthew, Jeremy, Christopher. BS, Sterling Coll., 1975; MD, U. Kans., Kansas City, 1978. Diplomate Am. Bd. Family Practice. Resident in family practice Meth. Med. Ctr., Peoria, Ill., 1978-81; family physician Princeville (Ill.) Med. Ctr., 1981—. Mem. Am. Acad. Family Physicians. Home: 10721 N Sleepy Hollow Rd Peoria IL 61615 Office: Princeville Med Ctr 223 E Main St Princeville IL 61559

ERICKSON, VIRGINIA BEMMELS, chemical engineer; b. Sleepy Eye, Minn., June 19, 1948; d. Gordon Boothe and Marion Mae (Rieke) Bemmels; m. Larry Douglas Erickson, Sept. 6, 1969; children: Kirsten Danielle, Dean Michael. Diploma in Nursing, Swedish Hosp. Sch. Nursing, 1969; BSChemE, U. Wash., 1983, MChemE, 1985. RN. Asst. head nurse N. Meml. Hosp., Mpls., 1970-73; intensive care RN Swedish Med. Ctr., Seattle, 1973-83; research asst. U. Wash., Seattle, 1983-85; instrumentation and control engr. CH2M Hill, Bellevue, Wash., 1985—, mgr. dept., 1988-93, mgr. info. mgmr., 1994—, v.p., 1995—; cons. instrumentation and control engr. Mem. editorial adv. bd. Control. Leader Girl Scouts U.S., Seattle, 1985; supt. Seattle Ch. Sch., 1983; rep. United Way, 1986—. Recipient Cert. Achievement, Soc. Women Engrs., 1983, Teenfeed, 1990. Mem. AICE, NAFE, Instrument Soc. Am., Tau Beta Pi. Democrat. Mem. United Methodist Ch. Home: 6026 24th Ave NE Seattle WA 98115-7009 Office: CH2M Hill 777 108th Ave NE PO Box 91500 Bellevue WA 98009-2050

ERICKSON, WHITNEY JAYE, critical care nurse; b. Williams AFB, Ariz., July 6, 1966; d. Morris Edward and Donna Sue (Wilson) Norsworthy; m. Curtis Allen Erickson, Mar. 10, 1992. ADN, Texarkana Coll., 1988; BSN, U. Ark. Med. Scis., 1991, MNSc, 1992; postgrad., Rush U., 1994—. Staff nurse med.-surg. Wadley Regional Med. Ctr., Texarkana, Tex., 1987-88; staff nurse burn/trauma Univ. Hosp., Little Rock, 1989-90; rsch. nurse coord. Dr. John Eidt, Little Rock, 1990-92; staff nurse ICU Sierra Vista (Ariz.) Community Hosp., 1992, Univ. Med. Ctr., Tucson, Ariz., 1993-94. Mem. AACN, ANA, Am. Assn. Nurse Anesthetists, Am. Pain Soc., Ark. Nurses Assn., Sigma Theta Tau. Mem. RLDS Ch. Home: 1597 S Moorland Rd # 101 New Berlin WI 53151

ERICKSON-WEERTS, SALLY ANNETTE, dietetics educator; b. Phoenix, Oct. 18, 1952; d. Dennis Lee and Ann Marie (Conklin) E.; children: Matthew, Alexander, Kyle. BS, Mankato State U., 1973; MS, Kans. U., 1976. Registered dietitian, Minn. Clin. dietitian Saga Food Svc., Pitts., 1975-76; pub. health nutritionist Minn. Dept. of Health, Mpls., 1976-77; prof. Lakewood (Minn.) C.C., 1977-79; fed. nutritionist Indian Health Svcs./Pub. Health Svc., Anchorage, 1979-85; pvt. practice Monkato, Minn., 1986-89; pres. Dietary Care Systems, Inc., Mankato, Minn., 1989-92; asst. prof. Mankato State U., 1992—; cons. in field. Author: One Menu System, Nutritional Care System, Lite Weight, Diet Care Seminars, 1989-92. Mem. PEO, Am. Dietetic Assn. Office: Mankato State U Box 44 Mankato MN 56001

ERICSON, PHYLLIS JANE, counselor, psychotherapist, consultant; b. Ft. Worth, Aug. 16, 1947; d. John H. and Charlotte Marie (Turner) E.; divorced; children: Colleen Nichole Murphy Pass, Sean Matthew Murphy Pass. B. Gen. Studies in Bus. Mgmt. and Advt., U. Tex., Arlington, 1981; MA in Psychology and Psychotherapy, Antioch U., 1990; postgrad., Union Inst., Cin., 1992—. Registered and cert. hypnotist, Calif.; cert. chem. dependency counselor, Tex.; lic. profl. counselor, marriage and family therapist, chem. dependency counselor, Tex.; cert. nat. and neuro-linguist programming master strategist. Clk.-typist Gen. Dynamics Corp., Ft. Worth, 1965-69; counselor Snelling & Snelling Pers., Ft. Worth, 1970-72; account exec. Ft. Worth Star Telegram, 1972-79; v.p., prin. Ericson Assocs., Inc., Hurst, Tex., 1979-83; account exec. L.A.Times, Times Mirror Corp., 1983; nat. advt. dir. Baker Comm., Beverly Hills, Calif., 1984; owner, prin., builder GE Rehabs, Ft. Worth, 1984-86; counselor Comprehensive Counseling (later Ctrl. Psychol. Svcs.), Hurst, 1988-91; dir., counselor, cons. Ctrl. Psychol. Svcs., Bedford, Tex., 1988—; counselor J. Marszalek & Assoc., Dallas, 1984-87, Wynrose Outpatient Program, Arlington, Tex., 1988-89, HCA Richland Hosp., North Richland Hills, Tex., 1988-89; crisis intervention counselor Suicide and Crisis Ctr., Dallas, 1987-88; pvt. practice Ctr. for Counseling Devel. Svcs., Ft. Worth, 1987-88; group facilitator, clin. cons. Bedford Meadows Hosp., 1989-91; instr. psychology dept. Tex. Wesleyan U., 1989; mem. allied staff, group facilitator Charter Hosp.-Grapevine, Tex., 1991-92. Mem. ACA, Am. Assn. for Group Counseling, Nat. Assn. Alcohol and Drug Abuse Counselors, Tex. Assn. Alcohol and Drug Abuse Counselors, Internat. Soc. for Study Multiple Personality Disorders, North Tex. Assn. for Study Multiple Personality Disorders. Office: Ctrl Psychol Svcs 1901 Central Dr Ste 450 Bedford TX 76021-5830

ERICSON, RUTH ANN, psychiatrist; b. Assaria, Kans., May 15; d. William Albert and Anna Mathilda (Almquist) E. Student, So. Meth. U., 1945-47; BS, Bethany Coll.; MD, U. Tex., 1951. Intern, Calif. Hosp., L.A., 1951-52; resident in psychiatry U. Tex. Med. Br., Galveston, 1952-55; psychiatrist Child Guidance Clinic, Dallas, 1955-63; clin. instr. Southwestern Med. Sch., Dallas, 1955-72; practice medicine specializing in psychiatry, Dallas, 1955—; cons. Dallas Intertribal Coun. Clinic, 1974-81, Dallas Ind. Sch. Dist., U.S. Army, Welfare Dept., Tribal Concerns, Alcoholism, Adv. Bd. Intertribal Coun. Fellow Am. Geriatrics Assn., Royal Soc. Medicine, Royal Soc. Medicine; mem. So. Med. Assn., Tex. Med. Assn., Dallas Med. Assns., Am. Psychiat. Assn. (life), Tex. Psychiat. Assn., North Tex. Psychiat. Assn., Am. Med. Women's Assn., Dallas Area Women Psychiatrists, Alumni Assn. U. Tex. (Med. Br.), Navy League (life), Air Force Assn., Tex. Archaeol. Soc. (life mem.), Dallas Archaeol. Soc. (hon. life mem., pres. 1972-73, 82-84, 89-91, archival rschr.), South Tex. Archaeol. Soc., El Paso Archeol. Soc., N.Mex. Archaeol. Soc., Dallas Archeol. Soc. (hon. life, active archaeol. project), Paleopathology Soc., Internat. Psychogeriatric Assn. (Famous Women of the 20th Century), Alpha Omega Alpha, Delta Psi Omega, Alpha Psi Omega, Pi Gamma Mu, Lambda Sigma, Alpha Epsilon Iota, Mu Delta. Lutheran. Home: 4007 Shady Hill Dr Dallas TX 75229-2844 Office: 3026 Mockingbird Ln # 101 Dallas TX 75205

ERICSSON, SALLY CLAIRE, federal agency administrator; b. Madison, Wis., Jan. 16, 1953; d. William H. and JoAnn (Finnell) E.; m. Thomas A. Garwin, Oct. 7, 1979; children: Rachel, Benjamin. B in Urban and Regional Planning, U. Ill., 1976; M in Pub. Policy, Harvard U., 1980. Legis. analyst Dem. Steering and Policy Com, Washington, 1982-87; adminstr. asst. Rep. Sam Geidenson U.S. Ho. Reps., Washington, 1987-89; legis. asst. to Sen. John F. Kerry U.S. Senate, Washington, 1989-90; asst. to pres. for policy and rsch. Svc. Employees Internat. Union, Washington, 1990-93; assoc. under sec. for econ. affairs U.S. Dept. Commerce, Washington, 1993—. Home: 1805 Monroe St NW Washington DC 20010 Office: US Dept Commerce Econ & Stats Adminstrn 4836 Herbert C Hoover Bldg Washington DC 20230

ERIE, GRETCHEN ANN, cardiovascular clinician; b. Mason City, Iowa, June 18, 1945; d. Donald W. and Eloise M. Schultz; m. Thomas H. Erie, Aug. 19, 1990; stepchildren: Aaron, April. BSN, U. Iowa, 1967. RN; cert. basic life support, St. Paul. Staff nurse U. Iowa Hosp., Iowa City, 1967-68, Meth. Hosp., Houston, 1968-69; staff nurse cardiovascular surgery U. Minn. Hosp., Mpls., 1969-72, insvc. nurse cardiovascular surgery, 1972-75, head nurse cardiovascular surgery, 1975-81; nurse clinician Cardiac Surg. Assn., Mpls., 1981—; speaker U. Minn. Hosp. Community Edn. Dept., various cities in Minn., 1975-81, United Hosp., St. Paul, 1982, 87. Pianist Pleasant

Hills Nursing Home, St. Paul, 1987-89; flutist North Heights Luth. Ch., St. Paul, 1987—; patterning exerciser Handicapped Toddler, St. Paul, 1987-88; leader singles group North Heights Luth. Ch., 1984-88. Mem. AACN, Am. Heart Assn. Republican. Lutheran. Home: 3220 Orchard Ct White Bear Lake MN 55110 Office: Cardiac Surg Assn 920 E 28th St Ste 420 Minneapolis MN 55407-1139

ERIKSEN, JAN PAQUETTE, education educator; b. Columbus, Ohio, July 24, 1950; d. Jack Kenneth and Jane Audrey (Russell) Paquette; m. Mark John Eriksen, Oct. 10, 1975. BA in English, Ohio State U., 1972, MA in Journalism, 1981, MA in Counselor Edn., 1985, PhD in Adult Edn., 1990. Lic. profl. counselor, S.D. Customer svc. rep. Graybar Electric Co., Columbus, Ohio, 1972-75; copy dir., account exec. Howard Swink Advt. and Pub. Rels., Columbus, 1975-80; grad. adminstrv. assoc. to v.p. regional campuses, dean coll Ohio State U., Columbus, 1980-81, acad. advisor univ. coll., 1980-84, bridge program coord. Office Continuing Edn., 1984-90; asst. prof. dept. counseling and human resource devel. Coll. Edn. and Counseling, S.D. State U., Brookings, 1990-94; coord. gen. studies SUNY Buffalo State Coll., 1994—; presenter various confs., meetings, colls. and univs. throughout U.S. Referee editorial bd. Nat. Acad. Advising Assn. Jour., 1990-93; referee editorial bd. Dakota Counselor, 1990-94; contbr. articles to profl. jours. Mem. adv. bd. older workers program Career Learning Ctr., Brookings, S.D. Recipient scholarship Women in Comm. Inc., 1982-83, Profl. Devel. scholarship Nat. Acad. Advising Assn., 1987, Student Rsch. award Nat. Acad. Advising Assn., 1990. Mem. ACA, Am. Coll. Pers. Assn., Assn. Adult Devel. and Aging, Assn. Counselor Educators and Suprs., Nat. Acad. Advising Assn. (commn. on advising adult learners 1985—, task force on advising grad. students 1992—), Nat. Career Devel. Assn., No. Rocky Mountain Ednl. Rsch. Assn., S.D. Counseling Assn., S.D. Coll. Pers. Assn. (state coll. rep., conf. planning coms. 1993-94), S.D. Assn. Adult Devel. and Aging (pres.-elect 1993-94), S.D. Assn. Counselor Educators and Suprs. Office: Buffalo State Coll Lifelong Learning Ctr TR100 1300 Elmwood Ave Buffalo NY 14222-1095

ERION, CAROL ELIZABETH, music educator; b. Quincy, Ill., Jan. 16, 1943; d. Alva Eugene and Margaret Althea (Kaempfer) McKenney; m. David F. Erion, June 19, 1965; children: Elizabeth Celia Erion Brewer, Paul Frederick. MusB, Oberlin Coll., 1965; MusM, New England Conservatory Music, 1982; cert., U. Toronto, Ont., Can., 1978, Mozarteum Acad. Music, Salzburg, Austria, 1979. Music tchr. Montessori Sch. No. Va., Annandale, 1972-84, St. Agnes Episcopal Sch., Alexandria, Va., 1984-85, The Sidwell Friends Sch., Washington, 1985-87; music and fine arts tchr. Arlington (Va.) Pub. Schs., 1988—; music dir. All Saints Episcopal Ch., Alexandria, 1983-90; workshop clinician various music edn. orgns. in U.S., 1980—; adj. prof. George Mason U., Fairfax, Va., 1983—; cons. WETA-TV, Washington, 1987. Author: Tales to Tell, Tales to Play, 1982; contbr. articles to profl. jours. Humanities fellow Coun. Basic Edn., 1989. Mem. NEA, AAUW, ASCD, Am. Recorder Soc., Am. Orff Schulwerk Assn. (pres. 1993—). Democrat. Episcopalian. Home: 19 W Linden St Alexandria VA 22301-2621

ERLANSON, DEBORAH MCFARLIN, state program administrator; b. Watertown, N.Y., Oct. 17, 1943; d. Raymond Thomas and Alberta Antoinette (Schultz) McF.; m. David Norman Erlanson, Sept. 10, 1966; 1 child, Joshua David. AA in Liberal Arts, Dutchess Community Coll., 1964; BA in Psychology, Am. Internat. Coll., 1966; MS in Edn., So. Ill. U., 1972. Occupancy tng. coordinator Decatur (Ill.) Housing Authority, 1975-76, target projects program coordinator, 1976-77, spl. services coordinator, 1977-78, asst. dir. planning, 1978-82, dir. program devel., 1982—; speaker various convs., 1978—; cons. Piatt County Housing Authority, Monticello, Ill., 1985-89, Woodford Homes, Inc., Decatur, 1985-86. Steering com. Near West Restoration and Preservation Soc., Decatur, 1985-86, bd. dirs. 1986—, v.p. 1992—; steering com. Communities in Partnership, 1991—, bd. dirs. 1993—; mem. Decatur Advantage 20/20, 1993, Macon County Literacy Coun., 1992—; parent group counselor Macon County Parents Anonymous, Decatur, 1976-80; mem. health div. Decatur Coun. Community Svcs., 1978-84; bd. dirs. YWCA, Decatur, 1992—. Mem. Nat. Assn. Housing/Redevel. Ofcls. (Nat.: bd. govs. 1987—, profl. devel. com. 1983-93, vice-chair, 1987-89, v.p. profl. devel. 1987-89, task force product devel. 1987, task force elderly housing issues 1990-91, profl. devel. trainer 1986—, award of Excellence Jury 1991—, task force family self-sufficiency 1992-93; Regional: pres. 1993—, Charles A. Thompson award 1991, State: exec. bd. 1983-93, pres. 1984-87, William R. Hammond award 1993), Decatur Women's Network, Internat. City Mgmt. Assn. Home: 465 W Macon St Decatur IL 62522-3122 Office: Decatur Housing Authority 1808 E Locust St Decatur IL 62521-1596

ERLEBACHER, ARLENE CERNIK, lawyer; b. Chgo., Oct. 3, 1946; d. Laddie J. and Gertrude V. (Kurdys) Cernik; m. Albert Erlebacher, June 14, 1968; children: Annette Doherty, Jacqueline Erlebacher. B.A., Northwestern U., 1967, J.D., 1973. Bar: Ill. 1974, U.S. Dist. Ct. (no. dist.) Ill. 1974, U.S. Ct. Appeals (7th cir.) 1974, Fed. Trial Bar, 1983, U.S. Supreme Ct. 1985. Assoc. Sidley & Austin, Chgo., 1974-80, ptnr., 1980—. Bd. dirs. Legal Assistance Found. Chgo. Fellow Am. Bar Found.; mem. ABA, Ill. Bar Assn., Chgo. Bar Assn., Chgo. Council Lawyers, Order Coif. Office: Sidley & Austin 1 First Nat Plz Chicago IL 60603

ERLENBORN, MARY ENA, company financial official, accountant; b. Chgo., May 18, 1959; d. Wilton H.J. and Irene C. (Ziarko) E.; m. Thomas E. Templeton, June 11, 1988. BBA, Loyola U., Chgo., 1981; M Mgmt., Northwestern U., 1984. CPA, Calif. Audit mgr. Deloitte & Touche, San Diego, 1981-90; fin. cons., San Diego, 1990-92; bus. mgr. Sci. Applications Internat. Corp., San Diego, 1992—. Mem. AICPA, Inst. Mgmt. Accts. (cert.), Am. Soc. Women Accts. (chpt. pres. 1988-89, nat. bd. dirs. 1989-93, nat. v.p. 1991-93). Office: SAIC-ITER Joint Work Site 11025 N Torrey Pines Rd La Jolla CA 92037

ERLENMEYER-KIMLING, L., psychiatric and behavior genetics researcher, educator; b. Princeton, N.J.; d. Floyd M. and Dorothy F. (Dirst) Erlenmeyer; m. Carl F. E. Kimling. B.S. magna cum laude, Columbia U., 1957, Ph.D., 1961. Sr. research scientist N.Y. State Psychiat. Inst., N.Y.C., 1960-69; assoc. research scientist N.Y. State Psychiat. Inst., 1969-75, prin. research scientist, 1975-78, dir. div. devel. behavioral studies, 1978—, acting chief med. genetics, 1991—; asst. in psychiatry Columbia U., 1962-66, rsch. assoc., 1966-70, asst. prof., 1970-74, assoc. prof. psychiatry and genetics, 1974-78, prof., 1978—; vis. prof. psychology New Sch. Social Research, 1971—; Mem. peer rev. group NIH, 1976-80; mem. work group on guidance and counseling Congl. Commn. on Huntington's Disease, 1976-77; mem. task force on intervention Pres.'s Commn. on Mental Health, 1977-78; mem. initial rev. group NIMH, 1981-85; adv. bd. Croatian Inst. Brain Rsch., 1991—. Editor: Life-Span Research in Psychopathology, 1986; issue editor: Differential Reproduction, Social Biology, 1971, Genetics and Mental Disorders, Internat. Jour. Mental Health, 1972, Genetics and Gene Expression in Mental Illness, Jour. Psychiat. Rsch., 1992, Measuring Liability to Schizophrenia: Progress Report 1994, Schizophrenia Bull., 1994; mem. editorial bd. Social Biology, 1970-79, Schizophrenia Bull., 1978—, Jour. Preventive Psychiatry, 1980-84, Croatian Med. Jour., 1991—, Neurology/Psychiatry/Brain Research, 1991—, Neuropsychiat. Genetics, Am. Jour. Med. Genetics, 1992—. Recipient Merit award NIMH, 1989-96; grantee NIMH, 1966-69, 71-96, Scottish Rite Com. on Schizophrenia, 1970-74, 84-87, 89-94, W.T. Grand Found., 1978-86, MacArthur Found., 1981. Fellow APA, Am. Psychopath. Assn., Am. Psychol. Soc.; mem. AAAS, Am. Soc. Human Genetics, Behavior Genetics Assn. (mem.-at-large 1972-74, Theodosius Dobzhansky award 1985), Internat. Soc. Psychiat. Genetics, Soc. Study Social Biology (bd. dirs. 1969-84, 92-96, sec. 1972-75, pres. 1975-78), Scientists Ctr. for Animal Welfare, Phi Beta Kappa, Sigma Xi.

ERLICHSON, MIRIAM, fundraiser; b. Bronx, N.Y., July 26, 1948; d. Jack and Bess (Hyatt) E.; m. Walter Forman, Sept. 26, 1970 (div. 1975); m. Victor Petrusewicz, July 17, 1980. BA in English, CCNY, 1969; postgrad., Hunter Coll., 1970-71; MA, CCNY, 1976; JD, Pace U., 1993. Cert. secondary tchr., N.Y. Tchr. English Intermediate Sch. 84, Bronx, 1972-78; coord. ann. giving N.Y. Hosp.-Cornell Med. Ctr., N.Y.C., 1979-90; bd. dirs. 77th Settler Corp. Mem. Jane Austen Soc. (Eng.), Phi Beta Kappa.

ERNST, AMY L., artist; b. S. Norwalk, Conn., Apr. 26, 1953; d. Jimmy and Edith Dallas (Brodie) E.; m. Eric Donald Johnson, June 10, 1979 (div. June 1989). BS in Theatre and Arts, Emerson Coll., 1977; MA in Arts Adminstrn., Ind. U., 1984; student, Pratt Inst., Venice, Italy, 1992. Opera set designer various cos., Boston, 1975-80; curator Ernst Family Found. Exhbns. include Guild Hall Mus., E. Hampton, N.Y., 1991, 92, 93, Ward-Nasse Gallery, N.Y.C., 1991, 92, 93, Ashwagh Hall, Springs, N.Y., 1992, 93, Clayton & Liberatore Gallery, Bridgehampton, N.Y., 1992, Carolyn J. Roy Gallery, N.Y.C., 1993, Synchronicity Gallery, N.Y.C., 1993, Odeon Gallery, Sag Harbor, N.Y., 1993, Anita Shapolsky Gallery, N.Y.C., 1993, Galerie Delacroix, Tangier, Morocco, 1993, Brooke Alexander Gallery, N.Y.C., 1993, BWAC, N.Y.C., 1994, The Prince Bldg., N.Y.C., 1994, Fine Arts Gallery Mantee Community Coll., Fla., 1994. Vol. tchr. Met. Mus. Art; bd. dirs. Rimrock Found., E. Hampton, N.Y., 1992. Mem. Artist Equity, Jimmy Ernst Artist Alliance, Orgn. Ind. Artists, Guggenheim Mus., Reverse Renaissance (co-founder, chmn. 1993). Home: 808 Broadway New York NY 10003

ERNST, ANNA LOUISE, counselor; b. St. Louis, July 6, 1947; d. Lawrence Henry Sullentrup and Eleanor Lydia Biermann Sullentrup Berger; m. Donald E. Ernst, May 31, 1970; 1 child, Susan. BS in Edn. (Spanish), Ctrl. Mo. State U., 1969; MS in Edn., Ill. State U., 1977. Lic. high sch. counselor (bilingual). Fgn. lang. tchr. Union (Mo.) High Sch., 1969-70, Clinton (Mo.) High Sch., 1970-74; counselor Joliet (Ill.) Ctrl. High Sch., 1974—; crisis trainer/counselor Critical Incident Stress Debriefing, St. Joe's Med. Ctr., Joliet, 1991—; TeenLine coord. Joliet Ctrl. High Sch., 1987—. Contbr. articles to profl. jours. Mem. Multi-Agy. Survivor Svcs., Joliet, 1991-93. Mem. Am. Assn. Suicidology, Am. Counseling Assn., Ill. Alliance for Info. and Referral Systems, Nat. Alliance for Info. and Referral Systems. Office: Joliet Ctrl High Sch 201 E Jefferson Joliet IL 60432

ERNST, KATHRYN FITZGERALD, management, marketing consulting firm executive, author; b. N.Y.C., Nov. 12, 1942; d. Joseph Michael and Helen Ann (Dougherty) Fitzgerald; m. John Lyman Ernst, Dec. 7, 1971 (div. Apr. 1977). BA in Econs., Wells Coll., Aurora, N.Y., 1963; postgrad N.Y. U., 1964. Portiolio analyst Donaldson, Lufkin & Jenrette, N.Y.C., 1966-68; asst. v.p. Prentice-Hall, Englewood Cliffs, N.J., 1968-74; v.p. Franklin Watts/Grolier, N.Y.C., 1975-77; mktg. mgr. ITT, N.Y.C., 1977-80: mng. dir. Warburg, Paribas Becker, N.Y.C., 1980-82; pres., owner Ernst Assocs., Inc., N.Y.C., 1982—. Author: Danny and His Thumb, 1972, Mr. Tamerin's Trees, 1978 (Nat. Sci. Tcrh.s award 1979), Owl's New Cards, 1979 (ALA-Children's Choice award 1980), Charlie's Pets, 1980, Indians: The First Americans, 1981, ESP McGee & The Mysterious Magician, 1984, The Complete Calorie and Carbohydrate Counters for Dining Out, 1987. Recipient Outstanding Achievement award Fed. Govt., 1966, Pub. Achievement award Christopher Soc., 1973, Acad. Women Achievers YWCA, 1979. Mem. Direct Mktg. Assn. (Echo award 1985), Nat. Adv. Coun. for Artss for Am., Williams Club. Avocations: bridge, chess, golf, modern art, jazz. Office: Ernst Assocs Inc 120 E 56th St Ste 500 New York NY 10022-3607

ERNST BOGDAN, JANET LEE, interior designer; b. Winston-Salem, N.C., Apr. 16, 1955; d. William Lee Ernst and Marie Keith (Shouse) Snyder; m. Nica Bogdan, Aug. 19, 1994. BS in Home Econs., Interior Design, U. N.C., Greensboro, 1977. Instr. arts and crafts Craft Showcase, Winston-Salem, 1977-78; display design The Ltd., Inc., N.C. and S.C., 1978-79; designer ind. retail stores Winston-Salem, 1977-81; head design dept. Butler Enterprises, Inc., Winston-Salem, 1981-86; design prin. Carolina Contract Design, Winston-Salem, 1986—; pres. Triad Design Concepts, Inc., Winston-Salem and Greensboro, 1988-90; cons. design, catalog line drawings, photography contract furniture and lighting mfrs., N.C. and Ga.; mentor student interns U. N.C., Greensboro, 1983-84, 87-90; propr. Carolina Carpet Svcs., 1992. Vol. Humane Soc., Winston-Salem, 1977-78; bd. dirs. Jamestowne Homeowners Assn., 1991-94, treas., 1993, pres., 1994; invited participant citizen amb. program Comml. Interior Design Del. to People's Republic of China. Mem. Inst. Bus. Designers (affiliate, ednl. com. 1987), Nat. Trust Hist. Preservation. Republican. Moravian. Office: Carolina Contract Design The Keystone 1386-F Westgate Center Dr Winston Salem NC 27103

ERNSTER, SISTER JACQUELYN, college president; b. Salem, S.D., Oct. 3, 1939; d. John Ernster and Eleanor (Bie) Ingalls. B.A., Mount Marty Coll., 1965; M.A., Ind. U., 1969; Ph.D., Ohio State U., 1976. Mem. faculty Mount Marty Coll., Yankton, S.D., 1970-76, v.p. acad. affairs, 1976-83, pres., 1983—; speaker S.D. Commn. on Humanities Pub. Issues Forum, 1980-82. Corp. bd. dirs. Sisters of Sacred Heart Convent, Yankton, 1976-82; trustee Madonna Profl. Care Ctr., Lincoln, Nebr., 1977-82. Mem. editorial bd. Yankton Press and Dakotan, 1984. Bush Found. fellow, 1982-83. Mem. Am. Council on Edn. (nat. identification program 1979, nat. com. on women in higher edn. 1984—), Nat. Assn. Ind. Colls. and Univs. (bd. dirs. 1989-91), Council for Ind. Colls., S.D. Pvt. Coll. Found., Consortium for Mid-Am. (chmn. pres. 1988-89), Delta Kappa Gamma (pres. 1980-82). Club: Interchange (bd. dirs. 1985) (Yankton), Kiwanis (bd. dirs. Yanktown chpt. 1990). Office: Mt Marty Coll Office of the President 1105 W 8th St Yankton SD 57078-3724

ERRICKSON, BARBARA BAUER, electronic equipment company executive; b. Pitts., Apr. 5, 1944; d. Edward Ewing Bauer and Margaret J. McConnell; m. James Jay Burcham, June 30, 1966 (div. May 1972); children: James Jay II, Linda Lee; m. William Newel Errickson, Apr. 9, 1976 (div. Feb. 1987). BA, U. Ill., 1966; MBA, So. Meth. U., 1981. Programming trainee Allstate Ins. Co., Northbrook, Ill., 1973; programmer, team leader Motorola, Inc., Chgo., 1974-78; supr. systems Tex. Instruments, Dallas, 1978-81, product line mgr. worldwide shipping systems, 1981-83, product line mgr. shipping, inventory systems, 1983-84, mgr. mktg. info. systems, 1985, mgr. benefit systems, 1986-89, mgr. S.W. case cons. and edn., 1990-92, western area advanced practices mgr., 1992—; dir., billing and software developer Spring Park Home Owners, Garland-Richardson, Tex., 1984—, pres. and chmn. fin., 1985, v.p. legal, 1986. Active Dallas Women's Ctr., 1984—; mem. bus. adv. council So. Meth U. Bus. Adv. Program; mem. bus. adv. coun. El Centro Coll. Rehab. for Physically Challenged Through Data Processing, 1987—; chmn. control and adminstrn./mktg. United Way, 1986-89. Recipient Women in Leadership cert. YWCA Met. Chgo., 1977. Mem. Am. Mgmt. Assn., Am. Women in Computing (bd. dirs. 1987—, pres. 1989), Community Assns. Inst., So. Meth. U. MBA Soc., Spring Park Racquet Club, Beta Gamma Sigma. Republican. Presbyterian. Home: 6702 Lake Shore Dr Garland TX 75044-2044 Office: Tex Instruments Inc PO Box 869305 6620 Chase Oaks Blvd Plano TX 75086

ERRICO, CYNTHIA BOYLAN, tax preparer, bookkeeper; b. Miami, Fla., May 18, 1954; d. Stanley William and Irene Harriet (Schaeffer) Boylan; m. Carl Albert Errico, May 12, 1974 (div. Jan. 1993). AA, Brookdale C.C., 1986; student, Richard Stockton Coll. N.J., 1994—. Bank teller N.J. Nat. Bank, West Long Branch, 1972-74; head teller Jersey Shore Bank, Long Branch, 1976-78; bookkeeper Aliotta, Fritsch & Walsh, West Long Branch, 1978-80; semi-sr. staff acct. Rudolf, Cinnamon & Calafato, Ocean, N.J., 1980-91; bookkeeper, tax preparer All Purpose Bookkeeping and Tax Svc., Long Branch, 1991—. Mem. Nat. Assn. Tax Practitioners, Delta Mu Delta (Zeta Alpha chpt.). Republican. Episcopalian. Home and Office: 910 Orlando Dr Forked River NJ 08731

ERSWELL, ANGELA BENNETT, insurance analyst; b. Hammond, Ind., Mar. 15, 1964; d. Richard Douglas and Stephanie Lee (Arnold) Bennett; m. Michael T. Maguire Jr., Mar. 5, 1983 (div. July 1985); 1 child, Katie Kristina; m. Dennis C. Erswell, Apr. 25, 1994. Parkland Jr. Coll.; A of Data Processing, Parland Jr. Coll., 1984; B of Communications, Ill. State U., 1991. Analyst State Farm Ins., Bloomington, Ill., 1985—. Office: State Farm Ins 1 State Farm Plz Bloomington IL 61701-4300

ERVIN, ARDITH ANN, psychiatric social worker; b. St. Charles, Ill., June 13, 1935; d. Arden J. and Helen Mildred (Carlson) Zollers; m. Don L. Ervin, Sept. 25, 1954 (div. Mar. 1975); children: Ann Lee, Mark Richard, Daniel Arden; m. Bill D. Toland, Dec. 31, 1983 (div. Aug. 1987). Student, Presbyn. Hosp. Sch. Nursing., 1953-54; RN, Community Coll. of Denver, 1973; BSW magna cum laude, Met. State Coll., 1974; MSW magna cum laude, U. Denver, 1984. With Jefferson County Dept. Social Services, Lakewood, Colo., 1972-75, Larimer County Dept. Social Services, Ft. Collins, Colo., 1975-83; pvt. practice social work Colo., 1976-78; psychiat. social worker S.E. Wyo. Mental Health Ctr., Cheyenne, 1984-87; founder with others The Jacob Center, Inc., 1988. Organizer Parents Anonymous Groups, Ind., 1975, leader; v.p. Child Protective Service Workers, 1979-80; bd. dirs. United Day Care Ctr., Ft. Collins., 1978-79, Larico Youth Home, Ft. Collins., 1978-80, Youth Shelter Care, Ft. Collins, 1980-82. Vol. Service award, Jefferson County; named one of Agency of Yr., 1992. Mem. Nat. Assn. Social Workers. Lutheran. Home: 1217 Village Ln Fort Collins CO 80521-4232

ERVIN, DORIS J., bank officer; b. San Angelo, Tex., June 22, 1951; d. Bernard Charles and Ruth Earlyne (Snowman) Hastings; m. Craig W. Ervin, July 24, 1976; children: Rebecca Ruth McMahon, Heather Marie. Teller supr., sales People Heritage Bank, Thomaston, Maine, 1983-85, 90—; town clk. Town of Thomaston, 1989-90. Organist Thomaston Assembly of God Ch., 1983—, Sunday sch. tchr., 1988—, asst. treas., 1986-87, women's ministries leader, 1980-83, sec. to bd. dirs., 1987-88; troop leader Kennebec Coun. Girl Scouts Am., 1986-87; sec. Thomaston C. of C., 1985-87; mem. Richard Simoneau election campaign, Knox County, 1993; organizer Candidates Night Debate, Thomaston, 1993; chairperson Maine Sch. Adminstrv. Dist., Thomaston, 1991-94, dir. 1988-94, strategic planning com. mem., 1992-93, chair curriculum com., 1990-91, chair screening com. supt. search, 1993. Republican. Home: 33 Main St Thomaston ME 04861 Office: Peoples Heritage Bank 115 Main St Thomaston ME 04861

ERVIN, MARGARET HOWIE, elementary educator, special education educator; b. L.A., May 13, 1924; d. James Stanley and Margaret (Goff) H.; m. E. Frank Ervin, Mar. 22, 1947 (div. 1957); children: Frank, Daniel, Charles. BA, Fresno (Calif.) State U., 1958; grad. student, Purdue U., 1965-66, San Francisco State U., 1974-75. Cert. elem. and spl. edn. tchr. Elem. tchr. Clovis (Calif.) Schs., 1958-60, Fremont (Calif.) Unified Schs., 1960-83; spl. tchr. in summers Dominican Coll., San Rafael, Calif., 1972-78; asst. dir., cons. Arena Sch. and Learning Ctr., San Rafael, 1974-75; dir. Ervin Sch. and Learning Ctr., San Rafael, 1983-88; researcher, tchr. Primaria Sch. #110 PRI9745, Celaya, Mex., 1988; elem., spl. tchr. Napa (Calif.) City/County Schs., 1989—; diagnosis cons. Ervin Learning Ctr., Napa, 1989—; spl. edn. guest speaker various cities, U.S., Can., 1974—; learning seminar Parents and Tchrs., Mexico, summer 1992, Psycho-motor Tgn. Don Bosco Home for Girls, Mexico, summer 1993. Vol. Option Inst. and Fellowship, "Sonrise" autism/devel. disabilities, Sheffield, Mass., summer 1994; pres. Children Handicapped Learning Devel., Calif., 1971-72, tchr. parents, 1970-80, 94—; bay area rep. Calif. Tchrs. Assn., Burlingame, 1970-74. Recipient cert. of merit Calif. Tchrs. Assn., Burlingame, 1974, $5,000 gift to Ervin Sch. Calif. Assn. Neurol. Handicapped Children, Fremont, 1984. Mem. AAUW, NOW, Assn. Children With Learning Disabilities (trustee). Democrat. Unitarian. Home and Office: Ervin Learning Ctr 1695 Pine St # 9 Napa CA 94559-3852

ERVIN, PATRICIA MARIE, human resources supervisor; b. Phila., Feb. 19, 1965; d. Robert Kenneth and Patricia Agnes (Haggerty) Edney; m. Francis X. Ervin, Jr., Apr. 11, 1992. BS, Phila. Coll. Textiles and Sci., 1987. Auditor/cons. Laventhol & Horwath, Phila., 1987-90; human resources supr. Cooper and Lybrand, Phila., 1990—. Recipient Sr. award AICPA, 1987. Mem. Coopers and Lybrand Profl. Women's Forum, Soc. Human Resource Mgmt. Roman Catholic. Home: 110 Mimosa Dr Cherry Hill NJ 08003 Office: Coopers & Lybrand 2400 Eleven Penn Ctr Philadelphia PA 19103

ERWAY, NANCY ANGELIA, nurse; b. Cooperstown, N.Y., Jan. 5, 1944; d. Victor and Angelia Rezen; m. Harold L. Erway, Aug. 10, 1963; children: Victor, Patti, Eric. AAS, Orange County C.C., 1963. RN Mary Imogene Bassett, Cooperstown, N.Y., 1961-65, 78-93, Pub. Health Nurse, Cooperstown, 1965-68, Headstart Program, Cooperstown, 1968-78; owner Nancy's Old and New, Cherry Valley, N.Y. Pres., v.p. Cherry Valley Ctrl. Sch. Bd., 1973-86; bd. dirs. Cherry Valley Health Ctr., 1983-93; chair for reenactment of Cherry Valley massacre, 1993, Ann. Meml. Day Peddlers Market, 1992, 93, 94; dir. Cherry Valley Youth Ctr. Mem. Cherry Valley C. of C. (pres. 1994—). Home: RR 1 Box 55 Cherry Valley NY 13320-9523

ERWIN, BETTE JANE, clinical psychologist; b. Rochester, Minn., Nov. 23, 1937; d. Benjamin Lyle and Miriam Evelyn (Sheldon) E.; m. Forrest Wahl, July 4, 1959 (div. 1964). BA, Macalester Coll., 1959; MA, Wayne State U., 1970, PhD, 1973. Lic. psychologist, Mich. Practice psychology Beverly Hills, Bloomfield Hills, Mich., 1972—; faculty Wayne State U., Detroit, 1972-74, U. Mich., Dearborn, 1974-78, Merrill Palmer Inst., Detroit, 1979-81, Ctr. for Humanistic Studies, Detroit, 1981-85. Co-author: Test without Trauma, 1973. Mem. Am. Psychol. Assn., Mich. Psychol. Assn., Mensa. Libertarian. Home: 16015 Kirkshire Beverly Hills MI 48025

ERWIN, JUDITH ANN (JUDITH ANN PEACOCK), writer, photographer, lawyer; b. Decatur, Ga., Jan. 4, 1939; d. Milo Eugene and Lucy Isabelle (Simpson) Peacock; m. William Wofford Erwin, Sept. 5, 1959 (div. Mar. 1982); children: William Wofford Jr., Allison Sheridan (Norton). AA, Fla. C.C., 1987; BA summa cum laude, Jacksonville U., 1989; JD, U. Fla., 1993. Photography instr., freelance writer Jacksonville, Fla., 1986-91, freelance dance photographer, 1984-91; theater and dance critic Folio Weekly, Jacksonville, Fla., 1987-89; writer dance VUE mag.; founder On Our Own, 1991; lawyer Inman & Fernandez; pres. Ballet Guild, Jacksonville, 1973-75, Ballet Repertory Jacksonville, 1979-80; freelance costume designer, Jacksonville, 1981-86. Mem. editorial staff Kalliope, Jour. Women's Art, 1989-91; editor-in-chief U. Fla. Jour. of Law and Pub. Policy, fall 1993. Mem. del.'s council Art's Assembly Jacksonville, 1979-80. Mem. AAUW, ATLA, Nat. Soc. ARts and Letters, Nat. League Am. Pen Women, Fla. Bar Assn., Jacksonville Bar Assn., Jacksonville Women Lawyers Assn., Assn. Family Conciliation Cts., Phi Kappa Phi, Phi Theta Kappa. Democrat. Episcopalian.

ERWIN, KATHIE TANNER, psychotherapist, geriatric services professional; b. Memphis, July 21, 1950; d. Felix Gordan and Rosan Zermina (Ricossa) Tanner; m. Bert F. Erwin, Aug. 23, 1981; children: Robin and Kelly (twins). BA, Eckerd Coll., 1981; MBA, Calif. Coast U., 1985, PhD, 1986; MA, Liberty U., 1989. Lic. mental health counselor; nat. cert. counselor, gerontol. counselor. Dir. pub. affairs Sta. WLCY-AM-FM, St. Petersburg, Fla., 1972-73, Sta. WPCV-FM, Winter Haven, Fla., 1977-80; news and consumer editor Sta. WRBQ-FM, Tampa, Fla., 1973-77; exec. news prodr. Sta. WTOG-TV, St. Petersburg, 1976-77; mktg. specialist Sta. WGTO-AM, Cypress Gardens, Fla., 1980-81; cert. fin. planner Erwin Fin. Strategies, Largo, Fla., 1982-90; co-dir. KEC Clinic, Clearwater, Fla., 1990-91; dir. Geriatric Support Programs, Largo, 1991—; pvt. practice Clearwater, 1992—. Author: How to Start and Manage a Counseling Business, 1993. Trustee Eckerd Coll., St. Petersburg, Fla., 1990-92. Mem. ACA, Am. Mental Health Counselors Assn., Am. Assn. Christian Counselors (conf. dir.), Assn. Specialists in Group Work, Inst. Cert. Fin. Planners, Eckerd Coll. Alumni Assn. (pres. 1987-90, Outstanding Leadership and Vision award 1990). Southern Baptist. Office: Charter-Medfield Resource Ctr 12775 Seminole Blvd Largo FL 34648

ESCHETE, MARY LOUISE, internist; b. Houma, La., Feb. 8, 1949; d. Marshall John and Louise Esther (Davis) E.; m. Lorphy Joseph Bourque, July 7, 1979. BS, La. State U., 1970; MD, La. State U. Med. Ctr., Shreveport, 1974. Diplomate, Am. Bd. Internal Medicine. Resident in internal medicine La. State U. Med. Ctr., Shreveport, 1974-77; staff instr. La. State U. Med. Ctr., 1979, fellow in infectious disease, 1979; pvt. practice Houma, 1980-83; staff, dept. internal medicine South La. Med. Assocs., Houma, 1983—; chmn. infection control, Terrebonne Gen. Hosp., 1981—, South La. Med. Ctr., 1983—. Contbr. articles to med. jours. Bd. dirs. Houma Battered Women's Shelter, 1983-87, Houma YWCA, 1987-94; mem. Roche Nat. AIDS Adv. Bd., 1993; Triparish vol. activist, 1994. Named Citizen of Yr. Regional and State Social Workers, 1992. Mem. ACP, AAAS, AMA, Infectious Disease Soc., Am. Soc. Microbiology, So. Med. Assn. (grantee 1978), N.Y. Acad. Sci., La. State Med. Soc., Terrebonne Parish Med. Soc. (sec. 1982-83, v.p. 1993-94, pres. 1994-95), Krewe of Hyachinthians (pres. 1989-90, 94-95, bd. dirs. 1990-94), Houma Jr. Women's Club (reporter 1988-89, rec. sec. 1989—, pres.-elect 1991-93, pres. 1993-95), Alpha Epsilon Delta. Democrat. Roman Catholic. Home: 3387 Little Bayou Black Dr Houma LA 70360-2840 Office: South La Med Ctr 1978 Industrial Blvd Houma LA 70363-7055

ESCOBAR, MARISOL See MARISOL

ESFANDIARY, MARY S., federal agency administrator, physical scientist; b. Passaic, N.J., June 27, 1929; d. Peter J. and Veronica R. (Kida) Nieradka; m. Mohsen S. Esfandiary; children: Homayoun Austin, Dara S. BS in Chemistry, St. John's U., 1951; postgrad., Polytechnic Inst. N.Y., 1955-56. Research chemist Picatinny Arsenal, Dover, N.J., 1951-56; supr. phys. sci. Bur. Mines, Washington, 1956-61; asst. to dir. research Nat. Iranian Oil Co., Tehran, 1961-64; lectr. U. Tehran and Aryamehr Inst. Tech., Tehran, 1961-64, 69-73; dir. internat. affairs Acad. of Scis., Tehran, 1977-79; chief geog. names br. Def. Mapping Agy., Washington, 1981-86, chief prodn. mgmt. office, 1986-87, chief support div., chief inventory mgmt. div., 1987-90, chief product mgmt. dept., 1990-92, dep. dir. distbn. mgmt. ops. Combat Support Ctr., 1993, chief, co-prodn. mgmt. divsn., 1993-94, chief divsn. internat. ops. coprodn. mgmt., 1993—. Contbr. papers and articles to tech. jours., 1952-78. Pres. UN Delegations Women's Club, N.Y.C., 1967-69, v.p., program dir., 1964-67; pres. Diplomatic Corps. Com. for Red Cross, Bangkok, Thailand, 1974-76; v.p., bd. dirs. Found. for Blind of Thailand, Bangkok, 1973-77; mem. Edn. Working Group ARC, 1989-90. Recipient Badge of Honor for Social Service, Thailand, 1975, 1st Class medal Red Cross, Thailand, 1976. Mem. AAAS, Mensa. Democrat. Home: 4401 Sedgewick St NW Washington DC 20016-2713 Office: Def Mapping Agy Lee Hwy Fairfax VA 22030

ESH, DALIA REGINA, insurance educator, financial planner; b. May 15, 1950; d. Yedidya Mizrahi and Orah (Debby) Mizrahi Malka; m. David Esh; children: Odelia, Roy, Amanda, Scott (twins). Cert. proficiency in English, Cambridge U., Eng., 1969; BA, Bar Ilan U., 1972, teaching cert., 1976; postgrad., U. Mo.-St. Louis, 1981-82, Washington U., St. Louis, 1983-84; MS in Mgmt., Am. Coll., 1989. CLU, LUTCF; chartered fin. cons. English tchr. Lady Davis Sch., 1973-80; tchr. Epstein Acad., St. Louis, 1981-82; sales rep. Met. Ins. Co., St. Louis, 1982-85, mktg. specialist, instr., Tulsa, 1985-86, br. mgr., Carrollton, Dallas, Tex., 1986-93, br. mgr. Des Plains, 1993—. Recipient Career Builders award Met. Ins. Co., 1982, Leader's Conf. award, 1984, Nat. Quality award, 1984, 85, Mgmt. Conf. award, 1989, 90, 91, Sales Office of Yr award, 1990. Mem. Nat. Assn. Life Underwriters, Internat. Assn. Fin. Planning, NAFE, Am. Soc. CLU, GAMA. Avocation: folk dancing, tennis. Office: Met Ins Co 999 E Touhy Ave Ste 120 Des Plaines IL 60018

ESHOO, ANNA GEORGES, congresswoman; b. New Britain, Conn., Dec. 13, 1942; d. Fred and Alice Alexandre Georges; children: Karen Elizabeth, Paul Frederick. AA with honors, Canada Coll., 1975. Chmn. San Mateo County Dem. Ctrl. Com., Calif., 1978-82; chair Human Rels. Com., 79-82; mem. Congress from 14th Dist. Calif., 1993—; mem. com. on commerce Congress from 14th Calif. dist., 1995—; regional minority whip 5; chief of staff Calif. Assembly Speaker Leo McCarthy, 1981; mem. Com. on Commerce; regional majority whip No. Calif., 1993—. Co-founder Women's Hall of Fame; chair San Mateo County (Calif.) Dem. Party, 1980; active San Mateo County Bd. Suprs., 1982-92, pres., 1986; pres. Bay Area Air Quality Mgmt. Dist., 1982-92; mem. San Francisco Bay Conservation Devel. Commn., 1982-92; chair San Mateo County Gen. Hosp. Bd. Dirs. Roman Catholic. Office: US Ho of Reps Office Of House Mems Washington DC 20515

ESHOO, BARBARA ANNE RUDOLPH, academic official; b. Worcester, Mass., Sept. 27, 1946; d. Charles Leighton and Irene Isabella (Wheeler) Rudolph; divorced: 1 child, Melissa Clinton; m. Robert Pius Eshoo, July 11, 1981. Student, Morehead State U., 1964-66, U. N.H., 1974, 75; BA, New Eng. Coll., 1976. Asst. to dir. Currier Gallery Art, Manchester, N.H., 1976-78, coord. pub. rels., 1979-82; dir. pub. rels. Daniel Webster Coll., Nashua, N.H., 1982-88, chief advancement officer, 1988—; mem. faculty Currier Art Ctr., Manchester, 1977-79; bd. advisers New Eng. Coll. Art Gallery, Henniker, N.H., 1989-91. Adviser on planned giving United Way, Nashua, 1989-90; com. mem. Manchester Mayor's Task Force on Youth Affairs, 1986-88, Manchester Bd. of Sch. Commn., 1986-90; del. N.H. Sch. Bds. Assn., 1988-90; trustee Manchester Historic Assn., 1989—; mem. Mayor's Com. on Leadership, Manchester, 1988-91; bd. dirs. Swiftwater coun. Girl Scouts U.S.; chair parents com. Bennington Coll. Mem. Nat. Soc. Fund Raising Execs. (bd. dirs., v.p. pub. affairs N.H./Vt. chpt.), Advt. Club N.H. (bd. dirs., v.p. 1980-82), Nashua Rotary West. Democrat. Home: 47 Amoskeag Pl Manchester NH 03101-1237 Office: Daniel Webster Coll 20 University Dr Nashua NH 03063-1300

ESHRAGH, PAMELA JEANNEAN, human resources specialist; b. Mt. Pleasant, Tex., Sept. 25, 1951; d. Jimmie Lee and Helen Marguerite (McBrayer) Justiss; m. Hamid Eshragh, Sept. 1, 1978; children: Jennifer Leigh, Natalie Elizabeth, Jessica Christine. Student, Stephen F. Austin State U., 1970-72; Assoc. degree, Massey Bus. Coll., 1974. Adminstrv. asst. to athletic dir./head coach Stephen F. Austin State U., Nacogdoches, Tex., 1971-77; asst. mgr. mgmt. sys. Am. Gen. Capital Mgmt., 1977-78; corp. recruiting, tng. mgr. Tex. Instruments, Inc., 1978-81; corp. mgr., pers. and adminstrn. Oceaneering Internat., Inc., 1981-84; cert. pers. cons. Quest Pers., 1984-86, Steitz and Corbett, 1987; owner, cert. pers. cons. Pers. Resources, 1987-92; human resource mgr. Nat. Contract Staffing, 1992-93; area mktg. mgr. Norrell Svcs., Inc., Las Vegas, Nev., 1993—; cons. Eshragh Pers. Resources, Houston, 1987-89; instr. Harris County C.C., Houston, 1985-89. Mem. Nat. Assn. Pers. Cons. (cert. pers. cons.), Nat. Assn. Temporary Svcs., Soc. Human Resource Mgmt. (sr. profl. human resources, conv. chmn. 1992), So. Nev. Assn. Temporary Svcs., So. Nev. Human Resource Assn. (chmn. publicity 1993, sec. 1994), Toastmasters Internat. Office: Norrell Svcs Inc 4560 S Eastern B-16 Las Vegas NV 89119

ESKOW, BONNIE MICHELE, food company executive; b. Bklyn., Sept. 18, 1966; d. Martin and Iris Blossom (Krell) E. BA cum laude in Econs., CUNY, 1988; MBA in Computer and Info. Tech., Hofstra U., 1991. Sales mgr. Courier life Publs., Bklyn., 1983-86; pres., founder Competitive Edge Inc., Bklyn., 1986-91; assoc. product mgr., total quality mgmt. facilitator Kraft Foods, White Plains, N.Y., 1992—; spkr. Grad. Bus. Sch. Hofstra U. Recipient Recognition for Sponsoring Telemktg. Campaign, Books For Kids, N.Y.C., 1988. Mem. NAFE, Am. Mktg. Assn., Assn. MBA Execs., Assn. Collegiate Entrepreneurs Bklyn. Coll. (founder, alumni advisor, regional leader, pres. 1986), Direct Mktg. Assn., Soc. Computing and Info. Processing, Spl. Interest Group Artificial Intelligence, Spl. Interest Group Bus. Data Processing and Mgmt., Am. Soc. Quality Control. Office: ET-3 250 North St White Plains NY 10625

ESPAÑA, CAROLINE SOPHIE, computer company executive; b. Mexico City, Oct. 24, 1965; d. Roger Henri and Marie Christiane (Jaques D'Hont) E. BA in Advt., UDEC, Mexico City, 1983-87. Adminstrv. asst. C. Steel & Co., Phoenix, 1982-83; sub dir. Ashton Internat. de Mexico, Mexico City, 1987-88; v.p. fin. Ashton Internat., S.A. de C.V., Mexico City, 1988-90, pres., 1990—; bd. dirs. Sources S.A. de C.V., Mexico City, Ashton Internat. Corp., Chula VistaCalif.; v.p. LDVI Corp., Chula Vista, 1992—; sec./treas. IOEC Corp., Chula Vista, 1989—, AI-AI-AI, S.A. de C.V., Mexico City, 1991—. Roman Catholic. Office: LDVI Corp PO Box 1175 Chula Vista CA 91912-1175

ESPERIAN, KALLEN ROSE, soprano; b. Waukegan, Ill., June 8, 1961; d. Arthur Kalouste Esperian and Mary Anna (Haynes) Parquette; m. Thomas Michael Machen, Nov. 24, 1982; 1 child, John. MusB in Voice, U. Ill., 1983. Winner Opera Co. Phila./Luciano Pavarotti Internat. Voice Competition, 1985, debut with co. as Mimi in La Boheme, 1986, further performances in Modena and Genoa, Italy and with Genoa Opera Co. in Beijing, also appeared in documentary film of trip, Distant Harmony; debut as Mimi with Deutsche Oper, West Berlin, 1986, new prodn., 1988-89, Lyric Opera Chgo., 1987, Teatro Colon, Buenos Aires, 1987, Vienna State Opera, 1986, Hannover Opera, 1987, Met. Opera, N.Y.C., 1988, Salzburg Landestheater, 1989; debut as Luisa Miller Teatro Filharmonico, Verona, Italy, Vienna State Opera, 1986, La Scala Opera, Milan, Italy, 1989; debut as Michaela in Carmen Opera Theatre St. Louis, 1987; debut as Nedda in Pagliacci Conn. Opera Co., 1988; appeared in Paverotti Plus concert Avery Fisher Hall, N.Y.C., televised live from Lincoln Ctr.; other concerts include benefit Carnegie Hall, 1988, as Leonora in Il Trovatore with Met. Opera Co. in Met in the Parks program, 1988, in Rossini's Petite Messe Solonnelle at Montreal Internat. Festival, 1989, spl. benefit with Domingo for Opera Omaha and Fresno Philharmonic, 1989-90; other engagements include Elena in I Vespri Siciliani at La Scala, Mimi in La Boheme with Met. Opera, Deutsche Oper, Salzburg, Austria, also Munich and Zurich, Switzerland, 1989-90, Elvira in Don Giovanni with Utah Opera Co., Rossini Stabat Mater, Opera Bastille, Paris, Margerite in Faust, Festival of Orange, Desdemona in Otello, Salzburg, Opera Bastille, 1990, Palermo, 1991, Luisa Miller, Met. Opera, 1991, Verdi Requiem, Opera Bordeaux, Collegiate Chorale, Detroit Symphony, debut with L.A. Opera in La Boheme, 1993, opening night of Metropolitan Opera in gala Otello, Maria Stuarda Bologna Opera, 1994, Otello, Bilbao, Spain, 1994. Mem. Am. Guild Mus. Artists. Democrat. Methodist. Home: 514 Lindseywood Cv Memphis TN 38117-1936 Office: Hans Boon care Herbert H Breslin Inc 119 W 57th St New York NY 10019-2303*

ESPINAL, MARIA EMILIA, mental health counselor; b. Havana, Cuba, Mar. 4, 1963; came to U.S., 1968; d. Humberto Julian and Irma Fredina (Sosa) E. BA in Psychology and Edn., U. Miami, Coral Gables, Fla., 1984, MS in Edn., 1993. Rsch. study coord. Bascom Palmer Eye Inst., U. Miami (Fla.) Sch. Medicine, 1985-89, CMV retinitis trial coord., 1989-92; group facilitator Safe Space: Battered Women's Shelter, Miami, 1992-93; sch. counselor Miami Springs (Fla.) Elem. Sch., 1992-93; staff therapist Inst. Family Living, U. Miami, Coral Gables, 1992-93; program specialist Parent Resource Ctr., Miami, 1993-94; family P.A.C.T. counselor Switchboard of Miami, 1994—; mem. steering com. Studies of the Ocular Complications of AIDS-Cytomegalovirus Retinitis Trial, Balt., 1989-92; nat. rep. for study coord. Johns Hopkins U., Balt., 1989. Contbr. articles to profl. jours. Vol. Big Bros./Sister, Miami, 1981-90, Juvenile Alt., Miami, 1981-83, In Transition, Miami, 1986. Mem. ACA, Am. Mental Health Counselors, Assn. Specialists in Group Work, Internat. Assn. Marriage and Family. Republican. Roman Catholic. Office: Switchboard of Miami 75 SW 8th St Miami FL 33130

ESPOSITO, AMY SKLAR, lawyer; b. Bklyn., Nov. 9, 1955; d. Sidney and Rhoda (Weiner) Sklar; m. Francis Benedetto Esposito, May 4, 1985; children: Melissa, Anthony. BA, U. Vt., 1977; JD, Hofstra U., 1980. Bar: N.Y. 1981, Fla. 1983. Assoc. Herman & Natale, Esqs., Garden City, N.Y., 1980-81, Law Offices of Gabriel Kohn, Mineola, N.Y., 1981-84; ptnr. Ostor & Sklar, Esqs., Deer Park, N.Y., 1984-93; pvt. practice Deer Park, 1993-94; assoc. Naiburg & Rosenblum, Hauppauge, N.Y., 11550. Coach mock trials Nassau County (N.Y.) High Schs., 1984-86. Mem. N.Y. State Bar Assn., Nassau-Suffolk Women's Bar Assn. (assoc., speaker on matrimonial law). Jewish. Office: Naiburg & Rosenblum 222 Veterans Meml Hwy Hauppauge NY 11788 also: Rosenblum & Naiburg 64 Hilton Ave Hempstead NY 11550

ESPOSITO, BONNIE LOU, marketing professional; b. Chgo., July 20, 1947; d. Ralph Edgar and Dorothy Mae (Groh) Myers; m. Frank Merle Esposito, Aug. 15, 1969 (div. Sept. 1985); children: Mario Henry, Elizabeth Ann. BA, George Williams Coll., 1969. Caseworker Little Bros. of the Poor, Chgo., 1969-72; dir. Little Bros.-Friends of the Elderly, Mpls., 1972-78; organizer Community Crime Prevention, Mpls., 1978-81; owner Espo Inc./Mario's Ristorante, Mpls., 1978-85; mktg. mgr. City of Mpls. Energy Office, 1981—; dir. mktg. and tng. The Energy Collaborative, 1987-93; dir. mktg. Ctr. for Energy and Environment, Mpls., 1989—; v.p., bd. dirs. Resource Alternatives, Inc. Mem. NAFE (bd. dirs. Monday Night Network 1988), Midwest Direct Mktg. Assn., Minn. Multi-Housing Assn., Nat. Apt. Assn., Profl. Assn. for Consumer Energy Edn. (bd. dirs. 1993—, chmn. fin. com.). Office: Ctr Energy Environment 100 N 6th St Ste 412A Minneapolis MN 55403

ESPOSITO, CHERYL LYNNE, lawyer; b. Cleve., Dec. 13, 1964; d. John N. and Patricia A. (Manilla) E.; m. John J. Nebel III, Oct. 20, 1990; 1 child, Deanna Teresa. BA in Polit. Sci., U. Pitts., 1986, cert. in East Asian studies, 1986, JD, 1989. Bar: Pa. 1989, U.S. Dist. Ct. Pa. 1989. Assoc. Riley & DeFalice, P.C., Pitts., 1989-93, Cauley & Conflenti, Pitts., 1993-94; Marshall, Dennehey, Warner, Coleman & Goggin, Pitts., 1994—. Soprano U. Pitts. Choral Soc., 1986-91; cantor St. James Ch., Wilkinsburg, Pa., 1991-92, St. Maurice Ch., Forest Hills, Pa., 1992—; mem. steering com. Tribute for First 100 Women Lawyers in Allegheny County, 1992, Tribute to the Female Judiciary of Pa., 1993-94. Mem. ABA (tort and ins. div.), Pa. Bar Assn., Allegheny County Bar Assn., Am. Inn of Ct. (charter), Japan-Am. Soc. Pitts., St. Thomas More Soc. Roman Catholic. Office: Marshall Dennehey Coleman & Goggin 2900 USX Tower 600 Grant St Pittsburgh PA 45219

ESQUIVEL, LAURA, writer; b. Mexico, 1951; d. Julio Caesar and Josephina E.; m. Alfonso Arau; 1 child, Sandra. Author: Como agua para chocolate, 1989, Like Water for Chocolate, 1991; (screenplays) Chido One, 1985 (Ariel award nominee for Best Screenplay Mexican Acad. of Motion Picture, Arts and Scis.), Like Water for Chocolate, 1993, Little Ocean Star, 1994. Office: Doubleday 666 Fifth Ave New York NY 10103*

ESSA, LISA BETH, educator; b. Modesto, Calif., Nov. 19, 1955; d. Mark Newyia and Elizabeth (Warda) Essa. B.A., U. Pacific-Stockton, 1977, M.A. in Curriculum and Instrn. Reading, 1980. Cert. tchr. elem., multiple subject and reading specialist, Calif. Tchr. primary grades Delhi (Calif.) Elem. Sch. Dist., 1978-80; reading clinic tutor San Joaquin Delta Community Coll., Stockton, Calif., 1980; tchr. primary grades Hayward (Calif.) Unified Sch. Dist., Supr., San Francisco host com. Dem. Nat. Conv., 1984. Femmes Club scholar, 1973; U. Calif. Optometry Alumni Assn. scholar, 1973; Jobs Daughters scholar, 1974. Mem. Internat. Reading Assn., Calif. Tchrs. Assn., Hayward Unified Tchrs. Assn., San Francisco Jr. C. of C., Jr. League San Francisco. Democrat. Episcopalian. Home: 1960 Clay St Apt 109 San Francisco CA 94109-3435

ESSIG, KATHLEEN SUSAN, university official, controller; b. Denver, July 5, 1956; d. Robert and Ethel (Sutherland) Essig. BS in BA, Colo. State U., 1979, MS, 1987. CPA, Colo. Personal fin. planner, v.p. fin. Successful Money Mgmt., Ft. Collins, Colo., 1987-88; accts. payable technician Colo. State U., Ft. Collins, 1980-81, supr. comml. accts. receivable, 1981-83, gen. acct. II, 1983-85, supr. student loans, 1985-87, supr. accts. receivable, acct. II, 1988-89, cost acct. III, 1989-94, contr., 1994; sr. cons. KPMG Peat Marwick, Denver, 1994—. Mem. Am. Bus. Women's Assn. (v.p. 1985, Woman of Yr. 1985), Nat. Assn. Accts.

ESSINGER, SUSAN JANE, special education educator; b. Paris, Ill., Oct. 7, 1952; d. Rex Milburn and Virginia Ellen (White) E. BS in Edn., Ea. Ill. U., Charleston, 1973; MS in Edn., Ind. State U., 1980. Cert. learning disabilities, elem., educationally mentally handicapped with early childhood endorsement. Elem. tchr. Havana (Ill.) Sch. Dist., 1973-74; tchr. early childhood spl. edn. Paris Sch. Dist. 95, 1974—. Mem. NEA, Assn. for Edn. Young Children, Ill. Edn. Assn., Paris Tchrs. Assn., Coun. for Exceptional Children. Home: 1104 S Main St Paris IL 61944 Office: Paris Sch Dist 95 S Main St Paris IL 61944

ESSLINGER, KIMBERLY MARIE, retail store administrator; b. Balt., July 23, 1960; d. Leslie John Jr. and Mary Agnes (Bittel) E. Student, Barbizon Sch., Towson, Md., 1976-78. Asst. store mgr. Ups & Downs div. U.S. Shoe, Balt., 1981-83; store mgr. Petrie Stores Corp., Balt., 1980-83; area sales mgr., mdse. planner Woodward & Lothrop, Washington, 1983-92; divisional sales mgr. Bon Ton Stores Inc., York, Pa., 1992—. Mem. NAFE. Republican. Roman Catholic.

ESSLINGER, NELL DANIEL, singer, choral director, writer; b. Huntsville, Ala., June 13, 1903; d. William Francis and Blanche (Russell) E.; m. Raymond G. Miller, Aug. 18, 1979. Vocal cert., Agnes Scott Coll., 1922; BA, U. Ala., 1954; MMus., U. Ill., 1962. Dir. Huntsville Music Study Club Chorus, 1938-39, 48-50, Male Chorus, 1948, Tri-Choral, 1950, Music Appreciation Club, 1950; dir., instr. voice Koch Sch. Music, Rocky River, Ohio, 1963-64; tchr. voice Baldwin Wallace Coll., Berea, Ohio, 1965-66; tchr. voice, choral dir. N.E. State Jr. Coll., Rainsville, Ala., 1966-69; owner, CEO The Notation Press, Ala., 1965—. Debut Carnegie Hall Chambers, N.Y., 1925; ch. and oratorio soloist, 1919-39, guest soloist Waldorf Astoria, N.Y., 1924, 25, Kenilworth Inn, Battery Park Inn, AShveville, N.C., 1926; appeared in theatre prodns. ADrienne, 1924, Roxy's Gang, N.Y., 1925; radio shows Mr. Naftzeger's Morning Hour, N.Y., The House by the Side of the Rd, others; author: (textbook) Revised Notation, 1965, 87 (award for Creative Achievement Ga. Sci. and Tech. Commn. 1968), The Variety of Voice, 1989; also poetry. Recipient awards Ala. Writers Conclave, Ala. State Poetry Soc., 1989-90. Mem. NAFE, Ala. Assn. Inventors, Huntsville Music Study Club (hon. life), Bus. & Profl. Women's Club (charter Rainsville, Ala.), Alpha Epsilon Rho. Home and Office: 624 E Moulton St Decatur AL 35601

ESTABROOK, ALISON, breast surgeon, surgical oncologist, educator; b. N.Y.C., Oct. 29, 1951; d. Edwin Burke Estabrook and Shirley (Butler) Wood; m. William Neelis Harrington, June 13, 1981. BA cum laude, Barnard Coll., 1974; MD, NYU, 1978. Diplomate Am. Bd. Surgery. Resident in surgery Columbia-Presbyn. Med. Ctr., N.Y.C., 1978-81, 82-84, fellow in surg. oncology, 1981-82, asst. prof. surgery, 1984—, Florence Irving asst. prof., 1989-92; assoc. prof., 1992—; dir. Breast Clinic Columbia-Presbyn. Med. Ctr., N.Y.C., 1985—; chief breast surgery, 1991—. Contbr. articles to med. jours. Recipient Blakemore prize for rsch. Columbia-Presbyn. Med. Ctr., 1982, 84; Florence and Herbert Irving grantee, 1989-92. Fellow ACS; mem. AMA, Am. Med. Women's Assn., Am. Assn. Acad. Surgeons, Am. Fedn. Clin. Rsch., Am. Soc. Clin. Oncology, Nat. Surg. Advancement Breast Project, N.Y. Surg. Soc., N.Y. Met. Breast Cancer Group. Office: Columbia-Presbyn Med Ctr 161 Ft Washington Ave New York NY 10032-3713

ESTEFAN, GLORIA MARIA, singer, songwriter; b. Havana, Cuba, Sept. 1, 1957; came to U.S., 1959; d. Jose Manuel and Gloria G. (Garcia) Fajardo; m. Emilio Estefan, Jr., Sept. 1, 1979; children: Nayib Emil, Emily Marie. BA in Psychology, U. Miami, Fla., 1978, MusD (hon.), 1993. Composer: (popular songs) Anything for You, 1987, Live for Loving You, 1991, Can't Forget You, 1991, Coming Out of the Dark, 1991, Always Tomorrow, 1992, Go Away, 1993; performer songs for Olympics in Korea, 1987, World Series Baseball, St. Louis, 1987, Pan Am. Games, 1988, Superbowl Halftime, Mpls., 1992; albums: Primitive Love, 1986, Let It Loose, 1987, Cuts Both Ways, 1990, Coming Out Of The Dark, 1991, Greatest Hits, 1992, Mi Tierra, 1993. Benefactress Children's Home Soc., Miami, 1991, Leukemia Soc., 1991, United Way, 1991, United Negro Coll. Fund, 1992, Community Alliance Against AIDS, Miami, 1992, Hurrican Relief Fund, So. Fla., 1992-93; pub. mem. U.S. Del. to 47th Gen. Assembly UN. Recipient Am. Music award, 1987, Victory award, 1991, Songwriter of Yr. award BMI, 1991, Humanitarian of Yr. award B'nai Brith, 1992, Casita Maria Gold Medal award, 1993, Hispanic Heritage award, 1993, Hearst Found. Gold Medal award, 1992, Ellis Island Congl. Medal of Honor, 1993.; named Billboard's Best New Pop Artist and Top Pop Singles Artist, 1986; also numerous Grammy award nominations, 1988-91. Office: Estefan Enterprises Inc 6205 Bird Rd Miami FL 33155-4885

ESTELL, DORA LUCILE, retired educational administrator; b. Ft. Worth, Mar. 3, 1930; d. Hugh and Hattie Lucile (Poole) E. BA, East Tex. Bapt. U., 1947; MA, U. North Tex., 1959; EdD, East Tex. State U., 1988. Tchr. Mission (Tex.) Ind. Sch. Dist., 1951-53; tchr., adminstr. Marshall (Tex.) Ind. Sch. Dist., 1953-68; dep. dir. Region VII Edn. Svc. Ctr., Kilgore, Tex., 1968-94, ret., 1994. Contbr. articles to profl. jours. Mem. Phi Delta Kappa. Baptist. Home: 611 W Bell Rockdale TX 76567

ESTEP, SARAH VIRGINIA, association executive; b. Altoona, Pa., Mar. 1, 1926; d. Benner Marshal and Helen Rebecca (Sellers) Wilson; m. Charles Sheldon Estep, Apr. 12, 1952; children: Cynthia Jane, Rebecca Anne, Robert Wilson. BA, Mary Washington U., Fredericksburg, Va., 1947. Social worker Blair County Childrens's Aid Soc., Altoona, Pa., 1947-52; tchr. Anne Arundel Bd. Edn., Annapolis, Md., 1952-75; pvt. camp dir. Hartford County, Md., summer 1963; camp dir. Girl Scouts of Cen. Md., Balt., summer 1964; dir. camping Camp Fire Girls Md., Balt., 1966-67; founder, dir. Am. Assn. Electronic Voice Phenomena, Severna Park, Md., 1982—; cons. in field; lectr. in field; conductor workshops in field. Author: Voices of Eternity, 1988; editor/pub. quar. newsletter, AA-EVP News, 1982; contbr. articles to profl. jours.

ESTERLINE, SHIRLEY JEANNE, lithograph company executive; b. Paulding, Ohio, June 6, 1936; d. George Gary and Catherine Genevieve (Durbin) Sontchi; m. Meredith Esterline, Apr. 1, 1956; children: Gordon Alan, Amy Jeanne. Cert. med. technologist, Elkhart U., Ind., 1956. Lab technician, Fort Wayne, Ind., 1956-57; sec. Zollner Corp., Fort Wayne, 1957-58, Magnavox Corp., Fort Wayne, 1958-61; sales coord. Doty Lithograph Inc., Fort Wayne, 1975-77; sales mgr. Dot Line div. Dot Corp., Auburn, Ind., 1977-87, Midwest sales mgr. Falco/Sunbelt div. FL Cos., Nashville, 1987-89; pvt. cons., 1989—. Recipient Top Sales award Dot Corp., 1985. Mem. Specialty Advt. Assn. Internat. (suppliers com. 1983—, cert. advt. specialist 1985, master advt. specialist 1986, chmn. 100 club 1983—, seminar facilitator calendar advt. coun. 1985-89, CAS Alumni 1985—, mgmt. awards 1984, 85, 86). Methodist. Avocations: reading, gardening.

ESTERLY, JULIET KING BINDT, counselor, educator, social worker for the blind; b. L.A., May 31, 1912; d. Roy Brooks and Cora May (Hurley) King; m. Henry M. Bindt, May 30, 1937 (div. 1942); m. Everett E. Esterly, Oct. 30, 1971 (dec. 1981). BA, Scripps Coll., 1934; MA in Social Svc., U. Calif., Berkeley, 1939; cert. to teach blind, U. Wash., 1948; postgrad. in rehab., U. San Francisco. Social worker for blind Alameda County Welfare Dept., Oakland, Calif., 1939-40; home tchr. Calif. State Libr., 1940-52; counselor tchr. Calif. Dept. Rehab., 1952-72; cons. on blindness Magnificent Obsession, Universal Studios, 1936; sec. div. home tchrs. Am. Assn. Workers for Blind, 1944-46; charter pres. Western Conf. Home Tchrs. of Blind, 1958-52, Assoc. Blind Calif., 1958-63, Braille Revival League Calif., 1987-92; nat. v.p. Braille Revival League, 1990-92; bd. dirs. Am. Coun. Blind. Author: Handbook for the Blind, 1952. Legis. chair Women's Internat. League for Peace and Freedom, 1936-38; active Hollywood and Berkeley LWV, 1935-39; pres. Berkeley chpt. Nat. Fedn. Bus. and Profl. Women's Clubs, 1951-52, chmn. state scholarship com., 1953; mem. gen. adv. com. Medic Alert Internat., 1966-86; pres. Rossmoor Residents' Assn., 1976-78. Recipient Citizen of Merit award Rossmoor Retirement Community, 1985, Cert. for Significant Contbr. to Community award Delta Kappa Gamma, 1991, Commendation Outstanding Record of Community Svc. Pres. George Bush, 1991, Commendatory Proclamation Svc. to Community and Blind Walnut Creek City Coun., 1991; Juliet King Esterly scholarship endowed in her honor Scripps Coll., 1954. Mem. AAUW, Am. Assn. Ret. Persons (chpt. pres. 1983-86), Am. Coun. of Blind (Amb. award 1978), Am. Assn. Edn. and Rehab. of Blind, Ret. Pub. Employees Assn. (chpt. pres. 1988-92), Coun. Rehab. Specialists (nat. pres. 1984-88, 92—). Democrat. Home: 2408 Ptarmigan Dr Unit 1 Walnut Creek CA 94595

ESTERLY, NANCY BURTON, physician; b. N.Y.C., Apr. 14, 1935; d. Paul R. and Tanya (Pasahow) Burton; m. John R. Esterly, June 16, 1957; children: Sarah Burton, Anne Beidler, John Snyder, II, Henry Clark, II. AB, Smith Coll., 1956; MD, Johns Hopkins U., 1960. Intern, then resident in pediatrics Johns Hopkins Hosp., 1960-63, resident in dermatology, 1964-67; instr. pediatrics Johns Hopkins U. Med. Sch., 1967-68; instr., trainee La Rabida U. Chgo. Inst.; also dept. pediatrics U. Chgo. Med. Sch., 1968-69; asst. prof. Pritzker Sch. Medicine, U. Chgo., 1969-70, asso. prof., 1973-78; asst. prof. dermatology Abraham Lincoln Sch. Medicine, U. Ill., 1970-72, asso. prof. dermatology and pediatrics, 1972-73; dir. div. dermatology, dept. pediatrics Michael Reese Hosp. and Med. Ctr., Chgo., 1973-78; prof. pediatrics and dermatology Northwestern U. Med. Sch., 1978; head div. dermatology, dept. pediatrics Children's Meml. Hosp., Chgo., 1978-87; prof. pediatrics and dermatology Med. Coll. Wis., Milw., 1987—; head div. dermatology, dept. pediatrics Children's Hosp. Wis., Milw., 1987—. Contbr. numberous articles to profl. jours. Mem. Internat. Soc. Pediatric Dermatology, Am. Acad. Dermatology, Am. Dermatol. Assn., Wis. Dermatol. Soc., Soc. Investigative Dermatology, Am. Acad. Pediatrics, Soc. Pediatric Rsch., Soc. Pediatric Dermatology, Women's Dermatol. Soc., Wis. Pediatric Soc., Sigma Xi. Office: MACC Fund Rsch Ctr Dept Pediatrics 8701 W Watertown Plank Rd Milwaukee WI 53226-4801

ESTES, ELAINE ROSE GRAHAM, librarian; b. Springfield, Mo., Nov. 24, 1931; d. James McKinley and Zelma Mae (Smith) Graham; m. John Melvin Estes, Dec. 29, 1953. BSBA, Drake U., 1953, tchg. cert., 1956; MSLS, U. Ill., 1960. With Pub. Libr. Des Moines, 1956-95, coord. extension svcs., 1977-78, dir., 1978-95, ret., 1995; lectr. antiques, hist. architecture, libraries; mem. conservation planning com. for disaster preparedness for libraries. Author bibliographies of books on antiques; contbr. articles to profl. jours. Mem. State of Iowa Cultural Afairs Adv. Council, 1986-94, Nat. Commn. on Future Drake U., 1987-88; chmn. Des Moines Mayor's

Hist. Dist. Commn.; bd. dirs. Des. Moines Art Ctr., 1972-83, hon. mem., 1983—; bd. dirs. Friends of Library USA, 1986-92, Henry Wallace House Found.; mem. Iowa Libr. Centennial Com., 1990-91), nominations rev. com. Iowa State Nat. Hist. Register, 1983-89; chmn. hist. subcom. Des Moines Sesequecentennial com., 1993, Iowa Sister State Commn., 1993—; mem. 45th anniversary com. Des Moines Art Ctr., 1993; mem. com. 40th anniversary Drake U. alumni weekend, 1993. Recipient recognition for outstanding working women—leadership in econs. and civic life of Greater Des Moines YWCA, 1975, Disting. Alumni award Drake U., 1979, Woman of Achievement award YWCA, 1989. Mem. ALA, Iowa Libr. Assn. (pres. 1978-79), Iowa Urban Pub. Libr. Assn., Libr. Assn. Greater Des Moines Metro Area (pres., chmn. 1992), Iowa Soc. Preservation Hist. Landmarks (bd. dirs. 1969—), Terrace (Gov.'s Mansion) Soc. (v.p. 1991-93, pres. 1993—), Links Club, Quester's, Inc. Club (pres. 1982, state 2nd v.p. 1984-86), Rotary. Office: Pub Libr of Des Moines 100 Locust St Des Moines IA 50309-1775

ESTEY, AUDREE PHIPPS, artistic director; b. Winnipeg, Man., Can., Jan. 7, 1910; d. Robert and Anna (Harrington) Phipps; student Immaculate Heart Coll., 1927-29, Ernest Belcher Ballet Sch., 1928-31, Robert Major Drama Sch., 1929-31, Koslov Ballet Sch., 1930-31; m. L. Wendell Estey, Sept. 18, 1933; children: Lawrence Mitchell, Carol.Dancer Ernest Belcher Ballet Co., L.A., 1930, Fanchon and Marco Co., L.A., 1930-31; actress-dancer Fox Studio, Hollywood, Calif., 1931-32; ballet tchr. Lawrenceville and Princeton, N.J., 1938-80, Perry Mansfield Camp, Steamboat Springs Colo., summers 1949-50; head dance dept. Les Chalets Francais, Deer Isle, Maine, 1951-73; founder non-profit Princeton (N.J.) Ballet Soc., 1954, dir., cons.; founder Princeton Regional Ballet Co., 1963; founder profl. co., Princeton Ballet, 1979, Am. Repertory Ballet Co. Host Northeast Regional Ballet Festival-Princeton, 1968; coordinator Northeast Regional Ballet Festival-Jacob's Pillow, 1970. Apptd. by gov. N.J. State Commn. to Study Arts, 1968, trustee N.J. Sch. of the Arts, 1980; bd. dirs. Sarasota Ballet of Fla., 1989-91, co-chair resource com., 1992-93, mem. artistic com., 1993—. Recipient Rutgers U. award for contbn. to arts in N.J., 1982. Mem. N.E. Regional Ballet Assn. (pres., 1967-68, exec. v.p., 1968-71), Sarasota-Manatee Dance Tchrs. Assn. (pres. 1990-93). Episcopalian. Choreographer over 20 ballets for children and young dancers including: Festival of the Gnomes, Pastels, Peter and the Wolf, Sleeping Beauty, Cinderella, Pied Piper, The Nutcracker (choreography for Act I currently used by Princeton Ballet), Chanson Innocente, Graduation Ball, Coppelia. Office: 262 Alexander St Princeton NJ 08540

ESTIN-KLEIN, LIBBYADA, advertising executive, medical writer; b. Newark, July 13, 1937; d. Barney and Florence B. (Tenkin) Straver; m. Harvey M. Klein, Sept. 9, 1984. Student Syracuse U., 1955-57; BS, Columbia, 1960; RN, Columbia-Presbyn. Med. Ctr., 1960; cert., N.Y. Sch. Interior Design, 1962. Med. rsch. tech. writer, N.Y.C., 1960-62; pres. Libbyada Estin Interiors, N.Y.C., 1962-65; v.p. advt. and pub. relations Behrman/Estin Inc., N.Y.C., 1965-67; account exec., dir. pub. rels. J.S. Fullerton, Inc., N.Y.C., 1967-68; med. writer L.W. Frohlich & Co., Intercon Internat. Inc., N.Y.C., 1968-69, Kallir Philips Ross Inc., N.Y.C., 1969-71; copy supr. William Douglas McAdams Inc., N.Y.C., 1971-75, Sudler & Hennessey Inc., N.Y.C., 1975-80; v.p., exec. adminstr., creative dir. Grey Med. Advt. Inc., N.Y.C., 1980-84; founder, ptnr. Estin Sandler Comm. Inc., N.Y.C., 1984; v.p. Barnum Comm. Inc., N.Y.C., 1984-86; sr. v.p. ICE Comm., Inc., Rochester, N.Y., 1986-87; pres. Estin-Klein Comm. Inc., Rochester and Pittsford, N.Y., 1987—; dir. health group Roberts Comm., Inc., East Rochester, N.Y., 1993—; bd. dirs. Grief Resource Info. Edn. Forum, Inc. Mem. Pub. Rels. Soc. Am., Advt. Women N.Y., Am. Advt. Fedn., Advt. Coun. of Rochester, Rochester Sales and Mktg. Execs. Club, Mktg. Communicators of Rochester, Am. Med. Writers Assn., Pharm. Advt. Coun., Healthcare Bus. Women's Assn., Am. Nurses Assn., Allied Bd. Trade, Columbia-Presbyn. Hosp. Alumnae Assn., Columbia U. Alumnae Assn., Syracuse U. Alumnae Assn., Sigma Theta Tau, Delta Phi Epsilon. Home and Office: 289 Garnsey Rd Pittsford NY 14534-4540

ESTIS, LISA ROBIN, psychologist; b. East Meadow, N.Y., Feb. 21, 1955; d. Irwin Louis and Rosalie (Levine) Lubin; m. Monty Estis, Aug. 25, 1985; children: Ian Scott, Brad Gary. BS, Johns Hopkins U., 1977; MS, U. Miami, 1980, PhD, 1982. Clin. psychologist Children's Psychiat. Ctr., Eatontown, N.J., 1982-85, Assocs. in Psychol. Svcs., Somerville, N.J., 1985-87; pvt. practice adult, adolescent and child psychol. svcs. Mendham, N.J., 1987-90; clin. psychologist Colo. Biodyne, Denver, 1990-91; pvt. practice adult, adolescent and child psychol. svcs. Aurora, Colo., 1991—; facilitator Regis U. Without Walls, Denver, 1992—. Recipient Regents scholarship N.Y. Regents, East Meadow, 1973. Mem. APA, Colo. Psychol. Assn., Assn. for the Advancement Psychology, Colo. Women Psychologists, Colo. Neuropsychol. Soc. Home: 7174 S Chapparal Crl East Aurora CO 80016 Office: Eating Treatment Ctr Ste 560 8400 E Prentice Ave Englewood CO 80111

ESTRICH, SUSAN RACHEL, law educator; b. Lynn, Mass., Dec. 16, 1952; d. Irving Abraham and Helen Roslyn (Freedberg) E.; m. Martin Kaplan. BA, Wellesley Coll., 1974; JD, Harvard U., 1977. Law clk. to Hon. J. Skelly Wright U.S. Ct. Appeals, Washington, 1977-78; law clk. to Hon. John P. Stevens U.S. Supreme Ct., Washington, 1978-79; dep. nat. issues dir., spl. asst. Kennedy for Pres. campaign, Washington, 1979-80; sr. policy advisor Mondale-Ferraro campaign, 1984; of counsel Tuttle & Taylor, L.A., 1986-87; campaign mgr. Dukakis for Pres. campaign, Boston, 1987-88; asst. prof. law Harvard Law Sch., Cambridge, Mass., 1981-86, prof. law, 1986-90; Robert Kingsley prof. law and polit. sci. U. So. Calif., 1990—; host talk show Sta. KABC, L.A. Author: Real Rape, 1987; co-author: Dangerous Offenders, 1985; columnist L.A. Style mag.; weekly columnist USA Today; contbg. editor L.A. Times Opinion Sect.; pres. Harvard Law Rev.; contbr. articles to numerous jours. Mem. Dem. Nat. Com., Washington, 1984-88, ACLU (nat. bd.), pres. Boston chpt., 1985-86; mem. nat. governing bd. Common Cause, 1983-89. Mem. D.C. Bar, Calif. Bar, U.S. Supreme Ct. Bar. Jewish. Office: U So Calif Law Ctr Los Angeles CA 90089-0071

ESTRIN, DEBORAH PERRY, human resources executive; b. Waynesboro, Va., Dec. 28, 1948; d. James William and Annie Lee (Miller) Perry; m. Abbott Simon Estrin, Feb. 6, 1982. BS in Humanities, U. Tenn., 1982; MBA, Fairleigh Dickinson U., 1988. Dir. human resources Ciba Geigy Pharms., Summit, N.J., 1983-89; v.p. human resources Geneva Pharms. divsn. Ciba Geigy Pharms., Broomfield, Colo., 1989-91, USPCI subs. Union Pacific, Houston, 1991-94, N.Y. Power Authority, White Plains, 1994—; adj. prof. Audrey Cohen Coll., 1994—. Office: NY Power Authority 123 Main St 7th Flr White Plains NY 10601

ESTRIPEAUT, JENNY CECILIA, medical radiology technologist; b. Panama, Republic of Panama, Jan. 9, 1963; came to U.S., 1988; d. Ricardo Gaspar and Cecilia Clarita (Wright) E. BS in Radiology Tech., Creighton U., 1985. Registered radiology technician; cert. radiographer, mammographer. Radiology technologist San Fernando Hosp., Panama, 1985-88; CT technologist Mt. Sinai Hosp., Miami, Fla., 1988, 92-93; chief technologist ultrafast CT Ultrafast CT Assoc., Miami, 1988-92; mammographer Bapt. Hosp., Miami, 1992—; chief technologist Med. Imaging, Miami, 1993—; trainer CT scanner, Costa Rica, 1994, Miami, 1993; spkr. in field. Home: 4630 NW 102d Ave # 104 Miami FL 33178

ETCHISON, KATHLEEN MARIE, magazine editor; b. Tipton, Ind., Oct. 21, 1963; d. Dallas Franklin and Marilyn (Cotton) E. BA in English Lit. summa cum laude, Butler U., 1986. Editl. assoc. Norden Labs., Lincoln, Nebr., 1987, sci. writer, 1988, editor Norden News, 1989-90; editor Topics in Veterinary Medicine, Pfizer Animal Health, formerly SmithKline Beecham Animal Health, Exton, Pa., 1990—. Sponsor child Christian Children's Fund, 1987—. Recipient APEX award Comm. Concepts, 1994, Clarion award Women in Comm., Inc., 1994. Mem. Internat. Assn. Bus. Communicators (EPIC award 1994), Phi Kappa Phi. Office: Pfizer Animal Health 812 Springdale Dr Exton PA 19341

ETHERIDGE, MELISSA, singer, songwriter; b. Leavenworth, KS, 1962. Student, Berklee Coll. of Music, Boston, 1970. Wrote songs for the film, Weeds; albums include Melissa Etheridge, 1988, Brave and Crazy, 1989, Never Enough, 1992, Yes I Am, 1993. Named Entertainer of Year Can. Acad. Recording Arts and Scis., 1990; Grammy award, Best Female Rock Vocal for "Aint It Heavy," 1993, Female Rock Vocal Performance for "Come to My Window," 1994. Office: care Island Records 14 E 4th St New York NY 10012-1155*

ETSITTY, SYLVIA MAE, administrator; b. Ganado, Ariz., July 23, 1957; d. Benjamin William Harding and Evelyn (Lee) McCabe; 1 child, Bryant Loren. AA, Bacone Jr. Coll., Muskogee, 1978; student, U. N.Mex., Albuquerque, 1982-83, Ariz. State U. Researcher Navajo Nation Jud. Branch, Window Rock, Ariz., 1978-78; police planner Div. Pub. Safety, Window Rock, 1979-80; mgmt. analyst Navajo Nation Div. Soc. Services, Window Rock, 1981-81; personnel analyst Navajo Nation Personnel Dept., Window Rock; prog. analyst Navajo Nation Vet. Office, Window Rock, 1984-84; project dir. Navajo Dept. Health, 1984—; bd. dirs. Ft. Defiance (Ariz.) Hosp. Steering Cmty., 1984—, health planner Navajo Divsn. Health; organizer Navajo Nation Vietnam Vet. Symposium, Window Rock, 1987-84. Author: Short Story, 1975, 89, Poetry, 1978. Vice-chmn. Local Planning Bd. Ganado, Cornfields Ariz., 1988; tech. advisor Ft. Defiance Steering Com. Window Rock, 1988; Native Am. Child Welfare Advocate. Recipient Excellence in Svc. award Dept. of Health, 1986, Disting. Svcs. award Ft. Defiance Hosp. Window Rock, 1987, Photography awards Navajo Nation Window Rock, 1988, 89, Disting. Svc. award The Navajo Nation Govt. Mem. Red Cross Navajo Chpt. Window Rock. Democrat. Presbyterian. Home: PO Box 1432 Window Rock AZ 86515-1432 Office: Navajo Nation Dept Health PO Box 1390 Window Rock AZ 86515-1390

ETTER, SELMA CATHERINE, librarian; b. Scranton, Pa., Sept. 18, 1948. AB, Muhlenberg Coll., 1970; MLS, Rutgers U., 1971; MA, U. Mass., 1990. Cataloger King's Coll., Wilkes Barre, Pa., 1971-78; indexer H.W. Wilson, Bronx, 1978-79; supr. OCLC Inc., Columbus, Ohio, 1979-80; ref. libr. Geisinger Med. Ctr., Danville, Pa., 1980-87; sci. ref. libr. U. Mass., Amherst, 1987—. Master tutor, tutor trainer Susquehanna Adult Literacy Coop., Danville, Pa., 1980-87. Mem. AAUW, MLA, Med. Libr. Assn. Office: U Mass Amherst MA 01003

ETTER, ZANA CLAIRE, media library director; b. Camden, N.J., June 6, 1950; d. Clair V. and Zana Irene (Clapper) Cathers; m. D.W. Early, June 29, 1974 (div. July 1981); m. Markus Ernst Etter, May 28, 1988; 1 child, Erich. Student, U. Lausanne, Switzerland, 1970; BA in French, Rutgers U., 1972, MEd, 1979, MLS, 1986. Cert. French, German and ESL tchr., N.J. Cataloguer Princeton (N.J.) U., 1973-79; info. specialist Edn. Improvement Ctr., Princeton, 1979-82; supr., libr. assoc. Rutgers U. Tech. Svcs., New Brunswick, N.J., 1982-87; dir. media libr. univ. medicine and dentistry Robert Wood Johnson Med. Sch., Piscataway, N.J., 1987—; tchr. ESL West Windsor-Plainsboro (N.J.) Schs., 1978, YMCA, Princeton, 1981; tchr. French East Windsor Adult Sch., Hightstown, N.J., 1981; pvt. practice tutoring English, Plainsboro, N.J., 1981-84. Contbr. articles to profl. jours. Mem. Med. Libr. Assn., Health Scis. Libr. Assn. N.J. Office: Robert Wood Johnson Med Sch 675 Hoes Ln Piscataway NJ 08854-5635

ETTINGER, AMY BETH, electronic information manager; b. Orleans, France, July 20, 1958; came to U.S., 1960; d. Joseph Alan Ettinger and Diane Rae Frank. BS, Northern Ariz. U., 1981. Owner, pres. At Last Audio Video, Inc., Flagstaff, Ariz., 1981-83; account exec. KSTM-FM Radio, Mesa, Ariz., 1983-84; account rep. KOY-AMRadio, Phoenix, Ariz., 1984-85; sales mgr. KSTM-FM Radio, Mesa, Ariz., 1985-87; mktg. mgr. The Talking Phone Book, Phoenix, Ariz., 1987-89; audiotex mgr. The Ariz. Republic, Phoenix Gazette, Phoenix, Ariz., 1989—; bd. advisors 4th Media/Newspapers and Voice, Phoenix, 1991-92. Enrollment supr. The Experience, Phoenix, 1991-93; event coord. The Victory Fund, Phoenix, 1993; sponsor Save The Children, Phoenix, 1994. Recipient Silver Ingot Phoenix Newspapers, 1991. Mem. Interactive Newspaper Network. Democrat. Jewish. Office: The Ariz Republic & Phoenix Gazette 120 E Van Buren Phoenix AZ 85004

ETTINGER, JAYNE GOLD, physical education educator; b. N.Y.C., Oct. 18, 1954; d. Benjamin and Joan Louise (Hyman) Gold; m. Brian K. Ettinger, July 10, 1988; 1 child, Bradley Joseph. AA, Green Mountain Coll., Poultney, Vt., 1973; BS, Cortland State Coll., 1975; MS, Western Conn. State Coll., 1981. Lic. phys. edn. tchr., N.Y. Phys. edn. tchr. Lakeland Cen. Schs., Shrub Oak, N.Y., 1975—; volleyball ofcl. Hudson Valley Bd. of Ofcls., 1984-88, pres., 1987-89. Coord. Jump Rope for Heart, Mohegan Lake, N.Y., 1988—, Basketball Shoot Contest, Easter Seal Soc., 1989—, Hopping-Disability Awareness, 1992—. Mem. AAHPERD, N.Y. State Assn. Health, Phys. Edn., Recreation and Dance, Lakeland Fedn. Tchrs. (sec. 1985—), Kappa Delta Pi. Office: George Washington Elem Sch 3634 Lexington Ave Mohegan Lake NY 10547

ETTINGER, JUDITH MERLE, academic director; b. Comden, N.J., Jan. 5, 1948; d. Sigmund Joel and Betty (Dworkin) E.; m. Mr. Rodenstein (div. May 1991); children: Betsy, Shanna, David. BA, Case Western Res. U., 1970; MS, U. Wis., 1976, PhD, 1980. Adminstrv. asst. Mass. Coll. Pharmacy, Boston, 1973-74; rsch. asst. Guidance Inst. for talented Students, Madison, Wis., 1976-78; dir. career counseling U. Wis., Eau Claire, 1978-80; project dir. Ctr. on Edn. and Work U. Wis., Madison, 1980—; cons. and trainer in field. Author: Micro Computers in Vocational Education, 1986, Resource and Planning Guide, 1990; author and editor: Improved Career Decision Making, 1991; contbr. numerous articles to profl. jours. Recipient Cert. of Appreciation, Dept. of Pub. Instruction, 1990, Contbn. award Nat. Occupational Info. Coordination Com., 1992. Mem. ACA, Nat. Career Devel. Assn. (bd. dirs., trustee 1993—), Wis. Career Devel. Assn., Wis. Counseling Assn. Home: 1105 Chapel Hill Rd Madison WI 53711-3101

ETZ, LOIS KAPELSOHN, architectural company executive; b. Newark, Feb. 7, 1944; d. Sol D. and Matilda (Zlotnick) Kapelsohn; m. Leonard Etz, Dec. 4, 1967 (dec. May 1976); children: Rachel Jennie, Rebecca Sarah. BA, Mount Holyoke Coll., 1966; MA, Seton Hall U., 1968. Counselor N.J. Rehab. Commn., Trenton, 1966-68; pvt. antique dealer Princeton, N.J., 1968-78; pres. Nat. Code Cons., Princeton, 1971-78; dir. purchasing, aux. svcs. Mercer County Community Coll., Trenton, 1978-81; v.p. Hillier Group Architects, Princeton, 1981—. Bd. dirs. Vols. in Probation, Princeton, 1981, N.J. Printmaking Coun., Princeton Arts Coun., Mercer County Spl. Svc. Com., Hadassah; v.p. McCarter Theatre Assocs., Princeton, 1986-89; bd. dirs. McCarter Theatre Trustees, Princeton, 1989-91; past v.p., bd. dirs. Jewish Ctr. Commendation Chief Justice N.J. Supreme Ct., 1982. Commendation Chief Justice N.J. Supreme Ct., 1982. Mem. Mt. Holyoke Alumnae Assn. (past pres. Princeton chpt.), Record Mgmt. Assn. (founding officer), Princeton Pers. Assn. Democrat. Jewish. Home: 1038 Princeton Kingston Rd Princeton NJ 08540 Office: The Hillier Group CN23 500 Alexander Pk Princeton NJ 08540

EU, MARCH KONG FONG, state official; b. Oakdale, Calif., Mar. 29, 1922; d. Yuen and Shiu (Shee) Kong; children by previous marriage: Matthew Kipling Fong, Marchesa Suyin Fong; m. Henry Eu, July 30, 1973; stepchildren: Henry, Adelina, Yvonne, Conroy, Alaric. Student, Salinas Jr. Coll.; B.S., U. Calif.-Berkeley; M.Ed., Mills Coll., 1951; Ed.D., Stanford U., 1956; postgrad., Columbia U., Calif. State Coll.-Hayward; LL.D., Lincoln U., 1984. Chmn. div. dental hygiene U. Calif. Med. Center, San Francisco; dental hygienist Oakland (Calif.) Pub. Schs.; supr. dental health edn. Alameda County (Calif.) Schs.; lectr. health edn. Mills Coll., Oakland; mem. Calif. Legislature, 1966-74, chmn. select com. on agr., foods and nutrition, 1973-74; mem. com. natural resources and conservation, com. commerce and pub. utilities, select com. med. malpractice; sec. state State of Calif., 1975—, chief of protocol, 1975-83, sec. of state, 1975-94; Ambassador to Federated States of Mironesia U.S. Dept. of State, Washington, 1994; chmn. Calif. State World Trade Commn., 1982-87; spl. cons. Bur. Intergroup Relations, Calif. Dept. Edn.; ednl., legis. cons. Sausalito (Calif.) Pub. Schs., Santa Clara County Office Edn., Jefferson Elementary Union Sch. Dist., Santa Clara High Sch. Dist., Santa Clara Elementary Sch. Dist., Live Oak Union High Sch. Dist.; mem. Alameda County Bd. Edn., 1956-66, pres., 1961-62, legis. adv., 1963. Mem. budget panel Bay Area United Fund Crusade; mem. Oakland Econ. Devel. Council; mem. tourism devel. com. Calif. Econ. Devel. Commn.; mem. citizens com. on housing Council Social Planning; mem. Calif. Interagy. Council Family Planning; edn. chmn., mem. council social planning, dir. Oakland Area Baymont Dist. Community Council; charter pres., hon. life mem. Howard Elementary Sch. PTA; charter pres. Chinese Young Ladies Soc., Oakland; mem., vice chmn. adv. com. Youth Study Centers and Ford Found. Interagy. Project, 1962-63; chmn. Alameda County Mothers' March, 1971-72; bd. councillors U. So. Calif. Sch. Dentistry, 1976; mem. exec. com. Calif. Democratic Central Com., mem. central com., 1963-70, asst. sec.; del. Dem. Nat. Conv., 1968; dir. 8th Congl. Dist. Dem. Council, 1963; v.p. Dems. of 8th Congl. Dist., 1963; dir. Key Women for Kennedy, 1963; women's vice chmn. No. Calif. Johnson for Pres., 1964; bd. dirs. Oakland YWCA, 1965. Recipient ann. award for outstanding achievement Eastbay Intercultural Fellowship, 1959; Phoebe Apperson Hearst Disting. Bay Area Woman of Yr. award; Woman of Yr. award Calif. Retail Liquor Dealers Inst., 1969; Merit citation Calif. Assn. Adult Edn. Adminstrs., 1970; Art Edn. award; Outstanding Woman award Nat. Women's Polit. Caucus, 1980; Person of Yr. award Miracle Mile Lions Club, 1980; Humanitarian award Milton Strong Hall of Fame, 1981; Outstanding Leadership award Ventura Young Dems., 1983; Woman of Achievement award Los Angeles Hadassah, 1983, Outstanding Leadership award Filipino-Am. C. of C., 1985, CARE award, 1985, Disting. Svc. award Republic of Honduras, 1987, Polit. Achievement award Calif Dem. Party Black Caucus, 1988, JFK Am. Leadership award Santa Ana Dem. Club, 1989, L.A. County Good Scout award, Boy Scouts Am., 1989; named Woman of Yr., Dems. United, San Bernadino, 1989, Woman of Distinction, Soroptimist Internat., Monterey Park, 1987, Woman of Achievement, Santa Barbara Legal Secs. Assn. and County Bar Assn., 1987, one of Am.'s 100 Most Important Women, Ladies Home Jour., 1988; recipient Community Leadership award Torat-Haijun Hebrew Acad., 1990, Special Appreciation U. Vietnamese Student Assns. So. Calif., 1990, Nat. Assn. Chinese-Am. Bankers, 1990, Orange County Buddhist Assn., 1990, Internat. Bus. award, West Coast U., 1992. Mem. Am. Dental Hygienists Assn. (pres. 1956-57), No. Calif. Dental Hygienists Assn., Oakland LWV, AAUW (area rep. in edn. Oakland br.), Calif. Tchrs. Assn., Calif. Sch. Bd. Assn., Alameda County Sch. Bd. Assn. (pres. 1965), Alameda County Mental Health Assn., So. Calif. Dental Assn. (hon.), Bus. and Profl. Women's Club, Chinese Retail Food Markets Assn. (hon.), Delta Kappa Gamma.

EUBANKS-POPE, SHARON G., real estate entrepreneur; b. Chgo., Aug. 26, 1943; d. Walter Franklyn and Thelma Octavia (Watkins) Gibson; m. Larry Hudson Eubanks, Dec. 20, 1970 (dec. Jan. 1976); children: Rebekah, Aimée; m. Otis Eliot Pope, June 7, 1977; children: O. Eliot Jr., Adrienne. BS in Edn., Chgo. Tchrs. Coll., 1965; postgrad., Ill. Inst. Tech., 1967, John Marshall Law Sch., 1970, Governor's State U., 1975-76. Educator, parent coord. Chgo. Bd. Edn., 1965-77; owner, ptnr. Redel Rentals, Chgo., 1977—; realtor ERA Diversified Real Estate, Hazel Crest, Ill., 1990—. Adminstrv. bd. St. Mark United Meth. Ch., Chgo., 1967, bd. trustees, 1988; com. chair Englewood Urban Progress Ctr., Chgo., 1973; coord., educator League Women Voters, Chgo. (Outstanding Community Law Class award 1975), 1975-76. Named Outstanding Sch. Parent Vol., Chgo. Bd. Edn., 1977; recipient Christian Leadership award United Meth. Women, Chgo., 1985. Mem. NAFE, NAACP, Am. Soc. Profl. and Exec. Women, Nat. Assn. Realtors, Greater South Suburban Bd. Realtors, Jack and Jill Am., Inc. (Chgo. chpt. journalist 1989-91, Mid-western region sec./treas. 1993—, founder Parents for Parity in Edn. 1992, pres. Eubanks-Pope constrn. 1993, parliamentarian of Parity 1991), Alpha Beta Gamma. Office: Redel Rentals 4338 S Drexel Blvd Chicago IL 60653-3536

EUFINGER, CHARLOTTE COLEMAN, lawyer; b. Marysville, Ohio, Feb. 16, 1947; d. William L. and Rose Anna (Green) Coleman; m. John M. Eufinger, Sept. 4, 1971; children: Anthony William, Mary Katherine. BA, Miami U., Oxford, Ohio, 1969; JD, Ohio State U., 1972. Atty. at law Coleman & Eufinger, Marysville, Ohio, 1972—. Trustee Ohio U., 1989—, chair bd. trustees, 1993-94, Internat. Family Ctr., Marysville, Union County Meml. Hosp. Assn., Marysville, Marysville High Sch. Alumni Scholarship, 1991—, pres., 1994—; trustee Children, Inc., Marysville, past pres., Ohio U. Found. Bd., 1994—; active Inter - U. Coun., 1991-94, community adv. coun. Americom Bank, 1994. Recipient Athena award Marysville C. of C., 1988; named to Acad. Rev. Bd., U.S. Congress, 1991-92. Mem. ABA, Ohio State Bar Assn., Ohio Trial Lawyers Assn., Union County Bar Assn. (pres. 1976). Democrat. Lutheran. Office: Coleman & Eufinger 110 S Court St PO Box 266 Marysville OH 43040

EURICH, NELL P., educational consultant; b. Norwood, Ohio, July 28, 1919; d. Clayton W. and Adah (Palmer) Plopper; m. Alvin C. Eurich, Mar. 15, 1953 (dec. 1987); children: Juliet Ann, Donald Alan; m. Maurice Lazarus, 1988. AA, Stephens Coll., 1939; BA, Stanford U., 1941, MA, 1943; PhD, Columbia U., 1959. Dir. student union U. Tex., 1942-43; resident counselor Barnard Coll., 1944-46; asst. to pres. Woman's Found., 1947-49; officer charge pub. relations State U. N.Y., 1949- 52; acting pres. Stephens Coll., 1953-54; asst. prof. English NYU, 1959-64; academic dean New Coll., Sarasota, Fla., 1965; dir. project to reorganize curriculum Aspen (Colo.) Pub. High Sch., 1966; dean faculty, prof. English Vassar Coll., 1967-70; provost, dean faculty, prof. English; provost, dean faculty, prof. English, v.p. acad. affairs Manhattanville Coll., N.Y., 1971-75; sr. cons. Internat. Council for Ednl. Devel., 1975-82, Acad. for Ednl. Devel., 1982-88; mem. nat. selection com., chmn. Rocky Mountain regional com. Nat. Endowment Humanities, 1966-67, cons., 1970-71; mem. Middle States commn. Marshall Scholarships, 1967-68; chmn. Northeastern region, 1969-71; mem. U.S. Commn. on Ednl. Tech., HEW, 1968-69; mem. overseer's vis. com. on summer sch. and univ. extension Harvard, 1969-75; mem. panel of judge's Fed. Woman's award, 1969; cons. Acad. for Ednl. Devel., 1970-71; mem. career minister rev. bd. U.S. Dept. State, 1972; participant Ditchley Conf. V, 1973; mem. Rhodes Scholarship Selection Com., 1976; moderator exec. seminar Aspen Inst. for Humanistic Studies, 1977, 79, 80; dir. Adult Learning Project Carnegie Found. for Advancement Teaching, 1985-90; advisor Nat. Acad. of Engring., 1987-88; acad. advisor Cambridge Coll., 1990—; vis. com. Neuro Scis., Mass. Gen. Hosp. Author: Science in Utopia, 1967, Higher Education in Twelve Countries: A Comparative View, 1981, (with B. Schwenkmeyer) Great Britain's Open University, 1971, Corporate Classrooms, 1985, The Learning Industry, 1991; contbg. author: (Alvin Toffler) Learning for Tomorrow, 1974, From Parnassus: Essays for Jacques Barzun, 1976; contbr. articles to profl. jours. Past trustee Bank Street Coll., Salisbury Sch., Hudson Guild Neighborhood House, Colo. Rocky Mountain Sch., Bennington Coll., Carnegie Coun. on Policy Studies in Higher Edn., 1977-80, Carnegie Found. for Advancement Teaching, 1978-84; trustee New Coll. Found., Internat. Coun. for Edn. Devel. Mem. MLA, Am. Assn. Colls. (spl. com. on liberal studies 1966-70), World Soc. Ekistics, Nat. Coun. Women (hon.), Century Assn. N.Y.C. Home: 144 Brattle St Cambridge MA 02138-2202

EUSTER, JOANNE REED, librarian; b. Grants Pass, Oreg., Apr. 7, 1936; d. Robert Lewis and Mabel Louise (Jones) Reed; m. Stephen L. Gerhardt, May 14, 1977; children: Sharon L., Carol L., Lisa J. Student, Lewis and Clark Coll., 1953-56; B.A., Portland State Coll., 1965; M.Librarianship, U. Wash., 1968, M.B.A., 1977; Ph.D., U. Calif.-Berkeley, 1986. Asst. libr. Edmonds Community Coll., Lynnwood, Wash., 1968-73, dir. libr.-media ctr., 1973-77; univ. libr. Loyola U. of New Orleans, 1977-80; libr. dir. J. Paul Leonard Libr., San Francisco State U., 1980-86; univ. libr. Rutgers State U. N.J., New Brunswick, 1986-89, v.p. info. svcs., 1989-91, v.p. univ. librs., 1991-92; univ. libr. U. Calif., Irvine, 1992—; cons. Coll. S.I., Union Ejidal, La Penita, Nayarit, Mexico, 1973, Univ. D.C., 1988; co-cons. Office of Mgmt. Svcs. Assn. of Rsch. Librs., 1979—; bd. regents, Kansas; mem. adv. coun. Hong Kong U. Sci. and Tech. Librs., 1988—, Princeton U. Libr., 1988-92, U. B.C., Can., 1991—. Author: Changing Patterns of Internal Communication in Large Academic Libraries, 1981, The Academic Library Director, Management Activities and Effectiveness, 1987; columnist Wilson Libr. Bull., 1993—; contbr. articles to profl. jours. Mem. ALA, Calif. Libr. Assn., Assn. Coll. and Rsch. Librs. (pres. 1987-88), Am. Assn. for Higher Edn., Rsch. Librs. Group (chmn., bd. dirs. 1991-92). Office: Univ Calif Main Libr PO Box 19557 Irvine CA 92713-9557

EUSTIS, PAMELA JOAN, fund raising executive; b. N.Y.C., Mar. 11, 1959; d. Richard Wood and Shirley Kendall (Tunison) E. AB, Smith Coll., 1981. cert. fund raising exec., 1990. Asst. for spl. events Met. Mus. Art, N.Y.C., 1981-87, assoc. for social events, 1987-88; merchandising svcs. mgr. Modern Bride mag., N.Y.C., 1988-89; dir. spl. events and fund raising coord. The Brit.-Am. C. of C., N.Y.C., 1989—. Bd. dirs. Coun. of Protocol Execs., 1991—; active The Blue Hill Troupe. Mem. Women in Fin. Devel. Republican. Episcopalian. Office: Brit-Am C of C 52 Vanderbilt Ave New York NY 10017

EUTO, JEWEL ELIZABETH, counselor; b. Balt., Aug. 24, 1952; d. Vincent Kail and Mabel (Bowers) Bishop; m. Neil Joseph Euto, Dec. 10, 1971; 1 child, Daniel John. BS in Human Devel., SUNY, Saratoga, 1981; MEd in Counseling, St. Lawrence U., 1986; postgrad., Saybrook Inst., San Francisco, 1987-89; EdD in Vocat./Tech./Occupational Edn., Nova U., 1994. Cert. addiction profl., nat. cert. counselor, cert. guidance counselor, Ala., Fla.; lic. profl. counselor, Ala. Program dir. Sunmount Devel. Ctr., Tupper Lake, N.Y., 1986-88; addictions instr. Mater Dei Coll., Ogdensburg, N.Y., 1986-89; counselor, fin. aid dir. Withlacoochee Tech. Inst., Inverness, Fla., 1989—; clin. dir., v.p., cons. Tri-County Rehab., Inc., Lecanto, Fla., 1990—; cons. Interlink, Colo., 1991, Heritage, Beverly Hills, Fla., 1990. Vice chair St. Lawrence County Dem. Club, Canton, N.Y., 1980-83; 21 county regional del. N.Y. State Women's Dem. Party, Albany, N.Y., 1980-85; spkr. various cmty. orgns.; active VFW. With U.S. Army, 1991, Persian Gulf. Named one of the Outstanding Young Women in Am., 1988; edn. grantee Citrus County Sch. Dist., 1993. Mem. Internat. Assn. Addictions and Offender Counselors, Am. Assn. Counseling and Human Devel., Fla. Assn. Counseling and Human Devel., Am. Legion. Office: Rt 3 Box 210AA Somerville AL 35670-9802

EUTSLER, THERESE ANNE, physical therapist; b. Jasper, Ind., Sept. 11, 1959; d. Joseph Martin and Viola Agnes (Rasche) Wagner; m. Mark Leslie Eutsler, Oct. 3, 1987. BS, Ind. U., 1982. Physicial therapist Reid Meml. Hosp., Richmond, Ind., 1982-84; physical therapist Cen. Convalescent Services, Crawfordsville, Ind., 1984-85, St. Elizabeth Hosp., Lafayette, Ind., 1985-86, 95—; clinical coord. St. Elizabeth Hosp., Lafayette, 1986-92; with Indsl. Rehab. of Crawfordville, 1992-94. Bd. dirs. Arthritis Found. Tippecanoe unit, Lafayette, 1986-89, John T. Conner Ctr. for U.S.-USSR Reconciliation, 1989—; del. Ind. State Dem. Conv., Indpls., 1988. Mem. Am. Physical Therapy Assn. Orthopedic Sect., Jaycees. Roman Catholic. Home: 207 Main St Linden IN 47955

EVAGUES, KATHERINE ANN, nurse; b. Bay Shore, N.Y., Apr. 18, 1948; d. ARthur Robert and Katherine (Weber) Kirchner; m. Jeffrey Evagues, Oct. 5, 1991. AAS in Nursing, Suffolk County Community Coll., 1968; BS in Nursing, C.W. Post Coll., 1976; MA in Health Care magna cum laude, SUNY, Stony Brook, 1986. RN, N.Y.; credentialed alcoholism counselor. Staff nurse Southside Hosp., Bay Shore, 1968-69, staff nurse oper. rm., 1974-76, 81-89; insvc. instr. Boston Hosp. for Women, Brookline, Mass., 1969-70; staff nurse med.-surg. Newton Wellesley Hosp., Newton Lower Falls, Mass., 1970-71; nurse-in-charge Univ. Hosp., Boston, 1970-74; nursing team leader Straub Hosp., Honolulu, 1976-80; alcoholism counselor Lighthouse Counseling Ctr., Riverhead, N.Y., 1989-92; nursing care coord. Eastern L.I. Hosp., Greenport, N.Y., 1989-91; pub. health nurse Suffolk County Riverhead (N.Y.) County Ctr. Bur. Pub. Health Nurses, 1991-93; nurse Dept. Social Svcs., Med. Assessment Bur., Hauppauge, N.Y., 1993—. Assn. Oper. Rm. Nurses scholar, 1974; HEW grantee, 1975. Mem. N.Y. State Nurses Assn., N.Y. Fedn. Alcoholism Counselors. Lutheran. Office: Dept Social Svcs Med Svcs Bur PO Box 2000 Hauppauge NY 11788

EVANGELISTA, PAULA LEE, public policy and communications director; b. N.Y.C., Sept. 16, 1955; d. Frank Marino and Mary Louise (Denning) E.; m. Ralph Frederick Frakes, Dec. 8, 1984. BA in History and Creative Writing, Carnegie Mellon U., 1977. Mgr. pub. policy and comm. Hoffmann-La Roche Inc., Nutley, N.J., 1986-90, asst. dir., 1990-92, dir., 1992—. Bd. dirs. Soc. Progressive Supranuclear Palsy, Balt., 1990—; bd. dirs., trustee Boys and Girls Club, Clifton, N.J., 1991-92. Democrat. Roman Catholic. Home: 28 Twinlight Ter Highlands NJ 07732

EVANISKO, CATHERINE ANN, human resources executive; b. Passaic, N.J., Jan. 16, 1951; d. Alfred Frank and Ruth (Stephens) Moll; m. Thomas F. Evanisko, Oct. 16, 1971; children: Matthew C., Vanessa S. Student Bus. Adminstrn., Bergen C.C., Paramus, N.J., 1975, Ramapo Coll., 1984. Sr. pers. rep. Litton Automated Bus. Systems, Carlstadt, N.J., 1968-73; dir. transportation Dwight Englewood (N.J.) Sch., 1983-89; asst. v.p. human resources Mellon Securities transfer Svcs., Ridgefield, N.J., 1989-94; asst. v.p. Human Resources AFCO, N.Y.C, 1994—. Softball coach, Northvale, N.J., 1982-86. Mem. Soc. Human Resource Mgmt., The Human Resource Exchange, Human Resource Coun. of N.J. Roman Catholic. Office: AFCO 10 Hanover St New York NY 10004

EVANS, ANGELA MARIE, religious organization executive; b. L.A., Sept. 25, 1956; d. Frederick K.C. and Betty Ruth (Scott) P.; m. A. Michael Evans, Feb. 28, 1976; children: Alan Michael, Adrian Marie. Student, West L.A. City Coll., 1974-75; cert. in mgmt. effectiveness, U. So. Calif., 1988; BA in Church Adminstrn., Friends Internat., 1992. Exec. sec., office mgr. Crenshaw Christian Ctr., L.A., 1977-80, exec. asst., 1980-84, exec. adminstr., 1984-88, exec. v.p., 1988—; corp. sec. Crenshaw Christian Ctr., L.A., 1983—. Employee Med. Fund/Assist Fund, L.A., 1984-85; bd. dirs. Frederick K.C. Price III Sch. Bd., L.A., 1985—. Supporter Traditional Value Coalition, Orange County, Calif., 1990—, Life Chain of So. Calif., Orange County, 1990—, Christian Legal Soc., Annandale, Va., 1988—. Recipient Outstanding Svc. award Lung Assn., 1979, Appreciation award FKCP III Child Care Ctr., 1986; named Outstanding Young Woman of Am., 1986. Mem. Christian Mgmt. Assn. Democrat. Office: Crenshaw Christian Ctr PO Box 90000 Los Angeles CA 90009-9201

EVANS, BEVERLY ANN, school administrator, state legislator; b. Tod Park, Utah, Jan. 26, 1944; d. Elias Wilbur and Geraldine Vilate (Rigby) Cook; m. Stephen R. Evans, July 31, 1965; children: Lorie Ann, James. MA, Utah State U, 1968. Tchr. Duchesne (Utah) Sch. Dist., 1965-70; instr. Uintah Basin Applied Tech. Ctr., Roosevelt, Utah, 1970-73, adminstr., 1973—; instr. Utah State U., Logan, 1968—; rep. Utah Legislature, Salt Lake City, 1986—; cons. Utah State U., 1980—. Recipient Award of Merit, Nat. Safety Coun., Chgo., 1985-87, Alumni award Nat. 4-H, 1989, Bus. Woman of Yr award Utah BPW, 1990, Pub. Servant award Duchesne County C. of C., 1993. Republican. Mem. LDS Ch. Home: HC 65 Box 36 Altamont UT 84001-9704*

EVANS, BILLIE ARNELL, rehabilitation nurse, radiologic technologist; b. Oceanside, Calif., Jan. 20, 1952; d. William Amos and Peggy Joyce (Steele) Mann; m. Craig Evans Jr., Sept. 28, 1990. Radiology Technologist, Norfolk Gen. Sch. Radiology, Va., 1975; ASN, Tidewater C.C., Portsmouth, Va., 1983; BS in Health Care Adminstrn., St. Joseph's Coll., 1989; MS in Health Care Adminstrn., Cen. Mich. U., 1990. Registered radiologic technologist; RN, Va., N.C.; cert. rehab. nurse; cert. renal lithotripsy specialist. Radiology technologist Norfolk Gen. Hosp., 1976-83; shift head nurse Brain Injury unit Med. Coll. of Va., Richmond, 1984-89; staff nurse Southeastern Regional Rehab., Fayetteville, N.C., 1989-90; staff primary nurse stroke acute care unit Duke Med. Ctr., Durham, N.C., 1990-91; clin. charge nurse II Cysto Ste. U. N.C., Chapel Hill, 1991-92, nurse edn. clinician divsn. neurosurgery, 1992—. Recipient Nursing Process award Med. Coll. Va., 1987, Excellence in Adminstrv. Practice award, 1988. Mem. Assn. for Rehab. Nursing, Am. Urol. Assn. (nursing mem.), Am. Registry of Radiologic Technologists, Am. Congress of Rehab. Medicine, Nat. Head Injury Found., N.C. Assn. Rehab. Nursing, N.C. Head Injury Found., Am. Lithotripsy Soc., Sigma Iota Epsilon. Roman Catholic. Home: 506 Snowcrest Trail Durham NC 27707 Office: U NC CB 7060 Divsn Neurosurgery Rm 148 Burnett-Womack Blvd Chapel Hill NC 27514

EVANS, CAREN SUE, accounting administrator; b. Festus, Mo., Dec. 20, 1965; d. Ralph Virgil and Deloris Jane Harmon; m. Marty Lavern Evans, Aug. 20, 1983. Student, Mineral Area Coll., 1984-85, 92-93. Keypuncher The Leader Jour., St. James, Mo., 1983-84, Mineral Area Coll., Flat River, Mo., 1984-85; accounts payable supr. Purcell Tire and Rubber Co., Potosi, Mo., 1985—. Office: Purcell Tire and Rubber Co 300 Hall St Potosi MO 63664

EVANS, CAROL ROCKWELL, nursing administrator; b. New Orleans, Jan. 8, 1953; d. Daniel Raymond Sr. and Helen (Fischer) Rockwell; divorced; children: Nikki Elizabeth, Mimi Michelle. ADN, La. State Med. Ctr., 1990. RN, La.; cert. ACLS, BLS, cert. case mgr.; lic. life and health ins. agent. Life and health ins. agt. La. Ins. Agts. Assn., New Orleans, 1975—; dir. case mgmt. and utilization rev. Associated Med. Rev. Svcs., Metairie, La., 1986—; charge nurse med-surg. telemetry unit Elmwood Med. Ctr., Jefferson, La., 1990—; RN specialist II med.-surg. telemetry unit St. Charles Genl. Hosp., New Orleans, 1993—. Lobby La. Health Care, Baton Rouge, 1991. Mem. ANA, Individual Case Mgmt. Assn., Assn. Rehab. Nurses Case Mgmt. Soc. Am., Am. Assn. Respiratory Care, New Orleans Continuity Care, La. Managed Healthcare Assn. (edn. com. 1992—). Republican. Roman Catholic. Home: 6002 Mitchell Ave Metairie LA 70003 Office: Assoc Med Rev Svc 2821 Richland Ave Metairie LA 70002

EVANS, CAROLYN JOYCE, employment counselor; b. New Albany, Ind., Jan. 4, 1945; d. Joseph Gordon and Minnie Belle (Johnson) Kime; m. Robert Gene Leffler, June 14, 1960 (dec. Jan. 1969); children: Robert, Tina Leffler Fields, Kevin; m. John Douglas Evans, Feb. 27. 1970; children: Kimberly Evans Mayfield, Scott. BA in Psychology, Ind. U. S.E., 1987, MS in Counseling, 1994. Machine operator Air Guard Industries, New Albany, 1965-77; coord. family svcs. Floyd County Head Start, New Albany, 1978-87; case mgr. Floyd County Welfare Dept., New Albany, 1987-91; employment counselor Floyd County Job Tng. Partnership Act Program and Ind. Dept. Employment and Tng. Svcs., New Albany, 1991—; mental health counselor, New Albany; peer reviewer Floyd County Head Start, New Albany, 1985—; cons. State of Ind. Dept. Employment and Tng. Svcs., Indpls., 1993—. Recipient State Recognition award Adult Literacy Program, 1988, Adult Literacy Vol. of Yr. award Ind. State Adult Literacy Program, 1988. Mem. Am. Counseling Assn. (assoc.), Am. Assn. Marriage and Family Therapists. Office: 430 Pearl St Ste 17 New Albany IN 47150

EVANS, CATHERINE GULLEY, librarian; b. Orange, Tex., Oct. 9, 1950; d. Walter Raleigh Jr. and Elizabeth Whitfield (Walker) Gulley; m. Wayne Lea Randall, Jan. 18, 1969 (div. 1981); children: Mary Helen, Wayne Lea Jr.; m. John Edward Evans, June 25, 1983. BS, Miss. U. for Women, 1972; MS, Memphis State U., 1981; MLS, U. Tenn., 1994. Libr. Motley Sch., Columbus, Miss., 1972-75, Heritage Acad., Columbus, 1975-77, Northside Elem. Sch., Natchez, Miss., 1979-80, Magnolia Heights Acad., Senatobia, Miss., 1980-81; libr. Memphis U. Sch., 1981-90, head libr., 1990—; dir. Memphis Assn. Ind. Schs. Libr. Consortium, 1990—. Contbr. articles to profl. jours.; producer videos. Mem. altar guild, flower guild, clothes closet Holy Apostles Episcopal Ch., Memphis, 1983-88. Mem. ALA, Assn. for Ednl. Communication and Tech., Southeastern Libr. Assn., Tenn. Libr. Assn. (chair local arrangements 1989, chair honors and awards 1990, 91, 94, chair sch. libr. divsn. 1987, chair libr. instrn. roundtable 1994, Louise Meredith award 1990, James E. Ward Libr. Instrn. award 1993), TENN-SHARE (bd. dirs.), On-Line Audio-Visual Catalogers, Memphis Libr. Coun. (v.p. 1992, pres. 1993). Republican. Episcopalian. Office: Memphis Univ Sch 6191 Park Ave Memphis TN 38119-5399

EVANS, CHARLOTTE MORTIMER, writer, communications consultant; b. Newton, N.J., Nov. 26, 1933; d. Karl Otto and Wilhelmina (Otterbach) Pfau; student Douglass Coll., 1952-54; B.S., R.N., Columbia U. Presbyn. Hosp., 1957, postgrad., 1957-59; postgrad. N.Y.U., 1959-60; M.P.A., Coll. of Notre Dame, 1979; m. John Atterbury Mortimer, Nov. 20, 1964; children: Meredith Elizabeth, Mandy Leigh; m. G. Robert Evans, Sept. 4, 1982. Spl. assignment nurse Columbia-Presbyn. Med. Center, N.Y.C., 1957-59; med. advt. copywriter Paul Klemtner & Co., N.Y.C., 1959-61, William Douglas McAdams Agy., N.Y.C., 1961-62; account exec. Arndt, Preston, Chapin, Lamb & Keen, N.Y.C., 1962-63; Rocky Mountain corr. Med. World News, Denver, 1963-64; owner Publicite, Denver; gen. mgr. Center Mktg. Assn., Palo Alto, Calif., 1964-66; freelance writer, pub. rels. and mgmt. cons., Woodside, Calif., 1966-85; pres. Communications for Youth, 1979—. Mem. Palo Alto-Stanford Hosp. Aux., 1968-72; pub. rels. assistance Peninsula Children's Ctr., Palo Alto, 1968-73, Triton Mus. Art, San Jose, Calif., 1966-70; chmn. citizens adv. com. San Mateo County Juvenile Social Svcs.; health component Early Childhood Com., Woodside Elem. Sch. Dist.; mem. adv. com. South County Youth and Family Svcs. Program; mem. Statewide Citizens Adv. Com. on Child Abuse and Neglect Ill. Dept. Children and Family Svcs., 1987—; past chair, mem., bd. dirs. ct.-apptd. spl. advocate program CASA-Kane County, 1989—; chair adv. com. to Congressman Dennis Haskert on Family and Child Legis., 1990—; bd. dirs. N.J. Jr. C. of C./UNICEF/African Project, 1960-61; mem. San Mateo County Mental Health Adv. Bd., Friends of Woodside Libr. Bd, 1983-85; mem. Rep. Senatorial Inner Circle, 1982—; vol. Nat. Com. for Prevention Child Abuse and Neglect, 1987—; acting chair, founder Media & Children, 1993—. Home and Office: PO Box 710 Wayne IL 60184-0710

EVANS, DIANE JOSEPH, banker; b. Milford, Del., Nov. 8, 1956; d. Richard Beebe and Mary Prudence (Green) Joseph. High sch. diploma, Georgetown, Del. Bookkeeper Baltimore Trust Co., Selbyville, Del., 1974-75, receptionist, 1975-76, teller, 1976-85, sec. to v.p., 1985-87, loan support, 1987-89, loan rep., 1989-91, collection officer, 1991—. Mem. Fin. Women Internat. Republican. Wesleyan. Home: PO Box 288 Dagsboro DE 19939-0288 Office: Baltimore Trust Co PO Box 470 Selbyville DE 19975-0470

EVANS, ELIZABETH ANN WEST, real estate agent; b. Xenia, Ohio, Mar. 28, 1933; d. Millard Stanley and Elizabeth Denver (Johns) West. BA, Ohio U., 1966, MA, 1968; grad., Realtor Inst., 1993. Sec. various orgns., Ohio, 1952-61; tchr. Ohio U., Athens, 1966-67, Zanesville, 1968-72; tchr. Collier County Pub. Schs., Naples, Fla., 1972-77; sales Helen's Hang Ups, Naples, 1978-79; mgr. pvt. practice Wilmington, Ohio, 1979-87; adminstrv. asst. Powell Assocs., Cambridge, Mass., 1987-90; real estate agt. Bill Evans Realty, Inc., Naples, 1989-90, Howard Hanna Real Estate Svcs., Naples, 1991-93, Downing-Frye Realty, Inc., Naples, Fla., 1993—. Mem. AAUW, Nat. Assn. Realtors, Greater Naples Alumnae Panhellenic (pres. 1984-86), Nat. Soc. DAR (chaplain 1988-90, chmn. Motion Picture, Radio and TV 1992-94, asst. chaplain 1994—), Naples-Marco Kappa Alpha Theta Alumnae Club (treas. 1990-92), Phi Beta Kappa, Phi Kappa Phi, Phi Sigma Iota. Republican. Presbyterian. Home: 15117 Royal Fern Ct Apt A200 Naples FL 33963-8081 Office: Downing-Frye Realty Inc 3411 Tamiami Trl N Naples FL 33940-3702

EVANS, G. ANNE, lawyer; b. Eastland, Tex., Feb. 24, 1954; d. Travis Clay and Maude Velma (DeMoss) E.; children: Courtney Faith, Alexandria Brooke. BA in Psychology, U. Nebr., Omaha, 1988; JD, U. Nebr., Lincoln, 1991. Bar: Nebr. 1991, U.S. Dist. Ct. Nebr. 1991, U.S. Ct. Appeals (8th cir.) 1992. Pvt. practice, Omaha, 1992—. Mem. ABA (vice chair solo practitioners/small firm com.), Assn. Trial Lawyers Am., Nat. Assn. Criminal Def. Attys., Nebr. Assn. Trial Attys., Nebr. Criminal Def. Attys. Assn., Am. Inns of Ct. (co-founder Omaha chpt.), Golden Key, Phi Alpha Delta, Psi Chi. Democrat. Roman Catholic. Home: 11926 Wakeley Plz # 11 Omaha NE 68154 Office: 105 S 17th St Ste 717 Omaha NE 68102

EVANS, GAIL HIRSCHORN, television news executive; b. N.Y.C., Dec. 17, 1941; d. David Louis and Violet Ideta (Burkart) Hirschorn; m. Robert Mayer Evans, Mar. 13, 1966; children: Jason, Jeffrey, Julianna. BA, Bennington Coll., 1963. Aide to rep. William Fitts Ryan U.S. Congress, Washington, 1960-63, aide to rep. James Roosevelt, 1963-64; exec. asst. senator Harrison Williams U.S. Senate, Washington, 1964-65; legis. asst. The White House, Washington, 1965-66; owner, ptnr. Global Rsch. Svcs., Atlanta, 1976-80; prodr. CNN, Atlanta, 1980-87, v.p., 1987-91, sr. v.p., 1991—; bd. trustees Radio TV News Dirs. Found., Washington, 1993—; mem. adj. faculty Emory U. Bus. Sch., Atlanta, 1994—. Participant Leadership Atlanta, 1978-79; bd. dirs. Atlanta Clean City Commn., 1976-79, Ga. Endowment for Humanities, Atlanta, 1976-80; chairperson Ga. Endowment for Humanities, Atlanta, 1980-81. Democrat. Jewish. Home: 4700 Paran Valley NW Atlanta GA 30327 Office: CNN 1 CNN Ctr Atlanta GA 30348

EVANS, JANE KEEGAN, opera and music theatre producer; b. Milw., Oct. 24, 1956. BA in Econs., U. Wis., Milw., 1980. Dir. pub. rels. Milw. Symphony Orch., 1980-85; dir. mktg. Skylight Comic Opera, Milw., 1985-87; dir. communications Opera Am., Washington, 1987-89; gen. dir. Skylight Opera Theatre, Milw., 1989-92; mng. dir. Lyric Opera Cleve., 1993—. Office: PO Box 06198 Cleveland OH 44106

EVANS, JANET, Olympic athlete; b. Aug. 28, 1971. 3 time Gold medalist, 400m Freestyle, 800m Individual Medley Seoul Olympic Games, 1988; Gold medalist, 800m Freestyle Barcelona Olympic Games, 1992, Silver medalist, 400m Freestyle, 1992; winner 40th nat. title-400m Freestyle Phillips 66 Nat. Swimming Championships, Indpls., 1994. Named U.S. Swimmer of Yr., 1987. Address: US Olympic Committee 1750 E Boulder St Colorado Springs CO 80909*

EVANS, JO BURT, communications executive, rancher; b. Kimble County, Tex., Dec. 18, 1928; d. John Fred and Sadie (Oliver) Burt; m. Charles Wayne Evans II, Apr. 17, 1949; children: Charles Wayne III, John Burt, Elizabeth Wisart. BA, Mary Hardin-Baylor Coll., 1948; MA, Trinity U., 1967. Owner, mgr. Sta. KMBL, Junction, Tex., 1959-61; real estate broker, Junction, 1965-74; staff economist, adv. on 21st Congl. Dist., polit. campaign Nelson Wolff, 1974-75; asst. mgr., bookkeeper family owned ranches and rent property, Junction, 1948—; gen. mgr. TV Translator Corp., Junction, 1968—, sec.-treas., 1980—. Treas., asst. to coordinator Citizens for Tex., 1972; historian Kimble Hist. Soc.; mem. Com. of Conservation Soc. to Save the Edwards Aquifer, San Antonio, 1973; homecoming chmn. Sesquicentennial Year, Junction; treas., asst. coordinator New Constitution, San Antonio, 1974; legis. chair Hill Country Women, Kimble County, 1990—. AAUW scholarship named in honor, 1973; named an outstanding Texan, Tex. Senate, 1973. Mem. Nat. Translator Assn., AAUW, Daus. Republic Tex., Tex. Sheriffs Assn., Nat. Cattlewomens Assn., Internat. Platform Assn., Bus. and Profl. Women (pres. 1981-82). Republican. Mem. Unity Ch. Home: PO Box 283 Junction TX 76849-0283 Office: 618 Main St Junction TX 76849-4635

EVANS, JOAN, accountant; b. Springfield, Ill., Jan. 5, 1955; d. Ray Franklin and Annis Burdene (Garrison) Tracy; m. John Michael Lewis, June 15, 1980 (div. 1986); 1 child, Maris Jene Lewis; m. James William Evans, June 1990. BBA, Lamar U., 1990. CPA, Tex. Gas plant acct. Union Texas Petroleum, Houston, 1990-91; sr. staff acct. Trident NGL, Inc., The Woodlands, Tex., 1992—; ptnr. Am. Info. Source, The Woodlands, 1993—. Acct. free tax preparation VITA-IRS, Beaumont, Tex., 1987-90, Liberty, Tex., 1991—. Mem. Inst. Mgmt. Accts., Beta Alpha Psi, Beta Gamma Sigma, Phi Kappa Phi, Alpha Lambda Delta. Home: Rte 4 Box 150 Dayton TX 77535 Office: Trident NGL Inc 10200 Grogan's Mill Rd Spring TX 77380

EVANS, JUDY ANNE, health center administrator; b. Elmira, N.Y., Mar. 29, 1940; d. Hugh Kenneth and Mary (Faul) Leach; m. Nolly Seymour Evans, Feb. 18, 1965; children: Samantha, Meredydd, Clelia, Nolly III. BS, Cornell U., 1962; MBA, Syracuse U., 1992. Fin. analyst Morgan Guaranty Trust Co., N.Y.C., 1962-66; bus. adminstr. SUNY Health Sci. Ctr., Syracuse, 1983-89, adminstr. dept. pediatrics, 1990—. Mem. allocations com. Children Miracle Network, Syracuse, 1990—; children's hosp. steering com. Crouse Irving/Univ. Hosp., Syracuse, 1990—; bd. dirs. Syracuse Friends of Chamber Music, 1983-89, Syracuse Camerata, 1982-88. Mem. Assn. Adminstrs. of Acad. Pediatrics. Home: 26 Lyndon Rd Fayetteville NY 13066-1016 Office: SUNY Health Sci Ctr 750 E Adams St Syracuse NY 13210-2306

EVANS, LINDA, actress; b. Hartford, Nov. 18, 1942; m. John Derek (div.); m. Stan Herman, 1976 (div.). Appearances include (films) Twilight of Honor, 1963, Those Calloways, 1964, Beach Blanket Bingo, 1965, The Klansman, 1974, Avalanche Express, 1979, Tom Horn, 1980, Dead Heat, 1988; (TV series) The Big Valley, 1965-69, Wonder Woman, Hunter, 1977, Dynasty, 1980-88 (Emmy award nominee 1983); (TV movies) Nakia, 1974, The Big Ripoff, 1975, Nowhere to Run, 1978, Standing Tall, 1978, Bare Essence, 1982, I'll Take Romance, 1983 (also exec. prodr.), Dynasty Reunion, 1991, The Gambler Returns: The Luck of the Draw, 1991; (TV miniseries) include Bare Essence, 1982, North and South Book II, 1986, The Last Frontier, 1986; sr. prodr.: Yanni in Concert: Live at the Acropolis, 1994; author: Linda Evans Beauty and Exercise Book, 1983. Office: William Morris Agy 151 El Camino Beverly Hills CA 90212*

EVANS, LINDA KAY, publishing company executive; b. Tipton, Ind., June 16, 1945; d. Walter K. and Helen S. (Fakes) E. BA in English, Purdue U., 1968. Asst. to mng. editor Random House Pubs., N.Y.C., 1969-71; asst. to dir. editorial svcs. Sch. div. McGraw-Hill Book Co., N.Y.C., 1971-75, mgr. state contracts and inventory dept., 1975-88; bookstore owner, pres. The Literary Bookshop, N.Y.C., 1988-93; prodn. mgr. trade div. Simon & Schuster, N.Y.C., 1994—; pub. cons. for sch. textbooks Prentice-Hall Book Co., Englewood Cliffs, N.J., 1992-93. Recipient Holiday Window Display award to Lit. Bookshop, Greenwich Village C. of C., 1990. Office: Simon & Schuster Trade Div 1230 Ave of the Americas New York NY 10020

EVANS, LOIS LOGAN, investment banker, government official; b. Boston, Dec. 1, 1937; d. Harlan deBaun and Barbara (Rollins) Logan; m. Thomas W. Evans, Dec. 22, 1956; children: Heather, Logan, Paige. Student, Vassar Coll., 1954-55; BA, Barnard Coll., 1957. Alt. chief del. UN Commn. on Status Women, N.Y.C., 1972-74; bd. dirs. U.S. Commn. to UNESCO, Washington, 1974-78; pres. Acquisition Specialists, Inc., N.Y.C., 1975—, chmn. bd. dirs.; asst. chief protocol U.S. State Dept., N.Y.C., 1981-83; chmn. bd. Fed. Home Bank, N.Y.C., 1986-88, mem. bd. dirs., 1984-88; mem. adv. bd. U.S. Export-Import Bank, 1988-90, Nat. Fin. Com.; mem. George Bush Nat. Fin. Com.; mem. Nat Policy Coun. Vice chair devel. council Williams Coll., N.Y., 1979-81; co-chair Reagan-Bush Campaign, N.Y., 1984; bd. dirs. Bklyn. Jr. League, 1968-72, mgmt. decision lab NYU, 1992—; U.S. rep. South Pacific Commn., 1990-92. Mem. Women's Forum, Econ. of N.Y. Club. Republican. Episcopalian. Office: Acquisition Specialists Inc 919 3rd Ave # 21flr New York NY 10022-3903

EVANS, LUCY LEE GRIMES, family planning activist; b. N.Y.C., June 16, 1945; d. Charles Pennybaker and Louise Davis (Ireland) Grimes; m. Craig Carlton Evans; children: James Ireland, Natalie Dana, Daphne Decourcy, Peter Davis. BA with honors, Radcliffe Coll., 1967; postgrad., U. Chgo., 1968-69. Asst. tchr. Brearley Sch., N.Y.C., 1970-71; English tchr. Chapin Sch., N.Y.C., 1971-72; editorial asst. Saturday Rev. World Mag., N.Y.C., 1973-74, William Morrow and Co., N.Y.C., 1974-76; mgmt. trainee Mfrs. Hanover Trust Co., N.Y.C., 1976-80; cons. Western Hemisphere region Internat. Planned Parenthood, N.Y.C., 1993—; vol. Internat. Planned Parenthood, 1991—; mem. population and the environment com. Planned Parenthood of Conn., 1994—; mem. Challenge Partnership Com., co-editor Challenge Partnership Newsletter. Contbr. articles to newspapers. Dem. del. Tex. State Conv., Houston, 1992; mem. Dem. Town Com., New Canaan, Conn., 1993-94; Dem. cand. Bd. Edn., New Canaan, 1993; participant UN Internat. Conf. on Population and Devel., Cairo, 1994, also spkr., Bringing Cairo Home Conf. Dept. of State, 1994, Yale Conf. on Population, Consumption and the Environment, 1994. Mem. NOW, ACLU, Zero Population Growth, Planned Parenthood Fedn. of Am., Sierra Club, AAUW, Audubon Soc., Natural Resources Def. Coun., LWV, Cousteau Soc., Population Comm. Internat., The Feminist Majority, Pub. Citizen Forum for World Affairs, Harvard Clubs of Fairfield County and So. Conn., Union of Concerned Scientists.

EVANS, MARGARET A., civic worker; b. N.Y.C., Jan. 20, 1924; d. Bernard J. and Katherine (Walsh) Markey; B.A., Coll. Mt. St. Vincent, Mt. St. Vincent-on-Hudson, N.Y., 1944; postgrad. Columbia U.; m. John Cullen Evans, Jr., Nov. 24, 1951. Rep. N.Y. Telephone Co., 1944; personnel office Sak's 34th, N.Y.C., 1944-45, tng. supr., selling and non-selling depts., 1945-49, spl. assignment for store mgr. 1949-50; non-selling tng. supr. Gimbel Bros., 1950-51; rep. Gimbels and Sak's 34th at NCCJ Retail Group meeting, 1949-50. Instr. textile painting for ARC, Chelsea Navy Hosp., 1952-54, ARC vol., 1980—; bd. dirs. Marblehead Hosp. Aid Assn., 1954, pres., 1955-58; sec. Mass. Hosp. Assn. Council of Hosp. Auxiliaries, 1957-59, chmn. North Shore region, 1959-61, chmn.-elect, 1961-62, state chmn., 1962-64; exofficio trustee Salem Hosp.; trustee Mary A. Alley Hosp., 1956-79, chmn. bd., 1974-79; mem. Welcome Wagon of Fairfield/Easton (Conn.), 1979-83; chmn. Fairfield/Easton Theater Group, Fifth Wheel Club of Fairfield, 1983-85 . Mem. Alumnae Assn. Coll. Mt. Saint Vincent, Arrangers of Marblehead (chmn. garden therapy 1967-79). Clubs: Marblehead Women's Newcomers (pres. 1953). Home: 108 Cedarwood Ln Fairfield CT 06432-1308

EVANS, MARGARET ANN, human resources administrator, business owner; b. Great Bend, Kans., Dec. 26, 1947; d. Freddy Florence and Peggy (Hawkins) Green; m. Carl Evans, Aug. 13, 1972; children: Carl André, Christopher Dion. B in Psychology, U. Mo., 1971, MPA, 1972. Pers. specialist Met. Jr. Coll., Kansas City, Mo., 1972-73; employee rels. specialist Amoco Oil Co., Kansas City, 1973-74; classification specialist Richards-Gebaur AFB, Mo., 1974-75; employee rels. officer Govt. Employee Hosp. Assn., Kansas City, 1977-84, mgr. pers., 1984-87, dir. human resources, 1987—; mem. pers. com. Sta. KKFI, Kansas City, 1989—; mem. cert. bd. Human Resource Inst. Sec. and v.p. Booster Club, Hickman Mills High Sch., Kansas City, 1989—. Ford Found. fellow U. Mo., 1971; recipient

Contbr. of Yr. award Human Resource Mgmt. Assn., 1992, Pres. award 1993. Mem. NAFE, Soc. Human Resources Mgmt. (pers. rsch. com. Kansas City chpt. 1989—, nat. com. 1990—, sec.-treas. Mo. state coun. 1992-93, area IV bd. mem.), Pers. Mgmt. Assn. (co-chmn. coll. rels. 1981), Urban League, NAACP, Links, Inc., ASPA, ASTD, Alpha Kappa Alpha. Home: 10216 E 96th St Kansas City MO 64134-2309 Office: Govt Employee Hosp Assn 35 W 40th St Kansas City MO 64111-2219

EVANS, MARI-LYNN CURRENCE, television and video producer; b. Buckhannon, W.Va., July 3, 1959; d. William Dale and Virginia LaVon (Mick) Currence; m. Marvin Doak Evans, Apr. 22, 1983; 1 child, William Zachary Mick. BA in Psychology, U. Akron, 1982, cert. in lifespan devel., gerontology, 1982. Counselor Akron (Ohio) Ctr., 1980-82; pres. MLE Cons., Akron, 1982-84, AdultCare, Akron, 1984-89; dir. SUMMA Health System, Akron, 1989-91; CEO Evening Star Prodns., Lakewood, Ohio and London, 1989—, London, Eng., 1989—; mem. adv. com. Area Agy. on Aging, Akron, 1989-94, Alzheimer's Assn., Akron, 1989-91, v.p., 1986-88; chair OASIS, Akron, 1989—; cons. Geriatric Assocs., Akron, 1991-94; mem. Am. Sch. in London Aging Conf., London, Henley Ctr./Age Cancer Concern, Eng., 1994, Am. Embassy, Eng., 1994. Contbg. author: Insights, 1991. Pres. Summit AIDS Housing Corp., Akron, 1988-92, exec. com. 1993—; v.p. Women's History Project, Akron, 1989-91; adv. mem. Ohio Atty. Gen. Health Ins. Info. Program, Columbus, 1989-91; mem. social svcs. adv. bd. County of Summit, Ohio, 1995; active Oasis, 1989, Women's Entrepreneur Growth Orgn., 1995. Recipient award of recognition Women's History Project, 1986, award of appreciation Joseph P. Kennedy Found., 1989. Mem. NAFE, Nat. Assn. Sr. Living Industries, Am. Health Edn. Consortium, N.E. Ohio Gerontol. Soc., Am. Geriatric Soc., Am. Soc. in London, Women's Network. Office: Evening Star Prodns 219 Overwood Rd Akron OH 44313 also: Evening Star Prodns, 19 Bracknell Gdns Ste 111, London England

EVANS, MARSHA JOHNSON, naval officer; b. Springfield, Ill., Aug. 12, 1947; d. Walter Edward Johnson and Alice Anne (Field) Staffansson; m. Gerard Riendeau Evans, June 30, 1979. AB, Occidental Coll., 1968; MA, Fletcher Sch., 1977, MA in Law & Diplomacy, 1977; postgrad., Nat. War Coll., 1988-89. Commd. ensign USN, 1968, advanced through grades to real admiral, 1993; mideast policy officer Commander-in-Chief, U.S. Naval Forces, Europe, London, 1977-79; spl. asst. to sec. treasury U.S. Treasury Dept., Washington, 1979-80; staff analyst Office of Chief Naval Ops., Washington, 1980-81; dep. dir. Pres. Commn. on White House Fellowships, Washington, 1981-82; exec. officer Recruit Tng. Command, San Diego, 1982-84; commanding officer Naval Tech. Tng. Ctr., San Francisco, 1984-86; battalion officer, sr. lectr. polit. sci. U.S. Naval Acad., Annapolis, Md., 1986-88; chief of staff San Fransisco Naval Base, 1989-91, Naval Acad., West Point, N.Y., 1991-92; exec. dir. of the standing com. on mil. and civilian women Dept. of the Navy, 1992-93; comdr. Navy Recruiting Command, Washington, 1993—. White House fellow, 1979; Chief Naval Ops. scholar, 1976. Mem. Mortar Bd., Phi Beta Kappa.

EVANS, MARY EILEEN, state administrator, researcher, nurse; b. Sellersville, Pa., Sept. 30, 1942; d. Emlyn Thomas Evans and Mary Elizabeth (Fasbenner) Gerheart. RN, Lankenau Hosp. Sch. Nursing, Phila., 1963; BS in Edn., Temple U., 1965; MS in Nursing, U. Pa., 1969; PhD in Sociology, SUNY, Albany, 1976. Staff nurse North Penn Hosp., Lansdale, Pa., 1963-65; office nurse H. Karl Dimlich, MD, Lansdale, 1963-65; instr. Wilkes-Barre (Pa.) Gen. Hosp. Sch. Nursing; asst. prof. Sch. Nursing, SUNY, Albany, 1969-76; prin. rsch. scientist N.Y. State Office Mental Health, Albany, 1976-87, interim dir. Bur. Survey and Evaluation Rsch., 1987-88, asst. dir. Bur. Evaluation and Svcs. Rsch., 1988—; bd. dirs. Analytica, Albany; cons. VA Med. Ctr., Albany, 1976-88; assoc. prof. Albany Coll. Pharmacy, 1976-84, Union Coll., Schenectady, 1981, 85; assoc. prof., lectr. SUNY, Albany, 1986-90, adj. assoc. prof. Sch. Pub. Health, 1992—; trustee Found. N.Y. State Nurses Assn., 1988—; mem. editorial bd. Jour. Emotional and Behavioral Disorders; reviewer several jours. Co-author: Pharmacological Aspects of Nursing Care, 1984, 4th edit., 1993, Pharmacological Aspects of Nursing Care in Australia; mem. editorial bd. Jour. Child and Family Studies; contbr. articles to profl. jours., chpts. to books. Maj. U.S. Army, 1975-79. Fellow Am. Acad. Nursing; mem. APHA, Am. Sociol. Assn., Am. Statis. Assn., Am. Evaluation Assn., Soc. Rsch. in Nursing Edn., N.Y. State Nurses Assn. (editorial bd. The Jour. 1988-93), N.Y. State Sociol. Assn., Ea. Evaluation Rsch. Soc., Nat. Assn. for Rural Mental Health, Assn. Health Svcs. Rsch., Sigma Theta Tau, Pi Lambda Theta, Alpha Kappa Delta. Office: NY State Office Mental Hlth 44 Holland Ave Albany NY 12229-0001

EVANS, MARY JOHNSTON, corporate director; b. Shawnee, Okla., Feb. 28, 1930; d. Paul Xenophon and Helen Elizabeth (Alford) Johnston; children by previous marriage: Marcy Benson, Paul Johnston Head, Eric Talbott Head; m. James H. Evans, 1984. Student, Wellesley Coll., 1947-48, U. Okla., 1949. Dir. Amtrak, 1974-80, vice chmn., 1975-79; bd. dirs. Household Internat., Inc., Saint-Gobain Corp., The Sun Co., Inc., Baxter Internat. Inc., Delta Air Lines, Inc., Dun and Bradstreet Corp.; mem. adv. bd. Morgan Stanley & Co. Pres. Jr. League Oklahoma City, 1968-69; trustee Nat. Council Crime and Delinquency, 1971-75, Presbyn. Med. Center, Oklahoma City, 1969-75, Brick Presbyn. Ch., 1985-89; bd. dirs. St. Anthony Hosp., 1973-75; bd. visitors U. Pitts. Grad. Sch. Bus., 1978-85; trustee Mary Baldwin Coll., Staunton, Va., 1976-83, Carnegie Hall, 1985-92. Recipient Law Day award-Liberty Bell award Oklahoma Bar Assn., 1971, Disting. Service award U. Okla., 1981; named one of Top 100 Corporate Women Bus. Week mag., 1976; named to Okla. Hall of Fame, 1978. Mem. Conf. Bd. (Sr.), Pi Beta Phi. Presbyterian (elder). Clubs: Colony, River; Maidstone (East Hampton, N.Y.). Address: 920 Fifth Ave New York NY 10021-4160 also: Windmill Ln PO Box 488 East Hampton NY 11937

EVANS, ORINDA D., federal judge; b. Savannah, Ga., Apr. 23, 1943; d. Thomas and Virginia Elizabeth (Grieco) E.; m. Roberts O. Bennett, Apr. 12, 1975; children: Wells Cooper, Elizabeth Thomas. B.A., Duke U., 1965; J.D. with distinction, Emory U., 1968. Bar: Ga. 1968. Assoc. Fisher & Phillips, Altanta, 1968-69, ptnr., 1974-79; ptnr. Alston, Miller & Gaines, Atlanta, 1974-79; judge U.S. Dist Ct. (no. dist.) Ga., Atlanta, 1979—; adj. prof. Emory U. Law Sch., 1974-77; counsel Atlanta Crime Commn., 1970-71. Recipient Emory Univ. Law Sch. Distinguished Service awd., 1968, Better Business Bureau Distinguished award, 1972. Mem. Atlanta Bar Assn. (dir. 1979). Democrat. Episcopalian. Office: Richard B. Russell Fed Bldg & US Courthouse 75 Spring St SW Rm 1988 Atlanta GA 30303-3309*

EVANS, PAMELA R., marketing executive; b. Hoisington, Kans., Aug. 25, 1957; d. John Roy and Sarah Mace (Alder) E. BS in Bus., U. Kans., 1980. Sales rep. Home & Automotive Products div. Union Carbide Corp., Seattle, 1981; dist. sales mgr. Home & Automotive Products div. Union Carbide Corp., Syracuse, N.Y., 1981-82; mktg. assoc. Home & Automotive Products div. Union Carbide Corp., Danbury, Conn., 1982-84, assoc. product mgr., 1984; asst. product mgr. Grocery Products div. Ralston Purina, St. Louis, 1984-85, product mgr., 1985-86; product mgr. Eveready Battery Co. subs. Ralston Purina, St. Louis, 1986-88, group dir. mktg., 1988-90; dir. mktg. Consumer Products div. Esselte Pendaflex, 1990-91; dir. new bus. devel. Olympus Am., Inc., Woodbury, NY, 1991-92; v.p. mktg. consumer products group Olympus Am., Woodbury, NY, 1992-95; pres. Evans Cons., 1995—. Home: 6803 Upper York Rd New Hope PA 18938-9511 Office: 6803 Upper York Rd New Hope PA 18938

EVANS, PATRICIA ELLEN BURNS, culinary expert; b. Chgo., Oct. 5, 1956; d. Daniel Francis Burns and Mary Elizabeth (Lynott) Burns Corcoran; m. Frederick John Evans, Nov. 26, 1993. Grad., Notre Dame High Sch., 1974. Owner Pepper's Pantry, Lawrenceville, N.J., 1987—; freelance hist. researcher for authors Lawrenceville, 1990—. Recipient Honor for Mktg. Innovative Small Bus., Princeton C. of C., 1992. Mem. Exch. Club of Greater Princeton (pres., chmn. bd. dirs. 1992-93), 24 Club of Princeton (pres., chmn. bd. dirs. 1991, 92, 94), Nat. Exch. Club (cons., advisor to bd. 1992-93). Home and Office: 37 Fairway Ct Lawrenceville NJ 08648-1468

EVANS, PAULINE D., physicist, educator; b. Bklyn., Mar. 24, 1922; d. John A. and Hannah (Brandt) Davidson; m. Melbourne Griffith Evans, Sept. 6, 1950; children: Lynn Janet Evans Hannemann, Brian Griffith. BA, Hofstra Coll., 1942; postgrad., NYU, 1943, 46-47, Cornell U., 1946, Syracuse U., 1947-50. Jr. physicist Signal Corps Ground Signal Svc., Eatontown, N.J., 1942-43; physicist Kellex Corp. (Manhattan Project), N.Y.C., 1944; faculty dept. physics Queens Coll., N.Y.C., 1944-47; teaching asst. Syracuse U., 1947-50; instr. Wheaton Coll., Norton, Mass., 1952; physicist Nat. Bur. Standards, Washington, 1954-55; instr. physics U. Ala., 1955, U. N.Mex., 1955, 57-58; staff mem. Sandia Corp., Albuquerque, 1956-57; physicist Naval Nuclear Ordnance Evaluation Unit, Kirtland AFB, N.Mex., 1958-60; programmer Teaching Machines, Inc., Albuquerque, 1961; mem. faculty dept. physics Coll. St. Joseph on the Rio Grande (name changed to U. Albuquerque 1966), 1961—, assoc. prof., 1965—, chmn. dept., 1961—. Mem. AAUP, Am. Phys. Soc., Am. Assn. Physics Tchrs., Fedn. Am. Scientists, Sigma Pi Sigma, Sigma Delta Epsilon. Achievements include patents on mechanical method of conical scanning (radar), fluorine trap and primary standard for humidity measurement Home: 730 Loma Alta Ct NW Albuquerque NM 87105-1220 Office: U Albuquerque Dept Physics Albuquerque NM 87140

EVANS, ROSEMARY HALL, civic worker; b. Lenox, Mass., Mar. 25, 1925; d. Alfred A. and Rosamond (Morse) Hall; m. Richard Morse Colgate, Jan. 1, 1949; children: Jessie Morse, Margaret Auchincloss, Pamela Morse; m. James H. Evans, July 1, 1972 (div. 1984). Trustee Menninger Found., Topeka, Princeton (N.J.) Theol. Sem., Santa Barbara City Coll., Nat. Recreation Found., N.Y.C.; founding mem., life trustee Nat. Recreation and Park Assn., Washington; past dir. Nat. Audubon Soc., N.Y.C., Joffrey Ballet, N.Y.C. and L.A., Simon's Rock of Bard Coll., Gt. Barrington, Mass., Westminster Choir Coll., Princeton; former mem. Green Acres Commn., N.J.; former mem. Equine Adv. Bd. N.J. Morgan Horse Assn.; former collaborator Nat. Park Svc. Mem. Colony Club (N.Y.C.), Tarratine Club (Dark Harbor, Maine), Birnam Wood Golf Club (Montecito, Calif.), Lenox (Mass.) Club, Profile Club (Sugar Hill, N.J.). Republican.

EVANS, ROSEMARY KING (MRS. HOWELL DEXTER EVANS), librarian, educator; b. Forsyth, Ga., Nov. 16, 1924; d. Wiley Gwin and Mary (Goggans) King; B.S., Tift Coll., 1957; librarian's certificate Woman's Coll. of Ga., 1963; M. Library Edn., U. Ga., 1972, postgrad. in library edn., 1975; m. Howell Dexter Evans, June 29, 1945; children—Joseph William, Curtis McKenney. Tchr. elementary sch., Forsyth, Ga., 1946-48, 54-62; librarian Mary Persons High Sch., Forsyth, 1962-73; catalog librarian Tift Coll., Forsyth, 1973-74; head librarian Stratford Acad., Macon, Ga., 1974-77; head librarian, assoc. prof. Gordon Jr. Coll., Barnesville, Ga., 1977-87; chmn. regents' acad. com. libraries State Bd. Regents Univ. System of Ga.: Mem. Ga. State Bd. Certification of Librarians. Author; The Christmas Tree Farm, 1989. Spiritual edn. chmn. PTA, 1960-61; mem. Monroe County Hosp. Authority, 1988—, Monroe County Libr. Bd., 1990—. Named Star Tchr., 1966. Mem. Nat., Ga., Monroe County (sec. 1959-60, v.p. 1961-62, pres. 1962-63) edn. assns., Ga. (dis. pres. 1965), ALA, Southeastern library assns., Ga. Library Assn. Methodist (chmn. local edn. bd. 1964-65, chmn. commn. on Christian vocation 1965—, exec. com., tchr. adult Bible class). Author: Backhome Cuisine, 1984. Home: Evans Rd Smarr GA 31086

EVANS, ROXANNE ROMACK, retired military officer, hospital administrator; b. Idaho Falls, Idaho, Feb. 14, 1952; d. Richard Edward and Anne Elizabeth (Browning) R.; m. Paul Evans. BS, U. Idaho, 1974; postgrad., U. Md., 1979; MHA, Baylor U., 1982. Registered dietitian, Tex., S.C., Va., Okla. Commd. 2d lt. U.S. Army, 1974, advanced through grades to lt. col., 1990; dietetic intern Brooke Army Med. Ctr., Ft. Sam Houston, Tex., 1974-75; staff dietitian Walter Reed Army Med. Ctr., Washington, 1975-77; chief food service div. Kimbrough Army Hosp., Ft. George G. Meade, Md., 1977-80; adminstrv. resident Tripler Army Med. Ctr., Hawaii, 1981-82, chief clin. dietetics br., 1982-85; chief nutrition care div. Moncrief Army Community Hosp., Ft. Jackson, S.C., 1985-87; chief clin. dietetics div. Nutrition Care Directorate Walter Reed Army Med. Ctr., Washington, 1987-89; chief procurement activity Army Med. Specialist Corps, Dental Corps, Vet. Corp, 1989-92; chief nutrition care divsn. Reynolds Army Community Hosp., Ft. Still, Okla., 1992-93; hosp. adminstrn. Reynolds Army Cmty. Hosp., Fort Sills, Okla., 1993-94; retired U.S. Army, 1994, ret., 1994. Asst. leader cub scouts Boy Scouts Am., Columbia, S.C., 1985-86. Mem. Am. Dietetic Assn., Am. Coll. Healthcare Execs. (diplomate).

EVANS, RUBY ELAINE, accounting educator; b. Steens, Miss., Jan. 22, 1948; d. Verner O'Neal and Frances Louise (Sanders) Logan; m. Robert Earl Evans, Feb. 21, 1969; children: Sharon Elaine, Karen Ruth, Anita Lynn, Sydney Rachel, Matthew Robert. BS, Miss. U. for Women, 1971, MS, 1979; postgrad., Miss. State U., 1987—. CPA, Miss. Transfer clk. Miss. U. for Women, Columbus, 1971-75, acctg. supr., 1976-86, prof., 1986—. Mem. AICPA, Inst. Mgmt. Accts. (student activities dir. 1993—), Am. Soc. Women Accts (pres. 1982-83, Outstanding Woman Accountant 1986), Miss. Soc. Pub. Accts., Am. Acctg. Assn. Republican. Mem. Ch. of Christ. Office: Miss Univ for Women W Box 940 Columbus MS 39701

EVANS, SUSAN MARSTON, preschool director; b. Corpus Christi, Tex., Mar. 25, 1950; d. Arthur Albert and Opal Rosa (Roscher) Marston; m. Michael Lynn Evans, July 7, 1973; children: Kimberly Michelle, Lorelei Marston, Gregory Howard. BA in English, So. Meth. U., 1972, MA in English, 1973; secondary tchr. cert., Coll. Santa Fe, 1974; postgrad. early childhood adminstrn., Houston C.C., 1993. Cert. secondary tchr., presch. adminstr. Coll. residence hall dir. So. Meth. U., Dallas, 1972-73; coll. English/humanities instr. prison program Coll. Santa Fe, N.Mex., 1973-76; coll. prep. instr. prison program N.Mex. State U., Santa Fe, 1974-76; jr. high tchr. Los Alamos (N.Mex.) Ind. Sch. Dist., 1976-79; tutor Missouri City, Tex., 1981-92; presch. dir. Southminster Presbyn. Ch. Early Learning Ctr., Missouri City, 1989—; bd. mem. Southminster Presbyn Ch. Early Learning Ctr. Sch. Bd., Missouri City, 1990—, mem. bldg. com., 1992, mem. budget com., 1993; mem. spl. edn. adv. bd. Fort Bend Ind. Sch. Dist., Sugarland, Tex., 1990—. Editor: (poetry collectin) Cumbres Jr. High Creative Writing Collection, 1977; writer, editor Lantern Ln. Elem. Sch. PTO Newsletter, 1982-87. City chmn. Mothers March, March of Dimes, Missouri City, 1982-83; deacon Southminster Presbyn. Ch., Missouri City, 1982-85; sec. PTO, Lantern Ln. Elem. Sch., Missouri City, 1984-87; leader South Tex. Girl Scout Assn., Missouri City, 1983-92; v.p. Elkins High Sch. Band/Dance Team Booster Club, 1992—; den leader Tiger Cubs, Tomahawk Dist., Missouri City, 1993—. Named Outstanding Tchr. Prison Coll. Svc. Club/Jaycees, Santa Fe, 1974. Mem. AAUW, Nat. Assn. Edn. Young Children, Ft. Bend County Panhellenic Assn., So. Meth. U. Alumnae Assn., Ft. Bend County Zeta Tau Alpha Alumnae Assn., Phi Beta Kappa, Mortar Bd. Home: 3531 Point Clear Dr Missouri City TX 77459-3702 Office: Southminster Presbyn Ch 2310 Brightwater Dr Missouri City TX 77459-1800

EVANS, TRELLANY VICTORIA THOMAS, entrepreneur; b. Georgetown, S.C., Apr. 18, 1959; d. Abraham Lincoln and Jannie Ruth (Brown) Thomas; m. Leroy Michael Evans, Sr., June 18, 1983; children: Leroy, Jr., Thomas, Trellany Janiece. BS, S.C. State U., 1980; MBA, MHA, Pfeiffer Coll., 1995. Instr. Horry-Georgetown (S.C.) Tech. Coll., 1982-83, Big Bend C.C., Bad Kreuznach, Germany, 1986-87; statistician U.S. Govt.-Europe, Bad Kreuznach, Germany, 1987-89; budget analyst U.S. Govt.-Europe, Baumholder, Germany, 1989-91; acct. U.S. Govt.-DeCA, Fort Lee, Va., 1991; pres., CEO Abraham & Evans Assocs., Huntersville, N.C., 1990—; program dir. Charlette (N.C.) Self Employment Project Ctr. for Cmty. Self-Help and Self-Help Credit Union, 1994—; cons. Abraham and Evans Assocs., Huntersville, 1990—; part-time computer applications instr. Mitchell C.C., Mooresville, N.C., 1994-95; grad. rsch. asst. Pfeiffer Coll., 1994. Mem. NAFE, Am. Soc. for Quality Control, Order of Eastern Star. Baptist. Office: Abraham and Evans Assocs PO Box 142 15312 Curling Ct-1020 Huntersville NC 28078

EVANS, VIRGINIA ANN, marketing professional, real estate salesperson; b. Bunkie, La., Sept. 29, 1940; d. James Godby Sr. and Virginia (Jordan) Guinn; m. Scottie Neal Evans, Dec. 22, 1963; children: Vicki Lynn, Patti Rachael, Mandi Joan. Student, Northwestern Coll., Natchitoches, La., 1958-59. Real estate salesperson Bill. Stanton Realty, Jackson, Miss., 1979, Stan Weber & Assocs., New Orleans, 1980-86, Latter & Blum, Inc., New Orleans, 1986—; mktg. rep. Delta Title Corp., New Orleans, 1986—; mem. all coms. Real Estate Bd. New Orleans, 1980—; treas. WestBank Comml. Group, New Orleans, 1989-91. Vocalist at Constn. Week, New Orleans, 1992, U.S.S. Indiana (BB-58) Reunion, New Orleans, 1988, and with profl. orgns. and at nat. convs. Mem. So. Bapt. Hosp. League, New Orleans, 1980—. Mem. Women's Coun. of Realtors (sec. 1989, Outstanding Mem. 1988, Allen H. Johness award 1991, Pres.'s award 1991), New Orleans Realtors Assn. (Max J. Derbes Meritorious award 1992), Delta Aimees. Republican. Christian.

EVANS-O'CONNOR, NORMA LEE, secondary school educator, consultant; b. Vanceburg, Ky., Sept. 4, 1952; d. Herbert Martin and Nellie Irene (Parker) E.; 1 child, Karen. AB, Morehead State U., 1975; MEd, Xavier U., 1982. Cert. tchr. Fla., Ky., Tenn., Ohio. Tchr. Forest Hills Sch. Dist., Cin., 1977-83, Osceola County Schs., Kissimmee, Fla., 1983—; cons. Walt Disney World, Lake Buena Vista, Fla., 1991—; bd. mem. Nat. Assn. Secondary Sch. Prins. Student Coun. Bd., Va., 1990-91; movie checker Theatrical Enetertain Svcs., L.A., 1990—; security guard Walt Disney World Co., Lake Buena Vista, Fla. 1988—. Mem. NEA, Nat. Assn. Workshop Dirs., Osceola County Tchrs. Orgn. Democrat. Roman Catholic. Office: Osceola County Schs 420 S Thacker Ave Kissimmee FL 34741

EVANSON, BARBARA JEAN, middle school education educator; b. Grand Forks, N.D., Aug. 15, 1944; d. Robert John and Jean Elizabeth (Lommen) Gibbons; m. Bruce Carlyle Evanson, Dec. 27, 1965; children: Tracey, John, Kelly. AA, Bismarck State Coll., 1964; BS in Spl. and Elem. Edn., U. N.D., 1966. Tchr. spl. edn. Winship Sch., Grand Forks, 1966-67, Simle Jr. High, Bismarck, 1967-70; tchr. Northridge Elem. sch., Bismarck, 1980-86, Wachter Middle Sch., Bismarck, 1986—; workshop facilitator Brass Found., Chgo., 1988—, Dept. Pub. Instrn., Bismarck, 1988—, Chpt. I, Bismarck, 1989—, McRel for Drug Free Schs., Denver, 1990—. Co-founder The Big People, Bismarck, 1978—, Our Kids Need to Know, Bismarck, 1983; mem. task force Children's Trust Fund, N.D., 1984; senator N.D. Legislature, Bismarck, 1989—; mem. N.D. Bridges Adv. Bd., 1991—, DPI English Adv. Com., 1993—; co-facilitator Lead Mid. Sch. for Carnegie, 1994—; bd. dirs. Caring for Children, 1993-94; mem. Gov.'s Task Force on Edn., 1993-94, N.D. Art Edn. Task Force, 1992-93;, N.D. Health Adv. Coun., 1993-94. Recipient Gold award Bismarck Norwest Bank, 1985; named Tchr. of Yr., N.D. Dept. Pub. Instrn., 1989, Legislator of Yr., Children's Caucus, 1991, Outstanding Alumnae, Bismarck State Coll., 1991. Mem. Nat. Edn. Assn., N.D. Edn. Assn., Bismarck Edn. Assn., N.D. Reading Assn., Internat. Reading Assn., Assn. Curriculum Devel., Alpha Delta Kappa (state treas. 1984—). Republican. Home: 723 N Washington St Bismarck ND 58501 Office: Wachter Middle Sch 1107 S 7th St Bismarck ND 58504

EVANSON, ELIZABETH MOSS, editor; b. Dallas, Oct. 13, 1934; d. Clifton Lowther and Virginia (Spence) M.; m. Jacob T. Evanson, Apr. 8, 1958; children: Evan A., Virginia M. BA with high honors, Swarthmore Coll., 1956; MA, Columbia U., 1957. Ency. and book editor Columbia U. Press, N.Y.C., 1957-61; adminstrv. asst. New Haven (Conn.) Redevel. Agy., 1961-63; freelance editor Yale U. Press, New Haven, 1964-69; editor Ctr. for Studies of John Dewey, Carbondale, Ill., 1971-72, U. Wis. Press, Madison, 1975-80; editor Inst. for Rsch. on Poverty U. Wis., Madison, 1980—, conf. organizer, 1984—; asst. dir. pub. info. Inst. for Rsch. on Poverty, Madison, 1989—, sr. editor, 1986—. Translator: The French Revolution, 1962; contbr. articles and essays on poverty rsch. Mem. Acad. Staff Pub. Representation Orgn., Phi Beta Kappa. Unitarian. Office: Inst for Rsch on Poverty 1180 Observatory Dr Madison WI 53706-1393

EVANS-SILMAN, JILL MARIE, personnel executive; b. Tulsa, May 1, 1961; d. Max Hubert and Mary Lou (Newberry) Evans; m. Michael Brian Silman, Apr. 9, 1989. B of Journalism, U. Tex., Austin, 1983. With Adia Pers. Svcs., various locations, 1983-89; br. mgr. Temps & Co., Houston, 1990, Talent Tree, Houston, 1990-91; gen. mgr. Add A Temp/Exec. Employment, Woodlands, Tex., 1991-92, owner, pres., 1992—; adv. dir. Inter City Temporary Svcs., Inc., 1992—. Contbr. articles to profl. publs. Chmn. bd. dirs. Tim Hearn Meml. Found., 1991-92; mem. Edn. for Tomorrow Alliance, Woodlands, 1992. Mem. Nat. Assn. Pers. Consultants, Tex. Assn. Pers. Consultants, Houston Area Assn. Pers. Consultants, Wives of Houston Police Officers (pres. 1991-92), Tex.-Exes, C. of C., Alpha Xi Delta. Republican. Office: 25025 Interstate 45 The Woodlands TX 77380-3034

EVDOKIMOVA, EVA, prima ballerina assoluta, choreographer, director, producer; b. Geneva, Dec. 1, 1948; parents Am. citizens; m. Michael Gregori, 1982. Student, Munich State Opera Ballet Sch., Royal Ballet Sch., London; studied privately with Maria Fay (London), Vera Volkova (Copenhagen), Natalia Dudinskaya (Leningrad). pres. of jury First Rudolf Nureyev Internat. Ballet Competition, Budapest, 1994. Debut Royal Danish Ballet, Copenhagen, 1966; Prima Ballerina Assoluta, Deutsche Oper Berlin, 1969-90; artistic dir. National Ballet of America, Inc.; frequent guest artist with numerous major ballet cos. worldwide including London Festival Ballet, English Nat. Ballet, Am. Ballet Theatre, Paris Opera Ballet, La Scala, Kirov Ballet, Tokyo Ballet, Teatro Colon, Nat. Ballet of Can., and all other major nat. ballet cos.; premiered roles in all Rudolf Nureyev's classical ballet prodns.; appeared in over 16 classical and modern ballets with Rudolf Nureyev across the world; repertoire of more than 125 roles includes Swan Lake, Giselle, La Sylphide, Sleeping Beauty, Romeo and Juliet, Don Quixote, La Bayadere, Onegin, Raymonda; created roles in many contemporary ballets for stage, film and TV; film appearances include The Nutcracker, La Sylphide, Cinderella, A Family Portrait, The Romantic Era, Invitation to the Dance, Portrait of Eva Evdokimova, and others. Recipient Diploma, Internat. Ballet Competition, Moscow, 1969; winner Gold medal Varna Internat. Ballet competition, 1970; awarded title Prima Ballerina Assoluta, Berlin Senate, 1973, Berlin Critic's Prize, 1974; first fgn. mem. Royal Danish Ballet, first Am. and Westerner to win any internat. ballet competition, first Am. to perform with Kirov Ballet, 1976, first Am. to perform in Peking after the Cultural Revolution, 1978, first and only Am. dancer with portrait in permanent collection, Mus. Drama and Dance, Leningrad, only Am. performer ever to be honored in a German opera house, Grand Défilé ceremony, 1990 Deutsche Oper Berlin; recipient letter for meritorious svc. from Pres. Bush, 1990, numerous other awards; holder world record for 67 curtain calls with 40 minute standing ovation, Berlin, 1990. *

EVEN, JAN, newspaper editor; b. Oak Park, Ill., Apr. 18, 1950; d. Francis A. and Margaret Hope (Herrick) E.; m. Thomas E. Osborne, Feb. 13, 1988. BS in Edn., Northwestern U., 1972, MSJ, 1978; MA in Eng., U. Ill., 1973; postgrad., Oxford U., 1972, U. Cin., 1973. Tchr., 1973-76; editorial asst. Rand McNally Pub. Co., 1976-77; freelance reporter Lerner Newspapers, Chgo., 1977-78; reporter The Herald, Arlington Hgts., Ill., 1978-79; reporter newsfeatures dept. Seattle Times, 1980-81; reporter, copyeditor Tacoma News Tribune, 1981-83; copy editor, editorial dept. Seattle Times, 1984-86, copy editor, news desk, 1986-87, zone news editor, 1987, night news editor, 1987-90, arts and entertainment editor, 1990—; secondary sch. tchr., 1973-76; instr. Pacific Luth. U., Tacoma, Wash., 1985-86. Office: The Seattle Times PO Box 70 Fairview Ave N & John St Seattle WA 98111

EVENCHIK, CAROLE S., insurance company executive; b. Canton, Ohio, May 23, 1957; d. Martin Roy and Lois (Wasserman) E. BS in Urban Affairs Adminstrn., U. Cin., 1978; CLU, Am. Coll., 1989, ChFC, 1991. Asst. v.p. Lincoln Agy. of United Banks, Denver, 1979-85; cash mgmt. cons. United Banks of Colo., Denver, %; agent, registered rep., cons., owner The Principal Fin. Group, Denver, 1985-88; mktg. cons. The Principal Fin. Group, Des Moines, 1988-91; brokerage sales mgr. The Principal Fin. Group, Mpls., 1991-92; mktg. rep. Minn. Mutual, St. Paul, 1992—. Mem. bd. trustees Shir Tikvah Congregation, St. Paul, 1992-94, social action chair. mem. Am. Soc. of CLU, ChFC, Soc. Chartered Life Underwriters and Chartered Fin. Cons. Office: Minn Mutual 400 Robert St N 20-3731 Saint Paul MN 55101

EVERETT, CAROL NAN, public relations executive; b. Pasadena, Tex., Dec. 22, 1944; d. Calvin Ferrell and Dorothy Ernestine (Taylor) Gage; children: Joe Bob, Kelly Kay. Student, Durham's Bus. Coll., Austin, Tex. Credit mgr. Holy Cross Hosp., Austin; office mgr. Howard Burk, M.D., Austin, W. F. Wisner, M.D., Garland, Tex.; dir. North Dallas Woman's Clinic; adminstr. Dallas Med. Clinic; owner Promenade Meat Ctr.; with Bowles Green; pub. rels. staff Life Network Inc., Dallas. Author: Blood Money, 1992; prodr. video: Light of Life, 1991. Office: Life Network Inc Ste 206 17430 Campbell Dallas TX 75252

EVERETT, DIANA JEAN, university athletics administrator; b. Durant, Okla., Aug. 20, 1949; d. William Price and Francis Imogene (Harris) E. BA in Phys. Edn., U. Tex., Arlington, 1974; MS in Phys. Edn., Baylor U., 1978; PhD in Sports Adminstrn., Tex. Woman's U., 1995. Cert. adminstrn. and teaching. Tchr., head coach Midlothian (Tex.) Ind. Sch. Dist., 1974-77; instr. Baylor U., Waco, Tex., 1977-78; tchr., head coach San Marcos (Tex.) Ind. Sch. Dist., 1978-80, Clear Creek Ind. Sch. Dist., League City, Tex., 1985-91; asst. dir. athletics Tex. Woman's U., Denton, 1991-95; exec. dir. Nat. Assn. Girls and Women in Sports, Reston, Va., 1995—; mem. host com. Dallas Internat. Sports Commn., 1994-95. Site dir. Tex. State Spl. Olympics, Denton, 1993; tournament dir. Nat. Women's Wheelchair Basketball, Dallas, 1994; active Nat. Girls and Women Sport Day, Denton and Dallas, 1991-95; sec. Exec. Women's Golf League, Denton, 1994-95; site facilitator Elk's Youth Basketball Shoot-Out, Denton, 1991-95; vol. Disabled Sports Assn. North Tex., Dallas, 1994. Mem. AAUW, Am. Assn. Health, Phys. Edn., Recreation and Dance, Nat. Assn. Coll. Women Athletic Adminstrs., Nat. Assn. for Girls and Women Sports, Bay Area Women's Athletic Network (v.p. 1989-93), Delta Psi Kappa. Home: Rte 1 Box 92B Bridgeport TX 76426 Office: Nat Assn Girls and Women in Sports 1900 Association Dr Reston VA 22091

EVERETT, DONNA RANEY, business educator; b. Corpus Christi, Tex., May 30, 1939; d. Donald Wayne and Zora Lee (Wynne) Raney; div.; 1 child, Donna Melinda. BA, Phillips U., Enid, Okla., 1961; MS, U. Houston, 1983, EdD, 1988. Various positions various orgns., Tex., 1965-80; adj. prof. U. Houston, 1983-88; asst. prof. bus. Tex. Tech U., Lubbock, 1988-89, Lamar U., Beaumont, Tex., 1989-90; asst. prof. bus. edn. Tex. Tech U., Lubbock, 1990-93; assoc. prof. bus. and mktg. edn. Ea. N.Mex. U., Portales, 1993-94; asst. prof. bus. and mktg. edn. U. Mo., Columbia, 1994—; sponsor Zeta Kappa chpt. Pi Omega Pi. Troop leader Girl Scouts U.S., Ft. Worth and Lake Jackson, Tex., 1964-80, dir. tng. Lake Jackson coun., 1980-82. Recipient curriculum devel. award Tex. Higher Edn. Coordinating Bd., 1987-88, outstanding article award Nat. Assn. Bus. Tchrs. Edn. Rev., 1992; named Outstanding Faculty Mem., Tex. Tech U., 1991. Mem. Am. Ednl. Rsch. Assn. (bus. edn. and info. sys. spl. interest group), Internat. Soc. Tech. in Edn., Tex. Bus. Edn. Assn. (editor 1988-93, collegiate bus. tchr. of yr. dist. 4 1988, dist. 17 1992), Nat. Bus. Edn. Assn., Tex. Computer Edn. Assn., Mo. Bus. Edn. Assn., S.W. Fedn. Adminstrv. Disciplines (Disting. Paper award 1989, 93), Am. Vocat. Assn. (com. mem. 1990—), Delta Pi Epsilon (pres. Alpha Gamma chpt. 1988-89).

EVERETT, PAMELA IRENE, legal management company executive, educator; b. L.A., Dec. 31, 1947; d. Richard Weldon and Alta Irene (Tuttle) Bunnell; m. James E. Everett, Sept. 2, 1967 (div. 1973); 1 child, Richard Earl. Cert. Paralegal, Rancho Santiago Coll., Santa Ana, Calif., 1977; BA, Calif. State U.-Long Beach, 1985; MA, U. Redlands, 1988. Owner, mgr. Orange County Paralegal Svc., Santa Ana, 1979-85; pres. Gem Legal Mgmt. Inc., Fullerton, Calif., 1986—; co-owner Bunnell Publs., Fullerton, Calif., 1992—; instr. Rancho Santiago Coll., 1979—, chmn. adv. bd., 1980-85; instr. Fullerton Coll., 1989—, Rio Hondo Coll., Whittier, Calif., 1992-94; advisor Nat. Paralegal Assn., 1982—, Saddleback Coll., 1985—, North Orange County Regional Occupational Program, Fullerton, 1986—, Fullerton Coll. So. Calif. Coll. Bus. and Law; bd. dirs. Nat. Profl. Legal Assts. Inc., editor PLA News. Author: Legal Secretary Federal Litigation, 1986, Legal Secretary Bankruptcy, 1987, Going Independent-Business Planning Guide, Fundamentals of Law Office Management, 1994. Republican. Office: 406 N Adams Ave Fullerton CA 92632-1605

EVERETT, PATRICIA PEDEN, art consultant; b. Santa Monica, Calif., May 28, 1952; d. Edward Delano and Edith May (Smith) Peden; m. Edward Bruce Everett, May 16, 1987. BA in Fine Art, Calif. State U., Northridge, 1978, MA in Fine Art, 1981. Freelance photographer L.A., 1976-82; assoc. art cons. Anne Goodman Art Cons., Marina Del Rey, Calif., 1982-87, exec. v.p., 1986-88; owner, dir. Corp. Fine Art, Chatsworth, Calif., 1989—. Mem. Woodland Hills C. of C. (bd. dirs. 1995). Democrat. Office: Corp Fine Art 9274 Franklin St Chatsworth CA 91311

EVERETT, VIRGINIA SAUERBRUN, counselor; b. Newark, N.J., Mar. 24, 1939; d. Arthur Gordon and Elwyna (Van Alen) Sauerbrun; m. Chandler H. Everett, Sept. 14, 1963 (div. Feb. 1986); children: Chandler P., Alexander U. BA, Coll. Wooster, 1961; MS in Gen. Counseling, Seattle Pacific U., 1990. Cert. chem. dependency counselor I. Counselor South King County Drug & Alcohol Recovery Ctrs., Seattle, 1990—; counselor Seattle Mental Health Inst., 1988-89, King County Perinatal Treatment Program, 1992-93, King County Pub. Health Dept., 1991—. Treas. Pacific N.W. Ballet League, Seattle, 1983; chmn. publicity Seattle Opera Guild, 1984; mem. work com. Washington State Coalition on Women's Substance Abuse Issues, 1990. Mem. ACA, Nat. Assn. Alchoholism and Drug Abuse Counselors, Chem. Dependency Profls. Wash. Republican. Episcopalian. Home: 8408 NE 19th Pl Bellevue WA 98004 Office: South King County Recovery Ctrs 15025 4th Ave SW Seattle WA 98166

EVERETT, WENDY ANN, toy designer; b. East Lansing, Mich., May 6, 1950; d. Donald Franklin and Mary Margaret (Marshall) E. BA in Edn., Fine Arts, Mich. State U., 1972; M in Early Childhood Devel., Fairfield (Conn.) U., 1989. Elem. sch. tchr. Fraser (Mich.) Pub. Schs., 1973-77; creative dir. WFR Ribbon Corp., N.Y.C., 1977-79; pres. Wendy Everett Creations, Westport, Conn., 1979—. Author: The Gift Book, 1986, Active Bulletin Boards, 1979; composer (children's musical) The Vegetable Garden, 1973 (children's TV show) The Dream Makers, 1990; regular guest (TV show) Our Home; contbr. articles to mags.; designer Barbie Doll Fashions, 1983—, Care Bears, Strawberry Shortcake, Cabbage Patch Doll Clothes, Americana Crafts, ET Quilt, ET Wallhanging, 1983, Stenciling Hunt Mfg. Co. Kits, 1979—, Pastime Industries Crafts, 1990, Bath Buddies toy line, 1989—, ednl. toys for Princess Fabrics, N.Y.C., 1992—. Mem. Cooper Hewitt Mus., Southport Trinity Episc. Ch. Mem. Am. Craft Assn., Nat. Arts Club (N.Y.C.), Phi Beta Kappa. Home: 1123 Sasco Hill Rd Fairfield CT 06430

EVERITT, ALICE LUBIN, labor arbitrator; b. Washington, Dec. 13, 1936; d. Isador and Alice (Berliner) Lubin; BA, Columbia U., 1968, JD, 1971. Assoc. firm Amen, Weisman & Butler, N.Y.C., 1971-78; spl. asst. to dir. Fed. Mediation and Conciliation Svc., Washington, 1978-81; editor Dept. Labor publ., 1979, pvt. practice labor arbitration, Washington, N.Y.C. and Petersburg, Va., 1981—; dean admissions Hofstra U. Sch. Law 1985-89; mem. various nat. mediation and arbitration panels including Fed. Mediation and Conciliation Svc., U.S. Steel and United Steelworkers. Mem. Am. Arbitration Assn., Soc. Profls. Dispute Resolution, Indsl. Rels. Rsch. Assn., Civil War Roundtable of Washington, N.Y.C. and Richmond. Office: 541 High St Petersburg VA 23803-3859

EVERLY, BARBARA ANN, court official; b. Glen Haven, Wis., Jan. 4, 1931; children: Nancy Everly Persons, Becky Everly Smiley, Rocky. Student, Bayless Coll. Bus., Dubuque, Iowa, 1951. Asst. pers. mgr. A.Y. McDonald Mfg., Dubuque, 1961-63; adminstr. County Atty.'s Office, Dubuque, 1963-65; clk. U.S. Bankruptcy Ct. for No. Dist. Iowa, Cedar Rapids, 1965—; mem. faculty Fed. Jud. Ctr., Washington, 1966-86; orgn. devel. leader Adminstrv. Office, U.S. Cts., Washington, 1968-86; chmn. Bankruptcy Seminars Iowa, Inc., Cedar Rapids, 1969—; pres. Gt. Plains Bankruptcy Conf., Cedar Rapids, 1990—. Author: (booklet) Leadership, 1974. Fellow Am. Bankruptcy Coll., Inst. Ct. Mgmt.; mem. Am. Bankruptcy Inst. (bd. dirs. 1992—). Home: 4405 Pepperwood Hl SE Cedar Rapids IA 52403-1029 Office: Clk US Bankruptcy Ct PO Box 74890 Cedar Rapids IA 52407-4890

EVERS, JEAN GRAF, editor, writer, publicist; b. Columbus, Ohio, Dec. 27, 1917; d. Ray W. and Marie A. (Dooley) Arms; B.A. magna cum laude, Northwestern U., 1940; m. Don Graf, May 15, 1947 (dec., 1962); m. 2d Carl G. Evers, Jan. 22, 1964. Assoc. editor House and Garden mag., N.Y.C., 1942-45, Life mag., N.Y.C., 1945-47; partner Graf and Graf, pub. relations, 1947-63; public relations Am. Carpet Inst., N.Y.C., 1955-57; public relations dir. Galbraith Hoffman, N.Y.C., 1958-60; guest editor Herald Tribune Decorating Supplements and Sunday mag., Today's Living, 1960-61; dir. interior furnishings Mohair Council, Kairella Agy., N.Y.C., 1966-68; asst. editor Voices, regional weekly newspaper six towns, Southbury, Conn., 1973-74, editor, 1974-87; guest home furnishings editor Modern Bride, 1955; freelance writer, contbr. articles to nat. women's and decorating mags. including Good Housekeeping, Parents; author: Practical Houses for Contemporary Living, 1954; Doubleday Decorating Books, 1972. Press chmn. Southbury Tercentennial Celebration, 1973. Recipient Vogue Prix de Paris, Conde Nast Publs., 1940. Mem. Nat. Home Fashions League (nat. dir., N.Y. chpt., 1972-73, nat. pres., 1975-76, adv. council, 1977-79), Am. Soc. Interior Designers (press), Phi Beta Kappa, Delta Gamma. Home: 738B Heritage Vlg Southbury CT 06488-1312

EVERSOLE, SANDRA JOY, operating room nurse; b. Leesville, La., Nov. 15, 1955; d. Marvin Henry and Joy Marie (Caraway) Miller; m. Robert Dean Eversole, July 6, 1974; children: Brandi, Jennifer, Brian. ADN, Brazosport-Galveston Coll., 1977. cert. oper. rm. nurse, 1988. Staff nurse med.-surg. Sweeny (Tex.) Community Hosp., 1977-78; staff nurse oper. rm. Sweeny (Tex.) Cmty. Hosp., 1978-82; staff nurse oper. rm. Polly Ryon Hosp., Richmond, Tex., 1982-91, asst. mgr. oper. rm., 1991—; preceptor Polly Ryon Hosp., Richmond, 1992—, mem. safety and infection control com., Richmond, 1992—. Designer intraoperative record, 1990. Mem. PTA Needville Elem. Sch., Band Boosters Club; mem. United Ch. of Christ. Mem. Assn. Oper. Rm. Nurses (cert.), Live Oak Club. Home: 15426 John Miller Rd Guy TX 77444-9516 Office: Polly Ryon Hosp 1705 Jackson St Richmond TX 77469-3289

EVERSON, DIANE LOUISE, publishing executive; b. Edgerton, Wis., Mar. 27, 1953; d. Harland Everett and Helen Viola (Oliver) E. BS, Carroll Coll., 1975. Co-pub. Edgerton (Wis.) Reporter, 1976—; v.p. Silk Screen Creations, 1981—. Pub. Career Directors newspaper, 1981—, Directions mag., 1981—, Career Waves Newsletter, 1989—, Coll. and Univs. Directories. Trustee Carroll Coll., 1987—. Mem. Nat. Newspaper Assn. (regional dir. bd. dirs.). Democrat. Lutheran. Home: 114 Kellog Rd Edgerton WI 53534-9352 Office: Directions Pub 21 N Henry St Edgerton WI 53534-1821

EVERSON, NINA MARIE BRODE, small business owner, preschool educator; b. Marietta, Ohio, Aug. 21, 1949; d. Edward Van and Mary Isabelle (Moore) Perry; m. Gary Allen Brode, Sept. 1, 1972 (div. June 1980); 1 child, Jonathan Andrew; m. Larry Austin Everson, May 2, 1990; stepchildren: Austin James, Amber Dawn. BA, Glenville (W.Va.) State Coll., 1986; cert. in Montessori pre-primary, Carlow Coll., 1987; MA in Early Childhood Edn., W.Va. U., 1990. Cert. pre-primary tchr. AMS. Owner, artist Art Unltd., Davisville, W.Va., 1978-89; ad layout artist Cox's Dept. Store, Parkersburg, W.Va., 1979-83; preparer bank deposits Montgomery Ward, Parkersburg, 1981-91; ad exec. Sta. WIBZ, Parkersburg, 1983; counselor Open Door Home, Marietta, Ohio, 1984-85, 86; tchr. De Sales Heights Acad., Parkersburg, 1984-91; owner, tchr. Montessori Experience Pre-Sch., Parkersburg, 1991—; docent Parkersburg Art Ctr., 1978-81; pvt. tutor, Parkersburg, 1989-91; guest speaker in field, 1987-91. C&P Telephone Co. scholar, 1984-85. Mem. Am. Montessori Soc. (tchr.), Field Painter's Assn. (artist), Glenville State Coll. Alumni Assn. Roman Catholic. Home: 507 Ellis Ave Parkersburg WV 26101 Office: The Montessori Experience 1701-19th St Parkersburg WV 26101-3597

EVERS-WILLIAMS, MYRLIE, cultural organization administrator; b. Vicksburg, Miss., Mar. 17, 1933; m. Medgar Evers (dec. June 1963); m. Howard Williams; 3 children. Student, Alcorn State U.; BA in Sociology, Pomona Coll., 1968. Mem. staff, sec. NAACP; dir. planning Claremont (Calif.) Colls., 1968-70; v.p. Seligman & Latz, N.Y.C.; dir. consumer affairs Atlantic Richfield Co.; commr. Pub. Works Bd., L.A., 1987-95; chairwoman NAACP, 1995—; civil rights leader. Author: For Us the Living, 1967. Candidate for Congress in Calif., 1970; candidate for L.A. City Coun., 1987. Office: NAACP 4805 Mt Hope Rd Baltimore MD 21215*

EVERT, CHRISTINE MARIE (CHRIS EVERT), retired professional tennis player; b. Ft. Lauderdale, Fla., Dec. 21, 1954; d. James and Colette Evert; m. John Lloyd, Apr. 17, 1979 (div.); m. Andy Mill, July 30, 1988; 1 child, Alexander James. Amateur tennis player, until Dec. 1972, profl. tennis player, 1972-89, ret. from tennis, 1989; owner Evert Enterprises/IMG, Boca Raton, Fla., 1989—; Olympics commentator CBS Sports, 1992; commentator NBC Sports tennis events; winner numerous tournaments including U.S. Jr. Championship, 1970, 71, U.S. Open, 1975, 76, 77, 78, 80, 82, Wimbledon Singles, 1974, 76, 81, doubles, 1976, Australian Open, 1982, 84, French Open Singles, 1974, 75, 79, 80, 83, 85, 86, Virginia Slims, 1972, 73, 75, 77, 87, European Women's Open, Geneva, 1987, Eckerd Open, 1987; spl. advisor to U.S. Nat. Tennis Team by U.S. Tennis Assn.; bd. dirs. Internat. Tennis Hall of Fame; trustee Womens Sports Found. Star 3 vols. VCR instrnl. tennis tapes, 1991—; corp. spokesperson and rep., appearing in TV commls. and print advertisements; host and organizer Chris Evert Pro-Celebrity Tennis Classic, 1989, 90, 92, 93. Founder Chris Evert Charities, Inc., Healthy Start. Recipient Lebair Sportsmanship trophy, 1971; named Female Athlete of Yr. AP, 1974, 75, 77, 80, Athlete of Yr. Sports Illustrated, 1976, Greatest Woman Athlete of Last 25 Years Women's Sports Found., 1985, Flo Hyman award Women's Sports Found., 1990, Providencia award Palm Beach County Conv. and Visitors Bur., 1991; named one of Top 10 Romantic People of 1989, Korbel; inducted Madison Sq. Garden Walk of Fame, 1993. Mem. U.S. Lawn Tennis Assn. (Top Women's Singles Player award 1974), Nat. Honor Soc., Fla. Sports Found. (bd. dirs.), Women's Tennis Assn. (pres. 1982-91, exec. com., Sportmanship award 1979, Player Svc. awards 1981, 86, 87). Address: Evert Enterprises/IMG 7200 W Camino Real # 310 Boca Raton FL 33433-5511

EVERTON, MARTA VE, ophthalmologist; b. Luling, Tex., Nov. 12, 1926; d. T.W. and Nora E. (Eckols) O'Leavy; B.A., Hardin-Simmons U., 1945; M.A., Stanford U., 1947; M.D., Baylor U., 1955; postgrad. N.Y.U.-Bellevue Hosp., 1956-57; m. Robert K. Graham, Oct. 15, 1960; children: Marcia, Christie, Leslie Fox. Intern, Meth. Hosp., Houston, 1955-56; resident in ophthalmology Baylor Affiliated Hosps., Houston, 1957-59; clin. instr. ophthalmology Baylor U., 1959-60; asst. clin. prof. ophthalmology Loma Linda U., 1962-73; practice medicine specializing in ophthalmology, Houston, 1959-60, Pasadena, Calif., 1961-74, Escondido, Calif., 1974—. Mem. Calif. Med. Assn., Am. Acad. Ophthalmology, Alpha Omega Alpha. Home: 3024 Sycamore Ln Escondido CA 92025-7433 Office: 820 E Ohio Ave Escondido CA 92025-3421

EVEY, LOIS REED, psychiatric nurse; b. Burgettstown, Pa., Aug. 23, 1925; d. Harry Lemoyne and Willa Blanche (Miller) Reed; diploma Presbyn. Hosp. Sch. Nursing, Pitts., 1946; B.Nursing Edn., U. Pitts., 1959, M.Nursing Edn., 1963, postgrad., 1978; m. Raymond Cuervo, Sept. 1946; 1 son, Craig Dale; m. 2d, Kenneth George Evey, Aug. 20, 1959. Successively staff nurse, relief head nurse Women's Hosp., Pitts., 1946-53; staff nurse, then head nurse, asst. bldg. supr. Woodville (Pa.) State Hosp., 1953-59; med.-surg. nursing instr. St. Margaret Meml. Hosp., Pitts., 1959-61; psychiat. staff nurse Council House, Inc., Pitts., 1962-66, acting exec. dir., 1966, exec. dir., 1966-80; exec. dir. VA Med. Center, Pitts., 1982—, coordinator in-patient psychosocial rehab. program, 1984-85; lectr. community mental health workshops; mem. nurse adv. bd. Pitts. Planned Parenthood; mem. Task Force to Establish Domiciliary Care, Community Human Service Center, Pitts.; mem. Greater Pitts. Rehab. Council; mem. Pitts. chpt. Gov.'s Com. Employment of Handicapped; mem. citizens council bd. St. Francis Gen. Hosp., Western Psychiat. Inst. and Clinics; bd. dirs. continuing edn. for nurses U. Pitts., Indiana U. of Pa., Carlow Coll. Author: (with others) Rehabilitating the Mentally Ill in the Community. Served with Cadet Nurse Corps, U.S. Army, 1943-46. USPHS grantee, 1961-63. Mem. Am. Orthopsychiat. Assn., Internat. Assn. Psycho-Social Rehab. Services (co-founder, dir.), Pa. Assn. Mental Health and Mental Retardation Service Providers, Nat. Council Therapy and Rehab. Through Horticulture, Am. Nurses Assn. (legis. com.), Pa. Nurses Assn., Nat. Assn. Mental Health Adminstrs., Pa. Assn. Mental Health Adminstrs., Am. Public Health Assn., Pa. Public Health Assn., United Mental Health, Nat. Assn. Retarded Citizens, Pa. Assn. Retarded Citizens, Western Pa. Aftercare Assn., Health and Welfare Planning Assn., Pitts. Exec. Women's Council (charter), U. Pitts. Alumni Assn., Presbyn. U. Hosp. Alumni Assn. (past pres.; life), Sigma Theta Tau, Alpha Tau Delta. Republican. Mem. United Ch. of Christ. Club: East Hills (life) (Pitts.). Home: 305 Lougeay Rd Pittsburgh PA 15235-4502

EVSTATIEVA, STEFKA, opera singer; b. Rousse, Bulgaria, May 7, 1947; d. Evstati Bojanov Nedev and Maria Nikolai (Dencheva) Nedeva; m. Mladen Hristov Kovatchev, Oct. 28, 1973; 1 child, Valeria. Grad., State Conservatory, Sofia, Bulgaria, 1971. Spinto soprano Opera House-Rousse, 1971-79; dramatic soprano National Opera, Sofia, 1979—. Appeared in leading operatic roles at Met. Opera N.Y., San Francisco Opera, Washington Opera, Covent Garden, London, Grand Opera, Paris, La Scala, Milano, Stadts Opera, Vienna. Recipient 2d prize 5th Chaikovski Competition, Moscow, 1974, Grand Prix award Competition for Belcanto-Belgium Radio and TV, 1978, Competition for Young Opera Singers, Sofia, 1979, Giovanni Zanatello award Verona Festival, 1982.

EWELL, MIRANDA JUAN, journalist; b. Beijing, Apr. 25, 1948; d. Vei-Chow and Hsien-fang Yolanda (Sun) J.; m. John Woodruff Ewell Jr., Feb. 20, 1971; children: Emily, David, Jonah. BA summa cum laude, Smith Coll., 1969; postgrad., Princeton U., 1971, U. Calif., Berkeley, 1981-82. Staff writer The Montclarion, Oakland, Calif., 1982-83; with San Jose (Calif.) Mercury News, 1984—, staff writer; now correspondent San Jose (Calif.) Mercury News, San Francisco Bureau. Recipient Elsa Knight Thompson award Media Alliance, San Francisco, 1984, George Polk award L.I. U., N.Y., 1989, Heywood Brown award Newspaper Guild, Washington, 1989. Mem. Asian-Am. Journalists Assn. *

EWERS, ANNE, opera company director. Gen. dir. Boston Lyric Opera, 1984-89, Utah Opera, Salt Lake City, 1990—; panelist Nat. Endowment for Arts; freelance stage dir. San Francisco Opera, N.Y.C. Opera, Can. Opera Co., Minn. Opera, Vancouver Opera, numerous others. Dir. nearly fifty opera prodns. including La Giaconda, Un Ballo in Maschera, La Rondine, The Merry Widow, Ring Cycle, Salome, Dialogues des Carmelites, Eugene Onegin; dir. Dame Joan Sutherland's North American Farewell, Dallas Opera. Bd. dirs. Opera Am., 1993—. Office: Utah Opera 50 W 2d South Salt Lake City UT 84101

EWERS, PATRICIA O'DONNELL, university administrator; b. Chgo., July 22, 1935; d. Patrick Brenden and Johanna Marie (Galvin) O'D.; m. John Leonard Ewers, July 26, 1958; children: John P., Michele M. Ewers DeCesare. BA in English summa cum laude, Mundelein Coll., 1957; MA in English, Loyola U., Chgo., 1958, PhD in English, 1966. Instr. English Mundelein Coll., Chgo., 1964-66; asst. prof. English DePaul U., Chgo., 1966-69, assoc. prof. English, 1969-76, dir. humanities divsn. gen. edn. program, 1969-73, chair dept. English, 1973-76, prof. English, 1976-90, dean Coll. Liberal Arts and Scis., 1976-80, v.p., dean faculties, 1980-90; pres. Pace U., N.Y.C., 1990—; ptnr. N.Y.C. Ptnrs., 1990—; chmn., mem. North Ctrl. Assn. Accreditation Teams, 1977-90; mem. nat. identification program for women in higher edn. Ill. State Com. for Am. Coun. on Edn., 1983-86; commr.-at-large North Ctrl. Assn. Colls./Schs., 1984-87; mem. com. on study of undergrad. edn. State of Ill. Bd. Higher Edn., 1985-86, 1989-90; mem. Commn. Minorities in Higher Edn., Am. Coun. Edn., 1990-93; mem. N.Y.C. Workforce Devel. Commn., 1993; mem. human resources bd. AT&T Corp., Basking Ridge, N.J., 1994; mem. adv. coun. on postsecondary edn. State Dept. Edn., 1994—. Trustee Riverside (Ill.) Pub. Libr., 1980-86, Cath. Theol. Union, Chgo., 1985-90, sec., 1986-90, N.Y. Downtown Hosp., 1991—, Our Lady of Mercy Med. Ctr., Bronx, N.Y., 1993—; chmn., bd. trustees Commn. Ind. Colls. and Univs./N.Y. State Commn. Ind. Colls. and Univs., 1992—; bd. dirs. Cath. Charities, 1984-90, Com. on Social Svc., 1986-90, subcom. on employer assistance programs, 1986-88, Am. Brands, 1991—, Phoenix Theatre, 1992—, Drama League, N.Y.C., 1993—, Richard Tucker Music Found., 1993—, Westchester County Assn., 1993—; bd. trustees Coun. for Adult and Experimental Learning, 1992, El Museo del Barrio, N.Y.C., 1994—; mem. Chgo. Network, 1986-90, steering com. Assn. Colls. and Univs./N.Y. State Commn. Ind. Colls. and Univs., 1992—, individual investors adv. com. to bd. dirs. N.Y. Stock Exch., 1994—; co-chmn. com. on higher edn. and econ. develop. State of N.Y. Budget Dir.'s Adv. Coun., 1994—. Recipient Outstanding Alumna award Loyola U., Chgo., 1984. Mem. Nat. Assn. Ind. Colls. and Univs. (bd. dirs. 1995—), Regional Plan Assn. (coun. for the region tomorrow 1990-93), Downtown Lower Manhattan Assn., Inc. (bd. dirs. 1991—), Women's Forum, Inc., Fin. Women's Assn., Econ. Club of N.Y., Univ. Club, Met. Club, St. Andrew's Golf Club, Phi Gamma Mu, Beta Gamma Sigma, Alpha Lambda Delta, Delta Epsilon Sigma. Roman Catholic. Office: Pace U Office of Pres Pace Plz New York NY 10038

EWING, CATHARINE VAUGHAN, political science educator; b. Washington, Aug. 11, 1944; d. George M. and M. Alice (Jones) E. BA, Rice U., 1966; MA, Vanderbilt U., 1969; PhD, U. Okla., 1977. Instr. U. Oklahoma, Norman, 1971-72; asst. prof. Phillips U., Enid, Okla., 1972-80, assoc. prof., 1980-87, prof., 1987—, dir. Sweden semester, 1978, chair social sciences, 1985-88, dir. faculty summer devel. program, 1990; book reviewer Slavic Rev., 1978, 80, Russian Rev., 1991, 92. Author: (with Stanley Vardys) Constitutions of Special Sovereignties: Lithuania, 1978. Mem. YWCA, Enid, 1986—, Oklahomans for Choice, Enid, 1988—. Grantee NSF, 1992, NEH, 1980. Mem. LWV, Am. Political Sci. Assn., Am. Assn. for Advancement of Slavic Studies, S.W. Social Sci. Assn., Okla. Polit. Sci. Assn. (exec. com. 1993-94). Democrat. Presbyterian. Office: Phillips U 100 S University Ave Enid OK 73701-6439

EWING, MARY EILEEN, radiologic technologist; b. Morning Sun, Iowa, Aug. 26, 1926; d. Frank Leeman and Myrtle Marguerite (Mehaffy) Steele; m. Dean Willard Ewing, Mar. 29, 1952; children: John, Eileen, Diane, Denise. BS in Radiologic Tech., St. Louis U., 1948. Registered technologist. Staff technologist Mo. Pacific Hosp., St. Louis, 1948-52; staff technologist Blanchard Valley Hosp., Findlay, Ohio, 1968-69, asst. chief technologist, 1969-80, asst. dir. dept., 1980-90; clin. instr. Lima (Ohio) Tech. Coll., 1978-90; sec. N.W. Libr. Dist. Exec. Bd., 1988—. Library trustee McComb (Ohio) Pub. Libr., 1957—; pres. Libr. Bd., McComb, 1967—; elder ck. of session, 1994—. Mem. Am. Soc. Radiologic Techs., Ohio Soc. Radiologic Techs., World Orgn. China Painters, Internat. Porcelain Artists and Tchrs., Philomath Club (pres. 1958, 95), Mansfield China Painters, NSDAR (Ft. Findlay chpt. sec. 1993-94, regent 1995). Democrat. Presbyterian. Home: 103 W South St Mc Comb OH 45858

EWING-WILSON, DEBORAH LOUISE, neurologist; b. Seattle, Aug. 6, 1955; d. Elwin Stanley Ewing and Mary Alice Castleman; m. Fredrick Paul Wilson, Sept. 26, 1982; children: Victoria, Katherine. BA, Wellesley Coll., 1978; DO, Chgo. Coll. Osteo. Medicine, 1983. Diplomate Am. Bd. Psychiatry and Neurology, Am. Bd. Electrodiagnostic Medicine. Intern Brentwood Hosp., Cleve., 1983-84; resident Cleve. Clinic Found., 1984-87; staff section neurology Ohio Permanent Med. Group, Cleve., 1987—, chief neurology, 1992—; staff Cleve. Clinic found., 1992—, Metrohealth St. Luke's Med. Ctr., Cleve., 1992—; clin. prof. neurology Ohio U., Athens, 1989—. Contbr. articles to profl. jours. Fellow Am. Assn. Electrodiagnostic Medicine; mem. AMA, Am. Acad. Neurology, Am. Osteo. Assn., Ohio Osteo. Assn., Cleve. Acad. Medicine, Epilepsy Found. N.E. Ohio, Cleve. (mem. profl. adv. bd. 1991—). Episcopalian. Office: Ohio Permanente Med Group 3733 Park East Dr Cleveland OH 44122-4311

EXUM, ANNETTE HENRIETTA, corporate training executive; b. Raleigh, N.C., Apr. 27, 1950; d. George Cliftonand Marguerita (Girardeau) E. BA in Psychology/Human Resource Devel., N.C. State U., 1972; Masters Cert. in Psychology, U. N.C., Chapel Hill, 1973, M.Social Found. of Edn., 1975, ABD, 1980. Dir. child care svcs. Migrant and Seasonal Farm Workers Assn., Raleigh, 1973-75; social planner City of Raleigh, 1975-76; spl. asst. to assoc. commr. for EEOP-HEW/Ednl. Policy Fellow George Washington U., Washington, 1976-77; legis. advocate and program dir. Coun. of the Great City Schs., Washington, 1977-79; dir. fed. programs Wake County Pub. Schs., Raleigh, 1980-81; owner United Wholesales Industries, Houston, 1981-82; office mgr. Exum Real Estate Co., Raleigh, 1982-83; registered rep. Prudential Fin. Svcs. Corp., Houston, 1983-87; pres. Citizens Fin. Corp., Raleigh, 1987-94, Total Quality Tng. Assocs., Raleigh, 1994—; human rights writer/lectr. Bd. dirs. N.C. Black Caucus, 1994—, African-Am. Dance Ensemble, 1994—, Smart Star.; advocate for world-wide human rights; founder The Voter Solidarity Com.; mem. Early Childhood Leadership Devel. Program, 1993. Fellow Leadership Raleigh, 1992, Inst. of Polit. Leadership, 1993—. Mem. Delta Sigma Theta. Democrat. Office: Total Quality Tng Assocs 808 Quarry Rock Rd Raleigh NC 27610

EYERLY, GLORIA A., lawyer; b. Mansfield, Ohio, Aug. 8, 1951; d. Richard Charles and Evelyn Mae (Erickson) Eyerly; m. Kevin P. Mulrane,

May 20, 1978. BA, Ohio State U., 1973, JD, 1976. Bar: Ohio. Asst. prosecuting atty. Richland County, Mansfield, Ohio, 1976-78; staff atty. Franklin County Pub. Defender, Columbus, Ohio, 1979-81, supervising atty., 1981-86; ptnr. Sunbury, Underwood & Eyerly, Columbus, Ohio, 1986-89; staff atty. Ohio Pub. Defender, Columbus, Ohio, 1989-91, supervising atty., 1991-93, chief counsel, 1993-94, interim pub. defender, 1994, chief counsel, 1994. Author (with others) Ohio Appellate Practice, 1983, Ohio Post Conviction Manual, 1987. Named Top Ohio Women Litigator Ohio Law Newsletter, 1991. Mem. ABA, Columbus Bar Assn. (chair court of appeals com. 1986-88, nom. com. 1988), Ohio Assn. Criminal Defense Lawyers (founding mem., bd. dirs. 1987-89, chair Amicus com. 1989, Pres. award 1988, 89), Ohio State Bar Assn., Nat. Assn. Criminal Defense Lawyers, Nat. Legal Aid & Defender Assn., Franklin County Women Lawyers, Phi Beta Kappa, Phi Alpha Theta. Office: Ohio Pub Defender 8 E Long St 11th Fl Columbus OH 43215

EYFELLS, KRISTIN HALLDORSDOTTIR, painter, sculptor; b. Reykjafjordur, Iceland, Sept. 17, 1917; came to U.S., 1945; d. Halldor and Maria Jenny (Jonasdottir) Kristinsson; m. Johann Eyfells, Sept. 26, 1949. Student, Rudolf Schaefer Sch. Design, San Francisco, 1945-46, Hofstra U., 1957-60; BA in Psychology, U. Fla., 1962, BFA in Art, 1964. Founder, owner, dress designer Fix Dress Shop, Reykjavik, Iceland, 1942-74; painter, sculptor, photographer Reykjavik, 1964-69, Orlando, Fla., 1969—; sculpture instr. Maitland (Fla.) Art Ctr., 1979. One woman shows include U. Fla., Gainesville, 1963, Ch. St. Sta. Gallery, Orlando, Fla., 1979, Women in Art House, Orlando, 1981, Orlando Mus. of Art, 1987, Herr-Chambliss Fine Arts, Hot Springs, Ark., 1990; husband and wife exhibitions at John Maeder Fortress, New Smyrna Beach, Fla., 1973, The Maitland (Fla.) Art Ctr., 1975, Osceola Ctr. for Arts, Kissimmee, Fla., 1987, Herr-Chambliss Fine Arts, 1989, Gaier Contemporary Gallery, Orlando, 1994; also numerous regional, nat. and internat. group shows, and pvt. exhbns. Founding mem. Women in Art House, Orlando, 1983. Recipient 2d prize sculpture Internat. Airport, Orlando, 1986. Mem. Nat. Mus. Women in Arts, Orlando Mus. Art, Maitland Art Ctr., Living Art Mus. (Iceland), Assn. Icelandic Sculptors, Assn. Icelandic Artists. Home: 2011 Tuskawilla Rd Oviedo FL 32765

EYMAN, SUSANNE KOHN, clinical psychologist; b. L.A., Oct. 3, 1956; d. Abraham Joseph and Wila (Rottstein) Kohn; m. James Randall Eyman, June 5, 1982; children: Adrianne Sarah, Ethan James. BA, U. So. Calif., 1977; PhD, U. Nev., 1984. Lic. psychologist, Kans. Asst. prof. Washburn U., Topeka, 1983-85; staff psychologist Topeka State Hosp., 1985-86; postdoctoral fellow Menninger Clinic, 1986-88; pvt. practice Southwind Counseling Svcs., Manhattan, Kans., 1989—. Contbr. articles to profl. jours., chpts. to books. Mem. Am. Psychol. Assn., Kans. Psychol. Assn. Democrat. Jewish. Office: Southwind Counseling Svcs 225 Southwind Pl Manhattan KS 66502-3186

EYRE, PAMELA CATHERINE, army officer; b. Chgo., Nov. 3, 1948; d. Francis Thomas and Jane (Burd) E. BA, Ctrl. State U. Okla., 1972; MPA, U. Okla., 1976. Commd. 2d lt. U.S. Army, 1973, advanced through grades to lt. col., 1991; test and evaluation officer Ft. Gordon, Ga., 1982-85, rsch. and devel. coord. Ft. Monmouth, N.J., 1985-88, with army gen. staff Pentagon, Washington, 1988-91, acquisition policy staff officer Army Secretariat Pentagon, 1991-94; asst. project mgr. Def. Telecomm. Svc., Washington, 1994—. Fellow Armed Forces Communications Electronics Assn. Home: 100 Harbor View Dr # 2209 Baltimore MD 21230

EYSTER, MARY ELAINE, hematologist, educator; b. York, Pa., Mar. 21, 1935; d. Charles Gable and March Viola (Schriver) E.; m. Robert E. Dye, Jan. 2, 1965; children: Robert E., Charles. AB, Duke U., 1956, MD, 1960. Intern. N.Y. Hosp.-Cornell Med. Coll., N.Y.C., 1960-61, resident in medicine, 1961-63, fellow in hematology, 1963-66, instr. medicine, 1966-67, asst. prof. medicine, 1967-70; asst. prof. medicine Milton S. Hershey Med. Ctr. Pa. State U., Hershey, 1970-73, assoc. prof. Milton S. Hershey Med. Ctr., 1973-82, prof. Milton S. Hershey Med. Ctr., 1982—, chief hematology div., dept. medicine Coll. Medicine, 1973—; bd. dirs. Hemophilia Ctr. Cen. Pa., 1973—, AIDS Clin. Trials Unit Pa. State U., 1987—; faculty rsch. assoc. Am. Cancer Soc., 1966-71; mem. State Hemophilia Adv. Com., 1973—, chmn., 1977-79, 1988-90; mem. policy bd. Coop. F VII inhibitor study Nat. Heart, Lung and Blood Inst., 1975-79; mem. med. and sci. adv. coun. Nat. Hemophilia Found., 1976-77, 82—, chmn. med. adv. com. Del. Valley chpt., 1979-82; co-investigator, mem. multi-agy. task force on AIDS HHS, 1982-83; mem. blood products adv. com. FDA, 1985-89; exec. com. NIH-NIAID Clin. Trials, 1988-90. USPHS grantee, 1976—. Fellow ACP; mem. Pa. Med. Soc., Am. Fedn. Clin. Rsch., World Fedn. Hemophilia, Am. Soc. Hematology, Am. Assn. Blood Banks, Internat. Soc. Thrombosis and Haemostasis, Internat. Soc. Hematology, Pa. Soc. Hematology, Oncology (bd. dirs. 1982-85), Am. Heart Assn. Coun. on Thrombosis, Phi Beta Kappa, Alpha Omega Alpha. Office: Milton S Hershey Med Ctr PO Box 850 Hershey PA 17033-0850

EZELL, MARGARET PRATHER, information systems executive; b. New Orleans, Aug. 12, 1951; d. Bluford and Mildred Winston (Seab) E. BS, Brigham Young U., 1973; MS, Utah State U., 1975; PhD, Mich. State U., 1982. Asst. prof., extension specialist Coop. Extension Svc., Pa. State U., University Park, 1982-85; So. regional computer coord. Coop. Extension Svc./USDA, Athens, Ga., 1985-88; cons. info. tech. Coop. Extension Svc./USDA, Clemson, S.C., 1988-89; info. tech. cons., instructional designer Atlanta, 1989—; adminstr. info. svcs., ea. region Resolution Trust Corp./FDIC, Atlanta, 1990-93; mgr. database FDIC/RTC, Atlanta, 1994—. Named one of Outstanding Young Women in Am., 1983; Mich. State U. scholar, 1981, Marie Dye scholar, 1981. Mem. Am. Assn. Family and Consumer Scis. (grantee 1983, family econ./home mgmt. sect., pre-conf. local arrangements chmn. 1984-85, mem. nat. electronic tech. com. 1986-89), Ga. Assn. Family and Consumer Scis. (dist. vice chmn. 1986-87), Cen. Pa. IBM-PC Assn. (charter, treas. 1983-84), Agrl. Communicators in Edn. (Excellence in Computers award 1989), Assn. Banyan Users Internat. (ATlanta chpt., pres. 1991), World Futures Soc., Epsilon Sigma Phi, Kappa Omicron Nu.

EZELL-GRIM, ANNETTE SCHRAM, business management educator, academic administrator; b. West Frankfort, Ill., June 19, 1940; d. Woodrow C. and Rosa (Franich) Schram; m. John R. Grim, III; BS U. Nev., 1962, MS in Physiology, 1967, postgrad., 1969; EdD in Pub. Adminstrn., Brigham Young U., 1977; children: Michael L., Rona Maria. Mem. staff Washoe Med. Ctr., Reno, 1962; teaching asst. U. Nev., Reno, 1962-63, instr., 1963-64, 1965-67, asst. prof., 1967-71; curriculum specialist U. Nev. Med. Sch., 1971-72, project mgr. Fed. Grant Intercampus Edn. Project, 1969-71, assoc. prof., curriculum specialist rural practitioner program, 1971-73, staff assoc. Mountain States Regional Med. Program, 1974-75; cons. Nev. Dept. Edn., 1975-77; asst. dean acad. affairs U. Utah, Salt Lake City, 1977-80; acting Dean, 1981, dir., prof. doctoral program Edn. Adminstrn.; prof., dept. head Coll. Human Development, Pa. State U., 1982-85; dean Coll. Profl. Studies, prof. bus. adminstrn. U. So. Colo., Pueblo, 1985-87; sr. asst. to pres. Towson State U., Balt., 1987-94, assoc. prof. mgmt. sch. bus., 1994—; cons. higher edn., TV edn., research methology; adviser to various research, polit. and ednl. bds. Mem. Am. Ednl. Research Assn., AAAS, Am. Acad. Arts and Scis., AAUP, Am. Council on Edn., Am. Assn. Higher Edn., Soc. for Coll. & Univ. Planning, Decision Scis. Inst., Sigma Xi, Phi Kappa Phi, Delta Kappa Gamma. Home: 314 Oyster Cove Dr Grasonville MD 21638 Office: Towson State U Towson MD 21204

FAATZ, JEANNE RYAN, state legislator; b. Cumberland, Md., July 30, 1941; d. Charles Keith and Myrtle Elizabeth (McIntyre) Ryan; B.S., U. Ill., 1962; postgrad. (Gates fellow) Harvard U. Program Sr. Execs. in state and local Govt., 1984; M.A., U. Colo.-Denver, 1985. children: Kristin, Susan. Instr. Speech Dept., Met. State Coll., Denver, 1985—; sec. to majority leader Colo. Senate, 1976-78; mem. Colo. Ho. Reps. from Dist. 1, 1978—, asst. majority leader. Past pres. Harvey Park (Colo.) Homeowners Assn., Southwest Denver YWCA Adult Edn. Club; Southwest met. coord. UN Children's Fund, 1969-74; mem. citizens adv. coun. Ft. Logan Mental Health Center; bd. mgrs. Southwest Denver YMCA. Mem. Bear Creek Rep. Women's Club. Home: 2903 S Quitman St Denver CO 80236-2208 Office: State Capitol Denver CO 80203

FABACHER, DIANE HAINS, psychiatric social worker; b. Baton Rouge, June 9, 1941; d. James Hubert and Frances (Gremillion) H.; m. Edward B. Fabacher, Jr., Feb. 9, 1963 (div. Feb. 1980); children: Edward B. III, Todd, Scott, Stacy, Julie. BS in Social Counseling, Our Lady of Holy Cross Coll., 1984; MSW, Tulane U., 1984. Adolescent, women's place social worker Greenbriar Hosp., Covington, La., 1968-88; dir. YWCA Parent Aide Program, New Orleans, 1985-86; pvt. practice Covington, 1988—. Mem. Nat. Assn. Social Workers, Northshore Social Workers Assn., La. Soc. Clin. Social Workers, Nat. Assn. Female Execs., NOW. Republican. Home: 204 W 15th Ave Covington LA 70433-3356 Office: Greenbriar Hosp Greenbriar Dr # 1836 Covington LA 70433-4602

FABARES, SHELLEY, actress; b. Santa Monica, Calif., Jan. 19, 1944; d. James Fabares; m. Mike Farrell, Dec. 1984; stepchildren: Mike, Erin. Began career as child model and actress; earned gold record for 1962 single Johnny Angel; early TV work includes adaptation of Our Town, Matinee Theatre, Playhouse 90; regular cast member The Donna Reed Show, 1958-63; appeared in TV movie Brian's Song, 1971, ABC, (other TV movies) Memorial Day, Run Till You Fall, Deadly Relations, 1993, ABC; other TV work includes (series) The Practice, The Little People, Forever Fernwood; co-star for five years One Day At A Time, CBS; co-star Coach, ABC, 1989— (Emmy nomination, Supporting Actress - Comedy, 1993, 94); (films) Never Say Goodbye, Rock Pretty Baby, Marjorie Morningstar, Summer Love, A Time to Sing, Hot Pursuit, Love or Money, Ride the Wild Surf, Hold On, Clambake, Spinout, Girl Happy. *

FABIAN, JEANNE, entrepreneur, executive recruiter; b. Wilkes Barre, Pa., June 25, 1946; d. Joseph A. and Dorothy (Cannon) F.; m. Christopher Sykes, Sept. 7, 1968 (div. Mar. 1979). BBA, Baruch Coll., N.Y.C., 1969; MBA, Hofstra U., Hempstead, N.Y., 1979. CPA, N.Y. Auditor Arthur Andersen & Co., N.Y.C., 1969-73; planning analyst Avon Products, Inc., N.Y.C., 1973-75; fin. analyst Revlon, Inc., N.Y.C., 1975-77; acctg. mgr. Am. Standard, Inc., N.Y.C., 1977-78; sr. fin. analyst Texaco, Inc., Harrison, N.Y., 1979-82; asst. dir. Harper & Row Pubs., Inc., N.Y.C., 1983-86, exec. recruiter, 1986-89; v.p., promoter Malka Records Inc., N.Y.C., 1990-93; owner Fabian Assocs., Inc., N.Y.C., 1989—. Treas., bd. dirs. Stanwix Apts. Corp., Forest Hills, N.Y., 1983—. Mem. AICPA, N.Y. State Soc. CPAs. Office: Fabian Assocs Inc PO Box 1624 New York NY 10017

FABRIZIO, MARGARET MARY, county official; b. L.A., Apr. 6, 1954; d. Nadir Alfred and Sheila Marie (Chartrand) F. BA, U. Calif., Santa Cruz, 1976. Office mgr. Dave Richards Bail Bonds, Santa Cruz, 1977-80; family support officer Office of Dist. Atty., Santa Cruz, 1980-85; dir. info. svcs., asst. office adminstr. Grunsky, Pybrum, Ebey and Farrar, Watsonville, Calif., 1985-88; owner M. Fabrizio & Assocs., Capitola, Calif., 1988-94; dir. Ctrl. Collections divsn. County of Santa Cruz, Calif., 1994—; mayor City of Capitola, 1994—. Co-chmn. Santa Cruz County Women's Commn., 1986-91; mem., pres. Capitola Hist. Mus., 1991-92; bd. dirs. Santa Cruz Cmty. Action Bd., 1991—, treas., 1991—, pres., 1994; chair Women's Commn. subcom. on GAIN, 1987-92; mem. Capitola City Coun., 1992—. Recipient Charley Parkhurst award, 1992. Democrat. Roman Catholic.

FACEY, SOPHIA GABRIELLE, community health nurse; b. Jamaica, West Indies, Sept. 8, 1963; d. Illonka Doreen (Anderson) Chang. Student, Rutgers U., 1981-84; AS, RN, Hahnemann U., 1991. RN; cert. BLS instr., Pa. Flight attendant Continental Airlines, Houston, 1985-88; staff nurse, surgical trauma, med. ICU Albert Einstein Med. Ctr., Phila., 1991-93; vis. nurse Vis. Nurse Assn. Greater Phila., 1993—. Activist Nat. Abortion Rights League, Phila., 1992; membership recruiter NAACP, Phila., 1989—; mem. Super Cities adv. com. Greater Del. Valley chpt. Nat. Multiple Sclerosis Soc., 1993. Mem. ANA. Democrat. Roman Catholic. Home: Apt 171D 801 Cooper St Deptford NJ 08096

FACKLER, NANCY GRAY, head nurse; b. Norfolk, Va., Jan. 24, 1941; d. Albert Edward and Rita Marie (Murray) Gray; m. Martin L. Fackler, Sept. 29, 1964. BSN, Fla. State U., 1962; postgrad., San Francisco State U., 1988, Golden Gate U., 1989-91; M of Pub. Adminstrn. and Health Svcs. Mgmt., Golden Gate U., 1991; postgrad., U. Fla., 1993-94. RN, Fla.; lic. pvt. and comml. pilot.; gerontology cert., U. Fla. Commd. ensign USNR, 1962, advanced through grades to rear adm. Nurses Corps, 1994; nursing assignments U.S. Naval Hosps. USNR, U.S., Japan, 1962-86; with N.W. Region, mem. navy med. command NW region policy bd. USNR, Oakland, Calif., 1986-89; readiness command nurse USNR, San Francisco, 1989-91; DON Univ. Nursing Care Ctr., Gainesville, Fla.; originator res. same day surgery program USN Hosp., Jacksonville and USN Hosp., Oakland, Calif. Mem. Sec. of Navy Nat. Navy Res. Policy Bd.; active Alachua County Health Care Coalition. Mem. ANA, Nat. Naval Res. (policy bd.), Nat. Gerontol. Nursing Assn., Naval Res. Assn., Am. Tennis Assn., Fla. Tennis Assn. Home: RR 4 Box 264 Hawthorne FL 32640

FADER, SHIRLEY SLOAN, writer; b. Paterson, N.J.; d. Samuel Louis and Miriam (Marcus) Sloan; m. Seymour J. Fader; children: Susan Deborah, Steven Micah Kimchi. BS, MS, U. Pa. Writer, journalist, author Paramus, N.J., 1956—; chmn., coord. ann. writers seminar Bergen C.C., 1973-76. Author: (books) The Princess Who Grew Down, 1968, From Kitchen to Career, 1977, Jobmanship, 1978, Successfully Ever After, 1982 (Brit. edit. 1985), Wait a Minute: You Can Have It All, 1993, paperback edit., 1994; (columns) Jobmanship, People and You, Family Weekly mag., 1971-82, How to Get More From Your Job, Glamour mag., 1978-81, Start Here, Working Woman mag., 1980-88, Work Strategies, Working Mother mag., 1987-88, Women Getting Ahead, Ladies Home Jour., 1980-90, How Would You Handle It, New Idea mag., 1984—, Moving Up, Woman mag., 1989-90, Career Expert "Ask the Experts", Woman's World mag., 1992—; contbg. editor Family Weekly, 1971-82, Glamour mag., 1978-81, Working Woman mag., 1980-88, Working Mother mag., 1987-88, Ladies Home Jour., 1980-90, Woman mag., 1989-90; contbr. articles to mags. worldwide. Mem. Authors Guild, Am. Soc. Journalists and Authors (chmn.-moderator ann. writer's conf. 1971-95, nat. v.p., 1976-77, mem.-at-large nat. exec. coun. 1976-78, 83-86, nat. sec., mem. exec. coun. 1995-96), Nat. Press Club. Address: 377 McKinley Blvd Paramus NJ 07652

FADLEY, ANN MILLER, English language and literature educator, writer; b. Ft. Worden, Wash., Nov. 22, 1933; d. Albert Delmar and Helen Elizabeth (Bush) Miller; m. Mit Rowley White, June 19, 1953 (div. Apr. 1977); children: Don M., Sharon L. White Patterson, Barbara A. White Salzman, Brian A.; m. John Lewis Fadley, Oct. 13, 1979. Student, Denison U., 1951-53; BA cum laude, Ohio State U., 1974, MA, 1976, PhD, 1986. Lectr. Ohio State U., Columbus, 1981-84; instr. Ohio Dominican Coll., Columbus, 1984-87; asst. prof. English Marshall U., Huntington, W.Va., 1987-88, Fla. So. Coll., Lakeland, 1988—; adj. prof. Ohio U., Ironton, 1988; panelist pub. TV, Columbus, 1985; chmn. Nat. Poetry Day, 1991—; chmn. vis. creative writers Fla. So. Coll., Lakeland, 1994—. Author: (fiction and poetry) Onionhead, 1989, 95, (poetry) Birmingham Poetry Review, 1992, Heartbeat, 1994, also articles and lit. criticisms; asst. editor Ohio Jour., 1975-76; founder, editor Cantilever Jours., 1989—. Organizer, pres. Tri-Village Jr. C. of C. Wives Club, Columbus, 1959-60; past awards chmn. Young Musicians' competition; chair Ruth Flower Brown Scholarship, Huntington, 1988; contest supr., mem. com. SCORE, 1988; judge VFW Voice of Democracy contest, Lakeland, 1990, 91, 92, Fla. state judge, 1992; mem. bldg. com., organ fund task force, trustee Christ United Meth. Ch., Lakeland, 1991—, sec. trustees, 1991-93; judge creative writing Polk County Citrus Festival, 1993. Recipient Merit award Fla. Poets Competition, WORDART Soc., 1990, Distinction award, 1991, hon. mention for poems; recipient hon. mention Nat. League Am. Pen Women, Lakeland, 1993, 94; grantee Fla. Endowment for Humanities, 1991, award hanging poetry Arts in the Park, Lakeland, 1993, 94, hanging poetry display Lake Morton Libr., 1994. Mem. MLA, South Atlantic MLA, Southeastern Renaissance Conf., Renaissance Soc. Am., Nat. Coun. Tchrs. English (chair session 1990), Fla. State Poets Assn. (head Lakeland workshop 1991, 92), Popular Culture Assn. (chair session 1992), Delta Delta Delta. Republican. Office: Fla So Coll Dept English 111 Lake Hollingsworth Dr Lakeland FL 33801-5698

FAFOGLIA, BARBARA ANN, school administrator; b. Springfield, Ill., Feb. 16, 1951; d. Robert Frank and Nina Marie (Hashman) Wanless; 1 child, Erin Elizabeth. BA in Edn., So. Ill. U.; MA in Health Edn. Adminstrn., Sangamon State U. Cert. tchr., Ill.; cert. relapse prevention specialist. Tchr. English/lang. arts Ball-Chatham (Ill.) Unit Dist. #5, 1974-85; ednl. cons. Ctrl. Ill. Day Care Providers Assn., Springfield, 1985-88; communications specialist Ill. Prevention Resource Ctr., Springfield, 1985-90; consulting writer, editor So. Ill. U. Sch. of Medicine, Springfield, 1985-90; drug-free programs coord. Springfield Pub. Schs. Dist. 186, 1990—. Mem. NEA, AACD, ASCD, Ill. Edn. Assn., Nat. Coun. Tchrs. English, Nat. Soc. DAR, Am. Guidance Svc. (book reviewer), Ill. Alcoholism and Drug Dependence Assn., Nat. Prevention Coalition, nat. Prevention Network, Springfield Youth Network, Am. Counseling Assn., Ill. Assn. Student Assistance Profls., Nat. Assn. Leadership for Student Assistance Programs, Am. Guidance Svc.(book reviewer), Kappa Delta Pi Internat. Honor Soc.

FAGERSTEN, BARBARA JEANNE, special education educator; b. San Francisco, Feb. 29, 1924; d. Ernest Mauritz and Louise (Hopkins) F.; m. Harold Gurish, Feb. 7, 1950 (div. 1970); children: Michael, Matthew, Jonathon. BA, San Francisco State U., 1951; MS, Dominican U., 1973, degree in spl. edn., 1975; degree in adminstrn. and supervision, 1976, degree in community coll. instruction, 1981. Personnel sec. Arabian Am. Oil Co., San Francisco, 1944-45; union sec. Jeweler's Union, San Francisco, 1946-48; med. sec. Mt. Zion Hosp., San Francisco, 1949-50; spl. edn. tchr. Marin Office Edn., San Rafael, Calif., 1967-92; bd. dirs. DeWitt Learning Ctr., San Rafael, 1969. Bd. dirs. Marin Tchrs. Credit Union, San Rafael, 1978-93, Marinwood Cmty. Svcs., San Rafael, 1986-87; commr. Parks and Recreation Marinwood, San Rafael, 1983-86. Mem. Calif. Assn. Neurol. Handicapped Children (trustee 1973-74), Phi Delta Kappa. Democrat. Home: 272 Blackstone Dr San Rafael CA 94903-1508

FAGIN, CLAIRE MINTZER, nursing educator, administrator; b. N.Y.C.; d. Harry and Mae (Slatin) Mintzer; m. Samuel Fagin, Feb. 17, 1952; children: Joshua, Charles. BS, Wagner Coll., 1948; MA, Tchrs. Coll. Columbia, 1951; PhD, N.Y. U., 1964; DSc (hon.), Lycoming Coll., 1983, Cedar Crest Coll., 1987, U. Rochester, 1987, Med. Coll. Pa., 1989, U. Md., 1993, Wagner Coll., 1993; DHL, Hunter Coll., 1993; LLD (hon.), U. Pa., 1994. Staff nurse, clin. instr. Sea View Hosp., S.I., N.Y.; clin. instr. Bellevue Hosp., N.Y.C.; psychiat. nurse cons. Nat. League for Nursing, N.Y.C.; asst. chief psychiat. nursing svc. clin. ctr. NIH; rsch. project coord. dept. psychiatry Children's Hosp., Washington; instr., assoc. prof. psychiat.-mental health nursing NYU, N.Y.C., dir. grad. programs in psychiat. mental health nursing, 1965-69; chmn. nursing dept., prof. Herbert H. Lehman Coll., CUNY, N.Y.C., 1969-77; dir. Health Professions Inst., Montefiore Hosp. and Med. Ctr., 1975-77; Margaret Bond Simon dean sch. of nursing U. Pa., Phila., 1977-92, Leadership chair prof., 1992—, interim pres., 1993-94; bd. dirs. Solomon Inc., CMAC; mem. task force Joint Commn. Mental Health of Children, 1966-69; gov.'s com. on children N.Y. State, 1971-75; pres. Coun. on Deans of Nursing, Sr. Colls. and Univs. N.Y. State, 1974-76; cons. to many pub. and private univs. and health care agys.; cons. Pan Am. Health Nursing, Washington, 1972-74, NIMH, HEW, 1974-76, NIMH, 1979, 83; mem. expert adv. panel on nursing WHO, 1974—; mem.-at-large Nat. Bd. Med. Examiners, 1980-84; dir. Provident Mut. Ins. Co., 1977—, audit com., 1978—, chmn., 1985—, exec. com., 1986—; dir. Salomon Inc., 1994—, CMAC, 1994—; mem. nat. adv. mental health coun. NIMH, 1983-88; speaker profl. convs., radio and TV; bd. dirs. Daltex Corp., 1984-91, compensation com. Contbr. articles to profl. publs. .ecipient Achievement award Wagner Coll., 1956, Achievement award Tchrs. Coll., 1975, Disting. Alumna award NYU, 1979, Founders award Sigma Theta Tau, 1981, Hon. Recognition award ANA, 1988, Woman of Courage award Womens Way, 1990, Alumni Merit award U. Pa., 1991, Trustee Coun. Pa. Women First Leadership award, 1991, Caring award Vis. Nurses Assn., 1992, Hildegard Peplau award outstanding contbn. psych-nursing, 1994, Barbara Thoman Curtis award ANA, 1994; named NIMH fellow, 1950-51, 60-64, Am. Nurses Found. Disting. scholar, 1984, Disting. Dau. Pa., 1994. Fellow Coll. Physicians Phila.; mem. Inst. Medicine of NAS (governing coun. 1981-83, chmn. bd. health promotion and disease prevention 1991-94), Am. Acad. Nursing (governing coun. 1976-78), Am. Orthopsychiat. Assn. (bd. dirs. 1972-75, exec. com. bd. dirs. 1973-75, pres. 1985-86), Nat. League for Nursing (pres. 1991-93). Office: U Pa 354 NEB Philadelphia PA 19104-6096

FAGNANT-LOUGHMAN, SUZANNE CLAIRE, graphic artist, designer; b. Holyoke, Mass., June 22, 1960; d. Rene Victor and Claire Margaret (Goulet) F. BA in Comml. Art and History, Notre Dame Coll., Manchester, N.H., 1982. Freelance artist Chicopee, Mass., 1982-84; mgr., designer Ampad Corp., Holyoke, Mass., 1984-88, 4M Corp./Fonda Group, Springfield, Mass., 1988-89; dir. mktg. svcs. and design, graphic designer, design cons. Reynold's Am. Mfg. Co., Holyoke, 1988-89; owner, designer la Collection Suzanne, 1988—. Mem. Western Mass. Ad Club. Democrat. Roman Catholic.

FAGUNDO, ANA MARIA, creative writing and Spanish literature educator; b. Santa Cruz de Tenerife, Spain, Mar. 13, 1938; came to U.S., 1958; d. Ramón Fagundo and Candelaria Guerra de Fagundo. BA in English and Spanish, U. Redlands, 1962; MA in Spanish, U. Wash., 1964, PhD in Comparative Lit., 1967. Prof. contemporary lit. of Spain and creative writing U. Calif., Riverside, 1967—; vis. lectr. Occidental Coll., Calif., 1967; vis. prof. Stanford U., 1984. Author 8 books of poetry including Invención de la Luz, 1977 (Carabela de Oro poetry prize Barcelona 1977), Obra Poetica: 1965-90, 1990, Isla En Si, 1992, Antología, 1994, La Miriada de Los Sonambulos, 1994; founder, editor: Alaluz, 1969—. Grantee Creative Arts Inst., 1970-71, Humanities Inst., 1973-74; Summer faculty fellow U. Calif., 1968, 77; Humanities fellow, 1969. Mem. Am. Assn. Tchrs. Spanish and Portuguese, Sociedad Gen. de Autores de Espana. Roman Catholic. Home: 5110 Caldera Ct Riverside CA 92507-6002 Office: U Calif Spanish Dept Riverside CA 92521

FAHEY, H.K., real estate agent; b. Lancaster, N.Y., Mar. 19, 1918; d. Andrew and Anna Kramek; m. JOseph A. Fahey, Nov. 22, 1946 (dec. Nov. 1991); 1 child, Brian A. Grad., Chowns Bus. Sch., 1939. Sec. Custiss Wright, Genesee-Cheektowaga, N.Y., Buffalo Jewelry Case; part-time agt. M.J. Peterson Co. Mem. Lancaster Art Soc. (pres.), Williamsville Art Soc., Cheektowaga Art Soc. (awards for watercolor and oil paintings), Niagara Water Frontier. Republican. Roman Catholic. Home: Bavarian Swan Estate 6211 Genesee Lancaster NY 14086

FAHNESTOCK, JEAN HOWE, retired civil engineer; b. Pitts., May 22, 1930; d. James Murray and Hazel Margaret (Alberts) F. AA, Stephens, 1950; BS in Civil Engring., Carnegie-Mellon, 1955. Registered profl. engr., Ill., Mich., Iowa. Sr. project mgr. De Leuw, Cather & Co., Chgo., 1955-92; design mgr. De Leuw, Cather & Co., Kuwait, 1978-81, Abu Dhabi, 1981-85, Kennedy Expy. and Elgin-O'Hare Expy., Chgo., 1985-92. Recipient Outstanding Performance award De Leuw, Cather & Co., 1981. Fellow ASCE (life); mem. NSPE (life), Ill. Soc. Profl. Engrs. Republican. Presbyterian. Home: 4606 W Bryn Mawr Ave Chicago IL 60646-6632

FAHRENBACK, MARGARET ELLEN, school system administrator; b. Akron, Ohio, Dec. 15, 1944; d. Kenneth L. and Ellen (Eddy) James; m. William N. Fahrenback, Feb. 3, 1965; children: Fredrick, Christine. BFA, Ohio U., 1968; MA, Kent State U., 1973, ednl. specialist, 1976. Psychologist Field Local Schs., Mogadore, Ohio, 1975-80, coord. spl. svcs., 1980-82, supr. spl. svcs., 1982—; mem. adv. coun. Mid-Eastern Ohio Spl. Edn. Regional Resource Ctr., Cuyahoga Falls, Ohio, 1982—, Portage County Coop. Learning Ctr., Ravenna, Ohio, 1986—. Mem. edn. commn. United Ch. of Christ, Kent, Ohio. Ohio Dept. Edn. grantee, 1988-90; Martha Holden Jennings Early Childhood Edn. grantee, 1992-94. Mem. Delta Kappa Gamma Internat. (Theta chpt. 2nd v.p. 1988-90, 1st v.p. 1990-92). Office: Field Local Schs 1473 Saxe Rd Mogadore OH 44260-9790

FAHRINGER, CATHERINE HEWSON, retired savings and loan association executive; b. Phila., Aug. 1, 1922; d. George Francis and Catherine Gertrude (Magee) Hewson; grad. diploma Inst. Fin. Edn., 1965; m. Edward F. Fahringer, July 8, 1961 (dec.); 1 child Francis George Beckett. With Centrust Bank (formerly Dade Savs. and Loan Assn.), Miami, 1958-85, v.p., 1967-74, sr. v.p., 1974-82, sec., 1975-79, head savs. personnel and mktg. div., 1979-83, exec. v.p. office of chmn., 1984, dir., 1984-90, co-chmn. audit com. of bd. dirs., 1990; referral assoc. Referral Network Inc., subs. Coldwell Banker, 1990—. Trustee United Way of Dade County (Fla.) 1980-87, chmn. audit com. 1982-84; trustee Pub. Health Trust, Dade County, 1974-84, sec. 1976, vice chmn., 1977-78, chmn. bd., 1978-81; mem. adv. coun. Womens'

Bus. Devel. Ctr., Fla. Internat. U., 1993—; mem. spl. steering com. Breast Cancer Task Force, Jackson Meml. Hosp., 1991; hon. bd. govs. U. Miami, Soc. for Rsch. in Med. Edn.; trustee South Fla. Blood Svc., Miami, 1979-84, vice chmn., 1980, chmn., 1981-84; trustee Dade County Vocat. Found., 1977-81; trustee Fla. Internat. U. Found., 1976-90, trustee emeritus, 1990, v.p. bd., 1978-81, pres., 1982-84; bd. dirs. Sta. WPBT-TV, 1984—, chmn. budget and fin com., 1986, mem. exec. com. 1985-92, sec. 1987, investment com., 1988-90, vice chmn. 1988-92, mem. fin. com., 1992, chmn. audit and control com., 1994; bd. dirs., mem. nominating com. Girl Scout Coun. Tropical Fla., 1985-89, chmn. 1988-89, mem. long range planning com., 1986-88; citizens oversight com. Dade County Pub. Sch. System, 1986-90, chmn. 1988-90; bd. dirs. New World Sch. of Arts, 1987-90, chmn. devel. com., 1987-90, mem. New World Sch. of Arts Found., 1989-90, chair New World Sch. of Arts Gala, 1990; mem. Disaster Relief Com., chair Hurricane Disaster Relief Distrbn. Ctr., 1992; mem. fin. commn., chmn. capital improvement fund com. Coral Gables Congrl. Ch., commd. Stephen min., 1995—; mem. grievance com. 11th Jud. Cir. Fla. Bar, 1988-92; bd. trustees United Protestant Appeal, 1994—. Named Woman of Yr. in fin. Zonta Internat., 1975, amb. Air Def. Arty., U.S. Army Air Def. Command, 1970, Woman of Yr. in Sports, Links Club, 1986; recipient Trail Blazer award Women's Coun. of 100, 1977, Community Headliner award Women in Communication, 1983, Outstanding Citizen of Dade County award, 1984, Honors and Recognition award Golden Panthers Club of Fla. Internat. U., 1989, Disting. Svc. and Leadership award Fla. Internat. U., 1990, Woman of Yr. award Fla. Internat. U., 1991, appreciation New World Sch. of the Arts, 1990, Meritorious Pub. Svc. award Fla. Bar, 1991; hon. BA U. Hard Knocks Alderson-Broaddus Coll., 1987. Mem. Dade Bus. and Profl. Women's Club (past pres., Woman of Yr. 1974), LWV, Inst. Fin. Edn. (life, nat. dir., past pres. Local Greater Miami chpt.), Savs. and Loan Mktg. Soc. South Fla. (past pres.), Savs. and Loan Pers. Soc. South Fla., Internat. Women's Alliance, Fla. Women's Alliance (bd. dirs. 1983-91, pres. 1987-89), Women's Union of Russia (conf. del. 1992), Coral Gables Country Club (treas. women's golf assn. 1988-89, sec., bd. dirs. 1993, found. trustee 1993, v.p. bd. dir. 1994), Links Fla. Internat. U. Club (bd. dirs., sec., v.p. 1992), Greenway Women's Golf Assn. (treas. 1988-89), Biltmore Women's Golf Assn., Greater Miami Women's Golf Assn., Golden Panther Club (bd. dirs. 1988—, v.p. 1991, pres. 1992-94), Fla. Internat. U. Athletics Club. Democrat. Contbr. articles to profl. jours.

FAHY, NANCY LEE, food products marketing executive; b. Schenectady, N.Y., Aug. 15, 1946; d. Christopher Mark and Frances (Lee) F.; m. Steven Neil Wohl, June 8, 1945 (div. Apr. 1978). BS cum laude, Miami (Ohio) U., 1968. Educator Palatine (Ill.) Pub. Schs., 1968-70, Glencoe (Ill.) Pub. Schs., 1970-78; sales rep. Keebler Co., Elmhurst, Ill., 1978-80, dist. mgr., 1980-82, account mgr., 1982-83, zone mgr., 1983-85, account mgr., 1985-89; regional mktg. mgr. Keebler Co., Elmhurst, 1989—. Vol. Lincoln Park Zool. Soc., Chgo., 1975-78. Mem. Food Products Club, Merchandising Execs. Club (bd. dirs. 1984-85), Grocery Mfgs. Sales Execs. Club (bd. dirs. 1984-85, asst. sec. 1987, treas. 1988, 1st v.p. 1989), Phi Beta Kappa. Office: Keebler Co 1135 Commerce Rd Morrow GA 30260-2913

FAILINGER, MARIE ANITA, law educator, editor; b. Battle Creek, Mich., June 29, 1952; d. Conard Frederick and Joan Anita (Lang) F.; children: Joanna, Kristina. BA, Valparaiso U., 1973, JD, 1976; LLM, Yale U., 1983; postgrad., U. Chgo., 1990. Bar: Ind. 1976, U.S. Dist. Ct. (no. dist.) Ind. 1976, U.S. Dist. Ct. (so. dist.) Ind. 1977, U.S. Ct. Appeals (7th cir.) 1979, Minn. 1984, U.S. Supreme Ct. 1980. Prof. of law Hamline U., St. Paul, 1983—, assoc. dean, 1990-93. Editor: Jour. of Law and Religion, 1988—; contbr. articles, book revs. to profl. publs. Bd. dirs. Crossroads Adoption Svc., Mpls., 1986—; pres. Midwest Ctr. for Arts, Entertainment, Lit. and the Law, 1992-95; treas. Am. Indian Rsch. and Policy Inst., 1993—; vice chair Grayling Inst. Mem. Minn. Women Lawyers (bd. dirs. 1989-90), Am. Assn. Law Schs. (chair poverty sect. 1984-88, law and religion sect. exec. com.), Nat. Equal Justice Libr. (bd. dirs. 1989—). Democrat. Mem. Evang. Luth. Ch. Am. Office: Hamline U Sch Law 1536 Hewitt Ave Saint Paul MN 55104-1205

FAIN, CHERYL ANN, translator; b. Providence, May 16, 1953; d. Harry and Pearl (Friedman) F. Student, U. Salzburg, Austria, 1973-74; BA with high distinction, U. R.I., 1975; MA, Monterey Inst. Internat. Studies, 1978, post graduate cert in translation English-German, 1978. Freelance German translator various govt. agys., burs., record co., others, Balt. and Monterey, Calif., 1976—; in-house German and French med. translator Social Security Adminstrn., Balt., 1984-94; German/French translator, asst. to counselor sci. and tech. Embassy of Switzerland, Washington, 1994—. Translator: Perspectives on Mozart, 1978, also various articles and liner notes. Mem. Am. Translators Assn. (accredited for translation from German-English, French-English), Phi Kappa Phi. Home: Calvert House Apts 2401 Calvert St NW Apt 421 Washington DC 20008-2646 Office: Embassy of Switzerland 2900 Cathedral Ave NW Washington DC 20008

FAIN, KAREN KELLOGG, history and geography educator; b. Pueblo, Colo., Oct. 10, 1940; d. Howard Davis and Mary Lucille (Cole) Kellogg; m. Sept. 1, 1961; divorced; 1 child, Kristopher. Student, U. Ariz., 1958-61; BA, U. So. Colo., 1967; MA, U. No. Colo., 1977; postgrad., U. Denver, 1968, 72-93, Colo. State U., 1975, 91, U. No. Ill., 1977, 83, Ft. Hayes State Coll., 1979, U. Colo., 1979, 86-87, 92, Ind. U., 1988. Cert. secondary tchr., Colo. Tchr. history and geography Denver Pub. Schs., 1967—; tchr. West H.S., Denver, 1992—; area adminstr., tchr. coord. Close Up program, Washington, 1982-84; reviewer, cons. for book Geography, Our Changing World, 1990. Vol., chmn. young profls. Inst. Internat. Edn. and World Affairs Coun., Denver, 1980—; mem. state selection com. U.S. Senate and Japan Scholarship Com., Denver, 1981-89, Youth for Understanding, Denver; mem. Denver Art Mus., 1970—; vol. Denver Mus. Natural History, 1989—; bd. overseas Dept. Def. Dependents Sch., Guantanamo Bay, Cuba, 1990-91. Fulbright scholar Chadron State Coll., Pakistan, 1975; Geog. Soc. grantee U. Colo., 1986; recipient award for Project Prince, Colo. U./Denver Pub. Schs./Denver Police Dept., 1992. Mem. Colo. Coun. Social Studies (sec. 1984-86), Nat. Coun. Social Studies (del. 1984), World History Assn., Fulbright Assn., Am. Forum for Global Edn., Rocky Mountain Regional World History Assn. (steering com. 1984-87), Colo. Geographic Alliance (steering com. 1986), Gamma Phi Beta, Kappa Kappa Iota. Democrat. Episcopalian. Home: 12643 E Bates Cir Aurora CO 80014-3315 Office: West High Sch 951 Elati St Denver CO 80204-3964

FAIR, MARY LOUISE, elementary school educator, retired; b. Emporia, Kans., July 16, 1931; d. Dale Franklin Fair and Beulah Fair (Emma) Martin. BA, Marymount Coll., 1953. Bus. edn. tchr. Geneseo (Kans.) High Sch., 1953-55, St. John (Kans.) High Sch., 1955-56; sec. YMCA, Salina, Kans., 1956-57; alumna sec. Marymount Coll., Salina, Kans., 1957-58; bus. edn. tchr. Hayden High Sch., Topeka, Kans., 1958-59; sec. Mental Health Assn., Denver, 1959-60; sec., substitute tchr. Denver Pub. Schs., 1960-62, elem. tchr., 1962-86. 1st v.p. AARP, Heather Gardens, Aurora, Colo., 1988-90, pres., 1991, parliamentarian, 1994, publs. com., 1994—; tutor Aurora and Cherry Creek elem. schs., 1987—. Mem. AAUW (Aurora br., historian 1993-94), Marymount Coll. Alumnae Assn. (pres. 1956-58), Alpha Delta Kappa (state sgt.-at-arms 1982-84, state pres. 1986-88, S.W. regional sgt.-at-arms 1989-91, internat. chmn. living meml. scholarship com. 1991-93, pres., chpt. pres. coun. 1994-96). Republican. Baptist. Home: 3022 S Wheeling Way Apt 311 Aurora CO 80014-5607

FAIRBROTHER, KATHRYN LOUISE, customer relations executive; b. Inglewood, Calif., Jan. 8, 1957; d. Edward McCullough Fairbrother and Carolyn (Howe) Stevens. BA in English Lit., UCLA, 1979; MBA, Calif. State U., Dominguez Hills, 1994. Asst. dept. mgr. Broadway, Westchester, Calif., 1978-79; customer svc. rep. Grand Rent A Car subs. First Gray Line Corp., L.A., 1979-82, supr. customer svc., 1982-84, mgr. charter sales, 1984-87, security investigator, 1987-88; mgr. charter sales Gray Line Tours subs. First Gray Line Corp., L.A., 1984-87; sr. supr. customer rels. Toyota Motor Sales, USA, Inc., Torrance, Calif., 1988—. Mem. AIDS project L.A. Mem. NAFE, Soc. Consumer Affairs Profls., Delta Mu Delta. Democrat. Presbyterian. Home: 5301-B Knowlton St Los Angeles CA 90045-2008

FAIRFIELD, CATHERINE ELIZABETH, minister; b. Indianapolis, May 25, 1951; d. James Patrick and Martha Elizabeth (Waggoner) F.; m. Alfred A. Merwald, Sept. 17, 1977 (div. 1987); children: Jennifer Anne, Elizabeth Martha. AB, Ind. U., 1973; MA, U. Chgo., 1977; DMin, Chgo. Theol. Sem., 1986. Ordained to ministry, Bapt. Ch., 1977. Asst. min. Univ. United Meth. Ch., Madison, Wis., 1977-78; chaplain resident Rush Med. Ctr., Chgo., 1978-80; Protestant chaplain Mercy Hosp., Aurora, Ill., 1980-81; staff therapist Ctr. for Life Skills, Chgo., 1981-87; dir. Genesis Therapy Ctr., Oak Forest, Ill., 1987—. Active Hyde Park Union Ch., Chgo., 1978—. Democrat. Home: 549 W Winchester Rd Chicago Heights IL 60411-1617 Office: Genesis Therapy Ctr 4931 W 158th St Oak Forest IL 60452-3513

FAIRLEIGH, MARLANE PAXSON, business consultant, educator; b. Three Rivers, Mich., Feb. 28, 1939; d. Ronald Edward and Evelyn May (Roth) Paxson; m. James Parkinson Fairleigh, June 25, 1960; children: William Paxson, Karen Evelyn. MusB, U. Mich., 1960; MBA, Jacksonville State U., 1986. Cert. econ. devel. fin. profl. Adj. faculty Providence Coll., 1976-80, R.I. Coll., Providence, 1978-80; grad. asst. news bur. and info. ctr. Jacksonville (Ala.) State U., 1983-84, grad. asst. Coll. Commerce, 1984-85, account exec. Small Bus. Devel. Ctr., 1985—; presenter various seminars. Contbr. articles to profl. jours. Chairperson Jacksonville State U. campus United Way Calhoun County, 1986-87; bd. dirs. 2nd Chance, Inc. Mem. Active Corps of Execs., Women's Exec. Network, Calhoun County Women's Empowerment Network (task force com.), Calhoun County C. of C., Jacksonville Coun. C. of C. (steering com. 1995). Home: 512 Fairway Dr SW Jacksonville AL 36265-3301 Office: Jacksonville State Univ Merrill Hall Small Bus Devel Ctr Jacksonville AL 36265

FAISON, HOLLY, communications professional; b. Sherman, Tex., Aug. 11, 1953; d. Ronald Miller and Ann (LaRoe) F. BA, Tex. A&M U., 1976. Dispatcher College Station (Tex.) Police Dept., 1976-77; police communications operator Tex. Dept. Pub. Safety, Bryan, 1977-83; supr. police communications facility Tex. Dept. Pub. Safety, Austin, 1983-85, Victoria, 1985-87; supr. police communications facility Tex. Dept. Pub. Safety, Bryan, 1987-92, regional supr. police communications, 1993—; mem. Brazos County Emergency Mgmt./Civil Def. Coun., Bryan, 1987-92. Producer video tng. tapes. Mem. Associated Pub. Safety Communications Officers, Exec. Women in Tex. Govt. Methodist. Home: 5500 DeSoto # 903 Houston TX 77091 Office: Tex Dept Pub Safety 10110 NW Freeway Houston TX 77092

FAITH, DONNA LYNN, assistant principal; b. Berkeley Springs, W.Va., Jan. 16, 1957; d. Donald Lee and Shirley Yvonne (Culp) F. AA, Hagerstown Jr. Coll., 1977; BS, Towson State U., 1979; MEd, Shippensburg State U., 1981; postgrad., U. Md., 1984—. Cert. elem. edn. tchr., tchr. gen. sci. and earth sci., adminstrn. and supervision. Sci. tchr. Washington County Bd. Edn., Hagerstown, Md., 1979-93, integration resource specialist, 1993-94; asst. prin. Windsor Knolls Mid. Sch., Ijamsville, Md., 1994—; insvc. trainer Washington County Bd. Edn., Hagerstown, 1984-94; teaching internship U. Md., College Park, 1985-86; cons., sci. educator Potomac Edison, Hagerstown, 1986-87; SAT coord. Ednl. Testing Svc., Princeton, N.J., 1989-94. Co-chairperson Gender Equity Roundtable, Hagerstown, 1993-94; mem. Washington County Commn. for Women, 1993—. Mem. AAUW, ASCD, Nat. Sci. Tchrs. Assn., Am. Legion Aux., Hagerstown Jr. Coll. Alumni Assn. (v.p. 1993-94, Best. Vol. 1993), Soroptimists, Alpha Delta Kappa (ways and means chair 1990-92). Democrat. Home: 54 E Irvin Ave Hagerstown MD 21742-3428 Office: Windsor Knolls Mid Sch 1150 Windsor Rd Ijamsville MD 21754

FAITH BHATIA, LORI ANN, educator; b. Madison, Wis., Mar. 14, 1967; d. James W. and Rita R. (Mitchell) Faith; m. Pradeep K. Bhatia, Dec. 31, 1993. BS in Edn., U. Wis., Whitewater, 1989, MBA, 1993. Outreach instr. U. Wis., Whitewater, 1993; tng. specialist Silton-Bookman Sys., Cupertino, Calif., 1994—; part-time instr. Stratton Coll., Milw., 1994, Gateway Tech. Coll., Racine, Wis., 1994, Waukesha County Tech. Coll., Pewaukee, Wis., 1990-94; tech. writer JI Case Corp., Racine, 1993-94; adminstrv. sec.-fin. Milw. Med. Ctr., 1990-91. Mem. Grad. Bus. Assn. (v.p. 1991-93), Beta Gamma Sigma. Home and Office: 4118 Washington Rd Apt 101 Kenosha WI 53144

FAJARDO, KATHARINE LYNN, public relations and marketing executive; b. Akron, Ohio, Mar. 19, 1951; d. Edwin Murray and Diane (Zabiegalski) Humphrey. BA, Johns Hopkins U., 1973; MBA, U. Calif., 1987. Dir. pub. affairs coun. Electronic Industries Assn., Washington, 1973-75; author Pension Benefit Guaranty Corp., 1975-76; pension cons. Proskauer, Rose, Goetz & Mendelsohn, N.Y.C., 1976-77; sr. mktg. cons. The Equitable Life Assurance Soc., N.Y.C., 1977-79; mgr. comm. and advertising St. Joe Minerals Corp., N.Y.C., 1979-82; mktg. and pub. rels. cons., 1982-87; v.p. Burson-Marsteller, 1988-91; pres. Cygnet Pub. Rels., Atlanta, 1991-92; v.p., dir. pub. rels. Sawyer, Riley, Compton, Inc., Atlanta, 1993-94; ptnr. Buffington and Rizzo, 1994—. Recipient Nicholson awards, 1979, 80, Big Apple awards, 1989, 90, 91, Silver Anvil award, 1991, 2 Bronze Anvil awards, 1990. Mem. NAFE, Pub. Rels. Soc. Am.

FAKRODDIN, NILOFER NABI, financial consultant; b. Springfield, Ill., July 17, 1959; s. Nabi Rasool and Zahida Nabi (Imam) F. B Fin., U. Ill., 1981. Sr. internat. acct. Continental Bank, Chgo., 1981-84; banking assoc. Continental Bank, Chgo. and Houston, 1984-86; fin. cons. Merrill Lynch, Chgo., 1986—, asst. v.p., 1994—. Fundraiser Chgo. Found. for Religious and Cultural Reflection, Chgo., 1990-93; mem. Internat. Visitor's Ctr., Chgo., 1993—; tutor underprivileged children in conjunction with Merrill Lynch's Scholarship Builder Program, Chgo., 1993—. Home: 535 N Michigan Ave Apt 1903 Chicago IL 60611-3810 Office: Merrill Lynch 225 W Wacker Dr Ste 1400 Chicago IL 60606

FALCAO, LINDA PHYLLIS, screenwriter; b. Lisbon, Portugal, June 1, 1960; came to U.S., 1961; d. John Moniz and Phyllis Margaret (Fleming) F.; m. Michael J. Salmanson, July 26, 1992; 1 child, Lauren N. BS in Econs., BA, U. Pa., 1982, JD, 1985. Assoc. Schnader, Harrison, Segal & Lewis, Phila., 1985-86; law clk. Hon. Phyllis W. Beck Superior Ct. Pa., 1986-88, 92; assoc. Dechert, Price & Rhoads, Phila., 1989-92; freelance writer Wynnewood, Pa., 1993—. Author: (screenplay) Pattern and Practice, 1993. Presdl. scholar Commn. Presdl. Scholars, Washington, 1978. Mem. Phi Beta Kappa, Beta Gamma Sigma.

FALCK, MARIA J., retail executive; b. Pitts., Jan. 16, 1962; d. Robert Charles and Penelope (Torlidas) F. BFA, SUNY, Purchase, 1984. Sales mgr. Macy's, N.Y.C., 1986-87, customer svc. mgr., 1987-88, budget mgr., 1988-89; assoc. mgr., ops. mgr. Banana Republic, N.Y.C., 1989-91; assoc. mgr. Tiffany & Co., N.Y.C., 1991-92; store mgr. Tiffany & Co., Troy, Mich., 1992-94; mgr. The Jr. League, 1993—; with Internat. Fashion Group, 1993-94; tng. mgr. Brooks Bros., N.Y.C., 1994—. Capt. Macy's Thanksgiving Day Parade, N.Y.C., 1987; bd. dirs. Alumni Orgn., Purchase, 1989-91, rep. Coll. Coun., Purchase, 1989-91. Greek Orthodox. Home: 23-66 32nd St Astoria NY 11105 Office: Brooks Bros 1120 Ave of the Americas New York NY 10036

FALCONE, NOLA MADDOX, financial company executive; b. Augusta, Ga., July 8, 1939; d. Louia Vernon and Geneva Elizabeth (Fox) Maddox; m. Charles Anthony Falcone, Dec. 6, 1968; 1 child, Charles Maddox. B.A., Duke U., 1961; M.B.A., U. Pa., 1966. Security analyst, portfolio mgr., investment officer, with pers. trust dept. Chase Manhattan Bank, N.Y.C., 1961-63, 66-70; portfolio mgr., registered rep. Lieber & Co., 1974-75; br. mgr., ptnr., dir. 13 Evergreen funds Evergreen Asset Mgmt. Corp., Arlington, Va., 1979—; ptnr. Lieber & Co., Arlington, 1981—; bd. dirs. Evergreen Asset Mgmt. Corp., Purchase. Mem. fin. com. Jr. League, Scarsdale, N.Y., 1972-75; bd. dirs. Ea. Sem., Pa.; bd. visitors Fuqua Sch. Bus., Duke U., Durham, N.C.; bd. dirs. Gordon Coll., Wyndham, Mass. Mem. Fin. Analysts Soc., CFA. Democrat.

FALK, BARBARA C., pediatrician; b. Wyandotte, Mich., Aug. 28, 1941; m. John Carl Falk, Oct. 11, 1975; children: Ann Marie, Carl. BS in Pharmacy, U. Mich., 1963; MD, Wayne State U., 1975. Intern Children's Meml. Hosp. Chgo., 1975-76, resident, 1976-79; pediatrician Mundie, Falk & Assoc., Evanston, Ill., 1979-86, Michael Reese Health Plan, Evanston, 1986-89, North Shore Pediatrics, Wilmette, Ill., 1990—. Fellow Am. Acad. Pediatrics. Office: Pediatric Assocs North Shore 1149 Wilmette Ave Wilmette IL 60091

FALK, DEAN, anthropology educator; b. Seattle, June 25, 1944; children: Sarah Falk Schofield, Adrienne Falk Dolen. Student, Antioch Coll., 1962-63, U. Wash., 1964-65; BA with honors, U. Ill., 1970, MA, 1972. Asst. prof. Rollins Coll., Winter Park, Fla., 1976-77, So. Ill. U., Carbondale, 1977-79; asst. prof. health scis. Boston U., 1979-80; investigator Caribbean Primate Rsch. Ctr., 1980-84, curator Cayo Santiago primate skeletal collection, 1982-86, assoc. researcher, 1984-86; asst. prof. anatomy Sch. of Medicine U. P.R., 1980-82, assoc. prof. anatomy Sch. of Medicine, 1982-86; assoc. prof. Purdue U., 1986-88; prof. SUNY, Albany, 1988—. Author: External Neuroanatomy of Old World Monkeys, Primate Brain Evolution: Methods and Concepts, 1982, Braindance: What New Findings Reveal About Human Origins and Brain Evolution, 1992; mem. panel referees Human Evolution; mem. editorial bd. Man, Advances in Human Evolution; contbr. articles to Jour. Neuroscis., Jour. Neurosci. Methods, Am. Jour. Phys. Anthropology, Internat. Jour. Primatology. Antioch Alumni Assn. scholar, 1962, Ctr. for Continuing Edn. of Women scholar, 1975, Alice C. Lloyd scholar, 1975; grantee NSF, 1970-71, 71-72, 78, 82, 84-86, 90-92, U. Mich., 1976, So. Ill. U., 1979, NIH, 1986-90. Fellow Am. Anthrop. Assn. (elected, sec., treas. biol. anthropology sect. 1989-91); mem. AAAS, Am. Assn. Phys. Anthropologists, Lang. Origins Soc., Sigma Xi. Home: 173 S Main Ave Albany NY 12208-2411 Office: SUNY Dept Of Anthropology Albany NY 12222

FALK, JOAN FRANCES, public relations executive; b. Flushing, N.Y., Jan. 15, 1936; d. Leo Carl Hjalmar and Frances Louise (Masin) F. Cert., Parsons Sch. Design, N.Y.C., 1955; BS, NYU, 1956, MBA, 1958. Assoc. editor Fairchild's Fin. Manual, N.Y.C., 1956-58; editor, costs mgr. Western Printing & Lithographing, N.Y.C., 1958-61; dir. rsch. and costs Grolier, Inc., N.Y.C., 1961-64; budget supr. Ted Bates & Co., N.Y.C., 1965-82; bus. mgr. N.W. Ayer Pub. Rels. (Div. of N.W. Ayer, Inc.), N.Y.C., 1982—, Diamond Info. Ctr. (Div. of N.W. Ayer, Inc.), N.Y.C., 1992—. Contbr. photographs to Grolier Internat., 1964, Encyclopedia Brittanica, 1970. Active Broadway Flushing Homeowners; vol. fundraiser pub. broadcast TV, WNET, N.Y.C., WLIW, L.I. Mem. Daus. of Nile (Queen of al Kahbay Temple # 22 1970, supreme temple officer 1980), Order Ea. Star (matron of Bayside Pleiades #737 1962, dist. dep. grand matron 1987), Orgn. Triangles (past queen of Rising Star #69), Nat. Leadership Coun. (Capital award 1991), Bayside H.S. Alumni Assn. (past rec. sec.). Republican. Lutheran. Home: 164-16 32d Ave Flushing NY 11358 Office: NW Ayer 825 8th Ave New York NY 10019-7416

FALK, JULIA S., linguist, educator; b. Englewood, N.J., Sept. 21, 1941; d. Charles Joseph and Stella (Sarafinovich) Sableski; m. Thomas Heinrich, Jan. 20, 1967; 1 child, Tatiana Prentice. BS, Georgetown U., 1963; MA, U. Wash., 1964, PhD, 1968. Instr. linguistics Mich. State U., East Lansing, 1966-68, asst. prof., 1968-71, assoc. prof., 1971-78, prof., 1978—, asst. dean Coll. of Arts and Letters, 1979-81, assoc. dean Coll. Arts and Letters, 1981-86; cons. on lang. and law, lang. and gender, bias-free communication, East Lansing. Author: Linguistics and Language, 1973, 2d revised edit., 1978; contbr. articles on lang. acquisition, history of linguistics to profl. jours. Fellow Woodrow Wilson Found., 1963, NDEA Title IV, 1963-66, NSF, 1965; recipient Paul Varg Alumni award for Teaching, 1993. Mem. Linguistic Soc. Am., N.Am. Assn. History of Lang. Scis. Home: 2100 Holt Rd Williamston MI 48895-9747 Office: Mich State Univ Dept Linguistics A-614 Wells East Lansing MI 48824

FALK, JUSTINA CHEN, advertising executive; b. Taipei, Republic of China, May 30, 1951; came to U.S., 1976; d. Liang Yih and Helen Y.Y. (Lee) Chen; m. Edward Falk. BBA in Acctg., Nat. Chengchi U., Taipei, 1973; M in Profl. Acctg., U. Tex., 1978. CPA, Tex. Systems analyst Ministry Fin., Taipei, 1973-76; auditor, cons. Price Waterhouse & Co., Houston, 1978-80; cons. CEXEC, Inc. for Dept. Energy, Houston, 1980-81; fin. analyst Hydril Co., Houston, 1981-82; asst. city controller City of Houston, 1982; pres. Graphics and Advt. Agy., Houston, 1983—; owner Gift World, Baytown, Tex., 1986—; Mem. U.S. Dept. Commerce's Nat. Adv. Bd. of Minority Bus. Devel. Agy. Publ., mng. editor mag. Asian Panorama, 1983-86; contbg. writer Issues Mag., 1981-86. Founder, 1st pres. Tex. Asian Rep. Caucus, 1985-86; exec. bd. dirs. Tex. Fedn. Rep. Women, 1985-86. Recipient Small Bus. award Houston Minority Bus. Devel. Agy., Houston, 1985. Mem. Tex. Soc. CPA's, Issues Research and Ednl. Found. (bd. dirs. 1981—). Methodist. Office: Graphics and Advt Agy 2600 SW Freeway Ste 1001 Houston TX 77098

FALK, PAMELA S., legislative staff member. MA in Politics, NYU, 1975, PhD in Internat. Rels. and Latin Am. Affairs, 1980; JD, Columbia U., 1992. Dir. Latin Am. affairs Americas Soc., 1979-85; assoc. prof. Hunter Coll., 1979-85, Columbia Coll., 1985-90, Sch. Internat. and Pub. Affairs; assoc. dir. Inst. Latin Am. and Iberian Studies; cons. Latin Am. issues CBS Evening News and CNN, 1989-91; with Latin Am. group Debevoise and Plimpton, N.Y.C.; staff dir. Subcom. Western Hemisphere Affairs Ho. Com. Fgn. Affairs. Author: Cuban Foreign Policy: Caribbean Tempest, 1986; editor, co-editor various publs.; contbr. articles to profl. jours. Mem. nat. adv. bd. Ctr. Study Presidency; bd. dirs. Caribbean Cultural Ctr. Stone scholar Columbia U. Mem. Coun. Fgn. Rels. Office: Subcom Western Hemisphere Affairs O'Neill House Office Bldg Rm 705 Washington DC 20515*

FALKENBERG, MARY ANN THERESA, realtor; b. Chgo., Dec. 8, 1931; d. Joseph and Catherine (Bausch) Haselsteiner; student Barat Coll., 1953; m. Charles V. Falkenberg, Jr., Apr. 9, 1955; children—Catherine, Grace Ann, Susan Marie, Charles V., Robert, Thomas, Martin, Mary, Elizabeth, Joseph. Tchr. piano, 1946-73; organist St. Thomas of Villanova Ch., 1960—, choir dir., 1960—; sales staff Quinlan & Tyson, Realtors, Inc., Palatine, Ill., 1970-77; pres., co-owner, broker, mgr. Assoc. Realty Corp., Palatine, 1978-91; mgr. Prudential Preferred Properties, 1991—. Named Palatine Woman of Yr., Suburban Press Found., 1962; cert. home protection cons. Mem. Women in Mgmt., Am. Mgmt. Assn., Ill. Assn. Realtors (life mem. two million dollar club, mem. three million dollar club, four million dollar club, five million dollar pres.'s club, Gold award 1988, leading edge award), Nat. Assn. Realtors (accredited profl. residential appraiser, cert. real property appraiser), Nat. Assn. Female Execs., N.W. Suburban Bd. Realtors (edn. com. 1977-78, non-resident com. 1982, broker-lawyer com. 1986-91, grievance com. 1988-90, chmn. 1990—), MAP (bd. dirs. 1986-90, sec. 1988-90, treas. 1990-91, v.p. 1991-92, pres. 1993—), Women in Sales, Barat Coll. Alumni Assn. Club: Women's. Republican. Roman Catholic. Home: 517 Warwick Ave Palatine IL 60067-3875 Office: 240 E Northwest Hwy Palatine IL 60067-8140

FALKENSTEIN, KARIN EDITH, elementary school principal; b. Michigan City, Ind., Feb. 12, 1950; d. Martin Victor and Helen Marion (Hedberg) Sandstrom; m. Chrles William Falkenstein Jr., July 13, 1985; 1 stepchild, Amanda Ann. BA in Elem. Edn., Spl. Edn., Mich. State U., 1972, MA in Reading Instrn., 1975. Spl. edn. tchr. Hesperia (Mich.) Pub. Schs., 1972-73; spl. edn. tchr. Buchanan (Mich.) Community Schs., 1973-79, elem. prin. Moccasin Sch., sch. farm coord., 1979-80; elem. prin. Ottawa Sch., Buchanan (Mich.) Community Schs., 1980—; dist. spl. edn. supr., 1980—; gifted and talented coord. Ottawa Sch., Buchanan (Mich.) Community Schs., 1980—, elem. coord., K-12 testing coord. and K-6 curriculum dir., 1993—; instr. Ind. U., South Bend, 1981—; presenter spl. edn. workshops. Mem. Big Bros./Big Sisters of Niles/Buchanan, Inc., 1982—, v.p., 1985, pres., 1986-87; mem. Coll. Edn. Alumni Bd., v.p., pres.; Sun. sch. tchr. First United Meth. Ch., 1982—, bd. trustees, 1986-91, Chrisian edn. chairperson, 1988-90; mem. Buchanan Fine Arts Coun., 1987—, treas., 1988-93; mem. Hospice Bereavement Care, 1987—; mem. Redbud Area Ministries LOVE, Inc., 1985-89, pres., 1988-89; bd. dirs. Berrien Coun. for Children, 1987—, mem. edn. com., 1984—; bd. dirs. Four Flags Samaritan Ctr., 1985—; mem. PTA, 1988—. Recipient Nat. Disting. Prin.'s award, 1989, Mich. Legis. recognition, 1989, Pres.'s award Mich. State U. Coll. Edn. Alumni Assn., 1987, Golden Nugget award for spl. edn., 1983, Milken Found. Family Educator award, 1993; named Mich. Outstanding Practicing Prin., 1988, Region 5 Prin. award, 1989. Mem. Mich. Elem. and Mid. Sch. Prins. Assn. (membership chair 1984-86, profl. devel. chairperson 1983-84, pres. 1987-88), ASCD, Coun. for Exceptional Children, Tri-County Coun. of Women in Ednl. Adminstrn. (profl. devel. chair 1983-84, pres. 1985-87, historian 1987-92), Spl. Edn. Dirs. and Coords. for Berrien County, Internat. Reading Assn., Mich. Reading Assn., Mich. Alliance for Gifted Edn., Mich. Assn. Learning Disabilities Educators, Mich. State U. Alumni Assn. (nat. bd. v.p. 1992-93, treas. 1991-

92, pres. 1993-94, Coll. of Edn. v.p. 1987, pres. 1988), Phi Delta Kappa. Office: Buchanan Community Schs 109 Ottawa St Buchanan MI 49107-1136

FALL, MARIJANE EATON, counselor, educator; b. Sanford, Maine, Oct. 4, 1940; d. Harold Vincent and Estella Anne (Prescott) Eaton; m. David William Fall (div. 1985); children: David Gregory, Gretchen, Amy. BA, Nasson Coll., 1963; MS, U. So. Maine, 1986; EdD, U. Maine, 1991. Lic. profl. counselor, Maine; lic. mental health counselor, Iowa; nat. cert. counselor. Counselor Wiscasset and Damariscotta (Maine) Pub. Schs., 1986-89; pvt. practice Westport Island, Maine, 1987-92, Iowa City, 1993—; lectr. II counseling U. So. Maine, Gorham, 1991-92; asst. prof. U. Iowa, Iowa City, 1992—; mem. adj. faculty U. Maine, Orono, 1990; cons. Big Bros. and Big Sisters, Damarcocotta, Maine, 1989-92, Iowa Test of Basic Skills, Iowa City, 1993—; supr. play therapists, Maine, then Iowa, 1992—. Mem. editorial bd. Sch. Counselor, 1993—; contbr. articles to profl. publs. Troop leader, cons. Girl Scouts U.S., Sanford, Maine, 1978-84; pres. bd. dirs. Sanford Young Men's Christian Assn., 1981—, hon. life mem., 1983. George Nasson scholar Nasson Coll., Springvale, Maine, 1963. Mem. ACA (cert.), North Cen. Assn. Counselor Edn. Suprs., Play Therapy Assn. Mem. Soc. of Friends. Office: Univ Iowa Lindquist Ctr # N364lc Iowa City IA 52242

FALLACI, ORIANA, writer, journalist; b. Florence, Italy, June 29, 1930; d. Edoardo and Tosca (Cantini) F. Grad., Liceo Classico Galileo Galilei, Italy; student, U. Florence Faculty Medicine, 1946-48; Litt.D. (hon.), Columbia Coll., Chgo., 1977. Editor and spl. corr. Europeo Mag., Milan, Italy, 1958-77; collaborator with major publs. throughout world, including Look mag., Life mag., The Washington Post, N.Y. Times, London Times; dir. Rizzoli Pubs. Corp. Author: (novels) Penelope at War, 1966, Letter to a Child Never Born, 1977, audio book read by author, 1993, A Man, 1979 (Viareggio Prize award), Inshallah, 1990 (Hemingway prize, Super Bancarella prize 1991), (non-fiction) If The Sun Dies, 1967, Nothing So Be It, 1972, (Bancarella award), Interview with History, 1976, (essays) The Useless Sex, 1964, The Egotists, 1965, (audio) Oriana Fallaci reads: Letter to a Child Never Born, 1993. Author: (novels) Penelope at War, 1966, Letter to a Child Never Born, 1977 (audio book read by author 1993), A Man, 1979 (Viareggio prize), Insciallah, 1990 (Superbancarella prize and Hemingway prize, Antibes Internat. prize 1993), (non-fiction) If The Sun Dies, 1967, Nothing and So Be It, 1972 (Bancarella award), Interview with History, 1976, (essays) The Useless Sex, 1964, The Egotists, 1965. Recipient St. Vincent award for journalism, 1971, 73. Office: Rizzoli 31 W 57th St Fl 4 New York NY 10019-3402 also: RCS Rizzoli Libri, Via Mecenate 91, 20138 Milan Italy

FALLETTA, JO ANN, musician; b. N.Y.C., Feb. 27, 1954; d. John Edward and Mary Lucy (Racioppo) F.; m. Robert Alemany, Aug. 24, 1986. BA in Music, Mannes Coll. Music, N.Y.C., 1976; MA in Music, Juilliard Sch., N.Y.C., 1982; PhD in Musical Arts, Juilliard Sch., 1989; Honorary Doctorate, Marian Coll., Wis., 1988. Music dir. Queens Philharmonic, N.Y.C., 1978-91, Den. Chamber Orch., Colo., 1983-92; assoc. condr. Milw. Symphony, Wis., 1985-88; music dir. Women's Philharmonic, San Francisco, 1986—, Long Beach Symphony, Calif., 1989—, Va. Symphony, Norfolk, 1991—. Stokowski Conducting Competition, Toscanini Conducting award. Office: Long Beach Symphony Orch 555 E Ocean Blvd Ste 106 Long Beach CA 90802-5048 Office: ICM Artists LTD 40 W 57th St New York NY 10019*

FALLIN, BARBARA MOORE, human resources director; b. Paducah, Ky., Nov. 12, 1939; d. James Perry Moore and Margaret Arminta (Winn) Kastner; m. Jon Ball, Jan. 21, 1961 (div. July 1963); m. Ralph Daniel Fallin, May 23, 1965; children: Wade, Cathi, Cindy Pergrim, Danielle. Student, Fla. Christian Coll., 1957-58. Cert. sr. profl. in human resource mgmt. Exec. asst. to contr. The Borden Co., Tampa, Fla., 1958-65; mktg. asst. Martin-Marietta Corp., Shalimar, Fla., 1965-71; asst. to pres. Browning-Marine, Ft. Walton Beach, Fla., 1973; pers. coord. Keltec Fla., Shalimar, 1974-78; pers. mgr. Metric Systems Corp., Ft. Walton Beach, 1979-87, pers. dir., 1987-92; dir. human resources Metric Sys. Corp., Ft. Walton Beach, 1992—; mem. Job Service Employer Com.. Ft. Walton Beach, 1985—; mem. adv. bd. Bay Area Vocat.-Tech. Ctr., Ft. Walton Beach, 1988—. First mistress Krewe of Bowlegs, Ft. Walton Beach, 1983-84, first lady to Cap'n Billy Bowlegs XXXII, 1986-87; mem. citizens adv. com. U. West Fla., Pensacola, 1991—; mem. funds distbn. com. Okaloosa County United Way, 1990-93. Mem. NAFE, Soc. Human Resouce Mgmt., Emerald Coast Pers. Mgmt. Assn. (pres. 1986-88, bd. dirs. 1988-92), Nat. Mgmt. Assn., Ft. Walton Beach C. of C. (hosts com. 1991—), Mardi Gras Club. Republican. Presbyterian. Office: Metric Sys Corp 645 Anchors St NW Fort Walton Beach FL 32548-3803

FALLIN, JOANNA ALICIA, occupational therapist; b. Alexandria, La., July 10, 1963; d. Henry Ford and Bette Jo (Roane) F. BS in Fin., La. Tech. U., 1984, MBA, 1985; M in Occupl. Therapy, Tex. Woman's U., 1994. CMA. Fin. analyst Electronic Data Sys., Dallas, Detroit, Antwerp, Belgium, 1985-89; fin. supr. Electronic Data Sys., Houston, 1989-90; fin. specialist Electronic Data Sys., Dallas, 1990-92. Vol. Child Abuse Prevention Coun., Houston, 1990, Equest-Horseback Riding for Persons with Disabilities, Wylie, Tex., 1992, 95, AIDS Svcs. Dallas, 1991-92. Mem. Inst. Cert. Mgmt. Accts., Am. Occupl. Therapy Assn. Baptist. Home: 5921 Harvest Hill # 2086 Dallas TX 75230

FALLIN, MARY COPELAND, state official; b. Warrensburg, Mo., Dec. 9, 1954; d. Jospeh Newton and Mary (Duggan) Copeland; m. Joseph Price Fallin, Jr., Nov. 3, 1984; children: Christina, Price. BS, Okla. State U., 1977. Bus. mgr. Okla. Dept. Securities, Oklahoma City, 1979-81; state travel coord. Okla. Dept. of Tourism, Oklahoma City, 1981-82; sales rep. Associated Petroleum, Oklahoma City, 1982-83; mktg. dir. Brian Head (Utah) Hotel & Ski Resort, 1983-84; dir. sales Residence Inn Hotel, Oklahoma City, 1984-87; dist. mgr. Lexington Hotel Suites, Oklahoma City, 1988-90; real estate assoc. Pippin Properties, Inc., Oklahoma City, 1992-94; state rep. Okla. Ho. of Reps., Oklahoma City, 1990-94; lt. governor State of Okla., Oklahoma City, 1995—. Mem. Okla. Fedn. Rep. Women; mem. Am. Legis. Exch. Coun., Nat. Conf. State Legislatures. Mem., del. Okla. Fedn. Rep. Women; mem. Am. Legis. Exch. Coun., Nat. Conf. State Legislatures. Named Nat. Legislator of the Yr., Okla. Ladies in the News, Guardian of Small Bus. award. Presbyterian. Home: 2521 NW 59th St Oklahoma City OK 73112 Office: State Capital Rm 211 Office of Lt Governor Oklahoma City OK 73105*

FALLON, KATHLEEN A., medical laboratory technician; b. West Palm Beach, Fla., Dec. 5, 1952; d. Edward Leon and Vivian Elaine (Fisher) F. Student, Broward C.C., 1971-84, Palm Beach C.C., 1980—. Lic. med. lab. technician, Fla.; lic. real estate, notary pub. Safety chair and med. lab. technician West Palm Beach, 1974—, trustee, 1992—; writer, inventor, author Kaaf, Inc., Boynton Beach, West Palm Beach, Fla., 1993—; bicycle safety instr. Nat. Safety Coun., West Palm Beach. voter registrar Voting Registration Office, West Palm Beach; vol. elem. sch. activities Fund Raising West Palm Beach. Mem. Exec. Females. Democrat. Roman Catholic. Home: 5409 Western Ave West Palm Beach FL 33405

FALLS, KATHLEENE JOYCE, photographer; b. Detroit, July 3, 1949; d. Edgar John and Acelia Olive (Young) Haley; m. Donald David Falls, June 15, 1974; children: Daniel John, David James. Student, Oakland Community Coll., 1969-73, Winona Sch. Profl. Photography, 1973-80; degree in photography, 1988, 90. Printer Guardian Photo, Novi, Mich., 1967-69; printer, supr. quality control N.Am. Photo, Livonia, Mich., 1969-76; free lance photographer Livonia, 1969-76; owner, pres. Kathy Falls, Inc., Carleton, Mich., 1976—; instr. digital imaging Monroe County (Mich.) C.C., 1994—; instr. Monroe County Community Coll. Continuing Edn., 1981-83; nat. artisan judge Congl. High Sch. Art Competition, 1985—; owner Picture Perfect, Carleton, 1987; co-owner Haleys Gift Shoppe, Dundee, Mich., 1989. Author: (booklet) Emergency Photo-Retouching for Photographers, 1988; contbr. articles to profl. jours. Represented in spl. categories in the Nat. Loan Collection, Profl. Photographers Am., 1980, 81, 83, 87; represented in permanent Collections Monroe County Hist. Mus., Archives Notre Dame. Catechist St. Patrick's Ch., Carleton, 1984-87; active Big Bros. and Big Sisters, Monroe, 1986-87; corr. sec. Monroe Women's Ctr, 1986-88. Recipient numerous awards granted by profl. photographic orgns. Mem. NAFE, Am. Soc. Photographers, Detroit Profl. Photographers Assn. (bd. dirs. 1987—, artisan chmn. 1981-82, Best of Show award 1981, 83), Profl. Photographers Mich. (artisian chairperson 1982-83, Best of Show award 1976, 81, Artist of Yr. 1980, 91), Profl. Photographers Am. (cert. profl. photog. specialist, photographic specialist degree 1988), Am. Photographic Artisans Guild (council mem., bd. dirs. 1987—, pres. 1992, Photographic Artisan degree 1989, Artisan Laurel degree 1991), Monroe County Fine Arts Council, Monroe C. of C. (chmn. council women bus. owners), Nat. Orgn. Women Bus. Owners, Profl. Photographers Am. (Photographic Craftsman degree 1990), Toastmasters, Internat. Club. Democrat. Roman Catholic. Club: Monroe Camera. Home and Office: 10779 Swan Creek Rd Carleton MI 48117-9324

FALLS, WALDTRAUT MARGRETE GOETZE, medical librarian; b. N.Y.C., June 28, 1941; d. Otto Paul and Anna Irma (Zander) Goetze; A.B., State U. N.Y. at Albany, 1963, M.A. (scholar), 1964; M.S., Columbia U., 1967; m. John Allen Falls, Jr.; children—John Francis, Michael Gregory. Asst. advt. librarian Curtis Pub. Co., N.Y.C., 1964-65; library asso. N.Y. U. Commerce Library, N.Y.C., 1965-67; librarian, instr. N.Y.C. Community Coll., Bklyn., 1967-69, 70, 73-75; med. librarian Victory Meml. Hosp., Bklyn., 1975-87, clin. librarian, U. Medicine and Dentistry N.J., Newark, 1987-88; info. mgr. otolaryngology Facial Plastic Surgery Assocs., 1988—. Mem. ALA, Med. Library Assn., Bklyn., Queens and S.I. Health Scis. Librarians, N.Y. Library Club (life). Home: 328 78th St Brooklyn NY 11209-3013 Office: Facial Plastic Surgery Assocs 7333 6th Ave Brooklyn NY 11209-2607

FALUDI, SUSAN C., journalist, scholarly writer. Formerly with West Mag., San Jose, Calif., Mercury News; with San Francisco Bur., Wall St. Jour.; spkr. in field. Author: Backlash: The Undeclared War Against American Women, 1991 (National Book Critics Circle award for general nonfiction 1992); contbr. articles to mags. Recipient Pulitzer Prize for Explanatory Journalism, 1991. Office: care Sandra Dijkstra Sandra Dijkstra Literary Agency 1155 Camino del Mar Ste 515 Del Mar CA 92014*

FALVEY, JUDITH NELL JONES, librarian, media specialist; b. Magnolia, Miss., Aug. 11, 1944; d. Jerry Judson and Vera Kathleen (Oglesby) Jones; m. Alvin Peyton Adams Jr., June 19, 1965 (div. 1984); m. Norman David Falvey, May 24, 1986; children: Stephen Elliot Adams, Peyton Seab Adams. BS in Libr. Sci., U. So. Miss., 1965, MS in Libr. Sci., 1976. Dir. Pike-Amite Libr. System, McComb, Miss., 1965-66; libr. North Pike High Sch., Summit, Miss., 1966-85; media supr. North Pike Pub. Schs., Summit, 1985—. Mem. Miss. Libr. Assn. Methodist. Home: PO Box 368 Summit MS 39666-0368 Office: North Pike Schs RR 4 Box 11aa Summit MS 39666-9103

FAMIGLIETTI, CHRISTINE A., police officer; b. Bklyn., Oct. 25, 1960; d. Carmine and Gloria Madaline (Hildenbrand) F. Grad., N.Y.C. Police Acad. Bankteller supv. Nat. Westminster Bank, Great Neck, N.Y., 1980-86; police officer N.Y. Police Dept., 1986—. Recipient Cmty. Svc. award 113 Precinct Cmty. Coun., 1992. Mem. Police Benevolent Assn., Police Woman's Endowment. Office: NYPD 113 Precinct 16702 Baisley Blvd Jamaica NY 11434

FAN, LINDA C., investment company executive; b. Princeton, N.J., Mar. 22, 1956; d. Chung-Teh and Mook-Lan (Mui) F.; m. William A. Schaefer, Aug. 9, 1985; children: Ralph, Fred. AB, Princeton U., 1978; MBA, U. Chgo., 1982. Assoc. Salomon Bros., N.Y.C., 1982-85; assoc. Morgan Stanley & Co., N.Y.C., 1985-87, v.p., 1987-91, prin., 1991—. Office: Morgan Stanley Co Inc 5th Fl 1221 Ave of The Americas New York NY 10020

FANCHER, MARY FRANK, music educator; b. Altus, Okla., Dec. 11, 1912; d. Oscar Franklin and James Ina (Wood) Penick; m. Camillo Houston Fancher, may 17, 1933; children: Suzanne Litman, Lonnie Frank, Jack Carroll, Mary Jeanne Moorman. BS in Edn., No. Tex. State U., 1967. Pianist, singer Elk City, Okla., 1928-35; tchr. various schs., Tex., 1930-39, Okla., 1945-46; piano tchr. various pvt. studios, 1946—. Organist St. Paul Episcopal Ch., Altus, Okla., 1950-51; dir. piano festivals, Altus, 1940-70; actress, singer, and dancer numerous community programs and prodns., 1982—. Docent Arts Guild, Denton, Tex., 1980—, Greater Denton Arts Coun., 1980—; active Denton Benefit League, 1973—, Denton County Dems., 1973—; vol. Friends of Symphony, Denton, 1980-87, Denton Community Theatre, 1973—, Denton Light Opera Co. Named to Hall of Fame Piano Guild USA, 1968; recipient Meritorious Service award March of Dimes, 1953-73. Mem. Altus MacDowell Club Allied Arts (pres., v.p. 1968-70), Denton Music Tchrs. Assn. (charter, archivist), Tex. Music Tchrs. Assn., Okla. Music Tchrs. Assn. (charter, v.p. Altus br., adjudicator piano contests 1953-54), Nat. Guild Piano Tchrs., Shakespeare Club (sec., v.p. fine arts dept. 1976-79, pres., v.p., sec. music dept. 1975-78), Ariel Club (del. music dept. 1989—). Baptist. Home: 1201 N Austin St Apt 2 Denton TX 76201-3183

FANELLE, CARMELLA, dentist; b. Camden, N.J., Jan. 15, 1960; d. Joseph and Sylvia Catherine (Manganaro) F.; m. Frederick Matthew Rojek Jr., Nov. 15, 1986; 1 child, Eva Noel Rojek. BS, Chestnut Hill Coll., Phila., 1982; DDS, Temple U., 1986. Lic. dentist, Pa., N.J. Pvt. practice Phila., 1987-89, Barrington, N.J., 1990—; dentist, cons. Temple U., Phial, 1990; dir. gen. dentistry Temple Hosp., Phila., 1990. Recipient Am. acad. Dental Radiology award, 1986. Fellow Acad. Gen. Dentistry; mem. ADA, Pa. Dental Assn., Phila. County Dental Assn., So. Dental N.J. Dental Assn. Roman Catholic. Office: 34 Clements Bridge Rd Barrington NJ 08007-1802

FANGEROW, KAY ELIZABETH, nurse; b. Thomas, Okla., June 27, 1952; d. Byron Frederick and Wilma Jean (Bickford) Mayfield; children: David Andrew, Sarah Elizabeth; m. Stephen Fangerow. Student Oral Roberts U., 1970-71; BS in Nursing magna cum laude, Calif. State U.-Long Beach, 1975; MS in Health Care Adminstrn., U. LaVerne, 1991. RN, Calif.; cert. pub. health nurse. Staff nurse pediatrics service Long Beach Meml. Hosp., 1974-75, Riverside (Calif.) Community Hosp., 1975-76, Parkview Community Hosp., Riverside, 1982-84; supervising pub. health nurse County Health Dept., San Bernardino, Calif., 1976—; cons. Am. Home Health, Santa Ana, Calif., 1986—. Instr. Inland Counties chpt. Am. Cancer Soc., Riverside, 1977—, also mem. pub. and profl. edn. coms. Mem. Am. Pub. Health Assn. (co-author abstract 1986, 87, 89, coordinator hypertension worksite project, diabetes control project, pub. health nursing homeless project, presenter ann. meeting 1986, 87, 89), Pub. Health Nurse Group (chmn. 1977-78, vice chmn. profl. preformance com. 1978, sec. peer rev. com. 1978), So. Calif. Pub. Health Assn., Pub. Health Advs., Vis. Nurse Assn. Pomona (West End utilization rev. com.). Democrat. Home: PO Box 3308 Running Springs CA 92382-3308

FANNIN, JUANITA JUDE, career planning administrator; b. Pilgrim, Ky., May 14, 1949; d. David Stepp and Ethel (Fredrick) Jude; m. Donald Ray Fannin, Aug. 19, 1967; children: Sherrie R., Stephanie L. AA, Prestonsburg C.C., 1985; AB, Morehead State U., 1985, MA, 1988, cert. in spl. edn., 1990. Cert. guidance counselor, Ky. Owner, mgr. RoSan Dress Shoppe, Kermit, W.Va., 1975-80; owner, dir. Inez (Ky.) Med. Clinic, 1980-81; tchr. spl. edn. Martin County Sch. System, Inez, 1986-88; guidance counselor Ky. Tech.-Mayo Campus, Paintsville, 1988—. Mem. ASCD, Am. Vocat. Assn., East Ky. Vocat. Assn. (pres.-elect 1991-92), East Ky. Counselor Assn., Ky. Counselor Assn. Baptist. Home: PO Box 1117 Inez KY 41224-1117 Office: Ky Tech Mayo Campus 513 3rd St Paintsville KY 41240-1032

FANNING, ELEANOR, lawyer; b. Warren, Ohio, May 19, 1949; d. Arthur and Irene Lillian (Elefant) F. BA, Syracuse U., 1968; JD, Temple U., 1974. Bar: Pa. 1974. Law clk. Isaac S. Garb, Pres. Judge Bucks County, Doylestown, Pa., 1974-75; mental health rev. officer County of Bucks, Doylestown, 1975—; sole practice law, Trevose, Pa., 1980—. V.p. Fedn. Mercer and Bucks Counties; bd. dirs. Abrams Hebrew Acad., Big Sister, Phila., 1982-84. Recipient Sara A. Shulman award Temple U. Law Sch., 1974. Mem. ABA, Pa. Bar Assn., Bucks County Bar Assn. Democrat. Office: Ste 204 Two Neshaminy Interplex Trevose PA 19053

FANNING, KATHERINE WOODRUFF, editor, journalism educator; b. Chgo., Oct. 18, 1927; d. Frederick William and Katherine Bower (Miller) Woodruff; m. Marshall Field, Jr., May 12, 1950 (div. 1963); children: Frederick Woodruff, Katherine Woodruff Stephen, Barbara Woodruff; m. Lawrence S. Fanning, 1966 (dec. 1971); m. Amos Mathews, Jan. 6, 1984. BA, Smith Coll., 1949; LLD (hon.), Colby Coll., 1979; LittD (hon.), Pine Manor Jr. Coll., 1984; LHD (hon.), Northeastern U., 1984; hon. degree, Harvard U., 1988, Smith Coll., 1988, Babson Coll., 1988, U. Alaska, 1989, Govs. State U., Ill., 1989. With Anchorage Daily News, from 1965, editor, pub., 1972-83; editor The Christian Science Monitor, 1983-88; fall fellow Inst. of Politics Harvard U., Cambridge, Mass., 1989; adj. prof. journalism Boston U., 1991—; dir. AP, 1988-89, Boston Globe Newspaper Co., 1992—; mem. nat. adv. com. Freedom Forum Media Studies Ctr.; sr. adv. bd. Joan Shorenstein Barone Ctr., Harvard U.; bd. dirs. Inst. for Global Ethics, Inst. for Journalism Edn. Trustee Kettering Found., Charles Stewart Mott Found.; bd. dirs. Ctr. for Fgn. Journalists, Boston Pub. Libr. Found.; bd. overseers Boston Symphony Orch. Recipient Elijah Parish Lovejoy award Colby Coll., 1979, Smith Coll. medal, 1980, Mo. medal of Honor, U. Mo. Journalism award, 1980. Mem. Am. Soc. Newspaper Editors (bd. dirs. 1981—, pres. 1987-88), Soc. Profl. Journalists, Coun. Fgn. Rels., St. Botolph Club (Boston), Badminton and Tennis Club (Boston). Home and Office: 330 Beacon St Boston MA 02116-1153

FANNY-DELL (FANNY-DELL HENDRICKS), artist, sculptor, educator; b. Trinidad, Colo., May 30, 1939; d. Troy Stephen and Madelene Leona (Ball) Swift; div. first husband; children: Dennis Howard, Kim Renee, Terry Don, Laura Beth Wigley; m. Cecil Gene Hendricks, Dec. 10, 1979; stepchildren: Richard, Elizabeth, Russell, K. Renee (dec.), Beverly. Student, South Oklahoma City Jr. Coll., 1978, Highline C.C., Seattle, 1980, Bellevue (Wash.) C.C., 1982-84. Freelance illustrator, 1978—; owner, artist Fannytastics, Seattle, 1983—; asst. instr. Bellevue C.C., 1984-90; vol. archaeol. field excavations, Okla., 1977-80; sec. to Okla. state archaeologist, Norman, 1977-78; exhibit preparer and coord. Spiro Mounds, Okla. State Pk. Visitor Ctr. Exhibits, 1978; asst. art lab. South Oklahoma City Jr. Coll., 1979; docent Cowboy Hall of Fame, Oklahoma City, 1979; artist, craftsman Bringloe Hist. Figures, Seattle, 1980-81. Shows include Bellevue (Wash.) Community Coll. Art Faculty Shows, 1986, 87, 88, 89, 90, St. David Religious and Fine Art Show, Lynwood, Mass., 1986, 87, 89, 93 (Best of Show cash award), Mercer Island Visual Arts League Summer Arts Festival, Mercer Island, Wash., 1982, 83, 85, 86, The Best and the Brightest, Scottsdale, Ariz., 1991; represented in permanent collections Pacific N.W. Mus. of Flight, Seattle, Okla. SPIRO Archaeol. State Park Interpretive Ctr., Stoval Mus. Okla. U., Norman; producer (videotapes) Wax Sculpture, 1988, Lost Wax Casting, 1988; commd. portraits of clay, bronze or concrete for pvt. collectors. Recipient 2d place award Art X 5 Show, Oklahoma City, 1979, 1st place medal SeaTac Visual Arts Olympics, 1984. Mem. Internat. Sculpture Ctr., Sculpture Source and Artist Trust, Western Art Assn., Exptl. Aircraft Assn. (historian 1982-88), Aircraft Owners and Pilots Assn. Office: Fannytastics 4735 S 158th St Seattle WA 98188

FANOS, KATHLEEN HILAIRE, osteopathic physician, podiatrist; b. Bremerhaven, Germany, Aug. 18, 1956; came to U.S., 1957; d. Homer Dantangelo and Ilse Helmar (Ochs) F. AAS in Music, Nassau C.C., Garden City, N.Y., 1976; BS in Music Edn., Hofstra U., 1978; D Podiatric Medicine, Coll. Podiatric Med. and Surg., Des Moines, 1987; DO, Coll. Osteo. Med. and Surg., Des Moines, 1994—. Tchr. music McKenna Jr. High Sch. and Eastlake Elem. Sch., Massapequa, N.Y., 1978-79; musician numerous profl. orgns., N.Y., Iowa, 1979—; preceptorship in podiatry Bayshore, N.Y., 1987-88; pvt. practice podiatry Hyde Park and Brookline, Mass., 1988-91; pvt. practice podiatry, Des Moines, 1991-92; ins. med. examiner Portamedic, Burlington, Mass., 1988-91. Mem. Phi Theta Kappa, Pi Kappa Lambda, Sigma Sigma Phi.

FANTALIS, MARYANNE, lawyer; b. Bethpage, N.Y., June 8, 1966; d. Pierre A. and Elfriede (Eisenhut) Lehmuller; m. Jeff Fantalis, May 27, 1990. BA in History, SUNY, Stony Brook, 1987; JD, Rutgers U., 1991. Bar: N.J. Jud. law clk. Marilyn Rhyne Herr, Flemington, N.J., 1991-92; assoc. atty. Skoloff & Nolfe, Livingston, N.J., 1992—.

FANTINI, JOANNE, multimedia executive; d. Dominick and Elizabeth (Murphy) F. BS in Engring., Lehigh U., 1986. Computer cons. Phila., 1982-90; asst. staff Lincoln Lab. MIT, Lexington, 1987-94; pres. Sound Image Multimedia, Cambridge, Mass., 1988—; mem. steering com. Electronic Guide Group, Cambridge, 1992—. Co-author (software) DNA Sequencer, 1992. Mem. Boston Computer Soc. (music dir. 1992-93). Office: Sound/Image Multimedia 107 South St Ste 605 Boston MA 02111

FANUS, PAULINE RIFE, librarian; b. New Oxford, Pa., Feb. 14, 1925; d. Maurice Diehl and Bernice Edna (Gable) Rife; m. William Edward Fanus, June 20, 1944; children: Irene Weaver, Larry William, Daniel Diehl. BS, State U., 1945; MLS, Villanova U., 1961; postgrad., Temple U., 1986—. Periodical librarian Tex. Coll. Arts Industries, Kingville, 1945; tchr. nursery sch. Studio Sch., Wayne, Pa., 1953-55; librarian circulation, reference Franklin Inst., Phila., 1963-66; asst. librarian Ursinus Coll., Collegeville, Pa., 1966; catalog librarian, instr. Eastern Coll., St. Davids, Pa., 1967-71; head libr. Agnes Irwin Sch., Rosemont, Pa., 1971-93, head libr. emeritus, 1993—. Book reviewer The Book Report. Mem. AAUP (chpt. sec. Eastern Coll. 1970-71), Pa. Library Assn. Home: Country Club Rd Phoenixville PA 19460 Office: Agnes Irwin Sch Ithan Ave Bryn Mawr PA 19010

FARACE, VIRGINIA KAPES, librarian; b. Hazleton, Pa., July 10, 1945; d. Elmer Bernard and Elizabeth E. (Kuntz) Kapes; m. Frank John Farace, May 9, 1970. BA, Rider U., 1967; MLS, Rutgers U., 1968. Reference and govt. documents librarian Hazleton Area Pub. Libr., 1968-70; libr. dir. Boynton Beach (Fla.) City Libr., 1970—; bldg. cons. Boynton Beach City Libr., 1973-74, 85-89, Palm Springs (Fla.) Pub. Libr., 1976, 86. Editor: (directory) Library Resources in Palm Beach County, 1979. Chair legis. com. Edn. Alliance, Palm Beach County, 1987-94; mem. strategic planning task force Palm Beach County Sch. Bd., 1990-91; chair job opportunity task force Project Mosaic, Palm Beach County, 1990-93, transition team 1993; chair budget com. Book Fest! A Literary Festival, Palm Beach County, 1990-93, mem. co-exhibitors com., 1994—; edn. com. Govs. Initiative for Teens, 1992—, sec. 1993—; mem. adv. coun. Santaluces High Sch., 1991—, chair, 1994—; mem. Congress Mid. Sch. Adv. Coun., 1992—; mem. Leadership Palm Beach County Class of 1994, mem. pub. issues com.; mem. task force Boynton Beach Historic Schs. Task Force, 1993; mem. community network Palm Beach County Sch. Bd., 1993—, safe schs. task force; mem. bd. dirs. Boynton Beach Hist. Soc., 1992—, chair by-laws com., 1993, chair nominating com., 1994-95. Mem. ALA, AAUW (v.p. Boynton Beach br. 1989—, state strategic planning com. 1990—, chair 1992, Woman of Change award 1991, state conv. planning com. 1992, chair credentials com. 1992, SE Fla. cluster rep. state bd., 1994—, chair state nominating com. 1994-95, mem. bylaws com. 1994-95), Southeastern Libr. Assn., Spl. Libr. Assn., Fla. Pub. Libr. Assn. (pres. 1989-90, chair library adminstrn. divsn., 1992-93, parliamentarian 1992-94, legis. com. 1993—, chair adult svcs. divsn. 1994-95), Palm Beach County Libr. Assn. (pres. 1979-80, citation for Leadership and Svc. 1980), Coop. Authority for Libr. Automation (treas. 1984-93, pres. 1993—), Boynton Beach C. of C. (chair edn. com. 1991—, mem. bd. dirs. 1992—, vice chair 1994—, parliamentarian 1993—, chair nominating com. 1994, outstanding com. chair 1992, Dir. of the Year 1993, 94), Alpha Xi Delta (pres. 1980-84). Roman Catholic. Home: Lake Clarke Shores 1841 Caribbean Rd West Palm Beach FL 33406 Office: Boynton Beach City Libr 208 S Seacrest Blvd Boynton Beach FL 33435-4499

FARAH, CYNTHIA WEBER, photographer, publisher; b. Long Island, N.Y., June 2, 1949; d. Andrew John and Aria Emma (Jelnikova) Weber; m. James Clifton Farah, Jan. 12, 1974 (div. 1992); children: Elise, Alexa. BA in Communications, Stanford U., 1971; MA, U. Tex., El Paso, 1992. Mem. prodn. staff Sta. KDBC-TV, El Paso, Tex., 1971-73; v.p. Sanders Co. Advt., El Paso, 1973-74, film critic El Paso Times, 1972-77; freelance photographer, El Paso, 1974—; pres. CM Pub., El Paso, 1981-89. Photographer, co-author: Country Music: A Look at the Men Who've Made It, 1982; author: Literature and Landscape: Writers of the Southwest, 1988; film critic Sta. KTEP, 1993—. Bd. dirs. N. Mex. State U. Mus. Adv. Bd., Las Cruces, 1982-90; dir., vice-chmn. Shelter for Battered Women, El Paso, 1981-86; active Jr. League, 1977-90, sustaining mem. 1990—, C. of C. Leadership El Paso Program, 1983-84; mem. El Paso County Hist. Comm., 1984-89, vice chmn., 1986, 87, El Paso County Hist. Alliance (v. chmn. 1986-88); trustee El Paso Community Found., 1984—; adv. bd. El Paso Arts Resources dept., 1987-93, chmn., 1991-93; mem. adv. bd. Tex. Film Alliance, 1991—, Tex. Ctr. for the

Book, 1987—; mem. literary adv. panel Tex. Commn. on Arts, 1991-93; mem. adv. coun. El Paso Bus. Com. for Arts, 1988-90; mem. adv. coun. Harry Ransom Humanities Rsch. Ctr. U. Tex., Austin; mem. Tex. Com. Humanities Bd., 1993—; mem. lit. panel Cultural Arts Coun. Houston, 1993. Recipient J.C. Penny Golden Rule award, 1989, Vol. Svc. award El Paso Bur. United Way, 1989, Clara Barton Medallion ARC, 1979, Conquistador award City of El Paso, 1991; named Outstanding Active Mem. Jr. League, 1987-88, Outstanding Sustaining Mem., 1993-94; named to El Paso Women's Hall of Fame, 1992. Mem. Western Lit. Assn., U. Tex. at El Paso Libr. Assn. (v.p. 1987-88, pres. 1989-91), Modern Lang. Assn., Stanford U. Alumni Assn. Episcopalian.

FARAN, ELLEN WEBSTER, publishing executive; b. Cambridge, Mass., June 17, 1951; d. James John and Ellen (Gallishaw) F. BA, Radcliffe Coll., 1973; MBA, Harvard U., 1981. Editorial asst. Folger Shakespeare Libr., Washington, 1974-77; editorial assoc. Internat. City Mgmt. Assn., Washington, 1977-79; gen. mgr. David R. Godine Pub., Boston, 1980-82; cons. Nat. Acad. Press, Washington, 1982-83; assoc. pub. Harper & Row, N.Y.C., 1983-90; chief fin. officer Farrar, Straus & Giroux, N.Y.C., 1990—; adj. faculty NYU Sch. of Continuing Edn., 1992—; speaker pub. course Radcliffe Coll., 1989—. Office: Farrar Straus & Giroux Inc 19 Union Sq W New York NY 10003-3304

FARBER, JACKIE, editor; b. Jersey City, Apr. 16, 1927; d. Herman B. and Pauline (Birnbaum) Levine; m. Samuel Farber, June 25, 1950 (div. 1981); children: Thomas Adam, John David; m. 2d Jay Topkis, Sept. 27, 1981. BA, Smith Coll., 1949. Editor Bernard Geis Assocs., N.Y.C., 1963-72; sr. editor Delacorte Press, N.Y.C., 1972-74, exec. editor, 1980-81, editor-in-chief, 1981-89, fiction editor, 1989—; sr. editor William Morrow, N.Y.C., 1974-78, Random House, N.Y.C., 1978-80; fiction editor Delacorte Press div. Bantam Doubleday Dell Pub. Group, 1980-91; v.p., fiction editor Delacorte Press divsn. Bantam Doubleday Dell Pub. Group, 1991—. Mem. Women's Media Group. Jewish. Home: 155 E 72d St New York NY 10021 Office: Bantam Doubleday Dell Pub Co 1540 Broadway New York NY 10036

FARBER, LILLIAN, retired photography equipment company executive; b. N.Y.C., Aug. 4, 1920; d. Louis and Fannie (Disraeli) Bachrach; m. Leonard L. Farber, Nov. 3, 1940 (div. 1975); children: Lindy Linder, Robert D., Peggy, Felicia Gervais. BA, NYU, 1940; MA, Sarah Lawrence Coll., 1966. Co-dir. Upward Bound Sarah Lawrence Coll., Bronxville, N.Y., 1966-70, dean student svcs., 1973-76; v.p., owner Zone VI Studios, Inc., Newfane, Vt., 1976-90, ret., 1990. One-woman photography shows include, Vt., N.Y. V.p. Greenburgh League Women Voters, Hartsdale, N.Y., 1955-63; state com. woman N.Y. State Dem. Com., 1968-70; family adv. Westchester Coun. of Social Agys., White Plains, N.Y., 1970-73; pres. bd. trustees Moore Free Libr., Newfane, 1977—; chmn. bd. trustees Marlboro (Vt.) Coll., 1978—; trustee Vt. Coun. on the Arts, 1992—; mem. Vt. Bicentennial Commn., 1990-91. Mem. ACLU. Home: Maple Hollow PO Box 265 Newfane VT 05345

FARBER, VIOLA ANNA, dancer, choreographer, educator; b. Heidelberg, Germany, Feb. 25, 1931; came to U.S., 1938, naturalized, 1944; d. Eduard and Dora (Schmidt) F.; m. Jeffrey Clarke Slayton, June 14, 1971. Student, Am. U., 1949-51, Black Mountain Coll., 1951-52. Instr. dance Adelphi U., Garden City, N.Y., 1953-65; dancer Merce Cunningham Dance Co., N.Y.C., 1952-65; instr. dance Adelphia U., N.Y.C., 1959-67, Bennington (Vt.) Coll., 1967-68, NYU, 1971-73; dir., tchr. Viola Farber Dance Studio, N.Y.C., 1969-84; also artistic dir., choreographer, dancer Viola Farber Dance Co., N.Y.C., 1969-86; chair dance dept. Sarah Lawrence Coll., 1988—; artistic dir. Centre National de Danse Contemporaine, Angers, France, 1981-83; dir. Found. Contemporary Performance Arts; tchr. Am. Dance Festival, Durham, N.C., 1987, ADF, Seoul, Korea, 1990; guest tchr. throughout U.S. and Europe including Holland, Germany, Denmark, others. Choreographer, Viola Farber Dance Co., Théâtre Contemporain d'Angers, France, Ballet Théâtre Français, Repertory Dance Theatre Utah, Manhattan Festival Ballet, Nancy Hauser Dance Co., Dance depts. Adelphi, NYU, Ohio State U. and U. Utah, Janet Gillespie and Present Co.; commd. by Heinz Found.; collaborated with Robert Rauschenberg and David Tudor on video tape Brazos River, 1976; choreographed Jeux Chorégraphique for Ballet Théâtre Français de Nancy, 1980, Extemporary Dance Co., London, Plymouth, Eng., 1984, London, 1986; performed Centre Pompidou, Paris, 1979; choreographer for Emlyn Claid, London, 1986, Pauline Daniels, London, 1986, Nat. Youth Dance Co., Eng., 1986, New Dance Ensemble, Mpls., 1988; choreographer Duet for Emmy and Karen, 1989; choreographed and performed Au Fil du Temps, Lyon, France, 1989, with Mathilde Monner Ainsi de Suite, Paris, 1992, Montpelier, 1994. Recipient Gold medal with Jeff Slayton, Paris Dance Festival, 1971; Guggenheim fellow, 1983-84; grantee NEA, 1975, 79, NEA, 1976, 81, N.Y. State Coun. on Arts, 1974-79, CAPS, 1974, 78, N.Y. Dept. Cultural Affairs, 1977. Office: Sarah Lawrence Coll Dept of Dance Bronxville NY 10708-5500

FARENTHOLD, FRANCES TARLTON, lawyer; b. Corpus Christi, Tex., Oct. 2, 1926; d. Benjamin Dudley and Catherine (Bluntzer) Tarlton; children: Dudley Tarlton, George Edward, Emilie, James Dougherty, Vincent Bluntzer (dec.). AB, Vassar Coll., 1946; JD, U. Tex., 1949; LLD, Hood Coll., 1973, Boston U., 1973, Regis Coll., 1976, Lake Erie Coll., 1979, Elmira Coll., 1981, Coll. of Santa Fe, 1985. Bar: Tex. 1949. Pvt. practice, 1949-65, 67-76, 80—; mem. Tex. Ho. of Reps., 1968-72; dir. legal aide Nueces County, 1965-67; asst. prof. law Tex. So. U., Houston; pres. Wells Coll., Aurora, N.Y., 1976-80; disting. vis. prof. Thurgood Marshall Tex. So. U., Houston, 1994-95. Mem. Human Relations Com., Corpus Christi, 1963-68, Corpus Christi Citizen's Com. Community Improvement, 1966-68; mem. Tex. adv. com. to U.S. Commn. on Civil Rights, 1968-76; mem. nat. adv. council ACLU; mem. Orgn. for Preservation Unblemished Shoreline, 1964—; Dem. candidate for Gov. of Tex., 1972; del. Dem. Nat. Conv., 1972, 1st woman nominated to be candidate v.p. U.S., 1972; nat. co-chmn. Citizens to Elect McGovern-Shriver, 1972; chmn. Nat. Women's Polit. Caucus, 1973-75; mem. Dem. platform com., 1988; trustee Vassar Coll., 1975-83; bd. dirs. Fund for Constl. Govt., Ctr. for Devel. Policy, 1983—, Mexican Am. Legal Def. and Ednl. Fund, 1980-83; chmn. Inst. for Policy Studies, 1986-91. Recipient Lyndon B. Johnson Woman of Year award, 1973. Mem. State Bar Tex. Office: 2929 Buffalo Speedway # 1813 Houston TX 77098

FARES-O'MALLEY, PATRICIA, psychotherapist; b. Chicago Heights, Ill., Oct. 24, 1947; d. Pasquale A. and Velma A. (Granno) Fares; m. James H. Kreske, Oct. 10, 1986; children: Christine, John F. O'Malley, Joshua Kreske. BA, St. Xavier Coll., 1969; MA, Gov.'s State U., 1981; postgrad., Valparaiso U. Pvt. practice Olympia Fields, Ill.; lectr. psychotherapy Chgo. State U., Prairie State Coll., Chicago Heights, Ill. Contbr. articles to profl. jours. Faculty scholar U. Southern Calif., 1981. Mem. Am. Psychol. Assn., Assn. Human Psychology, AACD.

FARGUES-MOORE, MONIQUE PIERRETTE, engineering educator; b. Bordeaux, Gironde, France, July 10, 1959; d. Pierre Marie and Marguerite (Denis) Fargues; m. Thomas Preston Moore, July 2, 1989. Engr., Ecole Superieure Engrs., Paris, 1982; MSEE, Va. Polytech. Inst., 1984, PhD, 1988. Asst. prof. elec. and computer engring. Naval Postgrad. Sch., Monterey, Calif., 1989—. Guide Monterey Bay Aquarium, 1992—. Mem. IEEE (reviewer 1987—, assoc. editor 1994—, ASILOMAR conf. on signals, systems and computers steering com. 1990—), Soc. Indsl. and Applied Math., Soc. Photo-Optical Instrumentation Engrs., World Wildlife Fund, Sierra Club, Am. Inst. for Cancer Rsch., Sigma Xi. Office: Naval Postgrad Sch 833 Dyer Rd Monterey CA 93943-5121

FARINELLI, JEAN L., public relations firm executive; b. Phila., July 26, 1946; d. Albert J. and Edith M. (Falini) F. BA, Am. U., Washington, 1968; MA, Ohio State U., Columbus, 1969. Asst. pub. relations dir. Dow Jones & Co., Inc., N.Y.C., 1969-71; account exec. Carl Byoir & Assocs., Inc., N.Y.C., 1972-74, v.p., 1974-80, sr. v.p., 1980-82; pres. Tracy-Locke/BBDO Pub. Relations, Dallas, 1982-87; pres. Creamer Dickson Basford, Inc., N.Y.C., 1987-88, chmn., chief exec. officer, 1988—; pres., chief exec. officer Eurocom Corp. & PR (U.S.), 1991, Corp. Graphics, Inc., 1992. Trustee Nat. Found. Infectious Diseases. Recipient PR CaseBook, PR Reporter, N.H., 1984, Silver Spur, Tex. Pub. Rels. Assn., Dallas, 1985, Matrix award Women in Comms., 1993. Mem. Pub. Rels. Soc. Am. (Silver Anvil award 1980-81, 85, Excalibur award Houston chpt. 1985, chmn. 1986 Silver Anvil awards, chmn. 1987 honors and awards com., chmn. 1989 Spring Conf. Counselors Acad., acad. exec. bd. 1990-91), Women in Comms. (Matrix award 1993), Nat. Investor Rels. Inst., Internat. Pub. Rels. Assn. (pub. rels. seminar), Arthur W. Page Soc. (trustee, treas.), Nat. Found. for Infectious Disease (trustee), The Wisemen. Home: 333 E 56th St New York NY 10022 Office: Creamer Dickson Basford 1633 Broadway New York NY 10019-6772

FARION, ANYA MARIA, sculptor; b. Glen Cove, N.Y., May 17, 1954; d. Dmytro and Maria Irena (Cybyk) F. Student, Istituto Statale dell'Arte, Massa, Italy, 1974; BFA, Manhattanville Coll., 1975. artist-in-resident N.Y. Found. for Arts, N.Y.C., 1986—. One woman shows Gallery OMYA, N.Y.C., 1984, 90; exhibited in group shows at Gen. Assembly Hall, UN, N.Y.C., 1977, Cork Gallery, Lincoln Ctr., N.Y.C., 1978, Ukrainian Cultural and Ednl. Ctr., Winnipeg, Can., 1981, The Pen and Brush, N.Y.C., 1985, Catharine L. Wolfe Art Club, Nat. Arts Club, N.Y.C., 1986, Warren Hotel, Spring Lake, N.J., 1987, Sensory Evolution Gallery, N.Y.C., 1988, Piazza Carducci, Seravezza, Italy, 1989, Biennial of Ukrainian Art Nat. Mus., Lviv, Ukraine, 1991, Ukrainian Inst. Am., N.Y.C., 1992, Gallery OMYA, N.Y.C., 1987, 93; represented in collections Nat. Mus., Kiev, Nat. Mus., Lviv, Ukraine, E. M. Warburg, Pincus & Co. Inc. and pvt. collections. Recipient 2d prize Internat. Sculpture Symposium, Ukraine, 1994; Fulbright grantee Bd. Fgn. Scholarships, Italy, 1988-89, artist grantee Com. for Visual Arts, 1984, 87, 90; child fund scholar Child Fund, Italy, 1989. Mem. Internat. Sculpture Ctr., Ukrainian Artists Assn. (gallery dir. 1991—), Ukrainian Art & Literary Club (v.p. 1993—). Home: # 5C 415 E 80th St New York NY 10021 Studio: 43 St Marks Pl New York NY 10003

FARKAS, CAROL GARNER, nurse, administrator; b. N.Y.C., Apr. 26, 1936; d. Charles Harry and Phyllis (Levine) Schotland; m. Theodore Arthur Garner, 1956 (dec. 1971); children: Charles Hugh Farkas Garner, Judi Beth Garner Farkas, Andrea Lee Garner Farkas Krupen; m. Robin Lewis Farkas, Oct. 17, 1972; adopted children: Bradford Lewis Farkas, Andrew Lawrence Farkas. BSN with distinction, Cornell U., 1976; MPH, Columbia U., 1980. Dir. Am. Inst. Life Threatening Illness & Loss, N.Y.C., 1980—; del. white House Conf. Aging, N.Y. State Gov.'s Conf. Aging; mem. N.Y. State Hospice Adv. Group, 1979-81; mem. adv. com. office health mgmt. N.Y. State Dept. Health, 1979-81; mem. select com. financing and licensure, com. legis. edn. Nat. Hsopice Orgn., 1980—, N.Y. task force on life and the law, 1994—; mem. Choice in Dying, 1991-92, Nat. Coun. Death and Dying, 1990-91, Soc. Right to Die, 1982-90; co-chair med. student conf. nursing com. Columbia Presbyn., N.Y.C., 1992. Co-editor: Nursing and Thanatology, 1982; contbr. articles to profl. publs. Mem. Sigma Theta Tau. Home: 730 Park Ave New York NY 10021-4945

FARKAS, EVA HAUSER, accountant; b. Chgo., June 20, 1941; d. Fred and Sylvia (Wolfson) Hauser; m. Martin Joseph Farkas, July 1, 1962; children: Earl Edward, Ronald Howard. BEd, Chgo. Tchrs. Coll., 1963; MS in Taxation, DePaul U., 1991. Tchr. 6th grade Sch. Dist. 152, Harvey, Ill.; bookkeeper Phillip Bernstein, CPA, Skokie, Ill.; acct. Walgreens, Deerfield, Ill., 1978; revenue agt. IRS, Chgo., 1978-88, mgr. revenue agt. group, 1988-89, tech. advisor to dist. dir., 1989—. Mem. Nat. Coun. of Jewish Women (life, fin. sec. 1992-93). Jewish. Home: 155 N Harbor Dr #3108 Chicago IL 60601 Office: IRS 230 S Dearborn Chicago IL 60604

FARLEY, BARBARA SUZANNE, lawyer; b. Salt Lake City, Dec. 13, 1949; d. Ross Edward Farley and Barbara Ann (Edwards) Farley Swanson; m. Arthur Hoffman Ferris, Apr. 9, 1982; children: Barbara Whitney, Taylor Edwards. BA with honors, Mills Coll., 1972; JD, U. Calif.-San Francisco, 1976. Bar: Calif. 1976. Extern law clk. to justice Calif. Supreme Ct., San Francisco, 1975; assoc. Pillsbury, Madison & Sutro, San Francisco, 1976-78, Bronson, Bronson & McKinnon, San Francisco, 1978-80, Goldstein & Phillips, San Francisco, 1980-84; ptnr., head litigation, Rosen, Wachtell & Gilbert, San Francisco, 1984-89; of counsel Lempres & Wulfsberg, Oakland, Calif., 1989—; arbitrator U.S. Dist. Ct. (no. dist.) Calif., San Francisco, 1981—, Calif. Superior Ct., San Francisco, 1984-89; judge pro tem San Francisco Mcpl. Ct., 1983—; probation monitor Calif. State Bar, 1990—; speaker Nat. Bus. Inst. Estate Adminstrn. Contbg. author Calif. Continuing Edn. of the Bar; mng. editor U. Calif.-San Francisco Constl. Law Quarterly, 1975-76; civil litigation reporter. Mills Coll. scholar, 1970-72, U. Calif.-San Francisco scholar, 1973-76. Mem. ATLA, San Francisco Bar Assn., Calif. Trial Lawyers Assn., San Francisco Trial Lawyers Assn., Alameda Bar Assn. Office: Lempres & Wulfsberg 300 Lakeside Dr Ste 2400 Oakland CA 94612-3539

FARLEY, CAROLE, soprano; b. Le Mars, Iowa, Nov. 29, 1946; d. Melvin and Irene (Reid) F.; m. Jose Serebrier, Mar. 29, 1969; 1 dau., Lara Adriana Francesca. MusB, Ind. U., 1968. Fulbright scholar Hochschule für Musik, Munich, 1968-69. (Musician of Month, Musical Am./Hi Fidelity 1977), Am. debut at Town Hall, N.Y.C., 1969, Paris debut, Nat. Orch., 1975, London debut, Royal Philharmonic Soc., 1975, S.Am. debut, Teatro Colon, Philharmonic Orch., Buenos Aires, 1975; soloist with, major Am. and European symphony orchs., 1970—, soloist, Welsh Nat. Opera, 1971, 72, Cologne Opera, 1972-75, Phila. Lyric Opera, 1974, Brussels Opera, 1972, Lyon Opera, 1976, 77, Strasbourg Opera, 1975, Linz Opera, 1969, N.Y.C. Opera, 1976, New Orleans Opera, 1977, Cin. Opera, 1977, Met. Opera Co., N.Y.C., 1977—, Zurich Opera, 1979, Chgo. Lyric Opera, 1981, Can. Opera Co., 1980, Düsseldorf Opera, 1980, 81, 84, Palm Beach Opera, 1982, Theatre Mcpl. Paris, 1983, Theatre Royale dela Monnaie Brussels, 1983, Teatro Regio, Turin, Italy, 1983, Nice Opera (France), 1984, 86, 87, 88, Cologne Opera, 1985, Teatro Comunale, Florence, Italy, 1985, BBC Opera, 1987, TeatroColon, Buenos Aires, 1987, 88, 89, Opera de Montpellier (France), 1988, 94, Theatre des Champs Elysees, Paris, 1988, Helsinki Festival, 1989, Tchaikovsky Opera Arias Pickwick/IMP Records, 1993, Met. Opera Premiere Shostakovich Opera Lady Macbeth of Mzensk, 1994, Theatre Capitole de Toulouse Wozzeck, 1994; on New Zealand Broadcasting Commn. Orchestral Tour, 1986; TV film for ABC Australia La Voix Humaine, also co-producer compact disc and video for BBC, London, 1990; co-producer compact disc and video The Telephone, 1990; recorded compact disc Weill, 1992, Metro. Opera Shostakovich: "Lady Macbeth", 1994, Strausslieder with Czech Philharmonic, 1995; recorded for Deutsche Gramophone, Chandos, CBS, BBC, ASV, RCA, Ricercar and Varese-Sarabande records, London/Decca Records, IMP Masters, Pickwick. Recipient Abiati prize for her role as Lulu, Italy, 1984, Deutsche Schallplatten award for recording Carole Farley Sings French Songs, 1988; named Alumni of Year, U. Ind., 1976. Mem. Am. Guild Mus. Artists. Home: 270 Riverside Dr New York NY 10025-5209

FARLEY, EDNA PEARL, retired educator, researcher; b. Graham, N.C., May 17, 1914; d. Edward Azariah and Daisy Bell (Covington) Everett; m. Lucien Farley, Dec. 27, 1947 (div. July 1971). BA, Bennett Coll., Greensboro, N.C., 1937; postgrad., U. N.C., 1945, Howard U., 1946-47, U. Cin., 1953-55. Cert. tchr. Tchr. Norwood (N.C.) High Sch., 1937-42, Olive Hill High Sch., Morganton, N.C., 1942-49, Blaenboro (N.C.) High Sch., 1949-50, Dyer Sch., Cin., 1950-61, Peaslee Sch., Cin., 1961-68, Rockdale Sch., Cin., 1968-81; ret. educator Edn. Civic Sch., Cin., 1981—; libr. Mt. Zion Meth. Ch., Cin., 1981—; fund raiser Marva Collins Sch., Cin., 1989—. Author: Teaching Reading, 1977, The Negro Heritage of Graham, N.C., 1990; editor commentaries Pride Mag., 1960; writer on edn. and civic subjects The Cin. Enquirer, 1990. Mem. Opera Guild, Cin., 1980—; pres. Nat. Coun. Negro Women, Cin., 1960. Recipient citation Ohio Ho. of Reps., 1993. Mem. AAUW (historian), Cin. Hist. Soc. (pub. rels.), Friends of Women's Studies (pub. rels.), Women's Classical Caucus (pub. rels.), Bennett Coll. Alumnae Assn. (sec.), Woman's City Club of Cin., Urban League of Cin., Phi Delta Kappa. Home: 39 Clinton Springs Ave Cincinnati OH 45217

FARLEY, IRENE HALÁSZ, secondary education educator; b. Budapest, Hungary, Feb. 10, 1942; came to U.S., 1957, naturalized, 1965; d. Nicholas and Elizabeth (Tenke) Halász; m. Robert James Farley, Mar. 17, 1966; children: Erin Elizabeth Farley Friday, Robin Margaret. BS, St. Joseph's U., Phila., 1965; MS, U. Pa., Phila., 1966, postgrad., 1970-80. Cert. tchr. math., Pa., tchr. social studies, Pa. Tchr. math. Ravenhill Acad., Phila., 1961-68, prin., 1968-73; tchr. math. Vero Beach (Fla.) Sr. High Sch., 1973-74, Lower Merion (Pa.) Sch. Dist., 1974-75; tchr. math., athletics coach Phila. High Sch. for Girls, 1975—; lectr. Chestnut Hill Coll., Phila., 1975; instr. Harcum Jr. Coll., Bryn Mawr, Pa., 1967-68; fgn. lang. monitor Radio Sta. WTEL, Phila., 1969-72; participant Dodge Faculty Devel. Seminar, Bryn Mawr, 1985-86. Mem. Penn Relay Carnival Officials U. Pa., 1975—, Gulph Mills (Pa.) Civic Assn., 1981—, Republican Party, Montgomery County, Pa., 1981—, Mother Divine Providence Ch., King of Prussia, Pa., 1981—. Recipient Ofcl. of Yr. award Greater Delaware Valley Track Ofcls. Coun., 1980, Olympic Ofcl. award The Athletics Congress and Internat. Amateur Athletics Fedn., 1984, Legion of Honor award Chapel of Four Chaplains, 1989; Acad. Yr. grantee NSF, 1965; U. Pa. scholar, 1966-68. Mem. U.S.A. Track and Field Assn., Nat. Coun. Tchrs. Math., Assn. Tchrs. Math. Pa. and Vicinity. Roman Catholic. Home: 189 Gypsy Ln Gulph Mills King Of Prussia PA 19406-3720 Office: Phila High Sch for Girls 1400 W Olney Ave Philadelphia PA 19141

FARLEY, JENNIE TIFFANY TOWLE, industrial and labor relations educator; b. Fanwood, N.J., Nov. 2, 1932; d. Howard Albert and Dorothy Jane (Van Wagner) Towle; m. Donald Thorn Farley Jr., June 16, 1956; children—Claire Hamlin, Anne Tiffany, Peter Towle. BA, Cornell U., 1954, MS, 1969, PhD, 1970. Mem. editorial staff Mademoiselle and Seventeen mags., N.Y.C., 1954-56; freelance writer, Eng., Sweden, Peru, 1956-67; lectr., research assoc., adj. asst. prof. Cornell U., Ithaca, N.Y., 1970-72, dir. women's studies, 1972-76, asst. prof. Sch. Indsl. and Labor Relations, 1976-82, assoc. prof., 1982-89, prof., 1989—, exec. bd. dirs. women's studies program, 1970—; vis. prof. Ctr. for Women Scholars and Research on Women Uppsala U., Sweden, 1985-86; trustee Cornell U., 1988-92. Author: Affirmative Action and the Woman Worker, 1979, Academic Women and Employment Discrimination, 1982; editor: Sex Discrimination in Higher Education, 1982, The Woman in Management, 1983, Women Workers in Fifteen Countries, 1985. Recipient Corinne Galvin award Tompkins County Human Rights Commn., 1987, Unsung Heroine award Cen. N.Y. NOW, 1991. Mem. AAUP, Ithaca AAUW (pres. 1980-82), Grad. Women in Sci., Sociologists for Women in Soc., Tompkins County NOW. Club: Cornell Women's of Tompkins County. Home: 711 Triphammer Rd Ithaca NY 14850-2504 Office: Cornell U Sch Indsl & Labor Rels Ithaca NY 14853

FARLEY, LOIDA LESLIE, healthcare administrator; b. Chgo., Oct. 21, 1953; d. Jesus Flecha and Martha (Lopez) Marcano; m. James Christopher Farley, June 4, 1977; children: Jonathan, Betsy, Anna. AA, Minn. Bible Coll., 1979; AS in Nursing, Rochester Community Coll., 1979. RN, Minn., Iowa. Nurse technician St. Mary's Hosp., Rochester, Minn., 1979; staff nurse Meth. Hosp., Rochester, 1979-82; nurse, houseparent Midwest Christian Children's Home, Peterson, Iowa, 1983-84; project coord. Bremer Care Facility Inc., Waverly, Iowa, 1985-86; svc. coord. Bremer County Care Facility, Waverly, Iowa, 1986-88, dir. nursing, coord. spl. olympics, asst. adminstr., 1988-90, asst. adminstr., dir. health svcs., 1991-94; instr. med. aide course Hawkeye Inst. Tech., Waterloo and Waverly, Iowa, 1988. Vol. CPR instr., Blackhawk chpt. ARC, 1987—, first aid instr., 1988—; vol. counselor Alternatives for Women Cirsis Pregnancy Ctr.; mem. Iowans for Life Nat. Right to Life, ARC Disaster Team; coord. Project Angel Tree of Prison Fellowship Ministries, 1991-92. Recipient commendation Bremer County Care Facility, 1986. Mem. Women's Fellowship, ARC (bd. dirs. Waverly chpt.). Office: Bremer Care Facility Inc 1951 Larrabee Ave Waverly IA 50677-9593

FARLEY, PATRICIA ANN, psychotherapist; b. Homestead, Fla., Sept. 7, 1950; d. Nicholas Tetro and Margaret Ann (Keffer) Moreo; m. A.J. Farley, Apr. 5, 1969 (div. June 1988); children: David, Kristen. BS magna cum laude, U. Houston, 1987, MA, 1990. Lic. chem. dependency counselor; cert. eating disorders therapist. Family counselor Rader Inst., Houston, 1987-89; facilitator Bay Area Coun., Houston, 1990-92; therapist The Meta Ctr., Houston, 1987—, pairs facilitator, 1989—; pvt. practice psychotherapist Houston, 1987—. Mem. Phi Kappa Phi, Alpha Chi. Office: 3730 Kirby Ste 250 Houston TX 77098

FARLEY, PEGGY ANN, finance company executive; b. Phila., Mar. 12, 1947; d. Harry E. and Ruth (Lloyd) F.; m. Reid McIntyre, Dec. 31, 1985 (div.); 1 child, Margaret Ruth Farley. AB, Barnard Coll., 1970; MA with high honors, Columbia U., 1972. Admissions officer Barnard Coll., N.Y.C., 1973-76; adminstr. Citibank NA, Athens, Greece, 1976-77; cons. Orgn. Resources Counselors, N.Y.C., 1977-78; sr. assoc. Morgan Stanley and Co. Inc., N.Y.C., 1978-84; mng. dir., chief exec. officer AMAS Securities Inc., N.Y.C., 1984—; also bd. dirs. AMAS Securities, Inc., N.Y.C.; bd. dirs. AMAS Group, London. Author: The Place Of The Yankee And Euro Bond Markets In A Financing Program For The People's Republic of China, 1982. Mem. Columbia U. Seminar on China-U.S. Bus., Rep. Senatorial Inner Circle, Fgn. Policy Assn. Mem. Asia Soc., China Inst., Met. Club, Econ. Club of N.Y. Republican. Presbyterian. Home: 146 E 89th St New York NY 10128 also: 908 Owassa Rd Newton NJ 07860-8920 Office: AMAS Securities Inc 520 Madison Ave New York NY 10022-4213

FARLEY, ROSEMARY CARROLL, mathematics and computer science educator; b. N.Y.C., Apr. 7, 1952; d. Joseph William and Nancy (Flaherty) C.; m. Dennis Michael Farley, Oct. 10, 1976; children: Christopher, Mary Ann, Brian, Nancy. BS, Coll. Mt. St. Vincent, 1974; MS, NYU, 1976, PhD, 1991. Instr. Fordham U., Bronx, N.Y., 1976-79; instr. Manhattan Coll., Bronx, N.Y., 1979-82, assoc. prof., 1989—; asst. prof. Coll. Mt. St. Vincent, Bronx, N.Y., 1982-88. Mem. Math. Assn. Am., Am. Math. Soc., Am. Statis. Assn. Democrat. Roman Catholic. Home: 120 Bennett Ave Yonkers NY 10701-6310 Office: Manhattan Coll Manhattan Coll Pky Bronx NY 10471

FARLEY, SARAH JANE, legal assistant; b. Evanston, Ill., Apr. 18, 1959; d. Donald Stephen and Georgia (Bark) F. BA in Polit. Sci., U. Minn., 1981; legal asst. cert., Roosevelt U., Chgo., 1981. Group leader status dept. West Pub. Co., Saint Paul, 1981-84; legal asst. Robins Zelle Larson & Kaplan, Mpls. and San Francisco, 1984-88, Zelle & Larson, San Francisco, 1988—. Mem. San Francisco Legal Asst. Assn., Bay Area Litigation Support Mgrs. Assn., Phi Beta Phi.

FARMER, DEBORAH KIRILUK, marketing professional; b. Richmond, Va., June 6, 1956; d. Curtis Wayne Kiriluk and Lilan Baltz Starford; m. Roger Paul Schatzel, Oct. 1993. Student, J. Sargeant Reynolds Community Coll., 1974-78, Va. Commonwealth U., 1978-79, John Tyler Community Coll., 1986. Paralegal asst. Hunton Willams, Richmond, 1974; coord. office svcs. Va. Housing Devel. Authority, Richmond, 1975-78; dist. adminstr. Lanier Bus. Products, 1978-80; exec. asst. Old Dominion Emergency Med. Svcs. Alliance, Richmond; asst program dir. Sta. WRVA-AM, Richmond, 1981-83; coord. local sales Stas. WRNL-AM and WRXL-FM, Richmond, 1983-84; sr. account exec. Sta. WTVR-FM, Richmond, 1984-85; mgr. nat. sales Sta. WQSF-FM, Richmond, 1985-88; nat. account exec. HNW&H, Atlanta, 1988-89; mgr. local sales Sta. WTKN/WHVE, St. Petersburg, Fla., 1989-90; gen. sales mgr. WFNS-AM, Tampa, Fla., 1990-91; sr. acct. exec. Staff Leasing Group, Tampa, 1991—; cons. mem., gov. adv. bd. EMS Pub. Info. Edn., Richmond, 1986; bd dirs. Travelers Aid Soc. Va., 1987-88, sec., mem. exec. comm., 1988; mem. task force study of women Va. Power, Richmond, 1988. Contbr. articles to profl. jours. CPR instr. ARC, Richmond, 1979-87, mem. VOAD com., 1994; emergency medical technician Manchester Vol. Rescue Squad., Richmond, 1979-86, sec. bd. dirs., 1979-81, pub. rels. officer, 1985-86; dir. disaster relief Tampa Bay Bapt. Assn., 1993—; chair pub. rels. com. FBC Brandon, 1990—. Am. Bus. Women's Assn. scholar, 1975. Mem. Am. Women in Radio and TV (charter, v.p. 1987-91). Republican. Baptist.

FARMER, ELAINE FRAZIER, state legislator; b. New Castle, Pa., Mar. 14, 1937; d. John R. and Pearle (McLure) Frazier; m. Sterling N. Farmer, Aug. 22, 1959; children: Heather, Drew. BBA, Case Western Reserve U., 1958, MEd, 1964. Employment supr. Stouffer Corp., Cleve., 1958-60; tchr. Lakewood Schs., Cleve., 1960-64; subs. tchr. North Allegheny Schs., Pitts., 1972-77; agt. Howard Hanna Real Estate Services, Pitts., 1977-86, mgr., 1983-86; elected mem. Ho. of Reps., Harrisburg, Pa., 1986—; state dir. Women in Govt. Councilman Town of McCandless, Pa., 1980-86; trustee Northland Libr., Pitts., 1980-85, North Hills Passavant Hosp., 1990-92; liaison McCandless Planning Commn., 1984-86; mem. comty. adv. bd. St. Barnabas Nursing Home, coun. Pitts. Cancer Inst., 1994—. Mem. Nat. Order Women Legislators, Am. Legis. Exch. Coun., North Hills C. of C. Republican. Presbyterian. Office: House of Reps PO Box 197 Harrisburg PA 17120-2020

FARMER, HELEN SWEENEY, psychology educator; b. Ottawa, Can., Dec. 23, 1929; d. Henry Bertrum and Mabel Sarah (Switzer) Sweeney; m. James A. Farmer, Jan. 25, 1955; children: James Sweeney, David Sargent, Paul Alexander. BA, Queens U., Can., 1952; BD, Union Theol. Sem., 1955; MA, Columbia U., 1969; PhD, UCLA, 1972. Lic. psychologist, Ill. Dir. evaluation services INSGROUP, Long Beach, Calif., 1971-74; asst. prof. counseling psychology U. Ill., Urbana, 1974-81, assoc. prof., 1981-87, prof., 1987—. Author: (with Tom Backer) New Career Options for Women: Counselor's Sourcebook, 1977, New Career Options for Women: A Woman's Guide, 1977; contbr. articles to profl. jours. Queens U. scholar, 1949, Can. govt., 1949-52; grantee Nat. Inst. Edn., 1974, 76, 78; grantee NSF, 1991. Fellow APA (div. sec.), Am. Psychol. Soc.; mem. AACD, Am. Ednl. and Rsch. Assn. (div. v.p. 1984-86). Home: 2204 S Staley Rd Champaign IL 61821-9763 Office: U Ill Sch Edn Dept Ednl Psychology Champaign IL 61820

FARMER, JANENE ELIZABETH, artist, educator; b. Albuquerque, Oct. 16, 1946; d. Charles John Watt and Regina M. (Brown) Kruger; m. Michael Hugh Bolton, Apr. 1965 (div.); m. Frank Urban Farmer, May, 1972 (div.). BA in Art, San Diego State U., 1969. Owner, operator Iron Walrus Pottery, 1972-79; designer ceramic and fabric murals, Coronado, Calif., 1979-82; executed commns. for clients in U.S.A., Can., Japan and Mex., 1972—; designer fabric murals and bldg. interiors; painter rare and endangered animals, Coronado and La Jolla, Calif., 1982—; tchr. Catholic schs., San Diego, 1982-87, Ramona Unified Sch. Dist., 1988—; instr. U. Calif., San Diego, 1979-83, 92—, resident artist. Mem. Coronado Arts and Humanities Coun., 1979-81. Grantee Calif. Arts Coun., 1980-81; U. San Diego grad. fellow dept. edn., 1984. Mem. Am. Soc. Interior Designers (affiliate). Roman Catholic. Home: 4435 Nobel Dr Apt 35 San Diego CA 92122-1559

FARMER, JUDY FOLEY, educator, special education; b. Roanoke, Va., July 8, 1946; d. Trevor Monroe and Mayme (Thompson) Foley; children: Troy Norman, Sean Neil. BA in English, Edn., Randolph-Macon Women's Coll., 1969; MEd in Diagnostic and Prescriptive Teaching/Learning Disabilities, Coll. William & Mary, 1978; postgrad. in Spl. Edn., Adminstrn., Va. Polytech. Inst., 1980—. Cert. tchr. English, Spl. Edn., Va. Tchr. Henry County Schs., Collinsville, Va., 1969-70; libr. Va. Western C.C., Roanoke, Va., 1970-73; tchr. learning disabled Hampton (Va.) City Schs., 1979-80, Montgomery County Schs., Christiansburg, Va., 1980-82, Roanoke County Schs., Salem, Va., 1982-83; coord. spl. svcs. Bland (Va.) County Pub Schs.; tchr. learning disabled Botetort County Pub. Schs., Fincastle, Va., 1987-88, Roanoke City Schs., 1988—; instr. Upward Bound Roanoke Coll., Salem, Va., 1992—; adj. instr. Dominion Bus. Sch., Roanoke, 1992—. Author: (book of poetry) Life Goes On and On and On; developer of ednl. materials (tests, learning packages); presenter at profl. seminars and workshops. Mem. NAFE, Va. Middle Sch. Assn., Va. Assn. Edn. Gifted, Peninsula Orgn. for Exceptional Children, Coun. for Exceptional Children (v.p. New River chpt. 1982-83, pres. 1983-84, sec. Va. Fedn., 1983-84), Internat. Reading Assn. (bd. dirs. Newport News 1975-78). Home: 328 E Cleveland Ave Vinton VA 24179-2625

FARMER, LESLEY SUZANNE JOHNSON, library director; b. Spokane, Wash., June 15, 1949; d. Leslie Harlan and Emma Cecelia (Johnson) Johnson; m. Mark Lesley Farmer; 1 child, Christopher. BS in English, Whitman Coll., 1971; MLS, U. N.C., 1972; EdD, Temple U., 1981. Cert. tchr., Calif. Info. specialist Balt. County Pub. Library, Randallstown, Md., 1972-73; tech. libr. Singer Bus. Machines, San Leandro, Calif., 1974-75; instr., libr. Peace Corps, Tunis, Tunisia, 1975-77; media specialist Archdiocese Phila., 1977-81; asst. prof. Va. Commonwealth U., Richmond, 1981-82; young adult libr. Meml. Libr. Radnor Twp., Wayne, Pa., 1982-83; libr. dir. San Domenico Sch., San Anselmo, Calif., 1984-93; tchr. libr. media Redwood High Sch., Lakespur, Calif., 1993—; adj. prof. Villanova (Pa.) U., 1982-83, San Jose State U., 1988—, U. San Francisco, 1990—; speaker Calif. Libr. Assn., 1987-93, Calif. Med. Libr. Assn., 1991—; cons. Va. Dept. Edn., 1981-82, Marin County (Calif.) Office Edn., 1984-87. Author: Cooperative Learning Activities in the Library Media Center, 1991, I Speak Hyper Card, 1992, Young Adult Services in the Small Library, 1992, Creative Partnerships, 1992, When Your Library Budget Is Almost Zero, 1993; editor: Media and the Young Adult, 1985; contbr. articles to profl. jours. Chair S. Marin County Girl Scouts USA, 1986-88. Grantee NEH, 1986, Marin County Computer Edn. Consrotium, 1984-86, Libr. Svcs. and Constrn. Act, 1992, U.S. Dept. Edn., 1993, 94, Carolina Disting. Alumnus award, 1994. Mem. ALA (chmn. rsch. com. young adult svcs. dir. 1985-88, computer applications com. 1985-88, media selective com. 1991-92, Hanne rsch. award 1990), Young Adult Libr. Svcs. (bd. dirs. 1993-96), Calif. Libr. Assn., Calif. Media and Libr. Educators (sect. editor), Cath. Libr. Assn. (sect. pres. 1989-91, editor 1992-93). Democrat. Roman Catholic. Home: 135 Golden Hinde Passage Corte Madera CA 94925-1909 Office: Redwood High Sch 395 Doherty Dr Lakwspur CA 94933

FARMER, MARTHA KNIGHT, academic administrator, executive; b. Roanoke, Ala., July 21, 1938; d. Edward Wilson Jr. and Bobbie (Neely) Knight; m. Claude William Farmer Jr., Oct. 10, 1958; children: Claude William III, Andrea Elizabeth. BS, U. Ala., 1960, MSc, 1965; PhD, U.S.C., 1977. CPA, Ga. Tchr. math. Aiken (S.C.) Jr. High Sch., 1964-66; from instr. to prof. Sch. of Bus. Adminstrn., Augusta (Ga.) Coll., 1966-94, coord. acctg., MIS and bus. law depts., 1982-85, acting assoc. dean, 1985-86, acting dean, 1986-88, dean, 1988-91, 93-94; acting pres. Augusta (Ga.) Coll., 1991-93; staff acct. Baird and Co., CPAs, Augusta, 1970-71; pres. Castleton State Coll., 1994—; editorial advisor Soc. for Advancement of Mgmt. Advanced Mgmt. Jour., North Dalmouth, Mass., 1990-92. Bd. dirs. Augusta chpt. ARC, 1991-92; mem. cmty. adv. bd. Jr. League Augusta, 1992-94. Mem. Am. Acctg. Assn. (com. rels. 2-yr. faculty), Ga. Soc. CPAs (sec.-treas., v.p., program chair Augusta chpt., pres. 1983-87), So. Bus. Adminstrn. Assn. (exec. com. 1988-94, sec.-treas. 1990-92, v.p. for programs 1993-94), Edn. Found. Ga. Soc. CPAs (bd. dirs. 198-94), Augusta C. of C. (econ. devel. com. 1988-92, chair existing industry com. 1989-90, bd. dirs. 1989-91, vice chmn. edn. com. 1991, exec. com. 1992-93, treas. 1994), Rotary, Phi Kappa Phi (editorial advisor Nat. Forum 1989-93). Home: PO Box 1425 Castleton VT 05735-1425 Office: Castleton State Coll 2500 Walton Way Castleton VT 05735

FARMER, MARY BAUDER, small business owner; b. San Diego, Nov. 30, 1953; d. Chester Robert and Dixie (Cook) Bauder; m. L. Michael Dowling, July 1990. BS, Auburn U., 1986; postgrad., Ga. State U., 1992—. Exec. dir. Birmingham Woman's Med. Clinic, Ala., 1975-80; pres. Beacon Clinic, Montgomery, Ala., 1980-83; ptnr. Hill, Rose and Farmer, Atlanta, 1988-90; owner, mgr. Mary Farmer Fine Art, Atlanta, 1990—; v.p. Global Interests Inc., 1990—. Author, pub.: The Landlord's Primer for Georgia: A Self-Help Guide for Inexperienced Landlords. Bd. dirs. Planned Parenthood Greater Atlanta; mem. pub. rels. com. Project Open Hand, Ga. Citizens for Arts; mem. Bus. Com. for Arts. Mem. LWV (action com. 1982-86), Ga. Women's Agenda (founder), Omicron Delta Kappa. Democrat. Home: 690 Greystone Park Atlanta GA 30324

FARMER, PAMELA LYNN, physician; b. Elwood, Ind., Feb. 4, 1958; d. George Patrick and Olive Ruth (Colman) F. BA with honors, U. N.C., 1980; MD, East Carolina U., 1989. Resident in family practice Duke U. Med. Ctr., Durham, N.C., 1990-92; commd. med. officer USPHS, 1992, advanced through grades to lt. comdr., 1992; physician Mammoth Clinic, Yellowstone Nat. Park, Wyo., 1992-95. Mem. Am. Acad. Family Physicians, Am. Med. Women's Assn., Physicians for Social Responsibility.

FARMER, SUSAN LAWSON, broadcasting executive, former secretary of state; b. Boston, May 29, 1942; d. Ralph and Margaret (Tyng) Lawson; m. Malcolm Farmer, III, Apr. 6, 1968; children: Heidi Benson, Stephanie Lawson. Student, Garland Jr. Coll., 1960-61, Brown U., 1961-62. Mem. Providence Home Rule Charter Commn., 1979-80; sec. of state State of R.I., Providence, 1983-87; chief exec. officer, gen. mgr. Sta. WSBE-TV, Providence, 1987—; spl. adv. R.I. Family Ct., 1978-83; mem. nat. voting standards panel Fed. Election Commn. co-chmn. Nat. Voter Edn. Project; mem. electoral coll., 1984; chmn. Gov.'s Com. on Ethics in Govt., 1985-86; mem. teaching facility and adv. panel Internat. Ctr. on Election Law and Adminstrn.; mem. natl. edn. adv. com. Pub. Broadcasting System, 1987—; trustee Eastern Ednl. TV Network, 1987—. Bd. dirs. Justice Resources Corp., Marathon House, Inc., R.I. Council Alcoholism, R.I. Hist. Soc., Planned Parenthood (R.I. chpt.), R.I. Rape Crisis Ctr., The Newport Inst.; mem. Mayor's Task Force on Child Abuse, R.I. Film Commn.; v.p. Miriam Hosp. Found.; mem. adv. com. Women in Polit. and Govtl. Careers Program, U. R.I., 1985—; mem. adv. bd. Com. for Study of Am. Electorate-Ford Found. Project-Efficacy in State Voting Laws, 1986; mem. Commn. to Study Length of Election Process, 1985—; steering com. Nat. Fund for America's Future, Project Vote R.I.; bd. dirs. Dawn for Children Tng. Thru Placement; pres. Channel 36 Found.; bd. dirs. R.I. Anti-Drug Coalition Exec. Com. Named Woman of Yr., Nat. Women's Polit. Caucus, 1980. Mem. LWV, N.E. Assn. Schs. and Colls. (com. on tech. and course instns.), So. Ednl. Comms. Assn. (bd. dirs. 1993—), R.I. Women's Polit. Caucus (Woman of Yr. 1980), Bus. and Profl. Women (Woman of Yr. 1984), Common Cause, Save the Bay, Women for Non-nuclear Future, Providence Preservation Soc., Orgn. State Broadcasting Execs, Agawam Hunt Club, Mill Reef Club (Antigua, West Indies). Home: 147 Lloyd Ave Providence RI 02906-1552 Office: Sta WSBE-TV 50 Park Ln Providence RI 02907-3145

FARNHAM, MARY GLADE SIEMER, artist; b. Ross, Calif., Nov. 1, 1924; d. Albert Henry and Mabel Meta (Jones) Siemer; children: Thomas Ross, Evan Neil, Gwen Marie, William Blair, Hugh Porter. Student Marin Jr. Coll., 1942-43, Goucher Coll., 1943-44; B.A., U. Calif.-Berkeley, 1947. Profl. athlete, Curry Co., Yosemite, Calif., 1945; advt. prodn. mgr. City of Paris/Hale's, San Francisco, 1947; advt. artist Lipman Wolfe, Portland, Oreg., 1947-48; advt. layout artist Meier & Frank, Portland, 1948; art dir. Olds & King, Portland, 1948-50; free lance comml. artist, Portland, 1950-56; pres. Marin County Devel. Co., San Anselmo, Calif., 1963-78; pres., designer Mary Farnham Designs, Inc., Portland, 1983-89. Exhibited in 14 one woman shows and numerous group shows, U.S. & abroad. Mem. pub. art selection panel II, Met. Arts Commn., Portland, 1982-83; bd. dirs. N.W. Artists Workshop, Portland, 1977-78; sec. Artist Membership, Portland Art Assn., 1973-74. Episcopalian. Club: Multnomah Athletic. Avocations: swimming; diving.

FARQUHAR, KAREN LEE, commercial printing company executive, consultant; b. Warwick, N.Y., May 27, 1958; d. Wesley Thomas and Margaret Anne (Storms) Kervatt; m. David W. Farquhar, July 17, 1982 (div. Feb. 1990); 1 child, Lauren Nichole. Assoc. Sci., Roger Williams Coll., 1978, BS cum laude, 1980. Office mgr. Price-Rite Printing Co., Dover, N.J., summer 1975-76; cons. SBA, Bristol, R.I., 1978-80; account exec. P.M. Press Inc., Dallas, 1980-90, sales trainer, 1984-85; v.p. KDF Bus. Forms Inc., Dallas, Tex., 1984-90; account exec. Jarvis Press, Dallas, 1990—; pres. Print Trends, Dallas, 1990—. Printer, Tex. Aux. Charity Auction Orgn., Dallas, 1985, Crescent Gala, Dallas, 1986, Cystic Fibrosis, Dallas, 1989-93, L.E.A.P. Found., 1992—, Dallas Soc. of Visual Comm., 1992, AIDS Resources Com., Dallas chpt. Cerebral Palsy, 1994, Hoyd-Paxton AIDS Benefit, 1994, Loyd-Paxton AIDS Charity, Cerebal Palsey Charity. Recipient various awards Clampitt Paper Co., Dallas, 1982, P.M. Press Inc., 1983-89, Mead Paper Co., 1985-89. Mem. Printing Industry in Am. (recipient Judges Favorite award 1992, Best of Show Hon. Mention award 1994), Internat. Assn. Bus. Communicators, Nat. Bus. Forms Assn. Republican. Baptist. Avocations: piano, aerobics. Home: 325 Brooks Lane Coppell TX 75019

FARQUHAR, MARILYN GIST, cell biology and pathology educator; b. Tulare, Calif., July 11, 1928; d. Brooks DeWitt and Alta (Green) Gist; m. John W. Farquhar, June 4, 1952; children: Bruce, Douglas (div. 1968); m. George Palade, June 7, 1970. AB, U. Calif., Berkeley, 1949, MA, 1952, PhD, 1955. Asst. rsch. pathologist Sch. Medicine U. Calif., San Francisco, 1956-58, assoc. rsch. pathologist, 1962-64, assoc. prof., 1964-68, prof. pathology, 1968-70; rsch. assoc. Rockefeller U., N.Y.C., 1958-62, prof. cell biology, 1970-73; prof. cell biology Sch. Medicine Yale U., New Haven, 1973-87, Sterling prof. cell biology and pathology, 1987-90; prof. pathology div. cell molecular medicine U. Calif., San Diego, 1990—, coord. div. cellular and molecular medicine, 1991—. Mem. editorial bd. numerous sci. jours.; contbr. articles to profl. jours. Recipient Career Devel. award NIH, 1968-73, Disting. Sci. medal Electron Microscope Soc., 1987. Mem. NAS, Am. Acad. Arts and Scis., Am. Soc. Cell Biology (pres. 1981-82, E.B. Wilson medal 1987), Am. Assn. Investigative Pathology, Am. Soc. Nephrology (Homer Smith award 1988). Home: 12894 Via Latina Del Mar CA 92014-3730

FARQUHARSON, PATRICE ELLEN, primary school educator; b. West Haven, Conn., Feb. 10, 1956; d. Robert Douglas and Margaret Ellen (Dietle) F. BS in Edn., U. Conn., 1978; MS in Edn., So. Conn. State U., 1984; postgrad., Nova Southeastern U., 1992. Cert. tchr., Conn. Asst. dir. West Haven (Conn.) Child Devel. Ctr., 1978-82, exec. dir., 1982—; edn. cons. dept. pediatrics div. child and family studies U. Conn., 1993—; cons. early childhood edn., workshop presenter, nat. and New Eng., 1987—; profl. cheerleader The New Eng. Patriots football team, 1980; dir., ptnr. New Eng. Cheerleading Camp, West Haven, 1982-84; cheerleading coach U. New Haven, 1982-90. Scholar Conn. Early Childhood Edn. Coun., 1993, 94. Mem. Nat. Assn. Edn. Young Children, Conn. Assn. Edn. Young Children, Early Childhood Coop. Orgn., Coalition for Children, Dirs. Forum, Gov. Adv. Coun. Early Childhood Edn., South Ctrl. Conn. Agy. on Aging (adv. coun.). Home: 5 Sunflower Cir West Haven CT 06516-6229 Office: West Haven Child Devel Ctr 201 Noble St West Haven CT 06516-6099

FARR, LONA MAE, non-profit executive; b. Phila., June 4, 1941; d. Alonzo Schroeder and Lillyan (Nickels) F.; m. Malcolm J. Gross, Aug. 24, 1963 (div. Mar. 1976); children: Andrea Lillyan, Stacey Jane, John Farr; m. David V. Voellinger, Sept. 27, 1981. AB in History and English, Muhlenberg Coll., 1962; MS in Edn., Temple U., 1968. Advanced cert. in fund raising. Tchr. Swain Sch., Allentown, Pa., 1962-63, St. Monica's Sch., Berwyn, Pa., 1963-65, Hebrew Day Sch., Scranton, Pa., 1965-66; pub. rels. assoc. Muhlenberg Coll., Allentown, 1973-75, dir. alumni affairs, 1975-77; dir. devel. and pub. rels. Allentown Coll. St. Frances de Sales, Allentown, 1977-81; dir. pub. rels. Good Shepherd Home, Allentown, 1981-84, dir. devel., 1984-87, group exec., v.p. instnl. devel., 1987-92; v.p. instl. devel. Luth. Home at Topton, Pa., 1992—. Prodr. (films) More Than a Name, 1983 (Golden Eagle award 1984), Venture of Faith, 1984 (silver medal N.Y. Film Festival 1985), Spirit of Good Shepherd Day, 1987, Aspects of Topton, 1993 (1st place PANPHA), Topton New Century, 1993 (1st place PANPHA), They Came to Topton, 1994, (video) The Best You Can Be, 1988. Bd. dirs. Muhlenberg Coll., Kids Peace, Orefield Symphony, Baum Sch. Art, Allentown, United Way Lehigh County (WELD Silver Bowl award 1993); founding bd. dirs. Lehigh Valley Interfaith TV; adviser Lehigh County Human Svcs., Allentown, 1986-91. Recipient Disting. Sales award Sales and Mktg. Execs. Lehigh Valley, 1984, Weld Silver Bowl award United Way, 1993. Mem. Pub. Rels. Soc. Am., Nat. Soc. Hosp. Devel., Nat. Soc. Fund Raising Execs. (chair cert. bd., rep. nat. bd. dirs. 1987—, founding pres. Ea. Pa. chpt. 1986-88, Outstanding Exec. award 1988, Fund Raising Exec. of Yr. 1988, United Way Weld award 1993, Nat. Cert. Bd. Appalachian Health Care Pub. Rels./Mktg. Assn. (pres. 1987), Ea. Pa. BBB (bd. dirs.), Muhlenberg Coll. Alumni Assn. (pres. 1981-85), Rotary (bd. dirs. Allentown 1988—, pres. 1993-94), Quota Club (pres. Allentown 1986-88). Home: 2238 W Chew St Allentown PA 18104-5548 Office: Lutheran Home at Topton 1 S Home Ave Topton PA 19562-1399

FARR, PATRICIA HUDAK, librarian; b. Youngstown, Ohio, Mar. 10, 1945; d. Frank Francis and Anna Frances (Tylka) Hudak; m. William Howard Farr, Aug. 28, 1971; children: Jennifer Anne, William Patrick. BA, Youngstown State U., 1970; MLS, U. Md., 1980. Children's libr. Pub. Libr. Youngstown and Mahoning (Ohio), 1970-71; asst. Fla. State U. Libr. Tallahassee, 1971-73; rsch. asst. John Hopkins U. Sch. Hygiene and Pub. Health, Balt., 1974-76; asst. Mary Washington Coll. Libr., Fredericksburg, Va., 1976-79; children's libr. Cen. Rappahannock Regional Libr., Fredericksburg, 1980-84, young adult svcs. coord., 1984-89, youth svcs. libr., 1989-91, young adult svcs. coord., 1991—. Revision editor HEW pub. Thesaurus of Health Edn. Terminology, 1976; compiler Health Edn. Monographs, 1974-76. Youngstown State U. scholar, 1963-64; R.V. Lowery Meml. scholar, 1979-80. Mem. ALA, Va. Libr. Assn. Democrat. Episcopalian. Club: Rappahannock Twirlers Square Dance. Home: 618 Kings Hwy Fredericksburg VA 22405-3156 Office: Cen Rappahannock Regional Library 1201 Caroline St Fredericksburg VA 22401-3701

FARR, REETA RAE, special education administrator; b. Edhube, Tex., Jan. 15, 1926; d. Paul Ray and Verna (Biggerstaff) Wright; m. Gerald Edward Self, June 1, 1946 (dec. Dec. 1977); children: Eddie, Lee; m. Barnie B. Farr Jr., Dec. 28, 1978. BS, Southeastern Okla. State U., 1959, MS, 1963. 1st grade tchr. Sherman (Tex.) Pub. Schs., 1959-61; 1st grade tchr. Denison (Tex.) Pub. Schs., 1961-64, spl. edn. tchr., 1964-72, spl. edn. counselor, 1972-76, spl. edn. diagnostician, 1976-85, dir. spl. edn., 1985—. Named Educator of Yr. Denison Edn. Assn., 1991. Mem. NEA, AAUW (pres. 1981-83), Tex. State Tchrs. Assn. (local pres. 1971), Tex. Ednl. Diagnostician Assn., Tex. Assn. Counseling and Devel., Phi Delta Kappa (sec./treas. 1983, del. 1978-93), Delta Kappa Gamma. Mem. Ch. of Christ. Home: PO Box 135 Denison TX 75021-0135

FARR, SIDNEY SAYLOR, editor, author; b. Stoney Fork, Ky., Oct. 30, 1932; d. Wilburn and Rachel (Saylor) S.; m. Leon Lawson, Feb. 23, 1947 (div. July 1967); children: Dennis Wayne, Bruce Alan; m. Grover V. Farr, Jan. 24, 1970. BA, Berea Coll., 1980. Assoc. editor Coun. of the So. Mountains, Berea, Ky., 1964-69; editor This Week in Asheville (N.C.) Daniels Graphics, 1970-71; editor Appalachian Heritage Berea Coll., 1985—. Author: (annotated bibliography) Appalachian Women, 1981; (narrative cookbook) More Than Moonshine, 1983, Table Talk: Appalachian Meals and Memories, 1995; (biography of near-death experiencer) What Tom Sawyer Learned from Dying, 1993. Mem. AAUW, Kiwanis (pres. Berea club 1992-93). Democrat. Home: 109 High St Berea KY 40403-1520 Office: Berea Coll Berea KY 40403

FARRAN, JACQUELINE LEE, consultant; b. Mt. Holly, N.J., May 28, 1955; d. Ralph Joseph and Dorothy Farran. AA, Asnuntuck Coll., Enfield, Conn., 1977; BA in Human Svcs. Adminstrn., Columbia Pacific U., San Rafael, Calif.; paralegal, Am. Inst. Paralegal Studies, 1987. Columnist Vol. Action Ctr., Hartford, Conn., 1977-79; proofreader Thrifty Reminder Newspaper, 1977-78; outreach worker Town of Windsor Locks, Conn., 1979-81; program dir. Bickford Home, Windsor Locks, 1981-83; facilitator workshops, events and programs in govt. reform field, 1980's—. Columnist Conn. Needs You, 1970s; editor Coop. Edn. Bull., 1975-77; contbr. articles to profl. publs. Del. Dem. Town Com., Windsor Locks, 1985-91; facilitator Castle Cancer Support Group, 1983-86; writer Amnesty Internat., West Hartford, 1980—; mem., assoc. Dem. Nat. Com., 1994—. Named Hometown Hero, Conn. Celebration 350 Inc., Enfield, 1986, Hon. Native Am. for contbns. to human rights, 1990. Mem. ACLU, LWV (pres. local chpt. 1986-88), Conn. Civil Liberties Union, Am. Mus. Women in Art (charter), World Affairs Coun. (host family 1980-82), Children in Placement for Adoption (advisor 1987-88), Habitat for Humanity (ptnr. 1992—), Gen. Fedn. Women's Clubs Conn. (Windsor Locks br.). Home: 11 Concorde Way Unit B 3 Windsor Locks CT 06096-1534

FARRAR, ELAINE WILLARDSON, artist; b. L.A.; d. Eldon and Gladys Elsie (Larsen) Willardson; BA, Ariz. State U., 1967, MA, 1969, PhD, 1990; children: Steve, Mark, Gregory, JanLeslie, Monty, Susan. Tchr., Camelback Desert Sch., Paradise Valley, Ariz., 1966-69; mem. faculty Yavapai Coll., Prescott, Ariz., 1970-92, chmn. dept. art, 1973-78, instr. art in watercolor and oil and acrylic painting, intaglio, relief and monoprints, 1971-92; grad. advisor Prescott Coll. Master of Arts Program, 1993—. One-man shows include: R.P. Moffat's, Scottsdale, Ariz., 1969, Art Center, Battle Creek, Mich., 1969, The Woodpeddler, Costa Mesa, Calif., 1979; group show Prescott (Ariz.) Fine Arts Assn., 1982, 84, 86, 89, 90-94, N.Y. Nat. Am. Watercolorists, 1982; Ariz. State U. Women Images Now, 1986, 87, 89, 90, 91, 92; works rep. local and state exhibits; supt. fine arts dept. County Fair; com. mem., hanging chmn. Scholastic Art Awards; owner studio/gallery Willis Street Artists, Prescott. Mem. AAUW, Mountain Artists Guild (past pres.), Ariz. Art Edn. Assn., Nat. Art Edn. Assn., Ariz. Coll. and Univ. Faculty Assn., Ariz. Women's Caucus for Art, Women's Nat. Mus. (charter Washington chpt.), Kappa Delta Pi, Phi Delta Kappa. Republican. Mormon. Home: 535 Copper Basin Rd Prescott AZ 86303-4601

FARRAR, MARTHA ANN, lay worker, retired gift shop owner; b. Victoria, Tex., July 13, 1943; d. Warrington Siebert and Byrd Lillian Bertha (Dreyer) F. Student, Victoria Coll., 1961-63; cert., Baldwin Bus. Coll., 1964; cert. in nursing, Renger Hosp. Sch. Nursing, 1966. Reporter Zion Luth Ch. Women, Mission Valley, Tex., 1970-76, sec., 1976-78, pres., 1980-82, mem. adult choir, 1957-61, 72-84, Sunday sch. tchr., 1982-93, mem. altar guild, 1990-94; ret., 1993; owner Martha' Gift Shoppe, Victoria, 1972-93; mem. choir Spirit of Zion Ch., Mission Valley, 1985-94; mem. Rebecca Cir. Bible Study Group, Mission Valley, 1981-93, pres., 1990-91; mem. Christian Fellowship Bowler's League, Victoria, 1990-93, sec., treas., 1994—. Co-organizer, sec. Golden Crescent Region Interaction Mayor's Com., 1994—, chmn. parade com., 1994—. Democrat.

FARRELL, ANNETTE ANGELA, nurse administrator; b. Queens, N.Y., July 31, 1950; d. Charles II and Patrina Bea (Cito) Cantasano; m. George Ryan Farrell, June 23, 1977. AAS, CUNY, 1973; postgrad., New Sch. RN, N.Y. Nurse Lenox Hill Hosp., 1970-72; mgr. Myron I. Buckman M.D., P.C., N.Y.C., 1972-79, Barnes & Noble Bookstores, N.Y.C., 1979-85; adminstr. Ea. Women's Med. Ctr., N.Y.C., 1985-89; exec. dir. Choices Women's Med. Ctr., N.Y.C., 1989—. Mem. NARAL, Nat. Women's Health Network, Nat. Abortion Fedn., N.Y. Assn. for Ambulatory Care, Nat. Coalition Abortion Providers. Roman Catholic. Home: 218 W 10th St 6C New York NY 10014-2997

FARRELL, DIANA TRACY, parole officer; b. East Orange, N.J., Aug. 19, 1960; d. Richard Joseph and Jeanette MacDonald (Nobes) F.; m. Brian Joseph Duddy, Oct. 13, 1984. BA in Psychology, Washington Coll., Chestertown, Md., 1981; AAS, Brookdale C.C., 1992. Counselor Marion House, Belmar, N.J., 1981-83; community svc. investigator Monmouth County Probation Dept., Freehold, N.J., 1983-84, probation officer, 1984; parole officer Bur. Parole Dept. Corrections State of N.J., Red Bank, 1984-91, sr. parole officer, 1991—; vol. Prisoners Self Help Legal Clinic, Newark, 1993. Mem. AAUW. Democrat. Methodist.

FARRELL, EILEEN, soprano; b. Williamantic, Conn., Feb. 13, 1920; d. Michael John and Catherine (Kennedy) F.; m. Robert V. Reagan, Apr. 4, 1946; children: Robert V., Kathleen. Degrees hon., U. R.I., Loyola U., U. Hartford, Notre Dame Coll., N.H., Wagner Coll., Cin. Conservatory. Vis. prof. Hartford U. Made debut as singer, Columbia Broadcasting Co., 1941; singer own program, CBS, 6 yrs; made opera debut with San Francisco Opera in Il Trovatore, 1951; singer with major symphony orchs. in, U.S.; toured throughout, U.S. and in S.Am.; performer pops, blues and jazz with symphony orchs.; rec. artist, ABC Dunhill, Columbia, RCA, London, Angel records; recordings include Eileen Farrell as Medea (Grammy award nomination 1958), I've Gotta Right to Sing the Blues (Grammy award nomination 1960), Arias in Great Tradition (Grammy award nomination 1960), Bach: Cantatas No. 58 and No. 202 (Grammy award nomination 1961), Wagner: Gotterdamerung, Brunnhilde's Immolation Scene; Wesendonck: Songs (Grammy award 1962). Address: ICM Artists Ltd 40 W 57th St New York NY 10019*

FARRELL, FRANCINE ANNETTE, psychotherapist, educator; b. Long Beach, Calif., Mar. 26, 1948; d. Thomas and Evelyn Marie (Lucente) F.; m. James Thomas Hanley, Dec. 5, 1968 (div. Dec. 1988); children: Melinda Lee Hanley, James Thomas Hanley Jr. BA in Psychology with honors, Calif. State U., Sacramento, 1985, MS in Counseling, 1986. Lic. marriage, family and child counselor, Calif.; nat. cert. addiction counselor. Marriage, family and child counselor intern Fulton Ct. Counseling, Sacramento, 1987-88; pvt. practice psychotherapist Sacramento, 1988—; instr. chem. dependency studies program, Calif. State U., Sacramento, 1985—, acad. coord. chem. dependency studies program, 1988-90; trainee Sobriety Brings a Change, Sacramento, 1986-87; assoc. investigator, curriculum coord. Project S.A.F.E., Sacramento, 1990-91; presenter Sacramento Conf., ACA, 1986, 88, 89, 91, 92, Ann. Symposium on Chem. Dependency, 1993. Presenter (cable TV series) Trouble in River City: Charting a Course for Change, 1991. Mem. Nat. Coun. on Alcoholism, Calif. Assn. Marriage and Family Therapists, Calif. Assn. Alcoholism and Drug Abuse Counselors (bd. dirs. region 5, 1988-90), Phi Kappa Phi. Roman Catholic. Office: 2740 Fulton Ave # 100 Sacramento CA 95821-5108

FARRELL, JUNE ELEANOR, retired middle school educator; b. Ft. Atkinson, Wis., Dec. 31, 1916; d. Isaac Leslie and Thora Eleanor (Huppert) Winter; m. Martin Joseph Farrell, Sept. 21, 1946; children: Leslie June

Kathryn, Robert Joseph. BA, DePauw U., Green Castle, Ind., 1939. Cert. secondary tchr. English, Latin, and drama, Fla. Tchr. English, Latin and drama Elmore (Ind.) Twp. High Sch., 1939-41; tchr. Latin and English Beach Grove High Sch., Indpls., 1941-46; v.p. Farrell Foods Inc., 1948-66; tchr. English Ft. Atkinson (Wis.) Jr. High Sch., 1966-67, Venice (Fla.) Jr. High Sch., 1967-82; tchr. sci. Venice Area Mid. Sch., 1982-89, ret., 1989. Contbr. articles to profl. jours. Bd. dirs. AARP, Venice, Fla., 1994—; pres. Friends of Venice Cmty. Ctr., 1984—. Mem. Sarasota County Reading Coun. (pres. 1974-76), Sarasota County Tchrs. English (treas. 1975-79), Alpha Delta Kappa (pres. chpt. 1976-78, altruistic chmn. 1986-93), Delta Zeta. Republican. Methodist. Home: 640 W Venice Ave Venice FL 34285-2031 also: 603 Van Buren St Fort Atkinson WI 53538-1715

FARRELL, JUNE MARTINICK, public relations executive; b. New Brunswick, N.J., June 30, 1940; d. Ivan and Mary (Tomkovich) M.; B.S. in Journalism, Ohio U., 1962; M.S. in Public Relations, Am. U., Washington, 1977; m. Duncan G. Farrell, July 31, 1971. Public relations asst. Corning Glass Works, N.Y.C., 1963-65; assoc. beauty editor Good Housekeeping mag., N.Y.C., 1966; public relations specialist Gt. Am. Ins. Co., N.Y.C., 1967-68; assoc. editor Ea. Airlines, N.Y.C., 1968-82, regional public relations mgr., Washington, 1976-82; public relations dir. Nat. Captioning Inst., Falls Church, Va., 1982-83; dir. internat. pub. rels. Marriott Corp., 1984—; staff cons. Office of Public Liaison, White House, 1981-82. Creator, condr. spl. career awareness program for inner city youth, Washington, 1979-80; mem. public relations com. Jr. Achievement, 1979; motivational counselor for youth Nat. Alliance of Businessmen, 1979; adj. prof. tourism and pub. rels. George Washington U., 1992—; bd. dirs. Am. Mgmt. Svcs., 1985—; trustee, mem. devel. quality assurance coms. Nat. Hosp. Orthopedics and Rehab., 1984-92; mem. membership com. U.S. Travel Data Svc.; mem. adv. com. Tampa-Westborough Conv.-Visitors Bur.; mem. planning com. Travel Industry Coalition. Mem. Soc. Am. Travel Writers, Am. Soc. Travel Agts., Travel Industry Assn. Am. (nat. conf. planning com., chair pub. relations com., Discover Am. task force), Women in Communication, Phi Mu. Republican. Club: Internat. Aviation. Home: 6630 Lybrook Ct Bethesda MD 20817-3029 Office: Marriott Internat One Marriott Dr Washington DC 20058

FARRELL, KAROLYN KAY MCMILLAN, adult education educator; b. Springfield, Mo., June 23, 1938; d. Octa H. and Ruth Marie (Funkhouser) McMillan; m. Donald Paul Farrell, June 19, 1960; children: Shawn McMillan, Beth Melanie. BS in Edn. cum laude, SW Mo. State U., 1960; M Adult Edn., U. Ark., 1983, EdS, 1991; postgrad., U. Mo., 1964. Cert. adult edn. adminstr. Instr. art, sci., vocat. home econs. Indian Head High Sch., Charles County, Md., 1960-62; instr., cons. Kansas City (Mo.) Bd. Edn., 1962-63, cons. enrichment, 1963-68; instr. art Fayetteville (Ark.) Arts Gallery, 1973-77; artist in residence Butterfield Sch., Fayetteville, 1973-77; creator, developer Curriculum Disseminating Ctr., U. Ark., Fayetteville, 1979-82; dir. community and adult edn. Fayetteville Community Schs., 1979—; dietary asst. Trinity Luth. Hosp., Kansas City, 1962-63;instr. health Fayetteville High Sch., 1976-79; freelance artist, Fayetteville, 1980—. Vol. visual arts com. Walton Arts Ctr., 1980—; vol. Nelson Atkins Mus., Friends of Art, Kansas City, 1988—; co-chmn. NW Ark. Project Literacy U.S., 1988—. Levi grantee, Fayetteville, 1983-85; recipient numerous art awards. Mem. Am. Assn. Adult and Continuing Edn., Ark. Assn. Adminstrs. Adult Edn. (pres. 1989-91), Nat. Community Edn. Assn., Ark. Assn. Pub. Continuing and Adult Edn. (facilitator), Rotary (fellowship com.), Phi Delta Kappa (found. com. 1988—). Baptist. Home: 1567 Anson Pl Fayetteville AR 72701-3705

FARRELL, NAOMI, editor, journalist, medical writer, nurse researcher, poet; b. Glasgow, Scotland, Apr. 21, 1941; came to Can., 1949, USA, 1963; d. Louis and Minnie (Przestrzeleniec) F. AAS with honors, CUNY, 1970; BSN, Hunter Coll., 1973; UN studies cert., L.I. U., 1978, MS in Social Sci. and Internat. Affairs, 1979. RN; cert. med.-surg. specialist, 1991. TV performer Can., 1959-63; adminstr. Health Ins. Plan, N.Y.C., 1964-65; nurse, researcher Cornell Med. Ctr., N.Y.C., 1977-80; assoc. editor Al Hoda, New Lebanese Am. Jour., N.Y.C., 1979—; UN corr., freelance writer Globe and Mail of Can., Al Ahram Weekly, Egypt, Technion U. Report, Israel; mideast corr. UN Observer and Internat. Report, 1993—; UN corr. The New Middle East Mag., 1994—; cons. Internat. Med. Tourism, 1985. Author numerous articles and poems for newspapers and mags. Mem. internat. adv. bd. Symphony for UN, 1986. Research paper on world hunger accepted by UN Research and Tng. Library and used in Presdl. Commn. on World Hunger, Washington, 1979. Mem. UN. Corrs. Assn. (assoc. editor 1985—), Soc. Writers of UN (v.p. 1985-86), Fgn. Press Assn., UN Assn. (citation for position paper 1978), Soc. Internat. Devel., N.Y. Acad. Scis., Am. Nurses Assn., Voices-English Poets Soc. (Israel). Home: 321 E 48th St Apt 3A New York NY 10017 also: care Golan, 14/8 Second November St, Haifa Israel

FARRELL, SHARON ELAINE, real estate broker; b. Boston, Nov. 8, 1941; d. Winston Cushman and Evelyn (Murphy) Lawson; m. James E. Waldron, Oct. 15, 1961 (div. Apr. 1987); children: Peter M., Kathleen M.; m. Richard J. Farrell, May, 1994. AA, Massasoit Community Coll., 1984; grad., Realtors Inst., 1987. Cert. residential specialist. Staff asst. student life office Massasoit Community Coll., Brockton, Mass., 1983—; assoc. broker Anderson Real Estate, Inc., East Bridgewater, Mass., 1984—. Den mother Cub Scouts Boy Scouts Am., East Bridgewater, 1972-76, den leader, coach, 1976-78; mem. com., 1978-79. Mem. Am. Soc. Notaries (life), Nat. Assn. Realtors, Mass. Assn. Realtors, Nat. Assn. Cert. Residential Specialists, Mass. Assn. Cert. Residential Specialists, Green Key Soc. Roman Catholic. Home: 1725 Washington St East Bridgewater MA 02333-2219 Office: Anderson Real Estate Inc 324 N Bedford St East Bridgewater MA 02333-1146

FARRELL-LOGAN, VIVIAN, actress; b. N.Y.C.; m. Harvey Lewis, Aug. 5, 1979 (dec. Aug. 1980); m. Tracy Harrison Logan, June 3, 1984. BS in Edn., Syracuse U.; MA in Theatre, NYU. Tchr. elem. sch. Levittown (N.Y.) Schs., 1965-75; tchr. workshops Coll. of Cape Breton, N.S., Can., 1977-79. Appearences include (stage) Gateway Playhouse, Bellport, N.Y., Playhouse 3200, Richmond, Va., Bartke's Dinner Theatre, Tampa, Fla., (film) Impulse; narrator for Nutcracker, Eglevsky Ballet Co. with L.I. Symphony Orch., Nassau Coliseum, Uniondale, N.Y., 1978-79; appeared as The Musical Storyteller, Lincoln Ctr., N.Y.C., Carnegie Recital Hall, N.Y.C., 1978-80, also in various libraries and schs., N.Y. area; performer, 1978—, writer, performer (album) The Musical Storyteller, 1978; author: (children's book) Robert's Tall Friend: A Story of the Fire Island Lighthouse, Island-Metro Publs., Inc., 1987; appearing numerous schs., librs. in Author Narrates Her Book Robert's Tall Friend, 1989—; appearing N.Y.C schs. and on tour in one-woman play Amelia, My Courageous Sister, 1993—. Nassau County (N.Y.) Office Cultural Devel grantee, 1986—, N.Y. State Coun. on the Arts grantee, 1986—. Mem. Actors Equity Assn., Screen Actors Guild, AFTRA, Twelfth Night Club, Ninety-Nines, Alpha Psi Omega, Zeta Phi Eta. Office: PO Box 734 Lindenhurst NY 11757-0734

FARRELLY, MAUREEN PATRICIA, medical-surgical nurse; b. Mt. Holly, N.J., Feb. 27, 1969; d. George Joseph and Mary Margaret (Tierney) F. BSN, Thomas Jefferson U., Phila., 1991. Staff nurse Jefferson Park Hosp., Phila., 1991-94; vol. U.S. Peace Corps, Asuncion, Paraguay, 1994—. Mem. Sigma Theta Tau. Office: Jefferson Park Hosp 2 Rotunda 3905 Ford Rd Philadelphia PA 19131

FARRER, CLAIRE ANNE RAFFERTY, anthropologist, educator; b. N.Y.C., Dec. 26, 1936; d. Francis Michael and Clara Anna (Guerra) Rafferty; 1 child, Suzanne Claire. BA in Anthropology, U. Calif., Berkeley, 1970; MA in Anthropology, U. Tex., 1974, PhD in Anthropology, 1977. Various positions, 1953-73; fellow Whitney M. Young Jr. Meml. Found., N.Y.C., 1974-75; arts specialist, grant adminstr. Nat. Endowment for Arts, Washington, 1976-77; Weatherhead resident fellow Sch. Am. Research, Santa Fe, 1977-78; asst. prof. anthropology U. Ill., Urbana, 1978-85; assoc. prof., coord. applied anthropology Calif. State U., Chico, 1985-89, prof., 1989—; dir. Multicultural and Gender Studies, 1994; cons. in field, 1974—; mem. film and video adv. panel Ill. Arts Coun., 1980-82; mem. Ill. Humanities Coun., 1980-82; vis. prof. U. Ghent, Belgium, spring 1990. Author: Living Life's Circle: Mescalero Apache Cosmovision, 1991, Play and Inter-Ethnic Communication, 1991, Thunder Rides a Black Horse: Mescalero Apaches and the Mythic Present, 1994; co-founder, co-editor Folklore Women's Communication, 1972; editor spl. issue Jour. Am. Folklore, 1975, 1st rev. edit., 1986; co-editor: Forms of Play of Native North Americans, 1979, Earth and Sky: Visions of the Cosmos in Native North American Folklore, 1991; contbr. numerous articles to profl. jours., mags. and newspapers, chpts. to books. Recipient 10 awards, fellowships and grants. Fellow Am. Anthrop. Assn., Royal Anthrop. Inst. (U.K.), Soc. for Applied Anthropology, Assn. Anthrop. Study of Play; mem. Am. Ethnol. Soc., Am. Folklore Soc., Am. Soc. Ethnohistory. Mem. Soc. of Friends. Office: Calif State U Dept Anthropology Butte 311 Chico CA 95929-0400

FARRIGAN, JULIA ANN, small business owner, educator b. Albany, N.Y., July 19, 1943; d. Charles Gerald and Julia Tryon (Shepherd) F. BS in Elem. Edn., SUNY, Plattsburgh, 1965; MS in Curriculum Planning and Devel., SUNY, Albany, and U. Manchester, Eng., 1973; postgrad. in adminstrv. svcs. Calif. State U., Fresno, 1976-78. With Monroe-Woodbury Ctrl. Sch. Dist., Monroe, N.Y., 1965-90; dist. coordinator gifted programs The Pine Tree Sch., 1979-90; ptnr. Baskets Plain and Fancy; adj. prof. Gifted Edn. Contbr. articles to profl. jours. Pres. United Meth. Women, Jackson United Meth. Ch.; bd. dirs., Butts County Hist. Soc., docent, editor newsletter; chmn. Hist. Dist. Commn. City Jackson; coord. blood drive ARC Butts County. Mem. DAR (regent William McIntosh chpt., state chmn.), AFT, ASCD, NYUFT, Nat. Assn. for Gifted Children, Coun. Exceptional Children, Monroe-Woodbury Tchr's. Assn., Hawthorne Garden Club (officer), Kiwanis (mem. bd. dirs.), Delta Kappa Gamma (officer Upsilon chpt., state officer). Democrat. Methodist.

FARRINGTON, BERTHA LOUISE, nursing administrator; b. Poteet, Tex., Jan. 20, 1937; d. Leonard Gilbert and Janie (Hernandez) Lozano; m. James Charles Farrington, Jan. 30, 1965; children: Mark Hiram, Robert Lee. BSN, Tex. Women's U., 1960; NP, U. Tex., 1984. RN, Tex. Charge nurse emergency rm. Parkland Meml. Hosp., Dallas; head nurse emergency rm./day surgery Bapt. Meml. Hosp., Pensacola, Fla.; asst. dir. health svcs. U. Tex. Southwestern Med. Ctr., Dallas, dir. student health svcs. Mem. Tex. NPs Assn.

FARRINGTON-HOPF, SUSAN KAY, plumbing and heating contractor; b. Seattle, Dec. 17, 1940; d. Donald Robert and Dorothy May (Graf) Little; m. Edwin Terry Farrington, Sept. 4, 1959 (div. Apr. 1972); children: Cathe T., Jacqueline M.; m. William Desmond Hopf, Nov. 20, 1983. BA cum laude, U.S. Internat. U., 1975, MA, 1976. Program speaker AMR Internat., N.Y.C., 1977-82; pres. Dawson Plumbing & Heating Co., Seattle, 1979—; tng. cons. Fred Sherman, Inc., San Marcos, Calif., 1982—; cons. Pacific S.W. Airlines, San Diego, 1977, Dept. Labor Job Corps, Moses Lake, Wash., 1978. Developer assertive mgmt. workshop, 1976. Mem. Seattle Execs. Assn. (bd. dirs., treas., v.p., pres. 1993—), Am. Soc. Tng. and Devel., Nat. Assn. Plumbing Heating Cooling Contractors, Women Own Bus. Avocations: skiing, sailing, gardening. Home: 16419 261st Ave SE Issaquah WA 98027-8214 Office: Dawson Plumbing & Heating Co 1522 12th Ave Seattle WA 98122-3908

FARROW, MARGARET ANN, state legislator; b. Kenosha, Wis., Nov. 28, 1934; d. William Charles and Margaret Ann (Horan) Nemitz; m. John Harvey Farrow, Dec. 29, 1956; children—John, William, Peter, Paul, Mark. Student Rosary Coll., 1952-53; B.S. in Polit. Sci., Marquette U., 1956, postgrad., 1975-77. Tchr., Archiodese of Milw., 1956-57; trustee Elm Grove Village, Wis., 1976-81, pres., 1981-86; mem. Wis. State Assembly, 1986-89, State Senate, 1989—. asst. majority leader, 1993—; mem. joint com. on fin., 1993—; mem. Senate com. on environ. and energy, 1993—; co-chair joint survey com. on retirement systems, 1993—. Legis. Coun., 1991-93, Wisc. Jobs Coun., 1991—, Gov.'s Commn. For Quality Workforce, 1990-91; chair Wisc. Women's Coun., 1989-93. Home: 14905 Watertown Plank Rd Elm Grove WI 53122-2332 Office: Wis State Capitol Senate House Madison WI 53702*

FARROW, MIA VILLIERS, actress; b. Los Angeles, Feb. 9, 1945; d. John Villiers and Maureen Paula (O'Sullivan) F.; m. Frank Sinatra, July 19, 1966 (div. 1968); m. Andre Previn, Sept. 10, 1970 (div. Feb. 1979); children: Matthew Phineas and Sascha Villiers (twins), Fletcher, Lark, Daisy, Soon-Yi, Moses Amadeus, Dylan O'Sullivan, Satchel O'Sullivan, Tom, Isaiah, Gabriel Wilk. Student pub., pvt. schs. Actress appearing in TV and films. Debut in The Importance of Being Earnest, N.Y.C., 1964; starred in TV series Peyton Place; films include Hurricane, Rosemary's Baby, 1968, See No Evil, 1971, The Public Eye, 1972, The Great Gatsby, 1974, A Wedding, 1978, Death on the Nile, A Midsummer Night's Sex Comedy, 1982, Zelig, 1983, The Purple Rose of Cairo, 1985, Broadway Danny Rose, 1984, Supergirl, 1984, Hannah and Her Sisters, 1986, September, 1987, Radio Days, 1987, Another Woman, 1988, Oedipus Wrecks, 1989, Crimes and Misdemeanors, 1989, Alice, 1990, Shadows and Fog, 1992, Husbands and Wives, 1992, Widows' Peak, 1994, Miami Rhapsody, 1995; appeared in stage plays Romantic Comedy, Mary Rose, The Three Sisters, The House of Bernarda Alba, Ivanov; joined Royal Shakespeare Co., London, 1974. Recipient Golden Globe award, 1967; Best Actress award French Acad., 1969; Rio de Janeiro Film Festival award, 1969; Italian Academy award, 1970; D. W. Griffith award for best actress, 1990. *

FARWELL, MARCIA TIMS, real estate broker, editor, publisher; b. Newton, Mass., Jan. 3, 1940; d. Leonard C. and Margaret B. (Bailey) Tims; m. Clarence L. Farwell, June 17, 1961; children: Gerald G., Randall L., Tobin K. BS, U. N.H., 1962. Pvt. practice editor and pub. local newspaper, Brookline, N.H., 1966—; pvt. practice real estate broker Greater Nashua (N.H.) Bd. Realtors, 1985—. Overseer of pub. welfare Town of Brookline, N.H., 1970—; mem., vice chair, treas. Supervisory Adminstrv. Unit, Sch. Bd., Hollis, Brookline, 1973—; chmn. Sch. Bd. Brookline, 1973—. Mem. So. N.H. Multiple Listing Svc., Greater Nashua Bd. Realtors. Democrat. Home: Stonehedge Rd Brookline NH 03033 Office: Farwell Real Estate 104A Rte 13 Brookline NH 03033

FASKE, DONNA See KARAN, DONNA

FASSIHI, THERESA CARMELA, journalist; b. L.A., Sept. 12, 1959; d. John Harrison Simons and Sally Elisa Graham; m. Mohammad Reza Fassihi, July 14, 1984; children: Mansoor Reza, Samad Reza Donaciano. BA in Econs. and Journalism, Stanford U., 1981; postgrad., Tulsa U., 1992—. Copy editor, reporter Dallas Morning News, 1981-84; feature writer Tulsa Tribune, 1985-87; corr. Adweek mag., Dallas, 1986-90; co-editor Tulsa Women, 1990-91; editorial adviser S mag., Tulsa, 1985-86. pub. rels. cons. ARC, Tulsa, 1989. Mem. Women in Communications, Tulsa Exec. Exch. (v.p. 1987-88). Democrat.

FASSINGER, ELIZABETH AYNNA, physical therapist. BA in Econs. and Acctg., Westminster Coll., 1973; cert. in phys. edn., Slippery Rock State U., 1974; MSEd in Exercise Physiology, U. Pitts., 1976; postgrad., U. So. Calif., 1977-81; BS in Phys. Therapy, Mt. St. Mary's Coll., 1983; PhD in Healthcare Adminstr., Southwest U., 1994. Registered phys. therapist, Calif.; cert. phys. edn. tchr., Calif., Pa.; cert. gerontology specialist. Student tchr. Bethel Park Park Sch. System, Pitts., 1973-74; mem. staff Presbyn. Hosp. Cardiac Rehab. Program, Pitts., 1974-76; head rsch. asst. Andrus Gerontology Ctr. U. So. Calif., L.A., 1979-81; clin. intern in phys. therapy numerous hosps., Calif., 1981-83; with inpatient and outpatient clinics VA Med. Ctr., Sepulveda, Calif., 1983-84; staff rsch. assoc., ednl. coord. U. Calif., Irvine, 1984-85; owner, operator care phys. therapy, ind. contractor Fullerton, 1985—. Contbr. articles to profl. jours. Mem. Orange County chpt. Am. Heart Assn., rehab. sect. com., 1984-85, vol. for sch. health programs, vol. for community programs. Grantee GM Corp. Westminster Coll., Am. Heart Assn. U. Pitts.; rsch. grantee U. So. Calif., Found. for Phys. Therapy, 1984. Mem. AAUW, NAFE, Am. Arthritis Assn., Am. Biofeedback Soc., Am. Coll. Sports Medicine (Southwestern sect.), Am. Phys. Therapy Assn. (Calif. chpt.), Soc. Orthopedic Medicine, Orthopedic Rsch. Soc., Orange County Women's Network, Nat. Golf Found. for Golf Coaches. Home: 1943 N Sunnycrest Dr # 105 Fullerton CA 92635-3627

FASSLER, MARGOT ELSBETH, music educator, religious studies educator; b. Oswego, N.Y.; d. Frank B. Fassler and Susan Cooper Fassler Babcock; m. Peter Jeffery; children: Joseph Fassler, Frank Jeffery. MA, Syracuse U., 1976; MPhil, Cornell U., 1980, PhD, 1983. Asst. prof. Mills Coll., Oakland, Calif., 1982-83; asst. prof. Yale U., New Haven, 1983-89, prof., 1994—; dir. Yale Inst. Sacred Music, New Haven, 1994—; assoc. prof. Brandeis U., Waltham, Mass., 1989-94. Author: Gothic Song, 1993; contbr. articles to profl. jours. Recipient Elliott prize Medieval Acad. Am., 1985, Kinkeldey award Am. Musicological Soc., 1994. Mem. Am. Musicological Soc. (bd. dirs. 1989-92). Office: Yale Inst Sacred Music 409 Prospect St New Haven CT 06511

FASTABEND, GLORIA J., secondary education educator; b. San Diego, Calif., June 7, 1951; d. Arthur George and Faith June (Davis) F. BA, Boise State U., 1973; MEd, Coll. of Idaho, 1987. Advanced secondary teaching cert., Idaho; lic. profl. counselor, Iraho; cert. clin. hypnotherapist. Right-hand man Hoffman's Greenhouse & Nursery, Nampa, Idaho, 1965-84; social studies tchr. South Jr. High, Nampa, 1973-87; tchr. govt. and psychology, advisor Associated Student Body Nampa Sr. High Sch., 1987—, coach ski team, 1987—; mental health counselor, pvt. practice Nampa and Caldwell, Idaho, 1987—; trainer Nat. Diffusion Network IPLE, 1991—. Bd. dirs. Mercy House, Nampa, 1987-91. Mem. NEA, Am. Mental Health Counselors Assn., Am. Sch. Counselors Assn., Am. Counseling Assn., Idaho Mental Health Counselors Assn. (bd. dirs.), Idaho Soc. Counselors Assn., Idaho Edn. Assn., Nampa Edn. Assn. (bldg. rep. 1974-77), Nat. Coun. Social Studies, others. Office: Nampa High Sch 203 Lake Lowell Ave Nampa ID 83686-6654

FATUM, DELORES RUTH, school counselor; b. Kingston, N.Y., Aug. 1, 1945; d. Robert and Dorothy Beatrice (Van Demark) F. BS, Winthrop Coll., 1968; MEd, Ga. Coll., Milledgeville, 1973. Cert. couselor, Ga.; practice tchr. supr. Sch. couselor Laurens County Bd. of Edn., Dublin, Ga.; regional coordinator Outdoor Edn., Ga. Dept. of Natural Resources, Atlanta. Author: (manuals) Georgia Outdoor Education, Student Services for Laurens County. Mem. Am. Counseling Assn., Am. Sch. Counselors Assn., Nat. Mid. Sch. Assn., Profl. Assn. Ga. Educators. (v.p. Laurens county chpt.), Ga. Sch. Counselors Assn. (chair U.S. Congl. Dist. 8). Home: 573 Coleman Ln Dublin GA 31021-8122 Office: W Laurens Mid Sch 332 W Laurens School Rd Dublin GA 31021-9525

FAUCETTE, NANCY LEE, human resources manager; b. Exeter, N.H., Apr. 3, 1958; d. Neve Arhtur Dimock and Eloise (Clancey) Brown; m. Todd Joseph Faucette, June 21, 1986. BS in Internat. Rels. Latin Am., The Am. U., 1979, M of Pub. Adminstrn., Internat. Devel., 1980. Adminstrv. aide U.S. Senate, Washington, 1977; adminstrv. asst. Nat. Coun. of La Raza, Washington, 1978; spl. asst. to pres. Am. Univ., Washington, 1979; human resource mgr. CIA, Washington, 1980-87, 90—; adminstrv. officer U.S. Army, Frankfurt, Germany, 1987-89. Named summer fellow Georgetown U., 1979; mem. Presidential Mgmt. Intern Program, White House, Washington, 1980-82. Mem. NAFE, AAUW. Republican. Home: 206 Whitney Pl NE Leesburg VA 22075-4834

FAUGHT, LYNDA MARIE, elementary education educator, real estate broker; b. Detroit, Aug. 20, 1948; d. Sylvester Joseph and Mary Ann (Wierzbicki) Krogol; m. Harry Edward Keffer, June 30, 1966 (div. Jan. 1980); children: Kelley Ann, Todd Alan, Sean Kyle. BA, U. Detroit, 1992, postgrad., 1992—. Hair stylist, lic. cosmetologist Detroit, 1966—; realtor Clarkston, Mich., 1979—; tchr. Clarkston Comty. Schs., 1992—; cons. in real estate investments, Oakland County, Mich., 1980—. Crisis counselor Common Ground, Royal Oak, Mich., 1993. Jesuit's scholar U. Detroit, 1990. Mem. ASCD, Nat. Assn. of Edn. of Young Children, Nat. Assn. Realtors, Mich. Assn. Realtors, Mich. Reading Assn. Home: 6950 Patrick Ct Clarkston MI 48346-2273

FAUGHT, STEPHANIE ROBIN, art educator; b. Indpls., Dec. 18, 1951; d. Edward Francis and Dorothy Marie (Teague) F. BFA, Montclair (N.J.) State U., 1973, postgrad., 1974-76. Substitute tchr. Woodbridge (N.J.) Twp. Bd. of Edn., 1971-73, elem. art tchr., 1973-84, 85-86; middle sch. art tchr. Colonia (N.J.) Middle Sch., 1984-85; high sch. art tchr. Woodridge High Sch., 1986-90; middle sch. art tchr. Avenel (N.J.) Middle Sch., 1990-94; art tchr. John F. Kennedy H.S., Iselin, N.J., 1994—; spkr. Woodbridge River Watch, 1991; pvt. art tchr., 1983-93; advisor Avenel Middle Sch. Yearbook, 1991—. Illustrator (book) Care of the Lower Back, 1975, Touching All the Bases, 1993. Campaign vol. Rep. Party, Woodbridge, 1992; sec. to the producer Fgn. Broadcast Svc. Dem./Rep. Nat. Convs., Miami, 1972. Recipient Gov.'s Tchr. Recognition award State Dept. of Edn., 1992, Excellence in Edn. award C. of C., 1992. Mem. Woodbridge Twp. Fedn. of Tchrs. (v.p. 1980-83, pres. 1983—, Cert. of Merit, 1982), Art Educators of N.J., Met. Mus. of Art, Ecology Club (advisor 1990—). United Methodist. Home: 2702 Madaline Dr Avenel NJ 07001-1367 Office: John F Kennedy HS Washington Ave Iselin NJ 08830

FAUL, JUNE PATRICIA, education specialist; b. Detroit; d. John William and Shirley Olive (Block) Lynch; m. George Johnson Faul, Dec. 22, 1949; two children. BA, U. Calif., Berkeley, 1952. Cert. elem. tchr., Calif. Tchr. Tulare County (Calif.) Schs., 1945-46, Tulare City Schs., 1946-48, Visalia (Calif.) City Schs., 1948-49, Richmond (Calif.) City Schs., 1951-52, Pacific Grove (Calif.) Sch. Dist., 1965-85; designated English teaching specialist State of Calif., 1969—; cons. Leo A. Meyer Assocs., Inc., Hayward, Calif., 1993—; prin. Group Four Assocs.; lectr. Calif. State U., Fresno, 1969, U. Calif., Santa Cruz, 1970. Apptd. mem. first human relations commn. City of Richmond, 1962-64; mem. adv. bd. Family Resource Ctr.; founding mem., 1st pres. Monterey (Calif.) Peninsula Child Abuse Prevention Council, 1974; hon. life mem. Calif. PTA; bd. dirs. Carmel Cultural Commn., 1964-67, Harrison Meml. Library, Carmel, Calif., 1978-84; mem., chmn. bd. Monterey Peninsula Airport Dist., 1980—. Mem. Am. Assn. Airport Execs., Friends of Hopkins Marine Station (founder, bd. dirs.) Carmel Heritage (founder, bd. dirs.), Monterey NAACP (life), Monterey Mus. Art (life), Monterey Symphony Guild (life). Democrat. Avocation: writing. Home: PO Box 4365 Carmel CA 93921-4365

FAULCONER, KAY ANNE, communications executive; b. Shelbyville, Ind., Aug. 19, 1945; d. Clark Jacks and Charlotte (Tindall) Keenan; children: Kevin Lee, Melissa Lynne. BA in English, Calif. State U., Northridge, 1968; MBA, Pepperdine U., 1975, MA in Comm., 1976; EdD in Higher Edn., U. So. Calif., 1993. Pres., Kay Faulconer & Assocs., Oxnard, Calif., 1977—; instr. Oxnard Coll., U. LaVerne; dir. bus. adminstrn. of justice programs, Ventura (Calif.) Coll., dean econ. and cmty. devel. Former pres., founder Oxnard Friends of Libr.; former exec. bd. Ventura County March of Dimes; mem. PTA; officer, bd. dirs. Oxnard Girls Club. Named Businesswoman of Yr., Ventura Bus. and Profl. Women's Club, 1976; Woman of Achievement, Oxnard Bus. and Profl. Women's Club, 1973, recipient Career Woman award, 1974.Mem. Am. Soc. Tng. and Devel., Am. Assn. Women in Community and Jr. Colls. (Leaders for 80's program), Ventura County Profl. Women's Network. Club: Oxnard Jr. Monday (past pres., hon. life). Home and Office: PO Box 5643 Oxnard CA 93031

FAULKNER, ADELE LLOYD, interior designer, color consultant; b. Los Angeles, Dec. 26, 1911; d. Lloyd Lawrence and Coralynn (DeVoe) Lloyd; m. William Garl Quinn, Dec. 22, 1963 (dec. Mar. 1988); 1 child by previous marriage, Lloyd Nelson Faulkner (dec.). Grad., Woodbury Coll., 1932. Pres. Adele Faulkner & Assos., Inc.; syndicated columnist Copley News; dir. Los Angeles Community Design Ctr., 1972-76; tchr. interior design UCLA, 1987-91; former tchr. UCLA extension, U. Calif.-Irvine; mem. adv. council UCLA, bd. visitors Fiden Nat. Accrediting Body for Univs. Teaching Interior Design. Bd. dirs. Interval House, 1983—, Found. for People, 1982-90; founder Huntington Harbor League, 1985. Recipient award of merit Women in Design, 1980, nat. design awards Am. Soc. Interior Design, 1968-69; disting. svc. award Interval House, 1985, Women of Distinction award, 1989, 1st annual award disting. contbn. to design edn. Designer West Mag., 1986, Sr. Citizen Vol. award Vol. Ctr. Greater Orange County, 1990, vol. of distinction award L.A. Times Orange County, 1993. Fellow Am. Soc. Interior Designers (life, accredited, chpt. pres. 1957-59, v.p. nat. bd. govs. 1956-63, 72-76, sec.-treas. 1957-58, regional v.p. 1971-75, nat. membership chmn. 1973-76, regional v.p. 1971-75). Office: Adele Faulkner & Assocs Inc PO Box 1216 Sunset Beach CA 90742-1216

FAULKNER, MARILYN HAUCH, consumer products company executive; b. St. Joseph, Mich., May 9, 1942; d. Ernest and Doris Esther (Obendorfer) Hauch; B.A., Northwestern U., 1964; M.A., U. Mich., 1965; m. Bert L.

Rondelli, Dec. 27, 1966 (div.); 1 son, Michael Louis; m. David Faulkner. Reference librarian Chgo. Public Library, 1965, J. Walter Thompson Co., Chgo., 1965-67; asso. librarian Schering Corp., Bloomfield, N.J., 1967-70; info. scientist Ortho Pharm. Corp., Raritan, N.J., 1974-75; librarian Ortho Diagnostics, Inc., Raritan, 1975-80; mgr. bus. and tech. info. Johnson & Johnson Baby Products, Skillman, N.J., 1980—; mgr. bus. and tech. info. ctr. Johnson & Johnson Consumer Products, Inc., 1989—; cons. Schering Corp., 1972-73. Active United Way. Mem. Spl. Libraries Assn., Gamma Phi Beta. Office: Johnson & Johnson Consumer Products Grandview Rd Skillman NJ 08558-1308

FAURIOL, SANDIE, nonprofit agency executive; b. Tokyo, Japan, June 19, 1949; d. William Arthur and Betsy Ross (Moore) Ellis; m. Georges Alfred Fauriol, Apr. 16, 1977 (div. 1993). Student, U. N.C., 1967-69; BA, Ohio U., 1971; postgrad., Georgetown U., Wash., 1980. Resource devel. officer, exec. dir. Planned Parenthood of Met., Washington D.C., 1976-79; v.p. for devel. Martineau Corp., Washington D.C., 1979-80; campaign dir., dir. nat. salute Vietnam Vets. Meml. Fund, Washington D.C., 1980-83; dir. devel. Youth for Understanding, Washington D.C.; co-founder, exec. dir. Project on the Vietnam Generation, Washington D.C., 1985-87; founder, 1st pres. Ctr. for The New Leadership, 1987-90; campaign dir. Nat. Mus. Health and Medicine, 1990-91; fundraising cons., 1987-92; dir. devel. Asbury Methodist Village, 1992-94; exec. dir. Asbury Found., 1994—; pres. Nat. Council Career Women, 1980-81, mem. adv. bd., Pub. Leadership Edn. Network, Wash., 1988--. Author: Enduring Legacies: Expressions from the Hearts and Minds of the Vietnam Generation, 1987. Mem. Nat. Soc. Fund Raising Execs. (pres. Greater Washington D.C. area chpt., 1988-90). Methodist. Office: Asbury Found 201 Russell Ave Gaithersburg MD 20877

FAUSETT, V. LOUISE, realtor, educator; b. Polk County, Mo., July 16, 1936; d. Leonard and Marie (Griffith) Cates; m. Norman L. Fausett, Aug. 12, 1955 (div. 1991); children: Mark Lee, Anita Marie Cates. Student, U. Mo., 1955-56; BS in Home Econs. cum laude, S.W. Mo. U., 1958; cert. real estate broker, Johnson Sch., Parkville, Mo., 1973; postgrad., Rockhurst Coll., 1982. Tchr. Marionville (Mo.) Schs., 1958-59, Western (Mo.) Schs., 1068-76; realtor Gene Wright Real Estate, Platte City, Mo., 1977-83, Era Martin House, Platte City, 1983-91, Gaslight Realtors, Platte City, 1991-94; mem. Kansas City Real Estate Bd., 1993. Dir. SIA, Mo., 1991. Mem. Mo. Assn. Realtors (life), Mo. Million Dollar Club (life), Kappa Omicron Phi. Republican. Baptist. Home: PO Box 553 Platte City MO 64079-0553 Office: ERA Martin House 301 Marshall Platte City MO 64079

FAUST, MARJORIE ALICE, animal science educator; b. Allentown, Pa., Jan. 18, 1962; d. Gerald Paul and Alice Jeannette Faust. BS, Pa. State U., 1983; MS, N.C. State U., 1988, PhD, 1991. Asst. herdsperson Rothrock Golden Holsteins, Kempton, Pa., 1983-85; grad. rsch. and teaching asst. N.C. State U., Raleigh, 1985-91; asst. prof., ext. specialist dairy Iowa State U., Ames, 1991—; mem. dairy decisions support systems com. USDA, 1992—; cons. dairy, Ea. Europe, 1993—. Mem. Am. Dairy Sci. Assn. (extension and edn. com., breeding and improvement com. Midwest sect. 1993—, sec./treas. Midwest sect. 1994), Am. Soc. Animal Sci. Office: Iowa State U 4 Kildee Hall Ames IA 50011

FAUST, NAOMI FLOWE, educator, poet; b. Salisbury, N.C.; d. Christopher Leroy and Ada Luella (Graham) Flowe; AB, Bennett Coll.; MA, U. Mich., 1945; PhD, N.Y. U., 1963; m. Roy Malcolm Faust, Aug. 16, 1948. Elem. tchr. Pub. Schs. Gaffney (S.C.); tchr. English, French, phys. edn. Atkins High Sch., Winston-Salem; instr. English, Bennett Coll. and So. U., Scotlandville, La., 1944-46; prof. English, Morgan State Coll., Balt., 1946-48; tchr. English, Greensboro (N.C.) Pub. Schs., 1948-51, N.Y.C. Pub. Schs., 1954-63; prof. edn. Queens Coll. of City U. N.Y., Flushing, 1964-82; lectr. in field; writer, lectr., poetry readings, 1982—. Named Tchr.-Author of 1979, Tchr.-Writer; cert. of Merit for poem Cooper Hill Writers Conf., 1970; Achievement award L.I. br. AAUW, 1985. Mem. AAUP, Nat. Coun. Tchrs. English, Nat. Women's Book Assn., Nat. Assn. Univ. Women (L.I. br.), World Poetry Soc. Intercontinental, N.Y. Poetry Forum, NAACP, United Negro Coll. Fund, Alpha Kappa Alpha, Alpha Kappa Mu, Alpha Epsilon. Author: Discipline and the Classroom Teacher, 1977; (poetry) Speaking in Verse, 1974, All Beautiful Things, 1983, And I Travel by Rhythms and Words, 1990; contbr. poetry to jours. Home: 11201 175th St Jamaica NY 11433-4135

FAVARO, MARY KAYE ASPERHEIM (MRS. BIAGINO PHILIP FAVARO), pediatrician; b. Edgerton, Wis., Sept. 30, 1934; d. Harold Wilbur and Genevieve Catherine (Hyland) Asperheim; B.S., U. Wis., 1956; M.S., St. Louis Coll. Pharmacy, 1965; M.D., U. Wis., 1969; m. Biagino Philip Favaro, May 31, 1969; children—Justin Peter, Gina Sue. Instr. pharmacology St. Louis U. and St. Mary's Hosp. Sch. Practical Nurses, 1959-64; staff pharmacist U. Hosps., Madison, Wis., 1964-65; intern Albany (N.Y.) Med. Center, 1969-70, resident, 1970-71; resident in pediatrics U. S.C., Charleston, 1971-72, asst. prof. pediatrics, 1973-75; pvt. practice pediatrics, 1974—. Mem. A.M.A., Am. Med. Women's Assn. Roman Catholic. Author: Pharmacology, an Introductory Text, 1992; The Pharmacologic Basis of Patient Care, 1985. Home: 1866 Capri Dr Charleston SC 29407-7606 Office: 5390 Dorchester Rd Charleston SC 29418-5652

FAVREAU, SUSAN DEBRA, management consultant; b. Cleve., Dec. 15, 1955; d. Donald Francis and Helen Patricia (Rafferty) F. Cert., N.Y. State Police Acad., 1974; student, Cornell U., 1984, SUNY, 1986. Communications specialist N.Y. State Police, Loudonville, 1974-87; communications specialist div. hdqrs., 1987—; mgmt. cons., sec.-treas., dir. Don Favreau Assocs., Inc., Clifton Park, N.Y., 1983-86, v.p., 1986—; adj. faculty Internat. Assn. Chiefs of Police; NYSPIN coord. FBI/Nat. Crime Info. Ctr. cert. program, 1986—. Author: Teamwork in the Telecommunication Center, 1986, One More Time: How to be a Mature and Successful Telcommunications Manager, 1987, Law Enforcement Terminal Security, 1991; also NYSPIN cert. manuals. Recipient Dirs. commendation N.Y. State Police Acad., 1977, commendation N.Y. State Police, 1978, Supt.'s commendation, 1986. Mem. NAFE, N.Y. State Civil Svc. Assn., Emergency Communicators Profl. Assn. (adv. bd.), Colonie Police Benevolent Assn. (hon.), Am. Soc. Law Enforcement Trainers, Assoc. Pub. Safety Communications Officers (planning commn. Atlantic chpt. 1991, registration chair ann. NE conf. 1991), N.Y. State Troopers Police Benevolent Assn. (hon.), Nat. Bus. Women Am., Internat. Assn. Chiefs Police, Am. Horse Shows Assn., Am. Soc. Law Enforcement Trainers, Capital Dist. Hunter/Jumper Coun. Republican. Roman Catholic. Home: 4D Hollandale Ln Clifton Park NY 12065 Office: Hdqrs NY State Police State Office Bldg Campus Bldg # 22 Albany NY 12226

FAWCETT, FARRAH LENI, actress, model; b. Corpus Christi, Tex., Feb. 2, 1947; d. James William and Pauline Alice (Evans) F.; m. Lee Majors, July 28, 1973 (div. 1982); 1 son, Redmond James. Student, U. Tex. at Austin. Works as model. Movie debut in Myra Breckenridge, 1970; other film appearances include Love is a Funny Thing, 1970, Logan's Run, 1976, Somebody Killed Her Husband, 1978, Sunburn, 1979, Saturn 3, 1980, Cannonball Run, 1981, Extremities, 1986, See You in the Morning, 1989, Man ofthe House, 1995; TV movie appearances include Charlie's Angels, 1976, Murder in Texas, 1981, The Red Light Sting, 1984, The Burning Bed, 1984, Between Two Women, 1986, Nazi Hunter: The Beate Klarsfeld Story, 1986, Margaret Bourke-White, 1989, The Substitute Wife, 1994; regular on TV series Charlie's Angels, 1976-77, Good Sports, 1991; other TV appearances include Harry O, McCloud, The Six Million Dollar Man, Marcus Welby, M.D., Apple's Way; N.Y.C. Stage debut (off-Broadway) Extremities, 1983; TV miniseries appearances include Poor Little Rich Girl: The Barbara Hutton Story, 1987, Small Sacrifices, 1989, Children of the Dust, 1995. Mem. Delta Delta Delta. *

FAWCETT, LOUISE CROZIER, occupational therapist, educator; b. Devils Lake, N.D., June 11, 1948; d. Robert Maywood and Margaret (Running) Fawcett; m. Varick Lee Olson, June 20, 1992. BS, U. N.D., 1970; MHS, U. Fla., 1978; PhD, U. Minn., 1990. Cert. occupational therapist. Staff occupational therapist to sr. occupational therpist U. Minn. Hosps., Mpls., 1971-73; program coord. Macalester Satellite Program St. Paul's Devel. Achievement Ctr., 1974-77, infant worker Ramsey County Infant Program, 1978, coord., 1978-80; asst. prof. St. Mary's Jr. Coll., St. Paul, 1978-80; dir., asst. prof. occupational therapy asst. program Coll. St. Catherine, Mpls., 1981-88, asst. prof. dept. occupational therapy, 1988-90, asst. prof. and dir. M.A. program occupational therapy, 1990-92, assoc. prof., dir. M.A. program occupational therapy, 1992-93; faculty mem., grad. thesis advisor MHA/MPH Ind. Study Program in Hosp. Adminstrn., U. Minn., Mpls., 1986-87; rsch. dir. Lazarus Project Consultation Project, Augustana Home, Mpls., 1989-92; faculty program in long-term care adminstrn., U. Minn., Mpls., 1988-93, conductor workshops in field; mem. Commn. on Edn. Steering Com., 1992-95; assoc. dean for grad. programs Coll. of St. Catherine, 1993—. Contbr. articles to profl. jours. Med. ednl. policies com. St. Mary's Jr. Coll., 1981-86, chair, 1982-83; adv. com. on role of occupational therapy in pub. sch. spl. edn. programs Minn. Dept. Edn., 1985-86; bd. dirs. North Suburban Devel. Achievement Ctr., 1983-86, vice chair 1984-86; bd. dirs. Summit Hill Townhouse Condominium Assn., 1988-91, 92—, sec., 1988, pres., 1989-91. Recipient Alice Jantzen award U. Fla., 1978. Mem. Am. Occupational Therapy Assn. (mem. accreditatio com. 1986-92, vice chair 1987-92, roster of accreditation evaluators 1984-92, acad. rep. commn. on edn. 1981-88), Minn. Occupational Therapy Assn. (sec. 1981-82, co-chair program com. 1983 state conf.), Minn-Dak Occupational Therapy Edn. Coun. (acad. rep. 1981-88), Phi Kappa Phi, Pi Theta Epsilon. Office: Coll of St Catherine 2004 Randolph Ave Saint Paul MN 55105-1789

FAWCETT, MARIE ANN FORMANEK (MRS. ROSCOE KENT FAWCETT), civic leader; b. Mpls., Mar. 6, 1914; d. Peter Paul and Mary (Stepanek) Formanek; m. Roscoe Kent Fawcett, Mar. 16, 1935; children: Roscoe Kent, Peter Formanek, Roger Knowlton II, Stephen Hart. Grad. high sch., Mpls.; cert. Harvard U., 1976, 77, 78, 79, 80, 81, 82, 83. Chmn. of vols. Merry Go Round Club House and Mews, Greenwich, Conn., 1949-92, trustee, 1948-90, v.p., bd. dirs., 1949—, corr. sec., 1992—, chmn. entertainment, 1970-90; bd. dirs., vol. chmn., corr. sec. Nathaniel Witherell Hosp., Greenwich, 1952-92, chmn. vols., 1956-89, corr. sec. aux. bd. 1956-94; chmn. vols. Greenwich Hosp., 1953-54; dist. chmn. ARC, Community Chest, Mental Health, 1946-50; vol. mentally retarded children Milbank Sch., Greenwich, 1958-92. Bd. dirs. Cerebral Palsy, Greenwich Symphony, 1956—, Greenwich Symphony Guild, 1956—, Putnam Indianfield Sch., Nathaniel Witherell Auxiliary, 1994—, Merry Go Round Mews, 1994—, Multiple Sclerosis Soc., 1948—, v.p., 1970, corr. sec., 1958—; active drives for ARC, Community Chest, Leukemia, Muscular Dystrophy, Mental Health, Mentally Retarded Children Milbank Sch.; participating mem. Huxley Inst. Biosocial Rsch.; mem. polo com. Susan Cancer Fund, Pegasus Therapuetic Riding and Rusk Inst. Rehab. Medicine. Named Woman of Year, Soroptomist Club, 1967; recipient Community Svc. award United Cerebral Palsy Assn. Fairfield County, 1972, Fund Drive award Cerebral Palsey, 1970, citations for 36 yrs. outstanding vol. svcs. Nathaniel Witherell Hosp. Aux., Conn. Dept. Health, 1977. Mem. Internat. Platform Assn., The Woman's Club of Greenwich, Travel Club of Greenwich (corr. sec., bd. dirs. 1982—). Address: 515 E Putnam Ave Greenwich CT 06830-4813

FAWELL, BEVERLY JEAN, state legislator; b. Oak Park, Ill., Sept. 17, 1930. BA, Elmhurst Coll., 1970; postgrad., No. Ill. U., 1974. Mem. Ill. Ho. of Reps., Springfield, 1981-83, Ill. Senate, Springfield, 1983—. Republican. Office: 213 Wesley Ste 105 Wheaton IL 60187

FAWSETT, PATRICIA COMBS, federal judge; b. 1943. BA, U. Fla., 1965, MAT, 1966, JD, 1973. Pvt. practice law Akerman, Senterfitt & Edison, Orlando, Fla., 1973-86; commr. 9th Cir. Jud. Nominating Commn, 1973-75, Greater Orlando Crime Prevention Assn., 1983-86; judge U.S. Dist. Ct. (mid. dist.) Fla., Orlando, 1986—. Trustee Loch Haven Art Ctr., Inc., Orlando, 1980-84; commr. Orlando Housing Authority, 1976-80, Winter Park (Fla.) Sidewalk Festival, 1973-75; bd. dirs. Greater Orlando Area C. of C., 1982-85. Mem. ABA (trial lawyers sect., real estate probate sect.), Am. Judicature Soc., Assn. Trial Lawyers Am., Fla. Bar Found. (bd. dirs. grants com.), Commn. on Access to Cts., Fla. Coun. Bar Assn. Pres.'s (pres., bd. dirs. 9th cir. grievance com.) Osceola County Bar Assn., Fla. Bar (bd. govs. 1983-86, budget com., disciplinary rev. com., integration rule and bylaws com., com. on access to legal system, bd. of cert., designation and advt., jud. adminstrn., selection and tenure com., jud. nominating procedures com., pub. rels. com., ann. meeting com., appellate rules com., spl. com. on judiciary-trial lawyer rels., chairperson midyr. conv. com., bd. dirs. trial lawyers sect.), Orange County Bar Assn. (exec. coun. 1977-83, pres. 1981-82, trustee Legal Aid Soc. 1977-81), Order of Coif, Phi Beta Kappa. Office: US Dist Ct Federal Bldg 80 N Hughey Ave Rm 611 Orlando FL 32801-2231*

FAY, MARY SMITH, genealogist; b. Burnt Prairie, Ill., Aug. 27, 1915; d. William Logan and Mary Myrtle (Hunsinger) S.; m. Charles Hemphill Fay, Sept. 4, 1969 (dec.). BS, U. Ill., 1936, MS, 1937. Cert. genealogist. Tchr. math and gen. scis. Crossville (Ill.) High Sch., 1937-38; hosp. adminstr. U. Mich., Ann Arbor, 1939-48, Monmouth Meml. Hosp., Long Branch, N.J., 1965-67; supr., tech. info., exploration and prodn. Rsch. Lab. Shell Oil Co., Houston, 1948-69; freelance genealogist, 1969—. Author: War of 1812 Veterans in Texas, 1979 (1st prize Tex. State Geneal. Soc. 1980), rev. 1994, Edwin Fay of Vermont and Alabama 1794-1876: His Origins from 1656 and his Descendants to 1987, 1988. Mem. nat. bd. Med. Coll. Pa., Phila., 1989—. Fellow Tex. State Geneal. Soc.; mem. DAR (former regent, Ann Poage chpt.), Colonial Dames of Am., Daus. Am. Colonists (Daniel Braman chpt.), Geneal Speakers Guild, U.S. Daus. 1812 (hon. nat. v.p.), Tex. Navy (hon. admiral). Episcopalian. Home: 5403 Beverly Hill Ln # 1 Houston TX 77056-6918

FAY, SISTER MAUREEN A., university president. BA in English magna cum laude, Siena Heights Coll., 1960; MA in English, U. Detroit, 1966; PhD, U. Chgo., 1976. Tchr. English, speech, moderator student newspaper, student council St. Paul High Sch., Grosse Pointe, Mich., 1960-64; chairperson English dept., dir. student dramatics, moderator student publs. Dominican High Sch., Detroit, 1964-69; co-dir. Cath. student ctr. Adrian (Mich.) Coll., 1969-71; instr. English Siena Heights Coll., Adrian, 1969-71; evaluators inst. criminal justice execs. U. Chgo., 1971-73; instr. English U. Ill., Chgo., 1971-74; dir. evaluation sch. new learning DePaul U., Chgo., 1974-75; fellow in acad. adminstrn. Saint Xavier Coll., Chgo., 1975-76, dean. grad. studies, 1979-83, dean continuing edn., 1976-83; asst. prof. No. Ill. U., Dekalb, 1980-83; pres. Mercy Coll. Detroit, 1983-90, U. Detroit Mercy, 1990—; v.p. VAUT Corp. bd. dirs. four inner city high schs., Archdiocese Chgo.; mem. exec. com. Assn. Mercy Colls.; adv. com. Adult Learning Svcs., The Coll. Bd., Met. Affairs Corp. of Detroit and S.E. Mich., cons. Nat. Assn. for Religious Women, 1974-75, North Cen. Assn. Colls. and Schs., evaluator commn. on higher edn.; trustee Rosary Coll., River Forest, Ill., New Detroit, Inc., 1993; emeritus mem. div. bd. Mercy Hosps. and Health Svcs. of Detroit; bd. dirs. Nat. Bank of Detroit., Detroit Econ. Growth Corp., 1992; mem. Nat. Commn. Ind. Higher Edn., 1993; commr. North Centrl Assocs., Commn. on Instns. of Higher Edn., 1993. Asst. editor: (book rev.): Adult Education, A Journal of Research and Theory, 1971-74. Bd. dirs. United Way SE Mich., 1991, Assn. Catholic Colls. and Univs., 1992; Steering com. Metro Detroit GIVES; exec. com., edn. task force Detroit Strategic Planning com., 1987; trustee Mich. Opera Theatre; bd. dirs. Greater Detroit Interfaith Round Table Nat. Conf. Christians and Jews, Inc., The Detroit Symphony; mem. Nat. Bipartisan Commn. on Ind. Higher Edn. in U.S., 1993. Mem. Am. Assn. Higher Edn., North Cen. Assn. (cons., evaluator commn. on higher edn.), Nat. Assn. Ind. Colls. and Univs. (bd. dirs.), Assn. Ind. Colls. and Univs. of Mich. (exec. com., chairperson), Am. Assn. Cath. Colls. and Univs., AAUW, Pi Lambda Theta. Office: U Detroit Mercy Office of the President 4001 W Mcnichols Rd Detroit MI 48221-3038

FAY, NANCY ELIZABETH, nurse; b. Fulton, N.Y., May 10, 1943; d. Harold and Jean (Junker) Sant; m. Ronald George Fay, July 30, 1966; step children: Rory Patrick, Ronald George Jr. R.N., Genesee Hosp., Rochester, N.Y., 1964. Cert. gerontology nurse practitioner; cert. physician's asst., cert. diabetes educator. N.Y. Head maternity nurse St. Luke's Hosp., Utica, N.Y., 1975-78, diabetes clinician, 1978-82, co-dir. diabetes out-patient clinic, 1980-82; nurse practitioner, physician's asst. Slocum Dickson Med. Group, Utica, 1982-86; gerontol. nurse practitioner Masonic Home, Utica, 1988—; diabetes educator Upstate N.Y. Spl. Profl. Pregram Eli Lilly and Co., 1988—. Chair ann. Gerontol. Teaching Day Masonic Home, 1988-94, N.Y. State Physicians Diabetes Teaching Day A.D.A., 1983-90. Recipient Extra Mile award St. Luke's Hosp., 1979, Outstanding Citizenship award Am. Legion, Utica, 1982; Diabetes research grantee Diabetes Project, Ctr. Disease Control Utica, 1980-82, 21st Ann. Scroll award Cen. N.Y. Acad. Medicine, . Fellow Acad. Medicine Cent. N.Y.; mem. Am. Diabetes Assn. (pres. Utica chpt. 1983—, Outstanding Vol. of Yr. 1978, bd. dirs. N.Y. State affiliate 1983—, 1st v.p. 1986-87, Program award 1985-86, profl. edn. chmn. 1983—, chair patient and pub. edn. Upstate Affiliate, 1987—, 1st v.p., 1988-89, applicant nat. com. patient and pub. and profl. edn. 1988-89, pres.-elect N.Y. State Affiliate 1987-89, pres. 1990-92, immediate past pres. 1992-94, Sp. Svc. award N.Y. Upstate Affilliate Am. Diabetes Assn., 1994), Am. Acad. Physician's Assts., Am. Assn. Diabetes Educators, Womens Health and Edn. Referral Service St. Luke's Hosp. (bd. dirs. 1987—), N.Y. State Coalition Nurse Practitioners. Republican. Methodist. Avocations: doll collecting, dancing, poetry, bike riding. Home: Valley Rd PO Box J Oriskany NY 13424-0710 Office: Masonic Home 2150 Bleecker St Utica NY 13501

FAY, TONI GEORGETTE, communications executive; b. N.Y.C., Apr. 25, 1947; d. George E. and Allie C. (Smith) Fay. B.A., Duquesne U., Pitts., 1968; M.S.W. (NIMH fellow 1970-72), U. Pitts., 1972, M.Ed., 1973; cert. Yale U. Drug Dependence Inst., 1973. Caseworker, N.Y.C. Dept. Welfare, 1968-70; regional commr. Gov. Pa. Council Drugs and Alcohol, 1973-76; dir. social services Pitts. Drug Abuse Ctr., 1972-73; dir. planning and devel. Nat. Council Negro Women, 1977-79; exec. v.p. D. Parke Gibson Assocs., 1979-82; mgr. community relations Time Inc. (name now Time-Warner Inc.), N.Y.C., 1982-83, dir. corp. community rels. and affirmative action Time Warner, Inc., 1983-93; v.p., corp. officer, Time Warner, Inc. 1993—. Bd. dirs. UNICEF, Congressional Black Caucas Found., NAACP Legal Def. Fund. Bd., Franklin and Eleanor Inst. Named Woman of Yr., Pitts. YWCA, 1975; recipient Twin award YWCA of USA, 1987; named one 100 Top Women in Bus., Dollars and Sense Mag., 1986. Mem. Exec. Leadership Council, Nat. Coun. Negro Women (v.p.), Alpha Kappa Alpha. Office: Time Warner Bldg 75 Rockefeller Plz New York NY 10019

FAYER, JANE CAROLYN, information services professional; b. Phila., Oct. 29, 1958. BA, Harvard U., 1980; MBA, Drexel U., 1992. Rsch. asst. Children's Hosp. of Phila., 1983-88, Thomas Jefferson U., Phila., 1988-91; biologist Berlex Labs., Cedar Knolls, N.J., 1991-92; project data coord. Berlex Labs., Wayne, 1992-93; assoc. dir. info. svcs. Innapharma, Suffern, N.Y., 1993—. Contbr. articles to profl. jours. Office: Innapharma 75 Montebello Rd Suffern NY 10901

FAYNE, GWENDOLYN DAVIS, air force officer, English educator; b. Toledo, Dec. 8, 1951; d. Robert Louis and Marietta Beatrice (Sautter) Davis; m. Barry Dennis Fayne, Jan. 6, 1979; children: Ashleigh Elizabeth, Zachary Alexandur-John. BFA, So. Meth. U., 1972; MEd, U. North Tex., 1978; MA, U. Denver, 1987. Cert. tchr., Tex., Ala. Substitute tchr. Toledo and Dallas, 1972-73; film dir. Channel 39 Christian Broadcasting Network, Dallas, 1973-75; engr., air operator Channel 40 Trinity Broadcasting Network, Tustin, Calif., 1978; commd. 2d lt. USAF, 1978, advanced through grades to maj., 1989; mgr. western area Hdqrs. USAFR Officers Tng. Corp., Norton AFB, Calif., 1979-81; chief tng. systems support Hdqrs. Air Force Manpower Pers. Pentagon, Washington, 1981-84; pers. policies officer J1, Orgn. of Joint Chiefs of Staff Pentagon, Washington, 1984-85; asst. prof. English, dir. forensics USAF Acad., Colorado Springs, Colo., 1987-92; adj. faculty mem. dept. English Auburn U., Montgomery, Ala., 1994—; adj. faculty mem. dept. arts and scis. Troy State U., Montgomery, 1994—; assoc. editor The Airpower Jour., Maxwell AFB, Ala., 1992-94, mil. doctrine analyst, 1994—; chair mil. affairs Jr. Officer's Coun., Norton AFB, 1981; invited speaker in field. Editor: Parliamentary Debate: The Jour. of Nat. Parliamentary Debate Assn.; assoc. editor The Airpower Jour., Maxwell AFB, 1992-94; contbr. articles to profl. jours. Teacher, mem. choir, soloist various chs., 1973; chair publicity com. Birthright, Inc., Woodbridge, Va., 1983. Named Command Jr. Officer of Yr., Hdqrs. USAFR Officers Tng. Corps, 1979. Mem. Speech Comm. Assn., Cross Exam. Debate Assn. (chmn. program devel. com. for nat. orgn. 1990-91), Am. Forensics Assn., Nat. Parliamentary Debate Assn. (co-founder, editor Parliamentary Debate jour. 1992—), Phi Upsilon Omicron. Republican. Methodist. Home: 8200 Harrogate Hill Montgomery AL 36117 Office: Airpower Rsch Inst Coll Aerospace Doctrine Rsch Edn Maxwell AFB Montgomery AL 36112

FAY-SCHMIDT, PATRICIA ANN, paralegal; b. Waukegan, Ill., Dec. 25, 1941; d. John William and Agnes Alice (Semerad) Fay; m. Dennis A. Schmidt, Nov. 3, 1962 (div. Dec. 1987); children: Kristin Fay Schmidt, John Andrew Schmidt. Student, L.A. Pierce Coll., 1959-60, U. San Jose, 1960-62, Western State U. of Law, Fullerton, Calif., 1991-92. Cert. legal asst., Calif. Paralegal Rasner & Rasner, Costa Mesa, Calif., 1979-82; paralegal, adminstr. Law Offices of Manuel Ortega, Santa Ana, Calif., 1982-92; sabbatical, 1992-94; mem. editorial adv. bd. James Pub. Co., Costa Mesa, 1984-88. Contbg. author: Journal of the Citizen Ambassador Paralegal Delegation to the Soviet Union, 1990. Treas., Republican Women, Tustin, Calif., 1990-91; past regent, 1st vice regent, 2d vice regent NSDAR, Tustin, 1967-92; docent Richard M. Nixon Libr. and Birthplace, 1993—, bd. dirs. Docent Guild, 1994—; docent Orange County Courthouse Mus., 1992-94. Mem. Orange County Paralegal Assn. (hospitality chair 1985-87). Roman Catholic. Home: 13571 Hewes Ave Santa Ana CA 92705

FAZZINI, GEORGIA CAROL, corporate executive, business owner; b. Chicago Heights, Ill., Feb. 17, 1946; d. George and Corella A.T. (Roggeveen) Tjemmes; m. Dan Fazzini, Dec. 31, 1964; 1 child, Daniel Edward. Student, Ill. State U., Normal, 1963-64, Nat. Beauty Coll., 1979. Sec. Marshall Erdman & Assocs., Madison, Wis., 1972-73, U. Wis., Madison, 1973-74, Waukegan (Ill.) Devel. Ctr., 1974-75; br. adminstr. Universal Bus. Machines, Boise, Idaho, 1982-83; owner Substitute Sec. Typing Svc., Boise, 1983-87, Revisions Resume Writing Svc., 1987-90; chief exec. officer Diamond Devel. Ctr., Boise, 1988—; cons. Nat. Multiple Sclerosis Soc., Boise, 1983-85; instr. resume writing dept. Community Edn. Boise Schs., 1986-90, Caldwell Schs., 1989-90; resume cons. Tulsa Psychiat. Ctr., Corp. Assistance Program, 1988, Simplot Aquaculture, Caldwell, Idaho, 1991; lectr. resume writing, Tulsa, 1988, Boise, 1989-91. Pres. New Neighbors' League, Canton, Ohio, 1978-79 (Rose of Month award 1979); vice chmn., bd. dirs., sec., cons. Nat. Multiple Sclerosis Soc., Boise, 1982-86; mem. Idaho Assn. Pvt. Devel. Disability Ctrs., 1989—; guest speaker Miss Teen Pageant, Boise, 1983-84; lobbyist Boise Secretarial Svcs., 1985-86, Idaho Devel. Disability Ctrs., 1989. Mem. Idaho Assn. Pvt. Devel. Disability Ctrs., Nat. Fedn. Ind. Bus., People to People Internat, Citizen Amb. Delegation to China, Women in Mgmt. Home: 1519 Aquarius Ct Nampa ID 83651-1422 Office: Diamond Devel Ctr 1119 Caldwell Blvd Nampa ID 83651-1719

FEAR-FENN, MARCIA BELL, educational program administrator; b. Youngstown, Ohio, June 2, 1952; d. Paul Raymond Fear Sr. and Shirley Jean (McLaughlin) Rice; m. Thomas Peter Fenn, Aug. 11, 1984; children: Jessica Jean Fenn, Danielle Nicole Fenn. BA cum laude, Youngstown State U., 1975, MS, 1980; PhD, Ohio State U., 1988. Nat. cert. counselor. Tchr. East High Sch., Youngstown, 1975-77; crisis counselor Help Hotline, Inc., Youngstown, 1976-80; counselor Mahoning County Work Adjustment Ctr., Youngstown, 1978-79; grad. asst. Youngstown State U., 1979-80; grad. assoc. Ohio State U., Columbus, 1980-85, adj. asst. prof., 1989—, sex equity program dir., 1985-94; cons. Ohio Dept. Edn., 1994—; reviewer Am. Coll. Testing Program, Iowa City, Iowa, 1992, ERIC Clearinghouse on Adult, Career and Vocat. Edn., Columbus, 1992; mem. K-12 career edn. team Ohio Dept. Edn., Columbus, 1990-91. Author monographs; producer pub. svc. announcements and videotapes, 1986-90; creator, patent holder Symbol Spirit for '76, 1975. Mem. Nat. Coalition for Sex Equity in Edn., Clinton, N.J., 1990-92; mem. Wider Opportunities for Women, Washington, 1990-92. Sex Equity Program grantee Ohio Dept. Edn., 1985-92; recipient commendation Youngstown City Coun., 1976. Mem. Am. Assn. for Counseling and Devel., Am. Vocat. Assn., Ohio Assn. for Counseling and Devel. (sec. 1984-85, archives chair 1985-86), Ohio Vocat. Assn. (constn. and bylaws chair 1986-88), Phi Kappa Phi. Methodist. Home: 2300 Byerly Mill Rd West Jefferson OH 43162-9740 Office: Ohio State U 1900 Kenny Rd Columbus OH 43210-1016

FEARS, LOUISE MATHIS, parochial school educator; b. Washington, Ga., Dec. 31, 1935; d. Ambrose Powell Jr. and Sarah Louise (Moon) Mathis; m. Henry Beane Fears, June 22, 1958; children: Scott Powell, Douglas Edward, Leslie Fears Carter. BA, Shorter Coll., 1958; MEd, Ga. State U., 1977. Cert. Profl. Tchr., Ga. Evaluator Ga. State Dept. Ed., Atlanta, 1958-60; asst. Pers. Dept. City of Atlanta, 1960-61; tchr. DeKalb County Ga., Bd. Edn., Decatur, 1977-90; ednl. dir. Learning Solutions Gwinnett Pl. Ctr., Duluth, Ga., 1990-91; tchr. Christ the King Sch., Atlanta, 1991—. Author:

A Limousine is a Magazine About Lemons, 1987. Trustee Shorter Coll., 1987-92, 94—; U.S. del. joint U.S./Chinese Early Childhood Edn. Conf., Beijing, 1993. Mem. Ga. Assn. Young Children, So. Early Childhood Assn., Nat. Assn. Edn. Young Children. Democrat. Baptist.

FEATHER, LISA KAY, nursing administrator; b. Mt. Vernon, Ill., Sept. 14, 1963; d. Fred E. and D. June (McKinney) Bradford; m. Kenneth R. Feather, Oct. 2, 1981; children: Randall Ray, Brandi Jo. ADN, Frontier C.C., 1982; BSN, So. Ill. U., 1988. Cert. CPR, Am. Heart Assn.; cert. ACLS instr., BTLS instr.; cert. trauma nurse specialist, emergency nurse. Staff RN ortho/neuro unit Good Samaritan Hosp., Mt. Vernon, Ill., 1982-85, staff RN emergency dept., 1985-88, staff RN ICU/CCU, 1988; PRN office nurse Drs. Sahni and Chow, Mt. Vernon, 1988-90; staff RN emergency dept., dir. emergency dept and Emergency Med. Svcs.coord. Good Samaritan Regional Health Ctr., Mt. Vernon, 1990—; EMT lead instr. Rend Lake Coll., 1991. Mem. Ill. Coun. Nurse Mgrs., Emergency Nurse Assn., Sigma Theta Tau (Epsilon Eta). Office: Good Samaritan Regional Health Ctr 605 N 12th St Mount Vernon IL 62864-2801

FEATHERMAN, SANDRA, political science educator; b. Phila., Apr. 14, 1934; d. Albert N. and Rebe (Burd) Green; m. Bernard Featherman, Mar. 29, 1958; children: Andrew Charles, John James. BA, U. Pa., 1955, MA, 1978, PhD, 1978. Asst. prof. dept. polit. sci. Temple U., Phila., 1978-84, assoc. prof., 1984-91, asst. to pres., 1986-89, pres. faculty senate, 1985-86, dir. Ctr. for Pub. Policy, 1986-91; vice chancellor acad. adminstrn., prof. polit. sci. U. Minn., Duluth, 1991—; bd. dirs. Phila. Ranger Corp., 1990-94. Author: Jews, Blacks and Ethnics, 1979; contbr. articles to profl. jours. Mem. Sch. Bd. Nominating Panel, Phila., 1969-71, 79-81; bd. dirs. Citizens Com. Pub. Edn. in Phila., 1977-89, pres., 1979-81; pres. Pa. Fedn. Community Coll.; trustee C.C. Phila., 1970-92, chmn. bd. trustees, 1984-86; life trustee Samuel Fels Found.; bd. dirs. United Way SE Pa., 1977-89, United Way Pa., 1981-84; mem. commn. jud. selection and evaluation Phila. Bar Assn., 1979-81; pres. Girls Clubs Am., Phila., 1971-73, mem. nat. bd., 1971-74; mem. Pa. Coun. on Arts, 1979-83; nat. bd. dirs. Women and Founds.-Corp. Philanthropy, 1986-91; v.p. Jewish Community Rels. Coun., 1982-89; speaker Commonwealth of Pa. Humanities Coun., 1988, 90, 91; life trustee, v.p. Samuel Fels Fund. Recipient Brooks Graves award Pa. Polit. Sci. Assn., 1982, City of Phila. Community Svc. award, 1984, Women's Achievement award YWCA, 1989. Mem. Am. Assn. Univ. Women (bd. dir. Phila. chpt. 1975-78, 80-91, pres. 1984-86, nat. chair internat. fellowships panel 1987-91, Outstanding Woman award 1986, bd. dirs. nat. bd. 1993—), Am. Polit. Sci. Assn., Am. Soc. Pub. Adminstrn. Recipient Adminstr. of the Yr. award Minn. Women in Higher Edn., 1994. Office: U Minn 420 Adminstrn Bldg 10 University Dr Duluth MN 55812-2403

FEBO, NILDA LUZ, pediatrics and psychiatric-mental health nurse; b. Rio Piedras, P.R., Feb. 26, 1947; d. José Febo Febo and Petra Pastrana Diaz; children: Annette K. Cancel, Melissa S. Stepherson. Diploma, Meth. Hosp. Sch. Nursing, Bklyn., 1971; student, Empire State Labor Coll., N.Y.C., 1975-76, Hunter Coll., 1976-77; BSN, U. P.R., Rio Piedras, 1984. RN, N.Y., P.R.; cert. in gen. nursing practice. Pub. health nurse N.Y.C. Dept. Health and Rubella Project, 1971-77; office nurse, physician's asst. Dr. Vargas, Carolina, P.R., 1977-78; staff nurse med. and psychiat. ICU VA Hosp., San Juan, P.R., 1978-88; staff nurse pediatrics unit Mt. Sinai Hosp., N.Y.C., 1988-92; prof. practical nursing San Juan, P.R., 1993—. With USAF, 1966-67. Mem. N.Y. State Nurses Assn., P.R. Nurse's Assn. Home: RR 2 Box 1568 San Juan PR 00926

FEDERER, BLAZENA ANTONIE, chemical engineer, chemist; b. Smilkov, Czechoslovakia, July 18, 1947; came to U.S., 1978; d. Antonin Alois and Blazena (Jaksicova) Kriz. MS Chem. Engr./Chemistry magna cum laude, Coll. of Chem. Engring, Prague, Czech Republic, 1967. Plant mgr. Astrid n.p., Prague, 1967-71; sr. rsch. chemist Beiersdorf A.G., Hamburg, Germany, 1971-78; sr. process engr. Avon Products, Inc., Suffern, N.Y., 1979-85; mgr. process devel. Max Factor, Paramus, N.J., 1985-87; mgr. quality engring. L&F Products, Montvale, N.J., 1987-94, mgr. consumer satisfaction, 1994—; mem. exec. com. for selection of candidates for internat. exch. program Ga. Tech., Atlanta, 1978-79. Carl Duisberg Soc. fellow, Köln, Germany, 1978-79. Mem. NAFE, Chemists Club, Am. Soc. for Quality Control. Home: 15 Cathy Ln Waldwick NJ 07463

FEDOROFF, NINA VSEVOLOD, research scientist, consultant; b. Cleve., Apr. 9, 1942; d. Vsevolod N. and Olga S. (Snegireff) Stacy; m. T. Patrick Gaganidze, June 18, 1966 (div. 1978); children: Natasha, Kyr; m. M. Broyles, 1990. B.S., Syracuse U., 1966; Ph.D., Rockefeller U., 1972. Asst. mgr. transl. bur. Biol. Abstracts, Phila., 1962-63; flutist Syracuse (N.Y.) Symphony Orch., 1964-66; acting asst. prof. UCLA, 1972-74; postdoctoral fellow UCLA and Carnegie Inst. Washington, Los Angeles and Balt., 1974-78; staff scientist Carnegie Inst. Washington, Balt., 1978—; prof. dept. biology Johns Hopkins U.; mem. devel. biology panel NSF, Washington, 1979-80, sci. adv. panel Office of Tech. Assessment, Congress, Washington, 1979-80, recombinant DNA adv. com. NIH, Bethesda, Md., 1980-84, sci. adv. com. Japanese Human Frontier Sci., 1988, mem. adv. com. Directorate for Biol. Scis., 1994—; sci. adv. com. Competitive Rsch. Grants Office, USDA; mem. commn. on life scis., basic biology bd. NRC, NAS, Washington, 1984-90; bd. dirs. Genetics Soc. Am.; mem. bd. overseers Harvard U., 1988-91; trustee BIOSIS, Phila., 1990—; mem. NAS Coun., 1991-94; dir. Internat. Sci. Found., 1992-93. Editor: Gene, 1981-84; editor, bd. rev. editors Sci., 1985, sci. adv. bd. The Plant Jour., 1991—; editor Perspectives in Biology and Medicine, 1991—; contbr. chpts. to books, articles to profl. jours., book editor various publs. Recipient Merit award NIH, 1990; grantee NSF and USDA, 1979-84, NIH, 1984—, NSF, 1992—. Mem. AAAS, NAS, Am. Acad. Arts and Scis., Phi Beta Kappa (vis. scholar 1984-85), Sigma Xi (Howard Taylor Ricketts award 1990). Home: 110 W 39th St Apt 1106 Baltimore MD 21210 Office: Carnegie Inst of Washington Dept Embryology 115 W University Pky Baltimore MD 21210-3399

FEENEY, JOAN N., judge. BA in French and Govt., Conn. Coll., 1975; MA, Amherst Coll.; JD, Suffolk Univ. Law Sch., 1978. Law clk. to Judge Harold Lavien U.S. Bankruptcy Ct. Mass., 1978-79, law clk. to Judge James N. Gabriel, 1978-79, 82-86; assoc. Feeny & Feely, Boston, 1979-82; ptnr. Hanify & King P.C., Boston, 1988-92; bankruptcy judge U.S. Bankruptcy Ct. Mass., Boston, 1992—; editor Suffolk Univ. Law Review, 1976-78, Suffolk Transnational Journal, 1977-78; with Suffolk Voluntary Defenders, 1977-78, Volunteer Lawyer's Project. Mem. Mass. Bar Assn., Boston Bar Assn., Mass. Assn. of Women Lawyers. Office: Thomas O'Neill Federal Bldg 10 Causeway St Rm 1101 Boston MA 02222-1074*

FEENEY, MARY KATHERINE O'SHEA, retired public health nurse; b. Niagara Falls, N.Y., July 10, 1934; d. James T. and Mary Elizabeth (Woodside) O'Shea; m. Gerald E. Feeney, Apr. 27, 1957; children: Patricia, Elizabeth, Susan, Kathleen. BSN, Niagara U., 1956; MS in Mgmt., SUNY, Binghamton, 1981. RN, N.Y.; hypnotherapist; Assessment Modified Reflexology for Nurses. Pub. health nurse Herkimer County (N.Y.) Pub. Health Nursing Svc.; ret.; past coord. Herkimer County Long Term Health Care; bd. dirs. Oneida/Herkimer Coalition for Tobacco Control. Home: RR 3 Box 329 Little Falls NY 13365-9556

FEENEY, MARYANN MCHUGH, human resources professional; b. Bklyn., July 9, 1948; d. Michael Daniel and Mary Bridget (Hourican) McH.; m. Brian Francis Feeney, Sept. 21, 1974 (dec. Mar. 1992); 1 child, Michael. BA, Marymount Manhattan Coll., 1980. Human resources mgr. Muir Cornelius Moore, Inc., N.Y.C., 1977-84; dir. human resources Statue of Liberty-Ellis Island Found., N.Y.C., 1984-88; pres. The Taft Inst., N.Y.C., 1988—. Exec. producer Your Vote Video, 1991 (nominated ACE award 1991). Bd. dirs. Bklyn. Conservatory of Music, 1992—, SFX-Prospect Park Baseball, Bklyn., 1988—. Recipient Community Svc. award SFX-Prospect Park Baseball, 1992. Mem. Am. Polit. Sci. Assn., Am. Irish Cultural Soc. Democrat. Roman Catholic. Office: The Taft Inst 420 Lexington Ave New York NY 10170

FEENEY, PAULETTE CARMEL, academic program administrator; b. Munich, Germany, Oct. 12, 1948; came to U.S., 1951; d. Richard Thomas and Paule-Aimee (Bailly) F. BA in Religion, Carleton Coll., 1971; M in Religious Studies, Chgo. Theol. Sem., 1974; MBA, U. Hawaii, 1992. Clin. coord. U. Chgo. Hosps. and Clinics, 1972-73; counselor specialist Planned Parenthood Assn., Nashville, 1974-80, counseling dir., 1980-82, acting clin. dir., 1981-82; gen. mgr. Dolphin Galleries, Inc., Lahaina, Hawaii, 1983-91; program specialist U. Hawaii, Honolulu, 1993—, program specialist Coll. Continuing Edn. and Cmty. Svc.; mem. planning com. Women in Bus. Com., SBA, Honolulu, 1993—; grants rev. panelist State Found. on Culture and Arts, Honolulu, 1993. Home: 2507 Henry St Honolulu HI 96817-1136 Office: U Hawaii 2530 Dole St # D405 Honolulu HI 96822-2310

FEENKER, CHERIE DIANE, law librarian; b. Birmingham, Ala., Nov. 14, 1950; d. Marshall Ross and Joy (Martin) F. BA, U. Montevallo, 1971; MLS, U. Ala., 1979; JD with honors, Birmingham Sch. Law, 1989. Periodical libr. sci. and tech. dept. Birmingham Pub. Library, 1971-73, br. head, 1973-80, reference libr. tech. and bus. dept., 1980-84; law libr. Lange, Simpson, Robinson & Somerville, Birmingham, 1984—; firm rep. Exec. Women Internat., 1990—, historian 1991, pub. dir., 1993, bd. dirs. Mem. vestry St. Andrew's Parish, Birmingham, 1985-87. Mem. ABA, Ala. Bar Assn. (mem. faculty Continuing Legal Edn. 1987), Birmingham Bar Assn. (pub. rels. project com. 1992-93, pub. svc. com. 1994), Ala. Libr. Assn. (mem. faculty roundtable 1986-88, moderator 1987-88), Am. Assn. Law Librs., Libr. Sch. Assn. (bd. dirs. 1991-94), Law Libr. Assn. Ala., Beta Phi Mu. Episcopalian. Home: 4052 Brentwood Dr Irondale AL 35210-3505 Office: Lange Simpson Robinson & Somerville 1700 1st Ala Bank Bldg 417 N 20th St Birmingham AL 35203-3272

FEHIR, KIM MICHELE, oncologist, hematologist; b. Chgo., Aug. 31, 1947; d. William Frank and Beatric Mae (Mc Glaughlin) Debelak; m. John Stephen Fehir, Dec. 24, 1974. BS, Mich. State U., 1969; MS, U. Ill., Chgo., 1973, PhD, 1975; MD, Rush Med. Sch., Chgo., 1978. Diplomate Am. Bd. Internal Medicine. Intern, resident John Hopkins Hosp., Balt., 1978-81; fellow in oncology Meml. Sloan Kettering Cancer Ctr., N.Y.C., 1981-83; dir. med. oncology Stehlin Oncology Clin., Houston, 1983—; asst. prof. medicine Bayler Coll., Houston, 1983—. Contbr. to profl. jours. Mem. AMA, Am. Med. Soc. Hematologist, Am. Med. Soc. Clin. Oncology. Republican. Office: Stehlin Oncology Clinic 1315 Calhoun #1800 Houston TX 77002

FEHLER, POLLY DIANE, neonatalogy, nursing educator; b. Harvard, Ill., Jan. 6, 1946; d. Arthur William and Charlotte (Stewart) Eggert; m. Gene L. Fehler, Dec. 26, 1964; children: Timothy, Andrew. AS, summa cum laude, Kishwaukee Coll., 1974; BSN, magna cum laude, No. Ill. U., DeKalb, 1977, MSN, summa cum laude, 1980. Cert. BLS, neonatal resuscitation instr. Obgyn. staff nurse Kishwaukee Hosp., 1977; community health nurse DeKalb County Health Dept., 1977-79; grad. teaching asst. No. Ill. Univ., 1978-80; adj. maternity instr. Auburn Univ., Montgomery, Ala., 1980-81; maternal/newborn nurse USAF Regional Hosp. Maxwell, Montgomery, Ala., 1980-81, nurse internship coord., 1981-83; edn. coord. USAF Hosp., Bergstrom, Austin, Tex., 1983-87; neonatal ICU & transport RN St. Mary's Hosp., Athens, Ga., 1988-90; nursing instr. Tri-County Tech. Coll., Pendleton, S.C., 1990—; EMT, course lectr. U. Tex., Austin, 1984-86; counselor, vol. Hospice, 1984-87; sec., v.p. Shared Resources for Nurses, Austin, 1985-86; CPR instr.-trainer Am. Heart Assn., Tex., 1984-87, high blood pressure instr.-trainer, 1986-87; home health staff nurse Interim Health Care, Anderson, S.C., 1991-94; expert witness St. Mary's Hosp., Athens, 1991-92; coord. NCLEX rev. course Health Edn. Systems, Inc., 1993—; lectr. on interculturalism in nursing, 1993—. Nursing textbook reviewer Addison Wesley Pubs., 1993—. Nurse, med. evaluator Mass Casualty Exercises, Austin, 1984-87; tchr., sec. United Meth. Chs., Ill., Ala., Ga., S.C., 1970—; mem. alumni bd. No. Ill. Alumni, DeKalb, 1979-80; mem. Malta Dist. Bd. Edn., 1979-80; judge Austin Sch. Dist. Sci. and Math. Fair, Austin, 1983-84; S.C. Gov.'s Guardian ad Litem Vol. Capt. USAF, 1980-87. Recipient Sr. Nursing Class of Tri-County Tech. Coll. Instr. of the Yr. award, 1992. Mem. AAUW, ANA, S.C. Nurses Assn., S.C. Assn. Perinatal Nurses, S.C. Tech. Edn. Assn., Nursing Faculty Orgn. (v.p. 1991-94), United Meth. Women, S.C. Internat. Ednl. Consortium, Delta Kappa Gamma, Sigma Theta Tau. Meth. Home: 106 Laurel Ln Seneca SC 29678 Office: Tri-County Tech Coll PO Box 587 Pendleton SC 29670

FEIGEN, BRENDA S., lawyer, motion picture producer; b. Chgo., July 7, 1944; d. Arthur Paul Feigen and Shirley (Bierman) Feigen Kadison; m. Marc S. Fasteau (div.); 1 child, Alexis Feigen-Fasteau. BA in Math. cum laude, Vassar Coll., 1966; JD, Harvard U., 1969. Bar: Mass. 1970, N.Y. 1971. Chief analyst Boston Redevel. Authority, 1969; assoc. firm Rosenman, Colin, Kaye, Petschek, Freund & Emil, N.Y.C., 1970; coordinating dir. Women's Action Alliance, N.Y.C., 1970-72; dir. Nat. Women's Rights project ACLU, N.Y.C., 1972-74; ptnr. firm Fasteau and Feigen, N.Y.C., 1974-80; assoc. firm Hess, Segall, Guterman, Pelz & Steiner, N.Y.C., 1980-81; atty., motion picture agt. William Morris Agy., N.Y.C., 1982-87; film producer and atty., Beverly Hills, Calif., 1987—; pres. Brenda Feigen Prodns., N.Y.C. and L.A., 1987—; ptnr. Baxter/Feigen Prodns., 1991-92; ptnr. Berton & Feigen, Beverly Hills, 1992-94; pvt. practice, N.Y.C., 1992—; of counsel Berton & Donaldson, Beverly Hills, 1994—; adj. instr. law Coll. of New Rochelle, 1976; prof. UCLA Extension 1990; guest speaker; panelist numerous confs., seminars; co-chair Practicing Law Inst. Seminars on Entertainment Law; panelist AFI/Cinetex Conf., 1990, SAG Women's Conf., 1990; bd. dirs. Show Coalition, L.A., 1990-92; emerita mem. bd. dirs. Women's Action Alliance. Producer (film) NAVY SEALS, 1990; co-founder Ms Mag.; contbr. articles to mags., chpt. to book. Mem. adv. bd. Working Women United, nat. adv. bd. Take Our Daughters to Work, 1993—; bd. dirs. Film Forum, 1986-90; candidate for N.Y. State Senate, 1978. Hon. Pres.'s fellow Columbia U., 1977, 78, also mem. program social sci. rsch. on sex roles and social change; participant Exec. Seminar, Aspen Inst., 1979. Mem. NOW (nat. legis. v.p., bd. dirs. 1970-71), Show Coalition (bd. govs. 1990-92), N.Y. Women in Film (bd. dirs. 1985-86), Women's Action Alliance (co-founder, dir.), Nat. Women's Polit. Caucus (nat. adv. com.), Hollywood Women's Polit. Com. Democrat. Office: 9595 Wilshire Blvd Ste 711 Beverly Hills CA 90212 also: 49 E 68th St New York NY 10021-5012

FEIGENBAUM, HARRIET, sculptor; b. Bklyn., May 25, 1939; d. Samuel and Sarah (Spector) F.; m. Neil W. Chamberlain, Aug. 9, 1968. Student, Nat. Acad. Sch. Fine Arts, 1959-61, Colombia U., 1968-72. Prin. works include sculpture Holocaust Meml., Appellate Courthouse, N.Y.C., 1990; exhibited in group shows at Everhart Mus., Scranton, Pa., 1987, Edith Blum Art Inst., 1984, Mus. Am. Art, N.Y.C., 1978, Inst. Contemporary Art, Phila., 1978, Whitney Mus. Am. Art, N.Y.C.; solo exhbn. Pa. Acad. Fine Arts, Phila., 1986. Recipient Excellence in Design award Art Commn. of City of N.Y., 1991, grant Nat. Endowment for Arts, 1984, 87. Home and Office: 49 W 24th St New York City NY 10010

FEIGIN, BARBARA SOMMER, advertising executive; b. Berlin, Germany, Nov. 16, 1937; came to U.S., 1940, naturalized, 1949; d. Eric Daniel and Charlotte Martha (Demmer) Sommer; m. James Feigin, Sept. 17, 1961; children: Michael, Peter, Daniel. BA in Polit. Sci., Whitman Coll., 1959; cert. of Bus. Adminstrn., Harvard-Radcliffe Program Bus. Adminstrn., 1960. Mktg. rsch. asst. Richardson-Vick Co., Wilton, Conn., 1960-61; market rsch. analyst SCM Corp., N.Y.C., 1961-62; group rsch. supr. Benton & Bowles, Inc., N.Y.C., 1963-67; assoc. rsch. dir. Marplan Rsch. Co., N.Y.C., 1968-69; exec. v.p. strategic svcs. Grey Advt. Inc., N.Y.C., 1969—, mem. agy. policy council; bd. dirs. VF Corp., Circuit City Stores, Inc., PHH Corp. Contbr. articles to profl. jours. Bd. overseers Whitman Coll.; bd. advisors Catalyst. Recipient Women Achievers award YWCA, 1987. Mem. Advt. Rsch. Found. (bd. dirs. 1987, past chmn.). Office: Grey Advt Inc 777 3rd Ave New York NY 10017-1301

FEIGON, JUDITH TOVA, ophthalmologist, surgeon, educator; b. Galveston, Tex., Dec. 2, 1947; d. Louis and Ethel (Goldberg) F.; m. Nathan C. Goldman; children: Michael G., Miriam G. AB, Barnard Coll., Columbia U., 1970; postgrad., Rice U. and U. Houston, 1970-71; MD, U. Tex.-San Antonio, 1976. Diplomate Am. Bd. Ophthalmology. Intern Mt. Auburn Hosp., Cambridge, Mass. Intern and clin. teaching fellow, Harvard U. Med. Sch., 1976-77; resident in ophthalmology, Baylor Coll. Medicine, Houston, 1977-80, fellowship in retina, 1980-82, clin. instr., 1982—; asst. prof. ophthalmology U. Tex. Med. Br., Galveston, 1982-85, clin. asst. prof., 1985-91, clin. assoc. prof., 1992—; pvt. practice medicine specializing in ophthalmology, vitreoretinal diseases and surgery, Houston, 1983—; physician advisor to Houston br. Tex. Soc. to Prevent Blindness, 1987-89, also bd. dirs.; mem. staff Meth., St. Lukes, Tex. Children's, John Sealy, St. Joseph's Hosp., Park Pla. Contbr. articles to profl. publs. Mem. AMA, Assn. Am. Physicians and Surgeons, Am. Acad. Ophthalmology, Tex. Med. Assn., Tex. Opthal. Soc., Houston Opthal. Soc., Harris County Med. Soc., U. Tex.-San Antonio Alumni Assn., Harvard Med. Sch. Alumni Assn., Vitreous Soc. Office: 7515 Main St Ste 650 Houston TX 77030-4519

FEIL, LINDA MAE, tax preparer; b. Dallas, Oreg., Apr. 9, 1948; d. Fred Henry and Ruth Irene (Hoffman) F. AA, West Valley Community Coll., 1975; student, Golden Gate U. Ctr. for Tax Studies, 1975, Menlo Coll. Sch. Bus. Adminstrn., 1978. Enrolled agt. IRS; cert. in fed. taxation. Income tax preparer, office mgr. H & R Block, Inc., Santa Clara, Calif., 1972-74, asst. area mgr., 1974-76; propr. L.M. Feil Tax Service, Santa Clara, 1976-80; ptnr. Tennyson Tax Service, Santa Clara, 1980-81; owner McKeany-Feil Tax Service, San Jose, Calif., 1981-83; owner Feil Tax Service, San Jose, 1983-90, Richmond, Calif., 1990—. Mem. Nat. Soc. Pub. Accts., Nat. Assn. Enrolled Agts. (chpt. sec. 1981-83, chpt. v.p. 1983-84), Mission Soc. Enrolled Agts. (pres. 1984-85, Enrolled Agt. of Yr. 1985), Calif. Soc. Enrolled Agts. (bd. dirs. 1985-86). Home: 4843 Silver Creek Rd Fairfield CA 94533 Office: Feil Tax Svc 3065 Richmond Pky # 108 Richmond CA 94806-1904

FEILER, JO ALISON, artist; b. Los Angeles, Ca., Apr. 16, 1951; d. Alfred Martin and Leatrice Lucille Feiler. Student, UCLA, 1969, Art Ctr. Coll. Design, L.A., 1970-72; BFA, Calif. Inst. Arts, 1973, MFA, 1975. Asst. dir. Frank Perls Gallery, Beverly Hills, Calif., 1969-70; photography editor Coast Environ. mag., L.A., 1970-72; art dir. Log/An Inc., L.A., 1975-82. One-woman shows Inst. Contemporary Art, London, 1975, Calif. Inst. Arts, Valencia, 1975, NUAGE, L.A., 1978, Susan Harder Gallery, N.Y.C., 1984; exhibited in numerous group shows, 1975—; represented in permanent collections including Nat. Portrait Gallery, London, Victoria and Albert Mus., London, Met. Mus. Art, N.Y.C., Mus. Modern Art, N.Y.C., Los Angeles County Mus. Art, Internat. Mus. Photography, Rochester, N.Y., Santa Barbara Mus. Art, Oakland Mus., Mus. Fine Arts, Houston, Bibliotheque Nat., Paris, Musee D'Art Moderne De La Ville De Paris, Fondation Vincent Van Gogh, Arles, France, others. Recipient cert. art excellence Los Angeles County Mus. Art, 1968, award Laguna Beach Mus. Art, 1976; Calif. Inst. Arts scholar, 1974. Mem. Royal Photog. Soc. Gt. Britain, Friends of Photography. Democrat. Office: 251 E 51st St Ste 19G New York NY 10022

FEIN, LINDA ANN, nurse anesthetist, consultant; b. Cin., Dec. 10, 1949; d. Joseph and Elizabeth P. (Kannady) Stofle; m. Thomas Paul Fein, Dec. 11, 1971. Nursing diploma, Miami Valley Hosp. Sch. Nursing, Dayton, Ohio, 1971, Wright State U., Dayton, 1969; postgrad. U. Cin. Med. Ctr., 1978. Nursing asst. Miami Valley Hosp., Dayton, 1969-71; staff nurse operating room Cin. Children's Hosp. and Med. Ctr., 1971, 73, Peninsula Hosp., Burlingame, Calif., 1972-73; staff nurse operating room and emergency room Doctors Hosp., San Diego, 1972; staff nurse emergency room Ohio State U. Hosps., Columbus, 1973-75, head nurse operating room, 1975-76; staff nurse anesthetist Bethesda Hosps., Cin., 1978-86; staff nurse anesthetist Mercy Hosp. of Fairfield, Cin., 1986—; locum tenens anesthetist Good Samaritan Hosp., Dayton, Ohio, 1993—; staff nurse, anesthetist Fort Hamilton-Hughes Hosp., Hamilton, Ohio, 1995—. childbirth educator psychoprophylactic method, 1975—; critical care nursing cons. Med. Communicators & Assocs., Salt Lake City, 1985-89; ind. nursing cons., 1989—; co-owner Exec. Shops, Cin., 1982-85; speaker in field. Mem. search com. Cin. Gen. Hosp. Sch. of Anesthesia for Nurses, 1981-82; bd. dirs. YWCA, 1988-91, Children's Diagnostic Ctr., 1989—, pres. bd. dirs., 1994, Planned Parenthood, 1992—. Recipient Recognition of Profl. Excellence, First Nurse Anesthesia Faculty Assocs., 1982. Mem. Miami Valley Hosp. Sch. of Nursing Alumni Assn., Cin. Gen. Hosp. Sch. Anesthesia for Nurses Alumni Assn., Nurse Anesthetists of Greater Cin., Ohio Assn. Nurse Anesthetists, Am. Assn. Nurse Anesthetists, Am. Assn. Operating Room Nurses, Am. Assn. Critical Care Nurses, Nat. Registry of Cert. Nurses in Advanced Practice (cert.), Ohio Coaliation of Nurses with Specialty Cert., Am. Soc. Critical Care Medicine, Am. Trauma Soc., NAFE, Altrusa Internat. (officer 1985-92). Republican. Methodist. Lodge: Eastern Star. Avocations: antiques, gourmet cooking, African violets, roses, swimming. Home: 650 History Bridge Ln Hamilton OH 45013-3659

FEIN, SHEILA CAROL, artist; b. N.Y.C., Jan. 16, 1956; d. Saul Israel and Mae (Libsky) Eisenberg; married; children: Jenna, Kara, Caitlin and Amanda (twins). BS in Graphic Design, SUNY, Buffalo, 1977. Comml. artist, instr. C.E.T.A. Program N.Y. C. of C., Schenectady, 1977-78; free-lance illustrator & design, 1978-83; fine artist Gallery Assns., N.Y., Pa., Washington, Rome, Conn., L.A., 1983—; art dir. Bob Gail Orch. & Entertainment, Beverly Hills, Calif., 1994—. Painter (portraits) Pres. Clinton, 5 Marx Bros., prominent mems. L.A. cmty. Mem. Beverly Hills Art League, Fusion Art L.A.

FEINBERG, GLENDA JOYCE, restaurant chain executive; b. Louisville, Feb. 8, 1948; d. Harold and Winnie Esther (McIntosh) F.; divorced; 1 child, Anthony John. Student, Purdue U., 1967-68, Ind. U., 1977-79. Cert. in restaurant and personnel mgmt. Beverage mgr. Don Ce Sar Beach Hotel, St. Petersburg Beach, Fla., 1979-80; catering dir. Best Western-Skyway Inn, St. Petersburg, Fla., 1980-83; gen. mgr. Village, Inc., St. Petersburg Beach, 1983-86; banquet mgr. Tradewinds Resort Hotel, St. Petersburg Beach, 1986-87; exec. mgr. Ponderosa, Inc., Clearwater, Fla., 1987-90; food and beverage dir. Days Inn Island Beach Resort, St. Petersburg Beach, 1990-92; owner, mgmt. cons., pvt. caterer G.F. Sans, Marengo, Ind., 1992—. Bd. dirs. AIDS Coalitions Pinellas, 1990. Mem. NOW, World Wildlife Fedn., Nat. Geographic Soc., Greenpeace, Amnesty Internat., Environ. Def. Fund, Nat. Audubon Soc., Nat. Arbor Day Found. Democrat.

FEINBERG, GLORIA GRANDITER, psychologist; b. N.Y.C., Dec. 18, 1923; d. David and Ray (Davis) Granditer; B.A., U. Pa., 1944; M.A., N.Y. U., 1947; m. Mortimer R. Feinberg, June 22, 1947; children—Stuart Andrew, Todd E. Asst. psychologist Grasslands Hosp., Valhalla, N.Y., 1948-51; cons. BFS Psychol. Assos., N.Y.C., 1960-77, pres., 1977—. Mem. Am. Psychol. Assn., Phi Beta Kappa, Pi Gamma Mu. Author: Leavetaking, 1978. Home: 34 Brook Ln Cortlandt Manor NY 10566-6502 Office: 666 5th Ave New York NY 10103-0001

FEINBERG, MARY STANLEY, judge. AB, Mt. Holyoke Coll., 1970; JD, Univ. of Va., 1973. Bar: W. Va., U.S. Dist. Ct. (so. dist.) W. Va., U.S. Ct. Appeals (4th cir.). Atty. Columbia Gas Transmission Corp., 1973-76; law clk. to Judge Dennis R. Knapp, 1976-77; asst. U.S. atty. Charleston, W. Va., 1977-92; magistrate judge U.S. Dist. Ct. (so. dist.) W. Va., Bluefield, W. Va., 1992—. Mem. Am. Bar Assn., W. Va. Bar Assn., Kanawha County Bar Assn. Office: US Courthouse PO Box 4190 Bluefield WV 24701*

FEINER, ARLENE MARIE, librarian, researcher, consultant; b. Spring Green, Wis., Mar. 23, 1937; d. Herman Joseph and Cecelia Margaret (Meixelsperger) F. BA in History, Alverno Coll., 1959; MA in Libr. Sci., Rosary Coll., 1971; MA in Orgnl. Devel., Loyola U., Chgo., 1985. Gen. office worker USIA, Washington, 1959-60; adminstrv. sec. Nat. Coun. Cath. Women, Washington, 1960-62; asst. libr. Munich campus, U. Md., Fed. Republic Germany, 1962-64; preliminary cataloger, 1st editor MARC Pilot Project, Libr. of Congress, Washington, 1965-67; head libr. Acad. of the Holy Cross, Kensington, Md., 1967-70, Jesuit Sch. of Theology Libr., Chgo., 1971-79, coord. serial activities; women's studies bibliographer, Loyola U., Chgo., 1979-86; tech. svcs., collection devel. cons. DuPage Libr. System, 1986-91; contract adminstr. Wabash Nat. Fin., Arlington Heights, Ill., 1992—. Editor: (bibliography) Current Serials, 1980-85; compiler: (bibliography) Guide to Women's Studies Sources, 1985; contbr. articles to profl. jours. Bd. dirs. Women's World Ctr., Chgo., 1985-88. Assn. of Theol. Schs. in U.S. and Can. grantee, 1976. Mem. ALA, NAFE, Nat. Mus. Women in Arts, C.G. Jung Inst. Chgo. Roman Catholic. Avocations: poetry, hiking, music. Home: 336 W Wellington Ave Apt 2102 Chicago IL 60657-5614

FEINGOLD, JANICE ANN, elementary education educator; b. Jersey City, Mar. 18, 1955; d. Thomas Patrick and Norma Grace (Hultman) Sheehy; m. L. Hillen, June 19, 1976 (div. 1982); 1 child, Adrienne Grace; m. I. Richard Feingold, May 17, 1987. BA, Jersey City State Coll., 1977; student, Fairleigh Dickinson U., 1978-80; EdM, Rutgers U., 1992; postgrad., Nova Southeastern U., 1993—. Cert. elem. tchr., supr. grades K-12, N.J. Tchr. 2d grade Roosevelt Sch., Union City, N.J., 1977-88, tchr. math., 1988—. Com. woman Dem. Com., Hudson County, N.J., 1985-86. Mem. ASCD, AAUW,

Nat. Coun. Tchrs. Math., Assn. Math. Tchrs. N.J., Kappa Delta Pi, Phi Delta Kappa. Republican. Home: 63 Telegraph Hill Rd Holmdel NJ 07733 Office: Roosevelt Sch 4507 Hudson Ave Union City NJ 07087

FEINMAN, LYNN BETH, market research professional; b. Washington, May 16, 1951; d. Edward Ronald and Maxine Jane (Oppleman) F. BA in Edn., Simmons Coll., Boston, 1973. Supr. Burke Mktg. Rsch., Boston, 1975-78; mgr. Internat. Data Corp., Waltham, Mass., 1978-80, Burke Mktg. Rsch., Oakland, Calif., 1981-83; field dir. Burke Mktg. Rsch., Cin., 1983-85, mgr. spl. project, 1985-86; mgr. market rsch. field Kenner Products, Cin., 1986—. Trustee, mem. devel. com. United Cerebral Palsy, Boston, 1978-81, trustee, chair spl. events com., Cin., 1985—; copywriter, capt. PBS Action Auction, Cin., 1990—; mem. speakers bur. Am. Cancer Soc., Cin., 1993—; vol., ringmaster Winton Woods/Hamilton County Parks Riding Ctr., Cin., 1985-91. Mem. Mktg. Rsch. Assn.

FEINMAN, VALERIE JACKSON, librarian, educator; b. Hamilton, Ontario, Can., June 28, 1937; d. Cecil Thomas and Eulah Marguerite (Robison) Jackson; m. Robert David Feinman, June 3, 1967; children: Vanessa Jennifer, Alexander Conrad. BA in Sci. Studies, McMaster U., 1963; MS in Libr. Sci., Syracuse U., 1966; MBA, Adelphi U., 1989. Physics libr. Syracuse (N.Y.) U., 1964-66; editor N.Y. State union list Upstate Med. Ctr., Syracuse, 1966-69; cataloguer bus. Columbia U., N.Y.C., 1969-70; serials libr. Adelphi U., Garden City, N.Y., 1970-83, acad. techs. dept., 1983-85, coord. libr. instrn., assoc. prof., 1985—. Editor; N.Y. State Union List of Serials, 1966, 68, N.Y. Union List of Serials, 1967; contbr. articles to profl. jours. Mem. ALA, Libr. Info. Tech. Assn., Assn. Coll. and Rsch. Librs. (N.Y. chpt. regional chmn. 1980-82, Bibliography Instrn. Sect.), Libr. Instrn. Round Table of ALA, Nassau County Libr. Assn., Beta Phi Mu, Delta Mu Delta. Home: 119 Schenck Ave Great Neck NY 11021-3818 Office: Adelphi Univ Librs South Ave Garden City NY 11530

FEINN, BARBARA ANN, economist; b. Waterbury, Conn., Feb. 16, 1925; d. David Harris and Dora (Brandvein) F.; m. Steven L. Wissig, Jan. 10, 1991. AB magna cum laude, Smith Coll., 1946. MA (univ. scholar), Yale U., 1947, PhD (univ. fellow), 1952; cert. Oxford (Eng.) U., 1949. Rsch. economist First Nat. City Bank, N.Y.C., 1953-54; assoc. economist Office Messrs. Rockefeller, N.Y.C., 1954-61; asst. to dir. N.Y. State Office for Regional Devel., N.Y.C., 1961-62; cons. economist Nelson A. Rockefeller, N.Y.C., 1963-64; pvt. cons., 1965-68; sr. coun. economist N.Y. State Coun. Econ. Advisers, N.Y.C., 1969-72; chief economist Office S.C. Gov., Columbia, 1972-74; chief economist State of S.C., 1974—; mem. bd. econ. advisors, 1976-88 , sec. bd. econ. advisors, 1986-88, exec. dir. bd. econ. advisors, 1988— ; adj. prof. bus. adminstrn. U. S.C., Columbia, 1972-74. Ofcl. participant White House Conf. on Balanced Nat. Growth and Econ. Devel., 1978; del. meetings on nat. balanced growth Nat. Govs. Assn., Leesburg, Va., 1977; mem. S.C. Gov.'s Task Force on the Economy, 1980-84; mem. productivity measurement com. S.C. Coun. on Productivity, 1981-84. Dir. Smith Coll. Alumnae Fund Program, N.Y.C., 1965-66, mem. spl. gifts com., 1971, class v.p., 1986-91; del. assembly Assn. Yale Alumni, 1983-86, 91—. Recipient Wilbur Lucius Cross medal Yale U., 1987. Mem. Am. Econ. Assn., Nat. Assn. Bus. Econs., Soc. Govt. Economists, Downtown Economists Luncheon Group, Western Econ. Assn., N.Y. Assn. Bus. Economists, Atlanta Econ. Club, Carolinas Econ. Assn., Phi Beta Kappa. Clubs: Yale (N.Y.C. and cen. S.C.); Summit, Wildewood (Columbia, S.C.); Sea Pines (Hilton Head Island, S.C.); Smith Coll. (Columbia). Contbr. articles to profl. jours. Home: 50 Mallet Hill Ct Columbia SC 29223-3126 Office: Govs Office Columbia SC 29201

FEINSTEIN, BEVERLY, psychiatrist, psychoanalyst; b. N.Y.C., Dec. 11, 1943. BA, Barnard Coll., 1964; MD, NYU, 1968; PhD in Psychoanalysis, So.Calif. Psychoanalytic Inst., 1988. Diplomate in psychiatry Am. Bd. Psychiatry and Neurology; lic. physician, Calif. Intern Bellevue Hosp, N.Y.C., 1968-69; resident in psychiatry UCLA Neuropsychiat. Inst., 1969-72; fellow UCLA Brain Rsch. Inst., 1971-72; staff psychiatrist, biofeedback and insomnia rsch. Sepulveda (Calif.) VA Hosp., 1972-76; asst. clin. prof. UCLA, 1972—; assoc. staff St. John's Hosp., Santa Monica, Calif., 1976—, Westwood Hosp., L.A., 1976-93. Contbr. articles to profl. jours.; presenter in field. Co-originator, co-dir. UCLA Methadone Maintenance Clinic, 1970-72; cons. Am. Inst. Family Rels., 1977-78, Jewish Family Svc., 1984-85; bd. dirs. Children with Attention Deficit Disorders, 1990-92. So. Calif. Psychoanalytic Soc. grantee to lecture in Israel, 1983. Mem. Am. Psychiat. Assn., Am. Psychoanalytic Assn., So. Calif. Psychoanalytic Inst. and Soc. (chmn. ethics com. 1991-92), So. Calif. Psychiat. Soc. (councillor 1990-92, sec. 1992-93, pres.-elect 1994—). Address: 586 E Channel Rd Santa Monica CA 90402

FEINSTEIN, DIANNE, senator; b. San Francisco, June 22, 1933; d. Leon and Betty (Rosenburg) Goldman; m. Bertram Feinstein, Nov. 11, 1962 (dec.); 1 child, Katherine Anne; m. Richard C. Blum, Jan. 20, 1980. BA History, Stanford U., 1955; LLB (hon.), Golden Gate U., 1977; D Pub. Adminstrn. (hon.), U. Manila, 1981; D Pub. Service (hon.), U. Santa Clara, 1981; JD (hon.), Antioch U., 1983, Mills Coll., 1985; LHD (hon.), U. San Francisco, 1988. Fellow Coro Found., San Francisco, 1955-56; with Calif. Women's Bd. Terms and Parole, 1960-66; mem. Mayor's com. on crime, chmn. adv. com. Adult Detention, 1967-69; mem. Bd. of Suprs., San Francisco, 1970-78, pres., 1970-71, 74-75, 78; mayor of San Francisco, 1978-88, U.S. senator from Calif., 1992—; mem. exec. com. U.S. Conf. of Mayors, 1983-88; Dem. nominee for Gov. of Calif., 1990; mem. Nat. Com. on U.S.-China Rels. Mem. Bay Area Conservation and Devel. Commn., 1973-78. Recipient Woman of Achievement award Bus. and Profl. Women's Clubs San Francisco, 1970, Disting. Woman award San Francisco Examiner, 1970, Coro Found. award, 1979, Coro Leadership award, 1988, Pres. medal U. Calif., San Francisco, 1988, Scopus award Am. Friends Hebrew U., 1981, Brotherhood/Sisterhood award NCCJ, 1986, Comdr.'s award U.S. Army, 1986, French Legion of Honor, 1984, Disting. Civilian award USN, 1987; named Number One Mayor All-Pro City Mgmt. Team City and State Mag., 1987. Mem. Trilateral Commn., Japan Soc. of No. Calif. (pres. 1988-89), Inter-Am. Dialogue, Nat. Com. on U.S.-China Rels. Office: US Senate 331 Senate Hart Office Bld Washington DC 20510

FEIRSTEIN, JANICE, real estate executive; b. Binchester, Eng., Dec. 3, 1942; came to U.S., 1967; d. Edward Mons and Mary (Watson) Walmsley; m. Laurence Feirstein, Aug. 27, 1967; 1 child, Douglas. Grad. in bus., Christison U., Spennymoor, Eng., 1961; grad. in mgmt., Inst. Fin. Edn., Ft. Lauderdale, Fla., 1980. Mgr. gift and gourmet cookware store, Lauderhill, Fla., 1977-78; exec. asst. Werbel Roth Sec., Ft. Lauderdale, 1978-79; from teller to new accounts rep. to asst. br. mgr. to br. mgr. Broward Fed. Savs. and Loan, Ft. Lauderdale, 1979-82; v.p., resort mgr. Broward Ocean View Properties, Inc., Ft. Lauderdale, 1982-88; pres. Daily Mgmt. Inc., Ft. Lauderdale, 1988—; shareholder Daily Mgmt. Inc., Pompano Beach, Fla., 1990—; owner Light House Cove Resort Mgmt. Inc., Pompano Beach, 1988—; bd. dirs. Inst. Fin. Edn., 1981-83; mem. fin. com. Am. Resort and Recreational Devel. Assn., 1986. Vol. Gen. Hosp., Plantation, Fla., 1977-78; mem. adv. com. Broward County Sch. Bd., 1982; active Coop. Bus. Edn., Broward County, 1980-81, Nat. Adoption Ctr., 1986, Outreach Broward, 1986, Light House Condominium Community Assn., bd. dirs, v.p., sec. 1983-89. Mem. NAFE, Am. Bus. Women's Assn., Fla. Community Assn. Mgrs. Inc., Am. Resort Devel. Assn. (ednl. com. 1991—), Ft. Lauderdale C. of C., Pompano Beach C. of C. Office: 202 Bonaventure Blvd Fort Lauderdale FL 33326

FEIS, CAROLYN L., policy analyst; b. Steubenville, Ohio, Mar. 6, 1959. BA, U. Calif., Berkeley, 1981; MA, Mich. State U., 1983, PhD, 1990. Evaluation specialist Mich. Dept. Mental Health, Lansing, 1983-89; sr. social sci. analyst U.S. Gen. Acctg. Office, Washington, 1989—. Mem. Am. Psychol. Assn., Soc. for Community Rsch. and Action (nat. coord. 1994—), Soc. for Psychol. Study of Social Issues, Phi Beta Kappa.

FEIST-FITE, BERNADETTE, international and business education consultant; b. Linton, N.D., Sept. 28, 1945; d. John K. and Cecilia (Nagel) F.; m. William H. Fite. BS in Dietetics, U. N.D., Grand Forks, 1967; MS in Edn., Troy (Ala.) State U., 1973; EdD U. So. Calif. Commd. officer USAF, 1965, advanced through grades to maj., 1983; prof. health and fitness Nat. Def. U., Ft. McNair, Washington, 1989—; pres. Feist Assocs., 1989—; instr. seminars, workshops, researcher on internat. bus. and edn. issues; mgr. Coffeehouse Unitarian Ch. Mem. Alexandria Little Theatre. Decorated Air Force Commendation medal, Dept. Def. Meritorious Svc. medal. Mem. NAFE, VFW, Soc. Internat. Edn., Tng. and Rsch., Am. Dietetic Assn., Nat. Assn. Women Bus. Owners, Women in Defense, Japan-Am. Soc. Washington, Dietitians in Bus. and Industry, Sports and Cardiovascular Nutritionists, Andrews Officers Club. Home: 2442 Cerrillos Rd Ste 312 Santa Fe NM 87505-0105 Office: Feist Assocs PO Box 7105 Alexandria VA 22307-0105

FEITIS, MARJORIE CAROLINE, translation service company executive; b. Bellingham, Wash.; d. Clarence and Margaret (Chambers) Still; m. Peter Feitis. BA, U. Wash., 1962; MA, Ohio State U., 1964; postgrad., Institut d'Etudes Politiques, Paris, 1967-68. Owner, chief exec. officer SCITRAN (Scientific Translation Service) Co., Santa Barbara, Calif., 1972—. Transl. numerous publs from 45 different langs. Active Santa Barbara Environ. Resources Coun.; mem. Santa Barbara Land Use Bd.; bd. dirs. Montecito (Calif.) Assn., Leadership 1990, Santa Barbara Mus. Art. Named del. to U.S.-China Joint Session on Industry, Trade and Econ. Devel., Beijing, 1988; named one of 40 Outstanding Women in Govt. Procurement SBA, 1981. Mem. Am. Translators Assn., AAUW, Nat. Womens' Edn. Fund, LWV. Club: Four Seasons Hotel (bd. dirs.). Office: SCITRAN Co 1482 E Valley Rd Santa Barbara CA 93108-1200

FELD, KAREN IRMA, columnist, journalist, public speaker; b. Washington, Aug. 23, 1947; d. Irvin and Adele Ruth (Schwartz) F. Student, U. Pitts., 1965-67; BA, Am. U., 1969. Columnist, reporter Roll Call Newspaper, Washington, 1969-74; nat. pub. relations coordinator Ringling Bros./ Barnum & Bailey Circus, Washington, 1971-74; publicist Twentieth Century Fox, Los Angeles, 1974-75; pub. relations account exec. Harshe, Rotman & Druck, Los Angeles, 1975; freelance writer, broadcaster, 1970—; corr. People mag., Washington, 1980-85; broadcaster Voice of Am., 1984; columnist, contributing editor Capitol Hill mag., Washington, 1980-89; columnist Washington Times, 1986-87, Universal Press Syndicate, 1988-89, Creators Syndicate, 1989-90; syndicated columnist Capital Connections, 1990—; Prodigy polit. columnist, 1990-93; adj. instr. Kent State U. Pol. Campaign Mgmt. Inst., 1981; radio/TV commentator, 1993—; lectr. in field, 1990—. Contbr. articles to People mag., Money mag., Time mag., Vogue mag., Los Angeles Times Syndicate, others. Recipient Health Journalism award Am. Chiropractic Assn., 1991. Mem. AFTRA, Nat. Fedn. Press Women (Excellence in Journalism awards 1984-94), Women in Comms., Capital Press Women (v.p. 1985-91, Excellence in Journalism awards 1984-94), Am. Soc. Journalists and Authors, Nat. Press Club, Capitol Hill Club, Woodmont Country Club (Rockville, Md.), U.S. Senate Press Gallery White House Corr. Assn., Am. Newswomen's Club, Sigma Delta Chi. Jewish. Home and Office: 1698 32d St NW Washington DC 20007

FELD, KATHERINE PHOEBE, lawyer; b. Summit, N.J., June 9, 1958; d. Frank Kernan and Phoebe Elizabeth (Driscoll) Ward; m. Jeffrey Scott Feld, June 20, 1985; children: Deborah Phoebe, James Stuart. BA, U. Va., 1979; MBA, Cornell U., 1982, JD, 1983. Bar: N.Y. 1984, N.J. 1985. Assoc. Brown & Wood, N.Y.C., 1983-84; assoc. counsel Oppenheimer Mgmt. Corp., N.Y.C., 1984—, corp. sec., 1987—; v.p. Oppenheimer Mgmt. Corp., 1990—. Mem. Phi Beta Kappa. Office: Oppenheimer Mgmt Corp 2 World Trade Ctr New York NY 10048

FELDER, JIMMIE ROBINSON, library director; b. Hayneville, Ala., Mar. 27, 1925; d. Arthur Will and Fannie (Hulett) Robinson; m. John Richard Felder, June 5, 1955; 1 child, Jamelle Bernice. BS, Ala. State Tchrs. Coll., 1947; MEd, Ala. State Coll., 1954; MLS, Vanderbilt U., 1969. Cert. libr., English tchr. Math tchr. Merritt High Sch., Midway, Ala., 1947-48; elem. tchr. Morningstar Jr. High Sch., Lowndesboro, Ala., 1948-49; tchr. English Lowndes County Tng. Sch., Hayneville, Ala., 1949-50, Gordonville (Ala.) Ctr. Sch., 1950-56; tchr. English, libr. Central High Sch., Hayneville, 1956-62; asst. libr. George W. Carver High Sch., Montgomery, Ala., 1962-70; head libr. media ctr. George W. Carver High Sch., Montgomery, 1976-89; tchr. English Sidney Lanier High Sch., Montgomery, 1970-73, asst. libr., 1973-76; libr. dir., founder, organizer Hayneville/Lowndes Pub. Libr., 1990—; vol. Carver Elem. Media Ctr., Montgomery, Trenholm State Tech. Coll., Montgomery; pres. Montgomery Assn. Classroom Tchrs., 1983-84; dir. dist. 7 Southeastern Region Assn. Classroom Tchrs., 1984-89. Organizer Tots and Teens, Hayneville, Ala. and Tuskegee, Ala., 1986; youth dir. Day Street Bapt. Ch., 1983-90; faculty rep. Montgomery County Edn. Assn., 1977-89; block rep. March of Dimes, 1980—, Muscular Dystrophy, 1980—, Leukemia Soc., 1980—. Recipient Outstanding Achievement award Carver Creative and Performing Arts, 1986, 87, 88, Nat. Tots and Teens, Inc., 1975-81, 83, Hayneville Town Coun., 1992, Alpha Kappa Alpha, 1993, Day Street Bapt. Ch., 1991, 92, 1st Bapt. Ch., 1993, Ala. Assn. Classroom Tchrs., 1989, Citizen of Yr. award Delta Sigma Theta, 1991, George Peabody Coll. Tchrs., 1992, Hayneville Mid. Sch., 1993, 94, Ruth H. Johnson award Ala. Instrnl. Media Assn., 1993; named Woman of Yr., Zeta Phi Beta, 1992, Woman of Achievement Montgomery Advertiser, 1993, Sr. of Achievement, 1993. Democrat. Baptist. Home: 2042 Early St Montgomery AL 36108-3428 Office: Hayneville/Lowndes Pub Libr 4 S Washington St Hayneville AL 36040-2726

FELDHUSEN, HAZEL J., elementary education educator; b. Camp Douglas, Wis., Feb. 20, 1928; d. Vincent O. and Helen (Johnson) Artz; m. John F. Feldhusen, Dec. 18, 1954; children: Jeanne V., Anne M. B, U. Wis., 1965; M, Purdue U., 1968. Tchr. Suldal Sch., Mauston, Wis., 1947-50, Lake Geneva (Wis.) Schs., 1950-55, West Lafayette (Ind.) Schs., 1965-91; cons. World Conf., Hamburg, 1985, Juneau (Alaska) Schs., 1986, Connersville (Ind.) Schs., 1987, Vancouver (B.C., Can.) Schs., 1990, Norfolk (Va.) Schs., 1991, Taiwan Nat. U., 1992, U. New South Wales, Sydney, Australia, 1993, New Zealand Schs., Auckland, 1993; 2d Nat. Conf. Gifted, Taiwan, 1992. Author: Individualized Teaching of the Gifted, 1987; contbr. articles to profl. jour. Mem. Tchr. of Yr. Com., West Lafayette, 1988. Recipient Outstanding Tchr. award Elem. Tchrs. Am. 1974, Appreciation award U. Stellenbosch 1984, Appreciation award Australian Assn. for the Gifted 1987; winner Golden Apple Teaching award Greater Lafayette C. of C., 1989. Mem. NEA, Ind. State Tchrs. Assn., West Lafayette Edn. Assn. (Outstanding Achievement award 1984), Phi Delta Kappa, Delta Kappa Gamma (v.p 1983-85). Home: 2411 Trace 24 West Lafayette IN 47906-1887

FELDMAN, ADRIENNE ARSHT, lawyer, broadcasting company executive, banking executive; b. Wilmington, Del., Feb. 4, 1942; d. Samuel and Roxana (Cannon) Arsht; m. Myer Feldman, Sept. 28, 1980. BA, Mt. Holyoke Coll., 1963; JD, Villanova U., 1966. Bar: Del. 1966. Assoc. Morris, Nichols, Arsht and Tunnell, Wilmington, 1966-69, Bregman, Abel and Kay, Washington, 1979-84; dir. govt. affairs TWA, N.Y.C., 1969-79; pres., chmn. bd. Land Title & Escrow Corp., Washington, 1981-86; v.p. Ardman Broadcasting Corp., Washington, 1984—, also bd. dirs.; chmn. bd. Totalbank Corp. Fla., Miami, 1986—, also bd. dirs.; chmn. Eve Stillman Corp., N.Y.C., 1989—, also bd. dirs.; bd. dirs. Ardman, Inc., Washington, Capital Broadcasting, Inc., Kansas City, Mo., Trade Nat. Bank, Miami. Bd. dirs. Washington Opera Co., 1982-84, Am. Ballet Theatre, N.Y.C., 1984-90; founder, chmn. Van Guard Found., Washington, 1987-94, Fit and Fabulous, Washington, 1992-93; mem. exec. com. Lombardi Cancer Ctr., Washington, 1988-92; cons. Best Buddies, Washington, 1991—; mem. Com. of 200. Named Woman of Yr., Am. Ballet Theatre, 1989. Mem. Del. Bar Assn., Women's Internat. Forum, Potomac Tennis Club (Md.), Gov.'s Club (Palm Beach, Fla.). Office: Ardman Broadcasting Corp Ste 700 1250 Connecticut Ave NW Washington DC 20036

FELDMAN, ANNETTE YOUNG, civic worker; b. Hoopeston, Ill., July 23, 1916; d. Reuben and Ida (Horvitz) Yonkelowitz; m. Jerome Feldman, Oct. 19, 1941 (dec. 1986); children: Jill Feldman Crane, Robert. Student, Northwestern U., 1934-36; BS, U. Chgo., 1938, MS, 1940. Nutritionist ARC, Chgo., 1940-41; nutrition cons. Med. Coll. Va., Richmond, 1941-42; specialist food and nutrition U. Ill. Extension Svc., Champaign, 1943-45; tutor East Bay Literacy Coun., 1990—; historian Alameda Contra Costa Med. Aux. Dist. II, 1990—. Editor cookbooks for philanthropic orgns. Chmn. fund drives and disaster food ARC, Hayward, Calif., 1948, bd. dirs., 1954-58; chmn. bldg. fund St. Rose Hosp., Hayward, 1956; chmn. heart fund drive Am. Heart Assn., Hayward, 1958; mem. adult edn. com. Congregation Beth Jacob, Oakland, Calif., 1965; chmn. fund-raising events Scholarships, Inc., Hayward, 1969; pres. Alameda-Contra Costa Med. Aux., 1961-62, condr. nutritional symposium, 1975; charter assoc. Children's Hosp. Found. Circle of Friends, 1985—; life mem. Hayward Sch. Dist. PTA, Hayward Forum Arts; mem. Friends of Hayward Edn. Fund, World Affairs Coun., Women's Am. Orgn. for Rehab. Through Tng., Judah Magnes Mus.; mem. Tamarack br. Children's Med. Ctr. No. Calif.; tutor Inter Bay Literacy Coun., 1990. Recipient Appreciation award Alameda-Contra Costa Med. Aux., 1962. Mem. Am. Dietetic Assn. (life; registered), Bay Area Dietetic Assn., Eden Hosp. Found., AAUW, Chgo. Alumni Assn., Hill and Valley Club, Order of Ea. Star, Hadassah (life mem. Eden chpt., Svc. award 1960). Home: 22119 Prospect St Hayward CA 94541-2627

FELDMAN, ARLENE BUTLER, aviation industry executive. BA cum laude in Polit. Sci., U. Colo., 1975; JD, Temple U. Sch. Law, 1978. Supervising atty. U.S. Railway Assn., Phila., 1977-82; dir. divsn. aeronautics N.J. Dept. Transp., Trenton, 1982-84; from acting dir. to dep. dir. tech. ctr. FAA, Atlantic City, N.J., 1984-86; dep. dir. Western-Pacific region FAA, L.A., 1986-88; regional adminstr. N.Eng. Region FAA, Burlington, Mass., 1988-94; eastern regional adminstr. FAA, Jamaica, N.Y., 1994—; panelist, guest spkr. Women in Aviation Conf., 1992, 93; adv. bd. U. So. Calif. Chairwoman Boston Federal Exec. Bd. Saving Bond, 1993. Mem. Air Traffic Control Assn. (dir., exec. bd., conf. panel moderator 1993, 91, spkr. 1993), Am. Assn. Airport Execs., Am. Assn. State Hwy. and Transp. Ofcls., Am. Helicopter Soc., Helicopter Assn. Internat., Nat. Assn. State Aviation Ofcls., Nat. Coun. Women in Aviation Aerospce, Internat. Aviation Women's Assn., Profl. Women Controllers, Inc., Pi Sigma Alpha. Office: FAA JFK Internat Federal Bldg Jamaica NY 11430

FELDMAN, CARYN SUE, clinical psychologist; b. Chgo., Nov. 2, 1957; d. Irving and Pearl Lee (Davis) F. BA in Psychology with honors, So. Ill. U., 1981; PhD in Clin. Psychology, U. S.C., 1989. Lic. psychologist. Adminstr., rehab. asst. disabled student svcs. U. S.C., Columbia, 1983-85, Mental Health Clinic, U. S.C., Columbia, 1986-87; psychology intern Springdale & Joseph Kershaw Schs., Camden, S.C., 1985-86, VA Med. Ctr., Durham, N.C., 1987; psychology intern outplacement Duke U. Diet & Fitness Ctr., Durham, 1987-88; coord. psychology pre-release unit S.C. State Hosp., Columbia, 1990; lic. psychologist Pain Evaluation & Treatment Inst.- U. Pitts. Med. Ctr., 1990—; co-chair behavioral medicine com. Pa. Cancer Pain Initiative, Hershey, 1982-83. Co-Author: (with others) The Contribution of Psychological Variables, 1992, Facilitating The Use of Non-Invasive Pain Management Strategies with The Terminally Ill, 1992; co-editor: Noninvasive Approaches to The Management of Pain in The Terminally Ill, 1992; contbr. chpts. to books. Pres.'s scholar So. Ill. U., 1981; Biomed. Rsch. grantee NIH, 1988. Mem. APA, Greater Pitts. Psychol. Assn., Phi Beta Kappa. Office: Pain Evaluation & Treatment Inst 4601 Baum Blvd Pittsburgh PA 15213

FELDMAN, LILLIAN MALTZ, education consultant; b. N.Y.C.; d. Jacob and Ida (Burko) Maltz; m. Harry A. Feldman, June 14, 1939 (dec. Jan. 1985); children: Ronald, Donna Feldman Weisman, Jeffrey, Robert. AB, George Washington U., 1937, MA, 1939; EdD in Early Childhood Edn., Syracuse U., 1987; HLD (hon.), SUNY, 1993, DHL (hon.), 1993. Cert. tchr., guidance counselor, sch. adminstr., N.Y. Elem. sch. guidance counselor Syracuse (N.Y.) Sch. Dist., 1963-65, Kindergarten tchr., 1957-63, dir. early children edn., 1965-83; dir. Syracuse Head Start, summers 1968-70; cons. early childhood edn. Syracuse, 1985—; adj. instr. child, family and community studies Syracuse U., 1988-89, adj. prof. child and family studies, 1990-91. Author invited papers in early child devel. and care, 1988, 89. Child care adv. com. Cen. N.Y. Community Found., Syracuse, 1989—; adv. com. Dr. Martin Luther King Community Sch., Syracuse, 1988—; bd. dirs. Nat. Coun. Jewish Women, Syracuse, 1988—. Named Woman of Achievement in Edn., Post-Standard, Syracuse, 1969; recipient Hannah G. Solomon Award Nat. Coun. Jewish Women, Syracuse, 1979, Honoree Na'amat USA 1988, Friend of Children award Women's Commn. Task Force on Children, 1992. Mem. Syracuse Assn. for Edn. Young Children (Outstanding Early Childhood Educator award 1984), Consortium for Children's Svcs. (Silver Dove award 1985, Friend of Family award 1992), Onondaga County Child Care Coun. (Community Svc. award 1983, Friend of Children award 1992), Delta Kappa Gamma, Phi Delta Kappa. Democrat.

FELDMAN, MIRIAM ELLIN, nursing home administrator, nurse; b. N.Y.C., Dec. 12, 1924; d. Charles and Ida (Novick) Ellin; m. Herbert Feldman, Mar. 23, 1958; children: Leslie Ellin, Peter Hilton, Madeleine Elyse. RN, N.Y. State U., 1965; AAS, Queens Coll., 1965; BS, SUNY, 1974. Asst. adminstr. Five Towns Nursing Home, Woodmere, N.Y., 1963-65; cons. nursing service, N.Y., 1967-73; adminstr., developer Cerebral Palsy Domiciliary Care Program, N.Y., 1973-79; adminstr. Woodmere Health Care Ctr., N.Y., 1979—; cons. gerontology and the handicapped. Producer ednl. video tapes Patient Abuse Series, 1979-81. Recipient Outstanding Service award United Cerebral Palsy Assn., 1981. Fellow Am. Coll. Health Care Adminstrs.; mem. Am. Nursing Assn., Assn. for Help of Retarded Children. Club: Hadassah. Office: 39 Burton Ave Woodmere NY 11598-1747

FELDMAN, NAN HASS, artist, educator; b. Bklyn., May 6, 1950; d. Samuel Aaron and Marietta (Meshberg) Hass; m. Alan Grad Feldman, Oct. 22, 1972; children: Rebecca Lee, Daniel Gabriel. BFA, SUNY, Buffalo, 1972; postgrad., Framingham State Coll., 1973, 74, 84; MA, Goddard Coll., 1987; MFA, Vt. Coll., 1993. Tchr. art Brophy Pub. Sch., Framingham, Mass., 1972-74; artist tchr. Danforth Mus. Art, Framingham, 1975-92, DeCordova Mus., Lincoln, Mass., 1985-86, Worcester (Mass.) Art Mus., 1982—; instr. art Framingham State Coll., 1987—; artist-in-resident Babson Coll., 1976, pub. schs., Mass., 1981, 85, 86; judge scholastic art awards Boston Globe, 1989-95; artist mentor Art All-State, Worcester, 1994. One-woman shows include Worcester Art Mus., 1990, Jefferson Cutter Gallery, Arlington, Mass., 1993-94, Cove Gallery, Wellfleet, Mass., 1994; exhibited in group shows, including Worcester Art Mus., 1975, 85, 87, 88, 90, 92, Danforth Art Mus., 1975, 78, 82, 84, 86, 88, 90, 93, Fitchburg (Mass.) Art Mus., 1976, 77, Mass. Coll. Art, 1981, Newport (R.I.) Mus. Art, 1984, Boston Ctr. for Arts, 1989, 90, Cove Gallery, 1991, 92, 93, Chase Gallery, Boston, 1991, Arden Gallery, Boston, 1994, others; represented in pvt. and pub. collections including Fidelity Investment Corp., Veryfine Products, Inc., Warner Bros. Movie Studios, Brigham and Women's Hosp., Mass., Metro West Hosp., Mass., St. Elizabeth's Hosp., Mass. Recipient liquitex fine art achievement award Binney and Smith, Inc., 1987; grantee Framingham Arts Lottery, 1987, Mass. Arts Lottery, 1990; Frances A. Kinnicutt fgn. travel grantee Worcester Art Mus., 1987, 95. Mem. Coll. Art Assn. Democrat. Home and Studio: 399 Belknap Rd Framingham MA 01701

FELDMAN, SUSAN CAROL, neurobiologist, anatomy educator; b. Bklyn., Oct. 1, 1943; d. Saul Feldman and Ann Richmanl 2 children. BA, Hofstra U., Hempstead, N.Y., 1963; MS, Rutgers U., 1967; PhD, CUNY, 1976. Rsch. technician med. sch. Cornell U., N.Y.C., 1963-64; grad. teaching asst. CUNY, 1964-74; postdoctoral fellow Albert Einstein Coll. Medicine, Bronx, N.Y., 1975-77; postdoctoral fellow, instr. anatomy Columbia U., N.Y.C., 1977-79; asst. prof. anatomy N.J. Med. Sch., Newark, 1979-86, assoc. prof., 1986—. Contbr. articles to profl. jours. Mem. AAAS, Soc. Neurosci., Am. Assn. Anatomists, Am. Soc. Cell Biology, NOW. Office: Univ Med Dental NJ NJ Med Sch 185 S Orange Ave Newark NJ 07103-2714

FELDMAN, VALERIE MICHELE, marketing professional; b. Chgo., Nov. 6, 1934; d. Bernard and Florence (Schwartzman) Berger; m. Leon, Mar. 25, 1956; 1 child, Suzanne Lynn. BA in Journalism magna cum laude, U. Wis., 1955. Copywriter Montgomery Ward & Co., Chgo., 1955-59; public rels. writer Am. Hosp. Assn., Chgo., 1959-60; advt. mgr. Maling Shoes, Inc., Chgo., 1960-65; free-lance copywriter Chgo., 1971-78; copy chief Clarkson Assocs., Wash., 1979-81; v.p. creative svcs. Levy/Zimberg Assocs., 1981-82; account exec. Pallace, Inc., Silver Spring, 1982-83; mktg./advt. cons. Chevy Chase, 1983-89; asst. mgr. comm. The Acacia Group, Washington, 1989-94; mgr./sr. editor United Svcs. Life Ins., Arlington, Va., 1994—. Recipient Highest Readership Award Cons. Engr. Mag., Cons. Engr., Computer Decisions Mag., Awards of Excellence Employment Mgrs. Assn. Mem. Am. Mktg. Assn., Women Advt. and Mktg. (2nd v.p., bd. dirs.), Wash. Ind. Writers, Internat. Assn. Bus. Communicators, Direct Mktg. Assn. Wash. Home: 4620 N Park Ave Bethesda MD 20815-4549 Office: United Svcs Life Ins 4601 Fairfax Dr Arlington VA 22203

FELDSTEIN, CLAIRE SZEP, psychotherapist; d. Edward and Margaret (Schiffer) Szep; children: Leslie Tory, Jamie Bisignano, Susan Feldstein. BA, Hunter Coll., 1975; MSW, Barry U., 1979. Lic. clin. social worker, Fla.; diplomate in clin. social work Am. Bd. Forensic Examiners. Preferred provider HMOs, EAPs and ins. cos., pvt.; pvt. practice North Miami, Fla. Menninger Found. fellow. Mem. NASW, Nat. Assn. Accreditaion Psychoanalysis, Fla. Soc. Clin. Social Work, Fla. Alcohol and Drug Abuse Assn., Psi Chi. Office: 2450 NE 135th St Apt 911 North Miami FL 33181-3535

FELECOS, SYLVIA, secondary school educator; b. Chgo., Dec. 9, 1954; d. Demetrios Peter and Sophia (Nikolopoulou) F. BA, U. Ill., Chgo., 1977; MA, Roosevelt U., Chgo., 1978. High school English tchr. Amundsen High Sch., Chgo., 1978-79, Lake Ctrl. High Sch., St. John, Ind., 1979—. Recipient Nat. Merit award medal VFW, 1968. Republican. Greek Orthodox. Home: 5711 128th St Crestwood IL 60445-3815

FELICIANO-WELPE, DIANE, microelectronics laboratory director; b. Utica, N.Y., Oct. 10, 1956; d. Anthony Salvatore and Teresa (Montrose) Feliciano; m. Frank C. Welpe Jr., Sept. 12, 1981. AS, Mohawk Valley Community Coll., Utica, 1976; BS, Cornell U., 1978; MBA, Rensselaer Poly. Inst., 1990. Staff scientist Oneida Rsch. Svcs., Inc., Whitesboro, N.Y., 1979-81; group leader Oneida Rsch. Svcs., Inc., Whitesboro, 1981-84, tech. mgr., 1984-88, dir., 1988—. Named Woman of Merit, Nat. Women's History Mohawk Valley Chpt., Utica, 1987. Mem. Internat. Soc. for Hybrid Microelectronics, Internat. Reliability Physics Symposium (mgmt. com.), Joint Electron Device Coun. Office: Oneida Rsch Svcs Inc One Halsey Rd Whitesboro NY 13492

FELIX, ELAINE SAWTELLE, retail executive; b. Richmond, Va., June 24, 1958; d. Curtis Rucker and Dorothy (Daniels) Sawtelle; m. Brian David Felix, July 30, 1983; 1 child, Kristen Paige. AA in Retailing, Va. Intermont Coll., Bristol, 1981, BA in Merchandising, 1981. With Kings Dominion, Doswell, Va., 1977-80, Miller & Rhoads, Richmond, 1980-81; store mgr. Life Uniform & Shoe Shop, Richmond, 1981, Bethesda, Md., 1981-82; store mgr. The Children's Pl., Gaithersburg, Md., 1982-83, Miami, Fla., 1983-84, Williamsburg, Va., 1984-85; dist. ops. dir. The Children's Pl., Richmond, 1985-90; owner jewelry and T-shirt design bus. Designs by Elaine, 1991—; part-time svcs./sales rep. Barrington Distbrs., 1993-95; indep. distbr. NuSkin Internat. and Interior Design Nutritionals, 1993—; svc. rep. BMP (book mktg.), 1995—. Leader Girl Scouts Am., Fredericksburg, Va., 1976. Lions Club scholar. Mem. Nat. Assn. Female Execs., Alpha Chi. Republican. Methodist. Home and Office: 5516 Windy Ridge Dr Midlothian VA 23112-6376

FELIX, PATRICIA JEAN, steel company purchasing professional; b. Baptistown, N.J., Dec. 13, 1941; d. Dmitri and Rosalia (Hryckowian) F. Student, Pratt Inst., 1960-61, Moravian Coll., Bethlehem, Pa., 1961-63. Pricing analyst Riegel Paper Corp., N.Y.C., 1966-69; placement mgr. Gardner Assocs., N.Y.C., 1969-72; buyer Bethlehem Steel Corp., 1973-78, buyer exempt, 1978-84, sr. buyer, 1984, purchasing supr., 1984-94, mem. raw materials team, 1994—. Sec. Coun. St.Nicholas Russian Orthodox Ch., Bethlehem, 1982-85, mem. coun., 1985-91, bldg. com., 1992-93, Bethlehem-Tondabayashi Sister City Commn., 1988-91, sec., 1989-90, chmn., 1991-93. Home: 1721 Millard St Bethlehem PA 18017-5142 Office: Bethlehem Steel Corp 1170 Eighth Ave Bethlehem PA 18016

FELL, DONNA EILEEN, computer scientist; b. Trenton, N.J., Aug. 22, 1961; d. Donald Alan and Eileen Joan (Notarian) F. BA in Math., Rider Coll., 1983. Math. tutor Rider Coll., Lawrenceville, N.J., 1981-83; seasonal asst. N.J. Dept. Transport., Trenton, 1980-82; sr. computer scientist Naval Air Warfare Ctr., Trenton, 1983—. Mem. alumni bd. Pennington (N.J.) Sch., 1986—. Office: Naval Air Warfare Ctr Aircraft Div 1440 Parkway Ave Ewing Township NJ 08628-3087

FELLENSTEIN, CORA ELLEN MULLIKIN, retired credit union executive; b. Edwardsville, Ill., June 2, 1930; d. Russell K. and Elberta Mable (Rheude) Mullikin; m. Charles Frederick Fellenstein, Feb. 24, 1951; children: Keith David, Kimberly Diane. Student Community Coll., 1980-83. Cert. consumer credit exec. Teller, loan officer, office mgr. Credit Union of Johnson County, Lenexa, Kans., 1976-84, 1st v.p., supr. lending, collections and Mastercard depts., 1984-86, exec. v.p., 1987-94. Author: Moore Family History, 1987. Precinct committeewoman Johnson County Reps., Olathe, Kans., 1976-92; vol. Cerebral Palsey, 1957-66, Olathe Community Hosp., 1976-92, Shawnee Mission (Kans.) Med. Ctr., 1986-90. Mem. NAFE, Internat. Credit Assn., Kans. Credit Assn., Credit Profls. (dir. 1983-92), Exec. of Yr. Johnson County chpt.), DAR (treas. 1966-86), Daus. Am. Colonists (treas. 1976-86), Friends of Historic Mahaffie Farmstead, Soroptomist Internat., Beta Sigma Phi. Mem. Christian Ch. Avocations: genealogy, philately, numismatics, camping. Home: 2000 E Arrowhead Dr Olathe KS 66062-2467

FELLERS, RHONDA GAY, lawyer; b. Gainesville, Tex., July 20, 1955; d. James Norman and Gaytha Ann (Sanders) F.; m. Bruce C. Hinton, Oct. 15, 1981 (div. Oct. 1985). BA, U. Tex., 1977, JD, 1980; LLM in Taxation, U. Denver, 1987. Bar: Tex. 1981, Colo. 1981, U.S. Dist. Ct. (no. dist.) Tex. 1982, U.S. Dist. Ct. Colo. 1985, U.S. Tax Ct. 1985, U.S. Ct. Appeals (5th cir.) 1986, U.S. Ct. Appeals (10th cir.) 1989, U.S. Supreme Ct. 1993, U.S. Ct. Claims 1993. Assoc. Walters & Assocs., Lubbock, Tex., 1981-83; gen. counsel Security Nat. Bank, Lubbock, 1983; sole practice Lubbock, 1983-87; assoc. Melvin Coffee & Assocs., P.C., Denver, 1984-85, 87-90; atty. adviser U.S. Tax Ct., Washington, 1990—. Mem. State Bar Tex., Colo. Bar Assn., Colo. Women's Bar Assn. Office: US Tax Ct 400 2d St NW Washington DC 20217

FELLIN, OCTAVIA ANTOINETTE, retired librarian; b. Santa Monica, Calif.; d. Otto P. and Librada (Montoya) F. Student U. N.Mex., 1937-39; BA, U. Denver, 1941; BA in L.S., Rosary Coll., 1942. Asst. libr., instr. libr. sci. St. Mary-of-Woods Coll., Terre Haute, Ind., 1942-44; libr. U.S. Army, Bruns Gen. Hosp., Santa Fe, 1944-46, Gallup (N.Mex.) Pub. Libr., 1947-90; post libr. Camp McQuaide, Calif., 1947; freelance writer mags., newspapers, 1950—; libr. cons.; N.Mex. del. White House Pre-Conf. on Librs. & Info. Svcs., 1978; dir. Nat. Libr. Week for N.Mex., 1959. Chmn. Red Mesa Art Ctr., 1984-88; pres. Gallup Area Arts Coun., 1988; mem. Western Health Found. Century Com., 1988, Gallup Multi-Model Cultural Com., 1988—; v.p., publicity dir. Gallup Community Concerts Assn., 1957-78, 85—; organizer Gt. Decision Discussion groups, 1963-85; co-organizer, v.p. chair fund raising com. Gallup Pub. Radio Com., 1989—; mem. McKinley County Recycling Com., 1990—; mem. local art selection com. N.Mex. Art Dirs., 1990; mem. Gallup St. Naming Com., 1958-59, Aging Com., 1964-68; chmn. Gallup Mus. Indian Arts and Crafts, 1964-78; mem. Eccles. Conciliation and Arbitration Bd., Province of Santa Fe, 1974; mem. publicity com. Gallup Inter-Tribal Indian Ceremonial Assn., 1966-68; mem. Gov's. Com. 100 on Aging, 1967-70; mem. U. N.Mex.-Gallup Campus Community Edn. Adv. Coun., 1981-82; N.Mex. organizing chmn. Rehobeth McKinley Christian Hosp. Aux., pres., 1983, chmn. aux. scholarship com., 1989—, chmn. cmty. edn. loan selection com. 1990—, bd. dirs., corr. sec., 1991—; mem. N.Mex. Libr. Adv. Coun., 1971-75, vice chmn., 1974-75; chmn. adv. com. Gallup Sr. Citizens, 1971-73; mem. steering com. Gallup Diocese Bicentennial, 1975-78, chmn. hist. com., 1975; chmn. Trick or Treat for UNICEF, Gallup, 1972-77, Artists Coop, 1985-89; chmn. pledge campaign Rancho del Nino San Huberto, Empalme, Mex.; active Nat. Cath. Social Justice Lobby; bd. dirs. Gallup Opera Guild, 1970-74; bd. dirs., sec., organizer Gallup Area Arts Council, 1970-78; mem. N.Mex. Humanities Council, 1979, Gallup Centennial Com., 1980-81; mem. Cathedral Parish Council, 1980-83, v.p., 1981, century com. Western Health Found., 1988-89; active N.Mex. Diamond Jubilee/U.S. Constn. Bicentennial Gallup Com., 1986-87, N.Mex. Gallup Campus 25 Silver Anniversary Com., 1994. Recipient Dorothy Canfield Fisher $1,000 Libr. award, 1961, Outstanding Community Service award for mus. service Gallup C. of C., 1969, 70, Outstanding Citizen award, 1974, Benemerenti medal Pope Paul VI, 1977, Celebrate Literary award Gallup Internat. Reading 8 Assn., 1983-84, Woman of Distinction award Soroptimists, 1985, N.Mex. Disting. Pub. Svc. award, 1987, finalist Gov's award Outstanding N.Mex. Women, 1988, Edgar L. Hewett award Hist. Soc. N.Mex., 1992; Octavia Fellin Pub. Libr. named in her honor, 1990. Mem. ALA, N.Mex. Library Assn. (hon. life, v.p., sec., chmn. hist. materials com. 1964-66, salary and tenure com., nat. coordinator N.Mex. legislative com., chmn. com. to extend library services 1969-73, Librar. of Yr. award 1975, chmn. local and regional history roundtable 1978, Community Achievement award 1983, Membership award 1994), AAUW (v.p., co-organizer Gallup br., N.Mex. nominating com. 1967-68, chmn. fellowships and centennial fund Gallup br., chmn. com. on women), Plateau Scis. Soc., N.Mex. Folklore Soc. (v.p. 1964-65, pres. 1965-66), N.Mex. Hist. Soc. (dir. 1979-85), Gallup Hist. Soc., Gallup Film Soc. (co-organizer, v.p. 1950-58), LWV (v.p. 1953-56), NAACP, Pax Christi U.S.A., Women's Ordination Conf. Network, Gallup C. of C. (organizing chmn. women's div. 1972, v.p. 1972-73), N.Mex. Women's Polit. Caucus, N.Mex. Mcpl. League (pres. libr.'s div. 1979—), Alpha Delta Kappa (hon.). Roman Catholic (Cathedral Guild, Confraternity Christian Doctrine Bd. 1962-64, Cursillo in Christianity Movement, mem. of U.S. Cath. Bishop's Adv. Council 1969-74; corr. sec. Latin Am. Mission Program 1972-75, sec. Diocese of Gallup Pastoral Council 1972-73, c. liturgical commn. Diocese of Gallup 1977). Author: Yahweh the Voice that Beautifies the Land, A Chronicle of Midposts: A Brief History of the University of New Mexico Gallup Campus. Home and Office: 513 E Mesa Ave Gallup NM 87301-6021

FELSHER, CELIA ANN, lawyer; b. N.Y.C., Jan. 24, 1955; d. Hal C. and Beatrice A. (Fink) F.; m. John Lawrence Cecil, June 27, 1982; children: Rachel, Edward. BA, Princeton U., 1976; JD, Columbia U., 1979. Assoc. Milbank, Tweed, Hadley & McCloy, N.Y.C., 1979-87, ptnr., 1988—. Mem. ABA. Democrat. Jewish. Home: 521 Eagle Knolls Rd Larchmont NY 10538-3908 Office: Milbank Tweed Hadley & McCloy 1 Chase Manhattan Plz New York NY 10005-1401

FELSTED, CARLA MARTINDELL, librarian, travel writer; b. Barksdale Field, La., June 21, 1947; d. David Aldenderfer Martindell and Dorthe (Hetland) Horton; m. Robert Earl Luna, Aug. 24, 1968, (div. 1972); m. Hugh Herbert Felsted, Nov. 2, 1974. BA in English, So. Meth. U., 1968, MA in History, 1974; MLS, Tex. Woman's U., 1978. Cert. secondary tchr., Tex.; cert. learning resources specialist, Tex. Tchr. Bishop Lynch High Sch., Dallas, 1968-72, Lake Highlands Jr. High Sch., Richardson, Tex., 1973-75; instr. Richland Coll., Richardson, Tex., 1973-76; library asst. So. Meth. U., Dallas, 1977-78; librarian Tracy-Locke Advt., Dallas, 1978-79; corp. librarian Am. Airlines, Inc., Ft. Worth, 1979-84; research librarian McKinsey & Co., Dallas, 1984-85; reference librarian St. Edward's U., Austin, Tex., 1985—, assoc. prof., 1994—; ptnr. Southwind Info. Svcs. and Southwind Bed-Breakfast, Wimberley, Tex., 1985-92; bd. dirs. S.W. Fed. Credit Unit, 1978-81. Editor, compiler: Youth and Alcohol Abuse, 1986; co-editor Mexican Meanderings, 1991—; contbr. to Frommer's travel guides, 1991—. Mem. adv. bd. Sch. Libr. and Info. Scis., Tex. Women's U., Denton, 1982-84; mem. curriculum com. Wimberley Ind. Sch. Dist., 1986; bd. dirs. Hays-Caldwell Coun. on Alcohol and Drug Abuse, San Marcos, Tex., 1986-88, Inst. Cultures for Wimberley Valley, 1989-91, Tex. Alliance Human Needs, 1992—. Grantee St. Edward's U., 1986-89. Mem. ALA, Tex. Libr. Assn. (dist. program com., membership com. 1986-88, Tex.-Mex. rels. com. 1992—), Wimberley C. of C. (bd. dirs. 1987-88). Unitarian. Home: PO Box 33057 Austin TX 78764-0057

FELTEAU, ANNE L., nursing consultant; b. Benton Harbor, Mich., Mar. 16, 1942; d. Frank and Anne (Figlus) Graziano; m. Leonel Felteau, Aug. 31, 1963; children: Leonel, Wesley, Douglas. Diploma in nursing, Meml. Hosp., South Bend, Ind., 1963; BBA, Mercer U., 1984; MBA, Ga. Coll., 1986. RN, Ga., Mich.; C.N.A.A. cert. Staffing mgr. Med. Ctr. of Cen. Ga., Macon; project coord. nursing info. systems Gwinnett Hosp. System, Lawrenceville, Ga.; product mgr., nursing info. systems, nurse cons. SunHealth Corp., Atlanta; program mgr. nursing svcs. HBO & Co., Atlanta; dir. bus. affairs, nursing Grady Health System, Atlanta, dir. nursing bus. affairs. Mem. ANA, Am. Coll. Healthcare Execs., Am. Orgn. Nurse Execs., Healthcare Info. Mgmt. Systems Soc., Ga. Nurses Assn., Ga. Assn. Nurse Execs., Healthcare Fin. Mgmt. Assn., Sigma Theta Tau. Home: 1578 Greyson Ridge Marietta GA 30062-7203

FELTON, CYNTHIA, principal; b. Chgo., Apr. 1, 1950; d. Robert Lee Felton Sr. and Julia Mae (Cheton) Felton-Phillips. BA, Northeastern, 1970; MEd, National Coll., 1984; MA, DePaul U., 1988; PhD, Loyola U., Chgo., 1992. Cert. tchr, adminstrv., Ill. Tchr. Chgo. Pub. Schs., 1971-86, adminstr., 1986-89, asst. prin., 1989-92, prin., 1992—. Mem. ASCD, Nat. Coun. Tchrs. Math, Nat. Coun. Suprs. Math, Ill. Coun. Tchrs. Math (bd. dirs. 1992—). Office: Orr High Sch 730 N Pulaski Rd Chicago IL 60624

FELTON, PATRICIA ANN, nurse, hospital administrator; b. Birmingham, Ala., Nov. 10, 1949; d. Perry Lee and Frankie (Walton) Brown; m. Herman Felton, Jan. 28, 1971; children: Kenneth, Karla, Felicia. Assoc. Nursing Arts, Wayne County Community Coll., 1974; B Nursing Sci., Madonna Coll., 1981; M Adminstrn., Marygrove Coll., 1987; postgrad., Mercy Coll.; MBA, U. Detroit-Mercy, 1992. RN, Mich. Staff nurse oper. rm. Sinai Hosp., Detroit, 1980-82; asst. dir. Meharry Allied Health Learning Ctr., Detroit, 1982-84; dir. of nursing Universal Variable Staffing Systems, Detroit, 1982-83; clin. instr. Highland Pk. (Mich.) Community Coll., 1983-85, Mercy Coll., Detroit, 1983-85, Westland (Mich.) Med. Ctr., 1984-85; patient care educator staff devel. Grace Hosp., Detroit, 1985-87; dir. surg. svcs. Mercy Meml. Hosp., Monroe, Mich., 1988-91; dir. surg. svcs., anesthesia St. Luke's Hosp., Saginaw, Mich., 1991—; cons. Kitch, Saurbier, Drutchas, Wagner and Kenney, P.C., Detroit, 1986-89. Mem. NAFE, Assn. Oper. Rm. Nurses, Black Nurses Assn., Wayne County Community Coll. Nurse Alumni (sec. 1984), Mich. Assn. Nurse Execs. Democrat. Baptist. Home: 25096 Lindenwood Ln Southfield MI 48034-6188 Office: St Lukes Hosp 700 Cooper Ave Saginaw MI 48602-5399

FELTY, AMY PATRICIA, computer scientist, researcher; b. Columbus, May 19, 1962; d. Evan Jerome and Elvira Rosemary (Maneri) F. BA, Colgate U., 1984; MSE in Computer Sci., U. Pa., 1986, PhD in Computer Sci., 1989. Teaching asst. U. Pa., Phila., Spring 1985, rsch. fellow, 1984-89; vis. rschr. INRIA (Nat. Inst. for Rsch. in Computer Sci. and Automation), Rocquencourt, France, 1989-91; rsch. scientist Software Prins. Rsch. Dept., AT&T Bell Labs., Murray Hill, N.J., 1991—; lectr. in field; condr. workshops in field; organizing com. mem. IEEE Symposia on Logic in Computer Sci., 1993—. Contbr. articles to profl. jours. Charles A. Dana scholar Colgate U., 1982; recipient Rubinoff Award for outstanding dissertation U. Pa., 1990. Mem. ACM, NOW, Am. Assn. for Artificial Intelligence, European Assn. for Theoretical Computer Sci., Women at AT&T, Phi Beta Kappa. Democrat. Office: AT&T Bell Labs 600 Mountain Ave Murray Hill NJ 07974

FENDERSON, CAROLINE HOUSTON, psychotherapist; b. East Orange, N.J., June 17, 1932; d. George Cochran and Mary Bullard (Saunders) Houston; m. Kendrick Elwell Fenderson, Jr.; 1 child, Karen Sibley. BA, Vassar Coll., 1954; MA, U. So. Fla., 1973. Lic. mental health counselor, Fla.; diplomate Am. Bd. Cert. Managed Care Providers; cert. Nat. Bd. Clinical Hypnotherapists; cert. trainer, development of human capacities Found. for Mind Rsch.; ordained to ministry of edn. Unitarian Univeralist. Dir. of religious edn. Unitarian Universalist Ch., St. Petersburg, Fla., 1960-80; min. of religious edn. Unitarian Universalist Ch., Clearwater, Fla., 1981-83; counselor and staff devel. cons. Pinellas County (Fla.) Schools, 1973-83; pvt. practice Clearwater and Palm Harbor, Fla., 1983—. Author: Life Journey, 1988; (with Kendrick Fenderson Jr.) Magnets, 1961, Southern Shores, 1964; (with others) Man the Culture Builder, 1970, U.U. Identity, 1979; contbr. articles to profl. jours. Pub. affairs chmn. St. Petersburg Jr. League, 1960; founder Childbirth and Parent Edn. League of Pinellas County, 1960-70, pres., v.p., com. chair, tchr.; v.p. Child Guidance Clinic, St. Petersburg, 1960. Mem. ACA, Liberal Religious Edn. Dirs. Assn. (v.p. 1980-81), Assn. Transpersonal Psychology, Assn. Humanistic Psychology, Internat. Transpersonal Assn., Unitarian Universalist Assn. (com. mem. 1975-79), Phi Beta Kappa, Kappa Delta Pi. Home: 29 Freshwater Dr Palm Harbor FL 34684-1106 Office: 25 400 US 19 N Ste 172 Clearwater FL 34623

FENN, SANDRA ANN, program support administrator; b. Sugar Land, Tex., Oct. 31, 1953; d. William Charles and Helen Maxine (Kyle) F.; m. Jimmie Dan Watts, May 21, 1973 (div. June 22, 1988); 1 child, Gabriel Nathaniel; life ptnr. David Alfredo Garza; 1 child, Lindsay Nichelle. A in Gen. Studies, Alvin (Tex.) C.C., 1994. Shampoo asst. LaVonne's Salon of Beauty, Houston, 1972-73; coding clk. Prudential Ins. Co., Houston, 1974-75; word processing operator MacGregor Med. Assn., Houston, 1983-85; computer applications analyst Computer Scis. Corp., Houston, 1987-92; program support adminstr. Sci. Applications Internat. Corp., Houston, 1992—. Mem. Phi Theta Kappa. Home: 107 Clearview # 1206 Friendswood TX 77546 Office: Sci Applications Internat Corp 16511 Space Center Blvd Houston TX 77058

FENN, SHERILYN, actress; b. Detroit, Feb. 1, 1965. TV series: Twin Peaks, 1990 (Emmy award nomination best supporting actress in a drama series); TV movies Silence of the Heart, 1984, Dillinger, 1991; TV specials Divided We Stand, 1988, A Family Again, 1988; film appearances The Wild Life, 1984, Just One of the Guys, 1985, Out of Control, 1985, Thrashin', 1986, The Wraith, 1986, Zombie High, 1987, Two Moon Junction, 1988, Crime Zone, 1988, Wild at Heart, 1990, Backstreet Dreams, 1990, Ruby, 1992, Desire and Hell at Sunset Motel, 1992, Diary of a Hitman, 1992, Of Mice and Men, 1992, Twin Peaks: Fire Walk With Me, 1992, Three of Hearts, 1993, Boxing Helena, 1993, Fatal Instinct, 1993. Office: care Phyllis Carlyle 639 N Larchmont Ste 207 Los Angeles CA 90007*

FENNELL, DIANE MARIE, marketing executive, process engineer; b. Panama, Iowa, Dec. 11, 1944; d. Urban William and Marcella Mae (Leytham) Schechinger; m. Leonard E. Fennell, Aug. 19, 1967; children: David, Denise, Mark. BS, Creighton U., Omaha, 1966. Process engr. Tex. Instruments, Richardson, 1974-79; sr. process engr. Signetics Corp., Santa Clara, Calif., 1979-82; demo lab. mgr. Airco Temescal, Berkeley, Calif., 1982-84; field process engr. Applied Materials, Santa Clara, 1984-87; mgr. product mktg. Lam Rsch., Fremont, Calif., 1987-90; dir. sales and mktg. Ion & Plasma Equipment, Fremont, Calif., 1990-91; pres. Fennell Assocs., Inc., Half Moon Bay, Calif., 1991—; founder, coord. chmn. Plasma Etch User's Group, Santa Clara, 1986-88; tchr. computer course Adult Edn., Half Moon Bay, Calif., 1982-83. Founder, bd. dirs. Birth to Three program Mental Retardation Ctr., Denison, Tex., 1974-75; fund raiser local sch. band, Half Moon Bay, 1981-89; community rep. local sch. bd., Half Moon Bay, 1982-83. Mem. Am. Vacuum Soc., Soc. Photo Instrumnentation Engrs., Soc. Women Engrs., Material Rsch. Soc. Home: 441 Alameda Ave Half Moon Bay CA 94019-1365

FENNELL ROBBINS, SALLY, writer; b. Greensburg, Pa., Feb. 17, 1950; d. Clifford Seanor and Charlotte Louise (Hoffman) Fennell; m. John W. Robbins, Sept. 22, 1984. BS in Journalism, cum laude, Ohio U., 1972; MA in Journalism, magna cum laude, Marshall U., 1974. Intern, reporter Tribune-Rev., Greensburg, Pa., 1972; prodn. asst. Harper's Bazaar, N.Y.C., 1972; reporter UPI, Birmingham, Ala., 1972-73; reporter, dept. editor HFD-Retailing Home Furnishings, Fairchild Pubs., N.Y.C., 1975-77; account exec. supr., client svc. mgr., v.p. Burson-Marsteller, N.Y.C., 1977-83; group mgr., v.p. pub. rels. div. Ketchum Communications, 1983-84; freelance writer, editor, 1984-89; dir. retail communications Deloitte & Touche Retail Svcs. Group, N.Y., 1989-93; writer, 1993—. grad. teaching asst. Sch. Journalism/Reporting, Marshall U., Huntington, W.Va., 1973-74. Home and Office: 237 E 20th St New York NY 10003-1812

FENNER, ESTELLE YVONNE, accounting manager; b. Richmond, Va., Dec. 12, 1955; d. Moses Trim and Sara Elizabeth (Hobson) F. BS, Va. Commonwealth U., 1977. Sr. examiner State Corp. Commn., Richmond, 1979-85; sr. acct., fin. analyst dept. of accounts Commonwealth of Va., Richmond, 1985-87, acctg. mgr. dept. of treasury, 1987—. Leader Girl Scouts U.S., Richmond, 1985—. Mem. Am. Soc. Women Accts. (pres. Richmond chpt. 1991—), Soc. Fin. Examiners (cert.), Inst. Mgmt. Accts., Govt. Fin. Officers Assn. Democrat. Baptist. Home: 10408 Natick Ct Richmond VA 23236-3762 Office: Commonwealth of Va Dept Treasury 101 N 14th St Richmond VA 23219-3684

FENNING, LISA HILL, federal judge; b. Chgo., Feb. 22, 1952; d. Ivan Byron and Joan (Hennigar) Hill; m. Alan Mark Fenning, Apr. 3, 1977; 4 children. BA with honors, Wellesley Coll., 1971; JD, Yale U., 1974. Bar: Ill. 1975, Calif. 1979, U.S. Dist. Ct. (no. dist.) Ill., U.S. Dist. Ct. (no., ea., so. & cen. dists.) Calif., U.S. Ct. Appeals (6th, 7th & 9th cirs.), U.S. Supreme Ct. 1989. Law clk. U.S. Ct. Appeals 7th cir., Chgo., 1974-75; assoc. Jenner and Block, Chgo., 1975-77, O'Melveny and Myers, Los Angeles, 1977-85; judge U.S. Bankruptcy Ct. Cen. Dist. Calif., Los Angeles, 1985—; bd. govs. Nat. Conf. Bankruptcy Judges, 1989-92; pres. Nat. Conf. of Women's Bar Assns., N.C., 1987-88, pres.-elect, 1986-87, v.p., 1985-86, bd. dirs; lectr., program coord. in field; bd. govs. Nat. Conf. Bankruptcy Judges Endowment for Edn., 1992—. Mem., bd. advisors: Lawyer Hiring & Training Report, 1985-87; contbr. articles to profl. jours. Durant scholar Wellesley Coll., 1971; named one of Am's. 100 Most Important Women Ladies Home Jour., 1988. Fellow Am. Bar Found., Am. Coll. Bankruptcy; mem. ABA (mem. commn. on women in the profession 1987-91, Women's Caucus 1987—, Individual Rights and Responsibilities sect. 1984—, Bus. Law sect. 1986—, Bus. Bankruptcy com.), Nat. Assn. Women Judges (Nat. Task Force Gender Bias in the Cts. 1986-87, 93-94), Nat. Conf. Bankruptcy Judges (mem. endowment edn. bd.), Am. Bankruptcy Inst. (bd. steering com. statis. project 1994—), Calif. State Bar Assn. (chair com. on women in law 1986-87), Women Lawyers' Assn. L.A. (ex officio mem., bd. dirs., chmn, founder com. on status of women lawyers 1984-85, officer nominating com. 1986, founder, mem. Do-it Yourself Mentor Network 1986—), Phi Beta Kappa. Democrat. Office: US Bankruptcy Ct 255 E Temple St Rm 1682 Los Angeles CA 90012-3334

FENSTERSTOCK, JOYCE NARINS, financial executive; b. N.Y.C., Dec. 30, 1948; d. Charles S. and Frances D. (Kross) Narins; m. Blair C. Fensterstock; children: Michael Bayard, Evan Steele, Laurel Sage. BA in Psychology, Wellesley Coll., 1970; MBA, Harvard U., 1973. Assoc. corp. fin. Goldman, Sachs & Co., 1973-78, Warburg Paribas Becker Inc., Chgo., 1974-75; past sr. v.p. corp. fin., mng. dir. Paine Webber Inc., N.Y.C.; past pres. Paine Webber Mut. Funds, N.Y.C.; now pres. PaineWebber Atlas Global Growth, N.Y.C. Mem. Fin. Women's Assn., Harvard Club (N.Y.C.). Home: 120 E 75th St New York NY 10021-3278 Office: PaineWebber Atlas Global Growth 1285 Ave of the Americas New York NY 10019*

FENTON, MARJORIE, university official, consultant; b. Warren, Ohio, Feb. 7, 1935; d. Leland Reed and Elma Arlene (Gotthardt) Titus; m. Harold W. Fenton, June 11, 1955 (div. Sept. 1984); children: Brian, Amy. BS in Edn., Kent State U., 1985, M in Edn. Adminstrn., 1988. Treas. Champion Local Sch. Dist., Warren, 1967-80, Trumbull County Joint Vocat. Sch. Dist., Warren, 1980-89; pres., cons. Sch. Mgmt. Svcs., Inc., Southington, Ohio, 1989—; coord. Ashland U., Ohio, 1989—; cons. Ohio Dept. Edn., Columbus, 1980-84, 89—, Kemper Securities, Inc., 1993—; trustee Champion Cmty. Sr. Housing, Inc., Warren, 1982-90. Mem. Trumbull County Bd. Edn., Warren, 1968-93. Recipient Exemplary Service to Edn. award Champion Local Schs., Warren, 1980. Mem. Ohio Assn. Sch. Bus. Ofcls. (state pres. 1979-80, state legis. chmn. 1980-89, Pres.'s Disting. Svc. award 1984, Recognition Outstanding Svc. 1985), Assn. Sch. Bus. Ofcls. Internat. (chair profl. devel. rsch. com.), Ohio Sch. Bds. Assn., Phi Delta Kappa.

FENTON, MONICA, grant writer; b. Elizabeth, N.J., Mar. 2, 1944; d. Edward B. and Veronica (Kryszczuk) Zacharczyk; m. C. Gerald Bischoff (div. 1971); m. Roger A. Fenton, July 30, 1983. Student, Union Coll., Cranford, N.J., 1962-66. Sr. rsch. tech. Bristol-Myers Co., Hillside, N.J., 1963-75; tech. adminstr., electron microscopist Albert Einstein Coll. Medicine, Bronx, N.Y., 1975-88; asst. to dir. Ctr. Rsch. Occupational & Environ. Toxicology Oreg. Health Sci. U., 1988—. Mng. editor Third World Med. Rsch. Found., N.Y.C., 1987—, editorial cons., 1990—; copy editor (proc.) The Grass Pea: Threat and Promise, 1989, Nutrition, Neurotoxins and Lathyrism, 1994, (transcripts) Toxicity of Cycads, 1988; contbr. tech. rsch. articles and abstracts to profl. jours., ghost writer 4 rsch. revs. Mem. Electron Microscopy Soc. Am., Nat. Soc. Fundraising Execs. Home: 54 W Shore Rd Mountain Lakes NJ 07046 Office: Oreg Health Sci U 3181 SW Sam Jackson Park Rd Portland OR 97201-3011

FERBER, LINDA S., museum curator; b. Suffern, N.Y., May 17, 1944. BA cum laude, Barnard Coll., 1966; MA, Columbia U., 1968, PhD in Art History, 1980. Curator Am. painting and sculpture The Bklyn. Mus., 1982—, chief curator, 1985—. Author: William Trost Richards (1833-1905): American Landscape and Marine Painter, 1980, Tokens of a Friendship:

Miniature Watercolors by William T. Richards, 1982, (with others) The New Path: Ruskin and the American Pre-Raphaelites, 1985, Never at Fault: The Drawings of William T. Richards, 1986, (with others) Albert Bierstadt: Art and Enterprise, 1991; also articles on 19th and 20th century Am. art history. Wyeth Endowment for Am. Art fellow, 1976-77. Mem. Coll. Art Assn., Am. Assn. Mus., Phi Beta Kappa. Office: Brooklyn Mus 200 Eastern Pky Brooklyn NY 11238-6052

FERDICO, DIANE C. LEON, artist; b. N.Y.C., Dec. 17, 1945; m. John Ferdico, Sept. 15, 1979. BA, N.Y.U., 1991, postgrad. instr. N.Y. Open Ctr., 1993, Greenwich Village Art Ctr., 1984-92. One-person shows include Colegio Farmaceuticos de Alicante, 1984, LaGuardia Community Coll., 1992; two-person shows include Studio 18 Visual Arts Ctr., 1985; group exhibitions include Gallery II West, 1984, Greenwich Cillage Art Ctr., 1986, Manhattan Graphics Ctr., 1988, Studio 18 Visual Arts Ctr., 1981-90, Banco Hispano Americano, 1990, Mus. for Contemporary Arts, 1990, Wetherholt Gallery, 1991, The Art Directors Club, 1992, Tribeca 148 Gallery, 1992, Ward-Nasse Gallery 1992; represented in permanent collections N.Y.U., The N.Y. Pub. Libr., Kunstlerinnenarchiv, Nurnberg, Germany, Colegio Farmaceuticos de Alicante, Spain, Internat. Women Artists Archive Acquisitions; contbr. articles and reviews to jours. in field. Studio asst. Met. Mus. of Art Young People's Programs, 1985-86. Home: 99-34 67 Rd Forest Hills NY 11375

FERENCE ABRAMS, PATRICIA SUSAN, nurse; b. N.Y.C., Nov. 19, 1950; d. Edward Joseph Ference and Ann Carol (Fox) Gray. RN, Misericordia Hosp. Sch. Nursing, Bronx, N.Y., 1974. Nurse Montefiore Hosp., Bronx, 1974-77, North Shore Univ. Hosp., Manhasset, N.Y., 1977—. Mem. Am. Nurses Assn., N.Y. State Nurses Assn. Address: 9854 Nob Hill Ln Sunrise FL 33351

FERETIC, EILEEN SUSAN, editor; b. N.Y.C., Aug. 31, 1949; d. Joseph Anthony and Eileen Helen (Sohl) F.; m. William Kulakoski; 1 child, Shannon. B.A., Fordham U., 1971. Editor Manpower Edn. Inst., N.Y.C., 1970-72; editor UTP div. Hearst Bus. Communications, L.I., N.Y., 1972-90; editorial dir. FM Bus. Pub., Garden City, N.Y., 1990-92; editor Corporate Systems mag., 1975-80, Office Products News, 1972-82, Today's Office, 1982-92; also editorial dir. Office Group, 1978-92; editor in chief Beyond Computing mag., N.Y.C., 1992—; industry rep. U.S. Dept. Commerce, 1980, 83; mem. Pres.'s Pvt. Sector Survey on Cost Control/Office Automation Task Force, 1982. Co-author textbook on adminstrv. procedures in electronic office, 1979; co-producer, host (TV series) Office Automation; contbr. World Book Ency. Recipient N.Y. Daily News award journalism, 1970; Long Island Press Club Writing award. Mem. Am. Soc. Bus. Press Editors Assn. (writing award, Apex award for editorial writing, award for best new mag.). Home: 115 Rita Dr East Meadow NY 11554-1326 Office: Beyond Computing IBM Corp 590 Madison Ave New York NY 10022-2521

FERETIC, GERALDINE ANN MARIE, program coordinator; b. Poughkeepsie, N.Y., Sept. 26, 1958; d. Nicholas Frank and Catherine (Cerrito) F. AAS, Farmingdale U., 1978; BA in Psychology, Adelphi U., 1982, MA in Psychology, 1984, MSW, 1991. Cert. social worker, ACSW. Psychologist Montefiore Hosp. Med. Ctr. Riker's Island Prison, East Elmhurst, N.Y., 1984-89; psychologist Suffolk Child Devel. Ctr., Smithtown, N.Y., 1989-91; program coord. Devel. Disabilities Inst., East Hills, N.Y., 1991—. Mem. APA, NASW, Assn. for Behavior Analysis. Office: Devel Disabilities Inst 210 Forest Dr Greenvale NY 11548-1206

FERGES, ROSE D., nursing educator; b. Balt., Feb. 8, 1930; d. Walker H. and Bessie E. (Dorsey) Dawson; m. Joseph H. Ferges Sr., Jan. 2, 1953; children: Frances, Toney, Joseph Jr., Paula. AA, Essex Community Coll., Balt., 1972; BS, U. Balt., 1979; MS, Coppin State U., 1991. Nursing supr. Highland Health Facility, Balt.; supr. Spring Grove Hosp., Balt., Veterans Adminstrn. Ft. Howard, Balt.; Instr. nursing edn. Dept. Veterans Affairs, Balt. Mem. Md. Nurses Assn., NAACP, Blacks in Govt. (rsch. com.), Toastmaster (charter; chair data validation com.).

FERGUS, PATRICIA MARGUERITA, English language educator emeritus, writer, editor; b. Mpls., Oct. 26, 1918; d. Golden Maughan and Mary Adella (Smith) F. B.S., U. Minn., 1939, M.A., 1941, Ph.D., 1960. Various pers. and editing positions U.S. Govt., 1943-59; mem. faculty U. Minn., Mpls., 1964-79, asst. prof. English, 1972-79, coord. writing program conf. on writing, 1975, dir. writing centre, 1975-77; prof. English and writing, dir. writing ctr., assoc. dean Coll. Mt. St. Mary's Coll., Emmitsburg, Md., 1979-81; dir. writing seminars Mack Truck, Inc., Hagerstown, Md., 1979-81; writer, 1964—; editorial asst. to pres. Met. State U., St. Paul, 1984-85; coord. creative writing, writer program notes for Coffee Concerts, The Kenwood, 1992-94; dir. Kenwood Scribes Presentation, 1994; speaker and cons. in field; dir. 510 Groveland Assocs.; bus. mgr. Eitel Hosp. Gift Shop. Author: Spelling Improvement, 5th edit., 1991; contbr. to Midwest Chaparral, Downtown Cath. Voice, Mpls., Mountaineer Briefing, ABI Digest; contbr. poems to Minn. English Jour., Mpls. Muse, The Moccasin, Heartsong and Northstar Gold, The Pen Woman, Midwest Chaparral, Rhyme Time; contbr. short stories to anthologies. Mem. spl. vocal octet St. Olaf Ch. Choir, St. Olaf Parish Adv. Bd. Recipient Outstanding Contbn. award U. Minn. Twin Cities Student Assembly, 1975; Horace T. Morse-Amoco Found. award, 1976, Golden Poet award, World of Poetry, 1992; Ednl. Devel. grantee U. Minn., 1975-76; Mt. St. Mary's Coll. grantee, 1980; 3d prize vocal-choral category Nat. Music Composition Contest, Nat. League Am. Pen Women, speaker and Bronze Medalist, 13th Internat. Biographical Congress, 1986. Mem. AAUW, Am. Biog. Inst. (dep. gov.), Internat. Biog. Ctr. (hon. mem. adv. coun.), Nat. Coun. Tchrs. English (regional judge, 1974, 76-77, state coord. 1977-79), Minn. Coun. Tchrs. English (chmn. career & job opportunities com., spl. com. tchr. licensure, sec. legis. com.), Nat. League Am. Pen Women (1st pl. Haiku nat. poetry contest 1992), World Lit. Acad., Mpls. Poetry Soc. (numerous poetry prizes), League Minn. Poets, Midwest Fedn. Chaparral Poets (numerous poetry prizes, 1st prize 1993). Roman Catholic. Home and Office: 701 E High St Apt 311 Charlottesville VA 22902

FERGUSON, BRENDA, educational administrator; b. Macedonia, Ill., Jan. 30, 1942; d. Bill and Earlene (Boyles) Fisher; m. Jeff Ferguson, Jan. 18, 1963; children: Terri Rotz, Tamala Ferguson. BS, U. Ill., 1963, MEd, 1967; cert. in elem. edn., So. Ill. U., 1964, cert. in adminstrn., 1985. Recreation dir. U. Ill. Ext. Svc., Kankakee, Ill., 1960, West Frankfort, Ill., 1961-62; tchr. kindergarten Rantoul (Ill.) Schs., 1963-64, Champaign (Ill.) Schs., 1965-66, Belleville (Ill.) Schs., 1966-67; asst. ext. advisor U. Ill. Ext. Svc., Belleville/East Saint Louis, 1967-69; tchr. home econs. Herrin (Ill.) Schs., 1970-87; adminstrv. dir. Williamson County (Ill.) Regional Sys., 1987—. Mem. ASCD, Ill. Prins. Assn., Ill. Womens Adminstrs. Assn. (v.p. 1993-94), Ill. Vocat. Home Econs. Tchrs. Assn. (state pres., state conf. chair, state bd. dirs., Educator of Yr. 1991), Ill. Vocat. Assn. (bd. dirs. 1989-90), Am. Vocat. Dirs., Beta Sigma Phi. Home: 1117 E Poplar Herrin IL 62948 Office: Williamson County Reg Voc 700 N 10th St Herrin IL 62948

FERGUSON, DEBORAH LEA, maternal health nurse; b. Bainbridge, Md., May 15, 1953; d. Howard D. and Doris F. (Light) Bechthold; 1 child, Amy Lynn Ferguson. ADN, Odessa (Tex.) Coll., 1974. RN, Tex.; cert. in neonatal resuscitation. Staff nurse Roper Hosp., Charleston, S.C., 1974-76, St. Joseph Hosp., College Station, Tex., 1976-78; med. coord. med.-surg. unit HCA Med. Ctr. Plano, Tex., 1978-79, asst. administrated supr., 1979-80, staff nurse, 1980-84, head nurse newborn nursery, 1985—, head nurse spl. care nursery, 1986-90. Mem. NAFE, Assn. Women's Health, Obstet. and Neonatal Nurses. Office: 3901 W 15th St Plano TX 75075

FERGUSON, FRANCES HAND, volunteer, civic worker; b. N.Y.C., Apr. 9, 1907; d. Learned and Frances (Fincke) Hand; m. Robert Munro Ferguson, Nov. 10, 1933; children: Patty M., Robert H.M., Phyllis M. AB, Bryn Mawr Coll., 1929; MA in Psychology, Columbia U., 1931, postgrad., 1933-35. Tchr. Brearley Sch., 1936-38; dir. courses N.Y. chpt. Am. Women's Vol. Svc., 1939-40; successively N.Y. chpt. pres., nat. chmn. field com., exec. com. Planned Parenthood Fedn. Am., 1940-51, pres., 1953-56, chmn., 1st pres., 1959-65; vol. rsch. technician Meml. Hosp., 1941-42; bd. dirs. Internat. Planned Parenthood Fedn., 1953—, v.p., 1959-62, treas., 1970-73; bd. dirs. Euthanasia Soc., 1955-62, Am. Eugenics Soc., 1957-63; mem. nat. com. Maternal Health, 1957-63, Human Betterment Assn., 1956-64, Assn. for Vol. Sterilization, 1964-85, Assn. for Study Abortion, 1967-70, Assn. for Vol. Surg. Contraception, 1985—. Recipient Disting. Svc. award Bryn Mawr Coll., 1960, Dirs. award Planned Parenthood Fedn. Am., 1965, Internat. Planned Parenthood, 1992. Mem. Assn. for Vol. Surg. Contraceptive. Home: 1035 5th Ave New York NY 10028-0135

FERGUSON, KATHARINE ADELE, librarian; b. Tulare, Calif., Apr. 6, 1941; d. Paul Andrew and Dora Gladys (Skidmore) Hancock; m. Lonnie L. Ferguson, May 15, 1966 (div. Aug. 1982); children: Tonya, Keith. AA, Bakersfield Coll., 1960; BA, Lewis and Clark Coll., 1962; MLS, U. Calif., Berkeley, 1963. Reference librarian U.S. Army, Korea, 1963-64; catalog librarian Calif. Poly. U., San Luis Obispo, 1964-66, Colorado Coll., Colorado Springs, 1970-72; pub. services librarian Mary Hardin Baylor Coll., Belton, Tex., 1972-77; acquisitions librarian U.S. Army, Ft. Huachuca, Ariz., 1981-87; chief librarian U.S. Army, Yuma, Ariz., 1987—. Pub. relations vol. Parents Without Ptnrs., Sierra Vista, Ariz., 1984-87. Mem. ALA, Spl. Library Assn., Ariz. State Library Assn. Office: Post Libr Yuma Proving Ground AZ 85365

FERGUSON, KATHRYN CUCCIA, judge; b. New Brunswick, N.J.. BA, Rutgers Coll., N.J., 1980; JD, Rutgers Sch. of Law, N.J., 1983. Law clk. to Judge Judith H. Wizmur U.S. Bankruptcy Ct. (N.J. dist.), 1985-86; atty. Markowitz & Zindler, 1986-93; judge U.S. Bankruptcy Ct. (N.J. dist.), 3rd circuit, Trenton, 1993—. Office: US Post Office & Courthouse 402 E State St Trenton NJ 08608*

FERGUSON, KELLIE GAIL, business advisor; b. Dobbs Ferry, N.Y., June 2, 1941; d. Charles Willard and Doris (Mosher) Wilson; m. Donald Wesley Ferguson; children: Dawn Ferguson-Whitman, Laurie L. Ferguson. BSBA, Post Coll., 1980. Dir. data processing Choate Rosemary Hall Found., Inc., Wallingford, Conn., 1975-89; dist. mgr. for office automation Kelly Temporary Svcs., Detroit, 1989-90; sr. bus. advisor Distributor Info. Systems Corp., Farmington, Conn., 1990—; auditor ISO 9000. Contbr. articles to jours. Office: Disc 135 South Rd Farmington CT 06034

FERGUSON, MADELYN KRISTINA, education educator; b. Miami Beach, Fla., July 14, 1948; d. Francis Robb and Shirley Anne (Walsh) F.; m. Eugene Francis Zenobi, June 25, 1988. AA, Miami Dade Jr. Coll., 1968; BA in Edn., Fla. Atlantic U., 1975; MEd in Reading, U. LaVerne, Calif., 1981. Tchr. elem. edn. Sumner County Pub. Schs., Gallatin, Tenn., 1975-77; tchr. elem. edn. Dade County Pub. Schs., Miami, 1977-78, tchr. compensatory edn., 1979-81, tchr. elem. edn., 1981-83, tchr. acad. excellence, 1983—; leader Dade County 4-H, Miami, 1984— mem. coun. adv. com., 1989—; mem. overall adv. com. Fla. Coop. Extension, Miami, 1989—. Co-author, editor: Hands on Science Activities, 1988; editor: Miami Celebrity Cookbook, 1987. Member Urban League, Miami, 1984-95, ACLU, Miami, 1989-95. U. Fla. grantee, 1986, 87; Dade Pub. Edn. Fund grantee, 1989; Chevron/U. Fla. grantee, 1990, Nat. Gardening Assn. youth garden grantee, 1994; 4-H Cmty. Pride grantee, 1994; named Leader of Yr. Dade County 4-H, 1987, Tchr. of Yr. Lorah Park Elem. Sch., 1987; recipient Commendation, U.S. Congl. Record, 1991, Outstanding Vol. award Metro Dade County Coop. Ext., 1994. Mem. ASCD, Nat. Sci. Tchrs. Assn., League Environ. Educators of Fla., Fla. Assn. for the Gifted, Nature Conservancy, Friends of Va. Key (bd. dirs. 1991—). Democrat. Home: 3942 SW 5th St Miami FL 33134-2035

FERGUSON, MARGARET GENEVA, author, publisher, real estate broker; d. James B. and Dollie (McCloud) F. Student, Kansas City Jr. Coll., 1949, YMCA Real Estate Inst., 1960, Bryant and Stratton Bus. Coll., 1962, Ill. Inst. Tech., 1969. Sec. Cook County Grand Jury, 1979; acting mgr. internal svc. dept. Xerox Corp., 1985-86; tutor reading and math., 1988; host Black Image Prodn. Cable 19, 1989; interviewed on various TV shows, including PM Mag., 1983; active pub. rels. newspapers, Chgo., Detroit, Kansas City, St. Louis, 1970-91; conductor workshops in field, 1970-92; participant Pan Meth. Pilgrimage to Eng., 1984, World Meth. Conf., Nairobi, Kenya, 1986. Author, pub.: The History of St. Paul CME Church 1907-1988, 1989, Books in Print, 1989-90, This Is Your Life Dr. Owens, 1991. Co-chmn. fund raiser Citizens for Mayor Harold Washington, Chgo., 1987; treas. St. Paul Mortgage Fund, 1984; vol. Am. Cancer Soc., Salvation Army, Lighthouse for the Blind; bd. dirs. Hyde Park Co-op Soc. Inc., 1992-94; dist. pres. Christian Methodist Episcopal Ch. Nat. Women's League, 1980-86, nat. fin. sec., 1980-92; officer St. Paul Christian Methodist Episcopal Ch., 1954—; v.p. lay ministry, 1987-92, pres. 1992—; sec. Christian Methodist Episcopal Long Range Planning Commn., 1982-86; mem. Chgo. State Street Women's Coun. Recipient History Writing award Christian Meth. Episcopal Ch., 1990, Gold Coaster Kiwanis Club award, 1983, Black on Black Love award, 1988; named to Cultural Citizens Found. Hall of Fame, 1990, Vol. of Yr. Chgo. Lighthouse, 1982, 1st Lady award V-103 FM, 1991, Citizens award, 1994, others. Mem. NAACP, Nat. Coun. Negro Women, People United to Serve Humanity (prison ministry award 1991), Chgo. Bd. Realtors, S.W. Suburban Bd. Realtors, Lambda Kappa Nu. Home: 727 E 60th St Apt 808 Chicago IL 60637-2539

FERGUSON, MARTHA ANN, elementary school educator; b. Pitts., Apr. 3, 1947; d. Edward Lawrence and Mary I. (Livingston) Hora; m. June 14, 1969 (div.); 1 child, Matthew Lawrence. BA in English, Calif. State U., Long Beach, 1969; postgrad., UCLA, Pepperdine U., 1970—, Marymount Loyola U., 1987—; Cert. Lang. Devel., 1994. Lang. devel. spl. cert. Tchr. kindergarten Lawndale (Calif.) Sch. Dist., 1970-73, tchr. first grade, 1973-74, early childhood educator, 1974-81, tchr. intermediate, 1981-92, tchr. bilingual, 1992—; math. chair Lawndale Sch. Dist., 1987—, math. mentor, 1987-90; trainer Tchr. Expectations and Student Achievement, 1980—; family math. trainer L.A.C.O.E., 1988—; master tchr. Loyola Marymount and Calif. State U., Dominguez, 1985—; equals math. trainer, 1989—. Mem. NEA, 1978—, NEA Polit. Action Com., Washington, 1980—, NEA Equity Watch, Washington, 1984—. Recipient scholarship Valley Forge Freedom Found., 1987. Mem. AAUW, Nat. Coun. Tchrs. Math., Lawndale Tchrs. Assn. (pres. 1979-84, grievance chair 1987-91, negotiations chair 1980-86, v.p. 1989-91), Calif. Tchrs. Assn. (state coun. rep. 1981-94, credentials and profl. devel. com. 1983-94, appointed to elections and credentials com. 1994). Democrat. Home: 810 E Grand Ave #A El Segundo CA 90245 Office: William Green Elem Sch 4520 W 168th St Lawndale CA 90260

FERGUSON, MARY FRANCES GEORGE, accountant, tax preparer; b. Lynchburg, Va., Dec. 10, 1944; d. Mike Herman and Mary Edward (Reed) George; m. Sanford Lewis Ferguson, Mar. 29, 1969. A in Bus., Ctrl. Va. C.C., 1989; BA, Lynchburg Coll., 1991. CPA, Va. Pvt. practice acctg. and tax preparation Lynchburg, dealer antiques and fine arts; ptnr. Heritage Promotions, Lynchburg. Mem. Ins. Mgmt. Accts. (bd. dirs. 1994—), Phi Theta Kappa, Gold Key, Phi Kappa Phi. Home: 1103 Cosby St Lynchburg VA 24504

FERGUSON, PAMELA ANDERSON, mathematics educator, educational administrator; b. Berwyn, Ill., May 5, 1943; d. Clarence Oscar and Ruth Anne (Stroner) Anderson; m. Donald Roger Ferguson, Dec. 18, 1965; children: Keith, Amanda. BA, Wellesley Coll., 1965; MS, U. Chgo., 1966, PhD, 1969. Asst. prof. Northwestern U., Evanston, Ill., 1969-70, U. Miami, Coral Gables, Fla., 1972-77; assoc. prof. U. Miami, 1978-81, prof. math., 1981-91, dir. honors program, 1985-87, assoc. provost, dean Grad. Sch., 1987-91; pres. Grinnell Coll., Iowa, 1991—. Contbr. over 50 articles to refereed jours. Mem. Iowa Rsch. Coun., 1993—. NSF grantee. Mem. Am. Math. Soc., Am. Women in Math., Wellesley Club, U. Chgo. Club, Sigma Xi, Phi Beta Kappa, Omicron Delta Chi. Lutheran. Office: Grinnell Coll Office of the Pres 1121 Park St PO Box 805 Grinnell IA 50112-0810

FERGUSON, SUSAN KATHARINE STOVER, nurse, psychotherapist, consultant; b. Warsaw, Ind., Mar. 11, 1944; d. Robert Eugene and Barbara Louise (Swaney) Stover; m. Philip Charles Ferguson, Oct. 2, 1965 (div.); children: Scott Duane, Shawn Alaine, Erin Kirsten. Diploma in nursing, Meth. Hosp., 1966; BA in Psychology, Purdue U., 1988; MSW, Smith Coll., 1991; advanced cert. in Psychoanalytic Psychotherapy, Psychoanalytic Psychotheraphy Ctr., 1993-94. Staff nurse, health hazard appraiser Meth. Hosp. of Ind., Indpls., 1966-68; staff nurse USPHS, Bethel, Alaska, 1968-70; instr. childbirth preparation Wabash, Ind., 1973-83; nurse Family Physicians Associated, Wabash, 1976-83; rsch. asst. Purdue U., Ft. Wayne, Ind., 1986-88; staff nurse, self-awareness seminar coord. Charter Beacon Hosp., Ft. Wayne, Ind., 1988-89; intern clin. social work Clifford Beers Guidance Ctr., New Haven, Conn., 1990-91; psychiat. nurse Yale-New Haven Hosp., 1990-91; pvt. practice Citadel Psychiat. Clinic, Ft. Wayne, Ind., 1991-93; dir. social svcs. Charter Northridge Behavioral Health sys., Raleigh, N.C., 1993-94; dir. social svcs., clinician adult psychiatry Charter Northridge Hosp., Raleigh, 1993-94; pvt. practice Raleigh, 1993—. Bd. dirs. Hoosiers for Safety Belts, Indpls., 1987-88, Ind. Med. Pol. Action Com., Indpls., 1986-87; coordinator, founder Safe Start Infant Safety Seat Loan Program, Wabash, 1981-87; participant in leadership devel. com. Wabash County C. of C., 1983; workshop leader Wabash County Hosp. Stop Smoking Program, 1982-83. Mem. NASW (family rels. coun.), Charles F. Menniger Soc., N.C. Psychoanalytic Soc., Kappa Kappa Kappa. Republican.

FERGUSON, SYBIL, franchise business executive; b. Barnwell, Alta., Can., Feb. 7, 1934; came to U.S., 1938, naturalized, 1976; d. Alva John and Xarissa (Merkley) Clarke; m. Roger N. Ferguson, July 10, 1952; children: Debra Kay, Michael David, Wade Clarke, Lois Christine, Julie Xarissa. Ed. pub. schs. Founder Diet Ctr. Inc., Pitts., 1970—; co-owner Golden Eagle Ranches, Crystal Springs Cannery. Author: The Diet Center Program, Lose Weight Fast and Keep It Off Forever, 1983, Diet Center Cookbook. Charter mem. women's aux. Madison Meml. Hosp., Resburg; founding sponsor Children's Miracle Network Telethon; past mem. nat. adv. coun. Brigham Young U., adv. bd. Ricks Coll., Boise State U.; mem. Rexburg Civic Assn. Recipient Bus. Leader of Yr. award Ricks Coll., 1980; named Great Figure of Franchising, 1987, to Community Leaders Am., one of Top 60 Women Entrepreneurs, Saavy mag., Idaho Bus. Leader of Yr., 1988, Woman of Distinction Birmingham So. Coll. Gala 9, 1989. Mem. Internat. Franchise Assn., Am. Entrepreneur Assn., Rexburg C. of C. (program dir. 1976), Com. of 200 (founder). Mem. LDS Ch. Lodge: Soroptimists (v.p. Rexburg chpt. 1975, award 1979). Office: PO Box 519 Rexburg ID 83440-0519

FERGUSON, TAMARA, clinical sociologist; b. The Hague, Netherlands; came to U.S., 1955; d. Simon and Sonia (Pokrowska) Van den Bergh; m. John D.A. Ferguson, Dec. 7, 1958. MA in Sociology, Columbia U., 1962, PhD, 1970. Asst. prof. U. Detroit, 1960-71; asst. prof., then assoc. prof. U. Windsor, Ont., Can., 1971-78; adj. assoc. prof. sociology Wayne State U. Med. Sch., Detroit, 1978—; assoc. med. staff dept. psychiatry Harper Hosp., Detroit, 1982—. Co-author: The Young Widow: Conflict and Guidelines, 1981; contbg. author: Clinical Sociology in Mental Health Setting, 1991. 2d lt. Free French armed forces, 1944-45, ETO. Mem. Am. Sociol. Assn., Found. Thanatology, Sociol. Practice Assn. (bd. dirs.). Office: Harper Hosp-Neuropsychiatry Day Treatment Program 50 E Canfield Detroit MI 48201

FERGUSON, WANDA RENEE, art educator; b. South Boston, Va., Dec. 6, 1954; d. Owen Coleman and Ruby Ann (Hall) F. BS in Art Edn., Radford U., 1976. Sales rep. W Atlee Burpee Co., Warminster, Pa., 1978-80; territory mgr. Am. Express Corp., Richmond, Va., 1980-84; regional sales mgr., asst. v.p. Signet Bank, Richmond, Va., 1984-86; account exec. Control Data Corp., Richmond, 1987-90; art educator Elkhardt Mid. Sch., Richmond, 1990—; art instr. Richmond City Schs. Artists of sculptures and paintings at various shows. Vol., Big Bros./Big Sisters, 1978-81, 84-86; steering com. Va. Environ. Assembly, Richmond, 1989, vol. chair, 1989. Mem. Richmond Craftsman's Guild (sec., bd. dirs. 1989—, pres. 1990-92), Metro. Artists Assn., Sierra Club (Chair polit. com. 1989—, exec. com. 1991-92), Control Data K Club. Methodist. Home: 3705 Floyd Ave Richmond VA 23221-2615 Office: Elkhardt Mid Sch 6300 Hull St Rd Richmond VA 23225

FERGUSON KENNEDY, BARBARA GEARHART BROWNELL, reporter; b. Essex, Conn., June 27, 1951; d. Edward John Joseph and Virginia (Gearhart) F.; m. Eugene Timothy Kennedy, June 1, 1993. AA, Colo. Women's Coll., 1971; BA, U. Minn., 1974; postgrad., Sorbonne U., 1975-77. Mng. editor, co-owner Internat. Mideast Tourist & Bus. Mag., Paris, 1984-88; corr. Saudi Gazette Newspaper, Paris, 1987-88, London, 1988-90; bur. chief Saudi Gazette Newspaper, Washington, 1990—; speaker in field. Contbr. articles to profl. jours. Lay minister All Souls Episcopal Ch., Washington, 1992—. Recipient Tihama Pub. Co. award for journalistic excellence, Jeddah, Saudi Arabia, 1988, Outstanding Support award U.S. Intelligence and Threat Analysis Ctr. Pentagon, 1990. Mem. Nat. Press Club, Fgn. Corrs. Assn. (v.p. 1990—, bd. dirs.), Fgn. Press Assn. London, Assn. de la Presse Etrangere (bd. dirs. 1985-88), Anglo-Am. Press Assn. Paris, DAR, Alpha Phi. Independent. Office: Saudi Gazette Newspaper 1145 Nat Press Bldg Washington DC 20045

FERGUSSON, FRANCES DALY, college president, educator; b. Boston, Oct. 3, 1944; d. Francis Joseph and Alice (Storrow) Daly. BA, Wellesley Coll., 1965; MA, Harvard U., 1966, PhD, 1973. Asst. prof. Newton Coll., Mass., 1969-75; assoc. prof. U. Mass., Boston, 1974-82, asst. chancellor, 1980-82; provost, prof. Bucknell U., Lewisburg, Pa., 1982-86; pres. Vassar Coll., Poughkeepsie, N.Y., 1986—. Trustee Mayo Found., 1988—, Ford Found., 1989—, Historic Hudson, 1990—; bd. dirs. Marine Midland Bank, Cen. Hudson Gas and Electric Corp. Recipient Founder's award Soc. Archtl. Historians, 1973. Office: Vassar Coll Office of the Pres Raymond Ave Poughkeepsie NY 12603-2312

FERHOLT, J. DEBORAH LOTT, pediatrician; b. New Rochelle, N.Y., Aug. 27, 1942; d. Sidney and Rose (Rubin) Lott; m. Julian Ferholt, June 19, 1963; children: Beth, Sarah. BS in Biology, U. Rochester, 1963, MD, 1967. Diplomate Am. Bd. Pediatrics. From instr. to assoc. prof. Yale Sch. Nursing, New Haven, Conn., 1969-90, lectr., 1990—, clin. assoc. prof. pediatrics, 1987—; pvt. practice pediatrics New Haven, Conn., 1982—. Author: (book) Health Assessment of Children, 1980 (Best Pediatric Book award 1981). Fellow Am. Acad. Pediatrics (mem. com. daycare State of Conn.). Office: 303 Whitney Ave New Haven CT 06511-7204

FERKINGSTAD, SUSANNE M., cosmetics executive; b. Red Wing, Minn., Aug. 19, 1955; m. Steve Ferkingstad, Oct. 19, 1991. Diploma Cosmetology, Ritter St. Paul Coll., 1974; grad., Bruno's, 1978. Instr. Ritter's St. Paul Coll., 1974-75; asst. mgr., mgr. Scot Lewis Inc., Bloomington, Minn., 1975-79; edn. dir. My Kind of Place, St. Paul, 1979-80; pres., co-owner Someone's Looking (formerly Charpentier's Inc.), St. Paul, 1980-86, owner, 1986—; styles dir. women's sect. Minn. Cosmetology Edn. Com. Fundraiser, chairperson Battered Women's Shelter, St. Paul, 1984, Children's Home Soc., St. Paul, 1985; vol. St. Paul Food Shelves Food Dr., 1985, 88; vol., model United Arts Fashion Show, 1986; vol. fundraiser pub. TV Action Auction, Ronald McDonald House, Food Shelf Drives Someone's Looking, St. Paul, MS Walkathon, 1988. Recipient numerous hairstyling awards. Mem. Nat. Cosmetologists Assn., Minn. Hairdressers and Cosmetologists Assn., St. Paul Cosmetologists Assn. (dir. 1981-83, pres. 1983-85), Hair Am., Minn. Hair Fashion Com. Home: 3111 Drew Ave N Robbinsdale MN 55422-3247 Office: Someone's Looking Inc 141 4th St E # 125 Saint Paul MN 55101-1627

FERLITA, THERESA ANN, clinical social worker; b. Pinar del Rio, Cuba, Sept. 8, 1944; came to U.S., 1945; d. Sam Marion and Maria (Garcia-Collia) F. AB in Sociology, Spalding Coll., Louisville, 1966; MS in Social Work, U. Louisville, 1972. Lic. clin. social worker, Fla. Various positions, 1966-70; sr. resource program developer Children's Bd. Hillsborough County, Tampa, Fla., 1990-92; supr. homefinding unit Ky. Dept. Child Welfare, Louisville, 1972-73; foster care worker Fla. Dept. Health and Rehabilitative Svcs., Tampa, 1974; homemaker supr. Family Counseling Ctr., Clearwater, Fla., 1974; sr. social worker, mem. intake team London Borough of Newham Social Svcs., 1976; clin. social worker Alcoholism Svcs. Hillsborough Community Mental Health Ctr., Tampa, 1977-78; clin. social worker The Children's Home, Inc., Tampa, 1978-80; case coord., coord. tng. and edn., supr. teen mother program The Child Abuse Coun., Inc., Tampa, 1980-90, clin. supr. Rainbow Family Learning Ctrs., 1989-90; pvt. practice family therapy, adults abused as children, 1991; social worker med.-surg. and trauma Tampa (Fla.) Gen. Hosp., 1992-95; mgr. family svcs. Hillsborough County Headstart Dept., Tampa, 1995—; adj. instr. Hillsborough C.C., Tampa, 1988; cons. The Spring Battered Spouse Shelter, Tampa, 1984; coord. Parents Anonymous Children's Group, Tampa, 1980-85; mem. state health adv. com. Redlands Christian Migrant Assn., Immokalee, Fla., 1982—; mem. policy coun. Hillsborough County Headstart, Tampa, 1986-89; mem. Cmty. Action Bd., Hillsborough County. Editor, compiler manuals for child abuse and neglect investigations, 1986, 87. Pres. Fair Oaks Condominium Assn.,

Tampa, 1990-91; past pres. Child Abuse Com., Fla., Inc.; bd. dirs., v.p. Centro Tampa, 1989-90. Mem. NASW (sec. Tampa Bay unit 1981-83, vice-chmn. 1990-91, Social Worker of Yr. award 1988, sec. Fla. chpt. 1986-88, del. assembly 1986-91), Acad. Cert. Social Workers, Nat. Network Social Work Mgrs. Democrat. Roman Catholic. Home: 3812 N Oak Dr Apt 21M Tampa FL 33611-2517 Office: Hillsborough County Headstart Dept County Ctr 801 E Kennedy Blvd 13th flr Tampa FL 33602

FERM, LOIS ROUGHAN, religious organization administrator; b. Buffalo, Feb. 5, 1918; d. Laurence Francis and Bertha Margaret Lucy (Jopp) R.; m. Robert O. Ferm, June 28, 1941; children: Lois Esther, Rebecca Ann, Paul Robert, Stephen John. BA, Houghton Coll., 1939; MA, U. Mich., 1955; PhD, U. Minn., 1972. Cert. tchr., N.Y. Tchr. Rushford (N.Y.) Cen. Sch., 1939-41; instr. library, sociology John Brown U., Siloam Springs, Ark., 1949-51; librarian Cuba (N.Y.) Cen. Schs., 1953-55; chmn. dept. edn. Houghton (N.Y.) Coll., 1955-57; instr. edn. U. Minn., Mpls., 1959-61, mgr. Coll. Edn. Library, 1961-64; personal asst. rsch., resource coord. Billy Graham Evangel. Assn., Mpls., 1973—. Pres., Riceville Property Owners Assn., Asheville, N.C., 1982, 83, 87, 88. Mem. Soc. Am. Archivists, Oral History Assn., Christian Women's Clubs, Pi Lambda Theta, Pi Alpha Theta. Republican. Baptist. Home: 27 Patriots Dr Asheville NC 28805-9730 Office: Billy Graham Evang Assn 1300 Harmon Pl Minneapolis MN 55403-1925

FERN, CAROLE LYNN, lawyer; b. Freeport, N.Y., Sept. 2, 1958; m. Tariq Rafique. BA, Johns Hopkins U., 1979; JD, Harvard U., 1983. Bar: N.Y. 1983, Calif. 1987. Assoc. Donovan, Leisure, Newton & Irvine, N.Y.C., 1983-87, Shearman & Sterling, N.Y.C., 1987-91; assoc. Berlack, Israels & Liberman, N.Y.C., 1991-92, ptnr., 1993—. Dep. counsel Dukakis for Pres. Mem. ABA, N.Y. State Bar Assn. (profl. liability com.), N.Y.C. Bar Assn., Am. Arbitration Assn. (panel of arbitrators), N.Y. County Lawyers Assn. (Supreme Ct. com.), Phi Beta Kappa. Democrat. Unitarian. Office: Berlack Israels & Liberman 120 W 45th St New York NY 10036

FERN, EMMA E., state official; b. Columbus, Ohio, July 22, 1927; d. Frederick and Wilhelmina (Boxheimer) Brauler; m. Joseph S. Fern, Mar. 31, 1956. AA in Criminal Justice, Miami-Dade Community Coll., 1975. Adminstrv. asst. Lucayan Beach Hotel, Bahamas, Loew's Hotels, Miami Beach, Fla.; intelligence analyst Metro-Dade Police Dept., Miami; crime intelligence analyst supr. Fla. Dept. Law Enforcement, Miami. Recipient award Fla. Dept. Law Enforcement for disting. contbn. to criminal justice, 1984, U.S. Dept. Justice award for pub. svc. Mem. Internat. Assn. Law Enforcement Intelligence Analysts (charter, pres. 1990-95). Home: 1365 NW 192nd Ter Miami FL 33169-3442

FERNAN, MARY BRIGID, lawyer; b. Kansas City, Mo., May 29, 1958; d. James Paul and Mildred Louise (Connor) F.; m. Mark Dwight Whitaker, May 28, 1983; children: Paul Connor, James Sullivan, Helen Foster Whitaker. BSN, George Mason U., 1982, JD, 1987. Bar: Va. 1987, Pa. 1995. Nurse George Washington Med. Ctr., Washington, 1980-82, Mt. Vernon Hosp., Alexandria, Va., 1982-84; atty. Legal Svcs. No. Va., Arlington, 1987, Office Rev. and Appeals, EEOC, Falls Church, Va., 1987-88; pvt. practice Annadale, Va., 1988-93, Pottsville, Pa., 1993—; adj. faculty paralegal program No. Va. C.C., 1992; counselor, mem. legal com. My Sister's Pl., Washington, 1987-93. Vol. ARC, Alexandria, 1987; vol. atty. Women's Legal Def. Fund, Washington, 1989-91; mem. Shelter Outreach Program, 1990-93; v.p. Ravensworth Bristow Civic Assn., 1990-93; head makeup design for community theatre troupe Camelot Players, 1990-91; tchr. 3d grade religious edn. St. Michael's Ch. Choir, 1991-92, tchr. 8th grade religious edn., 1992-93, mem. choir, 1992-93. Mem. ABA, Va. State Bar Assn., Fairfax Bar Assn., Phi Delta Phi. Roman Catholic. Office: 504 Hardwick Grn Pottsville PA 17901-4052

FERNANDES, FRANCES MARGARET, international business executive; b. Waimea, Hawaii, Jan. 12, 1941; d. William James and Dorothy (Lemes) F.; m. Gordon Sumner Jr., May 1, 1991; children: Lenore Ray, Adrienne Borrego, Valerie Appert. BA, Calif. State U., Fullerton, 1979; MBA, Coll. of Santa Fe, 1987. Mgmt. info. specialist Los Alamos (N.Mex.) Nat. Lab., 1979-92; pres. Fernandes Bus. Internat., Santa Fe, N.Mex., 1992—. Cantor St. Francis Cathedral, Santa Fe, 1986—; pres. Spanish Toastmasters, Los Alamos, 1983-85; singer musical programs. Mem. Am. Shortwave Listeners Club. Home: # 5 215 Camino de los Marquez Santa Fe NM 87505 Office: Sumner Assocs 100 Cienega St Ste D Santa Fe NM 87501-2003

FERNANDES SALLING, LEHUA, lawyer, state senator; b. Lihue, Hawaii, Dec. 6, 1949; d. William Ernest Fernandes and Evelyn (Ohai) Fernandes; m. Michael Ray Salling, Aug. 14, 1971; 1 child. BS, Colo. State U., 1971; JD, Cleveland Marshall Coll., 1975. Law Ptnr. Fernandes Salling & Salling, Kapaa Kauai, Hawaii, 1976—; mem. Hawaii Senate, 1982—. Mem. Hawaii State Bar Assn., Maile Bus. and Profl. Women's Club, Kamokila Canoe Club, Zonta. Office: Leipapa A Kamehameha Bldg 235 S Beretania St Honolulu HI 96813-2437

FERNANDEZ, ISABEL LIDIA, human resources specialist; b. Miami, Fla., Jan. 23, 1964; d. Rafael Juvencio and Lidia Rafaela (Morin) Fernandez. BBA, Fla. Internat. U., Miami, 1984, MS in Hospitality Mgmt., 1990. Personnel cons. Miami, 1984—; asst. dir. human resources Turnberry Isle Yacht & Country Club, Miami, 1985-87; dir. personnel Sheraton River House, Miami, 1987-88; program dir. hospitality mgmt. programs Miami-Dade Community Coll., 1988-89; dir. human resources Doubletree Hotel, Miami, 1989-91, Sky Chefs, Miami, 1991-93; trainer Barnett Technologies, Miami, 1993—. Editor newspaper The Sunblazer, 1983-84; contbr. articles to profl. jours. Named Employee of the Month, Coconut Grove Hotel, Miami, 1985. Mem. NAFE, Am. Hotel and Motel Assn. (pres. Greater Miami chpt.), Young Reps. Club (pub. rels. com.). Republican. Lutheran. Home: 8510 NW 3 Lane # 501 Miami FL 33126

FERNANDEZ, LINDA FLAWN, entrepreneur, social worker; b. Tampa, Fla., Sept. 14, 1943; d. Frank and Rose (D'Amico) F.; 1 child, Marci. B.S., U. South Fla., 1965; M.S., U. Nev., 1976. Social worker Hillsborough County, Tampa, Fla., 1965-67; parole officer adult div. Fla. Parole Commn., Tampa, 1967-69; dir. social services Sunrise Hosp., Las Vegas, Nev., 1969-78; ind. real estate investor, Fla. and Nev., 1965—; pres. Las Vegas Color Separations, Inc., 1978—, Las Vegas Typesetting, Inc., 1983—; LMR Enterprises, Inc., Las Vegas, 1984—; sec.-treas. Sierra Color Graphics, Inc., Las Vegas, 1983—. Founder, organizer Human Relations, pet mascots for elderly; team ofcl. girls' softball, 1985; mem. Clark County Citizens Com. Efficiency and Cost Reduction, 1991; vice-chmn. Citizens Com. Efficiency and Cost Reduction, 1992. Recipient numerous awards Ad Club Fedn. Mem. Las Vegas C. of C. (congl. com.) Women's Las Vegas C. of C., Ad Club Fedn., Citizens for Pvt. Enterprise, U.S. C. of C. Avocations: tennis; water skiing. Office: 3351 S Highland Dr Ste 210 Las Vegas NV 89109

FERNÁNDEZ, MAGALI, language educator; b. Havana, Cuba, Dec. 30, 1935; came to U.S., 1960; d. Andrés and Hortensia (Zamora) Hernández; m. Raimundo Rafael Fernández. BS in Edn., NYU, 1968, MA in Spanish Lit., 1970, PhD in Spanish Lit., 1984. Cert. tchr., N.Y. Bilingual sec. various orgns., N.Y.C., 1960-64, Spanish Mission to UN, N.Y.C., 1964-67; tchr. Newtown High Sch., Queens, N.Y., 1970-74, Ea. Dist. High Sch., Bklyn., 1974—; lectr. Spanish, Fordham U., N.Y.C., 1971, 72. Author: EL Collar, 1954, Rómulo Gallegos y Agustín Yañez: dos ensayos sobre literatura hispanoamericana, 1972, El Discurso Narrativo en la Obra de Ma. Luisa Bombal., 1988; contbr. lit. criticisms, articles to numerous publs. Mem. Am. Assn. Tchrs. of Spanish, NYU Alumni Assn.

FERNANDEZ, SONIA CISTERNE, psychotherapist; b. Mayari, Oriente, Cuba, Apr. 27, 1956; came to U.S., 1969; d. Juan Felipe and Sonia Rosa (Tuero) Cisterne; m. Albert Marco Fernandez, Jan. 10, 1981; children: Karih, Kristina. BA in Psychology/Spanish, Wayne State U., 1977, MA in Counseling and Guidance, 1980. Lic. profl. counselor; cert. social worker, Mich. Substance abuse therapist Latin Am. Community Against Substance Abuse, Detroit, 1978-80; supr., counselor Latin Ams. for Social and Econ. Devel., Detroit, 1980-84; family therapist Family and Neighborhood Svcs. Ctr. for New Options, Inkster, Mich., 1985; therapist S.W. Detroit Community Mental Health Svcs., Inc., Detroit, 1986—; mental health cons. Latino Family Svcs., Inc., Detroit, 1986—. Author: (booklet) Conducta Hiperactiva en Ninos y Adolescentes, 1994. Mem. Cuban Club of Detroit, 1972—. Recipient Cert. of Recognition Latino Family Svcs. and Ea. Mich. U. Dept. of Social Work, 1991. Mem. ACA, Mich. Counseling Assn., Detroit-Wayne County Interagency (com. adoption resources and edn.). Roman Catholic. Office: SWDCMH 1700 Waterman Detroit MI 48209

FERNANDEZ-POL, BLANCA DORA, psychiatrist, researcher; b. Buenos Aires, Mar. 5, 1932; came to U.S., 1967; d. Balbino Fernandez and Maria Remedios van Pol. MD, U. Buenos Aires, 1958. Diplomate Am. Bd. Psychiatry and Neurology. Intern N.Y. Polyclinic Med. Sch., 1967-68; resident in psychiatry UCLA/Brentwood Hosp., 1968-69, NYU/Bellevue Hosp., 1969-71; gen. practitioner Hosp. Espanol, Buenos Aires, 1959-62; forensic psychiatrist Criminoloy Inst., Buenos Aires, 1963-65; clin. attending psychiatrist Bellevue Psychiat. Hosp., N.Y.C., 1971-75; pvt. practice St. Petersburg, Fla., 1976-78; chief psychiat. svcs. USAF Hosp. Yokota, Tokyo, 1980, USAF Hosp., Homestead, Fla., 1981; chief continuing treatment program dept. psychiatry Bronx-Lebanon Hosp., Bronx, 1983—; prof. psychology U. Moran, Buenos Aires, 1962-67; asst. prof. psychiatry N.Y. Med. Coll., N.Y.C., 1972-74; clin. asst. prof. psychiatry Albert Einstein Coll. Medicine, Bronx, 1982—. Contbr. articles to profl. jours. Maj. USAF, 1978-81. Mem. Am. Psychiat. Assn., N.Y. Acad. Scis., Am. Acad. Psychiatrists in Alcoholism and Addictions, Res. Officers Assn. U.S., Assn. Mil. Surgeons U.S. Home: PO Box 21644 Brooklyn NY 11202-0036 Office: Bronx Lebanon Hosp 1285 Fulton Ave Bronx NY 10456-3401

FERRAINOLO, NANCY, mortgage investor; b. Pitts., Mar. 14, 1950; d. Anthony Joseph and Concetta (DiIorio) F. BA in History, Carlow Coll., 1972; MA in Old Testament, Pitts. Theol. Sem., 1976; BS in Acctg., Point Park Coll., 1980. Cert. mortgage investor; notary pub. Adminstrv. asst. Etna Equipment & Supply, Pitts., 1972-78; pers. acctg. adminstr. Envirotech Corp., Coraopolis, Pa., 1978-81; fin. analyst GE Corp., Stamford, Conn., 1981-83; mgr. qualified plan adminstrn. Mellon Bank N.A,, Pitts., 1984-89; sr. defined contbr. specialist Mockenhaupt, Mockenhaupt, Cowden & Parks, Inc., Pitts., 1989-93; cert. mortgage investor, dir. Toto & Assocs., Inc., Glenshaw, Pa., 1993—. Vol. and tour guide, Pitts. Coun. for Internat. Visitors, 1969—;. Mem. NRA (cert. instr.), Pa. Assn. Notaries, Nat. Assn. Fed. Lic. Firearm Dealers, Nat. Real Estate and Mortgage Investors Assn. Office: Toto & Assocs Inc 1403 Mount Royal Blvd # 28 Glenshaw PA 15116-2200

FERRANTE, JOAN MARGUERITE, English and comparative literature educator; b. N.Y.C., Nov. 11, 1936; d. Nicholas Henry and Josephine (Pisacane) F.; m. R. Carey McIntosh. Student, Brearley Sch., 1950-54, Radcliffe Coll., 1954-55; B.A., Barnard Coll., 1958; M.A., Columbia U., 1959, Ph.D., 1963. Asst. prof. English and comparative lit. Columbia U., N.Y.C., 1966-70; assoc. prof. Columbia U., 1970-74, prof. English and comparative lit., 1974—, chmn. English and comparative lit., 1988-91, dir. Ctr. for Italian Studies, 1977-80; lectr. modern langs. Swarthmore (Pa.) Coll., 1968; lectr. medieval studies Fordham U., N.Y.C., 1976; Andrew Mellon prof. humanities Tulane U., 1984. Author: The Conflict of Love and Honor, 1973, Guillaume d'Orange, Four Twelfth Century Epics, 1974, Woman as Image in Medieval Literature from the Twelfth Century to Dante, 1975, (with Robert Hanning) The Lais of Marie de France, 1978, The Political Vision of the Divine Comedy, 1984; editor: (with George Economou) In Pursuit of Perfection, Courtly Love in Medieval Literature, 1975, (with Robert Hanning) The Challenge of the Medieval Text, 1985; mem. adv. bd.: Speculum, 1975-78; cons. editor Records of Civilization, Columbia U. Press, 1975—. Am. Council Learned Socs. fellow, 1969-70; NEH fellow, 1980-81. Fellow Medieval Acad. Am. (councillor); mem. Dante Soc. Am. (councillor, v.p. 1978-83, pres. 1985-91), MLA (exec. coun. 1986-90), Internat. Arthurian Soc., Internat. Courtly Lit. Soc., Phi Beta Kappa (senator 1979—, v.p. 1988-91, pres. 1991-94). Office: Columbia U 616 Philosophy Hall New York NY 10027

FERRANTE, OLIVIA ANN, retired educator, consultant; b. Revere, Mass., Nov. 9, 1948; d. Guy and Mary Carmella (Prizio) F. BA, Regis Coll., 1970; MEd, Boston Coll., 1971, postgrad., 1977-81; postgrad., Middlebury Coll., 1974, Lesley Coll., 1982. Cert. history tchr., tchr. of blind. Chmn. Braille dept. Nat. Braille Press, Boston, 1971-74; tchr. of visually impaired, spl. needs dept. Revere High Sch., 1974-92; cons. Revere PTA, 1984—. Contbr. articles to profl. jours. Vol. Morgan Meml., Boston, 1983—, tchr. braille, 1993—, tchr. literacy program, 1993—, mem. Steven Rich scholarship com., 1993—; mem. Revere Com. for Handicapped Affairs, 1985—, Everett (Mass.) Chorus, 1974-76, Adult Music Ministry, 1989, Revere First Com., 1993; soloist Revere Music Makers, 1977-79; mem. partnership com. Internat. Year Disabled, 1980-81, mem. adult choir Immaculate Conception Ch., 1966—, mem. adv. bd. Mass. Commn. of Blind, 1988—, governing bd. on ind. living, 1989; access monitor Mass. Orgn. on Disability, 1988—; mem. adv. bd. Radio Reading Svc. for Blind, 1989; memtor Nat. Braille Literacy Project, 1992, mem. Friends of the Sick Children's Trust, 1992; vol. Birthright, 1992, ProLife Office, 1992; active Arts Coun. Coop, 1992—; mentor Vision Found., 1993—; friend Wang Ctr., 1993—, Boston Pub. Garden and Common, 1993—, Boston Pops, 1992—; mem. and publicist mobility adv. bd. Mass. Com. for Blind, 1994—; mem. Revere Soc. for Cultural and Historical Preservation, 1994—; mem. Historic Mass., 1994—, Cath. League, 1994—; friend Paul Revere House, 1994—. Mem. NEA, Mass. Tchrs. Assn. Revere Tchrs. Assn., Nat. Space Soc., Nat. Cath. Assn. for Persons with Visual Impairment, Cath. Daus.'s of Am., Friends of Revere Pub. Libr., Friend of Librs. For Blind, Friends of Boston Symphony Orch., Nat. Writers Union, Amnesty Internat., Soc. Creative Anachronism, Women Affirming Life, Michael Crawford Internat. Fan Assn. Democrat. Roman Catholic. Home: 115 Reservoir Ave Revere MA 02151-5825 Office: Revere High Sch Spl Needs Dept 101 School St Revere MA 02151-3099

FERRARA, BARBARA ELLEN, research administrator; b. Berkeley, Calif., Aug. 15, 1949; d. Gennaro and Dorathea (Lehman) F. BA, MacMurray Coll., 1971; MPA, Sangamon State U., 1989. Asst. to the dir. ctr. for policy studies/program evaluation Sangamon State U., Springfield, Ill., 1978-89; asst. to the exec. dir. inst. for pub. affairs Sangamon State U., Springfield, 1989—; mem. confr. facilities and activies rev. com., Sangamon Univ., 1993—, dep. speaker Univ. Assembly, 1986-87, mem. staff senate 1984-87, vice chair, 1986-87, employee of the month selection com., 1986-87, accreditation self-study subcom. on rsch. and creative activity, 1986, univ.-wide select com. to review affirmative action, 1984. Contbr. articles to profl. jours. Bd. dirs. North Washington Park Neighborhood Assn.; election judge Springfield Bd. of Election; mem. Springfield Area Arts Coun. Mem. Govtl. Rsch. Assn., Policy Evaluation Group, Policy Studies Orgn. Democrat. Office: Sangamon State Univ Shepherd Rd Springfield IL 62794-9243

FERRARI, JEAN K., accountant; b. Escanaba, Mich., Nov. 18, 1953; d. Eldred and Edna V. (Sattem) S.; m. John A. Ferrari Jr., April 13, 1974; children: Marissa, Angela, Lorraine. AS in Acctg., Kalamazoo Valley C.C., 1989; student, We. Mich. U. Acctg. clerk Comercia Bank, Kalamazoo, 1974-77; bookkeeper Minute Markets, Kalamazoo, 1977-81; acct. FEMA Corp., Portage, Mich., 1981—. Mem. Inst. Mgmt. Accts., Beta Gamma Sigma (sec. 1993). Methodist. Home: 54881 County Rd 657 Paw Paw MI 49079 Office: FEMA 6666 Lovers Ln Kalamazoo MI 49002

FERRARI, JODI MOREAU, systems transportation operations analyst; b. Charleroi, Pa., May 13, 1956; d. Joseph Eugene and Rose Marie (Vivio) F.; m. Frank Goldovsky, Nov. 19, 1991; 1 child, Adora Moreau Goldovsky. BS, Ind. U. of Pa., 1978; postgrad., Temple U. Mgr. customer ops. ctr. Conrail, Phila., 1978-89, mgr. customer svc., 1989-92, sr. transportation system ops. analyst, 1992—. Republican. Roman Catholic. Home: 1 Owl Ct Marlton NJ 08053 Office: 2201 Market St Philadelphia PA 19103

FERRARI, LINDA JOY, nurse, nursing administrator; b. Wausau, Wis., Aug. 28, 1960; d. Joel Darwin and Sharron (Junghans) Walter; m. Louis A. Ferrari Jr., Oct. 28, 1989; 1 child, Louis A. III. ADN, Rochester (Minn.) C.C., 1982. Cert. BLS, ACLS, CCRN, Wis. RN Theda Clark Regional Med. Ctr., Neenah, Wis., 1982-88; RN Door County Meml. Hosp., Sturgeon Bay, Wis., 1988—, supr., 1989—; supr. Dorchester Nursing Ctr., 1989—; staff nurse Baylake Outpatient Surgery Ctr., 1994—.

FERRARO, BETTY ANN, corporate administrator, state senator; b. Newport, Vt., Mar. 3, 1925; d. Clarence John and Mauretta Rowena (Potter) Morse; m. Dominic Thomas Ferraro, Oct. 8, 1964; children: Deborah, David, Susan, Barbara. Student, Mary Hitchcock Hosp. Sch. Nursing, Coll. St. Joseph, Rutland, Vt. Exec. sec. to asst. treas. Cen. Vt. Pub. Svc. Corp., Rutland, 1943-44; sec. to dean N.Y. Med. Coll., N.Y.C., 1944-46; model G. Fox Co., Hartford, Conn., 1947; corp. sec., office mgr. John Russell Corp., Rutland, 1970-80; exec. dir. Rutland Area Coordinated Child Care Com., Washington, 1977-79; adminstrv. asst. Hilinex of Vt., Rutland, 1981-83; owner Classic Connection Gift Shop, Rutland, 1983-87; adminstr. Vicon Recovery Systems, Inc., Rutland, 1987-90; owner, operator nursery sch., 1973-77; mgr. Day Care Ctr., 1978-80; alderman City of Rutland, 1984-86; resource dir. Rutland City, Vt. Emergency Mgmt. Team for State of Vt., 1984-90; mem. Cmty. Devel. Commn., 1986; lectr. St. Peter's Parish, Rutland. Chmn. Rutland City Rep. Com., 1991—, state committeewoman State Rep. Com., 1991—, rep.; rep. Rutland County Rep. Com.; state del. Rep. Nat. Conv., 1992; state rep., 1990-92; state senator, 1992-94, 95-97; mem. jud. nominating bd. Human Resource Investment Coun., Vt. Student Assistance Corp. Bd. Fleming Inst. fellow, 1995. Mem. Nat. Assn. Women in Constrn. (chartered, past pres.), Rutland County Rep. Women (founder). Republican. Roman Catholic. Home and Office: Condo 13 155 Dorr Dr Rutland VT 05701

FERRARO, GERALDINE ANNE, lawyer, former congresswoman; b. Newburgh, N.Y., Aug. 26, 1935; d. Dominick and Antonetta L. (Corrieri) F.; m. John Zaccaro, 1960; children: Donna, John, Laura. B.A., Marymount Manhattan Coll., 1956, hon. degree, 1982; J.D., Fordham U., 1960; postgrad., N.Y. U. Law Sch., 1978, hon. degree, 1984; hon. degree, Hunter Coll., 1985, Plattsburgh Coll., 1985, Coll. Boca Raton, 1989, Va. State U., 1989, Muhlenberg Coll., 1990, Briarcliffe Coll. for Bus., 1990, Potsdam Coll., 1991. Bar: N.Y. 1961, U.S. Supreme Ct. 1978. Pvt. practice, N.Y.C., 1961-74; asst. dist. atty. Queens County, N.Y., 1974-78; chief spl. victims bur., 1977-78; mem. 96th-98th Congresses from 9th N.Y. Dist.; sec. House Democratic Caucus; first woman vice presdl. nominee on Democratic ticket, 1984; fellow Harvard Inst. of Politics, Cambridge, Mass., 1988; mng. ptnr. Keck Mahin Cate & Koether, N.Y., 1993-94; appointed Amb. to UN Human Rights Commn., 1994, 95. Author: Ferraro, My Story, 1985, Changing History: Women, Power, and Politics, 1993. Chmn. Dem. Platform Com., 1984; bd. dirs. N.Y. Easter Seal Soc.; Dem. candidate U.S. Senate, 1992; U.S. President Clinton's appointee to UN Human Rights Commn. Conf., Geneva, 1993, World Conf., Vienna, Austria, 1993. Mem. Queens County Bar Assn., Queens County Women's Bar Assn. (past pres.), Nat. Dem. Inst. for Internat. Affairs (bd. dirs.), Coun. Fgn. Rels., Internat. Inst. Women's Polit. Leadership (former pres.). Roman Catholic.

FERREE, CAROLYN RUTH, radiation oncologist, educator; b. Liberty, N.C., Jan. 29, 1944; d. Numer Floyd and Mary Isabel (Glass) Black; m. Bill K. Ferree, Aug. 17, 1968 (div. 1980). BA, U. N.C., Greensboro, 1966; MD, Bowman Gray Coll., Winston-Salem, 1970. Diplomate Am. Bd. Radiation Oncology. Intern medicine N.C. Bapt. Hosp., Winston-Salem, 1970-71, resident in radiation oncology, 1971-74; instr. radiation oncology Bowman Gray Sch. Medicine, Winston-Salem, 1974-75, asst. prof., 1975-80, assoc. prof., 1980-87, prof., 1987—. Contbr. articles to profl. jours. Mem., v.p. County Bd. of Pub. Health, Winston-Salem, 1985-92; bd. dirs. U. N.C.-Greensboro Excellence Found., 1988—; med. dir. Forsyth County chpt. Am. Cancer Soc., 1975—. Fellow Am. Coll. Radiology; mem. Pediatric Oncology Group (radiotherapy coord.), N.C. Med. Soc. (sec.-treas. 1991—, 2nd v.p. 1990-91, del. to AMA), AMA, Am. Soc. Therapeutic Radiologists Orgn. Office: Bowman Gray Sch Medicine Med Center Blvd Winston-Salem NC 27157

FERREE, PATRICIA ANN, corporate managed care analyst, nurse; b. Middletown, N.Y., Oct. 5, 1947; d. William Harry and Florence Arlene (Sarr) Krenrich; m. Daniel Milton Ferree, Feb. 13, 1972; children: Patricia Ann, Daniel Milton Jr. AS, Cen. Fla. Community Coll., Ocala, 1969; BS in Nursing, Va. Commonwealth U., 1985. Cert. cardiac nurse therapist. Critical care nurse Fla. Hosp., Orlando, 1969-76, cardiac nurse therapist, 1976-80, head nurse cardiac rehab., 1980-82; nurse adminstrn., rsch. nurse Va. Heart Inst., Richmond, 1982-86; coord. health care cost containment Cir. City Stores, Inc., Richmond, 1986, mgr. health and safety, 1986-89, corp. mgr. workers' compensation and safety, 1989-93, corp. mgr. workers compensation, 1993-94, managed care corp. sr. analyst, 1994—. Choir dir. Courthouse Rd. Seventh-Day Adventist Ch., Richmond, 1983-89, min. music, 1989-94; mem. curriculum com. Richmond Acad. Home and Sch. Leader; chmn. cardiovascular task force Am. Heart Assn., 1984-85. Recipient svc. plaque cardiology dept. Fla. Hosp., 1982; Peggy Gibson Meml. nursing scholar, 1967, Fla. Bd. Edn. nursing scholar, 1967-69. Mem. Am. Assn. Occupational Health Nurses, Am. Soc. Safety Engrs., Soc. Nursing Profls., Am. Assn. for Cardiovascular and Pulmonary Rehab. (founding), Richmond Met. Soc. for Cardiac Rehab. (founding), Phi Kappa Phi, Sigma Zeta. Republican. Office: Cir City Stores Inc 9950 Mayland Dr Richmond VA 23233-1463

FERREIRA, JO ANN JEANETTE CHANOUX, consumer electronics manufacturing executive; b. Melrose Park, Ill., Dec. 3, 1943; d. John W. and June B. Chanoux; BS, Purdue U., 1965, MS (NSF fellow), 1969; m. G. Dodge Ferreira, Apr. 21, 1979 (div. Dec. 1993). With systems devel. research IBM, San Jose, Calif., 1965-67; asst. dir. mgmt. info. systems edn. Union Carbide Corp., N.Y.C., 1969; mgmt. cons. Touche Ross & Co., N.Y.C., 1970-72, Peat Marwick Mitchell, N.Y.C., 1974-75; dir. corp. devel. strategy cons. A.T. Kearney-Mgmt. Cons., Chgo., 1975-83; dir. Computer Devel. Center, United Airlines, 1983-88; pres. WSG Designs Inc., Northbrook, Ill., 1988-92, Accorde-Moraine Consulting, Inc., 1992-93; gen. mgr. acoustic rsch. divsn. Internat. Jensen, Inc., Lincolnshire, Ill., 1993—, v.p. bus. plans and internat. group liaison, 1994—; lectr. Purdue U., 1969, 73-74; guest lectr. Northwestern U., 1981; gen. mgr. acoustic rsch. divsn., exec. asst. to pres. Internat. Jensen, Inc., 1993—. Mem. Inst. Mgmt. Cons. (cert. mgmt. cons.), Am. Arbitration Assn. Phi Kappa Phi. Contbr. articles to profl. publs.; speaker various groups. Office: Internat Jensen Inc 25 Tri State Internat Ctr Lincolnshire IL 60069

FERRELL, STEPHANIE, journalist, writer; b. Radford, Va., June 4, 1963; d. Harold Orville Ferrell and Carol (Ward) Blake. AAS, 1983; BS in Comm., W.Va. State Coll., 1985. Pub. rels., model HBA Fur Corp., N.Y.C., 1986, 87; underwriting adminstr. Fiduciary Ins. Co. Am., N.Y.C., 1987, 88; journalist 361st/340th Pub. Affairs Detachment, Ft. Totten, N.Y., 1986-91; editorial asst. Dow Jones News Svc., N.Y.C., 1989-91; team leader 943d Replacement Detachment, Ft. Totten, 1991—; editor Who's News Wall St. Jour., N.Y.C., 1991—; model/actress Belinda Dale Modeling Agy., Charleston, W.Va., 1981-86. 2d lt. USAR, 1991—. Mem. NOW, Nat. Press Photographers Assn., Internat. Thespian Soc. (life). Democrat. Baptist. Office: Wall St Jour 200 Liberty St Fl 10 New York NY 10281-1099

FERREY-LAUGHON, BARBARA ELOYCE, journalist, newspaper editor; b. Bishop, Calif., Oct. 28, 1964; d. Robert Hayes and Sandra Lee (Jensen) F. BA, U. Nev., 1987. Staff writer Chalfant Press, Inc., Bishop, 1987-88, sr. staff writer, 1988-89, community news editor, editor spl. issue, 1989, city editor, 1989-90, news editor, 1990-92, editor, 1992—. Co-recipient 1st place award for recreation publs. Calif. Newspaper Advt. Execs. Assn., 1989, 93; recipient Altrusa Outstanding Svc. award, 1991-2. Mem. Soc. Profl. Journalists, Altrusa (rec. sec. 1993-94, 1st v.p. 1994—, pub. com. Bishop 1990—, Dedicated Svc. award 1991), Calif. Soc. Newspaper Editors. Office: Chalfant Press Inc 450 E Line St Bishop CA 93514-3506

FERRI, ALESSANDRA MARIA, ballet dancer; b. Milan, Italy, May 6, 1963; came to U.S., 1985; d. Carlo and Gian-Carla (Ghelfi) F.; m. Mauricio Orbecchi, Nov. 10, 1990. Scuola media superiore, Teatro Alla Scala, Milan; Liceo Linguistico, Francesco Sforza, Milan; student, Scuola Di Ballo Teatro Alla Scala, Milan, Royal Ballet Sch., London. Mem. corps de ballet The Royal Ballet, 1980-83, solo dancer, 1983-84, prin. dancer, 1984-85; prin. dancer Am. Ballet Theatre, N.Y.C., 1985—; guest star Nat. Ballet Can., 1988, Ballet Nat.de Marseilles, 1989-90, Ater-Balletto, 1990-92, Teatro All Scala, 1991-92, Opéra de Paris, 1992. Created roles in L'Invitatino au Voyale, Valley of Shadows, Isadora, Consort Lessons, Different Drummer, Chanson; danced in Napoli Divertissements, Illuminations, Return to the Strange Land, The Sleeping Beauty, Afternoon of a Faun, The Two Pigeons, Swan Lake, Mayerling, Manon, Romeo and Juliet, Voluntaries, Konservatoriet, Cinderella, La Bayadere, Les Biches, Seven Deadly Sins, Carmen; roles with ABT include La Bayadere, Fall River Legend, Giselle, Manon,

Other Dances, Pillar of Fire, Romeo and Juliet, Sinfonietta, The Sleeping Beauty, Some Assembly Required, La Sylphide, Les Sylphides, Bruch Violin Concerto No. 1; appeared with Ballet National de Marseill in Roland Petit's Le Diable Amoreux, 1989, with Ballet of Teatro alla Scala in Roland Petit's Suite Satie, 1994, with Nat. Ballet of Can. in Romeo and Juliet, with Paris Opera Ballet in Carmen. Recipient Prix De Lausanne, 1980, Sir Laurence Olivier award, London, 1984. Office: Am Ballet Theater 890 Broadway New York NY 10003-1211*

FERRI, MARGARET JEAN, counselor; b. Windsor, Ont., Can., June 21, 1953; came to U.S., 1980; d. Phillip Joseph and Isabel Jean (Holt) Moroun; m. Anthony Joseph Ferri, Sept. 10, 1976; children: Steven Anthony, Theresa Jean. AAS, Purdue U., Ft. Wayne, 1983, BA in Psychology, 1984; MS in Counseling, U. Nev., Las Vegas, 1991. Cert. case mgr., cert. rehab. counselor; cert. in early childhood spl. edn. Counselor Maryvale, Windsor, 1975-76, The Inn of Windsor, 1976-80; counselor, supr. Assn. for Retarded Children, Ft. Wayne, 1981-85; counselor Spl. Children's Clinic, Las Vegas, 1985-86; child devel. specialist, residential program coord. So. Nev. Mental Health Retardation Svcs., Las Vegas, 1986-90; mgr. traumatic brain injury program Univ. Med. Ctr., Las Vegas, 1990-91; rehab. counselor Intracorp, Las Vegas, 1991—. Mem. Jr. Mesquite, Las Vegas, 1986-88; mem. adv. bd. Community Rehab. Svcs. Nova Care, Las Vegas, 1991—. Mem. ACA, So. Nev. Head Injury Assn. (bd. dirs. 1991-92). Roman Catholic. Office: Intracorp 1771 E Flamingo # 216-B Las Vegas NV 89119

FERRIERO, LORI JEAN, nursing administrator; b. Pitts., Dec. 11, 1959; d. Joseph M. and Loretta C. (Manella) F. BSN, Carlow Coll., 1981; A in Anesthesia, Western Pa. Hosp. Sch. Nurse Anesthesia, 1985; MEd, Pa. State U., 1992. Cert. registered nurse anesthetist. Staff nurse delivery room West Penn Hosp., Pitts., 1981-82, staff nurse coronary care unit, 1982-83; staff nurse anesthetist Butler (Pa.) Meml. Hosp., 1985-86; staff nurse anesthetist Mercy Hosp., Pitts., 1986-90, asst. chief nurse anesthetist, 1990-94, supr. anesthesia svcs., chief nurse anesthetist same day surgery ctr., 1994—. Active mentor program Carlow Coll., Pitts., 1990—. Mem. Am. Assn. Nurse Anesthetists, Pa. Assn. Nurse Anesthetists, Alcoma Ladies Golf Assn. (sec.), Alcoma Golf Club. Roman Catholic. Office: Mercy Hosp Same Day Surgery Ctr 1400 Locust St Pittsburgh PA 15219

FERRIN, DEBORAH KAYE, child care coordinator, educator; b. San Diego, Sept. 26, 1952; d. Alfred Leonard and Kathryn Mae (Brice) Cabral; m. David Eugene Ferrin, July 26, 1981; 1 child, Jacob Zenas. AS in nursing sch. tng., Grossmont Coll., El Cajon, Calif., 1974; BS in Child Devel., San Diego State U., 1976; MBA, Nat. U., 1982. Dir. asst. Campus Care Child Care, El Cajon, 1971-74; tchr. Head Start, Otay, Calif., 1976-78; dir. Aka Head Start, El Cajon, 1978-81; instr. San Diego C.C., 1981-89, Grossmont Coll, El Cajon, 1981-89; child care coord. City of San Diego, 1989—; cons. Children's Hosp., San Diego, 1993—; presenter Nat. Assn. Edn. of Young Children's Local Govt.'s Role in Child Care, 1990. Pres., bd. dirs. East County Cmty. Clinic, El Cajon, 1972-81; pres. PTA, Meridian Sch., El Cajon, 1987-89; den leader, merit counselor Boy Scouts Am., El Cajon, 1988—. Mem. Nat. Assn. Edn. Young Children (presentor, validator 1976—), San Diego Assn. Edn. Young Children (publicity chair 1976), Calif. City County Child Care Coord. (conf. chair 1989, Recognition award 1992), Calif. Women in Govt., Women Employees Assn. (exec. com. 1992), Nat. Coun. Jewish Women (hon. Svc. award 1992). Democrat. Presbyterian. Home: 1408 Sunnyland Ave El Cajon CA 92019 Office: City of San Diego 1200 Third Ave Ste 924 San Diego CA 92101

FERRIS, EVELYN SCOTT, lawyer; b. Detroit, d. Ross Ansel and Irene Mabel (Bowser) Nafus; m. Roy Shorey Ferris, May 21, 1969 (div. Sept. 1982); children: Judith Ilene, Roy Sidney, Lorene Marjorie. J.D., Willamette U., 1961. Bar: Oreg. 1962, U.S. Dist. Ct. Oreg. 1962. Law clk. Oreg. Tax Ct., Salem, 1961-62; dep. dist. atty. Marion County, Salem, 1962-65; judge Mcpl. Ct., Stayton, Oreg., 1965-76; ptnr. Brand, Lee, Ferris & Embick, Salem, 1965-82; chmn. Oreg. Workers' Compensation Bd., Salem, 1982-89. Bd. dirs. Friends of Deepwood, Salem, 1979-82, Salem City Club, 1972-75, Marion County Civil Svc. Commn., 1970-75; com. mem. Polk County Hist. Commn., Dallas, Oreg., 1976-79; mem. Oreg. legis. com. Bus. Climate, 1967-69, Govs. Task Force on Liability, 1986. Recipient Outstanding Hist. Restoration of Comml. Property award Marion County Hist. Soc., 1982. Mem. Oreg. Mcpl. Judges Assn. (pres. 1967-69), Altrusa, Internat., Mary Leonard Law Soc., Western Assn. Workers Compensation Bds. (pres. 1987-89), Capitol Club (pres. 1977-79), Internat. Assn. Indsl. Accident Bds. and Commns. (pres. 1992-93), Phi Delta Delta. Republican. Episcopalian. Home: 747 Church St SE Salem OR 97301-3715 Office: Dept Ins and Fin Labor and Industries Bldg Salem OR 97310

FERRO, JEAN, photo artist; b. Phila., Oct. 28, 1944; d. Charles Joseph and Hilda Emma (Bernhardt) Radnetter; m. Alberto Ferro, Nov. 22, 1982 (div. July 1993); 1 child, Eric Etebari. Photo artist L.A., Paris, Rome, Tokyo, 1974—; art lectr. on creative self-portrature Art Ctr. Coll. Design, Pasadena, 1989—; presenter various workshops and lectrs. Self-portrait ltd. edit. Paris Photo Lab Presents Jean Ferro, 1989; contbg. artist Focus on AIDS IV, 1992, Focus on AIDS V, 1994; exhibited in group shows at Mus. Anthropology, Calif. State U., Chico, 1991, Paris Photo Lab., 1991, 92, Home Savs. Am., L.A., 1991, 92, 93, Lace Gallery, L.A., 1993, G. Ray Hawkins Gallery/Dirs. Guild, L.A., 1993, 94, Friends of Jr. Arts Ctr., 1993, Calif. Mus. Photography, U. Calif., Riverside, 1993-94, Mcpl. Art Gallery, L.A., 1995; contbr. articles to profl. jours. Recipient awards Fuji Film Corp., N.Y.C., 1989, Polaroid Corp., Cambridge, Mass., 1990, Bob Olsen Color Expansions, Hollywood, Calif., 1991, Popular Arts Entertainment, HOB, Hollywood, Calif., 1993, Zona Prodns., Beverly Hills, Calif., 1993, Paris Photo Lab., L.A., 1989—, A&I Color Lab., Hollywood, 1985—, Artist in the Cmty. award City of L.A. Cultural Affairs, 1992-93. Mem. Women in Photography Internat. (advisor 1989—). Studio: Jean Ferro Studio 419 N Larchmont Blvd # 64 Los Angeles CA 90004

FERRO-NYALKA, RUTH RUDYS, librarian; b. Chgo., June 2, 1930; d. Joseph F. and Anna (Serbenta) Rudys; BA, U. Chgo., 1950; MA in Library Sci., Rosary Coll., 1972; children: Keith A. Krisciunas, Kevin L. Krisciunas, Kenneth M. Krisciunas; stepchildren: Anita L. Abbate, Vincent A. Abbate. Tchr. elem. sch. Westmont, Ill., 1961-63; librarian Dist. 105 public schs., La Grange, Ill., 1972—, tchr. program for gifted children, 1979-81, 82-85, coordinator gifted program, 1981-82. Mem. ALA, NEA, Ill. Edn. Assn., Dist. 105 Tchrs. Assn. (pres. 1983-85, 91-93), AAUW. Roman Catholic. Home: 5800 Doe Cir Westmont IL 60559-2138 Office: 1001 S Spring Ave La Grange IL 60525-2760

FERRY, APRIL, costume designer. Films include: The Rose, 1979, Foxes, 1980, Cheech & Chong's Next Movie, 1980, The Best Little Whorehouse in Texas, 1982, One From the Heart, 1982, Mike's Murder, 1982 (also actress), Hammett, 1982, The Big Chill, 1983, Irreconcilable Differences, 1984, American Dreamer, 1984, Perfect, 1985, Gotcha!, 1985, Mask, 1985, Poltergeist II: The Other Side, 1986, Big Trouble in Little China, 1986, Planes, Trains, and Automobiles, 1987, Made in Heaven, 1987, She's Having a Baby, 1988, Child's Play, 1988, Three Fugitives, 1989, My Name is Bill W., 1989 (TV movie), Leviathan, 1989, Immediate Family, 1989, Almost an Angel, 1990, Decoration Day, 1990 (TV movie), Unlawful Entry, 1992, Radio Flyer, 1992, The Babe, 1992, Free Willy, 1993, Beethoven's 2nd, 1993, Rockford Files: I Still Love L.A., 1994 (TV movie), Maverick, 1994, Little Giants, 1994. Office: 1615 Shell Ave Venice CA 90291*

FERRY, JOAN EVANS, school counselor; b. Summit, N.J., Aug. 20, 1941; d. John Stiger and Margaret Darling (Evans) F. BS, U. Pa., 1964; EdM, Temple U., 1967; postgrad., Villanova U., 1981. Cert. elem. sch. tchr., elem. sch. counselor. Indsl. photographer Bucksco Mfg. Co., Inc., Quakertown, Pa., 1958-59; math. and German tutor St. Lawrence U., Canton, N.Y., 1959-61; research asst. U. Pa., Phila., 1963; tchr. elem. sch. Pennridge Schs., Perkasie, Pa., 1964-74, 75-77, elem. sch. counselor, 1981—; pvt. practice counselor, real estate partnership Perkasie, 1981—; chair child study team Perkasie Elem. Sch., 1988-94; tutor math., German, St. Lawrence U., Canton, N.Y., 1959-61; supervisory tchr. East Stroudsburg U., Pennridge Schs., 1971-74; research asst. U. Pa., Phila., 1963; mem. acad. coms. for Pennridge Schs.; adj. faculty Bucks County Community Coll., 1983—; instr. Am. Inst. Banking, 1982—; notary pub., 1986—; mcpl. auditor, sec. bd. auditors, 1984-90, mcpl. auditor 1990—, chmn. bd. auditors 1990—; cons. in field. Author (with others) Life-Time Sports for the College Student: A Behavioral Objective Approach, 1971, 3d rev. edit. 1978, Elementary Social Studies as a Learning System, 1976. Vol. elem. sch. counselor Perkasie, 1979-81; mem. Hilltown Civic Assn., 1965-70, 1992—; exec. com. chairperson Hilltown PTO, 1965-73; mem. soloist Good Shepherd Episcop. Ch. Choir, Hilltown, 1964-77; mem., steering com. Perkasie Sch., 1989—. NSF grantee, Washington, 1972-73, Philanthropic Edn. Orgn. grantee, Doylestown, Pa., 1982; recipient Judith Netzky Meml. Fellowship award B'nai B'rith, Phila., 1979; Durning scholar Delta Delta Delta, Arlington, Tex., 1981, Am. Mgmt. Assns. scholar, N.Y.C., 1982, Statesman's award World Inst. Achievement, 1989, Achievement award Women's Inner Circle, 1990, Golden Acad. award for lifetime achievement, 1991; named to Internat. Tennis Hall of Fame, 2000 Notable Am. Women Hall of Fame, 1989, Community Leaders of Am. Hall of Fame, 1990, Internat. Book of Honor Hall of Fame, 1990, Internat. Bus. & Profl. Women's Hall of Fame, 1994, Lifetime Achievement Acad. Humane Soc. of U.S., Outstanding Aux. Spring Mountain Ski Patrol, 1993. Fellow Internat. Biog. Assn.; mem. AAUW, NEA, NAFE, Humane Soc. U.S., World Inst. Achievement, Pa. State Edn. Assn. (polit. action com. for edn., chair Pennridge Schs. 1986—, del. leadership conf. 1987, 89), Pennridge Edn. Assn. (faculty rep 1986-88, exec. council 1986—, negotiations resource com. 1987-89, 91-93, steering com. Perkasie Sch. 1989—, chairperson Child Study Team, 1988-94, Instrnl. Support Team, 1992—), Am. Inst. Banking (chairperson 1987), U.S. Tennis Assn. (hon. life), Pa. and Middle States Tennis Assn. (hon. life), U.S. Profl. Tennis Registry, Mid. States Profl. Tennis Registry, Women's Internat. Tennis Assn., Nat. Ski Patrol, Pa. Elected Women's Assn., Bucks County Assn. of Twp. Ofcls., Pa. Sch. Counselors Assn., Pa. Assn. Notaries, Am. Soc. Notaries, Internat. Fedn. of Univ. Women, Internat. Platform Assn., Nat. Ski Patrol (Svc. Recognition award 1994), Am. Biog. Inst. Rsch. Assn., (rsch. bd. advisors, bd. govs. 1989—), World Inst. Achievement, Lifetime Achievement Acad., Rails-to-Trails Conservancy, Highpoint Racquet Club, Pennridge Community Rep. Club (recording sec. 1986-91, publicity chmn. 1991-92, Pen care chmn. 1992—), Mediterranean Club, Nockamixon Boat Club, Peace Valley Yacht Club, Highpoint Racquet Club, Kappa Delta Pi. Episcopalian. Clubs: Mediterranean, Nockamixon Boat, Peace Valley Yacht, Highpoint Racquet. Home: 834 Rickert Rd Perkasie PA 18944-2661 Office: Pennridge Schs 601 N 7th St Perkasie PA 18944-1507

FERSHTMAN, JULIE ILENE, lawyer; b. Detroit, Apr. 3, 1961; d. Sidney and Judith Joyce (Stoll) F.; m. Robert S. Bick, Mar. 4, 1990. Student, Mich. State U., 1979-81, James Madison Coll., 1979-81; BA in Philosophy and Polit. Sci., Emory U., 1983, JD, 1986. Bar: Mich. 1986, U.S. Dist. Ct. (ea. dist.) Mich. 1986, U.S. Ct. Appeals (6th cir.) 1987, U.S. Dist. Ct. (we. dist.) Mich. 1993. Assoc. Miller, Canfield, Paddock and Stone, Detroit, 1986-89; assoc. Miro, Miro & Weiner P.C., Bloomfield Hills, Mich., 1989-92; pvt. practice law Bingham Farms, Mich., 1992—; lectr. in field. Contbr. articles to jours. Bd. dirs. Franklin Cmty. Assn., 1989—, sec., 1991-92; mem. Franklin Planning Commn., 1993—, Franklin Charter Commn., 1993—. Mem. ABA (mem. planning bd. YLD litigation sect.), State Bar Mich. (exec. coun. young lawyers sect. 1989—, sec./treas. 1992-93, vice chair 1993-94), Fed. Bar Assn. (courthouse tours com. Detroit chpt.), Common Cause, Women Lawyers Assn. Mich., Mich. Women's Hist. Ctr. and Hall of Fame, Detroit Inst. Arts Founder's Soc., Detroit Zool. Soc., Nat. Mus. Women and Arts, Soc. Coll. Journalists, Phi Alpha Delta, Omicron Delta Kappa, Phi Sigma Tau, Pi Sigma Alpha. Home: 31700 Briarcliff Rd Franklin MI 48025-1273 Office: 30700 Telegraph Rd Ste 3475 Bingham Farms MI 48025-4527

FERTIG-DYKS, SUSAN BEATRICE, international media and business consultant; b. Panay, The Philippines, Jan. 9, 1944; d. Claude Edward and B. Laverne (Shockley) Fertig; m. George Middleton Dykes III, Sept. 18, 1965; children: George M. Dykes IV, Dirk Fertig Dykson. BA in Communications, U. Mo., 1982. Freelance writer, dir. producer Kansas City, Mo., 1981-83; dir. pub. svc. KSHB-TV, Kansas City, Mo., 1982-83; dir. broadcast svc. VA, Washington, 1983-86; pres., chief exec. officer Victoria Prodns., Ltd., Alexandria, Va., 1986-89; dir. media info. Bicentennial Presdl. Inaugural com., Washington, 1988-89; resume review Office Presdl. Personnel The White House, Washington, 1989; dir. policy, spl. projects Office Human Resources & Adminstrn. Dept. Vets. Affairs, Washington, 1989; dir. pub., visual comm. USDA, Washington, 1989-93; pres., CEO Fertig Comms., Alexandria, Croatia, 1993—; CEO, bd. dirs. Fertig & Assocs. Internat., Zagreb, Croatia, 1993—; dir., CEO ICA (Inst. Cultural Affairs Internat. Belgium)-Zagreb, Zagreb, 1993—; chmn. Philippine Festival Commn., Washington, 1992, 1st v.p. 1994, pres.-elect, 1995; pres.-elect, chmn. Internat. Gold Screen Film/Video Competition Nat. Assn. Govt. Communicators, 1994; talent, script cons. Hrvatska Radio-Televizija, 1994—; script cons. Jadran Film, Zagreb, 1994. Ofcl. U.S. observer XVI Internat. Film Competition, Berlin, 1990; judge XVII Internat. Film Competition, Berlin, 1992, Internat. Contest Agrarian Cinema & Video, Zaragosa, 1992; judge Golden Eagle awards Coun. Internat. Non-Theatrical Events (CINE), 1992—, adv. coun., 1993—; judge Festival Internat. du Court Metrages de Mons, Belgium, 1994. Chmn. coord. George Bush for Pres., Alexandria, 1987-88; surrogate speaker women's groups Bush/Quayle and Victory 88, Washington; campaign tours N.H. primaries, 1988; mem. Pres.'s Club Rep. Nat. Com., Washington, 1984; bd. dirs. Found. for Aid to the Philippines, 1991-92. Mem. NATAS, Assn. Philippine Am. Women (pres. 1991-93), Women in Film & Video, Fed. City Rep. Women, Filipino-Am. Rep. Coun., Philippine Heritage Fedn., Rep. Nat. Com. (life). Episcopalian. Home: 205 S Yoakum Pky Apt 1021 Alexandria VA 22304-3826 Office: 10 Bartula Kasica, 41 000 Zagreb Croatia also: Am Embassy Zagreb Dart Unit 1345 APO AE 09213-1345

FERZACCA, PAMELA ANN, special education educator; b. Detroit, Sept. 28, 1963; d. John Joseph and Lois Susan (Henson) F. BS, Grand Valley State Coll., Allendale, Mich., 1987. Cert. spl. edn. tchr. Substitute tchr. Almont (Mich.) Community Schs., 1987-88, bilingual tchr., 1988-90; 1st grade tchr. Almont Summer Migrant Edn. Program, 1988, tchr. kindergarten, 1989, 90, recruiter, 1990; tchr. 3d grade Almont Elem. Sch., 1990-94; tchr. educably mentally impaired Almont Jr./Sr. High Sch., 1994—. Mem. Nat. Assn. Migrant Educators, Coun. Exceptional Children, Mich. Edn. Assn., Almont Edn. Assn. Democrat. Roman Catholic. Home: PO Box 120 132 S Main St Almont MI 48003 Office: Almont Elem Sch 401 Church St Almont MI 48003-1030

FESHBACH, NORMA DEITCH, psychologist, educator; b. N.Y.C., Sept. 5, 1926; m. Seymour Feshbach; children: Jonathan Stephan, Laura Elizabeth, Andrew David. BS in Psychology, CCNY, 1947, MS in Ednl. Psychology, 1949; PhD in Clin. Psychology, U. Pa., 1956. Diplomate Am. Bd. Prof. Psychology; cert. in clin. psychology, Phila.; lic. clin. and ednl. psychologist, Calif. Tchr. Betsy Ross Nursery Sch., Yale U., 1947-48; clin. psychologist Yale U. Med. Sch., 1948; teaching asst. dept. psychology Yale U., 1948-51; research asst. human resources research office George Washington U., Washington, 1951-52; psychology intern Phila. Gen. Hosp., 1955-56; research assoc. dept. psychology U. Pa., 1959-61; research assoc. Inst. Behavioral Sci. U. Colo., 1963-64; assoc. research psychologist dept. psychology UCLA, 1964-65; clin. psychologist II UCLA Neuropsychiat. Inst., 1965; prof. Grad. Sch. Edn. UCLA, 1965—, prof. psychology dept., 1975-92, chmn. dept. edn., 1985-90, interim dean Grad. Sch. Edn., 1991-92, acting dir. Corinne A. Seeds Univ. Elem. Sch., 1985-89; Fulbright sr. lectr./researcher U. Rome, 1988; lectr. Jr. Coll. Phys. Therapy, New Haven, Conn., 1948-49, dept. psychology, U. Pa., 1956-57, UCLA Neuropsychiat. Inst., Calif. Dept. Mental Hygiene, Los Angeles, 1966-69; vis. asst. prof. Stanford U. dept. psychology, 1961-62, U. Calif. Berkeley, 1962-63; vis. scholar dept. exptl. psychology Oxford U., 1980-81; co-prin. investigator various projects and programs; co-prin. dir. and investigator NIMH Tng. Program in Applied Human Devel., 1986-91, co-dir. tng. grant in applied human devel., 1991—; clin. and research cons. Youth Services, Inc., Phila., 1955-61; also cons. various media orgns.; head program in Early Childhood and Devel. Studies, 1968-80; dir. NIMH Tng. Prog. in Early Childhood and Devel. Studies, 1972-82; prog. dir. Ctr. for Study of Evaluation, UCLA Grad. Sch. Edn., 1966-69; co-dir. UCLA Bush Found. Tng. Prog. in Child Devel. and Social Policy, 1978-82; chair grad. faculty UCLA Grad. Sch. Edn., 1979-80. Editorial cons., mem. editorial bd. psychology and ednl. research revs., contbr. numerous articles on child psychology to profl. jours. Mem. adv. coun. of Women's Clinic, Los Angeles, 1974-76; mem. adv. bd. Nat. Com. to Abolish Corporal Punishment in Schs., 1972-80, Nat. Ctr. for Study of Corporal Punishment and Alternatives in the Schs., 1976—; mem. profl. adv. com. on Child Care, Los Angeles Unified Sch. Dist., 1978-80; trustee EVAN-G Com. to End Violence Against the Next Generation, 1972-80; exec. bd. Internat. Soc. for Research in Agression, 1982-84. Recipient James McKeen Cattell Fund Sabbatical award, 1980, 81, Townsend Harris Medal, Disting. Alumnus award CCNY, 1982, Disting. Sci. Achievement in Psychology award Calif. Psychol. Assn., 1983, Achievements in Psychology award CUNY, 1989, GSE Faculty award Harold A. and Lois Haytin Found., 1991; named Faculty Mem. Woman of Yr. Nat. Acad. Profl. Psychologists, Los Angeles, 1973; U.S. Pub. Health Tng. fellow, 1953-56; rsch. grantee NIMH, 1972-77 (co-principal with D. Stipek), 77-82, 1986—, Hilton Found., 1985-86, Spencer Found. 1984-85, Child Help, USA, 1982-84 (co-principal with C. Howes), UCLA Acad. Senate, 1981—, Bush Found., 1978-83, 79-80, 80-81, 81-82, 82-83 (co-dir. with J.I. Goodlad), Adminstrn. for Children, Youth and Families, 1981-82 (co-dir. with J.I. Goodlad), NSF, 1976-77, 77-78, 78-80 (co-prin. with S. Feshbach), Com. on Internat. and Comparative Studies, 1973-74, 77-78. Fellow Am. Psychol. Assn. (officer var. coms., Disting. Contbn. Psychology and Media, Divsn. 42, 1992); mem. Assn. Advancement Psychology, AAAS, AAUP, Am. Bd. Profl. Psychologists, Am. Ednl. Research Assn., Calif. Assn. for Edn. Young Children, Nat. Assn for Edn. Young Children, Internat. Assn. Applied Psychology, Internat. Soc. for Research on Aggression, Internat. Soc. Study of Behavioral Devel., Internat. Soc. Prevention Child Abuse and Neglect, Nat. Register of Health Services Providers in Psychology, Sor Research in Child Devel., Western Psychol. Assn. (pres. 1979-80); Sigma Xi, Delta Phi Upsilon.

FESI-SULLIVAN, KATHLEEN ANN, finance and insurance consultant; b. Gary, Ind., July 30, 1953; d. Thomas Edward Sullivan and Carlene Lois (Norris) Lines; m. Michael Terry Fesi, June 24, 1973 (div. Oct. 1991); children: Michelle Loraine Fesi, Jennifer Marie Fesi. Student, Ind. U., 1982. Fin. and ins. cons. GM Acceptance Corp., Decatur, Ill., 1971—. Mem. Assn. Fin. and Ins. Profls. (cert., Women of the Yr award, 1995), Am. Bus. Women's Assn. (com. chair). Republican. Roman Catholic. Home: 4804 Baker Woods Ct Decatur IL 62521 Office: GM Acceptance Corp 2828 N Monroe St Decatur IL 62526

FESQ, LORRAINE MAE, aerospace and computer engineer; b. Pennsauken, N.J., June 26, 1957; d. John Fred Henry and Natalie Nicola (Nasuti) F.; m. Frank Tai, May 14, 1988. BA in Math., Rutgers U., 1979; MS in Computer Sci., UCLA, 1990, PhD in Computer Sci. and Astrophysics, 1993. Sci. programmer Systems and Applied Sci. Corp., Greenbelt, Md., 1979-81; computer engr./mgr. Ball Aerospace Systems Div., Boulder, Colo., 1981-86; systems engr. OAO, El Segundo, Calif., 1986-87; spacecraft systems engr. TRW, Redondo Beach, Calif., 1987—. Contbr. articles to IECEC Proceedings, AAS Proceedings, Diagnostic Workshop (DX-92) Proceedings, NASA Goddard Space Applications of Artificial Intelligence Proceedings. Mem. Playa Del Rey (Calif.) Network, 1988—. MS fellow TRW, 1988-89, PhD fellow, 1990-93. Mem. AIAA (sr., tech. com. mem. artificial intelligence tech. com. 1990—), Am. Astronautical Soc., Am. Assn. for Artificial Intelligence, Am. Astronomical Soc. Home: 6738 Esplanade St Playa Del Rey CA 90293-7525 Office: TRW MS M2/2375 1 Space Park Blvd Redondo Beach CA 90278-1001

FESSENDEN, ANN T., law librarian; b. Norman, Okla., Oct. 4, 1951; d. Wayne B. and Tula D. (McCarty) F.; m. Ronald F. Bock, June 6, 1992; 1 child, Michael F. Bunnell. BA in Jour., U. Okla., 1974, MLS, 1977; JD magna cum laude, U. Miss., 1984. Acquisitions asst. U. Okla., Norman, 1974-77; tech. svcs. libr. U. Miss., University, 1978-84, co-acting law libr., 1982; cir. libr. U.S. Ct. Appeals (8th cir.), St. Louis, 1984—. Contbg. author (book) Judicial Opinion Writing Manual, 1991; contbr. articles to profl. jours. Mem. Am. Assn. Law Librs. (chair placement com. 1989-90), Mid-Am. Assn. Law Librs. (v.p. & pres.-elect 1992-94), Beta Phi Mu. Office: US Ct Appeals Libr 1114 Market St Rm 650 Saint Louis MO 63101

FESSLER, PATRICIA LOU, library and media coordinator; b. Chgo., Dec. 1; d. Eugene Rickert and Dorothy May (Schmidt) McKeen; m. Kermit John Fessler, June 23, 1951; children: Barbara, Peter, James. BA, Cornell Coll., 1950; MS, Chgo. State U., 1970. Cert. tchr., supr., Ill. Tchr. phys. edn. Harlan (Iowa) Pub. Schs., 1950-51, Blue Island Community High Sch. Dist. # 218, Oak Lawn, Ill., 1960-63, 67-70; coord. library, media A.B. Shepard High Sch., Oak Lawn, Ill., 1971-93; mem. adv. coun. Grad. Sch. Libr. Scis. U. Ill., Champaign, 1977-80; mem. libr./media adv. coun. State Bd. Edn., Springfield, Ill., 1980-83. Deacon Palos Park (Ill.) Presbyn. Ch., 1991-93. Named as one of Those Who Excel Ill., State Bd. Edn., 1987. Mem. AAUW (ednl. found. honoree 1992), Assn. for Ednl. Comms. and Tech. (bd. dirs. 1981-84, Spl. Svc. plaque 1989, bd. trustees 1984—, found. sec. 1988—), Ill. Ednl. Comms. and Tech. (pres. 1977-78, 80-82, Disting. Svc. award 1982-84, Meritorious Svc. award A.V. Am. 1983).

FETNER, SUZANNE, small business owner; b. Fowlerville, Mich., May 4, 1929; d. Clayton Charles and Ferne Marie (Abbey) Fenton; m. William Clyde Peters, June 1950 (div. Aug. 1971); children: Randall Ray, Gregory Kim, Melinda Jane Peters Jones, Kelly Sue Peters Raymond; m. Eugene Macelee Fetner, Apr. 10, 1977. BS, Ea. Mich. U., 1967. Cert. early childhood edn., Fla. Tchr. kindergarten Fowlerville (Mich.) Pub. Schs., 1949-50, Horsebrook Sch., Lansing, Mich., 1950-51, Grand Ledge (Mich.) Pub. Schs., 1951-52, Manchester (Mich.) Pub. Schs., 1952-56, Holy Trinity Episcopal Sch., Melbourne, Fla., 1967-72; owner, tchr. Country Adventure, Inc., Melbourne, 1973-77; owner, dir. Woodlake Wonderland, Inc., Palm Bay, Fla., 1978-89, Country Beginnings, Inc., Palm Bay, 1985-93; mem. Presch. Adminstv. Consultants, Palm Bay, 1985—; adv. bd. Dist. Interagy. Coun. for Early Childhood Svcs., Brevard County, 1990—, South Brevard High Sch. Child Care, Melbourne, 1980—. Author: (booklet) Stepping Stones, 1984. Founder, coord. Read to Your Child Week, Melbourne, Palm Bay, 1978-92. Named Unforgettable Lady of 80's Soroptomist Club, Melbourne, 1989. Mem. Nat. Assn. Child Care Profls., Brevard Assn. Children Under Six (pres. 1981-82), Fla. Assn. Children Under Six, So. Assn. Children Under Six. Republican. Methodist. Home and Office: 567 Birch St West Melbourne FL 32904

FETRIDGE, BONNIE-JEAN CLARK (MRS. WILLIAM HARRISON FETRIDGE), civic volunteer; b. Chgo., Feb. 3, 1915; d. Sheldon and Bonnie (Carrington) Clark; m. William Harrison Fetridge, June 27, 1941; children: Blakely (Mrs. Harvey H. Bundy III), Clark Worthington. Student, Girls Latin Sch., Chgo., The Masters Sch., Dobbs Ferry, N.Y., Finch Coll., N.Y.C. Bd. dirs. region VII com. Girl Scouts U.S.A., 1939-43, nat. program com., 1966-69, nat. adv. bd., 1972-85, internat. commr.'s adv. panel, 1973-76, Nat. Juliette Low Birthplace Com., 1966-69; bd. dirs. Girl Scouts Chgo., 1936-51, 59-69, sec., 1936-38, v.p., 1946-49, 61-65, chmn. Juliette Low world friendship com., 1959-67, 71-72; mem. Friends Our Cabana Com. World Assn. Girl Guides and Girl Scouts, Cuernavaca, Mexico, 1969—, vice chmn., 1982-87; founder, pres. Olave Baden-Powell Soc. of World Assn. Girl Guides and Girl Scouts, London, 1984-93, bd. dirs., 1984—, hon. assoc., 1987; asst. sec. Dartnell Corp, Chgo., 1981-91, sec., 1991—, bd. dirs. 1989—; vice chmn. Dartnell Found., 1990—; bd. dirs. Jr. League of Chgo., 1937-40, Vis. Nurse Assn. Chgo., 1951-58, 61-63, asst. treas., 1962-63; women's bd. dirs. Children's meml. Hosp., 1946-50; v.p. parents coun. Latin Sch., 1952-54, bd. dirs. alumni assn., 1964-69; Fidelitas Soc., 1979; women's bd. U.S.O., 1965-75, treas., 1969-71, v.p., 1971-73; women's svc. bd. Chgo. Area coun. Boy Scouts Am., 1964-70, mem. nat. exploring com., 1973-76; staff aide and ARC Motor Corps, World War II. Recipient Citation of Merit Sta. WAIT, Chgo., 1971, Juliette Low World Friendship medal Girl Scouts U.S.A., 1989; 1st recipient Medal of Recognition World Assn.Girl Guides and Girl Scouts, 1993; Baden-Powell fellow World Scout Found., Geneva, 1983. Mem. Nat. Soc. Colonial Dames Am. (life; Ill. bd. mgrs. 1962-65, 69-76, 78-82, v.p. 1970-72, corr. sec. 1978-80, 1st v.p. 1980-84, state chmn. geneal. info. services com. 1972-76, hist. activities com. 1979-83, mus. house com. 1980-83, house gov. 1981-82), Chgo. Dobbs Alumnae Assn. (past pres.), Nat. Soc. DAR, Chgo. Geneal. Soc., Conn. Soc. Genealogists, New Eng. Historic Geneal. Soc., N.Y. Geneal. and Biog. Soc., Newberry Library Assocs., Chgo. Hist. Soc. Guild., Casino Club, The Racquet Club of Chgo., Chickaming Country Club (Lakeside, Mich.), Union League Club of Chgo. Republican. Episcopalian. Home: 2430 N Lakeview Ave Chicago IL 60614-2720

FETSKE, MELODY PACE, accountant; b. Charlottesville, Va., Dec. 8, 1949; d. George Minor and Florence Early (Duke) Pace; m. Albert Arthur Fetske II, June 30, 1973; 1 child, Virginia Michele. BA, Mary Wash. Coll., 1972; postgrad., George Mason U., 1979-83, No. Va. C.C., Annandale, 1983-

88. CPA. Loan interviewer Navy Fed. Credit Union, Vienna, Va., 1972-74; asst. treas. Comdial Fed. Credit Union, Charlottesville, 1974-78; contr. Cole Corette & Abrutyn, Washington, 1978-82, United Ski Industries Assn., McLean, Va., 1989-92, Ski Industries Am., McLean, Va., 1982-94, The Folger Shakespeare Libr., 1994—; owner Melody Fetske, CPA, Herndon, Va., 1993; cons. Sperry Fed. Credit Union, Charlottesville, 1975-76. Dir. plays The Glass Menagerie, 1973, Pied Piper of Hamlin, 1976, Godspell, 1977, Girls Guide to Chaos, 1990. Mem. Elden St. Players, Herndon Coun. of the Arts. Mem. AICPA, Inst. Mgmt. Accts., Am. Soc. Assn. Execs., Va. Soc. CPAs (No. Va. chpt.), Herndon C. of C. Home: 603 Austin Ln Herndon VA 22070-5101

FETTWEIS, YVONNE CACHÉ, archivist; b. L.A., Nov. 28, 1935; d. Boyd Eugene and Georgette Louisa (Tilmann) Adams; m. Maurice Lee Caché, Jan. 8, 1955 (div. 1962); children: Maurice C.B. II, Michele-Yvonne (Mrs. Vernon Young Sr.); m. Rolland Phillip Fettweis, July 22, 1967. BA, Wagner Coll., 1954; postgrad, Am. U., 1973, Bentley Coll., 1981. Legal sec., asst. Judge, Davis, Stern, Orfinger & Tindall, Daytona Beach, Fla., 1961-66; head rec. sect., bd. dirs. 1st Ch. Christ Scientist, Boston, 1969-71, rsch. assoc., 1971-72, adminstrv. archivist, 1972-78, sr. assoc. archivist, 1979-84, records adminstr., 1984-91, div. mgr. records mgmt./orgnl. archives, 1991-92, divsn. mgr. ch. history, 1992-95, divsn. mgr. ch. history healing ministry, 1995—. Exec. sec. Volusia County Goldwater campaign, Daytona Beach, 1964. Mem. Soc. Am. Archivists (editor The Archival Spirit), Automated Records and Techniques Task Force, Am. Mgmt. Assn., Orgn. Am. Historians, Ctr. for Study of Presidency, New Eng. Archivists, Assn. Records Mgrs. and Adminstrs. (bd. dirs. 1983—), Assn. Coll. and Rsch. Librs., Bay State Hist. League, Order Ea. Star, Order Rainbow (bd. dirs. 1972-77). Republican. Christian Scientist. Home: 42 Edgell Dr Framingham MA 01701-3181 Office: 1st Ch Christian Sci 175 Huntington Ave # A221 Boston MA 02115-3187

FEUER GEDZELMAN, CHERYL ILISE, educational services executive, elementary school educator; b. N.Y.C., Jan. 10, 1961; d. Martin Murray and Linda Jane (Corn) Feuer; m. Michael Jon Gedzelman, Mar. 20, 1994. BA, U. Chgo., 1982; M of Health Adminstrn., Tulane U., 1985; MA in Curriculum and Teaching, Columbia U., 1990. Cert. N-6, N.Y. Cons. Corson Group, N.Y.C., 1985-87; fin. analyst Mt. Sinai Hosp., N.Y.C., 1987-88; tchr. Rodeph Sholom Sch., N.Y.C., 1988-89, Barnard Sch., N.Y.C., 1989-92; editor, corr. Clinton Transition Team, Washington, 1992-93; owner, dir. Tutoring for Success, Oakton, Va., 1994—. Freelance writer Families Newspaper, Herndon, Va., 1994—. Newsletter writer, bd. dirs. Flint Hill Homeowners Assn., 1994—. Mem. Bus. and Profl. Women, Ctrl. Fairfax C. of C. Office: Tutoring for Success 3131 Valentino Ct Oakton VA 22124

FEUREY, CLAUDIA PACKER, not-for-profit executive; b. Pt. Hueneme, Calif., Apr. 24, 1949; d. Benjamin Ray and Phyllis Laura (McGrath) Packer; m. John J. Feurey Jr.; children: Matthew, Sarah, Nicholas. BA, Barnard Coll., 1970. V.p. comm. and corp. affairs Com. for Econ. Devel., N.Y.C., 1976—. Contbr: Wall St. Journal on Management, Successful Training Strategies. Mem. Mauweehoo Club. Republican. Presbyterian. Office: Com for Econ Devel 477 Madison Ave New York NY 10022-5802

FEUSS, LINDA ANNE UPSALL, lawyer; b. White Plains, N.Y., Dec. 9, 1956; d. Herbert Charles and Edna May (Hart) Upsall; m. Charles E. Feuss, Aug. 16, 1980; children: Charles Herbert, Anne Hart. BA, Colgate U., 1978; JD, Emory U., 1981. Bar: Ga. 1981, S.C. 1981. Assoc. Rainey, Britton, Gibbs & Clarkson, Greenville, S.C., 1981-83; counsel Siemens Energy & Automation, Atlanta, 1983-91; counsel Siemens Corp., Atlanta, 1991-93, sr. counsel, 1993-94, assoc. gen. counsel, 1994—; rep. law coun. II Mfr.'s Alliance Productivity and Innovation, Washington, 1995; rep. law com. Nat. Elec. Mfrs.' Assn., Washington, 1995. Bd. dirs. Am. Heart Assn., Greenville, 1981-93; mem. leadership com. Woodruff Arts Ctr. Campaign, Atlanta, 1985-90; vol. High Mus. Art, Atlanta, 1993—. Mem. ABA, Am. Corporate Coun. Assn. (dir. Ga. chpt. 1995), State Bar Ga., S.C. Bar, Atlanta Bar Assn., Colgate Club Am. (pres. 1986-88, bd. dirs. 1989—). Office: Siemens Corp 3333 State Bridge Rd Alpharetta GA 30202

FICHTER VESPERMAN, JANICE LOUISE, graphic artist; b. Mt. Kisco, N.Y., Oct. 28, 1965; d. Marvin Raymond and Virginia Hope (Sherman) Fichter; m. Richard Louis Vesperman, Sept. 8, 1990. AS in Bus. Adminstrn., Westchester Coll., 1986; paralegal cert., Manhattanville Coll., 1988; postgrad., Conn. Inst. Art, 1991-93. Lic. cosmetologist. Pharmacist's asst. Yorktown Pharmacy, Yorktown Hts., N.Y., 1982-84; mgr. Engraver's Block, Yorktown, N.Y., 1984-86; CRT oper N.Y. Tel., Rye Brook, N.Y., 1986; asst. to v.p. Fin. Insts. Retirement Fund, White Plains, N.Y., 1986-87; mgr., CEO OMB Enterprises, Mobile, Ala., 1987-89, Vesperman Typing & Graphics, Yorktown, 1991—; office mgr. Briarcliff Phys. Therapy, Briarcliff Manor, N.Y., 1990-91; English tutor Westchester Community Coll., Valhalla, N.Y., 1985-86; ceremonial hostess Conn. Inst. Art, Greenwich, 1992; motivational speaker, cons. in field. Author short stories Reflections mag., 1982-83 (cert.); columnist Reporter Dispatch, 1982-83; editor's asst. Yearbook, 1983-84; journalist Viking Newspaper, 1984-86 (contributor's Excellence award); inventor in field. Stage mgr. Community Theater, Garrison, N.Y., 1990-91; coord. Midway, Putnam (N.Y.) Hosp. Ctr., 1991; Sunday sch. tchr. St. Andrew's Luth. Ch., Yorktown Hts. Recipient Franchise Rights award Scentura Creations, Atlanta, 1988, God, Home Country award Boy and Girls Scouts Am. and Luth. Ch. of Am.

FICHTHORN, FONDA GAY, principal; b. Jamestown, Ohio, Sept. 4, 1949; d. Robert William and Evelyn Elizabeth (Schmitt) F. BS, Otterbein Coll., 1970; MEd, Wright State U., 1984. Cert. tchr., prin., supr., Ohio. Elem. tchr. Groveport (Ohio) Madison Schs., 1970-71; elem. tchr. Miami Trace Schs., Washington Court House, Ohio, 1971-92, prin., 1992—. Recipient Class Act award Sta. WDTN-TV, 1990. Republican. Home: 7313 St Rt 729 NW Washington Court House OH 43160-9526 Office: Wilson Sch 1604 St Rt 41 SW Washington Court House OH 43160

FICKEN, KAREN VALARIE, software executive; b. Dallas, Dec. 4, 1953; d. Roger Bedford and Alice May (Lee) Harlan; m. W. Curt Ficken, Sept. 10, 1977; children: Rob, Andrea. BBA, Stephen F. Austin State U., Nacogdoches, Tex., 1976. Sales rep. Classic BMW/Ferrari, Richardson, Tex.; supr. dental/med. benefits Rockwell Internat., Richardson; fin. analyst Bell No. Rsch., Richardson; software reliability engr. Bell No. Rsch.; sr. specialist Northern Telecom, Inc., 1991—. Mem. bd. adjustments, City of Fairview; trustee Lovejoy Ind. Sch. Dist., Allen, Tex., 1991—. Mem. DAR.

FICKEN, MILLICENT SIGLER, zoology educator; b. Washington, July 27, 1933; d. Phares Oscar and Helen Elizabeth (Richards) Sigler; m. Robert William Ficken, June 25, 1955 (div. 1989); children: John William, Carolyn Marie Ficken Powers. BS, Cornell U., 1955, PhD, 1960. Postdoctoral fellow Cornell U., Ithaca, N.Y., 1960-62; rsch. assoc. dept. zoology U. Md., College Park, 1963-67; asst. prof. zoology U. Wis., Milw., 1967-69, assoc. prof. zoology, 1969-75, prof. dept. biol. scis., 1975—, acad. program dir. field sta., 1967—. Contbr. articles on ornithology and animal behavior to sci. publs. NSF grantee, 1967-80, 87, 88. Fellow Animal Behavior Soc., Am. Ornithologists' Union; mem. AAAS, Soc. for Study of Evolution, Cooper Ornithol. Soc., Wilson Ornithol. Soc. Home: 1623 16th Ave Grafton WI 53024-2019 Office: U Wis Dept Biol Scis Milwaukee WI 53201

FIDALE, MARY SUSAN, medical/surgical/oncology nurse; b. Chgo., Nov. 5, 1954; d. Antonio and Gilda (Garelli) F. AAS, William Rainey Harper Coll., 1974; BSN, Elmhurst Coll., 1982; postgrad., Roosevelt U., 1991—. RN, Ill.; cert. med. office asst., Am. Assn. Med. Assts. Office asst. Dr. I. James Young, Arlington Heights, Ill., 1973-82; home health aide Concerned Care, Inc./Home Health Agy., Des Plaines, Ill., summer 1981; staff nurse med./surg./oncology Good Shepherd Hosp., Barrington, Ill., 1982—; initiator, facilitator The Nurses Support Group, Good Shepherd Hosp., 1988—, facilitator Cancer Patient Support Group; domestic violence adv. counselor, facilitator support group for abused women Turning Point Ctr. for Abused Women and Children, Woodstock, 1992—; domestic violence adv. counselor State of Ill., 1992—; inservice leader emergency room dept. Good Shepherd Hosp., 1992. Contbr. articles to profl. publs., including Ill. Nursing Spectrum. Vol. Save-A-Pet Animal Shlter NO-Kill, The Compassionate Friends-Bereaved Parent Support Group; mem. oversight com. for Vogelcei Teen Ctr., Hoffman Estates, Ill. Recipient Disting. Svc. award, 1988; Roosevelt U. acad. tuition grantee. Mem. ANA (cert. med.-surg. nurse), ACA, Ill. Coalition Against Domestic Violence, Am. Mental Health Counselors Assn., Ill. Nurses Assn., Oncology Nurses Soc., Am. Cancer Soc. (facilitator I Can Cope program), Animal Protection Inst. Am., Human Soc. U.S. Democrat. Roman Catholic. Office: Good Shepherd Hosp 450 W Rt 22 Barrington IL 60010

FIDLER, CAROL ANN, accountant; b. Sharon, Pa., Apr. 28, 1942; d. Thomas Daniel and E. Geraldine (Boyer) Bracken; m. Michael Lawrence Fidler, Aug. 23, 1969 (div. 1991); 1 child, Michael Lawrence Jr. Diploma, Akron City Hosp. Sch. Nursing, 1963; BS in Chemistry, Kent State U., 1967; MS in Preventive Medicine, Ohio State U., 1972, MBA, 1979. CPA, Ohio; RN, Ohio. Rsch. assoc. dept. preventive medicine Ohio State U., Columbus, Ohio, 1969-70; dir. Riverside Meth. Hosp. Sch. Nursing, Columbus, 1973-77; dir. nursing devel. Ohio Hosp. Assn., Columbus, 1977-79; sr. bus. analyst Borden Inc.-Chem. div., Columbus, 1979-81; fin. adminstr. Bank One, Columbus N.A., 1981-84; pres. Northwest Tax Svc., Columbus, 1984-86; sr. cons. Peat, Marwick, Mitchell, Columbus, 1985-86; sole practice acctg. Columbus, 1986-90; controller The Wood Co's., Columbus, 1987-88; co-owner Clem & Fidler CPAs, 1991-94; owner Carol A. Fidler & Assocs., CPAs, Columbus, 1994—; cons. in field, Columbus, 1984—; instr. Newton Becker CPA Rev., Columbus, 1988-90; dir., treas. Donovan Prodns. Inc., Columbus, 1989—. Vol. Arthritis Assn., Columbus, 1978-84; treas. Northside Child and Family Devel. Ctr., Columbus, 1987—, bd. dirs., 1986—. Mem. Ohio Soc. CPAs (chair MAP com. Columbus chpt. 1991-93, Cert. award 1986, Silver medal 1986), Inst. Mgmt. Accts. (dir. member attendance Columbus chpt. 1988-89, dir. tech. programs 1989-90, dir. student and acad. affairs 1990-91, dir. CMA program 1991-93, treas. 1993—, lead instr. CMA rev. course 1991—), Planning Forum (pres. Columbus chpt. 1986-87, v.p. fin. com. 1985-86, v.p. programs 1984-85, dir. 1987-90). Republican. Home: 4138 Winfield Rd Columbus OH 43220-4606

FIDLER, SHELLEY N., legislative director; b. Bklyn., Jan. 19, 1947; d. Jay William and Rhoda H. (Wander) F.; m. Curtis B. Gans, Sept. 23, 1979; 1 child, Aaron. BA, Brown U., 1968. Legis. asst. Rep. Philip Sharp, 1976-80; asst. to chmn. Subcom. Fossil and Synthetic Fuels Ho. Com. Energy and Commerce, 1980-86, asst. to chair Subcom. Energy and Power, 1987-94, staff dir., 1994—. Office: Subcom on Energy & Power 331 Ford House Office Bldg Washington DC 20515*

FIEL, MAXINE LUCILLE, journalist, behavioral analyst, lecturer; b. N.Y.C.; d. William Jack and Rowena (Burton) Stempel; m. David H. Fiel; children: Meredith Susan, Lisa Beth. Student in psychology and humanities, NYU. Nat. columnist, contbg. editor Mademoiselle Mag., N.Y.C., 1972—; nat. columnist Womens World, Englewood, N.J., 1979-89; contbg. editor Overseas Promotions, N.Y.C., 1979—; articles and features editor Japanese Overseas Press, 1976—; feature editor N.Y. Now, N.Y.C., 1980-91; contbg. editor Woman's World mag., 1979-89, Bella mag., Eng., 1987-89; nat. columnist First mag. for women, 1989-91; founder Starcast Astrological Svcs., Floral Park, N.Y., 1993—; cons. legal profession jury selection, 1984—; mktg. cons. Imperial Enterprises, Tokyo and Princeton, N.J., 1983—; cons. spokesperson Rowland Co., N.Y.C., 1972-81, Allied Chem. Co., N.Y.C., 1972-75; lectr., cons. Atlanta and Fla. Bar Assns., 1986—; creator Touch Game Parker Bros., Salem, Mass., 1971-76; behavior analystand communications advisor multi-nat. bus. corps.; cons. Chesebrough-Ponds, Footwear Coun., Grand Marnier Liquor; founder Starcast Astrological Svcs., 1993. Pioneer field polit. body lang., 1969; contbr. articles to News Am., L.A. Times, Newhouse News Svc., Newspaper Ent. Assocs., King Features; TV appearances on morning and afternoon shows (nationwide), People are Talking, The Regis Philbin Show, Eyewitness News, Cable News Network, Tonight Show, Today Show, Good Morning Am., Joan Rivers Show, Jenny Jones, Entertainment Tonight, Merv Griffin Show, BBC Breakfast Show, many others; daily segment on Good Morning Japan. Active Sister Cities, Tokyo and N.Y.C.; charter mem. Elem. Sch. Cultural Exchange, Toyko and N.Y.C., Ctr. Environ. Edn.; bd. dirs. Periwinkle Prodns. Anti-Drug Abuse, N.Y.C. Recipient Achievement award field behavioral sci. and photojournalism, Tokyo, 1974, Outstanding Rsch. award field psychology of gesture, Tokyo, 1976, Outstanding Achievement award Internat. Conf. Soc. Para-Psychology, 1974-75; honored guest at award dinner for involvement and support in the merging of Eye Rsch. Inst. Boston and Harvard Med. Sch., 1991. Mem. AFTRA, Internat. Found. Behavioral Rsch. (past v.p.), Nat. Writers Assn. (profl.), Authors Guild, Authors League, World Wildlife Fund, Whale Protection Fund, Cousteau Soc., Nature Conservancy, Greenpeace, People for Ethical Treatment Animals, Humane Assn. U.S., Guiding Eyes for Blind, Braille Camps for Blind Children, Save the Children, Lotos Club (N.Y.C.), East End Yacht Club (Freeport, N.Y.). Office: 338 Northern Blvd # 3 Great Neck NY 11021

FIELD, ANDREA BEAR, lawyer; b. New London, Conn., Nov. 30, 1949; d. Geurson Donald and Lorraine (Solomon) Silverberg; m. Thornton Withers Field, May 17, 1984; children: Benjamin, Geoffrey. Student, Wellesley Coll., 1967-69; BA, Yale U., 1971; JD, U. Va., 1974. Bar: Va. 1974, D.C. 1978, U.S. Ct. Appeals (3d, 4th, 5th, 7th, 8th and D.C. cirs.). Assoc. Hunton & Williams, Washington and Richmond, Va., 1974-81; ptnr. Hunton & Williams, Washington, 1981—. Mem. ABA (chair sect. natural resources, energy and environ. law 1989-90, coun. 1984-87, 90-91, chair. com. air quality 1982-84, com. environ. controls bus. law sect. 1990-91, vice chair com. environ. law, real property, probate and trust law sect. 1990-91, teleconf. com. 1991—; chair standing com. on natural conf. groups 1993-94, nat. conf. lawyers and scientists 1990-93, sect. ad hoc com. nat. insts. 1989-90, coun. sect. sci. and tech. 1991-92). Office: Hunton & Williams Ste 9000 2000 Pennsylvania Ave NW Washington DC 20036

FIELD, BARBARA A., architect, councilwoman; b. Miami, Fla., Feb. 21, 1941; d. Stanton Nathanial and Sylvia Jane (Kahanow) F.; m. Bruce Barrett Gruber, 1963; m. Richard Dexter Herndon, Sept. 1973; children: Erick Barnes Herndon, John Christopher Herndon; m. Christopher Karl Johansen, Sept. 4, 1983. Student, U. Miami, 1958-59; BArch, Ga. Inst. Tech., 1965. Registered architect, N.C., Ga. Intern architect John M. Johansen Assocs., New Canaan, Conn., 1966-68, Chris-Janer, Johansen, Kouzmanoff, New Canaan, 1967-68; architect, intern architect Benjamin Thompson Assocs., Inc., Cambridge, Mass., 1968-70; v.p. Earth Guild, Inc., Cambridge, 1970-76, Asheville, N.C., 1976—; assoc., project mgr. SPACEPLAN/Architecture, Interiors & Planning, PA, Asheville, 1980—. Prin. works include (John M. Johansen Assocs. Architect of Record) Clark Univ. Libr., Worcester, Mass., L. Francis Smith Elem. Sch., Columbus, Ind., Okla. Ctr. Theater, Oklahoma City, (Chris-Janer, Johansen, Kougmanoff Architects of Record) SUNY campus master plan, Stonybrook, N.Y., (Benjamin Thompson Assocs. Inc. Architect of Record) Prototype Housing for HUD, South End, Boston, Design Rsch. Bldg., Cambridge (Nat. Design award AIA), Kirkland Coll. Music and Art Bldg., Clinton, N.Y., (Spaceplan Architecture, Interiors & Planning, P.A. Architect of Record) Mt. Pisgah Acad. Adminstrn./Classroom Bldg., Candler, N.C., Meml. Mission Hosp. renovation and interiors, Asheville, Asheville Profl. Bldg., Pack Pl. Edn., Arts & Sci. Ctr., Asheville, Drhumor Bldg. hist. renovation, Asheville, Sand Hill-Venable Elem. Sch., Asheville. Set designer Boston Ballet Co.; designer sets, spl. effects and interiors Boston Tea Party; mem. design devel. Peachtree Beautification Project, Peachtree Ctr., Atlanta; com. mem. bd. dirs. Light Up Your Holidays, 1985-87, city coun. liaison, 1992—; active Asheville Art Mus., 1989—, The Health Adventure, 1989—, Colburn Gem And Mineral Mus., 1989—, Asheville-Buncombe Discovery, 1992-93; mem. South Pack Sq. Redevelopment Assn., 1990—, city coun. liaison, 1992; mem. Asheville Downton Commn., 1990—, Asheville Minority Bus. Commn., 1990-93, city coun. liaison, 1993—; mem. Asheville City Coun., 1991—. Buncombe County Tourist Devel. Authority, 1992—, Buncombe County Environ. Affairs Bd., 1992—, Buncombe County Solid Waste Com., 1992—, Asheville-Buncombe Crimestoppers, Inc., 1993—; mem. com. existing bldgs. N.C. Bldg. Code Coun., 1991—; city coun. liaison bd. dirs. Arts Alliance, 1991—, Pack Place, 1991—; chmn. Asheville HOME Regional Housing Consortium, 1991—, Asheville Urban Area Transp. Adv. Com., 1991—; mem. art-in-architecture panel U.S. Gen. Svcs. Adminstrn., Asheville, 1992; mem. mayor's com. Asheville Unified Devel. Ordinance, 1992—; mem. community and econ. devel. com. N.C. League Municipalities, 1993; mem. mayor's com. Asheville Housing and Community Devel. Com., 1994; city coun. liaison Asheville-Buncombe Mcpl. Svc. Dist. Bd., 1994; bd. dirs. Fayerweather Sch., Cambridge, 1974-76, Madison County Arts Coun., Marshall, N.C., 1978-80, Grove Arcade Pub. Market Found., 1992-93; bd. dirs. Asheville Downtown Assn., 1987—, mem. publs. bd., 1988—, chmn. issues com., 1989-91, mem. devel. com., 1990—, v.p., 1991. Mem. AIA (registered, sec./treas. Asheville sect. 1982, v.p., pres. elect 1988, pres. 1989, bd. dirs. N.C. chpt. 1990-92, PAC bd. dirs. 1993—, sec. 1994), Gamma Psi. Home: 33 Haywood St Asheville NC 28801 Office: SPACEPLAN/Architecture Interiors Planning PA 39 Patton Ave Asheville NC 28801

FIELD, CAROL HART, writer, journalist, foreign correspondent; b. San Francisco, Mar. 27, 1940; d. James D. and Ruth (Arnstein) Hart; m. John L. Field, July 23, 1961; children: Matthew, Alison. BA, Wellesley Coll., 1961. Contbg. editor, assoc. editor, asst. editor City Mag., San Francisco, 1974-76; contbg. editor New West/Calif. Mag., San Francisco, L.A., 1975-80, San Francisco Mag., 1980-82; fgn. corr. La Gola, Milan, Italy, 1990—; lectr. Smithsonian Inst., Washington, 1991; bd. dirs. Bay Package Prodns., 1994—. Author: The Hill Towns of Italy, 1983 (Commonwealth Club award 1984), The Italian Baker, 1985 (Internat. Assn. Culinary Profls. award 1986), Celebrating Italy, 1990 (Commonwealth Club award Internat. Assn. Culinary Profls. award 1991), Italy in Small Bites, 1993 (James Beard award), Focaccia: Simple Breads from the Italian Oven, 1994; contbr. articles to profl. jours. Mem. lit. jury Commonwealth Club Calif., San Francisco, 1987, 88, 92; bd. dirs. Women's Forum West, San Francisco, 1990-92, Bancroft Libr. U. Calif., Berkeley, 1991—, The Headlands Inst., San Francisco, 1992-93; bd. dirs. The Mechanics' Inst., San Francisco, 1987-92, pres., 1990-92; bd. dirs. Bay Package Prodns., 1994—. Recipient Internat. Journalism prize Maria Luigia Duchessa di City of Parma, Italy, 1987, Barbi Colombini prize Tuscany, 1991; named Alumna of Yr. Head Royce Sch., Oakland, Calif., 1991. Mem. Accademia Italia della Cucina, Authors Guild, Am. Inst. Wine and Food, Les Dames d'Escoffier, Internat. Assn. Culinary Profls. Home and Office: 2561 Washington St San Francisco CA 94115

FIELD, JOYCE FINEMAN, English language educator; b. Pitts., May 29, 1929; d. Archie and Bess (Karp) Fineman; m. Harold David Field Jr., Sept. 3, 1950; children: Stephen, Lawrence, Richard. BA, Wellesley Coll., 1950; MA, U. Minn., 1968, ABD, 1976. Tchr. West Haven (Conn.) schs., 1950-51; instr. in English Normandale C.C., Bloomington, Minn., 1969-94. NEH grantee, 1991. Mem. Brandeis U. Women's Orgn. (bd. dirs.). Home: 152 Groveland Ter Minneapolis MN 55403-1148

FIELD, KAREN ANN, real estate broker; b. New Haven, Jan. 27, 1936; d. Abraham Terry and Ida (Smith) Rogovin; m. Barry S. Crown, June 29, 1954 (div. 1969); children: Laurie Jayne, Donna Lynn, Bruce Alan, Bradley David; m. Michael Lehmann Field, Aug. 10, 1969 (div. 1977). Student Vassar Coll., 1953-54, Harrington Inst. Interior Design, 1973-74, Roosevelt U., 1987—. Cert. residential specialist. Owner Karen Field Interiors, Chgo., 1970-86, Karen Field & Assocs., Chgo., 1980-81; pres., ptnr. Field-Pels & Assocs., Chgo., 1981-86; with top sales volume Sudler-Marling, Inc., 1989; sales broker Koenig & Strey, Inc., Chgo., 1989—. Mem. Women's Coun. Camp Henry Horner, Chgo., 1960; bd. dirs., treas. Winnetka Pub. Sch. Nursery (Ill.), 1961-63; pres. Jr. Aux. U. Chgo. Cancer Rsch. Found., 1960-66, mem. exec. com. woman's bd., 1965-66; bd. dirs., sec. United Charities, Chgo., 1966-68, Victory Gardens Theatre, Chgo., 1979; co-founder, pres. Re-Entry Ctr., Wilmette, Ill., 1978-80; mem. br. Child Abuse Svcs., Chgo., 1981-89, Stop AIDS Real Estate Div., 1988, AIDS Walkathon Com., 1990; bd. dirs. The Chicago Ctr. for Self-Taught Art. Recipient Servian award Jr. Aux. of U. Chgo. Cancer Rsch. Found., 1966, Margarite Wolf award Women's Bd., U. Chgo. Cancer Rsch. Found., 1967, WAIT Woman of Day. Mem. Internat. Real Estate Fedn. (chmn. membership Chgo. chpt.), Chgo. Real Estate Bd., Chgo. Assn. Realtors, Chgo. Coun. Fgn. Rels., English Speaking Union (jr. bd. 1958-59), Carlton Club. Office: Koenig & Strey Inc 900 N Michigan Ave Chicago IL 60611

FIELD, SALLY, actress; b. Pasadena, Calif., Nov. 6, 1946; m. Steve Craig, Sept. 1968 (div. 1975); children: Peter, Eli; m. Alan Greisman, Dec. 1984, 1 son, Samuel. Student, Actor's Studio, 1973-75. Starred in TV series Gidget, 1965, The Flying Nun, 1967-69, The Girl With Something Extra, 1973; film appearances include The Way West, 1967, Stay Hungry, 1976, Heroes, 1977, Smokey and the Bandit, 1977, Hooper, 1978, The End, 1978, Norma Rae, 1979 (Cannes Film Festival Best Actress award 1979, Acad. award 1980), Beyond the Poseidon Adventure, 1979, Smokey and the Bandit II, 1980, Back Roads, 1981, Absence of Malice, 1981, Kiss Me Goodbye, 1982, Places in the Heart, 1984 (Acad. award for best actress 1984), Murphy's Romance (also exec. producer), 1985, Surrender, 1987, Punchline, 1987 (also prodr.), Steel Magnolias, 1989, Soapdish, 1991, Not Without My Daughter, 1991, Homeward Bound: The Incredible Journey, 1993 (voice only), Mrs. Doubtfire, 1993, Forrest Gump, 1994; TV movies include Maybe I'll Come Home In the Spring, 1971, Marriage: Year One, 1971, Home for the Holidays, 1972, Bridges, 1976, Sybil, 1976 (Emmy award 1977), A Woman of Independent Means, 1994; prodr. Dying Young, 1991.

FIELDER, BARBARA LEE, management leadership and communications trainer; b. Long Beach, Calif., Dec. 6, 1942; d. Thomas G. Coultrup and Elizabeth L. (Doran) Cox; m. Alford W. Fielder, Apr. 14, 1970; children: Kris, Kimberly, Brian. BSBA, Redlands U., 1979. Cert. tchr., Calif. Sr. compensation analyst Irvine Co., Newport Beach, Calif., 1973-76; pers. adminstr. Shiley divsn. Pfizer Co., Irvine, Calif., 1976-78; asst. dir. human resources BASF-Video Corp., Fountain Valley, Calif., 1978-79; pres. Barbara L. Fielder & Assoc., Roseville, Calif., 1979-89, Fielder Group, Ky., 1989—; instr. U. Calif., Irvine and Riverside, 1981-85, Davis, 1985-88; instr. Orange Coast Coll., Long Beach C.C., Coastline C.C.; workshop leader Inst. Applied Mgmt. and Law, 1981—, Nat. Seminars Group, 1989-94, Skill Path, 1994—. Contbr. articles to profl. publs., weekly articles on mgmt. and bus. to Tribune Courier Newspaper, monthly articles to Pro-Shop Mag.; author I'm Communicating But...Am I Being Heard?. Pres. Calif. Employers Coun., 1983-86; mem. Pvt. Industry Coun., Orange County, Calif., 1983-84; past mem. Foothill Adv. Bd., 1987-89; bd. dirs. Industry Edn. Coun. Calif., 1987-89. Recipient Outstanding Svc. award Interstate Conf. Employment Security Agys., Indpls., 1984. Mem. Nat. Speakers Assn., Tenn. Speakers Assn., Internat. Platform Assn., Lions Club. Presbyterian.

FIELDER, DOROTHY SCOTT, postmaster; b. Detroit, Apr. 20, 1943; d. William Lacy and Gertrude Elizabeth (Coddington) Davis; m. Douglas Stratton Fielder, July 13, 1968; 1 child, William Todd. AB, Randolph-Macon Woman's Coll., 1965; MA, Kent State U., 1968. Lab. instr. Mary Baldwin Coll., Staunton, Va., 1965-66, Hartwick Coll., Oneonta, N.Y., 1969-70; rsch. and teaching asst. Kent (Ohio) State U., 1966-68; high sch. tchr. biology Fairfax County Pub. Schs., Va., 1968-69; postal clk. U.S. Postal Svc., Maryland, N.Y., 1978-80, rural carrier, 1980-81; postmaster U.S. Postal Svc., Schenevus, N.Y., 1981—; coord. Benjamin Franklin Stamp Club, U.S. Postal Svc., Albany, N.Y., 1982-93. Author: Pictorial History of the Town of Maryland, N.Y., 1990, Otsego County Postal History, 1994. Vice chmn. Town of Maryland Planning Bd., 1989-93, chmn., 1993—. Mem. AAUW, Nat. Assn. Postmasters U.S., Town of Md. Hist. Assn. (pres. 1982—), Tri-County Postmasters Assn. (pres. 1990-94), Empire State Postal History Soc., Am. Philatelic Soc., Environ. Planning Lobby. Methodist. Home: RR 1 Box 1038 Maryland NY 12116-9703 Office: US Postal Svc 62 Main St Schenevus NY 12155

FIELDHOUSE, JILL MARIE, information manager; b. Paterson, N.J., Apr. 20, 1959; d. George David and Marjorie Ruth (Gillies) F. BA in Botany, Rutgers U., 1981, postgrad., 1989—. Teaching asst. Rutgers U., Newark, N.J., 1981-82; rsch. asst. Upjohn Co., Kalamazoo, 1983-85; staff immunologist Merck & Co., Inc., Rahway, N.J., 1985-88, sr. documentation specialist, 1988-92; mgr. regulatory info. Hoffmann-LaRoche, Nutley, N.J., 1992—. Contbr. articles to profl. jours.; patentee in field. Mem. career awareness day com. Hawthorne (N.J.) High Sch., 1989; deacon 1st Presbyn. Ch., Cranford, N.J., 1990, tutor. Rotary scholar, 1977. Mem. NAFE, Drug Info. Assn., Phi Beta Kappa, Beta Beta Beta. Home: 8 Pacific Ave Cranford NJ 07016

FIELDING, JEAN COLE, elementary education educator; b. Norfolk, Va., Dec. 5, 1946; d. John Carrington and Anna Catherine (Van Weelde) C.; m. Robert Edward Fielding, June 28, 1969; children: Bryan Lewis, Christopher David. BA in Edn., Lynchburg Coll., 1969, MEd in Elem. Edn., 1972. Cert. tchr., Va. Tchr. Yellowbranch-Campbell County Schs., Rustburg, W.Va., 1969-75; substitute tchr. Lynchburg (Va.) City Schs., 1983-86; tchr.

James River Day Sch., Lynchburg, 1986—; mem. Piedmont Area Reading Coun., Lynchburg, 1991—. Mem AAUW. Methodist.

FIELDS, ANITA, academic dean; b. Amarillo, Tex., Oct. 29, 1940; d. Dera and Mamie Maureen (Craig) Bates; 1 child, William Kyle. Grad. nursing, Jefferson Davis Hosp., 1962; BSN, Tex. Christian U., 1966; MSN, Northwestern State U. La., 1974; PhD, Tex. Women's U., 1980. C.E. coord., asst. prof. Northwestern State U., Shreveport; prof., dean McNeese State U., Lake Charles, La.; gov.'s appointee Southwest La. Hosp. Dist. Commn., 1989-91, chmn., 1989-91. Mem. allocations com. and loaned exec. United Way, 1991-92, Am. Heart Assn., Am. Cancer Soc., ARC. Recipient Ben Taub award, 1962, Ann Magnussen award ARC, 1977; named Nurse of Yr. SDNA, 1972, 80. Mem. ANA (del.), LSNA (past pres., past 1st v.p., Spl. Recognition award 1993), SDNA (bd. dirs., past pres.), LDONA (bd. dirs.), Nat. League for Nursing (agy. mem.), Sigma Theta Tau, Delta Kappa Gamma (Image of Nursing award 1993), Phi Kappa Phi. Home: 1723 Fox Run Dr Lake Charles LA 70605-6406

FIELDS, BARBARA P. LINDER, marketing executive; b. Bklyn., Jan. 29, 1950; m. Steven Linder (div.); m. Nolan I. Fields, Oct. 1980; children: Brent, Adam, Stephanie, Brittany. Student, Marjorie Webster Jr. Coll., 1968-70, Am. Musical and Dramatic Acad., 1971. Showroom, nat. sales dir. Faded Glory Jeans, N.Y.C., 1974-75; owner Blazing Sadie Inc., N.Y.C., 1975-76, Personal Connections Ltd., 1976-78; internat. mktg. sales dir. Multilite USA (div. Multilite, Can.), 1979; vice pres., co-owner Nu Fields Inc. (cons. lighting and giftware industry), 1980—; owner Simply Stoned Clothing and Art Designs, 1985-89; founding pres. C.H.A.D.D. of Nassau County (Children With Attention Deficit Disorders), Bellmore, N.Y., 1989—; owner Artistic Concepts, 1993—. Home: 183 Colony Dr Holbrook NY 11741-2847

FIELDS, DAISY BRESLEY, human resources development consultant; b. Bklyn.; student Hunter Coll., 1932-35, Am. U., 1949-53; m. Victor Fields, Aug. 2, 1936; 1 child, Barbara Fields Ochsman. Pers. officer USAF Base, Norfolk, Va., 1942-45; asst. pers. officer Dept. Agr., Phila., 1945-47; asst. dir. pers. Smithsonian Instn., Washington, 1954-60; chief spl. programs NASA, Washington, 1960-67; spl. asst. Fed. Women's Program, VA, Washington, 1967-70; sr. program assoc. Nat. Civil Svc. League, 1971-72; cons. Equal Employment Opportunity/Affirmative Action, 1972-75, 78—; exec. dir. Federally Employed Women, Washington, 1975-77; pres. Fields Assocs., Silver Spring, Md., 1978—; exec. dir. The Women's Inst., Am. U.; instr. Mt. Vernon Coll., 1979-80, Am. U., 1982; cons. USAID, 1990, 91, 92, 93. Author: A Woman's Guide to Moving Up in Business and Government, 1983; editor: Winds of Change: Korean Women in America, 1991; contbr. articles to profl. jours. Chmn., Montgomery County (Md.) Pers. Bd., 1972-78; chmn. legis. com. Comm. for Women in Pub. Adminstrn., 1976-79; commr. Md. Commn. for Women, 1973-77; commr. Montgomery County Commn. for Women, 1979-82; editor newsletter, past pres. Clearinghouse on Women's Issues; v.p., mng. editor Women's Inst. Press; bd. dirs. Nat. Woman's Party, 1989—. Recipient award UN Assn. U.S.A., 1980. Mem. NAFE, Nat. Coun. Career Women, Women's Equity Action League (pres. Md. 1972-74; award 1978), Federally Employed Women (pres. 1969-71, editor newsletter 1972-77, recipient award 1974, 78), Nat. Press Club, Am. News Women's Club, Internat. Women's Writing Guild, Washington Ind. Writers, Capital Press Women, Fedn. Orgns. Profl. Women (exec. coun. 1976-77, 80-82), Nat. Assn. Women Bus. Owners. Home and Office: 13905 N Gate Dr Silver Spring MD 20906-2218

FIELDS, HARRIET GARDIN, counselor, educator, consultant; b. Pasco, Wash., Feb. 25, 1944; d. Harry C. and Ethel Jenell (Rochelle) Gardin; m. Avery C. Fields; 1 child, Avery C. BS in Edn., S.C. State U., Orangeburg, 1966; MEd, U. S.C., 1974. Lic. profl. counselor and supr.; nat. bd. cert. counselor and career counselor. Tchr. Richaldn Sch. Dist., Columbia, S.C., 1966-67 73-76; counselor supr. S.C. Dept. Corrections, Columbia, 1971-73; counselor Techinal Edn. System, West Columbia, S.C., 1967-70; exec. dir. Bethlehem Community Ctr., Columbia, 1976-79; human rels. cons. Calhoun County Schs., St. Matthews, S.C., 1979-82; admission counselor Allen U., Columbia, 1982-83; pres., cons. H.G. Fields Assn., Columbia, 1983—; exec. dir. Big Bros./Big Sisters, Columbia, 1984-87. Mem. Richland County Coun., Columbia, 1989-92, chair, 1993, 94, 95; 2d vice chair Richland County Dem. Party, Columbia, 1984-88; sec. Statewide Reapportionment Com., 1990—. Recipient inaugural Woodrow Wilson award Greater Columbia C. of C., 1994, numerous human rels. and outstanding svc. awards. Mem. Am. Counselor Assn. (resolutions chair So. br. 1993-94), S.C. Assn. Counselors (chair govt. rels. 1985—, pres. 1982-83), Assn. Multicultural Counseling Devel., S.C. Coalition of Pub. Health, S.C. Assn. Counties, Nat. Assn. Counties (employment and steering com., taxation and fin. com.). Democrat. Methodist. Office: Richland County Coun PO Box 192 2020 Hampton St Columbia SC 29202

FIELDS, JENNIE, advertising executive, writer; b. Chgo., July 25, 1953; d. Ira Samuel and Belle Harriet (Springer) F.; m. Steven W. Kroeter, Aug. 28, 1983; 1 child, Chloe Melinda. BFA, U. Ill., 1974; MFA, U. Iowa, 1976. Copywriter Foote Cone & Belding, Chgo., 1977-79; v.p., copy supr. Needham Harper & Steers, Chgo., 1979-82, Young & Rubicam, N.Y.C., 1982-85; v.p., creative dir. J. Walter Thompson, Chgo., 1985-86; assoc. creative dir. Leo Burnett, Chgo., 1986-89; sr. v.p., group creative dir. Young & Rubicam, N.Y.C., 1989-93; sr. v.p. Lowe & Ptnrs., SMS, N.Y.C., 1993—; ptnr. Steven Fields Design Assoc., Chgo., 1983—. Author: Lily Beach, 1993, paperback edit., 1994 (Featured Alternate, Book of Month Club 1993). Recipient 2 Lions Cannes Internat. Festival, Clio award, Nat. Addy award, Effie award, Chgo. Addy Gold award. Home: 452 8th St Brooklyn NY 11215-3616 Office: Lowe and Ptnrs SMS 1114 Ave of the Americas New York NY 10105-0010

FIELDS, KATHY ANN, dermatologist; b. Waukegan, Ill., May 14, 1958; d. Maynard Bernard and Blanche (Telson) F.; m. Garry Rayant, Aug. 10, 1991. Student, Northwestern U., 1975-76; BS, U. Fla., 1979; MD, U. Miami, Fla., 1983. Diplomate Am. Bd. Dermatology. Intern in ob-gyn. Jackson Meml. Hosp., 1983-84; resident in dermatology Stanford (Calif.) U. Med. Ctr., 1984-87; laser specialist Sydney, Australia, 1987; pvt. practice San Francisco, 1988—. Creator acne skin care line with nat. market ProActiv Solution. Fundraiser Am. Cancer Soc., San Francisco, 1988—, Child Abuse Prevention, United Jewish Appeal, Women's Young Leadership Cabinet, 1991—, mosaic counsel. Fellow Am. Acad. Dermatology; mem. AMA, Calif. Med. Assn., San Francisco Med. Soc., San Mateo Med. Soc. Office: 350 Parnassus Ave San Francisco CA 94117-3608

FIELDS, SUZANNE, architect; b. Tallahassee, Jan. 15, 1949; d. Roger Gordon and Martha Ann (Sanders) F.; m. Alfred Thomas Lamb, June 8, 1968 (div. May 1974); 1 child, BonT Lamb. BArch, Fla. A&M U., 1981, MArch, 1990. Registered architect, Fla. Archtl. intern Copeland Consulting Engrs., Inc., Tallahassee, 1981-83, Mays Leroy Gray, AIA, P.A., Tallahassee, 1984-92; registered architect Fields Co. Architects, Inc., Tallahassee, 1993—. Damage assessment evaluator ARC, Fla., 1989—; sponsor Fla. Sheriff's Youth Ranch, Fla., 1990—; active Property Owners Assn. Mysterious Waters, Inc., Fla., 1991—. Mem. AIA (Nat. and Fla. chpt.), Nat. Trust Hist. Preservation, Rotary (sec. Wakulla County chpt. 1992-94, pres. 1994—). Office: Fields Co Architects Inc PO Box 6644 Tallahassee FL 32314

FIELDS, WENDY LYNN, lawyer; b. N.Y.C., Sept. 22, 1946; d. Sidney and Helen (Silverstein) F. BA, George Washington U., 1968, JD, 1976. Bar: D.C. 1976. Assoc. Arent, Fox, Kintner, Plotkin & Kahn, Washington, 1976-78; ptnr. Weissbard & Fields, Washington, 1978-83, Wilkes, Artis, Hedrick & Lane, Washington, 1983-86, Foley & Lardner, Washington, 1986—. Mem. Geroge Washington Law Rev., 1973-75. Mem. D.C. Bar. Assn. Office: Foley & Lardner 3000 K Street NW Ste 500 Washington DC 20007

FIELO, MURIEL BRYANT, space engineer, interior designer; b. Bklyn., Dec. 11, 1921; d. Harry and Minnie (Dick) Bryant; m. Julius Fielo, June 17; 1 child, Michael Kenneth. Student, CCNY, 1938-41, Rutgers U., 1965-69; cert. N.Y. Sch. Interior Design, 1970. Gen. mgr. Fidelity Discount Corp., Irvington, N.J., adv. supr. Lincoln Loan Cos., Essex County, N.J., 1941-49; interior designer Alex Fielo Interior Decorators, Newark, 1942-49, prin., 1949-69, owner, 1969—; designer, cons. space engr. MUDGE Interior Design Studios, East Orange, N.J., 1969—. Mem. adv. panel Interior Design Mag, 1977—. Essex County freeholder clk. Bd. Freeholders, 1972-76; commr. East Orange Bus. Devel. Authority, 1977-86; mem. U.S. adv. coun. SBA-Region II, 1980-81; active LWV, 1950-55; organizer, 1st pres. South Orange chpt. Women's Am. ORT, 1952-54, mem. nat. speakers bur., 1952-65, parliamentarian No. N.J. coun., 1955-65; pres. Amity chpt. B'nai B'rith, Newark, 1946-48, v.p. No. N.J. coun., 1948-49, various nat. and state positions, 1948-80; mem. nat. com. on sect. fund raising Nat. Coun. Jewish Women, 1979-81, nat. tour. chmn., 1979-81; trustee community svcs. coun. Oranges and Maplewood, United Way of Essex and West Hudson, 1981-83; bd. dirs. East Orange Central Ave. Mall Assn., 1979-83, chmn. new voter registration drive East Orange 2d Ward, 1955—, entire city, 1969; pres. East Orange Dem. Club, 1957-58, campaign coord. for Dem. mayoral candidate, 1969, calendar coord. Essex County Dem. Party, 1970-76; mem. N.J. Bipartisan Coalition for Women's Appts., 1981—. Named Outstanding Entrepreneur of 1984 N.J. Gov., Outstanding Orgn. Pres. Kean Coll. Profl. Women's Assn., 1985, Wonder Woman of 1986, Bus. Jour. of N.J., One of 8 Women to Watch in 1987 Jersey Woman Mag., 1987; also recipient various awards for civic svc.; named Bus. Person of Yr. East Orange C. of C., 1988. Mem. Internat. Soc. Interior Designers (bd. dir. 1981-85), Nat. Home Fashions League (N.J. membership chmn. N.Y. chpt. 1981-82), Interior Design Soc., N.J. Assn. Women Bus. Owners (state bd. 1979-82), Women Entrepreneurs N.J. (pres. 1981-85, chief exec. officer 1987—), N.J. Home Furnishings Assn. (bd. dirs. 1981-84, 86—), Constrn. Specifications Inst., N.J. Soc. AIA (profl. affiliate), Guild Designer Woodworkers, Women Bus. Ownership Ednl. Coalition (N.J. State pres. 1985-87, chief exec. officer 1987—, mem. steering com. interior designers for licensing in N.Y. 1985—), East Orange C. of C. (bd. dir. 1977—, v.p. 1981-85), Bus. and Profl. Women's Club of Oranges (bd. dir. 1958-66). Jewish. Home and Office: MUDGE Interior Design Studio 185 S Clinton St East Orange NJ 07018-3039

FIERING, SUSANNAH, art therapist, educator; b. N.Y.C., Mar. 18, 1934; d. Stephen and May (Cavin) Leeman; m. Alvin Fiering, Jan. 27, 1957 (div. 1984); children: Gina, Wendy, Chloe. BA, Bard Coll., 1955; MFA, Inst. Allende, Guanajuato, Mex., 1973; MEd, Lesley Coll., 1980. Registered art therapist. Instr. art, art history, art edn. Lesley Coll., Bunker Hill C.C., Stonehill Coll., Cambridge, Charleston, No. Easton, Mass., 1975-78; art therapist, intake specialist, case mgr. New Ctr. for Psychotherapies, Boston, 1977-81; instr. art therapy Lesley Coll. Grad. Sch., Cambridge, 1982; chairperson acad. coun. Beacon Coll., Boston, 1983-84; instr. psychology, art prison edn. project Curry Coll., Lancaster, Mass., 1983, 85; instr. art therapy Salve Regina U., Newport, R.I., 1985-92; expressive therapist Phase, Tavnton, Mass., 1986-88, Waltham (Mass.)/Weston Hosp., 1988-91; pvt. practice art therapy, counseling, 1980—; art therapist Charter Hosp. Austin, 1991-92; art and child therapist House of the Morning Star, Austin, 1993; workshop leader, staff devel. trainer numerous orgns., 1987—. Executed mural for Charter Hosp. Austin, 1992; sculptures reproduced in Woman Poets #3, 1974; woodcut prints reproduced in Magical Blend mag., 1993; exhibited in group shows at De Cordova Mus., 1986 and numerous others. Active Save our Springs, Austin, 1991-93. Mem. Am. Art Therapy Assn. Office: House of Morning Star 4401 Barrow Ave Austin TX 78751-3914

FIERROS, RUTH VICTORIA, retired secondary school educator; b. McRoberts, Ky., Mar. 29, 1920; d. Willie A. and Harriet (Wright) Cornett; m. Jose Fernando Fierros, Nov. 22, 1945 (dec.); children: Cedric Joseph, Philip Alonso, Stephen Michael. BA in English, Berea Coll., 1942; MA in English and Edn., Tex. A&I U., 1954. Cert. tchr., Tex. Tchr. Jenkins Ind. Schs., McRoberts, 1942-43, Laredo (Tex.) Ind. Schs., 1951-87; ret., 1987. Editor: Class '42 Yearbook, 1982, 87, 92; author: Upon the Easel of my Heart, 1982; contbr. poems to anthologies. Chairperson 50th and 55th anniversary reunions Berea Coll. Class of 1942; pres. Tuesday Music & Literature, 1986-88. With USN, 1943-46. Recipient Tchr. Excellence award U. Tex., 1987, Golden Apple award Alpha Delta Kappa, 1987, Golden Poet award, 1988, Cert. of Citation State of Tex. Ho. of Reps., 1987, Armed Forces award, 1988, Leadership award, 1988. Mem. AAUW (1st v.p. 1966-68), NEA, Gifted and Talented Assn., Nat. Coun. Tchrs. English, Tex. State Tchrs. Assn., World of Poetry, So. Poetry Assn. (Critics Choice award), Nat. Libr. of Poetry, Webb County Unit Ret. Tchrs. Assn. (2d v.p. 1994-95), Charles T. Morgan Soc., Delta Kappa Gamma (pres.). Democrat. Roman Catholic. Home: 1801 Fremont St Laredo TX 78043-2606

FIFE, BETTY H., librarian; b. Indpls., Mar. 31, 1925; d. Otho Cova and Mae Craddock (Paxton) Hay; m. James A. Fife, Aug. 30, 1945; children: Andrew, Marlie, John, Laurie. BS, Boston U., 1967, MS, 1969; student, Northeastern U. Classroom tchr., libr. Town of Hanover (Mass.); elem. libr. Town of Newburgh (N.Y.). Fellow Northeastern U. Mem. NCTE. Home: 174 Cedar Acres Rd Marshfield MA 02050-6036 Office: PO Box 115 Vails Gate NY 12584-0115

FIFE, JANET KAY, elementary school educator; b. Creston, Iowa, Dec. 26, 1944; d. Cleve Hoiser and Eiffle Laurene (White) Seley; m. Bruce D. Fife, Aug. 15, 1965 (div. Nov. 1977); 1 child, Menda S. AA, Creston Community Coll., 1965; BS in Edn., Western Ill. U., 1967; MA in Edn., N.E. Mo. State U., 1978. Sch. tchr. Keokuk (Iowa) Community Schs., 1967—. Sec., treas. Tri State Coalition Against Family Violence, 1983-93, dir., 1983—; city councilperson Keokuk City, 1986—; dir. Sister Cities, 1990-92, S.E. Iowa League of Municipalities, 1990—; trustee Southeastern C.C., Keokuk/Burlington, Iowa, 1992—, pres. 1994—; pres. YMCA, 1992-93, bd. dirs., 1992—; pres. Iowa Women's Polit. Caucus, 1994—. Mem. Internat. Reading Assn., Assn. Univ. Women, Bus. and Profl. Women (pres. 1992-94), Delta Kappa Gamma. Home: 1903 Fulton St Keokuk IA 52632-2827 Office: Keokuk Community Schs 727 Washington St Keokuk IA 52632-2438

FIFER, EDITH MARY CALDWELL, educational administrator; b. Chgo.; d. William and Earline (Harrell) Caldwell; m. James Franklin Fifer III, Aug. 17, 1968; children: James Franklin IV, Lisa Beth. BS in Edn., Chgo. State U., 1964; MA in Guidance and Counseling, Govs. State U., Park Forest South, Ill., 1975; EdD in Early Childhood Edn., Nova U., 1987. Cert. elem. tchr., K-12 adminstr., spl. edn., Ill. Tchr. Hinton Elem. Sch., Chgo. Pub. Schs., 1965-69, tchr. spl. edn., 1970-76, coord. spl. edn., 1976-81, tchr. instrnl. intervention Bur. Early Childhood Edn. of the Handicapped, 1981-84, coord. Bur., 1984-89, adminstr. early childhood edn. of handicapped, 1989—; mem. task force for autism Ill. Bd. Edn.; project liaison pilot mental health program Chgo. Pub. Schs., Mental Health Assn. Ill., U. Ill., Chgo.; founder, chairperson ICPS Core Planning Com. Mental Health Schs. Project; active Community Approach to Integrated Svc. System Com.; presenter in field. Contbr. to profl. publs. Mem. adv. com. Women's Treatment Ctr., Chgo.; pres. bd. dirs. Prevention First; mem. adv. bd. ednl. outreach Field Mus. Natural History, Chgo.; vol. Lincoln Park (Ill.) Zool. Assn.; active Com. Nat. Assn. Perinatal Addiction Rsch. and Edn. Mem. Coun. for Exceptional Children, Chgo. Coun. for Exceptional Children (adv. bd.), Coun. for Adminstrs. Spl. Edn., Doctorate Assn. N.Y. Educators, Phi Delta Kappa. Home: 8215 S Morgan St Chicago IL 60620-3132 Office: Chgo Bd Edn 1819 W Pershing Rd Chicago IL 60609-2317

FIFER CANBY, SUSAN MELINDA, library administrator; b. Stockton, Calif., Jan. 23, 1948; d. Reginald Dekovan and Shirley Rae (Canaday) Fifer; m. Thomas Yellott Canby, Oct. 9, 1982. BS, U. Nebr., 1970; MLS, U. Md., 1974. Circulation libr. Nat. Geog. Soc., Washington, 1975-81, asst. librarian, 1981-83, dir. Libr., 1983-94, dir. libr. and indexing, 1994—; bd. dirs. tech. com. D.C. Council Govts., 1985-88; bd. dirs. Capital Area Consortium, 1989—, chair, 1994—. Lay reader St. Luke's Ch., Brighton, Md., 1985—, mem. vestry, 1994—. Mem. ALA (John Cotton Dana award 1985, 89), Spl. Librs. Assn. (chmn. geography and map div. 1978, 85), D.C. Libr. Assn. (pres. 1991-92, v.p. 1990-91, sec. 1981-83, Disting. Svc. award 1993), Assn. Am. Geographers, Hort. Soc. Sandy Spring (v.p. 1987-88), Delta Delta Delta. Republican. Episcopalian. Avocations: gardening, reading. Home: 6855 Haviland Mill Rd Clarksville MD 21029-1308 Office: Nat Geog Soc Library 17th St # M St NW Washington DC 20036

FIGGINS, LETHA ARLENE (LETHA ARLENE DEHN), retired educator; b. Quenemo, Kans., July 16, 1916; d. Walter Frank and Louise May (Weis) Dehn; m. Byron Edward, Aug. 31, 1940; 1 child, Geri Sue Bauman. BA, Ottawa (Kans.) U., 1964; MS, Kans. State Tchrs. Coll., 1971. Cert. tchr., Kans. Tchr. Middleton Rural Sch., Quenemo, 1934-40, Chippewa Rural Sch., Ottawa, 1940-42, Spring Creek Rural Sch., Ottawa, 1946-66, Lincoln Elem., Ottawa, 1966-82; ret., 1982. Contbr. articles profl. jours. Mem. Pres. Reagan's Task Force, 1980-88, Pres. Bush's Task Force, 1989—; active Franklin County Rep. Women, Ottawa, 1986—, Nat. Rep. Congl. Com., Bus. Profl. Women; pres., v.p. Franklin County Tchrs. Orgns., Ottawa; v.p. Ottawa Edn. Assn., 1976, pres., 1977; vol. Phone Friend, 1988-89, 90—, Ottawa Univ.; pres. Elm Grove Homemaker's Unit, 1985-87; mem. Friends of Ottawa Libr.; tchr. Vacation Bible Sch. Bapt. Ch., 1950-60. Named Tchr. of Yr. Finalist, State of Kans., 1980. Mem. Alpha Delta Kappa (pres. 1951—), Bus. Profl. Women (Woman of Yr. Ottawa club, sec. 1988—), Ottawa Area Retired Tchrs. Assn. (historian 1985-89), AAUW (program leader), Assn. Childhood Edn. (past pres.), Rebekah Noble Grand (elected v.p. dist. 8, 1989, apptd. dist. dept. pres. #8 1990, 93, apptd. lodge dep.), Friendship Love Truth Club (past pres.). Republican. Baptist. Home: 416 E 14th St Ottawa KS 66067-3611

FIGGS, LINDA SUE, principal; b. Westhope, N.D., Dec. 19, 1946; d. Clifford James and Ethel Grace (Geise) Drake; m. Tom R. Figgs, Dec. 27, 1969. Student, Minot State U., 1964-66; B.Music Edn., U. Kans., 1968, M.Music Edn., 1972, EdD, 1978. Cert. secondary music tchr., ednl. adminstr., Kans., Iowa, Nebr., N.D. Music tchr. Jefferson County N. High Sch., Winchester, Kans., 1968-76, 89-91, supr. student tchrs., 1970-75; rsch. asst. to assoc. dean of edn. U. Kans., Lawrence; prin. McKinley Elem., Liberal, Kans., 1992—; bd. dirs. Am. Youth Symphony Band and Orch., Nebr., 1970-76; rsch. asst. Sch. Edn., U. Kans., Lawrence, 1977; piano tchr. Toon Shop, Atchison, Kans., Leavenworth, Kans.; music tchr. Little Flower Sch., Minot, N.D., Effingham, Kans.; mgr. music store Effingham; sec. humanities Minot State U.; counselor Internat. Music Camp, Dunseith, N.D., Midwestern Music and Art Camp, Lawrence; summer counselor, unit leader Nat. Music Camp, Interlochen, Mich.; sponsor 5th grade Positive Peer Group; mem. edn. adv. panel TeleKansas Alliance; mem. U.S. D480 Action Team Mem., McKinley Action Team Mem.; reader adv. bd. Southwest Daily Times; mem. residency coordinating team NEA; mem. tech. com. Quality Performance Accreditation Team; elem. adminstrn. rep. Stakeholders Com. Sch. Site Coun. Contbr. articles to profl. publs. Music dir. United Meth. Ch., Atchison; mem. choir United Meth. Ch., Liberal, 1992-94; choir dir. 1st Christian Ch., Liberal, 1995—; active McKinley Elem. PTA, S.W. Kans. Humane Soc.; bd. dirs. Comty. Concert, 1994—; bd. dirs., docent Baker Arts, 1994—; vol. Mid Am. Air Mus.; vol., mem. 500 Club; mem. Leadership Liberal, 1995—. Mem. ASCD, NEA, AAUW (edn. & scholarship com.), Nat. Assn. Elem. Sch. Prins., United Sch. Adminstrs., Kans. Assn. Sch. Adminstrs., Kans. Assn. for Supervision and Curriculum Devel., Kans. Assn. Elem. Sch. Prins., Kans. Edn. Assn., Nat. Mid. Sch. Assn., Kans. Assn. Mid. Level Edn., Kans. Reading Assn., Kans. Reading Coun., Profl. Devel. Coun. (co-pres., insvc. com.), U. Kans. Alumni Assn. (life), S.W. Symphony soc. (pres. 1993—), Sigma Alpha Iota, Pi Kappa Lambda, Phi Delta Kappa. Presbyterian. Home: 303 N Kansas Ave Ste 401 Liberal KS 67901-3339

FIGLAR, ANITA WISE, banker; b. Camas, Wash., Oct. 7, 1950; d. William Hulon and Mary Wise (Adkisson) Ward; m. Richard Bould Figlar, Aug. 7, 1976; children: Richard Bould II, David Wise. Student, U. Wash., 1968-70; BA in Intercultural Studies, Ramapo Coll., 1974. Mktg. coord. power and control ops. Gen. Cable Corp., Union, N.J., 1975-76, mktg. analyst power and control ops., 1976-78; various positions Potters Industries, Inc., Hasbrouck Heights, N.J., 1971-75; with highway safety programs dept. Potters Industries, Inc., Parsippany, N.J., 1981-82, mgr. highway safety programs dept., 1982-84, mgr. bus. devel., 1985-86, industry mgr. Highway Products div., 1986-89; with customer svc. United Jersey Bank, Hackensack, N.J., 1989; fin. svc. rep. United Jersey Bank, 1989-90, asst. br. mgr., bank officer, 1990-91; bank officer retail sales United Jersey Bank, Hackensack, N.J., 1991-92, bank officer retail sales mgr., 1992-94, v.p., mgr. retail sales, 1994—. Contbr. articles to many profl. and govtl. publs. Notary pub.

FIKE, CINDY JANE, pediatrics nurse; b. New Castle, Pa., July 25, 1957; d. Irvin Clifford and Dorothy Marie (Stevick) F. Diploma in Practical Nursing, Butler Community Coll., 1978, ADN, 1988; student, Pa. State U., 1991-93. RN; cert. pediatric safety and CPR. Nurse's aide St. John's Luth. Home, Mars, Pa., 1975-78, practical nurse, 1978-79; practical nurse Grove City (Pa.) United Community Hosp., 1979-88, staff nurse pediatrics, 1988—; chairperson/lectr. Parenting Classes for Area Pregnant and Parenting Teams, Grove City, 1990—; pediatric tour guide United Community Hosp., 1986—; participant Children's Health Fair, United Community Hosp., 1989—. Contbr. articles to profl. jours. Vol. Am. Cancer Soc., 1988—. Named Nurse of Hope, Mercer County, Pa., 1988-89. Democrat. Methodist. Home: 165 Main St Connoquenessing PA 16027 Office: United Community Hosp 40 # 1 Broad St Grove City PA 16127

FILCHOCK, ETHEL, education educator, poet. BS in Edn., Kent State U. Tchr. Cleve. Pub. Schs.; with EFC Creations, Solon, Ohio. Author: Voices in Poetics: Vol. 1, 1985 (Merit award), Hall of Fame: Ethel Filchock, Vol. 1, 1991 (book of poetry) Softer Memories Across a Lifetime, 1989, (poetry chapbook) A Glimpse of Love, 1991; composer: Praise God, The Lord is Coming; lyricist: (songs) He Is Born, 1991, An Old-Fashioned Christmas, Let's Wave the Stars and Stripes Forever, 1991, Be There for Me Music of America, 1993, Christmas Joy, Happy Holidays, 1993. Chmn. sch. United Way, 1985-86. Recipient Cert. of Achievement N.Y. Profl./Amateur Song Jubilee, 1986, Editor's Choice award Disting. Poets of Am., Outstanding Achievement in Poetry, Nat. Libr. of Poetry, 1993. Mem. NAFE, Am. Fedn. Tchrs. Roman Catholic. Club: Akron Manuscript.

FILER, EMILY SYMINGTON HARKINS, social services administrator; b. Balt., May 12, 1936; d. Frank Fife and Grace (Cover) Symington; m. George Archer Harkins, June 21, 1958 (div. 1982); children: Montgomery Fox, Emily Harrison (dec. Apr. 1978); m. Robert Hoagland Filer, June 24, 1989. Degree, Villa Julie Med. Sec. Sch., Balt., 1955. Cert. vol. adminstr. Registrar Johns Hopkins Hosp., Balt., 1955-57, sec. hearing and speech ctr., 1957-58; pres. Distaff Wives, San Francisco, Boston, 1958-63; v.p., bd. dirs. The Planning Council, Tidewater, Va., 1969-78; pres. Jr. League of Norfolk (Va.)-Virginia Beach, 1972-74; founder, coord. Lee's Friends, Norfolk, 1978-86, exec. dir., 1986—; chmn. Tidewater dist. Va. Council Soc. Welfare, 1985-87, Va. Council Social Welfare, 1988; bd. dirs. Va. Wesleyan Coll., Norfolk, 1979—, Olde Huntersville Devel., Norfolk, 1985-87. Lic. pastoral caregiver The Ch. of Good Shepherd, 1992—; bd. dirs. Westminster Canterbury of Virginia Beach, 1992—, exec. com. sec., 1993—. Lee's Friends recipient Community Svc. award Vol. Action Ctrs., 1981, Community Svc. award Jewish Community of Tidewater, 1982, Pres. Vol. Action award, 1982, Spl. Vol. Action award South Hampton Roads, 1988, 1989 Gov.'s Gold medal for Vol. Excellence, 1990 J.C. Penney Golden Rule award Hampton Roads, LF award, Women-In-Transition award YWCA, 1989, Spl. award as an Outstanding Bus. Woman of Hampton Roads, 1989, Disting. Merit citation NCCJ, Va. Vol. Adminstr. of Yr. award, 1992, Outstanding Orgn. award Tidewater Dist., 1992, Vol. of Distinction award Jr. Leagues Internat., 1994; named Great Citizen of Hampton Roads, 1987. Mem. Internat. Assn. for Vol. Adminstrs. (cert. liaison, region IV 1986, profl. devel. liaison assn. 1987-88, region IV 1987-88, 93-94, recertification chair 1990-92), Colonial Va. Assn. for Vol. Adminstrs. (dep. sec. 1986-87, pres. 1987-89), Tidewater Cancer Network (assoc. 1986), Nat. Hospice Orgn. (assoc.), Va. Assn. for Hospice Orgn. (assoc.), Jr. League of Norfolk-Va. Beach (sustainer). Episcopalian. Office: Lee's Friends 618 Stockley Gardens Norfolk VA 23507-2017

FILIPI, JOAN LEAHY (JODY FILIPI), medical association executive, speech pathologist; b. Park Falls, Wis., Nov. 29, 1950; d. James Joseph and Katherine A. (Lillestrand) Leahy; m. David H. Filipi, Nov. 28, 1975; children: Kristin Brita, James Bohdan. BS in Speech Pathology Edn., U. Nebr., Omaha, 1972, MS in Speech Pathology, 1974; Cert. of Clin. Competence in Speech/Lang. Pathology, The Am. Speech and Hearing Assn. Cert. speech pathologist, Nebr. Speech lang. pathologist Ednl. Svc. Unit #4, Auburn, Nebr., 1975, Ralston (Nebr.) Pub. Schs., 1975-78; adminstrv. asst. Nebr. Acad. Family Physicians, Omaha, 1987-89, interim exec. dir., 1989, exec. dir., 1989—; mng. editor Cornhusker Family Physician mag., 1990—; sec., exec. dir. Family Health Found. Nebr., 1990-93; exec. dir. Nebr. Acad. Family Physicians Found., Omaha, 1993—. Pres. Nebr. Children's Chorus, Omaha, 1985-90, designer T-shirt, 1985; bd. dirs. Nebr. Alliance for Arts Edn., Fremont, 1989-91, dir. vacation ch. sch. Dundee Presbyn. Ch., Omaha, 1985-87; asst. dir. LOGOS Program, 1993-94, dir., 1994—; mem. Christian

Edn. Council, 1995; mem. class 14 Leadership Omaha, 1991-92; mem. Leadership Omaha Community Boardmanship Course, YWCA Women of Distinction, Nebr. Safety Ctr. Adv. Coun., 1992—. Mem. Profl. Convention Mgmt. Assn., Am. Soc. Assn. Execs., Am. Assn. Med. Soc. Execs., Nebr. Soc. Assn. Execs., Nebr. Choral Arts Soc. (bd. dirs. 1987-91, outstanding svc. award Nebr. Children's Chorus 1988), The Great Navy of the State of Nebr. (admiral 1994), Leadership Omaha Alumni Assn. Office: Nebr Acad Family Physicians 7101 Newport Ave Ste 201 Omaha NE 68152-2153

FILIPPELLI, ALICE MARIE, special education educator; b. Paterson, N.J., Feb. 24, 1962; d. William Carl Jr. and Donna Marie (Altavilla) F. BA in Psychology, William Paterson Coll., Wayne, N.J., 1985, postgrad., 1985-88, 91—. Cert. tchr. of handicapped, N.J. Substitute tchr. United Cerebral Palsy League, Union, N.J., 1985; grad. asst. infant psychology program William Paterson Coll., 1985-87; classroom tchr. St. Patricks Spl. Classes Sch., Newark, 1985-88; spl. edn. tchr. Paterson Pub. Sch. # 27, 1988—; mem. ann. conv. Assn. Schs. and Agys. for Handicapped, Atlantic City, 1985-88. Vol. helper, fund raiser Eva's Kitchen/Homeless Shelter, Paterson, 1986—; polit. worker, poll worker Young. Dems. (Riverside) Assn., Paterson, 1978—. Recipient Sponsor Appreciation award Paterson PASS-PLAN Orgn., 1991. Mem. NEA, N.J. Edn. Assn., Passaic County Edn. Assn., Paterson Edn. Assn. (bldg. del. 1989—). Democrat. Roman Catholic. Home: 1036 E 24th St Fl 2 Paterson NJ 07513-1628 Office: Paterson Pub Schs No 27 250 Richmond Ave Paterson NJ 07502-1332

FILIPPINI, CHRISTINE MARIE, counselor; b. Norristown, Pa., Aug. 1, 1957; d. Nicholas John Caramenico and Christine (Dougherty) Stayton; m. Anthony John Filippini, May 26, 1989; children: Anthony, Christopher. AB, Muhlenberg Coll., 1979; MEd, Millersville (Pa.) U., 1980. Sch. counselor West Perry Sr. High Sch., Elliottsburg, Pa., 1980-84, READS Inc., Levittown, Pa., 1984-87; sch. counselor, coord. teen/parent program Methacton Sch. Dist., Fairview Village, Pa., 1987—; co-chair Montgomery County Teen/Parent Task Force, Norristown, 1991-93. Presenter Chester County (Pa.) Intermediate Unit, 1989, 94, March of Dimes Conf., Phila., 1990, Pa. Dept. of Edn., State College, 1991—. Mem. AACD (del. 1990), Pa. Sch. Counselors Assn., Pa. Counseling Assn. (exec. coun. on com.), Pa. Edn. Assn., Methacton Edn. Assn., Montgomery County Counselors Assn. (senator 1989-94), Pa. Counselors Assn. (exec. bd. 1989-94). Office: Methacton Sch Dist Kreible Mill Rd Fairview Village PA 19409

FILLEY, DOROTHY MCCRACKEN, museum consultant, antique costume restorer; b. St. Augustine, Fla., Mar. 22, 1915; d. Fred Wellman and Rozella May (Leith) McCracken; m. Marcus Lucius Filley IV, Sept. 11, 1937; children—Leith Child Filley Colen, Linda Derrick Filley Laguerre. BS in Fine Arts, Skidmore Coll. 1936; MA in Museology, SUNY-Oneonta, 1974. Founder, dir. Rensselaer County Jr. Mus., Troy, N.Y., 1954-59; exhibits cons. to N.Y. State historian N.Y. State Edn. Dept., Albany, 1956-57; mus. cons. Hist. Soc., Saratoga Springs, N.Y.-Park Casino, 1971-74; curator, coordinator Rockefeller Empire State Mall Art Collection, Albany, 1978-80; curator exhibits and collections Albany Inst. History and Art, 1974-81, mus. cons., 1981-87; mem. N.Y. State Council on the Arts Mus. Adv. Bd., N.Y.C., 1974-75; cons. compiling history Town of Colonie, Newtonville, N.Y., 1975; mem. adv. bd. Shaker Heritage Soc., Albany, 1981-88; cons. textiles and costumes Albany Inst. History and Art, 1983-89; cons. Troy Savs. Bank Oil Painting Collection of bank presidents from 1823 to 1987 for conservation, 1988; spl. research cons. History of SUNY Univ. Plaza Bldg., 1986; historian Village Improvement Soc., 1992. Author: Recapturing Wisdom's Valley, 1975. Mem. Cooperstown Grad. Assn., Jr. League Troy (pres. 1950-51). Avocations: gardening, tennis, swimming, wildlife preservation. Home: RR 1 Box 129B Yarmouth ME 04096-9710

FILLICARO, BARBARA JEAN, business owner, consultant; b. Chgo.; d. Frank and Lillian (Kosach) F. Student, DePaul U., 1974-78, BA in Bus. Mgmt., 1978. Cert. Wordperfect software instr. Exec. sec. Continental Bank, Chgo., 1962-68; supr. secretarial svcs. Morton Quality Products, Chgo., 1968-71; adminstrv. asst. Libby, McNeill & Libby, Chgo., 1971-76, purchasing agt., 1976-78; mktg. rep. TRW Fin. Systems, Orlando, Fla., 1978-82; dist. sales rep. Streamline Industries, N.Y.C., 1982-84; office automation specialist Microage Computer Stores, Lombard, Ill., 1984-86; applications software trainer, cons. Fillicaro & Assocs., Lombard, 1986—; mem. faculty Coll. of DuPage, Glen Ellyn, Ill., 1988—; multimedia tech. specialist S.t Augustine Coll., Chgo., 1993—; charter mem., chmn. advocacy com. DuPage County Women's Bus. Coun., 1992; spkr. Multimedia '95, Orlando, Fla., 1995. Mem. Art Inst., Chgo., 1975-78. Mem. Chgo. Orgn. Data Tng. Educators, Am. Mgmt. Assn., Women in Mgmt. (bd. dirs., program chmn. 1986-88), Am. Assn. Individual Investors, Assn. for Devel. of Desktop Pub. Technique, DePaul U. Alumni Coun., Zonta Internat. (charter mem., treas. 1979-80), Internat. Interactive Comm. Soc. Home and Office: 5108 W Winnemac Ave Chicago IL 60630-2330

FILLOY, BEVERLEE ANN HOWE, clinical social worker; b. Ogden, Utah, Mar. 11, 1926; d. Albert Herman Howe and Bernice Anna (Ewing) Howe Routt; m. Jose Antonio Filloy-Alvarez, Feb. 4, 1945 (dec. 1988); children: Richard Anthony, Emily Ann. BA with honors, U. Calif., Berkeley, 1947, MSW, 1954; PhD, Calif. Inst. Clin. Social Work, Berkeley, 1980. Bd. cert. diplomate clin. social work, sex therapist, clin. supr. Social caseworker Family Svc. Agy., Sacramento, Calif., 1959-63; cons., supr. Stanford Lathrop Meml. Home, Sacramento, 1964-69, Arnold Homes for Children, Sacramento, 1968-71; pvt. practice social work Sacramento, 1963—; faculty Calif. Soc. Clin. Social Work, Sacramento, 1979—, Calif. State U., Sacramento, 1956-58, 90; sec. Nat. Registry Providers of Health Care in Clin. Social Work, 1983-85, bd. dirs., 1980-86, treas. Nat. Fedn. for Socs. for Clin. Social Work, 1981-86. Founder, bd. Planned Parenthood of Sacramento, 1964. Fellow Calif. Soc. for Clin. Social Work (pres. 1983-85, bd. dirs. 1969-87, Mem. of Yr. award 1990); mem. ACLU, Calif. Inst. for Clin. Social Work (trustee, sec.-treas. 1976-88, v.p. 1989-94), Soc. for Sci. Study Sex, Amnesty Internat., Older Women's League, Am. Assn. Sex Educators, Counselors, Therapists, Phi Beta Kappa. Democrat. Office: 3525 Watt Ave Ste 1 Sacramento CA 95821-2617

FILOMIA, LISA, accountant; b. Bronx, N.Y., Dec. 19, 1963; d. Ralph and Marilyn (Cohen) F. BA in Bus. Adminstrn., SUNY, Buffalo, 1984, MBA in Fin. and Acctg., 1985. CPA, N.Y.; cert. mgmt. acct., N.Y. With Ernst & Young, N.Y.C., 1985—, now sr. mgr. Mem. AICPA, N.Y. State Soc. CPAs. Office: Ernst & Young 787 7th Ave New York NY 10019

FILTER, EUNICE M., business equipment manufacturing executive; b. Teaneck, N.J., Sept. 19, 1940. BA in Econs., CCNY, 1966. Security analyst Morgan Guaranty Trust Co. N.Y., 1966-70; sr. tech. analyst G.A. Saxton & Co., N.Y.C., 1970-73; mgr. Xerox Corp., Stamford, Conn., 1973-79, dir. investor rels., 1979-84, v.p., corp. sec., 1984—, treas., 1990—; dir. Baker Hughes, Inc., Houston, 1992—. Trustee Wells Colls., Aurora, N.Y., 1990—; bd. dirs. United Way Tri-State, N.Y.C., 1989-93, Westport-Weston (Conn.) United Way, 1989-93. Recipient Graham & Dodd award Fin. Analysts Fedn., N.Y.C., 1971; named to Acad. of Women Achievers YWCA of N.Y.C., 1981. Mem. Investor Rels. Assn. of N.Y. (pres. 1984-85), Nat. Investor Rels. Inst., Nat. Assn. Corp. Treas., Am. Soc. Corp. Secs., Fin. Women Assn. of N.Y., Nat. Assn. Corp. Treas. Office: Xerox Corp 800 Long Ridge Rd Stamford CT 06904

FINARELLI, MARGARET G., federal government administrator; b. Phila., Apr. 14, 1946; d. Benjamin Fessenden Jr. and Margaret (Taliaferro) Griffith; m. John David Finarelli, July 8, 1966; children: John Albert, Matthew Brian. BA magna cum laude with distinction, U. Pa., 1967; MS, Drexel U., 1969. Sci. analyst CIA, Langley, Va., 1969-77; physical sci. officer U.S. Arms Control and Disarmament Agy., Washington, 1977-79; sr. policy analyst Office Sci. Tech. Policy, Washington, 1979-81; chief internat. planning and program NASA, Washington, 1981-86, dir. policy div. office space sta., 1986-88, dep. assoc. adminstr. external rels., 1988-91, assoc. adminstr. policy coordination and internat. rels., 1991-93; asst. for strategic planning NASA, 1993—; bd. trustees Internat. Space U. Recipient Exceptional Svc. medal NASA, 1985, Exceptional Achievement medal, 1991, Presdl. Meritorious Rank U.S. Pres., Washington, 1988, Outstanding Achievement award Women in Aerospace, 1989. Mem. Am. Inst. Aeronautics and Astronautics (exec. coun. nat. capitol sect. 1988-89), Phi Beta Kappa. Office: NASA Office of Adminstr. 300 E St NW Washington DC 20546-0001

FINBERG, BARBARA DENNING, foundation executive; b. Pueblo, Colo., Feb. 26, 1929; d. Rufus Raymond and Velma Aileen (Hopper) Denning; m. Alan R. Finberg, June 21, 1953. B.A., Stanford U., 1949; M.A., Am. U. of Beirut, Lebanon, 1951. Intern U.S. Dept. State, Washington, 1949-50, fgn. affairs officer, Tech Coop. Adminstrn., 1952-53; program specialist, area chief Inst. Internat. Edn., N.Y.C., 1953-59; editorial assoc., program officer Carnegie Corp. N.Y., N.Y.C., 1959-80, v.p. program, 1980-88, exec. v.p., 1988—. Trustee Stanford U., 1976-86, v.p. bd. dirs., 1982-85; trustee N.Y. Found., 1979-91, vice chmn. bd. dirs., 1983-85, chmn., 1985-89; mem. accreditation com. Assn. Am. Law Schs., 1986-88; adv. com. Henry A. Murray Rsch. Ctr. for Study of Lives, Radcliffe Coll., 1986—; bd. dirs. The Hole in the Wall Gang Fund, Inc., 1987—, Investor Responsibility Rsch. Ctr. Inc., 1989—, vice chmn. bd. dirs., 1992-94, Ind. Sector, 1990—, chmn. mgmt. com., 1994—, Consortium for Advancement of Pvt. Higher Edn., 1992. Rotary Found. fellow, 1950-51; recipient Women of Vision awards N.Y. Women's Found., 1995. Mem. Am. Ednl. Research Assn., Soc. for Research in Child Devel., Council on Fgn. Relations. Club: Cosmopolitan of N.Y. Home: 165 E 72d St Apt 19L New York NY 10021-4351 Office: Carnegie Corp NY 437 Madison Ave New York NY 10022-7001

FINCH, CAROLYN-BOGART, speech and language pathologist, speaker, writer; b. Mineola, N.Y., June 24, 1938; d. Harold Edwin and Ruth (Waring) Bogart; m. Gordon M. Finch (div. Oct. 1982); children: David Harold, Martha Louise; m. Donald Hall Hulme; children: Wendy Harriet Hulme, Allison Elizabeth Hulme. BS, Elmira Coll., 1965; MS, Western Conn. State U., 1972; postgrad., Nova U., 1982. Cert. speech and lang. pathologist, early childhood edn., elem. edn. and communication. Speech therapist Elmira (N.Y.) City Schs., 1963-65; supervision therapist Speech and Hearing Clinic Elmira Coll., 1966-67; speech therapist Greenshire Residential Sch., Cheshire, Conn., 1968-69; speech pathologist Danbury (Conn.) City Schs., 1970-73; owner, dir. Peter Piper Sch. and Learning ctr., Brookfield Center, Conn., 1973-88, Speech Pathology Assocs., Danbury, 1974-87; mem. adj. faculty Western Conn. State U., Danbury, 1974-86, prof., 1986-87; pres. Apples and Oranges; profl. speaker Dunn & Bradstreet Bus. Edn. Svcs.; organizer, chmn. bd. Liberty Nat. Bank, Danbury; freelance lectr., 1986-88; pres., nat. speaker Bogart Comm., Inc., Danbury; acct. exec. V.R. Bus. Brokers, R. Zemper Assocs.; pres. comm. Fitness Internat. div. Bogart Comm.; nat. expert on body lang.; speaker on voice power, mind power and the multi-cultural workplace. Author: (multisensory articulation program) Portraits of Sounds, 1969, (book and posters) Survival Sign System, 1982, Universal Handtalk, 1988, Socks Says!, 1993. Dem. nominee Danbury Town Com., 1985; mem. adv. com. Fairfield County 4-H. Recipient Mayoral Proclamation for Survival Sign System, City of Danbury, 1986; named Woman of Yr. Bus. and Prof. Women, 1990. Mem. Women in Comm., New Eng. Speakers Assn., Nat. Speakers Assn., Women in Comm., John Cosentino Singers. Home and Office: Bogart Communications Inc 51 Cedar Dr Danbury CT 06811-3302

FINCH, DIANE SHIELDS, retail merchandising manager; b. Detroit, Aug. 25, 1947; d. Earl Arthur and Carrie (Steele) Shields; m. Glenn A. Finch III, Oct. 5, 1968; 1 child, Jennifer Lynn. AA, U. Houston, 1969; student, U. St. Thomas, 1970-73, Rice U., 1980. Apt. mgr. Moonmist Manor, Houston, 1972-75; sales merchandiser Mattel Toys, Houston, 1975-77; sales merchandiser Plough Sales, Houston, 1977-79, ter. mgr., 1979-80, area mdse. mgr., 1980-84, dist. sales mgr., 1984-86; dist. mdse. mgr. Schering-Plough Healthcare Product, Houston, 1986-92; dist. retail merchandising mgr. McNeil Consumer Products, Houston, 1992—. Area chmn. Assn. Community TV, Houston, 1985-87; mem. Friends of Ronald McDonald House; mem. Citizens Animal Protection. Mem. Nat. Assn. Female Execs., Am. Mgmt. Assn., Tex. Exec. Women (bd. dirs.), Houston Fedn. Profl. Women. Office: Johnson & Johnson Corp 5020 Longmont Houston TX 77056

FINCH, LUCILLE KAY, collections specialist; b. Winona, Minn., July 7, 1949; d. Donald Herman and Wilma Orlene (Northrup) Unnasch; m. Robert Lee Finch, Apr. 25, 1970; children: Laurie Ann, Paula Marie, Chad Henry. Student, Viterbo Coll., 1979-80. Telephone operator Centel Telephone Co., La Crosse, Wis., 1969-77; collector Credit Bur./La Crosse, 1977, Credit Bur. Data, La Crosse, 1978; mgr. Wis. Collection Sys., La Crosse, 1978-82; collection mgr. Cmty. Credit Union, La Crosse, 1984-90; collection specialist Trane Fed. Credit Union, La Crosse, 1990—. Methodist. Home: W5445 CTH-F # 32 La Crosse WI 54601 Office: Trane Fed Credit Union 2715 Losey Blvd S La Crosse WI 54602

FINCH, RUTH L., lawyer; b. Niagara Falls, N.Y., June 30, 1950; d. Charles W. and Helen (Pile) Pinches; m. Stephen B. Finch, Jr., Aug. 9, 1975 (div. 1982). BA, Wheaton Coll., 1972; JD, George Washington U., 1976. Bar: N.Y. 1977. From counsel to v.p. Chem. Bank, N.Y.C., 1977-85; v.p., counsel for credit cards Citibank, N.Y.C., 1985-86, v.p., group gen. counsel consumer-internat. group, 1986-87, v.p./gen. counsel pvt. banking group, global asset mgmt., 1988—. Pres. Water's Edge Property Owner's Assn., Plainsboro, N.J., 1987—; elder Nassau Presbyn. Ch., Princeton, N.J., 1989-91; mem. Women's Campaign Fund Leadership Cir. Mem. ABA, Fin. Women's Assn. (bd. dirs. 1989—, pres. 1993-94), Internat. Alliance (bd. dirs.). Republican. Office: Citibank 153 E 53d St New York NY 10043-0001

FINCH, RUTH W., photographer; b. Rochester, N.Y., Feb. 27, 1916; d. Orator Frank and Persis Earle (Davis) Woodward; m. E.C. Kip Finch, Nov. 24, 1951 (dec. Dec. 1988); children: Ruth Persis Simons, Earle Kip Finch. BA, Bryn Mawr (Pa.) Coll., 1937. Asst. editor Golf World, 1948-50; photographer Am. Indians, travel, nature. Treas. Conn. Conservation Assn., Bridgeport, Conn., 1988—. Mem. U.S. Golf Assn. (com. mem. 1953-62), Colonial Dames (N.Y.C.), New Canaan (Conn.) Country Club, New Canaan Garden Club. Republican. Episcopalian.

FINCHER, MICHELE SAKUYAKO, educator, counselor; b. Osaka, Japan, Oct. 13, 1965; came to the U.S., 1969; d. Clifton Franklin and Kazue (Terai) F. BS, USAF Acad., 1987; MS, Auburn U., 1993. Cert. counselor. Commd. 2d lt. USAF, 1987, advanced through grades to capt., 1991; asst. officer in charge of exercise devel. 602d Tactical Air Control Wing, Tucson, Ariz., 1987-88, officer in charge mission readiness ctr., 1988-89; chief maintenance 83d Tactical Control Squadron, Alamogordo, N.Mex., 1989-91; instr., counselor USAF Acad., Colorado Springs, 1993—. Coach USAFA Dance Team; sponsor USAFA Cadet Sponsor Program; vol. USAFA Women's Mentor Program. Mem. Am. Counseling Assn., Am. Coll. Personnel Assn., Phi Beta Delta, Phi Kappa Phi.

FINCHER, TINA MICHELLE, social service agency administrator; b. Rome, Ga., Mar. 29, 1967; d. Billy David and Paulette Marcia (McCown) F. BS, Kennesaw State U., 1988; MEd, West Ga. Coll., 1994. Sr. caseworker Floyd Family and Children Svcs., Rome, 1989-90, social svc. specialist I, 1990-91, social svc. specialist II, 1991-94; exec. dir. Exch. Club Family Resource Ctr., Rome, 1994—; group facilitator Heroes Great and Small, Rome, 1989—. Mem. Child Abuse Resource Effort, Rome, 1990-93; vol. Rome Rape Response, 1992—. Mem. Ga. Coun. on Child Abuse, Commn. on Children and Youth, Exch. Club. Home: 2240 N Bellview Rd Rockmart GA 30153-3402 Office: Exch Club Family Resource Ctr 306 Glen Milner Blvd Rome GA 30161-3204

FINDLEY, ELIZABETH JOAN, insurance company executive; b. St. Louis, Oct. 24, 1965; d. John Allen and Naomi Joan (Reker) F.; Craig O'Connor, Dec. 3, 1994. BS in Math., U. Mo., 1988. Actuarial analyst Blue Cross/Blue Shield of Ark., Little Rock, 1989-91; actuary asst. Blue Cross/Blue Shield of Mo., St. Louis, 1991-94, unit mgr. actuarial rsch., 1994; sr. actuarial analyst WF Coroon, St. Louis, Mo. Mem. St. Louis Actuaries Club. Office: WF Corroon 231 S Bemiston Ste # 400 Saint Louis MO 63105

FINE, DEBORAH JANE, researcher, librarian; b. Boston, May 16, 1942; d. Irving Horace and Muriel (Baer) F. BA, UCLA, 1965; MLS, Simmons Coll., 1967. Researcher Paramount Studios, Hollywood, Calif., 1968-69, Zoetrope Studios, L.A., 1972-77; dir. rsch. Lucasfilm Ltd., San Rafael, Calif., 1978—. Researcher (film) Godfather, Part II, 1974, Apocalypse Now, 1979, More American Graffiti, 1979, Return of The Jedi, 1983, Raiders of the Lost Ark, 1981, Indiana Jones and the Temple of Doom, 1984, Willow, 1987, Tucker, 1988, Indiana Jones and the Lost Crusade, 1989, (TV series) The Young Indiana Jones Chronicles, 1992—; producer's asst. (film) The Black Stallion, 1979. Mem. Acad. Motion Picture Arts and Sci., Spl. Libs. Assn. Office: Lucasfilm Ltd PO Box 2009 San Rafael CA 94912-2009

FINE, JO RENÉE, management executive, audio-visual production executive; b. Norfolk, Va., June 19, 1943; d. Ruby Arthur and Tillie Fern (Goldman) F.; BA, Smith Coll., 1965; MA, NYU, 1968, PhD, 1973; m. Edward Trieber, Apr. 12, 1981; 1 child, Jessica Fine Trieber. Probation officer N.Y.C. Office Probation, 1966; res. asst. N.Y.U., N.Y.C., 1966-68, assoc. res. scientist Inst. Devel. Studies, 1968-73, res. scientist, 1973-77, adj. asst. prof. dept. ednl. psychology, 1973-76; program analyst N.Y. State Dept. Mental Hygiene, N.Y.C., 1977-78; pvt. practice psychotherapy, N.Y.C., 1978-81; pres. CVM Prodns., Inc., N.Y.C., 1978—; dir. mgmt. training centers Cicatelli Assocs., 1992—. adj. asst. prof. ednl. communication and tech. NYU, 1988—; cons. to bds. edn., N.Y.C., also greater met. area, 1973—, tng. cons., 1990—. Mem. APA, ASTD, Am. Jewish Com. (v.p.). Co-author: The Synagogues of New York's Lower East Side, 1978. Home: 55 W 16th St New York NY 10011-6305 Office: Cicatelli Assocs 505 8th Ave Fl 20 New York NY 10018-6505

FINE, MARJORIE LYNN, lawyer; b. Bklyn., Aug. 14, 1950; d. Percy and Sylvia (Bernstein) F.; m. John Kent Markley, May 6, 1979; children: Jessica Paige Markley, Laura Anne Markley. BA, Smith Coll., 1972; JD, U. Calif., 1977. Bar: Calif. 1977. Assoc. to ptnr. Donahue Gallagher Thomas & Woods, Oakland, Calif., 1977-87; sr. counsel Bank of Am., San Francisco, 1987-89; assoc., gen. counsel Shaklee Corp., San Francisco, 1989-90; gen. counsel, v.p. Shaklee U.S., Inc., San Francisco, 1990—; judge pro tem Oakland Piedmont Emeryville Mcpl. Ct., 1982—; fee arbitrator Alameda Co. Bar Assn., 1980-87. Mem. ABA, Calif. Bar Assn. Jewish. Office: Shaklee Corp 444 Market St San Francisco CA 94111-5325

FINE, MIRIAM BROWN, artist, educator, poet, writer; b. Vineland, N.J., Mar. 8, 1913; d. Abraham and Katie (Walidarsky) Brown; m. Irvin Fine, Nov. 3, 1935; children: Ruth Eileen Fine, Adele Aviva Fine Gross. BFA, The U. the Arts (formerly Indsl. Sch. Arts) and U. Pa., 1935; postgrad., Cheltenham (Pa.) Art Sch., 1968-77, Temple U., 1976-91. Tchr. art and watercolor painting Phila. Pub. Schs., 1953-60; lectr., watercolor tchr. Assn. Ret. Profls. Temple U., 1976-92; pvt. tchr. art, Phila., 1952-77; geriatric poster contest judge and program cover design Pa. Podiatric Med. Assn., 1984—; tchr., vis. artist Abington Friends Com., 1989-90; tchr. watercolor N.E. Cultural Art Coun. Phila.1, 1987-90; tchr. watercolor, speaker poetry forum David G. Neuman Sr. Ctr., Jewish Community Ctr. Phila., 1991—. Executed 7 murals at Spruance Elem. Sch., Phila., 1951, Holocaust oils and watercolors displayed in Temple Sholom Synagogue, Oxford Cir. Synagogue, UN Women's Conf., Nairobi, Kenya, 1985—, Libr. Nat. Mus. Women in Arts, Washington, 1992—; 15 1-person exhbns.; author: (poetry and illustrations) Word and Drawings, 1984, Mom I Didn't Know It Was Like That, Family History, 1984, The Full Moon Energises My Creativity, 1988, You Are in My Galaxy, 1990, That's Life, 1992, Flowers I, 1993 (Nat. Mus. Women in Arts, Washington), Treasures of Miriam Brown Fine for You, 1993; author, illustrator: My Bible, 1994; contbr. watercolor paintings on boxs and book covers Continental Box Co., 1995. Did benefit for St. Christopher's Children's Hosp., Phila., 1984-87; mem. Torch of Life chpt. City of Hope, Phila., 1935—, mem. Herman chpt., 1992—. Recipient Phila. Art Tchrs. award, 1956, Chapel of Four Chaplains award Torch of Life chpt. City of Hope, 1964, 50 Yr. Svc. award 1981, 60 Yr. Svc. award 1991; Bd. Edn. Art scholar, 1931. Mem. NOW, Artists Equity Inc., Phila. Watercolor Club (hon.), Women's Caucus for Art, Univ. Arts Alumni Assn., Acad. Am. Poets, Nat. Fedn. State Poetry Socs., Writers Cadence Crafters, Poets Study Group, Nat. Mus. of Women in Arts, Temple U. Assn. Ret. Profls. (pres. emeritus, award), Pa. State Poetry Socs., Fight for Sight. Democrat. Jewish. Home and Studio: 1438 Devereaux Ave Philadelphia PA 19149-2701

FINE, RANA ARNOLD, chemical, physical oceanographer; b. N.Y.C., Apr. 17, 1944; d. Joseph and Etta (Kreisman) Arnold; m. Shalle Stephen Fine, June 20, 1965 (div. 1979); m. James Stewart Mattson, Jan. 5, 1983. BA, NYU, 1965; MA, U. Miami, 1973, PhD, 1975. Systems analyst Svc. Bur. Corp. subs. IBM, Miami, 1965-69; postdoctoral rsch. assoc. Rosenstiel Sch. U. Miami, 1976-77, rsch. asst. prof., 1977-80, rsch. assoc. prof., 1980-84, assoc. prof., 1984-90, prof. of marine and atmospheric chemistry, 1990—, chair divsn. marine and atmospheric chemistry, 1990-94; assoc. program dir. NSF, Washington, 1981-83; mem. div. polar programs adv. com. NSF, Washington, 1987-90; mem. geophys. study com. NAS, Washington, 1989-92, mem. ocean studies bd., 1992—; mem. adv. panel Tropical Ocean/Global Atmosphere Program, 1990-93. Contbr. articles to profl. jours. Vol. guide Vizcaya Mus., Miami, 1967-78. Grantee NSF, 1977—, NOAA, 1986—, Office of Naval Rsch., 1983-88, NASA, 1990—. Fellow Am. Geophys. Union (sec. oceanography sect. 1986-88, pres.-elect oceanography sect. 1994-96); mem. AAAS (nominating com. atmosphere and hydrology sect.), Am. Meterol. Soc., Oceanography Soc. Office: RSMAS/MAC/U Miami 4600 Rickenbacker Cswy Miami FL 33149-1031

FINELLO, TERRY LEE, communications educator; b. Trenton, N.J., Nov. 1, 1947; d. Curtis Gillikin and Joy (Urban) Rooy; m. Dennis John, June 23, 1973 (div. July 1985); 1 child, Elaine Marie. BS in Communications, Psychology, Edn., Murray State U., 1970, MS in Communications, 1971; postgrad., Cen. Conn. State U., New Britain, 1972. Tchr. Tchr., teaching asst. Murray State U., Murray, Ky., 1970-71; instr. adult edn. Wincester Bd. of Edn., Winsted, Conn., 1973-76; special lectr. Central Conn. State U., New Britain, Conn., 1975-85; lectr. communications dept. Tunxis Community Coll., Farmington, Conn., 1986–; communications lectr. U. Conn., Waterbury, 1986, Torrington, 1986—; English educator Wincester Bd. of Edn., Conn., 1971—; cons., lectr. Veteran's Hosp. Nursing Staff, Meridan, 1981, Bus. and Profl. Women, 1982; faculty cons. Conn. State Conf. Emergency Med. Techs., Hartford, 1988-94; presenter New England League of Middle Schs., Hyannis, 1988; cons. Pvt. Individuals Pub. Speaking Coach, 1976—. Mem. AAUP, NEA, Conn. Edn. Assn., Winsted Edn. Assn., Nat. Coun. Tchrs. English, New Eng. League of Middle Schs., Litchfield County Women's Network, Internat. Platform Assn. Home: 51 Pythian Ave Torrington CT 06790-3712 Office: Pearson Sch 2 Wetmore Ave Winsted CT 06098-1297

FINERMAN, WENDY, film producer. Prodr.: Hot to Trot, 1988, Forrest Gump, 1994 (Academy Award for Best Picture 1995); exec. prodr.: I Like It Like That, 1994. Office: Paramount Pictures 5555 Melrose Ave Los Angeles CA 90038-3197*

FINGER, PHYLLIS THOMAS, educator; b. Jacksonville, Fla., June 25, 1947; d. Charles Joseph and Avis Mary (Tacke) Thomas; m. Homer Ellis Finger III, Aug. 15, 1970; 1 child, Geoffrey Thomas. BA, Fla. So. Coll., 1969; MA, Syracuse U., 1970; EdD, Lehigh U., 1985. Cert. English, lang. arts tchr. Tchr., student coun. advisor Easton (Pa.) Area Sch. Dist., 1974—; tchr. English Lawrence Township Sch. Dist., Trenton, N.J., 1970-73; grad. inst. Lehigh U. Sch. Edn., Bethlehem, Pa., 1979-81; Am. English tchr. fellow Omiya, Japan, 1994-95; del. Pa. Tchr. Exch. to Omiya, Japan, 1989, 93; judge Odyssey of the Mind, Southeastern Pa. Vice chmn. Northampton County Bicentennial Constitution Commn. and Solid Waste Adv. Com.; elder 1st Presbyn. Ch., Easton, 1990-94, chairperson Christian edn. and mission com.; assoc. mem. Tokyo Union Ch.; bd. dirs. Cmty. Action Com., Lehigh Valley, Inc.; class agt. Fla. So. Coll., 1992—. Recipient Howard L. Klopp award for Excellence in Tchg., Cedar Crest Coll. Mem. AAUW, ASCD, LWV (pres. Easton 1987-89), Nat. Coun. Tchrs. English, Lehigh U. Alumni Assn. (pres. 1991-94), Hist. Easton, N.Y. Marathon, Swiss Alpine Marathon, Phi Delta Kappa (pres. 1985). Democrat. Home: 118 E Wayne Ave Easton PA 18042-1644 Office: Easton Area Sch Dist 12th & Northampton Sts Easton PA 18042

FINGERHUT, MARILYN ANN, federal agency administrator; b. Bklyn., Oct. 3, 1940; d. Robert Vincent and Marion (Carroll) F.; m. David W. Haartz, May 14, 1988; children: Margot, D. Bradley. BS in Cell Biology, Coll. of St. Elizabeth, Convent Station, N.J., 1964; PhD in Cell Biology, Cath. U. Am., 1970; MS in Occupational Health, Harvard U., Boston, 1981. Tchr. elem. schs., Jersey City, 1961-62, East Orange, N.J., 1964-65; instr. Coll. of St. Elizabeth, 1970-71; rsch. assoc. N.J. Coll. Medicine and Dentistry, Newark, 1971-72; asst. prof. to assoc. prof. St. Peter's Coll., Jersey City, 1973-80; researcher St. Joseph Med. Ctr., Paterson, N.J., 1977-80;

predoctoral fellow USPHS, 1966-69, commd. capt., 1989; epidemiologist Nat. Inst. for Occupational Safety and Health, Cin., 1981-88, br. chief, 1988-94; sr. scientist office of dir. Nat. Inst. for Occupational Safety and Health, Washington, 1994—. Contbr. articles to sci. jours. Founding mem. Women's R & D Ctr., Cin., 1987—. Recipient commendation medal USPHS, 1989, 92. Mem. APHA, Soc. for Epidemiologic Rsch. Democrat. Roman Catholic. Office: Nat Inst Occupl Safety & Health 200 Independence Ave SW Washington DC 20201

FINIZZI, MARGUERITE H(ELENE), secondary education educator; b. Allentown, Pa., Nov. 16, 1934; d. John Michael and Margaret Mary (Havrilla) Martin; BS in Secondary Edn., Kutztown State Coll., 1956; MA in English, Lehigh U., 1973; m. Joseph Anthony Finizzi, Nov. 19, 1954. Tchr. English, Harrison-Morton Jr. High Sch., Allentown, 1956-64, Louis E. Dieruff High Sch., Allentown, 1964-76, Allen High Sch., Allentown, 1976—; adviser pubs. Allen High Sch., 1978—, Quill and Scroll chpt., 1978, intramural bowling, 1992; instr. to develop. drug edn. competency for tchrs., Pa. dept. edn. Student Assistance Program and Intervention Team Tng., 1987, Lehigh U. Gifted Summer Inst., 1989—; mem. in-svc. coun. Allentown Sch. Dist., 1973-93; discussion leader for jr. classes Jewish Day Sch., 1969-71, peer coaching, 1989-90; v.p. Fearless Ladies Bowling League, 1986-89; coord. peer Leadership workshop, 1989, Traveling Ladies League, 1993-94, judge numerous acad. contests, Tchr. Expectations and Student Achievement (TESA), 1987-90, Allentown Sch. Dist. coord. for TESA Program, 1988, coord., 1989, lead tchr., 1990; leader workshops Kutztown U., 1993; workshop instr. Pa. State U. Summer Literary Mag., 1992; lectr., speaker in field; seminar discussion leader Council of Youth, 1980; adviser Student Newspaper Adv. Program; pres. Lehigh County (Pa.) Coordinating Coun., 1967-71; mem. steering com. Allentown Sch. Dist., 1984. Recipient Meritorious award Kutztown State Coll., 1956; Newspaper Fund fellow, 1981; Commonwealth Partnerships fellow for lit. Inst. Secondary Tchrs., 1985. Mem. NEA, AAUW (membership com. 1993—, rep. Pa. 1993-94), Nat. Council Tchrs. English (co-chmn. conf. 1985, judge nat. writing contest 1987-93), Pa. Council Tchrs. English (judge state writing advancement 1994), Pa. State Edn. Assn. (editor eastern region constn.), Allentown Edn. Assn. (social chairperson 1964-79, exec. sec. 1964-69), Allentown Women Tchrs. Club (editor constn. and by-laws, welfare chmn. 1986-89, pres.-elect 1990—, pres. 1994), Lehigh U. Alumni, Kutztown U. Alumni (pres. Lehigh County 1969-72), Columbia Sch. Press Assn. (adviser Reflector Sci. newsletter 1978-90, conf. workshops 1992, student oratorical judge 1992), Pa. Sch. Press Assn., Pa. Shakespeare Festival (sustaining, media coalition 1993). Home: 3025 Pearl Ave Allentown PA 18103-6424

FINK, CATHY DEVITO, small business owner; b. Jacksonville, Fla., Dec. 23, 1957; d. Pasquale and Kay Francis (Mentry) DeVito; m. Robert Thomas Fink, May 5, 1984; 1 child, Christopher DeVito Fink. AAS, Canton (N.Y.) Agrl. & Tech., 1978. Adminstv. asst. MPR Assocs., Washington, 1978-84; owner, dir. CDF Svcs., Falls Church, Va., 1984—; PAC mgr. Neece, Cator & Assocs., Inc., Washington, 1987—. Tchr. computers Haycock Elem. Sch., Fairfax, Va., 1986-87, pres. PTA; v.p. Capital Boys Hockey Club, Washington, 1987-89; bus. mgr. Women in Housing and Fin. Mem. NAFE, Nat. Economists Club (bus. mgr. 1988—), Nat. Economists Ednl. Found. (bus. mgr. 1988—), Bus. Network Internat. (pres. Falls Church chpt.). Republican. Roman Catholic. Office: CDF Svcs 6712 Fisher Ave Falls Church VA 22046

FINK, DIANE JOANNE, physician; b. Chgo., July 27, 1936; d. Roman John and Mary Frances (Obrzut) Paluszek; (widow); children—Laura, Janice. B.S., Stanford U., 1957, M.D., 1960. Rotating intern, then resident in internal medicine Kaiser Found. Hosp., San Francisco, 1960-63; resident in internal medicine, then research asso. immunohematology VA Hosp., San Francisco, 1963-66; chief oncology sect. VA Hosp., 1969-71, staff physician charge cancer chemotherapy sect., 1966-69, chmn. tumor bd., 1967-71; exec. sec., prin. investigator cancer chemotherapy group Pacific VA, 1966-71; program dir. chemotherapy, div. cancer research resources and centers Nat. Inst. Cancer, NIH, HEW, 1971-73, chief treatment br., then asso. dir. cancer control, cancer control program, 1973-74; dir. div. cancer control and rehab., 1974-79; asso. dir. Nat. Cancer Inst., 1979-81; v.p. Am. Cancer Soc., 1981—; mem. faculty U. Calif. Med. Center, San Francisco, 1967-71, asst. clin. prof. medicine, 1969-71; chmn. U.S. del. U.S.-USSR Exchange Cancer Control/Cancer Centers; mem. expert adv. panel on cancer WHO, 1977—; chmn. DES task force HEW, 1978; chmn. asbestos edn. task force HEW, 1978. Contbr. to med. jours. Recipient Gerard B. Lambert award Lambert Found., 1975; Superior Service Honor award NIH, 1975. Mem. Am. Assn. Cancer Research, Am. Assn. Cancer Edn., AMA, Am. Med. Women's Assn., Am. Soc. Clin. Oncology, Am. Soc. Hematology. Office: Am Cancer Soc 1710 Webster St Oakland CA 94612-3412

FINK, JOANNA ELIZABETH, art dealer; b. Boston, Aug. 8, 1958; d. Alan Donald and Barbara Emma (Swan) F. Student, Wellesley Coll., 1976-78; BA, NYU, 1980; MA, NYU, Inst. Fine Arts, 1983. Asst. dir. Nardin Gallery, N.Y.C., 1979-80; photographer, adminstrv. asst. NYU, Dept. Fine Arts, N.Y.C., 1980-82, instr. art history, 1982; registrar Estate of Milton Avery, N.Y.C., 1982; rsch. cons. Chase Manhattan Bank, N.Y.C., 1983; dir. Alpha Gallery, Boston, 1983—; hon. bd. mem. Artcetera Auction/Aids Action Commn., Boston, 1990-92. Author: Georg Baselitz, 1985, The Books of Anselm Kiefer, 1992; editor: Goya & British Satirical Prints, 1991; contbr. book revs. to profl. jours. Mem. Boston Art Dealers Assn. Office: Alpha Gallery Inc 14 Newbury St Boston MA 02116-3201

FINK, LOIS MARIE, art historian; b. Michigan City, Ind., Dec. 30, 1927; d. George Edward and Marie Helen (Hensz) F. B.A., Capital U., 1951; M.A., U. Chgo., 1955, Ph.D., 1970; H.H.D. (hon.), Capital U., 1982. Instr. Lenoir Rhyne Coll., Hickory, N.C., 1955-56; instr. Midland Coll., Fremont, Nebr., 1956-58; asst. prof. Roosevelt U., Chgo., 1958-70; curator Nat. Mus. of Am. Art, Smithsonian Instn., Washington, 1970-93; curator emeritus, 1993—; adv. com. Washington area Archives Am. Art, 1979—. Co-author: Academy: The Academic Tradition in American Art, 1975; contbg. author: Elizabeth Nourse: A Salon Career, 1983; author: American Art at the Nineteenth-Century Paris Salons, 1990; contbr. articles to profl. jours. Fellow The Soc. for the Arts, Religion, and Contemporary Culture; mem. Coll. Art Assn., Am. Studies Assn. Home: 10401 Grosvenor Pl Apt 1306 Rockville MD 20852-4640 Office: Nat Mus of Am Art Smithsonian Instn Washington DC 20560

FINKEL, CAROL BETH, psychologist; b. Boston, Jan. 20, 1953; d. Leonard and Minerva F.; m. Walter Nickelsberg, Sept. 1, 1991. BA, U. Del., 1975; MA, Fairleigh-Dickinson U., 1977; PhD, U. Notre Dame, 1981. Lic. psychologist, N.J. Staff psychologist Guidance Ctr., Cherry Hill, N.J., 1981-85; psychologist Washington Psychol. Svcs., Turnersville, N.J., 1985-86; counseling psychologist Counseling Program, Marlton, N.J., 1986-91; pvt. practice Haddon Heights, N.J., 1986—. Mem. APA, Phi Beta Kappa, Psi Chi. Office: 408 White Horse Pike Haddon Heights NJ 08035

FINKEL, MARION JUDITH, physician, pharmaceutical company administrator; b. N.Y.C., Nov. 2, 1929; d. Israel and Bella (Stillman) F.; premed. student L.I. U., 1945-48; M.D. (Howard Sloan Meml. scholar), Chgo. Med. Sch., 1952; m. Simon V. Manson, Sept. 12, 1954. Intern, Jersey City Med. Center, 1952-53; resident in internal medicine Bellevue Hosp., N.Y.C., 1954-56; med. editor Merck and Co., 1957-61; pvt. practice specializing in internal medicine, N.Y.C., 1956-57, N.J., 1961-63; with FDA, 1963-85, dir. div. metabolic and endocrine drugs, 1966-70, dep. dir. bur. drugs, 1970-71, 72-74, dir. office new drug eval., 1971-72, 74-82, dir. office orphan products devel., 1982-85; exec. dir. research and devel. Berlex Labs., Inc., 1985-88, v.p. drug registration and regulatory affairs Sandoz Pharms., Inc., 1988-94, v.p. corp. regulatory compliance, 1994—. Recipient award of merit FDA, 1974; Superior Service award USPHS, 1976, 84; Fed. Woman's award Fed. Govt., 1976, Meritorious Exec. award, 1980; named Disting. Alumnus, Chgo. Med. Sch., 1977, L.I. U., 1980. Mem. Am. Soc. Clin. Pharmacology and Therapeutics, Drug Info. Assn. Contbr. chpts., numerous articles to profl. pubis. Office: Sandoz Pharm Corp RR 10 East Hanover NJ 07936

FINKEL, SHEILA BERG, marketing professional; b. Houston, Sept. 13, 1947; d. Phillip Raymond and Anna (Roth) Berg; m. Steven M. Finkel (div. June 1979). BA, Washington U., St. Louis, 1969; MBA, Keller Grad. Sch. Mgmt., 1991. Lab. technician Jewish Hosp., St. Louis, 1969-70, Peoria (Ill.) Sanitary Dist., 1970-73; asst. to gen. mgr. Consol. Office Supply, Chgo., 1974, purchasing mgr., 1974-83; with Wilson Jones Co., Chgo., 1984-91, mktg. info. mgr., 1988-89, promotions and telesales mgr., 1989-90, sales promotion mgr., 1990-91; with Esselte Pendaflex Corp., Garden City, N.Y., 1990-91, dir. mktg., 1992—. Pres. Pattington Condominium Assn., Chgo., 1986, 90, sec., 1989. Mem. NAFE, Chgo. Assn. Direct Mktg.

FINKELDAY, KAREN LYNN, manufacturing executive; b. Orange, N.J., July 21, 1944; d. Gordon Dayton and Dorothy Laura (Chesseman) Mattoon; m. John Paul Finkelday, Nov. 16, 1963; 1 child, John Paul. Student, Glassboro State Coll., 1962-63, Ocean County Coll., 1978-83. Multiple listing svc. mgr. Ocean County Bd. of Realtors, Toms River, N.J., 1976-79; acct. supr. Paco Packaging Inc., Lakewood, N.J., 1980-83; office mgr. Warne Surgical Products Inc., Eatontown, N.J., 1983-84; sales mgr. TFX Medical Inc., Eatontown, N.J., 1984-86; coord. mktg. and sales Standard-Keil Mfg. Co., Allenwood, N.J., 1986-87; exec. asst. to pres. Standard-Keil Mfg. Co., Allenwood, 1987-89; mgr. United Refrigerated Svcs., Inc., Tarboro, N.C., 1989—. Creator: (advertisement) Signatures Series, 1987, Nat. Restaurant Assn., 1987, Ptnrs. for Progress, 1988; contbr. articles to profl. jours. Mem. Greenville Mus. Art. Mem. NAFE, Am. Mgmt. Assn., N.J. Bd. Realtors, U.S. Golf Assn., Greenville Country Club. Home: 3044 Dartmouth Dr Greenville NC 27858-6745 Office: United Refrigerated Svcs Inc PO Box 7006 Tarboro NC 27886-7006

FINKLER, KIRA, legislative counsel; b. Milw., Apr. 4, 1966. BA, U. Ariz., 1988; JD, Am. U., 1993. Tchr. English Taipei, Taiwan, 1988-89; law clk. Van Ness, Feldman and Curtis, 1992-93; counsel Subcom. Pub. Lands, Nat. Pks. and Forests, 1993—. Office: Subcom Pub Lands Nat Parks & Forests 308 Senate Dirksen Office Bldg Washington DC 20510*

FINLAYSON, LOUISE MARY, psychologist; b. Lackawanna, N.Y., Sept. 15, 1953; d. Bruce Lowell and Mary Jane (Milligan) Finlayson; m. James C. Tai, May 24, 1974 (div. Apr. 1979); m. Foster Charles Gesten, May 30, 1986; 1 child, Noah Finlayson-Gesten. BA, SUNY, Buffalo, 1982; MA, Mich. State U., 1985, PhD, 1990. Lic. psychologist. Therapist R.I. Rape Crisis Ctr., Cranston, 1986-87; clin. psychology fellow Harvard Med. Sch., Boston, 1987-90; psychologist Community Health Plan, Latham, N.Y., 1990-92; pvt. practice psychologist Albany, N.Y., 1992—. Mem. NOW, APA, N.Y. Psychol. Assn., Psychol. Assn. Northeastern N.Y., N.Y. State Coalition Against Sexual Assault. Office: Ten Eyck Psychotherapy 15 Ten Eyck Ave Albany NY 12209

FINLEY, DIXIE LEE, academic counselor; b. Lockwood, Mo., Jan. 11, 1941; d. Orville Leroy and Nellie Lorene (Hayter) Bird; m. Charles Byron Finley, Aug. 1, 1958; children: Gretchen Larisa, Angela Kay. BA, U. Mo., Rolla, 1968; MEd, U. Mo., 1975. Lic. prof. counselor; nat. cert. counselor. Tchr. Rolla Pub. Schs., 1973-74; counselor Rolla Pub. Sch., 1976—, Newburg (Mo.) Pub. Sch., 1975-76. Contbr. articles to profl. jours. Vice-chmn. Mo. Com. for Profl. Counselors, Jefferson City, 1986-88. Mem. ACA, Am. Sch. Counselors Assn. (program com. 1986—, governing bd. 1986—), Mo. Counseling Assn., Mo. Tchrs. Assn., Mo. Sch. Counselor Assn. (pres. 1984—). Presbyterian. Office: Rolla Pub Sch 1111 Soest Rd Rolla MO 65401

FINLEY, LUCY LAYNE, artist; b. Sanford, N.C., Jan. 31, 1937; d. James Oscar and Vera Jane (Banner) Layne; m. William Ronald Finley, Apr. 11, 1959; children: Peggy Ann, James Lloyd, Thomas Lee. AA in Fine Art magna cum laude, No. Va. C.C., 1981. Gallery artist Fishseale & Mousetooth, Manassas, Va., 1992—. Recipient Gold from the Guilds award Fairfax County Coun. of the Arts, 1981, Arschile Gorky award Waterford Found., 1983. Mem. The Art League (Exemplary award 1991), Arlington Arts Ctr., Manassas Art Guild (pres. 1981-82). Home: 13100 Ginger Ct Manassas VA 22111-4618

FINLEY, ROSE REYNOLDS, nurse; b. Jackson, Miss., Jan. 28, 1939; d. Craig Amacker and Rose Wells Reynolds; children: Joseph Thomas Lee, Stuart Duncan Lee. BA, Miss. Coll., 1962; MEd, Miss. State U., 1981; BSN, Miss. Univ. for Women, 1985. RN, Miss. Rsch. asst., counselor Miss. State U., Starkville, Miss., 1980-82; staff nurse Clay County Med. Ctr., West Point, Miss., 1985-86; nurse, counselor Sunhaven, Starkville, 1988—; parish nurse Trinity Presbyn. Ch., Starkville, 1993—; vis. nurse Alexander's Home Health Agy., Starkville, 1986-88. Elder Trinity Presbyn. Ch., Starkville, 1992—; facilitator Alzheimer's Support Group, Starkville, 1988-92. Mem. ACA, Health Ministries Assn., Alzheimers Assn., Arthritis Found., Sigma Tau Delta. Democrat. Home: 406 Chapin St Starkville MS 39759-2620 Office: Trinity Presbyn Ch 607 Hospital Rd Starkville MS 39759-2121

FINLEY, SARA CREWS, medical geneticist, educator; b. Lineville, Ala., Feb. 26, 1930; m. Wayne H. Finley; children: Randall Wayne, Sara Jane. B.S. in Biology, U. Ala., 1951, M.D., 1955. Diplomate Am. Bd. Med. Genetics; cert. clin. geneticist; cert. clin. cytogeneticist. Intern Lloyd Noland Hosp., Fairfield, Ala., 1955-56; NIH fellow in pediatrics U. Ala. Med. Sch., Birmingham, 1956-60; NIH trainee in med. genetics Inst. Med. Genetics, U. Uppsala, Sweden, 1961-62; mem. faculty U. Ala. Med. Sch., 1960—, co-dir. lab. med. genetics, 1966—, prof. pediatrics, 1975—, occupant Wayne H. and Sara Crews Finley chair med. genetics, 1986—; Disting. Faculty lectr. Med. Ctr., U. Ala. at Birmingham, 1983; mem. staff Univ., Children's hosps.; mem. ad hoc com. genetic counseling Children's Bur., HEW, 1966; mem. ad hoc rev. panel for genetic disease and sickle cell testing and counseling programs, 1980; mem. genetic diseases program objective rev. panel Bur. Maternal and Child Health and Resources Div., HHS, 1989, mem. adv. group on lab. quality assurance, 1989; Birmingham bd. dirs. Compass Bank. Author papers on clin. cytogenetics, human congenital malformations, human growth and devel. Mem. White House Conf. Health, 1965; mem. rsch. manpower rev. com. Nat. Cancer Inst., 1977-81; mem. Sickle Cell Disease Adv. Com., NIH, 1983-87; chairperson physician's campaign bd. dirs. United Way, 1993-95. Recipient Disting. Alumna award U. Ala. Sch. Medicine Alumni Assn., 1989, Med. award Ala. Assn. for Retarded Children, 1969, Turlington award Planned Parenthood of Ala., 1982, Nat. Outstanding Alumnae award Zeta Tau Alpha, 1992, Disting. Alumna award U. Ala. Nat. Alumni Assn., 1994; named Top Ten Women in Birmingham, 1989, Top 31 Most Outstanding Alumnae U. Ala., Tuscaloosa, 1993. Fellow AMA, Am. Coll. Med. Genetics; mem. Am. Soc. Human Genetics, Am. Fedn. Clin. Rsch., Soc. Exptl. Biology and Medicine, N.Y. Acad. Scis., So. Soc. Pediatric Rsch., Med. Assn. Ala., Ala. Assn. Retarded Children (Ann. Med. award 1969), Ala. Acad. Sci., Jefferson County Med. Soc. (pres. 1990), Jefferson County Pediatric Soc., Rotary Club of Birmingham, Phi Beta Kappa, Sigma Xi, Alpha Epsilon Delta, Omicron Delta Kappa, Phi Kappa Phi, The Harrison Soc., Zeta Tau Alpha. Home: 3412 Brookwood Rd Birmingham AL 35223-2023 Office: U Ala UAB Station Birmingham AL 35294

FINLEY, SARAH MAUDE MERRITT, social worker; b. Atlanta, Nov. 19, 1946; d. Genius and Willie Maude (Wright) Merritt; m. Craig Wayne Finley, Aug. 10, 1968; children: Craig Wayne Jr., Jarret Lee. BA, Spelman Coll., 1968; postgrad., Atlanta U., 1968-69. Job placement advisor Marsh Draughton Bus. Coll., Atlanta, 1971-72; child attendant Fulton County Juvenile Ct., Atlanta, 1972; social worker Fulton County Dept. Family and Children Svcs., Atlanta, 1972—, casework suprs., 1976—, Title VI customer svc. coord. Ctrl. City/North Area office, 1990—. Mem. Am. Pub. Welfare Assn., Ga. County Welfare Assn., Ga. Conf. on Social Welfare, Atlanta Pub. Schs. PTSA, Nat. Assn. Counties, Nat. Alumnae Assn. Spelman Coll. Baptist. Office: Fulton County Dept Family and Children Svcs 84 Walton St NW Atlanta GA 30303-2125

FINN, FRANCES MARY, biochemistry researcher; b. Pitts., May 6, 1937; d. Stephen B. and Geraldine H. (Weber) F.; m. Klaus Hofmann, Feb. 26, 1965. BS in Chemistry, U. Pitts., 1959, MS in Biochemistry, 1961, PhD in Biochemistry, 1964. Asst. rsch. prof. biochemistry U. Pitts., 1969-73, assoc. rsch. prof., 1973-80, assoc. prof. medicine, 1980-88, prof., 1988—. Mem. Am. Chem. Soc., Endocrine Soc., Am. Soc. for Biochemistry and Molecular Biology. Home: 1467 Mohican Dr Pittsburgh PA 15228-1613 Office: U Pitts Protein Rsch Lab 3550 Terrace St Pittsburgh PA 15261-0001

FINN, RUTH ANGELL, town official; b. Randolph, Vt., July 19, 1935; d. Philip Alvin and Alice Marion (Amee) Angell; m. Richard Murley Finn, June 18, 1960; children: Charles Philip, Carolyn Ruth. B.S., Simmons Coll., 1957; postgrad. N.E. Law Sch., 1958; grad. Vt. Real Estate Commn., 1972-88; Cert. mcpl. clk. Intern U.S. Dept. Budget, Washington, 1957; adminstrv. asst. John Marsh Agy., Barre, Vt., 1960-61; paralegal Angell & Angell, Randolph, Vt., 1968-84; clk.-treas. Town of Barre, 1984—. Co-chmn. ARC Blood Bank, Barre, 1966-70. Mem. Internat. Inst. Mcpl. Clks., Vt. Town Clks. and Treas. Assn., Vt. Clk. and Treas. Assn. (past pres.), Vt. Govt. Fin. Officers Assn. (past pres.), N.E. Clks. Assn., AAUW (pres. 1965-67), DAR (v.p. gen. 1993—). Club: Simmons. Lodge: Order Eastern Star. Avocations: music (piano and organ), skiing, genealogical history, tennis, golf. Home: 59 Windywood Rd Barre VT 05641-8334 Office: Town of Barre Municipal Bldg Websterville VT 05678

FINNBERG, ELAINE AGNES, psychologist, editor; b. Bklyn., Mar. 2, 1948; d. Benjamin and Agnes Montgomery (Evans) F.; m. Rodney Lee Herndon, Mar. 1, 1981; 1 child, Andrew Marshal. BA in Psychology, L.I. U., 1969; MA in Psychology, New Sch. for Social Rsch., 1973; PhD in Psychology, Calif. Sch. Profl. Psychology, 1981. Lic. psychologist, Calif. Rsch. asst. in med. sociology Med. Coll. Cornell U., N.Y.C., 1969-70; med. abstractor USV Pharm. Corp., Tuckahoe, N.Y., 1970-71, Coun. for Tobacco Rsch., N.Y.C., 1971-77; editor, writer Found. of Thanatology Columbia U., N.Y.C., 1971-76, cons. family studies program cancer ctr. Coll. Physicians &Surgeons, 1973-74; dir. grief psychology and bereavement counseling San Francisco Coll. Mortuary Scis., 1977-81; rsch. assoc. dept. epidemiology and internat. health U. Calif., San Francisco, 1979-81, asst. clin. prof. dept. family and community medicine, 1985-93, assoc. clin. prof., dept. family and community medicine, 1993—; chief psychologist Natividad Med. Ctr., Salinas, Calif., 1984—; asst. chief psychiatry svc. Natividad Med. Ctr., 1985—, acting chief psychiatry, 1988-89, vice chair medicine dept., 1991-93, sec.-treas. med. staff, 1992-94. Editor: (newspaper) The California Psychologist, 1988—; editor Jour. of Thanatology, 1972-76, Cathexis, 1976-81. Mem. gov.'s adv. bd. Agnews Devel. Ctr., San Jose, Calif., 1988—, chair, 1989-91, 94—. Mem. APA, Nat. Register Health Svc. Providers in Psychology, Calif. Psychol. Assn. (Disting. Svc. award 1989), Soc. Behavioral Medicine, Mid-Coast Psychol. Assn. (sec. 1985, treas. 1986, pres. 1987, Disting. Svc. to Psychology award 1993). Office: Natividad Med Ctr PO Box 81611 1330 Natividad Rd Salinas CA 93912-1611

FINNEGAN, JACQUETTA LYNN, treasurer; b. Hammond, Ind., Mar. 21, 1961; d. Donald Eugene and Betty L. (Vandergriff) Johnson; m. Scott William Finnegan, July 23, 1985; 1 child, Natalie J. Student, Ind. Coll. Commerce, Hammond, 1991—. Dental claims examiner Prudential Ins., Merrillville, Ind., 1979-82; radiology transcriptionist St. Anthony Med. Ctr., Crown Point, Ind., 1983-86; treas./bursar Credent Electric, Inc., Crown Point, 1990—. Pres. N.W. Ind. Pro Choice Alliance, Valparaiso, Ind., 1990—; mem. Dem. Women's Network, Washington, 1993—, Dem. Congl. Com., Washington, 1992—; mem. People for Am. Way, 1993—, Nat. Abortion Rights Action League, 1990—. Mem. NOW, Nat. Ct. Reporter Assn. Office: Credent Electric Inc PO Box 478 Crown Point IN 46307

FINNEGAN, MARY ELIZABETH O'DONNELL, classicist, educator; b. Lubec, Maine, Sept. 24, 1907; d. Edward Eugene and Mary Rysam (Sleight) O'Donnell; m. Reynold Edward Finnegan, Oct. 23, 1929 (dec. Jan. 1974); children: Maureen F. Landrigan, Edward William, Reynold Joseph. BA cum laude, Coll. New Rochelle, 1927; MA, Tufts U., 1980; PhD in Humanities, Fla. State U., 1991; DHL (hon.), U. System N.H., 1983. Tchr. Latin and French Lancaster (N.H.) Acad., 1927-29, 1932-33; tchr. social studies Berlin (N.H.) High Sch., 1943-46, tchr. English and fgn. langs., 1958-72, head langs. dept., 1970-72; tchr. English Gorham (N.H.) High Sch., 1946-58; tutor Tufts U., Medford, Mass., 1978-79; teaching asst. Fla. State U., Tallahassee, 1982-85; adj. prof. U. System N.H., Berlin, 1976—, prof. emeritus, 1991—; vis. asst. prof. Dartmouth Coll., Hanover, N.H., 1987-88; sch. vol., Gorham, N.H., summers 1976—; dir. ednl. workshops North Country Edn. Found.; lectr. CANE Inst., 1993. Contbr. book reviews to profl. jours.; contbr. articles to profl. jour. Mem. AAUW (Gift honoree 1985, Life Mem. award 1992), Am. Classical League (lectr. 1978, 89, 91), Classical Assn. New Eng. (mem. exec. bd., recipient Beach Barlow award 1982), N.H. Classical Assn. (bd. dirs. 1965-80), Ret. Tchrs. Assn., Berlin Bus. and Profl. Women Assn. (Women of Achievement award 1981), Nat. Fedn. Women's Clubs, Coll. New Rochelle Alumnae Assn. (alumnae coun. 1982, medalist), Eta Sigma Phi, Kappa Gamma Pi (alumnae coun. Coll. New Rochelle 1974—, official Francophone corr. 1994). Democrat. Roman Catholic. Home: Durand Rd W Randolph NH 03570 Office: PO Box 263 Gorham NH 03581-0263

FINNEGAN, SARA ANNE, publisher; b. Balt., Aug. 1, 1939; d. Lawrence Winfield and Rosina Elva (Huber) F.; m. Isaac C. Lycett, Jr., Aug. 31, 1974. B.A., Sweet Briar Coll., 1961; M.L.A., Johns Hopkins U., 1965; exec. program, U. Va. Grad. Sch. Bus., 1977. Tchr., chmn. history dept. Hannah More Acad., Reisterstown, Md., 1961-65; redactor Williams & Wilkins Co., Balt., 1965-66, asst. head redactory, 1966-71, editor book div., 1971-75, assoc. editor-in-chief, 1975-77, v.p., editor-in-chief, 1977-81, pres. book div., 1981-88, group pres., 1988-94; editor Kalends, 1973-78, 89-92; exec. sponsor jour. Histochemistry and Cytochemistry, 1973-77; dir. Passano Found., 1979-91. Trustee St. Timothy's Sch., Stevenson, Md., 1974-83; mem. adv. bd. Balt. Ind. Schs. Scholarship Fund, 1977-81; mem. adv. coun. grad. study Coll. Notre Dame of Md., 1983; bd. overseers Sweet Briar Coll., 1987-90, bd. dirs. 1990—, chmn.-elect, 1994, chmn., 1995. Mem. Assn. Am. Pubs. (exec. coun. profl. and scholarly pub. div. 1984-85), Internat. Sci., Tech. and Med. Pubs. Assn. (group exec. 1986-93, chmn.-elect 1988, chmn. 1989-92). Republican. Lutheran.

FINNERTY, FRANCES MARTIN, medical administrator; b. Asheville, N.C., Dec. 23, 1936; d. Robert James and Elizabeth Howerton (Babbitt) Martin; m. Richard Phillip Caputo, Sept. 23, 1961 (div. 1974); m. Frank A. Finnerty Jr., July 26, 1975; children: Jonathan, Robert, Richard. Student, Mary Washington Coll., 1954-55, Croft Coll., 1955-57. Dist. mgr. Bus. Census Dept. Commerce, Suitland, Md., 1969-71; program coord. Georgetown U. D.C. Gen. Hosp., Washington, 1972-76; clin. mgr. Hypertension Ctr. Washington, 1976-82; project dir. PharmaKinetic Clin. Rsch. Labs., Balt., 1983; dir. mktg. Classic Glass, Alexandra, Va., 1984-86; office adminstr. Frank A. Finnerty Jr., M.D., Washington, 1987—; cons. U.S. Census, U.S. Army, The Pentagon, Washington, 1969-70; cons. mapping ops. U.S. Census, Prince Georges County, Md., 1970; cons. paramedics pers. Merck Sharpe & Dohme, West Point, Pa., 1974. Contbr. articles to profl. jours. Recipient Cmty. Svc. award Dist. of Columbia, 1980. Mem. Am. Art League (Disting. Artist award 1993), Nat. Assn. Women in Arts, Dist. Med. Soc. Wives. Home: 5117 Albemarle St NW Washington DC 20016

FINNERTY, LOUISE HOPPE, beverage and food company executive; b. Alexandria, Va., Jan. 19, 1949; d. William G. and Ruth A. (Ehren) Hoppe; m. John D. Finnerty, May 21, 1988; 1 child, William Patrick Taylor. B.A., Va. Commonwealth U., 1971; postgrad., Am. U., 1972-73. Staff asst. to Dr. Henry Kissinger Nat. Security Council, Washington, 1971-73; adminstrv. asst. Nat. Petroleum Council, Washington, 1973-75; profl. staff mem. Senate Armed Service Com., Washington, 1976-81; spl. asst. Office Legis. Affairs, Dept. State, Washington, 1981-84, dep. asst. sec. of state, 1984-88; mgr. govt. affairs PepsiCo, Inc., Purchase, N.Y., 1988-91; dir. govt. affairs Pepsico Foods and Beverages Internat., Somers, N.Y., 1991—. Mem. Nat. Fgn. Trade Coun. (bd. dirs. 1991—), Spring Lake Bath and Tennis Club. Republican. Lutheran. Home: 400 Park Ave Rye NY 10580-1213 also: 506 2nd Ave Spring Lake NJ 07762-1107 Office: Pepsico Foods & Beverage Internat Pepsico Foods & Beverage Internat Somers NY 10589

FINNEY, BETTY JANE, psychology educator; b. N.Y.C., Apr. 11, 1926; d. James Phillip and Agnes Campbell (Fenwick) Mackey; m. Robert W. Finney, Dec. 16, 1948 (div. June 1971); children: Robbin L. Finney Hobbins, R. William Jr., Wendy, David C. BA, Flora Stone Mather Coll., 1946; MA, Western Res. U., 1958; PhD, Case Western Res. U., 1968. Tchr. pub. schs. Ohio, 1946-56; dean of girls Willoughby (Ohio)-Eastlake Jr. High Sch., 1956-58, asst. prin., 1958-63; instr. Cuyahoga Community Coll., Ohio, 1964-65; assoc. prof. psychology Millersville (Pa.) U., 1968-71, prof. psychology, 1971—; owner Psychol. Assocs., Pa., 1971-79; pvt. practice Lancaster, 1971—; rsch. cons. Lancaster Cleft Palate, 1969-71. Bd. dirs. Lancaster

Coun. Alcohol and Drug Abuse, 1979-83, Hospice, Lancaster, 1979-83, Housing for People with AIDS, Lancaster, 1988—, United Way Lancaster, 1988-92. Mem. APA. Democrat. Episcopalian. Home: 416 Stonegate Ct Millersville PA 17551-2102 Office: Millersville U Byerly Hall Millersville PA 17551

FINNEY, JOAN MCINROY, former governor; b. Topeka, Feb. 12, 1925; d. Leonard L. and Mary M. (Sands) McInroy; m. Spencer W. Finney, Jr., July 24, 1957; children: Sally, Dick, Mary. B.A., Washburn U., 1974. Mem. staff U.S. Senator Frank Carlson, Topeka and Washington, 1953-69; commr. elections Shawnee County, Kans., 1970-72; adminstrv. asst. to mayor of Topeka, 1973-74; treas. State of Kans., Topeka, 1974-91; gov. State of Kans., 1991-94. Pres. Interstate Oil and Gas Compact Commn., 1992; mem. women's adv. bd. Am. Cup, 1994; co-chair U.S. Term Limits Coun., 1994. Roman Catholic.

FINNEY, LINNEA RUTH, educator, tailor; b. Seattle, May 4, 1952; d. Donald Bruce and Ethel Ruth (Hagli) Deans; m. Raymond Howard Finney, Oct. 5, 1977; children: Sean Howard, Chelan Kimber. AA, AAS, Shoreline C.C., Seattle, 1995, A Arts and Scis. in Acctg., 1995. Dental asst., technician Dr. Donald Bruce Deans, Seattle, 1966-74; dental technician Zundel Dental Lab., Seattle, 1976-79; tailor Carol McClellan Suedes & Leathers, Seattle, 1982, 84; wardrobe asst. Diana Ross on Tour, Seattle, 1982, Harry Belafonte on Tour, Seattle, 1987, Rod Stewart on Tour, Seattle, 1988, Dream Girls Nat. Tour, Seattle, 1988; home tchr. Mukilteo (Wash.) Sch. Dist., 1991-94; tailor Haute Couture, Bothell, Wash., 1964-74, 81-84, Seattle, 1977-80, Everett, Wash., 1984—. Vol. Habitat for Humanity, Lynnwood, Wash., 1992. Home: 2 140th St SW Everett WA 98208-6907 Office: Dr Donald Bruce Deans 6334 NE 157th St Bothell WA 98011

FINNIE, DORIS GOULD, investment company executive; b. Mpls., Sept. 2, 1919; d. Earl Chester and Marie Ethelee (McGulpin) Gould; m. Donald Johnstone Finnie, May 23, 1939; children: Dianne Elaine Finnie Boggess, Denise Eileen. BA in Journalism, U. Denver, 1941. Office mgr. K&P, Inc., Golden, Colo., 1965-82; exec. dir. Rocky Mountain Coal Mining Inst., Lakewood, 1982—. Editor Procs. of Rocky Mountain Coal Mining Inst., 1982—. Founder City of Lakewood, 1968; dir. Alzheimer and Kidney Found., Denver, 1970-72. Recipient Ernest Thompson Seton award Camp Fire, Inc., 1963; named Woman of Yr. Denver Area Panhellenic, 1977. Mem. Colo. Soc. Assn. Execs., Rocky Mountain Assn. Meeting Planners (Humanitarian award 1992), Profl. Conv. Mgmt. Assn., Kappa Delta (Outstanding Alumnae Assn. award 1959, 74, Order of Emerald 1987). Office: Rocky Mountain Coal Mining Inst 3000 Youngfield St Ste 324 Lakewood CO 80215-6553

FINNIGAN, CLAIRE MARIE, media specialist, librarian; b. Putnam Valley, N.Y., Sept. 4, 1923; d. William Edward and Rose Ann (Crowell) F. BS, SUNY, Geneseo, 1945; MS, Columbia U., N.Y.C., 1952; postgrad., Columbia U., 1963, Westchester C.C., 1994. Sch. libr. Eden (N.Y.) Cen. Sch., 1945-47, New Paltz (N.Y.) High Sch., 1947-48; sch. libr. Peekskill (N.Y.) Elem. Schs., 1948-90, ret.; libr. U.S. Naval Air Sta., Atlantic City, N.J., summer 1948; assoc. prof. Queens Coll., Flushing, N.Y., summer 1955; cons. N.Y. State Ednl. Dept., Albany, 1953-57, Franciscan High Sch., Lake Mohegan, N.Y., 1984-86. Contbr. articles to profl. jours. Dir. RIF Program, Peekskill, 1972-87; sec., bd. dirs. City Libr., Peekskill, 1991-93, sec., 1993—; bd. dirs. City Mus., Peekskill, 1982-87; vol. Westchester Lighthouse for the Blind, 1992-94. Recipient Svc. award Home-Sch. Coun., 1984, Leadership award Bd. of Edn., 1987. Mem. N.Y. Sch. Libr. Media Specialists (pres., sec., treas. 1953-57, Svc. award 1987), Southeastern Sch. Libr. Media Specialists (bd. dirs., sec. 1985-87), Internat. Reading Assn. (award 1982), AAUW (sec., bd. dirs. Peekskill chpt. 1962-87, Woman Achievement award 1989), Women's Club of Peekskill (sec., treas., bd. dirs. 1962-87), Delta Kappa Gamma, Alpha Omicron (v.p. No. Westchester, N.Y. chpt. 1988-90, pres. 1990-92, communications state com. 1991-93, travel and study state com. 1993-95, treas. 1993-94). Home: 1 Lakeview Dr Apt 6L Peekskill NY 10566-2238

FINO, MARIE GEORGETTE KECK, real estate broker; b. Greenville, Pa., Jan. 30, 1923; d. Harvey I. and Winifred L. (Fuller) Keck; m. Alex F. Fino, Sept. 27, 1947; children: Timothy A., Jeffrey J. Cert. in real estate, Pa. State U., 1980; grad., Realtors Inst., Harrisburg, Pa., 1981. RN, Pa.; lic. real estate broker, Pa. Broker, owner 305 Realty, North Warren, Pa., 1983—; instr. Pa. State U., 1985—; treas. Warren County Bd. Realtors, 1981-84, v.p., 1984-86, pres., 1988. Patentee fuel storage vent. Treas. Northwestern Pa. Regional Planning Commn., 1985-92, exec. com., 1988-92, treas., 1991; bd. dirs. Warren County Devel. Assn., Warren County Crime Stoppers, 1989—. Named Woman of Yr. in Bus. and Industry, County of Warren, 1986, Citizen Amb. to China, 1994. Mem. Nat. Assn. Realtors, Pa. Assn. Realtors (bd. dirs. 1984-88, vice chmn. comml.-indsl. com. 1984-88, bd. dirs. 1992-93), Soc. Indsl. and Office Realtors (nat. bd. dirs. 1992—, dist. v.p. 1993-95), Warren County C. of C., Philomel Club (bd. dirs. 1978-80), Conewango Valley Club (Warren), Zonta. Republican. Roman Catholic. Office: 305 Realty 305 Market St Warren PA 16365-2335

FINSTAD, SUZANNE ELAINE, author, lawyer; b. Mpls., Sept. 14, 1955; d. Harold Martin and Elaine Lois (Strom) F. Student, U. Tex., 1973-74; BA in French, U. Houston, 1976, JD, 1980; postgrad., London Sch. Econs., 1980, U. Grenoble, France, 1979. Bar: Tex. 1981. Legal asst. Butler & Binion, Houston, 1976-78, law clerk, 1978-81, assoc., 1982; spl. counsel Ad Litem in the Estate of Howard Hughes Jr., Houston, 1981; mng. ptnr. Finstad & Assoc., Houston, 1990—. Author: Heir Not Apparent, 1984 (Frank Wardlaw award 1984), Ulterior Motives, 1987, Sleeping With the Devil, 1991, Queen Noor: A Biography, 1995; contbr. articles to various mags. Recipient Am. Jurisprudence award in climinal law U. Houston, 1979, named to Order of Barons, Bates Coll. Law, 1979-80. Democrat. Office: Joel Gotler Renaissance Agy 8523 Sunset Blvd Beverly Hills CA 90069

FIOCK, SHARI LEE, design entrepreneur, researcher; b. Weed, Calif., Oct. 25, 1941; d. Webster Bruce and Olevia May (Pruett) F.; m. June 6, 1966 (div. 1974); children—Webster Clinton Pfingsten, Sterling Curtis. Cert. Art Instrn. Sch., Mpls., 1964; pvt. student. Copywriter Darron Assocs., Eugene, Oreg., 1964-66; staff artist Oreg. Holidays, Springfield, 1966-69, part-time 1971; co-owner, designer Artre Enterprises, Eugene, 1969-74; design entrepreneur Shari & Assocs., Yreka, Calif., 1974— (retained as cons., devel. sec. Cascade World Four Season Resort, Siskiyou County, Calif., 1980-86); part time adminstrv. asst., coord. of regional catalog Great Northern Corp./U.S. Dept. Commerce and Econ. Devel., 1994—. cons., pres. Reunions, Family, Yreka, 1984—. Designer 5 ton chain saw sculpture, Oreg. Beaver, 1967; author: Goose Gabble, 1992; illustrator: Holiday Fun Book, 1978; author, illustrator Blue Goose Legend, 1995; co-creator Klamath Nat. Forest Interpretive Mus., 1979-91; owner Coyote Pub. Author, illustrator Family Reunions and Clan Gatherings, 1991. Residential capt. United Way, Eugene, 1972; researcher Beaver Ofcl. State Animal, Eugene, 1965-71; counselor Boy Scouts, 1983-91. Mem. Nat. Writers Club(founder, pres. Siskiyou chpt., past v.p. State of Jefferson chpt., N.W. rep.). Avocations: family activities; outdoor recreation; travel; theater; music. Home: 406 Walters Ln Box 1854 Yreka CA 96097-9704

FIORAVANTI, NANCY ELEANOR, banker; b. Gloucester, Mass., Apr. 10, 1935; d. Richard Joseph and Evelyn Grace (Souza) F. Grad. high sch. Various positions and depts. Bank of New Eng.-North Shore (formerly Cape Ann Bank and Trust Co., successor to Gloucester Safe Deposit & Trust Co.), Gloucester, 1953—, with trust dept., 1959-86, asst. trust officer, 1970-84, trust officer, 1984-86; trust officer Cape Ann Savs. Bank, 1986—, corporator, 1992—; past mem. and treas. adv. com. Gloucester Lyceum and Sawyer Free Libr., elected mem. of the corp., 1989. Home: PO Box 1638 Gloucester MA 01931-1638 Office: 109 Main St Gloucester MA 01930-5799

FIORE, MARY, magazine editor. Former editor Photoplay mag.; mng. editor Good Housekeeping mag. Office: Good Housekeeping 959 8th Ave New York NY 10019-3737*

FIORELLA, BEVERLY JEAN, medical technologist, educator; b. Owensboro, Ky., Oct. 29, 1930; d. Gabriel and Agnes Loretta (Kurz) F. BS, Webster Coll./St. Louis U., 1952; MA, Cen. Mich. U., 1976. Chief microbiology and blood bank St. Mary's Hosp., Kansas City, Mo., 1956-67; instr., asst. prof. med. lab. scis. dept. Coll. Assoc. Health Professions, U. Ill., Chgo., 1967-74, assoc. prof., 1974-80, prof., 1980—, assoc. head dept. med. lab. scis., 1977-90, acting dept. head, 1990-91, head, 1991—, grad. program coord., 1977-81, dir. grad. studies, 1990-93; mem. adv. panel on health ins. Subcom. Health of Com. on Ways and Means, Ho. of Reps., 1975-80; cons. lab. improvement sect. immunohematology divs. labs. Dept. Pub. Health State of Ill., 1975-85; cons. editor Clin. Lab. Scis., 1987-90. Mem. bd. editors Med. Tech.-A Series, 1970-74. Named Med. Technologist of Yr., Mo. Soc. Med. Technologists, 1967. Mem. Am. Soc. Clin. Lab. Sci. (pres. 1976-77), Am. Assn. Blood Banks, Ill. Clin. Lab. Sci. Assn. (exec. sec. 1987—, named Ill. Med. Technologist of Yr. 1976), Chgo. Soc. Med. Technologists (treas., dir. 1969-70), Chicagoland Blood Bank Soc. (v.p. 1975-76), Internat. Assn. Med. Lab. Technologists (coun. 1988—), Acad. Clin. Lab. Physicians and Scientists, Clin. Lab. Mgrs. Assn., Am. Soc. Allied Health Professions, Internat. Soc. Blood Transfusion, Alpha Mu Tau. Office: U Ill Chgo Dept Med Lab Scis 808 South Wood St Rm 690 Chicago IL 60612-7305

FIORELLA-RUSSO, DOROTHY CHRISTINE, elementary education and university educator; b. N.Y.C., July 24, 1931; d. Anthony Joseph and Assunta Mary (Moroni) Fiorella; m. Victor Donald Russo, Jr., Apr. 30, 1960. BA, Marymount Manhattan Coll.; MS, Fordham U., 1959; diploma in reading, Hofstra U., 1978, PhD, 1987, postgrad., 1987—; cert. in litigation, Adelphi U. and Nat. Ctr. for Paralegal Tng., 1980. Cert. elem. and secondary English tchr., N.Y., reading specialist, N.Y. Tchr. St. Margaret's Sch., Bronx, N.Y., 1955-56, Sacred Heart, Manhattan, N.Y., 1956-57, Bd. Edn., N.Y.C., 1957-60, Harborfields Dist. 6, L.I., 1960—; English instr. Marymount Manhattan Coll., N.Y. Bd. dirs. Marymount Alumnae Adv. Coun., N.Y., 1985—, Fordham U. Pres.'s Coun., Bronx, 1985-87, Fordham U. Recruitment Program, Bronx, 1983-87; campaign worker Dem. Party, N.Y.C., 1990, 92; Marymount rep. N.Y. State Bundy/Affairs Fund, 1982-83; L.I. rep. Marymount Recruitment Program, 1992; chmn. Ft. Salonga Assn., L.I., 1979-83; campaign worker Dem. Party, N.Y.C., 1990, 92, 94; vol. St. John's Hosp., L.I. Recipient Tchr.-Student Participation award Suffolk Reading Coun., 1991-94, Tchr.-Student Participation award 3d and 4th ann. N.Y. Senate Earth Day Competition, 1994, 95. Mem. APA, Guilford Internat. Soc. Intelligence Edn. (v.p. 1991—, bd. dirs. 1990—), N.Y. Acad. Scis., N.Y. Orton Dyslexia Soc., Nat. Dyslexia Rsch. Found., Coun. for Exceptional Children, World Coun. for Gifted and Talented Children, Am. Assn. Higher Edn. Roman Catholic. Home: 7 Bonnie Dr Northport NY 11768-1448

FIPPINGER, GRACE J., retired telecommunications company executive; b. N.Y.C., Nov. 24, 1927; d. Fred Herman and Johanna Rose (Tesio) F. BA, St. Lawrence U., 1948; LLD (hon.), Marymount Manhattan Coll., 1980; DCS (hon.), Molloy Coll., 1982; DHL, St. Lawrence U., 1990. Dist. mgr. N.Y. Tel. Co., South Nassau, 1957-65, div. mgr., 1965-71; gen. comml. mgr. N.Y. Tel. Co., Queens, Bklyn., 1971-74; v.p., sec., treas. N.Y. Tel. Co., 1974-82; v.p., treas., sec. NYNEX Corp., N.Y.C., 1982-90; ret., 1990; bd. dirs. Conn. Mut. Life Ins., Bear Stearns Co., Pfizer, Inc. Former mem. State Manpower Adv. Council; former mem. Gov.'s Econ. Devel. Adv. Council; past bd. dirs. Consumer Credit Counseling Service Greater N.Y., 1972—; hon. bd. dirs. Am. Cancer Soc., 1974—, YMCA Greater N.Y., 1975—; former dir. A.R.C., L.I., Nassau County Health and Welfare Council; trustee Citizens Budget Commn., 1974—; former dir. exec. bd. Nassau County Fedn. Republican Women. Named Woman of Yr., Bus. and Profl. Women Nassau County, 1969, Woman of Achievement, Flatbush Bus. and Profl. Women's Assn., 1974, Woman of Yr., Soroptimist Club Nassau County; hon. mem. Soroptimist Club Nassau County, 1974; recipient John Peter Zenger award Nassau County Press Assn., 1975, Outstanding Bus. Women of 1977 award Marymount Manhattan Coll., 1978; honoree Catalyst Inc., 1977, Women's Equity Action League, 1978, Republican Women in Bus. and Industry, Cath. Med. Ctr. Bklyn./Queens, 1983, Girl Scouts, 1984, Clark Garden, L.I., 1985. Mem. Am. Mgmt. Assn. (former trustee and mem. exec. com.), Nat. Assn. Corp. Treas., Fin. Execs. Inst., Am. Soc. Corp. Secs., Am. Soc. Corp. Treas. Inc., Fin. Womens Assn. N.Y., N.Y. Chamber Commerce and Industry (chmn. mems. council 1977-79), L.I. Assn., Nat. Women's Econ. Alliance., Ladies Profl. Golf Assn. (hon.). Clubs: St. Lawrence of L.I. (N.Y.C.).

FIRE, NANCY ANN, elementary educator; b. Bradford, Pa., Feb. 22, 1951; d. Francis John and Christine Ann (Ross) F. BS in Elem. Edn., Clarion (Pa.) State U., 1973; MEd in Acad. Curriculum and Instrn., Pa. State U., 1976. 3rd grade tchr. West Br. Sch. - Bradford Area Schs., 1973—, 2nd grade tchr., 1984-86; adj. instr. U. Pitts./Bradford Elem. Edn. Program, 1991—; cooperating tchr. Student Tchrs. for U. Pitts., Bradford, 1992. Prodr., dir. vocalist (dinner theatre) Broadway Revue, 1989; novelty song lyricist, 1992; solist A Musical Tribute to Ray Evans, 1993; prodr. Amahl and the Night Visitors Enchanted Mountain Players, 1993. Congrl. internship Congressman William F. Clinger Jr., Washington, 1985, campaign vol. to re-elect William Clinger, Bradford, 1986. Mem. AAUW (v.p. 1980-82, pres. 1988-90), NEA, Pa. State Edn. Assn. Roman Catholic. Office: West Branch Elem Sch 645 W Washington St Bradford PA 16701-2634

FIRESTONE, NANCY B., lawyer; b. Manchester, N.H., Oct. 17, 1952; d. Albert and Bernice (Brown) F. BA, Washington U., St. Louis, 1973; JD, U. Mo., 1977. Bar: Mo. 1977, U.S. Ct. Appeals (2d, 4th, 5th, 6th, 9th, 8th and 10th cirs.). Trial atty. U.S. Dept. Justice, Washington, 1977-85; asst. chief U.S. Dept. Justice, 1984-85, dep. chief environ. enforcement, 1985-89; assoc. dep. adminstr. EPA, 1989—, adminstrv. judge, 1992—; adj. prof. Georgetown U. Law Ctr., 1986—. Mem. ABA. Home: 6203 Beachway Dr Falls Church VA 22041-1401

FIRSTENBERG, JEAN PICKER, film institute executive; b. N.Y.C., Mar. 13, 1936; d. Eugene and Sylvia (Moses) Picker; m. Paul Firstenberg, Aug. 9, 1956 (div. July 1980); children—Debra, Douglas. BS summa cum laude, Boston U., 1958. Asst. producer Altman Prodns., Washington, 1965-66; media advisor J. Walter Thompson, N.Y.C., 1969-72; asst. for spl. projects Princeton (N.J.) U., 1972-74, dir. publs., 1974-76; program officer Markle Found., N.Y.C., 1976-80; dir. Am. Film Inst., L.A., Washington, 1980—; mem. com. L.A. Task Force on Arts; former chmn. nat. adv. bd. Peabody Broadcasting Awards; bd. dirs. Trans-Lux Corp. Trustee Boston U.; mem. adv. bd. Will Rogers Inst., N.Y.C., Big Sisters of Los Angeles; bd. dirs. Variety Club of Calif., Los Angeles; chmn., bd. advisors Film Dept. N.C. Sch. of Arts. Recipient Alumni award for disting. service to profession Boston U., 1982; seminar and prodn. chairs at directing workshop for women named in her honor Am. Film Inst., 1986. Mem. Women in Film (Los Angeles and Washington, Crystal award 1990), Trusteeship for Betterment of Women, Acad. Motion Picture Arts and Scis. Office: Am Film Inst 2021 N Western Ave PO Box 27999 Los Angeles CA 90027 also: Am Film Inst Kennedy Ctr Performing Washington DC 20056*

FISCHBARG, ZULEMA F., pediatrician, educator; b. Buenos Aires, Mar. 22, 1937; came to U.S., 1962; d. Naun and Esther (Pollner) Fridman; m. Jorge Fischbarg; children: Gabriel Julian, Victor Ernesto. MD, U. Buenos Aires, 1960. Pediatric intern Children's Hosp., Louisville, 1962-63, resident in pediatrics, 1963, chief resident in pediatrics, 1964; fellow hematology Michael Reese Med. Ctr., Chgo., 1964-66, Presbyn. St. Lukes Hosp., Chgo., 1966-67; fellow pediatric hematology Children's Meml. Hosp., Chgo., 1967-68; asst. clin. pediatrician U. Chgo., 1968-69; instr. in pediatrics Cornell U. Med. Sch., N.Y.C., 1970-72, asst. prof. in pediatrics, 1972-76, assoc. prof. pediatrics, 1978—; assoc. attending pediatrician N.Y. Hosp., 1979—; assoc. attending in pediatrics St. John's Hosp./Cath. Med. Ctr., N.Y.C.; med. specialist sch. health Dept. Health, N.Y.; instr. in medicine Ill. U., Chgo., 1967-68; asst. attending pediatrician, N.Y. Hosp., N.Y.C., 1972-76. Fellow Am. Acad. of Pediatrics, Queens Pediatric Soc.; mem. N.Y. Acad. of Medicine, N.Y. Soc. for the Study of Blood. Democrat. Jewish. Home: 175 E 62d St 6D New York NY 10021 Office: 37-51 72d St Jackson Heights NY 11372

FISCHER, BARBARA JOAN, state agency administrator; b. Bismarck, N.D., July 31, 1951; d. Edwin Elmer Telin and Luella Lenora (Maier) Miller; m. Floyd Alfred Fischer, Oct. 15, 1993. AA, Bismarck Jr. Coll., 1971; BS in Acctg., Mary Coll., 1973. CPA, N.D. Auditor-in-charge N.D. State Auditor's Office, Bismarck, 1973-75; publs. specialist Standard & Poors Compustat, Denver, 1976-80; auditor N.D. Dept. Human Svcs., Bismarck, 1980-85, audit supr., 1985-91, mgr. long term care and hosp. svcs., 1991—. Mem. Nat. Mgmt. Assn. (bd. dirs. 1992-94), State Bd. Nursing Home Adminstrs. (bd. dirs. 1991—). Office: ND Dept Human Svcs 600 E Boulevard Ave Bismarck ND 58505-0660

FISCHER, DALE SUSAN, lawyer; b. East Orange, N.J., Oct. 17, 1951; d. Edward L. and Audrey (Tenner) F. Student Dickinson Coll., 1969-70; BA magna cum laude, U. So. Fla., 1977; JD, Harvard U., 1980. Bar: Calif. 1980. Ptnr. law firm Kindel & Anderson, L.A., 1986—; judge pro tem L.A. Mcpl. Ct.; faculty Nat. Inst. Trial Advocacy; lawyer in classroom Constl. Rights Found.; moderator, panelist How to Win Your Case with Depositions. Mem. Legal adv. bd. Sr. Care Network. Mem. ABA, Am. Arbitration Assn. (mem. panel arbitrators), L.A. County Bar Assn., L.A. Complex Litigation Inn of Ct. Home: 3695 Hampton Rd Pasadena CA 91107-3004 Office: Kindel and Anderson 555 S Flower St Los Angeles CA 90071-2300

FISCHER, IRENE KAMINKA, retired research geodesist, mathematician; b. Vienna, Austria, July 27, 1907; came to U.S., 1941; d. Armand and Clara (Loewy) Kaminka; m. Eric Fischer, Dec. 21, 1930; children: Gay A., Michael M.J. MA, U. Vienna, 1931; postgrad., Georgetown U., 1950-57; D. in Enging., U. Karlsruhe, Karlsruhe, Fed. Republic Germany, 1975. Tchr. secondary schs. Vienna, 1931-38; tchr. secondary schs. and colls. Washington, D.C., Mass., N.Y., Mass, 1941-45; researcher MIT, Cambridge, Mass., 1942-44; rsch. geodesist Army Map Svc., Def. Mapping Agy., Washington, 1952-77. Author: Geometry, 1965, Basic Geodesy, The Geoid--What's That?, 1973; contbr. hundreds of articles to profl. jours. Recipient medals Dept. Army, 1957, 66, 67, Dept. Def., 1967, Def. Mapping Agy., 1971, Nat. Civil Svc. League Career award, 1976; named Fed. Retiree of Yr. Nat. Assn. Retired Fed. Employees, 1978. Fellow Am. Geophys. Union, Internat. Assn. Geodesy (sec. sect. V 1963-71, chmn. study groups 1963-75); mem. Nat. Acad. Enging. Home: 6060 California Cir Apt 210 Rockville MD 20852-4835

FISCHER, KAREN ANN, librarian; b. St. Paul, Mar. 10, 1947; d. Robert Fred and Dorothy Eva (Portz) F. BA, Hamline U., 1969; MLS, U. Minn., 1971; MA, Mont. State U., 1980. Monographic cataloger U. Iowa, Iowa City, 1971-73; head tech. svcs. Coll. of St. Benedict, St. Joseph, Minn., 1973-76; cataloger, reference libr. Mont. State U., Bozeman, 1976-84, cataloger, 1984-86; dir. libr. media svcs. Cen. Oreg. Community Coll., Bend, 1986-93; dir. Briggs Libr. U. Minn., Morris, 1993—. Mem. ALA, Assn. Coll. and Rsch. Librs., Libr. Adminstrn. and Mgmt. Assn., Minn. Libr. Assn., Mont. Libr. Assn. (pres. 1985-86, chair acad. and spl. librs. divsn.). Office: U Minn Morris Briggs Libr 600 E 4th St Morris MN 56267

FISCHER, KATHLEEN JOYCE, nursing educator; b. Yokohama, Japan, Jan. 19, 1947; (parents Am. citizens); d. F. W. and Florence (Davis) Lanard; m. Norman Erwin Fischer, Aug. 15, 1971; children: Brandon, Amy. BSN, U. Mich., 1969; MA, Ea. Mich. U., 1974. Cert. CNA; cert. Cin. Continuing Edn. and Staff Devel. Asst. dir. med. nursing U. Mich. Hosps., Ann Arbor, asst. dir. surg. nursing, ednl. nurse specialist, dir. ednl. svcs. nursing. Author: ANA Standards for Staff Development, 1990, Quality Improvement Indicators for Staff Development, 1992, Performance Improvement in Staff Development, 1995; past mem. editorial bd. Jour. Staff Devel. Mem. Nat. Nursing Staff Devel. Orgn. (bd. dirs., v.p.), Community Staff Devel. Orgn. (chairperson), Mich. Nurses Assn. (chairperson coun. continuing edn.).

FISCHER, LINDA, nursing educator; b. Paterson, N.J., Sept. 26, 1959; d. William Jr. and Marie (Bilz) F. BSN cum laude, Coll. Misericordia, 1981. RN, Pa.; BLS instr.; CCRN. Staff nurse cardiac intensive care unit Geisinger Med. Ctr., Danville, Pa., 1987-89, clin. nurse II cardiac intensive care unit, 1987—;, 1981-89; clin. instr. cardiac intensive care unit, cardiovascular spl. care unit Geisinger Med. Ctr., Danville, Pa., 1989—. Mem. AACN, Sigma Theta Tau.

FISCHER, LOIS MARIN, computer educator; b. N.Y.C., Dec. 21, 1935; d. Isidore and Ruth (Goller) Marin; m. Warren Herbert Fischer, Jan. 24, 1954 (dec. Mar. 30, 1971); children: Susan Paula, Robert Benjamin; m. Ove Ofteness Michaelsen, July 11, 1989. BFA in Painting and Drawing, Ariz. State U., 1981, MFA in Painting and Drawing, 1983. Cert. vocat. educator, secondary art educator, elem. educator, N.J.; cert. community coll. tchr., Ariz. Articulation coord., performing arts series coord., instr. South Mountain C.C., Phoenix, 1983-86, Rio Salado C.C., Mesa, Ariz., 1983-86; instr. math., bus. comm. Am. Bus. Inst., Newark, 1986-88, Drake/Sawyer Bus. Coll., Jersey City, 1986-88; instr. Pt. Pleasant (N.J.) Boro Adult Sch., 1987-91, Metuchen (N.J.) Adult Sch., 1987-91, Katharine Gibbs Sch., Montclair, Piscataway, N.J., 1987-92; instr., alumni coord. The Chubb Inst., Jersey City, 1990-95, dept. chair personal computer applications, 1995—; prop builder, painter Celebrity Theatre, Phoenix; electrician, scene shop asst. Sesame Street Live Road Show, Tempe, Ariz.; scenic artist, asst. to dir. Ariz. State U. Lyceum Theatre, Tempe, tech. dir., 1981-83; instr. theatre Maricopa C.C. Dist. All Employees Meeting, Phoenix Civic Ctr., 1985, South Mountain C.C., Phoenix, 1983-86. One-person exhbns. include Gault Gallery, Southfield, Mich., 1972, Elaine Horwitch Gallery, Scottsdale, Ariz., 1973, Steckler-Haller Galler, Scottsdale, 1974, Pot Pourri Gallery, Oakland, Calif., 1975, Berkeley City Hall, 1976, Gallery of Hawaii, 1977, U. Calif., Berkeley, 1978, Lucien Labaudt Gallery, San Francisco, 1979, Harry Wood Gallery, Ariz. State U., 1983, Lyceum Theatre, Ariz. State U., 1983, Phoenix Little Theatre, 1984, Gammage Ctr. for the Arts, Tempe, 1985; exhibited in group shows. Civil rights activist Mother Waddles Soc., Detroit, 1967-69; pres. Woman Image Now, Ariz. State U. art student orgn., Tempe, 1974; chair fine arts jury, gallery dir. Berkeley Artists' Assn., 1976-78; graphic designer City of Phoenix, Parks, Recreation and Libr. Dept., 1982; co-chair Exhbn. Com., Ariz. Women's Caucus for the Arts, Phoenix, 1983. Mem. MENSA, AAUW, Coll. Art Assn., N.J. Bus. Educators Assn., Smithsonian Instn. Democrat. Jewish. Home: 67 Westport Dr Whiting NJ 08759 Office: The Chubb Inst 40 Journal Sq Jersey City NJ 07306

FISCHER, MARSHA LEIGH, civil engineer; b. San Antonio, May 9, 1955; d. Joe Henry and Ellen Joyce (Flake) F. BSCE, Tex. A&M U., 1977. Enging. asst. Tex. Dept. Hwys. and Transp., Dallas, 1977-79; outside plant engr. Southwestern Bell Telephone Co., Dallas, 1979-82, staff mgr. for budgets, 1982-84; area mgr., enging. design Southwestern Bell Telephone Co., Wichita Falls, Tex., 1984-86; area mgr. Southwestern Bell Telephone Co., Ft. Worth, 1986-88; dist. mgr., local provisioning application Bell Communications Rsch., Piscataway, N.J., 1988-91; dist. mgr. enging. Southwestern Bell Telephone, Ft. Worth, Tex., 1992-94, dir. customer svcs., 1994—. Named one of Outstanding Women of Am., 1987. Mem. NSPE, Tex. Soc. Profl. Engrs., Tex. Soc. Civil Engrs., Profl. Engrs. in Industry, Tex. A&M Assn. Former Students. Republican. Home: 6724 Johns Ct Arlington TX 76016-3622 Office: Southwestern Bell Telephone 1255 Tavaros Ave Rm 220 Dallas TX 75218-4053

FISCHER, MARY CORNELIA (CONNIE FISCHER), army project director, operations research analyst; b. Richmond, Va., Apr. 5, 1944; d. Walter Edward and Doris (Mundy) F.; m. James Edward Detwiler, Dec. 19, 1974. BA, Radford U., 1965; M in Math., U. Tenn., 1970; MA, U. Ill., 1971, advanced cert., 1977; MBA, Western New Eng. Coll., 1980; PhD, Columbia Pacific U., 1989; grad., U.S. Army Commd., Gen. Staff Coll. Asst. prof. math. Embry Riddle Aero. U., Daytona Beach, Fla., 1972-75; prof. U. So. Colo., Pueblo, 1976-77, Western New England Coll., Ft. Deven, Hanscomb AFB, Mass., 1980-81, Troy State U.-Europe, Izmir, Turkey, 1983, U. Md.-Europe, Izmir, 1984; ops. rsch. analyst U.S. Army Combined Arms Command, Ft. Leavenworth, Kans., 1985-88; sr. ops. rsch. analyst, project mgr. Army Tng. Devices, Orlando, Fla., 1988-91; chief mgmt. info. U.S. Army Simulation, Tng. and Instrumentation Command, Orlando, 1991-93, project dir., 1993—. Mem. Mil. Ops. Rsch. Soc., Army Ops. Rsch. Soc. Office: PM CATT (STRICOM) Attention AMCPM-FAMS 12350 Research Pky Orlando FL 32826-3261

FISCHER, PAMELA SHADEL, public relations executive; b. Harrisburg, Pa., Feb. 28, 1959; d. Richard Lee and Pauline Louise (Nies) S.; m. Charles J. Fischer, Jr., June 11, 1983. BA in English, Lebanon Valley Coll., Annville, Pa., 1981. Pub. relations coordinator Pa. Optometric Assn., Harrisburg, 1981-83; pub. relations dir. Morris Center YMCA, Cedar Knolls, N.J., 1983-85; pub. relations coordinator Delta Dental Plan of N.J., Parsippany, 1985-86; pub. relations mgr. AAA N.J. Automobile Club, Florham Park, N.J., 1986-91, mgr. mem. svcs. and pub. affairs, 1991-94, asst. v.p. pub. rels. & safety, 1994—. Corp. capt. United Way of Morris County, Cedar Knolls, 1985-90, chmn. publs. com., 1989-90, chmn. mktg. com., 1991—, bd. dirs. of exec. com.; career counselor Lebanon Valley Coll., 1983—; bd. dirs. Morris Ctr. YMCA, 1992-94. Rotary Found. scholar, 1981; recipient Gold award United Way of Morris County, 1988. Mem. Pub. Rels. Soc. Am. (bd. dirs. 1995—), N.J. Press Assn., Internat. Assn. Bus. Communicators, Y's Club of Cedar Knolls (pres. 1986-91). Democrat. Roman Catholic. Office: AAA NJ Automobile Club 1 Hanover Rd Florham Park NJ 07932-1807

FISCHER, PATRICIA ANN, middle school educator; b. Cleve., Apr. 11, 1951; d. Norman Stanley and Teresa (Domagalski) Michaels; m. David Leland Stroh, June 1, 1973 (div. June 1977); m. Lawrence Joseph Fischer, June 14, 1986. BA in Edn., Ohio No. U., 1973; MBA in Edn., Mt. St. Joseph Coll., Cin., 1986; postgrad., Miami U., Oxford, Ohio, 1985—, Ohio State U., 1988. Cert. K-8 tchr., 7-12 history tchr., Ohio. Mid. sch. tchr. St. Gerard Sch., Lima, Ohio, 1973-79, Our Lady of Rosary Sch., Cin., 1980-89; mid. sch. tchr. Little Flower Sch., Cin., 1989—, coord. sci., 1989—. Recipient award Project Bus., Cin., 1986, 87, 88, 89, Civic Achievement award Burger King Corp., Cin., 1990, 91, 92, Sci. Tchr. award NSTA, 1993, 20-Yr. award for Cath. educator Diocese of Cin., 1994. Mem. Nat. Cath. Edn. Assn., Ohio Edn. Assn., European Am. Study Ctr. Alumni Assn., Order Ea. Star, Alpha Omicron Pi. Roman Catholic. Home: 5450 Cecilia Ct Cincinnati OH 45247 Office: Little Flower Sch 555 Little Flower Ave Cincinnati OH 45239

FISCHER, SUSAN LOIS, financial services company executive; b. N.Y.C., Mar. 18, 1947; d. Julius and Bertha (Sviridow) Kulman; m. Robert J. Fischer, July 11, 1976. BS in Edn., NYU, 1969, MA in Edn., 1971; MBA in Fin., L.I. U., Dobbs Ferry, N.Y., 1986. Cert. tchr., N.Y. Tchr. N.Y.C. Bd. Edn., 1969-84; fin. analyst Integrated Resources Equipment Group, Inc., N.Y.C., 1984-85, asst. v.p., 1985-87; v.p. Integrated Resources Capital Markets Group, Inc., N.Y.C., 1987-88; v.p. Integrated Resources Equipment Group, Inc., N.Y.C., 1989-92, exec. v.p., 1992—; v.p. Integrated Resources, Inc., N.Y.C., 1990-93, 1st v.p., 1993-94; sr. mgr. Concurrency Mgmt. Corp., N.Y.C., 1994—; v.p. Integrated Resources, Inc. Bd. dirs. Walden Wood Homeowners Assn., 1986-88; co-chmn. ACTS leadership team Marble Collegiate Ch., 1992-94; mem., vol. Soc. Meml. Sloan-Kettering Cancer Ctr. Recipient Disting. Alumni award L.I. U., Westchester Campus. Home: 345 E 81st St New York NY 10028-4005 Office: Concurrency Mgmt Corp 10 Union Sq E New York NY 10003-3314

FISCHER, ZOE ANN, real estate and property marketing company executive, real estate consultant; b. L.A., Aug. 26, 1939; d. George and Marguerite (Carrasco) Routsos; m. Douglas Clare Fischer, Aug. 6, 1960 (div. 1970); children: Brent Sean Cecil, Tahlia Georgienne Marguerite Bianca. BFA in Design, UCLA, 1964. Pres. Zoe Antiques, Beverly Hills, Calif., 1973—; v.p. Harleigh Sandler Real Estate Corp. (now Prudential), 1980-81; exec. v.p. Coast to Coast Real Estate & Land Devel. Corp., Century City, Calif., 1981-83; pres. New Market Devel., Inc., Beverly Hills, 1983—; dir. mktg. Mirabella, L.A., 1983, Autumn Pointe, L.A., 1983-84, Desert Hills, Antelope Valley, Calif., 1984-85; cons. Lowe Corp., L.A., 1985. Designer interior and exterior archtl. enhancements and remodelling; designed album cover for Clare Fischer Orch. (Grammy award nomination 1962). Soprano Roger Wagner Choir, UCLA, 1963-64. Mem. UCLA Alumni Assn. Democrat. Roman Catholic. Avocations: skiing, designing jewelry, interior, landscape and new home design, antique collecting.

FISCHLER, BARBARA BRAND, librarian; b. Pitts., May 24, 1930; d. Carl Frederick and Emma Georgia (Piltz) Brand; m. Drake Anthony Fischler, June 3, 1961; 1 child, Owen Wesley. AB cum laude, Wilson Coll., Chambersburg, Pa., 1952; MM with distinction, Ind. U., 1954, AMLS, 1964. Asst. reference librarian Ind. U., Bloomington, 1958-61, asst. librarian undergrad. library, 1961-63, acting librarian, 1963; circulation librarian Ind. U.-Purdue U., Indpls., 1970-76, pub. services librarian Univ. Library, sci., engring. and tech. unit, 1976-81, acting dir. univ. libraries, 1981-82, dir. univ. libraries, 1982—; vis. and assoc. prof. (part-time) Sch. Libr. and Info. Sci., Ind. U., Bloomington, 1972—, counselor-coord., Indpls., 1974-82; resource aide adv. com. Ind. Voc. Tech. Coll., Indpls., 1974-86; adv. com. Area Libr. Svcs. Authority, Indpls., 1976-79; mem. core com., chmn. program com. Ind. Gov.'s Conf. on Librs. and Info. Svcs., Indpls., 1976-78, mem. governance com., del. to conf., 1990; mem. Ind. State Libr. Adv. Coun., 1985-91; cons. in field. Contbr. articles to profl. jours. Fund-raiser Indpls. Mus. Art, 1971, Am. Cancer Soc., Indpls., 1975; vol. tchr. St. Thomas Aquinas Sch., Indpls., 1974-75; fund-raiser Am. Heart Assn., Indpls., 1985; bd. dirs., treas. Historic Amusement Found., Inc., Indpls., 1984-91; bd. advisors N.Am. Wildlife Park Found., Inc., Battle Ground, Ind., 1985-91, bd. dirs., 1991—; mem. adv. bd. Ind. U. Ctr. on Philanthropy, 1987-90. Recipient Outstanding Svc. award Cen. Ind. Area Libr. Svc. Authority, 1979; Outstanding Libr. award Ind. Libr./Ind. Libr. Trustee Assn., 1988, Louise Maxwell award for outstanding achievement, 1989. Mem. ALA, Libr. Adminstrn. and Mgmt. Assn. (vice chair and chair elect fund raising and fin. devel. sect. 1991-92), Ind. State Libr. Adv. Coun., Midwest Fedn. Libr. Assns. (chmn. local arrangements for conf. 1986-87, sec. 1987—, bd. dirs. 1987-91), Ind. Libr. Assn. (chmn. coll. and univ. div. 1977-78, chmn. libr. edn. div. 1981-82, treas. 1984-86), German Shepherd Dog Club of Cen. Ind. (pres. 1978-79, treas. 1988-89, v.p. 1989-90, pres. 1990-93, bd. dirs. 1993—), Wabash Valley German Shepherd Dog Club (pres. 1982-83), Cen. Ind. Kennel Club (bd. dirs. 1984-86), Pi Kappa Lambda, Beta Phi Mu. Republican. Presbyterian. Home: 735 Lexington Ave Apt 3 Indianapolis IN 46203-1000 Office: Ind-Purdue U 755 W Michigan St Indianapolis IN 46202-5195

FISCHLER, SHIRLEY BALTER, lawyer; b. Bklyn., Oct. 9, 1926; d. David and Rose (Shapiro) Balter; m. Abraham Saul Fischler, Apr. 9, 1949; children: Bruce Evan, Michael Alan, Lori Faye. BA, Bklyn. Coll., 1947, MA, 1951; JD, Nova U., Ft. Lauderdale, Fla., 1977. Bar: Fla. 1977, D.C. 1980, U.S. Ct. Appeals (D.C. cir.) 1980. Tchr., N.Y.C. Bd. Edn., 1948-50, Richmond (Calif.) Pub. Schs., 1965-66; assoc. Panza, Maurer, Maynard, Platow & Neel, Ft. Lauderdale, 1977—; pro bono atty. Broward Lawyers Care, 1982-86. Bd. dirs. Broward Ctr. Performing Arts, 1993—; bd. govs. Nova. U. Law Ctr., 1982—; mem. Commn. on Status of Women, Broward County, Fla., 1982-87, vice chair, 1983-84, PACERS Broward County Ctr. for Performing Arts. Mem. Fla. Bar Assn., D.C. Bar Assn., Broward County Bar Assn. Home: 5000 Taylor St Hollywood FL 33021-5839 Office: Panza Maurer Maynard & Neel 3081 E Commercial Blvd Fort Lauderdale FL 33308-4329

FISCINA, ELIZABETH GLADYS, hotel industry administrator; b. Kew Gardens, N.Y., Mar. 27, 1944; d. Elizabeth C. Gaddis; m. Peter J. Fiscina (dec.); children: Vincent P. Musac, Elizabeth D. Musac Metz. Grad., L.I. Beauty Sch., Hempstead, N.Y., 1978. Lic. hairdresser. Cosmetologist, 1978; adminstrv. asst. I.W. Industries, Melville, N.Y., 1983-85; exec. housekeeper Woodcrest Club, Syosset, N.Y., 1986-87; head housekeeper Seawanhaka Corinthian Yacht Club, Centre Island, N.Y., 1987-88; exec. housekeeper Royal Inn Motor Lodge, Manhasset, N.Y., 1989-92; housekeeping mgr., 1992—. Home: 7 E Main St Oyster Bay NY 11771-2405

FISH, BARBARA, psychiatrist, educator; b. N.Y.C., July 31, 1920; d. Edward R. and Ida (Citrin) F.; m. Max Saltzman, Dec. 12, 1953; children: Mark, Ruth Saltzman Deutsch. B.A. summa cum laude, Barnard Coll., Columbia U., 1942; M.D., NYU, 1945. Diplomate Am. Bd. Psychiatry and Neurology, Am. Bd. child psychiatry. Intern Bellevue Hosp., N.Y.C., 1945-47, resident in pediatrics, 1948-49, resident in psychiatry, 1949-52; resident in pediatrics N.Y. Hosp., N.Y.C., 1947-48; practice medicine specializing in child psychiatry N.Y.C., 1952-65; instr. psychiatry Med. Coll Cornell U., N.Y.C., 1955-60; instr. pediatrics Cornell U., 1955-56, asst. prof. clin. pediatrics, 1956-60; child psychiatrist dept. pediatrics N.Y. Hosp.-Cornell Med. Center, 1955-60; mem. faculty William A. White Inst. Psychoanalysis, N.Y.C., 1957-66; assoc. prof. psychiatry sch. medicine N.Y. U., N.Y.C., 1960-70; prof. N.Y. U., 1970-72, adj. prof., 1972—, dir. child psychiatry med. ctr., 1960-72; prof. psychiatry and behavioral sci. UCLA, 1972-89, Della Martin prof. psychiatry and behavioral sci., 1989-91, Della Martin prof. psychiatry and behavioral sci. emeritus, 1991—; mem. advisory com. mental health services for children N.Y.C. Community Mental Health Bd., 1963-72; mem. profl. advisory com. on children N.Y. State Dept. Mental Hygiene, 1966-72; mem. com. cert. child psychiatry Am. Bd. Psychiatry and Neurology, 1969-77; mem. clin. program projects research rev. com. NIMH, 1976-78. Contbr. articles on the antecedents of schizophrenia and other severe mental disorders, and on the psychiat. diagnosis and treatment of children; mem. editorial bd.: Jour. Am. Acad. Child Psychiatry, 1966-71, Jour. Autism and Childhood Schizophrenia, 1971-74, Child Devel. Abstracts and Bibliography, 1974-82, Archives Gen. Psychiatry, 1975-84. Recipient Woman of Sci. award UCLA, 1978; NIMH grantee, 1961-72, 78-88, Harriett A. Ames Charitable Trust grantee, 1961-66, William T. Grant Found. grantee, 1977-83, Scottish Rite schizophrenia rsch. grantee, 1979-87. Fellow Am. Psychiat. Assn. (Agnes McGavin award 1987), Am. Acad. Child Psychiatry, Am. Coll. Neuropsychopharmacology (charter); mem. Am. Psychopath. Assn. (v.p. 1967-68), Assn. for Research in Nervous and Mental Diseases, Soc. Research in Child Devel., Psychiat. Research Soc. Home: 16428 Sloan Dr Los Angeles CA 90049-1157 Office: UCLA Neuropsychiat Inst 760 Westwood Plz Los Angeles CA 90024-8300

FISH, BARBARA JOAN, investor, small business owner; b. Seattle, June 12, 1936; d. George Francis Linehan and Maureece Shirley (Frederick) McCullough; m. Ralph Edwin Fish, July 14, 1956 (dec. Nov. 1986). Grad. high sch., Portland, Oreg. Owner Sea and Sand R.V. Park, Depoe Bay, Oreg., 1977—; real estate investor State of Oreg. Active St. Augustine's Ch. Mem. Lincoln City C. of C., Depoe Bay C. of C. Republican. Roman Catholic. Home and Office: Sea and Sand RV Park 4985 N Hwy 101 Depoe Bay OR 97341

FISH, HELEN THERESE, educator, author; b. Mpls., Mar. 17, 1944; d. John Howard and Helen Therese (Ochs) Berg; m. Ronadl Bruce Fish, Oct. 13, 1967 (div. May 1994); children: Eric James, Angela Diane, Christine Ann. BS, U. Minn., Mpls., 1966; postgrad., U. Minn., Mankato, 1969-70, U. Wis., Whitewater, 1970-72; MEd, Brenau Coll., 1986; EdS U. Ga in Admnistrn., U. Ga., 1992, postdoctoral, 1994. Cert. elem. tchr., Minn., Wis., Ill., Kans., Ga. Tchr. kindergarten Lincoln Hills Sch., Mpls., 1966-68, Mapleton (Minn.) Pub. Schs., 1968-69; tchr. 1st grade Hoover Sch., Mankato, 1969-70; kindergarten tchr. Todd Sch., Beloit, Wis., 1970-73; tchr. presch., K-1 Wilson Sch., Janesville, Wis., 1973-75; tchr. gifted and reading specialist (remedial) Lakewood Sch., Park Forest, Ill., 1975-77; tchr. kindergarten, 1st and 3d grades Sibley Sch., Albert Lea, Minn., 1977-82; tchr. kindergarten Most Pure Heart Sch., Topeka, 1983-85; tchr. kindergarten Enota Sch., Gainesville, Ga., 1985-88, chronicler Danforth grant, 1988-91; tchr. kindergarten Centennial Sch., Gainesville, Ga., 1992—; adj. asst. prof. Brenau U., Gainesville, Ga., 1988—, U. Ga., 1988—; cons. and field test tchr. Rsch. and Devel. Ctr. U. Wis., Madison, 1970-79, Ency. Britannica Edn. Corp.; workshop leader for adminstrs. and tchrs. in Pre-Reading Skills; demonstration tchr. Internat. Reading Assn. Conv., New Orleans, 1975. Author: Starting Out Well: A Parent's Approach to Exercise and Nutrition, 1989; editor Y's Menettes newsletter, 1971-75. Sec., treas. PTA, Mpls, Mankato, Albert Lea, Beloit, Janesville, Park Forest, Topeka, Gainesville; leader Girl Scouts U.S., Blue Birds, Topeka; softball coach, Gainesville. Recipient award for contbns. to edn. and participation in Tchr. in Space Program NASA, 1986; Cert. of World Leadership, Cambridge, Eng., 1990. Mem. Ga. Edn. Assn., Assn. for Supervision and Curriculum Devel., Ga. Presch. Assn., Internat. Platform Assn., Pi Lamda Theta (Hon. Teaching Soc. award). Republican. Roman Catholic. Home: 3650 Brown Well Ct Gainesville GA 30504-5774 Office: Centennial Sch Gainesville GA 30501

FISH, MARJORIA, quality assurance professional; b. Albany, N.Y., Dec. 16, 1958; d. Raymond Domenic and Arlene Marie (Kiciniski) F.; m. Richard Lawrence Weldon, Sept. 3, 1983 (div. Dec. 1988). BS in Biology and Psychology, Russell Sage Coll., 1980; MS in Health Svcs. Adminstrn., Sage Coll., 1994. Technologist Albany Med. Ctr. Hosp., 1981-83; rsch. asst. SUNY Rsch. Found., Albany, 1983-85; from rsch. scientist to quality assurance adminstr. II Sterling Winthrop Pharm., Rensselaer, N.Y., 1985-93; quality assurance mgr. Regeneron Pharm. Inc., Rensselaer, N.Y., 1993—. Mem. APHA, Am. Soc. Quality Control, N.E. N.Y. Pub. Health Assn., Parenteral Drug Assn. Democrat. Roman Catholic. Home: 34 Oakwood St Albany NY 12208 Office: Regeneron Pharm Inc 81 Columbia Tpke Rensselaer NY 12144

FISH, MICHELE LOYD, optical retailer; b. Belleville, Ill., Jan. 5, 1952; d. Delmer Edward and Patricia Ann (Marshall) Munie; m. Robert Wendelin Fish, May 25, 1973 (div. Feb. 1981). BS cum laude, U. Mo., 1973. Asst. buyer Famous-Barr, St. Louis, 1974-75, dept. mgr., 1975-76, buyer, 1976-81, store mgr., 1981-82; buyer Venture Stores, St. Louis, 1982-84, divsn. merchandise mgr., 1984-85, divsn. v.p., 1985-93; sr. v.p. Roman Co., St. Louis, 1993-94; sr. dir. merchandising and buying LensCrafters, Cin., 1995—; adv. bd. dept. textile and apparel mgmt. U. Mo., Columbia, 1987-94, chair, 1988-90. Active Olympic Festival Village, U.S. Olympic Festival, St. Louis, 1994, spl. venue mgr. Athlete's Village, 1994; dir. AMC Cancer Rsch. Ctr., 1986-94, also v.p., sec.; chair gifts Women's Event, 1988-94, chair gifts golf tournament, 1989-93, co-chair St. Louis Walks for Women, 1994; vol. Reach to Recovery, 1992-94; vol. coord. First Night St. Louis, 1994. Recipient Torch of Liberty award Anti-Defamation League, 1990, Citation of Merit, U. Mo., 1992. Republican. Roman Catholic. Home: 82 E Sherwood Dr Saint Louis MO 63114

FISH, NANCY, actress; b. N.Y.C.; d. Abraham Moses and Alice (Silver) Fisch; m. Ralph Harper Silver, July 6, 1968 (div. Dec. 1986); children: Natasha Silver, Light Silver; m. Walter Scott Perry II, Apr. 12, 1992. BA, Bennington Coll.; postgrad., Harvard U. Appeared in over 34 films including The Mask, Death Becomes Her, Terminator 2, Sleeping With the Enemy, The Exorcist III, Beethoven Birdy, Sudden Impact, The Conversation, Steelyard Blues, More American Graffiti; appeared in numerous stage prodns. including The Committee Revue, America Hurrah, Fedunn, Bleacher Bums; TV credits include recurring roles on Roseanne, Brooklyn Bridge, Hull High as well as guest star appearances in The Wonder Years, Thirtysomething, Head of the Class, Parenthood,. Mem. Acad. Motion Picture Arts and Scis., Actors Studio. Office: Camden ITG 822 S Robertson Blvd Los Angeles CA 90035

FISHBAUGH, CAROLE SUE, secondary school educator; b. Newark, Ohio, Mar. 11, 1938; d. Lawrence William Baird and Thelma Irene (Kennon) Baird-Thogmartin; m. Emerson LaVerna Fishbaugh, Sept. 11, 1961. BS in Edn., Ohio U., 1962; postgrad., Ohio State U., 1963-65, U. North Fla., 1985—, Jacksonville U., 1994. Cert. elem., K-12 reading tchr., K-12 tchr. mentally retarded, Fla. Elem. tchr. Greenfield (Ohio) Exempted Village Schs., 1958-60; elem. tchr. Newark Pub. Schs., 1960-61, tchr. mentally retarded, 1961-62. 63-65; tchr. mentally retarded Alexandria (Va.) Pub. Schs., 1962-63; vice prin. Lincoln Jr. High Sch., Newark, 1964-65; tchr. reading Nassau County Pub. Schs., Fernandina Beach, Fla., 1986-93; contact person reading dept. Fernandina Beach Mid. Sch., 1990-93, mem. sch. adv. coun., 1991—, contact person for alternative edn., chair dept. alternative edn., 1993-94, chair sch. improvement adv. counsel, 1994—, tchr. varied exceptionalities, 1994—, mem. dist. team, 1994—; mem. grant com. Fernandina Beach Mid. Sch., 1992—. Mem. ch. and soc. com., organizer drug abuse fight Meml. United Meth. Ch., Fernandina Beach, 1987; mem. adminstrv. coun. Meth. Children's Home Soc. for United Meth. ch., 1987—; mem. Fernandina Beach Task Force to Fight Crime, 1992—; dist rep. Sch. Adv. Coun., 1994-95. Mem. ASCD, AAUW, Nat. Mid. Sch. Assn., Fla. League Mid. Schs., Nassau Tchrs. Assn. (sch. rep. 1987-90, treas. 1988-90, rep. on sch. improvement 1992, sec. 1994), Order Eastern Star. Democrat. Office: Fernandina Beach Mid Sch 315 Citrona Dr Fernandina Beach FL 32034-2739

FISHBONE, VIVIAN MANPERL, artist; b. N.Y.C., July 13, 1926; d. Isidore and Rose (Kovner) Manperl; m. Stanley E. Zeeman, June 21, 1947 (div. July 1966); children: Susan Rogers, Wendy Blom; m. Herbert Fishbone, Oct. 23, 1966. AB, Skidmore Coll., 1946; postgrad., Lehigh U., 1964-66, Art Students League, N.Y.C., 1966-70. Rsch. asst. Rockefeller Inst., N.Y.C., 1946, Jefferson Med. Coll., Phila., 1947-50; rsch. asst. dept. phys. medicine U. Pa., Phila., 1947; tchr. Pennridge Jr. High Sch., Perkasie, Pa., 1965-66. Fifteen one-woman shows, 1978—, including Kemerer Mus., Bethlehem, Pa., 1986, Four Corners Gallery, Lambertville, N.J., 1987, 89, Touchstone Theater, Bethlehem, 1992; exhibited in group shows, 1978—, including Allentown (Pa.) Art Mus., 1978, 81, 89, Lehigh U., Bethlehem, 1980, Hunterdon Art Ctr., Clinton, N.J., 1981, 84, 86, 88, 89, Lehigh Art Alliance, Allentown, 1982, 84, Kemerer Mus., 1985, Muhlenberg Coll., Allentown, 1984, 86, 93; represented by Bixler Gallery, Stroudsburg, Pa. Bd. dirs. Kemerer Mus., 1987-90. Winner Easton (Pa.) Ctr. Square Show, 1979; recipient best of show award Easton Area Artists, 1971, 1st prize for portraiture, 1975; purchase prize Easton Pub. Libr., 1972, 1st prize for oil or acrylic Cmty. Art League, Easton, 1979, 1st prize Juried Mems. Show, Hunterdon Art Ctr., Clinton, N.J., 1994. Mem. A Family of Artists, Lehigh Valley Arts Coun., Lehigh Art Alliance (bd. dirs. 1970-75, floating award 1982), Women in Arts, Art Students League (life), New Arts Program. Home and Studio: 431 Paxinosa Rd E Easton PA 18042-1337

FISHER, ANDREA, art dealer; b. Pitts., Sept. 15, 1944; d. Andrew and Antoinette Lapitski; children: Andrew L., Derek M. AB, U. Calif., Berkeley, 1966. Cert. secondary sch. tchr. Calif., 1969. Buyer Emporium Capwell, San Francisco, 1966-68; tchr. Mt. Diablo Sch. Dist., Concord, Calif., 1969-72; pres. Serendipity Catering, Santa Fe, 1979-84; owner Fisher Enterprises, Santa Fe, 1979-85; mgr., buyer Case Trading Post Wheelwright Mus. Am. Indian, Santa Fe, 1985-93; owner Andrea Fisher Fine Pottery, Santa Fe, 1993—; cons. in field; lectr. in field. Bd. dirs. Santa Fe Cmty. Found., 1990-94, Wheelwright Mus. Am. Indian, Santa Fe, 1980-84, Coun. Internat. Rels., Santa Fe, 1979-81; coach Nat. Elem. Sch. Championship Chess Team, 1984; judge 8th No. Indian Pueblos Arts and Crafts Fair. Recipient Hort. Sweepsteaks, N.Mex. Coun. Garden Clubs, Santa Fe, 1981, Best Regional Dish award Am. Culinary Inst., N.Y., 1985; named N.Mex. State Women's Chess Champion, 1982. Mem. Nat. Mus. Store Assn. (chair Rocky Mountains, mem. nat. nominating com.), N.Mex. Mus. Found., Indian Arts & Crafts Assn., Friends Ethnic Art, Santa Fe Garden Club (hon.), Nat. Assn. Woman Bus. Owners. Home: Jacona Plaza Rte 5 Box 230 Santa Fe NM 87501-9309 Office: Andrea Fisher Fine Pottery 221 W San Francisco St Santa Fe NM 87501

FISHER, ANITA JEANNE, English language educator; b. Atlanta, Oct. 22, 1937; d. Paul Benjamin and Cora Ozella (Wadsworth) Chappelear; m. Kirby Lynn Fisher, Aug. 6, 1983; 1 child by previous marriage, Tracy Ann. BA, Bob Jones U., 1959; pstgrad., Stetson U., 1961, 87, U. Fla., 1963; MAT, Rollins Coll., 1969; PhD in Am. Lit., Fla. State U., 1975; postgrad., Writing Inst., U. Cen. Fla., 1978, NEH Inst., 1979, U. Cen. Fla., 1987, Stetson U., 1987, U. Fla., 1987, 90. Cert. English, gifted and adminstn. supr. Chmn. basic learning improvement program, secondary sch. Orange County, Orlando, Fla., 1964-65; chmn. composition Winter Park High Sch., Fla., 1978-80; chmn. English depts. Orange County Pub. Schs., Fla., 1962, 71; reading tchr. Woodland Hall Acad., Reading Rsch. Inst., Tallahassee, 1976; instr. edn., journalism, reading, Spanish, thesis writing Bapt. Bible Coll., Springfield, Mo., 1976-77; prof. English, S.W. Mo. State U., Springfield, 1980-84, instr. continuing edn., courses in music and creative writing, 1981-82, editor LAD Leaf; tchr. Volusia County Schs., Fla., 1984-88, gifted students, 1986-88; tchr. Lee County Schs., 1988—; adj. prof. Edison Community Coll., U. So. Fla., 1989—, Barry U., 1993—; mem. steering com. So. Assn. Colls. and Schs., 1989-90; speaker in field. Contbr. writings to publs. in field, papers to nat. profl. confs. Vol. Greene County Action Com., 1977, Heart Fund, 1982; book reviewer Voice of Youth Advs. Writing Program fellow U. Cen. Fla., 1978. Mem. Lee County Coun. Tchrs. Eng., Kappa Delta Pi, Phi Delta Kappa. Republican. Presbyterian.

FISHER, BARBARA TURK, school psychologist; b. Bklyn., Feb. 21, 1940; d. Jack and Reva (Miller) Turk; m. Ronnie Herbert Fisher, Aug. 15, 1961; children: Sylvia Kay, Mark Lee. BA, Fla. State U., 1961; MS, Barry U., 1966, EdS, 1977; EdD, Nova U., 1989. Coord. of counseling Immaculate La Salle High Sch., Miami, Fla., 1966-69; rehab. counselor Miami Adult Tng. Ctr., 1969-70; sch. psychologist Dade County Sch. Sys., Miami, 1970—; instr. Miami Dade C.C., 1991; presenter at profl. assn. meetings and social sci. seminars, 1993. Fellow AAUW; mem. Dade County Asns. Sch. Psychologists. Republican. Jewish. Home: 234 Antiquera Ave Apt 3 Miami FL 33134-2914 Office: Dade County BPI Region I Office 733 E 57th St Hialeah FL 33013-1357

FISHER, CAROL GARRETT, university administrator; b. Columbus, Ohio, June 26, 1940; d. Alfred Benjamin and Jessie (Campbell) Garrett; m. Alan Washburn Fisher, Aug. 24, 1963; children: Elizabeth, A. Christy, Garrett L. BA, Ohio Wesleyan Univ., 1962; MA, NYU, 1966, Mich. State U., 1976; PhD, Mich. State U., 1981. Instr. Lansing (Mich.) C.C., 1978-87; edn. coord. Kresge Art Mus., Mich. State U., East Lansing, 1985—; adj. prof. dept. of art Mich. State U., 1981, 84, 86, 91, 93; co-dir. Smithson Regional Tchrs. Workshop, East Lansing, 1991-93; cons. Pub. Broadcasting Sys., Channel 13, N.Y.C., 1986-87, Project on Art History in the Humanities, East Lansing High Sch., 1983-84; coord. edn. programs Kresge Art Mus., 1985—, vis. curator, 1981-82, 84, 91, instr. docent program, 1982, 84; coord. Medieval Symposium, 1986—. Asst. editor Kresge Art Mus. Bull., 1985-86, editor, 1987-92; contbr. numerous articles to profl. publs. Travel grant Nat. Endowment for the Humanities, 1990, Inst. of Turkish Studies, 1988-89. Mem. N.Am. Historians of Islamic Art (sec., treas. 1991—), Coll. Art Assn., Am. Inst. of Archaeology (pres., v.p. ctrl. Mich. 1987-89), Turkish Studies Assn., Middle East Studies Assn., Phi Soc., Phi Kappa Phi. Home: 830 Lantern Hill Dr East Lansing MI 48823 Office: Kresge Art Mus Mich State U East Lansing MI 48824

FISHER, CARRIE FRANCES, actress, writer; b. Oct. 21, 1956; d. Eddie Fisher and Debbie Reynolds; m. Paul Simon, 1983 (div. 1984); 1 child, Billie Catherine. Ed. high sch., Beverly Hills, Calif.; student, London Cen. Sch. Speech and Drama. Mem. chorus in Broadway musical Irene, 1972, also in Broadway prodn. Censored Scenes from King Kong; appeared in films Shampoo, 1975, Star Wars, 1977, Mr. Mike's Mondo Video, 1979, The Blues Brothers, 1980, The Empire Strikes Back, 1980, Under the Rainbow, 1981, Return of the Jedi, 1983, Garbo Talks, 1984, The Man with One Red Shoe, 1985, Hannah and Her Sisters, 1986, Hollywood Vice Squad, 1986, Amazon Women on the Moon, 1987, Appointment With Death, 1988, When Harry Met Sally..., 1989, The 'Burbs, 1989, Loverboy, 1989, She's Back, 1989, Sibling Rivalry, 1990, Drop Dead Fred, 1991, Soapdish, 1991, This Is My Life, 1992; TV movies include Come Back, Little Sheba, (spl.) 1977, Leave Yesterday Behind, 1978, Liberty, Sunday Drive, 1986, Sweet Revenge, 1990; author: Postcards from the Edge, 1987, (also screenplay, 1990), Surrender the Pink, 1990, Delusions of Grandma, 1994. Office: Kaufman 1201 Alta Loma Rd West Hollywood CA 90069*

FISHER, DENISE DANCHES, public relations executive, marketing consultant; b. Miami Beach, Fla.. AA, Miami Dade Coll., 1975; BA in Communcations, U. Miami, 1977. Asst. continuity dir. WSVN-Channel 7, Miami, 1972-73; trade practice cons. Better Bus. Bur., Miami, 1973-74; asst. sales promotion dir. John Donnelly & Sons, Miami, 1974-75; mktg. dir. Dadeland Mall, Miami, 1978-83; advt. dir. Galleria Novita, Miami, 1983-84; freelance cons. Miami, 1984—; community relations dir. Am. Lung Assn., Miami, 1986-91; community rels. coord. Hospice of Metro Denver. Tchr. Confrat. Christian Doctrine, St. Joseph's Ch., 1988—, Ch. of Risen Christ, 1991—. Recipient Addy awards, 1978, 80, Communications Excellence award Congress Lung Assn., 1989. Mem. Pub. Rels. Soc. Am. (accredited, chpt. bd. dirs.), Advt. Fedn. Republican. Office: Hospice of Metro Denver 3955 E Exposition Ave Ste 500 Denver CO 80209-5033

FISHER, ELLENA ALLMOND, librarian; b. Windsor, Va.; d. Calvin Percy and Oretha Mae (Eley) Allmond; m. Eddie Lee Fisher; children: Ellena II, Melba. BA cum laude, Va. Union U.; MS, Atlanta U. Lang. asst. Va. Union U., Richmond, tutor; libr. assoc. Atlanta U.; rsch. asst. Econ. Opportunity Atlanta; clk. typist West Employment Svc., River Forest, Ill.; monitor testing Pasadena (Calif.) Coll. Skills Ctr.; reference libr. L.A. Pub. Libr.; young adult libr. Mark Twain Libr., L.A.; mem. book com. L.A. Pub. Libr., 1990; founder teen writing club; founder Roger Williams Libr.; pres., CEO Ellena Calvin Enterprises; mem. adv. bd. Am. Biog. Inst. Mem. Castle Heights Sch. PTA, L.A., 1985-86; Doug Wilder supporter, Va. Named World Intellectual of 1993; named to Women's Inner Circle of Achievement, The 1st 500; hon. doctorate London Inst. for Applied Rsch., Third World Coll. (Paris). Mem. NAFE, Am. Investors Network, Calif. Librs., Our Authors Study Club, Young Adult Reviewers. Baptist. Home: 3507 Clyde

Ave Los Angeles CA 90016-5043 Office: Mark Twain Libr 9621 S Figueroa St Los Angeles CA 90003-3928

FISHER, HEIDI ALICE, librarian; b. Quakertown, Pa., Mar. 31, 1963; d. David Allen and Martha Catherine (Breisch) F. BA in Latin, St. Olaf Coll., 1985; MS, Drexel U., 1987. Grad. asst. Drexel U. Hagerty Libr., Phila., 1985-87; asst. order libr. LI order divsn. Princeton (N.J.) U., 1987-90, asst. order libr. LII Firestone Libr., 1990—. Mem. N.Am. Serials Interest Group. Home: 574 Doloro Dr Morrisville PA 19067-6833 Office: Princeton U Libr 1 Washington Rd Princeton NJ 08544-2002

FISHER, JEANETTE NELSON, communications executive; b. Wichita, Kans., Nov. 14, 1942; d. Russell Alan and Jean (Branch) Nelson; m. E. Gregory, M.D., June 15, 1963; children: Ted, Ann, Betsy, Matt, Kate. Student, Mt. Carmel Acad., Wichita, 1960; BA, Rosary Coll., River Forest, 1964. Chmn. 48er's Vols. Sta. WCET-TV, Cin., 1973-75; v.p. bd. dirs. Santa Maria Community Service, Cin., 1980-87; vol. coord. PRO Kids, Cin., 1986-87; chmn. Hamilton County Children's Trust Fund; reg. rep. Nat. CASA, 1988. Named Vol. of the Year Pro Kids, 1986. Mem. Hamilton County Children's, Pro Kids Bd. of Dirs., Cin. Women's Ins. Sales, Altrusa Women's Club. Democrat. Roman Catholic. Home: 1421 Herschel Ave Cincinnati OH 45208-2531 Office: Pro Kids 222 E Central Pky # 209A Cincinnati OH 45202-6207

FISHER, (MARY) JEWEL TANNER, retired construction company executive; b. Port Lavaca, Tex., Oct. 31, 1918; d. Thomas M. and Minnie Frances (Dunks) Tanner; grad. Tex. Luth. Coll., 1937; m. King Fisher, Aug. 13, 1937; children—Ann Fisher Boyd, Linda Fisher LaQuay. Sec. treas. King Fisher Marine Svc., Inc., Port Lavaca, 1959-82; dir., cons. King Fisher Marine Svc.; artist. Trustee Meml. Med. Ctr., 1976-81, 90-94, pres. bd. trustees, 1992-93; trustee Golden Crescent Coun. Govts., 1980-81, Crisis Hotline Calhoun County, 1985-93. Lic. pvt. pilot. Mem. DAR (regent Guadalupe Victoria chpt. 1986-88), Daus. Republic Tex., 99's, Internat. Orgn. Women Pilots. Home: PO Box 166 Port Lavaca TX 77979-0166 Office: PO Box 108 Port Lavaca TX 77979-0108

FISHER, JIMMIE LOU, state official; b. Delight, Ark., Dec. 31, 1941. Student, Ark. State U.; grad. John F. Kennedy Sch. Govt., Harvard U., 1985. Treas. Greene County, Ark., 1971-78; auditor State of Ark., Little Rock, 1979, treas., 1981—; sec. Ark. State Bd. Fin. Mem. Ark. Bd. Election Commrs.; trustee, ex-offico mem. Ark. Pub. Employees Retirement System, Ark. Tchr. Retirement System; trustee Ark. State Hwy. Retirement System; former vice chair Dem. State Com.; former mem. Dem. Nat. Com.; del. Dem. Nat. Conv., 1988; past pres. Ark. Dem. Women's Club. Mem. State Bd. Fin. (sec.), State Bd. Election Commrs., Nat. Assn. State Treas. (pres.). Office: Treasury Dept 220 State Capitol Bldg Little Rock AR 72201-1059*

FISHER, KATHI ANN, business owner; b. Ft. Bragg, N.C., Apr. 13, 1955; d. Eugene and Roberta Walmer; divorced; 1 child, William Curtis. Student, Ohio State U., 1982-84. With sales Gilardis Pizza, Sidney, Ohio, 1984-87, Diapaolo Sysco, Columbus, Ohio, 1987-88, Tricor Indsl., Wooster, 1989-91, B&G Supply, Akron, Ohio, 1992-94; owner 300 Below Zero, Wooster, 1994—. Mem. NAFE, Am. Soc. Metals. Office: 300 Below Zero 540 High St Wooster OH 44691

FISHER, LAURA LANI, physician, medical educator; b. East Orange, N.J., July 13, 1959; d. Hyman Wendell and Rosalie Jane (Joseph) F. BA in Biology and Biomed. Ethics, Brown U., 1981, MD, 1984. Intern in internal medicine N.Y. Hosp., 1984-85, resident in internal medicine, 1985-87, chief resident in medicine, 1989-90, dir. Lyme Disease Ctr., 1990—; from clin. to rsch. fellow in infectious diseases Mass. Gen. Hosp., Boston, 1987-89; dir. student health svc. Cornell Med. Coll., N.Y.C., 1990-93, asst. prof. medicine, 1990—; infectious disease cons. McAdams, Inc., N.Y.C., 1990—. Contbr. articles to profl. jours. Mem. nat. cabinet Israel Bonds-Young Leadership, U.S., 1992-94, mem. city bd. dirs., 1993-94; mem. Anti-Defamation League, N.Y.C., 1993-94; mem. Park East-Young Leadership, N.Y.C., 1994. Recipient Rsch. Scientist award NIH, 1988-89. Fellow ACP; mem. AMA, N.Y. Med. Soc., Mass. Med. Soc., Brown Med. Soc., Infectious Disease Soc. Am. Democrat. Jewish. Office: 449 E 68th St Ste 8 New York NY 10021

FISHER, LINDA ALICE, physician; b. Plainfield, N.J., Dec. 27, 1947; d. Alvin Edwin and Bertha Sophie (Steigmann) F. BA, Douglass Coll., New Brunswick, N.J., 1970; M in Med. Sci., Rutgers U., 1972; MD, Harvard U., 1975. Diplomate Am. Bd. Internal Medicine. Intern, then resident Jewish Hosp. St. Louis, 1975-78; dir. ambulatory care St. Luke's Hosp., St. Louis, 1978-84; chief med. officer St. Louis County Dept. Health, Clayton, 1984—; bd. overseers St. Louis Regional Med. Ctr., 1985—; chief physician St. Louis Met. Police Dept., 1978-88; instr. clin. medicine Washington U., St. Louis, 1978-94, asst. prof. 1994—; asst. prof. clin. medicine, St. Louis U., 1979—; cons. Ill. Local Govtl. Law Enforcement Officers Tng. Bd., 1988. Contbr. articles to profl. jours. Chmn. licensure com. Mo. Bd. Registration for Healing Arts, 1983-86; adv. coun. Girl Scouts U.S., 1986—. Fellow ACP; mem. AMA, APHA, Am. Med. Women's Assn. (chpt. pres. 1982-85), Nat. Assn. Physician Broadcasters, St. Louis Met. Med. Soc. (councilor 1982-84, sec. 1986, editor 1989-90), Mo. Women's Forum. Lutheran.

FISHER, LUCY J., motion picture company executive; b. N.Y.C., Oct. 2, 1949; d. Arthur Bertram and Naomi (Kislak) F.; m. Douglas Z. Wick, Feb. 16, 1986; children: Sarah, Julia, Tessa. BA, Harvard U., 1971. V.p. prodn. 20th Century Fox, L.A., 1979-80; v.p. worldwide prodns. Zoetrope Studios, Burbank, Calif., 1980-81; v.p., sr. prodn. exec. Warner Bros. Pictures, Burbank, 1981-87, sr. v.p., 1987-89, exec. v.p. prodn., 1989—. Mem. Hollywood Women's Polit. Com., L.A., 1988-90. Office: Warner Bros Pictures 4000 Warner Blvd Burbank CA 91522-0001*

FISHER, M. JANICE, hospital administrator; b. Phila., Dec. 16, 1937; d. Joseph John and Phyllis R. (Catarro) Ronollo. AS, Delaware County C.C., 1987. Dir. vol. resources Haverford (Pa.) State Hosp., 1971-86; liaison Friends of Haverford State Hosp., 1986—. Pres. Local 2347 Am. Fedn. State, County, Mcpl. Employees Cheney U., 1976-83, Local 2346, Haverford State Hosp., 1987-88. Mem. Am. Hosp. Assn., Assn. Dirs. Vol. Svcs., Lioness Club Aston Twp., Delt. Valley Assn. Dirs. Vol. Programs, M.L.B. Club (v.p.). Home: 250 Beverly Blvd Apt B-105 Upper Darby PA 19082

FISHER, MARY MARGARET, legislative staff member; b. Phoenix, Nov. 19, 1964. BBA, U. Notre Dame, 1987; JD, Am. U., 1990. Legis. aide Sen. Christopher S. Bond, 1991-93; minority counsel Senate Banking Com., 1993—. Office: Banking Housing & Urban Affairs G-08 Senate Dirksen Office Bldg Washington DC 20510*

FISHER, MARY MAURINE, federal agency official; b. Schenectady, N.Y., July 19, 1929; d. Maurice Lee and Beatrice Mae (Harris) Prescott; m. Eugene T. Fisher, Apr. 16, 1948 (dec. 1982); children: Gene Thomas, William Lee. BA, Strayer Coll., 1952; postgrad., U. Va., 1966-89. Credit mgr. Gen. Electric Credit Corp., Washington, 1950-70; with SBA, Washington, 1970—; mem. Pres.'s adv. com. on small and minority bus., 1979-85, on Native Am. affairs, 1979-80, on reservation devel., 1978-79, on Native Am. econ. devel., 1977-78. Mem. Fairfax (Va.) Little League, 1956-74, Fairfax Indsl. Devel. Authority, 1985—; treas. Warren Woods-Joyce Heights Civic Assn., Fairfax, 1958—; active Friends of Fairfax City. Mem. Nat. Contract Mgmt. Assn. Democrat. Methodist. Home: 4203 Lamarre Dr Fairfax VA 22030-5133

FISHER, NANCY, writer, producer, director; b. N.Y.C., Oct. 21, 1941; d. Seymour and Tema F.; 1 child, Sarah Olivia. B.A., Barnard Coll. Creative group head Benton & Bowles Advt., London, 1970-74, McCann Erickson Advt., N.Y.C., 1974-75; creative dir. Norman, Craig & Kummel Advt., N.Y.C., 1975-78; pres. Nancy Fisher Inc., N.Y.C., 1978—; pres. Creative Programming, Inc., N.Y.C., 1981-89. Author: Vital Parts, 1993, Side Effects, 1994. Creator, writer, producer TV series Womanwatch, 1982-89, Celebrity Chefs, 1983-89; numerous home video cassettes including Look Mom, I'm Fishing (Parents Choice award), The Annapolis Book of Seamanship Video Series (Cindy award), The Christmas Carol Video, Video Dog, Video Cat, Video Baby. Recipient 5 broadcast awards Network Documentary Series. Mem. Dirs. Guild of Am., Authors Guild, Wings (N.Y.C.). Office: 200 E 84th St New York NY 10028-2906

FISHER, NANCY LYNNE, medical/surgical nurse, pre-admission nurse; b. Pottstown, Pa., Sept. 14, 1947; d. Frank Keyser and Ruth May (Grater) Elliott; (div.); children: Ashley Brewer, Tara Brewer; m. James Christian Fisher, June 18, 1983; stepchildren: Sloan, Nicole. Diploma, Sch. of Nursing, St. Joseph's Hosp., Reading, Pa., 1981; BSN summa cum laude, Kutztown U., 1993. Med./surg., neuro. staff nurse Pottstown (Pa.) Meml. Med. Ctr., 1981-83, orthopedic staff nurse, 1983-87, med./surg., neuro staff nurse, 1987—, substitute pre-admission surg. nurse, 1990-93, outpatient surg. nurse, pre-admission surg. nurse, 1993—; student rep. to nursing faculty orgn. Nursing Forum of Kutztown, Pa., 1991-93. Recipient David Hottenstein award in nursing Kutztown U.; Berk's County Fedn. of Women's Club scholar, Reading, Pa., 1991. Mem. Assn. Ambulatory Care Providers Ea. Pa., Kutztown U. Honors Program, Nursing Honor Soc., Honors Club. Mem. Bible Fellowship Ch. Home: 202 Main St Oley PA 19547

FISHER, PATRICIA SWEENEY, business executive, lawyer; b. Chgo., Sept. 11, 1954; d. Michael C. and Mary J. (Moore) Sweeney. BA, Northwestern U., 1975; JD, Northwestern U., Chgo., 1978; postgrad., Harvard U. Sch. Bus., 1990. Bar: Ill. 1978, Ind. 1990. Assoc. Isham, Lincoln & Beale, Chgo., 1978-81; gen. atty. Amoco Corp., Chgo., 1981-90, asst. treas., 1990-93; v.p., treas. United Air Lines, Chgo., 1993—. Office: United Air Lines EXOTS PO Box 66100 AMF Ohare IL 60666

FISHER, SALLIE ANN, chemist; b. Green Bay, Wis., Sept. 10, 1923. BS in Chemistry, U. Wis., 1945, MS, 1946, PhD, 1949. Instr. Mt. Holyoke Coll., South Hadley, Mass., 1949-50; asst. prof. U. Minn., Duluth, 1950-51; group leader Rohm & Haas Co., Phila., 1951-60; assoc. dir. rsch. Robinette Rsch. Labs., Berwyn, Pa., 1960-72; v.p. Puricons, Inc., Malvern, Pa., 1972-76; pres. Puricons, Inc., Malvern, 1976—; mem. adv. bd. Internat. Water Conf., Pitts., 1976-91, Reactive Polymers, Netherlands, 1982-88. Contbr. chpts. to books and over 95 articles to profl. jours. Recipient award of merit Engring. Soc. Western Pa., Pitts., 1984. Fellow ASTM (vice-chmn. D-19 1972-78, award of merit 1974, Max Hecht award com. D-19 1975); mem. Soc. Chem. Industry, Am. Chem. Soc., Am. Waterworks Assn., Nat. Assn. Corrosion Engrs. Office: Puricons Inc 101 Quaker Ln Malvern PA 19355-2480

FISHER, SHIRLEY IDA A., photography and humanities educator; b. Cleve., Aug. 7, 1935; d. E. and I. (Morley) F. BFA, Ohio U., 1957, MFA, 1959; postgrad., U. Calif., Berkeley, 1964—, U. Calif., Santa Cruz, 1964—. Instr. Detroit Community Ctr., 1960-63; med. photographer Ford Hosp., Detroit, 1961-63; comml. photographer Detroit, 1960-63; photo producer San Jose State U., 1963-70, prof. photography, 1966-67; prof. digital photography and humanities, coord. dept. De Anza Coll., Cupertino, Calif., 1967—, founder digital photography dept., 1985—; photojournalist to Mexican, Ruerto Rican and Costa Rican dept. tourism; photographer in over 56 countries; owner Hispanic and Anglo Publs., San Jose, 1986—, World Images Photography, Cupertino, 1963—; 1st invited Am. photographer to Ecuador. Work represented in internat. mus., embassies, bi-nat. ctrs. and pvt. collections; author, editor: Argentine and Chilean Photo, 1984, Cinco de Mayo en San Jose, 1987; editor: Self Reflections, 1987. Am. participant USIS serving in Ecuador, Uruguay, Chile, Bolivia, Venezuela, Brazil, Argentina, 1981-86. Mem. Soc. Photog. Edn., Sister Cities San Jose (Calif.), Friends of Photography, Peninsula Advt. Photographers Assn., Adobe Users Group, Phi Theta Kappa, Kappa Alpha Mu. Home and Office: PO Box 1081 Cupertino CA 95015-1081

FISHER, SUSAN KAY, nuclear industry supply company executive, accountant; b. Atlanta, Apr. 12, 1948; d. Jack Eugene and Alma Louise (Ashley) Ferguson; m. Martin Prell Fisher, Aug. 19, 1972 (div. 1978); 1 child, Susan Ashley. BA, Samford U., 1970. CPA, Miss. Tchr. math. Franklin County Bd. of Edn., Rocky Mountain, Va., 1972-74; sr. acct. Koury, Ready & Lefoldt, Jackson, Miss., 1977-79; controller Patterson Enterprises, Ltd., Jackson, 1979-81; v.p. fin. and adminstrn. Fred. S. James of Miss., Jackson, 1981-83; pres., owner The Office Mgr., Jackson, 1983-85; v.p. Divesco Inc., Jackson, 1985—, also bd. dirs.; officer, bd. dirs. Divesco, Inc., Jackson. Bd. dirs. United Cerebral Palsy, Jackson, 1984, Make-a-Wish Found. Miss., 1986-87; bd. dirs. Friends of Children's Hosp., 1988-89; chair stewardship com. Rankin County Bapt. Assn., 1993, mem., 1994—. Mem. AICPA, Assn. Records Mgrs. and Adminstrs. (pres. 1984-85), Jackson Aquatic Club (treas. 1990-91), Am. Nuclear Soc., Am. Soc. Quality Control. Home: 27 Bastille St Brandon MS 39042-8551 Office: Divesco Inc 5000 Hwy 80 E Jackson MS 39208-4255

FISHER, WENDY ASTLEY-BELL, marketing executive; b. London, Jan. 23, 1944; came to U.S., 1947; d. Leonard Astley and Rita (Duis) Astley-Bell; m. Richard Van Mell, Mar. 21, 1970 (div. May 1980); m. Lester Emil Fisher, Jan. 23, 1981. Student, Hood Coll., 1961-63, U. Alta., Can., summer 1963; BA honors, Northwestern U., 1965; postgrad., U. Chgo., 1965-66. Lab. technician Northwestern U. Med. Sch., Chgo., 1966-67; designer Okamoto/London Studio, Chgo., 1967-71, Communications Internat., Chgo., 1971-72; freelance artist K&S Photographics, Chgo., 1972-76; dir. spl. projects Lincoln Park Zool. Soc., Chgo., 1976-81; mem. pub. rels. staff Field Enterprises, Chgo., 1981; pres., creative dir. Mailworks, Inc., Chgo., 1981—; speaker in field. Co-author: The First Hundred Years, 1975; contbr. articles to profl. jours. Bd. dirs. Jr. League Chgo., 1965-74, Vis. Nurse Assn. Chgo., 1978-82; mem. women's bd. Lincoln Park Zool. Soc., 1981-84; trustee Crow Canyon Archeol. Ctr., 1994—. Recipient Gold Cert. Chgo. Savs. and Loan Assn., 1973, Award of Merit Splty. Advt. Assn., 1979; named Outstanding Women Entrepreneur Chgo. chpt. Women in Communications, 1983. Mem. Nat. Soc. Fundraising Execs. (bd. dirs. Chgo. chpt. 1982-88, Pres.'s award 1987, cert. in fundraising), Chgo. Assn. Direct Mktg. (bd. dirs. 1982-87, bd. dirs. edn. found. 1985-87), Assn. Direct Response Fundraising Counsel, Direct Mktg. Assn. (Leadership award 1978), Am. Assn. Mus., Am. Assn. Zool. Parks and Aquariums, Econ. Club Chgo. Office: Mailworks Inc 230 N Michigan Ave Chicago IL 60601-5910

FISHERMAN, NINA YARLOVSKY, nursing administrator; b. Flin Flon, Man., Can., Oct. 5, 1955; d. Vasyl Nicolov and Milka Georgi (Krehtinkoff) Yarlovsky; m. Jay Richard Fisherman, June 26, 1983. BS, Roanoke Coll., 1977; postgrad., Autonomous U. Guadalajara, 1977-79; MS, Pace U. Grad. Sch. Nursing, 1982. Staff nurse oncology Yonkers (N.Y.) Gen. Hosp., 1982-83, Montefiore Med. Ctr., Bronx, N.Y., 1984-85; br. mgr., nursing supr. Staff Builders, Health Care Svcs., Inc., Flushing, N.Y., 1985-88; inpatient nurse mgr. Ritter-Scheuer Hospice, Bronx, 1988-90; supr. home care Jacob Perlow Hospice, Beth Israel Med. Ctr., N.Y.C., 1990; patient care mgr. Westmoreland Hospice, Greensburg, Pa., 1992-93; dir. clin. svcs. Olsten Kimberly Quality Care, Inc., White Plains, N.Y., 1993—; presenter AIDS conf. Mem. Nat. Hospice Orgn., N.Y. State Hospice Assn.

FISHER WHITMORE, EVE PHYLLIS, psychologist; b. Houston, Apr. 20, 1959; d. Seymour and Rhoda Lee (Feinberg) Fisher; m. Mark Denton Whitmore, Apr. 30, 1988. BA, U. Rochester, 1981; MA, Ohio State U., 1983, PhD, 1987. Postdoctorl clin. rsch. intern Ohio State U., Columbus, 1987-89; psychologist State of Ohio, Columbus, 1991—; adj. psychologist Columbus State C.C., 1989-90; vis. asst. prof. Ohio Wesleyan U., Delaware, Ohio, 1990-91. Contbr. articles to profl. jours. Mem. Am. Psychol. Assn., Ohio Psychol. Assn. (com. mem. 1991—), Columbus Ohio Psychol. Assn. Home: 3768 Darbyshire Dr Hilliard OH 43026

FISHKIND, LINDA SUSAN, counselor; b. N.Y.C., June 22, 1954; d. Demetrios and Athie (Poulos) Zouzoulas; m. Henry Herman Fishkind, Oct. 11, 1987. BA, Fla. Atlantic U., 1976; student, U. N.C., 1976-79; MA, U. Ctrl. Fla., 1992. Rsch. asst. U. N.C., Chapel Hill, 1976-79; pres., owner Eagle Rsch. & Comm., Boca Raton, Fla., 1980-83; v.p. comm. Broward Econ. Devel. Bd., Ft. Lauderdale, Fla., 1983-86; v.p. Fishkind & Assocs., Inc., Orlando, Fla., 1988—; psychology specialist UCF Counseling and Testing Ctr., Orlando, 1991—. Mem. ACA, Fla. Assn. Counseling, Fla. Audubon Soc. (chpt. rep. 1992—), Orange Audubon Soc. (bd. mem., pres. 1992—). Home: 604 W Palm Valley Dr Oviedo FL 32765 Office: UCF Counseling & Testing PO Box 163170 Orlando FL 32816-3170

FISHMAN, CLAIRE, media specialist; b. Croydon, Surrey, Eng.; came to U.S., 1968; d. Jack and Anne (Greenberg) Ritoff; m. Leon Fishman, Sept. 2, 1962 (dec. July 1976); children: Jonathan David, Simon Andrew. Cert. in edn., Bognor Regis Tchrs.' Tng. Coll. Southampton, Eng.; BA in History summa cum laude, U. Bridgeport; M. in Libr. Sci. and Tech., So. Conn. State U.; postgrad., Fairfield U. Cert. sch. libr., media specialist, elem. and secondary tchr. Tchr. Ecclesbourne Road Boy's Elem. Sch., Croydon, Bridge Road Elem. Sch., Willesden, Eng.; gen. subjects and libr. Caulfield High Sch., Melbourne, Australia, Ashburton Secondary Modern for Girls; pub. libr. Ferguson Libr., Stamford (Conn.) Pub. Schs., 1968-73; libr. Convent of the Sacred Heart, Noroton, Conn., 1973-74; media specialist, learning facilitator Dundee Elem. Sch., Cos Cob Elem. Sch., Greenwich (Conn.) Pub. Schs., 1974—. Mem. Bd. Reps., Stamford, chmn. pers. , charter revision, 1984-87; asst. sec., chmn. policy, ad hoc breakfast Stamford Bd. Edn., 1988-91; dist. rep. Stamford Dem. City Com., 1983-91, treas., 1992—; bd. dirs. First Night Stamford, 1988-90, pres., 1990; mem. Pub. Arts Adv. Panel, Stamford; bd. dirs. Congregation Agudath Sholom, Stamford; Justice of the Peace. Mem. Greenwich Edn. Assn. (computer adv. com., bd. dirs., profl. rights and responsibilities com., negotiation team, nat. del., state del.), Conn. Ednl. Media Assn., Alpha Sigma Lamba, Phi Alpha Theta, Delta Kappa Gamma. Jewish. Home: 1 Clover Hill Dr Stamford CT 06902-1601 Office: Cos Cob Elem Sch Boston Post Rd Cos Cob CT 06807

FISHTEIN, ELIZABETH (MARY BETH STONE), writer; b. N.Y.C., May 24, 1947; d. Oscar and Ruth (Cohen) F. Student, NYU, 1965-66, Baruch Coll., 1980-81. Lic. real estate salesperson, N.Y., tourguide, N.Y.C.; notary pub., N.Y. Owner Do the Write Thing!, N.Y.C.; co-owner Signature Tours, N.Y.C.; owner Big Mama Music, N.Y.C. Composer/lyricist: (song) Phoenix, 1989 (winner Billboard Ann. Songwriter's Contest). Congl. dist. coord. United We Stand America, N.Y.C., 1993-94. Mem. ASCAP, Songwriters Guild, Women in Music, Nashville Songwriters Assn. Internat., Nat. Acad. Popular Music. Democrat. Jewish. Home: 56 W 70th St New York NY 10023-4620 Office: Do The Right Thing! 56 W 70th St New York NY 10023-4620

FISK, CARMEL J., counsel; b. Liberal, Kans., Nov. 27, 1959; d. Bob G. and Mildred M. (Schram) Schulz; married. Student, U. Okla., 1978-79; BS in Fgn. Svc., Georgetown U., 1982, JD, 1989. Bar: D.C. 1989. Legis. rschr. Rep. Mickey Edwards, 1982-84; legis. dir. Rep. George C. Wortley, 1984-86, Rep. James M. Inhofe, 1987-89; cons. Internat. Found. Electoral Sys., 1989-91; minority counsel Subcom. Internat. Law, Immigration and Refugees Ho. Com. Judiciary, 1991—. Univ. scholar U. Okla., 1978-79. Roman Catholic. Office: Subcom on Internat Law Immigration & Refugees Rm B-351C Rayburn House Office Bldg Washington DC 20515*

FISS, CINTHEA KATHRIN, artist; b. N.Y.C., Nov. 16, 1955; d. Murray and Jenny (Scherer) F.; m. David R. Thompson, Dec. 20, 1980 (div.). BFA, Antioch Coll., 1978; postgrad., Nova Scotia Coll., 1979-80; MFA, Calif. Inst. Arts, 1993. Stationary engr. Shorenstein Co., San Francisco, 1982-88; facilities mgr. Headlands Ctr. for Arts, Sausalito, Calif., 1988-89; stationary engr. DeYoung and Asian Art Mus., San Francisco, 1992; tchg. asst. Calif. Inst. Arts, Valencia, 1991-93; art instr. William Grant Still Art Ctr., L.A., 1993; tchr. Sixth St. Photography Workshop, San Francisco, 1993-94; stationary engr. San Francisco Pub. Libr., 1994—; mem. faculty U. Ariz., Tucson, 1994—; curator The Eye Gallery, San Francisco, 1984-90. Recipient Artist Equipment award Bay Area Video Coalition, 1994; AAUW scholar, 1990; Am. Photography Inst. fellow, 1993; Western States Art Fedn./NEA regional fellow, 1994. Mem. Internat. Union Oper. Engrs. (class rep. 1984-86, Apprentice of Yr. award runner-up 1986), Tradeswomen, Coll. Art Assn. Home: 2714 E 8th St Tucson AZ 85716

FISZER-SZAFARZ, BERTA (BERTA SAFARS), research scientist; b. Wilno, Poland, Feb. 1, 1928; m. David Safars; children—Martine, Michel. M.S., U. Buenos Aires, 1955, Ph.D., 1956. Lab. chief Cancer Inst. Villejuif, France, 1961-67; vis. scientist Nat. Cancer Inst., Bethesda, Md., 1967-68; lab. chief Institut Curie, Orsay, France, 1969—; vis. scientist Inst. Applied Biochemistry, Mitake, Gifu, Japan, 1986; gen. sec. dep. French-Israel Assn. Sci. Rsch. and Tech., 1994. Contbr. articles to profl. jours. Mem. European Assn. Cancer Research, Am. Assn. Cancer Research (corres. mem.), N.Y. Acad. Scis., European Cell Biology Orgn., French Soc. Cell Biology. Office: Institut Curie-Biologie, Bat 110 Centre Universitaire, Orsay 91405, France

FITCH, BONNIE LYNN, music store owner; b. New Rochelle, N.Y., June 1, 1953; d. Harry H. and Nevair Isabelle (Gulbenkian) Shahdanian; m. Clyde James Fitch, July 22, 1978; children: James Andrew, Thomas William. BMus in Music Edn., SUNY, Potsdam, 1975. Cert. elem. and secondary music tchr., N.Y. Elem. music specialist Monticello (N.Y.) Sch. Dist., 1975-78; mgr. sheet music dept. So. Nev. Music Co., Las Vegas, Nev., 1979-81; owner Bonnie's Music Shoppe, Las Vegas, 1981—; Vocalist Saratoga Performing Arts Ctr., 1976. Named to Disting. Women in So. Nev., Careline, 1989, 90, 91, 92, 94. Mem. Retail Sheet Music Dealers Assn., Music Tchrs. Nat. Assn., So. Nev. Cmty. Concert Assn. (mem. exec. bd., historian 1988-93), Social Register of So. Nev. Mem. Armenian Orthodox Ch. Office: Bonnie's Music Shoppe 1500 E Sahara Ave Las Vegas NV 89104-3439

FITCH, LINDA BAUMAN, computer coordinator, educator; b. Elmira, N.Y., Jan. 6, 1947; d. Floyd Theodore Bauman and Wilma Mildred Rennie; m. H. Taylor Fitch, Feb. 15, 1969; children: Trevor Andrew, Matthew Taylor. BS, Keuka Coll., Keuka Park, 1969. Elem. tchr. Penn Yan Cen. Sch. Dist., Penn Yan, N.Y., 1972-73; computer coord. Fitch Auto Supply, Penn Yan, 1973—. Com. chmn. troop 48, Boy Scouts Am., Branchport, N.Y., 1986-92; v.p. Penn Yan Cen. Sch. Bd., 1984-92, pres. 1992—; chmn. pub. rels. Yates Day Care Ctr., Penn Yan, 1980-82; mem. Bd. Coop. Ednl. Svcs., 1992—. Mem. AAUW, Nat. Sch. Bds. Assn. (fed. rels. network 1988—), N.Y. State Sch. Bds. Assn. (state legis. network 1991—), Four County Sch. Bds. Assn. (legis. chmn., 2d v.p., 1st v.p., pres.). Republican. Presbyterian. Home: 3120 Kinneys Corners Rd Bluff Point NY 14478-9752 Office: Fitch Auto Supply F&W Parts 211 Clinton St Penn Yan NY 14527

FITCH, MARY KILLEEN, salary design and workers compensation specialist; b. Carroll, Iowa, July 15, 1949; d. Michael Francis and Mildred (Pauley) Killeen; m. David Paul Fitch, July 3, 1971; one child, Emily Grace. BS, Iowa State U., 1971, MS, 1975; postgrad. U. Minn., 1982—. Pers. adminstr. Control Data Corp., Roseville, Minn., 1976-77; sr. compensation analyst/employee rels. rep. Honeywell, Inc., Mpls., 1977-80; human resource mgr./compensation and benefits mgr. No. Telecom, Inc., Minnetonka, Minn., 1980-82; adj. instr., teaching asst. Lakewood Community Coll./U. Minn., Mpls., 1982-84; compensation cons. Gen. Mills, Wayzata, Minn., 1984-85; mgr. compensation Northwestern Nat. Life Ins., Mpls., 1985-87; prin. compensation specialist Comml. Bldgs. Group, Honeywell, Inc., Mpls., 1987-89; dir. compensation, HRIS, workers compensation, salary design, Nat. Car Rental System, Inc., Mpls., 1989—; cons. exec. compensation Honeywell Inc., Mpls., 1984; cons. human resources Les Kraus & Assocs., Edina, Minn., 1984; pres. Personnel Mgmt. Services of Twin Cities, St. Paul, 1983—. Author: (with Paul Muchinsky) Organization Behavior and Human Performance, 1975; (with John Fossum) Personnel Psychology, 1985. Former chmn., bd. dirs. Kathadin, United Way Agy., Mpls., 1985—; curriculum com. U. Minn., 1983-84. George Catt Iowa State U. scholar, 1970. Mem. AAUW, Assn. Human Resources Systems Profls., Am. Compensation Assn., Psi Chi, Phi Kappa Phi. Avocations: dressage, karate. Home: 1188 90th St E Inver Grove MN 55077-4206 Office: HR Nat Car Rental Systems Inc 7700 France Ave S Minneapolis MN 55435-5296

FITCH, NANCY ELIZABETH, historian; b. White Plains, N.Y., June 17, 1947; d. Robert Franklin and Nancy Elizabeth (Harvey) F. BA in Polit. Sci./English Lit., Oakland U., Rochester, Mich., 1969; MA in History, U. Mich., 1971, PhD in History, 1981. Danforth teaching intern dept. history U. Mich., Ann Arbor, 1970; asst. prof. history and lit. Sangamon State U., Springfield, Ill., 1972-74; sr. social sci. rsch. analyst The Congl. Rsch. Svc. of Libr. of Congress, Washington, 1975-78; asst. to the chmn./historian U.S. EEO Commn., Washington, 1982-89; asst. prof. history Lynchburg Coll. of Va., 1989-91; asst. prof. African Am. studies Temple U., Phila., 1991-92; Jesse Ball Dupont vis. scholar Randolph-Macon Woman's Coll., Lynchburg, Va., 1992-93; assoc. prof. history U. N.C. at Asheville, 1993—; chmn.'s rep. White House Inst. on Historically Black Colls. and Univs., U.S. Dept. Edn., 1985-89; pub. rels. vol. S. Africa Exhibit Project, Washington, 1986-88; mem. adv. com. DuPont Vis. Scholars Project, Va. Found. Ind. Colls., 1990-91; adj. prof. in history Shaw U., Asheville, 1994. Editorial assoc.: Jour. S. Asian Lit., 1969-79; editorial bd.: Diversity: A Journal of Multicultural Issues; book reviewer Jour. S. Asian Lit., Lit. East and West, The Historian,

Jour. Asian Studies; author: (series) Essays on Liberty, 1988; contbr. articles to profl. jours. Organizer, producer Ann. Dr. Martin Luther King Jr. Celebration prog., Washington, 1986-88; guest lectr. on history of Am. music Blue Ridge Music Festival, Lynchburg, 1991; participant Radio America African-Am. contbrs. to art and lit., 1990; vol./cons. The Holiday Project, Washington, 1986-88; mem. Widening Horizons Prog. of D.C. Pub. Schs., 1986-88. Recipient Achievement award Mt. Vernon Day Care Ctr., 1983, Spl. Commendation, U.S. EEO Commn., 1985-89, Ft. Drum Sgt. Maj.'s medal for svc. 10th Mountain div. Light Inf., Ft. Drum, N.Y., 1992; fellow Ford Found., 1971-72, Nat. Def. Fgn. Lagn., 1970, U. Mich., 1970-71, 78-79, John Hay Whitney Found., 1969-70. Mem. Assn. for Advancement of Core Curricula, Afro-Am. Archaeology Network, Friends of Benjamin Banneker Hist. Park, Phi Alpha Theta (faculty advisor 1990-91). Republican. Episcopalian/Buddhist. Office: Univ NC at Asheville Asheville NC 28804

FITCH, RACHEL FARR, health policy analyst; b. Deering, Mo., July 27, 1933; d. Allen Edward and Rosie Leola (Jones) Farr; R.N., St. Vincent Hosp., 1954; student Little Rock U., 1965-67; B.S., St. Louis U., 1974, M.S., 1976, Ph.D., 1983; m. Coy Dean Fitch, Mar. 31, 1956; children: Julia Anne, Jaquelyn Kay. Psychiat. staff nurse VA Ft. Root Hosp., North Little Rock, Ark., 1954-57; surg.-med. staff nurse St. Vincent Infirmary, Little Rock, 1957-65; acute care nurse Georgetown U. Hosp., Washington, 1968-69; public health nurse to adminstr. South office Vis. Nurse Assn. Greater St. Louis, 1970-73; cons. in edn. St. Louis City Health Dept., 1977-80; rsch. specialist Sen. John C. Danforth, St. Louis, 1980; owner RFF Assocs., 1983-86; project dir. study of infant mortality in city of St. Louis, 1978. Mem. community health edn. com. Am. Heart Assn., 1977-87; bd. dirs. LWV of Mo., 1984—, editor newspaper, 1984-87, dir. health issues, 1987—. Mem. Am. Public Health Assn., Acad. Polit. Sci. (pres. 1992-94), Grand Jury Assn. St. Louis (bd. dirs.), Womens Club (St. Louis U. Sch. Medicine), Sigma Theta Tau.

FITCH, SARAH KATHRYN, accountant; b. Gilmer, Tex., Jan. 30, 1940; d. Curtis Hicks and Estelle Manie (Gunn) Tress; m. Kyle Jones Fitch, Jr., Mar. 18, 1960; children: Kyle Mark, Julie Carol, Lori Page Fitch Busby. BS summa cum laude, East Tex. Bapt. U., 1985; postgrad., La. Tech. U., 1987. Ins. investigator Equifax, Inc., Tyler, Tex. and Shreveport, La., 1981-82; sec. East Tex. Bapt. U., Marshall, 1982-84, acct., 1984-86; adminstrv. clerk Thiokol Corp., Marshall, 1986-90, acct., 1990—; pvt. practice cosmetics distbr. Marshall, 1991—. Active United Way. Mem. Inst. Mgmt. Accts., Alpha Chi. Office: Thiokol Corp Hwy 43 PO Box 1129 Marshall TX 75671-1129

FITE, KATHLEEN ELIZABETH, education educator; b. Houston, June 26, 1948; d. Daniel Patrick and Edith Elizabeth (Burnett) F. BS in Edn., S.W. Tex. State U., 1969, MEd, 1970; EdD, N. Tex. State U., 1972. Cert. tchr. Prof. S.W. Tex. State U., San Marcos, 1973—, dir. Ctr. for Study of Basic Skills, 1980, dir. Race Integration Tng. Inst., 1982-83, dir. elem. edn. dept., 1983-84, assoc. dir. sponsored projects, 1984-86, dir. sponsored projects, 1986-87; cons. U.S. Dept. Edn., numerous pub. cos.; mem. adv. bd. Dushing Pub. Group, Inc. Co-author: A Few Favorites of the Total Teacher, The Super Ideas Book, Creative Art Ideas; asst editor SW Tex. U. Faculty Bull., 1977-78, editor, 1978-81; contbr. numerous articles, reports and book revs. to profl. jours. Mem. sr. citizens adv. com. San Marcos City Coun., Commn. for Women; facilitator, dir. numerous community workshops; pres. Jr. Svc. League; activity chmn. Tex. Spl. Olympics; numerous other civic activities. Named Ky. Col., 1975, to Hall of Fame, San Marcos Commn. for Women, 1991; grantee U.S. Dept. Edn., L.B. Johnson Inst., 1988, 89, also others. Mem. Nat. Assn. Edn. Young Children, Tex. Assn. Tchr. Educators, Kindergarten Tchrs. Tex., Tex. Computer Edn. Assn. (bd. dirs. 1984-87, publs. editor, state conf. asst. 1984-88), San Marcos Assn. for Edn. Young Children (treas.), S.W. Tex. State U. Alumni Assn. (Teaching award of honor, Key of Excellence award, Strutter Hall of Fame), Golden Key, Phi Delta Kappa (pres. 1981, v.p., faculty advisor, mem. ritual team 1986-89), Kappa Delta Pi (hon.). Methodist. Home: 602 Larue Dr San Marcos TX 78666-2410 Office: SW Tex State U Dept Curriculum & Instrn San Marcos TX 78666

FITHIAN, PATRICIA ANN, special education director; b. Waterbury, Conn., Mar. 19, 1946; d. Daniel Francis and Isabelle (Driscoll) Walsh; divorced; children: Warren Bruce, Bridget Marie. BS in Edn., So. Conn. State U., 1969, MS in Edn., 1972; postgrad., Chapman Coll., 1989. Tchr. severely handicapped Waterbury Pub. Schs., 1969-73; tchr. severely handicapped, learning handicapped-disabled Mariposa County Unified Schs., Mariposa, Calif., 1979-90, dir. spl. edn., 1990—. Mem. Community Adv. Coun.; bd. dirs. Sequoia Area 8 Devel. Disabilities, 1985-88. Mem. Calif. Assn. Resource Specialist, Calif. Tchrs. Assn., Spl. Edn. Adminstrs. County Offices, AAUW. Methodist. Office: Mariposa County Unified Schs 5081 Hwy 140 Mariposa CA 95338-9208

FITTING-GIFFORD, MARJORIE ANN, mathematician, educator, consultant; b. Detroit, Nov. 29, 1933; d. Ellis John and Dorothy Jennie Premo; m. George R. Pickering, Dec. 16, 1954 (div. 1964); children: William Russell, David Ellis, John Lawrence; m. Frederick N. Fitting, Feb. 25, 1972 (dec. 1985); m. Forrest W. Gifford, May 28, 1988. BS in Math., Mich. State U., 1954, PhD, 1968; MEd, Wayne State U., 1958; AM in Math., U. Mich., 1966. Cert. tchr., Mich., Calif. Tchr. math. secondary schs., Mich., 1954-61; instr. Lawrence Inst. Tech., Southfield, Mich., 1961-68; grad. asst. Mich. State U., East Lansing, 1966-68; prof. emeritus math. and computer sci. San Jose State U., Calif., 1968-92; instr. math U. Nev., Las Vegas, 1993-95; v.p. fin. Metra Instruments, San Jose, 1972-82; pres. Metier, Henderson, Nev., 1982—; cons. San Jose (Calif.) Unified Sch., 1969-71. Author: (software) Math Test Generation, 1983; co-author: (book series) Computer Literacy Series, 1983-85. Recipient Dean's award for teaching excellence San Jose State U., 1982; J.C. Plant scholar Mich. State U., 1954; NSF fellow, 1965-66, Fulbright sr. lectr./rsch. grantee, Portugal, 1985-86. Mem. Math. Assn. Am., Am. Math. Soc., Nat. Coun. Tchrs. Math. (review panel 1954—), Computer Using Educators, So. Nev. Tchrs. Math, Calif. Math. Coun., Zeta Tau Alpha. Democrat. Roman Catholic. Avocations: gardening, rafting, kayaking.

FITTS, C. AUSTIN, investment banker, former federal agency administrator; b. Phila., Dec. 24, 1950; d. William Thomas Jr. and Barbara Kinsey (Willits) F. AA, Bennett Coll., 1970; student, Chinese U., Hong Kong, 1971; BA, U. Pa., 1974, MBA, 1978. With Dillon, Read & Co., Inc., N.Y.C., 1978-89, sr. v.p., 1984-86, mng. dir., mem. bd. dirs., 1986-89; asst. sec. for housing, urban devel. and fed. housing commr. HUD, Washington, 1989-90; pres. The Hamilton Securities Group, Inc., Washington, 1990-94; bd. dirs. Student Loan Mktg. Assn. Sallie Mae; adv. bd. Fedn. Nat. Mortgage Assn. Fannie Mae, 1992-93; mem. emerging mkts. adv. com. SEC, 1990-93. Mem. graduate adv. bd. Wharton Sch., 1986—. Mem. Urban Land Inst., Nat. Multi-Housing Coun. (bd. dirs.), Coun. for Excellence in Govt. (prin. 1991—), Econ. Club N.Y., Wharton Sch. Club Washington (adv. bd. 1991—). Office: The Hamilton Securities Group 1410 Q St NW Washington DC 20009

FITTS, JANET SUE, emergency room nurse, paramedic, trauma nurse coordinator, educator; b. Kansas City, Mo., Apr. 7, 1963; d. George Humphrey and Peggy Jean (Thompson) Jones; m. Thomas Allen Fitts, Oct. 14, 1989; 1 child, Megan. BSN, St. Louis U., 1989; cert. EMT-paramedic, St. John's Mercy Med. Ctr., St. Louis, 1991. RN, Mo.; cert. CEN, BLS instr.-trainer, ACLS affiliate faculty, pediatric advaned life support provicer, neonatal advanced life support provider, pre-hosp. trauma life support instr., advanced burn life support provider; cert. trauma nurse specialist. Firefighter, nurse, paramedic Eureka (Mo.) Fire Protection Dist., 1988—; neonatal-obstetrics nurse Met. Med. Ctr.-West, Des Peres, Mo., 1989-90; paramedic supr. Medcor, Inc., Eureka, 1989-94; nurse emergency dept. St. John's Mercy Hosp., Washington, Mo., 1990—; trauma nurse coord. St. John's Mercy Hosp., Washington, 1994—, 1994—; nurse emergency dept. Mo. Bapt. Med. Ctr., St. Louis, 1991-93; owner, educator Emergency Med. Svcs. Edn. Programs, Eureka, 1990—; paramedic instr. East Ctr. Coll., Union, Mo., 1990—; instr. emergency nursing Forest Park C.C., St. Louis, 1992—; community/outreach educator Eureka Fire Protection Dist., 1990-94, dir. CPR program, 1991-94. Contbr. articles to profl. jours. Named Student Nurse of Yr., Mo. Student Nurses' Assn., 1987-88. Mem. ANA, Mo. Nurses Assn. (membership com. 1990-91), Emergency Nurses Assn. (cert. trauma nurse core course provider), Nat. Assn. EMTs, Mo. Emergency Med. Svcs. Assn., Firefighters Assn. Mo., Am. Heart Assn. (coun. on cardiopulmonary and critical care), Sigma Theta Tau, Sigma Alpha Iota. Home: 97 Oak Rdg Eureka MO 63025-3527 Office: St John's Mercy Hosp 200 Madison Ave Washington MO 63090

FITZGERALD, CAROL J., foundation administrator, association executive; b. Chgo., July 2, 1950; d. Lucien W. and Dian (Gorgas) F.; m. Douglas Paul Becknell, July 10, 1971; 1 child, Rachel Fitzgerald Becknell. BS in Edn., No. Ill. U., 1973; MA in French, Ill. State U., 1976. Tchr. Prophetstown (Ill.) High Sch., 1976-77; dir. program Sterling-Rock Falls YWCA, Ill., 1977-80; county coord. Highland Coll. CETA, Freeport, Ill., 1980-81; tchr. Sauk Valley Coll., Dixon, Ill., 1981-82; planner N. Cen. Ill. Coun. Govts., Princeton, 1982-83; exec. asst. Sterling C. of C., 1985; exec. dir. Sterling-Rock Falls YWCA, 1985—. Dir. Lincoln Land Chpt. ARC, 1986-91; adv. bd. Whiteside County Health Dept., Morrison, 1985—; founder Sauk Valley Chpt. NOW, Sterling, 1978, pres. 1978-79, 81-82; sec. Sterling-Rock Falls Ministerial Assn., 1986-87; steering com. mem. Daily Bread Food Co-op, 1980—; treas. Rock Valley Nuclear Freeze Coalition, 1982, Ill. Coalition Against Sexual Assault, Springfield, 1988—. Mem. NAFE, Coun. Ill. and St. Louis YWCAs (pres. elect 1994), Rock River Valley Pers. Assn. Unitarian. Office: YWCA 412 1st Ave Sterling IL 61081-3603

FITZGERALD, ELLA, singer; b. Newport News, Va., Apr. 25, 1918; m. Ray Brown (div. 1953); 1 child, Ray. Began singing with Chick Webb Orch., 1934-39; tours throughout U.S., Japan, Europe; with Jazz at the Philharmonic troupe, 1948-57; rec. artist for Decca, 1936-55, Verve, from 1956, now Pablo Records; appeared in motion picture Pete Kelly's Blues, 1955; nightclub appearances include Sahara Hotel, Caesar's Palace, both Las Vegas, Fairmont Hotel, San Francisco, Ronnie Scott's Club, London; appeared on TV in spls. with Frank Sinatra; also on All Star Swing Festival, 1972, concert with Boston Pops, 1972; later with more than 40 symphony orchs. throughout U.S.; records include At Duke's Place, 1966, Best, 1967, Clap Hands, 1961, Cote d' Azur, (with Ellington), 1967, Ella, Ella Fitzgerald; In Hamburg, 1965, Mack the Knife, Ella in Berlin, 1960, Sunshine of Your Love, Things Ain't What They Used to Be, Tribute to Porter, 1965, Whisper Not, 1966, Watch What Happens, 1972, Take Love Easy, 1975, Ella in London, 1975, Lady Time, 1978, A Perfect Match (with Count Basie), 1979, A Tisket a Tasket, 1985, Montreux Ella, The Intimate Ella, 1990, All That Jazz, 1990, Brighten The Corner, 1991, Misty Blue, 1991, Pure Ella, 1994, Verve Jazz Master 6: Ella Fitzgerald, 1994, numerous others. Recipient 12 Grammy awards, numerous popularity awards from Down Beat mag., Metronome mag., Musicians Poll, JAY Award Poll; named number 1 female singer 16th Internat. Jazz Critics Poll, 1968, Commander of Arts and Letters, Paris, 1990; recipient Am. Music award, 1978, Kennedy Center honor, 1979, Grammy award as best female jazz vocalist, 1981, 84; recipient Nat. Medal of the Arts, 1987. Office: care Norman Granz 451 N Canon Dr Beverly Hills CA 90210-4819*

FITZGERALD, GERALDINE, actress; b. Dublin, Ireland, Nov. 24, 1913; came to U.S. 1938, naturalized, 1954; d. William and Mary (Richards) F.; m. Stuart Scheftel, Sept. 10, 1946; children: Michael Lindsay-Hogg, Susan Scheftel. Student, Queens Coll., London. Appeared in numerous motion pictures, 1936—, including Wuthering Heights (Acad. award nomination), 1939, Dark Victory, 1939, Wilson, 1944, Three Strangers, 1946, 10 North Frederick, 1958, The Pawnbroker, 1964, The Mango Tree, 1977, Arthur, 1980, Easy Money, 1983, Pope of Greenwich Village, 1984, Poltergeist II, 1986, Arthur II, 1988; appeared on stage as Mary Tyrone in Long Days Journey into Night (Variety Critics award), 1971, The Lunch Girl; appeared in Broadway prodn. Touch of the Poet, 1980; directed play Mass Appeal, 1980; TV film appearance Do You Remember Love?, 1985, The Best of Everything, Dixie: Changing Habits, 1983, Kennedy, 1983, Street Songs, Circle of Violence, 1986, Night of Courage, 1986, Bump in the Night, 1991. Active N.Y. State Council Arts. Recipient Handel medallion N.Y.C., 1974. Mem. AFTRA, Screen Actors Guild, Actors Equity.

FITZGERALD, SISTER JANET ANNE, college president; b. Woodside, N.Y., Sept. 4, 1935; d. Robert W. and Lillian H. (Shannon) F. BA magna cum laude, St. John's U., 1965, MA, 1967, PhD, 1971, LLD (hon.), 1982. Joined Sisters of St. Dominic of Amityville, Roman Catholic Ch., 1953; NSF postdoctoral fellow Cath. U. Am., summer 1971; prof. philosophy Molloy Coll., Rockville Centre, N.Y., 1969—; pres. Molloy Coll., 1972—; trustee L.I. Regional Adv. Coun. on Higher Edn., 1972—, chmn. 1981-84; trustee Commn. on Ind. Colls. and Univs., 1981-84, 1989-92, Fellowship of Cath. Scholars, 1977—, v.p., 1977-80; trustee Cath. Charities, Diocese of rockville Centre, 1979-82; invited expert peritus Vatican Internat. Conf. on Cath. Higher Edn., Rome, 1989. Author: Alfred North Whitehead's Early Philosophy of Space and Time, 1979. Mem. bd. advisors Sem. of Immaculate Conception, 1975-80; mem. adv. bd. pre-theology program Dunwoodie Sem., Archdiocese of N.Y.; mem. pub. policy com. N.Y. State Cath. Conf., 1992—; mem. N.Y. State Edn. Dept.-Blue Ribbon Panel on Cath. Schs., 1992—; 1st women grand marshal St. Patrick's Day Parade, Glen Cove, 1992. Recipient Disting. Leadership award L.I. Bus. News, 1988, plaque of recognition L.I. Women's Coun. for Equal Edn. Tng. and Employment, 1989, Pathfinder award Town of Hempstead, 1990, Disting. Long Islander in Edn. award Epilepsy Found. L.I., 1991, Educator of Yr. award Assn. Tchrs. N.Y., 1980; honored by L.I. Cath. League for Religious and Civil Rights, 1989; named L.I.'s 100 Influentials, L.I. Bus. News, 1992, 93. Mem. Soc. Cath. Social Scis. (bd. advisors). Office: Molloy Coll Office of the President 1000 Hempstead Ave Rockville Centre NY 11570-1199

FITZGERALD, JANICE S., public relations executive, academic administrator; b. Poughkeepsie, N.Y., Nov. 2, 1948; d. Lloyd Raymond and Emily Mae (Anderson) Spinner. BA magna cum laude, Cheyney U. Pa., 1972, MEd, 1973; MA, Villanova U., 1980; postgrad., Carnegie Mellon U., 1979, Harvard U., 1992. Prof. Cheyney U. Pa., 1972-74; dir. pub. rels. Cheyney U. Pa., Cheyney, 1974-83; dir. pub. rels. Pa. State System of Higher Edn., Harrisburg, 1983—, exec. assoc. to chancellor, dir. communications, 1985-90, exec. deputy, 1990—; reader Nat. Edn. Assn.; pres. Correct Correspondence; free lance writer. Vol. radio reader, Tri-County Assn. of Blind, Suburban Guild, Community Gen. Osteo. Hosp.; pub. rels. coun. State System of Higher Edn. Named one of Outstanding Women in Am., 1981, named Alumnus of Yr. Nat. Assn. Equal Opportunity, 1985; recipient award Chapel of Four Chaplains, 1982, Valedictory and Alumni Key award Cheyney U. Pa., 1972. Mem. Am. Coun. Edn. (mem. nat. identification program for advancement of women, state planning com.), Coll. and Univ. Pub. Rels. Assn. of Pa., Pub. Rels. Soc. of Am., Edn. Writers Assn., Nat. Assn. Women in Edn. Office: Office of Chancellor Pa State Sys Higher Edn 2986 N 2nd St Harrisburg PA 17110

FITZGERALD, JUDITH KLASWICK, federal judge; b. Spangler, Pa., May 10, 1948; d. Julius Francis and Regina Marie (Pregno) Klaswick; m. June 5, 1971 (div. Dec. 1982); 1 child; m. Barry robert Fitzgerald, Sept 20, 1986; 1 child. BSBA, U. Pitts., 1970, JD, 1973. Legal researcher Assocs. Fin., Pitts., 1972-73; law clk. to pres. judge Beaver County (Pa.) Ct. Common Pleas, 1973-74; law clk. to judge Pa. Superior Ct., Pitts., 1974-75; asst. U.S. atty. U.S. Dist. Ct. (we. dist.) Pa., Pitts. and Erie, 1976-87; U.S. bankruptcy judge U.S. Dist. Ct. (we. dist.) Pa., Pitts., Erie and Johnstown, 1987—. Co-author: Bankruptcy and Divorce, Support and Property Division, 1991; editor: Pennsylvania Law of Juvenile Delinquency and Deprivation, 1976; contbr. articles to legal jours. Mem. Pitts. Camerata, 1978-80, Allegheny County Polit.-Legal Edn. Project, 1980, West Pa. Conservancy, 1990—, Mendelssohn Choir Pitts., 1982—; mem. coun. Program to Aid Citizen Enterprise, 1985-87. Recipient Spl. Achievement awards Dept. Justice, Spl. Recognition award Pittsburgh mag., Operation Exodus Outstanding Performance award Dept. Commerce, 1986. Mem. Allegheny County Bar Assn., Women's Bar Assn. of Western Pa., Nat. Conf. Bankruptcy Judges, Am. Bankruptcy Inst., Nat. Conf. Bankruptcy Clks., Comml. Law League of Am., Fed. Criminal Investigators Assn. (Spl. Svc. award 1988), Zonta. Republican. Lutheran. Office: US Bankruptcy Ct 1000 Liberty Ave Pittsburgh PA 15222-4002

FITZGERALD, LAURINE ELISABETH, university dean, educator; b. New London, Wis., Aug. 24, 1930; d. Thomas F. and Laurine (Branchflower) F. B.S., Northwestern U., 1952, M.A., 1953; Ph.D., Mich. State U., 1959. Instr. English, dir. devel. reading lab., head resident-dir. Wis. State Coll., Whitewater, 1953-55; area dir. residence and counseling Ind. U., 1955-57; teaching grad. asst. guidance and counseling, then instr., counselor Mich. State U., East Lansing, 1957-59; asst. prof. psychology and edn., assoc. dean students U. Denver, 1959-62; asst. prof. counseling psychology, staff counselor for Carnegie Found. project U. Minn., 1962-63; assoc. dean, assoc. prof. Mich. State U., 1963-70, assoc. dean students. prof. adminstrn. and higher edn., dir. div. edn. and rsch., 1970-74; dean Grad. Sch., prof. counselor edn., dir. N.E. Wis. Coop. Regional Grad. Ctr. U. Wis.-Oshkosh, 1974-85; dean/dir. Ohio State U.-Mansfield, 1986-87, prof. edn. policy and leadership, 1985-93, dir. student pers. asst. program, edn. policy and leadership, 1989-92; adj. prof. edn. policy and leadership Ohio State U., 1992-93; vis. lectr. U. Okla., Norman, 1961; vis. prof. Oreg. State U., 1977; cons. in field; vocat. expertwitness, 1962-95. Contbr. numerous articles to profl. jours.; co-author monographs, texts. Adv. bd. Mansfield Gen. Hosp., 1986-94; bd. dirs. Renaissance Theatre, 1986-87; exec. com. Ohio Consortium on Tng. and Planning, 1985-87; bd. dirs. New Beginnings, 1986-94; trustee Mt. Carmel Coll. Nursing, chmn. acad. affairs com., 1988—. Recipient Higher Edn. Rocky Mountain coun. Girl Scouts U.S., 1961, Evelyn Hosmer U. Denver, 1962, Merit award Northwestern Alumni Assn., 1993; named Old Master Purdue U., 1979, Most Disting. Women in Edn., Mich., 1973; Elin Wagner Found. fellow, 1963-64. Mem. AAUW, AAUP (chpt. treas. 1955-56), NEA, Am. Psychol. Assn., Mich. Psychol. Assn., Am. Pers. and Guidance Assn., Am. Coll. Pers. Assn. (sec. 1965-67, exec. bd. 1968-70, chmn. women's task force 1970-71, editor jour. 1976-82, Disting. Scholar award 1985, sr. scholars com. 1985-90, historian 1982-95, chmn. scholars com. 1986-87, sr. scholars diplomate 1990, awards and commendations com. 1988-89, pres.-elect 1989-90, pres. 1990-91, past pres. 1991-92), Assn. Counselor Edn. and Supervision, Am. Assn. Higher Edn., Nat. Assn. Women Deans, Adminstrs. and Counselors (rsch., ednl. by-laws programs, publs., univ. coms. 1959-72, v.p. 1972-74, KSP Trust Commn. 1979-81, pres. 1980-81, editorial bd. 1991—), Mich. Assn. Women Deans, Adminstrs. and Counselors (pres. 1967-69), Ohio Assn. Women Deans, Adminstrs. and Counselors, Mich. Coll. Pers. Assn., Wis. Coll. Pers. Assn., Midwest Assn. Grad. Schs. (pres. 1980-82), Intercollegiate Assn. Women Students (editorial bd., nat. advisor), Women's Equity Action League (past pres. Mich., nat. sec.-treas. legal and edn. def. fund), Bus. and Profl. Women's Club (chpt. pres. 1980, state officer 1981, Lena Lake Forest fellow 1966-67), Wis. Soc. for Higher Edn. (Achievement award 1985, Pres. award 1982), Altrusa Internat. (mem. bd. dirs. 1986-94), Mortar Bd., Shi-Ai, Beta Beta Beta, Psi Chi, Alpha Lambda Delta, Delta Kappa Gamma, Zonta (pres. Lansing club, chmn. internat. status of women com. 1960-85). Home: 812 Wyman St New London WI 54961-1771

FITZGERALD, PATRICIA ANN, university administrator; b. Elmira, N.Y., June 14, 1949; d. Leo Joseph FitzGerald and Catherine Elizabeth (Reed) Green; m. Gregory Joseph Dobrich, Nov. 15, 1991. BA, Syracuse (N.Y.) U., 1971, MLS, 1975; M in Pub. Mgmt., Carnegie Mellon U., 1988. Geology library supr. Syracuse U. Libraries, 1972-76, sci. reference librarian, 1976-78, acting chemistry librarian, 1978; assoc. reference librarian U. Del. Libraries, Newark, 1978-83; head sci. and tech. libraries Carnegie Mellon U. Libraries, Pitts., 1983-87, asst. dir. pub. svc., 1987-90; asst. dir. adminstrv. svc. Welch Med. Libr. Johns Hopkins U., Balt., 1990-92; mktg. cons. Sys. and Svc. Inc., Balt., 1993—. Trustee Pitts. Regional Libr. Ctr., 1988-90, treas., 1988-89, v.p., 1989-90. Mem. ALA, Am. Mgmt. Assn., Spl. Librs. Assn. (sec. info. tech. div. 1983-85, chmn. 1989—), Del. Online Users Group (founder, chmn. 1980-82). Office: 200 Orchard Ridge Dr Gaithersburg MD 20878

FITZHUGH, KATHRYN, law librarian; b. Little Rock, Feb. 4, 1950; d. Charles Edward and Billie Jean (Burns) Corrothers; m. Benjamin Dewey Fitzhugh, Nov. 28, 1970; 1 child, Erica Janine. BA, U. Ark., 1971; MSLS, U. Ill., 1976; JD, U. Ark., Little Rock, 1983. Bar: Ark. 1983, U.S. Dist. Ct. (ea. dist.) Ark. 1983. Sci./tech. libr. Grad. Inst. Tech., Little Rock, 1977-79; br. libr. U.S. Cts. Br. Libr., Little Rock, 1980-83, 89-92; law clk. Hon. George Howard Jr., Little Rock, 1983-84; ptnr. Fitzhugh & Fitzhugh, Little Rock, 1985-87; ref./circulation libr. U. Ark.-Little Rock/Pulaski County Law Libr., 1987-89, pub. svcs. libr., 1992—. Contbr. book: Handbook of Law for Arkansas Women, 1987. Mem. North Little Rock NAACP, 1990—, Arkansans for Gifted and Talented Edn., Little Rock, 1992—; active Ouachita Girl Scout Coun., 1986-88, Shorter Coll. Adult Edn. Bd., 1986-87, Carver Magnet Elem. Sch. PTA, 1993—. The Herbert Lehman Edn. Fund scholar, 1967-71; Am. Assn. Law Librs. travel grantee, 1988. Mem. ABA, ALA, Am. Assn. Law Librs., Pulaski County Bar Assn., Ark. Bar Assn., Ark. Assn. Women Lawyers (corr. sec. 1989-90), Soc. Southwest Archivists, Delta Sigma Theta. Methodist. Home: 4715 Darragh Dr Little Rock AR 72204-8425 Office: U Ark at Little Rock Pulaski County Law Libr 1203 McAlmont St Little Rock AR 72202-5142

FITZHUGH, SUSAN ISACKS, photographer; b. New Orleans, Nov. 6, 1942; d. Leonard Smith Isacks and Susan Nickerson (Bryan) White; m. Donald Lewis Fitzhugh Jr., Mar. 19, 1965 (div. Aug. 1971); 1 child, Lisa. Student, La. State U., 1960-61. Photographer of edn., healthcare and human svcs., 1980—. Recipient Merit award Communication Arts Mag., 1985, 86, 87, Gold award Coun. of Advancement and Support of Edn., 1988. Mem. Am. Soc. Mag. Photographers (bd. dirs. Mid-Atlantic chpt. 1991-94). Democrat. Office: Susie Fitzhugh Photographer 3406 Chestnut Ave Baltimore MD 21211-2516

FITZPATRICK, BLANCHE, author, economics professor; b. Medford, Mass.; d. Joseph Leo and Elizabeth Dorothy (Bresnahan) F. AB summa cum laude, Tufts U., 1945; AM, Stanford U., 1950; PhD, Harvard U., 1966. With labor rels. dept. Raytheon Mfg. Co., Newton, Mass., 1945-46; labor economist U.S. Dept. Labor, Boston and Washington, 1946-53; dir. sales analysis Polaroid Corp., Cambridge, Mass., 1953-58; prof. econs. Lesley Coll., Cambridge, 1958-64, Calif. State U., Fullerton, 1964-65; vis. prof. Calif. State U., 1977-78; prof. econs. Boston U., 1965—; vis. prof. Goucher Coll., Balt., 1980-82. Author: Women's Inferior Education, 1976, Woman Traveler: How to Get Over the Economic Hurdles Along Life's Way, 1990, Getting a Living, Getting a Life, 1994. Mem., com. chmn. Mass. Gov.'s Commn. on Status of Women, 1971-74, Mass. Bd. Higher Edn., 1975-76; trustee U. Lowell (Mass.), 1975-78; mem. faculty adv. com. Md. Bd. Higher Edn., 1981-82. Mem. Am. Econ. Assn., Phi Beta Kappa. Democrat. Office: Pemberton Publishers PO Box 441558 Somerville MA 02144-0013

FITZPATRICK, CHRISTINE MORRIS, legal administrator, former television executive; b. Steubenville, Ohio, June 10, 1920; d. Roy Elwood and Ruby Lorena (Mason) Morris; student U. Chgo., 1943-44, U. Ga., 1945-46; m. T. Mallary Fitzpatrick, Jr., Dec. 19, 1942; 1 child, Thomas Mallary III. BA, Roosevelt U., 1947; postgrad. Trinity Coll., Hartford, Conn., 1970. Assoc. dir. Joint Human Rels. Project, City of Chgo., 1965-66; tchr. English, Austin Sch. for Girls, Hartford, 1966-70; promotion coord. Conn. Pub. TV, Hartford, 1971-72, dir. community rels., 1972-73, v.p., 1973-77; pub. rels./pub. affairs cons. Commonwealth Edison Co., Chgo., 1977-79; dir. spl. events Chgo. Public TV, 1979-84; v.p. Fitzpatrick Group, Inc., Chgo., 1986-88; adminstrv. dir. Fitzpatrick Law Offices, 1988-94, Fitzpatrick Eilenberg & Zivian, 1994—; v.p. Pub. Rels. Clinic Chgo., 1980-81. Bd. advisers Greater Hartford Mag., 1975-77; bd. dirs. World Affairs Ctr., Hartford, 1975-77; mem. adv. coun. Am. Revolution Bicentennial Commn. Conn., 1975-77. Mem. Pub. Rels. Soc. Am. (dir. Conn. Valley chpt. 1976-77), Am. Women in Radio and TV (New Eng. chpt. pres. 1976-77), LWV (Chgo. chpt. pres. 1962-64, Hartford chpt. v.p. 1971-73). Home: 5518 S Harper Ave Chicago IL 60637

FITZPATRICK, CHRISTINE Y., academic adminstrator, educator; b. Muncie, Ind., Dec. 14, 1952; d. Danny Lee Young and Greta Elizabeth (Nelson) Payne; m. Don Robert Fitzpatrick, June 2, 1979; children: Sarah E., Ryan M., Stephanie G. BS in English Edn., Ball State U., 1979, MA in English, 1981. Asst. to dir. Ball State London Ctr., 1980-81; asst. to dean for minority affairs Purdue U. Sch. Engring and Tech., Indpls., 1983-86, asst. dean., 1987—; Mem. Ind. Gender Equity Adv. Bd., Inpls., 1991-94. Co-author: Composing Technical Documents, 1991. Career Devel. grantee AAUW Ednl. Found., 1992. Mem. Midwest Modern Lang. Assn. (chmn. computer rsch. sect. 1990-91, sec. 1989-90), Phi Delta Kappa. Office: Purdue U Sch Engring and Tech 799 W Michigan St Indianapolis IN 46202

FITZPATRICK, ELLEN, economist, consultant; b. Newark, June 22, 1957; d. Robert and Joan M. (Tampany) F. BA, Rutgers U., 1979; MS, Poly. U.,

White Plains, N.Y. Asst. staff mgr. N.Y. Telephone, N.Y.C., 1980-82, staff specialist, 1982-84, staff mgr., 1984-86, assoc. dir., 1986-87; sr. cons. KPMG Peat Marwick, Short Hills, N.J., 1987-89, mgr., 1989-91, sr. mgr., 1991-93; sr. mgr. Arthur Andersen & Co., Chgo., 1993—. Mem. Am. Econ. Assn., Nat. Assn. Bus. Economists, N.Y. Assn. Bus. Economists. Home: 415 W Aldine Ave # 15-A Chicago IL 60657 Office: Arthur Andersen & Co 33 W Monroe St Chicago IL 60603

FITZPATRICK, GAYLE DANIEL, human resources professional; b. Sylvester, Ga., Feb. 5, 1941; d. Howard Alton and Gladys (Little) Daniel; m. Henry Harris Fitzpatrick, July 27, 1963; 1 child, Beth. BSBA, North Ga. Coll., 1964; MBA, George Washington U., 1974. Chief clk. spl. com nat. emergencies del. emergency power U.S. Senate, Washington, 1975-76, staff asst. temporary com. to study Senate com. system, 1976-77; office and personnel mgr. Resources for the Future, Washington, 1977-78; personnel mgr. Brookings Instn., Washington, 1978-81; employee devel. specialist U.S. Army Europe, Kaiserslautern, Germany, 1981-84; dir. for personnel and adminstrn. Clean Sites, Inc., Alexandria, Va., 1984-87; chief non-appropriated funds div. civilian personnel office U.S. Army South, Republic of Panama, 1987-89; mgr. dist. office U.S. Census Bur., Alexandria, 1989-90; sr. v.p. human resources Prison Fellowship, Reston, Va., 1991—. Mem. ASTD, Soc. Human Resources Mgmt. Methodist.

FITZPATRICK, KELLY MOIRA, career officer; b. Alexandria, Va., Dec. 17, 1959; d. Kevin Anthony and Pauline Colette (Beauregard) F. BA in Journalism, Boston U., 1980; MA in Philosophy, Johns Hopkins U., 1988. Commd. 2d lt. U.S. Army, 1980, advanced through grades to maj., 1992; adj./co. comdr. 2d Quartermaster Bn. U.S. Army, Korea, 1980-81; chief adminstrv. svcs. U.S. Army, Ft. Hood, Tex., 1981-83, chief pers. actions br., 1983-84, co. comdr. 2d Armored Divsn., 1984-85; prof. philosophy U.S. Mil. Acad., West Point, N.Y., 1988-91; adj. gen. 19th Support Command, Korea, 1991-93; pub. affairs officer 24th Infantry Div., Ft. Stewart, Ga., 1993—. Mem. Assn. of U.S. Army. Office: 24th Infantry Divsn Fort Stewart GA 31314

FITZPATRICK, LOIS ANN, library administrator; b. Yonkers, N.Y., Mar. 27, 1952; d. Thomas Joseph and Dorothy Ann (Nealy) Sullivan; m. William George Fitzpatrick, Jr., Dec. 1, 1973; children: Jennifer Ann, Amy Ann. BS in Sociology, Mercy Coll., 1974; MLS, Pratt Inst., 1975. Clk. Yonkers (N.Y.) Pub. Library, 1970-73, librarian trainee, 1973-75, librarian I, 1975-76; reference librarian Carroll Coll. Library, Helena, Mont., 1976-79, acting dir., 1979, asst. prof., 1979-89, dir., 1980—, assoc. prof., 1989—; chmn. arrangements Mont. Gov.'s Pre White House Conf. on Libraries, Helena, 1977-78; mem. steering com. Reference Point coop. program for librs., 1991; mem. adv. com. Helena Coll. of Tech. Libr., 1994—. Pres. elect Helena Area Health Sci. Libraries Cons., 1979-84, pres., 1984-88; bd. dirs. Mont. FAXNET; co-chmn. interest group OCLC; chmn. local arrangements Mont. Gov.'s Pre White House Conf.; mem. adv. bd. Helena Coll. of Tech. Mem. Mont. Library Assn. task force for White House conf. 1991). Democrat. Roman Catholic. Club: Soroptimist Internat. of Helena (2d v.p. 1984-85, pres. 1986-87). Home: 1308 Shirley Rd Helena MT 59601-6635 Office: Carroll Coll Jack and Sallie Corette Libr Helena MT 59625-0099

FITZPATRICK, NANCY S., advertising executive; b. 1930. V.p., sec. J. Walter Thompson Co., N.Y.C. Office: J Walter Thompson Co 466 Lexington Ave New York NY 10017-3140

FITZPATRICK, SUSAN G. BEAMAN, management consultant; b. Oct. 15, 1954; d. Ralph P. and Gloria D. (Nelmark) Beaman; m. John H. Fitzpatrick, June 15, 1985; children: Sarah, Kevin, Michael, Brian. B.S., registered O.T., U. Ill., 1976. Supr. outpatient services Rehab. Inst. of Chgo., 1976-79; br. mgr. Kemper Group, Chgo., 1979-80, div. mgr. Midwest, 1980-81, asst. dir. Natlsco Rehab. Mgmt., Inc., 1981-82, v.p., 1983-85; mgmt. cons. Coopers & Lybrand, Chgo., 1985-86; v.p., gen. mgr. Bensinger, DuPont & Assoc, 1986-88; mng. ptnr. Fitzpatrick Enterprises, 1988—; grants chmn., dir. Barrington Area Arts Coun., 1990-91; lectr. in field. Contbr. articles to profl. jours. Mem. Nat. Occupational Therapy Assn. Republican. Home: 391 N Valley Ct Barrington IL 60010-3432 Office: 391 N Valley Ct Barrington IL 60010-3432

FITZSIMMONS, SHARON, tobacco and food products company executive. Treas. Philip Morris Internat., Port Chester, N.Y. Office: Philip Morris Internat 800 Westchester Ave Port Chester NY 10573*

FITZSIMMONS, SOPHIE SONIA, interior designer; b. Paris, July 6, 1943; came to U.S., 1947; d. Oleg and Sophie (Ovsianico-Koulikovsky) Yadoff; m. J. Heath Fitzsimmons, Sept. 8, 1962; children: Gregory James, Raymond Heath, Douglas Paul. AAS with honors, Fashion Inst. Tech., N.Y.C., 1964; student, NYU Wagner Sch., 1994. Design intern Euster Assocs., Inc., Armonk, N.Y., 1964; prin. Sophie Y. Fitzsimmons Interior Design, N.Y., Conn, 1964-77; co-owner Avon (Conn.), Interiors, Inc., 1977-89; prin. Sophie Fitzsimmons Interior Design, N.Y.C., 1989—; guest exhibitor Fashion Inst. Tech. Symposium, 1984. Author: Salute. Chair ann. show Hope Benefit, Hartford, Conn., 1975; mem. Rep. Women's Club Conn., 1978-89; bd. dirs. Friends of Hartford Ballet, 1986-88; vol. N.Y. Commn. UN, Consular Corps and Internat. Bus., 1992—; vol. tchr. East Internat. Community Ctr., 1993—; pres., bd. dirs. Squadron Line PTAA, 1976; bd. dirs. Simsbury chpt. Federated Women's Club, 1976. Decorated Medal of Recognition, French Resistance Movement, World War II; recipient Award Edn. Civique Chevalier. Mem. Nat. Soc. Interior Designers (adv. panel 1967), Hartford State Co. Stagehands, World Affairs Coun. (exec. forum), Mark Twain Meml. Wadsworth Atheneum, Bushnell Meml., Simsbury Farms Golf Assn. (bd. dirs. 1989), Bamm Hollow Women's Golf Assn. (bd. dirs. 1992—). Office: Sophie Fitzsimmons Interior 55 Liberty St New York NY 10005-1015

FIX-ROMLOW, JEANNE KAY, hair care products company executive; b. Madison, Wis., June 29, 1947; d. Glen H. and Violet M. (Bohnsack) Fix; m. Paul James Romlow, Nov. 7, 1985. Student, Madison Area Tech. Sch., 1966. Mgr. Fashion Fabrics, Madison, 1973-74; promotion dir. Livesey Enterprises, Madison, 1976-77; sales assoc. First Realty Group, Madison, 1977-79; territory mgr. Aerial Beauty and Barber Supply, Madison, 1979-83; regional dir. John Paul Mitchell Systems, Santa Clarita, Calif., 1983-85, v.p., 1986-87, sr. v.p., 1987-91, exec. v.p., 1991—. Home: 11344W Bay Dr Lodi WI 53555 Office: John Paul Mitchell Systems 26455 Golden Valley Rd Santa Clarita CA 91350-2621

FLAATEN, RUBY CHERYL, nurse manager; b. Mason City, Iowa, Dec. 12, 1944; d. Truman Almer and Truly Zeola (Ones) Flaaten. Diploma in nursing, Meth.-Kahler Sch. Nursing, 1965. Staff nurse Ear, Nose and Throat Rochester (Minn.) Meth. Hosp., 1965-67, asst. head nurse Ear, Nose and Throat, 1967-69; head nurse, nurse mgr. ear, nose and throat, plastic surgery, oral surgery, gen. surgery ophthalmology, gen. surgery Rochester (Minn.) Meth. Hosp./Mayo Med. Ctr., 1969—. Mem. ANA, Minn. Nurses Assn., 6th Dist. Minn. Nurses Assn. (sec.-treas., del.), Am. Orgn. Nurse Execs. (coun. nurse mgrs.), Minn. Orgn. Leaders in Nursing, Dist. F. Orgn. Leaders in Nursing, Oncology Nurse Soc., Am. Soc. Plastic and Reconstructive Surgery Nurses, Soc. Otorhinolaryngology and Head-Neck Nurses, Acad. Med.-Surg. Nurses, Meth.-Kahler Alumni Assn. (treas.), Sons of Norway. Republican. Lutheran. Home: 1929 3rd Ave NE Apt 4 Rochester MN 55906-4031

FLAGG, E(LOISE) ALMA WILLIAMS, educational administrator; b. City Point, Va., Sept. 16, 1918; d. Hannibal Greene and Caroline Ethel (Moody) Williams; m. J. Thomas Flagg, Jr., June 24, 1942; children: Thomas L., Lois Luisa. BS, Newark State Coll., 1940, LittD (hon.), 1968; MA, Montclair (N.J.) State Coll., 1943; EdD, Columbia U., 1955. Tchr., Washington, 1941-43; with Newark Pub. Schs., 1943-83, vice-prin., 1963-64, prin., 1964-67, asst. supt., 1967-78, dir., 1978-83; cons. edn., 1972—; adj. instr., guest speaker various univs. and colls, poet-in-residence various pub. schs. Author: (poetry) Lines and Colors, 1979, Feelings, Lines, Colors, 1980, Twenty More with Thought and Feeling, 1981; editor: Cardiac Valve Bioprosthesis. Mem. Newark Bicentennial Commn.; life mem. NAACP. Recipient various profl. awards; E. Alma Flagg Sch. erected, 1984; E. Alma Flagg Scholarship Fund established, 1984. Mem. LWV (pres. Newark 1982-84), AAUW, N.J. Hist. Soc., Assn. Supervision and Curriculum Devel., Nat. Soc. Study of Edn., Nat. Coun. Tchrs. of English, Nat. Assn. Negro Bus. and Profl. Women's Clubs (recipient Truth award, 1985) Nat. Coun. Tchrs. of Math., Nat. Alliance Black Sch. Educators, Nat. Coun. Negro Women (life), Newark Sr. Citizen's Commn. (editorial cons. 1989—), Alpha Kappa Alpha (life), Kappa Delta Pi. Presbyterian. Home: 44 Stengel Ave Newark NJ 07112-2410

FLAGG, JEANNE BODIN, editor; b. N.Y.C., July 13, 1925; d. G. William and Joan (Lippoth) Bergquist; m. Allen Elias Flagg, Apr. 15, 1955 (div. 1967); children—Jennifer Andrea, Christopher Trevor. B.A., Barnard Coll., 1947; M.A., Columbia U., 1950. Tech. editor Reinhold Pub. Corp., N.Y.C., 1951-57; editor Barnes & Noble, Inc., N.Y.C., 1967-71, Harper & Row Pubs., N.Y.C., 1971-88; sponsoring editor McGraw-Hill Pub. Co., N.Y.C., 1989—. Mem. AAAS. Home: 1015 Old Post Rd Mamaroneck NY 10543-3901 Office: McGraw-Hill Pub Co 1221 Ave Of The Americas New York NY 10020-1001

FLAHERTY, GERLINDE M. (LYNN FLAHERTY), marketing professional; b. Stuttgart, Fed. Republic Germany, Feb. 19, 1942; came to U.S., 1959; d. Wilhelm and Frida (Lorenz) Klenk; m. Gerard Eugene Flaherty, June 9, 1962; children—Curt P., Wayne T. Ed., Germany. With Honeywell Corp., 1959-89, word processing coordinator, Ft. Washington, Pa., 1977-83, sr. systems rep. Bull HN Info. Systems (formerly Honeywell Inc.), Bala Cynwyd, Pa., 1983-89; exec. sec. clin. rsch. Rorer Pharm. Corp., Horsham, Pa., 1989-91; corp. sec. to CEO, mktg. coord. Nat. Med. Svcs., Willow Grove, Pa., 1991—. Mem. Assn. Info. Systems Profls. (pres. Ft. Washington chpt. 1982-86), Am. Bus. Women's Assn. (v.p. membership 1984, v.p. 1986, pres. 1987-88, 93-94, developer, organizer new chpt. 1988—, Woman of Yr. 1983), NAFE. Home: 1194 Emma Ln Warminster PA 18974-2634 Office: Nat Med Svcs 2300 Stratford Ave Willow Grove PA 19090-4123

FLAHERTY, SERGINA MARIA, ophthalmic medical technologist; b. Düsseldorf, Germany, Nov. 22, 1958; came to U.S., 1962; d. Austin W. and Evelyn (Kähl) F. Cert. ophthalmic med. technologist. Ophthalmic asst. U.S. Army, Ft. Rucker, Ala., 1978-82; ophthalmic technician Wiregrass Total Eye Care Clinic, Enterprise, Ala., 1983-86, Straub Hosp. and Clinic, Honolulu, 1986-90; ophthalmic technologist Sheldon Braverman and Assocs., San Antonio, 1993—. Mem. Assn. Tech. Pers. in Ophthalmology, Ophthalmic Photographer Soc., Hawaii Ophthalmic Assts. Soc. (pres. 1989-90, sec. 1987-89, founding mem.), Ophthalmic Pers. Soc. San Antonio (program dir. 1994—). Home: 5650 Grissom Rd Apt 807 San Antonio TX 78238-2251 Office: Sheldon P Braverman & Assoc 1100 N Main Ave San Antonio TX 78212-4712

FLAHERTY, TINA SANTI, corporate communications executive; b. Memphis; d. Clement Alexander and Dale (Pendergrast) Santi; m. William Edward Flaherty, Feb. 22, 1975. B.A., Memphis State U., 1961; hon. doctorate, St. John's U., 1979. Commentator host interview program Sta. WMC-TV, Memphis, 1960-61; newscaster, commentator Sta. WHER, Memphis, 1961-62; community rels. specialist Western Electric Co., N.Y.C., 1964-66; v.p. pub. rels. div. Grey Advt., N.Y.C., 1966-72; dep. dir. corp. rels. Colgate-Palmolive Co., N.Y.C., 1972-75; dir. corp. rels. Colgate-Palmolive Co., 1975-76, corp. v.p., v.p. in charge of communications, 1976-84; v.p. pub. affairs GTE Corp., Stamford, Conn., 1984-86; pres., chief exec. officer Image Mktg. Internat., N.Y.C., 1986—. Former chmn. Bus. Coun. of UN Decade for Women; bd. dirs. Nat. Jr. Achievement, 1978—, Hugh O'Brian Youth Found.; mem. adv. bd. Santa Fe Chamber Music Festival; mem. The White House Pub. Affairs Advisors; nat. bd. dirs. Animal Med. Ctr. Recipient Jr. Achievement Meml. award, 1984; Named One of N.Y.C.'s Outstanding Women of Achievement NCCJ, 1978; One of 100 Top Corp. Women Bus. Week, 1976, One of 73 Women Ready to Run Corp. Am., Working Woman, 1985; named Woman of Distinction Birmingham So. Coll., 1991. Mem. Com. of 200, Internat. Women's Forum. Home and Office: Image Mktg Internat 1040 Fifth Ave PH New York NY 10028

FLAKE, LEONE ELIZABETH, special education educator; b. New Orleans, Jan. 12, 1938; d. Alfred Charles and Ione (Mills) Ittmann; m. Allen Oliver Flake, July 25, 1959; children: Diana Lee, Alan Mark, Wendy Lynn. BA, St. Mary's Dominican, New Orleans, 1973; MEd, U. New Orleans, 1979, postgrad., 1980. Cert. elem. tchr., learning disabled, social maladjusted, emotionally disturbed, kindergarten, mild moderate, severe profound, computer literacy, La. Tchr. grade 2 Jefferson Parish Sch. Board, Metairie, La., 1973-74, tchr. grade 3, 1974-75, tchr. grade 1, 1975-79, spl. edn. tchr. emotionally disturbed, 1979-87, generic tchr., spl. edn., 1987—, spl. edn. tchr., exptl. tchr., 1991—; substitute prin. Marie Riviere Elem., Metairie, 1992—. Spl. edn. chair, Marie Riviere Elem., 1987—, sch. rep., 1987—, sch. dir. very spl. arts., 1987—, spl. needs tchr., 1991—, elem. discipline com., 1987—, sch. bld. level com. for project read, 1992—, elem. safety com., 1987—, sch. effectiveness action plan com., 1987—, sch. bldg. level com., 1987—, spl. program to upgrade reading task force, 1984-85; counselor, At Risk Students for Project Charlie, 1991—. Recipient cert. of Merit Jefferson Parish Coun. Of Charitable Involvement, 1985, Jefferson Parish key to the City, 1985, Appreciation cert. Coun. for Exceptional Children, 1991, Outstanding Tchr. award Am. Petroleum Inst., 1992-93. Mem. The Orton Dyslecic Soc., Internat. Reading Assn., La. Reading Assn., Coun. for Exceptional Children, Children Adults with Attention Deficit Disorders, J.C. Ellis Coop. Club (v.p. 1984-84), Phi Delta Kappa, Kappa Delta Pi, Beta Sigma Phi (internat. mem, preceptor 1973—),. Home: 3701 Wanda Lynn Dr Metairie LA 70002

FLANAGAN, ANITA MARIE, public relations professional, environmentalist; b. South Charleston, W.Va., Sept. 25, 1940; d. Henry August and Mary Margaret (Hodge) Thormahlen; m. Shaun Michael Flanagan; children: Michael Lawrance, Sheilah Mary Catherine. AB, Northeastern U., 1963; BS, Southeastern Mass. U., 1977; MS in Environ. Health Mgmt., Harvard U., 1983. Planning cons. Town of Duxbury (Mass.), 1983; mgr. Pub. Participation Program Mass. Dept. Environ. Mgmt., Boston, 1984-86; community relations dir. Clean Harbors Inc., Braintree, Mass., 1986-88, Flanagan-Thompson Assocs., Plymouth, 1988-89; sr. pub. info. rep. Boston Edison Co., Plymouth, Mass., 1989-95; asst. to pres. Bridgewater (Mass.) State Coll., 1995—; hazardous waste coord., mem. oil spill response team Town of Duxbury, 1980-85; presenter pub. info. mgrs.' conf. European Nuclear Soc., Annecy, France, 1992. Mem. APHA, AAAS, Soc. for Risk Analysis, Am. Nuclear Soc., Nat. Assn. Environ. Profls., Assn. for Women in Sci. (presenter USCEA Info '91, European Nuclear Soc. Pime '92, '93).

FLANAGAN, ANNE PATRICIA, art educator, artist; b. Methuen, Mass., Jan. 26, 1927; d. John Joseph and Kathryn Josephine (Conley) Kane; m. Robert William Flanagan, Dec. 27, 1951; children: Robert W. Jr., Kathryn A., Joan Marie. B in Music Edn., Boston U., 1948; BFA, U. N.H., 1982. Cert. tchr. Mass. Supr. music Town of Middetown, R.I., 1948-50; asst. supr. music Towns of Littleton, Harvard and Stow, Mass., 1951-52; adj. therapist music Bayberry Psychiat. Hosp., Hampton, Va., 1973-74; relief mgr. Fidelity House, Lawrence, Mass., 1979-82; asst. mgr. Fidelity House, Lawrence, 1982; instr. oil painting Adult Edn. Program, Derry, N.H., 1984-86; art tchr., dept. chair St. Joseph's Regional Sch., Salem, N.H., 1989—; charter mem. Alley Art Gallery, Portsmouth, N.H., 1982-84; mem. Art Group Gallery, Manchester, N.H., 1988-91. Exhibited works in numerous one-woman and group shows including Art Group Gallery, 1989, 88, Newburyport (Mass.) Art Assn., 1987 (1st prize), St. Matthew's Art Show, Windham, N.H., 1985 (1st prize), Alley Gallery, 1983-84, U. N.H., 1982. Vol. art tchr. St. Joseph's Regional Sch., Salem, 1989-91; vol. Korean Orphange, Seoul, 1966-67; vol. tchr. artistically gifted children after sch. program St. Joseph Regional Sch., 1991-94; tchr. art sr. citizens group Royal Crest, Andover, Mass., 1983-84; tchr. developmentally retarded adults Fidelity House, 1979-82. Recipient cert. of achievement Republic of Korea, Seoul, 1967, cert. of appreciation U.S. Army, 1976. Roman Catholic. Home: 138 Shadow Lake Rd Salem NH 03079 Office: St Josephs Regional Sch 40 Main St Salem NH 03079

FLANAGAN, BARBARA, journalist; b. Des Moines; d. John Merrill and Marie (Barnes) F.; m. Earl S. Sanford, 1966. Student, Drake U., 1942-43. With promotion dept. Mpls. Times, 1945-47; reporter Mpls. Tribune, 1947-58; women's editor, spl. writer Mpls. Star and Tribune, 1958-65; columnist Mpls. Star, 1965—. Author: Ovation, Minneapolis. Active Junior League Mpls., Womans Club Mpls.; bd. dirs. Minn. Opera., Friends of Mpls. Pub. Libr. Mem. Mpls. Soc. Fine Arts (life), Mpls. Inst. Arts (founding mem. Minn. Arts Forum), Kappa Alpha Theta, Sigma Delta Chi. Episcopalian. Home: 3200 W Calhoun Pky Apt 301 Minneapolis MN 55416 Office: Mpls Star Tribune 5th and Portland Sts Minneapolis MN 55488

FLANAGAN, DEBORAH MARY, lawyer; b. Hackensack, N.J., Sept. 17, 1956; d. Joseph Francis and Mary Agnes (Fitzsimmons) F.; m. Glen H. Koch, Aug. 27, 1983. BA summa cum laude, Fordham U., 1978, JD, 1981; LLM taxation, NYU, 1987. Bar: N.Y. 1982 and U.S. Dist. Ct. 1988. V.p., assoc. tax counsel McGraw-Hill Inc., N.Y.C., 1981—. Mem. ABA, N.Y. State Bar Assn., Assn. of Bar of City of N.Y., N.Y. County Lawyers Assn., Fordham U. Law Alumni Assn. Home: 201 Chestnut Ridge Rd Saddle River NJ 07458-2818 Office: McGraw-Hill Inc 1221 Ave Of The Americas New York NY 10020-1001

FLANAGAN, JUDITH ANN, marketing and entertainment specialist; b. Lubbock, Tex., Apr. 28, 1950; d. James Joseph II and Jean (Breckenridge) F. BS in Edn., Memphis State U., 1972. Area/parade supr. Entertainment div. Walt Disney World, Orlando, Fla., 1972-81; parade dir. Gatlinburg (Tenn.) C. of C., 1981-85; entertainment prodn. mgr. The 1982 World's Fair, Knoxville, 1982; cons. Judy Flanagan Prodns./Spl. Events, Gatlinburg, 1982—, Miss U.S.A. Pageant, Knoxville, 1983; prodn. coord. Nashville Network, 1983; dir. sales River Terr. Resort, Gatlinburg, 1985-86; account exec. Park Vista Hotel, Gatlinburg, 1986-88; project coord. Universal Studios, Fla., 1988-90; dir. spl. events in univ. rels. U. Tenn., Knoxville, 1990—; prodn. mgr. 1984 World's Fair Parades and Spl. Events, New Orleans, Neil Sedaka rock video, Days of Our Lives daytime soap opera. Mem. Memphis State U. Acad. Donor Fund. Named One of Outstanding Young Women Am., 1981; recipient Gatlinburg Homecoming award, 1986. Mem. Memphis State U. Alumni Assn. Roman Catholic. Home: 350 Bruce Rd Gatlinburg TN 37738-5612

FLANAGAN, NATALIE SMITH, state representative; b. Bradford, Mass., Aug. 6, 1913; d. Forrest Van Zandt and Blanche (Robbins) Smith; m. John Frances Flanagan, Sept. 20, 1944 (dec.). Grad. high sch., Vassalboro, Maine. Mem. N.H. Ho. of Reps., Concord, 1973—, chmn. constl. and statutory com., 1987—. Pres. Mass. chpt. Young Reps., 1930—; pres. bd. dirs. Haverhill (Mass.) Girls Club, 1940—; founder Rockingham (N.H.) Nutrition Program, 1979; mem. N.H. Bicentennial Commn., 1983—. Recipient Meritorious Pub. Svc. medal Sec. State, 1990. Congregationalist. Home: 132 Maple Ave Atkinson NH 03811-2245 Office: NH State Legis Legis Office Bldg Rm 302 Concord NH 03301*

FLANAGAN, THERESE ANN, real estate, roofing and construction executive; b. Chgo., Sept. 23, 1955; d. William Joseph and Margaret Eileen (McNellis) F. BA, U. Fla., 1984, MA, 1987. With First Fed. of Lake Worth, Fla., 1973-74, Fla. Nat. Bank, Palm Beach, Fla., 1974-75, 77-79; salesman Irish Realty, Inc., Lake Worth, 1979-81; asst. mgr. Sun Bay Apts., Gainesville, Fla., 1982; with Library Systems, U. Fla., Gainesville, 1982-86; pres. Flanagan & Assocs. Realty, Lake Worth, 1986—, The Flanagan Cos., Lake Worth, 1992—. Producer, dir.: (video) Zora Neale Hurston, 1986. Vol. Textbook Reading for the Blind, Gainesville, 1987, The Children's Pl., West Palm Beach, Fla., 1988-89, Project Literacy, West Palm Beach, 1988-89, Reading Tutor, 1991—. Mem. BBB, Am. Cmty. Assn. Mgrs., Real Estate Brokerage Mgrs. Coun., West Palm Beach C. of C., Russian Club (treas. 1983-84), Phi Kappa Phi. Democrat. Roman Catholic. Office: The Flanagan Cos 3939 S Congress Ave Lake Worth FL 33461-4119

FLANAGIN, MICHELE DIANE, marketing specialist; b. Aurora, Ill., Nov. 8, 1959; d. Lloyd Densmore and Hildegarde M. (Rehe) F. BA, Northwestern U., 1981, MM, 1986. Sales rep. Canon Inc., Chgo., 1981-82; mktg. rep. Internat. Imaging, Chgo., 1982-83, mktg. specialist, 1983-87; mktg. mgr. U. Chgo. Dept. Med., 1987-89; dir. of practice mktg., 1989—. Mem. Am. Hosp. Assn., Beta Gamma Sigma.

FLANARY, KATHY VENITA MOORE, librarian; b. Amherst, Tex., Jan. 15, 1946; d. Charles Edward and Jean (Willman) Moore; children: Suzanne Flanary, Charles Flanary. BA, U. Ill., 1972, MLS, 1974. Cert. profl. libr., N.Mex.; cert. tchr., N.Mex. Dir. children's libr. Hayner Pub. Libr., Alton, Ill., 1974-76; dir. Ruidoso (N.Mex.) Pub. Libr., 1978-80; libr. media specialist Horgan Libr., N.Mex. Mil. Inst., Roswell, 1985-93; libr. N.Mex. Sch. Visually Handicapped, Alamogordo, 1993—; workshop presenter Lewis & Clark Regional Libr. Systems, Ill., 1975; outreach programer Hayner Pub. Libr., 1974-76; del. Pre-White Ho. Conf., State of N.Mex., 1991. Contbr. articles to newspapers and profl. jours. Bd. dirs. Alton Symphony, 1975; mem. Altrusa, Ruidoso, 1979-84, Friend of Roswell Pub. Libr.; sec. Ruidoso Summer Festival, 1979; bd. dirs. Supts. Adv. Bd., Roswell, N.Mex., 1987-89; pres. Friends of Libr., Ruidoso, 1980-83, Parent Advocacy for Gifted Edn., 1990-92; v.p. Sunset PTA; bd. dirs. N.Mex. Libr. Found., 1992—. Recipient Svc. award Altrusa, 1979, Sunset PTA, 1989. Mem. N.Mex. Libr. Assn. (libr. devel. com., edn. tech. roundtable vice chair 1991, chair elect 1992, co-chair state conv. local arrangements 1990-91, 2d v.p. 1993-94, 1st v.p. 1994-95, pres. 1995-96), N.Mex. Acad. and Rsch. Librs. (vice chair 1992, pres. 1993), Kiwanis (bd. dirs. 1990-92).

FLANDERS, CATHY CHRISTIENNE, statistical and program consultant, researcher; b. Auburn, N.Y., Oct. 21, 1951; d. Russell Benson and Lillian (Pine) F. BS in Psychology cum laude, U. Md., College Park, 1990, postgrad., 1991—. Freelance artist Md., 1972-75; groom, exercize rider Md. Racing Assocs., Md., Del., N.Y., 1975-78; thoroghbred horse trainer Md. Racing Assocs., 1978-83; freelance writer Balt. News Am. Horseman's Jour., 1983-85; exec. dir. The Discovery Inst., 1991—; cons., rschr. psychology. Contbr. articles to profl. jours. Mem. Am. Psychological Assn., Phi Kappa Phi. Democrat. Home: 12703 Bermuda Ln Bowie MD 20715

FLANDERS, PAULA FREISE, public health service officer; b. Bismarck, N.D., Feb. 4, 1949; d. Hubert Richard and Marion Edith (Johnson) Freise; m. Marlow Lee Flanders, June 9, 1972; children: Trevor Jay, Bridgette Lynn, Ian Turner. BSN, Jamestown Coll., 1971. Adminstr., dir. nursing Golden Manor Nursing Facility, Steele, N.D., 1971-74; home health nurse Home Med. Resources, Bismarck, 1974-88; health faciltiy surveyor N.D. Dept. Health and Consol. Labs., Bismarck, 1988-92, mgr. licensure and cert., 1992—; mem. Kidder County Health Bd., Steele, 1975-88. Leader Farmerettes and Willing Workers 4-H Club, Pettibone, N.D., 1985—, county consumer choice judging coach, Kidder County, 1988—. Mem. N.D. Nat. Mgmt. Assn., N.D. Environ. Health Practitioners Assn. Home: HC 2 Box 115 Pettibone ND 58475 Office: ND Dept Health & Consol Lab State Capitol Jud Wing 600 E Boulevard Ave Bismarck ND 58505-0200

FLANIGEN, EDITH MARIE, materials scientist. Sr. rsch. fellow materials sci. UOP Tarrytown (N.Y.) Tech. Ctr. Recipient Perkin medal Am. Chem. Soc., 1992, Francis P. Garvan-John M. Olin medal Am. Chem. Soc., 1993. Office: UOP Tarrytown Tech Ctr 777 Old Saw Mill River Rd Rte 100 C Tarrytown NY 10591

FLANNELLY, LAURA T., mental health nurse, nursing educator, researcher; b. Bklyn., Nov. 7, 1952; d. George A. Adams and Eleanor (Barragry) Mulhearn; m. Kevin J. Flannelly, Jan. 10, 1981. BS in Nursing, Hunter Coll., 1974; MSN, U. Hawaii, 1984, postgrad., 1988—. RN, N.Y., Hawaii. Psychiat. nurse Bellevue Hosp., N.Y.C., 1975, asst. head nurse, 1975-77; psychiat. nurse White Plains (N.Y.) Med. Ctr., 1978-79; community mental health nurse South Beach Psychiat. Ctr., N.Y.C., 1979-81; psychiat. nurse The Queen's Med. Ctr., Honolulu, 1981-83; crisis worker Crisis Response Systems Project, Honolulu, 1983-86; instr. nursing U. Hawaii, Honolulu, 1985-92, asst. prof., 1992—; adj. instr. nursing Hawaii Loa Coll., Honolulu, 1988, Am. Samoa Community Coll., Honolulu, 1987, 89, 90; mem. adv. bd., planning com. Psychiat. Day Hosp. of The Queen's Med. Ctr., Honolulu, 1981-82; program coord. Premenstrual Tension Syndrome Conf., Honolulu, 1984; dir. Ctr. Psychosocial Rsch., Honolulu, 1987—; program moderator 1st U.S-Japan Health Behavioral Conf., Honolulu, 1988; faculty Ctr. for Asia-Pacific Exch., Internat. Conf. on Transcultural Nursing, Honolulu, 1990; mem. bd. dirs. U. Hawaii Profl. Assembly, 1994—. Contbr. articles to profl. jours. N.Y. State Bd. Regents scholar, 1970-74; NIH nursing trainee, 1983-84; grantee U. Hawaii, 1986, 91, Hawaii Dept. Health, 1990. Fellow Internat. Soc. Rsch. on Aggression; mem. AAAS, Am. Ednl.

Rsch. Assn., Am. Psychol. Soc., Am. Statis. Assn., Nat. League for Nursing, N.Y. Acad. Scis., Pacific and Asian Affairs Coun., Sigma Theta Tau. Home: 445 Kaiolu St Apt 1006 Honolulu HI 96815-2255 Office: U Hawaii Sch Nursing Webster Hall Honolulu HI 96822

FLANNERY, CAROLINE OLSON, real estate broker; b. San Antonio, Apr. 28, 1942; d. Marion Alfred and Martha (Pancoast) Olson; m. John Oge Flannery, Jr., May 21, 1977. BA, U. Tex., 1963; MA, Incarnate Word Coll., San Antonio, 1975. Cert real estate broker, tchr., Tex. Biology tchr. Alamo Heights High Sch., San Antonio, 1965-72; sales and mgmt. tng. supr. Tex. Pharmacal Co., San Antonio, 1972-79; sales assoc. Guy Chipman Co., San Antonio, 1979-81, office mgr., 1981-84; pres. CF Enterprises, San Antonio, 1984-87; mktg. dir. Kuper Realty, 1987-89; office mgr. Hallmark Bradfield Properties, San Antonio, 1989-90, Guy Chipman Co., San Antonio, 1990-94; tng. dir., mgmt. cons. Kuper Realty, San Antonio, 1994—; instr. Am. Coll. Real Estate, San Antonio Bd. Realtors, 1986-89. Author: Skin Care Training Manual, 1975. Co-chmn. Bexar County Women's Ctr. Assn. Annual Fund Raiser, San Antonio, 1988. Recipient Jr. Goodwill Amb. award Am. Red Cross 9 European Countries, 1958. Mem. Nat. Assn. Realtors, Tex. Assn. Realtors, San Antonio Bd. Realtors, Battle of Flowers Assn., Jr. League of San Antonio, S.W. Found. Forum, Lantana Garden Club (pres. 1986-87). Republican. Methodist. Home: 4 Plum Ln San Antonio TX 78218-6025 Office: Kuper Realty Corp 6606 N New Braunfels San Antonio TX 78209

FLANNERY, ELIZABETH MARIE, psychologist; b. Mauston, Wis., Nov. 18, 1954; d. Robert E. and Pauline M. (Dietrich) F.; m. Michael J. Swords, June 17, 1989; children: Liam James Flannery Swords, Colin Michael Flannery Swords. BS in Sociology, U. Wis., 1977, BS in Psychology, 1977, MSW, 1980, PhD in Psychology, 1986. Lic. psychologist, Maine, marriage and family therapist, Maine. Asst. clin. prof. U. Vt., Burlington, 1987-90; psychologist Portland, Maine, 1989—. Mem. Nat. Register of Health Care Providers Psychology, APA, Nat. Assn. Sch. Psychology. Office: 527 Ocean Ave Portland ME 04103

FLANNERY, ELLEN JOANNE, lawyer; b. Bklyn., Dec. 13, 1951; d. William Rowan and Mary Jane (Hamilla) Flannery. AB cum laude, Mount Holyoke Coll., 1973; JD cum laude, Boston U., 1978. Bar: Mass. 1978, D.C. 1979, U.S. Ct. Appeals (D.C. cir.) 1979, U.S. Ct. Appeals (4th cir.) 1981, U.S. Ct. Appeals (6th cir.) 1983, U.S. Ct. Appeals (3d cir.) 1987, U.S. Dist. Ct. D.C. 1980, U.S. Dist. Ct. Md. 1985, U.S. Supreme Ct. 1983. Spl. asst. to commr. of health Mass. Dept. Pub. Health, Boston, 1973-75; law clk. U.S. Ct. Appeals D.C. cir., Washington, 1978-79; assoc. Covington & Burling, Washington, 1979-86, ptnr., 1986—; lectr. ins. U. Va. Sch. Law, 1984-90, Boston U. Sch. Law, 1993, U. Md. Sch. Law, 1994; mem. Nat. Conf. Lawyers and Scientists, AAAS-ABA, 1989-92. Contbr. to articles to profl. jours. Mem. ABA (chmn. com. med. practice 1987-88, chmn. life scis div. 1982-84, 88-91, vice chair food and drug law com. 1991—, chmn. sect. sci. and tech. 1992-93, del. of sci. and tech. sect. to ho. of dels. 1993—). Office: Covington & Burling PO Box 7566 1201 Pennsylvania Ave NW Washington DC 20044

FLASHMAN-KNEPPER, ALBERTA ROSE, psychiatrist; b. Newark, Aug. 7, 1934; d. Samuel Julius and Raschen (Solomon) Cohen; m. Edward B. Frankel, 1958 (div. 1967); children: Rebecca Kron, Judith Cohen, Laura Frankel; m. Barry Paul Flashman, 1970 (div. 1980); m. William Edgar Knepper, Oct. 3, 1987. BA, UCLA, 1955; MD, U. So. Calif., 1960. Diplomate Am. Bd. Psychiatry. Intern L.A. County Gen. Hosp., L.A., 1961-62, resident in dermatology, 1962-65; resident in psychiatry St. Elizabeth Hosp., Washington, 1970-71, Inst. Psychiat. Human Behaviour, Balt., 1971-73; pvt. practice Annapolis, Md., 1973—. Mem. Am. Psychiat. Assn., Am. Group Therapy Assn., Md. Psychiat. Assn., Anne Arundel Med. Assn., Alpha Omega Alpha. Democrat. Jewish. Office: 99 Cathedral St Annapolis MD 21401

FLASKAMP, RUTH EHMEN STAACK, retired elementary education educator; b. Moline, Ill., Dec. 11, 1927; d. Henry Frederick and Tjiede Lena (Ehmen) Staack; m. Richard Kresse Flaskamp, June 10, 1950; children: Richard Henry, Thomas Marc. BA, Augustana Coll., 1949; MEd, Bowling Green State U., 1971. Tchr. elem. grades Lanark (Ill.) Consolidated Schs., 1949-50; tchr. elem. grades Sylvania (Ohio) City Schs., 1956-93, ret., 1993. Contbr. articles to profl. jours., various curriculum guides. Bd. dirs. Sylvania Pub. Libr., 1960-61; mem. edn1. adv. com. Toledo Edison, Toledo Zoo, 1986; active various polit. campaigns. Jennings scholar, 1982-83; recipient award for excellence in edn. NEA/Ladies Home Jour., 1990-91. Mem. NEA, Sylvania Edn. Assn. (sec. 1975-76, 89-90, pres. 1991), Ohio Edn. Assn. (rep.), N.W. Ohio Edn. Assn., Nat. Sci. Tchrs. Assn., Golden Emblem Club. Republican. Lutheran. Home: 4312 Holland-Sylvania Rd # 120 Toledo OH 43623 Office: Sylvania Stranahan Sch 3840 N Holland Sylvania Rd Toledo OH 43615-1008

FLATT, VICCI D'ANN, primary school educator; b. Ada, Okla., June 10, 1958; d. Forrest Wayne and Velma Ruth (Bullard) Mason; children: Leah Ruth, Sammy Dean Jr. BS, East Ctrl. U., 1988. Tchr. Big 5 Headstart, Ada, Okla., 1980-84, ECU Child Devel. Ctr., Ada, 1988-90; Carney (Okla.) Primary Pub. Schs. Carney (Okla.) Pub. Schs., 1990—. Mem. NEA, Okla. Edn. Assn., Okla. Reading Assn. Democrat. Mem. Ch. of Christ.

FLAX, FLORENCE ROSELIN, photographer; b. Brockton, Mass., June 23, 1936; d. Samuel and Aida (Liebowitz) Polinsky; m. Barry Melvin Flax, Mar. 23, 1963; children: Amy Rhonda, Matthew David. Student, Chandler Sch. for Women, Boston, 1955. Sec. Northeastern U., Boston, 1956-63; ind. artist, art dealer Vienna, Va., 1974-82; ind. photographer specializing in infrared and macro-photography Vienna, 1982—. Featured in group exhbns. Tartt Gallery, Washington, 1991, Internat. Platform Assn., Washington, 1991, 92 (judges choice award, 2d prize 1993, 1st prize 1994, 3d prize 1994), Ellipse Art Ctr., Arlington, Va., 1991, Capital Hill Art League, 1994; photo editor, photography columnist Old Dominion Sierran, 1993-94; contbr. photographs to 1995 Town of Vienna Calendar. Vol. Rep. Presdl. Campaign hdqrs., 1976, 80, 84; vol. Va. Chpt. Sierra Club, 1993—; mem. Women's Cabinet, Northeastern U., Boston, 1978. Mem. Am. Soc. Media Photographers (Mid Atlantic), Washington Figure Skating Club (charter), Sierra Club, World Wildlife Fund, Friends of the Nat. Zoo, Am. Film Inst., World Found. Successful Women (charter), Internat. Platform Assn., Capital Hill Art League. Home and Office: 104 Saratoga Waye NE Vienna VA 22180-3663

FLECHNER, ROBERTA FAY, graphic designer; b. N.Y.C., June 7, 1949; d. Abraham Julius and Evelyn (Medwin) F. BA, CCNY, 1970; MA, NYU, 1972; cert. Printing Industries Met. N.Y., N.Y.C., 1974, 75, 79. Researcher, asst. editor Arno Press, N.Y.C., 1970-73; free-lance editor Random House, N.Y.C., 1973-74, graphic designer/compositor coll. dept., 1984—; graphic designer Core Communications in Health, N.Y.C., 1974-76; prodn. mgr. Heights-Inwood News, N.Y.C., 1976-77; art dir., graphic designer Jour. Advt. Research, N.Y.C., 1976-81; prin., graphic designer/compositor Roberta Flechner Graphics, N.Y.C., 1976—; graphic designer/compositor W. W. Norton & Co., Inc., 1977—, McGraw Hill, Inc., 1990—; mech. artist Fawcett, N.Y.C., 1979-80; graphic designer Avon Internat., N.Y.C., 1982; art dir., compositor, layout artist Source: Notes in the History of Art, N.Y.C., 1982—; graphic designer John Wiley & Sons, Inc., N.Y.C., 1985. Designer stationery, 1979 (Art Direction mag., Creativity-cert. distinction 1979). Art dir. enviroNews, N.Y. State Atty. Gen.'s Environ. Protection Bur., N.Y.C., 1977-78. Mem. Graphic Artists Guild, NOW, Women's Nat. Book Assn. (cons.), Nat. Assn. Female Execs., Women's Caucus for Art, Am. Inst. Graphic Arts, CCNY Alumni, NYU Alumni. Office: 10615 Queens Blvd Flushing NY 11375-4365

FLEETWOOD, MARY ANNIS, education association executive; b. Winfield, Ala., July 31, 1931; d. George A. and Martha Ann (Perry) Sullivan; m. Lewis N. Fleetwood, Aug. 19, 1950; children: Juanita, Dexter Lewis, Melanie Louise. Student, HCC Community Coll., 1973-80. Gen. office staff Able Rose Mercentile Co., Birmingham, Ala., 1949-51; with auditing dept. Bank for Savs. & Trusts, Birmingham, Ala., 1951; account receivables clk. I.W. Phillips, Tampa, Fla., 1972-77; account clk. Sch. Bd. Hill County, Tampa, Fla., 1980, office mgr., 1981-90. V.p. PTA, 1961-62; pres. Woman's Missionary Union, Birmingham, 1963-64. Mem. Nat. Inst. Govt. Purchasing (cert. profl. buyer). Baptist. Home: 601 W Sylvan Dr Brandon FL 33510-3542

FLEEZANIS, JORJA KAY, violinist, educator; b. Detroit, Mar. 19, 1952; d. Parios Nicholas and Kaliope (Karageorge) F.; m. Michael Steinberg, July 3, 1983. Student, Cleve. Inst. Music, 1969-72, Cin. Coll.-Conservatory Music, 1972-75. Violinist Chgo. Symphony Orch., 1975-76; concertmaster Cin. Chamber Orch., 1976-80; violinist Trio D'Accordo, Cin., 1976-80; asst. prin. 2d violinist San Francisco Symphony Orch., 1980-81; assoc. concertmaster San Francisco Sympony Orch., 1980-89; acting concertmaster Minn. Orch., Mpls., 1988-89, concertmaster, 1989—; violinist Am. Piano Trio, San Francisco, 1984—; faculty mem. San Francisco Conservatory of Music, 1983-89, U. Minn., 1990-93; founder Chamber Music Sundaes, San Francisco, 1980-89. Performer World Premiere John Adams Violin Concerto with Minn. Orch., 1994; rec. artist CRI and Koch Classical Records. Democrat. Office: Minn Orch 1111 Nicollet Mall Minneapolis MN 55403-2406

FLEISCHER, CYNTHIA SILVERMAN, special education educator; b. Chgo., May 6, 1951; d. Herbert Sanford and Francine Patricia (Leeb) Silverman; m. Cary Steven Fleischer, June 3, 1973; 1 child, Holly Anne. BA, Washington U., St. Louis, 1973; MA, Northwestern U., 1974; cert. advanced study, Nat.-Louis U., Evanston, Ill., 1992. Cert. in elem. edn., early childhood edn., learning disabilities, behavioral disorders, gen. adminstv. and supervisory, Ill. Spl. edn. tchr. Julia Molloy Edn. Ctr., Morton Grove, Ill., 1974-79; dir., tchr. St. Elisabeth's Nursery Sch., Glencoe, Ill., 1984-85, 86-87; coord. Hillel Torah North Suburban Day Sch., Skokie, Ill., 1987-90; spl. edn. tchr. Sch. Dist. 29, Northfield, Ill., 1991—; at risk cons. Hillel Torah North Suburban Day Sch., 1990-91. Bd. dirs., mem.-at-large assoc. bd. Chgo. Lighthouse for the Blind, 1988-94; bd. dirs. PTO, Deerfield, 1987-92. Mem. ASCD, Orton Dyslexia Soc., Phi Beta Kappa. Office: Sch Dist 29 525 Sunset Ridge Rd Northfield IL 60093-1025

FLEISCHER, ELLEN LEE, real estate agent; b. Cin., Dec. 15, 1945; d. Leo Simon and Janet F. BA in Mgmt. Econs., U. Cin., 1968. Pub. rels. Cin. Gas and Electric CO., 1968-71; campaign coord. Taft for Senate, Cin., 1971-72; new bus. devel. profl. Fifth Third Bank N.A., Cin., 1973-77; mktg. mgr. Williamsburg Mgmt., Cin., 1984-86; real estate agt. Sibcy Cline Realtors, Ft. Mitchell, Ky., 1986-91, Re/Max Affiliates, Ft. Mitchell, 1992—; artist, Cin., 1979-86; mem. Kenton Boone Bd. Realtors, Northern Ky. Exhibitor watercolor abstracts various galleries in Cin., Naples and Coral Gables, Fla., N.Y.C.; author essay, Congl. Record, 1st pl. award, 1968. Mem. Ky. Assn. Realtors (mem. legis. devel. com. 1990), Million Dollar Club, Friends of Covington, No. Ky. Heritage League, Cin. Art Mus., Omicron Delta Epsilon. Home: 100 Riverside Pl Covington KY 41011-5711

FLEISCHER, MARTHA HESTER, lawyer, English educator; b. Portland, Maine; d. Carl Everett and Ruth (Jordan) Hester; m. Bruce Golden, 1962 (div. 1967); m. Stefan Fleischer, June 15, 1968; children: Katharine Anne, Victor Everett. BA, Duke U., 1958; MA, Columbia U., 1959, PhD, 1964; JD, SUNY, Buffalo, 1982. Bar: N.Y. 1983, U.S. Dist. Ct. (we. dist.) N.Y. 1983, Fla. 1983. Assoc. Nixon Hargrave Devans & Doyle, Rochester, N.Y., 1982-86, Lacy, Katzen, Mittleman & Ryen, Rochester, N.Y., 1986-87; v.p., assoc. counsel Mfrs. and Traders Trust Co., Buffalo, 1987—. Home: 114 Windsor Ave Buffalo NY 14209-1019 Office: Mfrs and Traders Trust Co One M & T Plaza Buffalo NY 14240

FLEISCHMAN, BARBARA GREENBERG, public relations consultant; b. Detroit, Mar. 20, 1924; d. Samuel J. and Theresa (Keil) Greenberg; BA, U. Mich., 1944; m. Lawrence A. Fleischman, Dec. 18, 1948; children: Rebecca, Arthur, Martha. Tchr., Detroit Public Schs., 1944-45, psychoanalyst's sec., Detroit, 1947-49; sec. Greenberg Ins. Agy., Detroit, 1947-49; customer/public relations cons. Kennedy Galleries, N.Y.C., 1976—. Bd. dirs. Detroit Artists Market, 1958-66; mem. women's com. Detroit Inst. Arts, 1957-66, founder, pres. vol. com., 1961-66; bd. dirs. Friends of Channel 13, 1968-80, pres., N.Y.C., 1975-79, chmn. auction, 1975, trustee, 1975-84; pres. Friends of N.Y. Pub. Library, 1979-84, trustee, 1980—, v.p. bd., 1987—; bd. dir. Am. Craft Coun., 1980-83; trustee The Acting Co., 1986-89, pres. 1988-89; governing bd. Off the Record Luncheons, Fgn. Policy Assn., 1978-85; assoc. producer Channel 13 Auction, 1978-80; trustee Mus. TV and Radio, 1988-92; mem. vis. com. Greek and Roman Dept. Boston Mus. Fine Arts, 1990—, Met. Mus., 1991—; bd. dirs. Planned Parenthood N.Y.C., 1990—. Mem. Cosmopolitan Club. Office: Kennedy Galleries Inc 40 W 57th St New York NY 10019-4001

FLEISHER, MARCY BETH, television reporter; b. Chgo., July 15, 1964; d. Richard Sheldon and Carol Sue (Sagett) F. BAS, U Mich., 1986. Reporter Sta. WAAM-NBC Radio, Ann Arbor, Mich., 1985-86; prodn. asst. NBC News, N.Y.C., 1986-87; anchorwoman, reporter Sta. WENY-ABC TV, Elmira, N.Y., 1987-88, Sta. WICZ-NBC TV, Binghamton, N.Y., 1988-89; reporter Sta. WTNH-ABC TV, New Haven, 1989-90, Sta. WBNS-CBS TV, Columbus, Ohio, 1990—. Mem. Young Jewish Profls., Sigma Delta Tau. Office: Sta WBNS-TV 770 Twin Rivers Dr Columbus OH 43215-1127

FLEISHMAN, WENDY RUTH, lawyer; b. Phila., Dec. 28, 1954; d. Harry and Sylvia (Laub) F. B.A., Sarah Lawrence Coll., 1974; J.D., Temple U., 1977; postgrad. U. Pa., 1981-83. Bar: Pa. 1977, U.S. Dist. Ct. (ea. dist.) Pa. 1984, N.Y. 1992. Asst. dist. atty. City of Phila., 1977-84; assoc. Ballard, Spahr, Andrews & Ingersoll, Phila., 1984-86; ptnr. Fox, Rothschild, O'Brien & Frankel, 1987-93; assoc. Skadden, Arps, Slate, Meagher & Flom, N.Y.C., 1993—. Bd. dirs. Women Organized Against Rape, Women's Way (both Phila.). Mem. ABA (editor torts and ins. practice Trial Techniques Newsletter 1993—, mem. adv. bd. on products liability Practicing Law Inst., mem. faculty Nat. Inst. Trial Advocacy, mem. criminal justice com.), Fed. Bar Assn., Am. Arbitration Assn. (arbitrator), Pa. Bar Assn. (mem. prof. responsibility com., atty. adv. com.), N.Y. Womens Bar Assn. Democrat. Jewish. Office: Skadden Arps et al 919 3rd Ave New York NY 10022

FLEMING, ALICE CAREW MULCAHEY (MRS. THOMAS J. FLEMING), author; b. New Haven, Dec. 21, 1928; d. Albert Leo and Agnes (Foley) Mulcahey ; m. Thomas J. Fleming, Jan. 19, 1951; children: Alice, Thomas, David, Richard. AB, Trinity Coll., 1950; MA, Columbia U., 1951. Author: The Key to New York, 1960, Wheels, 1960, A Son of Liberty, 1961, Doctors in Petticoats, 1964, Great Women Teachers, 1965, The Senator from Maine: Margaret Chase Smith, 1969, Alice Freeman Palmer: Pioneer College President, 1970, Reporters At War, 1970, General's Lady, 1971, Highways into History, 1971, Pioneers in Print, 1971, Ida Tarbell, The First of the Muckrakers, 1971, Nine Months, 1972, Psychiatry, What's it All About?, 1972, The Moviemakers, 1973, Trials that Made Headlines, 1974, Contraception, Abortion, Pregnancy, 1974, New on the Beat, 1975, Alcohol: The Delightful Poison, 1975, Something for Nothing, 1978, The Mysteries of ESP, 1980, What to Say When You Don't Know What to Say, 1982, The King of Prussia and a Peanut Butter Sandwich, 1988, George Washington Wasn't Always Old, 1991, What, Me Worry?, 1992, P.T. Barnum: The World's Greatest Showman, 1993; editor: Hosannah the Home Run!, 1972, America Is Not All Traffic Lights, 1976; contbr. articles to mags. Nat. bd. dirs., mem. bd. dirs. N.Y. region Medic Alert Found. U.S., past. chmn. N.Y. regional bd.; mem. pres.'s coun. United Hosp. Fund; voting mem. Empire Blue Cross and Blue Shield. Recipient Nat. Media award Family Svc. Assn. Am., 1973, Alumnae Achievement award Trinity Coll., 1979, Nat. Vol. of Yr. award Medic Alert Found., 1991. Mem. PEN, Authors Guild. Address: 315 E 72nd St New York NY 10021-4674

FLEMING, BECKY LYNN, production company executive; b. Corpus Christi, Tex., July 15, 1942; d. John David and Kathleen (Gilmore) Weaver; m. James R. Allen, Aug. 31, 1962 (div. May 1971); m. Art F. Fleming, July 4, 1977; children: Kim Reneé Woodring, Timothy Bryan Fleming. Assoc. degree, Tex. A&I U., 1964; postgrad., Durham's Bus. Coll., Corpus Christi, 1964. Adminstrv. asst. Neuhaus & Taylor, Dallas, 1970-72; pres. Bart Enterprises, St. Louis, 1972—; dir. meeting planners Altair Travel, St. Louis, 1990-91; exec. dir. Citrus County Abuse Shelter, Inverness, Fla., 1993—. Bd. dir. Alternative to Living in Violent Environ., Religious Heritage of Am. Mem. Univ. Women's Club (St. Louis), Am. Bus. Womens Assn., Meeting Planners Internat., Jr. League, Delta Theta, Beta Sigma Phi. Presbyterian.

FLEMING, GLORIA JEAN, gerontological nurse; b. Whitinsville, Mass., Jan. 23, 1946; d. Albert Theodore and Rita Maria (Bousquet) Girouard; m. Lloyd Grenville Elon Fleming, Sept. 12, 1971; children: Jason, Brian, Keith. ADN, Quinsigamond C.C., Worcester, Mass., 1971; BS in Health Studies, Anna Maria Coll., Paxton, Mass., 1975. Cert. gerontol. nurse. ANA. DON White Horse Village, Edgmont, Pa., 1990-91, Little Flower Manor, Dardy, Pa., 1991-92, Dunwoody Village, Newtown Square, Pa., 1992-94; cert. nurse Genex Cert. Svc., Wayne, Pa., 1994—. Home: 913 Pineview Dr West Chester PA 19380-1868

FLEMING, LISA L., lawyer; b. Louisville, Nov. 14, 1961; d. Joseph D. Ware. BA cum laude, Hanover (Ind.) Coll., 1982; JD, U. Louisville, 1985. Bar: Ind., U.S. Dist. Ct. (so. and no. dists.) Ind.; cert. mediator pursuant to Ind. Trial Rules. Dir. spl. projects Am. Comml. Barge Line Co., Jeffersonville, Ind.; career cons. Hanover Coll.; mem. Ind. Vocat. Tech. Coll. Devel. Coun., 1994—. With Ind. Vocat. Tech. Coll. Devel. Coun., 1994—; cons. Jr. Achievement; mentor Young Leaders Inst.; mem. Leadership So. Ind., 1990—, bd. dirs. 1992—; mem. appropriations and allocation com. Clark County Ind. United Way, 1993. Mem. NAFE, ABA (admiralty and corp. counsel coms.), Ind. State Bar Assn. (articles and by-laws com.), Clark County Bar Assn., Am. Corp. Counsel Assn. (bd. dirs., chpt. treas. 1992—), Environ. Law Inst., Jefferson County Pub. Sch. System Speakers Bur., River City Bus. and Profl. Women, Ky. Women Advs., Focus Louisville, Hanover Coll. Alumni Assn. (bd. dirs. 1990—, pres. elect 1991-92, pres. bd. dirs. 1992-93, past pres. 1993-94), So. Ind. C. of C. (chair govt. affairs debate subcom. 1991-95, women's bus. coun., 1991—, chair political skill workshop subcom. 1993—), Phi Mu (alumnae pres. Louisville chpt. 1985-91, advisor Rho chpt.). Address: 622 W Saint Catherine St Louisville KY 40203-3112

FLEMING, LOIS DELAVAN, librarian, educator; b. Toledo, Jan. 25, 1928; d. Millard Terry and Willa Metta (Symons) DeLavan; m. Philip Jefferson Fleming, May 15, 1952; children: Mark William, Philip Jefferson Jr., Morris Frederick. BA in Journalism, Fla. State U., 1950, MLS, 1965, AMD, 1968, PhD in Adult Edn., 1987. Asst. libr., instr. Strozier Libr., Fla. State U., Tallahassee, 1965-67; cmty. rels. libr. Palm Beach County Libr. Sys., West Palm Beach, Fla., 1970-72; pub. libr. cons. State Libr. Fla., Tallahassee, 1972-78; adminstr. Leon County Pub. Libr., Tallahassee, 1978-85; program coord. Fla. Lit. Initiative Dept. Edn., Tallahassee, 1988-90; owner, pres. Fleming Assocs., Tallahassee, 1990—; adj. prof. Sch. Libr. & Info. Fla. State U., 1980, 82, 88; mem. tech. assistance com. cmty. edn. Dept. Edn., 1975-78; mem. planning com. ednl. info. ctrs. project Fla. Dept. Edn., 1976-78; mem. pub. com. Gov. Conf. on Librs and Info. Sci., 1978; cons. NEH, 1978, Contract Rsch. Corp., 1979-80, U.S. Dept. Health, Edn. & Welfare, 1979; presenter workshops in field. Co-editor Sch. Media Quar., 1978, Drexel Libr. Quar., 1979; contbr. articles to profl. jours. Bd. dirs. Refuge House, 1981-83, vol., 1991—; bd. dirs. Creative Employment Found., Inc., 1984-85, The Homeless Shelter, 1993-94, Woodland Hall Academy/Dyslexia Rsch. Inst., 1990—, Project Literacy-US Plus, 1990-93. Mem. ALA (vice chmn., chmn-elect pub. libr. assn. alt. ednl. programs sect. 1977-78, chmn. 1978-79, others), ASTD, ESUBA (v.p.), NOW, Fla. Libr. Assn. (bd. dirs. 1978-81, chmn. adult svcs. caucus 1976-77, chmn. ad hoc stds. com. 1981-83, others), Nat. Assn. Parliamentarians, Fla. State Assn. Parliamentarians, Altrusa Internat., Tallahassee Writers Assn., Aircraft Owners & Pilot Assn., Coalition Against Domestic Violence, Fla. State U. Libr. Sch. Alumni Assn. (bd. dirs. 1990-93). Home and Office: Fleming Assocs 2601 Lucerne Dr Tallahassee FL 32303

FLEMING, MARY JOYCE THURSTON, nursing researcher; b. Delaware, Ohio, July 31, 1955; d. William Ralph and Shirley Marie (Russell) Thurston; m. Robert J. Fleming, Nov. 26, 1977; children: Marie Joyce, Melissa Jo, Michael James, Mark Joseph. Diploma, Grant Hosp. Sch. Nursing, Columbus, Ohio, 1977; BSN, Capital U., 1980. Cert. med.-surg. nurse, BLS instr.-trainer, ACLS instr. Staff nurse Ohio State U., Columbus, 1977-80; staff nurse Grady Meml. Hosp., Delaware, 1980-82, staff devel. instr., 1983-91, agrl. health coord., 1991—. Contbr. articles to profl. jours. Treas. North Ctrl. Ohio Regional Insvc. Com.; mem. Buckeye Valley Sch. Dist. Bd. Edn., 1988-91, v.p., 1989, pres., 1990, chair bond issue com., 1993, mem. strategic planning com., 1991—; chair Buckeye Valley Levy Com., 1988; mem. nursing adv. com. Marion Tech. Coll.; pres. Delaware County Bd. Am. Heart Assn.; pres., exec. com. Delaware County Sch. Bus. and Industry; chmn., exec. com. Ohio Farm and Home Safety Com.; vice-chmn. Home Health Care Bd. of Grady, Delaware County Jr. Achievement Bd.; bd. dirs. Delaware County United Way, 1994—; 4H adv. Ashley Jr. Farmers, 1993—. Recipient Ohio's Superior Rural Health Program award, 1993; William St. Found. grantee, Ohio Dept. Health grantee. Mem. Nat. Safety Coun., Nat. Inst. Farm Safety, Ohio Nursing Assn. (legis. com. 1976), Ohio Hosp. Assn. (edn. com. 1989-92), Ohio Young Farmers Assn. (grantee), Dist. 10 Jersey Breeder's Assn. (sec. 1992). Home: 4716 N Old State Rd Delaware OH 43015-9042

FLEMING, PATRICIA STUBBS, federal official; b. Phila., Mar. 17, 1936; d. Fredrick Douglass Stubbs and Marion Turner Stubbs Thomas; m. Harold S. Fleming, June 1958 (div. Feb. 1971); children: Douglass, Craig, Gordon. BA, Vassar Coll., 1957; postgrad., NYU, 1958-60, U. Pa., 1957-58, Phila. Acad. Fine Arts, 1957-58. Legis. asst. to reps. U.S. Ho. of Reps., Washington, 1971-77; asst. to sec. HEW, Washington, 1977-78, dir. intergovtl. and legis. affairs Office Civil Rights, 1979-80; asst. to sec. U.S. Dept. Edn., Washington, 1979-80, dep. asst. sec. legis., 1980-81; sr. pub. policy assoc. James H. Lowry & Assocs., Washington, 1981-83; chief staff Rep. Ted Weiss U.S. Ho. of Reps., Washington, 1983-86, profl. staff mem. subcom. human resources & intergovtl. rels, 1986-93; spl. asst. to sec. HHS, Washington, 1993-94; dir. Office Nat. AIDS Policy The White House, Washington, 1994—. One-person show NYU; exhibited in group shows in N.Y.C. and Washington. Democrat. Episcopalian. Home: 6009 Massachusetts Ave Bethesda MD 20816 Office: The White House 1600 Pennsylvania Ave Washington DC 20006

FLEMING, PAULA ELLEN, interior designer; b. Bklyn., Apr. 4, 1952; d. Frank Joseph and Rosalie Ellen (Tumminia) Saviano; m. Barry Rost, Jan. 20, 1974 (div. July 1978); 1 child, Eric; m. Howard Victor Fleming, Sept. 3, 1978; 1 child, Meredith. BFA, Pratt Inst., 1974. Office coord. Kaiser Broadcasting, N.Y.C., 1974-76; owner, designer Paula Fleming Interiors, East Rockaway, N.Y., 1976—; cons. in field. Featured in Homeowner mag., 1989. Bd. dirs. Waverly Pk. PTA, 1978-87, v.p. 1980-85, hon. mem. 1987. Mem. Am. Soc. Interior Designers, Allied Bd. Trade, Nat. Assn. Female Execs. Home and Office: Paula Fleming Interiors 17 Mallow Rd East Rockaway NY 11518-2224

FLEMING, SUZANNE MARIE, university official, chemistry educator; b. Detroit, Feb. 4, 1927; d. Albert Thomas and Rose E. (Smiley) F. BS, Marygrove Coll., 1957; MS, U. Mich., 1960, PhD, 1963. Joined Congregation of Sisters Servants of Immaculate Heart of Mary, Roman Catholic Ch., 1945. Chmn. natural sci. div. Marygrove Coll., Detroit, 1970-75, v.p., dean, 1975-78, acad. v.p., 1978-80; asst. v.p. acad. affairs Eastern Mich. U., Ypsilanti, 1980-82, acting assoc. v.p. acad. affairs, 1982-83; provost, acad. v.p. Western Ill. U., Macomb, 1983-86; vice chancellor U. Wis., Eau Claire, 1986-89; freelance writer, 1989—; vis. scholar U. Mich., 1989—; pres. Mich. Coll. Chemistry Tchrs. Assn., 1975; councilor Mich. Inst. Chemists, 1973-77; bd. dirs. Nat. Ctr. for Rsch. to Improve Postsecondary Teaching and Learning, 1988-90. Contbr. articles to profl. publs. NIH research grantee, 1966-69. Fellow Am. Inst. Chemists; mem. Am. Chem. Soc. (councilor, Detroit 1980-83, Petroleum Research Fund grantee, 1962-88), Am. Assn. Higher Edn., Sigma Xi. Home and Office: 2888 Cascade Dr Ann Arbor MI 48104-6659

FLEMMING, ARLENE JOAN DANNENBERG, social worker, psychotherapist; b. N.Y.C., July 21, 1940; d. Melvin and Helen (Ruthberg) Gelb; m. Richard Bruce Dannenberg, Dec. 25, 1962; children: Susan Joy, David Grant; m. Howard Charles Flemming Jr., Oct. 22, 1988; children: Howard Charles Jr., Craig Stephan. BA, SUNY, White Plains, 1984; MSW, Fordham U., 1988. Lic. social worker, N.Y. Intern in social work, alcoholism counselor The Sharing Community, Yonkers, N.Y., 1985-86, Yorktown Ctr. for Alcoholism and Psychotherapy, Yonkers, 1986-87; alcoholism counselor, psychotherapist Westchester County Med. Ctr., Yonkers, 1986-87; social worker, psychotherapist Middletown (N.Y.) Psychiat. Ctr., 1988-90; clin. social worker, psychotherapist Self Search Labs., Marlboro, N.Y., Newburgh, 1990—; adj. prof., tutor, SUNY, Empire, State Coll., 1988-94;

liaison profl. orgns. Am. Bd. Cert. Managed Care Providers, 1994. Mem. NASW, Mental Health Assn. Ulster County, N.Y. Fedn. Alcoholism and Chem. Dependency Counselors (pres. mid-Hudson region 1990-94, Counselor of Yr. award 1993, regional rep., 1994—, chair managed care com. 1994), Alcoholism and Substance Abuse Coun. Ulster County, Dutchess County Coun. Alcoholism and Chem. Dependency, Sullivan County Coun. on Alcoholism and Chem. Dependency, Alcoholism and Drug Abuse Coun. Orange County, Nat. Coun. Alcoholism and Other Drug Dependencies, Nat. Coun. Alcoholism and Other Drug Addictions Westchester, Rockland County Coun. on Alcoholism and Drug Addictions, N.Y. State Coun. on Alcholism and Other Drug Addictions, N.Y. Fed. Alcoholism and Substance Abuse Counselors, Hudson Valley Addictions Counselor's Assn., Nat. Assn. Alcoholism and Chem. Dependency Counselors (managed care com. 1994), Assn. Diagnostic Excellence and Brief Psychotherapy, N.Y. State Soc. Clin. Social Work Psychotherapists, Inc., Eastern Orange County C. of C. Republican. Home and Office: 108 Sunset Dr Newburgh NY 12550-2219

FLEMMING, NAOMI VERNETA, elementary school educator; b. Las Vegas, Nev., Oct. 13, 1953; d. James Major and Mable Audrey (Mack) F. BS in Edn., U. Nev., 1976. Inventory clk. Woolco Dept. Stor, Las Vegas, 1969; student aide U.S. AEC, Las Vegas, 1971-75; telephone sales person Sears, Roebuck & Co., Las Vegas, 1973-74; clk., typist U.S. Energy, Rsch. and Devel. Adminstrn., Las Vegas, 1975-77; div. sec. U.S. Dept. Energy, Las Vegas, 1977-79; investigator U.S. Office Personnel Mgmt., Las Vegas, 1979-85; employment security specialist State of Nev., Las Vegas, 1988; counselor NutriSystem Weight Loss Ctr., Las Vegas, 1988-89; tchr. Mabel Hoggard Sixth Grade Ctr. (name now to Mabel Hoggard Math & Sci. Magnet Sch.), Las Vegas, 1988—; mem. black history program com. Mabel Hoggard Sch., Las Vegas, 1989-90, student coun. advisor, 1990-91, tchr. liaison Parent Tchr. Student Assn., 1991-92, mem. Martin Luther King Jr. parade com. 1991-92, Just Say No To Drugs Computer Club advisor, 1992-93; Hoggard Magnet sch. lang. arts rep., drill team sponsor, Clark County Sch. Dist. mentor, 1993-94, Hoggard Magnet Sch. Title I reading tchr., 1994—. Mem. Martin Luther King Jr. Parade Com., 1991-92; advisor Just Say No To Drugs Club, 1992-93; chairperson hospitality com. Am. Bus. Women's Assn., 1976-77; mem. women's adv. com. U.S. Energy, R&D Adminstrn., Las Vegas, 1976-78; facilitator, vol. Fully Alive Self-Help Ctr., 1992, 93-94. Mem. Las Vegas Alumnae chpt. Delta Sigma Theta (publicist 1976-78). Democrat. Home: 1220 W Washington Ave Las Vegas NV 89106 Office: Mabel Hoggard Math & Sci Magnet Sch 950 N Tonopah Dr Las Vegas NV 89106

FLETCHER, BETTY B., federal judge; b. Tacoma, Mar. 29, 1923. B.A., Stanford U., 1943; LL.B., U. Wash., 1956. Bar: Wash. 1956. Mem. firm Preston, Thorgrimson, Ellis, Holman & Fletcher, Seattle, 1956-1979; judge U.S. Ct. Appeals (9th cir.), Seattle., 1979—. Mem. ABA (Margaret Brent award 1992), Wash. State Bar Assn., Am. Law Inst., Fed. Judges Assn. (immediate past pres.), Order of Coif, Phi Beta Kappa. Office: US Ct Appeals 9th Cir 1010 5th Ave Seattle WA 98104-1130

FLETCHER, BRADY JONES, vocational education specialist; b. Natchitoches, La., Apr. 17, 1928; d. Louis Benjamin and Isadore Hannah (Stephens) Jones; m. Donald Greene Fletcher, Aug. 13, 1950; children: Donald Bruce, Nathan Louis, Debra Patrice. BA, Clark Coll., 1950; MA (fellow), Howard U., 1953; postgrad. (NDEA fellow), Ind. U., 1965; EdS in Guidance, George Washington U., 1967, EdD, 1977. Tchr. math. and sci. Fairmont Heights (Md.) High Sch., 1951-54; tchr. math. and sci. Douglas High Sch., Upper Marlboro, Md., 1955-57, Prince George's County (Md.) Pub. Schs., 1951-59, Banneker Jr. High Sch., Washington, 1959-63; chmn. guidance dept. Garnet/Patterson Jr. High Sch., 1963-67; counselor Lincoln Jr. High Sch., D.C. pub. schs., 1967-69, Kensington (Md.) Jr. High Sch., 1969-73, Banneker Jr. High Sch., 1975-77; career edn. specialist Montgomery County (Md.) Schs., 1973-75; cons. Md. State Dept. Edn., 1973, Balt. City Pub. Schs., 1973, Balt. County Pub. Schs., 1973, D.C. Pub. Schs.; mem. adv. com. for spl. needs population Montgomery Coll., Rockville, Md., Am. Coll. Testing Bd., Md., DC, 1987—; project dir. InterAmerica Research Assos., Inc., Rosslyn, Va., 1977—. Editor: Career Edn., 1973-75; Increasing Collaboration in Career Education (2 vols.). Rep. to Community Action Bd. for Montgomery County Edn. Assn.; dir. D.C. Summer Youth Job Program, 1981; del. to Russia, Czech Republic and Poland citizen ambassador program People to People Internat., 1993. Inst. Ednl. Leadership fellow, summer 1984, Montgomery County Vocat. Assessment Ctr. (recipient dedicated service award 1987); recipient Educators award Clinton A.M.E. Ch., 1988, Multicultural Counseling award Founders of Orgn., 1987, award Montgomery County Coun., 1990; resolution in her honor Md. State Senate, 1990. Mem. AACD (Nat. award for govt. rels.), Am. Pers. and Guidance Assn. (Human Relations Com. award 1974, editor conv. newsletter 1983), Am. Assn. Specialists in Group Work (nat. chairperson human rels. 1993), Md. Pers. and Guidance Assn. (award 1975), Nat. Capital Pers. and Guidance Assn. (award 1975-76), Ind. Counseling Assn. (v.p. ctrl. chpt. 1992), Ind. Sch. Counselors Assn., Ind. Career Devel. Assn., Ind. Multicultural Assn., D.C. Assn. Counseling and Devel. (pres. 1986-87, del. to North Atlantic region assembly, recipient award distinguished profl. leadership 1987, award for profl. devel. of assn. 1986, trustee 1988-89, co-chairperson govt. rels. com., Nat. awards Govt. Rels. Com. Boston 1989 and Cin. 1990), Nat. Vocat. Guidance Assn., Assn. Non-White Concerns, Nat. Assn. Career Edn., Nat. Sch. Counselor Assn., Internat. Platform Assn., Indpls. Urban League, Alpha Kappa Alpha, Phi Delta Kappa. Home: 7340 Steinmeier Dr Indianapolis IN 46250-2567

FLETCHER, CATHY ANN, auditor; b. Barnesville, Ga., Aug. 23, 1949; d. John James and Dorothy Lee (Banks) Fletcher; 1 child, Lisa Faye. Student, Ohio State U., 1969-70; AS, Mass. Bay Community Coll., 1982; AS, Northeastern U., Boston, 1984, BS, 1984; MA in HumanResources Mgmt. Emmanuel Coll., Boston, 1993. Mail clk. Fed. Reserve Bank, Boston, 1971-72; office mgr. Breckenridge Sportswear, Boston, 1973-74; asst. dir. Whittier Street Health Ctr., Boston, 1974-81; sec. to dir. Northeastern U., 1981-84; auditor Def. Contract Audit Agy. N.E. Region, Boston, 1984—; sec., bd. dirs. Boston Tenant Policy Coun., 1977-79; mgr. northeastern region Fed. Women's Program, 1989—; mem. adv. bd. DCAA EEO, 1989—. Author: Softball Team Book, 1975. V.p., bd. dirs. Bromley Health Tenant Mgmt. Corp., Jamaica Plain, Mass., 1976-91; mem. fund-raising com. Com. to Elect Jesse Jackson Pres., Boston, 1984; apptd. fed. women program coordinator State of Mass., 1988; mem. women's opportunity com. Boston Fed. Exec. Bd., 1990—, mem. women's coun., 1994—; active Women's Ednl. Indsl. Union, 1993—; active NAACP. Mem. AAUW, NAFE, Profl. Coun., Nat. Tenants Orgn., Assn. Govt. Accts. (cert. govt. fin. mgr.), Federally Employed Women (treas. Greater Boston chpt. 1992-93, pres. 1994—), Hawkettes Social (pres., past mem. profl. coun. 1989), Elks, Sigma Epsilon Rho. Avocations: reading, swimming, cooking, walking, travel. Office: Def Contract Audit Agy Boston Br Office Thomas P Oneill Fed Bu Boston MA 02222

FLETCHER, DENISE KOEN, strategic and financial consultant; b. Istanbul, Turkey, Aug. 31, 1948; came to U.S., 1967, naturalized, 1976; d. Moris and Kety (Barkey) Koen; m. Robert B. Fletcher, Nov. 11, 1969; children—David, Kate. A.B. (Coll. scholar), Wellesley Coll., 1969; M.City Planning, Harvard U., 1972. Analyst Ea. div. Getty Oil Co., N.Y.C., 1972-73; sr. analyst Ea. div. Getty Oil Co., 1973-74, cash mgmt. and bldg. supr., 1974-76; cash mgmt. and bldg. supr. Getty Oil Co. (Eastern), 1976; asst. treas. N.Y. Times Co., N.Y.C., 1976-80; treas. N.Y. Times Co., 1980-88; pres. Fletcher Assocs. Inc., Larchmont, N.Y., 1988—; chief exec. officer Communication Venture Group, Ltd., N.Y.C., N.Y., 1989-90; bd. dirs. Software, Etx. Stores, Inc., 1991-94, Comml. Venture Group, Inc. Bd. dirs. Overseas Edn. Found. Internat., 1988, Boy Scouts Am., Exploring, 1991-93; bd. dirs., v.p. bd. dirs., mem. exec. com. YWCA, N.Y., 1987—; mem. budget com. City of Larchmont, N.Y., 1981-83, chmn. zoning bd. appeals, 1987—, mem. selection com., 1985-87; mem. alumni exec. coun. Harvard U. Sch. Govt., 1982-87. Mellon scholar, 1970. Mem. Fin. Execs. Inst., Fin. Women's Assn., Treasurers Club N.Y., Phi Beta Kappa. Club: Harvard (N.Y.C.). Office: Fletcher Assocs Inc PO Box 503 Larchmont NY 10538-4221

FLETCHER, LOUISE, actress; b. Birmingham, Ala., 1936; d. Robert Capers F. BA, U. N.C., 1957; student acting with Jeff Corey; LHD (hon.), Gallaudet U., 1982, Western Md. Coll., 1986. Films include Thieves Like Us, 1973, Russian Roulette, 1974, One Flew Over the Cuckoo's Nest, 1975 (Acad. award as best actress), Exorcist II: The Heretic, 1976, The Cheap Detective, 1977, The Magician, 1978, Natural Enemies, 1979, The Lucky Star, 1979, The Lady in Red, 1979, Strange Behavior, 1980, Brainstorm, 1981, Strange Invaders, 1982, Once Upon a Time in America, 1982, Firestarter, 1983, Overnight Sensation, 1983, Invaders from Mars, 1985, The Boy Who Could Fly, 1985, Nobody's Fool, 1986, Flowers in the Attic, 1987, Two Moon Junction, 1987, Blue Steel, 1988, Best of the Best, 1989, Shadowzone, 1989, Blind Vision, 1990, The Player, 1991, Return to Two Moon Junction, 1993, Tollbooth, 1993; TV appearances include Maverick, Wagon Train, The Law-Man, Playhouse 90, The Millionaire, Alfred Hitchcock, Thou Shalt Not Commit Adultery, 1978, A Summer To Remember, 1984, Island, 1984, Second Serve, 1985, Hoover, 1986, The Karen Carpenter Story, 1988, Nightmare on the 13th Floor, 1988, Twilight Zone, 1988, Final Notice, 1989, The Hitchhiker, 1990, Tales from the Crypt, 1991, In a Child's Name, 1991, Boys of Twilight, 1991, The Fire Next Time, 1992, Civil Wars, 1993, Deep Space Nine, 1994, 95, The Haunting of Cliff House, Dream On, 1994, Someone Else's Child, 1994, VR5, 1994, 95. Bd. dirs. Deafness Rsch. Found., 1980—. Mem. Nat. Inst. Deafness and Other Communicable Disorders (adv. bd.).

FLETCHER, MARJORIE AMOS, librarian; b. Easton, Pa., July 10, 1923; d. Alexander Robert and Margaret Ashton (Arnold) Amos; A.B., Bryn Mawr Coll., 1946; m. Charles Mann Fletcher, May 14, 1949; children: Robert Amos, Elizabeth Ashton, Anne Kennard. Asst. to dir. rsch., then rsch. asst. to pres. Penn Mut. Life Ins. Co., 1946-49; officer A.R. Amos Co., Phila., 1949-66; part-time tchr., 1965-68; librarian Am. Coll., Bryn Mawr, Pa., 1968-77, archivist, 1973—, dir. oral history collection, 1975—, lectr. on archives, 1975—, asst. prof. edn., 1973-87, dir. archives and oral history, 1977—; pres. pub. rels. MAF Enterprises, 1987—. Author articles in field. Recipient awards Phila. Flower Show, 1965—. Mem. Spl. Librs. Assn. (pres. Phila. 1977-78), Soc. Am. Archivists (chairperson oral history sect. 1981-87, award of merit 1987), Oral History Assn., Hist. Soc. Pa., U.S. Pony Club, D.A.R., Nat. Soc. Colonial Dames in Commonwealth of Pa., Emergency Aid Pa. Found., Phila. Skating Club, Davis Creek Yacht Club, Bridlewild Pony Club (sponsor), Bridlewild Trails Club (Gladwyne). Republican. Episcopalian. Home: 1135 Norsam Rd Gladwyne PA 19035-1419 Office: Am Coll Bryn Mawr PA 19010

FLETCHER, MARY LEE, business executive; b. Farnborough, Eng.; d. Dugald Angus and Mary Lee (Thurman) F.; B.A., Pembroke Coll., Brown U., 1951. Ops. officer C.I.A., Washington, 1951-53; exec. trainee Gimbels, N.Y.C., 1953-54; head researcher Ed Byron TV Prodns., N.Y.C., 1954; copywriter Benton & Bowles, Inc., N.Y.C., 1955-63; creative dir. Alberto-Culver Co., Melrose Park, Ill., 1964-66; v.p. advt. and publicity Christian Dior Perfumes, N.Y.C., 1967-71; v.p. Christian Dior-N.Y., N.Y.C., 1972-78, exec. v.p., dir., 1978-85. Home: 12 Beekman Pl New York NY 10022-8059

FLETCHER, SUZANNE WRIGHT, physician, educator; b. Jacksonville, Fla., Nov. 14, 1940; d. Robert Dean and Helen (Selmer) Wright; m. Robert H. Fletcher; children: John Wright, Grant Selmer. BA, Swarthmore Coll., 1962; MD, Harvard Med. Sch., 1966; MSc, Johns Hopkins U., 1973. Diplomate Nat. Bd. Med. Examiners, Am. Bd. Internal Medicine. Intern Stanford (Calif.) U. Med. Ctr., 1966-67, resident, 1967-68; physician 22nd med. detachment U.S. Army, New Ulm, Germany, 1969-70; asst. prof. epidemiology and health Mc Gill U., Montreal, Can., 1974-77, assoc. prof., 1977-78, asst. prof. medicine, 1973-78; dir. med. clinic dept. medicine N.C. Meml. Hosp., 1978-82; assoc. prof. medicine U. N.C., 1978-83, co-chief divsn. gen. medicine and clin. epidemiology dept. medicine, 1978-86, rsch. assoc. health svcs. rsch. ctr., 1978-90, vice chmn. clin. svcs., 1981-84, prof. medicine, clin. prof. epidemiology, 1983-90, program dir. faculty devel. gen. medicine and gen. pediatrics, 1985-90, co-dir. internat. clin. epidemiology network program Rockefeller Found., 1986-90; editor Annals of Internal Medicine, Phila., 1990-93; adj. prof. medicine U. Pa., Phila., 1990-93, Jefferson Med. Coll., 1991-93, U. N.C., 1992—; prof. ambulatory care and prevention Harvard Med. Sch.; chmn. NIH Tech. Assessment Conf., 1992, Nat. Cancer Inst. Internat. Workshop, 1993; active World Bank Seminar on Preventive Strategies in Med. edn., Hangzhou, China, 1986, Ad Hoc NCI Com. on BSE Cancer Detection Rsch. and Applications, 1986. Author: Clinical Epidemiology—The Essentials, 1982, 2nd edit., 1988; contbr. chpts. to books; contbr. articles to profl. jours. Rsch. grantee Conseil de la Recherche en Sante du Quebec, 1975-77; grantee Health and Welfare Can., 1976-78, Robert Wood Johnson Teaching Hosp. Gen. Medicine Group Practice Program, 1980-84, Nat. Ctr. Health Scis. Rsch. and Health Tech., 1985-89, Rockefeller Found. Clin. Epidemiology Resource and Tng. Ctr., 1986-90, NIH, 1987-90; recipient Can. Nat. Health Rsch. Scholar award Can. Govt., 1975-78. Fellow Am. Coll. Physicians (mem. med. knowledge self assessment program 1984-85, mem. clin. practice subcom. 1987, mem. pub. policy subcom. 1988-89), Am. Coll. Epidemiology (chairperson pub. com. 1992-94, bd. dirs. 1990-93), Coll. Physicians Phila.; mem. Soc. Gen. Internal Medicine (counsellor 1978-81, pres.-elect 1982-83, pres. 1983-84, mem. pub. com. 1990—, chair Glaser Award com. 1991, co-editor Jour. Gen. Internal Medicine, 1984-89), Inst. Medicine (mem. coun. 1993—, mem. exec. com. 1993—), So. Soc. Clin. Investigation, Am. Pub. Health Assn., Sydenham Soc., Phila. Epidemiology Soc., Phila. Med. Soc. Democrat. Unitarian. Office: Harvard Med Sch Dept Ambulatory Care/Prevention 126 Brookline Ave Ste 200 Boston MA 02215-3920

FLETTNER, MARIANNE, cultural organization administrator; b. Frankfurt, Germany, Aug. 9, 1933; d. Bernhard J. and Kaethe E. (Halbritter) F. MBA, Hessel Bus. Coll., 1953. Sec. various cos., 1953-61, Pontiac Motor Div., Burlingame, Calif., 1961-63; sec. Met. Opera, N.Y., 1963-74, asst. co. mgr., 1974-79; artistic adminstr. San Diego Opera, 1979—. Home: 4015 Crown Point Dr San Diego CA 92109-6254 Office: San Diego Opera PO Box 988 San Diego CA 92112-0988

FLICK, DEBORAH LYNN, diversity solutions consultant, educator; b. Cin., Feb. 9, 1949; d. Donald Michael and Lois Mae (Hilmering) F.; m. Sheldon Ira Becker, Dec. 12, 1992. BA in Bus. Adminstrn., Ohio U., 1971; MA in Psychology, Sonoma State U., 1975; PhD in Comm., U. Colo., 1985. Cmty. organizer, counselor York St. Ctr., Denver, 1975-77; founder, exec. dir. Denver (Colo.) Safe House for Battered Women, 1977-79; exec. dir. Boulder (Colo.) Women's Resource Ctr., 1979-80; instr. women studies U. Colo., Boulder, 1980-85, adj. asst. prof. women studies, 1985-93, lectr. women studies, 1993—; owner, CEO Deborah L. Flick & Assocs., Boulder, 1986—; cons. Hewlett Packard, Colo., 1990—, Agys. of the U.S. Govt., 1991—, Storage Tek, Louisville, Colo., 1992—, U.S. Westn, 1990—, AT&T, 1986—. Author: (brochure) Developing and Teaching an Inclusive Curriculum, 1993; editorial bd.: Frontiers: A Jour. of Women Studies, 1982-85. Co-founder, chairperson Colo. Assn. for Aid to Battered Women, Denver, 1977-79; bd. mem. Boulder (Colo.) Campus Com. on Sexual Harassment, U. Colo., 1983-94; bd. dirs. Boulder (Colo.) County Safehouse, 1984-87. Recipient Pub. Svc. Recognition award Boulder (Colo.) County Safehouse, 1981, Teaching Excellence award U. Colo., 1982. Mem. NOW, Internat. Soc. for Intercultural Edn., Tng. and Rsch., Golden Key. Office: Deborah L Flick & Assocs 663 Sky Trail Boulder CO 80302

FLIGNER, CORINNE LINA, pathologist, educator; b. Albuquerque, Dec. 8, 1951; d. Oscar M. and Suzanne (Schiess) F.; m. Mark Howard Wener, Aug. 8, 1982; children: Leah Suzanne, Zachary Benjamin. B Univ. Studies, U. N.Mex., 1973, MD, 1976. Diplomate Am. Bd. Pathology, Am. Bd. Anatomic, Clin. and Forensic Pathology. Resident in gen. surgery U. Wash. Affiliated Hosps., Seattle, 1976-78, resident in anatomic and clin. pathology, 1979-83; fellow in pediat. clin. pathology CHMC, Seattle, 1984-85; med. examiner King County Med. Examiner's Office, Seattle, 1984-93; asst. prof. pathology and lab medicine Sch. Medicine U. Wash., Seattle, 1985-93, assoc. prof. pathology and lab. medicine Sch. Medicine, 1993—; dir. autopsy svc. U. Wash. Med. Ctr., Seattle, 1993—. Contbr. articles to med. jours. Fellow Am. Acad. Forensic Scis. (program chmn. 1992), Nat. Assn. Med. Examiners, Phi Beta Kappa, Alpha Omega Alpha. Office: U Wash Med Ctr Hosp Pathology RC-72 1959 NE Pacific St Seattle WA 98195

FLING, JACQUELINE ANN, library administrator; b. Bethesda, Md., Aug. 13, 1947; d. Esther (Lanza) F. BS in Edn., Kent State U., 1970; MLS, U. Pitts., 1984. Sch. libr. Crestwood Pub. Schs., Manuta, Ohio, 1971-74; asst. libr. Urban Inst., Washington, 1977-82; dir. tech. svcs. Pitts. Pub. Schs., 1985-87; dir. census bur. libr. Census Bur., Washington, 1987-92; divsn. mgr. libr. and records mgmt. Garcia Cons., Inc., 1992—. U. Pitts. scholar, 1984. Mem. ALA, Spl. Libr. Assn., Beta Phi Mu. Office: Garcia Cons Inc 2361 Jefferson Davis Hwy Arlington VA 22202

FLINK, JANE DUNCAN, publisher; b. Atlanta, Feb. 17, 1929; d. James Archibald and Frances (Watkins) Duncan; m. Richard Albert Flink, Nov. 20, 1954; children: Jennifer, Elizabeth, Caroline, Charles Albert, James Duncan. Student Carleton Coll., U. Mo., Columbia (Mo.) Coll. Reporter, Tri-Town News, Greendale, Wis., 1958-61; reporter, photographer, feature writer, editor Cen. Mo. Rural and Farm Life mag., Centralia (Mo.) Fireside Guard, 1973-78, asst. editor, 1982-83; editor Bus. Briefs, MFA Oil Co., Columbia, Mo., 1977; editor Lifestyles, Kingdom Daily News, Fulton, Mo., 1978-82; assoc. editor Mo. Ruralist, Columbia, 1983-85; dir. external rels. Winston Churchill Meml. and Library, Westminster Coll., Fulton, Mo., 1985-89, dir., 1989-90; owner, pub. Boone County Jour., Ashland, Mo., 1986—. Rep. committeewoman Ward I, Centralia, 1972, 74, 76; mem. exec. bd. Friends of Churchill Meml., Fulton; mem. Boone County Commn. on Child Abuse, 1978-81, Boone County Hist. Soc.; bd. dirs., mem. pub. rels., devel., Maplewood coms. Walters-Boone County Mus. and Visitors Ctr.; mem. Boone County Govt. Rev. Task Force, 1991; chair So. Boone County Sch. Budget Rev. Task Force, 1991-92; pres. Lake Champetra Homeowners Assn., 1994-95, v.p., 1995—. Recipient numerous editorial awards. Mem. Nat. Fedn. Press Women (nat. achievement award 1982, bd. dirs. 1991-93, 21st century com. 1992-93), Mo. Press Women (dist. v.p. 1978-79, v.p. 1985-87, pres. 1991-93, chmn. honors, awards 1979-81, Woman of Achievement award 1988), Mo. Press Assn., Mo. soc. Newspaper Editors. Home: 7230 N Shore Dr Hartsburg MO 65039-9753 Office: Boone County Jour 104 W Broadway Ashland MO 65010

FLINN, ROBERTA JEANNE, management, computer applications consultant; b. Twin Falls, Idaho, Dec. 19, 1947; d. Richard H. and Ruth (Johnson) F. Student Colo. State U., 1966-67. Ptnr., Aqua-Star Pools & Spas, Boise, Idaho, 1978—, mng. ptnr., 1981-83; ops. mgr. Polly Pools, Inc., Canby, Oreg., 1983-84, br. mgr. Polly Pools, Inc., A-One Distributing, 1984-85; comptroller, Beaverton Printing, Inc., 1986-89; mng. ptnr. Invisible Ink, Canby, Oreg., 1989—. Mem. Nat. Assn. Female Execs., Nat. Appaloosa Horse Club, Oreg. Dressage Soc. (pres. North Willamette Valley chpt.) Republican. Mem. Christian Ch. Home: 24687 S Central Point Rd Canby OR 97013-9743

FLINNER, BEATRICE EILEEN, library and media sciences educator; b. Uledi, Pa., Feb. 8, 1924; d. Charles Robert and Esther Marjorie (Sickles) Jeffreys; m. Donald Allayaud, May 18, 1944 (killed in action World War II); m. Lyle P. Flinner, June 27, 1947; children: Donald Allayaud, Carol Jean Flinner Dorough. AB summa cum laude, Southern Nazarene U., 1974; MLS, U. Okla., 1977; MA in Social Studies, Southern Nazarene U., 1978, MA in Early Childhood, 1981. Cataloging dept. Asbury Theol. Sem., Wilmore, Ky., 1949-52; aquisitions Geneva Coll., Beaver Falls, Pa., 1959-62, audio visual coord., 1965-68; assoc. prof., head pub. svcs. Southern Nazarene U., Bethany, Okla., 1968—, assoc. prof. Libr. Scis., 1978—, adj. prof.grad. edn., 1981—; mem. adv. bd. Bethany Libr., rep. to Bd. Trustees, 1986-87. Book reviewer The Christian Librarian, 1980—; indexer Christian Periodical Index, 1988—; contbr. articles to profl. jours. Mem. AAUW, Okla. Libr. Assn., Assn. Christian Librs. (v.p. 1991-93, program chair internat. conf. 1992), Okla. Assn. Coll. and Rsch. Librs., Univ. Women's Club, U. Okla. Sch. Libr. Info. Sci. Alumni Assn., Assn. Christian Librs. (conf. coord. 1992-95), Phi Delta Lambda, Delta Kappa Gamma. Republican. Nazarene.

FLINT, CYNTHIA MARIA, nurse, administrator; b. Detroit, Aug. 29, 1956; d. Clyde Everette Burgess and Frances (Flint) Algee; m. Freddie Joseph Sherman, July 15, 1985 (div.). BS in Biology, Spelman Coll., 1981; MBA, Nat. U., 1985, MA in Human Behavior, 1987; BSN, St. Louis U., 1992. RN, Mich. Enlisted USAF, 1982, advanced through grades to staff sgt., 1985; adminstrv. specialist 307th Consol. Aircraft Maint. Squadron Strategic Air Command, Travis AFB, Calif., 1982-83, Mil. Airlift Command, Travis AFB, 1983-85, Base Comdr's Office, Travis AFB, 1985-87; info. technician 3415 Mission Support Squadron, Lowry AFB, Colo., 1987-91; nurse Nardin Park Substance Abuse Ctr., Detroit, 1993—; prin. New World Concepts, 1989-90. Vol. ARC David Grant Med. Ctr., Travis AFB, 1983-85, Adopt-A-Sch. Program Vaughn Elem. Sch., Aurora, Colo., 1987—. Mem. Spelman Coll. Glee Club Alumnae Assn., Nat. Alumnae Assn. Spellman Coll., Delta Sigma Theta. Home: 14179 Abington Detroit MI 48227-1303 Office: Nardin Park Substance Abuse Ctr 9605 Grand River Detroit MI 48204

FLINT, LOU JEAN, state education official; b. Ogden, Utah, July 11, 1934; d. Elmer Blood and Ella D. (Adams) F.; children: Dirk Kershaw Brown, Kristie Susan Brown Felix, Flint Kershaw Brown. B.S., Weber State Coll., 1968; M.Ed., U. Utah, 1974, Ed.S, 1981. Cert. early childhood and elem. edn., Utah Bd. Edn., 1968, edn. adminstrn., 1981. Master tchr. Muir Elem., Davis Sch. Dist., Farmington, Utah, 1968-77; edn. specialist Dist. I, Dept. Def., Eng., Scotland, Norway, Denmark, Holland, Belgium, 1977-79; ednl. cons. Office Higher Edn. State of Utah, Utah System Approach to Individualized Learning, Tex., S.C., Fla., Utah, 1979-81; acad. affairs officer Commr. Higher Edn. Office State of Utah, Salt Lake City, 1982—; mem. Equity Vocat. Edn. Bd., Women's Politics Caucus; adv. bd. Women and Bus. Conf.; mem. single parent employment demonstration project State of Utah, foster care citizen review pilot project State of Utah; pres. elect Utah Mental Health Assn. Named Exemplary Tchr., Utah State Bd. Edn., 1970-77, Outstanding Educator, London Central High Sch., 1979; recipient Appreciation award, Gov. of Utah, 1983-85, 93, Woman of Achievement award Utah Bus. and Profl. Women, 1985, Pathfinder award C. of C., 1988, Outstanding Educator award YWCA, 1989, Silver Apple award Utah State U., 1992. Mem. AAUW (Edn. Found. award given in her honor, 1986), Nat. Assn. Women's Work/Women's Worth (Disting. Woman award 1987), Women's Polit. Caucus (Susa Young Gates award 1987), Nat. Assn. Edn. Young Children, Utah Assn. Edn. Young Children (past pres.), Women Concerned About Nuclear War, Utah Jaycee Aux. (past pres. Centerville), Crones Coun., Math Sci. Network. Mormon. Author: The Comprehensive Community College, 1980; others. Office: State of Utah Office Commr Higher Edn 355 W North Temple # 3 Triad Salt Lake City UT 84180-1114

FLIPPEN, CHERIE DARLENE, artist, publisher; b. Welch, W.Va., Feb. 11, 1959; d. Robert Eugene Sr. and Loretta Jean (Lambert) F. BFA, Fla. State U., 1981. Artist, art dir. Rachesky Co. Advt., West Palm Beach, Fla., 1982-86; artist Jewelmasters, West Palm Beach, 1986-89, direct mail mgr., 1989-90, store mgr., 1991-92, advt. dir., 1992-94; owner Tropical Impressions Fine Art & Pub., West Palm Beach, 1993—. Fine artist, published many images including some used by Busch Gardens/Sea World, Humane Soc. Internat., other environ. orgns. Recipient 6 Addy awards Advt. Club of the Palm Beaches, 1982-85. Home: 5524 55th Way West Palm Beach FL 33409-7110

FLIPPIN, SHARON KAYE, analyst, statistician; b. Stuart, Va., Dec. 8, 1956; d. Bernie Walter and Patsy Ann (Goins) Chilton; 1 child, Jennifer Nichole. BS in Bus. summa cum laude, High Point U., 1993. With gen. office and sales Franklin Auto Parts, Inc., Mt. Airy, N.C., 1976-79; sr. acctg. clerk Integon Corp., Winston-Salem, N.C., 1980-83; sales agt. USAir, Inc., Winston-Salem, N.C., 1983-85, analyst, supr., 1985—; cons., organizer Princess House, Inc., North Dighton, Mass., 1977-80. V.p. PTO, Westfield, N.C., 1988; fundraiser Westfield First Responders, 1990, Multiple Sclerosis, Winston-Salem, N.C., 1992. Mem. Inst. Mgmt. Accts., Alpha Sigma Lambda, Alpha Chi (N.C. Nu chpt.). Baptist. Home: 5149 Westfield Rd Westfield NC 27053

FLOOD, ANN MARGARET, clinical psychologist; b. Eden, Wis., Aug. 18, 1950; d. Frank S. and Florence (O'Brien) F.; m. Barry R. Harrow, Dec. 21, 1992. BA cum laude, U. Wis., Oshkosh, 1973; MA in Clin. Psychology, The Fielding Inst., 1989, PhD in Clin. Psychology, 1992. Lic. clin. psychologist, Calif., Ariz. Pharm. salesperson Hoffmnn-La Roche, Inc., Kansas City, Mo., 1974-81; crisis counselor Interim, Inc., Salinas, Calif., 1987-89; counselor U. Calif., Santa Cruz, 1989-90; family/child counselor Family Svcs. Assn., Salinas, 1989-91; pvt. practice specializing in clin. and forensic psychology Salinas and Monterey, Calif., 1993—; clin. cons. Hospice, Salinas, 1991—; counselor at-risk youth Family Resource Ctr. Salinas, 1992—; panelist, speaker 30th anniversary conv. Assn. for Humanistic Psychology, San Francisco, 1992; speaker on ecology and human behavior to various orgns., 1992—; presenter in field. Bd. dirs. Carmel Valley (Calif.) Comty. Youth Ctr., 1992—, Child Abuse Prevention Coun., Salinas, 1993—; active ARC of Monterey County, 1990-92, Monterey County Task Force on Self-Esteem, 1988-90; vol. Fond du Lac (Wis.) Mental Health Clinic, 1971-73; mem. abused children program Johnson County Mental Health Ctr., Overland Park, Kans., 1st offender program, uprooted/new roots program, speakers forum asst., 1977-79; playground supr., Fond du Lac, summers 1969, 70. Recipient Direct Svc. award Child Abuse Prevention Coun., 1994; Alpha Phi fellow, 1972-73; Alpha Phi Grad. Found. scholar, 1973. Mem. APA, Calif. Psychol. Assn., Calif. Assn. Marriage and Family Therapists, Mid-Coast Psychol. Assn. (ethics com.), Children with Attention Deficit Disorder, Alpha Kappa Delta, Delta Tau Kappa, Psi Chi. Home: PO Box 1427 Carmel Valley CA 93924 also: Ste F 11 Maple St Salinas CA 93901 also: 9 Delfino Pl # 8 Carmel Valley CA 93924

FLOOD, DIANE LUCY, marketing communications specialist; b. Plainfield, N.J., June 13, 1937; d. William Edward and Lucy (Dycker) Flood. B.A., Vassar Coll., 1959; postgrad. Fontainebleau Sch. Fine Arts (France), 1961. Advt. prodn. aide indsl. chem. div. Am. Cyanamid Co., Wayne, N.J., 1959-62, prodn. supr., 1962-64, creative coord. organic chems. div. advt., 1964-66, design art and copy mgr., 1966-70, advt. rep., 1970-72, advt. rep. paper, process chems. and resins, indsl. chem. div., 1972-77, advt. coord. water treating, mining, paper and enhanced oil recovery chems., 1977-83, mgr. mktg. communications indsl. products div., 1983—, mgr. mktg. communications Venture Chems. div., 1986-87; Chem. Products and Indsl. Products divs., 1987-89, mgr. mktg. communications Chem. Products, Indsl. Products and Internat. Chems. div., 1989-90, mgr. mktg. communications Chem. Group, 1990-93, Cytec Industries, Inc., 1993—. Past dir., v.p., past pres. 103 Gedney St. Owners Co-op, 1985-92. Mem. Vassar Coll. Alumni Assn. Mem. Consistory of Reformed Ch. Club: Vassar of N.Y.C. Home: 103 Gedney St # 3C Nyack NY 10960-2238 Office: Cytec Industries Inc West Paterson NJ 07424

FLOOD, DOROTHY GARNETT, neuroscientist; b. Sayre, Pa., Oct. 7, 1951; d. James Murlin and Dorothy Garnett (Dietrich) F.; m. Paul David Coleman, Feb. 26, 1983. BA cum laude, Lawrence U., 1973; student, U. Ill., 1972-73; MS, PhD, U. Rochester, N.Y., 1980. Sr. instr. in anatomy U. Rochester, 1980-83, asst. prof. neurology, anatomy, 1984-90, assoc. prof. neurology, neurobiology, 1990-94; sr. sci. Cephalon, Inc., West Chester, Pa., 1994—. Contbr. to book chpts. and articles in field; editorial bd. Neurobiology of Aging, 1989—. Recipient Fenn award U. Rochester, 1980; grantee NSF, NIH, Office of Naval Rsch., 1979-94. Mem. Soc. Neurosci., Am. Assn. Anatomists, European Neurosci. Assn. Office: Cephalon Inc 145 Brandywine Pky West Chester PA 19380

FLOOD, (HULDA) GAY, editor, consultant; b. Plainfield, N.J., Aug. 14, 1935; d. William Edward and Lucy (Dycker) F.; BA, Smith Coll., 1957. Picture dept. Sports Illustrated, Time Inc., N.Y.C. 1957-58, letters dept., 1958-59, reporter, 1959-60, writer-reporter, 1960-71, assoc. editor, 1971-85, sr. editor, 1985-90; editor, cons., 1990—. Mem. Alumnae Assn. Smith Coll., Smith Coll. Students Aid Soc., Smith Coll. Club N.Y. Elder, chair fin. com. 1st Reformed Ch., Nyack, N.Y. Office: 103 Gedney St # 3C Nyack NY 10960-2238

FLOOD, JOAN MOORE, paralegal; b. Hampton, Va., Oct. 10, 1941; d. Harold W. and Estalena (Fancher) M.; 1 child by former marriage, Angelique. B.Mus., North Tex. State U., 1963, postgrad., 1977; postgrad. So. Meth. U., 1967-68, Tex. Women's U., 1978-79, U. Dallas, 1985-86. Clk. Criminal Dist. Ct. Number 2, Dallas County, Tex., 1972-75; reins. libr. Scor Reins. Co., Dallas, 1975-80; corp. ins. paralegal Assocs. Ins. Group, 1980-83; corp. securities paralegal Akin, Gump, Strauss, Hauer & Feld, 1983-89; asst. sec. Knoll Internat. Holdings Inc., Saddle Brook, N.J., 1989-90, 21 Internat. Holdings, Inc., N.Y.C., 1990-92; dir. compliance Am. Svc. Life Ins. Co., Ft. Worth., 1992-93; v.p., sec. Express Comm., Inc., Dallas, 1993-94; fin. transactions paralegal Thompson & Knight, Dallas, 1994—. Mem. ABA, Tex. Bar Assn., State Bar of Tex. Republican. Episcopalian. Home: PO Box 190165 Dallas TX 75219-0165

FLOOD, SELMA EBLE, psychologist; b. Phila., May 20, 1927; d. Louis M. and Friede M. (Lehmuth) Carlile. BA, Swarthmore Coll., 1949; MA, Temple U., 1951. Pub. rels. asst. Cayuga Savs. & Loan, Phila., 1951-53; sr. staff psychologist Devereux Found., Devon, Pa., 1953-75, Woods Svcs., Langhorne, Pa., 1981—; pvt. practice clin. psychologist Phila., 1975-81. Majority inspector 1st Dist., 5th Ward Election Bd., Phila., 1976—; bd. dirs. Tri County Fountain Ctr., Landsdowne, 1959-80. Mem. APA (life), Am. Assn. on Mental Retardation (life), Nat. Register Health Svcs. Republican. Unitarian. Home: Society Hill Towers # 26 D S Philadelphia PA 19106 Office: Woods Svcs Langhorne PA 19047

FLOOD-STOLLER, JOAN ELIZABETH, critical care nurse; d. Raymond Gabriel Flood and Anna Annoinette Augresani; m. Leslie Stoller, Feb. 8, 1964; children: Cheryl Ann R. Cole. RN, Laboure Coll., Boston, 1984; BS, Boston U., 1975; BSN, U. Mass., 1987. Formerly ICU-CCU nurse Lee Meml. Hosp., Ft. Myers, Fla.; Medicare clin. coord. Healthpark Care Ctr., Ft. Myers, 1994—. Mem. Amenisty Internat. Mem. ANA, Sigma Theta Tau. Home: PO Box 151201 Cape Coral FL 33915-1201

FLOOK, MARILYN HARRIGAN, real estate professional, housing developer; b. Pitts., Dec. 18, 1947; d. Jack W. and Madeline (Raineri) Harrigan; m. Frank D. Flook, June 20, 1976 (dec. Dec. 27, 1979). BS, Kans. State U., Pittsburg, 1972. Cert. econ. devel. profl. Constrn. analyst Housing and Urban Devel., Jacksonville, Fla.; community devel. specialist Housing and Urban Devel., Washington, housing specialist; affordable housing mktg. specialist Resolution Trust Corp., Kansas City, Mo., affordable housing monitor and compliance sect. chief. Home: 6224 Howe Dr Fairway KS 66205-3452 Office: Resolution Trust Corp 4900 Main St Kansas City MO 64112-2644

FLOOKS, RENEA KRISTEN, elementary education educator; b. Peckville, Pa., June 17, 1964; d. Robert Joseph and Elaine Diane (Prutisto) Caljean; m. Michael Raymond Flooks. BS, Temple U., 1986. Tchr. Phila. Sch. Dist., 1987-91, Dwight-Englewood Sch., N.J., 1991—. Mem. social com. Ind. Harbor Complex. Republican.

FLORA, CORNELIA BUTLER, sociologist, educator; b. Santa Monica, Calif., Aug. 5, 1943; d. Carroll Woodward and May Fleming (Darnall) Butler; m. Jan Leighton Flora, Aug. 22, 1967; children: Gabriela Catalina, Natasha Pilar. BA, U. Calif., Berkeley, 1965; MS, Cornell U., 1966, PhD, 1970. Asst. to full prof. Kans. State U., Manhattan, 1970-89, dir. population rsch. lab., 1970-78, univ. disting. prof., 1988-89; program adviser Ford Found., Bogota, Colombia, 1978-80; prof., head dept. sociology Va. Poly. Inst. and State U., Blacksburg, 1989-94; dir. North Ctrl. Regional Ctr. Rural Devels., prof. sociology Iowa State U., Ames, 1994—; cons. USAID, 1981-91, Inter Am. Devel. Bank, 1992, United Nations, 1992. Author: Rural Communities: Legacy and Change; editor: Sustainable Agriculture, 1990, Rural Policy for the 1990s; contbr. articles to sociol. publs. Chair bd. dirs. Cooper House, Blacksburg, 1990—. Mem. Rural Sociol. Soc. (pres. 1988-89, Outstanding Rsch. award 1987), Latin Am. Studies Assn. (bd. dirs. 1982-84, pres. Midwest sect. 1989-90), Am. Sociol. Assn. Mem. Church of Brethren. Office: Iowa State U N Ctrl Regional Ctr Rural Devels 317 East Hall Ames IA 50011-1070

FLORA JUNE See EHLERS, FLORENCE RAUSH

FLORENCE, CELESTE NORRIS, retired educator; b. Greenville, S.C., July 1, 1923; d. Harold Sullivan and Pauline (Miller) Norris; m. Harold Neal, Apr. 15, 1946; children: Harold Neal, Jr., Nan Celeste Parker. Student, Armstrong State Coll., 1943; BA, Berry Coll., 1966. Tchr. Tchr. Third Street Sch., Cedartown, Ga., 1947-50, Trion (Ga.) Elem. Sch., 1971-72. Trustee Chattooga County Libr., 1968-87, chmn., 1979-87; pres. Jr. Welfare League, Cedartown, 1950-52, Summerville (Ga.) Music Club, 1962-64; chmn. Trion Zoning Bd., 1980-91. Mem. DAR. Republican. Presbyterian. Home: 995 Central Ave Trion GA 30753-1126

FLORENCE, VERENA MAGDALENA, small business owner; b. Interlaken, Switzerland, Nov. 4, 1946; came to U.S., 1967; d. Paul Robert and Marie (Raess) Demuth; m. Kenneth James Florence, Dec. 10, 1967. BA, U. Calif., Berkeley, 1974; MS, UCLA, 1979, PhD, 1982. Research scientist Procter & Gamble, Cin., 1983; adminstr. Swerdlow & Florence, Beverly Hills, Calif., 1984-89; pres., chief exec. officer, chmn. of bd. Böl Designs, Inc., L.A., 1989—. Contbr. articles to profl. jours. Mem. L.A. Computer Soc. (SIG leader). Democrat. Home and Office: 1063 Stradella Rd Los Angeles CA 90077-2607

FLORES, ROBIN ANN, social worker, social services administrator; b. Allentown, Pa., Oct. 6, 1949; d. Norman Henry and Ann May (Huff) Flores. B.S. in Edn., Kutztown U., 1971; M.S. in Adminstrn., U. Scranton, 1983. Caseworker gerontology Lehigh County Area Agy. for Aging, Allentown, Pa., 1973-75, info. referral outreach coordinator, 1975-78, supr. community services, 1979—; lectr. community svcs., family care giving and on aging process, Lehigh County, Pa., 1978—; utilization community resources, Lehigh County, 1978—. Mem. adv. bd. Community Action Com. of Lehigh Valley, 1979-82, Elder Well, 1987—; Pa. del. White House Conf. on Aging, Hershey, Pa., 1981; bd. dirs. Vis. Nurse Assn. of Lehigh County, 1982—, Women Inc., 1983-87; adv. bd. Homecare, Inc., 1982—, Geriatric Edn. Modules, Allentown Osteo. Hosp., 1979; mem. profl. adv. com. Lehigh Valley Hospice, 1984—; mem. utilization and rev. bd. Vis. Nurse Assn., 1979—; consumer rep. Pa. Power and Light Co.; co-chmn. Human Services Tng. Coop., 1975-81. Mem. NAFE, Allentown Art Mus., Old Allentown Preservation Assn., Quota Internat. Home: 1255 Forest Rd Whitehall PA 18052-6217 Office: Lehigh County Area Agy on Aging 930 W Hamilton St PO Box 1548 Allentown PA 18105

FLORES-NAZARIO, MARGARITA, human resources director; b. Naguabo, P.R., Oct. 17, 1951; d. Juan and Victoria (Nazario) Flores; m. Antonio Rodriguez; children: Antonio IV, Diana Margarita. BA in Psychology, U. P.R., Rio Piedras, 1973, MPA, 1981. Cert. sr. human resources profl. Dir. fed. programs Municpality of Naguabo, 1973-77; pers. rep. BD Catheters Co., Canovanas, P.R., 1977-79; mgr. pers. Products Control Clorox Inc., Ceiba, P.R., 1979-81, Bard Cardiosurgery, Las Piedras, P.R., 1981-88; dir. human resources Whitehall Robins Labs., Guayama, 1988—. Mem. P.R. Mfrs. Assn. (bd. dirs. 1993, Mgr. of Yr. award 1986), Labor Practitioners P.R., Pharm. Industries Assn., Soc. Human Resources Mgmt. (pres. 1986). Home: Box 10162 CUH Sta Humacao PR 00792 Office: Whitehall Robins Labs PO Box 208 Guayama PR 00785

FLORESTANO, PATRICIA SHERER, university educator; b. Washington, Mar. 15, 1936; d. Wilbur L. and Virginia M. (Moriconi) F.; B.A. in Am. Civilization, U. Md., 1958, M.A. in Govt. and Politics, 1970, Ph.D. in Pub. Adminstrn. and Am. Govt., 1974; m. Thomas Florestano, Nov. 29, 1959; children—Leslie C., Thomas. Research staff State Legis. Commn. on Intergovt. Coop., 1972-75, State Gov.'s Commn. on Functions of Govt., 1973-75; staff asst. to pres. Md. Senate, 1975-78; asst. prof. Inst. Urban Studies, U. Md., College Park, 1974-79, dir. Inst. Govtl. Service, 1979-85, vice-chancellor govtl. relations, 1985-91; vis. prof. govt. Schaefer Ctr. Pub. Policy U. Balt., 1991-94, prof., 1994—, pub. adminstr., sr. fellow; cons. ednl. evaluation, mgmt. and survey research. Lector St. Elizabeth Ann Seton Ch., 1970-92; dir. Crofton (Md.) Gymnastics Program, 1972-74; vice chmn. Anne Arundel County (Md.) Commn. on Women, 1975; mem. Transition Exec. Com. for Gov. Elect. State Md., Dec. 1994- Jan. 1995; mem. Anne Arundel County Schs. Adv. Forum, 1975-76, chmn. nominations com., 1976-78. Recipient Outstanding Teaching award Students Assn. of U. Md., 1979. Mem. Am. Soc. Pub. Adminstrn. (pres. 1983-84, conf. fellow), Am. Polit. Sci. Assn., So. Polit. Sci. Assn., Urban Affairs Assn. (past chmn. governing bd.), So. Consortium Univ., Pub. Service Orgns. (former editor). Democrat. Roman Catholic. Author: (with other) The States and Metropolitan Areas, 1981; Attitudes of Special Interest Groups and the Public on Chesapeake Bay Areas, 1980; also articles. Home: 1516 Farlow Ave Crofton MD 21114-1516 Office: 1304 Saint Paul St Baltimore MD 21202-2713

FLORIAN, MARIANNA BOLOGNESI, civic leader; b. Chgo.; d. Giulio and Rose (Garibaldi) Bolognesi; BA cum laude, Barat Coll., 1940; postgrad. Moser Bus. Sch., 1941-42; m. Paul A. Florian III, June 4, 1949; children—Paul, Marina, Peter, Mark. Asst. credit mgr. Stella Cheese Co., Chgo., 1942-45; With ARC ETO Clubmobile Unit, 1945-47; mgr. Passavant Hosp. Gift Shop, 1947-49; pres., Jr. League Chgo., Inc., 1957-59; pres. woman's bd. Passavant Hosp., 1966-68; bd. dirs. Northwestern Meml. Hosp., 1974-81, mem. exec. com., 1974-79; pres. Women's Assn., Chgo. Symphony Orch., 1974-77, founder WFMT/CSO Radiothon, 1976; chmn. Guild Chgo. Hist. Soc., 1981-84, trustee Chgo. Hist. Soc., 1981-84; life trustee Orchestral Assn., v.p. 1978-82, vice chmn. 1982-86, mem. exec. com. 1978-87; mem. women's bd. U. Chgo.; mem. vis. com. dept. music U. Chgo., 1980-90; pres. bd. dirs. Antiquarian Soc. of Art Inst., 1989-91. Recipient Citizen Fellowship, Inst. Medicine Chgo., 1975, Presdl. Commendation for leadership and svc. Barat Coll., 1990. Clubs: Friday (pres. 1972-74), Contemporary; Winnetka Garden.

FLORIN, SHARON, artist; b. Bklyn., Feb. 16, 1952; d. Lawrence and Blanche Ina (Title) F. BA cum laude, Adelphi U., 1973; postgrad., Art Students League, 1969-77. Freelance artist, 1973—. Solo exhbns. at Noho Gallery, N.Y.C., 1982, 83, 85, 86, 89, 91; group exhbns. include Queens Mus., Flushing, N.Y., 1984, Hoyt Inst. Fine Arts, New Castle, Pa., 1990, Butler Inst. Am. Art, Youngstown, Ohio, 1991, Hudson River Mus., Yonkers, N.Y., 1982, 83, 91, Chautauqua (N.Y.) Instn., 1992, Alexandria (La.) Mus. Art, 1992, Michael Ingbar Gallery, N.Y.C., 1993, 94. Recipient Hon. Mention award Butler Inst. Am. Art, 1991. Mem. Nat. Assn. Women Artists (Elizabeth Erlinger Meml. award 1990, Elizabeth Stanton Blake Meml. award 1992), Women in the Arts, Inc., Women's Caucus for Art, Nat. Artists Equity, Orgn. Ind. Artists. Home: 339 E 19th St New York NY 10003-2825 Studio: 12-23 Jackson Ave Long Island City NY 11101

FLORY, MARGARET MARTHA, retired religious organization administrator; b. Wauseon, Ohio, May 13, 1914; d. Arthur Henry and Laura Grace (Gorsuch) F. BA, Ohio U., 1936, MA, 1938; postgrad., Union Theol. Seminary, 1940-43; LLD, Maryville Coll., 1988. Teaching fellow Ohio U., Athens, 1936-38, dir. Westminster Found., 1940-44; tchr. Bainbridge (Ohio) High Sch., 1938-39; mem. drama and speech faculty Ala. State Coll., Montevallo, 1939-40; Eastern area sec. Presbyn. Ch. Nat. Hdqrs., N.Y.C., 1944-51, staff student world rels., 1951-68, staff new dimension in mission, 1969-73; staff ecumenical sharing program dir. Presbyn. Ch. U.S.A., 1973-80, mem. Stony Point (N.Y.) ctr. program staff, 1981-87; ret., 1987. Author: Moments in Time, 1995; contbr. articles to profl. jours. Active Pres. Kennedy's Women's Com. on Civil Rights, 1963; trustee Maryville (Tenn.) Coll., 1963-78; pres. bd. trustees World Student Christian Fedn., N.Y.C., 1968-90; bd. ch. visitors Warren Wilson Coll., N.C., 1993—. Named Outstanding Alumnae Ohio U.; recipient Human Rights award Korean Christian Scholars, 1985, Woman of Faith award Presbyn. Women, 1987, Cert. of Appreciation Silliman U., 1981; conf. hall named in her honor John Knox Internat. Studies Ctr., Geneva, 1993. Mem. AAUW (exec. bd.), Assn. for Women's Edn. in Asia (pres. 1973-85), Ch. Relationships with Eastern Europe, Ch. Women United, Phi Beta Kappa. Home and Office: 1 College Row # 276 Brevard NC 28712-3155

FLOTT, NANCY LEE, librarian; b. Wichita, Kans., June 8, 1932; d. Henry A. Pribbenow and Lillian I. (Torkleson) Fate; m. Richard E. Flott Sr., May 29, 1954 (div. 1966); children: Paula, Rick, Larry, Karla. BS, Emporia State U., 1954, MS, 1962; PhD, Kansas State U., 1976. Sch. librarian Lab. Sch. Emporia (Kans.) State U., 1960-63; media specialist United Sch. Dist. #345, Topeka, 1963-72; program specialist Kans. St. Dept. Edn., Topeka, 1972-82; asst. prof. Emporia (Kans.) State U., 1982-88; library dir. Cottey Coll., Nevada, Mo., 1988—; founder coord. Kans. Online Group, 1975-83, chair tech. task force Kansas Library Network Bd., 1983-85; dir. Title IV-C Classroom Improvement Grants Progran, Kans., 1981, Kans. Ednl. Dissemination/Diffusion System Resource Component, 1974-82. Contbr. articles to profl. jours. Mem. Community Theatre Bd., 1987-88, Internat. Tng. Communication, 1986—; pres. Kan-Talk of Internat. Tng. im Emporia, 1983, v.p., 1985, sec., 1986; mem.leadership tng. Vernon County, Nevada, 1988-89. Mem. ALA, Spl. Library Assn., Kans. Library Assn., AAUW (treas. 1985-88, v.p. 1989-91), Bus. and Profl. Women's Club, Community Coun. for the Performing Arts (bd. dirs.), PEO, Soroptomist Internat. Home: 810 S Clay St Nevada MO 64772-3239 Office: Cottey Coll 1000 W Austin St Nevada MO 64772-2700

FLOURNOY, MELISSA, state legislator; b. Carthage, Tex., Sept. 16, 1961; d. Alfred Glenn Jr. and Nena (Courtney) F. BA, Hollins Coll., 1983; MPA, Columbia U., 1985; postgrad., La. State U. Mgmt. analyst U.S. Dept. Justice, Washington, 1985-87; exec. dir. The Light House Ednl. Ctr., Shreveport, La., 1987-90; dir. devel. Nesbitt Cos., Shreveport, 1990-92; v.p. Flournoy Davis & Assocs., Shreveport, 1992—; state rep. La. Ho. of Reps., Baton Rouge, 1992-96. Pres. Women's Polit. Fund, Shreveport, 1988—; mem. Jr. League Shreveport, 1988-91, Rivers Cities Network, Shreveport, 1990—. Named Pub. Servant of Yr., NASW, 1989, Outstanding Woman of Yr., Yonta Club Internat., 1992; recipient Pearl award for community contrbn. Vols. Am. of North La., 1989. Mem. YWCA, Shreveport Single Room Occupancy Inc. (pres. 1987-92), Univ. Club (bd. dirs. 1989-91). Democrat. Baptist. Office: La Ho of Reps State Capitol Baton Rouge LA 70804-0402 also: Flournoy Davis & Assocs 333 Southfield Rd Shreveport LA 71105-4154

FLOURNOY, NANCY, statistician, educator; b. Long Beach, Calif., May 4, 1947; d. Carr Irvine and Elizabeth (Blincoe) F.; m. Leonard B. Hearne, Aug. 28, 1978. BS, UCLA, 1969, MS, 1971; PhD, U. Wash., 1982. Statistician Regional Med. Programs, L.A., 1969-70; assoc. mem. S.W. Regional Lab. for Ednl. Rsch. and Devel., Los Alamitos, Calif., 1971-73; database mgr. U. Wash., Seattle, 1973-75; dir. clin. stats. Fred Hutchinson Cancer Rsch. Ctr., Seattle, 1974-86; affiliate asst. prof. U. Wash., Seattle, 1984-88; dir. stats. and probability NSF, Washington, 1986-88; prof. stats. The Am. U., Washington, 1988—, chair dept. math. and stats., 1993-95; mem. of corp. Nat. Inst. Statis. Scis., Research Triangle Park, N.C., 1990—. Co-author: Quality Control--Shared Multi-Disciplinary Databases, 1990; editor Multiple Stats. Integration, 1991. Mem. leadership com. Nat. Abortion Rights Action League, Washington, 1990—, Emily's List, 1993—; grant reviewer AAUW, NSF, NIH; faculty sponsor Students Against Sexual Violence. USPHS fellow, 1969-71; Nat. Cancer Inst. grantee, 1975-86, NSF grantee, 1989-90, Am. Math. Soc./Inst. of Math. Statistics/Soc. of Indsl. Applied Math. grantee, 1989, 92. Fellow AAAS (mem. nom. com.), Inst. Math. Stats. (outreach com. 1989), Am. Statis Assn. (com. of certification, publs. com. satis. and environment sect. 1991-92, rep. biopharm. sect. to coun. of sects. 1994, chair coun. sections), World Acad. Art & Sci., Washington Acad. Sci.; mem. AAUW, Caucus for Women in Stats., Internat. Stats. Inst., Biometric Soc., Internat. Assn. for Statis Computing, Assn. Women in Math. (joint com.), Math. Assn. Am., Washington Statis. Soc. (chair Elizabeth Scott award com., 1994). Democrat. Presbyterian. Office: Am U Dept Math and Stats 4400 Massachusetts Ave NW Washington DC 20016-8050

FLOWE, CAROL CONNOR, lawyer; b. Owensboro, Ky., Jan. 3, 1950; d. Marvin C. Connor and Ethel Marie (Thorn) Smith; children: Samantha Kathleen, Andrew Benjamin. BME magna cum laude, Murray State U., 1972; JD summa cum laude, Ind. U., 1976. Bar: Ohio 1977, D.C. 1981, U.S. Dist. Ct. (so. dist.) Ohio 1977, U.S. Dist. Ct. Md. 1983, U.S. Dist. Ct. D.C. 1981, U.S. Supreme Ct. 1987, U.S. Ct. Appeals (2d, 4th, 5th, 7th and D.C. cirs.). Assoc. Baker & Hostetler, Columbus, Ohio, 1976-80, Arent, Fox, Kintner, Plotkin & Kahn, Washington, 1980-87; deputy gen. counsel Pension Benefit Guaranty Corp., Washington, 1987-89, gen. counsel, 1989—. Co-author: EEO Handbook, 1986. Trustee, The Newport Schs., Kensington, Md., 1986-88. Mem. ABA, D.C. Bar Assn., Order of Coif, Alpha Chi, Phi Alpha Delta. Democrat. United Church of Christ. Home: 8608 Aqueduct Rd Potomac MD 20854 Office: Pension Benefit Guaranty Corp 1200 K St NW Washington DC 20005-4026

FLOWER, JULIANA DOUGLAS, arts administrator; b. Carlisle, Pa., Dec. 14, 1959; d. James Dunbar and Faith (Myers) F.; m. Mark Evans Lord, Dec. 27, 1991. BA, Swarthmore Coll., 1983; MA, Bryn Mawr Coll., 1992. Curatorial asst. Yale U. AA Gallery, New Haven, Conn., 1984-87; ops. mgr., admissions counselor Bryn Mawr (Pa.) Coll., 1987-91; adminstr. Phila. (Pa.) AA Alliance, 1992; asst. dir. Arts and Bus. Coun., Phila., 1993—; bd. dirs., co. mem. Potlatch, Phila., 1992—.

FLOWERS, CAROLYN DIANNE, drafting and plotting service executive; b. Culver City, Calif., Sept. 1, 1941; d. Guy Alford and Bethany June (Heaton) Cowart; m. Allen Kenneth Eagleman, Nov. 17, 1961 (div. Feb. 1984); children: Jeremy, Michelle Eagleman Nishimura, Jordan, Marlaine Eagleman Williams; m. Delbert Nyles Flowers, June 19, 1988. Student, Columbia Christian Coll., 1958-59, Pepperdine U., 1959-60. Contract clk. Telecommunication Cos., Calif. and Wash., 1972-79; various tech. positions Pacific Northwest Bell, Seattle, 1979-84; contract drafter Pacific Telephone, AT&T and other communications cos., Sacramento area, 1984-89; owner, drafter Pro Draft CADDrafting and Plotting Svc., Vacaville, Calif., 1989—; chmn. com. OPTIMA, Seattle, 1981-84. Mem. Solano Networking Group, Vacaville, 1990-94. Mem. NAFE, Nat. Assn. CAD-CAM Operators, N.Am. AutoCAD Users Group, Solano AutoCAD Users Group (pres. 1991-92), Am. Design Drafting Assn., Vacaville C. of C. Mem. Ch. of Christ. Office: Pro Draft CAD Drafting & Plotting Svc PO Box 5551 Vacaville CA 95696-5551

FLOWERS, CYNTHIA, investment company executive; b. N.Y.C., May 29, 1951; d. Bernard and Pearl (Davis) Heller; m. Robert Flowers, June 3, 1973; children: Perry, Lindsey. BS summa cum laude, Boston U., 1973; MBA with honors, NYU, 1976. Sr. mgr. portfolios Citibank NA, N.Y.C., 1973-82; v.p. Nat. Securities Corp., N.Y.C., 1982-87; pres. Stillrock Mgmt. Inc., N.Y.C., 1987-90; founder, pres. Flowers Capital Mgmt. Inc., N.Y.C., 1990—. Mem. N.Y. Soc. Security Analysts, Westside Tennis Club, Beta Gamma Sigma. Office: Flowers Capital Mgmt Inc 97 Groton St Forest Hills NY 11375-5956

FLOWERS, JUDITH ANN, public relations director; b. Oxford, Miss., Feb. 21, 1944; d. Woodrow Coleman and Ola Marie (Harding) Haynes; m. Sayles L. Brown Jr., Apr. 20, 1963 (div. Apr. 1974); children: Sayles L. III, Gregory A., Matthew C., Stephen W.; m. Taylor Graydon Flowers Jr., Apr. 27, 1979. Grad. high sch., Clarksdale, Miss. Office mgr. The KBH Corp., Clarksdale, 1964-69; office mgr., estimator Willis & Ellis Constrn., Clarksdale, 1969-75; with advt. prodn. Farm Press Pub., Clarksdale, 1975-79, advt. mgr., 1979-86, dir. advt. svcs., 1986-93; dir. mktg. and pub. rels. Cotton Club Casino, Greenville, Miss. Counselor County Youth Ct., Clarksdale, 1985—; sec. Keep Clarksdale Beautiful, 1990-92; bd. dirs. Delta Arts Coun., 1994—. Mem. NAFE, Bus. and Profl. Women (corr. sec. 1987-88, 2d v.p. 1988-89, 1st v.p. 1989-90, pres. 1992-93), Agri-Women Am., Nat. Agri-Mktg. Assn. (v.p. mid-south chpt. 1989-90, pres. 1990-91, nat. dir. 1991-93), Clarksdale C. of C. (chmn. agri-bus. comm. 1989—, bd. dirs. 1989-92), Greenville Hospitality Assn. (bd. dirs. 1993—), So. Garden History Soc. (bd. dirs. 1992—), The Garden Conservancy. Republican. Baptist. Home: PO Box 3126 Dublin MS 38739-0126 Office: Cotton Club Casino PO Box 1777 Greenville MS 38702

FLOWERS, KATIE VISHELL, entrepreneur, consultant; b. Scott Town, Mo., Aug. 14, 1967; d. Cleveland Jerome and Jessie Mae (Common) Turner; m. Pernell Robert Flowers; children: Kristen, Christopher, Pernell Robert II. Student, Art Inst. Chgo., 1994—. Tchr. Archdiocese of Chgo., 1987-90; adminstr. Chgo. Police Dept., 1990—; pres. Simply Arty Ink, Chgo., 1993—. Mem. 8th Ward Young Dems., Chgo., 1994, Am. Mus. Natural History, 1994. Mem. NOW, Coalition for Improved Edn. (adv. com. 1994—). Baptist. Home: 7024 S Paxton Apt 1B Chicago IL 60649 Office: Simple Arty Ink 7024 S Paxton Apt 1B Chicago IL 60649 also: Chgo Police Dept 1121 S State St Chicago IL 60605

FLOWERS, VIRGINIA ANNE, academic administrator emerita; b. Dothan, Ala., Aug. 29, 1928; d. Kyrie Neal and Annie Laurie (Stewart) F. BA, Fla. State U., 1949; MEd, Auburn U., 1958; EdD, Duke U., 1963. Teaching asst. Duke U., Durham, N.C., 1963; elem. and secondary sch. tchr., adminstr. Dothan and Dalton, Ga., 1949-61; asst. prof., then prof. edn., head dept. Columbia (S.C.) Coll., 1963-68, assoc. dean, then dean, 1969-72; prof. edn. Va. Commonwealth U., 1968-69; teaching asst. Duke U., 1963; assoc. dean, asst. provost, acting dean, vice provost Trinity Coll. Arts and Scis., Duke U., 1972-74, prof. edn., chmn. dept., asst. provost ednl. program devel., 1974-80; dean Sch. Edn., Ga. So. Coll., Statesboro, 1980-85; asst. vice chancellor acad. affairs Univ. System of Ga., Atlanta, 1985-88, vice chancellor, 1988-90, vice chancellor emerita, 1990—; ind. ednl. cons. Co-author: Law and Pupil Control, 1964, Readings in Survival in Today's Society, 2 vols, 1978; editorial bd.: Jour. Tchr. Edn, 1980-82, Ednl. Gerontology, 1979—; contbr. articles to profl. jours. Bd. dirs., mem. exec. com. Learning Inst. N.C., 1976-80; mem. bd. visitors Charleston So. U., 1992-93; adv. trustee Queens Coll., Charlotte, N.C., 1976-78; vice chmn. continuing commn. on study of black colls. related to United Meth. Ch., 1973-76. Delta Kappa Gamma scholar Duke U., 1963, State of Fla. scholar Fla. State U., 1949. Mem. NEA, Am. Ednl. Rsch. Assn., So. Assn. Colls. and Schs. (mem. commn. on colls.), Am. Assn. Higher Edn., Am. Assn. Colls. of Tchr. Edn. (pres. 1983-84, bd. dirs., mem. exec. com. 1979-84), Nat. Orgn. Legal Problems in Edn., Kappa Delta Pi, Phi Delta Kappa. Home and Office: PO Box 1603 Marianna FL 32447-5603

FLOYD, JENNETTE L., marketing executive; b. Kinston, N.C., May 31, 1958; d. Henry B. and Rubie M. (Fore) Floyd; m. Billy R. Kerley, Aug. 12, 1978 (div. Jan. 1983); m. L. Mark Godwin, Aug. 24, 1985 (div. July 1990). BSBA, U. Ala., 1979; cert. in exec. mgmt., Birmingham-Southern U., 1987; MBA, Vanderbilt U., 1992. Territory mgr. Burroughs Corp., Huntsville, Ala., 1979-81; account exec. So. Cen. Bell, Birmingham, Ala., 1981-82, AT&T-IS, Birmingham, 1983-84; asst. product mgr. Bell So. Svcs., Birmingham, 1984-85, market rsch. analyst, 1986-87; mgr., strategic market rsch. No. Telecom, Nashville, 1987-88, mgr. strategic analysis and rsch., 1988, mgr. strategic mktg. programs, 1988-89, mgr. program R&D, 1988-90, sr. mgr. rsch. and planning, 1990-91, sr. mgr. mkt. devel., 1991-93; advisor mktg. and tech. No. Telecom, Morristown, N.J., 1993—. Vol. Salvation Army, Birmingham, 1984-87, United Way, 1990-91, Buddies 1990, McNeilly Day Care Ctr. 1990, Jr. Achievement 1991. Recipient Wall Street Jour. award. Mem. Nat. Women's Polit. Caucus. Mem. Christian Ch. Home: 385 Ocean Blvd Apt 6M West End NJ 07740 Office: No Telecom Inc 465 South St Morristown NJ 07962

FLOYD, LINDA ANN, librarian; b. Columbia, Mo., Nov. 13, 1955; d. James Richard and Nancy Laverne (Mountjoy) Musgrave; m. Jimmy Floyd, Nov. 27, 1980; children: Allison Marie, William Colvin. BS, Auburn U., 1977; MLS, U. Ala., 1986. Cert. libr., Ga. Libr. dir. Andalusia (Ala.) Pub. Libr., 1981-86, Chattooga County Libr., Summerville, Ga., 1987-89; reference libr. Berry Coll. Meml. Libr., Mt. Berry, Ga., 1989-90, tech. svcs. libr., 1990—. Bd. mem. Chattooga Family and Child Ctr., Summerville, 1991—. Mem. AAUW, Phi Delta Kappa, Delta Kappa Gamma, Beta Phi Mu. Republican. Presbyterian. Office: Berry Coll Meml Libr Mount Berry GA 30149

FLOYD-TENIYA, KATHLEEN, business services executive; b. Berwyn, Ill., June 23, 1953; d. David James and Phyllis L. (Lyons) Floyd; m. Robert Don Teniya, June 20, 1982 (div. Oct. 1991); 1 child: James David. Cert. credit and fin. analyst, lic. realtor, Ill. Indsl. specialist Technicon Instrument Corp., Elmhurst, Ill., 1971-74, service contract adminstr., 1974-76; asst. to pres. Elmed, Inc., Addison, Ill., 1976-77; credit rep. mgr. Memorex Corp., Lombard, Ill., 1977-79; nat. sales rep. Midcontinent Adjustment Co., Glenview, Ill., 1979-83, asst. v.p. sales, 1983-86; pres., chief exec. officer, (Inteletek) Innovative Telemktg. Techniques Inc., Itasca, Ill., 1986—. Newspaper editor, publicity chmn. Dupage County chpt. Young Ams. for Freedom, 1969-70, pres.; mem. bd. edn. Trinity Luth. Sch., Lombard, Ill, 1989—; appointed mem. legal and fin., citizen advisor Village Bd., Bloomingdale, Ill., 1989—. Mem. Nat. Assn. Female Execs., Am. Soc. Profl. and Exec. Women. Lutheran. Clubs: Lombard Women's Rep., Ill. Fedn. Rep. Women. Home: 263 Evergreen Ln Bloomingdale IL 60108-1815 Office: Inteletek Innovative Telemktg Techniques Inc PO Box 163 Itasca IL 60143-0163

FLUCK, MICHELE M(ARGUERITE), biology educator; b. Geneva, Aug. 5, 1940; came to U.S., 1972; d. Wilhelm and Henriette Alice (Delaloye) F. MS, U. Geneva, 1964, 66, PhD, 1972. Rsch. assoc. N.Y. Pub. Health Rsch. Inst., N.Y.C., 1972-73; instr. Harvard Med. Sch., Boston, 1973-78, asst. prof., 1978-79; assoc. prof. Mich. State U., East Lansing, 1979-86, prof., 1986-90, disting. prof., 1990—. Contbr. articles to profl. jours. Recipient Young Investigator's award, Nat. Cancer Inst.; grantee Nat. Cancer Inst., 1979—, Am. Cancer Soc. grantee, 1987—. Fellow Leukemia Soc. Am. (scholar 1979-85); mem. AAAS, Am. Assn. virologists. Office: Mich State U Microbiology Dept Giltner Hall East Lansing MI 48824-1101

FLUELLEN, SHIRLEY ANN, optics researcher; b. Macon, Ga., Nov. 17, 1952; d. Alexander Hamilton and Mamie L. (Stanley) F. B.S., Fort Valley State Coll., Ga., 1973; postgrad. U. Mich. Dental Sch., 1973-74; O.D., Ind. U., 1979; specialist cert. Manila Central U., 1981. Cert. optometrist. Optometrist, Manila and Va., 1979—; optics research specialist Naval Space Surveillance System, Dahlgren, Va., 1982—. Chair polit. action group for Va., NAACP, 1985; organizer, pres. Fredericksburg Area Pan-Hellenic Council 1984—; mem. Nat. Council Negro Women, 1984—. Am. Fund Minority Dental Edn. scholar, 1972-74; Ga. Bd. Regents Scholar, 1969-72. Mem. Nat. Optometric Assn. (chair regional membership com.; Student Service award 1977), Beta Kappa Chi, Alpha Kappa Mu (chpt. v.p. 1972-73), Alpha Kappa Alpha, Ruby Bell Missionary Soc. Mem. Christian Methodist Episcopal Ch. Lodges: Order of Eastern Star, Daus. of Elks. Avocations: reading; travel; sewing; jogging. Home: 1292 Elmhurst Cir SE Atlanta GA 30316-2726 Office: 4800 Buford Hwy Atlanta GA 39901-0001

FLUGGER, PENELOPE ANN, banker; b. Chgo., June 26, 1942; d. William and Florence Bernadette (Brongiel) Grabos; B.S., U. Ill., 1964; M.B.A., Baruch Coll., 1971; CPA, N.Y., Ill.; m. Robert John Flugger, July 11, 1970. Sr. mgr. Price Waterhouse Co., N.Y.C., 1964-75; with Morgan Guaranty Trust Co., 1975—, auditor, 1982—, sr. v.p., 1982—, mng. dir., 1994; active Nat. Child Labor Com., Acctg. Edn. Change Commn., N.Y.C. Audit Com. Mem. Am. Inst. C.P.A.s, Nat. Assn. Accts., Fin. Execs. Inst., N.Y. State Soc. C.P.A.s, Ill. State Soc. C.P.A.s. Office: JP Morgan & Co 60 Wall St New York NY 10260-0060

FLUSHING, BARBARA VALIERE, counselor; b. Pontiac, Ill., May 8, 1950; d. Virgil Edward Tibbs and Shirley Olive (Adams) Tibbs-Carlin; m. David Vincent Flushing, June 14, 1975; children: Brett Aaron, Devon Vincent. AA, Winston Churchill Coll., 1970; BS in Edn., Ea. Ill. U., 1972; ME, U. Mo., 1993. Tchr. Crystal River (Fla.) Primary Sch., 1972-75, Alojandro Tapia, Aquadulce, Panama, 1976-77, Caribbean Sch., Ponce, P.R., 1984-85; counselor Mehlville Sch. Dist., St. Louis, 1992-93, High Ridge (Mo.) Elem. Sch., 1993—; supr. Washington Luth. Sch. Latchkey, St. Louis, 1990-91. Com. chair Boy Scouts Am., St. Louis, 1986-88. Mem. Am. Counselors Assn., Am. Sch. Counselor Assn., Mo. Sch. Counselor's Assn., Jefferson County Sch. Counselor's Assn., Chi Sigma Iota, Phi Kappa Phi. Home: 4849 Bogard Ct Saint Louis MO 63128-4409

FLYNN, CAROL, state legislator; b. Aug. 7, 1933; m. Richard L. Flynn; 2 children. Mem. Minn. State Senate, 1990—. Mem. Democratic Farm Labor Party. Office: Minn State Senate State Capital Saint Paul MN 55155*

FLYNN, CAROLYN ANN, sales executive; b. Camden, N.J., Oct. 30, 1948; d. Thomas and Carolyn (Goff) F. BA, Glassboro (N.J.) State Coll., 1975; MBA, St. Joseph's U., Phila., 1994. Tchr. Diocese of Camden, N.J., until 1978; sales adminstrn. acct. Mack Trucks Inc., Allentown, Pa., 1978-80, credit mgr., 1980-83, bus. mgr., 1983-85, sales rep., 1985-87, supr. sales, 1987-92; mgr. sales ops., 1992—; officer Mack Truck Sales of Queens, Mack Truck Sales of Tampa, Mack Truck Sales of No. Calif. Mem. NAFE, Alpha Phi (pres. alumna 1991-93). Roman Catholic.

FLYNN, DONNA STEELE, legislative staff director; b. Washington, Sept. 2, 1953. BS, U. Md., 1985; JD, George Mason U., 1991. Personal sec. Rep. Bill Archer, 1977-84, legis. dir., tax counsel, 1988—; legis. asst. Patton, Boggs & Blow, 1984-88. Office: Rep Bill Archer R-TX 1236 Longworth House Office Bldg Washington DC 20515*

FLYNN, ELIZABETH ANNE, advertising and public relations company executive; b. Washington, Aug. 21, 1951; d. John William and Elizabeth Goodwin (Mahoney) F. AA, Montgomery Coll., Rockville, Md., 1972; BS in Journalism, U. Md., 1976; postgrad. San Diego State U., 1976. Writer, researcher, Sea World, Inc., San Diego, 1977-79; sr. writer Lane & Huff Advt., San Diego, 1979-80; account exec. Kaufman, Lansky, Baker Advt., San Diego, 1980-82; mng. dir. Excelsior Enterprises, Beverly Hills, Calif., 1983-84; sr. account exec. Berkhemer & Kline, Inc., L.A., 1985; pres. Flynn Advt. & Pub. Rels., L.A., 1985—; cons. Coca-Cola Bottling Co. L.A., 1982-84; U.S. corr. Aeronovum mag., 1990—; v.p. mktg. Graffiti Prevention Systems, L.A., 1990-91; dir. new bus. devel. BBDO Hispanica, L.A., 1992-93; pub. rels. dir. Regional Organ Procurement Agy. So. Calif., L.A., 1994—. Bd. dirs. Friends of Reconstructive Surgery, Beverly Hills, 1983-89, Nat. Kidney Found., 1994, So. Calif. Coalition on Donation, 1994—, also mem. steering com. Recipient Distinction cert. Art Direction Mag., 1982. Mem. NAFE, Greater L.A. Press Club. Republican. Roman Catholic. Avocations: screenwriting, short stories, painting. Address: Flynn Advt & Pub Rels 1440 Reeves St Apt 104 Los Angeles CA 90035-2950

FLYNN, FAYE WILLIAMS, elementary school educator; b. Wellington, Tex., Sept. 13, 1913; d. Benjamin Franklin and Willie (Tibbets) Williams; m. Alton Lavoy Flynn Sr., Sept. 25, 1934 (dec. 1940); children: Alton Lavoy Jr., Nelda Louise Flynn Willis. Student, Tex. Women's U., 1933-34; BA, West Tex. State U., 1943, cert. in lang. and learning, 1973. Tchr. 1st and 2d grades Hopkins Elem. Sch., Pampa, Tex., 1943-47; tchr. 1st grade Sam Houston Elem. Sch., Pampa, 1947-58; resource tchr. 1st grade Sanborn Elem. Sch., Amarillo, Tex., 1960-62; tchr. 1st grade Cononado Elem. Sch., Amarillo, 1962-70; reading specialist Avondale Elem. Sch., Amarillo, 1970-76; tchr. 2d grade Whittier Elem. Sch., Amarillo, 1976-78, ret., 1978. Mem. AAUW (leader internat. rels. interest group Amarillo chpt. 1991-92), Amarillo Ret. Tchrs. Assn., Panhandle Plains Hist. Soc., Tex. Ret. Tchrs. Assn., Amarillo Fedn. Women's Club, Amarillo Internat. Club, Amarillo Art League (program dir. 1989-91), Book Rev. Club (past pres., reviewer). Democrat. Methodist. Home: 1111 Buena Vista St Amarillo TX 79106-4310

FLYNN, MARIE COSGROVE, portfolio manager; b. Honolulu, Jan. 1, 1945; d. John Aloysius and Emeline Frances (Cael) Cosgrove; m. John Thomas Flynn, Jr., June 3, 1968; children: Jamie Marie, Jacqueline Elizabeth. BA., Trinity Coll., 1966. Analyst U.S. Govt., Washington, 1967-70; coord. nat. reading coun. F.X. Doherty Assocs., N.Y.C., 1970-71; security analyst Corinthian Capital Co., N.Y.C., 1971-73; portfolio mgr. Clark Mgmt. Co., Inc., N.Y.C., 1973-78; v.p., sr. portfolio mgr. Lexington Mgmt. Corp., Saddle Brook, N.J., 1978—. Elected mem. Somerset County Rep. Com., 1994—. Mem. Fin. Analysts Fedn., Inst. Chartered Fin. Analysts, Fin. Women's Assn., N.Y. Soc. Security Analysts, Bus. and Profl. Women's Club. Home: 50 Pickle Brook Rd Bernardsville NJ 07924-1909 Office: PO Box 1515 Park 80 W Pla II Rochelle Park NJ 07662

FLYNN, PATRICIA MARIE, economics educator; b. Lynn, Mass.. BA in Econs., Emmanuel Coll., 1972; MA in Econs., Boston U., 1973, PhD in Econs., 1980. Rsch. assoc. Inst. for Employment Policy, Boston U., 1975-83; prof. econs. Bentley Coll., Waltham, Mass., 1976—; sr. rsch. fellow New Eng. Bd. Higher Edn., Boston, 1980-82; vis. sch. Fed. Res. Bd., Boston, 1983-84; exec. dir. Inst. for Rsch. & Faculty Devel., Bentley Coll., Waltham, 1986-90; assoc. dean faculty Bentley Coll., Waltham, Mass., 1991-92, dean grad. sch., 1992—; mem. faculty Inst. in Employment and Tng. Adminstrn. Harvard U., Cambridge, Mass., summers, 1979-81; cons. U. Mo., Columbia, 1983-84, First Security Svcs. Corp., Boston, 1985, Devel. Alternatives, Inc., Jakarta, Indonesia, summer, 1987, ABT Assocs., Cambridge, 1987-89; bd. dirs. Fed. Savs. Bank, Waltham, Mass. Co-author: Turbulence in the American Workplace, 1991, Technology Life Cycles and Human Resources, 1993; contbr. articles to profl. jours. Adv. panel mem. Office Tech. Assessment, U.S. Congress, Washington, 1989-91; accreditation team mem. New Eng. Assn. Schs. and Colls., 1985—; mem. Newton (Mass.) Econ. Devel. Commn., 1984-87. Grantee Dept. Labor, 1982-84, 88-89, Nat. Inst. Edn., 1982-83, NSF, 1990-93, Sloan Found., 1995—; recipient Gregory H. Adamian award for tchg. excellence Bentley Coll., 1986, Scholar of Yr., 1991. Mem. Am. Econ. Assn., Com. on the Status of Women in Econs. Professions, The Boston Club, The Boston Econ. Club. Home: 35 Pulsifer St Newton MA 02160-2220 Office: Bentley Coll 175 Forest St Waltham MA 02154-4713

FOARD, SUSAN LEE, editor; b. Asheville, N.C., Aug. 1, 1938; d. Carson Cowan and Anne (Brown) F. A.B., Salem Coll., 1960; M.A., William and Mary Coll., 1966. Asst. editor Inst. Early Am. Hist. and Culture, Williamsburg, Va., 1961-66; asso. editor Inst. Early Am. Hist. and Culture, 1966; editor U. Press of Va., Charlottesville, 1966—. Mem. Women Faculty and Profl. Assn. (U. Va.), Women in Scholarly Publishing of AAUP. Office: PO Box 3608 University Sta Charlottesville VA 22903-0608

FOCH, NINA, actress, creative consultant, educator; b. Leyden, The Netherlands, Apr. 20, 1924; came to U.S. 1927; d. Dirk and Consuelo (Flowerton) F.; m. James Lipton, June 6, 1954; m. Dennis de Brito, Nov. 27, 1959; 1 child, Dirk de Brito; m. Michael Dewell, Oct. 31, 1967 (div.). Grad., Lincoln Sch., 1939; studies with Stella Adler. Adj. prof. drama U. So. Calif., 1966-68, 78-80, adj. prof. film, 1987—; creative cons. to dirs., writers, prodrs. of all media; artist-in-residence U. N.C., 1966, Ohio State U., 1967, Calif. Inst. Tech., 1969-70; mem. sr. faculty Am. Film Inst., 1974-77; founder, tchr. Nina Foch Studio, Hollywood, Calif., 1973—; founder, actress Los Angeles Theatre Group, 1960-65; bd. dirs. Nat. Repertory Theatre, 1967-75. Motion picture appearances include Nine Girls, 1944, Return of the Vampire, 1944, Shadows in the Night, 1944, Cry of the Werewolf, 1944, Escape in the Fog, 1945, A Song to Remember, 1945, My Name Is Julia Ross, 1945, I Love a Mystery, 1945, Johnny O'Clock, 1947, The Guilt of Janet Ames, 1947, The Dark Past, 1948, The Undercover Man, 1949, Johnny Allegro, 1949, An American in Paris, 1951, Scaramouche, 1952, Young Man with Ideas, 1952, Sombrero, 1953, Fast Company, 1953, Executive Suite, 1954 (Oscar award nominee), Four Guns to the Border, 1954, You're Never Too Young, 1955, Illegal, 1955, The Ten Commandments, 1956, Three Brave Men, 1957, Cash McCall, 1959, Spartacus, 1960, Such Good Friends, 1971, Salty, 1973, Mahogany, 1976, Jennifer, 1978, Rich and Famous, 1981, Skin Deep, 1988, Sliver, 1993, Morning Glory, 1993; appeared in Broadway plays including John Loves Mary, 1947, Twelfth Night, 1949, A Phoenix Too Frequent, 1950, King Lear, 1950, Second String, 1960; appeared with Am. Shakespeare Festival in Taming of the Shrew, Measure for Measure, 1956, San Francisco Ballet and Opera in The Seven Deadly Sins, 1966; also many regional theater appearances including Seattle Repertory Theatre (All Over, 1972 and The Seagull, 1973); actress on TV, 1947—, including Playhouse 90, Studio One, Pulitzer Playhouse, Playwrights 56, Producers Showcase, Lou Grant (Emmy nominee 1980), Mike Hammer; series star: Shadow Chasers, 1985, War and Remembrance, 1988, LA Law, 1990, Hunter, 1990, Dear John, 1990, 91, Tales of the City, 1993; many other series, network spls. and TV films; TV panelist and guest on The Dinah Shore Show, Merv Griffin Show, The Today Show, Dick Cavett, The Tonight Show; TV moderator: Let's Take Sides, 1957-59; assoc. dir. (film) The Diary of Anne Frank, 1959; dir. (nat. tour and on-Broadway) Tonight at 8:30, 1966-67; assoc. producer re-opening of Ford's Theatre, Washington, 1968. Hon. chmn. Los Angeles chpt. Am. Cancer Soc., 1970. Recipient Film Daily award, 1949, 53. Mem. AAUP, Acad. Motion Picture Arts and Scis. (co-chair exec. com. fgn. film award, membership com.), Hollywood Acad. TV Arts and Scis. (bd. govs. 1976-77). Office: PO Box 1884 Beverly Hills CA 90213-1884

FODREA, CAROLYN WROBEL, educational researcher, publisher; b. Hammond, Ind., Feb. 1, 1943; d. Stanley Jacob and Margaret Caroline (Stupeck) Wrobel; m. Howard Frederick Fodrea, June 17, 1967 (div. Jan. 1987); children: Gregory Kirk, Lynn Renee. BA in Elem. Edn., Purdue U., 1966; MA in Edn., U. Chgo., 1973; postgrad., U. Colo., Denver, 1986-87. Cert. elem. tchr., Ind., Ill. Tchr. various schs., Ind., Colo., 1966-87; founder, supr., clinician Reading Clinic, Children's Hosp., Denver, 1969-73; pvt. practice in reading rsch. clinic Denver, 1973-87, Deerfield, Ill., 1973—; creator of pilot presch.-kindergarten lang. devel. program Gary, Ind. Diocese Schs., 1987—, therapist lang. and reading disabilities, 1987—; pvt. practice Reading Clinic, Highland, Ind., 1987—, Deerfield, Ill., 1988—; founder Ctr. for Rsch. in Ednl. Ecology, Deerfield, Ill., 1989—; conducted Lang. Devel. Workshop, Gary, Ind., 1988; pres. Lang. Comm. Strategies for the 21st Century Corp. Cons. Firm; tchr. adult basic edn. Dawson Tech. Sch., 1990, Coll. Lake County, 1991, Prairie State Coll., 1991—, Chgo. City Colls., 1991, R. J. Daley Coll., 1991, Coll. DuPage, 1991—; condr. adult basic edn. workshops for Coll. of DuPage, R. J. Daley Coll., 1992, Ill. Lang. Devel. Literacy Program. Author: Language Development Program, 1991, Comprehension Program, 1985, Presch. Kindergarten Lang. Devel. Program, 1988, A Multi-Sensory Stimulation Program for the Premature Baby in its Incubator to Reduce Medical Costs and Academic Failure, 1986, Predicting At-Risk Babies for First Grade Reading Failure Before Birth, Oral Language Development Program, Grades 1 to Adult, 1988, 92. Active Graland Country Day Sch., Denver, 1981-83, N.W. Ind. Children's Chorale, 1988—. Mem. NEA, Am. Ednl. Rsch. Assn., Internat. Reading Assn., Am. Coun. for Children with Learning Disabilities, Assn. for Childhood Edn. Internat., Colo. Assn. for Edn. of Young Children, Infant Stimulation Edn. Assn., AAUW, NAFE, Nat. Assn. for Women in Career-North Shore, Art Inst. Chgo., Smithsonian Instn., Cousteau Soc., U. Chgo. Alumni Club (Chgo. area ann. fund, Pres. fund com. 1988—, numerous positions Denver area chpt. 1974-87). Roman Catholic. Office: Lang Comm Strategy 280 Crestwood Village Northfield IL 60093-3402

FOEGE, ROSE ANN SCUDIERO, human resources professional; b. Bklyn., Aug. 22, 1941; d. Thomas Edward and Catherine Mary (Demarsico) Scudiero; m. William Henry Foege, Apr. 19, 1975. BA, Queens Coll., 1973; MS cum laude, Iona Coll., 1981. Cert. Am. Registry Radiologic Technologists. X-ray technician St. Clare's Hosp., N.Y.C., 196-61; supr. x-ray N.Y. Internat. Longshoremen's Assn. Med. Ctr., N.Y.C., 1960-67, Life Extension Inst., N.Y.C., 1967-73; radiologic technologist Exxon Corp., N.Y.C., 1973-81, coordinator systems and records, 1981-86; staff human resources specialist Exxon Rsch. & Engrs., Linden, N.J., 1986-93; sect. supr. human resources Exxon Chem. Co., Linden, N.J., 1994—. V.p Wykagyl Neighborhood Assn., New Rochelle, N.Y. Mem. NAFE, Soc. Human Resources Mgmt., Am. Mgmt. Assn., Am. Acad. Med. Adminstr., Am. Soc. Radiologic Technologists, Mensa, Iona Coll. Alumni Assn., Iona Coll. Pres.'s Club. Home: 149 Wykagyl Ter New Rochelle NY 10804-3124 Office: Exxon Chem Co Park and Brunswick Area Linden NJ 07036

FOGEL, J(OAN) CATHY, lawyer; b. Chgo., Mar. 18, 1943; d. Norman Jack and Esther Lois (Grobstein) Friedman; m. Jay Bernard Lichtenberg, June 29, 1968 (dec. Apr. 1981); 1 child, Ian Robert; m. Donald Benjamin Fogel, Sept. 27, 1987; children: Alexis Jill, D. Brandon. BS, U. Wis., 1964; JD, Cath. U., 1977. Bar: U.S. Ct.Appeals (D.C. cir.) 1977, D.C. 1978, U.S. Ct. Appeals (7th cir.) 1979, U.S. Ct. Appeals (2d cir.) 1979, U.S. Supreme Ct. 1981, U.S. Ct. Appeals (3d cir.) 1984. Research librarian Library Congress, Washington, 1964-66; legislative research specialist Am. Pub. Power Assn., Washington, 1966-71; assoc. Duncan, Miller & Pembroke, Washington, 1977-83, ptnr., 1983-88; ptnr. Verner, Liipfert, Bernhard, McPherson and Hand, Washington, 1989—; spl. asst. atty. gen. State of N.D., 1979-86. Contbr. articles to profl. jours. Mem. ABA, Women's Bar Assn., D.C. Bar Assn., Fed. Energy Bar Assn. (chmn. fed. power act parts I & II 1985-86, vice-chmn. power mktg. agys. 1988-89, chmn. power mktg. agys. 1989-90). Democrat. Jewish. Home: 3804 Woodbine St Bethesda MD 20815-4957 Office: Verner Liipfert Bernhard McPherson & Hand 901 15th St NW Ste 700 Washington DC 20005-2327

FOGGS-CRUMBLY, IRIS YVONNE, press secretary; b. Anderson, Ind., July 14, 1958; d. Edward Lewis and Joyce Delores (Stone) Foggs. BS, Ball State U., 1980. Legis. corr. office of congressman Joel Deckard U.S. Ho. Reps., Washington, 1980-82; comms. specialist Erie (Pa.) Ins. Group, 1983-85; acct. mgr. Pers. Pool of Am., Washington, 1986-87; dep. press sec. Pa. Dept. Corrections, Camp Hill, 1987-89, exec. asst. to commr., 1989-90; press sec. Pa. Dept. State, Harrisburg, 1990—; pub. chair 3d Nat. Conf. on Female Offenders, Pitts., 1989; intern reporter Sta. WISH-TV, Indpls., summer 1979. Prodr., host: (TV show) Images, 1992—. Cand. Pa. Ho. Reps., Harrisburg, 1992; bd. dirs. United Cerebral Palsy of Capital Region, United Way of Capital Region; mem. ctrl. Pa. campaign adv. bd. United Negro Coll. Fund; active Jr. League Harrisburg. Recipient Outstanding Profl. Contbns. award Affirmative Action Office of U.S. Postal Svc., 1990, Mayor's award for Disting. Pub. Svc., 1990. Mem. Nat. Assn. Black Journalists (v.p. local chpt., pres. Ctrl. Pa. Assn. Black Communicators 1993-94, founding mem.). Democrat. Mem. Ch. of God. Office: Pa Dept State 302 N Office Building Bldg Harrisburg PA 17120-0021

FOIT-ALBERT, BEVERLY, architect; b. Buffalo, Apr. 28, 1938; d. Franklin and Ruth Foit; m. Joseph Cox, Aug. 1986; children: James, Jeffrey, Richard. BArch, Cornell U., 1961; MArch, SUNY, Buffalo, 1975; PhD in Human Sci., Saybrook Inst. Registered architect, N.Y. Prin. Foit, Baschnagel & Assocs., Buffalo, 1970-77; assoc. prof. architecture SUNY, 1970—; pres. Foit-Albert Assocs., Buffalo, 1977—. Bd. dirs. Greater Buffalo Partnership, 1993, Erie and Niagara Counties Regional Planning Bd., Buffalo, 1992—, Erie County Preservation Bd., Buffalo, 1992—. Recipient Award of Distinction, Coun. Ednl. Facility Planners Internat., Toronto, Ont., Can., 1993, Small Bus. Svc. Sector award Bus. First/Greater Buffalo Partnership, 1993, Excellence in Parking Design award Instnl. and Mcpl. Parking Congress, Atlanta, 1993, Disting. Alumni award Cmty. Adv. Coun., SUNY, 1993; selected as 1 of 15 "Women Who Make A Difference, Minorities and Women in Bus. Mag. Mem. AIA (bd. dirs. 1990—), Himalayan Inst. (bd. dirs. 1989—), Buffalo Pl., Inc. (mem. com. 1991—). Office: Foit-Albert Assocs 763 Main St Buffalo NY 14203-1395

FOK, AGNES KWAN, cell biologist, educator; b. Hong Kong, British Crown Colony, Dec. 11, 1940; came to U.S., 1962; d. Sun and Yau (Ng) Kwan; m. Fok, June 8, 1965; children: Licie Chiu-Jane, Edna Chiu-Joan. BA in Chemistry, Coll. Great Falls, 1965; MS in Plant Nutrition and Biochemistry, Utah State U., 1966; PhD in Biochemistry, U. Tex., Austin, 1971. Asst. rsch. prof. pathology dept. U. Hawaii, Honolulu, 1973-74, Ford Found. postdoctoral fellow, anatomy dept., 1975, asst. rsch. prof. Pacific Biomed. Rsch. Ctr., 1975-82, assoc. rsch. prof., 1982-88, assoc. rsch. prof. biology program, 1985, rsch. prof., 1988—, grad. faculty, dept. microbiology, 1977—; dir. biology program Pacific Biomed. Rsch. Ctr., 1994—. Contbr. articles to profl. jours. Mem. Am. Soc. for Cell Biology, Soc. for Protozoologists, Sigma Xi (treas. Hawaii chpt. 1979—). Office: U Hawaii Dept Microbiology Honolulu HI 96822

FOL, MONIQUE ELIANE, educator; b. Courbevoie, France, June 20, 1933; came to U.S., 1957; d. Cornelius Maxime and Lucette (Adam-Mulhberg) F. Baccalaureat in Philosophy, Universite de Paris, 1952, Licence en Droit, 1955; MA, U. Calif., Berkeley, 1960; Doctorat, Universite de Nice, 1977. Councellor-at-law Paris, 1955-57; teaching asst. U. Calif., Berkeley, 1959-61, research asst., 1962-63; instr. Wellesley (Mass.) Coll., 1964-67; full prof. Boston Coll., Chestnut Hill, Mass., 1967—. Author: Jean de Boschere ou le chemin du retour, 1987, le Temps de la Confidence, 1990, les Mots pour l'écrire, 1990, Emile Zola/1991, Un Nouvel Engagement, 1992, Excavatio I, 1992, Excavatio II, III, 1993, Excavatio IV, 1994, Les Jambes Meurtries dans L'oeuvre d'Emile Zola, 1995; co-author: Un Certain Style, 1969, Un Style certain: Les Mots Pour l'Ecrire, 1988, Le Cheval Tentaculaire dans les Rougon-Macquart, 1995, Occident/Orient, rencontres; founder Les Nouvelles Presses Universitaires Weslof, Berkeley, Calif.; editor, founder Excavatio/Zola; contbr. articles to profl. jours. Founder, pres. A Will/A Way, Littleton, Mass., 1981, Boston br. Handicapped Organized Women, 1985. Bourses Ministere de l'Education Nationale Paris, 1952-55; Harbism and Burgess rsch. grantee Princeton U., 1958, Newhouse grantee U. Calif., 1958, rsch. grantee, 1961-62; Mellon Found. grantee, 1985-86; Ford Found. grantee, 1985; faculty teaching grantee Boston Coll., 1985, rsch. grantee, 1984-85, faculty fellow, 1987; Que. Govt. grantee, 1989; French Govt. grantee, 1991, 92, 93. Mem. MLA, Assn. Tchrs. French, Boston Inst. Psychology, Emile Zola Intercontinental Assn. (founder, pres.), Assn. Internationale Emile Zola et les Ecrivains Naturalistes a travers le Monde (founder, pres.). Democrat. Home and Office: Parkview Mobile Estates 226 Stone Ter Palm Springs CA 92264

FOLEY, HELEN CLAIBORNE, university administrator; b. Columbia, S.C., June 8, 1945; d. David Bartholemew and Helen Irving (DuBose) F. BS magna cum laude, U. S.C., 1984; MEd, Vanderbilt U., 1986. Staff asst. U. S.C., Columbia, 1971-77; assoc. dir. U. S.C. Alumni Assn., Columbia, 1977-80; dir. devel. coll. pharmacy U. S.C., Columbia, 1980-85; dir. devel. Va. Poly. Inst., Blacksburg, 1987-90; v.p. devel. Tenn. Performing Arts Ctr., Nashville, 1991-92, fundraising cons., 1992; dir. spl. gifts La. State U., Baton Rouge, 1992—. Vol. Richland Meml. Hosp., Columbia, 1970-75, Spl. Olympics, Columbia, 1976-78; tchr. Literacy Coun., Columbia, 1987. Named one of Disting. Alumni U. S.C., 1988. Mem. Rotary (chmn. mentor com. Blacksburg-Christiansburg chpt. 1989), Blacksburg C. of C. (chmn.

legis. com. 1989). Episcopalian. Home: 9024 Fox Run Ave Baton Rouge LA 70808

FOLEY, MRS. JOHN PORTER, JR. See ANASTASI, ANNE

FOLEY, KATHERINE ELIZABETH, librarian; b. Ludington, Mich., Feb. 13, 1946; d. James Horace and Mary Elizabeth (Parrott) Reynolds; m. Michael Glen Foley, June 1, 1968. BA, Whittier Coll., 1968; MLS, UCLA, 1971. Environ. engring. libr. Calif. Inst. Tech., Pasadena, 1971-75; sch. libr. Columbia (Mo.) Pub. Schs., 1976-78; reference libr. Mo. State Libr., Jefferson City, 1978-80; audio-visual libr. Richland (Wash.) Pub. Libr., 1980-84, libr. supr., 1984-90; assoc. dean libr. media svcs. Columbia Basin Coll., Pasco, Wash., 1990—; appointed mem. Wash. State Adv. Coun. on Librs., Olympia, 1989-90. Mem. ALA, Wash. Libr. Assn. (local arrangements co-chair 1990), Beta Phi Mu. Office: Columbia Basin Coll Libr 2600 N 20th Ave Pasco WA 99301

FOLEY, KATHLEEN M., neurologist, educator, researcher; b. Flushing, N.Y., Jan. 28, 1944; d. Joseph Cyril and Catherine (Cribbin) Maher; m. Charles Thomas Foley, Aug. 10, 1968; children: Fritz, David. BA in Biology magna cum laude, St. John's U., N.Y.C., 1965, DSc (hon.), 1992; MD, Cornell U., 1969. Diplomate Am. Bd. Psychiatry and Neurology (examiner 1980—); lic. physician, N.Y. Intern, then resident in neurology The N.Y. Hosp., N.Y.C., 1969-74; asst. attending neurologist, neuology dept. Meml. Sloan-Kettering Cancer Ctr., N.Y.C., 1974-79, assoc. attending neurologist, 1979-88, chief-pain svc., 1982—, attending neurologist, 1988—; attending neurologist Manhattan (N.Y.) Eye & Ear Hosp., 1974-83; instr. in neurology, Med. Coll. Cornell U., N.Y.C., 1974-75, asst. prof., 1975-79, assoc. prof., 1979-89, assoc. prof. pharmacology, 1979-89, prof. neurology and neuroscience, 1989—, prof. clin. pharmacology, 1990—; rsch. assoc. lab. neuro-oncology Sloan-Kettering Inst. Cancer Rsch., N.Y.C., 1981-84; vis. asst. physician, cons. in neurology Rockefeller U. Hosp., 1975-79, vis. assoc. physician, 1979—; cons. Calvery Hosp., 1982—; assoc. mem. Meml. Sloan-Kettering Cancer Ctr., 1985-88, mem. 1988—. Editor Clinical Jour. Pain, 1985-87, Jour. Pain and Symptom Mgmt., 1987—, Palliative Medicine Jour., 1993—. Patient Svcs. Adv. Group, Am. Cancer Soc. Genetic Training grant NIH, 1970-71, Program for Pain Rsch. grant Bristol-Myers, 1988-92; Neuro-Oncology spl. fellow Meml. Sloan-Kettering Cancer Ctr., 1975-78; recipient Jr. Faculty award Am. Cancer Soc., 1975-78, Disting. Svc. award, 1992, Nat. Bd. award The Med. Coll. Pa., 1986, Willaim M. Witter award U. Calif. San Francisco, 1987, Annie Blount Storrs award Calvery Hosp., 1988, Balfour M. Mount award Am. Jour. Hospice Care, 1988, Disting. Oncologist award Dayton Oncology Soc., 1990, Tenth Barbara Bohen Pfeifer award Am. Italian Found. for Cancer Rsch., 1993; named Outstanding Women Scientist Women in Sci. Met. N.Y. Chpt., 1987, A. Soriano Jr. Meml. Lectr. The Andres Soriano Cancer Rsch. Found. Inc., 1992. Mem. AAAS, AMA (ad hoc adv. panel mgmt. chronic pain, DATTA reference panel), NAS (Inst. Medicine), Acad. Hospice Physicians, Am. Acad. Neurology (chmn. long range planning com. 1990—, scientific program com. 1990, and other coms.), Am. Fedn. Clin. Rsch., Am. Med. Womens Assn., Am. Neurological Assn. (mem. com. 1984-85, councilor 1984, 94), Am. Pain Soc. (bd. dirs. 1980-82, pres. 1984-85, bylaws com. 1986-87 long range planning task force 1989—), Am. Soc. Clin. Onocology (program com. 1991-92, com. on care at the end of life 1993—, and other coms.), Am. Soc. Clin. Pharmacology and Therapeutics, Assn. Rsch. in Nervous and Mental Diseases, Children's Hospice, Children's Hospice Internat., Cornell U. Med. Coll. Alumni Assn. (bd. dirs., nominating com.), Eastern Pain Assn. (John J. Bonica award 1986), Harvey Soc., Internat. Assn. Study Pain (councilor 1984-90, edn. com. 1986-93, and various coms.), N.Y. Acad. Scis. (USP adv. panel on neurology 1990—), Soc. for Neuroscience, Alpha Omega Alpha. Office: Meml Sloan-Kettering Cancer Ctr 1275 York Ave New York NY 10021-6007

FOLEY, PATRICIA JEAN, accountant; b. Bridgeport, Conn., Jan. 12, 1956; d. John Edward and Louise (Caselli) F. AA, Housantonic Community Coll., 1978; BS, Cen. Conn. State Coll., 1980; postgrad., U. Hartford, 1992. CPA, Conn. Staff acct. Spitz, Sullivan, Wachtel & Falcetta, Hartford, Conn., 1981-82, client acct., 1982-85, sr. acct., 1985-87, supr., mgr., 1987—; mem. Acctg. Del. to Russia, Ukraine & Estonia Citizens Amb., 1993. Pres. Woodsedge Condominium Assn., Newington, Conn., 1989-92, treas., 1985-92. Mem. AICPA (mgmt. adv. svs. com. 1987-94, info. tech. divs., 1992—), Conn. Soc. CPAs, Am. Women Soc. CPAs, Community Assn. Inst. (membershp chair Conn. chpt. 1991-92). Home: 35 Woodsedge Dr Apt 1B Newington CT 06111-4271

FOLEY, RITA VIRGINIA, computer company executive; b. Boston, Mar. 20, 1953; d. Francis Michael and Rita Claire (Martin) F.; m. Peter G. Buckley, May 15, 1976; children: Michael E., Nathaniel R. Grad., U. Geneva, 1974; AB in Psychology, Smith Coll., 1975. Sales rep. Polaroid, St. Albans, England, 1975-77; br. mgr. Harris Lanier, N.Y.C., 1977-82; various mgmt. positions Digital Equipment Corp., N.Y., N.J., 1982-89; dist. mgr. Digital Equipment Corp., Piscataway, N.J., 1989-91, group mgr. northwest telecom & utilities, 1991-92; U.S. mktg. mgr. high performance systems Digital Equipment Corp., Marlboro, Mass., 1992-93; v.p. northeast regional ctr. Digital Equipment Corp., N.Y.C., 1993-94; v.p., regional mgr. western region Digital Equipment Corp., Santa Clara, Calif., 1994—. Head various coms. Pratt Area Cmty. Coun., Bklyn., 1982—, co-chair bd. dirs., 1983-85; mem. exec. devel. forum N.Y.C. C. of C., 1993; mem. svc. com. children with learning disabilities Mary McDowell Cmty. Ctr., Bklyn., 1990—; sponsor Spl. Olympics, N.Y. and Conn., 1990, 91; cmty. crime patroller Pratt Area Crime Patrol, Bklyn., 1983-89. Mem. Am. Womens Elec. Devel. Corp., Smith Coll. Club. Office: Digital Equipment Corp 2525 Augustine Dr Santa Clara CA 95054

FOLK, KATHERINE PINKSTON, English language educator, writer, journalist; b. Corsicana, Tex., Feb. 8, 1925; d. Lucian Albert and Katherine (Shell) Pinkston; m. Elmer Ellsworth Folk, Apr. 21, 1946 (div. Sept. 1985); children: Russell Harter, David Shell, Barbara Kay Folk Nowotny. BA in Journalism, Tex. Tech. U., 1946; postgrad., U. Houston, 1960-71. Reporter Scurry County Times, Snyder, Tex., 1946; dir. advt. Dunlaps Dept. Store, Lubbock, Tex., 1946; instr. English Odessa (Tex.) Coll., 1948-53; dir. communication, editor Viva Mag. Houston Met. Ministries, 1979-80; dir. communication for continuing edn. Houston Community Coll. System, 1989-90, instr. English, 1980—; auditor creative writing Rice U., Houston, 1966; tutor English Spring Br. Ind. Sch. Dist., Houston, 1970-75. Contbr. articles to popular mags. Ann. sponsor Odessa Coll., 1950-53; mem. Harris County Heritage Soc., Houston, 1985-91, Nat. Fedn. Rep. Women, Houston, 1987-94, Country Playhouse Little Theatre; bd. dirs. Spring Br. YMCA, Houston, 1990-91. Mem. AAUW, Jr. League Houston (patron tea rm.), Nat. Fedn. Press Women, Soc. Chldren's Book Writers, Romance Writers Am., Delta Delta Delta (chmn. scholarship com. 1972). Episcopalian. Office: Houston C C Sys 22 Waugh Dr Houston TX 77007-5898

FOLK, SHARON LYNN, printing company executive; b. Bellefontaine, Ohio, June 13, 1945; d. Emerson Dewey and Berdena Isabelle (Brown) F. A.A. in Liberal Arts, Sacred Heart Coll., 1965, L.H.D. (hon.), 1985; A.B. in Econs. and Bus. Adminstrn., Belmont Abbey Coll., 1968. Exec. v.p. Nat. Bus. Forms, Inc., Greeneville, Tenn., 1968-73, chmn. bd., pres., 1973—; sec., treas. Nat. Forms Co., Inc., Gastonia, N.C., 1969-73, chairperson, bd. dirs., pres., 1973—, SF Enterprises, Inc., Greeneville, 1987—, Andrew Johnson Golf Club, Inc., Greeneville, 1987—; mem. bus. adv. com. Bus. Ptnrs., Inc., Washington, 1987-89; bd. dirs. Andrew Johnson Bank, Greeneville, chairperson employee rels. com., Internat. Bus. Forms Industries, Arlington, Va., 1978-83. Mem. fin. com. YMCA, Greeneville, 1977-78, bd. dirs., 1977-80; bd. dirs. United Way, 1980-85, Greeneville, vice chmn., 1989-90; mem. presdl. steering com. U.S. Senator Howard Baker, 1979-80; mem. Rep. Presdl. Task Force, 1981—; life mem. Rep. Nat. Com., 1981—; mem. Rep. Senatorial Inner Circle, Washington, 1984-86; vice-chmn. parish coun. Notre Dame Cath. Ch., Greeneville, 1984-85, chmn., 1985-87; founding mem. Com. 200, Chgo., 1981—, vice chmn., membership chmn. S.E. region, 1983-84, bd. dirs. 1984-85, v.p., bd. dirs., 1985-86; mem. bd. advisors Belmont Abbey Coll., 1984-85, trustee, 1986-90, exec. com., 1989-90, chair fin. com., 1991-94, mentor fin. com., 1994—; trustee Sacred Heart Coll., Belmont, N.C., 1985-89; bd. dirs. Oak Grove Cemetery, Greenville, 1989—; bd. dirs. Am. Heart Assn., Greenville, 1989-91; bd. dirs. Jr. Achievement of Greeneville, Inc., 1991—; chair Takoma Adventist Found. Bd., 1992—; trustee Tusculum Coll., Greenville, 1989—; bd. dirs. Takoma /Adventist Hosp. Found., Greeneville, 1987—, vice chair, 1989-90. 2d lt. CAP, 1984—; maj. Civilian Guard, Middleboro, Ky., 1986—; oblate Order of St. Benedict, Our Lady Help of Christians Abbey, Belmont, 1967—. 1st lt. Search and Rescue Pilot Civil Air Patrol, Aux. USAF, Maxwell Air Force Base, Ala., 1984—. Mem. Nat. Bus. Forms Assn., Forms Mfrs. Credit Interchange, Am. Mgmt. Assn., Nat. Assn. Women Bus. Owners, Tenn. Bus. Roundtable (bd. dirs. 1986), Belmont Abbey Alumni Coll. Assn. (bd. dirs. 1986-94), U.S. Tennis Assn. (life), Airplane Owners and Pilots Assn. Avocations: tennis, airplane pilot, photography, golf, reading, water skiing. Home: 1131 Hixon Ave Greeneville TN 37743-5807 Office: Nat Bus Forms Co Inc PO Box 1750 Greeneville TN 37744

FOLLEY, CHERYL KOLB, paralegal; b. Buffalo, N.Y., Sept. 15, 1938; d. Charles Roy and Ruth Lucille (Schwartz) Kolb; m. John Frederick Folley III, Aug. 26, 1961; children: Eric Alan, Sarah Folley McMackin. BA in History, Denison U., 1960; paralegal cert., Nat. Ctr. for Paralegal Tng., Atlanta, 1993. Part-time rschr. ARC Rsch., Columbia, S.C., 1980; part-time merchandiser RN Koch, Providence, 1982-83; part-time secret shopper Piggly Wiggly, Charleston, S.C., 1983-85; paralegal Law Office of Adele Pope, Columbia, 1993—. Founder, sec., membership com. Murraywood Swim and Racquet Club, Columbia, 1974-79, 92-94; pres., sec., treas. Homeowners of Murraywood, Columbia, 1977-92. Mem. S.C. Assn. Legal Assts., Columbia Legal Asst. Assn., Phi Alpha Theta. Democrat. Home: 1525 Murraywood Dr Columbia SC 29212-1119

FOLMER, JOAN E., accountant; b. Lancaster, Pa., Nov. 13, 1944; d. John H. and Jean M. (Hershey) Kraybill; m. Roy R. Folmer, Aug. 12, 1967. BS in Biology summa cum laude, Elizabethtown Coll., 1967, postgrad., 1976-78. Sci. instr. Sch. Nursing Lancaster (Pa.) Gen. Hosp., 1968-79; staff acct. Hershey (Pa.) Chocolate N.Am., 1979-81, fin. acct., 1981-85, sr. fin. acct., 1985-86, mgr. fixed asset acctg., 1986—; mem. user adv. com. Dunn & Bradstreet Software, Atlanta, 1985-93. V.p. Oakmont Condominium Assn., Hershey, 1989-92. Mem. Inst. Mgmt. Accts. Home: 1186 Draymore Ct Hummelstown PA 17036 Office: Hershey Chocolate N Am 19E Chocolate Ave Hershey PA 17033

FOLSOM, WYNELLE STOUGH, retired wood products manufacturing executive; b. Bankston, Ala., July 19, 1924; d. Richard Carey and Ora Beatrice (Fowler) Stough; m. Eugene Bragg Folsom, Sept. 3, 1944; children: Don Wayne, Dana L. Student U. Ala., Livingston U., 1962-63, Draughan Bus. Coll., Montgomery, Ala., 1941-42, Alexander State Coll., Alexander City, Ala., 1967-68, Chilton Vocat. & Tech. Sch., Clanton, Ala., 1969-70. Sec., Ala. Power Co., Birmingham, 1942-44; med. librarian Santa Rosa Hosp., San Antonio, 1944-46; payroll clk. Dow Chem. Co., Freeport, Tex., 1946-48; with audit dept. Sears, Roebuck & Co., Selma, Ala., 1956-66; sec.-treas. Oakline Chair Co., Inc., Selma, 1967-83, pres., 1983-86. Chmn. publicity Cahaba Regional Libr. (Friends of the Libr.), Clanton, Ala., 1979; mem. Selma-Dallas County Historic Preservation Soc., 1982-87. Mem. Selma C. of C., Hemorcallis Garden Club (pres. 1979), Woman's Study Club (chmn. publicity 1967-69). Republican. Mem. Ch. of Christ. Avocations: needlework, fishing, reading, painting, gardening. Home: 803 Lay Dam Rd Clanton AL 35045-2923 Office: Oakline Chair Co Inc Hwy 31 N PO Box 1698 Clanton AL 35045-1698

FONDA, BRIDGET, actress; b. Jan. 27, 1964; d. Peter and Susan F. Films: Aria, 1987, You Can't Hurry Love, 1988, Shag, 1988, Scandal, 1989, Strapless, 1989, Frankenstein Unbound, 1990, The Godfather, Part III, 1990, Doc Hollywood, 1991, Out of the Rain, (also known as Remains), 1991, Single White Female, 1992, Singles, 1992, Bodies Rest and Motion, 1993, Point of No Return, 1993, Little Buddha, 1994, It Could Happen To You, 1994, Camilla, 1994, The Road to Wellville, 1994, Rough Magic, 1995, City Hall, 1995; TV appearances: (series) 21 Jump Street, 1989, Jacob Have I Loved, WonderWorks episode, 1989, (made for cable movie) Leather Jackets, 1991. Office: United Talent Agency 9560 Wilshire Blv 5th Floor Beverly Hills CA 90212*

FONDA, JANE, actress; b. N.Y.C., Dec. 21, 1937; d. Henry and Frances (Seymour) F.; m. Roger Vadim (div.); 1 child, Vanessa; m. Tom Hayden, Jan. 20, 1973 (div.); 1 child, Troy; m. Ted Turner, Dec. 21, 1991. Student, Vassar Coll. Appeared on Broadway stage in There Was a Little Girl, 1960, The Fun Couple, 1962; appeared in Actor's Studio prodn. Strange Interlude, 1963; appeared in films Tall Story, 1960, A Walk on the Wild Side, 1962, Period of Adjustment, 1962, Sunday in New York, 1963, In the Cool of the Day, 1963, The Love Cage, 1963, La Ronde, 1964, Cat Ballou, 1965, The Chase, 1966, Any Wednesday, 1966, The Game Is Over, 1967, Hurry Sundown, 1967, Barefoot in the Park, 1967, Barbarella, 1968, Spirits of the Dead, 1969, They Shoot Horses, Don't They?, 1969, Klute, 1970 (Acad. award best actress), Steelyard Blues, 1973, A Doll's House, 1973, The Blue Bird, 1976, Fun with Dick and Jane, 1976, Julia, 1977, also producer Coming Home, 1978 (Acad. award best actress), California Suite, 1978, Comes a Horseman, 1978, also producer The China Syndrome, 1979, Electric Horseman, 1979, Nine to Five, 1980, On Golden Pond, 1981, Rollover, 1981, The Dollmaker, 1984 (ABC-TV, Emmy award best actress), Agnes of God, 1985, The Morning After, 1986 (Acad. award nomination best actress), Old Gringo, 1988, Stanley and Iris, 1990, producer Lakota Woman, 1994; author: Jane Fonda's Workout Book, 1981, Women Coming of Age, 1984, Jane Fonda's New Workout & Weight-Loss Program, 1986, Jane Fonda's New Pregnancy Workout & Total Birth Program, 1989, Jane Fonda Workout Video, 12 additional videos. Recipient Golden Apple prize for female star of yr. Hollywood Women's Press Club, 1977, Golden Globe award, 1978; rated no. 1 heroine of young Ams., U.S. News Roper Poll., 1985, 4th most admired woman in Am., Ladies Home Jour. Roper Poll, 1985. Office: Fonda Films PO Box 5947 Beverly Hills CA 90209

FONG, ELAINE CHUN, principal; b. Honolulu, Feb. 9, 1936; d. James Tai Yee and Esther Chun; m. James Chuck Fong, Dec. 26, 1964; children: Margery Ann, Elizabeth Ann. BA, U. Hawaii, 1958; MA, U. San Francisco, 1975. Tchr. Dept. Edn. State of Hawaii, Honolulu, 1958-61; tchr. San Francisco Unified Sch. Dist., 1961-81; dir. San Francisco Tchr. Ctr., 1981-85; prin. San Francisco Unified Sch. Dist., 1985—; cons., trainer Calif. Schs. Leadership Acad., Sacramento, 1986—; trainer Tchr. Expectations and Student Achievement, San Francisco, 1987—. Bd. dirs. Learning Through Edn. in the Arts Project, San Francisco, 1985-92. Mem. AAUW, Calif. Assn. for Supervision and Curriculum Devel. (exec. bd. dirs. 1993—), Alpha Delta Kappa (pres. 1982-84, 92-94), Sigma Omicron Pi (v.p. 1990-92, pres. 1992-94), Phi Delta Kappa. Roman Catholic. Home: 2200 15th Ave San Francisco CA 94116-1823

FONS-COLVIN, MARY LYNN, medical researcher; b. Oak Creek, Wis., Feb. 26, 1963; d. Albert George and Dorothy Elise (Griffin) Fons; children: m. Scott Hall Colvin, June 25, 1988. BS in Biology and Psychology, Carroll Coll., 1985; cert. in small bus. operation, Waukesha County Tech. Coll., 1989. Lab. technician Cytogenetics Endocrine Lab., Waukesha, Wis., 1985-86; sr. rsch. technician Med. Coll. Wis., Milw., 1986-87; rsch. scientist Schwarz Pharma Kremers-Urban, Mequon, Wis., 1987-89, clin. rsch. scientist, 1989-91; med. rsch. assoc. Schering-Plough Pharms., Kenilworth, N.J., 1991-93; sr. clin. rsch. assoc. Coromed, Inc., Troy, N.Y., 1993-94; clin. rsch. cons. Clinimetrics Rsch. Assocs., San Jose, Calif., 1994—; v.p. Creative Houseworks, Inc., Milw., 1990-91; asst. lab. animal technician Am. Assn. Lab. Animal Sci., 1989. Author abstracts in field. Recipient cert. Ctr. for Profl. Advancement, 1990, 92. Mem. NAFE, Am. Heart Assn., Drug Info. Assn., Chautauqua Assn., Nat. Audubon Soc., Wilderness Soc., Environ. Def. Fund, Sierra Club. Democrat. Roman Catholic. Office: 203 Meadow Way Golden CO 80403-9542

FONTÁNEZ-PHELAN, SANDRA MARÍA, special education director, consultant; b. Las Piedras, P.R., June 1, 1952; came to U.S., 1955; d. Santos and Felicita (Velazquez) Fontánez; m. Patrick Mallon Phelan, July 23, 1983; children: Patrick Brandon, Cory Michael. Student, U. P.R., 1969-70; BA, U. Ill. at Chgo., 1973, MA in Edn., 1980; postgrad., So. Ill. U., Carbondale, 1986, Ill. State U., Normal, 1988—. Cert. tchr., adminstr., learning disabilities, behavior disorders, emotionally disturbed, educable mentally disabled, trainable mentally disabled, Spanish K-12, bilingual edn. and ESL tchr. Tchr. Spanish Chgo. Pub. Schs., 1974-77, tchr., counselor behavior disorders, 1977-80, tchr. home and hosp., 1980-81, resource tchr. bilingual learning disabilities, 1981, master tchr. bilingual spl. edn., 1981-83, ednl. diagnostician, 1983-85, dir. spl. edn., 1991—; tchr. communications Fermi Lab. Sci. and Engring. Program, Batavia, Ill., 1980; facilitator Chgo. Pub. Sch. Compliance and Due Process, 1985-89; grad. asst. Ill. State U., Normal, summer 1989; prin. John Hancock Elem. Sch., Chgo., 1989-91; dir. spl. edn. Chgo. Pub. Schs., 1991—; counselor Chgo. City Colls., 1982-85; hearing officer level I Ill. State Bd. Edn., Springfield, 1988—; cons. Bilingual and Spl. Edn. Issues, Chgo., 1988—; mem. adv. coun. Truman Coll., Chgo., 1988—; tchr. rep. U. Chgo. Mock Congress, Chgo., 1979, translator law offices, Chgo., 1979. Mem. adv. coun. Truman Coll., Chgo., 1988—, Dover St. Block Club, Chgo., 1983—, Sheridan Pk. Neighbors Assn., Chgo., 1983—, Our Lady of Lourdes Ch.-Womens Guild, Chgo., 1983—. Ill. Consortium for Ednl. Opportunity Ill. State U. fellow, 1989—; So. Ill. U. fellow, 1986. Mem. Nat. Conf. of P.R. Women (pres. 1990—), Ill. Coun. of Adminstrs. for Spl. Edn., Coun. for Exceptional Children, Chgo.'s Prin. Assn. (dist. 7 staff devel. 1989-90), Southwest Community Congress (edn. com. 1989-90), Nat. Assn. Bilingual Edn., Learning Disabilities Assn. Democrat. Roman Catholic. Office: Chgo Pub Schs 1819 W Pershing Rd Chicago IL 60609

FOOR, KATHY JANE, financial executive; b. Lakewood, Ohio, July 2, 1958; d. Ronald Foor and Patricia Foor Wolfe; 1 child, Jeffrey A. Student Point Park Coll., Pitts., 1993-94. Fin. analyst Intracorp, Pitts., 1985-93, sr. billing analyst, 1994—. Home: 25 High St Aliquippa PA 15001 Office: Intracorp 3200 Park Lane Dr Pittsburgh PA 15275

FOOTE, BARBARA AUSTIN, civic foundation executive; b. Seattle, Mar. 26, 1918; d. Edwin Charles and Marion (Roberts) A.; m. Robert Lake Foote, June 14, 1941; children: Markell Foote Kaiser, Marion Roberts, Helen Foote Schloerb. AB, Vassar Coll., 1940. Tchr. Shady Hill Sch., Cambridge, Mass., 1942-43, Madeira Sch., Greenway, Va., 1943-44, North Shore Country Day Sch., Winnetka, Ill., 1960-71; mem. exec. com. Chgo. Community Trust, 1970-85, chmn. exec. com., 1978-85; bd. dirs. Harris Bank, Glencoe and Northbrook, Ill., The New Eng. (name formerly New Eng. Mut. Life Ins. Co.), Boston. Author book of verse, 1948. Pres. Jr. League Chgo., 1947-49, Assn. Jr. Leagues Am., 1954-56, Glencoe Bd. Edn., 1957-63; trustee Vassar Coll., 1966-74; bd. dirs. Presbyn. Home, Evanston, Ill. Mem. Vassar Alumni Assn. (nat. pres. 1975-78), Phi Beta Kappa. Congregationalist. Clubs: Fortnightly of Chgo.; Cosmopolitan (N.Y.C.). Home: 587 Longwood Ave Glencoe IL 60022-1736 also: Wausaukee Club Box 8-A HCR Hwy 1 Athelstane WI 54104-9999

FOOTE, EVELYN PATRICIA, retired army officer, consultant; b. Durham, N.C., May 19, 1930; d. Henry Alexander and Evelyn Sevena (Womack) F. BA summa cum laude, Wake Forest U., 1953; student, U.S. Army Command & Gen. Staff Coll., Leavenworth, Kans., 1971-72, U.S. Army War Coll., Carlisle, Pa., 1976-77; MS in Govt. and Pub. Affairs, Shippensburg State U., 1977; student, U. Va. Sch. Bus. Adminstrn., 1980; LLD (hon.), Wake Forest U., 1989. Commd. 1st lt. U.S. Army, 1960, advanced through grades to brig. gen., 1986; platoon officer WAC U.S. Army, Ft. McClellan, Ala., 1960-61; officer selection officer 6th recruiting dist. U.S. Army, Portland, Oreg., 1961-64; comdr. WAC Co. U.S. Army Engr. Brigade, Ft. Belvoir, Va., 1964-66; student Adj. Gen. Officer Advanced Course, Ft. Benjamin Harrison, Ind., 1966; exec. officer, chief adminstrv. div. pub. affairs office U.S. Army, Vietnam, 1967; exec. officer, office personnel ops. WAC, Washington, 1968-71, plans and programs officer OFC, dir., 1972-74; personnel mgmt. officer U.S. Army Forces Command, Ft. McPherson, Ga., 1974-76; comdr. 2d basic tng. bn. U.S. Army Tng. Brigade and Military Police Sch., Ft. McCllellan, Ala., 1977-79; faculty mem. U.S. Army War Coll., 1979-82; student Fgn. Service Inst., Dept. of State, Washington, 1982-83; comdr. 42d Mil. Police Group, Mannheim, Fed. Republic of Germany, 1983-85; spl. asst. to comdg. gen. 32d Army Air Def. Command Hdqrs., Darmstadt, Fed. Republic of Germany, 1985-86; dep., insp. gen. for inspections Hdqrs. Dept. of the Army, Washington, 1986-88; dep. comdg. gen. Mil. Dist. Washington, comdr. Ft. Belvoir, Va., 1988-89; ret. U.S. Army, 1989; free-lance lectr., cons. in def. pers. and leadership, mem. or advisor numerous bds.; lectr. various U.S. Army and civilian groups. Contbr. articles to military jours. Bd. visitors Wake Forest U.; trustee U.S. Army War Coll.; bd. dirs. Nat. Woman's Party; mem. Am. Battle Monuments Commn., 1994—. Decorated D.S.M., Legion of Merit with oak leaf cluster, Bronze star, Meritorious Svc. medal with two oak leaf clusters, German Cross of Svc. 1st class; recipient Dist. Pub. Svc. award Wake Forest U., 1987. Mem. Army and Air Force Mut. Aid Assn. (bd. dirs.), Exec. Women in Govt., Am. Battle Monuments Commn., 1994, Zonta Internat. Democrat. Lutheran.

FOOTE, FRANCES CATHERINE, association executive, living trust consultant; b. Chgo., Apr. 3, 1935; d. Peter and Ellen Gertrude (Quinn) F. BS in Edn., Cardinal Stritch Coll., 1957; MS in Edn., Ill. State U., 1966. Cert. tchr., Ill. Tchr. Sch. Dist. 123, Oak Lawn, Ill., 1959-84; asst. prin. Sch. Dist. 123, Oak Lawn, 1971-80; pres. Am. Now, St. Petersburg, Fla., 1985—; instr. geography workshops for tchrs., 1967-70, use of newspaper in classroom workshops, 1973-75; co-chair social Studies Curriculum Revision; living trust cons. Accurate Bus. Assocs., Inc., St. Petersburg; ind. rep. Watkins Products. Officer PTA, Oak Lawn, 1973-76; mem. Rep. Nat. Com., Washington, vol. State of Fla. Guardian ad litem, St. Vincent de Paul Soc. Mem. Am. Fedn. Tchrs. Roman Catholic. Home: 280 126th Ave E Apt 203 Treasure Island FL 33706-4442

FOOTE, JEAN ANNETTE, nurse, educator; b. Portland, N.D., Sept. 17, 1938; d. E. Wallace and Jennie A. (Finell) Haugom; m. Denis D. Foote, Dec. 18, 1960; children: Heidi J., Kirsten A., Sonja J. BSN with distinction, U. Minn., 1961, MS, 1972; postgrad., Ariz. State U. Sch. nurse Moorhead (Minn.) Pub. Schs.; community health nurse Fargo (N.D.) Dept. Health; asst. prof. Ariz. State U., Tempe; assoc. prof. Grand Canyon U., Phoenix. Contbr. to profl. publs. Mem. ANA, Ariz. Nurses Assn. (bd. dirs.), Am. Pub. Health Assn., Sigma Theta Tau.

FOOTE, KARISSA JAYN, tennis pro; b. Ft. Worth, Aug. 16, 1959; d. Granville Raymond and Bobbie Jean (Whitiker) Foote. BS, Tex. Wesleyan U., Ft. Worth, 1982; postgrad., Tex. Wesleyan Coll., Ft. Worth, 1983. Head tennis coach Tex. Wesleyan U., Ft. Worth; asst. profl. Ceder Canyon Tennis Club, Lancaster, Tex., Center Tennis Club, Arlington, Tex.; asst. prof. to dir. tennis River Bend Athletic Club, Ft. Worth, 1983-90, dir. tennis, 1990-94; head tennis profl. East Chase Sports Club, Ft. Worth, 1994—; co-organizer Jr. Athletic Tennis Orgn.. Mem. U.S. Racquet Stringers Assn., U.S. Tennis Assn., Tex. Tennis Assn., U.S. Profl. Tennis Assn. Democrat. Episcopalian. Home: 5801 Hadley Fort Worth TX 76117 Office: East Chase Sports Club 9055 John T White Rd Fort Worth TX 76120

FOOTE, LINDA GASS, property management executive; b. Livingston County, Ky., Sept. 12, 1939; d. Norman W. and Ruby (Sunderland) Gass.; m. Phillip L. Foote, Nov. 13, 1959 (div. Aug. 1976); children: Phillip L. Jr., Gerard Stuart. BA cum laude, Western Ky. U., 1960, postgrad., 1970—. Tchr. English lang., Latin, history, speech Marshall County High Sch., Benton, Ky., 1961-62, Murray (Ky.) High Sch., 1962-66, Paducah (Ky.) Tilghman High Sch., 1966-68, Hardinsburg (Ky.) High Sch., 1970-71, Glasgow (Ky.) High Sch., 1971-72, Ea. High Sch., Louisville, 1972-78; real estate broker Louisville, 1972—, gen. contractor, 1976—; property mgr. Thompson Properties Inc., Louisville, 1981-85, I.R.E. Fin. Svcs., Louisville, 1985-92; owner, mgr. Foote Property Mgmt., Louisville, 1985—; real estate broker, Ohio, 1986—; owner, mgr. Linda Foote Constrn., Inc. Women's Bus. Enterprise, Louisville, 1993—; instr., conductor seminars Continuing Edn. Ctr. U. Louisville, 1988—. Vol. fundraiser Sta. KET-TV, 1988. Named Bldg Mgr. of Yr., Bldg. Owners and Mgrs., 1990. Mem. AARP, Bldg. Owners and Mgr. Inst. (instr. 1990). Democrat. Office: Profl Towers 4010 Dupont Cir Louisville KY 40207-4859

FOOTE, RUTH ANNETTE, business official, land developer; b. Riverside, Calif., Nov. 2, 1925; d. Edgar Wallace and Murrel (Sibrell) Thomas; m. Harold Dale Borregard, July 15, 1945 (div.); children: Linda Gail, Valerie Louise, Jennifer; m. Robert Earl Foote, June 24, 1951; children: Robin David, James Wayne. Student pub. schs., San Bernardino, Calif. Comml. closer M.P. Crum Co., Dallas, 1964-67, Trammel Crow Co., Dallas, 1967-69; developer Hidden Valley Airpark, Denton, Tex., 1969-70, exec. sec., 1969-73; escrow officer, mgr. Southwest Land Title, Denton, 1970-75; exec. v.p. Lawyers Title Co., Denton, 1975-80, Attorneys Title Co., Dallas, 1984; legal sec. Ray & Gilchrist, Lewisville, Tex., 1984-86; founder, co-owner Am. Title

Co. Dallas, Lewisville, Tex., 1986—; ins. agt. Alliance for Affordable Health Care, Dallas; assoc. Starcom, Inc.; owner, developer Whitehawk Valley, Denton, 1977—, Rainbow Valley, Denton, 1979—, Home Opportunities Made Easy, 1990; owner branch office Safeco Land Title Co., North Richland Hills, Tex., 1976-81; exec. v.p. Inpact Mortgage, Inc., 1993—. Mem. fund raising com., historian bd. dirs. Habitat for Humanity of Denton. Author: And the Truth Shall Set You Free, 1980. Mem. Women's Forum Dallas. Republican. Mem. LDS Ch. Pioneered (with Robert Foote) earth sheltered home communities which provide their own electricity, fuel and water. Home: RR 2 Box 1049 Sanger TX 76266-9525 Office: Impact Mortgage Inc 223 N Locust Denton TX 76201

FOOTE, SHERRILL LYNNE, manufacturing company technician; b. Marshalltown, Iowa, Apr. 19, 1940; d. Howard Raymond Ellis and Lois Ellen (Cooper) F.; m. Terry D. Downey, July 27, 1958 (div. 1978); children: Patrick L., Holly L. Harrelson; m. Frank H. Foote, Nov. 17, 1979 (div. 1989); stepchildren: Lauri K., Christopher R. Student, Marshalltown Community Coll., 1981—. Receptionist Drs. Long & Clawson, Marshalltown, 1958-59; clk. Fisher Controls, Marshalltown, 1963-73, cost estimating analyst, 1974-82, sr. cost estimator, 1982—. Contbr. limericks Des Moines Register (Contest Winner), 1976, Marshalltown Times Rep., 1986. Mem. Mensa (contbr. Bull. Wordplay 1981—, limerick editor M-Pressions Ctrl. Iowa newsletter 1989-91, local sec. 1991-93). Democrat. Methodist. Home: 702 Ratcliffe Dr Marshalltown IA 50158-3453

FORBES, CYNTHIA ANN, small business owner, marketing educator; b. Richmond, Calif., Dec. 27, 1951; d. James Martin and Mary Jane (Clafferty) Forbes; m. Larry Charles Osofsky, Mar. 20, 1970 (div. 1980); 1 child, Anna; m. William Charles Ham, Aug. 30, 1986. BA, U. Calif., 1977; MS, Golden Gate U., 1981. Research asst. U. Calif., Berkeley, 1975-77, Chevron Research, Richmond, 1977-79; specialist dealer affairs Chevron USA, San Francisco, 1979-80, sales rep., San Fafael, Calif., 1981-84, adminstrv. supr., San Ramon, Calif.; 1984-85, advt. mgr. Chevron Chem. Co., San Francisco, 1986-88; assoc. prof. Golden Gate U., San Francisco, 1981-92. Vol., lectr. child abuse prevention; bd. mem. Sierra Nev. Children's Svcs. Mem. ASTD. Democrat. Avocations: mountaineering, bicycling. Home: PO Box 165 Downieville CA 95936 Office: PO Box 2348 Nevada City CA 95959

FORBES, GEORGINA, artist, psychotherapist; b. Boston, Jan. 18, 1943; d. G. Donald and Faith (Fisher) F.; m. John Jacob Karol, Oct. 19, 1963 (div. Apr. 1977); children: Angelisse Forbes Karol, Christopher Hale Karol. Student, Regis Coll., 1962; MA in Counseling Psychology, Antioch U., 1978. Exec. officer Ministry of External Affairs Govt. Malawi, Zomba, 1965-67; interviewer, soundtechnician, asst. editor Apertura Films, Orford, N.H., 1968-74; nursing asst. Hanover (N.H.) Ter. Healthcare, 1974-75, social worker, 1975-76; psychotherapist outpatient svcs. Community Counseling Svcs., Lebanon, N.H., 1976-77; pvt. practice Boston, 1978-79, Thetford, Vt., 1979-89; outpatient psychotherapist Calvin Turley Assocs., Newton, Mass., 1979-81; dir. career counseling Women's Info. Svcs., Lebanon, 1987-89; outpatient clinician Healthcare and Rehab. Svcs., White River Junction, N.J., 1989-93. Exhibited in solo and group shows, East Coast and Carribean, 1972—. Dir., creator Peace Hunger Kitchen Project, Thetford, 1986-88; del. Ind. Party, Thetford, 1988. Mem. NOW, Alliance for Visual Arts, Women's Peace and Freedom Project (co-chair 1992-93), Women's Caucus for Art, Artemis' Bow (dir.). Home: Artemis Bow RR 1 Box 624 Windsor VT 05089-9719

FORBES, KAY PRESTON, accountant, tax consultant; b. Laredo, Tex., Feb. 26, 1953; d. Thomas J. R. Jr. and Margaret E. (Clem) Preston; m. Harris Bryant Forbes, Jan. 8, 1983; children: Joanna Elizabeth, Laura Preston. BA, Rice U., 1975, M of Acctg., 1976. CPA, Tex. Mem. tax staff Arthur Andersen & Co., Houston, 1976-77, mem. sr. tax staff, 1977-79, tax mgr., 1979-84, tax ptnr., 1984—; lectr. Jones Grad. Sch., Rice U., Houston, 1980-81; past chair Rice Acctg. Coun.; acad. affairs com. Houston Bus. Forum; planning com. 10th, 11th and 12th ann. nonprofit orgns. inst. U. Tex. Sch. Law; mem. dean search com. Jones Grad. Sch. Adminstrn., Rice U.; bd. dirs., parliamentarian Jones Grad. Sch. Alumni. Co-chair Founder's Soc. Mem. AICPA (Elijah Watt Sells award 1976), Tex. Soc. CPAs (Acctg. Excellence award 1976), Tex. Accts. and Lawyers for the Arts (pres., chair publs. com., adv. bd., projects com., chair vol. recruitment com., long range planning com., spl. events com., acct.'s adv. com.), Houston Chpt. CPAs. Office: Arthur Andersen & Co Ste 1300 711 Louisiana Houston TX 77002

FORBES, MARY GLADYS, educator; b. Bend, Oreg., June 19, 1929; d. Percy Lloyd and Bertha May (Gettman) F. BA in Edn. magna cum laude, Cascade Coll., 1951; BS in Edn., Western Oreg. State Coll., Monmouth, 1951, MS in Edn., 1968. Cert. tchr., Oreg. Tchr. Christian & Missionary Alliance, Mamou, Guinea, West Africa, 1952-54, Bend (Oreg.)-Redmond Christian Day Sch., 1954-56, Dalat Sch., Asia, 1956-76; tchr. Bend-LaPine Sch. Dist. 1, Bend, 1976—, adminstr., tchr., 1981-87, tchr. kindergarten, 1989—; cons. Chpt. I Program in Spl. Edn., 1976-88; supt. Sunday sch. Christian and Missionary Alliance, 1976-80, Faith Fellowship Four Sq., Madras, Oreg., 1981-88. Mem. Citizens for the Republic, Washington, 1989; mem. Rep. Nat. Com., 1990—. Recipient cert. of appreciation Hale Found., 1986, 87, Skyhook II Project, 1987, Concerned Women Am., 1987, Nat. Law Enforcement Officer Meml., 1991, Am. Indian Relief Coun., 1992. Mem. Am. Def. Inst., Nat. Right to Life Com., Inc., Coun. for Inter-Am. Security, Nat. Assn. for Uniformed Svcs., Concerned Women for Am., Capitol Hill Women's Club, Christian Coalition, Am. Ctr. for Law and Justice, Am. Life League, Oregon Citizens Alliance. Home: 181 NE 9th St Madras OR 97741-2618 Office: Bend LaPine Sch Dist 1 520 NW Wall St Bend OR 97701-2608

FORBES, NANCY MOGGIO, marketing research analyst, business planner; b. Northampton, Mass., Sept. 6, 1955; d. Armand Norman and Viola Katherine (Zack) Moggio; m. Patrick Frank Tria (div. Nov. 1987); m. Lewis J. Forbes Jr., Sept. 23, 1988; children: Zackary Lewis, Tyler Moggio. BA cum laude, Albertus Magnus Coll., 1977; MBA, U. Phoenix, 1984. Inventory analyst So. New England Telephone, New Haven, 1977-79; cost acct. IBM, Tucson, 1980-82, indsl. engr., 1982-84; fin. analyst IBM, Atlanta, 1984-88, bus. planner, 1989-91, mktg. analyst, 1991—. Editor newsletter Tng. Industry News, 1992—; author, creator Multiple Job Aids, 1990-93; developer course How to Obtain Competitive Info., 1992. Mem. Soc. Competitive Intelligence Profls. (advisor local chpt. 1991—), ASTD. Home: 3335 Hunterdon Way Marietta GA 30067-5003

FORBES, PATRICIA R., legislative counsel; b. Plainfield, N.J., Mar. 28, 1954. BA, Middlebury Coll., 1976; JD, U. So. Calif., 1981. Atty./advisor office gen. counsel U.S. SBA, 1982-86, chief counsel legislation and regulation, 1986-91; majority counsel Senate Small Bus. Com., 1991—. Office: Com Small Business 428-A Senate Russell Office Bldg Washington DC 20510*

FORCE, CRYSTAL ANN, school counselor; b. Atlanta, Jan. 4, 1947; d. Raymond Ralph and Mary Ellen (Sticher) Bennett; m. Edward James Force, June 26, 1971; children: Lane Bennett, Patrick Brendan. BA, Carson-Newman Coll., 1969; MEd, Fla. Atlantic U., 1971. Cert. sch. counselor, Ga. Tchr. English Clewiston (Fla.) High Sch., 1969-71, sch. counselor, 1971-72; sch. counselor Greenport (N.Y.) Sch., 1972-75; dir. after sch. program LaBelle Elem. Sch., Marietta, Ga., 1985-89; sch. counselor LaBelle and Fair Oaks Elem. Schs., Marietta, 1989-90, LaBelle and King Springs Elem. Schs., Marietta, Smyrna, Ga., 1990-91, King Springs Elem. Sch., Smyrna, 1991—; co-dir. Smart Kids Orgn., Smyrna, 1992—. Chair parent edn. com. Griffin Mid. Sch. Parent Teacher Student Assn., Smyrna, 1993-94, exec. bd. sec. 1988; mem. Citizens Adv. Coun., Smyrna, 1984-85, 93-94; mentor Campbell High Sch., Smyrna, 1992-93. Recipient Am. Hero in Edn. award Reader's Digest Assn., 1993, Today's Kids award Brawner Hosp., 1993, Elem. Sch. Counselor of Yr. for Cobb County, Ga., 1994. Mem. AAUW, Am. Counseling Assn., Am. Sch. Counselor Assn., Ga. Sch. Counselor Assn., Nat. Sch. Age Child Care Alliance, Ga. Sch. Age Child Care Assn., Cobb County Sch. Counselor Assn., Campbell High Sch. Booster Club. Republican. Baptist. Home: 4227 Deerwood Pkwy Smyrna GA 30082 Office: King Springs Elem Sch 1041 Reed Rd Smyrna GA 30082

FORCE, ELIZABETH ELMA, retired pharmaceutical executive, consultant; b. Phila., Sept. 6, 1930; d. Harry Elgin and Loretta G. (Werner) F. BA, Temple U., 1952; postgrad., U. Pa., 1965-67; MPh, George Washington U., 1972, PhD, 1973. Cons. sr. scientist Booz-Allen Hamilton, Bethesda, Md., 1967-68; rsch. cons. scientist GEOMET, Inc., Rockville, Md., 1968-70; profl. assoc. div. med. scis. NAS-NRC, Washington, 1970-74; mgr. clin. adminstrn. dept. clin. rsch. and devel. Wyeth Labs., Radnor, Pa., 1974-77; exec. dir. regulatory affairs Merck Sharp and Dohme Rsch. Labs., West Point, Pa., 1977-88; cons. Clin. Regulatory Systems, Sarasota, Fla., 1988—; asst. professorial lectr. epidemiology and environ. health Sch. Medicine George Washington U., Washington, 1972-74; vis. assoc. prof. cmty. health and preventive medicine Med. Coll. Jefferson U., Phila., 1981-83. Editor Clin. Rsch. Practice and Drug Regulatory Affairs, 1983-85, Drug Info. Jour., 1984-88; contbr. 60 articles to profl. jours. Pres. Women's Resource Ctr., Sarasota, 1992-94; pres., bd. dirs. Siesta Tower Condominium Assn., Sarasota, 1990-92; vice chmn. Com. for Minority Contracts, Sarasota County, 1991; chmn. adv. coun. bd. trustees Ringling Mus. of Art, 1991-95, Coun. on Violence, Sarasota County, 1994. Ruhland Pub. Health fellow George Washington U. Sch. Medicine, 1971-73. Mem. Drug Info. Assn. (pres. 1986-87, Outstanding Dir. award 1985). Office: 4822 Ocean Blvd Apt 3A Sarasota FL 34242-1304

FORCIER, RENÉE MARTEL, geriatrics, medical/surgical nurse; b. Balt., Aug. 29, 1947; d. Leonard George and Dolores Irene (Menchini) F. AA, Montgomery Jr. Coll., Takoma Park, Md., 1972; diploma in nursing, Wash. Adventist Hosp. Sch., Takoma Park, 1975; cert. edn. for parish svc. program, Trinity Coll., Washington, 1989; student, U. Md., 1991—. LPN, Md., D.C. Pvt. nurse practitioner Tri-Cities Nurses Registry, Chevy Chase, Md., 1976—; charge nurse Manor Care Nursing Home, Wheaton, Md., 1982-86; nursing adminstr., dir. nursing Medcall/Med. Staffing Svc., Inc., Silver Spring, 1989; home health nurse Montgomery Gen. Hosp., Olney, Md., 1992—. Author philosophy course Montgomery Jr. Coll., 1970; pub. Jour. Practical Nursing. Mem. Sodality-Coun. of Cath. Women, Silver Spring, 1984—; nurse-vol. Bethesda Cares Project-Mobile Med. Care Inc. for Homeless, Bethesda, 1991—; cert. nurse insvc. instr. Arthritis Found., Arlington, Va., 1988—; advocate for disabled St. Andrew Apostle Cath. Ch., 1989—, mem.-at-large parish coun., 1992; mem. Archdiocesan Com. on Ministry with Persons Who are Disabled, 1989—; vol. ARC. Recipient Cmty. Svc. award for vol. nursing govt. of Montgomery County, Rockville, Md., 1991, 93, Women of Influence award Pres.'s Commn. on Women's Affairs, 1993. Mem. Nat. Assn. Dirs. of Nursing Adminstrn. in Long-Term Care, Nat. Assn. Practical Nurse Edn. and Svcs., Golden Key, Mortar Bd., John Carroll Soc. Democrat. Home: 317 Chartwell Dr Silver Spring MD 20904-6301

FORCINIO, HALLIE EUNICE, editor; b. Cleve., Aug. 25, 1952; d. Quentin L. and Bertha W. (Bolman) Schirch; m. Robert K. Forcinio, Jan. 24, 1981. BA cum laude, Baldwin-Wallace Coll., Berea, Ohio, 1974. Traffic mgr. Jaeger Advt., Berea, 1975; editorial asst. Arthur G. McKee & Co., Cleve., 1975-78; comm. asst. Work Wear Corp., Cleve., 1978-82; assoc. editor HBJ Publs. (name now Advanstar Comm.), Cleve., 1982-84, mng. editor, 1984-91, editor in chief, 1991-92; freelance writer, editor Cleve., 1992—. Mem. Friends Cleve. Pub. Libr. Mem. Internat. Assn. Bus. Communicators (sec., editor), Am. Soc. Bus. Press Editors, Inst. Packaging Profls., Internat. Packaging Press Orgn., Cleve. Zool. Soc., Cleve. Mus. Natural History, Kappa Phi (editor 1976-83, pres. 1983-87, 89-91). Republican. Lutheran.

FORD, ANABEL, research anthropologist, archaeologist; b. L.A., Dec. 22, 1951; d. Joseph B. Ford and Marjorie Henshaw Skopecek; m. Michael A. Glassow, May 4, 1974. BA in Anthropology, U. Calif., Santa Barbara, 1974, MA in Anthropology, 1976, PhD in Anthropology, 1981. Teaching asst. dept. anthropology & environ. studies U. Calif., Santa Barbara, 1975-80, rsch. asst. archaeologist office of pub. archaeology, 1980-81, lectr. dept. archaeology, 1982—, asst. rsch. archaeologist Social Process Rsch. Inst., 1982-87, head MesoAmerican Rsch. Ctr., 1987—, asst. rsch. archaeologist Community Orgn. Rsch. Inst., 1987-91, assoc. rsch. archaeologist, 1991—; vis. asst. prof. dept. anthropology UCLA, 1987-89; guest lectr. various univs. including Ariz. State U., U. Ariz., Boston U., Columbia U., Harvard U., La. State U., Trent U., UCLA, York U., Univ. Nacional Autonoma de México; numerous archaeol. field and lab. activities. Contbr. over 30 articles to profl. jours.; presenter over 20 papers at profl. meetings & symposia; author various manuscripts. Pub. lectr. various schs. and orgns.; supr. Vol. Lab. and Field Program, 1978—. Humanities fellow U. Calif.-Santa Barbara (UCSB), 1989-90, 90-91; Fulbright rsch. scholar, 1986, 90; grantee UCSB, L.S.B. Leakey Found., NSF, NEH, Heinz Found., Wenner-Gren, CIRMA, CIES/USIS, Univ. Rsch. Expeditions Program, others. Mem. AAAS, Am. Anthropol. Assn., Soc. for Am. Archaeology, Assn. for Field Archaeology, Sociedad Mexicana de Antropologia, So. Calif. Mesoamerican Network, UCSB Affiliated Faculty Women, Assn. for Belizean Archaeology, Belize Ctr. for Environ. Studies, Sigma Xi. Office: CORI/MesoAmerican Rsch Ctr U Calif Santa Barbara CA 93106-2150

FORD, ANN SUTER, family nurse practitioner, health planner; b. Mineola, N.Y., Oct. 31, 1943; d. Robert M. and Jennette (Van Derzee) Suter; m. W. Scott Ford, 1964; children: Tracey, Karin, Stuart. RN, White Plains Hosp. Sch. Nursing (N.Y.), 1964; BS in Nursing with high distinction, U. Ky., 1967; MS in Health Planning, Fla. State U., 1971, PhD, 1975; MSN, Fla. State U., 1992. Nurse, U. Ky. Med. Ctr., 1964-65, Tallahassee Meml. Hosp., 1968-69; guest lectr. health planning dept. urban and regional planning Fla. State U., Tallahassee, 1973-76, health planner and research assoc., 1974-76, vis. asst. prof., 1976-77, asst. prof. and dir. health planning splty., 1977-83, assoc. prof., 1982-83; health care analyst and policy cons., 1983-86; med., health program analyst Aging and Adult Svcs. for State of Fla., 1986-90; coordinator Fla. Alzheimer's Disease Initiative, 1986-90; family nurse practitioner Capital Area Physicians' Svcs., 1993-94; assoc. prof. nursing Fla. A&M U., 1994—; bd. dirs. Regional Fla. Lung Assn., 1986-91; mem. exec. com. human services and social planning tech. dept. Am. Inst. Planners, 1977-83. Author: The Physician's Assistant: A National and Local Analysis, 1975; contbr. numerous articles on health edn. and health planning to profl. jours.; contbr. chpts. to books; author rsch. reports. USPHS grantee, 1965-67; HEW grantee, 1978; Univ. fellow Fla. State U., 1971-72; recipient Am. Inst. Planners' Student award, 1975. Mem. Am. Planning Assn. (charter mem. human services and social planning tech. dept. 1976-83, chmn. health planning session Oct. 1978, 79, health policy liaison 1979-83, author assn. health policy statement), Am. Health Planning Assn., Fla. Nurses Assn., Phi Kappa Phi, Sigma Theta Tau. Address: 2602 Cline St Tallahassee FL 32312-3110

FORD, BARBARA JEAN, library studies educator; b. Dixon, Ill., Dec. 5, 1946. BA magna cum laude with honors, Ill. Wesleyan U., 1968; MA in Internat. Rels., Tufts U., 1969; MS in Libr. Sci., U. Ill., 1973. Dir. Soybean Insect Rsch. Info. Ctr. Ill. Natural History Survey, Urbana, 1973-75; from asst. to assoc. prof. U. Ill., Chgo., 1975-84, asst. documents libr., 1975-79, documents libr., dept. head, 1979-84, acting audiovisual libr., 1983-84; asst. dir. pub. svcs. Trinity U., San Antonio, 1984-86, assoc. prof., assoc. dir., 1986-91, acting dir. librs., 1989, 91; prof., dir. univ. libr. svcs. Va. Commonwealth U., Richmond, 1991—; mem. women's re-entry adv. bd. U. Ill., Chgo., 1980-82, student affairs com., 1978-80, student admissions, records, coll. rels. com., 1981-84, univ. senate, 1976-78, 82-84, chancellor's libr. coun. svcs. com. 1984, campus lectrs. com. 1982-83; admissions interviewer for prospective students Trinity U., 1987-91, reader for internat. affairs theses, 1985-91, libr. self-study com., 1985-86, internat. affairs com., 1986-91, inter-Am. studies com., 1986-91, faculty senate, 1987-90; with libr. working group U.S./Mex. Commn. Cultural Coop., 1990. Contbr. articles to profl. publs., papers to presentations. Bd. dirs. Friends of San Antonio Pub. Libr., 1989-91. Celia M. Howard fellow Tufts U., 1969; sr. fellow UCLA Grad. Sch. Libr. and Info. Sci., 1993. Mem. ALA (conf. program com. 1985-91, libr. edn. assembly 1983-84, membership com. 1978-79, status of women in librarianship com. 1983-85, Lippincott Award Jury 1979-80, Shirley Olofson Meml. award 1977), AAUP, MLA (mid-Atlantic chpt.), Am. Assn. Higher Edn., Am. Assn. Info. Sci., ALA Coun. (at-large councilor 1985-89, chpt. councilor Ill. Libr. Assn. 1980-84, com. on coms. 1987-88, spl. coun. orientation com. 1982-83), Assn. Coll. and Rsch. Librs. (bd. dirs. 1989-92, pres.-elect 1989-90, pres. 1990-91, publs. com. 1990-91, conf. program planning 1990-91), Nat. Assn. State Univs. and Land Grant Colls. (commn. info. tech. 1992-94), Internat. Fedn. Libr. Assns. and Instns. (sec. official pubs. sect., gen. info. com. 1985 conf., moderator Latin Am. seminar on official pubs. 1991), Med. Libr. Assn., Mid. Atlantic Libr. Assn., Spl. Librs. Assn. (program com. 1976-77, 80-82, publicity com. 1977-79, chair 1978-79, chair spl. projects com. 1981-82, sec./treas. divsn. social sci. internat. affairs sect. 1984-86), Assn. Libr. Info. Sci. Edn. (chair local arrangements conf. planning com. 1988, 92), Ill. Libr. Assn. (chair election com. 1976-77, exec. bd. 1978-79, 80-84, bd. govt. documents round table 1976-79, chair 1978-79, long range planning com. 1980-84), Tex. Libr. Assn. (pubs. com. 1985-87, legis. com. 1986-87, judge best of exhibits award 1987, task force Amigos Fellowship 1990, del. conf. on librs. and info. svcs., 1991, Va. Libr. Assn. (ad hoc. com. distance learning 1992), Va. State Libr. and Archives (Va. libr. and info. svcs. task force 1991-93, steering com. Arbuthnot lecture 1992-93, coop. continuing edn. adv. com. 1992-94), Va. Assn. Fund Raising Execs., Chgo. Libr. Club (2d v.p. 1983-84), Richmond Acad. Libr. Consortium (v.p. 1991-92, pres. 1992-93), Beta Phi Mu, Phi Kappa Phi, Phi Alpha Theta, Kappa Delta Pi. Office: Va Commonwealth U Box 2033 901 Park Ave Richmond VA 23284-9056

FORD, BETTY BLOOMER (ELIZABETH FORD), health facility executive, wife of former President of United States; b. Chgo., Apr. 8, 1918; d. William Stephenson and Hortence (Neahr) Bloomer; m. Gerald R. Ford (38th Pres. U.S.), Oct. 15, 1948; children: Michael Gerald, John Gardner, Steven Meigs, Susan Elizabeth. Student, Sch. Dance Bennington Coll., 1936, 37; LL.D. (hon.), U. Mich., 1976. Dancer Martha Graham Concert Group, N.Y.C., 1939-41; model John Powers Agy., N.Y.C., 1939-41; fashion dir. Herpolsheimer's Dept. Store, Grand Rapids, Mich., 1943-48; dance instr. Grand Rapids, 1932-48; chmn. bd. dirs. The Betty Ford Ctr., Rancho Mirage, Calif. Author: autobiography The Times of My Life, 1979, Betty: A Glad Awakening, 1987. Bd. dirs. Nat. Arthritis Found. (hon.); trustee Martha Graham Dance Ctr., Eisenhower Med. Ctr., Rancho Mirage; hon. chmn. Palm Springs Desert Mus.; nat. trustee Nat. Symphony Orch.; trustee Nursing Home Adv. and Rsch. Coun. Inc.; mem. Golden Circle Patrons Ctr. Theatre Performing Arts; bd. dirs. The Lambs, Libertyville, Ill.; Sunday sch. tchr., 1961-64. Mem. Women in Senate and House. Episcopalian. Home: PO Box 927 Rancho Mirage CA 92270-0927*

FORD, DARLENE ANNETTE, computer operator; b. Oak Hill, Ohio, Mar. 10, 1957; d. Ralph Raymond and Rosetta (Sunderland) Ragland; m. Lowell Gene Ford, Feb. 21, 1976 (div. Sept. 1981); children: Lowell, Charles, Laurie, Michael McCarter. Student, Southeastern Bus. Sch., Jackson, Ohio, 1992-93. Cert. in micro-computer/data processing, jr. acctg., data entry. Computer operator Plum Run Corp., Jackson, 1993—. Computer tutor South St. Sch., Jackson, 1990-92; cub scout leader Boy Scouts Am., Jackson, 1992; asst. Girl Scouts USA, Jackson, 1993—; advisor 4H, 1994. Mem. NAACP (freedom fund com. 1993, community coord. 1993, labor/industry com. 1993, asst. sec. 1993—, Outstanding Svc. award 1993). Baptist. Home: 2034 Rock Run Rd Jackson OH 45640-9233 Office: Plum Run Corp 200 Broadway St Jackson OH 45640-1702

FORD, EILEEN OTTE (MRS. GERARD W. FORD), modeling agency executive; b. N.Y.C., Mar. 25, 1922; d. Nathaniel and Loretta Marie (Laine) Otte; m. Gerard William Ford, Nov. 20, 1944; children: Margaret (Mrs. Robert Craft), Gerard William, M. Katie, A. Lacey. B.S., Barnard Coll., 1943. Stylist Elliot Clarke Studio, N.Y.C., 1943-44, William Becker Studio, 1945; copywriter Arnold Constable, N.Y.C., 1945-46; reporter Tobe Coburn, 1946; co-founder Ford Model Agy., N.Y.C., 1946—, now chmn. bd. Author: Eileen Ford's Model Beauty, Secrets of the Model's World, A More Beautiful You in 21 Days, Beauty Now and Forever, 1977. Bd. dirs. London Philharmonic, 1948—. Recipient Harpers Bazaar award for promotion internat. understanding., Woman of Yr. in Advt. award, 1983. Office: Ford Modeling Agy 344 E 59th St New York NY 10022-1570*

FORD, E(MMA) JANE, public relations executive; b. Anderson, Ind., Mar. 25, 1918; d. Kenneth E. and Emma (Thomas) Griffith. BGS, Ind. U.-Purdue U. at Indianapolis, 1982. Advt. dir. Farm Bur. Ins., Indpls., 1956-73; pub. relations dir. Brulin & Co., Indpls., 1973-76; pub. info. dir. Ind. Arts Commn., Indpls., 1976-79, Indpls. Art League, Indpls., 1982-84; ret., 1984—; talent coord., moderator Indy Internat. Cable TV, Indpls.; past vice chmn. Service Corps of Retired Execs. Author: (play) An Evening With Zane Gray, 1985; sculpture Indpls. Mus. Art. Guide Eiteljorg Mus. Am. Indian and Western Art; nat. chmn. ann. conv. Women's Overseas Svc. League, 1994. Named Ad Woman of Yr. Ad Club of Ind., 1961. Mem. Women in Communications (past sec.), Woman's Press Club of Ind. (past sec.), Pub. Relations Soc. of Am., AAUW (assoc. editor). Republican. Episcopal.

FORD, JEAN ELIZABETH, former English language educator; b. Branson, Mo., Oct. 5, 1923; d. Mitchell Melton and Annie Estella (Wyer) F.; m. J.C. Wingo, 1942 (div. 1946); m. E. Syd Vineyard, 1952 (div. 1956); m. Vincent Michel Wessling, Feb. 14, 1983 (div. Dec. 1989). AA in English, L.A. City Coll., 1957; BA in English, Calif. State U., 1959; MA in Higher Edn., U. Mo., 1965. Cert. English tchr. Dance instr. Arthur Murray Studios, L.A., 1948-51; office mgr. Western Globe Products, L.A., 1951-55; pvt. dance tchr., various office jobs L.A., 1955-59; social dir. S.S. Matsonia, 1959; social worker L.A. County, 1959-61; 7th grade instr. Carmenita Sch. Dist., Norwalk, Calif., 1961-62; English instr. Leadwood (Mo.) High Sch., 1962-63; dance instr. U. Mo., 1963-66, SW Mo. State U., 1966-68, NW Mo. State U., 1970-76, Johnson County Community Coll., 1976-77; tax examiner IRS, Kansas City, Mo., 1978-80; tax acct. Baird, Kurtz & Dobson, Kansas City, Mo., 1981; substitute tchr. various sch. dists., 1976-85; dance chmn. Mo. Assn. Health, Phys. Edn. and Recreation, 1965-66, 68-69, ctrl. dist. AAHPER, 1972-73; vis. author Young Author's Conf., Ctrl. Mo. State U., 1987, 88, 89; speaker Am. Reading Assn., Grandview, Mo., 1990; real estate sales agt., Kansas City, 1980-84; real estate sales broker, Mo. and Kans., 1990—; pvt. practice tax acct., dance tchr., 1984—. Author, pub.: Fish Tails and Scales, 1982, 2d edit., 1988. Mem. Village Presbyn. Ch., Prairie Village, Kans. Mem. Am. Contract Bridge League, Kansas City Ski Club. Democrat. Presbyterian. Home and Office: 9528 Manning Ave Kansas City MO 64134-2229

FORD, JO-ANN, food products company executive. V.p., corp. sec. RJR Nabisco Holdings Corp., N.Y.C. Office: RJR Nabisco Inc 1301 Ave of the Americas New York NY 10019-6013*

FORD, JUDITH ANN, retired natural gas distribution company executive; b. Martinsville, Ind., May 11, 1935; d. Glenn Leyburn and Dorotha Mae (Parks) Tudor; m. Walter L. Ford, July 25, 1954 (dec. 1962); children: John Corbin, Christi Sue. Student, Wichita State U., 1953-55; student, U. Nev.-Las Vegas. Legal sec. S.W. Gas Corp., Las Vegas, 1963-69, asst. corp. sec., 1969-72, corp. sec., 1972-82, v.p., 1977-82, sr. v.p., 1982-88, also bd. dirs., dir. 7 subs. Bd. dirs. DesertView residence for handicapped, 1989—, treas., 1990-91, chmn., 1994—; trustee Nev. Sch. Arts, Las Vegas, 1979-90, chmn. bd. dirs., 1985-86; trustee Disciples Sem. Found., Claremont Sch. Theology and Pacific Sch. Religion, San Francisco, 1985-91, 92—, vice chmn., 1993-94, chmn., 1994—; mem. Ariz. Acad., Ariz. Town Halls, 1986-92. Mem. Am. Soc. Corp. Secs., Greater Las Vegas C. of C. (bd. dirs. 1979-85), Pacific Coast Gas Assn. (bd. dirs. 1984-88), Ariz. Bus. Women Owners (exec. com. 1985-88). Democrat. Mem. Christian Ch. (Disciples of Christ).

FORD, KAREN BALES, cosmetics executive; b. Knoxville, Tenn., Apr. 28, 1953; d. Charles Edward and Norma Marie (Cluck) Bales; m. Charles David Ford, Jr., Dec. 16, 1972; children: Alison Marie, Justin David. EdB, U. Ark., Little Rock, 1978. Tchr. Bullitt County Bd. Edn., Shepherdsville, Ky., 1978-87; sales dir. Mary Kay Cosmetics, Shepherdsville, Ky., 1988-89; sr. sales dir. Mary Kay Cosmetics, Roswell, Ga., 1989-93, exec. sr. sales dir., 1993—. Republican. Methodist. Home and Office: Mary Kay Cosmetics 285 Wexford Overlook Dr Roswell GA 30075

FORD, KAREN CLARK, systems engineer; b. Bluefield, Va., Sept. 27, 1963; m. Paul James Ford, Jr., May 11, 1991; 1 child, Paul James Ford III. BS, Emory and Henry Coll., Emory, Va., 1985. Sr. systems engr. Gen. Electric Aerospace/Martin Marietta, Reston, Va., 1985-92; Martin Marietta, Reston, 1992—.

FORD, KAY LOUISE, outplacement executive; b. Pontiac, Mich., Aug. 2, 1944; d. Norman Avery and Elsa Katherine (Wahlsten) F.; m. Billy Wayne Reed, Aug. 20, 1965 (div. Jan. 1979); children: Matthew Wayne Reed, Bradley Ford Reed. AB, U. Mich., 1965; MA, SUNY, Brockport, 1983.

Speech therapist Community Treatment Ctr., Bath, Maine, 1966-68; continuing edn. coord. SUNY, Brockport, 1974-78, grad. asst., 1978-79; contract tng. dir. Monroe Community Coll., Rochester, N.Y., 1979-86; exec. dir. Livingston Washtenaw Pvt. Industry Coun., Ann Arbor, Mich., 1986-91; dir. devel. McKinley Found., Ann Arbor, 1991-92; v.p. community rels. Regional Coun. Aging, Inc., Rochester, 1992-93; v.p. Drake Beam Morin, Inc., Rochester, 1993—; cons. KLF Personal PR Assocs., 1993—; contract trainer Cornell U., Rochester, N.Y., 1983-86, Learning Internat., Buffalo, 1984-87, Jannotta, Bray and Assocs., Chgo., 1992; field instr. U. Mich., 1988-92; adj. instr. SUNY, Brockport, N.Y., 1993—. Co-chmn. Internat. Spl. Olympics Ceremonies Com., Brockport, 1979-80, Washtenaw United Way Comm., Ann Arbor, 1987-91, Mich. Theatre Fund Raising, Ann Arbor, 1987-90; bd. dirs. Jazz for Life--On Stage for Kids, Ann Arbor, 1987-90, Peace Neighborhood Ctr., 1991-92; mem. bus. and labor leaders adv. com. Washtenaw C.C. Mem. ASTD, Nat. Soc. Fund Raising Execs., Planned Giving Coun. Upstate N.Y., Ann Arbor Pers. Assn., Rochester C. of C., Rotary, Huron Valley Fundraisers Network, Greater Brighton Area C. of C., Mich. Rehab. Svcs., Supported Employment, Washtenaw C.C. (mem. bus. and labor leaders adv. com.), Univ. Club Rochester, Rochester Women's Network.

FORD, LEE ELLEN (LEOLA FORD), scientist, educator, retired lawyer; b. Auburn, Ind., June 16, 1917; d. Arthur W. and Geneva (Muhn) Ford; BA, Wittenberg Coll., 1947; MS, U. Minn., 1949; PhD, Iowa State Coll., 1952; JD, U. Notre Dame, 1972. Bar: Ind. 1972. CPA auditing, 1934-44; assoc. prof. biology Gustavus Adolphus Coll., 1950-51; prof. and head biology dept. Anderson (Ind.) Coll., 1952-55; vis. prof. biology U. Alta. (Can.), Calgary, 1955-56; assoc. prof. biology Pacific Luth. U., Parkland, Wash., 1956-62; prof. biology and cytogenetics Miss. State Coll. for Women, 1962-64; chief cytogeneticist Pacific N.W. Rsch. Found., Seattle, 1964-65; founder, dir. Canine Genetics Consulting Svc., Parkland, Wash., 1963-69; pvt. practice, Ind., 1972-92. Founder, sponsor, trainer guide dogs for adult and child blind, mentally and physically handicapped Companion Collies for the Adult, Jr. Blind, 1955-65; founder, dir., rschr. Genetics Rsch. Lab., Butler, Ind., 1955-75, cons. cytogenetics, 1969-75; legis. cons., 1970-79; dir. chromosome lab. Inst. Basic Rsch. in Mental Retardation, S.I., 1968-69; founder, dir., rschr. Legis. Bur. U. Notre Dame Law Sch., 1969-72, editor New Dimensions in Legis., 1969-72; editor Butler Record Herald, 1972-76; founder, dir., writer Ind. Interreligious Commn. on Human Equality, 1976-80; exec. asst. to Gov. Otis R. Bowen, Ind., 1973-75; founder, sponser, bd. dirs. Ind. Commn. on Status Women, 1973-74; bd. dirs. Ind. Coun. Chs.; founder, editor, writer Ford Assocs. pubs., 1972-86; mem. Pres.'s Adv. Coun. on Drug Abuse, 1976-77. Admitted to Ind. bar, 1972. Adult counselor Girl Scouts U.S., 1934-40; founder, sponsor, bd. dirs. Ind. Task Force Women's Health, 1976-80; mem. exec. bd., bd. dirs. Ind.-Ky. Synod Lutheran Ch., 1972-78; bd. dirs., mem. coun. St. Marks Luth. Ch., Butler, 1970-76; mem. social svcs. pers. bd., 1970-76; mem. DeKalb County (Ind.) Sheriff's Merit Bd., 1983-87; founder, dir., pres. Ind. Caucus for Animal Legis. and Leadership, 1984-87. Mem. AAUW, AAAS, Genetics Soc. Am., Am. Human Genetics Soc., Am. Genetic Assn., Am. Inst. Biol. Scis., Am. Soc. Zoologists, La. Acad. Sci., Miss. Acad. Sci., Ind. Acad. Sci., Iowa Acad. Sci., Bot. Soc. Am., Ecol. Soc. Am., ABA (bd. dir.), Ind. Bar Assn. (bd. dir.), DeKalb County Bar Assn. (bd. dir.) Bar Assn., Humane Soc. U.S. (bd. dir. 1970-88), DeKalb County Humane Soc. (founder, bd. dirs. 1970-86), Ind. Fedn. Humane Socs. (bd. dir. 1970-84), Nat. Assn. Women Lawyers (bd. dir.), Bus. and Profl. Women's Club, Nat. Assn. Rep. Women (bd. dir.), Women's Equity Action League (bd. dir.), Assn. So. Biologists, Phi Kappa Phi. Club: Altrusa. Author: Lee's 7 Lives, 1992; founder, editor: Breeder's Jour., 1958-63; numerous vols. on dog genetics and breeding, guide dogs for the blind. Contbr. over 4000 sci., popular and rsch. publs. on cytogenetics, dog breeding and legal topics; contbr. articles to Am. Kennel Club Gazette, 1970-81, also others; Pioneer in research of identifying and isolating monoploid chromosomes of corn plants by use of cytology to give hybrid monoploid seeds thus quicker corn yeild; Pioneer in identifying and separating cytologically individual chromosomes in corn plants, oats, wheat, barley, animals. Home and Office: 336 Hickory St Butler IN 46721-1471

FORD, LORETTA C., retired university dean, nurse, educator; b. N.Y.C., Dec. 28, 1920; d. Joseph F. and Nellie A. (Williams) Pfingstel; R.N., Middlesex Gen. Hosp., New Brunswick, N.J., 1941; BS in Nursing, U. Colo., 1949, MS, 1951, EdD, 1961; DSc (hon.), Ohio State Med Coll.; LLD (hon.) U. Md., 1990; m. William J. Ford, May 2, 1947; 1 dau., Valerie. Staff nurse New Brunswick Vis. Nurse Service, 1941-42; supr., dir. Boulder County (Colo.) Health Dept., 1947-58; asst. prof., then prof. U. Colo. Sch. Nursing, 1960-72; dean Sch. Nursing, dir. nursing, prof. U. Rochester (N.Y.), 1972-86, acting dean Grad. Sch. Edn. & Human Devel., 1988-89; vis. prof. U. Fla., summer 1968, U. Wash., Seattle, 1974; mem. educators adv. panel GAO; dir. Security Trust Co., Rochester, Rochester Telephone Co.; internat. cons. in field. Bd. dirs. Threshold Alternative Youth Svcs., Easter Seal Soc., ARC, Monroe Community Hosp.; mem. adv. com. Commonwealth Fund Exec. Nurse Fellowship Program. Served with Nurse Corps, USAAF, 1942-46. Recipient N.Y. State Gov.'s award for women in sci., medicine and nursing, Modern Healthcare Hall of Fame award, 1994; named Colo. Nurse of Yr. Fellow Am. Acad. Nursing; mem. Nat. League Nursing (fellowship, Linda Richards award), Am. Coll. Health Assn. (Boynton award), Am. Nurses Assn., Am. Public Health Assn. (Ruth B. Freeman award), NAS Inst. Medicine (Gustav O. Leinhard award, 1990). Author articles in field, chpts. in books. Office: U Rochester Med Ctr 601 Elmwood Ave Box SON Rochester NY 14642

FORD, LUCILLE GARBER, economist, educator, college official; b. Ashland, Ohio, Dec. 31, 1921; d. Ora Myers and Edna Lucille (Armstrong) Garber; m. Laurence Wesley Ford, Sept. 1, 1946; children: Karen Elizabeth, JoAnn Christine. AA, Stephens Coll., 1942; BS in Commerce, Northwestern U., 1944, MBA, 1945; PhD in Econs., Case Western Res. U., 1967; PhD (hon.), Tarkio Coll., 1991. Cert. fin. planner. Instr. Allegheny Coll., Meadville, Pa., 1945-46, U. Ala., Tuscaloosa, 1946-47; personnel dir., asst. sec. A.L. Garber Co., Ashland, Ohio, 1947-67; prof. econs. Ashland U., 1967—, chmn. dept. econs., 1970-75; dir. Gill Ctr. for Econ. Edn. Ashland Coll., 1975-86, v.p., dean Sch. Bus., Adminstrn. and Econs., 1980-86, v.p. acad. affairs, 1986-90, provost, 1990-92; exec. asst. to pres., 1993—; commr. North Ctrl. Assn. Colls. and Schs.; bd. dirs. A. Schulman Co., Western Res. Econ. Devel. Coun., Morgan Freeport Corp., Ohio Coun. Econ. Edn.; lectr. in field. Author: University Economics-Guide for Education Majors, 1979, Economics: Learning and Instruction, 1981, 91; contbr. articles to profl. jours. Mem. Ohio Gov.'s Commn. on Ednl. Choice, 1992; candidate for lt. gov. of Ohio, 1978; trustee Stephens Coll., 1977-80; elder Presbyn. Ch.; bd. dirs. Presbyn. Found., 1982-88; trustee Synod-Presbyn. Ch., 1994—; active ARC. Recipient Outstanding Alumni award Stephens Coll., 1977, Outstanding Prof. award Ashland U., 1971, 75, Roman F. Warmke award, 1981. Mem. Am. Econs. Assn., Nat. Indsl. Research Soc., Am. Arbitration Assn. (profl. arbitrator), Assn. Pvt. Enterprise Edn. (pres. 1983-84), North Cen. Assn. Colls. & Schs. (commr.), Omicron Delta Epsilon, Alpha Delta Kappa. Republican. Home: 1717 Upland Dr Ashland OH 44805-3956 Office: Ashland U 401 College Ave Ashland OH 44805-3702

FORD, MARCYANNE ROSE, database analyst; b. New Britain, Conn., July 17, 1941; d. Stanley S. and Mildred (Koscieniak) S.; children: William, Todd, Christopher, Kerilee, Alyssa, Derrick. BA in Math., St. Joseph Coll., West Hartford, Conn., 1963; MS in Computer Sci., Rensselaer Poly. Inst. Tchr. math. St. Paul High Sch., Bristol, Conn., 1980-81; analyst telecommunications Hartford (Conn.) Ins. Group, 1981—. mem. mentoring program St. Joseph Coll., 1992. Republican. Roman Catholic. Home: 3 Summit Dr Burlington CT 06013-1511 Office: Hartford Ins Group Hartford Plz # 5 Hartford CT 06115-1701

FORD, MAUREEN MORRISSEY, civic worker; b. St. Joseph, Mo., July 1, 1936; d. Albert Joseph and Rosemary Kathryne (FitzSimons) Morrissey; student U. N.Mex., 1953-54, U. Bridgeport (Conn.), 1966-68; BS, Fairfield U., 1986, postgrad. in Applied Ethics, 1986—; m. James Henry Lee Ford, Jr., Feb. 12, 1954; children: Kathryne Elizabeth, Maryellen, James Henry Lee III, William Charles, Maureen Lee. Charity and sch. vol., 1959—; fundraiser for community causes, mus., agys., 1964—; active presdl. campaign Barry Goldwater, 1963-64, congressional campaign Senator Lowell Weiker, 1968; pre-sch. tchr. Nature Ctr. Environ. Activities, 1966-68, trustee, v.p. bd. dirs., 1968-75; assoc. program in applied ethics, Fairfield U., 1986—. Author: (with Lisa H. Newton) Taking Sides: Controversial Issues in Business Ethics, 3d edit., 1994—. V.p. Women's League, 1966-70; mem. exec. com. Republican Women's Club, Westport, 1967-68; leader, trainer Troops on Fgn. Soil br. Girl Scouts US, Caracas, Venezuela, 1971-72; founding trustee, treas. Kara Mus., Norwalk, Conn.; mem. adv. council Fairfield County (Conn.) for spl. edn. Staples High Sch.; bd. dirs. CLASP; mem. exec. com. Group Home Search; pres. Ind. Assocs. Cons. Firm, 1991—; cons., facilitator life planning workshops Merideth Assocs., Westport; v.p., bd. dirs. Isaiah 61:1, Inc., 1989—; active grants com. Bridgeport Pub. Edn. Fund and Devel. Commn.; mem. 1st selectmen's com. on recycling, 1974-75; bd. dirs. PTA, 1976-79; mem. YWCA of Bridgeport Com. of 100 and Task Force; v.p. bd. dirs. YWCA, 1980-87, pres., 1984-85; v.p. Conf. Women's Orgns., Bridgeport; founding mem. Concerned Women Colleagues of Bridgeport; pres. Jr. League Eastern Fairfield County, Inc., 1977-78; v.p., sec. J.H.L.F. Inc., Westport. Mem. Assn. Jr. League Am., Westport Tennis Assn. Roman Catholic. Home: 299 Sturges Hwy Westport CT 06880-1723

FORD, NANCY LOUISE, composer, scriptwriter; b. Kalamazoo, Oct. 1, 1935; d. Henry Ford III and Mildred Wotring; m. Robert D. Currie, June 7, 1957 (div. 1962); m. Keith W. Charles, May 23, 1964. BA, DePauw U., 1957; D of Arts (hon.), Eastern Mich. U., 1986. Composer: off-Broadway musicals (in collaboration with Gretchen Cryer) Now Is the Time for All Good Men, 1967, The Last Sweet Days of Isaac, 1970, I'm Getting My Act Together and Taking It on the Road, 1978, (Broadway mus.) Shelter, 1972; performer stage and TV prodns.; scriptwriter: (TV daytime serials) Love of Life, 1971-74, Ryan's Hope, 1975, Search for Tomorrow, 1981-82, Guiding Light, 1977-78, As the World Turns, 1978-80, 87—. Trustee DePauw U. Recipient Emmy awards, 1983, 84. Mem. Dramatists Guild, Writers Guild Am. East, AFTRA, Actors Equity, Am. Fedn. Musicians, League Profl. Theatre Women N.Y. (co-v.p.).

FORD, NAOMI RUTH, manufacturers representative; b. Red Boiling Springs, Tenn., Feb. 12, 1934; d. Dewey Sephus and Edith Irene (Lyons) Slate; m. Horace Jere Ford, Mar. 18, 1954 (div. 1971); children: Sharon Ford Hester, Horace Jeffrey. Student, Peabody Coll., 1950-53, Watkins Inst., 1972-75, Middle Tenn. State U., 1976. Sales rep. Fashion Furniture Mart, Nashville, 1971-76; mem. sales and design staff Tarkington Show Room, Nashville, 1976-81, McQuiddy Office Designers, Nashville, 1981-84; mfrs. rep. Jerry Ladich Assocs., Johnson City, Tenn., 1984-86; ind. mfrs. rep. Nashville, 1986—. Mem. Nat. Office Products Assn., Friend of Interior Bus. Designers. Republican. Baptist. Home: 437 Belle Point Dr Nashville TN 37221-3464 Office: NF Assocs PO Box 210909 Nashville TN 37221-0909

FORD, SUSAN COOPER, maternal/women's health nurse, air force officer; b. Columbia, S.C., Feb. 22, 1961; d. Edwin Jr. and Ethel R. (Jernigan) Galloway; married; children: Christian Nicole, Amanda Perry. BA, Columbia Coll., 1983; BS in Nursing with honors, Calif. State U., Bakersfield, 1989. Cert. in infant resuscitation and newborn assessment, ACLS, NALS. RN, staff nurse Antelope Valley Hosp./Med. Ctr., Lancaster, Calif., 1989-80; commd. 1st lt. USAF, 1990, advanced through grades to capt., 1994; nurse David Grant Med. Ctr., Travis AFB, Calif., 1990—; high risk labor and delivery nurse David Grant Med Ctr., Travis AFB, Calif., 1993—. Home: 118 Mcbride Ct Travis AFB CA 94535

FORD, VICTORIA, public relations executive; b. Carroll, Iowa, Nov. 1, 1946; d. Victor Sargent and Gertrude Francis (Headlee) F.; m. John K. Frans, July 4, 1965 (div. Aug. 1975); m. David W. Keller, May 2, 1981 (div. Nov. 1985); m. Jerry W. Lambert, Mar. 30, 1991. AA, Iowa Lakes Community Coll., 1973; BA summa cum laude, Buena Vista Coll., 1974; MA in Journalism, U. Nev., Reno, 1988. Juvenile parole officer Iowa Dept. Social Services, Sioux City, 1974-78; staff reporter Feather Pub. Co., Quincy, Calif., 1978-80; tng. counselor CETA, Quincy, 1980; library pub. info. officer U. Nev., Reno, 1982-84; pub. relations exec. Brodeur/Martin Pub. Relations, Reno, 1984-87; pub. relations dir. Internat. Winter Spl. Olympics, Lake Tahoe (Calif.) and Reno, 1987-89; owner Ford Factor Pub. Rels. cons. firm, Reno, 1989—. Contbr. articles to Range Mag., other profl. jours. Mem. adv. bd. Reno Philharm., 1985-87, Reno-Sparks Conv. and Visitors Authority, 1985-93; bd. dirs. Truckee Meadows Habitat for Humanity, 1992-93, half-time exec. dir., 1994; mem. Gov.'s Com. on Fire Prevention, 1991-92; mem. U. Nev. Reno Oral History Program, 1994; bd. dirs. Nev. Women's Archives, 1994—; mem. com. Nev. Writers Hall of Fam, 1993, 94. Mem. NOW, Pub. Rels. Soc. Am. (charter v.p. Sierra Nev. chpt. 1986-87, pres. 1987-88), Sigma Delta Chi. Democrat. Home: PO Box 6715 Reno NV 89513-6715 Office: The Ford Factor PO Box 6715 Reno NV 89513-6715

FORDE, ELAINE POHLSCHNEIDER, school counselor; b. Salem, Oreg., June 17, 1956; d. Alwin Frank and Mary Ida (Kaufmann) Pohlschneider; m. Charles E. Forde, Dec. 20, 1987. BS, Oreg. State U., 1978; M in Counseling, Portland State U., 1994. Tchr. Waldport (Oreg.) H.S., 1978-80; tchr., counselor Clackamas H.S., Milw., 1980-94; counselor Jesuit H.S., Portland, Oreg., 1994—; leadership camp counselor Oreg. Assn. Student Coun., Salem, 1986-93; camp dir. Nat. Cheerleading Assn., Dallas, 1988-94; co-dir. state cheerleading camp competition Oreg. Sch. Activities Assn., Salem, 1995. Mem. Oreg. Counseling Assn., Oreg. Cheerleading Assn., Bergfriende Ski Club (trip capt.). Roman Catholic.

FORDHAM, SHARON ANN, food company executive; b. Somerset, N.J., Jan. 30, 1952; d. Thomas Anthony and Gladys Maryann (Hagaman) F. BA in History with honors, Rutgers U., 1975; MBA in Mktg., U. Pa., 1977. Asst. product mgr. Bristol-Myers (Drackett Co.), Cin., 1977-78, product mgr., 1979; product mgr. Borden, Inc., Columbus, Ohio, 1979-81, Nabisco Brands Inc., East Hanover, N.J., 1981-82; group product mgr. Nabisco Brands, Inc., East Hanover, N.J., 1982-84, dir. mktg., 1984-86; sr. dir. new bus. Nabisco, Brands Inc., East Hanover, N.J., 1986-91, v.p. new bus., 1991—; v.p., gen. mgr. Life Savers Co. Originator, dir. Almost Home (Cookie Wars), 1983, Low Salt Nabisco Crackers, 1987, Teddy Grahams, 1988, Mr. Phipps, 1991, Tater Crisps, Snack Wells, 1992, Nabisco Breakfast Snack Line, 1994. Mem. Woodbridge (N.J.) Wind Ensemble, 1982-83, Hillsborough Wind Ensemble, Somerset, N.J., 1984-87. Recipient award Point of Purchase Advt. Inst. (POPAI), 1983, 89, gold Effie award Assn. Nat. Advertisers, 1986, 89, 92, new product of yr. award Bus. Week, 1988, Food and Beverage Mktg., 1988, 91, 93, new snack product of yr. award Consumer Network, 1988, Gorman Pub., 1988, 91. Mem. Mensa, Wharton Club N.Y. (bd. dirs.), Fiddler's Elbow. Republican. Roman Catholic. Office: Nabisco Biscuit Co PO Box 527 100 DeForest Ave East Hanover NJ 07936

FORDYCE, THERESA ROSE, mental health nurse; b. Andrews AFB, Md., June 7, 1960; d. Robert David Sr. and Patricia Anne (Bahm) F. BA in Psychology, Belmont Abbey Coll., 1982; AAS, Mercer County Community Coll., Trenton, N.J., 1987. Staff nurse Trenton Psychiat. Hosp., 1987-88, Greenville (S.C.) Hosp. Systems/Marshall Pickens, 1988-91, Chestnut Hill Psychiat. Hosp., 1991-92; RN supr. Magnolia Manor, 1992-94; RN, primary therapist Boys Home of the South, Belton, S.C., 1994—. Home: 144A Rasor Dr Greenville SC 29609 : Boys Home of the South 10612 Augusta Rd Belton SC 29627

FOREHAND, JENNIE MEADOR, state legislator; b. Nashville, Dec. 17, 1935; d. James T. and Estelle (Woodall) Meador; student Woman's Coll. of U. N.C., Greensboro, 1954-56; B.S. in Indsl. Relations, U. N.C., Chapel Hill, 1958; m. William E. Forehand, Jr., July 19, 1958; children: Virginia, John Bentley. Reporter, Charlotte (N.C.) News, 1954-56; probation counselor Juvenile Ct., Charlotte, 1958; tchr. Anne Arundel County (Md.), 1958-60; statis. analyst NIH, Bethesda, Md., 1961-62; edn. research project evaluator Montgomery County (Md.) Bd. Edn., 1973-74; interior designer, owner Antiques and Interiors, Rockville, Md., 1971—; state rep. Md. Gen. Assembly, 1978—; mem. Md. State Senate, 1995—. mem. appropriations com., joint capital budget com., health and environ. subcom., chair Montgomery County delegation transp. com., co-chair com. on mgmt. of pub. funds; co-chair Gov. Task Force on Sr. Citizen Ctrs., NIH Bio-Safety Com., Senate Judicial Proceedings Com.; vice chair Econ. and Culture Devel. Com. of So. Legis. Conf., 1994—; Planning bd. Montgomery County Health Systems; consumer rep. Rockville Econ. Devel. Council, Md. Community Mental Health Adv. Bd.; pres. local civic assn.; bd. dirs. Mid-Md. Lung Assn., Montgomery County Hist. Soc.; mem. Peerless Rockville Hist. Preservation, Ltd.; bd. dirs. Md. Coll. Art and Design, Rockville Arts Place, Asbury Meth. Homes. Recipient Bus. Leadership award Suburban Md. Tech. Coun.; named Outstanding Legislator Montgomery County Med. Soc. Mem. Women's Caucus of Md. Gen. Assembly (pres. elect.), AAUW, Women's Polit. Caucus. Democrat. Methodist. Office: State Senate 214 Senate Office Bldg Annapolis MD 21401

FOREHAND, MARGARET P., library director; b. Nov. 12, 1951; children: Lindsay Howell, Walker Harrison. BA in Edn., U. Richmond, 1973; MA in Edn., Va. Commonwealth U., 1974; MLS, U. Md., 1977. Libr. hdqrs. Chesapeake Libr. Systems, 1979-85, dir. librs. and rsch. svcs., 1985—. Bd. dirs. Tidewater ARC, 1980-83, Western Tidewater Area Health Edn. Ctr., 1980—, exec. coun. 1982—; v.p. Va. Stage Co., 1981-82, bd. dirs., 1979-85; bd. dirs. the Planning Coun. Cultural Alliance of Greater Hampton Roads, 1985—, exec. coun. 1986-88; bd. dirs. Am. Cancer Soc. Portsmouth-Chesapeake Bds., 1987—, pres., 1991—; mem. Mayor's Com. on Protocol, 1987, Mayor's Commn. on Bicentennial Constitution, 1987; co-chmn. Mayor's Task Force on Libr., 1989—, Gov.'s Rural Econ. Devel. Task Force, 1990-91. Named Outstanding Young Career Woman Va. Fedn. Bus. and Profl. Women's Clubs, 1978, Outstanding Bus. and Profl. Woman, 1993. Mem. ALA (Va. chair nat. libr. week 1985-86), Va. Libr. Assn. (coun.mem. 1978-86, chair Va. Pub. Libr. sect. 1978-79), Va. State Libr. Bd. (vice chmn. 9186-87, chmn. 1987-88, chmn. bldg. com. 1988—), State Adult Literacy Com. (chmn. 1989—), Chesapeake C. of C. (chmn. pub. rels. com. 1989—, planning coun., bd. dirs., UVA adv. bd., Hampton Roads Bd.), DAR (bd. dirs. Chesapeake chpt. 1983—). Office: Chesapeake Pub Libr 298 Cedar Rd Chesapeake VA 23320-5597

FOREMAN, CAROL LEE TUCKER, business executive; b. Little Rock, May 3, 1938; d. James Guy and Willie Maude (White) Tucker; A.A., William Woods Coll., Fulton, Mo., 1958; A.B., Washington U., St. Louis, 1960; postgrad. Am. U.; LL.D. (hon.), William Woods Coll., Fulton, Mo., 1976; m. Jay Howell Foreman, June 13, 1964; children: Guy Tucker, Rachel Marian. Rsch. asst. Com. on Govt. Ops., U.S. Senate, 1961; assoc. Fed. Counsel Assocs., 1961-63; instr. Am. govt. William Woods Coll., Fulton, 1963-64; exec. asst. to Rep. James Roosevelt, 1964; dir. rsch. and publs. Dem. Nat. Com., 1965-66; Congressional liaison aide HUD, 1967-69; chief info. liaison Ctr.for Family Planning Program Devel., Planned Parenthood-World Population, 1969-71; dir. policy coordination Commn. on Population and Am. Future, 1971-72; exec. dir. Citizens Com. on Population and Am. Future, 1972-73, Paul Douglas Consumer Rsch. Ctr., 1973-77, Consumer Fedn. Am., 1973-77; asst. sec. food and consumer svcs. Dept. Agr., Washington, 1977-81; pres. Foreman & Co., 1981-86, ptnr. Foreman & Heideprim, 1986-94; pres. Foreman & Heideprim, Inc., 1994—; coord. Safe Food Coalition, 1987—; bd. dirs. Adams Nat. Bank. Editor: Regulating for the Future, 1991. Exec. dir. Ctr. for Women Policy Studies, 1983-84; mem. Interdeptl. Task Force on Women; mem. D.C. Commn. on Status Women, 1973-74; bd. dirs. Consumer's Union, 1982-83, chmn., 1993—; bd. dirs. Food Rsch. and Action Ctr., 1983—, Christianity and Crisis, 1990—; vice-chmn. Ctr. Nat. Policy, 1982-84, bd. dirs., 1981—; trustee Washington U., St. Louis, 1987—. Recipient Disting. Alumni award Washington U., 1979. Mem. Women's Equity Action League (past pres. local chpt.), Nat. Planning Assn. (dir. 1985—), Woman's Nat. Dem. Club, Pi Beta Phi. Presbyterian. Home: 5408 Trent St Chevy Chase MD 20815 Office: Foreman & Heideprim Inc Ste 1030 1100 New York Ave NW Washington DC 20005

FOREMAN, LAURA, dancer, choreographer, conceptual artist, writer, educator; b. L.A.; d. Michael and Gladys (Charnas) F.; m. John Everett Watts. Dir. dance, physical fitness and recreation depts. and movement specialist cert. program, Foreman Dance Theatre artist-in-residence. New Sch. Social Rsch., N.Y.C., 1971—; founder, dir. Choreographers Theatre, N.Y.C.; artist-in-residence Channel 13 TV Lab., 1978, Holographic Film Found., N.Y.C., 1983; dance dir., bd. dirs. Composers and Choreographers Theatre, Inc.; mem. dance panel N.Y. State Council on Arts; cons. Nat. Endowment Humanities; mem. Artists Talk on Art, The Performance Project, N.Y. Theater Bridge, Writers Rm., N.Y.C.; visual arts panel Ill. Arts Council, documentary and arts panel, Nat. TV Emmy Awards; bd. dirs. Ear Inc., N.Y.C.; tchr. master classes New Sch., Parsons Sch. of Design, Art Student League, Met. Mus. Art. Choreography and performanc art includes Memorials, Study, A Time, Perimeters, Epicycles, SkyDance for skywriters and helicopters, Margins, Signals, Laura's Dance, Spaces (Collage I-IV), Locrian, Performance, a deux, Postludes, Monopoly, Program, Heirlooms, Entries, others.; video includes TimeCoded Woman I, II, III (2 silver, 1 gold award Houston Internat. Film Festival 1979, 80, 81, Bronze medal Internat. Film and TV Festival of N.Y., 1981); conceptual work (with John Watts) includes WallWork, crowd-created art work, 1981, Coney Island Cray-Pas, 1981, Concourse Cray-Pas, The Philadelphia Story, 1981; installations include Roomwork, 1981, WindoWork, 1982, 91; one-woman shows Portico Gallery, Phila., Limbo, N.Y.C., Souyun Yi Gallery, N.Y.C., Kleinert Arts Ctr., Woodstock, N.Y.; two-person shows Souyun Yi Gallery, Webb & Parsons Gallery, Vt.; over 50 group shows including Bronx, N.Y., Wustum., Wis., Hudson Highlands, N.Y., Chgo. Peace, Ill., and Pasadena, Calif., museums; permanent collections include Antwerp Mus.; off-Broadway shows City Junket, 1980; published in The Act, Downtown, Letters, Pinehurst Jour., Confrontation, ACM, Santa Clara Review, Up Front Muse Internat., Lamia, Ink mags., (short story collection) Pig Iron Anthology. Grantee CAPS, 1970, 73, N.Y. State Coun. Arts, 1970-74, Nat. Endowment Arts, 1971, 73, 77, 78, Vogelstein Found., 1985, Pub. Arts Commns., JBR Found., 1989; fellow Blue Mountain, 1985, 90, Dorset Colony, 1985, 88, MacDowell Colony, 1986, Djerassi Found., 1987, Vt. Studio Sch. and Colony, 1988, Act II Colony, 1988, Radgale Found., 1990, Watershed Ctr. for Ceramic Arts, Edward Albee Found., Byrdcliffe Arts Colony, 1991, Cummington Community for the Arts, 1992, Lookout Sculpture Park, 1994, Pallenville Found., 1994, Mary Anderson Ctr., 1994. Mem. Artists and Scis. in Collaboration (founder), Artists Talk on Art. Home: 94 Chambers St New York NY 10007-1826

FOREST, CHARLENE LYNN, cell biologist, educator; b. N.Y.C., Feb. 27, 1947; d. Harold Matthew and Sadie (Biller) Friedman; m. Richard Mark Forest, June 29, 1969. BS, Cornell U., 1968; MS, Adelphi U., 1972; PhD, Ind. U., 1976. Postdoctoral fellow Harvard U., Cambridge, Mass., 1976-79; asst. prof. Bklyn. Coll., CUNY, 1979-83, 84-86, assoc. prof., 1986—; prin. investigator, grant assoc. Rsch. Found. CUNY, Bklyn., 1983-84. Contbr. articles to profl. pubs. Grantee NIH, 1980-83, NSF, 1983-85, 85-88; recipient Career Advancement award NSF, 1989-90. Mem. AAAS, Am. Soc. Cell Biology, Genetics Soc. Am., Soc. Protozoologists, Assn. Women in Sci., Am. Soc. Plant Physiologists, N.Y. Soc. Electron Microscopists, N.Y. Acad. Scis., Sigma Xi. Office: Bklyn Coll Dept Biology 1600 Bedford Ave Brooklyn NY 11210

FORESTER, ERICA SIMMS, decorative arts historian, consultant, educator; b. N.Y.C., Feb. 13, 1942; d. Leon Marcus and Selma (Rosen) Simms; m. Bruce Michael Forester, Dec. 21, 1962; children: Brent Peter, Robin Ann, Russell Charles. BA, Cornell U., 1963; MA, Columbia U., 1964; cert., N.Y. Sch. Interior Design, 1973; AAS in Interior Design, Parsons Sch. Design, 1982. Owner Erica Forester, Interiors, Bronxville, N.Y., 1973—; mem. faculty Parsons Sch. Design, N.Y.C., 1982—; cons. in field, 1980—; lectr. Hudson River Mus., 1984, Eastchester Hist. Soc., 1989, Bartow Pell Mansion, 1990, Scarsdale Adult Sch., 1991; guest curator Scarsdale Hist. Soc., 1987. Author (with others): At Home in Westchester; Style and Design 1836-1886. Mem. adv. bd. Am. Field Svc. Rye Country Day Sch., 1984-88; mus. adv. bd. Scarsdale Hist. Soc. Mem. Allied Bd. Trade, Decorative Arts Trust, Assn. Ind. Historians of Art. Home and Office: 55 Northway Bronxville NY 10708-2325

FORESTER, MARIE-CHRISTINE, marketing and management consultant; b. Geneva, Switzerland, Aug. 5, 1943; came to U.S., 1964; d. Charles and Renee (Giovanna) Meynet; m. Russell Forester, Feb. 2, 1968; 1 stepchild, Lynn Forester. Degree in Arch., Ecole D'Architecture, Lausanne, Switzerland, 1964. Rschr. in hosp. arch. U. Mich., Ann Arbor, 1964-67; head rsch. dept. Bertrand Goldberg Assocs., Architects and Engrs., Chgo., 1967-68; v.p. Russell Forester, AIA, Inc., La Jolla, Calif., 1968-78; pres. The Space Factory, La Jolla, 1978—; prin. Christine Forester Catalyst, La Jolla, 1981—; cons. architect U. Mich. Med. Ctr., 1964-67; adv. bd. Internat. Savs. Bank, 1990—, cons., 1990—, mem. mktg. com., 1990—, mem. retail bank strategy task force, 1993. Author, illustrator and pub.: Let's face It!, 1984. Founding mem. Charter 100, 1978—, bd. trustees, 1978—, v.p., 1992—; bd. trustees Mus. Photographic Arts, 1981-86, chair archtl. com., 1981-86, chair nominating com., 1985-86; mem. adv. panel allocations programs commn.

San Diego Commn. for Arts and Culture, 1989; bd. trustees Mus. Contemporary Art, San Diego, 1992—, chair devel. com., 1992—, devel./mktg. strategy task force com., 1990—; bd. trustees San Diego Regional Cancer Ctr., 1991—, chair nominating com. 1991—, devel. com. Recipient San Diego Coun. on Youth Outstanding Contbn. award, 1978; NEH grantee, 1978-79. Mem. Rotary Club of San Diego (mem. mgmt. cons./reorgn. classification 1993—). Democrat. Home: PO Box 135 La Jolla CA 92038-0135 Office: Christine Forester Catalyst 2025 Soledad Ave La Jolla CA 92037

FORGIONE, KATHLEEN C., wellness author, consultant; b. Bklyn., Nov. 12, 1944. AAS, Bklyn. Coll., 1963, BA, 1967; MA, NYU, 1969. Dir. activity therapy Valley Psychiatric Ctr., Chattanooga, 1978-84; coord. adult programs Signal Ctrs., Chattanooga, 1985-89; dir. activity therapy Noreen McKeen Residence, West Palm Beach, Fla., 1989-92; faculty Fla. Internat. U., Miami, 1992-93; Lifetracks Seminars, West Palm Beach, 1993—; coord. activity course PBC Coll., 1993. Co-chmn. Gov.'s Com. on Employment, Chattanooga, 1988; chmn. N.Y. Recreation and Parks Svc., 1971. Mem. NAFE, Nat. Wellness Inst., Fla. Writers Assn., Fla. Health Assn. Home: 2000 N Congress Ave Lot 173 West Palm Beach FL 33409-6344

FORISTER, JEAN WHITBY, guidance counselor, consultant; b. Crowell, Tex., Oct. 31, 1935; d. Tom Mulry Whitby and Edith Catherine (Weatherall) Cogdell; m. Charles F. Russell, July 31, 1961 (div. 1966); m. Thomas Eugene Forister, Aug. 4, 1966; children: Thomas Eugene Jr., Jill. BA with honors, North Tex. State U., 1958; MEd with honors, U. Tex., 1966. Cert. tchr. and counselor, Tex.; lic. realtor, Tex.; lic. profl. counselor, N.Mex. Exec. sec. Humble Oil, Amarillo, Tex., 1958-59; tchr. Crowell Schs., Vernon and Dallas, 1959-65; psychol. and guidance counselor Houston Area Schs., 1966-75; owner TJs Ladies Store, Crowell, 1975-82; guidance counselor SEARCH, Amarillo, 1983-84, Humble (Tex.) Schs., 1984-87, Ruidoso (N.Mex.) Mcpl. Schs., 1990—; co-owner Santana, Ltd., Ruidoso, 1992—. Mem. Crowell City Coun., 1976-80; vice chmn., bd. dirs. United Meth. Ch., Crowell, 1976-80. Grantee Nat. Fed. Edn. Act, 1965-66. Mem. NEA, Alpha Delta Pi. Democrat. Office: Ruidoso Mcpl Schs 200 Harton Cir Ruidoso NM 88345

FORKAN, PATRICIA ANN, association executive; b. N.Y.C., June 13, 1944; d. Robert James and Elaine May (Van Horn) F.; BA in Polit. Sci., Pa. State U., 1966; postgrad. Am. U., 1968-69. Manpower analyst Dept. Labor, Washington, 1967-69; nat. coordinator Fund for Animals, N.Y.C., 1970-76; v.p. program and communications Humane Soc. of U.S., Washington, 1976-86, sr. v.p. 1987-91, exec. v.p., 1992—; bd. dirs. Solar Elec. Light Fund; mem. U.S. del. Internat. Whaling Commn., 1978, 93, 94 Re-negotiation of Conv. for Regulation of Whaling, 1978, U.S. del. North Pacific Fur Seal Commn., 1985; mem. U.S. Public Adv. Com. to Law of the Sea, 1978-83; bd. dirs. Coun. for Ocean Law; advisor, contbr. weekly TV show Living with Animals, 1985-91; advisor Animal Polit. Action Com.; sr. v.p. Humane Soc. Internat., 1991—; coun. woman Friendship Heights (Md.) Village, 1993—. Contbr. articles to environ. and animal welfare publs.; co-host weekly radio show, 1986-87. Office: Humane Soc of US 2100 L St NW Washington DC 20037-1525

FORMAN, BETH ROSALYNE, entertainment industry professional; b. N.Y.C., Oct. 15, 1949; d. Philip and Dorothy Lea (Vilensky) F. BA in English with honors, NYU, 1971; MA with honors, Columbia U., 1972; MBA in Fin., Rutgers U., 1980. Asst. to contr. Colin Hochstin Co., N.Y.C., 1971-78; instr. Columbia U., N.Y.C., 1974-76; adj. faculty Bergen Community Coll., Paramus, N.J., 1985-87; communications cons. B.R. Forman & Co., Paramus, 1981-87; proposal mgr. Ogden Svcs.Corp., N.Y.C., 1988-89; dir. tech. svcs. Ogden Entertainment Svcs., Rosemont, Ill., 1990-92; dir. mktg. comms. Ogden Entertainment Svcs., N.Y.C., 1993—. Bd. dirs. new leadership div. United Jewish Community Bergen County, River Edge, N.J., 1981-87, chmn. fundraiser, 1983, chmn. edn. com., 1983-86, treas., 1984-86; mem. steering com. Viewpoints div. Am. Jewish Com., 1991-93. Pres.'s fellow Columbia U., 1973; recipient Masters award Ogden Svcs. Corp., 1994. Mem. NAFE, Internat. Platform Assn., Women in Comm. (v.p. spl. programs 1992-93 Chgo. chpt.), Columbia U. Club of N.Y., Mensa. Democrat. Home: 421 Yuhas Dr Paramus NJ 07652-4125 Office: Ogden Entertainment 2 Pennsylvania Plz New York NY 10121

FORMAN, JEANNE LEACH, piano and voice educator; b. Los Angeles, Mar. 3, 1916; d. Rowland E. and Charlotte F. (Van Wickle) Leach; student U. Redlands, 1934-36, UCLA, 1937; m. Edward S. Forman, July 28, 1945; children: Bonnie Jeanne Forman Ottinger, Karen Lynn Forman Maginnis, Wendy K. Forman Bolduc. Pvt. tchr. piano, Pasadena, Calif., 1945-52, Tucson, 1952-58, Sunnyvale, Calif., 1958-75, Santa Barbara, Calif., 1976—; owner, dir. Jeanne Forman Studios, Sunnyvale; owner/dir. Jeanne Forman Enterprises (Music to Write By), 1982—; owner J. Forman Advt. Agy.; propr. Jeanne Forman Advt. and Enterprises; founder Classic Acts of Santa Barbara, 1991—; writer L.A. Times, 1978-80; columnist The Galeria Santa Barbara News Press, 1978; publicity writer Music Tchrs. Assn.; tchr. of blind Santa Clara County Assistance League; lectr. on blind techniques, vocal techniques, rapport in communications; free lance writer; gen. edn. staff Brooks Inst. Photography; voice specialist, 1990-91; Santa Barbara guest appearances There is a Way, Sta. KHJ-TV, L.A.; author, presenter seminars; voice specialist with speech difficulties or tonal problems. Author: Security, 1984, Secret of the Pig, 1984; composer: I Love to Hear the Bells, 1986, Christmas Is Here; compositions performed by U. Calif., Santa Barbara, 1971. Coach Civic Light Opera. Mem. Calif. Assn. Profl. Music Tchrs., Music Tchrs. Nat. Assn. Home: 1119 Alameda Padre Serra Santa Barbara CA 93103-2004

FORMAN, LINDA HELAINE, accountant; b. Chgo., July 15, 1943; d. Hymen and Rose (Klapman) Davis; divorced; children: David, Rachel. BBA, Loyola U., Chgo., 1969. CPA, Ill., Iowa. Ptnr., dir. health-care cons./employee benefits cons. depts. Gleeson, Sklar, Sawyers & Gumpata, LLP, Skokie, Ill., 1972—. Mem. AICPA (key person legis. contact 1994—), Ill. Soc. CPAs (bd. dirs. 1993-95, chair film subcom. 1984-86, speakers bur. 1986-88, pub. svc. announcements 1988-90, chair pub. rels. com. 1990-92, strategic planning com. 1992-93, legis. contact program 1993—, v.p. 1995—), Internat. Group Acctg. Firms (healthcare and tax groups 1986—), Nat. Assn. Women Bus. Owners (bd. dirs. 1986-90, co-chair Pub. Affairs Day 1991-92, mem. pub. affairs com. 1990—, nat. healthcare task force 1993—), Destiny Inst. (mentor 1992—), LaLeche League Internat. (Ill. state treas. 1974-76, budget chair 1992-93), Chgo. Ptnrs. Earned Income Credit (founding com. 1994—). Jewish. Office: Gleeson Sklar Sawyers & Cumpata LLP 5550 W Touhy Ave Ste 300 Skokie IL 60077-3254

FORMAN, LORI ANN, foundation adminstrator; b. Sioux Falls, S.D., Dec. 4, 1958; d. Richard William and Duaine Berenice (Erickson) F. BA, Augustana Coll., 1979; M in Pub. Policy, Harvard U., 1981. Cons. OILDECO, Sandvika, Norway, 1980; sr. polit. analyst Decision Making Info., Washington, 1981-83; spl. asst. U.S. Agy. Internat. Devel., Washington, 1983-87, sr. advisor, 1987-89, program officer, 1989-90; exec. v.p. Pacific Mgmt. Resources Inc., Honolulu, 1990; dir. Japan program Nature Conservancy, Arlington, Va., 1990—; lectr. in field. Reviewer; (book) Japan's Foreign Aid, 1990; contbg. reviewer (book) Yen for Development, 1990. Vol. Presdls. Youth for Ford, Kansas City, Mo., 1976, Saiki for Senate, Honolulu, 1992; vice chmn. Community Devel. Citizens Adv. Com., Sioux Falls, S.D., 1978-79; mem. internal audit com. Georgetown Luth. Ch., Washington, 1994. Harry S. Truman scholar Truman Found., 1979; ITT Internat. fellow Inst. Internat. Edn., 1980; named one of Ten Outstanding Young People Osaka Jr. C. of C., 1992. Mem. Soc. Internat. Devel., Japan-Am. Soc., Washington Area Bicycle Assn., Asia Soc., Sushi Club. Office: Nature Conservancy 1815 N Lynn St Arlington VA 22209

FORMAN-BELLO, JUDITH, clinical social worker; b. Boston, July 27, 1951; d. George William and Florence (Saberlinsky) Forman; m. Martin Glen Bello, Sept. 11, 1982. BA, Boston U., 1970; MSW, Boston Coll., 1972. Lic. ins. clin. social worker, Mass.; diplomate Am. Bd. Examiners in Clin. Social Work. Clin. social worker Cath. Charitable Bur., Boston, 1972-74; clin. social worker Boston City Hosp., 1974—, tchr. sociology high sch. program, 1985-86; pvt. practice, Boston, 1984—. Coord. Mass. Tenants' Union, 1988-89. Mem. NASW, Acad. Cert. Social Workers, Mass. Acad. Clin. Social Workers, Nat. Coun. Jewish Women, Jewish Women's College Club. Home: 89 Pleasant St Brookline MA 02146-3421 Office: Boston City Hosp 818 Harrison Ave Roxbury MA 02118-2999

FORNELL, MARTHA STEINMETZ, art educator, artist; b. Galveston, Tex., Dec. 19, 1920; d. Joseph Duncan and Martha Lillian (McRee) Steinmetz; m. Earl Wesley Fornell, Sept. 20, 1947 (dec. Mar. 1969). B.Mus. cum laude, U. Tex., 1943; postgrad. U. Houston, 1953-56, Lamar U., 1957-60. Music cons., fgn. program editor Voice of America, USIA, N.Y.C., 1944-46; advt. cons. fed. agys., San Antonio, 1946-47; tchr. music secondary schs., Houston, 1953-56; tchr. art Beaumont (Tex.) Ind. Sch. Dist., 1956-79; collages exhibited Galerie Paula Insel, N.Y.C., 1974-84, Ponce, P.R., 1976-79, 82, 84, 87; group show participant Ann. Am. Nat. Miniature Show, Laramie, Wyo., Beaumont Art Mus. Annual, 1960, Houston Art League Easter Annual, 1960, Austin Women's Club, 1961. Recipient Circuit awards Tex. Fine Arts Assn., 1962-64, Invitational awards, 1964-65. Mem. Tex. Fine Arts Assn., Mu Phi Epsilon. Contbr. articles to Am.-German Rev. Address: 2303 Evalon Ave Beaumont TX 77702

FORNERIS, JEANNE M., lawyer; b. Duluth, Minn., May 23, 1953; d. John Domenic and Elva Lorraine (McDonald) F.; m. Michael Scott Margulies, Feb. 6, 1982. AB, Macalester Coll., 1975; JD, U. Minn., 1978. Bar: Minn. 1978. Assoc. Halverson, Watters, Bye, Downs & Maki, Ltd., Duluth, Minn., 1978-81, Briggs & Morgan, P.A., Mpls. and St. Paul, 1981-83; ptnr. Hart & Bruner, P.A., Mpls., 1983-86; assoc. gen. counsel M.A. Mortenson Co., 1986-90, v.p., gen. coun., 1990—; instr. women's studies dept. U. Minn., Mpls., 1977-79. Author profl. edn. seminars, 1981; author, editor articles. Bd. dirs. Good Will Industries Vocat. Enterprises, Inc., 1979-81; chmn. bd. trustees Duluth Bar Library, 1981; mem. United Way Family and Individual Services Task Force, Duluth, 1981. Nat. Merit Assn. scholar, 1971. Fellow Am. Coll. Construction Lawyers; mem. ABA, Am. Arbitration Assn. (mem. large complex case panel), Minn. State Bar Assn., Hennepin County Bar Assn., Minn. Women Lawyers (bd. dirs.). Democrat. Roman Catholic. Office: MA Mortenson Co 700 Meadow Ln N Minneapolis MN 55422-4899

FORNES, MARIA IRENE, playwright, director; b. Havana, Cuba, May 14, 1930; came to U.S., 1945, naturalized, 1951; d. Carlos Luis and Carmen Hismenia (Collado) F. Ed. Havana pub. schs. Pres. N.Y. Theatre Strategy, 1973-80. Writer, director: (plays) The Successful Life of Three, 1965 (Obie award best script 1965), Promenade, 1965 (Obie award best script 1965), There! You Died (title changed to Tango Palace), 1965, A Vietnamese Wedding, 1967, The Annunciation, 1967, The Curse of Langston Hughes, 1972, Aurora, 1973, Dr. Kheal, 1973, Molly's Dream, 1973, Fefu and Her Friends, 1978 (Obie award best script 1978), Eyes on the Harem, 1979 (Obie award best direction 1979), Life is a Dream (translation and adaption of Calderon's play), 1981, A Visit, 1981, Mud, 1983 (Obie awards best script and direction 1984), Sarita, 1984 (Obie awards best script and direction 1984), The Danube, 1984 (Obie awards best script and direction 1984), The Conduct of Life, 1985 (Obie award best play 1985), Cold Air (translation and adaption of Piñera's play), 1985 (HBO Translation award 1986, Playwrights U.S.A. award 1986), Lovers and Keepers, 1986, Abingdon Square, 1987 (Obie award best new play 1988), Uncle Vanya (revision of Chekov's play), 1987, Hunger, 1988; writer: (plays) The Widow, 1963, The Office, 1965, The Red Burning Light: or Mission XQ3, 1968, Cap-a-Pie, 1975, Washing, 1976, Lolita in the Garden, 1977, In Service, 1978, Evelyn Brown (A Diary), 1980, Blood Wedding (translation and adaptation of Garcia Lorca's play), 1980, No Time, 1985, Drowning (adaption of Chekov play), 1985, The Trial of Joan of Arc on a Matter of Faith, 1986, The Mothers (title changed to Charley), 1986, Art, 1986, And What of the Night?, 1988, La Plaza Chica, 1994; director: (plays) Going to New England, 1980, Exiles, 1982; costume designer: Two Camps by Koutoukas, 1968; contributor: (music, lyrics) Carmines Sings Whitman Sings Carmines, 1985. Recipient Obie award for sustained achievement, 1982, Academy-Inst. award for literature Am. Acad. and Inst. of Arts and Letters, 1985; grantee John Hay Whitney Found., 1961-62, Centro Mexicano de Escrivatores, 1962-63, OADR U. Minn., 1965, Cintas Found., 1967-68, Yale Univ. 1968-69, Creative Artists Pub. Service Program, 1972, 75, Nat. Endowment for Arts, 1974, 84, 85; fellow Boston Univ.-Tanglewood, 1968, Rockefeller Found., 1971, Guggenheim Found., 1972-73. Address: 1 Sheridan Sq New York NY 10014*

FORNEY, VIRGINIA SUE, educational counselor; b. Little Rock, Sept. 15, 1925; d. Robert Millard and Susan Amanda (Ward) Tate; m. J.D. Mullen, Jr., Oct. 13, 1945 (div. 1966); children: Michael Dunn, Patricia Sue; m. Bill E. Forney, Apr. 29, 1967. Student Tex. State Coll. for Women, 1943-46; BFA, U. Okla., 1948; postgrad. Benedictine Heights Coll., Tulsa, 1957-58; M.Teaching Arts, Tulsa U., 1969; postgrad. Okla. State U., intermittently, 1969—. Cert. secondary tchr., sch. counselor, vis. sch. counselor, Okla. With Sta. WNAD, U. Okla., 1947-49; tchr. lang. arts Tulsa Bd. Edn., 1959-73; women's counselor Tulsa YWCA, 1980; vis. sch. counselor Tulsa County Supt. of Schs. Office, 1980-86; dir. spl. project Tulsa County Supt. Schs. Office, 1986-91; owner, dir. Svc. to Families in Bus. and Industry, 1991—. Mem. budget com. United Way Greater Tulsa, 1980-86, edn. com. Planned Parenthood Greater Tulsa, 1980-86; mem. Tulsa County adv. coun. Okla. State U., 1983-85; chairperson Tulsa Coalition for Parenting Edn., 1983-84; chairperson problems of youth study Tulsa Met. C. of C., 1984-85; mem. gen. bd. March of Dimes Greater Tulsa, 1985; pres. evening alliance All Souls Unitarian Ch. Mem. Am. Assn. for Counseling and Devel., Internat. Assn. Pupil Personnel Workers (state bd. dirs. 1982-86), Okla. Assn. Family Resource Programs (regional v.p. 1982-86, state pres. 1986-87), Program Internat. Ednl. Exchange (community coordinator for Tulsa 1986-90), LWV Okla. (chairperson juvenile justice study 1976-77), LWV Met. Tulsa (mem. exec. bd. 1993—). Democrat. Unitarian. Avocation: piano.

FORNILLO, JEAN MARY, small business owner; b. Williamsburg, N.Y., Nov. 20, 1942; d. William George and Margaret Frieda (Belcher) Bannwarth; m. Raymond John Fornillo, Jan. 9, 1967; children: Damien, Andrea. BA, Cedar Crest Coll., Allentown, Pa., 1964; postgrad., U. Hawaii, 1966; MA, Adelphi U., 1967. Cert. 7-12 social studies tchr., K-12 art tchr., N.Y. Probation officer Nassau County Probation Dept., Westbury, N.Y., 1964-65; tchr. social studies Boardman Jr. High Sch., Oceanside, N.Y., 1965-67, Freeport (N.Y.) High Sch., 1967-69; tchr. art Three Village Sch. Dist., Setauket, N.Y., 1977-79; tchr. English, N.Y. State Div. for Youth, South Kortright, 1979-80; assoc. editor Woman's World mag., Englewood, N.J., 1980-82; co-owner, mgr. PIP Printing 784, Binghamton, N.Y., 1983—, PIP Printing 9035, Endicott, N.Y., 1986—; co-chmn. legis. com. Small Bus. Coun., 1991—. Charter mem., parliamentarian, chair Police Community Rels. Adv. Bd., 1988—; bd. dirs., pres., treas. Broome County Coun. on Alcoholism, 1988—; chmn., facilitator Main Street Reconstrn. Adv. Com., Binghamton, 1989-91; mem. Project Pride, Broome County, N.Y., 1991—; chmn. Main Street Reopening Celebration, Binghamton, 1991; Rep. candidate for Broome County Legislature, 1990l; bd. dirs. Southern Tier Zool. Soc., 1995. Recipient award of excellence N.Y. State Dept. Transp., 1992, President's award for volunteerism Key Bank N.Y., 1992; scholar, grantee East-West Cultural Inst., Honolulu, 1966. Mem. Broome County C. of C. (chmn. Ambs. Club 1985-88, mem. accreditation com. 1988-89, mem., chmn. various coms. 1983—), Nat. Fedn. Ind. Bus., So. Tier Club Printing house Craftsmen, Washington Avenue Mchts. Assn., Leadership Broome Alumni Assn. (bd. dirs. 1988—), Phi Alpha Theta. Office: PIP Printing 53 Main St Binghamton NY 13905-3000

FORONDA, ELENA ISABEL, secondary school educator; b. N.Y.C., Jan. 15, 1947; d. Severino Deliso and LaVerne (Ibanez) F. BS in Music, Hunter Coll., CUNY, 1969, MA in Music Edn., 1971. Tchr. vocal music N.Y.C. Pub. Sch. System, 1970—; asst. dir. tchr. placement Hunter Coll., City U. N.Y., summers 1971-72; examination asst. N.Y.C. Pub. Sch. System Bd. Examiners, 1987-89. Sponsor children in Philippines and El Salvador, World Vision Internat.; del. Asian Am. Women's Caucus, 1977; mem. Hunter Coll. choirs, 1968-69, 71; pianist, minister of music Ch. of The Holy Spirit, Bklyn., 1988-90; lay reader, lay eucharistic minister L.I. Diocese Episcopal Ch., 1993. Dist. winner Nat. Piano Playing Auditions, 1965; recipient N.Y. State permanent cert. Dept. Edn., 1971. Mem. Music Educators Nat. Conf., Music Educators Assn. N.Y.C., N.Y. State Sch. Music Assn., Amateur Chamber Players (Vienna, Va.). Democrat.

FORREST, DIANE, data processing executive; b. Bayonne, N.J., Oct. 22, 1946; d. Max D. and Selma (Winter) Forrest; m. Nicholas John LaHowchic, Sept. 11, 1981. BA, Boston U., 1968; MBA, Pace U., 1982. Cert. prodn. and inventory mgmt. Programmer trainee Prudential Life Ins. Co., Newark, 1968-69; programmer analyst Computer Usage Corp., N.Y.C., 1970-71; systems analyst Plymouth Computers, Inc., N.Y.C., 1972-73; distbn. project leader T.J. Lipton Inc., Englewood Cliffs, N.J., 1973-74, fin. project leader, 1975-76, mgr. mktg. project, 1977-78; project mgr. mfg. Nabisco Brands, Inc., N.Y.C., 1978-80, corp. mgr. mfg. systems, 1981-82; mgr. mfg. cons. Peat Marwick Mitchell & Co., N.Y.C., 1982-83, sr. mgr. mfg. practice, 1984-85, sr. mgr. in charge Stamford/White Plains, 1986-87, editor newsletter, 1983-86; dir. mgmt. info. systems Tambrands Inc., White Plains, N.Y., 1987-89, v.p. info. svcs., 1989-94; sr. v.p.. chief info. officer Henry Schein, Inc., Port Washington, N.Y., 1994—. Contbr. articles to profl. jours. Mem. NAFE, ASME, Am. Prodn. and Inventory Control Soc., Data Processing Mgmt. Assn., Robotics Assn., Assn. Women Bus. Owners, Acad. Women Achievers. Office: Henry Schein Inc 5 Harbor Park Dr Port Washington NY 10706

FORREST, KATHLEEN, secondary education educator; b. Attleboro, Mass., Nov. 28, 1955; d. Joseph Paul and Josephine Joan (Dziedzic) Poholek; m. Wayne J. Forrest, Aug. 9, 1980. BA, Wheaton Coll., Norton, Mass., 1977; MEd, R.I. Coll., 1978. Cert. tchr. Spanish, French, bilingual edn., Mass., R.I. Foreign lang. tchr. Pawtucket (R.I.) School Dept., 1977—; adj. prof. R.I. Coll., Providence, 1990—; advisor Shea H.S. Key Club, Pawtucket, 1987-93. Home: 11 Doro Pl Rumford RI 02916

FORREST, MELBA JUNE, real estate broker, appraiser, educator; b. Melbourne, Ark., Mar. 31, 1931; d. William Turner and Mamie Mae (Felts) Clem; m. Cloyce Byram Forrest, May 5, 1951; children: Ruth Ann, James Byram. BA, U. Wichita, 1957; MEd, Wichita State U., 1970. Cert. real estate appraiser, residential real property appraiser, Kans. Real estate assoc. Bond Realty Investment Corp., Wichita, 1976-79; pres. Forrest Properties, Inc., Wichita, 1979—; instr. Wichita Pub. Schs., 1957-66, 68-75, Minneha Sch. Dist., Wichita, 1962-66; speaker in field. Author: Narrative Appraisal Report Writing, 1987. Mem. Nat. Assn. Realtors, Kans. Assn. Realtors, Nat. Assn. Ind. Fee Appraisers (designated 1988, pres. Wichita chpt. 1988-90, Kansas State dir. 1990—, named Kansas Coord. of Yr. 1988, Kansa Ind. Fee Appraiser of Yr. 1989). Home: 25 Laurel Dr Wichita KS 67206-2542 Office: Forrest Properties Inc 25 Laurel Dr Wichita KS 67206-2542

FORRESTER, ROSEMARY WELLINGTON, regional senatorial representative; b. Petoskey, Mich., Aug. 1, 1953; d. James Doud and Mary Margaret (Thompson) Wellington; m. Dan L., June 16, 1974; children: Jennifer Mary, Joshua Daniel. BS in Sociology, No. Mich. U., Marquette, 1977; postgrad., No. Mich. U., 1987—. Activities coordinator E.U.P. Mental Health Bd., Sault, Mich., 1978-80; client services asst. E.U.P. Mental Health Bd, Sault, 1980; assoc. dir. U.P. Health Systems Agy., Sault, 1980-82; U.P. field coordinator Riegle for Mich., Sault, 1982, Marquette, 1988; community educator Chippewa County Health Dept., 1983-84; legal asst. U.P. Legal Services, Sault, 1983-85; camp lic. cons. Mich. Dept. of Social Services, Mich., 1985-86; career cons. Six County Consortium for Employment, Marquette, 1985-92; regional rep. U.S. Senator Carl Levin, Escanaba, Mich., 1992—. Del. Mich. Dem. State Ctrl. Com., 1986-91; chair Marquette County Health Care Access project adv. com., 1987-90; publicity chair United Way Marquette County, 1987-89; mem. Marquette Women's Ctr. Life Skills adv. com., 1987-88; appointee Alger-Marquette Community Mental Health Bd., 1989-93; vice chmn., mem. fin. com. Marquette County Irwin for Congress, 1988, coord., 1988; mem. adv. bd. spl. projects No. Mich. U. Mem. Mich. Assn. Community Mental Health Bds. (del., legis. com.), U.P. Pers. Assn. Methodist. Home: 774 Lakewood Ln Marquette MI 49855-0985

FORSTER, SUSAN BOGART, computer educator; b. Hackensack, N.J., June 6, 1944; d. Charles William and Lillian (Vito) Bogart; m. John D. Forster, June 17, 1967; children: Gregory, Brian. BA, Mt. Holyoke Coll., 1966; MEd, George Mason U., 1985. Computer programmer MIT Draper Lab., Cambridge, Mass., 1966-68; computer programmer P.R.C., San Diego, 1968-71, Washington, 1972; tchr. adult edn. Fairfax (Va.) County Pub. Schs., 1983-84; programmer Fairfax County Pub. Schs., Annandale, Va., 1984-85; computer dir. Potomac Sch., McLean, Va., 1985-93; computer trainer, tchr. The Langley Sch., McLean, Va., 1994—; dir. computer Summer Inst., Washington, 1993—; program developer Adult Computer Literacy Program, McLean, 1991-92; adj. prof. edn. Marymount U., 1993—, George Mason U., Fairfax, Va., 1993—. Mem. Assn. for Advancement of Computing in Edn., Computer Assn. Ind. Schs. (program chair 1990-91). Home: 1900 Wintergreen Ct Reston VA 22091-5114

FORSTER, THERESA M., legislative staff director; b. Akron, Ohio, Jan. 16, 1955. BA, U. Akron, 1977. Mem. staff Senate Spl. Com. Aging, 1977-80; legis. aide Sen. David Pryor, 1980-88; cons. health care policy, 1988-91; dir. home care aide divsn. Nat. Assn. Home Care, 1991-93; staff dir. Senate Spl. Com. Aging, 1993—. Office: Spl Com Aging G-31 Senate Dirksen Office Bldg Washington DC 20510*

FORSYTHE, PATRICIA HAYS, development professional; b. Curtis, Ark.; d. John Chambers and Flora Jane (Eby) Hays; m. Kurt G. Pahl, Dec. 15, 1962 (div. Dec. 1980); children: Thomas Walter, Susan Clara; m. Robert E. Forsythe, June 20, 1981; 1 child, Nathaniel Ryan. BA, Calif. State U., Los Angeles, 1974; MSLS, U. So. Calif., 1976. Asst. to dir. devel. office The Assocs., Calif. Inst. Tech., Pasadena, 1978-81; exec. dir. Iowa City Pub. Library Found., 1982-89; dir. devel. Hoover Presdl. Libr. Assn., West Branch, Iowa, 1989-94, exec. dir., 1994—. Contbr. articles to profl. jours. Recipient Outstanding Fund Raising Exec. award Ea. Iowa, 1990. Mem. LWV (editor 1985-87), ALA, Nat. Soc. Fund Raising Execs. (bd. dirs. 1987-89, chmn. Ea. Iowa Philanthropy Day 1990-91, bd. dirs. Ea. Iowa chpt. 1986—), Iowa City C. of C., Iowa Life Shares Assn. (bd. dirs., pres.-elect 1994-95), Libr. Adminstrn. and Mgmt. Assn., I.C. & M. Club, Hancher Guild (audience devel. 1981-85, pres. 1985-86), Univ. Athletic Club, Rotary (program chair 1992-94). Congregationalist. Home: 1806 E Court St Iowa City IA 52245-4643 Office: Hoover Presdl Libr Assn PO Box 696 West Branch IA 52358-0696

FORTE, MURIEL ELIZABETH, nurse; b. Niagara Falls, N.Y., Nov. 11, 1940; d. Wilbur Francis and Dorothea Bloomingdale (Bradt) Connell; m. Francis Anthony Biancuzzo, May 23, 1970 (dec. Oct. 1971) m. Eugenio Forte, Apr. 9, 1988. BSN, U. Buffalo, 1963. Cert. diabetes educator. Staff nurse Meml. Med. Ctr., Niagara Falls, 1963-69, staff devel. instr., 1983—, diabetic teaching nurse, 1966-94; commd. capt. USAF, 1973, advanced through grades to lt. col., 1987; clin. nurse 914 Tactical Clinic, Niagara Falls, 1973-78, chief nurse, 1978-93; comdr. 914 Med. Squadron, Niagara Falls, 1993—; Active in Operation Desert Storm, 1991. Mem. nursing and health com. ARC, Niagara Falls, 1967—, disaster svcs. com., Niagara Falls, 1987—, mem. nominating com.; active election campaign Judge John Mariano, Niagara Falls, 1983; vestrywoman Ch. of the Epiphany, Niagara Falls; mem. nominating com. Nurse's House. Decorated Air Force Commendation medal, 2 Air Force Meritorious Svc. medals; recipient Good Neighbor award Tops Markets, Niagara Falls, 1993. Mem. ANA, DAR, Am. Assn. Diabetes Educators, N.Y. State Nurses Assn., Res. Officers Assn. (life), Friends of Air Force Mus., Aquarium of Niagara Falls, Humane Edn. Soc. Republican. Episcopalian. Home: 629 13th St Niagara Falls NY 14301

FORTENBAUGH, CATHY CAROL, oncology nurse, clinical nurse specialist; b. Trenton, N.J., May 31, 1959; d. Joseph Edward and Jocelyn Marjorie (Stout) Sickels; m. Richard Hall Fortenbaugh, May 1, 1982 (div. Feb. 1994); children: Patrick Thurman, Sean Richard. BSN, Widener U., 1981; MSN, U. Pa., 1982. RN, Pa.; cert. oncology nurse ANCC. Staff nurse med. oncology unit Hosp. of U. Pa., Phila., 1981-90, asst. head nurse, 1990-92, interim head nurse, 1992; nurse mgr. St. Mary Hosp., Langhorne, Pa., 1992-94; surg. oncology clin. nurse specialist Helene Fuld Med. Ctr., Trenton, N.J., 1994—. Mem. nurse of hope team Am. Cancer Soc., Bucks County, Pa., 1992-93. Mem. Oncology Nursing Soc. (mgmt. spl. interest group, asst. editor newsletter), Southeastern Pa. Assn. Nurse Mgrs. Home: 817 River Rd Yardley PA 19067 Office: Helene Fuld Med Ctr Med Arts Bldg 40 Fuld St Ste 301 Trenton NJ 08638

FORTENBERRY, CAROL LOMAX, real estate appraiser; b. Charlotte, N.C., Apr. 23, 1959; d. Henry Clyde and Anne Tristram (Holt) Lomax; m. Mark Kevin Fortenberry, July 14, 1984; 1 child, Liza Holt. BA in radio, TV, motion pictures, U. N.C., Chapel Hill, 1981; MBA, Queens Coll., Charlotte, 1988. Lic. real estate salesman, N.C.; cert. gen. real estate appraiser, N.C. Various positions Jefferson Pilot Communications Co., Charlotte, 1981-85; asst. show mgr. So. Shows, Inc., Charlotte, 1985-87; bus. mgr. Mark Fortenberry Photography, Charlotte, 1987-88; comml. real estate appraiser Stout-Beck & Assocs., Charlotte, 1988-94, Fitzhugh L. Stout & Assoc., Charlotte, 1994—. Coord. blood donor program, mem. outreach com. St. John's Episc. Ch., Charlotte, 1990. Mem. Comml. Real Estate Women (bd. dirs. N.C. chpt.), U. N.C. Alumni Assn., Nat. Bone Marrow Registry. Home: 128 Wonderwood Dr Charlotte NC 28211-4010 Office: Fitzhugh L Stout & Assoc 505 East Blvd Charlotte NC 28203-5175

FORTI, CORINNE ANN, corporate communications executive; b. N.Y.C., July 26, 1941; d. Wilbur Walter and Sylvia Joan (Charap) Bastian; B.A., CUNY, 1963; m. Joseph Donald Forti, Aug. 18, 1962 (dec.); 1 child, Raina. Adminstrv. asst. Ednl. Broadcasting Corp., 1963-65; adminstrv. asst. W.R. Grace & Co., N.Y.C., 1965-67, pub. relations rep., 1967-70, mgr. info. services, 1970-79, dir. info. services, 1980-86, dir. info. and advt., 1986-87; pres. Bastian-Forti Communications, 1988-89, Forti Communications Inc., 1989—; lectr. photography and graphics Am. Mgmt. Assn. Bd. dirs. YM/YWCA Day Care, Inc. Named to Acad. Women Achievers, YWCA, 1979; recipient citation award in communications Nat. Council of Women, 1979. Mem. Am. Women in Radio and TV, Chem. Mfrs. Assn., Am. Mgmt. Assn., Women Execs. in Pub. Relations. Republican. Roman Catholic. Home and Office: 1246 Calle Yucca Thousand Oaks CA 91360-2239

FORTI, LENORE STEIMLE, business consultant; b. Houghton, Mich., Sept. 9, 1924; d. Russell Nicholas and Agnes (McCloskey) Steimle; m. Frank Forti, May 29, 1950 (dec.). BBA summa cum laude, Northwood U., 1973, Dr.Laws, 1969. Asst. corp. sec., purchasing agt. Fed. Life & Casualty Co., Detroit, 1942-53; supr. sectl. J.L. Hudson Co., Detroit, 1953-57, adminstrv. asst. to exec. v.p., 1957-86; instr. Wayne State U. and U. Mich. Adult Edn., Detroit, 1958-71; creator, dir. Seminars for Profl. People, 1971—. Co-author: The Professional Secretary; contbr. articles to profl. jours. Asst. br. dir. planning City of Detroit for Civil Def.; chmn. bd. trustees PSI Rsch. and Ednl. Found.; trustee PSI Retirement Home Complex, Albuquerque; elected dir. Porperty Owners and Residents Assn., Sun City West Mcpl. Govt., 1994; pres. Women's Bd. Northwood U., Midland, Mich.; pres. parish coun. Our Lady of Lourdes Ch., Sun City West, Ariz., 1988, pres. ladies guild, 1990, pres. singles club, 1995; 1st v.p. Vol. Bur. of Sun Cities, 1989. Elected One of Detroit's Top Ten Working Women, 1969; elected to Exec. and Profl. Hall of Fame. Mem. Profl. Sec. Internat. (internat. pres. 1967-69), Future Secs. Assn. (nat. coord.), Lioness Club (pres. 1991-92), Sun City West Singles Club (pres. 1988, pres. Singles Club Ch. 1995). Republican. Roman Catholic. Home: 12613 Seneca Dr Sun City West AZ 85375-4635

FORTNER, BILLIE JEAN, small business owner; b. Tarrytown, Ga.; d. Willard and Sara (Beckworth) Burch; m. Randall Carroll; m. David Jones (div.); m. Robert F. Fortner, Jr., Sept. 20, 1981; children: Gina Sumner, Simone Dixon, Natalie Garner. AA summa cum laude, Brewton Parker Coll., 1970; BS, Ga. So. Coll., 1972, MEd, 1975, EdS, 1977. Math & sci. tchr. Toombs County Schs., Lyons, Ga., 1971-76, gifted tchr., 1976-81; gifted tchr. Montgomery County Schs., Mt. Vernon, Ga., 1985-88; ptnr. Rabbit's Quik Stop, Vidalia, Ga., 1985—, Rabbit's Cargo Inc., Vidalia, 1987—, Fortner Rentals, Vidalia, 1988—, Rabbit On the Strip, Vidalia, 1988—, Fortner Farms, Vidalia, 1989—; artist-in-residence, ptnr. F.C.F. Investments, Vidalia, 1992—; ptnr. Kipling B. Collins; artist-in-residence, Vidaliak, Ga. Troup leader Girl Scouts, Vidalia, 1972-76; block coord. Ga. Heart Assn., Vidalia, 1976. Mem. Phi Beta Kappa. Baptist. Home: 404 Slayton St Vidalia GA 30474 Office: Rabbit's Quik Stop Hwy 292 W Vidalia GA 30474

FORTSON-RIVERS, TINA E. (THOMASENA ELIZABETH FORTSON-RIVERS), social studies educator, computer training specialist; b. Anderson, S.C.; d. Thomas Henry and Mary (Oliver) Fortson; m. Michael M. Rivers, Sept. 12, 1962 (div. 1973); children: Michael II, George Thomas, Kashiya Elaine. BA, Spelman Coll., 1962; MEd, Bowie State U., 1979; MS, Johns Hopkin U., 1982. Cert. adminstrn., supervision, Md. Tchr. Tulip Grove Elem. Sch., Bowie, Md., 1973-79, Kenmoor Elem. Sch., Landover, Md., 1979-82; computer coord. Benjamin Stoddert Mid. Sch., Temple Hills, Md., 1982-86; computer tng. specialist Prince Georges County Pub. Schs., Upper Marlboro, Md., 1986—; ednl. cons. Wicat, Provo, Utah, 1985-91; design cons. Computer Lady, Capitol Heights, Md., 1990-92. Author: Education Software Correlation to PGCPS Socal Studies Curriculum, 1992. Mem. Com. of 100, Prince Georges County Schs., Upper Marlboro, 1985. Mem. Mid. States Coun. for Social Studies (bd. dirs. 1979-92, conf. program chair 1989, regional conf. coord. 1992-93, pres. 1994—), Md. Coun. for Social Studies (treas. 1982-83), Prince Georges County Coun. for Social Studies (pres. 1981-82), Nat. Coun. for Social Studies (chmn. membership com. 1994), Alpha Delta Kappa (sec. 1992—, membership chair, Md. dist. chair 1994, del. U.S./Russia Conf. on Edn. 1994). Methodist. Office: PG Co Pub Schs 8437 Landover Rd Landover MD 20785-3502

FORTUNE, LAURA CATHERINE DAWSON, elementary school educator; b. Louisville, Feb. 2, 1931; d. Lewis Harper and Zelma Ruth (Hocutt) Dawson; m. James Ralph Fortune, Jan. 10, 1950; children: Elaine, Jean, Tom, Joe. BS, R.I. Coll., 1969, MEd, 1972; postgrad., Longwood Coll., Farmville, Va., 1980-88, U. Va., 1977-90. Cert. math. tchr., elem. edn. tchr. Mid. sch. tchr. North Kingston (R.I.) Schs., 1969-74; 6th grade tchr. Campbell County Schs., Altavista, Va., 1974-92, sch. divsn. grantwriter, 1992—, instructional coord., 1987-91. Vice chair Rep. exec. com. Campbell County; chair NEA Rep. Educators Caucus; chmn. Rep. Tchr. Adv. Coun. Va.; leader Girl Scouts U.S., parent com., 1961-69; treas. Narrow River Preservation Assn., 1970-74; mem. Edn. Commn. of States; mem. Gov.'s Commn. on Champion Schs. Mem. NEA, Nat. Coun. Tchrs. Math., Va. Edn. Assn., Assn. for Supervision and Curriculum Devel., Campbell County Edn. Assn. (treas.), Piedmont Area Reading Coun., Phi Delta Kappa. Baptist. Address: Rte 2 Box 324 Evington VA 24550

FORWARD, DOROTHY ELIZABETH, legal assistant; b. Medford, Mass., Oct. 12, 1919; d. Roy Clifford and Julia (Lane) Hurd; student UCLA, 1964; m. Winston W. Forward, Sept. 29, 1942. Sec. nat. dir. fund raising ARC, Washington, 1943-46; legal sec. William W. Waters, Esq., Los Angeles, 1953-56; office mgr. Winston W. Forward, Ins. Adjuster, Arcadia, Calif., 1956-64; legal asst. John M. Podlech, Esq., Pasadena, 1964-79; dir. Calif. Probate Insts., Arcadia, 1970—; ind. probate legal asst., 1979—; condr. workshops in probate procedures, 1967-92. Recipient ARC Meritorious Service award, 1945. Mem. Nat. Assn. Legal Secs., Legal Secs. Inc., Calif. Assn. Legal Secs. (parliamentarian 1982-84), Pasadena Legal Secs. Assn. (Sec. of Yr. 1974, 75, 77, Freedom Through Edn. award 1975, pres. 1976-78), Los Angeles County Forum of Legal Secs. (chmn. 1978-80), Nat. Assn. Legal Assts. (charter), Arcadia Travelers Club (recording sec. 1993, 94). Contbg. author: Calif. Legal Secretary's Handbook, 1984, 85. Office: PO Box 660311 Arcadia CA 91066-0311

FORYST, CAROLE, mortgage broker; b. Chgo., Apr. 8; d. James M. and Marie V. (Votruba) F.; m. Anthony H. Cordesman, Feb. 14, 1976; children: Justin G., Alexander Scott. Student, Rosary Coll., 1958-61, Cite Universite de Grenoble, France, 1961, Hunter Coll., 1964-67, Roosevelt U., 1970-71. Fin. reporter Chgo. Sun-Times, 1969-72; fin. reporter Los Angeles Times, 1972; staff asst. to sec. U.S. Dept. Treasury, Washington, 1973-76; dep. dir. pub. affairs U.S. Dept. Interior, Washington, 1976; asst. v.p. Assn. Am. Railroads, Washington, 1977-78; v.p. AMTRAK, Washington, 1979-81; assoc. adminstr. budget and policy Urban Mass Transp. Adminstrn., Washington, 1981-84; comml. real estate broker Barnes, Morris & Pardoe, Washington, 1984-88, Larry Hogan & Assocs., Inc., Landover, Md., 1988-93; mortgage broker Mortgage Investment Corp., Vienna, Va., 1993-94, Windsor Mortgage Co, McLean, Va., 1994—; mem. fin. svc. com. Treas. Dept., Fed. Credit Union, 1991-93, Pub. Internat. Bus. Insights, 1991-93, Glbal Techs. Co., 1993—, Hotels and Comm. Real Estate Co., 1993—. Republican. Home: 960 Carya Ct Great Falls VA 22066-1929 Office: Windsor Mortgage Corp 1355 Beverly Rd McLean VA 22101

FOSBROKE, L. LINDLEY POWERS, communication and theatre arts educator; b. Albany, N.Y., Aug. 19, 1926; d. William Tibbits and Winifred Lispenard (Robb) Powers; AB, Smith Coll., 1948; MA in Speech, U. Wis., 1963, MFA in Theatre Directing, 1963, PhD in Theatre (E.B. Fred fellow), 1968; postdoctoral Episcopal Theol. Sch., 1972-74, Weston Coll. Sch. Theology, 1974-75; m. Davis Spencer, Mar. 5, 1949 (div. 1961); children: Eleanor Tibbits Spencer Tupper, Joseph Allen Powers Spencer; m. Gerald E. Fosbroke, Dec. 17, 1976. Children's libr. N.Y.C. Public Libr., 1948-49; tchr., Racine, Wis., 1959-61; dir. Wis. 4-H Drama Program, also rsch. asst. U. Wis., 1961-64; instr. U. Wis., 1964-65, 66-67, teaching asst. Sch. Music, 1965-66; asst. prof. drama Bridgewater (Mass.) State Coll., 1968-69; assoc. prof., dir. grad. study theatre edn. Emerson Coll., Boston, 1969-71, assoc. prof. fine arts, 1971-76, prof., 1977-79, founder, adviser creative svc. interdisciplinary program, 1974-79; adjunct prof. Art and Religious Studies The Union Inst., Cinn., 1992—. Condr. community and conv. workshops in theatre arts; lectr. to clergy and parishes on liturgical experience of myth and symbol; also active in ch. renovation and conducting classes for lay lectors and clergy Dioceses of N.J. and Mass. V.p., bd. dirs. Ch. Home Soc., Boston, 1973-84; sec. Iona Community New World Found., 1977-86; founder, sec., trustee Iona Cornerstone Found., Inc., 1981—, Iona Cornerstone Found. Ltd., 1982—; mem. Diocesan Ecumenical Commn., 1980-84, sec., 1980-82; mem. Mass. Council Chs. Jewish Community Coun. Dialogues, 1982-84; lay reader, eucharistic min. Episc. Ch. Mem. AAUP, Iona Community (asso.), Soc. St. John the Evangelist (asso.), Dobbs (dir., mem. exec. com. 1949-57, editor Bull., 1949-57), Smith alumnae assns., U. Wis. Alumni Assn., Conservation Law Found. Mem. Ch. of the Messiah. Author: Proclaim the Word, 1980, also drama ednl. materials. Home: 70 Carey Ln Quissett Harbor Falmouth MA 02540

FOSCARINIS, MARIA, lawyer; b. N.Y.C., Aug. 8, 1956; d. Nicolas and Rosa F. BA, Barnard Coll., 1977; MA, Columbia U., 1978, JD, 1981. Bar: N.Y. 1982, U.S. Dist. Ct. (so. and ea. dists.) N.Y. 1983, D.C. 1986, U.S. Dist. Ct. D.C., U.S. Ct. Appeals (D.C. cir.). Law clk. to judge U.S. Ct. Appeals (2d cir.), N.Y.C., 1981-82; assoc. Sullivan & Cromwell, N.Y.C., 1982-85; counsel Nat. Coalition for Homeless, Washington, 1985-89; founder and dir. Nat. Law Ctr. on Homelessness and Poverty, Washington, 1989—. Notes editor Columbia U. Law Rev., 1980-81. Harlan Fiske Stone scholar, 1978-79; John Dewey fellow. Mem. ABA (commr. Homelessness and Poverty). Home: 1444 Rhode Island Ave NW Washington DC 20005-5455 Office: Nat Law Ctr Homelessness & Poverty 918 F St NW Ste 412 Washington DC 20005-1105

FOSDICK, PATRICIA ANN, human resources director; b. Battle Creek, Mich., Apr. 7, 1937; d. Floyd Frank and Marie Delores (Wood) Eldridge; m. Roger Evan Fosdick, Sept. 27, 1957; children: Robert Lee, Deborah Sue Fox. AA in Bus., Kellogg C.C., Battle Creek, 1979; BA in Human Resources Mgmt., Spring Arbor Coll., 1990; vol. mgmt. cert., U. Colo.; postgrad., Western Mich. U., 1987. Asst. product mgr. Kraft-Gen. Foods Corp., Battle Creek, 1961-64; exec. dir. Area Coun. Chs., Battle Creek, 1977-79; dir. vol. personnel Calhoun County Red Cross, Battle Creek, 1979—; instr. Am. Red Cross, Washington, 1988—. Bd. dirs. Washington Heights Community Ministries, Battle Creek, 1986-91; v.p. bd. dirs. Altrusa Day Nursery, Battle Creek, 1986-92; pub. rels. chair Needlework Guild Am., Battle Creek, 1988—, Volunteerism In Action, Battle Creek, 1989-91, vol. mgmt. cons., 1990—. Grantee Am. Red Cross, Washington, 1989, 90; recipient ednl. scholarship Am. Bus. Women, Battle Creek, 1978, 79. Mem. NAFE, AAUW, Calhoun County Counseling Assn. (sec.-treas. 1992—), Mich. Assn. Vol. Adminstrs. (sec. bd. dirs. 1985-87). Home: 885 Riverside Dr Battle Creek MI 49015

FOSGATE HEGGLI, JULIE DENISE, producer; b. El Paso, Tex., Feb. 17, 1954; d. Orville Edward and Patricia (Ward) Fosgate; m. Bjarne Heggli, June 20, 1980; children: Elise Mai, Kristin April. BA in Broadcasting, U. So. Calif., 1976, MA in Journalism, 1978. On-board editor Royal Viking Line, San Francisco, 1978-80; editor Stentor, Trondheim, Norway, 1981; staff Grunion Gazette, Long Beach, Calif., 1981; news editor Nine Network Australia, Los Angeles, 1981-82; editor South Coast Metro News, Costa Mesa, Calif., 1981-82; v.p. The Newport Group, Newport Beach, Calif., 1982-85; exec. editor Orange County This Month, Newport Beach, 1985; exec. dir. mktg. Gen. Group Cos., Harbor City, Calif., 1985-87; sr. v.p. mktg. Automax Corp., L.A., 1987-88, Gen. Group Internat., Harbor City, Calif., 1988-90; assoc. producer Zoo Life Tv Spls., L.A., 1991; asoc. producer NBC News, Burbank, Calif., 1992-94; v.p. mktg. Western Nat., Scottsdale, Ariz., 1994—. Mem. Phi Beta Kappa. Home: # 2024 11333 N 92d St Scottsdale AZ 85260 Office: Western Nat 7272 E Indian School Rd Scottsdale AZ 85251

FOSHAY, MAXINE VALENTINE SHOTTLAND, civic worker, public relations executive; b. N.Y.C., Feb. 14, 1921; d. Maximillian Stanford and Violet Gertrude (Turner) Shottland; m. Robert Lethbridge Foshay, Mar. 16, 1956. B.A., Royal Acad. Dramatic Arts (London), 1943. Field rep. Am. Cancer Soc., N.Y.C., 1967-68; dir. fund raising and pub. rels. Preventive Medicine Inst., Strang Clinic 1969-71; dir. fund raising and pub. rels. Fedn. Handicapped, N.Y.C., 1971-72; exec. dir. Irvington House, 1972-73; chmn. group affiliates Meml. Sloan Kettering, 1960-66; v.p. Meml. Sloan Kettering Soc., 1966-67; vol. Meml. Sloan Kettering Cancer Soc., 1956-77; prin. Maxine V. Foshay and Assocs., 1977—; v.p. Victoria Home for Retired Men and Women, Ossining, N.Y., 1988—; bd. dirs. Elder Craftsman, N.Y.C.; dir. devel. Children's Asthmatic Found. N.Y. Mem. Daus. Brit. Empire State N.Y. (1st v.p. 1980-84, statewide pres. 1984-88, Medal Brit. Empire Her Majesty's Honours List 1987).

FOSLER, NORMA LORRAINE, counselor; b. Chgo., Jan. 26, 1930; d. Walter Frederick and Josephine L. (Graft) Apel; m. Jay Vincent Woosley, June 8, 1954 (dec. Feb. 1958); m. Gail Marvin Fosler, Aug. 4, 1967; 1 child, Scott Edwin. BEd, Nat. Coll. Edn., Evanston, Ill., 1951; MA, Stanford U., 1963. Cert. in elem. edn. 5th grade tchr. Santa Cruz (Calif.) City Schs., 1951-53; 6th grade tchr. Redwood City (Calif.) Sch. Dist., 1954-55; substitute tchr. Palo Alto (Calif.) Elem. Schs., 1955-56; coll. admissions counselor Nat. Coll. Edn., Evanston, Ill., 1958-62; coll. counselor Ladue (Mo.) Sch. Dist., 1964-66, New Trier Sch. Dist., Winnetka, Ill., 1966-67; counselor Parkland Coll., Champaign, Ill., 1967-69, 78-94; mem. H.S. Adv. Com. Champaign Sch. Dist., 1983-85; workshop dir. assertive tng. Champaign Sch. Dist., 1983-85. Election judge Champaign County Clks. Office, 1994—. Fellow Stanford U., 1963-64. Mem. ACA, Ill. Counseling Assn., U. Ill. Women's Club (v.p. Newcomers 1967-68). Presbyterian. Home: 1011 W Healey St Champaign IL 61821-3926

FOSNOCHT, REBECCA ANN, elementary education educator; b. Bryn Mawr, Pa., Feb. 10, 1966; d. Thomas Ashton and Mary Raymond (Lambert) F. BA, Amherst Coll., 1988; postgrad., Immaculata Coll., 1990-92, U. Pa., 1994—. Asst. tchr. PResbyn. Children's Village, Rosemont, Pa., 1989-90; tchr. ESL La. Comunidad Hispana, Kennett Swuare, Pa., 1989-91, Great Valley Sch. Dist., Malvern, Pa., 1992-94, Cheshire (Conn.) Sch. Dist., 1994—. Mem. NOW, Tchrs. English to Speakers of Other Langs., Marion Cricket Club.

FOSSLAND, JOEANN JONES, marketing professional, consultant; b. Balt., Mar. 21, 1948; d. Milton Francis and Clementine (Bowen) Jones; m. Richard E. Yellott III, 1966 (div. 1970); children: Richard E. IV, Dawn Joeann; m. Robert Gerard Fossland Jr., Nov. 25, 1982. Student, Johns Hopkins U., 1966-67; cert. in real estate, Hogan's Sch. Real Estate, 1982. Owner Kobble Shop, Indiatlantic, Fla., 1968-70, Downstairs, Atlanta, 1971; seamstress Aspen (Colo.) Leather, 1972-75; owner Backporch Feather & Leather, Aspen and Tucson, 1975-81; area mgr. Welcome Wagon, Tucson, 1982; realtor assoc. Tucson Realty & Trust, 1983-85; mgr. Home Illustrated mag., Tucson, 1985-87; asst. pub., gen. mgr. Phoenix, Scottsdale, Albuquerque, Tricities Tucson Homes Illustrated, 1990-93; pres. ADvantage Solutions Group, Cortaro, Ariz., 1993—; power leader Darryl Davis Seminars Power Program, 1995. Designer leather goods (Tucson Mus. Art award 1978, Crested Butte Art Fair Best of Show award 1980). Voter registrar Recorder's Office City of Tucson, 1985-91; bd. dirs. Hearth Found., Tucson, 1987—, pres., 1994; bd. dirs. Ariz. Integrated Residential & Ednl. Svcs., Inc., 1989—, pres. 1994—); mem. Hunger Project, Holiday Project. Mem. NAFE, Women's Coun. Realtors (Tucson chpt. pres. 1995, Tucson affiliate of yr. 1991, leadership tng. grad. designation 1989), Tucson Assn. Realtors (affiliate of yr. 1988). Democrat. Presbyterian. Office: Advantage Solutions Group PO Box 133 Cortaro AZ 85652-0133

FOSTER, BOBBIE DORE, newspaper editor; b. Abbeville, La., Nov. 28, 1938; d. Morris Allen and Mary Ann (Fontenette) Dore; m. Bernard Vance, July 28, 1979. Student, U. Washington, 1971-72, Western Washington State U., 1975-76, Portland State U., 1977-78; BA, U. Portland, 1989. Office mgr. The Skanner Newspaper, Portland, Oreg., 1977-78, copy editor, 1978-79, mng. editor, 1979-84, editor, 1984—; coord. Sch. Partnership Program: Journalism, Portland, 1990—. Bd. dirs. ARC Oregon Trail chpt., Portland, 1985-88, State Scholarship Commn., Eugene, Oreg., 1988-91, Community Action Agy., Portland, 1985-86; mem. Oreg. Peace Inst., 1988-89, Urban League Adv. Com., Portland, 1982-83. Recipient Edn. and Leadership in Politics, Edn. and Community Svc. award Oreg. Women's Polit. Caucus, Women of Color Task Force, Salem, Oreg., 1979, Support of Coop. Edn. Program award Portland Community Coll., 1985, Community Svc. award Black Women's Gathering, Portland, 1987, Svc. award ARC, Portland, 1988, 2nd pl. best editorial West Coast Black Pubs. Assn., Bakersfield, Calif., 1989. Mem. Women in Comm. (v.p. mem. 1984-85, v.p. profl. devel. 1988-89, Outstanding Cmty. Svc. award 1988, Offbeat award 1991), Black Cath. Lay Caucus (del. Nat. Black Cath. Congress 1988), Soc. Profl. Journalists (co-chmn. minority mentor program 1989-90), Nat. Assn. Black Journalists, Portland Assn. Black Journalists, Rotary Club (pres. 1993-94), Albina Club, Delta Sigma Theta Sorority Inc. (Women of Excellency award for cmty. svc. 1992). Roman Catholic. Office: The Skanner Group Newspapers 2337 N Williams Ave Portland OR 97227-1935

FOSTER, CATHERINE RIERSON, manufacturing company executive; b. Balt., Mar. 14, 1935; d. William Harman and Ella Fredericka (Magsamen) Rierson; m. Morgan Lawrence Foster, Nov. 17, 1957 (dec. Jan. 1990); children: Diana Kay, Susan Ann, Morgan Lawrence, Heather Lynne. Student, Balt. City Coll., 1955, Johns Hopkins U., 1956-57, Glendale Coll., 1962-63. Sec. Martin Co., Balt., 1956-57, adminstrv. sec., 1957-58; v.p., corp. sec. Fostermation, Inc., Meadville, Pa., 1971-90, pres., chmn. bd., 1990—, also bd. dirs.; mem. adv. com. Vocat./Tech. Sch., Meadville, 1982-86. Pres. La Crescents, La Crescenta, Calif., 1962; active City Hosp. Aux., Meadville, 1969-86, Rep. Women's Workshop, Glendale, Calif., 1966-68, Com. to Elect Ronald Reagan, Glendale, 1967; bd. dirs. YWCA, Meadville, 1988-89, also chmn. fin. com., 1988-89; bd. dirs. Jr. Achievement, Crawford County, Meadville, 1992-94. Mem. DAR (chpt. regent 1989-92), NAFE, Rotary, Zonta Internat., Order Eastern Star. Lutheran. Home: 1121 Lakemont Dr Meadville PA 16335-2826 Office: Fostermation Inc 200 Valleyview Dr Meadville PA 16335

FOSTER, CYNTHIA ANNETTE, business supply company owner; b. Dayton, Ohio, Mar. 17, 1939; d. Frederick Hughes II and Ruth Ann (Petry) Pfarrer; m. May 1, 1965; children: Cynthia Ann, Alyce Pfarrer. AB in Speech Pathology, Ind. U., 1961. Cert. clin. speech pathologist, ASHA. Initiator speech therapy program Boonville (Ind.) Sch. Corp., 1961, part-time speech therapist, 1961-62; part-time staff speech Rehab. Ctr., Evansville, Ind., 1961-62, staff speech therapist, 1962-66; co-owner Delta Supply Co. Evansville Inc., 1985—, v.p., sec., 1985—. Juror Circuit Ct., Evansville, 1989; vol. numerous orgsn., Evansville, 1969—; sec. McCutchanville Garden Club, Evansville, 1971. Mem. Jr. League Evansville (bd. dirs. 1972-78, editor newsletter 1974-75, treas. 1977-78, arrangements chair 1976-77), Gamma Phi Beta (treas. 1980-85, pres. 1985, Merit Roll cert. 1990), Sigma Alpha. Republican.

FOSTER, DIANE MARIE, elementary school counselor; b. St. Louis, June 17, 1946; d. Perry and Florence (Eubanks) F. AA, Meramec Jr. Coll., Kirkwood, Mo., 1966; BA, Webster Coll., 1968; MEd, U. Mo., 1975. Cert. classroom tchr., math specialist, counselor, psychol. examiner, sch. psychologist. Classroom tchr. Valley Park (Mo.) Sch. Dist., 1968-80, elem. sch. counselor, 1980—; chpt. I grant writer Valley Park (Mo.) Sch. Dist., 1980—, adminstrv. asst., 1981-82, student coun. sponsor 1981-86, 94, spl. edn. entitlement writer, 1982-85. Sunday sch. tchr. Manchester (Mo.) Heights Ch., 1977-78, Kirkwood (Mo.) Bapt. Ch., 1981-86. Mem. Am. Sch. Counseling Assn., Am. Counseling Assn. Home: 411 S Ballas Rd Kirkwood MO 63122 Office: Valley Park Elem Sch 356 Meramec Sta Rd Valley Park MO 63088

FOSTER, FRANCES, actress; b. Yonkers, N.Y., June 11, 1924; d. George Henry and Helen Elizabeth (Lloyd) Brown Davenport; m. Morton Goldsen, Sept. 11, 1982; m. Robert Standfield Foster, Mar. 29, 1941 (dec.); 1 son, Terrell Robert. Student, Am. Theatre Wing, N.Y.C., 1949-52. Artist in residence CCNY, N.Y.C., 1973-77; actress Negro Ensemble Co., N.Y.C., 1967-86. Appeared in plays throughout the world including, Munich Olympics, 1972; World Theatre Festival, London, 1969, Australia, 1977. Recipient Obie award, 1985. Mem. SAG, AFTRA, Actors Equity Assn. (councillor 1953-67). Democrat. Office: Marje Fields Inc 165 W 46th St New York NY 10036-2501

FOSTER, JOANNE MARY, librarian; b. Milw., June 1, 1946; d. Ray Arthur and Loretta Margaret (Cajski) Weslowski; m. Michael Alan Foster, June 14, 1969; children: Martha Hadley, Megan Hope. AB, Marquette U., 1968; MLS, U. Wis., Milw., 1969. Libr. Milw. Pub. Libr., Milw., 1970-71; head tech. svcs. Eureka (Ill.) Coll., 1977-90; libr. tech. svcs. Ill. Cen. Coll., East Peoria, 1990—. Trustee Ill. Prairie Dist. Pub. Libr., Metamora, 1978—, pres. bd. dirs., 1989—; bd. dirs. Ill. Valley Libr. System, Pekin, 1978-84. Mem. Amnesty Internat., Ill. Libr. Assn., Pax Christi. Roman Catholic. Home: RR 1 Metamora IL 61548-9801 Office: Ill Cen Coll 1 College Dr Peoria IL 61635-0001

FOSTER, JODIE (ALICIA CHRISTIAN FOSTER), actress; b. L.A., Nov. 19, 1962; d. Lucius and Evelyn (Almond) F. BA in Lit. magna cum laude, Yale U., 1985. Acting debut in TV show Mayberry, R.F.D, 1969; numerous other TV appearances including My Three Sons, The Courtship of Eddie's Father, Gunsmoke, Bonanza, Paper Moon, 1974-75; TV spl. The Secret Life of T.K. Dearing, 1975; TV movies Rookie of the Year, Smile, Jenny, You're Dead; motion picture appearances Napoleon and Samantha, 1972, Menace of the Mountain, One Little Indian, 1973, Tom Sawyer, 1973, Kansas City Bomber, 1972, Alice Doesn't Live Here Anymore, 1974, Taxi Driver, 1976 (Acad. award nominee for Best Supporting Actress), Echoes of a Summer, 1976, Bugsy Malone, 1976, Freaky Friday, 1976, The Little Girl Who Lives Down the Lane, 1977, Candleshoe, 1977, Foxes, 1980, Carny, 1980, O'Hara's Wife, 1982, Svengali, 1983, Hotel New Hampshire, 1984, The Blood of Others, 1984, Mesmerized, 1986, Siesta, 1986, Five Corners, 1986, Reckless Endangerment, Stealing Home, 1988, The Accused, 1988 (Acad. award for Best Actress, 1989), Backtrack, 1991, The Silence of the Lambs, 1991 (Golden Globe award for Best Actress in Drama, 1992, Acad. award for Best Actress, 1992), Shadows and Fog, 1992, Sommersby, 1993, Maverick, 1994; dir., actress: Little Man Tate, 1991; prodr., actress: Nell, 1994 (Acad. award nominee for Best Actress 1995). Recipient Golden Globe award, 1989. Office: care ICM 8942 Wilshire Blvd Beverly Hills CA 90211*

FOSTER, JOY VIA, library media specialist; b. Besoco, W.Va., Aug. 11, 1935; d. George Edward and Burgia Stafford (Earls) Via; m. Paul Harris Foster, Jr., Dec. 8, 1956 (dec. Dec. 1962); children: Elizabeth Lee, Michael Paul. BS, Radford Coll., 1971; MS, Radford U., 1979. Cert. pub. sch. libr., Va. Clk. Va. Tech. and State U., Blacksburg, 1955-57; clk. Christiansburg (Va.) Primary Sch., 1971-72, libr., 1972-85; libr. Auburn Mid. and High Sch., Riner, Va., 1985—. Meml. chmn. Am. Cancer Soc., Christiansburg, 1965-66; area chmn. Am. Heart Fund, Christiansburg, 1990-93, block worker, 1985-91. Mem. NEA, ALA, Am. Assn. Sch. Librs., Montgomery County Edn. Assn. (v.p. 1988-89, sec. 1989-91, bldg. rep. 1991—), Va. Ednl. Media Assn., Va. Ednl. Assn., Women of the Moose. Presbyterian. Office: Auburn Mid and H S 4163 Riner Rd Riner VA 24149

FOSTER, JOYCELON DAVIS, customer account executive; b. Bessemer, Ala., Oct. 22, 1957; d. Allie and Inell (Brown) Davis; m. Carl Edward Foster Sr., Dec. 29, 1979; children: Carl Edward Jr., Allison Inell. BA, U. Ala., 1979. Adminstrv. coord. Randall Pub. Co., Tuscaloosa, Ala., 1986-92; resource specialist Tuscaloosa (Ala.) County Juvenile Ct., 1992-93; customer svc. rep. Ala. Power Co., 1993-94; customer account exec. Comcast Cablevision, Tuscaloosa, Ala., 1994—. Copy editor: In Touch, 1991. Loaned exec. United Way, Tuscaloosa, 1991; asst. coord. Adopt-A-Sch., Tuscaloosa, 1991;

speaker C. of C. West Ala., Tuscaloosa, 1991; vol. staff Youth for Christ, Tuscaloosa, 1994. Mem. Nat. Mgmt. Assn., Ala. Power Svc. Orgn., Delta Sigma Theta Sorority Inc. (sgt.-at-arms 1991-93). Democrat. African Methodist Episcopal.

FOSTER, KATHRYN WARNER, newspaper editor; b. Charleston, S.C., Sept. 16, 1950; d. Jack Huntington Warner and Theodora (Heinsohn) Miller; m. William Chapman Foster, Sept. 11, 1971; children: William Huntington, Jonathan Chapman. BA in English, Newberry Coll., 1972. Obituary writer, TV editor Greenville (S.C.) News-Piedmont, 1971-72, asst. lifestyle editor, 1972-73, feature editor, 1973-78; Living Today copy editor Miami (Fla.) Herald, 1978-83, asst. weekend editor, 1984-86, asst. travel editor, 1986-91, editor in home and design dept., 1992-93, editor Getaways midweek travel page, 1993—; editor Miami Herald Dining Guide, 1988-91, asst. editor Destinations mag., 1990-91; speaker S.W. Fla. Writer's Conf., Ft. Myers, 1992. Contbr. articles to newspapers. Sec. Palmetto Elem. PTA, Miami, 1990-91. Recipient Penney-Mo. 1st pl. award for feature sects. U. Mo. Sch. Journalism, Columbia, 1978. Lutheran. Office: Miami Herald Travel Dept 1 Herald Pla Miami FL 33132-1689

FOSTER, LADESSA KAYE, counselor; b. Caldwell, Idaho, Apr. 21, 1964; d. Kenneth Wayne Hamilton and Tanya Marlene (Kearn) Pilote; m. Brian Wayne Foster, Sept. 24, 1988; children: Nicole Kaylee, Michael Wayne. BA in Psychology, Albertsons Coll. Idaho, 1985, MEd in Counseling, 1989. Lic. profl. counselor, Idaho. Psychol. assoc. Idaho State Sch. and Hosp., Nampa, 1989-91; social svc. designee Boise (Idaho) Samaritan Village, 1991-93; qualified mental retardation profl. Personal Care Svcs., Boise, 1991-93; counselor YWCA Crisis Ctr., Boise, 1991—; crisis counselor, sexual assault counselor Rape Crisis Alliance, Boise, 1991—. Author: (manual revision) Rape Crisis Alliance Manual, 1994. Mem. Am. Counseling Assn., Am. Mental Health Counselors Assn., Idaho Counseling Assn., Idaho Mental Health Counselors Assn. (bd. mem. 1993—, ethics chairperson 1993-94, profl. devel. chairperson 1994—), Idaho Victim Witness Assn. Office: YWCA Crisis Ctr 720 W Washington Boise ID 83702

FOSTER, LORRIE GAIL, training organization administrator; b. Tucson, Ariz., May 30, 1956; d. Frank N. and Madelyn (Petruso) F. AB in Diplomacy and World Affairs, Occidental Coll., 1978; MPA, Harvard U., 1992. Mgr. Pacific Telephone, L.A., 1978-83; loaned exec. L.A. Olympic Orgn. Com., 1983; mgr. pub. affairs and strategic planning AT&T Internat., Basking Ridge, N.J., 1983-88; exec. dir. Gov.'s Commn. on Internat. Trade, Newark, 1988-90; mktg. cons. Boston, N.Y. and N.J., 1990-93; mktg. dir. World Trade Inst., N.Y.C., 1993-94, exec. dir., 1994—; fgn. svc. officer intern USIA African Bur., Washington, 1977; bd. mem. Women in Internat. Trade, Washington, 1987-90. Adviser United Way, N.J., 1989-90; bd. mem. Resource Ctr. for Women and Their Families, Somerset, N.J., 1989-91. Mem. Am. Aritration Assn. (comml. arbitrator 1992—). Office: World Trade Inst 1 World Trade Ctr 55 New York NY 10048

FOSTER, LYNN, law librarian, lawyer; b. Chgo., Nov. 10, 1952; d. James Thomas and Janet Carol (Burkwest) F.; 1 child, Patrick Andrew. AB, U. Ill., 1973, MS, 1975; JD, So. Ill. U., 1982. Bar: Ill. 1983. Reader svcs. libr. So. Ill. U. Law Library, Carbondale, 1982-83; dir. law libr. Ohio No. U. Law Library, Ada, 1983-86, U. Ark. at Little Rock Law Libr., 1986—. Co-Author: Subject Compilations of State Laws, 1981 (Andrews award 1982), Legal Research Exercises, 1983, 4th rev. edit., 1992; author: Arkansas Legal Bibliography: Documents and Selected Commercial Titles, 1988. Mem. ABA, Am. Assn. Law Libraries, Mid Am. Assn. Law Libraries, S.W. Assn. Law Libraries. Office: U Ark at Little Rock Law Libr 1203 Mcalmont St Little Rock AR 72202-5142

FOSTER, MAMOSA BEWLEY, principal; b. Knoxville, Tenn., Apr. 23, 1949; d. Charles Thomas and Elizabeth (Brown) Bewley; m. John B. Foster, Jr., June 2, 1969; children: Shaunna Patrice, John B. III, Charles Adrian. BS in Edn., Knoxville Coll., 1971; MS in Curriculum and Instrn., U. Tenn., 1989, EdS in Adminstrn. and Supervision, 1991. Tchr. Knox County Schs., Knoxville, 1971-87, 88-89, curriculum facilitator, 1989-90, adminstrv. intern, 1990-91, asst. prin., 1991-93, prin., 1993—; career ladder evaluator Dept. Edn., State of Tenn., Nashville, 1987-88; faculty assoc. U. Tenn., Knoxville, 1986—; sci. cons. U. Tenn., Martin, 1989-90. Columnist Halls Shopper, 1990. Bd. dirs. Boys and Girls Clubs Am., Knoxville, 1993-94, Knox Housing Partnership, Knoxville, 1993-94; housing cons. Knoxville Area Urban League, 1993-94. Cultural Enrichment grantee City of Knoxville Dept. Parks and Recreation, 1993; recipient Best award for tchg. Greater Knoxville C. of C., 1990, Best award for prin. and sch., 1994. Mem. NEA (del. to rep. assembly), NAFE, Tenn. Edn. Assn. (del. to rep. assembly), Nat. Assn. Elem. Sch. Prins., Tenn. Assn. Elem. Sch. Prins., Knox County Edn. Assn. (chairperson minority affairs), Pi Lambda Theta. Home: 1426 Patricia Cir Knoxville TN 37914

FOSTER, MARCIA WILLIAMS, national account manager; b. Mobile, Ala., Sept. 28, 1950; d. D.V. and Erma Ganelle (Deese) Williams; m. Ronald Stewart Foster, Aug. 21, 1971 (div. Nov. 1987), remarried Sept. 1, 1990; children: Michael Stewart, Susan Genelle. Student, Spring Hill Coll., 1968-71; cert. gen. ins., Ins. Inst. Am., 1983. Cert. ins. profl., ins. counselor. Ins. sec., receptionist Millette & Assocs. Inc., Pascagoula, Miss., 1973-74; personal lines rep. Ross-King-Walker, Inc., Pascagoula, 1974-76; personal lines customer svc. Kennedy Ins. Agy., Inc., San Jose, Calif., 1978-79; personal lines customer svc. Baumhauer-Croom Ins., Inc., Mobile, 1976-78, underwriting sec., asst. to pres., 1980-82; adminstrv. asst. to pres. Lyon Fry Cadden Ins. Agy., Inc., Mobile, 1982-94; account mgr., nat. accounts Willis Corroon Corp. of Mobile, Mobile, Ala., 1994—. Vol. Cystic Fibrosis Found., Mobile, 1985-90, Matthews City Park, Ranger Babe Ruth, Mobile, 1989—. Named Ala. State Ins. Woman of Yr., Ala. Ind. Ins. Agts., 1985. Mem. Ins. Women of Mobile (ednl. course instr. 1987—, pres. 1986-87, Presdl. Svc. award 1984, Mobile Ins. Woman of Yr. 1985, Anna S. Loding Meml. award 1990), Nat. Assn. Ins. Women Internat. (chmn. Ala. state conf. 1992, asst. region III dir. 1986-87, mem. Ala. coun.), Soc. Cert. Ins. Counselors (cert.). Episcopalian. Home: 3584 Pepper Ridge Dr Mobile AL 36693-2555 Office: Willis Corroon Corp of Mobile PO Box 2407 Mobile AL 36652

FOSTER, MARY FRAZER (MARY FRAZER LECRON), anthropologist; b. Des Moines, Feb. 1, 1914; d. James and Helen (Cowles) LeCron; B.A., Northwestern U., 1936; Ph.D., U. Calif., Berkeley, 1965; m. George McClelland Foster, Jan. 6, 1938; children—Jeremy, Melissa Foster Bowerman. Research asso. dept. anthropology U. Calif., Berkeley, 1955-57, 75—; lectr. in anthropology Calif. State U., Hayward, 1966-75; mem. faculty Fromm Inst. Lifelong Learning, U. San Francisco, 1980. Fellow AAAS, Am. Anthropol. Assn.; mem. Linguistic Soc. Am., Internat. Linguistic Assn., Southwestern Anthrop. Assn., Soc. Woman Geographers. Democrat. Author: (with George M. Foster) Sierra Popoluca Speech, 1948; The Tarascan Language, 1969; editor: (with Stanley H. Brandes) Symbol As Sense: New Approaches to the Analysis of Meaning, 1980, (with Robert A. Rubinstein) Peace and War: Cross-Cultural Perspectives, 1986, (with Robert A. Rubinstein) The Social Dynamics of Peace, 1988 (with Lucy J. Botscharow) The Life of Symbols, 1990. Home: 790 San Luis Rd Berkeley CA 94707-2030

FOSTER, NANCY HASTON, columnist, author; b. Austin, Tex., June 7; d. Arch B. and Verlea (Jones) Haston; m. Joe D. Foster Jr. (div.). BJ, U. Tex., BA in Sociology. Writer, pub. rels. dept. Trinity U., San Antonio, Tex.; social worker pub. welfare dept. State of La., Lafayette; instr. sociology U. Tex., Austin; columnist San Antonio Light, 1982-83, San Antonio Express-News, 1989-90; freelance writer, 1977—. Co-author: San Antonio, A Texas Monthly Guidebook, 1983, rev. edit., 1989, 94; author: The Alamo and Other Texas Missions to Remember, 1984; contbg. editor, writer: Texas, Fodor's Travel Guides, 1985, rev. edit., 1991, Fodor's American Cities, 1986, rev. edit., 1988, Texas, A Texas Monthly Guidebook, 1993; contbr. articles to popular mags. Mem. Women in Communications, Phi Beta Kappa. Home and Office: 412 Cloverleaf Ave # 3 San Antonio TX 78209-4115

FOSTER, R. PAM, interior designer; b. Fleet, Hants, Eng., June 17, 1946; came to U.S., 1991; d. William Henry and Mabel (Selby) Melville; m. Ernest William Bracken, Feb. 4, 1991; children from a previous marriage: Paul Melville, Nina Kathleen. Student in Bus., Clark's Coll., Guildford, Surrey, Eng., 1964. From sec. to dir. sales Brit. Caledonian Airways, Gatwick, Eng., 1969-71, sr. mktg. exec., 1985-89; v.p. Transcontinental Svcs., London, 1973-81; owner, pres. Claremont Travel Ltd., Hurstpierpoint, Eng., 1981-85; mgr. interior design Brit. Airways, London, 1989-91; pres., owner House of Melville, Inc., Leesburg, Va., 1993—. Local organizer Cystic Fibrosis Rsch. Trust, Sussex, Eng., 1974-84. Office: House of Melville RR1 Box 361 Leesburg VA 22075

FOSTER, RUTH MARY, dental association administrator; b. Little Rock, Jan. 11, 1927; d. William Crosby and Frances Louise (Doering) Shaw; m. Luther A. Foster, Sept. 8, 1946 (dec. Dec. 1980); children: William Lee, Robert Lynn. Grad. high sch., Long Beach, Calif. Sr. hostess Mon's Food Host of Coast, Long Beach, 1945-46; dental asst., office mgr. Dr. Wilfred H. Allen, Opportunity, Wash., 1946-47; dental asst., bus. asst. Dr. H. Erdahl, Long Beach, 1948-50; office mgr. Dr. B.B. Blough, Spokane, Wash., 1950-52; bus. mgr. Henry G. Kolsrud, D.D.S., P.S., Spokane, 1958—, Garland Dental Bldg., Spokane, 1958—. Sustaining mem. Spokane Symphony Orch. Mem. Nat. Assn. Dental Assts., DAV Aux., DAV Comdr.'s Club, Wash. State Fedn. of Bus. and Profl. Women (dist. 6 dir.), Spokane's Lilac City Bus. and Profl. Women (pres.), Nat. Alliance Mentally Ill, Wash. Alliance Mentally Ill, Spokane Alliance Mentally Ill, Internat. Platform Assn., Spokane Club, Credit Women's Breakfast Club, Dir.'s Club, Inland N.W. Zool. Soc. Democrat. Mem. First Christian Ch. Office: Henry G Kolsrud DDS PS 3718 N Monroe St Spokane WA 99205-2850

FOSTER, RUTH SULLIVAN, state senator; b. Machias, Maine, Apr. 18, 1929; d. John Francis and Edith Meserve Sullivan; m. Charles Foster Jr. (div.); children: Jennifer Libby, Jacquelyn Dearborn. Student, U. Maine. Licensed real estate broker. Mem. Maine State Ho. Reps. from 127th dist., Maine State Senate from 12th dist. Former mem. city coun. Ellsworth, Maine; former mayor Ellsworth, 1978-81; active Hancock County Pub. Lands & Reservations; bd. dirs. Maine Coast Meml. Hosp. Republican. Home: 95 Main St Ellsworth ME 04605-1902 Office: Maine State Senate State Capitol Augusta ME 04330*

FOSTER, SCARLETT LEE, public relations executive; b. Charleston, W.Va., Dec. 14, 1956; d. William Christoph Foster, Jr. and Anne (Howes) Conway. B in Comm., Bethany Coll., 1979. Dir. pub. rels. Allergy Rehab. Found., Charleston, 1979-80; dir. pubs. Contractors Assn. W.Va., Charleston, 1980-82; comm. rep. Monsanto Co., Nitro, W.Va., 1982-84, 1984-87; mgr. environ. and community rels. Monsanto Co., St. Louis, 1987-89, mgr. pub. rels., 1989-91, mgr. fin. pub. rels., 1991-93, dir. pub. rels., 1993-94, dir. corp. pub. rels., 1994—. Bd. dirs. Sta. KWMU Pub. Radio, St. Louis, 1992—; trustee Bethany (W.Va.) Coll., 1994—. Named Outstanding Alumni of Achievement Bethany Coll., 1990. Mem. Internat. Assn. Bus. Communicators (Gold Quill award of Merit). Episcopalian. Office: Monsanto Co A2SP 800 N Lindbergh Blvd Saint Louis MO 63167

FOSTER, VERA A. CHANDLER, social worker; b. Indianola, Miss., Aug. 9, 1915; d. William Henry and Maria Grey Chandler; m. Luther Hilton Foster Jr., Aug. 27, 1941; children: Adrienne Foster Williams, L. Hilton. BA magna cum laude, Fisk U., 1936; MA, U. Nebr., 1941, U. Chgo., 1950; social work cert., U. Minn., 1941; LHD (hon.), Tuskegee U., 1981. Sec. to pres. Va. State U., Petersburg, 1936-39; dean women, sociology instr. Langston (Okla.) U., 1942-43; rsch. assoc. Tuskegee (Ala.) U., 1943-48, assoc. dir. Tuskegee Inst. Cmty. Edn. Program, 1966-68; mental hygienist Jaandrew Hosp., Tuskegee, 1950; social worker, supr. field instrn. Tuskegee VA Med. Ctr., 1950-81. Mem. World Coun. YWCA, N.Y.C., 1960-66, Nat. Bd. YWCA, N.Y.C., 1962-66, Ala. Law Enforcement Planning Agy., 1973-76, Ala. Youth Svcs. Bd., 1974-81, State Bd. of Social Work Examiners, 1977-80, No. Va. Group on Aging, 1992—; mem. Ala. adv. com. U.S. Civil Rights Commn., Montgomery, 1959-81; bd. dirs. Women's Internat. League for Peace & Freedom, Phila., 1962-66, Planned Parenthood, N.Y.C., 1966-72, Vol.-The Nat. Ctr., Washington, 1977-91, Common Cause, Washington, 1978-84, Ind. Sector, Washington, 1980-84, Alexandria (Va.) Cmty. "Y", 1983-87; del. White House Confs., Washington, 1951, 69, 70, 71, 81; cmty. svc. cons. to pres. Ala. Federated Women's Clubs, Tuskegee, 1964-67; cmty. svc. cons. S.E. Ala. Self-Help Assn., Tuskegee, 1968-78, Sr. Citizen's Program, Tuskegee, 1970-78; cons. to Ala. state dir. NAACP, Tuskegee, 1968-75; mem. Va. Gov. Adv. Commn. on Aging, Richmond, 1984-90. Rosenwald fellow Julius Rosenwald Fund, 1940-41, March of Dimes Found. fellow, 1949-50; recipient Alumni Pub. Svc. award U. Nebr., 1971, U. Chgo., 1972, Outstanding So. Women's award So. Women Archives, 1981. Mem. NASW (v.p. Ala. chpt. 1972-74, Ala. Social Worker of Yr. 1974), Sr. Citizens Employment Svcs. Alexandria (sec. 1992-94), The Links (25 Yr. Quality of Life Contbns. award 1992), Delta Sigma Theta, Phi Beta Kappa. Democrat. Episcopalian. Home: 309 S Yoakum Pky Apt 1507 Alexandria VA 22304-3905

FOSTER, VIRGINIA, retired botany educator; b. Joseph, Oreg., Feb. 4, 1914; d. Perry Alexander and Genevieve (Shain) F. BS, U. Wash., 1949, MS, 1950; PhD, Ohio State U., 1954. Prof. Judson Coll., Marion, Ala., 1956-58; prof. Miss. State Coll. for Women, Columbus, 1958-59, LaVerne (Calif.) Coll., 1959-60, Calif. Western U., San Diego, 1960-61, Pensacola (Fla.) Jr. Coll., 1962-84. Author: (lab. manual) The Botany Laboratory, 1976, rev. edit., 1985, 3d edit., 1991. Home: 9270 Scenic Hwy Pensacola FL 32514-8054

FOSTER VARGAS, KATHLEEN DIANE, legal administrator; b. Boston, Feb. 22, 1951; d. Joseph Ernest and Barbara Shirley (Dundas) Emge; children: Christian Andrew Fabian, Michelle Diane; m. Howard Vargas, 1995. BA in Anthropology/Archaeology, Pacific Luth. U., 1984, MA in Anthropology/Archaeology, 1984; JD, Am. Coll. of Law, 1989. Sec. New England Regional Primate Rsch. Ctr., Harvard Med. Sch., Southborough, Mass., 1969-72; typesetter Hudson Sun/Marlboro (Mass.) Enterprise, 1970-72, Framingham (Mass.) News, 1975-76, TOWN Crier, Wayland, Mass., 1975-77; tchr. English Castillo Escuela, Guadalajara, Mexico, 1972-74; rsch. asst. U. Calif., Irvine, 1978-80; rsch. assoc. Hoko River Archaeol. Project, Pullman, Wash., 1981-84; law clk., investigator Law Offices of Leonard Moen, Tacoma, 1984-86; law clk. Law Offices of Thomas Moga, Upland, Calif., 1986-90; hearing rep. Law Offices of Grant Lynd, Westminster, Calif., 1990—. Asst. (film) Battered Women/Convicted Killers, 1981. Asst. leader Brownies/Girl Scouts, Puyallup, Wash., 1981-85. Recipient Am. Jurisprudence award for appellate advocacy Lawyers Coop/Bancroft Whitney Pub., 1988, Am. Jurisprudence award for uniform comm. code, 1988. Mem. Bus. and Profl. Women's Assn., Nat. Notary Assn. Democrat. Office: Law Offices of Grant A. Lynd 14340 Bolsa Chica Rd # B Westminster CA 92635

FOTI, MARGARET ANN, association executive, editor; b. Phila., Dec. 15, 1944; d. Samuel A. and Margaret M. (DiBiase) F. B.A., Temple U., M.A. in Communications, 1985, postgrad, 1985—. Tech. editor U. Pa., Phila., 1962-64, asst. to bus adminstr., 1964-65; sr. editorial asst. Cancer Rsch. Jour., Phila., 1965-69, mng. editor, 1969—; exec. dir. Am. Assn. Cancer Rsch., Phila., 1982—, dir. publs., 1990—; adminstrn., pub. edn., devel., editorial and pub. cons., lectr. in field. Contbr. articles to profl. jours. Pres. Nat. Coalition for Cancer Rsch., 1994—. Recipient Cert. of Appreciation Am. Assn. Cancer Rsch., 1975, 85, 90, Coun. Biology Editors, 1984. Mem. AAAS, Am. Soc. Assn. Execs., Am. Assn. Cancer Research, European Assn. for Cancer Rsch., European Assn. Sci. Editors, Internat. Fedn. Sci. Editors, Soc. Sch. Publs., Soc. for Scholarly Publs. (pres.-elect 1994—), Council Biology Editors, Council Engrs. and Sci. Soc. Execs., AAAS. Democrat. Roman Catholic. Home: 220 Locust St Apt 24A Philadelphia PA 19106-3932 Office: Am Assn Cancer Rsch Pub Ledger Bldg Ste 816 150 S Independence Mall W Philadelphia PA 19106-3483

FOTOPOULOS, SOPHIA STATHOPOULOS, medical scientist, administrator; b. Kansas City, Mo., Nov. 6, 1936; d. Marinos G. and Stavroula (Fotopoulos) Stathopoulos; m. Chris K. Fotopoulos, Aug. 27, 1963 (div.). B.A., U. Kans., 1958, M.A., 1964, Ph.D., 1970. Diplomate Behavioral Scis. Regulatory Bd. State of Kans., Council for Nat. Register of Health Service Providers. Research asst. U. Kans. Med. Ctr., Kansas City, 1958-61; research assoc. Inst. Community Studies, Kansas City, Mo., 1965-66; lectr. U. Kans., Lawrence, 1969-70; dir. Psychophysiology-pharmacology Lab. Greater Kansas City (Mo.) Mental Health Found., 1970-73; staff assoc. neuropsychophysiology, 1973, Midwest Research Inst., Kansas City, Mo., 1974-75, head Psychophysiology Lab., 1975-77, assoc. dir. chem. scis. div., 1977-79, dir. life scis. div., 1979-84; dean, dir. rsch. Am. U., Washington, 1984-87; exec. v.p., CEO Immucomp, Inc., 1987-92; pres., CEO Bioactive Tech., 1992—. prof. dept. medicine Kansas U. Med. Ctr., 1987—; spl. rev. com. Nat. Cancer Inst., 1978—; mem. adv. com. Am. Cancer Soc., 1982—; lectr. U. Mo.-Kansas City Sch. Medicine, 1970-84. NIH research fellow, 1962-64, HHS research fellow, 1965-69; recipient Creative Scientist award Am. Inst. Research, 1971. Mem. AAAS, Claude Bernard Soc., Internat. Soc. for Antiviral Rsch., N.Y. Acad. Scis., Biofeedback Soc. Am., Mo. Biofeedback Soc. (pres. 1979-80), Sigma Xi. Greek Orthodox. Clubs: Zonta (pres. KCII 1983—). Contbr. articles to profl. jours. Office: Bioactive Tech 11850 W 85th St Shawnee Mission KS 66214-1581

FOUCHÉ, HELEN STROTHER, editorial design executive; b. Washington, Apr. 19, 1939; d. James Herschel and Elizabeth Ellen (Wright) Strother; m. Robert Michael Fouché, Oct. 20, 1962; children: James Michael, David Carroll, Stephen Charles. BA cum laude, Auburn U., 1960; student, Belles Artes, Managua, Nicaragua, 1964-65; student Intensive Lang. Tng., Fgn. Svc. Inst., 1961, 73; grad., Am. Transp. Inst., 1983. Asst. producer-dir. Internat. TV Svcs., U.S. Info. Agy., Washington, 1960-62; diplomatic svcs. with fgn. svc. husband U.S. Dept. of State, Europe, Africa, Cen./So. Am., 1963-81; art instr. for internat. children's classes La Paz, Bolivia, 1979; community liaison officer U.S. Embassy, La Paz, 1979-81; internat. group coord. Group Travel Unlimited, Alexandria, Va., 1983-84, mktg. creative/tech. writer, 1985-86; mng. editor Am. Leisure Industries, Lanham, Md., 1986-87; editor, cons. Washington Editorial Svcs., DC and Met. area, 1987-88; pres. Washington Editorial Svcs. Inc., Washington, Arlington, Va., 1988—; founding bd. dirs. Fgn. Svc. Youth Found., Washington, 1989-91; cons. Overseas Briefing Ctr., Fgn. Svc. Inst., U.S. Dept. of State, Arlington, 1981—; travel cons., tour mgr. Acad. Travel Abroad, Inc., 1990—, Travelcorp Inc., 1991—; media cons. designed slide shows, wrote scripts for non-profit causes. Contbg. editor, columnist: Diplomatic Digest, others; editor FS EYE for U.S. Dept. of State, 1991-94; mem. editorial bd. Fgn. Svc. Jour., 1989-92; executed murals, Crippled Children's Ward Managua (Nicaragua) Gen. Hosp., 1964, Montessori Sch., La. Paz, 1980; contbr. articles to profl. publs. Pres. Episcopal Ch. Women of St. Michael's, 1989-90, mem. vestry, 1990-94; mem. Altar Guild, 1982—, lector, 1984—; mem. Bus. Coun. Internat. Understanding. Recipient Vol. of Yr. award, Tampa, Fla., 1970; named for Exceptional Cross-Cultural Effectiveness, Fgn. Svc. Inst., Dept. of State, 1988, one of Outstanding Young Women of Am., 1973. Mem. AAUW, DAR, Assn. of Am. Fgn. Svc. Women (bd. mem., editorial com., newsletter editor), Nat. Press Club, Internat. Women's Media Found., Jamestown Soc., Order of Charlemagne, Alpha Gamma Delta Alumnae Assn. Democrat. Episcopalian. Home and Office: Washington Editorial Svcs 1509 N Kentucky St Arlington VA 22205-2824

FOULK, DEBRA LEE, financial executive; b. Estherville, Iowa, Oct. 15, 1956; d. Robert Jay and Helen Darlene (Hayes) Richey; m. George Fredrick Foulk, Apr. 26, 1977; children: Rochelle Ann, Jason Everett, Jennifer Lynn. AA, Suisun C.C., 1976. Journeyman clk. Lucky Stores, Inc., Richmond, Calif., 1977-80; data processing clk. Vallejo (Calif.) Gen. Hosp., 1979-81, acct., 1981-85; asst. to contr. Woodland (Calif.) Meml. Hosp., 1985-89, budget coord., 1989-92; budget mgr. Woodland Healthcare, 1992—. Active Friends of Dixon (Calif.) Libr., 1994. Mem. Healthcare Fin. Assn. Mgmt. (mem. long term care com. 1992-93). Home: 1620 Winfield St Dixon CA 95620-4249

FOULK, DOROTHY MARGARET, nurse; b. Springfield, Mo., June 18, 1946; d. Hugh Griff and Lillian M. (Pearson) DeBord; m. Gary Donald Foulk, May 22, 1964; children: Donald Ray, Laurene Ann. Student, SW Bapt. U., 1988-91; AS in Nursing, SW Mo. State U., 1990. RNC. Owner retail bus. Montier, Mo., 1968-89; nurse technician Ozark's Med. Ctr., West Plains, Mo., 1989, clin. coord. neuro-psych unit, 1990—. Mem. Bus. and Profl. Women. Baptist. Home: Highway 60 Montier MO 65546 Office: Ozarks Med Ctr Neuro-Psych Unit 1103 Alaska St West Plains MO 65775-2001

FOULKE, SARAH SYLVIA, home economist; b. Phila., May 31, 1940; d. John Ashley Roberts and Iva Smith Carll; m. Richard L. Foulke, Nov. 24, 1966 (div. Mar. 1984). BSc in Home Econs., Temple U., 1962; MSc in Life Span Devel., U. Del., 1980, PhD in Family Studies, 1989. Rsch. assoc. U. Del., Newark, 1978-80; coop. extension agt. Del. Coop. Extension, Georgetown, 1980-90; Sussex County coord. Del. Coop. Extension, Newark, 1985-87; asst. prof. dept. individual and family studies Coll. Human Resources, U. Del., Newark, 1989-90, rsch. asst. dept. individual and family studies, 1987-88; coop. extension agt., home econs. program leader Cornell Coop. Extension of Suffolk County, Riverhead, N.Y., 1990—; adj. prof. grad. program in gerontology dept. social sci. L.I. U., Southampton, N.Y., 1993—; presenter in field. Mem. editorial bd. Jour. for Nutrition of Elderly, 1993—; contbr. articles to profl. publs. Mem. program com. Del. Women's Conf., 1988; mem. county com. Read Aloud Del., 1988-90; mem. com. L.I. Nutrition Network, Families for Self Sufficiency Coalition, 1992—; mem. Suffolk County Perinatal Coalition, 1991—; mem. subcom. Hunger on L.I., 1992—; mem. adv. bd. Primary Care INitiative of Univ. Hosp., SUNY, Stony Brook, 1993—; bd. dirs., health svcs. com. L.I. Head Start Child Devel. Svcs., Inc., 1993—; bd. dirs. Sussex County Home Svcs., 1986-88, Arthritis Found., Del., 1985-86. Grantee EPA, 1991, 92-94, 92-93, Mid-Atlantic Fisheries, 1992-93, Nat. Consumer Credit Edn. and AT&T Fund, 1991-92, Wyandanch Union Free Sch., 1990-91; Mary Nell Greenwood fellow, 1987; recipient Vol. award Arthritis Found., 1983, Outstanding Svc. award Del. Pork Producers, 1984, Outstanding Community Support for Culinary Hearts Kitchen award Am. Heart Assn., 1984, Mid Career award Epsilon Sigma Phi, 1993, Outstanding Alumnae award U. Del. Coll. Human Resources, 1994. Mem. Nat. Coun. on Family Rels., Am. Home Econs. Assn., N.Y. State Nutrition Coun., Nutrition Coun. Greater N.Y., Groves Family Conf., N.Y. State Assn. Ext. Home Economists (bd. dirs., v.p. 1993-94, Spl. Svc. Agt. award 1993), N.Y. State Home Econs. Assn. (bd. dirs., ext. sect. chair 1992, 93, 94, bd. dirs. L.I. dist. 1991, 92, pres. 1992-93), Nat. Assn. Ext. Home Economists (arrangements com. 1989), Epsilon Sigma Phi, Kappa Omicron Nu. Office: Cornell Coop Extension 246 Griffing Ave Riverhead NY 11901

FOULKROD, SARAH SUTHERLAND, librarian; b. Clintwood, Va., Aug. 26, 1949; d. Benjamin Fulton and Sarah Neal (Cothron) Sutherland; m. Charles Bruce Foulkrod, Aug. 4, 1973; 1 child, Charles Matthew. BA, U. Ky., 1971; MLS, U. Pitts., 1972. Reference libr. Wilmington (Del.) Inst. Libr., 1972-77, coordinator, acquisitions, 1974-77; libr. Solebury Sch., New Hope, Pa., 1993—. Trustee Free Libr. of Northampton Twp., Richboro, Pa., 1981-87; mem. Dist. Adv. Com. for Bucks County Librs., Doylestown, Pa., 1987-91; sec. Friends of the Libr., Richboro, 1989-92. Mem. AAUW, Pa. Libr. Assn., Embroiderers Guild of Am. Republican. Methodist.

FOUNTAIN, ANNE OWEN, Spanish language educator; b. Buenos Aires, Aug. 30, 1946; d. George Earle and Margaret Frances (Richards) Owen; m. Alvin Marcus Fountain II, June 20, 1970; children: Catherine Anne, Elizabeth Moore. BA with honors in Spanish, Ind. U., 1966, MA, 1968; PhD, Columbia U., 1973, cert. in Latin Am. studies, 1973. Publs. asst. The Hispanic Soc. Am., N.Y.C., 1970-71; Spanish instr. Peace Coll., Raleigh, N.C., 1972-75, spl. studies coord., 1975-85, ind. study/honors coord., 1985-87, Alumnae Disting. prof. Spanish, 1988—; cons. Acad. Alliances, N.C. World Ctr., N.C. Global Lang. Camps Inc. Contbr.: Essays on Comedy and the Gracioso in Plays by Agustin Moreto, 1986; contbr. articles to profl. jours. Co-chair cultural exhibits Internat. Festival of Raleigh, 1990-91; vol. Meals on Wheels, Raleigh, 1985—; active Hillyer Meml. Christian Ch. Nat. def. fgn. lang. fellow Ind. U., Bloomington, 1966-67; faculty fellow Columbia U., N.Y.C., 1967-70. Mem. MLA, Am. Assn. Tchrs. Spanish and Portuguese (pres. N.C. chpt. 1984-86, Teaching award 1994), Assn. Depts. Fgn. Langs., S.E. Coun. L.Am. Studies (exec. coun. 1990—, pres.-elect 1992-93, pres. 1993-94, chmn. 1995-96), So. Conf. on Lang. Teaching (adv. bd., bd. dirs., vice chmn. 1993-94), Fgn. Lang. Assn. N.C. (hon. life, pres. 1987-89), Delta Kappa Gamma, Sigma Delta Mu (v.p. 1988-92, pres. 1992—). Home: 2620 Mayview Rd Raleigh NC 27607-6917 Office: Peace Coll 15 E Peace St Raleigh NC 27604-1194

FOUNTAIN, EUGENIA FERRIS, library director; b. 1959. BA, U. Conn., Storrs, 1981; MLS, Simmons Coll., 1985. Ref. libr. Essex Inst.,

Salem, Mass., 1985-88; dir. libr. svcs. Marian Ct. Coll., Swampscott, Mass., 1988—. Office: Marian Ct Coll 35 Littles Point Rd Swampscott MA 01907-2896

FOUNTAIN, KAREN SCHUELER, physician; b. Aberdeen, S.D., Oct. 14, 1947. BA, No. State Coll., Aberdeen, S.D., 1968; MD, U. Md., Balt., 1972. Diplomate Nat. Bd. Med. Examiners, Am. Bd. Radiology in Therapeutic Radiology. Intern Md. Gen. Hosp., Balt., 1972-73, resident in radiation oncology, 1973-74; fellow in radiation oncology Mayo Clinic, Rochester, Minn., 1974-76, cons. in oncology, 1976-81; clin. asst. prof. Columbia U., N.Y.C., 1981-83, residency program dir. dept. radiation oncology, 1981-93, clin. assoc. prof., 1983—; mem. med. bd. Presbyn. Hosp., N.Y.C., 1983-86; faculty coun. mem. Columbia U., 1982-89; del. N.Y. State Radiological Soc., N.Y.C., 1987—. Fellow Am. Coll. Radiology, N.Y. Acad. Medicine; mem. Am. Soc. Therapeutic Radiology and Oncology, Radiol. Soc. N.Am., Am. Radium Soc., Am. Soc. Clin. Oncology, N.Y. Roentgen Soc. (sec. chair 1989-90). Office: Columbia-Presbyn Med Ctr Rad Onc 622 W 168th St New York NY 10032-3702

FOUNTAIN, LINDA KATHLEEN, health science association executive; b. Fowler, Kans., Apr. 30, 1954; d. Ralph Edward and Ruth Evelyn (Cornelson) Young; m. Andre Fountain. BS in Nursing, Cen. State U., Edmond, Okla., 1976. RN, Okla. Staff nurse med./surg. and coronary care unit Presbyn. Hosp., Oklahoma City, 1976-79; mgr. nursing Hillcrest Osteo. Hosp., Oklahoma City, 1979-80; staff nurse, mgr. Oklahoma U. Teaching Hosp., Oklahoma City, 1981-82; pres. New Life Programs, Oklahoma City, 1981-88, Nursing Entrepreneurs, Ltd., Oklahoma City, 1988—; mgr. Internat. Health Supply, Oklahoma City, 1988—; coord. lactation cons. program State of Okla., 1981—, new life car seat rental program at various hosps., 1983—, also speaker Success Co., Oklahoma City, 1984—; owner Rainbows Overhead Graphic Media, Oklahoma City, 1984-91; speaker in field. Founder Praxis Coll., Oklahoma City, 1988. Named Mentor of Yr., Okla. Metroplex Childbirth Network, Oklahoma City, 1984. Mem. Am. Nurses Assn., Internat. Lactation Cons. Assn., Internat. Platform Assn., Bodyworkers and Wellness Therapies Assn. Office: Nursing Entrepreneurs Ltd PO Box 75393 Oklahoma City OK 73147-0393

FOURCARD, INEZ GAREY, foundation executive, artist; b. Bklyn.; d. George W. and Frances E. (MacDonald) Garey; student Pratt Inst., 1946-48; BFA, McNeese State U., 1963; diploma Maestro di Pittura Arti Modernea e Contemporaneo, Salsomaggiore, Italy, 1982. Waldren Arthur Fourcard, Aug. 7, 1948; children—Chrystal Frances, Sharon Lynn, Waldren Arthur, Andrea Renee, David Marquard, Anita Lynn. Exhibited in numerous one man shows throughout U.S., also in Eng., France and Spain; 3 paintings on loan to Gov. La., 1974-77; mem. gifted and talented sect. of Spl. Edn. State of La., 1971-73; mem. adv. council Child Centered/Parent Tutored Kindergarten Program, 1974—; mem. La. Task Force for Community Edn., 1974-75; v.p. La. Assn. for Sickle Cell Anemia, 1974—; named best statewide vol.; mem. Calcasieu Parish Bicentennial Com., 1974—; exec. dir., founder Southwestern Sickle Cell Anemia Found., Lake Charles, La., 1973—, producer, dir. 7 Sickle Cell Telethons, Sta. KPLC-TV, 1980-87; bd. dirs. World Sickle Cell Anemia Found.; del. to Dem. Nat. Convs., 1980, 84. Named Hon. Citizen of Fort Worth, 1977; recipient Award of Merit, Human Relations Council of Lake Charles Deanery, award for services to sickle cell disease Sigma Gamma Rho, award for community service Phi Beta Sigma, Gold medal first prize Accademia Italia della Arti e del Sarvo, Italy, 1980, Statua della Vittoria Centro Studie Richerche Delle Nazioni, Italy, 1985. Democrat. Roman Catholic. Important works include The Widow in pvt. collection Bertrand Russell Peace Found., London. Home: 1414 St John St Lake Charles LA 70601-2470 Office: 730 Enterprise Blvd Lake Charles LA 70601-4516

FOUREMAN, NANCY LEE, artist; b. Greenville, Ohio, June 24, 1944; d. LaVern Columbus and Adonia Pauline (Lane) Foreman; m. Richard Allen Foureman, June 29, 1963; children: Stacy Lee, Steven Allen. Student, Ind. State Tchrs. Coll., 1962; BFA in Art, Miami U., Oxford, Ohio, 1963; degree in painting, Art Instrn. Schs., Mpls., 1966. Owner, mgr. Studio Gallery Fine Arts, Greenville, 1970—, Ollie Lane Gallery, Rockport, Mass., 1989-90; dir. Darke County Fair Bd., Greenville, 1977—, Greenville Art Gallery, 1988-91; condr. freelance workshops and seminars, 11980—; mgr. Hatfield's Color Shop, Rockport, 1988-89; dir., chmn. over 50 exhibits in midwest region; chmn. Nat. Wildlife Exhbn., Greenville Guild Regional Exhbn. One-woman shows include Riverbend Art Ctr., Dayton, Ohio, Ind. U.; 2-woman shows Middletown Fine Arts Ctr., Parma Art Ctr., Cleve.; exhibited in group shows Am. Painters in Paris, Dayton Painters and Sculptors Exhbn., Hoosier Salon, Indpls., also others; represented in permanent collections Cleve. Mus. Natural History, also corp. collections. Trustee Darke County Ctr. for Arts, Darke County Ctr. for Arts, 1988—; cons. Greenville Sch.. Bd., 1990—; bd. dirs. Greenville Guild and Theater, 1970-83, Greenville City Art Sch., 1977; chmn. bd. Greenville Art Gallery. Recipient best of show award Art Instrn. Schs., 1970, Garst Mus., 1983, Burkner Nat. Exhibit, Troy, Ohio, 1990, judges award Oil Painters Am., Chgo., 1992; David Humphrey Miller award Wassenburg Art Ctr., May Van Landingham merit award Winchester Court House, Agnes T. Lontz merit award for watercolor, pastel award Lima Art Assn., watercolor award Middletown Fine Arts Ctr., 1st place in watercolor award Art Instrn. Schs., award Robert Simmons Inc., Lois and Shermann S. Brown Meml. merit award. Mem. North Shore Arts Assn., Am. Artists Profl. League, Tri Arts Profl. Woman Artists, Greenville Art Guild (pres. 1975-93), Darke County Agrl. Soc. (bd. dirs., sec. 1977-93), Preble County Art Assn., Art Assn. Richmond (Ind.) (hon.), Dayton Painters and Sculptors, Randolph County Art Assn., Western Ohio Watercolor Soc. Home and Studio: 6441 Daly Rd Greenville OH 45331-9410

FOURNIER, JULIANA J. ALGER, lawyer; b. Stanford, Calif., July 1, 1961; d. Thomas Mason Alger and Johanna Alice Fromm Buscher; m. Randy James Fournier, Apr. 21, 1990; 1 child, Gregory Ross. BS with distinction, U. Wis., 1983; JD with honors, U. Tex., 1986. Bar: Tex. 1986. Assoc. Akin, Gump, Strauss, Hauer & Feld, Dallas, 1986-90, Schlanger, Mills, Mayer & Grossberg, Houston, 1990-92, Sinex & Stephenson, Houston, 1992—; adj. prof. So. Meth. U., Dallas, 1987-89; lectr. on employment issues. Vol. Houston Attys. for Non-Profit Devel., 1992—. Mem. ABA, Tex. Bar Assn., Houston Young Lawyers Assn. (spl. olympics com.), Dallas Bar Assn. Office: 2323 S Shepherd Dr Houston TX 77019-7019

FOUSE, SARAH VIRGINIA, geriatrics nurse; b. Florence, Ala., Apr. 24, 1948; d. John E. and Violet (Chandler) Perkins; m. Alvin Fouse Jr., Feb. 9, 1967; children: Anthony, Alicia, Alvin III. LPN, Gateway Tech. Coll., 1975, ADN, 1984; BSN, Alverno Coll., 1987; MSN, U. Wis., Milw., 1992. Cert. psychiat.-mental health nurse; cert. gerontology nurse. Staff nurse VA Med. Ctr., North Chicago, Ill., LPN, nursing asst., head nurse, adminstrv. clin. nurse specialist. Mem. ANA, Kans. Nurses Assn., Wis. Nurses Assn., Kenosha-Racine Nurses Assn., Milw. Assn. Black Nurses, Sigma Theta Tau. Home: 1900-21st St Racine WI 53403

FOUT, MARY JANE, librarian, educator; b. East St. Louis, Oct. 26, 1937; d. William Pomeroy and Phebe Georgia (Anderson) Eaton; m. John Calvin Fout, Feb. 26, 1960 (div. May 1973); children: Justine Alyss, Elizabeth, John Eric. BA in German and History, U. Omaha, 1959, MA in History, 1963; M of Libr. and Info. Sci., U. Calif., Berkeley, 1977. Cert. tchr., Nebr., N.Y., Calif. Tchr. Indian Hills Jr. H.S., Omaha, 1959-60, Tech. Jr. High Sch., Omaha, 1962-64, Heidelberg Jr. H.S., Germany, 1964-65; archivist intern Social Welfare History Archives, U. Minn., Mpls., 1965-67; lectr. history U. Nebr., Omaha, 1967-68; interlibr. loan libr. Bard Coll., Annandale-on-Hudson, N.Y., 1971-73; career ctr./attendance clk. Armijo High Sch., Fairfield, Calif., 1974-76, career ctr./English Libr. libr., 1976-82, tchr. fgn. lang. and pub. svc., 1982-89, libr., 1989—; summer youth employment tng. program counselor, summers 1980—. Contbg. author: Social Welfare History archives Collection, 1972. Mem. AAUW (past pres.), World Affairs Coun. No. Calif., Calif. Media Libr. Educators Assn. (charter), Am. Field Svc. (dist. rep., past pres. chpt., Pat Lawrence award 1990), Overseas Brats, Commonwealth Club, Alpha Xi Delta, Delta Kappa Gamma. Democrat.

FOUTS, ELIZABETH BROWNE, psychologist, metals company executive; b. New Orleans, July 5, 1927; d. Donovan Clarence and Mathilde Elizabeth (Hanna) B.; m. James Fremont Fouts, June 19, 1948; children: Elizabeth, Donovan, Alan, James. BA, Tulane U., 1948; MS, N.E. La. U., 1973, postgrad., 1984. Cert. sch. psychologist, La.; cert. reality therapist, La. Instr. spl. ed., psychol. cons. N.E. La. U., Monroe, 1971-73; sch. psychologist Ouachita Parish Schs., Monroe, 1973-87; sec.-treas Fremont Corp., Monroe, 1967—, Auric Metals Corp., Salt Lake City, 1975—; dir. La Fonda Hotel, Santa Fe, N.Mex., 1993—; pres. Family Resource Ctr. N.E. La. U., 1993-94; pres. Sunbelt Reality Therapist, 1989-90; bd. dirs. La Fonda Hotel, Santa Fe. Mem. exec. bd. Episc. Diocese Western La., 1986-87, comm. ministry, 1987—; pres. family resource ctr. N.E. La. U., 1993-94; bd. dirs. Assn. for Retarded Citizens, Monroe, 1982-88, treas., 1984, pres., 1987. Named Outstanding Sch. Psychologist State of La., 1987. Mem. Nat. Assn. Sch. Psychologists, Coun. for Exceptional Children, La. Sch. Psychologists Assn. (pres. 1978-79, Outstanding Woman Sch. Psychologist 1984, newsletter editor 1988—). Avocations: biking, skiing, swimming. Home: PO Box 7070 Monroe LA 71211-7070 Office: 4002 Bon Aire Dr Monroe LA 71203-3015

FOWKE, EDITH MARGARET FULTON, author, English language educator emeritus; b. Lumsden, Sask., Can., Apr. 30, 1913; d. William Marshall and Margaret (Fyffe) Fulton; m. Franklin George Fowke, Oct. 1, 1938. Student, Regina Coll., 1929-31; B.A. with high honors in English and History, U. Sask., 1933, M.A. in English, 1938; LL.D. (hon.), Brock U., 1974, U. Regina, 1985; D.Litt., Trent U., 1975, York U., 1982. Editor Western Tchr., Saskatoon, Sask., 1937-45; assoc. editor Mag. Digest, Toronto, Ont., 1945-50; freelance writer CBC Radio, 1950-71; assoc. prof. English, York U., Downsview, Ont., 1971-77; prof. York U., 1977-83, prof. emeritus, 1983—. Author: Folk Songs of Canada, 1954, Folk Songs of Quebec, 1957, Songs of Work and Freedom, 1960, Canada's Story in Song, 1960, Traditional Singers and Songs from Ontario, 1965, More Folk Songs of Canada, 1967, Lumbering Songs from the Northern Woods, 1970, Sally Go Round the Sun, 1969, Penguin Book of Canadian Folk Songs, 1974, Folklore of Canada, 1976, Ring Around the Moon, 1977, Folktales of French Canada, 1979, Sea Songs and Ballads from Nineteenth Century Nova Scotia, 1981, Singing Our History, 1985, Tales Told in Canada, 1986, Red Rover, Red Rover: Children's Games Played in Canada, 1988, Canadian Folklore, 1988, A Family Heritage: The Story and Songs of LaRana Clark, 1994, Legends Told in Canada, 1994, Black Cats and Shooting Stars, 1995; editor: Songs and Sayings of an Ulster Childhood by Alice Kane, 1983, Can. Folk Music Jour., 1971—; co-editor: Bibliography of Canadian Folklore in English, 1982, Explorations in Canadian Folklore, 1985. Decorated Order Can. Fellow Am. Folklore Soc., Royal Soc. Can.; mem. Writer's Union Can. (life), English Folk Dance and Song Soc., Can. Soc. Children's Authors, Illustrators and Performers, Folklore Studies Assn. Can. (life), Can. Soc. Traditional Music (hon. pres.). Home: 5 Notley Pl, Toronto, ON Canada M4B 2M7

FOWLER, ARDEN STEPHANIE, music educator; b. N.Y.C., May 24, 1930; d. Arthur Simon and Lenore Irene (Strouse) Bender; m. Milton Fowler, Aug. 6, 1951; children: Stacey Alison, Crispin Laird. Student, Traphagen Sch., 1947-49; BA, Marymount Coll., Tarrytown, N.Y., 1976; MusM, U. So. Fla., 1978. Designer Rubeson's Sportswear, N.Y.C., 1949-51; free-lance designer Dobb's Ferry, N.Y., 1952-72; organist/choir dir. Children's Village, Dobb's Ferry, N.Y., 1972-74; music specialist Highland Nursery Sch., Chappaqua, N.Y., 1972-76; pvt. voice tchr., vocal coach, 1972—; music therapist Cedar Manor Nursing Home, Ossining, N.Y., 1974-76; founder, pres. Gloria Musicae Chamber Chorus, Sarasota, Fla., 1979-85, mng. dir., 1985-89; soloist various chs. and choruses, N.Y., Fla., 1953—; mem. faculty vocal music dept. St. Boniface Conservatory, Sarasota, 1979-81; music critic Sarasota Herald Tribune, 1986-91; lectr. music history Edn. Ctr., Longboat Key, Fla.; vol. music for early childhood Head Start. Freelance travel writer, 1985—. Mem. AAUW, Nat. Assn. Tchrs. Singing, Chorus Am., Assn. Profl. Vocal Ensembles, Friends of the Arts (hon.), Sigma Alpha Iota, Phi Kappa Phi. Democrat. Episcopal. Home: 4244 Marina Ct Cortez FL 34215-2518

FOWLER, BARBARA HUGHES, classics educator; b. Lake Forest, Ill., Aug. 23, 1926; d. Fay Orville and Clara (Reber) Hughes; m. Alexander Murray Fowler, July 14, 1956; children: Jane Alexandra, Emily Hughes. BA, U. Wis., 1949; MA, Bryn Mawr Coll., 1950, PhD, 1955. Instr. classics Middlebury (Vt.) Coll., 1954-56; asst. prof. Latin Edgewood Coll., Madison, Wis., 1961-63; mem. faculty U. Wis., Madison, 1963—; prof. classics U. Wis., 1976—, John Bascom prof., 1980—, prof. emeritus, 1991—. Author: The Hellenistic Aesthetic, 1989, The Seeds Inside a Green Pepper, 1989, Hellenistic Poetry, 1990, Archaic Greek Poetry, 1992, Love Lyrics of Ancient Egypt, 1994; also articles. Fulbright scholar Greece, 1951-52; Fanny Bullock Workman travelling fellow, 1951-52. Mem. Am. Philol. Assn., Archaeol. Inst. Am., Classical Assn. Middle West and South. Home: 1102 Sherman Ave Madison WI 53703-1620 Office: U Wis 910 Van Hise Hall Madison WI 53706

FOWLER, BETTY JANMAE, dance company director, editor; b. Chgo., May 23, 1925; d. Harry and Mary (Jacques) Markin; student Art Inst., Chgo., 1937-39, Stratton Bus. Coll., Chgo., 1942-43, Columbia U., 1945-47; B.A., Eastern Wash. U., 1984; 1 dau., Sherry Mareth Connors. Mem. public relations dept. Girl Scouts U.S.A., N.Y.C., 1961-63; adminstrv. asst. to editor-in-chief Scholastic Mags., N.Y.C., 1963-68; adminstrv. dir. Leonard Fowler Dancers, Fowler Sch. Classical Ballet, Inc., N.Y.C., 1959-78, tchr. ballet, 1959-61; pvt. practice Ecol. Lifestyle Advisor, 1980—; editor Bulletin, Kiwanis weekly publ., Spokane, Wash., 1978-82, adminstrv. sec. Kiwanis Club; instr. Spokane Falls Community Coll., 1978. Founder Safe Water Coalition Wash. State, 1988. Cert. metabolic technician Internat. Health Inst. Avocations: travel, reading. Address: 5615 W Lyons Ct Spokane WA 99208-3777

FOWLER, CECILE ANN, nurse, professional soloist; b. Paterson, N.J., Feb. 14, 1920; m. Chester A. Fowler, Mar. 9, 1942. Grad., Passaic (N.J.) Gen. Hosp. Nursing Program, 1941. Nurse Beth Israel Hosp., Newark, 1941-42, Orange (N.J.) Meml. Hosp., 1942-50; asst. receptionist Dr. Stokes, Urologist, East Orange, N.J., 1943-44; nurse Mountainside Hosp., Montclair, N.J., 1960-69, head nurse, premature and newborns, 1966-67; profl. soloist, 1952-69; part-time nurse Upper Three Hosps., 1950-60; co-founder The Oratorio Soc. of N.J., Montclair, 1952; mem. quartet First Baptist Ch., Montclair. Active various coms. PTA, 1951-62; co-founder CD, Little Falls, N.J., 1967; sponsor Met. Opera Guild N.Y., 1977—; child sponsor World Vision, 1983—; mem. Rep. Presdl. Task Force, 1987; founder Challenger Ctr. for Math., Space and Sci. Edn., 1990—, Ptnrs. in Hope: St. Jude's Rsch. Ctr., 1991—; mem. Friends of Richard Tucker Music Found., 1987—. Recipient Vocal Accomplishment award Griffith Music Found., 1944, 45, medal of Merit, Pres. Reagan, 1988, Pres. Bush, 1990, Rep. Presdl. Legion of Merit, 1992. Mem. Lincoln Ctr. for the Performing Arts, Friends of Carnegie Hall, Friends of Richard Tucker Music Found, Am. Biog. Inst. Am. (rsch. bd. advs. 1989—, dep. gov., life mem., fellowship, Commemorative Medal of Honor 1991), Heritage Found. (U.S. English mem. 1986—), U.S. Senatorial Club (preferred mem.), Little Falls Woman's Club (edn. chmn.), Montclair (gov. 1979-81), Montclair Operetta (various chairmanships 1943—, gov. 1990—). Republican. Roman Catholic. Home: 9 Lotz Hill Rd Clifton NJ 07013-2312

FOWLER, ELIZABETH MILTON, real estate executive; b. Watertown, Fla., Jan. 11, 1919; d. Arthur Wellington and Mattie Jean (Hodges) Milton; m. Albert L. Fowler, Jr., Aug. 6, 1948; children: Patricia Dawn Cecilia, Richard Gordon Sean. Student Bowling Green Bus. U., 1938-39; Cultural HHD (hon.), World U. Roundtable, 1988. Sec. to dir. Workmen's Compensation Div., Fla. Indsl. Commn., Tallahassee, 1940-41; sec. to supt. div. Gibbs Ship Yard Repair, 1942-44; sec. to elec. engrs. Reynolds, Smith & Hills, Architects and Engrs., 1946-49; sec. to pres. Aichel Steel Corp., Jacksonville, Fla., 1949-50; adminstr. office mgr. for prin., vice-prin. Am. Dependent Sch., Moron Air Base, Spain, 1961-63; owner, mgr. Elizabeth Properties, Jacksonville, 1956—. Chmn. ways and means com. Chattanooga High Sch. PTA, 1956-57; asst. den mother Cub Scout Troop, 1970; block worker Gov. Reagan's Presdl. Campaign. Recipient Spl. Appreciation award Eglin AFB, Fla., 1969. Mem. Nat. Assn. Female Execs., Am. Security Council (nat. adv. bd.), Dade County Crimewatch Orgn. Republican. Avocations: art and interior design, horseback riding, collecting fine porcelain, reading, politics and world affairs. Home and Office: 20101 SW 92d Ave Miami FL 33189

FOWLER, LINDA MCKEEVER, hospital administrator, management educator; b. Greensburg, Pa., Aug. 7, 1948; d. Clay and Florence Elizabeth (Smith) McK.; m. Timothy L. Fowler, Sept. 13, 1969 (div. July 1985). Nursing diploma, Presbyn. U. Hosp., Pitts., 1969; BS in Nursing, U. Pitts., 1976, M in Nursing Adminstrn., 1980; DPub Adminstrn., Nova U., 1985. Supr., head nurse Presbyn. Univ. Hosp., Pitts., 1969-76; mem. faculty Western Pa. Hosp. Sch. Nursing, Pitts., 1976-79; acute care coord. Mercy Hosp., Miami, 1980-81; asst. adminstr. nursing North Shore Med. Ctr., Miami, 1981-84, v.p. patient care, 1984-88, Golden Glades Regional Med. Ctr., Miami, 1988-89, Humana Hosp.-South Broward, Hollywood, Fla., 1989-91, assoc. exec. dir. nursing; assoc. adminstr./CNO HCA Bayonet Point/Hudson Med. Ctr., 1991—; mem. adj. faculty Barry U., Miami, 1984—, Broward Community Coll., Ft. Lauderdale, 1984—, Nova U., 1986—; cons. Strategic Health Devel. Inc., Miami Shores, Fla., 1986—. Bd. dirs. Pesco County Am. Cancer Soc., 1992—. Dept. HEW trainee, 1976, 79-80. Mem. Am. Orgn. Nurse Execs. (legis. com. 1988-90), Fla. Orgn. Nurse Execs. (bd. dirs. 1986-88), South Fla. Nurse Adminstrs. Assn. (sec. 1983-84, bd. dirs. 1984-86), U. Pitts. Alumni Assn., Presbyn. U. Alumni Assn., Portuguese Water Dog Club Am. (bd. dirs. 1988-89), Ft. Lauderdale Dog Club (bd. dirs. 1981-82, 83-85, v.p. 1982-83), AKC (dog judge), Sigma Theta Tau. Lutheran. Home: 10354 Armadillo Ct New Port Richey FL 34654-2602 Office: HCA Bayonet Point/Hudson Med Ctr 14000 Fivay Rd Port Richey FL 34667-7103

FOWLER, MARTI, secondary education educator; b. St. Louis, Mar. 25, 1952; d. Chester Felix and Emily (Kohout) Czarcinski; m. Robert Lee Fowler, Mar. 26, 1988. BA, So. Ill. U., 1973, MA, 1981. Cert. tchr. English, speech and theatre, Mo. Tchr. asst. Hazelwood Sch. Dist., St. Louis, 1974-76; instr. Jefferson Coll., 1991-92, St. Louis C.C. at Meramec, St. Louis, 1990—; tchr. Hazelwood E. High Sch., St. Louis, 1976—. Co-playwright/lyricist: (musical theatre) Difficult Choices, 1988; dir. and choreographer numerous prodns., 1973—. Mem. Am. Alliance for Theatre in Edn. (Mo. state chmn. 1993—), Theatre Edn. Assn. (Mo. State chmn. 1993—), Speech Theatre Assn. of Mo., Speech Comm. Assn., Internat. Thespian Soc., Zeta Phi Eta (pres. 1972-73). Home: 1221 Beaver Trail Dr Ferguson MO 63135-1249 Office: Hazelwood E High Sch 11300 Dunn Rd Saint Louis MO 63138-1098

FOWLER, SUSAN MICHELE, real estate broker, entrepreneur; b. East Liverpool, Ohio, Jan. 6, 1952; d. George Robert and Mary Helen (Gilliland) F.; m. Paul Joseph Cusumano, Nov. 5, 1988. BA, West Liberty Coll., 1973; postgrad., Kent State U., 1992—. Lic. real estate broker, Ohio. Sales rep. Tropic-Cal, L.A., 1974-76; project mgr. R&B Enterprises, L.A., 1977-80; regional leasing mgr. First Union Mgmt., Inc., Cleve., 1981-82; comml. real estate broker Adler, Galvin, Rogers, Inc., Cleve., 1983-86, Coldwell Banker Comml. Real Estate, Cleve., 1986-90; pres. Comml. Real Estate Co., Cleve., 1990—; owner Susan M. Fowler Comml. Real Estate Co., Chagrin Falls, Ohio, 1990—, Empower Yourself Seminars, Chagrin Falls, 1992—; pres. Christopher Real Estate Investment, Cleve., 1989—, Christopher Mgmt. Co., Cleve., 1989—; founder, speaker Empower Yourself Seminars, 1992. Trustee, pres. West Side Community Mental Health Ctr., Cleve., 1985—; trsutee, v.p. Child Conservation Coun., Cleve., 1988—; trustee Big Bros. and Big Sisters Greater Cleve., 1989, Visions for Youth, 1991; mem. Cleve. Mus. Art, Geauga County Humane Soc., Fairmount Arts Centre. Mem. Comml. Real Estate Women, Cleve. Area Bd. Realtors (speakers bur.), Nat. Assn. Realtors, Ohio Assn. Realtors, Cleve. Mus. Art, Pine Lake Trout Club. Home: 6 Circle Dr Chagrin Falls OH 44022-4206 Office: Empower Yourself Seminars PO Box 23255 Chagrin Falls OH 44023-0255

FOWLER, TERRI (MARIE THERESE FOWLER), artist; b. Decatur, Ga., Sept. 26, 1949; d. John Francis and Marjorie (Benson) Herndon; m. John Charles Fowler, July 29, 1972; children: Courtney Marie, Douglas Edwin. Studied with Carolyn Wyeth, Wyeth Sch. Art, 1972. speaker to arts groups, schools. One-man shows include Hampden Sydney Coll., 1973, Longwood, Coll., 1976, C&S Bank, Camden, S.C., 1979, Benfield Gallery, 1985-93; exhibited in cen. chpt. Va. Mus., 1973 (recipient award 1973), Colonial Williamsburg, 1974-77, Md. St. House, Md. St. Senate, 1983-85; works selected by Am. Heart Assn. for Holiday Card Series, 1986-87, commnd. Prince Edward County Bicentennial Com., 1976; represented in many nat. and internat. pvt. collections. Active Girl Scouts Am. cen. Md.; sec. citizens adv. com. Annapolis Mid. Sch. Mem. Balt. Watercolor Soc., Md. Fedn. Art. Annapolis Watercolor Club., San Diego Watercolor Soc., U.S. Naval Acad. Womens Club and Garden Club. Home: 123 Groh Ln Annapolis MD 21403-4008

FOWLER, TILLIE KIDD, congresswoman; b. Milledgeville, Ga., Dec. 23, 1942; d. Culver and Katherine Kidd; m. L. Buck Fowler, 1968; children: Tillie, Elizabeth. BA in Polit. Sci., Emory U., 1964, JD, 1967. Legis. asst. Rep. Robert G. Stephens, 1970-71; counsel White House Office of Consumer Affairs, 1982-83; mem. 103d-104th Congresses from 4th Fla. dist., 1993—. Pres. Jr. League Jacksonville, Fla., 1985-92, Fla. Humanities Coun., Jacksonville City Coun., 1989-90, mem. 1989-91. Republican. Office: US Ho of Reps 413 Cannon House Office Bldg Washington DC 20515

FOWLER, VIVIAN DELORES, insurance company executive; b. Knoxville, Tenn., Sept. 26, 1946; d. Rance James Pierce and Margaret Willadene (Crowe) Compton; m. James Hubert Fowler, May 12, 1979. Student, U. Tenn., Knoxville. CPCU. Clk. The Travelers Ins. Co., Knoxville, 1967-84, adminstv. staff, 1984, comml. mktg. asst., 1984-86; comml. account analyst The Travelers Ins. Co., Nashville, 1986-89, sr. account analyst, 1989-90, account mgr., 1990-93; regional asst. mgr. small bus. unit coml. lines The Travelers Ins. Co., Atlanta, 1993—, regional underwriting mgr. small bus. mktg., 1994. Lay witness speaker, United Meth. Ch., Knoxville 1979-82; charter mem. St. Thomas Hosp. Found. Soc., 1990; mem. Arthritis Found., 1991. Mem. NAFE, Soc. CPCU, Soc. Cert. Ins. Counselors (cert. 1987), Nat. Assn. of Ins. Women (cert. Profl. Ins. Woman 1975), Internat. Platform Assn. Republican. United Methodist. Home: 604 Ashley Forest Dr Alpharetta GA 30202-6133 Office: The Travelers Ins Co 211 Perimeter Ctr Pky Atlanta GA 30346

FOWLES, DEBORAH MARIE, controller; b. Rockland, Maine, Apr. 4, 1954; d. Donald Clyde and Cora M. (Rowling) F. BS in Youth Leadership, Brigham Young U., 1976; BS in Mgmt. Studies, U. Md., 1990. Corp. adminstr. Program Resources, Inc., Rockville and Annapolis, Md., 1976-83; mgr. acctg. and adminstrn. Pathology Assocs., Inc., Frederick, Md., 1983-89, contr., 1989—, also officer and bd. dirs. Mem. NAFE, Inst. Mgmt. Accts., U. Md. Alumni Assn. (vol. mentor 1992—). Republican. Office: Pathology Assocs Inc 15 Worman's Mill Ct Frederick MD 21701

FOX, AUDREY H., artist, educator; b. Phila., Sept. 14, 1954; d. Donald and Kay (Sklarz) F.; m. John Phillip Golden, Sept. 10, 1989. BFA, Tyler Sch. Art, 1976; postgrad., Barnes Found., 1976-80. Workshop coord., tchr. dept. urban outreach Phila. Mus. Art, 1972; coord., instr. art activities Lower Merion Twp. Dept. Recreation and Sch. Dist., 1972-74; designer murals (comml. and residential) Lower Merion Twp. Dept. Recreation, Lower Merion, 1978-79; designer murals, tchr. various programs Manayunk Ctr. for Arts, 1985-89; tchr. drawing and painting Notre Dame Acad., 1990; tchr. painting, sculpture printmaking, design and crafts, 1982—. Works exhibited in juried shows at Main Line Ctr. for Arts, 1977, Peddler's Art Gallery, Bryn Mawr, Pa., 1977, First Bank of U.S., Phila., 1977, Phila. Convention and Visitors Ctr., 1977, 78, 79, Vassar Coll., 1980, 82, West Chester State Coll., 1981, 91, Marketplace Designers' Resource Ctr., 1981, 84, Manayunk Ctr. for Arts, 1986, Temple U., Phila., 1986, 90, Kling Gallery, 1987, Am. Art Investment Gallery, Wayne, Pa., 1991, Am. Coll., 1993, 94, Sande Webster Gallery, 1993, Rosemont Coll., 1994, Berman Mus., 1994, APF Gallery, 1994, Jun Gallery, 1994, Vox Populi Gallery, 1994, Woodmere Art Mus., 1995; designer various newsletters and posters; executed mural City of Phila., 1983. Recipient Best in Show award Nat. League Am. Pen Women, 1981, award of excellence Manhattan Arts Internat., 1994. Mem. Art Guild Delaware Valley (Merit award 1986, 92), Artists Equity (Phila. br., Art in Pub. Places award 1982), Women's Caucus for Art. Home: 631 Righters Mill Rd Narberth PA 19072

FOX, BARBARA, artist, educator; b. Bklyn., Aug. 4, 1940; d. Edward J. and Gertrude (Smith) F. BA, U. Rochester, 1974, MA, 1976; MFA, Rochester Inst. Tech., 1981. Instr. SUNY, Brockport, 1981-85; lectr. U. Rochester, N.Y., 1985; asst. prof. art Nat. Tech. Inst. for Deaf/Rochester Inst. Tech., 1986—; vis. asst. prof. SUNY, Oswego, 1986; bd. advisors N.Y. Found. for Arts, N.Y.C., 1993—; coord., bd. dirs. Women's Resource Ctr.,

Rochester Inst. Tech.; mem. artists adv. panel Pyramid Arts Ctr., Rochester, 1982-86. One and two person shows include U. Rochester, 1985, Wells Coll., Aurora, N.Y., 1991, Geva Theatre, Rochester, 1993, Utica Coll. Syracuse U., 1995; represented in permanent collections at Mus. Modern Art, Albright Knox Art Gallery. Grantee Window Project Installation, 1990, Arts for Greater Rochester, 1990; recipient Purchase Prize award Wallace Meml. Libr., Rochester Inst. Tech., 1981. Mem. Women's Caucus for Art, Coll. Art Assn., Pyramid Arts Coun. Office: Rochester Inst Tech Nat Tech Inst for Deaf Rochester NY 14623

FOX, BETTY, insurance agent, consultant; b. Chgo., July 30, 1935; d. Abraham and Lucille (Manesewitz) Axelrod; m. Ira Rosenberg; children: Deborah Kravitz, Esther Fox Ham, Adam. Student, U. Ill., Chgo., 1953; CLU, The Am. Coll., 1989, ChFC, 1990. Art tchr. Suburban Fine Arts Ctr., Highland Park, Ill., 1963-75; commodities broker Rosenthal et al, Chgo., 1975-78; registered rep. The Equitable, Northbrook, Ill., 1978—; Painter represented in nat. collection (blue ribbon award 1971). Bd. dirs. Suburban Fine Arts Ctr., Highland Park, Ill., 1962—; vol Jewish Vocat. Svc., Chgo.; active Alliance for Mental Illness. Recipient Purchase prize Kemper Ins. Co., Nat. Wine Art Competition. Mem. Nat. Assn. Life Underwriters, Million Dollar Round Table, Chgo. Women Ins. Assn. (treas. 1989), Nat. Assn. Women Life Underwriters, Lake County Life Underwriters, 500 Club (pres. 1990, agy. CLU advisor 1989-92, chmn. Agts. Forum 1992—). Office: Equitable Life Assurance Co 500 Skokie Blvd Ste 300 Northbrook IL 60062-2897

FOX, CHOOWON, travel consultant; b. Hamhyung, Korea, July 10, 1947; came to U.S., 1984; m. Michael Anthony Fox, May 18, 1982; 1 child, David Yi. BA, Ewha Women's U., Seoul, 1970. Travel agt. TWA Airlines, Seoul, 1974-84; customer svc. agt. TWA Airlines, Washington, 1984-88; travel cons. Carlson Travel, Washington, 1988-89, U.S. Travel, Arlington, Va., 1989—. Named Million Dollar Agt., U.S. Travel, 1990, 91, 92, 93. Home: 4094 Championship Ct Annandale VA 22003 also: 4709 Chowen Ave S Minneapolis MN 55410

FOX, CYNTHIA ANN, accountant, consultant; b. Prospect, Conn., Feb. 18, 1960; d. George Arthur and Jane Ann (Coughlan) Pelzer; m. Edward Brian Fox, Sept. 26, 1987; 1 child, Catherine Kelley. BS in Fin., Cen. Conn. State U., 1983; MS in Fin. Mgmt., Fairfield U., 1993. Cert. mgmt. acct. Treas. Moore & Munger, Mktg. & Refining, Shelton, Conn., 1985-89; mgr. fin. reporting Nestle Foods Corp., Purchase, N.Y., 1989-92; cons. pvt. practice, Carmel, N.Y., 1992—. Vol. fin. budgeting for individuals, Carmel, 1992-93. Mem. Inst. Mgmt. Accts. Republican. Roman Catholic. Home and Office: Laurie Ln Carmel NY 10512

FOX, DAWNE MARIE, safety scientist; b. West Lafayette, Ind., Aug. 3, 1948; d. Gerhard P. and Betty M. (Norris) F.; m. Gerald C. Newmeyer, Oct. 4, 1969 (div. 1981); children: Mimie, Jerry. Grad. magna cum laude, Lord Fairfax, Middletown, Va., 1979; grad., Casper (Wyo.) Coll., 1985. Cert. environ. trainer Nat. Environ. Tng. Assn.; EPA cert. instr. in asbestos abatement, supr., inspector and mgmt. planner, project designer tng. courses; cert. instr. occupl. safety and health adminstrn., U.S. Dept. Labor, Nat. Tng. Inst. Regional safety coord. Milchem Inc., Casper, 1979-83; safety dir. Energy Insulation Inc., Casper, 1983-85; safety mgr. Western States Constrn., Loveland, Colo., 1985-86; safety officer Govt. of D.C., 1987-89; dir. safety, health svcs. Denver and Rio Grande R.R., Denver, 1989-90; safety mgr. Browning-Ferris Inc., Hyattsville, 1990-91; sr. safety scientist Gen. Physics Corp., Columbia, Md., 1991—; cons., Casper, 1983-85. Instr. ARC, Casper, 1981-85, Am. Heart Assn., Casper, 1982-85; spl. aide to Spl. Olympics, Casper, 1983-85. Mem. Nat. Safety Coun., Am. Soc. Safety Engrs. (v.p. 1982-83, pres. 1983-84, Safety Profl. award 1982), Assn. Am. Railroads Safety Coun. (past del.). Republican. Roman Catholic. Home: 11410 Edmonston Rd Beltsville MD 20705-1731

FOX, ELLEN ELIZABETH, internist, educator; b. Washington, Dec. 11, 1959; d. Bernard H. Fox and Mary Margaret (Wilkinson) Bradstock. BA summa cum laude, Yale U., 1981; MD, Harvard U., 1987. Diplomate Am. Bd. Internal Medicine. Resident in internal medicine Yale U., New Haven, 1987-90, chief resident dept. medicine, 1990-91; fellow in clin. med. ethics U. Chgo., 1991-92, instr. medicine, 1992-94; asst. prof. medicine and med. edn. U. Ill., Chgo., 1994—, dir. program clin. ethics, 1994—; dir. curriculum ethical and humanistic medicine Yale U., 1991—. Author: (curriculum) Yale Curriculum in Ethical & Humanistic Medicine, 1991; co-author: Curricular Guidelines in Ethics, 1994; contbr. articles to profl. jours. Founding dir. Care Homeless People Project, Chgo., 1993-94. Mem. Soc. Gen. Internal Medicine, Soc. Bioethics Consultation, Phi Beta Kappa. Office: U Ill Chgo M/C 787 840 S Wood St Chicago IL 60612

FOX, FRANCES JUANICE, retired librarian, educator; b. Vicksburg, Miss., Aug. 17, 1916; d. Willie Amercy Thaxton and Fannye Lou (Spell) Hepfer; m. Leonard John Fox, Feb. 25, 1937; children: Frances Juanice, L. John Jr., Kenneth L., Robert T., William E., Elizabeth Jean. AA, Phoenix Coll., 1959; BS in Edn., Ariz. State U., 1963, MS in Edn., Libr., 1972. Cert. kindergarten, primary, and elem. tchr., cert. libr., cert. religious edn. Diocese of Phoenix. Substitute tchr. Escambia County Sch. Dist., Pensacola, Fla., 1936-38; kindergarten tchr. Lollipop Ln. Sch., Phoenix, 1960-61, 1st United Meth. Day Sch., Phoenix, 1961-62; tchr. grade 3 Wilson Elem. Sch., Phoenix, 1962-63; summer libr. R.E. Simpson Elem. Sch., Phoenix, 1964, 65; preschool tchr. Jewish Community Ctr., Phoenix, 1967-68; libr. Audio Visual Ctr. Sts. Simon and Judge Elem. Sch., Phoenix, 1969-82; cataloger First United Meth. Ch. Libr., Phoenix, 1963, Baker Ctr. Ariz. State Univ. Meth. and Hillel Students Libr., Tempe, 1969. Co-compiler: (libr. manual) Diocese of Phoenix, 1980-81. Organizer, leader Girl Scouts Am., Birmingham, Ala., 1951, 52, Phoenix, 76-83; leader cubs Boy Scouts Am., Birmingham, 1950-52, Phoenix, 52-55; swim instr. ARC, Fla., Ariz., 1933, 34, 53, 54; dance instr. Circle Game and Beginning Dance, Wesley Community Ctr., Phoenix, 1966, 67. Recipient Gold Poet award World Book of Poetry, 1990, Honorable Mention, Poetic Voices of Am., 1990, Internat. Achievement award Cambridge, Edn., 1994; academic scholar Phoenix Coll., Ariz. State Coll., 1959. Mem. ALA, Ariz. State Libr. Assn. (com. on continuing edn. 1979-81), Gold Star Wines of Am., Inc. (past v.p. parlimentarian), DAV Aux. (life), Ariz. PTA (life mem., organizer, v.p.), Gold Star Wives Am. (pres. 1993-94), Phi Theta Kappa, Iota Sigma Alpha Honor Soc. Methodist. Home: 2225 W Montebello Ave Phoenix AZ 85015

FOX, GRETCHEN HOVEMEYER, staff assistant, freelance editor, genealogical consultant; b. Erie, Pa., Jan. 2, 1940; d. Ernst Henry and Marjory Etta (Hollister) Hovemeyer; m. Kenneth Roland Fox, Apr. 23, 1989. AB, Radcliffe Coll., 1961. Manuscript sec. Internat. Tax Program Harvard U. Law Sch., Cambridge, Mass., 1961-63; copy editor Internat. Tax Program Harvard U. Law Sch., Cambridge, 1963-65, editorial asst., 1965-66, publs. asst., 1966-76, editorial and pub. dir., 1976-89; freelance editor, cons. pub. and genealogy Cambridge, 1989—; database/rsch. asst. innovations program John F. Kennedy Sch. of Govt., Harvard U., Cambridge, Mass., 1991-93, staff asst. innovations program, 1993—. Co-compiler: Bibliography on Taxation of Foreign Operations and Foreigners: 1968-75, 1976, Bibliography on Taxation of Foreign Operations and Foreigners: 1976-82, 1983; contbr. articles on geneal. to prof. jours.; designer computer software. Mem. New Eng. Hist. Geneal. Soc., Orange County Geneal. Soc. (pub. cons. 1983-91), Sullivan County (N.Y.) Hist. Soc., DAR (chpt. registrar, chpt. historian 1978-83). Office: Harvard U John F Kennedy Sch Govt 79 JFK St Cambridge MA 02138

FOX, JANE ELLEN, librarian; b. DuQuoin, Ill., Oct. 29, 1947; d. Eugene Earl and Lois Jean (Beggs) Gross; m. Loren Fox, July 22, 1967; 1 child, Matthew Elliott. BS, So. Ill. U., 1969; MS in LS, U. Mich., 1979. Tchr. Dist. 2, Colorado Springs, Colo., 1969-71; libr. Henry Ford Centennial Libr., Dearborn, Mich., 1980—, supr. adult svcs., 1993—. Mem. AAUW (v.p. 1990-92), Mich. Libr. Assn. Office: 16301 Michigan Ave Dearborn MI 48126-2723

FOX, JO, media and marketing professional; b. Pitts.; d. James Joseph and Marion Delores (Brannan) F.; divorced; children: Barbara Lee Lindsay, Matthew Brannan Brosious, Sarah Krick Vaivoda. BA, Pa. State U.; MA, Georgetown U., 1981. Chief script writer Sta. KOMO AM & TV, Seattle; reporter Erie (Pa.) Times; reporter, sect. editor Bellingham (Wash.) Herald; editor Westport (Conn.) News, 1963-70; founder Capital Corresponse, 1965-75; founder, editor, pub. Fairpress, Westport, 1971-77; pres. Jo Fox, Inc., Westport, 1984—; media/mktg. dir. City of Bridgeport, Conn., 1991—; del. Pres. Coun. Small Bus., 1982; pub. rels. assoc. Hill & Knowlton, N.Y.C., 1983-94; publs. cons. Gannett/WRN Group, Westchester, N.Y., 1990; mem. mktg. Bridgeport Regional Bus. Coun. Bd. dirs. Westport Conservation Commn., 1969-72, Westport C. of C., 1984-86, Bridgeport (Conn.) Area Arts Coun., 1988—, Norwalk (Conn.) Symphony, 1991-94; mem. gov's. (Conn.) Panel on Environ. Policy, 1976; founder, mem. bd. dirs. ARTFORCE, 1993—. Recipient Brotherhood award NCCJ, 1972, 74, 76, Editorial Writing award Columbia Sch. of Journalism, Am. Trucker's Assn., New England Press Assn.; named one of 6 Most Important Women in Conn. U.N. Women's Year Com., 1976. Mem. Pub. Rels. Soc. Am., Fairfield County Hunt Club, Pa. State Alumni Club, Rotary (bd. dirs.). Home: 9 Sprucewood Ln Westport CT 06880 Office: City of Bridgeport 45 Lyon Ter Bridgeport CT 06604

FOX, JOAN MARIE, educator; b. Flint, Mich., July 8, 1948; d. Elmer William and Elizabeth (Fisher) Skolnik; m. Richard Charles Fox, Dec. 19, 1970; children: Elizabeth Grace, Julie Anne. BA in Edn., Mich. State U., 1970; postgrad., Ind. U., 1982-83; MEd, U. Md., 1988; postgrad., Loyola Coll., 1989—. Tchr. math. Dayton (Ohio) Pub. Schs., 1970-71; tchr. 5th grade Mt. Orab (Ohio) Elem., 1971-75; docent Indpls. Mus. of Art, 1979-81; substitute instrional aide Washington Twp. Schs., Indpls., 1981-83; ednl. cons. Mastery Edn. Corp., Watertown, Mass., 1983-85; tchr. Howard County Pub. Schs., Ellicott City, Md., 1985—; bd. dirs. Mt. Hebron Nursery Sch., Ellicott City, 1984—; employee recognition com. Howard County Pub. Schs., 1988—. Mem. Md Com. for Children, Balt., 1983—, Smithsonian, Washington, 1983—, ARC, Balt. Mem. NEA, Nat. Coun. Tchrs. of Math., Phi Delta Kappa (sec. 1985-86, v.p. 1986-87, pres. 1987-88). Democrat. Episcopalian. Home: 9990 Old Annapolis Rd Ellicott City MD 21042-5602 Office: Howard County Pub Schs 4200 Centennial Lane Ellicott City MD 21042

FOX, KELLY DIANE, financial advisor; b. Brockton, Mass., Sept. 9, 1959; d. James H. and Betty Jane (Calloway) F.; m. Alan David Goldberg, July 6, 1985; 1 child, Andrew Jason. B.A., Allegheny Coll., 1980; postgrad. in Bus. Adminstrn., Suffolk U., 1983-84; student Temple U., London, 1978, Syracuse U., London, 1979. Asst. mgr. Casual Male, Braintree, Mass., 1980, Hit or Miss, Braintree, 1981-82; merchandiser Foxmoor, West Bridgewater, Mass., 1982; distbr. Hill's Dept. Stores, Canton, Mass., 1982-85; asst. buyer BJ's Wholesale Club, Natick, Mass., 1985-92; fin. advisor, Am. Express Fin. Advisors, 1993—. Cheerleading coach Avon High Sch., Mass., 1982-83; co-chair enrichment program Falls Elem. Sch.; active John Woodcock Sch. Coun., 1993-94; treas., Attleboro Area Coun. for Children; bd. dir. Atteboro Area Parents Anonymous. Mem. NAFE. Methodist. Avocations: dance, exercise, cooking, art galleries.

FOX, LORRAINE SUSAN, marketing professional; b. L.A., Feb. 8, 1956; d. Robert Lazar and Valerie Joan (Barker) Fox; m. Clark Byron Siegel, July 19, 1981 (div. Nov. 1989). AB with distinction, Stanford U., 1979; MBA, U. Chgo., 1983. Sr. fin. analyst MacIntosh div., Apple Computer, Cupertino, Calif., 1983-84, Sun Microsystems Inc., Mountain View, Calif., 1984-85; mgr. fin. planning and analysis Sun Microsystems Inc., Mountain View, 1985-86, project mgr., 1986-88, mgr. project mgmt., 1988-90, sr. product mktg. mgr., 1990-93, mgr. mktg. strategy, 1993-95; dir. multimedia product mktg. new media divsn. Oracle Corp., Redwood Shores, Calif., 1995—. Vol. fundraiser Stanford (Calif.) U., 1983-88; vol. Sun Microsystems Community Vols., Mountain View, 1989—; alumni rep. undergrad. commn. on edn. Stanford U. Mem. Commonwealth Club, Stanford Profl. Women's Club, Churchill Club. Home: 707 Bryant St Palo Alto CA 94301-2554 Office: Oracle Corp 500 Oracle Pkwy Redwood Shores CA 94065

FOX, LYNN SMITH, federal government official; b. Spartanburg, S.C., Apr. 19, 1955; d. James Leonard and Dorothy Harriet (Wilson) Smith; m. William Lloyd Fox, Aug. 1, 1981; 1 child, Harriet Buffington. Student, Wofford Coll., 1974; BA cum laude, Smith Coll., 1977; MBA, George Washington U., 1982. Legis. asst. Rep. John J. LaFalce, Washington, 1982-83; profl. staff mem. Subcom. on Econ. Stabilization, Ho. Banking Com., Washington, 1983-85; congl. liaison asst. Fed. Res. Bd., Washington, 1986-88, spl. asst. to bd., 1992-94, dep. congl. liaison, 1994—; dir. corporate rels. Harvey Mudd Coll., Claremont, Calif., 1990-92. Vice chair Inland Hospice, Claremont, 1992; class officer Smith Coll. Alumnae, Northampton, Mass., 1993—; asst. troop leader Girl Scouts, Chevy Chase, Md., 1994—. Univ. fellow George Washington U., 1981-82. Mem. Women in Housing and Fin. (vice chair 1986). Home: 3526 Woodbine St Chevy Chase MD 20815 Office: Fed Res Bd 20th & Constitution Ave NW Washington DC 20551

FOX, MADELINE JOAN, speech and language pathologist; b. N.Y.C., Oct. 13, 1944. BA, Queens Coll., 1966; MS, U. Mich., 1967. Cert. clin. competence speech. pathologist. Speech lang. pathologist U. Md., Balt., 1966; pvt. practice, 1967—; instr. dept. surgery U. Md. Hosp., 1971—; speech and lang. therapy pvt. practice dir. Madeline Fox Assocs. Mem. Am. Speech Hearing Assn., Md. Speech Lang. Hearing Assn. Office: Madeline Fox Assocs Inc Baltimore MD 21208

FOX, MARGARET ANNE, community development specialist; b. Cin., Oct. 14, 1950; d. Raymond Arthur and Mary Margaret (Habig) F. BA in Sociology, Thomas More Coll., 1973; attended, Westminster Choir Coll., 1982-85. Social worker Cath. Charities, Cin., 1973-75; assoc. dir. Met. Area Religious Coalition of Cin., 1975-79, cons., 1981-82; organizational devel. cons. C-Major Vision, Princeton, N.J., 1985-87; exec. asst. Winsight, Inc., Princeton, 1987-88; immigration liaison Princeton Theol. Sem., 1988-91; urban ministry assoc. Presbytery of New Brunswick, Trenton, N.J., 1991-92; pres. Shared Vision, Princeton, 1992—; founder WomenFirst, Inc., Paterson, N.J., 1993—. Singer The Living Visions Ensemble, 1985-87; trustee C-Major Vision, Inc., 1985—; bd. dirs. Feminist Bd. of Greater Cin., 1978-79. Recipient Outstanding Svc. award NCCJ, 1978. Roman Catholic. Home: 261 Moore St Princeton NJ 08540-3403 Office: Shared Vision 261 Moore St Princeton NJ 08540-3403

FOX, MARY ANN WILLIAMS, librarian; b. Savannah, Ga., Jan. 16, 1939; d. Alton F. and Arthur (Colquitt) Williams; m. William Francis Fox, Dec. 26, 1960 (div. 1984); children: Katherine Frances, William Francis Jr. BA, U. Ga., 1960; MLS, Rutgers U., 1984. Libr. Metuchen (N.J.) Pub. Libr., 1983-85, Mable Smith Douglas Libr. Rutgers U., New Brunswick, N.J., 1984, Firestone Libr. Princeton (N.J.) U., 1985, The Hun Sch. of Princeton, 1985—; bd. dirs. Region 5 Libr. Coop., N.J., 1985-92. Trustee East Brunswick (N.J.) Pub. Library, 1979-92; bd. dirs., Cen. Jersey YWCA, New Brunswick, 1985-88, Cen. Atlantic Conf. United Ch. of Christ, 1985-88. Mem. ALA, N.J. Libr. Assn., N.J. Ind. Sch. Assn. (chair libr. sect. 1988—), Edn. Media Assn. N.J. (bd. dirs. 1987—), Librs. of Middlesex (pres.). Democrat. Mem. United Ch. of Christ. Home: 10 Redcoat Dr East Brunswick NJ 08816-2759 Office: Hun Sch Princeton Edgerstone Rd Princeton NJ 08540

FOX, MARYE ANNE, chemistry educator; b. Canton, Ohio, Dec. 9, 1947. BS, Notre Dame Coll. of Ohio, 1969; MS, Cleve. State U., 1970; PhD, Dartmouth Coll., 1974; postgrad., U. Md., 1974-76. Prof. chemistry U. Tex., Austin, 1976-91, Rowland Pettit Centennial prof., 1986-92, M. June and J. Virgil Waggoner regents chair chemistry, 1992—, v.p. rsch., 1994—; mem. Nat. Sci. Bd., 1991—, also vice-chair, 1994—. Assoc. editor Jour. Am. Chem. Soc., 1986-94; mem. adv. bd. Jour. Organic Chemistry, Chem. Engring. News, Chem. Review; contbr. numerous articles to profl. jours. Recipient Agnes Faye Morgan Rsch. award, Iota Sigma Pi, 1984, Arthur C. Cope scholar award Am. Chem. Soc., 1988; Garvan medal Am. Chem. Soc., 1988, Havinga medal Leiden U., 1991; named to Hall of Excellence, Ohio Found. Ind. Colls., 1987, The Best of the New Generation, Esquire Mag., 1984; Alfred P. Sloan Rsch. fellow, 1980-82, Camille and Henry Dreyfus tchr. scholar, 1981-85. Mem. Nat. Acad. Sci., Am. Acad. Arts and Sci. Home: 5203 Valburn Cir Austin TX 78731-1142 Office: Univ Tex Dept Chemistry Austin TX 78712

FOX, MAXINE RANDALL, banker; b. Yates Ctr., Kans., Feb. 18, 1924; d. Carey Holaday and Nettie Myrrl (Herder) Randall; m. Joseph Marlin Fox, Aug. 25, 1946 (dec. 1992); children: Kathryn Lynette Fox Wilz, Jonathan Randall Fox. A in Fine Arts, Colo. Woman's Coll., 1942; B Music Edn., U. Denver, 1946. Pub. sch. music. tchr. Barr Lake (Colo.), 1942-43, Independence Sch., Fort Lupton, Colo., 1943-44, Fowler Pub. Schs., Fowler, Colo., 1944-48, 1952-54; employee The Fox Ins. Agy., Fowler, Colo., 1948-55, co-owner, 1955-86; with The Fowler (Colo.) State Bank, 1949—, vice chmn. bd. dirs., 1987—. Former mem. Fowler Libr. Bd.; mem. PEO. Mem. AAUW, DAR, First Families Ohio, Descendants Colonial Clergy (life), Fowler Hist. Soc. (past treas.), Fowler C. of C., Friends of Libr., Fowler Women's Club, Order Ea. Star, Fowler Golf Club, Pueblo Golf and Country Club. Republican. Methodist. Home: 3308 Rd KK.75 Fowler CO 81039 Office: Fowler State Bank 201 S Main St Fowler CO 81039-1132

FOX, MIRIAM ANNETTE, state legislative fiscal analyst; b. Cuba, N.Y., May 27, 1959; m. Frederick S. Fox, Jan., 1991. BA in Polit. Sci., Idaho State U., 1984; MS in Pub. Mgmt. & Policy, Carnegie-Mellon, 1986. Semiconductor line technician Gould/AMI, Pocatello, Idaho, 1978-84; legal rsch. analyst Manning, Holmes And Winmill Law Firm, Pocatello, 1983-84; market rsch. intern Internat. Trade Adminstrn., Pitts., 1985; rsch. intern Health & Welfare Planning Assn., Pitts., 1985-86; acctg. clk. Carnegie Mellon U., Pitts., 1986; tax revenue analyst Pa. House Appropriations Com., Harrisburg, 1987-91, sr. tax revenue analyst, 1991-93, sr. fiscal analyst, 1993—; designee to Pa. Sch. Employees Retirement Sys. Bd., 1993—. Mem. Capitol Hill Dem. Women's Club, Phi Kappa Phi. Office: Pa House Reps Appropriations Com 512 E9 Main Capitol Bldg PO Box 54 Harrisburg PA 17108-0054

FOX, MURIEL, public relations executive; b. Newark, Feb. 3, 1928; d. M. Morris and Anne L. (Rubenstein) F.; m. Shepard G. Aronson, July 1, 1955; children: Eric R., Lisa S. Student, Rollins Coll., 1944-46; B.A. summa cum laude, Barnard Coll., 1948. Art critic, bridal editor Miami (Fla.) News, 1946; reporter U.P.I., 1946-48; polit. speechwriter, publicist, 1949-50; with Carl Byoir & Assos., N.Y.C., 1950-86; TV-radio writer Carl Byoir & Assos., 1950-52, dir. TV-radio dept., 1952-57, v.p., 1956-74, group v.p., 1974-76, exec. v.p., 1977-85; pres. subs. MediaCom Communications Tng., 1975-85, By/Media Inc., 1981-85; sr. cons. Hill & Knowlton, Inc., 1986-90; dir. Harleysville Ins. Co., Rorer Group Inc.; Co-chmn. Vice Presdl. Task Force on Women, 1968; mem. steering com. Women's Forum, 1974-79, pres., 1976-78; mem. Women's Econ. Adv. Com., N.Y.C., 1974-78; mem. nat. adv. com. Nat. Women's Polit. Caucus; mem. nat. adv. bd. Women Today, Ethnic Woman. Bd. dirs. N.Y. Diabetes Assn., 1956-66; bd. dirs. Holy Land Conservation Fund, United Way of Tri-State, Internat. Rescue Com., 1977-84; v.p. Rockland Ctr. for the Arts, 1985—. Named one of 100 Top Corp. Women Bus. Week mag., 1976; recipient Matrix award Women in Communications, 1977, Bus. Leader of Year award ADA, 1979; Disting. Alumna award Barnard Coll., 1985; Eleanor Roosevelt Leadership award, 1985. Mem. NOW (founder, v.p. 1967-70, chmn. bd. 1971-73, chmn. nat. adv. com. 1973-74, bd. dirs. legal defense and edn. fund 1974—, v.p. fund 1977-78, pres. 1978-81, chmn. bd. 1981—, Muriel Fox Communications Leadership award 1991), Am. Women in Radio and TV (bd. dirs. 1950-51, chmn. nat. publicity com. 1955-57, chmn. nat. pub. rels. com. 1957-59, Achievement award 1983), Am. Arbitration Assn. (bd. dirs. 1983-87). Home and Office: 66 Hickory Hill Rd Tappan NY 10983-1804

FOX, NANCY LOUISE, office nurse; b. Schenectady, N.Y., Feb. 22, 1949; d. Burton Marsh and Ruth Mary (Elliott) Ball; m. John Paul Fox Jr., May 10, 1969; children: Eric, Shannon. Student Sch. Nursing, Elliot Community Hosp., 1967-69. LPN, Mass. LPN Sturdy Meml. Hosp., Attleboro, Mass., 1974-82, Good Samaritan Hosp., Tampa, Fla., 1982-84, Dr. Beverly J. Vance, Tampa, 1984-85, Dr. David S. Stroud, Wareham, Mass., 1985—. Deaconess First Congl. Ch., Wareham, 1989—, choir mem., 1988—; co-chairperson The Diaconete, 1994-95. Home: 191 High St Wareham MA 02571 Office: Dr David S Stroud MD 53 Marion Rd Wareham MA 02571

FOX, PATRICIA ANN, school librarian, media specialist; b. Peekskill, N.Y., Nov. 9, 1942; d. Martin Van Deusen and Martha M. Hunt; m. Charles James Fox, Aug. 14, 1966; children: Jeffrey, Martin, Traci Lynn, Brandi Lynn. BA, SUNY, Albany, 1964. Cert. libr. media specialist. Tchr. social studies Gloversville (N.Y.) High Sch., 1964-66; elem. librarian Amsterdam (N.Y.) Sch. Dist., 1966-67; sch. libr. media specialist Greater Johnstown (N.Y.) Sch., 1967—, libr. media dept. chair, 1989—; mem. adv. coun. Hamilton Fultom Montgomery Sch. Libr. System,. Johnston, 1986—, chmn. adv. coun., 1988-90; mem. steering com. Knox Jr. High Sch., Johnstown, 1992. Mem. AAUW (v.p. membership Amsterdam br. 1984-85, pres. 1991—), Ecclectic Study Club (pres. 1987-88), Eastern N.Y. Libr. Assocs. Home: 119 Woodlawn Dr Gloversville NY 12078 Office: Knox Jr High Sch 400 S Perry St Johnstown NY 12095

FOX, PAULA (MRS. MARTIN GREENBERG), author; b. N.Y.C., Apr. 22, 1923; d. Paul Hervey and Elsie (de Sola) F.; m. Richard Sigerson (div. 1954); children: Adam, Linda, Gabriel; m. Martin Greenberg, June 9, 1962. Student, Columbia U. Condr. writing Seminars U. Pa. Author: 22 children's books and 6 novels, including How Many Miles to Babylon, 1966, Portrait of Ivan, 1968, Blowfish Live in the Sea, 1970; (novels) Poor George, 1967, Desperate Characters, 1970, The Western Coast, 1972, The Slave Dancer, 1974 (John Newbery medal), The Widow's Children, 1976, The Little Swineherd and Other Tales, 1978, A Place Apart, 1983 (Am. Book award), A Servant's Tale, 1984, One-Eyed Cat, 1985 (Newbery honor book 1985), Maurice's Room, 1985, The Moonlight Man, 1986, The Stone-Faced Boy, 1987, The Village by the Sea, 1988, Lily and the Lost Boy, 1989, The God of Nightmares, 1990, Monkey Island, 1991, Amzat and His Brothers, 1993, Western Wind, 1993. Recipient Arts and Letters award Nat. Inst. Arts and Letters, 1972, Hans Christian Andersen medal, 1978, fiction citation Brandeis U., 1984; Guggenheim fellow, 1972. Mem. P.E.N., Authors League. Address: care Robert Lescher 67 Irving Pl New York NY 10003

FOX, RENÉE CLAIRE, sociology educator; b. N.Y.C., Feb. 15, 1928; d. Paul Fred and Henrietta (Gold) F. A.B. summa cum laude, Smith Coll., 1949, L.H.D., 1975; Ph.D., Harvard U., 1954; M.A. (hon.), U. Pa., 1971; Sc.D. (hon.), Med. Coll. Pa., 1974, St. Joseph's Coll., Phila., 1978; D. honoris causa, Katholieke U., Belgium, 1978; LHD (hon.), La Salle U., Phila., 1988; DSc (hon.), Hahnemann U., 1991. Rsch. asst. Bur. Applied Social Rsch., Columbia U., 1953-55, rsch. assoc., 1955-58; lectr. dept. sociology Barnard Coll., 1955-58, asst. prof., 1958-64, assoc. prof., 1964-66; lectr. sociology Harvard U., 1967-69; rsch. fellow Center Internat. Affairs, 1967-68, research assoc. program tech. and soc., 1968-71; prof. sociology, psychiatry and medicine U. Pa., Phila., 1969—, Annenberg prof. social scis., 1978—, chmn. dept. sociology, 1972-78; sci. adviser Centre de Recherches Sociologiques, Kinshasa, Congo, 1963-67; vis. prof. sociology U. Officielle du Congo, Lubumbashi, 1965; vis. prof. Sir George Williams U., Montreal, Que., Can., summer 1968; Phi Beta Kappa vis. scholar, 1973-75; dir. humanities seminar med. practitioners NEH, 1975-76; maître de cours U. Liége, Belgium, 1976-77; vis. prof. Katholieke U., Leuven, Belgium, 1976-77; Wm. Allen Neilson prof. Smith Coll., Mass., 1980; dir. d' Etudes Associé, Ecole des Hautes Etudes en Sciences Sociales, Paris, summer 1989; mem. bd. clin. scholars program Robert Wood Johnson Found., 1974-80; mem. Pres.'s Commn. on Study of Ethical Problems in Medicine, Biomed. and Behavioral Research, 1979-81; dir. human qualities of medicine program James Picker Found., 1980-83; Fae Golden Kass lectr. Harvard U. Sch. Medicine and Radcliffe Coll., 1983, Kate Hurd Mead lectr. Med. Coll. Pa./Coll. Physicians Phila., 1990, Lori Ann Roscetti Meml. lectr. Rush-Presbyn.-St. Luke's Med. Ctr., Chgo., 1990; vis. scholar Women's Ctr., U. Mo., Kansas City, 1990, vis. scholar Case Western Reserve Sch. of Med., 1992; opening address 13th Internat. Conf. on Social Scis. and Medicine, Hungary, 1994, vis. prof. U. Calif., San Francisco Sch. of Med., 1994; lectr. founds. of medicine Faculty of Medicine McGill U., Montreal, Can., 1995. Author: Experiment Perilous, 1959, (with Willy DeCraemer) The Emerging Physician, 1968, (with Judith P. Swazey) The Courage to Fail, 1974, rev. edit. 1978, Essays in Medical Sociology, 1979, 2d edit., 1988, L'Incertitude Medicale, 1988, The Sociology of Medicine: A Participant Observer's View, 1989, (with Judith P. Swazey) Spare Parts: Organ Replacement in American Society, 1992, In the Belgian Château: The Spirit and Culture of European Society in an Age of Change, 1994; assoc. editor: Am. Sociol. Rev, 1963-66, Social Sci. and Medicine; mem. editorial com.: Ann. Rev. Sociology, 1975-79; assoc. editor Jour. Health and Social Behavior, 1985-87; mem. editorial adv. bd. Tech. in Soc., Sci., 1982-83; mem. editorial bd. Bibliography of Bioethics, 1979—, Culture, Medicine and Psychiatry, 1980-86, Jour. of AMA, 1981-94, Am. Scholar,

1994—, Current Revs. in Publs., 1994—; vice chair adv. bd. Am. Jour. Ethics and Medicine; contbr. articles to profl. jours. Bd. dirs. Medicine in Public Interest, 1979—; mem. tech. bd. Milbank Meml. Fund, 1979-85; mem. overseers com. to visit univ. health services Harvard Coll., 1979-86; trustee Russell Sage Found., 1981-87; vice chmn. bd. dirs. Acadia Inst., 1990—. Recipient E. Harris Harbison Gifted Teaching award Danforth Found., 1970, Radcliffe Grad. Soc. medal, 1977, Lindback Found. award for teaching U. Pa., 1989, Centennial medal Grad. Sch. Arts and Scis. Harvard U., 1993; Wilson Ctr., Smithsonian Instn. fellow, 1987-88, Guggenheim fellow, 1962; Fulbright Short-Term Sr. scholar to Australia, 1994. Fellow African Studies Assn., AAAS (dir. 1977-80, chmn. sect. K 1986-87), Am. Sociol. Assn. (council 1970-73, 79-81, v.p. 1980-81), Am. Acad. Arts and Scis. (co-chair Class III section I membership com., 1994—), Inst. Medicine (Nat. Acad. Scis., council 1979-82), Inst. Soc., Ethics and Life Scis. (founder, gov.); mem. AAUP, AAUW, Assn. Am. Med. Colls., Social Sci. Research Council (v.p., dir.), Eastern Sociol. Soc. (pres. 1976-77, Merit award 1993), N.Y. Acad. Scis., Soc. Sci. Study Religion, Inst. Intercultural Studies, 1969-93, (asst. sec. 1969-78, sec. 1978-81, 89-92, v.p. 1987-89), Am. Bd. Med. Specialists, Coll. of Physicians of Phila. (council, 1993—), Phi Beta Kappa (senate 1982-87). Home: 135 S 19th St Philadelphia PA 19103-4912

FOX, SARA, artist, sculptor; b. Haifa, Israel, July 4, 1949; came to U.S., 1956; d. Mark and Miriam (Brender) Auerbach; m. Carl Fox, Mar. 23, 1968; children: David, Jason. Owner Zeeks & Creations Inc., Lake Helen, Fla. Creator Zeeks (people sculptures) as seen in N.Y. Galleries, World Trade Ctr., N.Y.C., Columbus Day Parade, Orlando Mag., Ctrl. Fla. Mag., Orlando Sentinel, News Jour., Winter Park (Fla.) Art Festival, Jazzfest, DeLand Mus., others; commns. for murals include City of of Pontiac, Mich., N.Y. med. ctrs., pvt. homes and offices; creator unique props. for off-Broadway prodns.; stage design for nightclubs and theatrical prodns. Office: Zeeks & Creations Inc PO Box 55 Lake Helen FL 32744-0055

FOX, SARAH, lawyer; b. Buffalo, Dec. 12, 1951; d. Austin McCracken and Jean McLean (Coatsworth) F. BA, Yale U., 1973; JD, Harvard U., 1982. Reporter Buffalo Courier-Express, 1973-79; staff counsel Internat. Union of Bricklayers & Allied Craftsmen, Washington, 1982-90; chief labor counsel Senate Labor and Human Resources Com., Washington, 1990—. Office: Labor & Human Resources Com 428 Dirksen Senate Office Bldg Washington DC 20510

FOX, SELENA MARIE (SUZANNE BISSET CARPENTER), minister, priestess, psychotherapist; b. Arlington, Va., Oct. 20, 1949; d. Thomas Richard and Anne Elise (Fox) Bisset; m. Dennis Darrel Carpenter, June 7, 1986. BS in Psychology with honors, Coll. William and Mary, 1971; postgrad., Rutgers U., 1972, Madison Area Tech. Coll., Wis., 1973-75, U. Wis., 1991—. Min. Circle Sanctuary, Mt. Horeb, Wis., 1974—; guest min. Unitarian Universalists, Wis., others, 1980—; speaker chs. and spiritual communities, U.S. and Can., 1975—; speaker, organizer regional, nat., internat. ecospiritual/pagan festivals, 1977—; del., speaker World Coun. Chs. Conf., Toronto, 1988, Parliament of World's Religions, Chgo.,1993, others; guest speaker tchr. at univs., 1980—; founder, exec. dir. Circle Sanctuary Nature Preserve, 1983—; founder Sch. for Priestesses, 1986, Lady Liberty League, 1991; Wiccan civil rights leader. Author: Goddess Communion Rituals, 1988; cons. (Time-Life book series) Mysteries of the Unknown, 1990; founding editor Circle Guide to Pagan Groups, 1979, Circle Network News quar., 1980, Circle Guide to Pagan Arts, 1992; founder Circle's Worldwide Nature Spirituality Network, 1978, Wiccan Shamanism, 1979, Pagan Academic Network, 1992; contbr. articles and rituals to books and jours., 1975—; nat./internat. Nature Spirituality spokesperson on TV, and radio, for films, mags., newspapers, others, 1979—. Recipient Feature Writing Excellence award PROCOM/WABC, Madison, 1978. Mem. ACA, Am. Mental Health Counselors Assn., Assn. for Transpersonal Psychology, Am. Academy of Religion. Mem. Circle Sanctuary/Nature Spiritualist. Office: Circle Sanctuary PO Box 219 Mount Horeb WI 53572-0219

FOX-FREUND, BARBARA SUSAN, real estate executive; b. Rocky Mount, N.C., Jan. 17, 1949; d. Albert Richard and Anita (Levinson) Fox; m. James Coleman Freund, Jan. 12, 1985. Student, Centenary Coll., 1968, Boston U., 1970. Real estate broker Whitbread-Nolan, Inc., N.Y.C., 1972-80; v.p. Stribling and Assocs., Ltd., N.Y.C., 1980-82; exec. v.p. Cross and Brown Residentials, Inc., N.Y.C., 1982-88; pres. Fox Residential Group, Inc., N.Y.C., 1988—. Bd. dirs. Riverside Symphony, N.Y.C., 1989; bd. dirs., pres. 55 W. 73d St. Corp., N.Y.C., 1986—. Mem. Real Estate Bd. N.Y. (chmn. residential com. 1986-89, ethics com. 1989-92, bd. dirs. brokerage com. 1988-92, tchr. 1986—, chmn. inter-firm rels. com. 1991-93, bd. dirs. residential div. 1994—, bd. govs. 1994—). Republican. Jewish. Home: 55 W 73d St New York NY 10023 Office: Fox Residential Group Inc 1015 Madison Ave New York NY 10021-0204

FOXHOVEN, SISTER CHARLITA, nun, religious organization administrator; b. Earling, Iowa, Sept. 26, 1931; d. Henry M. and Frances M. (Kaufman) F. BA in Mgmt., Alverno Coll., 1976; MBA, Northwestern U., 1985. Bookeeper, acct. John W. Stang Corp., Omaha, 1950-56; acct. Sch. Sisters of St. Francis, Milw., 1958-69, treas. internat., 1980—. Bd. dirs. St. Francis Svc. Found., Milw., 1987-94, Alverno Coll., Milw., 1969-77, St. Mary's Hill Hosp., Milw., 1969-87. Mem. Nat. Assn. Religious Treasurers (presenter nat. conv. 1980, 86), Regional Assn. Religious Treasurers, U.S. Cath. Conf. (acctg. practices com. 1985, 86). Office: Sch Sisters St Francis 1501 S Layton Blvd Milwaukee WI 53215-1924

FOXXE, JOANNE LYNN, realtor; b. N.Y.C., Apr. 29, 1955; d. Stuart Morton and Edith Marcia (Brawer) Ratner. BA in Sociology, U. Calif., Santa Cruz, 1978; student, Grad. Realtor Inst., 1986. Cert. residential specialist, Calif. Realtor David Lyng & Assocs., Capitola, Calif., 1989—. Mem. Santa Cruz Bd. Realtors (profl. standards com. 1992-93), Women in Bus., Santa Cruz C. of C., David Lyng & Assocs. President's Club. Office: David Lyng & Assocs 2170 41st Ave Capitola CA 95010-2009

FRACKMAN, NOEL, art critic; b. N.Y.C., May 27, 1930; d. Walter David and Celeste (Barman) Stern; m. Richard Benoit Frackman, July 2, 1950; 1 child, Noel Dru Pyne. Student Mt. Holyoke Coll., 1948-50; BA, Sarah Lawrence Coll., 1952, MA, 1953; postgrad. Columbia U., 1964-67; MA, Inst. Fine Arts, NYU, 1976, PhD, 1987. Art critic Scarsdale Inquirer (N.Y.), 1962-67, Patent Trader, Mt. Kisco, N.Y., 1962-71; assoc. Arts Mag., N.Y.C., 1968—; lectr. Aldrich Mus. Contemporary Art, Ridgefield, Conn., 1967-75, Gallery Passport Ltd., N.Y.C., 1968—; contractual lectr. Met. Mus. Art, N.Y.C., 1994—; curator of edn. Storm King Art Ctr., Mountainville, N.Y., 1973-75; instr. continuing edn. div. SUNY, Purchase, 1988—; bd. dirs. Friends of the Neuberger Mus. Art, Purchase (N.Y.) Coll., Shah U. N.Y., 1994—. Author (catalogue) John Storrs, Whitney Mus. of Am. Art, 1986; contbr. articles and/or revs. to various mags. including: Arts Mag., Harper's Bazaar, Feminist Art Jour., Art Voices. Sarah Williston scholar, 1948-50; recipient 1st prize, coll. publs. contest Mademoiselle mag., 1961. Mem. Internat. Assn. Art Critics, Art Table Inc., Coll. Art Assn. Home: 3 Hadden Rd Scarsdale NY 10583-3327

FRAGNUL, RITA MARIE, artist; b. N.Y.C., Feb. 23, 1922; d. Andrew and Josephine (Ferrari) Drago; m. Daniel F. Fragnul, Aug. 29, 1964. BA in Studio Art, U. Md., 1985, BA in Art History, 1986. Radio actor Sta. WEVD, N.Y.C., 1944-51, Sta. WAAT, Newark, 1944-51; Freelance photographer N.Y.C., 1953-58, freelance painter, 1959-64; freelance painter Silver Spring, Md., 1968-90, Bethesda, Md., 1991—. Vol. staff congress U.S. House Reps., Washington, 1981-87. Mem. Nat. Mus. of Women in Arts. Democrat. Roman Catholic. Home: 4400 E West Hwy Bethesda MD 20814-4524

FRAHM, SHEILA, lieutenant governor, former state legislator; b. Colby, Kans., Mar. 22, 1945; m. Kenneth Frahm; children: Amy, Pam, Chrissie. BS, Ft. Hays State U., 1967. Mem. bd. edn. State of Kans., 1985-88; mem. Kans. Senate, Topeka, 1988-94, senate majority leader, 1993-94; lt. gov. State of Kans., 1995—. Mem. AAUW (Outstanding Br. Mem. 1985), Thomas County Day Care Assn., Shakespeare Fedn. Women's Clubs, Farm Bur., Kans. Corn Growers, Kans. Livestock Assn., Rotary (Paul Harris fellow 1988). Republican. Address: 985 S Range Ave Colby KS 67701-3504 also: Lt Gov's Office 2225 State Capitol Topeka KS 66612

FRAKER, BARBARA J., elementary education educator, school system administrator, middle school education educator; b. Kansas City, Mo., Apr. 22, 1950; d. Theodore and Donna Ruth (Beitman) Van Alden; children: Tamara Amanda, Everett Nathaniel. BS, Taylor U., Upland, Ind., 1972; MA, U. Mo., Kansas City, 1978, EdS, 1983. Cert. elem. tchr., K-12 reading tchr., elem. adminstr., mid. sch. social studies, 9-12 social studies and early childhood tchr., Mo. Tchr. Scarritt Elem. Sch., Kansas City, Mo., 1972-73, Richardson Elem. Sch., Kansas City, 1973-76, Willard Elem. Sch., Kansas City, 1976-80, Linwood Elem. Sch., Kansas City, 1980-81; title I tchr. Kalihi Waena Elem. Sch., Honolulu, Hawaii, 1981-82; instrnl. asst. to prin., tchr. C.A. Franklin Elem. Sch. Kansas City Sch. Dist., 1983-86; tchr., reading resource Lincoln Middle Sch., 1986-92; tchr. social studies resource Kansas City Sch. Dist., 1992-93; curriculum coord. Lincoln Middle Math/Sci. Magnet Sch., Kansas City, 1993—. Mem. ASCD (assoc.), Nat. Coun. Social Studies, Phi Delta Kappa (v.p. Zeta Delta chpt. membership 1991-92, pres. 1992—). Office: Lincoln Middle Sch 2012 E 23rd St Kansas City MO 64127-3702

FRALEY, PENNY KELLY, librarian; b. Springdale, Ohio, Oct. 4, 1946; d. Russell Ross and Katherine (Sims) Kelly; m. George Wayne Fraley, Aug. 17, 1968; children: Andrew, Julianne. BA in Edn., Morehead State U., 1970. Elem. libr. Steubenville (Ohio) City Schs., 1971-73; asst. libr. Mercy Hosp., Hamilton, Ohio, 1983-87; libr. Internat. Tech. Corp., Cin., 1987—. Mem. Spl. Librs. Assn. Office: Internat Tech Corp 11499 Chester Rd Cincinnati OH 45246-4012

FRAME, ANNE PARSONS, civic worker; b. Berkeley, Calif., Jan. 3, 1904; d. Reginald Hascall and Maude (Bemis) Parsons; A.B., Mills Coll., 1924; postgrad. Columbia, 1924-25; m. Frederic D. Tootell, Apr. 3, 1926 (div. July 1935); children: Geoffrey H., Natalie (Mrs. Oliver); m. Jasper Ewing Brady, Jr., July 31, 1935; (dec. Dec. 1944); 1 son, Hugh Parsons; m. Howard Andres Frame, Mar. 29, 1948 (dec. Dec. 1986). Dir. Parsons, Hart & Co., Seattle, Hillcrest Orchard Co., Seattle. Mem. bd. mgmt. Palo Alto br. A.R.C., 1955-61; trustee Children's Hosp. & Med. Ctr., Seattle, 1942-48; bd. dirs. Children's Health Coun., Palo Alto, Calif., 1953-63, 64-76, pres., 1954-58, assoc. mem., Seattle, 1986—; sponsor Nat. Recreation Assn., 1942-66, trustee, 1948-66; sponsor Nat. Recreation and Park Assn., 1966—, trustee, 1966-73; trustee Nat. Recreation Found., 1964—; 1st v.p. Children's Hosp. at Stanford Sr. Aux., 1965-67, bd. dirs. Hosp., 1967-85; former mem. adv. com. Holbrook-Palmer Park; trustee Mills Coll., 1952-62; bd. dirs. Holbrook-Palmer Recreation Park Found., 1968-86; bd. govs. San Francisco Symphony Assn., 1949-79; mem. Atherton (Calif.) Park and Recreation Commn., 1968-81. Mem. LWV, Bowne House Hist. Soc., San Mateo County, Seattle, Chgo., Calif. hist. socs., Calif. Heritage Council, San Francisco Mus. Art, Seattle Art Mus., Museum Soc., Nat. Trust for Historic Preservation, Nat. Soc. Colonial Dames Am. Episcopalian. Clubs: Sunset, Tennis (Seattle), Woodside-Atherton Garden (bd. dirs. 1966-68), Francisca (San Francisco), Menlo Country (Calif.), Seattle Garden Club.

FRAME, NANCY DAVIS, lawyer; b. Brookings, S.D., Dec. 13, 1944; d. Wilmer L. and Adele N. (Swensen) D.; m. J. Davidson Frame, Mar. 28, 1970; 1 child, Katherine Adele. BS, S.D. State U., 1966; MA, Georgetown U., 1968, JD, 1976. Bar: D.C. 1976. Atty., advisor AID, Washington, 1976-81, asst. gen. counsel, 1981-86; dep. dir. Trade and Devel. Agy., Washington, 1986—. Recipient Superior Honor award AID, 1984, Presdl. Rank award, 1993; Fulbright fellow , 1966, NDEA fellow, 1967. Mem. ABA, Fed. Bar Assn. Home: 5819 Magic Mountain Dr Rockville MD 20852-3231 Office: Trade and Devel Agy SA 16 Washington DC 20523

FRANANO, SUSAN MARGARET KETTEMAN, orchestra administrator, soprano; b. Kansas City, Mo., Sept. 30, 1946; d. Charley Gilbert and Mary Elizabeth (Bredehoeft) Ketteman; m. Frank Salvatore Franano, Dec. 20, 1969; 1 child, Domenico Frank. AA, Stephens Coll., Columbia, Mo., 1966, BFA, 1967; postgrad., U. Mo., Kansas City, 1967-68; MusM, So. Ill. U., Edwardsville, 1969. Gen. mgr. Kansas City (Mo.) Symphony Orch.; mgr. Lyric Opera Group, Kansas City, 1976-82; tour coordinator Lyric Opera Kansas City, 1978-85; dir. outreach Kansas City Symphony, 1982-84, asst. mgr., 1984-85, ops. mgr., 1985-86, gen. mgr., 1986—. Regional liaison Mo. Citizens for Arts, Kansas City, 1984-86; regional rep. Am. Guild Mus. Artists, Kansas City, 1977-81; regional ammenities task force mem. Mid-Am. Regional Coun., 1989—; panelist Nat. Endowment for the Arts, 1991. Mem. Am. Symphony Orch. League, Mo. Citizens for Arts, Symphony Women's Assn., Jr. Women's Symphony Alliance, Friends of Symphony, Kansas City Consensus, Cen. Exchange Club (Kansas City), Woodside Racquet Club (Shawnee Mission). Democrat. Roman Catholic. Office: Kans City Symphony 1020 Central Ste 300 Kansas City MO 64105*

FRANCA, CELIA, ballet director, choreographer, dancer, narrator; b. London, Eng., June 25, 1921; m. James Morton, Dec. 7, 1960. Student, Guildhall Sch. Music, Royal Acad. Dancing; LLD (hon.), Assumption U. of Windsor, 1959, Mt. Allison U., 1966, U. Toronto, 1974, Dalhousie U., 1976, York U., 1976, Trent U., Peterborough, Ont., Can., 1977, McGill U., 1986; DCL (hon.), Bishop's U., 1967; DLitt (hon.), Guelph U., 1976. Founder, artistic dir. Nat. Ballet Can., Toronto, 1951-74; co-founder Nat. Ballet Sch., Toronto, 1959; Mem. jury 5th Internat. Ballet Competition, Varna, Bulgaria, 1970, 2d Internat. Ballet Competition, Moscow, 1973. Debut: corps de ballet Mars, The Planets (Tudor), Mercury Theatre, London, 1936; soloist, Ballet Rambert, London, 1936-38, leading dramatic dancer, Ballet Rambert, 1938-39, guest artist, Ballet Rambert, 1950, dancer, Ballet des Trois Arts, London, 1939, Arts Theatre Ballet, London, 1940, Internat. Ballet, London, 1941, leading dramatic dancer, Sadler's Wells Ballet, 1941-46, guest artist, choreographer, Sadler's Wells Theatre Ballet, London, 1946-47, dancer, tchr., Ballets Jooss, Eng., 1947, ballet mistress, leading dancer, Met. Ballet, London, 1947-49, dancer, Ballet Workshop, London, 1949-51, prin. dancer, Nat. Ballet Can., 1951-59; prin. roles include Black Queen in Swan Lake; title roles in Lady from the Sea; choreographer: ballets, including Midas, London, 1939, Cancion, London, 1942, Khadra, London, 1946, Dance of Salome, BBC-TV, 1949, The Eve of St. Agnes, BBC-TV, 1950, Afternoon of a Faun, Toronto, 1952, Le Pommier, Toronto, 1952, Casse-Noisette, 1955, Princess Aurora, 1960, The Nutcracker, 1964, Cinderella, 1968, numerous others for CBC, Can. Opera Co.; author: The National Ballet of Canada: A Celebration, 1978. Hon. patron Osteoporosis Soc. Can. Decorated Order of Can.; recipient Key to City of Washington, 1955; Woman of Year award B'nai B'rith, 1958; award for outstanding contbn. to arts Toronto Telegram, 1965; Centennial medal, 1967; Hadassah award of merit, 1967; Molson award, 1974; award Internat. Soc. Performing Arts Adminstrs., 1979; twice visited China at invitation of Chinese govt. to teach; in Beijing mounted full-length Coppelia, 1980; honored as one of founders of Can.'s major ballet cos. at Alta. Ballet Co.'s 15th anniversary, 1981; recipient Can. Dance award, 1984; Gold Card IATSE local 58, 1984; diplôme d'honneur Can. Conf. Arts, 1986, Woman Yr. award St. George's Soc. Toronto, 1987, Order of Ont., 1987, Gov. Gen. award, 1994. Office: 203 350 Queen Elizabeth Dr, Ottawa, ON Canada K1S 3N1 also: 157 King St E, Toronto, ON Canada M5C 1G9*

FRANCES, LINDA KAY EDMONDS, medical technologist, artist; b. Lima, Ohio, Dec. 29, 1941; d. Dale Clair Edmonds and P.A. Leota (Lee) (McCurdy) Beard Keogh; m. Richard William Luedtke, Apr. 23, 1962 (div. Oct., 1979); children: Laura Linda (dec.), Lisa Ann, Richard Dale; m. Frederick D. DeMarais, Nov. 21, 1993 (div. Mar. 1995). BS in Med. Tech. cum laude, U. Toledo, 1963, BA in Painting summa cum laude, 1976; BFA, Bowling Green U., 1977, postgrad. studies in Art, 1978-82. Med. technologist St. Luke's Hosp., Maumee, Ohio. One-person show Van Cliff Gallery, Toledo, 1986; group shows include Sydney Rothman Gallery, Barnagut Light, N.J., 1987, Artageous Gallery, San Diego, 1986-87, Common Space Gallery, Toledo, Ohio, 1989-95, Galleries Ginza, Tokyo, 1991; group exhbns. include Toledo Artists Club Gold Medal Show, 1987, 91, 92, Art on the Rocks, Marquette, Mich., 1990, Toledo Fedn. Mus. Show, 1990, Art 'n Apples, Rochester, Mich., 1989, 90, Ludington Art Festival, 1991, Cin. Summerfair, 1991, Master Artists Tour, 1991-93, others. Home and Studio: 8622 Avenue Rd Perrysburg OH 43551-4013

FRANCHINI, ELISABETTA PAIGE, artist; b. Chgo., June 27, 1960; d. Marcello Gregorio and Barbara Jean (Ralston) F. Student, U. Paris, 1980-81; BA, Smith Coll., 1982; postgrad., Sch. Visual Arts, N.Y.C., 1983-84. One woman shows include Third Coast, Chgo., 1987, Monique's, Chgo., 1988, Artscape Gallery, Rockford, Ill., 1989, Galeria Marchetti, Chgo., 1989, 90, 91, Caldwell Snyder Gallery, San Francisco, 1992, 93, 94, 95, Jayson Gallery, Chgo., 1992, 94; exhibited in group shows, 1984—, including Newport (R.I.) Outdoor Art Festival, 1984, Evanston (Ill.) Lakeshore Arts Festival, 1985, North Shore Art League, Winnetka, Ill., 1986, Midwest Pastel Soc., St. Charles, Ill., 1988, 94, Art Miami Internat. Art Expn., Miami Beach, Fla., 1994; illustrator: Karen Brown's Italian Country Bed and Breadfasts, 1992, 2d edit., 1994. Recipient hon. mention Newport Outdoor Art Festival, 1984, Evanston Lakeshore Arts Festival, 1985. Mem. Chgo. Artists Coalition, Terra Mus. Am. Art, Nat. Mus. Women in Arts, NOW. Studio: 934 Elmwood Ave Wilmette IL 60091

FRANCHINI, ROXANNE, banker; b. N.Y.C., Mar. 20, 1951; d. Tullio and Jean (Brady) F. Student, Emerson Coll., Ricker Coll., New Sch. Social Rsch. With Princess Marcella Borghese div. Revlon, N.Y.C., 1972-73; stewardess TWA Airlines, 1973-74; asst. to pres. N.Y. Shipping Assn., N.Y.C., 1974-79; benefits mgr. Kidde, Inc., N.Y.C., 1979-83; 2d v.p. pension trust fin. svcs. Chase Manhattan Bank, N.A., N.Y.C., 1983-85, v.p. mgr. global securities, 1985-89; v.p., sales dir. global custody worldwide securities svcs. Citibank, N.Y.C., 1989-91; v.p. Mellon Bank, Pitts., 1991—. Chair fin. local fund raising campaigns. Mem. AAUW, Am. Mgmt. Assn., Fin. Women's Assn. of N.Y., Internat. Found. Employee Benefits, Internat. Ops. Assn., Nat. Investment Co. Svc. Assn., Nat. Assn. Colls. and Univ. Bus. Offices.

FRANCIOSI, BARBARA LEE, designer, fiber artist; b. Batavia, N.Y., Oct. 25, 1931; d. Henry Curtis and Ferne Marie (Jewitt) Parcells; m. Raymond Louis Cates, June 23, 1950 (div. 1960); children: Gwynne Cates Chandler, Edward Paul Cates; m. Pat Franciosi, Feb. 1, 1964. Grad., Ctrl. City Bus. Coll., Syracuse, N.Y., 1949. Med. sec., asst. Harold Courtney, MD, Syracuse, N.Y., 1949-51; dir., owner Barbara Schs. of Dance, Preble, N.Y., and Groton, Conn., 1951-63; legal asst. Melvin Scott, Atty., New London, Conn., 1961-75; designer, owner Fiber Artistry by Barbara Lee, Groton, 1978—. Sec. Dem. City Com., Groton, Conn., 1972-76; candidate dist. judge of probate State of Conn., 1974; vice chmn. Dem. Town Com., Groton, 1976-80; elected Groton Town Coun., 1971, Rep. Town Meeting, Groton, 1969-71, 77-79; mem. Lyman Allyn Art Mus. Recipient numerous 1st prizes. Mem. Am. Craft Coun., Coun. Am. Embroiderers, Mystic Art Assn., Soc. Conn. Crafts. (bd. dirs., corr. sec. 1983-86). Office: Fiber Artistry by Barbara Lee 30 W Elderkin Ave Groton CT 06340

FRANCIS, CAROLYN RAE, music educator, musician, author, publisher; b. Seattle, July 25, 1940; d. James Douglas and Bessie Caroline (Smith) F; m. Barclay Underwood Stuart, July 5, 1971. BA in Edn., U. Wash., 1962. Cert. tchr., Wash. Tchr. Highline Pub. Schs., Seattle, 1962-64; musician Olympic Hotel, Seattle, 1962-72; 1st violin Cascade Symphony Orch., 1965-78; tchr. Bellevue (Wash.) Pub. Schs., 1965-92; founder/pres. Innovative Learning Designs, Mercer Island, Wash., 1984—; profl. violinist for TV, recs., mus. shows, 1962-85; violist Eastside Chamber Orch., 1984-86; pvt. tchr. string instruments, 1959—; spkr. in-svc. workshops, convs., music educators numerous cities; adjudicator music festivals; instr. MIDI applications for educators, 1992—. Author-pub. Music Reading and Theory Skills (curriculum series), Levels 1, 2, 1986, Level 3, 1984; contbr. articles to profl. jours., 1984—. Mem. Snohomish Indian Tribe. Bellevue Schs. Found. grantee, 1985-86, 86-87, 89-90. Mem. NEA, Am. String Tchrs. Assn. (regional mem. chmn. 1992-94), Music Educators Nat. Conf., Music Industry Coun. Office: Innovative Learning Designs 7811 SE 27th St Ste 104 Mercer Island WA 98040-2979

FRANCIS, KAREN ELYDA, television producer, painter; b. Memphis, Apr. 27, 1950; d. Ben Porter and Marguerite Katherine (Marlowe) F.; children: Sarah Helfinstein, Ben Helfinstein. BA in Communication Arts, Rhodes Coll., 1971; MA, U. Mo., 1973. Cert. tchr., Tenn. Secondary sch. tchr. Memphis City Schs., 1971-72; speech tchr. U. Ga., Athens, 1973-75; dir. computer systems installations Planning Rsch. Corp., McLean, Va., 1976-78; dir. account mgmt. TDX Systems, Cable & Wireless, Vienna, Va., 1978-80; cons. telecommunications MCI, Washington, 1985-87; producer Fairfax Cable Access, Merrifield, Va., 1991—; owner Art Promotions, McLean, 1989—. Exhibited paintings in numerous group and one-woman shows including Clark & Co. Gallery, Washington, 1994, McLean Project for Arts, 1992, Hospice of No. Va. Auction Gala, 1992, Touchstone Gallery Benefit Auction, McLean, 1991, Great Falls Art Ctr., Va., 1990, many others; paintings represented in numerous pvt. collections. Active Family AIDS Housing Found., 1992, Hospice No. Va., 1991, 92, Friends of Vietnam Vets. Meml., 1992; founding bd. mem. Jobs for Homeless People, 1988-90. Office: Art Promotions PO Box 3104 McLean VA 22103

FRANCIS, LA FRANCIS DIANA, nursing administrator, career officer; b. Brewton, Ala., Nov. 30, 1955; d. Lucian Webster Jr. and Mary (McMillan) Johnson; m. Denis Hinds Francis, Oct. 25, 1980; children: Amanda Rachel, Vanessa Nicole. BSN, U. No. Colo., 1978. Med.-surg. staff nurse Penrose Community Hosp., Colorado Springs, 1978; gen. surg. staff nurse Meml. Hosp., Colorado Springs, 1978-81; PRN reg. staff nurse Alpha Nurse Registry PRN, El Paso, Tex., 1981; head nurse North Park Community Hosp., El Paso, Tex., 1982; lt. jr. grade, post-part. staff nurse Naval Hosp., San Diego, 1982-83; lt., 1984—; post-part. asst. charge nurse Naval Hosp., San Diego, 1983, ortho. staff nurse, 1984, maj. jnt. ortho. staff nurse, 1984-85, EENT asst. charge nurse, 1985; ortho.-neurol. charge nurse Meml. Hosp., Colorado Springs, 1985-86; staff nurse ICU Naval Hosp. Beaufort, S.C., 1986-87, staff nurse gen. med.-surg., 1987, asst. charge nurse gen. med.-surg., 1988-89, div. officer acute care, 1989-90, charge nurse sickcall, 1990-91, sr. nurse quality assurance/coord., 1991; div. officer sickcall Br. Med. Clinic Naval Sta. Va., Norfolk, Va., 1992; dept. head sickcall Br. Med. Clinic NAVSTA, Norfolk, Va., 1992—; total quality leadership facilitator/leader, BLS instr., 1990—. Contbr. articles of rsch. to profl. jours. Budget chair Religious Ministries, Parris Island, S.C., 1990-91; vol. Help of Beaufort, S.C. Recipient Help of Beaufort Vol. of Yr. award, 1991. Mem. ANA, Am. Acad. Ambulatory Nurse Adminstrs. Baptist. Home: 375 Courtney Arch Virginia Bch VA 23452-5701 Office: Br Med Clinic Naval Sta Norfolk VA 23511-6692

FRANCIS, MARY FRANCES VAN DYKE, real estate executive, editor; b. Sedalia, Mo., Nov. 17, 1925; d. Frank B. and Mary Irene (Sims) Van Dyke; student Central Mo. State Coll.; m. Harold E. Francis, Apr. 23, 1944 (div. 1980); children—David Eugene, Lois Irene Valero, Roland Wayne, Eric Brian. Tchr. grade sch. Pettis County, Mo., 1943-44; timekeeper Montgomery Ward & Co., Kansas City, Mo., 1944-45; instr. new operators Southwestern Bell Telephone Co., Independence, Mo., 1945-47; real estate salesman Russell Realtors, Independence, 1958-66; owner Mary Francis, Realtor, Independence, 1967—; exec. sec., editor Eastern Jackson County Bd. Realtors, 1962-68; exec. asst., pub. relations dir., editor Kansas City Realtor, 1968-71; marketing asst. South Central region Chgo. Title Ins. Co., Kansas City, 1971-75; pres. Maranco, Inc., real estate, 1975—; v.p. Raintree Lake Realty, 1980-83 . Cub Scout den mother council Boy Scouts Am. Recipient Outstanding Service award Eastern Jackson County Bd. Realtors, 1964, Salesmanship award, 1965, CPW Real Estate Exchange award, Expo, 1983. Mem. Nat. Assn. Real Estate Bds. (charter pres. Greater Kansas City chpt., gov., pres. Mo. Women's Council), Mo. Real Estate Assn. (mem. Speakers Bur.). Club: Soroptomist (past pres., Independence). Contbr. articles to realty publs. Address: PO Box 1158 Independence MO 64051-0658

FRANCIS, SANDRA JO, psychotherapist, educator, school counselor; b. Turlock, Calif., Apr. 22, 1941; d. Peter Alexander and Josephine Pauline (Abdallah) F. BA, Dominican Coll., San Rafael, Calif., 1964; MS, San Francisco State U., 1990. Cert. elem., secondary, cmty. coll. tchr., Calif.; lic. marriage, family and child counselor, Calif. Tchr. various elem./secondary schs. Calif., Rome and London, 1964-89; counseling intern Schs. of the Sacred Heart, San Francisco, 1987-88; part-time counseling intern Teenage Pregnancy/Parenting and Alcohol Counseling Ctr., San Francisco, 1988-89, Social Svcs. Dept. Presidio of San Francisco, 1988-90; counselor Redwood High Sch., Larkspur, Calif., 1990—; pvt. practice, San Francisco, 1990—; lectr. in field. Mem. Calif. Tchrs. Assn., No. Calif. Sandplay Assn., Calif. Assn. Marriage and Family Therapists (clin. mem. San Francisco and Marin County chpts.), Marin County Psychol. Assn. (hon.), Chi Sigma Iota. Home: 80 Ora Way Apt 301 San Francisco CA 94131-2512 Office: 4831 Geary Blvd San Francisco CA 94118-2910

FRANCIS, SHERRY SELF, cosmetology academy owner; b. Shelby, N.C., Apr. 5, 1951; d. Charles L. and Auley (Cantrell) Watson; children: Francis, Misti, Michelle. Merchandise mgr. Hudsons Dept. Store, Shelby, 1968-72; office mgr. Dicey Mills, Shelby, 1972-75; clerical engr. Shelby Supply Co., 1976-78; bookkeeper Bost Bakery, Shelby, 1979-82; office mgr. Carolina Artisans, Shelby, 1982-87; pres., owner Progressive Hairstyling Acad., Shelby, 1987—; co-owner, v.p., sec. O.E. Ford of Shelby, Inc., 1989—; co-owner, sec. Moss Lake Boat Storage, Shelby, 1980—. Pres. Cleve. Com. Home Builders, Shelby, 1992-94; active participant Miss Wheel Chair Padgent, 1991-94. Mem. Nat. Beauty Sch. Owners (pvt. beauty schs. women's coun.), N.C. Pvt. Beauty Sch. Owners. Republican. Methodist. Home: 164 Northshores Dr Cherryville NC 28021 Office: Franco Investments Inc Progressive Hairstyling Acad 814 S DeKalb St Shelby NC 28150

FRANCISCHINE, JANICE MARIE, pediatrics nurse; b. Bronx, N.Y., Sept. 14, 1966; d. Ronald James and Veronica Louise (Gorga) F. BSN, MS, Molloy Coll., 1988. Cert. BLS, ACLS, PALS, NALS Am. Heart Assn., PNP. Staff nurse adult medicine oncology L.I. Jewish Med. Ctr., New Hyde Park, N.Y., 1988-90, staff nurse pediatric emergency rm., 1991-92, mem. scheduling com., 1992, asst. nursing care coord. pediatric emergency rm., 1992—; PNP Office of Dr. Louis O. Pupo, MD, New Hyde Park, 1994—. Mem. Emergency Nursing Assn., Nat. Assn. PNPs. Roman Catholic. Home: 6 Bruce Ln Brentwood NY 11717 Office: LI Jewish Med Ctr Lakeville Rd New Hyde Park NY 11040

FRANCKE, GLORIA NIEMEYER, pharmacist, editor, publisher; b. Dillsboro, Ind., Apr. 28, 1922; d. Albert B. and Fannie K. (Libbert) Niemeyer; m. Donald Eugene Francke, Apr. 15, 1956. BS in Pharmacy, Purdue U., 1942; PharmD, U. Cin., 1971; postgrad. U. Mich., 1945; PharmD (hon.) Purdue U., 1988—. Pharmacist, Dillsboro Drug Store, 1943-44; instr. Sch. Pharmacy, Purdue U., Lafayette, Ind., 1943; asst. to chief pharmacist U. Mich. Hosp., Ann Arbor, 1944-46; assoc. editor Am. Jour. Hosp. Pharmacy, Washington, 1944-64; asst. dir. Div. Hosp. Pharmacy of Am. Pharm. Assn., Washington, 1946-56; exec. sec. Am. Soc. Hosp. Pharmacists, Ann Arbor, 1949-60; acting dir. dept. communications, Washington, 1963-64; drug lit. specialist Nat. Library Medicine, Bethesda, Md., 1965-67; clin. pharmacy teaching coordinator VA Hosp., Cin., 1967-71; asst. clin. prof. clin. pharmacy Coll. Pharmacy, U. Cin., 1967-71; chief program evaluation br. Alcohol and Drug Dependence Service, VA, Central Office, Washington, 1971-75; dir. Pharmacy Intelligence Ctr., Am. Pharm. Assn., Washington, 1975-85; mem. Roche Hosp. Pharmacy Adv. Bd., 1971-74; judge for ann. Lunsford Richardson Pharmacy awards, 1963, 64; mem. com. standards for drug abuse treatment and rehab. programs Joint Commn. Accreditation of Hosps., 1974-75. Author: (with D. E. Francke, C. J. Latiolais and N.F. H. Ho) Mirror to Hospital Pharmacy, 1964. Contbr. articles on hosp. pharmacy and clin. pharmacy to profl. jours. Recipient H.A.K. Whitney award Mich. Soc. Hosp. Pharmacists, 1953, Disting. Alumnus award Purdue U. Sch. of Pharmacy, 1985, Remington Honor medal, 1987, Career Achievement award Profl. Frat. Assn., 1991; also various commendations. Mem. Internat. Pharm. Fedn., Am. Inst. History of Pharmacy (exec. sec. 1966-78), Tex. Soc. Hosp. Pharmacists (hon.), Am. Pharm. Assn. (hon. chmn. 1986), Am. Soc. Hosp. Pharmacists, Drug Info. Assn., Kappa Epsilon, Rho Chi. Presbyterian. Home and Office: 3900 Cathedral Ave NW # 403A Washington DC 20016-5201

FRANCKE, LINDA BIRD, journalist; b. N.Y.C., Mar. 14, 1939; d. Samuel Curtis and Janet (King) Bird; m. G.D. Mackenzie, Jan. 12, 1961; 1 son, Andrew Mackenzie; m. Albert Francke III, Oct. 7, 1967; 2 daughters: Caitlin, Tapp. Student, Bradford Jr. Coll., 1958. Copywriter Young & Rubicam, Inc., N.Y.C., 1960-63, Ogilvy & Mather, Inc., N.Y.C., 1965-67; contbg. editor N.Y. Mag., N.Y.C., 1968-72, 80—; gen. editor Newsweek Mag., N.Y.C., 1972-77; columnist N.Y. Times, 1977—; TV news commentator Spl. Edit., 1978-79; dir. New Directions; juror Am. Book Awards, 1981; Co-chmn. Writer's Resource Center, Southampton, N.Y. Works in numerous anthologies, including, The New York Spy, 1967, The Power Game, 1970, Running Against the Machine, 1969, Women: A Book for Men, 1979, Hers: Through Women's Eyes, 1985, America Firsthand, Vol. II: From Reconstruction to the Present, 1994; author: The Ambivalence of Abortion, 1978, Growing Up Divorced, 1983; collaborator: First Lady from Plains, 1984, Ferraro: My Story, 1985, Q Woman of Egypt, 1987, Daughter of Destiny, 1989. Mem. Women's Commn. for Refugee Women and Children, Internat. Rescue Com. Inc.; chmn. East End Choice; candidate N.Y. State Assembly, 2d Dist., 1990; del. to Dem. Nat. Conv., 1992; bd. dirs. Bridgehampton Child Care & Recreational Ctr., Inc., The Retreat. Recipient award Cannes Film Festival, 1969, Nat. Clarion award, 1994. Mem. Authors Guild, Women's Media Group N.Y.C. Home: Sagaponack NY 11962

FRANCO, ANNEMARIE WOLETZ, editor; b. Somerville, N.J., Sept. 18, 1933; d. Frederick Franz and Bertha (Laugginger) Woletz; m. Frederick Nicholas Franco, June 11, 1977. Student, Wood Coll. of Bus. Editorial asst. Internat. Musician, then assoc. editor, 1965-88, ret., 1988. Republican. Presbyterian. Home: 166 Wellstone Dr Palm Coast FL 32164-4111

FRANCO, CAROLE ANN, international consultant; b. Hartford, Conn., Dec. 21, 1948; d. Nicholas Lawrence and Mary Elizabeth (LaRosa) F. BA in Spanish, Duke U., 1970; grad. cert. in edn., Trinity Coll., Hartford, 1971; postgrad. in French, Sorbonne, Paris, 1980; M Internat. Rels., Cambridge (Eng.) U., 1981. Tchr. West Hartford (Conn.) Pub. Schs., 1970-76; researcher on biography of Sumner Welles Washington, 1976-77; adminstr. Ctr. for Strategic and Internat. Studies, Washington, 1978-79; broker, mgr. Parks Capital Mgmt., N.Y.C., 1981-83; assoc., cons. Burgess Mgmt. Assocs., N.Y.C., 1984-88; producer, owner Kingdom Prodns., New Paltz, N.Y., 1988-93; internat. cons. Strategic Ptnrs. Internat., New Paltz, 1993—; polit. advisor N.Am. Petroleum Corp., Curacao, Netherlands Antilles, 1987—. Mem. Duke U. Alumni Assn. N.Y., Cambridge U. Alumni Assn. N.Y. (founder, bd. dirs. 1987—), United Oxford-Cambridge U. Club (London). Republican. Roman Catholic. Home: PO Box 36 New Paltz NY 12561-0036

FRANDEN, BLANCHE M., nursing educator; b. N.Y.C., June 9, 1923; d. Samuel and Rebekah (Stern) Randall; m. Robert Jacob Franden, Aug. 20, 1950; children: Richard Jules, Peter Herb, Daniel Ethan. Grad. Mass. Meml. Hosp. Sch. Nursing (now Boston U. Hosp.), 1945; B. in Vocat. Edn., Calif. State U., L.A., 1980. RN, Calif. dir. student health Mass. Meml. Hosp., Boston, 1947-49; staff nurse various hosps., N.Y., Calif., 1949-91; instr., coord. hosp. related occupations East San Gabriel Valley Regional Occupational Program, West Covina, Calif., 1973-90, program dir., instr. coord. EMT-ambulance, 1985—; program dir. EMTIA program La Puente Valley Regional Occupational Program, 1986-93; CPR instr.-trainer; mem. CPR com., local governing bd. Am. Heart Assn; com. mem. L.A. County Com. to Revise EMTIA Refresher Course Curriculum Program L.A. County, 1992—. Author student manual. Mem. AAUW, VFW Women's Aux., Calif. Assn. Regional Occupational Ctrs./Programs, Am. Vocat. Assn., Calif. Assn. Health Career Educators, Orange County Profl. and Bus. Jewish Women, L.A. County Assn. EMT Instrs. and Coords. Democrat. Jewish. Office: E San Gabriel Valley Regional Occupational Program 1024 Workman St West Covina CA 91790

FRANEY, BILLIE NOLAN, political activist; b. Eveleth, Minn., Sept. 17, 1930; d. Mark and Ann Murray Nolan; m. Neil Joseph Franey; children: Kathleen, Timothy, Nora, Colin, Patrick. Student, Carleton Coll., 1948-49, U. Minn., 1949-50; BA, Coll. St. Scholastica, 1952. Social worker Cath. Welfare, Mpls., 1952-53; Contbr. articles to profl. jours. Chair Indian Affairs, Minn. Mrs. Jaycees, 1962; mem. Charter Commn., White Bear Lake, Minn., 1962-65; pres. White Bear Lake LWV, 1965-67; lobbyist Common Cause of Minn., 1979, Minn. LWV, 1980, AAUW, 1987-89; mem. met. futures task force Met. Coun., 1988-89; co-chair Women Come to the Capitol, Minn. Women's Consortium. Named Outstanding Young Women of Am., 1966; revipient Sister Ann Edward Scholar award The Coll. of St. Scholostica, 1992. Mem. AAUW (pres. 1992-94, St. Paul program v.p. 1990-92, legis. pub. policy chair 1987-89, Minn. chpt. legis. pub. policy v.p. 1987-89, scholarship named for as a gift from St. Paul AAUW 1989, Women as Agts. of Change award 1991), Coun. Met. Area LWV (chair 1981-83, program and study chair 1979-81, bd. mem. 1978-79). Home: 1323 Hedmanway White Bear Lake MN 55110

FRANK, AGNES T., medical librarian; b. Budapest, Hungary; d. Julius Furedi and Maria Szlovak; m. Neil Frank (div. 1971). MLS, Columbia U., 1964. Dir. med. library French & Polyclinic Med. Sch. and Health Ctr., N.Y.C., 1970-74, St. Vincent's Hosp. and Med. Ctr., N.Y.C., 1974—. Mem. Med. Libr. Assn. (cert.). Home: 372 Central Park W Apt 16A New York NY 10025-8211 Office: St Vincent's Hosp Med Ctr 153 W 11th St New York NY 10011-8397

FRANK, ANN-MARIE, sales administration executive; b. Omaha, July 27, 1957; d. Joseph Anthony and Louise Virginia (DiMauro) Malingagio; m. Jon Lindsay Frank, July 13, 1985; 1 child, Jon L. BA in Fine and Communication Arts, Loyola Marymount U., L.A., 1980, MBA, 1988. Sr. mktg. clk. Telautograph Corp., L.A., 1981-84; advt. asst. Automotive Dealers Mktg., L.A., 1984-85; region adminstrv. mgr. Data Gen. Corp., Manhattan Beach, Calif., 1986-90; adminstrv. customer svc. mgr. Candle Corp., L.A., 1991-92, mgr. fin. svcs. western area, 1992-93; mgr. sales adminstr. nat. ops. Candle Corp., Santa Monica, 1993—. Dir., editor: (creative drama) Patchwork, 1982 (Rochester, N.Y. trophy). Republican. Roman Catholic. Home: 3311 Raintree Ave Torrance CA 90505 Office: Candle Corp 2425 Olympic Blvd Santa Monica CA 90404-4030

FRANK, BETTY POPE, editor; b. Detroit, Dec. 9, 1914; d. Melville S. and Belle O. (Oberfelder) Welt; m. Vernon K. Pope, Dec. 18, 1938 (div. 1961); children: John, Anne, Barbara; m. Morton Frank, Dec. 31, 1963. BA, Vassar Coll., 1936. Staff editor Look Mag., Des Moines, 1936-40; staff writer The Open Road, N.Y., 1940-41; freelance writer N.Y.C., 1941-59; articles editor Good Housekeeping, N.Y.C., 1960-77, contract writer, 1977-80; editor, cons. Family Circle, N.Y.C., 1980-87; ret., 1987—; bd. dirs. U. Bridgeport, 1978—. Mem. adv. com. Vassar Quar., 1960s and 70s. Bd. dirs. Planned Parenthood, Westchester County, 1951-60. Recipient Best Article published award Mag. Writers & U. Mo., 1979. Mem. Cosmopolitan Club (bulletin com. 1988-91). Democrat. Home and Office: 19-10 Meadow Lakes Hightstown NJ 18520

FRANK, BRENDA KAY, quality assurance professional; b. Marshfield, Wis., Sept. 2, 1954; d. Orval Clarence Matter and Violet A. (Walti) Koenig; m. John Frederick Frank, June 19, 1976. BS, U. Wis., 1976. Mech. engr. Kohler (Wis.) Co., 1976-82; quality control mgr. Bemis Mfg. Co., Sheboygan Falls, Wis., 1983—. Office: Bemis Mfg Co PO Box 901 Sheboygan Falls WI 53085-0901

FRANK, CARLA IRWIN, critical care nurse, consultant; b. Louisville, Jan. 26, 1953; d. William P. and Marjorie (Puckett) Irwin; children: R. Lee Frank Jr., Richard L. Frank. BS in Nursing, U. Evansville, 1975. RN, Ky.; cert. ACLS instr., CPR instr.-trainer, instr. in AIDS edn., first aid instr.-trainer; registered first aid tng. agy. for Nat. Safety Coun. Staff nurse progressive coronary unit, relief house supr. Suburban Med. Ctr., Louisville, 1975—; pres. Health and Safety First Inc.; cardiovascular nurse cons.; cons. on stress mgmt. for law enforcement. Mem. AACCN, Fraternal Order Police (assoc.), Louisville Police Officers Assn. (assoc.), Alpha Tau Delta. Baptist. Home and Office: 8913 Lethborough Dr Louisville KY 40299-1435

FRANK, DEBRA WILSON, sales, management trainer; b. Seattle, Nov. 14, 1961; d. Melvin Edmond W. and Deanna May Sanner; m. Thomas S. Frank, Aug. 6, 1994. BA in Bus. Adminstrn. cum laude, U. Wash., 1984. Asst. buyer, dept. mgr. Frederick & Nelson, Seattle, 1985-86; gen. mgr. Borders Book Shop, Indpls., 1986-87; regional mgr. Borders Book Shop, Ann Arbor, Mich., 1987-89, v.p. ops., 1989-92, mgmt. trainer, 1993—. Pres. Brownstones Condominium Assn., Ann Arbor, 1992-93. Mem. Am. Soc. Tng. & Devel., Phi Beta Kappa, Beta Gamma Sigma.

FRANK, ELIZABETH, English literature educator, author; b. Los Angeles, Sept. 14, 1945. d. Melvin G. and Anne R. Frank; 1 child, Anne Louise Buchwald. Student Bennington Coll.; BA, MA, PhD, U. Calif.-Berkeley. Joseph E Harry prof. modern langs. and English lit. Bard Coll., Annandale-on-Hudson, N.Y., 1982—. Author: Jackson Pollock, 1983, Louise Bogan: A Portrait (Pulitzer prize for biography 1986). Office: Bard Coll Dept of Language & Literature Annandale On Hudson NY 12504*

FRANK, JUDITH ANN (JANN FRANK), small business owner; b. Fresno, Calif., Feb. 10, 1938; d. Walter R. Frank and Ethel Joan (Klomburg) Brinkerhoff; m. David Rogers, Oct. 1956 (div. June 1973). BA, Calif. State U., Fullerton, 1989, postgrad., 1990-91; postgrad., Chapman U., 1991-93. Vault teller, new accounts, comml. Bank of Am., Fresno, 1956-64; new accounts and note teller Security First Nat. Bank, Fresno, 1965-68; br. bookkeeper, supr. Wells Fargo Bank, Santa Clara and San Jose, Calif., 1968-78; student asst. Fullerton Coll. Career Planning and Placement Ctr., 1982-83; owner, operator Distant Drums, Fullerton, 1994—. Phys. and occupational intern transitional tng. program for brain injured adults Rehab. Inst., So. Calif., Orange, 1978-80, vol., 1993; vol. Sr. Citizen's Transp., Lunch & Counseling Program, Fullerton, 1981-82, City Wide Disaster Drill, Whitter, Calif., 1987; vol. grad. Evolution of Psychotherapy Conf., Anaheim, Calif., 1990. Recipient Commendation for Vol. Svc. Orange County Coun. Women in C. of C., 1980, Disting. Svc. award Rehab. Inst. So. Calif., Orange, 1993; tuition scholarship grantee Chapman U., Orange, 1991. Mem. Native Am. Inst., Assn. Humanistic Psychology, Calif. Indian Art Assn., Golden Key, Alpha Gamma Sigma. Office: Distant Drums 3340 Topaz Ln # A8 Fullerton CA 92631

FRANK, KRISTY LOUISE, English educator; b. Oshkosh, Wis., June 29, 1942; d. Allan Theodore and Marian Virginia (Johnson) F.; married, Oct. 8, 1977, widowed, Jan. 1991. Student, Oshkosh State Coll., 1961-64; BA in English, U. Wis., Milw., 1967, MS in Ednl. Adminstrn. and Supervision, 1984; teaching cert., Marquette U., 1969. Tchr. English and Holocaust studies Juneau High Sch., Milw. Pub. Schs., 1967—; instr. in Holocaust studies McPherson Coll., Milw., 1993—. Active Simon Wiesenthal Ctr., Planned Parenthood, Raoul Wallenberg Com. Coun. for Basic Edn./Nat. Endowment for Arts fellow, 1987—; Honeywell grantee, 1987; recipient Gold Tchr. award Ameritech-Wis. Bell, 1992, Holocaust Teaching award Yom Hashoah Commemeration Com., 1992. Mem. NOW, ACLU, Milw. Tchrs. Assn. (v.p. 1993—, mem. various coms., bldg. rep., field staff mem.), Nat. Fedn. Interscholastic Spirit, Am. Soc. for Vad Vashem, U. Wis.-Milw. Alumni Assn. Democrat. Home: 4237 N 42nd St Milwaukee WI 53216-1617 Office: Juneau High Sch 6415 W Mount Vernon Ave Milwaukee WI 53213-4025

FRANK, LAURA JEAN, computer scientist; b. New Rochelle, N.Y., May 21, 1945; d. James Florian and Erma (Guttag) F. BA, U. Vt., 1967; MBA, Iona Coll., New Rochelle, 1971; postgrad. China Inst., N.Y.C., Polytechnic Inst., White Plains, N.Y. With Equitable Life Assurance Soc., N.Y.C., 1967-79, project leader, 1978-79; sr. planning specialist PHH Relocation, Wilton, Conn., 1979-80, project mgr., 1980-83, system mgr., 1983-88, mgr. office tech., 1988-91, founding prof. Homequity U., 1985-91; system's cons., LJF Assocs., 1991—. Editor Stamford First Nighter, bd. dirs. Tri-State Trainers; contbr. articles and featured in profl. jours. Mem. Stamford Hist. Soc., Friends of Stamford Symphony. Mem. NAFE, Women In Mgmt., Corp. Computing Mgmt. Assn. (bd. dirs.), Assn. Info. Systems Profls., Delta Mu Delta, Alpha Epsilon Phi. Republican. Jewish. Home: 20250 Soundview Ave Stamford CT 06902-7123

FRANK, MARY, sculptor, artist; b. London, Feb. 4, 1933; came to U.S., 1940; d. Edward and Eleanor (Weinstein) Lockspeiser; children—Andrea (dec.), Pablo. Pupil, Hans Hoffman, 1951, Max Beckman, 1950. Tchr. drawing New Sch. Social Research, N.Y.C., 1965-70; tchr. drawing and sculpture Queens Coll. Grad. Sch., N.Y., 1970—. One-woman exhbns. include Poindexter Gallery, N.Y.C., 1958, Stephen Radich Gallery, N.Y.C., 1961, 63, 66, Drawing Shop Gallery, N.Y.C., 1964, Boris Mirski Gallery, Boston, 1965, 67, Donald Morris Gallery, Detroit, 1964, 68, Richard Grey Gallery, Chgo., 1969, Zabriskie Gallery, N.Y.C., 1968, 71-73, 75, 77, 78, 79, 82, 84, 86, 89, U. Conn., Storrs, 1975, Proctor Art Ctr. Bard Coll., Annandale-on-the-Hudson, N.Y., 1975, Harcus Krakow Rosen Sonnabend Gallery, Boston, 1976, Cummings Art Ctr. Conn. Coll., 1976, Quay Gallery, San Francisco, 1982, Marsha Mataka Gallery, Washington, 1985, Neuberger Mus., Purchase, N.Y., 1978, Bklyn. Mus., 1987, Roger Ramsey Gallery, Chgo., 1987, DeCordova Mus., Lincoln, Mass., 1988, Everson Mus., 1988, Nielsen Gallery, Boston, 1988, De Cordova Mus., Lincoln, Mass., 1988, Dalshemier Gallery, Balt., 1988, Pa. Acad. Fine Arts, Phila., 1989, Everson Mus., Syracuse, N.Y., 1989, Rena Branstein Gallery, San Francisco, 1990, Art Awareness, Lexington, N.Y., 1991, Galerie Zabriskie, Paris, 1992, Allene Lapides Gallery, N.Y.C., 1992, Ctrl. Park Zoo Gallery, N.Y.C., 1992, Midtown Payson Galleries, N.Y.C., 1993; exhibited in group shows Guggenheim Mus., N.Y.C., 1972, Kent, Ohio, 1972, Gedok, Hamburg, Fed. Republic Germany, 1972, Whitney Mus., N.Y.C., 1972, 73, Phila., 1974, Portland (Maine) Mus., 1975, N.Y. Cultural Ctr., N.Y.C., 1975, Mpls. Inst. Arts, 1975, U. Houston Fine Arts Ctr., 1975, Marion Koogler McNay Art Inst., 1976, Phila. Coll. Art, 1976, Bklyn. Mus., 1977, 83, 93, Whitney Mus. Am. Art, 1977, 79, 80, 86, Art Inst. Chgo., 1977, Wave Hill, Bronx, 1978, 83, Allbright-Knox Gallery, Buffalo, 1978, Queens Mus., Flushing, N.Y., 1978, Pratt Manhattan Ctr., N.Y.C., 1980, Inst. Contemporary Art, Richmond, 1980, Grey Art Gallery, N.Y. U., N.Y.C., 1981, Md. Inst. Arts, Balt., 1981, The Am. Crafts Mus., N.Y.C., 1981, New Britain (Conn.) Mus. Am. Art, 1983, Contemporary Art Ctr., Cin., 1984, 85, de Saissaet Mus., Santa Clara, 1985, The Chrysler Mus., Norfolk, Va., 1985, Dayton (Ohio) Art Inst., 1985, The Jewish Mus., N.Y.C., 1988, Mus. Mod. Art, N.Y.C., 1988, Nat. Gallery of Art, Washington, 1990, Mus. Fine Arts, Boston, 1990, Nat. Mus. Contemporary Art, Seoul, Korea, 1990-91, Midtown Payson Galleries, N.Y.C., 1992, G.W. Einstein Co., N.Y.C., 1993, Nat. Acad. Design, 1993, Nielsen Gallery, Boston, 1993; represented in permanent collections Chgo. Art Inst., Kalamazoo Inst. Art, Mus. Modern Art, univs. N.C., Mass., N.Mex., Worcester Art Mus., Yale Wichita Art Mus., So. Ill. U., Bank Chgo., Whitney Mus., Joseph H. Hirshhorn Mus. and Sculpture Garden, Metropolitan Mus. Art, Akron (Ohio) Art Inst., Arnot Art Mus., N.Y., Balt. Mus. Art., Bank Chgo., Brown U., R.I., Conn. Coll., Crocker Bank, de Cordova Mus., Mass., Des Moines Art Ctr., Everson Mus. Art, The Jewish Mus., N.Y., The Libr. Congress, Washington, Michael C. Rockefeller Art Ctr. Gallery, Mus. Fine Arts, Boston, Neuberger Mus., N.Y., Storm King Art Ctr., N.Y., U. Bridgeport, Conn., Va. Mus. Art; illustrator books: Enchanted, 1968, Buddha, 1969, Son of-a-Mile-Long Mother, 1970, Shadows of Africa, 1992. Recipient award Nat. Inst.-Am. Acad. Arts and Letters, 1972; grantee Ingram Merril Found., 1961, Longview Found., 1962-64, Nat. Council Arts, 1968; Guggenheim fellow, 1973, 83. Office: Midtown Payson Galleries Inc 11870 SE Dixie Hwy eries Hobe Sound FL 33455*

FRANK, MARY LOU, educator; b. Cleve., May 18, 1915; d. William Henry and Martha Ann (Brown) Parsons; m. Russell Edward Frank, May 18, 1935; children: Richard Edward, James Russell. BS in Edn., Cleve. State U., 1960; MS in Edn., U. Akron, Ohio, 1967, Miami U., Oxford, Ohio, 1934-35; student, Baldwin-Wallace Coll., 1933-34. Cert. tchr., Ohio. Substitute tchr. Cleve. Pub. Schs., 1963; tchr. elem. Brecksville (Ohio) City Sch. Dist., 1953-71; tchr. elem. Lee County Bd. of Edn., Ft. Myers, Fla., 1971-74, ret., 1974; mem. ambassadors to China from Fla., Children's Palaces Homes Hosps., 1980. Martha Holden Jennings Found. scholar, 1963-64, grantee, 1965. Mem. U.S. Power Squadron Aux. (pilot), Collier Reading Coun., Delta Kappa Gamma. Home: 61 Impala Ct # 23 Fort Myers FL 33912-6338

FRANK, MARY LOU BRYANT, psychologist, educator; b. Denver, Nov. 27, 1952; d. W.D. and Blanche (Dean) Bryant; m. Kenneth Kerry Frank, Sept. 9, 1973; children: Kari Lou, Kendra Leah. BA, Colo. State U., 1974, MEd, 1983, MS, 1986, PhD, 1989. Tchr. Cherry Creek Schs., Littleton, Colo., 1974-80; from grad. asst. to dir. career devel. Colo. State U., Ft. Collins, 1980-86; intern U. Del., Newark, 1987-88; psychologist Ariz. State U., Tempe, 1988-93; assoc., lead prof. psychology Clinch Valley Coll. U. Va., Wise, 1992—; asst. acad. dean, 1993—; instr. Colo. State U., Ft. Collins, 1981-82, counselor 1984-85, 86-87; prof. Ariz. State U., Tempe, 1989-92; assoc. prof. psychology Clinch Valley Coll. U. Va., 1992—. Author: (program manual) Career Development, 1986; contbr. book chpts. on eating disorders and existential psychotherapy. Com. mem. Missions and Social Concerns, Gilbert, 1988—. Mem. APA, AACD, Phi Kappa Phi, Phi Beta Kappa, Pi Kappa Delta. Office: U Va Clinch Valley Coll Dept Psychology Wise VA 24293

FRANK, MYRA LINDEN, consultant; b. Richmond, Va., Oct. 26, 1950; d. J. C. and Myra Teresa (Lanzarone) Frank; m. Timothy Franklin Long (div. Jan. 1981); m. Robert Andrew Hudson (div. 1994). BA, Erskine Coll., 1972; student, Inst. Fin. Edn., 1982-88. Chief activities therapist S.C. Dept. Corrections, Columbia, 1973-75, acting prin., 1975-77, coll. coord., 1977-78; owner, operator Carolina Coast Seafood, Aiken (S.C.) and Beaufort (S.C.) 1978-80; from teller to savs. counselor Security Fed. Savs. & Loan, Aiken, 1981-83; customer svc. rep. Bankers 1st Savs. & Loans, Augusta, Ga., 1983-84, mgr. br. adminstrn., 1984-85; coord. automated teller machines, banking officer 1st Fed. Savs. Bank, Brunswick, Ga., 1985-88; ptnr., cons. electronic banking/software devel. RAH Systems, Brunswick, Ga., 1988-93; ptnr. specific application computer programming, software tng. Details & More, Greenville, S.C., 1989-90, ptnr. event planning, various mfg. positions and mktg./sales, 1989-91; cons. office and computer svcs. Mauldin, S.C., 1992-93; lectr. S.C. Edn. Tchrs. Assn., Columbia, 1974, S.C. Assn. Social Workers, Columbia, 1975, Bus. and Profl. Women's Club, Columbia, 1978; small bus. owner, distbr. Nuskin product line, 1987-90; ind. mktg. rep. Network 2000/U.S. Spring, 1988-92; computer specialist Top Food Svcs. Carolina, Inc., Duncan, S.C., 1989-9o; adminstrv./sales mgr. Custom Catering, Duncan, 1990; cons. Contract Office/Computer Svcs., Greenville, 1992—. Appeared with Aiken Community Theatre, 1981. Bd. dirs. Quest Soc., Greenville, 1992—; mem. hospice com. Am. Cancer soc., Augusta, 1981; lectr. St. John's United Meth. Ch., 1981-82. Democrat. Home and Office: PO Box 333 Mauldin SC 29662-0333

FRANK, PAULA FELDMAN, business executive; b. Tulsa; d. Maurice M. and Sarah (Bergman) Feldman; m. Gordon D. Frank, Dec. 15, 1955; children: Cynthia Jan, Margaret Jill. B.S., Northwestern U., 1954. Directed, wrote and appeared in TV films for Nat. Safety Coun., Chgo., 1954-55; appeared in TV commls., 1955-56; asst. prodn. mgr. Kling Films, Chgo., 1956; pres. Gaston Ave. Optical Inc., ret. 1992; Dallas. Social chmn. Baylor Hosp. Vol. Corp., Dallas, 1962—; asst. dir. Des Plaines (Ill.) Theater Guild, 1956-57, Pearl Chappell Playhouse, Dallas, 1962-63, Dallas Theater Center, 1964. Mem. Hockaday Alumni Assn., Tau Gamma Epsilon, Phi Beta, Sigma Delta Tau. Home: 7123 Currin Dr Dallas TX 75230-3645

FRANK, RUBY MERINDA, employment agency executive; b. McClusky, N.D., June 28, 1920; d. John J. and Olise (Stromme) Hanson; m. Robert G. Frank, Jan. 14, 1944 (dec. 1973); children: Gary Frank, Craig. student Coll. Mankato, Minn., Aurora (Ill.) U. Exec. sec., office mgr. Nat. Container Corp., Chgo., 1943-50; owner, pres. Frank's Employment, Inc., St. Charles, Ill., 1957—; corp. sec. Sta. WFXW-FM, Geneva, 1988—; chmn. Baker Hotel, 1989-91; sec. bd. trustees Delnor Hosp., St. Charles, 1959-78, chmn. bd., 1985-87; vocat. adviser Waubonsee Coll.; bd. dirs. Aurora U., corporate sec. 1994. Contbr. weekly broadcast Sta. WGSB, 1970-80, weekly interview program Sta. WFXW. Active mem. Women's aux.; vice chmn. Kane County (Ill.) Rep. Com., 1968-77; pres. Women's Rep. Club, 1969-77; local bd. Am. Cancer Soc.; adv. council Dellora A. Norris Cultural Arts Ctr.; bd. govs. Luth. Social Svc. Baker Hotel, sec. 1987, vice chmn. 1988, chmn. Baker Hotel, 1989-90; bd. dirs. St. Charles Hist. Soc., 1989, Ill. Chamber Symphony, Dorchester Assn.; co-vice chmn. Delnor Community Health System; bd. dirs., exec. bd. Aurora Found., 1989—, v.p., 1990-92, pres. 1993—. Recipient Exec. of Yr. award Fox Valley PSI; Charlemagne award for community service, 1982; Mentor of Bus. Women award, 1991. Mem. St. Charles C. of C. (pres., bd. dirs. 1976-82, amb.), Kane-DuPage Pers. Assn. (v.p. 1971—), Nat., Ill. employment assns., Ill. Assn. Pers. Cons. (dir.), Women in Mgmt., St. Charles Country Club, Execs. Club of Chgo., St. Charles Ambs. Club (pres.), The Club of Pelican Bay (Naples, Fla.). Lutheran. Home: 534 Longmeadow Cir Saint Charles IL 60174-2316 Office: Arcada Theater Bldg 12 S 1st Ave Saint Charles IL 60174-1947

FRANK, SHANNON L., sign designer; b. Kellogge, Idaho, Oct. 9, 1965; d. Alfred M. and Elizabeth A. (Ryser) McGuire. BA, Ea. Mont. Coll., Billings, 1993. Clk. UPS, Billings, 1990-92; camera tech. Miller Sterling Camera, Billings, 1988-93; assoc. Holiday Stationery, Billings, 1992-93; sign tech. Signs Now, Billings, 1993—. 2d lt. U.S. Army Nat. Guard., 1989—. Home: 2010 Central Ave Billings MT 59102

FRANKE, LINDA FREDERICK, lawyer; b. Mankato, Minn., Aug. 28, 1947; d. Cletus and Valeria (Haefner) Frederick; m. Willis L. Franke, Dec.

17, 1966; children: Paul W., Gregory J. BA, U. Mo., 1981, JD, 1984. Bar: Mo. 1985, U.S. Dist. Ct. (we. dist.) Mo. 1985. Rsch. assoc. Koenigsdorf, Kusnetzky and Wyrsch, Kansas City, Mo., 1984-85; asst. gen. counsel dept. revenue State of Mo., Independence, 1985-86; claims rep. workers' compensation Cigna Ins. Co., Overland Park, Kans., 1986-87; sr. claims rep. workers' compensation Gulf Ins. Co., Kansas City, Mo., 1987-88; worker's compensation atty. Fireman's Fund Ins. Co., Kansas City, 1988—; mem. Mo. Worker's Compensation Com. U. Mo. scholar, 1980, 81. Mem. Platte County Bar Assn., Kansas City Met. Bar Assn. (adv. bd. workers' compensation com.). Home: 8117 NW Eastside Dr Weatherby Lake MO 64152 Office: Firemans Fund Ins Co 2300 Main St Kansas City MO 64108-2415

FRANKEL, ALICE KROSS, physician, director; b. N.Y.C., Feb. 3, 1929; d. Isidor and Anna (Moscowitz) Kross; m. Julian B. Schorr, May 14, 1951 (div. 1963); children: David, Ellen; m. Marvin E. Frankel, Aug. 22, 1965; 1 stepchild, Eleanor Frankel Perlman; 1 child, Mara. BA, Oberlin (Ohio) Coll., 1949; MD, Columbia U., 1953. Pvt. practice N.Y.C., 1956-66, 85—, Larchmont, N.Y., 1966-85; assoc. clin. prof. psychiatry Med. Coll. Cornell U., N.Y.C., 1970-90; dir. Child Devel. Ctr. Jewish Bd. Family & Children's Svcs., N.Y.C., 1984—; supervising and tng. psychoanalyst Psychoanalytic Ctr. Tng. & Rsch. Columbia U., N.Y.C., 1984—. Mem. Am. Psychiat. Assn., Am. Psychoanalytic Assn., Am. Acad. Child and Adolescent Psychiatry, Assn. for Child and Adolescent Analysis, N.Y. County Med. Soc., N.Y. State Med. Soc. Democrat. Jewish. Office: Jewish Bd Family Childrens Svcs Child Devel Ctr 120 W 57th St New York NY 10019-3320

FRANKEL, BARBARA BROWN, cultural anthropologist; b. Phila., Dec. 24, 1928; d. Paul and Sarah (Magil) Brown; m. Herbert L. Frankel, Feb. 27, 1949 (dec. Sept. 1976); children: Claire R. Sholes, Joan L. Frankel, David S. Frankel; m. Donald T. Campbell, Mar. 19, 1983. PhB, U. Chgo., 1947; BA, Goddard Coll., 1966; MA in Anthropology, Temple U., 1970; PhD, Princeton (N.J.) U., 1974. Asst. prof. Lehigh U., Bethlehem, Pa., 1973-77, assoc. prof., 1977-85, assoc. dean arts and sci., 1981-83, prof. anthropology, 1985-93, prof. emerita, 1994—; rsch. assoc. prof. Boston U., 1980-81. Author: Childbirth in the Ghetto, 1977, Transforming Identities, 1989; contbr. articles to profl. jours. Bd. dirs. Pinebrook Svcs. for Children and Youth, Whitehall, Pa., 1987-93. Grad. fellowship for Women Danforth Found., Princeton U., 1969-73; predoctoral fellowship AAUW, 1971-72; rsch. grant Mellon Faculty Devel. Grant, Boston U., 1980-81, Provost's Rsch. award Lehigh U., 1987. Fellow Am. Anthropol. Assn., Royal Anthropol. Inst. (U.K.), Soc. for Applied Anthropology (chair ethics com. 1986-88); mem. AAAS, Soc. for Humanistic, Urban, Med. Anthropology, Social Studies of Sci. Assn., Phila. Anthropol. Soc. (pres. 1988), LWV (study com. chair 1994-95), Phi Beta Kappa (pres. Beta chpt. 1989-90). Democrat. Agnostic Jewish. Home: 637 N New St Bethlehem PA 18018-3936 Office: Lehigh U Sociology & Anthropology 681 Taylor St Bethlehem PA 18015-3169

FRANKEL, HELEN BRUCE, county executive; b. N.Y.C., June 1, 1925; d. Robert MacGregor Grant Bruce and Mary Gallagher; children: Marty Jean, Molly, David A., Berry, Robert A. BS, U. Calif., Berkeley, 1947. RN, Calif.; pub. health nurse. Vis. nurse Evanston (Ill.) V.N.A., 1954-56; instr., trainer ARC, L.A., 1957-65; asst. head nurse Holy Cross Hosp., San Fernando, Calif., 1963-65; faculty mem. Hitchcock Sch. Nursing, Hanover, N.H., 1966-68; clinic mgr. L.A. Planned Parenthood, Pomona, Calif., 1968-70; staff development Kern Med. Ctr., Bakersfield, Calif., 1974-76; cons., educator County of Kern, 1976-80; pub. health nurse County of Kern, Bakersfield, 1981-82, coroner, pub. adminstr., pub. guardian, 1983—; child death adv. bd. Calif. Dept. of Justice, Sacramento, 1989-90; chair Kern County Child Death Rev. Team, Bakersfield, 1988—. Allocations com. United Way of Kern County, 1988-92; v.p. Campfire Coun. of Kern County, 1986-90; v.p. Am. Cancer Soc. Kern Unit, 1975—, pres. 1993-94; del. Calif. State Dem. Party, 1991 (spl. lifetime achievement award, 1994). Recipient Doubenmier award Am. Assn. Pub. Adminstrs., 1988; named Outstanding Woman of Yr. Greater Bakersfield C. of C., 1987. Mem. LWV, AAUW (gift recipient 1991), Bus. and Profl. Women's Club (Woman of Yr. 1988), Kern County Mgmt. Coun., Calif. State Coroners Assn. (pres. 1989-90, bd. dirs. 1984-92), Calif. Pub. Adminstrs./Pub. Guardian/Pub. Conservator's Assn., Soroptimist Internat. (Women Helping Women award). Democrat. Office: Coroner's Office Pub Adminstr/Conservator 1832 Flower St Bakersfield CA 93305

FRANKEL, JENNIFER LYNN, corporate litigation paralegal; b. Red Bank, N.J., Oct. 21, 1969; d. Edward Irwin and Ann Ruth (Weinstein) F. BA, George Washington U., 1990; MA in Internat. Rels., NYU, 1992. Senatorial intern The Office of Senator Thomas Eagleton, Washington, 1985-86; pub. rels. intern Found. for Internat. Human Rels., Washington, 1986-87; office asst. Sullivan and Cromwell, Washington, 1988-89; rsch. asst. comm. dept. Nat. Inst. for Dispute Resolution, Washington, 1989; legis. specialist Arnold and Porter Cons. Group, Washington, 1990; temporary bilingual program asst. Africa divsn. World Bank, 1990; rsch. assoc. Mobley, Luciani & Assocs., N.Y.C., 1990-91; head instr., ednl. coord. Ronkin Ednl. Group, N.Y.C., 1991-92; corp. litigation paralegal Lehman Bros. Office of the Gen. Counsel, N.Y.C., 1992—; exec. editor The Thruston Tribune. Mem. NAFE, Paris C. of C. (french bus. lang. fluency cert. 1990) Phi Eta Sigma, Sigma Kappa. Democrat. Jewish. Home: 298 Mulberry St Apt 6-0 New York NY 10012-3331

FRANKEL, JUDITH JENNIFER MARIASHA, clinical psychologist; b. Bklyn., May 25, 1947; m. Anthony R. D'Augelli, Sept. 1, 1968 (div. 1985); children: Jennifer Hadley, Rebekah Lindsey. BA, New Coll. at Hofstra U., 1968; MA, U. Conn., 1971, PhD, 1972. Lic. psychologist, Pa. Rsch. psychologist Family Consultation Ctr., Roslyn, N.Y., 1968, Conn. State Dept. Mental Health, Hartford, 1969-71; staff intern VA Hosp., West Haven, Conn., 1971-72; asst. prof., dir. program devel. and evaluation Addiction Prevention Lab. Pa. State U., State College, 1972-81; pvt. practice psychology State College, 1976—; psychol. cons. PYRAMID Orgn., Walnut Creek, Calif., 1975-78, N.Y. Dept. Mental Health, 1976, Nat. Inst. Alcohol Abuse Prevention, Nat. Inst. Drug Abuse Prevention, Nat. Youth Alternatives Program, 1975-79, Meadows Psychiatric Ctr. Women's Program, 1993—; v.p. Mental Health Profls., State College, 1978-80, pres., 1980-82; exec. bd. Ctrl. Pa. Psychol. Assn., 1989-90. Author: Decisions Are Possible, 1975, Communication and Parenting Skills, 1976, Helping Others, 1980; contbr. articles to profl. jours. Campaigner Stein for Rep., 1982, Wachob for Congress, 1984, Radis for Rep., 1990; chair community action Congregation Brit Shalom, State College, 1985-87, coord. ednl. liaison, 1985-87; v.p. Jewish Community Coun. Women, 1988-90, pres., 1990-93, bd. dirs. Congregation Brit. Shalom, 1985-87, 90-93. USPHS fellow, U. Conn., 1969-71. Mem. APA, Eastern Psychol. Assn., Cen. Pa. Psychol. Assn. (exec. bd. 1989-90), Jewish Community Coun. Women (bd. dirs. 1990-94), Phi Beta Kappa, Phi Kappa Phi. Democrat. Jewish.

FRANKEL, MARLENE JOAN, clinical psychologist; b. N.Y.C., Feb. 4, 1953; d. Melvin Irwin and Frances Evelyn (Mondschein) F. BA, SUNY, Binghamton, 1975; PhD, Washington U., St. Louis, 1980. Lic. psychologist, N.Y., Colo. Clin. psychology intern Crestwood Children's Ctr., Rochester, N.Y., 1977-78; pediatric psychology trainee St. Louis Children's Hosp., St. Louis, 1978-79; asst. psychologist Behavioral Stress Ctr., Elmhurst, N.Y., 1981-82; staff psychologist Peninsula Counseling Ctr., Lynbrook, N.Y., 1982-85, South Shore Child Guidance Ctr., Freeport, N.Y., 1982-90; psychologist in ind. practice, Rockville Centre, N.Y., 1984-90, Denver, 1990—. Grad. scholar Washington U., 1976, 78. Mem. APA, Colo. Psychol. Assn., Colo. Soc. Psychologists in Pvt. Practice (co-sec. 1994—), Colo. Women Psychologists, Nat. Register of Health Svc. Providers in Psychology, Phi Beta Kappa. Office: 90 Madison St Ste 204 Denver CO 80206-5411

FRANKENTHALER, HELEN, artist; b. N.Y.C., Dec. 12, 1928; d. Alfred and Martha (Lowenstein) F.; m. Robert Motherwell, Apr. 5, 1958 (div.); m. Stephen DuBrul, Jr., July 1994. BA, Bennington Coll., 1949; LHD (hon.), Skidmore Coll., 1969, Hofstra U., 1991; DFA (hon.), Smith Coll., 1973, Moore Coll. Art, 1974, Bard Coll., 1976, NYU, 1979; DFA, Phila. Coll. Art, 1980, Williams Coll., 1980; DFA (hon.), Marymount Manhattan Coll., 1989, Adelphi U., 1989, Washington U., St. Louis, 1989; D.Art, Radcliffe Coll., 1978, Amherst Coll., 1979; D.Art (hon.), Harvard U., 1980; DFA (hon.), Yale U., 1981, Brandeis U., 1982, U. Hartford, 1983, Syracuse U., 1985, Dartmouth Coll., 1994. tchr., lectr. Yale U., 1966, 67, 70, Hunter Coll., 1970, Princeton U., 1971, Cooper Union, N.Y.C., 1972, Washington U. Sch. Fine Arts, 1972, Skidmore Coll., 1973, Swathmore Coll., 1974, Drew U., 1975, Harvard, 1976, Radcliffe Coll., 1976, Bard Coll., 1977, Detroit Inst. Arts, 1977, NYU, U. Pa., Sch. Visual Arts, Goucher Coll., Wash. U., Yale Grad. Sch., U. Ariz., 1978, Graphic Arts Council N.Y., 1979, Harvard U., 1980, Phila. Coll., 1980, Williams Coll., 1980, Yale U., 1981, Brandeis U., 1982, U. of Hartford, 1983, Syracuse U., 1985, Sante Fe Inst. Fine Arts, 1986, 90, 91; U.S. rep. Venice Biennale, 1966. One-woman shows include, Tibor de Nagy Gallery, N.Y.C., 1951-58, Andre Emmerich Gallery, N.Y.C., 1959-73, 75, 77, 78, 79, 81, 82, 83, 84, 86, 87, 89, 90, 91, 92, 93, Jewish Mus., N.Y., 1960, Everett Ellin Gallery, Los Angeles, 1961, Galerie Lawrence, Paris, 1961, 63, Bennington Coll., 1962, 78, Galleria dell'Ariete, Milan, 1962, Kasmin Gallery, London, 1964, David Mirvish Gallery, Toronto, 1965, 71, 73, 75, Gertrude Kasle Gallery, Detroit, 1967, Nicholas Wilder Gallery, Los Angeles, 1967, Andre Emmerich Gallery, Zurich, 1974, 80, Swarthmore (Pa.) Coll., 1974, Solomon R. Guggenheim Mus., N.Y.C., 1975, Corcoran Gallery Art, Washington, 1975, Seattle Art Mus., 1975, Mus. Fine Arts, Houston, 1975, 85, 86, Ace Gallery, Vancouver, B.C., Can., 1975, Rosa Esman Gallery, N.Y.C., 1975, 83, 89, 3d Internat. Contemporary Art Fair, Paris, 1976, 81, retrospective Whitney Mus. Am. Art, 1969, Whitechapel Gallery, London, Eng., 1969, Kongress-Halle, Berlin, Kunstverein, Hannover, 1969, Heath Gallery, Atlanta, 1971, Galerie Godard Lefort, Montreal, 1971, Fendrick Gallery, Washington, 1972, 79, John Berggruen Gallery, San Francisco, 1972, 79, 82, Portland (Oreg.) Art Mus., 1972, Waddington Galleries II, London, 1973, 74, Janie C. Lee Gallery, Dallas, 1973, Houston, 1975, 76, 78, 80, 82, Met. Mus. Art, N.Y.C., 1973, Gallery Diane Gilson, Seattle, 1976, Greenberg Gallery, St. Louis, 1977, Galerie Wentzel, Hamburg, Germany, 1977, Jacksonville (Fla.) Art Mus., 1977-78, Knoedler Gallery, London, 1978, 81, 83, USIA exhbn., 1978-79, Atkins Mus. Fine Art, William Rockhill Nelson Gallery Art, Kansas City, Mo., 1978, 80, Saginaw Art Mus., Mich., 1980, Gimpel and Hanover and Andre Emerich Galleries, Zurich, 1980, Gallery Ulysses, Vienna, 1980, Knoedler Gallery, London, 1981, 83, Buschlen/Mowalt Fine Arts, Vancouver, 1989, Mus. Modern Art, N.Y.C., 1989, Douglas Drake Gallery, N.Y.C., 1989, Mizografia Gallery, L.A., 1989, Gerald Peters Gallery, Santa Fe, 1990, Kukje Gallery, Seoul, Korea, 1991, Assn. Am. Artists, N.Y.C., 1992, Knoedler & Co., N.Y.C., 1992, 94, Nat. Gallery Art, Washington, 1993, San Diego Mus. Art, 1993, Mus. Fine Arts, Boston, 1994, Contemporary Arts Ctr., Cin., 1994, numerous others; exhibited in group shows including, Whitney Mus., 1958, 71, 75-79, 82, 89, Carnegie Internat., Pitts., 1955, 58, 61, 64, Columbus Gallery Fine Arts, 1960, Guggenheim Mus., 1961, 76, 80, 82, Seattle World's Fair, 1962, Art Inst. Chgo., 1963, 69, 72, 76, 77, 82, 83, San Francisco Mus. Art, 1963, 68, Krannert Mus., U. Ill., 1959, 63, 65, 67, 80, Washington Gallery Modern Art, 1963, Pa. Acad. Fine Arts, 1963, 68, 76, N.Y. World's Fair, 1964, Am. Fedn. Arts Circulating Exhbn., 1964, U. Austin Art Mus., 1964, Rose Art Mus. Circulating Exhbn., 1964, Detroit Inst. Arts, 1965, 67, 73, 77, U. Mich. Mus. Art, 1965, Md. Inst., 1966, Norfolk Mus. Arts and Scis., 1966, Venice Biennale, 1966, Smithsonian Instn., 1966, Expo '67, Montreal, 1967, Washington Gallery Modern Art, 1967, Ga. Mus. Art, Athens, 1967, U. Okla. Mus. Art, Norman, 1968, Philbrook Art Center, Tulsa, 1968, Cin. Mus., 1968, U. Calif. at San Diego, 1968, Mus. Modern Art, N.Y.C., 1969, 75, 76, 80, 82, Met. Mus., N.Y.C., 1969-70, 76, 79, 81, Va. Mus., Richmond, 1970, 74, 87, Balt. Mus. Art, 1970, 76, 89, Boston U., 1970, Boston Mus. Fine Arts, 1972, 82, 90, Des Moines Art Center, 1973, Mus. Fine Arts, Houston, 1974, 82, Smith Coll. Mus. Art, Northampton, Mass., 1974, El Instituto de Cultura Puertorriquena, San Juan, 1974, Basil (Switzerland) Art Fair, 1974, 76, Finch Coll. Mus. Art, N.Y.C., 1974, S.I. Mus., 1975, Denver Art Mus., 1975, Visual Arts Mus., N.Y.C., 1975, 76, Mus. Modern Art, Belgrade Yugoslavia, 1976, Chrysler Mus., Norfolk, Va., 1976, Everson Mus., Syracuse, N.Y., Galleria d'Arts Moderna, Rome, 1976, Grey Art Gallery, N.Y.C., 1976-78, 81, Bklyn Mus., 1976-77, 82, Edmonton Art Gallery, Alta., Can., 1977, 78, Albright-Knox Mus., Buffalo, 1978, Fogg Art Mus., Harvard U., 1978, 83, Art Gallery Ont., 1979, Hirshorn Mus. and Sculpture Garden, Washington, 1980, Phoenix Art Mus., 1980, Nat. Gallery Art, Washington, 1981, Tate Gallery, London, 1981, Walker Art Ctr., Mpls., 1981, Milw. Art Mus., 1982, Mus. Fine Arts, Boston, 1982, Whitney Mus. Am. Art , N.Y., 1982, St. Louis Art Mus., 1982, High Mus. Art, Atlanta, 1989, Nelson-Atkins Mus. Art, Kansas City, Nat. Gallery Can., 1990, Williams Coll. Mus. Art, Williamstown, Mass., 1991, Aldrich Mus. Contemporary Art, Ridgefield, Conn., 1992, Mus. Modern Art, Mexico City, 1992, Yokohama Mus. Art, Japan, 1992, Marugame Inokuma-Genichiro Mus. Contemp. Art, 1992, Mus. Modern Art, Wakayama, 1992, Tokushima Modern Art Mus., Japan, 1992, Hokkaido Obihiro Mus. Art, 1993, Whitney Mus. Am. Art, Stamford, Conn., 1993, Gallery One, Toronto, Can., 1994; represented in permanent collections, Bklyn. Mus., Met. Mus. Art N.Y., , Solomon R. Guggenheim Mus., NYU, Mus. Modern Art, Albright-Knox Art Gallery, Buffalo, Whitney Mus., N.Y.C., U. Mich., High Mus., Atlanta, Milw. Art Inst., Wadsworth Atheneum, Hartford, Newark Mus., Yale U. Art Gallery, U. Nebr. Art Gallery, Carnegie Inst., Pitts., Detroit Inst. Art, Balt. Mus. Art, Univ. Mus., Berkeley, Calif., Bennington (Vt.) Coll., Art Inst. Chgo., Cin. Art Mus., Cleve. Mus. Art, Columbus Gallery Fine Arts, Honolulu Acad. Arts, Contemporary Arts Assn., Houston, Pasadena Art Mus., William Rockhill Nelson Gallery Art, Kans. City, Kans., Kans. City Art Inst., Atkins Mus. Fine Arts, Kans. City, Kans., City Art Mus., St. Louis, Mus. Art, R.I. Sch. Design, Providence, San Francisco Mus. Art, Everson Mus., Syracuse, N.Y., Smithsonian Instn., Walker Art Inst., Mpls., Washington Gallery Modern Art, Wichita Art Mus., Brown Gallery Art, Nat. Gallery Victoria, Melbourne, Australia, Australian Nat. Gallery, Canberra, Victoria and Albert Mus., London, Eng., Tokyo Mus., Ulster Mus., Belfast, No. Ireland, Elvehjem Art Center, U. Wis., Israel Mus.-Instituto Nacional de Bellas Artes, Phila. Mus. Art, Phoenix Art Mus., Corcoran Gallery Art, Boston Mus. Fine Arts, Springfield (Mass.) Mus. Fine Arts, Witte Mus., San Antonio, Abbott Hall Art Gallery, Kendal, Eng., Mus. Contemporary Art, Nagaoka, Japan, Guggenheim Mus., N.Y.C., 1984, others; was subject of film Frankenthaler: Toward a New Climate, 1978. Trustee Bennington Coll., 1967—. Fellow Calhoun Coll., Yale U., 1968—; recipient 1st prize for painting Paris Biennale, 1959, Gold medal Pa. Acad. Fine Arts, 1968, Great Ladies award Fordham U., Thomas Moore Coll., 1969, Spirit of Achievement award Albert Einstein Coll. Medicine, 1970, Gold medal Commune of Catania, III Biennale della Grafica d'Arte, Florence, Italy, 1972, Garrett award 70th Am. Exhbn., Art Inst. Chgo., 1972, Creative Arts award Nat. Women's div. Am. Jewish Congress, 1974, Art and Humanities award Yale Women's Forum, 1976, Extraordinary Woman of Achievement award NCCJ, 1978, Alumni award Bennington Coll., 1979, N.Y.C. Mayor's award , 1986, Lifetiem Achievement award Coll. Art Assn., 1994. Mem. NEA, Am. Acad. (vice-chancelor 1991), Am. Acad. Arts and Scis., Nat. Coun. Arts, Nat. Inst. Arts and Letters. Office: M Knoedler & Co Inc 19 E 70th St New York NY 10021

FRANKIEWICZ, MARCIA JEAN, telemarketing executive; b. East Chicago, Ind., July 9, 1947; d. Edward Stanley and Bernice Jean (Pikula) F.; m. Richard Joseph Palchak, Apr. 22, 1989; children: Sarah Frankiewicz-Palchak, Jason Frankiewicz-Palchak. BS in Edn., Western Mich. U., 1969; MS in Spl. Edn., U. Wis., Whitewater, 1981. Tchr., unit leader Wilson Elem. Sch., Janesville, Wis., 1969-79; spl. edn. tchr. Brown Deer (Wis.) High Sch., 1979-84, trainer, 1983-84; spl. svcs. mgr. Braeger Chevrolet, Inc., Milw., 1984-85; telemktg. mgr. Gander Mountain, Inc., Wilmot, Wis., 1985-86; pres., owner MJ Dimensions, Milw., 1986—; guest WISN Radio, Milw., 1988; speaker and seminar leader in field. Advisor mktg. edn. adv. com. Milw. Pub. Schs., 1987—. Mem. Wis. Telemktg. Mgrs. Assn. (pres. 1987-89), Sales and Mktg. Execs. Milw. (v.p. programs 1989-90, bd. dirs. 1991-94), Internat. Assn. Pers. Women (bd. dirs. 1984-87), Pers. Indsl. Rels. Assn. Milw. (various coms.), Wis. Women Entrepreneurs, Alpha Omicron Pi, Kappa Delta Pi. Roman Catholic. Office: MJ Dimensions 2670 N Lake Dr Milwaukee WI 53211

FRANKING, HOLLY MAE, software publisher; b. Washington, D.C., May 13, 1944; d. Nelson W. and Dorothy Elizabeth (O'Connor) F.; m. John Robert Slegman, Aug. 16, 1986. BA in English, Mt. St. Mary's Coll., 1967; MA in English, Loyola U., L.A., 1970; MA in Philosophy, U. Kans., 1986, PhD in English, 1988. Cert. preschool, kindergarten, grades 1-12, adult tchr., Calif., jr. coll. tchr., Calif. Grade 3 tchr. Valley Sch., L.A., 1968-69; grade 4 tchr. St. Elizabeth Sch., Van Nuys, Calif., 1970-72, grades 5,6 tchr., vice prin., 1972-77; grades 7, 8 tchr. St. Mel. Sch., L.A., 1978-79; grade 6 tchr., vice prin. St. Elizabeth Sch., Van Nuys, 1978-82; grades 10-12 tchr. Taft High Sch., L.A., 1982-83; pres., co-founder, software pub., author Diskotech, Inc., Prairie Village, Kans., 1987—; faculty rep. for sch. bd. St. Elizabeth Sch., Van Nuys, 1973-78. Author: (computerized video novel) Negative Space, 1990, CD-Rom version 1995, Dr. Franking's Language Lessons, 1990; editor: Mae Franking's "My Chinese Marriage," 1991; pub.: How To Be Happily Employed in the 1990s, 1993; author, pub. software; pub. PCards (1st ever multimedia greeting cards, 1994; book reviewer Kansas City Star newspaper, 1994. Democrat. Home: 6240 Rosewood Shawnee Mission KS 66205 Office: Diskotech Inc 7930 State Line Rd Ste 210 Prairie Village KS 66208

FRANKL, RAZELLE, management educator. BA in English, Temple U., 1955; MA in Polit. Sci., Bryn Mawr Coll., 1966; MBA in Organizational Devel., Drexel U., 1973; PhD, Bryn Mawr Coll., 1984. Chair codes and ordinance com. Exec Com. Neighborhood Improvement Program, Lower Merion Twp., 1967-68; pres. LWV Lower Merion Twp., 1967-68; v.p. for organizational affairs LWV, Springfield, Mass., 1968-70; chair environ. quality com. LWV Radnor Twp., 1970-71; instr. applied behavioral sci. Drexel U. Sch. Bus., 1972-73; planner office of mental health/mental retardation Dept. Pub. Health, City of Phila., 1971-73, planner office of health planning, 1971-73; coord. for health programs Phila. '76 Inc. (Official Bicentennial Corp.), 1972-74; adj. faculty dept. mgmt. adminstrv. studies div. Sch. Bus. Rowan Coll. N.J. (formerly Glassboro State Coll.), 1974-77, 81-82; asst. prof. Glassboro (N.J.) State Coll., 1982-88, assoc. prof. dept. mgmt., 1988—; mem. comm. com. Nat. Bd. Med. Coll. Pa.; presenter in field. Author: Televangelism: The Marketing of Popular Religion, 1987, Popular Religion and the Imperatives of Television: A Study of the Electric Church, 1984; author: (with others) Religious Television: Controversies and Conclusions, 1990, Teleministries as Family Businesses, 1990;, New Christian Politics, 1984; contbr. articles to profl. jours. Dir. Nat. Bd. Med. Coll. Pa., chair spring program; chair, bd. dirs. Anti-Violence Partnership of Phila. Rsch. grantee Rowan Coll. N.J. (formerly Glassboro State Coll.), 1986-87, 90, 91, 93-94, 94-95, All-Coll. Rsch. grantee, 1987-88. Mem. Am. Acad. Mgmt. (chair membership com. div. mgmt. edn. and devel., chair media rels. com., div. women in mgmt.), Soc. for Human Resource Mgmt., Am. Sociol. Assn., Ea. Sociol. Soc., Assn. for Sociology Religion, Religious Rsch. Assn., Soc. for Sci. Study Religion (chair womens caucus), Internat. Sociol. Assn., Assn. for Rsch. on Non-profit Orgns. and Vol. Action. Home: 536 Moreno Rd Wynnewood PA 19096-1121

FRANKLIN, ARETHA, singer; b. Memphis, 1942; d. Clarence L. and Barbara (Siggers) F.; m. Ted White (div.); m. Glynn Turman, Apr. 11, 1978. First record at age 12; rec. artist with Columbia Records, N.Y.C., 1961, then with Atlantic records, now with Arista Records; albums include Aretha, 1961, Electrifying, 1962, Tender Moving and Swinging, 1962, Laughing on the Outside, 1963, Unforgettable, 1964, Songs of Faith, 1964, Running Out of Fools, 1964, Yeah, 1965, Soul Sister, 1966, Queen of Soul, Take it Like You Give It, 1967, Lee Cross, Greatest Hits, 1967, I Never Loved a Man, 1967, Once in a Lifetime, Aretha Arrives, 1967, Lady Soul, 1968, Greatest Hits, Vol. 2, 1968, Best of Aretha Franklin, Live at Paris Olympia, 1968, Aretha Now, 1968, Soul 69, 1969, Today I Sing the Blues, 1969, Soft and Beautiful, Aretha Gold, 1969, Satisfaction, I Say a Little Prayer, 1969, This Girl's in Love With You, 1970, Spirit in the Dark, 1970, Don't Play that Song, 1970, Live at the Fillmore West, 1971, Young Gifted and Black, 1971, Aretha's Greatest Hits, 1971, Amazing Grace, 1972, Hey Hey Now, 1973, Star Collection, 1978, First 12 Sides, 1973, Let Me Into Your Life, 1974, With Every Thing I Feel in Me, 1975, You, 1975, Sparkle, 1976, Ten Years of Gold, 1976, Sweet Passion, 1977, Almighty Fire, 1978, La Diva, 1979, Aretha, 1980, Who's Zoomin' Who, 1985, One Lord, One Faith, One Baptism, 1987, Aretha Sings the Blues, 1965, 85, Lady Soul, 1988, Through the Storm, 1989, What You See Is What You Sweat, 1991, Jazz to Soul, 1992; appeared in film: Blues Brothers, 1980; performer: (Showtime prodn.) Aretha, 1986; concert tours in U.S. and Europe. Named Top Female Vocalist, 1967; named Number One Female Singer 16th Internat. Jazz Critics Poll, 1968; recipient Grammy award for best female rhythm and blues vocal, 1967-74, 81, 85, 87, 88 for best rhythm and blues rec., 1967, for best soul gospel performance, 1972, for best rhythm and blues duo vocal (with George Michael, 1987); Am. Music award, 1984; Kennedy Center Honor, 1994. Address: 8450 Linwood St. Detroit MI 48206 Office: care Wm Morris Agency 151 El Camino Dr Beverly Hills CA 90212*

FRANKLIN, BARBARA HACKMAN, former U.S. Secretary of Commerce; b. Lancaster, Pa., Mar. 19, 1940; d. Arthur A. and Mayme M. (Haller) Hackman; m. Wallace Barnes, Nov. 29, 1986. BA with distinction, Pa. State U., 1962; MBA, Harvard U., 1964; D of Bus. Adminstrn. (hon.), Bryant Coll., 1973; D of Commerce (hon.), Drexel U., 1990; D of Comml. Sci., U. Hartford, 1994. Mgr. environ. analysis Singer Co., N.Y.C., 1965-68; asst. v.p. Citibank, N.Y.C., 1969-71; asst. on White House staff for recruiting of women to positions in govt., Washington, 1971-73; commr., vice chmn. U.S. Consumer Product Safety Commn., Washington, 1973-79; sr. fellow, dir. govt. and bus. programWharton Sch., U. Pa., Phila., 1979-88; pres., CEO Franklin Assocs., Washington, 1984-92; alt. rep., pub. del. 44th Session UN Gen. Assembly, 1989-90; sec. of commerce Dept. of Commerce, Washington, 1992-93; adviser to comptroller gen. U.S., 1984-92, 94—; bd. dirs., chair audit com. Aetna Life and Casualty Co., Dow Chem. Co.; bd. dirs. AMP, Inc.; chair task force on tax reform Adv. Com. Trade Policy and Negotiations, 1985-86, 89-92, 94—; pub. mem. Auditing Standards Bd. Planning Com., 1989; pub. mem., bd. dirs. Am. Inst. CPA's, 1979-86. Apptd. by Pres. Reagan then Bush to Pres.'s Adv. Com. Trade and Policy Negotiations, 1982-86, 89-92, chair task force on tax reform, 1985-86; co-chmn. Nat. Fin. Com. George Bush for Pres., 1985-88; bd. visitors Def. Systems Mgmt. Coll., Dept. Def., 1986-89; svcs. policy adv. Com. of U.S. Trade Representatives; apptd. by Gov. Thornburgh to State Bd. Edn., Commonwealth Pa., 1980-81; bd. regents U. Hartford, 1986-88. Trustee Pa. State U., 1976-92. Recipient Disting. Alumni award Pa. State U., 1972, Disting. Woman award Northwood Inst., 1972, Catalyst award for Corp. Leadership, 1981, Excellence in Mgmt. award Simmons Coll., 1981, Am. Assn. Poison Control Ctrs. award, 1979, cert. appreciation, Am. Acad. Pediatrics, 1979, Dirs. Choice award Nat. Women's Econ. Alliance, 1987, Corp. Social Responsibility award CUNY, 1988, John J. McCloy Auditing award, 1992, Womens Nat. Rep. Club award, 1993; Kappa Alpha Theta Graduate fellow, 1962, Edith Gratia Stedman, Harvard U., fellow, 1962; named one of 50 Most Influential Corp. Dirs. Am. Mgmt. Assn., 1990. Fellow Nat. Assn. Corp. Dirs.; mem. NACD (Blue Ribbon commn. bd. and CEO evaluation 1994), Women's Forum Washington, Nat. Women's Econ. Alliance Found. (bd. govs., Dir.'s Choice award 1987), Internat. Women's Forum (founding mem.), Coun. Fgn. Rels., Exec. Women in Govt. (founding mem., vice chmn. 1973), Bretton Woods Com., Washington Forum, Alumni Coun. Pa. State U., 1925 F Street Club, Washington (bd. govs.), Women's Nat. Rep. Club (bd. govs. 1969-71), Econ. Club N.Y., Econ. Club D.C. Congregational. Avocations: exercise, skiing, sailing, reading. Office: 2600 Virginia Ave NW Suite 506 Washington DC 20037 also: 1875 Perkins St Bristol CT 06010

FRANKLIN, BARBARA KIPP, financial planner, investment adviser; b. Jackson, Mich., Jan. 7, 1943; d. Robert Charles and Barbara Jean (Boardman) F.; m. Peter G. Stone. BBA, U. Mich., Ann Arbor, 1967. Chartered fin. analyst; cert. fin. planner. Freelance journalist various Mich. and Ohio newspapers, 1968-71; pub. relations rep. Bayerische Motoren Werke, Munich, Germany, 1969-71; acct. exec. Dean Witter Reynolds, Los Angeles, 1975-77; trust rep. First Interstate Bank, 1978-79; trust adminstr. Union Bank, Los Angeles, 1980-81; trust portfolio mgr. Fidelity Bank, Phila., 1981-84; trust portfolio mgr., v.p. Provident Nat. Bank, Phila., 1984-91; pvt. practice Del. and Pa., 1992—. Mem. Hist. Soc. Chester County; bd. dirs., exec. com., treas. Children's Country Week Assn., Chester County, 1988—. Mem. DAR, Internat. Assn. Fin. Planning, Assn. Investment Mgmt. and Rsch., Inst. Chartered Fin. Analysts, Inst. CFP, Nat. Assn. Life Underwriters, Delaware Valley Soc. CFP (bd. dirs. 1991-93, sec. 1993—), Chester County Chamber of Bus. and Industry, Estate Planning Coun. Chester County, Exch. Club So. Chester County (charter), Ctrl. Chester County C. of C., Phila. Securities Assn., Fin. Analysts Phila.

FRANKLIN, INGA SIVILLS KNUPP, special education educator; b. Norfolk, Va., Sept. 24, 1955; d. Stanley Allen and Margaret (DeVane) K.; m. John Walter Franklin, Aug. 21, 1976; 1 child, John Allen. BS in Spl. Edn., Pembroke State U., 1976; MEd, U. N.C. Chapel Hill, 1982; AG cert., St. Andrews, 1982. Cert. tchr., including H.S. sci., math. grades 6-9, lang. arts grades 6-9, learning disabilities, mentally handicapped, behavior/emotionally handicapped, N.C. Spl. edn. tchr. Bladen County Schs., Elizabethtown,

N.C., 1976—; co-owner Franklin's Finishing Touch; sch.-based com. chair, adminstrv. placement com., tchr. learning disabilities workshops. Contbr. article to profl. jour., 1985. Art. dir. VBS, First Bapt. Ch., Dublin, N.C., 1992-93, mem. children's com., 1990-93, crusader dir., 1992—; asst. leader Wieblo Scouts, 1992-93. Mem. Bladen County Coun. Exceptional Children (pres. 1985, 92, sec. 1993, Presdl. award 1992). Democrat. Home: 386 Lyons Landing Rd Dublin NC 28332

FRANKLIN, LYNNE, business communications consultant, writer; b. St. Paul, Minn., Aug. 24, 1957; d. Lyle John Franklin and Lois Ann (Cain) Kindseth; m. Lawrence Anton Pecorella, Sept. 2, 1989; 1 stepchild, Lauren. BA in Psychology and English, Coll. St. Catherine, 1979; MA, Hamline U., 1989. Residential treatment counselor St. Joseph's Home, Mpls., 1979-80; staff writer Comml. West Mag., Mpls., 1980-81; acct. exec. Edwin Neuger & Assocs., Mpls., 1981-83, Hill and Knowlton, Mpls., 1983-84; mgr. pub. rels. Gelco Corp., Eden Prarie, Minn., 1984-86; dir. financial rels. Dunstan & Assocs., Mpls., 1986; cons. MC Assocs., Chgo., 1986-87; v.p. Fin. Rels. Bd., Chgo., 1987—; principal Wordsmith, Glenview, Ill., 1993—; judge achievement awards Internat. Assn. of Bus. Communicators, Mpls., 1986, presenter fin. rels., 1990; judge achievement awards Publicity Club of Chgo., 1992-94; presenter annual report seminar Nat. Investor Rels. Inst., Chgo., 1992. Author: (novel) Second Sight, 1989. tchr. Great Books Program, St. Paul, 1976-79, Minn. Literacy Coun., 1985-87. Recipient Annual Report Excellence award Fin. World Mag., 1991-94, MerComm-ARC Competition, 1992-94. Office: Wordsmith 2019 Glenview Rd Glenview IL 60025

FRANKLIN, MARGARET LAVONA BARNUM (MRS. C. BENJAMIN FRANKLIN), civic leader; b. Caldwell, Kans., June 19, 1905; d. LeGrand Husted and Elva (Biddinger) Barnum; m. C. Benjamin Franklin, Jan. 20, 1940 (dec. 1983); children: Margaret Lee (Mrs. Michael J. Felso), Benjamin Barnum. B.A., Washburn U., 1952; student, Iowa State Tchrs. Coll., 1923-25, U. Iowa, 1937-38. Tchr. pub. schs. Union, Iowa, 1925-27, pub. schs., Kearney, Nebr., 1927-28, Marshalltown, Iowa, 1928-40; advance rep. Redpath-Vawter-Chautauquas, 1926, Associated Chautauquas, 1927-30. Mem. Citizens Adv. Com., 1965-69; mem. Stormont-Vail Regional Ctr. Hosp. Aux.; bd. dirs. Marshalltown Civic Theatre, 1938-40, pres. 1938-40; bd. dirs. Topeka Pub. Libr. Found., 1984-92; mem. Park Ave. Christian Ch., N.Y.C.; 1st sec. beautification com. City of Topeka, 1951. Recipient Waldo B. Heywood award Topeka Civic Theatre, 1967, Vol. Svc. award Topeka Pub. Libr., 1991. Mem. DAR (state chmn. Museum 1968-71), AAUW (50+ Yr. mem.), Gemini Group of Topeka, Topeka Geneal. Soc., Topeka Civic Symphony Soc. (dir. 1952-57, Svc. Honor citation 1960), Doll Collectors Am., Shawnee County Hist. Soc. (dir. 1963-75, sec. 1964-66), Stevengraph Collectors Assn., Friends of Topeka Public Libr. (dir. 1970-79, Disting. Svc. award 1980), PEO Sisterhood, Philanthropic and Ednl. Orgn. (pres. chpt. 1956-57, coop. bd. pres. 1964-65, chpt. honoree 1969), Native Sons and Daus. Kans. (life), Nonoso, Topeka Stamp Club, Western Sorosis Club (pres. 1960-61), Minerva Club (2d v.p. 1984-85), Woman's Club (1st v.p. 1952-54), Knife and Fork Club, Alpha Beta Gamma. Republican.

FRANKLIN, MARY ANN WHEELER, administrator, educator, higher education and management consultant; b. Boston; d. Arthur Edward Wheeler and Madeline Ophelia (Hall) Wheeler-Brooks; m. Carl Matthew Franklin; 1 child, Evangeline Rachel Hall Franklin-Nash. BS, U. N.H., 1942; MEd, U. Buffalo, 1948; EdD, U. Md., 1982. Cert. tchr., N.Y., Ga. Instr. edn. W.Va. State Coll., Institute, 1947; tchr. gen. sci. John Marshall Jr. High Sch., Bklyn., 1952; assoc. prof. sci. Elizabeth City (N.C.) State Coll., 1960; asst. dean coll. Morgan State U., Balt., 1967-77, asst. dean Coll. Arts and Scis., 1977-78, v.p. acad. affairs, 1978-82; asst. prof. bus. Catonsville (Md.) Community Coll., 1982; asst. to dean evening and weekend coll. So. U. New Orleans, 1983-92; cons. numerous locations Herford County Tchrs., Murfressboro, N.C., 1961, St. Catherine's Sch., Elizabeth City, 1962-64, Archbishop Keogh High Sch., Balt., 1970-80, Hampton Inst. Va. St. Paul Coll., 1972; bd. dirs. Archbishop Keough High Sch.; presenter confs.; speaker. Editor Academic Affairs Newsletter, 1980-82, Morgan State Coll. Cataloge, 1969-82; author: The How and Why of Testing at Elizabeth City State College, 1962, Report on Princeton University Program for Physics Teachers in HBCU's, 1964, Learning Summer Camp Code, National Library of Poetry, 1992, Interrogations of a Mumies Polity, 1993, Who Are We/ Who We Are, 1994. Mem. com. higher edn. Citizens League, Balt., 1979-81; assoc. dir. youth camp NCCJ, 1974-75, bd. dirs. 1969-80; dir., originator Vestibule Program and Parents Workshop for New Citizens and Residents; dir., originator Slino Summer Learning Camp, 1984-95;pres Lake Willow Homeowners Assn., 1994—. Fellow NSF, Harvard U., 1958-59, Carnegie-Ford-NSF, Princeton U., 1964; recipient Education award Am. Assn. of Coll. Tchrs., 1966. Mem. AAUW, Am. Mgmt. Assn., Nat. Coun. Negro Women (bd. dirs. 1984), Am. Assn. Higher Edn., Am. Assn. Coll. Higher Edn., Nat. Assn. Trainers and Educators for Alcohol and Substace Abuse Counselors (pres. accreditation coun.'s alcohol and drug counseling program), La. Assn. Continuing Higher Edn., Md. Assn. Higher Edn. (pres. 1976-78), Urban League, Delta Sigma Theta, Phi Sigma, Pi Lambda Theta.

FRANKLIN, MELISSA, physicist; b. Edmonton. BS, Univ. of Toronto; PhD, Stanford Univ., Calif. Asst. prof. Univ. of Ill., Champaign-Urbana; jr. fellow Harvard Univ., Cambridge, Mass., prof. physics, 1992—. Office: Harvard Univ Dept of Physics Jefferson Lab Cambridge MA 02138-6502*

FRANKLIN, PHYLLIS, professional association administrator; b. N.Y.C., Apr. 21, 1932; d. Matthew Pine and Helen Lutsky; m. Irwin Franklin, Apr. 21, 1958 (div. 1971); children: James, Jody. AB, Vassar Coll., 1954; MA, U. Miami, 1965, PhD, 1969; LHD (hon.), George Washington U., 1986. From asst. to assoc. prof. U. Miami, Coral Gables, 1969-80; spl. asst. to dean Coll. Arts & Scis. Duke U., Durham, N.C., 1980-81; dir. English programs MLA, N.Y.C., 1981-85, exec. dir., 1985—; adj. prof. English programs NYU, 1987-88. Editor ADE Bull., 1981-85, Profession, 1985—. Fellowship, Danforth Found., 1966-68, Am. Council on Edn., 1980-81; stipend NEH, 1971. Mem. USSR Acad. Scis., Am. Coun. Learned Socs. (bd. dirs. 1987-89, commn. on humanities and social scis. 1987-88, chair conf. secs. 1987-90), Nat. Humanities Alliance (bd. dirs. 1986-88, v.p. 1990-91, pres. 1991—), Nat. Fedn. Abstracting and Info. Svcs. (bd. dirs. 1994—). Democrat. Jewish. Office: Modern Language Assn 10 Astor Pl New York NY 10003-6935

FRANKLIN, RITA SIMS, retail executive; b. Selma, Ala., May 18, 1943; d. Emmett McClain and Mary Frances (O'Brien) Sims; children: Susan Lenore Sims Franklin, Sarah Louise Sims Franklin. Student, Judson Coll., 1961-62, Huntingdon Coll., Montgomery, Ala., 1962-65. Retail salesperson, acct. Sims Furniture & Interiors, Selma, Ala., 1965—. Councilwoman Selma City Council, 1980-84, 88—; mem. Old Depot Mus. Soc., Selma, 1976—; bd. dirs. Med. Family Practice Bd., Selma, 1980—, Easter Seal Rehab. Bd., 1980—; exec. bd. Community Action Agy., Selma, 1980—. Mem. Selma Dallas County Hist. Soc., Friends of the Selma Library, Selma Beautification Council, Women in Mcpl. Govt. (nat. bd. dirs.), others. Democrat. Baptist. Home: 1904 Tippett Dr Selma AL 36701-6641 Office: Sims Furniture PO Box 1058 Selma AL 36702-1058

FRANKLIN, SHIRLEY MARIE, marketing consultant; b. Kansas City, Mo., Apr. 13, 1930; d. Eric E. and Marie M. (Kilpatrick) Snodgrass; div. 1967; 1 child, Scot Wesley. BA, State U. Iowa, 1952; MS, Simmons Coll., 1954; MA, Kans. U., 1974. Cert. tchr., Kans., Mass., N.J., Ariz., Calif. Tchr., adminstr. various schs., 1952-76; gifted student program designer Leavenworth County (Kans.) Pub. Schs., 1976-77; sales cons., mgr. Sealight Co., Inc., Kansas City, Mo., 1978-82; dir. chain sales Haagen Dazs Ice Cream Co., Teaneck, N.J., 1982-87; program dir. case space mgmt. Ice Cream Industry, 1986-88; prin. Shirley Franklin Consulting, Basehor, Kans., 1987—; apptd. U.S. brands dir. Mövenpick Co., Zurich, Switzerland, 1990—; mktg. cons. Franklin & Assocs., 1994—; speaker at dairy industry meetings, seminars. Contbr. articles to profl. jours. and mags. Foster parent World Vision, Pasadena, Calif., 1986—; mem. nat. com. steering com. U.S. Congress Arts Caucus, Washington, 1988, 89; vol. ct. appointed spl. advocate for children in trouble, Kans., 1994. Recipient Excellence in Sales Promotions award Dairy and Food Industries Supply Assn. Mem. Internat. Ice Cream Assn. (mktg. coun. 1979—), Delta Delta Delta. Republican. Episcopalian. Home and Office: 3741 N 155th St PO Box 233 Basehor KS 66007-9205

FRANKOVELGIA, KYM, vocalist, entertainer; b. Chgo., Oct. 8, 1954; d. Nicholas Richard and Angela Camelita (Orvino) F.; m. Arthur Wlodarski, Apr. 6, 1985 (div. 1990). Student, U. No. Colo., 1972-74; floral designer, Am. Floral Art Sch., Chgo., 1985. Registered profl. florist. Vocalist, entertainer Delta Queen Steamboat Co., New Orleans, 1992-93; entertainer The Wellness House Benefit, Oak Brook, Ill., 1993; entertainer, vocalist charitable orgns., Chgo., 1993-94, Maui, 1994—. Author: So You Want to Become a Woman, 1984; performances include appearances with "The Dream Sisters", "Expresso", 1994. Home and Office: 150 Hauoli St Wailuku HI 96793

FRANKS, LUCINDA LAURA, journalist; b. Chgo., July 16, 1946; d. Thomas Edward and Lorraine Lois (Leavitt) F.; m. Robert M. Morgenthau, Nov. 1977; children: Joshua Franks Morgenthau, Amy Elinor Morgenthau. B.A., Vassar Coll., 1968. Journalist specializing youth affairs, civil strife in No. Ireland UPI, London, 1968-73, N.Y. Times, N.Y.C., 1974-77; freelance writer N.Y. Times Mag., N.Y. Times Book Rev., The Atlantic, The New Yorker, N.Y. mag., The Nation; Vis. prof. Vassar Coll., 1977-82; Ferris prof. journalism Princeton U., 1983. Author: Waiting Out A War: The Exile of Private John Picciano, 1974, Wild Apples, 1991. Recipient Pulitizer prize for nat. reporting, 1971, N.Y. Newspaper Writers Assn. award, 1971; Nat. Headliners award, Soc. Silurians journalism award, 1976. Mem. Am. PEN Club (membership bd.), Author's League, Coun. on Fgn. Rels., Writers Rm. Inc. (past pres.). Address: 1085 Park Ave New York NY 10028

FRANKSON-KENDRICK, SARAH JANE, publisher; b. Bradford, Pa., Sept. 24, 1949; d. Sophronus Ahimus and Elizabeth Jane (Sears) McCutcheon; m. James Michael Kendrick, Jr., May 22, 1982. Customer service rep. Laros Printing/Osceola Graphics, Bethlehem, Pa., 1972-73; assoc. editor Babcox Publs., Akron, Ohio, 1973-74; assoc. editor Bill Communications, Akron, 1974-75, sr. editor, 1975-77, editor-in chief, 1977-81; assoc. pub. Chilton Co./ABC Pub., Chgo., 1981-83, pub., 1983-89, group pub., Radnor, Pa., 1989-93; group v.p. Chilton Co., Radnor, Pa., 1993—; exec. MBA prof. Northwood U., mem. adv. coun. Recipient Automotive Replacement Edn. award Northwood Inst., 1983, award for young leadership and excellence Automotive Hall of Fame, 1984. Mem. Automotive Found. for Aftermarket (trustee), Automotive Parts and Accessories Assn. (bd. dirs., exec. com., sec. treas., strategic planning com., show planning task force, Disting. Svc. award 1993), Automotive Svc. Industry Assn. (bd. dirs. automotive divsn. com.). Republican. Club: Knollwood Country (Lake Forest, Ill.). Office: Chilton Co/ABC Pub 201 Chilton Way Radnor PA 19089

FRANSEN, LINDA G., museum curator; b. Jackson, Minn., Jan. 25, 1959; d. Russell Jarl and Merva Dell (Shover) F.; m. Thomas Lee Sanders, May 25, 1991. BA in History and Psychology, Gustavus Adolphus Coll., Minn., 1981; MA in Hist. Adminstrn., Eastern Ill. U., 1986. Curator, tour guide Jackson County Hist. Mus., Lakefield, Minn., 1980-82 summers; intern Minn. Hist. Soc., St. Paul, 1981, Rocky Mount Hist. Soc., Piney Flats, Tenn., 1982-83; mus. interpreter Lincoln Log Cabin Historic Site, Lerna, Ill., 1984 summer; grad. asst. Eastern Ill. U., Charleston, Ill., 1984-85; assoc. curator Conner Prairie, Fishers, Ind., 1985-90; mus. curator Am. Swedish Inst., Mpls., 1990—. Mem. Am. Assn. Mus., Am. Assn. Univ. Women (v.p. programs 1993-95), Assn. for State and Local History, Minn. Assn. Mus., Hist. Preservation, Smithsonian Inst. Lutheran. Office: Am Swedish Inst 2600 Park Ave Minneapolis MN 55407

FRANTZ, CECILIA ARANDA, psychologist; b. Nogales, Ariz., Aug. 6, 1941; d. Tomas Nävarro and Maria Guadalupe (Covarrubias) A.; m. Roger Allen Frantz, May 27, 1972; 1 child, Kimberly Marie Whelan. BA, U. Ariz., 1966; MA, Ariz. State U., 1972, PhD, 1975. Lic. clin. psychologist, Ariz., sch. psychologist, Va. Tchr. Wilson Sch. Dist., Phoenix, 1966-70; psychologist Child Evaluation Ctr., Phoenix, 1973-75; sch. psychologist Wilson Sch. Dist., Phoenix, 1975-78, spl. edn. dir., 1977-78, schs. supt., 1978-81; acting dir. Nat. Inst. Handicap Rsch. U.S. Dept. Edn., Washington, 1981-82, dep. asst. sec. dept. elm. and secondary edn., 1982-87; asst. dir. Bush's Nat. Steering Com. Campaign Hdqrs., Washington, 1987-88; pvt. practice Washington, 1988—; sch. psychologist Cath. Archdiocese of Arlington, Va., 1990-92; Arlington County Schs., Arlington, Va., 1992—; cons. U.S. Dept. Edn., Washington, 1987—. Mem. APA, Am. Assn Sch. Adminstrs., Ariz. State Psychol. Assn., Ariz. State Sch. Psychologists Assn., Maricopa Soc. Clin. Psychologists (sec. 1976-77). Republican. Roman Catholic. Home: 4501 Arlington Blvd Apt 609 Arlington VA 22203-2740

FRANTZ, GILDA GLORIA, Jungian analyst; b. Bklyn., Dec. 29, 1926; d. Jack Feldrais and Ruth (Gersten) Striplin; m. Kieffer Evans Frantz, Apr. 21, 1950 (dec. May 1975); children: Carl Gilbert (dec.), Marlene Maris. MA, Antioch U., L.A., 1978. Assoc. editor Psychol. Perspectives C.G. Jung Inst. of L.A., 1969-76, interviewer, adv. com. Matter of Heart, 1975-81, pres., 1980-83, chmn., 1980-83, tng. analyst, 1977—; adv. coun. Paul Brunton Philos. Found.; lectr. and workshop presenter in field. Editorial bd. Jour. of Contemporary Jungian Psychology; editorial adv. bd. Chiron, A Rev. of Jungian Analysis; contbr. articles to profl. jours. Co-facilitator support group for significant others of people with AIDS, Sherman Oaks (Calif.) Hosp.; keynote speaker Nat. Conf. Jungian Analysts, Lake Tahoe, 1994. Mem. Soc. of Jungian Analysts of So. Calif., Internat. Assn. Analytical Psychology, Internat. Symposium on Grief and Bereavement (adv. bd. 1983—), Nat. Archive for Rsch. in Archetypal Symbolism (exec. bd., sec. 1984-89), Nat. Assn. for Advancement of Psychoanalysis.

FRANTZVE, JERRI LYN, psychologist, educator, consultant; b. Huntington Beach, Calif., Sept. 9, 1942; d. Rolland and Marjorie (Ferrin) Weiland. Student, Purdue U., 1964-68; BA in Psychology and History, Marian Coll., 1969; MS in Organizational Psychology, George Williams Coll., 1976; PhD in Indsl. and Organizational Psychology, U. Ga., 1979. Case worker Marion County Welfare Dept., Indpls., 1970-71; sr. mktg. rsch. analyst Quaker Oats Co., Barrington, Ill., 1971-75; mgmt. cons. J.L. Frantzve & Assocs., Bklyn., 1978—; asst. prof. sch. of mgmt. SUNY, Binghamton, 1979-83; pers. rsch. and acad. affairs coord. Conoco/DuPont, Ponca City, 1983-86, dir. employee rels., 1986-88; cons. psychologist Mass., N.Y, 1988-89; assoc. prof. psychology Radford (Va.) U., 1989-94; cons. Brooklyn, N.Y., 1994—; instrn. cons. USAF, Rome, N.Y., 1979-83; dir. Israel Overseas Rsch. Program, Ginozar, Israel, 1982, Japanese Overseas Rsch. Program, Tokyo, 1983; coord. rsch. Ctr. for Gender Studies, Radford U., 1989-94. Author: Behaving in Organizations: Tales from the Trenches, 1983, Guide to Behavior in Organizations, 1983; contbr. articles to profl. jours. Bd. dirs. Broome County Alcoholism Clinic, Binghamton, N.Y., 1980-83, bd. dirs. Broome County Mental Health Clinic, Binghamton, 1981-83; del. Dem. Caucus, Okla., 1985. Mem. APA (com. on women in psychology 1986-88), AAUW, Acad. Mgmt. (placement dir. Ea. chpt. 1982), Internat. Pers. Mgmt. Assn., Assn. for Women in Psychology, Delta Sigma Pi. Home and Office: 1804 Glenwood Rd Brooklyn NY 11230

FRANZ, JULIE LISABETH, advertising executive; b. Chgo., Jan. 31, 1961; d. Oskar and Claudia (Langebartels) F. BA, Loyola U., Chgo., 1983; MBA, Northwestern U., 1991. Assoc. editor Modern Health Care and Advt. Age, Chgo., 1980-86; account exec. J. Walter Thompson, Chgo., 1986-89; account dir. Foote Cone & Belding, Chgo., 1989—; cons. Goodman Theater, 1990, Mus. Contemporary Art, 1991, Chgo. Arts Edn. Campaign, 1993-94, Chgo. Music Alliance, 1994. Recipient Cert. Ill. Alliance for Arts Edn., Chgo., 1994. Lutheran. Office: Foote Cone & Belding 101 E Erie St Chicago IL 60611-2811

FRANZ, WANDA, association administrator. Pres. Nat. Right to Life Com., D.C. Office: Nat Right to Life Com 419 7th St NW Ste 500 Washington DC 20004*

FRANZEN, JANICE MARGUERITE GOSNELL, magazine editor; b. LaCrosse, Wis., Sept. 24, 1921; d. Wray Towson and Anna Heldena (Renstrom) Gosnell; m. Ralph Oscar Franzen, Feb. 15, 1964. BS cum laude, Wis. State U., LaCrosse, 1943; MRE, No. Bapt. Theol. Sem., 1947. Tchr. history and social sci. Galesville (Wis.) High Sch., 1943-45; registrar Christian Writers Inst., Chgo., 1947-49; dir. Christian Writers Inst., 1950-63, dir. studies, 1964-86; fiction editor Christian Life Mag., Wheaton, Ill., 1950-63, woman's editor, 1964-72, exec. editor, 1972-86; mem. editorial bd. Creation House, Wheaton, 1972-86; with Christian Life Missions, Lake Mary, Fla.; speaker writers confs. Author: Christian Writers Handbook, 1960, 61, The Adventure of Interviewing, 1989; editor: Christian Author, 1949-54, Christian Writer and Editor, 1955-63; contbr. articles to various mags.; compiler/ contbr.: The Successful Writers and Editors Guidebook, 1977. Sec. Christian Life Missions, 1971—, v.p., 1971-91. Home: 3N455 Mulberry Dr West Chicago IL 60185-1185 Office: Christian Life Missions 177 E Crystal Lake Ave Lake Mary FL 32746

FRANZNICK, CATHY, public relations executive; b. Glen Cove, N.Y., Apr. 29, 1957; d. Philip and Barbara F. BS, SUNY, Brockport, 1979; MS, SUNY, Oswego, 1981. Conf. coordinator Mideast Am. Bus. Co., N.Y.C., 1978; media buyer Advt. Workshop, N.Y.C., 1980-81; asst. field specialist Youth Community Service, Oswego, 1981; v.p. pub. relations Franznick & Cusatis, N.Y.C., 1981—; cons. Jaworski Prodns., N.Y.C., 1984—, Nova Works Inc., N.Y.C., 1988, Illustrated Mag., Palm Beach, Fla., 1987—. Bd. dirs. Com. to Elect John Ravitz, N.Y.C., 1988. Mem. Pub. Relations Soc. Am., Ad Club N.Y., Publicity Club N.Y. Democrat. Roman Catholic. Home: 160 E 84th St Apt 4L New York NY 10028-2014 Office: Franznick & Cusatis 246 5th Ave New York NY 10001-7603

FRAPPIA, LINDA ANN, management executive; b. St. Paul, May 14, 1946; d. Orville Keith Ferguson and Marilyn Ardis (Morris) Bidwell; 1 child, Jennifer. Grad. high sch., Seattle. Cert. claims adminstr. Claims rep. Fireman's Fund Ins., L.A., 1965-68; adminstrv. asst. to v.p. Employee Benefits Ins., Santa Ana, Calif., 1969-72; claims specialist Indsl. Indemnity Ins., Orange, Calif., 1972-83; claims supr. CNA Ins., Brea, Calif., 1983-85; claims mgr. EBI Ins. Svcs., Tustin, Calif., 1985; v.p. United Med. Specialists, Santa Ana, Calif., 1985-91; chief exec. officer United Ind. Specialists, Santa Ana, 1990—; chief executive officer United Chiropractic Specialists, Santa Ana, 1987—; instr. Ins. Edn. Assn., Brea, 1988—; speaker Western Ins. Info. Svc., Orange, 1976-83. Mem. Calif. Mfrs. Assn., Pub. Agencies Risk Mgmt. Assn., Calif. Self-Insured Assn., Toastmasters Internat. (v.p. Orange chpt. 1978). Republican.

FRAPPIER, CARA MUNSHAW, school social worker; b. Grand Rapids, Mich., Feb. 13, 1942; d. Carroll Lambert and Ruth (Switzer) Munshaw; m. Calvin Leslie Frappier, July 30, 1966; 1 child, Arielle. BA, Mich. State U., 1963, MA, 1966, MSW, 1973. Lic. social worker, marriage and family counselor, Mich.; diplomate in clin. social work. Elem. tchr. Lansing (Mich.) Pub. Schs., 1963-65; sch. social worker Ingham Intermediate Sch. Dist., Mason, Mich., 1965—; bd. dirs. profl. staff assn. Ingham Intermediate Pub. Schs., 1981-85; founding mem. Family Therapy and Consultation Program for Sch. Social Workers. Mem. Nat. Assn. Social Workers, Am. Assn. Marriage and Family Counselors, Am. Orthopsychiat. Assn., Mich. Sch. Social Workers Assn. Democrat. Home: 5706 Bearcreek Dr Lansing MI 48917-1400 Office: Ingham Intermediate Sch Dist 2630 W Howell Rd Mason MI 48854-9398

FRARY, ELIZABETH LOEITA, retired banker; b. Tunbridge, Vt., July 24, 1926; d. Lesle E. Maxfield and Marguriete B. (Dodge) Richardson; m. Adrian W. Frary Jr., July 24, 1944; children: Ann Marie, Richard A., David L., Walter J. Grad. high. sch., South Royalton, Vt. Teller First Twin State Bank, White River Junction, Vt., 1965-67, clk., 1977-80, officer, 1980-85, mgr., officer, 1985-88. Mem. Emblem Club, Odd Fellows (mem. Rebekahs). Republican. Congregationalist. Home: RR 2 Box 84 South Royalton VT 05068-9315

FRASER, ARVONNE SKELTON, United Nations ambassador; b. Lamberton, Minn., Sept. 1, 1925; d. Orland D. and Phyllis (Du Frene) Skelton; m. Donald M. Fraser, June 30, 1950; children: Thomas, Mary MacKay, John Du Frene, Lois MacKay (dec.), Anne. Tallman (dec.), Jean Skelton Fraser. BA, U. Minn., 1948; LLD (hon.), Macalester Coll., 1979. Staff asst. Office Congressman Donald M. Fraser, 1963-70, adminstrv. asst., campaign mgr., 1970-76; regional coord. Carter-Mondale Com., 1976; counsellor office presdl. pers. The White House, 1977; coord. office women in devel. U.S. Agy. Internat. Devel., Washington, 1977-81; dir. Minn. and Chgo. coms. peace petition dr. Albert Einstein Peace Prize Found., Chgo., 1981-82; co-dir. ctr. on women and pub. policy Hubert H. Humphrey Inst. Pub. Affairs, U. Minn., Mpls., 1982-94; head U.S. del. Commn. On The Status of Women, UN, 1993-94, U.S. rep., amb., 1994—; bd. dirs. Nat. Dem. Inst. Internat. Affairs, Women's Econ. Devel. Corp., Nat. Women's Law Ctr., Washington Women's Network, Women's Campaign Fund, Nat. Women's Edn. Fund, Minn. DFL Edn. Found.; mem. U.S. del. UN Decade for Women World Conf., Copenhagen, 1980, Internat. Women's Yr. Conf., Mexico City, 1975, UN Commn. on Status of Women, 1974, 78, Internat. Bur. Edn. Conf., Geneva, 1977; cons. Kenya Women's Leadership Conf., 1984; organiser, chairperson Orgn. Econ. Coop. and Develp./Devel. Assistance com./Women in Devel. experts group for aid-donor nations, 1978-80; dir. Ford. Found. Women's Equity Action League Fund Intern Project and World Plan Project, treas. 1974-77, bd. dirs. 1970-77, 81-83, nat. pres. 1972-74, past legis. chairperson Washington office;. Author: U.N. Decade for Women: Documents and Dialogue, 1987; (with others) Women in Washington: Advocates for Public Policy, 1983. Trustee Macalester Coll., St. Paul, 1982-84; candidate Lt. Gov. Minn., 1986. Recipient Disting. Svc. award Women's Equity Action League, 1977, Superior Honor award U.S. Agy. Internat. Devel., 1981, Elizabeth Boyer award Women's Equity League, 1984, Leader of Leaders Outstanding Achievement award Mpls. YWCA, 1979, Resourceful Woman award Tides Found., 1992. Mem. Minn. Bar Assn. (maintenance guidelines com. 1991-93). Home: 821 7th St SE Minneapolis MN 55414-1331

FRASER, ELEANOR RUTH, radiologist, administrator; b. Woodlake, Calif., May 31, 1927; d. Morton William and Dorothy Jean (Harding) F. BA magna cum laude, Pomona Coll., 1949; MD, Stanford U., 1954. Diplomate Am. Bd. Radiology. Resident in radiology Los Angeles County Hosp., L.A., 1957; radiologist St. Joseph Hosp., Orange, Calif., 1957-61; pvt. practice Anaheim, Calif., 1961-78; radiologist Radiology Nuclear Med. Group, Bakersfield, Calif., 1978-85; dir. radiology Kern Valley Hosp., Lake Isabella, Calif., 1985—, chief of staff, 1992—. Mem. AMA, Calif. Med. Assn., Kern County Med. Assn., Soc. Nuclear Medicine, Kern Valley Exchange Club (sec. 1992-94), Phi Beta Kappa. Methodist. Home: 6120 Cougar Lake Isabella CA 93240 Office: 12424 Mount Mesa Rd Lake Isabella CA 93240 also: PO Box 1657 Lake Isabella CA 93240

FRATT, DOROTHY, artist; b. Washington, Aug. 10, 1923; d. Hugh and Martha (Holt) Miller; m. Nicholas Diller Fratt, Sept. 4, 1943 (div. 1965); children: Nicholas, Hugh, Gregory, Peter; m. Curtis Calvin Cooper, Nov. 3, 1972. Studied with Nicolai Cikovsky, 1940; student, Mt. Vernon Coll., 1940-42, Am. U., 1942-43, Phillips Collection Art Sch., 1942-43; studied with Karl Knaths, 1943. mem. commissioning panel for NEA grant, Scottsdale, Ariz., 1971; mem. adv. bd. U. Art Mus. Ariz. State U., Tempe, 1989—. Exhibited at UN Club Gallery, 1948, Desert Art Gallery, Scottsdale, Ariz., 1959, Tucson Art Ctr., 1964, Phoenix Art Mus., 1964, 75, Riva Yares Gallery, Scottsdale, 1965, 82, 89, 94, 95, Calif. Legion Honor, San Francisco, 1965, Mickelson Gallery, Washington, 1967, State-Wide Touring Exhibit, 1974, Scottsdale Ctr. for Arts, 1980, Carson-Sapiro Gallery, Denver, 1981, Thomas Beabor Gallery, La Jolla, Calif., 1985, U. Ariz. Gallery, Tucson, 1986; represented in pub. collections at Phoenix Art Mus., Tucson Mus., Ariz. State Mus., Tempe; represented in various corp. collections. Mem. Fine Arts Commn., Phoenix, 1965-71; mem. Sotheby Symposium Quality in Art, N.Y.C., 1990.

FRATTAROLI, BARBARA ANNE, assessor; b. Somerville, Mass., Nov. 30, 1937; d. Edward Francis and Dorothy Frances (Schultz) Brett; m. Louis Anthony Frattaroli Sr., June 18, 1960; children: Donna Marie, Joseph Francis, Diane Frances, Louis Anthony Jr. Accredited assessor, Mass. Jr. clk. Bd. Assessors, Medford, Mass., 1976-84, prin. clk., 1984-86, assessor, 1986—, chairperson, 1991—. Del. Dem. State Conv., Mass., 1990. Mem. Internat. Assn. Assessing Officers (Mass. chpt.), Mass. Assn. Assessing Officers, Middlesex County Assn. Assessing Officers. Roman Catholic. Office: Bd Assessors City Hall Medford MA 02155

FRAVEL, ELIZABETH WHITMORE, accountant; b. Hagerstown, Md., Oct. 17, 1951; d. John W. and Dorothy E. (McCullough) Whitmore; children: Christine E., John W. BBA, Bridgewater Coll., 1973. CPA. Jr. staff acct. Rockingham Meml. Hosp., Harrisonburg, Va., 1973-75; mgr. customer service Pentamation Enterprises Inc., Sparks, Md., 1975-83; sr. acct. Good

Samaritan Hosp., Balt., 1983-84; pvt. practice acctg. Balt., 1984-86, Annapolis, Md., 1986-87, 1989—; staff acct. Hammond & Heim Chartered Accts., Annapolis, Md., 1987-89; controller Smith Bros., Inc., Galesville, Md., 1989-94; CPA/office mgr. Mint Systems, Arnold, Md., 1994—. Treas. Belmont Condominium Assn., Balt., 1983-85. Mem. AICPAs, Md. Assn. CPAs, Md. Soc. Accts.

FRAVERT, COLLEEN MOHNIKE, health care consultant; b. Alhambra, Calif., Oct. 15, 1951; d. Louis A. and Ramona R. (Honey) Mohnike; m. Thomas G. Linvill, Nov. 25, 1972 (div. 1979); m. Edward J. Fravert Jr., Aug. 7, 1982; children: Ethan, Victoria, Kristen. BA, Lewis and Clark Coll., 1972. Promotion mgr. Pitman Learning, Inc., Belmont, Calif., 1978-81; production mgr. EDUCAT Pubs., Inc., Berkeley, Calif., 1982; loan closer Eureka Fed. Savs., San Carlos, Calif., 1983-84; branch mgr. Am. Home Mortgage, Virginia Beach, Va., 1984-85; v.p. Tidewater First Fin. Group, Virginia Beach, 1986-88; cons. Mgmt. Recruiters, Virginia Beach, 1988—. Democrat. Episcopalian.

FRAWLEY, SISTER CLAIRE, educator; b. Elmira, N.Y., Nov. 7, 1929; d. James Edward and Alice (Keating) Frawley. BS, Nazareth Coll., 1957, BA, 1966; postgrad., Siena Coll., 1967, U. Dayton, 1967-68, Cath. U., 1969-73; MRE, Divine Word, 1972. Sch. administr., tchr. Parish Schs., Rochester, Ithaca, Elmira, N.Y., 1950-80; founder, exec. dir. St. Claires Homes, Escondido Calif., homes for homeless women and children, youth minister, Escondido, established and administered program for youth and young adults. Recipient Women Helping Women award Soroptimists, Womens Internat. Living Legacy award; scholar Nat. U. Mem. NAFE, Assn. of Christian Therapists, Calif. Mental Health Assn., Womens Internat., Coalition of Human Svc. Agencies, Child Abuse Coalition, Inland Dirs. Coalition. Home: # 321 243 S Escondido Blvd Escondido CA 92025-4116

FRAYNE, HEATHER SUSAN, direct marketer, consultant; b. Jersey City, Jan. 25, 1947; d. Nathaniel Zebulan and Jeanne Rita (Olshan) F. BA, NYU, 1967, MA, 1968. Mgmt. supr. Grey Direct, N.Y.C., 1981-85; v.p., account supr. Rapp Collins Worldwide, N.Y.C., 1985-86; v.p. mgmt. supr. World Wide 1 on 1 (formerly Ayer Direct), N.Y.C., 1986-89; pres. Direct Marketers On Call, Inc., N.Y.C., 1989—; circulation mgr. Billboard Publs., Inc., N.Y.C., 1978-81. Contbr. articles to profl. jours. Mem., vol. N.Y.C. (N.Y.) Cares; vol. Ad Hoc Polit. Groups for Candidates, N.Y.C. Mem. Am. Women's Econ. Devel. Corp. Inc., Nat. Assn. Women Bus. Owners, Direct Mktg. Assn., Direct Mktg. Club N.Y., Woman's Direct Response Group. Home: 45 Christopher St New York NY 10014 Office: Direct Marketers On Call Inc 45 Christopher St New York NY 10014

FRAZEE, ELIZABETH LYNN, corporate executive; b. Princeton, N.J., Sept. 12, 1957; d. John Harold and Constance Jean (Clinton) F.; m. Olaf Paleos (div.). BSBA, Drexel U., 1984. Statis. asst. A.J. Wood Rsch. Co., Phila., 1980; rsch. tech. Response Analysis Corp., Princeton, 1981, rsch. asst., 1981-82, sr. rsch. asst., 1982-83, rsch. assoc., 1983-84; project dir. Matrix, Inc., Princeton, 1984-85, sr. account mgr., 1985-92; v.p., 1993—. Mem. Assn. Pub. Opinion Rsch., Nature Conservancy, Nat. Wildlife Fedn. Home: 12 Grandview Ave Trenton NJ 08648-1034 Office: Matrix Inc 3490 Us Highway 1 Bldg 11 Princeton NJ 08540-5920

FRAZER, ROBBIN WALSH, educational, travel planning and public relations consultant, training coordinator; b. Elnora, Alta., Can., May 31, 1920; d. George and Grace Mary (Lilley) Brock; m. Donn Frazer, July 8, 1944. Student, Ont. Ministry Colls. & Univs., 1964-66; grad., Can. Inst. for Orgn. Mgmt., 1969; BA in Social Communications, Ottawa U., 1982; postgrad., Dale Carnegie, 1984; student, U. Ottawa, Carleton U., Baniff Ctr., 1986, Algonquin Sch. Mgmt., Can., 1988. Office worker various Can. cos., 1940-50, 54-56; with White Pass & Yukon Rte., Vancouver, 1956-58, Pub. & Indsl. Rels. Ltd., Vancouver, 1958-59, Office Assistance Ltd., Vancouver, 1959-60, Crown Zellerbach Ltd., Can., 1960; mem. staff Banff Sch. Fine Arts Mgmt. Ctr., 1960-62; corr. Calgary Herald, Calgary Albertan, Edmonton Jour., 1960-64; CBC morning commentator Sta. CBW, Winnipeg, 1962; exec. sec. Jasper Park (Alta.) C. of C., 1963-64; exec. sec., rsch. and constituency asst. to cabinet mins. Can. Ho. of Commons, Ottawa, 1963-73; supr. pub. info., conf. coord. Conf. Bd. in Can., Ottawa, 1973-75; pres., cons. Spectrum Three Cons., Ottawa, 1975—; rsch. asst., coord. Alta. Industry and Resources 1980, 1979; Alta. provincial info. officer Can. Mortgage and Housing Corp., 1978-79; adminstr. nat. office Can. Pub. Pers. Mgmt. Assn., 1990; mem. faculty, instr. travel Algonquin Coll. Applied Arts and Tech., 1988-91; pres. World Bestravel Assocs., 1988—; dir. nat. client svcs. Govt. Leaders Tng. Inst.-Custom Learning Systems, 1991—. Author: Welcome To Greater Vancouver, 1969; author chpts.: Canada Handbook, 1975, Canada Yearbook, 1975; author other reports, proposals, user guides and papers; founding editor Performing Arts and Enertainment in Can. mag., 1961, assoc. editor, 1962-71, editor spl. projects, 1972—; contbg. editor Can. Assn. Ret. Persons News. Chmn. pub. rels. com. Salvation Army Red Shield Campaign; founding dir. publicity-pub. rels. Ottawa Symphony; dir. pub. rels. Can. Tulip Festival, Ottawa Festival of the Performing Arts, 6th N.E. Regional Ballet Festival of the U.S.; dir. publicity Friends of the Nat. Arts Ctr. Mem. Can. Pub. Rels. Soc., Can. Assn. for Distance Edn., Media Club Can., Can. Authors Assn., Tourism Industry Assn. Can., Ottawa Tourism and Conv. Authority, Ottawa-Carleton Bd. Trade, Can. Pub. Pers. Mgmt. Assn., Can. Study Parliament Group, Toastmasters, UN Assn., Royal Commonwealth Soc., Nat. Arts Ctr. Orch. Assn., Ottawa Symphony Orchestra Assn., Friends of the Nat. Gallery, Friends of the Can. Mus. of Civilization, Can. Assn. Mature People, Am. Assn. Ret. Persons. Office: World Bestravel Assocs, 530 Laurier Ave W Ste 1610, Ottawa, ON Canada K1R 7T1

FRAZIER, BARBARA ANNE, psychometrician; b. Balt., June 27, 1944; d. Arthur Alfred and Anne Catherine (Koerber) Douville; m. John Melvin Frazier, Mar. 20, 1965; children: Karen Elaine, Brian Douglas. BS in Psychology, Johns Hopkins U., 1967, MLA, 1974; CAS in Clin. Psychology, Loyola Coll., Balt., 1980. Psychometrician Psychology Cons. Assocs., Balt., 1978—, Rosedale Psychol. Svcs., Balt., 1986—; neuropsych clinician Johns Hopkins U. Sch. Medicine, Balt., 1987-90. Vol. Nature Conservancy, Habitat for Humanity; mem. Planned Parenthood, Handgun Control, Washington. Mem. APA.

FRAZIER, DEBORAH LYNN, nursing administrator; b. Columbia, S.C., Apr. 1, 1954; d. Earl R. and Barbara L. (Weech) Vickers; divorced, Sept. 1991; children: Anthony W. Jr., Shannon Lynn. BA, Fla. Tech., 1976; ADN, Memphis State, 1980. Staff RN labor and delivery City of Memphis Hosp., 1980-81; charge nurse labor and delivery/post-partum Virginia Beach (Va.) Gen. Hosp., 1981-88; head nurse Mary Immaculate Hosp., Newport News, Va., 1988-89; dir. maternal-child svcs. Humana Hosp. Bayside, Virginia Beach, 1989-91, Sentara Bayside Hosp., Virginia Beach, 1991-93; staff nurse labor and delivery Sacred Heart Hosp., Pensacola, Fla., 1993-94; dir. The Family Birthplace West Fla. Regional Med. Ctr., Pensacola, 1994—; educator Virginia Beach Emergency Med. Svcs., 1985-86; prepared childbirth instr. Drs. Elstein and Lackore, PC, Virginia Beach, 1987-89; active Escamlia County Healthy Start Coalition, 1995—. Mem. Healthy Start Coalition of Escambia County. Mem. Assn. Women's Health, Obstetric, and Neonatal Nurses (cert. inpatient obstet., chpt. coord. Tidewater chpt. 1987-91, legis. coord. 1991-93; coord. N.W. chpt. 1995—), Fla. Orgn. Nurse Execs. Home: 3501 Sea Horse Way 5612 Dove Dr Pace FL 32571

FRAZIER, JANICE LEE, medical technologist; b. Blue Island, Ill., Jan. 25, 1958; d. Maurice Lee and Janet Marian (Nagel) F. AS, Thornton C.C., South Holland, Ill., 1978; BA, Trinity Christian Coll., Palos Heights, Ill., 1980; cert. med. tech., St. Francis Sch. Med. Tech., Blue Island, Ill., 1981; MA, Wheaton Coll., 1987. Med. tech. Oak Forest (Ill.) Hosp., 1981-82, Glen Oakes Med. Ctr., Glendale Heights, Ill., 1983-88, Alexian Bros. Med. Ctr., Elk Grove Village, Ill., 1988-89; asst. dir. music tour group Outreach for Christ, Sioux Falls, S.D., 1982-83; lab. supr. Damon Clin. Lab., Oakbrook Terrace, Ill., 1989-90; lab. mgr. Damon Clin. Lab./Suburban Hosp., Hinsdale, Ill., 1990-91; lab. supr. night shift Denver Gen. Hosp., 1991—. Youth ministry asst. Fox Valley Presbyn. Ch., Geneva, Ill., 1989-90; assoc. dir. praise team bank Cherry Hills Cmty. Ch., Englewood, Colo., 1992-93; social activities dir. Bear Valley Ch., Lakewood, Colo., 1994—. Republican. Home: 2570 S Dayton Way # G107 Denver CO 80231

FRAZIER, KIMBERLEE GONTERMAN, veterinarian; b. St. Louis, Mar. 5, 1953; d. Joseph Wilbur Jr. and Melody (Engleman) Gonterman; m. Burk Ralph Frazier, Oct. 11, 1985; 1 child, Weston James. DVM magna cum laude, U. Mo., 1979. Vet. intern U. Mo. Coll. Vet. Medicine, Columbia, 1979-80; relief vet. St. Louis and Kansas City, Mo., 1980-84; account exec. Merrill Lynch, Clayton, Mo., 1984-85; owner, dir., small animal practitioner VET STOP Animal Clinics, St. Charles, St. Peters, Florissant, Kirkwood, St. Louis, Manchester, Mo., 1985—; owner, dir. HealthyPet Vet. Svcs. in PetsMart, St. Charles, Maplewood, Bridgeton, Town and Country, and O'Fallon, 1993—; advisor Math. Sci. Network, St. Louis, 1987. Frank Wells scholar U. Mo., 1978; First Pl. in Exhbn. Sport for synchronized swimming, Munich Olympics, 1972. Mem. AVMA, Mo. Vet. Med. Assn., St. Louis Vet. Med. Assn., Mo. Bot. Garden, Friends of Zoo, Gamma Sigma Delta, Phi Zeta. Republican. Home and Office: 4601 Maryland Ave Saint Louis MO 63108-1912

FRAZIER, PATRICIA ANN, psychologist, psychology educator; b. Oak Park, Ill., Sept. 12, 1957; d. Richard M. and Marion L. (Gustafson) F. BA, St. Olaf Coll., 1979; MA, U. Minn., 1984, PhD, 1988. Asst. prof. psychology U. Mo., Columbia, 1988-90; asst. prof. psychology U. Minn., Minneapolis, 1990-94, assoc. prof. psychology, 1994—; comm. mem. Am. Psychology Law Society, 1989-90, Am. Assn. Counseling and Devel., 1990-91, Int. Network on Personal Relationships, 1990-93, Am. Psychological Assn. div. 9, 17, 35 and 38, 1990-94. Mem. editorial bd. to sci. jours.; contbr. articles to profl. jours. Recipient Nat. Rsch. Svc. award Nat. Inst. Mental Health, 1986, Dissertation award Am. Psychological Assn., 1989, grantee Am. Psychological Assn., 1991, U. Minn., 1986, 1991, 1992, U. Mo., 1989, NIH, 1992—, Nat. Inst. Mental Health, 1992—. Mem. Am. Counseling Assn., Am. Psychol. Assn., Midwestern Psychol. Assn., Minn. Psychol. Assn., Int. Society for the study of Personal Relationships, Int. Network on Personal Relationships.

FRAZIER-MAULTSBY, LENORA I., principal; b. Washington, July 28, 1944; d. Leonard Douglas and Robnette Louise (Owens) Frazier; m. Oliver Williams, Jr. (div. Apr. 1973); m. Robert Lacy Maultsby, July 4, 1979; 1 child, LaChelle Reneé. BA, Hampton U., 1966; MA, Calif. State U., Sacramento, 1973; PhD, Union U., 1979. Tchr. emotionally and aurally handicapped, elem. and h.s. Sacramento City Unified Sch. Dist., 1967-73, 82-87, vice-prin. h.s., 1987-93; cons. affirmative action, ethnic programs, Title IX, pers. adminstr. Sacramento County Office Edn., 1973-82; prin. H.W. Harkness Elem. Sch., Sacramento, 1993—; commr. Sacramento County Office Edn., 1982—. Rockefeller Found. fellow, 1976. Mem. Calif. Assn. Pers. Commrs., Alpha Kappa Alpha, Phi Delta Kappa, St. Peter Claver. Roman Catholic. Office: HW Harkness Elem Sch 2147 54th Ave Sacramento CA 95822

FREASIER, AILEEN W., special education educator; b. Edcouch, Tex., Nov. 12, 1924; d. James Ross and Ethel Inez (Riley) Wade; m. Ben F. Freasier, Mar. 9, 1945 (dec.); children: Ben. C., Doretha J. Christoph, Barbara F. McNally, Raymond E., John F. BS HE, Tex. A and I Coll., 1945; MEd, La. Tech. U., 1966; postgrad. 90 hours, La. Tech. U. Tchr. Margaret Roane Day Care Ctr., Ruston, La., 1965-71; tchr. spl. edn. Lincoln Parish Schs., Ruston, 1971-81; I.E.P. facilitator Monroe (La.) SSD # 1, 1981-85; IEP facilitator LTI Monroe (La.) SSD # 1, 1985—, ednl. diagnostician, 1985—; mem. editl. bd. Jour. Correctional Edn., 1984—, learning tech. sect. editor, 1990—; newsletter editor spl. edn. network, 1991-94; chmn. spl. edn. spl. interest group Correctional Edn. Assn., 1994—; presenter in field; citizen amb. People Conf. on Edn., Beijing, 1992. Mem. editl. bd. Jour. Correctional Edn., 1984—, editor learning tech. sect., 1990—, newsletter editor spl. edn. network, 1991-94, chmn. spl. edn. spl. interest group, 1994—; contbr. articles to profl. jours. Treas. Ruston Mayor's Commn. on Women. Named Spl. Sch. Dist. #1 Tchr. of Yr., 1988; recipient J.E. Wallace Wallin Educator of the Handicapped award La. Fedn. CEC, 1994. Mem. ASCD, AAUW (sec. Ruston br., State co-chair diversity task force), Am. Assn. Mental Retardation, Coun. for Exceptional Children (treas. La. CEC Tech. and Media, sec. CEC-CASE), Phi Delta Kappa (pres.), Kappa Kappa Iota (state past pres. Loretta Doer award 1994), Ruston Mayor's Commn. on Women (treas.). Home: PO Box 1595 Ruston LA 71273-1595

FRECHETTE, MONIQUE S., respiratory therapist, rehabilitation services professional; b. Biddeford, Maine, Aug. 17, 1956; d. Leo Paul and Jacqueline Monique (Boucher) Mininni; m. James Claude Frechette, Aug. 17, 1973 (div. 1983); 1 child, Angela Marie. A in Allied Health Scis., So. Maine Vocat. Tech. Inst., 1983. Lic. registered respiratory therapist, 1988. Charge/staff therapist So. Maine Med. Ctr., Biddeford, 1981-91; v.p. Tech Med Inc., Biddeford, 1989—, dir. clin. svcs. and quality assurance, 1991—; pres., cofounder Maritime Med. Inc., Biddeford, 1993—. Editor: (quar.) The Commonwealth Gazette, 1994. Bd. dirs. Toys for Tots Christmas Social, Biddeford, 1992, 93, 95; spkr. Biddeford High Sch., 1992, 93, St. Joseph Coll., Portland, Maine, 1994, Southern Maine Med. Ctr., 1995. Recipient 1st place in class No. New England Bodybuilding Championships, Springfield, Mass., 1987, NPC Maine State Championship Bodybuilding, Sanford, 1988, 1st place overall AAU Maine State Championship Bodybuilding, Portland, 1988. Mem. NAFE, Am. Assn. Respiratory Care. Republican. Roman Catholic. Office: Tech Med Inc 376 Elm St Biddeford ME 04005

FREDERICH, KATHY W., social worker; b. Ashland, Ky., Apr. 19, 1953; d. James Greeley and Jo Ann (Sparks) Walker; divorced; m. Harry Donald Frederich, Sept. 5, 1987; stepchild, David Scott. BA with distinction, U. Ky., 1978; MS with honors, Ea. Ky. U., 1994. Tng. supr. Blue Grass Assn. for Retarded Citizens, Lexington, Ky., 1971-75, Bur. Vocational Rehab., Lexington, 1976-77; social worker Ky. Dept. for Social Svcs., Lexington, 1978-79, field office supr., 1979-85; social work/domestic violence prog. specialist, conf. coord. Ky. Dept. for Social Svcs., Frankfort, 1985—, tng. instr., 1987—; instr. Ky. Sheriff's Acad., 1986-92; cert. instr. Lexington Fayette div. police, 1981-87, 90-91; cons., trainer for field staff and related profls. statewide, Ky., 1983—; mem. adv. bd. Assn. for Older Kentuckians, 1989-93; mem. Ky. Law Enforcement Tng. Project, 1989-91; mem. Atty. Gen.'s Task Force on Domestic Violence Crime, 1991-93, KDVA Homicide-Suidide Task Force, 1990—, Legis. Task Force on Domestic Violence, 1994—; coord. 1st Nat. Teleconf. on Domestic Violence and Family Prevention Svcs., 1994. Contbr. to profl. publs. including Ky. Prosecutor's Manual on Domestic Violence, Ky. Hosp. Mag. on Abuse, Ky. Adult Abuse Med. Protocol, and others. Recipient Outstanding Svc. award Lexington Fayette div. of Police, 1984, Ky. Sheriff's Acad. Hon. Grad., 1989, tributes, 1986, 87, 88, Outstanding Kentuckian award Gov. Martha Layne Collins, 1987, Outstanding Young Am. Women award, 1987, Outstanding Victim Adv. award Lexington Urban County Govt., 1990, Outstanding Victim Advocacy award Ky. Victims' Coalition, 1993; named Ky. Col., 1985. Democrat.

FREDERICK, KATHLEEN ANNE, real estate executive; b. Berwyn, Ill., Dec. 11, 1950; d. Henry Clarence and Marion Elizabeth (Perryman) Bruck; m. James Gerard Frederick, Sept. 24, 1971; children: Jennifer, Christine, Timothy. Student, McHenry Jr. Coll., Crystal Lake, Ill., 1970-71, Coll. of DuPage, Glen Ellyn, Ill., 1974-83, Waubonsie Community Coll., Sugar Grove, Ill., 1985-89. Lic. residential appraiser, N.C. Mem. real estate sales staff Realty World-Carlson Realty, Batavia, Ill., 1982-85, Baird & Warner Real Estate, Geneva, Ill., 1985-88; mem. real estate sales/relocation staff Remax Profls. Real Estate, St. Charles, Ill., 1988-90, Remax Property Assocs., Raleigh, N.C., 1990-91; mgr. new homes and neighborhoods dept., relocation mgr. Accent Realty, Batavia, 1991-92; pres. RealPro Real Estate Buyers, Brokerage & Relocation Svcs., Sugar Grove, Ill., 1992—; with Foxfield Realty, Inc., Buyers Brokerage and Relocation Svcs., 1992. Mem. Nat. Orgn. Women in Constrn., Women's Coun. Realtors (referral and relocation com. 1990), Employee Relocation Coun. (cert. profl.), Toastmasters Internat., Optimists Club Internat. (charter). Home and Office: Real Pro Real Estate 703 Queensgate Cir Sugar Grove IL 60554-9211

FREDERICK, MYRNA SUE LABRY, sales executive, beauty consultant; b. Abbeville, La., Nov. 22, 1950; d. Noah and Jeanne (Vincent) LaBry; m. Conley J. Frederick, Jan. 22, 1972; children: Dawn M. Frederick Vincent, Shauri A., Ryan C., Brett J. Student, U. Southwestern La., Lafayette, 1968-69. Ins. office mgr. and cashier Kaplan, La., 1969-73; owner Baton Studio, Kaplan, 1973-79; mgr., fashion buyer, bookkeeper, cashier Kaplan, 1973-91, landscape artist, 1973—; ind. profl. sales dir. Mary Kay Cosmetics, 1992—; ind. profl. beauty cons., 1989—. Mem. Vermilion Arts Coun. Mem. Am. Bus. Women (sec., treas., v.p., pres. 1985-90, Outstanding Woman of Yr. 1990), Krew Chic Alapie (v.p., sec., treas., reporter), Kaplan Jaycee Jaynes (sec., treas., pres. 1974-79, Oustanding Woman of Yr. 1977, Dist. Woman of Yr. 1977-78). Democrat. Roman Catholic. Home: 115 Pelican St Kaplan LA 70548-5652

FREDERICK, NANCY, retired government official; b. Lakewood, Ohio, Aug. 23, 1932; d. Howard Peter and Marian Bissell (Slater) F.; m. Francis Liell Wenger. B.A., U. Colo., 1955; postgrad., George Washington U., 1962-63, U.S. Dept. Agr., 1964-65, Fgn. Svc. Inst., 1968. Reporter/photographer, city editor Robinson (Ill.) Daily News, 1956-61; area reporter UPI, 1956-61; spl. asst. to Congressman Peter Mack, Washington, 1961-62; with AID, 1962-91, info. officer/photographer, 1962-65; pres. Auto Internat. Repair Ctr., Ltd., Annapolis, Md., 1989—; editor Front Lines, 1966-68, program analyst devel. planning offices Latin Am. and Africa Burs., 1968-69, asst. desk officer Nigeria Relief and Rehab., 5 Cen. African countries, also Sahelian Drought Emergency Unit, 1969-74, human resources devel. officer Cen./West African Affairs, 1972-74, planning asst. to acting coord. Women in Devel. AID, 1974-77, program analyst to dep. dir. Am. Schs. and Hosps. Abroad, 1978-91; mem. AID Women's Adv. Com., 1973-75; AID adviser, U.S., del. UN World Conf. Internat. Women's Yr., Mexico City, 1975; U.S. del. UN Conf. Status of Women, Geneva, OAS Inter. Am. Conf. for Women, 1976; asst. founding spl. offices for women devel. activities, Peace Corps, WHO, FAO, World Bank; agy. speaker, panelist various confs., 1975-77; trustee Am. Ctr. for Oriental Rsch., Jordan, Am. U. in Bulgeria, 1991—. Author, co-author plans and papers in field; editor Environ. Protection Assn. Quar., 1979-89. Recipient five awards Fed. Editors Assn., 1966-69, various awards and citations AID, cert. Nat. Coun. of Negro Women, 1975, Recognition cert. Am. U. in Beirut, 1991, YWCA, 1991. Mem. Chesapeake Environ. Protection Assn. (trustee). Home: 1022 Shore Rd West River MD 20778

FREDERICK, NANCY ACKERMAN, real estate broker; b. Cleve., Apr. 1, 1942; d. William Houston Ackerman and Margaret Jorder (Ainslie) Post; m. Nicholas Frederick, June 26, 1965; children: Jacqueline, Barbara, Nicholas. BS in Elem. Edn., Taylor U., 1964; postgrad., Glassboro State U. Lic. real estate salesperson, N.J., real estate broker. Tchr. Kingston Elem. Sch., Cherry Hill, N.J., 1964-68; real estate salesperson Sterling Assocs., Somerdale, N.J., 1974-75, Bob Pritchett & Co., Cherry Hill, 1975-79; office mgr. Bob Pritchett & Co., Merchantville, N.J., 1980-81, Cherry Hill, 1981-82; sales rep., broker Fox & Lazo Realtors, Cherry Hill, 1982—; mem. social planning com., fellow Camden County Bd. Realtors, Cherry Hill, 1974-75; site mgr. Home Equity Relocation Co., Danbury, Conn., 1983—. Bldg. rep. Cherry Hill Edn. Assn., 1965-68; vol. officer Camden County Probation Dept., 1970-72; tchr. Sunday sch. Bethel Bapt. Ch., Cherry Hill, 1967-77; sec. bd. trustees Ocean Colony Condominium, Ocean City, N.J., 1988-89, mem. 5-yr. planning bd.; chmn. memberships Home and Sch. Assn., Cherry Hill, 1983; mem. Barclay Farm Civic Assn., Cherry Hill, 1985—. Fellow N.J. Assn. Realtors (Million Dollar Sales awards 1983-94); mem. AAUW, NAFE, Barclay Farm Swim Club. Republican. Home: 188 Pearlcroft Rd Cherry Hill NJ 08034-3341 Office: Fox & Lazo Realtors 100 Barclay Pavilion W Cherry Hill NJ 08034-2173

FREDERICK, VIRGINIA FIESTER, state legislator; b. Rock Island, Ill., Dec. 24, 1916; d. John Henry and Myrtle (Montgomery) Heise; B.A., U. Iowa, 1938; postgrad. Lake Forest Coll., 1942-43, LLD, 1994; m. C. Donnan Fiester (dec. 1975); children—Sheryl Fiester Ross, Alan R., James D.; m. 2d Kenneth Jacob Frederick, 1978. Free-lance fashion designer, Lake Forest, Ill., 1952-78; pres. Mid Am. China Exchange, Kenilworth, Ill., 1978-81; mem. Ill. Ho. of Reps., Springfield, 1979—, asst minority leader, 1990—. Alderman, first ward Lake Forest, 1974-78; del. World Food Conf., Rome, 1974. mem. Ill. Commn. on Status of Women subcom. pensions and employment, 1976-79; co-chmn. Conf. Women Legislators, 1982-85. Named Chgo. Area Woman of Achievement, Internat. Orgn. Women Execs., 1978. Recipient Lottie Holman O'Neal award, 1980, Jane Addams award, 1982, Outstanding Legislator award Ill. Hosp. Assn., 1986, VFW Svc. award, 1988, Joyce Fitzgerald Meml. award, 1988, Susan B. Anthony Legislator of the Yr. award, 1989, award Delta Kappa Gamma, 1991, Svcs. for Srs. award, Ill. Dept. Aging, 1991, Ethics in Pols. award, Rep. Women's Club, 1992, Woman of Achievement award YWCA North Eastern Ill., 1994, Ill. Women in Govt. award, 1994. Mem. LWV (local pres. 1958-60, state dir. 1969-75, mem. nat. com. 1975-76), AAUW (local pres. 1968-70, state pres. 1975-77, state dir. 1963-69, mem. nat. commns. 1967-69, Legislator of Yr. award 1993), UN Assn. (dir.), Chgo. Assn. Commerce and Industry (dir.). Methodist. Home: 1540 Greenleaf Ave Lake Forest IL 60045-1317

FREDERICKS, JOAN DELANOY, retired health science administrator; b. Dobbs Ferry, N.Y., Feb. 27, 1928; d. Robert Bert and Amelia (DeLanoy) F.; m. Stanley Whetstone, Mar. 20, 1993. BA, Skidmore Coll., Saratoga Springs, N.Y., 1949; MA, Syracuse U., 1954. Rsch. asst. C.F. Kettering Found., Yellow Springs, Ohio, 1949-50; rsch. tech. Syracuse (N.Y.) U. Med. Sch., 1950-54, Duke U. Med. Sch., Durham, N.C., 1954-58, NIH, Bethesda, Md., 1958-88; ret., 1988; chemist Nat. Inst. Arthritis and Metabolic Diseases, NIH, Bethesda, 1958-63, scientific grant asst. Nat. Inst. Heart, Lung and Blood Diseases, Bethesda, 1963-70, asst., program dir. Nat. Inst. Arthritis Metabolism and Digestive Diseases, 1970-81, exec. sec. div. Rsch. Grants, 1981-88; cons. in field. Vol. Sibley Meml. Hosp., Washington. Mem. Sumner Sq. Condominium Assn. (sec., v.p. 1988-92).

FREDERICKS, PATRICIA ANN, real estate executive; b. Durand, Mich., June 5, 1941; d. Willis Edward and Dorothy (Plowman) Sexton; m. Ward Arthur Fredericks, June 12, 1960; children: Corrine Ellen, Lorraine Lee, Ward Arthur II. BA, Mich. State U., 1962. Cert. Grad. Real Estate Inst., Residential Broker, Residential Salesperson; cert. real estate broker. Assoc. Stand Brough, Des Moines, 1976-80; broker Denton, Tuscon, 1980-83; broker-trainer Coldwell Banker, Westlake Village, Calif., 1984-90; broker, br. mgr. Brown, Newbury Park, Calif., 1990-94; dir. tng. Brown Real Estate, Westlake Village, Calif., 1994—; gen. mgr. Coldwell Banker Town & Country Real Estate, Newbury Park, Calif., 1994—; bd. sec. Mixtec Corp., Thousand Oaks, 1984-92. Contbr. articles to profl. jours. Pres. Inner Wheel, Thousand Oaks, 1991; bd. dirs. Community Leaders Club, Thousand Oaks, 1991, Conejo Future Found., Thousand Oaks, 1989-92, Wellness Community Ventura Valley, 1994—. Named Realtor of Yr., Conejo Valley Bd. Realtors, 1991. Mem. Calif. Assn. Realtors (dir. 1988-95), Conejo Valley Assn. Realtors (sec., v.p., pres.-elect 1989-92, pres. 1993), Pres.'s Club Mich. State U., Conejo Valley Assn. Realtors (pres. 1993), Com. 100, Inner Wheel of Thousand Oaks (pres. 1991), Community Concerts Assn., Alliance for the Arts, Conejo Valley Symphony Guild, Wellness Community, Indian Wells Country Club, North Ranch Country Club. Home: 48143 Vista Cielo La Quinta CA 92253 Office: Town and Country Coldwell Banker 2277 Michael Newbury Park CA 91320

FREDERICKS, SHARON KAY, nurses aide; b. Grand Rapids, Mich., July 12, 1942; d. Leroy and Edith Luella (Crawford) F. Student, LaSalle U., 1976; AAS, Community Svc. Asst., Kalamazoo Valley Coll., 1982; A in Bus. Mgmt., Davenport Coll., 1994, student, 1994—. Cashier Goodwill Industries, Battle Creek, Mich., 1963; dishwasher Woolworths, Kalamazoo, 1963; nurses aide Mary L. Bocher, Kalamazoo, 1964-69, Sisters St. Joseph, Nazareth, Mich., 1976—; kitchen aide Saga Foods, Kalamazoo Valley C.C., 1981-82, Saga Foods, Nazareth Coll., 1983-84. Vol. Portage Ctrl. Jr. and Sr. High Sch., 1961-62, Bronson Meth. Hosp., Kalamazoo, 1961-62; vol. nurse aide ARC, 1964-69, Bloodmobiles, 1970-75, Borgess Med. Ctr., 1977; sec.-treas. 3d Order St. Francis Secular, 1976-79, pres., dir. pub. rels. and bulls., 1979-81; participant neighborhood watch Vine Neighborhood, Kalamazoo, 1985-88; vol. Cath. Family Svcs., 1991—; vol., adminstrv. aide, Kalamazoo, 1991—. Named Vol. of Month, Kalamazoo Regional Psychiat. Hosp., 1976, Vol. of Week, Cath. Family Svcs., 1993; recipient John Edgar Hoover Gold medal, 1991; Thomas F. Reed Jr. scholar Davenport Coll. Mem. Nat. Spl. Child Advocates. Roman Catholic. Home: Apt 204 2310 Inverness Ln Apt 204 Kalamazoo MI 49001-1574

FREDERIKSEN, MARILYNN ELIZABETH CONNERS, physician; b. Chgo., Sept. 12, 1949; d. Paul H. and Susanne (Ostergren) Conners; m. James W. Frederiksen, July 11, 1971; children: John Karl, Paul S., Britt L. BA, Cornell Coll., 1970; MD, Boston U., 1974. Diplomate Am. Bd. Ob-Gyn., Am. Bd. Maternal-Fetal Medicine, Am. Bd. Clin. Pharmacology.

Pediatrics intern U. Md. Hosp., 1974-75, resident in pediatrics, 1975-76; resident in ob-gyn. Boston Hosp. for women, 1976-79; fellow in maternal fetal medicine Northwestern U., 1979-81, fellow clin. pharmacology, 1981-83; instr. ob-gyn. Northwestern U., Chgo., 1981-83, asst. prof. ob-gyn., assoc. clin. pharmacology, 1983-91, assoc. prof. ob-gyn., assoc. in clin. pharmacology, 1991—, sect. chief ob-gyn., 1993—; gen. faculty com. Northwestern U., Chgo., 1994—, ob-gyn. adv. panel, 1985—, USP Com. Revision, Rockville, Md., 1986—; del. USP conv. Northwestern U. Med. Sch., 1990, 95; gen. clinic rsch. ctr. com. NIH, 1989-93, chair, 1992-93; active Task Force Working Group on Asthma in Pregnancy NHLBI, 1991-92. Mem. editorial bd. Clin. Pharmacology & Therapeutics, 1993; contbr. numerous articles to profl. jours. Bd. dirs. Cornell Coll. Alumni Assn., Mt. Vernon, Iowa, 1986-90. Recipient Pharm. Mfrs. Assn. Found. Faculty Devel. award, 1984-86, Civil Liberties award ACLU, 1991. Fellow Am. Coll. Ob.-Gyn.; mem. Soc. Perinatal Obstetricians, Ctrl. Assn. Obstetricians and Gynecologists, Am. Med. Womens Assn., Am. Soc. Clin. Pharmacology and Therapeutics (chmn. sect. pediatric and pharmacology 1993—, bd. dirs. 1993—), Chgo. Gynecologic Soc. (treas. 1994—), Phi Beta Kappa. Republican. Episcopalian. Home: 2002 Devon Ave Park Ridge IL 60068-4306 Office: Northwestern U 680 N Lake Shore Dr Ste 1000 Chicago IL 60611-3057

FREDERIKSEN, PATIENCE ANN, librarian; b. Warwick, R.I., Aug. 21, 1957; d. Robert Christian and Winifred Holmes (Valentine) F.; 1 child, Christian Lawrence Klint. BA in Creative Writing/History, Carnegie Mellon U., 1979; MLS, Syracuse U., 1986. Reference libr. Anchorage Mun. Librs., 1986-88; reference coord. Juneau (Alaska) Pub. Librs., 1988-89; documents libr. Alaska State Libr., Juneau, 1989, collection devel. libr., 1989-91, head govt. publs. sect., 1991—. Recipient Nat. Merit Scholarship, Carnegie-Mellon U., Pitts., 1975-79. Mem. Alaska Libr. Assn. (editor Newspoke 1994—). Democrat. Home: 1310 4th St # 6 Douglas AK 99824-5323 Office: Alaska State Libr PO Box 110571 Juneau AK 99811-0571

FREDERIKSEN, PATRICIA E., family nurse practitioner; b. St. Louis, Oct. 6, 1956; d. Julius G. and Wanda L. (Guthrie) Kissel; divorced; 1 child, Jeremy Michael. ADN, St. Louis Community Coll., 1977; BSN, U. State N.Y., 1982; FNP, U. Colo., Denver, 1985. RN, Colo.; CNOR, CNRN; cert. family nurse practitioner. Med. case mgmt. supr. Intracorp., Denver; clin. mgr. Rehab. Svcs. Corp., Eureka, Calif.; family nurse practitioner Burre Clinic, Eureka; pvt. practice Eureka; dir. PM&R Marian Health Ctr., Sioux City, Iowa; family nurse practitioner Lebanon (Mo.) Med. Ctr. Mem. ANA (nursing scholar), ARN. Home: RR 8 Box 460 Lebanon MO 65536

FREDIANI, DIANE MARIE, graphic designer, interior designer; b. Bklyn., June 20, 1963; d. Albert Michael and Mary (Piantino) F. BFA in Graphic Design, Centenary Coll., 1985, teaching cert., 1991. Cert. graphic designer. Cashier, dept. supr. Reynolds, Hackettstown, N.J., 1982-85; window displays and promotions staff Reynolds, Hackettstown, 1985-86; clerical asst. AT&T, Basking Ridge, N.J., 1986-87; typesetter, bd. artist AT&T, Parsippany, N.J., 1988-89; project coord. interior design AT&T, Basking Ridge, 1989—; graphic designer St. Mary's Sch., Hackettstown, 1985—; nominee for White House Fellowship Com., 1994. Mem. Centenary Alumni Assn. (forensic judge oral speaking competition 1993, 94). Roman Catholic. Home: 109 Pleasant View Rd Hackettstown NJ 07840-1017 Office: AT&T 295 N Maple Ave Basking Ridge NJ 07920-1002

FREDRICK, SUSAN WALKER, tax company manager; b. Painesville, Ohio, Nov. 17, 1948; d. Floyd Clayton and Margaret (Merkel) Walker; m. Stephan Douglas Fredrick, Oct. 20, 1973. BS, Mt. Union Coll., Alliance, Ohio, 1970; MS, U. Conn., 1973. Research asst. Boyce Thompson Inst., Yonkers, N.Y., 1971-74; dir. quality control Lawley, Matusky, Skelly, Tappan, N.Y., 1974-75; field supr. Ecological Analysts, Middletown, N.Y., 1975-76; scientist Pandullo Quirk Assocs., Wayne, N.J., 1976-78; editor Biosis. Info. Service, Phila., 1978-80; tax preparer H&R Block, Inc., King of Prussia, Pa., 1978-80; dist. mgr. H&R Block, Inc., Malvern, Pa., 1980—; guest lectr. Temple U., 1981-86. Mem. NAFE, Nat. Assn. Enrolled Agts., Pa. Soc. Enrolled Agts., Nat. Assn. Underwater Instrs. (active instr.), Keystone Divers Club (West Chester, Pa.). Office: H&R Block Inc Great Valley Shopping Ctr # 18 Rtes 401 & 30 Malvern PA 19355

FREDRICKSON, SHARON WONG, accountant; b. Cleve., Nov. 24, 1956; d. Jack Don and Fung Suey (Chow) Wong; m. Brant M. Fredrickson, Mar. 19, 1988; children: Eric Brant, Saul Wong. BS in Acctg. summa cum laude, Case Western Res. U., 1978, MBA, 1987. CPA, Ohio. Acct. Price Waterhouse, Cleve., 1978-81, sr. acct., 1981-84; acctg. rsch. and planning analyst BP Am., Inc. (formerly Standard Oil Co.), Cleve., 1984-85, sr. fin. analyst rsch. and devel. acctg., 1985-88, bus. analyst, regional ctr. fin. reporting, 1989-93; fin. reporting analyst BP Oil Co., 1994—. Bus. advisor Inroads Cleve., Inc., 1982-84. Mem. Inst. Mgmt. Accts., Am. Inst. CPAs, Am. Woman's Soc. CPAs (Northeastern Ohio affiliate pres. 1985-86, v.p. 1984-85, sec. 1983-84), Ohio Soc. CPAs (state bd. dirs. 1985-86, 88-89, sec. Cleve. chpt. 1987-88, chpt. bd. dirs. 1986-87), Young Profls. Cleve. (trustee 1984-85). Office: BP Am Inc 200 Public Sq 15K Cleveland OH 44114-2375

FREDRIK, BURRY, theatrical producer, director; b. N.Y.C., Aug. 9, 1925; d. Fredric Kreuger and Erna Anita (Burry) Gerber; m. Gerard E. Meunier, Dec. 27, 1945 (div. 1949). Grad., Sarah Lawrence Coll., 1947. Ind. theatrical dir., producer U.S. and abroad, 1955—; lit. mgr., dir. Boston Post Road Stage Co., 1988-92; artistic dir. Fairfield County Stage Co. (formerly Boston Post Road Stage), 1992-93. Producer: (Broadway plays) Too Good To Be True, 1964-65 (nominated Tony award 1965), Travesties, 1975-76 (Tony award 1976), An Almost Perfect Person, 1977, The Night of the Tribades, 1978, To Grandmother's House We Go, 1981, The Royal Family, 1975-76, (off-Broadway plays) Thieves Carnival, 1955 (Spl. Tony award 1955), Exiles, 1956 (OBIE award 1956), Buried Child (Pulitzer prize 1980); dir.: (nat. tours) Misalliance, 1953, Milk and Honey, 1963, Dark at the Top of the Stairs, 1958, Dear Love, 1971, To Grandmother's House We Go, 1982, (off-Broadway prodns.) The Decameron, 1961, Catholic School Girls, 1981, (Broadway prodn.) Wild and Wonderful, 1972. Home: 51 Hillside Rd N Weston CT 06883-1513

FREE, ANN COTTRELL, writer; b. Richmond, Va.; d. Emmett Drewry and Emily (Blake) Cottrell; m. James Stillman Free, Feb. 24, 1950; 1 child, Elissa. Grad. Collegiate Sch. for Girls, Richmond, 1934; student Richmond div. Coll. William and Mary, 1934-36; AB, Barnard Coll. Columbia U., 1938. Reporter Richmond Times Dispatch, 1938-40; Washington corr., Newsweek, 1940-41, Chgo. Sun, 1941-43, N.Y. Herald Tribune, 1943-46; pub. information dir. UNRRA China Mission, Shanghai, 1946-47; corr. Middle and Nr. East and Europe, 1947-48; writer-photographer Marshall Plan, Washington and Western Europe, 1949-50; Washington corr. N.Am. Newspaper Alliance, 1955-80; contbg. editor Between the Species; contbr. newspapers and mags., including Washington Star and Washington Post; Washington editor EnviroSouth Quar., 1977-82; pres. Flying Fox Press. Mem. Friends of the Rachel Carson Nat. Wildlife Refuge (hon. founding mem.); chmn. Mrs. Roosevelt's Press Conf. Assn., 1943; cons. expert Rachel Carson Coun.; v.p. Vieques (P.R.) Humane Soc.; coord. Albert Schweitzer Summer Fellows Program; bd. dirs. Albert Schweitzer Fellowship; pres. Albert Schweitzer Coun. on Animals and Environment. Recipient Dodd Mead-Boys' Life Writing award, 1963, Albert Schweitzer medal, Animal Welfare Inst., 1963, Jr. Book award certificate Boys Clubs of Am., 1964; Humanitarian of Yr. awards Washington Animal Rescue League, 1971, Montgomery County Humane Soc., 1971, Washington Humane Soc., 1983, News Writing award Dog Writers Assn. Am., 1975, 78, Rachel Carson Legacy award, 1987, Disting. Alumni award The Collegiate Schs., 1992; recognition Dept. Interior, 1970. Mem. Soc. Woman Geographers, Nat. Press Club, Am. News Women's Club. Author: Forever the Wild Mare, 1963, Animals, Nature and Albert Schweitzer, 1982, No Room, Save in the Heart, 1987, Since Silent Spring: Our Debt to Albert Schweitzer and Rachel Carson, 1992. Home: 4700 Jamestown Rd Bethesda MD 20816-2923 also: Lantz Mill Edinburg VA 22824

FREE, HELEN M., chemist, consultant; b. Pitts., Feb. 20, 1923; d. James Summerville and Daisy (Piper) Murray; m. Alfred H. Free, Oct. 18, 1947; children: Eric, Penny, Kurt, Jake, Bonnie, Nina. BA in Chemistry, Coll. of Wooster, Ohio, 1944; DSc (hon.), Coll. of Wooster, 1992, Ctrl. Mich. U., 1993; MA in Clin. Lab. Mgmt., Central Mich. U., DSc (hon.), 1993 Cert. clin. chemist Nat. Registry Clin. Chemistry. Chemist Miles Labs., Elkhart, Ind., 1944-78, dir. mktg. services research products div., 1978-82, chemist, mgr., cons. diagnostics div. Miles Inc., 1982—; mem. adj. faculty Ind. U., South Bend, 1975—. Author: (with others) Urodynamics and Urinalysis in Clinical Laboratory Practice, 1972, 76. Contbr. articles to profl. jours. Patentee in field. Women's chmn. Centennial of Elkhart, 1958. Recipient Disting. Alumni award Coll. of Wooster, 1980, award Medi Econ. Press, 1986, Lab. Pub. Svc. Nat. Leadership award, 1994; named to Hall of Excellence, Ohio Found. Ind. Colls., 1992; named Woman of Yr. YWCA, 1993. Fellow AAAS, Am. Inst. Chemists (co-recipient Chicago award 1967), Royal Soc. Chemistry; mem. Am. Chem. Soc. (pres. 1993, bd. dirs., chmn. Chemistry Week task force, bd. com. pub. affairs and pub. rels., chmn. women chemists com. internat. activities com., grants and awards com., profl. and member relations com., nominating com., council policy pub. affairs and budget, Service award local chpt. 1981, councilor; Garvan medal 1980, co-recipient Mosher award, 1983), Am. Assn. for Clin. Chemistry (council, bd. dirs., nominating com. and pub. relations com., nat. membership chmn., profl. affairs coordinator, pres.), Assn. Clin. Scientists (diploma of honor 1992), Am. Soc. Clin. Lab. Sci. (chmn. assembly, Achievement award 1976), Nat. Com. Clin. Lab. Standards (bd. dirs.), Iota Sigma Pi (hon.), Sigma Delta Epsilon (hon.). Presbyterian. Lodge: Altrusa (pres. 1982-83, bd. dirs.). Home: 3752 E Jackson Blvd Elkhart IN 46516-5205 Office: Miles Inc Diagnostics Divsn PO Box 70 Elkhart IN 46515-0070

FREE, MARY MOORE, anthropologist; b. Paris, Tex., Mar. 6, 1933; d. Dudley Crawford and Margie Lou (Moore) Hubbard; m. Dwight Allen Free Jr., June 26, 1954 (dec.); children: Hardy (dec.), Dudley (dec.), Margery, Caroline. BS, So. Meth. U., 1954, MLA, 1981, MA, 1987, PhD, 1989. Instr. So. Meth. U., Dallas, 1982-89, prof. continuing edn., 1989-90, prof. Dedman Coll., 1990—, adj. asst. prof. dept. anthropology, 1990—; prof. Richland Community Coll., Dallas, 1986; house anthropologist Baylor U. Med. Ctr., Dallas, 1990—; adv. bd. geriatrics Vis. Nurse Assn., Dallas, 1984-91; presenter in field. Author: The Private World of the Hermitage: Lifestyles of the Rich and Old in an Elite Retirement Home, 1995; contbr. chpts. to sci. books and aricles to Anthropology Newsletter, Am. Jour. Cardiology, Cahiers de Sociologie Economique et Culturelle-Ethnopsycholie, Jour. Heart Failure, other profl. jours.; mem. editorial bd. Baylor U. Med. Ctr. Procs. Active various svc. and social orgns. Named one of Notable Women of Tex., 1984. Fellow Am. Anthrop. Assn., Inst. for Study of Earth and Man; mem. AAAS, Dallas Women's Club, Dallas Petroleum Club, Brook Hollow Golf Club, Pi Beta Phi. Methodist. Home: 4356 Edmondson Ave Dallas TX 75205-2602 Office: Baylor U Med Ctr 3500 Gaston Ave Dallas TX 75246-2088

FREE, RUTH MORGAN, librarian; b. Sunflower, Miss., Dec. 14, 1946; d. Sanderson George and Nora (Caraway) Morgan; m. Thomas Eugene Free, Dec. 17, 1973; 1 child, Elizabeth Caraway. AA, Miss. Delta C.C., Moorhead, 1967; BA in English, Delta State U., 1969, MEd in English, 1971; MLS, La. State U., 1974. Cert. Laubach Literacy, Human Effectiveness, Leadership Effectiveness. Libr. Ruleville (Miss.) Cen. High Sch., 1970-71; asst. dir. Sunflower County Librs., Indianola, Miss., 1971-87; dir. info. svcs., NASA tech. transfer grant writer Miss. Delta Community Coll., 1987-93; libr. Learning Resource Ctr., Tupelo (Miss.) Campus, Itawamba C.C., 1993—. Compiler: Automation and Networking in Mississippi Libraries, 1989; editor Automation and Networking Roundtable Newsletter, 1985; mem. editorial bd., reporter Miss. Librs. Jour., 1979. Group leader Miss. Gov.'s Conf. on Librs., 1978, asst. regional coord., 1991; mem. Miss. Gov.'s Task Force on Adult Edn., 1985-87, Sunflower County Literacy Coun., 1983-87; dir. Miss. Nat. Libr.-Week/Legis. Day, 1981; sec. Sunflower County Hist. Soc., 1983-87. Recipient John Cotton Dana Nat. Pub. Rels. award, 1972; journalism scholar U. Miss., 1967. Mem. AAUW, Miss. Libr. Assn. (chmn. 2-yr. roundtable 1993, past chmn. other coms.), Miss. Biomedical Libr. Consortium, Beta Phi Mu (Nat. continuing Edn. award 1980). Home: 135 Patterson Cir Saltillo MS 38866 Office: Itawamba CC Learning Resource Ctr 653 Eason Blvd Tupelo MS 38801-5955

FREED, LINDA RAE, critical care nurse; b. Fond du Lac, Wis., Aug. 27, 1957; d. Donald J. and Patricia R. (Ingalls) Wegener; m. Frank A. Freed, Aug. 22, 1981; children: Stephanie P., Courtney R., Matthew F. AS in Nursing, Weber State Coll., 1981; BS in Nursing, U. Utah, 1985. Cert. critical care registered nurse. Nurse aide Weber Meml. Hosp., Roy, Utah, 1977-79; nurse aide, float pool McKay-Dee Hosp., Ogden, Utah, 1979-80; practical nurse McKay-Dee Hosp., Ogden, 1980-81, staff nurse, charge nurse med. monitoring unit, 1981-86, staff nurse cardiac intensive care unit, charge nurse, 1986—; clin. faculty mem. Salt Lake C.C./Davis Applied Tech. Ctr., Kaysville, Utah, 1992—; preceptor in field. Mem. AACN (No. Utah chpt.), Sigma Theta Tau, Nu Nu. Home: 5832 Cedar Ln Ogden UT 84403-5253

FREED, RITA EVELYN, curator, Egyptologist, educator; b. Newark, June 29, 1952; d. Samuel David and Gertrude (Houseman) F. BA in Classical and Nr. Ea. Archaeology, Bibl. Studies, Wellesley Coll.; cert. in museology, NYU, MA, PhD. Exhbn. asst. Egypt's minor arts Mus. Fine Arts, Boston, 1978-82, curator dept. Ancient Egyptian, Nubian and Near Ea. Art, 1989—; curator Egyptian exhbn. univ. gallery Memphis State U., 1983, curator Egyptian antiquities, dir. Inst. Egyptian Art and Archeology, 1984-89, assoc. prof. dept. art, 1983-89; adj. prof. Wellesley Coll., 1991—; part-time rsch. asst. dept. Egyptian and classical art Bklyn. Mus., 1976-78; researcher Egyptian dept. Met. Mus. Art, 1977-78, lectr. dept. pub. edn., 1978; lectr. dept. art Adelphi U., 1978-79; mem. archaeol. survey team Idalion Excavations, Dhali, Cyprus, 1973; site supr. excavation of Philistine temple, Tel Qasile, Tel Aviv, 1973; field archaeologist, expdn. photographer Mendes Excavations, Ea. Delta, Egypt, 1977; small finds registrar Memphis Excavations, Mitrahineh, Egypt, 1988; epigrapher Giza Mastabas Project, Egypt, 1989; co-project dir. Boston-Penn Expdn., Bersheh, Egypt, 1990, Saqqara, Egypt, 1992. Contbr. articles and revs. to profl. jours. and books; author exhbn. catalogues. Ford Found. fellow, Slater Fgn. Study fellow; Trustee fellow and Durant scholar of Wellesley Coll.; NSF rsch. grantee. Mem. Am. Rsch. Ctr. in Egypt (bd. govs.), Soc. for Study Egyptian Antiquities, Egypt Exploration Soc., Egyptological Seminar, Internat. Assn. Egyptologists (N.Am. rep.), Internat. Coun. Mus. (Am. rep.), Am. Assn. Mus., Phi Beta Kappa. Jewish. Office: Mus Fine Arts 465 Huntington Ave Boston MA 02115-5519

FREED, RUTH S., anthropologist; Prof. anthropology Seton Hall U., South Orange, N.J., 1971-81, research assoc. Am. Mus. Natural History, N.Y.C., 1975—. Co-author (with Stanley A. Freed): Man From the Beginning, 1967, Shanti Nagar: The Effects of Urbanization in a Village in North India, vol. I, Social Organization, 1976, vol. II, Aspects of Economy, Technology and Ecology, 1978, vol. III, Sickness and Health, 1979; Rites of Passage in Shanti Nagar, 1980, Enculturation and Education in Shanti Nagar, 1981, The Psychomedical Case History of a Low Caste Woman of North India, 1985, Fertility, Sterilization, and Population Growth in Shanti Nagar, India: A Longitudinal Ethnographic Approach, 1985, Uncertain Revolution: Panchayati Raj and Democratic Elections in a North Indian Village, 1987, Ghosts: Life and Death in North India, 1993. Office: Am Mus Natural History Central Park West at 79th St New York NY 10026

FREEDGOOD, ANNE GOODMAN, editor; b. Mount Vernon, N.Y., Mar. 24, 1917; d. Jules Eckert and Mai Farr (Pfouts) Goodman; widowed; 1 child, Julia. B.A., Bryn Mawr Coll., 1938. Writer Office War Info., London, Paris, Munich, 1944-46; book editor N.Y. Star, N.Y.C., 1949-50; editor Harpers Mag., N.Y.C., 1950-58, Doubleday, N.Y.C., 1958-71, Random House, N.Y.C., 1971-87; cons. editor Summit Books, N.Y.C., 1988-91; sr. editor Harcourt Brace, N.Y.C., 1991-93; editor-at-large William Morrow & Co., N.Y.C., 1994—. Author short stories; contbr. articles to various publs. Home: 425 Riverside Dr New York NY 10025-7775

FREEDMAN, ANNE BELLER, public speaking and marketing consultant; b. Gardner, Mass., June 22, 1949; d. Gabriel Philip Freedman and Natalie Engler (Beller) Lyons; m. Edward A. Fischer, May 20, 1979; 1 child, Lynne Heather. BSJ U. Fla., 1971. Staff writer Coral Gables Times, Miami, 1972-73; reporter Miami News, 1973-74; assoc. editor Miami Phoenix, 1974-75; freelance writer, Miami, 1975-80; corr. Advt. Age, Miami, 1977-81; pres. Exec. S.O.S., Inc., Miami, 1980-90; pres. Speak Out, Inc., Coral Gables, 1990—; ptnr. Speak Out/Lewison-Singer, Inc., Coral Gables, 1991-94; instr. Fla. Internat. U. Producer cable TV show Not For Women Only, 1992, pub. rels., 1990-92; author: Unforgettable Speeches and Presentations in 8 Easy Steps, 1991. Bd. dirs. Miami/Bogota-Calé Sister Cities Program, 1983-85; host Focus South Cable TV Show, 1990-91. Mem. South Miami/Kendall C. of C. (editor monthly newsletter 1980-83, dir., 1982-85, chmn. bus. com. 1985-89, editor ann. directory and buyer's guide 1986-87, 89—, Presdl. award 1983, 89), Nat. Assn. Women Bus. Owners (chair public relations 1981, dir. tng. and devel. 1987—, dir. corp. ptnrs. 1988-89, v.p. 1989-91, co-chmn. Recognition awards, 1992, pub. rels. chair 1990-93, dir. tng. and devel. 1993-94, exec. chair 1994—), Coral Gables C. of C. (chmn., dir. 1993—), Greater Miami C. of C. Clubs: Toastmasters (pres. 1984). Home: 6721 SW 113th Pl Miami FL 33173-1954 Office: 6851 Yumuri St Ste 2 Coral Gables FL 33146-3609

FREEDMAN, ANNE ELLEN, political science educator, writer; b. Passaic, N.J., Apr. 6, 1938; d. Sidney and Mollie Klara (Kanter) Goldberg; m. Philip E. Freedman, Sept. 5, 1960; 1 child, Sharon Freedman Moore. BA in Polit. Sci., Rutgers U., 1959; MA in Polit. Sci., U. Calif., Berkeley, 1960; PhD in Polit. Sci., U. Iowa, 1964. Instr. Wheaton Coll., Norton, Mass., 1964-65; rschr. Bunting Inst., Radcliffe, Cambridge, Mass., 1964-66; from asst. to full prof. Roosevelt U., Chgo., 1966—. Co-author: Voluntary Associations, 1972, The Psychology of Political Control, 1975; author: The Planned Society, 1972, Patronage, 1994; contbr. articles to profl. jours. Active Ridgeville Neighborhood Assn. Recipient Dimock award Pub. Adminstrn. Rev., 1988; Woodrow Wilson Found. fellow, 1959-60. Mem. ASPA, Am. Polit. Sci. Assn., Internat. Pers. Mgmt. Assn. (v.p. Chgo. chpt. 1990-91, pres. 1993-94, bd. dirs. 1994—), Phi Beta Kappa (Douglass Coll. chpt.). Democrat. Home: 618 A South Blvd Evanston IL 60202 Office: Roosevelt U 430 S Michigan Chicago IL 60605

FREEDMAN, AUDREY WILLOCK, economist; b. Cleve., Nov. 25, 1929; d. Sylvester Rhodes and Hilda Louise (Reiber) Willock; m. Monroe H. Freedman, Sept. 24, 1950; children: Alice, Sarah, Caleb, Judah. BA in Econs., Wellesley Coll., 1951. Staff economist Communication Workers Am., AFL-CIO, Washington, 1958-60; staff economist Bur. Labor Stats., U.S. Dept. Labor, Washington, 1961-67, staff economist Manpower Adminstrn., 1968-71; mem. policy staff Cost of Living Coun., liaison U.S. Pay Bd., Washington, 1971-72; sr. cons. Orgn. Resources Counselors, N.Y.C., 1973-75; sr. rsch. assoc. Conf. Bd., N.Y.C., 1976-92; pres. Audrey Freedman & Assocs., N.Y.C., 1992—; chmn. bus. rsch. adv. coun., U.S. Bur. Labor Stats., 1992-94; bd. dirs. Manpower, Inc., mem. compensation com. Author: Security Bargains Reconsidered, 1978, Managing Labor Relations, 1979, Industry Response to Health Risk, 1981, The Changing Human Resource Function, 1991; contbr. articles to profl. jours. Recipient Disting. Svc. award U.S. Dept. Labor, 1967, Presdl. citation, 1972. Mem. Am. Fedn. Govt. Employees (v.p. local chpt. 1965-68, chmn. civil rights com. 1964-69), Am. Econ. Assn., Indsl. Rels. Rsch. Assn. Jewish. Home: 30-49 79th St Jackson Heights NY 11370 Office: 111 Broadway 5th Fl New York NY 10006

FREEDMAN, GAIL, financial analyst; b. Oyster Bay, N.Y., Dec. 26, 1963; d. Noble Aubrey and Dorothy Ann (Duffy) Langille; m. Jonathan Eric Freedman, Oct. 23, 1993. BA in Polit. Sci., Bethany (W.Va.) Coll., 1986; MBA in Mktg. and Fin., U. So. Calif., 1992. Legis. intern legis. affairs Dept. Treasury, Washington, 1985, adminstrv. asst. adminstrn., 1986, rsch. asst. legis. affairs, 1986-88; spl. asst. Congressman Thomas McMillen, Washington, 1988; sr. legal asst. Pepper, Hamilton & Scheetz, Washington, 1988-90; cons. L.A. County Dept. Transp., 1990-91; licensing intern Applause Co., Woodland Hills, Calif., 1991; mgr. rsch. unit Tobacco Control Program, L.A., 1992-93; health care fin. analyst L.A. County Dept. Health Svcs., PHP Fin. Mgmt., 1993—; mentor to students U. So. Calif. Grad. Sch. Bus., L.A., 1991—. Author: (poetry) Fortnight, 1981, The Harbinger, 1985; author commentary newspaper The Tower, 1985-86. Founder Sunday Sound, L.A., 1993. Mem. U. So. Calif. Commerce Assn., Kappa Delta Konnection. Home: 512 S Ogden Dr Los Angeles CA 90036-3231 Office: LA County Dept Health Svcs Pub Health Programs Fin Mgmt 5555 Ferguson Dr 1st Fl Los Angeles CA 90022

FREEDMAN, JOYCE, clinical psychologist; b. Providence, R.I., Sept. 5, 1947; d. Seymour and Ruth (Richman) F.; m. Mickey Lazarus, Oct. 23, 1988. PsyD, Mass. Sch. Profl. Psychology, 1984. Cert. marriage, family and sexual therapist. Psychologist N.E. Inst. Family and Sexual Rels., Framingham, Mass., 1978-85, Framingham Ct. Clinic, 1983-84; pvt. practice, 1985—.

FREEDMAN, JUDITH GREENBERG, state senator, importer; b. Bridgeport, Conn., Mar. 11, 1939; d. Samuel Howard and Dorothy (Hoffman) G.; m. Samuel Sumner, Dec. 24, 1964; 1 child, Martha Ann. Student, Boston U., 1957-58, U. Mich., 1958-59; BS, So. Conn. State U., 1961, MS, 1972. Tchr. Hollywood (Fla.) Pub. Schs., 1961-62, White Plains (N.Y.) Pub. Schs., 1962-64, Wilton (Conn.) Pub. Schs., 1964-66; tchr. Weston (Conn.) Pub. Schs., 1966-72, tutor, 1977-80, tchr., 1982-84; owner Judith's Fancy, Westport, Conn., 1984—; mem. Conn. Senate, 1987-88; ranking mem. human svcs. com., 1987-88, ins. com., 1987-88, ranking mem. appropriations com., 1989-94, chmn. program rev. and investigation, 1992-94, chmn. commn. on innovation and productivity, 1994—; dep. pres. pro tem Conn. State Senate, 1995—, chmn. edn. com., 1995—. Pres., v.p. Rep. Women's Assn., 1976-80; pres. Rep. Women of Westport, 1976-79; mem. Bd. Edn., Westport, 1983-87, 89—; treas. Conn. Order Women Legislators. Mem. Order of Women Legislators (treas.). Jewish. Home: 17 Crawford Rd Westport CT 06880-1823

FREEDMAN, SANDRA WARSHAW, mayor; b. Newark, Sept. 21, 1943; m. Michael J. Freedman; 3 children. BA in Govt., U. Miami, 1965. Mem. Tampa (Fla.) City Coun., 1974—, chmn., 1983-86; mayor City of Tampa, 1986—. Bd. dirs. Jewish Community Ctr., 1974-75, Boys and Girls Clubs Greater Tampa, Hillsborough Coalition for Health, Tampa Community Concert Assn.; mem. sports adv. bd. Hillsborough Community Coll., 1975-76; sec. Downtown Devel. Authority, 1977-78; bd. dirs., v.p. Fla. Gulf Coast Symphony, 1979-80; vice chmn. Met. Planning Orgn., 1981-82; corp. mem. Neighborhood Housing Service; bd. fellows U. Tampa; mem. steering com. Hillsborough County Council of Govt.'s Constituency for Children; mem. exec. bd. Tampa/Hillsborough Young Adult Forum; chmn. bd. trustees Berkeley Prep. Sch.; trustee Tampa Bay Performing Arts Ctr., Inc., Tampa Mus.; mem. ethics com. Meml. Hosp.; mem. Tampa Preservation, Inc., Tampa/Hillsborough County Youth Council, Davis Islands Civic Assn., Tampa Hist. Soc., Met. Ministries Adv. Bd., Rodeph Sholom Synagogue, Sword of Hope Guild of Am. Cancer Soc., Friends of the Arts. Recipient Spessard L. Holland Meml. award Tampa Bay Com. for Good Govt., 1975-76, Human Rights award City of Tampa, 1980, award Soroptimist Internat. Tampa, 1981, Status of Women award Zonta of Tampa II, 1986, Woman of Achievement award Bus. & Profl. Women; named to Who's Who and Why of Successful Fla. Women, 1984. Mem. Hillsborough County Bar Aux., Greater Tampa C. of C., C. of C. Com. of 100 (exec. com.), Fla. League of Cities (bd. dirs.), Tampa Urban League, Nat. Council Jewish Women, U. Miami Alumni Assn., Athena Soc., Hadassah. Office: Office of the Mayor 306 E Jackson St Fl 8 Tampa FL 33602-5208

FREEDMAN, SARAH WARSHAUER, education educator; b. Wilmington, N.C., Feb. 23, 1946; d. Samuel Edward and Miriam (Miller) Warshauer; m. S. Robert Freedman, Aug. 20, 1967; 1 child, Rachel Karen. BA in English, U. Pa., 1967; MA in English, U. Chgo., 1970; MA in Linguistics, Stanford U., 1976, PhD in Edn., 1977. Tchr. English Phila. Sch. Dist., 1967-68, Lower Merion High Sch., 1968-69; instr. English U. N.C., Wilmington, 1970-71; instr. English and Linguistics Stanford Univ., 1972-76; asst. and assoc. prof. English San Francisco State Univ., 1977-81; asst. prof. Edn. Univ. Calif., Berkeley, 1981-83, assoc. prof. Edn., 1983-89; dir. Nat. Ctr. for the Study of Writing and Literacy, 1985—; prof. Edn. Univ. Calif., 1989—; cons. Nat. Bd. of Profl. Teaching Standards, 1993; mem. nat. adv. bd. Children's TV Workshop program Ghostwriter, Nat. Standards in English Lang. Arts, 1993-94. Author: Exchanging Writing, Exchanging Cultures, Lessons in School Reform from the United States and Great Britain, 1994, Response to Student Writing, 1987; editor: The Acquisition of Written Language: Response and Revision, 1985; contbr. chpts. to books and articles to profl. jours. Recipient Richard Meade award for Pub. Rsch. in Tchr. Edn. Nat. Coun. Tchrs. English, 1989; fellow Nat. Conf. on Rsch. in English, 1986; Rockefeller Found. grantee Bryn Mawr Coll., 1992, Nat. Ctr. for

Study of Writing and Literacy grantee Office Ednl. Rsch. and Improvement, 1985—, Minority Undergrad. Rsch. Program grantee U. Calif., 1988, 89, 92, 93, numerous other grants. Mem. Nat. Coun. Tchrs. English (mem. standing com. on rsch. 1981-87, ex-officio 1987—, chair bd. trustees rsch. found. 1990-93), Am. Ednl. Rsch. Assn. (chair spl. interest group on rsch. in writing 1983-85, numerous other coms.), Linguistic Soc. Am., Am. Assn. Applied Linguistics, Internat. Reading Assn. Office: U Calif Dept Edn Berkeley CA 94720

FREEMAN, BETTY LOU, mortgage company executive; b. Miami, Fla., Aug. 23, 1946; d. Lucious Benjamin and Mary Lou (Bowe) Freeman; divorced; children: Betty LaVonn Hart, Willard Anthony Hart, Carlton Antonio Freeman. Diploma in medicine, U. Miami, Fla., 1965; student, Duke U., 1969, Cleve. State Coll., 1971, Biscayne Coll., Miami, Fla.; internat. cultural diploma of honor, Am. Bus. Inst. Supr. Histo-Pathologic Technologists, Miami, Fla., 1969-76; project dir. Health Manpower Tng. Program, Miami, Fla., 1977-78; instructional asst. II Miami Dade Community Coll., Miami, Fla., 1979; mng. dir. Universal Real Estate Corp., Houston, 1979-82; founder, owner, chief exec. officer FS Dove Mortgage Corp., Atlanta, 1985—; apptd. rsch. bd. advisors Am. Bus. Inst., 1992. Bd. dirs. Bible Way Full Gospel Missionary Bapt. Ch.; mem. choir Cathedral at Chapel Hill. Rsch. fellow Internat. Biog. Ctr., Cambridge, Eng., 1992, Diploma of Honor award, 1992, First 500 award, 1992; recipient Women's Inner Cir. of Achievement award Am. Biog. Inst., 1992, 2,000 Notable Am. Women award, 1992. Mem. NAFE, Am. Mgmt. Assn., Nat. Soc. Med. Technologists, Nat. Mortgage Brokers Assn., Nat. Soc. Am. Med. Tech., Nat. Soc. Histo-Technologists, Nat. Businesswomen's Leadership Assn., Nat. Mgmt. Assn. Republican. Office: FS Dove Mortgage Corp PO Box 462 Lithonia GA 30058-0462

FREEMAN, CORINNE, financial services, former mayor; b. N.Y.C., Nov. 9, 1926; d. Bernard J. Hirschfeld and Sidonie (Daxe) Lichtenstein; m. Michael S. Freeman, Mar. 14, 1948; children: Michael L., Stephan J. Adelphi Coll. Sch. Nursing, 1944-47. RN, N.Y., Mass. Nurse numerous hosps. in N.Y. and Mass., 1948-64; mayor St. Petersburg, Fla., 1977-85; mem. Pinellas County Sch. Bd., St. Petersburg, Fla., 1989—; fin. advisor Prudential Securities; bd. dirs. Goodwill Industries, Headstart, Creativity in Child Care. Chmn. Social Svc. Allocations Com., St. Petersburg, 1972-76, City Budget Rev. Com., 1973-76, Youth Svc. System, Pinellas County, 1975-76, West Coast Regional Water Supply Authority; past mem. community redevel. com. U.S. Conf. of Mayors; past pres. Fla. League Cities; past mem. Pinellas County Mayors Coun.; past mem. Nat. League of Cities Revenue and Fin. Task Force; pres. LWV, St. Petersburg, 1970-72, 75-76; trustee Fire Pension Bd., St. Petersburg, 1989-92, Bayfront Med. Ctr.; adv. com. Jr. League St. Petersburg, 1990-92. Recipient Disting. Alumni award Adelphi U. Mem. Fla. Nursing Assn. Republican. Home: 2101 Pelham Rd N Saint Petersburg FL 33710-3659 Office: 5858 Central Ave Saint Petersburg FL 33707-1728

FREEMAN, ELAINE LAVALLE, sculptor; b. Boston, May 22, 1929; d. John and Ellen (Tufts) Lavalle; m. Felix Joachim Freeman, Jr., June 16, 1951 (div. 1974); children: John Lavalle, William Baker, Ellen Candler. Student, NAD, 1973, Art Students League, N.Y.C., 1947-49, 70-73; BA, Fordham U., 1986. Profl. sculptor N.Y.C. and Southampton, N.Y., 1973—; instr. sculpture Sculpture Ctr. Sch., N.Y.C., 1977-81; vol. gallery asst. Sculpture Ctr., N.Y.C., 1979—; exec. com., sec., bd. trustees Sculpture Ctr., N.Y.C., 1985—; mem. Catherine Lorillard Wolfe Art Club, N.Y.C., Southampton (N.Y.) Artists. One woman shows include Wheeler Gallery, Providence, 1979, Sculpture Ctr., N.Y.C., 1977, Southampton Gallery, N.Y.C., 1975; exhibited in group shows including Nat. Acad., Audubon Artists, Allied Artists, Parrish Mus., Nat. Arts Club, Am. Standard Corp. Gallery, Sculpture Ctr. Gallery, Huntington Twp. Art League, East Edn Arts Coun., 1973—. Bd. dirs. Southampton Fresh Air Home for Crippled Children, 1980-86, sec., 1981-83, treas. 1980. Recipient Judges award Parrish Art Mus., Southampton, 1974, Am. Carving Sch. award, Allied Arts, N.Y.C., 1977, Anna Huntington Hyatt award, Catherine Lorillard Wolfe Art Club, N.Y.C., 1983, 1st prize sculpture, 1994. Mem. Colony Club, Meadow Club. Democrat. Episcopalian. Home: 119 W 77th St New York NY 10024-6927

FREEMAN, ELSBETH MEADE, psychologist; b. Kalamazoo, Mich., May 30, 1946; d. John David and Elizabeth Ann (Beilman) F.; m. Richard Lynn Terry, Sept. 4, 1965 (div. Jan. 1975); 1 child, Karianne Terry. BA, U. Tenn., 1979, PhD, 1986. Psychol. examiner Frazier Millington Mental Health Ctr., Memphis, Tenn., 1983, St. Mary's Med. Ctr., Knoxville, Tenn., 1982-86; psychol. examiner Knoxville, 1982-86, psychologist, 1986—; psychologist U. Tenn. Med. Ctr., Knoxville, 1993—. Mem. Tenn. Commn. on Children & Youth, Knoxville, Nashville, 1988—; steering coun. Tenn. Voices for Children, Nashville, 1993; bd. dirs. Tenn. Com. for Advancement of Psychology, 1992-94; instr. Disaster Mental Health Svcs., ARC, Knoxville, 1992—. Bacon-Beard fellow U. Tenn., Knoxville, 1979-80. Mem. APA, Tenn. Psychol. Assn. (pres. 1992-94, v.p. 1989-90), Knoxville Area Psychol. Assn. (sec. 1985-86, pres. 1987-89), Am. Profl. Soc. on Abuse of Children. Democrat. Episcopalian. Office: 4709 Papermill Rd Bldg 2 Knoxville TN 37909

FREEMAN, GERALDINE DELORIS, county official; b. Tampa, Fla., Aug. 30, 1951; d. Willie Fred and Rosa Lee (Brown) Live; m. Henry Jacob Freeman, Jr., Aug. 23, 1968; children: Henry Jacob III, Ronald David, Robin Annette. From printers helper to sr. printer Bd. County Commrs. Hillsborough County Govt., Tampa, Fla., 1973-91; printing svc. mgr. Hillsborough County Govt., Tampa, 1991—. Bd. dirs. Martin Luther King Jr. Scholarship Fund, Tampa; mem. Black Heritage Com., Tampa, 1991—, Thanksgiving Food Baskets, Tampa, 1978—; aux choir New Progress Missionary Bapt. Ch., 1990, 93, asst. ch. clk. 1991, fundraiser 1991. Named Govt. Mgr. of the Yr. Hillsborough Co., 1994. Mem. In-Plant Pub. Mgmt. Assn. (pres. Gulf Coast chpt., Mem. of Yr. 1989-90, regional chpt. Mem. of Yr. 1993). Democrat. Office: Hillsborough County Govt 1st Fl County Ctr 601 E Kennedy Blvd Tampa FL 33602-3500

FREEMAN, JANE GULLEDGE, small business owner; b. Albemarle, N.C., June 21, 1957; d. Marius Bailey Gulledge and Mary Alice Grizzell Wolfe; m. John Edward Freeman, Mar. 12, 1984; children: John Swindell, Bailey Jane. BS, U. N.C., Charlotte, 1979; MEd, Campbell U., Buies Creek, N.C., 1981. Tchrs. aide Albemarle City Schs., 1981-82; co-owner Freeman's Car Stereo Inc., Charlotte, 1983—. Republican. Methodist. Office: Freeman's Car Stereo Inc 6150 Brookshire Blvd Apt I Charlotte NC 28216-2443

FREEMAN, JILL MARIA, electrical contractor; b. Monticello, N.Y., May 20, 1961; d. William Peter and Ellen Mary (Fallon) Kitsos; m. Donald L. Freeman, Sept. 16, 1989; children: Jamie, Donald John, William. Student, Dutchess C.C., Poughkeepsie, N.Y., 1980-82, Adirondack C.C., Queensbury, N.Y., 1981, 90. Electrician John Lewis Contractor, Lake Luzerne, N.Y., 1984-86, Russell Brown Electric, Queensbury, 1986-88, Woodbury Devel., Queensbury, 1986-89, Warren County Dept. Pub. Works, Warrensburg, N.Y., 1989-91, Kitsman Contracting, Lake Luzerne, 1988—. Electrician, plumber Helping Hands, Corinth, N.Y. Mem. Nat. Ski Patrol (sr.).

FREEMAN, MARJORIE SCHAEFER, mathematics educator; b. Chevy Chase, Md., Sept. 23, 1924; d. Herbert Stanley and Helen (Hummer) Schaefer; m. John C. Freeman, June 14, 1947; children: John C. III, Walter H., Jill F. Hasling, Cathryn F. Disch, Helen Freeman, Paul D. AB, Randolph-Macon Womans Coll., 1946; MS, Brown U, 1949; postgrad., U. Houston, 1973-75. Computer asst. Inst. for Advanced Study, Princeton, N.J., 1949-50; rsch. asst. Tex. A&M Rsch. Found., College Station, 1954-55; instr. Tex. A&M U., College Station, 1955; cons. Gulf Cons., Houston, 1955-56; instr. South Tex. Jr. Coll., Houston, 1961-74; asst. prof. U. Houston-Downtown, 1974-90, asst. prof. emeritus, 1990—; systems analyst, programmer TERA, Inc., Houston, 1985; cons. Inst. for Storm Rsch., Houston, 1979-86; adv. bd. Weather Rsch. Ctr., Houston, 1987—. Mem. Math. Assn. Am., South Tex. Obedience Club, S.W. Tracking Assn., Am. Chesapeake Club. Home: 4404 Mount Vernon St Houston TX 77006-5814

FREEMAN, MARY LOUISE, state senator; b. Willmar, Minn., Oct. 21, 1941; d. James Martin and Luella Anna (Backlund) Hawkinson; m. Dennis Lester Freeman, June 10, 1962; children: Mark D., Sara L., Cary D., Maret S. BA, Gustavus Adolphus Coll., 1963. Substitute tchr. Arrowhead Edn. Assn., Storm Lake, Iowa, 1982-93; tchr., cons. Midwest Power, Des Moines, 1991-94; mem. Iowa Senate, Des Moines, 1994—; mem. early childhood intervention com., 1994—, mem. disaster prevention svcs. com., 1994—. Del. alt. Rep. Nat. Conv., Kansas City, 1976; active Midwest-Can. Relations Co., 1994—. Mem. Am. Legis. Exch. Coun., Nat. Coun. State Govt. Lutheran. Home: 311 E Lakeshore Dr Storm Lake IA 50558 Office: Iowa State Senate State Capitol Des Moines IA 50319

FREEMAN, MYRNA FAYE, county schools official; b. Danville, Ill., Oct. 30, 1939; d. Thomas Gene and Dorothy Olive (Chodera) F.; m. Lonnie Lee Choate, Aug. 16, 1959 (div. 1987); children: Leslie Rene, Gregory Lonn. BA in Pub. Adminstrn., San Diego State U., 1977, MA in Edn. Adminstrn., 1987. Employee benefits mgr. City of San Diego, 1974-84; asst. risk mgr. San Diego County Office Edn., San Diego, 1984—; instr. Sch. Bus. Mgrs. Acad., Assn. Calif. Sch. Adminstrs., 1985—, Ins. Edn. Assn., Cert. Employee Benefits Specialist courses, 1991—. Author: Book, Adm. Impact of Implement Leg. 1987; Author: Article Risk Mgmt.- Emp. Benefits 1985, Risk Mgmt. - Workers' Comp. 1986, Risk Mgmt. - Loss Control 1986. Mem. Kaiser Consumer Coun., 1977-84, pres., 1979-80; bd. dirs. S.D. County Affirmative Action Adv. Bd., 1985; mem. adv. com. Vista Health Plan Pub. Policy, 1994—; mem. adv. coun. Kaiser On-the-Job, 1994—. Recipient Award of Appreciation COMBO-Cultural Arts of San Diego 1977. Mem. Risk Ins. Mgmt. Soc. (pres. San Diego chpt. 1988), Calif. Assn. Sch. Bus. Ofcls. (chmn. risk mgmt. R&D comm. 1987-88), San Diego Group Ins. Claims Coun. (pres. 1987), S.D. Employers Health Cost Coalition (vice-chmn. 1987), Calif. Women in Govt. (bd. dirs. 1983-84), Calif. Assn. of Joint Powers Authority, Pub. Agys. Risk Mgmt. Assn., Pub. Risk Ins. Mgmt. Assn., Internat. Found. Employee Benefits Plans, San Diego Workers' Compensation Forum, Sigma Kappa, Phi Kappa Phi, Internat. Platform Assn. Republican. Methodist. Home: 4345 Cartulina Rd San Diego CA 92124-2102 Office: San Diego County Office Edn 6401 Linda Vista Rd # 405 San Diego CA 92111-7399

FREEMAN, NATASHA MATRINA LEONIDOW, nursing administrator; b. Nyack, N.Y., June 12, 1958; d. Paul and Matrina (Butich) L.; m. Douglas Edward Freeman, Oct. 20, 1990; children: Alexandra, Mary. AAS, Rockland C.C., 1979; BS in Nursing cum laude, SUNY Coll. Technology, Utica, 1982; MS in Nursing magna cum laude, Syracuse U., 1985. RN, N.Y.; cert. nurse adminstr. Staff nurse Englewood Hosp., N.J., 1979-80; charge nurse Mary Imogene Bassett Hosp., Cooperstown, N.Y., 1980-82, nursing service coordinator, 1983-86, asst. dir. systems devel., 1986-87; assoc. nursing practice coord. Strong Meml. Hosp.-U. Rochester, N.Y., 1987-88, asst. dir. nursing Bayfront Med. Ctr., St. Petersburg, Fla., 1988—. Translator: Excellence in Russian Language, 1976 (Otrada award). Served as 1st lt. USAFR, 1990-91, Persian Gulf War, Saudi Arabia. Mem. Am. Orgn. Nurse Execs., Fla. Orgn. Nurse Execs., Sigma Theta Tau. Office: Bayfront Med Ctr 701 6th St S Saint Petersburg FL 33701-4891

FREEMAN, PATRICIA ELIZABETH, library and education specialist; b. El Dorado, Ark., Nov. 30, 1924; d. Herbert A. and M. Elizabeth (Pryor) Harper; m. Jack Freeman, June 15, 1949; 3 children. BA, Centenary Coll., 1943; postgrad., Fine Arts Ctr., 1942-46, Art Students League, 1944-45; BSLS, La. State U., 1946; postgrad., Calif. State U., 1959-61, U. N.Mex., 1964-74; EdS, Peabody Coll., Vanderbilt U., 1975. Libr. U. Calif., Berkeley, 1946-47; libr. Albuquerque Pub. Schs., 1964-67, ind. sch. libr. media ctr. cons., 1967—. Painter lithographer; one-person show La. State Exhibit Bldg., 1948; author: Pathfinder: An Operational Guide for the School Librarian, 1975, Southeast Heights Neighborhoods of Albuquerque, 1993; compiler, editor: Elizabeth Pryor Harper's Twenty-One Southern Families, 1985; editor: SEHNA Gazette, 1988-93. Mem. task force Goals for Dallas-Environ., 1977-82; pres. Friends of Sch. Librs., Dallas, 1979-83; v.p., editor Southeast Heights Neighborhood Assn., 1988-93. With USAF, 1948-49. Honoree AAUW Ednl. Found., 1979; vol. award for outstanding service Dallas Ind. Sch. Dist., 1978; AAUW Pub. Service grantee 1980. Mem. ALA, AAUW (dir. Dallas 1976-82, Albuquerque 1983-85), LWV (sec. Dallas 1982-83, editor Albuquerque 1984-88), Nat. Trust Historic Preservation, Friends of Albuquerque Pub. Libr., N.Mex. Symphony Guild, Alpha Xi Delta. Home: 3016 Santa Clara Ave SE Albuquerque NM 87106-2350

FREEMAN, SHELLEY, financial services marketing executive, freelance editor and writer; b. Greensburg, Pa., Oct. 8, 1958; d. Martin Freeman and Felice (Oxman) Salsburg. Student, Muhlenberg Coll., 1976-80; BA in English, Wilkes Coll., 1982; postgrad., U. Pa., 1982-83. Publicity asst. Harper & Row, N.Y.C., 1983-84; mktg. assoc. E.F. Hutton & Co., N.Y.C., 1984-85, asst. v.p., 1985-87; sr. v.p., dir. fin. planning Shearson Lehman Bros., N.Y.C., 1988-92, dir. of sales support, 1992-93, dir. mktg., 1993—. Mem. Internat. Assn. for fin. Planning, Nat. Assn. Female Execs. Democrat. Jewish. Office: Shearson Lehman Bros 388 Greenwich St Fl 38 New York NY 10013-2375

FREEMAN, SUSAN TAX, anthropologist, educator; b. Chgo., May 24, 1938; d. Sol and Gertrude Tax.; m. Leslie G. Freeman, Jr., Mar. 20, 1964; 1 dau., Sarah Elisabeth. B.A., U. Chgo., 1958; M.A., Harvard U., 1959, Ph.D., 1965. Asst. prof. anthropology U. Ill., Chgo., 1965-70; assoc. prof. U. Ill., 1970-78, prof., 1978—, chmn., 1979-82; panelist NEH, Council for Internat. Exchange of Scholars; mem. anthropology screening com. Fulbright-Hays Research Awards, 1975-78; mem. ad hoc com. on research in Spain Spain-U.S.A. Friendship Agreement, various yrs., 1977-84; field researcher Mex., 1959, Spain, 1962—, Japan, 1983. Author: Neighbors: The Social Contract in a Castilian Hamlet, 1970, The Pasiegos-Spaniards in No Man's Land, 1979; asso. editor: Am. Anthropologist, 1971-73, Am. Ethnologist, 1974-76. Named to Inst. for the Humanities, U. Ill. Chgo., 1987-88; Wenner-Gren Found. for Anthrop. Research grantee, 1966, 83; NIMH grantee, 1967, 68-71; Nat. Endowment Humanities fellowships, 1978-79, 89-90. Fellow Am. Anthrop. Assn. (nominating com. 1981-82), Royal Anthrop. Inst. Gt. Britain and Ireland; mem. Soc. for Anthropology of Europe (exec. com. 1987-88), Soc. Spanish and Portuguese Hist. Studies (exec. com. 1990-92), Coun. European Studies (steering com. 1990-92), Internat. Inst. Spain (corporator, bd. dirs. 1982-87), Centro Estudios Sorians (hon.), Assn. Antropologia Castilla y Leon (hon.). Home: 5537 S Woodlawn Ave Chicago IL 60637-1620 Office: U Ill Dept Anthropology M/C 927 1007 W Harrison St Chicago IL 60607

FREEMAN, VERDELLE YVONNE, educator, multi-cultural studies consultant; b. Clewiston, Fla., Jan. 21, 1945; d. Theophilus Napoleon and Geneva Yvonne (Andrews) Hill; m. Alexander Walter Jones Jr., Oct. 26, 1987; children: Daphanne D. McCray, James Melvin Freeman Jr. BA in English, Fla. A&M U., 1965, BA in Libr. Sci., 1965, BA in Speech and Drama, 1965. Cert. tchr. secondary English, speech, drama, libr. grades K-12, N.J. Librarian South 2d St. Youth Ctr., Plainfield, N.J., 1972-74; tchr. English Piscataway (N.J.) High Sch., 1972—; program dir. Martin Luther King Ctr., Bridgewater, N.J., 1981-89; librarian Fairchilde Inernat., Plainfield, 1981-85; cons. Nat. Seed Project Curriculum Studies Wellesley (Mass.) Coll.; leader faculty devel. in-svc. tng. Piscataway Sch. Dist., dir. performing arts, 1990—, creator, dir. performing arts self esteem project; program dir. Judy Blume Reading Project, Bridgewater, 1988-91; dir. anti-drug project South 2d St. Yough Ctr., 1973-74. Contbr. articles to Nat. Seed Quar. newsletter, also profl. publs. Bd. dirs. Adult Literary Project, Urban League, New Brunswick, N.J., 1975-88, Commn. Black Cath. Ministry, Methen Diocese, 1988-90. Recipient Community Svc. and Achievement award Martin Luther King Jr. Ctr., 1988, N.J. State Parent's Assn., 1993. Mem. AAUW, NEA, ASCD, St. Martin dePorres Soc. (founder, pres. 1985—).Fla. A&M Alumni Assn. Home: 24 Phillips Rd Somerset NJ 08873-2032 Office: Piscataway High Sch 100 Behmer Rd/Hoes Ln Piscataway NJ 08854

FREEMAN, YVONNE JOUBERT, social worker; b. Dickinson, N.D., Sept. 26, 1940; d. Earl Francis and Esther Wilhelmina (Johnson) Joubert; m. Joe Mac Freeman, 1961 (div. 1963); children: Kristal Marie, Michael Earl, John Eric. BS in Secondary Edn., Carroll Coll., Helena, Mont., 1972; MSW, Ariz. State U., 1976. Social worker pub. welfare Lewis & Clark County, Helena, 1972-74; adult protective svcs. worker Ariz. State DES, Coolidge, 1976-77; emergency rm. social worker Maricopa County Hosp., Phoenix, 1977-79, social worker supr. psychol. emergency rm., 1979-81; social worker emergency rm. Maricopa Med. Ctr., Phoenix, 1981-86; social worker trauma ctr. Highland Gen. Hosp., Oakland, Calif., 1986-87; dir. social svcs. Good Shepherd Villa Nursing Home, Mesa, Ariz., 1987-93, Wickenburg (Ariz.) Cmty. Hosp. and Nursing Home, 1993—. Democrat. Roman Catholic. Office: Wickenburg Cmty Hosp PO Box 1388 Wickenburg AZ 85358

FREEMAN-BARAKA, RHONDA NICHELLE, business executive; b. Tuskegee, Ala., Mar. 9, 1962; d. Riley and Annie Mae (Lampkin) Freeman; m. Tony Colvin-Baraka, Dec. 24, 1985. BA in English, Talladega (Ala.) Coll., 1983. Reporter The Daily Home Newspaper, Talladega, 1982-83; intern reporter The Nat. Leader Newspaper, Phila., 1983; reporter The Tuskegee News, 1984, assoc. editor, 1985-86; editor, assoc. pub. The Tuskegee (Ala.) News, 1986-89; v.p., creative dir. Kuumba & Assocs. (name changed to T&R Communications, pub. rels. and consulting co.), Auburn, Ala., 1989—. Pub., editorial and creative dir. TAFRIJA mag. Mem. Ala. Press. Assn., Ala. Press Assn. Journalism Found. (bd. dirs.). Office: T&R Communications PO Box 450952 Atlanta GA 31145-0952

FREESE, BARBARA T., nursing educator; b. Kansas City, Mo., Oct. 1, 1944; d. Ernest M. and Marjorie (McIntosh) Tapp; m. Hal Freese, Feb. 3, 1968; 1 child, Tiffany Jo. BSN, U. Mo., 1967; MSN, Clemson U., 1980; EdD, U. Ga., 1989. Nursing faculty Lander U., Greenwood, dean sch. nursing. Contbr. articles to profl. jours. Fellow Royal Coll. Nursing, Australia; mem. ANA, Nat. League for Nursing, Mensa, Sigma Theta Tau., Kappa Delta Pi.

FREESE, KATHERINE, physicist, educator; b. Freiburg, Germany, Feb. 8, 1957; came to U.S., 1957; d. Ernst and Elisabeth Gertrude Maria (Bautz) F.; m. Fred Chester Adams, June 27, 1987; 1 child, Douglas Quincy Adams. BA, Princeton U., 1977; MA, Columbia U., 1981; PhD, U. Chgo., 1984. Postdoctoral fellow Harvard/Smithsonian Ctr. for Astrophysics, Cambridge, Mass., 1984-85, Inst. for Theoretical Physics, Santa Barbara, Calif., 1985-87, U. Calif., Berkeley, 1987-88; asst. prof. physics MIT, Cambridge, 1988-91; assoc. prof. physics U. Mich., Ann Arbor, 1991—; gen. mem. Aspen Ctr. for Physics, 1991—. Contbr. articles to profl. jours. William Rainey Harper fellow U. Chgo, 1982; Sloan Found. fellow, 1989; Presdl. Young Investigator NSF, 1990, rsch. grantee, 1991, 94; Presdl. fellow U. Calif., 1987. Mem. Am. Phys. Soc., Assn. for Women in Sci. Democrat. Office: U Mich Dept Physics Ann Arbor MI 48109

FREESE, MELANIE LOUISE, librarian, professor; b. Mineola, N.Y., May 12, 1945; d. Walter Christian and Agnes Elizabeth (Jensen) F. BS in Elem. Edn., Hofstra U., 1967, MA in Elem. Edn., 1969; MLS, L.I. U., 1977. Cert. tchr., N.Y. Bibliographic searcher acquisitions dept. Adelphi U. Swirbul Libr., Garden City, N.Y., 1973-79, res. desk libr., 1979-83; catalog libr., assoc. prof. Hofstra U. Axinn Libr., Hempstead, N.Y., 1984—; ch. librarian St. Peters Evang. Luth. Ch., Baldwin, N.Y., 1977—. Founder libr. Salvation Army Wayside Home and Sch. for Girls, Valley Stream, N.Y., 1993. Mem. ALA, Nassau County Libr. Assn. (corr. sec. acad. and spl. librs. divsn. 1986-88, v.p., pres.-elect 1989-90, pres. 1991), Bus. and Profl. Women's Club (pres. Nassau County chpt. 1990-92, Woman of Yr. 1994). Republican. Office: Hofstra U Axinn Library 1000 Fulton Ave Hempstead NY 11550-1009

FREETO, SHARON MAY, career officer, minister; b. Laconia, N.H., June 7, 1948; d. Neale Alvah and Barbara May (Papps) F.; m. William Robert Irwin, May 7, 1978. AB, Syracuse (N.Y.) U., 1970; ThM, Boston U., 1974; MA, Ball State U., 1981. Nat. cert. counselor; ordained minister Methodist Ch. Pastor People's United Meth., Fremont, N.H., 1974-76; commd. capt. USAF, 1976, advanced through grades to lt. col., 1989; Protestant chaplain USAF, Keesler AFB, Miss., 1976-79, Hahn AFB, Germany, 1979-82, Barksdale AFB, La., 1982-84; sr. Protestant chaplain USAF, Kelly AFB, Tex., 1984-86, Kunsan AFB, Korea, 1986-87; br. chief USAF, Lackland AFB, Tex., 1987-90; sr. chaplain USAF, Columbus AFB, Miss., 1990-93; chief budget and logistics, air edn. and tng. command USAF, Randolph AFB, Tex., 1993—; com. mem. Divsn. of Chaplains, Nashville, 1982-84. Mem. Am. Counseling Assn. Democrat. Office: HQAETC/HC 550D Street E Ste 2 Randolph AFB TX 78250

FREIBERGER, CHRISTINE HOLMBERG, educator; b. Southhampton, N.Y., June 4, 1935; d.Frank and Mildred (Anderson) Holmberg.; m. Walter F. Freiberger; Oct. 6. 1956; children: Christopher, Andrew, Nils. BA, Brown U., Providence, 1956, MAT, 1959. Cert. biology instr. Biology instr. Roger Williams Coll., Providence; sub. instr. Hope High Sch., Providence. Adv. coun. Salvation Army, Providence, 1991—. Republican. Episcopalian. Home: 24 Alumni Ave Providence RI 02906-2310

FREIBERGER, LINDA LOUISE, elementary education educator; b. Louisville, Oct. 19, 1946; d. Willis Marcus and Mary Carrie (Blessinger) F. MS, Ind. U., 1975. Tchr. St. Marks Sch., Indpls., 1965-66, St. James Sch., Cin., 1966-67, St. Ambrose Sch., Seymour, Ind., 1967-70, Galena Sch., New Albany, Ind., 1973—; salesperson Mary Kay Cosmetics. Mem. Ind. Reading Assn., Alpha Delta Kappa. Democrat. Roman Catholic. Home: 1714 Genung Dr Apt 24 New Albany IN 47150 Office: Galena Sch 6697 Old Vincennes Rd Floyds Knobs IN 47119

FREIDBERG, JOANNA MOORE, nurse practitioner; b. Easton, Md., Nov. 10, 1960; d. John William II and Evelyn (Williams) Moore. Diploma, MacQueen Gibbs Willis Sch., Easton, Med., 1985; BSN, U. Md., 1989; MSN, U. South Fla., 1993. CNOR; BCLS; RN, Md. Staff nurse Meml. Hosp. Easton, 1985-87; staff nurse oper. room Peninsula Gen. Med. Ctr., Salisbury, Md., 1987-90, Univ. Med. Ctr., Jacsonville, Fla., 1990-91, Doctor's Hosp., Sarasota, Fla., 1991-93; dermatology nurse practitioner Bradenton (Fla.) Dermatology, 1994; primary care nurse practitioner South Fla. Substance Abuse, Pompano Beach, 1994—. Nominated for Community Project Award, U. Md. Mem. AORN (bd. dirs. Delamar chpt. 1986-88, program workshop chmn. 1988, pres. elect Lower Shore of Md. chpt. 1989-90, program chmn. 1989-90, del. to congress 1990), Am. Acad. Nurse Practitioner, Fla. Nurses Assn. Home: #215 2820 SW 22nd Ave Delray Beach FL 33445-7292

FREIDENBERGS, INGRID, psychologist; b. Latvia, Aug. 6, 1944; came to U.S, 1951; d. Olgerts and Marta (Purvins) F.; m. Jack Feder, June 21, 1980; 1 child, Paul. BA, CCNY, 1966, MS, 1970; MA, L.I. U., 1973, PhD, 1975; cert. in psychoanalysis, NYU, 1983. Lic. psychologist, N.Y. Sch. psychologist Bur. of Guidance N.Y.C. Bd. Edn., 1971-73; intern in clin. psychology Bellevue Psychiat. Hosp., N.Y.C., 1973-74; with Inst. Rehab. Medicine NYU, N.Y.C., 1974—, dir. psychology intern program Inst. Rehab. Medicine, 1983-85, dir. psychol. svcs. Cancer Rehab. Svc., 1979—; adj. asst. prof. dept. counselor edn. NYU, 1978-82, clin. instr. dept. psychiatry NYU Med. Ctr., 1981—; presenter in field. Contbr. numerous articles to profl. jours. Mem. med. adv. bd. Skin Cancer Found. NSF fellow Yeshiva U., 1966, L.I. U. fellow, 1971-72. Mem. Am. Psychol. Assn., N.Y. State Psychol. Assn., Psychoanalytic Soc. of NYU, Assn. for the Advancement of Psychology. Office: 29 W 9th St New York NY 10011-8942

FREILICH, JOAN SHERMAN, utilities executive; b. Albany, N.Y., Nov. 3, 1941; d. Julius and Bess (Bergner) Sherman; m. Sanford J. Freilich, Jan. 24, 1965. AB in French magna cum laude, Barnard Coll., 1963; MA in French, Columbia U., 1964, PhD in French, 1971, MBA in Fin., 1980. Instr. CCNY, Columbia U., N.Y.C., 1965-75; tchr. Walden Sch., N.Y.C., 1970-74; asst. to the dean Coll. New Rochelle, N.Y., 1974-75, dir. admissions, 1975-78; sr. acct. Consol. Edison Co. N.Y., N.Y.C., 1978-81, mgr. acctg. rsch., 1981-82; contr. power generation Consolidated Edison Co. N.Y., N.Y.C., 1982-86, gen. mgr. power generation, 1986-89, exec. asst. to pres., 1989, asst. v.p. corp. planning, 1989-90, v.p. corp. planning, 1990-92, v.p., contr., chief acctg. officer, 1992—. Author: Paul Claudel's "Le Soulier de satin": A Stylistic, Structuralist and Psychoanalytic Interpretation, 1973; assoc. editor Claudel Studies, 1973-78; contbr. articles to profl. jours. Publ. grantee Humanities Rsch. Coun. Can., 1972; Pres.'s fellow Columbia U., 1964, Henry Todd fellow, 1967; recipient scholarship N.Y. State Bd. Regents, 1959, Nat. Merit Found., 1959, Columbia U., 1965. Mem. Fin. Execs. Inst., YWCA Acad. of Women Achievers, Phi Beta Kappa, Beta Gamma Sigma. Office: Consolidated Edison Co NY 4 Irving Pl New York NY 10003-3502

FREILICHER, JANE, artist; b. N.Y.C., Nov. 29, 1924; d. Martin and Bertha (Niederhoffer); m. Joseph Hazan, Feb. 17, 1957; 1 dau., Elizabeth. A.B., Bklyn. Coll., 1947; postgrad., Hans Hoffman Sch. Fine Arts, 1947; M.A., Columbia U., 1948. vis. lectr., critic art schs., colls. One-woman shows include Tibor de Nagy, 1952-68, John Bernard Myers Gallery, 1971, Fischbach Gallery, 1975, 77, 79-80, 83, 85, 88, 90, 92, 95, Utah Mus. Fine Arts, 1979, Lafayette Coll., 1981, Kansas City Art Inst., 1983, David Heath Gallery, Atlanta, 1990; group exhbns. include Met. Mus. Art, 1979-80, Denver Art Mus., 1979, Pa. Acad., 1981, Am. Acad. and Inst. of Arts and Letters, 1981, 84-85, Bklyn. Mus. 1984, Yale U., 1986, Tibor de Nagy Gallery, 1992, Whitney Mus., 1995; represented in permanent collections Met. Mus. Art, Hirschorn Mus., Bklyn. Mus., N.Y. U., Rose Art Mus., Whitney Mus., others; travelling retrospective in Currier Gallery Art, Parrish Mus., Contemporary Arts Mus., McNay Mus., 1986-87; illustrator Turandot and Other Poems, 1953, Paris Review, 1965. Recipient Eloise Spaeth award Guild Hall Mus., East Hampton, N.Y., 1991; AAUW fellow, 1974; Nat. Endowment Arts grantee, 1976. Mem. NAD (academician, Saltus Gold medal 1987), Am. Acad. and Inst. Arts and Letters. *

FREIMAN, LELA KAY, educator; b. Canton, Miss., Oct. 2, 1939; d. Lyle K. and Mae Susan (Billman) Linch; m. James F. Freiman, Sept. 5, 1965 (div. Feb. 1975); 1 child, Jennifer Leigh. Student, Northwestern State Coll., Natchitoches, La., 1957-59; BA, U. Iowa, 1962; MEd, U. Ariz., 1977. Tchr. speech, English and drama Sturgeon Bay (Wis.) High Sch., 1962-65; spl. edn. tchr. Naylor Jr. High Sch., Tucson, 1975-83; tchr. drama Sahuaro High Sch., Tucson, 1983—; summer camp dir. Sahuaro coun. Girl Scouts U.S.A., Tucson, 1977-87; mem. adv. coun. drama dept. U. Ariz., Tucson; participant Nat. faculty for Humanities, Santa Fe, Tucson, 1988-89. Fromer leader, trainer, camp dir. Girl Scouts U.S.A., Sturgein Bay, Wisconsin Rapids, Waukesha, Wis., Ariz., rep. Nat. Leadership Conf., Washington, 1983, bd. dirs. Sahuaro coun., 1992—; first aid com., instr. AFA, CPR ARC, Tucson, instr. CPR Am. Heart Assn.; Sunday sch. tchr., supt., mem. coun. Luth. Chrs., Wisconsin Rapids, Waikesha, now Tuscon; v.p. bd. dirs. S.W. Actors Studio, Tucson, 1987-92; adult mem. Ariz. State Thespian Bd. Recipient Thanks Badge, Sahuaro coun. Girl Scouts U.S.A., 1976, 88, Cross and Crown award Luth. Scouters So. Ariz., 1983, Mainstream Tchr. of Yr. award Assn. for Retarded Citizens So. Ariz., 1989. Mem. NEA, Am. Alliance for Theatre and Edn., Internat. Thespian Soc. of Ednl. Theatre Assn., Ariz. Theatre Educators Assn. (state sec. 1989-90, state treas. 1990-91, com. to draft curriculum guidelines for Ariz. Ho. of Reps., Theatre Educator of Yr. 1994-95), Ariz. Edn. Assn., Tucson Edn. Assn. Home: 7517 E Beach Dr Tucson AZ 85715-3649 Office: Sahuaro High Sch 545 N Camino Seco Tucson AZ 85710-3098

FRENCH, AMY JEAN, nurse; b. Pitts., June 16, 1961; d. Jerome Silverstein and Jean (Dunlop) Shields; m. Marc French, June 13, 1987. BN, Weidner U., 1989; postgrad., Our Lady of Lourdes Hosp., Camden, N.J. RN, Pa., N.J.; CCRN. Staff nurse surg. unit Presbyn. Hosp., Pitts., 1981-84; staff nurse coronary care unit Allegheny Gen. Hosp., Pitts., 1984-87; staff nurse SICU Lakenau Hosp., Phila., 1987-89, Deborah Heart & Lung Ctr., Brownshills, N.J., 1989—. Mem. Am. Assn. Critical Care Nurses, Am. Assn. Nurse Anesthetists. Presbyterian. Home: 319 Vincent Ct Tuckerton NJ 08087

FRENCH, BECKY RUSSELL, lawyer, educator; b. Charleston, Mo., Dec. 4, 1953; d. William C. and Billie (Summers) Russell; m. Robert R. French, Mar. 18, 1971 (div. 1978); m. William Dennis Harazin, Mar. 13, 1981. BSBA, Southeastern Mo. State U., 1976; JD, So. Ill. U., 1978; grad. Govt. Exec. Inst., U. N.C., 1982. Bar: Ill. 1979, N.C. 1982. Instr. Sch. Fin., So. Ill. U., 1978; legal asst. Sato & Tsuda, Tokyo, summer 1978; assoc. Kaufman & Litwin, Chgo., 1979; hearing officer State of N.C., Raleigh, 1979-80, dir. office adminstrv. hearings, 1980-84; adj. bus. law instr. N.C. State U., Raleigh, 1983—, contracts, patents officer, 1984-85, dir. Office of Tech. Adminstrn., 1985—, instr., 1982—, gen. counsel, 1986—; instr. So. Ill. U., 1977-78. Bd. dirs. Down-Town Housing Improvement Corp., Raleigh, 1983—. Mem. ABA, N.C. Bar Assn., Am. Judicature Soc., Ill. Bar Assn., Hist. Oakwood Assn., Rotary. Methodist.

FRENCH, CLAUDIA JEAN, psychologist, educator; b. Oakland, Calif., Sept. 24, 1959; d. Gilbert M. and Janet (Reimers) F.; m. James R. Allen, Apr. 28, 1990; children: Kai, Maya. BA in Psychology with honors, U. Iowa, 1981; MA in Clin. Psychology, U. Mont., 1988, PhD in Clin. Psychology, 1990. Lic. psychologist, S.D. Dir. Mineral County office, clinician Western Mont. Regional Mental Health Ctr., Superior, 1988-89; predoctoral intern in clin. psychology Richard H. Hutchings Psychiat. Ctr., Syracuse, N.Y., 1989-90; instr., adj. faculty dept. behavioral scis. U. Alaska, Fairbanks, 1991, counselor Ctr. for Health and Counseling, 1991; asst. prof. clin. tng. program psychology dept. U. S.D., Vermillion, 1991—, dir. Psychol. Svcs. Ctr., 1993—, clin. supr. hotline, 1991—, human rels. edn. com., 1993—. Contbr. articles to profl. jours. V.p. Clay County Child Protection Team, Vermillion, 1992—. Grantee U. S.D., 1991, 92, U. S.D.-Bush Found., 1993. Mem. APA (divsns. 12, 35, 45, and 48), Soc. for Indian Psychologists. Phi Beta Kappa. Office: U SD Dept Psychology 414 E Clark St Vermillion SD 57089

FRENCH, ELIZABETH IRENE, biology educator, violinist; b. Knoxville, Tenn., Sept. 20, 1938; d. Junius Butler and Irene Rankin (Johnston) F. MusB, U. Tenn., 1959, MS, 1962; PhD, U. Miss., 1973. Tchr. music Kingsport (Tenn.) Sympony Assn., 1962-64, Birmingham (Ala.) Schs., 1964-66; NASA trainee in biology U. Miss., Oxford, 1969-73; asst. prof. Mobile (Ala.) Coll. (name now U. Mobile), 1973-83, assoc. prof., 1983-94, prof., 1994—; orch. contractor Am. Fedn. Musicians, 1983—; 1st violin Kingsport Symphony Orch., 1962-64, Birmingham Symphony Orch., 1964-66, Knoxville Symphony Orch., 1965-68, Memphis Symphony Orch., 1970-73, Mobile Opera-Port City Symphony, 1974—. Violin recitalist Ala. Artists Series, 1978-81. Named Career Woman of Yr., Gayfer's, Inc., 1985. Mem. Assn. Southeastern Biologists, Human Anatomy and Physiology Soc. (nat. com. to construct standardized test on anatomy and physiology), Wilderness Soc., Ala. Acad. Scis., Ala. Ornithol. Soc., Mobile Bay Audubon Soc., Am. Fedn. Musicians, Ala. Fedn. Music Clubs (chmn. composition contest 1986—, historian 1991—), Schumann Music Club (pres. 1977-79, 85-87, 94—). Republican. Episcopalian. Home: 36 Ridgeview Dr Chickasaw AL 36611-1317 Office: U Mobile PO Box 13220 Mobile AL 36663-0220

FRENCH, GAYLE ANNE, accountant; b. Buffalo, June 24, 1952; d. Irving Henry and Ann Marie Virginia (Schifferli) Hackford; m. Roger Kenneth French, June 12, 1971 (div.); children: Shawn Roger, Kristian Roger. AA, Edison C.C., Ft. Myers, Fla., 1989; BS, U. South Fla., 1992, also postgrad. CPA, Fla. Bookkeeper Lehigh Bldg. Supply, Lehigh Acres, Fla., 1982-93; acct. Lee County Electric Coop. Inc., North Ft. Myers, Fla., 1993—. Vol. VITA, Ft. Myers, 1993, S.W. Regional C. of C., Ft. Myers, 1994. Mem. Inst. Mgmt. Accts., MBA Assn., Toastmasters (chpt. pres. 1994—), Beta Gamma Sigma. Home: 2112 Truman Ave Alva FL 33920 Office: Lee County Electric Coop Inc Bayline Dr North Fort Myers FL 33918

FRENCH, GEORGINE LOUISE, guidance counselor; b. Lancaster, Pa., May 15, 1934; d. Richard Franklin and Elizabeth Georgine (Driesbach) Beacham; BA, Calif. State U., San Bernardino, 1967; MS, No. Ill. U., 1973; DD, Am. Ministerial Assn., 1978; m. Barrie J. French, Feb. 4, 1956; children: Joel B., John D., James D., Jeffrey D. Ordained minister Am. Ministerial Assn., 1979; cert. counselor NCC bd.. pers. counselor Sages Dept. Store, San Bernardino, 1965-66; asst. bookkeeper Bank Calif., San Bernardino, 1964-65; tchr. Livermore (Calif.) Sch. Dist., 1968-69; guidance counselor Bur. Indian Affairs, Tuba City, Ariz., 1974-80, Sherman Indian High Sch., Riverside, Calif., 1980-82, Ft. Douglas Edn. Ctr., U.S. Army, Salt. Lake City, 1982-86; guidance counselor L.A. Air Force Sta., USAF, 1986-87, edn. svcs. officer, Comiso AFB, Italy, 1987-88; guidance counselor L.A. Air Force Base, 1989-93; extension tchr. Navajo Community Coll., Yavapai Jr. Coll.; personnel counselor USNR, 1976-86. Served with USAF, 1954-56. Cert. guidance counselor, secondary tchr. Mem. Am. Counselor Assn. (cert. counselor), Am. Assn. Retired Persons. Office: LA AFB SNC/DPUE 325 Challenger Way El Segundo CA 90245-4677

FRENCH, GERALDINE MARILYN, social worker, administrator, psychotherapist; b. L.A., Feb. 18, 1958; d. William and Geraldine (Zuccaro) F.; m. Joseph Peter Robitaille, Sept. 25, 1993. BS with distinction, U. Conn., 1979; MSW, NYU, 1984. Lic. ind. clin. social worker, Mass. Social work intern Bellevue Hosp. Ctr., N.Y.C., 1982-83, Yale U. Child Study Ctr., New Haven, 1983-84; crisis therapist Westfield (Mass.) Area Mental Health Clinic, 1984-85; therapist Child and Family Svcs. N.W., Torrington, Conn., 1984-85; diagnostic intake coord. Newington (Conn.) Children's Hosp., 1985-88, sr. social worker, 1988-89; clin. supr. The Children's Study Home, Springfield, Mass., 1989-90, dir. clin. svcs., 1990-94; adminstr. dept. psychiatry Baystate Med. Ctr., Springfield, 1994—; pvt. practice Springfield, 1991—; cons. mem. Westfield (Mass.) Area Coun. for Children, 1984-85; peer reviewer Coun. Accreditation of Svcs. for Children and Families, N.Y.C., 1992—. Asst. treas. Jr. League, Springfield, 1991—. Mem. NASW (bd. dirs. Conn. state 1987-89). Home: 1427 S Branch Pky Springfield MA 01129-2110 Office: Baystate Med Ctr Dept Psychiatry High St Springfield MA 01199

FRENCH, KATHLEEN PATRICIA, educational evaluator, consultant; b. Elizabeth, N.J., July 31, 1951; d. Raymond Patrick and Dorothy Ann (Gerber) F. BA, Kean Coll. N.J., 1974; MS in Edn., Fordham U., 1978. Cert. learning disabilities tchr.-cons., supr., spl. edn. tchr., elem. sch. tchr., N.J. Tchr. spl. edn. Elizabeth Sch. Dist., 1974-87; with pub. affairs dept. Merck and Co., Inc., Rahway, N.J., 1987-89; tchr. spl. edn. Woodbridge (N.J.) Twp. Sch. Dist., 1989-92; intervention strategist Phillipsburg (N.J.) Sch. Dist., 1992-93; adj. prof. Kean Coll. N.J., Union, 1992-94; learning cons. on child study team Union Twp. Sch. Dist., N.J., 1993—; alumni vol. to undergrad. admissions office Fordham U., N.Y.C., 1990—; adviser Union County Narcotics Bd., Elizabeth, 1992—. Mem. AAUW, NEA, N.J. Edn. Assn., Assn. Learning Cons., Coun. Exceptional Children (v.p. divsn. learning disabilities 1992—), N.J. Head Injury Assn., Kappa Delta Pi. Home: Apt 8 183 Gibson Blvd Clark NJ 07066-1455 Office: Union High Sch Child Study Team N 3d St Union NJ 07083-5085

FRENCH, LINDA JEAN, lawyer; b. Newark, N.Y., Nov. 12, 1947; d. Allyn B. and Willa E. (Cronk) Wrench; m. William J. French, Aug. 27, 1966; children: Mark W., David A. BA summa cum laude, William Jewell Coll., 1969; JD with distinction, U. Mo., 1978. Bar: Mo. 1978, U.S. Dist. Ct. (we. and ea. dists.) Mo. 1978, U.S. Ct. Appeals (8th and 10th cirs.) 1978, U.S. Ct. Appeals (D.C. cir.) 1979. Assoc. Blackwell Sanders Matheny Weary & Lombardi, Kansas City, Mo., 1978-82, ptnr., 1983-84; gen. counsel, sec. Payless Cashways Inc., Kansas City, 1984-86, v.p., gen. counsel/sec., 1986-91, sr. v.p., gen. counsel, sec., 1991—; lectr. U. Mo. Bus. Sch., Kansas City, 1991. Pres. Town and Country Homes Assn., Shawnee Mission, Kans., 1987, v.p., 1985-86; chmn. commn. adult and student recruitment William Jewell Coll., Liberty, Mo., 1984, chmn. commn. on comms., 1991, 92-93, mem. alumni bd. govs., 1987-93, v.p., 1991-93, exec. com., 1987-88, 91-93; bd. dirs. Legal Aid Western Mo., 1989-94, treas., 1991-93, exec. com., fin. com., audit com., 1992-93; bd. dirs. Greater Kansas City Jr. Achievement, 1985-86, Kansas City Tomorrow Leadership Program, 1988-89, alumni bd., 1991-92, alumni assn.; bd. dirs. ARC-Greater Kansas City chpt., 1992—, fin. com. 1992—, exec. com., 1993—, vice chair, 1994—; bd. dirs. Diastole, 1993—; bd. dirs. Trinity Luth. Hosp. Found., 1994—. Named one of Outstanding Young Women in Am., 1974, one of Top 100 Women in Corp. Am. Bus. Month, 1989, one of Top Women Execs. in Kansas City, 1992; recipient Citation of Achievement award William Jewell Coll., 1988. Mem. ABA (com. on labor and employment law, com. on bus. law), Mo. Bar Assn., Kansas City Met. Bar Assn. (vice chmn. then chmn. corp. house counsel com. 1986-88, lectr. continuing legal edn. program), Kansas City Assn. Women Lawyers, Am. Corp. Counsel Assn. (v.p. 1992-93), Am. Soc. Corp. Secs., Lawyers Assn. of Kansas City (bd. dirs. 1990—, sec. 1991—, pub. rels. com. chair 1990-91, program com. chair 1991-92, chair long range planning com. 1992-93, pres. elect 1993, pres. 1994), U. Mo. Kansas City Alumni Assn. William Jewell Alumni Assn., Kansas City Club. Presbyterian. Office: Payless Cashways Inc PO Box 419466 2300 Main St Kansas City MO 64108-2415

FRENCH, MARGO ANN, financial planner; b. Morehead City, N.C., Jan. 9, 1948; d. Robert Arthur and Dolores (Holtman) F.; m. Edwin A. Vogt, May 29, 1971 (div. Sept. 1975). Student, St. Petersburg Jr. Coll., Clearwater, Fla., 1975; BA, U. South Fla., 1984; postgrad., U. Tampa, 1985-87, Nat. Endowment for Fin. Edn., Denver, 1989—. Cert. fin. planner; registered respiratory therapist. Rsch. technician Merrell Nat. Labs., Cin., 1966-73; respiratory therapist Tampa (Fla.) Gen. Hosp., 1975-86; fin. planner IDS/Am. Express, Tampa, 1986-89; pvt. practice Riverview, Fla., 1989—; corp. dir. of respiratory svcs. The Mediplex Group, Wellesley, Mass., 1993—; adj. clin. instr. St. Petersburg Jr. Coll., 1978-79, Erwin Tech. Ctr., 1989-91. Mem. Phi Theta Kappa.

FRENCH, MARILYN, author, critic; b. N.Y.C., Nov. 21, 1929; d. E.C. and Isabel (Hazz) Edwards; m. Robert M. French, Jr., June 4, 1950 (div. 1967); children: Jamie, Robert. B.A., Hofstra Coll., 1951, M.A., 1964; Ph.D., Harvard U., 1972. Secretarial, clerical worker, 1946-53; lectr. Hofstra Coll., 1964-68; asst. prof. Holy Cross Coll., Worcester, Mass., 1972-76; Mellon fellow Harvard U., 1976-77; writer, lectr., 1967—. Author: (criticism) The Book as World: James Joyce's Ulysses, 1976, Shakespeare's Division of Experience, 1981; (novels) The Women's Room, 1977, The Bleeding Heart, 1981, Her Mother's Daughter, 1987, Our Father: A Novel, 1994; (non-fiction) Beyond Power: On Women, Men and Morals, 1985, The War Against Women, 1992; introductions to Edith Wharton's Summer and The House of Mirth, 1981. Mem. MLA, James Joyce Soc., Virginia Woolf Soc., Soc. for Values in Higher Edn. Office: care Summit Books 1230 Ave Of The Americas New York NY 10020-1513*

FRENCH, STEPHANIE TAYLOR, arts administrator; b. Newark; d. William Taylor and Connie V. French; B.A., Wellesley Coll., 1972; M.B.A., Harvard U., 1978; m. Amory Houghton, III, Sept. 8, 1979; 1 dau., Christina French Houghton. Traffic mgr. Radio Sta. KFRC, 1973-74; free-lance on-air performer, producer San Francisco and Oakland cable TV stas., 1973-76; dir. European Gallery, San Francisco, 1974-75; acct. exec. Young & Rubican, N.Y.C., 1978-79; acct. supr. Rives Smith Baldwin & Carlberg, Houston, 1980-81; mgr. cultural affairs and spl. programs Philip Morris Cos. Inc., N.Y.C., 1981-86, dir. cultural and contbns. programs, 1986-90, v.p. corp. contbn. ans cultural affairs bds., 1990—. Bd. dirs. The Joffrey Ballet, Photographers and Friends United Against AIDS, Lar Lubovitch Dance, Art Table, Am. Fedn. of Arts, Am. Council on Arts, Parsons Dance Co., Dance Theatre Workshop; co-chmn. producers council Bklyn. Acad. Music, Dance Theatre Workshop; co-chmn. Assocs. of Babies Hosp., Columbia Presbyn. Med. Ctr. Clubs: Harvard Bus. Sch., Wellesley. Home: 161 E 90th St Apt 2C New York NY 10128-2353 Office: Philip Morris Cos Inc 120 Park Ave New York NY 10017-5523

FRENKIEL, ANNAMAE MARY, multi-media specialist; b. Manchester, Conn., Dec. 28, 1941; d. Thomas Ewart and Ethel Mildred (Madden) Rollason; m. Richard Henry Frenkiel, Dec. 28, 1963; children: Scott Thomas, Kathleen Ann. BA, Tufts U., 1963; MLS, Rutgers U., 1991. Tchr. Bd. Edn., East Brunswick, N.J., 1963-66, Freehold, N.J., 1982-87; multi-media specialist Bd. Edn., North Brunswick, N.J., 1991—. Vice-chmn. Bd. Health, Manalapan, N.J., 1994, chmn. 1991-93; vice-chmn. Brookdale Coll. Search Com., Lincroft, N.J., 1987—. Mem. Ednl. Media Assn., AAUW (v.p. Freehold, N.J. chpt. 1992—), Beta Phi Mu. Republican. Office: North Brunswick High Sch Rt 130 South North Brunswick NJ 08902

FRESCH, MARIE BETH, court reporting company executive; b. Norwalk, Ohio, Jan. 16, 1957; d. Ralph Roy and Vonda Mae (Brunkhorst) Spiegel; m. James R. Fresch, Aug. 5, 1978; 1 child, Alexandra Jane. AS in Bus., Tiffin U., 1977; cert. in ct. reporting, Acad. Ct. Reporting, 1979. Registered profl. reporter, Ohio. Ofcl. reporter Seneca County Common Pleas Ct., Tiffin, Ohio, 1979-80; owner, operator Marie B. Fresch & Assocs., Norwalk, 1980—. Recipient Cert. of Merit, Nat. Ct. Reporters Assn., 1990. Mem. Nat. Ct. Reporters Assn., Ohio Ct. Reporters Assn. (student promotions and pub. rels. coms. 1986—), NOW (sec. Port Clinton chpt. 1984-86, treas. 1986-87, 91), Am. Legion Aux., Kappa Delta Kappa. Democrat. Methodist. Lodge: Order of Eastern Star (esther 1979-81). Home and Office: 47 Warren Dr Norwalk OH 44857-2447

FRETER, LISA, non-profit association administrator; b. Washington, Aug. 25, 1951; d. Theodore Henry and Elizabeth Crawford (Stout) Freter; m. David O'Shea Dawkins, Dec. 20, 1975; 1 child, Meghan Elizabeth. Student, Towson State Coll., 1969-70, U. de las Americas, Cholula, Puebla, Mex., 1972-73; BSBA, U. Phoenix, 1992. Owner B&B Liquors, Denver, 1979-81; dir. pubs. Gt. Western Assn. Mgmt., Denver, 1985-88; adminstrv. asst., conf. coord. Employment and Tng. divsn. Arapahoe County, Aurora, Colo., 1988-93; dir. confs. 3AI Affiliated Advt. Agys. Internat. Inc., Aurora, Colo., 1994—. Author: (poems) The San Miguel Writer, 1970, Xalli, 1971; exec. producer Law Enforcement Torch Run for Spl. Olympics Video, 1986, videotaped pub. svc. announcements, 1987; producer, dir. (video) Private Industry Council, 1989; contbr. articles to mags.; editor various newsletters. Exec. dir. Colleagues Police for Edn., Support, Denver, 1983-85; liaison Colo. Assn. Chiefs of Police, 1983-85; coord. Law Enforcement Torch Run for Spl. Olympics, 1986-88. Mem. Freedoms Found. Valley Forge (v.p. pub. rels. 1988-92, 93-94, pres. 1992-93), Colo. Gang Investigators Assn. (exec. dir. 1989-90, v.p. membership1993-94, newsletter editor 1994-95), Colo. Soc. Assn. Execs., Profl. Conv. Mgmt. Assn. Home: 1200 S Oneida St # 10-204W Denver CO 80224

FREUDENRICH, FRANCES MARIANNE, biology educator; b. Sewickley, Pa., Feb. 3, 1937; d. Nicholas and Stephanie (Narbesky) Feduska; m. Robert David Freudenrich, Oct. 22, 1960; children: David Robert, Connie Lee, Douglas Martin, Robert Scott. BS in Edn. and Biol. Scis., Indiana U. of Pa., 1959. Biology instr. Penn Hills (Pa.) Regional High Sch., 1959-61; mktg. rep. Feinman/Gottlieb, Inc., Valley Stream, N.Y., 1982—; substitute tchr. Glen Rock and Ridgewood (N.J.) Pub. Schs., 1981-90; Census Bur. supr. spl. places U.S. Dept. Commerce, Bergenfield, N.J., 1990; tchr. biology Queen of Peach High Sch., North Arlington, N.J., 1990—; peer rev. com. Earth Edn. Partnership Program, N.J., Costa Rica, 1994; mentor Gifted and Talented Soc., Glen Rock, 1987-89. Mem. Glen Rock Arboretum Com., 1990-91; mem., sec. Y.E.S. Youth Employment, Glen Rock, 1987-89; poll watcher Rep. Club, Glen Rock, 1985-89; co-chair Unified Scholarship Pops Concert, Glen Rock, 1988-89. Recipient Citizenship medal Am. Legion, Ambridge, Pa., 1948; Elks scholar, 1955, Suburbanites of Sewickley scholar, 1955; NSF grantee, 1960, Woodrow Wilson grantee, 1991, 92, 93, 94. Mem. N.J. Sci. Tchrs. Assn., N.J. Audubon Soc., Assn. N.J. Edn. for Environment, Cath. Lay Tchrs. Assn., Alliance for Biotech., Kappa Delta Pi, Omega Gamma Alpha, Sigma Tau. Home: 575 Rock Rd Glen Rock NJ 07452-1928 Office: Queen of Peace High Sch 191 Rutherford Pl North Arlington NJ 07031-6091

FREUND, CAROL MARGUERITE, clinical psychologist; b. Queens, N.Y., Feb. 15, 1957; d. Charles George and Doris Marguerite (Egeland) F. BA summa cum laude, SUNY, Geneseo, 1978; PhD, U. Nebr., 1985. Lic. expert parachutist. Clin. psychologist, asst. unit dir. South Beach Psychiat. Ctr., Staten Island, N.Y., 1985-87; clin. psychologist Forsyth-Stokes Mental Health Ctr., Winston-Salem, N.C., 1987-88; pvt. practice Atlanta, 1988-91; dir. adult psychiat. svcs. Cobb Hosp. and Med. Ctr., Austell, Ga., 1989-91. NIMH fellow, 1979-83; recipient Gold Wings award 12 Hour Free Fall award, 24 Hour Free Fall award, World Record feminine largest freefall formation Fedn. Aeronautique Internat. Mem. APA, Assn. Women in Psychology, U S. Parachute Assn. (24 Hour Free Fall award). Office: Ste 101 1700 Hospital South Dr Austell GA 30001

FREUND, EMMA FRANCES, medical technologist; b. Washington; d. Walter R. and Mabel W. (Loveland) Ervin; m. Frederic Reinert Freund, Mar. 4, 1953; children: Frances, Daphne, Fern, Frederic. BS, Wilson Tchrs. Coll., Washington, 1944; MS in Biology, Catholic U., Washington, 1953; MEd in Adult Edn., Va. Commonwealth U., 1988; cert. in mgmt. devel. Va. Commonwealth U., 1975, MEd, 1988; student SUNY, New Paltz, 1977, J. Sargeant Reynolds Community Coll., 1978. Cert. Nat. Cert. Agy. for Clin. Lab. Pers. Tchr. math. and sci. D.C. Sch. System, Washington, 1944-45; technician in parasitology lab., zool. div., U.S. Dept. Agr., Beltsville, Md., 1945-48; histologic technician dept. pathology Georgetown U. Med. Sch., Washington, 1948-49; clin. lab. technician Kent and Queen Anne's County Gen. Hosp., Chestertown, Md., 1949-51; histotechnologist surg. pathology dept. Med. Coll. Va. Hosp., Richmond, 1951—, supr. histology lab., 1970-88, mgr., supr. 1988—; mem. exam. coun. Nat. Cert. Agy. Med. Lab. Pers. Asst. cub scout den leader Robert E. Lee coun. Boy Scouts Am., 1967-68, den leader, 1968-70. Co-author: (mini-course) Instrumentation in Cytology and Histology, 1985. Mem. AAAS, NAFE, AAUW, Am. Soc. Med. Technology (rep. to sci. assembly histology sect. 1977-78, chmn. histology sect. 1983-85, 89-94), Va. Soc. Med. Technology, Richmond Soc. Med. Technologists (corr. sec. 1977-78, dir. 1981-82, pres. 1984-85), Va. State Soc. Histotechnology (pres. 1994—), Nat. Certification Agy. (clin. lab. specialist in histotech., clin. lab. supr., clin. lab. dir.), N.Y. Acad. Scis., Am. Assn. Clin. Chemistry (assoc.), Am. Soc. Clin. Pathologists (cert. histology technician), Nat. Geog. Soc., Va. Govtl. Employees Assn., Nat. Soc. Histotech. (by-laws com. 1981—; C.E.U. com. 1981—, program com. regional meeting 1984, 85, chmn. regional meeting 1987, program chmn. regional mtg. 1992), Am. Mus. Natural History, Smithsonian Instn., Am. Mgmt. Assn., Clin. Lab. Mgmt. Assn., Nat. Soc. Historic Preservation, Sigma Xi, Phi Beta Rho, Kappa Delta Pi, Phi Lambda Theta, Omicron Sigma. Home: 1315 Asbury Rd Richmond VA 23229-5305 Office: Med Coll VA Hosp Dept Surg Pathology PO Box 980240 Richmond VA 23298-0240

FREY, JUDITH LYNN, elementary education educator; b. Ashland, Ohio, Sept. 10, 1956; d. Lloyd Baeder and Norma Claire (Hostettler) Wygant; m. Daniel K. Frey, Nov. 21, 1981; children: Jennifer Lynn, Lynnette Danielle. BS in Edn., Otterbein Coll., 1978. Elem. remedial reading tchr. Norwalk (Ohio) City Schs., 1978-79; elem. remedial reading tchr. Bucyrus (Ohio) City Schs., 1979—, kindergarten tchr., 1981-87. Co-dir. Holy Trinity Cath. Ch. Pre-Sch. Religion, Bucyrus, 1987-92; co-leader Girl Scout Daisy Troop, Bucyrus, 1991-92. Mem. Internat. Reading Assn. (Crawford County chpt., bldg. rep. 1991-94). Home: 9940 County Highway 134 Nevada OH 44849-9763 Office: Lincoln Elem Sch 170 Plymouth St Bucyrus OH 44820-1627

FREY, MARGO WALTHER, career counselor, columnist; b. Watertown, Wis., July 1, 1941; d. Lester John and Anabel Marie (Bergin) Walther; m. James Severin Frey, June 29, 1963; children: Michelle Marie Frey Loberg, David James. BA in French, Cardinal Stritch Coll., 1963; MS in Counseling and Guidence, U. Wis., Milw., 1971; EdD in Adult Edn., Nova U., 1985. Nat. bd. cert. career counselor. Acad. counselor biology dept. Ind. U., Bloomington, 1975-76; dir. career planning and placement Cardinal Stritch Coll., Milw., 1977-89; pres. Career Devel. Svcs., Inc., Milw., 1989—; weekly columnist Milw. Sentinel, 1994—. Mem. Bloomington (Ind.) women's commn. com. on employment assessment Displaced Homemakers Task Force, 1975. Named to Practitioner's Hall of Fame, Nova U., 1985. Mem. ASTD (bd. dirs. 1992), Wis. Career Planning and Placement Assn. (bd. dirs. 1987), Wis. Assn. Adult and Continuing Edn. (bd. dirs. 1983-85), Milw. Coun. Adult Learning, Human Resource Mgmt. Assn., Tempo.

FREY, VIRGINIA ANN, minister; b. Urbana, Ohio, Mar. 22, 1942; d. Levi Jasper Dooley and Martha Jane (Blake) Braley; children: Debi Lynn, Charles Jeffrey, Tamara Janell. Student in nursing, Meth. Hosp., Indpls., 1960-61; MA in Christian Psychology, Kingsway Christian Coll. and Theol. Sem., Des Moines, 1984, ThD, 1989. Ordained to ministry, 1981; cert. behavior counselor. Evangelist, 1970-85, with Praise and Worship Indpls. Christian Fellowship, 1973-80; pastor His Tabernacle, Indpls., 1981-85; founder, pastor His Tabernacle, Princeton, Ind., 1986—; tour host mission trips to Israel, Mex., Haiti, Cen. Am., 1974-90; founder, dir. New Life Homes Drug Rehab. Ctr., Indpls., 1971-81; pastor, counselor Ind. Women's Prison, 1981-84; tchr. bus. adminstrn. Ind. Bus. Coll., 1994. Host, producer TV program Knowing Him, 1979-82; rec. Throne of Grace, 1981. Mem. Concerned Women Am., Women Aglow (regional sec., state pres. 1972-81), End-Time Handmaidens, Nat. Right to Life. Republican. Mem. Ind. Charismatic Ch. Home: 119 E Spruce St Princeton IN 47670-1773 Office: HIS Tabernacle 411 N Hart St Princeton IN 47670-1538

FREYD, JENNIFER JOY, psychology educator; b. Providence, Oct. 16, 1957; d. Peter John and Pamela (Parker) F.; m. John Q. Johnson, June 9, 1984; children: Theodore, Philip, Alexandra. BA in Anthropology magna cum laude, U. Pa., 1979; PhD in Psychology, Stanford U., 1983. Asst. prof. psychology Cornell U., 1983-87, mem. faculty coun. of reps., 1986-87; assoc. prof. psychology U. Oreg., Eugene, 1987-92, prof., 1992—; mem. dean's adv. com. U. Oreg., 1990-91, 92-93, mem. exec. com. Ctr. for the Study of Women in Soc., 1991-93, mem. child care com., 1987-89, 90-91; fellow Ctr. for Advanced Study in the Behavioral Scis., 1989-90; elected mem. faculty coun. of reps. Cornell U., 1986-87; mem. dean's adv. com. U. Oreg., 1990—, exec. com. Ctr. for Rsch. Study of Women in Soc., 1991-92, Inst. of Cognitive and Decision Scis., 1991—. Mem. editorial bd. Jour. Exptl. Psychology: Learning, Memory, and Cognition; guest reviewer Am. Jour. Psychology, Am. Psychologist, others; contbr. articles to profl. jours. Recipient Graduate fellowship NSF, 1979-82, Univ. fellowship Stanford U., 1982-83, Presdl. Young Investigator award NSF, 1985-90, IBM Faculty Devel. award, 1985-87, fellowship Ctr. for Advanced Study in the Behavioral Scis., 1989-90, John Simon Meml. fellowship Guggenheim Found., 1989-90, Rsch. Scientist Devel. award NIMH, 1989-94; other rsch. funding. Fellow AAAS, APA, Am. Psychol. Soc.; mem. Psychonomic Soc., Sigma Xi. Office: U Oreg 1227 Dept Psychology Eugene OR 97403-1227

FREYD, PAMELA PARKER, educational and research organization executive; b. Providence, July 7, 1938. BA in English, NYU, 1961; MS, U. Pa., 1968, PhD in Edn., 1981. Instr. U. Pa. Grad. Sch. Edn., 1982-85, coord., lectr. computer edn., 1986-89; rsch. assoc. Inst. Rsch. in Cognitive Sci. U. Pa., 1990—; dir. PENNlincs, U. Pa., Phila., 1989—; exec. dir. False Memory Syndrome Found., Phila., 1992—; cons. Learning Mag., 1985—; exch. tchr., Sydney, 1971, Shiraz, Iran, 1968; specialist Reading Lab., 1973; tchr. Albert M. Greenfield Sch., Phila., 1972-86; adj. prof. Chestnut Hill Coll., 1990; presenter various confs. and workshops. Contbr. articles to profl. jours. Grantee Phila. Bd. Edn., 1984, Phila. Alliance for Teaching Humanities, 1986-87, 88, ARCO, 1988-90, Phila. Renaissance in Sci. and Math., 1989, Rohm and Haas, 1989, Merck Sharp and Dohme, 1990, Literacy Rsch. Ctr., 1986, 88, Grad. Sch. Edn. Rsch., 1989, Nat. Coun. Tchrs. English Rsch. Found., 1989, Cognitive Sci. Inst., U. Pa., 1990, NSF, 1990, 92. Office: FMS Found 3401 Market St Ste 130 Philadelphia PA 19104 also: PENNlincs 3401 Walnut St Ste 400C Philadelphia PA 19104

FREYERMUTH, VIRGINIA KAREN, secondary art educator. BFA cum laude, Boston U., 1973, MFA, 1975; edn. cert., Suffolk U., 1975. Cert. art tchr., Mass. Grad. asst. Boston (Mass.) U., 1973-75; art tchr. Quincy (Mass.) Pub. Schs., 1975-76, Plymouth (Mass.) Pub. Schs., 1976-78, 83-85; painting tchr. Brockton (Mass.) Fuller Mus. Art, 1978-79; art coord. grades K-12 Duxbury (Mass.) Pub. Schs., 1985—; art reviewer Patriot Ledger, Quincy, 1975-85; dir. Freyermuth Fine Arts Ctr., Plymouth, 1990-94, Va. Freyermuth Resources, 1994—; mem. adv. coun. Mass. Field Ctr. Tchg. & Learning; tchr. in electronic residence Mass. Corp. Ednl. Telecom., Cambridge; instr. art Massasoit C.C., Brockton, 1991-92; dir. Helen Bumpus Gallery, Inc., Duxbury, 1992-94. Columnist Learning for Life, 1994. Mem. commn. on common core of learning Mass. Dept. Edn., 1993-94; mem. Mus. Fine Arts, Boston. Named Mass. Tchr. of Yr., Mass. Dept. Edn., 1994. Mem. NEA, Mass. Edn. Assn., Nat. Art Edn. Assn., Nat. State Tchrs. Yr., Mass. Alliance for Arts Edn. (bd. dirs. 1994—, Outstanding Art Educator in Mass. 1989), Kappa Delta Pi. Office: PO Box 6132 North Plymouth MA 02362

FREYTAG, SHARON NELSON, lawyer; b. Larned, Kans., May 11, 1943; d. John Seldon and Ruth Marie (Herbel) Nelson; children: Kurt David, Hillary Lee. BS with highest distinction, U. Kans., Lawrence, 1965; MA, U. Mich., 1966; JD cum laude, So. Meth. U., 1981. Bar: Tex. 1981, U.S. Dist. Ct. (no. dist.) Tex. 1981, U.S. Ct. Appeals (5th cir.) 1982. Tchr. English, Gaithersburg (Md.) High Sch., 1966-70; instr. English, Eastfield Coll., 1974-78; law clk. U.S. Dist. Ct. for No. Dist. Tex., 1981-82, U.S. Ct. Appeals 5th Cir., 1982; ptnr. litigation and appellate sect. Haynes and Boone, Dallas, 1983—, vis. prof. law Southern Meth. U., 1985-86; faculty Appellate Adv. program NITA. Editor-in-chief Southwestern Law Jour., 1980-81; contbr. articles to law jours. Woodrow Wilson fellow. Recipient John Marshall Constl. Law award. Mem. ABA (mem. litigation sect., chair subcom. on local rules), Fed. Bar Assn. (co-chmn. appellate practice and advocacy sect. 1990-91), Tex. Bar Assn., Dallas Bar Assn. (mem. appellate coun.), Dallas Mus. Art, Dallas Shakespeare Soc., Dallas Inn of Ct., Barristers, Order of Coif, Phi Delta Phi, Phi Beta Kappa. Lutheran. Office: Haynes & Boone 3100 NationsBank Plz Dallas TX 75202

FRIAUF, KATHERINE ELIZABETH, metal company executive; b. Balt., Oct. 13, 1956; d. John Beecher Friauf and Elizabeth Withers (Wilson) Struever. Student, Columbia Coll., Chgo., 1979-81. Cert. sound engr. Owner, operator Midwest Emery Freight System, Chgo., 1978-80; driver BCB Dispatch, Inc., Rochester, N.Y., 1980-88; dispatcher, systems analyst BCB Dispatch, Inc., LeRoy, N.Y., 1988-89; corp. controller Rochester Plating Works, Inc., 1988—; pres., co-owner Rochester Vibratory Inc., 1991—; dir. Rochester Plating Works, Inc., 1988—. Mem. NAFE, Rochester Women's Network (patron mem.). Presbyterian. Office: Rochester Vibratory Inc 4 Cairn St Rochester NY 14611-2416

FRICKER, BRENDA, actress; b. Dublin, Ireland, Feb. 17, 1945. Theatre work includes appearances with the Royal Shakespeare Co., London, Royal Court Theatre, London, Nat. Theatre, London; other appearances include (films) Quatermas Conclusion, Bloody Kids, Our Exploits at West Poley, My Left Foot, 1989 (Acad. award for Best Supporting Actress 1989), The Field, 1990, Home Alone 2: Lost in New York, 1992, Utz, 1993, So I Married an Axe Murderer, 1993, Angels in the Outfield, 1994, A Man of No Importance, 1994, Deadly Advice, 1994; (TV series) Casualty; (TV Movies) Licking Hitler, The House of Bernarda Alba, The Ballroom Romance; (miniseries) Brides of Christ, The Sound and the Silence. Office: United Talent Agy Inc 9560 Wilshire Blvd 5th Flr Beverly Hills CA 90212*

FRIDLEY, SAUNDRA LYNN, internal audit executive; b. Columbus, Ohio, June 14, 1948; d. Jerry Dean and Esther Eliza (Bluhm) F. BS, Franklin U., 1976; MBA, Golden Gate U., 1980. Accounts receivable supr. Internat. Harvester, Columbus, Ohio, San Leandro, Calif., 1972-80; sr. internal auditor Western Union, San Francisco, 1980; internal auditor II, County of Santa Clara, San Jose, Calif., 1980-82; sr. internal auditor Tymshare, Inc., Cupertino, Calif., 1982-84, div. contr., 1984; internal audit mgr. VWR Scientific, Brisbane, Calif., 1984-88, audit dir., 1988-89; internal audit mgr. Pacific IBM Employees Fed. Credit Union, San Jose, 1989-90, Western Staff Svcs., Inc., Walnut Creek, Calif., 1990—; internal audit mgr., 1990-92; dir. quality assurance, 1992—; owner Dress Fore the 9's, Brentwood, Calif., 1994—; pres., founder Bay Area chpt. Cert. Fraud Examiners, 1990. Mem. NAFE, Friends of the Vineyards. Mem. Internal Auditors Speakers Bur., Cert. Fraud Examiners (founder, pres. Bay area chpt.), Inst. Internal Auditors (pres., founder Tri-Valley chpt.), Internal Auditor's Internat. Seminar Com., Internal Auditor's Internat. Conf. Com. Avocations: woodworking, gardening, golfing. Home: 19 Windmill Ct Brentwood CA 94513 Office: Western Staff Svcs 301 Lennon Ln Walnut Creek CA 94598-2418 also: Dress Fore The 9's 613 First St Ste 9 Brentwood CA 94513

FRIDLEY DE BIGIT, JANE LAURA, marketing professional; b. St. Paul, Nov. 11, 1958; d. Russell William and Metta Gladwish (Holtkamp) Fridley; m. Carlos Alberto Bigit, Apr. 16, 1988; 1 child, Karina. BA with honors, Macalester Coll., 1980; M of Internat. Mgmt., Am. Grad. Sch. Internat. Mgmt., 1983. Spl. dep. Ft. McCoy Cuban Refugee Processing Ctr., U.S. Marshal Svc., Sparta, Wis., 1980; rsch. asst. Minn. Hist. Soc., St. Paul, 1981-82; internat. sales mgr. Carter-Day Internat., Inc., Mpls. and Charleston, S.C., 1984-88, 92-93; internat. sales rep. Carter-Day Internat., Inc., San Salvador, El Salvador, 1992. Mem. Am. Mgmt. Assn. Home and Office: Cons 740 Amber Dr Saint Paul MN 55126-4101

FRIED, ELAINE JUNE, business executive; b. L.A., Oct. 19, 1943; grad. Pasadena (Calif.) High Sch., 1963; various coll. courses; m. Howard I. Fried, Aug. 7, 1966; children: Donna Marie, Randall Jay. Agt., office mgr. Howard I. Fried Agy., Alhambra, Calif., 1975—; v.p. Sea Hill, Inc., Pasadena, Calif., 1973—. Publicity chmn., unit telephone chmn. San Gabriel Valley unit; past chmn. recipient certificate appreciation, 1987, Am. Diabetes Assn.; past publicity chmn. San Gabriel Valley region Women's Am. Orgn. for Rehab. Tng. (ORT); chmn. spl. events publicity, Temple Beth Torah Sisterhood, Alhambra, membership chmn., 1991-92, v.p. membership, 1991-93; former mem. bd. dirs., pub. relations com., pers. com. Vis. Nurses Assn., Pasadena and San Gabriel Valley, Recipient Vol. award So. Calif. affiliate Am. Diabetes Assn., 1974-77; chmn. outside Sisterhood publicity Congregation Shaarei Torah, 1993—, public rels. chair, 1993—. Co-recipient Ner Tamid award Temple Beth Torah. Contbr. articles to profl. jours. Clubs: B'nai B'rith Women, Hadassah, Congregation Shaarei Torah Sisterhood. Speaker on psycho-social aspects of diabetes, insurance and the diabetic, ins. medicine. Home: 404 N Hidalgo Ave Alhambra CA 91801-2640

FRIED, ELEANOR REINGOLD, psychologist, educator; b. Quantico, Va., Jan. 4, 1943; d. Morris and Eleanor (Wilson) R.; divorced, 1984; children: Joshua Mark, Noah Seth, Adam Lawrence. BS cum laude, Boston U., 1964; MS in Clin. Sch. Psychology, CUNY, 1971; postgrad. Fordham U., 1971-73; MA in Clin. Psychology, The Fielding Inst., 1980, PhD in Clin. Psychology, 1981. Lic. psychologist, N.J. APsychology intern Roosevelt Hosp., N.Y.C., 1971-73; cons. Inwood House, N.Y.C., 1971-83; staff therapist Univ. Consultation Center Mental Hygiene, Bronx, N.Y., 1974-79, clin. instr., 1976-80; sr. clin. psychologist moderate security unit North Princeton Developmental Ctr., 1983—; cons. Early Childhood Learning Center, Paramus, N.J., 1978-80, Found. for Religion and Mental Health, Briarcliff Manor, N.Y., 1979-82, Inwood House, N.Y.C., 1981-83, prin. clin. psychologist Ewing Residential Ctr., Trenton, N.J., 1987-88, Ind. Child Study Teams, East Orange, N.J; pvt. practice, Princeton, N.J. Mem. Am. Psychol. Assn. (assoc.), N.J. Psychol. Assn., Am. Bd. Forensic Examiners, Kappa Tau Alpha. Office: 601 Ewing St C-20 Princeton NJ 08540

FRIED, RONNEE, marketing research company executive; b. N.Y.C., Dec. 16, 1947; d. Phillip Frank Fried and Gloria Edith (Pfeffer) Sandow. B.A., George Washington U., 1969. Field dir. AHF Mktg. Research, N.Y.C., 1969-73; project dir. Decisions Ctr. Inc., N.Y.C., 1973-76, Ogilvy & Mather Advt., N.Y.C., 1977; assoc. group mgr. Data Devel. Corp., N.Y.C., 1977-81; ptnr., exec. v.p. Brown Koff & Fried Inc., N.Y.C., 1981—. bd. dirs. Chain Lightning Theatre Inc. Mem. speakers bur. Greater N.Y. Conf. Soviet Jewry, 1979—. Mem. Am. Mktg. Assn. (Effie Awards Judging co-chmn. 1982, membership com. 1981, Recognition award 1982, career counselor), Advt. Women N.Y. Jewish. Avocation: competitive ballroom dancing. Home: 454 Broome St New York NY 10013 Office: Brown Koff & Fried Inc 112 Madison Ave New York NY 10016

FRIEDAN, BETTY, author, feminist leader; b. Peoria, Ill., Feb. 4, 1921; d. Harry and Miriam (Horwitz) Goldstein; m. Carl Friedan, June 1947 (div. May 1969); children: Daniel, Jonathan, Emily. AB summa cum laude, Smith Coll., 1942, LHD (hon.), 1975; LHD (hon.), SUNY, Stony Brook, 1985, Cooper Union, 1987. Research fellow U. Calif. at Berkeley, 1943; lectr. feminism univs., women's groups, bus. and profl. groups in U.S. and Europe; founder NOW, 1st pres., 1966-70, chairwoman adv. com., 1970-72, mem. bd. dirs. legal def. and edn. fund; organizer Nat. Women's Polit. Caucas, 1971, Internat. Feminist Congress, 1973, First Women's Bank, 1973, Econ. Think Tank for Women, 1974; v.p. Nat. Assn. Repeal Abortion Laws, 1970-73; Disting. vis. prof. sch. journalism and studies of women and men in soc., U. So. Calif., 1987; vis. prof. sociology Temple U., 1972, Queens Coll., 1975; vis. lectr. Calhoun Coll., fellow Yale U., 1974; lectr. New Sch. Social Research, N.Y.C., 1971; sr. research assoc. Ctr. Social Scis., Columbia U., N.Y.C., 1979-81; bd. dirs. NOW Legal Defense and Education fund; co-chmn. Nat. Comms. Women's Equality; del. White Ho. Conf. on Family, 1980; del. UN Decade for Women Confs. in Mexico City, Copenhagen, Nairobi; mem. LORAN Commn. Harvard Community Health Plan; vis. scholar U. S. Fla., Sarasota, 1985; Disting. vis. prof. Sch. Journalism and Social Work Sch. U. So. Calif. Author: The Feminine Mystique, 1963, It Changed My Life: Writings on the Women's Movement, 1976, The Second Stage, 1981, new edit., 1986, The Fountain of Age, 1993; mem. editorial bd. Present Tense mag.; contbg. editor McCall's mag, 1971-74; contbr. Atlantic Monthly; contbr. articles to New York Times, Cosmopolitan, Saturday Rev., Family Circle, Good Housekeeping, and others; papers being collected by Schlesinger Libr. Harvard U. Mem. exec. com. Am. Jewish Congress, co-chair nat. commn. women's equality, 1984-85; mem. nat. bd. Girl Scouts USA, 1976-82; mem. N.Y. County Democratic Com. Recipient Humanist of Yr. award, 1975, Eleanor Roosevelt Leadership award, 1989; Inst. Politics fellow Kennedy Sch. Govt., Harvard U., 1982, rsch. fellow Ctr. Population Studies, Harvard U., 1982-83, Chubb fellow Yale U., 1985, Andrus Ctr. Gerontology fellow U. So. Calif., 1986. Mem. AFTRA, PEN, Author's Guild, Women's Ink, Women's Forum, Mag. Writers, Am. Soc. Journalists and Authors (1st recipient Mort Weisinger award for outstanding mag. journalism 1979, Author of Yr. 1982), Assn. Humanistic Psychology, Am. Sociology Assn., Gerontol. Soc. Am., Coffee House, Phi Beta Kappa. Address: 1 Lincoln Plz Apt 40K New York NY 10023-7141

FRIEDEL, HELEN BRANGENBERG, counselor, therapist; b. Kampsville, Ill., May 16, 1938; d. Carl Morris and Martha Marie (Zipprich) Brangenberg; m. John Laverne Friedel; children: Vincent Joseph, John Francis. BS, So. Ill. U., 1969, MS, 1973. Lic. profl. counselor, Mo. Educator Archdiocese of St. Louis, 1956-87; counselor Diocese of Belleville, Waterloo, Ill., 1988-89, Christian Bros. H.S., St. Louis, 1989—; pvt. practice Florissant, Mo., 1987—. Mem. parents adv. bd. St. Louis Prep. Sem., Florissant, 1973-79; youth moderator Sacred Heart Parish, Florissant, 1967-71, lector and eucharistic min. Mem. ACA, Mo. Counseling Assn. (bd. dirs. 1986-88, 90-93, sec. 1990, pres. 1992, legis. chair 1992-93, Kitty Cole Human Rights award 1993), St. Louis Counseling Assn., Mo. Multicultural Counselors, Mid Rivers Counseling Assn. (pres. 1986), Am. Sch. Counselors Assn., Mo. Sch. Counselors Assn., St. Louis Learning Disabilities Assn. (bd. dirs. 1994), Kappa Delta Pi. Roman Catholic. Home: 425 St Marie Florissant MO 63031 Office: Christian Bros Prep HS 6501 Clayton Rd Saint Louis MO 63117

FRIEDELL, ELLEN SILBERSTEIN, lawyer; b. N.Y.C., Nov. 5, 1948; d. Joseph Aaron and Sheila (Wright) Silberstein; m. Steven F. Friedell, July 2, 1978; children: Deborah, David. BA, Brandeis U., 1970; JD, Am. U., 1973. Bar: D.C. 1974, Pa., 1979, U.S. Dist. Ct., U.S. Supreme Ct. Sr. trial atty. CAB, Washington, 1973-76, U.S. Nuclear Regulatory Commn., Bethesda, Md., 1976-78; asst. gen. counsel Rohm & Haas Co., Phila., 1978—. Mem. ABA, Phila. Bar Assn. Democrat. Jewish. Home: 233 Monroe St Philadelphia PA 19147-3329 Office: Rohm & Haas Co Independence Mall W Philadelphia PA 19105

FRIEDEN, JANE HELLER, art educator; b. Norfolk, Va., Aug. 25, 1926; d. Samuel Ries and Saida (Seligman) Heller; m. Joseph Lee Frieden, Dec. 23, 1950 (dec. 1990); children: Nancy Frieden Crowe, Robert M., Andrew M. AA, Coll. of William and Mary, Norfolk, Va., 1945; BA, Coll. of William and Mary, Williamsburg, Va., 1947; MA, Columbia U., 1950. Lic. pvt. pilot. Tchr. art City of Norfolk Pub. Schs., 1947-48, Hudson Day Sch., New Rochelle, N.Y., 1948-49, Mt. Vernon (N.Y.) Pub. Schs., 1949-50, City of Norfolk Pub. Schs., 1950-51; prof. art Coll. William and Mary Extension, Williamsburg, 1957-72, U. Va. Extension, Norfolk, 1972-78, Community Colls. State of Va., Chesapeake and Hampton, 1978-82, St. Leo Coll., Norfolk, 1982—; travel agt., 1977-89. Author: (dictionary) A is For Art, 1978-82; artist water color paintings and ink drawings at several shows. Vol. Chrysler Mus. Art, Norfolk, 1991—, Va. Symphony Aux., 1992—, Norfolk Little Theatre Box Office, 1991—; tchr. drawing Ghent Venture, 1993. Mem. Internat. Orgn. Women Pilots (treas. 1978-85), Tidewater Artists Assn. (bd. dirs. 1975-80, 91—, treas. membership coun.), Tidewater Orchid Soc., Am. Orchid Soc., Norfolk Soc. Arts, United Daus. Confederacy, Hermitage Soc., Norfolk Ex Libris Soc. Coll. William & Mary (mem. steering com. 1993—), Va. Belles (reunion com. 1993—). Republican. Jewish. Home: 221 Oxford St Norfolk VA 23505-4354

FRIEDENBERG, KAREN ROSEN, real estate executive; b. Savannah, Ga., May 3, 1949; d. Emanuel F. and Thelma Z. (Reed) Rosen; 1 child, Jodi. BS in Mass Communications, Emerson Coll., 1971; student U. N.C., summer 1968, Harvard U., summer 1967, U. Ga., 1967-69. Exec. trainee Jordan Marsh, Boston, 1974-76; broadcast dir. Rich's, Atlanta, 1976-78; mktg. dir. Northlake Mall, Atlanta, 1978-80, Lenox Square, Atlanta, 1980-82; retail leasing assoc. Trammell Crow Co., Atlanta, 1982-85, Kern & Co., Atlanta, 1985-86, Retail Properties Group, 1986-89; mng. dir. Retail Realty Advisors, 1989-92; owner Comml. Real Estate Svcs., 1992—. with Re Max Achievers. Bd. dirs. Atlanta chpt. Nat. Coun. Jewish Women; patron High Mus. Art; mem. Temple Sinai. Mem. Internat. Coun. Shopping Ctrs., Atlanta Bd. Realtors, Comml. Real Estate Women, Midtown Bus. Assn., Buckhead Bus. Assn. (grad. Leadership Devel. 1990), Hadassah. Republican. Jewish. Avocations: aerobics, bicycling, hiking, rafting. Home: 4 Pendleton Pl Atlanta GA 30342

FRIEDHEIM, JAN V., education administrator; b. Corpus Christi, Tex., Oct. 20, 1935; d. Roy Lee Conyers and Bertha Victoria (Ostrom) Hamm; m. John R. Eisenhour, Nov. 22, 1962 (div. 1983); m. Stephen B. Friedheim, Sept. 1, 1984; children: Neenah, Stephen II, Robert. BS, U. Tex., 1957; Do of Ednl. Adminstrn. (hon.), The Constantinian U., Malta, 1994. Chmn. bd. Exec. Secretarial Sch., Dallas, 1960—; vice chmn. Tex. Vocat. Adv. Bd., Austin, 1979-86; mem. adv. com. Dept. Edn., Washington, 1980-84; commr. So. Assn. Colls. and Schs. Commn. on Occupationsl Edn. Instns., 1994—; mem. adv. com. State Postsecondary Rev. Entity, 1994; bd. dirs. Tex. Assn. Pvt. Schs. Mem. Assn. Ind. Colls. and Schs. (chmn. bd. dirs. 1980-81, commn. 1978-79, commr. 1974-79, Disting. Mem. 1974, 81, Mem. of Yr. 1979), Southwestern Assn. Pvt. Schs. (pres. 1982), Metroplex Assn. Pvt. Schs. (pres. 1989-90, 92-93), So. Assn. Colls. and Schs. (trustee 1981-85, commn. on occupational edn. instns. 1994—), Tex. Assn. Pvt. Schs. (bd. dirs. 1992—). Home: 6450 Patrick Dr Dallas TX 75214-2444

FRIEDLAND, BILLIE LOUISE, former human services administrator; b. Los Alamos, New Mex., Jan. 6, 1944; d. William Jerald and Harriet Virginia (Short) Van Buskirk; m. David Friedland. BS in Edn., Calif. U. of Pa., 1972, MS in Psychology, 1986; postgrad., W.Va. U., 1992—. Sales mgr., buyer Friedland's Ladies Ready-To-Wear, Monessen, Pa., 1969-72; tchr. Belle Vernon (Pa.) Area Schs., 1973-74; head social scis. dept. Yeshiva Achei Tmimim, Pitts., 1974-75; caseworker, outreach to children and their families Fayette County Mental Health and Mental Retardation Clinic, Uniontown, Pa., 1975; ctr. supr. Fayette County Mental Health and Mental Retardation Clinic, Outreach to Children & Their Families Project, Uniontown, 1976; case mgr., family support svcs. coord. Diverified Human Services Inc., Monessen, 1978-89; supr. community living arrangements Diversified Human Svcs., Inc., Monessen, Penn., 1989-92; grad. asst. W.Va. U. Affil. Ctr. for Devel. Disabilities, 1992-93; founded first Infant/Toddler Day Care Project, Fayette County, 1976-78. Mem. NAACP, Am. Assn. Mental Retardation, Coun. for Exceptional Children, Nat. Assn. Dual Diagnoses, Conf. on Black Basic Edn. Office: WVU Sch Human Resources Dept Spl Edn Morgantown WV 26506

FRIEDLANDER, PATRICIA ANN, marketing executive; b. Chgo., May 9, 1944; d. James Farrell and Therese Mary (Pfeiler) Crotty; m. Daniel B. Friedlander, July 3, 1971 (div. Apr. 1978); children: Michael Derek, David Colin; m. Denis R. Johnson, Feb. 24, 1994. BA, Cardinal Stritch Coll., 1966; MA, U. Wis., Milw., 1968; postgrad., U. Chgo., 1968-69, U. London, 1968—. Instr. U. Wis., Milw., 1966-68, Chgo. State U., 1968-71, Argo Community High Sch., Summit, Ill., 1971-73, Park Dist., Park Forest South, Ill., 1973-77; counselor Will County Mental Health Clinic, Park Forest South, 1977-78; sales rep. Prentice-Hall, Inc., Englewood Cliffs, N.J., 1978-84; nat. sales mgr. Dow Jones-Irwin, Homewood, Ill., 1984-87; dir. mktg. Nat. Textbook Co., Lincolnwood, Ill., 1987-88; mgr. mktg. Scott Foresman & Co., Glenview, Ill., 1988-90; corp. advt. dir. Giltspur, Inc., Itasca, Ill., 1990—; dir. Printer's Row Bookfair, Chgo., 1985; pub. cons.; speaker and author in trade show and pub. field. Den mother Cub Scouts Am., Park Forest South, 1981-84. Mem. Bus. Mktg. Assn., Am. Book Travelers, Midwest Book Travelers (pres. 1983-87), Chgo. Book Clinic, Chgo. Women in Pub., Am. Mgmt. Assn., Am. Mktg. Assn., Health Care Conv. & Exhibitors Assn., Internat. Exhibitors Assn. (del.), Exhibit Designers and Prodrs. Assn. (del.), Computer Exhibit Mgrs. Assn. Home: 2320 W Farwell Ave Chicago IL 60645-4735 Office: Giltspur Inc 500 Park Blvd Itasca IL 60143-3121

FRIEDMAN, BEVERLY RAE, food service director; b. Prineville, Oreg., Sept. 19, 1930; d. Clarence Erratt and Lenore Gwendolyn (Dunton) Kern; m. Jay Maynard, Nov. 18, 1967; children: David, Gail, Mark. BS, Oreg. State U., 1953; Dietetics degree, Mass. Gen. Hosp., Boston, 1954. Pediatric and rsch. dietitian Mass. Gen. Hosp., Boston, 1954-55; therapeutic dietitian Oreg. Med. Sch. Hosp., Portland, 1955-59, Children's Hosp., San Francisco, 1959-60, Kaiser Hosp., San Francisco, 1960-62; dietitian Jewish Home for Aged, Daly City, Calif., 1962-65; dietitian, therapeutic and adminstrn. French Hosp., San Francisco, 1965-68, Harkness Hosp., San Francisco, 1968-70; food svc. dir. Sequoia Union H.S. Dist., Redwood City, Calif., 1983—. Chmn. neighborhood Heart Assn., San Mateo, Calif., 1982-83. Mem. Alpha Phi. Republican. Jewish. Home: 3150 Casa De Campo # 6 San Mateo CA 94403-2108

FRIEDMAN, CHARLAINE, medical/surgical nurse; b. Cumberland, Md., Aug. 21, 1954; d. Charles Walter and Beulah (Shuck) Hughes; m. George Friedman, Jan. 20, 1982; children: Melanie Barbara, Raymond Charles. AD, Allegheny Community Coll., Cumberland, 1974; BSN, U. Md., 1981, MS, 1984. Head nurse City Hosp., Martinsburg, W.Va.; staff nurse Winchester (Va.) Med. Ctr.; nursing instr. Shepherd Coll., Shepherdstown, W.Va. Mem. ANA, Sigma Theta Tau. Home: 2003 Applewood Dr Martinsburg WV 25401-8004

FRIEDMAN, DEBORAH LESLIE WHITE, educational administrator; b. Grand Rapids, Mich., July 5, 1950; d. Edward Charles and Luella Jane (Carr) White; children: Karen Elizabeth, David Edward. BS, Cen. Mich. U., 1972; MBA, U. Toledo, 1980; mgmt. cert., N.C. State U., 1988, postgrad., 1991—. Traffic mgr. WTOL-TV, Toledo, Ohio, 1972-74; catering cons. Gladieux Food Svcs., Toledo, 1974-75; mktg. rsch. analyst Owens-Ill., Toledo, 1978; instr. Sampson C.C., Clinton, N.C., 1980-81, instr. in bus. adminstrn., 1980-81, chmn. acctg., bus. adminstrn., real estate, 1981—, pres. faculty senate, 1983-84; faculty advisor Phi Beta Lambda, 1981-88; adj. trainer N.C. Dept. Community Colls., Raleigh, 1989—. Bd. dirs. Clinton (N.C.) Found. for Edn., 1984-89, appropriations chmn., 1984-88, sec. , 1988-89; com. mem. Clinton City Schs. Com. on Standards of Excellence, 1986-87; vol. Girl Scouts Am., Clinton, 1983, 85; mem. N.C. Community Coll. Leadership Program, 1990. Named Outstanding Young Educator, Clinton Jaycees, 1985; recipient Outstanding Svc. award Clinton Student Govt. Assn., 1982, Excellence in Tchg. award N.C. State Bd. C.C., 1989, Cert. of Appreciation, State of N.C. for Vol. Svcs., 1987, EXCEL finalist, 1991, 93-94. Mem. Am. Assn. Women in Community and Jr. Colls. (membership dir. 1988-89), N.C. Assn. Bus. Chmn. and Dept. Heads, Bus.-Industry Assocs., Am. Bus. Women Assn. (pres. 1983-84, Sampson County Woman of Yr. 1984), Beta Gamma Sigma, Phi Kappa Phi. Home: 106 Tomahawk Trail Clinton NC 28328-3052 Office: Sampson C C PO Box 318 Clinton NC 28328-0318

FRIEDMAN, DIAN DEBRA, elementary education educator; b. Balt., June 12, 1943; d. Bernard Maurice and Sondra Seletta (Dolgoff) Jacobs; m. Irving Joel Friedman, June 24, 1965; children: Benjamin Aaron, Joshua Jason. AA, Miami (Fla.)-Dade Jr. Coll., 1963; BS in Elem. Edn., Fla. State U., 1965. With contracts and grants Fla. State U., Tallahassee, 1965-66; substitute tchr. Chicopee (Mass.) Sch. Systems, 1965-66; elem. tchr. City of Springfield, Mass., 1966-76; real estate salesperson Gene Kelly Real Estate, Suffield, Conn., 1985-87; ednl. tutor Suffield (Conn.) Sch. System, 1987—; curriculum coun. Suffield Sch. System, 1986-90; tchr. Computer Tots; substitute tchr. Agawan (Mass.) Mid. Sch. Bd. dirs. Child and Family Svcs., Inc., Hartford, Conn., 1986—, fin. resources com., 1988—; bd. dirs. Child and Family Charities, Inc., Hartford; chairperson Suffield Aux. Child and Family Svcs., 1978-80, mem. 1973—; mem. Citizens for Suffield, 1990—, Friends of Suffield Libr., 1973—. Mem. Fla. State Alumni Club, Suffield Woman's Club. Democrat. Jewish. Home: 119 Marbern Dr Suffield CT 06078-1542

FRIEDMAN, FRANCES, public relations executive; b. N.Y.C., Apr. 8, 1928; d. Aaron and Bertha (Itzkowitz) Fallick; m. Clifford Jerome Friedman, June 17, 1950; children—Kenneth Lee, Jeffrey Bennett. B.B.A., CCNY, 1948. Dir. pub. relations Melia Internat., Madrid, N.Y.C., 1971-73; sr. v.p. Lobsenz-Stevens, N.Y.C., 1973-75; exec. v.p. Howard Rubenstein Assocs., N.Y.C., 1975-83; pres., prin. Frances Friedman Assocs., N.Y.C., 1983-84; pres., chmn. bd. dirs. GCI Group Inc., N.Y.C., 1984-91, pub. rels. and editorial cons., 1991-93; mng. dir. L.V. Power & Assoc., Inc., 1993—. Bd. dirs. ACRMD-Retarded Children, N.Y.C., 1983-85, City Coll. Fund, N.Y.C., 1970-79; mem. adv. bd. League for Parent Edn., N.Y.C., 1961-65; editor South Shore Democratic Newsletter, North Bellmore, N.Y., 1958-61, press sec. N.Y. State Assembly candidate, 1965, N.Y. State Congl. candidate, 1968; officer Manhasset Dem. Club, N.Y., 1965-69; mem. adv. com. N.Y.C. Council candidate, 1985. U. New Haven Bartels fellow, 1993. Mem. Pub. Relations Soc. Am., Women in Communications (Matrix award for pub. relations 1989), The Counselors Acad., Pride and Alarm, City Club N.Y. Democrat. Jewish. Home: 860 5th Ave New York NY 10021-5856

FRIEDMAN, FREDRICA SCHWAB, editor, publisher; b. N.Y.C., Aug. 29, 1939; d. Joseph H. and Ruth (Landis) Schwab; m. Stephen J. Friedman, June 25, 1961; children: Vanessa V., Alexander S. BA, Vassar Coll., 1961; MA, Columbia U., 1963. Assoc. articles editor Holiday Mag., N.Y.C., 1966-68; contbg. editor Travel & Leisure Mag., N.Y.C., 1969-70; editorial cons. Saturday Rev. Mag., N.Y.C., 1971-74; sr. editor Reader's Digest Press, N.Y.C., 1974-77; sr. staff editor Reader's Digest Condensed Books, N.Y.C., 1977-84; sr. editor Little, Brown & Co., N.Y.C., 1985-88, exec. editor, assoc. pub., v.p., 1988—. Recipient Matrix award Women in Comm., 1992. Mem. Women's Forum, Women's Media Group, The Peer Group, Leadership Circle of Woman's Campaign Fund. Home: 1185 Park Ave New York NY 10128 Office: Little Brown & Co 1271 Avenue Of The Americas New York NY 10020-1300

FRIEDMAN, HELEN RUTH, clinical and media psychologist; b. Rome, N.Y., Dec. 30, 1951; d. Henry and Cecilia (Osipowitz) F. BS in Psychology cum laude, St. Lawrence U., Canton, N.Y., 1973; MS, Memphis State U., 1976, PhD, 1980. Cert. psychologist, Mo. Clin. psychologist St. Louis State Hosp., 1980-84; child sexual abuse treatment team mem. Child Guidance Ctr. Washington U. Sch. Medicine, St. Louis, 1983-84; pvt. practice clin. psychology St. Louis, 1981—; asst. prof. dept. interdisciplinary studies Fontbonne Coll., St. Louis, 1984-87; cons. Sexual Trauma unit St. Anthony's Psychiat. Ctr., St. Louis, 1990-94; lectr. mental health issues. Alternating host PsychTalk Sta. KDHX-FM, St. Louis, 1990—. Mem. Children's Mental Health Svcs. Coun., 1980-84; bd. dirs. Mental Health Assn. St. Louis, 1987-90, mem. profl. adv. bd. Mem. APA, Mo. Psychol. Assn. (chair profl. standards rev. com. 1985-87, mem. ad hoc com. on impaired psychologists 1984-86), St. Louis Psychol. Assn. (sec. 1981-83, pres. 1984-85, media coord. 1988—), Internat. Soc. for Study of Dissociation, Phi Beta Kappa. Office: 7750 Clayton Rd Ste 210 Saint Louis MO 63117-1342

FRIEDMAN, IRENE STERN, office administrator; b. N.Y.C., Oct. 8, 1950; d. Jacob Kurt and Claire (Weiser) Stern; m. Ellis Franklin Friedman, May 19, 1973; children: Abigail Stern, Marnie Alexis, Alexander Curtis. BA, Hunter Coll., 1971. English lang. and math tchr. N.Y.C. Bd. of Edn., 1970-72; proofreader Textronic Systems, N.Y.C., 1971-72; prodn. mgr. The Slide House, N.Y.C., 1972-73; reception/ins. supr. Reading (Pa.) Orthopedic Assocs., 1982-85; office mgr. Ellis & Friedman M.D., Wyomissing, Pa., 1985—. Contbr. articles to Shalom newspaper, 1974-94. Vol. Easter Seals, Reading, 1972-75, Reading Hosp., 1972-82; mem. United Synagogue Youth Commns., 1989-91, Principal's Advisory Coun., Wyomissing, 1989-92, Ad Hoc Sch. Facilities, Wyomissing, 1990-92; bd. mem. Kesher Zion Synagogue, Reading, 1988-94, exec. bd. mem., 1989-91, chair Hebrew sch., 1989-91, chair membership, 1991-94, Leagram chair, bd. mem. Sisterhood, 1994—. Mem. Hadassah (life), Phi Beta Kappa. Home: 1 Cardinal Pl Wyomissing PA 19610 Office: 320 Abington Dr Wyomissing PA 19610

FRIEDMAN, JANET TERI, finance company executive; b. Houston, Aug. 21, 1957; d. Ben and Susanna Ruth (Stern) F. BS in Elem. Edn. magna cum laude, U. Houston, 1978. Cert. real estate broker, tchr., airline sales agt., Tex., fraud examiner; expert witness. Sales rep. Continental Airlines/Tex. Internat. Airlines, 1978-82; pvt. practice real estate broker, buyer's agt., renovator, 1982; sr. residential loan originator Richard Gill Co./Gill Savs. and Loan, 1983-84; prodn. mgr., secondary mktg. coordinator, mem. orgn. team Devel. Mortgage Group, Inc., 1984-85; pres., mortgage broker, real estate and fin. cons. Friedman Fin. Services, Inc., Houston, 1985-94; prin. J. Friedman Mortgage, 1994—; sales cons. Marshall Homes, 1978, Victoria Wood Condominiums, 1978; expert witness; mem. bus. devel. bd. Lockwood Nat. Bank, Houston, 1990. Author: Safecracking the Mortgage Secrets: The Complete Guide to Home Loans, 1987; (syndicated column) Dear Ms. Mortgage; contbr. to jours. Vol. Crisis Intervention of Houston; chmn. Houston Proud's Continuing Edn. and C.A.R.E. seminars. Mem. Greater Home Builders Assn. of Houston, Houston Assn. Profl. Mortgage Women, Am. Bus. Women, Phi Kappa Phi, Kappa Delta Phi. Mem. Tex. Assn. Realtors (edn. com.), Houston Bd. Realtors (subcom. chmn. Burning Issues seminars, edn. com., speakers bur.). Office: 6060 Richmond Ave # 190 Houston TX 77057

FRIEDMAN, LINDA A., lawyer; b. Cleve., Oct. 6, 1952; d. Thomas John and Elaine (Urban) Bunsey; m. Doug Friedman, Aug. 6, 1978; children: Jessica, Rachel. Student, Sorbonne U., Paris, 1971-72; AB, Kenyon Coll., 1973; JD, Vanderbilt U., 1976. Law clk. U.S. Dist. Ct. (no. dist.) Ala., Birmingham, 1976-77; ptnr. Bradley, Arant, Rose & White, Birmingham, 1977—; legal editor Channel 6 TV, Birmingham, 1993—. Co-author: Protecting Intellectual Property, 1988, Unfair Competition in Alabama, 1989; editor: (chpts. in books) State Trademark and Unfair Competition, 1986, State Antitrust Practice and Statutes, 1991. Fundraiser March of Dimes, Birmingham, 1990; co-chmn. bus. leaders divsn. Birmingham Jewish Fedn., Birmingham, 1992, 93; VIP Starathon, United Cerebral Palsy, Birmingham, 1993. Named one of Top 40 under 40, Birmingham Bus. Jour., 1992. Mem. Ala. Bar Assn. (chmn. antitrust 1986-90, bd. bar examiners 1988-89, other offices, Continuing Legal Edn. award 1990), Am. Law Inst., Bus. and Profl. Women (steering com. 1992-93), Kiwanis. Office: Bradley Arant Rose & White 1400 Park Place Tower 2001 Park Pl Birmingham AL 35203-2709*

FRIEDMAN, LINDA ELLEN, clinical social worker; b. Newark, N.J., Feb. 26, 1955; d. Isadore Zival and Lorraine Harriet (Dlugitch) F. BA, Trenton State Coll., 1977; MSW, Rutgers U., 1981. Lic. clin. social worker. Social worker II Divsn. Youth and Family Svcs., Newark, 1978-80, social worker III, 1980-83; dir. social svcs. Pembroke Pines (Fla.) Cluster/Intermediate Care Facility-Mentally Retarded, 1983-85; adj. instr., clin. social worker U. Miami, Fla., 1985-92; qualified mental retardation profl. Interdisciplinary Program Cons., Inc., Miami, 1992-93, project dir., ind. support coord., 1993—. Vol. Metuchen (N.J.) Hot Line, 1979-80; chairperson dist. XI Human Rights Advocacy Ctr. for Developmentally Disabled, Miami, 1984-89; active mem. Dade County Community Com. for Developmentally Handicapped, Miami, 1985-92; mem., chairperson subcom. Dade County Presch. Interagy. Coun., Miami, 1987-92; mem. steering com. family support svcs. Fla. Devel. Disabilities Planning Coun., 1990; mem. adv. com. procedural safeguards Dept. of Edn. State of Fla., 1990; mem. adv. com. on personnel tng. and competencies Fla. Interagy. Coord. Coun. for Infants and Toddlers, 1990-92. Mem. NASW (Fla. chpt. 1983—). Home: 10330 Laurel Ct Pembroke Pines FL 33026 Office: Interdisciplinary Program Cons Inc 111 NW 183d St Ste 518 Miami FL 33169

FRIEDMAN, MARIA ANDRE, public relations executive; b. Jackson, Mich., June 12, 1950; d. Robert Andre and Mary MacLean (Thompson) Hoving; m. Stanley N. Friedman, July 22, 1973; children: Alexandra, Adam. BA cum laude, U. Md., 1972, MA, 1979; DBA, Nova U., 1993. Writer, U.S. Bur. Mines, Washington, 1973-78; head writer Nat. Ctr. for Health Svc. Rsch. and Health Care Tech. Assessment, DHHS, Rockville, Md., 1978-85, chief publs. and info. br. Agy for Health Care Policy and Rsch., 1986-89; dir. office pub. affairs Health Care Financing Adminstrn., Washington, 1990—, acting assoc. adminstr. for comm., 1992-93, sr. rsch. advisor,Balt., 1994—. Mem. Nat. Assn. Govt. Communicators, Acad. of Mgmt. Home: 12535 Heurich Rd Silver Spring MD 20902-1441 Office: Health Care Fin Adminstrn Rm 2224 Oak Meadows Bldg 6325 Security Blvd Baltimore MD 21207

FRIEDMAN, MILDRED, designer, educator, curator; b. L.A., July 25, 1929; d. Nathaniel and Hortense (Weinsveig) Shenberg; m. Martin Friedman; children: Lise, Ceil, Zoe. BA, UCLA, 1951, MA, 1952; DFA (hon.), Mpls. Coll. Art, 1984; DFA, Hamlin U., 1987. Instr. design L.A. City Coll., 1952-54; archtl. designer Cerny Assocs., Mpls., 1957-69; design curator Walker Art Ctr., Mpls., 1970-90; freelance cons. N.Y.C., 1990—; architecture and design panel Nat. Endowment Arts, 1975-78, policy panel design arts, 1979-82, presdl. design awards jury, 1991; vis. com. sch. architecture and planning MIT, 1985-88, grad. sch. design Harvard U., 1994—; bd. dirs. Internat. Design Conf., Aspen, 1989-91, Chgo. Inst. Architecture and Urbanism, 1990-93, Nat. Inst. Archtl. Edn., 1993—; design jury Am. Acad. Rome, 1991; guest instr. UCLA, 1992; jury to select architect for Whitehall Ferry Terminal, N.Y.C., 1992; vis. instr. Harvard U., 1993; cons. Battery Park City Authority, N.Y.C.; guest curator Bklyn. Mus., Cooper-Hewitt Nat. Mus. Design, Smithsonian Instn., Can. Ctr. Architecture. Editor Design Quar., 1970-91, numerous catalogues. Recipient Outstanding Achievement award YWCA, 1984, Outstanding Svc. award U. Minn., 1991; fellow Intellectual Interchange program Japan Soc., 1982; grantee Nat. Endowment Arts, 1992-93. Mem. AIA (hon., nat. awards jury 1981, 87, bd. dirs. Minn. chpt. 1984-86, Inst. Honors 1994).

FRIEDMAN, PAMELA RUTH LESSING, art consultant, financial consultant; b. N.Y.C., Jan. 15, 1950; d. Fred William and Helen D. (Kahn) Lessing; m. Neil David Friedman, May 28, 1972; children: Elizabeth Lessing, Paul Lessing. BA, U. Rochester, 1972; MSLS, U. N.C., Chapel Hill, 1974. Dep. libr. Am. Soc. Internat. Law, Washington, 1974-76; with edn. dept. Nat. Air and Space Mus., Smithsonian Inst., Washington, 1976-84; ind. cons. fin. and art Boulder, Colo., 1984—; pub. C.S.B. Co., Boulder, 1989—; lectr. in fields, 1989—; cons. Denver Art Mus., 1989-91, Asian Art Coordinating Coun., Denver, 1990—. Author: (reference book) Chinese Snuff Bottles, 1990; editor: (reference book) Flight Service Directory, 1975. Rep. S.E.V.A.B., Smithsonian Instn., 1979-81, mem. exec. bd. docent coun. Nat. Air and Space Mus., 1977-81; mem. trustee coun. U. Rochester, N.Y., 1992—, mem. visiting com. coll. of arts, 1994—; bd. dirs., mem. exec. com. bd., treas. Colo. Music Festival, Boulder, 1983-89; mem. exec. bd. Women's Incentive Fund Colo. U., Boulder, 1988—; rep. Leadership Boulder, 1986-87; v.p. bd. dirs. Lessing Found., N.Y., 1988—; mem. exec. bd. Interfaith Coun., Boulder, 1987-90; life mem. RAF Mus., 1977—. Recipient Internat. Gold Test Pin award Swiss Skiing Fedn., St. Moritz, 1975. Mem. Internat. Chinese Snuff Bottle Soc., Army and Navy Club (Washington), Beach Point Club (Mamaroneck, N.Y.). Home and Office: 503 Kalmia Ave Boulder CO 80304-1733

FRIEDMAN, PAULINE POPLIN, civic worker, consultant; b. Scranton, Pa., Apr. 2, 1930; d. Harry and Lillian (Kushner) Poplin; m. Sidney Friedman, Aug. 3, 1952; children: Anne Friedman Glauber, Robert. BS, Pa. State U., 1952. Cons. AID, Washington, 1993—. Trustee Temple Israel, 1985-87, Jewish Community Ctr., 1992—; mem. coun. King's Coll., 1992—; pres. Home Health Svcs.-Vis. Nurse Assn., Kingston, Pa., 1987-88, Coun. Family Agys., Harrisburg, Pa., 1987-88, Family Svc. Wyoming Valley, Wilkes-Barre, 1988-90; v.p. bd. dirs. Pa. State U., Wilkes-Barre, 1994—; mem. president's coun. Wilkes U., 1991—, King's Coll.; v.p. United Way; bd. dirs. Ethics Inst. N.E. Pa., Dallas, 1994—; v.p. Interfaith Coun. Wyo. Valley; bd. alumni coun. Pa. State U.; mem. Jewish Cmty. Bd. Wyo. Valley. Recipient humanitarian award Interfaith Coun. Wyoming Valley, 1989, Phillip Mitchell Cmty. Svc. award Pa. State U., University Park, 1990, Woman of Yr. award Family Svc. Wyoming Valley, 1993. Home: 796 Milford Dr Kingston PA 18704

FRIEDMAN, POLLY, public relations executive, marketing professional; b. Orange, N.J., Nov. 9, 1932; d. Sidney and Doris (Simons) Adler; m. Eugene M. Friedman, Jan. 14, 1954; children: Robert A. Friedman, Nancy Friedman Meagher. Student, Beaver Coll., 1951-53, NYU, 1953-54. Dir. pub. rels. Albert Einstein Med. Ctr., Phila., 1975-77, Pa. Coll. Optometry, Phila., 1977-79; mgr. media project devel. Sun Oil Co., Phila., 1979-86; dep. dir. Greater Phila. Econ. Coalition, Phila., 1986-88; exec. dir. The Nat. Constitution Ctr., Phila., 1992-94; pres. Polly Friedman & Assoc., Phila., 1988—; com. mem. White House Conf. on Small Bus., Pa.; hon. bd. mem. Nat. Archives Week, Phila., 1993; conf. speaker Nat. Park Svc., Washington, 1993, Nat. Parks & Conservation Assn., 1993 & 94, Nat. Newspaper Assn., 1993; mem. adv. com. Ambler Music Festival at Temple, Pa., 1992-94; mem. pub. rels. coun. Phila. Coalition on Domestic Violence, Phila., 1986, 87. Recipient Silver Anvil Best Pub. Rels. Event award Pub. Rels. Soc. of Am., 1979, Pepperpot award (Phila. chpt.), 1979, Best Pub. Affairs Radio Series Pa. Assn. Broadcasters, 1993. Office: Polly Friedman & Assocs PO Box 46 Spring House PA 19477

FRIEDMAN, RHONDA BETH, psychologist; b. N.Y.C., May 20, 1953; d. Bernard and Pearl (Indyck) F.; m. Kenneth W. Eckmann, July 2, 1978; children: Moshe, Ariel. BA, U. Pa., 1974; PhD, Mass. Inst. Tech., 1978. Postdoctoral fellow Boston U. Sch. Med., 1978-80, asst. rsch. prof. neurology, 1980-89; spl. expert NIH, Bethesda, Md., 1987-91; sr. rsch. assoc. NRH Rsch. Ctr., Washington, 1992—; clin. asst. prof. dept. neurology Georgetown U. Med. Ctr., Washington, 1991-93, adj. assoc. prof., 1993—; pres. Balt.-Washington Area Neuropsychology Group, 1992—. Mem. APA, Internat. Neuropsychol. Assn., Acad. Aphasia. Jewish. Office: Georgetown U Hosp Dept Neurology 3800 Reservoir Rd NW Washington DC 20007

FRIEDMAN, STEFFI, sculptor, educator; b. Berlin, Prussia, Germany, Mar. 10, 1925; came to U.S., 1940; d. Karl and Elise (Nachmann) David; m. Alvin Friedman; children: Gerald, Lawrence, Marjorie. Degree, Pratt Inst., 1946; student, Columbia U., Silvermine Sch. Art. Tchr. Steffi Friedman Sculpture Classes, Camp Terra Cotta, Vt.; represented by Images, Westport, Conn., Corp. Art Unlimited Inc., Westport, Aesthetics Collection Inc., San Diego, Martin Chasin, Fine Arts, Bridgeport, Conn., Corp. Art Source, Montgomery, Ala. One-person shows include Bauhaus II, Bell Gallery; Exhibited in group shows at Lynn. Art Assn. Galleries, Discovery Mus., Nat. Art Club, Homes Gallery, Tennis Hall of Fame, Madison Ave. Gallery, Jaro Galleries Inc., Nina's Choice Gallery, Cartier's Armstrong Gallery, Portrait Gallery, Robbins Gallery, Gump's Gallery, Rockfeller Collection Gallery, Brenner Gallery, Inc., Wilton Gallery, Images, DeLigney Art Galleries, and numerous others; prin. works include portrait relief and bust of Golda Meir Fed. Jewish Philanthropies, bicentennial medal State of N.Dakota, medallion Rensselaer Poly. Univ., statue Franklin Mint, statues Danbury Mint, portrait relief and relief plaques Gen. Electric Co., medallion and bldg. medallion Am. Jewish Com., N.Y.C., relief Weston Woods Film Studios, figure The Travelers Ins. Co., figures Disney, Orlando, Fla., relief Port Auth. N.Y. and N.J.; represented in private collections. Mem. Interna. Sculpture Ctr., Soc. Ct. Sculptors (bd. mem.), Nat. Sculptors Soc. (assoc. mem.), Allied Artists of Am., Westport Arts Ctr., The Am. Artists Profl. League, Knickerbocke Artists (assoc. mem.). Home: 9 Yankee Hill Rd Westport CT 06880

FRIEDMAN, SUE TYLER, technical publications executive; b. Nurenberg, Germany, Feb. 28, 1925; came to U.S., 1938; d. William and Ann (Federlein) Tyler (Theilheimer); m. Gerald Manfred Friedman, June 27, 1948; children: Judith Fay Friedman Rosen, Sharon Mira Friedman Azaria, Devora Paula Friedman Zweibach, Eva Jane Friedman Scholle, Wendy Tamar Friedman Spanier. Student, Beth Israel Sch. Nursing, 1941-43. Exec. dir. Ventures and Publs. Gerald M. Friedman, 1964—; owner Tyler Publs., Watervliet and Troy, N.Y., 1978-86; treas., dir. Northeastern Sci. Found., Inc., Troy, 1979—; treas. Gerry Exploration, Inc., Troy, 1982—; office mgr. Rensselaer Ctr. Applied Geology, Troy, 1983—. Pres. Pioneer Women/Na'amat, Tulsa, 1961-64, treas., Jerusalem, Israel, 1964, pres., Albany, N.Y., 1968-70; bd. dirs. Temple Beth-El, 1965—, dir. Hebrew Sch., 1965-80. Named Hon. Alumna, Dept. Geology, Bklyn. Coll. at CUNY, 1989; Sue Tyler Friedman medal for distinction in history of geology created in her honor Geol. Soc. London, 1988; recipient Disting. Svc. award Temple Beth-El, 1991, Scroll of Honor, State of Israel Bonds, 1981. Mem. Geology Alumni Assn. (hon.). Jewish. Home: 32 24th St Troy NY 12180-1915 Office: Northeastern Sci Found Inc Rensselaer Ctr Applied Geology 15 3rd St Troy NY 12180-3205

FRIEDMAN, SUSAN, executive recruitment firm executive; b. N.Y.C., June 28, 1936; d. Milton Friedman and Marian (Mendelson) Lustbader; m. James E. Fuller, Sept. 7, 1979 (div. Oct. 1982). BS, NYU, 1958; BFA, Parsons Sch. Design, 1958. Exec. fashion designer various firms including David Crystal and Jr. Cir., 1958-62; advt. recruiter Edwin B. Stern, N.Y.C., 1962-66, Judy Wald Agy., N.Y.C., 1966-75; ptnr., pres. Friedman Huss Visetlear Inc., advt. recruitment, N.Y.C., 1975-84; pres. Susan Friedman Ltd., N.Y.C., 1984—. Active various feeding the homeless orgns. Mem. GMHC, Nat. Gun Control. Democrat. Jewish. Office: 750 Lexington Ave New York NY 10022-1200

FRIEDMAN, SUSAN LYNN BELL, job training and community relations specialist; b. Lafayette, Ind., May 23, 1953; d. Virgil Atwood and Jean Loree (Wiggins) B.; m. Frank H. Friedman, July 31, 1976; 1 child, Alex Charles. B.A., Purdue U., 1975; M.S., Ind. State U., 1981. Asst. dir. pub. relations Vincennes U. Jr. Coll., Ind., 1977-83; dir. Knox County C. of C., Vincennes, 1983-84; asst. to pres. Am. Assn. Community and Jr. Colls., Washington, 1985-87; owner/pres. SBF Promotions, 1987—; mgr., program developer Family Resources, Inc., 1988-89; partnership coord. Beaufort (S.C.) County Sch. Dist., 1989-90; job tng. coord. Heart of Ga. Tech. Inst., 1990-92, econ. devel. v.p., 1992—; mem. Heart of Ga. Tech. Inst. Found., 1991—. Bd. dirs. Laurens County Am. Diabetes, Women in Need of God's Shelter, Inc., 1991—, Ga. Common Cause, 1992—, pres., 1993—; mem. Dublin-Laurens Leadership Class, 1994—; Hoosier scholar, 1971, 72; pres. Annandale BPW, Vincennes, Ind. and Beaufort, S.C.; v.p. BPW Dublin; bd. dirs. Beaufort-Jasper Comprehensive Health Services, Inc., 1988-90. Mem. NAFE, Am. Assn. Women in Community and Jr. Colls. (nat. liaison 1985-87), LWV (chpt. v.p. 1982-84), Ga. Assn. Women in Edn., ACLU. Democrat. Home: 300 Ridgecrest Rd Dublin GA 31021-4312

FRIEDMANN, ROSELI OCAMPO, microbiologist, educator; b. Manila, Nov. 23, 1937; came to U.S., 1968; d. Eliseo Amio and Generosa (Campana) Ocampo; m. Emerich Imre Friedmann ; children: Maria Roseli, Rodolfo. BSc in Botany, U. Philippines, 1958; MSc in Biology, Hebrew U. of Jerusalem, 1966; PhD in Biology, Fla. State U., 1973. Rsch. assoc. Inst. Sci. and Tech., Manila, 1958-67; rsch. asst. Queen's U., Kingston, Ont., Can., 1967-68; teaching asst. Fla. State U., Tallahassee, 1968-73, rsch. assoc., 1973—; asst. prof. dept. biology Fla. A&M U., Tallahassee, 1975-84, assoc. prof., 1984-87, prof., 1987—. Contbr. articles to sci. jours. Recipient Resolution of Commendation, State of Fla., Tallahassee, 1978, Antarctic Svc. medal U.S. Congress, Tallahassee, 1981. Mem. Soc. Phycologigue France, Phycological Soc. Am., Planetary Soc., AAAS, U.S. Fedn. Culture Collections, Am. Soc. Microbiology, Assn. Women in Sci., Sigma Xi. Office: Fla A&M U Martin Luther King Blvd Tallahassee FL 32307

FRIEDMAN PHILLIPS, PAULINE See VAN BUREN, ABIGAIL

FRIEDRICH, GLORIA JOY, school psychologist; b. Chgo., Feb. 20, 1936; d. George Anthony and Veronica Barbara K.; m. Robert, June 5, 1954; children: Christopher Lee, Jonathan Drew, James Todd. AA, Coll. of DuPage, Glen Ellyn, Ill., 1971; BA, Nat. Coll. of Edn., Evanston, Ill., 1982, MS in Edn., 1987; EdS, Nat. Coll. of Edn., 1990. Sch. Psychologist and Early Childhood Spl. Edn. Tchr. Tchr. St. John Luth., Darien, Ill., 1971-85, dir. Pre-Sch., 1972-85; sch. psychologist Community Unit Sch. Dist. 303, St. Charles, Ill., 1987—. Pres. LWV, Oak Lawn, Ill., 1961-62, DuPage County election judge, 1968-89; fellow Nat. Coll. Edn.; active Early Childhood Adv. Bd. Elmhurst (Ill.) Coll. Mem. Nat. Assn. of Sch. Psychologists, Ill. Sch. Psychologist Assn., West Suburban Sch. Psychologist Assn. (pres. 1990-91), DuPage Regional Unit of Chgo. Assn., Phi Delta Kappa. Lutheran. Office: Community Unit Sch Dist 303 201 S 7th St Saint Charles IL 60174-2664

FRIEDRICH, MARGRET COHEN, guidance and student assistance counselor; b. Balt., June 4, 1947; d. Joseph Cohen and Judith (Kline) Cohen Roisman; m. Jay Joseph Friedrich, May 16, 1971; children: David Benjamin, Marc Adam, Samantha Lauren. BEd, U. Miami, Fla., 1969, MEd, 1970. Cert. alcoholism and addiction counselor, alcoholism and drug counselor. Grad. asst. U. Miami, Coral Gables, Fla., 1969-70; tchr. Balt. Bd. Edn., 1970; guidance counselor Ridgewood Bd. Edn., N.J., 1970—; student asst. coord., 1986—, chmn. student assistance com., 1986—; alcoholism counselor Bergen County Dept. Health, Paramus, N.J., 1981-82; in-service tchr. Ridgewood Bd. Edn., 1983, supr., coordinator peer counseling program high sch., 1979—; with Assn. Mental Health and Counseling of No. N.J., 1985—; pres. BFH, 1987—, Maggie Assoc.; exec. officer BFPR; cons. N.J. Student Assistance Program, student asst. cons. N.J. Dept. Edn., chmn. student asst. com.; presenter Coll. Bd. Conf., 1992, CEEB Conf., Phila, 1992. Author tech. papers. Exec. bd. Hadassah, Ridgewood-Glen Rock, N.J., 1971—; youth leadership com. United Jewish Appeal, Bergen County, 1974-75; sec. Bergen County Youth Com. Substance Abuse, Paramus, 1980—, conf. coord. com., 1983; treas. Ridgewood Coalition Substance Use and Abuse, 1983-84, Ridgewood Substance Abuse Prevention Commn., 1989—; participant Pres.'s Drug-Free Am.; facilitator Gov.'s N.J. Drug-Free TeleConf.; co-chmn. fundraiser, treas. United Parents/Safe Homes, Ridgewood, 1984; mem. core com. Ridgewood Against Drugs; lectr./educator Passaic County Juvenile Conf. Com., Paterson, N.J., 1984. Reisman scholar, 1969; U. Miami teaching asst., 1970, recipient Recognition award, 1968, disting. Leadership award N.J. Assn. St. Asst. Profls. Mem. N.J. Assn. Alcoholism and Drug Counselors, Nat. Assn. Suicidology, N.J. Edn. Assn., Ridgewood Edn. Assn., Bergen County Edn. Assn., N.J. Task Force on Women and Alcohol, Nat. Assn. Coll. Adminstr. Counselors, N.J. Personnel and Guidance Assn., Women of Accomplishment, Sigma Delta Tau. (exec. bd. 1965-69). Democrat. Jewish. Office: Ridgewood High Sch Ridgewood NJ 07451

FRIEND, ELAINE BYRD, savings and loan executive; b. Smith County, Miss., Aug. 14, 1930; d. Clive Llewellyn and Annie Ruth (Husband) Byrd; m. Perry F. Friend, Jr., Mar. 28, 1953 (div. Apr. 1980); children: Melanie A. Taylor, Perry L., Susan V. Levens, Leah E. Gillespie. Cert., Fin. Inst. Edn., Chgo., 1971, 75-77, 80, Coun. on Mgmt., 1990. Lic. life ins. agt. Credit investigator Credit Bur. Laurel, Miss., 1948-52; credit mgr. Sherwin-Williams Paint Co., 1952-54; bookkeeper, teller Laurel Fed. Savs. and Loan Assn., 1954-58, mgr. savs. dept., 1959-61, with tax and ins. dept., 1968-74, sec. to the pres., 1974-79, asst. corp. sec., 1979-85, corp. sec., 1985—. Bd. dirs., mem. fin. com. United Way Pine Belt, Laurel, 1989—, chair metro campaign, 1992; sponsor Laurel Little Theater, 1965—; block chair Am. Heart Assn., 1992. Recipient Best 1st local campaign award Cystic Fibrosis Found., Little Rock, 1979. Mem. Fin. Women Internat. (Magnolia Group chair, sec., v.p. 1987-90, pres. 1990—), Nat. Assn. Bank Women (Miss. coun. Group Membership award 1989), Nat. Assn. Ins. Women (chair state conf. 1990), Ins. Women (chair state conf. 1990), Ins. Women Laurel (bd. dirs., numerous offices including pres. 1975—, chair long range planning com. 1992—, Ins. Woman of Yr. 1980, chmn. state conf. 1981), Laurel YWCA. Baptist. Home: 201 W Kingston St Laurel MS 39440-2970 Office: Laurel Fed Savs & Loan Assn 317 N 5th Ave Laurel MS 39440-3967

FRIEND, HELEN MARGARET, chemist; b. Lyndon, Ohio, Jan. 30, 1931; d. Maurice Chapman and Margaret (Beath) Mossbarger; m. William Warren Friend, Oct. 9, 1982. BA in Chemistry, Coll. of Wooster, 1953. Rsch. chemist Union Carbide Co., Cleve., 1953-56, asst. patent coord. battery products div., 1956-59, patent coord., 1959-86; patent coord. Eveready Battery Co., Westlake, Ohio, 1986-90, tech. patent assoc., 1990-95; mng. editor JEC Press-Internat. Battery Materials Assn., Cleve., 1978—. Mng. editor Progress in Batteries and Battery Materials, 1978—, JEC Battery Newsletter, 1987—; tech. editor Electrochem. Soc. Japan, U.S. br., 1975—. Mem. Am. Chem. Soc., Electrochem. Soc., Phi Beta Kappa. Presbyterian. Home: 576 Buckeye Dr Sheffield Lake OH 44054-1615 Office: Eveready Battery Co 25225 Detroit Rd Cleveland OH 44145-2536

FRIEND, MIRIAM RUTH, personnel company executive; b. Scranton, Pa., May 19, 1925; d. Benjamin and Etta (Weiss) Loewy; m. Sidney Friend, Aug. 27, 1950. BA, Syracuse U., 1947; cert., Inst. Pub. Welfare Tng. Cornell U., 1950. Social worker Child Placement div. N.Y. State Dept. Welfare, Binghamton and Ithaca, 1948-52; v.p. Office Help Temps., Yonkers, N.Y., 1954-83; pres. Friend & Friend Personnel Agy., Yonkers, N.Y., 1985—. Mem. Eliz Seton Coll. Adv. Council; pres. Pvt. Industry Council, Yonkers, 1981-82, Yonkers Gen. Hosp. Aux., 1983-84, Big Bros./Big Sisters, Yonkers, 1978-80; bd. dirs. Salvation Army, Yonkers, 1977—; publicity chmn. Sen. John E. Flynn Salute, 1986; chmn. breakfast com. Yonkers C. of C., 1978; chmn. Work Opportunities Referral for Kids, Wednesdays Together, 1993—; bd. dirs. Community Planning Council; trustee Yonkers Gen. Hosp., 1978—. Recipient Disting. Service award United Way, 1983, Community Service award Yonkers Council of Chs., 1984, Woman in Bus. award YWCA, 1986; named Pioneer of Industry Ind. Office Services, Hilton Head, S.C., 1984. Mem. Assn. Bus. Profl. Women, Psi Chi, Racquet Club, Amackassin Club (Yonkers), Soroptimists (pres. 1970-72), Rotary. Home: 11 Abbey Pl Yonkers NY 10701-1715 Office: Friend & Friend Pers Agy 11 Abbey Pl Yonkers NY 10701-1715

FRIES, HELEN SERGEANT HAYNES, civic leader; b. Atlanta; d. Harwood Syme and Alice (Hobson) Haynes; student Coll. William and Mary, 1935-38; m. Stuart G. Fries, May 5, 1938. Bd. mem. Community Ballet Assn., Huntsville, Ala., 1968—; mem. nat. nurses aid com. ARC, 1958-59; dir. ARC Aero Club, Eng., 1943-44; supr. ARC Clubmobile, Europe, 1944-46; mem. women's com. Nat. Symphony Orch., Washington, 1959—, chmn. residential fund drive for apts., 1959; bd. dirs. Madison

County Republican Club, 1969-70; mem. nat. council Women's Nat. Rep. Club N.Y., 1963—, chmn. hospitality com., 1963-65; bd. dirs. League Rep. Women, 1952-61; patron mem., vol. docent Huntsville Mus. Art, Huntsville Lit. Assn.; vol. docent Weeden House, Twickenham Hist. Preservation Dist. Assn., Inc., Huntsville; mem. The Garden Guild, Huntsville, The Collectors Guild Constn. Hall Village, Huntsville, Historic Huntsville Found., Hunstville Mus Art. Recipient cert. of merit 84th Div., U.S. Army, 1945. Mem. Nat. Soc. Colonial Dames Am., Daus. Am. Colonists, DAR, Nat. Trust Hist. Preservation, Va., Nat., Valley Forge (Pa.), Eastern Shore Va., Huntsville-Madison County hist. socs., Assn. Preservation Va. Antiquities, Greensboro Soc. Preservation, Tenn. Valley Geneal. Soc., Friends of Ala. Archives, Nat. Soc. Lit. and Arts, Va. Hist. Soc., English Speaking Union, Turkish-Am. Assn., Army-Navy Club, Washington Club, Capitol Hill Club, Army-Navy Country Club, Garden Club, Redstone Yacht Club, Huntsville Country Club, Heritage Club, Botanical Garden Club. Home: 409 Zandale Dr SW Huntsville AL 35801-3462

FRIES, MAUREEN HOLMBERG, English literature educator; b. Buffalo, July 14, 1931; d. Howard Henry and Margaret Teresa (Wiley) Holmberg; children: Jeb Stuart, Howard Gordon, John Pelham, Sheila Maureen. A.B. magna cum laude, D'Youville Coll., 1952; M.A., Cornell U., 1953; Ph.D., SUNY-Buffalo, 1969. Advt. copywriter Eastman Advt. Co., Ithaca, N.Y., 1953-54, Coe Advt. Co., Syracuse, N.Y., 1954; free-lance journalist, Buffalo, 1964-69; teaching fellow SUNY-Buffalo, 1965-69; asst. prof. N.Y. State U. Coll. at Fredonia, 1969-73, assoc. prof., 1973-77, prof. medieval Brit. lit., 1977-90, disting. teaching prof., 1990—; lectr. and cons. in field; participant, chmn. numerous confs. Editor: (with Jeanie Watson) The Figure of Merlin in the 19th and 20th Centuries, 1990, Approaches to Teaching the Arthurian Tradition, 1992; compiler A Biography By and About British Women Writers, 1971; contbr. articles to profl. jours., chpts. to books; mem. editorial bd. Quondam et Futurus: A Jour. of Arthurian Interpretations, 1984—. Reader various publs. Recipient Chancellor's award for Excellence in Teaching, 1977, Callista Jones award, 1982, D'Youville Coll. Alumni Svc. award, 1991; Kasling Meml. lectureship State U. of N.Y. Coll. at Fredonia, 1985; NEH fellow, 1975-76; State Univ. of N.Y. Faculty Research awards, 72, 73, 79, 80, Am. Philos. Soc., summer 1978, Am. Council Learned Socs. travel grant, summer 1978, NEH, 1979; Fulbright Research and Lecturing award, sr. professorship Universitat Regensburg, Fed. Republic Germany, Apr.-July 1984, other awards, grants, fellowships. Mem. Am. Classical League, Internat. Assn. Univ. Profs. of English, Internat. Courtly Lit. Soc., Medieval Acad. of Am., MLA (chairperson Arthurian Discussion Group, mem. exec. com. 1978-82, organizer, chairperson other ann. meetings northeastern and southeastern chpts.), Société Internationale Arthurienne. Democrat. Roman Catholic. Office: SUNY Coll 241 Fenton Hall Fredonia NY 14063*

FRIESEN, JANIS M., public relations executive; b. Wichita, Kans., Mar. 20, 1958; d. Gilbert G. and Ethel M. (Farha) F.; m. Butch Lowe. BA in Journalism, Wichita State U., 1980, MA in Comm., 1986. Pub. rels. coord. Mycro-Tek, Wichita, 1981-85; asst. v.p. advt. and comm. Bank IV, Wichita, 1985-91; pub. rels. dir. Sullivan Higdon & Sink, Wichita, 1991-93; pres. Friesen & Assocs., Wichita, 1993-94; ptnr. Allison-Friesen Advt. & Pub. Rels., Wichita, 1994—. Trustee Botanica, The Wichita Gardens, 1987—. Mem. Pub. Rels. Soc. Am. (past pres. 1991, Pub. Rels. Profl. Yr. 1991), Am. Fedn. Wichita. Office: Allison-Friesen PO Box 47691 Wichita KS 67201

FRIESNER, PHYLLIS LEA ELDRIDGE, genealogist; b. Waterloo, Iowa, Feb. 24, 1930; d. Lester Lyman and Edna Sylvia (Bruce) Eldridge; m. Theodore Edward Friesner, Sept. 19, 1948; children: Mark, Jay. Student, Des Moines Area C.C., 1979. Sec. receptionist Black's Dept. Store, Waterloo, 1948-56, Chapel of Memories Funeral Home, Waterloo, 1956-58; sec. Fed. Govt., Des Moines, 1975-76; exec. sec. Iowa Geneal. Soc., Des Moines, 1977-79; owner. libr., genelogist Tree Trackers Libr., Eagle Rock, Mo., 1985—; tchr. genealogy Adult Evening Edn., Des Moines, 1975-80; advisor The Adoption Experience, Des Moines, 1980-85; speaker in field. Mem. United We Stand, Mo., 1992. Mem. NOW, Daus. of Union Vets. (press corr. 1981-84, State award 1983), Iowa Geneal. Soc. (corr. sec. 1973-74), Feminine Majority, Tree Shakers Valley Junction co-founder, pres. 1975-79), Sons of Norway Lodge. Democrat. Home and Office: HCR-01 Box 1210 Eagle Rock MO 65641

FRIESON, CASSANDRA WARNER, hospital education coordinator; b. Jefferson County, Ala., Mar. 23, 1965; d. Thomas Roosevelt and Berta Mae (Oakes) W. BSN, U. Ala., Birmingham, 1987, MSN, 1992. RN, Ala. Staff nurse renal and liver transplant surg. units U. Ala., Birmingham. Juliet Nunn scholar, Ala. State nursing scholar. Mem. Sigma Theta Tau, Omicron Delta Kappa. Home: 1547 Delton Pl Midfield AL 35228

FRIGON, JUDITH ANN, electronics executive, office systems consultant; b. Wisconsin Rapids, Wis., Feb. 11, 1945; d. Harold Leslie and Muriel Alice (Berard) Neufeld; m. Gene Roland Frigon, June 17, 1967; children: Shane P., Shannon M., Sean M. Sec., office mgr. George Chapman D.D.S., Fairfax, Va., 1971-75; owner, operator Sunset Motel, Havre, Mont., 1976-78; sec. Wash. State U. Social Research Ctr., Pullman, 1978-80; adminstrv. sec. Wash. State U. Systems and Computing, Pullman, 1980-85, office automation cons., word processing trainer, IBM profl. office system adminstr., 1983-89, microcomputer cons. and trainer, 1989—; systems analyst, programmer Wash. State U. Computing Ctr., Pullman, 1985—; owner Computer Assistance, Tng. and Svcs., Pullman, 1992—. Pres. Pullman svc. unit Girl Scouts U.S., 1983-89, v.p. inland empire coun., Spokane, Wash., 1985-89, pres., 1989—; active Pullman Civic Trust, 1986—; mem-at-large Pullman United Way, 1988-93, admissions and allocations com., 1990-93, comm. com., 1990-93; host family for State of Wash. Jr. Miss Program, 1988—, local area judge Young Woman of Yr., 1985—. Mem. Profl. Secs. Internat., Jaycees (Jayceen of Yr. 1978), Pullman Kiwanis Club. Roman Catholic. Home: 1235 NW Davis Way Pullman WA 99163-2815 Office: Wash State U Computing Ctr 2120 Computer Sci Bldg Pullman WA 99164

FRISCH, ROSE EPSTEIN, population sciences researcher; b. N.Y.C., July 7, 1918; m. David H. Frisch; children: Henry J., Ruth Frisch Dealy. BA, Smith Coll., 1939; MA, Columbia U., 1940; PhD, U. Wis., 1943. Assoc. prof. population scis. Harvard U., Cambridge, Mass., 1984-92, assoc. prof. emerita, 1992—. Contbr. articles to profl. jours. John Simon Guggenheim Meml. fellow, 1975-76. Mem. AAAS, Endocine Soc. Am., Population Soc. Am., Sigma Xi (nat. lectr. 1989-90). Office: Harvard U Ctr Population Studies 9 Bow St Cambridge MA 02138-5103

FRISKOPP, ANNETTE M., satellite communications executive; b. Nebr., Feb. 18, 1964; m. Sharon Silverstein. BS in Acctg., U. Nebr., 1986; MBA, Harvard U., 1990. Acct. Price Waterhouse, N.Y.C., 1986-88; COO Boatracs Inc., San Diego, 1991—. Mem. Harvard Bus. Sch. Alumni. Home: 3525 Del Mar Heights Rd 384 San Diego CA 92130 Office: Boatracs Inc 6440 Lusk Blvd D 201 San Diego CA 92121

FRITJOFSON, SARAH MARIE, reporter, columnist; b. Roswell, N.Mex., July 8, 1908; d. Robert Seabury and Gena Vera (Nichols) Cook; m. Hjalmar Peter Fritjofson, Dec. 16, 1939 (dec. 1964). BA, Wellesley Coll., 1930; art studied with, Winhold Reiss, 1936-39; studied with, Hipolito Hidalgo de Caviedes, 1939-40, Adolf Spohr, 1950. Soc. editor Muscatine (Iowa) Jour., 1930-31; reporter, columnist Cody (Wyo.) Enterprise, 1962—; condr. seminars and workshops Buffalo Bill Hist. Ctr., Cody. Contbr. to Smithsonian Catalog on Winold Reiss Show, 1989, South Fork Jour., Smoke Signals. Lay reader Christ Ch., 1973—; pres. pub. Cody Music Club; patron Buffalo Bill Hist. Assn.; hon. mem. Cody Country Art League. Mem. AAUW (sec.), Wellesley Alumnae Assn. Republican. Episcopalian. Home: 1324 10th St Cody WY 82414-4101

FRITTS, LILLIAN ELIZABETH, retired nurse; b. N.Y.C., July 19, 1923; d. William Franklin and Elzora Jane (Hodge) Bowen; A.D.N., R.N., Central Peidmont Community Coll., 1969; m. Thurman Luther Fritts, Aug. 5, 1944; children—William Luther, Franklin Lee, George Allen. Emergency room nurse Lexington (N.C.) Meml. Hosp., 1953-58; office nurse James T. Welborn, M.D., Lexington, 1958-60; staff nurse Haven Nursing Ctr., Lexington, 1960-61; pvt. duty nurse, 1961-63; owner, ptnr. Buena Vista Nursing Ctr., Lexington, 1964-91, ret., 1991; adult extension tchr. Davidson County Community Coll., 1978, adv. bd. nursing program, 1969-79; pres. Piedmont dist. Long Term Nursing Dirs., 1986-88, Long Term Care Piedmont Nurses Assn., 1987-89. Mem. Am. Nurses Assn., N.C. Nurses Assn., Lic. Practical Nurse Orgn. (state sec. 1958-60), N.C. Lic. Practical Nurse Assn., Dist. 9 Nurse Assn. N.C., N.C. Health Care Facilities Services Assn., Gideons Internat. Baptist. Home: 797 Hill Everhard Rd Lexington NC 27292

FRITZ, BRIGITTE, interior designer, translator; b. Hameln, Germany, June 14, 1949; came to U.S., 1974; d. Paul and Walltraut (Krause) Dohmann; m. Harry Fritz, Dec. 22, 1973; children: Michael, Miriam, Melissa. Bus. cert., Handelschule Am. Langen Wall, Hameln, 1967; student, Sheffield Sch. Interior Design, 1990—. Legal sec. Dr. Jur. Schroeder, Hameln, 1970-73; co-owner H&B Fritz & Assocs., Milw., 1976-88, German is Our Splty., Sheboygan, Wis., 1988—; owner From House to Home Decorating, Sheboygan, 1990—. Co-author: (with Harry Fritz) The Unknown Visitor, 1979. Home: 641 Swift Ave Sheboygan WI 53081 Office: From House to Home Dec 641 Swift Ave Sheboygan WI 53081

FRITZ, ETHEL MAE HENDRICKSON, writer; b. Gibbon, Nebr., Feb. 4, 1925; d. Walter Earl and Alice Hazel (Mickish) Hendrickson; BS, Iowa State U., 1949; m. C. Wayne Fritz, Feb. 25, 1950; children: Linda Sue, Krista Jane. Dist. home economist Internat. Harvester Co., Des Moines, 1949-50; writer Wallace's Farmer mag., Des Moines, 1960-64; free-lance writer, 1960—. Chmn. Ariz. Council Flower Show Judges, 1983-85; media rels. Presdl. Inaugural Com., 1988. Accredited master flower show judge. Mem. Women in Communications (pres. Phoenix profl. chpt.; nat. task force com. 1980—), Am. Soc. Profl. and Exec. Women, Am. Home Econs. Assn., SW Writers' Conf., Ariz. Authors Assn., Phi Upsilon Omicron, Kappa Delta. Republican. Methodist. Club: PEO. Author: The Story of an Amana Winemaker, 1984, Prairie Kitchen Sampler, 1988, The Family of Hy-Vee, 1989.

FRITZ, JACQUELYNN, medical/surgical nurse; b. Youngstown, Ohio, Nov. 29, 1953; d. Louis and Elverna Anna Christina (Poese) F. Diploma in Nursing, Immanuel Hosp., Omaha, 1975; B Gen. Studies, U. Nebr., Omaha, 1988. Staff nurse med./surg. Immanuel Med. Ctr., Omaha, 1975-79, staff nurse orthopedics, 1979-80; staff nurse ICU St. Joseph Hosp., Omaha, 1980-82, staff nurse pulmonary endocrine, 1982-84, staff nurse progressive care, 1984-86, staff nurse telemetry/stepdown, 1986—; mem. nurse practice com. St. Joseph Hosp., 1991-92, recruitment and retention com., 1990-93; prsenter critical care classes, 1988-90, mem. critical care edn. com., 1994—. Mem. Disaster Action Team of ARC, Omaha, 1991, disaster health svcs. com., 1992. Mem. Nat. League for Nursing. Democrat. Home: 2730 Read St Omaha NE 68112-3122 Office: St Joseph Hosp 601 N 30th St Omaha NE 68131-2197

FRITZ, JEAN GUTTERY, writer; b. Hankow, People's Republic China, Nov. 16, 1915; d. Arthur Minton and Myrtle (Chaney) Guttery; m. Michael Fritz, Nov. 1, 1941; children: David, Andrea. BA, Wheaton Coll., Norton, Mass., 1937, LittD (hon.), 1987; LittD (hon.), Washington and Jefferson Coll., 1982. Author: Fish Head, 1954, The Late Spring, 1957, The Animals of Doctor Schweitzer, 1958, The Cabin Faced West, 1958, How to Read a Rabbit, 1958, Brady, 1960, I, Adam, 1963, Magic to Burn, 1964, Early Thunder, 1967, George Washington's Breakfast, 1969, Cast for a Revolution, 1972, And Then What Happened, Paul Revere?, 1973, Why Don't You Get a Horse, Sam Adams?, 1974, Where Was Patrick Henry on the 29th of May?, 1975, Who's that Stepping on Plymouth Rock?, 1975, Will You Sign Here, John Hancock?, 1976, The Secret Diary of Jeb and Abigail, 1976, What's the Big Idea, Ben Franklin?, 1976, Can't You Make Them Behave, King George?, 1977, Brendon the Navigator, 1979, Stonewall, 1979, Where Do You Think You're Going, Christopher Columbus?, 1980, The Man Who Loved Books, 1981, Traitor: The Case of Benedict Arnold, 1981, The Good Giants and the Bad Pukwudgies, 1981, Homesick: My Own Story, 1982 (Am. Book award 1983, Child Study Book award 1983, Honor Book, Newberry Medal Book 1983), China Homecoming, 1985, The Double Life of Pocahontas, 1983 (Boston Globe/Horn Book award 1984), Make Way for Sam Houston, 1986 (Western Writers award 1987), Shh! We're Writing the Constitution, 1987, China's Long March, 1988, The Great Little Madison, 1989, Bully for You, Teddy Roosevelt!, 1991, Around the World in 100 Years, 1994, Harriet Beecher Stowe and the Beecher Preachers, 1994. Recipient Christopher award Cath. Library Assn., 1982, Regina Medal Cath. Library Assn., 1985, Laura Ingalls Wilder award ALA, 1986. Home: 50 Bellewood Ave Dobbs Ferry NY 10522-2302

FRITZ, JOANNE LEE (JONI FRITZ), association executive; b. Bklyn., May 5, 1936; d. Theodore Roosevelt and Josephine (Chandler) L.; m. John D. Allen Jr., June 16, 1956 (div. Jan. 1970); children: John D. III, Cynthia Allen de Ramos, Victoria Lee Burnett; m. Nicholas Fritz Jr., July 4, 1970. Student, Cornell U., 1954-56; BA in Sociology with distinction, George Washington U., 1971. Tchr. Enon Elem. Sch., Chester, Va., 1958-59; med. records analyst Fairax (Va.) Hosp., 1962-66; med. asst. Drs. Apter and Morrissey Ltd., 1966-72; assoc. dir. Am. Network Community Options and Resources (formerly Nat. Assn. Pvt. Residential Resources), Falls Church, Va., 1972-76; exec. dir. Am. Network Community Options and Resources, Falls Church, Va., 1976—; panelist Office Human Devel., HHS, 1980-83, Health Care Financing Adminstrn., 1991; speaker pvt. residential svcs. nat. and state confs.; sec. Consortium for Citizens with Disabilities, 1974-82, chmn. housing task force, 1983-85, chmn. staff wage and hour task force, 1986-88; mem. steering com. Forum on Long Term Care, Washington, 1979-84; bd. dirs. Accreditation Coun. on Svcs. to People with Disabilities, 1979-80; mem. adv. panels various orgns. Author, editor, Links, 1976—. Trustee Commn. on Accreditation Rehab. Facilities, 1984-89, chmn. standards com., 1985-87. Recipient Ark. Traveler award; Ky. col. Mem. Am. Assn. Mental Retardation, Assn. Retarded Citizens, Nat. Head Injury Found., Nat. Assn. Women Execs., Nat. Fire Protection Assn. (subcom. bd. & care). Office: Am Network Community Options and Resources 4200 Evergreen Ln Ste 315 Annandale VA 22003-3255

FRITZ, MARY G., state legislator; b. Cambridge, Mass., May 8, 1938; d. Patrick John and Kathleen Sherry; m. William W. Fritz, Aug. 24, 1963; children: William Jr., Kathleen, Michael, Heather, Matthew, David. BA, Emmanuel Coll., Boston, 1959. Cert. tchr., Conn. Tchr. Wallingford (Conn.) Bd. Edn., 1979-83; dir., owner nursery sch., Yalesville, Conn., 1969-78; mgr. furniture store, Yalesville, 1977-81; legislator 90th dist. State of Conn., 1983-84, 87—. Bd. dirs. Wallingford Day Care, 1985—; adv. bd. Substance Abuse Coalition, Cheshire, Conn., 1985—; adv. coun. August Early Intervention Ctr., Cheshire, 1985—. Mem. Grange Club. Democrat. Roman Catholic. Home: 43 Grove St Wallingford CT 06492-1606*

FRITZ, SUZANNE EILEEN, critical care nurse; b. South Bend, Ind., Mar. 14, 1960; d. Harry F. and Dolores (Gemberzewski) Fritz. RN, Meml. Hosp. Sch. Nursing, South Bend, Ind., 1981; BSN, Ind. U., South Bend, Ind., 1990. Staff nurse ICU, CCU, OHR Meml. Hosp., South Bend, 1981-85; staff nurse cardiac catheterization lab. Meml. Hosp., 1985-87, staff nurse CCU, 1987-91; staff nurse cardiac catheterization lab.-spl. procedures St. Joseph's Med. Ctr., South Bend, Ind., 1991—. Mem. Ind. U. South Bend Student Nurses Assn. (sec.), Sigma Theta Tau. Home: 3600 N Main St Apt 7 Mishawaka IN 46545-3191

FRITZSCHE, DANA KAY, industrial rehabilitation specialist; b. Hamilton, Ohio, Oct. 15, 1962; d. Charles William and Carole Lou (Altman) F. BA, Miami U., Oxford, Ohio, 1985; MSc, cert. advanced study, Springfield Coll., 1987. Cert. rehab. counselor, ins. rehab. specialist. Rsch. asst. Springfield (Mass.) Coll., 1985-86, teaching asst., 1986-87; alcohol counselor intern VA, Northampton, Mass., 1987; psychology asst. Child & Adult Guidance Ctr., Columbus, Ohio, 1987-88; psychology asst. dept. corrections State of Ohio, Columbus, 1988-90, indsl. rehab. case mgmt. specialist bur. workers compensation, 1990—; instr. SCUBA Ctrl. Ohio Sch. Diving, Columbus, 1993—; fire warden J. Leonard Camera Ctr., Columbus, 1994. Vol. Citizens Humane Action, Westerville, Ohio, 1991—. Mem. 1199 Health Care and Social Svc. Union (union steward 1989-90), Purina Breeders Club. Home: 5042 Magnolia Blossom Blvd Gahanna OH 43230

FRIZZELL, LINDA DIANE BANE, exercise physiologist; b. Council Bluffs, Iowa, May 6, 1950; d. Howard Austin and Dorothy (Eyberg) Bane; m. Richard J. Frizzell, Sept. 5, 1971; children: William, Michelle, Audra, Austin. Cert. athletic trainer, John F. Kennedy Coll., 1970; BA, Parsons Coll., 1972; postgrad., U. Iowa, 1973; MS, Bemidji State U., 1988; PhD, U. N.D., 1991. Lic. phys. edn. tchr., coach, adaptive phys. edn. tchr., Minn.; cert. auto mech., nursing asst.; trained medication aide; water safety instr.; life guard tng. instr.; cert. leisure profl.; qualified mental retardation profl.; cert. personal trainer. Mgr. swimming pool, dir. swimming lessons Town of Oakland (Iowa), 1971; head cross country, men and women's track and field, asst. coach women's basketball, dir. women's instramurals, phys. edn. instr. Parsons Coll., Fairfield, Iowa, 1972-73; mgr. parts and svc. head mech. Winebrenner Ford, Walker, Minn., 1974-76; tchr., coach Laporte (Minn.) Sch., 1976-81; coach Cass Lake (Minn.) Sch., 1981-85; grad. asst. coach men and women track and field Bemidji (Minn.) State U., 1987; community edn. instr. Walker (Minn.)-Hackensack Schs., 1987—; mgr. warranty parts and svc. Walker Electric & Hardware, 1987-91; recreation dir. Town of Walker, 1991; therapeutic recreation specialist Ah-Gwah-Ching (Minn.) Nursing Home, 1987-91; grad. rsch. asst. Bureau Ednl. Svcs., U. N.D., Grand Forks, 1989-91; exec. dir. tng. facility developmentaly disable adults Deer River Hired Hands, 1991-92; cons. Bush Grant Study, U. N.D.; presenter at AAHPERD nat. conv. (conf. scholarship 1990, 91); adj. prof. Bemidji State U., 1993—; ind. cons. excercise physiology, rehabilitative therapy, leisure edn., health edn., 1991—; adminstrv. health planner. Tribal Health-Leech Lake Reservation, 1993—; speaker for various nat. orgns. on adult aging, devel. and exercise. Designed and copyrighted a wellness circuit for older adults; contbr. articles in field. Minn. rep. to Coun. on Aging and Adult Devel. Mem. Am. Assn. Leisure and Recreation (mem. com. on aging), Am. Coll. Sports Medicine (profl., govt. affairs com., Minn. rep.).

FRIZZELL, LUCILLE BRIDGERS, retired librarian; b. Yazoo City, Miss., Dec. 17, 1925; d. Thomas Alfred Bridgers and Maie Hollingsworth; m. Byron Waters Frizzell, July 24, 1952; children: Peter Graham, David Edward, Mark Dillard. BS, East Tenn. State U., 1977, MS, 1980. Sec. U.S. Steel Corp., 1946-53; libr. Steed Coll., Johnson City, Tenn., 1980-82, Bristol Coll., Johnson City, 1982-84, Draughons Jr. Coll., Johnson City, 1984-90. Mem. DAR (treas. Johnson City chpt. 1959-60), Tenn. Libr. Assn., Boone Tree Libr. Assn. (v.p. 1986-87), Nat. Soc. So. Dames (v.p. East Tenn. chpt. 1986-88, v.p. Tenn. state chpt. 1990-92), Watauga Assn. Genealogists (charter), Washington County Hist. Soc. (charter), Monday Club, Delta Kappa Gamma. Republican. Episcopalian. Home: 3320 Bondwood Cir Johnson City TN 37604-8907

FRIZZELL-DONNER, JUDITH, editor, writer, marketing professional; b. Woburn, Mass., Oct. 22, 1958; d. Norman Richard and Thelma Virginia (Josephson) Frizzell; m. Phillip Louis Donner, Aug. 12, 1984 (div. Aug. 1989). Grad. high sch., 1976. Editor, mktg. dir. Arnett Press, Downey, Calif.; asst. dir. creative svcs. The Nat. Assn. of TV Program Execs., L.A.; mng. editor audio/video interiors mag. CurtCo Pub., Woodland Hills, Calif.; mng. editor Mobile Office mag. CurtCo., Inc., Woodland Hills, Calif. Producer, editor Wild Wild West TV series, 1960. Mem. Nat. League of Am. Pen Women, Publ. Prodn. Club So. Calif. Democrat. Office: CurtCo Inc 21800 Oxnard St # 250 Woodland Hills CA 91367-3633

FRODI, ANN MARGARET, psychologist, educator; b. Göteborg, Sweden, June 21, 1944; came to U.S., 1974; d. Arne Torsten and Mary Crouse (Melvin) Frodi; m. Lawrence William Lundgren, July 11, 1981; 1 child, Annika Mary. BA, U. Lund, Sweden, 1967, degree in psychology, 1970; PhD, U. Göteborg, 1974, docent, 1978. Lic. psychologist, N.Y., Sweden. Field rschr. Ethiopia, Kenya, Tanzania, Zambia, 1968-69; head City of Göteborg Orphanage, 1969; clin. child psychologist City of Göteborg, 1970-71; lectr. U. Göteborg, 1971-73, rsch. fellow, teaching fellow, 1973-74; postdoctoral fellow U. Wis., Madison, 1974-76, rsch. assoc., 1976-77; asst. prof., then assoc. prof. U. No. Iowa, Cedar Falls, 1977-80, U. Rochester, N.Y., 1980-88; extern in family and marriage therapy dept. psychiatry U. Rochester Med. Sch., 1988-91; pvt. practice Rochester, 1990-91; psychologist Hamilton Assocs., Fairport, N.Y., 1993—; assoc. prof. psychology Nazareth Coll., Rochester, N.Y., 1993—; rsch. investigator Ctr. Human Growth and Devel., U. Mich., 1979-80; editl. cons. Psychol. Bull., Child Devel., Jour. Rsch. in Personality, Jour. Personality, others; grant reviewer NSF, Med. Rsch. Coun. N.Z. Contbr. numerous articles to profl. publs. Mem. APA, Internat. Soc. Rsch. on Aggression, Soc. Psychophysiol. Rsch., Soc. Rsch. in Child Devel., Merrill-Palmer Soc. Office: Hamilton Assocs 760 Perinton Hills Office Fairport NY 14450

FROEHLICH, MARY ELLEN, physical education educator; b. Trenton, N.J., Apr. 17, 1955; d. Frederick John and Mary Rose (Borosh) Froehlich; m. William Kirk Grooms, June 20, 1981 (div. July 14, 1993). Student, Slipper Rock (Pa.) State Coll., 1973-74; BS in Phys. Edn. with honors, U. Del., 1977; postgrad., Shippensburg State Coll., 1978, U. Md., 1979-83, Hood Coll., 1994—. Tchr. phys. edn. Bd. of Edn. of Washington County, Hagerstown, Md., 1977—, dir. sch. cmty. recreation ctr., 1977-82, phys. edn. dept. coord., 1977—, related arts team leader, 1991—. Vol. membership drives and capital campaign fund drives YMCA, Hagerstown, 1977-89. Recipient Helping Hand award Northern Middle Sch., Hagerstown, 1989. Mem. Md. Assn. Health, Phys. Edn., Recreation and Dance. Democrat. Roman Catholic. Home: 1015 Oak Hill Ave Hagerstown MD 21742 Office: Northern Middle Sch 701 Northern Ave Hagerstown MD 21742

FROELICH, BEVERLY LORRAINE, foundation director; b. Vancouver, B.C., Can., Oct. 23, 1948; came to U.S., 1968; d. Kenneth Martin and Ethel (Seale) Pulham; m. Eugene Leonard Froelich, Dec. 26, 1971; children: Craig, Grant. Cert. in fundraising, U. So. Calif., 1986; profl. designation in pub. rels., UCLA, 1987. Cert. fund raising exec. Contract analyst Universal Studios, Calif., 1968-71; exec. dir. Olive View, UCLA Med. Ctr. Found., Sylmar, Calif., 1987—; pres. Beverly Froelich Pub. Rels., Sherman Oaks, Calif., 1988-90; prin. Tracy Susman & Co., Sherman Oaks, 1986-88. Co-author: (program) Overcoming Chronic Arthritis Pain, 1989; contbg. writer hosp. earthquake preparedness guidelines Hosp. Coun. So. Calif., 1991. Founder San Fernando Valley br. Arthritis Found., Encino, 1983, pres., 1983-87, mktg. com.; exec. com. Jeopardy "Balancing the Odds" Found.; bd. dirs. health care com. VICA, Futures IV com., United Way; devel. com. Crespi H.S. Recipient Nat. Vol. Svc. award Arthritis Found., 1986, Jane Wyman Humanitarian award Arthritis Found., 1991, Disting. Svc. award Arthritis Found., 1990. Mem. Nat. Soc. Fund Raisers (exec. com. San Fernando Valley chpt.), Valley Industry and Commerce Assn., UCLA Alumni Assn., Publicity Club of L.A. Home: 14152 Valley Vista Blvd Sherman Oaks CA 91423 Office: Olive View Med Ctr Found 14445 Olive View Dr Cott M Sylmar CA 91423

FROELICH, SUSAN G., architect; b. Kansas City, Mo., Sept. 24, 1951; d. John Bohman and Alice Marguerite (Harris) Grow; m. W. Scott Pratt; children:Scottie, Alice, David, Laura. BArch, Kans. State U., 1973. Registered architect, Mich., Wis. Project architect Skidmore Owings & Merrill, Chgo., 1973-78, 83-85; project architect Murphy/Jahn, Inc., Chgo., 1978-82, 86—, now v.p.; project architect Froelich & Marik, L.A., 1982-83, Marshall & Brown, Kansas City, 1985-86. Prin. works include New World Ctr., Hong Kong, Group Repertory Theatre, North Hollywood, Calif., Bi State Indsl. Park, Kansas City, Mo., State of Ill. Ctr., Chgo., John Deere Harvester Works Office Facility, Moline, Ill., Two Liberty Pl., Phila., Livingston Pla., Bklyn., North Loop Block 37, Chgo., 1st and Broadway, L.A., Kudamm 119, Berlin, Cologne/Bonn Airport, Cologne, Jeddah Airport, Saudi Arabia, Sony European Hdqs., Berlin, Munich Airport Ctr., 21st Century Tower, Shanghai, China. Mem. AIA (corp. mem.). Office: Murphy/Jahn 35 E Wacker Dr Chicago IL 60601-2102

FROLICK, PATRICIA MARY, educator, retired; b. Portland, Oreg., May 17, 1923; d. Fred Anthony and Clara Cecelia (Riverman) F. BS in Edn., Marylhurst Coll., 1960; MS in Edn., Portland State U., 1970; student, U. Oreg., 1975; MA in Theology, St. Mary's Coll., Moraga, Calif., 1977. Joined Roman Cath. Order Sisters of Holy Names of Jesus and Mary, 1943. Left order in 1974. Elem. sch. tchr. Catholic Sch. System, Oreg., 1943-69; tchr., libr. Hood River Pub. Schs., 1970-74, Bend-La Pine (Oreg.) Pub. Schs., 1981-93; retired, 1993; part-time tchr's. asst., Portland, 1993—. Mem. NEA, Oreg. Edn. Assn., Met. Mus. Art (assoc.), Nat. Mus. Women in Arts (charter). Democrat. Roman Catholic. Home: 3465 SE 153rd Portland OR 97236-2265

FROMAN, ANN, sculptor. Student, New Sch. for Social Rsch., N.Y.C., 1967, Fashion Inst. Tech., N.Y.C., 1961, Art Students League, N.Y.C., 1970,

Nat. Acad. Sch. Fine Arts, N.Y.C., 1967, Palace Fontainebleau Sch. Fine Arts, France, 1961. Fashion, shoe designer, sculptor. Represented in numerous permanent collections including Survival, Time Warner, Inc., New Generation, March of Dimes, Bklyn. Coll., Butterfly, Shulamith Sch. for Girls, Bklyn., Lost Generation, Temple B'nai B'rith, Queen Esther, Iowa Jewish Home for the Aged, Des Moine, Sarah, Mus. Fine Art, Springfield, Mass., Three Dancers, Butler Mus. Art, Youngstown, Ohio, Jacob and the Angel, Slater Mus., Norwich, Conn., Ruth and Naomi, Richmond Library, Wichita, Kans., Temple Israel, Wilkes Barre, Pa., Out of the Ashes, Congregation Emanu-El, N.Y.C., Temple DeHirsch Sinai, Seattle, Culinary Inst. Am., Hyde Park, N.Y., Holy Family, St. Raphaels Ch., Livingston, N.J., Radcliffe Coll., Art Expo 1988-1992; numerous one woman shows include St. Raphaels Ch., Internat. Art Expo, N.Y., Beverly Hills, Calif., 1988, Artistic Investments, Atlanta, 1988, Jewish Community Ctr., Wilkes Barre, Pa., 1988, Great Artist Series, Miami, Fla., 1986, Bennington (Vt.) Mus., 1981, Judaica Mus., Phoenix, Ariz., 1979, Bodley Gallery, N.Y.C., 1978, Hebrew Coll., Boston, 1977, 82, Berkshire Mus., Pittsfield, Mass., 1977, Nat. Arts & Antiques Festival, N.Y.C., 1969, 73, Bacardi Gallery, Miami, 1971, Black Starr & Frost Lt. Gallery, N.Y.C., 1970, Leroy Fine Art, Sweden, 1991; numerous group shows including Internat. Arts Club, Nat. Arts Club, N.Y.C., Bklyn. Mus., Allied Artists Show, Vet. Artists Am., N.Y.C., Aleph Gallery, Mex. City, Ella Lerner Gallery, Lenox, Mass., Union Carbide, N.Y.C., Lever House, N.Y.C., Nelson Rockefeller Collection, N.Y.C., U.S. Customs Mus., N.Y.C., Bass Mus., Miami, Fla., Images Internat., Bethesda, Md. Recipient First Prize for Sculpture Salmagundi club, 1980, Cornavin Ltd. award Nat. Arts club, 1978, Watson Guptill award Nat. Arts Club, 1976, Ivan R. Lashin award Am. Soc. Contemporary Artists, 1975, Mortimer C. Ritter award Fashion Inst. Tech., 1971, Bklyn. Mus. Sculpture award, 1970, Shoe Design award, 1968, Packaging Design award Shoe Industry, 1965, Fashion Design award, 1959, Scholastic Mag. award, 1959. Studio: South Anson Rd Stanfordville NY 12581

FROMBERG, DONNA LYN, psychologist; b. Phila., Jan. 2, 1962; d. Carl Benjaman Fromberg and Helene J. (Levison) Wasserson. BA, Temple U., 1984; PsychD, U. Denver, 1992. Lic. clin. psychologist. Psychology intern McLean Hosp., Belmont, Mass., 1991-92, postdoctoral fellow in psychology of women, 1992-93, clin. adminstr. Women's Treatment Network, 1993—, co-dir. trauma lecture series, 1993-94; pvt. practice clin. psychology Belmont, 1993—. Mem. APA, NOW, Internat. Assn. for Study of Multiple Personality and Dissociation. Office: 115 Mill St Belmont MA 02178-1048

FROMM, HANNA, educational administrator; b. Nuremberg, W.Ger., Dec. 20, 1913; d. David and Meta (Stiebel) Gruenbaum; m. Alfred Fromm, July 4, 1936; children—David, Caroline Fromm Lurie. Grad. in choreography and music Folkwang Sch. Dancing and Music, Univ. Essen, Germany, 1934; D.Pub. Service (hon.), U. San Francisco, 1979. Served with ARC, World War II; exec. dir. and co-founder Fromm Inst. Lifelong Learning, U. San Francisco, 1975—. Co-founder Music in the Vineyards, Saratoga, Calif.; bd. dirs. Amnesty Internat., Nat. Council of Fine Arts Museums; former bd. dirs. Young Audiences, Community Music Ctr., Legal Aid to Elderly, San Francisco Chamber Music Soc.; coordinating com. geriatric curriculum and program U. Calif.-San Francisco; dir. Nat. Council on Aging. Recipient Living Legacy award Women's Internat. Ctr., 1990. Mem. Psychoanalytic Inst. of San Francisco Jewish. Club: Met. (San Francisco). Home: 850 El Camino Del Mar San Francisco CA 94121-1018 Office: 538 University Center 2130 Fulton St San Francisco CA 94117-1080

FROMSON, ANTOINETTE DUVAL, civic worker; b. Chgo., May 22, 1925; d. Ralph A. and Yvonne (Duval) Brown; Barnard Coll., 1947; m. Howard A. Fromson, Oct. 12, 1946 (div. Mar. 1991); children—Michele Yvonne, Michael Erik, Timothy Arthur, Brett Duval. Plaintiff, Women vs. Conn., legal action about the right of women to control their bodies, 1969; convenor, 1st chmn. Conn. Women's Polit. Caucus, 1970; organizer Westport-Weston (Conn.) chpt. NOW, 1972, organizer, convenor, pres. Southwestern conn. chpt., 1974-78; del. Conn. Democratic Conv., 1974; mem. Weston Town Dem. Com., 1972-74; bd. dirs. Westport YMCA, bd. trustess; bd. dirs. Conn. Planned Parenthood, Five Town Found., Greater Norwalk Community Coun.; lifetime mem. Nature Conservancys, Arlington, Va., Weston (Conn.) Hist. Soc. Mem. Unitarian-Universalists Women's Fedn., Barnard Alumni Assn., Nature Conservancy Arlington (life), Weston Hist. Soc. (life), Cedar Point Yacht Club, Aspetuck Valley Country Club, Fairfield Organic Gardening Club. Democrat. Unitarian. Home: PO Box 1151 Weston CT 06883-0151

FRONKO, SUZANNE ROSE, librarian, media specialist; b. Beaver Falls, Pa., Feb. 22, 1948; d. Matthew Joseph and Avelia (Primo) F. BS in Edn., Millersville U., 1968, Slippery Rock U., 1970; MLS, U. Pitts., 1973. Sch. libr., media specialist Moon Area (Pa.) Sch. Dist., 1970—. Mem. Dem. Nat. Com., 1993—, Pitt Golden Panthers, 1980—; vol. Animal Friends, Inc. Mem. NEA, Pa. State Edn. Assn., Moon Edn. Assn. (sec. 1982-84, treas. 1989-93, sec. 1993—), Pa. Sch. Librs. Assn. (assoc.), Beaver County Assn. Sch. Librs. Roman Catholic. Office: Moon Area Mid Sch Libr 1407 Beers School Rd Moon Township PA 15108-2509

FRONTIERE, GEORGIA, professional football team executive; m. Carroll Rosenblum, July 7, 1966 (dec.); children: Dale Carroll, Lucia; m. Dominic Frontiere. Pres., owner L.A. Rams, NFL, 1979—. Bd. dirs. L.A. Boys and Girls Club, L.A. Orphanage Guild, L.A. Blind Youth Found. Named Headliner of Yr., L.A. Press Club, 1981. Office: Los Angeles Rams 2327 W Lincoln Ave Anaheim CA 92801-5102*

FROOM, GEORGIA AMELIA, graphic designer, clarinetist; b. Eglin AFB, Fla., Feb. 22, 1944; d. Howard Oliver and Mavis Bernadine (Corbett) Powers; m. Charles Baumle Froom, Aug. 1, 1964 (div.); 1 child, Amelia Corbett. Student U. No. Iowa, Kansas City Art Inst., Mo. Media estimator Lambert & Feasley, N.Y.C., 1964-65; free lance artist, N.Y.C., 1966-77; owner Graphic People, N.Y.C., 1978—; class IV case supr. Celebrity Centre Ch. of Scientology, N.Y.C., 1990—; clarinetist Persphony Trio, N.Y.C., 1984-86. Class rep. Berkeley Carroll Street Sch., Bklyn., 1983-84, 1984-85. Mem. Soc. Illustrators (treas. 1982-85). Democrat. Avocations: skiing; painting; playing the clarinet; home renovation. Home: 197 St Johns Pl Brooklyn NY 11217-3405 Office: Graphic People 62 W 39th St New York NY 10018-3818

FROST, DIANA, lawyer; b. San Jose, Calif., Apr. 20, 1954; d. Richard George and Frances Edna (Atkins) Harkess; m. Douglas Edward Friedman, Sept. 14, 1980; children: Maxwell Douglas, Kyle Edward. BA, Bard Coll., 1976; JD, Fordham U., 1985. Bar: N.Y., U.S. Dist. Ct. (so., ea. dists) N.Y. Contracts mgr. St. Martin's Press, N.Y., 1980-82; litigation assoc. Coudert Bros., N.Y., 1986-91; sr. counsel Random House, Inc., N.Y., 1991—. Contbr. article to profl. jour. Office: Random House Inc 201 E 50th St New York NY 10022

FROST, ELIZABETH ANN, school counselor; b. Denver, July 24, 1963; d. Robert E. and Nettie L. (Jennings) Frost. BA, U. Wyo., 1987; MEd, U. Miss., 1993. Cert. EMT-intermediate defibrillation; cert. counselor K-12; cert. emergency/cardiac medications. Resource tchr. Alliance (Nebr.) High Sch., 1987-90, Afton (Wyo.) Elem. Sch., 1990-92, Staff Valley Jr. High, Afton, 1992-93; counselor Lincoln County Sch. Dist. # 2, Afton, 1993—. Named Outstanding Young Woman Am., 1987; recipient Meyman award Alliance Jr. C. of C., 1988, Disting. Svc. award, 1989, Educators Cultural Exch. Tour award Japan Travel Bur., 1994. Mem. NEA, ACA, Wyo. Edn. Assn.

FROST, ELIZABETH ANN MCARTHUR, physician; b. Glasgow, Scotland, Oct. 29, 1938; came to U.S., 1963; d. Robert Thomas and Anne M. (Ross) F.; m. Wallace Capobianco, Sept. 4, 1965 (dec. May 1988); children: Garrett, Ross, Christopher, Neil. MBChB, U. Glasgow, 1961. Diplomate Am. Bd. Anesthesiology, Royal Coll. Ob-Gyn., London. Intern in surgery Royal Infirmary, Glasgow, 1961-62; intern in medicine Victoria Infirmary, Glasgow, 1962; intern in obstetrics Royal Maternity Hosp., Glasgow, 1962-63; resident in internal medicine Englewood (N.J.) Hosp., 1963-64; resident in anesthesiology N.Y. Hosp., N.Y.C., 1964-66; instr. in anesthesiology Albert Einstein Coll. Medicine, Bronx, N.Y., 1966-68, asst. prof. to assoc. prof., 1968-81, prof. anesthesiology, 1981-91, mem. dept. history of medicine, 1973-91; prof., chmn. dept. anesthesiology N.Y. Med. Coll., Valhalla, N.Y., 1992—; dir. div. neuroanesthesia Albert Einstein Coll. Medicine and Affiliated Hosps. Book reviewer New Eng. Jour. of Medicine, 1983—; editor Preanesthetic Assessment, Anesthesiology News, 1984—, Gen. Surgery News, 1991; author/contbr. books; contbr. articles to profl. jours. Mem. N.Y. State Soc. Anesthesiologists, Am. Soc. of Anesthesiologists, Assn. of Univ. Anesthesiologists, Soc. of Neurosurg. Anesthesia and Neurologic Supportive Care, Am. Assn. of Neurol. Surgeons, Anesthesia History Assn., Internat. Trauma Anesthesia and Critical Care Soc. Office: NY Medical Coll Valhalla NY 10595

FROST, ELLEN ELIZABETH, psychologist, b. N.Y.C., July 16, 1947; d. John Joseph and Josephine Mary (Cornell) F.; m. Jerry Melnick, Jan 8, 1982; children: Mariel Frost, Matt James. B.A. magna cum laude, St. John's U., 1969; M.A. (N.Y. State regents fellow, 1969, USPHS fellow, 1969-72), Fordham U., 1981, Ph.D., 1982; candidate N.Y.U. Postdoctoral Program for Psychotherapy and Psychoanalysis, 1982-84. Clin. psychology intern Columbia-Presbyn. Psychiat. Inst., N.Y.C., 1972-73; asst. team leader, staff psychologist Bensonhurst inpatient unit, South Beach Psychiat. Center, Bklyn., 1973-75, sr. psychologist, Bensonhurst outpatient dept., 1975-81, assoc. psychologist, supr., 1982-89; clin. supr. New Hope Guild, Bklyn., 1983—; faculty L.I. Inst. Mental Health, 1990—, supr., 1993—. Mem. Am. Psychol. Assn., Sigma Xi. Office: 200 E 33rd St # 25 New York NY 10016-4874

FROST, ELLEN LOUISE, federal agency administrator; b. Boston, Apr. 26, 1945; d. Horace Wier and Mildred (Kip) F.; m. William F. Pedersen, Jr., Feb. 2, 1974; 1 son by previous marriage, Jai Kumar Ojha; children: Mark Francis Pedersen, Claire Ellen Pedersen. B.A. magna cum laude, Radcliffe Coll., 1966; M.A., Fletcher Sch. Law and Diplomacy, 1967; Ph.D., Harvard U., 1972. Teaching fellow, instr. Harvard U., Wellesley Coll., 1969-71; legis. asst. Office of Senator Alan Cranston, Washington, 1972-74; fgn. affairs officer Dept. Treasury, Washington, 1974-77; dep. dir. Office of Internat. Trade Policy and Negotiations, 1977; dep. asst. sec. of def. for internat. econ. and tech. affairs Dept. Def., Washington, 1977-81; dir. govt. programs Westinghouse Electric Corp., Washington, 1981-88; corp. dir., internat. affairs United Techs. Corp., Washington, 1988-91; sr. fellow Inst. for Internat. Econs., Washington, 1992-93; counselor to U.S. Trade Rep., Washington, 1993—. Author: For Richer, For Poorer: The New U.S.-Japan Relationship, 1987. Trustee Aspen Inst. Berlin, 1990-92. NSF trainee, 1967-69. Mem. Internat. Inst. Strategic Studies, Coun. Fgn. Rels., Phi Beta Kappa. Office: US Trade Rep Exec Office of President 600 17th St NW Washington DC 20506-0200

FROST, KAREN FRANCES, consultant; b. Chgo., Mar. 23, 1966; d. Albert Vincent and Ann Adeline (Adamkiewicz) Staroszczyk; m. Curtis Harvey Frost, Sept. 18, 1993. BA, Lake Forest Coll., 1988; MBA, U. Chgo., 1993. Flexible benefit adminstrn. cons. Hewitt Assocs., Lincolnshire, Ill., 1988-93; flexible benefits cons. Hewitt Assocs., Lincolnshire, 1993—. Mem. U. Chgo. Women's Bus. Group. Roman Catholic. Home: 1951 N Ricks Rd Apt 209 Palatine IL 60074-2535 Office: Hewitt Assocs 100 Half Day Rd Lincolnshire IL 60069-3242

FROST, ROSE, library executive; b. Saginaw, Mich., Jan. 20, 1950; d. Philip Raymond and Angeline Alice (Brink) Grybowski. AA, Delta Coll., 1969; BA, Mich. State U., 1971; MA, U. S. Fla., 1977. Cert. permanent profl. librarian, Mich. Library aide, librarian Orlando Pub. Library, Fla., 1973-78; sales rep. Baker & Taylor, Momence, Ill., 1978-81; pub. relations officer Saginaw Pub. Library, 1981-83; librarian Delta Coll., University Center, Mich., 1983-85; supr. user services Grace Dow Library, Midland, Mich., 1985-88; exec. dir. Presque Isle Dist. Library, Rogers City, Mich., 1988-93; dir. Ransom Dist. Libr., Plainwell, Mich., 1993-94; exec. dir. libr. svcs., Mt. Pleasant Vets. Meml. Libr., Mt. Pleasant, Mich., 1995—; chmn. Video Cassettes in Pub. Libraries Conf., 1986; chmn. adv. coun. Northland Library Coop., 1989-90; v.p. Tots Aboard Presch., 1992-93. Chmn. networking YWCA, Bay City, Mich., 1985; trustee Carrollton (Mich.) Pub. Schs., 1985-88. Mem. ALA, Mich. Libr. Assn. (pub. rels. com. 1981-84, chmn. intellectual freedom com. 1985-87, presenter Best of Show awards 1984, panel mem. conf. 1984, awards com. 1991-93), AAUW (newsletter editor 1983-84), Mich. Libr. Assn. (task force alternative funding 1990-94), Mich. Libr. Assn. Leadership Acad. Avocations: classical music, theater, travel, swimming, reading.

FROST CROCKETT, FELICIA DODEE, brokerage firm executive; b. Oklahoma City, Oct. 19, 1956; d. Carl S. Frost and Mikki (Matheny) Marcus; m. Billy Crockett. Student So. Meth. U., 1974-76. Gen. mgr. Keystone Readers Svc., Dallas, 1976-80; v.p. and sr. fin. cons. Merrill Lynch pvt. client, Dallas, 1980—. Bd. dirs. North Dallas Shared Ministries, 1988-91, Ronald McDonald Children's Charities, 1992—; mem. investment com. Dallas Womens Found., 1991-94. Mem. Dallas Opera (bd. dirs. 1991—), Dallas Securities Dealers Assn., Nat. Assn. Securities Dealers (gen. securities prin., mcpl. securities rulemaking bd. prin., registered options prin., bd. arbitrators), NYSE (com. mem.), Merrill Lynch Pres. Club (Smith fellow), Park Cities Exch. Club (charter, bd. dirs. 1991—), Chief Executive Officers Club. Republican. Office: Merrill Lynch Pierce Fenner and Smith 2000 Premier Pl 5910 N Central Expy Ste 2000 Dallas TX 75206-5152

FROSTIC, GWEN, paper company executive; b. Sandusky, Mich., Apr. 26, 1906; d. Fred Watson and Sara (Alexander) F. A in Teaching, Eastern Mich. U., 1965; BA, Western Mich. U., 1971; LLD (hon.), Ea. Mich. U., 1965; HHD (hon.), Western Mich. U., 1971; DFA (hon.), Mich. State U., 1973; DLitt (hon.), Alma Coll., 1977. Art tchr. Deabron (Mich.) Pub. Schs., 1927-39; tool designer Ford Motor Co., Dearborn, 1940-90; pres. Presscraft Papers, Benzonia, Mich., 1991—; mem. state bd. Bus. and Profl. Women, Wyandotte, 1930-60. Author: My Michigan, 1957, A Walk With Me, 1958, These Things Are Ours, 1960, A Place of Earth, 1962, To Those Who See, 1965, Wingborne, 1967, Wisps of Mist, 1969, Beyond Time, 1971, Contemplate, 1973, The Enduring Cosmos, 1976, The Infinite Destiny, 1978, The Evolving Omnity, 1981, The Caprice Immensity, 1983, Multiversality, 1985, Heuristic, 1987, Chaotic Harmony, 1989, Abysmal Acuman, 1991, Aggrandize, 1993. Recipient Southwest Mich. Mensa award, 1981, Franfort C. of C. award, 1981, Ohio Gov.'s Youth Art Exhbn. award, 1981, Huron Valley Mich. Botanical Club award, 1982, Crooked Tree Girl Scout Coun. award, 1982, Mich. Outdoor Edn. Assn. award, 1983, Internat. Assn. Printing House Craftsmen award, 1984, Mich. Capitol Girl Scout Coun. award, 1985, Women's Nat. Farm and Garden Club award, 1986; named to Mich. Womens Hall of Fame, 1986, Jr. Achievment Bus. Hall of Fame, 1991. Mem. Nat. Fedn. Garden Club, PEO, Order Ea. Star, Alpha Delta Kappa, Delta Kappa Gamma, Omicron Nu, Alpha Sigma Tau. Republican. Home and Office: 5140 River Rd Benzonia MI 49616

FRUCHTER, ROSALIE KLAUSNER, elementary school educator; b. Bklyn., May 1, 1940; d. Marcus and Sarah (Twersky) Klausner; m. Marvin Fruchter, Aug. 15, 1970; children: Marcus, Alexander. BA, Bklyn. Coll., 1960; MA, Nat. Louis U., Evanston, Ill., 1988; postgrad., U. Chgo., 1962-65. Tchr. William H. Ray Sch./Chgo. Bd. Edn., 1961—; cons. math project U. Chgo., 1985-87. Contbr. to math book: One Minute Math, 1990. Bd. dirs. Jewish Community Ctr. of Hyde Park, Chgo., 1978-84, Congregation KAM Isaiah Israel, Chgo., 1984-91, 93—; co-founder Nurit chpt. Hadassah, Hyde Park, 1980; mem. Hyde Park Neighborhood Club, Chgo., 1975—. Recipient Kate Maremont award Chgo. PTA, 1980; Chgo. Found. for Edn. grantee, 1990, 94. Mem. ASCD, Ill. Sci. Tchrs. Found., Acad. Econ. Edn., Nat. Coun. Tchrs. Math., Nat. Coun. Tchrs. English, Assn. for Childhood Edn. Internat., Chgo. Tchrs. Union (sch. del.), Pi Lambda Theta. Democrat. Home: 5434 S Hyde Park Blvd Chicago IL 60615-5815

FRUDAKIS, ROSALIE, small business owner; b. Bloomsburg, Pa., May 29, 1952; d. Jacob Louis and Mary (Kalish) Gluchov; m. Zenos Antonios Frudakis, Jan. 9, 1976. BA in Social Work, Elizabethtown Coll., 1973; postgrad., Temple U., 1974. Art therapist Inst. of Pa. Hosp., Phila., 1974-75; dir. art therapy Bacharach Rehab. Ctr., Pomona, N.J., 1975-76; cofounder, officer of found. Frudakis Acad. Fine Arts, Phila., 1976-85; founding ptnr., pres. Frudakis Gallery, Phila., 1976-85; founding ptnr. The Support System, Inc., Phila., 1984-87; ptnr. Frudakis Studio, Glenside, Pa., 1985—; devel. cons. Mus. at Drexel U., Phila., 1988-91. Patentee for game and method for encouraging self-improvement. V.p. fin. and adminstrn. Bach Festival, Phila., 1992-93; mng. dir. Convergence Dancers and Musicians, 1993—. Mem. Nat. Sculpture Soc. (allied profl. mem., devel. cons. 1985—, exhbn. project mgr. 1987). Home: 2355 Mount Carmel Ave Glenside PA 19038-4103

FRUEHLING, AURORA AVECILLA, civic volunteer; b. Honolulu, Nov. 3, 1934; d. Alfonso Ganaden and Angeles Managaser Avecilla; m. Royal Theodore Fruehling, June 26, 1960; children: Everett, Christine. Student, U. Philippines, Quezon City, 1952-54; BA, U. Hawaii, 1956; MA, Northwestern U., 1957. Com. sec. legis. and community affairs Hawaii Med. Assn., Honolulu, 1981-84. Active Honolulu County Com. on the Status of Women, 1980-88, chair, 1984-86; co-chair women's retreat com. 1st Presbyn. Ch. Honolulu, sec. worship and music commn., 1988-92, nominating com., pastor search com., 1987; rsch. and instl. rev. com. The Queen's Med. Ctr.; nat. bd. dirs. YWCA of U.S.A., 1988-94, nat. bd. officers nominating com., pub. policy com., racial justice com.; bd. dirs. YWCA of Oahu, 1987—, chair global edn. and advocacy com., past chair pub. policy com., membership com., nominating com., chair 1991 and 1994 Nat. Triennial Conv. preparation com. Mem. AAUW, (residence treas., exec. com., Wiki Kala investment club), MADD (Honolulu chpt., community adv. bd. 1988-90, nominating com. 1991), U.S.-China People's Friendship Assn., Pan-Pacific and S.E. Asia Womens' Assn. (2d v.p. 1988-90), Univ. Hawaii Women's Campus Club (councillor), Hawaii Alliance for Arts Edn. (sec. bd. dirs.), Honolulu Acad. Arts, Honolulu Theatre for Youth Stagehands, Filipino Hist. Soc. Hawaii. Home: 3549 Alani Dr Honolulu HI 96822

FRUEHWALD, KRISTIN G., lawyer; b. Sidney, Nebr., May 15, 1946; d. Chris U. and Mary E. (Boles) Bitner; m. Michael R. Fruehwald, Feb. 23, 1980; children: Laurel Elizabeth, Amy Marie. BS with highest distinction in History, U. Nebr., 1968; JD summa cum laude, Ind. U., 1975. Bar: Ind. 1975, U.S. Dist. Ct. (so. dist.) Ind. 1975. Assoc. Barnes & Thornburg, Indpls., 1975-81, ptnr., 1982—; speaker in field. Contbr. articles to profl. jours. Bd. dirs. Arts Ind., 1994—, Ind. Continuing Legal Edn. Forum, 1993—, Ind. Fed. Cmty. Defenders, Inc., 1993—, Indpls. Bar Found., 1992—, Arts Ind., Inc., Ind. affiliate Am. Heart Assn., 1977-81, Marion County chpt., 1978-81, vice chmn., 1981, Planning Giving Group Ind.; mem. evaluation com. United Way, mem. exec. women's group; gathering mem. Ind. Leadership Celebration; trustee Orchard County Day Sch., 1993—. Fellow ABA (chmn. distributable net income subcom. 1985-91 sect. taxation, mem. com. adminstrn. decedent's estates, mem. com. significant current legislation, real property, probate and trust sect.), Am. Coll. Trust and Estate Coun. (chmn. Ind. state laws com.), Ind. Bar Found., Ind. State Bar Assn. (bd. mgrs. 1989-90, chmn. probate, trust and real propert sects. 1987-88, mem. sect. taxation, 11th dist. del. Ho. Dels. 1987—); mem. Indpls. Bar Assn. (pres. 1993, chmn. estate planning and adminstrn. sect. 1982-83, chmn. long range fin. planning com. 1988-89), Indpls. Estate Planning Coun., Internat. Assn. Fin. Planners, Ind. Probate Code Study Commn. Office: Barnes & Thornburg 11 S Meridian St Ste 1313 Indianapolis IN 46204

FRUTH, BERYL ROSE, physician; b. Carey, Ohio, Mar. 27, 1952; d. Oscar W. and Alice (Arnett) Fruth. BA in Chemistry magna cum laude, Asbury Coll., 1973; MD, Ohio State U., 1977. Diplomate Am. Acad. Family Practice. Intern Grant Hosp., Columbus, Ohio, 1977-78, resident, 1978-79, chief resident, 1979-80; pvt. practice, Columbus, 1980-93; family physician Columbus Community Physicians, Inc., Grove City, Ohio, 1993—; asst. dir. family practice residency Grant Hosp., 1980-81; med. dir. Columbus Dispatch, 1983-93, St. Anthony Breast Evaluation Ctr., 1986—; lectr. Columbus Cancer Clinic, 1984; mentor family practice dept. Ohio State U., physician preceptor Sch. Medicine. Contbr. Ohio State U. Med. Sch. Learning Module in Alcoholism, 1983-84. Named Alumna of Yr., Vanlue Sch., Ohio. Fellow Am. Acad. Family Physicians; mem. AMA, Am. Med. Women's Assn., Acad. Family Practice. Office: 2041 Stringtown Rd Grove City OH 43123

FRY, ANNE EVANS, zoology educator; b. Phila., Sept. 11, 1939; d. Kenneth Evans and Nora Irene (Smith) F. AB, Mount Holyoke Coll., 1961; MS, U. Iowa, 1963; PhD, U. Mass., 1969. Instr. Carleton Coll., Northfield, Minn., 1963-65; asst. prof. Ohio Wesleyan U., Delaware, 1969-74, assoc. prof., 1974-80, prof., 1980—. Contbr. articles to profl. jours. Recipient Welch Teaching award Ohio Wesleyan U., 1976. Mem. AAAS, Am. Inst. Biol. Scis., Am. Soc. Zoologists, Ohio Acad. Sci., Soc. Devel. Biology, Sigma Xi. Office: Ohio Wesleyan U Delaware OH 43015

FRY, DORIS HENDRICKS, museum curator; b. Bristol, Pa., Jan. 20, 1918; d. John Reading and Mary Cordelia (Mariner) Hendricks; m. Wayne Franklin Fry, Aug. 30, 1944; children: Christine Mariner Bode, David Whiteley, Janet Margaret. Student, Temple U. Sch. Music, 1936-40. Cert. tchr. Hist. Soc. Early Am. Decoration, Inc. Art tchr. home studio Delmar, N.Y., 1957—; art tchr. The Arts Ctr., Albany, DN.Y., 1972-76, Albany Inst. History and Art, 1972-76; tchr. Mus. Hist. Soc. Early Am. Decoration, Albany, 1982-90, dir., curator, 1981-88; dir., curator Hist. Soc. Early Am. Decoration; trustee Mus. Hist. Soc. Early Am. Decoration, Albany, 1976-86, dir. Sch., 1979-81, chmn. tchr. cert. com., 1979-80; class coordinator Albany Inst. History and Art, 1972-76; lectr. Hitchcock Mus., Conn., Conn. Valley Mus., Mass., 1981-82, N.Y. State Mus. Contbr. articles to profl. jours. and popular mags. Recipient awards Hist. Soc. Early Am. Decoration, including Disting. Service award, 1986, Pres.'s award, 1989. Mem. PEO.

FRY, EVELYN LEONA, clinical social worker; b. Melrose Park, Ill., Feb. 6, 1952; d. James Herbert and Mary Grace (Anthony) Zimmermann; m. John David Fry, Nov. 9, 1974; children: Kathleen Ann, Jennifer Marie. BA in Psychology, So. Ill. U., 1975; MSW, Aurora (Ill.) U., 1987. Lic. clin. social worker, Ill. Pub. aid caseworker II, Ill. Dept. Pub. Aid, Aurora, 1980-81; social worker Carol Stream (Ill.) Police Dept., 1987-90, Cen. DuPage Hosp., Winfield, Ill., 1990; pvt. practice Warrenville, Ill., 1989-; social worker, clin. coord. Rapha Cristian Group, Forest Park, Ill., 1991-92; clin. dir. Living Hope Inst., Forest Park, Ill., 1993; psychotherapist in pvt. practice Peace of Mind, Roselle, Ill., 1993—, Maryville-Herrick House, Bartlett, Ill., 1993—; field instr. Aurora U., 1987-90; mem. adv. com. U-46 In Touch/Drug Free Task Force, Elgin, Ill., 1987-90; mem. steering com. Warrenville Youth and Family Svcs., 1989—; treas. NW DuPage Human Svcs. Coordinating Com., Bloomingdale, Ill., 1990—. Campaign worker Paul Simon for U.S. Senate, Lombard, Ill., 1980—; committeeman 27th precinct Winfield Twp. Dem. Orgn., Warrenville, 1985—; treas. Edgebrook Homeowners Assn., Warrenville, 1986-87; active local polit. campaigns, 1985, 89, 93; chmn. united thank officer Episcopal Churchwomen, St. Marks Ch., Geneva, Ill., 1989-90. Mem. NASW, Soc. Clin. and Exptl. Hypnosis (assoc.), Milton Erickson Inst. No. Ill. Office: Peace of Mind 17 Howard St Roselle IL 60172

FRY, MARION GOLDA, retired university administrator; b. Halifax, N.S., Can., Apr. 16, 1932; d. George W. and Marion I. (Publicover) F. Grad., U. King's Coll., 1953, DCL, 1985; MA, Dalhousie U., 1955; B of Lit., Oxford U., 1958; DLitt, Trent U., 1989. Asst. prof. philosophy, asst. dean of women Bishop's U., 1958-64; prin. Catharine Parr Traill Coll., Trent U., 1964-69, assoc. prof. philosophy, 1964-86, v.p., 1975-79; pres. U. of King's Coll., Halifax, 1987-93. Home: 652 Walkerfield Ave, Peterborough, ON Canada K9J 4W2

FRY, MILDRED HELEN, assistant regional library director; b. Canton, Ohio, Mar. 31, 1940; d. Homer D. and Freda A. (Heldman) Covey; m. James W. Fry, July 26, 1957 (div. 1985); 1 child, Christine Lee Fry Clarke. BA, Capital U., Columbus, Ohio, 1982; MLS, Kent (Ohio) State U., 1986. Libr. asst. Stark County Dist. Libr., Canton, 1958-61; asst. dir. Mayne Williams Pub. Libr., Johnson City, Tenn., 1965-66; circulation desk supr. Ohio State U. Libr., Edn. and Psychology, 1966-82; training coord. Online Computer Libr. Ct., Columbus, 1982-84; asst. dir. Cleve. Area Met. Libr. System, 1986—. Developer Libr. Leadership 2000 Inst., Ohio, 1993—. Mem. ASTD, ALA (exec. bd., sec. Continuing Libr. Edn. Network and Exch. Round Table 1990-92, mem. leadership devel. com. 1994—), Libr. Adminstrn. and Mgmt. Assn., Ohio Libr. Assn. (bd. dirs. 1990-93), Ohio Women Librs., First Families of Ohio. Democrat. Home: Ste 307 6511 Marsol Rd Cleveland OH 44124-3546 Office: Cleve Area Metro Libr 20600 Chagrin Blvd Ste 500 Cleveland OH 44122-5334

FRY, RITA ALIESE, lawyer; b. Memphis, May 28, 1946; d. McKinley and Lucile (Hoskins) High; m. Adelbert Fry; 1 child, Vincent J. BA, Loyola U., 1973; JD, Northwestern U., 1979. Bar: Ill. 1980, U.S. Dist. Ct. (no. dist.)

Ill. 1980, U.S. Ct. Appeals (7th cir.) 1993, U.S. Supreme Ct. 1993. Asst. pub. defender Office of Cook County Pub. Defender, Chgo., 1980-86; sr. supervising atty. City of Chgo. Dept. Law, Ill., 1986-88; 1st asst. pub. defender Office of Cook County Pub. Defender, Chgo., 1988-92; pub. defender of cook county Office of Cook County Pub. Defender, 1992—; mem. adv. bd. BNA Criminal Practice Manual, 1993, MacArthur Justice Ctr., 1993; mem. adv. com. Northwestern U. Sch. Law of Short Courses, 1993—; bd. dirs. Pub. Interest Law Initiative; bd. visitors No. Ill. U. Law Sch., 1992-94; exec. com. Cook County Criminal Justice Coordinating Coun.; mem. Cir. Ct. Liaison Com., 1993; mem. Ill. Supreme Ct. Subcom. on the Selection and Adminstrn. of Juries, 1993—, U.S. Senate Jud. Nominations Commn. for the State of Ill., 1993; many others. Recipient Ida Platt award Cook County Bar Assn., 1992, Kizzy award Kizzy Scholarship Fund Revlon, Inc., 1992, Sixth Amendment award Bill of Rights Bicentennial Celebration Indp. Voters of Ill., 1992. Mem. ABA (coun. mem. sect. of criminal justice), Am. Mgmt. Assn., Black Women Lawyers Assn., Chgo. Bar Assn. (bd. mgrs. 1992-94), Chgo. Conf. Black Lawyers, Chgo. Coun. Lawyers, Cook County Bar Assn., Ill. Pub. Defenders Assn. (bd. dirs.), Ill. State Bar Assn., Nat. Assn. for Criminal Def. Lawyers, Nat. Bar Assn., Nat. Lawyers Guild, Nat. Legal Aid and Defenders Assn., The Fellows of Am. Bar Found. Office: Cook County Pub Defender 200 W Adams Chicago IL 60606

FRYE, HELEN JACKSON, federal judge; b. Klamath Falls, Oreg., Dec. 10, 1930; d. Earl and Elizabeth (Kirkpatrick) Jackson; m. William Frye, Sept. 7, 1952; children: Eric, Karen, Heidie; 1 adopted child, Hedy; m. Perry Holloman, July 10, 1980 (dec. Sept. 1991). BA in English with honors, U. Oreg., 1953, MA, 1960, JD, 1966. Bar: Oreg. 1966. Public sch. tchr. Oreg., 1956-63; with Riddlesberger, Pederson, Brownhill & Young, 1966-67, Husband & Johnson, Eugene, 1968-71; circuit ct. judge State of Oreg., 1971-80; U.S. dist judge Dist. Oreg. Portland, 1980—. Office: US Dist Ct 706 US Courthouse 620 SW Main St Portland OR 97205-3037

FRYE, JUDITH ELEEN MINOR, editor; b. Seattle; d. George Edward and Eleen G. (Hartelius) Minor; student UCLA, 1947-48, U. So. Calif., 1948-53; m. Vernon Lester Frye, Apr. 1, 1954. Acct., office mgr. Colony Wholesale Liquor, Culver City, Calif., 1947-48; credit mgr. Western Distbg. Co., Culver City, 1948-53; ptnr. in restaurants, Palm Springs, L.A., 1948, ptnr. in date ranch, La Quinta, Calif., 1949-53; ptnr., owner Imperial Printing, Huntington Beach, Calif., 1955—; editor, pub. New Era Laundry and Cleaning Lines, Huntington Beach, 1962—; registered lobbyist, Calif., 1975-84. Mem. Textile Care Allied Trade Assn., Laundry & Dry Cleaning Suppliers Assn., Calif. Coin-op Assn. (exec. dir. 1975-84, Cooperation award 1971, Dedicated Svc.award 1976), Nat. Automatic Laundry & Cleaning Coun. (Leadership award 1972), Women Laundry & Drycleaning (past pres., Outstanding Svc. award 1977), Printing Industries Assn., Master Printers Am., Nat. Assn. Printers & Lithographers. Office: 22031 Bushard St Huntington Beach CA 92646-8409

FRYE, LAURIE ANN, air traffic controller; b. Providence, Aug. 6, 1957; d. John James and Alice May (Greaves) Jackson; 1 child, Jason Jackson. Machinist-pressman Bostitch, East Greenwich, R.I., 1976-83; air traffic contr. Dept. Def. 117 TCS, Savannah, Ga., 1983-87, FAA Jacksonville Ctr. Air Rte. Traffic Control Ctr., Hilliard, Fla., 1987—. Bd. mem. Code Enforcement Bd., Nassau County, Fla., 1993, 94. Republican. Methodist. Home: 39 Teal Ct Fernandina Beach FL 32034

FRYE, MARY CATHERINE, lawyer; b. Amarillo, Tex., Feb. 9, 1950; d. John Gristy and Estelle Angelina (Ashton) F.; m. Irwin Allen Popowsky, Dec. 18, 1977; children: Matthew Frye, Rebecca Susan. AB, Oberlin Coll., 1972; JD, U. Pa., 1977. Bar: Pa. 1977. Law clk. Phila. Orphans' Ct., 1977-79; assoc. Reager, Selkowitz & Adler, Harrisburg, Pa., 1980-89; staff atty. Pa. State Edn. Assn., Harrisburg, 1989-92; chief counsel Pa. Assn. Elem. and Secondary Sch. Prins., Harrisburg, 1992-94; chief civil divsn./asst. U.S. atty. U.S. Atty.'s Office (mid. dist.) Pa., Harrisburg, 1994—; adj. prof. law Widener U., Harrisburg, 1994—. Author: Sexual Harassment: A Guide for Administrators, 1993. Democrat. Home: 2091 North Dr Harrisburg PA 17110 Office: US Atty's Office 228 Walnut St Harrisburg PA 17108

FRYER, GLADYS CONSTANCE, nursing home medical director, educator; b. London, Mar. 28, 1923; came to U.S., 1967; d. William John and Florence Annie (Dockett) Mercer; m. Donald Wilfred Fryer, Jan. 20, 1944; children: Peter Vivian, Gerard John, Gillian Celia. MB, BS, U. Melbourne, Victoria, Australia, 1956. Resident Box Hill Hosp., 1956-57; postdoctoral fellow Inst. of Cardiology, U. London, 1958; med. registrar Queen Victoria Hosp., Melbourne, Australia, 1958; cardiologist Assunta Found., Petaling Jaya, Malaysia, 1961-64; fellow in advanced medicine London Hosp., U. London, 1964; clin. research physician U.S. Army Clin. Research Unit, Malaysia, 1964-66; physician to pesticide program U. Hawaii, 1967-68; internist Hawaii Permanente Kaiser Found., Honolulu, 1968-73; practice medicine specializing in internal medicine Honolulu, 1973-88; med. dir. Hale Nani Health Ctr., Honolulu, 1975-89, Beverly Manor Convalescent Ctr., Honolulu, 1975-89; vis. pediatric cardiac depts. Yale U., Stanford U., U. Calif., 1958; asst. clin. prof. medicine John Burns Sch. Medicine U. Hawaii, 1968-89; vis. geriatrics dept. U. Capetown, 1990; med. cons. Salvation Army Alcohol Treatment Facility, Honolulu, 1975-81; physician to skilled nursing patients VA, Honolulu, 1984-88; preceptor to geriatric nurse practitioner program U. Colo., Honolulu, 1984-85; lectr. on geriatrics, Alzheimer's disease, gen. medicine, profl. women's problems, and neurosci., 1961—; mem. ad hoc due process bd. Med. Care Evaluation Com., 1982-88, Hospice Adv. Com., 1982-88; mem. pharmacy com. St. Francis Hosp. Clin. Staff, 1983-89, chmn. 1983-84. Contbr. articles to profl. jours. Mem. adv. com. Honolulu Home Care St. Francis Hosp., 1974-87; mem. adv. bd. Honolulu Gerontology Program, 1983-89, Straub Home Health Program, Honolulu, 1984-87; mem. sci. adv. bd. Alzheimers Disease and Related Disorders Assn., Honolulu, 1984-89; mem. long term care task force Health and Community Svcs. Coun. Hawaii, 1978-84. Special Ops. Exec., War Office, London, 1943-44. Recipient Edgar Rouse Prize in Indsl. Medicine, U. Melbourne, 1955, Outstanding Supporter award Hawaii Assn. Activity Coordinators, 1987. Fellow ACP; mem. AAAS, Hawaii Med. Assn. (councillor 1984-89), Honolulu County Med. Soc. (chmn., mem. utilization rev. com. 1973-89), World Med. Assn., Am. Geriatrics Soc., N.Y. Acad. Sci. Episcopalian.

FRYER, JUDITH DOROTHY, lawyer; b. N.Y.C., Feb. 14, 1950; d. Jerome M. and Gloria (Abrams) F.; m. Daniel P. Biggs, June 4, 1972; chidren: Jeremy Fryer-Biggs, Zachary Fryer-Biggs. BA, Washington U., 1972; JD, Hofstra U., 1975. Bar: N.Y. 1976. Assoc. Carro, Spanbock, Fass & Geller, N.Y.C., 1978-82, ptnr., 1982-86; ptnr. Finley & Kumble, N.Y.C., 1987; counsel Kaye, Scholer, Fierman, Hays & Handler, N.Y.C., 1988-89, ptnr., 1989—; Bd. advisers Capital Sources for Real Estate newsletter, 1994—. Author: Roll-up Transactions-The Current Picture, 1992, Taking a REIT Public, 1994, Surprises in Recent REIT and Rollup Offerings, 1994; editor current devels.: Real Estate Securities & Capital Markets newsletter, 1989-90, editor, 1990-92. Fellow Am. Bar Found.; mem. ABA (chair subcom. equipment leasing programs 1988-91, chair subcom. on partnerships & REIT products 1991—, chair subcom. on partnerships, trusts and unincorporated assns. 1994—), Assn. of Bar of City of N.Y., Nat. Assn. Real Estate Investment Trusts (exec. com., bd. govs.), Investment Program Assn. (securities law and regulatory affairs com.), Real Estate Investment Assn. (founding mem). Office: Kaye Scholer Fierman Hays & Handler 425 Park Ave New York NY 10022-3506

FRYMYER, KAREN KAY, office administrator, business educator; b. Jackson Center, Ohio, June 19, 1941; d. Franklin Wesley and Phyllis Louise (Zwiebel) Judy; m. Merle L. Frymyer, 1959; 1 child, Jonathan Dale. Assocs., Lima Tech. Coll., 1984; B of Bus., U. Findlay, 1988. Cashier Interstate Securities Co., Inc., Kansas City, Mo., 1963-73; br. mgr. Interstate Securities Co., Inc., Lima, Ohio, 1973-75; realtor Century 21-Gary D. Smith & Co., Lima, Ohio, 1977-81; mortgage rep. Citizens Loan and Bldg. Co., Lima, Ohio, 1984-85; credit mgr. Moulton Gas Co., Wapakoneta, Ohio, 1985-88; relocation dir. The Gooding Co., Lima, 1988-90; instr. Northwest Coll., Lima, 1991, Lima Tech. Coll., 1984—; office mgr. Cowan HER Realtors, Lima, 1992—. Mem. Am. Bus. Women Assn. (pres. 1971-83, 84-86, Woman of Yr. 1971, 84), Lima Bd. Realtors (bd. dirs. 1979-93, Salesperson of Yr. 1981). Mem. United Ch. of Christ. Home: 2600 Shoreline Dr Lima OH 45805-3658

FRY-WENDT, SHERRI DIANE, psychologist; b. Clinton, Mo., Mar. 30, 1958; d. Charles Pierce and Norma Geraldine (Croft) Fry; m. Joseph Otto Wendt, May 24, 1980; children: Benjamin, Ethan, Nathaniel. BSE, Cen. Mo. State U., 1979, MS, 1981; PhD, U. Mo., 1989. Lic. psychologist, Mo. Mental health therapist Wyandot Mental Health Ctr., Kansas City, Kans., 1981-88; EAP contract psychologist Menninger Found., Topeka, 1988-89; contract psychologist Tri-County Mental Health Ctr., Kansas City, 1988-89; pvt. practice Kansas City, 1988—; trainer various workshops Wyandot Tng. Inst., 1985-88; expert witness State of Kans., 1985—. Youth group sponsor Hillside Christian Ch., Kansas City, 1982-86, children's choir dir., 1983-87, deaconess, 1983-93, dir. vacation bible sch., 1992, 93; deaconess Fairview Christian Ch., co-chair Christian edn.; bd. dirs. Northland Presch. Parents Club. Mem. APA, Internat. Soc. Study of Multiple Personality and Dissociation, Greater Kansas City Psychol. Assn., Phi Kappa Phi, Psi Chi. Office: 4901 Main St Ste 408 Kansas City MO 64112-2635

FRYXELL, GRETA ALBRECHT, botany educator, oceanographer; b. Princeton, Ill., Nov. 21, 1926; d. Arthur Joseph and Esther (Andreen) Albrecht; m. Paul A. Fryxell, Aug. 23, 1947; children: Karl Joseph, Joan Esther, Glen Edward. BA, Augustana Coll., 1948; MEd, Tex. A&M U., 1969, PhD, 1975. Tchr. math and sci. jr. high schs. Iowa, 1948-52; research asst. Tex. A&M U., College Station, 1968-71, research scientist, 1971-80, asst. prof. oceanography, 1980-83, assoc. prof., 1983-86, prof., 1986-94, prof. emeritus, 1994—; adj. prof. botany U. Tex., Austin, 1993—; vis. scientist U. Oslo, 1971; chmn. adv. commn. Provasoli-Guillard Ctr. for Culture Marine Phytoplankton, Bigelow Lab, Maine, 1985-87; hon. curator N.Y. Bot. Gardens, 1992—; courtesy prof. U. Oreg., 1994—. Editor: Survival Strategies of the Algae, 1983; contbr. articles to profl. jours. Recipient Outstanding Woman award Brazos County, College Station, 1979, Outstanding Achievement award Augustana Coll., Rock Island, Ill., 1980; Faculty Disting. Achievement award in rsch. Tex. A&M U., 1991, Geoscis. and Earth Resources Adv. Coun. medal, 1993; grantee NSF. Mem. AAAS, AAUW, ACLU, Phycol. Soc. Am. (editorial bd. 1976-79, 82-85, chairperson Prescott award com. 1991), Brit. Phycol. Soc., Internat. Phycol. Soc., Am. Soc. Limnology and Oceanography, Am. Soc. Plant Taxonomists, Internat. Diatom Soc. (bd. govs. 1986—), Tex. Assn. Coll. Tchrs. Democrat. Unitarian-Universalist. Office: U Tex Botany Dept Austin TX 78713-7640

FUCHS, ANNA-RIITTA, medical educator, scientist; b. Helsinki, Finland, Feb. 8, 1926; came to U.S., 1964; d. Martti Adolf and Rut Ester (Sario) Olsson; m. Fritz Fuchs, May 19, 1948; children: Anneli, Martin, Peter Erik, Lars Frederik. MS in Chemistry with honors, U. Helsinki, 1950; DSc, U. Copenhagen, 1978. Research assoc. Inst. Hygiene Med. Physiology, U. Copenhagen, 1952-62; adj. in reproductive physiology Inst. Med. Physiology, U. Copenhagen, 1962-65; research assoc. bio.-med. div. The Population Council, Rockefeller U., N.Y.C., 1965-71, staff scientist bio.-med. div., 1971-77; faculty mem. pharmacology Cornell U. Med. Sch., N.Y.C., 1973-80, assoc. prof. reproductive biology dept. ob-gyn and dept. physiol. biophysics, 1977-86, prof. reproductive biology dept. ob-gyn and dept. physiology and biophysics, 1986—; vis. scientist dept. ob-gyn. Fed. U. Bahia, Salvador, Bahia, Brazil, 1966; vis. prof. reproductive biology Dept. ob-gyn. Chulalongkorn U., Bangkok, 1972-73, 85; cons. dept. ob-gyn. Dept. Health U.S. Virgin Islands, St. Thomas, 1986. Mem. editl. bd.L Am. Jour. Physiology: Endocrinology and Metabolism, 1982-85, Clinica e Investigacion en Ginecologica y Obstetrica, Barcelona, Spain, 1977—; guest editor: Direction in Obstetric Perinatology, spl. issue Am. Jour. Perinatology, 1989; editor: (with F. Fuchs and P. Stubblefield) Preterm Birth, 1993; contbr. chpts. to books, more than 200 sci. articles to prof. jours. Elected friend N.Y.C. Commn. on the Status of Women, 1985. Served with Lotta Svard Finnish women's aux., 1939-44. Decorated Medal of Freedom of Finland, 1944. Fellow N.Y. Acad. Sci. (vice chmn., 1988, program chmn. com. for women in sci. 1982-88); mem. AAAS, Soc. for Gynecologic Investigation, Endocrine Soc., Soc. for the Study Reproduction, Soc. for the Study Fertility, Assn. for Women in Sci. (treas. 1978-80), Gynecol. Assn. Finland (hon.). Lutheran. Club: Larchmont (N.Y.) Yacht. Office: Cornell U Med Coll 1300 York Ave Rm S412 New York NY 10021-4805

FUCHS, ANNE SUTHERLAND, magazine publisher; b. Volta Redonda, Brazil, Apr. 19, 1947; d. Paul Warner and Evelyn Coffman; m. James E. Fuchs, Feb. 6, 1982. Student, U. Paris at Sorbonne, 1967-68, Western Coll. for Women, 1966-67; BA, NYU, 1969. V.p., pub. Woman's Day Spl. Interest Mags.-CBS Mags., N.Y.C., 1980-82, Cuisine Mag., CBS Mags., N.Y.C., 1982-84; v.p., pub. Woman's Day mag. DCI Comm., Inc., N.Y.C., 1985-88; sr. v.p., pub. ELLE mag., N.Y.C., 1988-90, Vogue, N.Y.C., 1990-94; group pub. Harper's Bazaar, N.Y.C., 1994—; chmn. mag. and print com. U.S. Info. Agy., 1989—. Chmn. women's bd. Madison Sq. Boys and Girls Club, N.Y.C.; mem. Com. 200, USIA; bd. dirs. N.Y.C. Partnership, N.Y.C. Partnership Found. Mem. Fin. Women's Assn. N.Y., N.Y. Jr. League, Advt. Women of N.Y., Women in Communications, Women's Forum, Com. of 200, Fin. Women's Assn. N.Y. Club: Economic (N.Y.C.). Office: Harper's Bazaar Hearst Mags 1700 Broadway 37th Fl New York NY 10019*

FUCHS, BETH ANN, research technician; b. Moberly, Mo., July 22, 1963; d. Larry Dale and Marilyn Sue (Summers) Williams; m. Fred Albano Fuchs Jr., Sept. 30, 1989. AA, Cottey Coll., 1983; BS in Engring., U. N.Mex., 1987. Bookkeeper, chemistry technician U. N.Mex., Albuquerque, 1984-88; rsch. engr. Sandia Nat. Labs., Albuquerque, 1988—. Mem. Am. Vacuum Soc. Republican. Home: 336 Espejo NE Albuquerque NM 87123

FUCHS, ELAINE V., molecular biologist, educator; b. Hinsdale, Ill., May 5, 1950; d. Louis H. and Viola L. (Lueck) F.; m. David T. Hansen, Sept. 10, 1988. BS in Chemistry with honors, U. Ill., Urbana, 1972; PhD in Biochemistry, Princeton U., 1977. Postdoctoral fellow dept. biology MIT, 1977-80; asst. prof. U. Chgo., 1980-85, assoc. prof., 1985-88, prof. dept. molecular genetics and cell biology, 1989—, Amgen prof. basic scis., 1993—, investigator, Howard Hughes Med. Inst., 1988—. Assoc. editor Jour. Cell Biology, 1993—, mem. editorial bd., 1988—; contr. numerous articles to profl. jours. Recipient R.R. Benseley award, Am. Assn. Anatomists, 1988, Searle Scholar award, Chgo. Community Trust, 1981-84, Presdl. Young Investigator award, NSF, Washington, 1984-89, NIF Merit award, 1993. Fellow Am. Acad. Arts & Scis.; mem. Am. Assn. Cell Biology, Am. Assn. Biol. Chemists, Phi Beta Kappa. Office: U Chgo Howard Hughes Med Inst Dept Molecular Genetics 5841 S Maryland Ave Rm 314N Chicago IL 60637-1470

FUCHS, KATHLEEN FITZGERALD, psychologist, educator; b. Chgo., May 24, 1946; d. Frank T. and Dorothy E. (Mills) Fitzgerald; m. Raymond P. Fuchs, June 27, 1970; children: Brian C., Laura E. BA cum laude, Barat Coll., 1968; MS, St. Louis U., 1971, PhD, 1975. Lic. psychologist, Wis. Psychologist II S.C. State Hosp., Columbia, 1973-74; cons. Richland Sch. Dist., Columbia, 1974; clin. psychologist Lansdowne Mental Health Ctr., Ashland, Ky., 1976-77; clin. psychologist Lawrence U., Appleton, Wis., 1977—, dir. counseling, 1989—; vis. assoc. prof. Lawrence U., Appleton, 1985-86, 87-88, lectr., 1992; adj. assoc. prof. psychology Lawrence U., 1993—. Mem. bd. edn. St. Pius Parish, Appleton, 1979-82. St. Louis U. fellow, 1968-69, NIMH fellow, 1969-70. Mem. Am. Psychol. Assn., Am. Coll. Pers. Assn., Kappa Gamma Pi, Delta Epsilon Sigma. Roman Catholic. Home: 2412 N Division St Appleton WI 54911-1960 Office: Lawrence U Counseling Ctr PO Box 599 Appleton WI 54912-0599

FUCHS, OLIVIA ANNE MORRIS, lawyer; b. Louisville, May 2, 1949; d. H.H. Morris Jr. and Betty Jean Wills Saltkill; m. Robert Edward Fuchs, Dec. 27, 1969. BA, U. Louisville, 1977, JD cum laude, 1980. Bar: Ky. 1980, U.S. Dist. Ct. (we. dist.) Ky. 1985, Ind. 1986, U.S. Dist. Ct. (so. dist.) Ind. 1987, U.S. Tax Ct. 1987. Assoc. Brown, Todd & Heyburn, Louisville, 1981-87; mem. Conliffe, Sandmann & Sullivan PLLC, Louisville, 1987—. Notes editor Jour. Family Law, 1979-80. Vol. advocate R.A.P.E. Relief Ctr., Louisville YWCA, 1981-87. Mem. ABA, Ind. Bar Assn., Ky. Bar Assn., Louisville Bar Assn. (probate sect. chmn. 1990, profl. responsibility com. chmn. 1988), U. Louisville Law Alumni Coun. (bd. dirs.), The Exec. Club. of Louisville, Jefferson Club, Univ. Club, Phi Alpha Delta (2d v.p. 1994—). Democrat. Presbyterian. Office: Conliffe Sandmann & Sullivan 621 W Main St Louisville KY 40202-2967 also: 141 E Spring St New Albany IN 47150

FUDGE, ANN MARIE, marketing executive; b. Washington, Apr. 23, 1951; d. Malcolm R. and Bettye (Lewis) Brown; m. Richard E. Fudge, Feb. 27, 1971; children: Richard Jr., Kevin. BA, Simmons Coll., 1973; MBA, Harvard U., 1977. Manpower specialist GE, Bridgeport, Conn., 1973-75; mktg. asst. Gen. Mills, Mpls., 1977-78, asst. product mgr., 1978-80, product mgr., 1980-83, mktg. dir., 1983-86; assoc. dir., strategic planning Gen. Foods, White Plains, N.Y., 1986-87, mktg. dir., 1987-89, v.p. mktg. and devel., 1989-91, exec. v.p., gen. mgr., 1991-94; pres. Maxwell House Coffee Co., White Plains, N.Y., 1994—; bd. dirs. Simmons Coll., Boston, Liz Claiborne, Inc., Allied Signal, Inc., Harvard Bus. Sch. Alumni Assn. , 1989-94. Bd. mem. Women's Economic Devel. Corp., St. Paul, 1984-86; chairperson Allocations Panel-United Way, Mpls., 1983-86; vol. Big Sisters/Big Bros., Fairfield County, Conn., 1988-90. Recipient Leadership award YWCA, Mpls., 1980, Black Achievers award Harlem YMCA, 1988, Candace award Nat. Coalition of 100 Black Women, 1991, 92, Corp. Women's Network award, 1994, She Knows Where She's Going award Girls, Inc., 1994. Mem. Exec. Leadership Coun. (pres.), Com. of 200, N.Y. Women's Forum. Office: Kraft Foods 250 North St White Plains NY 10625-0001

FUENTES, DAISY, television personality; b. Havana, Cuba, Nov. 17, 1966; d. Maria and Amado F.; m. Timothy Adams, Aug. 5, 1991. Bergen Comm. Coll., 1984-86. News reporter/weather anchor WXTV, New York, 1986-87; weather anchor WNJU-TV, New York, 1987-90; VJ MTV Networks, New York, 1988—. recipient: Outstanding Women in Media award, Latin Coalition for Fair Media, 1992. Office: MTV Networks 1515 Broadway New York NY 10036-1903*

FUENTES, MARIA ROSA, trade association executive; b. Spokane, Va., May 24, 1960; d. Gregorio Juan and Maria Rosa (Diaz) F. BS, Boston U., 1982; MBA, U. Maine, 1985. Asst. dir. Maine Advancement Program, Augusta, 1986-88; exec. dir. Maine Better Transp. Assn., Augusta, 1990—. Bd. dirs. United Valley ARC, Auburn, Maine, 1992—, So. Kennebec County Child Devel. Corp., Augusta, 1993—. Mem. Nat. Assn. Women in Constrn. (v.p. 1988—), U. Maine Alumni Assn. (bd. dirs. 1989—), Kennebac Valley Alumni of U. Maine (pres. 1988-92). Home: 21 Union St Hallowell ME 04347 Office: Maine Better Transp Assn 146 State St Augusta ME 04330

FUFUKA, NATIKA NJERI YAA, retail executive; b. Cleve., Feb. 21, 1952; d. Russell and Mindoro Reed. AA, AAB, Cuyahoga Community Coll., Cleve., 1973; BA, Mich. State U., 1975; postgrad., Cleve. State U. Asst. pers. dir. May Co., Cleve., 1975-78; merchandiser J.C. Penney, Cleve., 1978-80; sports mgr. Joseph Hornes, Cleve., 1980-81; fashion buyer Higbee, Cleve., 1981-86; merchandise exec. Fashion Bug, Euclid, Ohio, 1986-92; pres., CEO Mindy's Return to Fashion, Cleve., 1993—. Bd. dirs. Ohio Youth Adv. Coun.; vice chair Joint Com. on Medicad Provider Impact for State of Ohio, 1992; mem. Mayor's Census Task Force, Cuyahoga County Women Bus. Enterprise Adv. Coun., Cleve. Female Bus. Enterprise Adv. Coun., Displaced/Single Parent Homemakers Adv. Coun., Cuyahoga Community Coun., Cuyhoga Hills Boys Adv. Coun.; chair Centralized Resource Referral Svc. Panel United Way, 1993, mem. Gen. Assembly, 1993—; vice chair federated allocation panel United Way of Greater Cleve; bd. dirs. Women Community Found., 1993—, Career Beginning Program Bd., 1993—. Ford Found. scholar, 1975; recipient Jesse Jackson Voter Registration award, 1984, Leadership award United Way, 1991, Vol. Leadership recognition City of Cleve., 1991. Mem. NAFE, Assn. MBA Execs., Black Profl. Assn., Nat. Assn. Negro Bus./Profl. Women, Am. Profl. Exec. Women, Am. Women Bus. Assn., Nat. Assn. Black Female Entrepreneurs, Severance Merchant Mall Orgn., Op. Big Vote, Nat. Coun. Negro Women, Nat. Polit. Congress Black Women (nat. founder mem., founder mem. Ohio state chpt.), Nat. Hook-Up, 100 Black Women Coalition, Black Congl. Caucus Braintrust, Small Minority Bus. Braintrust, Corp. Braintrust, Black Women Agenda, Black Women Roundtable, Black Focus (pres. bd. trustees), 21st Congl. Dist. Caucus (exec. bd. mem., chair bus. women com., certs. of appreciation for outstanding svc. 1985, 86), Urban League Greater Cleve., Op. Push of Greater Cleve. (bd. dirs.), Project Vote (asst. dir., Voter Registration award 1984), Midwest Vote Project, Women Vote Project, Women-Space, United Black Fund, Greater East Cleve. Dem. Club, Minority Women Polit. Action Com., LWV, Cuyahoga Women Polit. Caucus, Ohio Pub. Interest Campaign, Ohio Rainbow Coalition, Ohio Dem. Women Com., Network Together, Black Elected Dem. Ofcls. Ohio, Cleve. City Club, 16th Dist. Club, Project M.O.V.E. Democrat. Pentecostal. Home: 12001 Martin Luther King Blvd Cleveland OH 44105

FUGATE, JUDITH, ballet dancer; b. Hamilton, Ohio, Nov. 23, 1956. Student, Sch. Am. Ballet. Dancer N.Y.C. Ballet, 1973—, soloist, 1979-86, prin. dancer, 1986—. Dancer numerous ballets including The Nutcracker, Don Quixote, A Midsummer Night's Dream, Concerto Barocco, Gounod Symphony, Valse-Fantaisie, Divertimento # 15, Fancy Free, Liebeslieder Walzer, Dances at a Gathering, The Fours, Seven by Five, A Fool for You, I'm Old Fashioned, Seven by Five, Ivesiana, Ma Mere l'Oye, N.Y.C. Ballet's Balanchine Celebration, 1993, Apollo, Coppélia, Jewels, Union Jack. Office: NYC Ballet Inc NY State Theater Lincoln Ctr Plz New York NY 10023 also: 1501 Strawberry Rd Mohegan Lake NY 10547-1046*

FUGELBERG, NANCY JEAN, educator; b. Tarentum, Pa., Mar. 6, 1947; d. Stanley and Mary (Struhar) Homer; m. Darrell Marvin Fugelberg, Aug. 27, 1977. Cert. master piano classes and music lit. Mozarteum, Salzburg, Austria, 1968; B in Music Edn., Mount Union Coll., 1969; postgrad. Kent State U., 1973-76; EdM in Curriculum and Instrn., Ashland U., 1989. Music tchr. Alliance Sch. Dist., Ohio, 1969-70, Minerva Sch. Dist., Ohio, 1970—; ch. organist First Imamnuel United Ch. of Christ, Alliance, Ohio, 1969-85. Pianist for musicals Carnation Players, Alliance, 1969-72; asst. organist, accompanist various chs. Recipient award for working with handicapped children Minerva Sch. Dist., 1981; Alumni Service award Mu Phi Epsilon, 1983, 84; named One of Outstanding Young Women Am., 1981. Mem. NEA, Minerva Tchrs. Assn., Ohio Edn. Assn., Mu Phi Epsilon (chpt. v.p. 1980-82, pres. 1982-84, historian and music therapy chmn. 1984—). Republican. United Ch. of Christ. Avocations: plants, traveling, playing keyboards shows. Address: 345 S Rockhill Ave Alliance OH 44601-2257

FUGGI, GRETCHEN MILLER, education educator; b. Westerly, R.I., Aug. 26, 1938; d. John Louis and Harriet (Schied) M.; m. William Joseph Fuggi, Aug. 15, 1960; children: Gretchen, Juliann, John, Kristen. BS, So. Conn. State U., 1960, MS, 1969, 6th yr. diploma, 1991, 6th yr. Ednl. Leadership diploma, 1994. Reading cons. Washington Magnet Sch., West Haven, Conn., 1974—; adj. prof. So. Conn. State U., New Haven, 1988—. Pres. Cath. Charity League of Greater New Haven, 1989-90; bd. dirs. New Haven Symphony Aux., 1992—. Mem. AAUP, Internat. Reading Assn., Conn. Reading Assn., Delta Kappa Gamma Soc. Internat. Roman Catholic. Home: 19 Westview Rd North Haven CT 06473-2013

FUJII, SHARON M., federal agency administrator. BA, U. Washington, 1966, M in Social Work, 1969; PhD, Brandeis U., 1975. Sr. v.p. Gerontological Planning Assn., 1975-77; prin. investigator Pacific-Asian Elderly Rsch. Project, 1977-79; program analyst Office of Refugee Resettlement, 1978-79, regional dir., 1979-80; regional adminstr., adminstrn. for children and families Dept. Health and Human Svcs., 1980-86, 86—; mem. Pres. Fed. Coun. on Aging, 1975-78. Health, Edn. and Welfare fellow, 1978-79. Office: Dept of Health & Human Svcs 50 United Nationa Plz Rm 450 San Francisco CA 94102*

FUJIWARA, ELIZABETH JUBIN, lawyer; b. New Orleans, Dec. 20, 1945; d. Otha Ernest and Yvette Marie (Jubin) Barron ; children: Jean Paul Jubin Toshiro, Maria Sachiko Yonahara, Cathleen Sumiko Yonahara. Student, U. Dallas, Irving, 1963-64; BA in Sociology, Loyola U., New Orleans, 1967; MSW, U. Hawaii, 1971, JD, 1983. Exec. dir. ACLU of Hawaii, Honolulu, 1975-77; specialist in equal edn. opportunity Hawaii Dept. Edn., Honolulu, 1977-78; asst. dir. Inst. Productive Behavior, Honolulu, 1978-80; faculty rsch. asst. William S. Richardson Sch. Law, U. Hawaii, Honolulu, 1981; law clk. to presiding justice Intermediate Ct. Appeals Hawaii, Honolulu, 1984-86; pvt. practice law Honolulu, 1986—. Editor: Women's Legal Rights in Hawaii, 1990, 2d edit., 1991, Our Rights, Our Lives, 1990. Active Hawaii Women's Polit. Action Caucus, 1983-85, 89—, Ad Hoc Com. Abortion Rights, 1977-79; organizer Coalition Against Capital Punishment, 1976-78; Peacer Corps trainee in P.R. and Guatemala, 1968. Named one of Outstanding Young Women of Yr. State Commn. on Status of Women, 1976, Outstanding Hawaii Woman Lawyer of Yr., 1988. Mem. Hawaii Bar Assn. (employment sect. officer 1993-94), Nat. Employment Lawyers Assn.

(founder and pres. Hawaii chpt. 1993-94), Assn. Trial Lawyers Am., Hawaii Women Lawyers (co-chair pay equity com. 1985-87, spouse abuse and women prisoners legal penal project 1985-88, mem. legis. com. 1985-87, bd. dirs.), Kappa Beta Gamma. Democrat. Buddhist. Office: 707 Richards St Ste 500 Honolulu HI 96813-4545

FULBRIGHT, HARRIET MAYOR, foundation administrator; b. N.Y.C., Dec. 13, 1933; d. Brantz and Evelyn (Griswold) M.; m. William Watts, Aug. 4, 1954 (div. 1975); children: Evelyn G. Ward, Shelby S. Watts, Heidi H. Mayor; m. J. William Fulbright, Mar. 10, 1990. BA, Radcliffe Coll., Cambridge, Mass., 1955; MFA, George Wash. U., 1975. Chair art dept. Maret Sch., Washington, 1975-80; asst. dir. Congl. Arts Caucus, Washington, 1980-82, Alliance of Ind. Coll. Art, Washington, 1982-84; exec. sec. Internat. Congress Art History, Washington, 1984-87; exec. dir. Fulbright Assn., Washington, 1987-91; pres. The Ctr. for Arts in the Basic Curriculum, Washington, 1991—; bd. dirs., vice-chmn. Coun. for Basic Edn., 1991—, World Learning, Inc., 1993—, Nat. Coun. for Internat. Visitors, 1993—. Author: How To Get Your Own Pre-School Play Group; editor: Fulbrighters Newsletter. Pres. Maret Sch. Bd. Honoree, Young Audiences, 1994. Mem. Nat. Coun. Stds. in the Arts. Office: Ctr for Arts in Basic Curriculum 1319 F St NW Ste 900 Washington DC 20004

FULKS, SARAH JANE See **WYMAN, JANE**

FULLER, ANNE ELIZABETH HAVENS, English educator, consultant; b. Pomona, Calif., Jan. 20, 1932; d. Paul Swain and Lorraine Elizabeth (Hamilton) Havens; m. Martin Emil Fuller, II, June 17, 1961; children: Katharine Hamilton, Peter David Takashi. A.B., Mount Holyoke Coll., 1953; B.A. (Fulbright scholar), Somerville Coll., Oxford U., 1955, M.A., 1959; Ph.D. (Univ. fellow), Yale U., 1958. Instr. English Mount Holyoke Coll., 1957-59; instr. Pomona Coll., 1959-61; asst. prof. U. Fla., Gainesville, 1961-63; lectr. U. Denver, 1964-68, 71-73; assoc. prof., chmn. center for lang. and lit. Prescott (Ariz.) Coll., 1968-70; tchr. Colo. Rocky Mountain Sch., 1970-71; dean of faculty Scripps Coll., Claremont, Calif., 1973-80; prof. English Scripps Coll., 1973-80; spl. asst. to pres., sec. to corp. Claremont U. Center, 1981-83; v.p. for acad. affairs Austin Coll., Sherman, Tex., 1982-84, faculty mem., 1984—; mem. SW dist. Rhodes Scholar Selection Com., 1975-83. Bd. dirs. Am. Council on Edn., 1979-81. Mem. Assn. Am. Colls. (dir. 1977-81, chmn. 1980-81), Am. Conf. Acad. Deans (dir. 1976-79), Commn. on Women in Higher Edn., Am. Assn. Higher Edn., Modern Lang. Assn. Am. Democrat. Episcopalian. Home: 605 Oxford Dr Sherman TX 75092-2433 Office: Austin Coll 900 N Grand Ave Sherman TX 75090-2433

FULLER, CAROL HUFFMAN, education researcher; b. Frankfort, Ind., Dec. 21, 1941; d. John Maurice and Helen Naomi (Eggers) H.; m. Jon Wayne Fuller, Feb. 15, 1969; children: Susan, Jon Geoffrey. BS, Ind. State U., 1963; PhD, Vanderbilt U., 1970. Rsch. asst. Vanderbilt U., Nashville, 1964-67; instr. psychology Davidson (N.C.) Coll., 1967-69, asst. prof., 1970-71; asst. prof. Sacred Heart Coll., Belmont, N.C., 1969-70; personnel rsch. psychologist Naval Personnel R & D Lab., Washington, 1972-73, CSC, Washington, 1973-74; rsch. assoc. Great Lakes Colls. Assn., Ann Arbor, Mich., 1985-89, Ind. Colls. Office, Washington, 1989-91; assoc. dir. Nat. Inst. Ind. Colls. and Univs., Washington, 1991—; cons. Nat. Ctr. Ednl. Stats., Washington, Luce Found., N.Y.C. Author: Scholarship and Service, 1991; contbr. reports and articles to profl. pubs. Home: 11108 Jolly Way Kensington MD 20895 Office: Nat Inst Ind Colls 1025 Connecticut Ave NW Washington DC 20036

FULLER, CASSANDRA MILLER, customer service executive; b. Norwalk, Conn., Dec. 10, 1965; d. George Louis and Bernice (Simmons) Miller; m. David Norman Fuller, Dec. 24, 1988. BS, S.C. State Coll., 1987; postgrad., U. Bridgeport. Interior decorator's apprentice Marty Rae Interiors, Orangeburg, S.C., 1984-85; asst. mgr. Dairy Queen, Orangeburg, S.C., 1986-87; day mgr. The Bedford, Stamford, Conn., 1987-88; dept. mgr. Burlington Coat Factory Warehouse, Danbury, Conn.; asst. mgr. Kidstuff, Inc., Orange, Conn., 1989-92; Postage By Phone customer assistance specialist Pitney Bowes, Stamford, Conn., 1992—; cons. Orangeburg Metro Transit 1987. Mem. Nat. Assn. Negro Bus. and Profl. Women's Clubs Inc., Nat. Black MBA Assn., NAFE, Kappa Omicron Phi. Democrat. Baptist. Office: Pitney Bowes Walter Wheeler Jr Dr Stamford CT 06902

FULLER, JUDITH ANN, art educator, artist; b. Xenia, Ohio, Dec. 3, 1942; d. Jesse Franklin and Edna Mae (Blangy) F.; children: Bryan Devon Tipple, Sean David Tipple. BFA in Painting, U. Dayton, 1965; MA in Art, Ball State U., 1972; PhD in Art Edn., The Ohio State U., 1987. Cert. tchr. Art tchr. K-6 Monroe Ctrl. Sch. System, Parker, Ind., 1966-67, art tchr. 7-12, 1967-69; instr. mus. children's program Dayton (Ohio) Art Inst., 1975-79, instr. workshop programs, 1976-77; instr. art appreciation, art history Capital U., Dayton, Ohio, 1984-87; instr. art appreciation, art edn. U. Dayton, Ohio, 1985-90, art history slide curator, 1989-90; asst. prof. Ctrl. Conn. State U., New Britain, Conn., 1990-92; adminstr., instr. summer studies program for U.S. Coll. Students Trinity Coll., Dublin, Ireland, 1989-92; chair, speaker conf. Three Perspectives on Aesthetics and Art Criticism Fordham U., N.Y.C., 1994; owner, mgr. People Uniting to Rescue the Arts, West Hartford, Conn., 1994. Prin. works exhibited in numerous shows including Ball State U. Gallery, Muncie, Ind., 1972, Rike Gallery Dayton (Ohio) Art Inst., 1979, Fine Arts Ctr., Springfield, Ohio, 1979, Gallery on the Green, Canton, Conn., 1990, Samuel T. Chen Art Gallery Ctrl. Conn. State U., New Britain, 1991, Fed. Plaza Gallery, N.Y.C., 1992, Lyman Ctr. for Arts So. Conn. State U., New Haven, 1992, Bank St. Coll., 1993, Conn. Women Artist, Inc., 1994, Gerald Quinn Libr. Gallery for Fordham U. at Lincoln Ctr., N.Y.C., 1994, Westbeth Gallery, N.Y.C., 1995. Mem. Coll. Art Assn., Nat. Art Edn. Assn. (speaker, 1986-95), Univ. Coun. for Art Edn. (exec. bd., sec. 1992—), Phi Kappa Phi. Home: PO Box 82 Farmington CT 06034

FULLER, KATHLEEN VIEL, insurance broker; b. Cin., May 22, 1949; d. Robert F. and Grace N. (Neubauer) Viel; children: Jennifer Blair DeMatteo, Melissa Marie. BA in Journalism, Memphis State U., 1971. Cert. ins. counselor. Comml. sales asst. Liberty Mut. Ins. Co., Memphis, 1971-73; sales rep. Corroon & Black, Nashville, 1974-76; underwriting supr. Nat. Life & Casualty, Nashville, 1976-79; personal lines mgr. Fi-Del Ins. Agy., Nashville, 1979-80; account exec. Physicians Shared Svcs., Nashville, 1987-88; account rep. Marsh & McLennan, Nashville, 1988—. Mem. Nat. Assn. Ins. Women. Office: Marsh & McLennan Inc PO Box 2545 Nashville TN 37219

FULLER, KATHRYN SCOTT, environmental association executive, lawyer; b. N.Y.C., July 8, 1946; d. Delbert Orison and Carol Scott (Gilbert) F.; m. Stephen Paul Doyle, May 29, 1977; children: Sarah Elizabeth Taylor, Michael Stephen Doyle, Matthew Scott Doyle. BA English, Am. Lit., Brown U., 1968, LHD (hon.), 1992; JD with honors, U. Tex., 1976; postgrad., U. Md., 1980-82; DSci. (hon.), Wheaton Coll., 1990; LLD (hon.), Knox Coll., 1992. Bar: Tex. 1977, D.C. 1979. Rsch. asst. Yale U., New Haven, Conn., 1968-69, Am. Chem. Soc., 1970-71, Harvard U. Mus. Comparative Zoology, Cambridge, Mass., 1971-73; law clerk Dewey, Ballantine, Bushby, Palmer & Wood and Vinson & Elkins, N.Y.C., Houston, 1974-76, U.S. Dist. Ct. (so. dist.), Tex., 1976-77; atty., advisor Office Legal Counsel Dept. Justice, Washington, 1977-79, atty. Wildlife and Marine Resources sect., 1979-80, chief Wildlife and Marine Resources sect., 1981-82; exec. v.p., dir. Traffic USA, pub. policy, gen. counsel World Wildlife Fund, Washington, 1982-89, pres., CEO, 1989—. Contbr. articles to profl. jours. Adv. com. Trade Policy and Negotiations; Pres'. Commn. Environ. Quality; bd. dirs. Brown U. Recipient William Rogers Outstanding Grad. award Brown U., 1990, UNEP Global 500 award, 1990; outstanding woman law student Tex. scholar, 1975. Mem. State Tex. Bar, D.C. Bar (coun. fgn. rels., internat. coun. environ. law, overseas devel. coun.), Zonta Internat. (hon.). Office: World Wildlife Fund 1250 24th St NW Washington DC 20037*

FULLER, MARILYN MORGAN, psychotherapist; b. Tecumseh, Mich., Aug. 25, 1932; d. Louis Earl and Henrietta Josephine (Morgan) Lindsley; m. John Hershel DeFoe, Sept. 12, 1951 (div. 1962); children: Kerry Irene, Susan Carol; m. Russell Eugene Greenfield, Mar. 17, 1964 (div. 1969); m. Marvin George Fuller, May 25, 1980. BA, Siena Heights Coll., Adrian, Mich., 1971, ME, 1972; PhD, Wayne State U., 1985. Nat. cert. counselor;cert. rehab. counselor. Counselor Mich. Dept. Social Svcs., Adrian, 1970-72, family svcs. worker, 1972-74; cons. Mich. Dept. Pub. Health, Detroit, 1974-81; pvt. practice psychotherapy Marietta/Atlanta, 1981-94. Fin. chmn. Rep. Party, Lisbon Falls, Maine, 1966-68; bd. dirs. Ct. Substance Abuse Bd., Adrian, 1972-74; v.p. bd. dirs. Mich. Alcohol and Addiction Assn., Detroit, 1978, bd. dirs., 1976-81. Recipient Bd. Dirs. award Mich. Alcohol and Addiction Assn., 1981. Mem. Am. Counseling Assn., Am. Group Counseling Assn. Jewish. Address: RR 1 Box 159 Orrs Island ME 04066-9707

FULLER, MARILYN TRIBBEY, accountant, educator; b. Maud, Okla., July 1, 1934; d. Thomas Henry and Ruth Margaruite (Dodson) Tribbey; divorced; children: John Stephen, Carole Ann Fuller Grant. BS in Acctg., Okla. State U., 1955; MBA, U. Ark., 1965, postgrad., 1968. CPA, Okla. Jr. acct. Williams, Hurst & Groth, Oklahoma City, 1955-56, John O. Moffitt & Co., Muskogee, Okla., 1959-62; sr. acct. Walter Theis & Co., Pine Bluff, Ark., 1962-64; acctg. instr. Paris (Tex.) Jr. Coll., 1968—; part-time instr. U. Ark., Fayetteville, 1965-66; part-time acct. Marilyn Fuller, CPA, Blossom, Tex., 1971-87. Author: (instructional package) Electronic Printing Calculator, 1976. Mem. Am. Acctg. Assn., Tex. Jr. Coll. Tchrs. Assn. Home: 1105 Ash St Blossom TX 75416 Office: Paris Jr Coll 2400 Clarksville St Paris TX 75460

FULLER, MARY FALVEY, management consultant; b. Detroit, Oct. 28, 1941; d. Lawrence C. and Mathilde G. Falvey; m. James W. Fuller, Aug. 22, 1981. BA in Econs. with honors, Cornell U., 1963; MBA, Harvard U., 1967. Systems engr. IBM Corp., N.Y.C., 1963-65; mgmt. cons. McKinsey & Co., Inc., N.Y.C., 1967-75; v.p. Citibank, N.A., N.Y.C., 1975-78, head asset servicing div., 1977-78; sr. v.p., dir., head adminstrn. div., mem. exec. com., mem. operating com. Blyth Eastman Dillon & Co., Inc., N.Y.C., 1978-80; pres. M.C. Falvey Assocs., Inc., N.Y.C., 1980-81; pres. Falvey Fuller & Assocs., 1982—; v.p. fin. Shaklee Corp., San Francisco, 1981-82; pres. Falvey Autos, Inc., Troy, Mich., 1978-93, also chmn., bd. dirs.; bd. dirs. Access Healthnet, Inc.; vis. prof. Cornell U. Johnson Grad. Sch. Mgmt., 1992; trustee Fed. Hosp. Ins. Trust Fund, Fed. Old Age and Survivors Ins. Trust Fund, Fed. Disability Ins. Trust Fund, 1984-89, Williamsburg Charter Found. 1988-89; dir. Tech. Funding Inc., 1983-91; mem. regional dealer adv. council Toyota Motor Sales Corp., 1986-88; mem. composite com. U.S. Med. Licensing Examination, 1995—. Mem. Com. for N.Y. Philharmonic, 1975-77; mem. 1979 Adv. Council on Social Security, 1979-80, Pres. Reagan's Transition Task Force on Social Security, 1979-80, Nat. Commn. on Social Security Reform, 1982-83; adminstrv. bd. Cornell U. Council, 1984-86; bd. dirs. St. Francis Hosp. Found., 1992—; trustee Cornell U., 1988—; mem. adminstrn. and legal processes adv. council Mills Coll., 1982-85; trustee San Francisco Performances, 1981-93, chmn. bd. trustees, 1984-91. Harvard Bus. Sch. grantee, 1965-67. Republican. Episcopalian. Mem. Global Econ. Action Inst. (internat. steering com. 1990-92), Harvard Bus. Sch. Assn. No. Calif. (dir.) Clubs: Commonwealth of Calif. (program com. 1983-85, chmn. Asia-Pacific study sect. 1985-86), Univ. (dir. San Francisco). Home: 1630 Dutton Rd Rochester MI 48306 Office: 2584 Filbert St San Francisco CA 94123-3318

FULLER, MARY LOUISE, sociology and criminology educator, mental health counselor; b. Aurora, Mo., Oct. 27, 1949; d. John Errol and Elizabeth Lenora (Fenton) F. BA, Drury Coll., 1987; MA, Western Ky. U., 1988; postgrad., So. Ill. U., 1989-92. Supr. acad. computer lab. Drury Coll., Springfield, Mo., 1984-87; counselor Rape Crisis, Springfield, 1985-87; rape survivor advocate, counselor Rape Crisis and Counseling, Bowling Green, Ky., 1987-88; crisis intervention counselor Barren River Mental Health, Bowling Green, 1987-88; instr. Western Ky. U., Bowling Green, 1987-88, So. Ill. U., Carbondale, 1989-92, Roosevelt U., Chgo., 1990. Author: Moody: A Poet's Progress, 1982, Obesity and Women, 1988. Mem. Mid-South Sociol. Assn., Midwest Sociol. Soc., Western Ky. Women's Studies Program, Phi Eta Sigma, Psi Chi, Alpha Kappa Delta. Democrat. Roman Catholic. Home: 1304 Edwards St Beardstown IL 62618-2022

FULLER, MAXINE COMPTON, retired secondary school educator; b. Tiny, Va., Aug. 23, 1921; d. Perry and Lillie (Sutherland) Compton; m. David Thompson Fuller Jr., 1946 (dec. Mar. 1975); children: Davine Miller, Patricia Machen, Shirley Brodeur, Dorothy Brunson, David Thompson III. BS, Longwood Coll., 1943; MA, U. Ala., 1966; AA in Edn., U. Ala., Birmingham, 1980. Receptionist Goodyear Tire and Rubber Co., Richmond, Va., 1943; office mgr. trainee Goodyear Tire and Rubber Co., Selma, Ala., 1943-44; office mgr. Goodyear Service, Bessemer, Ala., 1944-46; sec., ops. mgr. Birmingham So. Coll., 1966; tchr. Manpower-Bessemer State Tech. Coll., 1966-68, McAdory High Sch., 1968-71; bus. edn. coord. Hueytown High Sch., 1971-88, ret., 1988; vis. com. mem. So. Assn. Secondary Schs. and Colls., 1980, 84. Sunday sch. tchr. Pleasant Ridge Bapt. Ch., Hueytown, Ala., 1962-88, pers. com., 1980-83; mem. Hueytown High PTA, 1986-87; liaison officer Adopt-A-Sch. program Hueytown High/Lloyd Noland Hosp., 1987-88; chmn. bus. edn. dept. Hueytown High Sch., 1971-88. Mem. NEA, Am. Vocat. Assn., Nat. Ret. Tchrs. Assn., Ala. Edn. Assn., Ala. Vocat. Assn., Ala. Ret. Tchrs. Assn., Jefferson County Ret. Tchrs. Assn., Longwood Coll. Alumni Assn., Alpha Delta Kappa (corr. sec. Xi chpt. 1982-84), Delta Kappa Gamma (treas. Gamma Lambda chpt. 1976-80), Echo Book Club (Bessemer, pres. 1986-88), Hueytown Culture Club. Baptist.

FULLER, MOZELLE JAMES, clergywoman, retired nurse; b. Greer, S.C., Aug. 10, 1909; d. William and Julia (Lipscomb) James; m. James Henry Fuller, Mar. 12, 1928; 1 child, Shirley Lindsey Berkley. Diploma, Nat. Inst. Nursing; 2d semester cert., Howard U. Sch. Religion, 1968; DD (hon.), Universal Life Ch., Christ Mission, 1980, Christ's Instn. Inc., 1980. Ordained to ministry Pentecostal Bapt. Ch., 1967; Mut. Bapt. Missionary Assn., 1967. Personality Sta. WOL and Sta. WMMJ-FM, Washington; former religion editor Washington Daily Sun; bd. dirs. Internat. Found. for the Performing Arts; v.p. D.C. Sr. Citizens Clearinghouse Com., Inc., chaplain emeritus; chaplain Hair Expressions Beauty Salon, Acad. Sch. of Cosmetology by Hair Expressions. Former mem. D.C. Commn. on Aging; co-founder Ch. of What's Happening Now; missinary Peace Bapt. Ch., 1949—; founder Sr. Citizens United To Serve Humanity; nat. chaplain Radio One Network Inc., Washington, Balt.; co-founder Good Citizens Youth Assn., Inc., House of Imogene; chaplain Leroy Bukley Trio; mem. Young People Hour Inc. Recieved Nat. Black Monitor Hall of Fame Community Bldg. award, plaque ANC, 1990, cert. recognition Internat. Found. Performing & Creative Arts, 1991, Govt. of D.C. cert. Sr. Citizens Com., 1991; named Mother of Bus. Mothers Day 1989, BOTH Inc. Mem. Women Mins. Greater Washington, Mins. in Partnership, Am. Legion Aux. (life), Ellis Island Found. (charter), Amnesty Internat., Friends So. Poverty Law Ctr. Democrat. Baptist. Home: 624 17th St NE Washington DC 20002-4682

FULLER, NELL BENTON, medical librarian; b. Rock Hill, S.C., Apr. 6, 1917; d. James Newton and Annie Clementine (Bolling) Benton; A.B., U. N.C., Greensboro, 1940; M.S. in L.S., U. N.C., Chapel Hill, 1968; m. Henry Shepard Fuller, Dec. 15, 1962 (dec.). High sch. tchr., Stony Point, N.C., 1940-43; asst. librarian Bowman Gray Med. Sch., Wake Forest U., Winston-Salem, N.C., 1944-45, librarian, 1945-62; mem. faculty and staff Claude Moore Health Scis. Library, U. Va. Med. Center, Charlottesville, 1966-84, asst. prof., 1970-75, assoc. prof., 1975-84, head tech. services, 1970-84. Democrat. Presbyterian. Home: 1 Amberhill Ct Greensboro NC 27455-2208

FULLER, SUE, artist; b. Pitts.; d. Samuel Leslie and Carrie (Cassedy) F. B.A., Carnegie Inst. Tech., 1936; M.A., Columbia U., 1939. Producer: movies String Composition, 1970, 74; one-woman shows include Bertha Schaefer Gallery, McNay Art Inst., San Antonio, Norfolk Mus. Currier Gallery, Corcoran Gallery, Smithsonian Instn., others; exhibited in group shows including Aldrich Mus., Corcoran Gallery, Phila. Mus., Mus. Modern Art, Whitney Mus., Bklyn. Mus., Brit. Mus., London, others; represented in permanent collections Addison Gallery Am. Art, Larry Aldrich Mus., Chgo. Art Inst., Des Moines Art Ctr., Ford Found., Met. Mus., Guggenheim Mus., Whitney Mus. Am. Art, Tate Gallery London, Brit. Mus. London, Library of Congress, others; commd. works include Unitarian Ch. All Souls, N.Y.C., 1980, Tobin Library, McNay Art Mus., San Antonio, 1984. Recipient Alumni Merit award Carnegie Mellon U., 1974, CAA/WCA Nat. Honor award, 1986; Louis Comfort Tiffany fellow, 1948; Guggenheim fellow, 1949; Nat. Inst. Arts and Letters grantee, 1950; Eliot Pratt Found. fellow, 1966-68; Mark Rothko Found. grantee, 1973; U. Cin. Nat. Sculpture Conf.: Works by Women honoree, 1987. Home: PO Box 1580 Southampton NY 11969-1580

FULLER, TRACY ANNETTE, laboratory executive; b. Oklahoma City, Apr. 11, 1962; d. Billy Newton and Barbara Sue (Barnes) F. AA in Home Econs., Abraham Baldwin Coll., 1982; BS in Home Econs. & Journ, U. Ga., 1984. County agrl. agt., home economist Ga. Coop. Extension Svc., Douglas, 1984-87; territory mgr. sales Ross Labs. divsn. Abbott Labs., Marietta, Ga., 1987—. Contbr. articles to local newspaper; guest TV program, 1986 (Communication award). Recipient Young Profl. of Yr. award Ga. Home Econs. Assn., 1986. Mem. Cobb Area Pediatric Soc. (exec. sec. 1988—). Republican. Lutheran. Home and Office: Ross Labs 1119 S Cherokee St # 1846 Muskogee OK 74403-7012

FULLERTON, GAIL JACKSON, university president emeritus; b. Lincoln, Nebr., Apr. 29, 1927; d. Earl Warren and Gladys Bernice (Marshall) Jackson; m. Stanley James Fullerton, Mar. 27, 1967; children by previous marriage—Gregory Snell Putney, Cynde Putney Mitchell. B.A., U. Nebr., 1949, M.A., 1950; Ph.D., U. Oreg., 1954. Lectr. sociology Drake U., Des Moines, 1955-57; asst. prof. sociology Fla. State U., Tallahassee, 1957-60; asst. prof. sociology San Jose (Calif.) State U., 1963-67, asso. prof., 1968-71, prof., 1972-91, dean grad. studies and research, 1972-76, exec. v.p. univ., 1976-78, pres., 1978-91; ret., 1991; bd. dirs. Assoc. Western Univs., Inc., 1980-91; mem. sr. accrediting commn. Western Assn. Schs. and Colls., 1982-88, chmn., 1985-86; mem. Pres.'s Commn. Nat. Collegiate Athletic Assn., 1986-91; bd. dirs. Am. Coll. Assn., 1991. Author: Survival in Marriage, 2d edit, 1977, (with Snell Putney) Normal Neurosis: The Adjusted American, 2d edit, 1966. Carnegie fellow, 1950-51, 52-53; Doherty Found. fellow, 1951-52. Mem. Phi Beta Kappa, Phi Kappa Phi, Chi Omega. Home: 1643 Tompkins Hill Rd Fortuna CA 95540-9728

FULLIS, MARIAN ELIZABETH, nursing and hospital administrator; b. Holmesville, Pa.; d. Walter Edmund and Elizabeth Marian (Biscoe) Harnish; m. Charles William Fullis, July 21, 1956 (dec. Mar. 1991); children: Lisa M. Nicolo, Marsha A. Wetzel. Diploma in Nursing, Hosp. U. Pa., 1957; BBA, Gwynedd Mercy Coll., 1982; M in Health Adminstrn., St. Josephs U., Phila., 1984. Adminstrv. supr. Hosp. U. Pa., Phila., 1959-65; adminstrv. supr. critical care Warminster (Pa.) Gen. Hosp., 1975-76, asst. dir. critical care, 1976-77, asst. DON, 1977-82, assoc. DON, 1982-85, asst. adminstr. trauma adminstrn., 1985-86, assoc. adminstr. trauma adminstrn., 1987-88; mgr. nursing dept. Frank Ford Hosp., 1990-92; assoc. exec. dir. John F. Kennedy Hosp., Phila., 1992—. Mem. ANA (cert. nurse adminstrn., cert. legal nurse cons.), Am. Orgn. Nurse Execs., Exec. Coun. Nurse Adminstrs., Southeastern Pa. League Nursing, Pa. Nurses Assn., Southeastern Pa. Orgn. Nurse Execs., Am. Assn. Legal Nurse Consultants. Roman Catholic. Home: 915 Log College Dr Warminster PA 18974-1805 Office: John F Kennedy Meml Hosp Langdon St and Chelten Ave Philadelphia PA 19124

FULLWOOD, ALTBURG MARIE, women's health nurse; b. Scharbeutz, West Germany, May 6, 1933; d. Hans F. and Cacilie A. (Bliesmer) Burmann; m. Marvin Fullwood, Sept. 6, 1963; children: Randal O., Renée M. Diploma, St. Georg Hosp., Hamburg, West Germany, 1953, Kleemann Sch., Kiel, West Germany, 1954; ADN, U. N.C., Wilmington, 1984. RN, N.C.; cert. psychiat./mental health nurse. Nurse German Social Security System, Hamburg; exec. sec. to dir. Fla. State U., Eglin AFB; civil service pers. Dept. of Army, Southport, N.C.; psychiat. nurse New Hanover Regional Med. Ctr., Wilmington.

FULMER, LISA MICHELLE, marketing director, graphic arts consultant; b. Sacramento, July 9, 1962; d. Fred William and Scharlene Faye (Oling) F. BA in Mktg., Calif. State U. Stanislaus, Turlock, 1983. Promotions mgr. Unisource, Inc., Dublin, Calif., 1985-90, Noland Paper Co., San Jose, Calif., 1990; sales exec. Conservatree Paper, San Francisco, 1991; sales rep. Golden State Embossing, San Francisco, 1992; mktg. dir. Automatrix, Inc., San Francisco, 1993—; pvt. practice graphic arts cons. San Francisco, 1985—; bd. mem. Artists in Print, San Francisco, 1987-91; vis. lectr. Acad. Art Coll., San Francisco, 1987—; vol. Bus. Vols. for the Arts, San Francisco. Co-editor: Papers for Printing, 1991. Mem. San Francisco Creative Alliance, Western Art Dirs. Club, Print Buyers Assn. Democrat. Office: Automatrix Inc 530 Hampshire #401 San Francisco CA 94110

FULRATH, IRENE, corporate marketing executive; b. N.Y.C., Nov. 15, 1945; d. Logan and Grace (Sheehy) F. B.A., Wheaton Coll., Ill., 1967. Media exec. Doyle Dane Bernbach, N.Y.C., 1967-72; account exec., retail sales mgr. Sta. WABC, N.Y.C., 1972-84; account exec. Sta. WABC-TV, N.Y.C., 1984-86; corp. sales mgr., Am. Express Co., 1987—. Mem. Fin. Advt. and Mktg. Assn. (bd. dirs. 1981-84, sec. 1984-85, v.p. 1985-86, pres 1986-87). Republican. Presbyterian. Avocation: travel. Home: 150 E 56th St New York NY 10022

FULTON, ALICE, writer; b. Troy, N.Y., Jan. 25, 1952; m. Hank De Leo, 1980. BA in Creative Writing, Empire State Coll., 1978; MFA in Creative Writing, Cornell U., 1982; LittD (hon.), SUNY, 1994. Asst. prof. English Cornell U., Ithaca, N.Y., 1983-86, William Wilhartz prof., 1986-89; assoc. prof. English U. Mich., Ann Arbor, 1990-92, prof., 1992—; vis. prof. creative writing Vt. Coll., Montpelier, 1987; vis. prof. English, UCLA, 1991. Author: Anchors of Light, 1979, Dance Script with Electric Ballerina, 1983, Palladium, 1986, Powers of Congress, 1990, Sensual Math, 1995. Recipient Emily Dickenson award, 1980, Acad. Poets prize, 1982, Consuelo Ford award, 1984, Rainer Maria Rilke, award 1984, Bess Hokin prize, 1989, Ingrim Merrill Found. award, 1990; fellow MacDowell Colony, 1978, 79, MIllay Colony, 1980, Guggenheim, 1986-87, MacArthur Found., 1991, Yaddo Colony, 1987; grantee Mich. Coun. Arts, 1986, 91. Office: U Mich Dept English Ann Arbor MI 48109 Address: RR 13 2730 Le Forge Rd Ypsilanti MI 48198

FULTON, CARLA RAE, human resources manager; b. Clarion, Iowa, July 18, 1953; d. Don C. and Marietta (Walker) Greenfield; m. Kenneth W. Townsley, May 24, 1975 (div. 1987); m. James P. Fulton, July 17, 1994. BA, U. North Tex., 1975, MBA, 1982. Human resources specialist Mobil Oil Corp., Dallas, 1976-82; human resources mgr. S & A Restaurant Corp., Dallas, 1982-85; sr. compensation analyst Frito-Lay, Dallas, 1985-86; asst. dir. human resources Fed. Home Loan Bank, Dallas, 1986-89; sr. mgr. human resources DSC Communications Corp., Plano, Tex., 1989-92, Pier I Imports, Fort Worth, 1993—. Mem. Dallas Forty, 1990; mem. adv. coun. Seay Behavioral Ctr. Mem. Soc. Human Resource Profls., Dallas Human Resource Mgmt. (v.p. 1986-90), Nat. Human Resource Systems Profls. (sec. 1986), Dallas Human Resource Systems Profls. (founding mem., pres. 1985-86). Republican. Methodist. Home: 8812 Liptonshire Dr Dallas TX 75238-3642

FULTON, DEBRA ANN, nurse practitioner; b. Anne Arundel, Md., Dec. 16, 1961; d. William D. and Patricia A. (Rensel) F. BSN, U. Tex., Galveston, 1983, MSN, 1986. RN, Fla. Clin. nurse specialist Arnold Palmer Hosp. for Childen and Women, Orlando, Fla.; pediatric and internal medicine nurse practitioner Office of Dr. Shirley Nagel, Mt. Dora, Fla.; Medicare Part B project leader in med. policy/med. rev./fraud and abuse State of Fla., Jacksonville; med. cons., outreach educator/project mgr. Medicare Fraud Br. Fla. Home: 1210 Signal Point Dr Jacksonville FL 32225-6438

FULTON, ELEANOR MARIE, music educator; b. Morristown, Tenn., Aug. 9, 1939; d. Nyanza and Myrtle (Dockery) F. BA, Bennett Coll., 1961; grad., Manhatten Sch. of Music, 1969; postgrad., Haydn Conservatory, Eisenstadt, Austria, 1980. Music specialist New Haven Pub. Schs., 1965—; piano instr. Dixwell Children's Creative Art Ctr., New Haven, 1974-81; Orff instr. Neighborhood Sch. of Music, New Haven, 1980—; choir dir. children's chorus Yale U., New Haven, 1983-84; dir. Christian edn. Battell Chapel, Yale U., New Haven, 1984-85, asst. organist, 1991—; interim organist-choir dir. Ctr. Church on the Green, New Haven, 1986-87; cons. M. L. King Concert, New Haven Symphony Orch., 1979-83, narrator Young People's Concert, 1990-91; choir dir. All City Chorus, New Haven, 1979. Co-author Let's Slice the Ice, 1979; contbr. to Music for Children, 1977. Cons. United Cerebral Palsy, Conn., 1986-91. Mem. Am. Guild Organists, Orff Schulwerk, Am. Fedn. Tchrs. Congregationalist.

FULTON, GLORIA JEAN, librarian, educator; b. Sterling, Ill., Nov. 20, 1940; d. Reese H. and Aldine (Hansen) Hinton; m. Lloyd Griffiths Fulton, Mar. 26, 1977 (div. 1984); 1 child, Alexander. BA, UCLA, 1963, MLS, 1968; MA, Humboldt State U., 1976. Cons. RAND Corp., Santa Monica, Calif., 1965-66; librarian Santa Monica Pub. Library, 1969-70; librarian Humboldt State U., Arcata, Calif., 1970—, prof. Russian lang., 1979-89; libr. Coll. of Redwoods, Eureka, Calif., 1970-72; cons. Oscar Larson Internat., Eureka, 1990-91. Coun. Libr. Resources fellow, 1976-77, Nat. Def. Edn. Act fellow, 1963, Higher Edn. Act fellow, 1967-68, Woodrow Wilson Found. fellow, 1963, Inst. Internat. Edn. fellow U. Zagreb, Yugoslavia, 1964-65, ALA/USIA fellow Yugoslavia, 1991-92. Mem. ALA, Am. Assn. for Advancement Slavic Studies, Phi Beta Kappa. Home: 879 Union St Arcata CA 95521-6034 Office: Humboldt State U Library Catalog Dept Arcata CA 95521

FULTON, KATHRYN, federal agency administrator; b. New Haven, Mar. 1, 1961; d. James Francis and Anne Marie (Ahern) F. BA magna cum laude, Amherst Coll., 1979-83. V.p. govt. rels. Morgan Stanley and Co., Inc., 1983-91; dir. legis. affairs, office legis. affairs Securities and Exchange Commn., Washington, 1991—. Mem. Paul Hill Chorale. Mem. Amherst Assn. of Washington. Office: Securities and Exchange Commn 450 5th St NW Washington DC 20549*

FULTON, SANDRA MARIA, human resources development specialist; b. Panama City, Ancon, Panama, May 21, 1962; came to U.S., 1980; d. James Louie F. and Ana Sonia (Canas) Valley. BA, Fla. State U., 1984; MA, U. West Fla., 1987. Tng. coord. Ednl. Rsch. & Devel. Ctr., Pensacola, Fla., 1987-88; orgn. devel. specialist Martin Marietta, Balt., 1988-90; tng. specialist Helix System, Balt., 1990-91; sr. tng. specialist Johnson & Johnson Critikon, Tampa, Fla., 1991-94; mgr. employee rels. Johnson & Johnson Med., Inc., Tampa, 1994—. Editor: Conference Planning, 1987. Mem. NAFE, Am. Soc. Tng. & Devel., Orgn. Devel. Network. Office: Critikon PO Box 15400 Tampa FL 33684-5400

FULTON-MARTINEZ, KATHLEEN, health insurance company official; b. Kansas City, Kans., Sept. 20, 1960; d. Clarence Davy Crockett and Shirley Frances Fulton; m. Daryl Gerard Martinez, May 14, 1994. BA in Bus., Baker U., 1994. Ins. processor Mut. Benefit Life Ins. Co., Kansas City, Mo., 1978-81; lab. technician II, U. Kans. Med. Ctr., Kansas City, 1981-87; office rep. Mid-Am. Cardiology, Kansas City, Mo., 1987-88; ins. claims rep. Blue Cross Blue Shield Kansas City, 1988-93, electronic media claims ins. field rep., 1993—; cons., Kansas City, 1992—. Com. asst. League Dem. Women Voters, Kansas City, 1982, 84, 90. Mem. NAFE, Am. Bus. Women's Assn., Phi Theta Kappa. Methodist. Office: Blue Cross Blue Shield Kansas City 2301 Main St Kansas City MO 64108

FULWEILER, MARIE-LOUISE, lawyer; b. N.Y.C., Dec. 15, 1949; d. Spencer Biddle and Patricia Louise (Platt) F.; m. Douglas Finlay Allen, Jr., Sept. 10, 1977; children: Douglas Finlay Allen III, Spencer Platt Allen. AB, Radcliffe Coll., 1971; JD, Boston U., 1976. Bar: N.Y. 1977. Assoc. atty. White & Case, N.Y.C., 1976-84, Debevoise & Plimpton, N.Y.C., 1984-86; sr. assoc. counsel, v.p. Chase Manhattan Bank, N.A., N.Y.C., 1986—. Office: Global Corp Finance 1 Chase Manhattan Plz 25th Fl New York NY 10081

FULWEILER, PATRICIA PLATT, civic worker; b. N.Y.C., Mar. 19, 1923; d. Haviland Hull and Marie-Louise (Fearey) Platt; m. Spencer Biddle Fulweiler, Oct. 5, 1946; children: Marie-Louise Fulweiler Allen, Pamela Spencer, Hull Platt, Spencer Biddle. AB cum laude, Bryn Mawr Coll., 1945; MBA, Columbia U., 1950. Jr. copywriter, asst. account exec. Dorland Internat. Pettingell & Fenton, N.Y.C., 1945-46; statistician, fin. staff treas.'s office GM, N.Y.C., 1950-52; asst. account mgr. investment dept. Fiduciary Trust Co., N.Y.C., 1953-61; bd. dirs. Chapin Brearley Exchange, Inc., 1964-74, treas., 1966-71, pres., 1971-73. Bd. dirs. Knickerbocker Greys, 1965—, treas., 1970-75; bd. dirs., treas. City Gardens Club, N.Y.C., 1974-79, chmn. ways and means com., 1974-81; bd. dirs. Nat. Soc. Colonial Dames State N.Y., 1973-82, asst. treas., 1973-82; mem. fin. com. Alumnae Assn. Bryn Mawr Coll., 1970-76; bd. dirs. Daus. of Cin., 1974-81, scholarship adminstr., 1976-81; pres. Ladies Christian Union, 1982-87, chmn. fin. com., 1987-94; rec. sec. Women's Assn. St. James Ch., N.Y.C., 1972-75, co-chmn. Spring Festival, 1974-75, chmn., 1975-76, treas., 1976-81, mem. Altar Guild, 1975—; treas. Churchwomen's League for Patriotic Svc., 1982-86; mem. scholarship com. Youth Found., 1981—, pres., 1990—; membership chmn. Huguenot Soc. Am., registrar, 1986—. Mem. Soc. Sponsors of USN, Alumnae Coun. Spence Sch., Colonial Dames Am. (bd. dirs. 1987-93), Nat. Soc. Colonial Dames, Colony Club, Thursday Evening Club, Wilson Point Beach Assn. Club. Republican. Home: 158 E 83d St New York NY 10028

FUNG, AMY SHU-FONG, accountant; b. Hong Kong, Sept. 23, 1949; came to U.S., 1970; d. Wing-Chee and Fung-Siu (Tsang) Leung; m. Gee-You Fung, Mar. 17, 1970; children: Alice, Deborah. BS in Acctg., CUNY, 1982. Acct. Cath. Charities Diocese of Bklyn. Inc., N.Y.C., 1982-83; sr. acct. Beth Israel Med. Ctr., N.Y.C., 1983-85, St. John Episcopal Home for Aged and Blind, N.Y.C., 1986-87, Internat. Ctr. for Disabled, N.Y.C., 1988-91, United Jewish Appeal-Fedn. Jewish Philanthropies N.Y., N.Y.C., 1992-94. Home: 359 Colon Ave Staten Island NY 10308-1415

FUNG, KITTY KIT-YI, financial planning and analysis executive; b. Hong Kong, Hong Kong, Nov. 26, 1963; came to U.S., 1987; d. Chow and Cheung Yuen (Leung) F. B of Social Sci., Chinese U., Hong Kong, 1986; MBA in Fin. and Mktg., Ind. U., 1988; Advanced Profl. Degree in Pub. Acctg., Pace U., 1990. CPA, Md.; cert. mgmt. acct. Exec. officer trade dept. Hong Kong Govt., 1986-87; sr. fin. analyst Kraft Gen. Foods, White Plains, N.Y., 1988-91; dir. fin. planning and analysis Grolier, Inc., Danbury, Conn., 1991—. Mem. fin. com. Chinese for Christ N.Y. Ch., Bronx, 1992—. Mem. AICPA, Inst. Mgmt. Accts. (dir. newsletter 1992-93, dir. mem. acquisition 1993-94, v.p. mktg. and membership 1994-95, Svc. award 1993, Perfect Attendance award 1993). Office: Grolier Inc Sherman Turnpike Danbury CT 06811

FUNG-CHEN-PEN, EMMA TALAUNA SOLAITA, librarian, program director; b. Pago Pago, Am. Samoa, Sept. 4, 1951; d. Talauna and Ema (Tauoa) S.; m. Ioelu T. Fung-Chen-Pen, Nov 1, 1971; children: John Kevin, Juliet Ruth, Jacqueline Josie, Jennifer Lorna, Jonathan Emosi. AA Gen. Edn., Am. Samoa C. C., 1973, AS Libr. Studies, 1974; BA, Brigham Young U., Honolulu, 1977; MS in Librarianship, U. Hawaii, 1979. Libr. clerk Libr. Svcs., Pago Pago, 1971-74, libr. technician, 1974-76, libr. II, 1976-79, program dir., 1980—. Sec. Seventh Day Adventist Leone (Am. Samoa) Ch., 1990-94; dir. Seventh Day Adventist Leone Pathfinder, 1993—; pres. Parent-Tchr. Assn.-Sch., 1992; active SDA Sch. Bd., 1991—. Home: PO Box 1952 Pago Pago AS 96799-1952 Office: Am Samoa-Office of Lib Svcs PO Box 1329 Pago Pago AS 96799-1329

FUNICELLI, BETTY LYNN, accountant; b. Altoona, Pa., Mar. 20, 1963; d. Ray Joseph and Donna Jean (DeLancey) F. BS in Acctg., Pa. State U., 1985. CPA, Pa. Sr. mgmt. acct. Guy J. Landolfi, CPA, Altoona, 1985-90; pres. Betty Lynn Funicelli, PC, Altoona, 1990—. Mem. worship com., adminstrv. coun., choir dir., ch. pianist Greenwood United Meth. Ch., Altoona, 1985—, jr. youth asst. leader, 1989—, chmn. ch. pastor-parish rels. com.; mem. Cen. Pa. Youth Ministries, Duncansville, 1989—; bd. dirs. treas., chmn. fin. com. Tri-County unit Epilepsy Found. Western Pa., Altoona, 1991-93. Scholar Altoona Area Sch. Dist., 1981, Espy scholar Pa. State U., 1982-83. Mem. AICPA, Pa. Inst. CPA's, Am. Bus. Women's Assn. (treas. Horseshoe Curve chpt. 1991-92, chmn. hospitality com. 1990-91, Woman of Yr. award 1991), Altoona C. of C., Quota Club, Internat. Order Rainbow (life), Alpha Lambda Delta. Home: 1618 Princeton Rd Altoona PA 16602-7437 Office: The Pines Plaza Unit II 1637 E Pleasant Valley Blvd Altoona PA 16602-7337

FUNICELLO, LINDA ROSE, information systems project administrator; b. Jamestown, N.Y., Apr. 5, 1948; d. Nicholas Anthony and Lena (Goldstein) F.; m. Robert Martin Sugarman, June 28, 1980. BA, Skidmore Coll., 1994. Corr. Bank N.Y., N.Y.C., 1970; corr. N.Y. Life Ins. Co., N.Y.C., 1971-74, programmer trainee, 1974-76, programmer analyst, 1976-81, project leader, 1981-89, project mgr., 1989—. Mem. NOW, Microcomputer Mgrs. Assn. Home: 63 Pitt St Apt 1R New York NY 10002 Office: NY Life Ins Co 51 Madison Ave New York NY 10010

FUNK, DOROTHEA, public health nurse; b. St. Louis, Oct. 26, 1916; d. John Arthur and Pearl M. (Dial) Johnson; m. Frank E. Funk, Jan. 3, 1941. Diploma, Leo N. Levi Meml. Hosp., Hot Springs Nat. Park, Ark. RN, Ark. Asst. dir. nursing svc. Helena (Ark.) Hosp.; nurse-investigator Little Rock Health Dept.; pub. health nurse Clark County Health Dept., Arkedelphia, Ark.; nurse coord. for health manpower recruitment Ark. State Nurses Assn.; patient-coord. and liaison nurse Medi-Ctr. of Am., Inc.; health manpower coord. Ark. Nursing Assn., Little Rock, 1970-73. Vol., field rep. Women's Meml.-Meml. Found. Ind., Arlington, Va.; mem. Ark. Gov.'s Commn. on Status of Women; mem. Spl. Task Force on Delivery of Health Care; active ARC, Ark. Red Cross. Lt. Nurse Corps, U.S. Army, World War II. Recipient Health Planning award in Ark., 1979, Jerome S. Levy award Ctr. Ark. Health Systems Agy., 1983, Lifetime Achievement award Ark. Nurses Coalition, 1994. Mem. ANA, Ark. State Nurses Assn. (pres. Dist. 10 1971-73, state pres., state treas., chmn. pub. health nursing), Ark. Pub. Health Assn. (hon. life mem.), Bus. and Profl. Women's Club (co-dir. S.W. Ark. Fedn., club pres.), Altrusa Internat. (club treas. 1969-71), Am. Bus. Women's Assn., North Little Rock Women's City Club. Home: 7A Lakewood House 4801 North Hills Blvd North Little Rock AR 72116-7604

FUNK, ELLA FRANCES, genealogist, author; b. Domino, Ky., Apr. 7, 1921; d. Roy William and Edna Rene (Cummins) Roach; m. Eugene Boyd Funk, June 20, 1942; children: Susan Teresa, Eugene Boyd. B of Liberal Studies, Mary Washington Coll., 1982. Exec. sec. Lang. Labs., Inc., Bethesda, Md., 1969-70; office mgr. legal firm Donovan Leisure Newton & Irvine, Washington, 1970-76; genealogist, hist. researcher, writer, 1976—; class lectr., bd. dirs. Mary Washington ElderStudy Program; vol. Assn. Preservation Va. Antiquities; mem. Lake of the Woods Ch. Named Exec. of Week, Sta. WGMS, Washington, June 1975; recipient Blue Ribbon winner for poem Va. Fedn. Women's Clubs, 1994. Life mem. Nat. Geneal. Soc.; mem. Hist. Fredericksburg Found., DAR, Alpha Phi Sigma, Sigma Phi Gamma. Club: Woman's (Fredericksburg, Va.). Lodge: Order Eastern Star. Author: Cummins Ancient, Cummins New, vol. 1, 1978, vol. 2, 1980, Joseph Funk, a biography, 1984, Benjamin's Way, 1988, (short stories) Christmas In The Abbey, 1988 (ribbon winner 1989), Dangerous Mission (Va. Fedn. Women's Clubs ribbon 1991), The Phobia (Va. Fedn. Women's Clubs ribbon 1994. Recipient ribbon for poem "The Good Ship", 1990. Home: 4405 Turnberry Dr Fredericksburg VA 22408

FUNK, VICKI JANE, librarian; b. Frankfurt am Main, Hesse, Fed. Republic of Germany, Apr. 7, 1951; d. George N. and Maymie Lou (Harrell) F.; m. David Robert Koble, July 11, 1986. BS, Ind. State U., 1971; MLS, Okla. U., 1975; cert. in comparative libraries, Oxford U., Eng., Summer 1978; cert. in Scottish lit., St. Andrews U., Scotland, Summer 1985. Elem. open concept team tchr. Plainfield (Ind.) Pub. Schs., 1971-72; media specialist, tchr. elem. schs. Enid (Okla.) Pub. Schs., 1972-73, librarian, 1973-74; libr. media specialist Bartlesville (Okla.) Sr. H.S., 1975—; chmn. library evaluation teams North Cen. Assn., Okla., 1982-86; pres. V.I.E.W. adv. bd. Okla. State Dept. Vocat. Edn., 1980-81; tchr. pub. library continuing adult edn. program, Bartlesville, 1986. Storyteller Ednl. TV Bartlesville Cable, 1975-77, Oral Children's Program Pub. Library, 1985-86; book reviewer Okla. State Dept. Libraries "Gushers and Dusters", 1986-87; mem. book rev. selection com. Bartlesville Pub. Library. V.P. Friends of the Pub. Library, Bartlesville, 1986. Recipient Outstanding Svc. award Okla. Dept. Vocat. Edn., 1981; Emiline Libr. scholar Ind. State U., 1970; Innovative Edn. grantee Bartlesville Pub. Edn. Found., 1990, 91. Mem. NEA, AAUW (edn. officer 1980-81), Okla. Edn. Assn., Bartlesville Edn. Assn., Bartlesville Art Assn., Okla. Libr. Assn., Kappa Kappa Iota (v.p. 1990-91). Democrat. Presbyterian. Office: Bartlesville Sr High Sch 1700 Hillcrest Dr Bartlesville OK 74003-5899

FUNKE, DONNA JEAN, nurse anesthetist; b. Dearborn, Mich., July 24, 1962; d. Donald Paul and Norma Marie (Stuligross) F. BSN, Madonna U., 1984; MS in Mgmt. Human Resources, Golden Gate U., 1990; MS in Anesthesia, Wayne State U., 1992. Cert. ACLS, BCLS. Nursing asst. Garden City (Mich.) Hosp., 1979-80, Livonia (Mich.) Nursing Home, 1981, Providence Hosp., Southfield, Mich., 1982-84; staff nurse med. floor Hutzel Hosp., Detroit, 1984-85, staff nurse surg. ICU, 1985-86, staff nurse med. ICU, 1986-87; staff nurse, preceptor/instr. cardiovascular ICU Humana Hosp., Phoenix, 1987-91; instr. critical care Detroit Recieving Hosp., 1991-94; nurse anesthetist Hutzel Hosp., Detroit, 1994—; presenter in field. Vol. Detroit Symphony Orch., 1991—, Detroit Inst. Arts, 1991—. Grad. Profl. scholar Wayne State U., 1992-93. Mem. AACCN, ARC, Am. Soc. Pain Mgmt., Am. Assn. Nurse Anesthetists, Organ Procurement Agy. Mich. Roman Catholic. Home: 6024 Ternes St Dearborn MI 48126-2012 Office: Hutzel Hosp Anesthesia Dept 4707 St Antoine Detroit MI 48201

FURGIUELE, MARGERY WOOD, educator; b. Munden, Va., Sept. 28, 1919; d. Thomas Jarvis and Helen Godfrey (Ward) Wood; B.S., Mary Washington Coll., 1941; postgrad. U. Ala., 1967-68, Catholic U. Am., 1974-76, 80; m. Albert William Furgiuele, June 19, 1943; children—Martha Jane Furgiuele MacDonald, Harriet Randolph. Advt. and reservations sec. Hilton's Vacation Hide-A Way, Moodus, Conn., 1940; sec. TVA, Knoxville, 1941-43; adminstrv. asst., ct. reporter Moody AFB, Valdosta, Ga., 1943-44; tchr. bus. Edenton (N.C.) High Sch., 1944-45; tchr. bus., coordinator Culpeper (Va.) County High Sch., 1958-82; ret., 1982; tchr. Piedment Tech. Edn. Center, 1970—. Co-leader Future Bus. Leaders Am., Culpeper, mem. state bd., 1979-82; state advisor 1978-79, Va. Bus. Edn. Assn. Com. chmn., 1978-79. Certified geneal. record Searcher; author of two books, contbr. articles to profl. jours. Mem. Nat., Va. Bus. Edn. Assns., Am., Va. Vocat. Assns., Smithsonian Assos. Club: Country (Culpeper). Home: 1630 Stoneybrook Ln Culpeper VA 22701-3336

FURLOW, MARY BEVERLEY, English language educator; b. Shreveport, La., Oct. 14, 1933; d. Prentiss Edward and Mary Thelma (Hasty) F.; divorced, 1973; children: Mary Findley, William Prentiss, Samuel Christopher; m. William Peter Cleary, Aug. 1, 1989. BA, U. Tenn., 1955, MEd, 1972; MA, Governors State U., 1975; cert. advanced study, U. Chgo., 1987. Mem. faculty Chattanooga State Community Coll., 1969-73, Moraine Valley Community Coll., Palos Hills, Ill., 1974-78; English faculty Pima Community Coll., Tucson, 1978—; cons. in field. Contbr. author: Thinking on the Edge, 1993. Named one of Outstanding Educators of Am., 1973. Fellow Internat. Soc. Appraisers; mem. Internat. Soc. Philos. Enquiry, Ariz. Antiquarian Guild, Pi Beta Phi, Cincinatus Soc., Jr. League, Mensa, Holmes Socs., Clan Chattan Soc., DAR, Daughters of the Confederacy, Alpha Phi Omega (Tchr. of Yr. 1973). Democrat. Episcopalian. Home: 1555 N Arcadia Ave Tucson AZ 85712-4010 Office: Pima Community Coll 8202 E Poinciana Dr Tucson AZ 85730-4645

FURNEY, LINDA JEANNE, state legislator; b. Toledo, Sept. 11, 1947; d. Robert Ross and Jeanne Scott (Hogan) F. BS in Edn., Bowling Green State U., 1969. Tchr. Washington Local Schs., Toledo, 1969-72, Escola Americano do Rio de Janiero, 1972-74; asst. mgr. banquets Holiday Inn, Perrysburg, Ohio, 1976-77; tchr. Springfield Schs., Holland, Ohio, 1977-83; council mem. City of Toledo, 1983-86; mem. Ohio State Senate, Columbus, 1987—; ranking minority mem. Reference and Oversight Com. Pres. Ohio NOW, 1979-81; Dem. precinct committeewoman Toledo, 1980-90; mem. Toledo Bd. Edn., 1982-83. Congregationalist. Home: 2626 Latonia Toledo OH 43606 Office: State House Senate Columbus OH 43215*

FURR, SUSAN HILARY, business executive; b. Washington, Apr. 26, 1960; d. Lloyd Bell and Ruby LYdia (Pryor) F. BA, U. Md., 1984. Photo archivist Dumbarton Oaks Mus., Washington, 1983-85; photo curator Smithsonian Instn., Washington, 1984-85; photo editor/archivist Naval Procs. U.S. Naval Inst., Annapolis, Md., 1985-86; info. systems cons. Birch & Davis Assocs., Silver Spring, Md., 1987-92; assoc. exec. dir. Nat. Assn. for Interactive Svcs., Washington, 1992-94; pvt. practice info. systems cons. Washington, 1992—; exec. dir. Interactive Techs. Resource Ctr., Washington, 1994; CEO Virtual Arts Online Systems, Inc., Washington, 1994. Community activist, organizer, Washington, 1994. Smithsonian Instn./Art Conservation fellow, 1985; recipient Humanitarian award Washington Humane Soc., 1992. Mem. NAFE, Am. Soc. Assn. Execs., Interative Svcs. Assn., Phi Kappa Phi.

FURSE, ELIZABETH, congresswoman, small business owner; b. Nairobi, Kenya, 1936; came to U.S., 1958, naturalized, 1972; m. John Platt; 2 children (from previous marriage). BA, Evergreen State Coll., 1974; student, U. Wash., Northwestern U. Dir. Western Wash. Indian program Am. Friends Svc. Com, 1975-77; coord. Restoration program for Native Am. Tribes Oreg. Legal Svc., 1980-86; co-owner Helvetia Vineyards, Hillsboro, Oreg.; mem. 103rd Congress from 1st Oreg. dist., Washington, D.C., 1993—. Co-founder Oreg. Peace Inst., 1985. Office: 316 Cannon Washington DC 20515

FURSETH, LINDA CHARLENE, management professional; b. Wichita, Kans., Feb. 10, 1949; d. Emmett Sylvester and Mildred Rae (Jennings) Mishler; divorced. Mgr. US West, Seattle. Mem. Renton C. of C., Kent C. of C., VFW Ladies Aux., Eastern Star, Nat. Notary Pub. Assn.

FURSTMAN, SHIRLEY ELSIE DADDOW, advertising executive; b. Butler, N.J., Jan. 26, 1930; d. Richard and Eva M. (Kitchell) Daddow; grad. high sch.; m. Russell A. Bailey, Oct. 1, 1950 (div. Oct. 1967); m. William B. Furstman, Dec. 24, 1977. Asst. corporate sec. Hydrospace Tech., West Caldwell, N.J., 1960-62; sec. to pres. R.J. Dick Co., Totowa, N.J., 1962-63, Microlab, Livingston, N.J., 1963; asst. corporate sec. Astrosystems Internat., West Caldwell, N.J., 1963-65; corporate sec. Internat. Controls Corp., Fairfield, N.J., 1965-73; sec. to pres. Global Financial Co., Nassau, Bahamas, 1974-75; office mgr. Internat. Barter, Nassau, 1975-76; sec. to pres., corp. sec. Haas Chem. Co., Taylor, Pa., 1976-77; asst. to pres., pub. Am. Home mag., N.Y.C., 1977-78; v.p., office mgr. Gilbert, Whitney & Johns, Inc., Whippany, N.J., 1979—. Home: 11A Foxwood Dr Morris Plains NJ 07950-2650

FURTH, YVONNE, advertising executive. Pres. Kobs and Draft Advt., Chgo. Office: Kobs & Draft Advt Inc 142 E Ontario St Chicago IL 60611-2818*

FUSCIARDI, KATHERINE, nursing administrator; b. Highland Park, Mich., Aug. 15, 1965; d. William Charles and Geraldine May (Revoldt) Freigruber; m. Antonio Fusciardi, July 11, 1987; 1 child, Samantha Nicole. BSN, Oakland U., Rochester, Mich., 1987. Cert. BCLS instr., NALS instr. Staff nurse William Beaumont Hosp., Royal Oak, Mich.; staff nurse, head nurse Shady Grove Adventist Hosp., Rockville, Md.; staff nurse, asst. clin. mgr. St. Joseph's Mercy Hosp., Mt. Clemens, Mich.; staff nurse Mercy Hosp. South, Charlotte, N.C.; mem. clin. faculty Salisbury (Md.) State U., 1994—. Mem. NAACOG, Sigma Theta Tau.

FUTRELL, MARY ALICE HATWOOD, education association administrator; b. Alta Vista, Va., May 24, 1940; d. Josephine Austin; m. Donald Lee Futrell. BA, Va. State U., 1962; MA, George Washington U., 1968, EdD, 1992; postgrad., U. Md., U. Va., Va. Poly Inst. and State U.; DHL (hon.), Va. State U., George Washington U., 1984, Spellman Coll., 1986, Cen. State U., 1987; DEd, Eastern Mich. U., 1987; hon. doctorates, U. Lowell, Adrian Coll.; EdD, George Washington U., 1992. Bus. edn. tchr. Parker-Gray High Sch., Alexandria, Va., 1963-65; bus. edn. tchr., dept. chmn. George Washington High Sch., 1965-80; pres. NEA, Washington, 1983-89, Edn. Internat., Washington, 1992—; sr. fellow, assoc. dir. George Washington U. Ctr. for the Study of Edn. and Nat. Devel., 1989-92; dir. Inst. for Curriculum Stds. and Tech., Washington, 1992—; mem. adv. com. on tchr. cert. State of Va., 1977-82, adv. com. to U.S. Commn. on Civil Rights, 1978; mem. Gov.'s Com. on Edn. of Handicapped, 1977; state rep. to Edn. Commn. of States, 1982; mem. Carnegie Found.'s Nat. Panel on Study of Am. High Sch., Carnegie Forum on Edn. and Economy, task force on teaching as profession; mem. edn. adv. council Met. Life Ins. Co.; trustee Joint Council on Econ. Edn.; mem. study commn. on Global Perspectives in Edn.; mem. Va.-Israel Commn., Nat. Select Com. on Edn. Black Youth; mem. Nat. Bd. for Profl. Teaching Standards; chairperson edn. com. Nat. Council for Accreditation Tchr. Edn.; mem. task force on educationally disadvantaged Com. for Econ. Devel. Mem. editorial bd. ProEdn. mag.; bd. advisers Esquire Register, 1985. Mem. women's council Democratic Nat. Com., Dem. Labor Council; former pres. ERAmerica, nat. chairperson; mem. U.S. Nat. Commn. to UNESCO; mem. adv. council Internat. Labor Rights Edn. and Research Fund; mem. Nat. Dem. Inst. for Internat. Affairs, Nat. Labor Com. for Democracy and Human Rights; bd. advisers Project VOTE; mem. Martin Luther King Jr. Fed. Holiday Commn.; trustee Nat. History Day; bd. dirs. U.S. Com. for UNICEF, Nat. Found. for Improvement Edn., Citizen-Labor Energy Coalition. Recipient Human Rights award NCCJ, 1976, cert. of appreciation UN Assn., 1980, Disting. Service medal, Columbia Univ., 1987, Schull award Ams. for Dem. Action, Pres.'s award NAACP, numerous others; named Outstanding Black Bus. and Profl. Person, Ebony mag., 1984, One of 100 Top Women in Am., Ladies Home Jour. mag., 1984, One of 12 Women of Yr., Ms. mag., 1985, One of Top 100 Blacks in Am., Ebony mag., 1985-89; Ford Found. and Nat. Com. on U.S.-China Relations grantee, 1981. Mem. NEA (bd. dirs. 1978-80, task force on sch. vols. 1977-78, head human relations com. to 1980, sec.-treas. 1980-83) (Creative Leadership in Women's Rights award 1982), Edn. Assn. Alexandria (pres. 1973-75), Va. Edn. Assn. (pres. 1976-78) (Fitz Turner Human Rights award 1976), Edn. Internat. (pres. 1993—), World Confedn. Orgns. of Teaching Profession (pres. 1990-93, exec. com., v.p. 1988—, chmn. women's caucus, 1984—, women's concerns com., chmn. fin. commn., 1986-89, pres. 1990), Am. Assn. Colls. Tchr. Edn., Am. Assn. State Colls. and Univs. Office: George Washington U 2134 G St NW Washington DC 20052

FUTTER, ELLEN VICTORIA, museum administrator; b. N.Y.C., Sept. 21, 1949; d. Victor and Joan Babette (Feinberg) F.; m. John A. Shutkin, Aug. 25, 1974; children—Anne Victoria, Elizabeth Jane. Student, U. Wis., 1967-69; AB magna cum laude, Barnard Coll., 1971; JD, Columbia U., 1974, LLD (hon.); LLD (hon.), Hamilton Coll., N.Y. Law Sch.; DHL (hon.), Amherst Coll., Hofstra U. Bar: N.Y. 1975. Assoc. Milbank, Tweed, Hadley & McCloy, N.Y.C., 1974-80; acting pres. Barnard Coll., N.Y.C., 1980-81, pres., 1981-93; president American Museum of Natural History, New York, NY, 1993—; bd. dirs. Bristol Myers Squibb, CBS, Inc., Consol. Edison of N.Y.; trustee Am. Mus. Natural History, Coun. on Econ. Devel. Ptnr. N.Y.C. Partnership; bd. dirs. The Am. Assembly. Recipient Spirit of Achievement award Albert Einstein Coll. Medicine/Yeshiva U., Abram L. Sachar award Brandeis U., Elizabeth Cutter Morrow award YWCA, Distinction medal Barnard Coll., Excellence medal Columbia U. Mem. ABA, Am. Acad. Arts and Scis., N.Y. State Bar Assn., Assn. Bar City N.Y., Nat. Inst. Social Scis., Coun. Fgn. Rels., Cosmopolitan Club, Century Club, Phi Beta Kappa. Office: Am Mus Natural History Central Park West at 79th New York NY 10024

FUTTER, JOAN BABETTE, former school librarian; b. N.Y.C., Nov. 15, 1921; d. Samuel S. and Helen (Mosher) Feinberg; m. Victor Futter, Jan. 26, 1943; children: Jeffrey Leesam, Ellen Victoria Futter Shutkin, Deborah Gail Futter Cohan. AB, NYU, 1941; MS, L.I. U., 1966. Sch. libr. Carrie Palmer Weber Jr. High Sch., Port Washington, N.Y., 1966-91. Mem. LWV, AAUW, L.I. Sch. Media Assn., C.W. Post Libr. Assn., Cold Spring Harbor Beach Club, Manhasset Bay Yacht Club. Home: 17 Sunnyvale Rd Port Washington NY 11050-4519

FUZEK, BETTYE LYNN, elementary school educator; b. Knoxville, Tenn., Oct. 24, 1924; d. Wallace Paul and Bess (Wallace) Bean; m. John F. Fuzek, May 31, 1943; children: Mary Ann, Mark Lynn, Martha Elizabeth. Student, U. Tenn., 1944-45, East Tenn. State U., 1959-64; BS, Milligan Coll., 1966; postgrad. summers, various schs., 1966—. Cert. tchr., Tenn. Sci. tchr. Dobyns-Bennett High Sch., Kingsport, Tenn., 1969-72; subs. tchr. Sullivan County High Schs., Kingsport, 1973-86; violin tchr. Symphony Assn. of Kingsport Talent Edn. Prog., 1973-80, Kingsport Suzuki Assn., 1980-90; pvt. tchr. violin, 1990—; violinist Kingsport Symphony Orch., 1980-85. Tchr. Literacy Coun. Kingsport, Inc., 1990—. Mem AAUW, DAR. Presbyterian. Home: 4603 Mitchell Rd Kingsport TN 37664-2125

FYLER, PATRICIA ANN, nurse, small business owner; b. Pittsfield, Mass., Aug. 20, 1928; d. Clarence Augustus and Elaine Agnes (Carruthers) McConkey; m. Robert Parmelee Fyler, Oct. 4, 1949; children: Deborah, Rebecca, Pamela, Nancy, Cynthia. BS, U. Redlands, 1985. Staff to head nurse Berkshire Med. Ctr., Pittsfield, 1949-54; staff nurse, operating room St. Francis Hosp., Lynwood, Calif., 1954-57; staff nurse, operating room St. Jude Hosp., Fullerton, Calif., 1958-62, relief charge nurse, 1962-67, charge nurse, 1967-78, asst. supr. emergency dept., 1978-80; mgr. emergency dept. St. Jude Hosp., Yorba Linda, Calif., 1980-89; owner, pres. Fyler Assocs./ Multi-Specialty Legal Nurse Cons., Brea, Calif., 1990—; staff RN St. Jude

Med. Ctr., Fullerton, 1989—. Active local sch. bd., PTA, youth orgns. Mem. Am. Assn. Legal Nurse Cons., Emergency Nurses Assn. (numerous offices, CEN). Office: Fyler Assocs 2138 Westmoreland Dr Brea CA 92621-6059

GAALOVA, BARBARA HELOISE, banker; b. Newport News, Va., Mar. 24, 1953; d. Robert Joseph and Jeanne Margaret (Boublis) Kanzler; 1 child, Tatiana Alexandra. Student, Boston U., 1971-73, U. Bridgeport, 1985-90. Customer rels. rep. Union Trust Co., Shelton, Conn., 1973-76; sales coord. Carlan, Inc., Stamford, Conn., 1976-80; mktg. mgr. Union Trust Co., Shelton, Conn., 1973-76; mgr. sales and tng. Union Trust Co., Norwalk, Conn., 1984-87, asst. v.p., compliance officer, 1987-93; asst. v.p., compliance officer First Fidelity Bank, Stamford, Conn., 1994—; asst. v.p. and compliance officer First Fidelity Bank NA-NY, Hawthorne, N.Y., 1994—; founding mem., dir Bank Compliance Assn. Conn., 1989—; former chmn. Edn. Com.; speaker in field. Active Newtown (Conn.) Animal Welfare Soc., 1989—. Office: First Fidelity Bank 637 West Ave Norwalk CT 06850-4004 also: First Fidelity Bank 3 Skyline Dr Hawthorne NY 10532

GAAR, MARILYN AUDREY WIEGRAFFE, political science educator; b. St. Louis, Sept. 22, 1946; d. Arthur and Marjorie Estelle (Miller) W.; m. Norman E. Gaar, Apr. 12, 1986. AB, Ind. U., 1968, MA, 1970, MS, 1973. Mem. faculty Stephens Coll., Columbia, Mo., 1971-73, Johnson County Community Coll., Overland Park, Kans., 1973—; interviewer Fulbright Hayes Tchr. Exch. fellowship candidates, Kansas City, Mo., 1982-92; state selection com. Congress Bundestag Youth Exch. Program, Kans., 1985; pres. faculty del. Kans. Assn. Community Colls., 1984-85; govs. appointee, admissions interviewer, mem. selection panel U. Kans. Sch. Medicine, 1991—; mem. admissions criteria and admissions process review com. U. Kans. Med. Sch., 1992. Author: Profile of Kansas Government, 1990; contbg. editor to instr.'s manual Am. Democracy (by Thomas Patterson). Pres. LWV of Johnson County, Kans., 1987-89, producer 1990 Candidates Forum. mem. governing bd., 1993—; mem. Johnson County Elder Net Coalition, 1988; mem. governing bd. Johnson County Mental Health Ctr., 1981-86, chmn. 1985-86; vol., translator Russian Refugee Resettlement Program of Jewish Family and Children Svcs., Kansas City, 1979-81; alt. mem. Rep. Party State Com., Kans., 1984-86; chmn. Rep. Party City Com., Shawnee, Kans., 1982-86; bd. dirs. Substance Abuse Ctr., Johnson County, 1983-85; treas. Heart of Am., Japan Am. Soc., 1979; program chmn. Kans. Fedn. Rep. Women, 1984-87; hon. dir. Rockhurst Coll., Kansas City; bd. dirs. Huntington Farms Homes Assn., Leawood, Kans., 1993—. Grantee Europaische Akademie, West Berlin, 1984, 92, Fulbright Hayes, Netherlands, 1982, Japan, 1985; Univ. fellow NEH, 1990. Mem. C.C. Humanities Assn., Kans. Polit. Sci. Assn., Internat. Rels. Coun., People to People, Soc. Fellows, Nelson-Atkins Mus. Arts, Mus. Contemporary Art L.A., Norton Simon Mus., Friends of Huntington Libr., Dobro Slovo Nat. Slavic Honor Soc., Phi Beta Kappa, Phi Sigma Alpha. Episcopalian. Office: Johnson County C C 12345 College Blvd Shawnee Mission KS 66210-1283

GABARDI, LISA, psychologist; b. Vineland, N.J., May 21, 1962; d. Daniel Mark and Jean (Marchese) G.; m. Gregory George Bishop, Aug. 8, 1993. BA with distinction, U. Del., 1984; MS, Colo. State U., 1987, PhD, 1990. Lic. psychologist, Oreg. Study skills coord. Colo. State U., Ft. Collins, 1987-88, instr., 1988-89; counselor Univ. Counseling Ctr., Ft. Collins, 1988-89; psychology intern Tualatin Valley Mental Health Ctr., Portland, Oreg., 1989-90; psychology resident Delaunay Mental Health Ctr., Portland, 1990-91; staff psychologist, Portland, 1991-92, adult outpatient coord., 1992—; psychologist in pvt. practice Portland, 1992—; clin. asst. prof. Grad. Sch. Psychology, Fuller Theol. Sem., Pasadena, Calif., 1993-94. Contbr. articles to profl. jours. Bd. dirs. Multnomah County Child Abuse Coalition, 1992—. Mem. APA, Oreg. Psychol. Assn. (legis. com. 1990—), Mortar Board, Phi Beta Kappa. Office: Delaunay Family of Svcs 5215 N Lombard St Portland OR 97203-4325

GABAY, ELIZABETH LEE, infectious diseases physician; b. Milw., Oct. 20, 1951; d. George Gerald and Margaret Louise (Tracy) G.; m. Stephen K. Liu, June 29, 1974; children: Katherine Liu, Margaret Liu. BS, U. Wis., Milw., 1973; MD, U. Wis., 1976. Diplomate Am. Bd. Internal Medicine, Am. Bd. Infectious Diseases, Am. Bd. Geriatrics. Internatl medicine physician FHP, Long Beach, Calif., 1981-90, chmn. infectious disease dept., 1990—. Contbr. articles to profl. jours. Fellow ACP; mem. Am. Soc. Microbiology, Am. Geriatric Soc. Roman Catholic. Office: FHP 2925 N Palo Verde Ave Long Beach CA 90815

GABBARD, PAMELA KAYE, school counselor; b. New Castle, Ind., Dec. 25, 1946; d. Euil and Mary Ruth (Faubion) Reynolds; m. David Clark Randall, June 14, 1968 (div. May 1984); children: Christopher Clark, Mathhew Faubion; m. Harry Vernon Gabbard, June 9, 1984. BS in Elem. Edn., Taylor U., 1969; MA in Ednl. Counseling Psychology, U. Ky., 1985, Rank 1 Ednl. Counseling Psychology, 1988. Cert. counselor, tchr., Ky. Elem. sch. tchr. Stevenson Elem., Bellevue, Wash., 1969-71, Curtis Bay Elem., Balt., 1972-74; dir. Christian edn. Park United Meth. Ch., Lexington, Ky., 1978-83; elem. guidance counselor Huntertown Elem./Woodford County, Versailles, Ky., 1987—; camp dir. and coord. children's activities, Westminister House Presbyn. Mission Svc., New Castle, Ind., 1968; substitute tchr. Fayette County Pub. Schs., Lexington, 1986-87. Mem. Am. Counseling Assn., Am. Sch. Counseling Assn. (elem. v.p. 1994—), Ky. Counseling Assn., Ky. Sch. Counseling Assn., others. Republican. Methodist. Office: Huntertown Elem 785 Huntertown Rd Versailles KY 40383-9185

GABEL, EMMA MARGARET, retired librarian; b. Perkasie, Pa., Aug. 10, 1928; d. William U. and Mary Amanda (Kramer) G. BS in Edn., Kutztown U., 1950; MS Libr. Sci., Syracuse U., 1957. Libr. Morrisville (Pa.) High Sch., 1950-52; asst. libr. Susquehanna U., Selinsgrove, Pa., 1952-56, Indiana U. of Pa., 1956-66; head cataloger, asst. to dir. of libr. High Libr., Elizabethtown (Pa.) Coll., 1966-94; ret., 1994. Mem. Elizabethtown Hist. Soc., 1980—, Dem. Party Orgn., Elizabethtown. Mem. ALA, Pa. Libr. Assn. ,Lancaster County Libr. Assn., Pa. Citizens for Better Librs., AAUP, Am. Assn. Higher Edn., Delta Kappa Gamma Soc. Internat. 9state pres. Alpha Alpha state 1987-89). Lutheran.

GABEL, KATHERINE, academic administrator; b. Rochester, N.Y., Apr. 9, 1938; d. M. Wren and Esther (Conger) G.; m. Seth Devore Strickland, June 24, 1961 (div. 1965). AB, Smith Coll., Northampton, Mass., 1959; MSW, Simmons Coll., 1961; PhD, Syracuse U., 1967; JD, Union U., 1970; bus. program, Stanford U., 1984. Psychol. social worker Cen. Island Mental Health Ctr., Uniondale, N.Y., 1961-62; psychol. social worker, supt. Ga. State Tng. Sch. for Girls, Atlanta, 1962-64; cons. N.Y. State Crime Control Coun., Albany, 1968-70; faculty Ariz. State U., Tempe, 1972-76; supt. Ariz. Dept. of Corrections, Phoenix, 1970-76; dean, prof. Smith Coll., 1976-85; pres. Pacific Oaks Coll. and Children's Sch., Pasadena, Calif., 1985—; advisor, del. UN, Geneva, 1977; mem. So. Calif. Youth Authority, 1986—. Editor: Master Teacher and Supervisor in Clinical Social Work, 1982; author report Legal Issues of Female Inmates, 1981, model for rsch. Diversion program Female Inmates, 1984. Vice chair United Way, Northampton, 1982-83; chair Mayor's Task Force, Northampton, 1981. Mem. Nat. Assn. Social Work, Acad. Cert. Social Workers, Nat. Assn. Edn. Young Children, Western Assn. Schs. and Colls., Pasadena C. of C., Athenaeum, Pasadena Rotary Club. Democrat. Presbyterian. Office: Pacific Oaks Coll 5 Westmoreland Pl Pasadena CA 91103-3592

GABERT, NORI LAUREN, lawyer; b. Houston, Aug. 15, 1953; d. Lenard Morris and Dahlia (Edelstein) G. BA, U. Houston, 1975, JD, 1979. Bar: Tex. 1980, U.S. Dist. Ct. (so. and ea. dists.) Tex. 1980. Staff atty. securities bd. State of Tex., Houston, 1980-81; v.p., assoc. gen. counsel, sec. Am. Capital Asset Mmgt. Inc., Houston, 1981—. Mem. ABA, Houston Bar Assn. Office: Am Capital Asset Mgmt Inc 46th Fl 2800 Post Oak Blvd Houston TX 77056*

GABRIELSEN, CAROL ANN, employment consulting company executive; b. Oak Park, Ill., Aug. 8, 1951; d. George Kenneth and Mary Jo (Martin) G. Student, Harper Jr. Coll., 1970-71. Regional mgr. Reed Roberts Assn., Ill., Wis., Pa., 1972-79; account rep. The Gibbens Co., Schiller Park, Ill., 1980-81; CEO Unemployment Consultants, Inc., Arlington Heights, 1981-94; tech. advisor Gov. Edgar Unemployment Task Force, 1990-94. Author: Manufacturer's Guide to the New Unemployment Law, 1987, rev. edit., 1992. Vol. Bush/Quayle campaign, Arlington Heights, 1988; chairwoman golf outing Spl. Leisure Svcs. Found., 1992-94; legis. com. Greater Ohare Assn., 1992-94. Mem. Assn. Unemployed Tax (v.p. 1989, pres. 1990), Ill. Mfrs. Assn., Employers Assn. Ill., Our Lady of the Wayside Alumni Assn. (pres. 1990-92), Arlington Heights C. of C. (bd. dirs. 1987-92, v.p. 1991), Arlington Heights Rotary (chair youth exch. 1987-94, chair membership com. 1994). Roman Catholic. Office: Unemployment Consultants 1020 S Arlington Heights Rd Arlington Heights IL 60005-3108

GABRIELSON, SHIRLEY GAIL, nurse; b. San Francisco, Mar. 17, 1934; d. Arthur Obert and Lois Ruth (Lanterman) Ellison; m. I. Grant Gabrielson, Sept. 11, 1955; children: James Grant, Kari Gay. BS in Nursing, Mont. State U., 1955. RN, Mont. Staff and operating room nurse Bozeman (Mont.) Deaconess Hosp., 1954-55, 55-56; staff nurse Warm Springs State Hosp., 1955; office nurse, operating room asst. Dr. Craft, Bozeman, 1956-57; office nurse Dr. Bush, Beach, N.D., 1957-58; pub. health nurse Wibaux County, 1958-59; staff and charge nurse Teton Meml. Hosp., Choteau, Mont., 1964-65; staff pediatric and float nurse St. Patrick Hosp., Missoula, Mont., 1965-70; nurse, insvc. dir. Trinity Hosp., Wolf Point, Mont., 1970-79; ednl. coord. Community Hosp. and Nursing Home, Poplar, Mont., 1979—; coord. staff devel. Faith Luth. Home, Wolf Point, 1980-81; CPR instr. ARC, Am. Heart Assn., Great Falls, Mont., 1979—; condr. workshops and seminars; program coord., test proctor for cert. nursing assts., 1989—; preceptor for student nurses in rural health nursing clin. U. N.D., 1993—. Author: Independent Study for Nurse Assistants, 1977. Former asst. camp leader Girl Scouts U.S.A.; former mother advisor, bd. dirs. Rainbow Girls; pres. Demolay Mothers Club, 1977; bd. dirs. Mont. div. Am. Cancer Soc., 1984-90, mem. awards com., 1986-89; founder Tri-County Parkinson's Support Group, N.E. Mont. Recipient Lifesaver award Am. Cancer Soc., 1987, Svc. award ARC, 1989, Health and Human Svcs. award Mont. State Dept., 1990, U.S. Dept. Health award, 1990, Outstanding award, U.S. HHS, Mont. Health Promotion award Dept. Health and Environ. Scis. Mem. Am. Nurses Assn., Mont. Nurses Assn. (mem. commn. on continuing edn. 1977-91, chmn. 1984-86), Order Eastern Star, Alpha Tau Delta (alumni pres. 1956). Presbyterian. Home: 428 Hill St Wolf Point MT 59201-1244 Office: Community Hosp-Nursing Home PO Box 38 Poplar MT 59255-0038

GACH, LYDIA ANDREA, event planner; b. Bridgeport, Conn., Oct. 12, 1963; d. John and Edeltraud G. AA, Fashion Inst. Design/Mdsing., San Francisco, 1981-83. Owner, mgr. Party Productions, L.A., 1986—. Home: PO Box 9083 Marina Dl Rey CA 90295-1483

GADOLA, RITA URSULA, executive secretary, small business owner; b. Metuchen, N.J., Apr. 24, 1930; d. Louis Charles and Mary Concetta (Dente) DeMaio; m. John Henry Gadola, Jan. 20, 1950 (div. Feb. 1966, dec. Sept. 1986); children: Jonathan, Bruce, Gregory, Maureen, Susan, Daniel, Christopher. AA, Cumberland County Coll., 1990. Office mgr. South Jersey Glass of Vineland, 1971-75, Dept. Law & Pub. Safety, Divsn. on Civil Rights, Vineland, 1981-92, Motor Vehicle Dept. Regional Office, Deptford, N.J., 1992-93; ret., 1993; owner Mail & More, Vineland, 1994—. Office: Mail & More 1811 N Delsea Dr Vineland NJ 08360

GADSDEN, MARIE DAVIS, educational agency administrator; b. Douglas, Ga., Apr. 27; d. Thomas Jethro Sr. and Louella Helen (Mayberry) Davis; m. Benjamin Franklin Cochrane (div. 1948); m. Robert Washington Gadsden Jr., 1954 (dec. Mar. 24, 1993). BS in Biology, Ga. State Coll., 1939; MA in English/Communications, Altanta U., 1945; postgrad., Oxford (Eng.) U., 1951-53; PhD in English/Lang., U. Wis., 1954, LHD (hon.), 1982; LHD (hon.), U. New Eng., 1991. Cert. English, ESL tchr. Tchr. pub. schs. Cairo, Thomasville and Albany, Ga., 1939-43; tchr. Reed's Bus. Coll., Atlanta, 1943-45; asst. prof. drama, English So. U., Baton Rouge, 1945-47; assoc. prof. Dillard U., New Orleans, 1953-54, Howard U., Washington, 1954-57; researcher, prof. teaching English as a fgn. lang. Am. U., Washington, 1956-59; coordinator, specialist TEFL English Lang. Services, Inc., Conakry, Guinea, 1959-61; chmn. dept. humanities Alcorn U., Lorman, Miss., 1961-63; tng. officer, coordinator TEFL U.S. Peace Corps, Washington, 1963-65; vis. prof., supr. with Tchrs. Coll., Columbia U. U.S. Peace Corps, Nairobi (Kenya) and Kampala (Uganda), 1965-67; tng. coordinator Africa region U.S. Peace Corps, Washington, 1967-70; country dir. U.S. Peace Corps, Lome, Togo, 1970-72; prof. Tchrs. English to Speakers of Other Langs. dept. Am. Lang. Inst., Georgetown U., Washington, 1972; v.p., exec. dir. Phelps-Stokes Fund, Washington, 1972-83; conf. coordinator Africare, Washington, 1983-84; dep. dir. Nat. Assn. Equal Opportunity Higher Edn./AID Coop. Agreement, Washington, 1984-89; ret., 1989; mem. overseas liaison com. Am. Coun. on Edn., Washington, 1978-80; team cons. internat. edn. transition team U.S. Dept. Edn., Washington, 1980; bd. dirs. fgn. svc. selection bds. U.S. Info. Agy. Author: Minor Playwrights of the Abbey Theatre 1899-1914, 1953, Aesthetic of John Addington Symonds, 1964; editor: Update-NAFEO/AID Quar., 1984-89. Chair panel mem. Africa panel Coun. for Internat. Exch. of Scholars, Washington, 1975-78; pres., treas. Emergency Svc. for African Students, Washington, 1978-92; bd. dirs. Acad. for Ednl. Devel., N.Y.C. and Washington, 1978—; chair Oxfam Am., 1981-89. Recipient citation Philomathians, 1979, White House Presdl. Award for Outstanding Achievement in Internat. Devel. Assistance, 1990. Disting. Alumni award U. Wis., 1988; honoree Nat. Assn. Coll. Deans, Registrars, Admissions Officer, 1978, Club 20, 1983; named one of Top 50 Women in U.S. Govt. Pres. of U.S., 1963; named to Ga. Hall of Fame Chatham County (Ga.) Lions, 1979; named one of Women of Achievement Sta. WETA Radio-TV, 1981; Atlanta U. scholar, 1943-45; fellow La. State Dept. Edn., 1947-51, U.S. Council for Internat. Exchange of Scholars, 1951-53, UNESCO, 1952. Mem. AAUW, MLA, Nat. Coun. Tchrs. English, Nat. Coun. Negro Women (internat. honoree 1982), Teaching English to Speakers of Other Langs., African Am. Women's Assn. (chair edn. and scholarship com. 1973—). Democrat. Mem. A.M.E. Ch.

GAEDE, JANE TAYLOR, pathologist; b. Washington, July 8, 1941; d. Raleigh Colston and Margaret (Lamb) Taylor; m. William Hanks Gaede, Feb. 12, 1966; children: Geoffrey Terence, Bruce Lucas. BA, U. Miss., 1962; MD, Duke U., 1966. Diplomate Am. Bd. Pathology. Intern in surgery N.C. Bapt. Hosp., Winston-Salem, N.C., 1966-67; resident in pathology Duke Med. Ctr., Durham, N.C., 1967-71, asst. prof. pathology, 1974—; asst. prof. pathology Med. Univ. S.C., Charleston, 1971-74; staff pathologist VA Med Ctr., Durham, 1974—. Author: Clinical Pathology for the House Officer, 1982. Fellow Am. Soc. Clin. Pathologists; mem. DAR (1st vice regent local chpt. 1992-94), N.C. Soc. Pathologists. Presbyterian. Office: Duke Univ Med Ctr Dept Pathology PO Box 3712 Durham NC 27710

GAETA-HARPER, THERESA, psychotherapist; b. Altoona, Pa., July 6, 1955; d. Joseph D. and Anna M. (Malfara) Gaeta; m. Kevin W. Harper, Oct. 16, 1982. BA in Psychology, St. Francis Coll., 1977; grad. cert., Roosevelt U., 1986, MA in Clin. Psychology, 1989. Clinically cert. substance abuse counselor. Clin. therapist Family Guidance Ctr., Chgo., 1985-86, counseling coord., 1986-87, dir., clin. therapist, 1987-89; pvt. practice psychotherapy Chgo., 1989-91; mgr. vol. dept., clin. therapist Howard Brown Health Ctr., Chgo., 1989—; seminar/workshop trainer and educator Howard Brown Health Ctr., Chgo., 1989—, nat. trainer and educator, 1991-94. Producer video Active Duty, 1992. Vol. Guild for the Blind, Chgo., 1990-94, Cris Radio, Chgo., 1987-88; bd. dirs. Lakeview Mental Health Ctr., Chgo., 1989-91. Recipient Friend for Life award Howard Brown Health Ctr., 1992, Hon. Recognition PWA Support award, 1991; finalist Internat. Health and Med. Film Festival, 1994. Mem. ACA, Am. Mental Health Counselors, Midwestern Psychol. Assn., Coalition Ill. Counselors. Democrat. Roman Catholic. Office: Howard Brown Health Ctr 945 W George Chicago IL 60657

GAFFNEY, BERYL, Canadian legislator; d. Heath and Mary Clark; m. J. Cuthbert Gaffney, June 14, 1952; children: Michael, Kenneth, Patti, Gail, Alyson. Regional councillor City of Nepean, Regional Municipality of Ottawa-Carleton, Ont., Can., 1978-88; M.P. Ho. Commons, 1988. Liberal. Office: House of Commons, Offices of House Members, Ottawa, ON Canada K1A OA6

GAFFNEY, JUDITH, administrator; b. Yonkers, N.Y., Dec. 3, 1947; d. Morris and Anna (Mizar) Pollack; divorced; children: Michael, Daniel, Christopher. BA, CUNY, 1968, postgrad., 1968-69. Instr. biology Bklyn. Coll., 1968-69; technologist hematology, bone marrow Sloan-Kettering Cancer Ctr., N.Y.C., 1969-70; rsch. technologist immunology Albert Einstein Coll. Medicine, Bronx, 1970-77; rsch. assoc. hematology U. Conn. Health Ctr., Farmington, 1981-87, flow cytometry specialist, 1987-89, supr. bone marrow processing lab., 1989—; cons. in field. Contbr. articles to profl. jours. Chmn., bd. dirs. Pine Grove Nursery Sch., Avon, Conn., 1982; den coord., leader Boy Scouts Am., Avon, 1985-86. Mem. Am. Assn. Blood Banks, Internat. Soc. Hematotherapy & Graft Engrng. Office: U Conn Health Ctr 263 Farmington Ave Farmington CT 06030-0002

GAFFNEY, SUSAN, federal official. BA, Wilson Coll., 1965; MA in Advanced Internat. Studies, John Hopkins. Staff analyst to dep. commr. Dept. Housing Preservation and Devel., City of N.Y., 1970-79; dir. policy, plans and programs Office of Inspector Gen., Agy. for Internat. Devel., 1979-82; asst. inspector gen. Gen. Svcs. Adminstrn., 1982-87, dept. inspector gen., 1987-91; chief mgmt. integrity br. Office of Mgmt. and Budget, 1991-93; inspector gen. Dept. Housing and Urban Devel., 1993—. Recipient Presdl. Meritorious Rank award, Disting. Honor award, Disting. Leadership award Joint Fin. Mgmt. Improvement Program. Office: HUD Office of the Inspector General 451 7th St SW Rm 8256 Washington DC 20410

GAFFREY, KIM RENEE, critical care and home intravenous therapy nurse; b. Syracuse, N.Y., Apr. 10, 1963; d. William A. and Elaine (Levy) G.; m. Thomas S. Moroz, May 26, 1990; 1 child, Ryan Andrew. BSN, Russell Sage Coll., 1985. Cert. critical care nurse, intravenous, BLSC. Critical care nurse St. Peter's Med. Ctr., New Brunswick, N.J., 1984-87; home intravenous nurse Commun. Care Med., Princeton, N.J., 1987-90; critical care nurse Favorite Nurses, Union, N.J., 1987-92; home intravenous nurse Phoenix Health Care, Tenafly, N.J., 1991—; neuro ICU nurse Univ. Medicine and Dentistry of N.J., Newark, 1991-93; critical care nurse Princeton (N.J.) Med. Ctr., 1991-93; charge nurse Middlesex County Adult Corrections Ctr., North Brunswick, N.J., 1993—. Mem. AACN. Home: 62 Gregory Ln Franklin Park NJ 08823-1675

GAGEL, BARBARA JEAN, health insurance administrator; b. Celina, Ohio, Nov. 19, 1943; d. Vincent James and Theresa Barbara (Goettermoeller) G. BA, Miami U., 1965; MBA, U. Chgo., 1977. Asst. dir. for internat. trade State of Ill., Chgo., Brussels, Hongkong and Sao Paulo, Brazil, 1973-76; dir. office of mgmt. and planning Office Human Devel. Svcs., Chgo., 1976-79; dep. regional adminstr. Health Care Financing Adminstrn., Chgo., 1979-82, regional adminstr., 1982-87; dir. bur. of prog. ops. Health Care Financing Adminstrn., Balt., 1987-92; dir. health stds. and quality bur. Health Care Fin. Adminstrn., Balt., 1992—. Recipient Presdl. Disting. Rank award 1988, Presdl. Meritorious Rank award 1987, 92; named Fed. Exec. of Yr., 1987. Home: 2901 Boston St Unit 211 Baltimore MD 21224-4887 Office: Health Care Financing Admin 6325 Security Blvd # 30D Baltimore MD 21207-5161

GAGNE, ANN MARIE, special education educator; b. Elmont, N.Y., Feb. 21, 1956; d. Wilfred Alfred and Anita Agnes (Henne) G. BA in Edn., U. Miss., 1978, MEd, 1979; postgrad., Nicholl State U., 1982-85, U. Memphis, 1989-92. Tchr. learning disabled So. Elem. Sch., Southaven, Miss., 1979-82; tchr. spl. edn. Labodieville (La.) Elem. Sch., 1982-84, Bayou Bay (La.) Elem. Sch., 1984-86; tchr. of physically disabled/mentally fragile Shrine Sch., Memphis, 1986—; career ladder II tchr., 21st century classroom tchr.; athletic sports coach Spl. Olympics, wheelchair events dir. Active human rights com. Open Arms Corp. Mem. Coun. Exceptional Children, Memphis Jr. C. of C., Friends of Orpheum, Open Arms Corp. Human Rights Com., Delta Kappa Gamma. Roman Catholic. Home: 6850 Club Ridge Circle # 97 Memphis TN 38115

GAGNON, EDITH MORRISON, ballerina, singer, actress; b. Chgo., Apr. 8; grad. Chalif Sch. Dancing, N.Y.C.; student Northwestern U.; voice student Forest Lamont of Chgo. Opera Co.; grad., trained with Ivan Tarasoff Chalif Sch. of N.Y.; m. Alfred Gagnon, Feb. 3, 1977; children by previous marriage—Joyce, Morton. Premiere ballerina Pavley and Oukrainsky Russian Ballet of Chgo., performer with Chgo., Met., Ravinia Opera Cos.; appeared Birthday of Infanta, Greenwich Follies, The Five O'Clock Girl; founder, dir., instr. Sch. of Dance, St. Louis; singer in concert, Carnegie Hall; commentator radio programs Women on the Home Front, Sta. KSD, St. Louis, and CD program Sta. WEW, St. Louis U.; voice coach, producer, performer benefit performances, St. Louis, San Francisco area. Pres. Pets Unlimited, San Francisco; bd. dirs. Artists Embassy. Mem. Pacific Musical Soc. (v.p. San Francisco), Equity Guild. Clubs: Burlingame Country; International Embassy, Francisca

GAHAN, KATHLEEN MASON, small business owner, retired educational counselor, artist; b. Long Beach, Calif., May 23, 1940; d. Robert Elwyn and Jean Mason (Campbell) Fisher; m. Keith Victor Gahan, Apr. 21, 1961; children: Carrie Jean, Christie Sue. BA, Calif. State U., Long Beach, 1962, MA, 1967; student, Studio Arts Ctrs. Internat., Florence, Italy, 1992. Cert. gen. secondary educator, adminstr., Calif. Tchr. Long Beach Unified Sch. Dist., 1963-70; tchr. Porterville (Calif.) Union High Sch. Dist., 1970-76, counselor, 1976-95, ret., 1995; coord. gifted and talented edn. Porterville High Sch., 1976-83, coach acad. decathlon team, 1977-82, 85; adminstr. Counseling for Collegeable Hispanic Jrs., Porterville, 1988-90, Counseling for Ptnrship. Acad. in Bus., 1990-95; tchr. faculty and staff computer workshop Porterville High Sch., 1992-94; proprietor El Mirador Ranch, Strathmore, Calif., 1978—; salesman real estate, Porterville, 1981-82; income tax return preparer, Lindsay, Calif., 1983-84; organizer SAT preparation workshop, 1981-83. Editor: (cookbook) Mexican Cooking in America, 1974; editor (craft patterns) Glory Bee, 1979-84; group exhibits photography Porterville Coll., 1989, oil paintings, Coll. of Sequoias, 1992; one woman show Porterville Coll., 1995. Leader 4-H, Lindsay, 1971-79; mem. exec. com. Math. Sci. Conf. for Girls, Tulare County, 1982-85; adminstr. Advanced Placement Program, Porterville, 1979-95; mem. bible study Ch. of Nazarene; charter mem. Tulare County Herb Soc., 1983-85. Recipient 1st pl. Mus. Art, Long Beach, 1961, Orange Blossom Festival Art Show, Lindsay, 1988, 2d pl. Coll. of Sequoias Art Show, Visalia, 1988, Hon. mention Orange Blossom Festival Art Show, Lindsay, 1992, commendation Gov. Bd. and Dist. Adminstrsn., Porterville, Calif., 1975, 82; named Coach of Champion Acad. Decathlon Team, Tulare County, 1982, 85. Mem. AAUW, Am. Assn. Individual Investors, Calif. Tchrs. Assn., Women in the Senate and House, Porterville Educators Assn. Republican. Home: 1032 Mountain View Dr Lindsay CA 93247-1626

GAHS, DEBORAH JEAN, marketing professional; b. Balt., Dec. 17, 1953; d. Lockered S. and Thurley M. (Buchter) G. BA, U. Md., 1975; postgrad., George Wash. U., 1983, Towson State U., 1993. Membership coord. Wash./Md. Svc. Sta. Assn., Greenbelt, 1975-80; govt. affairs asst. Direct Mktg. Assn., Washington, 1980-84; dir. retail divsn. Soc. Am. Florists, Alexandria, Va., 1984-87; dir. floral divsn. Produce Mktg. Assn., Newark, Del., 1988-92; mktg. specialist Employee Assistance program Sheppard Pratt Health System, Balt., 1993—. Mem., trainer Depression and Related Affective Disorders Assn., Johns Hopkins U., Balt., 1992—; mem. Exec. Women's Network, Balt., 1992—. Recipient cert. Success Leadership Program, 1987, Basic Direct Mktg. Inst., 1980. Mem. Am. Soc. Assn. Execs.

GAIL, KRISTINE MARIE, accountant, consultant; b. Detroit, Oct. 12, 1963; d. Edward and Lillian Dolores (Kwasnivck) Kasprzyk; m. Kurt Kyle Gail, Aug. 8, 1986. Student, Eastern Mich. U., 1983-85; BBA in Acctg., Walsh Coll., 1987. CPA, Mich.; cert. insolvency and reorganization acct. Acct. Parker, Bohl & Assocs., Southfield, Mich., 1988-90; assoc. Jay Alix & Assocs., Southfield, 1990—. Mem. AICPA, Mich. Assn. CPAs, Assn. Insolvency Accts., Inst. Mgmt. Accts. (bd. dirs. 1993-94), Walsh Coll. Alumni Assn. (vol.). Office: Jay Alix & Assocs 4000 Town Ctr Ste 500 Southfield MI 48075

GAILEY, JOAN DALE, business management educator; b. Beaver Falls, Pa., May 10, 1940; d. Irvin D. and Elizabeth Jane (Hollander) Anderson; m. Ronald L. Gailey, Aug. 15, 1957; 1 child, Ronald. BSBA, Geneva Coll., 1975; MBA, Youngstown State U., 1980; PhD, U. Pitts., 1987. Libr. tech. Community Coll. Beaver County, Monaca, Pa., 1969-74; customer liaison, floor supr. LTV Steel, Aliquippa, Pa., 1975-79; instr. Youngstown (Ohio) State U., 1980-83; asst. prof. bus. mgmt. Kent State U., East Liverpool, Ohio, 1984-91, assoc. prof. bus. mgmt., 1992—; cons. in bus. mgmt., 1988—; coord. Kent State East Liverpool Bus. Resource Ctr. Contbr. articles to profl. jours. Mem. Rochester (Pa.) Area Planning Commn., 1989, Rochester Area Mktg. Com., 1990; tutor Adult Lit. Coun., Monaca, 1984-91; mem. adv. bd. Ret. Sr. Vol. Program, Lisbon, Ohio, 1990-94, vice chair, 1993—, facilitator Columbiana County Mini-Loan Fund, 1994—. Recipient Kent State Teaching Devel. award, 1990, Kent State Profl. Devel. award, 1992. Mem. Am. Ednl. Rsch. Assn. (editor newsletter 1993-94, program chair 1992), Midwest MLA, Ohio Bus. Tchrs. Assn., Humanities and Tech. Assn., Alpha Mu (Outstanding Mktg. Tchr. 1983). Office: Kent State U 400 E 4th St East Liverpool OH 43920-3402

GAILLARD, MARY KATHARINE, physics educator; b. New Brunswick, N.J., Apr. 1, 1939; d. Philip Lee and Marion Catharine (Wiedemayer) Ralph; children: Alain, Dominique, Bruno. BA, Hollins (Va.) Coll., 1960; MA, Columbia U., 1961; Dr du Troiseme Cycle, U. Paris, Orsay, France, 1964, Dr-es-Sciences d'Etat, 1968. With Centre National de Recherche Scientifique, Orsay and Annecy-le-Vieux, France, 1964-84; maitre de recherches Centre National de Recherche Scientifique, Orsay, 1973-80; maitre de recherches Centre National de Recherche Scientifique, Annecy-le-Vieux, 1979-80, dir. research, 1980-84; prof. physics, sr. faculty staff Lawrence Berkeley lab. U. Calif., Berkeley, 1981—; Morris Loeb lectr. Harvard U., Cambridge, Mass., 1980; Chancellor's Disting. lectr., U. Calif., Berkeley, 1981; Warner-Lambert lectr. U. Mich., Ann Arbor, 1984; vis. scientist Fermi Nat. Accelerator Lab., Batavia, Ill., 1973-74, Inst. for Advanced Studies, Santa Barbara, Calif., 1984, U. Calif., Santa Barbara, 1985; group leader L.A.P.P., Theory Group, France, 1979-81, Theory Physics div. LBL, Berkeley, 1985-87; sci. dir. Les Houches (France) Summer Sch., 1981; cons., mem. adv. panels U.S. Dept. Energy, Washington, and various nat. labs. C0-editor: Weak Interactions, 1977, Gauge Theories in High Energy Physics, 1983; author or co-author 140 articles, papers to profl. jours., books, conf. proceedings. Recipient Thibaux prize U. Lyons (France) Acad. Art & Sci., 1977, E.O. Lawrence award, 1988, J.J. Sakurai prize for theoretical particle physics, APS, 1993; Guggenheim fellow, 1989-90. Fellow Am. Acad. Arts and Scis., Am. Physics Soc. (mem. various coms., chairperson com. on women, J.J. Saburai prize 1993); mem. AAAS, NAS. Office: U Calif Dept Physics Berkeley CA 94720

GAINER, BARBARA JEANNE, radiology educator; b. Omaha, Dec. 9, 1938; d. Merrill Lester and Ressie (Kirby) Steele; m. Glenn Thomas Gainer, Oct. 26, 1968; 1 child, Kelly Jeanne Gainer Holmes. BA, Austin Coll., 1960; MD, U. Tex. Southwestern, 1966. Diplomate Am. Bd. Radiology. Rotating intern Meth. Hosp. Dallas, 1966-67; chief radiology RE Thomason Gen. Hosp., El Paso, Tex., 1971-77; resident in diagnostic radiology Meth. Hosp. Dallas, 1967-70; pvt. practice Radiology Cons., El Paso, 1977-78; from asst. to assoc. prof. radiology Tex. Tech. Health Scis. Ctr., El Paso, 1978-90, prof., 1990—; med. advisor radiologic tech. program El Paso C.C., 1979—; chief med. staff Thomason Gen. Hosp., 1989-90. Bd. dirs. Planned Parenthood, El Paso, 1983-86. Mem. AMA, Am. Coll. Radiology (alt. councilor), Radiol. Soc. N.Am., Tex. Radiol. Soc., Tex. Med. Assn., Assn. Univ. Radiologists. Republican. Presbyterian. Home: 8727 Marble Dr El Paso TX 79904 Office: Tex Tech Health Scis Ctr at El Paso 4800 Alberta St El Paso TX 79905

GAINES, ANNE PRESTON, publication executive; b. Charleston, W.Va., July 25, 1950; d. William Thomas and Elizabeth (Tupper) Griffiths; m. William Maxwell Gaines, Feb. 21, 1987 (dec.). BFA, U. Colo., 1972. Sec. N.Y. Bailliage Confrerie de la Chaine des Rotisseurs, N.Y.C, 1976-81; asst. to pub. Mad Mag.-E.C. Publs., N.Y.C, 1980-92, gen. mgr., 1992—. Mem. Wine and Food Soc. N.Y., John More Assn. (bd. dirs. 1980-86), Ison Soc. (charter mem.). Office: Mad Mag 1700 Broadway New York NY 10019

GAINES, BABETTE, county agency adminstrator; b. Bklyn., Apr. 21, 1927; d. Louis Samuel and Carlotta (Sabath) Lowenfeld; m. Jules Gaines, July 2, 1950 (dec. Oct. 1969); children: Leonard, David. BBA, Adelphi U., 1973, MBA, 1978. Converter's asst. various cos., N.Y.C., 1944-52, William Heller, Inc., N.Y.C., 1952-56; adminstrv. asst. Adelphi U., Garden City, N.Y., 1973-76, Nassau County Dist. Atty.'s Office, Mineola, N.Y., 1976-83; dir. fiscal and pers. Nassau County Dept. Sr. Citizen Affairs, Mineola, 1983—. Recipient Citation for Religious Dedication, Suburban Temple, 1971. Mem. Delta Mu Delta. Jewish. Home: 389 Wellington Rd East Meadow NY 11554 Office: Nassau County Dept Sr Citizen Affairs 400 County Seat Dr Mineola NY 11501

GAINES, BLAIR RIEPMA, mass communications educator, publisher; b. Washington, May 17, 1945; d. Siert F. and Marva L. Blair Riepma; m. Robert Anderson Gaines, June 11, 1966; children: Robert R., Elizabeth L. BA in History, Coll. of William and Mary, 1967; MA in Journalism, Ind. U., 1972. Writer, editor Bur. Land Mgmt., Washington, 1966-69; asst. to editor Jour. Mktg. Rsch., Bloomington, Ind., 1969-72; editor So. Rural Devel. Ctr., Starkville, Miss., 1973-78; ad dir. Aronov Realty Co., Montgomery, Ala., 1977-78; asst. prof. mass comm. Auburn U., Montgomery, 1978—; chmn. Univ. Bd. Publs., Montgomery, 1980—; designer Alliance Advt., Montgomery, 1990—. Publicity chmn. Aid to Inmate Mothers, Montgomery, 1985-93, Friends of Auburn U. Libr and Fall Book Harvest, Montgomery, 1991—; docent Montgomery Mus. Fine Arts, 1989—. Mem. Pub. Rels. Soc. Am., Phi Beta Kappa, Phi Alpha Theta, Pi Delta Phi, Omicron Delta Kappa. Home: 331 Landmark Dr Montgomery AL 36117-2703 Office: Auburn Univ Montgomery AL 36117

GAINES, JANICE MAE, association administrator; b. Berkeley, Calif., Jan. 26, 1958; d. Grant Robert and Jacquelyn Maurine (Melcher) G. BA, Western Wash. U., 1981, MEd, 1993. Ednl. program mgr. Internat. Soc. Optical Engring., Bellingham, Wash., 1989-91, asst. to tech. dir., 1991-92, mgr. tech. programs and edn., 1992-93, dir. ednl. svcs., 1993—. Grantee NSF, 1991, 93. Mem. Am. Soc. Assn. Execs., Am. Soc. Engring. Edn. Democrat.

GAINES, JEAN HUNT, healthcare administrator; b. L.A., Dec. 12, 1932; d. Robert George and Phyllis Julia (Tracy) Hunt; m. Kenneth Carnahan Gaines Jr., June 26, 1954; children: Katharine A., Elizabeth T. Gaines Pavloff. BA, UCLA, 1954; cert., U. Calif., Irvine, 1993. Assoc. dir. Delta Delta Delta Fraternity, Arlington, Tex., 1974-78, fin. dir., 1978-80, v.p. collegiate pers., 1980-84, pres., 1984-88, del. nat. Panhellenic conf., 1988-93, cons., 1993—; dir. vols. Community Hospice Care, Sherman Oaks, Calif., 1993—; area advisor So. Calif. Nat. Panhellenic Conf., Indpls., 1988-93; bd. dirs. Gamma Sigma Alpha, L.A. Author: (manuals) Advisory Committee Manual, 1973, House Corporation Guide, 1976; editor: (manuals) Finance Manual, 1980, Delta Delta Delta Chapter Manual, 1984. Chair svc. unit Orange County coun. Girl Scouts Am., 1974-78; bd. dirs. Nat. Charity League, South Coast, Calif., 1975—, Assistance League, Long Beach, Calif., 1976-91. Mem. AAUW, Nat. Assn. Female Execs., Hospice Vol. Mgrs. Assn., So. Calif. Assn. Dir. of Vol. Svcs., Phi Beta Kappa. Republican. Episcopalian.

GAINES, KENDRA HOLLY, English language educator, editorial and writing consultant; b. Chgo., Dec. 6, 1946; d. Reuben B. and Frances P. Gaines; m. Kenneth C. Wolfgang, Feb. 18, 1989. BA with distinction, Mt. Holyoke Coll., 1968; MA with honor, Claremont Grad. Sch., 1971; MA, Northwestern U., 1974, PhD, 1982. Cert. life secondary and community coll. tchr., Calif. Tchr. English, Claremont (Calif.) Collegiate Sch., 1969-72; teaching asst. Northwestern U., Evanston, Ill., 1975-78; instr. English, U. Mich., Ann Arbor, 1978-79; assoc. editor Scott, Foresman Co., Glenview, 1983-85; instr. English, career tutor U. Ariz., Tucson, 1985—; editorial cons., freelance writer, 1969—. Contbr. articles to various publs.; writer radio scripts Holiday World of Travel, 1969—. Elected to The Imperial Russian Order of St. John of Jerusalem Ecumenical Found. (Knights of Malta), N.Y.; grantee State of Calif., 1970; Mills fellow, 1971; fellow Northwestern U., 1973-76. Mem. MLA, Nat. Coun. Tchrs. English, AAUW. Home: 925 N Jerrie Ave Tucson AZ 85711-1153 Office: U Ariz Humanities Adminstrn Tucson AZ 85721

GAINES, PAMELA J., accountant; b. Clinton, Ind., July 27, 1962; d. Ronald David Gaines and Donna Rose (DeBolt) Hill; m. Steven D. Peak, May 30, 1987 (div. Dec. 1991); m. David Alan Fagan, Dec. 27, 1992. BBA, Belmont Coll., 1984. CPA, Tenn. Staff-supr. acct. Kraft Bros., CPAs, Nashville, 1984-91; ptnr. Gaines & Oakley, CPAs, Nashville, 1991—. Named Vol. of Week, The Tennessean, 1992. Mem. AICPA, Am. Woman's Soc. CPAs (pres. 1993-94), Nat. Assn. Self-Employed, Tenn. Soc. CPAs, Inst. Mgmt. Accts. (dir. spl. activities 1992-93, dir. student activities 1993—), Country Music Assn., Nashville Entertainment Assn. Home: 515 Derby Trace Nashville TN 37211 Office: Gaines & Oakley CPAs 50 Music Sq W # 404 Nashville TN 37203

GAINES, SARAH FORE, retired library science educator; b. Roxobel, N.C., Aug. 21, 1920; d. Stonewall Jackson Fore and Ethel Gattis; m. Clyde Ritchie Bell (div. 1974); m. John Coffman Gaines. AB, U. N.C., 1941, MA, 1944, PhD, 1968, MLS, 1982. Instr. U. N.C., Greensboro, 1967-69, asst. prof., 1970-75, assoc. prof., 1976-85, assoc. prof. emeritus, 1985—. Author: Charles Nodier, 1971; also articles, book revs. Home: 3017 Robin Hood Dr Greensboro NC 27408-2618

GAINEY-ARTIS, TERESA L., federal official; b. High Point, N.C., Dec. 23, 1958; d. Napoleon and Bessie Pearl (Evans) Gainey; 1 child, Jessica Michelle. AA in Bus., Columbia U., 1981; BS in Bus., U. N.C., 1985; MA, Webster U., 1991. Contract specialist U.S. Dept. Commerce, Silver Spring, Md., 1992—. Capt. USAF, 1985-89. Mem. Nat. Contract Mgmt. Assn., Blacks in Govt. (NOAA chpt.), Delta Sigma Theta. Office: US Dept Commerce 1325 E West Hwy Silver Spring MD 20910-3280

GAIPA, NANCY CHRISTINE, pharmacist; b. Benton Harbor, Mich., Oct. 11, 1949; d. Frank Thomas and Anne Marie (Scardina) G. BS, Marygrove Coll., Detroit, 1971; BS in Pharmacy, Wayne State U., 1992. Registered pharmacist, Mich.; cert. secondary educator, Mich. Educator Regina High Sch., Harper Woods, Mich., 1971-88; staff pharmacist Perry Drugs, Northville, Mich., 1993, Meijers, Inc., Westland, Mich., 1993—. Vol. Detroit Welfare Reform Coalition, 1989-91, Maral, Southfield, Mich., 1991. State of Mich. scholar, 1967-71. Mem. Am. Pharm. Assn., Mich. Pharmacists Assn., Golden Key Nat. Honor Soc., Iota Gamma Alpha, Rho Chi.

GAISSER, JULIA HAIG, classical educator; b. Cripple Creek, Colo., Jan. 12, 1941; d. Henry Wolseley and Gertrude Alice (Lent) Haig; m. Thomas Korff Gaisser, Dec. 29, 1964; 1 son, Thomas Wolseley. A.B., Brown U., 1962; A.M., Harvard U., 1966; Ph.D., U. Edinburgh (Scotland), 1966. Asst. prof. Newton Coll. (Mass.), 1966-69, Swarthmore Coll. (Pa.), 1970-72, Bklyn. Coll., 1973-75; assoc. prof. dept. Latin Bryn Mawr Coll. (Pa.), 1975-84, prof., 1984—, editor Bryn Mawr Latin Commentaries, 1983—. Mem. Mid-East selection com. Marshall Scholarships, Washington, 1975—, chmn., 1984-89; mem. mng. com. Intercollegiate Ctr. for Classical Studies in Rome, Stanford, Calif., 1984—, chmn. 1988-92. Author: Catullus and His Renaissance Readers, 1993. Decorated MBE. Marshall scholar, U. Edinburgh, 1962-64; NEH summer stipend, 1977; research grantee Am. Philosophical Soc., 1980, 93; ACLS Travel grant, 1985, fellow 1989-90; NEH sr. fellow, 1985-86, 93-94; resident Rockefeller Study and Conf. Ctr., Bellagio, Italy, 1994. Mem. Am. Philological Assn. (dir. 1985-88), Renaissance Soc. Am., Internat. Neo-Latin Soc. Office: Bryn Mawr Coll Dept Latin Bryn Mawr PA 19010

GAJDA, PATRICIA ANN, history educator; b. Cleve., Jan. 24, 1941; d. Thaddeus J. and Rose M. (Rusnaczyk) Gajda. BS, St. John Coll., 1962; MA, Case Western Reserve U., 1966, PhD, 1972; BA, U. Tex., Tyler, 1988. Tchr. Cleve. Catholic Sch., 1962-65; tchr., alt. prin. U.S. Dept. Def. Overseas Dependents Sch., Gelnhausen, Germany, 1965-67; instr. Dyke Coll., Cleve., 1968-70; vis. lectr. Digby Stuart Coll., London, 1970-71; lect. John Carroll U. and Cuyahoga Community Coll., Cleve., 1972-74; asst. prof. history Univ. Tex., Tyler, 1974-77, assoc. prof., assoc. v.p., 1976-83, dir. internat. program, 1977-86; prof. history U. Tex., Tyler, 1983—; cons. jr. coll., 1977—. Author: Faces of Tyler, 1979, Postscript to Victory, 1982. Precinct chair Dem. Party, Tyler, 1980; mem. Sister Cities; mem. Tyler Hist. Preservation Bd., 1992—. Mem. Tex. Cath. Hist. Soc. (past pres.), Tex. State Hist. Assn., East Tex. Hist. Assn. (editl. bd.), World History Assn., Polish-Am. Hist. Assn. (past 3d v.p., past mem. bd. dirs.), Am. Cath. Hist. Assn. Roman Catholic. Office: U Tex 3900 University Blvd Tyler TX 75799

GAJDOS, KATHLEEN CURZIE, psychologist; b. Phila., Oct. 21, 1945; d. William Donald and Katherine (Dmochowski) Curzie; m. Lawrence John Gajdos, May 30, 1970. BA, Holy Family Coll., 1967; MA, U. Dayton, 1971, Duquesne U., 1974; PhD, U. Pitts., 1983. Psychotherapist Face Addiction Program, Pitts., 1972-73, Mon Yough Mental Health/Mental Retardation, McKeesport, Pa., 1973-76, St. Francis Meth. Unit, Pitts., 1976; psychotherapist, cons. psychologist, supr. Irene Stacey Mental Health/Mental Retardation, Butler, 1976-85; psychologist Pa. Hosp. Counseling Program, Phila., 1986-87; clin. dir. Exton (Pa.) Psychol. Assocs., 1987-88; pvt. practice Chadds Ford, Pa., 1988—; adj. prof. Pa. State U., Media, 1991—; workshop seminar leader Temenos Retreat Ctr., West Chester, Pa.; book reviewer. Mem. APA, Pa. Psychol. Assn., Del. Psychol. Assn., Am. Family Therapy Acad., Amnesty Internat. Roman Catholic.

GAJL-PECZALSKA, KAZIMIERA J., surgical pathologist, pathology educator; b. Warsaw, Poland, Nov. 15, 1925; came to U.S., 1970; d. Kazimierz Emil and Anna Janina (Gervais) Gajl; widowed; children: Kazimierz Peczalski, Andrew Peczalski. Student, Jagiellonian Univ., Cracov, Poland, 1945-47; MD, Warsaw U., Poland, 1951, PhD in Immunopathology, 1964. Diplomate Polish Bd. Pediatrics, Polish Bd. Anatomic Pathology, Am. Bd. Pathology. Attending pediatrician Children's Hosp. for Infectious Diseases, Warsaw, Poland, 1953-58, head, pathology lab., 1958-65; adj. prof. Postgrad. Med. Sch., Warsaw, Poland, 1965-70; fellow U. Minn., Mpls., 1970-72, asst. prof. dept. pathology, 1972-75, assoc. prof. dept. pathology, 1975-79, prof. dept. pathology, 1979—, dir. immunophenotyping and flow lab., 1974—, dir. cytology dept. pathology, 1976—. Author chpts. to book; contbr. of numerous papers to profl. jours. Fellow WHO, Paris, 1959, London, 1962, Paris, 1967, U.S. Pub. Health Svcs. fellow, 1968-69; recipient Scientific Com. award Polish Ministry of Health and Social Welfare, 1964. Mem. Am. Soc. Experimental Pathology, Am. Soc. Cytology, Internat. Acad. Pathology, British Soc. Pediatric Pathology, Polish Soc. Pathology, Polish Soc Pediatricians. Roman Catholic. Office: U Minn Dept Pathology U Health Ctr PO Box 609 Minneapolis MN 55455

GAJUS, AUDREY BERGMAN, corporate executive; b. Loma Linda, Calif., July 3, 1956; children: Bill, Greg, Benjamin. BA, BS, U. Md., 1978; MBA, Northwestern U., 1979. Brand asst. Procter & Gamble, Cin., 1978-83; mktg. dir. Citicorp, Fla., Miami, 1983-89; owner, pres. A&B Gajus Corp. dba Play Away Babysitting Ctr., Coral Springs, Fla., 1989—; speaker numerous child care confs., 1994. Mem. Coral Springs C. of C. (chmn. in-sch. chamber 1989—, dir. ann. toys charity drive 1989—).

GALANTI, CHRISTINA BRIGITTA, fiber optic engineer; b. Lackawanna, N.Y., Dec. 3, 1959; d. John Joseph and Hildegard M. (Kleine) G. BS, Clarkson Coll. Tech., 1981, MS, 1983. Sr. engr. GTE Govt. Systems, Needham, Mass., 1983-84; prin. devel. engr. Telco Systems Fiber Optic Corp., Norwood, Mass., 1984—. Clarkson Presdl. scholar, 1980. Mem. Optical Soc. Am., Tau Beta Pi, Eta Kappa Nu. Independent. Roman Catholic. Office: 63 Nahatan St Norwood MA 02062

GALBRAITH, FRANCES LYNN, educational administrator; b. Phila., Jan. 16, 1950; d. Noble Galbraith and Frances J. Griffin; divorced; 1 child, Frances Lynn Witucki; m. Spencer McPherson Kuhn, June 23, 1989; children: Arthur McPherson, Edward James. BA, Rutgers U., Camden, N.J., 1974; EdD, Rutgers U., New Brunswick, N.J., 1986; MA, Glassboro State Coll., 1977. Tchr. of English Lenape Regional High Sch., Medford, N.J., 1974-90, community rels. coord., 1977-90, supr. curriculum, 1990—; adj. prof. Rutgers U., New Brunswick, 1981—; chmn. writing com., test devel. N.J. Dept. Edn., Trenton, 1982—, chmn. writing, com. 1987—, cons. N.J. Div. Gen. Acad. Edn.; reader, table leader, Ednl. Testing Svc., Princeton, N.J., 1981—; mem. reading and writing adv. coun. N.J. Dept. Higher Edn., 1980-81; manuscript reviewer Harcourt, Brace, Jovanovich; test devel. cons., item developer, Nat. Evaluation Systems, Westinghouse/Am. Coun. on Edn.; cons., workshop presenter Ednl. Info. Resource Ctr. South, 1987—; presenter in field, others. Manuscript reviewer Harcourt, Brace, Jovanovich. Mem. Nat. Coun. Tchrs. English (mem. commn. on composition 1986-90, writing achievement awards adv. com. 1984-87; chmn. numerous confs., asst. editor Quarterly Rev. of Doublespeak, 1980-84, other), N.J. Coll. English Assn. (presenter 1983 spring conf.), NEA (presenter conf. 1983), N.J. Edn. Assn., N.J. Assn. Learning Cons., N.J. Assn. Supervision and Curriculum Deve. (exec. bd. 1980-81, editor FOCUS newsletter 1980-81, other offices), Assn. South Jersey English Depts., others. Home: 245 Fishing Creek Rd Cape May NJ 08204 Office: Lenape Regional High Sch 235 Hartford Rd Medford NJ 08055

GALBRAITH, NANETTE ELAINE GERKS, forensic and management sciences company executive; b. Chgo., June 15, 1928; d. Harold William and Maybelle Ellen (Little) Gerks; m. Oliver Galbraith III, Dec. 18, 1948; children: Craig Scott, Diane Frances Galbraith Ketcham. BS with high honors with distinction, San Diego State U., 1978. Diplomate Am. Bd. Forensic Document Examiners. Examiner of questioned documents San Diego County Sheriff's Dept. Crime Lab., San Diego, 1975-80; sole prop. Nanette G. Galbraith, Examiner of Questioned Documents, San Diego, 1980-82; pres., examiner of questioned documents Galbraith Forensic & Mgmt. Scis., Ltd., San Diego, 1982—; one of keynote speakers Internat. Assn Forensic Scis., Adelaide, South Australia, 1990. Contbr. articles to profl. jours. Fellow Am. Acad. Forensic Scis. (questioned documents section, del. to Peoples Rep. of China 1986, USSR, 1988); mem. Am. Soc. Questioned Document Examiners, Southwestern Assn. Forensic Document Examiners (charter), U. Club Atop Symphony Towers, Phi Kappa Phi. Republican. Episcopalian. Office: Galbraith Forensic & Mgmt Scis Ltd Ste 400 4370 La Jolla Village Dr San Diego CA 92122

GALDI-WEISSMAN, NATALIE ANN, secondary education educator; b. N.Y.C., Nov. 28, 1948; d. Alphonse Vincent and Jean (Banek) Galdi; m. David Allen Weissman, Feb. 7, 1987. BA, Adelphi U., 1970, MA, 1971; PhD, NYU, 1978. Tchr. Jr. High Sch. 101, N.Y.C., 1971-81, Evander Child High Sch., N.Y.C., 1981-82, South Bronx High Sch., N.Y.C., 1982—; adj. prof. Mercy Coll., Dobbs Ferry, N.Y., 1976-88; prep. coord. South Bronx High Sch., acad. olympics coach, 1985-87. Mem. Union Fedn. Tchr.

GALE, CONNIE R(UTH), lawyer; b. Cleve., July 15, 1946; m. Curtis S. Gale, Dec. 20, 1967. Student, Miami U., Oxford, Ohio, 1964-66; BA with distinction, U. Mich., 1967, JD, 1971; MBA, Mich. State U., 1981. Bar: mich. 1971. Law clk. to presiding justice Mich. Supreme Ct., Lansing, 1971-72; asst. atty. gen. State of Mich., Lansing, 1973; corp. counsel Chrysler Corp., Highland Park, Mich., 1973-81; assoc. gen. counsel Fed.-Mogul Corp., Southfield, Mich., 1981-86; v.p., gen. counsel, sec. Allnet Communication Svcs., Inc. (subs. ALC), Bingham Farms, Mich., 1987—, ALC Communications Corp., Bingham Farms, 1987—. Mem. ABA (meetings com. bus. law sect.), Mich. Bar Assn. (chmn. in-house counsel com. 1984-93, chair bus. law sect. 1991, alt. dispute resolution com. 1986-89), Am. Corp. Counsel Assn. (chmn. securities law com. Detroit chpt. 1990, chmn. membership 1991, treas. 1992, sec. 1993, v.p. 1994, pres. 1995), Phi Kappa Phi. Office: Allnet Communication Svcs Inc 30300 Telegraph Rd Ste 350 Bingham Farms MI 48025

GALE, MICHELLE SUE, clinical psychologist; b. Bklyn., Feb. 14, 1954; d. Aaron and Irene (Meizel) G. BA in Folklore, U. Pa., 1976; MA in Psychology, Ga. State U., 1985, PhD in Clin. Psychology, 1991. Lic. psychologist, Ga. Instr., grad. teaching asst. psychology Ga. State U., Atlanta, 1986-87; counselor Atlanta Women's Counseling Collective, 1984-88; psychology intern Counseling and Testing Ctr. U. Ga., Athens, 1990-91; postdoctoral fellow Hub Counseling and Edn. Ctr., Tucker, Ga., 1992-93; staff psychologist Crescent Pines Hosp., Stockbridge, Ga., 1993—; pvt. practice Stockbridge, Ga., 1993—. Author: f-News, 1993. Mem. APA, Assn. for Women in Psychology, Ga. Psychol. Assn. Democrat. Jewish. Office: Michelle Gale PhD PC 7454 Hannover Pky S Ste 210 Stockbridge GA 30281

GALINSKY, DEBORAH JEAN, county official; b. Oakland, Calif., Jan. 22, 1951; d. Jerome James and Barbara Ann (Ball) G.; divorced; 1 child, Lauren Rachel Lipscomb. BSW, Bowie State U., 1978. Cert. housing counselor. Substitute tchr. Anne Arundel County Schs., Ft. Meade, Md., 1972-74; addictions counselor Dept. of Health, Ellicott City, Md., 1977-78; coord. dept. Citizens Svcs., housing program specialist Housing and Cmty. Devel., Ellicott City, 1979; coord. youth teen devel. County of Howard, Ellicott City, 1978—; rep. Inter-Agy. Com., Ellicott City, 1990-93. Author homeownership programs. Vol. Bethany United Meth. Ch., Ellicott City, 1987. Fellow Nat. Assn. Housing and Revel. Ofcls.; mem. Nat. Fedn. Housing Counselors, Assn. Cmty. Svcs. (counselors rep.). Democrat. Home: 6801 Oakhill Ln Box 6028 Columbia MO 21045 Office: County of Howard Housing & Comm Devel Dept 3450 Courthouse Dr Ellicott City MD 21043

GALITZ, LAURA MARIA, earth science educator; b. Chgo., Apr. 16, 1951; d. John Anthony and Barbara Jean (Bunche) Lauzon; m. Richard Allen Galitz, June 17, 1973; children: Melissa Jean, Kimberly Anne. BS in Biology, DePaul U., 1973. Cert. tchr., Ill. Tchr. St. Viator H.S., Arlington Heights, Ill., 1973-76; sales rep. E.R. Squibb & Sons, Princeton, N.J., 1976-77; fin. analyst Motorola, Inc., Schaumburg, Ill., 1978-81; substitute tchr. Palatine, 1990; substance abuse prevention coord. Lake Zurich (Ill.) Schs., 1991-94; earth sci. tchr. Grant Twp. H.S., Fox Lake, Ill., 1994—. Mem. Lake Zurich Mid. Sch.-North, PTO Bd., 1981—, sec. 1994-95, music parent coord., Seth Paine Sch. PTO Bd., 1993-94, vol. coord., 1992-93; vol. tchr. Palatine and Lake Zurich Schs., 1989—; project co-dir. Ela Area Cmty. Partnership, Lake Zurich, 1991—; referendum co-chairperson Citizens for New Schs., 1990-91, spkrs. com. head, 1991; dep. registrar Lake County, Ill. Recipient Partnership award Lake County Fighting Back Project, 1991. Office: Grant HS 285 E Grand Ave Fox Lake IL 60020

GALIZZI, MONICA, economics researcher; b. Piacenza, Italy, Nov. 12, 1961; came to U.S., 1987; BS, U. Cattolica, Milan, Italy, 1986; M in Polit. Economy, Boston U., 1990, PhD in Econs., 1994; D in Polit. Economy, U. Milan, Italy, 1990. Rsch. asst. dept. econs. Cath. U., Milan, Italy, 1986-87; instr. micro- and macro-economics, dept. econs. Boston U., 1989-92; postdoctorate rsch. fellow in econs. of labor markets U. Limburg, Maastricht, The Netherlands, 1993-94; economist Workers Compensation Rsch. Inst., Cambridge, Mass., 1994—. Home: 31 Pickman Dr Bedford MA 01730-1009 Office: Workers Compensation Rsch Inst 101 Main St Cambridge MA 02142

GALL, BETTY BLUEBAUM, dating service executive; b. Williamson, W.Va., June 11, 1944; d. Thomas Jefferson Bluebaum and Ollie Mae (Moore) Bluebaum Walker; Charles B. Walker (stepfather); 1 child, Thomas Ethan. Ptnr., dir. Chicagoland Register, dating service, Chgo., 1974-84; cooking instr. Elizabeth Benson Internat. Cooking Lessons, 1978-84; owner Ethnic Party People Catering, 1981—, Phone-A-Friend Dating Service, Chgo., 1984-90. Mem. communications dept. Little City Found., 1989-91, Betty Gall Office Svcs., 1991—. Home: 6314 N Troy St Chicago IL 60659-1414

GALL, LENORE ROSALIE, educational administrator; b. Bklyn., Aug. 9, 1943; d. George W. Gall and Olive Rosalie (Weekes) Gall Bryant. AAS, NYU, 1970, cert. tng. and devel., 1975, BS in Mgmt., 1973, MA in Counselor Edn., 1977; EdM and EdD, Columbia U., 1988. Various positions Ford Found., N.Y.C., 1967-75; dep. dir. career devel. Grad. Sch. Bus., NYU, N.Y.C., 1976-79; dir. career devel. Pace Lubin Sch. Bus., N.Y.C., 1979-82; dir. career devel. Sch. Mgmt., Yale U., New Haven, 1982-85; asst. to assoc. provost Bklyn. Coll., 1985-88, asst. to provost, 1988-91; asst. to v.p. acad. affairs Fashion Inst. Tech., 1991-94, asst. provost curriculum & instrn. N.Y.C. Tech. Coll., 1994—; adj. asst. prof. LaGuardia Community Coll., L.I. City, N.Y., 1981—, Sch. Continuing Edn. NYU, 1983-84; dir., sec. devel. workshop Coll. Placement Services, Bethlehem, Pa., 1978-81. Bd. dirs. Langston Hughes Community Library, Corona, N.Y., 1975-83, 86-92, chair, 1975-79, 82-83, 89-92, 2d v.p., 1986, 1st v.p., 1987-88, chair awards com. Dollars for Scholars, Corona, 1976—; active audience devel. task force Dance Theatre of Harlem, 1992—, honorary co-chmn., 1994-95. Recipient Concerned Women of Bklyn., Inc., 1994; Jewish Federation for the Edn. of Women grantee, 1986-87. Mem. AAUW, Assn. Black Women in Higher Edn. (exec. bd., membership chair, pres.-elect 1988, pres. 1989-93), Am. Assn. Univ. Adminstrs., Nat. Assn. Univ. Women (chaplain 1987-88, 2d v.p. 1988, 1st v.p. 1988-92, dir. northeast sect. 1993—), Nat. Assn. Women in Edn., Black Faculty and Staff Assn. Bklyn. Coll. (1st vice-chair 1986-87, chair 1987-88), New Haven C. of C. (chmn. women bus. and industry conf. 1984), Nat. Coun. Negro Women Inc. (life, 1st v.p. North Queens sect. 1986-89, pres. 1989-93), Nat. Assn. Negro Bus. & Profl. Women's Club (Sojourner

Truth award 1991), Phi Delta Kappa, Kappa Delta Pi, Pi Lambda Theta. Mem. A.M.E. Ch. Office: NYC Tech Coll 300 Jay St Brooklyn NY 11201-2983

GALLAGHER, ANNE PORTER, business executive; b. Coral Gables, Fla., Mar. 16, 1950; d. William Moring and Anne (Jewett) Porter; m. Matthew Philip Gallagher, Jr., July 31, 1976; children: Jacqueline Anne, Kevin Sharkey. BA in Edn., Stetson U., 1972. Tchr. elem. schs., Atlanta, 1972-74; sales rep. Xerox Corp., Atlanta, 1974-76, Fed. Systems, Rosslyn, Va., 1976-81; sales rep. No. Telecom Inc. Fed. Systems, Vienna, Va., 1981-84, account exec., 1984-85, sales dir., 1985-87, mktg. dir., 1987-94; v.p. Fed. Pub. Sector Timeplex Fed. Systems, Inc., Fairfax, Va., 1995—. Exec. com. N. Va. United Way. Mem. NAFE, Info. Tech. Assn. of Am., Armed Forces Communications and Electronics Assn., Pi Beta Phi. Episcopalian. Avocations: skiing, aerobics. Home: 4052 Seminary Rd Alexandria VA 22304-1646 Office: Timeplex Fed Systems Inc 12150 Monument Dr Fairfax VA 22033

GALLAGHER, JANICE STOREY, school system administrator; b. Houston, Feb. 21, 1941; d. Jesse E. and Clara P. (Theurer) Storey; m. Philip T. Gallagher, Oct. 3, 1970. BS, Southwest Tex. State U., 1962; MEd, Trinity U., San Antonio, Tex., 1965. Lic. profl. counselor; cert. elem./secondary edn. tchr., vocat.-edn. tchr. and counselor, Tex. Vocat. home econs. tchr. Harlandale Ind. Sch. Dist., San Antonio, 1962-69, counselor, 1969-89, adminstr., 1989—. Co-author: (manual) Crisis Management, 1990, (handbook) Action-Oriented Research, 1992. Chmn. Bexar County Scholarship Clearing House, San Antonio, 1990—. Counselor of Yr., Tex. Counseling Assn., 1992. Mem. So. Tex. Counseling Assn. (pres. 1992-93, 90-91), Am. Sch. Counselors Assn. (profl. devel. chmn. 1993-94), Cavaliers of the Midwest (pres. 1988-91). Office: Harlandale Ind Sch Dist 102 Genevieve Dr San Antonio TX 78214-2902

GALLAGHER, JEAN KAREN, artist, art educator; b. Hackensack, N.J., June 4, 1953; d. Robert James and Jennie (Marchese) G.; m. James Angevine Lewis, Mar. 17, 1989. BFA, U. S.C., 1975, MFA, 1980; D of Art, NYU, 1993. Asst. prof. art U. Tenn., Chattanooga, 1980-84; chair, asst. prof. art Converse Coll., Spartanburg, S.C., 1984-87; asst. dean Univ. of the Arts Phila. Coll. Art and Design, 1989; assoc. prof. art Calif. State U., Chico, 1990—. One-woman shows include Columbia Coll., 1980, U. of South, Sewanee, Tenn., 1982, Milliken Gallery, Spartanburg, S.C., 1984, P.S. 1 Mus., L.I., 1986, Spirit Sq. Ctr. for the Arts, Charlotte, N.C., 1987, Louis Abrons Arts for the Living Ctr., N.Y.C., 1987-88, Nexus Contemporary Art Ctr., Atlanta, 1988, Pyramid Arts/Ctr. for Visual and Performance Art, Rochester, N.Y., 1990, Phila. Coll. of Art and Design, 1990, 1078 Gallery, Chico, Calif., 1991, Works/San Jose, 1991, Inst. Design and Experimental Art, Sacramento, Calif., 1992, MACE Space for Art, San Francisco, 1994, Cabrillo Coll., Aptos, Calif., 1995; group exhbns. include Columbia (S.C.) Mus. Art, 1975, Smithsonian Inst., Washington, 1977, Lauren Rogers Mus. Art, Laurel, Miss., 1979, Soc. of Four Arts, Palm Beach, Fla., 1979, Stanislaus Art Gallery, Turlock, Calif., 1980, Milliken Gallery, 1980, Farthing Art Gallery, Boone, N.C., 1980, Centennial Art Ctr., Nashville, 1980, E.H. Little Gallery, Memphis, 1980, Art Gallery Weber State Coll., Ogden, Utah, 1981, Southwest Tex. U., San Marcos, Tex., 1981, Alternative Mus., N.Y.C., 1983, Rudolph E. Lee Gallery Clemson (S.C.) U., 1984, 85, Internat. Soc. Copier Artists, N.Y.C., 1984-85, The Upstair Gallery, Tryon, N.C., 1986, Germanow Gallery, Rochester, N.Y., 1986, Art Inst. Chgo., 1986, Weekend Gallery, Columbia, S.C., 1987, Atlanta Arts Festival, 1988, Muse Gallery, Phila., 1990, Forum Gallery, Jamestown, N.Y., Newport (R.I.) Art Mus., 1991, Continental Art Gallery, N.Y.C., 1991, Tyler Art Gallery, Herkimer, N.Y., 1991, 92, The Gallery at Los Patios, San Antonio, 1992, Erb Meml. Union Gallery, Eugene, Oreg., 1992, Mpls. Coll. Art and Design, 1993, 59 Franklin St., N.Y.C., 1993, Huntington Beach (Calif.) Arts Ctr., 1995; permanent collections include Lauren Rogers Mus. Art, U. S.C., Aiken, U. Tenn., Chattanooga, Chattanooga State Coll. Art Collection, S.W. Tex. State U. Art Collection, San Marcos, S.C. State Art Collection, Highways, Santa Monica, Calif. Recipient Purchase award for State Art Collection, S.C. Arts Commn., 1979, 81, Best in Show and Purchase award, 1986, 1st pl. in mixed media, 1986, finalist So. Arts Fedn./Nat. Endowment for Arts, 1988, Calif. State U., 1992; grantee P.S. 1 Mus., 1986, Converse Coll., 1987, N.C. Arts Coun., 1987, S.C. Arts Commn., 1987-88, Artists Space, 1987-88, Nat. Endowment for Arts, 1988, Calif. State U., 1991. Mem. Coll. Art Assn., Intersoc. for the Electronic Arts (assoc.), Orgn. Ind. Arts. Office: Calif State U Dept Art Ayers Hall Chico CA 95929

GALLAGHER, LINDY ALLYN, banker, financial consultant; b. Kalamazoo, Sept. 27, 1954; d. Karl P. Joslow and Audrey S. Phillips; m. Thomas J. Gallagher, Nov. 29, 1975; children: James Allyn Buckley, Phillip Graham, Charles Bedloe. BS, U. Pa., 1975; MBA, Columbia U., 1982. Faculty, researcher U. Pa., Phila., 1976-80; corp. banking officer Bank of Montreal, N.Y.C., 1982-84; v.p. Citibank NA, N.Y.C., 1984-89; v.p. manager Chase Manhattan Bank, N.Y.C., 1989-90; pres. The Allyn Co., New Canaan, Conn., 1990—; treas., dir. 957 Lexington Corp., 1981-87. Editor Columbia Jour. World Bus., 1980-82. Mem. Women's Nat. Rep. Club, 1986—; commr. Town of New Canaan, 1991—; treas., sec. Young Women's League New Canaan, Inc., 1992-94. Mem. Stanwich Club, The Penn Club (N.Y.C.). Republican. Episcopalian.

GALLAGHER, MARGARET PARR, sales executive; b. Balt., Apr. 5, 1939; d. Guy Hudson and Margaret Gormley (Sutherland) Parr; m. John Scott Gallagher, Sept. 5, 1959; children: Andrew Carlton, Anne Barlow. Student, Sweet Briar Coll., 1957-58; BS, Towson U., 1961. Grad. Realtors Inst.; cert. residential broker. Tchr. Howard County Schs., Ellicott City, Md., 1961-63; real estate broker Russell T. Baker, Ellicott City, 1972-78; tng. dir., asst. mgr. Cortland Ltd., Columbia, Md., 1978-79; mgr. Melbourne Feagin & Hammersmith, Laurel, Md., 1979-83; v.p. Long & Foster, Columbia, 1983—; bd. dirs. Dalton Alliances, Owings Mills, Md. Sec. Econ. Forum, Howard County, Md.; bd. dirs. Fells Point Corner Theatre, Balt. Mem. LWV, Howard County Assn. Realtors. Office: Long & Foster 10724 Little Patuxent Pky Columbia MD 21044-3106

GALLAGHER, NANCY ANNE, college official; b. Henniker, N.H., July 15, 1952; d. Bernard Leon and Theresa Marie (Damour) Young; m. Joseph John Gallagher, Oct. 2, 1971; children: Jennifer Joan, James Joseph. Student, St. Anselm Coll., 1986—. Clk. bus. office New Eng. Telephone, Manchester, N.H., 1970-74; operator switchbd. St. Anselm Coll., Manchester, 1978-87, dir. telecommunications, 1987—. Tchr. St. Raphael Ch., Manchester, 1986-90; vol. libr. St. Raphael Sch., Manchester, 1974-76. Mem. NAFE, Assn. Coll. and Univ. Telecom. Adminstr. (state coord.), N.H. Telecom. Assn. (program v.p.), N.H. Women in Higher Edn. Assn. Roman Catholic. Office: St Anselm Coll 100 Saint Anselms Dr Manchester NH 03102-1310

GALLAGHER, PAULA MARIE, real estate appraiser; b. Omaha, Nov. 10, 1959; d. Kenneth Leroy and Phyllis Virginia (Stopak) G. Diploma, Nebr. Coll. Bus., 1978-79; student, Met. Tech. Community Coll., Omaha, 1979-81, U. Nebr., Omaha, 1981-85, 91, Coll. St. Mary, Omaha, 1986-90; B of Profl. Studies, Bellevue Coll., 1993. Lic. real estate appraiser and broker, Nebr. Legal sec. McCormick Cooney Mooney & Hillman P.C., Omaha, 1979; word processor Firstier Bank, Omaha, 1979-83, staff asst., 1983-84; appraiser trainee Morrissay Appraisal Svcs., Omaha, 1985-88, real estate appraiser, 1988—; residential mem. Am. Inst. Real Estate Appraisers. Mem. Appraisal Inst. (sr. residential appraiser), Am. Bus. Women's Assn. (rec. sec. 1984-85, treas. 1988-89, Woman of Yr. award 1989), Omaha Women's C. of C. (edn. com. 1990-92, fin. com. 1991, dir. community recognition 1992, dir. edn. 1993). Roman Catholic. Home: 10321 N 186th Ave Bennington NE 68007-6137 Office: Morrissey Appraisal Svcs 11314 Davenport St Omaha NE 68154-2630

GALLAGHER, ROSANNA BOSTICK, elementary educator, administrator; b. Kingman, Ariz., May 16, 1949; d. Charles Topp and Mary (Lisalda) Bostick; m. Richard Kent Gallagher, June 18, 1971; children: Richard Jonathon, Ryan Charles. BA in Elem. and Spl. Edn., U. Ariz., 1971, MA in Bilingual Adminstrn., 1986. Cert. tchr., spl. edn. tchr., adminstr., Ariz. Tchr. learning disabled students Tucson (Ariz.) Unified Sch. Dist., 1973-75, curriculum specialist Davis Sch., 1975-77, multi-cultural resource tchr., 1979-81, curriculum generalist, 1981-87, prin. Drachman Primary Magnet Sch., 1987-93, prin. Robins Elem., 1994—; mentor Prescott Coll., Tucson, 1988—; instr. U. Phoenix, Tucson, 1988—; nat. cons., presenter Curriculum Assocs. Pub., 1990—; GAPS adv. bd. Pima County Health Dept., Tucson, 1991—; pres. Teaching Rainbow Publs., Tucson,1 980-83. Author: Rainbow of Activities, 1982, Chalkboard Activities, 1985, Counting Creatures, 1990, Abracadabra ABCs, 1990, Tantos Niñoto/So Many Children, 1993, Rub-a-Dubb-Dub/Uno Dos Tres, 1993. Adv. bd. Tucson area Girl Scouts U.S.A., 1988; choir mem. St. Mark's Meth. Ch., Tucson, 1988-92, coord. Time-With-Children program, 1991-93; com. mem. Pima County Interfaith Coun. Edn., Tucson, 1992. Recipient Outstanding Adminstr. award Tucson Assn. Bilingual Edn., 1990, Copper Letter award City of Tucson, 1994; named Tucson Woman on the Move YWCA, 1989. Mem. Tucson Adminstrs. Assn. (bd. dirs. 1988-89), Tucson Assn. Bilingual Adminstrs. Home: 867 W Placita Mesa Fria Tucson AZ 85704-4746 Office: Robins Elem Sch 3939 Magnetite Ln Tucson AZ 85745

GALLAHER, CAROLYN COMBS, secondary education educator; b. Lakewood, Ohio, June 27, 1939; d. Andrew Grafton and Wilhelmina D. (Jackson) Combs; m. Thomas F. Gallaher, Apr. 2, 1966; children: Andrew Brooks, Sloan T.F., Sarah Jane Bloodworth. BA, Duke U., 1961; MA, Columbia U., 1965; postgrad., Manhattanville Coll. Cert. history and Spanish tchr., N.Y. Tchr. Am. High Sch., San Salvador, El Salvador, 1961-62; Peace Corps vol. Ednl. TV, Colombia, South America, 1965-67; tchr. Tarrytown (N.Y.) High Sch., 1969-70, The Masters Sch., Dobbs Ferry, N.Y., 1979-93; dept. head, Lightner endowed history chair The Masters Sch., Dobbs Ferry, 1988-93; grad. asst. ESL inst. Manhattanville Coll., Purchase, N.Y., 1994—; originator ann. Con. for Advanced Placement Students; curriculum cons.; presenter Western Europe Inst. Workshop Columbia U. Mem. various bds. Life Ctr.-Environ. Organ, Larchmont, N.Y., 1976—; vestry St. John's Episcopal Ch., Larchmont, 1986-89. Recipient Fulbright grant U.S. Govt., Yugoslavia, 1989, NEH grant U.S. Govt., Dept. Edn. grant U.S. Govt. Mem. Nat. Coun. Social Studies, Westchester Coun. Social Studies, Phi Delta Kappa. Home: 2 Lyons Pl Larchmont NY 10538-3810

GALLAMORE, BETTY LOU, nurse; b. Poplar Bluff, Mo., Nov. 23, 1951; d. Virgil Luther and Alta Elaine (Dickerson) Groves; m. James Dewey Gallamore, June 27, 1970 (div. 1979); 1 child, Deborah Lynn; m. Jerry L. Capes, May 28, 1988 (div. 1993). AAS, Belleville Area Coll., Ill., 1979; BSN, St. Mary Coll., Leavenworth, Kans., 1987; MS in Nursing, U. Mo., Kansas City, 1991. RN, Kans.; cert. ARNP; clin. nurse specialist in gerontology. Office nurse Met. Orthopedics Ltd., St. Louis, 1973-81; dir. nursing Gardner (Kans.) Skilled Facility, 1982-84; staff nurse Bethany Med. Ctr., Kansas City, Kans., 1984-88; staff nurse-ICU Munson Army Hosp., Ft. Leavenworth, 1985-88; nurse coordinator VA Hosp., Leavenworth, 1988-90; staff nurse Bethany Med. Ctr., Kansas City, Kans., 1989-93, Trinity Luth. Hosp., Kansas City, Mo., 1990—; edn. coord. Kansas City Presbyn. Manor, 1991—; nurse Coffeyville (Kans.) Regional Med. Ctr., 1993—, Mercy Hosp., Independence, Kans., 1993-94; conductor workshop in field; affiliate faculty U. Mo., Kansas City, 1992—. Mem. ANA, AACN, Kans. Nurses Assn., Eagles, Nightingale Nursing Honor Soc. (fellow in nursing sci.), Sigma Theta Tau. Home: PO Box 1601 Coffeyville KS 67301

GALLANT, MAVIS, author; b. Montreal, Que., Can., Aug. 11, 1922. Hon. doctoral degree, U. St. Anne, N.S., Can., 1984, York U., Toronto, 1984, U. Western Ont., 1990; hon. doctoral degree, Queen's U., 1992. Writer-in-residence U. Toronto, 1983-84. Author: Green Water, Green Sky, 1959, 60, A Fairly Good Time, 1970; short stories The Other Paris, My Heart Is Broken: 8 Stories and a Short Novel (Brit. title An Unmarried Man's Summer), 1964, The Affair of Gabrielle Russier; introductory essay, 1971; The Pegnitz Junction, a Novella and Five Short Stories, 1973, The End of the World and Other Stories, 1974; short stories From the Fifteenth District, 1979, Home Truths, 1981, Overhead in a Balloon, 1985; play What Is To Be Done? (produced Toronto 1982), 1984, Paris Notebooks: Essays and Reviews, 1986, (short stories) In Transit, 1989, (short stories) Across the Bridge, 1993; The Moslem Wife and other stories, 1994; contbr. to New Yorker, 1951—. Decorated Order of Can.; recipient Gov.-Gen.'s Lit. award, 1982. Fellow Royal Soc. Lit.; fgn. hon. mem. Am. Acad. and Inst. Arts and Letters. Home: 14 rue Jean Ferrandi, Paris VI, France

GALLANT, SANDRA KIRKHAM, psychologist; b. Dallas, July 15, 1933; d. Eugene Raley and Anita Bernice (Brandenburg) Kirkham; AB, Hollins Coll., 1954; MS, Va. Commonwealth U., 1956; m. Wade Miller Gallant, Jr., Sept. 15, 1979 (dec. Dec. 1988). Psychologist aide Lynchburg Tng. Sch. and Hosp., 1954-56, Rehab. Center of Rapides Parrish, 1956; clin. psychologist Bowman Gray Sch. Medicine, Wake Forest U., 1956-64, staff psychologist, acting dir. reading, speech and psychology ctr., 1962-64; staff psychologist Reading Speech and Psychology Ctr., part-time 1964-74; sch. psychologist Winston-Salem/Forsyth County Schs., part-time, 1974-75; clin. psychologist Child Guidance Clinic, Winston-Salem, N.C., 1975-82; ptnr. Triad Psychol. Assocs., 1982—; cons. to various community orgns. and agys. Bd. dirs. Family Svcs., 1964-66; bd. dirs. Little Theatre, 1963-66, pres., 1964-65; trustee to exec. com. Arts Council, 1965-68, v.p., 1967-68; bd. dirs. Mental Health Assn. Forsyth County, 1971-77, 79-85, pres., 1974-75; bd. dirs. Mental Health Assn. N.C., 1975-82, sec., 1977-79, v.p., 1979-81. Named Vol. of Yr., Mental Health Assn. Forsyth County, 1976; co-recipient Forsyth Mental Health Bell award, 1981. Mem. Am. Psychol. Assn., N.C. Psychol. Assn. Episcopalian. Home: 2534 Warwick Rd Winston Salem NC 27104-1944 Office: Triad Psychol Assocs 840 W 4th St Winston Salem NC 27101-2502

GALLAWAY, GLADYS MCGHEE, elementary education educator; b. Detroit, Oct. 5, 1931; d. William A. and Elsie P. (Cooper) McGhee; m. Lowell E. Gallaway, Dec. 18, 1953; children: Kathleen, Michael, Ellen. BSc, Ohio State U., 1953; student, U. Minn., Ohio U. Cert. elem. edn. Instr. Ohio U., Athens; tchr. grade 5 Athens City Schs.; pres. conf. Coun. Tchrs. English, 1988, conf. Ohio Reading Coun., 1988. Author: Take Me To Your Leaders, 1993. Martha Holden Jennings grantee, 1984; Martha Holden Jennings scholar, 1989; recipient Literacy award Appalacian Reading Coun., 1992. Mem. Appalachian Reading Coun. (past pres.), Internat. Reading Assn., OCIRA (field rep. area 9), Ohio Coun. for Social Studies (Tchr. of Yr. 1989), Phi Delta Kappa (hon.). Home: 33 Longview Heights Rd Athens OH 45701-3335

GALLAWAY, MARTHINE S., artist; b. Oakland, Calif., June 15, 1913; d. Hector Lorillard and Alma Amelia (Steffensen) Solares; m. Howard Murray Gallaway, June 14, 1936; children: Heather, Bruce, Brian, Kent, Kirk. BA, U. Nev., 1934. Muralist on ceramic tiles. Developer high-fired ceramic glazes allowing refined detail in tile commns.; artist numerous tile commns. churches, restaurants, pvt. homes.; tile commns. published in numerous mags. Past pres. Arundel (Calif.) PTA, Carlmont High Sch. PTA, San Carlos, Calif.; libr. bldg. com. San Carlos, 1965, city hall bldg. com. 1960; vol. Woodside (Calif.) Store County Mus. Mem. Am. Soc. Interior Designers, Hist. Preservation Com. Designers, AAUW (charter mem., pres. 1955), Nat. Mus. of Women in the Arts (charter), Cap & Scroll, Zeta Tau Alpha. Home: 1400 Native Sons Rd Woodside CA 94062-4731

GALLEY, VIOLET URSULA, textile designer; b. Sale, Cheshire, Eng.; came to U.S., 1971, naturalized 1976; d. Herbert and Violet Hudson (Allen) Proctor; m. Charles Maurice Galley, Apr. 28, 1970 (dec. July 1979). Student, Manchester Coll. Art. Textile designer The Calico Printers Assn., Manchester, Eng., 1944-67, Fields & Currie Co. Ltd., Montreal, Que., Can., 1968-71, Cohn Hall Marx Ameritex, N.Y.C., 1972-76, Aquarius Fabrics Inc., N.Y.C., 1973-76, Dae Woo Internat., N.Y.C., 1973-81, Qualfab Inc., N.Y.C., 1984, Qualitex Inc., N.Y.C., 1985-86, Lowenstein Inc., N.Y.C., 1986-88, Reflections Inc, N.Y.C., 1988-89; Textile designer Andre Charles Ltd. (now Bombay Industries), N.Y.C., 1982-90; textile designer Cranston Print Works, Millworth Fabrics Inc., N.Y.C., 1990-92, Burlington Industries, N.Y.C., 1992-93; Textile designer Charming Shoppes of Del., Inc., Bensalem, Pa., 1993-94. Contbr. poems to books. Recipient Editors Choice award Nat. Libr. Poetry, 1993, 94, 3d prize Nat. Libr. Poetry, 1994. Mem. Internat. Soc. Poets (life, Internat. Pen award 1991).

GALLIAN, VIRGINIA ANNE, educator; b. St. Louis, Dec. 29, 1933; d. Martin Charles and Flora Olinda (Rocklage) Schake; children: John Charles, Paige Renee. BS, U. Mo., 1955, MS, 1966; student, U. San Jose, Calif., 1961, U. North Tex., Denton, 1971. Tchr. Hazelwood (Mo.) Pub. Schs., 1955, Ft. Dix Post Sch., Trenton, N.J., 1956, Ft. Bragg Post Sch., Fayetteville, N.C., 1956-58, Fergusen-Florrisant (Mo.) Pub. Schs., 1958-59; music supr. Jefferson City (Mo.) Pub. Schs., 1959-60; tchr. Union Sch. Dist., San Jose, 1960-63, 67, 68, Bridgeport (Calif.) Pub. Schs., 1963-65, Columbia (Mo.) Pub. Schs., 1965-67; music tchr. Denton Ind. Sch. Dist., 1970—; instr. U. North Tex., 1995. Mem. Tex. State Tchrs. Assn. (lobbyist 1985—, bd. dirs. 1988-93), Denton Edn. Assn. (chmn. 1985—), Sigma Alpha Iota (chaplin 1972-74), Phi Delta Kappa. Republican. Methodist.

GALLICHIO, KATHLEEN ANNE, lawyer, insurance and financial services company executive; b. Chgo., Jan. 30, 1955. BA, Loyola U., Chgo., 1976; JD, DePaul U., 1980. Bar: Ill. 1980. Counsel Kemper Group, 1981—; gen. counsel Kemper Corp., Long Grove, Ill., 1990—. Office: Kemper Corp 1 Kemper Dr Long Grove IL 60047-9108

GALLIK, JANICE SUSAN, finance executive; b. Akron, Ohio; d. Emil John and Antoinette Mary (Verdi) G.; children: Thomas Butowicz II, Elizabeth Henshaw. BS cum laude, U. Akron, 1965; postgrad., St. Francis Coll., 1978; MS, Ind. U., 1981; EdD, Seattle U., 1988. Mng. ptnr., treas., dir. pub. rels. Buckeye Group, Inc., Orion Inc., 1977-81; contr. D.S. Willett, Inc., 1982-85; mgr. acctg. G. Raden & Sons, Inc., 1986-89; cons. J. Gallik & Assocs., 1985—; controller Merit Steamship Agy., Inc., 1988-91; dir. fin. Seattle Children's Home, 1991—; adj. faculty Seattle Pacific U. Contbr. articles to profl. jours. Trustee, bd. dirs. Columbus 500 Com., 1989—; bd. dirs. Lit. Ctr., 1988-89; bus./community rels. Bellevue Art Mus., 1983-85; bd. dirs., com. mem., dir. pub. rels. Ft. Wayne Philharmonic, 1978-81; treas., pres. Aboite River Women's Club, 1980-81; bd. dirs. Izaak Walton's League, 1980; area rep. Girl Scouts Am.; bd. dirs., pres. Zelienople Jr. Women, 1974-76; med. team search com. Zelienople, Pa., 1976. Scholl scholarship St. Francis, 1978; rsch. grant NYU Ctr. for Entrepreneurship, 1986. Mem. Seattle C. of C., Acad. Mgmt., Seattle U. Alumni Assn. (bd. govs.), Phi Delta Kappa, Alpha Delta Pi. Office: Seattle Children's Home 2142 10th Ave W Seattle WA 98119-2899

GALLINGER, LOIS MAE, medical technologist; b. Hibbing, Minn., Sept. 5, 1922; d. Clarence Adolph and Dorothy Mae (Stoller) Belanger; m. Ben Elton Gallinger, Sept. 1, 1956; children: Carol Elda, Gregory John. BS, U. Minn., 1946; Med. Tech. Intern, Coll. St. Scholastica, 1948-49. Cert. med. technologist. X-ray technologist Leigh Clinic, Grand Forks, N.D., 1946-47, Nicollet Clinic, Mpls., 1947-48; med. technologist Little Traverse Hosp., Petoskey, Mich., 1949-52; med. and x-ray technologist Lakeside Med. Ctr., Duluth, Minn., 1952-60; med. technologist St. Mary's Med. Ctr., Duluth, 1961-87; retired, 1987. Treas. Benedictine Health Ctr. Aux., Duluth, 1984—, Women's Assocs. Duluth Symphony, 1986—; cookie chmn. No. Pine Girl Scouts USA, Duluth, 1969; bd. dirs. St. Paul's Episc. Women's Club, Duluth, 1970s, greeter's chmn., 1970s, corr. sec., 1990-94, publicity chmn., 1994; vol. Am. Cancer Soc., 1993—, Am. Lung Assn., 1993. Mem. AAUW, Am. Soc. Med. Tech., Minn. Soc. Med. Tech. (regional historian 1969), Duluth Women's Club, St. Paul's Episc. Women's Club (corr. sec. 1990-94, pub. chmn. 1994—). Home: 364 Leicester Ave Duluth MN 55803-2203

GALLINOT, RUTH MAXINE, educational consultant; b. Carlinville, Ill., Feb. 16, 1925; d. Martin Mike and Augusta (Kumpus) G. BS, Roosevelt U., Chgo., 1971, MA with honors, 1974; PhD, The Union Inst., Cin., 1978. Adminstrv. asst., exec. sec. Karoll's Inc., Chgo., 1952-66; asst. dean Cen. YMCA Community Coll., Chgo., 1966-81, dir. life planning inst., 1979-80; pres. Gallinot & Assocs., Chgo., St. Louis and Bethalto, Ill., 1980—; mem. task force Office Sr. Citizens and Handicapped, City of Chgo., 1971-79; mem. criteria and guidelines com. Internat. Assn. for Continuing Edn. and Tng., 1983-86, survey and rsch. com., 1984-88; team chair accreditation evaluation team Accrediting Commn. Ind. Colls. and Schs., Washington, 1983-88; instr. U.S. Office Pers. Mgmt., 1984—, Coun. Rehab. Affiliates, Chgo., 1985—. Developer leisure time adult edn. time series for elderly Uptown model cities area dept. human resources City of Chgo., 1970; editor: Certified Professional Secretaries Review, 1983; reporter Greater Alton Pub. Co., 1987-89; contbr. articles to profl. jours. Chmn. Commn. Status of Women in State of Ill., 1963-68; del. White House Conf. on Equal Pay, 1963, White House Conf. on Civil Rights, 1965, City of Chgo. White House Conf. on Info. and Library, 1976, State of Ill. White House Conf. Info. Services and Library Services, 1977; life mem. Mus. Lithuanian Culture, Chgo., 1973—; pub. mem. Fgn. Service Selection Bd. U.S. Dept. State, 1984; bd. dirs. Luths. for Chgo., 1978-83, also founding member; member adv. edn. com. Chgo. Commn. Human Relations, 1968-75 fundraising chmn. Bethalto (Ill.) Sr Citizens new bldg. furnishings, 1990-91, pres. 1995—. Recipient Leadership in Civic, Cultural and Econ. Life of the City award YWCA, Chgo., 1972, Achievement in Field Edn. award Operation P.U.S.H., Chgo., 1975. Mem. Profl. Secs. Internat. (past pres., ednl. cons. 1980-84), Edn. Network Older Adults (v.p., sec. 1979-86), Nat. Assn. Parliamentarians (Ill. and Chgo. chpts.), Literacy Coun. Chgo. (bd. dirs. 1979-86), Zonta of Alton (treas. Chgo. club 1965-66). Lutheran. Home and Office: Gallinot & Assocs 210 James St Bethalto IL 62010-1318

GALLO, PIA, art historian; b. N.Y.C., May 10, 1956; d. Thomas Joseph and Maria Dolores (Daniele) Gallo; m. Peter Van Wagner, Sept. 2, 1989. Student, John Cabot Coll., Rome, 1974-76; BA in English, Hiram (Ohio) Coll., 1978; postgrad., U. Chgo. Pvt. art dealer specializing in old master and modern prints Chgo., 1981—, N.Y.C., 1995—. Author catalogues: Pietro Testa, 1989, Recent Acquisitions, 1986, Herman Armour Webster, 1983, American Prints, 1981. Mem. Internat. Fine Print Dealers Assn., Arts Club of Chgo. Office: PO Box 261 Hastings On Hudson NY 10706

GALLOWAY, EILENE MARIE, national and international outerspace consultant; b. Kansas City, Mo., May 4, 1906; d. Joseph Locke and Lottie Rose (Harris) Slack; student Washington U., St. Louis, 1923-25; AB, Swarthmore Coll., 1928; postgrad. Am. U., 1937-38, 43; LLD (hon.), Lake Forest Coll., 1990, Swarthmore Coll., 1992; m. George Barnes Galloway, Dec. 23, 1924; children: David Barnes, Jonathan Fuller. Tchr. polit. sci. Swarthmore Coll., 1928-30; editor Student Svc., Washington, 1931; staff mem., edn. div. Fed. Emergency Relief Adminstrn., 1934-35; asst. chief info. sect., div. spl. info. Library of Congress, 1941-43, editor abstracts Legis. Reference Svc., 1943-51, nat. def. analyst, 1951-57; specialist in nat. def., 1957-66; sr. specialist internat. rels. (nat. security) Congl. Rsch. Svc., 1966-75; cons. internat. space activities, 1975—. staff mem. Senate Fgn. Rels. Com., 1947; profl. staff mem. U.S. group Interparliamentary Union, 1958-66; cons. Senate Armed Svcs. Com., 1953-74, Ford Found., 1958; spl. cons. spl. Senate Com. on Space and Astronautics, 1958; spl. cons. to Senate Com. on Aero. and Space Sci., 1958-77; cons. to Senate Com. on Commerce, Sci. and Transp., 1977-82; chmn. com. edn. and recreation Washington, 1937-38; forum leader 1976-79; guest Soviet Acad. Sci., 1982, adult edn. U.S. Office Edn., 1938; mem. Internat. Inst. Space Law of Internat. Astronautical Fedn., 1958—, U.S. mem. bd. dirs., v.p., 1967-79, hon. dir., 1979—, Fedn. ofcl. observer at sessions UN Com. on Peaceful Uses Outer Space and legal subcom., 1970-94, mem. com. for rels. with internat. orgns., 1979—; mem. Am. Rocket Soc.'s Space Law and Sociology Com., 1959-62; mem. adv. panel Office Gen. Counsel, NASA, 1971; adviser outer space del. U.S. Mission to UN Working Group on Direct Broadcast Satellites, 1973-75; observer UN Conf. Exploration and Peaceful Uses of Outer Space, Vienna, 1982; lectr. Nat. Acad. Sci., 1973, U.S. CSC, Exec. Seminar Center, Oak Ridge, 1973, 74, 75, 76, 78; ednl. counselor Purdue U., 1974; lectr. Inst. Air and Space Law McGill U., 1975, Inter Am. Def. Coll., 1977, 78, U. Akron, 1984, 91; mem. panel on solar power for satellites and U.S. space policy Office Tech. Assessment, 1979-80, 82-86, cons., 1982; cons. COMSAT, 1983, FCC Commn. on U.S. Telecommunications Policy, 1983-87. Pres., Theodore Von Karman Meml. Found., 1973-84; mem. alumni council Swarthmore Coll., 1976-79; mem. organizing com., author symposium on Conditions Essential For Maintaining Outer Space for Peaceful Uses, Peace Palace, Netherlands, 1984; bd. advisers Students for Exploration and Devel. of Space, 1984—. Rockefeller Found. scholar-in-residence, Bellagio, Italy, 1976; elected to Coun. of Advanced Internat. Studies, Argentina, 1985, Uruguayan Centro de Investigacion y Difusion Aeronautica-Expacial, 1985. Recipient Andrew G. Haley gold medal Internat. Inst. Space Law, 1968; dist. svc. award Libr. Congress, 1975; NASA Gold Medal for Pub. Svc., 1984, USAF Space Command plaque, 1984; Internat. Acad. Astronautics' Theodore Von Karman award, 1986, Women in Aerospace Lifetime Achievement award, 1987, Lifetime Achievement award Internat. Inst. Space Law, 1989; Wilton Park fellow, Eng., 1968. Fellow Am. Astronautical Soc.; mem. LWV (chmn. study groups housing, welfare in D.C., 1937-38, mem. tech. com. on law and sociology task force on legal aspects 1979—), AIAA (tech. com. on legal aspects of aeros. and astronautics 1980-84, internat. activities com. 1985—), World Peace Through Law Ctr., Am. Soc. Internat. Law, Am. Astronautical Soc., Lamar Soc. Internat. Law, Internat. Acad. Astronautics (trustee, chmn. sect. on social scis. 1982-93, Mars exploration sub-com., 1991—), Internat. Law Assn., Phi Beta Kappa, Delta Sigma Rho, Kappa Alpha Theta. Episcopalian. Author: Atomic Power: Issues Before Congress, 1946; (with Bernard Brodie) The Atomic Bomb and the Armed Services, 1947; History of United States Military Policy on Reserve Forces, 1775-1957, 1957; Guided Missiles in Foreign Count57; The Community of Law and Science, 1958; United Nations Ad hoc Committee on Peaceful Uses of Outer Space, 1959; Satellites: A Force for World Peace, World (Security and the Peaceful Uses of Outer Space), 1960; International Cooperation and Organization for Outer Space, 1965; Space Treaty Proposals by the United States and U.S.S.R., 1966; Treaty on Principles Governing the Activities of States in the Exploration and Use of Outer Space, Including the Moon and Other Celestial Bodies: Analysis and Background Data, 1967; Remote Sensing of the Earth by Satellites: Satellites: Legal Problems and Issues, 1973, 75; The Future of Space Law, 1976; Consensus as a Basis for International Space Cooperation, 1977; The Role of the United Nations in Earth Resources Satellites, 1972; Consensus Decisionmaking by the UN Committee on the Peaceful Uses of Outer Space, 1979; Settlement of Space Law Disputes, 1980; Agreement Governing the Activities of States on the Moon and Other Celestial Bodies, 1980, Perspectives of Space Law, 1981; Conditions for Success of International Space Institutions, 1982; Space Manufacturing, 1981; U.S. Space Policy and Programs, 1982; Space Station, 1986; U.S. National Space Legislation and Peaceful Uses Of Outer Space, 1987; Expanding Article IV of 1967 Space Treaty, 1982; History and Development of Space Law, 1982, Definition of Space Law, 1989, Law, Science and Technology for the Moon/Mars Missions, 1990, Legal and Regulatory Framework for Solar Power Satellites, 1992, The Space Agy. Forum and Internat. Coop., 1993; editor: Space Law Symposium, 1958; The Legal Problems of Space Exploration, 1961; United States International Space Programs, 1965; International Cooperation in Outer Space: A Symposium, 1972, Use of the Geostationary Orbit, 1988; assoc. editor Advances in Earth Oriented Applications of Space Tech., 1978-82, Acta Astronautica Jour., Space Technology: Industrial and Commercial Applications; mem. editorial adv. bd. Jour. Space Law, U. Miss. Law Sch., Space Communication and Broadcasting, 1984-89. Home: 4612 29th Pl NW Washington DC 20008-2105

GALLOWAY, LILLIAN CARROLL, modeling agency executive, consultant; b. Hazard, Ky., Sept. 23, 1934; d. William Zion and Clemma (Lewis) Carroll; m. Thomas Roddy Galloway, Dec. 21, 1957; children: David Junkin, Scott Thomas, Donald Lewis. Student, Cumberland Coll., 1955, Ea. U., Richmond, Ky., 1956, U. Cin., 1958, John Robert Powers Sch., Cin., 1958. Tchr. Vandalia (Ohio) Elem. Sch., 1954-56, Kenwood Elem. Sch., Louisville, 1956-57, Cin. Pub. Schs., 1957-64; founder, pres. Fairfax Model Agy., Washington, 1964-67, Cin. Model Agy. Internat., 1967—, Lillian Galloway Modeling Acad., Cin., 1971—, Children Model Agy. Internat., Cin., 1985—; cons., co-owner John Robert Powers Modeling Sch., Cin., 1957-64; pres. Student Model Bds., Cin., 1984—; dir. Career Day, Cin., 1967—. Mem. Cin. Better Bus. Bur., 1967—; trustee Knox Presbyn. Ch., Cin. Named Cin.'s Outstanding Bus. Woman, Sta. WCPO-TV, 1985, Outstanding Alumni, Cumberland Coll., 1988. Mem. DAR, Modeling Assn. Am. (chmn. convs. 1975-77), Am. Modeling Assn. Internat. (pres. 1976-77), Cin. Advertisers Club (membership and program coms., Outstanding Bus. Women award 1985), Exec. Women Internat. (program com., chmn. bd. dirs. 1986, Woman of Achievement award 1986), Cin. C. of C., Cumberland Coll. Alumni Assn. (pres. 1982), English Speaking Union, Order Ky. Cols., Cin. Woman's Club (bd. dirs. 1992—, lecture/entertainment chmn. 1992—), Town Club (bd. dirs. 1988—), Order Ea. Star (organist 1953—). Republican. Home: 6027 Stirrup Rd Cincinnati OH 45244-3917 Office: 6047 Montgomery Rd Cincinnati OH 45213-1611

GALLOWAY, P(ATRICIA) MARIA, gallery owner; b. Statesville, N.C., July 2, 1958; d. Howard John and Barbara Jacqueline (Robbins) G.; m. Michael Gordon Secrest, June 28, 1982; 1 child, Jacob Paul. Owner, buyer, clk. PM Gallery, Columbus, Ohio, 1980—. Editor Italian Village Newsletter, 1985-87, contbr., 1983—. Trustee Artreach, Columbus, 1983-86. Mem. Short North Bus. Assn. (trustee 1986-87, Vol. of Yr. 1990), Italian Village Soc. (treas. 1993, v.p. 1984, pres. 1985). Democrat. Office: PM Gallery 726 N High St Columbus OH 43215-1426

GALLUP, JANET LOUISE, business official; b. Rochester, N.Y., Aug. 11, 1951; d. John Joseph and Mildred Monica (O'Keefe) VerHulst; m. Robert Hicks Gallup, June 26, 1982 (div. Nov. 1985); 1 son, Jason Hicks. BA, Hofstra U., 1973; MA (grad. asst.), Calif. State U., Long Beach., 1979. Asst. trader E.F. Hutton, N.Y.C., 1973-75, Los Angeles, 1975, instr. Calif. State U., Long Beach, 1978-79; fin. analyst Rockwell Internat., Seal Beach, Calif., 1979-85, coordinator mgmt. and exec. devel. and succession planning, 1985-91; mgr. orgn. and employee devel. activities, Hughes Aircraft, 1991—. Vol. Cedar House Ctr.-Child Abuse, Long Beach, 1976. Democrat. Roman Catholic. Office: Hughes Aircraft 1901 W Malvern Ave Fullerton CA 92633-2100

GALLUPS, VIVIAN LYLAY BESS, federal contracting officer; b. Vicksburg, Miss., Jan. 14, 1954; d. Vann Foster and Lylay Vivian (Stanley) Bess; m. Ordice Alton Gallups, Jr., July 12, 1975. BA, Birmingham So. Coll., 1975, MA in Mgmt., 1985; MA in Edn., U. Ala., Birmingham, 1975. Cert. purchasing mgr. Nat. Assn. Purchasing Mgmt. Counselor Columbia (S.C.) Coll., 1975-76; case mgr. S.C. Dept. Social Services, Lexington, 1976; benefit authorizer, payment determination specialist then recovery reviewer Social Security Adminstrn., Birmingham, 1977-85; contract adminstr., now contracting officer U.S. Dept. Def., Birmingham, 1985-92; adminstrv. contracting officer U.S. Dept. Def., Alexandria, Va., 1992-94; contract specialist Def. Logistics Agy., U.S. Dept. Def., Alexandria, Va., 1994—. Hospice vol. Bapt. Med. Ctr.-Montclair, Birmingham, 1982; trustee, treas. Resurrection House, Birmingham, 1984-85; vol. counselor Cathedral Ch. of Advent, Birmingham, 1987. Mem. Nat. Contract Mgmt. Assn. (cert. profl. contracts mgr., chpt. sec. 1987, pres. 1990-93, nat. dir. 1993-94). Lutheran. Home: apt 1110 14203 MacFarlane Green Ct Upper Marlboro MD 20772 Office: US Def Dept Def Logistics Agy Cameron Station Alexandria VA

GALOTTI, DONNA, publishing executive; b. Mountainside, N.J., Feb. 8, 1955; d. Jack and Analid Kalajian; m. Ron Galotti, Oct. 14, 1981. BS, Penn State U., 1975. Internat. credit analyst Irving Trust Co., N.Y.C., 1976-77; ad sales rep. BMT Pub., N.Y.C., 1977-79; ad sales rep. Woman's Day Mag., N.Y.C., 1979-81, cosmetics mgr., 1981-83, ea. mgr., 1984-87; v.p., ad dir. Ladies' Home Jour., N.Y.C., 1987-89, v.p., pub., 1989—. Home: 100 Park Ave New York NY 10017-5516 Office: Ladies' Home Jour 100 Park Ave New York NY 10017-5516*

GALVAN, MARY THERESA, business and economics educator; b. Rockford, Ill., Dec. 19, 1957; d. Dino F. and Ida M. Dal Fratello; m. John D. Galvan, June 27, 1987; children: Marie K., John M., Kathleen T. BA, Rockford Coll., 1979; MA, No. Ill. U., 1981, PhD, 1988. Instr. No. Ill. U., DeKalb, 1979-81; asst. prof. Rockford Coll., 1981-87; assoc. prof. bus. and econs. St. Xavier Coll., Chgo., 1987-92; assoc. prof. mktg. North Ctrl. Coll., Naperville, Ill., 1992—, dir. Ctr. for Rsch., 1994—; cons. Fed. Res. Bank Chgo., 1988—. Lector, St. Elizabeth Seton Parish, Naperville, 1987—, pres. Women's Network. Earhart Found. fellow, 1988; Hegelar Carus scholar, 1987.. Mem. AAUW, Am. Econs. Assn., Am. Mktg. Assn., Am. Statis. Assn. (v.p. 1994—), Western Econs. Assn. Internat., Midwest Bus. Adminstrn. Assn., Midwest Econs. Assn., Phi Delta Kappa, Omicron Delta Epsilon. Office: North Ctrl Coll 30 N Brainard St Naperville IL 60540-4607

GALVANI, CHRISTIANE MESCH, English as a second language educator, translator; b. Kiel, Fed. Republic Germany, Jan. 19, 1954; came to U.S., 1977; d. Edgar and Elisabeth (Depken) Mesch; m. Paul Andrew Galvani, Dec. 19, 1979; 1 child, Jacqueline. BA, U. London, 1977; MA, Rice U., 1986. Freelance translator Houston, 1979—; instr. English, German, French Berlitz Sch. Langs., Houston, 1981-82, interpreter, translator, 1981-84, prodn. coord., 1982-84; ESL instr. Tex. So. U., Houston, 1989—; instr. Rice U., Houston, 1990 (summer). Translator: The Flowing Light of the Divinity, 1991. Named to Outstanding Young Women of Am., 1986. Mem. MLA, Am. Tranlators Assn., Am. Lit. Translators Assn., Houston Profl. Translators Forum (dir. 1982-83), Houston Humane Soc. Guild. Home: 8126 Western Trail Dr Houston TX 77040-2638 Office: Tex So Univ 3100 Cleburne St Houston TX 77004-4501

GAMACHE, KATHLEEN ANNE, law librarian; b. Detroit, July 5, 1956; d. Joseph Anthony and Pauline (Bradley) G. BA, Oakland U., 1979; MSLS, Wayne State U., 1981. Asst. libr. Detroit Coll. Law, 1982-84; libr. Clark, Klein & Beaumont, Detroit, 1984—. Mem. Am. Asns. Law Libraries. Office: Clark Klein & Beaumont 1600 First Fed Bldg Detroit MI 48226

GAMBARDELLA, ROSEMARY, federal judge. BA, JD, Rutgers U. Admitted to bar, 1980. Judge U.S. Bankruptcy Ct. for Dist. N.J., Newark. Office: US Bankruptcy Ct M L King Jr Fed Bldg 50 Walnut St Newark NJ 07102-3506

GAMBEE, ELEANOR BROWN, writer, lecturer, civic worker; b. N.Y.C., Apr. 10, 1904; d. Robert Rankins and Elizabeth (Turner) Brown; m. A. Sumner Gambee, June 1, 1928; children: Sumner Brown, Craig, Eleanor Fay, Robert Rankin. AB, Vassar Coll., 1925; postgrad., Columbia U., 1926. Free-lance writer, lectr. on herbs, horticulture, plants in industry various orgns., 1961—; cons. sect. herbs Nat. Geographic mag., 1983, Reader's Digest Guide to Gardening, 1978; researcher, chmn. Chemurgic Garden. Contbr. numerous articles to hort. publs.; editorial bd. Vassar Alumnae Mag., 1954-56. Trustee Dwight Sch., Englewood, N.J., 1957-63, First Presbyn. Ch., Englewood, 1992—; publicity chair Maternal Health Ctr. Bergen County, Englewood, 1934-38; v.p., mem. bd. Planned Parenthood Assn. Bergen County, 1938-46; publicity chair No. Valley chpt. ARC, 1939-43; mem. spl. honor friends of Horticulture, Wave Hill, 1993; 1st v.p. Social Svc. Fedn., Englewood, 1948-52; Englewood Hosp. Devel. Com., 1965-75; publs. com. Hort. Soc. N.Y., 1972-75. Recipient Garden Club Am. Hort. award, 1962, Merit award, 1979, Disting. Svc. award N.Y. Bot. Garden, 1980, Spl. honor The Friends of Horticulture Wave Hill, 1993. Mem. Herb Soc. Am. (past pres.), Corp. N.Y. Bot. Garden, Garden Club Englewood (past pres., hon. mem.). Home: 133 E Palisade Ave # H Englewood NJ 07631-2249

GAMBRELL, LUCK FLANDERS, corporate executive; b. Augusta, Ga., Jan. 17, 1930; d. William Henry and Mattie Moring (Mitchell) Flanders; m. David Henry Gambrell, Oct. 16, 1953; children: Luck G. Davidson, David Henry, Alice Kathleen, Mary G. Rolinson. AB, Duke U., 1950; diplome d'etudes françaises, L'Institut de Touraine, Tours, France, 1951. Chmn. bd. LFG Co., 1960—. Mem. State Bd. Pub. Safety, 1981-90; bd. dirs. Atlanta Symphony Orch., 1982-85; mem. Chpt. Nat. Cathedral, Washington, 1981-85; mem. World Service Council YWCA, 1965—, council Presbytery Greater Atlanta, 1988; elder First Presbyn. Ch., Atlanta; chmn. bd. dirs. Student Aid Found., Atlanta, 1992—; mem. Bd. Councilors The Carter Ctr., Emory U. Mem. Atlanta Jr. League, Alpha Delta Pi.

GAMBRELL, SARAH BELK, retail executive; b. Charlotte, N.C., Apr. 12, 1918; d. William Henry and Mary (Irwin) Belk; B.A., Sweet Briar Coll., 1939; D. Humanities (hon.), Erskine Coll., 1970, U. N.C.-Asheville, 1986; m. Charles Glenn Gambrell (dec.); 1 child, Sarah Belk. Officer, dir. Belk Stores, various locations, 1947—. Hon. trustee emeritus Princeton (N.J.) Theol. Sem.; trustee Johnson C. Smith U., Charlotte, N.C., Warren Wilson Coll., Swannanoa, N.C.; bus. adv. com. N.C. Sec. State, Raleigh, N.C.; trustee nat. bd. YWCA; bd. dirs. Parkinson's Disease Found., N.Y.C., N.C. Community Found., Raleigh, N.C.; bd. trustees Florence Crittenton Svcs., Charlotte, N.C.; hon. trustee Cancer Research Inst., N.Y.C.; hon. bd. dirs. YWCA, N.Y.C.; trustee Hezekiah Alexander Found., Charlotte, Found. for Good Bus., Raleigh. Mem. Fashion Group, Inc., Jr. League N.Y.C., Nat. Soc. Colonial Dames, DAR. Home: 300 Cherokee Rd Charlotte NC 28207-1908 Office: 6100 Fairview Rd Ste 640 Charlotte NC 28210-3277

GAME, ANNE ZIPP, management consultant; b. Ft. Worth, June 26, 1961; d. Arthur Neil and Hope (Worsham) Z. BA, Vanderbilt U., 1983; MBA, Harvard U., 1986. Research assoc. TCS Mgmt. Group, Nashville, 1983-84; personnel planning intern IBM Corp., Armonk, N.Y., 1985-86; mgmt. cons. Deloitte & Touche, Atlanta, 1986—. Trustee Diamond Jubilee Found. Alpha Omicron Pi; mem. Atlanta Symphony Assocs., 1986—, Am. Cancer Soc., Atlanta. Republican. Presbyterian. Home: 2004 Snowmass Trail Marietta GA 30062 Office: Deloitte & Touche Ste 300 285 Peachtree Center Ave NE Atlanta GA 30303-1229

GAMMELL, GLORIA RUFFNER, sales executive; b. St. Louis, June 19, 1948; d. Robert Nelson and Antonia Ruffner; m. Doyle M. Gammell, Dec. 11, 1973. AA in Art, Harbor Coll., Harbor City, Calif., 1969; BA in Sociology, Calif. State U., Long Beach, 1971. Cert. fin. planner. Bus. analyst Dun & Bradstreet, Los Angeles, 1971-81; sales rep. Dun & Bradstreet, Orange, Calif., 1971-93; rep. sales Van Nuys, Calif., 1981-90; pres., sec. bd. dirs. Gammell Industries, Paramount, Calif., 1993—. Mem. Anne Banning Assistance League, Hollywood, Calif., 1981-82; counselor YWCA, San Pedro, Calif., 1983-84; fundraiser YMCA, San Pedro, 1984-85; mem. womens adv. com. Calif. State Assembly, 1984-89. Recipient Best in the West Presdl. Citation, 1981-86, 89, 90. Home: 991 W Channel St San Pedro CA 90731-1415

GAMMON, MARYLOU, school system administrator, educator; b. Elmira, N.Y., Dec. 13, 1941; d. Victor Leon and Mary (Trivanovich) Bender; m. Henry Victor Baldi, June 6, 1964 (div. July 1971); m. John Henry Gammon Jr., Jan. 8, 1977; children: Marisa, Mariela. BA, U. Ariz., 1964, PhD, 1981; MEd, U. Wis., 1971. Cert. elem. and secondary tchr. English tchr. Sunnyside Sch. Dist., Tucson, 1964-66; Peace Corps vol. Univ. de Oriente, Cumaná, Venezuela, 1966-68, head English dept., 1968-69; grad. asst. U. Wis., Madison, 1969-70; tchr., reading cons. Jefferson Mid. Sch., Madison, 1970-72; English and reading tchr. Sahuarita (Ariz.) Sch. Dist., 1972-76; supt. Bonita Sch. Dist., Willcox, Ariz., 1981-94; assoc. county sch. supt. Coconino County, Flagstaff, Ariz., 1994—; adj. asst. prof. U. Ariz., Tucson, 1977-87; part-time assoc. prof. No. Ariz. U., Flagstaff, 1986—; cons., trainer Nat. Park Svc., Tucson, 1974-79. Contbr. articles to profl. jours. Precinct committeewoman Rep. Orgn., Graham County, Ariz., 1990—. Recipient Golden Bell award Ariz. Sch. Bds. Assn., 1989. Mem. Nat. Rural Edn. Assn. (del., exec. bd. dirs. 1992—), Ariz. Small and Rural Schs. Assn. (pres., co-founder 1986-88, exec. bd. dirs., 1986—), Ariz. Sch. Adminstrs. (com. chmn. 1981—, Small and Rural Supr. Yr. award 1993), Internat. Reading Assn., Phi Delta Kappa (sec. 1974—). Office: Coconino County Sch Office 100 E Birch St Flagstaff AZ 86001

GAMPEL, ELAINE SUSAN, investment management analyst and consultant; b. New Haven, Apr. 12, 1950; d. Stanley Irwin and Marion (Levine) G.; m. Alan Joseph Tedeschi, Sept. 9, 1984; children: Zachary Joseph Tedeschi Matthew Samuel Gampel Tedeschi. BS in Spl. Edn., Boston U., 1972; MS in Counseling, So. Conn. State U., New Haven, 1975. Cert. investment mgmt. analyst Wharton Sch. Bus., Investment Mgmt. Cons. Assn. Spl. edn. tchr. Ansonia (Conn.) Pub. Schs., 1972-77; v.p., investment mgmt. cons. Paine Webber Inc., Denver, 1977-89; 1st v.p. investments Dean Witter Reynolds, Denver, 1993; bd. dirs. the Denver Nuggets. Bd. dirs. United Cerebral Palsy of Denver, 1984-93; mem. outside editorial bd. Denver Post, 1991—; mem. investment com. Women's Found. of Colo., Denver, 1992—. Mem. Investment Mgmt. Cons. Assn. (cert. com. 1990—). Office: Dean Witter Reynolds 370 17th St Ste 5100 Denver CO 80202-5651

GAMSIN, SHARON L., public relations executive; b. N.Y.C., Mar. 8, 1949; d. Irving and Rita Gamsin. BS in Journalism, Boston U., 1971. Energy editor Jour. Commerce, N.Y.C., 1972-78; N.Y. corr. The Oil Daily, Washington, 1978-81; N.Y. bur. chief Petroleum Info. Internat., Houston, 1981-83; v.p. communications N.Y. Stock Exch., N.Y.C., 1983-92; v.p. corp. communications-Europe SmithKline Beecham, London, 1992—. Recipient Acad. Women Achievers award YWCA, 1988. Mem. N.Y. Fin. Writers' Assn. (bd. govs. 1979-85, 89-92, pres. 1983-84), Fin. Women's Assn., Women in Communications, Women Execs. Pub. Rels. Office: SmithKline Beecham, 1 New Horizons Ct, TW8 9EP Brentford Middlesex, England

GAMSON, ANNABELLE, dancer; b. N.Y.C., Aug. 6, 1928. Debut with Dunham group Cafe Soc. Uptown; Broadway debut Michael Kidd's Finian's Rainbow, 1947; appearances include Arms and the Girl, Make Mine Manhattan, Pipe Dream, l'Histoire du Soldat, Mother, Sonata Pathetique, Shifting Landscape, (Am. Ballet Theatre) Rodeo, (Ballet Theatre Workshop) La Muerte Enamorada; choregrapher: First Movement, 1976, Five Easy Pieces, 1976, Portrait of Rose, 1976, Dances of Death, 1978, Two Dances, 1979, The Women of Union Square, 1993, Semele, 1994; writer, editor, narrator: On Dancing Isadora's Dances, PBS, 1990. Recipient Brandeis U. Creative Arts award for dance, 1990, N.Y. Dance and Performance award (Bessie) spl. achievement award reconstruction dances of Isadora Duncan, 1990. Office: Sheldon Soffer Mgt Inc 130 W 56th St New York NY 10019 also: Hillandale Rd Rye Brook NY 10573*

GANAWAY, NORMA JEAN, vocational counselor; b. South Bend, Ind., Apr. 9, 1927; d. Welvin Sr. and Alphia (Bond) G. Grad., Thomas Comml. Sch., 1947; cert. in bus., Ind. U., 1980, cert. in supervisory devel., 1980. Sec. to contr. Robertson's Dept. Store, South Bend, 1947-62, sec. to divsnl. mgr. mdse., 1962-68; dir. Urban Tech. Asst. Project, South Bend, 1971; asst. dir. Neighborhood Assn. Model Cities, South Bend, 1971-74; client svc. specialist CETA Program, South Bend, 1974-83; vocat. counselor Workforce Devel. Svcs. No. Ind., South Bend, 1983—. Sec. Sunday Sch. Pilgrim Bapt. Ch., 1942-43, 50, pres. fellowship club, 1968-69, active red circle; bd. dirs. St. Joseph County YWCA, 1968-71, chmn. Y teenage com 1969-70; bd. dirs., pub. rels. com. Campfire Girls, 1969, 2d v.p., 1972; sec. bd. dirs. Hansel Ctr. Neighborhood Svcs., 1972-73; nat. bd. dirs. YWCA of U.S.A, N.Y.C., 1973-76; apptd. by mayor Commn. Status of Women, 1975, 76; housing commr. City of South Bend Pub. Housing, 1991—; active, past bd. dirs. South Bend Urban League; Rep. committeewoman, South Bend; dir. dist. # 2 St. Joseph County Rep. Women, 1994—. Recipient Woman of Yr. award South Bend-Mishawaka C. of C., 1970, Counselor award Ind. Vocat. Tech. Coll., 1990; Ganaway scholarship named in her honor, Workforce Devel. Svcs., 1993. Mem. NAACP (nat. life; state chair 1969—, Ind. conf., Achievement award 1990, Sorelle Entre Nous Club (pres., organizer 1951—, chair Ebony Fashion Show 1992), Order Ea. Star (grand chpt. Ind., dist. dep. grand matron 1968, Dist. Yr. award 1988-91, exec. dir. pub. rels. 1993-94), Imperial Ct. Daus. Isis (illustrious commandress 1962, imperial NAACP coord. 1967-89, Community Leader Am. award 1971). Home: 214 N Birdsell St South Bend IN 46628 Office: Workforce Devel No Ind Ste 400 PO Box 1048 Gateway Ctr South Bend IN 46628

GANDHI, BHANUMATI BHAGWANDAS, anesthesiologist; b. Bombay, India, Jan. 12, 1926; came to U.S., 1969; s. Bhagwandas Jasraj and Godvari (Mehta) G. LCPS, Topiwalla Nat. Med., Bombay, 1949; MBBS, Grant Med. Coll., Bombay, 1952, DGO, 1952. Attending anesthesiologist North Ctrl. Bronx (N.Y.) Hosp., 1969—. Fellow Am. Coll. Anesthesiologists. Home: 209 Garth Rd Apt 6E Scarsdale NY 10583 Office: North Ctrl Bronx Hosp 3424 Kossuth Ave Bronx NY 10467

GANDY-DIAMOND, JOYCE ANN, business administrator, former dance educator; b. Picher, Okla., Feb. 5, 1937; d. Sheppard Levi and Naydeen Maxine (Phillips) G.; m. Bernard Diamond, Aug. 2, 1985. AA, Parsons Jr. Coll., 1957; dance student of Thalia Mara, Gertrude Edwards Jory, Yurik Lazowsky, Robert Joffrey, Luigi, Frank Wagner. Cert. Cecchetti Coun. Am. Owner, tchr. Joyce's Dance Studio, Parsons, Kans., 1953-66; gen. sec. Nat. Acad. Ballet and Theatre Arts, N.Y.C., 1966-72; sec., adminstrv. asst., conv. mgr. Am. Inst. Steel Constrn., N.Y.C., 1973-79, office mgr., Chgo., 1979-80, personnel adminstr., Chgo., 1980-81; bus. adminstr. Bernard Diamond, D.D.S., Vinalhaven, Maine, 1983—. Recipient various dance grants, 1949-66. Mem. NAFE, Internat. Platform Assn. Mem. Ch. of Christ. Avocations: drawing, music, dance, gardening. Office: PO Box 293 Vinalhaven ME 04863

GANGAROSA, MARIA ELLEN, psychologist; b. Rochester, N.Y., May 28, 1962; d. Louis Paul, Sr. and Clara (Amalfi) G. BS in Psychology, Augusta Coll., 1984, AA in Criminal Justice, 1984; MS in Neuropsychology, Drexel U., 1987; PhD Candidate in Ednl. Psychology, U. Ga., 1991—. Cert. pastoral counselor. Mgr. Cole Nat. Key Concession, Cleve., 1981-83; teaching asst. Drexel U., Phila., 1984-85; neuropsychology intern Hosp. of U. Pa., Phila., 1985-87; devel. specialist Med. Coll. of Ga., Augusta, 1988—; clinic coord. Sch. Psychology Clinic/U. Ga., Athens, 1993—; consulting psychologist Dept. Infectious Diseases, Ctr. for Disease Control, Atlanta, 1987, 88, 90; part-time counselor, asst. Atlanta Bibl. Counseling Ctr., Atlanta, 1987-91. Contbr. abstracts and articles to profl. publs. Helping vol. United Way, Augusta, 1983-84. Mem. Internat. Neuropsychology Soc., Nat. Acad. Neuropsychology, Am. Counseling Assn., Nat. Assn. Nouthetic Counselors (cert. pastoral counselor), Psi Chi. Republican. Presbyterian. Office: Med Coll Ga Pediatrics/Neonatology Augusta GA 30912

GANGELL, BERNADETTE ANNE, librarian, writer, biologist; b. Hartford, Conn., Aug. 14, 1959; d. Lawrence Justus and Madeline Elizabeth (Clark) G. BA, St. Joseph Coll., 1983, postgrad., 1985-90; MA, Nat. U., Dublin, Ireland, 1992. Teaching asst. Mary Walsh Sch. Dance, Bloomfield, Conn., 1975-77; clerical asst. Ct. Jud. Dept., Hartford, 1978-83; asst. to law libr. Robinson & Cole, Esqs., Hartford, 1985-87; tech. asst. Prosser Pub. Libr., Bloomfield, Conn., 1983-91; med. toxicologist Keverly Labs., Inc., Bloomfield, 1990-91; researcher, writer Dublin, 1991-93; libr. Newington (Conn.) Libr., 1994—, Bristol (Conn.) Pub. Libr., 1994—; writer, craft designer Bloomfield, 1994—. Scholar, State of Conn., 1978. Mem. Irish No. Aid, Conn. Guild Craftsmen. Republican. Roman Catholic. Home: 32 Wintonbury Ave Bloomfield CT 06002

GANGEMI, MARIE, management consultant; b. N.Y.C., Jan. 28, 1948; d. Rosario and Clara (Scandura) G. BA, Bard Coll., 1969; MA, U. N.C., 1975. Mng. editor Praeger Pubs., N.Y.C., 1972-77, dir. prodn., 1977-85; pvt. practice mgmt. cons. N.Y.C., 1986—. Mem. Oratorio Soc. N.Y. (dir. mktg. 1985-93, bd. dirs. 1987—, treas. 1990—).

GANGITANO, ELIZABETH ANNE, insurance company executive; b. Quincy, Mass., May 14, 1950; d. Charles Terrell and Betty Mae (Richards) Phelps; m. Anthony Saldator Gangitano, May 3, 1969; children: Gina Elizabeth, Paul James, Bryan Anthony. Grad., North Quincy (Mass.) High Sch., 1969. Office mgr. Peerless, Inc., Stoughton, Mass., 1980-85, Ingle & Smith, CPAs, Boston, 1985-87; portfolio underwriter Nellie Mae, Braintree, Mass., 1987—. South Shore C. of C., Nat. Bus. Women's Leadership Assn., Toastmasters. Democrat. Methodist. Office: Nellie Mae 50 Braintree Hill Park Braintree MA 02184-8724

GANGLE, SANDRA SMITH, lawyer, arbitrator, mediator; b. Brockton, Mass., Jan. 11, 1943; d. Milton and Irene M. (Powers) S.; m. Eugene M. Gangle, Dec. 21, 1968; children: Melanie Jean Greenberg, Jonathan Rocco. BA, Coll. New Rochelle, 1964; MA, U. Oreg.; JD, Willamette U., 1980. Bar: Oreg. 1980. Instr. French, Oreg. State U., Corvallis, 1968-71, Willamette U., Salem, Oreg., 1971-74; instr. ESL, Chemeketa Community Coll., Salem, 1975-79; labor arbitrator Salem, 1980—; mem. Oreg., Idaho, Wash., Mont. Arbitration Panels; pvt. practice Salem, 1980-86; ptnr. Depenbrock, Gangle & Greer, 1986—; ptnr. Alternative Solutions, Inc., 1989—; clin. prof. Portland State U., 1981-84; cons. State Oreg., 1981. Contbr. articles to profl. jours. Land-use chmn. Faye Wright Neighborhood Assn., Salem, 1983-84; mem. Civil Svc. Commn., Marion County Fire Dist., Salem, 1983-89; mem. U.S. Postal Svc. Expedited Arbitration Panel, 1984-91; mem. Salem Neighbor-to-Neighbor Panel; mem. panel Fed. Mediation and Conciliation Svc., 1986—, domestic and internat. comml. arbitration panels Brit. Columbia Internat. Arbitration Ctr., 1988—; mem. Marion County Cir. Court Meditation Commn., 1993—; trustee Salem Peace Plaza. NDEA fellow, 1967. Mem. Am. Arbitration Assn. (arbitrator), Soc. Profls. in Dispute Resolution, Marion County Bar Assn. Office: Depenbrock Gangle & Greer 831 Lancaster Dr NE Ste 209 Salem OR 97301-2930

GANGSTEAD, SANDRA KAY, physical education educator, administrator; b. Ft. Dodge, Iowa, Dec. 12, 1950; d. James Elliott and Beverly Jean (Patton) G. BS with highest honors, U. Wis., LaCrosse, 1973; MS, U. Wyo., 1979; PhD, U. Utah, 1982. Cert. tchr., Wyo. Grad. asst. phys. edn. U. Wyo., Laramie, 1973-74; instr. Albany County Sch. Dist., Laramie, 1974-79; teaching fellow U. Utah, Salt Lake City, 1979-81, instr., 1981-82; asst. prof. Okla. State U., Stillwater, 1982-85, assoc. prof., 1986-87, coord. phys. edn., 1987-90; coord. Sch. Human Performance & Recreation, U. So. Miss., Hattiesburg, 1990-91, asst. dir., 1991-92, dir., 1992—. Assoc. editor editorial rev. bd. Phys. Educator, 1989-92, Phys. Edn. Index, 1988-91; editor Okla.

Assn. Health, Phys. Edn., Recreation and Dance Jour., 1984-90; author video tape prodn. Utah Skills Analysis Tests I and II, 1981, 82. Active Miss. Coalition for Disabled Individuals, Jackson, 1992-93, Coalition for Youth Miss., Jackson, 1992—, Miss. Gov.'s Commn. on Phys. Fitness and Sport, 1993—, chair higher edn. sub.-coun., amend IV task force. Nat. Youth Sports grantee Nat. Collegiate Athletic Assn., 1991-94; recipient Outstanding Faculty award Okla. State U., 1986. Mem. AAHPERD, Nat. Assn. for Phys. Edn. in Higher Edn., So. Dist. Assn. of Health, Phys. Edn. and Recreation, Miss. Assn. for Health, Phys. Edn., Recreation and Dance (coll. sect. chair 1992—, v.p. gen. 1994—, coll. sect. chair 1992-94), Okla. Assn. for Health, Phys. Edn., Recreation and Dance (v.p. 1989-90, coll. sect. chair 1988-89, rsch. sect. chair 1986-87, Presdl. citation 1987), Sigma Xi. Democrat. Office: U So Miss Sch Human Performance & Rec Southern Sta 5142 Hattiesburg MS 39406-5142

GANN, JO RITA, social services administrator, association executive; b. Talihina, Okla., June 2, 1940; d. Herbert and Juanita Rita (Fields) G. BS, Okla. Bapt. U., 1962; M Theatre Arts, Portland State U., 1970. Tchr. Oklahoma City Pub. Schs., 1962-64; teen dir., dir. health edn. YWCA, Oklahoma City, 1964-67; camp dir., teen dir. YWCA, Portland, Oreg., 1967-72; asst. dir., program coordinator YWCA, Flint, Mich., 1972-75; exec. dir. YWCA, Salem, Oreg., 1975—; chair N.W. regional staff YWCA, 1983, mem. constn. commn. YWCA, 1981-84, nat. com. to study purpose, 1988-91, del. to World Coun., Norway, 1991; CEO bus. panel Oregonian's Pub. Co. Co-author: A New Look at Supervision, 1980. Del. UN Conf. for Non-Govtl. Orgns.; internat. study del. on world econ. interdependence to Ghana, Africa; speaker Global Concerns, Salem and Portland, 1981—; mem. pres.'s council Salem Summerfest, 1985, 86. Mem. Nat. Assn. YWCA Exec. Dirs., Nat. Orgn. Female Execs., United Way Agy. Execs. (chair 1987, 88). Democrat. Office: YWCA 768 State St Salem OR 97301-3849

GANNON, SISTER ANN IDA, retired philosophy educator, former college administrator; b. Chgo., 1915; d. George and Hanna (Murphy) G. A.B., Clarke Coll., 1941; A.M., Loyola U., Chgo., 1948, LL.D., 1970; Ph.D., St. Louis U., 1952; Litt.D., DePaul U., 1972; L.H.D., Lincoln Coll., 1965, Columbia Coll., 1969, Luther Coll., 1969, Marycrest Coll., 1972, Ursuline Coll., 1972, Spertus Coll. Judaica, 1974, Holy Cross Coll., 1974, Rosary Coll., 1975, St. Ambrose Coll., 1975, St. Leo Coll., 1976, Mt. St. Joseph Coll., 1976, Stritch Coll., 1976, Stonehill Coll., 1976, Elmhurst Coll., 1977, Manchester Coll., 1977, Marymount Coll., 1977, Governor's State U., 1979, Seattle U., 1981, St. Michael's Coll., 1984, Nazareth Coll., 1985, Holy Family Coll., 1986, Keller Grad. Sch. Mgmt., Our Lady of Holy Cross Coll., New Orleans, 1988. Mem. Sisters of Charity, B.V.M.; tchr. English St. Mary's High Sch., Chgo., 1941-47; residence, study abroad, 1951; chmn. philosophy dept. Mundelein Coll., 1951-57, pres., 1957-75, prof. philosophy, 1975-85, emeritus faculty, 1987—, archivist, 1986—. Contbr. articles philos. jours. Mem. adv. bd. Sec. Navy, 1975-80, Chgo. Police Bd., 1979-89; bd. dirs. Am. Coun. on Edn., 1971-75, chmn., 1973-74; nat. bd. dirs. Girl Scouts USA, 1966-74, nat. adv., 1976-85; trustee St. Louis U., 1974-87, Ursuline Coll., 1978-92, Cath. Theol. Union, 1983-89, DeVry, Inc., 1987—, Duquesne U., 1989-91, Montay Coll., 1993—; bd. dirs. Newberry Libr., 1976—, WTTW Pub. TV, 1976—, Parkside Human Svcs. Corp., 1983-89. Recipient Laetare medal, 1975, LaSallian award, 1975, Aquinas award, 1976, Chgo. Assn. Commerce and Industry award, 1976, Hesburgh award, 1982, Woman of Distinction award Nat. Conf. Women Student Leaders, 1985, Outstanding Svc. award Coun. Ind. Colls., 1989, Woman of History award for edn. AAUW, 1989; named One of 100 Oustanding Chgo. Women, Culture in Action, 1994. Mem. Am. Cath. Philos. Assn. (exec. coun. 1953-56), Assn. Am. Colls. (bd. dirs. 1965-70, chmn. 1969-70), Religious Edn. Assn. Am. (pres. 1973, chmn. bd. 1975-78), North Cen. Assn. (commn. on colls. and univs. 1971-78, chmn. exec. bd. 1975-77, bd. dirs.), Assn. Governing Bds. Colls. and Univs. (bd. dirs. 1979-88, hon. bd. dirs. 1989-92). Office: Loyola U Coffey Hall 6525 N Sheridan Rd Chicago IL 60626-5311

GANNON, PAMELA MARIE, molecular biologist; b. Bronx, N.Y., May 25, 1962; d. Francis M. and Carol (Sachs) G.; m. David Charles Douglas, Sept. 8, 1994; 1 child, Madison Marie Douglas. BS, MIT, 1984; PhD, Tufts U., 1992. Rsch. asst. Med. Sch., Boston U., 1984; postdoctoral fellow MIT, Cambridge, Mass., 1992—. Contbr. articles to profl. jours. Predoctoral fellow NIH, 1986-88, Postdoctoral fellow Am. Cancer Soc., 1992-94. Mem. AAAS, Am. Soc. Microbiology (Pres. fellow 1990), Alpha Phi (pres. ho. corp. bd. 1990—, Found. scholar 1985). Home: 13 Concord Greene # 4 Concord MA 01742

GANOZA-BECKER, MARIA CLELIA, biochemistry educator; b. Lima, Peru, Oct. 24, 1937; came to U.S., 1950; d. Julio A. Ganoza and Clelia H. Finney; m. Andrew J. Becker; 1 child, Monica. BSc, Rollins Coll., 1959; PhD, Duke U., 1964; postgrad., Royal Acad. Scis., Can., 1983. Instr. Rollins Coll., Fla., 1957-59; rsch. assoc. Rockefeller U., N.Y.C., 1966-68; assoc. prof. U. Toronto, Ont., Can., 1968-74, career investigator Med. Rsch. Coun., 1968—, prof. biochem., 1974—, prof. microbiology, 1979—; vis. scientist Nat. Cancer Inst., Md., 1986. Assoc. editor Molecular Biology Reports (The Netherlands), 1974-90; contbr. articles to profl. jours.; contbg. author: Plasma Membrane Metabolism, 1970, Energy, Biosynthesis and Regulation, 1974, Cellular Regulation and Malignant Growth, 1985, The Roots of Modern Biochemistry, 1988, Ribosomes and Protein Synthesis A Practical Approach, 1990. Recipient Ayerst award Biochem. Soc. (Can.), 1976; rsch. grantee Med. Rsch. Coun. Can., 1968—, Nat. Cancer Inst. Can., 1969-73, Bickel & Connaught Founds., 1969—. Fellow Royal Soc. Can.; mem. Am. Fedn. Biol. Chemists, Can. Fedn. Biol. Chemists, N.Y. Acad. Scis., Sigma Xi. Office: U Toronto CH Best Inst, 112 College St, Toronto, ON Canada M5G 1L6

GANS, CAROL DICICCO, psychotherapist; b. Boston, Jan. 11, 1947; d. Henry Richard and Mary Teresa (Lena) DiC.; m. Nathan Gans, June 7, 1969 (div. Dec. 1992). BA in European History, Conn. Coll., 1969; MA in Psychology, West Ga. Coll., 1975. Tchr. music, art and phys. edn. Eugenia Hamilton Elem. Sch., Macon, Ga., 1969-70; tchr. social studies Clark Lane Jr. High Sch., Waterford, Conn., 1970-74; exec. dir. Colo. Fedn. Tchrs., Denver, 1976-79; tng. coord. Urban Inst., Devner, 1979-80; counselor, team leader Employ-Ex, Denver, 1980-82; clin. dir. Par Programs, Denver, 1982-84; human resources officer N.W. Banks Colo., Denver, 1984-91; pvt. practice psychotherapy Arvada, Colo., 1991—; adj. faculty Front Range C.C., Westminster, Colo., 1991-92; adminstr. employee assistance Land Title Guarantee Co., Denver, 1993—. Mem. ACA, Colo. Human Resources Assn., Colo. Wellness Coalition, Employee Assitance Profl. Assn., Employee Assistance Svcs. N.Am. Office: 6475 Wadsworth # 212 Arvada CO 80003

GANTMAN, GERALDINE ANN, marketing executive, consultant; b. N.Y.C., Jan. 14, 1945; d. Robert Marquette and Mary (Terrazzi) Rhynus. BA in History, CUNY, 1965. Project dir. Audits & Surveys, Inc., N.Y.C., 1966-68; sr. v.p. CCI, Inc., N.Y.C., 1968-80; v.p., account supr. N.W. Ayer, Inc., N.Y.C., 1980-83; exec. v.p. Tel. Mktg. Resources, Inc., N.Y.C., 1983-88; co-founder, sr. ptnr. Oetting & Co., Inc., N.Y.C., 1983—. Mem. Direct Mktg. Assn. (chmn. tel. mktg. coun. 1987-89). Office: Oetting & Co Inc 1995 Broadway New York NY 10023-5882

GANTT, REBECCA ESLER, writer; b. Phila., Sept. 14, 1909; d. Alexander Esler and Anna (Virginia) Musselman; m. Reginald Beswick Bromiley, Aug. 7, 1936 (div. 1949); m. William Andrew Horsley Gantt, Aug. 3, 1965. Student, U. B.C., Can., 1931-32, 34-36, Johns Hopkins U., 1945. Asst. Pavlovian Lab. Johns Hopkins Med. Sch., Balt., 1936-58; sec. Pavlovian Lab. Psychiat. Hosp., Perry Point, Md., 1959-65; researcher, speaker on religion and sci. at seminars. Mem. Pavlovian Soc. (W. Horsley Gantt medal 1988). Home: 807 Fairway Ave Catonsville MD 21228-5303

GANTZ, NANCY ROLLINS, nursing administrator, consultant; b. Buffalo Center, Iowa, Mar. 7, 1949; d. Troy Gaylord and Mary (Emerson) Rollins. Diploma in Nursing, Good Samaritan Hosp. and Med. Ctr., Portland, Oreg., 1973; BSBA, City Univ., 1986; MBA, Kennedy-Western U., 1987, PhD, 1991. Nurse ICU, Good Samaritan Hosp., 1973-75; charge nurse Crestview Convalescent Hosp., Portland, 1975; dir. nursing svcs. Roderick Enterprises, Inc., Portland, 1976-78, Holgate Ctr., Portland, 1978-80; nursing cons. in field of adminstrn., 1980-84; coord. CCU; mgr. ICU/CCU Tuality Community Hosp., Hillsboro, Oreg., 1984-86; head nurse intensive care unit, cardiac surgery unit, coronary care unit, Good Samaritan Hosp. & Med. Ctr., Portland, 1986-88, mgr. critical care units, 1988-92, asst. v.p. patient care svcs., 1992-93, dir. heart ctr. Deaconess Med. Ctr., Spokane, Wash., 1992-93; exec. asst. King Faisal Specialist Hosp. and Rsch. Ctr., Riyadh, Saudia Arabia, 1994—; mem. speakers bur. Nurses of Am.; mem. task force Oreg. State Health Div. Rules and Regulations Revision for Long Term Health Facilities and Hosps., 1978-79; numerous internat. and nat. speaking presentations. Contbr. chpts. to books and articles to profl. jours. Mem. Am. Nurses Assn. (cert.), Nat. League Nursing, Am. Assn. Critical Care Nurses (pres. elect greater Portland chpt. 1985-86, pres. 1986-87, bd. dirs. 1985—), Am. Heart Assn., Oreg. Heart Assn., Geriatric Nurses Assn. Oreg. (founder, charter pres.), Clackamus Assn. Retarded Citizens, AACN (chpt. cons. region 18 1987-89, mgmt. SIC region 18, 1990-92), AONE Coun. Nurse Mgrs. (bd. dirs. Region 9 1991-92, Sigma Theta Tau. Home: 15821 NW 19th St Vancouver WA 98684-4517

GANTZ, SUZI GRAHN, special education educator; b. Chgo., May 17, 1954; d. Robert Donald and Barbara Edna (Ascher) Grahn; m. Louis Estes Gantz, July 11, 1976; children: Christopher, Joshua. BS in Edn., U. Ill., 1976. BS in Edn. of Deaf and Hard of Hearing A.G. Bell Sch., Chgo., 1976-80, 88—; sales asst. Bob Grahn & Assocs., Chgo., 1982-84; with sales dept. Isis/My Sisters Circus, Chgo., 1984-86; interpreter Glenbrook North High Sch., Northbrook, Ill., 1986-87; interpreter, aide Lake Forest (Ill.) Dist. 67, 1987-88. Mem. Northbrook Citizens for Drug and Alcohol Alliance, 1988—; cubmaster Boy Scouts Am., Northbrook, 1990-93. Mem. Ill. Tchrs. of the Hearing Impaired, A.G. Bell Soc., Coun. on Exceptional Children. Home: 485 Laburnum Dr Northbrook IL 60062-2259 Office: AG Bell Sch 3730 N Oakley Ave Chicago IL 60618-4813

GANULIN, JUDY, public relations professional; b. Chgo., May 2, 1937; d. Alvin and Sadie (Reingold) Landis; m. James Ganulin, June 23, 1957; children: Stacy Ganulin Clark, Amy. BA in Journalism, U. Calif., Berkeley, 1958. Copywriter-sec. Joe Connor Advt., Berkeley, 1958; exec. sec. Prescolite Mfg. Co., Berkeley, 1958-59; info. officer Office of Consumer Counsel, Sacramento, 1959-61; pub. rels. positions various polit. campaigns, Fresno, Calif., 1966; adminstrv. asst., editor, mktg. Valley Pubs., Fresno, 1971-80; staff asst. to county supr. Bd. Suprs., Fresno, 1980-82; field rep. Assemblyman Bruce Bronzan, Fresno, 1982-84; prin. Judy Ganulin Pub. Rels., Fresno, 1984—; speaker new bus. workshop SBA/Svc. Corps Ret. Persons, Fresno, 1990—. Active Hadassah, Fresno, 1975—; pres. Temple Beth Israel Sisterhood, Fresno, 1976; panelist campaign workshop Nat. Women's Polit. Caucus, Fresno, 1994; bd. dirs. Temple Beth Israel, Fresno, 1972-75, Planned Parenthood Ctrl. Calif., Fresno, 1986-91. Mem. Pub. Rels. Soc. Am. (accredited pub. rels. practitioner, pres. Fresno/Ctrl. Valley chpt. 1994), Am. Mktg. Assn. (pres. ctrl. Calif. chpt.-ctrl. 1987-88), Calif. Press Women, Fresno Advt. Fedn., Pub. Rels. Roundtable (v.p., pres. 1991-93), Fresno C. of C. (mem. mktg. com. 1988—). Democrat. Office: Judy Ganulin Pub Rels 1117 W San Jose Fresno CA 93711

GANZ, PATRICIA ANNE, medical educator, physician; b. L.A., Mar. 23, 1948; d. Raymond W. and Ida (Shrier) Conn; m. Tomas Ganz, Aug. 16, 1970; children: David, Rebecca. BA magna cum laude, Harvard-Radcliffe, 1969; MD, UCLA, 1973. Diplomate Am. Bd. Internal Medicine, Am. Bd. Med. Oncology. Chief resident in medicine med. ctr. UCLA, 1977-78; from asst. to assoc. prof. medicine San Fernando Valley program UCLA, Sepulueda, 1978-90, prof., 1990-92; prof. schs. medicine and pub. health UCLA, 1990—; dir. divsn. cancer prevention and contorl rsch. Jonsson Comprehensive Cancer Ctr., L.A., 1993—. Office: UCLA Divsn Cancer Prevention & Control Rsch 1100 Glendon Ave Ste 711 Los Angeles CA 90024

GAPE, SERAFINA VETRANO, decorative artist and designer; b. Villa Franco, Sicily, Italy, Oct. 4, 1945; came to U.S., 1947; d. Augustino and Maria (Tramuta) Vetrano; m. William Evan Gape, Jan. 27, 1965; children: William Edward, Andrea Marie. BA, SUNY, Utica, 1982. Apprentice/journeyman/master Augustino Vetrano, New Hartford, N.Y., 1955-70; artist N.Y., 1970—; owner, designer Decorative Painting/Lit. Restoration Co., N.Y., 1980—; art tchr. Mohawk Valley C.C., Utica, N.Y., 1988; arts guide Fountain Elms/Hist. HouseMus., Utica, 1985—; cons., lectr. various chs., businesses, art orgns. Exhibited in group and one-woman shows including Italian Cultural Ctr., Utica, 1987, Ctrl. N.Y. Cmty. Arts Coun., N.Y.C., 1985 (awarded in a variety of mediums including oil, watercolor, acrylic and pastels); represented in pvt. collections in U.S., Can., Eng.; works include restoration and redesign of interiors of numerous chs. throughout Ctrl. N.Y. State, includes Our Lady of Lourdes, Utica, N.Y., 1994, Sts. Peter & Paul, Passaic, N.J., 1993, others. Mem. Munson-Williams-Proctor Inst., Kirkland Art Ctr., Utica Art Assn. (pres. 1984-87), Italian Cultural Ctr., Leatherstocking County Stencillers (v.p. 1990-91, pres. 1993-94), Stencil Artisans League. Home: 652 Daytona St Utica NY 13502-1110

GAPEN, DELORES KAYE, librarian, educator; b. Mitchell, S.D., July 1, 1943; d. Lester S. and Lena F. G. B.A., U. Wash., 1970, M.L.S., 1971. Gen. cataloger Coll. William and Mary, Williamsburg, Va., 1971-72; instr., asst. head Quick Editing Ohio State U., Columbus, 1972-74; head Ohio State U., 1974-77; asst. dir. tech. services Iowa State U., Ames, 1977-81; dean, prof. univ. libraries U. Ala., University, 1981-84; dean gen. library system U. Wis., Madison, 1984-91; exec. com. Council U. Wis. Libraries, 1985-87; cons. Northeast Mo. State U., 1980, Assn. Research Libraries task force on bibliog. control, 1981, Pa. State U., 1982, Conn. Coll., 1982; chmn. Coun. U. Wis. Librs., Madison, 1989-90; dir. libr. Case Western Res. U., 1991—; vice chmn. exec. com. of bd. trustees U. Wis. Online Computer Library Ctr., Madison, 1984-86, also mem. research libraries adv. com. (chair task force on Future of Research Library Coop. in Changing Techs. Environment, 1986-89, chmn. com. short cataloging records, 1983-84), 1989; cons. Bryn Mawr Coll. Online System Planning, 1983, Council Library Resources Edn. Task Force on Future of Library Sch. Edn., 1983, Tex. A&I U. reaffirmation team cons. for So. Assn. Colls. and Schs., 1984, Dickinson Coll. Library Autocat System, 1987; chair Assn. of Research Libraries Task Force for Govt. Info. in Electronic Form, 1986-87; mem. Assn. of Research Libraries Task Force on Scholarly Communication, 1983-87; nat. cons. scholar librarian, IBM, 1989-90. Contbr. articles to profl. pubs. Mem. AAUP, ALA, Southeastern Libr. Assn., Ala. Libr. Assn., Assn. Rsch. Librs. (chmn. task force govt. info. in electronic form 1986-87, bd. dirs. 1987-90), Bus. and Profl. Women's Assn., Beta Phi Mu, Alpha Lamba Delta. Democrat. Roman Catholic. Home: 13956 Cedar Rd # 139 Cleveland OH 44118-3204 Office: Case Western Res U Libr 10900 Euclid Ave Cleveland OH 44106-1712

GARBACZ, PATRICIA FRANCES, school social worker, therapist; b. Hamtramck, Mich., Nov. 26, 1941; d. Stanley and Frances (Harubin) G. BS, Siena Heights Coll., 1969; M. Pastoral Counseling, St. Paul U., Ottawa, Can., 1972; ThM, St. John Provincial Sem., 1983; MSW, Wayne State U., 1989. Cert. social worker Acad. Cert. Social Workers; cert. sch. social worker. Assoc. dir. vocations Archdiocese of Detroit, 1975-77; co-dir. of inst. for women Archdiocese of Lusaka (Zambia), 1977-78; pastoral minister Archdiocese of Detroit, 1979-80, assoc. dir. preformation, 1980-84; tchr., ministry coord. Bishop Borgess High Sch., Redford, Mich., 1984-86; tchr., dept. chair Aquinas High Sch., Southgate, Mich., 1986-88; therapist Community Coun. on Drug Abuse/Livonia (Mich.) Counseling, 1988-89; substance abuse therapist Oxford Inst., St. Clair Shores, Mich., 1989-91; sch. social worker Lakeshore Pub. Schs., St. Clair Shores, 1990—; therapist Macomb Child Guidance, 1989—. Mem. NASW.

GARBER, JANICE WINTER, retired advertising executive; b. N.Y.C., July 25, 1950; d. Irving and Frances (Edelman) Winter; stepdau. of Daniel Friedman; m. Dale Wayne Garber, Nov. 30, 1978. B.A., Queens Coll., 1979. Prodn. asst. P & F Graphics, N.Y.C., 1969-73; guest service mgr. Sheraton Corp., N.Y.C., 1973-76; advt. mgr. Am. Specialty Corp., N.Y.C., 1976-79; mng. editor VPO Industry News, 1979; advt. mgr. B & M Automotive Products, 1980-81; advt. mgr. Toyota Indsl. Equipment div. Toyota Motor Sales, U.S.A., Inc., Torrance, Calif., 1981-87, ret. 1987 . Mem. Bus./Profl. Advt. Assn. (dir. Los Angeles chpt. 1981), Am. Mktg. Assn. (Marsy award So. Calif. chpt. 1983).

GARBER, JOY BUCKLEY, insurance consultant; b. N.Y.C., Mar. 22, 1931; d. Floyd Thomas and Juliet Dorothea Buckley; m. Harry Douglas Garber, June 29, 1957; children: Deborah MacKelcan, Juliet Wong, John T. II, Buckley C. BS in Biology and Chemistry, Queens Coll., Flushing, N.Y., 1953. CLU. Lab. chief Charles Pfizer, Bklyn., 1953-57; ins. agt., benefits cons. Equitable Life Assurance Soc. of U.S., N.Y.C., 1981—. Dem. committeewoman, 1968—; pres. Dem. Club of Garden City, 1972-76; pres. Garden City Internat. Student Exch., 1980-88. Mem. Nassau County Soc. CLUs. Home: 76 Mulberry Ave Garden City NY 11530

GARBO, GRETA MARIA, biochemist, educator; b. Venice, Italy, Apr. 7, 1957; came to the U.S., 1984; d. Angelo and Annamaria (Stasioli) G.; m. Alan Raymond Morgan, July 8, 1988. MS in Biology, U. Padua, Italy, 1981, PHD in Biochemistry, 1983. Postdoctoral fellow U. Padua, 1983-84; rsch. assoc. Med. Coll. Ohio, Toledo, 1984-87; rsch. assoc. U. Toledo, 1987-88, rsch. asst. prof., 1988-92; product devel. scientist PDT Pharms., Santa Barbara, Calif., 1993—; prin. investigator NIH, 1990. Patentee in field. Mem. Am. Chem. Soc., European Soc. Photobiology, AAAS, Am. Assn. Photobiology, Ohio Acad. Sci., Sigma Xi.

GARCHIK, LEAH LIEBERMAN, journalist; b. Bklyn., May 2, 1945; d. Arthur Louis and Mildred (Steinberg) Lieberman; m. Jerome Marcus Garchik, Aug. 11, 1968; children—Samuel, Jacob. B.A., Bklyn. Coll., 1966. Editorial asst. San Francisco Chronicle, 1972-79, writer, editor, 1979-83, editor This World,, 1983-84, columnist, 1984—; also author numerous book and movie reviews, features and profiles; Author: San Francisco; the City's Sights and Secrets, 1995; panelist (radio quiz show) Mind Over Matter; contbr. articles to mags. Panelist (radio quiz show) Mind Over Matter; contbr. articles to mags. Vice pres. Golden Gate Kindergarten Assn., San Francisco, 1978; pres. Performing Arts Workshop, San Francisco, 1977-79. Recipient 1st prize Nat. Soc. Newspaper Columnists, 1992. Mem. Deutsche Music Verein, Media Alliance, Newspaper Guild, ACLU (bd. dirs. San Francisco chpt. 1977-79). Democrat. Jewish. Home: 156 Baker St San Francisco CA 94117-2111 Office: San Francisco Chronicle 901 Mission St San Francisco CA 94103-2988

GARCIA, EDNA I., secondary education educator; b. Humacao, P.R., Feb. 16, 1951; d. Agustin and Benigna Garcia; children: Clemente, Myrna. BA, Internat. Inst. of Ams., Hato Rey, P.R., 1983; postgrad., U. Bridgeport, 1985, Housatonic Coll., Bridgeport, Conn., 1989, Fairfield U., 1990—; student paralegal studies, Profl. Career Devel. Inst., Atlanta, 1990—. Notary pub.; cert. Spanish tchr. Coord. social sci., outreach worker Spanish Am. Devel. Agy., Bridgeport, 1973-79; tchr. English Dept. Pub. Edn., Carolina, P.R., 1979-83; ESL tchr. Bassic High Sch., Bridgeport, Conn., 1985—. Mem. citizens adv. com. on contract compliance Mayor's Office; state rep. 128th Dist. Conn., 1993—; mem. Dem. Town Com., 1994—; bd. dirs. The Kennedy Ctr., Inc., 1994—. Recipient Humanitarian award Conn. Edn. Assn., 1988, Jefferson award Sta. WTNH-TV Channel 8, 1991, Outstanding Achievement award The Hispanic Soc., Inc., 1991. Mem. NAFE, NOW, ASPIRA (founding mem.), ATENEO (founding mem.), Latinos for Progress, Nat. Assn. Latino Elected Officials. Democrat. Home: 1465 E Main St Apt 2B Bridgeport CT 06608-1120

GARCIA, JANE DAVIS, occupational health nurse, administrator; b. Mooresville, N.C., July 2, 1947; d. Charlie Moore and Colleen (Robbins) Davis; m. Ruben M. Garcia; children: Mikel Scott Hubbard, Julia Alicia Hubbard. ADN, Cen. Piedmont Community Coll., Charlotte, N.C., 1967; BS, Nova U., Ft. Lauderdale, 1987. Cert. adult nurse practitioner, occupational health nurse. Occupational health nurse practitioner Burlington Industries, Stonewall, Miss.; nurse practitioner otolaryngologist's office, Lansing, Mich.; DON EMSA Ltd. Partnership, Ft. Lauderdale. Mem. ANA, NPACE, Am. Assn. Occupational Health Nurses, Am. Acad. Nurse Practitioners, Fla. Nurses Assn., Emergency Nurses Assn. Home: 9140 Old Orchard Rd Davie FL 33328-6708

GARCIA, JUNE MARIE, library director; b. Bryn Mawr, Pa., Sept. 12, 1947; d. Roland Ernest and Marion Brill (Hummel) Traynor; m. Teodosio Garcia, July 17, 1928; children: Gretchen, Adrian. BA, Douglass Coll., 1969; MLS, Rutgers U., 1970. Reference libr. New Brunswick (N.J.) Pub. Libr., 1970-72, Plainfield (N.J.) Pub. Libr., 1972-75; br. mgr. Phoenix Pub. Libr., 1975-80, extension svcs. adminstr., 1980-93; dir. San Antonio Pub. Libr., 1993—. Recipient Productivity Innovator award City of Phoenix, 1981. Mem. ALA (life, mem. coun. 1986-90, 93—), REFORMA, Tex. Libr. Assn., Freedom Read Found. (bd. dirs. 1993—), Pub. Libr. Assn. of ALA (pres. 1991-92, mem. new standards task force 1983-87, mem. goals, guidelines and standards com. 1986-90, chairperson goals, guidelines and standards com. 1987-90), Libr. Adminstrn. and Mgmt. Assn. of ALA, Assn. Libr. Svc. Children of ALA, Young Adult Svcs. Divsn. ALA, Ariz. State Libr. Assn. (pres. 1984-85, Libr. of Yr. award 1986, Pres.'s award 1990), Beta Phi Mu. Home: 3731 Twisted Oaks Dr San Antonio TX 78217 Office: San Antonio Pub Library 203 S Saint Marys St San Antonio TX 78205-2726

GARCIA, KATHERINE LEE, comptroller, accountant; b. Portland, Oreg., Nov. 4, 1950; d. Gerald Eugene and Delores Lois (Erickson) Moe; m. Buddy Jesus Garcia; Nov. 19, 1977; children: Kevin, Brett, Rodd. BS cum laude, U. Nev., 1976. CPA, Idaho, Nev. Retail clk. Raleys, Food King, Reno, 1968-76; sr. acct. Pieretti, Wilson and McNulty, Reno, 1976-78, Deloitte Haskins and Sells, Boise, Idaho, 1979-81; sr. acct. Washoe County, Reno, 1981-83, chief dep. comptr., 1983-94, comptroller, 1994—. Treas., bd. dirs. Friends of 4 (pub. TV), Boise, 1979-81. Recipient Cert. of Excellence in Fin. Reporting, Govt. Fin. Officer's Assn., 1982—. Mem. AICPA, Nev. Soc. CPAs (chmn. state and local govt. com. 1992-93), Govt. Fin. Officers Assn. (mem. spl. rev. com. 1989—, state rep.), Nev. Govt. Fin. Officers Assn. (treas. 1989-91, reader for blind 1992—). Republican. Home: 655 W Joy Lake Rd Reno NV 89511-8712 Office: Washoe County PO Box 11130 Reno NV 89520-0027

GARCIA, LEEANN DAWN, governmental legislative and business affairs consultant; b. Pueblo, Colo., Aug. 31, 1962; d. Dallas Wayne and Leigh (Scholes) Overstreet; m. Henry T. Garcia, July 4, 1992. BA, Calif. State U., San Bernardino, 1984, MA, 1987, MPA, 1987. Planner II Riverside (Calif.) County Planning Dept., 1987-89; adminstrv. analyst II City of Fontana, Calif., 1989-91; asst. city mgr. City of Beaumont, Calif., 1991-92; congl. asst. Congressman George E. Brown Jr., Colton, Calif., 1992-95; prin., pres. Garcia Overstreet & Assocs., Grand Terrace, Calif., 1992—. Mem. planning commn. City of Grand Terrace, Calif., 1994. Mem. Am. Planning Assn., Calif. Assn. Local Govt. Econ. Devel., World Future Soc. Home: 22997 Jensen Ct Grand Terrace CA 92313-5578

GARCIA, MARY JANE MADRID, state legislator; b. Dona Ana, N.Mex., Dec. 24, 1936; d. Isaac C. and Victoria M. Garcia. A.A., San Francisco City Coll., 1956; B.S., N.Mex. State U., 1982, B.A. in Anthropology, 1983, M.A. in Anthropology, 1985. Interpretor, translator to USAF Capt., Hotel Balboa, Madrid, Spain, 1962-63; exec. sec. to city mgr. City of Las Cruces, N.Mex., 1964-65; adminstrv. asst. RMK-BRJ, Saigon, Socialist Republic Vietnam, 1966-72; owner Billy the Kid Gift Shop, Mesilla, N.Mex., 1972-81; pres., owner Victoria's Night Club, Las Cruces, 1981—; state senator Dist. 38, N.Mex.; with archaeol. excavations N.Mex. State U. Anthropology Dept., summer 1982, spring 1983. Bd. dirs., sec-treas. Dona Anna Mutual Domestic Water Assn.; mem. Subarea Council Health Systems Agy., 1979; bd. dirs. Sun Country Savings Bank, Las Cruses, 1985; treas. Toney Anaya for U.S. Senate, 1978; active Toney Anaya for N.Mex. Gov., 1979-82. Mem. N.Mex. Retail Liquor Assn. Democrat. Roman Catholic. Home: Isaac Garcia St PO Box 22 Dona Ana NM 88032-0022 Office: Senate of N Mex State Capital Santa Fe NM 87501*

GARCIA, OFELIA, college president; b. Havana, Cuba, Feb. 12, 1941; d. Ramon Garcia-Castro and Nieves (Gomez de Molina) Garcia. Student, Escuela de Bellas Artes, Havana, 1958-60; BA, Manhattanville Coll., 1969; MFA, Tufts U., 1972; postgrad., Duke U., 1973-75; D. Fine Arts (hon.), Atlanta Coll. Art, 1991. Asst. prof., art dept. chair, div. dir. humanities and fine arts Newton (Mass.) Coll., 1969-75; dir. studio art Boston Coll., Chestnut Hill, Mass., 1975-76; exec. dir. The Print Club, Phila., 1978-86; critic Pa. Acad. Fine Arts, Phila., 1982-86; pres. Atlanta Coll. Art, 1986-91, Rosemont (Pa.) Coll., 1991—; visual arts panelist State Coun. of the Arts, Pa. and N.J., 1985-86, Ga., 1990-91; mem. vis. com. dept. art and architecture Lehigh (Pa.) U., 1990—; bd. mgrs. Haverford Coll.; external reviewer Mid. States Assn. Colls. and Schs. Artist exhibitions of prints and drawings; curator, juror numerous nat. and internat. or regional art exhibitions. Nat. pres. Women's Caucus for Art, 1984-86, Am. Coun. on Edn., 1993—; co-chair Mayor's Commn. for Women, City Phila., 1992—; Arts Adv. Com. Barnes Found. Bd., 1992—. Recipient Am. Bookbuilders prize Boston Mus. Sch., 1969, Park Found. award, 1974; Kent fellow Danforth Found., 1975-80. Fellow Soc. for Values Higher Edn.; mem. Coll. Art Assn. Am. (bd. dirs. 1986-90, bd. coms. 1986-92), Commn. on Women in Higher Edn., Am. Coun. on Edn. (chair 1990-91), So. Assn. Colls. and Schs. (accreditation evaluator 1990-91), ArtTable, Inc. Roman Catholic. Office: Rosemont Coll Office of the President Rosemont PA 19010

GARCIA, SANDRA JOANNE ANDERSON, law and psychology educator; b. Buffalo, Aug. 10, 1939; d. James Edwards and Thelma Harriet (Crawford) Anderson; m. Gerard L. Garcia, Jr., June 11, 1960 (div. 1968); 1 child, Robert Vincent. BA, Tex. Western Coll., 1966; MA, U. Tex., El Paso, 1968; PhD, U. So. Calif., 1971; JD, Stetson U. Coll. Law, 1985. Rsch. assoc. Human Rsch. Office, George Washington U., El Paso, 1967-68; rsch. assoc. SW Regional Lab. for Ednl. Rsch. and Devel., Inglewood, Calif., 1968-69; asst. prof. English dept. UCLA, 1970-74; asst. prof. psychology U. South Fla., Tampa, 1974-80, assoc. prof., 1989-90, prof., 1990—; prof. interdisciplinary arts and scis. U. South Fla., 1992—. Editor: Bionic Babies in High-Tech Families: New Issues in Child Psychology, 1988; co-editor: Current Perspectives in Legal, Psychological, and Ethical Issues, 1990. Recipient Equal Opportunity award U. South Fla., 1976; rsch. fellow Ford Found., Jerusalem, 1973-74, Am. Bar Found., 1989, 90, McKnight Found., 1989-90, Nat. Ctr. for State Cts., 1990—, Fla. Commn. on Human Rels., 1992—. Democrat. Home: 807 Lorena Rd Lutz FL 33549-4527

GARCIA C., ELISA DOLORES, lawyer; b. Bklyn., Nov. 8, 1957; d. Vincent Garcia, Jr. and Dolores Elizabeth (Canedo) Marmo; m. John Jay Hasluck, Feb. 28, 1987; 1 child, Brooke Elisabeth. BA, MS, SUNY, Stony Brook, 1980; JD, St. John's U., 1985. Cons. Energy Devel. Internat., Pt. Jefferson, N.Y., 1980-83; assoc. Willkie Farr & Gallagher, N.Y.C., 1985-89; sr. counsel GAF Corp./Internat. Specialty Products, Wayne, N.J., 1989—. Chair Glen Rock, N.J. Planning Bd., 1994—, mem., 1992—; mem. Glen Rock Rep. Club, 1989—; active cmty. affairs. Mem. ABA, N.Y. State Bar Assn. Roman Catholic. Office: Internat Speciality Products 1361 Alps Rd Wayne NJ 07470

GARD, BEVERLY J., state legislator; b. N.C., Mar. 8, 1940; m. Donald Gard; children: David, Doug. BS, U. Tenn. Biochemist Eli Lilly & Co.; councilwoman City of Greenfield, Ind., 1976-88; mem. Ind. State Senate from 28th dist., 1988—. Mem. Hancock Assn Retarded Citizens, Ind. Assn. Cities and Towns. Republican. Methodist. Office: State Senate State Capital Indianapolis IN 46204*

GARDE, SUSAN REUTERSHAN, accountant; b. Southampton, N.Y., Sept. 5, 1953; d. Robert Gordon and Ann Patricia (Cronin) Reutershan; m. John Franklin Garde III, May 20, 1989; children: John Franklin IV, Sean Robert. BS, Skidmore Coll., 1975; MBA, Fla. Inst. Tech., 1983, MS in Mgmt., 1991. Budget analyst Grumman Aerospace Corp., Bethpage, N.Y., 1975-76, program planner, 1976-79; sr. budget planner Grumman Aerospace Corp., Stuart, Fla., 1979-81, program planner, 1981-82; adminstr. rsch. ctr. United Technologies, West Palm Beach, Fla., 1982-86; sr. adminstr. United Technologies Inc., West Palm Beach, 1986-87, United Technologies Optical Systems Inc., West Palm Beach, 1988-94; cost acct. Harbor Br. Oceanog. Inst., Inc., Ft. Pierce, Fla., 1994—. Mem. NAFE, Am. Bus. Women's Assn. (pres. Orchid chpt. 1986-87, Sailfish chpt. 1985), Nat. Wildlife Fedn., Skidmore Alumni Assn., Skidmore Club S.E. Fla. Republican. Roman Catholic. Home: 5100 9th St Vero Beach FL 32966 Office: Harbor Br Oceanog Inst 5600 US 1 North Fort Pierce FL 34946

GARDEBRING, SANDRA S., judge. Grad., Duke U. and Harvard U.; JD, U. Minn. Dir. EPA; commr. Minn. Pollution Control Agy., Minn. Dept. Human Svcs.; judge Minn. Ct. Appeals; assoc. justice Minn. Supreme Ct., 1991—; chmn. bd. regional planning agy. Met. Coun. Mem. Ctr. Victims of Torture; mem. lawyers com. Internat. Human Rights, LWV; past bd. dirs. St. Paul United Way, Camp DuNord, Project Environment Found., Clean Sits. Office: Minn Supreme Ct 248 Minn Jud Ctr 25 Constitution Ave Saint Paul MN 55155-6102

GARDENIER, EDNA FRANCES, nurse; b. Teaneck, N.J., June 30, 1935; d. Andrew Cairns and Edna Frances (Manney) O'Neil; B.S. in Nursing, Seton Hall U., S. Orange, N.J., 1965; M.Ed., Tchrs. Coll. Columbia U., 1970; EdD SUNY, Albany, 1990; m. Harvey James Gardenier, Aug. 25, 1961; children—Andrew, William. Staff nurse N.J. hosps., 1955-65; public health nurse, 1965-70; mem. nursing faculty Dutchess Community Coll., Poughkeepsie, N.Y., 1970—, program chmn. nursing, 1971-83, acting head dept. health technologies, 1979-80, head nursing dept., 1983—; mem. overall nursing faculty N.Y. State Regents Coll., 1981-92; mem. nurse edn. com. SUNY; mem. Dutchess County chpt. Am. Heart Assn., 1974-90 ; nutrition adv. council Dutchess County Coop. Edn., 1970-79. USPHS trainess, 1968-70. Mem. Am. Assn. Women in Jr. and Community Colls., N.Y. Assn. Degree Nurse Council, N.Y. State Nurses Assn., N.Y. State Two Year Coll. Assn., Sigma Theta Tau. Home: Rd 1 Box 85 Holsapple Rd Dover Plains NY 12522 Office: Dutchess C C Pendell Rd Poughkeepsie NY 12601

GARDINER, SUSAN NIVEN, purchasing director; b. N.Y.C., Aug. 28, 1956; d. Robert MacPherson Gardiner and Janet (Eaton) Gardiner Glover; m. René Raul Trespalacios, Oct. 12, 1991. BA in French Lang. and Lit., Smith Coll., 1978. Prodn. mgr. Wunderman, Ricotta & Kline, N.Y.C., 1978-79; prodn. supr. Random House Enterprises, N.Y.C., 1979-81; print svcs. mgr. Esquire Mag., N.Y.C., 1981-82; purchasing agt. Playtex, inc., Stamford, Conn., 1982-84; purchasing buyer Gen. Foods Corp., White Plains, N.Y., 1984-86; asst. v.p. promotional purchasing Lancome, Inc., N.Y.C., 1986—. Mem. Assn. Graphic Arts (judge 1991—). Home: 8 Brandywine Terr Morristown NY 07960 Office: Lancome Inc 575 Fith Ave New York NY 10017

GARDNER, ANN L., social anthropologist, researcher; b. Dayton, Ohio, Sept. 21, 1961; d. Owen Ben and Gladys Elizabeth (Brown) G. BA, Friends World Coll., 1982; non-degree work in Arabic lang., Am. U., Cairo, Arab Republic of Egypt, 1983-85; MA in Anthropology, U. Tex., 1987, PhD, 1994. Teaching asst. Ctr. Mid. Ea. Studies or dept. anthropology U. Tex., Austin. Rsch. grantee Nat. Geog. Soc., 1990, NSF, 1989-91, Wenner-Gren, 1990, U.S. Info. Agy. adminstered by Am. Rsch. Ctr. in Egypt, 1989-90; Arabic lang. fellowship U. Tex., summer 1988, Am. U. Cairo, 1984-85. Home: 3026 Clay St San Francisco CA 94115-1624

GARDNER, CARYN SUE, lawyer; b. Queens, N.Y., Mar. 9, 1960; d. Louis Arthur and Rhoda (Madonick) G. BA in Environ. Sci. and Urban Planning, SUNY, Binghamton, 1982; JD, DePaul U., 1985. Bar: Ill. 1985, U.S. Dist. Ct. (no. dist.) Ill. 1987, U.S. Ct. Appeals (7th cir.) 1987. Assoc. Rivkin, Radler, Dunne & Bayh, Chgo., 1985-86, Rudd & Kim, Schaumburg, Ill., 1986-87, Schain, Firsel & Burney, Schaumburg, 1987-92, Bickley & Bickley, Schaumburg, 1992-93, Bickley, Hart & Gardner, Schaumburg, 1993—; asst. instr. Harper Coll., Palatine, Ill., 1987-92, prof., 1992—; atty. Assn. Condominium, Townhouse and Homeowners Assns., Schaumburg, 1987, Assn. Condominium Edn., South Barrington, Ill., 1990—. Mem. ABA, Chgo. Bar Assn., Am. Trial Lawyers Assn. Office: Bickley Hart & Gardner 937-39 S Roselle Rd Schaumburg IL 60193

GARDNER, FRANCESCA MARROQUIN, lawyer, consultant; b. New Haven, Aug. 17, 1940; d. John William and Aida (Marroquin) G.; m. John Robert Reese, Sept. 5, 1964 (div. 1986); children: Jennifer Marie, Justine Francesca. BS in Math., Stanford U., 1962, LLB, 1965. Bar: Calif. 1966, U.S. Dist. Ct. Calif. 1966, U.S. Ct. Appeals (9th cir.) 1966. Legal assoc. Crist Peters Donegan & Brenner, Palo Alto, Calif., 1965-66, Covington & Burling, Washington, 1967, Heller Ehrman White & McAuliffe, San Francisco, 1969-72; mng. ptnr. Gardner Reese Co., San Francisco, 1980-90; program officer James Irvine Found., San Francisco, 1986-92; cons., lawyer The Gardner Group, San Francisco, 1993—; mem. Coun. for the Humanities and Scis., Stanford (Calif.) U., 1982-90; part time rschr. Hambrecht & Quist, San Francisco, 1984-85; bd. dirs. Life Plan Ctr., San Francisco. Co-editor: (book of quotations) Know or Listen to Those Who Know, 1974. Mem. Calif. Bar Assn., Town and Country Club, Stanford Assocs., Stanford Alumni Assn. Home: 3970 Clay St San Francisco CA 94118 Office: The Gardner Group 177 Post St Ste 910 San Francisco CA 94108

GARDNER, GWENDOLYN SMITH, retail executive; b. Bristol, Va., Mar. 2, 1948; d. Julian B. and Margaret Smith; m. Clyde Eugene Gardner Jr., July 20, 1968; children: Jennifer Ellen, Julie Anne. Student, U. N.C., Charlotte, 1966-67, King's Bus. Coll., Charlotte, 1967-68, Cen. Piedmont Community Coll., 1969. Cert. store profl. Asst. bookstore mgr., textbook mgr. Cen. Piedmont Community Coll., Charlotte, 1969-90; bookstore mgr. Davidson (N.C.) Coll., 1990—; tchr. facilitator Nat. Assn. Coll. Stores, Oberlin, Ohio, 1990-91, store evaluator, 1993. Mem. Am. Assn. Women Cmty. and Jr. Colls., Nat. Assn. Coll. Stores (nominating com. 1991, cert. com. 1991, chair 1993-94, 94-95, store evaluator 1993, Pres.'s award 1994), Coll. Stores Assn. N.C. (pres. 1990). Office: Davidson Coll Bookstore Main St Davidson NC 28036-9086

GARDNER, JEWELLE BAKER, business executive, interior designer; b. Ayden, N.C., May 23, 1925; d. Roland Ray and Helen Wingate (Jackson) Cannon; m. Paul Thomas Baker, July 25, 1956 (dec. 1963); children: Paula Jewelle Baker Bryan, Paul Thomas; 1 stepchild, Blanche Baker Miller; m. Fred Calvin Gardner, Apr. 19, 1969 (dec. May 1983); 1 stepchild, Angela Gardner Jones. Student Woods Bus. Sch., New Bern, N.C., 1942-45; BA, Am. Sch. Design, N.Y.C., 1948; BFA, U. N.C., Greensboro, 1950. Dept. head Navy Supply, Cherry Point, N.C., 1941-45; ptnr. Cannons Paint & Wallpaper Co., Ayden, 1945-70; exec. v.p. Baker Furniture Co., Kinston, N.C., 1950-63; operator Cannon Farms, Ayden, 1956—; pres., treas. Baker Furniture Co., Kinston, 1963-69; with consumer program Drexel Co., 1965-66; owner Jewelle Baker Cons., Kinston, 1969—; v.p. Gardner Homes, Elizabeth City, N.C., 1972-81; bus. cons. Gardner Constrn. Co., Kinston, 1975-81; bus. cons. Lenoir Plumbing & Heating Co., Kinston, 1975-81; chief exec. officer Gardner Homes, Elizabeth City, 1982—; chmn. bd., chief exec. officer Lenoir Plumbing & Heating Co., 1982—, Gardner Constrn. Co., 1982—; cons. Carolina Power & Light, 1963-65, N.C. Solar Energy Assn., 1977-79, Nutritional Therapy, Durham, 1979-81; lectr., 1950-63; del. U.S.-China Joint Session on Industry, Trade, and Econ. Devel., Beijing, 1988. Mem. Devel. Auth. of Neuse River Council of Govts., 1984-85. Columnist, Ayden Dispatch and Greenville News Leader, 1940-56; producer Performer Baker's Commls., 1960-69. Mem. C. of C. Kinston (bd. dirs., v.p., chmn. retail mchts. div.), So. Retail Furniture Assn., Nat. Retail Furniture Assn., N.C. Mchts. Assn., N.C. Farm Assn., Assoc. Gen. Contractors Am., Community Council for the Arts, Internat. Platform Assn., N.C. Zool. Assn., N.C. Art Soc., Kinston Country Club, Coral Bay Club, Pineknoll Golf and Country Club, Sea Water Marina Club. Democrat. Mem. Ch. Disciples of Christ. Home: 1708 Elizabeth Dr Kinston NC 28501-3416 Office: Gardner Constrn Co PO Box 856 Kinston NC 28502-0856

GARDNER, JOAN, medical, surgical nurse; b. Ft. Worth, Oct. 5, 1950; d. Bert and Pearl (Sandgarten) G. BS in Edn., U. Tex., 1972, BS in Communication, 1976; diploma, Brackenridge Hosp., 1982. RN, Tex. Trust asst. Austin (Tex.) Nat. Bank; tchr. English and reading Columbus (Tex.) Ind. Schs.; staff orthopedics nurse Seton Med. Ctr., Austin, 1982-83, staff nurse gyn. surgery and post partum, 1983-84, staff nurse post partum, 1984-85, staff nurse gyn. surgery and ear, nose, throat, and eye, 1986, charge nurse gen. surgery, 1988-92, staff nurse short-term surgery, 1992—. Home: 1602 Leigh St # A Austin TX 78703-2452 Office: 1201 W 38th St Austin TX 78705

GARDNER, JUDITH STURGEN, nursing administrator, educator; b. Harrisburg, Pa., Nov. 28, 1939; d. George W. Sr. and Gladys E. (Lenker) Sturgen; children: Scott, Alan, Wendy. Student, Fayetteville Community Coll., 1974; BS, Pa. State U., Middletown, 1986. Cert. CPR and BLS instr. Head nurse Aspen Ctr., Dauphin County, Harrisburg, Pa.; instr. Acad. Med. Arts, Harrisburg; asst. dir. First Step program Goodwill Idustries of Cen. Pa., Inc., Harrisburg; case mgr. physicians health program Edn. and Sci. Trust of the Pa. Med. Soc., Harrisburg; case mgr. job health program Cmty. Gen. Osteo. Hosp., Harrisburg, Pa.; managed care analyst Pa. Blue Shield, Harrisburg. Mem. Pa. Nurses Assn. (past bd. mem.). Address: 3211 Elm St Harrisburg PA 17109-5746

GARDNER, KAREN ANN, sales executive; b. Springfield, Mo., Apr. 14, 1962; d. John H. Schopp and Alice Jo Ogborn Loehr; m. Edwin Forrest Gardner, May 15, 1993; 1 child, Rachel Lynn. AA, Ocean County Coll., Toms River, N.J., 1982; BS, Rutgers U., 1985, MBA, 1988. Account rep. MetLife, Somerset, N.J., 1988—. Mem. NAFE, Nat. Assn. Life Underwriters. Republican. Roman Catholic. Office: MetLife 100 Franklin Square Dr # 206 Somerset NJ 08873-4109

GARDNER, KATHLEEN D., gas company executive, lawyer; b. Fayetteville, Ark., July 14, 1947; d. Harold Andrew and Bess (Gunn) Dulan; m. Robert Gardner, June 7, 1969 (dec. Sept. 1974); 1 child, Christina Ann. BS, U. Ark., 1969, JD, 1978; MA, U. Ala., 1972. Atty., corp. officer SW Energy Co., Fayetteville, 1978-85; asst. gen. counsel, asst. v.p. Ark. La. Gas Co., Little Rock, 1985-86, gen. counsel, v.p., 1986—; chmn. Regional Tng. Program, Birmingham, Ala., 1972-75. Bd. dirs. The New Sch. Fayetteville, 1978-79, Robert K. Gardner Meml. Fund, Fayetteville, Keep Ark. Beautiful Commn.; past bd. dirs. Ballet Ark., Ark. Mus. Sci. and History, Vis. Nurse Corp. Named Outstanding Young Woman Fayetteville Jaycettes, Ark. Jaycettes; recipient Woman of Achievement in Energy award, 1990. Mem. ABA, Ark. Bar Assn. (sec. natural resources sect. 1981), Pulaski County Bar Assn., Am. Gas Assn., DAR, Ark. Assn. Def. Counsel, Am. Arbitration Assn. (Ark. adv. coun.), Alpha Delta Pi. Episcopal. Office: Ark La Gas Co 400 E Capitol Ave Little Rock AR 72202-2418

GARDNER, LEE ROBBINS, psychiatrist; b. Balt., June 6, 1934; d. Bernard S. and Lee (Fraidin) Robbins; m. Robert Williams, Oct., 1990; children: Andrew, Nancy, Julie. BA, Barnard, 1956; MD, Columbia U., 1959, cert. adult psychoanalysis, 1979, cert. child psychoanalysis, 1981. Intern St. Luke Hosp., 1959-60; resident N.Y. State Psychiat. Inst., N.Y.C., 1962-66; attending psychiatrist N.Y. State Psychiat. Inst., 1966—; asst. clin. prof. psychiatry Columbia Coll. Physicians and Surgeons, N.Y.C., 1982—; collaborating faculty Columbia Psychoanalytic Ctr., Columbia U., 1980—; bi-annual lectr. N.J. Coll. Medicine & Dentistry. Jewish.

GARDNER, LINDA DIANE, speech pathologist; b. Bethel, N.C., Aug. 3, 1951; d. Bruce C. and Melvin B. (Mizelle) G. BS, East Carolina U., 1973, MS, 1976. Cert. of clin. competence in speech-lang. pathology. Speech pathologist Pitt County Schs., Greenville, N.C., 1976-78, 88-91, Pitt County Mental Health Ctr., Greenville, 1978-81, Lenoir Meml. Hosp., Kinston, N.C., 1981-82, Lenoir County Schs., Kinston, 1982-83, Nat. Speech and Hearing Assn., Greenville, 1983-87, InSpeech, Greenville, 1987-88, Devel. Evaluation Clinic, Greenville, 1991—. Co-author brochure. Vol. Spl. Olympics, Greenville, 1992. Mem. Am. Speech and Hearing Assn., N.C. Speech-Lang. and Hearing Assn., N.C. Assn. Suprs. in Speech Pathology and Audiology (treas. 1991-93). Office: Devel Evaluation Clinic Irons Bldg Charles Blvd Greenville NC 27858

GARDNER, LINDA FAY, gallery director; b. Elmira, N.Y., Dec. 19, 1947; d. Joseph Alva and Vivian Lenore (Lusk) Comfort; m. Allen D. Shaw, June 22, 1968 (div. July 1975); children: John Gregory Shaw, Lisa Anne Shaw; m. Thomas W. Gardner, Nov. 21, 1975; 1 child, Jesse Lynne. Grad., Elmira Bus. Inst., 1966. Med. sec. Dr. Gerald P. Schneider, Elmira, 1966-77; mgr., owner, fram designer Corning (N.Y.) Art & Frame, 1977-92; dir. West End Gallery, Corning, 1989—. Mem. Arnot Art Mus., Arts of the So. Finger Lakes, Rockwell Mus. Office: West End Gallery 2d Fl 87 W Market St Corning NY 14830

GARDNER, LISA ANN, risk management and insurance educator, consultant; b. Ottumwa, Iowa, June 8, 1962; d. Ronald Eugene and Mary Ann (Bloss) G. AA, Indian Hills C.C., Ottumwa, 1981; BS, U. Wyo., 1984; MBA, Drake U., 1988; PhD, Ga. State U., 1992. Residence hall dir. Indian Hills C.C., Ottumwa, 1985-87; acad. advisor Buena Vista Coll., Ottumwa, 1985-87; grad. rsch. asst. Drake U., Des Moines, 1987-88; grad. rsch. asst. Ga. State U., Atlanta, 1988-90, grad. teaching asst., 1990-92; asst. prof. Old Dominion U., Norfolk, Va., 1992-93, U. Nev., Las Vegas, 1993—; pvt. practice cons. Las Vegas, 1993—. Contbr. articles to profl. jours. Recipient Program Devel. grant AEtna Life and Casualty Found., 1987, Doctoral Dissertation Rsch. award State Farm Cos., 1991, Program Devel. grant Va. Chpt. Risk and Ins. Mgmt. Soc., 1993, Rsch. grant Old Dominion U., 1993; named Bell South scholar Ga. State U., 1988-92, Helen C. Leith fellow Ga. State U., 1988-92, Spencer Ednl. Found. scholar Atlanta Chpt. Risk and Ins. Mgmt. Soc., 1990. Mem. Am. Risk and Ins. Assn. (strategic planning com., Wright-Kulp Book awards com., nominations com.), Am. Fin. Assn., So. Risk and Ins. Assn., Inst. for Ins. and Risk Mgmt. (adv. bd., co-chair 1993—, external rels. com.), Beta Gamma Sigma (Delta chpt. of Ga.). Episcopalian. Office: Univ Nev Las Vegas Dept Fin 4505 S Maryland Pky Las Vegas NV 89154-9900

GARDNER, LIZ See WEDDINGTON, ELIZABETH GARDNER

GARDNER, SANDRA BEYER, sales manager; b. Shawano, Wis., June 2, 1960; d. David O. and Ernestine Alice (Hodel) Beyer; m. Stuart Charles Gardner, Dec. 12, 1992. BS in Agr. and Food Sci., U. Wis., 1982. Quality assurance technologist The Larsen Co., Green Bay, Wis., 1982-84; tech. coord. Schepps Inc., Dallas, 1984-85; tech. sales rep. Crest Foods Co., Ashton, Ill., 1985-88; regional sales mgr. Nat. Sea Products, Portsmouth, N.H., 1988-89; dist. sales mgr. J.M. Smucker Co., Orrville, Ohio, 1989-91, nat. accounts mgr. west, 1991—. Presbyterian. Office: 2131 N Collins St Ste 433 Arlington TX 76011-2811

GARDNER, SHERYL PAIGE, obstetrician/gynecologist; b. Bremerton, Wash., Jan. 24, 1945; d. Edwin Gerald and Dorothy Elizabeth (Herman) G.; m. James Alva Beat, June 20, 1986. BA in Biology, U. Oreg., 1967, MD cum laude, 1971. Diplomate Am. Bd. Ob-Gyn. Intern L.A. County Harbor Gen. Hosp., Torrance, Calif., 1971-72, resident in ob-gyn., 1972-75; physician Group Health Assn., Washington, 1975-87; pvt. practice Mililani, Hawaii, 1987—; med. staff sec. Wahiawa (Hawaii) Gen. Hosp., 1994—. Mem. Am. Coll. Ob-Gyn., Am. Soc. Colposcopy and Cervical Pathology, Hawaii Med. Assn., Sigma Kappa, Alpha Omega Alpha. Democrat. Office: 95-1249 Meheula Pkwy B-10A Mililani HI 96789-1762

GARDNER, TERRY LYNN, quality control inspector; b. Artesia, Calif., Oct. 26, 1951; d. Leslie Wilson and Velva Amy (Dufur) G. AA, Cypress Coll., 1983; Assoc. of Applied Sci., ITT Tech. Sch., 1992. Ordained reverend World Christian Ministries, 1993. Tchr. piano Community Christian Day Sch., Anaheim, Calif., 1970-79; assembler Lear Siegler, Inc., Anaheim, 1980-81; quality control inspector Apple Computer, Garden Grove, Calif., 1983-85, Allen Bradley, Fullerton, Calif., 1985-86, Innovative Sensors, Inc., Anaheim, 1986-88, McDonnell Douglass, Santa Ana, Calif., 1989; receiving inspector U.S. Divers, Santa Ana, 1989-90; quality control inspector ITT Cannon, Santa Ana, 1991-93; engrng. lab. technician McGaw, Irvine, Calif., 1993. Contbr. poetry: Great Poems of the Western World, 1990 (Golden Poet award 1990). Pres. Sci. Fiction Club of Cypress Coll., 1982-83. Republican. Home: PO Box 4427 North Hollywood CA 91617

GARELICK, MAUREEN PATRICIA JANE, editor; b. London, Apr. 9, 1960; arrived in U.S., 1981; d. Lewis Isaac and Deborah Beryl (Zecanowsky) G. BA in Social Sci. with honors, Bristol (Eng.) Poly. U., 1981; MA in Polit. Sci., U. Calif., Santa Barbara, 1983, CPhil, 1985. Promotion coord. UCSB Arts & Lectures, Santa Barbara, Calif.; editor ABC-Clio, Santa Barbara, 1989—. Contbr. articles to profl. jours. Commr. Payso Soccer League, Santa Barbara, 1992-93; mem. com. Kristiansen Classic Charity Soccer Tournament, Santa Barbara, 1992-93; active youth project planning com. Santa Barbara Gay and Lesbian Resource Ctr. Regent's fellow U. Calif., 1985-86. Office: ABC-Clio 130 Cremona Goleta CA 93117

GARFIELD, JOAN BARBARA, statistics educator; b. Milw., May 4, 1950; d. Sol. L. and Amy L. (Nusbaum) G.; m. Michael G. Luxenberg, Aug. 17, 1980; children: Harlan Ross and Rebecca Ellen (twins). Student, U. Chgo., 1968; BS, U. Wis., 1972; MA, U. Minn., 1978, PhD, 1981. Assoc. prof. ednl. psychology The Gen. Coll., U. Minn., Mpls., 1981—, coord. rsch. and evaluation, 1984-87. Mem. Am. Ednl. Rsch. Assn., Math. Assn. Am., Nat. Coun. Tchrs. of Math., Nat. Psychology Math. Edn., Internat. Assn. for Statis. Edn., Am. Statis. Assn., Internat. Study Group on Learning Probability and Stats. (sec. 1987—). Jewish. Office: U Minn Gen Coll 140 Appleby Minneapolis MN 55455

GARFIELD, NANCY ELLEN, marketing and advertising professional; b. Cin., Sept. 18, 1954; d. M. Robert and Pegge (Gerber) G. BA in Econs., Rollins Coll., 1976; MBA, Xavier U., 1980. Mktg. svcs. specialist Am. Standard, Inc., Cin., 1977-81; mktg. specialist F.H. Lawson Co., Cin., 1982-83; dir. mktg. Talsol Corp./Mar-Hyde subs. RPM Inc., Cin., 1983-88; mktg. and advt. cons. Cin., 1988—. Mgmt. advisor Cin. Jr. Achievement, 1978-81; bd. dirs. Cin. sect. mem. Nat. Coun. Jewish Women, 1992—, v.p. community svc., 1993—; mem. Cin. Civic Confederation, 1991—; mem. recruitment com. Big Bros./Big Sisters Assn. Cin., 1992—. Mem. Losantiville C. of C. (ltd. bd. dirs. 1986-89, pres. 1989), Cin. Indsl. Advertisers, Chi Omega.

GARFIELD, PHYLLIS HELEN, educational consultant; b. Columbus, Nebr., Aug. 21, 1950; d. Carl and Wilma (Phillips) Rafferty; m. Alan J. Garfield, Sept. 2, 1979; children: Eliot, Margaret, Carolan. AA, Platt C.C., Columbus, Nebr., 1972; BA, Midland Luth. Coll., Fremont, Nebr., 1974; student, Phillips U., Marburg, Germany, 1973-74; postgrad., Creighton U., 1975-79. Asst. to dean of students Marycrest Coll., Davenport, Iowa, 1980-83; cons. and v.p. Digigraphic Systems, Inc., Davenport, 1985—; internat. travel advisor Digigraphic Systems, Inc., Meenaleck, Ireland, 1992—; internat. study advisor Teikyo Marycrest U., Davenport, 1981—. Pres. Temple Emanuel Sisterhood, Davenport, 1993—. Fulbright fellow, Marburg, 1973-74. Home: 34 Oak Ln Davenport IA 52803-3124

GARGIULO, ANDREA W., lawyer; b. Hartford, Conn., Apr. 26, 1946; d. Charles M. and Irma S. (Rubin) Weiner; m. Richard A. Gargiulo, Nov. 26, 1975; 1 child, John K. BA, Smith Coll., 1968; JD cum laude, Suffolk U., 1972. Bar: Mass. 1972, U.S. Dist. Ct. Mass. 1975, U.S. Ct. Appeals (11th cir.) 1981, U.S. Supreme Ct. 1983. Asst. dist. atty. Middlesex County, Mass., 1972-75; chmn. Boston Fin. Commn., 1975-77; counsel Gargiulo, Rudnick, & Gargiulo, Boston, 1976—; chmn. Boston Licensing Bd., 1977-89; master U.S. Dist. Ct. Mass., Boston, 1976-83; lectr. Northeastern U. Coll. Criminal Justice, Boston, 1978, 80; bd. dirs. Arbella Mut. Ins. Co.; host TV show Women Today. Commr. Mass. Ethics Commn., 1985-88; bd. overseers Children's Hosp., Boston, 1983—, mem. bd. of bar overseers, 1992—. Mem. Boston Bar Assn. (coun. 1982-85), Assn. Trial Lawyers Am., Mass. Acad. Trial Attys., Mass. Bar Assn., Bay Club, Beacon Hill Garden Club, Harvard Mus. Assn., Wianno Yacht Club, Univ. Club. Democrat. Home: 13 W Cedar St Boston MA 02108-1211 Office: 66 Long Wharf Boston MA 02110

GARIBALDI, MARIE LOUISE, state supreme court justice; b. Jersey City, Nov. 26, 1934; d. Louis J. and Marie (Serventi) G. BA, Conn. Coll., 1956; LLB, Columbia U., 1959; LLM in Tax. Law, NYU, 1963. Atty. Office of Regional Counsel, IRS, N.Y.C., 1960-66; assoc. McCarter & English, Newark, 1966-69; ptnr. Riker, Danzig, Scherer & Hyland, Newark, 1969-82; assoc. justice N.J. Supreme Court, Newark, 1982—. Contbr. articles to profl. jours. Trustee St. Peter's Coll.; co-chmn. Thomas Kean's campaign for Gov. of N.J., 1981, mem. transition team, 1981; mem. Gov. Byrne's Commn. on Dept. of Commerce, 1981. Recipient Disting. Alumni award NYU Law Alumni of N.J., 1982; recipient Disting. Alumni award Columbia U., 1982. Fellow Am. Bar Found.; mem. N.J. Bar Assn. (pres. 1982), Columbia U. Sch. Law Alumni Assn. (bd. dirs.). Roman Catholic. Home: 34 Kingswood Rd Weehawken NJ 07087-6930

GARISON, LYNN LASSITER, real estate executive; b. El Dorado, Ark., Dec. 19, 1954; d. Robert Weaver and Iris Amy (Horton) Lassiter; m. James Wallace Garison, Jr., Dec. 11, 1982. Student, Randolph-Macon Woman's Coll., 1973-76; BS, Tex. A&M U., 1978. Lic. real estate broker, Ark., Okla., Tex. From broker assoc. to regional mgr. J. B. Goodwin, Realtors, Residential, Inc., Austin, Tex., 1979-82; comml. broker assoc. Christon Co., Realtors, Inc., Dallas, 1983-87; v.p. Dallas Mkt. Ctr., Dallas, 1987-89; regional v.p. Tenenbaum and Assocs., Inc., Dallas, 1989-92; pres. Artemis Co., Dallas, 1992—; bd. dirs. Consumer Credit Counseling Svc. Bd. dirs. Dallas Coun. World Affairs; mem. Mayor's Task Force on Child Abuse, Highland Pk. Presbyn. Ch. Mem. DAR, Daus. of the Republic of Tex., Nat. Assn. Corp. Real Estate, Cert. Comml. Investment Mem., Urban Land Inst., Rotary Internat. (bd. dirs. Park Cities club). Home: 4317 Greenbrier Dr Dallas TX 75225-6640

GARLAND, HILARY DUQUE, mental health therapist; b. L.A., May 21, 1966; d. William May and Louise Fleming (Grant) G.; m. Philip Luethi Ritcheson, Oct. 19, 1991. BA in Classics, Scripps Coll., Claremont, Calif., 1989; MS in Edn., U. So. Calif., 1991; MA in Psychology, Marymount U., 1992, postgrad., 1993—. Cert. tchr., Calif. Tchr. L.A. Unified Sch. Dist., 1989-92; counselor Fairfax Juvenile Detention Ctr., Fairfax, Va., 1992-93; vocat. therapist Green Door, Washington, 1993—; therapist Family Preservation Svcs., Inc., Alexandria, Va., 1993—. Mem. APA, ACA, NEA, Phi Delta Kappa, Psi Chi. Democrat. Roman Catholic.

GARLAND, JOAN BRUDER, social worker, psychologist; b. Cleve., Sept. 30, 1931; d. Henry Ignatius and Mary (Maher) Bruder; A.B., Mt. Holyoke Coll., 1952; postgrad. Wellesley Coll., 1952-53, U. Sao Paulo (Brazil), 1965-66; M.S., Sarah Lawrence Coll., 1974; M.S. in Social Work, Columbia U., 1977, PhD in Psychology, The Union Inst., 1986; Diplomate Clin. Social Work. m. Paul Griffith Garland, Aug. 28, 1954; children—Bonnie (dec.), Patrick, John, Cathryn. Grad. asst., chemistry dept. Wellesley (Mass.) Coll., 1952-53; chemist Polaroid Corp., Cambridge, Mass., 1953-54, 55-56; CAPES research fellow U. Sao Paulo, 1954-55; clin. instr. retardation N.Y. Med. Coll., Valhalla, 1978-80; social worker, psychiat. day treatment program Jewish Child Care Assn., Pleasantville (N.Y.) Cottage Sch., 1980; family research investigator Albert Einstein Coll. Medicine, Bronx, N.Y., 1982-86; pvt. practice, 1992—. Founder, v.p. Crime Victims Assistance Agy., Inc., 1981-83. Treas. council Girl Scouts, Sao Paulo, 1965-67; bd. dirs. PTA, 1972-73; bd. deacons Scarsdale (N.Y.) Congregational Ch., 1975; patient rep. White Plains (N.Y.) Med. Center, 1977. Lic. psychologist, clin. social worker, Fla.; cert. in family therapy, Center for Family Learning, Phila. Child Guidance Ctr.; cert. ind. social worker, Conn. Fellow Soc. Clin. Social Work Psychotherapists; mem. APA, Nat. Assn. Social Workers, Acad. Cert. Social Workers. Clubs: Mt. Holyoke, Wellesley (Palm Beach County). Home: 2156 Date Palm Rd Boca Raton FL 33432-7918

GARLAND, KIMBER AILINE, federal agency administrator; b. Lorain, Ohio, Sept. 4, 1963; d. Samuel David Garland and Helen (Middlebrooks) Sharp. BS, U. Akron, 1986; MS, George Mason U., 1991. Programmer/analyst CBS Records, Inc., Terre Haute, Ind., 1986-88; project mgr. Ctrl. Imagery Office, U.S. Govt., Washington, 1988-94; help desk svc. mgr. Ctrl. Imagery Office, U.S. Govt., Dunn Loring, Va., 1995—. Bd. dirs., sec. Bread for the City, Washington, 1993; mentor Youth at Risk, Washington, 1989—. Named Committed Ptnr. of the Month, Washington Area Project for Youth, 1990, Super Hooper Supporter, Hoop it Up-Nat. Tour, 1989. Mem. Assn. for Computing Machinery, Nat. Soc. Black Engrs. Democrat. Baptist. Home: 5716 Sweetway Ter Capital Hts MD 20743-5525

GARLAND, LARETTA MATTHEWS, educational psychologist, nursing educator; b. Jacksonville, Fla.; d. Wilburn L. and Clyde-Marian (Chamberlin) Matthews; diploma Fla. State Sch. Nursing, 1942; BSN, Emory U., 1950, MEd, 1953; BA in Edn., U. Fla., 1951; cert. cardiovascular nurse specialty Tex. Med. Center, 1965; EdD, U. Ga., 1975; postgrad. in counseling and guidance Ga. State U., 1969, grad. cert. in gerontology, 1981; Cert. nat. counselor, 1986; m. John B. Garland, Mar. 2, 1946; children: John Barnard, Brien Freeling, Amy-Gwin. Office and staff nurse, Lakeland, Fla., 1942, 45; nurse ARC, Buffalo, 1956; asst. prof. nursing Med. Coll. Ga., 1965-67; instr. Emory U., 1952-54, assoc. prof., 1967-71, prof., 1972-86; prof. emeritus, 1987—; ednl. psychologist, dir. gerontol. nurse practitioner program, 1978-80, asst. to dean, 1983-86. Author: (with Carol Bush) Coping Behavior and Nursing, 1982; editor: Gerontological Nursing Handbook, 1993; contbr. articles to profl. jours. Served with Nurse Corps, U.S. Army, 1942-45. Decorated Bronze Star; recipient Outstanding Teaching award Emory U. Sch. Nursing Grad. Srs., 1977, appreciation award So. Region Constituent Leagues, Nat. League for Nursing award, 1987, Mabel Korsell award of appreciation Ga. League for Nursing, 1987, Spl. Recognition award Ga. Nurses Assn., 1988, 90, Nurse of Yr. award, 1992, appreciation Ga. Assn. Nursing Students, 1990, Van de Vrede award Ga. League Nursing, 1993; HEW fellow, 1967-68. Mem. APA, AACD, Am. Nurses Assn., Ga. Assn. Nursing Students (hon.), Nat. League Nursing, Bus. and Profl. Women, China Burma India VA Assn., Hump Pilots Assn., Fla. Fed. Garden Clubs, Fla. Fed. Womens Clubs, Nat. Assn. Women Vet. (steering com.), Alpha Chi Omega, Sigma Theta Tau, Kappa Delta Pi, Alpha Kappa Delta, Omicron Delta Kappa. Methodist. Office: Emory U Nell Hodgson Woodruff Sch Nursing Atlanta GA 30322

GARLAND, MEG, advertising executive; b. Ft. Worth, Sept. 19, 1946; d. Robert Neal and Mary Jewell (Saul) G.; m. David Sterlin Barnard, June 10, 1967; children: Blayn Elizabeth, Mary Blayr. B.Advt.Art and Design, Tex. Tech U., 1969. Teaching asst. Tex. Tech U., Lubbock, 1968; graphic designer Storm Printing Corp., Dallas, 1969; art dir. Ratcliff Advt., Dallas, 1969-71; owner, prin. Triad Assocs., Waco, Tex., 1972—; bd. dirs. Kalyn/Siebert Inc., Gatesville, Tex. Scholarship grantor Tex. Tech. U., 1988—; bd. dirs. Am. Cancer Soc., Waco and McLennan County, 1989-91, Freeman Ctr., 1994—. Recipient Spl. award Waco Assn. Retarded Citizens, 1976, Tex. Assn. Retarded Citizens, 1977, Pathfinders, YWCA, 1988, varous design awards, 1966—. Mem. Hewitt C. of C. (pres. 1994), Waco Founder Lions Club. Methodist. Office: Triad Assocs 7702 Woodway Dr Waco TX 76712-3802

GARLAND, SYLVIA DILLOF, lawyer; b. N.Y.C., June 4, 1919; d. Morris and Frieda (Gassner) Dillof; m. Albert Garland, May 4, 1942; children: Margaret Garland Clunie, Paul B. BA, Bklyn. Coll., 1939; JD cum laude, N.Y. Law Sch., 1960. Bar: N.Y., 1960, U.S. Ct. Appeals (2d cir.), 1965, U.S. Ct. Claims, 1965, U.S. Supreme Ct., 1967, U.S. Customs Ct., 1972, U.S. Ct. Appeals (5th cir.), 1979. Assoc. firm Borden, Skidell, Fleck and Steindler, Jamaica, N.Y., 1960-61, Fields, Zimmerman, Skodnick & Segall, Jamaica, 1961-65, Marshall, Brater, Greene, Allison & Tucker, N.Y.C., 1965-68; law sec. to N.Y. Supreme Ct. justice, Suffolk County, 1968-70; ptnr. firm Hofheimer, Gartlir & Gross, N.Y.C., 1970—; asst. adj. prof. N.Y. Law Sch., 1974-79; mem. com. on character and fitness N.Y. State Supreme Ct., 1st Jud. Dept., 1985—, vice chmn., 1991—. Author: Workman's Compensation, 1957; Wills, 1959; Labor Law, 1962; contbg. author: Guardians and Custodians, 1970; editor-in-chief Law Rev. Jour., N.Y. Law Forum, 1959-60 (service award 1960); contbr. article to mag. Trustee N.Y. Law Sch., 1979-90, trustee emeritus, 1991—; pres. Oakland chpt. B'nai Brith, Bayside, N.Y., 1955-57. Recipient Disting. Alumnus award, N.Y. Law Sch., 1978. Mem. ABA (litigation sect.), N.Y. State Bar Assn., Queen's County Bar Assn. (sec. civil practice 1960-79), N.Y. Law Sch. Alumni Assn. (pres. 1976-77), N.Y. Law Forum Alumni Assn. (pres. 1963-65). Jewish. Home: 425 E 58th St New York NY 10022-2300

GARMAN, TERESA AGNES, state legislator; b. Ft. Dodge, Iowa, Aug. 29, 1937; d. John Clement and Barbara Marie (Korsa) Lennon; m. Merle A. Garman, Aug. 5, 1961; children: Laura Ann Garman Hansen, Rachel Irene Garman Coder, Robert Sylvester, Sarah Teresa Garman Powers. Grad. high sch., Ft. Dodge. With employee relations dept. 3M Co., Ames, Iowa, 1974-86; mem. Iowa Ho. of Reps., Des Moines, 1986—. Asst. majority leader, mem. platform com., del. Rep. Nat. Conv., 1988, del., mem. platform com., 1992; mem. Iowa Rep. Ctrl. Com. Mem. Rep. Farm Policy Coun., Story County Rep. Women, Story County Pork Prodrs., Farm Bur., Story City C. of C., Nev. C. of C. Roman Catholic. Home: RR 2 Ames IA 50010-9802 Office: State Capitol Des Moines IA 50319

GARMEL, MARION BESS SIMON, journalist; b. El Paso, Tex., Oct. 15, 1936; d. Marcus and Frieda (Alfman) Simon; m. Raymond Louis Garmel, Nov. 28, 1965 (dec. Feb. 1986); 1 child, Cynthia Rogers. Student, U. Tex., El Paso, 1954-55; BJ, U. Tex., 1958. Exec. sec. Nat. Student Assn., Phila., 1958-59, pub. rels. dir., 1960-61; sec. World Assembly Youth, Paris, Brussels, 1959-60; dictationist Wall Street Jour., Washington, 1961; libr., staff writer Nat. Observer, Silver Spring, Md., 1961-70; art critic Indpls. News, 1971-91, editor Free Time sect., 1975-91, critic radio and TV, 1991—. Mem. Nat. Fedn. Press Women (1st Place Critics award 1974), Hadassah Women's Zionist Orgn. Am. (life), Women's Press Club Ind. (1st Place Critics award 1993). Jewish. Home: 226 E 45th St Indianapolis IN 46205-1712 Office: Indpls News 307 N Pennsylvania St Indianapolis IN 46204-1811

GARMIRE, ELSA MEINTS, electrical engineering educator, consultant; b. Buffalo, Nov. 9, 1939; d. Ralph E. and Nelle (Gubser) Meints; m. Gordon P. Garmire, June 11, 1961 (div. 1975); children: Lisa, Marla; m. Robert Heathcote Russell, Feb. 4, 1979. AB in Physics, Harvard U., 1961; PhD in Physics, MIT, 1965. Rsch. scientist NASA Electronics Rsch. Ctr., Cambridge, Mass., 1965-66; rsch. fellow Calif. Inst. Tech., Pasadena, 1966-73; sr. rsch. scientist U. So. Calif. Ctr. for Laser Studies, L.A., 1974-78, prof. elec. engring. and physics, 1981-92, assoc. dir. Ctr. for Laser Studies, 1978-83, dir., 1984—, William Hogue prof. of engring., 1992—; vis. fellow Standard Telecommunication Labs., Eng., 1973-74; cons. Aerospace Corp., L.A., 1975-91, sci. adv. bd. Air Force, Washington, 1985-89, TRW, L.A., 1988-89, McDonnell Douglas, St. Louis, 1990-93. Contbr. over 200 sci. papers and articles to profl. publs.; patentee in field. Recipient Soroptimist Achievement award Soroptimist Club L.A., 1970, K.C. Black Award N.E. Electronics Rsch. and Engring. Meeting, 1972, Soc. Women Engrs. Achievement award 1994, U. So. Calif. Rschr. award, 1994; named Mademoiselle Women of Yr. Mademoiselle Mag., 1970. Fellow IEEE (bd. dirs. 1985-89), Optical Soc. Am. (bd. dirs. 1983-86, pres. 1992, pres. 1993), Am. Phys. Soc. (bd. dirs. 1994—); mem. NAE (life), Soc. Women Engrs. (sr., life), Harvard Radcliffe Club (v.p. 1984-86). Democrat. Office: U So Calif Ctr for Laser Studies DRB17 Los Angeles CA 90089-1112

GARNER, CARLENE ANN, orchestra administrator; b. Dec. 17, 1945; d. Carl A. and Ruth E. (Mathison) Timblin; m. Adelbert L. Garner, Feb. 17, 1964; children: Bruce A., Brent A. BA, U. Puget Sound, 1983. Adminstrv. dir. Balletacoma, 1984-87; exec. dir. Tacoma Symphony, 1987—; cons. Wash. PAVE, Tacoma, 1983-84. Treas. Coalition for the Devel. of the Arts, 1992-94; pres. Wilson High Sch. PTA, Tacoma, 1983-85; chmn. Tacoma Sch. Vol. Adv. Bd., 1985-87; pres. Emmanuel Luth. Ch., Tacoma, 1984-86, chmn. future steering com., 1987-93; sec.-treas. Tacoma-Narrows Conf., 1987—; trustee Tacoma Luth. Home. Mem. Northwest Devel. Officers Assn. (bd. mem.), Am. Symphony Orch. League, Jr. Women's Club Tacoma (pres. 1975-76, pres. Peninsula dist. 1984-86), Wash. State Fedn. Women's Clubs (treas. 1988-90, 3d v.p. 1990-92, 2d v.p. 1992-94, 1st v.p. 1994—, Clubwoman of Yr. 1977, Oustanding FREE chmn. Gen. Fedn.), Commencement Bay Woman's Club (pres. 1990-92, trustee), Pierce Country Club. Lutheran. Home: 1115 N Cheyenne St Tacoma WA 98406-3624 Office: Tacoma Symphony PO Box 19 Tacoma WA 98401-0019

GARNER, CAROL MURPHEY, nursing educator; b. Warrenton, Va., July 5, 1956; d. Randolph Clay III and Donna (Medberry) Murphey; m. James Luther Garner II, June 1, 1991. BS, Radford U., 1979; MSN, U. N.C., Greensboro, 1982, EdD, 1987. Staff nurse Rockingham Meml. Hosp., Harrisonburg, Va., 1979-80, U. N.C. Meml. Hosp., Chapel Hill, 1980-81; asst. head nurse Moses H. Cone Meml. Hosp., Greensboro, 1982-87; asst. prof. Radford (Va.) U., 1987-89; asst. prof. nursing Bradley U., Peoria, Ill., 1990-93, U. North Fla., 1993—; panelist, speaker for cmty./regional nat. nursing confs. and workshops. Mem. ANA, Fla. Nurses Assn., Sigma Theta Tau. Presbyn. Democrat. Home: 1713 River Oaks Rd Jacksonville FL 32207 Office: U North Fla Coll Health Dept Nursing 4567 St Johns Bluff Rd Jacksonville FL 32224

GARNER, CELESTE DIXON, etiquette consultant, writer; b. Birmingham, Ala., July 30, 1934; d. Joel Terrell and Margaret (Wright) Dixon.; m. Mabry E. Garner; 1 child, Ted A. Springer; stepchildren: Douglas M. Garner, Kathy G. Nelson, Gary L. Garner. Grad., U. Ala., 1991, Washington Sch. Protocol. Cert. etiquette cons. Owner, dir. Celeste Garner Sch. of Protocol. Author: The Special Irrevocable Trust Fund Program, 1973, The Special Trust Fund Program, 1978, The Biographical/Autobiographical Lecture Series. Mem. women's com. Ala. Symphony Assn., Women's Aux. Birmingham Human Soc., Birmingham Opera Guild, Rep. Women of the South, Women's Aux. to Salvation Army, Arlington Hist. Assn., Honors Day U. Ala.; sponsored exec. United Way, 1981. Mem. Jefferson County Med. Aux., Aux. to Med. Assn. State of Ala., AMA Aux., Birmingham Bot. Soc. Aux., Newcomen Soc., The Club, Summit Club, Birmingham Music Club, Triangle Honor Soc. Home: 2700 Lakeland Trl Birmingham AL 35243-3024

GARNER, GIROLAMA THOMASINA, educational administrator, educator; b. Muskegon, Mich., Sept, 15, 1923; d. John and Martha Ann (Thomas) Funaro; student Muskegon Jr. Coll., 1941; B.A., Western Mich. U., 1944, M.A. in Counseling and Guidance, 1958; Ed.D., U. Ariz., 1973; m. Charles Donald Garner, Sept. 16, 1944 (dec.); 1 dau., Linda Jeannette Garner Blake. Elem. tchr., Muskegon and Tucson, 1947-77; counselor Erickson Elem. Sch., Tucson, 1978-79; prin. Hudlow Elem. Sch., Tucson, 1979-87, adj. prof. U. Ariz., 1973—, Tuscon Pima Community Coll., 1981—, Prescott Coll., 1986—; mem. Ariz. Com. Tchr. Evaluation and Cert., 1976-78; del. NEA convs. Active ARC, Crippled Children's Soc., UNESCO, U.S.-China People's Friendship Assn., DAV Aux., Rincon Renegades; bd. dirs. Hudlow Community Sch., 1973-76. Recipient Apple award for teaching excellence Pima Community Coll., 1982. Mem. Nat. Assn. Sci. Tchrs., Tucson Edn. Assn., Ariz. Edn. Assn., NEA, Assn. Supervision and Curriculum Devel., AAUW, Tucson Adminstrs., Pima County Retired Tchrs., Delta Kappa Gamma, Kappa Rho Sigma, Kappa Delta Pi. Democrat. Christian Scientist. Home: 6922 E Baker St Tucson AZ 85710-2230 Office: 502 N Caribe Ave Tucson AZ 85710-2242

GARNER, JO ANN STARKEY, educator; b. Ft. Hamilton, N.Y., Dec. 25, 1934; d. Joseph Wheeler and Irene Dorothy (Vogt) Starkey; m. James Gayle Garner, Mar. 2, 1957; children: Mary Vivian Pine, Margaret Susan Gillis, Kathryn Lynn. BA in History, Govt., Law, U. Tex., Austin, 1956; postgrad., Trinity U., 1973. Cert. deaf edn. and elem. tchr., Tex. Kindergarten tchr. Platenstrasse Internat. Sch., Frankfurt, Fed. Republic Germany, 1964-66; tchr. of deaf Sunshine Cottage Sch. for Deaf, San Antonio, 1966—; speech cons. Trinity U., 1978, cooperating tchr., 1978-87. Mem. San Antonio Fiesta Commn. Mem. Tex. Alexander Graham Bell Assn. (charter), Tex. State Geneal. and Hist. Soc., San Antonio Geneal. and Hist. Soc., The Bright Shawl, Rep. Nat. Com., Sunshine Sch. for Deaf (supporting mem.), German-Texan Heritage Soc., Ind. Hist. Soc., Pioneers of Ind., Alpha Delta Pi, Ill. Geneal. Soc., Pioneers of Ill. Republican. Roman Catholic. Home: 2027 Edgehill Dr San Antonio TX 78209-2023 Office: Sunshine Cottage Sch for Deaf 103 Tuleta Dr San Antonio TX 78212-3196

GARNER, MARY JANE, cosmetics company executive; b. Terre Haute, Ind., Oct. 6, 1916; d. Thomas Law and Myra (Short) Kemp; m. William Stanley Garner, Jan. 11, 1941 (div. Nov. 1965); 1 child, William Stanley. Student Lindenwood Coll. for Women, 1935, John Heron Art Sch., 1936-38; grad. Parsons Sch. Design, 1940, Planning for Preservation Inst. of Govt., U. N.C., 1972; student writers workshop Ind. U., 1967. Model made-to-order dept. Bergdorft Goodman, N.Y.C., 1940-41; asst. buyer Crystal Room, Indpls., 1965-66; proof cons. fact Inc., St. Louis, 1968-69; pres., founder Mary Jane Garner Cosmetics, Chapel Hill, N.C., 1985—. Sec. Chapel Hill Hist. Soc., 1973-74, bd. dirs., 1973-75; mem. N.C. Bicentennial Com., 1974-78, also mem. grants com.; mem. Chapel Hill Bicentenial Commn., 1974-76; Republican precinct chmn., Chapel Hill, 1972; co-chmn. Holshouser for Gov., Orange County, N.C., 1972; Rep. precinct registrar, Chapel Hill, 1973-75; pres. Rep. Women's Club, Chapel Hill, 1973-74; chmn. state conv. N.C. Fedn. Rep. Women, 1974, Bicentennial chmn., 1974-76, legis. chmn., 1976-77, area v.p., 1978-80, pub. relations chmn., 1981-83, mem. credentials com. for nat. conv., 1980; mem. U.S. Senate Minority Leader's Citizens Adv. Com., 1974-76; mem. nat. adv. bd. Am. Security Council, 1978-79; mem. bldg. com. N.C. Rep. Hdqrs., 1978; mem. Nat. Presdl. Adv. Commn., 1989—. Recipient cert. appreciation Am. Revolution Bicentenial, 1976, Spl. Recognition award Am. Security Council, 1979, Presdl. Achievement award Pres. Reagan, 1982; named most improved golfer Golf Digest Mag., 1978. Club: Chapel Hill Country (bd. govs. 1975-76). Office: Mary Jane Garner Cosmetics 100 Howell Ln Chapel Hill NC 27514-3246

GARNER, MELANIE ANN, trainer, writer, editor; b. Cin., Aug. 14, 1942; d. Arthur Henry and Esther Jeannette (Denny) Klotter; m. Ronald Louis Garner, Dec. 26, 1964 (div. June 1982); children: Erin Kathleen, Shannon Colleen, Sean Brendan; m. Michael Cody Berry, July 6, 1985. BS in Edn., U. Cin., 1964, MA in English Lit., 1980. Cert. secondary sch. tchr., Ohio, Skills for an Empowered Workforce and Performance Mgmt. instr. Tchr. Cin. Pub. Schs., 1964-68; instr. English U. Cin., 1980-86, mng. editor Urban Resources, 1984-89; mgr. tng. svcs., environ. svcs. dept. U. Cin. Hosp., 1990-94; edn. coor. for patient focused care Christ Hosp./Univ. Hosp./Franciscan Health Care Systems, Cin., 1994—; freelance writer/editor, Cin., 1976—; bd. dirs., com. chair Literacy Network of Greater Cin., 1993—. Contbg. author: Minorities in America: Annotated Bibliography, 1976, 77, 78. Founding mem., bd. pres. Women's Rsch. and Devel. Ctr., Cin., 1987-93. Recipient Gov.'s Workplace Literacy award State of Ohio, 1993. Mem. Assn. for Women Adminstrs. (bd. dirs. 1992-93). Democrat. Methodist. Office: Christ Hosp Cincinnati OH 45219

GARNER, MILDRED MAXINE, retired religious studies educator; b. nr. Liberty, N.C., Mar. 15, 1919; d. Robert Monroe and Maize (Kimrey) G. B.A., U. N.C., Greensboro, 1939; M.A., Union Theol. Sem., N.Y.C., 1946; Ph.D., U. Aberdeen, Scotland, 1952. Tchr. English, history, journalism Roanoke Rapids, N.C., 1939, 41-42; asst. editor Bibl. Recorder, Raleigh, N.C., 1940; dir. religious activities Woman's Coll., U. N.C. at Greensboro, 1942-50; assoc. prof. religion Meredith Coll., Raleigh, 1952-58; prof. religion Sweet Briar (Va.) Coll., 1958—, Wallace Eugene Rollins prof. religion, 1969-84, prof. emeritus, 1984—, chmn. dept., 1961-62, 63-72, 74-78, 81-84; fellow summer seminar history and culture India U. Va., 1964, summer seminar history and culture China, 1965; summer seminar South Asia Duke U., 1966, summer seminar Banaras Hindu U., Varanasi, India, 1977; Fulbright scholar U. Aberdeen, 1950-51, 51-52; program advanced religious studies fellow Union Theol. Sem., 1955-56; Am. Inst. Indian Studies fellow, Poona, India, 1962-63, Inst. Judaism, Vanderbilt Div. Sch., Nashville, 1979; deacon Pullen Meml. Bapt. Ch., Raleigh, 1952-58. Author: First Baptist Church, Liberty, North Carolina, 1886-1986, 1986. Trustee 1st Bapt. Ch., Liberty, N.C., 1991—, Chatham Hosp., Siler City, N.C., 1992-94; chmn. adv. com. Liberty Sr. Adults Assn., 1993—; grand marshall Holiday Parade, Liberty, 1991. Mem. Fulbright Alumni Assn., Phi Beta Kappa. Republican. Baptist. Lodge: Rotary (hon. Liberty chpt.). Home: PO Box 427 Liberty NC 27298-0427

GARNER, PAMELA WATKINS, psychology educator; b. Roswell, N.Mex., Oct. 6, 1961; d. Eddie Jr. and Bonnie Jean (Harris) Watkins; m. George Robert Garner, May 22, 1985. BSW, U. Tenn., 1982; MA, U. Houston, 1988; PhD, Tex. A&M U., 1992. Predoctoral fellow U. Tex. Med. Sch., Houston, 1989-92; postdoctoral fellow U. Houston, 1992-93; asst. prof. psychology U. Houston-Clear Lake, 1993—. Contbr. articles to profl. publs. Presch. tchr. Wheeler Ave. Bapt. Ch., Houston, 1991, 92, 93. NIH grantee, 1994. Mem. APA, Soc. Rsch. in Child Devel., Internat. Soc. on Infant Studies. Office: U Houston-Clear Lake 2700 Bay Area Blvd Houston TX 77058-1002

GARNES, JANE E., photographer, educator; b. Balt., Apr. 18, 1943. BFA, Ohio Wesleyan U., 1965, cert. in student edn., 1967; MA summa cum laude, William Paterson Coll., 1982. Assoc. editor Jour. Audio Engring. Soc. Harvey Assocs., N.Y.C., 1965-66; mem. art faculty No. Highlands, Allendale, N.J., 1967—; owner, pres. Garnes Mktg. Svcs., Inc., Ramsey, N.J., 1980—; mem. English faculty Fondation Permanent, Epernay, France, 1974-75. Author: The Complete Handbook of Leathercrafting, 1981; contbr. articles to profl. publs.; exhbns. in jours., newspapers, U.S. and France, 1977—; photographs in jours., newspapers, books, publs., and art catalogues, U.S., France, and Venezuela, 1978—. Mem. NAFE, AAUW, NOW (sec. N.J. chpt. 1986-92), Profl. Photographers Am., N.J. Orgn. Women Bus. Owners, Nat. Mus. Women in the Arts (charter), Kappa Delta Pi. Office: Garnes Mktg Svcs Inc Ten Elbert Ct Ramsey NJ 07446-1011

GARNETT, DEBBIE JANE, controller; b. Columbus, Ga., Apr. 2, 1964; d. Nelson Colson and Kazue (Tanaka) Peacock; m. James Scott Garnett, July 2, 1981; 1 child, Joseph Daulton. B in Acctg. magna cum laude, Troy State U., 1992. Mgmt. reporter Tom's Foods, Columbus, 1981-89; auditor Dougherty, McKinnon & Luby, Columbus, 1989-94; asst. contr. Hughston Orthopaedic Clinic, Columbus, 1994; contr. Victory Developers, Columbus, 1994—. Vol., chmn. allocation com. United Way, Columbus, 1992-94. Mem. AICPA, Ga. Soc. CPAs, Inst. Mgmt. Accts. (dir. of program 1992-93, 93-94). Republican. Methodist. Home: 65 Lee Rd 519 Phenix City AL 36867 Office: Victory Developers Inc 506 45th St Ste B-5 Columbus GA 31904

GAROFALO, DENISE ANNE, librarian, automation consultant; b. Norwich, N.Y., July 26, 1959; d. John Andrew and Irene Anne (Boucher) Listovitch; m. James Anthony Garofalo, Aug. 29, 1987. BA, SUNY, Albany, 1980, MLS, 1982. Libr. Pawtucket (R.I.) Pub. Libr., 1982-85; head tech. svcs. and automated systems Warwick (R.I.) Pub. Libr., 1985-87; automation cons. N.H. State Libr., Concord, 1987-89; automated systems mgr. Mid-Hudson Libr. System, Poughkeepsie, N.Y., 1989—; speaker N.H. Libr. Assn., N.Y. Libr. Assn., Computer in Librs. Editor: G Whiz!, 1988-89; reviewer Libr. Jour., 1983—, Libr. Resources and Tech. Svcs. mag., 1989—, Info. Today, 1990—, Public Library Quarterly, 1991—; mem. editorial bd. Footnotes, 1990-91; contbr. articles to profl. jours. Bd. dirs. Woodside Commons, 1987-89; mem. com. Milford Town Hall Auditorium Renovation, 1989, N.Y. State Libr. Automation Plan Biennial Rev. Com., 1992—. Mem. ALA (impact evaluations and tech. advocacy suubcom. tech. in pub. librs. com. 1991—, electronic doorway libr. implementation plan task force 1993—), Am. Soc. Info. Sci., New Eng. Libr. Assn., N.Y. Libr. Assn. (speaker), NAFE, AAUW, Nat. Trust for Hist. Preservation, Nat. Audubon Soc. Democrat. Roman Catholic. Office: Mid-Hudson Libr System 103 Market St Poughkeepsie NY 12601-4029

GARONZIK, SARA ELLEN, stage director; b. Phila., Jan. 12, 1951; d. Milton and Bernice (Kohn) G. BA in Spanish cum laude, Temple U., 1972. Producing artistic dir. The Phila. Theatre Co., 1980—. Bd. dirs. Greater Phila. Cultural Alliance, Artreach, Citizens for the Arts in Pa. Recipient prize Sigma Delta Pi, 1972. Office: Phila Theatre Co Bourse Bldg 111 S Independence Mall E Philadelphia PA 19106

GARR, TERI (ANN), actress; b. Lakewood, Ohio, 1952; m. John O'Neil, Nov. 1993; 1 adopted child, Molly. Began career as dancer performing with San Francisco Ballet at age 13; in original road show co. of West Side Story; stage appearences include One Crack Out, 1978, Broadway, 1978, Ladyhouse Blues, 1979, Night of 100 Stars II, 1985; appeared in films including Viva Las Vegas, Head, 1968, Maryjane, 1968, Moonshine War, 1970, The Conversation, 1974, Young Frankenstein, 1974, Won Ton Ton, The Dog Who Saved Hollywood, 1976, Oh God!, 1977, Close Encounters of the Third Kind, 1977, Mr. Mike's Mondo Video, 1979, The Black Stallion, 1979, Honky Tonk Freeway, 1981, The Escape Artist, 1982, Tootsie, 1982, One From the Heart, 1982, The Sting II, 1983, The Black Stallion Returns, 1983, Mr. Mom, 1983, Firstborn, 1984, After Hours, 1985, Miracles, 1987, Out Cold, 1988, Let It Ride, 1989, Short Time, 1990, Waiting for the Light, 1990, Mom and Dad Save the World, 1992, Dumb and Dumber, 1995; TV movies include Doctor Franken, 1980, Prime Suspect, 1982, The Winter of Our Discontent, 1983, To Catch a King, 1984, Intimate Strangers, 1986, Fresno, 1986, Pack of Lies, 1987, Teri Garr in FlapJack Floozie, 1988, Drive, She Said (Trying Times), 1987, Mother Goose Rock n Rhyme, Stranger in the Family, 1991, Deliver Them From Evil: The Taking of Alta View, 1992, Fugitive Nights: Danger in the Desert, 1993; regular on TV series The Sonny and Cher Comedy Review, 1974, Good and Evil, 1991, Good Advice, 1994, The Women of the House, 1995—; other TV appearances include Law and Order, 1976, Fresno, Late Night with David Letterman, The Frog Prince, Tales from the Crypt, Duckman (voice). Office: care Brillstein/Grey 9150 Wilshire Blvd Ste 350 Beverly Hills CA 90212*

GARRET, PAULA LYN, publishing company executive; b. N.Y.C., Oct. 17, 1951; d. Norman and Sandra (Gilden); m. James T. Ferrise, Sept. 13, 1987. BS in Communications summa cum laude, Boston U., 1973; MBA, Case Western Reserve U., 1982. Dir. print media Stern/Frank Advt., Boston, 1973-76; dir. advt. Am. Soc. Assn. Execs., Washington, 1976-80; mktg. cons. PG & Assocs., Cleve., 1980-82; assoc. dir. advt. Calif. State Bar Assn., San Francisco, 1982-83; dir. mktg. and advt. Cars & Parts mag. div. Amos Press, Sidney, Ohio, 1983-84, dir. mktg. sales, 1984-87; v.p., pub. Amos Press, Inc., Sidney, Ohio, 1987-92; assoc. pub. Hemmings Motor News, Bennington, Vt., 1992—. Co-author: (monograph) Effective Business to Business Advertising, 1982. Mem. Am. Mktg. Assn., Direct Mail Mktg. Assn., Am. Mgmt. Assn., Splty. Equipment Market Assn., Automotive Restoration Market Assn. (mem. select coun., chair comms. com.). Office: Hemmings Motor News Rt 9 Bennington VT 05201

GARRETSON, BONNIE MARIE, cardiac nurse; b. San Diego, Aug. 7, 1954; d. Neil E. Arney and Doris M. (Leslie) Arney Huff; m. William Cedric

Garretson, Jr., Sept. 3, 1972; children: Eric William, Jason Alan, Jeremy Edward. BSN, U. Tulsa, 1993; postgrad., U. Okla., 1994—. Clin. nurse II cardiac specialty St. Francis Hosp., Tulsa, 1989—. Vol. ARC, Tulsa; mem. quality assurance coun. St. Francis. Hillcrest Merit scholar, 1992, faculty scholar U. Tulsa, 1992, Philanthropic Edn. Org. scholar, 1992—. Mem. Sigma Theta Tau. Republican. Pentecostal. Home: 502 W 44 St Sand Springs OK 74063

GARRETT, CYNTHIA SUE, modeling agency and apparel company executive; b. Toledo, Feb. 9, 1957; d. Johnnie Harrison and Dorothy Vestina (Taylor) G. Degree in cosmetology, Tenn. State Bd. Vocat., 1980; grad., C.L.S. Advanced Acad., 1983; degree in computer and advanced art, U. Tenn., 1991; degree in advanced model tng., Sentell/Carson, 1992. Dept. mgr. Ardan Catalog Showroom, Knoxville, Tenn., 1980-82; mgr. Command Performance, Knoxville; hair designer Hair Works Inc., Knoxville; model various profl. orgns., throught U.S., 1981—; instr. model tng. Model Search, Sevierville, Tenn., 1990-91; instr. and dir. model tng. All Occasion Photo & Prodn., Sevierville, 1992; pres., CEO Divine Appointment Apparel, Knoxville, 1992—; founder, pres., prodr. Model Showcase U.S.A., Knoxville, 1992—; founder, pres., dir. instr. Fashion Showcase U.S.A., Tulsa, 1992—; speaker in field to various chs., confs. and profl. orgns., 1992—. Writer, dir., prodr.: (video) Model Showcase U.S.A., 1993—; author: Divine Appointment; mistress of ceremony: (TV spl.) Model Showcase U.S.A., 1992—. Vol. D.A.R.E., Tulsa, 1994, STREET Ministry, Tulsa, 1994, Prison Min., Tulsa, 1994. Mem. NAFE, Christian Bus. Womens Assn., Tulsa Bus. Women, Purity with Purpose (alumni 1993). Home: PO Box 35143 Tulsa OK 74153-0143 Office: Model Showcase USA Ste 205 7984 S Sheridan Tulsa OK 74133

GARRETT, DONNA IRVIN, librarian; b. Nashville, Nov. 4, 1946; d. Donald and Violet Loucile (Nelson) Irvin; m. Billy Gene Garrett, July 14, 1979. BA, Tenn. Tech. U., 1969; MS, Memphis State U., 1976, student, 1977-79. Cert. libr. and tchr., Tenn. Tchr. Met. Nashville Schs., 1970-73, Shelby County Schs., Germantown, Tenn., 1973-75; libr. Shelby County Schs., Memphis, 1975—. Recipient Career Ladder III Libr. award Tenn. State Dept. of Edn., 1986—; named S.W. Tenn. Region Tchr. of Yr., 1993. Mem. ALA, NEA, Tenn. Assn. Sch. Librs. (v.p. 1992-93, pres. 1993-95), Tenn. Edn. Assn., Shelby County Edn. Assn. (Outstanding Tchr. award 1985), Soc. Sch. Librs. Internat., Memphis State U. Alumni (Disting. Edn. Alumni award 1986), Delta Kappa Gamma (treas. 1990-92). Mem. Ch. of Christ.

GARRETT, ELIZABETH, legislative director, counsel; b. Oklahoma City, June 30, 1963; d. Robert D. and Jane (Thompson) G. BA in History with spl. distinction, U. Okla., 1985; JD, U. Va., 1988. Bar: Tex. 1988, D.C. 1989. Law clk. to Hon. Stephen Williams U.S. Ct. Appeals (D.C. cir.), 1988-89; law clk. to Hon. Thurgood Marshall U.S. Supreme Ct., 1989-90; legal adviser to Hon. Howard M. Holtzman Iran-U.S. Claims Tribunal, The Hague, The Netherlands, 1990-91; legal counsel, legis. asst. Senator David L. Boren, 1991-93, legis. dir., tax counsel, 1993—. Articles editor U. Va. Law Rev.; contbr. articles to profl. jours. Ewing fellow U. Okla. Mem. ABA, Fed. Bar Assn., Tex. Bar Assn., D.C. Bar Assn., Order of Coif, Mortar Bd., Phi Beta Kappa, Chi Omega. Office: Sen David L Boren D-Okla 453 Senate Russell Office Bldg Washington DC 20510*

GARRETT, GLORIA SUSAN, social services professional; b. Tampa, Fla., Nov. 30, 1951; d. Howard Leon and Marie Leonora (Garcia) G.; m. Michael Thomas McClain, May 16, 1973; children: Molly Kathleen Garrett McClain, Andrew Michael Garrett McClain. Student, Agnes Scott Coll., 1969-71, U. South Fla., 1971-72; BA, Ga. State U., 1977, MEd, 1979. Sr. caseworker DeKalb County Dept. Family and Children Services, Decatur, Ga., 1979-80, 82-84, prin. caseworker, 1980-82, 84-85, casework supr., 1985-86, sr. casework supr., 1986-91; disability adjudicator Ga. Disability Adjudication Sect., Decatur, 1991-93, sr. disability adjudicator, 1993-94; case cons., 1994—. Mem. Nat. Assn. Disability Examiners, Ga. Assn. Disability Examiners. Office: Disability Adjudication PO Box 1187 Decatur GA 30031-1187

GARRETT, JILL HOPE, broadcast journalist; b. N.Y.C., Aug. 7, 1954; d. Carlton Ray and Mary Hope (Jackson) G. Grad. high sch., Wilkes-Barre, Pa., 1972. Clk.-stenographer EEOC, Washington, 1973; ministry, 1974-76; sec. prodn. asst. Sta. WBAX Radio, Edwardsville, Pa., 1976-77; photographer, reporter Sta. KJAC-TV, Port Arthur, Tex., 1977-79; news producer Sta. WVIA-TV, Pittston, Pa., 1979-80; reporter Sta. WNYT-TV, Albany, N.Y., 1980-83; morning anchor/reporter Sta. WCPO-TV, Cin., 1983-90; anchor, producer Sta. WNEP-TV, Scranton, Pa., 1990—. Former vol. Cin. Zoo. Home: 438 S River St Wilkes Barre PA 18702-2338 Office: Sta WNEP TV 16 Montage Mountain Rd Scranton PA 18507-1700

GARRETT, KATHRYN ANN (KITTY GARRETT), legislative clerk; b. Antlers, Okla., July 10, 1930; d. Stansell Harper and Vena Clifford (Crawford) Byers; m. William Donald Garrett, Jan. 13, 1955 (dec. June 1992); children: William Mark, Amy Kathryn, Ann Elizabeth Garrett Jenni. Student, Okla. A&M U., 1948-50. Sec. Garform Industries, Wagoner, Okla., 1951-52; sec. to exec. sec. Okla. Edn. Assn., Oklahoma City, 1952-55; sec. revenue and taxation com. Ho. Reps., State of Okla., Oklahoma City, 1969-76, bill clk./ins. clk., 1976-84, asst. chief clk./jour. clk., 1985-93; ret., 1994. Mem. Am. Soc. Legis. Clks. and Secs. (assoc.), Okla. Heritage Assn., Sooner Book Club. Democrat. Home: 1429 Wilburn Dr Oklahoma City OK 73127-3253

GARRETT, LINDA SILVERSTEIN, financial planner; b. Pitts., May 14, 1949; d. Maurice J. and Mary H. (Reagan) Silverstein; m. Mark B. Garrett, Apr. 1, 1978 (div. Aug. 1987). BS in Social Work, W.Va. U., 1972. CFP, Fla.; registered rep. N.Y. Stock Exch., Nat. Assn. Securities Dealers. Group worker, dir. Miami Jewish Home & Hosp. for the Aged, 1976-80, registered rep., 1980-84; rsch. asst. Prescott, Ball & Turben, North Miami, Fla., 1980-84; acct. exec. Prudential Securities, Ft. Lauderdale, Fla., 1984-88; v.p. Morgan Keegan, Ft. Lauderdale, 1988-89; fin. cons. Merrill Lynch, Ft. Lauderdale, 1989-94; v.p. Dean Witter, Plantation, Fla., 1994—. Instr., lectr. Assn. Women CPA, Ft. Lauderdale, 1985; cons. Jr. Achievement, Broward County, Fla., 1993; counselor Switchboard Miami, 1976-80; active Archdiocese Miami Planned Giving Coun. 1988-90, lectr. 1988-89. Mem. Internat. Assn. Fin. Planners, Nat. Coun. Aging. Democrat. Jewish. Home: 544 NE 17th Way Fort Lauderdale FL 33301 Office: Dean Witter Reynolds Cornerstone 1 1200 S Pine Island RP Plantation FL 33324

GARRETT, MARILYN RUTH, registered nurse; b. Columbia, Mo., Mar. 28, 1957; d. Charles Filmore and Mable Ruth (Rice) Pasley; m. Donald Bruce Garrett, June 9, 1983 (div. 1994); children: Patrick Bryan, Christopher Ryan. ADN, Cen. Meth. Coll., 1985. Cert. psychiat. and mental health nurse. Staff nurse Fulton (Mo.) State Hosp., 1985-89, clin. nursing supr., 1989-91, overall nursing supr., 1991-92, nurse educator, nursing edn. and staff devel., 1992-94, psychosocial rehab. tng. specialist coord., 1994—; instr. CPR, 1987—; aggressive mgmt. tng. instr., 1990—; chair nurse recruitment and retention com., Mo., 1991-93. Mem. vol. task force team Callaway County unit Am. Cancer Soc.; mem. panel Smoking Cessation Group for County Health Svcs. Named Employee of the Month State of Mo., Dept. Mental Health, 1991. Home: 1015 Bluff St Fulton MO 65251 Office: Fulton State Hosp 600 E 5th St Fulton MO 65251-1798

GARRETT, MELISSA JO, elementary education educator; b. Sewickley, Pa., Mar. 2, 1956; m. Allen McCain Garrett, Jr., June 23, 1977; children: Allayna McCain Garrett, Mitchell Joseph Garrett. BS in Therapeutic Recreation, Temple U., 1976; elem. cert., U. Pitts., 1986; MEd, Slippery Rock (Pa.) U., 1988; ABD in Curriculum and Instrn., Indiana U. Pa., 1993. Cert. elem. edn., reading specialist. Ins. broker, recreation instr., tutor Phila., 1976-79; kindergarten tchr. Pitts., 1985-86; remedial reading and math. coord. Monaca (Pa.) Sch. Dist., 1986-88; tutor, instr. Youngstown (Ohio) State U., 1988—; asst. prof. critical reading and thinking, freshman seminar Slippery Rock U., 1989—; asst. dir. Advisement Ctr., 1993—; presentations at Post-secondary Pedagogy Conf., 1991, Conf. of Freshman Yr. Experience, 1992; cons. schs. and industry for issues of diversity. Contbr. articles to profl. jours. Mem. Patterson Heights (Pa.) Borough Coun., 1987-91, chmn. recreation and shade trees coms.; announcer, chmn. ways and means Chippewa Indians Football, Beaver Falls, Pa., 1989—; scorekeeper Blackhawk Basketball and Baseball, 1990—; bd. dirs. Patterson Recreation and Blackhawk Recreation, Beaver Falls. Mem. ASCD, Internat. Reading Assn., Keystone State Reading Assn., Pa. Assn. for Devel. Educators, Pa. Assn. Colls. and Tchr. Educators, Leotta Hawthorne Reading Assn. (com. chmn. 1987-89), Coll. Reading Assn. (presenter conf. 1992), Assn. Pa. State Coll. and Univ. Faculties, AAUW (chmn. 1988-89), NYCLSA (presenter conf. 1992). Republican. Presbyterian. Home: 504 4th Ave Beaver Falls PA 15010-3212

GARRETT, NANCY ROBERTS, editor; b. Terre Haute, Ind., Dec. 5, 1954; d. Jack Richford and Anne Marie (Dennison) Roberts; m. William H. Garrett Jr., Jan. 2, 1978 (div. Sept. 1986). BS in Journalism cum laude, Ind. State U., 1977. Sports reporter Terre Haute Tribune-Star, 1975-76; sports reporter Paris (Ill.) Daily Beacon-News, 1977-80, reporter, photographer, 1981-85, mng. editor, 1985—; editor Marshall (Ill.) Independent, 1980-81; corr. Sta. WTWO-TV, Terre Haute, 1978-89; media adviser State Sen. Harry Woodyard, Chrisman, Ill., 1983-89; advt. cons. Rep. William Black, Danville, Ill., 1986-88. Author, editor Series Clark County Park Dist., 1980-81 (2d pl. award Ill. Press Assn.). Deacon Paris Presbyn. Ch., 1982, elder, 1985-92; commr. to 202d gen. assy. United Presbyhn. Ch., 1990; co-chmn. Bicentennial Fund, Presbyn. of Southeastern Ill., 1990—; mgr. Paris Youth Ctr., 1981-86; pres. Edgar County Young Rep., Paris, 1987-89; dir. Community Concert Assn.; cheer coord. Mayo Mid. Sch., 1987-88; drama dir. Paris High Sch., 1987—, cheerleading coord., 1989—; Rep. precinct committeeman, 1990—; dir. Edgar County Fair Queen Pageant, 1992—. Mem. Assn. Soc. Profl. Journalists, Ind. State U. Nat. Alumni Coun., Ill. Pageant Dirs. Assn., Sigma Delta Chi. Presbyterian. Home: 416 N Jefferson St Paris IL 61944-1424 Office: Paris Daily Beacon-News North Main St Paris IL 61944

GARRETT, SANDY LANGLEY, school system administrator; b. Muskogee, Okla., Feb. 8, 1943; 1 child, Charles Langley (Chuck). BS in Elem. Edn., Northeastern U., Tahlequah, Okla., 1968, MS in Counseling, 1980; grad. John F. Kennedy Sch. Govt., Harvard U., 1989. Lic. tchr., adminstr., supt. std., Okla. Tchr. Hillsdale Schs., Muskogee, Okla., 1968-80, coord. gifted program, 1980-82; coord. gifted and talented State Dept. Edn., Oklahoma City, 1982-85, dir. rural edn., 1985-87, exec. dir. ednl. svcs., 1987-88, state supt., 1991—; sec. edn. Gov.'s Office, Oklahoma City, 1988—; chair State Bd. Edn., Oklahoma City, 1991—, State Vo-Tech. Edn., Oklahoma City, 1991—; bd. dirs. So. Regional Edn. Bd.; regent Okla. Colls., 1991—; mem. Nat. Coll. Bd. Equality Project; chair. Okla. Lit. Initiatives Commn.; mem. So. Regional Ednl. Bd. Co-author: (curriculum guide) Gifted Galaxy; mem. editorial bd. Rural and Small Schs.; contbr. articles to profl. jours. Co-chair Dem. Party, Muskogee, 1978; del. Dem. Nat. Conv., N.Y.C., 1980, 82; mem. Leadership Okla., 1990. Recipient Cecil Yarbrough award, 1989, Claude Dyer Legis. award, 1989. Mem. Muskogee County Ednl. Assn., Delta Kappa Gamma, Phi Delta Kappa, Delta Kappa Gamma. Methodist. Home: Apt 2410 11300 N Pennsylvania Ave Oklahoma City OK 73120-7773 Office: State Dept Edn 2500 N Lincoln Blvd Oklahoma City OK 73105-4503*

GARRETT, SHIRLEY GENE, nuclear medicine technologist; b. Evanston, Ill., Apr. 19, 1944; d. Nathan and Emma Louise (Uecker) G. AA, Oakton Community Coll., 1977; AS in Nuclear Medicine, Triton Coll., 1980; BA, Northeastern Ill. U., 1983; MA, Gov.'s State U., University Park, Ill., 1985. Cert. nuclear medicine technologist. Nuclear medicine technologist Chgo. Osteopathic Hosp., 1980-88, Little County of Mary Hosp., Evergreen Park, Ill., 1989, Lutheran Gen. Hosp., Lincoln Park, Ill., 1989, Mt. Sinai Hosp., Chgo., 1990-92; technologist nuclear medicine Swedish Covenant Hosp., Chgo., 1992-93; pres. Providence Hosp. of Cook County, Chgo., 1994—. Contbr. articles to profl. jours. Vol. Ravenswood Hosp., Chgo., 1986—, Mt. Sinai Hosp., 1990-92. Mem. Soc. Nuclear Medicine (technologist sect., bylaws com. Ctrl. chpt. 1982-83, 85-86, 92—, continuing edn. com. 1986-87, chmn. nominating com. 1987-88, 92-93, chmn. edn. com. 1988-89, pres.-elect 1989-90, bd. govs. 1990-92, pres. 1991-92, chmn. bylaws com. 1992-93), Assoc. and Tech. Affiliates Chgo. Area (coord. edn. 1981-84, adv. bd. 1983-84, 87-88, pres. 1985-87, chmn. nominating com. 1987-89). Lutheran.

GARRETT, SUSAN LENORA, elementary educator; b. Arlington, Va., Sept. 5, 1955; d. Richard Henry and Virginia Ann (Hockman) Feigley; m. Theodore Edward Garrett, June 20, 1981; children: Jenna LeeAnn, Thad Edward; 1 stepchild, Lori Darlene. BA in Secondary Edn., Shepherd Coll., 1976; MEd, James Madison U., 1980. Elem. media specialist Hardy County Schs., Moorefield, W.Va., 1976—; speech instr. Shepherd Coll., Shepherdstown, W.Va., 1990—. Bd. dirs. Moorefield (W.V.) Active Caring, 1990—; treas. Duffey Meml. United Meth. Ch., Moorefield, 1992-94, Moorefield Elem. Sch. PTA, 1993—, Moorefield Vol. Fire Co. Aux., 1995—; svc. unit mgr., trainer, troop leader Shawnee coun. Girl Scouts U.S.A., 1991—. Recipient Appreciation Pin, Girl Scouts U.S.A., 1991, God and Svc. award Girl Scouts U.S.A., 1992, Honor Pin, Girl Scouts U.S.A., 1993. Mem. AAUW (pres. Moorefield br. 1988-90), DAR (Am. history essay chmn. South Br. Valley chpt. 1991—). Republican. Office: Moorefield Elem Sch 400 N Main St Moorefield WV 26836

GARRETT, TERESA ANN HOLLENBECK, geriatrics nurse, consultant; b. Idaho, May 27, 1960; d. Neal Lyle and Winnie May (Relk) Hollenbeck; m. E. Brian Garrett, July 11, 1985; children: Aaron Christopher, Kimberly Ann. BSN, U. Utah, 1982, MSN, 1992. Registered gerontol. nurse, intravenous nurse. Staff nurse, patient care coord. Community Nursing Svc., Salt Lake City; profl. svcs. cons. HealthCare Network, Tustin, Calif.; area nurse cons. Hill Haven Corp., Tacoma; dir. nursing resources MediSave Pharmacies, Inc.; clin. dir. Community Nursing Svcs. Mem. ANA, Utah Nurses Assn., Intravenous Nurses Soc., Nat. Vascular Access Network, Utah Geriatric Soc., Sigma Theta Tau, Gamma Rho (treas.), Phi Kappa Phi. Home: 1716 Logan Ave Salt Lake City UT 84108-2630

GARRETT, TERRI MELINDA, health promotion professional; b. Oxford, Colo., Nov. 25, 1948; d. Eugene Norman and Ethel Bea (Cotten) G. AA, Fashion Merchandising, Albuquerque, 1975; MBA, U. Chgo., 1974; BS, N.Mex. Inst. Mining and Tech., 1990. Cert. human resources mgr., health promotion dir., compensation mgr., adjudicator, contract mgr. Job club trainer, counselor State of Colo. Div. of Labor, Denver, 1976-84; compensation mgr. City of Aurora, Colo., 1984-87; mgmt. tng. dir. Denver Health and Hosps., 1987-88, 1988-89, sr. health planner, 1989-91, orgnl. devel. dir., 1991-92, health promotion, disease prevention mgr., 1992—; community educator Colo. Women's Cancer Control Initiative, Denver, 1992-94; active Hypertension Com., Denver, 1992-94; adminstr. Montbello CVD/HTN Prevention Project, 1993—. Author three-vol. study of compensation system with design of pay plan, 1985. Mem. Black Reps., Denver, 1993; chair Gov.'s Task Force on Diabetes in Hi Risk Populations, Colo., 1992-94; bd. treas. Theatre Assocs. Group for Denver Ctr. Theatre, 1989—; bd. dirs. City Women, 1987-94. Grantee Colo. Trust, 1993, Ctrs. for Disease Control, Montbello, 1993. Mem. ASTD, Soc. for Mktg. in Healthcare, Am. Soc. Correctional Healthcare, Colo. Health Edn. Coun., Heart Assn., Colo. Wellness Coalition. Office: Community Health Svcs 777 Bannock St # 1914 Denver CO 80204-4507

GARRIGAN, KATHLEEN, packaging executive; b. South Orange, N.J., Sept. 21, 1961; d. John Joseph and Kathleen (Valli) Garrigan. BS in Mktg. and Mgmt., Seton Hall U., 1983. Account mgr. Shell Packaging Group, Springfield, N.J., 1983-85, Accurate Box Co., Paterson, N.J., 1985-86; prin., dir. sales and marketing Source Packaging, Hackensack, N.J., 1986—. Roman Catholic. Office: Source Packaging 279 Huyler St South Hackensack NJ 07606-1407

GARRIOTT, LOIS JEAN, clinical social worker, educator; b. Avon Park, Fla., Mar. 22, 1944; d. John Arnold and Katherine Faith (Morton) G.; m. Bertram Paul Martin, Mar. 9, 1963 (div. Dec. 1978); children: Heidi, Ivy, Kurt, Aaron. AA, Macomb County Community Coll., Warren, Mich., 1969; BA in Psychology, U. Mich., Dearborn, 1974; MSW in Group Work, Wayne State U., 1978. Family therapist Cath. Social Svcs., Port Huron, Mich., 1978-79; specialist St. Clair County Community Mental Health, Algonac and Marine City, Mich., 1979-80; clinician St. Clair County Community Mental Health, Algonac and Marine City, 1980-85, clin. supr., 1985-88; clinician Ctr. for Personal Growth, Port Huron, Mich., 1986—; pvt. practice Roseville, Mich., 1988—; adj. lectr. Wayne State U., Detroit, 1987-89, mem. faculty, 1990—. Mem. Acad. Cert. Social Workers (diplomate). Office: Wayne State U Thompson Home Rm 418 Detroit MI 48202

GARRISON, ALTHEA, government official; b. Hahira, Ga., Oct. 7, 1940; d. Charles and Lenora Mae (Davis) G. AS, Newbury Jr. Coll., 1978; BS, Suffolk U., 1982; cert. in social studies, Harvard U., 1986; MS, Lesley Coll., 1984. Counselor, supr. Charlotte House Dorchester (Mass.), 1977-77; with EDP dept., sr. assessor Mass. Dept. Revenue, Boston, 1979-81; sr. examiner Office State Compt., Boston, 1982-90; human resource mgr. Office of State Comptr. Commonwealth of Mass., 1991—; state rep. gen. ct. 5th suffolk Rep. Dist., Mass., 1992-95; bd. dirs. Uphams Corner Health Ctr., Dorchester, 1983—, v.p., 1987—, Disting. Svc. award, 1991. Charter mem. adv. bd. Christian Record Braille, Lincoln, Neb., 1983; mem. alumna coun. Lesley Coll. Grad. Sch., Cambridge, Mass., 1986-88; mem. Nat. Rep. Congl. Com., 1988—; life mem. Rep. Presdl. Task Force, 1989—; charter founder Ronald Reagan Rep. Ctr., Washington, 1989; nominee city coun. Dorchester, 1989; nominee state rep. Rep. Primary, 1990; town com. woman Ward 13; apptd. to Nat. rep. Senatorial com., Presdl. commn., 1992; elected mem. Ward com. Ward 13 of Boston, 1992, vice chair Ward 13 commn. Recipient Senator's citation Commonwealth of Mass., 1982, medal of merit Rep. Task Force, 1989, cert. of appreciation Mass. Rep. Party, Outstanding Vol. award Suffolk U., 1991, Cert. Achievement Conf. New Legislators, 1993; hon. fellow John F. Kennedy Libr., 1987-90; named One of 100 Women Making History North Shore Women's Coalition; named to Rep. Presdl. Legion of Merit Honor Roll, 1993. Mem. Am. Mgmt. Assn., Nat. Assn. Govt. Employees (negotiator, organizer 1979-81), Suffolk U. Gen. Alumni Assn. (bd. dirs. 1986-89), Heritage Found., Nat. Found. Cancer Rsch. (hon., citation 1991), DAV Comdrs. Roman Catholic. Home: 18 Jerome St Apt 2 Dorchester MA 02125-2021 Office: Office State Comptr Rm 540 State House 9th fl Boston MA 02133-1099

GARRISON, BETTY BERNHARDT, mathematics educator; b. Danbury, Ohio, July 1, 1932; d. Philip Arthur and Reva Esther (Meter) Bernhardt; m. Robert Edward Kvarda, Sept. 28, 1957 (div. 1964); m. John Dresser Garrison, Jan. 17, 1968; 1 child, John Christopher. BA, BS, Bowling Green State U., 1954; MA, Ohio State U., 1956; PhD, Oreg. State U., 1962. Teaching asst. Ohio State U., Columbus, 1954-56; instr. Ohio U., Athens, 1956-57, San Diego State Coll., 1957-59; teaching asst. Oreg. State U., Corvallis, 1959-62; asst. prof. San Diego State U., 1962-66, assoc. prof., 1966-69, prof., 1969—. Reviewer of articles and books, 1966—; contbr. articles to profl. jours. NSF fellow, 1960-61, 61-62. Mem. Am. Math. Soc., Math. Assn. Am. Home: 5607 Yerba Anita Dr San Diego CA 92115-1027 Office: San Diego State U Math Dept San Diego CA 92182

GARRISON, EVA HEIM, school counselor; b. Dettingen, Bavaria, Germany, Sept. 23, 1940; came to U.S., 1964; d. Josef Fridrich and Barbara Fridericke (Vogt) Heim; m. Floyd Garrison, Sept. 15, 1962; children: Cindy Elizabeth, Michele Maria. AA, Solano C.C., 1973; BA, Ctrl. Wash. U., 1983; MEd, City U., Bellevue, Wash., 1994. Police officer Vallejo (Calif.) Police Dept., 1970-77; interim sch. instr. Ctrl. Kitsap Sch. Dist., Silverdale, Wash., 1983-84, interim sch. coord., 1984-87, instr. h.s. German, 1987-88, substance abuse coord., 1992-93; coord. in-sch. suspension program Camden County H.S., St. Mays, Ga., 1988-89. Mem. Substance Abuse Adv. Bd., Kitsap County, Wash., 1989-92, At-Risk Task Force, Kitsap County, 1987-88, Teen Pregnancy Task Force, Kitsap County, 1985-87; chair Ctrl. Kitsap Comty. Coalition, Silverdale, 1989-93. Recipient Gov.'s award in substance abuse prevention, 1992. Mem. Wash. State Sch. Counselors Assn., Wash. Mental Health Counselors Assn. Home: 4709 Chico Way Bremerton WA 98312

GARRISON, LAURA ANN, artist; b. Warwick, R.I., Nov. 16, 1958; d. Harold Francis and Bette Lou (Fortune) Quagan; m. Gregory Owen Garrison, Oct. 7, 1981; children: Amanda Rose Garrison, Gabrielle Kruse Garrison. Student, Vesper George Sch. of Art, Boston, 1976-77; BFA in Painting, U. Mass., 1992. Owner LG Novelties, Springfield, Mass., 1989-91; statue restoration St. Anne's Ch., Turners Falls, Mass., 1992-93; painting instr. Montague (Mass.) Parks and Recreation, 1992-93. Solo exhbns. include NADA/Mason Gallery-Bolger Art Ctr., Northfield Mt. Hermon Sch., Northfield, Mass., 1993, Shea Theaer, Turners Falls, 1993, Channing L. Bete Co., Inc. lobby and garden exhibit, South Deerfield, Mass., 1992. Collaborative shows include still life paintings and a group of paintings by students at Montague Parks and Recreation Dept., Greenfield (Mass.) Pub. Libr., 1993, Springfield Art League Invitational, 1993. Work also on display at Hart Gallery, Northampton, Mass., 1993. Bd. dirs. Friends of the Parks and Recreation Dept., Montague, 1993; mem. Ladiesof St. Anne, Turners Falls, 1993. With U.S. Army, 1981-84. Mem. Arts Coun. of Franklin County, Springfield Art League (publicity chairperson 1988-91). Home: 27 Randall Wood Dr Montague MA 01351

GARRISON, MARGUERITE CHERYL, military officer; b. Buffalo, Nov. 30, 1959; d. John Peter and Jean Marie (Collins) McDonald; m. Kevin Garrison, Aug. 16, 1986; children: Sean Patrick, Kieran Jerome. BS, Saint Bonaventure U., N.Y., 1981; student, U.S. Army Command and Gen. Staff Coll., Fort Leavenworth, 1993-94. Commd. 2d lt. U.S. Army, 1981, advanced through grades to maj., 1993; platoon leader 194th Mil. Police Co., New Ulm, Germany, 1983-84; asst. ops. officer 385th Mil. Police Bat., Kornwestheim, Germany, 1984-85; co. comdr. 630th Mil. Police Co., Bamberg, Germany, 1985-87; force structure officer Forces Command, Provost Marshal Office, Fort McPherson, Ga., 1987-90; exec. officer Forces Command, Provost Marshal Office, Fort McPherson, 1991-92; asst. sec. to joint staff Hdqrs. Forces Command, Fort McPherson, 1990-91; dep. program dir. 1993 World U. Games, Buffalo, 1992-93; exec. officer 705th Mil. Police Battalion, Fort Leavenworth, Kans., 1994—. Mem. Assn. of the U.S. Army, Mil. Police Regimental Assn., Am. Soc. for Indsl. Security, FBI Nat. Acad. Assocs. Home: 534 S Bittersweet Ln Lansing KS 66043-6243 Office: 705 Mil Police Battalion 300 McPherson Ave Bldg 429 Fort Leavenworth KS 66027

GARRISON, SUSAN KAY, lawyer; b. Renton, Wash., Sept. 6, 1952; d. Walter Raymond and Rose Faye (Wilson) G.; m. William W. Mayer Jr., Aug. 4, 1973 (div. July 1988); 1 child, Jonathan W.; m. Michael J.J. Campbell, Oct. 22, 1993. BA in Sociology cum laude, Gettysburg Coll., 1974; JD, Villanova U., 1980, LLM in Taxation, 1988. Assoc. Dechert Price and Rhoads, Phila., 1980-83, Surrick and Gollatz, Media, Pa., 1983-86; pvt. practice Media, 1986—; exec. trustee Garrison Family Found., Media, 1990—; pres., bd. mem. Nat. Abortion Rights Action League Pa., Phila., 1986-94. Com. mem. Middletown Twp. (Pa.) Open Space Commn., 1984-86; bd. mem. Clara Bell Duvall Edn. Fund, Phila., 1987-90; nat. coord. Nat. Evang. Women's Caucus, Chgo., 1990-91; commr. Del. County Women's Commn., Media, 1989-92; pres. Friends of Del.County Women's Commn., Media, 1990—; trustee, rec. clk. Media-Providence Friends Sch., 1988-94. Mem. ABA, Nat. Assn. Women and Law, Nat. Women History Network, Del. County Estate Planning Coun., Pa. Bar Assn., Delco Bar Assn. Republican. Presbyterian. Office: 339 W State St Media PA 19063

GARRISON, WANDA BROWN, environmental consultant; b. Madison County, N.C., Sept. 16, 1936; d. Roy Lee Brown and Zella Arizona (Miller) Brown Hannah; m. Charles Mitchell Garrison, July 9, 1955; children—Roy Lee, Marsha Joan; 1 step-son, Charles Mitchell, Jr. Student air-line hostess Weaver Airlines, St. Louis, 1954-55; student Haywood Tech. Coll., Clyde, N.C., 1967-68; student IBM, Asheville, N.C., 1977; student in data processing Agy. Record Control, Atlanta, 1978. Operator Day Co., Waynesville, N.C., 1954-57; driver Haywood County Schs., Waynesville, 1970-71; operator Am. Enka, N.C., 1972-75; bookkeeper L. N. Davis Ins. Co., Waynesville, 1975-80; stock preparation Champion Internat., Canton, N.C., 1980-89; cons. Garrison and Assocs. Environ. Solutions, Pensacola, Fla. Sec./treas. James Chapel Baptist Ch., Haywood County, N.C., 1965-77; pres. Fire Dept. Aux., Crabtree, N.C., 1973—; pres. Women Mission Union, Crabtree Bapt. Ch., Haywood County, 1977-80; v.p. Gideon Aux., Haywood County, 1982-84, pres., 1984-87; state aux. follow-up rep., 1984-87, state zone leader, 1987-88. Recipient Life Saving plaque Lion's Club, Waynesville, 1972. Mem. AFL-CIO. Republican. Home: 513 S 2nd St Pensacola FL 32507-3313

GARROTE, MARY JOSEPHINE, apparel designer, merchandiser, manufacturer; b. Jamaica, N.Y., Nov. 23, 1949; d. Giusseppe and Ida Nancy (Gullo) Linarello; m. Eugene Rafael Garrote, June 26, 1970 (div. Mar. 1985);

children: Eugene, Joseph, Kristin, Lauren. Student, SUNY, Oneonta, 1967-69, Fla. Atlantic U., Boca Raton, 1970-72, Fashion Inst. Tech., N.Y.C., 1975. Cert. elem. educator. Dir. merchandising, designer raquettes and activo Active Sportswear Lines, Miami, Fla., 1973-75; v.p., gen. merchandising mgr., design dir. Margee Sportswear, Inc., Miami, 1975-84; dir. mfg. Lemon Drop, Inc./Hang Ten Children, Miami, 1984-89; dir. ops. KMart Apparel Buying of Miami Corp., 1989-92; pres. Express-It Unltd., Miami, 1992—; cons. Guatemalan Trade Assn., 1986-89. Republican. Roman Catholic.

GARROTT, FRANCES CAROLYN, architectural technician; b. Bowling Green, Ky., Mar. 10, 1932; d. Irby Reid and Carrie Mae (Stahl) Cameron; m. Leslie Othello Garrott, Oct. 12, 1951 (dec. Feb. 1978); children—Dennis Leslie, Alan Reid; adopted children—Carolyn Maria, Karen Roxana; m. Raymond William Scerbo, May 31, 1978 (div. Oct. 1990). Student Fla. State U., 1951, St. Petersburg Jr. Coll., 1962-74; grad. Pinellas Vocat. Tech. Inst., 1975. With Sears, Roebuck and Co., Rapid City, S.D., 1951-52, St. Petersburg, Fla., 1961-62; bookkeeper Ohio Nat. Bank, Columbus, 1953-54, Sunbeam Bakery, Lakeland, Fla., 1955-56; with Christies Toy Sales, Pennsauken, N.J., 1958-60; exec. sec. Gulf Coast Automotive Warehouse, Inc., Tampa, Fla., 1970-73, office mgr., 1975-78; sec., treas., chief pilot, co-owner Tech. Devel. Corp., St. Petersburg, Fla., 1970-78; freelance archtl. draftsman and designer, archtl. cons., constrn. materials estimator, 1975—, Fla. state judge Vocat. Indsl. Clubs of Am. Skills Olympics, 1986. Nat. Assn. Women in Constrn. scholar, 1974. Mem. Nat. Assn. Women in Constrn., Alpha Chi Omega. Democrat. Home and Office: 1500 Sunset Rd Bldg F Unit 7 Tarpon Springs FL 34689-2749

GARROTT, IDAMAE T., state senator; b. Washington, Dec. 24, 1916; married; 2 children. AB, Western Md. Coll., 1936, LLD (hon.). Mem. Md. Ho. of Dels., 1979-87, mem. ways and means com., joint com. on energy; mem. Md. State Senate, 1987—, econ. and environ. affairs com., chmn. joint com. fed. rels., chmn. adv. com. on fed.-state local rels.; vice chair Montgomery County Senators. Author: Paying Our Way, Maryland State Taxes and You, 1958. Mem. Montgomery County Coun., 1966-74, chmn. planning com., 1970-74, pres., 1971; bd. dirs. Washington Met. Area Transit Authority, 1972-74; bd. dirs. Washington Suburban Transit Commn., 1971-74, chmn., 1972; bd. dirs. Met. Washington Coun.Govts., pres., 1974, chmn. land use com., 1969-74; chmn. Solid Waste Mgmt. Agy. Met. Washington, 1969-74; pres. Montgomery County Humane Soc., 1976-77; bd.dirs. Wheaton Rescue Squad, 1982-84. Recipient John Dewey award, 1982, Humanitarian award Montgomery County Humane Soc., 1983, Horn Book award Montgomery County Edn. Assn., 1985, also awards from Thomas B. Cook, 1987, Md. Assn. of Deaf, 1987, Md. Gerontol. Assn., 1991, Planned Parenthood, 1992, Md. Common Cause, 1993, Md. Profl. Animal Workers, 1994, Sierra Club, 1994, Md. Fed. Nat. Assn. Retired Fed. Employees, 1994, Md. Conservation Coun., 1994, Md. Commn. for Children, 1994, Allied Civic Group, 1994, Audubon Soc., 1994. Mem. Md. Assn. of Deaf, Md. Gerontol. Assn., Md. Profl. Animal Workers, Md. Fedn. Nat. Assn. Ret. Fed. Employees, Md. Com. for Children, Audubon Naturalist Soc, Sierra Club. Office: Md State Senate State House Annapolis MD 21401

GARSIDE, MARLENE ELIZABETH, advertising executive; b. Newark, Dec. 1, 1933; d. Abraham and Shirley (Janow) Carnow; BS in Commerce and Fin., Bucknell U., 1955; m. Stanley Kramer, Aug. 7, 1955 (dec. 1967); children: Deborah Frances, Elizabeth Anne; m. Martin Lutman, Aug. 27, 1969 (dec. 1981); m. Michael J. Weinstein, Apr. 9, 1983 (dec. 1984); m. Normand Garside, Apr. 5, 1986. Asst. rsch. dir. Modern Materials Handling Co., Boston, 1955-57; econ. analyst, project adminstr. United Rsch. Co., Cambridge, Mass., 1957-58; free lance tech. writer, econ. analyst, 1958-66; asst. mgr. survey planning and market rsch. IBM, White Plains, N.Y., 1967-69; mgr. rsch. svcs. McKinsey & Co., Cleve., 1969-72; former v.p., dir. Am. Custom Homes, former dir. Liberty Builders, Inc., Cleve.; owner, v.p., dir. Am. Custom Builders Inc., Cape Coral, Fla., 1978—; ptnr., dir. Star Realty Inc., Cape Coral, 1980—; account exec. Media Graphics, Inc., Naples, Fla., 1984; advt. mgr. Fox Electronics, Ft. Myers, Fla., 1984-86; v.p. Langdon Advt., Ft. Myers, 1987-88; asst. mgr. facility svcs. State of Fla. Dept. Health and Rehabilitative Svcs., Ft. Myers, 1988-90, facility svcs. mgr., 1990-92, gen. svcs. mgr., 1992—. Mem. Econ. and Indsl. Devel. Task Force, City of Cape Coral, 1979. Mem. Nat. Assn. Homebuilders, Bldg. Industry Assn., Constrn. Industry Assn., Nat. Bd. Realtors. Home: 1482 Sautern Dr Fort Myers FL 33919-2744 Office: State of Fla Dept Health Rehab Svcs 2295 Victoria Ave Fort Myers FL 33901-3884

GARSON, GREER, actress; b. No. Ireland, Sept. 29, 1908; d. George and Nina Sophia (Greer) G.; m. Edward A. Snelson (div.); m. Richard Ney, 1943 (div.); m. E. E. Fogelson, 1949 (dec. 1987). BA with honors, London U.; student, Grenoble U.; HHD (hon.), Rollins Coll., 1950; D of Communication Arts (hon.), Coll. of Santa Fe, 1970; LittD (hon.), Ulster U., 1977. Actress Birmingham (Eng.) Repertory Theatre, 1932-33. Appeared numerous London plays in lead roles; films include Goodbye Mr. Chips, Pride and Prejudice, When Ladies Meet, Blossoms in the Dust, Mrs. Miniver (Acad. award), Random Harvest, Madame Curie, Mrs. Parkington, Julius Caesar, The Law and the Lady, Her Twelve Men, Sunrise at Campobello (Golden Globe award), Strange Lady in Town, The Singing Nun, The Happiest Millionaire; plays include Auntie Mame, Tonight at 8:30, Captain Brassbound's Conversion; also appeared in pioneer British TV and Am. TV. Prin. founding donor Fogelson Forum Dallas Presbyn. Hosp., Fogelson Libr., Greer Garson Theatre, Garson Communications Ctr. and Studios Coll. of Santa Fe, Fogelson Pavillion at Meyerson Symphony Ctr., Dallas; Greer Garson Theatre at So. Meth. U., Dallas. Co-recipient U.S. Dept. of Interior Conservation Svc. award, 1981, many internat. awards.

GARTH-LEWIS, KIMBERLEY ANNE, political science consultant; b. Sacramento, Jan. 21, 1960; d. Nat Garth and Frances (Hopkins) Garth Bradley; m. Ronald Lewis, Jan. 16, 1980; children: Shavaugn I., Veronica G. BS, U. San Francisco, 1981; MPA, Golden Gate U., 1985, DPA, 1993. Lic. tchr., Calif. Pvt. cons. Sacramento, 1985—; founder, pres. rsch. firm KAGL & Affiliates, Inc., 1991—; adj. prof. U. San Francisco, Humphrey's Coll.; lectr. in U.S., Can. and Eng., 1985—. Contbr. articles to reports and transcripts. Ind. rschr. advocate Calif. Correctional Peace Officers Assn.; cons. Legis. Penal Code Comm., 1990; aide to State Senator Robert Presley; staff support state task force Blue Ribbon Commn., 1989; advisor Little Hoover Commn., 1993-94, others; mem. Sch. Site Coun., 1991-95. Recipient golden state Minority award, 1989, NAFE appreciation award, 1991, outstanding Women award, 1992-93. Mem. IARCA, ASPA, NAFE (chair sect. membership 1991-92), Polit. Sci. Soc., Black Chamber, Beta Phi. Republican. Home: 8480 Cutler Way Sacramento CA 95828 Office: 1228 N St Sacramento CA 95814

GARTNER, JESSIE LEE, emergency nurse; b. St. Paul, Kans., Feb. 7, 1940; d. Herbert Lee and Lela V. (Shouse) Moore; m. Billy C. Couey, June 18, 1960 (dec. Feb. 1981); m. Gary E. Gartner, Dec. 10, 1988. AAS with honors, Coffeyville C.C., 1986; ADN with honors, Labette County C.C., 1987; postgrad., Oxford U., 1991; BSN, Mo. Southern State Coll., 1992. Cert. emergency nurse. Clk.-typist Pittsburg (Kans.) State U., 1957-62, Jayhawk Distbrs., Independence, Kans., 1962-64; office mgr., asst. compt. Starcraft Corp., Independence, 1964-74; bookkeeper, parts sales rep. O'Malley Equipment, Independence, 1975-77; sec. Guaranty Performance, Independence, 1977-78; sec., bookkeeper Independence Community Coll., 1978-81; paramedic Coffeyville (Kans.) Regional Med. Ctr., 1981-87; clin. nurse St. John Regional Med. Ctr., Joplin, Mo., 1987—; CPR instr. Coffeyville Regional Med. Ctr., 1984-87; TNCC instr. St. John Regional Med. Ctr., 1991—; vol. asst. Kans. Bd. of Emergency Medicine, Coffeyville, 1981-87. Vol. Nat. Multiple Sclerosis Found., Joplin, 1989-91, Over 60 Olympics, Joplin, 1990, Spl. Olympics State Bowling Tournament, 1993. Mem. Emergency Nurses Assn. (trauma com., treas. 1993-94), Nursing Honor Soc., Order Ea. Star (past matron, Grand Chpt. Page award 1962, 91, chmn. state nursing com. 1994), St. Johns Hundred Club. Home: 415 S Connor Ave Joplin MO 64801-2927 Office: St John Regional Med Ctr 2700 Mc Clelland Blvd Joplin MO 64804-1623

GARVEY, DALE JEANE, recreational facility director; b. Monticello, Ill., Nov. 20, 1958; d. James Dale and Rosemary Mae (Traxler) G. BFA, U. Ill., 1979. Mgr. Kerasotes Theatres, Decatur, Ill., 1980-83; city mgr. Kerasotes Theatres, Champaign, Ill., 1983-85; dist. mgr. GKC Theatres, Springfield, Ill., 1985-91; exec. v.p. ops. GKC Theatres, Springfield, 1991—. Office: GKC Theatres 500 First Nat Bank Bldg Springfield IL 62701

GARVEY, EVELYN JEWEL, mental health nurse; b. Carrizozo, N.Mex., Aug. 23, 1931; d. Everett E. and Jewel A. (Bullard) Bragg; m. Robert J. Garvey, July 10, 1949; children: Nancy, Annie, Catherine, Robert, Michael, Betty. AD, Ea. N.Mex. Coll., 1972. RN, N.Mex.; cert. EMT., N.Mex. Staff nurse N.Mex. Rehab. Ctr., Roswell, 1972; staff nurse Villa Solano State Sch., Roswell, 1972-79, DON, 1979-81; staff nurse Ft. Stanton (N.Mex.) Hosp., 1981—.

GARVEY, JEANNE WOLTER, state legislator, realtor; b. Bridgeport, Conn., Jan. 13, 1939; d. Henry Adolph and Bertha Helen (Morazes) Wolter; m. Henry Hulton Garvey, Jr., Apr. 28, 1962; children: Henry Hulton, III, Kendra Garvey Owen, Colleen Elizabeth. Student, Western Conn. State U., Mattatuck C.C. Grad. Real Estate Inst. Rsch. lab. asst. Nestle Co., New Milford, Conn., 1957-63; realtor, appraisor DeVoe Realty Co., New Milford, 1976-93, Settlers and Traders Realtors, New Milford, 1993—; state rep. Conn. Legislature, Hartford, 1993—; mem. various coms. New Milford Bd. Realtors, 1976—, Conn. Bd. Realtors, Hartford, 1976—. mem., past. dir. New Milford Hist. Soc., 1971—; mem. New Milford Rep. Town Com., 1993—. Mem. Nat. Order Women Legislators, Nat. Assn. Realtors (various coms. 1976—). Roman Catholic. Office: Conn Legis Office Bldg Capital Ave Hartford CT 06106

GARVEY, JOANNE MARIE, lawyer; b. Oakland, Calif., Apr. 23, 1935; d. James M. and Marian A. (Dean) G. A.B. with honors, U. Calif., Berkeley, 1956, M.A., 1957, J.D., 1961. Bar: Calif. bar 1962. Assoc. firm Cavaletto, Webster, Mullen & McCaughey, Santa Barbara, Calif., 1961-63, Jordan, Keeler & Seligman, San Francisco, 1963-67; ptnr. Jordan, Keeler & Seligman, 1968-88, Heller, Ehrman, White & McAuliffe, 1988—; bd. dirs. Mexican-Am. Legal Def. and Ednl. Fund; chmn. Law in a Free Soc., Continuing Edn. of Bar; mem. bd. councillors U. So. Calif. Law Center. Recipient Paul Veazy award YMCA, 1973, Internat. Women's Yr. award Queen's Bench, 1975, honors Advs. for Women, 1978, CRLA award. Fellow Am. Bar Found.; mem. ABA (state del., chmn. SCLAID, chmn. delivery of legal svcs.), Calif. State Bar (v.p., gov., tax sect., del., Jud Klein award, Joanne Garvey award), San Francisco Bar Assn. (pres., pres. Barristers), Am. Law Inst., Calif. Women Lawyers (founder), Order of Coif, Phi Beta Kappa. Democrat. Roman Catholic. Home: 16 Kensington Ct Kensington CA 94707-1010 Office: 333 Bush St San Francisco CA 94104-2806

GARVEY, KATHERINE HESTON, gerontology nurse; b. Galesburg, Ill., Dec. 28, 1944; d. Ernest Edwin and Eunice Corinne (Hollister) Heston; m. Edward Anthony Garvey, Nov. 25, 1967; children: Travler Franklin, Edward Anthony II, Anne Elizabeth. BS, U. Md., 1981; MA, John F. Kennedy U., 1993. RN, Calif. Staff nurse ICU Children's Meml. Hosp., Chgo., 1967-68; staff nurse pediatrics St. Joseph's Hosp., Chgo., 1968-70; staff nurse neonatal ICU Prentice Woman's Hosp., Chgo., 1970-73; staff nurse newborn nursery Anne Arundel Gen. Hosp., Annapolis, Md., 1974-82; advisor/counselor Group Health, Washington, 1982-83; patient/home care educator John Muir Med. Ctr., Walnut Creek, Calif., 1984-92; minimun data set coord. Jewish Home for Aged, San Francisco, 1992—. Youth educator St. John Vlanney Ch., Walnut Creek, 1985; vol. St. Anne's Crisis Nursery, Concord, Calif., 1993. Recipient Contbg. scholarship Contra Costa Alternative Sch., Orinda, Calif., 1988-93. Mem. AAUW (sec. 1985, 86, membership v.p. 1987, 88, program v.p. 1989, 90). Roman Catholic.

GARVIN, FLORENCE WARD, management consultant; b. Ft. Sam Houston, Tex., Oct. 6, 1928; d. Edward Joseph and Florence Emily (Bock) Ward; BA, Our Lady of Lake U., San Antonio, 1949; postgrad. Trinity U., San Antonio, 1949-50; m. Sheldon R. Rappaport, Mar. 2, 1950 (div. July 1969); children—Bruce Ward, Lisa Lynn; m. 2d, Stefan J. Garvin, Oct. 3, 1981. Co-founder, asst. to pres. Pathway Sch., Norristown, Pa., 1961-68; adminstrv. dir. Neurosurg. Clinic for Children, Media, Pa., 1968-70; v.p. for devel. Vanguard Schs., Haverford, Pa., 1970-72; asst. to pres. Elwyn (Pa.) Inst., 1972-75; pvt. practice mgmt. cons., Media, 1976-78; cons. employee relations dept. E.I. DuPont de Nemours & Co., Inc., Wilmington, Del., 1978-85, sr. bus. assoc. internat. dept., 1985-89, mgr. bus. rels. devel., 1989-90, mgr. internat. human resources devel. human resources dept., 1990-94; pvt. practice, Media, Pa., 1994—. Pres. bd. dirs. Montgomery County Mental Health Clinics, 1965-68; bd. dirs. Phila. United Fund, 1969-72; bd. mgrs., sec. Garrett-Williamson Found., 1973-85; bd. dirs. Mary Campbell Center, Wilmington, 1978-81, trustee Wilmington Coll., 1981—; trustee Curtis Inst. Music, 1985-92; mem. devel. com. Mercy Haverford Hosp., 1994—; mem. policy coun. Del. County Head Start, 1994—; pres. bd. dirs. AIDS Task Force/Phila. Community Health Alternatives, 1994—; bd. dirs. Pacific Rim Bus. Coun., 1994—. Home: 2 Yarmouth Ln Media PA 19063-4327

GARWIG, ANN ELIZABETH, development director; b. Oneida, N.Y., June 9, 1950; d. Eugene Taylor and Esther A. (Fowler) Adams; m. Ronald Peter Savoie, June 10, 1972 (div. Dec. 1990); 1 child, Marc Savoie; m. Lee Roy Garwig, Mar. 16, 1991; stepchildren: Amy, Tina. BA, Mt. Holyoke Coll., 1972; MBA, Rider Coll., 1989. Corp. bus. mgr. Bevmar Industries, Middletown, R.I., 1980-82; office mgr. Bergman Hatton Assocs., Princeton, N.J., 1983-87; mgr. human resources EDUCOM, Princeton, 1987-88, cons. mgr., 1988-90; dir. devel. Mercer St. Friends Ctr., Trenton, N.J., 1990—; v.p. finance & devel. Boheme Opera Co., Trenton, 1993—, vol. asst. stage mgr. Chmn. stewardship Presbyn. Ch. of Lawrenceville, N.J., 1988-91, clk. of session, 1992—; publicity chmn. Greater Trenton Choral Soc., 1990-93. Mem. Women in Devel., Mercer County C. of C. (membership com. 1994), Nat. Soc. Fund Raising Execs., Mt. Holyoke Club. Home: G6 Shirley Ln Lawrenceville NJ 08648-1424 Office: Mercer St Friends Ctr 151 Mercer St Trenton NJ 08611

GARY, GRACE ELIZABETH, non-profit administrator; b. Nashville, May 14, 1954; d. Dan Carmack and Grace Elizabeth (Dietzel) G. AB, Randolph-Macon Woman's Coll., 1976; M Archtl. History, U. Va., 1980. Field rep. Nat. Trust Historic Preservation, Oklahoma City, 1981-82; asst. dir. Nat. Trust Historic Preservation, Denver, 1982-84; regional dir. Nat. Trust Historic Preservation, Phila., 1984-86; exec. dir. Preservation Pa., Lancaster, 1986-94; v.p. mem. svcs. U.S. Hist. Soc., Richmond, Va., 1994—; vice-chmn. Preservation Action, Washington, 1991—. Author: Rescuing Historic Resources: How to Respond to a Preservation Emergency, 1991, Organizing for Change, 1993. Chmn. designation com. Phila. Hist. Commn., 1985-86; vice-chmn. Please Touch Mus. for Children, Phila., 1985-90; mem. Gov.'s Cultural Front, Harrisburg, Pa., 1987-91. Named Alumnae of Distinction Randolph-Macon Woman's Coll., Lynchburg, 1986; USA fellow Design Arts Nat. Endowment Arts, 1990. Mem. Pa. Assn. Environ. Profls., Va. Preservation Alliance, Athenaeum of Phila., Nat. Trust Historic Preservation, Preservation Pa. Office: US Hist Soc First and Main St Richmond VA 23219

GARY, JULIA THOMAS, minister; b. Henderson, N.C., May 31, 1929; d. Richard Collins and Julia Branch (Thomas) G. BA, Randolph-Macon Woman's Coll., 1951; MA, Mt. Holyoke Coll., 1953; PhD in Chemistry, Emory U., 1958; MDiv cum laude, Candler Sch. Theology, 1986. Ordained to Meth. Ch. as deacon, 1986, as elder 1989. Instr. Mt. Holyoke Coll., South Hadley, Mass., 1953-54, Randolph-Macon Woman's Coll., Lynchburg, Va., 1954-55; from asst. prof. to prof. chemistry Agnes Scott Coll., Decatur, Ga., 1957-84, dean, 1969-84; pastor-in-charge St. Matthew United Meth. Ch., East Point, Ga., 1987-92; bd. dirs. Global Health Action, Inc., Atlanta, treas., 1991—; chair coord. coun. Decatur Area Emergency Assistance Ministry, 1995—. Contbr. articles to profl. jours. Recipient Alumnae Achievement award Randolph-Macon Woman's Coll., 1990. Mem. Zonta of Atlanta (pres. 1979-81, Zonta of the Yr. 1988), Phi Beta Kappa, Sigma Xi. Home: 117 Bruton St Decatur GA 30030-3767

GARY, NANCY ELIZABETH, nephrologist, academic administrator; b. N.Y.C., Mar. 4, 1937; d. Walter Joseph and Charlotte Elizabeth (Sayer) G. BS, Springfield (Mass.) Coll., 1958; MD, Med. Coll. Pa., 1962. Diplomate Am. Bd. Internal Medicine, Am. Bd. Nephrology. Resident Nassau County Med. Ctr., East Meadow, N.Y., 1962-64; resident St. Vincent's Hosp. and Med. Ctr., N.Y.C., 1964-65, chief renal sect., 1967-74; fellow in nephrology Georgetown U. Med. Ctr., Washington, 1965-67; instr. medicine NYU Sch. Medicine, N.Y.C., 1968-74; asst. prof. U. Medicine and Dentistry of N.J.-Rutgers Med. Sch., Piscataway, 1974-76, assoc. prof., 1976-81, prof., 1981-88, assoc. dean, 1981-87, exec. assoc. dean, 1987-88; dean Albany (N.Y.) Med. Coll., 1988-90; sr. med. adv. to adminstr. health care financing HHS, Washington, 1990-92; clin. prof. medicine George Washington U. Sch. Medicine, 1991—; prof. medicine, exec. v.p., dean Sch. Medicine Uniformed Svcs. U. Health Scis., Bethesda, Md., 1992—; clin. prof. Howard U. Coll. Medicine, Washington, 1992—. Contbr. chpts. to books, articles to profl. jours. Robert Wood Johnson Health Policy fellow NAS Inst. Medicine, 1987-88; recipient Joseph F. Boyle, M.D. award for Disting. Pub. Svc., Am. Soc. Internal Medicine, 1992. Mem. ACP (Master), AMA, Assn. Am. Med. Colls. (coun. deans), Am. Soc. Nephrology, Alpha Omega Alpha. Office: Uniformed Svcs U Health Sci Deans Office Sch Medicine 4301 Jone Bridge Rd Washington DC 20008-2957

GARZA, DEBORAH JANE, educational administrator; b. L.A., July 25, 1952; d. Nicholas and Mary Jane (Hover) Maloof. AA in Gen. Edn., Rio Hondo Coll., 1973; BA in Sociology, Calif. State U., Fullerton, 1978; MS in Sch. Mgmt., U. La Verne, 1988. Calif. life teaching credential; bilingual cert. competence; cert. sch. adminstr.; profl. adminstr. svcs. credential. Bilingual classroom tchr. Norwalk (Calif.)-La Mirada Unified Sch. Dist., 1981-87, 89—, categorical aid program specialist, 1987-88; instrnl. specialist Whittier (Calif.) City Sch. Dist., 1987-88; master tchr. Norwalk (Calif.)-La Mirada Unified Sch. Dist., 1985-90, dist. mentor tchr., 1989-90, presenter/instr., 1991—; panel mem. ednl. tv. broadcast Schooling and Language Minority Students, 1990. Treas. Edmondson Sch. PTA, Norwalk, 1989—. Recipient Merit Scholarship award U. of La Verne (Calif.) Faculty, 1991, Hon. Svc. award Edmondson Sch. PTA, Norwalk, 1992; named Tchr. of Yr., Edmondson Sch., 1990. Mem. Calif. Assn. for Bilingual Edn., Assn. Calif. Sch. Adminstrs., Norwalk-La Mirada Adminstrs. Assn.

GARZA, HELEN ESTRADA, registrar; b. San Antonio, Sept. 18, 1934; d. Raymond and E. (Estrada) G. BA, St. Mary's U., 1969, MA, 1972. Lic. profl. counselor, Tex.; lic. real estate agent, Tex. Asst. registrar St. Mary's U., San Antonio, 1969-72, assoc. registrar, fgn. student adviser, 1972—; mem. student loan com. Minnie Stevens Piper Found., San Antonio, 1989—. Author: Four-Year College and the Minority Student: An Appraisal of Some Efforts to Provide Equal Educational Opportunities for Ethnic and Minority Students, 1974. Mem. Am. Assn. Collegiate Registrars and Admissions Officers (rep. to social security adminstrn. 1974), Tex. Assn. Collegiate Registrars and Admission Officers (treas. 1978-79, chmn. 1979, local arrangements com. 1979), Nat. Assn. Fgn. Student Affairs, Phi Alpha Theta (pres. Kappa Zeta chpt. 1989-91). Democrat. Home: 915 Mt Serolod San Antonio TX 78213 Office: St Marys U One Camino Santa Maria San Antonio TX 78228-8576

GARZA, NORA, systems engineer; b. Jacksonville, Fla., Aug. 23, 1943; d. Luiz and Nora (Lusero Martinez) G.; m. Ronald Roger Holland, Feb. 12, 1971; 1 child, Michael Jackson Conn. BS, SUNY, Brockport, 1977. Supervising anaylyst Eastman Kodak Co., Rochester, N.Y., 1977-94; mgr. end user svcs. Xerox Corp., Rochester, 1994—. Asst. chair conf. program Internat. Alliance Women's Networks, 1991; bd. dirs., v.p. YWCA, Rochester, 1992-94; steering com. Hispanic Leadership Devel. Program, 1994; co-chair Rochester Grantmakers Forum; mem. task force Diversity Resource Directory, 1994; bd. dirs., treas. Chances and Changes, 1987-88. Mem. Soc. Hispanic Profl. Engrs. (v.p. 1994), Rochester Women's Network, Latinas Unidas, Hispanic Assn. for Profl. Advancement. Roman Catholic. Home: 47 French Woods Circle Rochester NY 14618

GARZA, OLIVIA, realtor, property manager; b. San Antonio, Aug. 2, 1930; d. Jesus Montemayor Caballero and Isabel Alvarado Caballero; m. Gilbert P. Garza, Mar. 31, 1951 (dec. Nov. 1972); children: Caroljean Garza McCarthy, Gilbert P.; m. V. Carl McNamee, June 3, 1977. Grad., high sch., 1948. Grad. Real Estate Inst. Sales staff Naylor Real Estate, San Antonio, 1973-79; office and property mgr. Condominium Locators, Houston, 1980-84; sales staff Ashford Realty, Houston, 1989—; owner Best Property Mgmt., Houston, 1984—. Charter mem., 1st pres. Bridge Emergency Shelter, San Antonio, 1976-79; trustee Baylor Coll. Dentistry, 1982-86; pres. Harris County Children's Protective Svcs., 1988-90; chmn. Region 11 Coun. Child Welfare Bds., 1986-89; mem. Tex. Coun. Welfare Bds., 1986-91; mem. adv. com. Tex. Child Protective Svcs., 1988-92; mem. advocacy and pub. policy com. Chld Abuse Prevention Network, 1992—; bd. dirs. nat. Am. Humane Assn., 1992—; mem. dist. bd. mgrs. Harris County Hosp., 1993—, numerous other civic activities. Mem. Nat. Assn. Realtors, Tex. Assn. Realtors, Houston Bd. Realtors. Home: 13052 Trail Hollow Dr Houston TX 77079-3741

GARZARELLA, PATRICIA NANCY, retail executive; b. Phila., Sept. 24, 1962; d. Anthony and Ersilia (Iacovella) G. BS in Mgmt., St. Joseph's U., 1984. With sales dept. Silo, Pa., 1984-87; mgr. territory Raymond Rosen, Pa., Del., 1988-89; with sales mgmt. div. Circuit City, Pa., N.J., 1989—. Mem. NAFE. Home: 126 W Berkley Ave Clifton Heights PA 19018-2504

GARZARELLI, ELAINE MARIE, economist; b. Phila., Oct. 13, 1952; d. Ralph J. and Ida M. (Pierantozzi) G.; BS, Drexel U., 1973, MBA, 1977, doctorate, 1992. With A.G. Becker, N.Y.C., 1973-84, v.p., economist, 1975-84, mgn. dir., 1984; ptnr., portfolio mgr. Lehman Bros. Inc., 1984-94; prin. Garzarelli Internat. Inc., Boca Raton, Fla., 1994—; lectr. in field. Named Businesswoman of Yr. Fortune Mag., 1987, # 1 in Quantitative Analysis, Instl. Investor Annual Contest. Mem. Nat. Assn. Bus. Economists, Women's Fin. Assn., Am. Statis. Assn., Women's Bond Assn. Developer Sector Analysis (econometric model for predicting industry profits and stock price movements, also predicted stock market crash of 1987). Office: Garzarelli Internat Inc 16661 Echo Hollow Boca Raton FL 33434

GARZELL, SANDRA JO, oncology nurse; b. Bay City, Mich., May 3, 1960; d. Roy Clarence and Doris Elaine (LaPan) Kernstock; m. James Joseph Garzell, May 30, 1987; children: Joseph Roy, Melissa Jo. BSN, Saginaw State U., 1982; MA, Cen. Mich. U., 1991. RN, Mich.; cert. oncology nurse. Nursing asst. Tri-City Nursing Ctr., Bay City, 1978-82; RN, staff nurse Bay Med. Ctr., Bay City, 1982-86, RN, nursing supr., 1986-90, RN, nursing mgr., 1990—; mem. Continuing Edn. Adv. Bd., Bay City, 1985—; adj. nursing instr. Saginaw (Mich.), Valley State U., Delta Coll., Bay City, 1990-91; bd. mem. Bay-Am. Cancer Soc. Adv. Bd., Bay City, 1991, Bay Regional Oncology Ctr., 1994—. Mem. Oncology Nursing Soc., Am. Cancer Soc. (med. dir. 1992-93), Am. Coll. Oncology Adminstrs. Home: 3130 Haberland Dr Bay City MI 48706 Office: Bay Med Ctr 1900 Columbus Ave Bay City MI 48708

GASAWAY, LAURA NELL, law librarian, legal educator; b. Searcy, Ark., Feb. 24, 1945; d. Merel Roger and Carnell (Miller) G. BA, Tex. Woman's U., 1967, MLS, 1968; JD, U. Houston, 1973. Bar: Tex. 1974. Catalog libr. U. Houston, 1968-70, catalog-circulation libr., 1970-72, asst. law libr., 1972-73, law libr., asst. prof. law, 1973-75; dir. law libr., prof. law U. Okla., Norman, 1975-85; dir. law libr., prof. law U. N.C., 1985—; copyright cons. Recipient Calvert prize U. Okla., 1978, 81, Compton award Ark. Librs. Assn., 1986. Fellow Spl. Librs. Assn. (H.W. Wilson award 1983, John Cotton Dana award 1987, Fannie Simon award, 1992); mem. ABA, State Bar Tex., N.C. Bar Assn.,, Am. Assn. Law Librs. (pres. 1986-87). Democrat. Author: (with Maureen Murphy) Legal Protection for Computer Programs, 1980; (with James Hoover and Dorothy Warden) American Indian Legal Materials, A Union List, 1981, (with Bruce S. Johnson and James M. Murray) Law Library Management during Fiscal Austerity, 1992, (with Sarah K. Wiant) Libraries and Copyright: A Guide to Copyright in the 1990s, 1994. Office: U NC Law Libr CB #3385 Chapel Hill NC 27599-3385

GASE, MARY ELLEN, music teacher; b. Saginaw, Mich., Sept. 17, 1937; d. Louis A. and Blanche A. (Pelkey) G. BS in Music Edn., St. Mary-of-the-Woods Coll., 1959; MHumanities, Calif. State U., Carson, 1978, Calif. State U., Carson, 1981. Cert. tchr. K-12, Mich.; registered music educator Music Educators Nat. Conf. Music tchr. South Intermediate Sch., Saginaw, 1959-81; music tchr. in summer sch. Saginaw Schs.; music tchr. Ctr. for the Arts and Scis., Saginaw, 1981—. Editor: Keys to Success, Piano Books Vol. I and II, 1992, 93; author articles on music. Mem. Jr. League, Saginaw, 1962—. Recipient Nat. Guitar Curriculum award, 1980, 81, Excellence in Teaching award Saginaw (Mich.) Pub. Schs. Bd. Edn., 1993; Northwestern U. Sch.

Music grantee, 1984. Republican. Roman Catholic. Home: 1559 Wenonah Ln Saginaw MI 48603

GASKELL, CAROLYN SUZANNE, librarian; b. Glen Cove, N.Y., Aug. 14, 1954; d. Duane Uson and Betty Jane (Slabach) G. BA, Pacific Union Coll., 1976; MA, U. Denver, 1977. Circulation libr. Walla Walla Coll., College Place, Wash., 1978-89, dr. librs., 1989—. Mem. ALA, Assn. Seventh-day Adventist Librs. (pres.-elect 1991-92, pres. 1992-93). Office: Walla Walla Coll Peterson Meml Libr 204 S College Ave College Place WA 99324-1139

GASKINS-CLARK, PATRICIA RENAE, dietitian; b. Ft. Sill, Okla., July 24, 1959; d. Jay Frank and Iwana (Robinson) Gaskins; m. Gene Martin Clark, June 6, 1986; 1 child, Taylor Renae. BS, Cameron U., 1982; MS, Cen. State U., 1986. Cert. home econ.; registered dietitian. Nutrition specialist William E. Davis & Sons, Inc., Oklahoma City, 1985-87; dietitian intern Okla. Teaching Hosps., Oklahoma City, 1987; clin. dietitian Grady Meml. Hosp., Chickasha, Okla., 1987-89; chief clin. dietitian Presbyn. Hosp., Oklahoma City, 1989-90; mgr. nutrition svcs. Norman (Okla.) Regional Hosp., 1990—. Mem. Am. Dietetic Assn., Cameron U. Alumni Assn., Oklahoma City Dist. Dietetic Assn., Okla. Dietetic Assn., Cen. State U. Alumni Assn., Phi Upsilon Omicron. Republican. Baptist. Office: Norman Regional Hosp 901 N Porter Ave Norman OK 73071-6482

GASPAR, ANNA LOUISE, retired elementary school teacher, consultant; b. Chgo., May 12, 1935; d. Miklos and Klotild (Weiss) G. BS in Edn., Northwestern U., 1957. Cert. elem. tchr., Calif. Tchr. 6th grade Pacific Palisades Elem. Sch., L.A., 1957-58; tchr. 1st grade Eastman Street Elem. Sch., L.A., 1959, Glassell Park, L.A., 1959-62, Stoner Ave. Elem. Sch., L.A., 1962-67; 2nd-4th grade tchr. Brentwood Elem. Sch., L.A., 1967-78; tchr. 4th and 5th grades Brockton Avenue Elem. Sch., L.A., 1978-90; est. The Swakopmund Tchrs. Resource Ctr., Namibia, 1991-93; English tchr. The Atlantic Sr. Primary Sch., Swakopmund, Namibia, 1992; career info. cons. Peace Corps., 1991—; substitute tchr. various schs., Las Vegas, 1994—. Mem. Internat. Platform Assn., Calif. Ret. Tchrs. Assn., So. Nev. Ret. Tchrs. Assn., Hadassah, Northwestern Univ. Alumni Assn., Lindblad Intrepid Club. Democrat. Jewish.

GASPARICH, MARGARET JO, interior designer; b. Bristol, Pa., Oct. 24, 1957; d. Leon Richard and Dixie Lee (Fitzpatrick) Robinson; m. Anthony Francias Gasparich, Nov. 25, 1978; children: Aaron Christopher, John Thomas, Rachelle Lindsay. AA, Art Inst., Pitts., 1977; postgrad., Franklin and Marshall U., 1989, Albright Coll., 1990. Sales rep., display mgr. Bed & Bath Shoppe, Langhorne, Pa., 1978; interior designer Ethan Allen, Langhorne, 1978-80; designer, mgr. Pomeroy's, Langhorne, 1980; interior designer B. Altman & Co., Willow Grove, N.Y.C., Pa., N.Y., 1981-84; pres. Middle Creek Design Group Inc., Lititz, Pa., 1989—; mktg. cons. Schreiter Pediatric Rehab. Ctr. Lancaster County, 1989—. Publicity chair, bd. dirs. Lancaster Symphony Orch., 1994—. Recipient Addy awards Ad Club of Cen. Pa., 1991. Mem. Am. Bus. Women Assn. (com. chmn. 1992-93), Lancaster C. of C. (com. 1993—). Republican. Methodist. Home: 216 Market St Lititz PA 17543-1133 Office: Middle Creek Design Group 216 Market St Lititz PA 17543-1133

GASPARRINI, CLAUDIA, publishing company executive, scientist, writer; b. Genova, Italy, Apr. 25, 1941; came to U.S., 1984; d. Corrado and Tina (Pizzuti) G. D in Earth Scis., U. Rome, 1965; cert. in English, U. Cambridge, Eng., 1965, Pitman Inst., London, 1965. Sr. tech. U. Toronto, Can., 1966-67; rsch. asst. U. Toronto, 1967-70, rsch. assoc., 1970-72; phys. scientist II Geol. Survey Can., Ottawa, 1973; rsch. scientist Nat. Inst. for Metallurgy, Johannesburg, South Africa, 1974-75; ind. cons. Toronto, 1976; pres., owner Minmet Sci. Limited, Toronto, 1977—, Jacksonville, Fla., 1982-86, Tucson, 1986—; pres., owner The Space Eagle Pub. Co., Inc., Toronto, Tucson, 1986—, 88—. Author: Gold and Other Precious Metals-The Lure and the Trap, 1989, How to Get the Most Out of the Legal System Without Spending a Fortune, 1990, Gold and Other Precious Metals-From Ore to Market, 1993, Murder of the Mind-The Practice of Subtle Discrimination, 1993, When You Make the Two One, 1994, (as Gloria J. Duv) How to Run a Successful Mail Order Business by Defrauding the Public, 1995; contbr. articles to profl. jours. and books. Scientist Sci. by Mail Program, Boston Mus. Sci., 1991-92; mem. rsch. bd. advisors Am. Biog. Inst., Raleigh, N.C., 1990—; hon. mem. Internat. Biog. Ctr. Adv. Coun., Cambridge, Eng., 1992—. Recipient Cert. Appreciation Outstanding Svc. Internat. Precious Metals Inst., 1994. Mem. Can. Inst. Mining and Metallurgy, Internat. Precious Metals Inst., Soc. for Geology Applied to Mineral Deposits, Assn. Women in Sci., Ariz. Geol. Soc. Home: 6651 N Campbell #102 Tucson AZ 85718 Office: Minmet Sci Limited PO Box 41687 Tucson AZ 85717 also: 2 Lansing Sq Ste 703, Willowdale, ON Canada M2J 4P8 also: Via Ugo de Carolis 62, Rome 00136, Italy

GASPARRO, MADELINE, banker; b. Jersey City, Oct. 5, 1928; d. Donato and Anna (D'Urso) D'Achille; m. Dominick J. Gasparro, Apr. 30, 1949; children: Dorothy, Joseph, Donato, Frank. Grad. high sch., Jersey City. Salesperson credit dept. and employee sales J.C. Penney, Parlin, N.J.; head teller Amboy Madison Nat. Bank, Old Bridge, N.J., bank mgr. Chpt. chmn. South Amboy Hosp., mem. fin. com.; eucharist minister St. Bernadette Ch. of Parlin. Mem. NAFE, Nat. Assn. Bank Women (past hostess), Fin. Women Internat. (chmn. membership Raritan Bay group 1990-91, v.p. 1991-92, pres. 1992-93), Altar Rosary Soc. (past pres.). Address: 17 Parkway Pl Parlin NJ 08859-1905

GASPER, RUTH EILEEN, real estate executive; b. Valparaiso, Ind., July 16, 1934; d. Reuben John and Effie (Wesner) Tenpas; m. Ralph L. Gasper, May 25, 1957. Student Purdue U., 1952-56; BA, Govs. State U., 1982. Analyst computer systems Leo Burnett Advt., Chgo., 1958-69; nat. adminstr. registrars Sports Car Club Am., Denver, 1977-79; pres. Ainslie, Inc., Chgo., 1982—; mem. North River Commn. Housing Com., Chgo., 1982-83, fin. com. Mayor's Task Force on Homelessness City of Chgo. Area coordinator Concerned Action Party, Lansing, Ill., 1977; chief race registrar Ind. Northwest Region Sports Car Club Am., 1969-80. Mem. Chgo. Property Owners Assn., Single Room Operators Assn. (co-founder, treas.), Albany Park C. of C., Condominium Assn. (bd. dirs. Fantasy Island II, sec. Single Room Assistance Corp.). Avocations: sports car racing, classical music.

GASPERINI, ELIZABETH CARMELA (LISA GASPERINI), advertising professional, graphic designer; b. Newark, Sept. 26, 1961; d. Enrico Caesar and Wanda Claudia (Stanziale) G. BFA, Caldwell (N.J.) Coll., 1983. Advt. specialist J.C. Penney Corp., Wayne, N.J., 1982-83; asst. prodn. mgr. Internat. Postal Mktg. Corp., Montville, N.J., 1983-84; art dir. Healy, Dixcy & Forbes, W. Caldwell, N.J., 1984-86; sr. mktg. specialist Am. Varityper Corp., E. Hanover, N.J., 1986-88; product promotion mgr. Brother Internat. Corp., Somerset, N.J., 1988-90; mktg. specialist Ishida USA Inc., Lincoln Park, N.J., 1990-91; mktg. svcs. coord. Castrol Inc., Wayne, N.J., 1991-92; mktg. promotions mgr. Nat. Electronic Info. Corp., Secaucus, N.J., 1992—; telemktg. specialist Sears, Roebuck & Co., Fairfield, N.J., 1984—; owner, cons. Gasperini Graphics, Towaco, N.J., 1984—; art cons. Italico Pubs., Livingston, N.J., 1982—. Mem. N.J. Art Assn., N.J. Italian-Am. Assn. (cons. 1982—). Democrat. Roman Catholic. Home: 10 Willard Ln Towaco NJ 07082-1517

GASPERONI, ELLEN JEAN LIAS, interior designer; b. Rural Valley, Pa.; d. Dale S. and Ruth (Harris) Lias; student Youngstown U., 1952-54, John Carrol U., 1953-54, Westminster Coll., 1951-52; grad. Am. Inst. Banking; m. Emil Gasperoni, May 28, 1955; children: Sam, Emil, Jean Ellen. Mem. Coeurde Coeur Heart Assn., Orlando Opera Guild, Orlando Symphony Guild. Mem. Jr. Bus. Women's Club (dir. 1962-64), Sweetwater Country Club (Longwood, Fla.); Lake Toxaway Golf and Country Club (N.C.). Presbyterian. Home: 1126 Brownshire Ct Longwood FL 32779-2209

GASQUE, DIANE PHILLIPS, personnel director; b. Madison, Wis., Mar. 31, 1954; d. Codie Odel and Ruth Elaine (Oimoen) Phillips.; m. Wyndham Henry Burriss, Feb. 5, 1977 (div. 1979); m. Allard Harrison Gasque, Nov. 14, 1992; 1 child, Folline Elaine Gasque. BA, Midlands Tech., Columbia, S.C. Cert. Notary S.C. With inventory control Oxford Industries, Columbia, S.C.; processing agent NCR, Columbia, S.C.; comml. loan officer S.C. Nat., Columbia, S.C.; personnel dir. Witten Sales, Columbia, S.C. Mem. The Order of the Confederate Rose. Republican. Presbyterian. Home: 1825 St Julian Pl Apt 3L Columbia SC 29204

GASS, GERTRUDE ZEMON, psychologist, researcher; b. Detroit; d. David Solomon and Mary (Goldman) Zemon; m. H. Harvey Gass, June 19, 1938; children: Susan, Roger. BA, U. Mich., 1937, MSW, 1943, PhD, 1957. Lic. clin. psychologist, Mich. Mem. faculty Merrill-Palmer Inst., Detroit, 1958-69, lectr., 1967; mem. faculty Advanced Behavioral Sci. Ctr., Grosse Pointe, Mich., 1969-72; pvt. practice clin. psychology Birmingham, Mich., 1972—; adj. prof. psychology U. Detroit, 1969-75; cons. Continuum Ctr. Oakland U., Rochester, Mich., 1961-77, Traveler's Aid, Detroit, 1959-75; pres. Shapero Sch. Nursing, Detroit, 1967-72, cons. 1958-78; psychol. cons. Physician's Ins. Co. of Mich., 1988—, mgt. Mich. Bell Telephone, 1979-82. Mem. Adv. Com Sch. Needs, 1954-56; trustee Sinai Hosp. Detroit, 1972—; bd. dirs. Tribute Fund United Community Services, 1955-67. Fellow Am. Assn. Marriage-Family, Am. Orthopsychiatric Assn. (v.p. 1975-76), Mich. Psychol. Assn.; mem. Am. Psychol. Assn., Psychologists Task Force (v.p. 1977-84), Mich. Inter-Profl. Assn. (pres. 1976-78), Mich. Assn. Marriage Counselors (1979-80), Mental Health Adv. Svc., Blue Cross and Blue Shield of Mich., Phi Kappa Phi, Pi Lambda Theta. Office: 30200 Telegraph Rd Bingham Farms MI 48025

GAST, ILENE FRANCES, research psychologist; b. Perth Amboy, N.J., June 14, 1950; d. Jerome Alvin and Sandra Hariette (Gillespie) G.; m. Jay Rosenberg, Oct. 24, 1976 (div. May 1980); m. Raymond Francis Colangelo, Aug. 11, 1984. BA, Am. U., 1972; MPhil, George Washington U., 1981, PhD, 1987. Employee devel. specialist CSC, Washington, 1972-77; instr. George Washington U., Washington, 1982; rsch. fellow U.S. Army Rsch. Inst., Alexandria, Va., 1982-85, pers. psychologist, 1985-88; pers. rsch. psychologist U.S. Office Pers. Mgmt., Washington, 1977-82, 88—; owner, mgr. Millefiori, Vienna, Va., 1990—. Contbg. author: Leaders and Managers, 1984. Recipient dir.'s award for meritorious svc. U.S. Office Pers. Mgmt., 1990, Pendleton award for pub. svc., 1992; grantee NATO, Oxford, Eng., 1982; fellow Consortium of Univs., 1982-85. Mem. APA, Soc. for Indsl. and Orgnl. Psychology, Internat. Pers. Mgmt. Assn. (assessment coun., bd. dirs. 1992-93), Pers. Testing Coun. Met. Washington (v.p. 1986-87, pres. 1987-88, exec. bd. 1988-89). Home: 9507 Rockport Rd Vienna VA 22180 Office: US Office Pers Mgmt 1900 E St NW Washington DC 20415

GAST, LINDA KAY, accountant, financial executive; b. San Antonio, Apr. 15, 1949; d. Jerry Joseph and Dolores Mae (McCurry) Rasmussen; m. Steven Alan Schwartzberg, Apr. 19, 1970; m. Johnny R. Gast, Jan. 8, 1994; 1 child, Laurie Rachelle; stepchildren: Laura Lee, Stacy Jo, Josh Daniel. BS, Lindenwood Coll., 1987. CPA, Mo. Office mgr. Coopers & Lybrand, St. Louis, 1982-84; controller The Type House, Inc., St. Louis, 1984-86; cons. Arthur Young & Co., St. Louis, 1986-87; v.p. fin. Amedco Health Care, Inc., Wright City, Mo., 1987-90; CFO RAPCO Internat., Inc., Jackson, Mo., 1990-94, exec. v.p., CFO, 1995—; bd. dirs. RAPCO Holding Co. Pres. bd. trustees Congregation B'nai Torah, St. Charles, Mo., 1987-90; bd. dirs. Hidden Valley, Burfordville, Mo. Mem. Wright City C. of C., Beta Sigma Phi (v.p. St. Peters, Mo. chpt. 1988-89, Woman of Yr. 1988-89). Home: 241 Clay Ln Whitewater MO 63785

GASTEYER, CARLIN EVANS, museum administrator, museum studies educator; b. Jackson, Mich., Mar. 30, 1917; d. Frank Howard and Marian (Spencer) Evans; student Barnard Coll., 1934-35; B.A., CUNY, 1983; m. Harry A. Gasteyer, Jan. 8, 1944; 1 dau., Nancy Catherine. Clk., First Nat. City Bank, 1939-42; statistician Bell Telephone Labs., 1942-45; dir. asst. S.I. Mus., 1956-61; bus. mgr. Mus. of the City of N.Y., 1961-63; mus. adminstr., 1963-66; asst. dir. Monmouth (N.J.) Mus., 1966-67, Mus. of City of N.Y., 1967-70; vice dir. adminstrn. Bklyn. Mus., 1970-74; dir. planning Snug Harbor Cultural Center, S.I., N.Y., 1975-79; cable TV Cons., 1980—; adj. lectr. mus. studies Coll. S.I. CUNY, 1985—. Active Girl Scouts. Co-founder, pres. Jr. Mus. Guild, S.I. Mus., 1956-58. Mem. N.Y.C. Local Sch. Bd. 54, 1960-61. Mem. Am. Assn. Mus., Mus. Council of N.Y.C. Home: 50 Fort Pl Staten Island NY 10301

GASTON, MARY EVELYNA TIDWELL, medical/surgical and critical care nurse; b. Nashville, May 24, 1953; d. Vernon and Nettie Mae Christina (Cunningham) Tidwell; children: Christina Hope, Victoria Marie, Robert Michael Clarence. ASN, Tenn. State U., 1987. Lic. RN, Tenn.; cert. nursing asst., critical care nurse, ACLS; CPR provider. Nursing asst. Metro Bordeaux Hosp., Nashville; med., surg. charge nurse II Nashville Gen. Hosp. Active Just Say No to Drugs program; v.p. Alex Green Elem. Sch. PTA, 1986, pres. 1987. Recipient award Civiton, 1963, 68. Baptist. Home: 3947 Dry Fork Rd Whites Creek TN 37189 Office: Nashville Gen Hosp 72 Hermitage Ave Nashville TN 37207

GASWICK, CAROLYN JEAN, librarian; b. York, Nebr., Dec. 14, 1942; d. Paul H. and Helen Alberta (Teale) Myers; m. Dennis Charles Gaswick, June 14, 1964; children: Christina, Wyatt. BS in Edn. and English, Nebr. Wesleyan U., 1964; MLS, Western Mich. U., 1972. Tchr. Oak Creek Sch., Albany, Oreg., 1965-67, Three Village Sch. Dist., Stony Brook, N.Y., 1968-69; libr. Litchfield (Mich.) Schs., 1972-73; reference libr. Kellogg Community Coll., Battle Creek, Mich., 1980-81; serials and documents libr. Albion (Mich.) Coll., 1981—. Active Sheridan Twp. Bd. Rev., 1990—, Sheridan Twp. Planning Commn., 1994—. Mem. ALA (N.Am. Serials Interest Group), AAUW (chair Mich. ann. meeting 1992), Mich. Libr. Assn., Govt. Documents Roundtable Mich. (sec. 1988-89, v.p., program chmn. 1989-90, pres. 1990-91), PEO (pres. 1978-80), Phi Kappa Phi, Kappa Delta Pi, Beta Phi Mu. Home: 123 Bushong Dr Albion MI 49224-9202 Office: Albion Coll Libr 602 E Cass St Albion MI 49224-1879

GATES, BARBARA LYNN, school administrator, educator; b. Billings, Mont., May 13, 1954; d. Joseph Isacc and Ima Evelyn (Daugherty) G. B.S. in Elementary Edn., Eastern Mont. Coll., 1976. Cert. tchr., Mont. Tchr., Union Sch., Lindsay, Mont., 1976-79, Greycliff Sch., Mont., 1979-80; supr. Alliance Christian Sch., Lewistown, Mont., 1981-83, prin., supr., 1983-86; prin., supr. Paradise Christian Acad., Lewistown, Mont., 1986-91.

GATES, CHERYL RENEE, quality engineer; b. L.A., Mar. 1, 1962; d. George Henry Jr. and Loretta Mae (Jackson) Howard; m. Max Lee Mangold, May 9, 1980 (div. Nov. 1991); 1 child, Keith; m. Thomas Arthur Gates, Aug. 22, 1994; q child, Lisa. Student, Ind. U., South Bend, 1983-89. Quality inspector Exptl. Nylon Products, Osceola, Ind., 1987; R&D lab. technician Mastic Corp., South Bend, 1987-89; R&D process engr. Alcoa Bldg. Products, Sidney, Ohio, 1989-93, corp. quality coord., 1993, corp. quality engr., 1993—. Mem. Soc. Plastics Engrs., Am. Soc. Quality Control. Home: 2134 Broadway Ave Sidney OH 45365-1918 Office: Alcoa Bldg Products 2615 Campbell Rd Sidney OH 45365-8845

GATES, DEBORAH WOLIN, petroleum company executive, lawyer; b. Jan. 20, 1955; m. Stephen A. Gates. BA, Coll. William & Mary, 1976; JD, U. Va., 1979; LLM, U. Wash., 1986. Bar: Va. 1979, Wash. 1982, Ky. 1990. Atty. EPA, Seattle, 1979-89; sr. atty. Ashland Petroleum Co. (divsn. Ashland Oil Co.), Russell, Ky., 1989-90, sr. group counsel, 1990-92, v.p. environ. and health dept., 1992—; adj. prof. U. Puget Sound Law Sch., Tacoma, 1986-89; active API Subcom. on Environ. and Health Law, Washington, 1990—. Bd. dirs. The Nature Conservancy of Ky., Lexington, 1992—, Cmty. Hospice, Ashland, Ky., 1993—. Recipient Tristate Women in Industry award YWCA, 1994. Mem. ABA (vice chair Native Am. resources sect. 1985-89), Ky. Bar Assn. (mem. corp. counsel sect. Ky. 1990—). Home: PO Box 472 Russell KY 41164 Office: Ashland Petroleum Co Environ and Health Dept 2000 Ashland Dr Russell KY 41164

GATES, DOROTHY LOUISE, educator; b. National City, Calif., Feb. 21, 1926; d. Harold Roger and Bertha Marjorie (Lippold) Gates. BA, U. Calif., Santa Barbara, 1949; MA, U. Hawaii, 1963, PhD, 1975; postdoctoral student U. Uppsala (Sweden), 1976, Bedford Coll., London, 1978, Cuban Ministry of Justice, 1979, Cambridge U., Eng., 1986. Dept. probation officer, Riverside County, Calif., 1950-54, 55-61; dir. La Morada, probation facility, Santa Barbara County, 1963-65; prof. sociology San Bernardino Valley Coll. (Calif.), 1965-87, prof. emeritus, 1987—; part-time tchr. criminology U. Redlands, Calif.; chmn. Riverside County Juvenile Justice and Delinquency Prevention Commn., 1971-88. Pres. Women's Equity Action League, Hawaii, 1972; mem. adv. group Riverside County Justice System, 1982. bd. dirs. San Bernardino County Mental Health Assn., Symphony Guild, Cooper Burkhart House, Riverside, Alzheimer Assn., Riverside & San Bernardino counties; mem. adv. council Ret. Sr. Vol. Program, San Bernardino; acad. pres. San Bernardino Valley Coll., 1986; pres., trustee Riverside Community Coll., 1989—. Recipient Cert. of Recognition, Riverside YWCA; named Citizen of Achievement, San Bernardino LWV, 1985; NEH fellow U. Va., 1977; named Outstanding Prof. San Bernardino Valley Coll., 1987. Mem. AAUW, LWV, Western Gerontology Assn., Am. Soc. Criminology, State of Hawaii Sociol. Soc., Calif. Probation, Parole and Correctional Assn. (award 1969), Calif. Women's Assn. Edn. and Rsch., Urban League, Kiwanis (past pres.). Address: 4665 Braemar Pl #212 Riverside CA 92501

GATES, JODIE, dancer; b. Sacramento. Scholarship student, The Joffrey Ballet Sch., 1981. Dancer Joffrey II Dancers, N.Y.C., 1981-83, The Joffrey Ballet, N.Y.C., 1983—. Appeared in TV series Dance in America. Active mem. Dancers Responding to AIDS. Home: 499 Fort Washington Ave # 2F New York NY 10033 Office: The Joffrey Ballet 130 W 56th St New York NY 10019-3818*

GATES, MADI, interior designer; b. Salix, Iowa, Aug. 13, 1938; d. Ralph Fredrick Madison and Joyce Elaine (Rugger) King; m. James Roland Gates, Dec. 30, 1962; children: Kirsten Ann. BS in Nursing Edn., U. Minn., 1963; student interior design program, Calif. Poly. State U., 1983. Staff nurse Winnebago (Nebr.) Indian Reservation, 1959-60; intensive care nurse U. Minn. Hosp., Mpls., 1960-63; head nurse Sierra Vista Hosp., San Luis Obispo, Calif., 1963-64, "float" nurse, 1966-80; owner, designer Madi Gates Interiors, San Luis Obispo, Calif., 1983—. Mem./seamstress Altar Guild St. Stephen's Episc. Ch., San Luis Obispo, 1968-80; mem. Children's Home Soc., San Luis Obispo, 1971—; chmn. Achievement House Workshop for the Disabled, San Luis Obispo, 1980-81, bd. dirs.; pres. Rep. Women, San Luis Obispo, 1969-70; mem. Archtl. Rev. Commn. City of San Luis Obispo, 1988—; kitchen designer Showcase House San Luis Obispo, 1990. Recipient scholarship Sioux City (Iowa) Med. Aux., 1956-59; named Nurse of Yr., U. Minn., 1962. Mem. Cen. Coast Interior Designers, Am. Soc. Interior Designers (allied, cert. masters level), San Luis Obispo C. of C. Clubs: Ninety-nines (San Luis Obispo) (treas. 1979-80), Pharmacy Aux. (pres. 1963-64). Home and Office: 125 Serrano Heights Dr San Luis Obispo CA 93405-1748

GATES, MARTHA MEYER, architect; b. St. Paul, June 4, 1914; d. Adolph Frederick and Ethel Rose (McGilvra) Meyer; m. Marshall DeMotte Gates, Jr., Sept. 9, 1941; children: Christopher, Catharine, Marshall III, Virginia. Student/exch. scholar, Archtl. Assn., London, 1935-36; cert. in architecture, Smith Coll., 1937. Registered architect, N.Y. Architect design/drafting Waasdorp & Northrup, Rochester, 1950, Walzer & Miller, Rochester, 1958-63; architect design/drafting and specifications Epping, Whitney, Fox, Rochester, 1964-74; architect design/drafting Handler & Grosso, Rochester, 1974-75; architect, draftsman Rochester Products (GM), 1975-77; pvt. practice Rochester, 1976—; lectr. on solar energy Rochester Mus. and Sci. Ctr., 1978-81, Pittsford Sch. Continuing Edn., 1982-84, Solar Utilization in N.W. N.Y., 1978-90. Pres. Pittsford Cmty. Com., 1953-54; pres., sec. Pittsford Recreation Commn., 1954-63; leader, trainer Girl Scouts USA, 1957-85; trustee, bd. dirs. YWCA, 1985-91. Recipient Solar House Design award N.Y. State R&D Authority, 1978. Mem. AIA (bd. dirs. Rochester chpt., v.p. pres. 1976), Ctr. for Environ. Info. (v.p., bd. dirs. 1984—, Hartwell Vol. award 1994), Am. Solar Energy Assn., N.E. Sustainable Energy Assn. Home and Office: Martha M Gates Architect 41 W Brook Rd Pittsford NY 14534

GATES, MARTINA MARIE, food products company executive; b. Mpls., Mar. 19, 1957; d. John Thomas and Colette Clara (Luetmer) G. BSBA in Mktg. Mgmt. cum laude, Coll. St. Thomas, 1984, MBA in Mktg., 1987. Tchrs. asst. Mpls. Area Vocat. Tech. Inst., Mpls., 1978-79; sec., regional sales mgr. Internat. Multifoods, Mpls., 1979, sec. bakery mix, mktg. mgr., 1979-80, sec., v.p. sales and new bus. devel., 1980, customer svc. rep. regional accounts, 1980-81, customer svc. rep. nat. accounts, 1981-82, credit coordinator indsl. foods div., 1982-85, asst. credit mgr. consumer foods div., 1985, advt./sales promotion mgr. indsl. foods div., 1985-86, asst. credit mgr. fast food and restaurant div., 1986-87, dir. devel. USA and Can. franchise area, 1987-89; dir. franchise devel. FIRSTAFF, Inc., Mpls., 1989-90; dir. adminstrn. Robert Half Internat., Inc., Mpls., 1990-94; dir. client svcs. The NPD Group, Inc., Chgo., 1994—. Vol. seamstress Guthrie Theater Costume Shop, Mpls., 1975—; alumni mem. New Coll. Student Adv. Council St. Thomas, St. Paul, 1984—; vol. Mpls. Aquatennial, 1987. Mem. Omicron Delta Epsilon.

GATES-COHEN, LISA, small business owner, chef, caterer; b. Washington, July 11, 1955; d. Chester Robert and Peggy Jean (Dalton) Gates; m. Sergio Vivoli, Nov. 3, 1978 (div. Nov. 1, 1984); m. Mitchell Cohen, Sept. 21, 1987. AA, Fleming Coll., Florence, Italy, 1974. Dir. The Am. Sch. in Switzerland, Lugano, 1974-80; counter person Bar Gelateria Vivoli, Florence, 1978-80; costumer, choreographer, scene designer English Theatre of Florence, 1978; tchr. Dance Sch. Theatre, Florence, 1978-81; sec., treas. Vivoli Da Firenze, Inc., L.A., 1981-82; event coord. Calif. Catering Co., Beverly Hills, Calif., 1983; chef, sales rep. St. Germain To Go, West Hollywood, Calif., 1984; chef, cons. Posh Affair Catering Co., L.A., 1984-87; owner, chef, party planner Lisa Gates-Vivoli Catering, L.A., 1985—; catering mgr. Maple Drive Restaurant, Beverly Hills, 1990-91; pvt. chef, 1991—. Mem. Mus. Contemporary Art, L.A., L.A. County Mus. Art, L.A. Theatre Ctr., NOW, L.A., Music Ctr. Unified Fund. Recipient Outstanding Achievement in Art award Bank of Am., Miraleste, Calif., 1972. Mem. NAFE, Am. Inst. Wine and Food, Da Camera Soc. (patron), Roundtable for Women in Foodsvc. Democrat. Home and Office: 1227 N Orange Grove Ave West Hollywood CA 90046-5311

GATEWOOD, JUDITH ANNE, roofing company administrator; b. Wichita, Kans., May 28, 1944; d. Alec Hunter and Mary Louise (Grecian) Stratton; m. Charles Eugene Gatewood, Jan. 26, 1962; children: Lori Lynn Gatewood Murphy, Charles Hunter. Cert. bus. communication, Topeka High Sch., 1983, cert. micro-computer ops., 1986. Clk. typist State of Kans., Topeka, 1964; exec. sec. H.M. Goodman and Co., Topeka, 1965-71; payroll supr. Hwy. Oil, Inc., Topeka, 1971—; corp. sec., treas. Gatewood Roofing, Inc., Topeka, 1983—. Commr. Mayor's Commn. Status of Women, Topeka, 1987-93, elected chair, 1990-91; Fortune 100 mem. Everywoman's Resource Ctr., 1993; deacon Westminster Presbyn. Ch., 1993. Mem. NAFE, Am. Bus. Women's Assn. (pres. Panache chpt. 1985-86, Echo chpt. 1984-85, sec.-treas. Topeka area coun. 1987-88, v.p. exec. chpt. 1988-90, Woman of Yr. Echo chpt. 1984, Exec. chpt. 1990, Star in Your Crown award Nat. Hdqrs. 1985, chmn. bull. receiving West Ctrl. Spring Conf. 1986, pres. area coun. 1990-91, elected gen. chair West Ctrl. Spring Conf. of 1994, pres. exec. chpt.1989-90, nat. v.p. dist. III 1994-95), Pi Tau Omega. Democrat. Presbyterian. Home: 3829 SE 23rd Ter Topeka KS 66605-1804 Office: Highway Oil Inc Bank Iv Towers Fl 12 Topeka KS 66603

GATHMAN, JAN DENISE, interior designer; b. Williston, N.D., Aug. 24, 1954; d. John W. and Margaret J. (Bearce) Fougner; m. Steve P. Gathman, July 15, 1977 (div. Apr. 1989); children: Heidi Jo, Todd Michael. AAAS in Interior Design, U. N.D., 1976; BS in Edn., Minot State U., 1994. Designer & color cons. Sherwin-Williams Co., Williston, N.D., 1975-77; design cons. Tollegson's of Minot, N.D., 1977-79; instr. U. N.D., Williston, 1979-92; design specialist Gaffaney's of Minot, 1992—; mem. adv. bd. N.D. Home Econs. Bd., Bismark, 1981-85; chair Faculty Women and Wives, U. N.D., 1985-90. Mem. Am. Bus. Womens Assn. (v.p. 1982-92, Woman of Yr. awards 1985, 86), Interior Design Soc., Delta Kappa Phi. Methodist. Home: 1325 27th St SE Minot ND 58701

GATI, TOBY T., federal official; b. Bklyn., July 27, 1946; m. Charles Gati; 2 children; 3 stepchildren. BA, Pa. State U.; MA, Columbia U., M in Internat. Affairs. Rsch. asst, project dir., dep. v.p., v.p., sr. v.p. UN Assn. of the U.S.A., 1972-93; spl. asst. to the pres. for nat. security affairs Nat. Security Coun., 1993; sr. dir. for Russia, Ukraine and Eurasian States Nat. Security Coun., UN, 1993; asst. sec. for intelligence and rsch. Dept. State, Washington, 1993—; cons. ABC World Tonight, 1986, Ford Found., 1987-89, BDM Internat., 1989; mem. Coun. on Fgn Rels., Internat. Inst. for

Strategic Studies. Office: Intelligence & Rsch Bureau Dept. State Rm 6531 2201 C St NW Washington DC 20520-6510

GATIPON, BETTY BECKER, medical educator, consultant; b. New Orleans, Sept. 8, 1931; d. Elmore Paul and Theresa Caroline (Sendker) Becker; m. William B. Gatipon, Nov. 22, 1952 (dec. 1986); children: Suzanne, Ann Gatipon Sved, Lynn Gatipon Pashley. BS, Ursuline Coll., New Orleans, 1952; MEd, La. State U., 1975, PhD, 1983. Tchr. Diocese of Baton Rouge, 1960-74, edn. cons. to sch. bd., 1974-78; dir. Right to Read program Capital Area Consortium/Washington Parish Sch. Bd., Franklington, La., 1978-80; dir. basic skills edn. Capital Area Consortium/Ascension Parish Sch. Bd., Donaldsonville, La., 1980-82; instr. Coll. Edn. La. State U., Baton Rouge, 1982-84; evaluation cons. La. Dept. Edn., Baton Rouge, 1984-85; dir. basic skills edn. Capital Area Basic Skills/East Feliciana Parish Sch. Bd., Clinton, La., 1985-86; program coord. La. Bd. Elem. and Secondary Edn., New Orleans, 1987-89; dir. divsn. of med. edn., dept. family medicine Sch. Medicine La. State U. Med. Ctr., New Orleans, 1989—; evaluator East Feliciana Parish Schs., 1982-86; presenter math. methods workshops Ascension Parish Schs., 1980-84. Author curriculum materials, conf. papers; contbr. articles to edn. jours. Curatorial asst. La. State Mus., New Orleans, 1987—; soprano St. Louis Cathedral Concert Choir, New Orleans, 1988—; chmn. Symphony Store, New Orleans Symphony, 1990—; lector St. Angela Merici Ch. Mem. Am. Ednl. Rsch. Assn., Assn. Am. Med. Colls., Midsouth Ednl. Rsch. Assn., La. Ednl. Rsch. Assn., Soc. Tchrs. Family Medicine, New Orleans Film and Video Buffs, Phi Kappa Phi, Phi Delta Kappa. Roman Catholic. Home: 105 Tenth St New Orleans LA 70124 Office: LA State U Med Ctr Sch Medicine 1542 Tulane Ave New Orleans LA 70112-2825

GATISON, BARBARA BAIN, telecommunications executive, association executive; b. N.Y.C., Jan. 22, 1952; d. Lawrence and Isabelle Bain; m. Lenward Gatison, Apr. 22, 1983; 1 child, Lenward II. BS in Life Scis. with distinction, Worcester Poly. Inst., 1974. Staff asst. data systems So. New Eng. Telecomm., New Haven, 1974-76, sr. engr. systems planning, 1976-78; mgr. test/assignment So. New Eng. Telecomm., West Hartford, Conn., 1978-79; mgr. installation/repair SNET Am. Inc., West Hartford, Conn., 1979-81; product mgr. network svcs. SNET Am. Inc., New Haven, 1981, dist. staff mgr. bus. svc. ctr. methods, 1981-82, divsn. staff mgr. planning and creative resources, 1982-85, divsn. mgr. consumer svcs., 1985-89, v.p. consumer svcs., 1989-92, v.p. spl. assignment, 1992-93; pres. SNET Am., Inc., North Haven, Conn., 1993—; mem. Greater New Haven adv. bd. Fleet Bank, N.A. Co-chair Citizens' Task Force Fighting Substance Abuse, New Haven; active New Haven chpt. Links, Inc.; pres. bd. dirs. YWCA Greater New Haven; trustee Worcester Poly. Inst.; bd. dirs. Clifford W. Beers Guidance Clinic, Inc., New Haven. Recipient Ichabod Washburn award Worcester Poly. Inst., 1984, Bus. award Elm City Sr. Club, 1991, Milestone award south ctrl. Conn. chpt. Nat. Coalition 100 Black Women, Inc., 1992, Bus. Leadership award Omega Psi Phi, 1993; named one of Women Who Make a Difference, New Haven Register, 1991; inductee Acad. of Women Achievers, YWCA, N.Y.C., 1991; subject of profile Barbara Gatison is a Trailblazer, The Inquirer, 1994. Mem. NAACP, NAFE.

GATRELL, JOSELLE BERNSTEIN, government official; b. Long Branch, N.J., Sept. 7, 1942; d. Benjamin and Theresa Bernstein; m. Jacob W. Gatrell (div. Nov. 1982). BS, U. Md., 1964; cert. in stats. of health scis., Yale U., 1966; MS, Am. U., Washington, 1974. Statistician, programmer Nat. Ctr. for Health Stats., Rockville, Md., 1967-73; sect. chief Nat. Inst. Drug Abuse, Rockville, 1975-78, chief info. resources mgmt. br., 1978-82, asst. dir. Info. Resources Mgmt., 1982-83; chief data mng. br. Office Toxic Substances EPA, Washington, 1983-85, info. mgmt. specialist Info Resources Mgmt., 1985-86; statistician Nat. Inst. Mental Health, Rockville, 1965-67, chief info. mgmt. and analysis br., 1986-88; statistician FDA, Rockville, 1973-75, dir. div. regulatory info. systems, 1988—. Mem. Phi Kappa Phi. Home: 7244 Lanham Ln Fort Washington MD 20744 Office: FDA 5600 Fishers Ln Rockville MD 20857-0001

GATTO, JANICE, lawyer; b. Hackensack, N.J., May 26, 1960; d. Nello and Ann (Laterza) G. BS, Fairfield U., 1982; JD, Villanova U., 1985. Bar: N.J. 1985, U.S. Dist. Ct. N.J. 1985. Sr. assoc. Melli & Wright, P.C., Paramus, N.J., 1985-89; ptnr. Law Offices of Gatto & Low, Montvale, N.J., 1989—; pub. defender Borough of Wood-Ridge, 1993-94; pub. defender Borough of Maywood, N.J., 1987-90; spl. counsel Borough of Teterboro, N.J., 1990—. Sec. Saddle Brook (N.J.) Zoning Bd. of Adjustment, 1984-85; charter mem. Statue of Liberty Ellis Island Found., Inc., N.Y.C., 1984—. Mem. ABA, N.J. Bar Assn., Bergen County Bar Assn., VFW, Am. Acad. Hosp. Atty.'s, Capitol Hist. Soc., Fairfield U. Alumni Assn., Villanova U. Alumni Assn. Home: 142 Henry St Hasbrouck Heights NJ 07604-1105 Office: Law Offices Gatto & Low 160 Summit Ave Montvale NJ 07645-1721

GATYAS, NANCY CAROL, education educator; b. Green Bay, Wis., Aug. 27, 1933; d. Bernard Charles and Leonora Petra (Jorgensen) Sleger; m. Frank Gatyas, Nov. 4, 1950; children: Frank, Kenton. Grad., Sheboygan County Tchrs. Coll., 1971; BA, Lakeland Coll., 1979; MA in Reading, Cardinal Stritch Coll., 1983. Cert. tchr., cert. reading specialist, Wis. Tchr. elem. schs. Plymouth, 1970-84; instr. speed reading U. Wis., Sheboyhan, Wis., 1984; reading specialist Riverview Middle Sch., Plymouth, 1982-84, Middleton-Cross Plains Schs., Wis., 1984—. Chmn. Plymouth Conservation Drives, 1974-81; active Dept. Agr. Mem. Wis. State Reading Assn. Republican. Lutheran. Clubs: Monroe Woman's, (program chmn. 1987, pres. 1988), Plymouth Woman's (pres. 1970-72), Sheboygan County Woman's (pres. 1972-74). Home: 3013 Irvington Way Madison WI 53713-3413

GAUDELIUS, YVONNE MADELAINE, art educator; b. Toronto, Ont., Can., July 21, 1957; d. Benardus Gaudelius and Sophia (Drewes) Carney; m. Nigel David Higson, June 7, 1991. BA, Queen's U., Kingston, Ont., 1980; postgrad., Sheridan Coll., 1981-83; BFA, N.S. Coll. of Art, 1986; PhD, Pa. State U., 1993. Cert. secondary sch. tchr., Ont. Art tchr. Epsom (Surrey, Eng.) Dist. Hosp., 1983-84; secondary sch. tchr. Halton Bd. Edn., Burlington, Ont., 1987-89; teaching asst. Pa. State U., University Park, 1990-93, instr., 1991-93, asst. prof. art edn. and women's studies, 1993—; conf. cons. Getty Ctr. for Edn. in Arts, L.A., 1992; editor NAEA Women's Caucus Report; mem. editorial bd. Pa. Art Edn. Jour. Contbr. articles to profl. publs. Mem. Nat. Art Edn. Assn., Am. Ednl. Rsch. Assn., Coll. Art Assn., Nat. Women's Studies Assn. Home: 711 Fairway Rd State College PA 16803-3411 Office: Pa State U Art Edn Dept 207 Arts Cottage Univ Park PA 16802-2905

GAUDIERI, MILLICENT HALL, association executive; b. East Liverpool, Ohio, Jan. 26, 1941; d. John Thompson and Sara (Pollock) Hall; m. Alexander V.J. Gaudiere, June 10, 1967; 1 son, Alexandre Barclay Everson. A.A., Centenary Coll., Hackettstown, N.J., 1961; postgrad., U. Pitts., 1962. Polit. researcher U.S. embassy, Paris, 1964-65; asst. to pres. RTV Internat., Inc., N.Y.C., 1966-71; exec. dir. Assn. Art Mus. Dirs., Montreal, Que., Can., 1973—. Bd. dirs. Ga. Pub. Radio, Savannah, 1978-79. Mem. N.Y. Jr. League (dir. 1973-75 Vol. of Yr. award), Am. Assn. Mus. Republican. Presbyterian. Office: Assn of Art Mus Dirs 41 E 65th St New York NY 10021

GAUDREAU, THERESE ANNE, educator; b. Fall River, Mass., Feb. 14, 1949; d. Louise Omer and Jeanne (Morneault) Chouinard; m. John Francis Gibney, Feb. 4, 1969 (div. 1980); 1 child, John Louis Gibney; m. William H. Gaudreau, Apr. 9, 1993. BS, Southeastern Mass. U., 1985. Asst. cashier Bank of New Eng. Bristol Co., Fall River, 1982-84, asst. v.p., 1984-86; v.p. Bank of New Eng. N.Am., Fall River, 1986-87, sr. v.p., 1987-90; adj. instr. Indian River C.C., Ft. Pierce, Fla., 1992—; bd. dirs. Southeastern chpt. Bank Adminstrn. Inst. Bd. dirs. Community Health Care Svcs., Fall River, 1986—, Jr. Achievement, 1988—, Boy Scouts Am., 1988—.

GAUGER, MICHELE ROBERTA, photographer, studio administrator, corporate executive; b. Elkhorn, Wis., Feb. 28, 1949; d. Robert F. and Christiane J. (Guiffaut) Marszalek; m. Richard C. Gauger, May 3, 1969 (div.). Student U. Wis., Superior, 1967-69, U. Wis., Whitewater, 1978-80, Winona Sch. Profl. Photography-Chgo., 1984-91; Degree in Photographic Craftsmenship, Profl. Photographers of Am., 1990, MA in Photography, 1994. Wedding photographer Fossum Studio, Elkhorn, 1973-78; owner Photography by Michele, Whitewater, 1978-81; pres., photographer, mgr., Michele Inc. of Wis., Whitewater, 1981—, Foxes Reg., 1987; speaker Wedding Photographers Internat. Conv., Las Vegas, Nev., 1987, 89, Nashville, 1988, 93, Tenn. Profl. Photographers Assn., Nashville, 1987, Twin Cities Profl. Photographers Assn., Mpls., 1987; lectr. Supra Color Seminar, Mpls., 1987, 89, San Francisco Profl. Photographers Assn., 1988, Monterey Profl. Photographers Assn., Nev. Profl. Photographers Assn., 1989, Mich. Profl. Photographers Assn., 1989, 94, Wis. Profl. Photographers Assn., 1993, 94. Contbr. articles to profl. jours.; works exhibited Chinese Nat. Gallery, Beijing, 1987, 88, 89, 91, 94. Mem. Nat. Arbor Found, Nebr., 1984—. Recipient 1st place Wedding Photography award Internat. Wedding Photography, 1983, 84, 87, 88 (two awards), 89, 91, 2nd place award, 1985, Grand award, 1988. Mem. Profl. Photographers Am. (Natl. Loan Collectional 1984), Exhibited Chinese Nat. Gallery, Beijing, China (2d place award 1988, Bronze medal 1989), Wis. Profl. Photographer Assn., Wedding Photographer Internat., Winona Sch. Profl. Photography Alumni Assn., Whitewater C. of C. Republican. Roman Catholic. Avocations: world travel, big game hunting, horseback riding, cooking. Home: RR 2 Whitewater WI 53190-9802 Office: Michele Inc RR 2 Whitewater WI 53190-9802

GAULIN, LYNN, social work educator; b. Chgo., Nov. 26, 1937. BA, U. R.I., 1979, MA in Adult Edn., 1991; MSW, Boston Coll., Newton, Mass., 1981. Lic. social worker, Mass. Planner King Philip Elder Svcs., Foxboro, Mass., 1981-84; field coord. U. R.I., Kingston, 1984—, instr. human sci. and svcs., 1988—. Chmn. North Attleboro (Mass.) Dem. Town Com., 1990-93; mem., chmn. sch. com. North Attleboro Pub. Schs., 1981-91; mem. North Attleboro Bd. Selectmen, 1991-94; mem. edn. com., chmn. leadership com. Commn. on Women, Providence, 1989—. Mem. Acad. Cert. Social Workers, New Eng. Assn. Coop. Edn. and Field Experience (bd. dirs. 1991-93), Assn. Profl. and Acad. Women, New Eng. Orgn. Human Svc. Edn. (bd. dirs. 1994—), Nat. Soc. Exptl. Edn., Phi Beta Kappa, Phi Kappa Phi (pres. URI chpt.). Democrat. Home: PO Box 664 605 Broadway North Attleboro MA 02760-1167 Office: U RI Taft Hall Kingston RI 02881

GAUTHIER, MARY ELIZABETH, librarian, researcher, secondary education educator; b. Tudor, Alta., Can., May 17, 1917; d. Harold Bertram and Mary Evelyn (Foley) Bliss; m. Louis Lyons Gauthier, May 31, 1947 (dec. 1976). PhB, Northwestern U., 1970; MA in Edn., Lewis U., 1976; EdD, Pacific States U., London, 1979. Clk. LaGrange (Ill.) Pub. Libr., 1956-57; package libr. AMA, Chgo., 1958-60; staff libr. Duff, Anderson & Clark, Chgo., 1960-63; libr./tchr. Fremont Sch. Dist. 79, Mundelein, Ill., 1970-75; substitute tchr. Valleyview Sch. Dist. 365-U, Romeoville, Ill., 1978-89; dormitory dir./tchr. Project Upward Bound, Romeoville, Ill., 1984-94, enrichment studies, 1991; ind. researcher South Bend, Ind., 1990-94; instr. Joliet (Ill.) Jr. Coll., 1986-89; cons. Wash. High Sch.; bd. of advisors Ivy Tech. Coll., Southbend, 1993. Contbr. monograph and articles to profl. jours.; author: Some Basic Principles of New Scientific Attitudes in Education, 1980. Active Manor Pk. Community Assn., Ottawa, Can., 1953. With RCAF, 1943-45. Recipient Gold medal Internat. Symposium on the Mgmt. of Stress, Monte Carlo, 1979; grantee Ill. State Bd. Edn., 1985, Ind. U. South Bend, 1992. Mem. AAAS, N.Y. Acad. Scis.

GAUTHIER, PAULE, lawyer; b. Joliette, Que., Can., Nov. 3, 1943; d. Gaétan and Mariette (Marchand) G. LLB, Laval U., Quebec, 1966, M in Bus. Law, 1969. Bar: Que. Ptnr. Desjardins Ducharme Stein Monast, Quebec, 1984—; bd. dirs. Royal Bank Can., Montreal, Celanese Can. Inc., Montreal, Royal Trust, Montreal. Bd. dirs. Laval U. Found., Quebec. Named to Queen's Coun., 1984, Privy Coun., 1988; named Officer of Order of Can., 1990. Mem. Can. Bar Assn. (pres. 1992-93). Home: 165 Grande-Alleé E #P-6, Quebec, PQ Canada G1R 2L1 Office: DesJardins DuCharme Stein Monast, 1150 Claire-Fontaine St Ste 300, Quebec, PQ Canada G1R 5G4

GAUVREAU, LAURIE, cleaning company executive; b. Hartford, Conn., Dec. 17, 1961; d. Donald Joseph and Eleanor Rose (Grignon) G. Bartending diploma, So. Maine Vocat. Tech. Inst., Portland, Maine, 1982. Cashier, shelf stocker Rogers Supa Dollar, Sanford, Maine, 1978-79; purchasing and sales staff Portsmouth Naval Shipyard, Kittery, Maine, 1979; receptionist, asst. R.J. Beaudoin, Jr., DDS, Sanford, 1979-80; various positions Sprague Electric Co., Sanford, 1980-82; transp. and equipment aide Webber Hosp., Biddeford, Maine, 1983-85; prep staff Ventrex Satellite Cyto Path. Lab, Sanford, 1983-85; sales staff Outdoor World, Moody, Maine, 1984-85; receptionist Dr. Carter F. Dillman, MD, Biddeford, 1985-89; owner The White Tornado, Shapleigh, Maine, 1989—. Home and Office: The White Tornado PO Box 294 Shapleigh ME 04076-0294

GAVIN, EILEEN ANN, psychology educator; b. Chgo., May 30, 1931; d. William Reton and Isabel Pavlowski G. BA in English, Coll. of St. Catherine, 1953; MA in Psychology, U. Minn., 1960; PhD in Psychology, Loyola U., Chgo., 1964. Tchng. asst. Coll. of St. Catherine, St. Paul, Minn., 1956-60, asst. prof., 1963-68, chmn. dept. psychology, 1967-79, assoc. prof., 1968-75, prof., 1975—. Contbr. articles to profl. jours., encyclopedias, and books. NDEA fellow Nat. Def. Edn. Act, 1960-63. Mem. APA (sec.-treas. divsn. 24 1975-78, sec.-treas. divsn. 26 1978-81, treas. divsn. 36 1989-92, pres. divsn. 36 1978-79, Disting. Svc. award 1989), Midwestern Psychol. Assn., Internat. Coun. Psychology, Phi Beta Kappa, Psi Chi, Delta Phi Lambda, Pi Gamma Mu, Psi Chi. Democrat. Roman Catholic. Office: Coll of St Catherine 2004 Randolph Ave Saint Paul MN 55105-1789

GAVIN, MARY JANE, medical, surgical nurse; b. Prairie Du Chien, Wis., Sept. 1, 1941; d. Frank Grant and Mary Elizabeth Wolf; m. Alfred William Gavin, Nov. 9, 1963; children: Catherine Heidi Elizabeth, Carl Alfred Eric. Student, North Cen. Coll., Naperville, Ill., 1959-61; BS, RN, U. Wis., 1964; postgrad., Deepmuscle Tng. Ltd., 1980; postgrad. in deep muscle therapy. RN, Wis. Staff nurse U. Wis. Hosps., Madison; RN home response VA, Milw. Unit chair Badger Girls State, 1991—; mem. Wis. Am. Legion Aus.; mem. task force for handicapped Eastside Wis. Evang. Luth. Ch., Madison, 1993. U. Wis. scholar. Mem. Monona Grove Am. Legion Aux. (pres. Unit 429). Home: 702 Fairmont Ave Madison WI 53714-1424

GAWEHN-FRISBY, DOROTHY JEANNE, retail sales company executive; b. Omaha, Jan. 20, 1931; d. Robert Floyd and Margaret Marie (Sitzman) Sealock; m. Kenneth Emil Gawehn, Apr. 17, 1951 (div. Jan. 1985); children: Marilyn Gawehn Jeffries, Kenneth M., Eric M., Celeste Gawehn-Yates; m. Charles Frisby, Mar. 17, 1990. Grad. high sch., Omaha. Systems technician Nat. Welding Co., Richmond, Calif., 1962-63; lead data entry operator United Grocers Co., Fresno, Calif., 1964-68, data processing mgr., 1968-72, computer operator shift supr., Oakland, Calif., 1972-76, documentation specialist, 1976-82; mgr. adminstrv. systems Baddour, Inc., Memphis, 1983-89; with Fed. Express Corp., 1989-91; sr. tech. writer Autozone, Memphis, 1991—; freelance writer; contract tech. writer with PED. Reader for the blind Sta. WTTL, Memphis, 1983-89; vol. worker Crisis and Suicide Intervention, Memphis, 1985-89, Docent for Ramesses exhibit, 1987. Recipient Key to Memphis. Mem. Internat. Tng. Communication (club pres. 1989-90, Communicator of Yr. award, Dixie region 1988-89, coun. 4 exec. bd. 1992-93), Data Processing Mgmt. Assn (Performance award 1973, Yosemite chpt.), Mensa (chmn. 1989-90). Republican. Roman Catholic. Avocations: backpacking, reading, writing, travel, hiking. Home: 6644 Elkgate Memphis TN 38141-1205 Office: Autozone 3030 Poplar Ave Memphis TN 38111-3552

GAY, ALEDA SUSAN, mathematician, educator; b. Frederick, Okla., Oct. 25, 1951; d. Paul W. and Evelyn (Tefertiller) G. BS, Okla. State U., 1973, MS, 1975, EdD, 1990. Cert. tchr., Okla. Tchr. math. Stillwater (Okla.) Pub. Schs., 1973-83; math. specialist Okla. Dept. Edn., Oklahoma City, 1983-89, computer cons., 1984-89; instr. Okla. State U., Stillwater, 1988-90; asst. prof. math. edn. U. Kans., Lawrence, 1991—; cons. math. textbook Houghton Mifflin, 1985-86; presenter panelist at profl. confs.; presenter workshops. Co-author: Principal Resources in Secondary Mathematics, 1985; developer high sch. algebra curriculum syllabus; contbr. articles to profl. jours. Mem. Assn. State Suprs. Math. (sec. 1988-90), Okla. Coun. Tchrs.Math. (v.p. 1982-84, rep. to Nat. Coun. Tchrs. Math. 1985-90, Outstanding Svc. award 1990), Math. Assn. Am., Nat. Coun. Suprs. Math., Kans. Assn. Tchrs. Math (v.p. colls.), Coll. Math. Educators Kans., N.E. Kans. Assn. Tchrs. Math., Assn. Math. Tchrs. Educators, Phi Delta Kappa. Office: U Kans Dept Curriculum and Instrn 202 Bailey Hall Lawrence KS 66045

GAY, FRANCES MARION WELBORN, private school educator; b. Charleston, S.C., Feb. 18, 1956; d. Melvin Floyd and Frances Helen (Looper) G. BA in English, Hollins Coll., 1979; MAT in English, The Citadel, Charleston, 1989. Cert. tchr. grades 5-12, S.C. Tchr. English, grades 7-8 Charleston Day Sch., 1986-87; tchr. grades 3-4 St. Paul's Acad., Ravenel, S.C., 1987-88; dir. devel. Charleston Day Sch., 1988-89, dir. devel. and admissions, 1989-92; tchr. science, grade 5 Ashley Hall, Charleston, 1992—, tchr. Lang. Arts, grade 6, 1992—. Editor: School Year Book, 1986-87; author/editor (bi-ann. newsletter) The CDS Gateway. Named one of Outstanding Young Women of Am., 1991. Mem. DAR, Hollins Alumnae Club of Charleston (pres. 1983—), Garden Club of Charleston , Jr. League of Charleston (chmn. violence on view 1989, corresponding sec 1992), Huguenot Soc. of S.C. (ch. docent 1985-86), English Speaking Union, Friends of the Confederate Home and Coll., Nat. Soc. Colonial Dames of the 17th Century. Episcopal. Home: 8 King St Charleston SC 29401-2714 Office: Ashley Hall 172 Rutledge Ave Charleston SC 29403

GAY, JUDITH ANN, accountant; b. Quincy, Ill.; d. Charles W. and Lucille M. (Robbins) Barnett; m. Carson J. Gay, Jan. 26, 1980; children: Michelle Riker, Melinda Riker, Jennifer. BS with high honors, Quincy (Ill.) Coll., 1978. CPA, Ill. Acct. Gray Hunter Stenn, Quincy, 1978—; corp. v.p., bd. dirs. Precision Plating of Quincy, Inc. Vol. Multiple Sclerosis, Quincy, 1988, Adams Sch. PTA, Quincy, 1989-93; treas., bd. dirs. Madonna House, 1994—. Mem. AICPA, Ill. CPA Soc., Inst. Mgmt. Accts., Nat. Assn. Accts. (v.p. com. 1980-81). Office: Gray Hunter Stenn 500 Maine St Quincy IL 62301-3932

GAY, MARILYN FANELLI MARTIN, television producer, talk show hostess; b. San Francisco, July 16, 1925; d. Louis and Gertrude (Dondero) Fanelli; m. William Thomas Martin, Jan. 11, 1953 (div. 1956); m. Mel Raymond Gay, May 3, 1963. Student U. Calif.-Berkeley, 1943-46, U. Oreg., 1946. Producer, hostess, writer TV show In God We Trust, Protestant Ch. Fedn., on Sta. KTLA, L.A., 1954-55, A Woman's World TV talk show on NBC TV outlet sta., Las Vegas, 1956, radio show Party with the Stars, L.A., 1958; writer Passing Parade Films, ABC-TV, 1958, Tel. Time; producer, hostess, writer The Marilyn Gay Show, Group W Cable, Valley Cable, Cox Cable, Century Cable, King Cable, Cablevision, Simmons Cable, Century Cable, Verdugo Hills TV, King Cable, Jones Intercable, Am. Cable, Copley Colony Cable, 1982—. Dir. spl. features, coord. radio and TV, Invest in America Campaign, 1957. Contbg. feature writer Los Angeles Times, 1957. Recipient award DAR, 1943, Commemorative medal of Honor Hallmark, 1985. Mem. Writers Guild Am.-West (founding), Internat. Platform Assn., U. Calif. Alumni Assn., Alpha Delta Pi. Mem. Ch. of Religious Science. Address: 1990 Ginger St #101 Oxnard CA 93030

GAYLE, MONICA, broadcast journalist; b. Wenatchee, WA, Mar. 3, 1960. BA Journalism, Wash. State U., 1982. Anchor, gen. assingment reporter KNSD-TV, San Diego, 1990-92; co-anchor CBS News Up to the Minute, 1992-93, CBS Morning News, 1993—. recipient 2 Emmys and 3 Sigma Delta Chi awards. Office: CBS Morning News 524 W 57th St New York NY 10019*

GAYLE-JONES, JEWELLE, human services educator, school system administrator; b. Palmetto, Fla., Nov. 26, 1938; d. Elmore and Lizzie Mae (Jones) Gayle; m. Ralph Jones Jr., Mar. 31, 1959 (div. 1992); children: Vicki Jones-Bell, Deborah Jones-Atkins, Wendy Jones. BA in Social Welfare, SUNY, Saratoga Springs, 1974; MEd, SUNY, Brockport, 1981; cert. adult edn., Harvard U., 1994. Tchr. Rochester (N.Y.) City Sch. Dist., 1971-75, v.p. bd. edn., 1992—; prof. human svcs. Monroe C.C., Rochester, 1975—; workshop facilitator Human Svc. Agys., Rochester, 1975—; adj. instr. Sch. Labor Rels., Cornell U., Rochester, 1978-80, SUNY, Brockport, 1981-82; mem. human rels. com. County of Monroe, Rochester, 1989-94; curriculum writer in field; spkr. in field. Sect. chair allocations United Way of Rochester, 1987-91; bd. dirs. Rochester chpt. Women's Fund of Monroe County, Rochester, 1988—, Wilson Commencement Park, Rochester, 1990—; chairperson children and family svcs. adv. com. Urban League of Rochester, 1990-94; pres. Rochester chpt. Links, Inc., 1994—; convenor Black Women's Roundtable, Rochester, 1994—, African-Am. Cir. of Sisterhood, Rochester, 1994—. Recipient Vol. Svc. award Met. Women's Network, 1981, Martin Luther King Commn., 1986-87, Citation award Jack and Jill of Am., 1987, Disting. Svc. cert. Urban League of Rochester, 1988, Appreciation cert. Monroe County Human Rels., 1991, Rochester Peace Edn., 1992. Mem. Delta Sigma Theta (Cmty. Svc. award 1993). Democrat. Mem. Unity Ch. of Rochester. Home: 165 N Water St # 306 Rochester NY 14604 Office: Monroe CC 228 E Main St Rochester NY 14604 also: 131 W Broad St Rochester NY 14614

GAYNOR, LEAH, radio personality, commentator, broadcaster; b. Irvington, N.J.; d. Jack and Sophia Kamish; AA, Miami Dade C.C., 1970; BA, Fla. Internat. U., 1975, postgrad., 1975—; m. Robert Merrill, Mar. 27, 1954 (dec.); children: Michael David (dec.), Lisa Heidi (dec.), Tracy Lynn (dec.). Owner, operator Lee Gaynor Assos., pub. relations, Miami, Fla., 1970-72; exec. dir. Ft. Lauderdale (Fla.) Jaycees, 1970-71; host interview program Sta. WGMA, Hollywood, Fla., 1971-73, stas. WWOK and WIGL-FM, Fla., 1973-79; occupational specialist Lindsey Hopkins Edn. Ctr. Dade County Pub. Schs., publicity-pub. rels., Miami, 1971-91; ednl. specialist Office Vocat., Adult, Career and Community Edn. Dade County Pub. Schs. 1991-94; broadcaster talk show sta. WEDR-FM, 1983-93; host, producer weekly half-hour pub. service talk program, The Leah Gaynor Show, 1985-94. Mem. Citizens Adv. Com. Career and Vocat. Edn., 1973; mem. adv. com. North Miami Beach High Sch., 1977-79; mem. publicity Com. Ctr. Fine Arts, Mus. Sci.; mem. Coalition Community Edn.; bd. dirs. Alternative Programs, Inc. Mem. Women in Comm., Am. Women in Radio and TV (dir. publicity Goldcoast chpt. 1974-76), Alliance Career Edn. (publicity chmn.). Democrat. Home: 1255 NE 171st Ter Miami FL 33162-2755

GAYNOR, MARGARET CRYOR, program director; b. Oak Park, Ill.; children: Andrew Thorp, Mary Leland. Student, Wellesley Coll., U. Ariz.; BA in Am. Studies, George Washington U., 1974; postgrad., Fed. Exec. Inst. Caseworker, spl. asst. U.S. Senate, Washington, 1962-65, 69-70; assoc. dir. for congl. rels. U. S. OEO, Washington, 1970-73; dir. Office of Govt. Rels. Smithsonian Instn., Washington, 1973-92, dir. Office of Policy and Program Devel., 1992—. Past treas. LEADER Fund of Women in Govt. Rels., bd. dirs.; mem. Alexandria Archaeology Commn. Home: 220 N Alfred St Alexandria VA 22314

GAYNOR-PETERSON, DEIDRE ANN, exercise physiologist; b. Superior, Wis., Oct. 14, 1959; d. Peter Emmett and Erma Cecilia (VanLandschoot) Gaynor; m. Brian Harter Peterson, June 14, 1990. BS, U. Wis., Superior, 1984; MS, U. Wis., La Crosse, 1988. Cert. Basic and Advanced Cardiac, Life Support qualifications, Am. Heart Assn. Wellness cons. Fit for Life, Duluth, Minn., 1988-89; health care specialist James River Corp. of Va., Richmond, 1989-91; fitness specialist Ctr. for Personal Fitness, Duluth, 1991-92; massage therapist Kintop Chiropractic Clinic, Superior, Wis., 1993-94; exercise physiologist Superior Meml. Hosp., 1993—. Bd. dirs. BMW Jaycees, Midlothian, Va., 1989-91; active Douglas County Dems., Superior, 1993—; mem. Head of the Lakes Fiar Bd., 1993—. Recipient Appreciation cert. March of Dimes, Richmond, Va., 1990. Mem. Nat. Wellness Assn., Am. Coll. Sports Medicine, Nat. Strength and Conditioning Assn., Superior Jaycees (bd. dirs. 1992-94). Home: 215 44th Ave E Superior WI 54880-4223

GDOWSKI, DIANA, tax specialist; b. Utica, N.Y., Aug. 16, 1951; d. Michael and Frances Mary (Carzo) G. BA, U. San Diego, 1972; MA, U. So. Calif., 1979, MBA, 1981, M Bus. Taxation, 1986. CPA, Calif. Instr. French lang. Bishop Montgomery High Sch., Torrance, Calif., 1973-76, U. So. Calif., L.A., 1977-79; auditor Ernst & Whinney, L.A., 1981-82, mgmt. cons., 1982-83; tax specialist Fox & Co., L.A., 1983-84; sr. tax specialist Kenneth Leventhal & Co., L.A., 1984-87; tax mgr. Deloitte, Haskins & Sells, Costa Mesa, Calif., 1987-88; mgr. tax acctg. Fluor Corp., Irvine, Calif., 1988—; instr. French lang. Torrance Unified Sch. Dist., 1988—. Vice-pres., Village Ct. Homeowners' Assn., L.A., 1982. Mem. AICPA, Calif. Soc. CPAs. Republican. Roman Catholic. Office: Fluor Corp 3333 Michelson Dr Irvine CA 92730-0001

GEALT, ADELHEID MARIA, museum director; b. Munich, May 29, 1946; came to U.S., 1950; d. Gustav Konrad and Ella Sophie (Daeschlein)

Medicus; m. Barry Allen Gealt, Mar. 15, 1969. BA, Ohio State U., 1968; MA, Ind. U., 1973, PhD, 1979. Registrar Ind. U. Art Mus., Bloomington, 1972-76, curator Western art, 1976—, acting dir., 1987-88, interim dir., 1988-89, dir., 1989—; adj. assoc. prof. Sch. Fine Arts, Ind. U., Bloomington, 1985-89, assoc. scholar, 1986, assoc. prof., 1989—. Author: Looking at Art, 1983, Domenico Tiepolo The Punchinello Drawings, 1986; co-author: Art of the Western World, 1989, Painting of the Golden Age: A Biographical Dictionary of Seventeenth-Century European Painters, 1993. Grantee Nat. Endowment for Arts, 1982, 83, Am. Philos. Soc., 1985, NEH, 1985. Mem. Assn. Art Mus. Dirs. Office: Ind U Art Mus 7th St Bloomington IN 47405-3024

GEANURACOS, ELSIE DA SILVA, foreign language educator; b. Bklyn., Dec. 29, 1922; d. John and Maria (Nascimento) Da Silva; m. George J. Geanuracos, Jan. 28, 1945; children: Constance, Patricia, James, Joan, John. BA, Hunter Coll., 1944; student Columbia U., 1944-47. 1st tchr. Portuguese lang. N.Y.C. Sch. System, 1945-50, Spanish tchr., 1945-50; prof. Spanish U. Bridgeport, Conn., 1969, 72, 73, Housatonic Community Coll., Bridgeport, 1970; founder, adviser Portuguese Scholarship Program, U. Bridgeport, 1973—, sec. Halsey Internat. Scholarship Program, 1974, mem. bd. assocs., instr. Spanish, Womens' Inst. U. Bridgeport; tutor Tutoring Ctr. Bridgeport. Com. mem. Womens' Aux. to Fairfield County Med. Assn., Am. Cancer Soc. Bridgeport chpt.; Chmn. dissemination com. Fairfield chpt. Autism Soc. Conn. translator Bridgeport Hosp. Aux.; mem. bd. assoc. U. Bridgeport; mem. Bklyn. Hist. Soc., Bklyn.; mem. Greater Bridgeport Symphony Guild. Recipient citation for community service Am. Cancer Soc. Bridgeport chpt.; citation as an internationalist UN Assn., 1975; 10-yr. service plaque Portuguese Scholar Ship Program of HISP, 1983. Mem. AAUW (treas. Fairfield chpt.), UN Assn., Judeo-Christian Women's Assn. (mistress of ceremonies first awards luncheon 1974), Alpha Delta Pi. Avocations: swimming, reading, drapery making, knitting, traveling. Home: 102 Lu Manor Dr Fairfield CT 06432-1434

GEARHART, MARILYN KAYE, mathematics and biology educator; b. Tucson, Apr. 11, 1950; d. Raymond Fred and Joan Gazelle (White) Hagerty; m. Lon David Gearhart, Mar. 22, 1975; children: Amanda Kaye, Shannon Leigh. BA in Elem. Edn. with dis, Manchester Coll., 1972; MS in Elem Edn. summa cum, Ind. U., 1976; BS in Math. with high hon, Tri-State U., 1985; postgrad., Ind. U., 1983-89. Substitute tchr. South Bend (Ind.) Community Sch. Corp., 1971-72; tchr. DeKalb County Ea. Community Sch. Dist., Butler, Ind., 1972-77; founder, tchr. Pleasant View Christian Early Learning Ctr., Angola, Ind., 1981-85; also bd. dirs. Pleasant View Christian Early Learning Ctr., Angola; micro computer tchr. Purdue U., Ft. Wayne, Ind., 1984; substitute tchr. Met. Sch. Dist. Steuben County, Angola, 1985; tchr. math. and biology DeKalb County Cen. United Sch. Dist., Auburn, Ind., 1985--. Author: (textbook) The Impossibility of Achieving and Maintaining an Utopia, 1971. Sponsor freshman class DeKalb H.S., 1987-89, sophomore class, 1989—, Students Against Drunk Driving, Auburn, 1985-90, Butler Elem. Little Hoosiers, 1973-77; mem. attendance and gifted and talented coms. DeKalb H.S., 1989-90; coach Acad. Decathlon and Hoosier Acad. Super Bowl, 1989—, Hoosier Spell Bowl, 1993—; leader Girl Scouts U.S., 1986-91, mem., coord. product sales Svc. Unit, 1989-90. Dir's. award Jr. Hist. Soc., 1981-85; maths. and sci. scholars Tri-State, 1985; grantee Tchrs. Retng. Fund. Ind.-State, 1983-85. Mem. NEA, AAUW (treas. 1987-89), Dekalb High Sch. Band and Show Choir Parents, Beta Beta Beta. Mem. Christian Ch. Home: 910 Duesenberg Rd Auburn IN 46706-3223 Office: DeKalb High Sch State Rd 427 Waterloo IN 46793

GEARY, ELIZABETH M., clinical social worker; b. Syracuse, N.Y., Oct. 24, 1961. BS, State U. Coll. Buffalo, 1983; MSW, SUNY, Albany, 1986. Cert. social worker, N.Y., sch. social worker, N.Y.; credentialled alcoholism counselor, N.Y. Chem. dependency social worker Bry-Lin Hosp.-Rush Hall, Buffalo, 1983-85; family specialist Alcoholism Coun. Niagara County, Lockport, N.Y., 1986-87; sch. social worker Orchard Park (N.Y.) Ctrl. Sch., 1987—; mem. policy devel. Fed. Drug-Free Schs.-Communities Act, Orchard Park Ctrl. Schs., 1991. Contbg. author (poems) Women of the Crooked Circle-Collections, 1995. Mem. Bertha Capen Reynolds Soc., 1992—, Community Network Inc., Buffalo, 1992—, women writers workshop Just Buffalo Lit. Ctr., Inc., 1991—; women's theater co. Community Network Inc., 1993—, Hallwall's Contemporary Arts Ctr., 1992—, Buffalo Inner City Ballet Guild, 1992—, NOW, 1989—. Writing fellow Canisius Coll. Western N.Y. Writing Project, 1993-94. Mem. N.Y. State Sch. Social Workers Assn. (bd. dirs. 1990-92). Democrat. Presbyterian. Office: Orchard Park Ctrl Sch Pupil Pers Svcs. Dept 3330 Baker Rd Orchard Park NY 14127 also: 334 Harris Hill Rd Williamsville NY 14221

GEARY, MARIE JOSEPHINE, art association administrator; b. Boston, Dec. 1, 1933; d. Vincent and Maryanne (DeAngelo) Bianco; m. John Francis Geary, Oct. 11, 1959; 1 child, John Francis Jr. Diploma, Medford High Sch., 1951. Registrar grad./postgrad. div. Tufts U. Sch. Dental Medicine, Boston, 1951-60; reporter, arts editor Chelmsford (Mass.) Newsweekly, 1970-82; owner, mgr. Village Sq. Art Gallery, Chelmsford, 1976-80; founder, owner A Way With Words, Chelmsford, 1980—; founder, dir. Eastcoast Quilters Alliance, Westford, Mass., 1988—; mktg. cons. Westford Regency Inn, 1991. Contbr. articles to profl. mags. Pub. rels. dir. New Eng. Quilt Mus., Lowell, 1986-88; founder, pres. Chelmsford Art Soc., 1970-75; founder, bd. dirs. Chelmsford Cultural Coun., 1980-84; founder, dir. pub. rels. Chelmsford Crafters, Inc., 1976-80; publicity dir. Chelmsford Town 4th of July Celebration, 1971-74; founder Women in Bus. Conf., 1994; adv. bd. Clear Lake Furniture. Mem. Am. Quilting Soc., Chelmsford Quilters (pres. 1985-89), New Eng. Quilters Guild (Compass editor 1985-88), Chelmsford Book Discussion Soc., Quilters Connection (Quiltations editor 1992-93, v.p. 1994—), Middlesex Women's Network, Women in Bus. (formed 1993, coord. 1st conf. 1994), Enterprising Women. Republican. Roman Catholic. Home: 38 Amble Rd Chelmsford MA 01824-1968 Office: Eastcoast Quilters Alliance PO Box 711 Westford MA 01886-0021

GEBBIE, KATHARINE BLODGETT, astrophysicist; b. Cambridge, Mass., July 4, 1932. BA, Bryn Mayr Coll., 1957; BSc, U. London, 1960, PhD, 1965. Rsch. assoc. astrophysics Joint Inst. Lab. Astrophysics, U. Colo., 1967-68, lectr. physics and astrophysics, 1974-77; astrophysicist Nat. Bur. Standards, 1968-85, supervisory physicist, 1985-89; dir. physics lab. Nat. Inst. Standards and Tech., 1990—; adj. prof. astrophys., planetary and atmospheric scis. U. Colo., 1977-89. Fellow Joint Inst. Lab. Astrophysics, Am. Phys. Soc.; mem. AAAS, Internat. Astron. Union, Internat. Com. Weights and Measures, Royal Astron. Soc., Sigma Xi. Office: Nat Inst Standards & Tech Physics Lab Bldg 221 Rte 270 Gaithersburg MD 20899

GEBBIE, KRISTINE MOORE, health science educator, health official; b. Sioux City, Iowa, June 26, 1943; d. Thomas Carson and Gladys Irene (Stewart) Moore; m. Lester N. Wright; children: Anna, Sharon, Eric. BSN, St. Olaf Coll., 1965; MSN, UCLA, 1968. Project dir. USPHS tng. grant, St. Louis, 1972-77; coord. nursing St. Louis U., 1974-76, asst. dir. nursing, 1976-78, clin. prof., 1977-78; adminstr. Oreg. Health Div., Portland, 1978-89; sec. Wash. State Dept. Health, Olympia, 1989-93; coord. Nat. AIDS Policy, Washington, 1993-94; assoc. prof. Oreg. Health Scis. U. Portland, 1980—; chair, U.S. dept. energy secretarial panel on Evaluation of Epidemiologic Rsch. Activities, 1989-90; mem. Presdl. Commn. on Human Imunodeficiency Virus Epidemic, 1987-88. Author: (with Deloughery and Neuman) Consultation and Community Orgn., 1971, (with Deloughery) Political Dynamics: Impact on Nurses, 1975; (with Scheer) Creative Teaching in Clinical Nursing, 1976. Bd. dirs. Luth. Family Svcs. Oreg. and S.W. Wash., 1979-84; bd. dirs. Oreg. Psychoanalytic Found., 1983-87. Recipient Disting. Alumna award St. Olaf Coll., 1979; Disting. scholar Am. Nurses Found., 1989. Fellow Am. Acad. Nursing; mem. Assn. State & Territorial Health Ofcls., 1988 (pres. 1984-85, exec. com. 1980-87, McCormick award 1988), Am. Pub. Health Assn. (exec. bd.), Inst. Medicine, N.Am. Nursing Diagnosis Assn. (treas. 1983-87), Am. Soc. Pub. Adminstrn. (adminstrn. award II 1983). Office: 2737 Devonshire Pl NW #315 Washington DC 20008

GEBICKE, NANCY ALBERTA, analytical services company executive; b. Washington, Sept. 11, 1944; d. Wilber C. and Lillian G. (Landis) Cheek; m. William A. Gebicke Jr., July 12, 1965; children: Brian A., Melanie A. Student in mgmt. technologies, Montgomery Coll., 1989—. Exec. asst. EG&G Washington Analytical Svcs. Ctr., Inc., Suitland, Md., 1965—, facility/contract security officer, 1983—. Mem. Am. Fedn. Astrologers. Office: EG&G Washington Analytical Svcs Ctr Inc 5211 Auth Rd Ste 204 Suitland MD 20746

GEBO, EMMA MARIE JOKI, education educator; b. Billings, Mont., Jan. 1, 1945; d. Waino August and Vera H. (Luoma) Joki; m. David Ray Gebo, Sept. 12, 1964; children: Lorri D., Paul A., Robyn J. BS in Home Econs., Mont. State U., 1966; MEd, U. Mont., 1971; PhD Vocat. Edn. Adminstrn., Colo. State U., 1988. Cert. secondary tchr., Idaho. Substitute tchr. various cities, Idaho, Mont., 1967-74; adult instr. Fashion Fabrics, Pocatello, Idaho, 1975-76; instr. clothing and tchr. edn. Idaho State U., Pocatello, 1975-80, chmn. dept. tchr. edn., 1980-92, prof., 1992-93, 94—; pres., COO Crafts, Inc., Ben Franklin franchise; sec.-treas., COO Super Save Drug, Inc., The Outlet, Inc.; mem. Idaho Coun. on Vocat. Edn., 1992—. Editor: Idaho Adult Living/Teen Living, 1986, Idaho Cooperative Vocational Education, 1984, 86, Curriculum Guides for Home Economics, 1987. Named Outstanding Young Women of Am., 1978-81, Pocatello Disting. Young Woman, Jaycettes, 1981; Am. Vocat. Assn. fellow, Ellen S. Richards fellow, 1987. Mem. Idaho Home Econs. Assn. (pres. 1983-85, Disting. Home Economist award 1985), Home Econs. Edn. Assn. (sec. 1989-91, publs. bd. 1986-87), Nat. Assn. Tchr. Educators Vocat. Home Econs. (newsletter editor 1986, sec. 1989-90, publs. bd. 1992—), Am. Home Econs. Assn. (by-laws com. 1983-85), Am. Vocat. Assn., Nat. Future Homemakers Am. (hon. Idaho chpt., tchr. task force 1984-88), Greater Pocatello C. of C. (pres. 1993-94), Pocatello Chiefs. Methodist. Home: 2409 S Fairway Dr Pocatello ID 83201-2044 Office: Super Save Offices PO Box 1669 Pocatello ID 83204-1669

GECEL, CLAUDINE, financial analyst; b. Brookline, Mass., July 31, 1957; d. Joseph and Sally Gecel. BS cum laude, SUNY, Albany, 1979; postgrad., Boston U., 1981, NYU, 1981-83. CFA. Investment analyst Dreyfus Corp., N.Y.C., 1981-85, Quadrex Group, London and N.Y.C., 1986; fin. analyst Disclosure, Inc., N.Y.C., 1987—. Friend White Columns Alt. ARt Space, N.Y.C., 1986—, New Mus. Contemporary Art, N.Y.C. 1987—; fundraiser Met. Opera Assn., 1991—. Recipient Cert. Appreciation Rensallaer County Dept. Probation, 1979. Mem. N.Y. Soc. Securities Analysts, Assn. Investment Mgmt. Rsch., Fgn. Policy Assn., French Alliance, N.Y. Road Runners Club. Home: 227 E 59th St New York NY 10022-1424 Office: Disclosure Rsch 83 Maiden Ln # 11 New York NY 10038-4812

GEDDES, BARBARA SHERYL, communications executive, consultant; b. Poughkeepsie, N.Y., May 27, 1944; d. Samuel Pierson and Dorothy Charlotte (Graham) Brush; m. James Morrow Geddes, Feb. 24, 1968 (div. Dec. 1980); 1 child, Elisabeth. BA, Skidmore Coll., 1968. Project leader Four-Phase Systems, Cupertino, Calif., 1976-77, Fairchild Co., San Jose, Calif., 1979-80; mgr. tech. publs. Mohawk Data Scis., Los Gatos, Calif., 1977-79, Sytek Inc., Mountain View, Calif., 1981-83; project mgr. Advanced Micro Computers, Santa Clara, Calif., 1980-81; v.p. communications systems Strategic Inc., Cupertino, 1983-86; pres., mng. ptnr. Computer and Telecommunications Profl. Services, Mountain View, Calif., 1986—; v.p. corp. mktg., sec. First Pacific Networks, Sunnyvale, Calif., 1988-94; chief exec. officer Comtech Applications Partnership Co., Sunnyvale, 1994—; cons. H-P, Varian, Aydin Energy, Chemelex, also others, 1972—; v.p. Conf. Recorders, Santa Clara, 1975-77; advisor Tele-PC, Morgan Hill, Calif., 1983—. Editor: Mathematics/Science Library, 7 vols., 1971. Contbr. numerous articles to mags. Mem. Santa Clara County Adoptions Adv. Bd., 1971-73, Las Cumbres Archtl. Control Commn., Los Gatos, 1983; advisor Los Altos Hills Planning Commn., Calif., 1978-79. N.Y. State Regents merit scholar, 1962. Mem. Assn. for Computing Machinery (editor 1970-72), Nat. Soc. for Performance and Instrn., Bus. and Profl. Advt. Assn., Women in Communications (pres. San Jose 1983—). Democrat. Home: 910 Mockingbird Ln Palo Alto CA 94306-3719

GEDDES, LADONNA MCMURRAY, speech educator; b. DuQuoin, Ill., May 20, 1935; d. Walter Allen and Cora Ruth (Schwinn) McMurray; m. John Kennedy Geddes Jr., Sept. 8, 1973. BS, So. Ill. U., 1957, MS, 1961; PhD, U. So. Calif., 1975. Cert. cons. in ethics and corp. compliance. Instr. Portland (Oreg.) State U., 1963-67; asst. prof. Ctrl. Wash. State Coll., Ellensburg, 1967-68, Calif. State U., L.A., 1973-74; justice planner Exec. Office of Staff Svc., Frankfort, Ky., 1975-76; staff asst. Ky. Bur. Corrections, Frankfort, 1976-78; assoc. prof. Ky. State U., Frankfort, 1978-79, dir. Pub. Svc. Inst., 1979-81; chairperson Ky. State U., 1981-83; dean N.W. Mo. State U., Maryville, 1983-86, prof., 1986-94; mgmt. cons., pres. Geddes & Assocs., Frankfort, 1994—. Author: Intro to Classical Rhetoric, 1991; author poetry (Poet of Merit 1989); contbr. articles to profl. jours. Tutor Adult Basic Edn. Literacy Program, Maryville, Mo., 1987-94; vol. Am. Cancer Soc., 1989—. Mem. AAUP, NAFE (network dir. 1983-87), Am. Soc. Trial Cons., Assn. for Comm. Adminstrn., Speech Comm. Assn., Am. Soc. Profl. and Exec. Women, Mo. Writers Guild, Speech and Theatre Assn. Mo. (mem. bd. govs. 1992—, editor jour. 1991—), Am. Legion Aux., Sigma Kappa, Pi Kappa Delta, Zeta Phi Eta. Home and Office: 525 Alfa Dr Frankfort KY 40601-4403

GEE, IRENE, food products executive; b. N.Y.C., Aug. 17, 1950; d. Jimmy Set and Lin Fung (Ng) G.; B.A., Hunter Coll., 1971; M.S. in Family and Consumer Studies, Lehman Coll., 1974, M.S. in Guidance and Counseling, 1978, M.S. in Adminstrn. and Supervision Coll. New Rochelle; m. Oct. 17, 1981. Tchr., Olinville Jr. High Sch., Bronx, N.Y., 1971-75, Lehman Coll., Bronx, 1975-77, Harry Eiseman Jr. High Sch., Bklyn., 1978-80; asst. prin. adminstrn. A. Philip Randolph Campus High Sch.; food stylist, recipe developer Ladies Home Jour., 1977-78; food stylist, recipe developer Woman's Day Mag., 1979—, home economist, 1980—; owner, operator Irene's Catering, 1984—; food coordinator Evander Childs High Sch.; food cons. Corn Products Corp., 1978—; food stylist Nabisco, 1978, also Perdue Co.; reciper writer, judger natural food contsts Scholastic Mag.; judge nat. contests Choices mag.; developer recipe booklets various cos. including Progresso and Fla. Mushrooms; cons. food cos. and publs.; comml. model Mauna Loa Macadamia Nuts, Lewis & Neale; recipe developer Lipton Co. Food exhibitor Avant Grade Foods; contbr. articles to Forecast and Choices mags. Mem. Am. Home Econs. Assn., Home Economists in Bus., Am. Counseling Assn., Omicron Nu. Contbr. articles Woman's World mag. Cert. secondary prin.

GEE, JULIA THERESA, artist; b. Council Bluffs, Iowa, July 23, 1954; d. Robert A. and Lucille K. (Laughlin) Jardon; m. Gil N. Gee, Apr. 24, 1976; children: Wesley Brice, John Robert. BA, Tarkio Coll., 1981; MSEd, N.W. Mo. State U., 1990; MFA in Painting, U. Nebr., 1993. Tchr. art Shenandoah (Iowa) High Sch., 1981-90, 94—; grad. teaching asst. U. Nebr., Lincoln, 1990-93. One-woman shows at Tarkio Coll., 1981, 84, N.W. Mo. State U., 1990, U. Nebr., 1993; exhibited in group shows at Tarkio Coll., 1984, Sioux City (Iowa) Art Ctr., 1986, Artist's Gallery, Des Moines, 1988, N.W. Mo. State U., 1989, 90, U. Nebr., 1990, 91, Coll. of St. Mary, Omaha, 1994, Dana Coll., Blair, Nebr., 1994, Hearst Ctr. for Arts, Cedar Falls, Iowa, 1994, Heritage Gallery, Des Moines, 1994 (Juror's award). Mem. coun. St. Mary's Ch., Shenandoah, 1988-90. Recipient juror's mention award Iowa Art Tchrs. Exhbn., U. Iowa, 1987, Carl Druart Fox meml. purchase award Art Educators Iowa, 1988, juror's choice award N.W. Mo. State U. Regional Art Tchrs. Exhbn., 1990, Disting. Alumni citation Tarkio Coll., 1991. Democrat. Home: RR 1 Box 193 Farragut IA 51639-9754 Studio: 610 W Thomas Shenandoah IA 51601

GEE, LINDA MARIE, respiratory therapist, polysomnographic technician; b. Wellsboro, Pa., Feb. 25, 1958; d. Norman Robert and Ann Mae (Petticrew) Butler; m. Richard P. Gee Jr., March 13, 1976 (div. Feb. 1992); children: Christina Marie, Tanya Lynn. AAS, Calif. Coll. Health Scis., 1988. Respiratory therapist St. Joseph's Hosp., Elmira, N.Y., 1983—; polysomographic tech. Sleep Disorders Ctr. St. Joseph's Hosp., Elmira, 1990—; respiratory therapist, profl. adv. Chemung County Health Dept., 1988—. mem. Nat. Bd. Respiratory Care, Assn. Polysomnographic Technicians. Home: 513 Broadway Apt B Elmira NY 14904

GEE, PHYLLIS ANN, critical care nurse; b. Cin., July 27, 1964; d. Albert Thomas and Catherine Ann (Kersker) Veith; m. Ricky Leroy Gee, Jan. 26, 1986 (div. June 1988); 1 child, Justin Thomas; m. Michael Edward Leder, Feb. 1, 1991 (div. Aug. 1992); 1 child, Jonathan David. Cert. in diversified health occupations, Warren County Career Ctr., Lebanon, Ohio, 1982; diploma, Community Hosp. Sch. Nursing, Springfield, Ohio, 1985. RN, Ohio; cert. ACLS. Nursing asst. III pulmonary ICU Community Hosp., Springfield, 1983-85; staff nurse, charge nurse ICU Clermont Mercy Hosp., Batavia, Ohio, 1985-89; staff nurse ICUICU Upjohn Agy. Univ. Hosp., Cin., 1991; staff nurse cardiovascular ICU The Christ Hosp., Cin., 1989—; mem. insvc. com. CV ICU The Christ Hosp., 1990—, mem. quality assurance com., 1993—, mem. peer rev. com., 1993—, mem. re-engring. com., 1994—. Tchr. Sunday sch. True Faith Holiness Ch. of God, South Lebanon, Ohio, 1990—; vol. Goshen (Ohio) Libr., 1992-93. Mem. AACN. Office: The Christ Hosp 2139 Auburn Ave Cincinnati OH 45219-2906

GEE, SHELLEY S., sales professional; b. Auburn, Calif., May 7, 1955; d. George and Ruby G. AA, Sierra Coll., 1975; BA, U. Calif., Berkeley, 1978. Retail merchandiser Ore-Cal Corp., L.A., 1983-84, sales and mktg. mgr., 1984-86, regl. sales mgr., 1986-89, nat. sales mgr., 1989—. Mem. Calif. Seafood and Fisheries Inst., Roundtable for Women in Foodsvc., Soc. Foodsvc. Mgmt.

GEE, THERESA SUSAN, lawyer; b. Seoul, South Korea, July 25, 1960; came to U.S., 1965; m. Steven J. Gee, Sept. 7, 1991. AB in Am. History, U. Calif., Berkeley, 1982; JD, U. Calif., San Francisco, 1988. Bar: Calif. 1988. Co-founder, editor Tri-Athlete, Inc. (sports mag.), Oakland, Calif., 1983-84; law clk. Kincaid, Gianunzio, Caudle & Hubert, Oakland, summer 1986; atty. Severson & Werson, San Francisco, 1988-89, Brown & Wood, San Francisco, 1989-90, Lillick & Charles, San Francisco, 1990-94, U.S. Dept. Labor, San Francisco, 1994—. Office: US Dept Labor Office of the Solicitor San Francisco CA

GEE-MCAULEY, KAREN SUZANNE, public relations executive; b. L.A., Apr. 30, 1962; d. Melvin and Ellen (Tom) G.; m. Skeet McAuley, June 25, 1994. BA in Journalism and Internat. Rels., U. So. Calif. Pub. rels. asst. J.W. Robinson's, L.A., 1982-85; jr. acct. exec. Madeline Zuckerman Pub. Rels., Tustin, Calif., 1985-86; from acct. exec. to v.p. Ruder Finn, L.A., 1986-90; from v.p. to exec. v.p. The Blaze Co., Venice, Calif., 1990—. Mem. Town Hall. Mem. Pub. Rels. Soc. Am., Am. Inst. Wine and Food (bd. dirs.). Home: 3516 Madera Ave Los Angeles CA 90039 Office: Blaze Co 228 Main St Ste 4 Venice CA 90291

GEERTZ, HILDRED STOREY, anthropology educator; b. N.Y.C., Feb. 12, 1927; d. Walter Rendell and Helen (Anderson) Storey; m. Clifford Geertz, 1948 (div. 1979); children: Erika, Benjamin. BA, Antioch Coll., Yellow Springs, Ohio, 1948; PhD, Radcliffe Coll., 1956. Lectr. U. Chgo., 1963-68; from assoc. prof. to prof. anthropology Princeton (N.J.) U., 1970—; chmn. dept. anthropology Princeton U., 1972-77, 86, 88-89. Author: The Javanese Family, 1961, Kinship in Bali, 1974, Images of Power: Balinese Paintings Made for Gregory Bateson and Margaret Mead, 1994, (with Lawrence Rosen) Meaning and Order in Moroccan Society, 1979; editor: State and Society in Bali, 1992. Office: Princeton Univ Dept Anthropology Princeton NJ 08544

GEESLIN, SARA CHAMBERS, sales executive; b. Memphis, June 17, 1948; d. Macie Marion and Sarah (Hendrix) Chambers; m. Robert Dewey Knight, Aug. 17, 1969 (div. July 1981); children: Macy Marian, Robert Miles; m. Gary L. Geeslin, June 30, 1988. BBA in Banking and Fin. cum laude, U. Miss., 1970; grad., Inst. of Banking, 1972. Mgmt. trainee Deposit Guaranty Nat. Bank, Jackson, Miss., 1970-72; asst. tng. mgr. Deposit Guaranty Nat. Bank, Jackson, 1971-72; office mgr. Holiday Inn, Columbus, Miss., 1972-77, Old South Coors, Inc., Columbus, 1981-82; sales rep. J.L. Teel Co., Inc., Columbus, 1982-85; mgr. sales Teel Bus. Sys., Columbus, Miss., 1985-90, br. mgr., 1990—. Mem. Columbus Jr. Aux., 1978—. Mem. Am. Bus. Women's Assn., U. Miss. Alumni Assn., Krewe of Bacchus, Presidents Club, Woodland Garden Club (Columbus), Old Waverly Golf Club (West Point, Miss.), Phi Kappa Phi, Beta Gamma Sigma, Delta Gamma Alumni Assn. (pres. N.E. Miss. chpt. 1980-81). Republican. Episcopalian. Home: 220 Huckleberry Hls Columbus MS 39701-1619 Office: Teel Bus Sys Highway 45 N Hwy 45 N Columbus MS 39701

GEFFEN, BETTY ADA, theatrical personal manager; b. Lachine, Que., Can., May 12, 1911; came to U.S., 1942, naturalized, 1945; d. Joseph and Minnie (Illievitz) Gottheil; student public schs., Montreal, Que.; m. Jacob N. Geffen, Dec. 23, 1944; 1 child, JoAnn Merle. Sec., Saul Cohen/Trustee in Bankruptcy, Montreal, 1926-28, Maxwell Cummings Real Estate, 1928-30, Monroe Abbey, Atty., 1930-31; with Tic-Toc, Stanley Grill and Chez Maurice, Montreal, 1931-41; sec. H.L. Green, N.Y.C., 1941-44; pvt. personal mgr., casting cons., N.Y.C., 1950—; v.p., sec. Mor-Lite Corp., 1994—; cons. Consab Assocs. Corp., N.Y.C., 1977-95. Trustee Israel Cancer Research Fund.; vol. Floating Hosp. Mem. NATAS, Women of the Motion Picture Industry, Motion Picture Pioneers, Internat. Platform Assn., The Nat. Mus. Women in the Arts (charter). Democrat. Clubs: Variety Women N.Y. (v.p. 1977-81, pres. 1982-86, chmn. bd. 1986-88), Brandeis U. Home and Office: 17 W 71st St Apt 7A New York NY 10023-4142

GEFFIN, WENDY, systems analyst; b. Flushing, N.Y., May 13, 1960; d. Gerald Geffin and Corinne Lola (Keyser) Petry. BS in Math. cum laude, SUNY, Stony Brook, 1983. Employment agent Career Builders, N.Y.C., 1983-85; actuarial analyst Am. Internat. Group, N.Y.C., 1985-88; MIS project mgr. Johnson & Higgins, N.Y.C., 1988—. Regents scholar N.Y. State Regents Bd. Mem. Arista Soc. Office: 125 Broad St 3d Flr New York NY 10004

GEFFNER, DONNA SUE, speech pathologist, audiologist, educator; b. N.Y.C.; d. Louis and Sally (Weiner) G. BA magna cum laude, Bklyn. Coll., 1967; MA, N.Y. U., 1968, PhD (NDEA fellow), 1970, postgrad., Advanced Inst. Analytic Psychotherapy, 1973-75. Asst. prof. Lehman Coll., 1971-76; assoc. prof. dept. speech St. John's U., 1976-81, prof., 1982—, dir. Speech and Hearing Ctr., 1976—, chmn. dept. speech communication scis. and theater, 1983-92, developer M.A. program in speech pathology and audiology; pvt. practice, 1980—; cons. to corp. execs.; TV producer and hostess NBC, 1977-78, CBS, 1978-79. Contbr. articles to profl. jours. and textbooks; issue editor Jour. Topics in Lang. Disorders, 1980; editor ASHA monograph, 1987. Active N.Y. State Licensure Bd., 1993—. Emmy nominee for Outstanding Instrnl. Program, 1978; recipient award Pres.'s Com. on Employment of Handicapped, Pres'. medal for Outstanding Faculty Achievement St. Johns U., 1987, Dist. Achievement award NYC Speech Lang.-Hearing Assn., 1994; N.Y. State Edn. Dept. grantee, 1976-78, CUNY Rsch. Found. grantee, 1972. Fellow Am. Speech, Lang. and Hearing Assn. (legis. councillor 1978-87, 90-94, Ednl. Standards Bd., v.p. acad. affairs 1995—); mem. N.Y. State Speech and Hearing Assn. (pres. 1978-80), Audiology Study Group N.Y. Office: St John's U Speech and Hearing Ctr 8000 Utopia Pkwy Jamaica NY 11439

GEHLHAUSEN, ELIZABETH ANN, social service program executive; b. Indpls., May 25, 1961; d. Donald Kenneth Steele and Jo Etta (Smith) Sanich; m. Thomas Lee Gehlhausen, Apr. 13, 1985; children: Brandon Thomas, William Cody. BA, Ind. U., 1983; grad., Ind. Law Enforcement Acad., 1982. Cert. probation officer. Police officer Ind. U. Police Dept., Bloomington, 1982-83; security officer Wm. H. Block Co., Indpls., 1983-84; probation officer Hamilton County Probation Dept., Noblesville, Ind., 1984-86; exec. dir., founder PREVAIL, Inc., Noblesville, 1986—; new programs cons. for victim assistance programs State of Ind.; presenter, trainer in field for various law enforcement, judicial, med., ednl. and religious profls. and grounds at local, state and nat. levels; cons. U.S. Dept. Justice Office for Victims of Crime. Mem. adv. bd. Hamilton County United Way, 1989-95; mem. com. policy plan task force United Way Ctrl. Ind., 1989-90; mem. benchmarking com. City of Noblesville; mem. progress com. Hamilton County, 1995—, Hamilton County Future Search Conf. Planning Com.; grad. Hamilton County Leadership Acad., 1994. Named Citizen of Yr., Am. Bus. Women's Assn., Noblesville, 1987, Disting. Hoosier, Gov. Ind., Indpls., 1988; recipient Cert. Appreciation, U.S. Dept. Justice, Washington, 1989, Ruth Ann Popcheff Human Svcs. award, 1994; honoree Girls, Inc., Indpls., 1991. Home: 12477 Bentley Blvd Fishers IN 46038-1222 office: PREVAIL Inc 942 N 10th St Noblesville IN 46060-1801

GEHLMANN, SHEILA CATHLEEN, psychologist, research analyst; b. Lorain, Ohio, Mar. 25, 1958; d. Donald Eugene and Barbara Ann (Elder) G. BSBA and Psychology, Aquinas Coll., 1986; MS in Applied Indsl./Orgnl. Psychology, Stevens Inst. Tech., 1991. Cons. Naqui & Assocs.,

Grand Rapids, Mich., 1985-86; grad. intern selection and testing divsn. AT&T, Morristown, N.J., 1989-90; projects mgr. Stevens Inst. Tech., Hoboken, N.J., 1988-90; test and measurement specialist Dept. Pers. City of New York, 1990-91; rsch. analyst APA, Washington, 1991—. Author: (with others) Stress and Well Being at Work: Assessments and Interventions for Occupational Mental Health, 1992. Vol. Sta. WCTC Cable Channel 9, Wyoming, Mich., 1980-85; participant K-9 walk, Muscular Dystrophy Assn., Fairfax, Va., 1993-94. Named one of Outstanding Women of Am., 1988. Mem. APA (assoc.), NAFE, Am. Psychol. Soc., Mid-Atlantic Camaro Club. Roman Catholic. Home: 3249 Martha Custis Dr Alexandria VA 22302 Office: APA 750 First St NE Washington DC 20002

GEHM, DENISE CHARLENE, ballerina, arts administrator; b. Miami, Fla., Dec. 14, 1951; d. Charles William and Verna Mae (Wiley) Gehm; m. Gary Edward MacDougal, June 15, 1992. BA cum laude, NYU, 1994; studied ballet with, George Milenoff, Thomas Armour. Soloist ballerina Harkness Ballet Co., N.Y.C., 1970-71, Nat. Ballet Washington, 1971-73; prin. ballerina Chgo. Ballet, 1974, Ballet de Caracas, Venezuela, 1975; featured ballerina Joffrey Ballet, N.Y.C., 1976-91. Appeared in Broadway plays West Side Story, 1979, Phantom of the Opera, 1988; with Rudolf Nureyev in Nijinsky's L'Apres-Midi d'Un Faune, 1979; prin. dancer Homage to Diaghilev, Broadway and State Theatre N.Y., 1979; featured roles include Joffrey's Nutcracker, Arpino's Suite St.-Saens, Cranko's Taming of the Shrew, Ashton's Midsummer Night's Dream, Robbin's N.Y. Export Opus Jazz; performed in numerous maj. cities, theatres and festivals including Champs Elysees in Paris, Herod Atticus Odeon, Athens, An der Vien, Vienna, and Spoleto (Italy)/U.S.A. festivals; featured in numerous TV comms. and print. Recipient Founders Day award NYU, 1994; Harkness House for Ballet and Arts scholar, 1969.

GEHRING, AMY MEHALICK, artist; b. Kinston, N.C., Nov. 27, 1954; d. William Thomas and Harriet L. (Kalbfleisch) Mehalick; m. Robert Joseph Gehring, Aug. 11, 1978; children: Kate, Jim. BFA in Painting, Miami U., Oxford, Ohio, 1976; MA/MFA in Painting, Bowling Green State U., 1978. Graphic artist Harte-Hanks Inc., Cin., 1979-82; lectr. U. Cin., 1980-88, adj. assoc. prof., 1987-89; free lance artist Cin., 1982—; adminstrv. asst. Sullivan Electric Co., Cin., 1991-93, NHP Mgmt. Co., Cin., 1993—. Represented in galleries; represented in permanent corp. collections IBM, AT&T, Xerox. Bd. mem., chair Madeira (Ohio) Recreation and Park Bd., 1994-95, bd. mem., 1991—. Recipient numerous awards. Roman Catholic. Home: 8154 Maxfield Ln Cincinnati OH 45243

GEHRKE, KAREN MARIE, accountant; b. Gaylord, Minn., Apr. 12, 1940; d. Stanley Henry and Frieda Marie (Hammel) Ostermann; m. Orville Raymond Gehrke, Oct. 21, 1961 (div. Aug. 1994); children: Kimberly, Karla, Kent. Grad. high sch., Gaylord, 1958. Inspector Fingerhut Mfg., Gaylord, 1959-60; rewinder 3M, Hutchinson, Minn., 1960-61; packer 3M, Hutchinson, 1971-72; sec. Boehmke Ins. Agy., Gaylord, 1961-63, Law Office of H.A. Knobel, Gaylord, 1964-68; teller First State Fed. Savs. and Loan, Hutchinson, 1969; sec. Wally's Tire Shop, Hutchinson, 1970, Lyle R. Jensen, CPA, Hutchinson, 1974-84; owner Karen M. Gehrke L.P.A., Hutchinson, 1984—. Mem. Nat. Assn. Female Execs., Nat. Soc. Pub. Accts., Minn. Assn. Pub. Accts., Hutchinson Area C. of C.

GEIBEL, SISTER GRACE ANN, college president; b. Sept. 17, 1937. BA in Piano and Music Edn., Carlow Coll., 1961; MA in Music Edn., U. Rochester, 1967, PhD in Music, 1975. Tchr. elem. and high schs., 1959-67, ch. musician, 1972-80; assoc. prof. and co-chmn. music dept. Carlow Coll., Pitts., 1981-82, acting acad. dean, 1982-83, dean, 1983-88, v.p. acad. affairs, 1984-88, pres., 1988—; mem. pres.'s coun. Pitts. Coun. on Higher Edn., numerous other ednl. orgns. Bd. dirs. Program for Female Offenders, Girls Hope of Pitts., PItts. Rsch. Inst., United Way of Allegheny County, Action Housing, Inc., Oakland Cath. High Sch.; mem. adv. bd. Mom's Ho.; trustee Mercy Hosp.; bd. advisors Pitts. Symphony Soc. Mem. Pitts. Athletic Assn., Duquesne Club, Zonta Club (mem. internat. bd.). Office: Carlow Coll Office of the President 3333 5th Ave Pittsburgh PA 15213-3165

GEIER, LISA LYN, audiologist; b. St. Joseph, Mo., May 11, 1961; d. Carolyn Ann (Moyer) Pratt; m. David Lee Geier, May 6, 1988. BGS, U. Kans., 1984, MA, 1990, postgrad. Cert. clin. audiologist, Mo. Audiologist Midwest Ear Inst., Kans. City, Mo., 1988-94; tech. writer, clin. monitor Advanced Bionics, Sylmar, Calif., 1994—; profl. advisor Kans. City, Mo. chpt. Self Help for Hard of Hearing, 1987. Contbr. articles to profl. jours. St. Luke's Hosp. Aux. scholar, 1991, 92, U. Kans. Grad. Student Rsch. Travel scholar, 1990, 92, Zonta Internat. scholar, 1986. Mem. Am. Speech Lang. Hearing Assn. (cert., ACE award 1990-93), Nat. Hearing Conservation Assn. (pub. rels. com. 1988), Sertoma Club (editor newsletter 1992, 93, scholar 1985), Greene County Med. Alliance.

GEIER, MARCIA H., technical writer; b. Newark, Jan. 22, 1955; d. Frank and Betty Sylvia (Saxon) G. BA in English, Rutgers U., Newark, 1976; cert. in electronics, Women's Tech. Inst., 1982; MA in Tech. and Profl. Writing, Northeastern U., 1986. Advt. copywriter Channel Home Ctrs., Parsippany, N.J., 1977-78, Morton Shoes, Boston, 1978-79; freelance photographer Boston, 1980-81; adminstrv. asst. Gilmore & Iandoli, Boston, 1981-82; test technician Teradyne, Boston, 1982-83; engring. technician Analog Devices, Wilmington, Mass., 1983; tech. writer Fish & Richardson, Boston, 1984; prin. tech. writer Xylogics, Inc., Burlington, Mass., 1984—; freelance copywriter Syndicated Ad Features, Newton, Mass., 1993—. Exhibited in numerous photography shows. Mem. Soc. Tech. Comm. Office: Xylogics Inc 53 3d Ave Burlington MA 01803

GEIGER, ANNE ELLIS, secondary educator; b. Washington, Jan. 20, 1932; d. George Joseph and Katherine Martha (Johnson) Ellis; m. John James Gallagher, June 12, 1954 (div. 1972); children: Sean James Jr., Michael William, Anne Cecilia Gallagher Jones; m. Gerald Lewis Geiger, May 28, 1983. BA, Trinity Coll., Washington, 1953; MEd, U. Md., 1972. Cert. tchr., Md. Social studies tchr. Notre Dame Acad., Washington, 1953-54; assoc. dir. Office of Edn., Laon (France) AFB, 1954-56; elem. tchr. Our Lady of Lourdes Sch., Bethesda, Md., 1956-57; social studies tchr. Albert Einstein Sr. High Sch., Kensington, Md., 1968-76; social studies tchr., head dept. Randolph Jr. High Sch., Rockville, Md., 1976-79, Argyle Jr. High Sch., Silver Spring, Md., 1979-81, Eastern Mid. Sch., Silver Spring, 1981—; mem. title IX adv. com. Montgomery County Pub. Schs., Rockville, 1977-78; cons. Nat. Geog. Soc., Washington, 1991-92. Chmn. econs., v.p., dir. focus women project Montgomery County Commn. for Women, Rockville, 1976-80. Recipient Meritorious Civilian Community Svc. award Republic of France, 1956. Mem. Montgomery County Ednl. Assn. (del. 1977-81), Rockville Bus. and Profl. Women's Club (pres. 1982-83), Phi Alpha Theta. Home: 5011 Westport Rd Chevy Chase MD 20815 Office: Eastern Mid Sch 300 University Blvd E Silver Spring MD 20901

GEISELHART, LORENE ANNETTA, elementary education educator; b. Rake, Iowa, June 28, 1929; d. Charles Tobias and Altha May (Mills) Knutson; m. James Willis Geiselhart, June 1, 1947 (div. 1971); children: Nancy Joyce, Larry Paul, Richard Ray, Kathleen Ann. Cert., Luther Coll., 1949; BA, U. No. Iowa, 1965, MA, 1989; postgrad., U. Iowa, 1990—. Pub. sch. tchr. Postville, Iowa, 1947-48; adminstrv. asst. to county supt. schs. Decorah, Iowa, 1948-49; pub. sch. tchr. Galesville and Trempealeau, Wis., 1949-51, Iowa Braille and Sight-Saving Sch., Vinton, 1959-70, South Winneshiek Community Sch., Ossian, Iowa, 1970-94; student tchr. supr. Luther Coll., Decorah, 1971-94. Sec. Calmar (Iowa) Improvement Assn., 1987-92; active Calmar Luth. Ch. Coun., 1975-80, 89-91, mem. choir, 1975-80, pres. Ch. Circle, 1975-77, 88-92. Mem. AAUW (pres. 1969-70, sec. 1990-92), NEA, Iowa Reading Coun., Iowa State Edn. Assn., NE Iowa Rosemaling Assn. (sec. 1991-94), Delta Kappa Gamma (pres. Beta Eta chpt. 1978-81, state fellowship com. 1982-84, grantee 1988). Democrat.

GEISELMAN, PAULA JEANNE, psychologist; b. Ohio, June 30, 1944; d. Paul and Rosemary (Dawson) Parsley. AB in Psychology with honors, Ohio U., 1971, MS in Exptl. Psychology, 1976; PhD in Physiol. Psychology, UCLA, 1983. Adj. asst. prof. UCLA, 1986-91; dir. psychophysiol. rsch. UCLA Sch. Medicine, 1986-91; assoc. prof. dept. psychology La. State U., 1991—; adj. assoc. prof. Pennington Biomed. Rsch. Ctr., 1991—; lectr. in field. Reviewer for Sci. Jour., Am. Jour. Physiology, Physiology and Behavior, Brain Research Bulletin, Appetite: Determinants and Consequences of Eating and Drinking; contbr. numerous articles to profl. jours. Mem. Soc. Neurosci., AAAS, N.Am. Assn. Study of Obesity, Women in Neurosci., Assn. Acad. Women, Am. Psychol. Assn., Am. Psychol. Assn., Eastern Psychol. Assn., Western Psychol. Assn. (head of physiol. psychol., chair. Animal Feeding and Behavior paper session 1981), Assn. Advancement Psychology, Internat. Brain Research Orgn., World Fedn. Neuroscientists, Brit. Brain Research Assn. (hon.), European Brain and Behavior Soc. (hon.), N.Y. Acad. Scis., Sigma Xi, Psi Chi. Office: La State U Dept Psychology 236 Audubon Hall Baton Rouge LA 70803-5501

GEISENDORFER, ESTHER LILLIAN, former nurse; b. Ferryville, Wis., May 18, 1927; d. Peter C. and Christie G. (Quamme) Walker; m. James V. Geisendorfer, Sept. 23, 1949; children: Jane Stokke, Karen Geisendorfer-Lindgren, Lois Buchnis. Student, U. Wis.-LaCrosse, 1944-45; RN, Fairview Hosp. Sch. Nursing, Mpls., 1948. Staff nurse Worthington (Minn.) Clinic, 1948-50; pvt. duty nurse, Sioux Falls, S.D., 1950-51; obstet. nurse Fairview Hosp., Mpls., 1951-53; staff nurse St. Anthony Hosp., Rock Island, Ill., 1953-54; obstet. nurse Fairview Hosp., Mpls., 1954-58, post anesthesia recovery nurse, 1958-62, emergency room nurse, 1962-66, obstet. nurse, 1966-68, head nurse obstetrics, 1968-76; staff devel. instr., clinician, Bellin Meml. Hosp., Green Bay, Wis., 1976-92, ret.; instr. in prenatal and Lamaze classes Ob-Gyn Assocs. of Green Bay Ltd.; editorial cons. Krames Communications. Mem. Wis. Assn. Perinatal Care, Nordfjord Laget in Am., Wis. Nurses Assn. (Disting. Svc. award 1981), Nurses Assn. Am. Coll. Obstetrics and Gynecology (cert., founder Northeast Wis. chpt.), Wis. Acad. Scis., Arts and Letters, Nat. Perinatal Assn. Lutheran. Home: 1001 Shawano Ave Green Bay WI 54303-3020 Office: Bellin Meml Hosp 744 S Webster Ave Green Bay WI 54301-3581

GEISER, ELIZABETH ABLE, publishing company executive; b. Phillipsburg, N.J., Apr. 28, 1925; d. George W. and Margaret I. (Ross) G. A.B. magna cum laude, Hood Coll., 1947. Promotion mgr. coll. dept. Macmillan Co., N.Y.C., 1947-54; promotion mgr. R.R. Bowker, N.Y.C., 1954-60; sales mgr. R.R. Bowker, 1960-67, dir. mktg., 1967-70, v.p., 1970-73, sr. v.p., 1973-75, sr. v.p., pub. book divsn.; adj. prof., dir. U. Denver Pub. Inst., 1976—; sr. v.p. Gale Rsch. Co., 1976-91, cons., 1991—; cons. Excerpta Medica, Elsevier, 1976-82; lectr. pub. procedures Radcliffe Coll., 1966-75; lectr. schs. libr. sci. U. Wash., U. So. Calif.; panel mem. TV series Living Library, 1970. Editor: The Business of Book Publishing, 1985. Contbr. Manual of Bookselling, 1969. Mem. bd. trustees Hood Coll., 1993—. Inducted into Publishing Hall of Fame, 1988. Mem. Assn. Am. Pubs. (exec. coun. prof. and scholarly pub. div. 1989-91, adv. coun. Frankfurt book fair 1971, sch. and libr. promotion and mktg. com. 1972-76, bd. dirs. 1982-85), ALA (pres. exhibits roundtable 1968-70, bd. dirs. exhibits roundtable 1968). Presbyterian. Home: 24 Forest Dr Springfield NJ 07081-1124 Office: 335 E 51st St Ste 5H New York NY 10022-6765

GEISINGER, JANICE ALLAIN, accountant; b. Iroquois County, Ill., June 21, 1927; d. Carl Oliver and Constance Kathryn (Risser) Irps Allain; m. Robert Bond Geisinger, Oct. 17, 1947 (div. 1976); children: Jacque K., Holly D., Terry Joe. AA, Blackburn U., Carlinville, Ill., 1947. Lab. technician Mich. Health Lab., East Lansing, 1947-48; with Southwestern Bell Telephone, Tulsa, 1948-49; bookkeeper Geisinger Ent., Dallas, 1951-69; salesman Earl Page Real Estate, Irving, Tex., 1969-71; food purchaser Town & Country vending, Dallas, 1971-75; bookkeeper/sec. Belco C & I Wiring Inc., Irving, 1976-85; leasing bookkeeper Copiers Etc., Inc., Dallas, 1985-89; bookkeeper Kennedy Elec. Inc., Mesquite, Tex., 1989; ret., 1990; cons. Ross Mech., Irving, 1989—. Crew leader Census Bur., Dallas, 1990. Mem. Am. Contract Bridge Assn. Home: 1216 E Grauwyler Rd Irving TX 75061-5031

GEISLER, LINDA LEE, artist; b. Salt Lake City, Jan. 5, 1964; d. Fenton L. and Marlene Juanita (Kelson) Anderson; m. Allen Jay Geisler, Sept. 17, 1982; children: Jessica Lee, Tashina Marie, Seth Kimball. Student, Utah State U., 1982-83, Mesa C.C., 1986; ind. studies European arts-architecture, Paris, Madrid, Toledo, Spain, London, 1988-92. Co-owner Vienna Fine Arts Agy., Fairborn, Ohio, 1993—; art slide libr. Utah State U., Logan, 1982-83. Exhibited in group shows at Salt Lake Ctr. of Arts, Salt Lake City, 1981, Springville (Utah) Mus. Art, 1982, The Sun Gallery, Park City, Utah, 1986, The Jireh Gallery, Scottsdale, Ariz., 1986, Sue Malinski Gallery, Surprise, Ariz., 1986-87, Stanek House Artists Assn., Spokane, Wash., 1992, 4th Ann. Invitational Spokane Western Art Show and Auction, 1993, Issaquah (Wash.) Gallery Art, 1993, Amy Burnett Gallery, Bremerton, Wash., 1994; represented by Colburn's Gallery, Spokane, Wash., 1993—, Worldly Goods Gallery, Leavenworth, Wash., 1994—, The Gallery, Coeur d'Alene, Idaho, 1994—. Publicity, artist for minority heritage weeks Williams AFB, Chandler, Ariz., 1985-86; youth camp leader women's camp program LDS Ch., Spokane, 1993-94, pub. rels. rep., Cheney, Wash., 1993. Recipient 1st pl. painting category USAF Nat. Art Competition, 1992. Mem. Am. Soc. Classical Realism, Art Soc. Ea. Wash. (newsletter editor 1993-94), N.W. Pastel Soc. (spl. award of merit 1993), Stanek House Artists Assn. (bd. mem. 1993—, award of merit 1992), Oil Painters of Am. (assoc.), Women's Caucus for Art. Home and Office: 5282 Sycamore Fairchild Air Force Base WA 99011-2035

GEIST, JILL MARIE, process development engineer; b. Oak Park, Ill., Nov. 11, 1959; d. Raymond Joseph and Julia Theresa Weiner: m. Mark Harold Geist, Aug. 24, 1985; children: Samantha Rae, Jacob Lee. Student, Coll. of Lake County, Grayslake, Ill., 1982-86. Line worker Zenith Microcircuits, Elk Grove, Ill., 1978, inspector, 1978, prodn. screen specialist, 1978-79, group leader screen print, 1979-80, process control inspector, 1980-81, engring. technician, 1981-83; engring. specialist Abbott Labs., Abbott Park, Ill, 1983-89, process devel. engr., 1989-93; new product coord. Abbott Labs., Abbott Park, Ill., 1993—. Patentee in field. Pres., co-founder Abbott Parent Network, Abbott Park, Ill., 1989-91, pres. emeritus, 1992. Office: Abbott Labs D-90E AP 31 200 Abbott Park Abbott Park IL 60064

GEIST, KARIN RUTH TAMMEUS MCPHAIL, educator, realtor, musician; b. Urbana, Ill., Nov. 23, 1938; d. Wilber Harold and Bertha Amanda Sofia (Helander) Tammeus; m. David Pendleton McPhail, Sept. 7, 1958 (div. 1972); children: Julia Elizabeth, Mark Andrew; m. John Charles Geist, June 4, 1989. BS, Juilliard Sch. Music, 1962; postgrad., Stanford U., 1983-84, L'Academia, Florence and Pistoia, Italy, 1984-85, Calif. State U., 1986-87, U. Calif., Berkeley, 1991, 92. Cert. tchr., Calif.; lic. real estate agt., Calif. Tchr. Woodstock Sch., Musoorie, India, 1957, Canadian, Tex., 1962-66; tchr. Head Royce Sch., Oakland, Calif., 1975-79, 87—, Sleepy Hollow Sch., Orinda, Calif., 1985—; realtor Freeholders, Berkeley, Calif., 1971-85, Northbrae, Berkeley, Calif., 1985-92, Templeton Co., Berkeley, 1992—; organist Kellogg Meml., Musoorie, 1956-57, Mills Coll. Chapel, Oakland, 1972—; cashier Trinity U., San Antonio, 1957-58; cen. records sec. Riverside Ch., N.Y.C., 1958-60; sec. Dr. Rollo May, N.Y.C., 1959-62, United Presbyn. Nat. Missions, N.Y.C., 1960, United Presbyn. Ecumenical Mission, N.Y.C., 1961, Nat. Coun. Chs., N.Y.C., 1962; choral dir. First Presbyn. Ch., Canadian, Tex., 1962-66; assoc. in music Montclair Presbyn. Ch., Oakland, 1972-88; site coord., artist, collaborator Calif. Arts Coun. Artist; cons. music edn. videos and CD Roms Clearvue EAV, Chgo., 1993—. Artist; produced and performed major choral and orchestral works, 1972-88; prodr. Paradiso, Kronis Quartet, 1985, Magdalena, 1991, 92, Children's Quest, 1993—. Grantee Orinda Union Sch. Dist., 1988. Mem. Berkeley Bd. Realtors, East Bay Regional Multiple Listing Svc., Calif. Tchrs. Assn., Commonwealth Club (San Francisco). Democrat. Home: 7360 Claremont Ave Berkeley CA 94705-1429 Office: Templeton Co 3070 Claremont Berkeley CA 94705

GEIZHALS, JUDITH SUSAN, psychologist; b. N.Y.C., Nov. 2, 1949; d. Harold Gustav and Charlotte (Rothowitz) Rotkin; m. Benjamin Geizhals, Sept. 1, 1973; children: Charles, Emily. BA in Art History, NYU, 1971; MS in Occupational Therapy, Columbia U., 1973; MA in Psychology, Hofstra U., 1977, PhD in Clin. and Sch. Psychology, 1980. Lic. psychologist, occupational therapist. Occupational therpaist Albert Einstein Coll. Medicine, N.Y.C., 1973-74; dir. day ctr. Riverdale Mental Health Clinic, N.Y.C., 1974-76; pvt. practice occupational therapy Riverdale and Port Washington, 1974-81; psychologist Port Washington (N.Y.) Sch. Dist., 1980-81, South Shore Ctr. Psychology, Merrick, N.Y., 1980-82; pvt. practive psychology Port Washington, 1982—; lectr. Parent Resource Ctr., Port Washington, 1982-84, Parent and Child Edn., Manhasset, N.Y., 1983-85. Mem. Residents for a More Beautiful Port Washington, 1985—, Friends of Library, Port Washington, 1983—, Friends of the Arts, Locust Valley, N.Y., 1984—. Mem. Am. Psychol. Assn., Nassau County Psychol. Assn. Democrat. Jewish.

GELARDEN, MARTHA JANE, sculptor; b. Beech Grove, Ind., Jan 15, 1954; d. Robert and Mary Elizabeth (Davis) G.; m. William Frederick Schanz, Jan. 20, 1978. BFA, Eastern Mich. U., 1985, MA, 1987, MFA, 1987. Train mgr. Artrain, Inc., Ann Arbor, Mich., 1977-78; registrar Waldorf Inst. Mercy Coll., Detroit, 1978-79; registrar, gallery mgr. Pewabic Pottery, Detroit, 1978-82; art tour guide Detroit Upbeat, Inc., 1982-86; program coord. Henry Ford C.C. Art Dept., Dearborn, Mich., 1987-89; gallery dir. Eastern Mich. U., Ypsilanti, 1990-94, 94—; adj. prof. Henry Ford C.C. Art Dept., 1987-89, Toledo (Ohio) Mus. Art, U. Toledo, 1989; vis. lectr. Eastern Mich. U., 1987—; art lectr. Landmark Travel, Saline, Mich., 1993, 94. Prin. works include What a Relief sculpture, Saxual Structures sculpture. Recipient Purchase award Grad. Sch. Eastern Mich. U., 1987; named to Nat. Dean's List, 1987. Mem AAUW, Nat. Mus. Women in Arts, Internat. Sculpture Source, Mich. Potters Assn. (newsletter editor 1982-84, jour. editor 1984, empty bowls benefit 1992, 93), Coll. Art Assn. Office: Eastern Mich U Art Dept 114 Ford Hall Ypsilanti MI 48197

GELB, JUDITH ANNE, lawyer; b. N.Y.C., Apr. 5, 1935; d. Joseph and Sarah (Stein) G.; m. Howard S. Vogel, June 30, 1962; 1 child, Michael S. B.A., Bklyn. Coll., 1955; J.D., Columbia U., 1958. Bar: N.Y. 1959, U.S. Dist. Ct. (so. dist. and ea. dist.) N.Y. 1960, U.S. Ct. Appeals (2d cir.) 1960, U.S. Ct. Mil. Appeals 1962. Asst. to editor N.Y. Law Jour., N.Y.C., 1958-59; confidential asst. to U.S. atty. ea. dist. N.Y., Bklyn., 1959-61; assoc. Whitman & Ransom, N.Y.C., 1961-70, ptnr., 1971-93; ptnr. Whitman Breed Abbott & Morgan, N.Y.C., 1993—. Mem. ABA (individual rights sect., real property & trust law sect.), Fed. Bar Counsel, N.Y. State Bar Assn. (trusts and estates com.), N.Y. State Dist. Attys. Assn., Assn. of Bar of City of N.Y., Columbia Law Sch. Alumni Assn. (bd. dirs.), Girls, Inc. (resources com.), Princeton Club. Home: 169 E 69th St New York NY 10021-5163 Office: Whitman Breed Abbott & Morgan 200 Park Ave New York NY 10166-0001

GELLAS, BONNIE, employee benefits communications executive; b. Trenton, N.J., July 21, 1949; d. George G. and Dorothy (Skokos) G. BA in History, Wilkes U., 1971; MA in Curriculum Devel., Columbia U., 1975. Tchr. secondary sch. social studies Newburgh (N.Y.) Free Acad., 1971-73, The Baldwin Sch., N.Y., 1974-75; curriculum developer Life Office Mgmt. Assoc., N.Y., 1975-78; comm. cons. Martin E. Segal Co., N.Y., 1978-82, Johnson & Higgins, N.Y., 1982-85; sr. comm. cons. Marjorie Gross & Co., N.Y., 1985-90; v.p., dir. comm. The Segal Co., N.Y., 1990—. mem. bd. dirs. Greater N.Y. Bridge Assn., 1991—. Mem. WEB, Internat. Found. Employee Benefit Plans, 1990—. Office: The Segal Co One Park Ave New York NY 10016-5895

GELLER, DIANE JOYCE, lawyer; b. Glen Cove, N.Y., Aug. 6, 1953; d. Isadore and Rose (Herskovitz) Goldstein; m. Joseph H. Geller, July 4, 1973; 2 children. BA, C.W. Post Coll., 1975; JD, Hofstra U., 1978. Bar: N.Y. 1978, U.S. Dist. Ct. (ea. and so. dists.) N.Y. 1978, U.S. Supreme Ct. 1990, Tenn. 1991. V.p. adminstrn. Counsel Synergy Group, Farmingdale, N.Y., 1978-83; gen. counsel, assoc. risk mgr. LRF Risk Mgmt., Great Neck, N.Y., 1984-85; gen. counsel Alpha Surg. Enterprises, Inc., White Plains, N.Y., 1985-86; v.p., gen. counsel Am. Med. Ins. Co., Hicksville, N.Y., 1986-89; counsel, corp. sec. Uniforce Temp. Pers., Inc., New Hyde Park, N.Y., 1989—; bd. advisors lawyers assistance program Adelphi U. Bd. Advisors, Garden city, N.Y.. Mem. ABA, Nassau County Bar Assn. Home: 32 Broadfield Pl Glen Cove NY 11542-2004 Office: Uniforce 1335 Jericho Tpke New Hyde Park NY 11040*

GELLER, FAYE-MERRILL, artist, educator; b. New Britain, Conn., July 12, 1948; m. Steven Andrew Geller, Dec. 19, 1987; children: Rebecca Jane Geller Wechter, Lauren Elizabeth, Jared Adam. Grad. high sch., New Britain. Pvt. tchr. painting Keene, N.H., 1990—; pvt. tchr. quilting Keene, 1992—. Exhibited in group shows at Art Walk, Keene, 1990, 91, 92, Lupine Gallery, Monhegan Island, Maine, 1991—, Shaw Gallery, Keene, 1992, Yikes Gallery, Center Harbor, N.H., 1993, Thorne-Sagendorf Gallery Keene State Coll., 1993, 94, Monadnock Artisans Gallery, Westmoreland, N.H., 1993—. Vol. Hospice, Keene, 1994; sponsor Monadnock Regional Humane Soc., 1987—. Mem. Copley Soc. Boston, Keene Art Assn., Omega Arts Network. Home and Office: 19 Skyview Circle Keene NH 03431

GELLER, JANICE GRACE, nurse; b. Auburn, Ga., Feb. 25, 1938; d. Erby Ralph and Jewell Grace (Maughon) Clack; m. Joseph Jerome Geller, Dec. 23, 1973; 1 child, Elizabeth Joanne. Student, LaGrange Coll., 1955-57; BS in Nursing, Emory U., 1960; MS, Rutgers U., 1962. Psychiat. staff nurse dept. psychiatry Emory U., Atlanta, 1960; nurse educator Ill. State Psychiat. Inst., Chgo., 1961; clin. specialist in mental retardation nursing Northville, Mich., 1962; faculty Coll. Nursing Rutgers U., Newark, 1962-63, faculty Advanced Program in Psychiat. Nursing, 1964-66; faculty Coll. Nursing U. Mich., Ann Arbor, 1963-64; faculty, Teheran (Iran) Coll. for Women, 1967-69; clin. specialist psychiat. nursing Roosevelt Hosp., N.Y.C., 1969-70; faculty, guest lectr. Columbia U., N.Y.C., 1969-70; supr. Dept. Psychiat. Nursing Mt. Sinai Hosp., N.Y.C., 1970-72; pvt. practice psychotherapy N.Y.C., 1972-77, Ridgewood, N.J., 1977—; faculty, curriculum coord. in psychiat. nursing William Alanson White Inst. Psychiatry, Psychoanalysis and Psychology, N.Y.C., 1974-84; mem. U.S. del. of Community and Mental Health Nurses to People's Republic of China, 1983. Contbr. articles to profl. jours.; editorial bd. Perspectives in Psychiat. Care, 1971-74, 78-84; author: (with Anita Marie Werner) Instruments for Study of Nurse-Patient Interaction, 1964. Committeewoman Bergen County Rep. Com., 1989; mem. Rep. County Com., Bergen County, N.J. Recipient 10th Anniversary award Outstanding Clin. Specialist in psychiat.-mental health nursing in N.J., Soc. Cert. Clin. Specialists, 1982; Fed. Govt. grantee as career tchr. in psychiat. nursing, Rutgers U., 1962-63; cert. psychiat. nurse and clin. specialist, N.J., N.Y. Mem. AAAS, ANA (various certs.), N.J. Nurses Assn., Soc. Cert. Clin. Specialists in Psychiat. Nursing (chmn.), Coun. Specialists in Psychiat. Mental Health Nursing, Am. Group Psychotherapy Assn., Am. Assn. Mental Deficiency, World Fedn. Mental Health, Friends of Hermitage, Soc. Valley Hosp. of Ridgewood, AMA Aux., Bergen County Med. Soc. Aux., Coll. Club, Sigma Theta Tau. Address: 159 Fairmount Rd Ridgewood NJ 07450-1422

GELLICI, JANET ANN, writer; b. Astoria, N.Y., Aug. 24, 1957; d. Paul and Dolores (Franchak) G. BA, U. Iowa, 1979. Pub. info. dir. Western Gov.'s Assn., Denver, 1980-82, Colo. Sch. Mines, Golden, 1982-83; pres. Market Comm., Wheat Ridge, Colo., 1983—; contbg. editor Internat. Bulk Jour., Surrey, England, 1986—; pres. Coal Market Strategies, Wheat Ridge, 1989—; columnist Denver Post, Wheat Ridge, 1990—; exec. dir. Western Coal Coun., Wheat Ridge, 1991—; ptnr. Bus. Affairs Unltd., Denver, 1994—; dir. Rocky Mountain Inventors & Entrepreneurs Congress, Denver, 1994. Office: Coal Market Strategies PO Box 2018 Wheatridge CO 80034

GELLMAN, ESTELLE SHEILA KLITTNICK, education educator; b. Bklyn., July 27, 1941; d. Jack and Ida (Frankel) Klittnick; m. Yale H. Gellman, Aug. 23, 1964; children: Douglas, Russell, Beth. BA in Psychology, CUNY, 1962; MA, Columbia U., 1965, PhD, 1968. Lic. psychologist, N.Y. Lectr. Hofstra U., 1966-67, asst. prof., 1968-72, assoc. prof., 1972-79, dir. PhD program in ednl. rsch., 1978-79, chairperson dept. counseling, psychology and rsch. in edn., 1979-88, prof., 1979—, acting assoc. dean. sch. edn., 1990; presented numerous workshops in field; evaluation cons. Teacher Corps Project Hofstra U., 1977, Title I project Massapequa (N.Y.) Pub. Schs., 1978. Author: Descriptive Statistics for Teachers, 1973, Statistics for Teachers, 1973; contbr. articles to profl. jours. Trustee Great Neck Community Sch., 1975-80, recording sec., 1975-76, vice chairperson, 1976-77, chairperson, 1977-79; chairperson Task Force on Individualized Instrn. Great Neck Pub. Schs., 1974-75, mem. citizens' budget adv. com., 1978-80, chairperson, 1979-80, mem. United Parent Tchr. Coun., pres., 1988-90, 2d v.p., 1986-88, 1st v.p., 1983-85, chairperson legis. com., 1981-85; pres. PTA Great Neck South Middle Sch., 1985-86; mem. study group on financing of edn. Great Neck LWV, 1981-83. Mem. Am. Assn. U. Profs. (mem. exec. com., dist. 8 rep. 1993—), Am. Ednl. Rsch. Assn., Ea. Ednl. Rsch. Assn., Am. Psychol. Assn., Ea. Psychol. Assn., Nat. Coun. on Measurement in Edn., Sigma Xi, Psi Chi. Home: 131 Schenck Ave Great

Neck NY 11021-3818 Office: Hofstra U Dept Counseling 212 Mason Hall Hempstead NY 11550

GELLMAN, GLORIA GAE SEEBURGER SCHICK, marketing professional; b. La Grange, Ill., Oct. 5, 1947; d. Robert Fred and Gloria Virginia (McQuiston) Seeburger; m. Peter Slate Schick, Sept. 25, 1978 (dec. 1980); 2 children; m. Irwin Frederick, Gellman, Sept. 9, 1989; 3 children. BA magna cum laude, Purdue U., 1969; student, Lee Strasberg Actors Studio; postgrad., UCLA, U. Calif.-Irvine. Mem. mktg. staff Seemac, Inc. (formerly R.F. Seeburger Co.); v.p. V.I.P. Properties, Inc., Newport Beach, Calif. Profl. actress, singer; television and radio talk show hostess, Indpls., late 1960s; performer radio and television commls., 1960s—. Mem. Orange County Philharm. Soc., bd. dirs. womens com.; mem. Orange County Master Chorale, Orange County Performing Arts Ctr., v.p., treas. Crescendo chpt. OCPAC Ctr. Stars, 1st v.p. membership; bd. dirs. Newport Harbor (Calif.) Art Mus., v.p. membership, mem. acquisition coun.; bd. dirs., mem. founders soc. Opera Pacific, mem. exec. com. bd. dirs.; patron Big Bros./Big Sisters Starlight Found.; mem. Visionaries Newport Harbor Mus., Designing Women of Art Inst. Soc. Calif.; pres. Opera Pacific Guild Alliance; immediate past pres. Spyglass Hill Philharm. Com.; v.p. Pacific Symphony Orch. League; mem. U. Calif. Irvine Found. Bd., mem. devel. com.; chmn. numerous small and large fundraisers. Recipient Lauds and Laurels award U. Calif., Irvine, 1994, Gellman Courtyard Sculpture honoring contbn. to Sch. of Humanities, U. Calif., Irvine. Mem. AAUW, AFTRA, SAG, Internat. Platform Assn., Actors Equity, U. Calif.-Irvine Chancellor's Club, U. Calif.-Irvine Humanities Assocs. (founder, pres., bd. dirs.), Mensa, Orange County Mental Health Assn., Balboa Bay Club, U. Club, Club 39, Islanders, Covergirls, Alpha Lambda Delta, Delta Rho Kappa. Republican. Home: PO Box 1993 Newport Beach CA 92659-0993

GELMAN, ELAINE EDITH, nurse; b. Bklyn., Feb. 16, 1927; d. Michael Levi and Shirley (Drezner) Rodkinson; m. David Graham Gelman, Apr. 6, 1952; children: Eric, Andrew, Amy. BS, CUNY, Queens, 1946; RN, NYU, 1948. Cert. PNP. Operating room staff, supr. Queens Gen. Hosp., Bellevue, Beth-El Hosp., N.Y.C., 1948-61; labor and delivery room staff, supr. Georgetown Hosp., Washington, 1962-66; pub. health nurse N.Y.C. Dept. Pub. Health, 1966-72; pediatric nurse practitioner child and youth program Roosevelt Hosp., N.Y.C., 1972-82; pvt. practice N.Y.C., 1982—. Mem. Dem. County Com., N.Y.C., 1984—; apptd. to N.Y. State Bd. of Nursing, 1990. Named Nurse of Distinction N.Y. State Legis., 1991; recipient Spl. Presdl. award N.Y. State Coalition of Nurse Practitioners, 1991. Fellow Nat. Assn. Pediatric Nurses Practitioners (legis. chmn. 1986-88, cert. recognition 1986, 87), Coalition of Nurse Practitioners, Inc. (pres. 1984-85, 87-88). Jewish. Home: 229 W 78th St New York NY 10024-6638 Office: Pediatric Practice 241 Central Park W New York NY 10024-4530

GELMO, MARLENE JANETTE ROSALIE, insurance executive, entrepreneur; b. Boston, Oct. 11, 1959; d. Marvin P. Gelmo and Benina (Mackinnon) Kemp; m. J. Mark Halan, Aug. 7, 1986. Student, Boston Conservatory, 1982-83, SUNY, Purchase, 1983-84; BS, SUNY, Binghamton, 1992. Lic. real estate broker, N.Y. Property mgr. Binghamton, 1986-92, Binghamton Mgmt. Assocs., 1989-90, Binghamton Realty and Mgmt. Group, 1990-92; ins. salesperson Met. Life Ins. Co., Binghamton, 1994—; cons. M&M Enterprises, Inc., Binghamton, 1991-92, Laural Assocs., New Canaan, Conn., 1991-92, Precious Constrn., Binghamton, 1990-92. Inventor Optimizer, Eatskies, Mappie, Detail. Mem. AAUW, Property Mgmt. Assn., So. Tier Pub. Rels. Soc., Golden Key Nat. Honors Soc. Home: 162 Bigelow St Binghamton NY 13904 Office: Met Life Ins 4500 Old Vestal Rd Vestal NY 13851

GELPI, BARBARA CHARLESWORTH, English literature and women's studies educator; b. El Centro, Colombia, Dec. 17, 1933; came to U.S., 1951; d. Lionel Victor and Frances Ardelle (Heins) Charlesworth; m. Albert Joseph Gelpi, June 14, 1965; children—Christopher, Adrienne. A.B., U. Miami, Fla., 1955, M.A., 1957; Ph.D., Radcliffe Coll., Cambridge, Mass., 1962. Asst. prof. U. Calif.-Santa Barbara, 1962-64; asst. prof. Brandeis U., Waltham, Mass., 1964-67; lectr. Stanford U., Calif., 1967-81, assoc. prof., 1981-92, prof., 1992—. Author: Dark Passages, 1965, Shelley's Goddess: Maternity, Language, Subjectivity, 1992; editor: Adrienne Rich's Poetry, 1975, Adrienne Rich's Poetry and Prose, 1993, Feminist Theory, 1982, Signs: Jour. of Women in Culture & Society, 1980-85; The Lesbian Issue, 1985; Women's Poverty, 1986; assoc. editor: Victorian Women, 1981. Mem. MLA (program com. 1981-84), Nat. Women's Studies Assn., Philol. Assn. Pacific Coast. Democrat. Roman Catholic. Home: 870 Tolman Dr Palo Alto CA 94305-1026 Office: Stanford U Dept English Stanford CA 94305

GELPI, GAIL ANN, principal; b. New Orleans, Oct. 31, 1940; d. Edwin Harry and Rita Marie (Belson) G. BA in Elem. Edn., Holy Cross Coll., New Orleans, 1962; MEd in Adminstrn./Supervision, Lady of the Lake, San Antonio, 1972; postgrad., U. New Orleans, 1985. Prin. St. Andrew the Apostle, New Orleans, 1968-72; asst. supt. Office of cath. Schs., New Orleans, 1972-74; prin. St. Gregory Barbarigo Sch., Houma, La., 1974-76, St. Angela Merici Sch., Metairie, La., 1976-78, St. James Major, New Orleans, 1978-85, Our Lady of Divine Providence, Metairie, 1985—; ednl. cons. Vezina and Assocs., Gretna, La., 1980-85; instr. Holy Cross Coll., New Orleans, 1980-90. Bd. dirs. Christian Bros., 1988—. Mem. Elem. Prins. Assn. (pres. 1983-85), Nat. Cath. Edn. Assn. (exec. 1979-80), Phi Delta Kappa. Office: Our Lady of Divine Providen 917 N Atlanta St Metairie LA 70003-5801

GELTNER, SHARON FANNIE, book editor; b. Lakeland, Fla., Dec. 10, 1958; d. Bernard Benjamin and Gail (Bergad) G. AA, Wm. Rainey Harper Coll., 1978; BJ, U. Ill., 1980. Editor White House Weekly Feistritzer Publs., Washington, 1980, Instl. Investor, Washington, 1981-83; freelance writer Alexandria, Va., 1984-90; feature writer, investigative reporter, fgn. corr. Knight Ridder Newspapers, Boca Raton, Fla., 1990-92; book editor Weiss Rsch., Palm Beach Gardens, Fla., 1994—; writer, researcher The Naisbitt Group, Washington, 1985-86; legal researcher David James Ltd., Bethesda, Md., 1986-87; invited panelist The Poynter Inst. Media Studies, 1992. Author: (with others) Weekends Away from Washington, D.C., 1989, Fodor's Wall Street Journal Guide to Business Travel, 1991; contbr. articles to Quill, Washington Journalism Rev., Media Bus. Quar., Am. Writer. Participant Women's March on Washington, 1986; fundraiser United Jewish Appeal, Washington, 1986-88.; rep. D.C. writers in Bangkok Royal Thai Embassy, Washington, 1986, Palm Beach County, Fla., Yellow Feathers gridiron, 1990-91. Recipient Nat. Headliner award for outstanding news reporting Press Club of Atlantic City, 1993. Mem. NOW, Washington Ind. Writers (Michael Halberstam award 1983), House and Senate Periodical Corrs., Amnesty Internat., Fla. Press Assn., Nat. Writers Union (del. nat. conv. 1994), Regional Reporters Assn., Nat. Women's Art Mus. (charter), U. Ill. Alumni Assn. Investigative Reporters and Editors. Home: 1441 Brandywine Rd # 500 I West Palm Beach FL 33409 Office: Weiss Rsch 4176 Burns Rd Palm Beach Gardens FL 33410

GELTZER, SHEILA SIMON, public relations executive; b. N.Y.C.; d. Sidney E. and Bertie (Rome) Simon; m. Howard E. Geltzer, Sept. 10, 1967; children: Jeremy Niles, Gabriel Lewis. BA, Queens Coll., 1961. With Philip Lesly Co., N.Y.C., 1962-63, Benjamin Co., N.Y.C., 1963-68; ptnr. Simon and Geltzer, Inc., N.Y.C., 1968-74, Ries and Geltzer, N.Y.C., 1974-79; prin. Geltzer and Co., Inc., N.Y.C., 1979—. Mem. Pub. Relations Soc. Am. (counselors acad.), Women in Communications, Women in Pub. Relations, Nat. Council of Women. Office: Geltzer & Co Inc 1180 Ave Of The Americas New York NY 10036-8401

GEMMELL-AKALIS, BONNI JEAN, psychotherapist; b. Lansing, Mich., Mar. 11, 1950; d. James Stewart Gemmell and Alpha Alice (Hackenberg) Vanden Bosch; m. Thomas Joe Akalis, Dec. 14, 1974 (div.); children: Scott Aaron, Ty Alexander, Zachary Alan. BS, Cen. Mich. U., 1972, MA, 1974. Ltd. lic. psychologist; cert. social worker. Clin. psychologist, sr. mental health therapist Lincoln Ctr. for Emotionally Disturbed Children & Youth, Lansing, 1974-77; outpatient psychologist Grand Rapids (Mich.) Child Guidance Clinic, 1978-81; pvt. practice Grand Rapids Psychiat. Svcs., 1981-88; pvt. practice Associated Therapists, Inc., Grand Rapids, 1988—, pres., 1989-90. Grad. fellow Cen. Mich. U., 1972-73. Mem. Mich. Psychoanalytic Coun., Mich. Women Psychologists, Mich. Assn. Profl. Psychologists, Am. Group Psychotherapy Assn., Grand Rapids Area Psychology Assn., Psi Chi. Home: 632 Duxbury Ct SE Grand Rapids MI 49546-9605 Office: Associated Therapists Inc 2959 Lucerne SE Grand Rapids MI 49546-7121

GEMMILL, ELIZABETH H., corporate executive; b. Phila., Dec. 7, 1945; d. Kenneth W. and Helen H. G.; m. Douglas B. Richardson, July 15, 1977; children—Katherine Preston Richardson, Hollis Bentley Richardson. A.B., Bryn Mawr Coll., 1967; J.D., Boston U., 1970. Bar: Mass. 1970, Pa. 1973. Assoc. firm vom Baur, Coburn, Simmons & Turtle, Boston, 1970-71; staff atty. Cape Cod Legal Services, Inc., Hyannis, Mass., 1971-73; asst. dist. atty. City of Phila., 1973-74; atty., asst. sec. Girard Bank, Phila., 1974-75; sec., treas., counsel Girard Bank, 1975-76, v.p. cust. svcs., 1976-78, v.p., gen. auditor, 1979-81, sr. v.p. pers. dept., 1981-83, sr. v.p., regional banking group head, 1983-85; v.p. Drexel U., Phila., 1986-87; v.p., sec. Tasty Baking Co., Phila., 1988—; bd. dirs. Am. Water Works, Inc., Phila. Facilities Mgmt. Corp. Bd. dirs. Met. YMCA Phila. and Vacinity, 1979-88, 90—, Presbyn.-U. Pa. Med. Ctr., 1982—, WHYY Inc., 1981-94, Phila. Coll. Textiles and Sci., Salvation Army, Forum Exec. Women. Mem. ABA, Pa. Bar Assn., Phila. Bar Assn., Am. Soc. Corp. Secs. (pres. Mid. Atlantic group), Nat. Investors Rels. Inst., Pa. Chamber Bus. and Industry. Office: Tasty Baking Co 2801 W Hunting Park Ave Philadelphia PA 19129-1392

GENDREAU, MARGOT LYNN, lobbyist; b. Deer Park, N.Y., Feb. 19, 1952; d. Raymond and Helen Louise (Schmidt) G. Pharmacy Technician, Baylor U., 1973-74; BFA, U. Mo., 1981. Registered pharmacy technician. Chief pharmacy tech. Columbia Regional Hosp., Columbia, Mo., 1976-77, Ellis Fischel State Cancer Hosp., Columbia, Mo., 1977-79; pharmacy tech. Harry S. Truman VA Hosp., Columbia, 1981-82; profl. products rep. Hoffman-La Roche, Nutley, N.J., 1982-86; profl. products rep. Boehringer-Ingelheim Pharm. Inc., Columbia, Mo., 1986-88, mgr. state govt. affairs, 1988—. Bd. dirs. Abuse Assault Rape Crisis Ctr., Columbia, 1981; Mem. Health Care Task Force, 1991—, Am. Legion Exch. Coun., Washington, 1991—, Mo. Dem. Party, 1993—, Mo. C. of C., 1993—, Tex. C. of C., Austin, 1993—. With U.S. Army, 1973-75, USAR, 1976-82. Named Traveler of Yr., Mo. Pharmacy Assn., 1988. Mem. Am. Legis. Exch. Coun., Kans. Parmacy Assn., Midwest Pharmacy Technicians Assn. (pres. 1980), Mo. Pharm. Travelers Assn. (pres. 1985-86), sec./treas. 1986—), Pharm. Mfrs. Assn. (chairperson Kans. task force 1991-93, S.D. task force). Roman Catholic. Office: Boehringer Ingelheim Pharm PO Box 10230 Columbia MO 65205-4003

GENDRON, MICHÈLE MARGUERITE MADELEINE, librarian; b. Paris, Mar. 15, 1947; came to U.S., 1950; d. Gerard Joachim and Denise Marie Louise (Le Morvan) G. BA, Orlinda Pierce Coll. for Women, Athens, Greece, 1969; MS, U. Ill., 1971. Libr. Free Libr. Phila., 1971-75, head, Kingsessing Br., 1975-76, head, Ramonita G. de Rodriguez Br., 1976-91, curator spl. collections ctrl. children's dept., 1991-92, head, lit. dept., 1992—; cons. devel. Hist. Children's Lit. Collection Montgomery County-Norristown (Pa.) Pub. Libr., 1993-94; organizing mem. Pa. Libr. Assn.'s 1st Conf. Svcs. to Youth, Harrisburg, Pa., 1987-89, Women's Network's 1st Conf. on P.R. Woman in Phila., 1981. Author: (bibliographies) Booklist, 1983; contbr. bibliographies Destination World, 1979, Stories to Share, 1985. Trustee Legal Svcs. Fund Dist. Coun. 47-Am. Fedn. State, County and Mcpl. Employees, 1985—. Recipient Charles Scribner award Scribner Pub., 1976, Nat. Security Forum award Air War Coll., 1985. Mem. ALA (Assn. Libr. Svcs. Children, Mildred Batchelder award selection com. 1979-81, 85-87, internat. rels. com. 1981-85, chair 1984-85, libr. instrn. round table 1991-93), Pub. Libr. Assn. (mktg. to pub. librs. 1991—, svcs. to multicultural populations 1991), Alliance Francaise de Phila., Beta Phi Mu. Roman Catholic. Office: Free Libr of Phila Lit Dept 1901 Vine St Philadelphia PA 19103-1116

GENEREUX, ANN MARIE, accountant, international examiner; b. Woonsocket, R.I., Oct. 31, 1960; d. Richard Alfred and Lorraine Claire (Levasseur) G. BSBA, Bryant Coll., 1982, MBA, 1983, MST, 1989. CPA, Mass. Staff acct. N.E. Apparel Inc., Braintree, Mass., 1983-84; revenue agt. IRS, Marlboro, Mass., 1984-87, 89-92, Boston, 1987-89; internat. examiner IRS, Marlboro, Mass., 1992—; acctg. instr. Newbury Coll., Hopedale, Mass., 1992—. Democrat. Office: IRS 1 Montvale Ave Stoneham MA 02180-3564

GENOVESI, MARIA E., marketing professional; b. N.Y.C., Aug. 29, 1960; d. Vincent D. and Rose C. (Macaloso) Comperchio; m. Joseph Genovesi, June 7, 1992. BA, CUNY, 1982. V.p. assoc. media dir. Lintas: Worldwide, N.Y.C., 1982-92; mktg. dir. Vogue Mag., N.Y.C., 1992-94; dir. mktg. svcs. Victoria Mag., N.Y.C., 1994—. Address: 2 Glen Oaks Dr Rye NY 10580

GENOVICH-RICHARDS, JOANN, health care services consultant, educator; b. Detroit, July 23, 1954; d. Steven Edward and Catherine Ann (Malaspina) Genovich; m. David Edward Richards, Aug. 15, 1975. BSN, U. Mich., 1976; MSN, Wayne State U., 1978; MBA, Oakland U., 1985; PhD, U. Mich., 1993. Mental health coord. Midland (Mich.) Hosp. Ctr., 1978-79; outpatient nursing supr. Henry Ford Hosp., Detroit, 1979-82; adminstrv. dir. nursing St. John Hosp. Macomb Ctr., Mt. Clemens, Mich., 1986; dir. quality svcs., cons., dir. nursing Mercy Health Svcs., Farmington Hills, Mich., 1983-89; instr. nursing Oakland U., Rochester, Mich., 1985-92, interim dean Nursing Sch., 1992; asst. prof. Sch. Nursing and Pub. Health, U. N.C., Chapel Hill, 1993; asst. v.p. planning and devel. Nat. Com. Quality Assurance, 1993—; bd. dirs. Sisters of St. Joseph Health System, Ann Arbor; clin. faculty Joint Commn. on Accreditation of Healthcare Orgns., Chgo., 1986-90. Contbr. chpt. to book and articles to profl. jours. Recipient Project grant, Inst. of Medicine, 1989. Mem. ANA, Mich. Nurses Assn., Nat. Assn. Quality Assurance Profls., Am. Soc. for Quality Control, Aircraft Owners and Pilots Assn. Roman Catholic. Home: 12322 Prairie Dr Sterling Heights MI 48312-5230

GENRICH, JUDITH ANN, real estate executive; b. Milw., Mar. 10, 1949; d. Einar and Eleanor Svea (Russell) Barnes; m. Nathan Mark Genrich, Oct. 23, 1971; children: Krista Svea, Erik Leif. BA, Gustavus Adolphus Coll., 1970; grad., Wis. Sch. Real Estate, Milw., 1979; postgrad., Carroll Coll., 1980, U. Wis., 1978-80, 92. Tchr. Oak Grove Middle Sch., Bloomington, Minn., 1970-71, Mukwonago (Wis.) High Sch., 1971-72; sales mgr. Lincoln Park Homes, West Allis, Wis., 1972-73, v.p., 1973-74, pres., 1974—; chmn. Mfrd. Housing Subdivision Sec., Madison, 1978-80; sec. Southeastern Wis. Housing, Milw., 1981-82, treas., 1982-84. Bd. dirs. Waukesha YMCA, 1985-87, v.p., 1987-89; bd. dirs. Waukesha County United Way, 1984-87; mem. alumni bd. Gustavus Adulphus Coll., St. Peter, Minn., 1974-80; trustee The Cooper Inst., Naples, Fla., 1987-93, mem. adv. bd., 1993—. Recipient Dedicated Svc. award Wis. Mfrd. Housing, 1975-84, 88. Mem. West Allis C. of C., Wis. Mfrd. Housing Assn. (bd. dirs. 1975-80), Ind. Bus. Assn. Wis. (trustee University Lake 1991—), Merrill Hills Country Club (chair golf 1991), Milw. Women's Dist. Golf Assn. (bd. dirs. 1993, v.p. 1994), Vasa Lodge, Eagle Creek Country Club. Republican. Lutheran. Home: 5219 N Hwy 83 Hartland WI 53029-9306

GENSHEIMER, ELIZABETH LUCILLE, software specialist; b. Louisville, Jan. 25, 1955; d. Theodore Rudolph and Florence Virginia (Nieder) G.; m. Eric Grant Schnoebelen. BS in Computer Sci., U. Louisville, 1976, postgrad., 1977-78; postgrad., U. Tex., Dallas, 1993—. Weapons analyst CIA, Washington, 1975-76; engr. software Tex. Instruments, Dallas, 1978-81, Northern Telecom, Inc., Richardson, Tex., 1981-83; mem. sci. staff Bell No. Rsch., Richardson, 1983-88, magnet mgr. univ. interrels. program U. Southwestern La., 1986-88, mgr. product test Meridian Data Network Systems, 1988-89; mgr. devel. software test Convex Computer Corp., Richardson, Tex., 1989-93; software cons. Ft. Worth Techs. Cons., 1993—. Mem. Am. Bus. Women's Assn., Nature Conservancy, Nat. Geol. Soc., Whale Watch Soc., Mensa. Home and Office: PO Box 796005 Dallas TX 75379-6005

GENTILCORE, EILEEN MARIE BELSITO, elementary school principal; b. Glen Cove, N.Y.; d. Samuel Francis and Nellie Theresa (McKenna) Belsito; m. James Matthew Gentilcore, Aug. 4, 1951; children: Kevin, John, Scott. BS in Edn., SUNY, Potsdam, 1951; MS in Edn., Hofstra U., 1968, profl. diploma, 1976, EdD, 1979. Tchr., first grade Sea Cliff (N.Y.) Schs., 1951-52; tchr., pre-K Germany Officers Sch., Munich, 1952-53; tchr., first grade Peekskill (N.Y.) Schs., 1953-54; tchr., second grade Syosset (N.Y.) Ctrl. Sch. Dist., 1954-55, reading cons., 1970-84, head tchr., 1974-84, principal, 1985—; bicentennial adv. bd. Syosset Community, 1976; adv. bd. mem. Telicare, Uniondale, N.Y., 1978-80. Author: Developmental Learning, 1979. N.Y. State PTA fellow (1971, 72, 73); Hofstra fellow, 1971; recipient Jenkins award PTA, 1968, Hon. Life, 1976, Pius X, 1985, Rotary Paul Harris, 1992 award Rockville Ctr. Diocese. Mem. Syosset Prins. (pres. 1992), Syosset-Woodbury Rotary (pres. 1993-95), Gift of Life Rotary (dist. 7250 bd. dirs. 1992—, v.p. 1994—, govs. aide 1995—), Kappa Delta Pi, Alpha Sigma Omicron. Roman Catholic.

GENTRY, ALMA P., finance coordinator; b. Ft. Worth, Nov. 15, 1954; d. Claud and Amanda (Dilliard) Pink; m. Roy L. Gentry, Aug. 29, 1975; children: Lisa, Roy Jr., Randall. Student, Abilene Christian U., 1973-75, U. Ky., 1990-91; AA, Lexington (Ky.) C.C., 1994. Svc. rep. South Ctrl. Bell/AT&T, Winchester, Ky., 1977-84; br. sec. U.S. Govt., Lexington, 1986-89; staff sec. fin. East Ky. Power Coop., Winchester, 1989-90, fin. coord., 1990—. Active Clark County Edn. Found., Winchester, 1992; coach Little League Girls Softball, Winchester, 1992, 94; vice-chmn. textbook com. Strode Sta. Elem., Winchester, 1993-94; vice-pres. Girls Basketball Boosters, Winchester, 1994. Mem. East Ky. Employees Assn. (sec. exec. bd. 1991-92, v.p. 1993-94, treas. 1994—), Toastmasters (Clark County chpt.). Democrat. Mem. Ch. of Christ. Office: East Ky Power Coop 4758 Lexington Rd Winchester KY 40391

GENTRY, JEANNE LOUISE, lecturer, writer; b. Portland, Oreg., Sept. 12, 1946; d. Louis Darell and Mary Louise (Lane) G.; m. Gini Mario Martini, June 13, 1965 (div. 1968); children: Deborah Corinna Martina, Darell James Martini; m. David Guy Gorrell, Feb. 19, 1982 (div. 1994). Student, Northwestern Coll. Bus., Portland, 1968, Mt. Hood Community Coll., Gresham, Oreg., 1986. Receptionist, sec. to pres. Met. Printing Co., Portland, 1969-73; adminstrv. asst. Lifespring, Inc., Portland, 1974-77; cons. Jeanne Mort Co., Boring, Oreg., 1978-80; office mgr. Beef Palace Provisioners, Gresham, 1980-82; bus. cons. Boring, 1983-90; owner Good As New Doll Hosp., Boring, 1990-92; sec. Profl. Svc. Industries, Portland, 1992—. Co-compiler: Lebanon Pioneer Cemetery, 1991, rev. edit. 1995. Mem. Geneal. Coun. Orgn. (sec. 1991-94), Nat. Geneal. Soc., Fellowship of Brethren Genealogists, Geneal. Forum of Oreg. (Newsletter staff), Ind. Geneal. Soc. (charter), East Tenn. Hist. Soc., Oreg. Hist. Cemeteries Assn. (pres. 1992—), Pellissippi Geneal. and Hist. Soc., Lebanon Geneal. Soc. Home: 16385 SE 232D Dr Boring OR 97009

GENTRY, VICKI PAULETTE, museum director; b. Bessemer, Ala., June 2, 1952; d. Gerald Vance and Marjorie Jean (Bush) George; children: Alissa Hubbard, Rebecca Hubbard. Office worker Mining Corp. of the South, Vance, Ala., 1978-79; artist, sign painter Bob's Sign Shop, Midfield, Ala., 1979-80; dir. Iron & Steel Mus. of Ala., McCalla, 1980—; program completion Office of Mus Programs, Smithsonian, Washington, 1987. Artist (book) Tannehill Crafts, 1982. Events Planner Ala. Reunion State of Ala., Montgomery, 1989. Recipient Top 20 Events in the South East award SE Tourism Soc., Atlanta, 1986-87, 88, 91, Head Start Vol. award, 1994. Mem. Ala. Preservation Alliance, Soc. Indsl. Archaeology, Nat. Trust for Hist. Preservation, Birmingham Area Mus. Assn., Am. Assn. State and Local History (program completion 1980), Am. Assn. Mus., Ala. Mus. Assn. (sec.-treas. 1983-85, Meritorious Svc. award 1983), Ala. State Employees Assn. (pres. Tannehill chpt. 1993-95). Democrat. Baptist. Home: 16920 Brooke Dr Mc Calla AL 35111-8504 Office: Tannehill Historical State Park 12632 Confederate Pky Mc Calla AL 35111-9508

GENUNG, SHARON ROSE, pediatrician; b. Williamsport, Pa., Oct. 6, 1951; d. Joseph Patrick and Jeanette (Mossendew) Lynch; m. Norman Bernard Genung, June 9, 1973; children: Jeffrey, Sarah. BS in Microbiology cum laude, Mich. State U., 1973; MS in Clin. Microbiology, U. Ark., 1979, MD, 1984. Lic. physician, Wash., Ark. Clin. resident in pediatrics Wright State U./Children's Med. Ctr., Dayton, Ohio, 1987; dir. pediatrics USAF Hosp. Fairchild, Spokane, Wash., 1987-88, dir. med. svcs., 1988-91; pvt. practice in pediats. Kapstaffer, Maixner & Genung, Spokane, 1991—; instr. in pediatric advanced life support, neonatal resuscitation. Contbr. articles to profl. jours. Maj. USAF M.C., 1980-91. Fellow Am. Acad. Pediatrics; mem. So. Med. Assn., Wash. State Soc. Pediatrics, Spokane Med. Soc., Spokane Pediatric Soc., Spokane Women's Assn. Physicians, Alpha Omega Alpha. Office: Kapstaffer Maixner & Genung 105 W 8th Ave Ste 318 Spokane WA 99204-2399

GEOGHEGAN, PATRICIA, lawyer; b. Bayonne, N.J., Sept. 9, 1947; d. Frank and Rita (Mihok) G. BA, Mich. State U., 1969; MA, Yale U., 1972, JD, 1974; LLM, NYU, 1982. Bar: N.Y. 1975. Assoc. Cravath, Swaine & Moore, N.Y.C., 1974-82, ptnr., 1982—. Mem. ABA, N.Y. State Bar Assn., Assn. of Bar of City of N.Y. Office: Cravath Swaine & Moore 825 8th Ave New York NY 10019-7416

GEO-KARIS, ADELINE JAY, state legislator; b. Tegeas, Greece, Mar. 29, 1918; student Northwestern U., Mt. Holyoke Coll.; LLB, DePaul U. Bar: Ill. Founder Adeline J. Geo-Karis and Assocs., Zion, Ill.; former mcpl., legis. atty. Mundelein, Ill., Vernon Hills, Ill., Libertyville (Ill.) Twp., Long Grove (Ill.) Sch. Dist.; justice of peace; former asst. state's atty.; mem. Ill. Ho. of Reps., 1973-79; mem. Ill. Senate, 1979—, asst. minority leader, 1988—; mayor, City of Zion, Ill. Served to lt. comdr. USNR., Res. ret. Recipient Americanism medal DAR; named Woman of Yr. Daughters of Penelope, Outstanding Legislator Ill. Fedn. Ind. Colls. and Univs., 1975-78, Legis. award Ill. Assn. Park Dists., 1976. Sponsor Guilty but Mentally Ill Law. Greek Orthodox. Office: Ill State Senate State Capitol Springfield IL 62706*

GEORGE, CAROLE SCHROEDER, computer company executive; b. Bloomington, Ind., Mar. 20, 1943; d. Melburne Evert and Neva Mae (Bechtel) Gibson; m. Richard D. White, Aug. 31, 1962 (div. 1972); 1 child, Kenneth Donald; m. Charles R. Schroeder, Apr. 7, 1973 (div. 1983); m. Thomas H. George III, May 4, 1991. BS in Pharmacy, Wayne State U., 1972; postgrad., Va. Commonwealth U., 1980-83. Registered pharmacist, Mich. Va. Staff pharmacist St. Joseph Hosp., Pontiac, Mich., 1972-73; dir. pharmacy St. Mary Hosp., Livonia, Mich., 1974-76; resident Detroit Receiving Hosp., 1977-78; clin. faculty pharmacy Med. Coll. of Va., Richmond, 1978-83; dir. pharmacy ops. Med. Coll. Va. Hosps., Richmond, 1978-83; mktg. mgr. TDS Healthcare Systems Corp., Atlanta, 1983-86; sr. cons. Gerber Alley, Norcross, Ga., 1986; dir. product mgmt. Baxter Healthcare Systems, Reston, Va., 1986-89; sr. v.p. Integrated Systems Tech. Inc., Reston, 1989—. Mem. Am. Soc. of Hosp. Pharmacists, Am. Pharm. Assn., Nat. Assn. for Healthcare Quality, Rho Chi.

GEORGE, CONNIE MARIE, insurance underwriter; b. Girard, Kans., July 31, 1959; d. Philip Andrew and Rosemary Lillian (Crager) G.; m. Jesse Misao Board, June 6, 1986; children: Danielle, Harrison, Maxwell. Grad., Colgan High Sch., 1977. Lic. property and casualty ins. agt.; cert. assoc. in underwriting; cert. profl. ins. woman; cert. assoc. in mgmt. Rater Cimarron (Kans.) Ins. Co., 1979-80, comml. underwriter, 1981-90; claims sec. Lauren Jones Ins., Dodge City, Kans., 1980-81; multi-lines underwriter EMC Ins. Cos., Wichita, Kans., 1990—. Mem. Ins. Women of Wichita, Nat. Assn. Ins. Women (bull. chair 1994, pub. rels. com.), Wichita Downtown Toastmasters Club. Democrat. Roman Catholic. Home: 9105 Westlawn St # 3 Wichita KS 67212-5332 Office: EMC Ins Cos 245 N Waco St Ste 330 Wichita KS 67202-1111

GEORGE, DEANNE MARIE, marketing consultant; b. Belleville, Ill., Oct. 30, 1967; d. Joseph William and Carolyn (Bruce) Knepper; m. Aaron Lewis George, Jan. 7, 1989. BS, MacMurray Coll., 1989; postgrad., Chapman U., 1993—. Tchr. elem. sch. Brent Internat. Sch., Baguio City, Philippines, 1990-91; mktg. cons. Clovis (N.Mex.) News Jour., 1991-92, Curry County Broadcasting, Clovis, 1992-94; publicist U.S. Govt. RAF, Lakenheath, England, 1994—. Case work dir. ARC, Camp John Hay, Philippines, 1990-91. MacMurray Coll. Honor scholar, Jacksonville, Ill., 1985-89. Mem. NAFE, Clovis Jr. Women's Club.

GEORGE, DENISE CHRISTINE, computer scientist; b. Chgo., Mar. 22, 1946; d. Daniel and Penelope (Cherimpes) Pavis; m. James Edward George, Dec. 20, 1970; children: Michael James, Christina Danielle. AB, U. Mich., 1966; MS, U. Ill., 1968. Applications programmer Argonne (Ill.) Nat. Lab., 1967-68; systems programmer Stanford (Calif.) Linear Acceleration Lab., 1969-71; computer cons. Colo. State U., Ft. Collins, 1972-75; staff scientist Los Alamos (N.Mex.) Nat. Lab., 1975—; bd. dirs. N.Mex. Network Women in Sci. Engring., Los Alamos. Mem. AAUW (bd. dirs. 1991-94, Equity award 1993). Office: LANL T-2 MS B243 Los Alamos NM 87545

GEORGE, DIANE ELIZABETH, librarian, educational technology and computer education educator; b. L.I., N.Y., July 12, 1952; d. Arnold J. and Jeanette A. (Hester) G. BS, So. Conn. State U., 1974, MS in Libr. Sci., 1976, MS in Ednl. Tech., 1977. Cert. intermediate adminstr., libr. media specialist K-12, elem. edn. 1-8, driver's edn. Libr. media specialist New Canaan (Conn.) Pub. Schs., 1976-77, North Haven (Conn.) Pub. Schs., 1977-80, Branford (Conn.) Pub. Schs., 1980—; ednl. cons. to SEED Project, New Haven; Conn. del. N.E. Regional Ednl. Leadership Conf., 1983; participant forum Linking Children with Nature, Roger Tory Peterson Inst., 1988. Recipient Faculty Excellence award Branford Intermediate Sch., 1985-86. Mem. Assn. for Supervision and Curriculum Devel., Conn. Educators Computer Assn. (bd. dirs. 1989—), Conn. Ednl. Media Assn. (bd. dirs. 1984-85, cert. of appreciation 1984). Office: Branford Intermediate Sch 185 Damascus Rd Branford CT 06405-6107

GEORGE, JOYCE JACKSON, judge emeritus, lawyer; b. Akron, Ohio, May 4, 1936; d. Ray and Verna (Popadich) Jackson; children: Michael Eliot, Michelle René. BA, U. Akron, 1962, JD, 1966; postgrad. Nat. Jud. Coll., Reno, 1976, NYU Sch. Law, 1983; LLM, U. Va., 1986. Bar: Ohio 1966, U.S. Dist. Ct. (no. dist.) Ohio 1966, U.S. Ct. Appeals (6th cir.) 1968, U.S. Supreme Ct. 1968. Tchr. Akron Bd. Edn., 1962-66; asst. dir. law City of Akron, 1966-69, pub. utilities advisor, 1969-70, asst. dir. law, 1970-73; sole practice, Akron, 1973-76; referee Akron Mcpl. Ct., 1975, judge, 1976-83; judge 9th Dist. Ct. Appeals, Akron, 1983-89; judge, Peninsula, Ohio, 1989; U.S. atty. No. Dist. Ohio, 1989-93; v.p. administrn. Telxon Corp., Akron, Ohio, 1993—; tchr., lectr. Ohio Jud. Coll., Nat. Jud. Coll.; cons. in field. Author: Judicial Opinion Writing Handbook, 1981, 2d edit, 1986, 3d edit., 1993, Referee's Report Writing Handbook, 1992; contbr. articles to profl. publs. Recipient Outstanding Woman of Yr. award Akron Bus. and Profl. Women's Club, 1982; Alumni Honor award U. Akron, 1983, Alumni award U. Akron Sch. Law, 1991; Dept. Treasury award, 1992; named Woman of Yr. in politics and govt. Summit County, Ohio, 1983. Mem. ABA, Ohio Bar Assn.

GEORGE, KATIE, lawyer; b. Chillicothe, Ohio, Sept. 4, 1953; d. Harry Paul and Tina Lillian George; m. Nov. 25, 1972 (div. Nov. 1983); 1 child, Alison; m. Timothy John Nusser, June 30, 1985. BBA, U. Toledo, 1983, JD, 1986, MBA, 1989. Bar: Ohio 1987, U.S. Dist. Ct. (no. dist.) Ohio 1993, Fla. 1994. Law clk. Allotta, Singer & Farley, Co., LPA, Toledo, 1985-86; mgmt. specialist Dept. Pub. Utilities City of Toledo, 1987-91, acting commr. Dept. Health, 1992-93, acting mgr. Dept. Pub. Safety, 1991-94; pvt. practice Toledo, 1987—; part-time instr. U. Toledo, 1987-88. Bd. dirs. City of Toledo BlockWatch, 1993. Mem. Ohio State Bar Assn., Toledo Bar Assn., Toledo Women's Bar Assn. Home: PO Box 178166 Toledo OH 43617-0166 Office: Katie George Atty at Law 3119 Central Park West Ste F Toledo OH 43617-1083

GEORGE, MARY KURIAN, internist; b. Trivandrum, Kerala, India, Jan. 18, 1966; came to U.S., 1967; d. Malayil Philip and Aleyamma (George) Kurian: m. Jose Thomas George, Oct. 13, 1990. BA/MD, U. Mo., Kansas City, MD. Resident in internal medicine Loyola U. Med. Ctr., Chgo., 1990-94; clin. instr. in divsn. gen. internal medicine Loyola U. Med. Ctr., Maywood, Ill., 1994—. Mem. AMA, Am. Coll. Physicians. Home: 180 Rosedale Ct Bloomingdale IL 60108

GEORGE, MARY SHANNON, state senator; b. Seattle, May 27, 1916; d. William Day and Agnes (Lovejoy) Shannon; B.A. cum laude, U. Wash., 1937; postgrad. U. Mich., 1937, Columbia U., 1938; m. Flave Joseph George; children—Flave Joseph, Karen Liebermann, Christy, Shannon Lowrey. Prodn. asst., asst. news editor Pathe News, N.Y.C., 1938-42; mem. fgn. editions staff Readers Digest, Pleasantville, N.Y., 1942-46; columnist Caracas (Venezuela) Daily Jour., 1953-60; councilwoman City and County of Honolulu, 1969-74; senator State of Hawaii, 1974-94, asst. minority leader, 1978-80, minority policy leader, 1983-84, minority floor leader, 1987, minority leader, 1987-94, chmn. housing com., 1993, transp. com., 1981-82; mem. Nat. Air Quality Adv. Bd., 1974-75, Intergovtl. Policy Adv. Com. Trade, 1988-93, White House Conf. Drug Free Am., 1988. Vice chmn. 1st Hawaii Ethics Commn., 1968; co-founder Citizens Com. on Constl. Conv., 1968; vice-chmn. platform com. Republican Nat. Conv., 1976, co-chmn., 1980; bd. dirs. State Legis. Leaders Found., 1993-94, Hawaii Planned Parenthood, 1970-72, 79-86, Hawaii Med. Services Assn., 1972-86; mem. adv. bd. Hawaii chpt. Mothers Against Drunk Driving, 1984—. Recipient Jewish Men's Club Brotherhood award, 1974, Disting. Svc. award Hawaii Women Lawyers, 1991, Mahalo award Friends of Libr. Hawaii, 1991; Outstanding Legislator of Yr. award Nat. Rep. Legislators Assn., 1985; named Woman of Yr., Honolulu Press Club, 1969, Hawaii Fedn. Bus. and Profl. Women, 1970; Citizen of Yr., Hawaii Fed. Exec. Bd., 1973, 76. Mem. LWV (pres. Honolulu 1966-68), Mensa, Phi Beta Kappa. Author: A Is for Abrazo, 1961. Home: 782G N Kalaheo Ave Kailua HI 96734-1973

GEORGE, SHIRLEY H., city librarian; b. Elgin, Ill., Dec. 29, 1938; d. Edwin William and Nora (Wiese) Hattendorf; m. Melvin R. George; children: Catherine, Elizabeth. BA, Valparaiso U., 1960; MLS, U. Minn., 1969; MBA, U. Chgo., 1982. Ref. libr. Elmhurst (Ill.) Pub. Libr., 1971-73; head ref. dept. Helen M. Plum Meml. Libr., Lombard, Ill., 1973-75; adminstrv. libr. Maywood (Ill.) Pub. Libr., 1975-84; asst. state libr. State Libr. Oreg., Salem, 1985-87; state libr. State Libr. Iowa, Des Moines, 1987-91; city libr. Beaverton (Oreg.) City Libr., 1992—. Mem. ALA, PNLA, Oreg. Libr. Assn. Episcopalian. Office: Beaverton City Libr 12500 SW Allen Blvd Beaverton OR 97005-9595

GEORGE-LEPKOWSKI, SUE ANN, medical technologist; b. Altoona, Pa., Sept. 17, 1948; d. Charles Frederick and E. Anita (Haller) G.; m. Walter Lepkowski. AS, BS in Agronomy, Pa. State U., 1968, 70, MEd in Agronomy, Biol. Scis., Edn., 1972; PhD, Columbia & Columbia Pacific U., 1980; DS, Columbia Pacific U., 1981. Internship echocardiology West Pa. Hosp., Pitts., 1979-80; echocardiology tech. Bronson Meth. Hosp., Kalamazoo, 1981-82; technologist Nalle Clinic, Charlotte, 1983-85; tech. dir. Carolina Cardiology, Asheville, N.C., 1985-86; chief echocardiolography technologist Candler Gen. Hosp., Savannah, Ga., 1986-88; echocardiolography, clin. specialist, technical spl. edn. specialist, chief technologist Self Meml. Hosp., Greenwood, S.C., 1988—; cons. in field, researcher; lectr. in field. Contbr. articles to profl. jours.; co-author: Clinical 2-D Echocardiography. Mem. choir Carolina Mountain Brass, Gospell Quartet; percussionist Images; edn. chmn. Greenwood Lupus Group, pres.; edn. chmn. S.C. Lupus Found. Recipient ACP award, Berkeley-Whittinger award for rsch. and acad. excellence. mem. Am. Soc. Ultrasonic Tech. Specialist, Am. Inst. Ultrasonic Medicine, Soc. Diagnostic Med. Sonographers, Am. Registry Diagnostic Med. Sonographers (registered diatnostic med. sonographer, registered diagnostic cardial sonographer), Altoona/Pa. State U. Alumni Assn., Columbia Pacific U. Alumni Assn., Altoona High Alumni Assn., IPTAY, S.C. Ultrasound Soc., Am. Soc. Echocardiology, Pa. State Carolina Club, Phi Epsilon Phi. Dutch Reformed. Home: 531 Willson S # 3 Greenwood SC 29649-1554 Office: Self Meml Hosp 1325 Spring St Greenwood SC 29646-3875

GEORGINO, SUSAN MARTHA, city redevelopment services administrator; b. Phila., Apr. 1, 1950; d. Joseph Francis and Eleanor (Kelly) Boyle; m. Richard Romano (div.); 1 child, Sean; m. Victor Georgino, Oct. 2, 1988; 1 child, Michael. BA, Calif. State U., L.A., 1975, MPA, 1983. Adminstrv. officer Maravilla Found., Montebello, Calif., 1978-81; adminstrv. analyst City of Burbank (Calif.), 1982-84, project mgr., 1984-87, asst. dir. community devel., redevel. adminstr., 1987-89; dir. redevel. svcs., deputy exec. dir. City of Brea (Calif.), 1989—; bd. dirs. Calif. Redevel. Assn. Bd. officer Soroptomist Internat., Brea, 1991; active La Providencia Guild, Burbank, 1990, Parks and Recreation Commn., Burbank, 1991; mem. City of Burbank's Performing Arts Grand Awards Program. Mem. Nat. Assn. Redevel. and Housing Ofcls. (bd. dirs. 1986-87), Calif. Assn. Econ. Devel. Ofcls., Orange County Consortium (bd. dirs.), Lambda Alpha Internat. (bd. dirs.). Roman Catholic. Office: City of Brea One Civic Ctr Circle Brea CA 92621

GEORGOPOULOS, MARIA, architect; b. Moussata, Cefalonia, Greece, Apr. 2, 1949; came to U.S., 1973; d. Vassilios and Joulia Georgopoulos; m. Demetrios Georgopoulos (div. 1974). BArch, Nat. Poly. Sch. Greece, Athens, 1972; MS, Columbia U., 1976. Registered architect, N.Y., Greece. Project mgr. Architects Design Group, N.Y.C., 1976-79, Griswold, Heckel & Kelly, N.Y.C., 1979-80; project dir. Lehman Bros., Kuhn Loeb Inc., N.Y.C., 1980-85; v.p. L.F. Rothschild Inc., N.Y.C., 1985-89, sr. project mgr., 1989-90; dir. of facilities mgmt. Dreyfus Corp., N.Y.C., 1990—. Mem. AIA, Am. Women Entrepreneurs, Greek Inst. Architects. Greek Orthodox. Club: Douglaston (N.Y.). Home: 14 Melrose Ln Douglaston NY 11363-1221 Office: The Dreyfus Corp 200 Park Ave New York NY 10166-0001

GERACE, MARY KATHRYN, accountant, financial consultant; b. Baton Rouge, July 8, 1958; d. Joseph Raymond and Norma Evelyn (Ford) G. Student, Richmond (Eng.) Coll., 1975, Am. Sch., Innsbruck, Austria, 1977; BS, St. Mary Dominican Coll., 1979; MBA, La. State U., 1984. CPA, La., Tex., Ga. Page and Senate aid La. State Legislature, Baton Rouge, 1972-80; with internat. banking and fin. planning dept. Republic Bank, Houston, 1985-87; ptnr. Gerace & Witherspoon, CPAs, Baton Rouge, 1987-93; fin. cons. Dem. Nat. Conv., Atlanta, 1988; pres., owner Geramco Internat. Trading, Baton Rouge, 1988—; owner Mary K. Carleton CPAs, Baton Rouge, 1994—. Dep. dir. technology Dem. Nat. Conv., N.Y., 1992; ofcl. Presdl. Inaugural Com., Washington, 1993. Mem. AICPA, La. Soc. CPAs, Tex. Soc. CPAs, Ga. Soc. CPAs, Nat. Soc. U.S. Daus. 1812, United Daus. of Confederacy, DAR, Flora Adams Darling Dau. Roman Catholic. Office: Mary K Carleton CPA 5800 One Perkins Place Baton Rouge LA 70808-9107

GERACI, PAULINE MARIE, military officer, educator; b. Lawton, Okla., May 18, 1959; d. John Francis and Nancy Katherine (Brown) G. BA in Elem. Edn., U. South Fla., 1984; MEd, U. Fla., 1993. Cert. tchr. elem. edn., reading specialist. Commd. 2d lt. U.S. Army, 1985-86, advanced through grades to capt., 1989; asst. prof. mil. scis. Army ROTC U. Fla., Gainesville, 1990-94; GED instr. New River Correctional, 1994—. Editor: (newsletter) Van Fleet Times, 1992 (Journalism award 1992); photojournalist: (mag.) The Guardsman, 1988-90 (Journalism award 1988). Pres. Family Support Group, 53d Inf. Brigade, Tampa, Fla., 1986; officer Christian Fellowship, 1991—. Mem. Internat. Reading Assn., Nat. Guard Officers Assn., Fla. Nat. Guard Officers Assn., Fla. Nat. Guard Enlisted Assn., Officers Club, Kappa Delta Pi. Office: U Fla Army ROTC Gainesville FL 32611

GERAGHTY, MARGARET KARL, financial consultant, portfolio manager; b. Bklyn., May 31, 1947; d. Edward H. and Margaret Honora (Miller) Karl; m. John Matthew Geraghty, Sept. 9, 1972; 1 child, Elizabeth. BA, Marymount Coll., Tarrytown, N.Y., 1969; MA, Hunter Coll., 1974; advanced profl. cert., NYU, 1978. Fin. analyst GM, N.Y.C., 1969-73; dir. fin. analysis Equitable, N.Y.C., 1973-77; asst. v.p. Equitable Life Holding Corp., N.Y.C., 1977-79, Equitable Life Assurance Soc., N.Y.C., 1979-84; v.p. Equitable Capital Mgmt. Corp., N.Y.C., 1984-91; fin. and investment cons. in pvt. practice, 1991—; bd. dirs. Equico Securities. Trustee Marymount Coll., 1984—, chmn. fin. com., 1988—; trustee St. Dominic Acad., Caldwell, N.J., 1987-90; treas. Cath. Big Bros., N.Y.C., 1987-91; co-chmn. Centennial Scholarship Fund, 1986-89; mem. Friends of Ridgewood Libr., Family Counseling Aux. Recipient Gloria Gaines award Marymount Coll., 1979, Golden Dome award Cath. Big Bros., 1994. Mem. Fin. Women's Assn., Coll. Club Ridgewood, Rep. Club. Home and Office: 250 Palmer Ct Ridgewood NJ 07450-2316 also: 400 East Ave Bay Head NJ 08742-4706

GERALD, PAMELA B., insurance company executive; b. Covington, La., Apr. 27, 1955; d. Arthur B. and Ana T. (Revollo) G.; m. John A. Rapanos, Nov. 26, 1977 (div. Mar. 1985). B of Profl. Studies magna cum laude, Barry U., 1988. Cert. ins. counselor, profl. ins. woman. Underwriter Fryer Ins. Agy., Coral Gables, Fla., 1972-75; account rep. Johnson & Higgins Fla., Inc., Miami, 1975-76; v.p. Frank R. MacNeill & Son, Inc. subs. Jardine Ins. Brokers Internat., Ltd., Miami, 1976—; assoc. dir. Glanvill Enthoven N.A., Ltd. subs. Jardine Ins. Brokers Internat., Ltd., Miami, 1994—; dir., asst. v.p. Cypress Ins. Co., Miami, 1989—; cons. MacNeill Fla. Residential Property & Casualty Joint Underwriting Dept., Miami, 1993-94, Retail Ins. Agy., Miami, 1994; panelist Ins. and You Cable Tap TV Access Prodn.; expert witness ins. ct. cases State Farm Ins. Co., Birmingham Fire Ins. Co.; past pres. MacNeill Employees Credit Union; bd. dirs. Property and Casualty Ins. Co. Mem. Nat. Assn. Ins. Women Internat., Nat. Assn. Profl. Surplus Lines Offices, Profl. Ins. Agents Fla., Inc., Fla. Assn. Ind. Agents, Ins. Women South Dade (past dir. edn.). Republican. Roman Catholic. Office: Glanvill Enthoven NA Ltd 9690 NW 41 St Miami FL 33178

GERARD, BERTHA MARIE POIRIER, artist; b. St. Martinville, La., Feb. 26, 1939; d. Leopold Paul and Emelie Poche Poirier; m. Allen Gerard; children: Felecia Marie, Mitchell John. Student, U. Southwestern La., 1980-85. Art works represented in pvt. and pub. collections. Active Feed the Children, St. Dominic's Home, Missionary Servants of the Most Blessed Trinity, Christian Appalacian Project, Father Flanagan's Boys Town, Missionaries of Africa, Habitat for Humanity Internat., U.S. Holocaust Mus., Washington, Nat. Wildlife Fedn., Washington, Project Hope, Millwood, Va., UN Assn. U.S.A., Better World Soc. Recipient Achievement cert. Nat. Wildlife Fedn., 1993. Mem. Nat. Mus. Women in Arts. Roman Catholic. Home: 101 Alpha Dr Lafayette LA 70506

GERARD, JEAN BROWARD SHEVLIN, former ambassador, lawyer; b. Portland, Oreg., Mar. 9, 1938; d. Edwin Leonard and Ella (Broward) Shevlin; m. James Watson Gerard, June 20, 1959 (dec. 1987); children: James W., Harriet C. AB, Vassar Coll., 1959; JD, Fordham U., 1977; LLD (hon.), U. S.C., 1983. Bar: N.Y. 1978, Fla. 1978, D.C. 1979, U.S. Dist. Ct. (ea. and so. dists.) N.Y. 1978. Atty. Cadawalader, Wickersham & Taft, N.Y.C., 1977-81; ambassador, permanent rep. of U.S. to UNESCO, Paris, 1981-85; U.S. ambassador to Luxembourg, 1985-89; bd. dirs. Banca di Roma Internat., S.A. (Luxembourg). Editor: Fordham Internat. Law Forum, 1977. Bd. govs. Women's Nat. Rep. Club, 1967-73, 74-80, pres., 1971-73; hon. del. Rep. Nat. Conv., N.Y.C., 1972; alt. del. 18th Congl. Dist. N.Y., N.Y.C., 1980; v.p. exec. bd. UNESCO, 1983-85; bd. dirs. Youth Found., 1985—, N.Y. Geneal. and Biological Soc., 1985—., Child Health Found., 1991—. Decorated SAR medal, 1970, medal of honor VFW, 1982, Medaille d'Or French Senate, Outstanding Civilian Svc. medal U.S. Army, 1990, Grand Croix of Ordre Grand Ducal de la Couronne de Chene (Luxembourg). Mem. N.Y. County Lawyers Assn., Assn. Bar City of N.Y. Presbyterian. Clubs: Colony; City Midday (N.Y.C.); Capitol Hill (D.C.); Cercle de l'Union Interalliee (Paris).

GERBERDING, GRETA ELAINE, lawyer; b. Ft. Wayne, Ind., Aug. 17, 1960; d. Miles Carston G. and Ruth (Hostrup) G. BS with high distinction, Ind. U., 1982; JD cum laude, 1985. Bar: Ind. 1985, U.S. Dist. Ct. (so. dist.) Ind., CPA, Ind., CEBS. Sr. tax cons. Ernst & Whinney, Indpls., 1985-87; assoc. Klineman, Rose, Wolf and Wallack P.C., Indpls., 1987-89, Hall Render Killian Heath & Lyman P.C., Indpls., 1989—; presenter at seminars. Author: (with G.P. Gooch) Trust and Estate Income Tax Reporting and Planning, 1985; contbr. chpts. to books. Chmn. hospitality area Virginia Slims Tennis Tournament, Indpls., 1987-89; vol. Jello Tennis Classic Tennis Tournament, Indpls., 1990-91; coord. Hospitality and Ball Kids, 1990, Jr. Jamboree GTE Tennis Tournament, Indpls., 1990; vol. Ctr. for Exploration The Children's Mus., Indpls., 1991—; mem. com. on funding Vision 2002 Luth. Camp Assn., Inc., 1993—. Glen Peters fellow Ind. U., 1984. Mem. ABA (com. martial deduction legis. real property and probate sect. 1986-87, tax section, gen. income tax com. 1987-89, employee benefits com. 1988—, subcom. health plan design and state regulation 1993—, health care task force 1994—), Ind. Bar Assn. (acct.-lawyers com. 1986-89, co-chmn. com. on legis. 1988-92, coun. tax sect. 1988—, sec.-treas. 1991-92, v. chmn. tax sect. 1992-93, chair elect 1993-94, chair 1994—), Indpls. Bar Assn., Indpls. Jaycees (treas. 4th Festival 1987 monthly dinner meetings 1988), West Indy Racquet Club (USTA Volvo Tennis Team 1986-87, RCA Tounament Credentials Com. 1993—), Indpls. Racquet Club (USTA Volvo Tennis Team 1988-91). Home: 7329 Harbour Pt Indianapolis IN 46240-3487 Office: Hall Render Killian Heath & Lyman PC PO Box 82064 Ste 2000 Indianapolis IN 46282

GERBERG, JUDITH LEVINE, human resource company executive; b. N.Y.C., Mar. 21, 1940; d. Murray Joseph and Pearl (Berens) Levine; m. Mort Gerberg, Feb. 1, 1969; 1 child, Lilia Anya Berens. BA in Comparative Lit., Columbia U., 1963, postgrad. in organizational devel., 1989; MA in Psychology and Art, NYU. Registered art therapist; cert. clin. mental health counselor; nat. cert. counselor. Program dir. Women's Selling Game, N.Y.C., 1979-84; mem. faculty Parsons Sch. Design, N.Y.C., 1979-85; pres. Judith Gerberg Assocs., N.Y.C., 1984—; orgnl. devel. mgmt. valuing diversity, team bldg., comm. skills, stress mgmt.; founder Powerhouse, 1st outplacement for creative profls. Co-author: The New York Women's Directory, 1973; contbr. articles and book revs. to various publs. Chmn. pub. rels. Profl. Women's Caucus, 1972; facilitator N.Y.C. Contr.'s Women's Econ. Task Force, 1994-95. N.Y. State scholar. Mem. Am. Art Therapy Assn. (life, bd. dirs. 1980-84), N.Y. Art Therapy Assn. (founding v.p. 1975), The Forum at Stephen Wise (co-chmn. 1986-87), Fin. Women's Assn., Women's Campaign Fund. Home: 35 W 82d St New York NY 10024 Office: 250 W 57th St Ste 1019 New York NY 10107-1019

GERDES, MICHELLE ANN, designer; b. Trenton, N.J., Sept. 23, 1961; d. Paul and Kathryn (Sinchock) Kaniuka; m. Christopher John Gerdes, Apr. 5, 1986; 1 child, Andrew Paul. BA magna cum laude, Kean Coll. N.J., 1983. Asst. art dir. Medecommunications (div. Med. Econs. Co.), Oradell, N.J., 1983-84; sr. designer mag. Med. Econs. Co., Oradell, 1984-85, asst. art dir. mag., 1985-86; asst. art dir. Butterfly Originals, Mt. Laurel, N.J., 1986-87; design coord. J.B. Lippincott Co., Phila., 1987-88; asst. art dir. TV Guide, Radnor, Pa., 1988-91; freelance art dir. Sewell, N.J., 1991-92; advt. designer Current Science, Phila., 1992—. Recipient Cert. of Excellence award Art Dirs. Club of N.J., 1986, Merit award, 1987. Roman Catholic. Home and Office: 2816 Breckenridge Blvd Norristown PA 19403

GEREAU, MARY CONDON, corporate executive; b. Winterset, Iowa, Oct. 10, 1916; d. David Joseph and Sarah Rose (Stack) Condon. Student, Mt. Mercy Jr. Coll., 1935-37; BA, U. Iowa, 1939, MA, 1941; m. Gerald Robert Gereau, Jan. 14, 1961. Program dir. ARC, India, 1943-45; dean of students Eastern Mont. Coll., 1946-48; supt. pub. instrn. state of Mont., 1948-56; sr. legis. cons. NEA, 1957-73; dir. legis. Nat. Treasury Employees Union, 1973-76; legis. asst. to Senator Melcher, Mont., 1976-86; pres. Woman's Party Corp., 1991—. Contbr. articles on state govt. and edn. to profl. jours. Co-chmn. Truman Commerative Com., 1994—. Mem. Coun. Chief State Sch. Officers (bd. dir. 1953-56, pres. 1956), Rural Edn. Assn. (exec. bd. 1953-56), Nat. Women's Party (v.p. 1984-91), Equal Rights Ratification Coun. (nat. chmn.), NEA. Named Conservationist of Yr. Mont. Conservation Coun., 1952, Roll Call Cong. Staffer of Yr., 1985; recipient Disting. Svc. award VFW, 1951, Disting. Svc. award, Chief State Sch. Officers, 1956. Mem. U.S. Congress Burro Club (pres. 1983-84).

GERGER, RICKI SUE, real estate corporation officer; b. Henderson, Tex., Nov. 22, 1946; d. Irving and Miriam (Schachter) Gerger; m. John Murry Starrels, Dec. 24, 1974 (div. 1982). BA, Washington U., St. Louis, 1968; MA, George Washington U., 1976. Asst. v.p. Shannon and Luchs Co., Washington, 1981-84; v.p. Merrill Lynch Realty, Washington, 1984-89, Prudential Preferred Properties, 1989-94, Long & Foster Real Estate, Inc., Washington, 1994—. Mem. Washington D.C. Assn. Realtors (treas. 1987, v.p. 1988, pres. elect 1989, pres. 1990, Realtor of Yr. 1992), Nat. Assn. Realtors (chmn. com. 1993, bd. dirs. 1989-94, regional v.p. 1991). Jewish. Home: 2725 Connecticut Ave NW Apt 708 Washington DC 20008-5300 Office: Long & Foster Real Estate Inc 5101 Wisconsin Ave NW Washington DC 20016

GERHARD, NANCY LUCILE DEGE, educator; b. St. Paul, July 23, 1939; d. Carl H. and Mildred L. (Toenjes) Dege; m. Rick A. Gerhard, June 25, 1960; children: Geoffrey Austin, Mark Alan. BS in Elem. Edn. magna cum laude, Gustavus Adolphus Coll., 1960; MA in Sch. and Guidance Counseling, Chapman U., 1978. Cert. English tchr., guidance counselor, elem. tchr., adminstr., Calif. Tchr. English Orange (Calif.) Unified Sch. Dist., 1987-93, mentor tchr., 1990-93, coach Middle Sch. Demonstration Program, 1990-93, h.s. counselor, 1993—; mem. Calif. Lang. Arts Instructional Materials Evaluation Panel, 1988; cons. UCI Writing Project, Calif. Lit. Project. Mem. ASCD, NEA, Coun. for Basic Edn., Calif. Tchrs. Assn., Orange Unified Edn. Assn. Office: Orange High Sch 525 N Shaffer St Orange CA 92667-6898

GERHARDT, KAREN ELIZABETH, designer, artist; b. Boulder, Colo., Mar. 30, 1965; d. Richard Basil and Rita Aurelia (Tureck) Egan; m. Steven G. Gerhardt, Nov. 14, 1992; children: Steven G. Jr., Zachary. BA in Art and Design, Saginaw Valley State U., 1987. Art dir. Optico Mfg. Co., Inc., St. Charles, Mich., 1987-90; artist, illustrator Creative Composition, Midland, Mich., 1990-91; electronic graphic artist, customer trainer Pendell Printing, Midland, 1991-93; publs. coord. Mackinac Ctr. for Pub. Policy, Midland, 1993—; prin. Sister Studio, 1993—. Mktg. agt., cons. Saginaw (Mich.) Home Builders Assn., 1993—. Roman Catholic.

GERHARDT, LILLIAN NOREEN, magazine editor; b. New Haven, Sept. 28, 1932; d. Victor Herbert and Lillian Angela (Beecher) G. BS, So. Conn. State U., 1954; MLS, U. Chgo., 1962. Children's libr. New Haven Pub. Libr., 1954-55; 1st asst. reference dept. Meriden (Conn.) Pub. Libr., 1955-58, head reference dept., 1958-61; assoc. editor Kirkus Svc., Inc., N.Y.C., 1962-66; exec. editor Sch. Libr. Jour. Book Rev., R.R. Bowker Co., Juvenile Projects, N.Y.C., 1966-71; editor in chief Sch. Libr. Jour., 1971—; v.p. Cahners Mags., N.Y.C., 1992—; lectr. Columbia U. Sch. Library Service, 1969-72. Sr. editor: Best Books for Children, 1967-70; sr. editor, project coordinator: SLJ Book Review Cumulative, 1969, Children's Books in Print, 1969, Subject Guide to Children's Books in Print, 1970; editor-in-chief Sch. Libr. Jour., v.p. Cahners magazines, 1992. Recipient Disting. Alumnus award So. Conn. State U. div. libr. sci., 1978, Cahners medal of excellence, 1993, 94, Jesse H. Neal award Am. Bus. Press, 1994. Mem. ALA (mem.-at-large council 1976-80, Mildred Batchelder award com. 1970, Newbery-Caldecott award com. 1970), Woman's Nat. Book Assn., Assn. Library Services to Children (pres. 1978-79). Office: Cahners Mags SLJ 249 W 17th St New York NY 10011-5300

GERHART, DOROTHY EVELYN, insurance executive, real estate professional; b. Monett, Mo., Apr. 20, 1932; d. Manford Thomas and Norma Grace (Barrett) Ethridge; m. Robert H. Gerhart, Apr. 11, 1952 (div. Dec. 1969); children: Sandra Gerhart Kreamer, Richard A., Diane Gerhart Lacey. Grad. high sch., Tucson; student, U. Ariz., 1950-53. Lic. real estate broker. Owner, pres. Gerhart Ins., Inc., Tucson, 1967-70, 89—; agt. Mahoney-O'Donnell Agy., Tucson, 1970-73, Gerhart & Mendelsoh Ins., Tucson, 1973-78; agt., mgr. personal lines dept. Tucson Realty and Trust, 1978-83; ins. agt. San Xavier Ins. Agy., Tucson, 1985-89; pres. Gerhart Ins., Inc., Tucson, 1989-93, Koty-Leavitt Ins., Inc. (formerly Gerhart Ins., Inc.), Tuscon, 1993—, Gerhart Realty, Inc., Tuscon, 1993—. Vol. Palo Verde Psychiat. Hosp. Mem. Nat. Fedn. Ind. Bus., Ind. Ins. Agts. Tucson (bd. dirs. 1973, 74, v.p. 1975, pres. 1976, First Woman Pres.), Fed. Home Life Ins. Co. (Pres.'s Club award 1986), Nat. Fedn. Small Bus., Altrusa Club of Tucson (bd. dirs. 1984, membership chmn. 1985, fund raising chmn. 1986). Republican. Address: PO Box 13421 Tucson AZ 85732 Office: Gerhart Realty Inc 3208 E Ft Lowell # 108 Tucson AZ 85716

GERHART, GLENNA LEE, pharmacist; b. Houston, June 11, 1954; d. Henry Edwin and Gloria Mae (Mrnustik) G. BS in Pharmacy, U. Houston, 1977. Registered pharmacist, Tex. Staff pharmacist Meml. City Med. Ctr., Houston, 1977-84, asst. dir. pharmacy, 1984—. Mem. Am. Pharm. Assn., Am. Soc. Hosp. Pharmacists, Tex. Pharm. Assn., Harris County Pharm. Assn., Plumeria Soc. Am., U. Houston Alumni Orgn. (life), Houston Cat Club, Nat. Cougar Club, Slavonic Benevolent Order of Tex., Greentrails Ladies Club, Kappa Epsilon. Republican. Methodist. Home: 19811 Cardiff Park Ln Houston TX 77094-3031 Office: Meml City Med Ctr 920 Frostwood Dr Houston TX 77024-2439

GERIKE, ANN ELIZABETH, psychologist; b. Casper, Wyo., Aug. 24, 1933; d. Marcus Gustav and Lillie Helene (Grobengieser) G.; m. John W. Robinson, Oct. 20, 1959 (div. Mar. 1978); children: David Gerike, Margaret Ann, Catherine Elizabeth. BA, U. Nebr., 1955, MA, 1956, PhD, 1983; postgrad., Glasgow U., 1957-60. Editor U. Nebr. Press, Lincoln, 1962-80; clin. psychologist Mental Health and Mental Retardation Authority Harris County, Houston, 1984-87; pvt. practice Mpls., 1988—; clin. psychologist Pyramid Mental Health Ctr., Mpls., 1988-93; aging specialist Employee Adv.

Resource, Control Data Corp., Mpls., 1988-89. Pres. Older Women's League, Houston, 1986; bd. dirs. Twin Cities Gray Panthers, Mpls., 1988—. Mem. APA, Minn. Psychol. Assn., Minn. Gerontol. Soc., Minn. Women Psychologists, Nat. Women's Studies Assn. (convenor Aging and Ageism Caucus 1986—). Democrat. Unitarian. Office: Midlife Counseling 5841 Cedar Lake Rd Ste 201 Saint Louis Park MN 55416

GERMAIN, NANCY ANN, school system administrator, consultant; b. Chgo., Jan. 5, 1941; d. Harold Wayne and Elizabeth Evartson (Halsey) Thrasher; m. Theodore Harry Germain, Dec. 30, 1977; children: Vicki, Jeffrey, Todd. BS, Wayne State U., 1973. Spl. edn. tchr. Mayville (Mich.) Cmty. Schs., 1973-87, tchr., cons., 1984-92, spl. edn. adminstr., 1987—, spl. edn. adminstr. sch. improvement, 1993—. Pres. Hoover Wrestling Club, Hazel Park, Mich., 1966-68, Concerned Citizens, 1981. Recipient Innovative Tchr. award Mich. Dept. Edn., 1984. Mem. Mich. Assn. Tchrs. Emotionally Disturbed Children, Mich. Assn. Adminstrs. Spl. Edn., Coun. for Exceptional Children, Jaycees (aux. pres. 1967, Outstanding Mem. award 1966). Office: Mayville Cmty Schs 6250 Fulton St Mayville MI 48744

GERMANOWSKI, JANET, women's health and medical/surgical nurse, educator; b. Augusta, Ga., Oct. 29, 1943; d. Leonard and Marion (Davis) Volkin; m. Peter J. Germanowski, Dec. 28, 1970; children: Peter, Lauren. BSN, U. Pitts., 1965, MSN, 1990. Project coord. Aminoguanidine Drug Trail, U. Pitts.; project nurse cholesterol lowering intervention program U. Pitts.; acting clin. instr. U. Pitts. Sch. Nursing; rsch. asst. dept. ob-gyn. Magee Women's Hosp., Pitts., head nurse, office mgr. dept. ob-gyn.; grad. student asst. U. Pitts. Sch. Nursing. Contbr. articles to profl. jours. Mem. ANA, NAACOG, Pa. Nurses Assn., Sigma Theta Tau. Home: 54 Ridgecrest Dr Pittsburgh PA 15235-4500

GERONEMUS, DIANN FOX, social work consultant; b. Chgo., July 4, 1947; d. Herbert J. and Edith (Robbins) Fox; BA with high honors, Mich. State U., 1969; MSW, U. Ill., 1971; 1 dau., Heather Eileen. Diplomate Am. Bd. Clin. Social Work; lic. clin. social worker, marriage and family therapist, Fla.; cert. case mgr. Social worker neurology, neurosurgery and medicine Hosp. of Albert Einstein Coll. Medicine, 1971-74; prin. social worker ob-gyn and newborn infant service Rush-Presbyn.-St. Luke's Med. Center, Chgo., 1974-75; social worker neurology, adminstr. Multiple Sclerosis Treatment Center, St. Barnabas Hosp., Bronx, N.Y., 1975-77, socio-med. researcher (Nat. Multiple Sclerosis Soc. grantee), dept. neurology and psychiatry, 1977-79, dir. social service, 1979-80; field work instr. Fordham U. Grad. Sch. Social Service, 1979-80; preceptor, social work program Fla. Atlantic U., Fla. Internat. U.; mem. edn. com., med. adv. bd., program cons. Nat. Multiple Sclerosis Soc., 1980-83, area service cons., 1983-86 ; pvt. practice psychotherapy; social work cons.; cons. in gerontology, rehab. and supervision, 1980—. Mem. Ombudsman Coun., 1992-94, vice chmn. 1993-94. Mem. NASW, Acad. Cert. Social Workers, Registry Clin. Social Workers, Am. Orthopsychiat. Assn. Jewish. Contbr. articles to profl. jours. Home: 833 NW 81st Way Fort Lauderdale FL 33324-1216

GERRISH, CATHERINE RUGGLES, food company executive; b. Winona, Minn., July 10, 1911; d. Clyde O. and Frances (Holmes) Ruggles; m. Hollis G. Gerrish, Sept. 10, 1946. AB, Radcliffe Coll., 1932, AM, 1934; PhD, Harvard U., 1937. Rsch. asst. Harvard U., 1937-39; instr., asst. prof. econs. U. Ill., 1939-42, assoc. prof., 1946; economist Bur. Budget, Exec. Office President, 1943-45; asst. editor Quar. Jour. Econs., 1951-69; treas., v.p. Squirrel Brand Co., Cambridge, Mass., 1966—. Bd. dirs. The Cambridge Homes, pres., 1990-91. Mem. Am. Econ. Assn., Nat. Tax Assn., Coll. Club of Boston (pres. 1948-51), Radcliffe Alumnae Assn. (pres. 1953-55). Home: 207 Grove St Cambridge MA 02138-1013 Office: 17 Boardman St Cambridge MA 02139-1927

GERRISH, LISA DEE, finance administrator, accountant; b. Kansas City, Mo., Nov. 1, 1958; d. Vaughan Carter and Marilyn Ruth (Simonds) G.; m. Frank J. Dattore, July 17, 1981 (div. Dec. 1991). BBA cum laude, U. Mass., Amherst, 1985; postgrad. in Bus. Adminstrn., Rollins Coll., 1993—. CPA, Mass. Audit supr., CPA Coopers and Lybrand, Boston, 1985-89; sr. acct.-in-charge Walt Disney World, Lake Buena Vista, Fla., 1989-90, acctg. mgr., 1990-92, sr. fin. analyst, 1992-93, fin. mgr., 1993—. Mem. ctrl. Fla. chpt. United Way, 1989-93. Mem. AICPAs, AAUW, Fla. Inst. CPAs, Inst. Mgmt. Accts., Acctg. Rsch. Found. Republican. Episcopalian. Home: 4350 S Lake Orlando Pky Orlando FL 32808-2259 Office: Walt Disney World PO Box 10 000 Lk Buena Vis FL 32830-1000

GERRITSEN, MARY ELLEN, vascular and cell biologist; b. Calgary, Alta., Can., Sept. 20, 1953; came to U.S., 1978; d. Thomas Clayton and Alice Irene (Minton) Cooper; m. Paul William Gerritsen, May 24, 1975 (div. 1977); m. Thomas Patrick Parks, Oct. 11, 1980; children: Kristen, Madelene. BSc summa cum laude, U. Calgary, 1975, PhD, 1978. Postdoctoral fellow U. Calif., San Diego, 1978-80; asst. prof. N.Y. Med. Coll., Valhalla, 1981-86, assoc. prof., 1986-90; sr. staff scientist Miles Pharms., West Haven, Conn., 1990-93; prin. staff scientist, 1993—; also head inflammation group Miles Pharms., West Haven, Conn., 1990—; cons. Insite Vision, Alameda, Calif., 1987-89, Boehringer Ingelheim Pharms., Ridgefield, Conn., 1985-88; adj. assoc. prof. N.Y. Med. Coll., 1990—. Mem. editorial bd. Microvascular Rsch., 1988—, Am. Jour. Physiology, 1993—; editor-in-chief Microcirculation, 1993—; contbr. articles to profl. jours. Vol., mem. peer rev. com. N.Y. State Heart Assn., Syracuse, 1986-90. I. W. Killam Found. fellow, 1976, Med. Rsch. Coun. Can. fellow, 1978. Mem. Am. Soc. for Pharmacology and Exptl. Therapeutics, Am. Physiol. Soc., Assn. Rsch. on Vision and Ophthalmology, Am. Soc. Investigational Pathology, Soc. Leukocyte Biology, Am. Soc. Cell Biology, Microcirculatory Soc. (coun. 1989-92, Mayr Wiedeman award 1985, Young Investigator award 1984, chair publs. com. 1991-93), N.Am. Vascular Biology Orgn. (steering com. 1993, coun. 1994—). Office: Miles Inc Inst for Bone Cartilage and Cancer 400 Morgan Ln West Haven CT 06516-4140

GERRY, DEBRA PRUE, psychotherapist; b. Oct. 9, 1951; d. C.O. and Sarah E. Rawl; m. Norman Bernard Gerry, Apr. 10, 1981; 1 child, Gisele Psyche Victoria. BS, Ga. So. U., 1972; MEd, Armstrong State U., 1974; PhD, U. Ga., 1989. Cert. Ariz. Bd. Behavioral Health Examiners. Spl. edn. tchr. Chatham County Bd. Edn., Savannah, Ga., 1972-74; edn. and learning disabilities resource educator Duval County Bd. Edn., Jacksonville, Fla., 1974-77; ednl. resource counselor spl. programs adminstr. Broward County Bd. Edn., Ft. Lauderdale, Fla., 1977-81; pvt. practice Scottsdale, Ariz., 1990—. Contbr. author coll. textbooks; contbr. articles to profl. jours. Vol., fundraiser, psychol. cons., group leader Valley AIDS Orgns., Phoenix, 1990-94; fundraiser Hosp. Health Edn. Programs, Scottsdale, 1992-93; mem. com. for women's issues Plz. Club, Phoenix, 1992-93; pres. Laissez Les Bon Temps Rouler, Wrigley Club, Phoenix, 1993-94. Recipient Rudy award Shanti Orgn., 1991. Mem. APA, NOW, Am. Counseling Assn., Nat. Assn. Women Bus. Owners, Assn. for Multicultural Coun., Assn. for Specialists in Group Work, Mensa, Phi Delta Kappa, Kappa Delta Epsilon, Sigma Omega Phi, Kappa Delta Pi. Office: 6210 E Thomas Ste 209 Scottsdale AZ 85251

GERSBACHER, EVA ELIZABETH, special education administrator; b. Carbondale, Ill., Dec. 31, 1949; d. Willard Marion and Eva (Oxford) G. BA, Hope Coll., 1970; postgrad., Grand Valley State Coll., 1971-73; MA, S.E. Mo. State U., 1974; postgrad., So. Ill. U., 1975-78. Cert. adminstr., tchr. learning disabilities, educable mentally impaired, severe mentally impaired, behavior disordered, physically handicapped, presch., elem. Tchr. Fairport (Mich.) Elem. Sch., summer 1970; support tchr. Day Sch. for Emotionally Disturbed, Carbondale, Ill., 1970-71, West Ottawa Sch. Dist., Holland, Mich., 1971-72, Ottawa Intermediate Sch. Dist., Grand Haven, Mich., 1972-73; diagnostic tchr. Tri-County Spl. Edn., Murphysboro, Ill., 1974-76; grad. asst. So. Ill. U., Carbondale, 1974-76, instr., 1976-78; coord. So. Ill. Ednl. Svcs. Ctr., Marion, Ill., 1978-82; prin. Tri-County Edn. Ctr., Anna, Ill., 1982-85; program adminstr. Tri-County Spl. Edn., Murphysboro, Ill., 1985—; cons. Head Start, So. Ill., 1975-77, So. Ill. Ednl. Svc. Ctr., 1976-77, Southwestern Ill. Regional Spl. Edn., 1977. Pres., treas., sec. Developmental Disabilities Protective Svc. Bd., Anna, Ill. Spl. edn. fellow Ill. Office Edn., So. Ill. U., 1976. Mem. Assn. Persons with Severe Handicaps, Assn. Citizens with Learning Disabilities, Assn. Behavior Analysis, Am. Assn. Mental Deficiency, Ill. Assn. Persons with Severe Handicaps (mem. governing bd. 1980-82), Coun. Exceptional Children (pres. 1990-93), Ill. Adminstrs. Spl. Edn., Ill. Women Adminstrs., Kappa Delta Pi, Phi Kappa Phi. Home: 1507 W Taylor Dr Carbondale IL 62901-2221 Office: Tri County Spl Edn 1725 Shomaker Dr Murphysboro IL 62966-2507

GERSHON, NINA, federal judge; b. Chgo., Oct. 16, 1940; d. David and Marie Gershon; m. Bernard J. Fried, May 15, 1983. BA, Cornell U., 1962; LLB, Yale U., 1965; postgrad., London Sch. Econs., 1965-66. Magistrate judge U.S. Dist. Ct. (so. dist.) N.Y., N.Y.C., currently. Fulbright scholar. Office: US District Court US Courthouse Foley Sq New York NY 10007-1501

GERSKE, JANET FAY, lawyer; b. Chgo., Nov. 14, 1950; d. Bernard G. Gerske and L. Fay (Knight) Capron; m. James P. Chapman, Dec. 5, 1982. BS, Northwestern U., 1971; JD, U. Mich., 1978. Bar: Ill. 1978, U.S. Dist. Ct. (no. dist.) Ill. 1978. Pvt. practice, Chgo., 1978-80, 84—; assoc. Jerome H. Torshen Ltd., Chgo., 1980-84. Chpt. chmn. Ind. Voters Ill./Ind. Precinct Orgn., Chgo., 1982-84; co-chmn. Ill. Women's Agenda Com., 1985-88, fin. officer, 1987-88; dir. Chgo. Abused Women Coalition, 1986-90, sec., treas., 1988-90. Mem. Women's Bar Assn. Ill. (co-chmn. rights of women com. 1985-86, dir. 1988-90), Chgo. Bar Assn. (co-chmn. legal status of women com. young lawyers sect.), Nat. Orgn. Social Security Claimants' Rep. Democrat. Home: 850 W Oakdale Ave Chicago IL 60657-5122 Office: 542 S Dearborn St Chicago IL 60605-1508

GERSONI-EDELMAN, DIANE CLAIRE, author, editor; b. Bklyn., Apr. 16, 1947; d. James Arthur and Edna Bernice (Krinski) Gersoni; B.A. cum laude, Vassar Coll., 1967; m. James Neil Edelman, Oct. 5, 1975; children—Michael Lawrence, Sara Anne. Asst. editor, then asso. editor Sch. Library Jour. Book Rev., 1968-72; free lance writer, 1972-74, 77—; writer, editor Scholastic Mags., Inc., N.Y.C., 1974-77; author: Sexism and Youth, 1974; Work-Wise: Learning About the World of Work from Books, 1980; cons., speaker in field. Club: Vassar (N.Y.C.). Contbr. articles, book revs. to anthologies, newspapers, mags. Home: care Edelman 301 E 78th St New York NY 10021-1322

GERST, ELIZABETH CARLSEN (MRS. PAUL H. GERST), university dean, researcher, educator; b. N.Y.C., June 10, 1929; d. Rolf and Gudrun (Wiborg) Carlsen; A.B. magna cum laude, Mt. Holyoke Coll., 1951; Ph.D., U. Pa., 1957; m. Paul H. Gerst, Aug. 3, 1957; children—Steven Richard, Jeffrey Carlton, Andrew Leigh. Instr. physiology Grad. Sch. Medicine, U. Pa., 1955-57, Cornell U. Med. Coll., N.Y.C., 1957-58; instr. Columbia Coll. Physicians and Surgeons, N.Y.C., 1959-61, asst. prof., 1961—, dir. Center Continuing Edn. in Health Scis., 1978-87, asst. dean continuing edn., 1984-87, spl. lectr., 1987—, dir. Office Med. Edn., N.Y. Acad. Med., 1987—; Authors: (with others) The Lung, Clinical Physiology and Pulmonary Function Tests, 1955, rev. edit., 1962. Pres. Citizen's Ednl. Council Tenafly, 1972-73; mem. Citizens Long-Range Planning Com., Tenafly Bd. Edn., 1973-77, chmn. supt. search, edn., tchr. hiring, personnel coms.; vice chmn. Tenafly Environ. Commn., 1972-77; trustee Tenafly Nature Center, 1972-80; bd. dirs., chmn. environ. quality Tenafly LWV, 1971-78; v.p. Bergen County LWV, 1973-75. Porter fellow Am. Physiol. Soc., 1956-57. Mem. Middle States Assn. Colls. and Schs. (team Commn. on higher edn., 1984—), Soc. Med. Coll. Dirs. of Continuing Med. Edn., Am. Physiol. Soc. (task force Women in Physiology 1973-75), N.Y. County Med. Soc. (com. on continuing med. edn. 1978—), Physiol. Soc. Phila., Harvey Soc., Biophys. Soc., Alliance Continuing Med. Edn., N.Y. Acad. Scis., AAAS, Phi Beta Kappa, Sigma Xi, Sigma Delta Epsilon. Unitarian. Home: 141 Tekening Dr Tenafly NJ 07670-1218

GERSTEIN, ELLEN CLAIRE, non-profit organization executive; b. Atlanta, Apr. 12, 1957; d. Joe Willie and Doris Renee (Florsheim) G.; 1 child, Tina Crooke. BA in Criminal Justice, U. Ga., 1979; M in Mgmt., U. Phoenix, 1991. Group home leader Cobb Emergency Shelter, Marietta, Ga., 1979-80; asst. counselor Physician/Surgeons Hosp., Atlanta, 1980-81; adminstr. OK Cmty., Phoenix, 1981-91; exec. dir. Gwinnett Coalition for Health and Human Svcs., Lawrenceville, Ga., 1991—; mem. adv. bd. Justice Ctr. of Gwinnett, Lawrenceville, 1994; bd. dirs. Christian Emergency Help Ctr., Atlanta, Gwinnett Cmty. Coun., Gwinnett County, Ga. Mem. adv. bd. Jr. League, North Fulton, Ga., 1994, Gwinnett Battered Women, 1993-94; mem. election com. Dem. Party, Duluth, Ga., 1994; bd. dirs. Head Start, 1994; initiating mem. Atlanta Regional Commn., 1994. Mem. Gwinnett C. of C. (mem. leadership com. 1994). Jewish. Home: 4094 Stillwater Dr Duluth GA 30136 Office: Gwinnett Coalition 250 Oak St Lawrenceville GA 30245

GERSTEIN, ESTHER, sculptor; b. N.Y.C., May 20, 1924; d. Leon and Lillian (Peretz) Grizer; m. Leonard B. Gerstein, Mar. 31, 1946; children: Lee Steven, Laurie Susan. Student, Pratt Inst., 1941-42, NYU, 1942-43; pvt. study, various sculptors; student, Cooper Union, 1946-48. Asst. tchr. Art Students League, N.Y.C., 1944-46; painting tchr. pvt. sch. Great Neck, N.Y., 1961-63; founder, instr. sculpture and painting Studio 33, Westbury, N.Y., 1964-72; sculptor and painter pvt. studios, N.Y.C. and Boca Raton, Fla.; lectr. Norton Mus., Palm Beach, Fla., 1985. Exhibited in group shows at Hecksher Mus., Huntington, N.Y., Norton Mus., Palm Beach, Fla., Kellenberg Gallery, C.W. Post Coll., L.I., Firehouse Gallery, Nassau Community Coll., L.I., Lever House, N.Y.C., Grace Bldg., N.Y.C., Hofstra U., Lighthouse Gallery, Tequesta, Fla., Montoya Art Gallery, Palm Beach, Del-Aire Country Club, Boca Raton, Fla., Bocaire Country Club, Boca Raton, Polo Country Club, Boca Raton, Nathan Rosen Gallery, Boca Raton, Lynn U., Boca Raton, Naza Gallery, Boca Raton, Naza Gallery, Boca Raton; one man show includes TV spl.; represented in numerous pvt. and corp. collections throughout U.S. Art Students League scholar, 1944, Cooper Union scholar, 1946. Mem. Artists Guild Norton Mus., Nat. League Am. Pen Women.

GERSTEL, JUDITH ROSS, film critic; b. Winnipeg, Man., Can., Dec. 19, 1944; d. Marvyn and Rachel (Kesten) Ross; m. Alan N. Gerstel, Nov. 6, 1963; children: Jennifer, Sasha (dec.). Student, U. Man., 1960-63; BA, U. Buffalo, 1964. Music and dance critic Buffalo Courier-Express, 1965; producer WGBH-FM, Cambridge, Mass., 1966-67; writer, critic Mpls. Star, 1968-71; writer, broadcaster CBC-TV, Windsor & Toronto, Can., 1974-77; TV producer CBC-TV, Can., 1977-81; asst. editor, feature writer Detroit Free Press, KRTN, 1988-91, film critic, 1991—. Recipient award for TV, Can. Music Coun., 1977; nominated for best documentary writer Assn. Can. TV and Radio Artists, 1979; Nat. Arts Journalism fellow U. So. Calif., 1994—. Mem. Nat. Soc. Film Critics. Office: Detroit Free Press 321 W Lafayette Blvd Detroit MI 48226

GERSTENBERGER, DONNA LORINE, humanities educator; b. Wichita Falls, Tex., Dec. 26, 1929; d. Donald Fayette and Mabel G. AB, Whitman Coll., 1951; MA, U. Okla., 1952, PhD, 1958. Asst. prof. English, U. Colo., Boulder, 1958-60; prof. U. Wash., 1960—, chmn. undergrad. studies, 1971-74, assoc. dean Coll. Arts and Scis., dir. Coll. Honors and Office Undergrad. Studies, 1974-76, chmn. dept. English, 1976-83, vice chmn. faculty senate, 1984-85, chmn. faculty senate, 1985-86; cons. in field; bd. dirs. Am. Lit. Classics; mem. grants-in-aid com. Am. Coun. Learned Socs.; chmn. region VII, Mellon Fellowships in Humanities, 1982-92; mem. adv. com. Grad. Record Exams, 1990-93, Coun. Internat. Exch. of Scholars, 1992—. Author: J.M. Synge, 1964, 2d edition, 1988, The American Novel: A Checklist of Twentieth Century Criticism, vols. I and II, 1970, Directory of Periodicals, 1974, The Complex Configuration: Modern Verse Drama, 1973, Iris Murdoch, 1974, Richard Hugo, 1983; editor: Microcosm, 1969, Swallow Series in Bibliography, 1974—; assoc. editor: Abstracts of English Studies, 1958-68; editor jour. Seattle Review, 1983—. Bd. dirs. N.W. Chamber Orch., Seattle, 1975-78, Wash. Friends Humanities, 1991—; trustee Wash. Commn. Humanities, 1985-91, pres., 1988-90; mem. vis. com. Lehigh U., 1987-92; pres. Am. Commn. for Irish Studies/West, 1989-91. Am. Council Learned Socs. grantee, 1962, 88; Am. Philos. Soc. grantee, 1963. Mem. MLA, Am. Com. Irish Studies. Office: U Wash GN-30 Dept English Seattle WA 98195

GERSTING, JUDITH LEE, computer science educator, researcher; b. Springfield, Vt., Aug. 20, 1940; d. Harold H. and Dorothy V. (Kinney) MacKenzie; m. John M. Gersting, Jr., Aug. 17, 1962; children: Adam, Jason. BS, Stetson U., 1962; MA, Ariz. State U., 1964, PhD, 1969. Assoc. prof. computer sci. U. Ctrl. Fla., Orlando, 1980-81; asst. prof. computer sci. Ind. U.-Purdue U., Indpls., 1970-73, assoc. prof., 1974-79, prof., 1981-93; prof. computer sci. U. Hawaii, Hilo, 1994—; staff scientist Indpls. Ctr. for Advanced Rsch., 1982-84. Author: Mathematical Structures for Computer Science, 1993, The Programming Process/Pascal, 1989; contbr. articles to computer sci. jours. Mem. Assn. for Computing Machinery, IEEE Computer Soc. Office: U Hawaii at Hilo 200 W Kawili St Hilo HI 96720

GERSTNER, DAWN MICHELLE, administrative secretary; b. Rochester, N.Y., May 27, 1970; d. David Glenn and Eloise Veronica (Morehouse) G. AAS in Office Tech., Monroe C.C., Rochester, 1990. Cert. profl. sec., N.Y. Clk. Fay's Drug Store, Rochester, 1986-93; sec. Eastman Kodak, Rochester, 1987-88, 89; legal asst. Hyatt Legal Svsc., Rochester, 1988-89; sec. Shearson Lehman Bros., Rochester, 1990; data control clk. Office of Clin. Practice Evaluation, U. Rochester, 1990-92, sec., 1992-94; adminstrv. sec. Rochester Group Mgmt., 1994—. Author: (with others) Creating a Community-Based Ambulatory Care Network in Rochester, N.Y., 1993. Mem. Profl. Secs. Internat. Home: 22 Old Pine Ln Rochester NY 14615 Office: Rochester Group Mgmt 2300 Buffalo Rd Bldg 200 Rochester NY 14624

GERSTNER, JOANNE C., sports journalist; b. Detroit, Apr. 27, 1971; d. Richard J. and Waltraud M. G. BA in Journalism with honors, Oakland U., 1993; postgrad., Northwestern U., 1994-95. Sports editor Oakland Post, Rochester, Mich., 1992-93; sports writer Flint (Mich.) Jour., 1993; asst. editor PGA Mag., NBA Inside Stuff, Troy, Mich., 1993-94. Detroit Soc. Profl. Journalists scholar, 1992. Mem. Women in Comm., Assn. for Women in Sports Media.

GERSTNER, MARY JANE, operating room nurse; b. Rochester, N.Y., June 27, 1953; d. Thomas J. and Jane E. Gerstner. Diploma, St. Joseph's Hosp. Health Ctr. Sch. Nursing, 1974; BSN, Nazareth Coll., 1982. RN, N.Y. Staff nurse operating rm. U. Rochester Med. Ctr./Strong Meml. Hosp., staff nurse ob.-gyn. unit; staff nurse operating rm. St. Mary's Hosp., Rochester, Genesee Hosp., Rochester. Mem. ARC. Mem. Assn. Operating Rm. Nurses, Am. Soc. Ophthalmolic RNs, Sigma Theta Tau.

GERTH, SHARON ANN, adult health nurse, educator; b. Boulder, Colo., Feb. 18, 1947; d. Robert John Sr. and Theresa Ann (Mozier) Seager; m. Aug. 29, 1970 (div. Jan. 1974); m. Frederick A. Gerth, June 4, 1977. BSN, So. Ill. U., 1970; MEd, U. Ill., 1976; MSN, Ind. U., Indpls., 1980, DNS, 1992. Staff nurse Christian Welfare Hosp., East St. Louis, 1970; staff nurse Lawrence and Meml. Hosp., New London, Conn., 1970-71, instr. Sch. Nursing, 1971-72; staff nurse, charge nurse Carle Found. Hosp., Urbana, 1973; coord., developer practical nursing program Parkland Coll., Champaign, Ill., 1973-79, nursing instr., 1973-80, nursing instr. ADN program, 1980-94; dept. chair/nursing Parkland Coll., Champaign, 1994—; adj. faculty U. Ill., Urbana-Champaign, 1991—; affiliate mem. nursing and patient care com. Carle Hosp., Urbana, 1991—. Host family program for fgn. students, U. Ill., Urbana, 1981—. Mem. ANA (med.-surg. coun. nursing practice), Am. Ednl. Rsch. Assn., Nat. League for Nursing (Ill. chpt.), Ill. Nurses Assn., Sigma Theta Tau, Kappa Delta Pi, Pi Lambda Theta, Phi Delta Kappa. Office: Parkland Coll 2400 W Bradley Ave Champaign IL 61821-1899

GERTIG, JUNE MUNFORD, lawyer; b. Chilliwack, B.C., Can., May 31, 1943; d. David Charles and Nell (Malott) Munford; m. Joseph Frank Gertig; children: Matthew Munford, Christopher Katherine, Joshua Shadwell. BA, Radcliffe Coll., 1965; JD, U. Wis., 1977. Bar: D.C. 1977. Assoc. Fried, Frank, Harris, Shriver, Jacobson, Washington, 1977-85, ptnr., 1985—. Office: Fried Frank Harris 1001 Pennsylvania Ave NW Washington DC 20004-2505

GERTNER, NANCY, federal judge; b. May 22, 1946. BA cum laude with honors, Columbia U., 1967; JD, Yale U., 1971; degree (hon.), New England Sch. Law, 1979. Law clerk to Hon. Luther M. Swygert U.S. Ct. Appeals (7th cir.), Chgo., 1971-72; ptnr. Silverglate, Gemer, Fine & Good, 1973-90, Dwyer, Collora & Gertner, 1990-94; judge U.S. Dist. Ct. Mass., Boston, 1994—; instr. Sch. Law Boston U., 1972-86, 87-90; vis. prof. Law Sch. Harvard U., 1985-86; mem. civic justice adv. com. to U.S. Dist. Ct., 1991; mem. adv. com. U.S. Ct. Appeals (1st cir.), 1991-92. Contbr. articles to legal jours. Bd. dirs. Women's Rights Com. Recipient Mass. Choice award, 1987, Black Educator's Alliance award Profl. Svc. to Edn., 1983, New England Hadassah award, 1992, Abigail Adams award Mass. Women's Polit. Caucus Edn. Fund., 1994. Mem. Assn. Trial Lawyers Am. (basic trial advocacy course com., vice chair 1985-86), Mass. Acad. Trial Lawyers, Mass. Half-Way Houses, Inc. (house com.), Mass. Civil Liberties Union (bd. dirs., Abraham T. Alper award for Excellence in Civil Liberties, 1980), Boston Bar Assn. (lawyers com. for civil rights under law, steering com. 1979—). Office: John W McCormack Courthouse 90 Devonshire St Rm 707 Boston MA 02109*

GERTRUDE, KATY See WILHELM, KATE

GERWELS, LAURENN BARKER, public relations executive, sculptor, artist; b. Morristown, Tenn., Mar. 17, 1945; d. George Herbert and Claire Hortense (Perkins) Prater; m. Rodney Gibson Russell, Aug. 27, 1967 (div.); children: Chelse Fore, Josh Barrett, Micaiah Lael; m. Paul Edward Barker, Feb. 16, 1981 (div.); m. John Gerwels, Oct. 2, 1993. Grad. cum laude, Mt. Vernon Sem., 1963; grad. Inst. Am. Univs., France, 1966; BA, So. Meth. U., 1967; postgrad. Dallas Art Inst., 1967. Cert. pilot, FAA. Graphic designer Taylor Pub., Dallas, 1968-69; art dir. First Nat. Bank-First Family mag., Dallas, 1969-70; graphic artist Tyler Courier Times (Tex.), 1971-74; dir. pub. rels. Marsco Engring., Tyler, 1974-79; owner R&L Design Studio, Tyler, 1979-81, Artworks/Presentation Plus Creative Agy., Austin, Tex., 1988-91; owner, Artworks Creative Agy., Knoxville, Tenn., 1991—; dir. pub. rels. Espey Huston & Assocs., Austin-Houston, 1981-88; design cons. S.W. Hist. Wax Mus., Arlington, Tex., 1979, Tex. Hist. Preservation Park, Austin, 1983; cons. pub. rels. Gallery Contemporary Southwestern Art, Dallas, 1983; cons.-art dir. Macintosh User's Monthly mag. Featured artist Tyler Courier Times, 1979, Tex. Hwys. State Mag., 1979, Austin Mag., 1981, 88, Ultra Mag., 1991, Knoxville News Sentinel, 1992, Sta. KLTV-TV, Longview, Tex., 1979, Sta. KTVV-TV, Austin, 1982, Sta. WBIR-TV, Knoxville, Tenn., 1992, Eyes of Tex. TV program, 1991. Mem. Travis County Susquicentennial Exhibit Com.; bd. dirs. Central Tex. March of Dimes, design cons. benefit, 1984—, East Tenn. Opera Guild, 1992—; bd. dirs., sec., participant Leadership Austin, 1986-87. Recipient State Rep. award Nat. Cherry Blossom Festival, Washington, 1966; U.S. Rep.-Bal de Petit Lits Blanc, Monte Carlo, Monaco, 1967; Design/Modeling award Neiman Marcus, Dallas, 1967; art fellow Vt. Studio Sch., Johnson, 1991. Mem. Nat. Mus. Women in Arts (Tenn. state com., exec. adv. com., bd. dirs.), Women in Comm., Inc., Tex. Presswomen's Assn., Glamour Mag. Orgn. Profl. Women, Austin Contemporary Visual Arts Assn., Soc. for Mktg. Profl. Svcs., Tex. Pub. Rels. Assn. Democrat. Episcopalian. Home: 21616 Beals Chapel Rd Lenoir City TN 37771-3845

GERWICK-BRODEUR, MADELINE CAROL, marketing and sales professional; b. Kearney, Neb., Aug. 29, 1951; d. Vern Frank and Marian Leila (Bliss) Gerwick; m. David Louis Brodeur; 1 child, Maria Louise. Student, U. Wis., 1970-72, U. Louisville, 1974-75; BA in Econs. magna cum laude, U. N.H., 1979; postgrad., Internat. Trade Inst., Seattle. Indsl. sales rep. United Radio Supply Inc., Seattle, 1980-81; mfrs. rep. Ray Over Sales Inc., Seattle, 1981-82; sales engr. Tektronix, Inc., Kent, Wash., 1982-83; mktg. mgr. Zepher Industries, Inc., Burien, Wash., 1983-85, Microscan Systems Inc., Tukwila, Wash., 1986.; market devel. URS Electronics, Inc., Portland, 1986-88; sr. product specialist Fluke Corp., 1989—; bd. dirs., sec. Starfish Enterprises Inc., Tacoma, 1984-87; com. chmn. Northcon, Seattle and Portland, 1984-86, 88, 90; speaker to Wash. Women's Employment and Edn., Tacoma, 1983—. Recipient Jack E. Chase award for Outstanding Svc. and Contbr. Northcon Founder's Orgn., 1988. Mem. Electronic Mfrs. Assn. (sec. 1982, sec.-treas. 1988, v.p. 1989), Inst. Noetic Scis., Phi Kappa Phi. Office: Fluke Corp MS270D PO Box 9090 Everett WA 98206-9090

GERWIN, LESLIE ELLEN, public affairs, community relations executive, lawyer; b. Los Angeles, May 18, 1950; d. Nathan and Beverly Adele (Wilson) G.; m. Bruce Robert Leslie, July 3, 1978; 1 child, Jonathan Gerwin Leslie. BA, Prescott Coll., 1972; JD, Antioch Sch. Law, 1975; MPH, Tulane

U., 1988. Bar: D.C. 1975, N.Y. 1981, U.S. Dist. Ct. D.C. 1977, U.S. Dist. Ct. (so. dist.) N.Y. 1980. Staff asst. Members of Congress, Washington, 1970-72; cons. Congressional Subcom., Washington, 1972-73; instr. U. Miami Law Sch., Coral Gables, Fla., 1975-76; assoc. prof. law Yeshiva U., N.Y.C., 1976-86; vis. assoc. prof. law Tulane Law Sch., New Orleans, 1983-84; pub. policy cons. New Orleans, 1987—; with Ariadne Cons., New Orleans, 1988-91; dir. devel. and community rels. Planned Parenthood La., Inc., New Orleans, 1989-90; legal advisor La. Coalition for Reproductive Freedom, 1990-92; exec. v.p. Met. Area Com., New Orleans, 1992-94; exec. dir. Met. Area Com. Edn. Fund, New Orleans, 1992-94; bd. dirs. Inst. for Phys. Fitness Rsch., N.Y.C., 1982-86, Challenge/Discovery, Crested Butte, Colo., 1977-80; cons. FDA, Washington, 1977-78, U. Judaism, L.A., 1974-75; mem. Met. Area Com. Leadership Forum, New Orleans, 1988. Contbr. articles to profl. jours. Mem. Ind. Dem. Jud. Screening Panel, N.Y.C., 1980; bd. dirs. New Orleans Food Bank for Emergencies, 1987-89; profl. adv. com. MAZON-A Jewish Response to Hunger, L.A., 1986-89; bd. dirs. Second Harvesters Food Bank Greater New Orleans, 1989-94, La. State LWV, 1990-91, Anti-Defamation League, New Orleans, 1989—, Jewish Endowment Found., 1987-93; trustee Jewish Fedn. Greater New Orleans, 1989—, Community Rels. Com., New Orleans, 1986—, Fed. Emergency Mgmt. Agy. Bd., Emergency Food and Shelter Program, S.E. La., 1988—; v.p. Tulane U. B'nai B'rith Hillel Found., 1987-90; steering com. Citizens for Pers. Freedom, 1989-91; steering com. Metro 2000, 1989-90; sec. New Orleans sect. Nat. Coun. Jewish Women, 1990-91, state pub. affairs chmn., 1992—; bd. Contemporary Arts Ctr., 1993—; bd. advocates Planned Parenthood La. Fellow Inst. of Politics, 1990-91; scholar Xerox Found., 1972-75; Decorated Order of Barristers; named One of Ten Outstanding Young Women of Am., 1987; recipient Herbert J. Garon Young Leadership award Jewish Fedn. Greater New Orleans, 1990; named YWCA Role Model, 1992. Mem. ABA, N.Y. Bar Assn., N.Y. Acad. Scis., Am. Pub. Health Assn., D.C. Bar Assn., Nat. Moot Ct. Honor Soc., Pub. Health Honor Soc., Calif. State Dem. Club (Key Svc. award 1988), Delta Omega.

GERWIN, MARY BERRY, legislative staff member, federal and state government lawyer; m. Edward F. Gerwin Jr.; children: Kathleen, Kristen. BA summa cum laude, U. Maine, 1977; JD cum laude, Georgetown U., 1980. Bar: D.C. Legis. aide to Senator William S. Cohen, Washington, 1981—; counsel sub-com. on oversight of govt. mgmt. Senate Com. on Govt. Affairs, Washington, 1981-86, minority staff dir. and chief counsel sub-com. on oversight of govt. mgmt., 1986-91; minority staff dir. and chief counsel Senate Special Com. on Aging, Washington, 1991—. Assoc. editor: Tax Lawyer Law Review. Pres. bd. dir. Senate Employee's Child Care Ctr. Mem. Alpha Kappa Delta, Phi Kappa Phi. Office: Special Com on Aging 628 Senate Hart Office Bldg Washington DC 20510*

GEST, KATHRYN WATERS, press secretary; b. Boston, Mar. 20, 1947; d. Mendal and Anna Hilda (Black) Waters; m. Theodore O. Gest, May 28, 1972; 1 child, David Mendal. B.S., Northwestern U., 1969; M.S., Columbia U., 1970. Reporter The Patriot-Ledger, Quincy, Mass., 1968; writer Europe desk Voice of Am., Washington, 1969; reporter St. Louis Globe-Democrat, 1970-77; reporter Congl. Quar., Washington, 1977-78, news editor, 1978-80, asst. mng. editor, 1980-83, mng. editor, 1983-87; St. Louis corr. Time Mag., 1975-77, The Christian Sci. Monitor, 1976-77; press sec. to Sen. William S. Cohen, Washington, 1987—; chmn., U.S. del. Internat. Labor Orgn. Tripartite Meeting on Conditions of Employment and Work of Journalists, Geneva, 1990. Recipient award for investigative reporting Inland Daily Press Assn., 1975. Mem. Soc. Profl. Journalists. Club: Nat. Press. Office: Office of Sen William S Cohen 322 Hart Senate Office Bldg Washington DC 20015

GETCHIUS, JUNE KATHERINE, customer service administrator; b. N.Y.C., Nov. 21, 1947; d. Nicholas nd Charlotte Feil. BS in Bus. Adminstrn., Fordham U., 1969; MA in Social Sci., Montclair State Coll., 1983; MBA, Pace U., 1994. Cert. tchr., N.J. Elem. tchr. St. Leo's Sch., Elmwood Park, N.J., 1969-81; office mgr. E. Loyas Ins., Garfield, N.J., 1981-83; customer rep. Nynex Mobile Comm., Pearl River, N.Y., 1983-85; collections supr. Nynex Mobile Comm., Pearl River, 1985-86, asst. mgr. CSC, 1986; mgr. resellers Nynex Mobile Comm., Orangeburg, N.Y., 1987-89; mgr. product planning Nynex Mobile Comm., Orangeburg, 1989-91, dir. methods and procedures, 1991-94, dir. customer svc. operating support, 1994—. Named Presdl. scholar Fordham U., 1965-69. Mem. Assn. Nynex Women, Mystic Seaport Mus., Phi Kappa Phi, Delta Mu Delta. Office: Nynex Mobile Comm 2000 Corporate Dr Orangeburg NY 10962-2624

GETMAN, SHERYL MARIE, artist; b. Kalispell, Mont., Dec. 31, 1947; d. Dannie E. Loutherback and Shirley Jean (Barry) Michaelson; m. Daniel William Getman, Jan. 21, 1952; children: Guy Young, Crescent. Student, Ea. Mont. State Coll., 1968, 69, Calif State Coll., Fullerton, 1970, Mont. State U., 1974, 75, 76, Flathead Coll., Kalispell Mt., 1977, 78, Art Student's League, N.Y.C., 1988. Artist Jorgensen Pottery & Art Studio, Coram, Mont., 1978-83; owner, mgr. Spruce Park Truck Stop, Coram, 1980-83; pres., artist Sky Jordan Graphics, Kalispell, 1983-86; pres. Sky Jordan Restaurant Inc., Kalispell Mt., 1983-86; pres., artist Artistic Urges, Inc., Princeton, N.J., 1986-92; propr. Whitney Mansion Gallery and Inn, Kalispell, 1992—; v.p. Sky Deco Inc., 1989—; feature writer Penington (N.J.) Post, 1989, also freelance writer; pres. Sky East Inc., 1990—; instr. Reevaluation Counseling, Creativity Seminars, 1989—; owner Getman Studio, Santa Monica, Calif. Author: Big House of Montana, 1993; illustrator: Memoirs of Montana Fisherman, Jelinski, 1993. Vol. Siddha Meditation Ctr. Mem. Nat. League Am. Pen Women, North Star Watercolor Soc. (bd. dirs. 1987-88). Unitarian. Office: Sheryl Getman Studios Lincoln Ctr Ste 421 2633 Lincoln Blvd Santa Monica CA 90405

GETSKE, KATHRINE, psychiatric social worker; b. Memphis, Jan. 19, 1937; d. Noble Owen and Annie Lou (Robertson) Fowler; m. Raymond Nicholas Getske, Nov. 27, 1965; children: Philip David, Raymond Nicholas Jr., Barbara Lynn, Virginia Kathrine. BS cum laude, Memphis State U., 1960; MA, Presbyn. Sch. Christian Edn., Richmond, Va., 1962; MSW, U. Tenn., 1989. Lic. cert. social worker, Tenn.; cert. dir. Christian edn. Dir. Christian edn. 1st Presbyn. Ch., Auburn, Ala., 1962-64; social worker ARC, Memphis, 1964-65, Dept. Human Svcs., Memphis, 1985-86; vol. coord. Johnson Aux. to the Regional Med. Ctr., Memphis, 1986-87; psychiat. social worker Memphis Mental Health Inst., 1990-91; med. and psychiat. social worker St. Joseph Hosp., Memphis, 1991-94. Pres. Johnson Aux. to Regional Med. Ctr., Memphis, 1985-86; mem. Dixon Gallery, Brooks Mus. League; elder Balmoral Presbyn. Ch. Mem. AAUW (pres. Memphis chpt. 1976-78, legis. chair 1990-91, named grant honoree 1985), Acad. Cert. Social Workers, Whitehaven Garden Club (sec., treas.), Kennedy Book Club. Republican. Home: 7607 Shady Rose Cv Memphis TN 38119-9109

GETTELMAN, ROBIN CLAIRE, media specialist; b. Milw., Jan. 6, 1952; d. Robert Otto and Virginia Mae (Proffit) G.; m. Ted Bayard Johnson, Sept. 25, 1976 (div. Jan. 1985). BS in Secondary Edn., U. Wis., 1974; MA in Librarianship, U. Denver, 1975. Dir. instructional material ctr. Cripple Creek (Colo.)-Victor Sch. Dist., 1975-81; dir. Franklin Ferguson Meml. Libr., Cripple Creek, 1975-81; dir. instructional materials ctr. D.C. Everest Jr. High Sch., Schofield, Wis., 1981—; dist. media coord. D.C. Everest Area Schs., Schofield, 1988—; reviewer Sch. Evaluation Consortium, Madison, Wis., 1986, Marshfield, Wis., 1987, reviewer, coord., Ashland, Wis., 1989; chair media com. D.C. Everest Area Schs., Schofield, 1988—. Recipient Svc. award of the Yr., Franklin Ferguson Meml. Libr., 1981. Mem. Wis. Sch. Libr. Media Assn. (chair profl. devel. com. 1983, chair 1984, 85 confs. exec. bd. 1985), Wis. Ednl. Media Assn., Wausau Area Jaycees (community dir. 1986-87, chair cancer ski-a-thon 1987, chair 4th of July concessions 1989, Project Chmn. of the Month 1987). Methodist. Home: 2405 Petunia Rd Wausau WI 54401-9351 Office: DC Everest Jr High Sch 1000 Machmueller St Schofield WI 54476-3811

GETTY, CAROL PAVILACK, government official; b. Wilmington, Del., Apr. 9, 1938; d. Frank Clifton and Maxine (Remaly) McGrew; m. Lawrence Lee Pavilack, Aug. 18, 1960 (div. 1980); children: Douglas Brooks, Joann Clements; m. James John Getty, May 8, 1985. BA, Wellesley Coll., 1960; MS in Criminal Justice, Ariz. State U., 1978; postgrad. U. S.C., U. Mo. Engring. aide Air Rsch., Phoenix, 1960-63; computer analyst Motorola, Phoenix, 1963; tchr. math. Phoenix County Day Sch., 1964-69; mem. Ariz. Bd. Pardons and Paroles, Phoenix, 1978-83; commr. U.S. Parole Commn., Kansas City, Mo., 1983-90, chmn., 1991-92, commr. 1992—; tech. adviser Maricopa County Alts. to Incarceration Commn., 1980-83. Treas., asst. treas., sec., impact community action, admissions and fin. Jr. League, 1970—; docent, treas. Phoenix Art Mus. League, 1968-79; vice chmn. Criminal Justice Adv. Com., Phoenix, 1973-78. Mem. Exec. Women in Govt., Am. Soc. Pub. Adminstrs., Assn. Patroling Authorities (regional v.p.), Ctrl. Exchange, Jr. League, Soroptimists (chancellor's adv. com. to the women's ctr. UMKC), Wellesley Club (fed. exec. bd.). Unitarian. Home: 7709 NW Westside Dr Kansas City MO 64152-1539 Office: US Parole Commn N Cen Reg Office N Pointe Tower Ste 700 10220 N Exec Hills Blvd Kansas City MO 64153

GETTY, ESTELLE, actress; b. N.Y.C., July 25, 1923; m. Arthur Gettleman, Dec. 21, 1947; children: Barry, Carl. Student, New Sch. for Social Rsch., Herbert Berghof Studios; studied with Gerald Russak. Appeared in numerous stage prodns. on and off Broadway including Death of a Salesman, The Glass Menagerie, All My Sons, 6 Rms Rv Vu, Blithe Spirit, Arsenic and Old Lace, I Don't Know Why I'm Screaming, Widows and Children, Torch Song Trilogy, 1981-83; film appearances include The Chosen, 1982, Tootsie, 1983, Mask, 1984, Protocol, 1984, Mannequin, 1987, Stop or My Mom Will Shoot, 1991; TV appearances include (series) The Golden Girls, 1987-92, (Emmy award as outstanding supporting actress in a comedy series 1988, Golden Globe award for best actress in a comedy, Am. Comedy award for best supporting actress in a series 1990), Golden Palace, 1992-93; (TV movies) No Man's Land, 1984, Victims for Victims: The Teresa Saldana Story, 1984, Copacabana, 1985; author: If I Knew Then What I Know Now...So What?, 1988. Office: Innovative Artists Talent and Literary Agency Los Angeles CA 90067 also: Green/Siegel & Associates 8730 Sunset Blvd Ste 470 Los Angeles CA 90069

GETZ, BETTINA, lawyer; b. Davenport, Iowa. BA with honors, Mich. State U., 1976; JD with honors, DePaul U., 1982. Judicial law clk. Ill. Appellate Ct., Chgo., 1982-84; assoc. atty. Isham Lincoln & Beale, Chgo., 1984-87; assoc. atty. Mayer Brown & Platt, Chgo., 1987-90, ptnr., atty., 1990—. Mem. Chgo. Inn of Ct. Office: Mayer Brown & Platt 190 S La Salle St Chicago IL 60603-3410

GETZENDANNER, SUSAN, lawyer, former federal judge; b. Chgo., July 24, 1939; d. William B. and Carole S. (Muehling) O'Meara; children—Alexandra, Paul. B.B.A., Loyola U., 1966, J.D., 1966. Bar: Ill. bar 1966. Law clk. U.S. Dist. Ct., Chgo., 1966-68; assoc. Mayer, Brown & Platt, Chgo., 1968-74, ptnr., 1974-80; judge U.S. Dist. Ct., Chgo., 1980-87; ptnr. Skadden, Arps, Slate, Meagher & Flom, Chgo., 1987—. Recipient medal of excellence Loyola U. Law Alumni Assn., 1981. Mem. ABA, Chgo. Council Lawyers. Office: Skadden Arps Slate Meagher Flom 333 W Wacker Dr Chicago IL 60606-1218

GEURTZE, DEBORAH ANN, artist; b. Albany, N.Y., Feb. 9, 1952; d. Harold H. Jr. and Pauline (Schwarze) G.; children: Peter Avery Geurtze Bird, Hanne Pauline Geurtze Walker. Student, RISD, 1970-71; BA, SUNY, Potsdam, 1974. Cartographer Adirondack Park Agy., Ray Brook, N.Y., 1975-76; tchr. Am. Sch. Tangier, Morocco, 1976-77, Vail (Colo.) Mountain Sch., 1977-78; owner, mgr. Deborah Geurtze Graphics Gallery, Cooperstown, N.Y., 1981-84, Real Estate Investment, Cooperstown, 1985—, Danny's Main St. Market, Cooperstown, 1990—; artist Deborah Geurtze Graphics, Cooperstown, 1980—. Exhbns. include Garrison Art Ctr., 1992, Everson Mus., 1993, Old Forge (N.Y.) Art Ctr., 1994. Mem. Cooperstown Art Assn. (co-pres. 1990-93, organizer nat. juried exhbn. 1989-92), Soc. Am. Graphic Artists, Albany Print Club. Home: RD 3 Box 225 Cooperstown NY 13326

GEVANTMAN, JUDITH, financial analyst, consultant; b. Pitts., May 25, 1949; d. Chaim and Charlotte Selma (Max) G. AB cum laude, Goucher Coll., Towson, Md., 1971; postgrad., NYU, 1971-74; MPA, Harvard U., 1977. Dep.dir. N.Y.C. Addiction Svcs. Agy., 1971-74; asst. v.p., supr. Moody's Investors Svc., N.Y.C., 1978-85; v.p., dir. mcpl. rsch. Wertheim, Schroder & Co., N.Y.C., 1986-87; v.p., mgr. fixed income rsch. Mabon, Nugent & Co., N.Y.C., 1988; ptnr. Rsch. Assocs., Bklyn., 1989—; chmn. bd. dirs. GemStone Investors Assurance Corp., 1990—; cons. Downstate Med. Sch., Bklyn.,1975, Harvard U. Med. Sch., Boston, 1976, Boston Mus. Sci., 1977. Bd. dirs. Bruekelen Owners Corp., Bklyn., 1982-83; alumni rep. Goucher Coll., 1985—; trustee Congregation Bnai Avraham, Brooklyn Heights, N.Y., 1988—. UN fellow U. Kans., 1970, Univ. fellow NYU, 1971-73; Senatorial scholar Md. Legislature, 1967-71; Urban Corp. grantee, 1970. Mem. Mcpl. Forum N.Y., Mcpl. Analyst Group N.Y., Harvard Club (N.Y.C.).

GEWIRTZ, GERRY, editor; b. N.Y.C., Dec. 22, 1920; d. Max and Minnie (Weiss) G.; m. Eugene W. Friedman, Nov. 11, 1945; children: John Henry, Robert James. B.A., Vassar Coll., 1941. Editor Package Store Mgmt., 1942-44, Jewelry Mag., 1945-53; freelance editor promotion dept. McCall's Mag., Esquire, 1953-56; free-lance fashion and gifts editor Jewelers Circular Keystone, N.Y.C., 1955-71; editor, pub. The Fashionables, 1971-74, The Forecast, 1974—. Nat. Jeweler, Ann. Fashion Guide, 1976-80; editor, assoc. pub. Exec. Jeweler, 1980-83; editor The Fashion Source (formerly Internat. Fashion Index), N.Y.C., 1984—; ptnr. Benefit Advantage, Inc., 1994. Corr. Internat. Mktg. News. Mem. exec. com. Inner City Council of Cardinal Cooke, N.Y.; chairperson women's task force United Jewish Appeal Fedn.; former bd. govs. Israel Bonds; former trustee Israel Cancer Research Fund, Central Synagogue; bd. dirs. Double Image Theater; former pres. women's aux. Brandeis U. Honored guest Am. Jewish Com., 1978; Israel Cancer Research Fund, 1978-81; recipient Disting. Community Service award Brandeis U., 1987; named to Jewellry Hall Fame, 1988. Mem. N.Y. Fashion Group, Nat. Home Fashions League (former pres.), Women's Jewelry Assn. (pres. 1983-87, named editor who has contbd. most to jewelry industry 1984). Home: 45 Sutton Pl S New York NY 10022-2444

GEWIRTZ, MINDY L., organizational and human relations consultant; b. N.Y.C., Mar. 19, 1951; d. Martin and Miriam (Altman) Lebovicz; m. Gershon C. Gewirtz, Sept. 7, 1971; children: Yussy, Henoch, Sora Leah, Adina, Doniel. MPS, N.Y. Inst. Tech., 1977; MSW, SUNY, Albany, 1981; PhD in Orgnl. Sociology, Boston U., 1995. Lic. ind. clin. social worker; diplomate Am. Bd. Clin. Social Workers. Project coord. Ringel Inst. Gerontology SUNY-Albany, 1980-82; coord. sr. adult dept. Jewish Family Svcs., Albany, 1983-84; dir. eldercare connection long distance caregiving svc. Jewish Family and Children's Svc., Boston, 1984-93; pres. Work and Life Balance Assocs., Boston, 1988—; postgrad. fellow orgnl. devel. & human resources cons. Boston Inst. Psychotherapy, 1990; adj. asst. prof. Boston U. Sch. Social Work; cons. Ibis Cons. Group, Cambridge, 1990—; orgn. and mgmt. cons. Boston Digital Equipment Corp., Boston, 1988-92; orgnl. cons. Malden Hills, Lawrence, Mass., 1992—; postgrad. fellow orgnl. devel. and human resources consultation Bost. Inst. Psychotherapy, 1990. Author: (with E. and N. Newman) Elderly Criminals, 1984; assoc. author: Human Dilemmas in Work Organizations; contbr. articles to profl. jours. and publs. Mem. Boston Work and Family Forum, New England Human Resources Assn., Greater Boston Orgnl. Devel. Network. Recipient Max Siporin Social Work fellow. Mem. NASW, ACSW (bd. cert. diplomate), Am. Assn. Bus. Women (career advancement fellow), New Eng. Human Resources Assn., Employee Assistance Profl. Assn., Phi Beta Kappa. Home: 23 Browne St Brookline MA 02146-3804

GEYER, CAROLYN KAY SMITH, college department head; b. Denton, Tex., Apr. 9, 1936; d. Elbert Geron and Hazel Beatrice (Lynn) Smith; m. Charles William Geyer, Aug. 23, 1959; children: Mark William, Thomas Hugh. BA in English, Augustana Coll., 1958; MA in English, Auburn U., 1965; PhD in Edn., U. Nebr., 1985. Intermediate tchr. Tex. Sch. for Deaf, Austin, 1958-59; lang. tchr. S.D. Sch. for Deaf, Sioux Falls, S.D., 1960-62; instr. English Auburn (Ala.) U., 1965-67, Augustana Coll., Sioux Falls, 1971-76; coll. rep. Harcourt Brace Jovanovich, Inc., 1976-77; tchr. English O'Gorman High Sch., Sioux Falls, 1977-80; asst. prof. English Augustana Coll., Sioux Falls, 1980-86, asst. acad. dean and assoc. prof., 1986-87, assoc. acad. dean, dir. adult learning, 1987-92, chair English and Journalism dept., 1992—, faculty rep. to bd. regents, 1992-94, prof. English, 1995—; regional mgr. Coun. of Adult and Exptl. Learning, N.D., S.D., Mont., 1985-90; S.D. state liaison for U.S. West's Pathways to the Future, 1990-91; vis. scholar dept. adult edn. Syracuse U., 1991; state corp. rep. Am. Coll. Testing, S.D., 1986-88; instl. rep. Coll. Bd., Augustana Coll., 1987-91. Contbr. articles to profl. jours. Mem. Tech. Info. Project on Environ. Issues in S.D., 1988—; bd. dirs. S.D. chpt. ARC, Sioux Falls, 1980-83. Recipient Faculty Growth award Am. Luth. Ch., 1983, Leadership grantee, 1986; U. Nebr. Regents fellow, 1984; Kellogg Found. project LEARN grantee, 1986-88, Devel. grantee Bush Faculty, S.D. Humanities Coun. grantee; recipient Granskou Award for Rsch., Augustana Coll. Alumni, 1990. Mem. NOW, AAUP, Luth. Women's Caucus (program com.), Feminists for Diversity in Luth. Colls. and Sems., Sierra Club, Nature Conservancy. Democrat. Lutheran. Office: Augustana Coll 2001 S Summit Ave Sioux Falls SD 57197

GEYER, GEORGIE ANNE, syndicated columnist, educator, author, biographer; b. Chgo., Apr. 2, 1935; d. Robert George and Georgie Hazel (Gervens) G. B.S., Northwestern U., 1956, LHD (hon.), 1993; postgrad. (Fulbright scholar), U. Vienna, Austria, 1956-57; Litt. D. (hon.), Lake Forest Coll., (Ill.), 1980, Chgo. State U., 1984, Coll. Mt. St. Joseph, 1986, St. Mary's of Notre Dame, 1986, Wilson Coll., 1987, Linfield Coll., 1987, St. Mary-of-the-Woods Coll., 1989, U. Indpls., 1991, Colby-Sawyer Coll., 1992, Franklin Coll., 1992; LHD (hon.), U. S.C., 1991, Rockhurst (Jesuit) Coll., Kansas City, 1992, Spring Hill Coll., 1993. Reporter Southtown Economist, Chgo., 1958; soc. reporter Chgo. Daily News, 1959-60, gen. assignment reporter, 1960-64, Latin Am. corr., 1964-67, roving fgn. corr. and columnist, 1967-75; syndicated columnist Los Angeles Times Syndicate, 1975-80, Universal Press Syndicate, 1981—; Lyle M. Spencer prof. journalism Syracuse U., 1977; regular news commentator PBS' Washington Week in Review; questioner on Presdl. debate, Oct., 1984; steering com. Aspen Inst. Latin Am. Governance Project, 1981-82; commentator on the BBC; regular panelist Voice of America; sent by Internat. Communication Agy. on 3 worldwide speaking tours on Am. journalism: Nigeria, Zambia, Tanzania and Somalia, 1979, Philippines and Indonesia, 1981, Iceland, Norway, Belgium and Portugal, 1982; rep. Fulbright scholar program 40th anniversary, New Zealand, 1987; commencement speaker various colls., univs. including U. S.Carolina, Rockhurst Coll., St. Mary's Notre Dame; sr. fellow Annenburg Washington, 1982-83, 92—; speaker, lectr. in field. Author: The New Latins, 1970, The New 100 Years War, 1972, The Young Russians, 1976; (autobiography) Buying the Night Flight, (Weintal prize citation Sch. Fgn. Svc. Georgetown U. 1984, Chgo. Found. for Lit. award 1984), 1983, Guerilla Prince, The Untold Story of Fidel Castro, 1981; subjects of interviews include Prince Sihanouk of Cambodia, Yassar Arafat, Anwar Sadat, King Hussein of Jordan, Pres. Khaddafy of Libya, the Ayatollah Khomeini, Sultan Qaboos of Oman, Pres. Juan Peron of Argentina, Pres. Siad Barre of Somalia, Prime Minister Mauno Koivisto of Finland, Anastasio Somoza, Jerzy Urban, Janusz Onyszkiewicz, Prime Minister Edward Seaga of Jamaica, Pres. Ronald Reagan, Pres. George Bush, others; discovered and had first interview with second most-wanted Nazi, Walter Rauff in Tierra del Fuego, Chile, 1966; found Dominican pres. Juan Bosch in hiding in P.R. during Dominican revolution, 1965; held by Palestinians as Israeli spy, 1973; imprisoned in Angola for writing about revolutionary government, 1976; contbr. chpts. to books, articles numerous pubs. Active Orgn. for S.W. Community Chgo., 1960-64; trustee Am. U., Washington, 1981-86; Coun. Fgn. Rels. Recipient 1st prize Am. Newspaper Guild, 1962; 2d prize Ill. Press Editors Assn., 1962; award for best writing on Latin Am. Overseas Press Club, 1966; Merit award Northwestern U., 1968; Nat. Headliner award Theta Sigma Phi, 1968; Maria Moors Cabot award Columbia U., 1970; Hannah Solomon award Nat. Council Jewish Women, 1973; Ill. Spl. Events Commn. Woman's award, 1975; Northwestern U. Alumni award, 1991; Woodrow Wilson fellow Rollins Coll., Winter Park, Fla., 1982; Presdl. Citation award Am. Univ., 1985; Disting. fellow Mortar Bd. Nat. Sr. Honor Soc., Am. U., 1982; Sr. fellow Annenberg Washington Program, Washington, 1982-83; fellow Soc. Prof. Journalists, 1992. Mem. Soc. Profl. Journalists, Women in Comm., Inst. Internat. Edn. (bd. dirs.), Midland Authors, Internat. Inst. Strategic Studies, Internat. Soc. Polit. Psychology, Women's Inst. for Freedom of Press, Washington Inst., Chgo. Coun. Fgn. Rels. (bd. dirs.), Gridiron Club, Cosmos Club (1st women mem.), Travern Club (1st woman mem.), Cliff Dwellers Club (hon.). Home and Office: 800 25th St NW Washington DC 20037-2207

GEYER, SIDNA PRIEST, secondary and business education educator; b. Anderson, Ind., Dec. 9, 1943; d. James Dale and Lavada Belle (Lantz) Priest; m. James Eugene Geyer, Aug. 29, 1965; children: Jonathan Andrew, Susan Leigh. BS in Edn., Ball State U., 1969; MS in Edn., U. Wis., Oshkosh, 1975; EdS, U. Wis., Stout, 1980. Cert. secondary tchr., post-secondary tchr., Wis.; lic. supr., coord., counselor, Wis. Tchr. 6th grade St. Mary's Sch., Charlotte, Mich., 1966-67; tchr. bus. edn. Oak Hill High Sch., Converse, Ind., 1969-70, Stockbridge (Wis.) High Sch., 1970-72; tchr. bus., counselor Fox Valley Tech. Coll., Appleton, Wis., 1972-83, assoc. dean bus. edn., 1983-87; tchr. bus., English, computer sci. Baraboo (Wis.) Sr. High Sch., 1988-90; dir. continuing edn. and performing arts U. Wis. Ctr. Baraboo-Sauk County, 1990—; evaluator bus. edn. U. Wis., Stout, 1981, N.E. Wis. Tech. Coll., Green Bay, 1985; mem. bus. adv. com. Brillion (Wis.) High Sch., 1983-87; mem. state-wide task force on develop curriculum for a sex equity course VTAE staff, 1983. Bd. dirs. Baraboo Literacy Coun., 1990-93; mem. bd. Baraboo Cmty. Scholarship Corp., 1993-94; mem. aux. bd. St. Clare Hosp., 1991—. Mem. ASTD, AAUW (bd. dirs. 1971—), Wis. Vocat. Assn. (mem. awards com.), Wis. East Ctrl. Assn. Vocat. Edn. (treas. 1984), Women in Mgmt. (mem. edn. com.), Am. Inst. Banking (mem. edn. com.), North Ctrl. Assn. (bus. edn. evaluator 1984, 87—), Wis. Assn. Adult and Continuing Edn. (bd. dirs. 1993-94). Methodist. Home: 880 Iroquois Cir Baraboo WI 53913-9999 Office: Univ Wis Ctr Baraboo-Sauk County 1006 Connie Rd Baraboo WI 53913-1015

GEZURIAN, DOROTHY ELLEN, accounting executive; b. N.Y.C., May 7, 1956; d. John and Surpug Susan (Sarkisian) G. BBA in Acctg., Econs. summa cum laude, CUNY, 1976. Sr. auditor Ernst & Ernst, N.Y.C., 1977-79; spl. asst. to v.p. fin. Olivetti Corp., N.Y.C., 1977-79; mgr. corp., bus. planning Olivetti Corp., Tarrytown, N.Y., 1979-82; treas., CFO The Ctr. for Humanities, Inc., Mt. Kisco, N.Y., 1982-85; contr., CFO 235 Main St. Assocs., affiliated cos., White Plains, N.Y., 1985-87; v.p. fin., CFO Mid-Atlantic Med. Svcs., Ft. Lee, N.J., 1987-90; contr. Med. Edn. Programs Ltd., Wilton Conn., Conn., 1991-93; v.p. fin., CFO Med. Edn. Programs, Ltd., Wilton, Conn., 1994—. Recipient N.Y. Soc. of CPA's award, 1976. Mem. Nat. Assn. Female Execs. Republican. Home: 10 Clearview Ave Danbury CT 06811-3333

GFELLER, DONNA KVINGE, clinical psychologist; b. Chgo., Jan. 15, 1959; d. Milton Melvin and Doris Ann (Chapman) Kvinge; m. Jeffrey Donald Gfeller, Aug. 2, 1986. BS in Biol. Scis., Ill. State U., 1980, MS in Clin. Psychology, 1984; PhD in Clin. Psychology, Ohio U., 1987. Lic. psychologist. Staff psychologist Cardinal Glennon Children's Hosp., St. Louis, 1986-87, sr. psychologist, 1988-89, dir. dept. psychology, 1990—. Mem. APA (divsn. clin. psychology, sect. on clin. child psychology), Soc. Pediatric Psychology, World Wildlife Fund. Office: Cardinal Glennon Children's Hosp 1465 S Grand Blvd Saint Louis MO 63104-1095

GFELLER, LISA ANNE, computer systems analyst; b. Aberdeen, Miss., May 24, 1959; d. Dewey Edward and Doris Louise (Ferguson) Gill; m. Daniel Dumitru Pope, May 12, 1979 (div. Sept. 1984); m. James Robert Gfeller, July 19, 1985; children: Jennifer, Kelly, Lindy, Melissa. Student, Judson Coll., 1977-79; BA in Math. and Computer Sci., So. Ill. U., 1981. Fin. planning asst. U.S. Planning Assn./Ind. Rsch. Assn., Jacksonville, N.C., 1982-84; mem. computer sales staff Computer Store, Jacksonville, N.C., 1984-85; sys. analyst Blue Cross/Blue Shield of Ala., Birmingham, 1985-93; ind. computer cons. Orlando, Fla., 1993—. Mem. career devel. com. Leadership Devel. Assn., Birmingham, 1992-93, adopt-a-sch. program tutor, 1990-92; poll watcher Bob McKee Election Campaign, Birmingham, 1986; discipleship tng. tchr. Eastside Bapt. Ch., Birmingham, 1990-93. Mem. Triplet Connection of Birmingham (pres. 1992, sec. 1993). Republican. Home and Office: 4857 Gorham Ave Orlando FL 32817

GHARIB, SUSIE, television newscaster; b. N.Y.C., Nov. 27, 1950; d. Ali and Homa (Razzaghmanesh) G.; m. Fereydoun Nazem, Jan. 20, 1973; children: Alexander, Taraneh. BA magna cum laude, Case Western Res. U., 1972; M in Internat. Affairs, Columbia U., 1974. Reporter Cleve. Plain Dealer, 1972-73; assoc. editor Fortune Mag., N.Y.C., 1974-83; anchor, reporter Bus. Times/ESPN, N.Y.C., 1983-85; bus. reporter ABC News, N.Y.C., 1986-87; anchor Fin. News Network, N.Y.C., 1989-90, CNBC Network, Ft. Lee, N.J., 1993—; moderator/host Xerox Corp., Stanford,

Conn., 1989—, KPMG Peat Marwick, N.Y.C., 1992—; cons. Adam Smith's Money World/PBS, N.Y.C., 1987. Bd. dirs. First Fortis, Inc., 1991—, Ice Theatre of N.Y., 1988-90. Mem. Overseas Press Club, Phi Beta Kappa, Sigma Delta Chi. Democrat. Home: 44 E 73d St New York NY 10021 Office: CNBC 2200 Fletcher Ave Fort Lee NJ 07024

GHATTAS, JANET LOUISE, secondary education educator, consultant; b. Bklyn., May 30, 1941; d. Najib Abraham and Josephne (John) G. BA, St. Lawrence U.; MAT, Ind. U.; postgrad., Harvard U., U. Madrid, Paris U., Cath. U. Vol. tchr. Peace Corps, Thies and Joal, Senegal, 1963-65; tchr. French and Spanish Weston (Mass.) Pub. Sch. Systems, 1967-94; cons. Intercultural Dimensions, Inc.; co-counselor Re-Evaluation Counseling. Contbr. articles to profl. jours. Sec. Cambridgeport Residents Against Crime, 1981-86; active Inst. Intercultural Comm., Jr. League. Fellow NDEA. Mem. N.E. Assn. Secondary Schs. and Colls. (evaluator), Boston Ctr. Internat. Visitors, Boston Area Returned Peace Corp Vols. (pres., editor), Appalachian Mt. Club. Office: Intercultural Dimensions Inc 276 Pearl St Unit J Cambridge MA 02139-4716

GHEN, EDYTHE SOLBERG, artist; b. Wakefield, Mass., May 1, 1922; d. Frederick Carl and Ethel (Keander) Solberg; m. William Russell Ghen; children: Karen, William Jr. Student, Mass. Coll. Art, 1940-41, Salem State Coll., 1974-78, Montserrat Sch. Art, 1984-86, 88-90. Sec., art editor War Dept., Boston, 1942-43; comml. artist Loudon Advt., Boston, 1943-44; sec. to pres. Benjamin Franklin Univ., Washington, 1944-45; art tchr. Beverly (Mass.) Adult Edn., 1958-60; art tchr. psychiat. div. J. B. Thomas Hosp., Peabody, Mass., 1970-72; pvt. practice Beverly, 1964—; lectr. various orgns., 1960—. Author two manuals on stained glass; author, illustrator children's picture books. Vol. Am. Lung Assn., pres., founder Essex County Fresh Air for Non-Smokers, 1992—. Recipient Beverly Arts Coun. awards, 1987, 88, Collidge awards Topsfield Fair, 1984, 87, vol. award Am. Lung Assn., 1976, Lifetime Achievement award Mass. Coll. Art, 1993, numerous others. Mem. Copley Soc. Boston (Sagendorf award 1992, Juror's Choice award 1994), Rockport Art Assn. (Moore award 1988, Wengenroth award 1991), North Shore Arts Assn. (Sketchgroup award 1988, Callow award 1988, Anderson award 1993), Acad. Artists Springfield (Guild Boston Artists award 1988), Guild Beverly Artists (Best of Show awards 1984, 90, 91), New Eng. Watercolor Soc. Methodist. Home: 42 E Corning St Beverly MA 01915-4735

GIALLION, DONNA LYNN, accountant; b. Passaic, N.J., Dec. 23, 1965; d. Glenn Ray and Lois Gail (Smith) G. BS, Montclair (N.J.) State Coll., 1989. Jr. acct. intern Organon Inc., West Orange, N.J., 1989-91, jr. acct., 1991-93, staff acct., 1994—. Mem. Inst. of Cert. Mgmt. Accts. Home: 85 Young Ave Cedar Grove NJ 07009-1431

GIANAKOS, PATRICIA ANN, social worker; b. Warren, Ohio, Oct. 14, 1948; d. Jimmie Lambros and Julie (Mougianis) G. BA in Pre-Profl. Social Work, Kent State U., 1970. Lic. social worker. Aid for aged workers Trumbull County Human Svcs. Dept., Warren, 1970-71, social svc. worker, 1971-88, adult svcs. worker, 1988—, mem. excellence com., 1991, 93, contbg. editor County Line newsletter, 1991—, mem. awards com., 1991-93, chmn. awards com., 1993—; mem. Trumbull County Task Force on Wellness in Later Yrs., Warren, 1991-92. Vol. St. Demetrios Festival, Warren, 1979—; mem. Dem. Nat. Com., Warren, 1992—, Ladies Philoptochos Soc., Warren, 1979—; co-founder, adviser Sr. Citizens Orgn. St. Demetrios Ch., Warren, 1979—. Mem. ACA, NASW, Am. Bus. Women's Assn., Assn. for Adult Devel. and Aging, Nat. Com. for Prevention of Elder Abuse. Greek Orthodox. Home: 1786 Dodge Dr NW Warren OH 44485-1823 Office: Trumbull Cou Human Svcs 150 S Park Ave Warren OH 44481-1018

GIANCOLA, HOLLY HARRINGTON, retail company executive; b. San Francisco, Feb. 1, 1961; d. Jonathan David and Coralie (Phelps) Harrington; m. Frank James Giancola, June 14, 1986; children: Michael Andrew, Angelina Elizabeth Dora. AS, Marymount U., Arlington, Va., 1981, BS cum laude, 1984; postgrad., Georgetown U. Law Ctr., 1985-86. RN, Va., D.C. Nurse Fairfax Hosp., Falls Church, Va., 1981-83; nurse Georgetown Hosp., Washington, 1983-84, clin. practitioner, 1984-88; pres. Harrington-Giancola Wardrobes Inc., Centreville, Va., 1988—; retail buyer Gt. Expectations Maternity, Centreville, 1989—; owner HG Designs, Centreville, 1994—; realtor Shannon and Luchs Realtors, Centreville, 1986-91; referral agt. Metro Referral, Fairfax, Va., 1993—; mktg. cons. Mercure Group, Clifton, Va., 1989-92; new bus. cons. Larry D. Worden, CPA, Clifton, 1989-92. Co-author: (pamphlet) Patient Guide to Angioplasty, 1985. Mem. Cabells Mill Neighborhood Watch, Centreville, 1989-93; vice chmn. Archtl. Control Bd., Va. Run HOA, 1994—; mem. Va. Run Elem. PTA, 1994—; mem. Poplar Tree Elem. Sch. PTA, 1990-93; class agt. Marymount U. Class of 1981, 91—; co-chmn. fundraising com. Centreville Day Ann. Celebration, WFCCA, 1994. Mem. NAFE, No. Va. Assn. Realtors, Cen. Fairfax C. of C., Fairfax County C. of C., Centreville Square Mchts. Assn. (pres. 1990—), Sigma Theta Tau. Republican. Episcopalian. Office: Gt Expectations Maternity 14200A Centreville Sq Centreville VA 22020-2355

GIANNELLI, CHRISTINA ROSE, lighting designer; b. N.Y.C., Sept. 14, 1960; d. Stanley and Karen (Kiil) Giannelli. BA, Yale Coll., 1982. From asst. lighting designer to designer/mgr. Williamstown (Mass.) Theater Festival, 1982-85; lighting designer, tech. supr. Balletap USA, N.Y.C., 1984-86; lighting dir. Houston Grand Opera, 1986-89; lighting supr. Houston Ballet, 1987-93, resident lighting dir., 1993—; resident lighting designer Cleve./San Jose Ballet, 1993—.

GIANNINI, CYNTHIA, dancer; b. San Francisco. Scholarship student, The Joffrey Ballet Sch., 1983-84. Dancer Joffrey II Dancers, N.Y.C., 1984-87, The Joffrey Ballet, N.Y.C., 1987—. Office: The Joffrey Ballet 130 W 56th St New York NY 10019-3818*

GIANNINI, GEMMA, photographer; b. Chgo., Sept. 21, 1951; d. Armando and Maria (Raffanti) G.; m. William Edward Schultz, Jan. 28, 1978. BA, U. Ill., Chgo., 1974, M of Health Professions Edn., 1981. Research asst. U. Ill., Chgo., 1974-78, instr., 1979-80; mgr. exams Am. Soc. Clin. Pathologists, Chgo., 1980-82, dir. exams, 1983; owner Signature Photography, Elk Grove Village, Ill., 1987—; intern Profl. Photographer's Am., Mt. Prospect, Ill., 1986; test cons. Michael Reese Hosp., Chgo., 1979. Author: articles, Evaluation & Health Profls., 1986, Med. Edn., 1981; reviewer Health Care Edn., 1979; video tape and manual, Interview skills, 1976. Instr. workshop Am. Dietetic Assn., Chgo., 1979. Mem. Advt. Photographers Am. Roman Catholic. Office: Gemma Giannini Photography PO Box 505 Medinah IL 60157-0505

GIBBARD, JUDITH R., library director; b. N.Y.C., Jan. 27, 1945; d. Charles J. and Esther (Polonsky) Popovits; m. Bruce Gregory Gibbard, June 19, 1966. AB in Edn., U. Mich., 1966, AM in English, 1968; MLS, Syracuse U., 1978. Cert. pub. libr., cert. secondary English/French tchr. Slide cataloger history of art dept. U. Mich., Ann Arbor, 1969-70; tchr. Assn. des Habitants de la Ville de Meyrin, Switzerland, 1970-71; cataloger Cornell U. Olin Libr., Ithaca, N.Y., 1972-78; head cataloging sect. Suffolk Coop. Libr. System, Bellport, N.Y., 1979-81; cataloging svcs. div. chief Suffolk Coop. Libr. System, Bellport, 1981-82; head tech. svc./automation Patchogue (N.Y.)-Medford Libr., 1983-89, asst. dir., 1989-90, dir., 1991—. Coord. Community Youth Com., Patchogue, 1992. Mem. Pub. Libr. Assn. (chair cataloging needs com. 1989-90), N.Y. Libr. Assn., Suffolk County Libr. Assn. (mem.-at-large 1988-89). Office: Patchogue-Medford Libr 54-60 E Main St Patchogue NY 11772

GIBBONEY, PAMELA CLAIRE, mathematics educator; b. McKeesport, Pa., Aug. 21, 1944; d. Herbert Vincent and Virginia Winifred (Lowry) Fredrickson; m. James Kearney Gibboney, 1969; children: Adam, Mija, Meredith. BS, Maryville (Tenn.) Coll., 1967; postgrad., Towson State U., 1973, Western Md. Coll., 1993—. Cert. tchr. Ch. organist various chs., 1960—; tchr. St. Mary's County Bd. Edn., Leonardstown, Md., 1967-68, Baltimore County Bd. Edn., Towson, Md., 1968-73; tchr. math., dept. chair Bd. Edn. Frederick County, Frederick, Md., 1973—; presentor Md. Math. Confs., Balt., 1990, 92, 94, Nat. Coun. Tchrs. Math., New Orleans, Seattle, 1991, 93, Pa. Mid. Schs., Hanover, 1993, Bendersville (Pa.) Elem. Sch., 1993; roundtable participant AAUW, Gettysburg, Pa., 1993-94, co-chairperson ednl. equity com. Co-author Coop. Integrated Reading and Comprehension curriculum materials Johns Hopkins U., 1990; co-writer spatial-skills workshops for math., 1992—; co-writer Lego Learning. Tchr., supt. coun. Bethlehem Luth. Ch., Bendersville, 1988—, facilitator Callahan Workshop, 1991; mem. Gov.'s Acad. State of Md., Balt., 1991. Grantee Washington Post, 1990, 91. Mem. NEA, Nat. Coun. Tchrs. Math., Md. Coun. Tchrs. Math., Md. State Tchrs. Assn., Frederick County Tchrs. Assn. Home: 1355 Coon Rd Aspers PA 17304-9618

GIBBONS, CELIA VICTORIA TOWNSEND (MRS. JOHN SHELDON), editor, publisher; b. Fargo, N.D.; d. Harry Alton and Helen (Haag) Townsend; student U. Minn., 1930-33; m. John Sheldon Gibbons, May 1, 1935; children—Mary Vee, John Townsend. Advt. mgr. Hotel Nicollet, Mpls., 1933-37; contbg. editor children's mags., 1935—; partner Youth Assos. Co., Mpls., 1942-65; pub. art dir. Mines and Escholier mags., 1954-65; founder Bull. Bd. Pictures, Inc., Mpls., 1954, pres., 1954—; founder Periodical Litho Art Co., Mpls., 1962, pres., 1962-65; artist Cath. Boy mag., 1938; artist, designer book Palaces That Went To Sea, 1990; chief photographer Cath. Miss mag., 1955. Mem. Women's aux. Mpls. Symphony Orch.; mem. Fort Lauderdale (Fla.) Art. Mus. Republican chairwoman Golden Valley, Minn., 1950; alternate del. Hennepin County Rep. Conv., 1962. Mem. Mpls. Inst. Arts, Internat. Inst., St. Paul Arts and Sci., Art Guild Boca Raton. Clubs: Woman's, Minikahda; Deerfield Beach Women's. Home: 1416 Alpine Pass Tyrol Hills Minneapolis MN 55416 Office: 1057 A # 1-a Hillsboro Beach FL 33441

GIBBONS, CONSTANCE KELLER, secondary school district administrator; b. St. Paul, Oct. 13, 1945; d. John Norman and Barbara K. (Walker) Oehler; m. Robert L. Keller, Mar. 15, 1969 (div. Oct. 1983); children: Wendy L. Keller Mowrer, Torie L. AA, Scottsdale C.C., 1977; BA in Edn., Ariz. State U., 1978; MA, U.S. Internat. U., 1986; EdD, Ariz. State U., 1994. Cert. tchr., prin., supt., Ariz., Calif. Tchr., coach Paradise Valley Sch. Dist., Phoenix, 1978-83, Fallbrook (Calif.) Union High Sch. Dist., 1984-88; adminstr. N.W. Arctic Borough, Kotzebue, Alaska, 1988-89; tchr. Alhambra Sch. Dist., Phoenix, 1989-94; adminstr. Brawley (Calif.) Union High Sch. Dist., 1994—; assoc. faculty mem. Ariz. State U., Tempe, 1993-94. Mem. AAUW, ASCD, Calif. Assn. Adminstrs. State Fed. Edn. Programs, Phi Theta Kappa, Phi Delta Kappa. Republican.

GIBBONS, JULIA SMITH, federal judge; b. Pulaski, Tenn., Dec. 23, 1950; d. John Floyd and Julia Jackson (Abernathy) Smith; m. William Lockhart Gibbons, Aug. 11, 1973; children: Rebecca Carey, William Lockhart Jr. B.A., Vanderbilt U., 1972; J.D., U. Va., 1975. Bar: Tenn. 1975. Law clk. to judge U.S. Ct. Appeals, 1975-76; assoc. Farris, Hancock, Gilman, Branan, Lanier & Hellen, Memphis, 1976-79; legal advisor Gov. Lamar Alexander, Nashville, 1979-81; judge 15th Jud. Cir., Memphis, 1981-83, U.S. Dist. Ct. (we. dist.) Tenn., Memphis, 1983—. Fellow Am. Bar Found., Tenn. Bar Found.; mem. ABA, Tenn. Bar Assn., Memphis Bar Assn., Nat. Assn. Women Judges, Order of Coif, Phi Beta Kappa. Presbyterian. Office: US Dist Ct 1157 Federal Bldg 167 N Main St Memphis TN 38103

GIBBONS, KATHLEEN GEMMA, medical/surgical nurse; b. Queens, N.Y., Apr. 2, 1952; d. William G. and Anna C. (Fiorillo) McGinn; m. Douglas M. Gibbons, Mar. 6, 1976; children: Melissa, Kyle, Michael. AAS in Nursing, Kingsborough Community Coll., Bklyn., 1972; BSN, C.W. Post Coll., L.I., 1980. RN, Colo. Acting asst. head nurse staff nursing Luth. Med. Ctr., Bklyn., 1972-79; staff nurse Balt. County Gen. & Greater Balt. Med. Ctr., 1980-81, Harrisburg (Pa.) Hosp., 1981-88; staff nurse, relief charge nurse surg. trauma unit Swedish Med. Ctr., Englewood, Colo., 1990-93; tchr. prenatal and postnatal classes Dr. Macalusos OB Office, Bklyn., 1978-79. Co-author: What You Should Know About Pid, 1986. Vol. to local sch. dist., cub scouts, youth athletics. Roman Catholic.

GIBBONS, LEEZA, television talk show host, entertainment reporter; m. Stephen Meadows; children: Lexi, Troy. Student, U. S.C. CEO Leeza Gibbons Enterprises; co-host Entertainment Tonight, Hollywood, Calif., 1984—, John and Leeza, Hollywood, 1993; host, exec. prodr. Leeza, 1993—; host/exec. prodr. syndicated radio programs Entertainment Tonight on Radio with Leeza Gibbons, The Entertainment Report, The Top 25 Countdown with Leeza Gibbons, The Leeza Gibbons' Superstar Music Spl. host Miss Universe Pageant, The Hollywood Christmas Parade; host, co-prodr. (series) Growing Up Together; film appearances include Robocop, 1987, Robocop 2, 1990, Soapdish, 1991, The Player, 1992, Last Action Hero, 1993. Office: Paramount TV 5555 Melrose Ave Los Angeles CA 90038-3149

GIBBONS, MARITZA, business development specialist; b. Miami, Fla., May 2, 1962; d. Carlos Francisco and Miriam (Estenger) Diaz Silveira; m. Winton Gary Gibbons Jr., Aug. 18, 1990. BS in Indsl. Engring., U. Miami, 1984; MS in Ops. Rsch., Columbia U., 1985; MBA, U. Chgo., 1989. Registered engr. in tng. Market analyst Burger King Corp., Miami, 1982-84; mem. tech. staff AT&T Bell Labs., Naperville, Ill., 1986-89, West Long Branch, N.J., 1984-86; assoc. A.T. Kearney, Chgo., 1989-91; asst. dir. Westinghouse Electric, Pitts., 1991-94; dir. bus. devel. Macmillan Computer Pub., Indpls., 1994—; summer assoc. IBM Corp., Franklin Lakes, N.J., 1983. Henry King Stanford scholar U. Miami, Coral Gables, Fla., Indsl. Engring. Alumni scholar, 1982-84; Fla. Acad. Fund scholar State of Fla., 1981-84, Nat. Hispanic Fund scholar Nat. Hispanic Assn., 1982-84. Mem. Beta Gamma Sigma, Tau Beta Pi, Alpha Pi Mu, Phi Kappa Phi. Home: 1284 Helford Ln Carmel IN 46032 Office: Macmillan Computer Pub 201 W 103d St Indianapolis IN 46290

GIBBONS, MARY PEYSER, civic volunteer; b. N.Y.C., Dec. 15, 1936; d. Frederick Maurice and Catherine Mary (McKelvey) Peyser; m. John Martin Gibbons, Dec. 26, 1955; children: Catherine Way, Mary Sloan, John, Fredericka Kerr, Myles. Ptnr. Gibbons & Bibow Assocs., Hartford, Conn., 1986-90; pres. Sefton & Sheil Ltd., Hartford, 1988—. Contbr. articles to profl. publs. Regent U. Hartford, 1988-94; trustee Hartford Art Sch., 1985—, v.p., 1991-92; pres. women's com. Wadsworth Atheneum, Hartford, 1978-80, trustee, 1981-90, 91—; bd. dirs. The Hartford Ballet, 1981—; vol. coms. Art Mus., U.S. and Can., 1982-91; active Am. Assn. Mus. Vols., 1982-90, pres., 1986-88, U.S. Found. World Fedn., Conn. Valley Girl Scout Coun., Inc., Friends of Museums. Mem. Hartford Club, Hartford Golf Club, Town and County Club. Office: Sefton & Sheil Ltd 1130 Prospect Ave Hartford CT 06105-1124

GIBBONS, SHEILA MARIE, aerospace company executive; b. N.Y.C., Mar. 31, 1931; d. Joseph Vincent and Edna Marie (McCarthy) MacAvoy; children: Laura Cecile Burns, Philip Damian, Sally Honora. BA in Art, Queens Coll., CUNY, 1952; JD, St. John's U., 1976. Bar: N.Y. 1977, Calif. 1977. Assoc. Carnahan & Freeman, Woodland Hills, Calif., 1977; asst. sec. Northrop Corp., L.A., 1978-80, sec., 1980-83, v.p., sec., 1983—. Honoree Tribute to Women in Internat. Industry, Nat. Bd. YWCA, Houston, 1983. Mem. ABA, L.A. Bar Assn. (subcom. fed. securities law), Am. Soc. Corp. Secs. (securities law com. 1981-84, adv. com. 1981-88, pres. L.A. chpt. 1984-88, ad hoc com. on tender offers 1984-85, bd. dirs. 1985-91, securities industry com. 1985-92, chmn. 1989-90), Am.-Irish Hist. Soc. Office: Northrop Corp 1840 Century Park E Los Angeles CA 90067-2101

GIBBS, BEATRICE ESTHER, librarian; b. Malden, Mass., Oct. 16, 1918; d. Joseph S. and Della N. (Rainen) G.; m. Howard Konowitch (dec. 1976); children: Paula, Bonnie, Marian, Ben. BA, Tufts U., 1969; MA, Glassboro State U., 1972. Tchr. Mid. Twp., Cape May Courthouse, N.J., 1964-75; libr. Cape May County Libr., Cape May Courthouse, 1975-84, Montgomery County Libr., Bethesda, Md., 1985—; appeared weekly WCMC TV program, 1976-84. Columnist: (book rev.) Gazette. Pres. PTA, Wildwood, N.J., 1964-70; leader Girl Scouts Am., Wildwood, 1964-70; dir. Coop Nursery, Wildwood, 1966-70. With USN, 1942-45. Mem. ALA, NCJW, Cape May County Art League (v.p. 1960-65), Cape May County Hist. Soc. (sec. 1965-68), Montgomery Libr. Staff Assn., Women in the Arts Mus., Tufts Alumni Assn., Internat. Reading Assn., Internat. Board Books for Young Children (del.). Home: 1111 University Blvd W Silver Spring MD 20902-3351 Office: Montgomery County Library 5501 Massachusetts Ave Bethesda MD 20816-1932

GIBBS, JUNE NESBITT, state senator; b. Newton, Mass., June 13, 1922; d. Samuel Frederick and Lulu (Glazier) Nesbitt; m. Donald T. Gibbs, Dec. 8, 1945; 1 child, Elizabeth. BA in Math., Wellesley Coll., 1943; MA in Math., Boston U., 1947; postgrad., U. R.I., 1981-84. Mem. Republican Nat. Com. from, R.I., 1969-80; sec. Republican Nat. Com., 1977-80; mem. R.I. State Senate, 1985—; mem. def. adv. com. Women in Services, 1970-72, vice chmn., 1972. Mem. Middletown Town Council, 1974-80, 82-84, pres., 1978-80. Served to lt. (J.G.) USNR, 1943-46. Home: 163 Riverview Ave Newport RI 02840-5324 Office: RI State Senate State Capitol Providence RI 02903

GIBBS, MARGARET CATHERINE, retired public administration educator; b. Hot Springs, Ark., Apr. 7, 1914; d. Leonard Everett and Kate (Ludwig) King; m. George Gibbs IV, June 27, 1942; children: George V., Thomas Ashley, Katherine Wellington Gibbs Gengoux, Sarah Randolph Gibbs Beetem. BA cum laude, U. So. Calif., 1936, MPA, 1941; PhD in Govt., Claremont Grad. Sch., 1973. Exec. sec. Univ. Religious Conf., L.A., 1937-38; mng. editor Palos Verdes Estates (Calif.) Bull., 1941-42; tchr. English to Latin Am. diplomats Washington, 1942; tchr. L.A. City High Schs., 1945-49; corr. L.A. Times, Claremont, Calif., 1950-62; lectr. pub. adminstrn. U. So. Calif., L.A., 1973-81; emeritus prof., chmn. dept. pub. adminstrn. Calif. State U., San Bernardino, 1975-80; cons. undergrounding com. League Calif. Cities, 1969; del. 2d U.S.-Japan Computer Conf., Tokyo, 1975, Inst. Adminstrv. Svcis., Mex., 1974, Abidjan, 1977. Contbr. articles to profl. jours. Bd. dirs. League Calif. Cities, 1962-70; mem. L.a. County Com. for Coord. Delinquency, 1964-66; trustee Citrus C.C., Glendora, Calif., 1974-81; mem. Claremont City Coun., 1962-70; mem. program adv. com. Calif. State U., San Bernardino, 1977-92; bd. councillors Sch. Edn., U. So. Calif., L.A., 1985-91; docent Rancho Santa Ana Bot. Garden, 1983-93. Recipient Beautiful Activist award Broadway Dept. Store and Germaine Monteil, 1972, merit award U. So. Calif., 1987; grantee Western Electric Fund, 1979. Mem. LWV, Am. Soc. Pub. Adminstrn. (nat. coun. 1979-82, Outstanding Achievement award Inland chpt. 1982), Trojan League, Internat. Congress Adminstrv. Sci., L.A. Philharmonic Assocs., Saturday Afternoon Club Ukiah, Alpha Kappa Psi. Democrat. Episcopalian. Home: 1199 S Dora St Apt B26 Ukiah CA 95482

GIBBS, MARY BRAMLETT, banker; b. Corona, Calif., Sept. 18, 1953; d. Kenneth Frank and Kathy Lee (Hill) Harris; m. Charles Merrill Gibbs, 1987; 1 child, Meryl Elisabeth. Student U. Md., 1974-77, Southwestern Grad. Sch. Banking. Br. mgr. Peoples Nat. Bank of Md., Suitland, 1972-77; with Post Oak Bank, Houston, 1977-82, asst. v.p. ops. mgmt., 1980-82; v.p. loan ops. First City Nat. Bank Houston, 1982-89; sr. v.p. First Interstate Bank Tex., 1989—. Bd. dirs., life mem. Big Sisters-Big Bros. of Houston; mediator Neighborhood Justice Ctr., 1981; mem. Christ Ch. Cath.; bd. dirs. Tex. So. U. Found., Houston Met. Ministries, Houston Area Urban League, Houston Fire Mus. Named Outstanding Young Houstonian, 1985, Woman on the Move, 1987; recipient Disting. Leadership award Nat. Assn. Community Leadership, 1990. Mem. Nat. Assn. Bank Women, NOW, Houston C. of C. (chair leadership Houston policy coun., chair Houston CRA officers coun. 1994—, bd. dirs. Project Print 1992—). Contbr. articles to profl. jours. Office: 1st Interstate Bank Tex 1000 Louisiana MS 519 Houston TX 77002

GIBBS, SARAH PREBLE, biologist, educator; b. Boston, May 25, 1930; d. Winthrop Harold and Edith Dorothea (Hill) Bowker; m. Robert H. Gibbs, June 9, 1951 (div. 1962); 1 dau., Elizabeth Dorothea; m. Ronald J. Poole, Feb. 2, 1963 (div. 1980); 1 son, Christopher Harold. A.B., Cornell U., 1952, M.S., 1954; Ph.D., Harvard U., 1962. Research assoc. Inst. Animal Genetics Edinburgh U., 1963-65; asst. prof. botany McGill U., Montreal, Que., Can., 1966-69; assoc. prof. biology McGill U., 1969-74, prof., 1974—. Recipient Darbaker prize Bot. Soc. Am., 1975; NSF fellow, 1958-61; NIH fellow, 1961-63. Fellow AAAS, Royal Soc. Can.; mem. Can. Soc. Cellular and Molecular Biology (pres. 1972-73), Am. Soc. Cell Biology, Internat. Phycol. Soc., Phycol. Soc. Am., Soc. Evolutionary Protistology, Can. Assn. Univ. Tchrs., Phi Beta Kappa, Sigma Xi, Phi Kappa Phi. Home: 70 Henley Ave, Montreal, PQ Canada H3P 1V3 Office: McGill U Dept Biology, 1205 Avenue Docteur Penfield, Montreal, PQ Canada H3A 1B1

GIBBS, VIRGINIA TURNBULL, materials engineer; b. Orlando, Fla., Jan. 19, 1960; d. Nathaniel Massie and Beverly (Adams) Turnbull; m. Daniel Leroy Gibbs, Apr. 13, 1991. BSE, Duke U., 1982; MBA, W.Va. U., 1989. Applications engr., mktg. devel. Borg-Warner Chems., Parkersburg, W.Va., 1982-85; application devel. engr. Borg-Warner Chems., Rancho Santa Margarita, Calif., 1985-88; account mgr. LNP Plastics, Rancho Santa Margarita, 1988-89; pres. Integrated Plastic Svcs., Peachtree City, Ga., 1989—. Mem. Soc. Plastics Engrs. (dir. decorating divsn. 1993—).

GIBBS-PICKETT, MARI ELIZABETH, artist, art educator; b. Cortland, N.Y., June 5, 1958; d. Donald Robert and Sarah Jeanette (Crawford) Gibbs; m. Dale I. Pickett, Aug. 24, 1980; children: Sarita Lorraine, Dale I. III. BA, SUNY, Cortland, 1987. Cert. tchr., N.Y. Propr. gallery Eden Arts, Cortland, 1982—; art educator Fingerlakes Adventist Sch., Cortland, 1982-93, Parkview Jr. Acad., Syracuse, N.Y., 1992—, local and pvt. workshops on Cape Cod, 1993—; author Atlantic Union Conf., South Lancaster, Mass., 1993—; illustrator Rainbow Pub. Illustrator: The Medic and the Mama San, 1993, Fragments of a Tapestry, 1994; author illustration periodical Atlantic Union Bull., 1993. Dir. community svcs. Seventh Day Adventist Ch., Cortland; fund raiser March of Dimes, Arthritis Found. Mem. N.Y. State Art Tchr. Assn. Home: 2146 E Homer Rd Cortland NY 13045-1208

GIBBY, MABEL ENID KUNCE, psychologist; b. St. Louis, Mar. 30, 1926; d. Ralph Waldo and Mabel Enid (Warren) Kunce; student Washington U., St. Louis, 1943-44, postgrad., 1955-56; B.A., Park Coll., 1945; M.A., McCormick Theol. Sem., 1947; postgrad. Columbia U., 1948, U. Kansas City, 1949, George Washington U., 1953; M.Ed., U. Mo., 1951, Ed.D., 1952; m. John Francis Gibby, Aug. 27, 1948; children—Janet Marie (Mrs. Kim Williams), Harold Steven, Helen Elizabeth, Diane Louise (Mrs. Roderick Rohrich), John Andrew, Keith Sherridan, Daniel Jay. Dir. religious edn. Westport Presbyn. Ch. Kansas City, Mo., 1947-49; tchr. elementary schs., Kansas City, 1949-50; high sch. counselor Arlington (Va.) Pub. Schs., 1952-54; counselor adult counseling services Washington U., 1955-56; counseling psychologist Coral Gables (Fla.) VA Hosp., 1956—; counseling psychologist Miami (Fla.) VA Hosp., 1956—, chief counseling psychology sect., 1982-86; sr. psychologist Office Disability Determination Fla. Hdqrs., 1987-94. Sec. bd. dirs. Fla. Vocat. Rehab. Found. Recipient Meritorious Service citation Fla. C. of C., 1965, President's Com. on Employment of Handicapped, 1965; commendation for meritorious service Com. on Employment of Physically Handicapped Dade County, 1965, named Outstanding Rehab. Profl., 1966, 81; named Profl. Fed. Employee of Year, Greater Miami Fed. Exec. Council, 1966; Outstanding Fed. Service award Greater Miami Fed. Exec. Council, 1966; Fed. Woman's award U.S. Civil Service Commn., 1968, Community Headliner award Theta Sigma Phi, 1968, Outstanding Alumni award Park Coll., 1968, Freedom award The Chosen Few, Korean War Vets. Assn., 1986; certificate of appreciation Bur. Customs, U.S. Treasury Dept., 1969, Fla. Dept. Health and Rehab. Services, 1970. Mem. Am., Dade County (past sec.) psychol. assns., Nat., Fla. (past dir. Dade County chpt.) rehab. assns., Nat. Rehab. Counseling Assn. (past sec.). Patentee in field. Home: 7107 Aberdeen Ave Dallas TX 75230

GIBBY-SMITH, BARBARA, psychologist, registered nurse; b. Woodburn, Oreg., Dec. 13, 1938; d. Chester Clifton and Marvel Elizabeth (Hill) Gibby; m. Roy Milton Smith, June 2, 1957 (div. June 1990); children: Thomas Clifton, Jeffery Shawn, Mark Anderson. ADN, Chemeketa C.C., Salem, Oreg., 1972; BS, SUNY, Albany, 1980; MS, Western Oreg. State Coll., 1982; D of Psychology, Pacific U., Forest Grove, Oreg., 1993. RN, Oreg. Adminstr. Birch St. Manor, Dallas, Oreg., 1973-81; disability determination specialist State of Oreg. Workers' Compensation Dept., Salem, 1983-85; counselor Women's Crisis Ctr., Salem, 1986-88; rehab. counselor Employer Rehab. Svcs., Portland, Oreg., 1985-87; therapist, counselor Pacific U., Hillsboro, Oreg., 1988-89, Forest Grove, 1989-91; intern psychology Portland State U., 1991-92, Kaiser-Permanente, Salem, 1991-92; resident psychology Tillamook (Oreg.) Counseling Ctr., 1993—; group therapy counselor Women's Crisis Ctr., Dallas, 1982-83; eating disorders group therapy facilitator, Salem, 1986-88. Active Women's Coalition Orgn., Salem, 1988—. Mem. APA. Democrat. Home: PO Box 64 1120 5th St Loop West Netarts OR 97143 Office: Tillamook Counseling Ctr 2405 Fifth St Tillamook OR 97141

GIBSON, ALTHEA, professional tennis player, golfer, state official; b. Silver, S.C., Aug. 25, 1927; d. Daniel and Annie B. (Washington) G.; m. William A. Darben, Oct. 17, 1965; m. Sydney Llewellyn, Apr. 11, 1983. B.S., Fla. A&M Coll., 1953; D. Pub. Service (hon.), Monmouth Coll., 1980; LittD (hon.), U. N.C., Wilmington, 1987; LHD (hon.), Upsala Coll., 1989. Amateur tennis player U.S., Europe, and S.Am., 1941-58; asst. instr. dept. health and phys. edn. Lincoln U., Jefferson City, Mo., 1953-55; made profl. tennis tour with Harlem Globetrotters, 1959; community rels. rep. Ward Baking Co., 1959; joined Ladies Profl. Golf Assn. as profl. golfer, 1963; apptd. to N.Y. State Recreation Council, 1964; staff mem. Essex County Park Commn., Newark, 1970; recreation supr. Essex County Park Commn., 1970-71; dir. tennis programs, profl. Valley View Racquet Club, Northvale, N.J., 1972; tennis pro Morven, 1973—; athletic commr. State of N.J., Trenton, 1975—; recreation mgr. City of East Orange, N.J., 1980; mem. N.J. State Athletic Control Bd., 1986; spl. cons. Gov.'s Coun. Phys. Fitness and Sports, N.J., 1988—; winner world profl. tennis championship, 1960, Wimbledon Women's Singles Championship, 1957, 58, Wimbledon Women's Doubles Championship, 1956-58, U.S. Women's Singles Championship, 1957, 58. Appeared in the movie The Horse Soldiers, 1958; author: I Always Wanted to Be Somebody, 1958. Named Woman Athlete of Yr., AP Poll, 1957-58; named to Lawn Tennis Hall of Fame and Tennis Mus., 1971, Black Athletes Hall of Fame, 1974, S.C. Hall of Fame, 1983, Fla. Sports Hall of Fame, 1984, Sports Hall of Fame of N.J., 1994. Mem. Alpha Kappa Alpha. Home: PO Box 768 East Orange NJ 07019-0768

GIBSON, DENICE YVONNE, telecommunications and computer executive; b. Grants Pass, Oreg., Apr. 6, 1955; d. Harry Charles Gibson and Bettye Yvonne Bentley Stein. BS in Psychology, U. San Francisco, 1980; MS in Systems Mgmt., U. So. Calif., 1982; postgrad., Stanford U., 1983; PhD in Instl. Mgmt., Pepperdine U., 1990. Documentation coord./systems analyst Argonaut Ins., Menlo Park, Calif., 1977-78; tech. ops. mgr. Amdahl Corp., Sunnyvale, Calif., 1978-85; sr. dir. worldwide mktg. Candle Corp., L.A., 1985-89; v.p. mktg. Panoramic Inc., San Jose, 1989-90; v.p. devel. Tandem Computers, Plano, Tex., 1990-92, v.p. devel. and support, 1992-93; v.p. devel. and support Tandem Corp., Cupertino, Calif., 1993—; adj. prof. info. systems mgmt. U. San Francisco, 1984-86; guest lectr. Stanford U., U. Calif., Berkeley, U. Calif., Santa Clara; adj. faculty U. Calif. at Santa Cruz, 1994, U. San Francisco, 1994; cons. Nat. Sch. Safety Ctr., 1987, Fed. Law Enforcement Tng. Ctr., 1987, Nat. Soc. Secs., 1986, Pacific Bell, 1985, Elxsi Computers, 1983, Trilogy, 1983. Contbr. articles to profl. jours. Mem. IEEE, Engring. Soc., Am. Soc. Tng. and Devel., Am. Mgmt. Assn., Internat. Platform Assn.

GIBSON, DOROTHY JEAN, chiropractor; b. El Dorado, Ark., Mar. 31, 1959; d. Benjamin Lecil and Gladys Dale (Blount) G. BA, So. Meth. U., 1981; MS, North Tex. State U., 1983; BS, Parker Coll. Chiropractic, Dallas, 1993, D of Chiropractic, 1993. Phys. edn. tchr., girls volleyball coach Richland C.C., 1983-84; sci. tchr., girls coach N. Carrollton (Tex.) Jr. H.S., 1984-86; sales rep., sales mgr. 7 Colors, Inc., Dallas, 1985-89; chiropractor Gibson Chiropractic Ctr., Fayetteville, Ark., 1993—. Instr. ARC, Fayetteville; girls coach, Fayetteville Girls Softball League. Mem. Am. Chiropractic Assn., Ark. Chiropractic Assn., Fayetteville C. of C., Washington County LWV, Exec. Women's Internat. Office: Gibson Chiropractic Ctr 60 E Township St Ste 7 Fayetteville AR 72703-2836

GIBSON, ELEANOR JACK (MRS. JAMES J. GIBSON), psychology educator; b. Peoria, Ill., Dec. 7, 1910; d. William A. and Isabel (Grier) Jack; m. James J. Gibson, Sept. 17, 1932; children: James J., Jean Grier. BA, Smith Coll., 1931, MA, 1933, DSc (hon.), 1972; PhD, Yale U., 1938; DSc (hon.), Rutgers U., 1973, Trinity Coll., 1982, Bates Coll., 1985, U. S.C., 1987, Emory U., 1990, Middlebury Coll., 1993; LHD (hon.), SUNY, Albany, 1984, Miami U., 1989. Asst., instr., asst. prof. Smith Coll., 1931-49; research assoc. psychology Cornell U., Ithaca, N.Y., 1949-66; prof. Cornell U., 1972—, Susan Linn Sage prof. psychology, 1972—; fellow Inst. for Advanced Study, Princeton, 1959-60, Inst. for Advanced Study in Behavioral Scis., Stanford, Calif., 1963-64, Inst. for Advanced Study, Ind. U., fall 1990; vis. prof. Mass. Inst. Tech., 1973, Inst. Child Devel., U. Minn., 1980; Disting. vis. prof. U. Calif., Davis, 1978; vis. scientist Salk Inst., La Jolla, Calif., 1979; vis. prof. U. Pa., 1984; Montgomery fellow Dartmouth Coll., 1986; Woodruff vis. prof. psychology Emory U., 1988-90. Author: Principles of Perceptual Learning and Development, 1967 (Century award), (with H. Levin) The Psychology of Reading, 1975, Odyssey in Learning and Perception, 1991. Recipient Wilbur Cross medal Yale U., 1973, Howard Crosby Warren medal, 1977, medal for disting. svc. Tchrs. Coll. Columbia U., 1983, Nat. Medal Sci., 1992, Lifetime Achievement award Internat. Soc. for Ecol. Psychology; Guggenheim fellow, 1972-73, William James fellow Am. Psychol. Soc., 1989. Fellow AAAS (div. chairperson 1983), Am. Psychol. Assn. (Disting. Scientist award 1968, G. Stanley Hall award 1970, pres. div. 3 1977, Gold medal award 1986); mem. NAS, Eastern Psychol. Assn. (pres. 1968), Soc. Exptl. Psychologists, Nat. Acad. Edn., Psychonomic Soc., Soc. Rsch. in Child Devel. (Disting. Sci. Contbn. award 1981), Am. Acad. Arts and Scis., Brit. Psychol. Soc. (hon.), N.Y. Acad. Scis. (hon.), Italian Soc. Rsch. in Child Devel. (hon.), Phi Beta Kappa, Sigma Xi. Home: RR 1 Box 265A Middlebury VT 05753-9705

GIBSON, ELISABETH JANE, principal; b. Salina, Kans., Apr. 28, 1937; d. Cloyce Wesley and Margaret Mae (Yost) Kasson; m. William Douglas Miles, Jr., Aug. 20, 1959 (div.); m. Harry Benton Gibson Jr., July 1, 1970. AB, Colo. State Coll., 1954-57; MA, San Francisco State Coll., 1967-68; EdD, U. No. Colo., 1978; postgrad. U. Denver, 1982. Cert. tchr., prin., Colo. Tchr. elem. schs., Santa Paula, Calif., 1957-58, Salina, Kans., 1958-63, Goose Bay, Labrador, 1963-64, Jefferson County, Colo., 1965-66, Topeka, 1966-67; diagnostic tchr. Cen. Kans. Diagnostic Remedial Edn. Ctr., Salina, 1968-70; instr. Loretto Heights Coll., Denver, 1970-72; co-owner Ednl. Cons. Enterprises, Inc., Greeley, Colo., 1974-77; resource coord. Region VIII Resource Access Project Head Start Mile High Consortium, Denver, 1976-77; exec. dir. Colo. Fedn. Coun. Exceptional Children, Denver, 1976-77; asst. prof. Met. State Coll., Denver, 1979; dir. spl. edn. N.E. Colo. Bd. Coop. Edn. Svcs., Haxtun, Colo., 1979-82; prin. elem. jr. high sch., Elizabeth, Colo., 1982-84; prin., spl. projects coord. Summit County Schs., Frisco, Colo., 1985—; prin. Frisco Elem. Sch., 1985-91; cons. Montana Dept. Edn., 1978-79, Love Pub. Co., 1976-78, Colo. Dept. Inst., 1974-75; cons. Colo. Dept. Edn., 1984-85, mem. proposal reading com., 1987—; pres. Found. Exceptional Children, 1980-81; pres. bd. dirs. N.E. Colo. Svcs. Handicapped, 1981-82; bd. dirs. Dept. Ednl. Specialists, Colo. Assn. Sch. Execs., 1982-84; mem. Colo. Title IV Adv. Coun., 1980-82; mem. Mellon Found. grant steering com. Colo. Dept. Edn., 1984-85; mem. Colo. Dept. Edn. Data Acquisition Reporting and Utilization Com., 1983, Denver City County Commn. for Disabled, 1978-81; chmn. regional edn. com. 1970 White House Conf. Children and Youth; bd. dirs. Advocates for Victims of Assault, 1986-91; mem. adv. bd. Alpine Counseling Ctr., 1986—; mem. placement alternatives commn. Dept. Social Svcs., 1986—; mem. adv. com. Colo. North Cen. Assn., 1988-91; sec. Child Care Resource and Referral Agy., 1992—; mem. Child Care Task Force Summit County, 1989—; mem. tchr. cert. task force Colo. State Bd. Edn., 1990-91; chair Summit County Interagy. Coord. Coun., 1989—. Recipient Vol. award Colo. Child Care Assn., 1992, Ann. Svc. award Colo. Fedn. Coun. Exceptional Children, 1981; San Francisco State Coll. fellow, 1967-68. Mem. Colo. Assn. Retarded Citizens, Assn. Supervision Curriculum Devel., Nat. Assn. Elem. Sch. Prins., North Cen. Assn. (state adv. com. 1988-91), Order Eastern Star, Kappa Delta Pi, Pi Lambda Theta, Phi Delta Kappa. Republican. Methodist. Author: (with H. Padzensky) Goal Guide: A minicourse in writing goals and behavioral objectives for special education, 1975; (with H. Padzensky and S. Sporn) Assaying Student Behavior: A minicourse in student assessment techniques, 1974; contbr. articles to profl. jours. Home: 600 W County Line Rd 23-103 Highlands Ranch CO 80126 Office: Summit County Schs Ctrl Office PO Box 7 Frisco CO 80443-0007

GIBSON, FLORENCE ANDERSON, talking book company executive, narrator; b. San Francisco, Feb. 7, 1924; m. V.H. Carlos Gibson, Aug. 30, 1947; children: Nancy Derwent, Christopher Carlos, Katherine Wayne Berrien, Diana Corona. Student, Finch Jr. Coll., N.Y.C., 1941-42; BA in Dramatic Lit., U. Calif., Berkeley, 1944; student, Neighborhood Playhouse, N.Y.C., 1944-45. Radio actress San Francisco, 1944, 46, 47; chmn. Washington com. Am. Field Svc., 1958-60, 62-65; founder, chmn. Peruvian Com. Am. Field Svc., Lima, 1960-62; treas., distbn. mgr. Living Garden and Concern 1975 calendars, 1971-75; sec. exec. com Fgn. Student Svc. Coun., 1973-76; narrator Talking Books Libr. of Congress div. for Blind and Physically Handicapped, 1975—; narrator Recorded Books, Inc., 1979; founder, pres. Audio Book Contractors, Inc., 1982—; narrator more than 645 unabridged books on cassettes. Actress, appearing in Blithe Spirit, 1945, Ah, Wilderness, 1946, Traffic Ct. TV series, others. Bd. dirs. Fgn. Student Svc. Coun., Concern, Inc., Rec. for the Blind, Children's Theater of Washington; vol. in occupational therapy Children's Hosp., Washington, 1949-50; vol. lobbyist student exch. program Am. Field Svc. Recipient 3 Parents' Choice awards, 1983, 84, 86; named Best Female Narrator, Book World; selected as A Notable Children's Recording, ALA, 1987, 88, 89. Home: 4626 Garfield St NW Washington DC 20007-1025 Office: Audio Book Contractors Inc PO Box 40115 Washington DC 20016-0115

GIBSON, JANE ELLEN, business executive; b. Milford, Conn., Mar. 24, 1947; d. Van R. and Josa Elizabeth (Marsh) G.; m. George L. Salazar, Sept. 27, 1969 (div. Feb. 1972); 1 child, Jason Eliot; m. J. Eliot Merk, July 13, 1972 (div. Dec. 1994). BA in Geography with honors, U. Hawaii, 1992, cert. in land use planning, 1992. Tech. illustrator GE Co., Syracuse, N.Y., 1966-68; structural steel drafting technician Acme Steel Co., Honolulu, 1969-70; book-keeper, sec. Hilo, Hawaii, 1974-75; cartographer Planning dept. County of Hawaii, Hilo, 1975-76; officer mgr., archtl. drafting technician MTZ Homes, Inc., Hilo, 1976-77; office mgr., concrete plant operator Merk's Works Ltd., Hilo, 1978-83; onwer, mgr. Ono Yogurt Meals & Munchies, Hilo, 1983-88; pres., owner Work Rite Systems, Inc., Hilo, 1988—; treas., bus. mgr., cartographic GIS technician, geographer MapTech, Inc., Hilo, 1992—; planner poacific Women's Conf., 1991. Vol. Hawaii County Fire Dept., Puna, 1974-75, Cmty. Mgmt. Assn., Volcano, Hawaii, 1991-92; del. Hawaii Bahai Nat. Conv., 1988, 91, 92, 94, 95. Mem. Am. Planning Assn., Assn. Am. Geographers, Navy League. Mem. Bahai Ch. Office: Work Rite Systems Inc 69 Railroad Ave Ste A19 Hilo HI 96720-4574

GIBSON, LOIS RAUCH, English language educator; b. N.Y.C., July 4, 1945; d. Morris and Ida E. (Cohen) R.; children: Michael, Jonathan. BA, Hunter Coll., 1966; MA, U. Pitts., 1968, PhD, 1975. Asst. prof. Coker Coll., Hartsville, S.C., 1978-82, assoc. prof., 1983-89, prof., chairperson dept. lang. and lit., 1990—; adj. lectr. Portland (Oreg.) State U., 1975-78, summers 1979, 80, 81, 83; mem. writing adv. com. S.C. Dept. Edn., Columbia, 1981—. Contbr. articles to profl. jours.; contbg. writer reference books, children's and adolescent lit., 1993—. Libr. vol. Forest Lake Elem. Sch., Columbia, 1987-88, 89—, Internat. Sch., Geneva, 1988-89. Oreg. Com. on Humanities grantee, Portland, 1975. Mem. MLA (South Atlantic br.), Nat. Coun. Tchrs. of English, Children's Lit. Assn. (guest editor issue quar. jour. 1991-92), S.C. Assn. Depts. of English (sec.-treas. 1990—). Office: Coker Coll Dept Lang And Lit Hartsville SC 29550

GIBSON, LOU ELLEN, computer systems analyst; b. Thomasville, Ga., Feb. 20, 1954; d. Elisha Wilburn and Elsie Inez (Hicks) G.; m. James Smith Ernest Sanchez, Apr. 22, 1972 (div. 1984); children: Marta Elena Ernest, Audrey Elisa Ernst, Jessica Anne Ernest. BS in Med. Tech., Canal Zone Coll., 1974; tech. degree computer programming, Byte S.A., Panama, 1979. Med. tech. Gorgas Hosp., Ancon, Panama Canal Zone, 1975-79, Gorgas Army Hosp., Ancon, Republic of Panama, 1979-80; computer programmer Panama Canal Commn., Balboa, Republic of Panama, 1980-84; computer systems analyst Panama Canal Commn., Balboa, 1984-91, project mgr., 1991—. Recipient U.S. Govt. Spl. Achievement awards Panama Canal Commn., Balboa, 1984, 86, U.S. Govt. Spl. Acts or Svc. award, 1990, U.S. Govt. Outstanding Performance award, 1991. Mem. Am. Soc. Clin. Pathologists. Home: PO Box 37301 # 242 Washington DC 20006 Office: Panama Canal Commn Divsn Data Processing Unit 2300 APO AA 34011-2300

GIBSON, LUCY WILLARD WEBB, psychologist; b. Richmond, Va., Jan. 9, 1947; d. Leroy and Mary Virginia (White) Webb; m. David Arthur Gibson, Feb. 4, 1967 (div. 1986); children: Amy Kristine, Mary Catherine. BSN, Fla. State U., 1971; MA in Psychology, U. Tenn., 1980, PhD in Indsl.-Organizational Psychology, 1988. Lic. indsl.-organizational psychology, Tenn. Outpatient psychiat. nurse, quality assurance coord. Ridgeview Psychiat. Hosp., 1972-85; chief operating officer, sr. cons. Lazarus Cons. Group, Knoxville, Tenn., 1991—; v.p., sr. cons. Resource Assocs., Inc., 1983-92; adj. instr. dept. psychology and mgmt. U. Tenn., 1982—; instr. applied organizational mgmt. program Tusculum Coll., 1986—; personnel specialist Oak Ridge Nat. Lab., 1983-86. Contbr. articles to profl. jours. Mem. Acad. Mgmt., Am. Soc. for Quality Control, Knoxville Assn. Women Execs. (pres. 1994), Am. Psychol. Assn., West Knoxville Rotary (chair community svc. com. 1993), Knoxville/Knox County LWV (2d v.p. 1988-92), Phi Kappa Phi, Beta Sigma Phi (pres. 1976). Office: Lazarus Cons Group Inc 8044 Ray Mears Blvd Ste 111 Knoxville TN 37919-5476

GIBSON, MELISSA, psychotherapist; b. San Francisco, Sept. 13, 1960; d. Bud and Gladys (Matter) Gibson; m. Michael Robert Macan, June 15, 1989; children: Rita, Maya. BA in Psychology, U. Calif., Berkeley, 1982, MSW, 1984. Lic. psychotherapist; cert. substance abuse counselor, eating disorders therapist. Social worker L.A. Child and Family Guidance Ctr., 1984-87; substance abuse counselor Randolph Treatment Ctr., Seattle, 1987-90; therapist eating disorders treatment program Women's Health Clinic, Seattle, 1990—; substance abuse prevention counselor Rivers Sch. Dist., Seattle, 1988-90. Author: Raising Happy and Healthy Daughters: A Parent's Guide to Teenage Self-Esteem, 1990; contbr. articles to profl. jours. Chair ann. fundraiser AIDS Action Ctr., Seattle, 1991—; vol. crisis intervention hotline Seattle Sexual Assault Ctr., 1992—; bd. dirs. Washington chpt. Planned Parenthood, 1994—. Mem. NASW, Nat. Assn. Eating Disorders Therapists (v.p. Seattle chpt. 1994—), Seattle Area Women's Issues Focus Group. Address: Werik Park North 7030 15th Ave NW Seattle WA 98117-5598

GIBSON, MICHELLE ANN, English language educator; b. Kansas City, Mo., Dec. 25, 1961; d. George Oram Gibson and Ann Christine (Wegner) Kelsey. AA in English, Hutchinson (Kans.) C.C., 1985; BA in Liberal Studies, Salisbury State U., 1987; MA in English, Ohio U., 1989, PhD in English, 1993. Office worker Hutchinson (Kans.) C.C., 1983-85; worker Hardee's, Hutchinson, 1983-85; instr. English Ohio U., Athens, 1987—; asst. prof. English U. Cin.; asst. dir. composition Ohio U., Athens, 1991, dir. jr. composition program, 1992; presenter in field. Author of articles and poems. Mem. AAUW, Nat. Coun. Tchrs. English, Coll. Composition and Comm. Democrat. Lutheran. Office: U Cin Dyer Hall Cincinnati OH 45221

GIBSON, NATALIE GAY, accountant; b. Gould, Ark., Dec. 14, 1963; d. Earnest Gibson and Felma Lavon (Watts) Evans. BS in Acctg., U. Ark., 1986. Accountant Ski and Scuba Acad. Houston, 1986-87; revenue agt. IRS, Houston, 1988—, vol. income tax coord. Coord. Gulf Coast Blood Dr., Houston, 1990-92, Fed. Contbns. Campaign, Houston, 1990-92. Mem. NAFE, Nat. Assn. Black Accountants (social and edn. chair 1989-94, various coms.), Assn. for Improvement Minorities, Federally Employed Women, Houston Area Urban League. Democrat. Baptist. Home: 311 Parramatta Ln Apt F307 Houston TX 77073-1010

GIBSON, PATRICIA ANN, library administrator; b. Joplin, Mo., Nov. 14, 1942; d. Arrell Morgan and Dorothy (Deitz) G. BA in English, U. Okla., 1963, MLS, 1966, PhD in Edn., 1977. English tchr. Norman (Okla.) Pub. Schs., 1963-65; pub. svcs. librarian U. Okla. Health Scis. Ctr., Oklahoma City, 1966-68, serials librarian, 1971-72, dir. media prodn., 1972-77; coord. library svcs. Okla. Regional Med. Program, 1968-70; head reference dept. Wichita State U., 1978-80; mgr. library devel. DataPhase Systems, Inc., Kansas City, Mo., 1980-82; v.p. program adminstrn., libr. dir. Am. Acad. Family Physicians Found., Kansas City, 1982—; cons. Am. Coll. Cardiology Library, 1986-87. Contbr. articles to profl. jours. Chmn. regional screening com. Am. Field Svc., Kansas City, 1987-89; bd. dirs. Midwest Ear Inst., 1993—. Kellogg Found. grantee, 1987-88. Mem. Med. Libr. Assn. (disting. mem. Acad. Health Sci. Librs., chmn. med. libr. edn. sect. 1985, libr. rsch. sect. 1989-90, med. soc. librs. sect. 1991-92), Kansas City Met. Libr. Network (pres. 1986, sec. 1987-89), Health Scis. Libr. Group Greater Kansas City (pres. 1992—), Nat. Network Med. Librs. (regional adv. com. midcontinental region 1991—, chmn. regional adv. com. 1994—). Democrat. Presbyterian. Office: Am Acad Family Physicians Found 8880 Ward Pkwy PO Box 8418 Kansas City MO 64114-0418

GIBSON, ROSE CAMPBELL, sociology educator; b. Detroit; d. John Henry and Lela Gertrude (Long) Campbell; m. Ralph M. Gibson, Dec. 31, 1947; children: Ralph M. Jr., John S. PhD, U. Mich., 1977. Rsch. asst. U. Mich., Ann Arbor, 1977, rsch. assoc./assoc. rsch. scientist, 1978-84, prof., 1984—. Co-author: Worlds of Difference, 1993, Health in Black America, 1994; author: Aging and the Life Course. Mem. Am. Statis. Soc., Gerontol. Soc. Am., Am. Psychol. Soc.

GIBSON, SARAH ANN SCOTT, art librarian; b. Harrisburg, Pa., Mar. 2, 1932; d. John Young Scott and Alice Virginia (Cooper) Rowe; m. Walter Samuel Gibson, Dec. 16, 1972. AB in History, Smith Coll., 1953; postgrad., Université de Strasbourg, France, 1953-54, École du Louvre, Paris, 1965-66; MLS, Case Western Reserve U., 1968, MA in Art History, 1972, PhD in Libr. and Info. Sci., 1975. Asst. cataloger Denison U., Granville, Ohio, 1958-69; asst. prof. U. Mich., 1972-73; asst. prof. Case Western Reserve U., 1975-82, asst. dean Sch. Libr. Sci., 1979-82, assoc. prof., 1982-86; exec. officer, assoc. prof. Matthew A. Baxter Sch. Info. and Libr. Sci., 1984-86; libr. Sterling & Francine Clark Art Inst., Williamstown, Mass., 1987—; vis. prof. Sch. Info. Studies Syracuse U., 1986. Author: (with Lois Swan Jones) Art Libraries and Information Services: Development, Organization and Management, 1986, (with others) Book Illustration From Six Centuries in the Library of the Sterling & Francine Clark Art Institute Library, 1990; assoc. editor RILA Internat. Repertory of Lit. of Art, 1986-87; contbr. articles to profl. jours. Fulbright fellow, 1953-54. Mem. Art Librs. Soc. N.Am., Jr. League Cleve., Princeton Club N.Y.C., Historians Netherlands Art. Home: RR 1 # 461H Mason Hill Rd Pownal VT 05261 Office: Sterling & Francine Clark Art Inst 222 South St Box 8 Williamstown MA 01267-0008

GIBSON, SHERI JO, clinical nurse specialist; b. Wagner, S.D., Sept. 28, 1959; d. John Berton and Elaine Ella (Mazourek) Weber; m. David John Gibson, Dec. 31, 1982; children: Daniel, Taylor. BSN, S.D. State U., 1981; MSN, Ariz. State U., 1989; FNP, S.D. State U., 1995. RN, S.D.; cert. CCRN; cert. case mgr. Ins. Rehab. Specialists Commn., ACLS provider, instr.; Pediatric Advanced Life Support provider; cert. Diabetes Team instr. Nurse technician cardiovascular ICU St. Mary's Hosp., Rochester, Minn., 1980; staff nurse McKennan Hosp., Sioux Falls, S.D., 1981-83, staff nurse ICU, 1983-84; staff nurse special care unit Valley Lutheran Hosp., Mesa, Ariz., 1984-87, 1988, adminstrv. coord., 1985-88, clin. nurse specialist critical care, 1988-91; clin. nurse specialist, dir. ctr. case mgmt. Sioux Valley Hosp., Sioux Falls, 1991—; chair Diabetes Team, 1986-88; adj. faculty Coll. Nursing Ariz. State U., 1991-92; presenter, rschr. in field. Mem. ANA, S.D. Nurses Assn., Sigma Theta Tau. Home: 1005 Plum Creek Rd Sioux Falls SD 57105 Office: Sioux Valley Hosp PO Box 5039 1100 S Euclid Ave Sioux Falls SD 57117-5039

GIBSON, VIRGINIA LEE, lawyer; b. Independence, Mo., Mar. 5, 1946. BA, U. Calif., Berkeley, 1972; JD, U. Calif., San Francisco, 1977. Bar: Calif. 1981. Assoc. Pillsbury, Madison & Sutro, San Francisco, 1980-83; ptnr. Chickering & Gregory, San Francisco, 1983-85, Baker & McKenzie, San Francisco, 1985—. Mem. ABA (employee benefits subcom. tax sect.), Internat. Found. Employee Benefit Plans, Am. Compensation Assn. (internat. compensation and benefits com.), Calif. Bar Assn. (exec. com. tax sect. 1985-88), San Francisco Bar Assn. (internat. and comparative law taxation sects.), Western Pension and Benefits Conf. (pres. San Francisco chpt. 1989-91, steering com. 1988—). Office: Baker & McKenzie 2 Embarcadero Ctr Ste 2400 San Francisco CA 94111-3909

GIBSON, WANDA D., computer specialist; b. Phoenixville, Pa., Oct. 5, 1948; d. Walter Norris and Cora Lee (Travis) Durden; m. Kenneth Gibson, Aug. 1, 1970; children: Wendy, Jeremy. BS, Ashland (Ohio) Coll., 1976; MEd, Wright State U., 1990. Ednl. coor. DRET Schs., Inc., Miamisburg, Ohio, 1983-89; registrar dept. head, instr. DRET Schs., Inc., Springfield, Ohio; tchr. Kenton Ridge High Sch., Springfield, 1990-91, Pioneer Joint Vocat. Sch., Shelby, Ohio, 1976-77; sec. Robert W. Lett, Esq., Ashland, Ohio, 1974-75; computer specialist Staunton (Va.) City Schs., 1991-92; instr. Dominion Bus. Sch., Harrisburg, Va., 1992—; adj. prof. Blue Ridge C.C., Weyers Cave, Va.; workshop leader on lesson plans devel. Mem. NEA, Staunton Edn. Assn., NAFE, Ohio Bus. Tchrs. Assn., Kappa Delta Pi. Home: 1161 Stuart St Harrisonburg VA 22801-2493

GIBSON, WENDY JOAN, lawyer; b. Englewood, N.J., Nov. 13, 1953; d. Robert Francis and Hilma Gertrude (Van Heek) Orr; m. Kenneth Lee Gibson, June 12, 1976; children: Christopher, Craig. BA, Principia Coll., 1975; JD, NYU, 1979. Bar: Ohio 1979, U.S. Dist. Ct. (no. dist.) Ohio 1980, U.S. Ct. Appeals (6th cir.) 1980; bd. cert. Bus. Bankruptcy Law Am. Bankrupcy Bd. of Certification. Assoc. Baker & Hostetler, Cleve., 1980-90, ptnr., 1990—. Mem. ABA, Ohio State Bar Assn., Cleve. Bar Assn., Am. Bankruptcy Inst. Office: Baker & Hostetler 3200 National City Ctr 1900 E 9th St Cleveland OH 44114-3303

GIDDENS, ZELMA KIRK, broadcast executive; b. Lafayette, Ala.; d. James William and Eunice (Rice) Kirk; grad. So. Union Jr. Coll., 1932; student Auburn U., 1934-35; m. Kenneth R. Giddens, May 19, 1934; children: Annsley Giddens Green, Therese Giddens Greer, Sara Kay Glenday. With Sta. WKRG-AM, 1947-55; with Sta. WKRG-AM-FM-TV, Mobile, Ala., 1955—, vice chmn., treas., 1960—. Founder, Mus. for Women's Art, Washington; trustee, Nat. Symphony. Mem. Smithsonian Assos., Mobile C. of C., Nat. Gallery Art Circle, Friends of Kennedy Ctr., Nat. Press Club, Am. Newspaper Women's Assn. Died Sept. 26, 1994. Home: 2555 N Delwood Dr Mobile AL 36606-1748 Office: 555 Broadcast Dr Mobile AL 36606-2936

GIDYNSKI, CHRISTINA BARBARA, clinical psychologist, researcher, clinician; b. Poznan, Poland, June 5, 1933; came to U.S., 1948; d. Joseph Casimir and Janina (Wozniak) G. AB, Guilford Coll., 1954; MA, Columbia U., 1955, PhD, 1972. Lic. clin. psychologist, N.Y. Rsch. fellow Cornell U. Med. Coll., N.Y.C., 1965-69; assoc. rsch. scientist NYU, N.Y.C., 1973-74; cons., psychol. rschr. Kittay Sci. Found., N.Y.C., 1974-77; pvt. practice N.Y.C., 1976—. Contbr. articles to profl. jours. Mem. APA, Nat. Register Health Svc. Providers. Mem. Soc. of Friends. Office: 315 W 57th St Ste 403 New York NY 10019-3158

GIEBNER, CARA RAE, trade association administrator; b. Cleve., Sept. 29, 1940; children: Catherine, Elaine, Christopher. BS, Ohio U., 1960. Exec. sec. Marcus Advt., Cleve., 1969-75; with personnel dept. Van Dorn Plastics, Strongsville, Ohio, 1975-80; exec. v.p. Suspension Specialists Assn., Medina, Ohio, 1980—; exec. sec. Heavy Duty Reps. Assn., Medina, 1986—. Newsletter editor Van Dorn Plastics Press, 1975-80, Spring Service Assn., 1981—, Gerspacher, 1981-85. Mem. Sales and Mktg. Execs. Cleve., Cleve. Area Meeting Planners, Fleet Maintenance Coun. of N.E. Ohio, Greater Cleve. Soc. Assn. Execs., Medina County Bd. Realtors, Alpha Delta Pi. Home and Office: 4015 Marks Rd Apt 2B Medina OH 44256-8316

GIER, AUDRA MAY CALHOON, environmental chemist; b. Bella Vista, Peru, Aug. 21, 1940; came to U.S., 1944; d. Nathan Moore and Olivia Cleo (Hite) Calhoon; m. Delta Warren Gier, Apr. 4, 1968. BA, Austin Coll., 1962; MS in Chemistry, Kans. State Coll., 1964; MA in History of Sci., U. Wis., 1974; postgrad., York U., Toronto, Can., 1974-79. Food technologist Midwest Rsch. Inst., Kansas City, Mo., 1963-64; chemist Mobay (formerly Chemagro), Kansas City, 1964-67; instr. chemistry St. Andrews Presbyn. Coll., Laurinburg, N.C., 1967-68; chemist Cardinal Chem. Co., Columbia, S.C., 1968; asst. prof. chemistry Lea Coll., Albert Lea, Minn., 1969-72; psychology intern emergency unit Thistletown Regional Centre for Children & Adolescents, Toronto, Ont., Can., 1975-77; assoc. prof. chemistry Cleveland Chiropractic Coll., Kansas City, 1979-84; adj. faculty Pk. Coll., Parkville, Mo., 1982-92; environ. chemist, quality assurance specialist Ecology & Environ., Inc., Overland Park, Kans., 1987—; pres. Delta and Assocs., Inc., Kansas City, 1988—; co-founder, v.p. Midwest Sci. Found., Kansas City, 1990—; adj. faculty Donnelly Coll., 1992—, dean adminstrn. health scis. program, 1992—; mentor tng. program Option Inst. and Fellowship, Sheffield, Mass., 1994—. Author: Highlights of Organic Chemistry, 1985; co-editor: (with D.W. Gier) History and Directory of Chemical Education, 1974, (with D.W. Gier) Peace is Something Speshl; co-inventor, copatentee acetylenic ketones as herbicides. Mem. adv. bd. Kansas City Interfaith Peace Alliance, 1980-95, bd. dirs., 1982-85, pres., 1985-86; bd. dirs.

Prairie Star Dist./Unitarian-Universalist Midwest (Upper), 1985-91; co-chair Bragg Symposium on Humanism, Kansas City, 1980-90; chair Social Responsibility Com., Prairie Star Dist. UUA, 1986-91; mem. N.Am. Com. for Humanism and Fellowship of Religious Humanists. Recipient Social Justice award Social Justice Com. Prairie Star Dist, 1985; named Woman of Yr., 1982, Humanist of Yr., 1987, All Souls Unitarian Ch., Kansas City. Mem. AAUW, ACLU, DAR, Am. Chem. Soc., Am. Soc. Quality Control (cert.), Inst. for Soc. Ethics and Life Scis., Midwest Bioethics Ctr., Planned Parenthood, NARAL, Hazardous Materials Control Rsch. Inst., Assn. for Quality and Participation, Alpha Chi. Democrat. Home: 421 W 99th St Kansas City MO 64114-3908

GIER, KARAN HANCOCK, counseling psychologist; b. Sedalia, Mo., Dec. 7, 1947; d. Ioda Clyde and Lorna (Campbell) Hancock; m. Thomas Robert Gier, Sept. 28, 1968. BA in Edn., U. Mo., Kansas City, 1971; MA Teaching in Math/Sci. Edn., Webster U., 1974; MA in Counseling Psychology, Western Colo. U., 1981; MEd Guidance and Counseling, U. Alaska, 1981; PhD in Edn., Pacific Western U., 1989. Nat. cert. counselor. Instr. grades 5-8 Kansas City-St. Joseph Archdiocese, 1969-73; ednl. cons. Pan-Ednl. Inst., Kansas City, 1973-75; instr., counselor Bethel (Alaska) Regional High Sch., 1975-80; ednl. program coord. Western Regional Resource Ctr., Anchorage, 1980-81; counselor U. Alaska, Anchorage, 1982-83; coll. prep. instr. Alaska Native Found., Anchorage, 1982; counselor USAF, Anchorage, 1985-86; prof. U. Alaska, Anchorage, 1982—; dir. Omni Counseling Svcs., Anchorage, 1984—; prof. Chapman Coll., Anchorage, 1988—; workshop facilitator over 100 workshops on the topics of counseling techs., value clarification, non-traditional teaching approaches, peer-tutor tng. Co-author: Coping with College, 1984, Helping Others Learn, 1985; editor, co-author: A Student's Guide, 1983; contbg. author developmental Yup'ik lang. program, 1981; contbr. photographs to Wolves and Related Canids, 1990, 91; contbr. articles to profl. jours. Mem. Am. Bus. Women's Assn., Blue Springs, Mo., 1972-75, Ctr. for Environ. Edn., World Wildlife Fund, Beta Sigma Phi, Bethel, Alaska, 1976-81. Recipient 3d place color photo award Yukon-Kuskokwim State Fair, Bethel, 1978, Notable Achievement award USAF, 1986, Meritorious Svc. award Anchorage Community Coll., 1984-88. Mem. Coll. Reading and Learning Assn. (editor, peer tutor sig leader 1988—, Cert. of Appreciation, 1986-93, bd. dirs. Alaska state, coord. internat. tutor program), AACD, Alaska Assn. Counseling and Devel. (pres. 1989-90), Alaska Career Devel. Assn. (pres.-elect 1989-90), Nat. Rehab. Assn., Nat. Rehab. Counselors, Greenpeace, Human Soc. of the U.S. Wolf Haven Am., Wolf Song of Alaska. Home and Office: Omni Counseling Svcs 8102 Harvest Cir Anchorage AK 99502-4682

GIERKEY, CHERYL ANN, counselor; b. South Bend, Ind., Apr. 16, 1965; d. Norman Ward and Georgann (Roggemann) G. BS, U. North Tex., 1988, MEd, 1992. Desk clerk Tex. Acad. Math. and Sci., Denton, 1988-89, asst. hall dir., 1989-91; Outreach counselor Women's Shelter, Arlington, Tex., 1992—. Vol. Big Bros. and Sisters, Ft. Worth, Tex., 1992—, Tex. Spl. Olympics, Arlington, 1994. Mem. ACA, Tex. Coun. Family Violence, Am. Mental Health Assn. Roman Catholic. Office: Family Violence Counseling Ctr 1241 Southridge Ct Ste 103 Hurst TX 76053

GIERLASINSKI, KATHY LYNN, accountant; b. Chewelah, Wash., May 21, 1951; d. John Edward and Margaret Irene (Seefeldt) Rail; m. Norman Joseph Gierlasinski, May 23, 1987. BBA, Gonzaga U., 1984. CPA, Wash. Legal sec. Redbook Pub. Co., N.Y.C., 1974-75, Howard Michaelson, Esquire, Spokane, Wash., 1975-76; sec. Burns Internat. Security Svcs., Spokane, 1977-79; sec. to contr. Gonzaga U., Spokane, 1979-81, acctg. asst., 1981-82; staff acct. Martin, Holland & Petersen, CPA's, Yakima, Wash., 1984-87; acct., supr. Strader Hallet & Co., P.S., Bellevue, Wash., 1988-91; acct. Miller & Co., P.S., Woodinville, Wash., 1991-93; pres. Gierlasinski & Assocs., P.S., Bothell, Wash., 1993—; treas. White Pass Ski Patrol, Nat. Ski Patrol Systems, Wash., 1987-90; editor, chmn. audit com. Mt. Spokane Ski Patrol, 1983-84. Mem. AICPA, Am. Soc. Women Accts. (charter, editor 1987), Wash. Soc. CPAs (sec. Sammamish Valley chpt. 1990-92, pres. 1992-93, pres. 1993-94, tax com., govt. affairs com.), Bus. and Profl. Women of Woodinville (treas. 1994—), Northshore C. of C. Republican. Lutheran. Home: 21730 2nd Ave SE Bothell WA 98021-8202

GIES, JANE MARIE, nurse; b. Elyria, Ohio, Mar. 10, 1963; d. Jerome Donald and Marilyn (O'Dor) Scheidler; m. Ronald Bruce Gies, Aug. 17, 1991. BSN summa cum laude, Kent State U., 1985. RN, Calif. RN cardiothoracic ICU Cleve. (Ohio) Clinic Found., 1985-87; RN cardiac surg. ICU Cedars-Sinai Med. Ctr., L.A., 1987-88, RN operating rm., BCLS instr., operating rm. peer instr., 1988—; mock code coord. Outpatient Surgery Ctr., Cedars Sinai Med. Ctr., 1992; presenter in field. Vol. instr. Kid Safe Saturday, Cedars-Sinai Med. Ctr., L.A., 1989, 90. Mem. Alpha Lambda Delta, Sigma Theta Tau. Roman Catholic (eucharistic minister). Home: 2512 Canyon Village Cir San Ramon CA 94583-6104

GIESBRECHT, MARGARET LOUISE, academic administrator; b. Rabbit Lake, Sask., Can., Apr. 18, 1937; came to U.S., 1960; d. Abraham and Helena (Goossen) Freisen; m. Francis Gerhard Giesbrecht, July 29,1960; children: Karen Lynn Giesbrecht Reed, Kathryn Marie. BS in Home Econs., Iowa State U., 1961; BS in Home Econ., U. Manitoba, 1963; MS in Child Devel., Iowa State U., 1963; PhD, U. N.C., 1977. Tchr. grade 2 Kelly (Iowa) Sch., 1962-63; child devel. instr. Iowa State U., Ames, 1963-64; psychology instr. Algonquin C.C., Ottawa, Ont., Can., 1969-70, Peace Coll., Raleigh, N.C., 1976-81; asst. prof. Campbell U., Buies Creek, N.C., 1981-88, from acting chair edn. dept. to dean Sch. Edn., 1988—; mem. N.C. State Dept. Pub. Instrn. evaluation teams, 1985-91, adv. coun. for Leadership Acad., 1992-93, N.C. State Evaluation Com., 1990—. Elder Cary (N.C.) Presbyn. Ch., 1988-91, trustee, 1991—. Recipient disting. vis. scholars grant State N.C., 1988-91, secondary project grant 1990-91. Mem. ASCD, Assn. Tchr. Educators, Nat. Assn. Edn. Young Children. Office: Campbell U Sch Edn 230 Taylor Hall Buies Creek NC 27506

GIESE, LOUISE JULIA, critical care nurse; b. Darby, Pa., Jan. 18, 1951; d. Marcellus Vincent and Louise (Collins) La Fleur; m. E. William Giese Jr., Sept. 9, 1972; children: Todd Andrew, Barton John. Diploma in nursing, Thomas Jefferson U., 1971, BSN, 1989, MSN, 1994. RN, N.J., Pa., Del., N.C., N.J.; cert. provider ACLS and BLS-C, Am. Heart Assn. Staff nurse ob-gyn. unit Fitzgerald-Mercy Hosp., Darby, 1971-72; staff nurse ICU Cooper Hosp., Camden, N.J., 1972-73; office nurse Yater Clinic, Washington, 1973; staff nurse Staff Builders, Balt., 1974-77; staff nurse CCU Howard County Hosp., Columbia, Md., 1974-77; staff nurse orthopaedic-neurol. unit Mt. Sinai Hosp., Balt., 1977; staff nurse ICU/CCU Underwood-Meml. Hosp., Woodbury, N.J., 1977-90; nurse mgr. CCU Newcomb Med. Ctr., Vineland, N.J., 1990-91, nurse mgr. post-ICU unit, 1991-92; staff nurse ICU West Jersey Health System, Voorhees, N.J., 1992—; clin. instr. C.C. Phila., 1994; clin. nurse specialist Med. Ctr. Del., Christiana, 1994—; clin. instr. C.C. of Phila., 1994—; participant Critical Care Nursing Delegation to Russia and Hungary, 1992. Del., People to People Citizen Amb. Program, 1992; vestry Ch. of the Good Shepherd, Pitman, N.J., 1989-92. Mem. AACN (cert., nat. and S.E. Pa. chpt.), Del. State Nurses Assn., N.J. State Nurses Assn. (mem. ednl. preparation com. 1989-91), Mid. Mgrs. So. N.J., Sigma Theta Tau. Episcopalian. Home: 200 Wilson Rd Turnersville NJ 08012 Office: Christiana Hosp PO Box 6001 4755 Ogletown-Stanton Rd Rm 4210 Newark DE 19718

GIFFIN, BARBARA HAINES, education coordinator; b. Mt. Holly, N.J., July 2, 1944; d. Harvey and Loris (Mantell) H.; m. Donald William Giffin, Mar. 25, 1967; children: Sherri Christine, Darrell Wesley. BS, Ind. U. of Pa., 1966; MEd, U. South Fla., 1982. Cert. tchr. Fla., N.J., Pa. Instr. No. Burlington (N.J.) County High Sch., 1966-68, Sterling High Sch., Sommerville, N.J., 1968-71, U. Tampa, Fla., 1975-77; instr., coordinator Pinellas Tech. Edn. Ctr., St. Petersburg, Fla., 1977—; instr., coord. Fire Chief's Assn., 1994—; Adv. bd. Operation Par., Inc., St. Petersburg, 1992-93; exec. bd. Pinellas Adult Vocat. Edn., St. Petersburg, 1991-92; v.p. Bus. Edn. Assn. Pinellas, 1988. Recipient Nat. Recognition award for Exemplary Vocat. Edn. Programs, 1991. Mem. Am. Vocat. Assn., Pinellas Adult Vocat. Edn. Assn. (treas. 1994-95), Shriners Aus., Fire Chiefs Assn. (coord. firefighter apprenticeship program for Pinellas County, SAC co-chmn. 1994). Democrat. Episcopalian. Home: 12338 Capri Cir N Treasure Is FL 33706-4974 Office: Pinellas Tech Edn Ctr 901 34th St S Saint Petersburg FL 33711-2209

GIFFIN, MARGARET ETHEL (PEGGY GIFFIN), management consultant; b. Cleve., Aug. 27, 1949; d. Arch Kenneth and Jeanne (Eggleton) G.; m. Robert Alan Wyman, Aug. 20, 1988; 1 child, Samantha Jean. BA in Psychology, U. Pacific, Stockton, Calif., 1971; MA in Psychology, Calif. State U., Long Beach, 1973; PhD in Quantitative Psychology, U. So. Calif., 1984. Psychometrist Auto Club So. Calif., L.A., 1973-74; cons. Psychol. Svcs., Inc., Glendale, Calif., 1975-76, mgr., 1977-78, dir., 1979-94; rschr. Social Sci. Rsch. Inst., U. So. Calif., L.A., 1981; owner Giffin Consulting Svcs., L.A., 1994—; instr. Calif. State U., Long Beach, 1989-90; mem. tech. adv. com. on testing Calif. Fair Employment and Housing Commn., 1974-80, mem. steering com., 1978-80. Mem. Am. Ednl. Rsch. Assn., Soc. Indsl. Organizational Psychology, Am. Psychol. Assn., Personnel Testing Coun. So. Calif. (pres. 1980, exec. dir. 1982, 88, bd. dirs. 1980-92). Home and Office: 260 S Highland Ave Los Angeles CA 90036-3027

GIFFIN, MARY ELIZABETH, psychiatrist, educator; b. Rochester, Minn., Mar. 30, 1919; d. Herbert Ziegler and Mary Elizabeth (Nace) G. BA, Smith Coll., Northampton, Mass., 1939; MD, Johns Hopkins, 1943; MS, U. Minn., 1948. Diplomate Am. Bd. Psychiatry and Neurology. Cons. in neurology and psychiatry Mayo Clinic, Rochester, 1949-58; med. dir. Josselyn Clinic, Northfield, Ill., 1948-89; pvt. practice psychiatry Northfield, 1989—; mem. faculty Inst. for Psychoanalysis, Chgo., 1963-89. Contbr. numerous articles to profl. jour. Mem. Ill. Psychiat. Soc., Am. Acad. Child Psychiatry. Republican. Mem. Am. Bapt. Ch. Home: 1190 Hamptondale Rd Winnetka IL 60093-1812 Office: 1 Northfield Pla Ste 300 Northfield IL 60093

GIFFORD, CINDA JEAN, educator, educational administrator; b. Aztec, N.Mex., Aug. 3, 1954; d. William Alvin and Allana Lee (McCoy) Lowman; m. Gerald Frederick Gifford, June 26, 1982. BS, Wayland Bapt. Coll., Plainview, Tex., 1976; MS, Utah State U., 1984. Cert. tchr./adminstr., Nev., N.Mex., Tex. Tchr. Tibbits Jr. High Sch., Farmington, N.Mex., 1976-80, Washoe High Sch., Reno, 1985-87; tchr. McQueen High Sch., Reno, 1987-93, coord. alternative edn., 1991—, dean students, 1992—, chmn. dept. alternative svcs. and career edn., 1992—; facilitator, speaker Inst. Day, Washoe County Sch. Dist., Reno, 1990, mem. prin.'s cabinet, 1990—, instr. tchr. insvc., 1993—, mem. supt.'s adv. bd., 1993—, mem. strategic planning com., 1990; mem. Coordinated At-Risk Edn. Adv. Bd., 1991—. Speaker Reno Leadership Conf., 1990; mem. Ptnrs. in Edn., Reno, 1990-92. Named Computer Tchr. of Yr. for No. Nev., 1990; Chpt. II block grantee State of Nev., 1988, 89, math. grantee Washoe County Sch. Dist., 1990, Best Idea '92 grantee 1st Interstate Bank, Reno, 1992. Mem. NAFE, Phi Delta Kappa. Baptist. Home: 3880 Squaw Valley Cir Reno NV 89509-5663 Office: McQueen High Sch 6055 Lancer St Reno NV 89523-1201

GIFFORD, KATHIE LEE, television personality; b. Paris, Aug. 16, 1953; d. Aaron Leon and Joan Epstein; m. Paul Johnson (div.); m. Frank Gifford, Oct. 18, 1986; children: Cody Newton, Cassidy Erin. Student, Oral Roberts U., Tulsa. Gospel singer; singer $100,000 Name That Tune Quiz Show; co-host Morning Show, 1985-88, LIVE with Regis and Kathie Lee, 1988—; author: The Quiet Riot, 1976, I Can't Believe I Said That, 1992; (with Regis Philbin) Cooking With Regis and Kathie Lee, 1993, Entertaining With Regis and Kathie Lee, 1994; marketer clothing collection Kathie Lee for Plaza South; album: Sentimental, 1993, It's Christmas Time, 1993. Office: Live With Regis & Kathie Lee WABC-TV Seven Lincoln Square New York NY 10023

GIFFORD, SUZANNE B., lawyer; b. Detroit, Nov. 5, 1938; d. Louis and Ruth Mildred (Babbitt) Balaze; m. Joseph A. Weiss, Dec. 27, 1975. BA, U. Mich., 1960, LLB, 1963. Atty. Sulmeyer & Kupetz, L.A., 1963-66; dep. city atty. City of Pasadena, Calif., 1966-72; asst. gen. coun. So. Calif. Rapid Transit Dist., L.A., 1972-88, gen. coun., 1988-93; co-gen. coun. Los Angeles County Metro Transit Authority, L.A., 1993-94; vice chair legal affairs com. Am. Pub. Transit Assn., Washington, 1994—. Home: 840 S Grand Ave Pasadena CA 91105

GIFFORD, VIRGINIA SNODGRASS, cataloger, bibliographer; b. Cottonwood, Idaho, June 15, 1936; d. John Howard and Virginia B. (Tibbs) S.; m. Guy A. Gifford, July 29, 1965 (div. Feb. 1973); 1 child, Stephen Jonathan. BA, Cen. Wash. U., 1957, MEd, 1959; MSLS, Cath. U. Am., 1969. Music cataloger Copyright Office, Washington, 1963-69; editor catalog publs. Libr. of Congress, Washington, 1969-73; music libr. Vassar Coll., Poughkeepsie, N.Y., 1973-80, performing arts cataloger copyright office, 1980-83; music cataloger spl. materials cataloging div. Libr. of Congress, Washington, 1983-92, computer files cataloger, 1992-93, music cataloger, 1993—; adj. prof. sch. of libr. and info. sci. Cath. U. Am., 1990—. Author: Music for Oboe, Oboe d'amore, English Horn at the Libr. of Congress, 1983. Mem. Music Libr. Assn. (chmn. N.Y.-Ont. chpt. 1975-77), Internat. Double Reed Soc. Democrat. Methodist. Home: 3801 Connecticut Ave NW # 803 Washington DC 20008-4530 Office: Libr of Congress Madison Building Rm 547 Washington DC 20011

GIFFUNI, CATHE, researcher, writer; b. N.Y.C., July 18, 1949; d. Joseph V. and Flora (Baldini) G. BA in Art History, Hollins Coll., 1970; postgrad., Columbia U., 1971-72. Author: Bessie Head: A Bibliography, 1986, A Bibliography of Louise Arner Boyd, 1986, James Courage: A Checklist of Published Primary and Secondary Sources, 1987, Joseph O'Neill: A Bibliography, 1987, Annie Smith Peck: A Bibliography, 1987, A Bibliography of the Film Scores of Ralph Vaughan Williams, 1988, Clarice Lispector: A Complete English Bibliography, 1988, Laura Z. Hobson: A Bibliography, 1988, Lajos Zilahy: A Bibliography, 1988, A Bibliography of the Mystery Writings of Leonardo Sciascia, 1989, Maurice Gee: A Bibliography, 1990, Witi Ihimaera: A Bibliography, 1990, Zofia Kossak: An English Bibliography, 1990, Iris Origo: A Bibliography, 1990, A Bibliography of the Mystery Writings of Elspeth Huxley, 1991, Joseph Roth: An English Bibliography, 1991, Leo Perutz: An English Biography, 1991, An English Bibliography of Alejo Carpentier, 1992, The Prose of David Malouf: A Bibliography, 1992, An English Bibliography of the Writings of Primo Levi, 1992, Zofia Kossak: An English Bibliography, 1992, A Bibliography of the Writings of Natalia Ginzburg, 1993, Catherine Drinker Bowen: A Bibliography, 1993. Home: 240 E 27th St New York NY 10016-9277

GIGUERE, BRENDA SUE, academic administrator; b. Rochester, Minn., July 18, 1959; d. Ida Mae (Myers) Holland; m. John Jay Bowers, Aug. 31, 1980 (div. 1983); m. John Wayne Giguere, Oct. 13, 1984. BA in Acctg., U. Akron, 1981. Cert. notary, Ohio. Acct., computer specialist, trainer McKinney Inc. (previously Bayless-Kerr & Palm Inc.), Cleve., 1981-86; adminstr. dept. Case Western Res. U., Cleve., 1986—; instr. adult edn. Lakewood (Ohio) Bd. Edn., 1991—, craft-n-flower basketry instr., calligraphy instr. Mem. Strictly Stitchin' Community Project, 1991-92, newsletter co-editor, 1992-94; mem. Cleve. Mus. Natural History. Mem. No. Ohio Atari Helpers (libr. 1991—), Toastmasters (sec.-treas. 1991-92, treas. 1992-93, area 15 gov. 1993-94, tng. com. chaor, v.p. pub., rels. club 7262, asst. divsn. E gov. 1994—, ATM 1994), Smithsonian Instn.

GILB, CORINNE LATHROP, history educator; b. Lethbridge, Alta., Can., Feb. 19, 1925; d. Glen Hutchison and Vera (Passey) Lathrop; m. Tyrell Thompson Gilb, Aug. 19, 1945; children: Lesley Gilb Taplin, Tyra. BA, U. Wash., 1946; MA, U. Calif., Berkeley, 1951, law student, 1950-53; PhD, Harvard U., 1957. History lectr. Mills Coll., Oakland, 1957-61; prof. humanities San Francisco State U., 1964-68; rsch. assoc. U. Calif., Berkeley, 1953-68; prof. history Wayne State U., Detroit, 1968-94, co-dir. Liberal Arts Urban Studies program, 1976-86; dir. planning City of Detroit, 1979-85; spl. cons. Calif. Legislature, 1963, 64; vis. scholar Hoover Instn., Stanford U., fall 1993. Author: Conformity of State to Federal Income Tax, 1964, Hidden Hierarchies, 1966, numerous chpts. in books; contbr. articles to profl. jours. Guggenheim fellow, 1957; grantee Social Sci. Rsch. Coun. Mem. Internat. Soc. Comparative Study of Civilizations (exec. council 1985—), No. Calif. World Affairs Council, various acad. assns. Presbyterian.

GILBERT, DIANE LYNN JEFFERSON, computer and data processing analyst; b. Arlington Heights, Ill., Nov. 23, 1962; d. Robert Wayne and Sally Ann (Wallace) Jefferson; m. David Allen Gilbert, Aug. 6, 1983; children: Jeffrey Robert, Jason David. BS in Edn., Western Ill. U., 1984; MS in Edn., Ill. State U., 1988. Elem. tchr. 6th grade Bloomington (Ill.) Sch. Dist. # 87, 1984-85, elem. tchr. 3d grade, 1985-88; data processing analyst State Farm Ins. Co., Bloomington, 1988—; customer svcs. rep. State Farm Disaster Customer Call Ctr., Bloomington, 1994—. Tchr. Sunday sch. Wesley United Meth. Ch., Bloomington, 1983—; active Northpoint PTA, 1992—; sec., mem. rep. citizens adv. coun. Unit 5 Sch. Dist., Normal, Ill., 1993—. Home: 16 Redstone Ct Bloomington IL 61704 Office: State Farm Ins Co 1 State Farm Plz Bloomington IL 61710

GILBERT, HEATHER CAMPBELL, manufacturing company executive; b. Mt. Vernon, N.Y., Nov. 20, 1944; d. Ronald Ogston and Mary Lodivia (Campbell) G.; BS in Math. (Nat. Merit scholar), Stanford U., 1967; MS in Computer Sci. (NSF fellow), U. Wis., 1969. With Burroughs Corp., 1969-82, sr. mgmt. systems analyst, Detroit, 1975-77, mgr. mgmt. systems activity, Pasadena, Calif., 1977-82; mgr. software product mgmt. Logical Data Mgmt. Inc., Covina, Calif., 1982-83, dir. mktg., 1983, v.p. bus. devel., 1983-84; v.p. profl. services, 1984-85; mgr. software devel. Unisys Corp., Mission Viejo, Calif., 1985—. Mem. Assn. Computing Machinery, Am. Prodn. and Inventory Control Soc., Stanford U. Alumni Assn. (life), Stanford Profl. Women Los Angeles County (pres. 1982-83), Nat. Assn. Female Execs., Town Hall. Republican. Home: 21113 Calle De Paseo Lake Forest CA 92630-7037 Office: Unisys Corp 25725 Jeronimo Rd Mission Viejo CA 92691-2711

GILBERT, JO, psychologist; b. L.A., July 25, 1949; d. Joseph Raymond and Rochelle Rose (Burdman) G.; divorced; 1 child, Branden Christopher Smale. BA in Psychology cum laude, UCLA, 1972; postgrad., U. Houston, 1971-72, William Marsh Rice U., 1972-77; PhD in Clin. Psychology, Calif. Sch. Profl. Psychology, 1980. Lic. psychologist, Calif.; qualified med. evaluator. Psychol. intern, researcher, then counselor Olive St. Bridge, Fresno, Calif., 1978-80; registered psychologist FCEOC Project Pride, Fresno, 1980-82; psychologist Fox, Pick and Assocs., Napa, Calif., 1982-85; pvt. practice Napa, 1985—; ptnr. Napa-Solano Psychotherapy Svcs., 1993—; adj. faculty in forensic psychology Calif. Sch. Profl. Psychology, Berkeley, 1987; faculty U. San Francisco, 1987-88; presenter at profl. confs.; mem. Sacramento County panel ct.-appointed psychologists, Yolo County panel ct.-appointed psychologists, Solano County panel ct.-appointed psychologists. Contbr. articles to profl. publs. Mem. APA, Calif. Psychol. Assn. (assoc. sec. 1994-95), Napa Valley Psychol. Assn. (past pres.), Soc. Personality Assessment. Democrat. Jewish.

GILBERT, JOAN STULMAN, petroleum company executive; b. N.Y.C., May 10, 1934; student Conn. Coll. for Women, 1951-53; m. Phil E. Gilbert, Jr., Oct. 6, 1968; children: Linda Cooper, Dana, Patricia. Br. coord. Vol. Service Bur., Westchester, N.Y., 1970-72; Westchester Lighthouse (pub. relations dir. 1972-76); exec. dir. Westchester Heart Assn., 1976-77; mgr. community rels. Texaco Inc., White Plains, N.Y., 1977—. Bd. dirs. Am. Heart Assn., Coll. Careers, Phoenix Theatre, ARC, Pvt. Industry Coun., Westchester Philharmonic, Choare-Rosemary Hall, United Way of Westchester; chmn. bd. The Street Theater; former trustee Westchester Coun. for the Arts; trustee Teatown Lake Reservation. Recipient awards Girl Scouts, Am. Heart Assn., Am. Diabetes Assn. Mem. Pub. Rels. Soc. Am. (chpt. pres. 1977), Advt. Club (dir.), Women in Comms., Public Issues Coun. of The Conference Bd., Sales and Mktg. Execs. Westchester (former dir.), Advertising Club of Westchester, Westchester County Assn. Home: The Croft Spring Valley Rd Ossining NY 10562-2002 Office: 2000 Westchester Ave White Plains NY 10650-0001

GILBERT, LIANE MARIE, research executive; b. Long Branch, N.J., June 20, 1949; d. Charles Wilson and Edith Doris (Johnson) Case; m. Roger William Gilbert, July 17, 1971; children: David Aaron, Charles Paul. BA in Psychology, Monmouth Coll., West Long Branch, N.J., 1972; MA in Teaching, Trenton State Coll., 1979. Cert. tchr. of handicapped, N.J. Tchr. spl. edn., dir. afternoon program S.E.A.R.C.H., Ocean, N.J., 1972-74; tchr. spl. edn. Jackson (N.J.) Twp. Sch. System, 1974-79; exec. dir. Otologic Edn., Inc., Shrewsbury, N.J., 1980-88; dir. clin. rsch. Nat. Patent Analytical Systems, Inc., Roslyn Heights, N.Y., 1983-86, v.p. rsch., 1986-88; pres. Westerman Rsch. Assocs., Inc., Shrewsbury, N.J., 1988—; participant numerous convs., profl. organs. and spl. interest groups, U.S.A., Israel and The Netherlands, 1974—; software devel. expert to knowledge engr. for Visual Perceptual System, 1984—; v.p. Otologic Edn., Inc., Shrewsbury, 1988—. Co-contbr. articles and chpts. to profl. publs.; U.S. and Can. patentee computer-aided drug-abuse detection. Fundraiser Am. Heart Assn., 1991; active MADD; activist Nat. Audubon Soc. Mem. Internat. Regulatory Affairs Profls. Soc., Nat. Graphic Soc., Assn. Clin. Pharmacologists, Regulatory Affairs Profls. Soc., Monmouth County Assn. Children with Learning Disabilities, Psi Chi, Sigma Xi. Office: Westerman Rsch Assocs Inc 499 Broad St Shrewsbury NJ 07702-4091

GILBERT, MELISSA, actress; b. Los Angeles, May 8, 1964; d. Paul and Barbara (Crane) G.; m. Bo Brinkman (div.); 1 son, Dakota; m. Bruce Boxleitner, Jan. 1, 1995. Student, U. So. Calif. Actress: (TV movies) Little House on the Prairie, 1974, Christmas Miracle in Caulfield, U.S.A., 1977, The Miracle Worker, 1979, The Diary of Anne Frank, 1980, Splendor in the Grass, 1981, Little House: Look Back to Yesterday, 1983, Choices of the Heart, 1983, Little House: Bless All the Dear Children, 1984, Family Secrets, 1984, Little House: The Last Farewell, 1984, Choices, 1986, Penalty Phase, 1986, Family Secrets, Killer Instincts, Without Her Consent, Forbidden Nights, 1990, Blood Vows: The Story of a Mafia Wife, Joshua's Heart, 1990, Donor, The Lookalike, 1990, , Conspiracy of Silence: The Shari Karney Story, 1992, With Hostile Intent, 1993, Shattered Trust, 1993, House of Secrets, 1993, Dying to Remember, 1993, Cries From the Heart, 1994, Against Her Will: The Carrie Black Story, 1994; (TV series) Little House on the Prairie, 1974-82, Little House: A New Beginning, 1983, Stand By Your Man, 1992, Sweet Justice, 1994— (TV spls.) Battle of the Network Stars, 1978, 79, 81, 82, Celebrity Challenge of the Sexes, 1980, Circus Lions, Tigers and Melissa, Too, 1977, Dean Martin Celebrity Roast, 1984, (stage prodns.) Night of 100 Stars, 1982, The Glass Menagerie, 1985, A Shayna Maidel, 1987 (Outer Critics Circle Award), (feature films) Nutcracker Fantasy, 1979, Sylvester, 1985, Ice House, 1989. Office: William Morris Agy 151 El Camino Beverly Hills CA 90212*

GILBERT, NANCY LOUISE, librarian; b. Norfolk, Va., Nov. 3, 1938; d. Oscar Linwood Jr. and Mary Margaret (Nicholls) Gilbert. BA, Greensboro Coll., 1961; MLS, U. North Carolina, 1968. Libr. Va. Beach (Va.) Pub. Libr., 1968, U.S. Army, Worms, Crailsheim and Mannheim, Fed. Republic Germany, 1968-74, Pentagon Libr., Washington, 1974-80, U.S. Army Mil. History Inst., Carlisle Barracks, Pa., 1980—. Mem. ALA, Spl. Librs. Assn., Mid-Atlantic Region Archives Conf.

GILBERT, RUTH ANN, library media specialist; b. Hackensack, N.J., Feb. 11, 1939; d. Barnet and Blanche (Starr) Shapiro; m. Stanley Robert Gilbert, June 19, 1960; children: Judith, David. BA, Trenton State Coll., 1960; postgrad., Kean Coll., Union, N.J., 1965, U. Vt., 1976, Syracuse (N.Y.) U., 1978. Permanent cert. N.Y. State Dept. Edn. Libr. media specialist elem. sch., Denville, N.J., 1965-68; reference libr. Morris County C.C., Randolph, N.J., 1969-72; libr. media specialist Salem (N.Y.) Ctrl. Sch., 1974—; profl. storyteller, N.Y., Vt., Mass., Mexico, 1984—; mem. adv. coun. Sch. Libr. System, Warren, Wash., Hamilton Essex, N.Y., 1987; presentor, workshop leader N.Y. State Reading Coun., N.Y. Libr. Assn., Lake Placid, Kiamesha Lake, N.Y., 1985, 87, 88, 90. Recipient Excellence in Pub. award Josten's Yearbook Co., 1985. Mem. NOW, PTA, Nat. Assn. Preservation and Perpetration of Storytelling, Nat. Storytelling Assn., N.Y. Libr. Assn., N.Y. State United Tchrs. (pres. 1991-94). Home: PO Box 112 West Rupert VT 05776-0112 Office: Salem Ctrl Sch E Broadway Salem NY 12865

GILBERT, RUTH ELIZABETH, inpatient obstetrics nurse; b. Damariscotta, Maine, Aug. 25, 1950; d. Harry Elwood and Dorothy May (Richards) Percival; m. Raymond Scott Gilbert, Nov. 16, 1974. BS in Edn., Portland Gorham U. of Maine, 1973; A. in Nursing, U. Maine, Augusta, 1975. RNC inpatient obstetrics; cert. BLS, neonatal resuscitation provider, nurses aide. Nurse aide Miles Hosp., Damariscotta, 1973-75, RN, 1975-77; RN Parkview Meml. Hosp., Brunswick, Maine, 1976—. Health officer Town of Alna, 1975-79. Mem. Wiscasset Yacht Club (sec. 1992-93, membership com. chmn. 1993-94, rear comdr. 1994-95).

GILBERT, SHANDEL SUE, reading educator, educational director; b. Wheeling, W.Va., Apr. 20, 1941; d. Meyer and Gertrude (Viess) Spiro; m. Sheldon Ian Gilbert, Dec. 23, 1967; children: John Harrison, Rebecca Jo. BA, Brandeis U., 1962; MEd, U. Pitts., 1964, reading specialist, 1992.

Editorial asst. Jewish Chronicle, Pitts., 1962-63; tchr. Pitts. Pub. Schs., 1965-67, Long Lots Jr. High Sch., Westport, Conn., 1964-65; instr. English C.C. Beaver County, Monaca, Pa., 1968-70; dir. Readers and Writers Workshop Beaver Falls, Pa., 1983-92, Pitts., 1993—; acad. counselor Academic Support Svcs. for Student Athletes, U. Pitts., 1992—, reading coord., 1993—; columnist News-Tribune, Beaver Falls, 1978-79. Assoc. editor: BEV and BEV N.Y., summer 1965; writer, pub.: (lang. arts newsletter) Letterbug, 1985-93. Pres. Beaver Valley Hadassah, 1975-77; co-chmn. State of Israel Bonds, Beaver Falls, 1976; bd. dirs. Merrick Free Art Gallery, 1986-91. Recipient Disting. Achievement award Ednl. Press Assn. Am., 1989. Mem. Children's Book Writers, Internat. Reading Assn. Home: 5600 Munhall Rd # 205 Pittsburgh PA 15217 Office: U Pitts Acad Support Svc Athletic Bldg 520 Pittsburgh PA 15213

GILBERT, SHIRLEY BERLIN, real estate developer, business owner; b. N.Y.C., Mar. 22, 1922; d. Philip and Clara (Donnenfeld) Rabach; m. Emanuel N. Berlin, 1945 (dec. 1961); 1 child, Jeffrey; m. Philip Gilbert. Asst. mgr. Winkelman's, Saginaw, Mich., 1954-59; co-owner Berlin Furniture and Appliances, Saginaw, 1959-61, owner, 1961-79; real estate developer various properties, 1964—; founder Berlin Realty, 1964. Campaign supporter Jeff Berlin for Rep. Candidate for Congress, 8th Dist., Mich.; vol. Juvenile Diabetes Found.; v.p., bd. dirs. Fla. Ctrl. region Hadassah, 1994, v.p. fundraising Collier County chpt., 1994, pres. Collier County chpt., 1989-91; mem. Sisterhood of Temple Shalom of Naples, chair fundraising major. event, 1987-88, blue book directory solicitor of ads, 1993-94. Named Outstanding Businesswoman of Yr., Altrusa Clubs Am., 1965. Home: PH # 1 4551 Gulf Shore Blvd N Naples FL 33940

GILBERT, SUZANNE HARRIS, advertising executive; b. Chgo., Mar. 8, 1948; d. Lawrence W. and Dorothea (Wilde) Harris; children: Kerry, Elizabeth, Gregory. B.S., Marquette U., 1965; MBA, U. Chgo., 1985. Fin. analyst Leo Burnett Co., Chgo.; sr. v.p. fin. adminstrn., sec.-treas. Clinton E. Frank Inc., Chgo., 1975-85; with Lintas Campbell-Ewald Co., Detroit, 1985—; formerly group sr. v.p., Lintas Campbell-Ewald, Warren, Mich., exec. v.p., chief fin. and adminstrv. officer, 1990—. Mem. Am. Assn. Advertising Agys. (fiscal control com.), Econ. Club Detroit, Fin. Execs. Inst., Better Bus. Bur. Office: Lintas Campbell Ewald 30400 Van Dyke Ave Warren MI 48093-2316

GILBERT BRYAN, SUSAN DEE, advertising and marketing executive; b. Miami, Nov. 16, 1951; d. Lawrence and Ruth (Stein) G.; 1 child, Vanessa Gilbert Bryan. BA in Edn., U. Fla., 1973. Dir. advt. and pub. relations Atlanta Internat. Film Festival, 1973-74; sales rep. RKO Radio Reps., Atlanta, 1974-75; dir. advt. ABC Record and Tape Sales Inc., Atlanta, 1975-76; account exec. Gerald Rafshoon Advt., Atlanta, 1976-77, Beber Silverstein and Ptnrs. Advt., Miami, 1977-78; pres., owner Susan Gilbert & Co., Inc., South Miami, Fla., 1979-91; sr. v.p., dir. mktg. Sunbank Miami, Fla., 1991-94; founder Susan Gilbert Inc., 1994—. Chmn. publicity Ronald McDonald House S.Fla., 1980—, bd. trustees, 1982—; mem. Dade county cabinet United Way, bd. dirs., 1989-93, bd. trustees, 1990—; pub. relations rep. Haven Sch. Mentally Handicapped, Miami, 1983-84; bd. trustees Bapt. Hosp., Miami, 1988—, Coconut Grove Playhouse, 1993—, Fla. Internat. U.; mem. exec. com. Fla. Commn. Status on Women, 1991—. Named Non-stop Achiever Germaine Monteil Cosmetics, 1985, Regional Honor Roll Women Advt. Adweek Mag., 1986. Mem. Advt. Fedn. Greater Miami (chmn. bd. dirs. 1985-86, trustee, Silver medal 1987, pres. 1984-85, cert. appreciation 1983-86), Am. Advt. Fedn. (fourth dist., sec. 1987-88, 3d lt. gov. 1988-89, 2nd lt. gov. 1989-90, 1st gov. 1990-91, gov.-elect 1991-92, gov. 1992-93, John Cummins Legis. award 1993), Greater Miami C. of C. (trustee), Coral Gables C. of C., 200 Soc. Profl. Women (chmn. publicity 1982—, exec. com. 1988), U. Fla. Alumni Assn. Office: Susan Gilbert Inc 801 Brickell Ave Ste 931 Miami FL 33131

GILBORNE, JEAN ELIZABETH, retired school educator, librarian; b. Bonfield, Ill., June 21, 1910; d. John V. and Anna Belle (Stroud) G. BEd, Ill. State U., 1937; M in English, U. Ill., 1944, MLS, 1951. Cert. secondary tchr.; libr. cert. Tchr. various rural schs., Kankakee County, Ill., 1928-38, Sheridan (Ill.) High Sch., 1938-39, Fillmore (Ill.) High Sch., 1939-40, Ashmore (Ill.) High Sch., 1940-42, Westfield (Ill.) U., 1942-44, Cerro Gordo (Ill.) High Sch., 1944-50; libr. Geneseo (Ill.) Unit Dist., 1951-75, retr., 1975. Mem. Cambridge Rebekah Lodge #517 (noble grand 1981—), Columbian Club, Ill. Retired Tchrs. (Henry-Stark Unit pres. 1990-91), Geneseo Bus. and Profl. Club (pres. 1959-61, 74-76), Gamma Omicron, Beta Sigma Phi, Beta Phi Mu. Republican. Methodist. Home: 607 S Center St # B Geneseo IL 61254-1678

GILCHRIST, ELLEN LOUISE, writer; b. Vicksburg, Miss., Feb. 20, 1935; d. William Garth and Aurora (Alford) G.; children—Marshall Peteet Walker, Jr., Garth Gilchrist Walker, Pierre Gautier Walker. BA in Philosophy, Millsaps Coll., 1967; postgrad., U. Ark., 1976; LittD (hon.), Millsaps Coll., 1987; LHD (hon.), U. So. Ill., 1991. Freelance writer, journalist; commentator, morning edit. of news Nat. Pub. Radio, Washington, 1984, 85. Author: The Land Surveyor's Daughter, 1979, In The Land of Dreamy Dreams, 1981, The Annunciation (Book of Month Club alternate in U.S. and Sweden), 1983, Victory Over Japan (Am. Book award 1984), 1984, Drunk With Love, 1986, Falling Through Space, 1987, The Anna Papers, 1988, Light Can Be Both Wave and Particle, 1989, I Cannot Get You Close Enough, 1990 (Miss. Inst. Arts and Letters award 1990, fiction award Miss. Libr. Assn. 1990), Net of Jewels, 1992, Starcarbon, 1994, Anabasis, A Journey to the Interior, 1994; (poems) Riding Out the Tropical Depression; contbr. short stories poems to literary publs. Recipient Poetry award U. Ark., 1976, Craft in Poetry award N.Y. Quar., 1978, Fiction award The Prairie Schooner, 1981, Poetry award Miss. Arts Festival, 1968, Saxifrage award, 1983, Fiction award Miss. Acad. Arts and Sci., 1982, 85, Am. Book award Victory Over Japan, 1984, J. William Fulbright prize U. Ark., 1985, Lit. award Miss. Inst. Arts and Letters, 1985, 90, 91; 2 Pushcart prizes; grantee NEA, 1979. Mem. Author's Guild.

GILDEA, KIMBERLY ANN, stockbroker; b. Altoona, Pa., July 22, 1961; d. Faber Charles and Joyce Ann (Bradley) Weakland. BS in Corp. Fin., W.Va. U., 1983; MS in Fin. Planning, Duquesne U., 1994. Cert. fin. planner. Stockbroker Anchor Fin. Svcs., Altoona, 1984-88, Kidder Peabody & Co., Altoona, 1988—; mem. estate planning coun. Kidder Peabody & Co., Altoona, 1992—. Bd. mem. Young Rep. Com., Altoona. Fellow Internat. Assn. Fin. Planners; mem. Inst. Managerial Accts. (bd. mem., membership com.), Rotary. Home: PO Box 2219 Altoona PA 16603 Office: Kidder Peabody 1331 12th Ave Altoona PA 16603

GILDENBLATT, ROSLYN WARSHOFSKY, nursing administrator; b. N.Y.C., Aug. 2, 1925; d. Isadore and Ida (Rosen) Warshofsky; m. Jule Gildenblatt, May 29, 1949; children: Stuart Alan, Daryl Lee, Nancy Gildenblatt Kahn. Diploma, RN, Jewish Hosp. Cin., 1947; BS in Psychology cum laude, Xavier U., 1970, MEd, 1972; postgrad., U. Cin., 1973, 74, 75. RN, Ohio. Supr. surg. areas The Jewish Hosp., Cin., 1961-68, asst. dir. nursing svc., 1968-78; dir. patient care Bethesda Hosp., Cin., 1979-80; supr. nursing svc. phys. therapy and respiratory therapy EPP Meml. Hosp., Cin., 1980-87, acting dir. nursing svc. phys. therapy & respiratory therapy, 1987-88; ret., 1988; vol. nurse ARC. Bd. dirs., sec. Jewish Nat. Fund, Cin., 1987—; bd. dirs., donor chair, Na' Amat U.S.A., Cin., 1990—, fundraising chair, 1990-93, donor chair, 1990—, pres., 1994, 95. Mem. ANA, NLN, Ohio Nurses Assn., Hadassah (life), Isaac M. Wise Temple Sisterhood (life). Jewish. Home: 11 Woodcreek Dr Blue Ash OH 45241

GILDOW, JANE ANN, secondary school educator, artist; b. Peoria, Ill., Dec. 14, 1942; d. Paul Frederick Sharpe and Gertrude Elizabeth (Hogg) Luce; m. Joseph William Gildow, June 22, 1968. BS, Ohio State U., 1965. Registered tchr., cert. K-12. Art tchr. grades 10-12 Kettering (Ohio) City Schs., 1965-68; art tchr. grades 1-6 Stow (Ohio) Pub. Schs., 1968-69; art tchr. grades 7-12 Mogadore (Ohio) Local Schs., 1969-76; art tchr. grades 6-12 Covington (Ohio) Exempted Village Schs., 1977-85, art tchr. grades 9-12, 1985—; seminar instr. Discover Art!, San Diego, 1994. Colored-pencil artist. Recipient 1st place award Masters of Colored Pencil Nat. Competition, 1993, others; Jennings scholar, 1975. Mem. Colored Pencil Soc. Am. (Eberhard Faber award 1993), Kappa Kappa Gamma. Republican. Home: 905 Copperfield Ln Tipp City OH 45371

GILE, MARY STUART, educational executive; b. Montreal, Que., Can., Mar. 24, 1936; d. William Gillies and Hazel Irene (Stuart) Sinclair; m. Robert Hall Gile, Mar. 29, 1974; children—D. Christopher, Julia Mary, John, Robertson Sinclair. BS, McGill U., 1957; MEd, U. N.H., 1971; EdD, Vanderbilt U., 1982. Specialist phys. edn. Protestant Sch. Bd. Greater Montreal, 1957-64, kindergarten tchr. White Mountains Sch. Bd., Littleton, N.H., 1965-67; dir. Open Door Kindergarten, Salem, N.H., 1967-69; coord. State Follow Through, State of N.H., 1969-80, N.H. Right to Read, 1973-74, U.S. Sec.'s Initiative in Excellence chpt. 1 Edn. Consol. and Improvement Act, 1983-84; sr. cons. edn. N.H. State Dept. Edn., Concord, 1969-85; v.p. edn. and devel. Acad. Applied Sci., Concord, 1985-90; prof., dept. head early childhood edn. N.H. Tech. Inst., Concord, 1990—; state dept. staff assoc. to U. N.H., Durham, 1970-74; mem. Gov.'s Task Force on Sexual Harassment, Concord, 1981-83; chair N.H. Trust Fund for Prevention of Child Abuse and Neglect, 1986-94, Commr.'s Com. on Alt. Work Schedules, Concord, 1982-84, gov. appt. state child abuse neglect prevention leadership team; commr.'s rep. State Day Care Adv. Com., Concord, 1984-85; commn. rep. N.H. State Held Care Adv. Com., 1994—. Contbr. articles to profl. jours. Pres. Concord Parents and Children, 1977-82; chmn. Citizens Adv. Bd. to Community Devel., 1978-82; chair Edn. Leadership Concord, 1993-94, chair selection com., 1994—; bd. govs. Merrimack County United Way, 1983-88; pres. N.H. Assn. for Mental Health, 1984-86. Recipient Appreciation cert. Maine Dept. Edn., 1984, cert. outstanding achievement N.H. State Bd. Edn., 1985, Imperial Oil Ltd. scholar, 1953; U. N.H. early childhood fellow, 1969; recipient Leo J. Rubin award United Way Merrimack County, 1993. Mem. N.H. Assn. for Edn. Young Children, Phi Delta Kappa. Congregationalist. Avocations: skiing, music, theater, hiking.

GILES, ANNE DIENER, flutist; b. Rochester, N.Y., Oct. 13, 1948; d. Frederick William and Alma Mary (Bastian) Diener; m. Allen Giles, Sept. 26, 1970; 1 child, Katherine Anne. BS, Juilliard Sch., 1970, MS, 1971. Prin. flutist L.A. Philharm. Orch., 1971—; tchr. of flute U. So. Calif., other univs., colls. Recording Music for Flute and Keyboard, Crystal Records, 1975; numerous recordings and performances as soloist with L.A. Philharm. Orch. and other orchs. Recipient Bronze medal Competition Internat., Geneva, Switzerland, 1973. Mem. Nat. Flute Assn. Office: L A Philharm Orch 135 N Grand Ave Los Angeles CA 90012-3013*

GILES, JEAN HALL, retired corporate executive; b. Dallas, Mar. 30, 1908; d. C. D. and Ida (McIntyre) Overton; m. Alonzo Russell Hall, II, Jan. 23, 1923 (dec.); children: Marjorie Hodges, Alonzo Russell III; m. Harry E. Giles, Apr. 24, 1928 (div. 1937); 1 child, Janice Ruth; 1 adopted child, Marjean Giles. Grad. Hamilton State U., PhD (hon.), 1973. comdg. officer S.W. Los Angeles Women's Ambulance and Def. Corps., 1941-43; maj., nat. exec. officer Women's Ambulance and Def. Corps, 1944-45; capt., dir. field ops. Communications Corps of the U.S. Nat. Staff, 1951-52; dir. Recipe of the Month Club. Active Children's Hosp. Benefit, 1946; coord. War Chest Motor Corps, 1943-44; dir. Los Angeles Area War Chest Vol. Corps and Motor Corps, 1945-46; realtor Los Angeles Real Estate Exchange, 1948—, now ret.; also partner Tech. Contractors, Los Angeles. Bd. dirs. Tchr. Remembrance Day Found. Inc. Mem. Los Angeles C. of C. (women's div.), A.I.M., Los Angeles Art Assn., Hist. Soc. So. Calif., Opera Guild So. Calif., Assistance League So. Calif., Needlework Guild Am. (sect. pres. Los Angeles), First Century Families Calif., Internat. Platform Assn. Clubs: Athletic; Town Hall, The Garden (Los Angles); Pacific Coast. Home: 616 Magnolia Ave Long Beach CA 90802-1243

GILES, MELVA THERESA, nursing educator; b. Balt.; 1 child, Meya Elizabeth. AA in Nursing, Catonsville (Md.) Community, 1970; BSN, Calif. State U., L.A., 1981; MSN, Calif. State U., Dominguez Hills, 1988; EdD, Pepperdine U., 1993. RN, Calif. Guest lectr. Rsch. Edn. Inst. UCLA; DON and in-svc. edn. CompCare Corp.; clin. nurse specialist, educator County of L.A.; assoc. prof. nursing L.A. Pierce Coll.; lectr. Calif. State U., Dominguez Hills Statewide Grad. Sch. Nursing. Fellow Nightingale Soc.; mem. Calif. Nurses Assn., Coun. Black Nurses, Future Soc., Assn. Pan-African Doctoral Scholars Inc., Phi Delta Kappa, Sigma Theta Tau, Chi Eta Phi (Delta chpt.).

GILES, SUSAN M., medical/surgical nurse; b. Inglewood, Calif., Mar. 28, 1965; d. Michael Paul and JoAnn Patricia (Margan) Stash.; m. Sept. 7, 1991. BSN, Westminster Coll., Salt Lake City, 1987. RN, Calif.; cert. med.-surg. Staff nurse gen. surg. unit St. Joseph Hosp., Orange, Calif., 1987-91; staff nurse gen. med. surg. unit Castle Med. Ctr., Kailua, Hawaii, 1992-94; staff nurse renal/pulmonary unit Mary Washington Hosp., Fredericksburg, Va., 1994—. Mem. ANA, Sigma Theta Tau.

GILFOYLE, NATHALIE FLOYD PRESTON, lawyer; b. Lynchburg, Va., May 4, 1949; d. Robert Edmund and Dorothea Henry (Ward) Gilfoyle; m. Christopher Y.W. Ma, Sept. 9, 1978; children: Olivia Otey, Rohan James. B.A., Hollins Coll., Roanoke, Va., 1971; J.D., U. Va., Charlottesville, 1974. Bar: Mass. 1974, D.C. 1977. Staff counsel Rate Setting Commn., Boston, 1974-76; ptnr. Peabody, Lambert & Meyers, Washington, 1976-84; ptnr. McDermott, Will and Emery, 1984—; bd. dirs. Washington Lawyers Com. Civil Rights Under Law, Washington, 1982—; participating counsel Vol. Lawyers for Arts, Boston, 1974-76, Washington, 1978—. Bd. dirs. ACLU Nat. Capital Area, Washington, 1980-83, Filmore Early Learning Ctr., 1977-81, St. Columba's Nursery Sch., 1992—, D.C. Bar Atty. Client Arbitration Bd. Mem. ABA, D.C. Bar Assn., Mass. Bar Assn., Women's Bar Assn. Episcopalian. Office: McDermott Will & Emery 1850 K St NW Washington DC 20006-2213

GILFOYLE, PHYLLIS JANE, human resources executive; b. Boston; d. J. Mark and Doris Jeanette (McGowan) Sherwood; children: Jennifer Freedman, Nancy White, Sandra Kutchins, Richard, Mark. BA, U. Chgo., MA, MLS, PhD. Chief libr. Bd. Libr. Dirs., Country Club Hills, Ill., 1964-71; libr. Blue Cross-Blue Shield, Chgo., 1971-76; mgr. regional pers. Marsh & McLennan, Inc., Chgo., 1976-79; asst. v.p. compensation and benefits Marsh & McLennan, Inc., N.Y.C., 1979-85; sr. v.p. human resources FPC Assocs., Chgo., 1985—; mgr. human resources The Midland Fin. Cos., Chgo., 1986—; cons. Forlty Plus, Chgo., 1985-90, Female Small Bus Owners, Chgo., 1985—, Ind. Labor Attys., Chgo., 1985—, Bus. and Profl. Women's Assn., 1986—, non-profit arts orgns. Contbr. articles to profl. jours. Mem. Bd. Edn. Dist. 160, Ill., 1968-71; bd. dirs. Suburban Libr. System, Ill., 1966-72; first v.p. Forty Plus, Chgo., 1987-89, bd. dirs., 1995; active Old Town Sch. of Folk Music, 1987—, Arts and Bus. Coun., Chgo., 1993—; bus. vol. for the arts, 1994—. Recipient State Civic Leader State of Ill., 1970. Mem. AAUW, NAFE, LWV (chair libr. unit 1986—), Am. Compensation Assn., Am. Soc. Pers. Adminstrs., Soc. Human Resource Profls. (policy and practice com. 1987—), Ill. Libr. Assn. (Freedom of Speech and Press award 1971), Ill. C. of C. (Health Care Reform com. 1994), Bus. and Profl. Women of Chgo. (chair network 1987—, pub. spkr., seminar condr.), Chgo. Compensation Assn. Mem. Soc. of Friends. Home: 1642 E 56th St Apt 517 Chicago IL 60637-1973

GILK, N. SUE, mental health counselor; b. Greeneville, Tenn., June 25, 1953; d. Carl and Annie B. (Powers) Bremson; m. Joel Martin Gilk, Oct. 9, 1983. Student, East Tenn State U., 1972-73; BA in English, So. Coll., Collegedale, Tenn., 1975; MA in Counseling, Andrews U., 1981. Lic. profl. clin. counselor, Ohio. Crisis intake counselor Riverwood Community Mental Health, St. Joseph, Mich., 1978-82; med. social worker Mercy-Meml. Med. Ctr., St. Joseph, 1982-85; pvt. practice St. Joseph, 1982-86; co-founder, sr. counselor Solomon Ctr. Counseling Svcs., Marion, Ohio, 1987—; trainer Personal Empowerment and Assertiveness Workshops, St. Joseph, Marion, 1982—; cons. Mercy-Meml. Med. Ctr., 1991, Turning Point Domestic Violence Shelter, Marion, 1993; presenter, speaker in field. Mem. adv. bd. Am. Cancer Soc., St. Joseph, 1985-86; mem. scholarship com. Marion Erie Credit Union, 1990-93. Recipient Meritorious Svc. award Youth Svc. Bur., 1978. Mem. Am. Counseling Assn., Assn. for Spiritual, Ethical and Religious Values in Counseling, Profl. Counselors' Network. Office: The Solomon Ctr Counseling Svcs 698 E Center St Marion OH 43302-4259

GILL, CAROLE O'BRIEN, family therapist; b. Providence, R.I., Apr. 7, 1946; d. Charles Warren and Angelina (Carcieri) O'Brien; m. Frank Ralston Gill, Oct. 17, 1964, (div. 1975); children: Michael Patrick, Peter Ralston. BA in Edn., U. R.I., 1978, BA in Psychology, 1984, MS in Marriage and Family Therapy, 1986. Cert. tchr.; cert. student assistance counselor; cert. prin. counselor; lic. marriage and family therapist. Tchr. East Greenwich Sch. System, R.I., 1978-79; counselor U. R.I., Providence, 1984; clin. asst., therapist Family Therapy Clinic, Kingston, R.I., 1984-86, family therapist, East Greenwich Ptnrs. in Psychotherapy, 1986-88, Children's Friend and Svc., 1988-90; student assistance counselor CODAC, 1990—; pvt. practice, East Greenwich, 1988—; supr. student-interns U. R.I., 1989-91; vol. Hotline/Sympatico, Wakefield, R.I., 1984; coord. Women's Connection U. R.I., 1984; co-facilitator women's abuse group Women's Resource Ctr., Wakefield, R.I., 1985-86. Mem. Friends of East Greenwich Pub. Libr., 1981—, R.I. Chpt. Nat. Com. for Prevention of Child Abuse. Mem. AAUW, Am. Assn. Female Execs., R.I. Marriage and Family Assn. (v.p. 1988-90, pres. student assoc. orgn. 1987-88), Am. Assn. Marriage and Family Therapy, Am. Psychol. Assn., New Eng. Psychol. Assn., R.I. Psychol. Assn. Avocations: archeology, anthropology, photography, needlework, music. Office: CODAC 1052 Park Ave Cranston RI 02910

GILL, DIANE LOUISE, psychology educator, university official; b. Watertown, N.Y., Nov. 7, 1948; d. George R. and Betty J. (Reynolds) G. BS in Edn., SUNY, Cortland, N.Y., 1970; MS, U. Ill., 1974, PhD, 1976. Tchr. Greece Athena High Sch., Rochester, N.Y., 1970-72; asst. prof. U. Waterloo, Ont., Can., 1976-78; asst. prof. U. Iowa, Iowa City, 1979-81, assoc. prof., 1981-86; assoc. prof. sport & exercise psychology U. N.C., Greensboro, 1987-89; prof. U. N.C., Greenboro, 1989—; assoc. dean U. N.C., Greensboro, 1992—. Author: (book) Psychological Dynamics of Sports, 1986; editor Jour. of Sport and Exercise Psychology, 1985-90; editorial bd. Jour. of Applied Sport Psychology, 1988—; contbr. articles to profl. jours. Fellow AAHPERD (rsch. consortium pres. 1987-89), APA, Am. Psychol. Soc., Assn. for Advancement of Applied Sport Psychology, Am. Acad. Kinesiology and Phys. Edn.; mem. N.Am. Soc. for Psychology of Sport and Phys. Activity (pres. 1988-91). Democrat. Office: U NC Dept Exercise and Sport Sci Greensboro NC 27412

GILL, E. ANN, lawyer; b. Elyria, Ohio, Aug. 31, 1951; d. Richard Henry and Laura (Beeler) G.; m. Robert William Hempel, Aug. 4, 1973; children: Richard, Peter, Mary. AB, Barnard Coll., 1972; JD, Columbia U., 1976. Bar: N.Y. 1977, U.S. Supreme Ct. 1982. Assoc. Mudge, Rose, Guthrie & Alexander, N.Y.C., 1976-77; assoc. Dewey Ballantine, N.Y.C., 1977-84, ptnr., 1985—. Mem. ABA, N.Y. State Bar Assn., Nat. Assn. Bond Lawyers. Home: 255 W 90th St New York NY 10024-1109 Office: Dewey Ballantine 1301 Ave Of The Americas New York NY 10019-6022

GILL, EVALYN PIERPOINT, editor, publisher; b. Boulder, Colo.; d. Walter Lawrence and Lou Octavia Pierpoint; student Lindenwood Coll., B.A., U. Colo.; postgrad. U. Nebr., U. Alaska, M.A., Cen. Mich. U., 1968; m. John Glanville Gill; children: Susan Pierpoint, Mary Louise Glanville. Lectr. humanities Saginaw Valley State Coll., University Center, Mich., 1968-72; mem. English faculty U. N.C., Greensboro, 1973-74; editor Internat. Poetry Rev., Greensboro, 1975-92; pres. TransVerse Press, Greensboro, 1981—. Bd. dirs. Eastern Music Festival, Greensboro, 1981—, Greensboro Symphony, 1982—, Greensboro Opera Co., 1982—, Weatherspoon Assn.; chmn. O. Henry Festival, 1985, 95. Mem. Am. Lit. Translators Assn., MLA, N.C. Poetry Soc., Phi Beta Kappa. Author: Poetry By French Women 1930-1980, 1980, Dialogue, 1985, Southeast of Here: Northwest of Now, 1986; editor: O. Henry Festival Stories, 1985, 87, Women of the Piedmont Triad: Poetry and Prose, 1989, Edge of Our World, 1990; contbr. poetry to numerous mags. Home: 2900 Turner Grove Dr N Greensboro NC 27455-1977

GILL, JANE PITTENGER, personnel management consultant, legal administrator; b. Phila., Dec. 16, 1932; d. Nicholas Otto and Cornelia (Chapman) P.; m. Stanley Jensen Gill, June 7, 1952 (dec. June 1991); children: Elizabeth Jensen, Stanley Chapman. BS in Edn., U. Ill., 1954; MA in Counseling, U. Colo., 1975. Staff dir. Boulder (Colo.) County Legal Svcs., 1975-77; legis. and program dir. Colo. Coaliton of Legal Svcs., Denver, 1977-81; dir. legal svcs. Colo. Bar Assn., Denver, 1981-87; cons., pres. Jane P. Gill & Assocs., Boulder, 1987—; mem., sec. bd. Colo. Lawyers Trust Account Found., 1983-89; mem. bd. Colo. Jud. Inst., 1989; mem. Nat. Legal Aid and Defender Program, 1975-92. Mem. Boulder Human Rels. Commn., 1992—, chmn., 1993, 94. Recipient Jacob Schaetzle award Colo. Bar Assn., 1989. Home and Office: Jane P Gill & Assocs 970 Grant Pl Boulder CO 80302

GILL, MARGARET GASKINS, lawyer; b. St. Louis, Mar. 2, 1940; d. Richard Williams and Margaret (Cambage) Gaskins; m. Stephen Paschall Gill, Dec. 21, 1961; children: Elizabeth, Richard. BA, Wellesley Coll., 1962; JD, U. Calif., Berkeley, 1965. Bar: Calif. 1966. Assoc. Pillsbury, Madison & Sutro, San Francisco, 1966-72, ptnr., 1973-94, mem. mgmt. com., 1973-94, head corp. securities group, mem. assoc., rev. com., 1981-91, chair assoc., rev. com., 1988-91; sr. v.p. legal, external affairs & sec. AirTouch Communications, San Francisco, 1994—; referee Calif. State Bar Ct., 1979-82. Mem. steering com. Trinity Episcopal Ch., Menlo Park, Calif., 1980-82, com. to revise constitution, Diocese Calif., 1981-82; trustee St. Luke's Hosp. Found., San Francisco, 1983-93; mem. adv. coun. Ch. div. Sch. of the Pacific, 1986; bd. dirs. Episcopal Diocese Calif., 1989—; trustee San Francisco Ballet, 1991—; bd. dirs., gen. counsel United Way Bay Area, San Francisco, 1993-94. Fellow Am. Bar Found.; mem. ABA (spl. com. on internat. practice 1979-82, spl. com. negotiated acquisition 1988-90), Calif. Bar Assn. (corp. com. 1982-85, chairperson 1985, exec. com. 1985-88, vice chairperson 1987-88, chair nominating com. bus. law sect. 1988), San Francisco Bar Assn. Republican. Episcopalian. Office: AirTouch Communications 425 Market St Fl 36 San Francisco CA 94105-2406

GILL, MARY MARGARET, critical care nurse; b. Ft. Wayne, Ind., July 24, 1961; d. James Anthony and Mary Kearney (Cameron) G. Diploma, Parkview Sch. Nursing, Ft. Wayne, Ind., 1982; BSN, Ball State U., 1991. RN, Ind.; cert. BLS, ACLS instr. Staff nurse oper. rm. Parkview Hosp., Ft. Wayne, Ind., 1983-85, nurse anesthesia, 1985-90, nurse coord. anesthesia, 1990-91, mgr. perioperative support svcs., 1991-93; nursing dir. emergency care ctr., 1993—. Mem. Assn. Operating Room Nurses, Nat. Assn. Pro-Life Nurses, Allen County Rigth to Life, Scottish Cultural Soc., Legion of Saint Michael, This'n That Antique Club, Sigma Theta Tau (Beta Rho chpt.). Roman Catholic. Office: Parkview Meml Hosp 2200 Randallia Dr Fort Wayne IN 46805

GILL, MELISSA D., development officer; b. Richmond, Va.; d. Harold B. and Margaret A. (Snell) G. BA, Coll. of William and Mary, 1982; MA, U. N.C., Chapel Hill, 1986. Asst. mgr. devel. Colonial Williamsburg (Va.) Fedn., 1986-88; advancement writer Coll. of William and Mary, Williamsburg, 1988-91; dir. corp. and fed. rels. The Citadel, Charleston, S.C., 1991; acting dir. devel. The Citadel, Charleston, 1991-92, assoc. dir. devel., 1992—. Mem. bd. dirs. Williamsburg Regional Library, 1991, United Way, Charleston, 1992. Office: The Citadel 171 Moultine St Charleston SC 29409

GILL, PATRICIA JANE, human resources executive; b. Mt. Vernon, N.Y., Jan. 20, 1950; d. J. Morgan and Magdalina (Manganiello) G. BA in History, St. Mary's Coll., 1971; MA in Counseling, NYU, 1973; MBA in Mktg., Fordham U., 1979; postgrad., Columbia U. Tchr., counselor Mt. Vernon Bd. Edn., 1970-74; tng. mgr. St. Luke's Hosp., N.Y.C., 1974-78; dir. personnel Bernard Hodes Advt., N.Y.C., 1978-80; mgr. mgmt. programs group Devel. Dimensions Internat., Pitts., 1980-82; v.p. Swan Cons., N.Y.C., 1982-83; nat. sales mgr. Reader's Digest, Pleasantville, N.Y., 1983-84; pres. Alexis-Gill Assocs., White Plains, N.Y., 1985; cons. in field. Author: Roleplaying, 1979. Worker Project Hope, New Rochelle, N.Y., 1986—. Mem. Am. Soc. Tng. and Devel. (pres. 1988), Nat. Speakers Assn. Episcopalian. Office: Alexis-Gill Assocs 222 Mamaroneck Ave Ste 207 White Plains NY 10605

GILL, RONNIE JOY, newspaper editor; b. Bklyn., Dec. 13, 1949; d. Robert and Frances (Noble) Ginsberg; m. Martin Harvey Gill, Nov. 24, 1971 (div. Nov. 1984). BA, Queens Coll., 1971. Adminstrv. asst. Technicolor, Inc., N.Y.C., 1971-72; daily TV listing editor Newsday, Inc., Melville, N.Y., 1972-74, TV book listing editor, 1974-79, editor, editing supr., 1979-87, editor, editing mgr., 1987-90, TV Plus editor, 1990-92; TV Plus/Entertainment listings editor, 1992—. Contbr. numerous articles to publs., 1973—. Jewish. Office: Newsday 235 Pinelawn Rd Melville NY 11747

GILL, WANDA EILEEN WAPLES, educational consulting firm executive, academic administrator, playwright; b. Burlington, N.J., Feb. 7, 1945; d. Thomas Garfield Jr. and Marian Marie (Jeffries) W.; m. Bruce Leon Gill, Dec. 24, 1969; children: Candace Ellen, Kimberly Lea. BS, Va. State U., 1967; MA, U. Cin., 1969; MEd, Bowie (Md.) State U., 1982; EdD, George Washington U., 1987. Coord. med.-dental health careers Georgetown U. Sch. Medicine, Washington, 1977-79; coord. student svcs. Bowie State U., 1979-80, dir. student svcs., 1980-93; assoc. dir. Middle States Assn. Commn. on Higher Edn., Phila., 1993-94; pres., CEO Diverse Ednl. Solutions, Inc., Mitchellville, Md., 1994—; cons. U.S. Dept. Edn., Washington, 1980-90; writer Metro Chronicle newspaper, Washington, 1987-88; proposal writer Coppin State Coll., Balt., 1989; mem. adv. bd. Planning A Needs Assessment Mgmt. System U. Ga., Athens, summer 1990. Author play The Cracker Box, 1990; also essays. V.p. Md. Women's Polit. Caucus, U. Md., 1988-90; pres. Cmty. Crisis Coalition, Prince George's County, Md., 1989—, Md. Exec. Coun. for Econ. Opportunity, 1991-93. Danforth Found. fellow, 1967-69; named Outstanding Young Woman of Am., Outstanding Young Women of Am., 1979. Mem. U. Md. System Women's Forum (sec. 1989-91), Mideastern Assn. Ednl. Opportunity Program Pers. (Outstanding Svc. award 1990). Democrat. Baptist.

GILLEM, ELISE MARIE (ELISE MARIE MICHAELS), radio and television personality; b. Kalamazoo, Dec. 24, 1958; d. Kenneth James and Mary Louise (Lemon) Fleckenstein; m. Mark Thomas Gillem; children: Charles Cortez, Gracie Lee. Grad. high sch., Kalamazoo. Radio personality Sta. KTIL, Tillamook, Oreg., 1983-84; personality/news dir. Sta. KXIQ/KGRL, Bend, Oreg., 1984-88, Sta. KLRR/KBND, Bend, Oreg., 1988-94; promotion dir. Sta. KTVZ-TV, Bend, Oreg., 1994—. Producer Living with Renal Failure, 1986 (hon. mention Oreg. AP); writer, host weekly TV show Your Next Home; creator, host, producer TV show The Earth Friendly Home. Bend coord. Oreg. Donor Program Miracle Mile Walk. Home: 19115 Pumice Butte Rd Bend OR 97702-8948 Office: Sta KTVZ 62990 OB Riley Rd Bend OR 97701

GILLEN, ANN, sculptor; b. Washington, Mar. 21, 1940; d. Vincent William and Irene Veronica (Maguire) G.; divorced; children: Katen Moore, L. Gordon Moore. BFA, Pratt Inst., 1961; MFA, Columbia U., 1969. curator sculpture; mem. art bd. Bellevue Hosp. Ctr., N.Y.C., 1986-90. One-woman shows include Vassar Coll. Art Gallery, Poughkeepsie, N.Y., 1976, Wave Hill, N.Y.C., 1977, Art Latitude Gallery, N.Y.C., 1979, U.S. Court Ho. Grand Lobby, N.Y.C., 1983, Bellevue Hosp. Park, N.Y.C., 1983-84, CUNY, Bklyn., 1984, Stamford (Conn.) Mus., 1984, 909 Third Ave, N.Y.C., 1987—, Elaine Benson Gallery, Bridgehampton, N.Y., 1990, Group Gallery, Provincetown, Mass., 1993, Atlantic Gallery, N.Y.C., 1994; exhibited in group shows including Storm King, N.Y., 1973-75, Berlin Arts Festival, 1976, Max Hutchinson's Sculpture Fields, 1990—, Lookout Sculpture Park, 1994—; represented in permanent collections including Lincoln Ctr Performing Arts, N.Y. Pub. Libr., N.Y.C. Bd. Edn., N.J State Arts Coun., Vogel Coll. of Memorabilia, Smithsonian Inst., Mus. Modern Art, N.Y.C., Continental Grain Corp., N.Y.C., others. Recipient work study Sculpture Space, N.Y., 1983, NEA, Olympics Commn., Lake Placid, N.Y., 1980; Hand Hollow Found. fellow, N.Y., 1983; Artist's Space of N.Y.C. grantee, 1991, Oto Marble, Philippines, 1991-92. Mem. Women's Caucus for Art. Home and Studio: 62 Grand St New York NY 10013

GILLES, JOANN, artist, educator; b. Pitts., Aug. 10, 1951; d. Alphonse Joseph and Dolores Marie (Amato) Broscious; m. Otis Steven Gilles, Oct. 29, 1971; 1 child, Kate Ellos. BS in Design, Portland State U., 1983, cert. tchr., 1983. Real estate agt. Tarbell, Lake Oswego, Oreg., 1976-79; real estate assoc. broker Tri West Properties, Wilsonville, Oreg., 1979-81; art tchr. Lake Oswego Schs., 1983-87; jewelery designer, mfr. JAG, Lake Oswego, 1987-91; textile designer Atelier, Portland, 1991-93; real estate broker Linda Borman Realty, West Linn, Oreg., 1993—; freelance artist Studio 216, Portland, 1983—, properties artist Oreg. Shakespeare Festival, Portland, 1987—; real estate broker JoAnn Gilles Real Estate, Lake Oswego, 1981-93. Prin. works exhibited in one-person shows including Acanthus Gallery, 1994, The Collector Gallery, Portland, 1990, Lakewood Gallery, Lake Oswego, 1987, The Attice Gallery, The Gango Gallery; paintings exhibited in group shows including All Oreg. Art Ann., 1988, Lake Oswego Festival Arts, 1987, 88. Vol. event planning Clinton Campaign for Pres., Portland, 1992; vol. Oreg. NARAL, Portland, 1991—. Mem. Portland Area Theatre Alliance, County Bd. Realtors. Office: Linda Borman Realty 18369 Willamette Dr West Linn OR 97068-1219

GILLESPIE, HELEN DAVYS, marketing/industry consultant, writer; b. San Jose, Calif., Nov. 23, 1954; d. Robert Bruce and Helen Davys (Street) G.; m. Nigel George Haden, May 1, 1982 (div. June 1986). BA in English with honors, Calif. State U., Chico, 1976; postgrad. in English, U. Sheffield, Eng., 1976-77, Calif. State U., Chico, 1977-78. Cert. bus. communicator. Bus. analyst Dun & Bradstreet, San Jose, 1978-80; personal asst. Times Computer Svcs., London, 1980; adminstr. Exec. Aviation, Palo Alto, Calif., 1981; sr. writer/editor Tymnet/McDonnell Douglas, San Jose, 1982-86; mgr. sales support Pactel Spectrum Svcs., Walnut Creek, Calif., 1987; mgr. product communications Varian Assocs., Inc., Sunnyvale, Calif., 1987-90; mgr. mktg. communications Allergan Humphrey, San Leandro, Calif., 1990-91; owner Write Away Comm., San Jose, Calif., 1987—, Isographics Internat., 1994—. Mem. Mus. Modern Art, San Jose. Mem. Bus. Mktg. Assn., Airline Owners and Pilots Assn., Writers Connection, Art Inst. Chgo., Mus. Soc. San Francisco, Commonwealth Club, Am. Soc. Quality Control.

GILLESPIE, JACQUELYN RANDALL, psychologist; b. Paris, France, Oct. 10, 1927; came to U.S., 1932; d. John Roberts and Hazel Maurine (Hammel) Hunter; m. Thomas Gilbert Gillespie, Apr. 27, 1947; children: Thomas Randall, Catherine Claire Gillespie Laroche. AB, Calif. State U., Long Beach, 1959; MS, Calif. State U., Fullerton, 1965; PhD, Calif. Grad. Inst., L.A., 1977. Lic. psychologist, psychoanalytic psychotherapist, Calif. Guidance cons. Lowell Sch. Dist., Whittier, Calif., 1963-69; psychologist Fullerton (Calif.) High Sch., 1969-82; pvt. practice Orange, Calif., 1976-90; assoc. prof. Calif. Grad. Inst., L.A., 1978-90. Author: Projective Use of Mother-and-Child Drawings, 1994; co-author: (reading text) Diagnostic Analysis of Reading Errors, 1981; contbr. articles to profl. jours. Grantee State of Calif., 1979; rsch. award Calif. Assn. Sch. Psychologists, 1972. Mem. APA (assoc.), Calif. Assn. Lic. Ednl. Psychologists (pres. 1983). Episcopalian. Home: 421-A Meadowlark Ave Naples FL 33942

GILLESPIE, MARY KREMPA, psychologist, consultant; b. New Haven, Oct. 31, 1941; d. Albert Charles and Marye (Bemis) Krempa; m. J. Joseph Gillespie, Sept. 1, 1962 (div. 1979); children: Carolyn Gillespie Kottmeyer, James Joseph III (dec.). AA in Classical Music cum laude, Mount Aloysius Coll., 1961; BA in Psychology cum laude, Immaculata (Pa.) Coll., 1973; MA in Clin. Psychology, West Chester (Pa.) U., 1974; postgrad., Temple U., 1976-80; PhD in Social Psychology, Walden U., 1988. Lic. psychologist Pa. Dir. tng. Rape Crisis Coun., West Chester, Pa., 1974-77; exec. dir. Open Door Counseling Ctr., West Chester, 1975-77; therapist Temple U. Community Counseling Clin., Phila., 1977-78; doctoral intern Coatesville (Pa.) Vets. Hosp., 1978-79; sr. psychologist Delaware Valley Psychol. Svcs., Phila., 1979-81; dir. Substance Abuse Programs Resource Spectrum, Phila., 1980-81; psychologist 1810 Counseling Ctr., Phoenixville, Pa., 1983-85, Ambler (Pa.) Psychol. Svcs., 1980-83; clin. supr., profl. mentor Eaglesmere Psychology Assocs., Malvern, Pa., 1980—, dir., 1983—; mem. staff Eugenia Hosp., Lafayette Hills, Pa., 1988—; dir. tng. Rape Crisis Coun., West Chester, Pa., 1974-77; vocat. counselor Haverford (Pa.) State Hosp., 1975; rsch. cons. Mind's Eye Ednl. Sys., Wayne, Pa., 1989-92; cons. The McGrail Group, Malvern, 1993—, corp. cons. in field, 1975—; clin. cons. Chester County Hosp., Occupational Health Ctr., 1988—, Children's Hosp. U. Pa., 1990—, The Reed Group, Rensselaer, N.Y., 1994—, Bus. Devel. and Tng. Ctr., Great Valley Ctr., Malvern, 1994—; occupational health psychologist Sterling-Winthrop Drugs, Collegeville, Pa., 1992—; expert witness in field; spkr. in field. Author: Outcome Study of an Innovative Paradoxical Treatment for Panic Attacks, 1988. Bd. dirs. Chester County Rape Crisis Coun., 1976-78; adminstr. U.S. Healthcare Managed Mental Health Care Capitation, 1979-90. Recipient Univ. fellowship Temple Univ., Phila., 1976-77. Mem. APA (field tester, master lectr., legis. network 1980—), Pa. Psychol. Assn. (legis. network 1980—), Am. Assn. Applied Psychophysiology and Biofeedback (cert. practitioner), Pa. Soc. Behavioral Medicine and Biofeedback, Am. Psychosomatic Soc., Sierra Club (legis. network 1985—), Audubon Club (legis. network 1985—), Phi Theta Kappa, Psi Chi. Home: RR 3 Box 2350 Malvern PA 19355-9803 Office: Eaglesmere Psychology Assoc 2350 Pheasant Hill Ln Malvern PA 19355-9712

GILLESPIE, PENNY HANNIG, counselor; b. Schenectady, N.Y., June 4, 1954; d. William Armand and Freda (Penney) H.; m. Kenneth Scofield Keyes, Jr., Sept. 2, 1984 (div. Aug. 1992). Student, U. Ariz., 1972-74. Cert. emergency med. technician Ariz., N.Y.; cert. in skills tng. for profls. in Hakomi psychotherapy, Oreg. Co-founder Ken Keyes Coll., Coos Bay, Ore., 1982-91; pvt. practice counseling Eugene, Ore., 1991—; founder, pres. The Wellness Network, Eugene, Oreg., 1994—. Co-author: Gathering Power Through Insight and Love, 1986, Handbook to Higher Consciousness: The Workbook, 1989; editor: How to Enjoy Your Life in Spite of It All, 1980, The Hundredth Monkey, 1982, Your Heart's Desire, 1983, Your Life Is a Gift, 1987, Discovering the Secrets of Happiness, 1988, PlanetHood, 1988, The Power of Unconditional Love, 1990. Bd. dirs. Living Love Ch., 1980-91, sec., v.p.; founding bd. dirs., sec., sec.-treas., v.p. The Vision Foundation, Inc., 1982-91; founding bd. dirs., sec., sec.-treas. Cornucopia, The Living Love Ch. of Ky., 1982-91. Recipient peace award Coalition for Justice and Peace, Ariz. State U. and the Inst. Peace Edn., 1989; award as site mgr. for Anne Frank exhibit Jewish Fedn. Lane County, Ore., 1993. Home: PO Box 21942 Eugene OR 97402

GILLETT, MARY CAPERTON, military historian; b. Richmond, Va., Apr. 28, 1929; d. Lewis Hopkins and Mary Caperton (Horsley) Renshaw; m. Richard Clark Gillett, June 7, 1949; children: Richard Clark Jr., Glenn Douglas, Mary Caperton, Priscilla Elizabeth, Blakeney Diana. Student, Wellesley Coll., 1946-49, BA, 1966, MA, 1971; PhD, Am. U., 1978. Historian U.S. Navy Dept., Washington, 1966-69, U.S. Dept. Army, Washington, 1972—. Author: The Army Medical Department, 1775-1818, 1981, The Army Medical Department, 1818-1865, 1988, 1865-1917, 1995; contbr. articles to profl. jours. Mem. Am. Assn. for History of Medicine, Am. Hist. Assn., Western Hist. Assn., The Westerners. Office: US Army Ctr of Mil History Washington DC 20374-5088

GILLETTE, ETHEL MORROW, columnist; b. Oelwein, Iowa, Nov. 27, 1921; d. Charles Henry and Myrne Sarah (Law) Morrow; student Coe Coll., 1939-41; BA, Upper Iowa U., 1959; MA, Western State Coll., 1969; m. Roman A. Gillette, May 6, 1944 (dec. 1992); children: Melody Ann, Richard Alan, William Robert (dec. 1993). Stenographer, Penick & Ford, Cedar Rapids, Iowa, 1941-43, FBI, Washington, 1943-44; tchr. Fayette (Iowa) High Sch., 1959-60, Jordan Jr. High Sch., Mpls., 1960-64, Montrose (Colo.) High Sch., 1964-68; family living, religion editor The News-Record, Gillette, Wyo., 1977-79, columnist Distaff Side, 1979-84. Mem. Western Writers Am., WestWind Writers/NMA (pres. 1994), Nat. Writers Club. Contbr. articles to various mags. Home: 1804 Locust Rd Montrose CO 81401-5825

GILLETTE, SANDRA ETTA, violinist; b. Boise, Idaho, Sept. 19, 1939; d. Lee Randolph and Gertrude Emily (Denney) Gillette; m. Gordon Donald Allen, June 9, 1959 (div. June 1976); children: Wendy Jo Jones, Michael Jay Allen; m. Eric Michael Schram, Jan. 25, 1985 (div. Aug. 1994). BA summa cum laude, Wash. State U., 1960; MA summa cum laude, U. Wash., 1966. Violinist Seattle Symphony Orch., 1967—, pers. mgr., 1984—; violinist Seattle Opera, 1967—, pers. mgr., 1984—. Chmn. fellowship and svc. Free Meth. Ch., Seattle, 1983-85. Mem. Am. Fedn. Musicians (union steward 1977-84), Internat. Guild of Symphony, Opera and Ballet Musicians, Phi Kappa Phi, Kappa Alpha Theta, Mu Phi. Republican. Office: Seattle Symphony Orch 305 Harrison St Seattle WA 98109

GILLETTE, SUSAN DOWNS, advertising executive; b. Phila., Mar. 4, 1950; d. George Woodrow and Ruth (McFarland) Downs; m. Raymond Gene Gillette, Oct. 6, 1979; children: Margaret Anne, Lindsay Ray. BA, No. Ill. U., 1972. Advt. asst. Wescom Inc., Downers Grove, Ill., 1972-73; copywriter Stern Walters Advt., Chgo., 1973-75; dir. creative services DDB Needham Worldwide, Chgo., 1975-90, pres., 1990—. Active AIDS pub. svc. campaign. Chgo. Dept. Pub. Health; tchr. local Sunday Sch.; active Mus. Broadcast Comm., Chgo. Coun. Fgn. Rels.; mem. adv. bd. No. Ill. U. Recipient Bronze Lion award Cannes Film Festival, 1978, Silver Lion award, 1987, Vol. award Am. Cancer Soc., 1986; named Creative Dir. of Yr., Ad-Week mag., 1986, Advt. Woman of Yr., Women's Advt. Club Chgo., 1990; honoree Women in Film, 1989. Mem. Chgo. Advt. Fedn., Women Film, Women's Advt. Club Chgo. Office: DDB Needham 303 E Wacker Dr Chicago IL 60601-5212

GILLETTE-BAUMANN, MURIEL DELPHINE, nurse; b. Pasadena, Calif., Nov. 10, 1945; d. Edwin and Jean Helen (Fremont) Gillette; m. Larry Houston Potter, Dec. 31, 1971 (dec. 1979); children: Melissa Darlene Genevieve Potter Stephens, Bryan Scott; m. Robert George Baumann Jr., Aug. 18, 1980; 1 child, Robert George III. Student, Western Coll. for Women, Oxford, Ohio, 1963-65; BSN, UCLA, 1968; M of Nursing, Oreg. Health Scis. U., 1991. Sch. nurse, health tchr. Hawthorne (Calif.) Intermediate Sch., 1969-70; nurse St. John's Hosp., Santa Monica, Calif., 1969-71; camp nurse L.A. Girl Scout Coun., 1969-71; nurse UCLA Med. Ctr., 1967-70; ICU/CCU/pediatrics nurse Mercy Med. Ctr., Roseburg, Oreg., 1971-79; nurse Umpqua Valley Community Hosp., Myrtle Creek, Oreg., 1981-91; health edn. dir. City of Myrtle Creek, 1986-91; nurse practitioner Umpgua Nat. Forest, Roseburg and Glide, Oreg., 1991-93; camp nurse, health coord. Oreg. Trail Boy Scout Coun., Roseburg, 1991—, Western Rivers Girl Scout Coun., Roseburg, 1984-90. Musician quartet, orch., soloist; artist in oils; poet. Bd. dirs. River 'N Dell Day Care Ctr., Myrtle Creek, 1983-85; trustee Augusta Bixler Farms, Inc., Stockton, Calif., 1976—; mem. Douglas County Cancer Screening Com. Capt. USAF, 1970-89. Umpqua Valley Hosp. Aux. scholar, 1989; L.A. Watercolor Soc. traveling art collection award, 1963. Mem. UCLA Alumni Assn., Umpqua Valley Hosp. Aux., Oreg. Health Sci. U. Alumni Assn., OES, Delta Zeta. Republican. Presbyterian. Home: PO Box 668 Myrtle Creek OR 97457-0104

GILLHAM, MARGARET ANN, artist agent; b. L.A., Sept. 29, 1961; d. James Percy and Ruth Monette (Gorman) G. BA in Art History, Ind. U., 1983; MA in Art History, U. Ill., 1985. Curatorial intern Cin. Art Mus., 1985; asst. curator William Howard Taft Nat. Hist. Site, Cin., 1985-86; mus. asst. High Mus. at Ga.-Pacific Ctr., Atlanta, 1986-87; curatorial asst. High Mus. Art, Atlanta, 1987-89; curator Art Mus. of South Tex., Corpus Christi, 1989-93; pvt. practice artist's agt., art cons. L.A., 1994—; adj. prof. art history Tex. A&M U., Corpus Christi, 1992. Author exhbn. catalogs, 1990-93. Home: 958 W Glenoaks Blvd Glendale CA 91202-2763

GILLHAM, MARTHA BETH, nutrition educator; b. Clarendon, Tex., July 29, 1940; d. John Rollins and Clara Rachel (Alexander) G. BS, Tex. Technol. Coll., 1962; PhD, Iowa State U., 1975. Registered and lic. dietitian. Dietitian St. Luke's Hosp., Denver, 1963-64; classroom tchr. Jefferson County Pub. Schs., Golden, Colo., 1964-67; asst. prof. dept. food and nutrition Iowa State U., Ames, 1971-75; asst. to assoc. prof. dept. human ecology U. Tex. at Austin, 1975—. Fellow Allied Health Inst.; recipient Katherine Ross Richards Teaching Fellowship, U. Tex. at Austin, 1989-90. Mem. Am. Dietetic Assn. (Medallion award 1991), Tex. Dietetic Assn. (Disting. Dietitian 1989), Austin Dietetic Assn., Sigma Xi (local v.p. 1982-84), Phi Kappa Phi, Phi Upsilon Omicron. Office: Dept Human Ecology Univ of Tex at Austin Austin TX 78712

GILLIAM, MARY, travel executive; b. Pampa, Tex., Apr. 18, 1928; d. Roy and Hylda O. (Bertrand) Brown; divorced; 1 child, Terry K. AA, Amarillo (Tex.) Bus. Coll., 1949. Flight attendant Braniff Internat. Airways, Dallas, 1950-53; from reservation agt. to mgr. passenger sales Trans-World Airlines, various locations, 1953-81; exec. v.p. Lakewood (Colo.) Travel, 1981; mgmt. cons. Bank One Travel, Columbus, Ohio, 1981-82; pres. Icaria Travel, Inc., Tucson, Ariz., 1986—, Intensive Trainers Inst., Tucson, 1983-92. Mem. Ariz. Rep. Com., 1978—. Recipient Award of Excellence Trans-World Airlines, N.Y.C., 1972, Pres.' Hall of Fame award, 1973. Mem. Am. Soc. Travel Agts. (Industry Svc. award 1980), Inst. Cert. Travel Agts., Ariz. Travel Agts. Assn. Republican. Methodist. Office: Icaria Travel Inc 2700 W Broadway Blvd Tucson AZ 85745-1715

GILLIAM, PAULA HUTTER, transportation company executive; b. N.Y.C.; d. Irving and Edna Phyllis (Manes) Hutter; m. Stanley Spencer Rolnick (div.); children: Jeffry Hutter Gilliam, Pamela Sara Bielory; m. Peter Gilliam, 1981. AA, Centenary Coll., 1961. Pres. Paula Rolnick Sales, N.Y.C., 1970-74; mdse. mgr. Kirby Block Internat., N.Y.C., 1974-78; pres. P.M.G. Internat. Ltd, N.Y.C., 1981—; v.p. Rical Air Express, Inc., N.Y.C., Rical Ocean Forwarding, N.Y.C.; ptnr. The Golden Unicorn Restaurant, 20 Mott St. Restaurant; mem. adv. bd. for internat. bus. Fashion Inst. Tech., 1991—. Producer (Broadway show) Stardust, 1987; exec. producer (plays) Long Days Journey Into the Night, 1988, Ah Wilderness. V.p. Murray Hill Com., N.Y.C., 1982—, chmn. bd., 1983-92; bd. advisors 132 E 35th St., N.Y.C., 1984-86; vol. aide Jun Eisland Coun. Women, Riverdale, N.Y., 1979—; bd. dirs. Theater Off Park, 1983-88, Black Goat Entertainment and Enlightenment, 1994—. Mem. Women in Internat. Trade (bd. dirs. 1991—), Women's Traffic Club, Met. Traffic Club. Democrat. Home and Office: 132 E 35th St New York NY 10016-3892

GILLIARD, JUDY ANN, broadcasting station executive; b. Ventura, Calif., Aug. 21, 1946; d. Sam Albert and Betty (Hardacre) G. A in Hotel and Restaurant Mgmt., Santa Barbara (Calif.) Community Coll., 1974. Calif. teaching credential. Supr. dining room Santa Barbara Biltmore, 1972-73; supr. food service, instr. dining room ops. Santa Barbara Community Coll., 1972-73; cons. J. Gilliard & Co., Santa Barbara, 1973-74; exec. mgr. Head of the Wolf Restaurant, Palm Springs, Calif., 1974-76; salesperson Indio (Calif.) Daily News, 1976-77; sales cons. Jurgensons Restaurant, Palm Springs, 1977-79; account exec. Sta. KPSI-FM, Palm Springs, 1978-84, gen. sales mgr., 1984-88, v.p., gen. mgr., 1988-92; owner, pres. JAG & Co., 1992—. Co-author: The Guiltless Gourmet, 1983, The Guiltless Gourmet Goes Ethnic, 1990, European Cuisine from the Guiltless Gourmet, 1991, Beyond Alfalfa Sprouts and Cheese, 1993; author: The Flavor Secret, 1994. Mem. Am. Heart Assn. (bd. dirs.), Nat. Spkrs. Assn., Palm Spring C. of C. (bd. dirs.), Desert Advt. Club (bd. dirs.), Am. Inst. Food and Wine, Internat. Food, Travel and Writers Assn., Internat. Assn. Cooking Profls. Home: 696 N Hermosa Dr Palm Springs CA 92262-6112

GILLICE, SONDRA JUPIN (MRS. GARDNER RUSSELL BROWN), sales and marketing executive; b. Urbana, Ill.; d. Earl Cranston and Laura Lorraine (Rose) Jupin; m. Gardner Russell Brown, Jan. 12, 1980; 1 child, Thomas Alan Gillice. BS, Lindenwood Coll.; MBA, Loyola Coll. Pers. officer N.Y. Citibank, 1968-70, 1st Nat. Bank of Chgo., 1970-72; mgr. human resources Potomac Electric Power Co., Washington, 1973-81; dir. pers. U.S. Synthetic Fuels Corp., Washington, 1981-86, v.p. human resources, Guest Svcs., Inc., 1987-90; v.p. sales and mktg., 1990-93; pres. Rus Son, Inc., 1994—; sr. v.p. govt. rels. Drake Beam Morin, Inc., 1994—. Mem. bd. govs. Loyola Coll., Nat. Coal Coun., mem. exec. com.; mem. nat. bd. Med. Coll. Pa.; mem. adv. coun. George Mason U.; bd. dirs. Restaurant Assn. Met. Washington. Mem. AAUW (pres. Falls Church br. 1976-78), Edison Electric Inst. (chmn. tng. and mgmt. devel. com.), Am. Soc. Pers. Adminstrs., Greater Met. Washington Bd. Trade, Soroptimists (pres. Washington chpt. 1979-80), DAR, Army Navy Country Club, Soc. Magna Charta Dames, Edgartown Yacht Club, The Arts Club, Georgetown Club. Republican.

GILLICK, BETSY BRINKLEY, financial analyst; b. Richmond, Va., May 11, 1959; d. Martha Lou (Caplinger) B. BBA, James Madison U., 1981, MBA, 1983. Procurement analyst Calculon Corp., Germantown, Md., 1983-85; agt. purchasing, subcontracts ORI/Calculon Corp., Rockville, Md., 1986-87; adminstr. contracts ORI/Calculon Corp., Rockville, 1987-89; sr. contracts adminstr. ARC Profl. Svcs. Group subs. ORI/Calculon Corp, Rockville, 1989-90, sr. fin. analyst, 1990-93; sr. fin. and contracts analyst Otsuka Am. Pharm. Inc., Rockville, 1993-94, fin. and contracts mgr., 1994—. Mem. Nat. Contract Mgmt. Assn. Democrat. Presbyterian. Home: 18420 Cape Jasmine Way Gaithersburg MD 20879-1054 Office: Otsuka Am Pharm Inc 2440 Research Blvd Rockville MD 20850

GILLIE, MICHELLE FRANCOISE, industrial hygienist; b. Phila., Oct. 24, 1956; d. Marino and Marcelle Jeannine (Boyer) Lazarich; m. Alan Deane Gillie, May 22, 1982; children: Patrick Alan, Caroline Elizabeth. BS, Pa. State U., 1977; MS, Drexel U., 1981. Diplomate Am. Bd. Indsl. Hygiene. Clin. chemist Pa. Hosp., Phila., 1976-80; indsl. hygienist Stewart-Todd Assocs., Wayne, Pa., 1981-82, S.W. Occupational Health Svcs., Houston, 1982-84; clin. toxicologist Smith-Kline-Beckman Labs., Houston, 1984-85; sr. indsl. hygienist Am. Analytical Labs., Akron, Ohio, 1985-88; indsl. hygiene cons. AMP Technical Svcs., Cleve., 1988-91; sr. indsl. hygienist Environ. Mgmt., Inc., Anchorage, 1991-92; indsl. hygiene cons. AMP Tech. Svcs., Bakersfield, Calif., 1992-94. Mem. Am. Indsl. Hygiene Assn. (pub. rels. com. chair Midnight Sun chpt. 1991-92). Home and Office: AMP Technical Svcs 711 E Boot Rd West Chester PA 19380-1229

GILLIGAN, CAROL, psychologist, writer; b. N.Y.C., Nov. 28, 1936; d. William Edward and Mabel (Caminez) Friedman; m. James Frederick Gilligan, June 12, 1960; children: Jonathan Mark, Timothy David, Christopher James. AB, Swarthmore Coll., 1958, hon. degree, 1985; AM, Radcliffe Coll., 1961; PhD, Harvard U., 1964; hon. degree, Regis Coll., 1983, Haverford Coll., 1987, Wesleyan U., 1992. Instr. U. Chgo., 1965-66; lectr. Harvard U., Cambridge, Mass., 1967-69, rsch. asst., 1969-70, asst. prof., 1970-78, assoc. prof., 1978-86, prof., 1986—; Laurie chair in Women's Studies Rutgers U., New Brunswick, N.J., 1986-87; Pitt Prof. U. Cambridge, Eng., 1992-93; founding mem. Harvard Project on Women's Psychology and the Devel. of Girls, 1987—; co-dir. The Company of Women and Girls, 1991—. Author: In a Different Voice, 1982, Mapping the Moral Domain: A Contribution of Women's Thinking to Psychological Theory and Education, 1988, Making Connections: The Relational Worlds of Adolescent Girls at Emma Willard School, 1990, (with Lyn M. Brown) Meeting at the Crossroads: Women's Psychology and Girls Development, 1992; editor: Women, Girls and Psychotherapy: Reframing Resistance, 1991. Bd. dirs. Ms Initiative in Girls, Facing History & Ourselves. Sr. rsch. fellow Spencer Found., 1984—; Mellon Faculty fellow Bunting Inst.-Radcliffe Coll., 1982-83; recipient Grawemayer award U. Louisville, 1992. Mem. APA, Assn. Women in Psychology. Democrat. Jewish. Office: Harvard U 503 Larsen Hall Appian Way Cambridge MA 02138

GILLIGAN, LINDA MIROSLAW, banker; b. Kansas City, Kans., Oct. 5, 1955; m. Thomas J. Gilligan, July 25, 1981; children: Emily, Molly, James. BBA, Washburn U., 1977; MBA, U. Mo., 1983. Chartered fin. analyst. Various analytical and supr. profl. Fed. Res. Bank, Kansas City, 1977-84; surveillance specialist Fed. Res. Bank, Mpls., 1984-85, sr. surveillance specialist, 1986-93, asst. v.p., 1993—. Mem. Twin Cities Soc. Security Analysts. Office: Federal Reserve Bank 250 Marquette Ave Minneapolis MN 55401-2171

GILLIGAN, MARY ANN, law librarian; b. Elizabeth, N.J., June 20, 1956; d. John Francis and Margaret Mary (Boyle) G. BA, Park Coll., 1977; MLS, Rutgers U., 1980. Asst. Time Inc., N.Y.C., 1981-83; law libr. Chubb & Son, Inc., Warren, N.J., 1985, Pennie & Edmonds, N.Y.C., 1985—. Mem. Am. Assn. Law Libraries, Special Libraries Assn., Law Library Assn. of Greater N.Y. Democrat. Roman Catholic. Office: Pennie & Edmonds 1155 Ave Of The Americas New York NY 10036-2711

GILLIGAN, SANDRA KAYE, private school director; b. Ft. Lewis, Wash., Mar. 22, 1946; d. Jack G. and O. Ruth (Mitchell) Wagoner; m. James J. Gilligan, June 3, 1972; 1 child, J. Shawn Gilligan. BS in Edn., Emporia State U., 1968, MS in Psychology, 1971; postgrad., Drake U., 1976, U. Mo., St. Louis, 1977-79. Tchr. Parklane Elem. Sch., Aurora, Colo., 1968-69, Bonner Springs (Kans.) Elem., 1970; stewardess Frontier Airlines, Denver, 1969; grad. teaching asst. Emporia (Kans.) State U., 1970-71; lead tchr. Western Valley Youth Ranch, Buckeye, Ariz., 1971-74; staff mem. program devel., lead tchr. The New Found., Phoenix, Ariz., 1974; ednl. therapist Orchard Pl., Des Moines, 1974-76; ednl. cons. Spl. Sch. Dist. of St. Louis County, 1976-79; founding dir. The Churchill Sch., St. Louis, 1979—; instr. Webster Coll., Webster Groves, Mo., 1978-80; adj. prof. Maryville Coll., St. Louis, summer 1985; mem. profl. adv. bd. Learning Disabilities Assn., St. Louis Learning Disabilities Assn.; keynote speaker Miss. Learning Disabilities Assn. Conv., 1991; site visitor blue ribbon schs. program U.S. Dept. Edn., 1992; cert. trainer Human Potential Seminars; presenter in field; bd. dirs. St. Louis Confederation Ind. Schs. Active St. Louis Ind. Schs. Mem. Learning Disabilities Assn., Orton Dyslexia Soc. Home: 14721 Greenleaf Valley Dr Chesterfield MO 63017-5514 Office: The Churchill Sch 1035 Price School Ln Saint Louis MO 63124-1533

GILLILAND, BARBARA DUKE, critical care nurse; b. Zuni, Va., Nov. 3, 1935; d. Marvin Lemuel and Martha Virginia (Galtress) Duke; div.; 3 children. Diploma, Va. Bapt. Hosp. Sch. Nursing, Lynchburg, 1956. Cert. critical care nurse, ACLS, BCLS instr. Staff nurse St. Elizabeth's Hosp., Washington; head nurse, pediatrics Community Health Ctr., Coldwater, Mich.; clinician, CCU Commonwealth Hosp., Fairfax, Va.; primary nurse Mt. Vernon Hosp., Alexandria, Va. Mem. AACCN (past treas., chpt. bd. dirs.), Carolina-Va. Soc. Critical Care Medicine. Home: 12668 Dulcinea Pl Lakeridge VA 22192-3148

GILLILAND, MARCIA ANN, nurse clinician, infection control specialist; b. Kansas City, Mo., Sept. 15, 1949; d. Robert Joseph and Mary Agnes (Paup) Caton; m. John Lee Gilliland, Mar. 28, 1974 (dec. Oct. 1983); children: Marcella Lyn, John Patrick, Devon Marie; m. Timothy J. Blow, Apr. 26, 1991. ADN, Kansas City C.C., 1979; BSN, Webster U., 1990. RN, Kans. Staff nurse U. Kans. Med. Ctr., Kansas City, 1979-84, infection control coord., 1984—, facilitator HIV/AIDS wellness group, 1991—; community health nurse Cath. Charities, Kansas City, 1980-82; pres., owner Kansas City Total Image, Overland Park, Kans., 1981-83. Active Rep. Committeewoman, Overland Park, 1994. Mem. Nat. Speakers Assn., Assn. Profls. in Infection Control and Epidemiology (pres. Kansas City chpt., 1993-94), Assn. Nurses in AIDS Care. Republican. Home: 9430 Riggs St Overland Park KS 66212-1443 Office: U Kans Med Ctr 3901 Rainbow Blvd Kansas City KS 66160-0001

GILLILAND, MARION CHARLOTTE S., volunteer; b. Duluth, Minn., Dec. 29, 1918; d. John Oscar and Jenny Olympia (Wangberg) Spjut; m. Charles Herbert Gilliland, Mar. 6, 1942; children: Charles Herbert Jr., Marion Charlotte Jr., Patricia Ann, Norman Paul, Cynthia Eileen. BA in Anthropology with honors, U. Fla., 1963, MA in Anthropology, 1965. Author: The Material Culture of Key Marco, Florida, 1976, Key Marco's Buried Treasure, 1989; contbr. articles to newspaper and profl. jours. Pres. Alachua County (Fla.) Childrens Com., 1959-61, Alachua County Scholarship and Loan Fund, 1960-62, Gainesville (Fla.) Womens Forum 1993-94; v.p. govtl. rels. div. Gainesville C. of C., 1977-79; health com. Human Svcs. Planning Coun., Gainesville, 1980-84; bd. dirs. Fla. Arts Celebration, Gainesville, 1984-91; sec. Friends of Music U. Fla., 1994—, pres., 1990-92; pres. Gainesville Women's Forum, 1993-94. Recipient Peggy Wilcox Svc. award State of Fla., 1985, Woman of Distinction award Santa Fe C.C., 1993. Mem. Fla. Med. Assn. Aux. (pres. 1969-70, bd. dirs. 1970-73), AMA Aux. (sec. 1975-76, v.p. so. regional 1976-78, historian 1978-79), Alachua County Med. Aux. (pres. 1960-61), So. Anthropol. Soc., Fla. Anthropol. Soc., Archael. Inst. Am., Nat. Assn. Underwater Investigators, Fla. Mus. Assocs., Fla. Women's Alliance (charter mem.), Mortar Bd. (hon.), Phi Kappa Phi. Home: 3031 SW 70th Ln Gainesville FL 32608-5216

GILLILAND, TERRI KIRBY, accountant; b. Tuscaloosa, Ala., Oct. 4, 1954; d. William Park and Bobbie (Fitts) Kirby; m. Glenn Scott Gilliland, Aug. 31, 1991; 1 child, Joshua Scott. BS in Commerce and Bus. Adminstrn., U. Ala., Tuscaloosa, 1977. CPA, Ala. Staff acct. Yeager & Christian CPAs, Tuscaloosa, 1979-84; chief acct. HealthSouth Rehab. Corporation, Birmingham, Ala., 1984-86; sr. acct. DeWitt & DeWitt CPAs, Tuscaloosa, 1986-93; acct. II-tax Hunt Refining Co., Tuscaloosa, 1993—; mem. regional adv. com. U.S. Small Bus. Adminstrn., Birmingham, 1991-93. Participant Leadership Tuscaloosa, 1988-89. Mem. AICPA, Am. Soc. Women Accts. (treas. West Ala. chpt. 1991-92, sec. 1992-93), Ala. Soc. CPAs, Inst. Mgmt. Accts. (acquisition dir.). Baptist. Home: 3015 1st Ct Tuscaloosa AL 35405 Office: Hunt Refining Co PO Box 038995 Tuscaloosa AL 35403

GILLIOM, JUDITH CARR, government official; b. Indpls., May 19, 1943; d. Elbert Raymond and Marjorie Lucille (Carr) G. B.A., Northwestern U., 1964; M.A., U. Pa., 1966. Feature writer, asst. women's editor Indpls. News, summers 1961-63; research asst. cultural anthropology Northwestern U., 1963-64, asst. instr. freshman English, 1964; editorial asst. to dir. div. cardiology Phila. Gen. Hosp., 1965-67; asst. to ophthalmologist-in-chief Wills Eye Hosp., Phila., 1967-69; editor, writer Nat. Assn. Hearing and Speech Agencies, Washington, 1969-70; free-lance speech writer White House Conf. Children and Youth, 1969-70; free-lance editor, writer, abstractor, 1971-78; free-lance speechwriter President's Com. Mental Retardation, 1971-78; dir. pubdls. Nat. Assn. Hearing and Speech Action, Silver Spring, Md., 1972-74; dir. communications Nat. Assn. Hearing and Speech Action, 1975-77; editor Hearing & Speech Action mag., 1969-70, 72-77; program mgr. Interagy. Com. on Handicapped Employees, 1978, dep. exec. sec., 1979-83; mgr. disability program Dept. Def., 1983—; cons. U.S. Archtl. and Transp. Barriers Compliance Bd., 1976-77, Office Ind. Living for Disabled, HUD, 1977-78, Office for Handicapped Individuals, HEW, 1978, Women's com. Pres.'s Com. Employment Handicapped, 1985-86. Mem. Nat. Spinal Cord Injury Assn., 1971-90, editor, pub. conv. jour., 1974-82, bd. dirs. D.C. chpt., 1975-81, 89-90, nat. trustee, 1975-81, nat. bd. dirs., 1978-79; bd. dirs. Nat. Ctr. for a Barrier-Free Environment, 1979-84, v.p., 1980-81, pres., 1981-82; nat. bd. dirs., treas. League Disabled Voters, 1980-85; local bd. dirs. Easter Seal Soc. Disabled Children and Adults, 1985-90; active Montgomery County Commn. on People with Disabilities, 1989—. Woodrow Wilson fellow, 1965. Mem. Phi Beta Kappa, Delta Delta Delta. Home: 901 Arcola Ave Silver Spring MD 20902-3401 Office: Dept Def The Pentagon Rm 3A272 Washington DC 20301-4000

GILLISON, JEANETTE SCOTT, elementary school educator; b. Phila., Aug. 17, 1931; d. Swinton O'Neal and Lillie (Roberts) Scott; m. Everett A. Gillison, Dec. 10, 1955 (div. Apr. 1965); children: Everett A. Jr., Sharida L., Katanya L. BA in Elem. Edn., Cheney State Tchrs. Coll., 1953. Elem. sch. tchr. Sch. Dist. Phila., 1953—, Meade Sch., Phila., 1953-58, Martha Washington Sch., Phila., 1960—; liaison tchr. for Sch. Dist. Phila., World Affairs Coun., 1969-73. Mem. adv. bd. Belmont YMCA educators to Africa, Phila., 1973—. Mem. NAACP (life), Nat. Coun. Negro Women (life), Black Women's Ednl. Alliance, Alpha Kappa Alpha (life). Home: 18 S 50th St Philadelphia PA 19139-3538

GILLMAN, GRETA JOANNE, physician; b. Montreal, Quebec, Can., Aug. 18, 1945; d. Hyman and Fanny (Izenberg) G.; m. Vic Bhoopat, Oct. 17, 1970; children: Lisa, Mitchell. MD, U. Calif., Irvine, 1969. Physician specialist L.A. County Hosp., 1973—; asst. clin. prof. UCLA, 1976—. Home: 13492 Grinnell Cir Westminster CA 92683 Office: LA County Hosp 10005 Flower St Bellflower CA 90706

GILLMAN, KAREN LEE, clinical psychologist; b. Wichita, Kans., Sept. 16, 1937; d. Raymond H. and Myra Ruth (Hudson) Hein; m. Louis Charles Thomason, Dec. 21, 1958 (div. 1980); children: Debra Lynn Roelke, Sandra Kim; m. Richard Earl Gillman, June 18, 1983. Student, Phillips U., 1955-58; BS, Okla. State U., 1959; MS, Va. Polytech. Inst., Blacksburg, 1974; PhD, SUNY, Albany, 1985. Lic. clin. psychologist, Maine, N.Y. Tchr. Washington Elem., Stillwater (Okla.) Jr. High Sch., Ponca City, 1959-64, West Hurley (N.Y.) Elem. Sch., 1971-72; therapist Family Svc. Ctr., Kingston, N.Y., 1974-77; sr. counselor Readiness Tng. Project Ulster County Community Coll., Stone Ridge, N.Y., 1978-79; clin. dir. Greene County Mental Health Clinic, Cairo, N.Y., 1979-84; dir. student assistance program Rens. County Dept. Mental Health, Troy, N.Y., 1984-86; dir. intensive day treatment St. Lawrence Psychiat. Ctr., Ogdensburg, N.Y., 1986-89; pvt. practice Dover-Foxcroft and Skowhegan, Skowhegan, Maine, 1989—; adj. prof. St. Lawrence U., Canton, N.Y., 1986; cons. Project Readiness Arbor Hill Dept. Labor, Albany, 1978, Overlook Pre-sch. Ctr., Woodstock, N.Y., 1974; vol. tchr. Ulster Acad., Kingston, 1974; music tchr. Headstart, Woodstock, 1970-71. newspaper columnist The Apple Polisher. Dir. Community Vacation Ch. Sch., Woodstock, 1967-70; Head of Day Family of Woodstock, Inc., 1974-77. Fellow NSF, 1961. Mem. APA, LWV (bd. dirs., editor 1967-69) Am. Assn. Marriage & Family Therapists, Soc. Psychologists in Addictive Behaviors, Maine Psychol. Assn. Democrat. Home: RR 2 Box 5215 Waterville ME 04901-9642 Office: Garland Rd Winslow ME 04901

GILLMOR, HELEN W., federal judge; b. 1942. BA, Queen's Coll. of CUNY, 1965; LLB magna cum laude, Boston Univ. Sch. of Law, 1968. With Ropes & Gray, Boston, 1968-69, Law Offices of Alexander R. Gillmor, Camden, Maine, 1970, Torkildson, Katz, Jossem, Fonseca, Jaffe, Moore & Hetherington, Honolulu, 1971-72; law clk. to Chief Justice William S. Richardson Hawaii State Supreme Ct., 1972; dep. pub. defender Honolulu, 1972-74; district court judge Family Ct., 1st circuit, State of Hawaii, 1977-83, Dist. Ct., 1st circuit, 1983-85; with Gillmor & Gillmor, Honolulu, 1985-94; district judge U.S. Dist. Ct. Hawaii, 9th circuit, 1994—; counsel El Paso Real Estate Investment Trust, El Paso, 1969; lectr. U.S. Agy. for Internat. Devel., Seoul, South Korea, 1969-70, Univ. of Hawaii, 1975. Office: Prince J K Kuhio Fed Bldg PO Box 50128 300 Ala Moana Blvd Rm C-414 Honolulu HI 96850*

GILLMOR, KAREN LAKO, state legislator, strategic planner; b. Cleve., Jan. 29, 1948; d. William M. and Charlotte (Sheldon) Lako; m. Paul E. Gillmor, Dec. 10, 1983; children: Linda D., Julie E., Paul M. BA cum laude, Mich. State U., 1969; MA, Ohio State U., 1970, PhD, 1981. Asst. to v.p. Ohio State U., Columbus, 1972-77, spl. asst. dean law, 1979-81; asst. to pres. Ind. Cen. U., Indpls., 1977-78; rsch. asst. Burke Mktg. Rsch., Indpls., 1978-79; v.p. pub. affairs Huntington Nat. Bank, Columbus, 1981-82; fin. cons. Ohio Rep. Fin. Com., Columbus, 1982-83; chief mgmt. planning and rsch. Indsl. Commn. Ohio, Columbus, 1983-86; mgr. physician rels. Univ. Hosps., Columbus, 1987-91; cons. U.S. Sec. Labor, Washington, 1990-91; mem. Regional Bd. Rev., Industrial Commn., Ohio, 1991-92; assoc. dir. Ctr. Healthcare Policy and Rsch. Ohio State U., 1991-92; mem. Ohio General Assembly, 1993—; legis. liaison Huntington Bancshares, Ohio, Ohio State U., Columbus. Grantee Andrew W. Mellon Found. 1978, Carnegie Corp. 1978; named Outstanding Freshman Legislator, Bulldog of the Treasury; recipient Pres. award Ohio State Chiropractic Assn., 1994. Mem. Women in Mainstream, Women's Roundtable, Ohio Fedn. Rep. Women, Am. Assn. Higher Edn., Coun. Advancement and Support Edn., DAR, Phi Delta Kappa. Methodist. Clubs: University (Columbus). Office: The Statehouse Columbus OH 43215-4276

GILLMOR, ROGENE GODDING, medical technologist; b. El Dorado, Kans., Jan. 25, 1939; d. Marc Antone and Verda May (Bogue) Godding; m. Charles Stewart Gillmor Jr., Nov. 28, 1964; children: Charles Stewart III, Alison Bogue. AA in Liberal Arts, Cottey Coll., 1958; BS in Biology, Stanford U., 1960; postgrad., Wesleyan U., U. Hartford, Foothills Coll. Rsch. asst. genetics Joshua Lederberg lab. Stanford U., 1960-62; assoc. scientist space biology/medicine Lockheed Missiles & Space Co., Palo Alto, Calif., 1962-64; rsch. asst. biology Princeton (N.J.) U., 1965-66, Wesleyan U., Middletown, Conn., 1967-69; lab. technician immunochemistry Hartford (Conn.) Hosp., 1978-84, instr. immunology clin. lab. edn. program, 1985-89, lab. supr. proteins/immunology dept. pathology and lab. medicine, 1986—; rschr. various labs, France and Switzerland, 1984-85. Contbr. articles to profl. jours. Leader Girl Scouts U.S., 1977-85; trustee, deacon Higganum (Conn.) Congl. Ch., 1980—. Recipient Achievement award Girl Scouts U.S., 1985. Mem. Am. Assn. Clin. Chemistry, Am. Soc. Clin. Pathologists (cert. immunology specialist), Am. Soc. Clin. Lab. Sci., Wesleyan Potters (pres. 1982-84), Haddam, Conn. Hist. Soc. (sec. 1970-72), Conn. Hist. Soc., PEO Sisterhood. Home: 29 Spencer Rd Higganum CT 06441-4034 Office: Hartford Hosp Dept Pathology & Lab Medicine 80 Seymour St Hartford CT 06102

GILLON, JEANNE MARIE, educator; b. Boston, May 27, 1937; d. Edward Thomas and Mabel Loretta (O'Shaughnessy) McGuiggin; m. John Charles Gillon, July 6, 1963; children: John Jr., Edward, Robert. BS magna cum laude, Boston Coll., 1959, MEd, 1960. Lic. tchr., Mass., N.Y. Elem. tchr. Cold Spring Harbor (N.Y.) Sch. Dist., 1960-66; dir. edn. Huntington (N.Y.) Arts Coun., 1986—; Suffolk County coord. imagination celebration N.Y. State Alliance Arts Edn.-N.Y. State Edn. Dept., Albany, Kennedy Ctr. Performing Arts, Washington, 1987—; grad. asst. Boston Coll. Grad. Sch., 1959. Trustee Beachcroft Assn., Huntington, N.Y., 1992—. Mem. AAUW (bd. mem. 1973-80, v.p. 1980-82, pres. 1982-84), N.Y. State Alliance for Arts Edn. (bd. mem. 1989-92). Democrat. Roman Catholic. Home: Inlet Pl Huntington NY 11743 Office: Huntington Arts Coun 213 Main St Huntington NY 11743

GILLOOLY, EDNA RAE See BURSTYN, ELLEN

GILMORE, JOANNE R., librarian; b. Phila., Oct. 18, 1952; d. John Leo and Sarah Rita (McGinley) G.; m. Michael O'Donnell, Nov. 11, 1978 (div.); m. Paul A. Grygier, Oct. 21, 1989. BA, Marywood Coll., 1974; MLS, Rutgers U., 1976. Reference & info. svc. libr. Cecil County Pub. Libr., Elkton, Md., 1977-82; mgr. ACCESS info. svc. Cumberland County Pub. Libr., Fayetteville, N.C., 1982, dept. head info. svcs., 1982-86; mgr. gen. reference Columbus (Ohio) Met. Libr., 1987-89, dir. tech. svcs., 1989—. Mem. ALA, Pub. Libr. Assn., Ohio Libr. Assn. (sec. tech. svc. 1992-94). Office: Columbus Metropolitan Libr 96 S Grant Ave Columbus OH 43215

GILMORE, JUDITH MARIE, physician; b. Houston, Dec. 28, 1942; d. Howard Ray and Mary Gardner (Currier) G.; m. Richard E. Kelley, July 21, 1974 (div. 1981); 1 child, Lisa Kelley. BA, U. Maine, 1965; MA, NYU, 1968; MD, Woman's Med. Coll., 1972. Diplomate Am. Bd. Internal Medicine, Am. Bd. Endocrinology. Resident St. Vincent's Hosp., N.Y.C., 1972-74; fellow in endocrinology St. Raphael's Hosp., New Haven, 1974-75, West Haven VA Hosp., New Haven, 1975-76; pvt. practice Bridgeport, Conn., 1976-80, Cranston, R.I., 1986—. Lt. comdr. USN, 1980-86. mem. staff St. Joseph's Hosp., Providence, 1986—; mem. consulting staff Newport (R.I.) Hosp., 1986—; mem. courtesy staff Roger Williams Hosp., Providence, 1994—. Mem. ACP, AMA, Am. Assn. Edn., Am. Diabetes Assn., R.I. Endocrine Assn. Office: 725 Reservoir Ave Ste 2 Providence RI 02910

GILMORE, JUNE ELLEN, psychologist; b. Middletown, Ohio, Oct. 22, 1927; d. Linley Lawrence and Elizabeth Kathleen (Barker) Wetzel; m. John Lester Gilmore, July 6, 1945; children: John Lester Jr., Michael Edward. BS, Miami U., Oxford, 1961; MS, Miami U., 1964. Lic. psychologist, Ohio. Intern in psychology Hamilton (Ohio) City Schs., 1963-64; psychologist Talawanda, Shiloh, Trenton Schs., Butler County, Ohio, 1964-66, Franklin (Ohio) City Schs., 1966-72, Wapakoneta (Ohio) City Schs., 1972-76, Cin. City Schs., 1978-86; pvt. practice psychology, 1975—; planner, evaluator Warren/Clinton Counties Mental Health Bd., Ohio, 1986-88; adj. instr. Wright State U., Dayton, Ohio, 1989-90. Co-author: Summer Children-Ready or not for School, 1986, The Rape of Childhood--No Time to be a Kid, 1990. Sec. Tri County Drug Coun., Lima, Ohio, 1975; chmn. Auglaize County Social Svcs., Wapakoneta, 1973-75; bd. dirs. Butler County Alcohol and Drug Addiction Svcs. Bd., 1990—, sec., 1992—. Mem. Ohio Sch. Psychologists Assn. (exec. bd. 1982-86), Southwestern Ohio Sch. Psychologist Assn. (pres.), Southwest Council Exceptional Children (Pres.), Nat. Assn. Sch. Psychologists, Ohio Psychol. Assn., Butler County 648 Mental Health Bd. (bd. dirs. 1978-86, pres. 1983-84). Republican. United Methodist. Home and Office: 6120 Michael Rd Middletown OH 45042-9201

GILMORE, LOUISA RUTH, retired nurse, retired firefighter; b. Pitts., Oct. 31, 1930; d. Albert Leonard and Bertha Christina (Birch) Huber; m. William Norman Kemp, May 27, 1950 (div. 1975); children: Janyce Louise Kemp Lipson, Barbra Lea Kemp Bilharz, Robert William, Paul Lee, Charles Albert; m. Robert James Gilmore, Sept. 1, 1989. Diploma in nursing, San Bernardino Community Coll., Needles, Calif., 1983. Office nurse Santa Fe Clinic, Needles, 1953-57; spl. duty nurse Needles Communities Hosp., 1957-62; nurse supr. Santa Fe Clinic, 1962-79; staff nurse in surgery Needles Desert Communities Hosp., 1979-90; ind. distbr. Reliv Products, Temple, Tex., 1991—; CPR instr. Needles Desert Communities Hosp., 1987-90; med. officer San Bernardino County Fire Dept., Needles, 1980-83, pub. info. officer 1983-90; ind. distbr. Reliv Products, 1991—. Mem. Calif. State Fireman Assn., Needles Firefighters Assn. (treas. 1987, 88), Beta Sigma Phi-Zeta Gamma (treas. 1966, sec. 1967, v.p. 1968, pres. 1969, named Sweetheart Queen 1969), Order of Rose (life).

GILMORE, MARJORIE HAVENS, lawyer, civic worker; b. N.Y.C., Aug. 16, 1918; d. William Westerfield and Elsie (Medl) Havens; AB, Hunter Coll., 1938; JD, Columbia, 1941; m. Hugh Redland Gilmore, May 8, 1942; children: Douglas Hugh, Anne Charlotte Gilmore Decker, Joan Louise. Admitted to N.Y. State bar, 1941, Va. bar, 1968; rsch. asst. N.Y. Law Revision Commn., 1941-42; assoc. firm Spence, Windels, Walser, Hotchkiss & Angell, N.Y.C., 1942, Chadbourne, Wallace, Parke & Whiteside, N.Y.C., 1942-43; atty. U.S. Army, Washington, 1948-53. Sec., Thomas Jefferson Jr. High Sch. PTA, 1956-58; chmn. by-laws rev. com., Long Point Corp., Ferrisburg, Vt., 1981-93; parliamentarian Wakefield High Sch. PTA, 1959-60, chmn. citizenship com., 1960-61; publicity chmn. Patrick Henry Sch. PTA, sec., 1964-65; parliamentarian Nottingham PTA, 1966-69; mem. extra-curricular activities com. Arlington County Sch. Bd.; area chmn. fund drive Cancer Soc., 1955-56; active Girl Scouts U.S.A., 1963-70; mem. '41 com. Columbia Law Sch. Fund. Recipient Constl. Law award Hunter Coll., 1938. Mem. Arlington Fedn. Women's Clubs (rec. sec. 1979-80), No. Dist. Va. Fedn. Women's Clubs (chmn. legis. com. 1986-88, chmn. pub. affairs No. dist. 1988-90), Columbia Law Sch. Alumni Assn., Alpha Sigma Rho. Presbyn. Club: Williamsburg Woman's of Arlington (corr. sec. 1970-72, 1st v.p. 1972-74, pres. 1974-76, chmn. communications 1981-82, chmn. legis. com. 1982-86, 90—). Home: 3020 N Nottingham St Arlington VA 22207-1268

GILMORE, PAMELA DARLENE, county administrator; b. Boaz, Ala., Jan. 19, 1958; d. Billy Gene Thompson and Marlene Rose (Robinson) Thompson Johnson; m. Keith Norman Gilmore, June 4, 1977; children: Joshua, Jeremy. Attended, Snead State Jr. Coll. Cert. county govt. adminstr. Bookkeeper Marshall County Commn., Guntersville, Ala., 1975-79, chief bookkeeper, 1979-83, chief clk., 1983-86, county adminstr., 1986—. Bd. dirs. North Ala. Health Care Bd., Huntsville, Ala., 1976-78, Cherokee-Dekalb-Marshall Child Devel., Ft. Payne, Ala., 1990—; sec. Emergency Food & Shelder Bd., Guntersville, 1983—, Marshall County Vocat. Coun., Guntersville, 1990—; fin. agt. E-911 Bd., Guntersville, 1993. Named Outstanding Young Women Am., 1984, 87. Fellow PTA, Ala. Reunion (bd. dirs., Outstanding Achievement award 1988), Aids Commn.; mem. Am. Cancer Soc. (bd. dirs., treas. 1985-87, cookbook chmn. 1985), Marshall County Employees Assn. (rep. 1987—), Assn. County Adminstrs. (bd. dirs. 1983, sec. 1994). Baptist. Home: 3505 Wyeth Dr Guntersville AL 35976-2651 Office: Marhsall County Commn 424 Blount Ave Guntersville AL 35976-1108

GILMORE, VANESSA D., federal judge; b. St. Albans, N.Y., Oct. 26, 1956. BS, Hampton U., 1977; JD, U. Houston, 1981. Fashion buyer Foley's Dept. Store, 1977-79; atty. Vickery, Kilbride, Gilmore & Vickery, Houston, 1981-85, 86-94, Sue Schecter & Assocs., Houston, 1985-86; judge U.S. Dist. Ct. (So. dist.) Tex., Houston, 1994—; chair Tex. Dept. Commerce, 1991-94; mem. adv. bd. St. John's Hosp.; bd. dirs. Post Oak Park Townhomes. Contbr. articles to legal jours. Bd. dirs. Tex. So. Univ. Found., Neighborhood Recovery Community Redevel. Corp., 1992—; chair African Am. Art Adv. Assn., Mus. Fine Arts; mem. scv. acad. nominations bd. Rep. Jack Fields, Tex., 1993; active Texans for NAFTA. Named One of Houston's Black Achievers, Human Enrichment of Life Program, 1989; recipient Citizen of the Month award Houston Defender, 1990, YWCA award, 1991, Austin Met. Resource Bus. Ctr. award, 1991, Houston Bus. and Profl. Men's Club award, 1992, Disting. Svc. award Nat. Black MBA Assn., 1994, Community Svc. award Holman St. Bapt. Ch., 1994. Mem. ABA, NAACP (chair chs. and orgns. com. Freedom Fund banquets 1989-93), Am. Trial Lawyers Assn., Am. Leadership Forum, Tex. Trial Lawyers Assn., Tex. Lyceum Assn., Houston Bar Assn., Houston Lawyuers Assn., U. Houston Law Alumni (bd. dirs. 1993—), W.J. Durham Legal Soc., Links, Inc. (Mo. chpt., chair LEAD substance abuse and teen prognancy prevention program 1990-91). Office: Fed Bldg 515 Rush Ave Rm 10026 Houston TX 77002*

GILROY, SUE ANN, state official. Sec. of state State of Ind., 1995—. Office: Office of the Sec of State State House Rm 201 Indianapolis IN 46204*

GILSON, BARBARA FRANCES, editor; b. Bklyn., May 6, 1946; d. Osmar Frank and Marie Elizabeth (Micka) G.; m. Robert Sawicki, June 29, 1962 (div. Sept. 1972); 1 child, Blake. BA in English, Smith Coll., 1976. Editor Literary Guild, Military Book Club Doubleday & Co., Inc., N.Y.C., 1968-78; sr. sponsoring editor McGraw-Hill Latinoamericana, Bogota, Colombia, 1978-83; sr. editor Barrons Edn. Series, Woodbury, N.Y., 1983-84; exec. editor Monarch Press Simon & Schuster, N.Y.C., 1984—, sr. editor Arco Pub., 1984—. Contbr. poems, articles, short story to profl. publs.

GILSON, ELIZABETH ANNE, editor; b. Lodi, Ohio, July 28, 1945; d. Elsworth Pratt and Mary Fern (Grimm) Allemang; m. Allen L. Gruber, Nov. 14, 1970 (div. Sept. 1975); 1 child, Jenny R.; m. Thomas L. Gilson, Aug. 8, 1988. BSBA, Ohio State U., 1968; BA in English, Writing, Adrian Coll., 1992. Copy writer Howard Swink Advt., Marion, Ohio, 1968-75, Hameroff and Assocs., Columbus, Ohio, 1976-77, freelance, Columbus, Ohio, 1977-79; sales promotion copy writer Fahlgren and Ferris, Toledo, 1979-80; copy writer freelance, Toledo, 1980-83; mktg. coord. Arnold Industries, Toledo, 1983-84; advt. mgr. Blackstone Art Studios, Toledo, 1984-85; asst. dir. pubs. Adrian (Mich.) Coll., 1987—. Program dir. Columbus Soc. Communicating Arts, 1977, 1st v.p., 1978; treas. N.W. Ohio Tourist Coun., Toledo, 1985; coord. pub. rels. Jamie Farr Toledo Classic LPGA Tournament, 1984. Mem. Coun. for Advancement and Support of Edn., Ohio State U. Alumni Assn., Lambda Iota Tau. Democrat. Home: 433 Carey St Deerfield MI 49238-9741 Office: Adrian Coll 110 S Madison St Adrian MI 49221-2575

GILSTRAP, LEAH ANN, media specialist; b. Seneca, S.C., Sept. 12, 1950; d. Raymond Chester and Eunice Hazel (Long) G. BA in History, Furman U., 1976, MEd, 1982; MLS, U. S.C., 1991. Cert. tchr., media specialist, S.C. Tchr., spl. edn. Greenville (S.C.) County Sch. Dist., 1978-79, tchr., 1979-92, media specialist, 1992—. Mem. NEA (del. 1991-94), ALA, S.C. Assn. Sch. Librs., S.C. Edn. Assn. (bd. dirs. 1994—), Greenville County Edn. Assn. (bd. dirs. 1988—, governance chair 1988—), Greenville County Coun. Media Specialists (bd. dirs. 1993-94). Democrat. Baptist. Home: 150 Howell Cir Apt 184 Greenville SC 29615 Office: Bryson Mid Sch 3657 S Industrial Dr Simpsonville SC 29681

GIMBERLINE, JACQUELINE L., accountant, internal auditor; b. Akron, Iowa, Sept. 21, 1946; d. John W. and Amelia May (Lambert) Henrich; m. Donald Dean Gimberline, Oct. 30, 1993; children: Kimberly J. Bitz McCleary, Sandra L. Bitz. MB, Morningside Coll., 1988; MBA, U. S.D., 1993. CPA, Iowa. Asst. mgr. Midwest divsn. Prices Fine Chocolate, Sioux City, Iowa, 1980-84; adminstrv. asst. Morningside Coll., Sioux City, 1984-88; acct. Midwest Energy, Sioux City, 1988-89; investment analyst Midwest Capital Group, Sioux City, 1989-90, adminstr., 1990-91; mgr. internal audit Midwest Power Systems, Sioux City, 1994—. Treas. Sioux Land Youth Symphony, Sioux City, 1994; bd. dirs. curriculum adv. bd. We. Iowa Tech., Sioux City, 1992-94. Mem. AICPA, Inst. Mgmt. Accts. Office: Midwest Power Systems 401 Douglas St Sioux City IA 51101

GIMBUTAS, MARIJA, archaeologist, educator; b. Vilnius, Lithuania, Jan. 23, 1921; came to U.S., 1949, naturalized, 1955; d. Daniel and Veronica (Janulaitis) Alseika; m. Jurgis Gimbutas, 1942; children: Danute, Živile, Rasa. MA, U. Vilnius, 1942; PhD, U. Tubingen, Germany, 1946; postgrad., U. Heidelberg and Munich, Germany, 1947-49; PhD (hon.), Calif. Inst. Integral Studies, San Francisco, 1988; Vytauas Magnus U., Kaunas, Lithuania, 1993. Research fellow Peabody Mus., Harvard U., Boston, 1955-63; lectr. dept. anthropology Peabody Mus., Harvard U., 1962-63; fellow Center for Advanced Study in Behavioral Scis., Stanford, Calif., 1961-62; prof. European archaeology and Indo-European studies UCLA, 1963-89; fellow Netherlands Inst. for Advanced Studies, 1973-74; project dir. excavations of Neolithic S.E. Europe, Obre, Bosnia, 1967-68, excavations at Sitagroi, N.E. Greece, 1968-69, excavations at Anza, Central Macedonia, 1969-70, at Achilleion, Thessaly, Greece, 1973-74, at Scaloria, nr. Manfredonia, Italy, 1979-80. Author: Die Bestattung in Litauen in der vorgeschichtlichen Zeit, 1946, Prehistory of Eastern Europe, 1956, Ancient Symbolism in Lithuanian Folk Art, 1958, The Balts, 1963, The Bronze Age Cultures of Central and Eastern Europe, 1965, The Slavs, 1971, The Gods and Goddesses of Old Europe, 1974, Neolithic Macedonia, 1976, The Goddesses and Gods of Old Europe, 1982, Die Balten, 1983, Baltai priešistoriniais laikais, 1985; co-editor: (with Colin Renfrew and Ernestine Elster) Excavations at Sitagroi. A Prehistoric Village in Northeast Greece, 1986, The Language of the Goddess, 1989, Achilleion, a Neolithic Village in Northern Greece, 6400-5600 B.C. Monumenta Archaeologica, UCLA, 1989, The Civilization of the Goddess, The World of Old Europe, 1991; editor: Jour.

Indo-European Studies, 1973—, Monumenta Archaeologica, 1976—. Recipient Woman of Yr. award L.A. Times, 1968; fellow NSF, 1959-60, 68-69, Smithsonian, 1967-71, Kress Found., 1967-72; grantee NEH, 1967, Ahmanson Found., 1973, 85, 92; subject of Festschrift Proto-Indo-European, The Archaeology of Linguistic Problems, 1987. Mem. Soc. Lithuanian Archaeologists (hon.), Lithuanian Acad. Sci. Home: 21434 Entrada Rd Topanga CA 90290-3539 *Died Feb. 2, 1994.*

GIMMESTAD, NANCY CORINNE, personal financial advisor; b. Dawson, Minn., Jan. 13, 1932; d. Bernard Arthur and Agnes (Omtvedt) G. BA, St. Olaf Coll., 1954; MA, Middlebury Coll., 1965; PhD, U. Mich., 1972. CFP, 1987. Tchr. English English Pelican Rapids (Minn.) High Sch., 1954-56; tchr. Northfield (Minn.) High Sch., 1956-58, Glendora (Calif.) High Sch., 1958-60, Edina (Minn.) High Sch., 1960-68; asst. prof. English U. Wis., Madison, 1971-75; adminstrv. aide Mpls. City Counc., 1978-84; fin. planner IDS Fin. Svcs., Inc., St. Paul, 1984-88; owner Gimmestad Fin. Svcs., Mpls., 1988—. Co-author: instructional program Poetry Unfolding, 1975. Candidate for Minn. State Sen., 1982. Mem. Nat. Assn. Scholars, Internat. Assn. Fin. Planning. Republican. Lutheran. Home and Office: 2645 Humboldt Ave S Minneapolis MN 55408-1023

GINN, CONNIE MARDEAN, nurse; b. Nevada, Mo., July 22, 1951; d. Walter Jess and Marjorie Dean (Bowman) Andrews; 1 child, Justin Andrew Hutchinson; m. Robert Bob Ginn, Feb. 18, 1978; 1 child, Heather Diane. LPN, Okla., Pa.; cert. gastrointestinal nurse clinician. Med./surgical nurse Jane Phillips Mem. Med. Ctr., Bartlesville, Okla., 1971-72, Baptist Med. Ctr., Oklahoma City, 1972-73; emergency rm. nurse Baptist Med. Ctr., 1973-75, with, 1975-77; with South Community Hosp., Oklahoma City, 1977-79; digestive disease nurse James L. Stammer, M.D. and area hosps., Oklahoma City, 1979-86; clin. coord. Regional Gastroenterology Assocs., Ben G. Lazarus, D.O., Lancaster, Pa., 1986-88; nurse Springer Clinic, Paul W. Hathaway, M.D., Tulsa, 1988-90; gastrointestinal clinician Hillcrest Med. Ctr., 1990—; dir. Okla. Ednl. Seminars, 1983-85, course coord., 1983-85. Presented articles on diseases and patient care to various confs. Vol. ARC Health and Safety. Mem. Soc. of Gastroenterology Nurses and Assocs. (regional del. to nat. seminars 1982-85, dir. at large 1984-86, co-div. chmn. regional socs. 1984, mem. program com. 1985, mem. shcolarship com. 1987-88), Regional Soc. Gastrointestinal Assts. (pres. elect Okla. and Ark. 1981-82, pres. Okla. 1980-85, founder and first pres. Okla. 1982), Northeastern Okla. Soc. Gastrointestinal Nurses and Assocs. (founder, bd. advisor 1991—), Pa. Soc. Gastrointestinal Assts., Nat. Soc. Gastrointestinal Nurses and Assocs., Nat. Assn. Lic. Practical Nurses, Lic. Practical Nurses Assn. of Pa., Nat. Soc. Physicians Nurses. Republican. Home: 11386 S Date St Jenks OK 74037-3240 Office: Family Med Care of Tulsa 7600 S Lewis Tulsa OK 74136

GINN, KATHLEEN, healthcare company executive; b. Holyoke, Mass., Sept. 24, 1948; d. Vincent E. and Nora (O'Neill) Johnson; m. Elmer Lee Ginn, Sept. 6, 1969; children: Vincent, Sean. Diploma, Providence Hosp. Sch. Nursing, Holyoke, Mass., 1969. Charge and staff nurse intensive care unit Providence Hosp., 1971-69; charge and staff nurse coronary intensive care unit Springfield Hosp., 1972-73; staff relief at various hosps. Med. Personnel Pool, 1972-76; surg. asst. Dr. Irving Meyer, 1976-78; staff operating rm. Nobel Hosp., 1979-80; owner, operator Bucket Brigade of West Springfield, Inc., 1980-84; dir. pediatrics Hampden County Nursing Svcs., 1984-86; charge nurse geriatrics unit Cresent Hill Nursing Home, 1985-86; owner, pres., adminstr. Compassionate Care Nursing Inc., West Springfield, Mass., 1986-91; mem. Kimberly Quality Care, 1991-92; mgr. para profl. dept., hospice devel. West Hills Health Care, 1992; mem. staff devel., infection control Genesis Health Ventures, 1992—. Bd. dirs. Combined Health Appeal; mem. med. adv. bd. program svcs. Mass. chpt. Nat. Multiple Sclerosis Soc., also peer counselor.

GINN, SUSAN B., training and educational specialist; b. Troy, Ala., Aug. 21, 1950; d. Robert Henderson and Idaleen (Hudson) Barr; m. Jerry Wesley Ginn, Aug. 9, 1989; children: Patrick, John, Dana. BS in Edn., Troy State U., 1972, MS in Sch. Adminstrn., 1983. Tchr. Dale City Bd. Edn., Ozark, Ala., 1972; edn. specialist Dept. Army, Ft. Rucker, Ala., 1979-89; tng. specialist Dept. Army, Ft. McPherson, Ga., 1989; force integration officer Dept. Army, Ft. Sheridan, Ill., 1990, transition svc. specialist, 1991; transition policy analyst pers. command Dept. Army, Alexandria, Va., 1992—. Recipient Profl. Woman of Yr. award U.S. Army Aviation Ctr., 1988. Mem. AAUW, AAAA, NAFE, Assn. U.S. Army (4th v.p. 1984-85), Federally Employed Women (v.p. local chpt. 1982-83), Beta Sigma Phi, Kappa Delta Pi, Gamma Beta Phi. Methodist. Home: 4626 E Rocky Slope Dr Phoenix AZ 85044-6074 Office: Dept of US Army Personnel Command Alexandria VA 22331

GINOSAR, D. ELAINE, elementary education educator; b. Red Lodge, Mont., June 14, 1937; d. Alvin Henry and Dorothy Mary (Roberson) Wedemeyer; children: Nathan B., Daniel M., David M. BA, Calif. State U., Northridge, 1964, MA, 1977. Cert. elem. tchr., reading and learning disabilities. Tchr. Sacramento City Unified Sch. Dist., 1977—; math. leader, 1992-95; owner, operator rental properties. Pres. Davis (Calif.) Flower Arrangers, 1993-95. Host family for U. Calif. Davis to 15 fgn. students from Japan, Thailand, Mexico, South Korea, 1990-95. Mem. AAUW (edn. equity chair 1993-95, edn. chair 1965-93, readers theater, women's history week 1990, 91), Calif. Tchrs. Assn. Republican. Presbyterian. Home: 3726 Chiles Rd Davis CA 95616

GINSBERG, BERNARDINE MARILYN, retired pharmacist; b. Buffalo, June 29, 1932; d. Jacob Maurice and Rosalind (Greenberg) Schwartz; B.S., U. Md., 1954; m. Marvin David Ginsberg, June 10, 1956; children—Cindy Lynn, Thomas Aaron. Registered pharmacist, Md. Pharmacist, Read Drug & Chem. Co., Balt., 1954-66; staff pharmacist Balt. County Gen. Hosp., 1966-80; staff pharmacist Howard-Morris Instl. Services, Timonium, Md., 1980-81; dir. pharmacy Balt. City Jail (PHP Corp.), 1981-84; dir. pharmacy Dept. Def., Ft. Meade, Md., 1985-90; sr. EEO investigator, Dept. Def., Ft. Meade, 1990-94; ret., 1994. Pres., Scotts Branch PTA, 1970-72, Sudbrook PTA, 1975-76, v.p. Milford Mill PTA, 1977-78, treas., 1978-79; chmn. unit memls. Am. Cancer Soc., 1980-86, state chmn. memls., 1981-85, unit treas., 1982-84, v.p., 1984-86, unit pres., 1986-87 , vice chmn. crusade, Md. div., 1985-87, chmn. 1987-89, chmn. field svc. div., 1989-91; vice chmn. pub. Edn., 1991-93, chmn. 1993-94; pres. greater Balt. unit, 1991-93; sec., bd. dirs. Md. div., 1990—; bd. dir. maricopa unit AZ divsn. Am. Cancer Soc. Recipient Vol. of Yr. award Am. Cancer Soc. Md. div., 1986-87, Martin Weil Leadership award, 1987-88, 93, Ruby Life Saver award, 1992. Democrat. Jewish. Home: 15715 Ballad Dr Sun City West AZ 85375

GINSBERG-FELLNER, FREDDA, pediatric endocrinologist, researcher; b. N.Y.C., Apr. 21, 1937; d. Nathaniel and Bertha (Jagendorf) Ginsberg; m. Michael J. Fellner, Aug. 27, 1961; children: Jonathan R., Melinda F. Bramwit. AB, Cornell U., 1957; MD, NYU, 1961. Diplomate Am. Bd. Pediatrics, Am. Bd. Pediatric Endocrinology. Intern Albert Einstein Coll. Medicine, N.Y.C., 1961-62, fellow in pediatrics, 1962-63, 64-65, 66-67, resident in pediatrics, 1963-64, 65-66, clin. instr. pediatrics, 1967; assoc. in pediatrics Mt. Sinai Sch. Medicine, N.Y.C., 1967-69, asst. prof., 1969-75, assoc. prof., 1975-81, dir. div. pediatric endocrinology, 1977—, prof. pediatrics, 1981—. Mem. med. scis. rev. com. Juvenile Diabetes Found., 1985-88, mem. scis. adv. bd., 1991—; mem. N.Y. State Coun. on Diabetes, Albany, 1988-89; chmn. Camp NYDA for Diabetic Children, Burlingham, 1977-89. Recipient Humanitarian award, Juvenile Diabetes Found., 1994; grantee NIH, 1977—, Am. Diabetes Assn., 1978, March of Dimes, 1983-87, Juvenile Diabetes Found., 1982-88, 93—, Wm. T. Grant Found., 1985-89. Fellow Am. Acad. Pediatrics; mem. Am. Diabetes Assn. (chmn. 1992-94, Outstanding Contbns. award 1991, Svc. award 1994), Soc. Pediatric Rsch., Am. Pediatric Soc., Endocrine Soc., Lawson Wilkins Pediatric Endocrine Soc., N.Y. Diabetes Assn. (pres.-elect 1985-87, pres. 1987-89, Svc. award Camp NYDA 1989, Max Ellenberg Profl. Svc. award 1993). Office: Mt Sinai Med Ctr Dept Pediatrics Box 1198 1 Gustave Levy Pl New York NY 10029-6504

GINSBURG, IONA HOROWITZ, psychiatrist; b. N.Y.C., Dec. 2, 1931; d. A. Eugene and Gertrude (Seidman) Horowitz; m. Selig M. Ginsburg, Aug. 15, 1954 (div. 1984); children: Elizabeth, Jessica. AB, Vassar Coll., 1953; MD, Columbia U., 1957. Diplomate Am. Bd. Psychiatry and Neurology. Pvt. practice N.Y.C., 1961—; instr. psychiatry Columbia U., N.Y.C., 1961-81, asst. clin. prof. psychiatry, 1981—; psychiatrist student health svc. NYU, N.Y.C., 1978—; cons.-liaison psychiatrist dept. dermatology Columbia Presbyn. Med. Ctr., N.Y.C., 1982—. Contbr. articles to profl. jours. Med. adv. bd. Nat. Psoriasis Found. Recipient Josie Bradbury Travel award Psoriasis Assn. Gt. Britain. Mem. Am. Soc. Adolescent Psychiatry, N.Y. Soc. Adolescent Psychiatry (pres. 1986, cert. of appreciation 1986), Am. Psychiat. Assn., Am. Psychosomatic Soc., Met. Coll. Mental Health Assn. (pres. 1980), Assn. Psychocutaneous Medicine N.Am. (sec.-treas. 1994—).

GINSBURG, RUTH BADER, U.S. supreme court justice; b. Brooklyn, N.Y., Mar. 15, 1933; d. Nathan and Celia (Amster) Bader; m. Martin David Ginsburg, June 23, 1954; children: Jane Carol, James Steven. AB, Cornell U., 1954; postgrad., Harvard Law Sch., 1956-58; LLB Kent scholar, Columbia Law Sch., 1959; LLD (hon.), Lund (Sweden) U., 1969, Am. U., 1981, Vt. Law Sch., 1984, Georgetown U., 1985, DePaul U., 1985, Bklyn. Law Sch., 1987, Amherst Coll., 1991, Rutgers U., 1991, Lewis and Clark Coll., 1992, Radcliffe Coll., 1994, NYU, 1994, Columbia U., 1994, Smith Coll., 1994, L.I. U., 1994; DHL (hon.), Hebrew Union Coll., 1988. Bar: N.Y. 1959, D.C. 1975, U.S. Supreme Ct. 1967. Law sec. to judge U.S. Dist. Ct. (so. dist.) N.Y., 1959-61; rsch. assoc. Columbia Law Sch., N.Y.C., 1961-62, assoc. dir. project internat. procedure, 1962-63; asst. prof. Rutgers U. Sch. Law, Newark, 1963-66, assoc. prof., 1966-69, prof., 1969-72; prof. Columbia U. Sch. Law, N.Y.C., 1972-80; U.S. Cir. judge U.S. Ct. Appeals, D.C. Cir., Washington, 1980-93; assoc. justice U.S. Supreme Ct., Washington, 1993—; Phi Beta Kappa vis. scholar, 1973-74; fellow Ctr. for Advanced Study in Behavioral Scis., Stanford, Calif., 1977-78; lectr. Aspen (Colo.) Inst., 1990, Salzburg Seminar, Austria, 1984; gen. counsel ACLU, 1973-80, bd. dirs., 1974-80. Author: (with Anders Bruzelius) Civil Procedure in Sweden, 1965; Swedish Code ofJudicial Procedure, 1968; (with others) Sex-Based Discrimination, 1974, supplement, 1978; contbr. numerous articles to books and jours. Fellow Am. Bar Found.; mem. AAAS, Am. Law Inst. (coun. mem. 1978-93), Coun. Fgn. Rels. Office: US Supreme Ct 1 1st St NE Washington DC 20543

GINSPARG, SYLVIA LEVINE, psychoanalyst; b. Chgo., July 22, 1931. AB in Psychology, Roosevelt U., 1951, AM in Clin. Psychology, 1953; PhD in Clin. Psychology, Washington U., 1956; grad. in theory of psychoanalysis, St. Louis Psychoanalytic Inst., 1982, grad. in child psychoanalysis, 1985. Lic. clin. psychologist, Mo. Clin. intern Mt. Sinai Hosp., Chgo., 1952-53; rsch. psychologist Malcolm Bliss Psychopathic Hosp. Washington U., St. Louis, Mo., 1953-54, psychol. intern Community Child Guidance Clinic, 1954-55; chief psychologist children's svc. Larue Carter Meml. Hosp., Indpls., 1956-57; cons. Family and Children's Svc. Greater St. Louis, 1957-60; rsch. psychologist Menninger Found., Topeka, 1960-65; staff psychologist Kans. Neurol. Inst., Topeka, 1965-66; staff psychologist Children's Hosp., div. Preventive Psychiatry Menninger Found., Topeka, 1966-76; pvt. practice Clayton, Ladue, Mo., 1976—; assoc. clin. prof. psychiatry and pediatrics St. Louis U. Med. Sch., 1977—; mem. faculty, supr. child devel. project and child and adolescent psychotherapy program St. Louis Psychoanalytic Inst., 1981—. Author: (with others) Children and the Death of a President, 1965, The Many Faces of Suicide, 1980; contbr. articles to Perspective, Nat. Observer. Fellow Sigma Xi; mem. APA, Am. Orthopsychiat. Assn. (editl. bd. 1973-81), Kans. Psychol. Assn. (chmn. social action com. 1970-71, bd. govs. 1975-76), Topeka Psychol. Assn., Mo. Psychol. Assn. (ins. com. 1981-82, legis. com. 1982-87), Psychologists Interested in Study of Psychoanalysis (program chmn. 1970-75, mem.-at-large 1973, pres. 1975-76, 93—, sec.-treas. 1990—), Am. Psychoanalytic Assn., Internat. Psychoanalytic Assn., N.Y. Freudian Soc., Inc., St. Louis Psychoanalytic Soc. Office: 141 N Meramec Ave # 216 Saint Louis MO 63105-3750

GINTER, DOLORES DENA (DEDE GINTER), public relations consultant; b. Chgo., Aug. 22, 1929; d. Benjamin and Dorothy Vera (Doroshow) Henner; m. Edward M. Ginter, Nov. 22, 1950; children—Susan Allyn, Barbara Ann. Student Northwestern U., 1948-49. Dir. pub. relations and programming Muckenthaler Cultural Ctr., Fullerton, Calif., 1970-73; dir. pub. relations Rubin Advt. Inc., Fullerton, 1975-78; pres. Ginter Assocs., Fullerton, 1978—. Author chpts. in book. Contbr. articles to jours. in field. Active Nat. Women's Polit. Caucus, Orange County, Calif., 1975—; campaign dir. local, county, city, state candidates, jud. candidates, 1960-80; chmn. Fullerton Bicentennial Commn., 1974-76; trustee Girls' Clubs of Orange County, 1981-85; trustee Mus. North Orange County, 1978-82; 83, 84; council on extended edn. Calif. State U.-Fullerton, 1982—, profl. adviser pub. relations sequence, 1984—. Recipient Outstanding Citizen award City of Fullerton, 1976. Mem. Pub. Relations Soc. Am. (accredited, fellow counselor's acad., Protos award 1980, 81, 82, 83, 84, 86, Disting. Service award, 1986, numerous awards of excellence, bd. dirs. 1980—, v.p. Orange County chpt. 1982-83, bd. dirs. 1984—), Publicity Club of Los Angeles. Democrat. Jewish. Club: Press of Orange County (Most Valuable Mem. award 1982). Office: Ginter Assocs 1816 Yermo Pl Fullerton CA 92633-1865

GINZBERG, ABIGAIL, video producer; b. N.Y.C., June 6, 1950; d. Eli and Ruth (Szold) G.; 1 child, Sasha Sesser-Ginzberg. Student, London Sch. Econs., 1969-70; BA, Cornell U., 1971; JD, U. Calif., San Francisco, 1975. Bar: Calif. 1975, D.C. 1979, U.S. Supreme Ct. 1979. Instr. Boalt Hall Law Sch., Berkeley, Calif., 1975-76; atty. Zaks and Harris, San Francisco, 1976-79; litigation counselor U.S. Dept. Labor, Washington, 1979-80; staff counsel Cal/OSHA/Dept. Indsl. Rels., San Francisco, 1979-80; instr. New Coll. Sch. Law, San Francisco, 1980-84; video prodr. New Directions Video, Albany, Calif., 1983—; pres. Nat. Lawyers Guild, San Francisco, 1988-91; cons. Dept. Labor, Washington, 1980-81, Dept. Health Svcs., Calif. and N.J., 1988-90, Bar Assn. of San Francisco, 1990-91. Prodr., dir.: (videos) Those Who Know Don't Tell, 1989 (Finalist award John Muir Med. Film Festival 1990, Silver Apple award Nat. Ednl. Film Festival 1990, Blue Ribbon award Am. Film and Video Festival 1990, Bronze award Houston Internat. Film Festival 1991, U.S. Environ. Film Festival award 1991), All Things Being Equal, 1989 (Golden Eagle award 1990, Finalist award Internat. Film and TV Festival N.Y. 1990), A Firm Commitment, 1990 (San Francisco AFTRA/SAG Am. Scene award 1991, silver plaque INTERCOM/Chgo. Film Festival 1991, Com. on Partnership award ABA 1992, Am. Scene award AFTRA/SAG 1992), All in A Day's Work, 1992 (E. Smythe Gambrell/ABA award 1993), Doing Justice: The Life and Trials of Arthur Kinoy, 1994 (Best of Festival award Vt. Internat. Film Festival 1994, CINE Golden Eagle award 1994, Silver Apple award Nat. Ednl. Film Festival, 1994), Inside/Out: A Portrait of Lesbian and Gay Lawyers, 1994, Breaking Down Barriers: Overcoming Discrimination Against Lawyers with Disabilities, 1994. Active Coalition for Civil Rights, San Francisco, 1988—; bd. dirs. Meiklejohn Civil Liberties Inst., 1991—; bd. advisors KPFA, 1986-92. Recipient Cert. Recognition, Calif. Assembly, 1988, award Alice Toklas Dem. Club, 1988, Award of Merit from Bar Assn. San Francisco, 1994. Mem. APHA, State Bar Assn. Calif., D.C. Bar Assn. Jewish. Home and Office: New Directions Video 1136 Evelyn Ave Albany CA 94706-2316

GIOLITTO, BARBARA, state representative; b. Elgin, Ill.; children: Kelly, Amy, Matt. BS in Sociology and Psychology, Rockford Coll., grad. in Human Rels. Sales rep. Chgo. Food Brokerage Co.; ins. agt. Pioneer Life; owner Environ. Concepts; state rep. State of Ill., 1993—. Dep. registrar, precinct com.-person Dem. Party; mem. Com. to Elect John Cox for Congress, Com. to Elect Mike Rotello, Com. to Elect Judge Ron Pirello, Com. to Elect Mary Tulley for County Bd.; mem. Project Self-Sufficiency, Women in Dem. Politics, LWV; chmn. Rockford Coalition for Reproductive Choice. Mem. AAUW (state bd. dirs.), Nat. Assn. Women in Careers (co-chair Crusader Clinic Art Auction 1991). Home: 807 Brae Burn Ln Rockford IL 61107-3805 Office: Ho of Reps 200 S Wyman St Ste 300 Rockford IL 61101-1234•

GIORDANO, CATHERINE KOWKABANY, nurse; b. Bklyn., Feb. 18, 1956; d. Emil and Madeline (Asmar) Kowkabany; m. William Lawrence Giordano, Feb. 2, 1985; 1 child, Lawrence William. ADN, L.I. Coll., 1978; BS in Adminstrn. cum laude, St. Francis Coll., Bklyn., 1982. RN, N.Y.; cert. apheresis nurse. Educator Downstate Med. Ctr., Bklyn., 1979-84; counselor ARC, Bklyn., 1981-84; head apheresis nurse Coney Island Hosp., Bklyn., 1982—. Office: Coney Island Hosp 2601 Ocean Pky Brooklyn NY 11235-7791

GIORDANO, JOAN AUGUSTA, artist; b. N.Y.C., Sept. 8, 1942; d. Vincent James and Antoinette (Narducci) Baldassano; m. Ben Giordano, Sept. 5, 1960; children: Jeffrey, Glenn. BA, Wagner Coll., 1962; MFA, Pratt Inst., 1978. Co-founder, adminstr. Art Lab. Workshop, Snug Harbor Cultural Ctr., 1975-80; founder, adminstr. Visual Exch., S.I., N.Y., 1980-83; curator The Sarah Inst., N.Y.C., 1980-85; asst. dir. Rockland Ctr. for Arts, Nyack, N.Y., 1985-87; dir. continuing edn. arts program Coll. of S.I., 1977-81, instr. fin arts painting, 1976-78; artist, instr. Studio in a Sch., N.Y.C., 1988-91; instr. LaGuardia C.C., CUNY, 1978-80, Union Coll., N.J., 1978-80; vis. artist U. South Fla., Tampa; workshop vis. artist Ringling Sch. Art, Sarasota, Fla.; lectr. Mauro Graphics Gallery, S.I., LaGuardia Coll., CUNY; curator Rockland Ctr. for Arts; resident Va. Ctr. Creative Arts, 1979, Yaddo Artists Colony, 1980. One-woman shows include Gallery DuBost, Paris, 1981, Sutton Gallery, N.Y.C., 1982, 84, Nuance Gallery, Tampa, Fla., 1987, Walter Wickiser Gallery, N.Y.C., 1993, 94, Queens Coll. Art Ctr., CUNY, Lamar Dodd Art Ctr. and Mus., Ga., 1995, Art Inst. for the Permian Basin, Tex., 1995; exhibited in numerous group shows, including Metropolitan Mus., N.Y.C., 1975, S.I. Mus., 1976, Sutton Gallery, 1981, U. Wis., Superior, 1983, Clayton Gallery, Tampa, 1990, A.J. Lederman Fine Arts, 1992, Alan Stone Gallery, 1986, 87, Feminine Dialouge UNESCO, Paris, 1982; represented in permanent collection of N.Y. Pub. Libr., numerous corp. and pvt. collections. Founder Urban Artists for Earth, N.Y.C., 1993. Recipient Julian Weissglass award for painting S.I. Mus., 1978; grad. fellow Hunter Coll., CUNY, 1973. Mem. N.Y. Artists Equity, Ironclad Artists (bd. dirs., sec. 1990-94). Home and Studio: 136 Grand St New York NY 10013

GIORDANO, LAURA ANN, quality management professional, nurse; b. Bronx, N.Y.; d. Joseph P. and Viola N. (Seymour) Morrissey; m. Joseph P. Giordano. BS in Nursing, Molloy Coll., Rockville Centre, N.Y., 1978; MBA, Adelphi U., Garden City, N.Y., 1985. RN, N.Y., Ariz.; cert. profl. in health care quality. Staff nurse Winthrop U. Hosp., Mineola, N.Y., 1978-79; staff nurse nursing supr. alcohol treatment ctr. Creedmoor Psychiat. Ctr., Queens, N.Y., 1979-80, asst. adminstr., cen. systems coord. acute admissions div., 1980-84, asst. dir. edn. and tng., 1984-85; community program rep. Office Community Behavioral Health Ariz. Dept. Health Svcs., Phoenix, 1985-87; clin. quality assurance coord. Ariz. State Hosp., Ariz. Dept. Health Svcs., Phoenix, 1987-90; dir. quality mgmt. svcs. div. behavioral health svcs. Ariz. Dept. Health Svcs., 1990-93; coop. projects specialist Health Svcs. Adv. Group Inc., Phoenix, 1994—. Mem. Am. Coll. Med. Quality, Ariz. Assn. for Healthcare Quality, Nat. Assn. for Healthcare Quality, Sigma Theta Tau, Delta Mu Delta.

GIORGI, ELSIE AGNES, physician; b. N.Y.C., Mar. 8, 1911; d. Anacleto and Maria (Maserati) G. BA, Hunter Coll., 1931; MD, Columbia U., 1949. Diplomate Am. Bd. Internal Medicine. Intern Cornell 2d med. div. Bellevue Hosp., N.Y.C., 1949-50, asst. resident in medicine Cornell 2d med. div., 1950-52, chief resident in medicine Cornell 2d med. div., 1952-53, chief gen. med. clinics Cornell 2d med. div., 1953-59, assoc. attending physician Cornell 2d med. div., 1953-62, physician, specialist in internal medicine, 1953-61; physician, specialist in internal medicine L.A., 1962—; psychiat. trainee Cedars of Lebanon Hosp., Los Angeles, 1961-62, assoc. attending physician, 1962—; dir. div. home care and extended care, Cedars-Sinai Med. Ctr., Los Angeles, 1962-66; chief adolescent clinic, med. dir. clinics Mt. Sinai Hosp., Los Angeles, 1962-66, assoc. attending physician dept. medicine, 1962-69, attending physician, 1970—; med. dir., coordinator U. So. Calif. Family Neighborhood Health Services Ctr. for Watts, 1966-67; attending physician Los Angeles County Hosp., U. So. Calif. Med. Ctr., 1966-71; assoc. mem. dept. internal medicine Orange County Med. Ctr., Calif., 1969—, dir. ambulatory care services, 1969-72; staff St. John's Hosp., Santa Monica, Calif., 1970—; asst. prof. clin. medicine, attending sr. physician internal medicine Cornell U. Med. Coll., 1957-62; asst. prof. clin. medicine UCLA, 1962-66, guest lectr. Sch. Social Welfare, 1964—, assoc. clin. prof. medicine and community medicine Sch. Medicine, 1972—, PRIMEX, 1972-73; asst. prof. medicine Sch. Medicine, U. So. Calif., 1966-69, adj. prof. medicine, community medicine, family medicine Coll. Medicine, U. Calif., Irvine, 1969-72; cons. Martin E. Segal Co., 1969—, VA Hosp., Long Beach, Calif., 1972—, Washington, 1972—; cons. health care sect. Social Security Adminstrn., Balt., Los Angeles County Health Dept., Calif. Council for Health Plan Alternatives, Burlingame, Regional Med. Care Program, 1971-73, Tb and Health Assn. of Los Angeles; mem. nat. adv. bd. Nat. Council Sr. Citizens, Washington; mem. adv. com. USPHS, Calif. Dept. Pub. Health; mem. med. adv. com. Vis. Nurse Assn., Los Angeles, 1976; mem. adv. bd. Life Extension Inst., N.Y.C.; mem. edn. com. Am. Cancer Soc., San Francisco; cons. ednl. films. Author sect. in textbook; contbr. articles to profl. pubs. Active Town Hall, Los Angeles; vol., bd. dirs. South Central Child Care Ctrs. for South Central Los Angeles; mem. nat. adv. bd. for legal research and services for elderly Nat. Council Sr. Citizens; mem. UCI-21 project com. U. Calif. Recipient Achievement award AAUW, 1968, Better Life award Am. Nursing Home Assn., 1974, lifetime commitment award Watts Health Found., 1987; named to Hall of Fame, Hunter Coll. Alumni Assn., 1976; feature This Is Your Life progam TV Sta. KNBC, 1984. Mem. AMA, New York County Med. Assn., Calif. Med. Assn., Los Angeles County Med. Assn., Los Angeles County Soc. Internists, Am. Pub. Health Assn. (med. care sect.), Gerontol. Soc., Western Gerontology Assn., Comprehensive Health Planning Assn., Nat. Acad. Scis., Inst. Medicine. Home: 153 S Lasky Dr Ste 3 Beverly Hills CA 90212-1769

GIOSEFFI, DANIELA, poet, author, educator; b. Orange, N.J., Feb. 12, 1941; d. Daniel Donato and Josephine (Buzevska) G.; m. Richard J. Kearney, Sept. 7, 1965 (div.) 1 child, Thea D.; m. Lionel B. Luttinger, June 6, 1986. BA, Montclair State Coll., 1963; MFA, Cath. U. of Am., 1966. Cons., poet Poets-in-the-Schs., Inc., N.Y.C., 1972-85; freelance writer, lectr. at numerous univs. throughout U.S. and Europe; appeared on Nat. Pub. Radio, CBC, BBC; speaker on world peace and disarmament, 1979—; keynote speaker Am. Forum for Global Edn. Nat. Conf., Miami, Fla., 1994. Author: (novel) The Great American Belly, 1977, 4th edit., 1979; (collection of poems) Eggs in the Lake, 1979, Word Wounds and Water Flowers, 1995; (non-fiction) Earth Dancing; Mother Nature's Oldest Rite, 1981, Women on War and Survival: International Voices for the Nuclear Age, 1988 (Am. Book award 1990), Dust Disappears: translations of Carilda Oliver Labra of Latin America, 1994, On Prejudice: A Global Perspective, 1993—; (plays) The Golden Daffodil Dwarf, Care of the Body, The Sea Hag in the Cave of Sleep, 1988; mem. editl. bd. Voices in Italian Americana, 1990—; short stories include Daffodil Dollars (PEN Short Fiction award 1990); contbr. poetry and fiction to numerous periodicals and anthologies; performer stage presentations of work throughout U.S. and Europe. Pres. Bklyn. Citizens for Sane Nuclear Policy, 1987-89; participant IV Feminist Internat. Bookfair, Barcelona, Spain, 1989, Miami Internat. Bookfair, 1990; mem. exec. bd., chmn. media watch com. Writers and Pubs. Alliance for Nuclear Disarmament, 1978-91. Recipient poetry and fiction award Creative Artists' Pub. Svc. Program, N.Y.C., 1971; grantee N.Y. State Coun. on Arts, 1972, 77, World Peace award Ploughshares Fund, 1989, Womens' Leadership Devel. Mem. PEN Am. Ctr., Acad. Am. Poets, Actors Equity Assn., Nat. Book Critics Cir., Poets' House, Skylands Writers and Artists Assn. (pres.). Address: PO Box 15 Andover NJ 07821

GIOVANNI, NIKKI, poet; b. Knoxville, Tenn., June 7, 1943; d. Jones and Yolande Cornelia (Watson) G.; 1 son, Thomas Watson. BA in History with honors, Fisk U., 1967; postgrad. in social work, U. Pa., 1967; LHD (hon.), Wilberforce U., 1972, Worcester U., 1972; DLitt (hon.), Ripon U., 1974, Smith Coll., 1975, Coll. Mt. St. Joseph on Ohio, 1983. Founder Nixtom Ltd., 1970; asst. prof. black studies Queens Coll., CCNY, 1968; assoc. prof. English Rutgers U., 1968-72; prof. creative writing Coll. Mt. St. Joseph on the Ohio, 1985; prof. Va. Poly Inst. and State U., Blacksburg, 1987—; vis. prof. English Ohio State U., 1984. Poet, writer, lectr.; author: Black Feeling, Black Talk, 1968, Black Judgement, 1968, Re: Creation, 1970, Poem of Angela Yvonne Davis, 1970, Spin a Soft Black Song, 1971, Gemini, 1971 (Nat. Book Award nomination 1973), My House, 1972 (Am. Libr. Assn. commendation 1973), A Dialogue: James Baldwin and Nikki Giovanni, 1973, Ego Tripping and Other Poems for Young Readers, 1973, A Poetic Equation: Conversations Between Nikki Giovanni and Margaret Walker, 1974, The Women and the Men, 1975, Cotton Candy on a Rainy Day, 1978, Vacationtime, 1980, Those Who Ride the Night Winds, 1983, Sacred Cows. . .and other Edibles, 1988 (Ohioana Book award 1988), Conversations with Nikki Giovanni, 1992, Racism 101, 1994, Grand Mothers, 1994, Knoxville, Tennessee, 1994; rec. artist: (album) Truth Is On Its Way, 1971 (Nat. Assn. Radio and TV Announcers award best spoken word album 1972), Like A Ripple on a Pond, 1973, The Way I Feel, 1974, Legacies: The Poetry of

Nikki Giovanni, 1976, The Reason I Like Chocolate, 1976, Cotton Candy on a Rainy Day, 1978, others; editor: Images of Blacks in American Culture, 1988, Appalachian Elders, 1991, Grand Mothers: Poems, Reminiscences, and Short Stories About the Keepers of Our Traditions, 1994; editor: Night Comes Softly, 1970, (with Jessie Carney Smith) Images of Blacks in American Culture, 1988, (with Cathee Dennison) Appalachian Elders: A Warm Heart Sampler, 1991; TV appearances include: Soul!, Nat. Ednl. TV network, numerous talk shows including the Tonight Show; participant Soul at the Center, Lincoln Center Performing Arts, N.Y.C., 1972. Vol. worker Nat. Council Negro Women, now life mem. Recipient Outstanding Achievement award Mademoiselle mag., 1971, Omega Psi Phi award outstanding contbn. arts and letters, 1971, Prince Matchabelli Sun Shower award, 1971, Meritorious Plaque Svc., Cook County Jail, 1971, Scroll, life mem. Nat. Coun. Negro Women, 1972, Woman of Yr.-Youth Leadership award Ladies Home Jour., 1972, Woman of Yr. award Cin. Chpt. YWCA, 1983, Post-Corbett award, 1986, Disting. Recognition award Detroit City Coun., 1986; elected Ohio Women's Hall of Fame, 1985; named Outstanding Woman Tenn., 1985; Ford Found. grantee, 1967, NEA grantee, 1968, Harlem Cultural Coun. grantee, 1969. Office: Va Poly Inst and State Univ Dept of English PO Box 0112 Blacksburg VA 24063-0112*

GIPSON, GAYLE, medical/surgical nurse; b. Scottsbluff, Nebr., Apr. 1, 1950; d. Raymond C. and Darline (Rohrick) Hartley; m. Mike S. Gipson, Jan. 4, 1971; children: Shawn, Kacey. AS, Ky. Wesleyan Coll., 1982; BSN, Coll. of Misericordia, 1992. Staff nurse orthopedics unit St. Joseph Hosp., Providence; staff nurse med. unit Oliver C. Anderson Hosp., Maryville, Ill.; nurse mgr., hosp. nurse recruiter med.-surg. orthopedics & pediatrics Tyler Meml. Hosp., Tunkhannock, Pa.; instr. trainer CPR. Mem. Am. Heart Assn., Northeastern Pa. Assn. Health Care Recruiters, Nightingale Soc., Sigma Theta Tau.

GIRA, CATHERINE RUSSELL, university president; b. Fayette City, Pa., Oct. 30, 1932; d. John Anthony and Mary (Stephen) Russell; m. Joseph Andrew Gira, July 17, 1954; children—Cheryl Ann, Thomas Russell. B.S., Calif. State U., 1953; M.Ed., Johns Hopkins U., 1957, M.L.A., 1972; Ph.D., Am. U., 1975. Tchr. Balt. County, Balt., 1953-60, head dept., 1958-60; writing cons. Md. State Dept. Edn., 1960-68; instr. Johns Hopkins U., Balt., 1964-65; from asst. prof. to prof. U. Balt., 1965-81, acting dean, 1981-82, provost, 1982-91; pres. Frostburg (Md.) State U., 1991—. Contbr. articles to profl. jours. Am. U. scholar, 1973-75. Mem. Am. Assn. Univ. Adminstrs. (bd. dirs. 1984-87, pres.-elect 1987, pres. 1988-90), Fedn. State Humanities Couns. (bd. dirs. 1990-94, vice-chair 1993-94), Md. Humanities Coun. (chmn. 1989-90), Md. Assn. Higher Edn. (bd. dirs. 1983-85, pres. 1986-87), Shakespeare Assn. Am., Edgar Allan Poe Soc. (bd. dirs. 1982—). Methodist. Home: 324 Braddock St Frostburg MD 21532 Office: Frostburg State U Office of Pres Frostburg MD 21532

GIRARD, ANDREA EATON, communication executive, consultant; b. N.Y.C., Oct. 16, 1946; d. Samuel Robert and Mimi (Eaton) G. Student, Syracuse U., 1964-66; BA cum laude, Finch Coll., 1968; MA, Columbia U., 1971. Talent coord./prodn. asst. Guber-Ford-Gross Prodns., N.Y., 1968-70; v.p. Charing Cross Press, N.Y.C., 1970-72; assoc. producer, talent dir.TV shows "To Tell the Truth" and "Snap Judment" Goodson Todman Prodns., N.Y.C., 1972-80; programming exec. David Letterman-NBC, N.Y.C., 1980; dir. of talent, producer Daytime/Arts and Entertainment Networks (Hearst/ABC Video Enterprises), N.Y.C., 1981-84; dir. current programming acquisition, sr. producer Lifetime Network (Hearst/ABC/Viacom Entertainment Svcs.), N.Y.C., 1984-86; pres. Girard Communications, N.Y.C., 1986—, dir. med. communications advantage internat., 1990-91, v.p. pub. rels., 1990-92; CEO Panache Communications Inc., N.Y.C., 1992—; judge Emmy awards Internat. Film and TV Festival; speaker pub. rels. coun. sch. of continuing edn. NYU; media cons. to med. industry, 1987—. Producer, writer (documentaries) Cave Dwellers of Crete, 1974, Sponge Divers of Kalymnos, 1979, Gypsies of the Camargue, 1983. Active fund raising bd. Jersey Wildlife Preservation Trust, N.Y.; active hospitality com. United Nations, N.Y., Big Apple Com. for the Benefit of the Image of N.Y. Mem. NATAS, Women in Radio and TV, Women in Comms., Nat. Assn. Women Bus. Owners, Internat. Assn. of Cooking Profls., Le Club. Office: Panache Comms 201 E 77th St Apt 7F New York NY 10021-2082

GIRARD, MARTHA LYNN, federal agency administrator; b. Olean, N.Y., Aug. 24, 1944. BA, Ladycliff Coll., N.Y., 1966. Various editorial and sr. mgmt. positions, 1966-88; dir. Office of the Fed. Register, Nat. Archives and Record Adminstrn., Washington, 1989—. Office: National Archives & Records 800 N Capitol St NW Washington DC 20408*

GIRARD, NETTABELL, lawyer; b. Pocatello, Idaho, Feb. 24, 1938; d. George and Arranetta (Bell) Girard. Student, Idaho State U., 1957-58; BS, U. Wyo., 1959, JD, 1961. Bar: Wyo. 1961, D.C. 1969, U.S. Supreme Ct. 1969. Practiced in Riverton, 1963-69; atty.-adviser on gen. counsel's staff HUD; assigned Office Interstate Land Sales Registration, Washington, 1969-70; sect. chief interstate land sales Office Gen. Counsel, 1970-73; ptnr. Larson & Larson, Riverton, 1973-85; pvt. practice Riverton, 1985—; guest lectr. at high schs.; condr. seminar on law for layman Riverton br. A.A.U.W., 1965; condr. course on women and law; lectr. equal rights, job discrimination, land use planning. Editor Wyoming Clubwoman, 1966-68; bd. editors Wyo. Law Jour., 1959-61; writer Obiter Dictum column Women Lawyers Jour., Dear Legal Advisor column Solutions for Seniors, 1988-94; featured in Riverton Ranger, 1994; also articles in legal jours. Chmn. fund dr. Wind River chpt. ARC, 1965; chmn. Citizens Com. for Better Hosp. Improvement, 1965; chmn. subcom. on polit. legal rights and responsibilities Gov.'s Commn. on Status Women, 1965-69, adv. mem., 1973—; rep. Nat. Conf. Govs. Commn., Washington, 1966; local chmn. Law Day, 1966, 67, county chmn. law day, 1994; mem. state bd. Wyo. Girl Scouts U.S., sec., 1974-89, mem. nat. bd., 1978-81; state vol. adviser Nat. Found., March of Dimes, 1967-69; legal counsel Wyo. Women's Conf., 1977. Recipient Spl. Achievement award UND, 1972, Disting. Leadership award Girl Scouts U.S.A., 1973, Franklin D. Roosevelt award Wyo. chpt. March of Dimes, 1985, Thanks Badge award Girl Scout Coun., 1987, Women Helping Women award in recognition of effective advancement status of women Riverton Club of Soroptimist Internat., 1990, Spl. award plaque in appreciation and recognition of 27 yrs. of svc. to State of Wyo., Wyo. Commn. for Women, 1964-92, Appreciation award Wyo. Sr. Citizens and Solutions for Srs., 1994. Mem. AAUW (br. pres.), Wyo. Bar Assn., Fremont County Bar Assn., D.C. Bar Assn., Women's Bar Assn. D.C., Internat. Fedn. Women Lawyers, Am. Judicature Soc., Assn. Trial Lawyers Am., Nat. Assn. Women Lawyers (del. Wyo., nat. sec. 1969-70, v.p. 1970-71, pres. 1972-73), Wyo. Fedn. Women's Clubs (state editor, pres. elect 1968-69, treas. 1974-76), Prog. Women's Club (pres.-elect 1994—), Riverton Chautauqua Club (pres. 1965-67), Riverton Civic League (pres. 1987-89), Kappa Delta, Delta Kappa Gamma (state chpt., hon.). Home: 224 W Sunset St PO Box 687 Riverton WY 82501 Office: 513 E Main St Riverton WY 82501-4440

GIRE, SHARON LEE, state legislator; b. Jan. 13, 1944; m. Dana A. Gire. BS in Edn., Ohio State U., 1965, postgrad. in counseling psychology, 1966; MSW, Wayne State U., 1975. Program dir. YWCA, Macomb, Mich., 1969-71, cons. ctrl. region teen program, 1971-73; commr. Macomb County, 1984-86; chairperson budget com., pers. com., data processing subcom., bldg. and grounds subcom.; state rep. Mich. Ho. of Reps., 1987—, co-chair human svcs., children com. and youth, mem. pub. health, housing and urban affairs com., mem. consumers econ. devel. and energy com.; mem. Mich. Assn. Counties Legis. Conf., Mich. Assn. Counties Ann. Conf., Mich. Assn. Counties Seminar County Govt., Mich. Mcpl. League State Legis. Confs., Mich. Mcpl. League Annual Confs., Mich. Mcpl. League Regional Meetings, Mich. Mcpl. League Workshops. Mem. Mt. Clemens Bd. Zoning Appeals, 1977-84; mem. Mich. Women in Mcpl. Govt., 1978-84; mem. comml. and indsl. devel. com., 1978-84; city liaison for student govt. day, 1979-84; mayor pro-tem City of Mt. Clemens, 1979-84; vice chairwoman Mich. Mcpl. League Region 5, 1982; dir. N.E. Interfaith Ctr., 1977-84. Home: 37567 Radde St Clinton Township MI 48036*

GIRLING, BETTIE JOYCE MOORE, home health executive; b. Midlothian, Tex., Feb. 10, 1930; d. Robert and Florence Irene (Shaw) Moore; B.S. in Edn., Daniel Baker Coll., 1952; M.S.S.W., U. Tex., Austin, 1956; m. Robert George William Girling, III, Sept. 2, 1960; children—Robert George William IV, Maria Julia Anastasia, Samuel Marcus Shaw, Katherine Susan Jane. Tchr., Clairemont (Tex.) Ind. Sch. Dist., 1952-53; caseworker Tex. Dept. Public Welfare, 1953-57, licensing supr., Dallas, 1960; caseworker Austin State Sch. for Mentally Retarded, 1957-60; with adoption intake Edna Gladney Home, Ft. Worth, 1961-65; researcher Child Welfare League Am., N.Y.C., 1966; organizer, exec. dir. Girling Home Care, Austin, 1967-69; asst. dir. agy. programs Girling Health Care, Inc., multi-state, comprehensive health care agy., 1967—; owner, operator child care facility, 1973-75; mem. long range planning com. Grad. Sch. Social Work, U. Tex.-Austin; mem. home health services adv. council Tex. Dept. Health; organizer, coordinator profl. workshops; Mem. Nat. Assn. Social Workers, Tex. Hosp. Assn., Tex. Home Health Agys., Nat. Assn. Home Health Agys., Women's Symphony League of Austin, Austin Symphony Orchestra Soc. (bd. dirs.). Recipient Ida Mae Hebert award Tex. Assn. for Home Care, 1994. Democrat. Baptist. Office: Girling Health Care Inc PO Box 4294 Austin TX 78765-4294

GIROLAMI, LISA S., film producer; b. Modesto, Calif., Sept. 13, 1960; d. Guido and Kristine (White) G. BA, Calif. State U., Long Beach, 1983. Assoc. prodn. exec. Walt Disney Pictures/Touchtone, Burbank, Calif., 1985-87; prodn. exec. Buena Vista Pictures, Burbank, Calif., 1987-89; producer Theme Park Prodns. div. Walt Disney, Burbank, Calif., 1989—; show designer Walt Disney Imagineering, Glendale, Calif., 1990-92; line prodr. Disney's Virtual Reality Attraction, 1992-94; mgr. prodn. Disney Interactive Software, Burbank, 1995—. Prodn. exec. films including Honey I Shrunk The Kids, Heartbreak Hotel, DOA, Disorganized Crime, Ernest Saves Christmas, Where the Heart Is, 1989; producer theme park films including the Lottery, Monster Sound Show; prodn. coord. films including Critters, 1985; set mgr. films Reanimator, 1985, Terminator, 1984; asst. dir. films including Summers End, Calling Home; sr. asst. to v.p. prodn. films including Ruthless People, Outrageous Fortune, Color of Money, Adventures in Babysitting, Who Framed Roger Rabbit?, Good Morning Vietnam, Tough Guys, Down and Out in Beverly Hills; prodn. mgr. numerous commls. Roman Catholic. Office: Walt Disney Studios 500 S Buena Vista Burbank CA 91221

GIROUARD, SHIRLEY ANN, nurse, policy analyst; b. New London, Conn., Jan. 16, 1947; d. Maxime Albert Girouard and Irene Barbara (Arnold) Reid. BA in Sociology, Ea. Conn. State Coll., 1972; MA in Sociology, U. Conn., 1974; MSN, Yale U., 1977; PhD in Policy Analysis, Brandeis U., 1988. Nurse Woodstock (Conn.) Pub. Health Assn., 1968-70; staff nurse Clinton (Conn.) Convalescent Ctr., 1970-72; ins. edn. coord. Middlesex Meml. Hosp., Middletown, Conn., 1973-75; clin. nurse specialist Dartmouth Hitchcock Med. Ctr., Hanover, N.H., 1977-83; staff nurse Dartmouth Hitchcock Med. Ctr., Hanover, 1983-84; legis. cons., lobbyist N.H. Nurses Assn., Concord, 1985-87; program officer Robert Wood Johnson Found., Princeton, N.J., 1987-92; exec. dir. N.C. Ctr. Nursing, 1992-93, Am. Nurse's Assn., 1993-94; health policy and nursing cons. Washington, 1994—; pvt. practice cons., 1983-87; profl. devel. cons., Lebanon, N.H., 1983-87; health policy and nursing cons. Author: (chpt.) Health Policy and Nurse Services, 1989; mem. editorial bd. Clin. Nurses Specialist Jour., 1986—; contbr. articles to profl. jours. State rep. N.H. Legislature, Concord, 1982-84; counselor City of Lebanon Coun., 1984-87. Fellow Am. Acad. Nursing; mem. ANA (project dir. 1986), N.C. State Nurses Assn., Sigma Theta Tau. Democrat.

GIROUX, CHRISTY ANNE HENDERSON, nurse, air force officer; b. Indpls., Nov. 30, 1956; d. Gentry D. and Bernese A. (Fodge) Henderson; m. Norman F. Gioux Jr., Feb. 22, 1983 (div. Nov. 1990); 1 child, Kathryn A. BSN, Ind. U., 1979; MA in Mgmt., Webster U., 1988. RN, Ind.; BLS instr.-trainer, ACLS instr. Asst. dir. nursing and health svcs. ARC, Indpls., 1979-80; commd. 2d lt. USAF, 1980, advanced through grades to maj., 1993; flight comdr., nurse program Air Force Health Professions, Indpls., 1992—. Pres., bd. dirs. Greenwood (Ind.) divsn. Am. Heart Assn., 1992-94. Mem. ANA, Ind. State Nurses Assn., Air Force Assn. Republican. Methodist. Office: Air Force Health Professions 9240 N Meridian St Ste 360 Indianapolis IN 46260-1822

GISRIEL-BRADFORD, BARBARA ANN, nurse administrator; b. Balt., Sept. 19, 1941; d. Robert G. and Gertrude C. (Hartman) Lessig; m. Daniel Joseph Bradford, Sr., May 14, 1983; children: Keith Clayton, Karen Marie. AA, Essex Community Coll., Balt., 1974; BSN, Coll. Notre Dame, Balt., 1982. Staff nurse med.-surg. ICU Balt. City Hosps.; staff nurse hemodialysis Balt. (Md.) City Hosps., coord. home hemodialysis program; asst. chief Kidney Disease Program Md., Balt., acting chief; acting asst. dir. spl. programs Dept. Health and Mental Hygiene, State of Md., Balt.; chief Kidney Disease Program of Md.; speaker in field. Mem. Am. Nephrology Nurses' Assn.

GISSEN, LINDA RUTH, sculptor; b. Newark, Aug. 16, 1937; d. Max R. and Ruth H. (Michaels) Mayer; m. Ira Gissen, July 29, 1956; children: Laura, Emily Gissen Dreyfus, David. BA, U. Cin., 1959; student, U. Mich., 1955-56; postgrad., Fairleigh Dickinson U. Tchr. art Open High Sch., Richmond, Va., Dwight Englewood (N.J.) Prep. Sch., Teaneck (N.J.) Arts Magnet Sch., Riverdell Adult Edn. Ctr., River Edge, N.J., Virginia Beach (Va.) Pub. Schs.; lectr. Muscarelle Mus. Art, Williamsburg, Va., Bergen Cmty. Mus., numerous others; art cons.; guest curator, juror, judge for art exhbns. One-woman shows include ArtSpace 1306, Richmond, Bergen Cmty. Mus., Paterson (N.J.) Mus., Robbins Gallery, South Orange, N.J., Working Gallery, Virginia Beach, numerous others; exhibited in group shows Am. Artists Profl. League, Am. Interfaith Inst., Beth Ahabah Mus., Richmond, Sculpture Ctr., N.Y.C., Valentine Mus., Richmond; represented in numerous permanent collections, including Newark Mus., Skirball Mus., Cin., Rockford (Ill.) Art Mus., The White House, also numerous pvt. collections; various commns. Pres. Jewish Cmty. Coun., Teaneck, 1982-84; mem. women's com. Brandeis U., 1981—. Recipient sculpture ribbons Met. Artists Assn., 1985-89, Woman of Achievement award Beth-El Richmond, 1989, merit award WHRO, 1992, bronze award Am. Interfaith Inst., 1992, Best in Show award Stockley Gardens Art Show, 1993, also others; commd. to create 1st Holocaust Meml. by Cath. Diocese, Richmond, 1987. Mem. Am. Craft Coun., Va. Artists Bus. Devel. Assn. (charter, juried). Home and Studio: 973 Larkaway Ct Virginia Beach VA 23464

GIST, MARILYN ELAINE, organizational behavior and human resource management educator; b. Tuskegee, Ala., May 9, 1950; d. Lewis A. and Grace (Perry) G. BA in Edn., Howard U., 1972; MBA, U. Md., 1982, PhD in Bus. Aminstrn. Organizational Behavior, 1985. Tchr. Montgomery County Pub. Schs., Rockville, Md., 1972-76; mgmt. intern NASA Goddard Space Flight Ctr., Greenbelt, Md., 1976-79; procurement mgr. NASA Goddard Space Flight Ctr., Greenbelt, 1980-81, staff asst. to dir. mgmt. ops., 1983-85; dir. contracts OAO Corp., Greenbelt, 1981-83; prof. organizational behavior U. N.C., Chapel Hill, N.C., 1985-87; prof. organized behavior and human resources U. Wash., Seattle, 1987—; staff cons. U. Md., Coll. Park, 1979-84, CIA, Langley, Va., 1984-85. Contbr. articles to profl. jours. Recipient Outstanding Student award Alumni Assn. Internat. U. Md., 1985, Alan Nash Outstanding Doctoral Student award U. Md., 1985; U. Md. Academic Research grantee, 1982-85. Mem. Acad Mgmt. (Outstanding Paper award 1987), Am. Psychological Assn., So. Mgmt. Assn. Democrat. Roman Catholic. Office: U Wash Sch Bus Adminstrn MacKenzie Hall DJ 10 Seattle WA 98195

GITELSON, SUSAN AURELIA, business executive, civic leader; b. N.Y.C.; d. Moses Leo and Miriam Evelyn (Silverman) G. BA, Barnard Coll.; MIA, Columbia Sch. Internat. Affairs; PhD, Columbia U. Trainee Rockefeller Found.; asst. prof. internat. rels. Hebrew U., Jerusalem; rsch. assoc. Columbia U., N.Y.C.; dir. internat. affairs and third world World Jewish Congress, N.Y.C.; pres. Internat. Cons., Inc., N.Y.C., S.J. Internat. Corp., N.Y.C. Author: Multilateral Aid for National Development and Self-Reliance; editor, author: Israel in the Third World; contbr. articles to profl. jours.; mem. editorial com. Jerusalem Papers on Peace Problems. Mem. nat. adv. coun. Ctr. for Study Presidency, N.Y.C.; mem. Columbia U. seminars; sponsor Gitelson Lecture on Human Rights and U.S. Fgn. Policy, Columbia U., Gitelson award for human values in internat. affairs Sch. Internat. and Pub. Affairs, Gitelson-Meyerowitz Human Rights essay award Columbia Ctr. for the Study of Human Rights, Gitelson Seminars on the UN, City U. Grad. Ctr., Gitelson Peace Prize, Gitelson Peace Papers and Publs., Truman Inst. of Hebrew Univ. of Jerusalem, Gitelson Essay awards, Ctr. for the Study of the Presidency; bd. overseers Truman Inst. of Hebrew Univ. of Jerusalem; mem. internat. bd. govs. Hebrew U. Jerusalem; mem., bd. dirs. Am. Friends of Hebrew U.; mem., bd. trustees Sutton Place synagogue. Recipient Outstanding Service award Columbia Sch. Internat. and Public Affairs; Alumni medal for conspicuous service Columbia U. Mem. Columbia Sch. Internat. and Public Affairs Alumni Assn. (pres. 1980-84), Soc. Internat. Devel. (pres.), Columbia U. Alumni Fedn. (exec. com., chmn. Alumni Trustee Nominating Com.), Internat. Studies Assn., Am. Polit. Sci. Assn., Am. Friends of Hebrew U., Am. Jewish Com. (internat. rels. commn.), UN Assn. of N.Y. (adv. coun.). Office: Internat Cons Inc 303 E 83rd St New York NY 10028-4318

GITNER, DEANNE, writer; b. Lyons, N.Y., Jan. 8, 1944; d. Myron and Mary (Kurland) Gebell; m. Gerald L. Gitner, June 24, 1968; children: Daniel Mark, Seth Michael. AB, Cornell U., 1966. Cert. English tchr. Tchr. English Gates (N.Y.) Chili Cen. Sch., 1966-68, Wantagh (N.Y.) Jr. and Sr. High Sch., 1968-70, F. Weiner Sch., Houston, 1980-81; writer Bellaire Texan, Houston, 1980; rep. sales McDougal Littel & Co., Chgo., 1981-83; writer Millburn Short Hills Ind., New Providence, N.J., 1987-93; comm. coord. Millburn Twp. (N.J.) Pub. Schs., Milburn, N.J., 1993—. Contbr. articles to profl. publs. Mem. Nat. Coun. Jewish Women (v.p. Houston sect. 1976-79, pres. 1980-81, v.p. Essex County N.J. sect. 1983-88, pub. rels. com. 1981-90, chmn. nat. bull. subcom. 1990-93, Vol. award), Soc. Profl. Journalists, Nat. Fedn. Press Women, N.J. Press Women (2nd prize comm. contest 1992, hon. mention 1990, 1st prize 1993, newsletter editor 1992), Cornell Club of No. N.J. (v.p. 1992, 93, pres. 1994, 95). Office: Millburn Twp Pub Schs 434 Millburn Ave Millburn NJ 07041 also: Millburn Twp Pub Schs 434 Millburn Ave Millburn NJ 07041

GITTLEN, ELAINE, art educator; b. Jeffersonville, Ind., Oct. 14, 1944; d. Bernard B. and Mollie (Raznik) Gaspas; m. Barry M. Gittlen, June 23, 1968; 1 child, Lisa Simone. BA in Edn., Wayne State U., 1966; MA in Edn., Loyola Coll., Balt., 1993. Cert. tchr., Md. Third grade tchr. Leonhard Sch., Southfield, Mich., 1966-68, Solomon Schechter Sch., Phila., 1968-69; tchr. of English YMCA Adult Program, Jerusalem, 1969-70; fourth grade tchr. Drexel Hill (Pa.) Elem., 1970-72; fourth grade tchr. Beth Tfiloh Cmty. Sch., Balt., 1972-74, art tchr., 1975—; lectr. in edn. Balt. Hebrew U., 1975—; art cons. Bd. Jewish Edn., 1981-85; lectr. Assn. Ind. Md. Schs., Balt.; lectr., workshop leader, Bd. Jewish Edn., Balt., 1980s. Author art curriculum. Pres. PTA of Schechter Sch., Balt., 1986-88; mem. PTA Coun. Chizuk Amuno, Balt., 1986-88; co-chair Balt. Jewish Book Fair, 1992; bd. dirs. PTSA Pikesville High Sch., Balt., 1993—. Mem. Nat. Art Educators Assn., Md. Art Educators Assn. Home: 7009 Plymouth Rd Baltimore MD 21208

GITTMAN, ELIZABETH, educational researcher, evaluator; b. N.Y.C., Mar. 15, 1945; d. Kallman and Rebecca (Santcroos) G.; m. Aug. 5, 1965 (div. 1977); children: Stephen Loeb, Leslie Loeb, Sherry Loeb; m. Victor Arnel, Mar. 5, 1981. BS, NYU, 1966; MS, CUNY, 1969; PhD, Hofstra U., 1979, Cert. Advanced Study, 1987. Cert. ednl. adminstr., N.Y. Tchr. N.Y.C. Bd. Edn., Kew Gardens, 1966-68; instr. New Sch. for Social Rsch., N.Y.C., 1980-81; ind. cons., 1981—; coord. instl. rsch. and evaluation Bd. Coop. Ednl. Svcs. of Nassau County, Westbury, N.Y., 1984-94; assoc. prof. N.Y. Inst. Tech., Old Westbury, 1994—; adj. prof. L.I. U., Brookville, N.Y., 1987-93. Mem. high risk youth rev. com. Ctr. Substance Abuse Prevention, U.S. Dept. Health & Human Svcs., 1990—; developer numerous ednl. programs. Hofstra U. Doctoral fellow, 1976. Mem. APA, Am. Ednl. Rsch. Assn., Am. Evaluation Assn., Nat. Coun. Measurement in Edn., Northeastern Ednl. Rsch. Assn. (membership com. 1989-90, nominating com. 1991, program co-chair 1993, program com. 1989-92, editor 1993—, bd. dirs. 1993—), L.I. ASCD, Kappa Delta Pi, Phi Delta Kappa (rsch. rep. 1990-91, sec. 1991-93, conf. co-chair 1992, v.p. 1993-94, pres.-elect 1994—). Republican. Jewish. Office: Sch Edn NY Inst Tech Old Westbury NY 11568

GIULIANTI, MARA SELENA, mayor, civic worker; b. N.Y.C., June 3, 1944; d. Leon and Bertha (Jablonky) Berman; m. Donald Giulianti, May 29, 1966; children: Stacey Alexander, Michael Alan. BA, Tulane U., 1966. Social worker L.A. County Social Svcs., 1966-68; adminstrv. asst. neurosurg. cons. D. Giulianti, MD, Hollywood, Fla., 1980-83; campaign mgr. City Commr. Suzanne Gunzburger, Hollywood, 1982; mayor City of Hollywood, 1986-90, 92—; vice chmn. Broward Employment and Tng. Adminstrn., 1987-89, 92—, chmn., 1989-90, 92—; mem. exec. bd. Fla. League Cities, Tallahassee, 1986-90, 92-94, bd. dirs., 1990-91, 94—; mem. econ. devel. task force Nat. League Cities, Washington, 1987-90, human devel. policy com., 1992-94, fin., adminstrn. and intergovtl. rels. steering com., 1994—; mem. Broward County Met. Planning Orgn., 1986-90. Contbr. articles to local newspapers. Pres. Women in Distress, Broward County, 1982-83, bd. dirs., 1983-90, trustee, 1994—; v.p. CHARLEE Family Care Homes, Broward County, 1986-88, bd. dirs., 1988-92; mem. Broward County Commn. on Status Women, 1984-86, Fla. Commn. on Drug and Alcohol Concerns, Tallahassee, 1984-85, Broward County Dem. Exec. Com., 1984-88; pres. Hills Dem. Club, 1991-94; bd. trustees Graves Mus. of Archeol. and Nat. History, Dania, Fla., 1993—. Recipient Hannah G. Solomon award, 1983, Giraffe Stick Your Neck Out award Women's Advocacy - the Majority/Minority 1986, Leadership award Leadership Hollywood Alumni, 1987, City of Peace award Israel Bonds, Broward County, 1987, Broward County Woman of Yr., Am. Jewish Congress, 1988; Menorah award Histadrut, 1990; named Woman of Yr. Women in Communications Inc., 1990. Mem. Nat. Coun. Jewish Women (nat. bd. dirs. 1985-89), Jewish Fedn. So. Broward (chair community rels. com. 1981-82, bd. dirs. 1982-90), Broward County Med. Aux. (br. pres. 1977-78), Nat. Jewish Community Rels. Adv. Coun. (exec. bd. 1985-87), Rotary. Democrat. Office: 2600 Hollywood Blvd Hollywood FL 33020

GIVEN, LINDA NASH, real estate broker; b. Walterboro, S.C., July 1, 1943; d. Robert Monroe Bennett and Vivian Marie (Priester) McKinney Bennett; m. Kemp Charles Nash Jr. (div.); children: Kemp Charles Nash III, Michael Bennett Nash; m. John Stanton Given. Student, Winthrop, 1961-63. Real estate saleswoman Anchor Realty Co., North Myrtle Beach, S.C., 1980-90, Re/Max So. Shores, North Myrtle Beach, 1990—. Mem. S.C. Assn. Realtors, Grand State Bd. Realtors (past pres., v.p., sec., Realtor Image award 1992, Realtor of Yr. 1994), North Myrtle Beach Woman's Club. Presbyterian. Home: 907 Pearlie St North Myrtle Beach SC 29582 Office: Re/Max So Shores 100 Hwy 17 S North Myrtle Beach SC 29582

GIVENS, CHARLENE KAY, wastewater services executive; b. Lebanon, Ind., Oct. 6, 1947; d. John Robert and Anna Mildred (Bowers) Whittaker; m. Ralph A. Givens, June 19, 1969; children: Maria Lynn. BA, Ind. U., 1969. Lab. technician City of Carmel, Ind., 1972-75; lab. technician City of Noblesville, Ind., 1975-82, supt. wastewater plant, 1982-85; owner Givens & Assocs. Wastewater Co., Inc., Cumberland, Ind., 1982—; program chmn. Ind. Vocat. Tech. Coll. pollution treatment, Indpls., 1982-85. Named Businesswoman of Yr., Hamilton chpt. Am. Bus. Women's Assn., 1982. Mem. Am. Businesswomen's Assn. (pres. 1980-81), Cen. Ind. Operators Assn. (pres. 1983-84), Ind. Soc. Cert. Operators (sec.-treas.), Ind. Water Pollution Control Assn. (pres. 1990-91), Water Environ. Fedn., Nat. Environ. Tng. Assn. Avocations: knitting, reading, antiques, exploring. Office: Givens & Assocs Wastewater Co. Inc 12010 E Washington St Cumberland IN 46229

GIVENS, JANET EATON, writer; b. N.Y.C., July 5, 1932; d. Irving Daniel and Matilda (Schmelzle) E.; m. Richard Ayres Givens, Aug. 24, 1957; children—Susan Ruth, Jane Lucile. B.A., Queens Coll., 1953; M.A., Columbia U., 1955. Lic. tchr., N.Y. Tchr. pub. elem. schs., Silver Spring, Md., 1953-55, Mamaroneck, N.Y., 1955-59; supr. prospective tchrs., part-time lectr. Queens Coll., N.Y.C., 1959-68. Author: The Migrating Birds, 1964; Something Wonderful Happened, 1982; Just Two Wings, 1984; contbg. author: Tensions Our Children Live With, 1959. V.p. PTA, Pub. Sch. 219, Queens, N.Y., 1972-73, del. to United Parents Assn., 1971-72, editor PS 219 News, 1971-73. Home: 14711 68th Rd Flushing NY 11367-1332

GIVHAN, CHRISTIN CHAFFIN, legislative staff member; b. Oxford, Miss., Mar. 28, 1965. BA, Vanderbilt U., 1987. Legis. asst. to Senator Richard Shelby, Washington, 1987-93; staff dir., sub-com. on econ. stabilization and rural devel. Senate Com. on Banking, Housing and Urban Affairs, Washington, 1993—. Office: Subcom on Econ Stblzn & Rural Dev Senate Hart Office Bldg Rm 534 Washington DC 20510*

GIVHAN, ROBIN DENEEN, journalist; b. Detroit, Sept. 11, 1964; d. Robert Earl and Stella Mae (Thompson) G. BA in English, Princeton U., 1986; MA in Journalism, U. Mich., 1988. Staff writer Detroit Free Press, 1988-92, San Francisco Chronicle, 1992-93; fashion editor Detroit Free Press, 1993—. Recipient Outstanding Achievement in Media award Nat. Coalition of 100 Black Women, 1992. Methodist. Office: Detroit Free Press 321 W Lafayette Blvd Detroit MI 48009

GIVNER, GAI ANTOINETTE, executive assistant; b. Pitts., Feb. 21, 1950; d. S.B. and Barbara Jean (Arrington) Thomas; divorced; 1 child, Barry. Student, Columbia U., NYU; BS, Vt. Coll., 1982; MS in Edn., Fordham U., 1985. Dir. promotions China Seas, N.Y.C., 1982-85; exec. asst. Family Circle, N.Y.C., 1985-86, ABC, N.Y.C., 1986-87, World Mktg. Alliance, Atlanta, 1993—. Founder Women in Crisis, N.Y.C., 1986—; stake missionary LDS Ch., Atlanta, 1994. Mem. Phi Delta Kappa. Democrat.

GLACEL, BARBARA PATE, management consultant; b. Balt., Sept. 15, 1948; d. Jason Thomas Pate and Sarah Virginia (Forwood) Wetter; m. Robert Allan Glacel, Dec. 21, 1969; children: Jennifer Warren, Sarah Allane, Ashley Virginia. AB, Coll. William and Mary, 1970; MA, U. Okla., 1973, PhD, 1978. Tchr. Harford County (Md.) Schs., 1970-71; tchr. Dept. Def. Schs., W.Ger., 1971-73; ednl. counselor U.S. Army, Germany, 1973-74; mgmt. cons. Barbara Glacel & Assocs., Anchorage, 1980-86, Washington, 1986-88; ptnr. Pracel Prints, Williamsburg, Va., 1981-85; sr. mgmt. tng. specialist Arco Alaska, Inc., 1984-85; gen. mgr. mgmt. programs Hay Systems, Inc., Washington, 1986-88; CEO VIMA Internat., Burke, Va., 1988—; 2d v.p., bd. dirs. Chesapeake Broadcasting Corp. Md.; adj. prof. Suffolk U., Boston, 1974-77, C.W. Post Ctr., L.I. U., John Jay Coll. Criminal Justice, N.Y.C., 1979-80, St. Thomas Aquinas Coll., N.Y.C., 1981, St. Mary's Coll., Leavenworth, Kans., 1981, Anchorage C.C., 1982; acad. adviser Ctrl. Mich. U., 1981-82; asst. prof. U. Alaska, Anchorage, 1983-85; mem. adj. faculty Ctr. for Creative Leadership, 1986—; guest lectr. U.S. Mil. Acad.; mem. U.S. Army Sci. Bd., 1986-90; mem. U.S. Dept. Def. Sci. Bd. Quality of Life Panel. Author: Regional Transit Authorities, 1983; (with others) 1000 Army Families, 1983, The Army Community and Their Families, 1989, Light Bulbs for Leaders, 1994. Chmn. 172d Inf. Brigade Family Coun. Recipient Comdr.'s award for pub. svc. U.S. Dept. Army, 1984, U.S. Army Patriotic Civilian Svc. award 1991, U.S. Army Forscom Svc. award 1993; AAUW grantee, 1977-78. Mem. ASTD (bd. dirs. Anchorage chpt.), Am. Psychol. Assn., Soc. for Indsl. and Organizational Psychology, Instrnl. Systems Assn. (v.p. 1993—), Soc. of Alumni Coll. of William and Mary (bd. dirs. 1992—). Home: 5617 Tilia Ct Burke VA 22015-1688 Office: VIMA Internat 5290 Lyngate Ct Burke VA 22015-1688 also: PO Box 31368, Braamfontein 2017, South Africa

GLAD, BETTY, government and international affairs educator; b. Salt Lake City, Sept. 27, 1929; d. Harluf Anderson and Edna Janette (Geertsen) G.; m. Irving T. Diamond, Sept., 1954 (div. Jan. 1957). BS magna cum laude, U. Utah, 1949; PhD, U. Chgo., 1962. Instr. Mt. Holyoke Coll., 1958-59; lectr., instr. Bklyn. Coll., 1960-64; from asst. prof. to assoc. prof. U. Ill., Urbana, 1964-72, prof., 1973-89, dept. head, 1972-73; prof. U. S.C., Columbia, 1989-93, Caroline disting. prof., 1993-95, Olin D. Johnston chair, 1995—; mem. hist. adv. com. U.S. Dept. State, Washington, 1990; rev. panelist NEH, Washington, 1980-83; chair Midwest Univs. Com. Seminar in U.S. Fgn. Policy, 1972; mem. promotions and tenure com. U. S.C., 1991-94; presenter in field. Author chpts. in books; mem. editl. bds., 1968-73; contbr. articles to profl. jours.; appeared on numerous TV and radio shows. Nat. Pub. Svc. fellow, 1952, Kappa Kappa Gamma nat. fellow, 1992. Mem. AAUW, Internat. Soc. for Polit. Psychology (program chair 1983, chair Harold Lasswell com. 1983-86, v.p. 1985-87, chair search com. for exec. dir. 1991, pres. 1993-94), Am. Polit. Sci. Assn. (treas. 1978-79, chair Woodrow Wilson com. 1984, v.p. 1994—, pres. Presidency Rsch. Group 1989-90, women's caucus, Mentor of Distinction award 1989), U. Utah Beehive Soc., Mortar Bd., Phi Beta Kappa. Democrat. Unitarian. Home: 1317 Belmont Dr Columbia SC 29205 Office: U SC Dept Govt & Internat Studies Columbia SC 29208

GLAD, SUZANNE LOCKLEY, retired museum director; b. Rochester, N.Y., Oct. 2, 1929; d. Alfred Allen and Lucille A. (Watson) Lockley; m. Edward Newman Glad, Nov. 7, 1953; children: Amy, Lisanne Glad Lantz, William E. BA, Sweet Briar Coll., 1951; MA, Columbia U., 1952. Exec. dir. New York State Young Reps., N.Y.C., 1951-57; mem. pub. rels. staff Dolphin Group, L.A., 1974-83; scheduling sec. Gov.'s Office, Sacramento, 1983-87; dep. dir. Calif. Mus. Sci. and Industry, L.A., 1987-94; ret. Mem. Calif. Rep. League, Flintridge, 1969—; mem. Assistance League of Flintridge, 1970—, Flintridge Guild Children's Hosp., 1969-89. Mem. Am. Assn. Mus., Sweet Briar Alumnae of So. Calif. (pres. 1972), Phi Beta Kappa, Tau Phi. Episcopalian.

GLADECK, SUSAN ODELL, social worker; b. Honesdale, Pa., Apr. 28; d. Lester Albert and Esther Grace (Fleming) Odell; children: Amy Frances, Esther Lena. BA with honors, Cedar Crest Coll., 1960; M. Social Svc., Bryn Mawr Coll., 1962. Lic. clin. social worker, Va.; cert. piano tchr. Social worker Family Svc. of Phila. and Family Svc. of Del. County, Media, Pa., 1962-63, Lehigh U. Child Devel. Ctr., Bethlehem, Pa., 1966, South Terr. Area Neighborhood Ctr., Bethlehem, Pa., 1969-71, Lehigh County Children's Bur., Allentown, Pa., 1971-73; social worker II Farifax (Va.) County Dept. Human Devel., 1987-90; sr. social worker adult svcs. Loudoun County Dept. Social Svcs., Leesburg, Va., 1990-94; pvt. practice McLean. Mem. NASW, Acad. Cert. Social Workers, Am. Coll. Musicians, Am. Guild Organists, Music Tchrs. Nat. Assn., Nat. Fedn. Music Tchrs., Va. Fedn. Music Tchrs., No. Va. Music Tchrs. Assn. Home and Office: 6516 Fairlawn Dr Mc Lean VA 22101-5235

GLADKI, HANNA ZOFIA, civil engineer, hydraulic mixer specialist; b. Krakow, Poland, Dec. 30, 1933; came to U.S., 1984; d. Stanislaw Wojtanowski and Maria (Ekiert) Wojtanowska; m. Jozef Gladki, July 2, 1955 (dec. 1982); 1 child, Ania. ScD, Tech. U., Warsaw, Poland, 1966; postgrad. degree, Agrl. U., Wroclaw, Poland, 1977. Asst. prof. Agrl. Acad. Krakow, 1966-70, assoc. prof., 1970-81, chair dept., 1973-83, dean of faculty, 1977-81, prof., 1981-85; hydraulic mixer specialist ITT Flygt Corp., Norwalk, Conn., 1985—; presenter at profl. confs. Contbr. articles to profl. publs. Mem. ASCE, AICE, Internat. Assn. Hydraulic Rsch. Roman Catholic. Home: 79 Melville St Stratford CT 06497-5723 Office: ITT Flygt Corp PO Box 1004 Trumbull CT 06611-0943

GLADSTONE, CAROL LYNN, assistant principal; b. N.Y.C., Aug. 14, 1944; d. Albert Ludwig and Jeanne (Eisner) Adler; m. Edward Gladstone, Nov. 20, 1973. BA, Hunter Coll., 1965; MA, CCNY, N.Y.C., 1967; PhD, Columbia Pacific U., 1988, postgrad., 1993-94. Cert. tchr. English, French, sch. dist. adminstr., Ariz., Conn., N.J., N.Y. English/reading tchr. Jr. High Sch. #120, N.Y.C., 1965-66; reading coord. Dewitt Clinton High Sch., Bronx, 1966-74; asst. chair John F. Kennedy High Sch., Bronx, 1974-85; asst. prin. James Monroe High Sch., Bronx, 1985—; prin. PM/Saturday Sch. James Monroe H.S., 1993-94; trainer of adminstrv. staff Bronx. Supt.'s Office, 1992—, Manhattan Supt.'s Office, 1989-90; adj. prof. Coll. of New Rochelle, N.Y., 1988-89, Lehman Coll., Bronx, 1987-88. Contbr. articles to profl. jours.; author: Competence in Cloze, 1989; author series of books: Gladstone Comprehensive Writing Program, 1986-88. Sec. Westchester (N.Y.) Alzheimer's Disease Assn., 1980-87; reporter Pub. Access Cable TV, Westchester, 1982-83. Named Supr. of Yr. Bronx Supt.'s Office, 1990-91, Educator of Yr. Assn. Tchrs. N.Y., 1987-88, 90-91, Educator as Writer Mayor of City of N.Y., 1986; N.Y. Inst. for Humanities fellow, 1994. Mem. ASCD (assoc. 1990—), N.Y. State English Coun. (Tchr. of Excellence 1992-93, regional dir. 1994—), N.Y. State Reading Assn., Bronx Asst. Prins. of English (standing com. on English 1995), Nat. Bd. for Profl. Tchg. Stds.

GLAESSMANN, DORIS ANN, county official; b. Northampton, Pa., Feb. 18, 1940; d. Frank G. and Theresa (Fischl) Zwikl; m. Edward Glaessmann, Sept. 1, 1962; children: Edward Jr., Robert F. Grad. high sch., Northampton, 1958. Sec., bookkeeper John F. Moore Agy., Inc., Allentown, Pa., 1958-64; ct. clk. Criminal div. Clk. of Cts. Office, Allentown, 1968-69, asst. dep. clk., 1969-76, chief dep. clk., 1976-82; clk. of cts., criminal and civil divsns. Lehigh County, Allentown, 1982—. Den mother, sec. Cub Scout Pack 140, Allentown, Pa., 1973-78; mem., past bd. dirs., 2d v.p. Quota Club Allentown, 1983—; mem. coun. St. Peter's Evang. Luth. Ch., Allentown, 1984-89. Mem. Nat. Assn. County Recorders and Clks., Internat. Assn. Clks., Recorders, Election Ofcls. and Treas., Pa. Prothonotaries and Clks. Assn. (past pres., treas. 1993—), Pa. Elected Women's Assn. (past sec.-treas. and pres. Lehigh Valley chpt.). Democrat. Home: 945 E Lynnwood St Allentown PA 18103-5250 Office: Lehigh County PO Box 1548 455 Hamilton St Allentown PA 18105-1548

GLAGOLA, HELEN WILSON, realtor; b. Hartville, Mo., June 21, 1939; d. James Layne Wilson and Vivianne L. (Pridgen) Houghton; m. Stephen Glagola, Sept. 10, 1961; children: Stephen, Mark, Douglas, Paul. BA, U. Calif., Berkeley, 1961. Lic. realtor. Interior designer Spokane, Balt., Frederick, Wash., Md., 1965-85; realtor Bach & Assocs., Frederick, 1987-89; realtor, relocation specialist Weichert Realtors, Frederick, 1987—. Co-chair Middletown Valley Preservation Assn., Frederick, 1983-89; active Hosp. Guild, Frederick, 1973-79, Jr. League, Spokane, Baton Rouge and Frederick, 1972-75. Recipient numerous awards Frederick Bd. Realtors. Mem. Nat. Assn. Realtors, Md. Assn. Realtors, Frederick County Assn. Realtors, Calif. Alumni Assn., Zeta Tau Alpha. Republican. Episcopalian. Home: 4192 Palomino Ln Middletown MD 21769 Office: Weichert Realtors 1065 W Patrick St Frederick MD 21702-3903

GLANCY, DOROTHY JEAN, lawyer, educator; b. Glendale, Calif., Sept. 24, 1944; d. Walter Perry and Elva T. (Douglass) G.; m. Jon Tobias Anderson, June 8, 1979. BA, Wellesley Coll., 1967; JD, Harvard Law Sch., 1970. Bar: D.C. 1971, Calif. 1976, U.S. Dist. Ct. D.C. 1971, U.S. Ct. Appeals (D.C. cir.) 1972. Assoc. Hogan & Hartson, Wash., 1971-73; counsel U.S. Senate Judiciary Subcomm. on Constitutional Rights, Wash., 1973-74; fellow in Law & Humanities Harvard U., Cambridge, Mass., 1974-75; asst. to assoc. prof. law Santa Clara U., Calif., 1975-82, prof. law, 1984—; vis. prof. law U. Arizona, Tucson, 1979; asst. gen. counsel U.S. Dept. of Agr., 1982-83; cons. Commn. Fed. Paperwork, Wash., 1976; dir. summer Law Study Program in Hong Kong, 1985-90; advisor Restatement, Third Property: Servitudes, 1986—. Dir. legal rsch. project regarding privacy and intelligent trnsp. systems Fed. Hwy. Adminstrn., 1993-95; mem. coun. Harvard Law Sch. Assn., 1991—; v.p. Presidio Hts. Assn. Neighbors, 1990—. Fellow Wellesley Coll., Harvard U. Mem. ABA (chair ethics com. of sect. on natural resources, energy and environ. law 1993—, chair-elect of sect. on real property, probate and trust law 1995—), State Bar Calif. (mem. environ. law sect., exec. com. property sect. 1995—), Assn. Am. Law Schs. (chair environ. law sect. 1992-93), Am. Law Inst., Calif. Women Lawyers, Soc. Am. Law Tchrs., Phi Beta Kappa. Democrat. Office: Santa Clara U Sch Law Santa Clara CA 95053

GLANERT, KAREN LOUISE, educator; b. Sheboygan, Wis., July 21, 1954; d. Alvin H. and Laverne E. (Haun) G. B.S. summa cum laude in Edn., U. Wis.-Whitewater, 1976, postgrad. Tchr., Lakeland (Wis.) Mfg. Co., 1972-76; instr. Sheboygan Pub. Schs., 1978—; counselor emotionally disturbed children; coach. Mem. Council Exceptional Children, Nat. Ret. Tchrs. Assn., Wis. Edn. Assn., Sheboygan Edn. Assn., PTA, Assn. Supervision and Curriculum Devel., Council Basic Edn., Luth. Women's League, Beta Sigma Phi. Lutheran. Home: 2427 Camelot Blvd Apt A Sheboygan WI 53081-7443 Office: Farmsworth Middle Sch 1017 Union Ave Sheboygan WI 53081-5936

GLANTZ, GINA, consultant; b. N.Y.C., Apr. 3, 1943; d. Nathan L. and Lillian (Rosenbaum) Stritzler; m. Ronald A. Glantz, Oct. 17, 1968; children—Amy Samantha, Peter Samuel. B.A., U. Calif.-Berkeley, 1965. Chief of staff County Exec. Peter Shapiro, County of Essex, N.J., 1978-82; owner, mgr. Gina Glantz Cons., Springfield, N.J., 1982-83; sr. cons. Mondale for Pres., Washington, 1984; nat. field dir. Mondale/Ferraro, Inc., Washington, 1984; ptnr. Martin & Glantz, Mill Valley, Calif. and Rosslyn, Va., 1985—. Home: 96 Avenue Del Norte San Anselmo CA 94960-2510 Office: Martin & Glantz 100 Shoreline Hwy Mill Valley CA 94941-3645

GLASBERG, PAULA DRILLMAN, advertising executive; b. Dusseldorf, Germany, Nov. 22, 1939; came to U.S., 1940, naturalized, 1942; d. Solomon and Regina (Rubin) Drillman; m. H. Mark Glasberg, June 19, 1960; children: Scot Bradley, Hilary Jennifer. B.A., Bklyn. Coll., 1957; M.A., New Sch. Social Research, 1959, Ph.D., 1962. Rsch. asst. McCann-Erickson, N.Y.C., 1962-64; v.p. Marplan, Inc., N.Y.C., 1964-70, Tinker/Pritchard Wood, Inc., N.Y.C., 1970-72; exec. v.p., chmn. exec. com. Rosenfeld, Sirowitz & Lawson, Inc., N.Y.C., 1972-78; exec. v.p., chmn. exec. com., dir. Marschalk Co. div. Interpublic Group of Cos., N.Y.C., 1978-1982; exec. v.p., dir., dir. strategic planning McCann-Erickson World Wide, Inc., 1983—, world wide exec. v.p., dir. strategic planning, 1990—; assoc. prof. Columbia U. Sch. Bus. Adminstrn., 1991—; bd. dirs. Stern Coll. for Women, 1987—; sponsor mem. Yeshiva U. Women's Orgn., 1985—. Fellow APA, NAS, Nat. Rsch. Coun., Nat. Assn. Psychologists; mem. Am. Assn. Advt. Agys., Am. Mktg. Assn., Advt. Rsch. Found., AAAS, Internat. Platform Assn. Home: 14 E 73rd St New York NY 10021-4128 Office: McCann-Erickson World Wide Inc 750 3rd Ave New York NY 10017-2703

GLASCO, KIMBERLY, ballet dancer. Grad., Nat. Ballet Sch. With Nat. Ballet of Can., 1979-83, 84—, 2nd soloist, 1981-82, 84-85, 1st soloist, 1982-83, 85-87, prin. dancer, 1987—; with Am. Ballet Theatre, 1983-84; guest appearances at Australian Spoleto Festival, 1987, World Ballet Festival (Japan), Verona (Italy) Festival. Created roles of Child Alice in Alice (Glen Tetley), and the Parlormaid in La Ronde (Glen Tetley), Swan Lake, Queen/Black Swan, Sleeping Beauty, Aurora, Valantanes (Killian Etudes), Transfigured Night, Elite Syncopations, Paquita, Merry Widow. Recipient Silver medal Moscow Internat. Ballet Competition, 1981. Office: National Ballet of Canada, 157 King St East, Toronto, ON Canada M5C 1G9 also: 252 W 76th St Apt 6E New York NY 10023-8230*

GLASER, VERA ROMANS, journalist; b. St. Louis; d. Aaron L. and Mollie (Romans); m. Herbert R. Glaser, Apr. 16, 1939; 1 dau., Carol Jane Barriger. Student, Washington U., St. Louis, George Washington U., Am. U., 1937-40. Reporter-writer Nat. Aero. mag., 1943-44; reporter Washington Times Herald, 1944-46; pub. relations specialist Great Lakes-St. Lawrence Assn., 1950-51; promotion specialist, writer Congl. Quar. News Features, 1951-54; writer-commentator radio sta. WGMS, Washington, 1954-55; mem. Washington bur. N.Y. Herald Tribune, 1955-56; press officer U.S. Senator Charles E. Potter, 1956-59; dir. pub. relations, women's div. Rep. Nat. Com., 1959-62; press officer U.S. Senator Kenneth B. Keating, 1962-63; Washington corr. N.Am. Newspaper Alliance, 1963-69, bur. chief, 1965-69; columnist, nat. corr. Knight-Ridder Newspapers, Inc., 1969-81; assoc. editor Washingtonian Mag., 1981-88, contbg. editor, 1988—; columnist Maturity News Svc., 1988-94; mem. Pres.'s Commn. on White House Fellows, 1969, Pres.'s Task Force on Women's Rights and Responsibilities, 1970; judge 1981 Robert Kennedy Journalism Awards. Free-lance writer nat. publs.; radio and TV appearances on Stas. WTOP-TV, ABC, PBS, C-SPAN. Mem. nat. bd. Med. Coll. Pa., 1977-88; bd. dirs. Washington Press Club Found., 1986-88; mem. exec. bd. Internat. Women's Media Found., 1990—. Mem. White House Corrs. Assn., Nat. Press Club (bd. govs. 1988, 89), Washington Press Club (pres. 1971-72), Overseas Press Club, Sigma Delta Chi. Unitarian. Home and Office: 5000 Cathedral Ave NW Washington DC 20016-2646

GLASPIE, APRIL CATHERINE, diplomat; b. Vancouver, B.C., Canada, Apr. 26, 1942. BA, Mills Coll., 1963; MA, Johns Hopkins U., 1965. With Foreign Service U.S. Dept. of State, 1966—; polit. officer U.S. Embassy, Cairo, 1973-77; asst. to Asst. Sec. State for Near Ea., S. Asian Affairs Washington, 1977-78; polit. officer U.S. Embassy, London, 1978-80, U.S. Mission to UN, N.Y.C., 1980-81; dir. lang. inst. U.S. Embassy, Tunis, Tunisia, 1981-83; polit. officer, dep. chief of mission U.S. Embassy, Damascus, Syria, 1983-85; dir., Office of Jordan, Lebanon, and Syrian Affairs U.S. Dept. of State, Washington, 1985-87; ambassador to Iraq, 1987—; dir. Office Southern African Affairs. Office: Office Southern African Affairs Dept of State 2201 C St Rm 4238 Washington DC 20520*

GLASS, DIANE, lawyer, association executive; b. Newark, Oct. 21, 1953; d. Henry and Ann (Kasianik) G.; m. John Hamilton Hardenbergh, May 11, 1985; children: Katherine, Nicholas, Alexander. BA cum laude, Rutgers U., 1976, JD, 1979. Bar: N.J. 1979, U.S. Dist. Ct. N.J. 1979, U.S. Ct. Appeals (3d cir.) 1984, N.Y. 1988, Pa. 1988. Jud. clk to judges Bachman and Appleby N.J. Superior Ct., New Brunswick, 1979-80; dep. atty. gen. Atty. Gen.'s Office State of N.J., Trenton, 1980—. Pres. bd. dirs. YWCA of Cen. Jersey, New Brunswick, 1986-88; nat. bd. dirs. YWCA of the U.S.A., N.Y.C., 1988-94. Mem. N.J. Bar Assn., Middlesex (N.J.) County Bar Assn., Middlesex County Women Lawyers. Roman Catholic. Home: 7 Renard Rd Belle Mead NJ 08502-2102 Office: Office Atty Gen of NJ Divsn Law Justice Hughes Complex CN 114 Trenton NJ 08625

GLASS, DOROTHEA DANIELS, physiatrist, educator; b. N.Y.C.; d. Maurice B. and Anna S. (Kleegman) Daniels; m. Robert E. Glass, June 23, 1940; children: Anne Glass Roth, Deborah, Catherine Glass Barrett, Eugene. BA, Cornell U., 1940; MD, Woman's Med. Coll. Pa., 1954; postgrad., U. Pa., 1960-61; DMS (hon.), Med. Coll. Pa., 1987. Diplomate: Am. Bd. Phys. Medicine and Rehab. (guest bd. examiner 1978, 89). Intern Albert Einstein Med. Center, Phila., 1954-55, clin. asst. dept. medicine, 1956-59, attending phys. medicine and rehab., 1968-70, chmn. dept. phys. medicine and rehab., sr. attending, 1971-85; chief rehab. medicine VA Med. Ctr., Miami, Fla., 1985—; clin. prof. dept. orthopaedics and rehab. U. Miami Sch. Medicine, 1985—, dir. resident tng. physical medicine and rehab., 1993—; Lois Mattox Miller fellow preventive medicine Woman's Med. Coll. Pa., 1955-56, instr. preventive medicine, 1956-59, instr. medicine, 1960-62; resident phys. medicine and rehab. VA Hosp., Phila., 1959-62, chief phys. medicine and rehab., 1966-68, cons., 1968-82; asst. clin. dir. Jefferson Med. Coll. Hosp., Phila., 1963-66, Camden County Stroke Program, Cooper Hosp., Camden, N.J., 1963-66; gen. practice medicine, Phila., 1956-59; asst. med. dir., chief rehab. medicine and rehab. Moss Rehab. Hosp., Phila., 1968-70, med. dir., 1971-82, sr. cons., 1982—; mem. active staff Temple U., Phila., 1968—, asso. prof. rehab. medicine, 1968-73, prof., 1973—, dir. residency tng. rehab. medicine, 1968-82; program dir. Rehab. Research and Tng. Center, 1977-80, chmn. dept. rehab. medicine, 1977-82; staff physician Hosp. Med. Coll. Pa., Phila., 1955-59, vis. asso. prof. neurology, 1973-79, clin. prof., 1977-82, vis. prof., 1982—; mem. cons. staff Frankford Hosp., Phila., 1968-82, Phila. Geriatric Center, 1975—; mem. active staff Willowcrest-Bamberger Hosp., Phila., 1980—; asso. phys. medicine and rehab. U. Pa. Sch. Medicine, Phila., 1962-66; asst. prof. clin. phys. medicine and rehab., 1966-68; asst. clin. dir. dept. phys. medicine and rehab. Jefferson Med. Coll., Phila., 1963-66. Contbr. articles to profl. jours. Mem. profl. adv. com. Easter Seal Soc. Crippled Children and Adults Pa., 1975-82; active Goodwill Industries Phila., 1973—, Community Home Health Services Phila., 1974-82, Eastern Pa. chpt. Arthritis Found., 1968—. Recipient Humanitarian Service Cert. Gov.'s Com. on Employment Handicapped, 1974, Outstanding Alumnae award Commonwealth Pa. Bd., Hosp. Med. Coll. Pa., 1975, Humanitarian award Pa. Easter Seal Soc., 1981, John Eiselie Davis award Am. Kinesiotherapy Assn., 1988. Mem. AMA, Am. Acad. Med. Dirs., Am. Acad. Phys. Medicine and Rehab., Am. Assn. Electromyography and Electrodiagnosis (asso.), Am. Assn. Sex Educators, Counselors and Therapists, Am. Burn Assn., Am. Coll. Angiology, Am. Coll. Utilization Rev., Am. Congress Rehab. Medicine (bd. govs., 2d v.p., Gold Key award 1989), Am. Heart Assn. (council on cerebrovascular disease), Am. Lung Assn. Phila. and Montgomery County (bd. dirs. 1977-79), Am. Med. Women's Assn., Assn. Acad. Physiatrists, Assn. Med. Rehab. Dirs. and Coordinators, Coll. Physicians Phila., Emergency Care Research Inst., Gerontol. Soc., Internat. Assn. Rehab. Facilities, Internat. Rehab. Medicine Assn., Pan Am. Med. Assn., Fla. Med. Assn., Fla. Soc. Phys. Medicine and Rehab. (pres. 1988-90), Pa. Acad. Phys. Medicine and Rehab. (pres. 1975-77), Pa. Med. Soc. (phys. medicine and rehab. adv. com. 1975—), Pa. Thoracic Soc., Delaware Valley Hosp. Council Forum, Philadelphia County Med. Soc., Phila. PSRO (bd. dirs. 1975-82), Phila. Soc. Phys. Medicine and Rehab. (pres. 1968-69), Laennec Soc. Phila., Martin County Med. Assn., Royal Soc. Health, Alpha Omega Alpha.

GLASS, JANICE LYNN, nurse; b. Norristown, Pa., Mar. 30, 1957; d. G. David and Eleanor (Lepre) Pascale; m. Marc Glass, Oct. 7, 1984; 1 child, Matthew David. AAS, Montgomery County C.C., 1984. RN, Pa. Psychiatric technician Norristown (Pa.) State Hosp., 1978-83; med.-surg. nurse Montgomery Hosp., Norristown, 1984-85, peritoneal dialysis nurse, 1985, oncology nurse, 1986-89, recovery rm. nurse, 1989—; drug and alcohol nurse Valley Forge Med. Ctr., Norristown, 1993—; legal nurse cons. Med.-Legal Cons. Inst., Houston. Contbr. editorials to newspapers, chpt. to book. Active Dem. Nat. Com., Nat. Abortion Rights Action League, Ams. United for Separation of Ch. and State, People for the Am. Way. Mem. NOW. Home: 2420 Norrington Dr Jeffersonville PA 19403

GLASS, JENNIFER LYNN, sociology educator; b. Dallas, May 29, 1957; d. Michael and Nancy Lou Glass; m. Bruce Gerard Juetten, June 3, 1984; children: Caitlin Rose, Annika Laurel. BA, New Coll., Sarasota, Fla., 1977; MS, U. Wis., 1979, PhD, 1983. Asst. prof. U. So. Calif., L.A., 1983-85; from asst. to assoc. prof. U. Notre Dame, South Bend, Ind., 1985-94; assoc. prof. U. Iowa, Iowa City, 1994—; cons. in field. Mem. editorial bd. Am. Sociol. Rev., 1992-95; contbr. articles to profl. jours. Recipient Reuben Hill award Nat. Coun. Family Rels., 1987; NSF grantee, 1991-94. Mem. Am. Sociol. Assn., Population Assn. Am., Sociologists for Women in Soc. Office: U Iowa Dept Sociology Iowa City IA 52242

GLASS, LAUREL ELLEN, gerontologist, developmental biologist, physician, retired educator; b. Selma, Calif., Oct. 1, 1923; d. Sydney L. and Marie (Damron) G. B.A., U. Calif.-Berkeley, 1951; Ph.D., Duke U., 1958; M.D., U. Calif., San Francisco, 1974. Teaching asst. zoology Duke U., 1953-56; research assoc. Pathology Research Lab., Med. Research Div., VA Hosp., Durham, N.C., 1957-58; part-time instr. anatomy Duke U. Med. Sch., 1958; instr. dept. anatomy U. Calif. Med. Sch., San Francisco, 1958-61; asst. prof. U. Calif. Med. Sch., 1961-66, assoc. prof., 1968-72, prof., 1972-89, prof. emeritus, 1989—, prof. psychiatry, 1984-89, prof. emeritus, 1989—, dir. Ctr. on Deafness, 1984-89; adj. prof. family and community medicine U. Calif. Med. Affiliate, Inst. on Health and Aging, U. Calif. Sch. Nursing, 1983-89; dir. project on adaptation to adult onset hearing loss Langley Porter Psychiat. Inst., U. Calif. Med. Sch., San Francisco, 1989-92; mem. San Francisco adv. com. Child Health and Disability Prevention Program, 1974-79; mem. exec. com., bd. dirs. Mission Neighborhood Health Ctr., 1974-77; mem. med. adv. com. Coalition for Med. Rights of Women, 1974-87; mem. adv. bd. P.R. Orgn. Women Health Edn. Project, 1976-78; v.p. Developmental Disabilities Programs, Inc., 1976-87. Mem. edn. commn. NAACP, Ocean View-Merced Heights Community Stblzn. and Improvement Project, exec. com. Ocean View-Ingleside Dist. Council, Bay Area Social Planning Council, 1969-73, adv. council Nat. Ctr. for Vision and Aging, 1986-94; bd. dirs. Service Com. on Pub. Edn., 1963-66, Constl. Rights Found., 1965-73, Deaf Counseling, Adv. and Referral Agency (DCARA), 1985-86, Hearing Soc. for the Bay Area, Inc., 1984-86, 93—; trustee Self-Help for Hard of Hearing People, Inc., 1986-89, Glide Found., 1966-75, Gallaudet U., Washington, 1986—; bd. govs. Pub. Advs. Inc., 1975-79; mem. San Francisco Bd. Edn., 1967-71, pres., 1969; regent Lone Mountain Coll., 1973-76; pres. United Meth. Congress of the Deaf, 1993—. Mem. Am. Assn. Anatomists, Gerontol. Soc. Am., Am. Soc. on Aging, Self Help for Hard-of-Hearing People, Inc., Assn. Late Deafened Adults, Am. Deafness and Rehab. Assn., NOW, Phi Beta Kappa, Sigma Xi. Democrat. Methodist. (adminstrv. bd.). Home: 1400 Geary Blvd #2210 San Francisco CA 94109-6574 Office: #2307 1400 Geary Blvd San Francisco CA 94109-6574

GLASSER, LYNN SCHREIBER, publisher; b. Chgo., Sept. 19, 1943; d. Alexander Paul and Beatrice (Bollard) Schreiber; m. Stephen A. Glasser, Dec. 30, 1965; children: Susan, Laura, Jeffrey, Jennifer. BA, Chatham Coll., 1965. Publs. editor Inst. CLE U. Mich. Law Sch., Ann Arbor, 1966-68; asst. to dir. Practising Law Inst., N.Y.C., 1968-71; v.p., COO Law Jour. Press and Law Jour. Seminars, N.Y.C., 1971-78; exec. v.p., pub. Law & Bus./Harcourt Jovanovich, Inc., N.Y.C., 1978-86; co-pres. Prentice Hall Law & Bus., Englewood Cliffs, N.J., 1986-94; cons. Simon and Schuster, N.Y.C., 1994—; organizer, originator over 1000 CLE seminars, 1986—; organizer Woman Advt. Conf., N.Y.C., Chgo. and San Francisco, 1993-94; chmn. Woman Bus. Lawyer Conf., N.Y.C. and San Francisco, 1994. Trustee N.J. Chamber Music Soc., Montclair, 1989—; co-donor Lynn & Stephen Glasser Scholarship Fund, Colgate U., 1988—, Bloomfield Coll., 1993—. Mem. Rockefeller Ctr. Club (N.Y.C.).

GLASSMAN, CAROLINE DUBY, state supreme court justice; b. Baker, Oreg., Sept. 13, 1922; d. Charles Ferdinand and Caroline Marie (Colton) Duby; m. Harry Paul Glassman, May 21, 1953; 1 son, Max Avon. LLB summa cum laude, Willamette U., 1944. Bar: Oreg. 1944, Calif. 1952, Maine 1969. Atty. Title Ins. & Trust Co., Salem, Oreg., 1944-46; assoc. Belli, Ashe, Pinney & Melvin Belli, San Francisco, 1952-58; ptnr. Glassman

& Potter, Portland, Maine, 1973-78, Glassman, Beagle & Ridge, Portland, 1978-83; justice Maine Supreme Judicial Ct., Portland, 1983—; lectr. Sch. Law, U. Maine, 1967-68, 80. Author: Legal Status of Homemakers in State of Maine, 1977. Mem. Am. Law Inst., Oreg. Bar Assn., Calif. Bar Assn., Maine Bar Assn., Maine Trial Law Assn. Roman Catholic. Home: 56 Thomas St Portland ME 04102-3639 Office: ME Supreme Jud Ct 142 Federal St Portland ME 04101-4151

GLASSMAN, GERALDINE JOAN, controller; b. Bronx, N.Y., Apr. 13, 1936; d. Louis Fuccillo and Doris Lane; m. Stanley B. Glassman, Feb. 23, 1958. Student, CUNY, 1954-55. Adminstrn. asst. computers Sleepwear Inc., N.Y.C., 1953-73; office mgr. Daniel D. Cole Inc., White Plains, N.Y., 1973-76; controller, v.p. fin. Paul Hardman Co., Mt. Vernon, N.Y., 1976—, also bd. dirs., 1987—. Republican. Jewish.

GLASSON, LINDA, hospital security and safety official, healthcare consultant; b. Nassawadox, Va., July 2, 1947; d. William Robert and Doris (Savage) G.; m. Charles William Lemon, Jr., Mar. 21, 1969 (div. 1973). Student Eastern Shore Br. U. Va., 1965-67, J. Sargent Reynolds Community Coll., 1976-80, Old Dominion U., 1981, Va. Wesleyan Coll., 1985. Cert. ambulance emergency med. technician. Clk.-typist G.L. Webster Co., Inc., Cheriton, Va., 1962-70; tchrs. aide Cape Charles High Sch., Va., 1970-72; dir. recreation and infirmary asst. United Meth. Children's Home, Richmond, Va., 1972-73; stockroom mgr. Flair Clothing Store, Richmond, 1973-74; with med. record dept. Richmond Meml. Hosp., 1974-75, asst. utilization rev. coord., 1975-80, hosp. police sgt., 1977-80; dir. safety and security Maryview Hosp., Portsmouth, Va., 1980—, chmn. hosp. safety com., 1980—, mem. disaster com., 1980—, chmn., 1986—. Contbg. author tng. manuals; contbr. articles to profl. publs. Instr. first aid and personal safety ARC, 1970-85, multimedia first aid instr., 1983-88, first aid chmn. bd. dirs. Henrico chpt., 1979-80, vol. emergency med. technician ambulance state fair annually 1974—. Mem. Internat. Assn. Hosp. Security (sr., chmn. Region III 1985, v.p., sec. 1985-88, spl. appointee to bd. 1988-89), Am. Soc. Indsl. Security (mem. nat. standing com. healthcare security 1979-84, v.p. 1983-84), Internat. Assn. Healthcare Security & Safety (pres.-elect 1990, pres. 1991-92, past pres. 93—), Internat. Healthcare Security and Safety Found. (pres. 1994). Baptist. Avocations: golf, softball, swimming, reading, classical music. Office: Maryview Hosp 3636 High St Portsmouth VA 23707

GLASTRIS, CAROLYN MOSES, floral company executive; b. Mpls., Apr. 16, 1960; d. Charles Albin and Linda (Foster) Moses; m. William Vlasios Glastris, Jr., July 7, 1984. BA, Northwestern U., 1982, MusM, 1989; MBA, NYU, 1984. Banker Harris Bank, Chgo., 1984-87; inventory mgr. McMaster-Carr, Elmhurst, Ill., 1989-90, adjustment mgr., 1990-91; pres. North Shore Floral Svcs., Wilmette, Ill., 1991—. Mem. Ill. Florist Assn., Ill. Orchid Assn., Bus. and Profl. Orgn. of Chgo. Symphony Orch. (chmn. Centennial Project 1990-91), Chgo. Bot. Garden, Lincoln Park Zoo, Quadrangles Assn. (pres. 1990-92), Delta Delta Delta (v.p. house corp. 1990-92). Office: Towne Flowers 1227 Green Bay Rd Wilmette IL 60091-1643

GLATMAN-STEIN, MARCIA, executive search company executive; b. N.Y.C., Feb. 28, 1944; d. Martin and Jean (Bykowsky) Eisenberg; m. Allan Glatman, June 27, 1965 (div. 1979); children: Jill, Kim; m. Seymour Stein, Nov. 22, 1983. BA, Hunter Coll., 1965, MA, 1969. Cert. tchr., N.Y. Tchr. N.Y.C. Bd. Edn., 1965-70; counselor Rockland Community Coll., Suffern, N.Y., 1976-77; acct. mgr. Alexander Ross Assoc., N.Y.C., 1978-80; sr. acct. mgr. Stevenson Group, N.Y.C., 1981-83; v.p. Richards Cons., N.Y.C., 1983-84, E.G. Todd Assocs., N.Y.C., 1984-88; pres. HRD Cons., Inc., Clark, N.J., 1989—. Pub. (newsletter) Trends in Human Resources. Mem. ASTD, Internat. Assn. of Corp. and Profl. Recruiters, Am. Compensation Assn., Human Resource Planning Assn., Soc. for Human Resource Mgmt. Office: HRD Cons Inc 60 Walnut Ave Clark NJ 07066-1606

GLAVIN, A. RITA CHANDELLIER (MRS. JAMES HENRY GLAVIN, III), lawyer; b. Schenectady, May 11, 1937; d. Pierre Charles and Helen C. (Fox) Chandellier; m. James H. Glavin, III, June 1, 1963; children—Helene, James, Rita, Henry. A.B. cum laude, Middlebury Coll., 1958; J.D., Union U. Albany Law Sch., 1961. Bar: N.Y. 1961, U.S. Dist. Ct. (no. dist.) N.Y. 1961, U.S. Tax Ct. 1965, U.S. Supreme Ct. 1978. Assoc. Eugene Steiner, Albany, N.Y., 1961-64, Helen Fox Chandellier, Schenectady, 1965-76; mem. Glavin and Glavin, Waterford, Schenectady, and Albany, N.Y., 1965-86, 87—; del. 4th Jud. Dist. Nominating Conv., 1966-67; confidential law clk. presiding justices N.Y. State Ct. Claims, 1968-71; surrogate judge Saratoga County, 1986. Bd. dirs., chmn. fin. com. Schenectady YWCA, 1979-81; mem. Univ. Council, SUNY, Albany, 1985—; tech. advisor HSA of Northeastern N.Y. Maternity and Pediatric Com., 1976; bd. dirs. Schenectady Jr. League, 1974, 76, Assn. Coun. Mem. and Coll. Trustees, SUNY, 1991—; del. N.Y. State Jr. League Pub. Affairs Com., 1976; sec. Bellevue Maternity Hosp., Inc., 1966—, bd. dirs. 1966-83, bd. advisers, 1984—; trustee Middlebury Coll., 1978-88, chmn. law com., 1982-88, vice chmn. bd. dirs., 1986-87. Mem. N.Y. State Bar Assn. (del. ho. of dels. 1987-88, nominating com. 1988-90), Saratoga County Bar Assn. (exec. com. 1981—, v.p. 1985, pres. 1986), Schenectady County Bar Assn., Phi Beta Kappa, Kappa Kappa Gamma. Mem. editorial bd. Albany Law Rev., 1960-61. Office: Glavin & Glavin 69 2nd St # 40 Waterford NY 12188-2422

GLAZE, LYNN FERGUSON, development consultant; b. Oakland, Calif., May 24, 1933; d. Kenneth Loveland and Constance May (Pedder) Ferguson; m. Harry Smith Glaze, Jr., July 3, 1957; children: Catherine, Charles Richard. B.A., Stanford U., 1955, M.A., 1966. Devel. dir. Greenwich Acad., Conn., 1982-84; devel. cons. Del. Learning Ctr., Brandywine Mus., Opera Del., Ctr. for Creative Arts St. Michael's Day Nursery, 1984—. Pres. Darien-Norwalk YWCA, Conn., 1973-76; sec. Darien Republican Town com., Darien, 1974-79; dist. chmn. Darien Rep. Meeting, 1974-76, mem. Rep. Nat. Conv. Platform Com., 1988; vestry St. Luke's Ch., Darien, 1979-82; justice of the peace, Darien, 1981-84; bd. dirs. Ingleside Homes, Inc., 1986-92; mem. Gov.'s Small Bus. Council, 1987, EEOC, New Castle County, 1991-94. Fellow Coro Found., 1981.

GLAZER, REA HELENE See KIRK, REA HELENE

GLAZOV, BEVERLY, controller; b. St. Louis, Aug. 11, 1943; d. Leo and Dorothy (Eiche) Gibstein; divorced; children: David, Kenneth, Michelle. Student, UCLA, 1985. Stockbroker Oppenheimer & Co., L.A., 1980-91; adminstr. asst. El Pollo Loco, L.A., 1991—; contr. Citiwide Cellular, L.A., 1992-94; adminstr. Western Internat. Media Corp., 1994; pres. Westside Investors Group, L.A., 1994—; fin. advisor Baraban Securities, L.A., 1980—. Office: Western Internat Media & Baraban Securities 11611 San Vicente Blvd Los Angeles CA 90049

GLEASON, CAROL ANN, rehabilitation nurse; b. Franklin, N.H., June 17, 1950; d. Adam Victor and Rita T. (Robichaud) Novak; m. William J. Gleason, Aug. 24, 1974; 1 child, Stephen Bryan. Diploma, St. Elizabeth Hosp., Boston, 1971. RN, Mass.; CCRN, CCM; lic. rehab. counselor. Surg. nurse St. Elizabeth Hosp., Boston, 1971-73; pvt. nurse for chief of otolaryngology Mass. Eye and Ear Infirmary, Boston, 1973-74; pvt. duty nurse Met. Nurses, Inc., Boston, 1975; liaison, mktg. RN Spaulding Rehab. Hosp., Boston, 1975-81; admissions nurse Shaughnessy-Kaplan Rehab. Hosp., Boston, 1982-86; mktg. assoc. New Medico Head Injury System, Lynn, Mass., 1986-88; asst. regional mgr. New Medico, Lynn, 1988-90; rehab. specialist Cost Containment Mgmt., Braintree, Mass., 1990-91; sr. rehab. cons. N.Am. Health and Rehab. Svcs., Nashua, N.H., 1991; sr. mktg. assoc. Greenery Rehab. Group, Newton, Mass., 1992-94; dir. admissions Transitional Hosps. Corp., Boston, 1994—; speaker Mass. Passenger Safety Bur., Boston, 1988—; participant Nurse in Washington Internship, 1991. Contbg. author: The Speciality Practice of Rehabilitation Nursing, A Core Curriculum, 3d edit., 1993; editorial/mktg. cons. Pertinent Legislation Affecting Nurses newsletter, 1991—; contbr. articles to profl. jours. Cert. vision/hearing tester Mass. Dept. Pub. Health, Boston, 1990-93; bd. dirs. Marblehead (Mass.) Festival of Arts, 1989-91, Jr. Aid Soc. Inc., Marblehead, 1979—; mem. MADD, Boston, 1990—. Recipient Occupant Safety award Mass. Nurses Assn., 1989, She Know's Where She's Going award Girls Inc., 1989. Mem. Nat. Head Injury Found., Nat. Assn. Rehab. Profl. In The Pvt. Sector (chpt. bd. dirs. 1987-90), Pro-Mass (chpt. bd. dirs. 1990-93), Mass. Coun. Nursing Orgns. (bd. dirs. 1986—), Assn. Rehab. Nurses (chmn. mktg./pub. rels. 1990-91, health policy 1988—, vice chmn. health policy 1991-92, chmn. health policy 1992-93, , pres. bd. dirs. New England chpt. 1988-89), Ins. Rehab. Nurses New Eng. (bd. dirs., co-pres. 1992-94, advisor 1994—, legis. chair 1990-92), Am. Nurses Assn., Mass. Nurses Assn. Democrat. Roman Catholic. Office: THC-Boston 15 King St Peabody MA 01960

GLEASON, CYNTHIA S., public relations executive, educator; b. Portage, Wis., Mar. 2, 1949; d. Walter E. and Arleen (Slette) G.; m. William J. Kostka, Jr., Apr. 6, 1974; children—Jennifer Kostka, William Kostka III. B.A. in Journalism, U. Wis., 1972. Intern, U. Wis.-Madison Med. Ctr. Office of Pub. Info., 1970, State of Wis. Dept. Natural Resources, Madison, 1971; writer-researcher, jr. account exec. William Kostka & Assocs., Denver, 1972—, sr. account exec., 1974-77, v.p., 1977-79, sr. v.p., 1979-81, exec. v.p., 1981—; instr. dept. journalism U. Colo. Bd. dirs. Juvenile Offenders In Need, Inc., Denver; active Guardians Ad Litem. Recipient Pub. Relations Person of Year award Southland Corp., 1976. Mem. Pub. Relations Soc. Am. (accredited; counselors acad.), Denver Press Club. Home: 13955 E Hamilton Dr Aurora CO 80014-3942 Office: William Kostka & Assocs 1407 Larimer St Denver CO 80202-1723

GLEASON, HARRIET HALL, nurse; b. Otranto, Iowa, May 11, 1923; d. Roy Francis Sr. and Amy Ruth (Read) G. RN, Kahler Sch. Nursing, Rochester, Minn., 1947; BS, Hartwick Coll., 1956. RN, Colo. Office nurse Mayo Clinic, Rochester, 1947-53, various hosps., Oneonta, N.Y., 1953-56; instr. Fairview Hosp., Mpls., 1956-57; clin. instr. Swedish Hosp., Mpls., 1958-59; supr. sick children unit Mt. Sinai Hosp., 1959-60; ward nurse various temp. agys., N.Y.C., 1960-82; gen. and spl. duty nurse various assignments, Morgantown, W.Va., 1982—. Author: (cookbook) Therapeutic Diets, 1980, 94, (essays) I Understand, 1994. Active ARC; membership com., vol. Rep. Party Caucus, Mpls., N.Y.C. and W.Va., 1960-82, 92, 93. Mem. AAUW, Tri Beta, Zeta Tau Alpha (Pan Hellenic rep.).

GLEASON, JEAN WILBUR, lawyer; b. St. Louis, Oct. 31, 1943; d. Ray Lyman and Martha (Bugbee) W.; m. Gerald Kermit Gleason, Aug. 28, 1966 (div. 1987); children: C. Blake, Peter Wilbur; m. Kurt Stromberg, Jan. 3, 1993; 1 child, Kristoffer Stromberg. B.A., Wellesley Coll., 1965; LL.B. cum laude, Harvard U., 1968. Bar: Calif. 1969, D.C. 1978. Assoc. Brobeck, Phleger & Harrison, San Francisco, 1969-72; spl. counsel to dir. div. corp. fin. SEC, 1972-76, assoc. dir. div. investment mgmt., 1976-78; of counsel Fulbright & Jaworski, Washington, 1978-80; ptnr. Fulbright & Jaworski, 1980—; mem. adv. panel on legal issues GAO, NASD select com. on Nasdaq, 1994—. Mem. ABA (chmn. subcom. on securities and banks, corp. laws com., bus. sect.), D.C. Bar Assn. (chmn. steering com. bus. sect. 1982-84), Fed. Bar Assn. (chair exec. coun., securities com.), Am. Bar Retirement Assn. (bd. dirs. 1986-90, 94—), Phi Beta Kappa. Home: 3411 Woodley Rd NW Washington DC 20016-5030 Office: Fulbright & Jaworski 801 Pennsylvania Ave NW Washington DC 20004-2615

GLEASON, JOANNA, actress; b. Toronto, Ont., Can., June 2, 1950; d. Monty and Marilyn (Plotell) Hall. Grad., UCLA. Broadway debut I Love My Wife, Ethel Barrymore Theatre, 1977; Broadway appearances include Hey! Look Me Over, 1981, The Real Thing, 1984, A Hell of a Town, 1984, A Day in the Death of Joe Egg, 1985, It's Only a Play, 1985, Social Security, 1986, Into the Woods, Old Globe Theatre, San Diego and Martin Beck Theatre, N.Y.C., 1987 (Antoinette Perry award for leading actress in a mus., N.Y. Outer Critics Circle award, Drama Desk award), Nick and Nora, 1991; appeared in films Heartburn, 1986, Hannah and Her Sisters, 1986, Crimes and Misdemeanors, 1989, FX2: The Deadly Art of Illusion, 1991; TV appearances include Why Us?, 1981, Great Day, 1983, Still the Beaver, 1983, Life Under Water, 1989, The Boys, 1991, For Richer, For Poorer, 1992, Born Too Soon, 1993, For The Love of Aaron, 1994, series Hello, Larry, 1979-80, Chain Reaction, 1980, Love and War, 1992. Mem. Actors' Equity Assn. Office: ICM 40 W 57th St New York NY 10019*

GLEASON, LAURA ANN, paralegal; b. Cape Canaveral, Fla., June 29, 1965; d. Joseph Allen and Joan Marie (Ressel) Gleason; m. John Wiley Whisler, Oct. 27, 1990; 1 child, Alexander Erik. BA cum laude, U. Mo., St. Louis, 1987. Teaching asst. U. Mo., St. Louis, 1985; intern Mo. Hist. Soc., St. Louis, 1986; arbitral agt./paralegal Am. Film Mktg. Assn., L.A., 1988—. Author: Handbook of Architectural Styles, 1986. Bd. dirs. L.A. Ctr. for Internat. Comml. Arbitration, 1993—, sec. exec. com. 1993—). Democrat. Roman Catholic. Office: American Film Mktg Assn 12424 Wilshire Blvd Ste 600 Los Angeles CA 90025-1040

GLEASON, LINDA MARY, geriatrics nurse; b. Baldwin, Wis., July 3, 1956; d. George Christian and Mary Agnes (Geraghty) Hop; m. James John Gleason, Sept. 23, 1978; 4 children. Student, U. Wis., Eau Claire, 1974-75, Augsburg Coll., 1975-76; diploma in nursing, Abbott Northwestern Sch. Nursing, 1978; student, U. Wis., River Falls, 1993-94. Staff nurse Baldwin Community Meml. Hosp., 1978-79; dir. nursing Glenhaven, Inc., Glenwood City, Wis., 1979-80; staff nurse Am. Heritage Care Ctr., Hammond, Wis., 1980-84, insvc. dir., 1984-88, staff nurse, 1988-94, nurse mgr., 1994, dir. nursing, 1994—. Treas. Local Minn. Student Nurse's Assn., Mpls., 1977-78; religious edn. tchr. St. Patrick's Cath. Ch., Erin, Wis., 1987-88; co-leader jr. Girl Scout troop 1117 St. Croix Valley coun. 476 Girl Scouts U.S., Baldwin, 1990-94; tchr.'s aide, vol. Greenfield Elem., Baldwin, 1989-94, vol. presch. screening, 1989-94. Recipient Outstanding Leader award Girl Scouts U.S.A. Coun., 1992. Roman Catholic. Home: 1380 9th Ave Baldwin WI 54002

GLEATON, HARRIET E., retired anesthesiologist; b. Altoona, Pa., Aug. 25, 1937; d. Munsey Sinclair and Anna Morgan (Scofield) G. BA, Franklin & Marshall Coll., 1959; MD, Temple U., 1962. Diplomate Am. Bd. Anesthesiology. Intern Mt. Sinai Hosp., N.Y.C., 1962-63; resident in anesthesiology Hosp. U. Pa., 1963-65; fellow Hosp. U. Pa., Phila., 1965-66, instr. anesthesiology, 1966-69; clin. anesthesiologist Michael Reese Hosp., Chgo., 1969-71; assoc. prof. U. Okla., Oklahoma City, 1971-81; clin. anesthesiologist Jane Phillips Episcopal Meml. Med. Ctr., Bartlesville, Okla., 1981-92; pvt. practice, 1992. Mem. AMA, Am. Soc. Anesthesiologists, Nature Conservancy, World Wildlife Fedn., Environ Def. Fund, Sierra Club.

GLEATON, MARTHA MCCALMAN, English language educator; b. Troy, Ala., Oct. 29, 1943; d. Isaiah Williams and Martha Frances (McCalman) G.; m. Ansley Giddens Brown, Jr., Feb. 11, 1967 (div. 1986); children: Anne Martha, Ansley Giddens III. BS, Troy State U., 1967; MA, U. N.C., Greensboro, 1975; PhD, U. N.C., 1980. Asst. prof. Bennett Coll., Greensboro, N.C., 1985-89; asst. prof. High Point (N.C.) U., 1989-94, assoc. prof., 1994—; faculty advisor Alpha Gamma Delta, High Point, 1990—, Jr. Yr. Abroad Westminster Coll., Oxford, England, 1991—. United Negro Fund grantee, 1986, 88. Mem. Nat. Coun. Tchrs. of English, Coll. Composition Comm., Southea. Am. Soc. 18th Century Studies.

GLEESON, CATHLEEN JEANNE, psychologist, educator; b. Pasadena, Calif., July 6, 1948; d. John Conway and Barbara Jeanne (Dart) G.; m. Bruch Kochis, Sept. 4, 1971 (div. 1980); children: Alexander Gleeson, Katherine Gleeson; m. David Maughan, Oct. 11, 1986. BGS, U. Mich., 1974; MA, U. Nebr., 1980; PhD, Wash. State U., 1986. Lic. psychologist, Vt. Sch. counselor Cath. Social Svcs. Bur., Lincoln, Nebr., 1976-78; dir. social svc. dept. Tabitha Nursing Home, Lincoln, 1979-81; individual and family therapist Luth. Social Svcs., Spokane, Wash., 1981-83, Human Affairs, Inc., Spokane, 1983-86; rsch. asst. Coll. Edn. Wash. State U., Pullman, 1984-85, counseling asst. Counseling Ctr., 1984-85; adminstr. Univ. Health Ctr., Burlington, Vt., 1986-91; asst. prof., dir. behavioral sci. program Dept. Family Practice, Coll. Medicine, U. Vt., Burlington, 1988-93; clin. rsch. prof. Dept. Family Practice, Coll. Medicine, U. Vt., 1993—; pvt. practice Behavioral Medicine Svcs., 1993—; adj. prof. dept. prof. psychology Antioch/New Eng. Grad. Sch., Keene, N.H., 1988-91; mem. planning com. Vt. AIDS, 1990—; mem. steering com. Vt. AIDS Consortium, 1993, 94; lectr., presenter, cons. in field. Coord. AIDS edn. in Vt. New Eng. AIDS Edn. and Tng. Ctr., 1988—; vol. Dem. Nat. Com., Burlington, Vt., 1993. Mem. APA, Vt. Psychol. Assn. (exec. com. 1993—), Soc. Tchrs. in Family Practice. Office: Behavioral Medicine Svc 86 Lake St Burlington VT 05401

GLEESON, CLARE ANN, pharmacist; b. Pitts., Mar. 7, 1956; d. Patrick M. and Theresa (DiMaggio) Gleeson; m. James M. Prata, Aug. 16, 1980; children: Adam, Daniel and Kristen Gleeson-Prata. BS in Pharmacy, Duquesne U., 1979. Registered pharmacist, Pa., Va., Ohio. Registered mgr. Peoples Drugs, Fairfax, Va., 1979-80; staff pharmacist Thomas Jefferson U. Hosp., Phila., 1980-82, mfg. pharmacist, 1982-83; pharmacist Allegheny Gen. Hosp., Pitts., 1983-84, St. Clair Hosp., Pitts., 1984-86, HMSS, Inc., Cleve., 1988—, Marcs Pharmacy, Cleve., 1986—; assoc. prof. Phla. Coll. pharmacy and Sci., 1980-83. Mem. Levy Com., Solon, Ohio, 1993. Mem. APHA, Am. Soc. Hosp. Pharmacists, We. Pa. Soc. Hosp. Pharmacists, No. Ohio Pharmacists Assn. Republican. Roman Catholic. Home: 32832 Springside Ln Solon OH 44139-2067 Office: HMSS Inc Cleveland OH 44124

GLEESON, ROSLYN M., pediatrics nurse; b. New Haven, Mar. 2, 1952. BS, U. Conn., 1974; MSN, U. Pa., 1979. RN, Pa., Del.; cert. pediatric nurse, child and adolescent nurse ANCC. Staff nurse, charge nurse St. Christopher's Hosp. for Children, Phila., 1974-77; staff nurse, charge nurse pediatrics, neonatal ICU Med. Coll. Pa., Phila., 1978-79; pediatric clin. specialist in spinal dysfunction Alfred I. duPont Inst., Wilmington, Del., 1979—; instr. Neumann Coll. Sch. Nursing, Aston, Pa., 1991; mem. pediatric test devel. com. ANCC; clin. instr. Temple U., Phila., 1977, Delaware County C.C., 1982, U. Del. Sch. Nursing, 1989—, Thomas Jefferson U. Sch. Nursing, Phila., 1991—; cons. in field; presenter at profl. confs. Mem. ANA (nurses in advanced practice coun. 1992—), Sigma Theta Tau. Office: Alfred I duPont Inst Box 269 1600 Rockland Rd Wilmington DE 19803-3616

GLEICH, CAROL S., health professions education executive; b. Kewanee, Ill., Jan. 18, 1935; d. Carl and Edna (Krause) Gleich BA, U. Iowa, 1958, MS, 1967, PhD in Health Sci. Edn., 1972. From instr. to asst. prof. pathology U. Iowa, 1971-77; program dir. med. tech. program, asst. prof. dept. pathology U. Iowa, Iowa City, 1972-77; edn. specialist divsn. adminstrv. health, 1977-88; chief resident devel. sec., 1988-90; health manpower edn. officer, physician manpower and credentialing , chief spl. projects and data analysis br. div. medicine, exec. sec. coun. on grad. med. edn., 1991, Bur. Health Professions, Health Resources and Services Adminstrn., HHS, Rockville, Md., from 1977, allied health cons. to Egypt; dir. Geriatric Edn. Ctrs. of PHS; adj. assoc. prof. U. Md. Sch. Medicine; mem. Iowa Health Manpower Com., 1976—; cons. U. Wis. System Acad. Affairs, 1976; panelist and participant workshops; presenter and del. to internat. congress. Cert. clin. chemistry technologist, Nat. Registry Clin. Chemistry. Mem. Am. Soc. Allied Health Professions, Nat. Council for Internat. Health, Am. Soc. Clin. Pathologists (assoc.; cert. med. technologist; sec. ASCP Bd. Registry, 1975-77), Am. Soc. Clin. Lab. Sci., D.C. Soc. Med. Tech. (Outstanding Med. Technologist of Yr. 1975), Beta Beta Beta, Alpha Mu Tau. Assoc. editor Am. Jour. Med. Tech., 1974-83, Jour. Allied Health, 1982-85; contbr. articles to profl. publs., papers to confs. Home: 14800 Rocking Spring Dr Rockville MD 20853-3635 Office: Parklawn Bldg Room 9A-27 5600 Fishers Ln Rockville MD 20857-0001

GLEIM, KATHY MARIE, music educator, performer, composer; b. Hammond, Ind., May 17, 1956; d. Erwin Albert and Elizabeth Ann (Raimey) Gleim; m. David Blake Hill, Dec. 17, 1983 (div. June 8, 1992); 1 child, Joshua Blake. B.Music in Piano Performance, Furman U., Greenville, S.C., 1978; M.Music in Piano Performance, U. Cin., 1981. Organist St. Michael's Luth. Ch., Doraville, Ga., 1972-74; grad. teaching asst. U. Cin., 1978-80; organist First Ch. of Christ Scientist, Vienna, Austria, 1982; piano instr. (Klavierlehrerin) Musikschule Neulengbach, Austria, 1982; sec. Internat. Atomic Energy Agy., Vienna, 1982-83; organist Prince of Peace Luth. Ch., Alpharetta, Ga., 1984-86; bilingual sec. ER-WE-PA USA, Ltd., Marietta, Ga., 1986-88; organist Eastminster Presbyn. Ch., Marietta, Ga., 1991-93; ind. piano instr. KG Ent., 1980—; freelance keyboardist, 1989—. Composer: (choral work) Psalm 23, 1993, (piano works) Improvisations for Piano, 1993, Sonic Stream, 1990, (electronic media) Metal Weave I, 1993, Mixolydian Crickets, 1990, Call of 5, 1990, Shakuhachi Jam, 1990, others. U. Cin. scholar, 1978-80, Furman U. music scholar, 1974-78. Mem. NOW, Atlanta Fedn. Musicians, Music Tchrs. Nat. Assn.

GLEITSMANN, MICHELE ELCANO, psychiatric nurse; b. Monterey, Calif., Apr. 20, 1947; m. Fred Gleitsmann, Oct. 27, 1984; 1 child, Kevin. BSN, U. Nev., Reno, 1969; MSN, U. Calif., San Francisco, 1970. RN, Md.; cert. clin. specialist in adult psychiat. and mental health nursing ANCC; cert. nurse psychotherapist, Md. Staff nurse, charge nurse Washoe Med. Ctr., Reno, 1969; rsch. nurse St. Elizabeth's Hosp., Washington, 1971; nursing instr. Marymount Jr. Coll., Arlington, Va., 1971-72; staff nurse, charge nurse Psychiat. Inst., Washington, 1972-73, nursing unit adminstr., nurse therapist, 1973-81; nursing unit adminstr. Psychiat. Inst., Rockville, Md., 1981-83; dir. of nursing Dominion Hosp., Falls Church, Va., 1983-85; instr. Charles County C.C., La Plata, Md., 1989-92; cons. emergency psychiat. svc. Calvert Meml. Hosp., Prince Fredrick, Md., 1992; sch. counselor Archbishop Neale Sch., La Plata, Md., 1992—; nurse psychotherapist, 1992—. Flutist So. Md. Concert Band; sec., bd. dirs. Homeowners Assn., Waldorf, Md., 1988-90, The Jude House, Bel Alton, Md., 1987-88, sec. Mem. ANA, Md. Nurses Assn.

GLENCER, SUZANNE THOMSON, science educator; b. Monongahela, Pa., Feb. 7, 1942; d. John Cuddy and Sue Elizabeth (DeForrest) Thomson; m. May 9, 1970 (div.). BS in Zoology, Pa. State U., 1964; MEd in Biology, Calif. (Pa.) State U., 1968; postgrad., U. Pitts., 1970-84. Biology, health instr. Allegheny Community Coll., Pitts., 1969-85; instr. Pa. State U., New Kensington, 1978-84; sci. tchr. Northgate Sch. Dist., Bellevue, Pa., 1967—, also drug/alcohol coord., 1978—; cons. area sch. dists., Pitts., 1990—; speaker numerous local orgns., Pitts., 1985—. Author: Adventures of Atom, 1985, Concepts in Kindness, 1987; contbr. articles to local newspaper, 1980—; writer and presenter numerous grants. Bd. dirs. Animal Friends, Pitts., 1974-84, Am. Cancer Soc., Pitts., 1979-83, Teen Recreation Fedn., Bellevue, 1989—; mem. adv. bd. Citizens Against Substance Abuse, Bellevue, 1990—. Named Outstanding Young Educator, North Hill's Jaycees, 1979, Pa. Outstanding Young Educator, State of Pa. Jaycees, 1979, Pa. State Tchr. of Yr., Dept. Edn., 1982, Citizen of Yr., Pitts. City & Suburban Life, 1982, Citizen of Yr., Pa. Police, 1989; recipient Nat. Drug Free Sch. award Pres. Bush, 1989, Citation Pa. Ho. of Reps., 1993. Mem. NEA, Pa. State Edn. Assn. Republican Roman Catholic. Home: The Ter RR 1 Box 617 Fombell PA 16123-9740 Office: Northgate Sch Dist 589 Union Ave Pittsburgh PA 15202-2958

GLENN, ANDREA POUTASSE, editor; b. Cleve., Sept. 13, 1951; d. Eugene Francis Poutasse and Helen (Kingston) Ingram; m. Grant Matthew Glenn, Aug. 4, 1973; children: Alexander, Charles, Margaret. BS, Kans. State U., 1973. Advt. copywriter Emerson/Franzke Advt., Topeka, 1973-78; editor Kansas! mag. Kans. Dept. Commerce, Topeka, 1978—. Author, editor: Kansas In Color, 1981. Mem. Auburn-Washburn Bd. Edn., 1991—; active Jr. League Topeka, 1981-92; bd. dirs. Mulvane Art Ctr., Topeka, 1987-92, Hist. Topeka, Inc., 1985-88. Mem. Regional Pubs. Assn. Episcopalian. Home: 7828 SW 37th St Topeka KS 66614-4939 Office: Kans Dept Commerce Ste 1300 700 SW Harrison Topeka KS 66603-3925

GLENN, BETH, sales and marketing executive; b. Petersburg, Va., Sept. 3, 1952; d. William Francis and Helen Elizabeth (Martin) G. BA cum laude, Kent State U., 1976. Systems analyst Raytheon, N.Y.C., 1980-81; office mgr. Chem. Bank, N.Y.C., 1981-82; sr. mktg. cons. Honeywell, Boston, 1982-87; worldwide mktg. mgr. Groupe Bull, Paris, 1987-91; dir. internat. sales Nynex, White Plains, N.Y., 1991—. Mem. NAFE, Assn. Mgmt. Women, Alliance Francais Newport, Millbrook Equestrian Ctr., Nat. Trust for Hist. Preservation, Preservation Soc. Newport, Friends of Vielles Maisons Francaises. Episcopalian.

GLENN, CLETA MAE, lawyer; b. Clinton, Ill., Sept. 24, 1921; d. John and Mattie Sylvester (Anderson) Glenn; BS, U. Ill., 1947; JD, DePaul U. Coll. Law, 1976; m. Rex Eugene Loggans, Sept. 3, 1948 (div.); 1 child, Susan. Real estate builder, developer, 1959-69; communications dir. Transp. Rsch. Ctr., Northwestern U., Evanston, Ill., 1969-72. Bar: Ill. 1977. Pvt. practice law, Chgo., 1977—; lectr. Assn. Trial Lawyers Am., John Marshall Law Sch. With USN, 1943-59. Recipient Real Estate Humanitarian award Kislak Co., Miami, Fla., 1962. Mem. ABA, Ill. Bar Assn. (assembly rep., mem. standing com. on traffic laws and cts., family law sect. council), Chgo. Bar Assn., Assn. Trial Lawyers Am., Ill. Trial Lawyers Assn., Lex Leggio, Phi Alpha Delta. Editor: Collective Bargaining and Technological Change in American Transportation, 1979; contbr. articles to profl. publs. Home: 200 E

Delaware Pl Chicago IL 60611-1757 Office: Glenn Law Offices 200 W Madison St Ste 2850 Chicago IL 60606-3416

GLENN, CONSTANCE WHITE, art museum director, educator, consultant; b. Topeka, Oct. 4, 1933; d. Henry A. and Madeline (Stewart) White; m. Jack W. Glenn, June 19, 1955; children: Laurie Glenn Buckle, Caroline Glenn Galey, John Christopher. BFA, U. Kans., 1955; postgrad., U. Mo., 1964-69; MA, Calif. State U., 1974. Dir. Univ. Art Mus. & Mus. Studies program, from lectr. to prof. Calif. State U., Long Beach, 1973—; art cons. Archtl. Digest, L.A., 1980-89. Author: Jim Dine Drawings, 1984, Roy Lichtenstein: Landscape Sketches, 1986, Wayne Thiebaud: Private Drawings, 1988, Robert Motherwell: The Dedalus Sketches, 1988, James Rosenquist: Time Dust: The Complete Graphics 1962-92, 1993; contbg. editor: Antiques and Fine Arts, 1991-92. Vice-chair Adv. Com. for Pub. Art, Long Beach, 1990—; chair So. Calif. adv. bd. Archives Am. Art, L.A., 1980-90; mem. adv. bd. ART/LA, 1986—, chair, 1992; mem. adv. bd. Decorative Arts Study Ctr., San Juan Capistrano, Calif., 1990—. Recipient Outstanding Contbn. to Profession award Calif. Mus. Photography, 1986. Mem. Am. Assn. Mus., Assn. Art Mus. Dirs., Coll. Art Assn., Art Table, Long Beach Pub. Corp. for the Arts (arts adminstr. of yr. 1989), Long Beach Opera Ring, Kappa Alpha Theta. Office: Univ Art Mus 1250 N Bellflower Blvd Long Beach CA 90840-0004

GLERUM, ELLEN, nurse, nursing educator; b. Bronx, N.Y., Nov. 12, 1958; m. Mark B. Glerum, Mar. 12, 1988. Student, SUNY, Stony Brook, 1976-80; BSN, Alfred U., 1982. RN, N.Y.; cert. neonatal intensive care nurse, Nat. Cert. Corp. for Obstet., Gynecol. and Neonatal Nursing Specialties; cert. neonatal resuscitation hosp. based instr., Am. Acad. of Pediatrics. Staff nurse in pediatrics White Plains Hosp. Med. Ctr., White Plains, N.Y., 1982-85; staff RN in neonatal ICU Westchester County Med. Ctr., Valhalla, N.Y., 1985-91; neonatal nurse clinician Westchester County Med. Ctr., Valhalla, 1991—; instr. neonatal concepts Care Series Confs., Westchester County Med. Ctr. Mem. Nat. Assn. Neonatal Nurses, N.Y. State Nurses Assn.

GLESMANN, SYLVIA-MARIA, artist; b. Spardorf/Erlangen, Germany, June 8, 1923; arrived in the U.S., 1925; d. Rolf-Joseph and Auguste (Schultheiss) Hoffmann; m. John Brainerd Glesmann, Apr. 30, 1948; children: Glenn M., Eric B., Jonathan M. Degree, Acad. Fine Arts, Nurnberg, Germany, 1940, Acad. Fine Arts, Munich, 1944. instr. Somerville Adult Edn. Classes. Paintings exhibited in group shows including Carrier Clinic, 1993, Bergen Mus., 1993, Morris Mus., 1993, Nabisco Brands, 1993, Tribute to Spring Cultural and Heritage Gallery, Somerville, N.J., 1993, 94, 95, Salmagundi Juried Mems. Show, 1994, Garden State Water Color Assn., Princeton, N.J., 1994, Barrons Art Ctr., 1993, Art on the Ave. Group Show of Flowers, 1991, Nat. Assn. Women Artists Show, N.Y.C., 1991, The "Big Picture" NAWA, N.Y., 1994, "105 Exhibition" SoHo, 1994, others; exhibited paintings in more than 21 one woman shows including Childrens Specialized Hosp., Mountainside, N.J., N.U.I. Corp., Bridgewater, N.J., 1987, others. Recipient over 50 awards in water color. Mem. Am. Artists Profl. League (pres. N.J. chpt. 1988-91), Nat. Assn. Woman Artists, Raritan Valley Arts Assn. (pres. 1976-78), Somerset Art Assn. (chairwoman 10th outdoor art show), Nat. Assn. Women Artists, Salmagundi Club, Nat. Mus. for Women in Arts. Lutheran. Home and Office: 36 Twin Oaks Rd Bridgewater NJ 08807-2343

GLESS, SHARON, actress; b. L.A.; m. Barney Rosenzweig. Student, Gonzaga U. Appeared in TV series Faraday and Company, 1973-74, Marcus Welby, M.D., 1974-75, Switch!, 1975-78, Turnabout, 1979, House Calls, 1981-82; star TV series Cagney and Lacey, 1982-88 (6 Emmy nominations 1982-88, Emmy award 1986, 87, Golden Globe award 1985), The Trials of Rosie O'Neill, 1990-92 (Golden Globe award 1990, Emmy nomination 1991, 92); appeared in TV miniseries The Immigrants, 1978, Centennial, 1978, The Last Convertible, 1979; numerous other guest appearances in TV series; TV movies include All My Darling Daughters, 1972, My Darling Daughters' Anniversary, 1973, Clinic on 18th Street, 1974, Richie Brockelman: The Missing 24 Hours, 1976, The Islander, 1978, Crash, 1978, Kids Who Knew Too Much, 1979, Moviola: The Scarlett O'Hara War, 1980, Revenge of the Stepford Wives, 1980, Hardhat and Legs, 1980, The Miracle of Kathy Miller, 1981, Palms Precinct, 1982, Hobson's Choice, 1983, The Sky's No Limit, 1984, Letting Go, 1985, The Outside Woman, 1989, Honor Thy Mother, 1992, Separated by Murder, 1994, Cagney and Lacey: The Return, 1994; motion pictures include The Star Chamber, 1983; theatrical debut in Watch on the Rhine, 1989; theater: Misery (London), 1992-93; films include Airport 1975, 1974, The Star Chamber, 1983. Recipient Genii award Hollywood Women in Radio and TV, Best Actress award Viewers for Quality TV, Milestone award, 1988, SI award, 1991, Crystal Airwaves Media award Coalition for Clean Air, 1987, Gideon Media award, 1992, Disting. Artist award, 1992; named Woman of Yr., Ms mag., NCA Woman of Year, 1987, Entertainer of Yr., 1987. Office: William Morris Agy 151 El Camino Dr Beverly Hills CA 90212*

GLICK, CYNTHIA SUSAN, lawyer; b. Sturgis, Mich., Aug. 6, 1950; d. Elmer Joseph and Ruth Edna (McCally) G. AB, Ind. U., 1972; JD, Ind. U.-Inpls., 1978. Bar: Ind. 1978, U.S. Dist. Ct. (so. dist.) Ind. 1978, U.S. Dist. Ct. (no. dist.) Ind. 1981. Adminstrv. asst. Gov. Otis R. Bowen, Ind., 1973-76; dep. pros. atty. 35th Jud. Cir., LaGrange County, Ind., 1980-82, pros. atty., 1983-90. Campaign aide Ind. Rep. State Cen. Com., Indpls., 1972-73. Named Hon. Speaker Ind. Ho. of Reps., 1972, Sagamore of the Wabash, Gov. Ind., 1974. Fellow Ind. Bar Found.; mem. ABA, Ind. State Bar Assn., LaGrange County Bar Assn. (pres. 1983-86), DAR, Bus. and Profl. Women's Club, Order of Ea. Star, Phi Delta Phi, Delta Zeta. Republican. Methodist. Home and Office: 113 W Spring St Lagrange IN 46761-1843

GLICK, JANE MILLS, biochemistry educator; b. Memphis, Nov. 26, 1943; d. Albert Axtell Jr. and Mary Louise (Baynes) Mills; m. John Harrison Glick, May 25, 1968; children: Katherine Anne, Sarah Stewart. AB, Randolph-Macon Woman's Coll., 1965; PhD, Columbia U., 1971. Postdoctoral trainee NIH, Bethesda, Md., 1971-73; postdoctoral fellow Sch. of Medicine Stanford (Calif.) U., 1973-74; rsch. asst. prof. biochemistry Sch. Dental Medicine U. Pa., Phila., 1974-77; asst. prof. biochemistry Med. Coll. Pa., Phila., 1977-82, assoc. prof. biochemistry, 1982-90, prof. biochemistry, 1990-94; sr. rsch. investigator Inst. Human Gene Therapy, U. Pa. Sch. Medicine, 1994—; mem. metabolism study sect. NIH, 1993—. Assoc. editor: Jour. Lipid Rsch., 1985-86, mem. editorial bd., 1987—; contbr. articles to profl. jours. Trustee Episcopal Acad., Merion, Pa., 1989—. Recipient Rsch. Svc. award NIH, 1975-77, Young Investigator award, 1980-83, Teaching award Lindback Found., 1985. Mem. AAAS, AAUP (sec. 1990-92), Arteriosclerosis Coun. Am. Heart Assn. (program com. 1990-93), Am. Soc. for Biochemistry and Molecular Biology, Am. Soc. for Human Genetics, Phi Beta Kappa, Sigma Xi. Presbyterian. Office: U Pa Med Coll Inst Human Gene Therapy 3400 Spruce St Maloney 601 Philadelphia PA 19104-4283

GLICK, JULIE LYNN, costumer; b. L.A., Mar. 27, 1959; d. Michael S. and Gail Harriet (Seligman) G. BS in Merchandising & Fashion Promotion, U. Ariz., 1980. Costumer Western Costume Co., L.A., 1981-82. Costuming supr.: (TV) thirtysomething, 19881-91 (Emmy award 1988-89, Emmy award nomination 1990-91), Brothers, Still the Beaver, Seinfeld, (film) Groundhog Day; costumer: (films) Geronimo, What About Bob?, The Doctor, Rocky 5, The Bounty, Caddyshack 2, Last of the Mohicans, Lost in America, Deadly Force, This is Spinal Tap, (TV) Knight Rider, Scarecrow and Mrs. King, Family Ties, Dreamfinders (TV movie) Flamingo Kid. Vol. mem. AIDS Project L.A., 1992-93. Mem. Internat. Alliance Theatrical and Stage Employees (key costumer). Democrat. Jewish.

GLICK, KAREN LYNNE, college administrator; b. Bucyrus, Ohio, Sept. 2; d. Phillip Dole and Bernice Grace Glick; BSJ, Bowling Green State U., 1967, MA, 1979; children: M. Todd, K. Christine. Editor, Bowling Green (Ohio) State U., 1972-74; account exec. Howard E. Mitchell, Jr., Advt., Findlay, Ohio, 1974-77; asst. to dir. Student Devel. Program, Bowling Green State U., 1977-79; dir. pub. info. Bluffton (Ohio) Coll., 1980-83; asst. to v.p. for instl. advancement Findlay (Ohio) Coll., 1983-85; assoc. dir. devel. Bluffton Coll., 1985-90; assoc. dir. divisional support Miami U., Oxford, Ohio, 1990-93; regional dir. devel. U. Ill. Found., Urbana, 1993—. Anglican. Club: Bowling Green U. Press (charter mem. 1983). Office: U Ill Found Harker Hall 1305 W Green St Urbana IL 61801

GLICKENHAUS, SARAH BRODY, speech therapist; b. Mpls., Mar. 8, 1919; d. Morris and Ethel (Silin) Brody; BS, U. Minn., 1940, MS, 1945; m. Seth Morton Glickenhaus, Oct. 23, 1944; children: James Morris, Nancy Pier. Speech therapist Davison Sch. Speech Correction, Atlanta, 1940-42; speech pathologist U. Minn., Mpls., 1945-46; speech therapist Queens Coll., N.Y.C., 1946-48; speech therapist VA, N.Y.C., 1949-50; pvt. practice, New Rochelle, N.Y., 1950-71; speech therapist Abbott Sch. United Free Sch. Dist. 13, Irvington, N.Y., 1971-79; pvt. practice, Scarsdale, N.Y., 1979—; tutor learning disabled children New Rochelle Public Schs., 1968-71. Mem. AAAS, Am. Speech Hearing & Lang. Assn., N.Y. State Speech &Hearing Assn., Westchester Speech & Hearing Assn. Club: Harvard (N.Y.C.). Jewish. Home and Office: 100 Dorchester Rd Scarsdale NY 10583-6051

GLICKMAN, MARLENE, social organization administrator; b. Evansville, Ind., May 13, 1936; d. Morris Jack and Sarah (Krawll) Foreman; m. Marshall Levi Glickman, Jan. 9, 1956; children: Cynthia Anne, Joseph Leonard. Student, Ohio State U., 1954-56. Area dir. The Am. Jewish Com., Buffalo, 1982—. Pres. Human Rights Adv. Coun., Western N.Y., 1988—; bd. dirs. YWCA, Buffalo and Erie County, 1990—, Sheehan Meml. Hosp., Inc., 1994—, Buffalo Fedn. Neighborhood Ctrs., Inc., 1994—; co-pres., bd. dirs. Western N.Y. Martin Luther King Jr. Commn., 1991—; mem. United Way Agy. Allocations Com.; chairwoman Towns and Villages div. United Way, 1981; pres. N.E. Lakes Coun. Union Am. Hebrew Congregations, 1982-86, Meals on Wheels of Buffalo and Erie County, 1981-83, Coun. Congl. Pres.-Erie County, 1979-81, Temple Beth Am., 1978-80 (1st woman pres.), Sisterhood Temple Beth Am., 1969-71, 76-77; vice chair gen. campaign United Jewish Appeal, 1980, chair woman's div., 1979; active western N.Y. vision for tomorrow-200V C. of C./Buffalo Partnership. Recipient Abraham Pugash Community Rels. award for establishing Kosher Meals on Wheels, Jewish Family Svc., Buffalo and Erie County, N.Y., 1975. Mem. Union Am. Hebrew Congregations (bd. dirs. 1982—, exec. com.), Commn. on Synagogue Music Facilitators, Joint Cantorial Placement Commn., Hadassah (life), Assn. Reform Zionists Am. (del. to Israel 1987), Brandeis Women's Com., Nat. Coun. Jewish Women (life, Hannah G. Solomon award 1985), Assn. Jewish Comty. Rels. Workers, Jewish Communal Svc. Assn. Office: The Am Jewish Com 3407 Delaware Ave Buffalo NY 14217-1421

GLIDDEN, MARIANNA PAGE, human resouces administrator; b. Meriden, Conn., Dec. 28, 1940; d. Leon Stanley and Antoinette Barbara (Misiorski) Paluszewski; m. Kenneth Paul Glidden, May 17, 1975. BFA, U. Conn., 1964; MS, Columbia U., 1971. Cert. social worker. Nat. dir. of nat. juvenile justice program collaboration Nat. Assembly, N.Y.C., 1976-81; dir. program devel. N.Y.C. Human Resources Adminstrn., 1981-88, asst. dep. adminstr., 1988-92, dep. adminstr., 1992—; adj. prof. social svcs. Fordham U., N.Y.C., 1989-91. Author: (with others) Community Collaboration, 1974; editor and author: (with others) Working Together, Advocating for Change, 1976; contbr. articles to Proceedings of the Conf. on Privitization: Myths and Realities, N.Y.C., 1992, 93. Bd. dirs. Yorktown Community Players, Yorktown Heights, N.Y., 1979—; trustee Town of Yorktown Mus., Yorktown Heights, 1980-90. Office: NYU Human Resources Adminst Office of Budget 151-155 W Broadway New York NY 10013

GLIER, INGEBORG JOHANNA, German language and literature educator; b. Dresden, Germany, June 22, 1934; came to U.S., 1972; d. Erich Oskar and Gertrud Johanne (Niese) G. Student, Mt. Holyoke Coll., 1955-56; Dr. phil. (Studienstiftung des deutschen Volkes), U. Munich, Germany, 1958; Dr. phil., Habilitation, 1969; M.A. (hon.), Yale U., 1973. Asst., lectr. U. Munich, 1958-69, universitätsdozentin, 1969-72; vis. prof. Yale U., 1972-73, prof. German, 1973—, chmn. dept., 1979-82, chmn. Medieval studies, 1986-93, sr. faculty fellow, 1974-75; vis. prof. U. Cologne, Germany, 1970-71, U. Colo., Boulder, spring 1983, U. Tubingen, summer 1984. Author: Struktur und Gestaltungsprinzipien in den Dramen John Websters, 1958, Deutsche Metrik, 1961, Artes amandi, Untersuchung zu Geschichte, Überlieferung und Typologie der deutschen Minnereden, 1971; contbr. articles, book reviews to profl. jours. Mem. Internationaler Germanisten-Verband, Modern Lang. Assn., Mediaeval Acad. Am., Am. Assn. Tchrs. German, Internat. Courtly Lit. Soc., Wolfram von Eschenbach Gesellschaft. Home: 111 Park St Apt 12T New Haven CT 06511-5412 Office: Yale Univ Dept Germanic Langs PO Box 208210 New Haven CT 06520-8210

GLIK, BRENDA-FAY, counselor, researcher; b. St. Louis, July 7, 1964; d. Morris and Eileen Shirley (Gliner) Tamsky; m. Jeffrey W. Glik, July 9, 1988; 1 child, Andrea. BA, Ind. U., 1986; MA, U. Mo., St. Louis, 1988, EdD, 1994. Author: (with others) Introduction to Counseling, 1994. Democrat. Office: 501 N Lindbergh Blvd Saint Louis MO 63141-7829

GLOCK, JACQUELYN MARIE, association executive; b. Jersey City, May 1, 1944; d. George Henry and Estelle Jacqueline (McBride) G.; 1 child, Jared. BA in English, Caldwell Coll., 1966; MSW, Rutgers U., 1970. Dir. planning and rsch. divsn. City of Jersey City, N.J., 1972-77; pres. Glock Assocs., Inc., Point Beach, N.J., 1977—; exec. dir. YWCA of Plainfield/North Plainfield, N.J., 1991—; devel. dir. Trinity Ch./Windmill Alliance, 1990—; devel. dir. Mental Health Assn. in N.J., 1991-94. Sec. Plainfield Bus. Devel. Corp., 1992—. Mem. Nat. Soc. Fundraising Execs., Rotary of Plainfield (cmty. svc. chair 1995). Democrat. Roman Catholic. Home: 410 Elizabeth Ave Point Pleasant Beach NJ 08742-4132 Office: YWCA of Plainfield/N Plainfield 232 E Front St Plainfield NJ 07060-1319

GLOE, DONNA, critical care nurse; b. Moberly, Mo., Apr. 24, 1951; d. James F. and E. Emogene (Semones) Osborn; m. Lloyd R. Gloe, Feb. 14, 1975; children: Darin Robert, Leslie Renee. BA, U. Mo., 1973; MEd, Lincoln U., Jefferson City, Mo., 1977; diploma, St. John's Sch. Nursing, Springfield, Mo., 1983; BSN, S.W. Bapt. U., 1991. Cert. critical care nurse. Family therapist Burrell Mental Health Ctr., Springfield; edn. coord., staff nurse surg. ICU St. John's Regional Health Ctr., Springfield; adj. faculty S.W. Bapt. U., 1992. Contbr. articles to profl. jours.; author video. Mem. AACN, Nat. Nursing Staff Devel. Orgn., Mo. Assn. Hosp. Educators. Home: HC 88 Box 4 Marshfield MO 65706-9005

GLOMB, DIANA, state legislator. BS, Northeast La. U., 1969; MSW, La. State U., 1974. Former social worker; mem. Nev. State Senate, 1991—. Mem. NASW, Nev. Rainbow Coalition. Democrat. Office: Nev State Senate State Capital Carson City NV 89710*

GLOSUP, LORENE See DEAN, DEAREST

GLOVER, FLORENCE WALKER, probation officer; b. Waynesboro, Ga., Nov. 5, 1942; d. Lenon and Julia Pearl (Johnson) Walker; m. Rudolph Waldon, Nov. 7, 1961; children: Anthony Angelo, Waldron Guy, Jeffrey Rudolph. BAA, Southwest Tex. State U., 1983. Child care worker II Bexar County Juvenile Detention Ctr., San Antonio, 1984-89, program coord., 1989-90, supr., 1990—. Mem. Order Eastern Star, Psi Beta. Home: 8 Flintstone Ct San Antonio TX 78213

GLOVER, JANET STOLLER, education educator; b. St. Clair, Pa., June 14, 1935; d. Millan Daniel and Pauline Margaret (Botto) Stoller; m. James Donald Glover, June 10, 1958; children: Carole Janet, Susan Margaret. BS in Biology, Grove City Coll., 1955; MA in Eng. Bible, Presbyn. Sch. Christian Edn., 1961; MEd in Early Childhood Edn., Ednl. Adminstrn., U. N.C., Charlotte, 1975; PhD in Adminstrn., Supervision, U. So. Miss., 1988. Dir. Christian edn., children's choirs Davis Meml. Presbyn. Ch., Elkins, W.Va., 1956-58, 1st Presbyn. Ch., Bloomfield, N.J., 1958-60; tchr. biology Richmond (Va.) City Schs., 1961-63, Kinston (N.C.) City Schs., 1965; tchr. biology and math. Lenoir County Schs., Kinston, 1966-68; dir. Week-Day Presch. Englewood Presbyn. Ch., Rocky Mount, N.C., 1970-71; dir. Week-Day Kindergarten Trinity Episcopal Ch., Statesville, N.C., 1974-75; tchr. kindergarten, educable mentally retarded, learning disabled, adminstrv. intern Iredell County Sch. Sys., Statesville, 1975-78; tchr. remedial lang. arts Fairview Elem. Sch., Fairview Sch. Dist., West Plains, Mo., 1978-79; prin. Koshkonong Elem. Sch. Koshkonong (Mo.) R-III Sch. Dist., 1980-81; tchr. 1st, 5th grades Biloxi (Miss.) Mcpl. Separate Sch. Dist., 1981-87; adj. asst. prof. dept. curriculum & instrn. Memphis State U., 1988-90; asst. prof. coord. secondary edn., dept. curriculum & instrn. Ga. Coll., Milledgeville, 1990—; adv. Student Profl. Assn. Ga. Educators; judge Oconee Regional Social Science Fair, 1991, 92, 93, state finals Nat. Competition Constn. and Bill of Rights, 1993; presider 3d Ann. Youth-at-Risk Conf., Savannah, Ga., 1992. Vol. Ctrl. State Hosp., Milledgeville, 1990—, tchr. Mother Love Classes, Parenting Ctr. Memphis, 1988-91, counselor presch. screening Shelby County Bd. Health, Memphis, 1988-91; mem. numerous Presbyn Chs., 1964—; corr. sec. Women of the Ch. Presbyterial, 1968-74; mem. edn. com. Commn. Human Rels., Rocky Mount, 1968-74; pres. bd. dirs. Meals on Wheels, Iredell County, N.C., 1974-77; bd. dirs. New Schoolhouse of the Arts, Davidson, N.C., 1974-77; chmn. bd. United Ministeries in Edn., 1978-80; coun. Synod of Mid-Am. Presbyn. Ch. (US), 1978-81; mem. gen. assembly mission bd. Presbyn. Ch. (US), 1978-81; mem. Gulf Coast Opera Chorus, Biloxi, Miss., 1981-87; coun. So. Miss. Presbytery, 1983-86, Miss. Presbytery, 1986-87; ordained elder clk. of session Convenant Presbyn. Ch., Biloxi, 1985-86; mem. nurture com. NE Ga. Presbytery, Presbyn. Ch. (US), 1993—. NSF fellow E. Carolina U., 1968. Mem. CWENS, AAUW (v.p. 1993—), ASCD (nat., Ga.), Kappa Delta Pi, Phi Delta Kappa (pub. rels. com.), Alpha Theta Mu (now Mortar Bd.). Home: PO Box 1220 Milledgeville GA 31061-1220 Office: Ga Coll Cbx # 071 Milledgeville GA 31061

GLOVER, KAREN E., lawyer; b. Nampa, Idaho, Apr. 14, 1950; d. Gordon Ellsworth and Cora (Frazier) G.; m. Thaddas L. Alston, Aug. 17, 1979; children: Samantha Glover Alston, Evan Glover Alston. AB magna cum laude, Whitman Coll., 1972; JD cum laude, Harvard U., 1975. Bar: Wash. 1975, U.S. Dist. Ct. (we. dist.) Wash. 1975. Assoc. Preston, Thorgrimson Ellis & Holman, Seattle, 1975-80; ptnr. Preston Gates & Ellis, Seattle, 1981—. Chmn. bd. dirs. United Way King County, Seattle, 1993-94; chair bd. overseers Whitman Coll., Walla Walla, Wash., 1995—; mem. bd. trustees King County Libr. Sys., Seattle, 1992—. Mem. Wash. State Bar Assn. (corp. and tax sects.), Seattle Pension Roundtable, Columbia Tower Club, Sand Point Country Club, Rainier Club. Episcopalian. Office: Preston Gates & Ellis 701 5th Ave # 5000 Seattle WA 98104-7078

GLOVER, LISA MARIE, transportation company executive; b. Detroit, Oct. 14, 1963; d. Ronald and Denise (Wellons) G. BS, Tuskegee U., 1986; MS, Morgan State U., 1988. Lic. real estate agt. Summer intern IBM, Charlotte, N.C., 1982, GM, Pontiac, Mich., 1983, 84, 85, Turner Constrn., Detroit, 1986; grad. intern State of Md., Dept. Transp., Balt., 1987-88; planner Dept. Transp., Detroit, 1988-90, asst. to dir., 1990-91, mgr. Office of Contract Compliance, 1991-93; transp. engr., cons. M2 Internat., Detroit, 1993-94; owner Trans. Svcs., Inc., 1994—; rep. Detroit Dept. Transp. SEMCOG, Transp. Adv. Coun., Detroit, 1988-93, Labor Mobility Project Steering Com., Detroit, 1991. Mem. Civic Ctr.-Optimist Club, 1992—, mem. 14th Congl. Dist. Young Dems., spl. projects com., 1992, young adults com. NAACP, 1989-91. Mem. NAFE, Assn. Gen. Contractors Am. (pres. 1985-86), Conf. Minority Transp. Ofcls., Tuskegee Nat. Alumni Assn., Morgan State Student Transp. Assn. (sec. 1986-87), Trade Union Leadership Coun. Young Adults, Alpha Kappa Alpha (sponsor teen group 1989—). Democrat. Mem. African Meth. Episcopal Ch. Office: 16238 Kentucky Detroit MI 48221-2987

GLOVER, MAGGIE WALLACE, state legislator; b. Florence, S.C., Aug. 29, 1948; d. Fulton and Ethel (Greene) Wallace. 1 child, Marisa. BA, Fayetteville St. U., 1970; MEd, Marion Coll., 1982. Former mem. S.C. Ho. of Reps., dist. 62; mem. S.C. Senate. Active sch. bd. trustees, Florevce Sch. Dist., 1983-86, 86-89. With AUS 1974-77. Mem. NAACP. Democrat. Home: PO Box 8000F Florence SC 29501 Office: Senate House State House Columbia SC 29211*

GLOVSKY, SUSAN G. L., lawyer; b. Boston, Apr. 16, 1955; d. Leonard B. and Marilyn S. (Shapiro) Loitherstein; m. Steven M. Glovsky, May 25, 1980; 1 child, Lowell Eliott. BS in Chemistry, U. Vt., 1977; JD, Boston U., 1980. Bar: Mass. 1980, Mich. 1980, N.Y. 1982, U.S. Dist. Ct. (ea. dist.) Mich. 1980, U.S. Patent Office 1981, U.S. Dist. Ct. Mass. 1982, U.S. Ct. Appeals (1st cir.) 1982, U.S. Ct. Appeals (fed. cir.) 1991. Assoc. Levin, Levin, Garvett & Dill, Southfield, Mich., 1980-81, Ladas & Parry, N.Y.C., 1981-82, Dahlen & Gatewood, Boston, 1982-83; ptnr. Dahlen & Glovsky, Boston, 1983-85; sole practice Boston and Salem, Mass., 1985-93; of counsel Hamilton, Brook, Smith & Reynolds, Lexington, Mass., 1993—. Mem. ABA (litigation sect.), Mass. Bar Assn., Boston Bar Assn., Boston Patent Law Assn. (chmn. inventor recognition com. 1987-89, chmn. litigation com. 1989—, bd. govs. 1990—, sec. 1993-94, treas. 1994—), Am. Arbitration Assn. (panel arbitrators 1985—). Jewish. Home: 131 Federal St Salem MA 01970-3242 Office: Hamilton Brook Smith & Reynolds 2 Militia Dr Lexington MA 02173

GLÜCK, LOUISE ELISABETH, poet; b. N.Y.C., Apr. 22, 1943; d. Daniel and Beatrice (Grosby) G.; m. Charles Hertz (div.); 1 child, Noah Benjamin; m. John Dranow, 1977. Student, Sarah Lawrence Coll., 1962, Columbia U., 1963-65; LLD (hon.), Williams Coll., 1993. Vis. poet Goddard Coll., U. N.C., U. Va., U. Iowa; Elliston prof. U. Cin., 1978; vis. faculty Columbia U., 1979; faculty M.F.A. program Goddard Coll., also Warren Wilson Coll., Swannanoa, N.C.; Holloway lectr. U. Calif., Berkeley, 1982; vis. prof. U. Calif.-Davis, 1983; Scott prof. poetry Williams Coll., 1983, faculty, 1984—; Regents prof. poetry UCLA, 1985-88; delivered Phi Beta Kappa poem Harvard U. commencement, 1990; baccalaureate spkr. Williams Coll., 1993; mem. vis. faculty Harvard U., spring 1995. Author: Firstborn, 1968, The House on Marshland, 1975, Descending Figure, 1980, The Triumph of Achilles, 1985, Ararat, 1990, The Wild Iris, 1992 (Pulitzer Prize for poetry 1993), Proofs and Theories (collected essays), 1994. Recipient lit. award Am. Acad. and Inst. Arts and Letters, 1981, award in poetry Nat. Book Critics Cir., 1985, Melville Cane award Poetry Soc. Am., 1986, Sara Teasdale Meml. prize Wellesley Coll., 1986, Bobbitt Natil prize Libr. Congress, 1992, Pulitzer prize, 1993, William Carlos Williams award, 1993; named Poet Laureate of Vt., 1994; grantee Rockefeller Found., Nat. Endowment for Arts, 1969-70, 79-80, 88-89, Guggenheim Found., 1975-76, 87-88, NEA, 1988-89. Fellow Am. Acad. Arts and Scis.; mem. Phi Beta Kappa (hon.).

GLUECK, MARY A., psychiatric and mental health nurse, administrator; b. Bridgetown, Barbados; came to U.S., 1952; d. Hubert and Christina Cumming; m. Stephen G. Glueck (dec.). Grad. sch. nursing, St. Joseph's Mercy Hosp., Georgetown, Guyana. RN, Calif. Clin. svcs. mgr. med.-surg., geropsychiat. rehab. Crystal Springs Rehab. div. San Mateo County Gen. Hosp., San Mateo, Calif. Mem. Mid. Mgrs. Assn., Am. Psychiat. Nurses Assn. Home: 4505 Sandra Ct Union City CA 94587-4853

GLUECK, SYLVIA BLUMENFELD, writer; b. Tulsa, Dec. 23, 1925; d. Maurice and Sina (Turk) Blumenfeld; m. Norton Shushan Glueck, June 15, 1947; children: Nancy Eisen, Milton Glueck. BJ, U. Mo., Columbia, 1949. Publicity dir. Sta. WDSU, New Orleans, 1946-47; advt. copywriter Swiftway Direct Mail, New Orleans, 1961; freelance writer and author New Orleans and San Antonio, 1965—. Author book, 1990; contbr. fiction articles to mags. and newspaper features, 1984-85, 90 (Golden Pro award 1986). Mem. AAUW, Women in Communication, San Antonio Writers Guild (publicity chmn.), Alamo Writers, San Antonio Profl. Writers Group, Mensa. Home and Office: 309 W Magnolia Ave Apt 1 San Antonio TX 78212-3216

GLYMPH, DIANNE TYLER, librarian; b. Burlington, N.C., Sept. 10, 1958; d. Earle Goodson and Mayme Alcora (Ellis) Tyler; m. Michael Joe Glymph, Sept. 26, 1981. BA cum laude, Presbyn. Coll., 1980; MLS, Univ. S.C., 1981. Head libr. Christ Ch. Episc. Sch., Greenville, S.C., 1981-83; reference libr. Greenville County Libr., 1983-90, br. mgr., 1990; reference libr. Midlands Tech. Coll., Columbia, S.C., 1991-94; ch. libr. Trinity Luth. Ch., Greenville, 1987-90. Contbr. to profl. jours. Singer Greenville Chorale, 1982-90; bd. dirs. Walter Johnson Club of Presbyn. Coll., 1987-89, Pebble Ridge Homeowners Assn., 1989-90. Mem. S.C. Libr. Assn. (sec. archives and spl. collections 1987-88), Piedmont Libr. Assn., Staff Assn. Greenville County Libr. (pres. 1987-88). Home: 15 Jamaica Dr Charleston SC 29407

GLYNN, MARY ANN THERESA, management educator; b. N.Y.C., Mar. 25, 1951; d. Francis P. and Nora T. (Broderick) G.; married, Jan. 8, 1972 (div. 1979); 1 child, Kathryn Elizabeth. BA, Fordham U., 1972; MA, Rider Coll., 1978; MBA, L.I. Univ., 1982; PhD, Columbia U., 1988. Dir. grad. admissions L.I. Univ., Westchester, N.Y., 1978-83; prof. mgmt. devel. program Smith Coll., Northampton, Mass., 1991—; asst. prof. Sch. of Orgn. and Mgmt. Yale U., New Haven, 1987-93; assoc. prof. Emory Bus. Sch.

Emory U., Atlanta, 1993—. Cons. editor Jour. Applied Behavioral Sci., 1991—, Jour. Mgmt.; contbr. articles to profl. jours. Fellow Columbia U., 1983-88. Mem. Acad. Mgmt., Strategic Mgmt. Soc., Beta Gamma Sigma, Delta Mu Delta. Office: Emory U Bus Sch 1602 Mizell Dr Atlanta GA 30322

GNIADEK, CHERYL LYNN, industrial services executive; b. Chgo., Feb. 21, 1947; d. Theodore Edward and Elsie Amelia (Grasmick) Whiffen; m. Richard Lawrence Gniadek, Nov. 15, 1969 (dec. Feb. 1979). BSBA, Ill. State U., 1969. Prodn. sec. Universal Tng. Systems, Lincolnwood, Ill., 1969-71; exec. sec. Alliance Am. Insurers, Chgo., 1971-78; temp. sec. Kelly Svcs., Grand Rapids, Mich., 1978-79; sec. Honeywell, Inc., Grand Rapids, Mich., 1979-80, sales corr., 1980-81; adminstr. customer quality Honeywell, Inc., Ft. Washington, Pa., 1981-84; rep. customer service Honeywell, Inc., Valley Forge, Pa., 1984-88; fin. acct. Honeywell, Inc., Ft. Washington, 1987-91; br. support supr. Honeywell, Inc., Valley Forge, 1991-92; supr. Regional Customer Svc. Ctr. Honeywell, Inc., Ft. Washington, Pa., 1992-95; field svcs. mgr. Honeywell, Inc., Valley Forge, Pa., 1995—. Mem. NAFE, Am. Bus. Women's Assn. (New Directions Charter chpt., pres. 1986, Woman of Yr. 1985), Instrument Soc. Am. (treas., edn. com. Phila. sect., sec., treas., 3d v.p., 2d v.p., 1st v.p., pres. 1994-95). Democrat. Roman Catholic. Home: 857 Thoreau Ct Warminster PA 18974-2057 Office: Honeywell Inc 1100 Virginia Dr Fort Washington PA 19044

GOBLE, ELISE JOAN H., pediatric ophthalmologist; b. Winnipeg, Man., Can., Jan. 23, 1932; d. Michael Samuel and Sarah (Corbin) Hollenberg; m. John Lewis Goble, Oct. 4, 1956; children: John Robert, Michael William. Assoc. in Music, U. Man., 1949, MD, 1956. Resident Columbia Presbyn. Eye Inst., N.Y.C., 1956-59; pvt. practice pediatric ophthalmology San Mateo, Calif., 1959—. Mem. San Mateo Sch. Health Com.; mem. Coordinating Coun. Developmental Disabilities, San Mateo; founder San Mateo chpt. Nat. Assn. Autistic Citizens. Fellow ACS, Am. Bd. Ophthalmology, Am. Bd. Pediatrics; mem. Am. Assn. Pediatric Ophthalmology & Strabismus (charter mem.), San Mateo County Med. Soc., Calif. Med. Assn. Home: 2007 New Brunswick Dr San Mateo CA 94402-4012 Office: 100 S Ellsworth Ste 507 San Mateo CA 94401

GOCEK, MATILDA ARKENBOUT (MRS. JOHN A. GOCEK), librarian; b. Hoboken, N.J., Feb. 18, 1923; d. Jacob Richard and Mathilda (Meyer) Arkenbout; m. Harry Francis Decker, May 15, 1939 (div. Nov. 1955) children: Ruth Ann Decker Robinson, Dianne Karen Decker McKinstrie; m. John A. Gocek, Nov. 18, 1956; 1 son, John Jacob. AA, Orange County Community Coll., 1961; BA, SUNY, New Paltz, 1964; MLS, SUNY, Albany, 1967. Libr. dir., Monroe (N.Y.) Free Libr., 1958-61, Tuxedo Park (N.Y.) Libr., 1963-76; historian Town of Tuxedo, 1973-76; dir. Suffern Free Libr., 1977-90; pres., chief exec. officer Libr. Rsch. Assocs. Inc., 1990—; libr. cons. Tuxedo Union Free Sch., 1967-69. Editor: Libr. Rsch. Assocs., 1968. Vice chmn. Montgomery Expdn. Meml. Observance, 1973. Bd. dirs. Tuxedo Park Sch.; trustee, pres. Mus. Village of Orange County (N.Y.), 1980-83. Mem. Orange-Sullivan Pub. (pres. 1967-70), N.Y. Library Assn., Southeastern N.Y. Libr. Reference Resource Coun., Libr. Assn. Rockland County (N.Y.) (goals com. 1977, exec. bd. 1980-83), Ramapo Catskill Libr. System Assn. (exec. bd. 1986-88). Home: RD 6 Box 41 Dunderberg Rd Monroe NY 10950 Office: Dunderberg Rd Monroe NY 10950

GOCHNAUER, ELISA ANNE, marketing executive; b. Bellefonte, Pa., Sept. 4, 1960; d. Theodore Frank and Doris Lee (Smith) Schneider; m. Dean Joe Gochnauer, Apr. 23, 1994. Student, Shippensburg U., 1978-80; BA, Millersville U., 1982. Cert. nursing asst. Sales svc. coord. Fleur de Lait Foods, Ltd., New Holland, Pa., 1982-87; sales adminstr. Northfield Specialty Foods, Lancaster, Pa., 1987-88; mktg. asst. Charles Chips Corp., Lancaster, 1988-89; dir. mktg. svcs. Charles Chips, Corp., Lancaster, 1989-93; with inside sales R/W Connection, Lancaster, 1994; mktg. asst. Red Rose Transit Authority, Lancaster, 1994—. Republican. Lutheran. Home: 748 Lawrence Blvd Lancaster PA 17601-1418 Office: Red Rose Transit Authority 45 Erick Rd Lancaster PA 17603

GOCKLEY, BARBARA JEAN, corporate professional; b. Pitts., July 26, 1951; d. William Ervin and Dorothy Marie (Wolf) Cain; m. William Lee Gockley, Mar. 29, 1975 (div. Aug. 1989); children: Ervin Cain, Marianne Cain, William Cain, Malinda Cain. Student, Indiana U. Pa., 1969-71, Thomas Edison State Coll., 1986-88; BA in Bus. Mgmt. and Mktg. Mgmt., Alvernia Coll., 1993. Cert. in purchasing mgmt. Asst. materials mgr. Redman Mobile Homes, Ephrata, Pa., 1972-75; mgr. inventory control Gym-Kin, Inc., Reading, Pa., 1975-77; supr. prodn./inventory control Wyomissing Converting, Reading, 1979-82; mgr. prodn./inventory control Dorma Door Controls, Inc., Reamstown, Pa., 1982-85, project mgr., 1985-86; materials mgr. Powder Coatings Group-Morton Internat., Reading, 1986-94; dir. purchasing Dexter Corp., Waukegan, Ill., 1994—; dir. programs Congress for Progress Inc., 1984-88, vice chmn., 1988-89, chmn., 1989-90; dir. programs Pansophic/ASD User Group Internat. Conf., 1991, 92; instr. Berks Campus, Pa. State U., Reading, 1985-86. Dir. Reinholds (Pa.) PTA, 1978-81; bd. dirs. Cocalico Sch. Bd., Denver, Pa., 1985-89. Mem. Am. Prodn. and Inventory Control Soc. (cert. prodn. and inventory mgmt., treas. Schuylkill Valley chpt. 1981-82, pres. 1982-84, dir. membership region IX 1985-86, asst. v.p. 1987, v.p. 1988-89, Internat. Vol. Svc. award 1986), Nat. Assn. Purchasing Mgrs., Assn. Mfg. Excellence, NAFE, Am. Bus. Women's Assn., Soc. Mfg. Engrs., Mothers of Twins Club (nominating chmn. Lancaster, Pa. 1977-78). Republican. Presbyterian. Office: Dexter Corp East Water St Waukegan IL 60085

GOCLAN, GERRI GENEVIEVE, marketing professional; b. Chgo., Nov. 27, 1949; d. Joseph John and Ann (Zake) G. BA magne cum laude, De Paul U., 1972; MBA, U. Pitts., 1987. Prodn. asst. Hirsch, Aarons & Williams Graphic Design, Chgo., 1973-75; advt. prodn. mgr. Chemetron Corp., Chgo., 1975-79; mgr. product promotion Allegheny Internat., Pitts., 1979-82, mgr. product advt., 1982-87; mgr. mktg. communications Redshaw, Inc., Pitts., 1987-88; founder, prin. The Goclan Group, Pitts., 1989—. Bd. dirs. Countryside Manor Homes Assn., Robinson, Twp., Pa., 1991—. Mem. NAFE, Pa. Small Business, Am. Mktg. Assn. (dir., chairperson 1990-91, 93-94, v.p. membership, 1991-92, newsletter editor, 1992-94). Office: The Goclan Group 102 Countryside Dr Mc Kees Rocks PA 15136

GODAGER, JANE ANN, social worker; b. Blue River, Wis., Nov. 29, 1943; d. Roy and Elmyra Marie (Hood) G. BA, U. Wis., 1965; MSW, Fla. State U., 1969. Lic. clin. social worker. Social worker III State of Wis. Dept Corrections, Wales, 1965-71; supervising psychiat. social worker I State of Calif., San Bernardino, 1972-75, La Mesa, 1975-77; psychiat. social worker State of Calif., San Bernardino, 1978-85; supr. mental health services Riverside (Calif.) County Dept. Mental Health, 1985-86; mental health counselor Superior Ct. San Bernardino County, 1986—; mem. adv. bd. Grad. Sch. Social Work Calif. State U., San Bernardino. Mem. Nat. Assn. Social Workers, Acad. Cert. Social Workers (diplomate), Kappa Kappa Gamma Alumnae Assn. Office: Office Mental Health Counselor 700 E Gilbert St Bldg 1 San Bernardino CA 92415-0920

GODBEY, HELEN KAY, city official; b. Ft. Worth, Jan. 18, 1946; d. Paschal Lee and Ester Katherine (Williams) Godbey; children: Tammy Denise Thompson, Shelly Rae Thompson. AAS, Tarrant County Jr. Coll., 1985; B in Career Arts Dallas Bapt. U., 1987; MPA, U. Tex., Arlington, 1991. Cert. mcpl. clk., Tex. peace officer. Ct. clk. City of Ft. Worth, 1966-68; transcriber for ct. reporters, Dallas and Tarrant Counties, 1970-75; sec. City of Euless Police Dept., Tex., 1975-81; city sec. Euless, 1981-89; asst. city mgr., 1989-93; city mgr., Burleson, Tex., 1993—; speaker, instr. police report writing Tex. A&M U., Tarrant County Jr. Coll. Police Acad., 1979-81; speaker IBM, various computer groups, Tex., Calif., 1983—, North Tex. State U. Ctr. for Community Svcs., Denton, 1984, 87—. Recipient Disting. Svc. awards Euless Police Dept., 1976, 79. Mem. Internat. Inst. Mcpl. Clks. Advanced Acad. (co-chair 1989-90, com. on technol. devel. 1984-89, constl. revisions), Tex. Mcpl. Clks. Assn. Inc. (trustee officer 1987-88, treas. com. 1989, v.p. 1990), Internat. City Mgmt. Assn., North Tex. City Mgmt. Assn., Tex. City Mgmt. Assn. (pub. rels. & membership com., profl. devel. com.), Internat. City Mgmt. Assn. (academe affairs com. 1992—), Kiwanis (v.p. Mid-Cities chpt. 1989-90). Baptist. Avocations: golf, hiking, skating. Home: 355 NW Hillery # 521 Burleson TX 76028 Office: 141 W Renfro Burleson TX 76028

GODDARD, CAROL ANN, newspaper editor; b. Chgo., Mar. 26, 1941; d. Robert Charles and Cecilia Margaret (Vonesh) Bosh; m. Joseph S. Goddard Jr., Feb. 9, 1966 (div. Mar. 1981); children: Laura Anne, Leslie Elizabeth. BA, DePauw U., 1963; postgrad., Northwestern U., 1964, U. Ill., 1979, No. Ill. U., 1980-81. Adminstrv. asst. A.G. Becker, Chgo., 1963-67; owner P&C Mktg., Hinsdale, Ill., 1975-79; reporter Doings newspaper, Hinsdale, 1979-82, assoc. editor, 1982-84, mng. editor, 1984-86; mng. editor Pioneer Press, Oak Park, Ill., 1986-90; exec. editor Pioneer Press, Park Ridge, Ill., 1990-91; bur. chief Lake County Pioneer Press, Bannockburn, Ill., 1992—. Chmn. Hinsdale Concert Com., 1989, Hinsdale Plan Commn., 1989-91; trustee Village of Hinsdale, 1991—; bd. dirs. Sarah's Inn (abused women's shelter), Oak Park, 1989-91. Mem. Suburban Press Club Chgo. (bd. dirs. 1980—, treas. 1980-81, pres. 1986-87, editorial awards), Zonta. Roman Catholic. Home: 219 W Maple St Hinsdale IL 60521-3311 Office: Pioneer Press 2201 Waukegan Rd Bannockburn IL 60015

GODDARD, DIANNE EDMONDS, lawyer; b. Indpls., June 13, 1949; d. Anthony and Mary Frances Guidone; m. Dennis Alan Edmonds, Aug. 22, 1970; children: Aleksander, Colin, Sarah. BA, Ball State U., 1970; JD, Ind. U., 1976. Bar: Ind. 1976, N.Mex. 1977, Wash. 1979. Asst. dist. atty. San Juan County Dist. Attys. Office, Farmington, N.Mex., 1977-79; deputy prosecutor Skagit County Prosecutors Office, Mt. Vernon, Wash., 1979-81; atty. pvt. practice, Mt. Vernon, Wash., 1981—; instr. Skagit Valley Coll., 1988—. Founder San Juan County Rape Crisis Ctr., Farmington, 1978; co-founder Skagit Rape Relief and Battered Women's Ctr., Mt. Vernon, 1980-81; chair Rob Johnson State Congress, Skagit County, 1990; bd. dirs. Skagitron, Burlington, Wash., 1985-87, Cmty. Homewell, Mt. Vernon, 1988-89. Mem. Wash. State Bar Assn. (sec. 1980-81), Wash. Women Lawyers, Skagit County Bar Assn. (sec. 1980-81), Alliance Holistic Lawyers. Buddhist. Office: 321 W Washington Ste 329 Mount Vernon WA 98273

GODDARD, SANDRA KAY, elementary education educator; b. Steubenville, Ohio, Oct. 31, 1947; d. Albert Leonard and Mildred Irene (Hill) G. BS in Edn., Miami U., Oxford, Ohio, 1969; MEd, Miami U., 1973. Tchr. elem. grades Gregg Elem.-Edison Local Schs. Dist., Hammondsville, Ohio, 1969—; former mem. health curriculum com. Jefferson County Sch., Steubenville; worked with Spl. Olympics, 1992, 93. Publicity chmn., rec. sec., box office chmn. Steubenville Players, 1981-83; mem. Edison Local Adv. Coun. on Drug Edn., 1987—; mem. Edison Local Curriculum Instrn. Com., 1993—; state judge Ashland Oil Tchr. Achievement awards, 1988-90; regional and state judge Odyssey of the Mind, 1992—, bd. dirs. region XI, 1993-94, regional dir. Region II, 1994—; mem. exec. com. Gregg Elem. PTO, 1990-92; instr. first aid and cmty. CPR, ARC, 1990—, instr., trainer, 1993—. Martha Holden Jennings scholar, 1972-73; mini-grantee Jefferson County Schs., 1991. Mem. NEA (del. to rep. assembly 1979, 85, 86, 87, 88), Ohio Edn. Assn. (exec. com. 1983-89, pres.'s cabinet 1985-87, appeals bd. 1994—), Ea. Ohio Edn. Assn. (pres. 1978-79, exec. com. 1983-89), Edison Local Edn. Assn. (pres. 1974-75, v.p. 1986-88, 89-91, exec. com. 1991—), Ohio Valley UNISERV Coun. (treas. 1986-92), Delta Kappa Gamma (legis. chair 1990-92). Democrat. Methodist. Home: 200 Fernwood Rd Apt 11 Steubenville OH 43952-9200 Office: Gregg Elem Sch RR 1 Bergholz OH 43908-9801

GODDEN, JEAN W., columnist; b. Stamford, Conn., Oct. 1, 1933; d. Maurice Albert and Bernice Elizabeth (Warvel) Hecht; m. Robert W. Godden, Nov. 7, 1952 (dec. Dec. 1985); children: Glenn Scott, Jeffrey Wayne. BA, U. Wash., 1974. News editor Univ. Dist. Herald, Seattle, 1951-53; bookkeeper Omniarts Inc., Seattle, 1963-71; writer editorial page Seattle Post-Intelligencer, Seattle, 1974-80, editorial page editor, 1980-81, bus. editor, 1981-83, city columnist, 1983-91; city columnist Seattle Times, 1991—. Author: The Will to Win, 1980, Hasty Put Ins, 1981. Mem. LWV (dir. 1969-71), Wash. Press Assn. (Superior Performance award 1979), Soc. Profl. Journalists, Mortarboard, City Club, Phi Beta Kappa. Office: The Seattle Times PO Box 70 Seattle WA 98111-0070

GODDESS, LYNN BARBARA, commercial real estate broker; b. N.Y.C., Mar. 3, 1942; d. Eugene Daniel and Hazel Cecile (Kinzler) G.; divorced. BS, Columbia U., 1963, postgrad., 1964-66. Coord. John M. Burns Assembly Campaign, N.Y.C., 1963; dir. spl. events, projects Kenneth B. Keating Senatorial Campaign, N.Y.C., 1964; dist. dir. fund raising Muscular Dystrophy Assn. Am. Inc., N.Y.C., 1965-66; exec. acct. fund raising, pub. relations Victor Weingarten Co., N.Y.C., 1966-67, Oram Group (formerly Harold L. Oram Inc.), N.Y.C., 1967-70; dir. devel. City Ctr. Music Drama Inc., N.Y.C., 1970; sales person Whitbread-Nolan, N.Y.C., 1971-73; from asst. v.p. to sr. v.p. Cross and Brown Co., N.Y.C., 1973-1985; sr. dir. Cushman & Wakefield, Inc., N.Y.C., 1985—. Trustee Young Adult Inst. Mem. Nat. Soc. Fund Raisers, Assn. Fund Dirs., Real Estate Bd. N.Y. (named Most Ingenious Broker Yr. 1975), Women's Forum (bd. dirs.). Office: Cushman & Wakefield Inc 51 W 52d St New York NY 10019-6178

GODFREY, ALINE LUCILLE, music specialist, church organist; b. Providence, R.I., Dec. 4, 1943; d. Bernard Almasse and Rita Linda (Laramee) Brindamour; m. George Ruben Godfrey, Aug. 22, 1981; 1 child, Murray Aaron. BA, Rivier Coll., 1970; cert. of attendance, Am. Conservatory of Music, Fontainebleau, France, 1972; M of Music, U. Notre Dame, 1975. Cert. tchr. profl. all level music, provisional elem.-gen., Tex. Choir dir. Scituate (R.I.) High Sch., 1970-74; tchr. grade 4 McDowell Intermediate Sch., Hondo, Tex., 1974-75; tchr. grade 5 Wilson Elem. Sch., Harlingen, Tex., 1975-76; organist St. Albans Episcopal Ch., Harlingen, 1977-80; music specialist St. Mary's Sch. and Immaculate Conception Sch., Brownsville, Tex., 1977-79; choral accompanist Harlingen H.S., 1979-80; tchr. grade 6 Sam Houston Sch., Harlingen, 1980-81; music dir. St. Alban's Episcopal Sch., Harlingen, 1987-90; choral accompanist Marine Military Acad., Harlingen, 1988-90; tchr. Stuart Place Elem. Sch., Harlingen, 1990-91; msic specialist Harlingen Ind. Sch. Dist., 1991—; organist St. James Ch., Manville, R.I., 1972-74, First United Meth. Ch., Mercedes, Tex., 1987-93; pianist, accompanist Cardinal Chorale, Harlingen, 1980-81. Composer: Songs for Tots, 1983; playwright: (musical) Why the Bells Rang, 1988; arranger, dir. (musicals) Across the U.S.A., 1988, Around the World at Wilson School, 1992; dir. Under the Big Top, 1989, United We Stand, 1991. Vol. Hosts Program, Harlingen, 1981, Riofest, 1983, Dishman Spring Festival, Combes, Tex., 1993, 94; dir. Crockett Sch. dedication, 1993. Mem. Tex. State Tchrs. Assn., Tex. Music Educators Assn., Smithsonian Instn., PEO Sisterhood (historian), Am. Assn. Ret. Persons. Home: PO Box 875 Combes TX 78535 Office: Wilson Elem Sch Primera Rd Harlingen TX 78552

GODFREY, EUTHA MAREK, elementary school educator, consultant; b. Balt., Mar. 25, 1937; d. Louis Joseph and Estelle Virginia (Stickels) Marek; m. Stanley I. Lewis (div. June 1970); children: Mark W. Lewis, Ronald A. Lewis, Kari S. Howard; m. Carl Godrey Sr., Nov. 20, 1983 (dec. July 1993). BM in Music Edn., Peabody Conservatory John's Hopkins U., 1959; postgrad., N.C. A & T State U., 1972-75, U. N.C., 1974-76. Cert. early childhood edn. Tchr. Murray County Schs., Chatsworth, Ga., 1959-60, Fulton County Schs., Roswell, Ga., 1960-62; music tchr. Balt. County Schs., Baltimore, Md., 1962-63; band, chorus tchr. Guilford County Schs., Greensboro, N.C., 1963-67, kindergarten tchr., 1967-73; cons., early childhood State Dept. Pub. Instruction, Raleigh, N.C., 1972-76; early childhood tchr. Peeler and Erwin Magnet Schs., Greensboro City Schs., N.C., 1973-91; cons. Divsn. of Reading, State Dept. Pub. Instruction, Raleigh, N.C., 1976-82; dir. music Palm Coast United Methodist Ch., Palm Coast, Fla., 1993—; cons., presenter, Individually Guided Edn., St. Louis, 1977; workshop presenter, Greensboro City Assn. for Edn. of Young Children, 1980-90; accreditation team, Southern Assn. of Schs. and Colls. State of N.C., 1977-91. Bd. dirs. Family Life Ctr., Palm Coast, 1992, 93; mem. state exec. com., Dem. Party, Greenboro, N.C., 1975; vol., Flagler County Pub. Libr., Palm Coast, Fla., 1992-93; mem. Fellowship of United Meth. Musicians in Worship, Music and Other arts. Greensboro Pub. Sch. Fund grantee, 1987-88; Full Competative scholar Peabody Conservatory, 1955. Mem. AAUW, N.C. Ret. State Employees, Nat. Edn. Assn. Retired, N.C. Assn. of Ret. Educators, Fellowship of United Methodist Musicians in Worship, Music & Other Arts, Am. Guild English Handbell Ringers, Choristers Guild, Mu Phi Epsilon. Home: 39 Westmore Ln Palm Coast FL 32164-4031

GODFREY, JOYZELLE EFFIE, economic development and small business consultant; b. Ft. Thompson, S.D., Jan. 18, 1942; d. Lawrence Michael and Nina Mae (Menzie) Gingway; m. Gene Rilling, Sept. 1963 (div. May 1970); children: Rodney, Mike, Neil, Nicolle, Yvette; m. Jerry Dean Godfrey, Sept. 1985 (div. Nov. 1993). BS, Black Hill State U., 1973; MPA, U. S.D., 1985. Mgr. Lakota Devel. Coun. St. Joseph's Indian Sch., Chamberlain, S.D., 1989—; small bus. cons. to Native Am. enterpreneurs. Author of poetry and short stories. Humanities scholar. Mem. Lambda Iota Tau Soc. Home: PO Box 257 Fort Thompson SD 57339 Office: Lakota Devel Coun Saint Joseph Indian Sch Chamberlain SD 57236

GODFREY, MARIAN ANGELL, arts administrator; b. Boston, Mar. 22, 1947; d. Thomas Barham Angell and Susan Sturgis (Strong) G. BA in English Lit. magna cum laude, Radcliffe Coll., 1970; MFA in Theater Adminstrn., Yale U., 1975. Mng. dir. Ensemble Studio Theater, N.Y.C., 1977-80; mgr. Mabou Mines, N.Y.C., 1980-83, producer, cons., 1985-89; dir. devel. Dance Theater Workshop, N.Y.C., 1983-85; N.Y. rep. La Jolla (Calif.) Playhouse, 1986-89; program dir. for culture Pew Charitable Trusts, Phila., 1989—; cons. Found. for Extension and Devel. of Am. Profl. Theater, N.Y.C., 1984-89; theater cons. AT&T, N.Y.C., 1986-89. Producer feature film Dead End Kids, 1986; contbr. articles to profl. publs. Mem. Mayor's Adv. Com. on Culture, Phila., 1992—; mem. nat. adv. com. Nat. Arts Policy Ctr. of Am. Coun. of Arts, 1992-93; co-chair theater cos. panel Nat. Endowment for Arts, Washington, 1992—; mem. arts and humanities task force Exec. Br. Agys., 1992-93; chair Delaware Valley Grantmakers Arts Task Group, 1990—; bd. dirs. Grantmakers in the Arts. Recipient Outstanding Mgmt. of Mabou Mines award Villager, 1981, Outstanding Achievement in Theater award Drama-Logue, 1980. Mem. Harvard Club N.Y.C. Office: Pew Charitable Trusts 2005 Market St Ste 1700 Philadelphia PA 19103

GODING, JUDITH GERMAINE, residential facility administrator, musician; b. Lynchburg, Va., Mar. 8, 1947; d. John Lewellyn and Louise Irene (McCormick) G. BA in Music, Lynchburg Coll., 1969, MEd in Spl. Edn., 1975; EdD in Sch. Adminstrn., Vanderbilt U., 1984. Cert. tchr., Va. Tchr. Cen. Va. Tng. Ctr., Lynchburg, 1969-79, program coord., 1979-82, ctr. dir., 1982—; tchr. Cen. Va. Community Coll., Lynchburg, 1978, 86; organist, choirmaster Peakland United Meth. Ch., Lynchburg, 1970-79, 84-87; interim organist, choir dir. Madison Hts. (Va.) Bapt. Ch., 1990-91; interim organist First Christian Ch., Lynchburg, 1989-90, Euclid Christian Ch., Lynchburg, 1991—; pianist Piedmont Club, Lynchburg, 1975—; presenter workshops. Contbr. articles to profl. jours. Recipient Edith Carrington award Lynchburg Fine Arts Ctr., 1988, Outstanding Achievement of Accomplishment in Human Svcs. Mgmt., Devel. Disabilities Svcs. Mgrs., Inc., 1989, Disting. Alumni award Lunchburg Coll., 1993, others. Mem. Cmty. Concerts Assn., Ctrl. Va. Alumni Club (pres. 1990—), Lynchburg Coll. Alumni Assn. (pres. 1994). Home: 1911 Mimosa Dr Lynchburg VA 24503-2329 Office: Cen Va Tng Ctr PO Box 1098 Lynchburg VA 24505-1098

GODSHALL, BARBARA MARIE, special education educator; b. Newark, N.Y., Jan. 5, 1958; d. Edward Franklin and Joan Marie (Moon) Moll; m. Clark J. Godshall, Oct. 26, 1985. AS, Cazenovia Coll., 1978; BS summa cum laude, Keuka Coll., 1989; MS, Nazareth Coll., 1991; CAS in Adminstrn., SUNY, Brockport, 1992. Cert. spl. edn. and elem. tchr., adminstr. Tchr. elem. Penn Yan (N.Y.) Ctrl. Sch. Dist., 1988-89, Niagara-Wheatfield Ctrl. Sch. Dist., Sanborn, N.Y., 1989-91; spl. edn. tchr. Lockport (N.Y.) Ctrl. Sch. Dist., 1991-92, Barker (N.Y.) Ctrl. Sch. Dist., 1992-93; pres., edn. cons. (elem., secondary and spl. edn.) BMG Cons., Lockport, 1989—. Bd. dirs. ARC, Lockport, 1990—, Lockport Pub. Libr., 1990—. N.Y. State scholar, 1991. Mem. ASCD, Coun. for Exceptional Children, Phi Delta Kappa. Home and Office: 5494 Forest Hill Rd Lockport NY 14094

GODWIN, GAIL KATHLEEN, author; b. Birmingham, Ala., June 18, 1937; d. Mose Winston and Kathleen (Krahenbuhl) G.; m. Douglas Kennedy, 1960 (div. 1961), m. Ian Marshall, 1965 (div. 1966). Student, Peace Jr. Coll., Raleigh, N.C., 1955-57; B.A. in Journalism, U. N.C., 1959; M.A. in English, U. Iowa, 1968, Ph.D., 1971. News reporter Miami Herald, 1959-60; rep., cons. U.S. Travel Service, London, 1961-65; editorial asst. Saturday Evening Post, 1966; instr. Univ. Iowa, Iowa City, 1967-71; lectr. Iowa Writer's Workshop, 1972-73, Vassar Coll., 1977, Columbia U. Writing Program, 1978, 81. Author: (novels) The Perfectionists, 1970, Glass People, 1972, The Odd Woman, 1974 (Nat. Book award nomination 1974), Violet Clay, 1978 (Am. Book award nomination 1980), A Mother and Two Daughters, 1982 (Am. Book award nomination 1982), The Finishing School, 1985, A Southern Family, 1987, Father Melancholy's Daughter, 1991, The Good Husband, 1994; (short stories) Dream Children, 1976, Mr. Bedford and The Muses, 1983;editor: (with Shannon Ravenel) The Best American Short Stories 1985, 1985; librettist: (with Robert Starer) The Last Lover, 1975, Journals of a Songmaker, 1976, Apollonia, 1979, Anna Margarita's Will, 1981, Remembering Felix, 1987. Recipient Thomas Wolfe Meml. award Lipinsky Endowment of Western N.C. Hist. Assn., 1988, Janet Kafka award U. Rochester, 1988; fellow Center for Advanced Study, U. Ill., Urbana, 1971-72; Am. specialist USIS, 1976; Nat. Endowment Arts grantee, 1974-75; Guggenheim fellow, 1975-76; recipient award in lit. Am. Acad. and Inst. of Arts and Letters, 1981. Mem. PEN, ASCAP, Authors Guild, Authors League. Home: PO Box 946 Woodstock NY 12498-0946*

GODWIN, JOYCE ANN, health and business services consultant; b. Washington, July 25, 1943; m. Earl R. Godwin. BA in Govt., Fla. State U., 1965; MA in Polit. Sci. and Pub. Adminstrn., George Washington U., 1967. Dir. inquiry service Nat. League Cities, Washington, 1965-68; mem. polit. sci. faculty Calif. State Coll., San Jose, 1968-71; mgr. govtl. and pub. affairs San Jose (Calif.) C. of C., 1968-69, gen. mgr., 1969-70, acting exec. v.p., 1970-71; dir. staff devel. Meml. Med. Ctr., Corpus Christi, Tex., 1971-73; dir. edn. Southwest Community Health Svcs., Albuquerque, 1973-74, dir. pers., 1974-79, v.p. mgmt. svcs., 1979-85, v.p. diversification, 1985-86, sec. corp., bd. dirs., 1982-93, v.p. bus. devel. and external rels., 1989-93; pres. Southwest Bus. Ventures Inc., 1986-93, Vanguard Properties Inc., 1986-93; bd. dirs. Pub. Svc. Co., N.Mex., 1989-91chmn. spl. litigation com., 1989, chmn. compensation com., 1990-91, chmn. corp. and pub. responsibility com., 1990—; v.p. Southwest Health Found., 1981-93. Contbr. articles to profl. publs. Chmn. orch. rels. com. N.Mex. Symphony Orch., 1985-87, exec. com., 1985-87, bd. dirs., 1983-89; assoc. gen. chmn. United Way, 1987, campaign chmn., 1988, bd. dirs., 1987-89. Named one of Outstanding N.Mex. Women, Gov. of N.Mex., 1988; recipient leadership award Leadership Albuquerque Alumni Assn., 1990. Mem. Greater Albuquerque C. of C. (chmn. roadrunners, bd. dirs., exec. com. 1984, chmn. statewide econ. devel. task force 1985, officer 1985-91, v.p. econ. affairs div. 1985, v.p. ednl. affairs div. 1986, v.p. membership 1987, chmn.-elect 1988-89, chmn. 1989-90).

GODWIN, KIMBERLY ANN, lawyer, federal agency administrator; b. Fargo, N.D., July 18, 1960; d. Robert Chandler and Kathryn Marie (Haney) G. BA in Polit. Sci., U. N.H., 1980; MS in Mass Comm., Boston U., 1984, JD, 1984. Bar: D.C. 1984, U.S. Supreme Ct. 1990. Legal intern Army Corps of Engrs., Waltham, Mass., 1983-84; assoc. Booz, Allen & Hamilton, Inc., Bethesda, Md., 1986-88; cons. Dept. State, Washington, 1984-86, asst. dir. comm. interagy. affairs, 1988-92, chief of policy diplomatic telecom. svc., 1992—; cons. Elton Assocs., Inc., Arlington, Va., 1984—. Mem. ABA (vice chmn. internat. comm. com. 1989—), Phi Beta Kappa, Pi Sigma Alpha. Home: 6215 Walhonding Rd Bethesda MD 20816-2138 Office: Dept State DTS -PO 2201 C St NW Washington DC 20520-0001

GODWIN, LINDA M., physicist, astronaut; b. Cape Girardeau, Mo., July 2, 1952; d. James M. Godwin. BS in Mathematics, Southeast Mo. State U., 1974, BS in Physics, 1974, MS, 1976; PhD, U. Mo., 1980. lic. private pilot. Flight controller, payloads officer Mission Ops. Directorate NASA, 1980-85, astronaut candidate, 1985, astronaut, 1986—, mission specialist on shuttle Atlantis flight STS-37, 1991, payload comdr. Space Radar Lab.-01, 1992—; astronaut Shuttle Endeavour, STS-59, 1993. Contbr. articles to profl. jours. Mem. Am. Physical Soc., Space City Chpt. of Ninety-Nines, Inc. Address: NASA Johnson Space Ctr Astronaut Ofc Houston TX 77058

GODWIN, MARY JO, editor, librarian consultant; b. Tarboro, N.C., Jan. 31, 1949; d. Herman Esthol and Mamie Winifred (Felton) Pittman; m. Charles Benjamin Godwin, May 2, 1970. BA, N.C. Wesleyan Coll., 1971; MLS, East Carolina U., 1973. Cert. libr., N.C. From libr. asst. to asst. dir. Edgecombe County Meml. Library, Tarboro, 1970-76, dir., 1977-85; asst. editor Wilson Library Bull., Bronx, N.Y., 1985-89, editor, 1989-92; dir. govt. sales The Oryx Press, Phoenix, 1993—; mem. White House Conf. on Librs.

and Info. Svcs. Task Force; bd. dirs. Libr. Pub. Rels. Coun., 1992—. Bd. dirs. Friends of Calvert County Pub. Libr., 1994. Recipient Robert Downs award for intellectual freedom U. Ill. Grad. Sch. of Libr. Sci., 1992. Mem. ALA (3M/Jr. Mem. Roundtable Profl. Devel. award 1981), N.C. Libr. Assn. (sec. 1981-83), Info. Futures Inst., Ind. Librs. Exchange Roundtable (v.p., pres. elect 1994). Democrat. Episcopalian. Office: The Oryx Press PO Box 83 Dowell MD 20629-0083

GODWIN, SARA, writer; b. St. Louis, Feb. 18, 1944; d. Robert Franklin II and Annabelle (Palkes) G.; children: Jane, Josh; m. Charles D. James, May 1, 1990. BA, Calif. State U., 1967; postgrad., UCLA, 1968-70, U. Calif., Berkeley, 1970-71, W.I. Inst. Fairleigh Dickinson U., St. Croix, V.I., 1971-72; MA, Dominican Coll., 1974. Writer, editor Ortho Books Standard Oil of Calif., San Francisco, 1975-77; writer, editor Gannett Corp., San Rafael, Calif., 1977-79; sr. writer Shaklee Corp., San Francisco, 1979-88; freelance writer Marin County, Calif., 1988—; featured speaker Ask the Gardener, Sta. KSFO, San Francisco, 1980-81. Author: Seals, 1990, Gorillas, 1990, Scott's See and Do: Lawns and Groundcovers, 1995, (with others) The Sea, 1993; scriptwriter (documentary) Discover Canada, Discovering the USA; contbg. editor Last Puff, 1990 (Lit. Guild selection), The Angler's Companion, 1991, Hummingbirds, 1991, The Gardener's Companion, 1992 (N.Y. Times Rev. garden book club selection), Landscaping Decks and Patios, 1994; manuscript editor All About Perennials, 1992; prin. lexicographer The Nat. Gardening Assn. Dictionary of Horticulture, 1994; contbr. cover stories and feature articles to numerous U.S. and fgn. mags. Recipient 1st prize Calif. Press Women, for travel writing, 1982, corp. communications, 1983, personal column, 1984. Mem. Pacific Asia Travel Assn., Authors Guild, Am. Soc. Journalists and Authors, Garden Writers Assn. Am. Home: PO Box 1503 Ross CA 94957-1503

GOEBEL, JIL THERESE, marketing consultant; b. San Diego, Apr. 5, 1958; d. Robert Louis and Mary Kathryn (Beard) G.; m. Randel Ross Castleberry, Aug. 26, 1985. BBA, U. San Diego, 1980, MBA, 1982. Market researcher Phillips Ramsey Advt. and Pub. Rels., San Diego, 1980-81, Cen. Fed. Savs. & Loan, San Diego, 1981; supr. product promotion LSI Products div. TRW, San Diego, 1981-85; mgr. mktg. communications Honeywell Inc., Colorado Springs, Colo., 1985-86; co-founder, co-owner Origin Systems, Inc., Colorado Springs, 1986—; programs com. San Diego Electronics Network, 1984-85. Moderator East San Diego Presbyn. Ch., 1984-85; com. mem. Women's Opportunities Week, San Diego, 1981-83; sec. Marina Park Condominium Assn., San Diego, 1983. Mem. Am. Mktg. Assn. (pres. 1984-85), Bus. and Profl. Advt. Assn. (charter), Colorado Springs MARCOM Network (charter), Colorado Springs Software Roundtable (com. mem. 1993—), San Diego Electronics Network, San Diego Women's Opportunities Network (mem. com. 1984-85), Delta Epsilon Sigma, Kappa Gamma Pi, Alpha Kappa Psi (v.p. 1980-84). Republican. Avocations: reading, music, dance, hiking. Office: Origin Systems Inc 3630 Sinton Rd Ste 300 Colorado Springs CO 80907-5098

GOEBIG, MARLENE M., secondary education educator; b. Phila., June 9, 1959. Attended, Université de Fribourg, Switzerland, 1979-80; BA, LaSalle U., 1981; MA, Villanova U., 1986. Cert. English and Theater Arts/Comm., Pa. Tchr. English West Cath. H.S., Phila., 1981-82; tchr. 5th and 6th grades Incarnation Sch., Phila., 1982-86; tchr. life skills Chas. A. Carroll H.S., Phila., 1986-87; tchr. reading, John B. Stetson Middle Sch., Phila., 1987-88; tchr. English Alternative Sch. for Middle Yrs., Phila., 1988-89; tchr. English and Drama Franklin Learning Ctr., Phila., 1989—; tchr., rschr. Women in World History Project, Phila., 1993—. Playwright: The Show Must Go On, 1994. Mem. Nat. Coun. Tchrs. of English, Ednl. Theater Assn. Office: Franklin Learning Ctr 15th & Mt Vernon Sts Philadelphia PA 19130

GOEDE, DONNA NELSON, elementary school counselor; b. St. Louis, Jan. 3, 1957; d. Paul Rex and Nadine Catherine (Greer) Nelson; m. Gary R. Goede, Oct. 14, 1978; children: Heather Jyll, Kelly Jeanine. BS in Edn., Harris-Stowe State Coll., St. Louis, 1979; MEd in Counseling, U. Mo., St. Louis, 1983; MA in Ednl. Processes, Maryville U., St. Louis, 1989. Cert. elem. tchr., early childhood educator, guidance counselor. Elem. tchr. N.W. R-1 Sch. Dist., House Springs, Mo., 1979-89, elem. guidance counselor, 1989—. Leader brownies and jr. scouts Girl Scouts U.S., House Springs, 1990-94; coun. mem. Job's Daus., Bethel 43, Fenton, Mo., 1985-87, 93-94; tchr. Sunday sch. St. Lucas United Ch. of Christ, St. Louis, 1983-93; coord. local Jump for Heart, Am. Heart Assn., House Springs, 1991-94. Mem. NEA (local negotiator and chair of tchrs. rights), Am. Sch. Counselor Assn., Mo. Sch. Counselor Assn., Jefferson County Sch. Counselor Assn., Gateway Storytellers, Order Ea. Star. Office: Northwest R-1 Schools PO Box 500 House Springs MO 63051-0500

GOEGLEIN, GLORIA J., state legislator; b. Ft. Wayne, Ind., Jan. 13, 1931; d. Alton F. and Nellie I. (Black) Woods; m. Leonard O. Goeglein, Oct. 17, 1954; children: Julia, Chris, Mark. Auditor Allen County, Ind., 1979-86; purchasing dir. City of Ft. Wayne, 1988-90; mem. Ind. Ho. of Reps., Indpls., 1990—; mem. ways and means com., 1993—, govtl. affairs com., 1991, cities and town com., 1991-92, Autism Commn., 1991—, Local Govt. Fin. Study Commn., 1991-94, Mental Health Commn., 1994—, interim study com. on state govt. mgmt. issues, 1994, local govt. com. 1995—. Mem. Allen County Coun., 1974-78, v.p. 1975-78. Home: 9339 Maysville Rd Fort Wayne IN 46815-5820

GOEHNER, DONNA MARIE, university dean; b. Chgo., Mar. 9, 1941; d. Robert and Elizabeth (Cseke) Barra; m. George Louis Goehner, Dec. 16, 1961; 1 child, Michelle Renee. BS in English, So. Ill. U., 1963; MSLS, U. Ill., 1966, CAS in L.S., 1974; PhD in Edn., So. Ill. U., 1983. Rsch. assoc. U. Ill., Urbana, 1966-67; high sch. librarian St. Joseph-Ogden Sch. System, St. Joseph, Ill., 1967-68; curriculum lab librarian Western Ill. U., Macomb, 1968-73, periodicals librarian, 1974-76, coordinator for tech. svcs., 1977-78, acquisitions and collection devel. librarian, 1979-86, acting dir. library, 1986, dean library svcs., 1988—; assoc. Univ. librarian for tech. and adminstrv. svcs. Ill. State U., Normal, 1986-88. Contbr. articles to profl. jours. Mem. ALA, Assn. Coll. and Rsch. Libraries (chmn. univ. libraries sect. 1988-89), Ill. Assn. Coll. and Rsch. Libraries (pres. 1985-86), Ill. Library Assn. (Acad.Librarian of Yr. 1989). Home: 1001 Wigwam Hollow Rd Macomb IL 61455-1007 Office: Univ Library Western Ill U Macomb IL 61455

GOEHRING, MAUDE COPE, retired business educator; b. Persia, Tenn., Jan. 5, 1915; d. James Lawrence and Bobbie C. (Ross) Cope; m. Harvey John Goehring Jr., Aug. 12, 1950 (dec. Mar. 1992). BS in Edn., Ind. U. of Pa., 1948; MEd, U. Pitts., 1950; student, Lebanon Valley Coll., 1944-45. Tchr. Penn Hills Sr. High Sch., Pitts., 1948-68; tchr. U. Pitts., 1959-60, ret., 1968; vol. chmn. ICU, operating rm. info. desk Margaret R. Pardee Meml. Hosp., Hendersonville, N.C., 1989-95; vol. Carolina Village Health Ctr., 1994—; coord. Henderson County Ct. House Vols., Hendersonville, 1983-89; cons., counselor tax aid program Am. Assn. Ret. Persons, Hendersonville, 1981—. Neighborhood chmn. Girl Scouts U.S., Butler County Pa., 1976-79; bd. dirs. ARC, Hendersonville, 1986-91; sec.-treas., bd. dirs. Crime Stoppers of Henderson County, 1991—; nat. bd. dirs. Second Wind Hall of Fame, 1991—. Mem. AAUW (officer 1975-76), Gideon Internat. Aux. (pres., sec. 1969-70), Delta Pi Epsilon (life, Gamma chpt., pres., sec. 1956-59, nat. del. 1957). Republican. Lutheran. Home: 21 Kestrel Ct Hendersonville NC 28792-2838

GOELZ, ELIZABETH ZETTELMAN, social services executive; b. Evanston, Ill., Dec. 2, 1934; d. Henry Joseph and Elsa (Oldberg) Zettelman; m. Richard Henry Goss, June 5, 1956 (div. Apr. 1970); children: Margaret Elizabeth Goss Owens, Richard Henry Eric Goss, Emily Charlotte Goss Crona; m. Edgar Louis Goelz, Jr., Nov. 24, 1974 (dec. Mar. 1993). BA, Wellesley Coll., 1956; postgrad., Nat. Coll. Edn., 1969-72. Cert. tchr. grades K-8, Ill. Tchr. Wilmette (Ill.) Sch. Dist., 1967-75; dir. Estes Park (Colo.) Victim Assistance Program, 1989—; lectr. Mallinckrodt Coll., Wilmette, 1972-73; cons., tchr. various schs., Chgo., 1970-75. Author: Robert Raley & His Descendants, 1991. Sec. Larimer County Domestic Abuse Intervention Project, 1993—; mem. Social Action Coun., Estes Park, 1990—. Mem. LWV, Jr. League (Evanston, Clearwater, Fla., Ft. Collins, Colo.). Democrat. Episcopalian. Home: 1740 Braeside Ln Box 883 Estes Park CO 80517 Office: Estes Park Victim Assistance Program Box 1287 Estes Park CO 80517

GOERS, SARAJANE, community education nurse; b. Clinton, Iowa, Apr. 5, 1946; d. Charles Maurice and Sarah Mardelle (Nichols) Cavanagh; m. Donald Fred Goers, Sept. 22, 1972 (dec. Mar. 1991); children: Christine M., Sarah E., Donald E. Diploma, Mercy Sch. Nursing, Iowa City, 1966; student, U. Iowa, 1969-71. RN, Ill., Iowa. Staff Mercy Hosp., Clinton, 1964-66, staff, nursing relief supr., 1966-68; staff, nursing relief supr. U. Iowa Hosp. Clinics, Iowa City, 1968-69, head nurse, 1969-71; with surg. intensive care Rockford (Ill.) Meml. Hosp., 1971-74, head nurse, 1974-77; patient edn./nursing supr. Freeport (Ill.) Meml. Hosp., 1977-90, RN community edn./svc., 1990—. Advisor Stephenson County Sr. Ctr., Freeport, 1991—. Mem. Am. Lung Assn. (bd. dirs. 1988—), Am. Cancer Soc. (bd. dirs., svc. chairperson, reach/recovery trainer 1980—), Am. Bus. Woman's Assn. (sec. 1987-90, pres. 1993, Woman of Yr. 1992), Am. Ostomy Assn., Am. Diabetes Assn., Quota Club Internat. Home: 22 N Stewart Ave Freeport IL 61032-3754 Office: Freeport Meml Hosp 1045 W Stephenson St Freeport IL 61032-4899

GOETZ, ANGELLA MARIE, infection control nurse, researcher; b. Stamford, Conn., Dec. 2, 1935; d. James Vincent and Mary (Marciano) Preteroti; m. Albert Frank Goetz, Oct. 12, 1963; 1 child, Lisa Marie. Diploma, Allegheny Gen. Hosp. Sch. Nursing, Pitts., 1956; BSN, U. Pitts., 1975, M Nursing Edn., 1977. RN, Pa. Staff nurse Allegheny Gen. Hosp., 1956-58, 59, head nurse, 1959-64, team leader, 1967-72; staff nurse Multnomah County Hosp., Portland, Oreg., 1958-59, Hotel Dieu Hosp., El Paso, 1964-66; instr. Western Pa. Hosp. Sch. Nursing, Pitts., 1977-78, infection control nurse, 1978-81; infection control nurse VA Med. Ctr., Pitts., 1981—, dir. IV team, 1991—; adj. instr. U. Pitts., 1991—; researcher in field. Mem. editorial bd. Am. Jour. Infection Control, 1987—, Infection Control and Hosp. Epidemiology, 1987-90; contbr. articles, abstracts and revs. to profl. jours. Mem. ANA, Assn. for Profls. in Infection Control and Epidemiology (cert., budget and fin. com. 1985—, Carole DeMille Achievement award 1994), Assn. Nurses in AIDS Care, NLN. Office: VA Med Ctr University Dr # C Pittsburgh PA 15213

GOETZ, CECELIA HELEN, lawyer, retired judge; b. N.Y.C.; d. Isador and Sylvia (Cohen) G.; m. Jack I. Spiegel; children—Matthew I. Spiegel, Robert Spiegel. B.A. cum laude, N.Y. U., 1940, LL.B., 1940, LL.M. in Taxation, 1957. Bar: N.Y. 1940, U.S. Dist. Ct. (so. and ea. dists.) N.Y. 1951, U.S. Ct. Appeals (2d cir.) 1958, U.S. Ct. Appeals (1st cir.) 1952, U.S. Ct. Appeals (9th cir.) 1967. Atty. claims div. (now civil div.) Dept. Justice, Washington, 1943-46; assoc. counsel Office Chief of Counsel for War Crimes, Nuremberg, Ger., 1946-48; ptnr. Goetz & Goetz, N.Y.C., 1949-51; asst. chief counsel Office Price Stblzn., Washington, 1951-52; spl. asst. to atty. gen., tax div., Dept. Justice, Washington, 1952-53; assoc. Weisman, Celler, Allan, Spett & Sheinberg, N.Y.C., 1953-58, Kaye, Scholer, Fierman, Hays & Handler, N.Y.C., 1958-64; ptnr. Herzfeld & Rubin, P.C., N.Y.C., 1964-78; judge U.S. Bankruptcy Ct., Eastern Dist. N.Y., Bklyn., 1978-93; of counsel Herzfeld & Rubin, P.C., N.Y.C., 1994—. Mem. Assn. Bar City N.Y., N.Y. State Bar Assn., ABA, N.Y. County Lawyers Assn., NYU Law Rev. Alumni Assn., N.Y. Women's Bar Assn., Women's Bar Assn. State N.Y. Nat. Conf. Bankruptcy Judges, Nat. Assn. Women Judges (founding), Assn. Women Judges State N.Y., Women's City Club N.Y. Office: 40 Wall St New York NY 10005

GOETZKE, GLORIA LOUISE, social worker, income tax specialist; b. Monticello, Minn.; d. Wesley and Marvel (Kreidler) G. BA, U. Minn., 1964; MSW, U. Denver, 1966; MBA, U. St. Thomas, 1977. Cert. enrollment to practice before IRS. Social worker VA Med. Ctr., L.A., 1980—; master tax preparer and instr. H&R Block, Santa Monica, Calif.; clin. instr. UCLA Grad. Sch. of Social Welfare; adj. prof. Calif. State U., Long Beach Grad. Sch. of Social Work. Mem. Nat. Assn. Social Workers (cert.). Lutheran.

GOFORTH, MARY ELAINE DAVEY, secondary education educator; b. Barnesville, Ohio, Sept. 9, 1922; d. Frederick Richard and Lola (Knox) Davey; m. Richard Eugene Goforth, Sept. 9, 1944; 1 child, Diane Lynell Goforth-Ohning. B.M.Ed., Oberlin Coll., 1944; MA in Edn., Coll. of Mt. St. Joseph, 1987. Cert. edn. Music tchr. Leipsig, Ohio, 1944-45, Perry Local, 1945-47; English tchr. Ohio No. Univ., 1946; English and music tchr. Perry Sch., Lima, Ohio, 1945-47; English tchr. Stone Creek, Ohio, 1947-51, Barnesville, Ohio, 1952-53, Tuscarawas, Ohio, 1957-59; English tchr. Conotton Valley Sch., Bowerston, Ohio, 1960-62; English tchr. New Philadelphia, Ohio, 1964-68, Indian Valley, Midvale, Ohio, 1973-88, Indian Valley, Gnadenhetten, Ohio, 1988-93. Author poems. Pres. New Philadelphia (Ohio) Tchrs.' Assn., 1967. Named Indian Valley Tchr. of Yr., 1985, Candidate for Ohio Tchr. of the Yr., 1985; Martha Holden Jennings scholar, 1985. Home: 2123 E High Ave New Philadelphia OH 44663-3323

GOGAN, CATHERINE MARY, dental educator; b. Buffalo, Feb. 9, 1959; d. John Francis and Mary Louise (Solomon) G. BA, SUNY, Buffalo, 1981, DDS, 1985, MS, 1995. Resident Erie County Med. Ctr., Buffalo, 1985-86, attending dentist, 1986—, dental residency coord., 1987—, dental dir. skilled nursing facility, 1989—; pvt. practice Buffalo, 1986—; clin. instr. SUNY, Buffalo, 1987-88, asst. prof., 1988—. Editor mag. UB Dental Report, 1989— (Golden Scroll award); contbr. articles to profl. jours. Fellow Am. Assn. Hosp. Dentists; mem. ADA, Am. Assn. Dental Schs., Orgn. Tchrs. Oral Diagnosis, Acad. Dentistry for Handicapped, Am. Soc. Geriatric Dentistry, U. Buffalo Dental Alumni Assn. (sec. 1988-989, v.p. 1989-90, pres. 1990-91), Mt. Mercy Acad. Alumni Assn. (bd. dirs. 1990-91), Omicron Kappa Upsilon (v.p. Lambda Lambda chpt). Roman Catholic. Office: SUNY at Buffalo Dept Oral Medicine 355 Squire Hall Buffalo NY 14214

GOGATE, SHASHI ANAND, pathologist; b. Indore, India, July 9, 1938; d. Kashinath M. and Manorama R.; M.B.B.S., M.G.M. Med. Coll., 1962; M.S., Ohio State U., 1969; m. Anand B. Gogate, June 20, 1962; children—Sangita, Soniya, Sanjay. Instr., research asso. Ohio State U., 1970-73, asst. prof. pathology, 1973-75, asst. clin. prof., 1975-87; assoc. clin. prof. 1987—; dir. lab. Columbus Pathology Lab., 1975-79; chief pathologist Lancaster-Fairfield Community Hosp., 1976—; pres. S.A. Gogate M.D., Inc., 1978—. Mem. adv. bd. Internat. Mediation Soc., Columbus. Fellow Coll. Am. Pathologists, Am. Soc. Clin. Pathologists; mem. AMA, Ohio Med. Assn., Franklin County Med. Soc., Fairfield County Med. Soc., Internat. Acad. Pathology, Republican. Hindu. Contbr. articles to profl. jours. Home: 6112 Sedgwick Rd Columbus OH 43235-3321 Office: Fairfield Med Ctr PO Box 1900 Lancaster OH 43130-6255

GOGGIN, JOAN MARIE, school system specialist; b. Boston, Nov. 15, 1956; d. Richard and Florence Muriel (Stone) G. BS in Edn., Westfield State Coll., 1978; MS in Edn., Lesley Coll., 1981. Spl. needs tchr. Supervisory Union # 53, Pembroke, N.H., 1978-79; grad. intern, head tchr. Ednl. Collaborative Greater Boston, Brookline, Mass., 1979-80; vocat. counselor Charles River Assn. for Retarded Citizens, Needham, Mass., 1981-83; dir. vocat. svcs. Community Assistance Corp., New Orleans, 1983-84; tchr. of pre-sch. children with severe spl. needs St. Charles Parish Pub. Schs., Luling, La., 1985-88; career placement and tng. specialist Plymouth (Mass.) Carver Regional Sch. Dist., 1988-93, inclusion facilitator, 1989-91, program adminstr., 1992-93; inclusion facilitator Plymouth Pub. Schs., 1992—; ednl. cons. Ednl. Performance Sys., 1994—; cons. on self advocacy Mass. Assn. for Retarded Citizens, 1980-83; ednl. cons. Human Devel. Ctr., La. State U., New Orleans, 1984-85, D.K. Hollingsworth & Assocs., Metairie, La., 1984-88; vocat. cons. United Cerebral Palsy, Harahann, La., 1984-85; program coord. JTPA Project, Plymouth Sch. Dist., 1989-91, program. adminstr., 1991-93, exec. prodr. Bridging the Gap, We All Belong Together, 1991-93. Exec. prodr.: Bridging the Gap: Transition to Independence, We All Belong Together. Active Mass. Dept. Edn. Task Force on Criteria for Spl. Edn. Svcs., 1992-93, mem. com. Individual Edn. Plan, 1990-93. Recipient Hon. Mention Tchr. of Yr. award Mass. Coun. Exceptional Children; grantee Mass. Dept. Edn., 1988-94. Mem. ASCD, NEA, Assn. for Severely Handicapped. Democrat. Office: Mt Pleasant Sch Pupil Pers Svcs Whiting St Plymouth MA 02360

GOGGINS, CONNIE LEE LAWRENCE, budget officer; b. Birmingham, Ala., July 13, 1959; d. Jimmie Levi and Nancy Lee (Walton) Lawrence; m. Jerry Lee Goggins, July 13, 1976; children: Jared Lawrence, Connor Lee. BS in Bus. Acctg. magna cum laude, U. Ala., Birmingham, 1992; postgrad., U. Ala., 1992—. Receptionist Ins. Store, Alabaster, Ala., 1977-78; customer svc. rep., bookkeeper Inst. Store, Inc., Alabaster, Ala., 1978-84; sec., receptionist, analyst U. Montevallo (Ala.), 1984-87, staff asst., 1987-89; adminstrv. asst. U. Ala., Birmingham, 1989; budget analyst U. Ala., 1990-93, budget officer, 1993—. Bd. dirs. Montevallo Dixie Youth Baseball Assn., 1992-94. Pearce, Bevill, Leesburg & Moore scholar, 1991-92. Mem. Inst. Mgmt. Accts. (assoc. dir. 1993-94, scholar 1991-92), Golden Key Honor Soc., Phi Kappa Phi, Beta Gamma Sigma. Home: 131 Cardinal Crest Montevallo AL 35115 Office: U Ala Univ Sta Birmingham AL 35294

GOGOLIN, MARILYN TOMPKINS, educational administrator, language pathologist; b. Pomona, Calif., Feb. 25, 1946; d. Roy Merle and Dorothy (Davidson) Tompkins; m. Robert Elton Gogolin, Mar. 29, 1969. BA, U. LaVerne, Calif., 1967; MA, U. Redlands, Calif., 1968; postgrad., U. Washington, 1968-69; MS, Calif. State U., Fullerton, 1976. Cert. clin. speech pathologist; cert. teaching and sch. adminstrn. Speech and lang. pathologist Rehab. Hosp., Pomona, 1969-71; diagnostic tchr. L.A. County Office of Edn., Downey, Calif., 1971-72, program specialist, 1972-74, cons. lang., 1975-76, cons. orgns. and mgmt., 1976-79, dir. adminstrv. affairs, asst. to supt., 1979—; cons. lang. sch. dists., Calif., 1975-79; cons. orgn. and mgmt. and profl. assns., Calif., 1976—; exec. dir. L.A. County Sch. Trustees Assn., 1979—. Founding patron Desert chpt. Kidney Found., Palm Desert, Calif., 1985. Doctoral fellow U. Washington, 1968; named One of Outstanding Young Women Am., 1977. Mem. Am. Mgmt. Assn., Am. Speech/Hearing Assn., Calif. Speech/Hearing Assn., Am. Edn. Research Assn. Baptist. Office: LA County Office Edn 9300 Imperial Hwy Downey CA 90242-2813

GOHEEN, JANET MOORE, counselor, sales professional; b. Everett, Mass., Sept. 29, 1945; d. Franklin Pierce and Virginia Louise (Murphy) Moore; m. Peter Arthur Goheen, Apr. 2, 1967; children: Kevin Murphy Moore Goheen, Andrew Hudson Moore Goheen. BA, Ohio Wesleyan U., 1967; MS, U. Bridgeport, 1979. Cert. profl. guidance counselor, Ohio. Tchr. English Nordinia Hills High Sch., Macedonia, Ohio, 1967-69, White Plains (N.Y.) High Sch., 1969-71, Hudson (Ohio) High Sch., 1982-83; tchr. emotionally disturbed Palisades Learning Ctr., Paramus, N.J., 1986-87; sales cons. The Longaberger Co., Dresden, Ohio, 1983-84, br. advisor, 1984-90, regional advisor, 1990—; middle sch. counselor Hudson Middle Sch., 1988—; tchr. ESL Hitchcock Presbyn. Ch., Scardsale, N.Y., 1976-79, Aurora (Ohio) City Schs., 1979-81, Hudson Local Schs., 1980-82. Mem. Jr. League of Scarsdale, 1976-79, Jr. League of Akron, 1979-82, Jr. League No. N.J., Ridgewood, 1983-85; mem. alumni bd. dirs. Ohio Wesleyan U., Delaware, Ohio, 1990-93. Mem. Am. Sch. Counselors Assn., Ohio Sch. Counselors Assn., Kappa Kappa Gamma, Kappa Delta Pi. Home: 97 Manor Dr Hudson OH 44236 Office: Hudson Middle Sch 77 N Oviatt St Hudson OH 44236

GOIN, OLIVE BOWN, biologist; b. Pitts., Dec. 2, 1912; d. Charles Elmer and Anne Louise (Hay) Bown; m. Coleman Goin, June 7, 1940 (dec.); children: Lynda, Coleman Jr. AB, Wellesley Coll., 1934; MS, U. Pitts., 1936. Asst. lab. mammalogy Carnegie Mus., Pitts., 1934-40; lab. instr. to asst. prof. U. Fla., Gainesville, 1942-46; rsch. assoc. Mus. of No. Ariz., Flagstaff, 1971-80; ret. Author: World Outside My Door, 1955, Introduction to Herpetology, 1962, Comparative Vertebrate Anatomy, Man and the Natural World, 1970, Introduction to Herpetology, 2d edit., 1971, Journey Onto Land, 1974, Man and the Natural World, 2d edit., 1975 (all with C.J. Goin); (with C.J. Goin and George Zug) Introduction to Herpetology, 3rd edit., 1978; contbr. numerous articles to profl. jours.

GOINS, FRANCES FLORIANO, lawyer; b. Buffalo, Jan. 30, 1950; d. William and Anita (Graziano) Floriano; m. Gary Mitchell Goins; children: Matthew W., Mark W. MusB, Cleve. Inst. Music, 1971; MusM, Case Western Res. U., 1973, JD, 1977. Bar: Ohio 1977, U.S. Dist. Ct. Ohio 1978, U.S. Ct. Appeals (6th cir.) 1979, N.Y. 1984, U.S. Ct. Appeals (2d cir.) 1991. Law clk to Hon. Frank J. Battisti U.S. Dist. Ct. (no. dist.) Ohio, Cleve., 1977-78; ptnr. Squire, Sanders & Dempsey, Cleve., 1986—; mem. vis. com. bd. overseers Case Western Res. U., Cleve., 1984—; faculty Nat. Inst. Trial Advocacy, Cleve., 1991-92; faculty, lectr. trial advocacy seminar Cleve. State U. Sch. Law, 1989-90. Editor-in-chief law rev. Case Western Res. Sch. Law, 1976-77. Trustee, chairperson devel. com. Lyric Opera Cleve., 1985-92; trustee Shoreby Club Cleve., 1989-91; v.p. bd. trustees Bay Village Montessori Sch., 1994—. Mem. ABA (bus. law sect., mem. fed. regulation of securities com., mem. subcom. on civil litigation and SEC enforcement matters 1992—), Ohio State Bar Assn. (mem. ad hoc com. on bus. cts. 1994—), Cleve. Bar Assn. (mem. com. on women and the law 1987—, mem. ethics com. 1988-90, mem. securities law inst. 1991, 92, 93). Democrat. Roman Catholic. Office: Squire Sanders & Dempsey 4900 Society Ct 127 Public Sq Cleveland OH 44114

GOKTEPE, JANET ROSE, financial analyst; b. Anniston, Ala., Nov. 27, 1950; d. Clifton Frank and Bertha Ezel (Yates) Yeager; m. Omer Faruk Goktepe, Aug. 30, 1973; children: Katherine Emel, Joy Saadet. BS in Bus. & Mgmt. magna cum laude, U. Md., 1976, MBA with honors, 1979, PhD in Bus. & Mgmt. with honors, 1986. Sec. dept. of justice FBI, Washington, 1969-72, Dept. of Treasury, Washington, 1972-75; rsch. analyst Comptroller of Currency, Washington, 1975-77, fin. analyst, 1977; fin. analyst Interstate Commerce Commn., Washington, 1978-86, Farm Credit Adminstrn., McLean, Va., 1986—; lectr. bus. Montgomery Coll., Rockville, Md., 1979-80, U. Md., College Park, 1980-82, U. Md. Grad. Sch., College Park, 1988-89. Author: (with others) Small Groups and Social Interaction, 1983; contbr. articles to profl. jours. Co-chair fed. women's program Interstate Commerce Commn., Washington, 1980-81; vol. Seven Locks Elem. Sch., Bethesda, Md., 1986-94; chair child care task force Farm Credit Adminstrn., McLean, 1989-90. Recipient Outstanding Vol. Svc. certs. Seven Locks Elem. Sch., 1987, 91, 94, Commendation letter Pres. Gerald Ford, 1974. Mem. Nat. Assn. Female Execs., Nat. Capitol Women's Network, Beta Gamma Sigma, Phi Kappa Phi. Home: PO Box 341141 Bethesda MD 20817 Office: Farm Credit Adminstrn 1501 Farm Credit Dr Mc Lean VA 22101

GOLANN, CECIL P., writer, editor, researcher; b. N.Y.C., Jan. 20, 1921; d. Daniel L. and Ethel (Block) G. BA summa cum laude, Barnard Coll., 1941; MA, Columbia U., 1942, PhD, 1952. Lectr. in English Hunter Coll., N.Y.C., 1953-55; dir. Mass Media award program Thomas Alva Edison Found., N.Y.C., 1955-57; editorial rschr. NBC-TV Sales Dept., N.Y.C., 1958-62; assoc. editor Macmillan Pub. Co., N.Y.C., 1962-66, sr. editor, 1966-70; freelance editor, writer N.Y.C., 1970—. Author: Our World: The Taming of Israel's Negev, 1970; contbr. over 100 articles to profl. jours. Fulbright grantee U.S. Govt., Italy, 1952-53; Univ. fellow Columbia U., 1942-43; Dibblee scholar Barnard Coll., 1941-42. Mem. Women's Nat. Book Assn., Editorial Freelancers Assn., English Speaking Union, N.Y. Pub. Libr., Planned Parenthood, NOW, Met. Opera Guild, N.Y.C. Opera Guild. Democrat. Unitarian.

GOLASHESKY, CHRYSA ZOFIA, telecommunications company executive; b. Bayonne, N.J., Feb. 16, 1957; d. John Stanley and Margaret Walterine (Stanko) G. BS, Pa. State U., 1978; MBA, Rutgers U., 1980. Cert. Christian Founds. for Ministry. Mktg. analyst ITT - Domestic Transmission Systems, Inc., N.Y.C., 1980-81; market rsch. analyst ITT - U.S. Transmission Systems, Inc., N.Y.C., 1981-82; project mgr., market researcher ITT - U.S. Transmission Systems, Inc., Secaucus, N.J., 1982-85, mktg. mgr., 1985-86; product mgr. Metromedia Long Distance, Inc., Secaucus, 1986-87, dir. product mgmt., 1987-88, dir. mktg., 1988-89; dir. product mktg. Metromedia/ITT Long Distance, Inc., Secaucus, 1989-91; v.p. product mktg. Metromedia Communications Corp., East Rutherford, N.J., 1991—. Mem. edn. com. OLA Parish, Bayonne, N.J., 1986—; mem. Christian Founds. for Ministry, Irvington, N.J., 1988-91. Roman Catholic. Home: 101 W 24th St Bayonne NJ 07002-2701 Office: Metromedia Comm Corp 1 Meadowlands Plz East Rutherford NJ 07073-2137

GOLD, ARLINE, educational administrator. EdD. Prin. George W. Miller Elem. Sch., Nanuet, N.Y. Recipient Elem. Sch. Recognition award U.S. Dept. Edn., 1989-90, Internat. Invitational Sch. award, 1990-91. Office: George W Miller Elem Sch 50 Blauvelt Rd Nanuet NY 10954

GOLD, LOIS MEYER, artist; b. N.Y.C., June 2, 1945; d. Seymour Roy and Carol (Rubin) Meyer; m. Leonard Marshall Gold, Oct. 14, 1971; 1 child, Eric Marshall. BA, Boston U., 1967; MA, Columbia U., 1970. Tchr. Lenox Sch., N.Y.C., 1972-84, Columbia Grammar Sch., N.Y.C., 1975-76; artist, free-lance N.Y.C., 1976—; represented by Lizan-Tops Gallery, N.Y.C.,

Summa Gallery, N.Y.C. Prin. works appear in permanent mus. collections including Herbert F. Johnson Mus. Art, Ithaca, N.Y., corp. collections, including Bklyn. Union Gas Co., Bristol Myers Squibb, Imperial Oil, others; featured artist The Artists Mag., 1993 (Landscape award 1993). Recipient Artists Mag. Landscape award, 1991, 93, Pastel Soc. Am. Juried Scholarship award, 1994-95. Mem. Pastel Soc. Am., Nat. Assn. of Women Artists (Pauline Law award 1988, Works on Paper award 1988), Cassatt Pastel Soc., Studio Ctr. Artist's Assn. Home: 45 E End Ave New York NY 10028

GOLD, PHRADIE KLING See KLING, PHRADIE

GOLD, RUTH HELEN, retired elementary education educator, volunteer; b. Bklyn., Feb. 2, 1928; d. Meyer and Augusta (Yachelson) Bernstein; m. Isadore Roy Gold, Dec. 28, 1949; children: Matthew David, Jennifer Ellen Gold Levy, Daniel Marshall. BA, Smith Coll., 1949; MA, Columbia U., 1950. Cert. brailist Libr. of Congress; cert. elem. tchr., N.Y. Tchr. early childhood N.Y.C. Pub. Schs., 1950's-70's, ret., 1970's; office mgr. Physicians Office, N.Y.C., 1980's, caregiver, 1990's. Literary braillist Helen Keller Inst., Libr. of Congress, 1970—. Mem. Nat. Coun. Jewish Women (Bklyn. sect. bd. dirs., 1950's—, past Bklyn. sect. v.p., nat. standimg com. bylaws, 1982-90, nat. spl. com. quota 1985-86, northeast dist. chair by laws 1984-86, action line vol. 1993—, Outstanding Dedication and Commitment award 1991), Nat. Braille Assn., Alumnae Assn. Smith Coll.

GOLD, SHIRLEY JEANNE, state legislator, labor relations specialist; b. N.Y.C., Oct. 2, 1925; d. Louis and Gussie (Lefkowitz) Diamondstein; BA in Music, Hunter Coll., 1945; MA in Behavioral Sci. (Crown-Zellerbach Corp. scholar), Reed Coll., 1962; m. David E. Gold, June 22, 1947; children: Andrew, Dana. Tchr., Portland (Oreg.) Public Schs., 1954-68; pres. Portland Fedn. Tchrs., Am. Fedn. Tchrs./AFL-CIO, 1965-72, pres. Oreg. Fedn. Tchrs., 1972-77; cons. labor relations, 1977-80; mem. Oreg. Ho. of Reps., Salem, 1980-88, majority leader, 1985-88, chmn. legis. rules, ops. and reform, human resources com., 1983-84, revenue com., 1987-88, policy and priorities com., com. of edn., commn. of states, from 1987, campaign fin. reform com., from 1987; now state senator Oreg. Senate; senate chair Revenue and Edn. Coms.; senate mem. Rules Electronics Com., Oreg. Comm. for Child Care; mem. Oreg. Tchr. Tenure Rev. Bd., 1965-72; mem. Nat. Multi-State Consortium, 1974; mem. Speak Out Oreg. com. to White House and Congress, 1978; mem. Oreg. Task Force on Tax Reform; mem. Solid Waste Regional Policy Commn., 1989-91; AFL-CIO scholar George Meany Inst., 3 times, 1976-77; commr., nat. vice chmn. Edn. Commn. of States, 1988-90; mem. Oreg. Commn. on Women. Chairperson precinct com., conv. del. Oreg. Democratic Party, 1960-80, dist. leader, chairperson edn. com., 1978-80; charter mem., mem. exec. bd., v.p. Oreg. Council for Cts., 1977-80. Named to Hunter Coll. Hall of Fame, 1985, Citizen of Yr., 1985. Mem. Hunter Coll. Alumni Assn., Reed Coll. Alumni Assn., Pacific N.W. Labor History Assn., Portland Fedn. Tchrs., Oreg. Fedn. Tchrs., Oreg. Fedn. Dem. Women, Oreg. Coalition for Nat. Health Security, Oreg. Women's Polit. Caucus, Com. on Drug Abuse, Northwest Oreg. Health System, ACLU, Coalition Labor Union Women. Jewish. Contbr. articles on labor relations to Willamette Week newspaper, 1977-80; editor Oreg. Tchr. newspaper, 1970-72. Office: S217 State St Salem OR 97301-3445

GOLDAPER, GABRIELE GAY, clothing executive, consultant; b. Amsterdam, The Netherlands, May 4, 1937; came to U.S., 1949; d. Richard and Gertrud (Sinzheimer) Mainzer; married, 1957; children: Carolyn, Julie, Nancy. BA in Econs., Barnard Coll., 1959; BS in Edn., U. Cin., 1960; postgrad., Xavier U., 1962. V.p. planning, systems and material control High Tide Swimwear div. Warnaco, Los Angeles, 1974-79; v.p., customer support cons. Silton AMS, Los Angeles, 1979-80; exec. v.p., ptnr. Prisma Corp., Los Angeles, 1980-84; exec. v.p. Mindstar Prods., Los Angeles, 1984-85; gen. mgr. Cherry Lane, Los Angeles, 1985-86; dir. inventory mgmt. Barco Uniforms, Los Angeles, 1986; mgmt. cons. to clothing industry Santa Monica, Calif., 1986—; dir. corp. operation svcs. Authentic Fitness, L.A., 1993; exec. v.p. corp. LCA Intimates, 1994—; instr. Calif. State U., 1978-79, UCLA Grad. Bus. Mgmt. Sch., 1979-86, Fashion Inst. Design and Merchandising. 1985—; chmn. data processing com. Calif. Fashion Creators, 1980; mediator Los Angeles County Bar Assn.; cons. Exec. Service Corps; lectr. various colls. Author: A Results Oriented Approach to Manufacturing Planning, 1978, Small Company View of the Computer, 1979; also articles. Elected mem. Commn. on Status Women, 1985-89. Mem. Apparel Mfrs. Assn. (mgmt. systems com. 1978-80), Calif. Apparel Industries Assn. (exec. com., bd. dirs. 1980), Am. Arbitration Assn. Home: 37 Village Pky Santa Monica CA 90405

GOLDBERG, ANNE CAROL, physician, educator; b. Balt., June 12, 1951; d. Stanley Barry and Selma Ray (Freiman) G.; m. Ronald M. Levin, July 29, 1989. AB, Harvard U., 1973; MD, U. Md., 1977. Diplomate Am. Bd. Internal Medicine, Am. Bd. Endocrinlolgy and Metabolism. Intern in medicine Michael Reese Hosp., Chgo., 1977-78; resident in medicine Michael Reese Hosp., 1978-80; fellow in endocrinology Washington U., St. Louis, 1980-83, instr. medicine, 1983-85, asst. prof. medicine, 1985-94, assoc. prof. medicine, 1994—, clin. dir. lipid reseach clinic, 1987—. Mem. steering com. Cholesterol Coalition, St. Louis, 1988-93. Mem. ACP, AMA, Am. Diabetes Assn., Am. Heart Assn., Am. Fedn. Clin. Rsch., Am. Med. Women's Assn., Alpha Omega Alpha. Democrat. Jewish. Office: Washington U Med Sch 4566 Scott Ave PO Box 8046 Saint Louis MO 63110

GOLDBERG, JOLANDE ELISABETH, law librarian, lawyer; b. Pforzheim, Germany, Aug. 11, 1931; came to U.S., 1967; d. Eugen and Luise Rosa (Thorwarth) Haas; m. Lawrence Spencer Goldberg, Sept. 7, 1969; children: Daniel Scott, Elisa Miriam, Clarissa Anna. Referendar, U. Heidelberg, 1957, PhD, 1963; postdoctoral, U. London, 1976-77. Bar: Germany 1961. Mem. rsch. staff Acad. Scis. and Humanities, Heidelberg, 1961-67; rsch. assoc. U. Heidelberg, 1964-67; cataloger, law specialist Libr. of Congress, Washington, 1967-72, asst. law classification specialist, 1972-80, law classification specialist, 1980—; sculptor, potter Torpedo Factory Art Ctr., Alexandria, Va., 1974—; lectr. Smithsonian Inst., Washington, 1988—. Author: Probschlag & Meistersignatur, 1963; contbr. articles to profl. jours. Exec. bd. dirs. Friends Torpedo Factory Art Ctr., Alexandria, 1987—. Named Volkswagenwerk Found. rsch. fellow, Fed. Republic of Germany, 1964-65, German Rsch. Assn. fellow, 1966, German Libr. Inst. grantee, 1981. Mem. Internat. Waterlily Soc., Internat. Soc. for Knowledge Orgn., Am. Assn. Law Librs. (TS SIS exec. bd. dirs. 1987—, citation for exceptional contbn. 1992), German Assn. Law Librs., Torpedo Factory Artist Assn., The Art League, Friends of Nat. Arboretum. Democrat. Jewish. Office: Libr of Congress Washington DC 20540

GOLDBERG, LEE WINICKI, furniture company executive; b. Laredo, Tex., Nov. 20, 1932; d. Frank and Goldie (Ostrowiak) Winicki; student San Diego State U., 1951-52; m. Frank M. Goldberg, Aug. 17, 1952; children: Susan Arlene, Edward Lewis, Anne Carri. With United Furniture Co., Inc., San Diego, 1953-83, corp. sec., dir., 1963-83, dir. environ. interiors, 1970-83; founder Drexel-Heritage store Edwards Interiors, subs. United Furniture, 1975; founding ptnr., v.p. FLJB Corp., 1976-86, founding ptnr., sec. treas., Sea Fin., Inc., 1980, founding ptnr., First Nat. Bank San Diego, 1982. Den mother Boy Scouts Am., San Diego, 1965; vol. Am. Cancer Soc., San Diego, 1964-69; chmn. jr. matrons United Jewish Fedn., San Diego, 1958; del. So. Pacific Coast region Hadassah Conv., 1960, pres. Galilee group San Diego chpt., 1960-61; supporter Marc Chagall Nat. Mus., Nice, France, U. Calif. at San Diego Cancer Ctr. Found., Smithsonian Instn., L.A. County Mus., San Diego Mus. Contemporary Art, San Diego Mus. Art; pres. San Diego Opera, 1992-94. Recipient Hadassah Service award San Diego chpt., 1958-59; named Woman of Dedication by Salvation Army Women's Aux., 1992, Patron of Arts by Rancho Sante Fe Country Friends, 1993. Democrat. Jewish.

GOLDBERG, LUELLA GROSS, business executive; b. Mpls., Feb. 26, 1937; d. Louis and Beatrice (Rosenthal) Gross; m. Stanley M. Goldberg, June 23, 1958; children: Ellen Goldberg Luger, Fredric, Martha Goldberg Aronson. BA, Wellesley Coll., 1958; postgrad. in philosophy, U. Minn., 1958-59. bd. dirs. Northwestern Nat. Life Ins. Co., Mpls., TCF Banking and Savs., Mpls., TCF Fin. Corp., Mpls., Piper Jaffray Investment Trust, Mpls., Am. Govt. Income Fund, Mpls., Hormel Foods Corp., Mpls. Pres. Minn. Orch. Women's Assn., Mpls., 1972-74; regent St. John's U., Collegeville, Minn., 1974-83; trustee U. Minn. Found., Mpls., 1978—; chmn. Minn. Orch. Assn., Mpls., 1980-83; mem. bd. overseers Sch. Mgmt., U. Minn., Mpls., 1980—; chmn. bd. trustees Wellesley (Mass.) Coll., 1985-93, acting pres., 1993; bd. dirs. Mpls. chpt. United Way, 1978-88, Ind. Sector, Washington, 1984-90; trustee Northwest Area Found., 1994—. Recipient Disting. Svc. award Minn. Orch. Assn., 1983, Community Svc. Leadership award Mpls. YWCA, 1986, Disting. Svc. to Higher Edn. award Minn. Pvt. Coll. Coun., 1992, Humanitarian award NCCJ, 1992. Mem. Nat. Women's Econ. Alliance, Minn. Women's Econ. Round Table, Phi Beta Kappa. Club: Cosmopolitan (N.Y.C.). Home: 7019 Tupa Dr Minneapolis MN 55439-1643

GOLDBERG, PAMELA WINER, strategic consultant; b. Boston, Oct. 14, 1955; d. Arthur Leonard and Marilyn (Miller) Winer; m. Marc Evan Goldberg, June 11, 1983; children: Frederick Warren, Alyssa Rachel, Meredith Hayley. BA, Tufts U., 1977; MBA, Stanford U., 1981. Day care dir. Community Action Inc., Haverhill, Mass., 1977-79; lending assoc. Bankers Trust Co., N.Y.C., 1980-81; mgr., bank officer, corp. fin. dept. Citicorp, N.Y.C., 1981-82; assoc. dir., mergers and acquisitions group State Street Bank, Boston, 1983-85; ind. strategic cons. Wellesley, Mass., 1986-93; exec. v.p. Concert Prodns., Inc., Boston, 1994; cons. Simon Mgmt., Wellesley, Mass., 1994—. Mem. exec. bd. Friends Beth Israel Hosp., Boston, 1987—; mem. exec. bd. trustees Temple Beth Elohim, Wellesley, 1992—; trustee Recuperative Ctr., Boston, 1988—; bd. dirs. PTO, Hunnewell Sch., 1991—. Home: 31 Lathrop Rd Wellesley MA 02181-7011 Office: Simon Mgmt 1 Washington St Wellesley MA 02181

GOLDBERG, RITA MARIA, foreign language educator; b. N.Y.C., Oct. 1, 1933; d. Abraham Morris and Hilda (Weinman) G. B.A. (N.Y. State Regents scholar), Queens Coll., 1954; M.A., Middlebury Coll., 1955; Ph.D., Brown U., 1968. Mem. faculty Queens Coll., N.Y.C., 1956, Oberlin (Ohio) Coll., 1957; mem. faculty St. Lawrence U., Canton, N.Y., 1957—; Dana prof. modern langs. St. Lawrence U., 1975—, chmn. dept., 1972-75, 83-91; chmn. Regional Conf. Am. Programs in Spain, 1979-81; mem. Nat. Fulbright Selection Com., 1990-92; mem. advanced placement test devel. com. for Spanish, Ednl. Testing Svc., 1993—. Author: Tonos a lo divino y a lo humano, 1981, Poesias barias y recreacion de buenos ingenios, 1984, Nuevos documentos y glosas cortesianos, 1987, Visiones, 1988; translator: A Priest Confesses (Jose Luis Martin Descalzo), 1960; contbr. articles to profl. jours. Spanish Ministry of Fgn. Affairs scholar, 1954-56; Danforth grantee, 1960-62, 63-64; Brown U. scholar, 1960-62. Mem. Am. Assn. Tchrs. Spanish and Portuguese, AAUP, MLA, Am. Council Teaching of Fgn. Langs., N.E. Modern Lang. Assn., N.Y. State Assn. Fgn. Lang. Tchrs., Phi Beta Kappa, Sigma Delta Pi. Roman Catholic. Home: 45 Judson St Canton NY 13617-1146 Office: St Lawrence U Dept Modern Langs Lits Canton NY 13617

GOLDBERG, WHOOPI (CARYN JOHNSON), actress; b. N.Y.C., Nov. 13, 1955; d. Robert and Emma (Harris) Johnson; m. David Claessen (div.); m. Lyle Trachtenberg, Oct. 1, 1994; 1 child, Alexandrea Martin. Mem. San Diego Repertory Theatre, 1975-80, Blake St. Hawkeyes, Berkeley, Calif., 1980-84. Appeared in one-person show Whoopi Goldberg on Broadway, 1984-85, Living on the Edge of Chaos, 1988 (Calif. theatre award outstanding achievement); films include The Color Purple, 1985, Jumpin' Jack Flash, 1986, Burglar, 1986, Telephone, 1987, Fatal Beauty, 1987, Clara's Heart, 1988, Beverly Hills Brats, 1989 (cameo), Homer and Eddie, 1989, The Long Walk Home, 1990, Ghost, 1990 (Acad. award best supporting actress, 1991), Soapdish, 1991, House Party 2 (cameo), The Player, 1992, Sister Act, 1992, Wisecracks, 1992, Sarafina!, 1992, Made in America, 1993, National Lampoon's Loaded Weapon 1, 1993, Sister Act 2: Back in the Habit, 1993, The Lion King, 1994 (voice), The Little Rascals, 1994, Naked in New York (cameo), 1994, Corrina, Corrina, 1994, Star Trek: Generations, 1994, The Pagemaster, 1994 (voice), Boys on the Side, 1995; TV film: Kiss Shot, 1989, My Past Is My Own; TV series: Star Trek: The Next Generation, 1988-94, Bagdad Cafe, CBS, 1990; TV specials include: Tales from the Whoop: Hot Rod Brown, Class Clown, 1990; host TV talk show The Whoopi Goldberg Show, 1992-93. Named NAACP Entertainer of the Yr., 1990, Humanitarian of Yr. Starlight Found., 1989; recipient, Hans Christian Andersen Award for outstanding achievement by a dyslexic, 1987. *

GOLDBERGER, BLANCHE RUBIN, sculptor, jeweler; b. N.Y.C., Feb. 2, 1914; d. David and Sarah (Israel) Rubin; m. Emanuel Goldberger, June 28, 1942; children—Richard N., Ary Louis. B.A., Hunter Coll., N.Y.C., 1934; M.A., Columbia U., 1936; Certificat d'Etudes, Sorbonne, Paris, 1936; postgrad. Westchester Arts Workshop Sculpture and Jewelry, White Plains, 1961-70, Silvermine Coll. Arts, 1962, Nat. Acad. Arts, N.Y.C., 1968. Tchr. French and Hebrew, N.Y.C. High Sch. System, Scarsdale Jr. and Sr. High Schs. One-woman shows include: Bloomingdale's, Eastchester, N.Y., 1975, Scarsdale Pub. Library, N.Y., 1976, Temple Israel, White Plains, N.Y., 1975, Greenwich Art Barn, Conn., 1972 Westlake Gallery, White Plains, N.Y., 1981; exhibited in group shows at Hudson River Mus., Yonkers, N.Y., 1978, Silvermine-New Eng. Ann., Silvermine, Conn., 1979; represented in permanent collection at Scarsdale High Sch. Library, N.Y.; sculpture commn. Jewish Community Ctr. White Plains, N.Y., 1988; commn. Manchester, Vt.; also pvt. collections. Recipient award Beaux Arts of Westchester, White Plains, N.Y., 1967, First Prize, White Plains Art Show, Holocaust Meml. Bronze Plaque for Synagogue Congregation Israel; various commns. for calli collis calligraphic collages. Mem. Nat. Assn. Women Artists, Nat. Assn. Tchrs. French, Scarsdale Art Assn. (bd. dirs.; first prizes for sculpture). Jewish. Avocations: lecturing on sculpture, reading contemporary lit. in Hebrew, the violin, classical music concerts.

GOLDBERG KENT, SUSAN, library director; b. N.Y.C., Mar. 18, 1944; d. Elias and Minnie (Barnett) Solomon; m. Eric Goldberg, Mar. 27, 1966 (div. Mar. 1991); children: Evan, Jessica, Joanna; m. Rolly Kent, Dec. 20, 1991. BA, SUNY, Binghamton, 1965; MS, Columbia U., 1966. Libr. N.Y. Pub. Libr., 1965-67, br. mgr., 1967-68; reference libr. Bklyn. Pub. Libr. 1971-72; reference libr. Finkelstein Meml. Libr., Spring Valley, N.Y., 1974-76; coord. adult svcs. Tucson Pub. Libr. Ariz., 1977-80, dep. dir., 1980-87; mng. dir. Ariz. Theatre Co., Tucson, 1987-89; cons., Tucson, 1989-90; dir. Mpls. Pub. Libr., 1990-95; dir. L.A. Pub. Libr., Calif., 1995—. mem. adj. faculty Pima Community Coll., Tucson, 1978, U. Ariz., Tucson, 1978-79; commr. Ariz. Commission on the Arts, 1983-87; bd. dirs. Tejo Foster Found. Tucson, 1994—; chmn. strategic directions com. Urban Librs. Coun. Evanston, Ill., 1993—, bd. dirs. Editor: Courtly Love in the Shopping Mall, 1991; contbg. author: Critical Issues Conference 8, 1979; Public Librarianship, 1982; Reorganization in the Public Library, 1984, Against All Odds, 1994. v.p. Cultural Alliance of Tucson, 1981-82; chmn. arts and culture com. Tucson Tomorrow, 1982-87. Mem. ALA (mem. coun. 1990—), NOW (pres. Rockland County br. 1974-76), Minn. Libr. Assn., Pub. Libr. Assn. (pres. 1987-88, chmn. 1994 Nat. Convention, exec. bd. Urban Linrs. Coun., 1994—). Office: LA Pub Libr 630 W 5th St Los Angeles CA 90071

GOLDBRONN-GALLAGHER, CAROLYN, school superintendent; b. Jersey City, Aug. 22, 1945; d. Frederick and Mary (Peltier) Goldbronn; divorced; children: Amy, Jed. BA, Jersey City State Coll., 1968; MA, Hunter Coll., 1971. Spl. edn. tchr. Union City (N.J.) Bd. Edn., 1969-72, Newark Bd. Edn., 1972-76; spl. edn. tchr. Jersey Bd. Edn., 1977-82, coord. P.S. # 31, 1982-85; prin. George Wash. Sch., Edgewater, N.J., 1985-89; supt. of schs. Youth Consultation Svc., Newark, 1989—; cons. various orgns. and bd., 1984—; adj. prof. Jersey City State Coll., 1986-88. Contbr. articles to profl. jours. Bd. dirs. N.J. Ctr. for Outreach and Svcs. for the Autistic Cmty., Inc., 1991-93, sec., 1993—. Recipient Adminstr. of Yr. award Very Spl. Arts, 1994, Gov.'s award, 1994. Mem. Assn. of Schs. and Agys. for the Handicapped (bd. dirs. 1991—, region I chair 1993—). Office: VH Sawtelle Learning Ctr 208 S Mountain Ave Montclair NJ 07042

GOLDEEN, DOROTHY ANN, art gallery owner; b. San Francisco, Nov. 12, 1948; m. Scott Morgan, Oct. 1986. BA, U. Calif., 1972. With Hansen-Fuller, San Francisco, 1972-78; prin. Hansen, Fuller & Goldeen, San Francisco, 1978-81, Fuller-Goldeen, San Francisco, 1982-87; pres. Dorothy Goldeen Gallery, Santa Monica, Calif., 1987—; presenter numerous seminars in field. Contbr. articles to profl. jours. and essays to exhbn. catalogs. Mem. Santa Monica Art Dealers Assn. (pres. 1989, 90), San Francisco Art Dealers Assn. (bd. dirs. 1979-80), Art Dealers Assn. Am., Soc. for the Encouragement of Contemporary Art, Artable (pres. 1992-94), Curators Coun. Office: 2224 Main St Santa Monica CA 90405

GOLDEN, BETH, community college administrator; 1 child, Molly E. Student, Eureka Coll., 1970; BA, U. N.C., Asheville, 1985; postgrad., Western Carolina U., 1993. Instr. adult basic edn. Blue Ridge C.C., Flat Rock, N.C., 1988, 90-91; tng. rep. Blue Ridge C.C., Flat Rock, 1989-90, compensatory edn. and spl. populations specialist, 1990-91, coord. spl. populations office, 1991—; cognitive retraining therapist Thomas Rehab. Hosp., Asheville, 1988-89, cons. in field. Chair Mayor's Com. for Persons with Disabilities; chair respite care com. Parents' Assistance League. Grantee State of N.C., 1985, Ednl. Found., 1991, 92, 93, Melvin Lane Charitable Trust, 1992, 93. Mem. N.C. Head Injury Found. (profl. coun.), Henderson County Coun. on Women (pres. 1991-93), Job Devel. Coun. Henderson County, Inter-Agy. Coun. Office: Blue Ridge C C College Dr Flat Rock NC 28731

GOLDEN, BONNIE JANE, counselor; b. Chgo., Apr. 5, 1956; d. Ted and Dorothy (Kranz) Schultz; m. Norman Scott Golden, Aug. 20, 1978; 1 child, Samuel Golden. AA, S.W. Coll., Chgo., 1975; BS, U. Ill., 1977; MEd, U. Ariz., 1978. Counselor, coord. U. Ariz., Tucson, 1978-83; counselor Pima Coll., Tucson, 1987—, EEO coord., 1984-87. Co-author: Building Self-Esteem: Strategies for Success in School, 1994. Mem. Assn. Psychol. Type, Nat. Counseling Assn., Nat. Career Devel. Assn. Office: Pima CC 1255 N Stone Tucson AZ 85709

GOLDEN, KIMBERLY KAY, critical care, flight nurse; b. Munich, July 31, 1961; came to U.S., 1961; d. Henry Davis and Mary Walker G. AA, Hinds Jr. Coll., Raymond, Miss., 1980, ASN, 1984; BSN, U. Miss., Jackson, 1987, AS in EMT-Paramedic, 1990. Cert. ACLS instr., Pediatric Advanced Life Support instr., emergency nurse, critical care RN; cert. paramedic, Miss., Tex., U.S. Staff nurse neuro ICU U. Miss. Med. Ctr., 1984-85, staff nurse surg. ICU, 1985-87; staff nurse emergency rm. Rankin Gen. Hosp., Brandon, Miss., 1987-88; flight nurse Lifestar Helicopter Flight Svc., 1988-91; staff nurse emergency rm., ICU Nightingale Nursing, Jackson, 1988-91, Riveroaks Hosp., Jackson, 1990-91; staff RN emergency rm., Aerovesta flight Midland Meml. Hosp., Tex., 1991-93; flight nurse Hosp. Wing BTLS, Memphis, Tenn., 1993—; examiner Nat. Registry EMT-P; advanced trauma life support station instr.; affiliate faculty paramedic program U. Miss. Faculty scholar Hinds Jr. Coll., 1983. Mem. AACN, Nat. Flight Assn., Emergency Nurses Assn. Baptist. Office: PO Box 140466 Austin TX 78714

GOLDEN, LAURIE GAY, corporate lawyer; b. Memphis, Oct. 17, 1961; d. Haschal and Julie (Douglas) G. BA in Acctg., U. Miss., 1983; JD, U. Memphis, 1986. Bar: Tenn. 1986; CPA, Tenn. Tax acct. Touche Ross & Co., Memphis, 1985-88; atty. Farris, Hancock, Gilman, Memphis, 1988-89; corp. counsel Perkins Family Restaurants, Memphis, 1989—. Mem. ABA, Tenn. Bar Assn., Memphis Bar Assn. Republican. Mem. Ch. Christ. Office: Perkins Family Restaurants 6075 Poplar Ave Ste 800 Memphis TN 38119-4709

GOLDEN, LESLIE BLACK, real estate agent; b. Dallas, Aug. 21, 1955; d. Aubrey C. Jr. and Martha (Cartwright) Black; m. G. Hawkins Golden II, Sept. 21, 1985; children: G. Hawkins III, John Houston. BBA, U. Tex., 1977. Advt. prodn. asst. Neiman Marcus, Dallas, 1977-78; group account exec. Registry Hotel, Dallas, 1978-80, sales mgr., 1982-83; sales mgr. Doubletree Inn., Dallas, 1980-82, Sheraton Park Cen., Dallas, 1983-85; real estate agt. Golden-King Properties, Dallas, 1985—. Mem. Jr. League Dallas, 1988—; bd. dirs. Innovators of Dallas Symphony Orch., 1986-89, chmn. arrangements, 1988, chmn. coloring book fundraiser, 1989, hon. trustee Dallas Symphony Orch., 1988-89; chair phone com., auditor chmn. jr. group Dallas Garden Club, 1983—, bd. dirs., 1987-89; bd. dirs. Yellow Rose Gala com. Multiple Sclerosis, Dallas, 1985-89; chmn. Easter egg hunt Dallas So. Meml., 1987—, bd. dirs. 1987-89; docent Dallas Zoo, 1989-93; vol. Freedom Ride Found., 1987; Highland Park Presbyterian Day School Parents Coun., 1990—, auctin solicitations com.; with Dallas Children's Theatre Guild, 1992—; vol. Equest, 1993—; co-chair Ridefest, 1994. Mem. The Science Pl., Dallas Mus. Art, Dallas Zoo, Channel 13, Dallas Childrens Theater Guild, Dallas Country Club, Park Cities Club, Kappa Alpha Theta Alumni. Office: Golden King Properties 8533 Ferndale Rd Ste 202 Dallas TX 75238-4401

GOLDEN, SANDRA JEAN, nurse; b. Portsmouth, Va., Nov. 18, 1954; d. Richard Elmer and Catherine Mae (Zenisek) Haungs; m. Gerald Thomas Golden, Jan. 18, 1980 (div. 1989); 1 child, Sarah Catherine. AAS, No. Va. Community Coll., 1974; postgrad., Shepherd Coll., 1980-81. Staff nurse, charge nurse surg. ICU/CCU Good Samaritan Hosp., Lebanon, Pa., 1974-77; staff nurse, charge nurse Jefferson Meml. Hosp., Alexandria, Va., 1977-78, City Hosp., Inc., Martinsburg, W.Va., 1978-79; office nurse Shenandoah Surg. Group, Inc., Martinsburg, 1980-87; case mgr., preceptor, home health Shenandoah Meml. Hosp., Woodstock, Va., 1988—. Mem. AACN. Republican. Roman Catholic. Office: Home Care of Shenandoah Memorial Hosp PO Box 3 Woodstock VA 22664

GOLDEN, SOMA, newspaper editor; b. Washington, Aug. 27, 1939; m. William Behr; 2 children. BA, Radcliffe Coll.; MA, Columbia U. Mem. econs. staff Bus. Week Mag., Washington, 1962-73; with The New York Times, 1973—, mem. editorial bd., 1977-82, editor Sunday bus. sect., 1982-87, nat. news editor, 1987-93, asst. mng. editor, 1993—; adj. prof. Columbia U., N.Y.C., 1961-76. Office: The New York Times Co 229 W 43rd St New York NY 10036-3913

GOLDENBERG, ELIZABETH LEIGH, bank officer; b. Dayton, Ohio, Oct. 29, 1963; d. Neal and Myrna (Gallant) G. AB in Philosophy and Politics, Mount Holyoke Coll., 1985. Intern, spokeswoman The White House, Washington, 1984; trainee Nat. Westminister Bank USA, N.Y.C., 1985-86, asst. to v.p. fin. and strategic planning ops. div., 1986-87; asst. dealer Toronto-Dominion Bank, N.Y.C., 1987-88, dealer money markets, 1988-90, sr. dealer money markets, 1990-91, sr. dealer, sr. mgr. short term asset trading, 1991-93; sr. dealer, sr. mgr. short term loan participation trading and sales ba & cd trading, 1993—. Contbr. articles and photographs to mags. Bd. dirs. USA Rugby Met. N.Y., N.Y.C., 1987-89; publicist, spokesperson, com. on image and mktg., 1993; U.S.A. Eagles publicist USA Rugby, Colorado Springs, Colo., 1989-94; chair Youth Rugby for Harlem Devel. Com., 1994—. Mem. N.Y. Amateur Sports Alliance, Pub. Securities Assn. (chmn. money market com. 1990-92, bd. dirs. 1990-92, mem. polit. action com. 1990-92, program com. 1990-92, awards com. 1991-93). Home: 355 6E S End Ave New York NY 10280

GOLDENBERG, HELEN ALPERT, computer programmer; b. N.Y.C., July 6, 1943; d. Milton and Lillian (Tzeses) Alpert; m. Harvey J. Goldenberg, July 29, 1964 (dec. 1991); children: Ilene Bonnie, Audrey Bliss. BA, Brandeis U., 1964; MLS, Simmons Coll., 1967; cert. computer applications in bus., Russell Sage Coll., 1981. Libr. trainee Boston Pub. Libr., 1965-67; libr. Simat Helliesen & Eichner, Boston, 1968-69, SUNY, Albany, 1970-73; computer programmer State of N.Y., Albany, 1982—. Project fund raising chair Colonie (N.Y.) Hadassah, 1971—; steward Pub. Employees Fedn., Albany, 1988-94. Jewish. Office: NY State Employees Ret Sys Alfred Smith State Office Bldg Albany NY 12244

GOLDENBERG, LINDA (LINDA ATKINSON), librarian, author; b. Bklyn., Mar. 3, 1941; d. Harry Louis and Sara (Nathanson) G.; children: William C. Murphy, Sara H. Atkinson. MA in Philosophy, NYU, 1964; MLS, CUNY, 1989. Libr. Chambers Sch., Kingston, N.Y. Author: Mother Jones: The Most Dangerous Woman in America (Notable Children's Trade Book in Social Science 1979), Alternatives to College, 1980, Psychic Stories: Strange But True, 1981, Hit and Run, 1981, Incredible Crimes, 1982, Your Legal Rights as a Minor, 1982, Have We Lived Before?, 1983, Women in the Martial Arts: A New Spirit Rising, 1983 (Best Books for Teenage award N.Y. Libr. Assn. 1984), In Kindling Flame: The Story of Hannah Senesh, 1984 (Nat. Jewish Book award 1985, Kenneth B. Smilen award 1985). Mem. NOW, N.Y. Libr. Assn., Sch. Libr. Media Specialists of Southeastern N.Y., Nat. Women's Studies Assn. Jewish.

GOLDENBERG, MYRNA GALLANT, English language and literature educator; b. Bklyn., Mar. 8, 1937; d. Harry and Fay (Solomon) Gallant; m. Neal Goldenberg, Jan. 27, 1957; children: Elizabeth, David Brian, Eve Lisa. BS cum laude, CCNY, 1957; MA, U. Ark., 1961; PhD, U. Md., 1987.

Faculty, dept. English Montgomery Coll., Rockville, Md., 1971—, chmn. dept., 1979-81, coord. gen. edn., 1981-90, coord. women's studies program, 1990-94; adj. faculty humanities dept. Johns Hopkins U., judaic studies, women's studies, honors coll. English U. Md.; dir. project to integrate scholarship on women and minorities into the curriculum Ford Found., 1993-94; co-dir. project integrating scholarship of women in curricula of selected Md. C.C.s, FIPSE, 1988-90; chmn. Montgomery County Commn. on Humanities, 1984-91; chmn. Title IX adv. com. Montgomery County Pub. Schs., 1985-89; lectr. in field. Contbr. author/author: Common and Uncommon Concerns: The Complex Role of Community College Department Chairpersons/Enhancing Department Leadership, 1990, Different Horrors/Sane Hell: Women Remembering the Holocaust, Thinking the Unthinkable: Human Meanings of the Holocaust, 1990, Writing Everybody In: Two-Year College English: Essays for a New Century, 1994; contbg. editor: Belles Lettres, 1989—; editor: C.C. Humanities Rev.; contbr. articles to profl. jours. Recipient Disting. Humanities Educator award C.C. Humanities Assn., 1989, Outstanding Faculty Mem. award Montgomery Coll., 1990, Teaching award Md. Assn. for Higher Edn., 1991; acad. adminstrn. fellow Am. Coun. on Edn., 1981-82; Lowenstein Wiener fellow U. Md., 1983. Mem. MLA (sec.), Nat. Women's Studies Assn. (sec.), Assn. Jewish Studies, Nat. Coun. Tchrs. English, History Edn. Soc., Phi Kappa Phi. Home: 9328 Garden Ct Rockville MD 20854-3962

GOLDFARB, JOAN RACHEL, lawyer; b. Cin., May 30, 1963; d. Lee I. and Theresa (Eckman) G. BA, Wesleyan U., 1985; JD, Boston Coll., 1991. Bar: Mass. 1992, D.C. 1994. List and media coord. Cinamon Assocs. Inc., Boston, 1985-87; staff atty. Dept. Interior, Washington, 1991—. Mng. editor Boston Coll. Environ. Affairs Law Rev., 1990-91. Mem. ABA.

GOLDFARB, MURIEL BERNICE, marketing and advertising consultant; b. Bklyn., Mar. 29, 1920; d. Barnett Goldfarb and May (Steinberg) Goldfarb Oshman; BA, U. Miami, Coral Gables, Fla., 1942; postgrad. CCNY, 1950. Pub. info. asst. UNESCO, Paris, 1946-47; advt. mgr. Majestic Specialties Co., N.Y.C., 1947-50; retail promotion mgr. Glamour Mag., 1955-61; advt. dir. Country Tweeds Co., N.Y.C., 1961-65; advt. dir. S. Augstein & Co., N.Y.C., 1966-72, Feature Ring Co., Inc., Gotham Ring Co., Inc., Fidco Inc., N.Y.C., 1972-77; dir. advt. and promotion Wasko Gold Products Corp., N.Y.C., 1977-81; advt. and mktg. cons. specializing in promotions and sale of vintage jewelry and Bric á Brac. Served to lt. WAVES, 1943-46. Mem. Fashion Group N.Y. Inc., Women's Jewelry Assn. (corr. sec. 1983-85). Jewish.

GOLDFINE, BEATRICE, artist; b. Phila., Aug. 17, 1923; d. Samuel and Esther (Sacks) Rubin; m. Leonard Goldfine, May 22, 1955; children: Carole Goldfine Ben-Maimon, Neil. Cert. in art history, Barnes Found., 1967; cert. in art, Pa. Acad. Fine Arts, Phila., 1980; student, Cheltenham Sch. Fine Arts, Phila., 1970; studied with Morris Blackburn, Phila., 1980-94. Studio Phila., 1980—. Art works include bronze bust of Golda Meir (Jewish Cmty. Rels. Com. award 1984), Winston Churchill (Technion-Israel Inst. tech. award 1982). Bd. dirs. Bezelel Sch. Art and Design, Israel, 1990. Recipient Bok award Harrisburg Mus. Art, 1984, Selected Artist award Lind Creed Breast Cancer Found., 1994. Fellow Pa. Acad. Fine Arts (Mary Butler Meml. award 1992); mem. Pastel Soc. Am., North Light Book Club (Cover Competition award 1994), Artist's Cultural Exch. (Outstanding Achievement award 1988), Phila. Sketch Club (1st prize 1985), Woodmere Mus. Art (1st prize 1979), Friends of Barnes Found. Home: 1424 Melrose Ave Elkins Park PA 19027 Office: 1010 Arch St Philadelphia PA 19107-3003

GOLDIN, CLAUDIA DALE, economics educator; b. N.Y.C., May 14, 1946; d. Leon and Lucille (Rosansky) G. BA magna cum laude, Cornell U., 1967; MA, U. Chgo., 1969, PhD, 1972; MA (hon.), U. Pa., 1985, Harvard U., 1990; DHL (hon.), U. Nebr., Lincoln, 1994. Asst. prof. econs. U. Wis., Madison, 1971-73; asst. prof. Princeton (N.J.) U., 1973-79, vis. fellow indsl. relations sec., 1987-88; vis. lectr. Harvard U., Cambridge, Mass., 1975-76, prof., 1990—; assoc. prof. U. Pa., Phila., 1979-85, prof., 1985-90; vis. fellow The Brookings Instn., 1993-94; mem. Inst. Advanced Study, Princeton, 1982-83; rsch. assoc., project dir. Nat. Bur. Econ. Rsch., Cambridge, 1979—. Author: Urban Slavery in the American South, 1976, Understanding the Gender Gap, 1990; editor: Strategic Factors in 19th Century American Economic History, 1992, The Regulated Economy, 1994, Jour. Econ. History; edtl. bd. Am. Econ. Rev., 1985-91, Quar. Jour. Econs., 1992—, Rev. Econs. & Statistics; contbr. articles to profl. publs. Guggenheim fellow, 1987-88; NSF award, 1975-77, 79-81, 81-82, 84-86, 87-89. Fellow Econometric Soc.; mem. Am. Acad. Arts and Scis., Am. Econ. Assn. (v.p. 1990-91), Econ. History Assn. (trustee 1984—, v.p. 1988-89). Office: Harvard U Dept Econs Cambridge MA 02138

GOLDING, CAROLYN MAY, government administrator; b. Essex County, N.J., July 1, 1941; d. Wesley Irwin and Florence Grace (Smith) G.; m. Gary Anthony Derosa, Oct. 18, 1975 (div. Sept. 1982). B.A., Duke U., 1963, postgrad., 1965-66. Tchr. English, Parkersburg High Sch. (W.Va.), 1963; asst. to registrar Duke U., Durham, N.C., 1963-65; mgmt. intern Dept. Labor, Washington, 1966-67, in various other positions, 1967-72, dep. assoc. regional adminstr. Employment and Tng. Adminstrn., San Francisco, 1972-77, comptroller, Washington, 1977-78, regional adminstr., San Francisco, 1979-82, dir. Unemployment Ins. Service, Dept. Labor, Washington, 1982-87, adminstr. employment security, Dept. Labor, 1987-88, dep. asst. sec. employment and tng., 1988—. Recipient Disting. Career Service award Dept. Labor, 1979, Fed. women's Career award Sec. Labor, 1983, Presdl. Meritorious rank, 1987, Philip Arnow award, U.S. Dept. of Labor, 1988. Mem. Internat. Women's Forum, Women's Forum of Washington, Am. Civil Liberties Union, NOW, The Writer's Ctr., Pi Sigma Alpha. Episcopalian. Office: Dept Labor Employment & Training Adminstrn 200 Constitution Ave NW Washington DC 20210-0001

GOLDING, SUSAN, mayor; b. Muskogee, Okla., Aug. 18, 1945; d. Brage and Hinda Fay (Wolf) G.; children: Samuel, Vanessa. Cert. Pratique de Langue Francaise, U. Paris, 1965; BA in Govt. and Internat. Rels., Carleton Coll., 1966; MA in Romance Philology, Columbia U., 1974. Asssoc. editor Columbia U. Jour. of Internat. Affairs, N.Y.C., 1968-69; teaching fellow Emory U., Atlanta, 1973-74; instr. San Diego Community Coll. Dist., 1978; assoc. pub., gen. mgr. The News Press Group, San Diego, 1978-80; city council mem. City of San Diego, 1981-83; dep. sec. bus., transp., housing State of Calif., Sacramento, 1983-84; county supr. dist. 3 County of San Diego, 1984—; mayor City of San Diego, 1992—; founder Internat. Trade Commn., San Diego, 1985; chmn. San Diego Drug Strike Force, 1987-88, Alcohol and Drug Abuse Prevention Task Force, 1988, San Diego Earthquake Preparedness Com., 1986—, San Diego Unified Disaster Council, 1989—, San Diego Regional Justice Facility Financing Agy., 1989—, Calif. Environ. Quality Act Task Force, San Diego County Bd. Suprs., 1989—; dir. Svc. Auth. for Freeway Emergencies, San Diego, 1987; mem. Gov.'s Pub. Infrastructure Task Force, Mortgage Capital Task Force, Calif. Housing Fin. Agy., Calif. Coastal Commn.; mem. San Diego County Commn. on the Status of Women; bd. dirs. San Diego County Water Authority; trustee So. Calif. Water Com., Inc.; founder Mid City Comml. Revitalization Task Force; chair Pub. Svcs. and Safety Com. San Diego City Coun., Select Com. on Affordable Rental Housing; co-chair City County Reinvestment Task Force; vice-chair Transp. and Land Use Com. of City Coun. Bd. dirs. Child Abuse Prevention Found., San Diego Conv. and Vis. Bur., Crime Victims Fund, United Cerebral Palsy, San Diego Air Quality Bd., San Diego March of Dimes, Rep. Assocs.; adv. bd. Girl Scouts U.S.; trustee So. Calif. Water Comm.; mem. Rep. State Cen. Com.; co-chair com. Presidency George Bush Media Fund, Calif.; chair San Diego County Regional Criminal Justice Coun., race rels. com. Citizens Adv. Com. on Racial Intergration, San Diego Unified Sch. Dist.; hon. chair Am. Cancer Soc's. Residential Crusade, 1988. Named one of Ten Outstanding Rep. County Ofcls. in U.S.A., Rep. Nat. Com., 1987, San Diego Woman of Achievement Soroptimists Internat., 1988, One of San Diego's Ten Outstanding Young Citizens, 1981; recipient Calif. Women in Govt. Achievement award, 1988, Alice Paul award Nat. Women's Polit. Caucus, 1987, Willie Velasquez Polit. award Mex. Am. Bus. and Profl. Assn., 1988. Mem. Nat. Assn. of Counties (chair Op. Fair Share, mem. taxation and fin. com.), Nat. Women's Forum, Kiwanis, Sigma Delta Chi. Jewish. Office: Office of the Mayor City Administration Bldg 11th Fl 202 C St San Diego CA 92101-4806*

GOLDMAN, ARLENE LESLIE, distribution company executive; b. Paterson, N.J., July 7, 1956; d. Jacob and Bertha (Deck) G.; student Am. U., 1974. Asst. store mgr., asst. buyer Latt's Country Squire, Washington, 1976-77; ops. mgr. Complement, Washington, 1977-78; with Bidermann Industries, 1978-83, prodn. mgr. Jean-Paul Germain div., N.Y.C., 1979-80, dir. ops., 1980-81, v.p., 1981-83; nat. sales mgr. Ralph Lauren div., 1984-86; ind. cons., 1986; v.p. adminstrn. N.E. region KNP BT Office Products Inc., N.Y.C., 1986—; bd. dirs. Yeshiva U. Mem. Friend Whitney Mus., Met. Mus. Art (sustaining mem.), ORT. Home: 23 E 10th St Apt 608 New York NY 10003-6136 Office: BT Summit Office Products Inc 303 W 10th St New York NY 10014-2521

GOLDMAN, BARBARA DEREN, film producer, interior decorator; b. Bridgeport, Conn., Dec. 22, 1949; m. James Goldman, Oct. 25, 1975. Pres. Barbara Deren Assocs., N.Y.C., 1975—, Raoulfilm Inc., N.Y.C., 1979—; co-pres. Magellan Entertainment, 1994—; v.p. Trans-Internat. Revisions, 1980—. Co-author: Where to Eat in America, 1987; contbr. to book Feast of Wine and Food, 1987.

GOLDMAN, DEBBIE JOY, psychotherapist; b. Flushing, N.Y., Sept. 8, 1954; d. Jack Bernard and Sandra (Pentasky) Landis; m. Marshall S. Goldman, June 9, 1974; children: Joseph, Vanessa, Jarred. BA in Psychology cum laude, Alfred U., 1978; MS in Counseling, Nova U., 1988. Lic. mental health counselor, Fla. Therapist, intern Drug Abuse Treatment Assn., North Palm Beach, Fla., 1987; contract therapist Ctr. for Family Svcs., West Palm Beach, Fla., 1989; program dir., expressive therapist wellness unit inpatient Human Hosp., West Palm Beach, 1989-90; co-founder, v.p. Creative Potentials, Inc., Lake Park, Fla., 1990—; pvt. practice Lake Park, 1990—; founder, coord. Mother's Connection, North Palm Beach, 1983-85, group facilitator, guest lectr., 1985—, bd. dirs.; condr. workshops in field. Office: Creative Potentials 600 Sandtree Dr # 308 Lake Park FL 33403

GOLDMAN, JANICE GOLDIN, psychologist, educator; b. Phila., Feb. 15, 1938; d. Samuel and Dorothea (Berenson) Goldin; m. Arthur S. Goldman, Aug. 31, 1958; children: Jill Ann Goldman-Callahan, Joshua N., Jennifer S. BA, U. Pa., 1960, MA, 1962; MS, Hahnemann Med. Coll., 1972, D in Psychology, 1975. Lic. psychologist, Pa. Chief psychologist Charles Peberdy Child Psychiatry Ctr. Hahnemann U., Phila., 1975-87, from clin. asst. to assoc. prof., 1985-87; pvt. practice Jenkintown, Pa., 1977—; cons. Haverford (Pa.) State Hosp., 1982, Assn. for Mental Health Affiliates with Israel, 1984, 86; mem. profl. adv. bd. Pub. Radio Sta WHYY, Phila., 1984-86; workshop leader Women's Ctr. of Montgomery County, Jenkintown, 1982—. Contbr. articles to profl. jours. Board dirs. Assn. for Mental Health Affiliate with Israel, nationwide, 1984-88, Or Hadash Synogogue, Wyncote, Pa., 1989. Mem. APA, Am. Family Therapy Acad., Nat. Register Health Svc. Providers, Phila. Soc. Clin. Psychology (sec. 1977-79), Pa. Psychol. Assn., Internat. Soc. for Study Dissociation, Greater Phila. Soc. Clin. Hypnosis, Am. Soc. Clin. Hypnosis, Amnesty Internat., Phi Beta Kappa. Democrat. Office: Foxcroft Sq Apts 1250 Greenwood Ave Jenkintown PA 19046-2901

GOLDMAN, JILL MINKOFF, management consultant executive; b. Kansas City, Mo., July 12, 1953; d. Julius Burt and Eloise Joy (Shlensky) Minkoff; m. Barry Charles Goldman, Jan. 30, 1982; children: Joshua Scott, Elise Lynn. Certificat D'Assiduite, Université de Grenoble (France), 1968; BA, Pomona Coll., 1974. Mktg. rep. IBM, Riverside, Calif., 1974-77, San Francisco, 1978-79; dir. store systems Neiman Marcus, Dallas, 1979-81; dir. end-user computing services. Marion Labs., Kansas City, Mo., 1982-89, dir. info. systems data and techs., 1989—; dir. corp. info. systems Marion Merrell Dow Inc., 1989-91; dir. Bus. Process Improvement, 1992-93; pres. Visions Connections, Inc., Kans., 1993—. bd. dirs. Trenchancy, Inc., Creative Courseware. Sch. pres. ARC, Kansas City, Mo., 1966-67; v.p. chpt. B'nai B'rith Girls, Kansas City, 1968-69. Mem. Silicon Prairie Tech. Assn., Am. Technion Soc. (bd. dirs.). Home: 5406 State Line Rd Shawnee Mission KS 66208-1154 Office: Vision Connections 4210 Shawnee Mission Pkwy 100A Shawnee Mission KS 66205

GOLDMAN, JUDY ANN, contemporary fine arts curator, consultant, appraiser; b. N.Y.C., Nov. 20, 1942; d. Benjamin and Grace (Shamamian) G. BA, Brandeis U., 1964; postgrad., NYU Inst. of Fine Arts, 1964-67; cert. appraisal studies, NYU Sch. of Continuing Edn., 1993. Libr. Mus. of Modern Art, N.Y.C., 1968-72; editor RILA, Williamstown, Mass., 1972-73; registrar Harvard Law Sch., Art Collection, Cambridge, Mass., 1973-77; dir. Thomas Segal Gallery, Boston, 1980-92. Editor (exhib. catalogue) Barnett Newman, 1971, Richard Hunt, 1971, Romare Bearden, 1971; contbr. articles to profl. jours. Mem. Rose Mus. (chair collections com. 1992), Appraisers Assn. of Am., Coll. Art Assn. of Am., Boston Mus. of Fine Arts, Mus. of Modern Art, Harvard U. Art Mus.

GOLDMAN, LISA EACHUS, health facility administrator; b. Waltham, Mass., June 24, 1955; d. George Bloomfield and Genivive (Foti) Gallub; m. Edward Elliot Goldman, July 1, 1984; children: Melissa Ann, Audrey Carol. BS, Barry U., 1983, MBA, MPA, 1994. Tchr. Dade County and Miami (Fla.) Tech. Inst., 1982-84; v.p. Point Adult Communities, North Miami Beach, Fla., 1984-92; CFO, ptnr. Fla. Behavioral Network, Pembroke Pines, 1993—; pres. Statewide Mgmt. & Fin. Svcs. Corp., Pembroke Pines, 1993—; exec. v.p. Assocs. in Geriatric Psychology, Inc., Pembroke Pines, 1992—; ptnr. Goldsel Inc., Fort Lauderdale, Fla., 1990-92; real estate investor, Miami, 1976-88. Co-author: Bi-Lingual Resource Jour., 1990, 91. Active Miami Shores Performing Theater; mem. bd. overseers U. Miami. Mem. Alzheimer's Assn. (v.p. 1993), Fla. State Coun. on Alzheimer's Disease, Nat. Long Term Care Com. (bd. dirs. Dade County chpt. 1991), Nat. Coun. Jewish Women (v.p. 1989-91), S.O.A.R.I.N.G. (chpt. pres.), Infants in Need Inc. Home: 20801 NE 21st Ct N Miami Bch FL 33179-1616 Office: Fla Behavioral Network 3 SW 129th Ave Pembroke Pnes FL 33027-1778

GOLDMAN, MARY CECILE, marketing executive; b. Houston, June 10, 1956; d. James Cecil and Mary Elizabeth (Nelms) Rotenberry; m. Gary Lawrence Cohen, Apr. 22, 1989 (div. May 1994); 1 child, Eric Alexander. BA, Rice U., 1978; M in Mgmt., Northwestern U., 1980. Cons. Arthur Andersen, Chgo., 1980-81; product mgr., sr. product mgr., sr. ops. analyst Baxter Internat., Deerfield, Ill., 1981-86; dir. sales and mktg. Premier Health Alliance, Westchester, Ill., 1986-90; owner, pres. Babychic, Inc., Denver, 1990-92; mgr. market intelligence group Valleylab/Pfizer, Boulder, Colo., 1992—; cons. mktg. Access Technologies, Inc., Englewood, Colo., 1994. Mem. Colo. Mountain Club. Republican. Office: Valleylab/Pfizer 5920 Longbow Dr Boulder CO 80301

GOLDMAN, PATRICIA BAIRD, educator, trainer, counselor; b. Charleston, W.Va., Sept. 10, 1938; d. William Albert and Genevieve Mary (Lowpine) Baird; m. Richard M. Goldman, June 24, 1979; children: Bruce, Leigh, Crissy, John. BA in English, U. Charleston, 1961; MA in Counseling, W.Va. Grad. Coll., Institute, 1994. Asst. editor W.Va. Edn. Assn., Charleston, 1959-60; tchr. Kanawha County Schs., Charleston, 1961-62, Norfolk (Va.) City Schs., 1963-64, Fairfax County Schs., 1964-78, Tucker County Schs., Parsons, W.Va., 1984-86; tchr., coll. lectr. Davis & Elkins (W.Va.) Coll., 1987-90; exec. dir. Act II Retreat Ctr., St. George, W.Va., 1993—; mem. adj. faculty dept. counseling W.Va. Grad. Coll. Inst., 1995. Contbr. articles to profl. jours. Chair pub. awareness and edn. com. Tucker County Devel. Authority, Parsons, W.Va., 1986-90; pres., founder. Tucker County Literacy Vols. Am., Parsons, 1987-89. Ogden Meml. scholar, 1957-58. Mem. AAUW (state pres. and v.p. 1990—, grantee 1990-91), ACA, Am. Mental Health Counselors Assn., Internat. Assn. Marriage and Family Counselors, Assn. for Humanistic Edn. and Devel., Alpha Delta Kappa, Phi Mu Gamma. Home and Office: 1 Dogwood Ln Saint George WV 26290

GOLDMAN, PHYLLIS E., psychology educator. BA, Rutgers U., 1966; MA, Seton Hall U., 1969; MS, Stevens Inst. Tech., 1978; EdD, Seton Hall U., 1983. Rsch. asst. Rutgers Univ., Newark, 1965-66; counselor N.J. Dept. of Labor and Industry, Newark, 1967-69; prof., psychology County Coll. of Morris, Randolph, N.J., 1969—; pvt. practice cons., 1978—. Editor: (book) Dimensions of Work and Human Behavior, 1980, 85, (jour.) Morris Manager, 1988, 89, 90; contbr. articles to profl. jours. Mem. speakers bur. County Coll. of Morris, Randolph, 1976—; bd. advisors Cath. Community Svcs., Newark, 1978-80. Mem. Am. Psychological Assn., Psi Chi, Kappa Delta Pi, Phi Delta Kappa. Office: County Coll of Morris Rt 10 & Center Grove Rd Randolph NJ 07869

GOLDMAN, RACHEL BOK, civic volunteer; b. Phila., Mar. 28, 1937; d. W. Curtis and Nellie Lee (Holt) Bok; m. James Nelson Kise, Dec. 20, 1958 (div. May 1974); children: Jefferson B, C. Curtis; m. Allen S. Goldman, Nov. 28, 1981; stepchildren: Jonathan, Benjamin Allen, Adam Louis. Student, Sweet Briar (Va.) Coll., 1955-57; BA in Art History, U. Pa., 1977. Bd. dirs. Arts Exchange mag., 1977-79, chmn. bd. dirs., 1977-79. Mem. collector's circle Pa. Acad. Fine Arts, 1983-85, exhbn. selection com. Morris Gallery, 1979-82; mem. Rittenhouse Sq. Women's Com. Pa. Orchestra, 1979-85; mem. Indian com. Pa. Yearly Meeting, 1971-75; mem. ladies' com. Powel House, 1965-69; founder, pres. Friends of Curtis Inst. Music, 1982—, chmn. 1982-85; bd. dirs. Mary Louis Curtis Bok Found., 1982—, The Curtis Inst. Music, 1982—, The Buten Mus., 1982-84, Brady Cancer Rsch. Inst. 1983—, Settlement Music Sch., 1984-87, The Phila. Award, 1970—, Elfreth's Alley Assn., 1962-65, sec. 1963-65; bd. dirs. The Am. Found., 1955-83, sec.-treas., 1980-83; bd. dirs. The Community Sch. of Phila., 1971-74, chmn. bd. dirs., co-founder, adminstr.; bd. dirs. Women in Transition, 1973-78, div. counselor, 1974-76; bd. dirs. Friends of Phila. Mus. Art, 1977-83, sec., 1979-81, program chmn., 1981-82, co-chmn., 1982-83; bd. dirs. Samuel Yellin Found., 1977—, co-founder, sec., 1977-84; mem. com. Soc. for Contemporary Art, Art Inst. Chgo., 1988-90, exhibitrix-selection subcom., 1987-88; collectors' group Mus. Contemporary Art, Chgo., 1986-92; bd. dirs. Art Resources in Teaching (A.R.T.), 1987-93, Craniofacial Ctr., 1989—, AboutFace, 1993—, Bay Chamber Concerts Inc. 1993—. Democrat. Clubs: Camden Yacht (Maine), Cosmopolitan of Phila. (house com. 1981-84).

GOLDMAN, SHERRY ROBIN, public relations executive; b. Queens, N.Y., Mar. 2, 1958; d. Daniel and Alice (Epstein) G. BA, Hofstra U., 1980. Assoc. editor Gralla Publs., N.Y.C., 1980-84; account supr. G.S. Schwartz & Co. Publs., N.Y.C., 1984-87; v.p. Ruder-Finn, Inc., N.Y.C., 1987-95, sr. v.p., 1992-95; cons., 1995—. Mem. Pub. Rels. Soc. Am. (bd. dirs. N.Y. chpt. 1993—, Silver Anvil award 1991), Internat. Assn. Bus. Communicators, Nat. Assn. Profl. Environ. Communicators.

GOLDMAN, SUSAN JOSEPH, public relations executive; b. Newark, N.J., Oct. 4, 1957; d. Joseph and Deborah (Shapiro) Firkser; m. Richard G. Goldman, March 22, 1992. BS in Journalism, Northwestern U., 1979. Asst. editor Chicagoland Monthly, Chgo., 1979; feature editor Chgo. Daily Law Bulletin, 1980; acct. exec. Leigh Communications, Chgo., 1981; dep. press sec. Stevenson for Gov., Chgo., 1982; acct. exec. Carl Byoir & Assocs., Chgo., 1983-85; sr. acct. exec., acct. supr., acct. group supr., v.p. Golin/Harris Communications, Chgo., 1985-93, sr. v.p., 1993—. Researcher (book) Women's Networks, 1979. Recipient Silver Anvil award Pub. Rels. Soc. Am., 1986, Silver Trumpet award Publicity Club of Chgo., 1986, 87, 90, 92. Office: Golin/Harris Comms 500 North Michigan Ave # 200 Chicago IL 60657

GOLDSMITH, CAROLINE L., arts executive; b. N.Y.C., Nov. 25, 1925; d. Reuben and Gladys (Garf) Steinholz; m. Mortimer M. Lerner, Dec. 1, 1948 (div. Nov., 1968); children: Lawrence, David; m. John F. Goldsmith. BA, Cornell U., 1946. Pres. dir. Gallery Passport Ltd., N.Y.C., 1960-66; sr. v.p. Ruder Finn Arts and Comm. Counselors, N.Y.C., 1966—; exec. dir. Arttable, Inc., N.Y.C., 1980—. Mem. Community Bd., N.Y.C., 1987—. Mem. Am. Assn. Mus., Am. Fedn. Arts, Internat. Coun. Mus. Coll. Art Assn., Smithsonian Inst., Century Assn., Internat. Women's Forum (bd. dirs.). Democrat. Jewish. Home: 375 West End Ave New York NY 10024 Office: Ruder Finn Arts & Comm Counselors 301 E 57th St New York NY 10022

GOLDSMITH, CAROLYN THOMAS, artist; b. Gainesville, Fla., July 27, 1943; d. Sidney J. and Laura (Odom) Thomas; m. Maurice Leon Goldsmith, Sept. 4, 1964; children: Maurice Alexander, Thomas Michael, Richard Thomas. AA, Stephens Coll., 1963. represented by Abstein Gallery, Atlanta. One woman shows include U. of the South, Sewanee, Tenn., 1979, 80, Jr. League Hdqrs., Birmingham, Ala., 1980, Culligan Gallery, Huntsville, Ala., 1982, Town Hall Gallery, Birmingham, 1984, Atchison Gallery, Birmingham, 1985, Bargainer, McKee, Sims, Montgomery, Ala., 1986, Birmingham Pub. Libr. Gallery, 1987, Gallery at the Symphony, Birmingham, 1989, Edgewood, Montgomery, Ala., 1989, Monty Stabler Gallery, Birmingham, 1990, 91, 92, 93, 94, also numerous group exhbns. Democrat. Episcopalian. Office: Carolyn T Goldsmith Studio 1603 Wellington Rd Birmingham AL 35209-4020

GOLDSMITH, CATHY ELLEN, special education educator; b. N.Y.C., Feb. 18, 1947; d. Eli D. and Gertrude A. G. BS, NYU, 1968, MA in Elem. Edn., 1971, MA in Ednl. Psychology, 1974. Cert. phys. handicapped, K-6 elem. edn. tchr., N.Y. 2d grade tchr. N.Y.C. Bd. Edn., 1968-69, tchr. learning disabled students (spl. edn.), 1969-86, tchr. emat. disturbed learning disabled students, 1986-87, tchr. learning disabled students, 1987-88, tchr. trainable retarded students, 1988—. Represented in permanent collections Bobst Libr. NYU. Recipient Charles Oscar Maas Essay award in Am. History, 1968, Disting. Alumni Svc. award NYU, 1987. Mem. Nat. Profl. Assn. in Edn., Coun. for Exceptional Children, Coun. for Learning Disabilities, Found. for Exceptional Children, Orton Dyslexia Soc., N.Y. State-N.Y.C. Assn. Tchrs. Handicapped, NYU Alumni Leadership Coun. (rec. sec.), Pi Lambda Theta (past pres.). Home: 3 Washington Square Vlg New York NY 10012-1835

GOLDSMITH, ETHEL FRANK, medical social worker; b. Chgo., May 31, 1919; d. Theodore and Rose (Falk) Frank; m. Julian Royce Goldsmith, Sept. 4, 1940; children: Richard, Susan, John. BA, U. Chgo., 1940. Lic. social worker, Ill. Liaison worker psychiat. consultation service U. Chgo. Hosp., 1964-68; med. social worker Wyler Children's Hosp., Chgo., 1968—. Treas. U. Chgo. Service League, 1958-62, chmn. camp Brueckner Farr Aux., 1966-72; pres. Bobs Roberts Hosp. Service Commn., 1962; bd. dirs. Richardson Wildlife Sanctary, 1988—; mem. Field Mus. Women's Bd., 1966—; bd. dirs. Hyde Park Art Ctr., 1964-82, Chgo. Commons Assn., 1967-77, Alumni Assn. Sch. Social Service Adminstrn., 1976-80, Self Help Home for Aged, 1985—. Recipient Alumni Citation Pub. Service, U. Chgo., 1972. Mem. Phi Beta Kappa. Home: 5631 S Blackstone Ave Chicago IL 60637-1827 Office: Wyler Hosp Dept Social Svc 5841 S Maryland Ave Chicago IL 60637-1463

GOLDSMITH, KAREN LEE, lawyer; b. Bridgeport, Conn., Jan. 10, 1946; d. James Joseph and Marjorie (Crowley) Minto; m. Michael Goldsmith, Oct. 12, 1968 (dec. May 1979); children: Susan Chapman, Pamela S., Neil J.; m. Jeffery S. Hooie, June 13, 1980. AA summa cum laude, Seminole Jr. Coll., 1969; BA summa cum laude, U. Cen. Fla., 1975; JD cum laude, U. Fla., 1978. Bar: Fla. 1979, U.S. Dist. Ct. (mid. dist.) Fla. 1979, U.S. Dist. Ct. (so. and no. dists.) Fla. 1981, U.S. Ct. Appeals (11th cir.) 1981. Assoc. Pitts, Eubanks & Ross P.A., Orlando, Fla., 1978-80; assoc. Dempsey & Slaughter P.A., Orlando, 1980-83, ptnr., 1983; ptnr. Dempsey & Goldsmith P.A., Orlando, 1984-90, Goldsmith & Grout, P.A., Winter Park, Fla., 1990—; lectr. Interhome '86, Ft. Lauderdale, Fla., 1986—, health care related legal issues various orgns., 1978—; speaker profl. meetings, 1982—; speaker Harborside Healthcare Annual Convention, 1992, 94. Author: Advance Directives in Florida, 1993; sr. editor U. Fla. Law Rev., 1978; contbr. articles to profl. jours. Mem. ABA, Am. Health Care Assn. (legal subcom. 1991—, lectr. ann. symposium), Fla. Bar Assn. (chmn. state law week 1985, 86), Orange County Bar Assn. (outstanding chmn. 1982), Nat. Health Lawyers Assn. (speaker 1982, 85, 87, 88), Nat. Conv. Med. Dirs. Assn. (speaker 1992), Fla. Assn. Dirs. Nursing (speaker 1992), Fla. Health Care Assn. (various seminars 1992, 93, 94, 95), U. Cen. Fla. Alumni Assn. (bd. dirs., exec. com., sec. 1988), Am. Soc. Assn. Execs., Order of Coif, Phi Kappa Phi. Roman Catholic. Office: Goldsmith & Grout PA PO Box 2011 1420 Gene St Winter Park FL 32790-2011

GOLDSMITH, KATHLEEN MAWHINNEY, accountant; b. Bklyn., July 16, 1957; d. James R. and Carmela (Ditria) Mawhinney; m. Marc Bruce Goldsmith, Oct. 7, 1979; children: James Ryan, Jaclyn Samantha. BS, Alfred U., 1979; MBA, U. Conn., 1986. CPA, Conn. Acct., Price Waterhouse, Stamford, Conn., 1979-83; contr. OCE Bus. Systems Inc., Stamford, 1983-89; dir. planning and control Gestetner, Greenwich, Conn., 1989-90, dir. adminstrn., 1990-91, dir. ops., 1991-92; dir. Gestetner Svcs., 1992-93, dir ops. and corp. contr., 1993-94, CFO, 1994—. Adv., Jr. Achievement, 1980-81. Named one of Outstanding Young Women of Am. Mem. Am. Inst.

CPAs, Conn. Soc. CPAs, Phi Kappa Phi, Delta Mu Delta. Home: 24 Lamppost Dr West Redding CT 06896-1120 Office: Gestener Corp 599 W Putnam Ave Greenwich CT 06830-6005

GOLDSMITH, MAXINE IRIS, library administrator; b. Tarrytown, N.Y., Apr. 25, 1947; d. Abraham Herman and Florence (Levinsky) Kaplan; m. Brian P. Goldsmith, Apr. 3, 1971; children: Scott, Leslie. BS, Russell Sage Coll., 1969; MLS, Rugers U., 1970. Reference librarian McGraw-Hill, Inc., N.Y.C., 1970-71; periodicals librarian N.J. State Libr., Trenton, 1971-76; librarian N.J. Div. Criminal Justice, Trenton, 1976-77; libr. admistr. N.J. Dept. Higher Edn., Trenton, 1978-94, N.J. Dept. Ins., Trenton, 1994—; bd. dirs. adv. com. Sch. Communications, Info. & Libr. Svc., Rutgers U., New Brunswick, N.J.; bd. dirs. B.T.C. Mgmt. Corp. Editor: (index) Popular Periodicals Index, 1975-91; author: (bibliography) Going to College in New Jersey, 1978, 80, 91, 94. Bd. dirs. After Sch. program, Hopewell Valley, Pennington, N.J., 1988-94. Mem. Spl. Librs. Assn. (pres. Princeton-Trenton chpt. 1985-86, sec.-treas. edn. div. 1989-91, chair edn. div. 1992-93), Hadassah (fin. sec. Lawrence chpt. 1987-94, pres. 1994—). Jewish. Home: 16 Brandon Rd Trenton NJ 08638-1126 Office: NJ Dept of Ins 20 W State St CN325 Trenton NJ 08625

GOLDSMITH, NANCY CARROL, business and health services management educator; b. Conemaugh, Pa., May 11, 1940; d. John and Mary (Appley) Stinich; m. Sidney Goldsmith, Apr. 2, 1966. RN, Temple U., 1961; Assoc. summa cum laude, C.C. Phila., 1984; BS in Health Care Mgmt. summa cum laude, Phila. Coll. Textiles and Sci., 1986; MA in Health Care Adminstrn. summa cum laude, Antioch U., Yellow Springs, Ohio, 1988; PhD in Health Svcs. and Hosp. Adminstrn. summa cum laude, Southwest U., New Orleans, 1990. Nurse, head nurse to med. surg. supr. Temple U. Hosp., Phila., 1961-67; nursing rsch. assoc. Smith Klein & French, Inc. and Ames Med. Co., Phila. and Elkhart, Ind., 1967-69; sr. nursing rsch. assoc. NIH, Washington, 1969-75; adminstrv. supr. nursing svcs. Rolling Hill Hosp. and Diagnostic Ctr., Elkins Park, Pa., 1975-87, lectr. legal aspects nursing, 1980-90, dir. cost containment strategies, 1987-89, lectr. in health svcs. mgmt., 1989—, asst. dir. nursing svcs., 1988-89, nursing svcs. dir., 1989-90; prof. health svcs. adminstrn. and svcs. Phila. Coll. Textiles and Scis., 1991—, prof. bus. mgmt., 1992—; mem. adv. bd. health and wellness programs Phila. Coll. Textiles and Sci., 1993—; lectr. Sr. Edn. League, 1992—; lectr. in healthcare fin. and health svcs. adminstrn. Pa. State U., 1994; lectr. in health svcs. reform C.C. Phila., 1993—, Free Libr. Phila., 1994—; instr. med./surg. nursing Temple U. Sch. Nursing, 1964-67, chmn. ann. fundraising, 1978-86. Author 2 books. Inventor use of dextrostix in hypoglycemic range, 1972 (Rsch. award 1974); co-patentee multipurpose biopsy needle, 1972; mem. editorial bd. Coll. Textiles Newletter, 1993—. Recipient Mayor's Liberty Bell award City of Phila., 1978, Legion of Honor award Chapel of Four Chaplains, 1981, Capitol award Nat. Leadership Coun., 1991, Excellence in Teaching Highest award Pa. Coll. Textiles and Sci., 1993; named to Hall of Fame, Internat. Profl. and Bus. Women's Assn., 1994. Mem. Am. Hosp. Assn., Am. Mgmt. Assn., Temple U. Nurse's Alumni Assn. (bd. dirs., v.p. 1991-92, pres. 1993-94, dir. continuing edn. com. 1986—), Temple U. Gen. Alumni Assn. (bd. dirs. 1980-88, 93—, Disting. Svc. award 1984), Downtown Club Temple U., Phi Beta Kappa, Phi Theta Kappa (pres. Delta of Pa. chpt. 1991-94, Honors Hall of Fame 1991). Jewish. Office: Phila Coll Textiles & Sci School House Ln Henry Ave Philadelphia PA 19144

GOLDSTEIN, BARBARA JOAN, sculptor; b. Chgo.; d. Charles Martin and Constance Evangeline (Bredeson) Kaplan; m. Michael Louis Goldstein, June 18, 1967; children: Rachel Rebecca, Elizabeth Caroline, Adam Charles. BA, Conn. Coll. for Women, 1967; MA, U. Chgo., 1969; postgrad., U. Utah, 1986-88. Child therapist Pritzker Sch., Chgo., 1969-70, Santa Clara County Health Dept., San Jose, Calif., 1970-71; sculptor Salt Lake City, 1970—. Represented in permanent collections U. Utah Med. Ctr., Nat. Kidney Found. Utah, Jewish Cmty. Ctr. Denver, Utah Mus. of Fine Arts, Salt Lake City Art Ctr., among others. Past pres. Salt Lake City Jewish Cmty. Ctr.; bd. dirs. Salt Lake City Art Ctr., 1992-93; Salt Lake City rep. Interfaith Forum on Religion, Art and Arch., 1992—. Mem. NASW, Phi Beta Kappa. Home and Office: 2720 Shadybrook Ln Salt Lake City UT 84121-1539

GOLDSTEIN, CHARLOTTE L(IPSON), marketing professional, public relations executive; b. Boston, Aug. 1, 1929; d. George Lipson and Frances (Feldstein) L.; m. Norman R. Goldstein, Sept. 15, 1948; children—Sue, David, Julie. Student Mary Brooks Coll., 1945-47. Pres. Engineered Inspection System, Robbinsville, N.J., 1970—. Contbr. articles to profl. jours. Bd. dirs. Congregation Beth Chaim, 1977-82, Sunday Sch. tchr., 1952-69, adult edn. com., mem. bd. continuing edn., caring coms.; charter mem. West Windsor Library Commn., 1981-85; mem. West Windsor Twp. Commn. on Aging. Mem. Middlesex County (N.J.) Bd. Realtors (assoc.), Mercer County Bd. Realtors, Hunterdon County Bd. Realtors, So. Monmouth County Bd. Realtors, Somerset County Bd. Realtors, Burlington County Bd. Realtors, Pa.-Bucks County C. of C. Princeton C. of C., Mercer C of C. Republican. Jewish. Clubs: Hadassah (pres. 1952-53), B'nai B'rith (bd. dirs. 1968-70). Avocations: china painting, cooking, traveling, bridge, reading. Home: 10 Jeffrey Ln Princeton Junction NJ 08550-1608 Office: Engineered Inspection System Inc 1200 Route 130 Robbinsville NJ 08691

GOLDSTEIN, DORIS MUELLER, librarian, researcher; b. Somerville, N.J., Mar. 11, 1942; d. Henry Frederick and Sophie (Lages) Mueller; m. Steven Morris Goldstein, July 4, 1971. BA, U. Nebr., 1964, MA, 1966; cert., Goethe U., Frankfurt, Fed. Republic Germany, 1966; MLS, U. Md., 1973. Vol., instr. Peace Corps, Addis Abeba, Ethiopia, 1966-68; cataloger Libr. of Congress, Washington, 1968-69; instr. Bowie (Md.) State Coll., 1969-72; libr. Kennedy Inst. of Ethics Georgetown U., Washington, 1973-81, dir. libr. and info. svcs., 1981—, dir. Nat. Reference Ctr. for Bioethics Lit., 1984—; cons. dept. nursing George Mason U., Fairfax, Va., 1984-89; adj. faculty mem. in libr. sci. U. Md., 1990. Author: Bioethics: A Guide to Information Sources, 1982; editor Scope Note Series, 1985—; contbr. articles to profl. jours. Ford Found. grantee, 1964. Mem. Spl. Librs. Assn., Med. Libr. Assn., D.C. Libr. Assn., Phi Beta Kappa, Alpha Lambda Delta, Delta Phi Alpha, Beta Phi Mu. Office: Georgetown U Kennedy Inst Ethics Washington DC 20057

GOLDSTEIN, ELEANOR, artist, social worker; b. N.Y.C., May 2, 1935; d. Benjamin and Gertrude (Bober) Kronish; m. Alvin Goldstein, Dec. 27, 1959; children: Eric, Michael, Eileen. BA, Bennington (Vt.) Coll., 1957; MSW, Columbia U., 1981. Cert. social worker, N.Y. Asst. dir. Westchester Student Adv. Coalition, White Plains, N.Y., 1981-82, exec. dir., 1982-85; free lance artist Hastings-on-the-Hudson, N.Y., 1985—. Bd. dirs. Hastings-on-the-Hudson Recreation Commn., 1976-78; v.p. Hastings Learning Disabilities Com., 1974-76; organizer Hastings Com. for Youth, Inc., 1976-79. Mem. Hudson River Contemporary Artists, Nat. Assn. Women Artists, Hastings League Women Voters (bd. dirs. 1973-75). Home and Office: 1 Chester Ter Hastings On Hudson NY 10706-3907

GOLDSTEIN, ELISABETH HARLOW BUCK, artist, graphic designer, educator; b. Boston, Feb. 25, 1954; d. Robert Day and June Merry (Schirmer) Buck; m. Allen Goldstein, Sept. 6, 1980. BFA, Mass. Coll. Art, 1976; cert., Parsons Sch. Design, 1982, Pratt Inst., 1983, Pocono Pines Workshops, 1991. Art dir. Dow Jones Pub., N.Y.C., 1976-77, Am. Heritage, N.Y.C., 1978, Danskin, N.Y.C., 1978-82, Lisa Buck Graphic Design, N.Y.C., 1982-85, Leavitt Advt., N.Y.C., 1985-88; tchr. Pa. Ctr. for Art, Stroudsburg, 1992-93; bd. dirs., chair gallery com., chair members exhbn. Monroe County Arts Coun., Stroudsburg, 1990—. Solo exhbns. include East Stroudsburg (Pa.) U., The Madelon Powers Art Gallery of Fine and Performing Arts, 1989; group shows include Lehigh U., Bethlehem, Pa., 1990, James Morgan Gallery, Pocono Pines, Pa., 1990, Abbington Art Galleries, Easton, Pa., 1990, Salmagundi Club Galleries, N.Y.C., 1990, 92, 93, 94, N.Y.C., 1993, Art Inst. Phila., 1990, Woodmere Art Mus., Phila., 1990, 91, 92, 94, Widener U. Mus., Chester, Pa., 1991, Bethlehem (Pa.) City Hall Rotunda Gallery, 1992, Nat. Arts Club, N.Y.C., 1994, Muhlenberg Coll., Allentown, Pa., 1994, Wayne (Pa.) Ctr. for Arts, 1994, numerous others; co-editor: (video) Where Are We Going, Artistic Expression Moving Towards the Turn of the Century, 1991. Curator Sherman Arts Ctr., Stroudsburg, 1991-93; chair Student Portfolio Seminar with Nancy Bossart, Stroudsburg, 1993; juror student exhbn. Monroe County Arts Coun., 1993, 94. Recipient Hazleton Art League award, 1992, 94, Best of Show award Pocono Manor Fine Art Exhbn., 1992. Mem. Am. Artist Profl. League, Pa. Watercolor Soc. (Keystone award 1993), N.Y. Artist Equity Assn., Lehigh Art Alliance (Binney & Smith award 1993), Phila. Watercolor Club (exhibiting, Dana Meml. award 1992, Strathmore Paper Co. award 1994), W.Va. Watercolor Soc. Home: RR 4 Box 4014 Stroudsburg PA 18360

GOLDSTEIN, JUDITH SHELLEY, reading and learning specialist; b. Bklyn., Mar. 5, 1935; d. Maurice and Mary (Goldstein) G. BA, Adelphi U., 1956; MA, Columbia U., 1957; EdD, Hofstra U., 1984. Cert. permanent tchr. in reading, spl. and elem. edn., N.Y. Early childhood tchr. N.Y.C. Sch. System, Bklyn., 1957-80; reading specialist Southampton (N.Y.) Unified Sch. Dist., 1981-87; spl. edn. tchr. Amagansett (N.Y.) Sch., 1987-88; mem. adj. faculty C.W. Post Campus, L.I. U., Brookville, N.Y., 1984-88; supr. clin. practice Southampton Campus L.I. U., 1988—; exec. dir. nursery sch. Jewish Ctr. of Hamptons, East Hampton, N.Y., 1988-89; bd. dirs. Alternatives East End Counseling Project, Southampton, 1989—; adj. assoc. prof. Southampton Campus L.I.U., 1989—, Dowling Coll., 1990-92, Suffolk County C.C., 1989—. Mem. Guild Hall, East Hampton, 1980—; v.p. edn. Hadassah, East Hampton, 1989-92; chair Am. Affairs, 1993—; tchr. religious ch. Jewish Ctr. of the Hamptons, 1990—. Mem. ASCD, AAUW (v.p. programming 1987-89, sec. 1993—), Internat. Reading Assn. Democrat. Home: 138 Windward Rd East Hampton NY 11937-3189

GOLDSTEIN, LAURA ROSE, executive; b. Phila., Apr. 30, 1951; d. Joseph and Tybie J. (Jackins) G. BA, U. Denver, 1974; BSN, Widener Coll., 1979. RN, Fla., Pa. Nurse Riddle Meml. Hosp., Media, Pa., 1979-80, Chester-Crozer Med. Ctr., Chester, Pa., 1980-82, Biomed. Community Dialysis Ctr., Beverly Hills, Calif., 1982-83; exec. asst., treas., supr. sales Transfermania, Inc., Hialeah, Fla., 1983—. Docent Zool. Soc. Fla., Miami, 1986-88; vol. Red Cross Hurricane Shelter, Miami, 1984-85, Am. Heart Assn., Media, 1977-79; leader Girl Scouts Am., Denver, 1974-76. Mem. Internat. Assn. Counselors & Therapists (cert. hypnotherapist 1992—), Psi Gamma Mu. Independent. Jewish. Office: 3240 W 16th Ave Hialeah FL 33012-4606

GOLDSTEIN, LINDA NEWMAN, publishing executive; b. Newark, May 2, 1945; d. Daniel and Beatrice (Birnbaum) N. m. Neil Goldstein, 1986. BA, U. Pitts., 1966. Pub. rels. dir. N.Y.C. Dept. Cultural Affairs, N.Y., 1968-70; N.Y. State Council Arts, 1970-74; communication dir. N.Y.C. Bicentennial, 1974-76; v.p., advt. dir. Omni mag., N.Y.C., 1978-89; v.p., assoc pub., 1989—; cons. in field. Fund raising coord., Mayor Ed Koch, N.Y., 1976; mem. young leadership council United Jewish Appeal, N.Y., 1983-84; career conf. chmn. Advt. Women of N.Y., 1984; fund raiser N. Am. Conf. Ethiopian Jewry, N.Y., 1985; Advt. Club N.Y. (mem. com. 1987, 88, 89). Avocations: snow skiing, tennis. Office: Omni Mag 1965 Broadway New York NY 10023-5904

GOLDSTEIN, LYNDA GARNER, county legislator; b. Rochester, N.Y., May 15, 1953; d. Reuben and Mary (Garson) Garner; m. Richard Goetz Goldstein, Oct. 29, 1977; children: Mollie, Zachary. BA, U. Rochester, 1974. Asst. dir. devel. Rochester (N.Y.) Philharm. Orch., 1975-77; manpower prodn. coord. City of Rochester, 1978-80; town council mem. Town of Brighton, N.Y., 1990-92; county legislator County of Monroe, N.Y., 1993—; dir. pub. affairs Adam Walsh Ctr., 1994—. Chair, CEO, bd. dirs. Rochester Broadway Theatre League, 1986—; bd. dirs. Brighton Edn. Fund, 1992—, Brighton Parkland Fund, 1993—, Rochester Family Resource Network, 1994—. Mem. Brighton Kiwanis (bd. dirs. 1994). Democrat. Home: 260 Danbury Cir N Rochester NY 14618

GOLDSTEIN, MARCIA LANDWEBER, lawyer; b. Bklyn., Aug. 7, 1952; d. Jacob and Sarah Ann (Danovitz) Landweber; m. Mark Lewis Goldstein, June 3, 1973. AB, Cornell U., 1973, JD, 1975. Bar: N.Y. 1976, U.S. Dist. Ct. (so. and ea. dists.) N.Y., U.S. Ct. Appeals (2d, 7th and 9th cirs.). Assoc. Weil, Gotshal & Manges, N.Y.C., 1975-83, ptnr., 1983—; visiting lectr. Yale U. Mem. ABA (com. on creditors' rights, corp. counse. com.), Assn. of Bar of City of N.Y. (bankruptcy and reorgn. com.), Practicing Law Inst. (ALI-ABA panels, NYU bankruptcy workshop panel), Nat. Bankruptcy Conf. Office: Weil Gotshal & Manges 767 Fifth Ave New York NY 10153-0001

GOLDSTEIN, MARSHA FEDER, tour company executive; b. Chgo., July 7, 1945; d. Charles S. and Geraldine (Shulman) Feder; m. Michael Warren Goldstein, Dec. 26, 1966; 1 child, Paul Goldstein. B.A., Roosevelt U., Chgo., 1967. Tchr. art Chgo. Pub. Schs., 1967-68; free-lance artist, Chgo., 1968-71; tchr. architecture Brandeis U., Northfield, Ill., 1974-80; tour guide My Kind of Town Tours, Highland Park, Ill., 1975-79, owner, 1979—; owner, Tours at the Mart, 1992—; art cons. Randall Pub. Co., Inc., 1984—. Editor: Highland Park by Foot or Frame, 1980. Contbr. to book in field. Chmn., commr. Highland Park Hist. Preservation Commn.; bd. dirs. Roosevelt U., Chgo.; charter mem. Nat. Mus. Women in the Arts. Recipient Cert. of Completion, Chgo. Arch. Found., 1975; Cert. of Appreciation, Machinery Dealers Nat. Assn., 1982. Mem. Nat. Assn. Women Bus. Owners (bd. dirs. Chgo. chpt., pres.), Women's Exec. Network, Chgo. Assn. Commerce & Industry (active youth motivation program), Chgo. Conv. and Tourism Bd. (mem. devel. com.), Chgo. Soc. Assn. Execs., Milw. Conv. and Tourism Bd., The Auditorium Bldg. Soc. (founder, chmn. 1994). Republican. Jewish. Club: Brandeis U. Nat. Women (bd. dirs., v.p. 1977—). Home: 1585 Tara Ln Lake Forest IL 60045-1221 Office: My Kind of Town Tours PO Box 924 Highland Park IL 60035-0924

GOLDSTEIN, MARY KANE, physician; b. N.Y.C., Oct. 24, 1950; d. Edwin Patrick and Mary Kane; m. Yondel Noah Goldstein, June 24, 1979; children: Keira, Gavi. Philosophy degree, Columbia U., 1973, MD, 1977; MS in Health Svcs. Rsch., Stanford U., 1994. Resident Duke U. Med. Ctr., Durham, N.C., 1977-80; asst. prof. medicine U. Calif., San Francisco, 1980-84; staff physician Cowell Student Health Ctr. U. Calif., Santa Cruz, 1984-85, clin. instr. dept. family and cmty. preventive medicine, 1984-85; staff physician Mid-Peninsula Health Svc., Palo Alto, Calif., 1986-88; dir. grad. med. edn. Stanford (Calif.) U., 1986-93, Agy. for Health Care Policy Rsch. fellow Sch. Medicine, 1991-94; sect. chief for gen. internal medicine Palo Alto (Calif) VA Med. Ctr., 1994—; editor Computer Ctr. Pubs., N.Y.C., 1971-72; computer programmer Columbia U., N.Y.C., 1972-73; faculty assoc. Stanford Sch. Medicine, 1992; chair ethic com. U. Calif./Natividad Med. Com., San Francisco, 1984. Author chpt. to book; contbr. articles to profl. jours. Recipient Rsch. award Far West HSR & D, 1990, Expanding Rsch. award Charles H. Dana Found., 1990, Cost Implications award Hartford Found. Geriatric Ctr., 1991, Preference Assessment in Geriatrics award Palo Alto Inst. for Rsch. and Edn., 1992. Fellow Am. Geriatrics Soc.; mem. Am. Bd. Family Practice (bd. dirs. 1993—), Am. Fedn. Clin. Rsch., Geriatric Test Com. Office: Palo Alto VA Med Ctr/Stanford U 3801 Mirande Ave Palo Alto CA 94304

GOLDSTEIN, PAMELA ELIZABETH, public relations executive; b. Orange, N.J., Apr. 24, 1945; d. William and Jewel Elizabeth (Thomas) G.; m. Robert N. Kornberg, April 14, 1974. BS in Journalism, Boston U., 1967. Reporter Courier News, Plainfield, N.J., 1963-64; adminstrv. asst. Action for Boston (Mass.) Community Devel., 1964—; publicity dir. Am. Program Bur., Boston, 1964—; mem. pub. rels. staff Gubernatorial Candidate, Boston, 1970; writer Statehouse News Svc., Boston, 1970; pub. rels. placement dir. Bryant & Stratton Jr. Coll., Boston, 1970-72; pub. rels. cons. Bruno Assocs., Newark, N.J., 1973-76; mem. pub. rels. office Newark City Coun., 1976-86; pub. rels. mgr., press sec. to mayor City of Newark, 1986—; pub. affairs rels. cons. Mental Health Assocs., East Orange, N.J., 1984—; workshop facilitator and panelist. vice chair Roseland Dem. Party, 1984—; coord. for N.J. Boston U. Alumni Sch. Com., 1975—; mem. Channel 13 N.J. Adv. Bd., 1986—; mem. City Without Walls Gallery, 1980—; mem. bd. dirs. Essex County Am. Cancer Soc., 1993—. Mem. Pub. Rels. Soc. Am. Jewish. Home: 19 Stonegate Dr Roseland NJ 07068 Office: City of Newark 920 Broad St Newark NJ 07102

GOLDSTEIN, PEGGY R., sculptor; b. N.Y.C., Jan. 16, 1921; d. Francis Mortimer and Ruth (Schram) Rosenfeld; m. E. Ernest Goldstein, June 22, 1941; children: Susan Lipsitch, Daniel Frank. AB, Smith Coll., 1941; student, Art Inst. Chgo., 1941-42, Corcoran Sch. Art, 1951-52, Acad. de la Grand Chaumière, Paris, 1952-53, Atelier 17, Paris, 1953, 66-67, Acad. de Peinture Orientale, Paris, 1973-75. tchr. Anacostia Neighborhood Mus., Smithsonian Instn., Washington, 1967-68, Am. Coll., Paris, 1976-77. One woman shows include Creative Gallery, N.Y.C., 1951, 53, Springfield Mus. Fine Arts, Mass., 1956, SW Tex. State Coll., San Marcos, 1960, Laguna Gloria, Austin, 1956, 61, Maison du Décor, Washington, 1968, Gottesman and Ptnrs., London, 1976, Galerie Lambert, Paris, 1970, 73, 77, 78, Galerie de la Cathédrale, Fribourg, 1981, Galerie Cimaise, Lausanne, 1983, Galerie Cardas, Lausanne, 1983, Galerie Valentine, Bex, 1984, Galerie Farel, Aigle, 1982, 85, Le Vieux Bourg, Denges, 1987, Galerie Motte, Geneva, 1989; exhibited in group shows at Salon de la Jeune Sculpture, 1961, 71-76, Salon de Mai, 1970, 72, 73, 77, Galerie Horizon, 1978—, Galerie Picpus, Montreux, 1981, Biennale of Fedn. Internat. de la Médaille, 1983, 85, 87, Création 85, Montreux, 1986, France-Chine, Marseille, 1987, Gravure, Paris, 1987, Galerie Siret, Paris, 1987—, U. Fribourg, 1988, La Fondation Taylor, Paris, 1990, Galerie Les Hirondelles, Coppet, 1990, Bibliothèque Nationale, Paris, 1992; U.S. Info. Agy. exhbns. Latin Am.; represented in permanent collections Bibliothèque Nationale, Paris, Nat. Archives, Washington, Musée Jenisch, Vevey, Bibliothèque Nationale, Berne; also pvt. collections; executed bronze outdoor sculpture, Nat. Hdqrs. Am. Camping Assn., Ind., 1987, 2 bronze mural sculptures, Austin, 1988; designer 20 medals Adminstrn. des Monnaies et Médailles, Ministère de Fin., Paris, 1973-86; illustrator: At Home After 1840, 1965; author, calligrapher: Lóng is a Dragon: Chinese Writing for Children, 1990 (Gold award Parents Choice 1991); author, calligrapher, illustrator: Ma Ma Hu Hu, An Introduction to Chinese Writing, 1995; contbr. articles to jours. Recipient Sculpture prize Soc. Washington D.C. Artists, 1954, Small Sculpture award Ball State Tchrs. Coll., 1961, Prize, UPFS Concours de Masque, 1977; Préfecture de Paris grantee, 1971. Fellow Creation 85, Le Bois Grave, Headliners Club (Austin, Tex.). Home: 1619 Northumberland Rd Austin TX 78703

GOLDSTEIN, SUSAN BETH, communications educator; b. N.Y.C., Oct. 3, 1944; d. Eli and Gertrude (Wasserman) G.; m. Martin Kenneth Goldstein, Dec. 5, 1982; 1 child, Gregory Eli. BA cum laude, Bklyn. Coll., 1965; MS, U. Mich., 1966. Cert. communications specialist. Speech and language cons. Columbia Presbyn. Hosp., N.Y.C., 1966-67; lectr. speech Baruch Coll., 1969—; therapist in communications-centered activities Ctr. for Mental Help, N.Y.C., 1970-73; cons. Susan B. Goldstein & Assocs., N.Y.C., 1985—; pub. speaker Fed. Trade Commn., N.Y.C., 1982, Met. Mus. Art, 1986-87, Dept. Aging, 1986, Am. Jewish Com., 1986, Fordham U., 1986. Co-author: The Communication Contract, 1974; contbr. articles to profl. jours. Organizer Siddha Yoga Dham Assn. Found. UN, 1978-80; v.p. Brandeis U. Women's Com., 1986-87. Vocat. Rehab. Assn. fellow, 1965. Mem. Am. Soc. for Tng. and Devel. Democrat. Jewish. Home: 429 E 52nd St New York NY 10022-6430

GOLDSTON, BARBARA M. HARRAL, editor; b. Lubbock, Tex., Jan. 26, 1937; d. Leonard Paul and Olivette (Stuart) Harral; m. John Rowell Toman (div. 1963); 1 child, Stuart Rowell; m. Olan Glen Goldston, 1989. BE, Tex. Christian U., 1959; MLS, U. Hawaii, 1968; postgrad., Golden Gate U., 1980-82. Tchr. pub. elem. schs., various cities, Tex. and Hawaii, 1959-66; contracts abstractor, indexer Champlin Oil Co., Ft. Worth, 1963-64; adminstrv. asst. engring. Litton Industries, Lubbock, Tex., 1964-65; mgr. rsch. library Hawaii Employers' Coun., Honolulu, 1968-72; rsch. cons. Thailand Hotel Study, Touche-Ross Assocs., Honolulu, 1974; dir. med. library U. S.D.-Sacred Heart Hosp., Yankton, 1977-79; editor, adminstrv. coord. book div. ABC-Clio, Inc., Santa Barbara, Calif., 1981-88; free-lance rsch./editorial cons. Albuquerque, 1988-89; instr. Santa Fe Community Coll., 1989—; owner Sandbar Prodns., Albuquerque, 1993—; ptnr. Broome-Harral, Inc., Albuquerque, 1989—. Author, editor with others Hist. Periodical Dir., 5 vols., World Defense Forces compendium. Contbr. Boy's Ranch, Amarillo, Tex., 1987—; mem. Lobero Theater Group, Santa Barbara, 1975-76; mem., treas. Yankton Med. Aux., 1977-79. Mem. ALA, Spl. Libraries Assn., Med. Libraries Assn., Am. Soc. Info. Sci., Albuquerque C. of C., Albuquerque Conv. and Visitors Bur., Better Bus. Bur. Albuquerque, Tex. Christian U. Alumni Assn., Delta Delta Delta. Republican. Episcopalian. Home: 9300 Seabrook Dr NE Albuquerque NM 87111-5863 Office: PO Box 3824 Albuquerque NM 87190-3824

GOLDTHWAITE, MARY JANE, lawyer; b. Cleve., Jan. 3, 1947; d. Allen Benson and Margaret Goldthwaite. B.A., Smith Coll., 1969; J.D., Ohio State U., 1973. Bar: Ohio 1973, U.S. Dist. Ct. (so. dist.) Ohio, 1974. Assoc. Porter, Wright, Morris & Arthur, Columbus, Ohio, 1973-78, ptnr., 1979; v.p., chief adminstrv. officer, gen. counsel, sec. ChemLawn Corp., Columbus, 1980-88; sr. v.p., chief adminstrv. officer, gen. counsel, sec. The Kobacker Co., 1992-94. Bd. dirs. Columbus U.S.A. Assn., 1983-84. Mem. ABA, Ohio State Bar Assn., Columbus Bar Assn., Am. Corp. Counsel Assn. (pres. Columbus chpt. 1985-86), Am. Soc. Corp. Secs. Office: Kobacker Co 6606 Tussing Rd PO Box 16751 Columbus OH 43216-6751

GOLDWASSER, SHIRLEY WHITEMAN, educational psychologist; b. Atlanta, June 25, 1935; d. Ben W. and Sarah R. (Abelman) Whiteman; m. M. Robert Goldwasser, June 24, 1956; children: Elise S., Kenneth L. BA, Ga. State U., 1976, MEd, 1978, PhD, 1988. Grad. rsch. asst. Ga. State U., Atlanta, 1978-79, assoc. grant dir., 1981-82, instr., 1979-83, program devel. specialist, 1984-86; edn. cons. Galloway Sch., Atlanta, 1986-88; prof. Piedmont Coll., Demorest, Ga., 1990-93; ednl. psychologist Raleigh, N.C., 1993—; presenter in field. Co-editor: Minimum Competency Education: Issues, Methodology and Policy for Local Sch. Systems, 1982. Docent N.C. Mus. Art, Raleigh, 1993—; mem. speaker's bureau Prevent Child Abuse N.C., Raleigh, 1993—. Teaching fellow Ga. State U., 1979-83. Mem. APA, Nat. Women's Studies Assn., Southeastern Psychol. Assn., Psy Chi. Home and Office: 33 Renwick Ct Raleigh NC 27615

GOLEC, JENNIFER JANE, insurance underwriter; b. Hartford, Conn.; d. Edward John and R. Jane (Bancroft) G. BA, Ctrl. Conn. State U., 1987; MBA, U. Conn., 1990; postgrad., U. Mo., 1994—. Tax analyst The Travelers, Hartford, Conn., 1987-90, auditor, 1990-91; fin. planner The Travelers, Farmington, Conn., 1991-92; customer svc. rep. The Travelers, Walnut Creek, Calif., 1992-94; underwriter, mem. sales staff The Travelers, Overland Park, Kans., 1994—. Mem. Mothers Against Drunk Drivers, Conn., 1989-92. Office: Travelers 7500 College Blvd Overland Park KS 66212

GOLLER, SUE LYNNE, political worker; b. Jefferson City, Mo., Oct. 22, 1961; d. David Rudolph and Dorothy Eda (Linhardt) G. BSBA, U. Mo., 1984. CPA, Mo. Staff Mo. Rep. party, Jefferson City, 1981; intern U.S. Senator John Danforth, Washington, 1983; staff Hansen-Beck and Co. CPAs, Columbia, 1984; auditor Mo. State Auditor's Office, Jefferson City, 1984-86; spl. asst. to state treas. State of Mo., Jefferson City, 1986-88; adminstrv. asst. Rep. caucus Mo. Ho. of Reps., Jefferson City, 1988-92, adminstrv. asst. to Rep. floor leader, 1992-94. Mem. Mo. Soc. CPAs, Assn. Govt. Accts., Jaycees, Mystical Seven, Omicron Delta Kappa. Lutheran.

GOLLIN, SUSANNE MERLE, cytogeneticist, cell biologist; b. Chgo., Sept. 22, 1953; d. Harvey A. and Pearl (Reiffel) G.; m. Lazar M. Palnick; 1 child, Jacob Hillel Palnick, Oct., 1991. BA in Biology, Northwestern U., 1974, MS, 1975, PhD, 1980. Diplomate Am. Bd. Med. Genetics, Clin. Cytogenetics. Postdoctoral fellow U. Rochester Med. Ctr. (N.Y.), 1979-81; rsch. assoc. in cell biology Baylor Coll. of Medicine, Houston, 1981-83, rsch. assoc. in genetics, 1983-84; asst. prof. dept. pathology and pediatrics U. Ark. Med. Scis., 1984-87; dir. cytogenetics lab. Ark. Children's Hosp., 1984-87; assoc. mem. Pitts. Cancer Inst., 1987—; asst. prof. human genetics U. Pitts., 1987—, dir. clin. cytogenetics lab., 1988—; mem. pediatric oncology group., mem. exec. com. Ark. Genetics Program, 1984-87; mem. organizing com. Am. Cytogenetics Conf., 1990—; mem. Allegheny County Bd. Health, 1992—, clin. lab. improvement adv. com. Ctrs. Disease Control and Prevention, HHS, 1994—. Contbr. articles to profl. jours. Mem. deans' adv. com. Pa. Sch. Excellence for Healthcare Profls., 1991—; mem. faculty senate exec. com. U. Pitts. Grad Sch. Pub. Health, 1992-94, pub. health affirmative action com., 1992-94, v.p. faculty senate, 1994—; vol. Lighthouse for the Blind, Houston, 1983; chmn. med. ethics and civil liberties com. ACLU, Pitts., 1989-91; alt. del. Dem. Nat. Conv., 1992. Fellow Am. Coll. Med. Genetics (founder); mem. AAAS, Am. Soc. Human Genetics, Am. Soc. Cell Biology, Soc. Analytical Cytology, Pitts. Cancer Inst., Southwest Oncology Group (core com. cytogenetics), Pitts. Cytogenetics Club (founder, coord. 1989), Sigma Xi. Avocations: gardening, photography, pulled thread embroidery. Office: U Pitts Dept Human Genetics 130 DeSoto St Pittsburgh PA 15261

GOLLIS, ELAINE SANDRA, nurse; b. Fall River, Mass., Mar. 30, 1938; d. Harold and Esther (Packer) G.; m. Pasquale Margiotta, May 16, 1968 (div. Oct. 1986); children: Ellen, Mark. Nurse, Worcester City Hosp., 1959; BS, Post Coll., 1989; MS, Hartford Grad. Ctr., 1992. Dir. nursing Hebrew Home and Hosp., Hartford, Conn., 1963-68, Jewish Home for Aged, San Francisco, 1968; clin. supr. Hebrew Home and Hosp., Hartford, 1989-92, coord. patient care, 1981-82, clinic coord. ambulatory care, 1982-84, ombudsman, 1984, acting dir. nursing, 1984-85, asst. dir. nursing, 1985—; clin. assoc. dept. behavioral sci. Sch. Dental Med. U. Conn., Farmington, 1986—, geriodontic seminarian, 1986—. Mem. ANA (cert. nurse adminstr.), North East Orgn. for Nursing. Jewish. Office: Hebrew Home and Hosp 1 Abrahms Blvd West Hartford CT 06117-1525

GOLLIVER, CHERYL RENA, nurse; b. St. Louis, Feb. 5, 1955; d. Howard James and Nolia Lavelle (Shaw) G. BSN, U. N. Ala., 1978. Staff nurse, charge nurse NICU Regional Med. Ctr., Memphis; staff nurse, newborn Kapiolani Med. Ctr., Honolulu; staff RN med./surg. Hinds Gen. Hosp., Jackson, Miss.; transport nurse newborn ICU Regional Med. Ctr., Memphis. Home: 7074 Windsor Dr Horn Lake MS 38637

GOLLY, LYNETTE ALICE, certified employee benefits specialist; b. Little Folks, Minn., Oct. 6, 1957; d. Leo Edward and Phyllis Catherine (Otremba) Stumpf; m. John Dean Golly, Jan. 20, 1979; children: Amanda, John Jr., Tanya, Kiel. Cert. Completion, Willmar Tech. Coll., 1976; cert. employee benefits specialist, Wharton Sch. Fin., Pitts., 1989. With Fredrickson Law Firm, Mpls., 1976-77; legal asst. Wausau Ins., Edina, Minn., 1977-78, Rinke-Noonan, St. Cloud, Minn., 1978-84; pension officer Zapp Bank, St. Cloud, Minn., 1984-87; chief exec. officer EBSC, Sauk Rapids, Minn., 1987—. Mem. Fin. Women Internat. (Cen. Lakes cpt. pres. 1988, state v.p. 1991, state pres. 1992), Fin. Planners Group, Cen. Minn. Estate Planning Coun. (sec. 1985-86), Midwest Pension Conf., Internat. Found. of Cert. Employee Benefit Specialists, Kiwanis. Roman Catholic. Office: EBSC 100 2nd Ave S # 202 Sauk Rapids MN 56379-1410

GOLOWAY, ANNE JEANNINE, marketing executive; b. Balt.; d. Stanley Alexander and Mary Lou (Pyrene) G. MAS, Johns Hopkins U., 1983; BS, Va. Poly. Inst. and State U., 1978. With prodn. mgmt. dept. Joseph E. Seagram & Sons, Inc., Balt., 1978-83; mktg. exec. Joseph E. Seagram & Sons, Inc., N.Y.C., 1983-86, Fleischmann Distilling Co., Lake Success, NY, 1986-88, Nat. Foods, Inc., Bronx, N.Y., 1988-90, Gross/Kufeld & Co., N.Y.C., 1990-91, BIC Corp., Milford, Conn., 1991-92, Del Pharm., Inc., Plainview, N.Y., 1992—.

GOLSAN, WANDA FAY LEA, education educator, writer; b. Pueblo, Colo., Oct. 6, 1941; d. Amos L. and Goldie C. (Cotter) Lea; m. William Gordon Golsan, Feb. 17, 1963; children: William Gordon, III, Kristine Lea Golsan Hoyt. BS, So. Nazarene U., 1963; MA, Adams State Coll., 1974. Cert. tchr., Colo., Calif. Tchr. Yukon (Okla.) Schs., 1963-67, Monte Vista (Colo.) Schs., 1968-89; tchr. lang. arts resources Lemon Grove (Calif.) Schs., 1989-93; tchr. lab., preschool Point Loma Nazarene Coll., San Diego, 1993-94, prof. edn., 1994—; workshop presenter Ch. of Nazarene, San Diego, 1989-94; student tchr. supr. Point Loma Nazarene Coll., 1994—. Author: Kinder Kare Power Pack, 1994. Recipient Outstanding Young Educator award Kiwanis Civic Club, 1971. Nazarene. Home: 4110 Loma Riviera Ln San Diego CA 92110 Office: Point Loma Nazarene Coll 3900 Lomaland Dr San Diego CA 92106-2889

GOLTRA, PHYLLIS HOLST, psychologist; b. Elkhart, Ind., June 23, 1942; d. Raymond Carl Hilmer and Helen Irene (Edquist) Holm; m. John Frederick Holst, Apr. 14, 1962 (div. 1976); children: Michael John Holst, Peter Raymond Holst; m. David Dwight Goltra, Aug. 31, 1981. BA, No. Ky. U., Highland Heights, 1981; MEd, Temple U., 1983, PhD, 1991. Lic. psychologist, Pa. Adult tng. facilitator Brighton Ctr., Newport, Ky., 1976-78; tng. officer Longview State Hosp., Cin., 1978-82; grad. asst. Temple U., Phila., 1983-86; psychotherapist Glorinda G. Margolis & Assocs. P.C., Phila., 1984-91, psychologist, 1991—. Mem. APA, Am. Group Psychotherapy Assn., Delaware Valley Group Psychotherapy Assn., Greater Phila. Soc. for Clin. Hypnosis, Am. Soc. for Clin. Hypnosis, Soc. for Advancement of Field Theory (exec. bd., conf. co-chair 1992). Office: Glorinda G Margolis & Assoc 1015 Chestnut St Ste 1500 Philadelphia PA 19147

GOLUB, SHARON BRAMSON, psychologist, educator; b. N.Y.C., Mar. 25, 1937; m. Leon M. Golub, June 1, 1958; children: Lawrence E., David B. Diploma, Mt. Sinai Hosp. Sch. Nursing, 1957; BS, Columbia U., 1959, MA, 1966; PhD, Fordham U., 1974. Head nurse Mt. Sinai Hosp., N.Y.C., 1957-59; contbg. editor RN Mag., Oradell, N.J., 1967-74; asst. prof. psychology Coll. New Rochelle, N.Y., 1974-79, assoc. prof., 1979-86, prof., 1986—, dir. women's studies, 1978-79, chmn. dept. psychology, 1979-82; pvt. practice individual and group psychotherapy Harrison, N.Y., 1976—; adj. prof. psychiatry N.Y. Med. Coll., Valhalla, 1980-94. Editor: Menarche, 1983 (Assn. Women in Psychology Disting. Pub. award 1984, Book of Yr. award Am. Jour. Nursing 1984), Lifting the Curse of Menstruation, 1983, Health Care of the Female Adolescent, 1984, Health Needs of Women as They Age, 1984, PERIODS from Menarche to Menopause, 1992; (with Rita Jackaway Freedman) Psychology of Women: Resources for a Core Curriculum, 1987; editor Women and Health, 1982-86, mem. editorial bd., 1986—; mem. editorial bd. Psychology of Women Quar., 1989—. Grantee Nat. Libr. Medicine, 1983-84; NIH rsch. fellow, 1971-74. Fellow Am. Psychol. Assn. (chmn. task force on teaching psychology of women 1980-83), Am. Psychol. Soc., Am. Assn. Applied and Preventive Psychology; mem. Soc. for Menstrual Cycle Rsch. (pres. 1981-83, bd. dirs. 1981-93), Assn. Women in Psychology, Phi Beta Kappa, Sigma Xi, Psi Chi. Office: Coll New Rochelle Dept Psychology New Rochelle NY 10805

GOMES, MARIA FERNANDES, accountant; b. Guarda, Portugal, Nov. 28, 1950; came to U.S., 1960; d. Manuel Da Costa and Leonilda (Teles) Fernandes; m. Antonio Gomes, June 22, 1968; 1 child, Jennifer Marie. BSBA summa cum laude, Western New Eng. Coll., 1981, MBA, 1984. CPA, Mass. Gen. mgr. Remillard Ins. Agy., Inc., Ludlow, Mass., 1968-81; sr. acct. Fred Wright Co., Inc., Springfield, Mass., 1981-87; pres. and prin. Gomes, Bramucci & Co., P.C., Ludlow, 1987—; adj. prof. acctg. Am. Internat. Coll., Springfield, Mass., 1987—, Elms Coll., Chicopee, Mass., 1989—. Pres., chmn. bd. Luso Fed. Credit Union, Ludlow, 1990; treas. Assn. for Cmty. Living, Springfield, 1985-90; bd. dirs. Ludlow Boys and Girls Club, Inc., asst. treas., 1992—; trustee, asst. treas. Ludlow Boys and Girls Club Charitable Trust, 1993. Mem. AICPA, NAFE, Mass. Soc. CPAs, Am. Woman's Soc. CPAs, Springfield Tax Club. Home: 105 Higher Brook Dr Ludlow MA 01056-1424 Office: Gomes Bramucci & Co PC 77 Winsor St Ludlow MA 01056-3469

GONA, M. JAYAKUMARI, nuclear medicine physician; b. Renigunta, India; d. Ratnam and Gnanaratnamma (Gali) Bolleddu; m. Chandrashaker R. Gona, Oct. 19, 1972; children: Suman F., Roopa S. MBBS, Guntur Med. Coll., India, 1954-59. Chief nuclear medicine svcs. VA Med. Ctr., Buffalo, 1986—; clin. assoc. prof. nuclear medicine svcs. SUNY, Buffalo, 1989—. Mem. Nuclear Medicine Chief's Assn., Soc. Nuclear Medicine. Office: VA Med Ctr 3495 Bailey Ave Buffalo NY 14215-1129

GONCE, NANCY CUMMINGS, librarian, educator, researcher; b. Birmingham, Ala., May 21, 1939; d. Truman and Mozelle (Brown) Cummings; m. Robert L. Gonce; children: Nancy Suzanne, Elizabeth Mozelle. BS in Library Sci., U. Ala., 1961; MS in Library Sci., Geroge Peabody Coll., 1961. Area librarian Ala. Pub. Library Service, Tuscaloosa, Ala., 1961-62; area librarian Ala. Pub. Library Service, Florence, Ala., 1962-64, field rep., 1964-67; librarian Riverbend Ctr. Mental Health, Florence, 1972-78; program coord. U. North Ala. Coop. Campus Ministry, Florence, 1980-82; librarian Webster Elem. Sch., Muscle Shoals, Ala., 1984-90; mem. steering com. U. North Ala. Coop. Campus Ministry, 1988-89, chmn. bd., 1989-90; libr. Muscle Shoals (Ala.) Bd. Edn., 1982-83, 1984-90; program devel. coord. Shoals, Inc., Florence, 1985-84; owner Gonce and Assocs., Florence, 1984—; del. Ala. Govs conf. on Librs., 1967, White House Conf. on Librs. and Info. Sci., 1979; adv. Ala. State Com. on Libr. Devel., 1973; mem. com. for regional confs. Ala. Govs. Conf. on Librs. and Info Svcs.; cons. Ala. Music Hall of Fame, Muscle Shoals, 1985—; exec. dir. W.C. Handy Music Festival, Florence, 1985—, music camp 1992—; founding bd. dirs., grants writer Safeplace, Inc., Florence, 1985; columnist arts/cultural affairs-Fanfare Times Daily, 1989—. Author arts column Times Daily, 1989—. Mem. founding mem. bd. Gingerbread Playhouse, Florence, 1976, Music Presentation Soc., Inc., 1980—; adv. bd. Kennedy-Douglass Ctr. for Arts, Florence, 1980-82, MainSt., 1992—; bd. dirs., 1992—; bd. dirs. Florence Ballet Co., 1979-83, Downtown Florence Unlimited, 1990—; adv. com. WomanHealth, Birmingham, Ala., 1981-83 state conf. del. Nat. Conf., Internat. Women's Yr., Ala., 1978-79, U. Ala. Sch. Libr. Info. Studies 1993—; mem. dept. of ch. and soc. Episcopal Dicoese, Birmingham, 1980-84, Ala. recruiter NBC Election Unit, 1980-90; bd. dirs. Muscle Shoals Concerts, Inc., 1990—; sec.-treas. Muscle Shoals Concert Guild, 1990—; project dir., sec. Frank Lloyd Wright/Rosenbaum House Found., 1991—; sec., bd. dirs. Shoals Comm. Theater, 1992—. Mem. AAUW (Outstanding Service award 1981), Ala. Library Assn. (various state coms.), C. of C. of Shoals (co-chmn. edn. com. and cultural affairs comm.). Democrat. Home: 321 Palisade Dr Florence AL 35630-5915 Office: Gonce and Assocs 115 1/2 E Mobile Florence AL 35630

GONDEK, THERESE MARIE, auditor; b. Muskegon, Mich., Oct. 2, 1950; d. Joseph George and Philomene Marie (La Pres) Schiller; m. Stephen Paul Gondek, May 19, 1973; children: Aaron Christopher, Adam Stephen. BS, No. Mich. U., 1973. Cert. internal auditor, trust auditor, fraud examiner; chartered fiduciary svcs. auditor. With audit staff Price Waterhouse, Detroit, 1974-76; with corp. audit staff K-Mart Corp., Troy, Mich., 1976-79; audit officer, sr. Ind. Nat. Corp., Indpls., 1980-86; auditor Boatmen's Trust Co., St. Louis, 1986—; v.p. trust audit Boatmen's Bancshares, Inc., 1991—. Mem. Bank Adminstrn. Inst., Inst. Internal Auditors (1st v.p. Indpls. chpt. 1985-86, pres. 1986-87, bd. govs. St. Louis chpt. 1988-89, 91-92, internat. conf. com. 1990, chmn. audit com. 1994-95), Am. Cancer Soc. (bd. dirs. Ill. divsn. area VIII), Nat. Assn. Cert. Fraud Examiners, Nat. Assn. Trust Auditors. Roman Catholic. Home: 8601 Colonial Acres Rd Troy IL 62294-2734 Office: Boatmen's Trust Co 510 Locust St Saint Louis MO 63101-1888

GONET, JUDITH JANU, pediatric nurse; b. Cleve., Sept. 27, 1947; d. John D. Sr. and Betty J. (Kurtz) Janu. Diploma in nursing, Mt. Sinai Hosp., Cleve., 1969; BSN, Ursuline Coll., Cleve., 1991; postgrad., Notre Dame Coll., Cleve., 1994. Cert. neonatal intensive care nurse, neonatal resuscitation, instr. Asst. head nurse adolescent medicine U. Hosps. of Cleve.; staff nurse maternity surgery Fairview Gen. Hosp., Cleve.; staff nurse pediatric ICU, Univ. Hosps. of Cleve.; nurse mgr. spl. care nursery Meridia Hillcrest Hosp., Mayfield Heights, Ohio; legal nurse cons., 1994-95. Mem. NAACOG, Am. Assn. Legal Nurse Cons., Nat. Assn. Neonatal Nurses. Home: 1137 Orchard Heights Dr Mayfield Heights OH 44124

GONG, CAROLYN LEI CHU, real estate agent; b. Visalia, Calif., July 10, 1949; d. Robert C. and Lynn P. (Low) G. BA in Health Sci., Calif. State U., Long Beach, 1973; MA in Sociology, Calif. State U., L.A., 1980. Cert. jr. coll. tchr., Calif. Social worker County of L.A., El Monte, Calif., 1974-76, children treatment counselor, 1976-81; children svcs. worker County of L.A., Norwalk, 1981-89; real estate agt. Coldwell Banker, Diamond Bar, Calif., 1989-90, First Team Real Estate, Dana Point, Calif., 1991-92, Grubb & Ellis Real Estate, Dana Point, Calif., 1994—, 1994—. Mem. NAFE, Nat. Assn. Realtors (Mult-million Prodn. award 1989—), Calif. Assn. Realtors, Asian Bus. League, Tennis Connection. Republican. Home: 33144 Ocean Ridge Dana Point CA 92629 Office: Grubb & Ellis Real Estate 34105 Coast Hwy Dana Point CA 92629

GONG, MAMIE POGGIO, educator; b. San Francisco, June 26, 1951; d. Louis and Mary Lee (Lum) G.; m. Andy Anthony Poggio. BA, U. Calif., Berkeley, 1973, postgrad., 1981-83, MEd, 1982. Tchr. Oakland (Calif.) Unified Sch. Dist., 1974-84, Palo Alto (Calif.) Unified Sch. Dist., 1984—; cons., writer Nat. Clearinghouse for Bilingual Edn., Washington, 1984; cons. ARC Assocs., Oakland, 1983; rsch. asst. dept. edn. Stanford U., 1987-89. Co-author: Promising Practices: A Teacher Resource, 1984. Recipient Kearney Found. award, 1969, others. Mem. Tchrs. English to Speakers Other Langs. (presenter 1990 conf.), Calif. Assn. Tchrs. English to Speakers Other Langs. Democrat. Office: Palo Alto Unified Sch Dist 25 Churchill Ave Palo Alto CA 94306-1099

GONNELLA, NINA CELESTE, biophysical chemist; b. Phila., Dec. 22, 1953; d. Anthony and Antoinette E. Gonnella. BA, Temple U., 1975; PhD, U. Pa., 1979; postdoctoral, Calif. Inst. Tech., 1979-81, Columbia U., 1981-83; research assoc., Yale U., 1984. Sr. rsch. scientist CIBA Geigy Pharm. Co., Summit, N.J., 1983-88, staff scientist II, 1989-93, rsch. fellow I, 1993-94, mgr., 1994—; vis. scientist Yale U., 1984 (Merck award 1975); invited lectr. CCNY, CIBA Geigy, Basel, Temple U., Varian Assocs. Contbr. articles to profl. jours. NSF fellow, 1976-79. Mem. ACS, Phi Lambda Upsilon. Office: Ciba Geigy 556 Morris Ave Summit NJ 07901

GONSALVES, PATRICIA E., surgical nurse; b. N.Y.C., Oct. 28, 1943; d. John A. Gonsalves and Julia Rivera Brosa. Diploma in practical nursing, Caledonian Hosp., Bklyn., 1963; student, Cornell Med. Ctr., 1965-66, L.I. U., 1971, SUNY, L.I., 1988. Lic. practical nurse; cert. surg. technologist, preceptor, oper. rm., med. photographer. Lic. practical nurse Luth. Med. Ctr., Bklyn.; assoc. primary nurse, lic. practical nurse Maimonides Med. Ctr., Bklyn., lic. practical nurse, surg. technologist. Contbr. articles to profl. jours. Guild del. Local 1199, Freedom of Health Choice, polit. Dem. endorser. Mem. NAACOG (Outstanding Leadership Recognition award), Nat. Assn. Practical Nurse Edn. and Svc., Nat. Surg. Asst. Assn., Soc. Peripheral Vascular Nursing, Assn. Surg. Technologists (pres. Metro 047 chpt. 1994, nat. bd. dirs. 1993-94, apptd. mem. exam. rev. com. Outstanding Leadership Honorable Mention Recognition award Med. Photographer award 1992), Nat. Ctr. Homeopathy, Found. for Advancement of Innovative Medicine. Home: 814 57th St Apt 2A Brooklyn NY 11220-3631

GONSOULIN GHATTAS, WENDY ANN, choreographer, dancer; b. New Iberia, La., Jan. 14, 1965; d. Claude Cleaveland and Margaret Ann Gonsoulin; m. Rony Joseph Ghattas, June 26, 1987. BFA, U. Southwestern La., 1988, postgrad. in speech-language pathology. Sales assoc. Zales Jewelers, LaFayette, La., 1986-92; choreographer The Performing Art Cons., Ltd., New Iberia, 1989—; instr. creative dance Cathy's Daycare Ctr., New Iberia, 1990—. Prin. dancer (musical) Cajun Odyssey, 1990, (concert with symphony) An Evening with the Acadiana and State of La Danse, 1991. Dance instr. for deaf students Daspit Elem. Sch., New Iberia, 1990—; bd. dirs. New Iberia Community Concert, 1991—; mem. svc. commn. Our Lady of Wisdom Cath. Ch., LaFayette, 1991—; founder PAC Reperatory Ensemble Modern Dance Co. Mem. Am. Bus. Women Assn. (nominee Outstanding Young Woman award 1991), Profl. Dance Tchr. Assn., Nat. Student Speech-Lang.-Hearing Assn., New Iberia Downtown Merchants Assn., Dance Educators Am., Delta Delta Delta (libr. 1983-84, marshall 1984-85). Democrat. Home: PO Box 43031 Lafayette LA 70504-3031 Office: The Performing Arts Cons Lt 101 Julia St PO Box 9125 New Iberia LA 70562

GONZALES, LUCILLE CONTRERAS, educational administrator; b. Colton. Calif., Nov. 30, 1937; d. Antonio Colunga and Ramona (Arroyo) Contreras; AA, San Bernardino Valley Coll., 1958; BA, U. Calif., Santa Barbara, 1960; MA, Claremont Grad. Sch., 1969; m. Enrique Gonzales, Aug. 27, 1960; children: Leticia Maria, Cecilia Maria. With Chino (Calif.) Public Schs., 1960-85, bilingual classroom tchr., 1970-74, bilingual coordinator, 1974-76, coordinator consol. application-intergroup relations, 1976-78, supr. spl. projects, 1978, adminstr. spl. projects, 1978-82, dir. spl. projects, 1982-85; dir. state and fed. programs Pomona Pub. Schs., Calif., 1985-88; edn. programs cons., restructuring waiver specialist Calif. Dept. Edn., 1988—; lead reviewer Calif. Sch. Recognition Program Schs; mem. High Sch. Accredation Team, Goals 2000 State Devel. Team; reader, interviewer Calif. Demonstration Restructuring Sch. Proposals and Sch. Teams; trainer State Dept. Edn. for Program Quality Review Trainers and Reviewers for Elem., Middle Grades, and Reviewers for Secondary in Edn., Master Trainers for Program Quality Rev.; mem. State Supts. Regional Adv. Hispanic Council, State Supts. Middle Grade Task Force, State Dept's. Middle Grades Program Quality Criteria Task Force, State's Supt. Adv. Com. on Gifted Edn. Mem. Migrant Regional Exec. Bd.; mem. Bilingual Dirs. Task Force; mem. Expanded Curriculum Cons. Steering Com.; rep. Calif. State Dept. Edn. Mem. NAFE, San Bernardino County Assn. Compensatory Edn. Dirs. (pres., v.p.), P.E.O., Assn. Secondary Spl. Projects, Assn. Calif. Sch. Adminstrs., Calif. Assn. of Adminstrs. of State and Fed. Ednl. Programs, Nat. Assn. Fed. Ednl. Program Adminstrs., Am. Assn. Sch. Adminstrs., Assn. State and Fed. Adminstrs. of Programs, Los Angeles County Bilingual Dirs., Large Urban Dirs., Assn. Large Urban Dirs., Pi Lambda Theta, Delta Kappa Gamma, Phi Delta Kappa. Lodge: Soroptimist. Home: 4955 Tyler St Chino CA 91710-3434 Office: 721 Capitol Mall Sacramento CA 95814-4702

GONZALES, NELIA LIMIAC, nurse; b. Tarlac, Philippines, Apr. 2, 1953; came to U.S., 1982; d. Sixto Lugue Limiac and Dolores (DeGuzman) Sicangco; m. Sebastino Dizon Gonzales, Sept. 30, 1975 (div. June 1984); children: Alexander, Ryan Oliver, Neil Johnson, Kimberly Anne. BSN, Far Eastern U., 1975. RN, N.Y., Calif. Clin. instr. Dagupan (Philippines) U., 1976-78; staff nurse Hosp. of Sacred Heart, Baguio, Philippines, 1978-79; nurse instr. St. Louis U., Baguio, 1979-82; staff nurse Glengariff Nursing Home, Glencove, N.Y., 1983-84, nurse supr., 1984-89; pvt. duty nurse Best Care Svcs., Garden City, N.Y., 1984-86, Kimberly-Quality Care, Hicksville, N.Y., 1985—, Samaritan at Home Svcs., West Islip, N.Y., 1987—, Home Care for Children, 1993—; vis. nurse supr. Star Multi Care Svcs., Hicksville, 1990-91; nurse supr. Kimberly-Quality Care, 1992—. Mem. PTA, Hicksville, 1993-94, Nat. Arbor Day Found., Nebr., 1994. Mem. ANA. Roman Catholic.

GONZALES, STEPHANIE, state official; b. Santa Fe, Aug. 12, 1950; 1 child, Adan Gonzales. Degree, Loretto Acad. for Girls. Office mgr. Jerry Wood & Assocs., 1973-86; dep. sec. of state Santa Fe, 1987-90, sec. of state, 1991; bd. dirs. N.Mex. Pub. Employees Retirement, N.Mex. State Convassing Bd., N.Mex. Commn. Pub. Records. Mem. exec. bd. N.Mex. AIDS Svc.; mem. Commn. White House Fellowships. Mem. Nat. Assn. Secs. State, Women Execs. in State Govt., United League Until Latin Am. Citizens (women's coun.). Office: Office of the Sec of State State Capital Rm 420 Santa Fe NM 87501

GONZALEZ, IRMA ELSA, federal judge; b. 1948. BA, Stanford U., 1970; JD, U. Ariz., 1973. Law clk. to Hon. William C. Frey U.S. Dist. Ct. (Ariz. dist.), 1973-75; asst. U.S. atty. U.S. Attys. Office Ariz., 1975-79, U.S. Attys. Office (ctrl. dist.) Calif., 1979-81; trial atty. antitrust divsn. U.S. Dept. Justice, 1979; ptnr. Seltzer Caplan Wilkins & McMahon, San Diego, 1981-84; judge U.S. Magistrate Ct. (so. dist.) Calif., 1984-91; ct. judge San Diego County Superior Ct., 1991-92; dist. judge U.S. Dist. Ct. (so. dist.) Calif., San Diego, 1992—; adj. prof. U. San Diego, 1992. Trustee San Diego Mus. Man; pres. Girl Scout Women's Adv. Cabinet. Mem. ABA, Calif. Bar Assn., San Diego County Bar Assn., Ariz. Bar Assn., Pima County Bar Assn., Nat. Assn. Women Judges, Nat. Coun. U.S. Magistrates, Lawyers' Club San Diego, Calif. Judges Assn., Thomas More Soc., La Raza Lawyers, Am. Inns of Ct. Office: Edward J. Schwartz US Courthouse 940 Front St Rm 11 San Diego CA 92101*

GONZALEZ, MARIA DEL CARMEN, translator, fitness and nutrition consultant; b. Havana, Cuba, Aug. 22, 1956; came to U.S., 1967; d. Raul and Esther (Almeida) G.; children: Katerina Avila, Kyle Anthony Avila. BA cum laude, U. Miami, 1977; postgrad., Fla. Internat. U., 1980-81. Lic. real estate agt., Fla.; cert. securities series 7 and 63; lic. group I and variable ins. agt. Staff writer Buenhogar Editorial Am., Miami, 1977-78; adminstrv. asst. to Commr. Armando La Casa Miami, 1978-79; interpreter, translator Assoc. Interpreters, Miami, 1980-85; real estate agt. Internat. Mktg. Realty, Miami, 1981-82; mgr., owner Angelini Imported Children's Wear, Miami, 1982-85; fin. rep. United Resources, Dallas, 1985-87; acct. exec. Dean Witter, Dallas, 1987-88; fin. cons. Merrill Lynch, San Antonio, 1988-90; pres. Translating Concepts, Inc., Internat. Networking Concepts, San Antonio, 1990—; v.p. R-U-Fit Fitness and Nutrition Ctr., San Antonio; judge UTSA Fgn. Lang. Contest, San Antonio, 1990-93. Vol. interpreter City of San Antonio, 1990-91. Mem. Phi Kappa Phi, Pi Delta Phi, Sigma Delta Pi. Roman Catholic. Home and Office: Translating Concepts 2333 NW 1st St Miami FL 33125-5203

GONZALEZ, MARIA NINA, music coordinator; b. Queens, N.Y., June 25, 1952; d. Simon Reinaldo and Esperanza Noemi (Garcia) G. Student, CCNY, 1971, Katherine Gibbs, N.Y.C., 1971-73, Inst. Audio Rsch., 1984-85. Exec. prodn. sec. McCann-Erickson, Inc., N.Y.C., 1973-83, asst. music producer, 1983—. Mem. The Spanish Inst., Nat. Assn. Female Execs. Home: 7100 Blvd E 12D Guttenberg NJ 07093 Office: McCann Erickson Inc 750 3rd Ave New York NY 10017-2701

GONZALEZ, NELIDA, physician; b. S. del Estero, Argentina, July 24, 1939; came to U.S., 1961; AB, Hunter Coll., 1967; MD, Georgetown U., 1971; MPH, Johns Hopkins U., 1983. Diplomate Am. Bd. Internal Medicine, Am. Bd. Geriatric Medicine. Intern Washington VA Hosp./Georgetown U. Med. Ctr., 1972-73; resident Georgetown U. Med. Ctr., 1972-74; physician Group Health Assn., Washington, 1974-94; physician M.T. Med. Group, Washington, 1994—, assoc. chair dept. internal medicine, 1994—; asst. clin. prof. George Washington U. Sch. Medicine, Washington, 1988—. Mem. AMA, D.C. Med. Soc., So. Med. Assn. Roman Catholic. Office: 700 New Hampshire Ave NW # 815 Washington DC 20037

GONZALEZ, RAQUEL MARIA, pharmacist; b. Veguitas, Oriente, Cuba, June 1, 1952; d. Ernesto Esteban and Evora Cristina (Ramirez) G. BS in Biology, Ga. Coll., 1974; BS in Pharmacy, Mercer U., 1977. Registered pharmacist, Ga., Fla., Tenn.; registered pharmacist cons., Fla. Staff pharmacist Cobb Gen. Hosp., Austell, Ga., 1978; staff pharmacist VA Hosp., Nashville, 1978-79, Decatur, Ga., 1979-81; staff pharmacist Lewisburg (Tenn.) Community Hosp., 1981-89; pharmacist Pharmacy Staffing Svcs. Inc., Brentwood, Tenn., 1989—; chief pharmacist Super D Drug Store # 50, Fayetteville, Tenn., 1989-93, Fred's Discount Pharmacy, Lewisburg, Tenn., 1993—; relief pharmacist Farmer's Market Pharmacy (Kroger), Nashville, 1989—. Mem. Ducks Unltd. Republican. Roman Catholic. Club: Atlanta Ski. Home: RR 1 Box 35 Belfast TN 37019-9801 Office: Pharmacy Staffing Svcs Inc 1413 Bowman Ln Brentwood TN 37027-6922 Office: Fred's Discount Pharmacy 1800 Mooresville Rd Lewisburg TN 37091

GONZALEZ-RUBIO, ELISA, soft drink company marketing executive; b. Barranquilla, Colombia, Nov. 4, 1954; came to U.S., 1975; d. Elberto and Dorothy Josephine (Harrison) G.-R. BBA, Ga. State U., 1977, MBA, 1979. Mktg. and bus. devel. specialist AMTAR, Atlanta, 1980-81; ter. sales mgr. S.W. Tex. Coca-Cola USA, 1981-84, mgr. market devel. North Tex., 1984-87; dist. mgr. program Coca-Cola USA, Atlanta, 1987-88; mgr. market executive Coca-Cola USA, Dallas, 1988-89, market execution mgr., 1989-90, Hispanic consumer market mgr. S.W. U.S., 1990—. Bd. dirs. Civil Rights Commn., Atlanta. Mem. Nat. Soc. Hispanic MBA (treas., orgnl. com. Dallas 1993, treas. 1994). Roman Catholic. Office: Coca-Cola USA 12270 Merit Dr Ste 914 Dallas TX 75251

GOOCH, CAROL ANN, psychotherapist consultant; b. Meridian, Miss., Apr. 17, 1950; d. James Tackett and Chris M. Page; (div.); 1 child, Aaron Patrick Gooch. BS, Fla. State U., 1972, DS, 1975; MS, Troy State U., 1974. Lic. profl. counselor, Tex.; lic. chem. dependency counselor, Tex.; lic. marriage and family therapist, Tex.; cert. chem. dependency specialist, Tex.; cert. compulsive gambling counselor, Tex. Tchr. Okaloosa Sch. Dist., Fort Walton, Fla., 1972-77; counselor USAF, Osan AFB, Korea, 1977-79; sch. counselor Tomball (Tex.) Sch. Dist., 1983-90; cons. Montgomery (Tex.) Sch. Dist., 1992—; psychotherapist pvt. practice, Houston, 1990—; cons. school systems, Houston, 1990—; coord. sr. program Forest Springs Hosp., Houston, 1993—, Cypress Creek Hosp., 1994—. Vol. cons. PTO, Woodlands, Tex., 1990. Recipient fellowship Fla. State U., Tallahassee, 1973, Nat. Disting. Svc. award Ex Coun. U.S. Pubs., N.J., 1989; named Outstanding High Sch. Counselor, Tomball Ind. Sch. Dist., 1989. Mem. ACA, ASCD, Tex. Sch. Counselors Assn., Am. Mental Health Counselors Assn., Tex. Mental Health Counselors Assn., Am. Bus. Women's Assn., Fla. State U. Alumni Assn., Kappa Delta Pi. Home and Office: Carol A Gooch MS LPC PO Box 8456 The Woodlands TX 77387

GOOCH, CAROLYN FRANCES, school nutrition services company executive; b. Louisiana, Mo., July 4, 1951; d. Kenneth Porter and Frances Carolyn (Geujen) Morris; m. William Ronald Gooch, Jan. 29, 1977; children: Angela Marie, Christina Carolyn. BS in Home Econs., U. Mo., 1973. Home economist Amana (Iowa) Refrigeration, 1973-75; youth specialist Mo. Coop. Extension, Higginsville, 1975-77; sec., tchr.'s aide Poplar Bluff (Mo.)

High Sch., 1978-79; area home economist Mo. Coop. Extension, Buffalo, 1980-82; mktg. specialist Mo. Dept. Agr., Jefferson City, 1983-87; supr. sch. food svc. Mo. Dept. Elem. and Secondary Edn., Jefferson City, 1987-90; dir. ops. Opaa Food Mgmt., Chesterfield, Mo., 1990-94; dir. tech. sales Sch. Nutrition Svcs., Zartic, Inc., Rome, Ga., 1994—; owner The Care Basket, Vandalia, Mo., 1988—; cons. Mo. Soybean Merchandising Coun., Jefferson City, 1988-90; recipe developer Nat. Pork Producers Assn., Des Moines, 1991; presenter workshops in field. Mem. NAFE, Am. Sch. Food Svc. Assn. (Mktg. award 1990), Mo. Sch. Food Svc. Assn. (local arrangement co-chair 1988-89, newsletter editor 1990), Am. Home Econs. Assn., Mo. Home Econs. Assn. (sec. 1989-91), Home Economists in Bus., Beta Sigma Phi (pres. 1988-89, Girl of Yr. 1988-89). Home: 211 N 6th St Vandalia MO 63382 Office: Zartic Inc 438 Lavender Dr Rome GA 30165

GOOCH, LEE AVA RUTH, elementary school educator; b. Hawthorne, Calif., July 6, 1957; d. Bill Barton Stout and Ava Lee (Robertson) Kerby; m. Russell Timothy Harris, Sept. 1976 (div. June 1977); m. Ron Gene Gooch, May 23, 1981; 1 child, Naomi Joy. B in Elem. Edn., Ctrl. State U., 1988. Cert. elem. edn. Tchr. Okla. City Pub. Schs., 1989—. Vol., female escort CAP, Okla. City, 1993-94; trainer Sooner Coun. Girl Scouts, 1982-94. Recipient Commendation for Saving a Student's Life Govt. Okla. Mem. Am. Fedn. Tchrs. (vol. sch. bd. elections 1991-94, award for Svc. Above and Beyond the Call of Duty), Kappa Delta Pi. Republican. Home: 8104 S Indiana Ave Oklahoma City OK 73159 Office: Madison Elem Sch 3117 N Independance Ave Oklahoma City OK 73112

GOOCH, PATRICIA CAROLYN, cytogeneticist; b. Michie, Tenn., Mar. 28, 1935; d. James Lide and Mary Frances (Hyneman) G. BS, U. Tenn., Knoxville, 1957. Tchr. sci. Knoxville City Sch. System, 1957-58; biologist Oak Ridge Nat. Lab., 1958-70, 73-94; ret. 1995; research assoc. Grad. Sch. Biomed. Sci., U. Tex., Houston, 1970; sr. research analyst Northrop Corp., NASA-Johnson Space Ctr., Houston, 1970-72; organizing com. sci. confs. Contbr. articles to profl. jours. Named Outstanding Tenn. Woman, U. Tenn. Pan-Hellenic Assn., 1974, one of Outstanding Young Women of Am., 1968. Mem. Anderson County Dem. Women's Club (membership chmn. 1985-86). Mem. AAAS, Am. Genetic Assn., Genetics Soc. Am., Environ. Mutagen Soc., U. Tenn. Alumni Assn. (chpt. treas. 1980-81, chpt. sec. 1981-82, chpt. v.p. 1982-83, chpt. pres. 1983-84, nat. bd. govs. 1984-87, chpt. sec./treas. 1992-93, chpt. v.p. 1993-94, chpt. pres. 1994-95), Oak Ridge Pan-Hellenic Assn. (benefit chmn. 1961), Delta Gamma Alumni Assn. (pres. Knoxville Area 1959-61, 67-69), Sigma Xi (chpt. admissions com. 1977-79). Mem. Ch. of Christ. Club: Big Orange (sec. 1978-80, 82-84). Home: 226 Tusculum Dr Oak Ridge TN 37830

GOOD, DEBORAH ANNE, psychotherapist; b. Chgo., Feb. 20, 1951; d. Julian H. and Lois (Goldstien) G. AA, Parkland Jr. Coll., Champaign, Ill., 1975; BA, Nat. Coll. Edn., Chgo., 1983; MEd in Early Childhood Devel., Erikson Inst., Chgo., 1992; postgrad., Inst. Psychoanalysis, Chgo., 1991—. Cert. to interpret for hearing impaired. Interpreter Dept. Vocat. Rehab., Champaign, 1973-81; profl. interpreter for hearing impaired Champaign H.S., 1973-74; child care specialist Edison Park Children's Home, Park Ridge, Ill., 1981-82; profl. tchr., coord. Tuesday's Child, Chgo., 1983-89; grad. intern U. Chgo., 1989-90, before sch. program head, 1990-91, profl. tchr., 1990-91; child/tchr. cons. Tuesday's Child, Chgo., 1991—, child psychotherapist, 1991—; freelance interpreter for hearing impaired, Champaign, 1973-81. Mem. ACA, Assn. Child Psychotherapists. Home: 450 W Briar Pl # 4E Chicago IL 60657

GOOD, LINDA LOU, elementary education educator; b. Zanesville, Ohio, May 30, 1941; d. John Robert and Alice Laura (Fulkerson) Moore; B.S. in Elem. Edn., Ohio U., 1964; m. Larry Alvin Good, Jan. 11, 1964; children—Jason (dec.), Alicia and Tricia (twins), Amy Jo. Tchr., West Muskingum Sch. Dist., 1962-64; 1st grade tchr., Bellevue, Ohio, 1964-68, 2d grade tchr., Zanesville Sch. System, 1970—; head tchr. Munson Sch., Zanesville. Co-chmn. Zane Trace Commemoration; pres. Munson-Garfield Schs. PTA; mem. Trinity Presbyn. Ch. Mem. NEA, Ohio Edn. Assn., Zanesville Edn. Assn., Eastern Ohio Tchrs. Assn. Presbyterian.

GOOD, MARJORIE THOMAS, Methodist minister; b. Wauneta, Nebr., Feb. 24, 1931; d. James W. and Addie Agnes (Decker) Thomas; m. Loren George Good, Aug. 17, 1951; children: Glen, George, Gena, Gayla, Glee-Ann. Student, Nebr. Wesleyan U., 1949-50; BSc, U. Nebr., 1951; MDiv., Iliff Sch. of Theology, Denver, 1981. Instr. home econ. Perkins County High Sch., Grant, Nebr., 1953-56; substitute tchr. Akron (Colo.) High Sch., 1969-75; lay assoc. pastor Christ United Meth. Ch., Sterling, Colo., 1975-79; pastor Howard Meml. United Meth. Ch., Woodrow, Colo., 1980-83, Merino (Colo.) United Meth. Ch., 1983-89, Christ United Meth. Ch., Casper, Wyo., 1989-90, Ovid/ Julesburg (Colo.) United Meth. Ch., 1990-93, Peetz (Colo.) United Meth. Ch., 1993—; mem. bd. of ordained ministry and joint rev. com. Rocky Mt. Conf. United Meth. Ch., Denver, 1982-90. Leader 4H Club Colo. State U. Extension Svcs., Washington County, Colo., 1967-87. Recipient Road-Runner award Rocky Mt. Conf. United Meth. Ch., Denver, 1986, Svc. award 4H Club Colo. State U. Extension Svc., 1987. Mem. AAUW (charter, pres. Sterling br. 1992-93). Home: 603 Logan Peetz CO 80747 Office: Peetz United Meth Ch 595 Logan Peetz CO 80747

GOOD, MARTHA GAIL, educational administrator; b. Great Bend, Kans., Dec. 12, 1943; d. John F. and Keeta E. (Strong) Stoskopf; m. Jack R. Good, Aug. 23, 1965; children: Tereasa D., Catherine D. BS in Elem. Edn. magna cum laude, Troy State U., 1977; M in Adminstrn., Okla. U., 1990. Cert. adminstrn., tchr., Kans., Okla. Airline stewardess Am. Airlines, Nashville, 1963-65; sec. Am. Life Inst., Lexington, Ky., 1965-67; registrar Boston U., Bremerhaven, Germany, 1977-80; tchr. Nativity Blessed Virgin Mary, Biloxi, Miss., 1980-83, Truman & Dunbar Elem. Sch., Oklahoma City, 1983-89; adminstrv. intern Eugene Field Elem. Sch., Oklahoma City, 1989-90; adminstr. Danforth Prin. Preparation Program, 1988-89; adminstr. Westwood Elem. Sch., Junction City, Kans., 1990-92, Auburn Elem. Sch., Auburn-Washburn Sch. Dist., Topeka, Kans., 1992—; mem. Effective Schs. Cadre with Unified Sch. Dist. 437, Topeka. Presented at Nat. Conv. of Am. Assn. Sch. Adminstrs., 1994, United Sch. Adminstrs. Conf., 1994. Mem. United Sch. Adminstrs., Pi Beta Phi, Phi Delta Kappa, Delta Kappa Gamma. Office: Auburn Elem Sch PO Box 9 810 N Commercial Auburn KS 66402-0009

GOOD, MARY LOWE (MRS. BILLY JEWEL GOOD), government official; b. Grapevine, Tex., June 20, 1931; d. John W. and Winnie (Mercer) Lowe; m. Billy Jewel Good, May 17, 1952; children: Billy, James. BS, Ark. State Tchrs. Coll., 1950; MS, U. Ark., 1953, PhD, 1955, LLD (hon.), 1979; DSc (hon.), U. Ill., Chgo., 1983, Clarkson U., 1984, Ea. Mich. U., 1986, Duke U., 1987; hon. degree, St. Mary's Coll., 1987, Kenyon Coll., 1988, Stevens Inst. Tech., 1989, Lehigh U., 1989, Northeastern Ill. U., 1989, U. S.C., 1989, N.J. Inst. Tech., 1989; hon. law degree, Newcomb Coll. of Tulane U., 1991; DSc (hon.), Manhattan Coll., 1992, Ind. U., 1992; LLD (hon.), Coll. of William and Mary, 1992; DSc (hon.), SUNY, Binghamton, 1994, Rensselaer Polytechnic Inst., 1994. Instr. Ark. State Tchrs. Coll., Conway, summer 1949; instr. La. State U., Baton Rouge, 1954-56; asst. prof. La. State U., 1956-58; asso. prof. La. State U., New Orleans, 1958-63; prof. La. State U., 1963-80; Boyd prof. materials sci., div. engring. research La. State U., Baton Rouge, 1979-80; v.p., dir. research UOP, Inc., Des Plaines, Ill., 1980-84; pres. Signal Research Ctr. Inc., 1985-87; pres. engineered materials research div. Allied-Signal Inc., Des Plaines, Ill., 1986-88; sr. v.p.-tech., Allied-Signal Inc., Morristown, N.J., 1988-93; under sec. of commerce for technology Dept. of Commerce, Washington, DC, 1993—; chmn. Pres.'s Com. for Nat. Medal Sci., 1979-82; mem. Nat. Sci. Bd., 1980-91 (chmn. 1988-91), chmn., 1988-90; mem. adv. bd. NSF Chemistry Sect., 1972-76; mem. com. medicinal chemistry NIH, 1972-76, Office of USAF Rsch., 1974-78, chemist div. Brookhaven and Oak Ridge Nat. Labs., 1973-83, chem. tech. div. Oak Ridge Nat. Lab., catalysis program Lawrence-Berkeley Lab.; catalysis program coll. engring. La. State U.; vice chmn. Nat. Sci. Bd., 1984, chmn., 1988-90; bd. dirs. Cin. Milacron Inc., bd. dirs. Ameritech. Contbr. articles to profl. jours. Mem. Nat. Sci. Bd., 1980-91; mem. Pres.' Coun. Advisors for Sci. and Tech., 1991-93, chmn., 1988-91. Recipient Agnes Faye Morgan rsch. award, 1969, Disting. Alumni citation U. Ark, 1973, Scientist of Yr. award Indsl. R&D Mag., 1982, Delmer S. Fahrney medal Franklin Inst., 1988, N.J. Women of Achievement award Douglass Coll., Rutgers U., 1990, Indsl. Rsch. Inst. medal, 1991, Disting. Svc. award NSF, 1992, Roe award ASME, 1993; AEC tng. grantee, 1967, NSF Internat. travel grantee, 1968, NSF rsch. grantee, 1969-80. Fellow AAAS, Am. Inst. Chemistry (Gold medal 1983), Chem. Soc. London; mem. NAE, Swedish Acad. Engring., Am. Chem. Soc. (1st woman dir. 1971-74, regional dir. 1972-80, chmn. bd. 1978, 80, pres. 1987, Garvan medal 1973, Herty medal 1975, award Fla. sect. 1979, Charles Lathrop Parsons award 1991), Internat. Union Pure and Applied Chmistry (pres. inorganic div. 1980-85), Zonta (past pres. New Orleans club, chmn. dist. status of women com. and nominating com., chmn. internat. Amelia Earhart scholarship com. 1978-88, pres. internat. Found. 1988-93, mem. internat. bd. 1988-90), Phi Beta Kappa, Sigma Xi, Iota Sigma Pi (regional dir. 1967-93, hon. mem. 1983). Home: 3321 O St NW Washington DC 20007-2814 Office: Dept of Commerce Office Tech Admn 14th and Constitution Ave NW Washington DC 20230

GOOD, VIRGINIA JOHNSON, real estate executive; b. Onancock, Va., Mar. 1, 1919; d. Obed Wilbur and Sallie Mildred (Deyerle) Johnson; m. William Dennis Good, Jan. 14, 1941 (dec. Apr. 1970). Bus. cert., Elon College, N.C., 1937; real estate cert., U. Miami, 1973; student, Montgomery County Jr. Coll., 1974. Acct. Carolina Biol. Supply Co., Elon College, N.C., 1935-39, Sears Roebuck, Richmond, Va., 1939-40, Ritchie Electric, Charlottesville, Va., 1940-41; mgmt. investor Dr. & Mrs. William D. Good Real Estate, Washington and Gaithersburg, Md., 1941-70, Good Properties, Washington and Miami Beach, Fla., 1970—, Dennis Apts., Miami Beach, Fla., 1972—; Mem. D.C. Apt. Owners/Mgmt. Assn., Washington, 1970-84, Miami Beach Apt. Owners Assn., 1970-86, North Shore Apt. Owners Assn., Miami Beach, 1986-88. Exec. com. Anti Rock Quarry, Dawsonville, Md., 1959, Save Our Coast, Miami Beach, 1982-86; mem. Montgomery County Hist. and Geneal. Soc., Rockville, Md., 1977—, Nat. Geneal. Soc., 1980—, Greater Miami Geneal. Soc., Miami, 1982—, Va. Hist./Geneal. Soc., Richmond, 1988—, Bradley Blvd. Civic Assn., Bethesda, Md., 1989. Mem. La Gorce Country Club, Miami Beach, Columbia Country Club (Chevy Chase, Md.), DAR, Nat. Soc. So. Dames, United Daus. of Confederacy, Nat. Soc. Colonial Dames of XVII Century, Nat. Huguenot Soc. Mem. United Church of Christ. Home: 5310 Lagorce Dr Miami FL 33140-2134 Office: 5723 Bradley Blvd Bethesda MD 20814-1033

GOODALE, JOANN OLSON, rehabilitation nurse; b. Huron, S.D., Mar. 6, 1937; d. Robert H. and Maxine (Biggerstaff) Olson; m. Eugene Clark Goodale, Dec. 15, 1957; children: Diane Kay Goodale Renz, Julie Ann, Michael Eugene. BSN, S.D. State U., 1959; MS in Rehab. Adminstrn. Mgmt., Depaul U., 1987. TN, S.D., Va., Ohio, Ill.; cert. ins. rehab. specialist, rehab. nurse, case mgr. Pvt. duty nurse U.S. Mil. Hosp., Madrid, Spain, 1959-60; staff nurse, acting head nurse No. Va. Hosp., Arlington, 1961-63; staff nurse, charge nurse, hosp. relief supr., employee health, staff devel. Kettering (Ohio) Meml. Hosp., 1965-75; rehab. nurse, case mgr. Liberty Mutual Ins. Co., Peoria, Ill., 1981-92; program dir. Midwest Acquired Brain Injury Rehab. Ctr. Meth. Med. Ctr., Peoria, Ill., 1992-94; mem. ins. adv. com. Rehab. Inst. Chgo., 1990-92. Mem. Pekin (Ill.) Mayor's Adv. Com. for Persons with Disabilities, 1992-95; mem. adult Christian edn. com. 1st Presbyn. Ch., Pekin, 1985-87. Mem. AAUW, Occupational Health Nurses Ill., Assn. Rehab. Nurses. Presbyterian. Home: 614 Washington St Pekin IL 61554-4238

GOODALL, FRANCES LOUISE, nurse, production company assistant; b. Gove, Kans., Apr. 30, 1915; d. Francis Mitchell and Ella Aurelia (Brown) Sutcliffe; m. Richard Fred Goodall, Feb. 22, 1946; children: Roy Richard, Gary Frederick. Student, U. Kans., 1932-33, Ft. Hays State Coll., 1933-34; BS in Nursing, U. Wash., 1939. RN, Wash. Nurse King County Hosp. System, Seattle, 1939-41; office nurse Dr. Cassius Hofrictor, Seattle, 1941-42; founder Goodall Prodns., Seattle, 1971—. Pres. Hawthorne Elem. Sch. PTA, Seattle, 1960-61, Caspar Sharples Jr. High Sch. PTA, Seattle, 1967-68; historian Seattle Coun. PTAs, 1964-65, 68-69; den mother Boy Scouts Am., Seattle, 1963-67; active United Good Neighbors, Seattle, 1964-68; treas. Women's Overseas Svc. League, Seattle, 1970-74, treas., 1987-91. 1st lt. Nurses Corps, AUS, 1942-46, PTO. Recipient vol. award King County Hosp. System, 1964, Acorn award Franklin High Sch. PTA, 1965, Woman Achievement Cert. award Past Pres. Assembly, 1992. Mem. U. Wash. Alumni Assn. (v.p. 1966-70), U. Wash. Nursing Alumni Assn., Seattle Mus. Art Soc. (assoc., social com., bd. dirs.), Pres's. Forum, Seattle Fedn. Women's Clubs (chmn. community improvement program 1990—), Seattle Geneal. Soc., Lake City Emblem Club, Order Eastern Star, Seattle Sorosis (pres. 1990—), Sigma Sigma Sigma, Kappa Delta (pres. Seattle alumni 1954-55, sec. alumnae coop. bd. 1963-82), Nat. Assn. Parliamentarians (pres. parliamentary law unit 1989-93, treas. 1960-61, 64-66, 75-89, 93-94), Am. Legion (life mem. Fred Hancock post #19 Renton, Wash.). Republican. Presbyterian. Home: 4111 51st Ave S Seattle WA 98118-1265

GOODART, NAN L., lawyer, educator; b. San Francisco, Apr. 4, 1938. BA, San Jose State U., 1959, MA, 1965; JD, U. of the Pacific, 1980. Bar: Calif. 1980, U.S. Dist. Ct. (ea. dist.) Calif. 1981. Tchr. Eastside Union High Sch., San Jose, Calif., 1960-65; counselor San Jose City Coll., 1965-75; atty. Sacramento, 1981—; speaker numerous seminars throughout no. Calif. and other western states, 1988—. Author: Who Will It Hurt When I Die? A Primer on the Living Trust, 1992 (Nat. Mature Media award 1993), The Truth About Living Trusts, 1995. Judge pro tem Sacramento County Small Claims Ct., 1988—; instr. continuing edn. of bar Am.'s Legal Ctr., Sacramento, 1992—. Mem. Nat. Acad. Elder Law Attys., Calif. State Bar Assn., Sacramento County Bar Assn. Office: Law Offices Nan L Goodart 7230 S Land Park Dr # 121 Sacramento CA 95831

GOODCHILD, ROSINA ANN, community health nurse; b. Streator, Ill., Nov. 28, 1963; d. David Floyd and Reita Mae (Keith) Allen; m. Robert Joseph Goodchild, June 4, 1988; children: Christopher Robert, Matthew James. AAS in Nursing, Ill. Valley Community Coll., 1984; BSN, Bradley U., 1988. RN, Ill. Camp nurse, counselor YMCA/CETA, Streator, 1983; pvt. duty nurse Streator, 1982-85; staff nurse emergency/trauma dept. St. James Hosp., Pontiac, Ill., 1984-88; charge nurse Bloodmobile ARC, Peoria, Ill., 1988-94; immunization nurse La Salle County Health Dept., Ottawa, Ill., 1992-94; mem. nursing adv. com. Heart of Ill. Blood Svcs., ARC, 1985-88. Exec. bd. dirs., sec. LaSalle County Ill. Am. Heart Assn., 1993—. Mem. ANA, Ill. Nurses Assn., Emergency Nurses Assn. Home: PO Box 233 400 Sylvan Ave Grand Ridge IL 61325-0233

GOODE, ERICA TUCKER, internist; b. Berkeley, Calif., Mar. 25, 1940; d. Howard Edwin and Mary Louise (Tucker) Sweeting; m. Bruce Tucker (div. 1971); m. Barry Paul Goode, Sept. 1, 1974; children: Adam Nathaniel, Aaron Benjamin. BS summa cum laude, U. Calif., Berkeley, 1962, MPH, 1967; MD, U. Calif., San Francisco, 1977. Diplomate Am. Bd. Internal Medicine. Chief dietitian Washington Hosp. Ctr., 1968; pub. health nutritionist Dept. Human Resources, 1969-73; intern Children's Hosp. (now Calif. Pacific Med. Ctr.), San Francisco, 1977-78, resident, 1978-80, chief med. resident internal medicine, 1979-80; pvt. practice internal medicine San Francisco, 1980—; expert witness med.-legal issues, Calif., 1990—; lectr., tchr. med. house staff Children's Hosp., 1982—; mem. teaching faculty U. Calif., San Francisco, 1984—. Contbr. articles to profl. publs. Co-chair Physicians for Clinton, No. Calif., 1992. Mem. AMA, ACP, Calif. Med. Assn., Calif. Soc. Internal Medicine, San Francisco Med. Soc., U. Calif. Alumni Assn. (del.), Alpha Omega Alpha. Office: Goode Brayer Dobrow Watanabe & Liberman 3801 Sacramento St # 100 San Francisco CA 94118-1625

GOODE, JANET WEISS, elementary school educator; b. Chattanooga, Tenn., Sept. 3, 1935; d. Albert H. and Dorothy E. (Crandall) Weiss; m. Gene G. Goode, June 11, 1961; children: Jennifer E., Amy V. BS in Biology, Carson-Newman Coll., 1957; MA in Botany, Vanderbilt U., 1959; MEd, Lynchburg Coll., 1980. Cert. postgrad. profl. tchr., Va. Instr. gen. biology, botany, zoology, animal ecology Carson-Newman Coll., Tenn., 1959-61; tchr. biology, chemistry Salem Acad., Winston-Salem, N.C., 1961-64; tchr. chemistry Wade Hampton High Sch., Greenville, S.C., 1964-65; tchr. sci. Va. Treatment Ctr. for Children, Richmond, 1966; tchr. biology Quantico (Va.) H.S., 1969-70; pvt. tutor Madison Heights, Va., 1980-85, James River Day Sch. and Seven Hills Sch., Lynchburg, Va., 1980-85; reading specialist chpt. I reading program Monelison Mid. Sch., Madison Heights, 1985-93; reading specialist Amherst County Adult Basic Edn. Program, 1992-94; reading specialist Chpt. I Reading Program and Reading Recovery Program Pleasant View Elem. Sch., Monroe, Va., 1993—; vis. instr. U. Chattanooga, summer 1960; mem. learning disabilities del. to Russia and Lithuania, Citizen Amb. Program, 1993; tchr. advisor Weekly Reader Publs. Editor: (newsletter) Topics for Chapter I; author: Can You Read a Baseball Card?; co-author: Transitional Intervention Program. Sponsor sch. lit. mag. Monellson Mid. Sch.; organist, co-chair Sunday svcs. com., newsletter editor for Ptnr. Ch. com., First Unitarian Ch.; mem. Friends of Libr., Madison Heights Br. Libr., helper ann. book sale. Recipient Reading Tchr. of the Year Piedmont Va. Area Reading Coun., 1993-94. Mem. NEA, Va. Edn. Assn., Amherst Edn. Assn., Orton Dyslexia Soc., Piedmont Area Reading Coun. (newsletter editor, past treas.), Va. State Reading Assn., Internat. Reading Assn., Lynchburg Stamp Club, Kappa Delta Pi, Phi Delta Kappa (past sec.). Office: Pleasant View Elem Sch Rt 2 Box 477 Monroe VA 24574

GOODE-HADDOCK, CELIA ROSS, title company executive; b. Bryan, Tex., May 22, 1950; d. Phillip Barron and Sara June (Council) Goode; m. Wallace Leonard Williams, Jan. 13, 1968 (div. 1969); 1 child, Quinn Williams; m. Robert Sherman Stallings, Aug. 19, 1972 (div. 1986); children: Ashley, Leigh; m. Billy Dan Haddock, Dec. 11, 1994. BS, Tex. A&M U., 1972. Sec. Univ. Title Co., College Station, Tex., 1972-77; mgr. Univ. Title Co., 1977-83; pres., 1983—; adv. com. Ticor Title Ins., Dallas, 1988-90; mem. adv. com. for continuing edn. State Bd. Ins., Austin, 1989-91. Election judge Brazos County, Tex., 1983—; loan com. Community Devel. Loan Com., College Station, 1988-91; commr. Brazos County Cen. Appraisal Dist., 1985—; adv. com. Congressman Joe Barton, 1987-92; bd. dirs. Humana Hosp. of Brazos Valley, 1988-91, Brazos Valley Med. Ctr., 1994—; pres. Brazos Valley Devel. Coun. Revolving Loan Fund; mem. bd. dirs., publicity chmn. Family Outreach, 1988-90; vol. Sta. KAMU-TV, 1979—, active in past numerous civic, polit. orgns.; mem. Operation Child Save Task Force, 1990-92; divsn. leader Brazos County United Way, others. Winner 1994-95 of Bryan Rotary Club Newman 10 award. Mem. Tex. Land Title Assn. (legis. chmn. 1990—, Outstanding Young title Person 1982), Bryan/College Station Bd. Realtors (Affiliate of Yr. 1985), Bryan College Station Homebuilders Assn., Bryan/College Station C. of C. (v.p. for leadership 1994—), Tex. A&M/Bryan College Station Coun Bd., Opera and Performing Arts Guild (chmn.). Methodist. Office: Univ Title Co 1021 University Dr E College Station TX 77840-2120

GOODEN, BARBARA ANN, credit union executive; b. Waycross, Ga., July 14, 1946; d. James William and Juanita Christine (Davis) G. A.A. in Psychology, A.A. in Bus. Adminstrn., A.A. in Edn., Waycross Jr. Coll.; grad. Sch. Fin. Counseling, Fla. State U., 1986; student Cert. Credit Union Execs. Cert. consumer credit executive. With Eli Witt Co., Tampa, Fla., 1968-80, credit union rep., 1974-80; credit card coord. 1st R.R. Community Fed. Credit Union F/K/A Waycross Seaboard System Fed. Credit Union, 1980-84, collection coord., 1984—; owner Craftmasters, 1987—. Contbr. articles on consumer credit to Waycross Jour. Herald, 1985. Women's rep. Southeast Area Employment and Tng. Council, Waycross, 1972-80. Mem. Waycross Credit Women (charter pres. 1984-85), Soc. Cert. Consumer Credit Execs., Ga. Soc. Credit Union Loan and Collection Coords. (charter), League Credit Unions. Baptist. Club: Okefenokee Bus. and Profl. Women's (v.p. 1972-74). Avocations: reading, cake decorating, floral art, crafts, cooking. Home and Office: 513 Riverside Dr Waycross GA 31501-5316 Office: 1st RR Community Fed Credit Union F/K/A Waycross Seaboard System PO Box 1256 Waycross GA 31502-1256

GOODERHAM, KATHRYN LEIGH, consultant; b. Sioux Falls, S.D., Dec. 15, 1950; d. Howard J. and Mary Kathryn (Price) Peckham; m. Kenneth John Gooderham, July 3, 1982. BA in English and History, U. S.D., 1972. Tchr. Lee County Schs., Ft. Myers, 1973-76; adminstrv. asst. South Seas Beach Improvement, Captiva, Fla., 1980-82; assoc. Stevens & Assocs., Ft. Myers, 1982-86; cons., owner Gooderham & Assocs., Ft. Myers, 1986—; active Econ. Devel. Coaltion, Ft. Myers, 1986. Pres. Fla. Women's Polit. Caucus, 1985—, S.W. Fla. Women's Polit. Caucus, 1985-91; chair Youth Connection Leadership Lee County, Ft. Myers, 1990—; campaign mgr. Campaign for Connie Allegra, 1990; treas. Fla. Commn. on Status of Women, 1993—; bd. dirs. Lee Alliance for Responsible Adolescent Parenting, 1994; active Cypress Lake United Meth. Ch., 1989—, Cape Coral Rep. Women's, Fla., 1991. Home: 2266 Chandler Ave Fort Myers FL 33907 Office: Gooderham & Assocs 6296 Corporate Ct SW B-201 Fort Myers FL 33919

GOODHART, KAREN STEPHAN, sales executive; b. Bklyn., Jan. 14, 1947; d. Frank Herman and Bernadette (Brady) S.; m. James Stanley Goodhart, June 7, 1969 (div. Jan. 1983); children: Kristen Stephanie, Erika Lee. BA, Alvernia Coll., 1969. Elem. tchr. Schuylkill Valley Sch., Leesport, Pa., 1969-78; mgr. sales Radio Shack, Reading, Pa., 1978-84, The Computer Source, Reading, 1984; buyer Boscov's, Reading, 1985-86; with sales dept. Info. Mgmt., Blue Bell, Pa., 1986; mgr. sales Bio-Med Pa., Inc., Allentown, 1986-87, v.p. sales, 1987-88; v.p. sales Med. Disposal Services, Inc., Reading, 1988-89; v.p. nat. mktg. Nat. Med. Waste Inc, 1989-92; pres., CEO Enviro Med, Balt., 1992-94; environ. cons. K K and R Assocs., Wyomissing, Pa., 1994—; bd. dirs. Nat. Solid Waste Mgmt. Assn. Mem. Am. Soc. Health Care, Nat. Exec. Housekeeping, Assn. Practitioners Infection Control. Democrat. Roman Catholic. Office: K K and R Assocs PO Box 7002 Wyomissing PA 19610

GOODHART, VICTORIA ANN, theater educator, performing company executive; b. Waterville, Maine, June 2, 1961; d. Ted Nathan Shiro and Alice Myra (Kay) Goodhart. Studied with Milton Katselas, 1982-84; apprenticed with Shelly Winters, Actor's Studio, L.A., 1985. Tchr., coach acting classes L.A., 1986-89; founder, creative dir. Public Alley 421 Theatre Co., Boston, 1991—; tchr. acting classes No Frills, Boston; instr. Mass. Coll. Art, Boston, The Actors Workshop, Boston. Appearances films, TV, commercials, music videos, theatre prodns., L.A., N.Y., Boston, 1980—. Debbie Reynolds scholar. Home: 101 Beacon St Boston MA 02116

GOODHUE, MARY BRIER, lawyer, former state senator; b. London, 1921; naturalized, 1942; d. Ernest and Marion H. (Hawks) Brier; m. Francis A. Goodhue, Jr., May 15, 1948 (dec. Sept. 1990); 1 child, Francis A. III. BA, Vassar Coll., 1942; LLB, U. Mich., 1944. Bar: N.Y. 1945. Assoc. Root, Clark, Buckner & Ballantine, N.Y.C., 1945-48; asst. counsel N.Y. State Crime Commn., N.Y.C., 1951-53, Moreland Commn., N.Y.C., 1953-54; mem. firm Goodhue, Arons & Neary and predecessors, Mt. Kisco, 1955—; mem. N.Y. State Assembly from 93d Dist., 1975-78, N.Y. State Senate, 1979-92. Trustee Katonah Mus. Art, Vis. Nurse Assn., Hudson Valley, John Jay Homestead; N.Y. del. Nat. Women's Conf., Houston, 1977. Mem. ABA, West Bar Assn., No. Westchester Bar Assn. Office: 126 Barker St Mount Kisco NY 10549-1500 also: Rock Gate Farm Rd Mount Kisco NY 10549

GOODIN, GENEVA BURTON, social worker, consultant; b. Columbia, Ky., Nov. 16, 1932; d. Forest and Elzada (Streeval) Burton; m. Jack Vitus Goodin, May 13, 1950; children: Veronica, Julia, Cynthia, Jackie. AA, Lindsey Wilson Coll., Columbia, 1979; BSW, Spalding U., Louisville, 1982; MSW, U. Ky., 1984. Lic. social worker, Ky. Social svc. aide Social Svcs., Columbia, 1975-82, social worker prin., 1982-89, social worker clinician, 1989-90; tchr. human svcs. Lindsey Wilson Coll., 1990—; social worker cons. Westlake Cumberland Hosp., Columbia, 1982—, Westlake Home Health, Columbia, 1982—, Russell County Hosp., Russell Springs, Ky., 1986-90. Martha Davis scholar U. Ky., 1983. Mem. NASW, Ky. Human Svc. Assn., Kappa Gamma Pi. Republican. Baptist. Home: 473 Little Cake Rd Columbia KY 42728-9154 Office: Social Svcs PO Box 288 Columbia KY 42728-0288

GOODIN, JULIA C., medical investigator, state official, educator; b. Columbia, Ky., Mar. 10, 1957; d. Vitus Jack and Geneva (Burton) G. BS, Western Ky. U., 1979; MD, U. Ky., 1983. Diplomate Am. Bd. Clin. and Anatomic Pathology, Am. Bd. Forensic Pathology. Intern Vanderbilt U. Med. Ctr., Nashville, 1983, resident in anatomic and clin. pathology, 1984-87; fellow in forensic pathology Med. Examiner's Office, Balt., 1987-88; asst. med. examiner Office of Chief Med. Examiner, Balt., 1988-90; dep. chief med. examiner State of Tenn., 1990-94; asst. med. examiner Nashville, 1990-93, chief med. examiner, 1993-94; asst. med. investigator State of N.Mex., Albuquerque, 1994—; asst. prof. U. N.Mex., Albuquerque, 1994—; clin. prof. U. Md. Med. Sch., Balt., 1988-90, Vanderbilt U. Med. Ctr., 1990-94. With USNR, 1985—. Mem. Am. Acad. Forensic Sci., Assn. Mil. Surgeons of U.S., AMA, Nashville Acad. of Medicine, So. Med. Assn., Tenn. Med. Assn. Home: Apt A112 3901 Indian School Rd NE Albuquerque NM 87110 Office: Office Med Investigator Univ Of New Mexico NM 87131

GOODIN, JULIE ANN, business owner; b. Lafayette, Ind., June 7, 1958; d. Robert Charles and Betty Jean (Swatts) Mennen; m. John William Goodin, June 14, 1980; children: Janae, John, James. Lic. in real estate, Bill Miller Sch., Lafayette, 1986; student, Fashion Inst. Tech., N.Y.C., 1978; BS, Purdue U., 1980. With Paul Harris Stores, Lafayette, 1974-80; with dept. sales Lord & Taylor, N.Y.C., 1978, sales mgr. Estee Lauder, 1980-82; sales cons., sr. sales dir. Mary Kay Cosmetics, Dallas and San Antonio, 1982-88; adminstrv. asst. Century 21 Mennen Realty, Lafayette, 1986-87; owner Baskets Unique, Marietta, Ga., 1988—; real estate closing transaction coord., 1994—. Vol. Children's Restoration Network, 1993. Mem. Beta Sigma Phi (v.p. Theta Iota chpt. 1990-91, pres. 1991-92, Woman of Yr. 1992, corr. sec. 1993—, vol. 1988—). Lutheran. Office: Baskets Unique 3297 Hutton Walk Marietta GA 30066-1624

GOODING, GRETCHEN ANN WAGNER, physician, educator; b. Columbus, Ohio, July 2, 1935; d. Edward Frederick and Margaret (List) Wagner; m. Charles A. Gooding, June 19, 1961; children: Gunnar Blaise, Justin Mathias, Britta Meghan. BA magna cum laude, St. Mary of the Springs Coll., Columbus, 1957; MD cum laude, Ohio State U., 1961. Diplomate Am. Bd. Diagnostic Radiology. Intern Univ. Hosps., Columbus, 1961-62; rsch. fellow Boston City Hosp., 1962-63, Boston U., 1963-65; with dept. radiology U. Calif., San Francisco, 1975—, assoc. prof. in radiology, 1981-85, prof., vice chmn., 1986—; asst. chief radiology VA Med. Ctr., San Francisco, 1978-87, chief radiology, 1987—, chief ultrasonography, 1975—; chair com. acad. pers. U. Calif., San Francisco, 1993-94; speaker in field. Co-editor Radiologic Clinics of N.Am., 1993—; mem. editorial bd. San Francisco Medicine, 1986-92, Applied Radiology, 1987-89, Current Opinion in Radiology, 1992-93, The Radiologist, 1993—, Emergency Radiology, 1993—; contbr. articles to profl. jours. Fellow Am. Coll. Radiology (mem. commn. on ultrasound 1984-92), Am. Inst. Ultrasound in Medicine (bd. govs. 1981-84, chair convention program 1986-88, Presdl. Recognition award 1984); mem. AMA, San Francisco Med. Soc. (chmn. membership com. 1992-94, bd. dirs. 1995), RSNA (course com. 1984-88, tech. exhibit com. 1992-94), Bay Area Ultrasound Soc. (pres. 1979-80), Soc. Radiologists Ultrasound (chair membership com. 1991-93), ARRS, AUR, CRS, Calif. Med. Assn., Am. Assn. Women Radiologists (pres. 1984-85, trustee 1991-94), VA Chiefs of Radiology Assn. (pres.-elect, pres. 1994-95), San Francisco Radiological Soc. (pres. 1990-91), Hungarian Radiological Soc. (hon.). Office: VA Med Ctr Radiology Svc 4150 Clement St San Francisco CA 94121-1598

GOODKIN, DEBORAH GAY, internal management consultant; b. Oceanside, N.Y., Dec. 8, 1951; d. Harold and Rose (Mostkoff) G.; m. Glenn Richard; children: Samuel Goodkin Richard, Sarah Goodkin Richard. BA, Syracuse U., 1972; M. Urban Planning, NYU, 1977. Planner, Nassau-Suffolk Planning, Hauppauge, N.Y., 1972; asst. to treas. Nat. Assn. Savs. Banks, N.Y.C., 1973; planning aide Dept. City Planning, N.Y.C., 1973-79; planner, real property mgr. N.Y.C. Bd. Edn., 1979-81, dir. Capital Budget Bur., 1981-85; supervising mgmt. engr. Port Authority N.Y. & N.J., 1985-90, mgr. fin. systems, 1989—; cons. C Corp., L.A., 1983—. Security cons. Dem. Nat. Com., N.Y.C., 1980. Recipient C.F.O. Award of Excellence, 1987, 92. Mem. Women in Govt. (guest lectr. 1983), Syracuse U. Alumni Assn., NYU Alumni Assn. Author: (zoning law) Bay Ridge Zoning Dist., 1978. Artist: Show of Selected Works, Sireuil, France, 1983. Office: Port Authority One World Trade Ctr New York NY 10048

GOODLATTE, JOYCE SWING, physician; b. Boston, Apr. 10, 1950; d. Raymond and Nell-Karen (Swing) G.; 1 child, Gabriel Rey-Goodlatte. BA, SUNY, Stony Brook, 1973; MD, U. Vt., 1978; cert. in family therapy, Family Inst. Chgo., 1988, Evanston (Ill.) Family Therapy Ctr., 1993. Diplomate Am. Bd. Family Practice, Nat. Bd. Med. Examiners. Resident in family practice Cook County Hosp., Chgo., 1978-81; staff physician ANCHOR HMO, Chgo., 1982-89; pvt. practice Chgo., 1988—; mem. faculty Hinsdale (Ill.) Family Practice Residency Program, 1989-92, Chgo. Ctr. Family Health, 1990—; cons. Chgo. Women's Health Ctr., 1979-83; med. cons. dept. communicative disorders Ctr. Rehab & Tng. of Persons with Disabilities, Chgo., 1981-89. Active Project Unity, Oak Park, Ill., 1993—. Mem. Am. Assn. Marriage and Family Therapists, Soc. Tchrs. Family Medicine. Office: Chgo Ctr Family Health 445 E Illinois Ste 651 Chicago IL 60611

GOODMAN, ABBIE REBECCA, state agency executive; b. Pitts., Jan. 17, 1961. BA, Chatham Coll., 1982. Pub. outreach coord. Mayor's Office Cable Communications, Boston, 1982-84; project mgr. Mass. Corp. Ednl. Telecommunications, Boston, 1984-86, mktg. dir., 1986-88; cons. Mass. Office Internat. Trade and Investment, Boston, 1988-91, exec. dir., 1991-93; exec. dir. Mass. Office Travel and Tourism, Boston, 1993—; cons. Bishoff-Solomon Communications, Boston. Pres. Mass. Women's Polit. Caucus, Boston, 1989-90; bd. dirs. Jackson Mann Cmty. Sch., Boston, 1984-88; life mem. Hadassah, Boston, 1983—; mem. bd. Discover New England, 1993—; mem. Gov.'s Sports Adv. Coun., 1993—. Office: Mass Office Travel and Tourism 100 Cambridge St Fl 13 Boston MA 02202-0001

GOODMAN, BEVERLY H(ALLQUIST), child psychiatrist; b. Mpls., Feb. 28, 1938; m. Warren H. Goodman, Nov. 27, 1970; children: Karyn, Alyssa. BA, MaCalester Coll., St. Paul, 1959; MD, U. Minn., 1963. Diplomate Am. Bd. Psychiatry and Neurology, Am. Bd. Adult and Child Psychiatry. Intern Brookdale Hosp. Ctr., Bklyn., 1963-64; resident in psychiatry Hillside Hosp., Glen Oaks, N.Y., 1964-67; fellow in child psychiatry Jewish Bd. Guardians, N.Y.C., 1968-70, staff psychiatrist, 1970-71; pvt. practice Great Neck, N.Y., 1970—; physician-in-charge, cons. and liaison child psychiatry North Shore U. Hosp., Manhasset, N.Y., 1991—; vol. attending psychiatrist L.I. Jewish Med. Ctr., New Hyde Park, N.Y., 1970—, North Shore U. Hosp., 1980—; asst. prof. Cornell Med. Coll., N.Y.C., 1991—. Mem. Am. Psychiatric Soc., Am. Acad. Child and Adult Psychiatry, Nassau Psychiatric Soc. (bd. dirs. 1988—), Physicians for Social Responsibility. Office: North Shore U Hosp 300 Community Dr Manhasset NY 11030

GOODMAN, BONNIE M., marketing executive; b. Phila., June 20, 1959; d. Albert Carl and Evelyn Ruth (Ross) Powell; m. Howard Bruce Goodman, Oct. 27, 1990; 1 child, Jillian Tawna. BA, UCLA, 1981. Rsch. asst. Hill and Knowlton, L.A., 1982, asst. acct. exec., 1982-83, acct. exec., 1983-84, sr. acct. exec., 1984-86, acct. supr., 1986-88, group supr., 1988-90, v.p., 1990-91, sr. v.p., 1991—. Recipient Adweek Spl. Events Mktg. award Adweek, 1989. Mem. Pub. Rels. Soc. Am. (Prism award 1993), Ad Club L.A., Hispanic Pub. Rels. Assn. Office: Hill and Knowlton 6500 Wilshire Blvd Los Angeles CA 90048

GOODMAN, CAROLYN, advertising executive; b. Chatham, Kent, U.K., Dec. 10, 1956; came to U.S., 1983; d. Dudley Cyril Harry and Barbara June (Le Lievre) Francis; m. Peter Earl Goodman, Apr. 15, 1989; 1 child, Robert Francis. BA, Carleton U., Ottawa, Ont., Can., 1977; Diploma of Creative Advertising, Algonquin Coll., Ottawa, 1980. Typesetter, paste-up artist The Ottawa Jour., 1979; copywriter, prodr. Sta. CFCN-TV, Lethbridge, Alta., 1980; account exec. Cockfield Brown, Inc., Calgary, Alta., 1980-83, Chiat/Day Inc., San Francisco, 1983-84; sr. account exec. DDB Needham Inc., San Francisco, 1984-88; v.p., mktg. mgr. 1st Nationwide Bank, San Francisco, 1988-90; v.p., group product mgr. Bank of Am., San Francisco, 1990; v.p., mgmt. supr. Ogilvy & Mather Direct, San Francisco, 1990-92; v.p., acct. dir. Cohn & Wells, San Francisco, 1992-93; sr. v.p., gen. mgr. Cohn & Wells, Toronto, 1994-95; direct mktg. cons. Bell Can., BC Tel., 1995—. Cons. Sierra Club, Can. Parks and Wilderness Soc. Home: 6 Rancho Dr San Anselmo CA 94960-1313

GOODMAN, D. SUZANNE, library media specialist; b. Lynnwood, Calif., Oct. 6, 1951; d. Roy Garness and Emma Jean (Foord) G. BA in English with teaching endorsement, U. Mont., 1975; K-12 libr. media endorsement, Mont. State U., 1992. Cert. tchr. English, Anthropology and libr. media, Mont. Tchr. English Upward Bound Missoula, Mont., summer 1974, 75; tchr. English Park High Sch., Livingston, Mont., 1975-79; tchr. reading Livingston Mid. Sch., 1980-82; libr. clerk Livingston Pub. Libr., 1985-88, young adult libr., 1988-92; head libr. media specialist Park High Sch. Libr., Livingston, 1992—; chair libr. subcom., Livingston, 1990-91; mem. Dist. Tech. Com., Livingston, 1992-93; chmn. Libr. Media Curriculum, Livingston, 1993-94. Contbr. book and video reviews to profl. jours. Facilitator Crazy Paradise Wilderness Group, Livingston, 1990. Fellow Mont. Writing Project, 1979; Mature Woman scholar Bus. and Profl. Women, 1991; joint We. Libr. Assn. and Mont. Libr. Assn. Internet Tng. grantee, 1994. Mem. We. Libr. Network, Pacific N.W. Libr. Assn., Mont. Libr. Assn. (svcs. to youth and children 1989—, sch. libr. media divsn. 1991—, retreat site coord. 1994, Continuing Edn. grantee 1990-91). Office: Park High Sch Libr McLeod Island Livingston MT 59047

GOODMAN, ELIZABETH ANN, lawyer; b. Marquette, Mich., Aug. 11, 1950; d. Paul William and Pearl Marie Goodman; m. Herbert Charles Gardner, Sept. 24, 1977. Student, U. Munich, 1970-71; BA cum laude, Alma (Mich.) Coll., 1972; JD cum laude, U. Mich., 1977. Bar: Minn. 1978, Mich. 1978, U.S. Dist. Ct. Minn. 1979. Cert. real property law specialist, real property sect. Minn. Bar Assn. High sch. tchr. Onaway (Mich.) High Sch., 1973-74; assoc. Dorsey and Whitney P.L.L.P., Mpls., 1978-82, ptnr., 1983—. Mem. Minn. Bar Assn., Hennepin County Bar Asnn. Office: Dorsey & Whitney PLLP 220 S 6th St Minneapolis MN 55402

GOODMAN, ELLEN HOLTZ, journalist; b. Newton, Mass., Apr. 11, 1941; d. Jackson Jacob and Edith (Weinstein) Holtz; m. Robert Levey; 1 dau., Katherine Anne. B.A. cum laude, Radcliffe Coll., 1963; hon. degrees, Mt. Holyoke Coll., Amherst Coll., U. Pa., U. N.H. Researcher, reporter Newsweek Mag., 1963-65; feature writer Detroit Free Press, 1965-67; feature writer columnist Boston Globe, 1967-74, assoc. editor, 1986—; syndicated columnist Washington Post Writers Group, 1976—; radio commentator Spectrum, CBS, 1978-80, NBC, 1979-80; commentator NBC Today Show, 1979-81. Author: Close to Home, 1979, Turning Points, 1979, At Large, 1981, Keeping in Touch, 1985, Making Sense, 1989, Value Judgments, 1993. Trustee Radcliffe Coll. Nieman fellow Harvard U., 1974; named New Eng. Newspaper Woman of Year New Eng. Press Assn., 1968; recipient Catherine O'Brien award Stanley Home Products, 1971, Media award Mass. Commn. Status Women, 1974, Columnist of Year award New Eng. Women's Press Assn., 1975, Pulitzer Prize for Commentary, 1980, prize for column writing Am. Soc. Newspaper Editors, 1980, Hubert H. Humphrey Civil Rights award, 1988, William Allen White award 1995. Office: Globe Newspapers Co 135 Morrissey Blvd Dorchester MA 02125-3338

GOODMAN, ERIKA, dancer, actress; b. Phila.; d. A. Allan and Laura (Baylin) G. Student, Sch. of Am. Ballet, 1961-63; BA in Theatre and Dance, Empire State Coll., 1993; master classes, Princeton Ballet, 1994. Mem. faculty Actors and Dirs. Lab., N.Y.C., 1979—; founding mem. ensemble theater co. The Barrow Group, N.Y.C., 1986—; mem. dance faculty CCNY, 1990; mem. dance faculty CCNY, 1990; guest tchr. ballet Balettakademein, Stockholm, 1986, 89; instr. master classes Rutgers U., East Carolina U., 1989, Hofstra U., U. Kans., 1990, Harvard U., summer 1993, Cornell U., Skidmore Coll., Vassar Coll., 1992—, Conn. Coll.; vis. prof. ballet, head ballet dept. CCNY, 1992—, lectr. world arts, 1993—. Dancer N.Y.C. Ballet Co., 1964-65, prin. dancer Joffrey Ballet, N.Y.C., 1966-75; performer (with Barrow Group) Seymour in the Heart of Winter, Perry St. Theatre, N.Y.C., 1986, When You Comin' Back Red Rider, 1987, Feather Hat, Three Sisters, 1989; casting dir. (films) Hazing in Hell, Neon Red; dir. ballet rehearsal Ballet Hispanico. Richard Porter Leach fellow, 1992-93.

GOODMAN, EVELYN KITTENPLAN, retired bank officer; b. Richmond, Va., Dec. 30, 1924; d. Philip and Hannah (Harfeld) K.; m. Bernard Stuart Goodman, June 15, 1947; children: Debra Sue, John William. Grad., Rutgers U. Stonier Grad. Sch. Banking, 1973; B in Commerce, U. Richmond, 1981. Proof transit clk. Cen. Nat. Bank, Richmond, 1941-43, proof transit mgr., 1943-45, acctg. clk., 1945-51, collateral custodian, 1957-62, with trust dept. investments, 1963-65, with trust dept., acctg. control, 1966-68, ops. officer, mgr., wire transfer, 1968-76, with methods, procedures, 1976-92, asst. v.p., 1978; ret., 1992. Bd. dirs. Sauer's Garden Civic Assn., Richmond, 1981-83; v.p. Temple Beth-El, Richmond, 1986-88, v.p. adminstrn. Sisterhood, 1993—; charter bd. dirs. Literacy Coun. Met. Richmond, 1982-90, 93—, sec., 1987-90; v.p. membership Shalom group Richmond chpt. Hadassah, 1993—; v.p. ways and means Beth Sholom Home Aux., 1993-94. Mem. Am. Inst. Banking (hon., pres. Richmond chpt. 1968-69, Banker of Yr. 1975), Nat. Assn. Bank Women (pres. 1970-71), Altrusa Internat. Club of Richmond (pres. 1973-75, dist. 2 treas. 1978-80, dist. chmn. fin. com. 1980-82, bd. dirs. 1993—). Jewish.

GOODMAN, FRANCES ROSALIND, mechanical engineer; b. Montreal, Ont., Can., Feb. 9, 1967; came to U.S., 1976; d. David Abraham and Mary (Barnes) G. BSME, Rensselaer Polytechnic Inst., 1989. Mech. engr. Krebs Engrs., Menlo Park, Calif., 1987-89, Lightwave Electronics, Mountain View, Calif., 1990—. Sec. homeowners bd. Willow West, Menlo Park, 1993—. Mem. ASME, Soc. Women Engrs., Soc. Mech. Engrs. Home: 21 Willow Rd # 38 Menlo Park CA 94025-5735 Office: Lightwave Electronics 1161 San Antonio Rd Mountain View CA 94043

GOODMAN, GAIL BUSMAN, small business owner; b. N.Y.C., Feb. 8, 1953; d. Irving Laurence and Harriet (Topol) Busman; m. Laurence Goodman, June 17, 1979 (div. 1987). Student, Northwestern U., 1970-72; BS magna cum laude, Tufts U., 1975. Staff occupational therapist St. Joseph's Hosp., Yonkers, N.Y., 1975-77; sr. occupational therapist N.Y. Hosp., White Plains, 1977-79; chief occupational therapist Phelps Hosp., Tarrytown, N.Y., 1979-80; occupational therapy cons. Elmwood Manor Nursing Home, Nanuet, N.Y., 1982-83; v.p. tng. Facelifters, Bklyn., 1981-86; pres. Visual Impact, Rye, N.Y., 1987—, ConsulTel, Rye, 1988—; guest speaker Columbia U., N.Y.C., 1977, 78, 79, 82. Mem. Women in Sales (pres. Westchester chpt. 1989-91). Democrat. Jewish.

GOODMAN, GAIL M., critical care and pediatric nurse; b. Chgo., Mar. 29, 1956; d. Jesse Williams; m. Napoleon Goodman; children: Marie, Mia, Justin, Michelle. Lic. practical nurse diploma, Chgo. Bd. Edn.; student, Chgo. State U., 1973-76, Governors' State U.; AS in Nursing, Olive-Harvey Coll., Chgo., 1984. RN, Ill.; cert. ACLS, TNCC, PALS instr. Practical nurse pediatrics unit U. Chgo. Hosps.; nurse emergency nurse South Chgo. Hosp.; relief charge nurse obstetrics and emergency room Roseland Hosp., Chgo., nurse emergency room; nurse mgr. emergency rm. Roseland Hosp., 1991-92; nurse mgr. pediatrics and emergency rm. St. Mary Med. Ctr., Gary, Ind., 1992—; seminar participant in field.

GOODMAN, GERTRUDE AMELIA, civic worker; b. El Paso, Tex., Oct. 24, 1924; d. Karl Perry and Helen Sylvia (Pinkiert) G. BA, Mills Coll., 1945. Pres. El Paso chpt. Tex. Social Welfare Assn., 1963-65, bd. dirs. 1965-70, state bd. dirs., 1965-70; state bd. dirs. Pan-Am. Round Table, El Paso, 1966—, bd. dirs. 1970-71, sec., 1973-74, life mem.; founder, 1st chmn. El Paso Mus. Art Mem. Guild, 1962-68; bd. dirs. Mus. Art Assn., 1962-69, also v.p.; chmn. dir. El Paso C. of C. women's Dept., 1976-77, Rio Grande Food Bank, 1988-94; pres. bd. dirs. El Paso Pub. Libr., 1978-80; pres. El Paso County Hist. Soc., 1981-82, bd. dirs., 1986-92; mem. planning com. El Paso United Way, 1953—; bd. dirs. El Paso Pub. Libr., 1972-80; mem. El Paso Mus. Art Bd. Coun. Recipient Hall of Honor award El Paso County Hist. Soc., Nat. Human Rels. award NCCJ, 1981, numerous awards for civic vol. work. Home: 905 Cincinnati Ave El Paso TX 79902-2435

GOODMAN, GRACE ANN, lawyer; b. Calais, Maine, May 13, 1936; d. Edward and Olive (Mott) G. BA in English, U. Redlands, 1957; MA in English, U. Wis., 1958; JD, Columbia U., 1978. Bar: N.Y. 1979, U.S. Dist. Ct. (so. dist.) N.Y. 1979, U.S. Dist. Ct. (ea. dist.) N.Y. 1979, U.S. Ct. Appeals (2d cir.) 1981. Press officer Am. Bapt. Demon. Hdqs., N.Y.C., 1958-59, asst. editor Crusader Mag., 1959-62; asst. for radio-TV Coun. of Chs. of N.Y.C., 1962-64; rsch. writer, Presbyn. Bd. Nat. Missions, N.Y.C., 1964-73; dir. evaluation Program Agy. United Presbyn. Ch. USA, N.Y.C., 1973-75; assoc. Rosenman & Colin, N.Y.C., 1978-84; asst. corp. counsel City of New York, 1984—. Author: Rocking the Ark, 1968; editor: Division in the Protestant House, 1976, author, producer: (TV series) Biographies of Three Theologians, 1963. Officer, mem. N.Y. Women's Chorus, N.Y.C., 1982-89; v.p. Dan Wagoner Dance Found., N.Y.C., 1988-92; mem. county com. Democrat Orgn., N.Y.C., 1982-84. Recipient Persuasive Writing award Forest Lawn Inc., 1957; fellow U. Wis., 1958. Mem. Assn. Bar of City of N.Y. (com. legal problems of elderly 1989-91, com. on immigration law 1981-84), Coun. of N.Y. Law Assocs. (dir. 1986-89). Democrat. American Baptist. Home: 156 W 77th St New York NY 10024 Office: City of New York Law Dept 100 Church St New York NY 10007

GOODMAN, GWENDOLYN ANN, nursing educator; b. Davenport, Iowa, Aug. 7, 1955; d. Merle Erwin and Loraine Etta (Mahannah) Langfeldt; m. Mark Nathan Goodman, Oct. 24, 1982; children: Zachary Aaron, Alexander Daniel. BS in Nursing, Ariz. State U., 1977. RN, Ariz. Staff nurse surg. fl. and intensive care unit St. Luke's Hosp. and Med. Ctr., Phoenix, 1977-81; staff nurse intensive care unit Yavapai Regional Med. Ctr., Prescott, Ariz., 1981-82; instr. nursing Yavapai Coll., Prescott, 1982-88, cons., 1986; part-time staff nurse Ariz. Poison Control Ctr., Phoenix, 1980-81; mem. profl. adv. com. Home Health Agy. Yavapai Regional Med. Ctr., 1988-93. Mem. Sigma Theta Tau. Democrat. Home: PO Box 450 Prescott AZ 86302-0450

GOODMAN, JOAN FRANCES, avionics manufacturing executive; b. N.Y.C., Oct. 25, 1941; d. Jack and Evelyn (Fine) G.; m. Stephen Gordon Glatzer, Oct. 2, 1982 (dec. Dec. 1987). BS, Alfred U., 1963; MA, NYU, 1967. RN, N.Y. Psychiatric liaison nurse Hosp. Albert Einstein Coll. Medicine, N.Y.C., 1968-73; nursing care coord. United Hosp., Port Chester, N.Y., 1974-80; asst. to pres. Glatzer Industries, New Rochelle, N.Y., 1980-87; pres., chief exec. officer Glatzer Industries Corp., New Rochelle, 1987—, Emergency Beacon Corp., New Rochelle, 1987—, ELTS Ltd., Inc., New Rochelle, 1987—. Mem. ANA, Nat. League Nursing, Chief Exec. Network (Westchester and Rockland County chpts.), Westchester Assn. Women Bus. Owners, Am. Women's Econ. Corp., Nat. Coun. Women in Aviation. Office: Glatzer Industries Corp 15 River St New Rochelle NY 10801-4351

GOODMAN, KAREN LACERTE, financial services executive; b. Mesa, Ariz., Nov. 9, 1946; d. Howard Lee and Margaret (Duncan) G.; m. Grant A. Lacerte, Feb. 1, 1964; children: Arthur Grant Jr., Arcel Leon Rene. Student, George Washington U., 1974-76. Prodn. mgr. Data Corp. of Am., Reston, Va., 1967-73; pres. Transco Leasing Co., Washington, 1974-78; sec., treas. to v.p. Certa Data Corp., Orlando, Fla., 1989—; pres. Fin. Rsch. Assocs., Inc., Orlando, 1979—; cons. in field, 1979—; dir. statis. seminars in field. Editor, pub.: Financial Studies of the Small Business (annual publ.), 1976—. Mem. Am. Heart Assn., Winter Haven, Fla., MADD, 1985—. Mem. Greater Orlando C. of C. Republican. Home: 6759 Winterset Gardens Rd Winter Haven FL 33884-3154 Office: Financial Rsch Assocs 510 Avenue J SE Winter Haven FL 33880-3781

GOODMAN, MARGARET GERTRUDE, government administrator; b. East Troy, Wis., Aug. 29, 1947; d. Andrew J. and Florence M. (Zinn) G.; 1 child, Mary Zinn. BA, Beloit Coll., 1969; MA, Johns Hopkins U., 1971. Legis. asst. to Rep. Clement J. Zablocki Ho. of Reps., Washington, 1971-73, staff cons. Com. Fgn. Affairs, 1977-93; fgn. policy analyst Congl. Rsch. Svc., Libr. Congress, Washington, 1973-77; regional dir. for Asia and Pacific Peace Corps, Washington, 1993—. Mem. Soc. Internat. Devel. (pres. Washington chpt. 1982-84, internat. v.p. 1988-91), Women in Fgn. Policy Assn., Asia Soc. Democrat. Office: Peace Corps 1990 K St NW Rm 7616 Washington DC 20526

GOODMAN, MYRNA MARCIA, school nurse; b. Bklyn., Mar. 5, 1936; d. Louis and Anna R. (Bernowitz) Sheinberg; m. Stanley M. Goodman, June 30, 1957; children: Farrell Jay, Blayne Barrie, Devin Josh, Danica Janine. Diploma, L.I. Coll. Hosp., Bklyn., 1956; B in Elected Studies, Thomas More Coll., 1980; postgrad., Xavier U., 1984-86. Cert. sch. nurse, Ohio. Sch. nurse, supr. health and wellness svcs. L.I. Coll. Hosp., 1956-58; nurse, office mgr. Pediatric Assocs. of Fairfield (Ohio), Inc., 1962-72; nurse Fairfield City Sch. Dist., 1972-89, dir. health svcs., 1989-92, supr. health and wellness svcs., 1992—; sec. Fairfield City Safety Coun., 1987-90; mem. Intervention Team for At-Risk Students, 1987-90, Del. to Study Sch. Health, Australia, 1989; keynote speaker Ohio Comprehensive Sch. Health Conf., 1991; conf. speaker Ohio Assn. Health, Phys. Edn., Recreation and Dance, 1990, Nat. Sch. Bds. Assn., 1993. Mem. adv. coun. Butler County Mental Health Assn., Drug Free Schs. and Community, 1988, Am. Heart Assn.; chairperson sch. site com. Am. Heart Assn., 1991—; past pres. Fairfield Tempo Club, 1976; com. mem. Fairfield Sister City Program; mem. Modern Music Masters, 1976; mem. adv. coun. Daytime Ctr. for Girls; bd. dirs. Greater Hamilton Safety Coun., Am. Heart Assn., 1988; coord. Heart-at-Work Program; co-chairperson Emplyee Wellness Com.; chairperson Comprehensive Sch. Health; adv. com. Fairfield Pub. Presch.; chairperson adv. com. Fairfield Schs. Food Svc.; spkr. del. assembly Ohio affiliate Am. Heart Assn., 1992, rep., 1994, co-pres. elect Hamilton/Fairfield divsn. bd. dirs. Recipient Outstanding Svc. award Fairfield Cen. Sch., 1974, 77, 78, 89, Letters of Recognition for Outstanding Svc. to Fairfield Sch. Dist. Supt., 1980, 86, 89, 90, March of Dimes, Am. Lung Assn., 1980, Am. Heart Assn., 1988, 89, 90, Hall of Fame award Am. Heart Assn., 1992, co-recipient Cert. of Appreciation, Am. Heart Assn. Sch. Site Task Force, 1992. Mem. NEA, ASCD, Ohio Edn. Assn., Ohio Assn. Sch. Nurses (conf. speaker 1993), S.W. Ohio Sch. Nurses Assn. (sec. 1987-90), Am. Sch. Health Assn., Nat. Assn. Sch. Nurses, Parents and Tchrs. for Children, Ohio Assn. Secondary Sch. Adminstrs., Nat. Assn. Secondary Sch. Adminstrs. Home: 5180 Suwannee Dr Fairfield OH 45014-2482 Office: Fairfield City Sch Dist 211 Donald Dr Fairfield OH 45014-3095

GOODMAN, VALERIE DAWSON, psychiatric social worker; b. Bluefield, W.Va., Feb. 2, 1948; d. Francis Carl and Lesly (Collett) Dawson; m. David William Goodman, June 9, 1985; 1 child, Amanda Lynn. BS, W.Va. U., 1970, MS, 1972; MSW, U. Md., 1980. Lic. clin. social worker, Md. Social worker Md. Children's Aide Family Svcs. Soc., Balt., 1972-78; social worker III Montgomery County Dept. Social Svcs., Rockville, Md., 1980-81; clin. social worker Johns Hopkins Hosp., Balt., 1981-83; part-time pvt. practice Balt., 1986—; supr. Johns Hopkins Hosp., 1983-86, chair Brogden com., 1984-85, spl. events com. depression and related affective disorders dept. psychiatry, 1994; spkr. in field. Parent vol. Park Sch. Mem. Kappa Delta. Home: 54 Bellchase Ct Pikesville MD 21208-1300

GOODMAN, YETTA M., educator; b. Cleve., Mar. 10, 1931; d. William and Dora (Shapiro) Trachtman; B.A. in History, Los Angeles State Coll., 1952, M.A. in Elem. Edn., 1956; Ed.D. in Curriculum Devel., Wayne State U., 1967; m. Kenneth S. Goodman, 1952; children: Debra, Karen, Wendy. Elem. and secondary tchr., public schs., Los Angeles, 1952-63; supr. pre-service teaching experiences Wayne State U., 1963-67; asst. to prof. U. Mich., Dearborn, 1967-75; prof. edn., co-dir. program in lang. and literacy U. Ariz., 1975—; regents prof., U. Ariz., 1990—; speaker, cons. lang. and lit. devel. Active in orgns. concerned with censorship and children's rights. Recipient Faculty Recognition award Tucson Trade Bur., 1978, Outstanding Tchr. Educator of Reading award Internat. Reading Assn., 1983. Mem. Nat. Council Tchrs. English (bd. dirs. 1976—, pres. 1978-79, Disting. Svc. award 1994), Center Expansion of Lang. and Thinking (bd. dirs. 1972—, pres. 1976-79), Internat. Reading Assn. (chairperson and active mem. various coms. 1962—, bd. dirs. 1994—, elected into Reading Hall Fame 1994), Internat. Assn. Supervision and Curriculum Devel., Am. Ednl. Research Assn., Assn. Childhood Edn. Internat. (bd. dirs. internat. centre for study literacy processes 1988—). Jewish. Author: How Children Construct Literacy: Piagetian Perspectives, 1990; (with C. Burke and B. Sherman) Reading Strategies: Focus on Comprehension, 1981; (with D. Watson and C. Burke) Reading Miscue Inventory: Alternate Procedures, 1986, (with K. Goodman and Wendy Hood) The Whole Language Evaluation, 1989, Organizing for Whole Language, 1991; (with K. Goodman and L. Bird) The Whole Language Catalogue, 1991; (with S. Wilde) Literacy Events in a Community of Young Writers, 1992, (with K. Goodman and L. Bird) The Whole Language Catalogue: Supplement on Authentic Assessment, 1992, The Language Catalogue: Forms for Authentic Assessment, 1994; contbr. numerous articles, chpts. to profl. publs.; also audio tapes scripts video, films. Home: 5649 E 10th St Tucson AZ 85711-3268 Office: U Ariz Coll Edn Program in Lang and Literacy Tucson AZ 85721

GOODSON, CAROL FAYE, librarian; b. Detroit, Mar. 28, 1947; d. Norman Elwood and Wilma Mary (Harmon) G.; m. Lawrence J. Price, May 10, 1974 (div. 1977). BA, SUNY, Buffalo, 1970, MLS, 1972. Libr. SUNY, Buffalo, 1970-72, St. Louis Pub. Libr., 1973-77; community sch. dir. St. Louis Bd. Edn., 1977-80; reference libr. Ga. Dept. Edn., Atlanta, 1981-84; head pub. svcs. Atlanta campus Mercer U., Chamblee, Ga., 1985; mem. Dominican Sisters of Nashville, 1985-90; asst. dir. Clayton County Libr. System, Jonesboro, Ga., 1990-91; coord. off-campus libr. svcs. West Ga.

Coll., Carrollton, 1991—; state coord. GA. Summer Reading Club, 1991; owner and moderator, ALA-PLAN listserv. Pres. Tower/Literacy Vols. Am., Clayton County, 1991; active Leadership Clayton, 1990-91. Mem. AAUP (exec. com. 1994—), ALA, Ga. Libr. Assn., Southeastern Libr. Assn., Libr. Info. Tech. Assn. (program planning com. 1992—, sec. 1993—), Assn. Coll. Rsch. Librs. (clip notes com. 1992—, extended campus libr. svcs. sect., comm. com. 1994—), Beta Phi Mu. Home: 210 Oak Ave Carrollton GA 30117-3726 Office: West Ga Coll Ingram Libr Carrollton GA 30118

GOODSON, MONA KAY, home economics educator; b. Tribune, Kans., Mar. 11, 1967; d. Lester Lew Sr. and Lyla Kay (Rowton) Burch; m. Thomas Mitchell Goodson, Dec. 30, 1989; children: Lacey Kay, Kaitlyn Marie. Assoc., Ea. Okla. State Coll., 1987; BS, East Ctrl. U., 1990. Vocat. home econs. educator Strother High Sch., Seminole, Okla., 1990—. Mem. Okla. Edn. Assn., Okla. Vocat. Assn., Strother Edn. Assn. Roman Catholic.

GOODSON, SHANNON LORAYN, behavioral scientist, author; b. Beaumont, Tex., May 26, 1952; d. James Ernest and Lorayn (Miller) G. BS in Psychology, Lamar U., 1974, MS in Organizational Psychology, 1977. Co-founder, pres., CEO Behavioral Scis. Rsch. Press, Inc., Dallas, 1979-92, pres., 1992—; presenter in field; guest on various radio talk shows. Co-author: (with G.W. Dudley) Earning What You're Worth?, 1992, Psychology of Call Reluctance, 1986; contbr. articles to profl. jours. and periodicals. Mem. SE Psychol. Assn. Office: Behavioral Scis Rsch Press 12803 Demetra Dr Dallas TX 75234

GOODSPEED, BARBARA, artist; b. Gardner, Mass., Sept. 1, 1919; d. George Daniel and Bernice (Lucas) G. Diploma Stoneleigh Coll., 1939, Famous Artist Schs., Westport, Conn., 1955. Free-lance photographer, N.Y.C., 1941-52, Christmas card designer, Sherman, Conn., 1952-69, oil and watercolor, fine arts artist, Sherman, 1969—. Illustrator: Forever Flowers, 1979. Recipient Merit award Sheffield Art League, 1979, 81, 83, others; named Artist of Yr., Art League of Harlem Valley, 1981. Fellow Am. Artists Profl. League (John Dole Meml. award, Parsons award 1991); mem. Salmagundi Club(Jane Peterson Meml. award), Hudson Valley Art Assn., Acad. Artists, Nat League Am. Pen Women, Kent Art Assn., Inc. (pres. 1970-72, 80-83, 85-88, 91-93, medal of Merit 1979, Grumbacher Gold medal 1989, 91), Housatonic Art League (v.p., bd. dirs. 1977-83), Catharine Lorillard Wolfe Art Club (bd. dirs. 1990-93, Corp. award). Avocations: camping, crafts. Home and Studio: 11 Holiday Point Rd Sherman CT 06784

GOODSTADT, SUZANNE LOUISE, artist; b. Boston, Nov. 28, 1950. Degree in fine arts, Accademia DiBelle Arti, Florence, Italy; degree in fashion design, Garland Jr. Coll., Boston; student, Mus. Fine Arts, Boston, Mass. Coll. Art, Boston, Sch. Visual Arts, N.Y.C., Art Students League, N.Y.C. Owner gallery N.Y.C.; instr. Fairleigh Dickinson U., Guggenheim Mus., 1985; fine art cons. Dyansen Gallery, N.Y., 1985, Boston Mus. of Sci., 1988, Brodney Gallery of Fine Arts, Boston, 1988-90; promotion cons. Manhattan Theater Club, 1985; art dealer European artists; art cons. TV, Channel D, 1980, Lee Ansel, 1980. Exhibited in group shows at Palazzo Strozzi Il Centro D'Incontro Per Stranieri, Florence, 1971, Mus. of Fine Arts, Boston, Mass. Coll. of Art, Boston.

GOODSTONE, ROSEMARY ANN, photographer; b. Wauwatosa, Wis., Feb. 2, 1947; d. Mary Ann (Bielicki) Fryt; m. Alan M. Goodstone, Nov. 27, 1968; 1 child, Julie R. Grad. high sch., Franklin, Wis. Receptionist, bookkeeper Family Fin., Milw., 1966-67; credit investigator Mortgage Assocs., Milw., 1967-68; sec., word processor IBM Corp., Milw., 1968-73; color artist Goodstone Candids, Franklin, Wis., 1974-84; photographer Goodstone Photography, Franklin, 1984—. Mem. Franklin Sch. Bd. Coms., 1982—; leader Girl Scouts U.S.A., Franklin, 1985; bd. dirs. Childbirth Edn. Assn., Milw., 1973-78; pres., bd. dirs. Parent Tchr. Orgn., Milw. and Franklin, 1978-85. Mem. Profl. Photographers Am., Wis. Profl. Photographers Assn. (various coms., bd. dirs. 1989-93, editor newsletter 1991-92, Scholar 1987, Cert. of Appreciation 1989, assoc. fellow 1992), S.E. Wis. Profl. Photographers Assn. (various coms., editor newsletter 1990, treas. 1991, sec. 1992, v.p. 1993, pres. 1994, Competition ribbons, Svc. award 1993, 94, 95), Wis. Bus. and Profl. Women, Nat. Fedn. Ind. Bus., Franklin C. of C. (v.p. 1992, pres. 1993, chmn. 1994, editor newsletter). Roman Catholic. Office: 7121 S 76th St # B Franklin WI 53132-9736

GOODWILL, JANET V. (CALI), psychotherapist; b. Winthrop, Mass., Sept. 10, 1943; d. Anthony and Virginia (Briana) Cali; m. Robert James Goodwill, Apr. 20, 1963; children: Debora Goodwill Choquette, Donna M. Goodwill. BA, U. Lowell, 1990; MA, U. Mass., 1992. Lic. marriage and family therapist. Cmty. devel. specialist Cmty./Univ. Partnership, Lowell, Mass., 1992-93; psychotherapist Ctr. for Family Devel., Lowell, Mass., 1993—; founder, dir. The Women's Connection, Lowell, 1992—; instr. U. Mass., Lowell, 1992—, Middlesex C.C., Lowell, 1993—; cons. Family Connection, Lowell, 1992—. Co-author copywright Student Success game, 1993; contbr. articles to profl. jours. Trustee Chelmsford (Mass.) Edn. Found., 1989—; bd. dirs. Rape Crisis Svcs. Greater Lowell, 1991—. Mem. APA, Mass. Tchrs. Assn. Home: 428 Wellman Ave North Chelmsford MA 01863 Office: Ctr for Family Devel 45 Merrimack St Lowell MA 01852

GOODWIN, BARBARA A., retired nurse, military officer; b. Phila., Dec. 23, 1938. Diploma, Boston City Hosp. Sch. Nursing, 1959; BS, U. Pa., 1968; MS, U. Colo., 1972; grad., Sq. Officer Sch., 1973, Air Command & Staff Coll., 1974, Air War Coll., 1977. Commd. officer USAF, advanced through ranks to brig. gen., 1988, nurse, 1962—; staff nurse USAF, Otis AFB, Mass.; clinic nurse USAF Clinic, Naha Air Base, Okinawa, Japan, 1963-65; clinic staff nurse USAF Hosp., Minot AFB, N.D., from 1965; flight nurse Aeromed. Evacuation Squadron, Rhein-Mein AFB, Frankfurt, Fed. Republic Germany, 1968-71; charge nurse med. unit USAF Med. Ctr., Scott AFB, Ill., 1972-73; clin. nurse specialist Malcolm Grow USAF Med. Ctr., Andrews AFB, Md., 1973-74, surg. nursing practice coord., from 1974; asst. chief nurse USAF Regional Hosp., Lakenheath, Eng., 1974-76; adminstrv. staff officer Office of Chief Air Force Nurse Corps, Bolling AFB, D.C., 1979-83; chmn. dept. nursing David Grant USAF Med. Ctr., Travis AFB, Calif., 1983-84; asst. for nursing svcs. Hdqrs. Mil. Airlift Command, USAF Med. Ctr., Scott AFB, Ill., 1984-88; chief USAF Nurse Corps, Office Surgeon Gen., USAF Hdqrs., Washington, 1988-91; ret., 1991. Decorated D.S.M., Legion of Merit with one oak leaf cluster. Mem. ANA, Aerospace Med. Assn., Assn. Mil. Surgeons of USAF Assn., Bus. and Profl. Women., Sigma Theta Tau.

GOODWIN, BARBARA LEE, school system administrator; b. Glendale, Tex., July 13, 1939; d. Charlie Wise and Maude Muller (Johnson) W.; m. Alfred Vern Goodwin, Mar. 30, 1957; children: Charles, Douglas, Elyse, Faylinn. BA, Howard Payne Coll., 1961; MEd, Stephen A. Austin U., 1973; student, Sam Houston State U., 1984. Cert. tchr. and counselor, Tex. Tchr. Channelview (Tex.) Schs., 1961-67, Lukin (Tex.) Schs., 1967-74; ednl. diagnostician Corsicana (Tex.) Schs., 1974-78; counselor elem. Huntsville (Tex.) Schs., 1978-81, prin., 1981-87, coord. elem. edn., 1987—. Office: Huntsville Sch Dist 441 Fm2821 Huntsville TX 77340

GOODWIN, JEAN MCCLUNG, psychiatrist; b. Pueblo, Colo., Mar. 28, 1946; d. Paul Stanley and Geraldine (Smart) McClung; m. James Simeon Goodwin, Aug. 8, 1970; children: Laura (dec.), Amanda Harding Goodwin, Robert Caleb, Paul Joshua, Elizabeth Cronin Goodwin. BA in Anthropology summa cum laude, Radcliffe Coll., 1967; MD, Harvard U., 1971; MPH, UCLA, 1972. Diplomate Am. Bd. Psychiatry and Neurology, Am. Bd. Forensic Psychiatry. Resident in psychiatry Georgetown U. Hosp., Washington, 1972-74; resident in psychiatry U. N.Mex. Sch. Medicine, 1974-76, asst. dir., dir. psychiat. residents tng., 1979-85; prof. Med. Coll. Wis., 1985-92, U. Tex. Med. Br., Galveston, 1992—; from inst. to assoc. prof. dept. psychiatry U. N.Mex. Sch. Medicine, 1976-85; cons. protective services Dept. Human Services, N.Mex., 1976-84; lectr. profl. groups. Author: Effects of High Altitude on Human Birth, 1969, Sexual Abuse: Incest Victims and Their Families, 1982, 2d edit., 1989, Rediscovering Childhood Trauma: Historical Casebook and Clinical Applications, 1993, Mischief and Mercy, 1993; mem. editl. bd. Jour. Traumatic Stress, 1985-93, Dissociation, 1988—; contbr. numerous articles on child abuse to profl. jours. Chmn. work group on child sexual abuse Surgeon Gen.'s Conference on Violence and Pub. Health, Leesburg, Va., 1985; mem. adv. bd. Nat. Resource Ctr. on Child Sexual Abuse, 1989—. Recipient Saville Prize in Family Planning, UCLA Sch. Pub. Health, 1972, Esther Haar award Am. Acad. Psychoanalysis, 1990, Cornelia Wilbur award Internat. Soc. for Study of Dissociation, 1994; Nat. Cen. Child Abuse and Neglect grantee, 1979-82, Nat. Inst. Aging grantee, 1980-85. Fellow Internat. Soc. Study Multiple Personality Dissociative Disorders (exec. com. 1991—), Am. Psychiat. Assn. (dist. br. treas., sec. N.Mex. br. 1980-82, exhibits and programs subcoms. 1985-91); mem. Am. Profl. Soc. on Sexual Abuse in Children (bd. dirs. 1986-90), Am. Med. Women's Assn. (state dir. N.Mex. 1978-80). Democrat. Roman Catholic. Office: U Tex Med Br Dept Psychiatry And Be Galveston TX 77555

GOODWIN, MARYELLEN, state legislator; b. Providence, Sept. 27, 1964. Student, R.I. Coll. mem. 12th Ward Dem. Com., R.I. Young Dems. Mem. state senate State of R.I., 1986—. Roman Catholic. Home: 325 Smith St Providence RI 02908-3759 Office: R I State Senate State Capital Providence RI 02903*

GOODWIN, NANCY LEE, corporate executive; b. Peoria, Ill., Aug. 11, 1940; d. Raymond Darrell and Mildred Louise (Brown) G. B.A. (Nat. Meth. scholar, Nat. Merit scholar), MacMurray Coll., 1961; M.A., U. Colo., 1963; Ph.D., U. Ill., 1971. Tchr. Roosevelt Jr. High Sch., Peoria, 1961-62; counselor U. Ill., Urbana, 1963-66; staff assoc., asst. prof. edn. measurement U. Ill., Chgo., 1967-71; asst. v.p., assoc. prof. stats. Fla. Internat. U., Miami, 1971-78; pres. Greenfield (Mass.) Community Coll., 1978-82, Arapahoe Community Coll., Colo., from 1982; corp. owner MTF Enterprises; prof. Nat. U.; owner C.A.T.S. Inc., 1987—; corp. mgr. DRM Enterprises; dir. Cons. Mid-Am. Computer Corp., First Chance Network U.S. Office Edn., 1972-78. Mem. Com. on Ill. Govt., Higher Edn. Task Force; mem. Vol. Action Center, Miami, 1972-78; active Girl Scouts U.S.A.; mem. Franklin/Hampshire Area Service Planning Team, 1978; incorporator Franklin County (Mass.) United Way, Farren Meml. Hosp.; adv. Franklin County Public Hosp.; bd. dirs. Women's Inst. Fla., Franklin County Arts Council, Franklin County Devel. Corp., Western Welcome Week, Inc.; bd. dirs., mem. fin. monitoring com. New Eng. Soy Dairy, 1980. Recipient Merit award Chgo. Tchrs. Assn., 1969; citation Girl Scouts U.S.A., 1973. Mem. NEA, Am. Assn. Higher Edn., Am. Ednl. Research Assn., Assn. Instl. Research, Centennial C. of C. (dir. 1983). Home: 5228 Del Rey Ave Las Vegas NV 89102-1414

GOODWIN, SHARON ANN, academic administrator; b. Little Rock, May 19, 1949; d. Jimmy Lee and Eddie DeLois (Cluck) G.; m. Mitchell Shayne Mick, May 4, 1968 (div. Mar. 1973); 1 child, Heather Michelle; m. Raymond Eugene Vaclavik, June 24, 1974 (div. Aug. 1982); 1 child, Tasha Rae Vaclavik. BA in Psychology, U. Houston-Clear Lake, 1980; MEd in Higher Edn. Adminstrn., U. Houston, 1990. Various clerical positions Gen. Telephone Co., Dickinson, Tex., 1969-80; state dir. Challenge, Inc., Oklahoma City, 1980-82; gen. mgr. Mr. Fix It, Houston, 1982-85; assoc. dir. admissions U. Houston, Tex., 1985-92; adminstr. Inst. for the Med. Humanities U. Tex. Med. Br., Galveston, 1992—. Legis. com. Comm. Workers, Dickinson and Austin, 1975; mem. centennial choir U. Tex. Med. Br., Galveston, 1992; vol. Dickens on the Strand, Galveston, 1993. Recipient Honorable Mention, World of Poetry, 1986, Golden Poet award World of Poetry, 1987. Mem. AAUW, Assn. of Am. Med. Colls.-Group on Institutional Planning. Home: PO Box 517 League City TX 77574 Office: Univ Tex Med Br Inst for the Med Humanities 301 University Blvd Galveston TX 77555-1311

GOODWIN, S(HEILA) DIANE, drug information scientist; b. Durham, N.C., Jan. 19, 1958; d. Leon Jackson and Mattie (Wilson) G. BS in Pharmacy, U. N.C., 1981; PharmD, Med. Coll. Va., 1986. Registered pharmacist, N.C., Va., Colo. Staff pharmacist Durham (N.C.) County Gen. Hosp., 1981-84; asst. prof. U. Fla. Coll. Pharmacy, Gainesville, 1988-89; clin. rsch. pharmacist Duke U. Med. Ctr., Ctr. AIDS Rsch., Durham, 1990-91; asst. prof. U. Colo., Sch. Pharmacy, Denver, 1991-94; drug info. sci. Burroughs Wellcome Co., Research Triangle Park, N.C., 1994—; cons., reviewer, researcher, lectr. in field. Contbr. articles to profl. and sci. jours. Clin. pharmacy fellow Duke U. Med. Ctr., 1986-87, Millard Fillmore Hosp., 1987-88. Mem. Am. Coll. Clin. Pharmacy (chmn. pub. and profl. rels. com. 1991-92, Schering rsch. grantee 1990), Am. Soc. Hosp. Pharmacists, Am. Soc. Microbiology, Am. Assn. Colls. Pharmacy, Soc. Infectious Diseases Pharmacists, Am. Med. Writers Assn., Am. Pharm. Assn., Kappa Epsilon, Rho Chi. Democrat. Baptist. Office: Burroughs Wellcome Co 3030 Cornwallis Rd Durham NC 27709

GOOGINS, SONYA FORBES, state legislator, retired banker; b. New Haven, Nov. 9, 1936; d. Edward and Madeline Forbes; m. Robert Reville Googins, June 21, 1958; children: Shawn W. and Glen. R. BE, U. Conn., 1958; postgrad., Dartmouth Inst., 1978. Tchr. Manchester (Conn.) High Sch., 1958-61; pres. Colonial Printing Co., Glastonbury, 1971-76; br. mgr., bank officer Conn. Nat. Bank, Hartford, 1982-89; mem. Conn. Ho. of Reps., 1994—. Mayor, Town of Glastonbury, 1983-85, 87-91, 93-95; mem. Town Coun., 1979-94; former mem. Econ. Devel. Commn., Youth Svcs. Commn., Rep. Town Com.; active policy bd. Capitol Region Coun. Govts., 1983-91, chmn., 1989-94; chmn. govt. divsn. Great Hartford United Way, 1992; bd. dirs. Conn. Capitol Region Growth Coun., 1992—; active Adv. Commn. Intergovtl. Rels., 1992—. Recipient Outstanding Svc. award Friends of Glastonbury Youth, 1990, Disting. Svc. award Capitol Region Coun., 1994; named Glastonbury Rep. of Yr., 1992. Mem. Nat. Assn. Regional Couns. (bd. dirs. 1993—), Greater Hartford Automobile Assn. Am. (bd. dirs.), Glastonbury Bus. and Profl. Women (past pres. and founder, Woman of Yr. 1988), Glastonbury C. of C., Glastonbury Jr. Woman's Club (past pres.). Roman Catholic. Home: 74 Forest Ln Glastonbury CT 06033-3918

GOOLD, FLORENCE WILSON, occupational therapist; b. Chgo., Aug. 26, 1912; d. Frank Elmer and Marie Louise (Walker) Wilson; m. Robert Charles Goold, Dec. 28, 1938; children: Frances Louise Goold Felty, Nancy Jean, Elizabeth Jane Ill, Robert Charles Jr. Student, U. Wis., 1934; BA, Boston Sch. Occupational Therapy, 1936. Occupational therapist Ypsilanti (Mich.) State Hosp., 1936-40, Michael Reese Hosp., Chgo., 1940-42, DuPage County Easter Seal Ctr., Villa Park, Ill., 1959-62; dir. occupational therapy Hinsdale (Ill.) Sanitarium and Hosp., 1962-71, Marianjoy Rehab. Hosp., Wheaton, Ill., 1971-73, Cen. DuPage Hosp., Winfield, Ill., 1972-73, Royal Oak Convalescent Home, Oak Park, Ill., 1973, Highland House Nursing Home, Downers Grove, Ill., 1973-75, St. Charles Med. Ctr., Aurora, Ill., 1975-78, Westmont (Ill.) Health Ctr., 1978-80, Americana Health Care Ctr., Naperville, Ill., 1981-84, Med. Pers. Pool, Chgo., 1985-89, Midwest Rehab. Svcs., Hindsdale, 1986-95. Pres. bd. dirs. DuPage County Easter Seal Ctr., Villa Park, 1942-59; bd. dirs. Community Adult Day Care, Downers Grove. Named Citizen of Yr., Downers Grove, 1987. Mem. PEO, Am. Occupational Therapy Assn., Ill. Occupational Therapy Ass. (past pres., Occupational Therapist of Yr. 1988), Phi Mu. Episcopalian. Home: 6582 Willowwood Ct Downers Grove IL 60516-3045 Office: Ill Occupational Therapy Assn 715 Lake St Ste 710 Oak Park IL 60301-1416

GOOLKASIAN, PAULA A., psychologist, educator; b. Methuen, Mass., Aug. 9, 1948; d. Paul K. and Sadie T. (Touma) G.; m. Francis C. Martin, July 29, 1978; 1 child, Christopher. BA, Emmanuel Coll., 1970; MS, Iowa State U., 1972, PhD, 1974. Asst. prof. U. N.C., Charlotte, 1974-79, assoc. prof., 1979-85, prof. psychology, 1985—, pres. faculty, 1989—; cons. in field. Contbr. articles to profl. jours. Nat. Def. Ednl. Act. fellow, 1971-74; grantee NSF, NIH, and numerous others. Mem. AAAS, APA, Psychonomics Soc., Ea. Psychol. Assn., Internat. Soc. Psychophysics, Soc. for Computers in Psychology (sec.-treas. 1989-91, pres. 1994), Sigma Xi, Phi Kappa Phi. Home: 7107 Preston Ct Charlotte NC 28215-3625 Office: U NC Dept Psychology Charlotte NC 28223

GOOREY, NANCY JANE, dentist; b. Davenport, Iowa, May 8, 1922; d. Edgar Ray and Glenna Mae (Williams) Miller; m. Douglas B. Miller, Sept. 12, 1939 (div. 1951); children: Victoria Lee, Nickola Ellen, Douglas George, Melahna Marie; m. Louis Joseph Roseberry Goorey, Feb. 22, 1980. Student, Wooster (Ohio) Coll., 1939-40; DDS, Ohio State U., 1955. Cert. in gen. anesthesiology. Mem. faculty coll. dentistry Ohio State U., Columbus, 1955-86, dir., chmn. div. dental hygiene coll. dentistry, 1969-86, asst. dean coll. dentistry, 1975-86, mem. grad. faculty colls. dentistry and medicine, 1980—, asst. dean, prof. emeritus colls. dentistry and medicine, 1986—; moderator, prodn. chmn. Lifesavers 40 Prodns., 1981—. Producer, video program Giving Your Mouth a Sporting Chance, 1990. Chmn. State Planning Com. for Health Edn. in Ohio, Columbus, 1976-77, 87-88; founder, chmn. Coun. on Health Info., Columbus, 1981-85, pres., 1985-86; trustee Mayor's Drug Edn. and Prevention Program, Columbus, 1980—; mem. edn. com. Franklin County Rep. Com.; mem. exec. com. Franklin County Rep. Party, 1993—. Recipient Vol. of Yr. award Columbus Health Dept., 1988-89, Dental Hygiene award Ohio State U., 1988. Fellow Am. Coll. Dentists (pres.-elect 1989-90), Am. Soc. Dental Ansthesiology, Internat. Coll. Dentists; mem. ADA (nat. consumer advisor 1975-78), Am. Assn. Dental Schs. (v.p., pres. 1972-77), Ohio Dental Assn. (cons. 1979—, mem. subcoun. on dentists concerned for dentists 1994—, chmn. subcoun. chem. dependency, Ohio Disting. Dentist 1983), Columbus Dental Soc. (pres. bd. dirs. 1986-87, 89-91, chmn. coun. on constn. and bilaws on jud. affairs 1989—), Ohio State U. Starling Womens Club (pres. 1982-83), Ohio State U. Faculty and Profl. Womens Club (pres. 1971-72), The Found. of the Acad. of Medicine (v.p. 1993-94), Ohio State Med. Assn. Alliance (chmn. state com. legis. affairs 1993-94, chmn. state health promotions com. 1994—), Acad. of Medicine Aux. (pres. 1992—, 93), Omicron Kappa Upsilon. Republican. Episcopalian. Office: Ohio State U Coll Dentistry 305 W 12th Ave Columbus OH 43210-1267

GOOTMAN, PHYLLIS MYRNA, educator; b. N.Y.C., June 8, 1938; d. Albert and Ida (Krieger) Adler; m. Norman Gootman, June 1, 1958; children: Sharon Hillary, Craig Seth. BA cum laude, Barnard Coll., 1959; PhD, Yeshiva U., 1967. Rsch. assoc. dept. physiology and biophysics U. Wash., Seattle, 1963; instr. dept. physiology Albert Einstein Coll. Medicine, Bronx, N.Y., 1968-70, asst. prof., 1970-73; asst. prof. SUNY, Bklyn., 1973-75, assoc. prof., 1975-81, prof., 1981—; vis. asst. prof. dept. physiology Albert Einstein Coll. Medicine, Bronx, 1973-76, vis. prof. dept. Physiology and Biophysics, 1984-92; mem. clin. campus, 1989—. Contbr. articles to profl. jours.; mem. editorial bd. Jour. of Developmental Physiology, 1986—. Recipient Hendel Family award Brandeis U., 1957; John Miles Davidson fellow in physiology Albert Einstein Coll. Medicine, 1973; recipient numerous grants. Fellow Royal Soc. Medicine; mem. AAAS, Soc. for Neurosci., Biophys. Soc., Am. Physiol. Soc., Am. Heart Assn., Am. Inst. Biol. Scis., Am. Autonomic Soc., Microcirculatory Soc., Soc. for Exptl. Biology and Medicine, Am. Assn. Lab. Animal Sci., Internat. Soc. for Devel. of Neuroscis. Office: SUNY Health Sci Ctr Bklyn Dept Physiology/Biophysics 450 Clarkson Ave Brooklyn NY 11203-2098

GOPLEN, DONNELLE, mental health services administrator; b. Loco, Okla., Nov. 5, 1936; d. Allen R. and Dorothy R. (Carmichael) Bean; B.A. with honors, U. N.Mex., 1974, M.A., 1977; postgrad. Family Therapy Inst., 1981-82; m. Bruce C. Goplen, Sept. 26, 1969; children: Stephen Harvey, Donald Harvey. State welfare worker State Welfare Agy., N.Mex., 1975-77; counseling intern Presbyn. Hosp., Albuquerque, 1977; social worker State of N.Mex., 1977-78; vol. mental health aide Prince William County (Va.) Community Mental Health Center, 1978-79, coordinator Social Activity Center; program coordinator mental health family services program Community Services Bd. of Prince William County, Prince William Women For... (founding mem. 1992—). Mem. Nat. Cert. Counselors. Home: 18414 Cedar Dr Triangle VA 22172-1416 Office: Prince William Cmty Svcs Bd 7969 Ashton Ave Manassas VA 22110

GORDIMER, NADINE, author; b. Republic of South Africa, Nov. 20, 1923; d.Isidore and Nan (Myers) Gordimer; m. Reinhold Cassirer, Jan. 29, 1954; children: Oriane, Hugo. Ed., Convent Sch., Springs, Republic of South Africa. Author: (story collections) Face to Face, 1949, The Soft Voice of the Serpent, 1952, Six Feet of the Country, 1956, Friday's Footprint, 1960, (W.H. Smith and Son Literary award 1961), Not for Publication, 1965, Livingstone's Companions, 1971, Selected Stories, 1975, Some Monday for Sure, 1976, A Soldier's Embrace, 1980, Town and Country Lovers, 1980, Something Out There, 1984, Crimes of Conscience, 1991, Jump, 1991, Why Haven't You Written?, 1992; (polit. and lit. essays) The Essential Gesture, 1988, Three in a Bed, 1991; (literary criticism) The Black Interpreters, 1973; (novels) The Lying Days, 1953, A World of Strangers, 1958, Occasion for Loving, 1963, The Late Bourgeois World, 1966, A Guest of Honour, 1970 (James Tait Black Meml. prize 1973), The Conservationist, 1974 (Booker prize for fiction Nat. Book League 1974), Burger's Daughter, 1979, July's People, 1981, A Sport of Nature, 1987, My Son's Story, 1991, None to Accompany Me, 1994; (other) On the Mines, 1973, Lifetimes Under Apartheid, 1986; editor: (with Lionel Abrahams) Southern African Writing Today, 1967. Decorated comdr. de l'Ordre des Arts et des Lettres (France), 1986; recipient Thomas Pringle award English Acad. South Africa, 1969, CNA award, 1974, 79, 81, 91, Grand Aigle d'Or, 1975, Disting. Svc. in Lit. Commonwealth award, 1981, MLA award, 1982, Nelly Sachs prize (Germany), 1985, Malaparte award (Italy), 1986, Bennett award, 1986, Benson medal, 1990, Nobel Prize for Literature, 1991; Neil Gunn fellowship Scottish Arts Coun., 1981. Fellow Royal Soc. Lit.; mem. AAAS, Com. European Authors, Am. Acad. (hon.), Inst. Arts and Letters (hon.), PEN (v.p.). Address: care Russell & Volkening 50 W 29th St New York NY 10001*

GORDIN, JOANNE, artist, educator; b. Allentown, Pa., Oct. 26, 1947; m. Stephen J. Gordin, June 22, 1975; 1 child, Eli. BA, Pa. State U., 1970; cert., Pa. Acad. Fine Arts, Phila., 1980; MFA, Pa. Acad. Fine Arts, 1993. Painting instr. Del. County C.C., Media, Pa., 1993-94; life drawing instr. Woodmere Art Mus., Phila., 1993-94; interim MFA coord. Pa. Acad. of the Fine Arts, Phila., 1994. One-woman shows include Thomas Jefferson U., Phila., 1984, Suzanne Gross Gallery, Phila., 1986, St. Joseph's U., Phila., 1991; exhibited in group shows at Pace U., N.Y.C., 1987, Butler Inst. Am. Art, Youngstown, Ohio, 1987, 88, Rutgers U., Camden, N.J., 1990, Cheltenham (Pa.) Art Ctr., 1985, 93, Beaver Coll., Glenside, Pa., 1985, 93, Pa. Acad. of the Fine Arts, Phila., 1980—. Mem. Fellow of Pa. Acad. of the Fine Arts (Purchase prize 1988).

GORDLY, AVEL LOUISE, state legislator, community activist; b. Portland, Oreg., Feb. 13, 1947; d. Fay Lee and Beatrice Bernice (Coleman) G.; 1 child, Tyrone Wayne Waters. BS in Adminstrn. of Justice, Portland State U., 1974. Phone co. clk. Pacific West Bell, Portland, 1966-70, mgmt. trainee, 1969-70; work release counselor Oreg. Corrections Divsn., Portland, 1974-78, parole and probation officer, 1974-78; dir. youth svcs., dir. youth gang programs Urban League of Portland, 1979-83; dir. So. Africa program Am. Friends Svc. Com., Portland, 1983-89, assoc. exec. sec., dir. Pacific N.W. region, 1987-90; freelance writer Portland, 1988-90; program dir. Portland House of Umoja, 1991; state rep. Dist. 19 Oreg. State Legis., Portland, 1991—, mem. joint ways and means com., adv. mem. appropriations com., rules and reorgn. com., low income housing com., energy policy rev. com., others; mem. joint ways and means com. on edn., mem. adv. bd. appropriations, mem. gov. drug and violent crime policy bd., mem. Oreg. liquor control commn. task force, mem. sexual harrassment task force, mem. Hanford waste bd., mem. gov. commn. for women; mem. Gov.'s Commn. for Women, Gov.'s Drug and Violent Crime Policy Bd.; originator, producer, host Black Women's Forum, 1983-88; co-producer, rotating host N.E. Spectrum, 1983-88. Mem. corrections adv. com. Multnomah Community; mem. adv. com. Oregonians Against Gun Violence; mem. Black Leadership Conf.; treas., bd. dirs. Black United Fund; co-founder, facilitator Unity Breakfast Com.; co-founder Sisterhood Luncheon; past project adv. bd. dirs. Nat. Orgn. Victims Assistance; past citizen chair Portland Police Bur.; past coord. com. Portland Future Focus Policy Com.; past coord. Community Rescue Path; past vice chair internat. affairs Black United Front.; past. sec. Urban League Portland, past vice chair, past exec. com.; past adv. com. Black Ednl. Ctr.; past vice chair Desegregation Monitoring, past adv. com., past chair curriculum com., other past orgns. coms. Recipient Outstanding Community Svc. award NAACP, 1986, Outstanding Women in Govt. award YWCA, 1991, Girl Scout-Community Svc. award, 1991, N.W. Conf. of Black Studies-Outstanding Progressive Leadership in the African-Am. Community award, 1986, Community Svc. award Delta Sigma Theta, 1981, Joint Action in Community Svc.-Vol. and Community Svc. award, 1981, Quality of Life Photography award Pacific Power & Light Co., 1986; Am. Leadership Forum Sr. fellow, 1988. Mem. NAACP.

GORDON, ALICE JEANNETTE IRWIN, secondary and elementary education educator; b. Detroit, Mar. 18, 1934; d. Manley Elwood and Jeannette (Coffron) Irwin; m. Edgar George Gordon, Feb. 4, 1967; children: David Alexander, John Scott. BA in Elem. Edn., Mich. State U., 1956; MA in Child Devel., U. Mich., 1959, EdS in Ednl. Psychology, 1967, MA in

Reading, 1990. Cert. K-12 tchr., Mich. Elem. tchr. Detroit Pub. Schs., 1956-67, reading tchr., 1967-68; secondary tchr. English and reading Parchment Pub. Schs., 1989-94; secondary reading specialist Kalamazoo Pub. Schs., 1994—; reading supr. Western Mich. U., Kalamazoo, 1992—; mem. alumni bd. Mich. State U. Coll. Edn., 1990—. Chmn. Century Ball, Nazareth Coll., Kalamazoo, 1987; co-chmn. Evening of Nte, Kalamazoo Symphony, 1989; precinct del. Kalamazoo Rep. Com., 1989, 92; mem. spelling and the adult learner Mich. Adult Edn. Practitioner Inquiry Project. Fellow U. Mich., 1963, 66; coop. learning grantee Mich. Dept. Edn., 1990. Mem. Internat. Reading Assn., Mich. Reading Assn., Homer Carter Reading Assn., P.E.O., Jr. League, Kappa Delta Pi, Phi Delta Kappa, Alpha Omega Pi. Presbyterian. Home: 4339 Lakeside Dr Kalamazoo MI 49008 Office: Loy Norrix High Sch 606 E Kilgore Rd Kalamazoo MI 49008

GORDON, ANNE KATHLEEN, editor; m. Phillip L. Berman. BA, U. Denver, 1979; postgrad., Columbia Grad. Sch. Journalism, 1983. Fin. writer Rocky Mountain Bus. Jour., Denver, 1981; fin. writer Sun-Tattler, Hollywood, Fla., 1982-83, fin. editor, 1983; asst. bus. editor Ft. Lauderdale (Fla.) News, 1983-85; bus. editor The Denver Post, 1985-88, asst. mng. editor, 1988; news cons. Sta. KCNC-TV, Denver, 1988-89, assignment mgr., 1989-90; editor Jackson Hole News, 1990-92; editor Sunday Mag. The Plain Dealer, Cleve., 1993—. Author: A Book of Saints, 1994. Recipient Best of Show award Colo. Press Assn., 1981, 86, Woman of Yr. award Broward County Bus. and Profl. Women's Assn., 1983, 1st Pl. Spot News award Colo. Associated Press, 1986, 1st Pl. Breaking News award Colo. Press Assn., 1986, Gen. Excellence award Wyo. Press Assn., 1991, Gen. Excellence award Nat. Newspaper Assn., 1992. Home: 1060 Erie Cliff Dr Lakewood OH 44107 Office: The Plain Dealer 1801 Superior Ave Cleveland OH 44104

GORDON, AUDREY KRAMEN, university administrator; b. Chgo., Nov. 18, 1935; d. Edward J. and Anne (Levin) K.; children: Bradley, Dale, Holly. BS with highest distinction, Northwestern U., 1965, MA, 1967, postgrad., 1971; MA, U. Chgo., 1970; PhD, U. Ill., Chgo., 1991. Cert. in clin. pastoral edn. Lectr. Northwestern U., Evanston, Ill., 1966-74; vis. asst. prof. Beloit (Wis.) Coll., 1974-75; research specialist U. Ill., Chgo., 1983-86, dir. continuing edn. Sch. Pub. Health, 1986-91, lectr. community health scis., 1988-91, dir. coll. advancement Sch. Pub. Health, 1991-92; coord./counselor Jewish Hospice, Chgo., 1984-89; asst. prof. community health scis. Sch. Pub. Health U. Ill., Chgo., 1992—; sr. rsch. specialist Ctr. for Pub. Health Practice, Sch. Pub. Health, U. Ill., 1992—; lectr. Loyola U. Stritch Sch. Medicine, Maywood, Ill., 1982—; pres. Rainbow Hospice Orgn., 1984-88, mem. profl. adv. bd., 1988—. Co-author: They Need To Know: How To Teach Children about Death, 1979. Recipient Northwestern Univ. Alumni Merit award, 1993. Mem. APHA, Ill. Pub. Health Assn., Ill. Hospice Orgn. (pres. 1989-90), Nat. Hospice Orgn. (coun. of profls.), Alpha Sigma Lambbda, Alpha Kappa Lambda, Delta Omega.

GORDON, BETTY L., health services administrator; b. Sayre, Pa., Apr. 4, 1947; d. Manley and Helen (Featherman) Rockman; m. Alan F. Gordon, Dec. 29, 1972. BSN, Russell Sage Coll., 1964; postgrad., Boston U., 1973-74; MPH in Health Svcs. Adminstrn., John Hopkins U., 1981. RN, Mass., N.Y. Gen. staff nurse Robert Packer Hosp., Sayre, Pa., 1968; staff nurse, team leader Vis. Nurse Assn. Allegheny County, Pa., 1968-71; nurse pub. health Vis. Nurse Assn. Boston, 1971; staff continuing care coord. Faulkner Hosp., Jamaica Plain, Mass., 1972-74; nurse pub. health, home health coord. Arlington County Dept. Human Resources, Va., 1974-78; dir. patient care svcs. Hospice Met. Denver, 1978-80; project site dir. long term care channeling demonstration City Balt., 1981-83; sr. v.p. clin. svcs. Kimberly Quality Care, Boston, 1983-94; sr. mgr. Simione & Simione Mgmt. Adv. Svc., Framingham, Mass., 1994—. Home: 151 Coolidge Ave Apt 713 Watertown MA 02172-2847 Office: 550 Cochituate Rd Framingham MA 01701

GORDON, BONNIE HEATHER, writer, editor; b. Phila., Oct. 18, 1952; d. Herman E. and Jean (Twersky) G.; m. Ed Kaplan, Apr. 2, 1978; 1 child, Philip Gordon Kaplan. BA in English, Temple U., 1975. Pub.'s rep. Columbia U. Press, N.Y.C., 1975-76; asst. editor mag. div. Dun-Donnelly Corp., N.Y.C., 1976-78; asst. editor High Times mag. Tixeon Inc., N.Y.C., 1978-79; staff editor Nat. League for Nursing, N.Y.C., 1981-82; freelance writer and editor N.Y.C., Cin., Phila., N.J., 1982-91; editor Law Sch. Admission Svcs., Newtown, Pa., 1991—. Author: Thus May Be Figured in Numberless Ways, 1985; editor, pub. Sapiens, 1981; writer, producer (documentary video) Which is Why Poetry is Weightlifting, 1991. Mem. bus. and profl. br. Nat. Coun. Jewish Women, 1989-90. Winner Blue Chip Cable Access award, 1992. Mem. Editorial Freelancers Assn., Women in Communication, Phi Beta Kappa.

GORDON, CAROLANN, oncological nurse, community health nurse; b. Hackensack, N.J., May 8, 1947; d. Henry Alfred and Irene Anne (Bielawski) Prell; m. Bruce Anthony Gordon, Mar. 3, 1967. LPN, Bergen Pines Hosp., Paramus, N.J., 1966; AAS, Dutchess C.C., Poughkeepsie, N.Y., 1985; BSN, SUNY, New Paltz, 1993. Staff nurse Columbia Presbyn. Hosp., N.Y., 1972-73, Alexander Linn Hosp., Sussex, N.J., 1974-75, Vassar Bros. Hosp., Poughkeepsie, 1978-86; asst head nurse, oncology No. Westchester Hosp. Ctr., Mt. Kisco, N.Y., 1987-93; nurse St. Francis Home Care Agy., Poughkeepsie, 1993—. Mem. Oncology Nurse Soc., Nat. Oncology Nurse Soc. (Hudson Valley chpt.), Dutchess C.C. Alumni Assn., SUNY New Paltz Nursing Alumni Assn. Office: St Francis Home Care Aby Rte 9G Poughkeepsie NY 12601

GORDON, DENA WALTERS, information specialist; b. Corpus Christi, Tex., Sept. 18, 1950; d. Edward Earl and Audyne (Warren) Walters. BA, U. Houston, 1971; MLS, U. Tex., 1975. Reference and data svcs. libr. Tex. Dept. Water Resources, Austin, 1976-77; coord. Energy Search Ctr. Tex. Indsl. Commn., Austin, 1977-80; mgr. tng. and devel. UMI/Data Courier, Louisville, 1980-85; head user svcs. dept. BIOSIS, Phila., 1985-93; editor-in-chief database publs. W.B. Saunders Co., Phila., 1993—; mem. bd. cons. Marquis Who's Who Directory of Online Profls., Chgo., 1984. Contbr. articles to profl. jours. Mem. Nat. Fedn. Abstracting and Info. Svcs. (chair edn./seminar com. 1987-89, chair conf. arrangements com. 1989-92, mem. info. policy and copyright com. 1992-93, Cert. of Appreciation 1989), Beta Phi Mu, Phi Kappa Phi, Sigma Tau Delta, Psi Chi, Spl. Librs. Assn. Office: WB Saunders Co Curtis Ctr Independence Square W Philadelphia PA 19106-3399

GORDON, ELLA DEAN, women's health nurse; b. Chgo., Jan. 19, 1947; d. Ed and Mozelle (Jordan) Hall; m. Starling Alexander Gordon, Aug. 2, 1969; children: Gerald Alexander, Dana Rolean. Diploma, Grady Meml. Hosp., 1968; student, Ga. State U., 1969-75; BSN, Med. Coll. Ga., 1976; M in Health Sci., Armstrong State Coll., 1983. RN, Ga., Tex. Charge nurse pediatrics evenings Grady Meml. Hosp., Atlanta, 1968-71; staff nurse pediatrics Dr.'s Meml. Hosp., Atlanta, 1971; charge nurse Pediatricians Office, Decatur, Ga., 1971-72; staff nurse VA Hosp., Atlanta, 1972-76; nurse primary care med. ICU VA Hosp., San Antonio, 1983; charge nurse, army nurse corps Eisenhower Army Med. Ctr., Ft. Gordon, Ga., 1976-79; staff nurse obstet. Noble Army Hosp., Ft. McClellan, Ala., 1984; instr. clin. nursing Jacksonville (Ala.) State Coll. Nursing, 1984-85; clin. nurse obstet. Gorgas Army Hosp., Republic of Panama, 1987-89; charge nurse oncology days Eisenhower Army Med. Ctr., Ft. Gordon, Ga., 1989-90; charge nurse obstet. Brooke Army Med. Ctr., Ft. Sam Houston, Tex., 1990—; cons. health edn. ETOWAH County Clinics, Gadsden, Ala, 1985; health educator Cardiovascular Coun. of Savannah, Ga., 1983, Parent/Child Devel. Svcs., Savannah, 1982. Contbr. articles to profl. jours. Instr. ARC, Ft. McClellan, 1985-86, chmn., vols., 1986-87. Capt. U.S. Army, 1976-79; col. USAR, 1991. Named One of Outstanding Young Women in Am., 1979, 83. Mem. Assn. Mil. Surgeons, Assn. of Women's Health, Obstets. and Neonatal Nurses, Res. Officer Assn., Officers Wives Club (publicity chmn. 1982-83), Sigma Theta Tau. Democrat. Home: 12810 El Marro San Antonio TX 78233 Office: Brooke Army Med Ctr Fort Sam Houston TX 78234

GORDON, ELLEN RUBIN, candy company executive; d. William B. and Cele H. (Travis) Rubin; m. Melvin J. Gordon, June 25, 1950; children: Virginia, Karen, Wendy, Lisa. Student, Vassar Coll., 1948-50; B.A., Brandeis U., 1965; postgrad., Harvard U., 1968. With Tootsie Roll Industries, Inc., Chgo., 1968—, corp. sec., 1970-74, v.p. product devel., 1974-76, sr. v.p., 1976-78, pres., COO, 1978—, also dir.; v.p., dir. HDI Investment Corp.; bd. dirs. CPC Internat., Inc.; mem. coun. on divsn. biol. scis. and Pritzker Sch. Medicine U. Chgo. Mem. adv. coun. J.L. Kellogg Grad. Sch. Mgmt. at Northwestern U., Stanford U. Grad. Sch. Bus.; mem. bd fellows Harvard U. Med. Sch.; mem. univ. resources and overseers com. Harvard U.; trustee, mem. Com. for Econ. Devel., Northwestern U. Assocs.; active Pres. Export Coun. Recipient Kettle award, 1985. Mem. Nat. Confectioners Assn. (bd. dirs.). Office: Tootsie Roll Industries Inc 7401 S Cicero Ave Chicago IL 60629-5818

GORDON, EMMAJEAN ELIZABETH, farmer, investor, consultant; b. Fresno, Calif., Dec. 10, 1920; d. John Peter and Emilie (Kromberg) Wagenleitner; div. 1976; children: Marilyn Gordon Johnson, Glenda Rouzaud Farrer. Bus. cert., 4 C's Bus. Sch., 1941; provision teaching credential, Fresno State U., 1942; BA, Chico State U., 1955, MA, 1963. Lic. tchr., supervision, adminstr. edn., life credentials. Tchr. Fresno (Calif.) County Schs., 1945-47, Shasta County Schs., Redding, Calif., 1947-49, Enterprise Elem. Sch., Redding, 1949-58; tchr. team sports and crafts Redding Recreation Dept., 1945-47, 49-58; tchr. Redding Elem. Sch., Bonneyview, 1958-59; tchr., counselor Enterprise High Sch., Redding, 1959-63, counselor, 1963-83; beauty cons. Mary Kay Cosmetics, Fresno, 1988—; farmer Fresno, 1978—; investor E.J. Gordon Enterprises, Fresno, 1976—; mem. salary com. Shasta-Union High Dist., Redding, 1973-75. Ch. choir leader Redding Ch., 1948-52; bd. mem., chmn. Redding Jr. Acad., 1973-76; chmn. county sr. adv. Shasta Coll., Redding, 1983-84, mem. med. adv. bd., 1979-82; mem. adv. bd. Shasta County Woman's Refuge, Redding, 1980-83. Named Gold Star Foster Parent, Shast County Foster Parent Assn., 1968, 86; recipient Golden Nike award Bus. and Profl. Women, Redding, 1983. Mem. NEA (life), AAUW (life), NAFE, Women in Agr. and Raisen Wives, Shasta Retired Tchrs. Assn. (life), Fresno Bus. and Profl. Women (scholarship chmn. 1989—, sec. 1990), Calif. Fedn. Fig Garden Women's Club, Profl. Women's Bowling Club, Palm Lakes Women's Golf Assn., Edison Social Club Women's Aux., Woodard Esec. Estates Condo Assn. (beautification chmn. 1989-91). Republican.

GORDON, GERD STRAY, retired historian, educator, writer; b. Stavanger, Norway, Nov. 15, 1912; came to U.S., 1948; d. Johannes and Ella (Stray) Johansen; m. Johan Vogt (div.); children: Mette Wernøe, Gerd Ada Vogt, Christina Isaksen; m. Raymond Gordon; 1 child, Karen Allyn. Student, Oslo U., 1937-41; BA, Fla. State U., 1960; MA, U. Pitts., PhD, 1978. Cert. tchr., Fla., Pa. Accredited corr. Aftenposten-Norsk Dameblad, Oslo, 1948-55; tchr. Panama C.Z. Schs., Panama Episc. Sch., 1960-61, Am. Coop. Sch., Tunis, Tunisia, 1962-64; tchr. Am. Internat. Sch., Bangkok, 1965-68, Djakarta, Indonesia, 1968-69; tchr. Am. Sch., New Delhi, India, 1969-70, Pitts. Pub. Sch. System, 1970-83; freelance lectr., 1983—; lectr. Slippery Rock (Pa.) U., U. Kans., Lawrence, Vanderbilt U., Nashville; presenter Symposium of Scandinavian Historians. Author: Kvinnen Idag (Woman Today), 1952; contbr. articles to numerous publs including Dictionary of Scandinavian History, 1986. Dem. ofcl., Denver, 1952-57, election judge, 1954-58; bd. dirs., rep., Planned Parenthood, Denver and Pitts., 1952-89; participant Citizen Day Com. signed S.P. Kinney II Denver Woman's Press Club, 1965, Senate of Pa., 1985. Resistance worker during German occupation of Norway, World War II. Recipient Outstanding Citizen award Norwegian Resistance; Ella Lyman Cabot Trust grantee U. Pitts. Mem. Denver Women's Press Club (bd. dirs. 1952—), Pitts. U. Historian Alumnae Orgn., Fla. State U. Alumnae Assn., AAUW (bd. dirs. Pitts. chpt. 1984—), LWV (past bd. dirs. Denver and Pitts. chpts.), Countryside Garden Club (bd. dirs. 1970—). Home: 224 Rockingham Rd Pittsburgh PA 15238-3014

GORDON, IRENE MARLOW, radiology educator; b. White County, Tenn., May 21, 1943; d. Paul Terah and Mary Eva (Holloway) Marlow; m. Shigern Chino, July 14, 1969 (div.); children: Hatsuyo Mary Chino, Kazumi Elaine Chino, Junzo Paul Chino, Hazuki Carol Chino, Fumiko Catherine Chino; m. James Robert Gordon, Sept. 6, 1979. BS, U. Dayton, 1966; MD, Ohio State U., 1970, MS, 1974. Intern in medicine and pediat. St. Lukes Hosp., San Francisco, 1970-71; resident in gen. radiology Ohio State U. Hosp., 1971-74; fellow in radiation and oncology U. Calif., Irvine; clin. instr. dept. radiology Ohio State U., Columbus, 1971-74; asst. clin. prof. divsn. radiation therapy U. Calif., Irvine, 1976-78, acting chief divsn. radiation therapy, 1976-77; asst. clin. prof. divsn. radiation therapy Harbor-UCLA Med. Ctr., L.A., 1981-82; clin. asst. prof. radiology, radiation oncology Ind. U. Med. Ctr., Indpls., 1992—; bd. dirs. Health Talents Internat., Sentinel Med. Rev. Orgn., sec., 1985-89, Hoosier Oncology Group, mem. exec. com., 1993—; mem. staff St. Joseph & Children's Hosp., Orange, Calif., 1974-82, Long Beach Meml. Med. Ctr., 1979-82; dir. radiation oncology St. Elizabeth Hosp. and Med. Ctr. Regional Treatment Ctr., Lafayette, Ind., 1982—. Translator for deaf Ouabache Ch. of Christ, Lafayette, 1993—; bd. dirs. Tippecanoe County chpt. ARC, 1992—. Mem. AMA, Am. Coll. Radiology (cert.), Am. Soc. Therapeutic Radiology and Oncology, Radiology Soc. N.Am., Am. Endocurie Soc., Am. Coll. Radiation Oncology, Am. Soc. Clin. Oncology, Tippecanoe County Med. Assn. (pres. 1994—), Ind. 9th Dist. Med. Assn. (pres. 1994). Office: Regional Treatment Ctr 1116 N 16th St Lafayette IN 47906

GORDON, JANINE M., advertising agency executive; b. N.Y.C., Oct. 2, 1946; d. Moses Fortune and Emma (Leo) Mager. B.A., U. Pa., 1968. Asst. buyer Bloomingdale's, N.Y.C., 1968-69; fashion credits editor Harper's Bazaar, N.Y.C., 1969-72; assoc. dir. pub. relations Cotton, Inc., N.Y.C., 1972-73; press officer Harrods Ltd., London, 1973-74; project mgr. J.C. Penney Co., Inc., N.Y.C., 1974-75; dir. pub. relations Bozell, Inc., N.Y.C., 1975-77; exec. v.p. corp. comm., mem. oper. com. Saatchi & Saatchi Advt., 1977-94; pres. Saatchi & Saatchi Pub. Rels., 1987-94, Janine Gordon Co., 1994—. Mem. Pub. Rels. Soc. Am., Advt. Women N.Y., Cosmopolitan Club.

GORDON, JUDITH, communications consultant, writer; b. Long Beach, Calif.; d. Irwin Ernest and Susan (Perlman) G.; m. Lawrence Banka, May 1, 1977. BA, Oakland U., 1966; MS in Libr. Sci., Wayne State U., 1973. Researcher Detroit Inst. of Arts, 1968-69; libr. Detroit Pub. Libr., 1971-74; caseworker Wayne County Dept. Social Svcs., Detroit, 1974-77; advt. copywriter Hudson's Dept. Store, Detroit, 1979; mgr. The Poster Gallery, Detroit, 1980-81; mktg., corp. communications specialist Bank of Am., San Francisco, 1983-84; mgr., consumer pubs. Bank of Am., 1984-86; prin. Active Voice, San Francisco, 1986—. Contbr. edit. The Artist's Mag., 1988-93; contbr. to book Flowers: Gary Bukovnik, Watercolors and Monotypes, Abrams, 1990. Vol. From the Heart, San Francisco, 1992, Bay Area Book Festival, San Francisco, 1990, 91, Aid & Comfort, San Francisco, 1987, Save Orch. Hall, Detroit, 1977-81, NOW sponsored abortion clinic project. Recipient Nat. award Merit, Soc. Consumer Affairs Profls. in Bus., 1986, Bay Area Best award, Internat. Assn. Bus. Communicators, 1986, Internat. Galaxy award, 1992. Mem. Internat. Assn. Bus. Communicators, Nat. Writers Union, Freelance Editorial Assn., AAUW, Graphic Arts Coun., Women's Nat. Book Assn., Media Alliance, Friends of City Arts and Lectrs., Friends of ZYZZYVA. Office: 899 Green St San Francisco CA 94133-3788

GORDON, JULIE ANN, accountant; b. Washington, Mo., June 5, 1961; d. Robert Clifton and Laverne Amanda (Kimker) Pierce; m. Timoth Lane Gordon, Aug. 22, 1981; children: Amber Kaye, Amanda Karen. AA, East Ctrl. Coll., Union, Mo., 1981; BS, Okla. Christian Coll., 1984. Acctg. clk. Maritz Inc., Fenton, Mo., 1985-88; fin. reporting acct. Maritz Inc., Fenton, 1988-92, acctg. supr., 1992—. Youth coun. mem. First Bapt. Ch. of St. Clair, Mo., 1991—; girl scout leader Greater St. Louis Girl Scout Coun., St. Clair, 1992-93. Mem. Inst. Mgmt. Accts., Order of Ea. Star (Worthy matron 1991), Bapt. Young Women (sec. 1992-93). Office: Maritz Inc 1375 N Highway Dr Fenton MO 63099

GORDON, JUNE, psychology educator, consultant, artist; b. Oshkosh, Wis., June 17, 1929; d. Felix and Harriet (Fero) Staerkel; m. Donald Emmanuel Gordon, Feb. 6, 1951; children: Bonita, Judy, Teresa, Thomas, Alexander, Philip. BS, Rollins Coll., 1971, MEd, 1974; EdS, U. Fla., 1976; EdD, Fla. State U., 1979; advanced study Jung Inst., Switzerland, 1982, U. Wis., 1984; imagery tng., London, 1985. Cert. sch. psychologist, Fla., hypnotherapy tng., Ill.; lic. mental health counselor. Freelance artist, Calif., Fla., Wis., Ala., 1958-74; coord. women's program Seminole Community Coll., Sanford, Fla., 1974-84; adj. prof. psychology Rollins Coll. and Seminole Community Coll., Winter Park, Fla., 1974—; pvt. practice counseling mental health svc., Sanford, 1984—; bd. dirs. Project Wedge, Cen. Fla. Ednl. Consortium for Women, Orlando; cons. in field. Artist: painting Mother, Mother, The CIA is Coming (Wis. Blue Ribbon 1967), The Skaters (Merit award, Oviedo, Fla. 1985); author: (with others) Divorce, 1977; Legal Rights, 1979; author, artist: New Goddess Odyssey collection 1985-92, 1992; contbr. articles to profl. jours. Founder Cen. Fla. Commn. on Status of Women, 1975; pres. Seminole County Mental Health Ctr., Inc., Fla., 1980-81, 91-92, bd. dirs., 1989—; bd. dirs. Met. Alcohol Coun., Orlando, 1981-83, Citrus coun. Girl Scouts U.S., 1984-88; committeewoman Dem. Exec. Com. of Seminole County, 1981-84; gov.'s appointee East Cen. Fla. Regional Planning Coun., 1983-86. Recipient Fannie Lou Hamers Human Rights award NOW, 1980, Best of Jewelry award Seminole Community Coll., Sanford, Fla., 1989. Mem. AAUW (pres. 1983-85, bd. dirs. Fla. state div. 1986-89), Nat. Wellness Assn., Jung Soc. North Fla., Fla. Assn. Community Colls., Future Soc. Avocations: all artistic and creative activities, designing, traveling, gardening. Home: 309 Idyllwilde Dr Sanford FL 32771-3638

GORDON, LEE DIANE, librarian; b. Lafayette, Ind., Oct. 30, 1948; d. Henry Charles and Leonora (Brower) G.; m. James J. Thomas, Aug. 27, 1977. BA, Calif. State U., Long Beach, 1970; MEd, U. Nev., Las Vegas, 1980. Cert. tchr., Nev., Calif.; cert. libr., Nev. Tchr. Carmenita Jr. High Sch., Cerritos, Calif., 1971-77; tchr. Jim Bridger Jr. High Sch., North Las Vegas, Nev., 1977-79, libr., 1979-84; libr. Eldorado High Sch., Las Vegas, Nev., 1984—. Co-author: The Overworked Teacher's Bulletin Board Book, 1981; filmstrips, 1983; author: World Historical Fiction Guide for Young Adults, 1995; contbr. articles to profl. jours. Mem. Am. Assn. Sch. Librs. (affiliate del., various coms. 1987—), Nev. Assn. Sch. Librs. (chair 1987), Clark County Sch. Librs. Assn. (pres. 1987-88), Delta Kappa Gamma (Iota chpt. pres. 1990-92). Office: Eldorado High Sch 1139 Linn Ln Las Vegas NV 89110-2628

GORDON, MARGARET LOUISE, former education educator; b. Norfolk, Va.; d. Daniel D. and Mary E. (Giddings) G. BS, Va. State U., 1938; MA, Howard U., 1944. Asst. prof. edn. Va. State U., Petersburg; elem. tchr. Norfolk City Sch. Bd.; prin. Jacox Jr. High Sch., 1957-67; jr. high sch. prin. Norfolk City Sch. Bd.; assoc. prof. secondary edn. Norfolk State U., 1967-76. Recipient Disting. Svc. award Howard U., award Omega Psi Phi. Mem. ASCD, Nat. Assn. Secondary Sch. Prins., Alpha Kappa Alpha.

GORDON, MARY CATHERINE, author; b. L.I., N.Y., Dec. 8, 1949; d. David and Anna (Gagliano) G.; m. James Brain, 1974 (div.); m. Arthur Cash, 1979; children: Anna Gordon, David Dess Gordon. BA, Barnard Coll., 1971; MA, Syracuse U., 1973. Tchr. English Dutchess Community Coll., Poughkeepsie, N.Y., 1974-78, Amherst (Mass.) Coll., 1979-80, Barnard Coll., 1988—. Author: (novels) Final Payments, 1978, The Company of Women, 1981, Men and Angels,1985, The Other Side, 1989, The Rest of Life, 1993, (short stories) Temporary Shelter, 1987, Good Boys and Dead Girls and Other Essays, 1991, The Rest of Life: Three Novellas, 1993. Recipient Kafka prize for Fiction, 1979, 82. Roman Catholic. Office: Viking Penguin Publicity Dept 375 Hudson St New York NY 10014-3658 also: Barnard Coll Dept of English 606 West 120th St New York NY 10027-5706*

GORDON, NANCY M., congressional administrator; b. Thunder Bay, Ont., Can., Nov. 10, 1943; came to U.S., 1959; d. Walter Ernest and Hilda May Gordon. BA in Econs., U. Calif., Berkeley, 1964; PhD in Econs., Stanford U., 1970. Asst. prof. Carnegie Mellon U., Pitts., 1969-74; econ. policy fellow Brookings Instn., Washington, 1975-76; sr. rsch. assoc. The Urban Inst., Washington, 1976-79; exec. dir. task force on women The White House, Washington, 1979, sr. advisor to asst. to pres., 1979-80; asst. dir. health and human resources Congl. Budget Office, Washington, 1980—. Author: (with others) The Subtle Revolution, 1979; contbr. chpts. to profl. jours. Pres., bd. dirs. Worldwide Assurance Employees Pub. Agys., 1987-90. Woodrow Wilson Found. fellow, 1964, IBM fellow, 1965, Stanford-Wilson Dissertation fellow Stanford U., 1967. Mem. Am. Statis. Assn. (chair com. on status of women in econ. profession, vice chair com. on women in sci.), Am. Econ. Assn. Home: 5500 Friendship Blvd Bethesda MD 20815 Office: Congl Budget Office/US Congress Second and D Sts SW Washington DC 20515

GORDON, RENA JOYCE, health services researcher, educator; b. Detroit, Mar. 4, 1936; d. Joseph Lazar and Edna Dorothy (Rosenfeld) Feigelman; m. Leonard Gordon, Dec. 25, 1955; children: Susan Melinda, Matthew Seth, Melissa Gail. BS with honors, Wayne State U., 1957; MA, Ariz. State U., 1971, Ariz. State U., 1978; PhD, Ariz. State U., 1983. Resource tchr. Detroit Pub. Schs., 1966-67; faculty assoc. Ariz. State U., 1971-76; rsch. stat. analyst Ariz. Dept. Health Svcs., Phoenix, 1981-82; rsch. asst. prof. dir. Phoenix Rural Health Office Coll. Medicine U. Ariz., 1983-89; exec. dir. Ariz. Coun. for Mothers and Children, 1992—; rsch. cons. Clin. Gerontology Unit, St. Lukes Hosp., Phoenix, 1982-83; adj. prof. dept. geography Ariz. State U., 1988—; vis. prof. Am. Grad. Sch. Internat. Mgmt., Glendale, Ariz., 1989; lectr. dept. family and cmty. medicine, U. Ariz. Coll. Medicine, Tucson, 1989—. Author: Arizona Rural Health Provider Atlas, 1984, 87; contbr. chpts. to books and articles to profl. jours. Mem. Camelback Hosps. Coun. Ctr., adv. com. 1982-88, chmn. 1983-84, St. Luke's Behavioral Health Ctr., 1988-92, bd. trustees, Phoenix. Recipient various awards U. Mich., Ariz. State U., challenge grant The Flinn Found. Mem. AAUW (bd. dirs. 1987-88), APHA., Ariz. Pub. Health Assn. (bd. dirs. 1986-88), Assn. Am. Geographers (med. geography sect.). Home: 13660 E Columbine Scottsdale AZ 85258

GORDON, RONNIE R., pediatrics educator, consultant; b. N.Y.C., June 29, 1923; d. Maurice and Margaret (Leizer) Klein; divorced; children: Lyn Leslie, Barbara Simmons. BA in Math., Hunter Coll., 1944; MS in Child Devel., Bank St. Coll., 1963; postgrad., NYU. Mathematician Manhattan Project, Los Alamos, 1944-47; dept. dir. Rusk Inst. Rehab. Medicine NYU Med. Ctr., 1962-85; project dir. grant Bureau Edn. Hand in Dept. HEW, 1969-78; project dir. presch. and infant devel. programs Katherine Lilly Conroy Learning Lab. Infant Sch. Therapeutic Playground, 1962-85; asst. prof. clin. rehab. medicine Sch. Medicine NYU, 1970-74, assoc. prof. clin. rehab. medicine pediatrics, 1974-86; dir. presch. and infant svcs. and rsch. dept. Inst. Rehab. Medicine NYU Med. Ctr., 1962-86; cons. pvt. practice N.Y.C., 1986—; presented at confs., seminars, and workshops at univs., annual meetings of nat. and internat. related assns. in Eng., Wales, France, Norway, Germany, Austria, Nova Scotia, Venezuela, Trinidad, Denmark, Sweden, Israel, Can., Netherlands, China, Hong Kong, Hawaii, Yugoslavia, Japan. Filmmaker: Special Children, Special Needs, 1972 (1st prize award), Special Children, Different Needs-Growing Up Handicapped, 1980 (award), Special Children 25 Years Later; co-author: Educational Programming for the Severely and Profoundly Handicaped, 1977; contbr. articles to Developmental Medicine and Child Neurology, Jour. Spl. Edn., Am. Sch. and Univ., Archtl. Forum, others; contbr. chpt. to books. Bd. dirs. Louise Wise Svcs. for Children, 1984—, subcom. preventive svcs. Recipient Contbn. award Hong Kong Rehab. Ctr., 1982, award State of N.Y. Dept. of Parks, 1973-74; grantee Evan F. Lilly Found., 1966-85, HEW, 1970-72, 72-75, 75-78; named to Hall of Fame, Hunter Coll., 1994. Mem. World Orgn. for Presch. Edn. (N.Y.C. liaison for the U.S. Nat. Com.), Assn. for Children with Learning Disabilities, Assn. for Childhood Edn. Internat., Am. Soc. of Law and Medicine. Home and Office: Apt 15 3 Washington Square Vlg New York NY 10012-1808

GORDON, RUBY DANIELS, retired nursing educator, counselor; b. Camden, Ark., Dec. 28, 1927; d. Fred Jewell and Etta Matilda (Watson) Daniels; m. DeVore Basil Gordon, Sept. 1, 1946 (div. 1950); children: Sally Ann Gordon, Lynne Gordon. Diploma, St. Monica's Hosp., Phoenix, 1949; BS, Ariz. State U., 1959, MA, 1962, PhD, 1975. Instr. basic scis. St. Joseph Hosp. Sch. Nursing, Phoenix, 1962-67; chairperson dept. nursing Glendale (Ariz.) C.C., 1967-80; prof. Phoenix Coll., 1980-92; counselor Glendale C.C., 1993—. Mem. ANA, NEA, ACA, Ariz. Nurses Assn., Nat. League for Nursing, Ariz. League for Nursing, Am. Soc. Aging, Am. Assn. for the History of Nursing, Nat. Coun. on the Aging, Assn. for Adult Devel. and Aging, Nat. Career Devel. Assn.

GORDON, SANDY GALE COMBS, medical/surgical nurse, community health nurse; b. Lafollette, Tenn., Sept. 8, 1950; d. Wise and Edna Leona (Boshears) Combs; m. Ralph William Gordon, Aug. 30, 1975. Diploma, Middletown Hosp., 1971. RN, Ohio. Pub. health nurse Bur. Pub. Health, Middletown, Ohio, 1979-82; staff nurse Middletown Hosp., 1971-79. Named

Internat. Women of Yr., 1994-95. Mem. Middletown Hosp. Alumni Assn. Home: 1107 Ellen Dr Middletown OH 45042-3341

GORDON, SHERIE GAY, special education educator, educational consultant; b. Washington, July 7, 1954; d. James Edward Sr. and Gene Southall; divorced; 1 child, Michael A. Gordon; m. Robert Robey; children: Robert E. Robey, Jamie L. Robey. BS in Edn., U. Md., 1976; MS in Human Devel., George Washington U., 1988. Cert. in spl. edn., adminstrn. and supervision, Md. Tchr. resource program St. Mary's County (Md.) Schs., 1979-82, tchr. emotionally disturbed program, 1982-84; tchr., chmn. dept. Chopticon High Sch., Morganza, Md., 1984-90, tchr., 1990—; sales cons. Ednl. Cons., Waldorf, Md., 1987—; coach Odyssey of the Mind, Charles County, Md., 1988—. Mem. exec. bd. Teachers of Tomorrow; pres. Bannister Neighborhood Swim Team, 1992—. U. Md. scholar; George Washington U. grantee, 1989; recipient coaching awards. Mem. NEA, Edn. Assn. St. Mary's County, Assn. Secondary Suprs. and Adminstrs., Coun. for Exceptional Children. Home: 2615 Ferguson Ct Waldorf MD 20602-1700 Office: Chopticon H S Waldorf MD 20602

GORDON, TINA, sculptor, art therapist; b. N.Y.C.; d. Abraham and Rose (Scoff) Schapiro; m. Norman B. Gordon (div.); children: Jane, Judith, Marc. BA in Fine Arts, Goddard Coll., 1972; postgrad., NYU, 1978-80; student, Nat. Acad. Art, N.Y.C., 1981-83, Parsons Sch. Design, N.Y.C., 1983-88. Art tchr. East River Montessori Sch., N.Y.C., 1969-72; instr. Nassau Community Coll., 1973-76; art therapist Manhattan Psychiat. Ctr., N.Y.C., 1977-87; curator ann. juried non-member exhbn. sculpture and photography. Exhibited in shows at Nat. Acad. Art, 1977, 78, 80, Nat. Art Club, N.Y.C., 1978, 79, 80, 83, 88, Thompson Gallery, N.Y.C., Salamagundi Art Club, N.Y.C., 1979-90, Pen and Brush, N.Y.C., 1984-89, L.I. Artists Guild, 1970, 71, 72, numerous others; commns. for Manhattan Psy. Ctr. Recipient Philip Isenberg 1st prize in Sculpture, Salmagundo Art Soc., 1994. Mem. Salmagundi Art Soc. (curator, chmn. ann. open juries exhbn. 1994), Elliot Liskin award in sculpture 1984, 86, First Prize Sculpture award), Nat. Assn. Women Artists, Pen and Brush (bd. dirs., 1994, Merit award 1985, 87, 88, 89), Am. Soc. Contemporary Artists, Burr Artists, Allied Artists, Knickerbocker Artists (Roman Bronze award 1981, 83), Nat. Sculpture Soc. (assoc.). Home: 24 Fifth Ave New York NY 10011-8858

GORDON-MOUNTIAN, LESLEY DARA, office manager, dancer; b. New Haven, Conn., Mar. 21, 1954; d. David Cole and Pearl Doris (Greenberg) G.; m. Vassilii Vladimirovich Mountian, Mar. 3, 1991. BA with honors, Northwestern U., 1976. Sr. asst. buyer I. Magnin, San Francisco, 1978-81; dancer Khadra Internat. Folk Ballet, San Francisco, 1986-91; dir., v.p., mem. exec. com. Khandra Internat. Folk Ballet, San Francisco, 1989-91; office mgr. Banque Paribas, San Francisco, 1981-94, office mgr., loan adminstr., 1994—; Choreographer Duquesne U. Tamburitzans. Bd. dirs. Calif. Artists Series, San Francisco, 1989-90; coord. Hartley House Food Dr., N.Y.C., 1972, Soviet Jewish Emigre Svcs., San Francisco, 1991; solicitor Casa de las Madres, San Francisco, 1991—, Americares, New Canaan, Conn., 1993—. Recipient Richter Internat. scholarship Northwestern U., Paris, 1975, Regents scholarship SUNY, 1971, scholastic award Alpha Lambda Delta. Jewish. Office: Banque Paribas 101 California St Ste 3150 4D San Francisco CA 94111

GORE, GENEVIEVE WALTON, company executive; b. Salt Lake City, Mar. 23, 1913; d. Thaddeus and Ethel May (Arnold) Walton; m. Wilbert Lee Gore, Jan 1, 1935 (widowed July 1986); children: Robert, Susan, Virginia, David, Elizabeth. Student, U. Utah, 1933, Henninger Bus. Coll., 1935; HHD in Humanities, Westminster Coll., 1982; D in Bus. Adminstrn., Goldey-Beacom Coll., 1991. Sec., treas. W.L. Gore & Assoc., Inc., Newark, Del., 1958—; dir. W.L. Gore & Assoc., Scotland, West Germany, India, Del. State C. of C., Wilmington. Co-founder W.L. Gore & Assoc., Inc., 1958. Bd. counselors Goldey-Beacom Coll., Wilmington, Del., 1991; bd. govs. Winterthur (Del.) Mus., 1991. Recipient Medal Distinction, U. Del., Newark, 1983, Bavarian Order of Merit, Germany, 1988, Disting. Performance in Mgmt. award Widener U., Wilmington, 1986; named Del. Women's Hall of Fame, Dover, 1989, Del. Bus. Leaders Hall of Fame, 1991. Mem. Girl Scouts Pres.Adv. Coun., Chesapeake Bay Girl Scouts, Independence Sch., Boy Scouts Am. Home: 487 Paper Mill Rd Newark DE 19711-7511 Office: WL Gore & Associates Inc 555 Paper Mill Rd Newark DE 19711-7513

GORE, TIPPER (MARY ELIZABETH GORE), wife of vice president of the United States; b. Washington, Aug. 19, 1948; m. Albert Gore Jr., May 19, 1970; children: Karenna, Kristin, Sarah, Albert III. BA in psychology, Boston U., 1970; MA in psychology, George Peabody Coll. Freelance photographer; chmn. Congl. Wives Task Force, 1978-79. Author: Raising PG Kids in an X-Rated Society, 1987. Co-founder Parents Music Resource Ctr., Arlington, Va., 1985. Office: Old Exec Office Bldg Rm 273 Washington DC 20501*

GORELICK, JAMIE SHONA, lawyer; b. N.Y.C., May 6, 1950; d. Leonard and Shirley (Fishman) G.; m. Richard E. Waldhorn, Sept. 28, 1975; children: Daniel H., Dana E. BA, Radcliffe Coll., 1972; JD, Harvard U., 1975. Bar: D.C. 1975, U.S. Dist. Ct. D.C. 1976, U.S. Tax Ct. 1976, U.S. Ct. Claims 1976, U.S. Ct. Appeals (D.C. cir.) 1976, U.S. Ct. Appeals (5th cir.) 1977, U.S. Supreme Ct. 1979, U.S. Ct. Appeals (Fed. cir.) 1982, U.S. Ct. Internat. Trade 1984, U.S. Dist. Ct. Md. 1985, U.S. Ct. Appeals (4th cir.) 1986, U.S. Ct. Appeals (3d. cir.) 1988. Assoc. Miller, Cassidy, Larroca & Lewin, Washington, 1975-79, 80, ptnr., 1981-93; asst. to sec., counselor to dep. sec. U.S. Dept. Energy, Washington, 1979-80; gen. counsel Dept. Def., Washington, 1993-94; dep. atty. gen. Dept. Justice, Washington, 1994—; chmn.'s adv. coun. U.S. Senate Jud. Com., 1988-93; teaching mem. trial advocacy workshop Harvard Law Sch., Cambridge, Mass., 1982, 84; mem. overseers com. to visit Harvard Coll, 1989-93; vice chmn. task force evaluation of audit investigative inspection components Dept. Def., Washington, 1979-80; mem. sec.'s transition team Dept. Energy, Washington, 1979; bd. dirs. Found. for Change, Nat. Women's Law Ctr., Mental Health Law Project. Bd. editors Corp. Criminal Liability Reporter, 1986-93, Rico Litigation Reporter, 1986-93; adv. bd. RICO Law Reporter, Corp. Criminal Liability Reporter; co-author: Destruction of Evidence, 1989; contbr. articles to profl. jours. Fellow Am. Bar Found.; mem. ABA (chmn. complex crimes litigation com. litigation sect. 1984-87, vice chmn. complex crimes litigation com. 1983-84, sec. litigation sect. 1988-90, coun. mem. 1990-93, com. on profl. discipline, house of delegates 1991-93), D.C. Bar (pres. 1992-93, bd. govs. 1982-88, sec. bd. govs. 1981-82, bar found. advisors 1985-93, legal ethics com.), Womens Bar Assn., Am. Law Inst. Office: Dep Atty Gen US Dept Justice Rm 4111 MAIN 10th & Constitution Ave NW Washington DC 20530-0001

GORELICK, MOLLY CHERNOW, psychologist, educator; b. N.Y.C., Sept. 17, 1920; d. Morris and Jean (Zabraun) Chernow; m. Leon Gorelick, Apr. 12, 1941; children: Walter, Peter. AB, UCLA, 1948, MA, 1955, EdD, 1962. Tchr., counselor Los Angeles City Bd. Edn., 1948-61; instr., chief guidance svcs. Exceptional Children's Found., Los Angeles, 1963-70; prof. Calif. State U., Northridge, 1970-91, prof. emeritus, 1991—; research project dir. Vocat. Rehab. Adminstrn. HEW, Los Angeles, 1964-66, project dir., 1971-75; owner, dir. Hi-Ho Day Camp, 1950-57; cons. Riverside County Schs., 1962-70, Kennedy Child Study Ctr., 1975-79; researcher Preschool Integration of Children with Handicaps, 1971-75. Co-author: Rescue series, 5 vols., 1967-68; contbr. articles to profl. jours. Former mem. adv. bd. Calif. State Regional Diagnostic Ctr. Children's Hosp., Mirman Sch. Gifted Children, Calif. Ednl. Ctr., Friendship Day Camp; adv. bd. UCLA Sch. Social Welfare. Mem. Am. Psychol. Assn., Western Psychol. Assn., NEA, Council Exceptional Children, Am. Assn. Mental Deficiency, Phi Beta Kappa, Pi Lambda Theta, Pi Gamma Mu. Office: Calif State U Northridge CA 91330

GOREN, DENISE LYNNE, deputy mayor; b. Phila., Oct. 4, 1952; d. Norman T. and Berniss (Rappoport) G.; m. Steven Robert Waxman, Oct. 6, 1977; children: Marisa, Adrianne, Rebecca. BA, Simmons Coll., 1973; JD, Temple U., 1976. Bar: Pa. 1976. Atty. advisor Defense Logistic Agys. Defense Personnel Support Ctr., Phila., 1976-84; asst. mng. dir. City of Phila., 1984-88, dir. mayor's office transp., 1988-92, deputy mayor transp., 1992—; commr. bd. Del. Val. Regional Planning Ctr., Phila., 1984—; treas. Del. River Ferry Co., Phila., 1988—; chair Regional Air Quality Policy Com., Phila., 1992—, City/SEPTA Transit First Com., Phila., 1988—; speaker in field. Recipient Govt. Svc. award Phila. Sect. ASCE, 1992. Mem. Women's Transp. Sem. (WTS Phila. award 1993). Office: City of Phila 1600 Arch St Fl 5 Philadelphia PA 19103-2028

GOREN, JUDITH ANN, psychologist; b. Detroit, Apr. 5, 1933; d. Herman and Evelyn (Apple) Wise; m. Robert Goren, Dec. 20, 1953; children: Gary, Steven, Nancy. BA, Wayne State U., 1954, MEd, 1972; PhD, Union Grad. Sch., 1983. Lic. psychologist, Mich. Author: (poetry) Coming Alive, 1975, Traveling Toward the Heart, 1994; contbr. poetry to jours., anthologies. Mem. Am. Psychol. Assn., Mich. Psychol. Assn., Assn. for Transpersonal Psychology.

GOREN, LEAH NATHAN, artist; b. Houston, Feb. 10, 1918; d. Max Henry and Rebecca (Sakowitz) Nathan; m. Jack Goren (dec. Mar. 10, 1973); children: Robert Nathan, Joan Goren Brannon, John Alan. BA, U. Tex., 1938; postgrad., So. Meth. U., 1974-76. Dancer, choreographer, 1938-61; artist Dallas, 1975—. One-woman shows include Allen St. Gallery, Dallas, 1976, Eastfield Coll., Dallas, 1978, So. Meth. U., Dallas, 1979, The William Campbell Gallery, Ft. Worth, 1979, Clifford Gallery, Dallas, 1982, 77, Plaza of the Americas Gallery, Dallas, 1988, Gallery Gopal, Dallas, 1989, Gallery 93, Dallas, 1994; exhibited in group shows including Tex. Regional Art Show, Dallas, 1975, Ark. Art Ctr., Little Rock, 1977, Meadows Mus., Shreveport, La., 1978, Laguna Gloria Mus., Austin, Tex., 1979, Art Ctr., Waco, Tex., 1992; represented in permanent collections in Country Clubs of Am., W.R. Grace & Co., Harris Meth. Hosp., Enserch Co., Vantage Cos., First City Bank. Recipient Third prize Tex. Regional Art Show, Dallas, 1975, Top award All Media Art Competition, Houston, 1977, Fletcher Thorne-Thomsen award Meadows Mus., Shreveport, 1978, Citation award Laguna Gloria Mus., Austin, 1976, 79. Mem. Dallas Artist Rsch., Dallas Art Mus. League, Dallas Women's Caucus for Art. Home: 11334 D Park Central Pl Dallas TX 75230 Studio: 2416 1/2 McKinney Ave Dallas TX 75201

GORENCE, PATRICIA JOSETTA, judge; b. Sheboygan, Wis., Mar. 16, 1943; d. Joseph and Antonia (Marinsheck) G.; m. John Michael Bach, July 11, 1969; children: Amy Jane Bach, Mara Jo Bach, John Christopher Bach. BA, Marquette U., 1965; MA, U. Wis.-Madison, 1968, JD cum laude, 1977. Bar: Wis. 1977, U.S. Dist. Ct. (ea. and we. dists.) Wis. 1977, U.S. Ct. Appeals (7th cir.) 1979, U.S. Supreme Ct. 1980. Writer/researcher Alverno Coll., Milw., 1970-71; writer/editor Council on Urban Life, Milw., 1970-73; instr. Carroll Coll., Waukesha, Wis., 1973-74; law clk. U.S. Dist. Ct. (ea. dist.) Wis. 1977-79; asst. U.S. atty. Dept. Justice, Milw., 1979-85, 88-89, 1st asst. U.S. atty., 1985-87, 89-91, U.S. atty., 1987-88; dep. atty. gen. State of Wis., 1991-93; lawyer Gimbel, Reilly, Guerin & Brown, Milw., 1993-94; U.S. magistrate judge (ea. dist.), 1994—; mem. adv. com. on local ct. rules U.S. Dist. Ct. (ea. dist.) Wis., 1984-91. Mem. ABA, 7th Cir. Bar Assn., State Bar Wis. (chairperson spl. com. on profls. 1988—, sec. 1990-92, chair rules and practices com. 1991—), Milw. Bar Assn., Profl. Dimensions, Assn. Women Lawyers, Slovenian Arts Council, Milw. Dance Theatre (bd. dirs. 1993—). Roman Catholic. Home: 3028 N Hackett Ave Milwaukee WI 53211-3444 Office: US Dist Court 517 E Wisconsin Ave Rm 264 Milwaukee WI 53202*

GORHAM-SMITH, R(OSELLA) DORITA, direct mail and marketing company executive & owner; b. Washington, Mar. 2, 1948; d. Herman Homer and Julia Rosella (Corker) Gorham; children: Shannon W. Smith, S. Joline Smith. AA, St. Louis Inst., Clayton, Mo., 1966; student, No. Va. Community Coll., Saddleback Valley Community; advanced cert., Alexandria (Va.) Sch. Music, 1968. Tchr. Alexandria Sch. Music, 1963-64, asst. dir., 1966-76; mgr. Deese Cosmetics, Beltsville, Md., 1976-78; R&D rep. Nat. Assn. Broadcasters, Washington, 1978-80; pres., owner U.S. Mail & Mktg. Corp., Paramount, Calif., 1990—. Coord. Inner City Music Appreciation, Alexandria, 1968-70; vol. Alexandria/Laguna Hills Pub. Schs., Va., Calif., 1975-89; activist Learning Disabled Programs, Va., 1980-86; mem. scholarship bd. Oakwood Sch., Annandale, Va., 1982-84; mem. Bd. Edn., Laguna Hills, Calif., 1987. Winner Guild Piano Competition, Washington, 1966; recipient Am. Lyricist award, 1978; St. Louis Inst. Music scholar, 1965; Top 100 L.A. Women-Owned Businesses, 1994. Mem. Direct Mail Club Calif., Nat. Assn. Women Bus. Owners, L.A. and Paramount C. of C., Pi Mu. Office: US Mail & Mktg Corp 7027 Motz St Paramount CA 90723-4842

GORKOS, SUSAN BROWN, nurse; b. Akron, Ohio, Aug. 1, 1948; d. William D. and Floyette (Caley) Brown; m. Joseph Roy Gorkos, Sept. 5, 1970; children: John, Joan. Diploma, Akron City Hosp. Sch. Nursing, 1969; BSN, Longston U., 1989; MS in Nursing, U. Okla., 1993. RN. Staff nurse Green Cross Hosp., Cuyahoga Falls, Ohio, 1969, Akron (Ohio) City Hosp., 1969-70, Mary Mount Hosp., Garfield Heights, Ohio, 1970-71, Monmouth Med. Ctr., Long Branch, N.J., 1971; staff, charge nurse Bedford (Ohio) Mcpl. Hosp., 1973-75, St. John Med. Ctr., Tulsa, 1978-83; staff nurse St. Francis Hosp., Tulsa, 1986-90, clin. instr., 1990-93, clin. nurse specialist gerontology, 1993-94; clin. nurse specialist gerontology St. John Med. Ctr., Tulsa, 1994—. Program com. Oasis-Adult Day Care, Tulsa, bd. dirs. Mem. ANA, Nat. Assn. Geriatric Nurses, Okla. Assn. Clin. Nurse Specialists, Okla. Pub. Health Assn., Acad. Med.-Surg. Nurses. Mem. Christian Ch. Home: 13026 E 46th St Tulsa OK 74134-5850 Office: St John Med Ctr 1923 S Utica Tulsa OK 74104

GORLIN, RENA ANN, writer; b. Bklyn., Dec. 27, 1957; d. Philip and Sylvia (Levy) G.; m. Raymond R. Plante, 1991. BA magna cum laude, Brandeis U., 1979; JD, Am. U., 1982. Legal editor and reporter U.S. Law Week, Washington, 1983-86; legal editor and reporter BNA's Patent, Trademark and Copyright Jour. Bur. Nat. Affairs, Inc., Washington, 1983, sr. copywriter, 1986—; freelance editor and copywriter, Washington area, 1986—. Author: Codes of Professional Responsibility, 1986, 2d edit., 1990, 3d edit., 1994. Mem. law com. Anti-Defamation League B'nai Brith, Washington, 1980; vol. Big Sisters, Waltham, Mass., 1976-78; moot ct. judge Cath. U. Law Sch. competitions, Washington, 1985—. Mem. Washington Ind. Writers, Soc. for Health and Human Values. Office: BNA Sales and Mktg Div 1231 25th St NW Rm 4-332M Washington DC 20037-1157

GORMAN, BRIDGET KIM, corporate communications specialist; b. Madison, Wis., Jan. 25, 1956; d. Edward James and Elizabeth Ann (Kane) Gahan; m. Jeffrey B. Gorman, May 12, 1979 (div. Feb. 1991); children: Shannon E., Erin K. BS in Polit. Sci., Milw. Area Tech. Coll., 1994. Long distance operator Wis. Bell, Madison, 1974-83; repair answerer Ameritech, Milw., 1983-85, maintenance adminstr., 1985-91, svc. technician, 1991—. Vol. Spl. Olympics, Pioneers of Am., Milw., 1974—. Mem. Ballys Vic Tanny. Roman Catholic. Home: 8616 W Lancaster Ave Milwaukee WI 53225 Office: Ameritech 7721 W Fond du Lac Ave Milwaukee WI 53218

GORMAN, CAROL ANN, women's health nurse, ultrasonographer; b. Washington, Ind., Jan. 22, 1946; d. Albert Earl and Agnes Eileen (Gootee) Mangin; m. Gerry Alan Gorman, Apr. 20, 1968; children: Kelly Ann, Jeffrey Alan, Kerry Ann. Diploma, St. Mary's Sch. Nursing, Evansville, Ind., 1966. RN, Ind.; cert. in reproductive endocrinology; registered diagnostic med. sonographer. Staff nurse labor and delivery St. Mary's Hosp., 1966-68; office nurse Evansville, 1968-69, physician's asst., 1970-75; infertility nurse coord. St. Mary's Med. Ctr., Evansville, 1990-91; antepartum testing nurse Evansville Ob-Gyn. Assocs., Inc., 1974-91, clin. supr., 1990-91, chief ob-gyn. ultrasonographer, 1978—; faculty lectr. Serono Symposia, U.S.A., Norwell, Mass., 1989-90; mem. repro/endo-infertility test com. Nat. Cert. Corp., Chgo., 1991—. Mem. NAACOG (sec.-treas. chpt. 1978, chair ultrasound task force 1992), Am. Fertility Soc., Am. Inst. Ultrasound in Medicine (mem. exec. com.). Roman Catholic. Office: Evansville Ob-Gyn Assocs 700 Cherry St Evansville IN 47713-1831

GORMAN, DEBORAH EWING, minister; b. Cleve., Oct. 22, 1946; d. John Sargeant and Susan (Marquis) Ewing; m. Paul Vincent Gorman Jr., June 8, 1968; children: Rachael Carrie, Paul Vincent III. BA, Conn. Coll., 1968; M in Arts and Religion, Ashland Theol. Sem., 1981. Ordained to ministry United Meth. Ch., 1985. Dir. youth and vol. mins. Rockport United Meth. Ch., Rocky River, Ohio, 1981-83; dir. Christian edn. North Olmsted (Ohio) United Meth. Ch., 1983-86; diaconal min. Christian edn. Westlake (Ohio) United Meth. Ch., 1987-93; dir. Christian edn. and programming First United Meth. Ch., Cleve., 1994—; leader tng. for ch. leaders, clergy, ch. sch. tchrs., youth workers and local chs., 1975-90; mem. East Ohio Conf. Coun. on Children's Ministries, 1980-84, chairperson, 1984-88; mem. East Ohio Youth Ann. Conf., 1981—; mem. East Ohio Ann. Conf., 1985—; mem. monitoring and evaluation coms. East Ohio Conf., 1984-88, coun. on ministries, 1984-88, mem. worship com., 1988-89, vice chairperson bd. diaconal ministry, 1988-90, chairperson lab. com., 1990-92; mem. Cleve Dist. Coun. on Ministries, 1988-91; chairperson edn. com. East Ohio Conf. Mem. Lakewood Hist. Soc., 1973-75, West Shore Concerts Bd., Cleve., 1974-75, PTA, Rocky River, Ohio, 1974-85. Recipient John Lennon Meml. award E. Ohio conf. United Meth. Ch., 1991. Mem. Religious Edn. Assn., Christian Educators Fellowship. Democrat. Office: First United Meth Ch 3000 Euclid Ave Cleveland OH 44115

GORMAN, DENISE, financial manager; b. N.Y.C., Apr. 13, 1959; d. Louis Arthur and Mary Ann (Aversano) Gamberale; m. Stephen Michael Goramn, July 18, 1981. BBA, San Diego State U., 1981; MBA, Calif. State U., Long Beach, 1988. Internal auditor Ford Aerospace Corp., Newport Beach, Calif., 1981-83, cost acct., 1983, acctg. payroll mgr., 1983-85, corp acctg. mgr., 1986-88, acctg. specialist, 1988-90; corp. acctg. mgr. Allergan Inc., Irvine, Calif., 1990-93, fin. mgr., 1993—. Mem. Inst. Mgmt. Accts. Office: Allergan Inc 2525 DuPont Dr Irvine CA 92715

GORMAN, IDA NIEBAUER, medical policy coordinator; b. Fairview, Pa., Dec. 7, 1949; d. Ferdinand Oscar and Julia Catherine (Bausch) Niebauer; m. Philip Thomas Gorman, June 14, 1975; children: Jennifer Lynn, Chad Michael. BA in Biology, Mercyhurst Coll., 1971; postgrad., Pa. State U., Hershey. Jr. rsch. technician dept. surgery M.S. Hershey (Pa.) Med. Ctr., 1971-73, rsch. technician, 1973-78; monitoring/telemetry cons. Intermedics, Inc., Freeport, Tex., 1974-83; sr. rsch. pacemaker technician M.S. Hershey (Pa.) Med. Ctr., 1978-83, rsch. technician dept. radiology, 1984, sr. rsch. technician, 1984-86, rsch. support asst. dept. radiology, 1986-89; magnetic resonance tech., spectroscopist York (Pa.) Imaging Ctr., 1989-93; med. policy coord. KHP Svcs./Pa. Blue Shield, Camp Hill, Pa., 1994—. Author: (manual) Basic Index and Troubelshooting Guide to Cardiac Pacing, 1983, (manuscript) T2 Weighted Image Manipulation to Accent Pathology, 1991, (computer software program) SPECTROSCOPY, 1992; contbr. articles to profl. jours. Sec. St. Theresa Home/Sch. Assn., New Cumberland, Pa., 1987-89; lector St. Theresa Ch., New Cumberland, 1989-91, St. Joseph's Ch., Mechanicsburg, Pa., 1992—. Scholar Mercyhurst Coll., 1967-71. Mem. AAAS, Am. Chem. Soc., N.Y. Acad. Sci. Roman Catholic. Home: 5004 Balmoral Ct Mechanicsburg PA 17055-8307

GORMAN, KAREN MACHMER, optometric physician; b. Poughkeepsie, N.Y., June 4, 1955; d. James Andrew and Joan (Benton) Machmer; m. D.L. McCartney III, Aug. 16, 1976 (div. June 1982); m. N. David Gorman, Oct. 16, 1985; 1 stepchild, Danette Y. Gorman. BS in Optometry, U. Houston, 1976, OD, 1978; therapeutic pharm. lic., U. Mo., St. Louis, 1993. Diplomate Nat. Bd. Examiners Optometry; lic. optometrist, Colo., Mo., Tex. Pvt. practice Dallas, 1978-83, 1984-85, Hurst, Tex., 1984-85, St. Joseph, Mo., 1986—; charter mem. optometric adv. panel Pearle, Inc., 1991-93; lectr. on eyecare to community groups. Contbr. poetry to lit. jours., articles to profl. jours.; lead actress (play) None Come Back Innocent, Robidoux Resident Theatre, St. Joseph, 1990, Hay Fever, 1991, The Best Man, 1992, Wedded But No Wife, 1993, Mousetrap, 1993, Diary of Anne Frank, 1994. Vol. Dallas Humane Soc., 1981, YWCA Women's Abuse Shelter; patron Robidioux Resident Theatre, St. Joseph, 1988-92, Ice House Theatre, St. Joseph, Kemper Albrecht Art Mus., St. Joseph, St. Joseph Animal Shelter; sponsor, coach, cheerleader and drill team Mo. Western State Coll., St. Joseph, 1985-86; legis. corr. Humane Soc. of U.S., 1990-92. Recipient Optometric Recognition awards Pearle, Inc., 1986-90; U. Houston scholar, 1972-76. Mem. U. Houston Alumni Assn, CWENS, Tau Sigma.

GORMAN, MARCIE SOTHERN, personal care industry franchise executive; b. N.Y.C., Feb. 25, 1949; d. Jerry R. and Carole Edith (Frendel) Sothern; m. N. Scott Gorman, June 14, 1969 (div.); children: Michael Stephen, Mark Jason; m. Mark Gordley, June 26, 1994. AA, U. Fla., 1968; BS, Memphis State U., 1970. Tchr., Memphis City Sch. System, 1970-73; tng. dir. Weight Watchers of Palm Beach County and Weight Watchers So. Ala., Inc., West Palm Beach, Fla., 1973—, area dir., then pres., 1977—; pres. Markel Ads, Inc. Cubmaster Troop 130. Hon. lt. col. a.d.c. Ala. Militia. Mem. Women' Am. ORT (program chmn. 1975), Optometric Soc. (sec. 1973), Weight Watchers Franchise Assn. (chair mktg. com., mem. advt./mktg. coun., chairperson region IV bd. dirs., treas., 2d v.p. 1991, 1st v.p.), Nat. Orgn. Women, Exec. Women of the Palm Beaches, Am. Bus. Women's Assn., Nat. Assn. Female Execs., Zonta. Home: 429 N Country Club Dr Lake Worth FL 33462-1003 Office: 2459 Congress Ave S West Palm Beach FL 33406-7613

GORMAN, MAUREEN J., lawyer; b. Rockford, Ill., Dec. 17, 1955; d. John William and Joanne Mary (Ollman) G.; m. Alan O. Sykes, 1980. BA, Coll. William and Mary, 1978; JD, Yale U., 1981. Bar: D.C. 1983, Ill. 1987. Law clk. to Hon. Warren W. Eginton U.S. Dist. Ct. Conn., 1981-82; assoc. Caplin & Drysdale, Washington, 1982-85; legis. atty. joint com. on taxation U.S. Congress, Washington, 1985-86; assoc. Mayer, Brown & Platt, Chgo., 1986-88, ptnr., 1988—. Mem. ABA (chairperson subcom. tech. corrections, employee benefits com., tax sect. 1987-91). Home: 343 E 1st St Hinsdale IL 60521 Office: Mayer Brown & Platt 190 S La Salle St Chicago IL 60603-3410*

GORMAN, SHIRLEY ANN, educator, consultant; b. Topeka, Jan. 18, 1950; d. Dale William and Ann E. (Hadl) Honig; m. James Michael Gorman Jr., Oct. 2, 1970; children: Sheila Ann, Jonathan Michael. BBA, Washburn U., 1986. Office mgr. Stryker Co., Topeka, 1987-88; asst. dir. Small Bus. Devel. Ctr., Washburn U., Topeka, 1988—; bd. mem. Human-Kind, Inc., Topeka, 1990-92. Contbr. articles to profl. jours. Organizer, facilitator Assn. Women Entrepreneurs, Topeka, 1993. Mem. Phi Beta Lambda (advisor 1991-94, Gold chpt. award). Lutheran. Home: 4825 SW 33rd Ter Topeka KS 66614-3705 Office: Washburn Univ SBDC 17th And College Topeka KS 66621

GORMLEY, NANCY H., lawyer, electric power industry executive. BA, U. Mass., 1953; LLB, Harvard U., 1956. Bar: Conn. 1957, N.Y. 1958, Pa. 1976. Dir. legal svcs., asst. sec. Allegheny Power Svc. Corp., N.Y.C., 1975-86, gen. solicitor, 1986-89, asst. v.p., gen. solicitor, 1990, v.p., corp. counsel, 1990—. Office: Allegheny Power Svc Corp 12 E 49th St New York NY 10017*

GORNEY, KAREN LYNN, actress; b. L.A.; d. Jay and Sondra (Karyl) G. BFA, Carnegie Mellon U.; MFA, Brandeis U. Actress roles include (soap opera) (Tara) All My Children, 1970-76, (film) Saturday Night Fever, 1977 (People's Choice award 1979), The Dean's List, 1987 (People's Choice award 1988), The Hard Way, 1990, (play) Dr. Faustus, 1990, (theatre prodns.) Evening of Infidelity Alice's Theatre/Theatre Row, N.Y.C., 1991, Academy Street, 1992-93, No Small Miracle, 1992-93, Shattered Mirror, 1993, The West Bank Downstairs Theatre, 1994, The Love Museum, 1994, Something to Eat, 1995, FAP SAP RAP, 1994, (TV series) Law and Order, 1993; writer, actress Unconditional Communication. Brandeis U. fellow; Carnegie Mellon scholar; recipient Bronze award Bravo mag., 1978. Mem. SAG, AFTRA, Equity. Office: c/o Jerry Kahn Agy 853 7th Ave New York NY 10019

GORSALITZ, JEANNINE LIANE, elementary school educator; b. Appleton, Wis., Sept. 22, 1939; d. Gustav Herman and Viola Rachel (Wiedenhaupt) G. BS, Dr. Martin Luther Coll., 1961; MA, U. Wis., Oshkosh, 1969. Cert. elem. tchr., Wis. Tchr. Palos Luth. Sch., Palos Heights, Ill., 1959-60; tchr., prin. St. Peter's Luth. Sch., Freedom, Wis., 1960-65; tchr. Grace Luth. Sch., Neenah, Wis., 1965-68, Gegan Elem. Sch., Menasha, Wis., 1968-93, Butte des Morts Elem. Sch., Menasha, 1993—; coord. elem. social studies Menasha Schs., 1988—; advisor Wis. Coun. for Local History, Madison, 1987—; lectr. Sch. Edn., U. Wis. Author/co-author ednl. curriculum (various awards). Vol. 1st Responder, Ellington, Wis., 1981-86, ARC, 1988—; block capt. Neighborhood Watch, Neenah, 1989—; active State Hist. Soc., Madison. Recipient Outstanding Contbn. award State Hist. Soc., 1980, Excellence in Edn. award U.S. Sec. Edn., Washington, 1989, Excellence award Nat. Coun. Econs., N.Y.C., 1990. Mem. Nat. Fedn. Tchrs., Wis. Fedn. Tchrs., Wis. Coun. for Environ. Edn., Wis. Coun. for Econ. Edn., Kiwanis. Lutheran. Home: 440 E Peckham St

Neenah WI 54956-4168 Office: Butte des Morts Elem Sch 501 Tayco St Menasha WI 54952-2732

GORSKI, SUE MUSSELWHITE, school librarian; b. Americus, Ga., Mar. 3, 1940; d. James Olan Musselwhite and Margaret Cornelia (Johnson) Spears; s. Stanley Paul Gorski, Dec. 16, 1962; children: Stanley Paul Jr., Margaret Elaine. AA, Ga. Southwestern U., 1960; BS in Elem. Edn., Auburn U., 1961; MSEd in Libr. Sci., Old Dominion U., 1984. Tchr. Muscogee County Schs., Columbus, Ga., 1961-63; libr. St. Mary's Sch., Hampton, Va., 1975-81, Booker Elem. Sch., Hampton, 1981-84, Phoebus High Sch., Hampton, 1984—. Sponsor Future Tchrs. Am.; mem. Suicide Crisis Team; driver Meals on Wheels, Hampton; area supr. Cancer Crusade, Hampton. Mem. Hampton Edn. Assn. (bd. dirs.), Hampton Librs. Assn. (pres., v.p.), Peninsula Area Librs. (pres.), Va. Edn. Media Assn. Office: Phoebus High Sch 100 Ireland St Hampton VA 23663-2199

GORSKI, SUSAN CLAIRE, medical devices manufacturing company official; b. Evanston, Ill., Aug. 26, 1955; d. Albert Lewis and Claire Maria (DeFren) Weber; 1 child, William Scot Molthop; m. Richard William Gorski, Aug. 22, 1988. BA in Bus., Loyola U., Chgo., 1990; cert., Mfg. Engring. Cert. Inst., Dearborn, Mich., 1990; M in Project Mgmt., Keller Grad. Sch., Chgo., 1994. With renal div. Baxter Healthcare Corp., Round Lake, Ill., 1976-91, various engring. positions in product devel., 1982-87, program mgr. product devel., 1987-90, mgr. hemodialysis product devel., 1990-91; project mgr. incontinence Hollister Inc., Libertyville, Ill., 1991-93, sr. project mgr. incontinence and wound care, 1993—. Patentee in field. Active Meals on Wheels. Mem. Soc. Mfg. Engrs., Soc. Project Mgmt. Roman Catholic.

GORSKI CROISSANT, KATHLEEN, occupational therapist; b. Cleve., July 27, 1958; d. Michael Robert and Marian Frances (Doubrava) G.; m. Ronald B. Croissant, Apr. 1993; children: Deandra Croissant, Kevin Croissant. AAS, Cuyahoga Community Coll., Cleve., 1981; BS, Ea. Mich. U., 1983. Reg. occupational therapist; cert. aerobics instr., personal trainer. Activity dir. Dover Nursing Home, Westlake, Ohio, 1981-82; staff therapist U. Hosps. of Cleve., 1984-86, sr. therapist, 1986-87, clin. specialist, 1989-90, clin. mgr., 1990—; pres. Kathleen Gorski Rehab., Westlake, Ohio, 1989—; occupational therapist UPS, Cleve., 1987-89. Named Outstanding Clinician, Cleve. Dist. O.T. Assn., 1988; recipient Humanitarian award Ea. Mich. U., 1983. Mem. Cleve. Dist. Occupational Therapists Assn., Ohio Occupational Therapists Assn., Am. Occupational Therapists Assn. Republican. Roman Catholic. Office: U Hosps of Cleve 2074 Abington Rd Cleveland OH 44106-2602

GORTNER, SUSAN REICHERT, nursing educator; b. San Francisco, Dec. 23, 1932; d. Frederick Leet and Erida Louise (Leuschner) R.; m. Willis Alway Gortner, Aug. 25, 1960; children: Catherine Willis, Frederick Aiken. AB, Stanford U., 1953; M Nursing, Western Res. U., 1957; PhD, U. Calif., Berkeley, 1964; postgrad., Stanford U., 1983. Staff nurse, instr., supr. Johns Hopkins Hosp. Sch. Nursing, Balt., 1957-58; instr. to asst. prof. Sch. Nursing U. Hawaii, Honolulu, 1958-64; staff scientist, rsch. adminstr. div. nursing USPHS, Bethesda, Md., 1966-78; assoc. dean rsch. Sch. Nursing U. Calif., San Francisco, 1978-86, acting chmn. dept. family health, 1982, prof. dept. family health care nursing, 1978-94; prof. emerita, 1994—; fellow, assoc. faculty mem. Inst. Health Policy U. Calif., San Francisco, 1979-94, affiliated faculty mem. Inst. for Aging and Health, 1981-94; adj. prof. internal medicine dept. gen. medicine Sch. Medicine, 1989-94, dir. cardiac recovery lab. Sch. Nursing, 1987—, spl. asst. to dean, 1993—; Fulbright lectr., rsch. scholar Norwegian Fulbright Commn., Oslo, 1988. Contbr. articles, papers to profl. publs., chpts. to books. Health advisor N. Fork Assn., Soda Springs, Calif., 1981—. Disting. scholar Nat. Ctr. Nursing Rsch., 1990; named Disting. Alumna Frances Payne Bolton Sch. Nursing, 1983. Fellow Am. Acad. Nursing; mem. ANA (chair exec. com., coun. nurse rsch. com. 1976-80, cabinet on nursing rsch. 1984-86), Am. Heart Assn. (coun. cardiovascular nursing exec. com. 1987-91, coun. epidemiology 1989—, Katharine A. Lembright award 1991, fellow in cardiovascular nursing coun. 1992), Sigma Theta Tau Internat. (Alpha Eta chpt., Marghetta W. Styles award 1990). Home: Box 1056 Soda Springs CA 95728 Office: U Calif N411Y 4th And Parnassus # N411Y San Francisco CA 94143

GORUM, VICTORIA, computer engineer; b. Tucson, Ariz., Dec. 30, 1951; d. Alvin E. and Virginia L. (Don Carlos) G. BS in Zoology, U. Mass., 1974; MS in Math., Elec. Engring., U. Nev., 1982. Rsch. asst. Worcester Found. for Exptl. Biology, Shrewsbury, Mass., 1974-76, Stanford Rsch. Inst., Menlo Park, Calif., 1976-77; sr. rsch. asst. Lawrence Berkeley (Calif.) Labs., 1977-79; tech. writer Lynch Communications, Reno, 1981-82; cons. CPL Inc., Sunnyvale, Calif., 1982-83; mgr. software support Zilog, Inc., Campbell, Calif., 1983-85; mgr. network support Sun Microsystems, Mountain View, Calif., 1986-90; mgr. net. info. systems Next Computer, Inc., Fremont, Calif., 1990-93; mgr. network ops. Adobe Systems, Mountain View, Calif., 1993-94; cons. Break Away Tech. Svcs., 1994—. Mem. Assn. for Computing Machinery, IEEE, Am. Needlepoint Guild, Embroidery Guild Am. Home: 14737 Clayton Rd San Jose CA 95127-5213

GORYN, SARA, textiles executive, real estate developer, psychologist; b. Lima, Peru, Dec. 28, 1944; came to U.S., 1988; d. Ricardo and Lola (Braiman) Grunfeld; m. Jorge Goryn, June 18, 1966 (dec. Sept. 1985); children: Karen, Monica, Lea. B in Psychology, Cath. U., Lima, 1978, M in Psychology, 1985; BA in Bus., Queens Coll., 1989-91. Sec. Inst. Internat. Edn., Lima, 1963-66; head dept. clin. psychology Coll. Leon Pinelo, Lima, 1978-85; pvt. practice Lima, 1978-85; founder Nido Picaflores, Lima, 1980; gen. mgr. Fabritex Peruana, Lima, 1985-88, Michelle Textiles, Charlotte, N.C., 1989—; v.p. Monica Investment, Charlotte, 1990-93, pres., 1993—; pres.; bd. dirs. Fabritex Peruana, Lima, MLK Internat., Charlotte, N.C., 1993. Author learning disabilities curriculum, 1980. Mem. Soc. Israelita Peru, Lima, 1966—, Hebraica, Lima, 1966—. Mem. Peru Psychol. Soc. Democrat. Home: 3600 Castellaine Dr Charlotte NC 28226-6386

GOSCHY-SCHOENBERG, JULIANA LEE, marketing analyst; b. Elmhurst, Ill., Sept. 21, 1962; d. Joseph Peter and Carol Ann (Kotvica) Goschy; m. Mark Howard Schoenberg, May 25, 1987; 1 child, Mary Elizabeth Goschy Schoenberg. Student, Coll. of Lake County, 1986-88; AS in Bus. Adminstrn., DeAnza Coll., 1991, AS in Mktg., 1991. Mail clk. Kemper Group, Long Grove, Ill., 1980-81, Centura Software, San Jose, Calif., 1988-89; agts. commn. specialist Kemper Life Ins., Long Grove, 1981-86, premium acctg. supr., 1986-87; mail list maintenance clk. Quill Office Supply, Lincolnshire, Ill., 1987-88; sales support coord. Compuware Corp., Los Gatos, Calif., 1988-94. Author, editor newsletter Xpediter Futures, 1993; author newsletter Compuware Corp-IAD Divsn., 1993—. Mem. United We Stand Am., San Jose, 1993. Mem. NAFE, Friends of Wis. Roman Catholic. Home: 2785 S Bascom Ave Apt 40 Campbell CA 95008-6264 Office: Compuware Corp 983 University Ave Los Gatos CA 95030-2305

GOSE, CELESTE MARLENE, writer; b. Laramie, Wyo., Jan. 2, 1959; d. Richard Vern Gose and Agnes Jean (Allen) McGreggor. BS, U. Wyo., 1984; student, U. UNA, Belo Horizonte, Brazil, 1982. Freelance writer freelance, Scottsdale, Ariz., 1990—. N.Mex. prodn. coord. (feature movies) Twins, 1988, Young Guns, 1988, (cable) The Tracker, 1987, asst. prodn. coord. (feature movies) Outrageous Fortune, The Sunday Disney Movie; asst. unit publicist The Milagro Beanfield War, 1986; casting asst. (television) Lonesome Dove, 1988, Sparks, 1989, The Fantastiks, 1995; author: Your Daggar or Mine?, 1991, (song lyrics) Awake Inside a Dream, 1990, Caught in Eternity, 1990, Drum Sticks on the Moon, 1990, Sometimes, Somewhere, 1994, Stardust and Loneflower, 1994, Coyotes Don't Bark, 1995. Active Nat. Abortion Rights Action League, Phoenix, 1991. Mem. Ariz. 602-Film Prodr's. Warehouse, Women in Comm., Internat. Arabian Horse Assn., Brazilian Inst. Ariz., Ariz. Club. Republican. Home and Office: 31206 N 65th St Cave Creek AZ 85331-6126

GOSE, KAREN KAMARA, state arts administrator; b. Seattle, July 4, 1955; d. Alvin Frederick Jr. and Donna Muriel (Malde) Kamara; m. Michael Gordon Gose, Mar. 20, 1978; children: John Michael, Elisabeth Jane. BA, The Evergreen State Coll., 1982. Adminstrv. asst. to v.p. and provost The Evergreen State Coll., Olympia, Wash., 1983-86; arts program mgr. II Wash. State Arts Commn., Olympia, 1986-88, 1988-90, asst. dir., 1990-93, acting exec. dir., 1993-94, exec. dir., 1994—; bd. dirs. Western States Arts Fedn., Santa Fe. Editor: Peoples of Washington, 1989. Office: Wash State Arts Commn 234 E 8th Ave Olympia WA 98504-2675

GOSHIEN, DEBORAH PURCELL, lawyer; b. Two Rivers, Wis., Mar. 26, 1941; d. Edward and Ethel (Lohman) Purcell; children: Nana Nash Duarte, Rowena Purcell, David B. Goshien; m. Donald D. Weisberger, June 23, 1991. BA, U. Chgo., 1962; JD magna cum laude, Cleve. State U., 1970; MS in Libr. and Info. Sci., Case Western Reserve U., 1971. Bar: Ohio 1970. Pres. Deborah Purcell Goshien Co., L.P.A., Cleve., 1970—. Mem. Nat. Assn. Women Lawyers, Ohio State Bar Assn., Mensa. Home: 3391 Superior Park Dr Cleveland Heights OH 44118 Office: 75 Public Sq Ste 1401 Cleveland OH 44113

GOSLAWSKI, VIOLET ANN, nurse, substance abuse counselor; b. Bangor, Mich., Aug. 31, 1929; d. George and Ethel Pikal; m. Stephen T. Goslawski, Jan. 18, 1975; children: John F. Cappetto, Steve Goslawski, Carol Smurawski. AAS in Nursing, Morton Coll., 1986; AAS in Mental Health, Loop Coll., 1987. RN, Fla., Ill.; clin. nurse specialist; cert. substance abuse counselor; nat. cert. addictions counselor, internat. cert. addictions counselor. Psychiat. nurse and addictions counselor HCA Riveredge Hosp., Forest Park, Ill.; psychiat. nurse, counselor Choices of Pinellas Community Hosp., Choices of Pinellas Park, Fla., 1990—, Medfield/Charter Psychiat. Hosp., Largo, Fla., 1990—, Rader Inst., Seminole, 1990.

GOSS, GEORGIA BULMAN, translator; b. N.Y.C., Dec. 1, 1939; d. James Cornelius and Marian Bright (McLaughlin) Bulman; m. Douglas Keith Goss, Dec. 21, 1957; children: Kristin Anne, David. BA, U. Mich., 1961. Libr., High Altitude Obs., Boulder, Colo., 1963-64, U.S. Bur. Standards, Boulder, 1964-65; cons. editor Spanish lang. pilots' tng. manual, 1981-82; freelance translator, Englewood, Colo., 1982—. Mem. U. Mich. Alumni Assn., Phi Sigma Iota. Republican. Episcopalian. Home and Office: D-1 # 105 7755 E Quincy Ave Denver CO 80237-2312

GOSS, MARTHA CLARK, insurance company executive; b. Glen Ridge, N.J., May 31, 1949; d. David Ormiston and Marion Jane (Drury) Clark; m. Richard Keith Dentel, Dec. 29, 1972 (dec. Feb. 1974); m. Joseph Coyle Briley, Mar. 25, 1978 (div. May 1993); children: Christopher Briley, Alexis Briley; m. David Charles Goss, June 18, 1994. AB, Brown U., 1971; MBA, Harvard U., 1978. CLU, ChFC. Trainee, credit analyst Chase Manhattan Bank, N.Y.C., 1972-74, asst. treas., 1974-76, 2d v.p., 1976, v.p., team leader, 1978-81; v.p. corp. fin. Prudential Ins. Co. Am., Newark, 1981-83, v.p., treas., 1983-89; pres., CEO Prudential Power Funding Assn., Newark, 1989-92; pres. Prudential Asset Mgmt. Co., Newark, 1992-94; sr. v.p., enterprise integrated control officer Prudential Ins. Co. Am., Newark, 1994—; bd. dirs. Dexter Corp., Windsor Locks, Conn., Foster Wheeler Corp., Clinton, N.J. Active Women's Campaign Fund, Washington, 1989—; trustee Ind. Coll. Fund N.J., 1984—, chair; trustee Brown U., 1987—, treas.; trustee Stuart Country Day Sch. of Sacred Heart, 1989—. Mem. Fin. Women's Assn., Com. of 200. Republican. Presbyterian. Office: The Prudential 751 Broad St Newark NJ 07102-3777

GOSSELL, TERRY RAE, advertising agency executive, small business owner; b. Rockford, Ill., Jan. 24, 1947; d. Virgil Houston and Wilma Beatrice (Cox) Pierce; m. Ronald Richard Gossell, Mar. 3, 1979 (div. Apr., 1983); children: Cameo Ann Elliott, Ronica Rae. Grad. high sch., Loves Park, Ill.; arts cert., U. Kans., 1962. Artist Rockford (Ill.F) Silk Screen Process, 1967-72, Grocery Co-op Advt., Ocala, Fla., 1973-74; art dir. Carlson & Co. Advt., Rockford, Ill., 1975; co-owner R.S.S.P. Graphics & Typesetting, Rockford, 1975-76; owner Graphic Comm., Inc., Rockford, 1976-79, T.R. Gossell Advt., Rockford, 1979-82; owner The Gossell Agy., Phoenix, 1982-88, Rockford, 1988—. Author, artist: (comic book) The Gang from Carl Hayden High Sch., 1986-87. Advisor No. Ill. Advt. Coun. Explorer Post #423, Rockford, 1990-92. Recipient Merit and 1st Place awards Rockford Advt. Club, 1978, 79, 1st Place and award of Excellence Nat. Assn. Pers. Cons., San Diego, 1985, Cert. of Merit, BMA Tower awards, 1994. Mem. No. Ill. Advt. Coun. (pres. 1992-94, merit, 1st and 2d pl. awards 1981, 91, 93, 94), Am. Advt. Fedn. Democrat. Lutheran. Office: The Gossell Agy 5002 Sherwood Forest Ln Rockford IL 61109-2735

GOSSETT, KATHRYN MYERS, language professional, educator; b. Baltimore, Ohio; d. Charles Edgar and Vera Mae (Good) Myers; m. William Thomas Gossett, June 30, 1984. BA summa cum laude, Ohio U., 1931, MA, 1936. Cert. tchr., Ohio, Pa., Mich. Latin and English tchr. Beccaria Twp. High Sch., Coalport, Pa., 1931-32; French, Latin and English tchr. Buford (Ohio) High Sch., 1932-36; tchr. fgn. langs. Oak Hill (Ohio) High Sch., 1936-42; critic tchr. Ohio U. and Athens High Sch., 1942-43; English and Spanish tchr. Eastern High Sch., Lansing, Mich., 1943-45; French tchr. Kingswood/Cranbrook Pvt. Sch., Bloomfield Hills, Mich., 1945-55, chmn. fgn. lang., 1955-75; Fulbright tchr. Lycée de Jeunes Filles, Annecy, France, 1953-54. Contbr. articles to profl. jours. Decorated chevalier des Palmes Academiques (France); recipient Cranbrook Founders medal, 1976; U. Besancon (France) scholar. mem. AAUW, Am. Assn. Ret. Persons, Eastern Star, Bloomfield Hills County Club, The Ocean Club of Fla. (Ocean Ridge), The Little Club (Gulf Stream, Fla.), The Village Club (Bloomfield Hills), Phi Beta Kappa. Republican. Episcopalian. Home: 1276 Covington Rd Bloomfield Hills MI 48301-2365

GOSSETT, SUSAN DIANNE, counselor educator; b. Atlanta, July 1, 1953; d. Herman R. and Edna (Hart) G. BS in Bus., Judson Coll., 1974; cert. elem. tchr., Berry Coll., 1975; MS in Guidance and Counseling, Jacksonville State U., 1979; EdD in Counselor Edn., U. Ala., 1992. Nat. cert. counselor, nat. cert. sch. counselor, cert. AA sch. counselor K-12, Ala., cert. tchr. class B K-8, Ala., sch. psychometrist, Ala.; lic. profl. counselor, Ala. Tchr. elem. edn. Spring Garden (Ala.) High Sch., 1976-79; guidance counselor Cherokee County Schs., Centre, Ala., 1979-90; grad. asst. instr., doctoral intern U. Ala., Tuscaloosa, 1990-91, asst. prof., 1991, rsch. asst., 1992; sch. counselor Centre Mid. Sch., 1992-93; asst. prof., coord. sch. counseling program Troy State U., Phenix City, 1993—; head start tchr. Spring Garden High Sch., summer 1976; freshmen counselor, summer 1987, 88, 89; freshmen counseling supr., summer 1990; adj. faculty U. Ala., Tuscaloosa, 1992; presenter Am. Sch. Counselor Nat. Conf., Little Rock, 1989, Nat. Mid. Sch. Assn. Regional Conf., Birmingham, Ala., 1989. Thelma J. M. Smith scholar, 1990-91. Mem. ACA, Am. Sch. Counseling Assn., Am. Assn. Specialists in Group Work, Am. Assn. Counselor Edn. and Supervision, So. Assn. Counselor Edn. and Supervision (presenter conf. 1991), Ala. Counseling Assn. (grad. student com. 1991-92), Ala. Sch. Counselors Assn., Ala. Assn. for Specialists in Group Work (sec. 1989-90), Chpt. III Ala. Assn. for Counseling and Devel. (presenter confs. 1987, 91, 92), Kappa Delta Pi, Chi Sigma Iota, Phi Kappa Phi. Democrat. United Methodist. Office: Troy State U One University Pl Phenix City AL 36869

GOTCH, JOAN MARY, systems analyst; b. Manchester, Conn., Oct. 30, 1933; d. Theodor Carl and Mary Dorothy (Sikora) Berkenkamp; m. Francis Edmond Gotch, Apr. 1, 1958; children: Stephen Michael, Kathryn Anne, Gregory Alan, Susanne Marie. AS, Arlington State Coll., 1953; BA in Math., U. Tex., 1955; postgrad., So. Meth. U., 1956-57, Wright State U., 1980-82. Computer programmer Chance Vought Aircraft, Dallas, 1955-58; computer scientist Logicon, Dayton, Ohio, 1979-92; sr. systems analyst Systems Rsch. Corp., Dayton, 1993—. Home: 297 Honey Jane Dr Beavercreek OH 45434-5712

GOTLIEB, JAQUELIN SMITH, pediatrician; b. Washington, Oct. 20, 1946; d. Turner Taliaferro and Lois Barbara (Fisk) Smith; m. Edward Marvin Gotlieb, June 25, 1970; children: Sarah Ruth, Aaron Franklin, David Jacob. BS in Zoology, Duke U., 1968; MD, Med. Coll. Va., 1972. Diplomate Am. Bd. Pediatrics. Rotating intern Med. Coll. Va. Hosps.-Va. Commonwealth U., Richmond, 1972-73, resident in pediatrics, 1973-74; pvt. practice Richmond, 1974-75, Stone Mountain, Ga., 1976-86, 87—; resident in pediatrics U. Colo., Denver, 1975-76; med. dir., cons. CIGNA Healthplan Ga., Atlanta, 1986-87; sch. physician Richmond City Schs., 1974-75. Troop leader Boy Scouts Am., Atlanta, 1988; bd. dirs. Ga. Health Found., Atlanta, 1985—. Fellow Am. Acad. Pediatrics; mem. Med. Assn. Ga., DeKalb Med. Soc. (com. chmn. 1976), Atlanta Women's Network. Office: Pediatric Ctr 5405 D Memorial Dr Stone Mountain GA 30083-3258

GOTSCH, AUDREY ROSE, environmental health sciences educator, researcher; b. Milw., May 30, 1939; d. Carlos Louis and Florence Olga (Clausing) Grandy; m. Thomas Gotsch, June 20, 1959; children: Christine Anne Robinson, Allison Lorraine. BS, Ind. U., 1963; MPH, U. Mich., 1966; DrPH, CHES, Columbia U., 1976. Pvt. practice as dental hygienist Lafayette, Ind., 1962-63, Springfield, Ill., 1963-65; health educator Ill. Dept. Health, Springfield, 1966-67, N.J. Dept. Health, Trenton, 1968; assoc. prof., chief dept. environ. and cmty. medicine U. Medicine and Dentistry N.J. Robert Wood Johnson Med. Sch., Piscataway, N.J., 1978-93, prof., chief dept. environ. and cmty. medicine, 1993—; acting chairperson dept. environ. and community medicine U. Medicine and Dentistry N.J. Robert Wood Johnson Med. Sch., 1994-95; dir. Pub. Edn. and Rsch. Com. Divsn.. Environ. and Occupational Health Scis. Inst., 1983—; cons. Nat. Hospice Demonstration Programs, 1980, Hospice of Ctrl. N.Y., Syracuse, 1980, Nat. Cancer Inst., 1981—, Fox Chase Cancer Ctr., Phila., 1983, Medcom, Inc., Calif., 1985, NIH, Heart, Lung and Blood Inst., Bethesda, Med., 1985—, and others; assoc. mem. grad. faculty, Rutgers U., New Brunswick, N.J., 1984—; mem. Outreach Task Force, The Cancer Inst. N.J., 1991—; assoc. mem. Inst. for Health, Health Care Policy and Aging Rsch., Rutgers, 1992; councilor, Coun. on Edn. for Pub. Health, 1990—, pres., 1993—. Author: (with others) Education for Health: Strategies for Change, 1987, Communication of Risk, 1992, also others; author ednl. curricula and videos; mem. editl. bd. Health Edn. Quar., 1986-89; editor-in-chief INFOletter: Environ. and Occupl. Health Briefs, 1988-95; contbr. numerous reports, articles and abstracts to profl. jours. and newspapers. Mem. N.J. Pub. Health Coun., Trenton, 1987—, sec., 1992-94, vice chair, 1994-95; task force Gov.'s Conf. on Aging, 1980-81. USPHS fellow, 1965-66, 1972-74hip award, 1962; grantee Nat. Inst. Environ. Health Scis., 1987—, NSF, 1991-92, 1992-95, N.J. Bus. Roundtable, 1989-90, 1990-91, 1991-92, N.J. Dept. Edn., 1991-92, U.S. EPA, 1991-95, N.J. Dept. Environ. Protection and Energy, 1991-92, numerous others; recipient C.V. Mosby scholarship award, 1962, Sec.'s award U.S. Dept. Health and Human Svcs., 1988, Statewide Faculty Recognition award N.J. Bd. Higher Edn., 1989. Mem. Am. Pub. Health Assn. (Pub. Health Edn. and Health Promotion sect., Occupational Safety and Health sect.), Assn. for the Social Scis. in Health, Assn. Tchrs. of Preventive Medicine, Soc. for Pub. Health Edn. (Greater N.Y., N.J. chpts.), Internat. Union for Health Edn., Soc. Toxicology (Mid-Atlantic chpt.), Nat. Ctr. for Health Edn., Nat. Hospice Orgn., N.J. Hospice Orgn. (bd. trustees 1980-82), N.J. Pub. Health Assn., Soc. for Pub. Health Edn., Soc. for Risk Analysis, Sigma Phi Alpha, Sigma Xi. Lutheran. Office: U Medicine & Dentistry NJ Robert Wood Johnson Med Sch EOHSI 681 Frelinghuysen Rd Piscataway NJ 08855-1179

GOTT, MARJORIE EDA CROSBY, conservationist, former educator; b. Louisville; d. Alva Baird and Nellie (Jones) Crosby; m. John Richard Gott, Jr., Mar. 12, 1946 (dec. Sept. 1993); 1 child, J. Richard III. AB in Math., U. Louisville, 1934; postgrad., U. Ky., 1938-42. Nationally accredited flower show judge, landscape design critic and judge. Underwriter Commonwealth Life Ins. Co., Louisville, 1934-37; tchr. English Hikes Sch., Buechel, Ky., 1937-43; civilian chief statis. control unit Materiel Command, Army Air Force, Dayton, Ohio, 1943-46; tchr. psychology Bapt. Hosp. and Gen. Hosp., Louisville, 1950-52; dedicated Ky.'s Floral Clock to All Kentuckians Who Take Pride in the Beauty of Their State Commonwealth of Ky.,1961. Author: (booklet) How a Garden Club Beautifies a City, 1967. Pres. Young Women's Rep. Club of Louisville and Jefferson County, 1938-40; pres. Beautification League, Louisville and Jefferson County, 1963-64; co-chair Keep Ky. Cleaner-Greener, 1963-68; bd. dirs. Scenic Ky., Inc., 1989—, Nat. Coun. State Garden Clubs, 1961-83. Recipient Conservation award of merit Commonwealth of Ky., 1963, Landscape Design Critics award Nat. Coun. State Garden Clubs, 1979. Mem. Woman's Club of Louisville (pres. 1973-75, hon. 1991—), Garden Club of Ky. (pres. 1961-63), Nat. Assn. Parliamentarians (Louisville unit, founder, pres. 1961-63). Presbyterian. Home: 136 Indian Hills Trail Louisville KY 40207

GOTTLIEB, JANE ELLEN, librarian; b. Bklyn., Dec. 8, 1954; d. Eli David Gottlieb and Edythe (Schwartz) Rosenberg. BA in Music, SUNY, Binghamton, 1976; MLS, Columbia U., 1978. Librarian Am. Music Ctr., N.Y.C., 1978-82; reference librarian Lincoln Ctr. Performing Arts, N.Y.C., 1982-83; head librarian Mannes Coll. Music, N.Y.C., 1983-86, The Juilliard Sch., N.Y.C., 1986—; judge Paul Revere Awards, Music Publishers Assn., 1987. Assoc. editor: The Musical Woman: An International Perspective, 1983—; contbr. articles to The New Grove Dictionary of American Music, 1986; contbr. book and music revs. to Notes: Quarterly Jour. of Music Libr. Assn. Mem. Music Libr. Assn. (bd. dirs. 1991-93, v.p./pres. elect 1994, pres. 1995—), Internat. Assn. Music Librs. Office: Juilliard Sch Lila Acheson Wallace Libr 144 W 66th St New York NY 10023-6547

GOTTLIEB, KRISTA, lawyer; b. Prague, Czechoslovakia, June 26, 1955; came to U.S., 1965; d. Paul and Krista (Podzimkova) G.; m. F. Joseph Coveney, Oct. 11, 1980; 1 child, David O. BA in Polit. Sci. cum laude, Barnard Coll., 1976; JD, Albany Law Sch., 1979. Bar: N.Y. 1980, U.S. Dist. Ct. (so., ea., we., no. dists.) N.Y. 1980, U.S. Ct. Appeals (2d cir.). Assoc. Fisher & Fisher, Bklyn., 1979-82, Reich, Rosen, Barrison & Felzen, N.Y.C., 1982-83, Moritt, Wolfeld & Resnick, Garden City, N.Y., 1983-85; ptnr. Mattar & D'Agostino, Buffalo, 1986—. Mem. NAFE, Women's Bar Assn., N.Y. State Bar Assn., Ask Women, Erie County Bar Assn. Office: Mattar & D'Agostino 17 Court St Ste 600 Buffalo NY 14202

GOTTLIEB, MARGARET ANNE, lobbyist; b. Cin., Dec. 28, 1955; d. Lester and Mary Patricia (Nolan) G.; m. Edward Joseph Goedecke, Apr. 17, 1982. BA, U. Cin., 1978; JD, Cleveland Marshall U., 1986. Legis. fellow Ohio Ho. Reps., Columbus, 1978-80; legis. asst. Congressman Douglas Applegate, Washington, 1980-81; mgr. govt. policy Cleve. C. of C., 1981-84; dir. legis. Am. Legislative Exchange Coun., Washington, 1987-88; dir. state govt. relations Direct Mktg. Assn., Washington, 1988—; prin. Exec. Solutions, Cleve., 1984-86. Mem. editorial adv. bd.: Lobbying and Influence, 1991—. Recipient Leadership Am. award Found. Women's Resources, 1988, Successfully Managing People award Leader Found., 1988. Mem. Washington Area State Relations, Women in Govt. Relations (co-chmn. corp. governance task force 1988), LWV (bd. dirs. 1983), Phi Beta Kappa. Democrat. Roman Catholic. Home: 1091 Paper Mill Ct NW Washington DC 20007-3619

GOTTLIEB-ROBERTS, MARILYN PATRICIA, artist, art educator; b. Rome, Ga., Apr. 18, 1939; d. John Treadwell and Mary Georgina (Crichton) Roberts; m. Norman Gottlieb, June 6, 1964 (div. Sept. 1975); children: Eric, Karla. BA in Painting and Lit., Goddard Coll., 1975; MFA in Painting and Drawing, U. Miami, Fla., 1977. Instr., Sch. Arts and Humanities, coord. visual arts dept. Miami (Fla.)-Dade C.C., 1980-93, prof., Sch. Arts and Humanities, 1993—. Exhibited one week residency and interactive installation: Harvard U., Cambridge, Mass., Real Art Ways, Hartford, Conn., 1984-87, Mobius, Boston, 1984-87, AVA Gallery, Hanover, N.H., 1984-87, The Currier Gallery of Art, Manchester, N.H., 1984-87, The Clocktower, N.Y.C., 1984-87; residencies and site sculptures Mobius, Boston, 1988-89, Birmingham Mus of Art, Ala., 1988-89, Columbus Mus. Art, Ga., 1988-89, Contemporary Art Ctr., New Orleans, 1988-89; Exhibited at The Drawing Ctr., N.Y.C., 148 Duane, N.Y.C., Frances Wolfson Gallery, Miami, Fla. Ctr. for Contemporary Art, Tampa, Fla., New Gallery U. Miami, Coral Gables, Fla., East Campus Gallery Valencia C.C., Orlando, Fla., Moon Gallery Berry Coll., Rome, Ga., many others; represented in permanent collections U. Miami Law Libr., Miami-Dade Pub. Libr., Martex Corporation, others. Bd. dirs. Tigertail Prodns., Miami, 1982-94, South Fla. Art Ctr., 1986-88; bd. dirs. Miami Beach (Fla.) Devel. Corp., trustee, 1990—; founding bd. dirs. Alliance for Media Arts, Miami Beach, 1983—; active South Fla. Art Ctr. Alternative Arts Adv. Bd., 1992—; others. Recipient Project grant State of Fla., Tallahassee, 1988, Henry Luce Found. grant Birmingham (Ala.) Mus., 1989, New Forms Fla. award NEA/Rockefeller Found., Miami, 1990, grant for artistic project Atlanta (Ga.) Art Festival, 1992-93, Endowed Tchg. chair Miami (Fla.)-Dade C.C., 1993; others. Office: Miami-Dade CC Wolfson Campus 300 NE 2nd Ave Miami FL 33132-2204

GOTTOVI, KAREN ELIZABETH, state legislator, political consultant, researcher; b. Rochester, N.Y., Feb. 2, 1941; d. Richard Allan Eckberg and Vivian Emma (Chall) Eckberg; m. Daniel Gottovi, June 23, 1962; children: Daniel Richard, Peter Andrew, Nancy Christine. BA, Wells Coll., 1962; MS in LS, U. N.C., 1972. Tchr. English, Pittsford (N.Y.) Cen. High Sch., 1962-65, 66; reference libr. Wilmington (N.C.) Pub. Libr., 1972-75; commr. New

Hanover County, Wilmington, 1976-84; polit. cons. Ind. Opinion Rsch. & Communications, Inc., Wilmington, 1985-91; mem. N.C. Ho. of Reps., Raleigh, 1990-94; mem. N.C. Coastal Resources Commn., Raleigh, 1980-88; bd. dirs. N.C. Ctr. for Pub. Policy Rsch., Raleigh, 1978-90. Bd. dirs. Lower Cape Fear United Way, Wilmington, 1976-84; mem. New Hanover Bd. Social Svcs., Wilmington, 1977-84, Pub. Libr. Adv. Bd., Wilmington, 1989-94, Women's Forum N.C., Raleigh, 1977—; committeewoman Dem. Nat. Com., Washington, 1980-88; mem. N.C. Commn. for Nat. and Community Svcs., 1994—. Recipient Susan B. Anthony award New Hanover NOW, 1985; named Legislator of Yr. N.C. Wildlife Fedn., 1994. Mem. Nat. Conf. State Legislatures (communications com. 1991—), Am. Assn. Polit. Cons., LWV (pres. New Hanover 1973-75), Phi Beta Kappa. Unitarian. Home: 116 Martingale Ln Wilmington NC 28409-2020

GOTTSCHALK, SHARON JAYNE, parks and recreation director; b. Paso Robles, Calif., July 31, 1943; d. Albert Eber Gardner and Leah Blanche Hinds; m. Dempsey D. Gottschalk, Aug. 6, 1966; children: Gretchen Gardner, Friederich Albert. AA, William Woods U., 1963; BS in Edn., Ariz. State U., 1965. Instr. elem. music Tina (Mo.)-Avalon Schs., 1967-68, Lawton Pub. Schs., 1968-69, Richmond (Mo.) Schs., 1971-85; asst. dir. Richmond Parks & Recreation, 1986—. Mem. alumni bd. William Woods U., Fulton, Mo., 1974—; treas. Ray County Child Protection Coun., Richmond, 1985—, Ray County United Way, Richmond, 1990—. Mem. Order Ea. Star, Optimist Club. Republican. Methodist. Home: 1106 Southview Richmond MO 64085 Office: Richmond Parks & Recreation 303 S Thornton Richmond MO 64085

GOTTSCHALL, JOAN B., judge; b. Oak Ridge, Tenn., Apr. 23, 1947; d. Herbert A. and Elaine (Reichbaum) G. BA cum laude, Smith Coll., Mass., 1969; JD, Stanford Univ., Calif., 1973. Bar: Ill. 1973. Assoc. Jenner & Block, 1973-76, 78-81, ptnr., 1981-82; staff atty. Fed. Defender Program, 1976-78, Univ. of Chgo., Office of Legal Counsel, 1983-84; magistrate judge U.S. Dist. Ct. (no. dist.) Ill., Chgo., 1984—; mem. vis. com. Divinity Sch., Univ. of Chgo.; mem. vis. com. on coll. and student activities Univ. of Chgo., co-vice-chmn. Chgo. Bar Assn. Alliance for Women; bd. dirs. Just the Beginning Found.; mem. com. Seventh Cir. Judicial Conf. Mem. Am. Bar Assn., Chgo. Bar Assn., Law Club of the City of Chgo., Am. Inns of Ct., Am. Law Inst. Office: Everett McKinley Dirksen Bldg 219 S Dearborn St Rm 2490 Chicago IL 60604*

GOUGE, BETTY MERLE, family therapist; b. Colbert, Okla., Nov. 8, 1937; d. Clifford Carlton and Cleo (Sims) Gage; m. W. Frank Wolfenbarger, July 26, 1980; children: Carol, Jeff, Gretchen Gouge Wolfenbarger. BS, Tex. Womans U., 1968, MS, 1971, PhD, 1975. workshop leader shcs. and profl. orgns. Co-author: Choices! Choices! Choices!, 1985, Wonderful You, 1985, My Feelings and Me, 1985, Let's Share, 1985, Land of Listening, 1985, The Feeling Fun House, 1985, A Lasting Friend, 1985, Rules at my House, 1986, An Island Adventure, 1986. Mem. APA, AACD, DGPA, AGPA, DAMFT, Am. Assn. Marriage and Family Therapy. Office: Family Counseling Ctr Ste 400 2925 Lyndon B Johnson Fwy Dallas TX 75234-7614

GOUGÉ, SUSAN CORNELIA JONES, microbiologist; b. Chgo., Apr. 18, 1924; d. Harry LeRoy and Gladys (Moon) Jones; student Am. U., Washington, 1942-43, La. Coll., 1944-45; BS, George Washington U., 1948; postgrad. Georgetown U., 1956-58, 66-69, Vt. Coll. of Norwich U., M.A. in Pub. Health, 1984; m. John Oscar Gougé, Aug. 7, 1943; children: John Ronald, Richard Michael (dec.), Claudia Renée Gougé Carr. Med. technician Children's Hosp. Research Lab., Washington, 1948-49; bacteriologist George Washington U. Research Lab., D.C. Gen. Hosp., 1950-53; med. microbiologist Walter Reed Army Inst. Research, Washington, 1953-61; research asst. Dental Research, Walter Reed Army Med. Ctr., 1961-62; microbiologist antibiotics div. FDA, 1962-63; supr. quality control John D. Copanos Co., Pharms., Balt., 1963-64; research tng. asst. infectious diseases and tropical medicine Howard U. Med. Sch., 1964-65; research assoc. Georgetown U. Lab. Infectious Diseases, D.C. Gen. Hosp., 1966-69; mycologist Georgetown U. Hosp. Lab., 1969-70; microbiologist Research Found. of Washington Hosp. Ctr., 1971-73; dir. quality control Bio-Medium Corp., Silver Spring, Md., 1973-76; microbiologist Alcolac, Inc., Balt., 1976-77; microbiologist div. labs., dept. human resources Community Health and Hosps. Adminstrn., Washington, 1978-79; microbiologist div. ophthalmic devices, Office Device Evaluation Ctr. for Devices and Radiol. Health, FDA, Rockville, Md., 1979—. Sec. to exec. bd. Bethesda Project Awareness, 1970-71; vol. lead poisoning detection testing project, D.C. Office Vols. Internat. Tech. Assistance, 1970-71; vol. Zacchaeus Free Clinic, Washington, 1979-84, Winchester Med. Ctr., 1994—. Mem. Nat. Capital Harp Ensemble, 1941-65; mem. parish social concerns com. Roman Cath. Ch., 1972-84; mem. Winchester Med. Ctr. Aux., 1994—. Recipient medal community service; registered microbiologist Nat. Registry Microbiologists; specialist microbiologist Am. Acad. Microbiology. Mem. AAAS, VITA, Am. Soc. for Microbiology, Am. Inst. Biol. Scis., Am. Chem. Soc., Internat. Union Pure and Applied Chemistry, N.Y. Acad. Scis., Am. Pub. Health Assn., Bus. and Profl. Women (Capital Club, rec. sec. 1973-74, 1st v.p. 1974-75, pres. 1975-76), Winchester Bus. and Profl. Women, World Affairs Council of Washington D.C., Winchester-Frederick County Hist. Soc., Toastmasters Internat. (charter sec. BMD Club #3941 1979-80), Pi Kappa Delta, Sigma Xi. Methodist. Office: FDA Div Ophthalmic Devices Office Device Evaluation 9200 Corporate Blvd Rockville MD 20850-4332

GOUGH, CAROLYN HARLEY, library director; b. Paterson, N.J., Sept. 23, 1922; d. Frank Ellsworth and Mabel (Harrison) Harley; m. George Harrison Gough, Sept. 21, 1944; children: Deborah Ann Gough Bornholdt, Douglas Alan. B.A., Coll. William and Mary, 1943; M.L.S., Drexel U., 1966. Research asst. Young and Rubicam, Inc., N.Y.C., 1943-44; library dir., asst. prof. Cabrini Coll., Radnor, Pa., 1966-81; chmn. Palm Beach County Library Bd., 1984-86. Mem. resources study com. Tredyffrin Twp. Library, 1964-65; docent Henry Morrison Flagler Mus., 1982—. Mem. Tri-State Coll. Library Coop. (v.p. 1973-74, pres. 1974-75), Assn. Coll. and Research Libraries (dir. 1978-81), AAUP, DAR (Palm Beach chpt.), Beta Phi Mu, Kappa Delta. Republican. Episcopalian. Clubs: Questers, Inc. (1st nat. v.p. 1964-66), Atlantis Golf, Atlantis Women's (co-pres. 1982-83), Sir Robert Boyle Soc. Home: 458 S Country Club Dr Atlantis FL 33462-1238

GOUGH, JESSIE POST (MRS. HERBERT FREDERICK GOUGH), retired education educator; b. Nakon Sri Tamaraj, Thailand, Jan. 26, 1907 (parents Am. citizens); d. Richard Walter and Mame (Stebbins) Post; B.A., Maryville Coll., 1927; M.A. in English, U. Chgo., 1928; Ed.D., U. Ga., 1965; m. Herbert Frederick Gough, June 30, 1934; children: Joan Acland (Mrs. Alexander Reed), Herbert Frederick. Tchr. English, Linden Hall, Lititz, Pa., 1930-32; tchr. Fairyland Sch., Lookout Mountain, Tenn., 1955-64; rsch. asst. English curriculum studies ctr. U. Ga., 1964-65; asso. prof. elem. edn. LaGrange (Ga.) Coll., 1965-73, prof., 1973-75; prof. N.W. Ga. area tchr. edn. svcs., 1969-71. Mem. Walker County (Ga.) Curriculum Coun., 1959-61, Walker County Ednl. Planning Bd., 1958-60. Mem. Am. Ednl. Rsch. Assn., Internat. Reading Assn., Nat., Ga. edn. assns., Delta Kappa Gamma. Home: 8111 Savannah Hills Dr Ooltewah TN 37363-9103

GOUGH, PAULINE BJERKE, magazine editor; b. Wadena, Minn., Jan. 7, 1935; d. Luther C. and Zita Pauline (Halbmaier) Bjerke; BA, U. Minn., Mpls., 1957; BS, Moorhead (Minn.) State Coll., 1970; MS, Ind. U., Bloomington, 1972, EdD, 1977; children: Mary Pauline, Sarah Elizabeth, Philip Clayton. Reporter women's page San Jose (Calif.) Mercury-News, 1957-58; with rsch. dept. Campbell-Mithun Advt., Mpls., 1958-60; tchr. Univ. Elem. Sch., Bloomington, 1970-79; freelance writer Agy. Instructional TV, Bloomington, 1974-80; mem. adj. faculty Ind. U.-Purdue U., Indpls., summers 1976, 77; asst. editor Phi Delta Kappan, Bloomington, 1980-81, mng. editor, 1981-88; editor, 1988—; mem. profl. staff Phi Delta Kappa, 1981—, also leader insts. on writing for publ. Recipient Disting. Alumna award Moorhead State U., 1982. Mem. Phi Beta Kappa, Phi Delta Kappa. Author articles in field. Home: 3570 S Oakridge Dr Bloomington IN 47401-8926 Office: Phi Delta Kappa PO Box 789 408 N Union Bloomington IN 47402

GOUGH, SHIRLEY MAE PREBIL, insurance underwriter, costume designer; b. DeKalb, Ill., Aug. 11, 1951; d. Joseph and Alberta Mae (Rhodes) Prebil; m. Stephen T. Gough, June 27, 1970 (dec. Mar. 1980). Student, U. Ky., 1974. CPCU; lic. property and casualty ins. agt., Ky. Broodmare foreman Hobeau Farm, Ocala, Fla., 1974-75; yearling foreman North Ridge Farm, Lexington, Ky., 1978-80; thoroughbred horse sales mgr. Fred Seitz, Brookdale Farm, Versailles, Ky., 1980-84; sr. prodn. underwriter Am. Bankers Ins. Co., Lexington, 1985—; costumer designer Shedrow Shirley Equine Designs; instr. equine ins. class Midway (Ky.) Coll., 1993; v.p., bd. dirs. Ky. Equine Inst. at Ky. Horse Park, Lexington, 1991—. Mem. World Sidesaddle Fedn. (trustee 1990—), Internat. Sidesaddle Orgn., Costume Soc. Am., Bluegrass Mensa (bd. dirs. 1980—, Lexington Vintage Dance Assn. (bd. dirs. 1994—), Woodord County Saddle Club (bd. dirs. 1992—), Alpha Zeta. Home: PO Box 241 Versailles KY 40383 Office: Am Bankers Ins Co PO Box 4238 Lexington KY 40544

GOULD, BONNIE MARIE, realtor; b. Cleve., Sept. 3, 1947; d. Edward Louis and Frances Dee (Pavlovich) Marincic; m. Wayne William Gould, June 7, 1969; 1 child, Scott Robert. Student John Carroll U., 1965-66, 76-78. Asst. prodn. mgr. Nelson Stern Advt., Cleve., 1966-73; sec. acctg. S. James Dubin & Assoc., Eastlake, Ohio, 1976-78; sec., atty. James Todoroff, Andrews & Todoroff, Eastlake, 1977-78; realtor sales Century 21-Baur, Euclid, Ohio, 1978-82; relocations dir., mgr. Century 21, Euclid, 1979-82; realtor assoc., relocation dir. Century 21-Malone, Inc., Willowick, Ohio, 1982-83, Century 21-William T. Byrne, Euclid, 1983-84, Smythe, Cramer Co., Euclid, 1984-86; v.p., corp. mgr. Acacia Realty Profls., Inc., 1986—; pres., treas., interior design coord. Acacia Design & Trade Profls., Inc., Gen. Contractors, 1990—. Mem. Realtors Polit. Action Com., Cleve., 1981—; vice chmn. local taxation and legislation com. Cleve. Area Bd. Realtors, 1983-84, vice chmn. polit. affairs, 1987—, chmn. home and flower, 1986, mem. enlarged legis. com., 1986—, internat. rules and fin. com., 1993-95, chmn., 1995. Sec., trustee Euclid Gateway Found., 1987—. Recipient Disting. Svc. award Cleve. Bd. Realtors, 1983, 87, Woman of Yr. award 1990. Mem. Cleve. Bd. Realtors (dir. 1984-86, 93—, 2nd v.p. 1994, treas. 1995, gov. Northern Ohio multiple listings svc., 1992—, contract and fin. com. 1992—), Ohio Assn. Realtors (trustee 1981—), Nat. Assn. Realtors, Women's Coun. Realtors (treas. Cleve. chpt. 1986-87, v.p. 1987-88, pres. 1989, chmn. nominating com. 1990, Woman of Yr. 1990), North East Roundtable (sec. 1980, chair 1981), Euclid C. of C. (trustee). Republican. Roman Catholic. Office: Acacia Realty Profls Inc 21801 Lake Shore Blvd Cleveland OH 44123 also: Acacia Design & Trade Profls Inc Euclid OH 44123

GOULD, CHARLENE JEANETTE, theater educator; b. Dodge City, Kans., Feb. 19, 1954; d. E. C. and Pauline C. (Mattingly) Burton; m. Richard S. Gould, July 24, 1976; children: Jennifer, Megan, Kaitlin. BS in Edn., Kans. State U., 1976; MA in Comm.-Theater, Wichita State U., 1980; PhD, U. Kans., 1995. Cert. secondary tchr., Kans. Theater, English, speech tchr. Eisenhower Jr. H.S., Topeka, Kans., 1976-77, Wichita (Kans.) H.S. East, 1977-83; theater instr. Avila Coll., Kansas City, Mo., 1983—, dir. human resource ctr., 1983-84, dir., 1983-94; comm. cons. Realty Info. Systems, Lenexa, Kans., 1985, St. Luke's Hosp., Kansas City, 1986—. Dir. various plays, including Cat on a Hot Tin Roof, 1988, Death of a Salesman, 1987, Streetcar Named Desire, 1992, Cherry Orchard, 1994. Troop leader, asst. Girl Scouts U.S., Overland Park, Kans., 1987—; active PTA, Blue Valley, 1990—. Mem. P.E.O., Assn. for Theatre in Higher Edn. Home: 5916 W 157th Terr Overland Park KS 66223 Office: Avila Coll 11901 Wornall Rd Kansas City MO 66245

GOULD, JOANN CARTER, accountant; b. Washington, Jan. 2, 1961; d. Roy Carter and Susie Fayetta (Boone) Carter Jackson; m. Raymond Tyrone Gould, Sr., Sept. 29, 1984; children: Jené Colette, Raymond Tyrone, Jr. BS in Acctg., U. Md., 1983. Staff acct. Folks & Co., Chartered, Washington, 1983-84; acct. Lawrence Johnson & Assocs., Washington, 1984-85; staff II acct./conversion team NCHP Property Mgmt., Washington, 1985-86; sr. assoc., acctg. supr. Brown & Co., CPAs, Washington, 1986-89; acctg. supr. Quadrangle Devel. Corp., Washington, 1989—. Active campaign com. Friends of Ron Russell, Prince George's County, Md., 1994. Mem. Inst. Mgmt. Accts. (meetings assoc. dir. 1993-94, membership acquisition assoc. dir. 1992-93), Delta Sigma Theta (mem. coms.). Home: 700 Etna Dr Upper Marlboro MD 20772 Office: Quadrangle Devel Corp 1001 G St NW Ste 700 Washington DC 20001

GOULD, MARILYN KAY JONES, advertising executive; b. Columbus, Ohio, July 11, 1953; d. Paul O. and Lynn A. (Pace) Jones; m. Glenn Hunting Gould III, Apr. 1, 1983; children: Courtney, Angela. BS in Comm., Taylor U., 1975; MS in Comm., Purdue U., 1978. Dir. pub. rels. Ohio State Funeral Dirs. Assn., Columbus, 1975-76; dir. Batesville (Ind.) Casket Co., 1978-82; pres. MKJ Mktg., Largo, Fla., 1982—. Author: Adult Death Education, 1976, Professional Funeral Service, 1985; prodr., creative dir. TV commls.; dir. video Planning Ahead, 1980. Mem. Am. Advt. Fedn. Republican. Baptist. Office: MKJ Mktg 1501 Belcher Rd Bldg B Largo FL 34641

GOULD, MARTHA BERNICE, retired librarian; b. Claremont, N.H., Oct. 8, 1931; d. Sigmund and Gertrude Heller; m. Arthur Gould, July 29, 1960; children: Leslie, Stephen. BA in Edn., U. Mich., 1953; MS in Library Sci., Simmons Coll., 1956; cert., U. Denver Library Sch. Community Analysis Research Inst., 1978. Childrens librarian N.Y. Pub. Libr., 1956-58; adminstr. library services act demonstration regional library project Pawhuska, Okla., 1958-59; cons. N.Mex. State Libr., 1959-60; childrens librarian then sr. childrens librarian Los Angeles Pub. Libr., 1960-72; acctg. dir. pub. srvices, reference librarian Nev. State Libr., 1972-74; pub. services librarian Washoe County (Nev.) Libr., 1974-79, asst. county librarian, 1979-84, county librarian, 1984-94; ret., 1994. Contbr. articles to jours. Treas. United Jewish Appeal, 1981; bd. dirs. Temple Sinai, Planned Parenthood of Nev.; trustee RSVP, North Nevadans for ERA; No. Nev. chmn. Gov.'s Conf. on Libr., 1990; mem. bd. Campaign for Choice, No. Nev. Food Bank, Nev. Women's Fund (Hall of Fame award 1989); mem. No. Nev. NCCJ, Washoe County Quality Life Task Force, 1992—; chair Sierra (Nev.) Cmty. Access TV; presdl. appointee Nat. Commn. on Librs. and Info. Sci., 1993-97; mem. adv. bd. Partnership Librs. Washoo County. Recipient Nev. State Libr. Letter of Commendation, 1973, Washoe County Bd. Commrs. Resolution of Appreciation, 1978, Freedom's Sake award AAUW, 1989, Leadership in Literacy award Sierra chpt. Internat. Reading Assn., 1992, Woman of Distinction award 1992, Nev. Libr. Assn. Libr. of Yr., 1993. Mem. ALA (bd. dirs., intellectual freedom roundtable 1977-79, intellectual freedom com. 1979-83, coun. 1983-86), ACLU (bd. dirs. Civil Libertarian of Yr. Nev. chpt. 1988, chair gov.'s conf. for women 1989), Nev. Libr. Assn. (chmn. pub. info. com. 1972-73, intellectual freedom com. 1975-78, govt. rels. com. 1978-79, v.p., pres.-elect 1980, pres. 1981, Spl. Citation 1978, 87, LIbr. of Yr. 1993).

GOULDER, CAROLJEAN HEMPSTEAD, psychologist; b. Houston, Minn., Apr. 9, 1933; d. Orson George and Jean Helen (Lischer) Hempstead; m. L. Lynton Goulder, Jr., May 26, 1956 (div. 1978); children: Jean Virginia, David Thomas, Ann Rachel; m. John T. Blake, Apr. 12, 1986. BS, Hamline U., 1956; CAGS, R.I. Coll., 1975, MA in Sch. Psychology, 1972; postgrad., Nova U., 1977-78. Cert sch. psychologist, R.I. Dept. head, instr. Highsmith Hosp., Fayetteville, N.C., 1956-57; instr. nursing New Eng. Deaconess Hosp., Boston, 1957-58; dir. psychol. svcs. Burrillville Sch. Dept., Harrisville, R.I., 1972-79, sch. psychologist, 1972—; coord. presch. handicapped, 1985-86; lectr. pediatric problems Sturdy Meml. Hosp., Attleboro, Mass., 1970-72; cons. Wheeler Sch., Providence, 1970-73. Chmn. 2d Congl. Ch. Sch., Attleboro, Mass., 1962-65, mem. religious edn. com., kindergarten com. and choir, 1965; active 1st Unitarian Ch., Providence, 1982—. Mem. R.I. Sch. Psychologists Assn., Nat. Assn. Sch. Psychology, Am. Psychol. Assn. (assoc.), Mass. Psychol. Assn. (assoc.), Delta Kappa Gamma. Office: AT Levy Sch Spl Svcs Office Harrisville RI 02830

GOULDING, JAYNE MARIE, accountant; b. Oakland, Calif., Mar. 12, 1957; d. Dean Payne and Anita Marie (Stanton) Phillips; m. Donald Rea Goulding, Jan. 31, 1987. AA in Acctg., Sierra Coll., 1979. Acct. clk., sr. acct. clk. Placer County Auditor-Controller, Auburn, Calif., 1974-77, acct.-auditor I and II, 1977-82, acct.-auditor III, tax mgr., 1982-90, supervising acct.-auditor, 1990—; lectr. in field. Recipient Cert. Placer County Human Rels. Commn., 1979. Mem. Calif. Tax Mgrs., Nat. Abortion Rights Action League, World Wildlife Fund (Wash. chpt.), Internat. Primate Protection League, Conservation Internat., Internat. Wildlife Coalition, Wildlife Conservation Internat., Bat Conservation Internat., U.S. Humane Soc. (Wash. chpt.), Am. Humane Soc., Am. Mus. Natural History, Nat. Geographic Soc., Nat. Arbor Day Found., Animal Protection Inst. Am. (Sacramento, Calif. chpt.), Calif. Marine Mammal Ctr., Californians Against Waste, Environ. Def. Fund (N.Y. state chpt.), People for the Ethical Treatment of Animals, The Wilderness Soc., Sacramento Zool. Soc. Friends of the Tolson Zoo, Ctr. for Marine Conservation, Whale Adoption Project, Save the Manatees, The Nature Conservancy, The Smithsonian Instn., League of Conservation Voters, Vegetarian Resource Group, Co-op Am., Divide Humane Soc., Gorilla Found., Greenpeace, Rainforest Action Network. Home: 5061 Reservoir Rd Greenwood CA 95635-9606 Office: Placer County Auditor-Contr 135 Fulweiler Ave Auburn CA 95603-4507

GOULDING, NORA See **CLARK, SUSAN**

GOULET, LORRIE, sculptor; b. Riverdale, N.Y., Aug. 17, 1925. Student, Inwood Potteries Studios, N.Y.C., 1932-36, Black Mountain Coll., N.C., 1943-44. One-woman shows Clay Club Sculpture Ctr., N.Y.C., 1948, 55, Cheney Libr., Hoosick Falls, N.Y., 1951, Contemporaries Gallery, N.Y.C., 1959, 62, 66, 68, Rye Art Ctr., N.Y., 1966, New Sch. Assocs., N.Y.C., 1968, Temple Emeth, Teaneck, N.J., 1969, Kennedy Galleries, N.Y.C., 1971, 73, 75, 78, 80, 82, 86, Carolyn Hill Gallery, N.Y.C., 1988, 91, Caldwell (N.J.) Coll., 1989; group shows include Mus. Natural History, 1936, Whitney Mus. Am. Art, N.Y.C., 1948, 49, 50, 53, 55, Met. Mus. Art, N.Y.C., 1951, Detroit Inst. Arts, 1960, Pa. Acad., 1950, 51, 52, 54, 59, 64, NAD, N.Y.C., 1966, 75, 77, Corcoran Gallery, Washington, 1966, Hofstra Mus., N.Y.C., 1990, The McNey Mus., 1990, The Copley Soc., Boston, 1991, The Spanish Inst., 1992, Lehigh U. Art Gallery, 1992, Iowa State U. Brunne Gallery, 1992, Paine Art Ctr., Oshkosh, Wis., 1992, Mitchell Art Gallery St. John's Coll., Annapolis Md., 1992, Revealed Form, Erie Art Mus., Erie, Pa., 1995; represented in permanent collections Hunter Mus., Chattanooga, Tenn., N.J. State Mus., Wichita Mus. Art, Hirschhorn Sculpture Mus., Washington, also pvt. collections. Tchr. Mus. Modern Art, 1957, 64, Scarsdale Studio Workshop, 1959, 61, New Sch., 1961-75, Art Students League, 1981—. Recipient numerous art awards, various commns. Fellow Nat. Sculpture Soc. (coun.); mem. Artists Equity, Audubon Artists, Sculptors Guild, Visual Artists and Galleries Assocs., Nat. Acad. Design (academician 1989, mem. coun. 1994), Fedn. Arts (del. 1992-93, bd. dirs.).

GOURLEY, PAULA MARIE, book arts educator, artist, designer bookbinder; b. Carmel, Calif., Apr. 29, 1948; d. Raymond Serge Voronkoff and Frances Eliseyvna (Kovtynovich) G.; m. David Clark Willard, Feb. 10, 1972 (div. Oct. 1973). AA, Monterey (Calif.) Peninsula Coll., 1971; BA, Goddard Coll., 1978; MFA, U. Ala., 1987. Radiologic technologist Cen. Med. Clinic, Pacific Grove, Calif., 1970-71, Community Hosp. of Monterey, 1972-75, Duke U. Med. Ctr., Durham, N.C., 1975-77; dept. head, ultrasound technologist Middlesex Meml. Hosp., Middletown, Conn., 1977-79; asst. prof. U. Ala., Tuscaloosa, 1985-93, assoc. prof., 1993—; asst. dir. Inst. for the Book Arts, U. Ala., 1985-88, coord., 1988—; U.S. rep. Les Amis de la Reliure d'Art, Toulouse, France, 1989—; corr. journalist for U.S. to Art et Metiers du Livre, Revue Internat., Paris. Editor (newsletter) First Impressions, 1988—; contbr. articles to profl. jours. Vol. PLUS Literacy Program, Tuscaloosa, 1991—. U. Ala. grantee, 1988, 89, 90, 92; recipient Diplome of honneur Atelier d'Arts Appliques, France, 1986, Craft fellowship Ala. State Coun. on Arts, 1993-94. Mem. Am. Registry Radiologic Technologists, Am. Registry Diagnostic Med. Sonographers, Guild of Bookworkers, Hand Bookbinders Calif., Bookbinders Internat. (v.p. U.S. 1989—), Pacific Ctr. for the Book Arts, Am. Craft Coun., Ala. Craft Coun., Can. Bookbinders and Book Artists Guild, Nat. Mus. Women in Arts. Home: 2811 6th St Tuscaloosa AL 35401-1759 Office: U Ala Main Libr # 517 Tuscaloosa AL 35487

GOURLIE, CAROL ELLEN, social sciences educator, academic advisor; b. Hartford, Conn., Dec. 24, 1933; d. William Henry and Lena (Conley) G. BA, Coll. New Rochelle, 1955; MA in Sociology, St. Joseph Coll., West Hartford, Conn., 1964, MA in Counseling, 1986; postgrad., Ctrl. Conn. State U., 1984-85. Med. social worker St. Francis Hosp., Hartford, 1955-67; instr. St. Joseph Coll., West Hartford, 1964-75, asst. prof., dir. acad. advisement, 1975—. Life mem. St. Francis Women's Aux.; bd. trustees New Hope Manor, 1973-77; bd. dirs. Infoline, 1972-74. Mem. AAUW (scholarship com. Hartford chpt.), Nat. Acad. Advising Assn., St. Peter Claver Women's Club. Roman Catholic. Office: St Joseph Coll 1678 Asylum Ave West Hartford CT 06117

GOUZE, MURIEL ENID, art educator; b. N.Y.C., Nov. 22, 1921; d. Elias and Birdye (Heller) Weinberg; m. Aug. 20, 1943 (dec. Jan. 31, 1973); children: Marshall, Judith. AB, Hunter Coll., 1943. Tchr. art Suffolk County Pub. Schs., N.Y.C., 1957-58; classroom substitute art tchr. Pinellas County Pub. Schs., St. Petersburg, Fla., 1958—. Mem. Suntan Art Ctr., Art Guild of Treasure Island, Art Club of St. Petersburg. Home: 12470 6th St E Treasure Is FL 33706

GOVER, FREDRICA JILL, psychologist; b. N.Y.C., Sept. 2, 1953; d. Hiram and Henrietta Gover; 1 child, Skye. BA, Sonoma State U., 1976, MA, 1983; PhD, Ctr. Psychol. Studies, 1989. Cert. tchr. Counselor Santa Rosa (Calif.) Jr. Coll., 1983, Vallejo (Calif.) Unified Sch. Dist., 1984-89; counselor, cons. Youth and Family Svcs., Vallejo, 1987—; psychol. asst. First Hosp. Vallejo, 1989; clin. psychologist Solano County Mental Health, Vallejo, 1990; drug/alcohol intervention specialist Vallejo Unified Sch. Dist., 1990—; pvt. practice Vallejo, 1994—; English/drama tchr. Nonesuch Sch., Analy Sch. Dist., Sebastopol, Calif., 1972-83; cons., trainer Adolescent Health Trainers Assn., El Sobrante, Calif., 1989—. Author: Coping with Teenage Stress, 1990, Helping Kids from Alcoholic Families, 1992. Solano County Mental Health mini-grantee, 1990. Mem. APA, Am. Assn. Suicidology, Assn. Counseling and Devel., Calif. Peer Counseling Assn. Democrat. Jewish. Office: Vallejo Unified Sch Dist 211 Valle Vista Vallejo CA 94590

GOW, LINDA YVONNE CHERWIN, travel executive; b. Plymouth, N.H., Dec. 15, 1948; d. Roger and Alice Mary (Theriault) Carignan; m. James T. Gow Jr., Aug. 29, 1987; 1 child, Alison. Student Rivier Coll., 1966-68, Whittemore Sch. Bus., 1976-79. Asst. mgr. Travel New Horizons, Peterborough, N.H., 1972-76; mgr. Garnsey Bros. Travel, Sanford, Maine, 1976-77; gen. mgr. R-W Travel, Dover, N.H., 1977-84; pres., owner The Travel Pro, Somersworth, N.H., 1984—; owner Cruise Quarters, Somersworth, 1988—. Sponsor Internat. Children's Festival, Somersworth, N.H., 1985—; mem. Gov.'s Pvt. Industry Council, 1987, 88. Mem. Am. Retail Travel Agts. Assn., Cruise Lines Internat. Assn., Rochester C. of C., Somersworth C. of C., Rotary Internat. (Somersworth N.H. chpt.). Office: The Travel Pro 394 High St Somersworth NH 03878-1420

GOWDY, MIRIAM BETTS, nutritionist; b. Nelsonville, Ohio, Jan. 9, 1928; d. Charles Donald and Lillian Mary (Liscott) B.; m. Robert Averill Gowdy, Oct. 12, 1950 (div. 1977); children: Carol Jo, Robert Jr., Bruce. BA in Home Econs., Ohio Wesleyan U., 1949; student, Duke U., 1949-50, Calif. State U., L.A., 1975-76. Registered dietitian. Dietitian L.A., 1977-91; cons. Nat.-in-Home Health, Van Nuys, Calif., 1984-87; clin. dietitian Lake Mead Hosp., 1991-94; pvt. practice cons. nutritionist Las Vegas, Nev., 1994—. Mem. Am. Diabetes Assn. (cons. San Fernando Valley Unit 1976-80, bd. dirs. N.W. chpt. 1977-82), So. Nev. Dietetic Assn. (mem. chmn. 1991-92, pres. 1993-94), Cons. Nutritionists (chmn.-elect So. Calif. chpt. 1979-81), Calif. Dietetic Assn. (chmn. diabetes care practice 1979-81), Am. Heart Assn. (mem. gov. bd. N.W. chpt. 1988-89), Sierra Club, Nat. Audubon Soc. Republican. Methodist. Home and Office: 9713 White Cloud Dr Las Vegas NV 89134-7840 Office: 9713 White Cloud Dr Las Vegas NV 89134

GOWENS, VERNEETA VIOLA, journalist; b. South Holland, Ill., Mar. 19, 1913; d. William and Mary Cawthorne (Fowler) Gibson; m. Albert Gowens, July 17, 1936; children: Victoria Ann Gowens Utke, Mary Ann Gowens Weiss. Educated public schs., Bryant and Stratton Bus. Coll. Clk., pub. rels. worker Chgo. and Riverdale Lumber Co., Chgo., 1934-45; feature writer, women's editor Tribune Publs., Harvey, Ill., 1960-62; feature writer, women's editor Star-Tribune, Williams Press, Chicago Heights, Ill., 1963-78; freelance writer; script writer variety shows Ship Ahoy, 1963, Fair 'n' Square, 1964; contbr. to Internat. Altrusan, 1974, Ch. Herald, 1977. Sunday sch. tchr., youth leader 1st Ref. Ch., South Holland; mem. editorial coun. Ch. Herald, Ref. Ch. in Am., 1976-82; pres. Dist. 150 PTA, 1965-66; adv. com. program in ltd. occupation tng. Thornton High Sch., 1963-69; mem. South Holland Indsl. Commn., 1965-68; bd. dirs. Family Svc. and Mental Health Ctr. of South Cook County, Ill., 1974-77; mem. South Holland unit Salvation Army, 1958—; judge Internat. Teen Pageant, 1969; mem. South Holland Community Chest, 1978-87; adv. bd. Thornton Community Coll. nursing program, 1976-83; mem. spl. events and publicity coms. South Holland Centennial, 1994; active South Holland Diamond Jubilee, 1969, South Holland Cable Commn., 1984—, South Holland Centennial Com., 1994. Recipient award South Holland C. of C., 1970, Genoa coun. K.C., 1974, Village of South Holland, 1969, 1st pl. in contest No. Ill. U., 1974, 75, award Suburban Press Found., 1969, 1st pl. award Ill. Press Assn., 1973, 50 other awards in writing. Mem. Ill. Women's Press Assn. (Woman of Yr. 1974, award 1978), Nat. Fedn. Press Women (1st pl. Sweepstakes award 1976). Home: 16830 S Park Ave South Holland IL 60473-2961

GOYAK, ELIZABETH F., public relations executive; b. Chgo., Oct. 7, 1922; d. Lewis Howard and Berenice Marie (Bowers) Fairbairn; m. Edward Anthony Goyak, May 20, 1951. BEd, So. Ill. U., 1943; MA, No. Ill. U., 1979. Reporter Internat. News Svc., Chgo., 1945-49, Chgo. Tribune, 1949-52; writer Gardner & Jones, Chgo., 1954-59, Aaron Cushman & Assocs., Chgo., 1959-60; v.p. Daniel J. Edelman, Chgo., 1960-76; mgr. pub. rels. Stone Container Corp., Chgo., 1976-82; pres. pub. rels. Chgo. Container, Matteson, Ill., 1982—. Dir. pub. rels. Dem. Women for Adlai Stevenson, 1952; founder, pres. bd. dirs. Matteson Pub. Libr., 1958-87; chmn. Matteson Bicentennial Commn., 1973-76. Mem. Pub. Rels. Soc. Am. (accredited, Silver anvil award 1975), Publicity Club Chgo. (sec., bd. dirs. 1964-76, Golden Trumpet award 1965, 66, 75), Chgo. Press Vets. Mem. United Ch. Christ. Home: 21310 Butterfield Pky Matteson IL 60443 Office: Chgo Connection 21310 Butterfield Pkwy Matteson IL 60443

GOYER, VIRGINIA L., accountant; b. Troy, N.Y., July 19, 1942; d. Clarence Archie and Edna Alice (Toussaint) G.; m. James Cobb Stewart, May 17, 1986. BS, Rochester Inst. Tech., 1975, MBA, 1976. Tax mgr. Deloitte Haskins & Sells, Rochester, N.Y., 1976-82; pres. Lamanna & Goyer, PC, CPAs, Rochester, 1982-89; owner Goyer & Assocs., CPAs, Rochester, 1989-93; pres. Virginia L. Goyer, CPA, P.C., Rochester, 1993—. Mem. adv. bd. Salvation Army, Rochester, 1985-88, Rochester Inst. Tech. Deferred Giving, 1988-89; mem. bd. Nat. Women's Hall of Fame. Mem. AICPA, Fla. Inst. CPA's, N.Y. State Inst. CPA's (bd. dirs. 1990-93, v.p. 1994-95, 1st woman pres. Rochester chpt. 1988-89), Rochester Women's Network, Nat. Assn. Women Bus. Owners (bd. dirs. 1992-93), Estate Planning Coun. (bd. dirs. 1987-89), NOW. Office: 354 Westminster Rd Rochester NY 14607-3233

GOYETTE-EWING, MICHELE, psychologist, researcher; b. Washington, Feb. 28, 1960; d. Romain Philip Goyette and Marcia Sprague Gallup MacDonald; m. Michael Francis Ewing, Aug. 19, 1989; 1 child, Grace Catherine Ewing. BA in Psychology with honors, Brown U., 1982; MS, Yale U., 1987, MPhil, 1988, PhD, 1992. Asst. tchr. Ottoson Jr. High Sch., Arlington, Mass., 1982-83; rsch. asst. U. Wash., Seattle, 1983-85, asst. tchr., 1984-85; fellow in clin. psychology Yale Child Study Ctr., New Haven, 1988-92, postdoctoral rsch. fellow, 1992-93, assoc. rsch. scientist, 1993—. NICHD grantee, 1993; Sterling Prize fellow, 1985. Mem. APA. Office: Yale U Box 208205 2 HIllhouse Ave New Haven CT 06520

GOZEMBA, PATRICA ANDREA, women's studies and English language educator, writer; b. Medford, Mass., Nov. 30, 1940; d. John Charles and Mary Margaret (Sampey) Curran; m. Gary M. Gozemba, Sept. 4, 1967 (div. Feb. 1975). BA, Emmanuel Coll., Boston, 1962; MA, U. Iowa, 1963; EdD, Boston U., 1975. Tchr. Waltham (Mass.) High Sch., 1963-64; prof. Salem (Mass.) State Coll., 1964—; vis. fellow East-West Ctr., 1995. Editor: New England Women's Studies, 1977-87; mem. editorial bd. Thought and Action, 1990-93; contbr. articles to profl. jours. Mem. NEA (standing com. 1982-93), NOW, NAACP, Nat. Women's Studies Assn. (gov. bd. 1977-89), Nat. Coun. Tchrs. English, Nat. Gay and Lesbian Task Force, Mass. State Coll. Assn. (editor 1982-90), Herb Soc. Am. Democrat. Home: 17 Sutton Ave Salem MA 01970 Office: Salem State Coll Salem MA 01970

GRABARSKY, S. W. (SHEILA PLASKON), artist; b. Bklyn., Dec. 2, 1945; d. Sidney H. (Grabarsky) Graybar and Vera (Fenster) Graybar; m. Martin B. Wallerstein, June 11, 1967 (div. 1987) m. Tom Plaskon, Jan. 9, 1991; children: Jolie Beth Doyle, Alison Joy Wallerstein. Student, Syracuse U., 1963-65, N.J. Ctr. for Visual Arts, 1978-89; studied with Philip Sherrod, N.Y.C., 1978-90. Represented by Ward-Nasse Gallery, N.Y.C., ArtSouth, Phila., ArtOne, Scottsdale, Ariz., Artemis, Bethesda, Md., Henk Van Hemert, The Netherlands. Exhbns. include Montserrat Gallery, N.Y.C., Ariel Gallery, N.Y.C., Straus Gallery, N.Y.C., Monmouth Coll. Gallery, Long Branch, N.J., Trenton (N.J.) Mus., Bergen Mus., Paramus, N.J., Middlesex County Mus., Piscataway, N.J., Johnson & Johnson, New Brunswick, N.J., Merck Corp. Gallery, Roseland, N.J., Jacob Javits Ctr., N.Y.C., Lever House, N.Y.C., Bucknell U., Pa., Cali Corp., Roseland, N.J., St. Lifer Gallery, Summit, N.J., others. Recipient numerous awards, commns., and invitationals. Mem. Nat. Women's Caucus for Art, Soc. Exptl. Artists, N.Y. Artists Equity Assn., Orgn. Ind. Artists, Shrewsbury Artists Guild, Art Alliance. Home and Studio: 295 Ocean Blvd # 4 Long Branch NJ 07740

GRABER, SUSAN P., judge; b. Oklahoma City, July 5, 1949; d. Julius A. and Bertha (Fenyves) G.; m. William June, May 3, 1981; 1 child, Rachel June-Graber. BA, Wellesley Coll., 1969; JD, Yale U., 1972. Bar: N.Mex. 1972, Ohio 1977, Oreg. 1978. Asst. atty. gen. Bur. of Revenue, Santa Fe, 1972-74; assoc. Jones Gallegos Snead & Wertheim, Santa Fe, 1974-75, Taft Stettinius & Hollister, Cin., 1975-78; assoc., then ptnr. Stoel Rives Boley Jones & Grey, Portland, Oreg., 1978-88; judge, then presiding judge Oreg. Ct. Appeals, Salem, 1988-90; assoc. justice Oreg. Supreme Ct., Salem, 1990—. Mem. Gov.'s Adv. Coun. on Legal Svcs., 1979-88; bd. dirs. U.S. Dist. Ct. of Oreg. Hist. Soc., 1985—, Oreg. Law Found., 1990-91; mem. bd. visitors Sch. Law, U. Oreg., 1986-93. Mem. Oreg. State Bar (jud. adminstrn. com. 1985-87, pro bono com. 1988-90), Ninth Cir. Jud. Conf. (chair exec. com. 1987-88), Oreg. Jud. Conf. (edn. com. 1988-91, program chair 1990), Oreg. Appellate Judges Assn. (sec.-treas. 1990-91, vice chair 1991-92, chair 1992-93), Am. Inns of Ct. (master), Phi Beta Kappa. Office: Oreg Supreme Ct 1163 State St Salem OR 97310

GRABINSKI, C. JOANNE, gerontologist, educator; b. Bend, Oreg., Dec. 8, 1941; d. Jack George and Helen Margaret (Thomsen) Huffman; m. Roger Neil Grabinski, Aug. 13, 1966; 1 child, Lawrence Neil. BS, MS in Home Econ. Edn., Oreg. State U., 1963, 68; MA in Family Rels., Cen. Mich. U., 1976, MA in Community Leadership, 1980; postgrad., Mich. State U., 1982-87. Dept. chair, tchr. home econs. Oakridge (Oreg.) Jr./Sr. High Sch., 1963-67, Briggs Jr. High Sch., Springfield, Oreg., 1967-68; prof. home econs. Lane C.C., Eugene, Oreg., 1968-69; residence hall dir., assoc. dir. Western Mich. U., Kalamazoo, 1970-72; dir., spl. interest coord. Mt. Pleasant (Mich.) Pub. Schs., 1976-77; money mgmt. counselor Coop. Ext. Svc./DSS, Mt. Pleasant, 1977-78; asst. prof. ednl. adminstrn./community leadership Cen. Mich. U., Mt. Pleasant, 1976, 77, asst. prof. home econs., 1980-86, dir./asst. prof. interdisciplinary gerontology program, 1984-91; pres., cons. cjgGERONTOLOGY, Mt. Pleasant, 1991—; project dir. Region 7 Alzheimer's Disease and Related Conditions Caregiver Edn. Project, Mich., Dept. Mental Health Cen., Mich. U., 1986-91; adj. prof. gerontology Western Mich. U., Kalamazoo, 1992-94; continuing edn. rep., lectr. gerontology Ea. Mich. U., 1992—. Editorial bd. AGHE Exchange, 1988-91, asst. editor, 1988-91; contbr. articles to profl. jours. Bd. dirs. Hospice of Cen. Mich., Mt. Pleasant, 1986-89, Cen. Mich. U. Dames, 1974-78, pres., 1976-77; bd. dirs. Mt. Pleasant Welcome Wagon Newcomers Club, 1972-76, pres., 1974-75; team mem. Bldg. Ties, Isabella County, Mich., 1983-84. Marie Dye Grad. fellow Mich. Home Econ. Assn., 1983; named Outstanding Faculty Mem., Ctrl. Mich. U. Mortar Bd. Mem. Am. Soc. on Aging, Gerontol. Soc. Am., Nat. Coun. on Aging, Mich. Coun. on Family Relations (bd. dirs. 1984-87), Nat. Coun. Family Rels., Mich. Soc. Gerontology, Kappa Omicron Nu, Omicron Nu, Kappa Omicron Phi, Phi Delta Kappa. Democrat. Lutheran. Home: 310 Apricot Ln Mount Pleasant MI 48858 Office: cjgGERONTOLOGY PO Box 868 Mount Pleasant MI 48804-0868

GRABNER, CAREN SUE, food service manager; b. Longview, Tex., Feb. 11, 1955; d. Keith C. and Patricia (Kuhn) Shaffer; m. Michael A. Grabner, Oct. 7, 1978 (div. Nov. 1989). Grad. high sch., Ft. Wayne, Ind. Exec. mgr. Ponderosa, Ft. Wayne, 1972-79; gen. mgr. Sizzler Steak House, Ft. Wayne, 1980-83; mgr. Pizza Hut, Ft. Wayne, 1984-86; sr. mgr. Burger King, Ft. Wayne, 1986-87; mgr. Ponderosa, Ft. Wayne, 1987-88; gen. bus. mgr. Taco Bell, Inc., Grand Rapids, Mich., 1988—.

GRABOSKY, TERRI JO, artist; b. Waukegan, Nov. 20, 1949; d. Joseph Vincent and Margaret D. (Schroeder) Morrissey; m. Hugh Francis Grabosky, July 23, 1985. BA in Art Edn., Carthage Coll., Kenosha, 1972, MEd in Creative Arts, 1984. Art teacher Jefferson J.H.S., Waukegan, 1974-79, Jack Benny Ctr. for the Arts, Waukegan, 1976-77; itinerant art teacher Waukegan Dist. #60, 1979-80; visual art specialist Cooke Magnet Sch., Waukegan, 1980-89; art tchr. Glencoe (Ill.) Sch. Dist., 1989—; presenter, State Gifted Convention, Chgo., 1981, State Convention of Ill. Music Edn. Assn., Springfield, 1982, Related-Arts Programs, 1981-87. Presenter BASIC workshop Sch. Art Inst., chgo., 1985; panelist State Art Region 1 Conf. Columbia Coll., 1987. Named Tchr. of the Yr., Waukegan Public Sch., Dist #60, 1984. Mem. Ill. Alliance for Arts Edn., Nat. Art Edn., Assn., Ill. Art Edn., Assn., Am. Craft Coun., Pi Lambda Theta. Episcopalian. Office: South Sch 266 Linden Ave Glencoe IL 60022-2199

GRACE, HELEN KENNEDY, foundation administrator; b. Beresford, S.D., Mar. 30, 1935; d. Walter James and Ethel Elvira (Soderstrom) Kennedy; B.S. in Nursing, Loyola U., Chgo., 1963; M.S. in Nursing, U. Ill., Chgo., 1965; Ph.D. in Sociology, Northwestern U., 1969, LLD Valparaiso U., 1992; DSc (hon.) S.D. State U., LHD (honoris causa) Loyola U., 1993; m. Elliott A. Grace, Nov. 20, 1961; 1 dau., Elizabeth Ann. Nursing adminstr. Ill. Dept. Mental Health, 1963-67; faculty Coll. of Nursing, U. Ill., Chgo., 1967-82, instr., 1967-69, asst. prof., 1969-71, assoc. prof., 1971-73, prof., assoc. dean for grad. study, 1973-77, dean coll. of Nursing 1977-82; program dir. W.K. Kellog Found., Battle Creek, Mich., 1982-86, coord. health programs, 1986-91, v.p. program, 1991—. Recipient Disting. Alumnus award Loyola U., Coll. of Nursing U. Ill., Centennial Alumni award Am. State and Land Grant Univs. Mem. Am. Nurses Assn., Nat. League for Nursing (governing bd. 1978-86), Am. Acad. of Nursing (governing council 1976-80), Am. Sociol. Assn. Author: Mental Health Nursing: A Psychosocial Approach, 1977, 2d edit., 1981; Families Across the Life Cycle: Family Studies for Nursing, 1977; The Development of a Child Psychiatric Treatment Program, 1971; Current Issues in Nursing, 1981, 4th edit. 1993. Office: 1 Michigan Ave E Battle Creek MI 49017-4005

GRACE, JULIANNE ALICE, manufacturing company executive; b. Riverdale, N.Y., Oct. 29, 1937; d. Arthur Edward and Julia May (McCarthy) Thompson; m. Daniel Vincent Grace, July 2, 1960; children: Daniel Vincent III, Deirdre Elizabeth. BA, Marymount Manhattan Coll., 1959; MA, Fordham U., 1960. Dir. admissions Marymount Manhattan Coll., N.Y.C., 1966-72; mgr. human resources The Perkin-Elmer Corp., Norwalk, Conn., 1972-78, dir. human resources, 1978-81, asst. sr. v.p. semiconductor equipment, 1981-83, asst. pres., 1983-85, v.p., asst. to chief exec. officer, 1985-86; v.p. adminstrn. The Perkin-Elmer Corp., Norwalk, 1986-90, v.p. corp. rels., 1990—. Bd. dirs. Norwalk and Wilton chpts. ARC, 1975-85, Metropool, 1991—, Waveny (Conn.) Care Ctr.; trustee Norwalk YMCA, 1986—; active Norwalk C.C. Found., 1986-90, Fairfield 2000. Woodrow Wilson Nat. Found. fellow, 1959-60. Mem. Econ. Soc. Conn., Nat. Investor Rels. Inst., Fairfield Pub. Rels. Assn., Women in Comm., Regional Plan Assn. (com.), Sports Car Club Am., Roton Point Club (Rowayton, Conn.), Wolfpit Running Club. Home: 54 Louises Ln New Canaan CT 06840-2120 Office: Perkin-Elmer Corp 761 Main Ave Norwalk CT 06859-0315

GRACE, MARCIA BELL, advertising executive; b. Pitts., July 29, 1937; d. Daniel Henry and Gertrude Margaret (Loew) Bell; m. Roy Grace, May 16, 1966; children: Jessica Bell, Nicholas Bell. AB, Harvard U., 1959. V.p., assoc. creative dir. Doyle Dane Bernbach, N.Y.C., 1964-77; sr. v.p., creative dir. Wells, Rich, Greene, Inc., N.Y.C., 1977-85, exec. v.p., creative dir., 1986-90; cons. Marcia Grace & Co., N.Y.C., 1990—. Recipient 1st Pl. ANDY award Advt. Club N.Y., 1968, 70, 72, 75, 1st Pl. Gold award The One Show, 1973, 78, Hall of Fame award The Clio Show, N.Y.C., 1982, 86.

GRACE, PRISCILLA ANNE, labor union executive; b. Ft. Worth, Mar. 20, 1943; d. John Paul and Pauline (Greer) G.; children: Kenneth C. Caldwell Jr., George E. Caldwell, Kristina Caldwell Henry. Grad. pvt. sch., Our Lady of Victory Sch., Ft. Worth. Telephone operator Southwestern Bell Telephone, Ft. Worth and Houston, 1968-70; letter carrier U.S. Postal Svc., Humble, Tex., 1973-85; officer local 283, Nat. Assn. Letter Carriers, Houston, 1984—; chmn. bd. dirs. Houston Postal Credit Union, 1990—; mem. exec. bd. Harris County AFL-CIO, Houston, 1988—. Editor Houston Letter Carrier Newsletter, 1978-84. Compeer vol. Houston Mental Health Assn., 1990-92. Mem. Nat. Assn. Letter Carriers (chmn. nat. election com. 1990, 94, Mem. of Yr. award local 283, 1978). Lutheran. Office: Nat Assn Letter Carriers 2414 Broadway St Houston TX 77012-3812

GRACE, SUE, state legislator; b. Milw.; m. Vincent Grace. Mem. Ariz. Ho. of Reps.; mktg. specialist. Named Legis. of Yr., Mental Health Assn., 1991. Republican. Office: Ariz House of Reps State Capitol Phoenix AZ 85007*

GRADE, LORNA J(EAN), medical writer and editor, medical business consultant; b. Milw., May 7, 1954; d. William H. and Carol A. (Kaczmarowski) Momberg; m. Scott F. Grade, Aug. 16, 1986; children: Aaron D. Hendrix, Anna T., Elena D. BA in Bus. and Communications, Alverno Coll., 1981. Supr. med. records Mt. Sinai Med. Ctr., Milw., 1974-79; mgr. cardiovascular disease sect. U. Wis. Med. Sch., Milw., 1980-89; freelance med. writer, Milw., 1989—; mgr. Definitive Health Svcs. Inc., Winter Park, Fla., 1992—, Milw., 1992—; mgr. Heart Study Ctr., Winter Park, Fla., 1981-89, Mobile Cardiovascular Testing, Milw., 1985-89, Mobile Diagnostic Svcs., Milw., 1987-89, Met. Imaging Ctr., 1988-89. Co-editor 4 med. ednl. newsletters; contbr. articles to profl. jours. Mem. Am. Med. Writers Assn. Roman Catholic. Home: 413 E Birch Ave Milwaukee WI 53217-5168

GRADER, PATRICIA ALISON LANDE, literary agent; b. L.A., Mar. 23, 1960; d. Frederick and Irma Rose (Davidson) L.; m. Scott P. Grader, Feb. 11, 1995. Student, Washington U., St. Louis, 1977-79; BA with high distinction, U. Calif., San Diego, 1982. Editorial asst. Crown Pubs., N.Y.C., 1982-83; asst. editor St. Martin's Press, N.Y.C., 1983-84; editor Atheneum Pubs., N.Y.C., 1984-87; v.p., sr. editor Simon & Schuster, Inc., N.Y.C., 1987-91; v.p., dir. IMG-The Julian Bach Literary Agy., N.Y.C., 1992—; mentor internship program Simon & Schuster, 1991; mem. adminstrv. com. IMG, 1992—; speaker in field. Mem. Women in Pub., Pi Beta Phi. Office: IMG-The Julian Bach Lit Agy 22 E 71st St New York NY 10021

GRADY, JANET LAURA, nurse educator; b. Monessen, Pa., Aug. 17, 1952; d. George and Delma (Picchiarini) Bindi; m. Kevin Patrick Grady, Apr. 30, 1976; children: Erika, Kevin, Christopher. Cert., U. Rouen, France, 1973; BA in Edn., U. Pitts., 1974; BSN, St. Francis Coll., 1986; MSN, U. Pitts., 1989. Cert. profl. Pa. Dept. Edn. Tchr. Cen. Cambria Sch. Dist., Ebensburg, Pa., 1974-80, Richland Sch. Dist., Johnstown, Pa., 1981-83; staff nurse Meml. Hosp., Johnstown, 1986-87; faculty and course coord. Conemaugh Sch. Nursing, Johnstown, 1987-93; faculty Sch. of Nursing U. Pitts., Johnstown, Pa., 1993—; adj. faculty Sch. Nursing U. Pitts., 1992-93; guest lectr. Conemaugh Outpatient Diabetes Edn. Program, Johnstown, 1989—. Active St. Benedict Edn. Coun., Johnstown, 1992—. Scholar St. Francis Coll., 1986. Mem. St. Francis Coll. Alumni Assn., St. Francis Coll. Sch. Nursing Alumni Assn., U. Pitts. Sch. Nursing Alumni Assn., U. Pitts. Johnstown Women's Assn. (exec. bd. 1990—), Sigma Theta Tau, Delta Epsilon Sigma. Home: 139 Peggy Ln Johnstown PA 15904 Office: U Pitts 227 Krebs Hall Johnstown PA 15904

GRAEBNER, DONNA R., funding company executive. V.p., treas., bd. dirs. J.C. Penney Funding Corp., Plano, Tex. Office: J C Penney Funding Corp 6501 Legacy Dr Plano TX 75024-3612*

GRAETTINGER, ELIZABETH SHOREY, volunteer; b. Oak Park, Ill., July 29, 1923; d. Clyde Everett and Elizabeth Dun (Douglass) Shorey; m. John Sells Graettinger, June 29, 1946; children: John S. Jr., William F., Alan M., Robert S., George D. AB, Wellesley Coll., 1945. With social svc. dept. ARC, Dublin, Ga., 1947-48; sec. Harvard U., Cambridge, Mass., 1948-49; bd. dirs. YWCA of Met. Chgo., Ill., 1971-93, pres., 1975-78; career vol. Nat. Bd., YWCA of USA, N.Y.C., 1979-91. Mem. Womens Bd. Rush Presbyn. St. Luke's Hosp., Chgo., Great Books Found., Chgo., 1978-94; chair women's com., bd. dirs. NCCJ, Chgo., 1964-80. Conf. Ctr. named in Her Honor YWCA Met. Chgo., 1988.

GRAF, DOROTHY ANN, business executive; b. Nashville, Mar. 21, 1935; d. Henry George and Martha Dunlap (Hill) Meek; student Montgomery Coll., 1979—; m. Peter Louis Graf, Oct. 28, 1971; children—Sidney E. Pollard, Deborah Lynn Pollard, Robert George Pollard, Michelle Joy Graf. Office mgr. Pa. Life Ins. Co., Miami and Dallas, 1957-72; exec. sec. to med. dir. Pitts. Children's Hosp., 1974; sec. G.E./TEMPO, Washington, 1974-76; adminstrv. asst. to sr. v.p. Logistics Mgmt. Inst., Washington, 1976-81, dir. adminstrv. services, 1981—; dir. KHI Services, Inc. Mem. Washington Tech. Personnel Forum. Democrat. Baptist. Home: 20404 Remsbury Pl Gaithersburg MD 20879-4369 Office: 2000 Corporate Ridge Mc Lean VA 22102-7805

GRAF, STEFFI, professional tennis player; b. 1969; d. Peter and Heidi Graf. Winner numerous profl. women's tennis tournaments including Italian Open, 1987, French Open, 1987, The Golden Grand Slam (Australian Open, French Open, Wimbledon, U.S. Open, Olympics), 1988, Berlin Open, 1988, Wimbledon, 1989, 91, 93, German Open, 1989, 91, U.S. Open, 1989, 91, 92, 93, U.S. Hardcourt Championship, 1989, 91, Australian Open, 1990, 94, Players Challenge, 1990, French Open, 1993; ranked no. 1 in world for more consecutive weeks than any other player in tennis history. *

GRAFENTIN, VICKI LEE, artist, educator; b. Omaha, July 2, 1951; d. Roland Erwin and Leona Marion (Falk) G. BFA in Drawing, U. Iowa, 1974; MA in Printmaking, U. Wis., 1990, MFA, 1991. Grad. asst. U. Hawaii, Honolulu, 1988, rsch. asst., 1989; teaching asst. U. Wis., Madison, 1989-90, 90-91, printer vis. artist program, Tandem Press, 1989, lectr., 1992; asst. prof. U. Wis., Milw., 1992—; printer and artist's asst. Warrington Colescott, Hollandale, Wis., 1991-92; panelist, lectr. advanced sculpture seminar U. Wis., Madison, 1990; vis. artist/lectr. U. Wis. Marathon Ctr., Wausau, 1991; portfolio participant Exch. Portfolio, Notre Dame U., 1991; guest instr. lithography U. Wis., Madison, 1991; vis. artist SUNY, New Paltz, 1991, U. S.D., 1992, U. Hawaii-Manoa, Honolulu, 1994, Davenport Mus. Art, 1995; panelist Printfest '93, Milw. Art Mus., 1993; lectr. U. Wis. Ctr.-Marshfield County. One-woman shows include: U. Wis. Marathon Ctr., Wausau, 1991, U. Hawaii-Manoa, Honolulu, 1994; exhibited in group shows at Honolulu Watercolor Soc., 1987, Honolulu Printmakers 61st Ann. Exhibit, 1988, Purdue U., West Lafayette, Ind., 1990, Milw. Art Mus., 1990, Artlink Contemporary Artspace, Ft. Wayne, Ind., 1990, 91, U. N.D., Grand Forks, 1991, Edna Carlsten Gallery, Stevens Point, Wis., 1991, Crossman Gallery, Whitewater, Wis., 1991, SUNY, Purchase, 1991, Cheekwood Mus. Art, Nashville, 1992, Harper Coll., Palatine, Ill., 1992, U. Nebr.-Lincoln, 1992, Univ. Wis.-Milw. Art Mus., 1993, Eppley Gallery, Sioux City, Iowa, 1993, Galleria del Conte, Milw., 1993, Bowling Green State Univ., 1993, Galleri Norske Grafikere, Oslo, Norway, 1993; exhibited at invitational; represented in permanent collections at Univ. S.D., Univ. Wis.-Parkside, Jim Gregg and Assocs., University, Miss., Bradley Univ., Univ. Dallas, Milw. Art Mus. Recipient Wis. Arts Bd. New Work award, 1993-94; Arts Midwest/NEA Regional Visual Arts fellow, 1992-93. Mem. Coll. Art Assn., L.A. Print Soc., So. Graphics Coun. Office: U Wis Sch Fine Arts Fine Arts Ctr Dept Art PO Box 413 Milwaukee WI 53202

GRAFF, BONITA LEE, accountant, investment advisor; b. Oshkosh, Wis., Aug. 14, 1962; d. Robert John and Leatrice Ann (Bahrke) G. BA, Lakeland Coll., 1984. CPA, Wis.; registered investment advisor. V.p. Advisory Investment Mgmt., Inc., Appleton, Wis., 1985—. Chair east ctrl. Wis. synod youth com. Evang. Luth. Ch. Am., Appleton, 1993. FEllow Wis. Inst. CPAs (chair personal fin. planning com. 1986—). Office: Advisory Investment Mgmt 811 N Lynndale Dr Appleton WI 54914-3085

GRAFF, CYNTHIA STAMPER, health care executive; b. Fairbanks, Alaska, May 22, 1953; d. Marshall Bernard and Nell (Buntyn) Stamper; m. Grant H. Van de Walker, July 13, 1974 (div. 1980); m. Dennis Alan Graff, July 10, 1990. BS in Fin., Calif. State U., Long Beach, 1975; LLB, York U., Toronto, 1985. Pres. MC Fin., Inc., Salt Lake City, 1976-82; founder, pres. The Road Butler, Toronto, 1985-86; house counsel Polyvoltec Inc., Toronto, 1986-87; v.p. Lindora Med. Clinics, Costa Mesa, Calif., 1988-91; pres. Lindora, Inc., Costa Mesa, 1992—. Mem. Am. Soc. Bariatric Physicians, Young Pres.'s Orgn. Republican. Home: 601 Lido Park Dr Newport Beach CA 92663-4411 Office: Lindora Med Clinics 3505 Cadillac Ave Ste N-2 Costa Mesa CA 92626-1433

GRAFF, MARNETTE KATHLEEN, writer, nurse; b. Oct. 8, 1951; d. Giovanni Laurance and Kathleen Marnette (Loschmidt) Travia; m. John J. Burk, July 28, 1973 (div. Mar. 1983); 1 child, Sean Christian Burk; m. Arthur Leonard Graff, May 4, 1991. AAS, Nassau C.C., 1971; student, NYU, 1987-90. RN, N.Y. Med.-surg. RN Mercy Hosp., Rockville Centre, N.Y., 1971-75; utilization rev. coord. Grandell SNF-HRF, Long Beach, N.Y., 1975-76; insvc. dir. to dir. nursing svcs. Port Jefferson (N.Y.) Nursing Home, 1977-79; utilization rev. coord. Island Peer Rev. Orgn., Hauppauge, N.Y., 1979; dir. utilization rev. J.T. Mather Meml. Hosp., Port Jefferson, 1979-88, utilization rev. cons., 1988—; v.p. Gallery of Two Sisters, Blithe Spirit, Ltd., Miller Place, N.Y., 1988-90; med. dir. Cinema World Movie Studios, Greenpoint, N.Y., 1990—; writer Nursing Spectrum, Hempstead, N.Y., 1989—; med. cons. ABC, N.Y.C., 1990—. Author: (screenplay) Building Blocks, 1989, Comin' Around Again, 1993; editor/author: (anthology) Feminine Intuition, 1991; contbr. articles to profl. jours. Episcopalian. Home and Office: Windmere Dunes 69 Harbor Beach Rd Miller Place NY 11764-1320

GRAFF, RANDY, actress; b. Bklyn., May 23, 1955. Grad., Wagner Coll. Profl. theater debut in Gypsy, Village Dinner Theater, Raleigh, N.C.; appeared in Godspell, Raleigh; other appearances include Pins and Needles, Roundabout Theatre, N.Y.C., 1978, Something Wonderful, Westchester Regional Theatre, Harrison, N.Y., 1979, Sarava, Mark Hellinger Theatre, N.Y.C., 1979, Coming Attractions, Playwrights Horizons, Mainstage Theatre, N.Y.C., 1980, Keystone, McCarter Theatre, Princeton, N.J., 1981, A... My Name is Alice, Village Gate Theatre, N.Y.C., 1984, Amateurs, Playhouse in the Park, Cin., 1985, Fiorello!, Goodspeed Opera House, East Haddam, Conn., 1985, Absurd Person Singular, Phila. Drama Guild, Phila., 1986, Les Miserables, Broadway Theatre, N.Y.C., 1987, City of Angels, Va. Theatre, N.Y.C., 1989 (Drama Desk award Featured Actress in Musical 1989, Tony award Supporting or Featured Actress in Musical 1990), Falsettos, 1993, Laughter on the 23d Floor, 1993; (TV shows) include Mad About You, Law & Order, Pros & Cons; (film) Key's to Tulsa, 1995. Recipient Drama Desk award, 1990, Antoinette Perry award for best featured actress in musical, 1990. Office: care Peter Strawn & Assocs 1501 Broadway New York NY 10036-4015

GRAFFEO, MARY THÉRÈSE, music educator, performer; b. Mineola, N.Y., Jan. 20, 1949; d. Michael Joseph and Florence Marie (Lonette) G. BA in Music Edn., Adelphi U., 1972; MusM in Vocal Performance, Kent State U., 1982. Cert. music tchr. N.Y. Tchr. music, therapist Nassau County Bd. Coop. Ednl. Svcs., Westbury, N.Y., 1972-85; tchr. music, developer curricula Great Neck (N.Y.) Pub. Schs., 1985-87; tchr. music Syosset (N.Y.) Pub. Schs., 1987-88, 89-90, Jericho (N.Y.) Pub. Schs., 1988-89; tchr. music, developer creative programs Lawrence (N.Y.) Pub. Schs., 1990-92; tchr. music Herricks Pub. Schs., New Hyde Park, N.Y., 1992-93, Hempstead (N.Y.) Pub. Schs., 1993—. Author: (curriculum) Music for the Trainable Mentally Retarded, 1973, (book) Creative Enrichment Programs/America: The First 100 Years in Song, 1990; co-author: The Remeidation of Learning Discrepancies Through Music, 1980; composer: (mus. play) Red Riding Hood's Day, 1993. Cultural adv. bd. Lawrence Pub. Schs., 1990-92, Hempstead Pub. Schs., 1993—; founding mem. United We Stand Am., Dallas, 1992—. Scholar Adelphi U., 1968-72, Blossom Festival Sch., Kent, Ohio, 1978-79. Mem. NEA, Music Educators Nat. Conf., N.Y. State United Tchrs., N.Y. State Sch. Music Assn., Nassau Music Educators Assn. Democrat. Roman Catholic. Home: 300 Edwards St Roslyn Heights NY 11577 Office: Early Childhood Ctr 436 Front St Hempstead NY 11550

GRAFFIS, JULIE ANNE, interior designer, entrepreneur; b. Houston, Jan. 4, 1960; d. Robert B. and Dorothy Gean (Weempe) Hyde; m. William B. Graffis, May 29, 1988; 1 child, Aaron James Hehr. Student, U. St. Thomas, Houston, 1977, Portland C.C., The Dalles, Oreg., 1984-85; AA, North

Seattle C.C., 1987. Cert. window fashions profl. assoc., specialist, master Window Fashions Cert. Program. Co-owner Mosier (Oreg.) Shell Svc., 1981-85; quality control mgr. Town & Country Jeep-Eagle, Seattle, 1986-87; cons. Giovi Ford-Mercury, Pullman, Wash., 1988-89; prin., CEO, Interiors by JAG, Vancouver, Wash., 1990—; mem. Allied Bd. of Trade; cons. Habitat for Humanity, Vancouver, 1992—; lectr., presenter interior design workshops. Bus. ptnr. Hough Elem. Found. and Sch.; patron Pilchuck Glass Sch. Mem. NAFE, Wondow Fashions Edn. and Design Resource Network, Greater Vancouver C. of C. (liaison bus. and edn. partnership 1992—, amb. 1993—), Inst. Managerial and Profl. Women. Office: Interiors by JAG 1605 F St Vancouver WA 98663-3445

GRAFTON, SUE, novelist; b. Louisville, Apr. 24, 1940; d. Cornelius Warren and Vivian Boisseau (Harnsberger) G.; children: Leslie Kirsten, Jay, Jamie; m. Steven Humphrey, Oct. 1, 1978. BA, U. Louisville, 1961. lectr. L.A. City Coll., Long Beach (Calif.) City Coll., U. Dayton (Ohio) Writers Conf., Midwest Writers Conf., Canton, Ohio, Calif. Luth. Coll., Thousand Oaks, Santa Barbara (Calif.) Writers Conf., L.A. Valley Coll., Antioch Writers Conf., Yellow Springs, Ohio, S.W. Writers Conf., Albuquerque, Smithsonian Campus on the Mall, Washington, and others. Author: (novels) Keziah Dane, 1967, The Lolly-Madonna War, 1969, "A" is for Alibi, 1982 (Mysterious Stranger award 1982-83), "B" is for Burglar, 1985 (Shamus award 1986, Anthony award 1986), "C" is for Corpse, 1986 (Anthony award 1987), "D" is for Deadbeat, 1987, "E" is for Evidence, 1988 (Doubleday Mystery Guild award 1989), "F" is for Fugitive, 1989 (Doubleday Mystery Guild award 1990, The Falcon award 1990), "G" is for Gumshoe, 1990 (Doubleday Mystery Guild award 1991, Anthony award 1991, Shamus award 1991), "H" is for Homicide, 1991 (Doubleday Mystery Guild award 1992), "I" is for Innocent, 1992 (Doubleday Mystery Guild award 1992, Mystery Scene Am. Mystery award 1993), Kinsey And Me, 1992, "J" is for Judgment, 1994, "K" is for Killer, 1994; editor: Writing Mysteries, 1992; author short fiction, short stories, screenplay, teleplay, TV episodes. Mem. Writers Gild Am. West, Mystery Writers Am. Inc. (pres. 1994), Private Eye Writers Am. (pres. 1989-90).

GRAHAM, BETSY JANE, school superintendent; b. Bartlesville, Okla., May 14, 1949; d. Karns Rufus Newman and Galela Marie Grissom; m. D. Bruce Graham, Dec. 20, 1969; children: Lee Ann, Jennifer Jane, Becky Lynn. BS, Bartlesville Wesleyan Coll., 1978; MS, Northeastern State U., 1982; EdD, Okla. State U., 1992. Tchr. elem. edn. Oologah (Okla.) Pub. Schs., 1978-85; prin. elem. edn. Copan (Okla.) Pub. Schs., 1985-89; prin. elem. edn. Coweta (Okla.) Pub. Schs., 1989-92, asst. supt., 1992-93; supt. Nowata (Okla.) Pub. Schs., 1993—; conf. presenter Nat. Assn. Elem. Prins., New Orleans, 1992. Bd. dirs. Nowata Hist. Main St., 1993—, treas. Presch. grantee Okla. State Dept. Edn., 1992. Mem. Nat. Assn. Sch. Adminstrs., Okla. Assn. Sch. Adminstrs., Okla. Schs. Adv. Coun. Mem., Okla. Comty. Edn. Assn., N.E. Okla. Interactive Video Consortium (bd. dirs. 1993—), Coop. Coun. Okla. Sch. Adminstrs., Nowata C. of C. (bd. dirs. 1993—), Nowata Rotary Club. Republican. Home: PO Box 263 Nowata OK 74048

GRAHAM, CAROLYN N., public administrator; b. Hattiesburg, Miss., Aug. 10, 1946; d. Roy Daniel and Doris Hazel (Garraway) Silver; 1 child, Kofi O. Graham. MEd, Antioch U., 1973; MPA, CUNY, 1986. Ordained min. Asst. dir. med. staff adminstrn. Emory U. Hosp., Atlanta, 1982-85; spl. asst. to dir. Human Svcs. Dept., Washington, 1985-86; exec. asst. to dir. State Health Planning Agy., Washington, 1986-88, acting dir., 1988-90, dir., 1990-92; dir. Human Svcs. Dept., Ft. Lauderdale, Fla., 1992—. Bd. dirs. Broward House, Ft. Lauderdale, 1993—, Fla. Healthcare Purchasing Coop., Tallahassee, 1993—, Broward Healthy Start, Ft. Lauderdale, 1993—; mem. Broward Women's Alliance, Ft. Lauderdale. Nat. Urban fellow, N.Y.C., 1985; Ford fellow Atlanta U., 1974; Urban Ministry scholar Wesley Theol. Sem., Washington, 1990-91. Democrat. Office: Dept of Human Svcs 115 S Andrews Ave # 433 Fort Lauderdale FL 33301

GRAHAM, CYNTHIA ARMSTRONG, banker; b. Charlotte, N.C., Jan. 3, 1950; d. Beverly Weller and Katherine (Anderson) Armstrong; m. Walter Raleigh Graham Jr., May 23, 1970. AB in Chemistry, Bryn Mawr Coll., 1971; MBA in Fin. with distinction, U. Pa., 1976. Computer programmer Philco-Ford, Ft. Washington, Pa., 1973-74; asst. dir. admissions Wharton Sch., U. Pa., Phila., 1974-76; asst. v.p. N.C. Nat. Bank, Charlotte, 1976-80; v.p. Barclays Am. Corp., Charlotte, 1980-86; sr. v.p. Barclays Bank Del., N.A., Wilmington, 1986-87, Barnett Banks, Inc., Jacksonville, Fla., 1987—; chmn., pres. Barnett Mcht. Svcs., Inc., Jacksonville, 1987-89, TeleCheck Southcoast, 1987-89, Barnett Card Svcs. Corp., Jacksonville, 1989—; bd. advisors Nat. DAta Corp., Atlanta, 1987-88; delivery sys. advisor VISA U.S.A., Inc., San Mateo, Calif., 1987-91; mcht. svcs. advisor MasterCard, Internat., N.Y.C., 1989-92; mem. U.S. regional bus. com. MasterCard, 1992—; card products advisor VISA U.S.A., Inc., San Mateo, 1991-94, VISA Internat., 1994, mem. mktg. com., 1994—; bd. dirs. Interlink Network, Inc. Mem. Jacksonville Women's Network, 1988-92, bd. dirs., 1991-92, treas., 1992; mem. bd. suprs. Spaceport Fla., 1990-92. Mem. Am. Bankers Assn. (exec. com. card divsn. 1991-94, vice chmn. 1993, chmn. 1994), Jacksonville C. of C. Office: Barnett Card Svcs Corp Bldg 400 9000 Southside Blvd Ste 400 Jacksonville FL 32256-0764

GRAHAM, DIANA, lawyer; b. N.Y.C., Mar. 2, 1959; d. John Francis and Dolores (DeCristofaro) G.; married. BA in Econs., Fairfield U., 1981; JD, NYU, 1984. Assoc. Law Offices of Thomas W. Gleason, N.Y.C., 1984-89; sr. atty. Witco Corp., Greenwich, Conn., 1989—. Mem. ABA, Am. Corporate Coun. Assn., N.Y. State Bar Assn., Chem. Mfrs. Assn. (tort litigation group). Democrat. Roman Catholic. Office: Witco Corp One American Ln Greenwich CT 06831

GRAHAM, DIANE SHAFER, art and architectural history educator; b. N.Y.C., Nov. 19, 1942; d. Raymond Philip and Jane Harris (Davies) Shafer; m. Ian Charles Strachan, July 29, 1967 (div. Oct. 1987); 1 child, Shona Elizabeth Strachan; m. Larry Allan Graham, Dec. 27, 1987. BA, Allegheny Coll., Meadville, Pa., 1964; MA, Sophia U., Tokyo, 1983; postgrad., Binghamton U., 1990—. Apptd. lectr. U. Hong Kong, 1983-84; adj. faculty SUNY, Brockport, 1988-90, Binghamton, 1990-92; rsch. cons. Altfield Gallery, Hong Kong, 1982-83; U.S. rep. Orientations Mag., Hong Kong and N.Y.C., 1982-90; adj. faculty Nazareth Coll., Rochester, N.Y., 1989-95; owner, dir. The Gallery, Geneseo, N.Y., 1993—; curatorial cons. Asian collection Meml. Art Gallery, Rochester, 1993—, Asian collection The Univ. Mus., Binghamton (N.Y.) U., 1994—; English lang. libr. Nat. Mus. Art, Bangkok, 1976-77; lectr., tour leader Coll. Women's Assn. Japan, 1980-82; lectr., seminar leader Nat. Mus. Art Vols., Bangkok, 1974-77. Mem. preservation com. Assn. for Preservation of Geneseo, 1991—; sec. Republicans Abroad, Tokyo, 1980-82; campaign vol. Polit. Campaigns of Raymond P. Shafer, Pa., 1957-67. Binghamton U. fellow, 1993-94, Nat. Fgn. Lang. fellow U. Pa., 1986. Mem. Coll. Art Assn., Soc. Archtl. Historians, Am. Assn. for Asian Studies, Nat. Com. for U.S.-China Rels., Nat. Trust for Historic Preservation, Oriental Ceramic Soc. of Hong Kong, The Siam Soc. Republican. Home: 61 2d St Geneseo NY 14454

GRAHAM, FRANCES KEESLER (MRS. DAVID TREDWAY GRAHAM), psychologist, educator; b. Canastota, N.Y., Aug. 1, 1918; d. Clyde C. and Norma (Van Surdam) Keesler; m. David Tredway Graham, June 14, 1941; children: Norma, Andrew, Mary. B.A., Pa. State U., 1938; Ph.D., Yale U., 1942. Acting dir. St. Louis Psychiat. Clinic, 1942-44; instr. Barnard Coll., 1948-51; research assoc. Sch. Medicine, Washington U., St. Louis, 1942-48, 53-57, U. Wis., Madison, 1957-64; asso. prof. pediatrics and psychology U. Wis., 1964-68, prof., 1968-86, Hilldale research prof., 1980-86; prof. U. Del., Newark, 1986-89, prof. emerita, 1989—; Disting. faculty lectr., U. Del., Newark, 1989; cons. Nat. Inst. Neurol. Diseases and Blindness perinatal research br.; mem. exptl. psychology research review com. NIMH, 1970-74, NRC, 1971-74; mem. bd. sci. counselors NIMH, 1977-81, chmn., 1979-81; mem. Pres.'s Commn. for Study of Ethical Problems in Medicine and Biomed. and Behavioral Research, 1980-82. Mem. editorial bd. Jour. Exptl. Child Psychology, 1964-67, Child Devel., 1966-68, Jour. Exptl. Psychology, 1968-73, Psychophysiology, 1968-73; contbr. articles to profl. jours. Recipient Rsch. Scientist award NIMH, 1964-89, Disting. Alumna award Pa. State U., 1983, Wilbur L. Cross medal Yale U., 1992. Fellow AAAS (chmn. sect. psychology 1979, mem. nominations com. 1992-95), APA (coun. 1975-77, pres. div. physiol. and comparative psychology 1978-79, G. Stanley Hall award 1982, Disting. Scientist award 1990); mem. NAS, Am. Psychol. Soc. (William James fellow 1990), Soc. Rsch. Child Devel. (council 1965-71, pres. 1975-77, Disting. Sci. Contbns. award 1991), Soc. Psychophysiol. Rsch. (dir. 1968-71, 72-75, pres. 1973-74, Disting. Contbns. award 1981), Soc. Exptl. Psychologists, Soc. Neurosci., Fedn. Behavioral Psychol. and Cognitive Scis. (exec. com. 1991-94), Psychonomic Soc., Acoustical Soc. Am., Internat. Soc. Devel. Psychobiology, Phi Beta Kappa, Sigma Xi. Home: 311 Dove Dr Newark DE 19713-1211

GRAHAM, GLORIA F., nurse educator; b. Angus, Nebr., Apr. 12, 1935; d. H.G. and Ethel A. (White) Darling; m. Richard L. Graham, June 19, 1954; children: Elizabeth, Jennifer. AS, Donnelly Jr. Coll., 1967; BSN, U. Kans., Kansas City, 1970; MA, U. Mo., Kansas City, 1976. Staff nurse Menorah Hosp., Kansas City, Mo.; sch. nurse Shawnee-Mission Schs., Overland Park, Kans.; instr. St. Luke's Hosp. Sch. Nursing, Kansas City, Mo. Sec. Community Housing Resource Bd. Mem. Phi Theta Kappa, Phi Delta Kappa.

GRAHAM, JAN, state attorney general; b. Salt Lake City. BS in Psychology, Clark U., Worcester, Mass., 1973; MS in Psychology, U. Utah, 1977, JD, 1980. Bar: Utah. Ptnr. Jones, Waldo, Holbrook & McDonough, Salt Lake City, 1979-89; soliciter gen. Utah Atty. Gen.'s Office, Salt Lake City, 1989-93; atty. gen. State of Utah, 1993—; adj. prof. law U. Utah Law Sch.; bar commr. Utah State Bar, 1991; master of bench Utah Inns Ct. VII; mem. Utah Commn. on Justice in 21st Century; bd. dirs. Jones, Waldo, Holbrook & McDonough; bd. trustees Coll. Law U. Utah (pres.). Fin. devel. chair YWCA; chair Ctrl. Bus. Improvement Dist.; mem. Salt Lake City Olympic Bid Com. 1988 Games. Named Woman Lawyer Yr. Utah, 1987. Mem. Am. Arbitration Assn. (nat. panel arbitrators), Women Lawyers Utah (co-founder, mem. exec. com.). Office: 236 State Capitol Building Salt Lake City UT 84114-1202*

GRAHAM, JEWEL FREEMAN, social worker, lawyer, educator; b. Springfield, Ohio, May 3, 1925; d. Robert Lee and Lula Belle Freeman; m. Paul N. Graham, Aug. 8, 1953; children: Robert, Nathan. BA, Fisk U., 1946; student, Howard U., 1946-47; MS in Social Svc. Adminstrn., Case Western Res. U., 1953; JD, U. Dayton, 1979; LHD (hon.), Meadville-Lombard Theol. Sch., 1991. Bar: Ohio; cert. social worker. Assoc. dir. teenage program dept. YWCA, Grand Rapids, Mich., 1947-50; coord. met. teenage program YWCA, Detroit, 1953-56; dir. program for interracial edn. Antioch Coll., Yellow Springs, Ohio, 1964-69, from asst. prof. to prof., 1969-92, prof. emeritus, 1992—; bd. dirs. Yellow Springs Instrument Co., 1981-93; commr. Ohio Commn. on Dispute Resolution and Conflict Mgmt., 1990-92. Mem. exec. com. World YWCA, Geneva, 1975-83, 1987—, pres. 1983; bd. dirs. YWCA of the U.S.A., 1970-89, pres. 1979-85. Named to Greene County Women's Hall of Fame, 1982, Ohio Women's Hall of Fame, 1988; named 1 of 10 Outstanding Women of Miami Valley, 1987; recipient Ambassador award YWCA of the U.S.A., 1993. Mem. ABA, Nat. Assn. of Social Workers (charter), Nat. Coun. of Negro Women (life), Alpha Kappa Alpha. Democrat. Unitarian Universalist. Office: Antioch Coll Livermore 51 Yellow Springs OH 45387

GRAHAM, JOANN, federal programs coordinator; b. Cin., July 19, 1956; d. Thomas Edgar and Mary Ellen (Mullen) G. Student, U. Cin., 1977—. Clk. typist U.S. Dept. Army, Cin., 1973-74, statis. clk., 1974-75; sec. Glenmary Home Missioners, Fairfield, Ohio, 1975-76; med. records technician USPHS, Cin., 1976-80; with U.S. Post Svc., 1980—; postmaster U.S. Post Svc., Mt. Olivet, Ky., 1985-86; affirmative action and EEO programs coord. U.S. Post Svc., Cin., 1986—; chairperson EEO com. Fed. Exec. Bd., Cin., 1988-89. Mem. ASTD, Nat. Career Devel. Assn., Am. Assn. for Counseling and Devel., Federally Employed Women. Democrat. Roman Catholic. Office: US Postal Svc 1591 Dalton Ave Rm 202T Cincinnati OH 45234-8991

GRAHAM, JORIE, author; b. N.Y.C., May 9, 1951; d. Curtis Bell and Beverly (Stoll) Pepper; m. James Galvin. BFA, NYU, 1973; MFA, U. Iowa, 1978. Asst. prof. Murray (Ky.) State U., 1978-79, Humboldt State U., Arcata, Calif., 1979-81; instr. Columbia U., N.Y.C., 1981-83; mem. staff U. Iowa, Iowa City, 1983—; poetry editor Crazy Horse, 1978-81. Author: Hybrids of Plants and of Ghosts, 1980 (Great Lakes Colls. Assn. award 1981), Erosion, 1983, The End of Beauty, 1987, Region of Unlikeness, 1991, Materialism, 1993; editor: (with David Lehman) The Best American Poetry 1990, 1990. Recipient Am. Acad. Poets award, 1977, Young Poet prize Poetry Northwest, 1980, Pushcart prize, 1980, 82, American Poetry Review prize, 1982; Bunting fellow Radcliff Inst., 1982, Guggenheim fellow, 1983, John D. and Catherine T. MacArthur Found. fellow, 1990; grantee Ingram-Merrill Found., 1981. Office: U Iowa Dept Creative Writing Iowa City IA 52242*

GRAHAM, KATHARINE, newspaper executive; b. N.Y.C., June 16, 1917; d. Eugene and Agnes (Ernst) Meyer; m. Philip L. Graham, June 5, 1940 (dec. 1963); children: Elizabeth Morris Graham Weymouth, Donald Edward, William Welsh, Stephen Meyer. Student, Vassar Coll., 1934-36; AB, U. Chgo., 1938. Reporter San Francisco News, 1938-39; mem. editorial staff Washington Post, 1939-45, mem. Sunday circulation and editorial depts., pub., 1969-79; pres. Washington Post Co., 1963-73, 77, chmn. bd., 1973-93, CEO, 1973-91, chmn. exec. com., 1993—; co-chmn. Internat. Herald Tribune; ind. trustee Reuters Founders Share Co. Ltd.; vice chmn. bd. dirs. Urban Inst.; mem. Coun. on Fgn. Rels., Overseas Devel. Coun.; past chmn. N.Y. Pubs. Assn. Life trustee U. Chgo.; hon. trustee George Washington U.; mem. collectors com. The Nat. Gallery of Art, Washington; active D.C. Com. Pub. Edn. Fellow Am. Acad. Arts and Scis.; mem. Am. Soc. Newspaper Editors, Nat. Press Club, Coun. Fgn. Rels., Overseas Devel. Coun., Met. Club, Cosmopolitan Club, 1925 F Street Club. Home: 2920 R St NW Washington DC 20007-2920 Office: Washington Post Co 1150 15th St NW Washington DC 20071-0002

GRAHAM, KENT HILL, philanthropist, museum guide; b. Winston-Salem, N.C., May 16, 1937; d. Charles Gideon and Nancy Critz (O'Hanlon) Hill; m. William Thomas Graham, Feb. 1, 1958; children: William Thomas, Ashton Cannon. Student, Duke U., 1955-58, U. Hawaii, 1958. Chmn. of vols., sec., sec. to exec. bd. Forsyth County chpt. ARC, asst. to nat. chmn. vols. Am. Nat. Red. Cross, Washington; bd. dirs. Centenary United Meth. Ch. Day Care Ctr.; bd. dirs. Am. Cancer Soc., Forsyth County, Little Theatre, Child Guidance Clinic; mem. Libr. Bd. of Forsyth County, 1970-77, chmn., 1975-77; Rep. candidate for alderman West Ward, Winston-Salem, 1965; vice chmn. N.C. Battleship Commn., 1973-77; bd. dirs. Winston-Salem Debutante Com., 1984-86, pres., 1985, nominating chmn., 1986; mem. exec. bd. Historic Winston, Inc.; trustee N.C. Sch. Arts, 1986-87; mem. N.C. Sentencing and Policy Adv. Com., Celebration N.C. Fin. Com. Capt. N.C. Naval Militia. Mem. Jr. League Nat. Fedn. Rep. Women, Order of the Long Leaf Pine, Twin City Garden Club (treas., 1st v.p., pres.), Garden Club Am. (zone VIII, bull. editor 1975-77, vice chmn. 1977-80, nominating com. 1979-80, water conservation coord. 1980-83). Home: 258 E Davie St Raleigh NC 27601-1865

GRAHAM, KIRSTEN R., computer science educator; b. Inglewood, Calif., July 20, 1946; d. Ray Selmer and Ella Louise (Carter) Newbury; m. Frank Sellers Graham, July 31, 1981. BS, U. Wis., Oshkosh, 1971; MS, U. Colo., 1980; postgrad., Army War Coll., 1987. Cert. Flight instr. Chief info. svc. Mont. State Dept. Labor and Industry, Helena, Mont.; dir., personal property and bus. lic. div. County of Fairfax, Va.; analyst officer U.S. Army Pentagon, Washington; battalion commdr. U.S. Army, Frankfurt, West Germany; assoc. prof. U.S. Army, West Point, N.Y.; del. People-to-People Women Computer Sci. Profls. program., China. Del. to People's Republic of China Citizen's Amb. Program, 1993. LTC U.S. Army, 1964-88. Mem. IEEE, Assn. for Computing Machinery, Am. Fedn. Tchrs.

GRAHAM, LAURIE, editor; b. Evanston, Ill., Nov. 22, 1941; d. Thomas Harlin and Mary Elisabeth (Stoner) Graham; m. George McKay Schieffelin, Dec. 12, 1980 (dec. Jan. 1988); m. Robert Dale Shearer, Apr. 6, 1994. Student, Mt. Holyoke Coll., 1959-61; BA, U. Colo., 1963. Editor Charles Scribner's Sons, N.Y.C., 1969-87. Author: Rebuilding the House, 1990; mem. editl. bd. Creative Nonfiction, 1994—, (press series) Emerging Writers in Creative Nonfiction, Duquesne U., 1994—. Mem. PEN, N.Y. Jr. League, Colony Club. Home: 1000 Grandview Ave Pittsburgh PA 15211-1362

GRAHAM, LOIS CHARLOTTE, retired educator; b. Denver, Mar. 20, 1917; d. James Washington Brewster and Martha Wilhemina (Raukohl) Plunkett; m. Milton Clinton Graham, June 30, 1940 (dec.); children: Charlotte, Milton, Charlene, James. Student, Okla. City U., 1935-36; AB, Ouachita Bapt. U., 1939; postgrad., U. Nev., Reno, 1953, 63, 68, Ark. State U., 1954, 59. Cert. tchr., Colo., Nev., Ark. Tchr. Fairmount Sch., Golden, Colo., 1939-40, Melbourne (Ark.) Sch., 1940-41, Blytheville (Ark.) Jr. H.S., 1944-45, Hawthorne (Nev.) Elem. Sch., 1952-81; substitute tchr. Mineral County Sch. Dist., Hawthorne, 1988-94; sr. resource cons. dept. geriatrics U. Nev.-Reno Med. Sch., 1988-90, del. to Rural Health Conf., Hawthorne, 1990; officer Mineral County Tchrs. Assn., 1955-65; ad hoc com. Nev. State Tchrs., 1965. Mem. Mineral County Emergency Planning Com., 1991—; asst. to pres. High Sch. PTA, Hawthorne, 1958, Elem. PTA, Hawthorne, 1961; pianist, choir dir., tchr. various chs., 1927—; active Older Am. Friends of Libr. Recipient Disting. Svc. award. Mem. AAUW (membership v.p. 1988-91, pres. 1991-95), Am. Assn. Retired Persons (pres. 1995—), Ret. Pub. Employees of Nev. (membership v.p.), Older Ams., Delta Kappa Gamma (v.p. 1991-92). Republican. Baptist. Home: PO Box 1543 Hawthorne NV 89415-1543

GRAHAM, MARILYN ANN, apparel designer; b. Jefferson, Iowa, Oct. 30, 1935; d. E. Duane and Leila M. (Goodwin) English; m. G. Robert Graham, Dec. 29, 1957; children: Mrs. Diann Andrews, Katherine, Debra S., Gregory R. BSBA, Drake U., 1957. Bus. edn. tchr. Schleswig (Iowa) High Sch., 1970-78; mgr. Pantry Supermarket, Ida Grove, Iowa, 1978-82; designer Marilyn Graham Designer Originals, Ida Grove, 1986—. Chmn. Ida County Republican Party, 1982-88; dir. Econ. Devel. Com. Status of Women, Ida Grove, 1992. Mem. P.E.O. (guard 1983-84, chaplain 1985-86, treas. 1987-88, sec. 1989). Methodist. Office: Marilyn Graham Designer Originals 503 First St Ida Grove IA 51445

GRAHAM, MARY ANNE, insurance company executive; b. Ft. Wayne, Ind., Apr. 12, 1947; d. George MacBeth and Edith Jean (Crawford) G.; m. John Chernyha, Oct. 11, 1980 (dec. Aug. 1989). BS, U. Wis., 1969. Claim customer liaison Conn. Gen. Life Ins. Co., Bloomfield, Conn., 1969-75, sr. nat. accounts coord., 1975-80, asst. dir., 1980-86; asst. regional dir. CIGNA Corp., Bloomfield, 1986-88, regional dir., 1988-89, asst. v.p., 1989-90, v.p. underwriting, 1990—. Guide Old State House, Hartford, Conn.; bd. dirs. Farmington Valley Arts Ctr., Avon, Conn., 1981-83, sec., 1981-82, treas., 1982-83; bd. dirs. Jr. League Hartford, 1984. Office: CIGNA Corp Routing B # 257B Hartford CT 06152

GRAHAM, NAN JONES, elementary school educator; b. Murfreesboro, Tenn., Apr. 2, 1953; d. Bobby Elisor and Peggy Nan (Wilkinson) Jones; m. William Newton Graham, Apr. 26, 1976; children: Benjamin Niles (dec. 1991), Boone Jones. BS in Edn., U. Tex., 1975, postgrad., 1977. Cert. tchr., Tex. Kindergarten tchr. Rockdale (Tex.) Elem. Sch., 1975-76; early childhood and kindergarten tchr. Elgin (Tex.) Primary Sch., 1976-78, kindergarten tchr., 1985-92; 4th grade tchr. Elgin Elem. Sch., 1992—; mentor tchr. Elgin Ind. Sch. Dist., 1992-93, mem. textbook com., 1992-93, team leader, 1987-88, mem. sch. improvement com., 1988-91, mem. accelerated sch. com., 1993—, mem. activities com., 1994—, active pilot project Class Within a Class, 1994—. Author: Starting Kindergarten, 1988. V.p., pres. Elgin Young Homemakers, 1978-85; v.p. Regional Young Homemakers, Elgin, 1985; coord. style show Am. Cancer Soc., Elgin, 1981, 82, 83, ANTS Project, 1993—. Named Outstanding Tchr. in Dist., Meadows Found., 1986, Outstanding Mem. Regional Young Homemakers, 1985. Mem. NEA, Tex. State Tchrs. Assn., Elgin Educators (treas. 1985-86). Home: RR 2 Box 160 Elgin TX 78621-9796

GRAHAM, PATRICIA ALBJERG, education educator, foundation executive; b. Lafayette, Ind., Feb. 9, 1935; d. Victor L. and Marguerite (Hall) Albjerg; m. Loren R. Graham, Sept. 6, 1955; 1 child, Marguerite Elizabeth. BS, Purdue U., 1955, MS, 1957, DLitt (hon.), 1980; PhD, Columbia U., 1964; MA (hon.), Harvard U., 1974; DHL (hon.), Manhattanville Coll., 1976; LLD (hon.), Beloit Coll., 1977, Clark U., 1978; DPA (hon.), Suffolk U., 1978, Ind. U., 1980; DLitt (hon.), St. Norbert Coll., 1980; DH (hon.), Emmanuel Coll., 1983; DHL (hon.), No. Mich. U., 1987, York Coll. of Pa., 1989, Kenyon Coll., 1991, Bank St. Coll. Edn., 1993; LLD (hon.), Radcliffe Coll., 1994. Tchr. high sch. Norfolk, Va., 1955-56, 57-58, N.Y.C., 1958-60; lectr., asst. prof. Ind. U., 1964-66; asst. prof. history of edn. Barnard Coll. and Columbia Tchrs. Coll., N.Y.C., 1965-68; assoc. prof. Barnard Coll. and Columbia Tchrs. Coll., 1968-72, prof., 1972-74; dean Radcliffe Inst., 1974-77; also v.p. Radcliffe Coll., Cambridge, Mass., 1976-77; prof. Harvard U., Cambridge, Mass., 1974-79, Warren prof., 1979—; dean Grad. Sch. Edn., 1982-91; pres. Spencer Found., Chgo., 1991—; dir. Nat. Inst. Edn., Washington, 1977-79, trustee Northwestern Mut. Life., 1980—. Author: Progressive Education: From Arcady to Academe, 1967, Community and Class in American Education: 1865-1918, 1974, S.O.S. Sustain Our Schools, 1992. Bd. dirs. Dalton Sch., 1973-76, Josiah Macy, Jr. Found., 1976-77, 79—; trustee Beloit Coll., 1976-77, 79-82, Found. for Teaching Econs., 1980-87; dir. Spencer Found., 1983—, Johnson Found., 1983—, Carnegie Found. for Advancement of Teaching, 1984-92. Am. Council on Edn. fellow Princeton U., 1969-70. Mem. Sci. Rsch. Assocs. (dir. 1980-89), Nat. Acad. Edn. (pres. 1985-89), Am. Hist. Assn. (v.p. 1985-89), Phi Beta Kappa. Episcopalian. Office: The Spencer Found 900 N Michigan Ave Ste 2800 Chicago IL 60611 also: Harvard Grad Sch Edn Cambridge MA 02138

GRAHAM, PAULA LEE, nurse; b. Genoa, Nebr., July 25, 1953; d. Arthur L. and Dorothy W. (Wheeler) Bourks; m. Richard R. Graham, Dec. 23, 1973; children: David, Timothy. AS in Nursing, Maria Coll., 1977; BS in Bus. Adminstrn., U. Phoenix, 1983, MSN, Pace U., 1993, postgrad. cert., 1993. RN charge nurse Valley Children's Hosp., Fresno, Calif., 1977-79, charge nurse pediatric ICU, 1979-81; staff nurse pediatric ICU Moffitt Hosp.-U. Calif., San Francisco, 1981-82; pediatric supr. Kaiser Found. Hosp., Hayward, Calif., 1982-84; Head Start nurse Westchester Community Opportunity Program, Port Chester, N.Y., 1990-91; per diem nurse in pediatrics unit Putnam Hosp. Ctr., Carmel, N.Y., 1992-93; grad. asst. in nursing lab. Pace U., Pleasantville, N.Y., 1992-93, also adj. prof., lectr., 1993-94; nurse-pediatric endocrinology metabolism and nutrition N.Y. Med. Coll., Valhalla, 1994—. Author, editor newsletter Child and Parent Edn. Soc., 1984-86. Den leader Cub Scouts, Pleasantville, 1992—, awards coord., 1994-95; tchr. Pleasantville Ecumenical Vacation Bible Sch., 1989—; tchr. Sunday Sch. Presbyn. Ch., Pleasantville, 1989—. Mem. ANA, AACN, N.Y. State Nurses Assn. (author newsletter dist. 16 1993), Nat. Assn. Pediat. Nurse Assocs. and Practitioners, Soc. Pediat. Nurses, Alpha Xi Delta, Sigma Theta Tau (mem. nominating com.). Home: 49 Brentwood Dr Pleasantville NY 10570-1220

GRAHAM, SCHARLEEN WALKER, counselor; b. Hazard, Ky., May 27, 1940; d. Elbert Walker and Delilia Henderson Tillman; m. Lewis Edward Graham, July 7, 1960; children: Dion Rashan, Natlie DeCarol, Gladys Marileen, Lisa Laniece. BS in Home Econs., U. Cin., 1964, BS in Edn., 1964, MEd, 1973, EdD, 1991. Home econs. tchr. Cin. Pub. Schs., 1964-71, home econs. supr. intern, 1971-73, multi-area job trainer/coord., 1973-74, adult vocat. supr., 1974-82, home econs. consumer edn. tchr., 1982-88, counselor, 1988—; tutor coord. Sch. for Creative and Performing Arts, Cin., 1989-91; coord. Just-Say-No Club, 1988—; advisor Future Educators Am.; mem. local sch. decision-making com., 1986—. Vol. Tour Crafts; adult leader Edn. Tour, Europe, 1992-93, Children Internat. Summer Village Interchange, Denmark, 1992-93. Mem. U. Cin. Alumni Assn., Tchr. Annuit Assn., Ohio Vocat. Assn., Am. Vocat. Assn., Delta Sigma Theta, Phi Beta Kappa, Kappa Delta Phi. Democrat. Baptist. Office: Sch for Creative/Perf Arts 1310 Sycamore St Cincinnati OH 45210-2022

GRAHAM, SYLVIA ANGELENIA, wholesale distributor, retail buyer; b. Charlotte, N.C., Mar. 27, 1950; d. John Wesley and Willie Myrl (Ray) White; m. James Peter Cleveland Fisher, Apr. 23, 1967 (div. Sept. 1972); 1 child, Wesley James Fisher; m. Harold Walker Graham, Sept. 14, 1972 (dec. June 1994); 1 child, Angelique Jane Graham. Cert., Naval Reserve Force Detachment Mgmt. Sch., 1985; air cargo specialist cert., Air U., 1987. Store owner Naval Air Terminal, Norfolk, Va., 1985-88; fleet liaison technician Naval Material Transp. Orgn., Norfolk, 1988-93; passenger svc. rep. Naval Material Transport Orgn., Norfolk, Va., 1988—; distbr. Blair Divsn. of Merchants, Lynchburg, Va., 1988—, Mason Shoe Co., Chippewa Falls, Wis., 1988—;

driver Greater Charlotte Transp. Co., 1988—, Watkins Products, Winona, Minn., 1992—, Citizens Def. Products, St. Joseph, Mo., 1993—; jewelry dealer Merlite Industries, N.Y.C., 1994; mem. Nat. Safety Coun., Charlotte, 1988—, "C" team Watkins Products, Lincoln, Nebr., 1992—; sec. Popular Club Plan, Dayton, N.J., 1990—; pubr. Citizens Def. Products, 1993—. Crusader Cancer Ctr. for Detection and Preventin Drive, Seattle, 1991—; blcok chmn. Easter Seal Soc., 1988—. With USN, 1991, Persian Gulf; USNR, 1992, Somolian Relief Effort; USN, 1993-94. Mem. Nat. Assn. Female Execs., Direct Selling Assn. Democrat. Pentecostal. Home: PO Box 16066 Charlotte NC 28297-6066

GRAHAM, SYLVIA SWORDS, educator; b. Atlanta, Nov. 15, 1935; d. Metz Jona and Christine (Gurley) Swords; m. Thomas A. Graham, Nov. 29, 1958 (div. 1970). BA, Mary Washington Coll., Fredericksburg, Va., 1957; MEd, W. Ga. Coll., Carrollton, 1980; SEd, W. Ga. Coll., 1981; postgrad., Coll. William and Mary, 1964-67. Tchr. Atlanta pub. schs., 1957-58, Newark County pub. schs., Newark, Calif., 1960-61; tchr. history Virginia Beach (Va.) pub. schs., 1964-75, Paulding County pub. schs., Dallas, Ga., 1976—; tour dir. Paulding High Sch. trips, Far East, 1985, USSR, 1989, Australia, 1988-89. County chmn. Rep. Party, 1987-89, county chmn. for re-election of Newt Gingrich, 1982; mem. Gingrich edn. com., 1983, 88; 1st vice chmn. 6th Congl. Dist., 1989-90; del. to 6th Dist. Conv., 1981—, State Rep. Conv., 1981—; chmn. 6th Congl. Dist., 1990-92, 7th Congl. Dist., 1992—; del. Nat. Rep. Convention, 1992. Named Star Tchr., Paulding County C. of C., Dallas, Ga., 1989. Mem. Dallas Woman's Club (pres. 1982-84, 1st v.p. 1986-88, pub. affairs chmn. 1986—, treas. for Civic Ctr. fund 1984—), Phi Kappa Phi. Republican. Baptist. Home: 204 Hart Cir Dallas GA 30132-1115

GRAHAM, TONI, writer; b. San Francisco, June 24, 1945; d. Joseph Foster and Maxine E. (Johnson) Avila; m. J. Richard Graham, Nov. 23, 1972 (div. 1987); 1 child, Salvatore Z. BA, New Coll. Calif., 1989; MA in English, San Francisco State U., 1992. Lectr. dept. creative writing San Francisco State U., 1992; thesis advisor lectr. MA in Writing program U. San Francisco, 1993—. Contbr. short fiction to mags., including Playgirl, Short Story Rev., Am. Fiction 88, Five Fingers Rev., Miss. Rev., Ascent, Clockwatch Rev., Miss. Mud, San Francisco Rev. Harrold scholar, 1986; recipient Calif. Short Story Competition award, 1987, Herbert Wilner Meml. Short Story award, 1994; story Shadow Boxing cited in Pushcart Prize XIV-Best of the Small Presses, 1989. Mem. MLA, Assoc. Writing Programs, Hemingway Soc., Golden Key Honor Soc. Home: 345 Prospect Ave San Francisco CA 94110-5509 Office: care Dijkstra Literary Agy 1237 Camino Del Mar Del Mar CA 92014-2505

GRAHN, BARBARA ASCHER, publisher; b. Chgo., Mar. 26, 1929; d. Harry L. and Eleanor (Simon) Ascher; m. Robert D. Grahn, Dec. 23, 1952; children: Susan Grahn Gantz, Nancy Lee, Wendy. BA, Miami U., Oxford, Ohio, 1950. Promotion dir. George Williams Coll., Chgo., 1950-52; sales mgr. Chatham Mfg., Chgo., 1952-54; research asst. Standard Rate and Data Service, Skokie, Ill., 1968-70, adminstr. editorial services, 1970-75, asst. editor, 1975-77; editor Wilmette, Ill., 1977-87, mng. editor, 1987-92; assoc. pub. Standard Rate and Data Service, Wilmette, Ill., 1992—. Precinct capt. Ill. Reps., 1956-58; pres. Cmty. Club of Jewish Women, Skokie, 1958-60; bd. dirs., treas. North Shore Towers Condo Assn., Skokie, 1986-90, 93—. Mem. NAFE, Chgo. Ad Club, Alpha Epsilon Phi. Office: SRDS 1700 Higgins Rd Des Plaines IL 60018

GRALA, JANE MARIE, securities firm executive; b. Phila.; d. Stanley Frank and Anna Stephanie (Yurkiewicz) G. BS, Rutgers U., Camden, 1976; MBA, Winthrop U., 1979; postgrad., Am. Mgmt. Assn., N.Y.C., 1980-82, Am. Inst. Real Estate Appraisers, Chgo., 1985. Mgr. acctg. dept. NDI Engring. Co., Pennsauken, N.J., 1968-72, project mgr., 1972-76; rep. sales Am. Cyanamid, Wayne, N.J., 1976-80; dist. mgr. Am. Appraisal Assocs., Phila., 1980-86; assoc. v.p. investments Prudential Securities Incorporated, Clearwater, Fla., 1986—; adj. prof. fin. area Tampa (Fla.) Coll., 1995—. Mem. Nat. Assn. Accts. (dir. advt. So. Jersey chpt. 1983-86), Assn. MBA Execs., Bus and Profl. Women's Assn., Nat. Assn. for Female Execs., Chi Delta, Phi Chi Theta. Republican. Office: Prudential Securities Inc 28100 US Highway 19 N Ste 100 Clearwater FL 34621-2656

GRALAPP, MARCELEE GAYL, librarian; b. Winfield, Kans., Nov. 2, 1931; d. Benjamin Harry and Lelia Iris G. B.A., Kansas State Teacher's Coll., 1952; M.A., U. Denver, 1963. Children's librarian Hutchinson Pub. Library, Kans., 1952-57, Lawrence Pub. Library, Kans., 1957-59; assoc. librarian Boulder Pub. Library, Colo., 1959-66, library dir., 1966—; vis. faculty U. Denver, 1965-66, 67, Kans. State Teacher's Coll., Emporia, 1965. Chmn. state plan for library devel. Libraries-Colo., 1974; city staff liaison Boulder Arts Commn., 1979—; bd. dirs. Boulder Ctr. for Visual Arts, 1975-79; treas. Irving Library Network, Inc. Recipient Governor's award Colo. Council on Arts and Humanities, 1981. Mem. ALA, Mountain Plains Library Assn., Colo. Library Assn. (legis. com. 1970-78, Lifetime Achievement award 1992), Boulder Hist. Soc., Boulder Philharm. Soc., Chautauqua Assn., Denver Art Mus., Delta Kappa Gamma. Democrat. Home: 3080 15th St Boulder CO 80304-2614 Office: Boulder Pub Libr PO Drawer H 1000 Canyon Blvd Boulder CO 80306

GRAMES, JUDITH ELLEN, building engineer and inspector, artist, educator; b. Inglewood, Calif., Feb. 7, 1938; d. Glover Victor and Dorothy Margaret (Burton-Bellingham) Hendrickson; divorced; children: Nansea Ellen Ryan, Amber Jeanne Shelly-Harris, Carolyn Angel Longmire, Susan Elaine Gomez, Robert Derek Shallenberger. Cert in journalism, Newspaper Inst. Am., N.Y.C., 1960; AA, Santa Barbara City Coll., 1971; BA, U. Calif., Santa Barbara, 1978, cert. in teaching, 1979. Cert. bldg. inspector, plumbing inspector, Calif. Editor, reporter, photographer Goleta Valley Sun Newspaper, Santa Barbara, 1968-71; editor, team asst. Bur. of Ednl. Rsch. Devel., Santa Barbara, 1971; bus. writer, graphics cons. Santa Barbara, 1971-77; art and prodn. dir. Bedell Advt. Selling Improvement Corp., Santa Barbara, 1979-81; secondary sch. tchr. Coalinga (Calif.) Unified Sch. Dist., 1981-83; bldg. inspector aide Santa Barbara County, Lompoc, 1983-88, from bldg. engring. inspector I to III, 1988—. Exhibited in group shows at Foley's Frameworks and Interiors, 1984, Grossman Gallery, 1984, Lompoc Valley Art Assn., 1984—, (numerous awards including Best of Show 1985, 1st place 1984, 94, 2d place 1984, 86, 88, 3d place 1987, 89, Hon. Mention 1986, 90, 91), featured artist Harvest Arts Festival, 1989, Cypress Gallery, 1994; contbr. poetry to anthologies. Mem. disaster response team Calif. Bldg. Ofcls., 1992—; exec. bd. dirs. Lompoc Mural Soc., 1991—. Delta Kappa Gamma scholar. Mem. NOW, Nat. Abortion Rights Action League, Nat. Mus. of Women in the Arts, Internat. Conf. Bldg. Ofcls., Engrs. and Technicians Assn., Lompoc Valley Art Assn., Toastmasters Internat. (Outstanding Speaker awards 1991-93). Office: Santa Barbara County 624 W Foster Rd Santa Maria CA 93455

GRANBORG, NANCY SUSAN, trust administrator; b. Jersey City, N.J., Feb. 18, 1939; d. Allen Conley and Susan Marie (Dixon) Mathias; m. Bertil S.M. Granborg, July 20, 1963; children: Susan, Mikael, Peter. BA, Wells Coll., 1960. Tax acct. Hawaiian Trust Co. Ltd., Honolulu, 1980-83, tax officer, 1983-85, trust officer, 1985-92, sr. trust officer, 1992-95. treas. Women's Campus Club U. Hawaii, 1992-95; dir. Honolulu Gerontology Program. Mem. Hawaii Soc. Enrolled Agents (dir., past pres. 1990-95), Hawaii Estate Planning Coun. Office: Hawaiian Trust Co Ltd PO Box 3170 Honolulu HI 96802

GRAND, GAIL LEVIN, guidance counselor, writer; b. N.Y.C., Sept. 21, 1943; d. Irving and Helen (Marcus) Levin; m. Harry Stephen Grand, July 11, 1965; children: Paul Marshall, Alissa Lynn. BA in Biology, CUNY, 1964; MS in Guidance and Counseling, Barry U., 1988. Cert. sch. guidance and counseling, sci., biology and gifted edn. tchr., Fla. Sci. tchr. Yonkers (N.Y.) Sch. Dist., 1964-65; biology tchr. Moorestown (N.J.) Sr. H.S., 1965-68; sci. tchr. Medford (N.J.) Twp. Mid. Sch., 1973-76; head sci. dept. Lehrman Day Sch., Miami Beach, Fla., 1976-88; dir. coll. counseling RASG Hebrew Acad., Miami Beach, 1988—; ind. coll. counselor, Miami, Fla., 1992—. Author: Student Science Opportunities, 1994. Mem. ACA, Am. Sch. Counselors Assn., Nat. Sci. Tchrs. Assn., Kappa Delta Pi. Office: RASG Hebrew Acad 2425 Pine Tree Dr Miami Beach FL 33140

GRANDIN, TEMPLE, livestock equipment designer, educator; b. Boston, Aug. 29, 1947; d. Richard McCurdy and Eustacia (Cutler) G. BA in Psychology, Franklin Pierce Coll., 1970; MS in Animal Sci., Arizona State U., 1975; PhD in Animal Sci., U. Ill., Urbana, 1989. Livestock editor Ariz. Farmer Ranchman, Phoenix, 1973-78; equipment designer Corral Industries, Phoenix, 1974-75; ind. cons. Grandin Livestock Systems, Urbana, 1975-90, Fort Collins, Colo., 1990—; lectr., asst. prof. animal sci. dept. Colo. State U., Fort Collins, 1990—; chmn. handing com. Livestock Conservation Inst., Madison, Wis., 1976—. Author: Emergence Labelled Autistic, 1986, Recommended Animal Handling Guidelines for Meat Packers, 1991, Livestock Handling and Transport, 1993; contbg. editor Meat and Poultry mag., 1987—; contbr. articles to profl. jours. Recipient Meritorious Svcs. award Livestock Conservation, Madison, Wis., 1986, Disting. Alumni award Franklin Pierce Coll., 1989, Industry Innovators award Meat Mktg. and Tech. Mag., 1994; named One of Processing Stars of 1990 Nat. Provisioner, 1990. Mem. Autism Soc. Am. (bd. dirs. 1988—, Trammel Crow award 1989), Am. Soc. Animal Sci., Am. Soc. Agrl. Cons. (bd. dirs. 1981-83), Am. Soc. Agrl. Engrs., Am. Meat Inst. (supplier mem.), Am. Registry of Profl. Animal Scis. Republican. Episcopalian. Home: Grandin Livestock Systems 2918 Silver Plume Dr C-3 Fort Collins CO 80526 Office: Colo State U Animal Sci Dept Fort Collins CO 80523

GRANE, NANCY LOUISE BENNETT, nursing and risk management consultant; b. Asheville, N.C., Nov. 15, 1949; d. Wade Thomas and Mary Catherine (Mekeel) Bennett; m. Wayne P. Grane, July 30, 1982; children: Alecia Kathleen, Bradford Mark, Courtney Dawn. Diploma in Nursing, Mercy Hosp. Sch. Nursing, Charlotte, N.C., 1970; BS in Pub. Adminstrn., St. Joseph's Coll., North Windham, Maine, 1986, postgrad. in Healthcare Adminstrn. RN, Ill., Ind., Mich., N.C. Staff nurse Mercy Hosp., Charlotte, 1970-72, Presbyn. Hosp., Charlotte, 1972-74; part-time plastic/reconstructive nurse asst. T. R. Giblin, M.D., Charlotte, 1974-75; pvt. duty nurse Med. Personnel Pool, Charlotte, 1975-76; risk management cons. McNeary Ins. Cons. Svc., Charlotte, 1976-79, Mich. Hosp. Assn. Mutual Ins. Co., Lansing, 1979-82; pvt. practice cons. Indian Head Park, Ill., 1982-87; risk mgr. St. Anthony Med. Ctr., Inc., Crown Pt., Ind., 1987-90; corp. claims and risk mgr. EHS Healthcare, Oakbrook, Ill., 1990—; case worker Vocat. Rehab., Charlotte, 1975-76; immunization and tng. officer N.C. Air NG, Charlotte, 1976-79; chief nurse Mich. Air NG, Battle Creek, 1979-87; clin. nurse AF Res. O'Hare Facility, Ill., 1988-91; now chief nurse, staff devel. officer IL/Air NG, O'Hare; lectr. in field; presenter seminars and workshops local, state, and nat. assns., 1979—. Contbr. articles to profl. jours. With USANG, 1974-87, lt. col. Ill. Air NG, 1991—. Mem. Am. Soc. Healthcare Risk Mgrs., Nat. Com. Risk Financing, Nat. Alliance Air Guard Flight Surgeons, Am. Assn. Legal Nurse Cons., Ind. Soc. Healthcare Risk Mgrs., Ind. Assn. Quality Assurance Profls., Res. Officers Assn., Air NG Nurses Assn. (life), Nat. Guard Assn. U.S. (life), Nat. Guard Assn. Ill. (life), Healthcare Risk Mgrs. of Met. Chgo. (mem. pub. com.), Mercy Hosp. Alumni Assn., St. Joseph's Coll. Alumni Assn. Home: 4 Nacona Ln Indianhead Park IL 60525

GRANGER, KATRINA SORAYA WARREN, social worker, consultant; b. West Palm Beach, Fla., Aug. 25, 1961; d. Willie James and Mary (Walker) W.; m. W. Oshea Granger, Nov. 12, 1988. AA, Palm Beach Jr. Coll., 1982; grad., U. West Fla., 1983; MSW, Barry U., 1987. Ctr. dir. Planned Parenthood Palm Beach Area, Belle Glade, Fla., 1983-85; educator Planned Parenthood Palm Beach Area, West Palm Beach, 1985-86, dir. counseling, 1986-87; advocate coordinator Healthy Mothers/Healthy Babies, West Palm Beach, 1987; with crisis intervention dept. Palm Beach County Schs. Roosevelt Elem. Sch., West Palm Beach, 1987-89; area specialist Palm Beach County Schs., 1989-90; ESE coord. Omni Mid. Sch., 1990-93; coord. ESE resource area 3 Palm Beach Lake H.S., 1993—; cons. Mental Health Assn., West Palm Beach, 1985—. Sec., bd. dirs. Urban League Palm Beach Country, 1985—. Mem. Nat. Assn. Social Workers, Nat. Assn. Exec. Females, N.Am. Christians in Social Work, Delta Sigma Theta. Democrat. Baptist. Home: 1517 43rd St West Palm Beach FL 33407-3607

GRANGER, KAY, mayor; b. Greenville, Tex., 1943; children: Jonh Dean, Chelsea, Brandon. Tex. Wesleyan U., 1964, U. Tex., Arlington, 1976. Mem. zoning com. City of Ft. Worth, 1980-88; mem. pvt. industry coun., 1988-89; councilwoman City of Ft. Worth, 1989-91, mayor, 1991—; owner Kay Granger & Assocs. Recipient Leadership award state of Tex., 1986, Woman of Yr. award, 1987, Bus. and Profl. Woman award, 1987. Mem. Am. Planning Assn., Internat. Sister Cities Assn., Women's Policy Forum (bd. dirs.), East Ft. Worth Bus. and Profl. Assn. (bd. dirs.), Ft. Worth Bus. and Estate Planning Coun., Meadowbrook Bus. and Profl. Womens Assn., East Ft. Worth C. of C. (vice chmn.). Methodist. Office: Office of the Mayor Municipal Bldg 3rd Fl 1000 Throckmorton St Fort Worth TX 76102-6311 Address: 308 Williams Rd Fort Worth TX 76120-1616*

GRANITZ, ADRIENNE DIANA, librarian; b. Sewickley, Pa., Nov. 10, 1946; d. Paul and Mary Ann Delores (Catizone) Hoko; m. Ronald George Granitz, Aug. 31, 1968; 1 child, Ronald George. BS, Edinboro State U., 1968; MS in Libr. Sci., Cath. U. Am., 1983. Libr. Reynolds Elem. Sch. Dist., Greenville, Pa., 1968-72; circulation libr. Piedmont Va. C.C., Charlottesville, 1974-92; libr. dir. Milliken Textile Libr., Inst. Textile Technology, Charlottesville. Mem. ALA, Va. Libr. Assn., Spl. Librs. Assn., Assn. Coll. and Rsch. Librs., Textile Info. Users Coun. Home: 1116 Holmes Ave Charlottesville VA 22901-3723 Office: ITT 2551 Ivy Rd Charlottesville VA 22903

GRANOF, CORINNE, curator, art historian; b. Milw., Feb. 4, 1961; d. Jack Charles and Rose (Bursak) G.; m. Vincent Paul Tomkiewicz, Sept. 11, 1986. BA, U. Wis., 1983, MA, 1986; PhD student, U. Chgo., 1988—. Curatorial asst. Slide Libr., U. Wis., Madison, 1983-85; instr. Mt. Senario Coll., Ladysmith, Wis., 1985-86; rsch. asst. U. Chgo., 1989-90; curator Mary and Leigh Block Gallery, Evanston, Ill., 1992-94; lectr. U. Chgo., 1994—. Bavarian State Govt. grantee, 1986-87; Fulbright scholar, 1986-87, Century scholar U. Chgo., 1988-92, DAAD scholar Direkt Akademische Austauschdienst, 1990-91, Visiting Com. Travel scholar U. Chgo., 1992. Mem. Coll. Art Assn., Fulbright Assn., Wis. Alumni Assn.

GRANROSE, CHERLYN SUE, psychology educator, researcher; b. Dearborn, Mich., Nov. 23, 1942; d. Lawrence Hilmer and Margaret Elizabeth (Gleason) Skromme; m. John Thomas Granrose, Apr. 14, 1963 (div. Dec. 1973); children: Karen Lynn Granrose Friend, Kathleen Rodriquez, Jonathan Lawrence Wesley. BS in Zoology, U. Mich., 1964, MS in Zoology, 1966; MS in Counseling Edn., Kans. State U., 1977; PhD in Psychology, Rutgers U., 1981. Rsch. asst. zoology U. Mich., Ann Arbor, 1966; adj. instr. biology U. Ga., Athens, 1967-72; biology instr. Kans. State U., Manhattan, 1974-78; psychology instr. Rutgers U., Newark, 1980; rsch. asst. AT&T, N.J., 1979-81; from asst. to assoc. prof. human resource adminstrn. Temple U., Phila., 1981-93; assoc. prof. mgmt. Clarkson U., Potsdam, N.Y., 1989; prof. psychology Claremont (Calif.) Grad. Sch., 1993—; cons. Development Dimensions Internat., Pitts., 1982-89, Phila. Suburban Water, 1986-90, A&P/SuperFresh Foods, Phila., 1982-84. Co-author: Science, Sex and Society, 1979, Job Saving Strategies, Worker Ownership and Quality of Work Life, 1989; contbr. articles to profl. jours. Mem. adminstrv. bd. First United Meth. Ch. of Germantown, Phila., 1986-88, LWV, Athens, Ga., 1966-72. Fulbright fellow, South Korea, Taiwan, 1988, Singapore, 1991, Radcliffe fellow H. Murray Ctr., 1991, Rackham fellow U. Mich., 1965-66, Danforth Found. fellow, 1968-72. Mem. APA, Am. Psychol. Soc., Soc. Indsl. Orgn. Psychologists, Assn. Internat. Bus., Acad. Mgmt. (divsn. bd. dirs. 1982-94), Phi Kappa Phi, Sigma Xi. Democrat. Home: 3603 Towne Park Cir Pomona CA 91767-1211 Office: Claremont Grad Sch Dept Psychology Claremont CA 91711

GRANT, AMY, singer, songwriter; b. Augusta, Ga., 1961; d. Burton Grant; m. Gary Chapman; 3 children: Matthew Garrison Chapman, Millie Chapman, Sarah Cannon Chapman. Student, Furman U., Vanderbilt U. Albums include Amy Grant, 1976, My Father's Eyes, 1977, Never Alone, 1978, Amy Grant in Concert, 1979, Amy Grant in Concert II, 1980, Age to Age (Grammy award), 1983, A Christmas Album, 1983, Straight Ahead, 1984, Unguarded (Grammy award), 1985, Lead Me On, 1988, Heart in Motion, 1991. Recipient 3 Dove awards Gospel Music Assn., Grammy award for contemporary gospel performance NARAS, 1982, for female gospel performance, 1983, 84, for female gospel vocal, 1985. Office: care A&M Records 1416 N La Brea Ave Los Angeles CA 90028-7563*

GRANT, ANN MARGARET, chemist; b. Perth Amboy, N.J., Dec. 21, 1943; d. James Joseph and Ruth Mabel (Schenk) G.; m. Kenneth Earl Goetz, July 16, 1965 (div. Mar. 1993); children: Jennifer Laurie Goetz, Annemarie Goetz. AB in Chemistry, Douglass Coll., 1965; PhD in Phys. Chemistry, Rutgers U., 1965. Assoc. scientist Hoffmann LaRoche, Nutley, N.J., 1965-69; lectr., rsch. assoc. Rutgers U., New Brunswick, 1974-77; rsch. fellow dept. pharmacology Case Western Res. U., Cleve., 1978-79; prin. chemist CPC Internat./Best Food, Union, N.J., 1979-82; sr. scientist analytical develop. Hoffmann LaRoche, Nutley, N.J., 1982-83, dir. analytical devel., 1983-92, sr. dir. pharm. process devel., 1991—; mem. dean's ind. adv. bd., chem. and biochem. engring. Rutgers U., 1992-94; mem. dean's adv. bd. Coll. Scis., Clemson (S.C.) U., 1993—; spkr. in field. Author: (edn. brochure) What is Mass Spectrometry?, 1989. Mem. exec. com. Columbia High Sch. Band Parents, Maplewood, N.J., 1992-94. Recipient Tribute to Women in Industry award Bergen County YWCA, 1992. Mem. Am. Chem. Soc. (chair North Jersey chpt. 1993, councilor 1985—, chair Am. Baekland award), Am. Soc. Mass. Spectrometry. Democrat. Home: 3604 Forest Lake Dr Florence SC 29501 Office: Roche Carolina Inc 6173 E Old Marion Hwy Florence SC 29506

GRANT, SISTER BARBARA LEE, hospital executive, nun; b. Jackson, Miss., Aug. 13, 1946; d. Robert Emmett and Patricia (Horan) G. BSN, Marillac Coll., 1970; M of Health Adminstrn., Washington U., St. Louis, 1980. Joined Sisters of Mercy, St. Louis, 1964. Staff nurse St. John's Mercy Med. Ctr., St. Louis, 1970-74; adminstrv. asst. St. Edward Mercy Med. Ctr., Ft. Smith, Ark., 1974-78; resident Mercy Health Svcs., Farmington Hills, Mich., 1980-81; asst. adminstr. Mercy Hosp., New Orleans, 1981-85, COO, 1985-87, CEO, 1987-94; exec. v.p. Mercy Bapt. Med. Ctr., New Orleans, 1994—. Trustee Mercy Regional Med. Ctr., Laredo, Tex., 1984-90, Mercy Med. Group S.W. Mo., Rolla, 1992-94; bd. dirs. St. Thomas Health Svcs., New Orleans, 1989-92; chairperson Met. Hosp. Coun., New Orleans, 1991; mem. exec. com. Met. Area Com.; trustee St. John's Regional Health system, 1994—. Mem. La. Cath. Health Assn. (pres. 1989-90). Office: Mercy and Bapt Med Ctr 2700 Napoleon Ave New Orleans LA 70115

GRANT, BEVERLY ELIZABETH, marketing consultant; b. Reading, Pa., May 18, 1948; d. Bernard E. and Bette A. (Strickler) Sauer; m. Armand Frederick Zigahn, Dec. 21, 1974 (div. 1984); children: Kimberly, Kristin. BS in Psychology, U. Pa., 1968, MBA, 1971. Registered scuba diver. V.p., account supr. Doyle Dane Bernbach, N.Y.C.; sr. v.p., mgmt. supr. Henderson Advt., Greenville, S.C.; mktg. mgr. Community Coffee, Baton Rouge; cons. Mobile Media Analyst, Baton Rouge; pres. Media Analysis Co., 1991-94. Vol. United Way, Greenville, 1988-90; treas. bd. dirs. Leadership Greenville. Mem. Am. Bus. Women Assn., Assn. Nat. Advertisers. Democrat. Episcopalian. Home: 16001 Antietam Ave Baton Rouge LA 70817

GRANT, CYNTHIA D., writer; b. Brockton, Mass., Nov. 23, 1950; d. Robert Cheyne and Jacqueline Ann (Ford) G.; m. Daniel Heatley; 1 child: Morgan; m. Erik Neel; 1 child, Forest. Author: Joshua Fortune, 1980 (Woodward Park Sch. annual book award 1981), Summer Home, 1981, Big Time, 1982, Hard Love, 1983, Kumquat May, I'll Always Love You, 1986, Phoenix Rising, 1989 (Mich. Libr. Assn. Young Adult Caucus best book of yr. 1990, PEN/Norma Klein award 1991, Detroit Pub. Libr. Author Day award 1992), Keep Laughing, 1991, Shadow Man, 1992, Uncle Vampire, 1993 (ALA best books for young adults list 1994). Recipient Book of Distinction award Hungry Mind Review, 1993. Mem. PEN (Norma Klein award 1991), Soc. Children's Book Writers and Illustrators. Home: Box 95 Cloverdale CA 95425 Office: care Atheneum Children's Books 866 3rd Ave New York NY 10022-6221

GRANT, HEDY P., lawyer; b. Bklyn., Aug. 1, 1946; d. Nelson A. and Anne (Novendstern) G.; m. M. David Burghardt, June 23, 1968 (div. Mar. 1976); m. Robert Lucania, July 1, 1988; 1 child, Sebastian. BA in French Lit., Bklyn. Coll., 1967; MS in Libr. Sci., Simmons Coll., 1972; JD, Franklin Pierce Law Ctr., Concord, N.H., 1979. Bar: N.J. 1980, N.J. 1982. Staff atty. N.H. Legal Assistance, 1979-82; editor N.Y. Coop. and Condo Newsletter, 1983; staff atty. Passaic County Legal Aid, 1984; sole practitioner Milford, N.J., 1985—. Trustee Jean Robertson Found., Bergen County, N.J., 1990—. Hebert Smith Found. regional fellow, 1979-81. Mem. Women Lawyers in Bergen County (v.p. 1988-90, pres. 1990-92), Bergen County Bar Assn. Office: 175 Boulevard New Milford NJ 07646

GRANT, JACQUELYN, minister, religion educator; b. Georgetown, S.C., Dec. 19, 1948; d. Joseph James and Lillie Mae (Ward) G. BA, Bennett Coll., 1970; MDiv, I.T.C., 1973; MPhil, Union Theol. Sem., 1980, PhD, 1985. Assoc. in rsch. Harvard Divinity Sch., Cambridge, 1977-79; grad. fellow Harvard U., Cambridge, 1979-80; prof. Interdenominational Theol. Ctr., Atlanta, 1980-88, 94—, assoc. prof., 1989-94, area chairperson, 1990—; vis. lectr. and prof. in field. Author: White Women's Christ and Black Women's Jesus, 1989; contbr. articles to profl. jours. Recipient Fellowship Am. Assn. Theol. Schs., 1987-88, Doctoral fellowship Rockefeller Found., 1973-75, Scholarship Interdenominational Theol. Ctr., 1970-73. Mem. Soc. for Study Black Religion, Black Theology Project, Ecumenical Assn. 3rd World Theologians, Am. Acad. Religion, World Coun. Churches (commn. mem.). African Methodist Episcopal.

GRANT, JOANNE CUMMINGS, public assembly facility administrator; b. N.Y.C., Oct. 12, 1947; d. Ivan Moxley and Antoinette Marie (Lomuscio) Chapman; m. Frank Bernard Cummings, Aug. 16, 1969 (div. Mar. 1977); 1 child, Matthew Colin; m. Rodney Clay Grant (div. May 1991). BA in Speech and History, Marshall U., 1969, MA in Speech Broadcasting, 1976. Adminstrv. asst. Gallup Orgn., Princeton, N.J., 1970; dir. prodn., continuity Sta. WGNT Radio, Huntington, W.Va., 1970-75, dir. news, 1976-78; asst. dir. Huntington Civic Ctr., 1978-82; mgr. bookings Orange County Conv. Ctr., Orlando, Fla., 1982-84; asst. dir. Ocean Ctr., Daytona Beach, Fla., 1984-87; mgr. events Orlando Centroplex, 1987-90, dir., 1990—; bd. dirs. Orlando/Orange County Conv. Bur., World Cup USA. Bd. dirs. Women's Resource Ctr., Light Up Orlando, co-chmn.; pres. Downtown Orlando Partnership, 1994. Named Downtown Woman of Yr. in Govt. Women's Exec. Coun., 1991, Facility Mgr. Yr. Performance Mag., 1993. Mem. Internat. Assn. Auditorium Mgrs. (chmn. exhibits and advt. com. 1984-85, 85-86, publs. and pub. rels. com. 1986-87, arenas com. 1987-88, 91-94, bd. dirs. dist. V 1990-91, 93-94, long range planning com. 1992-93, bd. dirs. 1994—, exec. com. 1994—), Am. Soc. Assn. Execs., Fla. Assn. Assn. Execs., Ctrl. Fla. Soc. Assn. Execs., Fla. Citrus Sports Assn. (exec. com., bd. dirs.). Democrat. Roman Catholic. Home: 1304 Lake Willisara Cir Orlando FL 32806 Office: Orlando Centroplex 600 W Amelia St Orlando FL 32801-1129

GRANT, JUANITA G., librarian; b. Princeton, W.Va., July 25, 1930; d. William Randle and Cora (Fitch) Grant; BS, Concord Coll., 1953; BS in Library Sci., U. N.C., 1955; M in Liberal Arts, Johns Hopkins U., 1970. Librarian, Spl. Services, U.S. Army, Germany, France, 1956-58; asst. librarian Carson Newman Coll., Jefferson City, Tenn., 1959-63; librarian Judson Coll., Marion, Ala., 1964-67; dir. Blount Library, Averett Coll., Danville, Va., 1967—; library adv. com. Va. Council Higher Edn., 1976-78; mem. adv. com. Danville Pub. Library, 1973-75; chmn. library com. Danville Mus. Fine Arts and History, 1976-80; mem. Louisa County Hist. Soc. Mem. ALA, Nat. Geneal. Soc., Va. Geneal. Soc., Va./N.C. Geneal. Soc., Southeastern Library Assn., Va. Library Assn., Am. Hist. Soc., Danville Hist. Soc., Book and Art Club, Wednesday Club, Phi Delta Kappa. Baptist. Home: 126 Primrose Ct Danville VA 24541-2604 Office: Averett Coll 420 W Main St Danville VA 24541-3692

GRANT, LAURIE LOUISE, physician assistant, health educator, consultant, biofeedback and neurofeedback therapist; b. York, Nebr., Dec. 24, 1953; d. Donald Eugene and Mae Louise (McDill) G.; m. Rory R. Hein, May 26, 1973 (div. Feb. 1993); children: Misty Louise, Miles Jeffrey. AS, Allegheny Coll., 1980; BA in Health & Natural Sci., La Roche Coll., 1981; MS, U. Colo., 1983; postgrad., Loyola U., New Orleans, 1990—. Physician asst. Vista Grande Family Medicine, Colorado Springs, Colo., 1980-84, Erindale Family Medicine, Colorado Springs, 1984-86, Front Range Family Medicine, Colorado Springs, 1986-88, Exec. Park Med. Arts, Colorado

Springs, 1988-94, USAF Acad. Hosp., Colo., 1994—; health educator, pres., founder Profl. Health Providers Health Consulting, Colorado Springs, 1984—; tchr., facilitator Nat. Inst. Inner Healing, Colorado Springs, 1991—; biofeedback/neurofeedback therapist, founder Awareness Assocs. Contbr. articles to profl. jours. Mem. pastoral coun. Corpus Christi Ch., Colorado Springs, 1991—, eucharistic min., 1990—; tchr. religious edn. seminars, Colorado Springs, 1986—; inner healing specialist Nat. Inst. Inner Healing, 1988—; co-founder Single Mothers and Children Found. Fellow Am. Acad. Physician Assts., Am. Coll. Sports Medicine; mem. Colo. Acad. Physician Assts., Nat. Inst. Inner Healing Specialists, Assn. Applied Psychophysiology and Biofeedback, Colo. Assn. Applied Psychophysiology and Biofeedback, Am. Counseling Assocs. Republican. Avocations: karate, teaching, cross-country skiing, scuba diving, snorkeling. Office: USAF Academy Hospital USAF Academy CO 80840

GRANT, LINDA KAY (LINDA KAY SCOTT), small business owner, sales executive; b. Galesburg, Ill., Oct. 15, 1949; d. Claire Arline Tabb and Addie Mae (Smith) Stedman; m. James G. Scott, Feb. 20, 1968 (div. Dec. 1977); children: Angela Cristine, Aaron Cristopher; m. Daryl Quinn Grant, Sept. 20, 1986; 1 child, Rachel Jane. Student, Balckhawk East Coll., 1984-86. Sec. Flynn Beverage, Inc., Rock Island, Ill., 1972-76, Lee's Place, Inc., Rock Island, 1976-81; merchandising rep. Polaroid Corp., Boston, 1981-84; sales rep. Drawing Bd. Greeting Cards, Dallas, 1984-86; owner Card Creations, Galva, Ill., 1986-90; mktg. rep. Q.C. Metall. Labs., Davenport, Iowa, 1989—. Mem. Dem. Women for Henry County, Cambridge, Ill., 1985—; pres. Galva/UA C. of C., 1988; advisor Galva/UA Econ. Devel. Com., 1989. Mem. NOW, Nat. Assn. for Female Execs. Methodist. Home: RR 1 Kewanee IL 61443-9801 Office: QC Metall Labs 17048 215th St Davenport IA 52804

GRANT, MARGARET M. DOYLE, lawyer; b. Columbus, Ohio, Apr. 13, 1957; d. Frederick Joseph and Mary Olga (Blaskovich) Doyle; m. Jeffrey D. Grant, May 19, 1990. BA, Coll. William & Mary, 1979; JD, U. Va., 1983. Bar: N.Y., D.C. Assoc. White & Case, N.Y.C., 1983-85, Washington, 1985-88; v.p., assoc. gen. counsel Riggs Nat. Bank, Washington, 1988-94; sr. comml. counsel Overseas Pvt. Investment Corp., Washington, 1994—. ESL tutor Sacred Heart Adult Edn., Washington, 1991—. Mem. Am. Soc. Internat. Law, N.Y. Bar Assn., D.C. Bar Assn. (vice chair in-house counsel com., sect. on corps., fin. and securities law 1994—). Roman Catholic. Office: Overseas Pvt Investment Corp 1100 New York Ave Washington DC 20524

GRANT, MIRIAM ROSENBLOUM, educator, journalist; b. Collinsville, Ala.; d. Harry M. and Rae (Rosenberg) Rosenbloum; m. Morton A. Grant, Nov. 17, 1952 (dec. 1967). AB, U. Ala., 1935; postgrad., U. Miami, 1968-69, Fla. Internat. U. Cert. tchr., Fla. Reporter Chattanooga Free Press., 1936-41, Birmingham (Ala.) Post, 1942; reporter, movie editor, drama critic Chattanooga News-Free Press, 1943-49; thcr., head journalism dept., newspaper and yearbook adviser North Miami (Fla.) Sr. High Sch., 1969-89. Recipient Golden Medallion Fla. Scholastic Press Assn., 1987, named life member, 1990, service award Coll. Fraternity Editors Assn., 1989. Mem. AAUW, U. Ala. Nat. Alumni Assn. (coun. mem.-at-large 1960-61), Ceramic League Miami (Corr. sec. 1963-64), Women's Panhellenic Assn. Miami (Sec. 1992-93), nat. Panhellenic Editors Conf. (vice chmn. 1986-87, chmn. 1987-89), Sigma Delta Tau (nat. pres. 1950-54, editor The Torch mag. 1968—, honor key 1988, scholarship named in her honor as 1st mem. to serve 50 yrs. on sorority nat. coun. 1991, archivist 1992—, CFEA recognition award as editor 1993), Theta Sigma Phi, Phi Lambda Pi, Rho Lambda, Sigma Delta Chi.

GRANT, PENNY, pediatrics educator; b. N.Y.C., Dec. 19, 1959; d. Stanley Charles and Hilda (Kleinerman) G.; m. Lee Mark Cohen, Feb. 28, 1987. BA, Columbia U., 1980; MD, N.Y. Med. Coll., 1984. Diplomate Nat. Bd. Med. Examiners, Am. Bd. Pediatrics. Intern N.Y. Hosp. Cornell Med. Ctr., N.Y.C., 1984-86; resident Jackson Meml. Hosp., U. Miami, Fla., 1986-88, dir. pediatric care network, 1989-90; pediatrician Pediatric Assocs., P.A., Hollywood, Fla., 1988-89; asst. prof. dept pediatrics U. Miami, 1989—; dir. Univ. Pediat. Assocs., Miami, 1993—. Mem. Am. Acad. Pediatrics. Office: Univ Pediatric Assocs 1150 NW 14 St Ste 711 Miami FL 33136-2113

GRANT, PHYLLIS MOORE, elementary education educator; b. Gordonsville, Ala.; d. William Jr. and Milie James (Black) Moore; m. James Grant, Sept. 5, 1970 (div. July 1987; children: Valarie Joy, Anne Sajo. BS in Music Edn., Ala. State U., Montgomery, 1964; MA in Elem. Edn., Eastern Mich. U., 1972, MA in Music Edn., 1978; EdS, Oakland U., Rochester, Mich., 1980; MA in Ednl. Admistnrn., Eastern Mich. U., 1992. Cert. elem. and secondary tchr., Mich. Sec. Alpha Alpha chpt. Gamma Phi Delta Sorority Alpha Alpha chpt., Montgomery, 1964-67; union rep. Huron Valley Assn., Milford, Mich., 1986-90; sec. Ala. State U. Alumni, Detroit, 1992—; test coord. Huron Valley Schs./Oxbow Elem. Sch., White Lake, Mich., 1990—; tchr. Huron Valley Sch. Dist., Highland, Mich., 1967—; tutor-tchr. Marygrove Coll., White Lake, 1967—. Sunday sch. tchr. Dexter Ave. Bapt. Ch., Detroit, 1977—, pianist, 1985—, dir., 1987—, coord. Sunday sch. programs, 1988—. Mem. ASCD, AAUW, Mich. Edn. Assn. (Svc. award 1986, 88), Huron Valley Edn. Assn. (Merit award 1974, 77), Nat. Staff Devel. Coun., Gamma Phi Delta sorority (Alpha Theta chpt.). Home: 16556 Sussex Detroit MI 48235 Office: Huron Valley Schs 100 Oxbow Lake Rd White Lake MI 48386

GRANT, RONNIE ANN, realtor, speaker; b. Detroit, Nov. 28, 1951; d. Ronald Thomas and Jewel Eloise (Horton) Offett; m. Willie Grant, June 23; children: Emmitt, Juliet, Jewel, Vanessa. Student, Wayne County C.C., Detroit, 1975-77, Lima Tech., 1988, Bliss Coll., 1991. Cert. real estate appraiser. Program dir. Day Care Ctr., Detroit, 1977-80; real estate sales woman North Western Ohio Land Co., Van Wert, Ohio, 1988—; spkr. Ohio Bd. Realtors, Columbus, 1991—. Bd. dirs. ARC, Van Wert, 1990-94; active Women that Win, Lima, Ohio, 1994; speaker for equal opportunity in housing Ohio Bd. Realtors. Mem. Nat. Bd. Realtors, Ohio Bd. Realtors, Van Wert Bd. Realtors (sec.-treas. 1989-90, v.p. 1990-91, pres. 1991-93, chairperson equal opportunity 1990-93). Home: 612 Shaffer Van Wert OH 45891 Office: North Western Ohio Land Co 147 E Main Van Wert OH 45891

GRANT, SHEILA SUE, graphic artist; b. Princeton, Ind., Jan. 24, 1961; d. Lowell Dean and Shirley Ann (Hughes) Grant. BA, Grand Rapids Baptist Coll., 1983; student, Kendall Coll. Art & Design, 1988—. Social worker Thumb Area Family Counseling, Caro, Mich., 1984-85, Tuscola County Juvenile Ct., Caro, 1985-86, Ottawa County Juvenile Ct., Grand Haven, Mich., 1986-88; graphic artist Richard Jones & Assoc., Grand Rapids, Mich., 1988-89, Valley City Sign, Comstock Park, Mich., 1989—. Office: Valley City Sign 5009 W River Dr Comstock Park MI 49321

GRANT, SHIRLEY MAE, business affairs director; b. Barberton, Ohio, Feb. 4, 1936; d. Chester Claude and Virginia Hutchison (Crispin) Culp; m. Stewart K. Grant, June 19, 1960 (dec. 1975); children: Michelle C. Grant Fontes, Sabrina K. Fox, Michael S. AA in Liberal Arts, Graceland Coll., 1956; BS in Edn. magna cum laude, Calif. State Ul., Long Beach, 1965, MS in Counseling/Student Affairs, 1974; AA in Real Estate, Fullerton Coll., 1979. Lic. real estate broker; cert. community coll. instr. Asst. registrar Graceland Coll., Lamoni, Iowa, 1956-58; adminstrv. asst., dean of students Calif. State U., Long Beach, 1958-61; tchr. Vista Unified/Rossmoor, Los Alamitos, Calif., 1965-70; asst. dean admissions and records Calif. State U., Long Beach, 1970-74; dir. sch. and coll. rels. Calif. State U., Fullerton, 1974-77; dir. sch. and coll. res. Calif. State U., Dominguez Hills, Carson, Calif., 1978-80; coord. tour and travel Knotts Berry Farm, Buena Park, Calif., 1980-85; chief info. officer Pro Value, Cerritos, Calif., 1985-89, Gen./Vascular Surg. Assocs., Long Beach, 1989-93; dir. bus. affairs Unyeway, Ramona, Calif., 1993—; cons. Systems Group, Ramona, Calif., 1979—. Steering com. Calif. Women in Higher Edn., Sacramento, 1977. Univ. scholar, Danforth scholar. Mem. Nat. Honor Soc. (pres. 1954). Home: 1448 Cedar St Ramona CA 92065-1326

GRANT, SUSAN IRENE, lawyer; b. N.Y.C., Apr. 27, 1953; d. Walter Arnold and Beatrice L. (Thalheimer) G.; m. Brian A. King, June 24, 1990; 1 child, Alexander Grant. BA, NYU, 1974; JD, Columbia U., 1977. Bar: N.Y. 1978, U.S. Dist. Ct. (so. and ea. dists.) N.Y. 1978. Assoc. Law Offices of Rita Eredics, Esq., Flushing, N.Y., 1977-78; staff atty. The Dreyfus Corp., N.Y.C., 1978-85; asst. gen. counsel Prudential-Bache Securities Inc., N.Y.C., 1985-89, asst. v.p., 1986-89; asst. gen. counsel, assoc. v.p. Prudential Mut. Fund Mgmt., Inc., N.Y.C., 1987-89; asst. counsel First Investors Corp., N.Y.C., 1989-94; sr. counsel, chief compliance officer Quest Adv. Corp., N.Y.C., 1994—. Bd. trustees Self Help Comty Svcs., Inc. Mem. ABA, N.Y. State Bar Assn., Am. Corp. Counsel Assn. Home: 11045 Queens Blvd Forest Hills NY 11375 Office: Quest Adv Corp 1414 Ave of the Americas New York NY 10019

GRANT, VIRGINIA ANNETTE, newspaper editor, journalist; b. Abilene, Tex., Jan. 21, 1941; d. Thomas Spenser and Dorris Barnett (Turner) G.; m. Steele Commager, Mar. 8, 1983 (dec. Apr. 1984). B.A., Brown U., 1963. Writer, editor Mademoiselle Mag., N.Y.C., 1965-68; reporter, feature writer Newsweek Mag., N.Y.C., 1968-69; asst. editor articles and fiction Seventeen Mag., N.Y.C., 1970-77; editor Living sect. N.Y. Times, N.Y.C., 1977-81, dep. style editor, 1981-82, editor Weekend sect., 1982-90, editor cultural affairs N.Y. Times Sunday Mag., 1990-94; art, architecture and photography editor Arts & Leisure, 1994—. Democrat. Office: NY Times 229 W 43rd St New York NY 10036-3913

GRANTER, SHARON SAVOY, restaurateur; b. Hammond, Ind., Oct. 21, 1940; d. Theodore Grummer and Marie Theresa (Vincent) Kocur; m. John Albert Savoy, Aug. 14, 1959 (div. Nov. 1974); children: Renee Savoy Heuss, Jennifer Lynn Savoy, Elizabeth Anne Savoy; m. Donald Ralph Granter, Feb. 10, 1979. Student, Ohio State U., 1958-59; grad., Lancaster Bus. Coll., 1959. Sec., bookeeper Manpower, Inc., Albany, N.Y., 1960-64; owner, operator, caterer Granter's Deli Catering Svc., Mansfield, Ohio, 1979-94; restaurateur, operator Perkins of Mansfield, 1989-94; broker Equinox Internat. Corp., 1994—. Editor newsletter NCO Rehab. Ctr., 1971-74. Vocalist Ohio State U. Jazz Forum Big Band, 1955-59; founder, dir. New Start Seminar, Mansfield, 1973-79; sec. Miss Ohio Scholarship Pageant, Mansfield, 1974-80, traveling companion, 1974-80, judge, 1974-86; mem. procurement com. Mansfield Gen. Hosp., 1973-74; pres. aux. AMA Riverside Hosp., Columbus, 1972. Mem. Nat. Restaurant Assn., Ohio Restaurant Assn. Republican. Home: 536 Chevy Chase Rd Mansfield OH 44907-1549 Office: 450 James Ave Mansfield OH 44907

GRANTUSKAS, PATRICIA MARY, elementary education educator; b. Irvington, N.J., Jan. 17, 1952; d. Albert L. and Mary D. (Gradeckis) G. BA summa cum laude, Kean Coll., Union, N.J., 1973, MA, 1977 and 1993, supr.'s cert., 1980. Cert. prin. supr., tchr., reading specialist, elem. tchr. Reading clinician Reading Inst., Kean Coll., 1977-80; instr. reading Newark Acad., Livingston, N.J., 1983—; reading specialist, test and basic skills coord. Garwood (N.J.) Bd. Edn., 1977-89; reading instr. Summer Clinic Pingry Sch., N.J., 1977-82; reading specialist, coord. basic skills Harrington Park (N.J.) Bd. Edn., 1989—; remedial reading tchr. Garwood (N.J.) Pub. Schs., 1973-77; pvt. tutor. Mem. YMCA. Mem. ASCD, N.J. ASCD, Nat. Coun. Tchrs. English, Internat. Reading Assn. (hon. coun., Pres.'s Club), N.J. Edn. Assn., N.J. Reading Assn. (bd. dirs. 1991-94, sec. bd. dirs. 1989-90), Garwood Tchrs. Assn., Harrington Park Edn. Assn., Suburban Reading Coun. (past pres.), Delta Kappa Gamma, Kappa Delta Pi, Phi Kappa Phi. Office: Harrington Park Sch 191 Harriot Ave Harrington Park NJ 07640-1401

GRANUM, NANCY JOHNSON, nurse; b. Guymon, Okla., Aug. 10, 1955; d. Walter Johnson and Elsie Irene (Coffman) Johnson Moore; m. Michael James Graum, Jan. 29, 1979; children: Angela, David. BS in Nursing, Okla. U., 1977. RN. Staff nurse Okla. Children's Meml. Hosp., Oklahoma City, 1977-80; clin. instr. Casper (Wyo.) Coll., 1982-84; office mgr. Michael J. Granum, M.D., Casper, 1984—. Bd. trustees Natrona County Sch. Dist. #1, Casper, 1992-94; dir. Wyo. Sch. Bds. Assn., Laramie, Wyo., 1993-94; vice chmn. bd. trustees Natrona County Sch. Dist. #1, 1994. Office: Michael J Granum MD 940 E 3rd St Ste 101 Casper WY 82601-3200

GRAPIN, JACQUELINE G., journalist; b. Paris, Dec. 15, 1942; came to U.S., 1985; d. Jean and Raymonde (Ledru) G.; m. Michel Le Goc, June 4, 1971; children: Claire, Julien. Degree, Institut d'Etudes Politiques, Paris, 1966; Degree in Law, U. Paris, 1967; Auditeur, Inst. des Hautes Etudes de Def. Nat., Paris, 1980. Staff writer LeMonde, Paris, 1967-81; dir.-gen. Interevia Pub. Group, Geneva, 1982-86; pres. The European Inst., Washington, 1989—; econ. corr. Le Figaro, Washington, 1987—; prof. Inst. d'Etudes Politiques, Paris, 1974-77. Author: Guerre Civile Mondiale, 1977, Radioscopie des Etats-Unis, 1980, Fortress America, 1984, Pacific America, 1987; assoc. editor World Paper, Boston, 1980-93; contbr. articles to profl. jours. Trustee Aspen Inst. for Humanistic Studies, N.Y.C., 1981—; bd. dirs. Internat. Women's Media Found., Internat. Action Against Hunger. Recipient Prix Vauban Inst. des Hautes-Etudes, Paris, 1977, Ordre de la Legion d'Honneur, 1993. Mem. Internat. Inst. Strategic Studies Longon, Swiss Soc. of the French Legion of Honor, Pen Club, Nat. Press Club, Kenwood Golf Club (Washington), Polo Club (Paris). Home: 4 Chernin Pont Perrin, 1231 Geneva Switzerland Office: The European Inst 4910 Massachusetts Ave NW Washington DC 20016-2345

GRAS, PATRICIA ELIZABETH, broadcast journalist, marketing consultant; b. Houston, Aug. 12, 1960; d. Hector Ricardo and Salome Amelia (Mdalel) G. BA in Econs., Tex. A&M, 1983; M Internat. Mgmt., Am. Grad. Sch. Internat. Mgmt., Glendale, Ariz., 1985; MBA, ESADE, Barcelona, Spain, 1985; MS in Journalism, Columbia U., 1990. Mktg. specialist Gallina Blanca Purina, Barcelona, 1985-87, Duquesne Purina, Paris, 1987; reporter, producer Sta. KTMD-TV, Houston, 1988-90; prodr., anchor, reporter Sta. KUHT-TV, Houston, 1990—; producer for med. show La Mujer y Su Sallud Prodsn., Miami, 1991; producer, anchor Usted que Opina, 1993. Singer, percussionist for Barandua, a Latin Am. folk music group. Master ceremonies Crisis Hotline, Houston, 1990-93; panelist Hispanic Women Leaders, 1991—. Recipient Excalibur for Excellence award Am. Soc.Pub. Rels., 1989, Houston Press Club award for coverage of town meetings on race and healthcare, 1992, Women in Comms. award for coverage of concerns of elderly, 1992; Group Study Exch. grantee Rotary Internat., 1994. Mem. Thunderbird Alumni Assn., Nat. Hispanic Journalists Assn., Houston Press Club, Houston Hispanic Journalists Assn., Hispanic Women's Leadership Com. Home: 15 E Greenway Plz Apt 6C Houston TX 77046-1503

GRASBERGER, ANNE SCOTT, nursing administrator; b. Ann Arbor, Mich., Jan. 17, 1961; d. Gerald Charles and Janet Louise (Ruediger) Scott; m. Bruce Lamont Grasberger, Oct. 1, 1988; children: Andrew Scott, Christopher Scott. BSN, U. Mich., 1983; MBA, U. Pa., 1993. RN, Md. Clin. nurse NIH, Bethesda, Md., 1983-88, nurse mgr., 1988-94. Contbr.: (with others) Mosby's Manual of Clinical Nursing, 1989. Home: 335 Meadowview Dr Trappe PA 19426

GRASH, VALERIE SUE, art historian; b. Waynesburg, Pa., July 13, 1965; d. Joseph George and Betty Jean (Piatt) G. BA in English and History, Slippery Rock U., 1987; MA in Art History, Pa. State U., 1991, postgrad., 1994—. Teaching asst., instr. art history Pa. State U., University Park, 1988-93; instr. art history Point Park Coll., Pitts., 1993—; guide Fallingwater, Bear Run, Pa., 1993—. Mem. Internat. Ctr. Medieval Art, Coll. Art Assn., Archaeol. Inst. Am., Vernacular Architecture Forum, Phi Alpha Theta, Alpha Sigma Alpha. Democrat. Home: 287 Huffman St Waynesburg PA 15370-1212 Office: Point Park Coll Dept Fine Arts 201 Wood St Pittsburgh PA 15222-1984

GRASMICK, NANCY S., superintendent of schools; b. Balt.; m. Louis J. Grasmick. BS in Elem. Edn., Towson State U., 1961; MS in Deaf Edn., Gallaudet U., 1965; PhD in Communicative Scis. with distinction, Johns Hopkins U., 1979; LHD (hon.), Towson State U., 1992, Goucher Coll., 1992. Tchr. deaf William S. Baer Sch., Balt., 1961-64; tchr. hearing and lang. impaired children Woodvale Sch., Balt., 1964-68; supr. Office Spl. Edn. Balt. County Pub. Schs., 1968-74; prin. Chatsworth Sch., Balt., 1974-78; asst. supt. Balt. County Pub. Schs., 1978-85, assoc. supt., 1985-89; sec. juvenile svcs. Dept. Juvenile Svc., Balt., 1991; spl. sec. children, youth and families Gov.'s Exec. Office, Balt., 1989-95; supt. schs. Md. Dept. Edn., Balt., 1991—; chmn. interagy. com. on sch. constrn. Gov.'s Subcabinet for Children, Yough and Families; mem. interagy. coordinating coun. Gov.'s Adv. Bd. Juvenile Justice, Gov.'s Workforce Investment Bd.; mem. profl. stds. and tchr. edn. bd. Md. Assocs. for Dyslexic Adults and Youth; mem. profl. adv. bd. Met. Balt. Assn. Learning Disabled Children. Trustee Md. Retirement and Pension Sys.; bd. dirs. Coll. Bound Found., Balt. Symphony Orch.; pres. Child Care Found.; mem. Md. Pub. Broadcasting Commn., Gov.'s Coun. Adolescent Pregnancy, Gov.'s Drug and Alcohol Abuse Commn. Trustee Md. State Retirement and Pension Systems; bd. Coll. Bound Found., Balt. Symphony Orch.; pres. Child Care Found.; mem. Md. Pub. Broadcasting Commn., Gov.'s Coun. Adolescent Pregnancy, Gov.'s Drug and Alcohol Abuse Commn. Recipient Medallion award Jimmy Swartz Found., 1989, Louise B. Makofsky Meml. award Md. Conf. Social Concern, 1990, Child Advocacy award Am. Acad. Pediatrics, 1990, Humanitarian award March of Dimes, 1990, Disting. Citizen's award Md. Assn. Non-pub. Spl. Edn. Facilities, 1991, Women of Excellence award Nat. Assn. Women Bus. Owners, 1991, Andrew White medal, Loyola Coll., 1991, Nat. Edn. Administr. of Yr. award Nat. Assn. Ednl. Office Profls., 1992, Nat. award computing to assist persons with disabilities Johns Hopkins U., 1992, Vernon E. Anderson Disting. Lecture award for Outstanding Leadership in Edn., Coll. Edn. U. Md., 1992, DuBois Circle Award of Honor, 1992, Disting. Alumna of Yr. award Johns Hopkins U., 1992, Pub. Affairs award Md. C. of C., 1994; named Communicator of Yr. by Speech and Hearing Agy., 1990, Marylander of Yr. by The Advt. and Profl. Club of Balt., 1990, Most Disting. Woman by Girl Scouts of Ctrl. Md., 1994. Mem. Phi Delta Kappa (Excellence in Edn. award), Pi Lambda Theta. Office: Md Dept Edn 200 W Baltimore St Baltimore MD 21201-2500

GRASSELLI, JEANETTE GECSY, university official; b. Cleve., Aug. 4, 1928; d. Nicholas W. and Veronica (Varga) Gecsy; m. Glenn R. Brown, Aug. 1, 1987. BS summa cum laude, Ohio U., 1950, DSc (hon.), 1978; MS, Western Res. U., 1958, DSc (hon.), 1995; DSc (hon.), Clarkson U., 1986; D Engring. (hon.), Mich. Tech. U., 1989; DSc (hon.), Wilson Coll., 1994, Notre Dame Coll., 1995. Project leader, assoc. Infrared Spectroscopist, Cleve., 1950-78; mgr. analytical sci. lab. Standard Oil (name changed to BP Am., Inc. 1985), Cleve., 1978-83, dir. technol. support dept., 1983-85, dir. corp. rsch. and analytical scis., 1985-88; Disting. vis. prof., dir. rsch. enhancement Ohio U., Athens, 1989—; bd. dirs. B.F. Goodrich Co., AGA Gas, Inc. USX Corp.; mem. bd. on chem. sci and tech. NRC, 1986-91; chmn. U.S. Nat. Com. to Internat. Union of Pure & Applied Chemistry, 1992-94; mem. joint high level adv. panel U.S.-Japan Sci. & Tech., 1994—. Author, editor 8 books; editor: Vibrational Spectroscopy; contbr. numerous articles on molecular spectroscopy to profl. jours.; patentee naphthalene extraction process. Bd. dirs. N.E. Ohio Sci. and Engring. Fair, Cleve., 1977—; trustee Ohio U., 1985-94, chmn., 1991-92; trustee Garden Ctr. Greater Cleve., 1990-93, chmn., 1995—; trustee Holden Arborteum, Cleve., 1988—, Edison Biotech. Ctr., Cleve., 1988—, Cleve. Playhouse, 1990, Cleve. Scholarship Program, 1992—, Mus. Arts Assn., 1991—, Gt. Lake Sci. Mus., 1991—, Cleve. Edn. Fund Sci. Collaborative, 1991—, Nat. Inventor's Hall of Fame, 1993—, Rainbow Babies and Children's Hosp., 1992—. Recipient Disting. Svc. award Cleve. Tech. Soc. Coun., 1985; named Woman of Yr. YWCA, 1980; named to Ohio Women's Hall of Fame State of Ohio, 1989, Ohio Sci. & Tech. Hall of Fame, 1991. Mem. Am. Chem. Soc. (chair analytical divsn. 1990-91, Garvan medal 1986, Analytical Chem. award 1993), Soc. for Applied Spectroscopy (pres. 1970, Disting. Svc. award 1983), Coblentz Soc. (bd. govs. 1968-71, William Wright award 1980), Royal Soc. Chemistry (Theophilus Redwood lectr. 1994), Phi Beta Kappa, Iota Sigma Pi (pres. fluorine chpt. 1957-60, nat. hon. mem. 1987). Republican. Roman Catholic. Home: 150 Greentree Rd Chagrin Falls OH 44022-2424

GRASSO, MARY ANN, theatre association administrator; b. Rome, N.Y., Nov. 3, 1952; d. Vincent and Rose Mary (Pupa) Grasso. BA in Art History, U. Calif., Riverside, 1973; MLS, U. Oreg., 1974. Dir. Warner Rsch. Collection, Burbank, Calif., 1975-84; mgr. CBS TV/Docudrama, Hollywood, Calif., 1984-88; exec. dir. Nat. Assn. Theatre Owners, North Hollywood, Calif., 1988—; instr. theatre arts UCLA, 1980-85, Am. Film Inst., L.A., 1985-88. Screen credits: The Scarlet O'Hara Wars, This Year's Blonde, The Silent Lovers, A Bunnies Tale, Embassy. Mem. Nat. Assn. Theatre Owners (exec. dir.), Bus. and Profl. Women's Assn. (Woman of Achievement award 1983), Acad. Motion Picture Arts and Scis., Friends of The Motion Picture Pioneers, Phi Beta Kappa. Democrat. Office: Nat Assn Theatre Owners 4605 Lankershim Blvd # 340 North Hollywood CA 91602-1818

GRAU, MARCY BEINISH, former banker, consultant, precious metals trader; b. Bklyn., Aug. 7, 1950; d. Joseph Beinish and Gloria (Rosenbaum) Bennett; m. Bennett Grau, Nov. 19, 1978; 2 children. AB with high honors, U. Mich., 1971; postgrad., Columbia U., 1972; N.Y. Inst. Fin., 1973. Asst. to chmn. Bancroft Convertible Fund, N.Y.C., 1973-75; precious metals trader J. Aron & Co., N.Y.C., 1975-81, mgr. metals mktg., 1981-83; v.p. Goldman, Sachs & Co/J. Aron, N.Y.C., 1983-88; investment banking cons., N.Y.C., 1988-90; bd. dirs. Ethical Fieldston Fund. Editor Precious Metals Rev. and Outlook, 1980—; contbr. article to profl. jours. Vol. worker pediatrics dept. Lenox Hill Hosp., N.Y.C., 1978-79; asst. The Holiday Project, The Hunger Project, N.Y.C., 1978-83; vol. Yorkville Common Pantry, N.Y.C., 1984; tutor Yorkville Neighborhood Assn., N.Y.C., 1984; assoc. Child Devel. Ctr., N.Y.C.; trustee Congregation B'Nai Jeshurun, 1989—, pres., 1991-94; trustee Ethical Fieldston Fund, 1994. Mem. Phi Beta Kappa. Democrat. Jewish. Home and Office: 300 West End Ave New York NY 10023-8156

GRAU, SHIRLEY ANN (MRS. JAMES KERN FEIBLEMAN), writer; b. New Orleans, July 8, 1929; d. Adolph and Katherine (Onion) G.; m. James Kern Feibleman, Aug. 4, 1955; children: Ian, James, Nora Miranda, William, Katherine. BA, Tulane U., 1950. Author: (short stories) The Black Prince and Other Stories, 1955, The Hard Blue Sky, 1958, The House on Coliseum Street, 1961, The Keepers of the House, 1964 (Pulitzer prize for fiction 1965), The Condor Passes, 1971, The Wind Shifting West and Other Stories, 1973, Evidence of Love, 1977, Nine Women, 1986, Roadwalkers, 1994; writer publs. including Holiday, New Yorker, New World Writing, Mademoiselle, Saturday Evening Post, Atlantic, The Reporter, 1954—. Mem. Phi Beta Kappa. Office: 210 Baronne St Ste 1120 New Orleans LA 70112-1713

GRAUER, EVA MARIE, sculptor, artist; b. Memphis, Jan. 13, 1925; d. Otto Franklin and Mary Eva (Nichols) Lyons. Student, Southwestern Coll., Memphis, Memphis Acad. Arts. Ind. sulptor, artist, archtl. restorer, art instr. Memphis, 1955—. Sculptures represented in permanent collections including: Overbrook Acad., Nashville, St. Jude Hosp., Memphis, St. Mary's Cathedral, Memphis, numerous pvt. collections; contbr. articles to numerous publs.; contbr. art, WKNO-TV, Memphis, Memphis Brooks Mus. Showcase. Mem. Brooks Art League. Episcopalian. Home and Studio: 1261 W Perkins Rd Memphis TN 38117-6120

GRAVATT, CHRIS-TINA MILLEN, heirloom miniature quilt maker; b. Trenton, N.J., Jan. 22, 1947; d. Edward George and Frances Claire (Ferber) Millen; divorced; children: Lisa Adele Gravatt McBryde, Carrie Anne Gravatt. Grad. high sch., Trenton, N.J., 1965. Seamstress Morrisville, Pa., 1968-75; quilt artist Morrisville, Phila., 1979-84; antique quilt restorer, conservationist Phila., 1980-90, maker heirloom miniature quilts, 1985—. Author: Heirloom Miniatures, 1990, Old Favorites in Miniature, 1993; exhibited in group shows at Mus. of Am. Folk Art, N.Y.C., 1991, Dollywood, Pigeon Forge, Tenn., 1991, Am. Quilt Soc. Mus., Paducah, Ky., 1991, Decatur Ho., Washington, 1991, Mus. of Am. Quilts and Textiles, San Jose, Calif., 1990-91, Handwerken Zonder Gretzen Needlework Fair, The Netherlands, 1990, The Golden Lion, Antwerp, Belgium, 1988, Houston Quilt Festival, Houston, 1987, Paisley (Scotland) Mus. and Art Galleries, 1986. Pres. Wild Geese Quilters, Phila., 1983-86, founder, 1981; co-pres. Head Ho. Craftsmen's Assn., Phila., 1984-86. Recipient over 50 awards, ribbons and prizes various quilt shows and contests, N.Y., Conn., Pa., Md., N.C., 1976—. Mem. Nat. Quilter's Assn., Am. Quilter's Soc., Am. Quilt Study Group, British Quilter's Guild, Heartstring Quilters. Home: 1308 E Columbia Ave Philadelphia PA 19125-3213

GRAVEL, TINA MARIE, sales executive; b. Springfield, Mass., July 22, 1960; d. Richard Armand Gravel and Dorothy Mary (Duggan) Messenger. BA, U. Mass., 1983. With tech. sales Mobil Chem. Co., Pittsford, N.Y., 1982-83; account mgr. McDonnell Douglas, St. Louis, 1983-88, acting mktg. dir., 1988-89; v.p. sales I.S. Internat., Dallas, 1989-90; exec. v.p. R & D Hamilton Taft, Dallas, 1990-91; exec. v.p. strategic planning and mktg. Agy. Mgmt. Svcs., Norwell, Mass., 1991-93; sr. account exec. Continuum, Austin, Tex., 1993—; account mgr. Sybase. Bd. dirs. Tex. chpt. Nat. Kidney

Found. Mem. Sales and Mktg. Execs. of Dallas, Southwest Ins. Assn., Dallas Safari Club. Republican.

GRAVELY, JANE CANDACE, computer company executive; b. Rocky Mount, N.C., Dec. 1, 1952; d. Edmund Keen and Janice Eleanor (Beavon) G.; m. Barney Ben Linthicum, July 13, 1985 (div. 1991). BS, N.C. Wesleyan Coll., 1974; MEd, Coll. William and Mary, 1980. Circulation and promotion mgr. Va. Gazette, Williamsburg, 1975-80; computer analyst, chief exec. officer Affordable Computer Systems, Rocky Mount, 1982-85, Goldsboro, N.C., 1985-95; instr. bus., math., computers Nash Tech. Coll., Rocky Mount, 1980-83; instr. math., computers N.C. Wesleyan Coll., Rocky Mount, 1983-85, instr. computers, 1985-89. Mem. NAFE, United Meth. Womens Circle (pres. 1990-91), Goldsboro C. of C. (Chamber Amb. Com. of 100, sec. 1994), Kiwanis, Goldsboro Club (2d v.p. 1994—), Omicron Delta Kappa. Republican.

GRAVES, BELLE L., accountant; b. Lincoln, Nebr., July 1, 1914; d. Fred T. and Hermina (Ruckert) G. BS in Bus., U. Nebr., 1937; MA, Columbia U., 1953. Cost acct. Woods Bros. Constrn. Co., Lincoln, 1937-40; comptroller Ben Simon & Sons, Lincoln, 1941-51; acctg. tchr. Lincoln Sch. Commerce, 1952-57; owner Graves Printing Co., 1958-69; acct. Nebr. Book Co., 1969-85; tax and fin. advisor Lincoln, 1985—. treas., mem. bd. dirs. Alzheimers Lincoln/Greater Nebr.; treas. generally yours Lincoln Gen. Hosp. Auxiliary Gift Shop; curator Gladys Lux Historical Gallery, 1988—. Named Vol. of Yr. by United Way, 1991; recipient Friend of the Coll. of Human Resources and Family Scientist award, 1995. Mem. Nat. Soc. Pub. Accts., Nebr. Pub. Accts., C. of C. of Lincoln (v.p. women's div. 1938-39), Toastmasters, Lincoln Doll Club (pres. 1986-88), Does, Kappa Phi. Republican. Methodist. Address: 501 Mulder Dr Lincoln NE 68510

GRAVES, CAROL KENNEY, construction company executive; b. Boise, Idaho, May 3, 1937; d. Elmer Kenney and M. Elizabeth (Rogers) Kenney Stolquist; m. Philip L. Graves, Aug. 6, 1955; children: Steven P., Kenton L., Cynthia M. Owner Carols, Peoria, Ill., 1975-78; realtor Clifton-Strode E.R.A., Peoria, 1978-83; pres. Little Red Hen Outlets Inc., Peoria, 1983-87, Asbestos Enviro-Clean Inc., Bartonville, Ill., 1988-93; pres. Enviro-Care Ins., Inc., 1988-93, Twice Over Clean, Inc., 1993—. Rep. precinct committeeperson Peoria, 1983-88; funds dir. YWCA, Oconomowoc, Wis., 1965; active Girls Scouts U.S., 1963—, ILNAC; mem. Kickapoo Twp. Assn., bd. dirs., 1984-88. Mem. Downtown Bus. Assn. (bd. dirs., pres. 1987-90), Heart of Ill. Food Svc. Assn., Nat. Radon Assn., Midwest Asbestos Coun., Nat. Lead Abatement Coun., Nat. Asbestos Coun., Profl. Assn. for Abestos Control, Nat. Lead Assn., Steel Structures Painting Coun., Nat. Air Duct Cleaners Assn., Nat. Assn. Demolition Contractors. Roman Catholic. Home: 4121 N Koerner Rd Peoria IL 61615-9626 Office: Twice Over Clean Inc 4405 Enterprise Dr Bartonville IL 61607-2756

GRAVES, JOY DAN, psychologist, consultant; b. Collinsville, Tex., Nov. 24, 1929; d. Tom Pryor and Fetna Pauline (Williams) Jackson; m. Robert Dean Graves, Apr. 4, 1952 (div. 1977); children: Kathleen Diane, Jeffrey Dale. BSN, Calif. State U., L.A., 1968; MS, UCLA, 1970; postgrad., Calif. State U., Long Beach, 1974-77; PhD, Calif. Sch. Profl. Psychology, L.A., 1980. RN, Calif.; lic. psychologist, Calif. Staff nurse coord. Riverside (Calif.) Community Hosp., 1960-65; nurse-therapist Orange County Hosp., U. Calif., Irvine, 1965-72; instr. North Orange County C.C. Dist., Fullerton, Calif., 1970-77; psychology intern Airport Marine Counseling Ctr., L.A., 1977-78; psychology intern L.A. Police Dept., 1978-81, staff psychologist, 1981-83; psychologist Didi Hirsch Community Mental Health Ctr., Culver City, Calif., 1981-91; asst. prof. U. Calif., 1978-84; pvt. practice, L.A. and Oceanside, Calif., 1982—; teaching asst. Calif. Sch. Profl. Psychology, 1978; pvt. practice clin. nurse specialist, 1970-82; mem. panel cons. div. disability evaluations Calif. Dept. Social Svcs., 1986—; mem. panel experts Superior Ct. County Los Angeles, 1982-93, Superior Ct. County San Diego, 1992—; lectr. U. Calif. Ext., 1978-84; mem. SCAN Team, multidisciplinary child abuse team; presenter in field, 1971—. Author: (with Joseph and Margaret Franks) Mathematical Concepts in Pharmacology: A Skills Workbook for the Health Scis., 1973, 5th edit., 1992; Early Intervention in Child Abuse: The Role of the Police Officers, 1983; contbg. author: Human Development, 1974, 79, Therapeutic Use of Self, 1989. Instr. first aid ARC; active Girl Scouts U.S.A., Boy Scouts Am., PTA. Grantee NIMH; nat. scholar P.E.O. Mem. APA, San Diego Psychol. Assn., Phi Kappa Phi. Democrat. Jewish. Home and Office: 3517 Roselle St Oceanside CA 92056-3825

GRAVES, KATHRYN LOUISE, dermatologist; b. Kansas City, Kans., Mar. 9, 1949; d. Jack Clair and Ruth Marjory (Prentice) Schroll; m. Jeffery Jackson Graves, Mar. 31, 1973; children: Jeffery Justin, Jonathon Tyler, Kathryn Camille. BA, U. Kans., 1971; MD, U. Kans., Kansas City, 1974. Diplomate Am. Bd. Dermatology. Intern St. Lukes Hosp., Kansas City, 1975-76, resident in internal medicine, 1976; resident dermatology Sch. Medicine U. Kans., Kansas City, 1976-79; dermatologist Hutchinson (Kans.) Clinic P.A., 1979—; mem. med. staff Hutchinson Hosp., 1979—. Fellow Am. Acad. Dermatology; mem. AMA, Kans. Dermatology Soc., Kans. Med. Assn., Reno County Med. Assn., Hutchinson C. of C., Gamma Phi Beta (standards chair 1973—). Republican. Methodist. Home: 211 Countryside Dr Hutchinson KS 67502 Office: Hutchinson Clinic 2101 N Waldron St Hutchinson KS 67502

GRAVES, LORRAINE ELIZABETH, dancer, educator, coach; b. Norfolk, Va., Oct. 5, 1957; d. Thomas Edward and Mildred Fayette (Odom) G. BS, Ind. U., 1978. Dancer, Regisseuse Dance Theatre of Harlem, N.Y.C., 1978—, ballet mistress, 1980—, prin. dancer, 1982—; guest tchr. N.C. Sch. of Arts, Winston-Salem, 1987, 93, Gov.'s Sch. for Arts, U. Richmond, 1990-94, Carlton Johnson Acad. of Dance, 1991-93, Okla. Summer Arts Inst., 1993-94, The Flint Sch. Performing Arts, Dance Theatre of Harlem, Kennedy Ctr. Residency Program, 1993-94; resident guest tchr. Gov.'s Magnet Sch. for Arts, Norfolk, Va., 1988-91. Appeared with Dance Theatre of Harlem as Princess of Unreal Beauty in live TV prodn. of Firebird, 1982, as Myrta, Queen of the Willis in NBC prodn. of Creole Giselle, 1987; performed at White House, 1981, also at the closing ceremonies of the 1984 Olympics, 1984, toured with Dance Theatre of Harlem, USSR, 1988, South Africa, 1992; guest artist Young People's Concert series, N.Y. Philharm., 1988, Detroit Symphony, 1989, River City Ballet, Memphis, 1991, 92; regisseuse Dance Theater of Harlem, 1989. Fellow Am. Guild Mus. Artists. Episcopalian. Office: Dance Theatre of Harlem PO Box 358 New York NY 10039-0358*

GRAVES, MAUREEN ANN, counselor; b. Sioux City, Iowa, July 10, 1946; d. Jack Milford and Elizabeth Mildred (St. George) Dryden; m. Thomas Darrel Graves, Oct. 9, 1965; children: Michael James, Lorrie Michelle. Grad., Gestalt Inst. Iowa, 1980. Cert. drug and alcohol counselor, Nebr.; cert. profl. asst., U. S.D.; cert. hypnotherapist. Counselor Siouxland Coun. on Alcoholism and Drug Abuse, Sioux City, 1979-81; counselor, co-founder New Hope Alcohol and Addiction Ctr., South Sioux City, Nebr., 1981—; cons. St. Luke Hosp. Addiction Ctr., Sioux City, 1987—; trainer Va. Satir-Internat. Tng. Inst., Crested Butte, Colo., 1988-89. Vol. co-facilitator Siouxland Coun. on Alcoholism and Drug Abuse, Sioux City, 1976-79; mem. exec. team couple World Wide Marriage Encounter, N.E. Nebr., 1979-82; trainer Va. Satir-Internat. Tng. Inst., Crested Butte, Colo., 1992; co-leader Satir Family Camp, San Jose, 1992, 93, 94; mem. Avanta Governing Coun., 1994-95. Mem. Avanta Network, Am. Mental Health Counselors Assn., Moscow Inst. for Profl. Devel. of Psychologists and Social Workers (founding), AACD. Roman Catholic. Home: 424 W 16th St South Sioux City NE 68776-2233 Office: New Hope Alcoholism & Addiction Ctr Inc PO Box 35 South Sioux City NE 68776-0035

GRAVES, NANCY STEVENSON, artist; b. Pittsfield, Mass.. BA, Vassar Coll., 1961; BFA, Yale U., 1961, MFA, 1964; PhD (hon.), Skidmore Coll., 1989; DFA, U. Md., 1992, Yale U., 1992. Numerous one-woman shows, including Whitney Mus. Am. Art, N.Y.C., 1969, Nat. Gallery Can., Ottawa, 1971, Neue Galerie der Stadt Aachen, Ger., 1971, Mus. Modern Art, N.Y.C., 1971, Inst. Contemporary Art, U. Pa., Phila., 1972, La Jolla (Calif.) Mus. Art, 1973, Art Mus. South Tex., Corpus Christi, 1973, André Emmerich Gallery, Inc., N.Y.C., 1974, 77, Janie C. Lee Gallery, Houston, 1977, 78, 83, 84, M. Knoedler & Co., 1979—, Richard Gray Gallery, Chgo., 1981, 86, Gloria Luria Gallery, Bar Harbor Islands, 1983, Greenburg Gallery, St. Louis, 1985, Heland Wetterling Gallery, Stockholm, 1988, 90, Gallery Mukai, Tokyo, 1988, Knoedler Kasmin, London, 1989, Linda Cathcart Gallery, Santa Monica, Calif., 1989, Locks Gallery, Phila., 1991, Meredith Long & Co., Houston, 1991, Irving Galleries, Palm Beach, Calif., 1992, Saff Tech. Arts, N.Y.C., 1992; retrospective show travelled to Albright Knox Gallery, Buffalo, Akron (Ohio) Art Inst., Contemporary Arts Mus., Houston, 1980, Brooks Art Gallery, Memphis, Neuberger Mus., Purchase, N.Y., Des Moines Art Center, Walker Art Center, Mpls., 1981, Hirschorn Mus., Washington, 1987, Modern Mus. Ft. Worth, Santa Barbara Mus., 1987, Bklyn. Mus., 1988; numerous group shows include Whitney Mus. Am. Art, N.Y.C., 1970, 76, 92, Corcoran Gallery Art, Washington, 1971, 76, Parc Floral, Paris, 1971, Neue Gallery, Kassel, Germany, 1972, Serpentine Gallery, London, 1973, Project 74, Colonge, Germany, 1974, Berlin Nat. Gallerie, 1976, Vancouver (B.C.) Art Gallery, Tehran (Iran) Mus. Contemporary Art, 1978, Am. Acad., Rome, 1979, Hudson River Mus., 1979, Helen Foresmand Specer Mus. Art, Kans., 1981, Mus. Fine Arts, Boston, 1982, 87, The Berkshire Mus., 1982, 83, Contemporart Arts Mus., Houston, 1982, Mus. Modern Art, Vienna, Austria, 1983, L.A. County Mus., 1984, Santa Barbara (Calif.) Mus., 1984, Toledo (Ohio) Mus. Art, 1984, Neuberger Mus., 1984, Bklyn. Mus., 1984, 86, Ludwig Mus., Cologne, Nelson-Atkins Mus., 1987, Balt. Mus., 1990, Palace of Budapest, Hungary, 1990, Mus. Fine Arts, Boston, 1992, Bellevue (Wash.) Art Mus., 1993, Mus. Modern Art, N.Y.C., 1994; permanent collections, Mus. Modern Art, N.Y.C., Whitney Mus. Am. Art, N.Y.C., Ludwig Mus., Cologne, Nat. Gallery Can., Ottawa, Des Moines (Iowa) Art Center, La Jolla Mus. Contemporary Art, Art Mus. South Tex., Corpus Christi, Berkeley (Calif.) Mus. Art, Albright-Knox Art Gallery, Buffalo, N.Y., Chgo. Art Inst., Met. Mus. Art, N.Y.C., Hirschorn Mus., Nat. Gallery Art, Washington, Akron (Ohio) Art Mus, Allem Meml. Art Gallery, Oberlin, Ohio, Berkshire Mus. Pittsfield, Birmingham (Ala.) Mus. Art, Bklyn. Mus., Brooks Meml. Art Gallery, Memphis, Corcoran Gallery Art, Washington, Ft. Worth Art Mus., L.A. County Mus., Mus. Contemporary Art, Chgo., Mus. Fine Arts, Houston, Mus. Fine Arts, Dallas, Mus. Modern Art, Vienna, Nelson-Atkins Mus. Art, Kansas City, Neuberger Mus, Purchase, N.Y., Neue Galerie in Alten Kurhaus, Aachen, Pa. Acad. Fine Arts, Phila., St. Louis Art Mus., Solomon R. Guggenheim Mus, N.Y.C., Univ. Art Mus., Berkeley, Calif., Vassar Art Mus., Poughkeepsie, N.Y., Walker Art Ctr., Mpls., Weatherspoon Art Gallery, Greensboro, N.C. . Vassar Coll. fellow, 1971-72; Fulbright-Hayes grantee, 1965-66; Paris Biennale grantee, 1971; Nat. Endowment for Arts grantee, 1972-73; Creative Artist Pub. Service grantee, 1974-75; recipient Skowhegan medal for Drawing and Graphics, 1980, Disting. Artistic Achievement award Yale U. 1985, Disting. award Vassar Coll., 1986, Am. Art award Pa. Acad. Art, 1987. mem. Am. Acad. and Inst. of Arts and Letters. Office: care Knoedler Contemporary Art 19 E 70th St New York NY 10021-4974

GRAVES, TINA MARIE, secondary education educator; b. Portales, N.Mex., Oct. 7, 1960; d. Buck Dewayne and Joyce Marie (Stephenson) Gossett; m. Robert G. Graves, May 24, 1985; 1 child, Joe. AA, South Plains Coll., Levelland, Tex., 1982; BS, Lubbock (Tex.) Christian Coll., 1984. Work study program Lubbock Christian Coll., 1983-84; substitute tchr. Anton (Tex.) Ind. Sch. Dist., 1983-84; tchr. secondary math. Smyer (Tex.) Ind. Sch. Dist., 1984-94, Frenship (Tex.) Ind. Sch. Dist., 1994—; tchr. math Lubbock Ind. Sch. dist., summer 1990. Mem. Nat. Assn. Secondary Sch. Prins., Tex. South Plains Coun. Tchrs. Math., Tex. Assn. Student Couns. (dist. pres. 1991-92, state v.p. 1992-93). Republican. Mem. Ch. of Christ. Home: 6807 Hyden Ave Lubbock TX 79424-2927 Office: Frenship Ind Sch Dist PO Box 100 Wolfforth TX 79382

GRAVES, VASHTI SYLVIA, computer analyst, consultant; b. Detroit, Mar. 22, 1967; d. James Graves and Sandra Horne Mcleod Graves Lewis. Student computer programming, Cass Tech. Sch., Detroit, 1981-85; BS in Computer Info. Systems, DeVry Inst. Tech., Chgo., 1988. Gen. officer worker Lenzip Mfg. Co., Chgo., 1985-86; programmer Safer Found., Chgo., 1986-89; programmer, user systems analysts Am. Automotive Assn., Dearborn, Mich., 1989-94; project adminstr. Comerica, Auburn Hills, Mich., 1994—; cons. GSA Advt., Chgo., 1988; owner, cons. Maze Advisors, Detroit, 1993; patron Internat. Inst. Active Alliance Française of Mich., 1995. Home: 14922 DuRussel Sterling Heights MI 48313

GRAY, ANN MAYNARD, broadcasting company executive; b. Boston, Aug. 22, 1945; d. Paul Maynard and Pauline Elizabeth MacFadyen; m. Richard R. Gray, Jr.; children: Richard R. Gray III, Dana Maynard. B.A., U. Mich., 1967; M.B.A., NYU, 1971. With Chase Manhattan Bank, N.Y.C., 1967-68, Chem. Bank, N.Y.C., 1968-73; asst. sec. Chem. Bank, 1971-73; asst. to treas., then asst. treas. ABC, Inc., 1974-76, treas., 1976-81, v.p. planning, 1979-86; v.p. Capital Cities/ABC, Inc. (merged 1986), 1986—; sr. v.p. fin. ABC TV Network Group, 1988-91; pres. Diversified Pub. Group Capital Cities/ABC, Inc., 1991—; bd. dirs. Am. Bus. Press, Neuberger & Berman Fixed Income Funds, Cyprus AMAX Minerals Co., Panhandle Ea. Corp. Trustee Martha Graham Ctr. of Contemporary Dance, N.Y.C., 1989-92, Cancer Care, Inc., 1991—, mem. pub. affairs com., 1990-92. Office: Capital Cities/ABC Inc 77 W 66th St New York NY 10023-6201

GRAY, AUDREY NESBITT, elementary education educator; b. Kalamazoo, Mich., Feb. 5, 1920; d. Walter Hale and Hazel Violet (Wriglesworth) Nesbitt; m. Llewellyn Wallace Gray, Apr. 22, 1943; children: Susan Nesbitt Moffitt, Deborah Llewellyn Gray-Olker, Gretchen Clarke Shannon. BS, Western Mich. U., 1943. Cert. elem. edn. tchr., Mich. Tchr. Three Rivers (Mich.) Pub. Schs., 1943-45; tchr. music Schoolcraft (Mich.) Pub. Schs., 1945-46; tchr. Comstock (Mich.) Pub. Schs., 1963-83, ret., 1983; bd. dirs. Mich. In Action for Drug Free Youth; mem. cons. team Drug Edn. Curriculum Guide, 1971, adv. com. Gov. Conf. Drug Free Schs. and Communities, 1990, steering com. for Med., Ednl., Legal Law Enforcement, State Bar Mich., 1991—, Mich alliance Drug Free Schs. and Communities, 1990-91; innovator, dir., advisor cmty. story hour program Juvenile Detention Facilities, Mich., 1993. Member Forum for Kalamazoo County, 1986—, Greater Kalamazoo Consortium, 1990—; mem. steering com. Nat. Issues Forum, Kalamazoo, 1989—; bd. dirs. Kalamazoo Area Families in Action, 1986-87; mem. State Bar of Mich. Task Force on Substance Abuse, 1991—. Recipient Top Tchr. award Grade Tchr. Mag., 1967, First Tchr. Appreciation award Nat. Honor Soc. Comstock High Sch., 1990. Mem. AAUW, Am. Lawyers Aux. (chair drug awareness com. 1990—, coun. state affiliates 1989-90, 91—, 2d v.p., 1991, pres., 1993), Gov.'s Conf. on Drug Free Schs. and Communities (adv. mem.), Mich. Lawyers Aux. (pres. 1987-88, drug awareness chair, 1989, co-chair statewide No Drug Use rally 1989), Kalamazoo Lawyers Aux. (pres., 1970-71, 88-89),. Republican. Presbyterian. Home: 1442 Prospect Hill Kalamazoo MI 49006-4446

GRAY, BARBARA BRONSON, registered nurse, writer; b. Van Nuys, Calif., June 3, 1955; d. Gerald M. and Jane Marie (Strauss) Bronson; m. Thomas Stephen Gray, Aug. 27, 1977; children: Jonathan Thomas, Katherine Marie. BS, UCLA, 1977, M in Nursing, 1981. RN, Calif. Staff nurse Valley Presbyn. Hosp., Van Nuys, Calif., 1977-80; asst. adminstr. Calif. Med. Ctr., L.A., Calif., 1981-84; freelance writer Agoura, 1984—; cons. St. John's Hosp. and Health Ctr., Santa Monica, Calif., 1986-90, Los Robles Regional Med. Ctr., Thousand Oaks, Calif., 1993—; lectr. UCLA Sch. Nursing, 1991—. Author: 120 Years of Medicine in Los Angeles County, 1991; contbr. articles to jours., mags. and newspapers; syndicated by L.A. Times Syndicate. Recipient Outstanding Achievement award Perinatal Newtork, Santa Clara County, Calif., 1994; named Writer of Yr., Nurseweek, 1991; Kellogg fellow, 1979-81. Mem. Nat. Assn. Sci. Writers, Sigma Theta Tau (Cert. of Appreciation 1994). Republican. Episcopalian. Home: 4909 Cardinal Way Agoura CA 91301-4762

GRAY, DAHLI, accounting educator and administrator; b. Grand Junction, Colo., Dec. 28, 1948; d. Forrest Walter and Mary (Crockett) G.; 1 child, Kimberly. BS, Ea. Oreg. State U., 1971; MBA, Portland (Oreg.) State U., 1976; D of Bus. Adminstrn., George Washington U., 1984. Instr. acctg. Portland State U., 1976-79, George Mason U., Fairfax, Va., 1980, George Washington U., Washington, 1981-82; asst. prof. Oreg. State U., Corvallis, 1983-86; research fellow U. Notre Dame, South Bend, Ind., 1986-88; assoc. prof. Am. U., Washington, 1988-90; chairperson, Walpert, Smullian & Blumenthal prof. Towson (Md.) State U., 1990-92; chairperson Morgan State U., Balt., 1992—. Contbr. articles to profl. jours. Named Tchr. of Yr., Alpha Lambda Delta, 1986; Peat Marwick Mitchell & Co. fellow, 1986-88. Mem. Internat. Assn. Acctg. Research and Edn., Am. Inst. CPA's, Nat. Assn. Accts. (Andrew Barr award 1982, 84, Cert. Merit 1982), Am. Acctg. Assn., Inst. Cert. Mgmt. Accts. Democrat. Home: 131 Versailles Cir Apt E Baltimore MD 21204-6926 Office: Morgan State U Sch Bus and Mgmt Acctg and Fin Dept Baltimore MD 21239

GRAY, DARLENE AGNES, nurse; b. Prince Frederick, Md., June 10, 1957; d. Reynold Jerome Gray and Ellen (Madaglene) Cooke. AA, Charles County Community Coll., 1988; student, U. Md., Balt., 1982. RN; cert. med. asst. Secretarial aide U. Md. Ea. Shore, Princess Anne, Md., 1979-82; med. surg. technician Calvert Meml. Hosp., Prince Frederick, Md., 1982—; nurse Homecall, Prince George, Md., 1985—. Mem. NAACP, Alpha Kappa Alpha, Alpha Beta Kappa.

GRAY, DAWN PLAMBECK, public relations/newletter publishing executive; b. Chgo., Aug. 23, 1957; d. Raymond August and Eunice Eve (Fox) Plambeck; m. Richard Scott Gray, Apr. 13, 1985; children: Zachary, Rae. BS, Northwestern U., 1979. Desk asst. Sta. WCFL, Chgo., 1979-80; writer UPI Internat., Chgo., 1980; asignment editor Cable News Network, Chgo., 1980-81; account exec. Aaron Cushman and Assoc., Chgo., 1981-83; account exec. Ruder Finn & Rotman, Chgo., 1983-84, account supr., 1984-86, dir. consumer group, 1986-87; dir. pub. rels. Tassani Communications, Chgo., 1987-90; v.p. Marcy Monyek & Assoc., Chgo., 1990; pres. Moments Inc., Chgo., 1991—. Mem. Ravinia Festival Assocs. Bd., Chgo., 1989—. Mem. Internat. Assn. Bus. Communicators (ednl. rels. com. 1987-88, seminar chairperson 1988—, pres. 1990-91, Silver Quill award 1987, 88). Office: Moments Inc 6 N Michigan Ste 1514 Chicago IL 60602

GRAY, DEBORAH DOLIA, business writing consultant; b. Elmo, Mo., Jan. 25, 1952; d. Gerald Lee and Rosalie (Thompson) G. BS in Music and Journalism cum laude, U. Nebr., 1976; MFA, Columbia U., 1988. Reporter The Lincoln (Nebr.) Star, 1975-78; spl. writer, feature projects The Fort Lauderdale (Fla.) News, 1978-79; reporter Miami (Fla.) News, 1979-80; curriculum specialist John Jay Coll. Criminal Justice, N.Y.C., 1980-84; tng. specialist Mgmt. Devel. Systems Inc., N.Y.C., 1985—; writing cons. various non-profit agys. and corps. Contbr. articles to profl. jours. Hollingsworth fellow Columbia U., 1985. Home: 200 W 93d St Apt 3-I New York NY 10024

GRAY, DEBORAH MARY, medical corporation executive; b. Sydney, N.S.W., Australia, Feb. 4, 1952; came to U.S., 1973; d. Anthony Eric and Mary Patricia (O'Mullane) Gray; m. Theodore Ralph Culbertson, July 31, 1971 (div. 1979); m. Scott Cameron Struthers, Jan. 31, 1981 (div. 1988). Student St. Petersburg Jr. Coll., 1978-85, Eckerd Coll., 1988-90. Fin. counselor Wuesthoff Meml. Hosp., Rockledge, Fla., 1973-75; adminstrv. dir. Dresden & Ticktin, MDs, P.A., St. Petersburg, Fla., 1976-80; exec. dir., v.p. Am. Med. Mgmt., Inc., Clearwater, Fla., 1980-90; pres., dir. All Women's Health Ctr., Inc., St. Petersburg, 1980-90, All Women's Health Ctr. North Tampa, Inc., Fla., 1980-90, All Women's Health Ctr. Tampa, Inc., 1980-90, Women's Ob-Gyn. Ctr. Countryside, Inc., 1984-90, All Women's Health Ctr. Sarasota, Fla., 1980-90, All Women's Health Ctr. Ocala, Fla., 1980-90, All Women's Health Ctr. Gainesville, Fla., 1981-90, Lakeland Women's Health Ctr., Fla., 1980-90, Ft. Myers Womens Health Ctr., Fla., 1980-90, All Women's Health Ctr. Jacksonville, Fla., 1980-90, Nat. Women's Health Svcs., Inc., Clearwater, Fla., 1983-90, D.M.S. of Ft. Myers, Inc., 1985-90, Alternative Human Svc., 1979; treas., v.p., dir. Birthing Mgmt. Inc., 1985-90; healthcare cons., 1990-92; N.Am. mgr. Cowra Wines, Australia, 1991—; owner, sole proprietor The Australian Wine Connection, Atlanta, 1992—; dir. Perinatal Ct. Ga. Bapt. Med. Ctr., 1990-92. Mem. bd. agy. that facilitates hard to place children adoptions One Ch. One Child, 1990-94.

GRAY, DIANE, dancer, choreographer; b. Painesville, Ohio, May 29, 1941; d. Gordon Dallas and Bettie (Kerr) G.; m. James William Viera, May 15, 1971; 1 child, James William II. BS, Juilliard Sch., 1963; MS in Edn., Hunter Coll., 1987. Chorus dancer Martha Graham Dance Co., N.Y.C., 1963-69, soloist, 1969-71, prin. dancer, 1972-79, assoc. artistic dir., 1993—; artist-in-residence various Univs., worldwide, 1965—; tchr. Martha Graham Sch., N.Y.C., 1963—; also dir. Martha Graham Sch., 1983—; dir. Dances by Diane Gray, N.Y.C., 1979-83. Mem. Kappa Delta Pi. Office: Martha Graham Sch 316 E 63rd St New York NY 10021-7702

GRAY, DOROTHY LOUISE ALLMAN POLLET, librarian; b. Billings, Mont., Dec. 17, 1945; d. Lee F. and Ruth H. (Behner) Allman; m. Michael Haslam Gray, Aug. 11, 1980; children: M. Alexander, Timothy Haslam. BA, U. Colo., 1969; MSLS, Syracuse U., 1972. Reference libr., bibliographer Libr. of Congress Div. Blind and Physically Handicapped, Washington, 1972-75; reference specialist Libr. of Congress Gen. Reference and Bibliography Div., Washington, 1975-77; ednl. liaison officer nat. programs Libr. of Congress, Washington, 1977-82; rsch. assoc. Nat. Commn. on Librs. and Info. Sci., Washington, 1982-88; info. ctr. mgr. Nat. Assn. Inveterate and Obdurate Politicos, Arlington, Va., 1988-92; info. svcs. libr. Nat. Sch. Bds. Assn., Alexandria, Va., 1992—. Editor: Sign Systems for Libraries, 1979; editor Leads, the newsletter of Internat. Rels. Roundtable, ALA, 1979-82. Recipient Superior Svc. award Libr. of Congress, Washington, 1981. Mem. ALA, CEC, Spl. Librs. Assn. Office: Nat Sch Bds Assn 1680 Duke St Alexandria VA 22314-3493

GRAY, EDNA JANE, elementary education educator; b. Stratford, Okla., July 29, 1941; d. Cooper and Margerine (Ragland) Coles; m. Joe Carl Gray, Dec. 16, 1961; children: Carl, Scott, Marjana Gray Tharp. AS, Murray State Coll., 1961; BS, East Cen. Okla. State Coll., 1965, MEd, 1982. Cert. elem. tchr., reading specialist, jr. high sci. and social studies tchr., Okla. 4th-6th grade tchr. Connerville (Okla.) Sch., 1965-68; 2d grade tchr. Vanoss Sch., Ada, Okla., 1978-80, reading tchr., 1980—. Recipient Tchr. of Today award Masons, 1992-93. Mem. NEA, Okla. Edn. Assn., Okla. Reading Coun., Pototoc County Reading Coun., Vanoss Classroom Tchrs. Assn., Delta Kappa Gamma (rsch. com. 1991-92, auditing and fin. com. 1992—). Democrat. Mem. Pentecostal Holiness Ch. Home: Rt 5 Box 219 Ada OK 74820 Office: Vanoss Sch Rt 5 Box 119 Ada OK 74820

GRAY, GWEN CASH, real estate broker; b. Cowpens, S.C., Oct. 24, 1943; d. Woodrow C. and Marie (Hamrick) Cash; m. Charles H. Gray, Oct. 24, 1987 ; children: Dianne Marie Young, Teena Michele Bulman. BS, Limestone Coll., Gaffney, S.C., 1984. Broker-in-charge, prin. Miller & Gray Real Estate, Spartanburg, S.C.; bd. dirs. Nations Bank Gaffney; lectr. in field. Contbr. articles to profl. jours. Advisor S.C. Peach Festival, Gaffney, 1977—, Clemson U. Extension Svc., 1987—. Named Woman of Yr. Bus. and Profl. Women, 1979, Woman of Yr. S.C. Rural Electric Coop., 1984. Mem. Am. Farm Bur., Nat. Bd. Realtors, S.C. Farm Bur., S.C. Bd. Realtors, Spartanburg Bd. Realtors, S.C. Hort. Soc. (bd. dirs.), S.C. Assn. Agr. Agts. (Friend of Extension award 1986), Spartanburg Multiple Listing Svc. (bd. dirs.). Republican. Baptist.

GRAY, HANNA HOLBORN, history educator; b. Heidelberg, Germany, Oct. 25, 1930; d. Hajo and Annemarie (Bettmann) Holborn; m. Charles Montgomery Gray, June 19, 1954. AB, Bryn Mawr Coll., 1950; PhD, Harvard U., 1957; MA, Yale U., 1971, LLD, 1978; LittD (hon.), St. Lawrence U., 1974, Oxford (Eng.) U., 1979, Washington U., 1985; HHD (hon.), St. Mary's Coll., 1974; LHD (hon.), Grinnell (Iowa) Coll., 1974, Lawrence U., 1974, Denison U., 1974, Wheaton Coll., 1976, Marlboro Coll., 1979, Rikkyo (Japan) U., 1979, Roosevelt U., 1980, Knox Coll., 1980, Coe Coll., 1981, Thomas Jefferson U., 1981, Duke U., 1982, New Sch. for Social Research, 1982, Clark U., 1982, Brandeis U., 1983, Colgate U., 1983, Wayne State U., 1984, Miami U., Oxford, Ohio, 1984, So. Meth. U., 1984, CUNY, 1985, U. Denver, 1985, Am. Coll. Greece, 1986, Muskingum Coll., 1987, Rush Presbyn. St. Lukes Med. Ctr., 1987, NYU, 1988, Rosemont Coll., 1988, Claremont U. Ctr. Grad Sch., 1989, Moravian Coll., 1991, Rensselaer Poly. Inst., 1991, Coll. William and Mary, 1991, Centre Coll., 1991, Macalester Coll., 1993, McGill U., 1993, Ind. U., 1994, Med. U. of S.C., 1994; LLD (hon.), Union Coll., 1975, Regis Coll., 1976, Dartmouth Coll., 1978, Trinity Coll., 1978, U. Bridgeport, 1978, Dickinson Coll., 1979, Brown U., 1979, Wittenburg U., 1979, U. Rochester, 1980, U. Notre Dame, 1980, U. So. Calif., 1980, U. Mich., 1981, Princeton U., 1982, Georgetown U., 1983, Marquette U., 1984, W.Va. Wesleyan U., 1985, Hamilton Coll., 1985, Smith Coll., 1986, U. Miami, 1986, Columbia U., 1987, U. Toronto, Can., 1991; LDH, U. Del., 1994. Instr. Bryn Mawr Coll., 1953-54; teaching fellow Harvard, 1955-57, instr., 1957-59, asst. prof., 1959-60, vis. lectr., 1963-64; asst. prof. U. Chgo., 1961-64, asso. prof., 1964-72; dean, prof. Northwestern

U., Evanston, Ill., 1972-74; provost, prof. history Yale U., 1974-78, acting pres., 1977-78; pres. U. Chgo., Ill., 1978-93; prof. dept. history U. Chgo., 1978—, Harry Pratt Judson Disting. Svc. prof. history, 1993—; bd. dirs. Cummins Engine Co., J.P. Morgan & Co., Morgan Guaranty Trust Co., Atlantic Richfield Co., Ameritech; fellow Center for Advanced Study in Behavioral Scis., 1966-67, vis. scholar, 1970-71; vis. prof. U. Calif., Berkeley, 1970-71. Editor: (with Charles Gray) Jour. Modern History, 1965-70; contbr. articles to profl. jours. Mem. Nat. Coun. on Humanities, 1972-78; trustee Yale Corp., 1971-74; bd. dirs. Andrew W. Mellon Found.; trustee Bryn Mawr Coll., Howard Hughes Med. Inst., Marlboro Sch. Music; bd. regents The Smithsonian Instn. Decorated Grosse Verdienstkreuz (Germany); fellow Newberry Libr., 1960-61, hon. fellow St. Anne's Coll., Oxford (Eng.) U., 1978—; Fulbright scholar, 1950-51; recipient Grad. medal Radcliffe Coll., 1976, Yale medal, 1978, Medal of Liberty award, 1986, Medal of Freedom, 1991, Frontrunner award Sara Lee, 1991, Laureate Lincoln Acad. Ill., 1988, Jefferson medal Am. Philos. Soc., 1993, Charles Frankel prize, 1993, Centennial medal Harvard U., 1994. Fellow Am. Acad. Arts and Scis.; mem. Renaissance Soc. Am., Am. Philos. Soc., Nat. Acad. Edn., Phi Beta Kappa (vis. scholar 1971-72). Office: U Chgo Dept History 1126 E 59th St Chicago IL 60637-1580

GRAY, KARLA MARIE, state supreme court justice. BA, Western Mich. U., MA in African History; JD, U. Calif., San Francisco, 1976. Bar: Mont. 1976, Calif. 1977. Law clk. to Hon. W. D. Murray U.S. Dist. Ct., 1976-77; staff atty. Atlantic Richfield Co., 1977-81; pvt. practice law Butte, Mont., 1981-84; staff atty., legis. lobbyist Mont. Power Co., Butte, 1984-91; judge Supreme Ct. Mont., Helena, 1991—. Mem. Mont. Supreme Ct. Gender Fairness Task Force. Fellow Am. Bar Found., Am. Judicature Soc., Supreme Ct. Hist. Soc.; mem. State Bar Mont., Silver Bow County Bar Assn. (past pres.), Nat. Assn. Women Judges. Office: Supreme Ct Mont Justice Bldg Rm 323 215 N Sanders St Helena MT 59601-4522

GRAY, KATHERINE, marriage and family counselor and support therapist; b. Los Angeles, July 6, 1941; d. Edward David and Marjorie (Graves) Ross; m. Daniel C. Gray, Feb. 5, 1965; children: Michael, Lisa. BA, Calif. State U., Sacramento, 1983, MS in Ednl. Cons. and Counseling, 1987, MS in Sch. Counseling. Instr. Shasta Coll., Redding, Calif., 1965-69; owner Water Ojai Valley Chapel, Ojai, Calif., 1971-77, Lipp & Sullivan, Marysville, Calif., 1977—; instr. Yuba Coll., 1988—; pres. Interagy. Council, 1988—; cons. and organizer various community outreach programs in edn. Contbr. articles to profl. jours. and newspapers. County coordinator, bd. dirs. Am. Cancer Soc., Marysville, 1980—; mem. exec. com., bd. dirs., com. chairperson Gateway Projects, Yuba City, Calif., 1980—; bd. dirs. Mercy Guild, Yuba City, 1980—, Easter Seals; past bd. dirs., com. chairperson Campfire Inc., Yuba City and Morro Bay, Calif., 1979-80; past pres. Ojai Valley-Oxnard Symphony Orch. Assn., Ventura County, Calif., 1975; Sacramento focus program coordinator 4-H, Yuba and Sutter Counties, 1985—; exec. officer, bd. dirs. Gateway Projects, 1985-87; pres. Interagy. Council of Yuba & Sutter Counties, 1988—. Mem. Calif. Funeral Dirs. Assn. (mem. legis. bd. com., edn., ethics and mem. bd. com.), Calif. Assn. for Counseling and Devel., Sacramento Area Gifted Assn., Children's Home Soc. (chpt. bd. sec.). Lodges: Soroptimists (past bd. dirs.), Rainbow for Girls (pres., bd. dirs. 1985-87). Avocations: music, art, travel, historical studies. Home: PO Box 611 Yuba City CA 95992-0611 Office: PO Box 148 629 D St Marysville CA 95901-5527

GRAY, KATHERINE WILSON, newspaper editor; b. Sumter, S.C., Aug. 23, 1940; d. Thomas III and Suzanne Barden (Winstead) Wilson; m. Kermit S. King (div. 1980); children: Suzanne E., John D.; m. Robert Faulkner Gray II, July 17, 1990. AB in Journalism cum laude, U. N.C., 1961. Reporter Charlotte (N.C.) Observer, 1961-62; advt. and news copywriter Sta. WWOK, Charlotte, 1962-63; advt. copywriter Belk, Charlotte, 1963-64; asst. dir. pub. rels. Winthrop Coll., Rock Hill, S.C., 1964-67; exec. women's editor The State and Columbia (S.C.) Record, 1968-69, reporter, 1979-84; assoc. editorial page editor Columbia Record, 1984-87, editorial page editor, 1987-88; assoc. editorial page editor The State, Columbia, 1988—. Bd. dirs. Greater Columbia Fighting Back Task Force against Alcohol and Drug Abuse, Columbia Commn. Children and Youth. Recipient Blue Cross-Blue Shield award, Media Person of Yr. award Animal Protection League, 1989; Tribute to Women in Industry honoree YWCA Midlands, 1991. Mem. Nat. Fedn. Press Women (award), Nat. Conf. Editorial Writers, Media Women S.C. (award, Media Woman of Yr. 1987), S.C. Press Assn. (award), Columbia Media Club, Summit Club, Phi Beta Kappa, Kappa Tau Alpha. Office: The State Record Co Inc PO Box 1333 Columbia SC 29202-1333

GRAY, LINDA, actress; b. Santa Monica, Calif., Sept. 12, 1940; m. Ed Thrasher (div. 1983); children: Jeff, Kelly. Studied with Charles Conrad. Appeared in: (TV series) All That Glitters, 1977, Dallas, 1978-91, Models, Inc., 1994—, (films) The Big Ripoff, 1975, Murder in Peyton Place, 1977, The Grass is Always Greener Over the Septic Tank, 1978, Two Worlds of Jennie Logan, 1979, Haywire, 1980, The Wild and the Free, 1980, Not in Front of the Children, 1982, The Entertainers, 1992, Highway Heartbreaker, Bonanza- The Return, 1993; other TV appearances include Marcus Welby, M.D., (host CBS Documentary) The Body Human: The Loving Process, 1981, Lovejoy, 1991, (co-host) Golden Globe awards, 1991; films include Under the Yum Yum Tree, 1963, Palm Springs Weekend, 1963, Dogs, Fun with Dick and Jane, 1977, Oscar, 1991. Emmy nominee for Dallas, 1981; recipient Bambi award for best actress Germany, 1982; Il Gato award for best actress Italy, 1983, 84; named Woman of Yr., Hollywood Radio and TV Soc., 1982. Office: care DePasse/Browning 5750 Wilshire Blvd Ste 640 Los Angeles CA 90036*

GRAY, MARGARET ANN, management educator, consultant; b. Junction City, Kans., Sept. 19, 1950; d. Carl Ray and Mayme Louise (Kopmeyer) G.; m. Dennis Wayne Stokes, June 9, 1973 (div. July 1981); m. Robert Frederick Carlson Jr., Nov. 21, 1987. BEd, Pittsburg State U., Kans., 1972; MBA, Wichita State U., 1981. Tchr., Sch. Dist. 1, Kansas City, Mo., 1972-73; tchr. Haysville Sch. Dist., Kans., 1974-81, dist. coord., 1979-81; instr. mgmt. Wichita State U., 1981-85; mgmt. devel. rep. Beech Aircraft Corp. a Raytheon Co., Wichita, 1985-87, mgr. mgmt. devel. and tng., 1988-91; tng. and devel. coord. MIT, Cambridge, 1991—; cons. Dartnell Inst., Chgo., 1983—; assoc. dir. Ctr. for Entrepreneurship, Wichita State U., 1984-85. Bd. dirs. Kans. Found. for partnerships in Edn., 1986—; mem. speaker's bur. United Way, 1986—, vol. tng. dir., 1987—, tng. com., 1987—, top leadership cabinet, 1989; bd. dirs. Kans. Literacy Group, 1989, Sedgwick County div. Am. Heart Assn., 1990; active Leadership 2000. Named Outstanding Young Alumnus Pitts. State U., 1991. Mem. ASTD (bd. dirs. Sunflower chpt.), Wichita C. of C. (bus. edn. success team 1988—), Rotary, Beta Gamma Sigma. Democrat. Roman Catholic. Club: Turnip (Wichita). Avocations: ballet, cross country skiing, classical music, hot air ballooning.

GRAY, NANCY ANN OLIVER, college administrator; b. Dallas, Apr. 23, 1951; d. Howard Ross and Joan (Dawkins) Oliver; m. Doyle P. Gray, Nov. 24, 1973 (div. Jan. 1985); children: Paul, Jeff, Scott; m. David Nelson Maxson, Oct. 5, 1985. BA, Vanderbilt U., 1973; MEd, North Tex. State U., 1975; postgrad., Vanderbilt U., 1976-79. Cert. fund raising exec. Tchr. Highland Park High Sch., Dallas, 1973-75; chmn. drama dept. Harpeth Hall Sch., Nashville, 1975-77; assoc. dir. devel. Vanderbilt U., Nashville, 1977-78, assist. dean students, 1978-80; dir. spl. gifts U. Louisville, 1982-86; dir. major gifts Oberlin (Ohio) Coll., 1986-90; dir. capital programs The Lawrenceville (N.J.) Sch., 1990-91; v.p. devel. and univ. rels. Rider U., Lawrenceville, 1991—; bd. dirs. Jr. Achievement Ctrl. N.J.; cons. United Way, Cleve., 1988-90, Oberlin Coll., 1990, Princeton Project '55, 1992—; guest lectr. Vanderbilt U., Nashville, 1987-88. Trustee Oberlin Libr. Bd. Trustees, 1989, Oberlin Sch. Endowment Bd., 1988-90, Oberlin Early Childhood Ctr., 1986-88, Vanderbilt U., Nashville, 1973-77; bd. dirs. Vanderbilt U. Alumni Assn., Nashville, 1984-85; mem. Jr. League, 1984-89, various coms. Named Outstanding Young Woman of Am., 1982, Outstanding Woman Achievement, Lorain County (Ohio) YWCA, 1988. Mem. Nat. Soc. Fund-Raising Execs. (pres. Louisville chpt. 1985-86), Coun. for Advancement Support to Edn. (conf. presenter). Home: 32 Laurel Wood Dr Trenton NJ 08648-1000 Office: Rider U Trenton NJ 08648-0125

GRAY, PHYLLIS ANNE, librarian; b. Boston, Jan. 2, 1926; d. George Joseph and Eleanor (Morrison) G. Ph.B., Barry Coll., 1947, M.B.A., 1979; MS in Libr. Sci., Cath. U. Am., 1950. Librarian U.S. Air Force Base, Miami, Fla., 1952-53; asst. librarian Brockway Meml. Library, Miami Shores, Fla., 1953-55; head librarian North Miami Pub. Library, 1955-59; supervising librarian Santa Clara County Library, San Jose, Calif., 1959-61; library dir. City of Commerce (Calif.) Pub. Library, 1961-68; adminstrv. librarian Miami Dade Pub. Library, 1969-76; library dir. Miami Beach (Fla.) Pub. Library, 1978-86; dir. Surf-Bal Bay Pub. Library, Surfside, Fla., 1987-91. Councilwoman Bal Harbour Village, 1979-83; treas. Women in Govt. Service, 1981-86, pres., 1988-89. Mem. ALA, Am. Soc. Pub. Adminstrn., Fla. Library Assn., Barry U. Alumni Assn., Fla. Pub. Library Assn. Democrat. Roman Catholic. Club: Pilot (rec. sec. 1981-82, pres. 1982-83). Home: 54 Park Dr Apt 6 Bal Harbour FL 33154

GRAY, SHEILA HAFTER, psychiatrist, psychoanalyst; b. N.Y.C., Oct. 19, 1930; m. Oscar Shalom Gray, Apr. 8, 1967. MD, Harvard U., 1958. cert. Washington Psychoanalytic Inst., 1969. Intern St. Elizabeths Hosp., Washington, 1958-59; resident McLean Hosp., Belmont, Mass., 1959-61; clin. and rsch. fellow Mass. Gen. Hosp., Boston, Mass., 1961-62; staff psychiatrist Chestnut Lodge, Inc., Rockville, Md., 1962-64; practice medicine, specializing in psychiatry and psychoanalysis Washington, 1964—; clin. asst. prof. psychiatry U. Md. Sch. Medicine, Balt., 1968-75, clin. assoc. prof., 1975-83, clin. prof., 1983—; instr. Washington Psychoanalytic Inst., 1971-75, teaching analyst, 1975—; mem. staff U. Md. Hosp., Balt.; physician mem. Commn. on Mental Health, Superior Ct. of D.C., 1972—; bd. govs. Nat. Capital Reciprocal Ins. Co., 1981—; treas. NCRIC Physicians Orgn., 1994—; cons. Walter Reed Army Med. Ctr., Washington, 1983—. Mem. Mayor's Adv. Com. on Mental Health Svcs. Reorgn., Washington, 1984; mem. adv. panel for Mayor's Environ. Design Awards Program, 1988-89; mem. exec. com. D.C. Fedn. Civic Assns., 1984—, asst. rec. sec., 1985, rec. sec., 1986-88, 2d v.p., 1989-90, pres., 1991-92, del.-at-large, 1993—; v.p. programs Women's Equity Action League Met. D.C., 1986; commr. D.C. Adv. Neighborhood Commn., 1986-88; mem. Met. Washington Coun. of Govt.'s Partnership for Regional Excellence, 1992—. Fellow Am. Psychiat. Assn.; mem. Am. Psychoanalytic Assn. (diplomate Bd. Profl. Standards), Washington Psychiat. Soc. (councillor 1981-83), Med. Soc. D.C. (exec. bd. 1982, ho. dels. 1992—), Washington Psychoanalytic Soc. (chmn. bd. dirs. psychoanalytic clinic and councillor ex officio 1987-90), Palisades Citizens Assn. (bd. dirs. 1980—, treas. 1983-84, pres. 1984-86). Office: PO Box 40612 Palisades Sta Washington DC 20016

GRAY, SUSANNE M. HARTMAN, medical/surgical nurse; b. Plainfield, N.J., Dec. 11, 1948; d. Wallace Harry Hartman and Gwendolyn (Pridmore) Hartman Riebeling. ASN, Essex County Coll., 1981; BSN, Bloomfield Coll., 1989. Cert. med-surg. nurse. Charge nurse East Orange (N.J.) Nursing Home, 1977-81; edn. instr. ARC, East Orange; staff nurse United Hosp. Med. Ctr., Newark; per diem staff nurse Pathways unit East Orange (N.J.) Gen. Hosp. Mem. ANA, Nat. League Nursing, N.J. State Nurses Assn., Assn. Nurses in AIDS Care, Alpha Chi. Office: United Hosp Med Ctr 15 South 9th St Newark NJ 07107

GRAY, SYLVIA INEZ, pallet manufacturing executive; b. Newport, Tenn., Oct. 30, 1946; d. Samuel Mitchell and Zina (Harvey) Frazier; children from previous marriage: Regina Aileen Owens, William Cluade Owens; m. Buster Doyle Gray, Jan. 5, 1984; 1 child, Samantha Nicole. Student, Walter's State Community Coll., 1981. Founder, pres. Cocke County Pallet Co., Inc., Newport, Tenn., 1985—. Chmn. Cocke County Rep. Jud. Com. 4th Dist., Tenn., 1990. Mem. Newport-Cocke County C. of C., Cocke County Rep. Women's Club (pres. 1989, treas. 1991, 93). Republican. Baptist. Office: Cocke County Pallet Co Inc 291 Chilton Rd PO Box 952 Newport TN 37821-0952

GRAY-LITTLE, BERNADETTE, psychologist; b. Washington, N.C., Oct. 21, 1944; d. James and Rosalie (Lanier) Gray; m. Shade Keys Little, Nov. 21, 1971; children—Maura, Mark. Asst. prof. psychology, U. N.C.-Chapel Hill, 1971-76, assoc. prof., 1976-82, prof., 1982—, chair dept., 1993—. NIMH fellow, 1967-68; Fulbright fellow, 1970-71; NRC fellow, 1982-83. Fellow Am. Psychol. Assn.; mem. Phi Beta Kappa. Office: U NC Psychology Dept Cb # 3270 Chapel Hill NC 27599

GRAY-NIX, ELIZABETH WHITWELL, occupational therapist; b. Milton, Mass., Apr. 9, 1956; d. Roland and Susan (Brooks) Gray; m. Ronald Harding Nix; 1 child, Roger Harrison Nix. BS, Utica Coll. of Syracuse U., N.Y., 1978. Reg. occupational therapist. Staff occupational therapist Walter E. Fernald State Sch., Waltham, Mass., 1978-82; head occupational therapist Walter E. Fernald State Sch., 1982-84, clin. supr., 1984—. Trustee Mass. Jaycees Charitable Trust, Mansfield, 1983-91; dir.-at-large South End Hist. Soc., Boston, 1983-85, fundraising dir., 1985-87; alumni rep. Beaver Country Day Sch., Brookline, 1974—, alumni sec., 1988—. Recipient Baystater award #060, Mass. Jaycees, 1984, Armbruster Keyman award, 1981, Award of Merit, Maddak, Inc., 1991, Jaycee Internat. Senatorship award, 1992. Mem. Mass. Occupational Therapists Assn., State Employeed Occupational Therapists Assn. (union rep.), Am. Occupational Therapists Assn., Jaycees Internat. (Mass. sec., pres. Riverside chpt. 1983, mem. coun. Newton chpt. 1979-82, state sec. 1994-95), Boston Ctr. for the Arts (mem. coun. 1979-84). Home: 90 Pelham Island Rd Sudbury MA 01776-3132 Office: Walter E Fernald State Sch 200 Trapelo Rd Waltham MA 02154

GRAYSON, GRACE RIETHMULLER, teacher, consultant; b. Johannesburg, Transvaal, South Africa, Apr. 21, 1917; came to U.S., 1946; d. Frederick Edward Christian and Martha Johanna (Broodrijk) Riethmuller; m. Lincoln Blaisdell Grayson, Nov. 10, 1946; children: David Arthur, Guy. Student, Tchrs. Coll., 1934; cert. tchr., U. Calif., Berkeley, 1969; student, Diablo Valley Coll., Berkeley, 1978-83. Master judge emeritus flower shows and landscape design. Supr. revenue posting dept. NSW Tramways, Sydney, Australia, 1939-46; freelance writer Australia and U.S.A., 1945-57; columnist Cooma (Australia)-Monaro Express, 1953-57; corr. Australian Broadcasting Commn., Sydney, 1954-57; pvt. practice crafts instr. Pleasant Hill, Calif., 1962-64; class instr. floral design Woolworths, Walnut Creek, Calif., 1966-69; tchr. arts and crafts Mt. Diablo (Calif.) Unified Sch. Dist., 1965-73; ret., 1973; curator accessories Mus. Fashion, Lafayette, Calif., 1987—; cons. in field. Contbr. articles to profl. jours. Supporting mem. Berkeley Repertory Theatre, 1975—; fundraiser Alexander Mus. Natural History, Walnut Creek, 1981—. Mem. Fan Assn. N.Am. (pres. 1986-88, chmn. rsch. com. 1988—), Fan Circle Internat. (corr.), Assn. Culturale "Il Ventaglio", Bologna (Italy) (hon. mem.), East Bay Fan Guild, Walnut Creek Civic Arts Assn., Diablo Women's Garden Club. Democrat. Episcopalian. Home: 2133 Pine Knoll Dr Apt 16 Walnut Creek CA 94595-2187

GRAYSON, SUSAN CUBILLAS, environmental health administrator; b. Miami, Fla., Oct. 10, 1946; d. Antonio Francisco and Betty Virginia (Evans) Cubillas; m. William James Grayson, July 1970 (div. 1978); 1 child, Jessica Virginia . BS, U. Ga., 1968, postgrad., 1968-70; postgrad., U. Cen. Fla., 1984-86. Tchr. high schs. Pickens County, Easley, S.C., 1970-71; bacteriologist Jennings Labs., Virginia Beach, Va., 1972-73; sanitarian Mecklenburg County Dept. Environ. Health, Charlotte, N.C., 1973-76; environ. health supr. Stanly County Health Dept., Albermarle, N.C., 1976-79; septage study supr. N.C. Div. Health Svcs., Raleigh, 1979-82; food sanitarian Walt Disney World Co., 1982-84; head food, lodging and instl. sanitation br. N.C. Dept. of Environ., Heath and Natural Resources, Raleigh, 1986—. Regional newsletter editor U.S. Pony Clubs, Inc., 1990-93. Named one of Outstanding Young Women in Am., 1983. Mem. Internat. Assn. Milk, Food and Environ. Sanitarians, Nat. Environ. Health Assn. (mem. jour. rev. com. 1982), N.C. Pub. Health Assn. (mem. newsletter com. 1989-91, mem. ednl. com. 1990-91), Conf. Food Protection (mem. uniformity com. 1990), Triangle Hunt Club, Raleigh Triangle Pony Club (sec. 1990-91, newsletter editor 1990—, dist. commr. 1993—). Democrat. Roman Catholic. Office: Food Lodging Instl Sanitation PO Box 27687 Raleigh NC 27611-7687

GRAZIANI, LINDA ANN, secondary education educator; b. Erie, Pa., Aug. 16, 1951; d. Edward and Christine (Karsznia) Grzelak; m. Richard Martin Graziani, Aug. 4, 1973; 1 child, Kristen Lynn. BS, Pa. State U., 1973; MBA, Gannon U., 1978. Asst. twsp. sec. Lawrence Park Twsp., Erie, Pa., 1968-73; bus. edn. tchr. Millcreek Sch. Dist., Erie, 1973-74, Fairview (Pa.) Sch. Dist., 1974-76, 83—, Girard (Pa.) Sch. Dist., 1976; adult edn. instr. Erie (Pa.) County Tech. Sch., 1978-85; active Bus. Adv. Coun., Millcreek, Pa., 1994—. Bd. dirs. Lake Erie Jr. Women's Club, Erie, 1977-83, St. Stephen's Preschool, Fairview, 1982-83; eucharistic min. Holy Cross Ch., Fairview, 1982—. Mem. Nat. Bus. Edn. Assn., Pa. State Edn. Assn., Pa. Bus. Edn. Assn., Erie County Bus. Edn. Assn., Inst. Mgmt. Accts., Phi Chi Theta. Democrat. Roman Catholic. Home: 680 Hawthorne Trace Fairview PA 16415 Office: Fairview HS 7460 McCray Rd Fairview PA 16415

GRAZIANI, N. JANE, communications executive, publisher; b. Pensacola, Fla., Apr. 25, 1958; d. Hamlet and Dolly (Fields) G. BA, La. State U., 1980, M in Journalism, 1984. Asst. editor Daily Reveille, Baton Rouge, 1978-79; with Cath. Commentator, Baton Rouge, 1979-80; bur. chief Capitol News Svc., Baton Rouge, 1981-83; adminstrv. asst. Common Cause, Baton Rouge, 1983-84; reporter Sanford (Fla.) Evening Herald, 1985; assoc. editor Inst. Internal Auditors, Altamonte Springs, Fla., 1985-86; dir. publs. Fla. Soc. Assn. Execs., Winter Park, 1986-88; dir. communications Orange County Med. Soc., Orlando, Fla., 1988-91; pub. King Publs., Orlando, Fla., 1991-92; editor Assn. Source, Casselberry, Fla., 1992-93, Car & Travel/Fla., Heathrow, 1993—; writer med. related issues Charisma mag., Lake Mary, 1989—. Team capt. March of Dimes Walk Am., Orlando, 1989. Recipient Med. Journalism award Sandoz Pharms., 1989. Mem. Soc. Profl. Journalists, Fla. Mag. Assn. (program com. 1987-89, trade show com. 1990, 91, bd. dirs. 1990-94, treas. 1991, pres. elect 1992, pres. 1993, past pres. 1994, Bronze award for Gen. Excellence 1989, Bronze award for Best Spl. Issue 1990, Bronze award for Gen. Excellence, 1994, First Place for Best Regular Editorial 1994), Ctrl. Fla. Soc. Assn. Execs. (comms. com. 1988-91), Fla. Soc. Assn. Execs., South Atlantic Karate Assn. (1st Kyu 1985—), Internat. Shotokan Karate Fedn. Republican. Presbyterian. Office: Car & Travel 1000 AAA Dr Box 73 Heathrow FL 32746

GRAZIANO, CATHERINE ELIZABETH, nursing educator; b. Providence, Dec. 2, 1931; d. William J. and Catherine E. (Keegan) Hawkins; m. Louis W. Graziano, Oct. 9, 1954; children—Mary Lou, William F., Catherine E., Paul, Carol. B.S., Salve Regina Coll., Newport, R.I., 1949-53, M.S., Salve Regina Coll., 1984; M.S., Boston Coll., 1965; PhD, Pacific Western U., 1988. Instr. nursing Salve Regina U., 1953-66, asst. prof., 1966-74, assoc. prof., 1974-82, prof., 1982—, chair dept. nursing, 1974-93; staff-charge nurse St. Joseph's Hosp., Providence, 1953-93, part-time faculty, 1960, 65; mem. R.I. Bd. Nurse Registration and Edn., 1970-79, pres., 1977-79; charter mem., sec. R.I. Health, Sci. and Edn. Council, 1972-78; adj. asst. prof. Coll. Nursing U. R.I., 1986—; mem. R.I. State Senate, 1992—. Active local and nat. senatorial campaigns. Mem. R.I. Nurses Assn. (pres. 1969-71, 73-75), Am. Nurses Assn., Women Educators (charter), Nursing Leadership Council R.I. (charter; chair 1981-82, sec. 1982—), Nat. League Nursing (accreditation site visitor 1990—), Sigma Theta Tau (R.I. State senator 1992—). Roman Catholic. Home: 42 Rowley St Providence RI 02909-5521 Office: Salve Regina U Ochre Point Ave Newport RI 02840

GRAZIOSI, CHERRY LYNN, journalist; b. Cleve., Oct. 28, 1957; d. Aldo and Margaret (Houlas) G. MA, Am. U., 1991. Anchor WFMD, Frederick, Md., 1985-88; freelance journalist Washington, 1988—. Pub. rels. dir. Frederick Women's Fair, Women's Ctr. Coun., Frederick, Md., 1988-89, Hatter for Congress, 1991, Jimmy Carter Work Project, Washington, 1992. Recipient numerous journalism awards, 1986-91. Republican. Roman Catholic. Home: 9802 Walker House Rd Gaithersburg MD 20879

GREASER, CONSTANCE UDEAN, automotive industry executive; b. San Diego, Jan. 18, 1938; d. Lloyd Edward and Udean Greaser. BA, San Diego State Coll., 1959; postgrad. U. Copenhagen Grad. Sch. Fgn. Students, 1963, Georgetown U. Sch. Fgn. Service, 1967; MA, U. So. Calif., 1968; Exec. MBA, UCLA, 1981. Advt., publicity mgr. Crofton Co., San Diego, 1959-62; supr. Mercury Publs., Fullerton, Calif., 1962-64; supr. engring. support services div. Arcata Data Mgmt., Hawthorne, Calif., 1964-67; mgr. computerized typesetting dept. Continental Graphics, Los Angeles, 1967-70; v.p., editorial dir. Sage Publs., Inc., Beverly Hills, Calif., 1970-74; head publs. RAND Corp., Santa Monica, Calif., 1974-90; mgr. communications Am. Honda Motors Co., Torrance, Calif., 1990—. Mem. nat. com. Million Minutes of Peace Appeal, 1986, Nat. Info. Standards Orgn., 1987-93, nat. com. Global Cooperation for Better World, 1988. Recipient Berber award Graphic Arts Tech. Found., 1989. Mem. Women in Bus. (pres. 1977-78), Graphic Comm. Assn. (bd. dirs. 1994—), Soc. for Scholarly Pubs. (nat. bd. dirs.), Women in Communication, Soc. Tech. Communication, Brahma Kumaris World Spiritual Orgn. Co-author: Quick Writer-Build Your Own Word Processing Users Guide, 1983; Quick Writer-Word Processing Center Operations Manual, 1984; editor: Urban Research News, 1970-74; mng. editor Comparative Polit. Studies, 1971-74; contbr. articles to various jours. Office: Am Honda Motor Co 1919 Torrance Blvd Torrance CA 90501-2746

GREATHOUSE, PATRICIA DODD, psychometrist, counselor; b. Columbus, Ga., Apr. 26, 1935; d. John Allen and Patricia Ottis (Murphy) Dodd; m. Robert Otis Greathouse; children: Mark Andrew, Perry Allen. BS in Edn., Auburn (Ala.) U., 1959, M in Edn., 1966, AA in Counselor Edn., 1975. Cert. secondary tchr., Ala., Ga. Tchr. Columbus High Sch., 1959-61, Phenix City Bd. Edn., 1957-58; tchr. pub. schs. Russell County (Ala.) Bd. Edn., Phenix City and Seale, 1961-69, 71-80, 82-83, counselor pub. schs., 1969-82, 83-93; psychometrist Russell County (Ala.) Bd. Edn., Seale, 1980-82; county psychometrist Russell County (Ala.) Bd. Edn., Phenix City, 1983-93. Editor: (ann.) Tiger Tales, 1973 (award 1980). Treas. Ladonia PTA, Phenix City, 1966-68, parliamentarian, 1987-88; leader Ladonia chpt. 4-H Club, Phenix City, 1961-80; active March of Dimes, Am. Heart Assn.; rep. Mardi Gras; tchr. Sunday Sch., Vacation Bible Sch. N. Phenix Bapt. Ch.; vol. Reach to Recovery Am. Cancer Soc., 1980—. Named Mardi Gras Queen Phenix City Moose Club, 1987, hon. life mem. Ladonia PTA, 1967, Outstanding Tchr. of Yr., 1972; recipient Silver Clover award 4-H Club, 1966, Outstanding PTA Performance award 1986-87; nominated to Tchr. Hall of Fame, 1980-81, 81-82, 82-83. Mem. NEA, AARP, Russell County Edn. Assn. (pres.-elect 1973), Ala. Edn. Assn., Ala. Pers. and Guidance Assn., Ala. Assn. Counseling and Devel., Coun. Exceptional Children, Am. Bus. Women's Assn. (pres. Phenix City charter chpt. 1986-87, woman of yr. 1987, Perfect Attendance award, treas. 1990—, tri-county coun.), Daus. of Nile (pres. Phenix City club 1980-81, 83-84, outstanding svc. award, sec. 1994—), Ret. Tchrs. Assn. (ctrl. sr. activities ctr. 1993), Jetettes (v.p. Phenix City club 1976, 80), Jaycettes, Order of Ea. Star (worthy matron 1981-82), Riverview Sr. Citizens, Delta Kappa Gamma (sec. 1979-80, pres. 1990-94), Kappa Iota. Democrat. Baptist. Home: 1502 Nottingham Dr Phenix City AL 36867-1941

GREATHOUSE-WREN, REBECCA HALE, counselor, secondary school educator; b. Carmel, Calif., May 19, 1959; d. David McLeod and Margarita (Amador-Lopez) Greathouse; m. William Robert Wren, Sept. 28, 1991. BFA, Sul Ross State U., 1980, all-level art cert., 1981, MEd in Counseling, 1984, MEd in School Adminstrn., 1986, MEd in Art, 1994; spl. edn. cert., U. Tex., Odessa, 1985; postgrad. in art therapy, U. Ill., Chgo., 1993—. Lic. profl. counselor Tex. Bd. Examiners; cert. all-level art, profl. counselor, profl. spl. edn. counselor, emotionally disturbed, generic spl. edn., spl. edn. supr., supr., mid-mgmt. and ESL, psychology health, composite social studies, Tex. Historian living history Fort Davis (Tex.) Nat. Historic Site, 1976-77; receptionist, mus. artist Mus. of the Big Bend, Alpine, Tex., 1978-79; advt. designer Alpine (Tex.) Avalanche, 1977-81; career counselor C.E.T.A. Manpower, Alpine, 1981-82; spl. edn. art tchr., asst. prin. High Frontier Sch.-Fort Davis (Tex.) Ind. Sch. Dist., 1982-85, prin., counselor, 1985-88; dist. sch. counselor, art tchr., ESL tchr. Fort Davis (Tex.) Ind. Sch. Dist., 1988—; contract counselor Alpine (Tex.) Women's Ctr.; pvt. practice counseling, Alpine. Educator St. Joseph Cath. Ch., Fort Davis, Tex. Mem. ACA. Democrat. Roman Catholic. Home: PO Box 1337 Fort Davis TX 79734-1337 Office: Fort Davis Ind Sch Dist PO Box 1339 Fort Davis TX 79734-1339

GREAVER, JOANNE HUTCHINS, mathematics educator, author; b. Louisville, Aug. 9, 1939; d. Alphonso Victor and Mary Louise (Sage) Hutchins; 1 child, Mary Elizabeth. BS in Chemistry, U. Louisville, 1961, MEd, 1971; MAT in Math., Purdue U., 1973. Cert. tchr. secondary edn. Specialist math Jefferson County (Ky.) Pub. Schs., 1962—; part-time faculty Bellarmine Coll., Louisville, 1982—, U. Louisville, 1985—; project reviewer NSF, 1983—; advisor Council on Higher Edn., Frankfort, Ky., 1983-86; active regional and nat. summit on assessment in math., 1991, state task force on math., assessment adv. com., Nat. Assessment Ednl. Progress standards com.; lectr. in field. Author: (workbook) Down Algebra Alley,

1984; co-author curriculum guides. Charter mem. Commonwealth Tchrs. Inst., 1984—; mem. Nat. Forum for Excellence in Edn., Indpls., 1983; metric edn. leader Fed. Metric Project, Louisville, 1979-82; mem. Ky. Ednl. Reform Task Force, Assessment Com., Math. Framework, Nat. Nat. Assessment Ednl. Progress Rev. Com. Recipient Presdl. award for excellence in math. teaching, 1983; named Outstanding Citizen, SAR, 1984, mem. Hon. Order Ky. Cols.; grantee NSF, 1983, Louisville Community Found., 1984-86. Mem. Greater Louisville Council Tchrs. of Math. (pres. 1977-78, 94—, Outstanding Educator award 1987), Nat. Council Tchrs. of Math. (reviewer 1981—), Ky. Coun. Tchrs. of Math. (pres. 1990-91, Jeff County Tchr. of Yr. award 1985), Math. Assn. Am., Kappa Delta Pi, Zeta Tau Alpha. Republican. Presbyterian. Avocations: tropical fish; gardening; handicrafts; travel; tennis. Home: 11513 Tazwell Dr Louisville KY 40241 Office: Gheens Acad 4425 Preston Hwy Louisville KY 40213

GRECO, ANN ELISABETH, home healthcare education services professional; b. Harper Woods, Mich., May 22, 1959; d. John Foster and Marie Elizabeth (Lewis) Crowell; m. James Francis Greco, June 6, 1981 (div. 1988). A in Bus. Adminstrn., Oakland C.C., Auburn Hills, Mich., 1982; BS in Mktg., Oakland U., 1984. Sr. program adminstr. Advt. Audit Svc., Inc., Bloomfield Hills, Mich., 1985-88; acct. exec., mgr. Beurmann Marshall Corp., Southfield, Mich., 1988-90; adminstrv. svcs. mgr. Budco, Detroit, 1990-91; disabilities rights specialist, editor Ctr. Independent Living, Detroit, 1991-94, Ctr. Independence Living, Sterling Heights, Mich.; vol. coord. Kenny Rehab., Rochester Hills, Mich., 1992-94; disability advocate Disability Advocates, Ltd., Keego Harbor, Mich., 1993—; cmty. educator Allen Home Health Care & Hospice, Southfield, 1994—; vol. for spkrs. bur. Kenny Rehab., 1994—; bd. dirs. Mich. Protection and Advocacy Svcs., Lansing, Mich., 1994—. Advocate, spkr. Mich. Deserves Better, Brighton, Mich., 1992-94. Roman Catholic. Home: 1175 Bamford Waterford MI 48328

GRECO, BARBARA RUTH GOMEZ, literacy organization administrator; b. Farifield, Calif., May 27, 1938; d. William Joseph and Ruth Marie (Fernandes) Gomez; m. Edward Fairfax Greco, Aug. 27, 1966 (div. Jan. 1995); children: Michelle, William. Assoc. degree cum laude, Lord Fairfax Community Coll., 1985; B, James Madison U., 1987, postgrad., 1987-93. Bd. dirs. Va. Literacy Coalition, Richmond, 1990, Region 4 Literacy Coordinating Com., Harrisonburg, Va.; pres. Literacy Vols. Am., Warren, 1988—; dir. mktg. and pub. rels. Wayside of Va. Inc., Strasburg, 1988; bus. cons. Echo Ridge Nursery, Winchester, 1990; owner Barbara Greco & Assocs. Contbg. writer North Valley Bus. Jour., Winchester, 1989-93. PTA chair County of Warren, 1974-78, mem. founding bd. coun. on domestic violence, 1980-88, vice-chair dem. com., 1981, pres. coun. on domestic violence, 1985-88, mem. crime commn., 1988; mem. textbook adoption com. Warren County High Sch., 1985; bd. dirs. Va. chpt. Am. Lung Assn., 1980-82; bd. dirs. United Way, 1984; Warren County coord. Patterson for State Senate, 1979; campaign coord. William A. Hall for Clk. of Ct., 1981; supr. phone bank Charles Robb Campaign, 1981; campaign treas. Michael Kitts for Town Coun., 1984; campaign vol. Gerald Lee Baliles for Gov., 1986; troop leader Girl Scouts U.S., 1970-71, area coord., 1971-72; com. mem. Warren County Strategic Planning Partnership, 1993. Mem. Shenandoah Valley Writer's Guild (past pres.), Phi Theta Kappa. Unitarian Universalist. Home: PO Box 1188 Front Royal VA 22630-1188

GREELEY, GALE ELIZABETH, psychiatrist; b. Portland, Oreg., Sept. 20, 1944; d. Charles Allison and Frances Elizabeth (MacBain) MacArthur; m. Robert Greeley, Jan. 24, 1967 (div. Feb. 1969); m. Burt J. Kempner, June 22, 1980; 1 child, Nathan Daniel. BA, Temple U., 1966; MD, Med. Coll. Pa., 1976. Diplomate Am. Bd. Psychiatry and Neurology. Instr. psychiatry Med. Coll. Pa., Phila., 1979-80; staff psychiatrist St. Elizabeths Hosp., Washington, 1981-85; asst. prof. U. South Fla., Tampa, 1985-88; pvt. practice Tampa, 1987—; staff psychiatrist Mental Health Care, Inc., Tampa, 1992—; asst. prof. George Washington U., Washington, 1983-85; mem. clin. faculty U. So. Fla., Tampa, 1987-94. Mem. Am. Psychiat. Assn., Am. Med. Women's Assn. Democrat.

GREEMON, TERESA GLANCE, accountant; b. Gastonia, N.C., July 27, 1950; d. William G. and E. Juanita (Rodden) Glance; m. C. Wayne Fortner, Aug. 24, 1968; children: Steven Dwayne, Tracy Lynne; m. Tony B. Greemon, June 20, 1981; children: Gregory Todd, Mark David. BA, Belmont Abbey Coll., 1988. Statis. clk. Homelite, textron, Gastonia, N.C., 1978-86; comml. credit staff First Union Nat. Bank, Charlotte, N.C., 1986-88; staff acct. Gaston County Dyeing Machinery Co., Stanley, N.C., 1988-91, mgr. fin. reporting, 1991—; adv. bd. mem. data 3 Software, Santa Rosa, Calif., 1991—. Mem. Gaston-Carlinas Inst. Mgmt. Accts. Office: Gaston County Dyeing Machine Co PO Box 308 Stanley NC 28164-0308

GREEN, ADELINE MANDEL, psychiatric social worker; b. St. Paul; d. Meyer and Eva Ulanove; B.S., U. Minn., M.S.W.; m. Nathan G. Mandel (div.); children—Meta Susan (Mrs. Richard Katzoff), Myra (Mrs. Jeffrey Halpern); m. Maurice L. Green. Past investigator, Ramsey County Mothers Aid and Aid to Dependent Children, Ramsey County Welfare Bd., St. Paul; then psychiat. social worker Wilder Child Guidance Clinic, St. Paul; then psychiat. social worker, supr. outpatient psychiatry clinic U. Minn. Hosps., Mpls., subsequently supr., clin. instr. psychiatry-social service, outpatient psychiatry clinic; currently in pvt. practice family and marriage counseling South Bay Clinic. Past pres. St. Paul sect. Council Jewish Women; past chmn. Diagnostic Clinic for Rheumatic Fever-Wilder Clinic, St. Paul; assoc. Family and Child Psychiat. Med. Clinic. Lic. clin. social worker. Mem. Nat. Assn. Social Workers, Acad. Certified, Social Workers, Minn. Welfare Conf., Am. Assn. Marriage and Family Counselors, Brandeis U. Women. Democrat. Home: 2365 Oakcrest Dr Palm Springs CA 92264-5020 Office: South Bay Psychiatric Clinic 14651 S Bascom Suite 225 Los Gatos CA 95030

GREEN, ALLISON ANNE, retired secondary education educator; b. Flint, Mich., Oct. 5, 1936; d. Edwin Stanley and Ruth Allison (Simmons) James; m. Richard Gerring Green, Dec. 23, 1961 (div. Oct. 1969). BA, Albion Coll., 1959; MA, U. Mich., 1978. Cert. tchr., Mich. Tchr. phys. edn. Southwestern High Sch., Flint, 1959-62; tchr. math. Harry Hunt Jr. High Sch., Portsmouth, Va., 1962-63; receptionist Tempcon, Inc., Mpls., 1963-64; tchr. phys. edn. and math. Longfellow Jr. High Sch., Flint, 1964-81, tchr. math., 1981-92, tchr. lang. arts and social studies, 1986-87. Mem. Fair Winds council Girl Scouts U.S., 1943—, leader Lone Troop, Albion, Mich., 1957, sr. tchr. aide adviser, 1964-67; mem. Big Sisters Genesee and Lapeer Counties, 1964-68; mem. adminstrv. bd. Court St. United Meth. Ch., vice chmn, 1995—; treas. edn. work area, mission commn., sec. council on ministries, mem. worship com. United Meth. Women Soc. Christian Service, also chmn. meml. com. Mem. NEA, Mich. Edn. Assn., Mich. Assn. Mid. Sch. Educators, United Tchrs. Flint (bldg. rep.), Delta Kappa Gamma (treas. 1982-88, profl. affairs chmn. 1978-80, legis. chmn. 1980-82, pres. 1988-90), Alpha Xi Delta (pres. Flint, alumnae, v.p., treas., corp. pres. Albion Coll., alumnae dir. province 1972-77, Outstanding Sr. Albion Coll. 1959), Embroiderers Guild Am. (sec. 1977-80, maps rep. 1980-82), Phi Delta Kappa (historian 1985-91, treas. 1991-92). Home: 1002 Copeman Blvd Flint MI 48504-7326

GREEN, BARBARA GRAHAM, church administrator; b. Wilmington, Del., July 12, 1950; d. Jesse Henry Jr. and Elizabeth Frances (Somers) G.; m. Alan Francis Geyer, Apr. 20, 1985; children: Christopher Donald Green Geyer and Elisabeth Frances Green Geyer (twins). BA, Coll. Wooster, 1972; student, U. Heidelberg, Germany, 1972-74; MDiv, Yale U., 1976. Ordained to ministry Presbyn. Ch., 1984. Liaison rep. to East German Ch. Fedn. Nat. Coun. Chs., Berlin, 1977-81; dir. disarmament Nat. Coun. Chs., N.Y.C., 1982; assoc. peacemaking Presbyn. Ch. (USA), Washington, 1983—; mem. internat. adv. com. German Protestant Kirchentag, Fulda, Germany; vice-chair Europe com. Nat. Coun. Chs., N.Y.C. Author: (with others) Peacemaking and Resistance, 1985; co-author: Lines in the Sand: Justice and the Gulf War, 1992; mem. editorial bd. Dietrich Bonhoeffer Soc. Internat. Grad. fellow Rotary Internat., 1972-73. Mem. Christians Associated Rels. Ea. Europe. Home: 5014 Smallwood Dr Bethesda MD 20816-2830 Office: Presbyn Ch (USA) 110 Maryland Ave NE Washington DC 20002

GREEN, BARBARA STRAWN, psychotherapist; b. Cleve., May 31, 1938; d. Charles Everard and Dorothy Haring (Strawn) G. BA, Pa. State U., 1960; MS, Columbia U., 1962; postgrad. in psychotherapy and psychoanalysis, Postgrad. Ctr. for Mental Health, N.Y.C., 1975. Cert. social worker, N.Y.; lic. social worker, Pa.; cert. Rutgers Summer Sch. Alcoholism Studies, 1982. Social worker VA, N.Y.C., 1962-66; sr. psychiat. social worker in child psychiat. Downstate Med. Ctr., Bklyn., 1966-71; staff therapist Inst. for Contemporary Psychotherapy, N.Y.C., 1971-73; social worker Lower East Side Service Ctr., N.Y.C., 1975-77; intake coordinator alcoholism program Postgrad. Ctr. for Mental Health, N.Y.C., 1981-82; program coordinator Bowery Residents Com., N.Y.C., 1984-86; pvt. practice psychotherapy N.Y.C., 1973—, Dingmans Ferry, Pa., 1994—; sec. alcoholism com. N.Y.C. chpt. NASW, 1987-89. Participant N.Y.C. Marathon, 1991, 92. Mem. Social Workers Helping Social Workers (chmn. 1982-84).

GREEN, BARBARA-MARIE, publisher, journalist, poet; b. N.Y.C., Mar. 21, 1928; d. James Matthew and Mae (McCarter) G. BA, CCNY, 1951, MA, 1955; ABD, NYU, 1978. Adminstr., tchr. English, 1952-82; tchr. English Newtown High Sch., Elmhurst, Queens, N.Y., 1961; asst. prin. Jr. High Sch. 142, Queens, N.Y., 1963; founder, pub. The "Creative" Record, Virginia Beach, Va., 1988-92; keynote speaker; pres. Bar 'JaMae Comm. Inc. Founder, publisher The Good News, East Elmhurst, N.Y., 1985-88; author poetry. Ch. and cmty. reporter N.Y. Voice; mem. libr. action com. Corona (N.Y.)-East Elmhurst, Inc.; mem. Langston Hughes Cmty. Libr. and Cultural Ctr., Corona, Harpers Ferry Hist. Assn., Va. Symphony League. Recipient Profl. award Nat. Assn. Negro Bus. and Profl. Women's Club Inc., 1964, Trophy "Career Woman of Yr.", County Line Guild of Career Women, 1967, Cert. of Appreciation Women's Equality Action League, 1978, Antioch Bapt. Ch., 1982, Cert. of merit City of N.Y., 1982, Community Svc. award Arlene of N.Y., 1990, N.Y. State Resolution commemorating the "Good" News, 1985, Participation award Coalition of 100 Black Women, Valuable Service citation Phi Delta Kappa; named Star Among Stars, 1991; named to African-Am. Biographies Hall of Fame, Atlanta, 1994. Mem. Nat. Assn. Negro Musicians (life; bd. dirs. Chgo. 1984-91, ea. region dir. 1990-91), Harpers Ferry Hist. Assn., Poetry Soc. Va., Nat. Assn. Black Journalists, Hampton Roads (Va.) Black Media Profls., Black Filmmakers, Zonta Internat., Va. Fedn. Bus. and Profl. Women's Clubs (corr. sec. 1992, 1st v.p. 1993, pres. 1993, chair coastal region pub. rels. com. state level 1994—, coastal region), N.Y.C. Ret. Suprs. Assn., Chesapeake, Va. C. of C., Phi Delta Kappa, Alpha Kappa Alpha, Zeta Phi Beta. Baptist. Office: Bar 'JaMae Comm Inc PO Box 64412 Virginia Beach VA 23467-4412

GREEN, BEVERLY JEAN, nurse; b. Ithaca, N.Y., Aug. 6, 1955; d. Arthur W. Sr. and Edna M. (Pearson) G. Diploma, Arnot-Ogden Sch. Nursing, 1977. RN, S.C.; cert. ACLS, CEN, trauma nursing care course, pediatric advanced life support. Staff RN Arnot Ogden Meml. Hosp., Elmira, N.Y., 1977-88; staff nurse Loris (S.C.) Comty. Hosp., 1988-94; staff RN, supr. Brunswick Hosp., Supply, N.C., 1988—. Mem. Emergency Nurses Assn. Home: 2140 Adams Circle Little River SC 29566

GREEN, BONNIE JEAN, early childhood administrator; b. Crookston, Minn., Oct. 23, 1950; d. Francis Romain and Dorothy Marion (Boatman) Bagne; m. Steven Douglas Wedger, July 21, 1973 (div. Feb. 1985); m. Charles Edward Green Jr., June 15, 1985; stepchildren: Andrew Green, Russell Green. BS in Edn. magna cum laude, U. N.D., 1972; cert. human rels., Minn. State U., 1973; postgrad., U. Minn., 1975-83. Cert. elem./early childhood edn. adminstr. Math/reading tutor bilingual students U. N.D., Grand Forks, 1969-71; 1st grade tchr. Park Rapids (Minn.) Ind. Sch. Dist., 1972-73; asst. dir./curriculum writer, tchr. Child Devel. and Learning Ctr., Burnsville, Minn., 1973-75, dir., 1975-87; caring ministry outreach Luth. Ch. of Incarnation, Davis, Calif., 1990—; facilitator-parent edn. program Dakato County Vo-Tech, 1973-78; advisor, cons. Dakota County Childcare Coun., 1977-83; advisor, tchr. cert. program Augsburg Coll., Mpls., 1977-78; supr. student tchrs. Coll. of St. Catherine, Augsburg, St. Paul, 1977-87; cons. Minn. Edn. for Young Children, 1978, State of Minn., 1979-81, Am. Luth. Ch., Mpls., 1981-83; cons., kindergarten curriculum Burnsville Sch. Dist., 1983; liaison coord. Head Start Program, Burnsville, 1985-87. Vol. Prince of Peace Luth. Ch., Burnsville, 1975-87 facilitator parents of divorce, 1984-87; vol. Yolo Wayfare Ctr., Woodland, Calif., 1992; bd. dirs. Riverwoods Homeowners Assn. Arch. Control, 1978-85; mem., vol. Holy Cross Luth., Wheaton, Ill., 1987-89, Luth. Ch. of Incarnation, Davis, 1989—, curriculum planner, 1989; publicity chair, bd. dirs. U. Calif. Farm Circle, Davis, 1989—; fundraiser Wheaton (Ill.) Newcomers, 1987-89. Mem. Nat. Assn. for Edn. Young Children, PEO (guard, treas.), Pi Lambda Theta. Home and Office: 39648 Lupine Ct Davis CA 95616-9756

GREEN, CAROL H., lawyer, educator, journalist; b. Seattle, Feb. 18, 1944; B.A. summa cum laude in History and Journalism, La. Tech. U., 1965; MSL, Yale U., 1977; JD, U. Denver, 1979. Intern, Shreveport (La.) Times, 1964, reporter, 1965-66; reporter Guam Daily News, 1966-67; city editor Pacific Jour., Agana, Guam, 1967-68; reporter, editorial writer, 1968-76, legal affairs reporter, 1977-79, asst. editor editorial page, Denver Post, 1979-81, house counsel, 1980-83, labor rels. mgr., 1981-83; assoc. Holme Roberts & Owen, 1983-85; v.p. human resources and legal affairs Denver Post, 1985-87; mgr. circulation sales and adminstrn., 1988-90, mgr. circulation, Newsday, 1990; gen. mgr. Distribution Systems Am., Inc., 1990-92; dir. labor rels., Newsday, 1992—; mem. corrections task force Colo. Criminal Justice Standards and Goals, 1985 speaker for USIA, India, Egypt; mem. Mailers Tech. Adv. Com. to Postmaster Gen., 1991-92. Bd. dirs. YWCA, Mile Hi Red Cross, Trans. Coun., Denver C. of C. Recipient McWilliams award for juvenile justice, Denver, 1971; award for interpretive reporting Denver Newspaper Guild, 1979. Mem. ABA (forum on communications law), Colo. Bar Assn. (bd. govs. 1985-87, chairperson BAR-press com. 1980), Newspaper Assn. Am. (mem. human resources and labor rels. com.), Denver Bar Assn. (co-chairperson jud. selection and benefits com. 1982-85, 1st v.p. 1986), Alliance Profl. Women (exec. com.), Colo. and Internat. Women's Forum, Leadership Denver. Clubs: Huntington Camera. Episcopalian. Office: Newsday 235 Pinelawn Rd Melville NY 11747

GREEN, CAROLE L., lawyer; b. Queens, N.Y., Mar. 17, 1959; d. Gerald Harry and Mary (Clark) G. AB cum laude with distinction, Dartmouth Coll., 1980; JD, Harvard Law Sch., 1983. Bar: N.Y. Congl. aide to rep. John Conyers U.S. House of Reps., Washington, 1980; assoc. real estate Kaye, Scholer, Fierman, Hays & Handler, N.Y., 1983-85, Richards & O'Neil, N.Y., 1985-87; gen. counsel Petrie Stores Corp., Secaucus, N.J., 1987-88; assoc. counsel Mfrs. Hanover Trust Co., N.Y., 1988-91; v.p., asst. gen. counsel Chemical Bank, N.Y., 1991—. Mem. ABA (mem. minority in-house counsel group 1994—), N.Y. State Bar Assn., Practicing Attys. for Law Students, Inc. (founding mem. 1986—), Black Alumni of Dartmouth Assn. Office: Chemical Bank 270 Park Ave 40th Fl New York NY 10017

GREEN, EDITH JUDITH, registered nurse; b. Camden, N.J., Jan. 28, 1937; d. Arthur William Fields and Emily Gladys (Heal) Glover; m. Edward Russell Green, Apr. 1958 (dec. Mar. 1975); children: Rachel, Edward, Thomas, Ellen, David, Russell. RN, Thomas Jefferson U., 1958; BS, Syracuse U., 1985; MPS, SUNY, New Paltz, 1991. RN. Staff nurse Vis. Nurse Assn., Utica, N.Y., 1982-84; psychiat. nurse St. Elizabeth Hosp., Utica, 1980-84; insvc. trainer Greystone Inc., Wappingers Falls, N.Y., 1988-89; counselor, educator Teen Parents Program YWCA, Poughkeepsie, N.Y., 1987-88; educator HIV and Sexuality Planned Parenthood, Poughkeepsie, 1990-93; staff nurse Prison Health Svcs., Poughkeepsie, 1989—; adj. prof. Dutchess C.C., Poughkeepsie, 1993—. Author: Ellery Queen Mystery Magazine, 1984. Active many local polit. groups. Mem. NOW (pres. 1987-90), Am. Assn. Sex Educator, Counselors and Therapists, Mystery Writer's Am., Family Planning Advocates, Internat. Women's Writers Group. Episcopalian. Office: Prison Health Svcs 150 N Hamilton St Poughkeepsie NY 12601

GREEN, ELEANOR MYERS, veterinarian, educator; b. Phila., Feb. 10, 1948; d. Wade Cooper and Eleanor Ruth (McWherter) Myers; m. George Ashby Green, Dec. 19, 1970; children: George Ashby Jr., Stacy Elizabeth, William Wade. Student, U. South Fla., 1965-67, U. Fla., 1967-69; DVM, Auburn U., 1973. Diplomate Am. Coll. Vet. Internal Medicine, Am. Bd. Vet. Practitioners (pres. 1993-95). Ptnrship, owner Guntown (Miss.) Vet. Clinic, 1973-76; asst. prof. Miss. State U., Starkville, 1976-84; assoc. prof. U. Mo., Columbia, 1984-91; prof. U. Tenn., Knoxville, 1991—. Mem. Am. Assn. Equine Practitioners, Tenn. Vet. Med. Assn., Am. Vet. Med. Assn., Internat. Soc. Vet. Perinatology, Tenn. Horse Coun., Am. Assn. Vet. Clinicians (pres.-elect 1994-95), Rotary Internat. Presbyterian. Office: Dept Large Animal Clin Scis Knoxville TN 37901

GREEN, FLORA HUNGERFORD, lactation consultant, nurse; b. Mason City, Iowa, June 23, 1941; d. Mac Willard and Ethel Elizabeth (Hill) Hungerford; m. Ronald Eugene Green, Aug. 3, 1974; children: Elizabeth Jane, Marjorie Ann. Diploma, Meth-Kahler Sch. of Nursing, 1963; BS in Biology, Westmar Coll., 1964; BS in Nursing, Case Western Res. U., 1968; MA in Edn. Media, U. Minn., 1971. RN, Idaho, Calif., Iowa; cert. lactation cons., lamaze instr. Ednl. programmer U. Wis., Milw., 1970-72; asst. prof. nursing Idaho State U., Pocatello, 1972-76; dir. ins-svc. and patient edn. Bingham Meml. Hosp., Blackfoot, Idaho, 1976-77; staff nurse St. Agnes' Hosp., Fresno, Calif., 1979-81, Eden Hosp., Castro Valley, Calif., 1981-83; pvt. practice lactation cons. Fremont, Calif., 1985—; staff nurse high risk ob. dept. Stanford U. Hosp., 1989-90, Kaiser Hosp.; obstetrics nurse Kaiser Permanente Med. Ctr., Hayward, 1991—; cons. media divsn. J.B. Lippincott Co., Phila., 1973-80; bd. dirs. Bay Area Lactation Assn., Daly City, Calif. Chmn. Blacow Sch. emergency and safety com., Fremont, 1987-88, 92-93; bd. dirs. Fresno Montessori Sch., 1980-81, Bannock County ARC, Pocatello, 1976-77; emergency svcs. disaster cons. Idaho State U., Bannock County Red Cross, Bannock County, Pocatello, Idaho, 1972-77. Mem. AAUW, NAACOG, So. Alameda ASPO (co-chairperson 1987-88), Internat. Lactation Cons. Assn., Internat. Childbirth Edn. Assn., Sons of Norway, Sigma Theta Tau. Lutheran.

GREEN, GLORIA JEAN, lawyer; b. Atlanta, Dec. 8, 1954; d. Alfred and Mattie Bell Green; 1 child, Avery Dyan Kelley. AB, Duke U., 1976; JD, Georgetown U., 1979. Bar: Ga. 1979. Atty. SEC, Washington, 1979-82; sr. atty. SEC, Atlanta, 1982-86; sr. atty. Fed. Home Loan Bank Atlanta, 1986-88, asst. v.p., 1988-90, v.p., 1990—. Dir. Wesley Cmty. Ctr., Atlanta, 1988—; vice chairperson bd. dirs. South DeKalb YMCA, Decatur, Ga., 1989—, DeKalb County Express, Decatur, 1991—; mem. adv. bd. Harper H.S. Mgmt. Program, 1990—; active Citizens for South DeKalb, Decatur, 1983-90, Decatur-DeKalb 100 Black Women, 1989-91. Recipient Outstanding Leadership award South DeKalb YMCA, 1992. Mem. ABA, Ga. Bar Assn., Ga. Assn. Black Women Attys., Gate City Bar Assn. Methodist. Office: Fed Home Loan Bank Atlanta 1475 Peachtree St NE Atlanta GA 30309

GREEN, GRACE DIANNE, small business owner, cake decorator; b. Abilene, Tex., Mar. 15, 1952; d. Carlton Douglas and Willie Elvee (Carey) Brooks; m. Bobby Gene Green, June 27, 1970; children: Amy Renee, Emily Michelle, April Suzanne, Amber Leanne. Diploma, Cooper H.S., Abilene, 1970. Mgr. in tng. Virginia Lee Pies, Abilene, 1976-86; mgr. The Cake Corner, Abilene, 1986-91; owner, cake decorator McKay's Bakery, Abilene, 1991—. Mem. hospitality com. Johnston PTA, Abilene, 1984-90; v.p. Abilene High Choir Boosters, 1992-94. Mem. Abilene C. of C., Abilene Downtown Assn. Home: 3761 Wilshire Dr Abilene TX 79603-4527

GREEN, JEAN RENEE, sales executive; b. Phila., Apr. 6, 1959; d. Norman Irwin and Anna (Newman) G. Student, Atlantic County Community Coll. Sales rep. Hombergers, Atlantic City, N.J., 1978-79; casino dealer Caesars Hotel & Casino, Atlantic City, 1979-81, casino floorperson, 1981-87, casino pit mgr., 1987-90; sales rep. PBM Distbrs., Atlantic City, 1990-91; v.p. sales, ops. ServiceMaster, Atlantic City, 1991—. Mem. Boardwalk Runners, Atlantic City Off Shore Racing Assn., Absecon Island Power Squadron. Home: 626 N Connecticut Ave Atlantic City NJ 08401-2716

GREEN, JENNIFER SHVONNE, accountant; b. N.Y.C., Jan. 12, 1970; d. Jessie Lee and Loretta (Sykes) G. BS, U. Va., 1992; posrgrad., Pace U., 1993—. CPA, N.Y. Acct. analyst IBM, White Plains, N.Y., 1992—. Rep. Popular, Mary Kay Cosmetics. Mem. Inst. Cert. Mgmt. Accts., Acctg. Soc. Home: 410 W 128th St Apt 31 New York NY 10027-2813

GREEN, JOANTA HERMION, electrical engineer; b. Cleve., Nov. 14, 1960; d. Joseph Ezkiel and Clarece Hermion (Marshall) G. BS in Chemistry and Biology, U. Md., 1983; MS in Econ. Devel., N.H. Coll., 1987; postgrad., U. Malaya, Kuala Lumpur, Malaysia, 1990; PhD in Energy Systems, U. Edinburgh, Scotland, 1992. Lab. tech. USDA, 1980-83; dep. headmistress, tchr. Chepareria (West Pokot, Kenya) Girl's Secondary Sch., 1983-86; project engr. renewable energy R & D div. Bechtel Group Inc., San Francisco, 1992—; ind. expert spl. energy program Deutsche Gesellschaft für Technische Zusammenarbeit GmbH, Eschborn, Germany, 1990-92; vis. fellow energy program Asian and Pacific Devel. Ctr., Kuala Lumpur, 1990-91; rsch. assoc. environmentally compatible energy strategies project Internat. Inst. Applied Systems Analysis Laxenburg, Austria, 1991-92; presenter in field. Contbr. articles to profl. publs. Mem. Assn. Energy Engrs., Inst. Energy (U.K.), NAFE. Office: Bechtel Group Inc 50 Beale St San Francisco CA 94105

GREEN, JOYCE, book publishing company executive; b. Taylorville, Ill., Oct. 22, 1928; d. Lynn and Vivian Coke (Richardson) Reinerd; m. Warren H. Green, Oct. 8, 1960. AA, Christian Coll., 1946; BS, MacMurray Coll., 1948. Pres. Warren H. Green, Inc., St. Louis, 1992—; exec. dir. Affirmative Action Assn. Am., 1977—; pres. InterContinental Industries, Inc., 1980—; chief exec. officer Pubs. Svc. Ctr. Mem. St. Louis C. of C., Jr. League Club, Media Club, Mo. Athletic Club, Media Club. Democrat. Methodist. Home: 12120 Hibler Rd Saint Louis MO 63141-6615 Office: 8356 Olive Blvd Saint Louis MO 63132-2814

GREEN, JOYCE HENS, federal judge; b. N.Y.C., Nov. 13, 1928; d. James S. and Hedy (Bucher) Hens; m. Samuel Green, Sept. 25, 1965 (dec.); children: Michael Timothy, June Heather, James Harry. B.A., U. Md., 1949; J.D., George Washington U., 1951. Bar: D.C. 1951, Va. 1956, U.S. Supreme Ct. 1956. Practice law Washington, 1951-68, Arlington, Va., 1956-68; ptnr. Green & Green, 1966-68; assoc. judge Superior Ct., D.C., 1968-79; judge U.S. Dist. Ct. for D.C., 1979—; bd. advisors George Washington U. Nat. Law Ctr. Co-author: Dissolution of Marriage, 1986, supplements, 1987-89; contbr. supplements Marriage and Family Law Agreements, 1985-89. Trustee D.C. div. Am. Cancer Soc., 1963-76; bd. adv. Nat. Law Ctr. George Washington U. Recipient Alumni Achievement award George Washington U., 1975, Profl. Achievement award, 1978, Outstanding Contbn. to Equal Rights award Women's Legal Def. Fund, 1976; named Woman Lawyer of Yr., 1979. Fellow Am. Bar Found.; mem. ABA (jud. adminstrn. div., exec. com., fed. trial judges), Fed. Judges Assn., Va. Bar Assn., Bar Assn. D.C., D.C. Bar, D.C. Women's Bar Assn. (pres. 1960-62), Exec. Women in Govt. (chmn. 1977), Lawyers Club of Washington; Kappa Beta Pi, Phi Delta Phi (hon.). Club: Lawyers' Club of Washington. Office: US Dist Ct US Courthouse 333 Constitution Ave NW Washington DC 20001*

GREEN, JUNE LAZENBY, federal judge; b. Arnold, Md., Jan. 23, 1914; d. Eugene H. and Jessie T. (Briggs) Lazenby; m. John Cawley Green, Sept. 5, 1936. JD, Am. U., 1941. Bar: Md. 1943, D.C. 1945. Claims adjuster Lumbermans Mut. Casualty Co., Washington, 1942-43, claims atty., 1943-47; pvt. practice Washington, 1947-68, Annapolis, Md., 1950-68; judge U.S. Dist. Ct. D.C., 1968—; mem. spl. ct. Regional Reorganization Railroad Act, 1987—; examiner bar, Washington, 1963-68. Named Woman Lawyer of Yr., 1965; recipient Lifetime Achievement award Alumni Assn. of Am. U., 1986. Mem. ABA, Md. Bar Assn., Bar Assn. D.C. (bd. dirs. 1966-68, award 1984), Women's Bar Assn. D.C. (pres. 1955-57), Federal Judges Assn., Am. Jud. Soc. Home: 464 W Joyce Ln Arnold MD 21012-2207 also: 550 N St SW Washington DC 20024-4643 Office: US Dist Ct US Courthouse 333 Constitution Ave NW Washington DC 20001-2802

GREEN, KAREN BLEIER, marketing professional; b. N.Y.C., Apr. 18, 1945; d. Benjamin and Sally (Karger) Bleier; m. Joseph H. Green, Sept. 3, 1966; children—Jessica, Adam. B.A., Simmons Coll., 1967; M.B.A, Harvard U., 1969. Media planner Ogilvy & Mather Inc., N.Y.C., 1969-71, asst. media dir., 1971-74, v.p., account supr., 1974-79, v.p., mgmt. supr., 1979-82, sr. v.p., mgmt. supr., 1982-90; advtg. dir., v.p. Citibank, N.A., 1990-91, strategic planning dir., v.p., 1991-93, dir. N.Y. mktg., 1994—. Office: Citibank NY Bank One Court Sq Long Island City NY 11120

GREEN, KATHY ELLEN, education educator; b. Detroit, May 23, 1950; d. Earl and Catherine Jeanette (Steczkowski) G. BS, U. Wis., 1974; MEd, U. Wash., 1977, PhD, 1981. Postdoctoral fellow Victoria U., Wellington, New Zealand, 1981-83; asst. prof. U. Wyo., Laramie, 1983-87; assoc. prof. edn. U. Denver, 1987—; chair AERA SIG: Survey Rsch., Washington, 1991-93, program chair, 1989-91. Editor: Educational Testing, 1991; contbr. articles to profl. jours. Nat. Merit scholar, 1968, Wis. Honor scholar, 1968. Mem. Nat. Coun. on Measurement in Edn. (co-dir. 1992), Am. Ednl. Rsch. Assn. Democrat. Home: 538 Detroit St Denver CO 80206 Office: U Denver Coll Of Edn Denver CO 80208

GREEN, LINDA GAIL, home healthcare consultant; b. Kalamazoo, Nov. 29, 1951; d. Jesse Floyd and Mattie Dean (Fulcher) G. BS in Nursing, Fla. State U., Tallahassee, 1974; postgrad., Nova U., Ft. Lauderdale, Fla. Cert. critical care nurse. Staff nurse med./surg. unit St. Mary's Hosp., West Palm Beach, Fla., 1974, staff nurse coronary care, 1974-75, relief charge nurse ICU, 1975-76, asst. nursing care coord. post anesthesia recovery rm., 1976-78, insvc. instr., 1978-81, asst. dir. staff devel. and edn., 1981-83; dir. insvc. H.H. Raulerson Hosp., Okeechobee, Fla., 1983-84; adminstr. Med. Personnel Pool, Palm Beach, Fla., 1984-90; regional exec. healthcare divsn. Interim Svcs., Inc. (formerly Pers. Pool of Am.), Ft. Lauderdale, 1990-93; pres. L.G.I. Consulting, 1993—. Bd. dirs. Vinceremos Riding Ctr., Inc. for Physically & Mentally Challenged. Mem. ANA, Fla. Nurses Assn., Palm Beach County Health Educators (past sec.), Palm Beach County Patient Educators (pres. 1989, Leadership and Spirit awards 1989), Royal Palm Beach Bus. Assn., Palms West C. of C. (v.p. 1987-88, Dedicated and Outstanding Svc. award 1989, Cert. of Appreciation 1986, 87), Zonta Internat. (past v.p. Palmes West chpt., del. to Zonta Internat. Conf., Hong Kong, 1992), Exec. Women of the Palm Beaches. Home: 5066 Coconut Blvd West Palm Beach FL 33411-9008 Office: PO Box 15301 West Palm Beach FL 33416-5301

GREEN, LINDA LOU, systems analyst; b. Cape Girardeau, Mo., Sept. 12, 1946; d. Barney Oldfield and Opal (Jeffries) G. BA, East Carolina U., 1967, MA, 1969; postgrad., U. Utah, 1969-70; grad., Naval War Coll., Newport, R.I., 1985, Command and Staff Coll., Ft. Leavenworth, Kans., 1990. Cert. in collegiate teaching. Asst. prof. history Jackson (Miss.) State U., 1970-72, Va. State U., Petersburg, 1972-74; commd. 1st lt. U.S. Army, 1974, advanced through grades to ltc., 1991; logistics engr. land systems div. Gen. Dynamics Corp., Warren, Mich., 1983-84; systems analyst Raytheon Svc. Co., Huntsville, Ala., 1984-86; pres. Green & Assocs. Inc., Huntsville, 1985-86; logistics engr., cost analyst, br. mgr. Applied Rsch. Inc., Huntsville, 1986-90; sr. ILS analyst Native Am. Svcs. Inc., Huntsville, Ala., 1990; sr. systems analyst BDM Internat. Inc., 1990; pres. Green and Assocs., Inc., Huntsville, 1990-91; sr. logistics analyst Sigmatech Inc., 1991—; instr. U. Md., Fed. Republic Germany, 1975-77, Calhoun Community Coll., Huntsville, 1990—; lectr. in field. Author: Study Guides for American History, 1969, The Family Tree, 1989, Logistics Engineering, 1991. Mem. Rep. Nat. Com., Washington, 1986-91. Mem. LWV, Soc. Logistics Engrs. (bd. dirs. TVC chpt. 1992-93, chpt. Logistician of Yr. 1993, recipient Nat. Field award in Integrated Logistics Support 1994), Assn. U.S. Army (bd. dirs. Redstone, Huntsville chpt. 1988-91), Res. Officers Assn., Ret. Officers Assn. Baptist. Office: Green and Assocs Inc 708 Lily Flagg Rd SE Huntsville AL 35802-3435

GREEN, LYNDA WARFEL, program director; b. Lancaster, Pa., Nov. 7, 1947; d. Walter K. and Elizabeth C. (Kleine) Warfel; children: Jonathan P., Courtney E. BA, Mt. St. Vincent Coll., 1969; MS, U. Hartford, 1984; postgrad., U. Conn. Cert. secondary English tchr., intermediate adminstr., Conn. English tchr. South Windsor (Conn.) Pub. Schs., 1970-80, Sir William Romney's Sch., Tetbury, England, 1976; grad. asst. U. Conn., Storrs, 1986-88; cons. State of Conn., Hartford, 1988-89; dir. curriculum Rocky Hill (Conn.) Pub. Schs., 1989—. Mem. ASCD, Conn. ASCD, New England League Middle Schs., AAUW. Home: 6 Tollgate Ln Simsbury CT 06070-1017 Office: Rocky Hill Bd Edn Church St Rocky Hill CT 06067

GREEN, MARJORIE, automotive distribution, import and manufacturing company executive; b. N.Y.C., Sept. 27, 1943; d. Benjamin Maxon and Harriet (Weslock) Gruzen; m. Thomas Henry Green, May 31, 1964. Student Antioch Coll., 1961-63, CCNY, 1964-65. Adminstrv. asst. edl. research U. Calif.-Berkeley, 1965-76; v.p., co-owner Automotion, Santa Clara, Calif., 1973—. Adv. bd. Import Car mag. Mem. Am. Fedn. State, County and Mcpl. Employees (pres. U. Calif. chpt. 1967), Porsche Club Am (v.p. Golden Gate region 1974, treas. region 1975). Home: 10666 W Loyola Dr Los Altos CA 94024-6513 Office: Automotion 193 Commercial St Sunnyvale CA 94086-5202

GREEN, MIRIAM BLAU, psychologist; b. New Castle, Pa., Sept. 21, 1932; d. Jacob Mont and Anne (Levine) Blau; m. Alvin Green, June 13, 1954; children: Andrew, Marie, Jennifer. BA with high honors, U. Mich., 1954; EdM, Harvard U., 1955; EdD, Columbia U., 1960. Lic. psychologist, N.Y.; diplomate Am. Bd. Profl. Psychology. Tchr. history Maimonides Sch., Boston, 1955-57; sch. psychologist Bur. Child Guidance, N.Y.C., 1960-67, Great Neck (N.Y.) Pub. Schs., 1967-81; instr. State U. Coll. Old Wesbury, Westbury, N.Y., 1982-85; fellow child psychoanalysis Postgrad. Ctr. Mental Health, N.Y.C., 1983-86, fellow family therapy, 1982-84, asst. coord. family program, 1985-89, dir. family and couples tng. program, 1989-91; mem. faculty, supr. Inst. for Child, Adolescent and Family Studies, 1991—; pvt. practice Great Neck and N.Y.C., 1983—; NIMH trainee Columbia U., 1958-60; lectr., instr. Queens Coll., CUNY, 1962-63; cons. Jewish Family Svc. of Bergen County, N.J., 1991-92; faculty supr. Postgrad. Ctr. Mental Health, 1991—. Mem. Am. Psychol. Assn. (div. sec. 1989—), N.Y. State Psychol. Assn., Nassau County Psychol. Assn., Psychol. Practioners L.I. (bd. dirs. 1987-89), Phi Beta Kappa. Jewish. Home: 22 Arleigh Rd Great Neck NY 11021-1338 Office: 145 E 48th St New York NY 10017-1254

GREEN, MONICA, peace organization director; b. Sydney, Australia, Apr. 29, 1959; d. Clifford James and Audley Jean Green; m. Richard S. West, June 6, 1992; children: Owen, Emma. BA with honors, Oberlin Coll., 1981. Counseling dir. Omni Health Ctr., Cleveland Heights, Ohio, 1981-85; exec. dir. Cleve. Nuclear Weapons Freeze Campaign, 1985-89; field dir. Sane/Freeze: Campaign for Global Security, Washington, 1989-90, exec. dir., 1990—. Office: Peace Action 1819 H St NW # 640 Washington DC 20006

GREEN, NANCY BALDWIN, marketing consultant; b. Cin., Oct. 25, 1947; d. Robert S. and Mary O'Neill (McDevitt) G.; children: Adrian Alexandra Burns, Alexander Anthony. BFA, Stanford U., 1970, MBA, 1975. Creative dir. Moorhead Mktg., Palo Alto, Calif., 1970-73; mng. dir. The Fields Investment Group, Mrs. Fields' Cookies, Portola Valley, Calif., 1975-83; prin. Green, Schleck & Stoller, Palo Alto, 1983-88, The William Baldwin Group, Palo Alto, 1988—. Co-author: Price Trends and Strategic Response, 1985. Office: The William Baldwin Group 2190 Saint Francis Dr Palo Alto CA 94303

GREEN, NANCY LOUGHRIDGE, higher education executive; b. Lexington, Ky.; d. William S. and Nancy O. (Green) Loughridge; BA in Journalism, U. Ky., 1964; MA in Journalism, Ball State U., 1971; postgrad. U. Ky., 1968, U. Minn., 1968. Tchr. English and publs. adv. Clark County High Sch., Winchester, Ky., 1965-66, Pleasure Ridge Park High Sch., Louisville, 1966-67, Clarksville (Ind.) High Sch., 1967-68, Charleston (W.Va.) High Sch., 1968-69; asst. publs. and pub. info. specialist W.Va. Dept. Edn., Charleston, 1969-70; tchr. journalism and publs. dir. Elmhurst High Sch., Ft. Wayne, Ind., 1970-71; adviser student publs. U. Ky., Lexington, 1971-82; gen. mgr. student publs. U. Tex., Austin, 1982-85; pres., pub. Palladium-Item, Richmond, Ind., 1985-89, News-Leader, Springfield, Mo., 1989-92; asst. to the pres., Newspaper Divsn. Gannett Co., Inc., Washington, 1992-94; exec. dir. coll. advancement Clayton State Coll., Morrow, Ga., 1994—; dir. Harte-Hanks urban journalism program, 1984; pres. Media Cons., Inc., Lexington, 1980; dir. urban journalism workshop program Louisville and Lexington newspaper pubs., 1976-82; sec. Kernel Press, Inc., 1971-82. Contbr. articles to profl. jours. Bd. dirs. Jr. League, Lexington, 1980-82, Manchester Ctr., 1978-82, pres., 1979-82; chmn. Greater Richmond Progress Com., 1986-87, bd. dirs. 1986-89; pres. Leadership Wayne County, 1986-87, bd. dirs., 1985-89; bd. dirs. Richmond Community Devel. Corp., 1987-89, United Way of the Ozarks, 1990-92, ARC, 1990-92, Springfield Arts Coun., 1990-91, Bus. Devel. Corp., 1991-92, Bus. Education Alliance, 1991-92, Caring Found., 1991-92, Cox Hosp. Bd., 1990-92, Springfield Schs. Found., 1991-92; mem. adv. bd. Ind. U. East, 1985-89, Richmond C. of C., 1987-89, Ind. Humanities Coun., 1988-89, Youth Communications Bd., 1988-92. Recipient Coll. Media Advisers First Amendment award, 1987, Carl Towley award Journalism Edn. Assn., 1988, Disting. Svc. award Assn. Edn. Journalism and Mass Comm., 1989; named to Ball State Journalism Hall of Fame, 1988, Coll. Media Advisers Hall of Fame, 1994. Mem. Student Press Law Ctr. (bd. dirs. 1975—, pres. 1985-87, 94—, v.p. 1992-94), Assoc. Collegiate Press, Journalism Edn. Assn., Nat. Council Coll. Publs. Advs. (pres. 1979-83), Disting. Newspaper Adv. 1976, Disting. Bus. Adviser, 1984). Columbia Scholastic Press Assn. (Gold Key 1980), So. Interscholastic Press Assn. (Disting. Service award 1983), Nat. Scholastic Press Assn. (Pioneer award 1982), Soc. Profl. Journalists.

GREEN, PATRICIA PATAKY, school system administrator, consultant; b. N.Y.C., June 18, 1949; d. William J. and Theresa M. (Digianni) P.; m. Stephen I. Green, Dec. 7, 1975. BS, U. Md., 1971, MEd, 1977, PhD, 1994. Tchr. Prince George's County (Md.) Pub. Schs., 1971-83; elem. instrnl. adminstrv. specialist Thomas Stone Sch., Mt. Ranier, Md., 1984-85, Glenridge Sch., Lanham, Md., 1984, Greenbelt (Md.) Ctr. Sch., 1983-84, Prince George's County Pub. Schs., 1985-91; prin. Columbia Park Sch., Landover, Md., 1991—; asst. supt. Prince George's County Pub. Schs., 1991—; cons. nationwide sch. systems, 1987—; seminar/workshop presenter in field. Editor, writer (newsletter) Tooth or Consequences, 1980—; featured in numerous mags. and on TV shows; contbr. articles to profl. jours. Recipient Nat. Sch. Recognition award U.S. Dept. Edn., 1988, Outstanding Adminstr. award Prince George's County C. of C., 1990. Mem. NAESP (Excellence of Achievement award 1988), ASCD, NEA, Nat. Sch. Bds. Assn., Nat. Assn. Secondary Sch. Prins., Phi Kappa Phi, Kappa Delta Pi.

GREEN, ROSE BASILE (MRS. RAYMOND S. GREEN), poet, author, educator; b. New Rochelle, N.Y., Dec. 19, 1914; d. Salvatore and Caroline (Galgano) Basile; m. Raymond S. Green, June 20, 1942; children: Carol-Rae Green Sadano, Raymond Ferguson St. John. BA, Coll. New Rochelle, 1935; MA, Columbia U., 1941; PhD, U. Pa., 1962; LHD (hon.), Gwynedd-Mercy Coll., 1979, Cabrini Coll., 1982. Tchr., Torrington High Sch., Conn., 1936-42; writer, researcher Fed. Writers Project, 1935-36; freelance script writer Cavalcade of Am., NBC, 1940-42; assoc. prof. English, univ. registrar Tampa U., Tampa, 1942-43; spl. instr. English, Temple U., Phila., 1953-57; prof. dept. English, Cabrini Coll., Radnor, Pa., 1957-70, chmn. dept., 1957-70. Author: Cabrinian Philosophy of Education, 1967, (criticism) The Italian-American Novel, 1972, (poetry books) To Reason Why, 1971, Primo Vino, 1972, 76 for Philadelphia, 1975, Woman, The Second Coming, 1977, Lauding the American Dream, 1980, Century Four, 1981, Songs of Ourselves, 1982, (transl.) The Life of Mother Frances Cabrini, 1984, The Pennsylvania People, 1984, Challenger Countdown, 1988, Five Hundred Years of America, 1492-1992, 1992; editor faculty jour. A-Zimuth, 1963-70. Exec. dir. Am. Inst. Italian Studies; dir. lit. com. Phila. Art Alliance; bd. dirs., trustee Free Libr. of Phila.; v.p., dir. Nat. Italian-Am. Found.; chair Nat. Adv. Coun. Ethnic Heritage Studies; adv. bd. Women for Greater Phila.; dir. Balch Inst. Phila. Decorated cavalier Republic of Italy; named Woman of Yr. Pa. Sons of Italy, 1975, Disting. Dau. of Pa., 1978; recipient Nat. Amita award for lit., 1976, Nat. Bicentennial award for poetry DAR, 1976, other awards for contbns. to lit. and edn. Fellow Royal Soc. Arts (London); mem. AAUW (dir.-at-large), Am. Acad. Polit. and Social Sci., Acad. Am. Poets, Acad. Polit. Sci., Am. Studies Assn., Ethnic Studies Assn., Nat. Council Tchrs. English, Am.-Italy Soc. (dir. 1952—), Eastern Pa. Coll. New Rochelle Alumnae (pres. 1951-54), Cosmopolitan Club, Franklin Inn Club (Phila.), Kappa Gamma Phi. Home: 308 Manor Rd Lafayette Hill PA 19444-1741

GREEN, RUTH MILTON, retired college administrator, consultant; b. Sioux City, Iowa, Feb. 29, 1924; d. John and Myrtle Alma (Phipps) Milton; m. Robert Wood Green, Dec. 31, 1943 (dec. July 1989): children: Robert William, Sandra Lou Green Montignani. Student, Morningside Coll., 1943-45. Registrar East High Sch., Sioux City, Iowa, 1943; acct. Buehler Bros., Iowa City, 1947-49; asst. dir. tchr. placement Morningside Coll., Sioux City, 1951-55, mem. staff registrar's office, 1960-65, asst. to registrar, 1965-70, dir. spl. project funding, 1971-81, dir. Title III Strengthening Devel. Institutions program, 1975-84, v.p. instl. research, planning and spl. projects, 1984-94; ret., 1994; asst. to prin. Ames (Iowa) High Sch., 1955-59; pvt. cons. for edn. and non-profit agys. in spl. project funding. Pres. First Congregational Ch., Sioux City, 1980; co-chair City Hall Site Selection Com., Sioux City, 1991-93; mem. Main St. Energy Greenway Com., co-chair fundraising com.; bd. dirs. Siouxland Mental Health Agy., 1983-89, v.p. bd. dirs., 1995; bd. dirs. Mary Treglia Community House, Waco, pres. bd. dirs., 1995 . Named Woman of Excellence Women Aware, 1986. Mem. PEO. Democrat. Home: 3801 6th Ave Sioux City IA 51106-2826

GREEN, RUTHANN, marketing and management consultant; b. Streator, Ill., July 14, 1935; d. John Joseph and Edna Marie (Peters) G. BS in Edn., U. Ill., 1957. Elem. tchr. Jefferson Sch., Davenport, Iowa, 1957-59; tchr. Hinsdale (Ill.) Jr. High Sch., 1959-62; ednl. cons. Harcourt Brace & World, Chgo., 1962-63; exec. sec. Everpure, Inc., Oakbrook, Ill., 1963-68; ednl. cons. Houghton Mifflin Co., Europe, 1968-69, Palo Alto, Calif., 1969-77; sr. mktg. mgr. Houghton Mifflin Co., Boston, 1977-87; v.p., nat. sales mgr. Riverside Pub. Co., Chgo., 1987-89; v.p., dir. mktg. McDougal, Littell & Co., Evanston, Ill., 1990-92; v.p., gen. mgr. Open Court Pub. Co., Chgo., 1992-94; pres. Peters & Green, Inc., Chgo., 1994—. Author: WSIL: Why Should I Listen, 1987, 93. Recipient Svc. award Am. Arbitration Assn., 1987, Golden Reel of Excellence Internat. TV Assn., 1983. Mem. Am. Mktg. Assn., Nat. Assn. Women Bus. Owners, Internat. Reading Assn., U.S. Bd. on Books for Young People, People for Am. Way, Common Cause, Am. Arbitration Assn. Home and Office: 1310 N Ritchie Ct Apt 21A Chicago IL 60610-2178

GREEN, SARAH LACK, resource specialist, educator; b. Germany, Jan. 26, 1949; d. Ben and Mere (Fein) Lack; 1 child, Krystal Robin Green. BA in Social Sci., San Jose State U., 1971, gen. elem. cert., 1972, secondary elem. cert., 1973; spl. edn. cert., Chico State U., 1989. Social studies tchr. Sequoia High Sch., Redwood City, Calif., 1974-75; tchr. Kingsbury Mid. Sch., Stateline, Nev., 1977-78; kindergarten/resource specialist tchr. Clear Creek Sch. Dist., Grass Valley, Calif., 1984—. Recreation leader San Jose (Calif.) Parks & Recreation Dept., 1970-73; dist. rep. Camp Fire Girls, Roseville, Calif., 1982-83. Grantee Nev. County Supt. Schs., 1993. Mem. Calif. Assn. Resource Specialists, Calif. Assn. Kindergarten Tchrs. Office: Clear Creek Sch 17700 McCourtney Rd Grass Valley CA 95949

GREEN, SHARON JORDAN, interior decorator; b. Mansfield, Ohio, Dec. 14, 1948; d. Garnet and L. Wynell (Baxley) Fraley; m. Trice Leroy Jordan Jr., Mar. 30, 1968 (dec. 1973); children: Trice Leroy III, Caerin Danielle, Christopher Robin; m. Joe Leonard Green, Mar. 13, 1978. Student, Ohio State U., 1966-67, 75-76. Typist FBI, Washington, 1968; ward clk. Means Hall, Ohio State U. Hosp., Columbus, 1970; x-ray clk. Riverside Hosp., Columbus, 1971; contr., owner T&D Mold & Die, Houston, 1988—; interior decorator, franchise owner Decorating Den, Houston, 1989-91; owner T&D Interior Decorator, Houston, 1992—. Tchr. aide Bedford Sch., Mansfield, Ohio, 1976-77, Yeager Sch., 1981-82; pres. N.W. Welcome Wagon, Houston, 1980-81, Welcome Club, El Paso, 1986-87; active North Houston Symphpny, 1992—, North Houston Performing Arts, 1993—, Mus. Fine Arts, Houston, 1993—, Edn. and Design Resource Network, 1993—, The Wellington Soc. for Arts, 1994. Republican. Home: 16247 Morningbrook Dr Spring TX 77379-7158

GREEN, SHARON JOYCE ALLIGOOD, broadcast executive; b. Kingsport, Tenn., Oct. 8, 1950; d. Lewis C. and Billie (Boggs) Alligood; m. Tony A. Green, Jan. 10, 1974 (div. July 1977); 1 child, Kevin Lewis. Student, Edmondson Bus. Coll., 1969; AB, Edmondson Jr. Coll., 1978. Sec. Sta. WTCI-TV, Chattanooga, 1970-71, traffic dir., 1971-83, program dir., 1983-89, membership devel. dir., 1990-92; membership devel. dir. Chattanooga Cable TV Co., 1993—; grad. asst. Dale Carnegie Courses, Chattanooga, 1987-88. Mem. Nat. Soc. Fund Raising Execs., Hamilton Pl. Rotary (info. chmn. 1990-91, sec. 1991-92, bd. dirs. 1992-95). Republican. Presbyterian. Home: 2300 David Cir Chattanooga TN 37421-1719 Office: Chattanooga Cable TV Co PO Box 182249 Chattanooga TN 37422-7249

GREEN, SHELLEY Z., lawyer, university counsel; b. N.Y.C.. AB, Vassar Coll., 1970; JD, Harvard U., 1974. Bar: N.Y. 1975, D.C. 1976, Pa. 1981, U.S. Supreme Ct. 1981. Assoc. Sutherland Asbill & Brennan, Washington, 1974-78; atty. advisor HEW, Washington, 1978-79; asst. gen. counsel U. Pa., Phila., 1979-80, assoc. gen. counsel, 1980-82, gen. counsel, 1982—. Office: U Pa 221 College Hall Philadelphia PA 19104

GREEN, SHIA TOBY RINER, therapist; b. N.Y.C.; d. Murray A. and Frances Riner; student CCNY; B.A., Antioch Coll., M.A., 1976; m. Gary S. Green, Sept. 4, 1957; children—Margot Laura, Vanessa Daryl, Garson Todd. Press. and legis. sec. U.S. Ho. of Reps., Washington, 1960-71; cons. Rehab. Services Adminstrn., Social and Rehab. Services, HEW, 1972-73; asst. dir. State of Md. Foster Care Impact Dmonstration Project, 1977-78; therapist Alexandria (Va.) Narcotics Treatment Program, 1979-84, Assocs. Psychotherapy Ctrs., Giburg, Md., 1984—; mem. treatment com. Alexandria Case Mgmt. and Treatment of Child Sexual Abuse. Mem. exec. bd. Children's Adoption Resource Exchange, Washington; vol. worker Girl Scouts U.S.A., also Boy Scouts Am., 1970-74. Mem. Am. Psychol. Assn., Md. Psychol. Assn., Am. Assn. Marriage and Family Therapy. Co-author: Permanent Planning in Maryland—A Manual for the Foster Care Worker. Home: One Lake Potomac Ct Potomac MD 20854 Office: 8915 Shady Grove Ct Gaithersburg MD 20877-1308

GREEN, SYLVIA FRAN, legislative staff member; b. Cleve., Miss., Aug. 2, 1944; d. Vernon Melvin Powell and Frances Louise (Allen) Smart; m. Charles Raymond Green; 1 child: Charles Darren. Student, Delta State U., 1962-64. Paralegal Alexander, Feduccia & Alexander, Cleve., 1964-72, Thomas, Price, Alston, Jones & Davis, Jackson, Miss., 1972-74, Binder, Lucas & Lohrman, Jackson, 1974-75; house staff Miss. Ho. of Reps., Jackson, 1975—. Home: 568 Oak Ridge Rd Brandon MS 39042 Office: Miss Ho of Reps PO Box 1018 Jackson MS 39215

GREEN, TOMIE TURNER, lawyer, state legislator; b. Jackson, Miss., Sept. 29, 1952; d. David Sr. and Lizzie Mae (McPherson) Turner; m. Cornelius Green Jr., Apr. 21, 1973; children: Nikisha Shontelle, Synarus Derron. BA, Tougaloo Coll., 1973; MS in Edn., Jackson State U., 1976; JD, Miss. Coll., 1984. Program counselor Jackson-Hinds Health Ctr., Jackson, 1975-77; program coord. Miss. Dept. Mental Health, Jackson, 1977-78; dir. testing Tougaloo (Miss.) Coll., 1978-84; sole practice law Jackson, 1984-85; jud. law clk. U.S. Dist. Ct., Jackson, 1985-86; asst. dist. atty. Dist. Atty.'s Office, Jackson, 1986-88; assoc. atty. Walker & Walker, Jackson, 1988-91; ptnr. Walker, Walker & Green, Jackson, 1991—; state rep. Miss. Ho. of Reps., Jackson, 1993—. Contbr. articles to profl. jours. Mem. ABA, Assn. Trial Lawyers Am., Magnolia Bar Assn., NAACP, Miss. Legis. Black Caucus, Phi Alpha Delta. Democrat. Mem. AME Ch. Home: 114 Pine Island Dr Jackson MS 39206-3234 Office: PO Box 22849 Jackson MS 32925*

GREENAWALT, PEGGY FREED TOMARKIN, advertising executive; b. Cleve., Apr. 27, 1942; d. Bernard H. and Gyta Elinor (Arsham) Freed; m. Gary Tomarkin, Aug. 7, 1966 (div. 1981); children: Craig William, Eric Lawrence; m. William Sloan Greenawalt, Oct. 31, 1987. BS, Simmons Coll., 1964. Asst. account exec. Howard Marks/Norman, Craig & Kummel, Inc., N.Y.C., 1964-66; account exec. Shaw Bros. Advt. Co., N.Y.C., 1966-67; copywriter Claire Advt. Co., N.Y.C., 1967; ptnr. Copywriters Coop., Hartsdale, N.Y., 1970-73; copy chief Howard Marks Advt., N.Y.C., 1973-80; sr. copywriter Wunderman, Ricotta & Kline, N.Y.C., 1980-82; v.p., assoc. creative dir. Ayer-Direct (N.W. Ayer), N.Y.C., 1982-84; sr. v.p., creative dir. D'Arcy Direct (D'Arcy, MacManus & Masius), N.Y.C., 1984-86; creative and mktg. cons., 1986—; pres. Tomarkin/Greenawalt, Inc.; judge Clio Awards, Echo Awards, Caples Awards. Author: Kiss, The Real Story, 1980. Dem. dist. Leader. Mem. Direct Mktg. Assn., Women in Communications , Direct Mktg. Club N.Y., Westchester Assn. Women Bus. Owners (past pres.). Office: 45 E 30th St New York NY 10016-7323

GREENAWALT, RUTH MARJORIE, librarian; b. Dunkirk, N.Y., Nov. 6, 1942; d. Vincent Prescott and Marjorie Mary (Kuhrt) Aldrich; m. Dale Elwood Greenawalt, July 27, 1976; children: Daniel Vincent, Trenton David. BS, SUNY, 1964; MLS, Syracuse U., 1965. Periodicals librarian SUNY, Fredonia, 1965-68; librarian James Madison U., Harrisonburg, Va., 1968-82; dir. library Bridgewater (Va.) Coll., 1984—. Contbr. articles to profl. jours. Mem. Va. Library Assn. Republican. Methodist. Home: RR 8 Box 101 Harrisonburg VA 22801-8531 Office: Alexander Mack Meml Library Bridgewater Coll E College St Bridgewater VA 22812-1503

GREENBAUM, CAROL ANN, librarian, educator; b. N.Y.C., June 2, 1947; d. Charles P. and Agnes M. (Wise) Byrne; m. Peter A. Greenbaum, Feb. 10, 1968; children: Peter A., James B. AAS, Suffolk County Community Coll., 1983; BA, SUNY, Stony Brook, 1984; MLS, CW Post U., 1989. Cert. tchr., libr. Libr. Islip (N.Y.) Pub. Libr., 1987-89, Deer Park (N.Y.) Pub. Libr., 1989—; libr., tchr. Deer Park Schs., 1989—; pub. libr. Half Hollow Hills Libr., Dix Hills and Melville, N.Y., 1991—; liaison mem. Bd. Coop. Ednl. Svcs. Libr., Lindenhurst, N.Y., 1989—, mem. coun., 1992—; workshop leader Libr. Conf., 1992. Co-author: Secondary School Library Media Curriculum, 1990; contbr. articles to libr. jours. Active WK Vanderbilt Hist. Soc., Oakdale, N.Y., 1979—, Dowling Coll. Restoration Com., Oakdale, 1986—, libr. div. Bd. Coop. Edn. Svcs., Lindenhurst, 1989—; high sch. coord./chairperson Human Understanding and Growth Seminar. Mem. L.I. Sch. Media Assocs., Inc., Sch. Libr. Media Specialists, Inc., Suffolk County Libr. Assn., Phi Theta Kappa, Alpha Beta Gamma. Democrat. Home: 171 Irish Ln Islip Terrace NY 11752-2109 Office: Deer Park High Sch 30 Rockaway Ave Deer Park NY 11729-3298

GREENBERG, ARLINE FRANCINE, artist, photographer; b. N.Y.C.; m. Sidney Greenberg. BA, Hunter Coll.; postgrad., NYU; AS, Parson Sch. Design, Pratt Inst. Ind. practice cons. firm in jewelry and design; v.p. Reliable Textile Co., N.Y.C.; fashion dir. Burlington Klopman Fabrics, N.Y.C., 1988-92; guest lectr. AWED and F.I.T. Contbr. fashion articles to newspapers. Recipient Medal in Fine Arts; scholar NYU. Mem. AATT, AWARE, Fashion Group, Fashion News Workship, The Info. Exch.. Home: 555 Kappock St Apt 15D Riverdale NY 10463-6458

GREENBERG, BLU, author; b. Seattle, Jan. 21, 1936; d. Sam and Sylvia (Genser) Genauer; m. Irving Greenberg; children: Jeremy, David, Deborah, Jonathan, Judith. BA, Bklyn. Coll., 1957; BA in Religious Edn., Yeshiva U., 1958; MA in Clin. Psychol., City U., N.Y.C., 1967; MS in Jewish History, Yeshiva U., 1977. Instr. Dept. Religious Studies Coll. Mt. St. Vincent, N.Y.C., 1970-77; lectr. Pardes Inst., Jerusalem, 1974-75; guest lectr. Harvard U., Princeton U., Dartmouth U., U. Ind., and various other colls. Author: How to Run a Traditional Jewish Household, 1983, On Women and Judaism: A View from Tradition, 1982; (poetry) Black Bread: Poems, After the Holocaust, 1994; mem. adv. bd. Lilith mag.; mem. editl. bd. Hadassah mag., 1986—. Mem. exec. bd. Coalition for Soviet Jews, 1987—; trustee Jewish Found. for Christian Rescuers, 1990—; mem. steering com. Women of Faith in 80's, 1988-91, The Dialogue Project, 1989—; pres. JWB Jewish Book Coun., 1983-86, mem. exec. bd.; mem. exec. bd. Fedn. Commn. on Synagogue Rels., 1976, chair, 1982-86, chair women's task force, 1976-80; co-founder, mem. exec. bd. U.S.-Israel Women to Women, 1978-93; chairperson Jewish Women Leaders Cons., 1988-91; mem. commn. on equality of women Am. Jewish Congress, 1981—, task force on bioethics, 1989—; mem. adv. bd. William Petschek Nat. Jewish Family Ctr., 1990—, Jewish Women's Resource Ctr., 1982—; bd. dirs. Covenant Found., 1991—. Named Woman Yr. United Jewish Appeal-Bronx Div., 1984, Woman Valor Riverdale Jewish Ctr. 1971; recipient Myrtle Wreath Lit. award Camden County Hadassah 1976, Nassau County, 1991, Lit. award B'nai Brith women 1981, Svc. award Am. Jewish Com., 1990, Women of Achievement memoirist, 1990, Riverdale Jewish Community Coun. Svc. award, 1988. Mem. Sh'ma (mem.editorial bd. 1979-93), Jewish Publ. Soc. (mem. editorial bd. 1985—), Jewish Women's Resource Ctr. (mem. adv. bd. 1982—), Jewish Book Council Am. (pres. 1983-86), Fedn. Commn. Synagogue Rels. (chmn. exec. bd. 1982-86), U.S.-Israel Women to Women (co-founder, mem. exec. bd. 1978—), Women Faith Eighties (mem. steering com. 1980—), B'nai B'rith Commn. Adult Edn. (mem. exec. bd.). Home and Office: 600 W 246th St Bronx NY 10471-3598

GREENBERG, BONNIE LYNN, music industry executive; b. Roslyn Heights, N.Y., May 22, 1955; d. Morris U. Greenberg and Rozlyn (Willner) Sadkin. BA, U. Denver, 1975; JD, Southwestern U., 1978. Bar: Calif. 1979, N.Y. 1980. Lawyer ABC Records, Inc., L.A., 1977-79; dir. bus. affairs MCA Records, Inc., Universal City, Calif., 1980-83, Paramount Pictures, 1984; chmn. Media MusiCons., L.A., 1988-93, Ocean Cities Entertainment, Inc., Santa Monica, Calif., 1986-93; judge anti drug video contest N.Y. Dept. Edn., 1988. Author: Negotiating Contracts in the Entertainment Industry,

1987, Music Volume; producer: Getting Through the Night, 1985; music supr. motion pictures include Hairspray, Book of Love, Menace II Society, Sister Act II, The Mask, Corrina, Corrina. Atty. Bet Tzedek, L.A., 1987, 94. Recipient Gov's. plaque N.Y., 1988. Democrat.

GREENBERG, CAROLYN PHYLLIS, anesthesiologist, educator; b. San Francisco, July 7, 1941. AB, Stanford U., 1962; MD, U. Calif., San Francisco, 1966. Diplomate Am. Bd. Anesthesiology. Rotating intern L.A. County Hosp., 1966-67; resident in anesthesiology Presbyn. Hosp., N.Y.C., 1967-69, vis. fellow in anesthesiology, 1969-70, asst. attending anesthesiologist, 1971-90, assoc. attending anesthesiologist, 1990—, med. dir. ambulatory surgery, 1986—; asst. attending anesthesiologist N.Y. Hosp., 1970-71; instr. anesthesiology Cornell Med. Sch., 1970-71; assoc. anesthesiology Columbia U., N.Y.C., 1971-74, asst. prof. clin. anesthesiology, 1974-90, assoc. prof. clin. anesthesiology, 1990—. Contbr. book chpts., articles to profl. jours. Mem. Am. Soc. Anesthesiologists, N.Y. State Soc. Anesthesiologists (Media award 1992), Med. Soc. N.Y., Soc. Ambulatory Anesthesia (treas. 1994—, Ambulatory Anesthesia Rsch. Found. award 1992), Malignant Hyperthermia Assn. of U.S. (hotline cons. 1983—). Jewish. Office: Presbyn Hosp Dept Anesthesiology 622 W 168th St New York NY 10032-3702

GREENBERG, ELINOR MILLER, college administrator, consultant; b. Bklyn., Nov. 13, 1932; d. Ray and Susan (Weiss) Miller; m. Manuel Greenberg, Dec. 26, 1955; children: Andrea, Julie, Michael. BA, Mt. Holyoke Coll., 1953; MA, U. Wis.-Madison, 1954; EdD, U. No. Colo., 1981; LittD (hon.), St. Mary-of-the-Woods, Ind., 1983; LHD (hon.), Profl. Sch. Psychology, Calif., 1987. Exec. dir. Arapahao Inst. for Community Devel., Littleton, Colo., 1969-71; founding dir. Univ. without Walls, Loretto Heights Coll., Denver, 1971-79, asst. acad. dean, 1982-84, asst. to pres., 1984-85; regional exec. officer Coun. for Adult and Experiential Learning, Chgo., 1979-91; founding exec. dir. US West Communications CWA, Pathways to the Future, 1986-91; rsch. assoc. Inst. for Rsch. on Adults in Higher Edn., U. Md., U. College., 1991, exec. dir. project Leadership, 1986—; pres., chief exec. officer EMG and Assocs.; cons. in field. Co-editor, contbr.: Educating Learners of All Ages, 1980; co-author: Designing Undergraduate Education, 1981, Widening Ripples, 1986, Leading Effectively, 1987, In Our Fifties: Voices of Men and Women Reinventing Their Lives, 1993; editor, contbr.: New Partnerships: Higher Education and the Nonprofit Sector, 1982, Enhancing Leadership, 1989, Weaving: The Fabric of a Woman's Life, 1991, Liberal Education Journal, 1992; guest editor Liberal Edn., 1992; feature writer Colo. Woman News, 1993—; contbr. Sculpting The Learning Organization, 1993; contbr. articles to profl. jours. Bd. dirs., exec. com. Anti Defamation League of B'nai B'rith, Denver, 1981—, chair women's leadership com., 1991-93, bd. dirs., 1985—; mem. Colo. State Bd. for Community Colls. and Occupational Edn., 1981-86, vice chair, 1984-85; bd. dirs. Internat. Women's Forum, 1986-88, Internat. Women's Forum Leadership Found., 1991—, Griffith Ctr., Golden, Colo., 1982-86, Colo. Bd. Continuing Legal and Jud. Edn., 1984—; pres. Women's Forum of Colo., 1986; v.p. Women's Forum Colo. Found., 1987; mem. adv. bd. Anchor Ctr. Blind Child, Colo. Coalition Prevention Nuclear War, Mile Hi Girl Scouts, Nat. Conf. on Edn. for Women's Devel., Community Adv. Bd. Colo. Woman News, adv. com. Colo. Pvt. Occupational Sch., 1990—; co-chair Gov.'s Women's Econ. Devel. Taskforce, Women's Econ. Devel. Coun., 1988—; mem. bd. visitors U. Hosp., U. Colo., 1990-91, gov. apptd. Colo. Math., Sci. and Tech. Commn., chair, 1991-93, co-telecom. adv. commn. TAC 14, chair, 1993—; founding steering com. Colo. Women's Leadership Coalition, 1988—. Named Citizen of Yr., Omega Psi Phi, Denver, 1966, Woman of Decade Littleton Ind. Newspapers, 1970; grantee W. K. Kellogg Found., 1982, Weyerhaeuser Found., 1986, Fund for Improvement of Post Secondary Edn., 1977, 80; recipient Sesquicentennial award Mt. Holyoke Coll. Alumni Assn., 1987, Minoru Yasui Community Vol. award, 1991. Mem. Am. Assn. for Higher Edn., Assn. for Experiential Edn. (editorial bd. 1978-80), Nat. conf. Women's Devel. Edn., Kappa Delta Pi. Democrat. Jewish. Home: 6725 S Adams Way Littleton CO 80122-1801

GREENBERG, EVA MUELLER, librarian; b. Vienna, Austria, July 19, 1929; came to U.S., 1939; d. Paul and Greta (Scheuer) Mueller; m. Nathan Abraham Greenberg, June 22, 1952; children: David Stephen, Judith Helen, Lisa Pauline. AB, Harvard/Radcliffe Coll., 1951; MLS, Kent State U., 1975. Head reference McIntire Libr., Zanesville, Ohio, 1978; with Lorain (Ohio) Pub. Libr., 1978-81; head reference Elyria (Ohio) Pub. Libr., 1981-82; reference libr. adult svcs. Cuyahoga County Pub. Libr., Strongsville, Ohio, 1983-89; head adult svcs. Oberlin (Ohio) Pub. Libr., 1989—. Contbr. articles to profl. jours. Grantee Ohio Humanities Coun. for Pub. Programs. Mem. ALA, Ohio Libr. Assn. (coord. community info. task force). Home: 34 S Cedar St Oberlin OH 44074-1520 Office: Oberlin Pub Libr 65 S Main St Oberlin OH 44074-1626

GREENBERG, GLORIA ULERT, clinical psychologist; b. N.Y.C., Jan. 25, 1925; d. Abraham and Anna (Lieberman) Ulert; children: Mark Alan, Meredith Cary. BA, Hunter Coll., N.Y.C., 1946; MS in Psychology, U. Miami, Fla., 1965, PhD in Psychology, 1968. Lic. psychologist, Fla. Staff psychologist Henderson Clinic, Ft. Lauderdale, Fla., 1968-69, Jackson Meml. Hosp., Miami, 1969-81; assoc. prof. psychology U. Miami, 1969-81; pvt. practice psychology Miami Beach, Fla., 1981—; psychol. cons. HRS, Miami, 1969-81; forensic psychologist, 1969-81; mental health dir. Stanley C. Myers Mental Health Ctr., Miami Beach, 1977-82. Bd. dirs. Miami Chamber Symphony Orch., 1978-82. Mem. Am. Psychol. Assn., Fla. Psychol. Assn., Dade County Psychol. Assn. Home and Office: 11 Island Ave Ste 2002 Miami FL 33139-1343

GREENBERG, HINDA FEIGE, library director; b. Bayreuth, Germany, Feb. 26, 1947; came to U.S., 1951; d. Samuel Leon and Sima (Schampagnere) F.; m. Joseph Lawrence, July 6, 1968; children: David Micah, Jacob Alexander. BA, Temple U., 1969; MLS, Rutgers U., 1981; postgrad., Drexel U., 1991—. Assoc. librarian Ednl. Testing Svc., Princeton, N.J., 1981-86; dir. info. ctr. Carnegie Found., Princeton, 1986—. Assoc. editor Jour. Reading, Writing and Learning Disabilities, 1984-86. Mem. Princeton/Trenton Spl. Librs. Assn. (pres. 1985-86). Office: Carnegie Found 5 Ivy Ln Princeton NJ 08540-7218

GREENBERG, JILL, accountant; b. Alexandria, Va., Nov. 3, 1970; d. Philip and Bonnie (Brozen) G. BS in Acctg., Va. Inst. Tech., 1992; postgrad. in bus. adminstrn., Salisbury State U., 1994—. CPA. Staff acct. Ernst & Young, Washington, 1992-93; sr. acct. Perdue Farms, Inc., Salisbury, Md., 1994—. Treas., mem. Rotaract, Salisbury, 1994—. Mem. Inst. Mgmt. Accts. (dir. meetings 1994). Office: Perdue Farms Inc Old O C Rd Salisbury MD 21802

GREENBERG, LENORE, public relations professional; b. Flushing, N.Y.; d. Jack and Frances Orenstein. BA, Hofstra U.; MS, SUNY. Dir .pub. rels. Bloomingdale's, Short Hills, N.J., 1977-78; dir. comms. N.J. Sch. Bds. Assn., Trenton, 1978-82; dir pub. info. N.J. State Dept. Edn., Trenton, 1982-90; assoc. exec. dir. Nat. Sch. Pub. Rels. Assn., Arlington, Va., 1990-91; pres. Lenore Greenberg & Assocs., Inc., 1991-94; pub. rels. dir. Petersons Pub. Co., Princeton, N.J., 1994—; adj. prof. pub. rels. Rutgers U. Freelance feature writer N.Y. Times; asst. editor Somerset Spectator. Mem. bd. assocs. McCarter Theatre, Princeton, N.J.; mem. Franklin Twp. Zoning Bd. Adjustment; mem. Franklin Twp. Human Rels. Commn.; chair Somerset County LWV; instr. Bus. Vols. for the Arts. Recipient award Am. Soc. Assn. Execs., award Women in Comms., award Internat. Assn. Bus. Communicators; Gold Medallion awrd Nat. Sch. Pub. Rels. Assn. Mem. Pub. Rels. Soc. Am. (accredited; pres. N.J. State chpt., nat. nominating and accreditation coms., Silver Anvil award), Nat. Health/Edn. Consortium. Home: 15 Tunnell Rd Somerset NJ 08873-2916

GREENBERG, SUSAN ANN, lawyer; b. Bklyn., Mar. 15, 1957; d. Irving Arthur and Betty (Mayo) G. BA in Econs., Boston U., 1978; JD, Bklyn. Law Sch., 1981; LLM in Labor Law, NYU, 1986. Bar: N.Y. 1982, U.S. Dist. Ct. (ea. and so. dists.) N.Y. 1982. Assoc. Law Offices of Bert W. Subin P.C., N.Y.C., 1981-82; atty. N.Y. Life Ins. Co., N.Y.C., 1982-83, asst. counsel, 1982, assoc. counsel, v.p., 1982—; sec., bd.dirs. N.Y. State Adv. Council Employment Law, N.Y.C., 1985—, mem. Equal Employment Adv. Council, 1983—. Bus. editor Bklyn. Jour. Internat. Law, 1980-81. Mem. ABA. *

GREENBERGER, ELLEN, psychologist, educator; b. N.Y.C., Nov. 19, 1935; d. Edward Michael and Vera (Brisk) Silver; m. Michael Burton, Aug. 26, 1979; children by previous marriage—Kari Edwards, David Silver. B.A., Vassar Coll., 1956; M.A., Harvard U., 1959, Ph.D., 1961. Instr. Wellesley (Mass.) Coll., 1961-63, asst. prof., 1963-67; sr. research scientist Johns Hopkins U., Balt., 1967-76; prof. psychology and social behavior U. Calif., Irvine, 1976—. Author: (with others) When Teenagers Work, 1986; contbr. articles to profl. jours. USPHS fellow, 1956-59; Margaret Floy Washburn fellow, 1956-58; Ford Found. grantee, 1979-81; Spencer Found. grantee, 1979-81, 87, 88-91. Fellow APA, Am. Psychol. Soc.; mem. Soc. Rsch. in Child Devel., Soc. Rsch. on Adolescent Devel. Office: Univ Calif Sch Of Social Ecology Irvine CA 92717

GREENBERGER, MARSHA MOSES, sales executive; b. Lakewood, N.J., Mar. 15, 1943; d. Bernard David and Ethel (Gordon) Moses; m. Paul Edward Greenberger (div. 1969); 1 child, Nathan Scott. Student, Kent (Ohio) State U., 1961-62. Mgr. gen. sales Ellison Products, Fairfield, N.J., 1972-79; gen. mgr. Indsl. Maintenance Corp., Cherry Hill, N.J., 1979-83; co-owner corp. sect. Ven-Mar Sales, Inc., Blairstown, N.J., 1983-89; pres. MGM Sales, 1989—. Office: MGM Sales 29 High Ridge Rd Randolph NJ 07869-1500

GREENBLATT, CHARLOTTE ELIZABETH, artist; b. Walpole, Mass., July 5, 1945; d. Arthur Warren and Harriett (McMahon) Bullard; m. William R. Greenblatt, 1965; children: James Marshall, Kathryn. Cert., Boston Conservatory of Music, 1963; student, Art Students League, N.Y.C., 1965-68. Rockette Radio City Music Hall, N.Y.C., 1963-65; potter, owner Canyon Pottery Malibu, Calif., 1982—; writer Symphony Pictures, Calabasis, Calif., 1982—. Author: (as Charlotte Green) (short stories) Ceramics Monthly, Crone Chronicles, 1993, (poetry) Parabola; artist, potter ceramic shows, commns., 1982—. Registrar League Women Voters, Malibu, 1992-93; driver Angel Food AIDS Project L.A., 1989—. Mem. NOW, Writer's Guild Am., Malibu Art Assn., Rockette Alumni Assn.

GREENBLATT, MIRIAM, author, editor, educator; b. Berlin; d. Gregory and Shifra (Zemach) Baraks; B.A. magna cum laude, Hunter Coll.; postgrad. U. Chgo., Spertus Coll.; m. Herbert Halbrecht (div. 1960); m. Howard Greenblatt, 1962 (div. 1978). Tchr., New Trier (Ill.) High Sch., 1978-81; editor Am. People's Ency., Chgo., 1957-58; editor Scott, Foresman & Co., Chgo., 1958-62; pres. Creative Textbooks, Evanston, Ill., 1972—. V.p. Chgo. Chpt. Am. Jewish Com., 1977-79, mem. nat. exec. council, 1980-84; treas. Glencoe Youth Services, 1981-83. Mem. Nat. Council Social Studies, Ill. Council Social Studies, Am. Hist. Assn., Nat. Coun. History Edn. Author: (with Chu) The Story of China, 1968, (with Cuban) Japan, 1971, The History of Itasca, 1976, (with others) The American People, 1986, James Knox Polk, 1988, Franklin Delano Roosevelt, 1989, John Quincy Adams, 1990, (with Jordan and Bowes) The Americans, 1994, (with Welty) The Human Expression, 1992, The War of 1812, 1994, (with Lemmo) Human Heritage, 1995, Cambodia, 1995; edit. cons. Peoples and Cultures Series, 1976-78; subject area cons. World Geography and Cultures, 1994; contbg. editor A World History, 1979. Jewish. Address: 550 Sheridan Sq Evanston IL 60202

GREENE, ADDIE LUE, English language educator, mayor, state legislator; b. Quinton, Ala., Jan. 21, 1943; d. Tom Greene and Mary (Williams) Treadwell; m. Melvin Lincoln, June 15, 1966 (div. 1973). BA, Stillman Coll., Tuscaloosa, Ala., 1965; MA, Fla. A&M U., 1973. Instr. English Palm Beach Pub. Schs., West Palm Beach, Fla., 1965-77; sr. instr. English Palm Beach Community Coll., Lake Worth, Fla., 1977—; vice mayor City of Mangonia Park, Fla., 1984-91, mayor, 1991—; mem. Fla. Ho. of Reps., 1993—. Mem. Big. Sister/Big Bros., West Palm Beach, 1981—. Named Role Model of Yr., Bus. and Profl. Women West Palm Beach, 1989, Unsung Hero, Vision mag., 1990, Woman of Excellence of Yr., Eta Phi Beta, 1993; recipient Black-on-Black Crime award, 1993, Leadership award Dem. Black Caucus, Outstanding Legislator award Fla. Acad. Trial Lawyers, Fla. Consortium Urban Leagues award. Mem. Fla. Conf. Black State Legislatures (sec.), Fla. League Cities, NAACP, Bus. and Profl. Women, Urban League, Gold Coast Voters League, Enterprise Fla. Innovative Partnership, Nat. Black Caucus State Legis. Leadership of Palm Beach County, Suncoast C. of C., No. C. of C. (Martin Luther King Jr. award), Haitian Am. Dem. Assn., Palm Beach County Human Rights Assn., 100 Black Women, Interstate Migrant Edn. Coun., Alpha Kappa Alpha. Democrat. Methodist. Home: 1617 Boardman Ave West Palm Beach FL 33407-2105

GREENE, ADELE S., management consultant; b. Newark; d. Adolph and Sara (Schubert) Shuminer; m. Alan Greene (div.); 1 child, Joshua. Student, Juilliard Sch. Music, 1942-44, NYU, 1942-44, New Sch. Social Research, 1944-47; diploma in mgmt., Harvard Bus. Sch., 1978. Account exec. Ruder and Finn Inc., N.Y.C., 1964-66, sr. assoc., 1966-68, v.p., 1968-72, sr. v.p., 1972-76; v.p. pub. affairs Corp. Pub. Broadcasting, Washington, 1976-78; pres., chief operating officer TV Program Group, Washington, 1978-80; pres. Greene and Assocs., N.Y.C., 1981—; exec. dir. Am. Friends of Brit. Mus., 1994—; instr. pub. relations and community affairs, NYU 1974-76; bd. dirs. Sci. Program Group, Washington 1976-81; treas., bd. dirs. Coliseum Park Apts. Co-author: Teen-Age Leadership, 1971. Advisor The Acting Co., Understudies, N.Y.C. 1987—; pres., chief operating officer Am. Craft Council 1980-81, trustee 1976-81; bd. dirs. Union Settlement, N.Y.C. 1987—; trustee Duke Ellington Sch. Arts, Washington, 1977-81. Mem. Pub. Relations Soc. Am. (silver anvil award 1971), Nat. Assn. Edn. Broadcasters, Am. Women Radio and TV. Home and Office: 30 W 60th St New York NY 10023-7902

GREENE, BARBARA ANN MARY, English educator; b. Pembroke, Ont., Can., Sept. 1, 1945; d. Aldred and Mary (Hutchinson) G.; 1 child, Caroline. BA in English, U. Toronto, Ont., 1966, postgrad., 1966-67, 86-87; MPA, Harvard U., 1981. Secondary tchr. English, media studies, dramatic arts North York (Ont.) Bd. Edn., Willowdale, Ont., 1967-72, 81-82, 1986-88; M.P. from Don Valley North Can. Ho. Commons, 1988-93; secondary tchr. English, media studies North York (Ont.) Bd. Edn., 1993—. Elected contr. City of North York, 1972-80, 82-85; mem. Met. Toronto Coun., 1972-80, 82-85, exec. mem., budget subcom. mem., 1974-80, 82-85; dep. mayor North York, 1974-80; mem. Parliament Ottawa, Ont., 1988—. Roman Catholic.

GREENE, ELIZABETH IVORY, real estate company official; b. N.Y.C., Jan. 17, 1929; d. Percy Van Eman Ivory and Elizabeth (Schofield) Post Price; m. James Benno Greene Jr. (dec.); children: Elizabeth Tylawsky, James Benno III, Edgar Charles Ivory. BA, Bennington Coll., 1952. Sculptor Hansen Lamps, N.Y.C., 1952-57; real estate agent Ely-Cruikshank Co., N.Y.C., 1968-70; prin. Greene Realty Ltd., N.Y.C., 1970—, Apocalyptic Holdings Ltd., N.Y.C., 1972—. Rep. candidate for N.Y. State Assembly, 1986, 88, 90, Libertarian candidate, 1986; leader Rep. Dist., N.Y.C., 1987—; bd. dirs. Community Rep. Club Greenwich Village; trustee City and Country Sch., N.Y.C., 1985, 89—; mem. Police Aux. N.Y.C.; mem. N.Y. State Rep. Com.; insp. N.Y.C. Bd. Elections, 1991. Recipient scholarship Bennington (Vt.) Coll., 1949-52. Mem. Small Property Owners Action Network (founder, pres. 1983—), Nat. Ctr. Neighborhood Enterprise, Village Visiting Neighbors (bd. dirs. 1987-89), DAR (John Jay chpt.), Greenwich Village C. of C. (bd. dirs.), Assn. Village Homeowners, N.Y. Mycological Soc. Home and Office: Small Property Owners Action 279 W 12th St New York NY 10014-1911

GREENE, FREDA, journalist, writer; b. London, Mar. 29, 1929; came to U.S., 1952; d. Philip and Stella (Tepper) H.; 1 child from previous marriage, Sheryl. Degree (hon.), Regent St. Poly., London, 1947. Owner Images Internat., L.A., 1978—; cons. pub. rels. Nat. Ctr. on Deafness, Calif. State U. Northridge, L.A., 1979-83. Author: How To Get A Job In Los Angeles, 1985 (Women's Referral Svc. award 1990); editor Changing Homes, 1987-88. Bd. dirs. Women's Referral Svc., 1989-90. Fellow World Literacy Acad.; mem. PEN (cons. L.A. chpt. 1979), Am. Soc. Journalists and Authors (v.p. 1987-88, cons. L.A. chpt. 1982), Women in Mgmt. (v.p. program 1989-90), Women's Nat. Book Assn. Office: Images Internat 6624 Newcastle Ave Reseda CA 91335-5634

GREENE, LYNNE JEANNETTE, fashion designer; b. Albany, N.Y., Aug. 27, 1938; d. Zebulon Stevens and Helen Matilde (Maier) Robbins; m. Stanley E. Greene, Jan. 31, 1962 (dec. June 27, 1987); 1 child, Stuart Nathaniel; m. Michael Alan Karlan, Sept. 29, 1991. Student, Goucher Coll., 1956-57; BA with honors, Parsons Sch. Design, 1960. Asst. designer Haymaker Sportswear (David Crystal), N.Y.C., 1959-61; designer Craig Craely Sportswear and Dresses, N.Y.C., 1961-63, Flair Lingerie, N.Y.C., 1964-66; designer, owner Kaleidoscope Lingerie, N.Y.C., 1966-67; head designer Contessa/Monique/Fisher Lingerie, N.Y.C., 1967-71; creative dir. Eye of the Peacock Sportswear, N.J., 1968-72; head designer, owner Lynne Greene Designs Retail, Montclair, N.J., 1972-74; designer, pres. Little Greene Apples Inc., Montville, N.J., 1971—; designer, dir. mktg. Lady Lynne Lingerie, Guy Laroche Lingerie, N.Y.C., 1973-93, Val Mode, N.Y.C., 1993—; lingerie critic Pratt Inst., 1984—. Patentee in field; illustrator books, pamphlets in fashion and packaging fields; commn. artist and illustrator. Active participant Montville Soccer Assn, 1972-88, fund drives for Am. Heart Assn., Cancer Inc. Mem. The Fashion Group. Republican. Unitarian Universalist.

GREENE, MARÍA CRISTINA, educational counselor; b. Rosario, Santa Fe, Argentina, Mar. 16, 1941; arrived in U.S., 1973; d. Norberto Ramón and Carmen (Ortega) Oroño; m. Homer Edwin Greene, July 24, 1967; children: Sharon Cristina, Brian David. BA in Lit., U. Nat. Rosario, 1966; MS in Edn., Western Ill. U., 1988. Cert. tchr. adult and secondary edn., Ill. Tchr. secondary edn. Academia Estudios Paralelos, Rosario, 1966-73; tchr. adult edn. Black Hawk Coll., Moline, Ill., 1979-83, career counselor, 1983-88, coord. pub. assistance program, 1989-90, counselor, assoc. prof., 1990—; mem. Ill. Quad Cities Higher Edn. Com., Moline, 1991—; mem. Comm. U. Bd. Dirs., Davenport, Iowa, 1992—; project advisor Hispanic Program for Ednl. Advancement of Western Ill. U., Moline, 1990—; mem. Regional Adv. Coun. for Hispanic Affairs, 1991—. Bilingual editor The Healing Journey, 1992—. V.p. Coun. Community Svcs., Moline, 1987-92; adminstr. Ch. Women United Ednl. Support Program, Moline, 1991—; mem. Ill. Migrant Coun. Regional Adv. Bd., East Moline, Ill., 1989—. Mem. ACA, Assn. for Multicultural Counseling and Devel., Ill. Counseling Assn. (Black Hawk chpt.), Nat. Acad. Advising Assn. Office: Black Hawk Coll 6600 34th Ave Moline IL 61265-5899

GREENE, NATALIE CONSTANCE, protective services official; b. Ft. Benning, Ga., Nov. 26, 1960; d. Wilbur Murray and Vernel Jeanette (Smalls) G. BS in Phys. Edn., East Stroudsburg U., 1983; AAS in Gen. Bus., Mercer County Community Coll., 1989, postgrad., 1991—; postgrad., Coll. of Air Force, 1991—. Mil. pay clk. Dept. Def.-U.S. Army, Trenton, N.J., 1984-85, Dept. Def.-USAF, McGuire AFB, N.J., 1985-86; spl. police officer Willingboro (N.J.) Police Dept., 1986-90; budget asst. Dept. Def., West Trenton, N.J., 1986-88; edn. planner, budget officer Dept. Edn., Edison, N.J., 1988-89; merchant svcs. clk. Chem. Bank, Cherry Hill, N.J., 1989-90; transit police officer Southeastern Pa. Transp. Authority, Phila., 1990—. Master sgt. USAFR, 1980—. Recipient Desert Shield/Storm award, 1992, Cert. of Appreciation, CAP, 1991, Willingboro Twp., 1991, Morton Elem. Sch., 1991, Outstanding Young Women of N.J., 1989. Mem. NAFE, VFW, Air Force Sgts. Assn., Air Force Assn., Fraternal Order Police, Fraternal Order Transit Police, Noncommd. Officers Acad. Grad. Assn., Ind. Brotherhood Transit Police, U.S. Res. Police Officers Assn., Inc. (sec. 1987—), Nat. Orgn. Black Law Enforcement, Nat. Polit. Congress Black Women. Baptist. Home: 132 Crestview Dr Willingboro NJ 08046-3538

GREENE, STEPHANIE HARRISON, marketing executive; b. Lake Forest, Ill., June 20, 1950; d. Howard Harrison and Gloria Juliet (Christensen) Greene. BA in Journalism and Advt., Syracuse U., 1972; MBA in Mktg., Cornell U., 1975. With Weeden & Co., Boston, 1972-73; product rep. Allis Chalmers, Matteson, Ill., 1975-76; asst. product mgr. Midwest Am./Am. Hosp. Supply, Des Plaines, Ill., 1976-77; product mgr. Borden, Inc., Columbus, Ohio, 1977-80; product line mgr. John Sexton & Co./Beatrice, Chgo., 1980-82; product mgr. non-foods PYA/Monarch/Sara Lee, Greenville, S.C., 1982-84; mktg. mgr. Fuller Brush/Sara Lee, Winston-Salem, 1984-89; pres. Corbett Harrison Greene, Mundelein, Ill., 1984—; mktg. mgr. The Greehill Corp., Libertyville, Ill., 1989—; bd. dirs. Career Pub., Mundelein, v.p., 1993—. Editor: The Quotation Dictionary, 1968. Active Winnetka (Ill.) Theatre, 1992-95, bd. govs., 1994-95, Wilmette (Ill.) Chorus, 1993-94, Village Follies, 1994. Mem. Print Prodn. Club, Cornell U. Alumnae Assn. (pres. Class of 1975), Johnson Club (amb. 1990, 91, pres. 1992-94), Holly Tree Garden Club (treas. 1983-84), Serendipity Garden Club (treas. 1978-79), Pi Beta Phi. Republican. Episcopalian. Home: 408 Hampton Ter Libertyville IL 60048-3334 Office: The Greehill Corp 15521 W Rockland Rd Libertyville IL 60048-9674

GREENE, WENDY SEGAL, special education educator; b. New Rochelle, N.Y., Jan. 9, 1929; d. Louis Peter and Anne Henrietta (Kahan) Segal; m. Charles Edward Smith (div. 1952); m. Richard M. Greene Jr. (div. Mar. 1967); children: Christopher S., Kerry William, Karen Beth Greene Olson; m. Richard M. Greene Sr., Aug. 29, 1985 (dec. 1986). Student, Olivet Coll., 1946-48, Santa Monica Coll., 1967-70; BA in Child Devel., Calif. State U., Los Angeles, 1973, MA in Elem. Edn., 1975. Cert. tchr., Calif. Counselor Camp Watitoh, Becket, Mass., 1946-49; asst. tchr. Outdoor Play Group, New Rochelle, 1946-58; edn. sec. pediatrics Syracuse (N.Y.) Meml. Hosp., 1952-53; with St. John's Hosp., Santa Monica, Calif., 1962-63; head tchr. Head Start, L.A., 1966-77; tchr. spl. edn. L.A. Unified Sch. Dist., 1977—, Salvin Spl. Edn. Ctr., L.A., 1977-85, Perez Spl. Edn. Ctr., L.A., 1986-; instr. mktg. rsch. for motivational rsch. Anderson-McConnell Agy., 1966; mentor tchr. L.A. Unified Sch. Dist., 1992—. Contbr. to house organ of St. John's Hosp.; co-editor of newspaper for Salvin Sch., L.A. and The Eagle, Perez Sch., L.A., 1988—. Bd. dirs. Richland Ave. Youth House, L.A., 1960-63, Emotional Health Assn., L.A., 1961-66, Richland Ave. Sch. PTA, 1959-63; vol. Hospice of St. Joseph Hosp., Orange, Calif., 1985—; mem. cmty. adv. com. spl. edn. Tustin Unified Sch. Dist., 1994. Mem. AAUW, So. Calif. Assn. Young Children, Olivet Coll. Alumni Assn. United Tchrs. Los Angeles, Kappa Delta Pi. Jewish. Club: Westside Singers (Los Angeles). Home: 14291 Prospect Ave Tustin CA 92680-2316

GREENE LLOYD, NANCY ELLEN, infosystems specialist, physicist; b. Worcester, Mass., Nov. 4, 1947; d. William Arthur II and Dorothy Goddard (Fuller) Green; 1 child, Ellen Dorothy; m. Stephen C. Lloyd, July 25, 1992. BS in Physics, Ohio State U., 1969, MS in Physics, 1971. Instr. physics U. Colo., Colorado Springs, 1971-73; physics programmer U. N.Mex., Albuquerque, 1973-76; data analyst Los Alamos (N.Mex.) Nat. Lab., 1975-77, programmer, 1977-78, mem. tech. staff controlled thermonuclear reaction divsn., 1978-81, mem. tech. staff Accelerator Tech. div., 1981-84, mem. tech. staff adminstrv. data processing divsn., 1984-85, mem. tech. staff dynamic experimentation divsn., 1985-94, staff mem. supr., 1989-90, acting sect. leader, 1990-91, acting dep. divsn. leader, 1992, chief ops. explosives tech. and applications divsn., 1992-94, mem. tech. staff environ., safety, and health divsn. Instl. Affairs Office, 1994—; speaker in field. Vol. Los Alamos Schs., 1980-88, Fountain Valley Sch., Colo., 1990-91. Nat. Merit scholar, Mich. State U., 1965, Nat. Defense Edn. Act Title IV fellow, Ohio State U., 1969. Mem. N.Mex. Digital Equipment Computer Users Soc. (exec. com. 1984-87, 88-90, registration chair computer conf. 1984-87, vice-chair 1988-89, publicity 1989-90), VAX Computer Local Users Group (chmn. 1981-82, sec. 1989-92), NAFE, IEEE, Toastmasters Internat. Office: Los Alamos Nat Lab PO Box 1663 # K491 Los Alamos NM 87545-0600

GREENFIELD, HELEN MEYERS, real estate executive, publishing company executive, inspection and testing service executive; b. Albany, N.Y., 1908; d. Stephen Ferencevich Meyers and Catherine (Bronkov) Ferencevich Meyers; m. Frank L. Greenfield, Apr. 1, 1929; children: Stuart Franklin, Val Shea. Grad., Baker's Bus. Sch., 1924. Accounts supr. George G. McCaskey Co., N.Y.C., 1924-29; spl. assignments purchasing dept. McCall's Pub. Co., N.Y.C., 1929, Fgn. Affairs Publs., Inc., N.Y.C., 1929-31; with purchasing dept. Glidden-Buick Corp., N.Y.C., 1931-32; interviewer U.S. Govt. Civil Works Adminstrn., N.Y.C., 1931-32; supr. filing and payroll systems Houston St. Project Ctr., N.Y.C., 1933-36; with dept. accounting Reuben H. Donnelley Co., N.Y.C., 1936-37; supr. layouts, makeup prins. of semi-monthly publs. Tide Publs., Inc., N.Y.C., 1939-41; asst. to purchasing agt., supr. maintenance perpetual inventory Hopeman Bros., N.Y.C., 1941-43; with money order divsn., corr. dept. U.S. Govt. P.O. Dept., N.Y.C., 1943-44; v.p. Frank L. Greenfield Co., Inc., N.Y.C., 1945-59, All Purpose Chair Corp., N.Y.C., 1950-55; pres. VAL Equipment, Inc., N.Y.C., 1950-62; v.p. Am. Testing Labs., Inc., N.Y.C., 1950-63; supr. personnel, purchases Irving Lampert Co., N.Y.C., 1951-52; account assignment coordinator, advt. contracts dept. Newsweek, N.Y.C., 1970-78; owner, operator Princess Helen Antiques, 1948-52; pres. Helen M. Greenfield Realty Corp., 1968-77; bus. cons., 1979—. Active New York Heart Assn.; founder, coord., show producer, dir. and hostess ann. banquet honor of Dr. Manuel Cabral, composer-dir. Mt. Laurel Ctr. Performing Arts, 1960-84; assoc. mem. Nat. Trust for Hist. Preservation; mem. Staten Island Hist. Soc., Staten Island Inst. of Arts and Scis.; mem. Statue of Liberty-Ellis Island Found. Inc. Named Hon. Princess Helene Evening Star by chief Rising Sun, Chief and High Priest of all N. and S. Am. Indian Tribes and Couns., 1947. Mem. Internat. Platform Assn. Club: Order Eastern Star (past matron).

GREENFIELD, MEG, journalist; b. Seattle, Dec. 27, 1930; d. Lewis James and Lorraine (Nathan) G. BA summa cum laude, Smith Coll., 1952; Fulbright scholar, Newnham Coll., Cambridge (Eng.) U., 1952-53; DHL (hon.), Smith Coll., 1978, Georgetown U., 1979, Wesleyan U., 1982, Williams Coll., 1987, Princeton U., 1990. With Reporter mag., 1957-68, Washington editor, 1965-68; editorial writer Washington Post, 1968-70, dep. editorial page editor, 1970-79, editorial page editor, 1979—; columnist Newsweek, 1974—. Recipient Pulitzer prize for editorial writing 1978. Mem. Am. Soc. Newspaper Editors, Phi Beta Kappa. Home: 3318 R St NW Washington DC 20007-2309 Office: Washington Post Co 1150 15th St NW Washington DC 20005-2780

GREENFIELD, SARAH C., school counselor; b. Rochester, N.Y., July 7, 1937; d. George Stoner and Margaret (Sidebotham) Curtice; m. James D. Greenfield, June 3, 1961. BA, U. Rochester, 1959; Ma in Edn., Ariz. State U., 1968, M of Counseling, 1970, PhD, 1975. Biochem. lab. technician Strong Meml. Hosp., Rochester, N.Y., 1959-61, Pabst Biochem. Lab., Milw., 1962-63; counselor, tutor Alum Rock Sch. Dist., San Jose, Calif., 1977; sch. counselor Chinle (Ariz.) Unified Sch. Dist., 1977—. Vol. crisis worker ADABI, Chinle, 1990—; vol. Heard Mus., Phoenix, 1965-75; mem. exec. bd. Interfaith Counseling N.W., Phoenix, 1970-72, Heard Mus. Gift Shop, 1970. Rockefeller Found. fellow, 1972. Mem. Am. Counseling Assn., Ariz. Counseling Assn. Presbyterian. Home: PO Box 1419 Chinle AZ 86503 Office: Chinle Jr High Sch PO Box 587 Chinle AZ 86503

GREENFIELD, W. M., management consultant, educator; b. N.Y.C., Feb. 15, 1944; d. Tobin and Beatrice (Goldstein) G. BA with honors in History cum laude, Brandeis U., 1965; MBA, Harvard U., 1977. Mgr. internat. dept., internat. editor EDP Industry Report, Internat. Data Corp., Newton, Mass., 1965-69; asst. rsch. dir. Harbridge House, Inc., Boston, 1969-72; mgr. info. and devel. Blue Shield Mass., Inc., Boston, 1972-75; pres., founder W. M Greenfield Assocs., Boston, 1975—; adj. asst. prof. mgmt. policy Boston Univ. Sch. Mgmt., 1977-84, 88—. Author: (with D. Curtin) Cash Flow Management, 1985; Accounting, 1986, Calculated Risk: A Guide to Entrepreneurship, 1986, 2d edit. pub. as Developing New Ventures, 1989, Successful Management Consulting: Building a Practice with Smaller Company Clients, 1987, Solve Your OWN Business Problems: Staying Sane while Staying Solvent, 1988; contbr. articles to profl. jours. Mem. U.S. Assn. for Small Bus. and Entrepreneurship (v.p. publs. 1991-93, program chairperson conf. ind. entrepreneurship divsn. 1995, divsn. v.p. 1995-96), Acad. Mgmt., Stamford C. of C. (Bus. Resource Coun. Vol. of Yr. 1994). Home: 455 Hope St Apt 4E Stamford CT 06906-1330 Office: 37 Lawrence St Boston MA 02116-6011

GREENHALGH, MARTHA MORRISON, accountant; b. Dearborn, Mich., Mar. 19, 1962; d. Richard Olcott and Geraldine E. (Schloff) Morrison; m. Donald Albert Greenhalgh, May 3, 1986; children: Sarah Margaret, Kevin Olcott. BS, Boston Coll., 1984. CPA, Mass. Acct. Laventhol & Horwath, Boston, 1984-87; pvt. practice Watertown, Mass., 1987—. Mem. AICPA, Mass. Soc. CPA's. Republican. Roman Catholic. Home: 144 Lovell Rd Watertown MA 02172-1225

GREENHOUSE, LINDA JOYCE, journalist; b. N.Y.C., Jan. 9, 1947; d. Herman Robert and Dorothy Eleanor (Greenlick) G.; m. Eugene R. Fidell, Jan. 1, 1981; 1 child, Hannah Margalit Fidell. BA, Radcliffe Coll., 1968; M of Studies in Law, Yale U., 1978; D.H.L. (hon.), Brown U., 1991; JD (hon.), Colgate U., 1993. Asst. to James Reston The N.Y. Times, N.Y.C., 1968-69, met. reporter, 1970-74, state polit. reporter, 1974-77; supreme ct. corr. The N.Y. Times, Washington, 1978-85, 88—, congl. corr., 1986-88. Bd. dirs. Yale Law Sch. Fund, New Haven, 1984-91. Fellow Am. Acad. Arts and Scis.; mem. Yale Law Assn. (exec. com. 1993—), Harvard Club Washington (bd. dirs. 1989-92). Office: The NY Times 1627 Eye St NW Washington DC 20006

GREENOUGH, MARTHA ALICE, finance executive; b. N.Y., June 10, 1952; d. William Croan and Doris Aileen (Decker) G.; m. David E. Pitt, Sept. 26, 1986; children: James Gabriel, Katharine Clarissa. BA, Harvard U., 1974, JD, 1977. Bar: N.Y. 1977. Atty. Kramer Levin Nessen, N.Y., 1977-80; cons. Bain & Co., Boston and London, 1980-84; mgr. fin. and banking The N.Y. Times Co., N.Y.C., 1984-92, dir. fin. and banking, 1992-93, asst. treas., 1993—. Mem. The Cosmopolitan Club. Unitarian. Office: The NY Times Co 229 W 43rd St New York NY 10036-3913

GREENSPAN-MARGOLIS, JUNE E., psychiatrist; b. N.Y.C., June 28, 1934; d. Benjamin Robert and Theresa (Cooperstein) Edelman; divorced; 1 child, Alisa Greenspan; m. Gerald J. Margolis. AB, Bryn Mawr Coll., 1955; MD, Med. Coll. Pa., 1959; grad., Inst Phila Assn Psychoanalysis, Bala Cynwyd, 1975. Intern Albert Einstein Med. Ctr., Phila., 1959-60; pvt. practice medicine specializing in pediatrics Cinnaminson, N.J., 1961-67; psychiat. resident Hahnemann Med. Coll., Phila., 1967-71; practice medicine specializing in adult and child psychiatry, psychoanalysis Jenkintown, Pa., 1971—; instr. U. Pa. Sch. Medicine, Phila., 1975-77, clin. assoc. 1977-81, clin. asst. prof. 1981-85, clin. assoc. prof. 1986—; tng. and supervisory analyst Inst. of the Phila. Assn. Psychoanalysis, Bala Cynwyd, Pa., 1986—. Fellow Am. Coll. Psychoanalysts; mem. AMA, Am. Psychiat. Assn., Am. Psychoanalytic Assn. (cert. adult and child psychoanalysis), Am. Acad. Child Psychiatry, Ctr. for Advanced Psychoanalytic Studies (Princeton). Office: Benson East Suite 223-C 100 Old York Rd Jenkintown PA 19046-3251

GREENWALD, CAROLINE MEYER, artist; b. Madison, Wis., Jan. 30, 1936; d. Frank Gustave and Lina Doris (Logemann) Meyer; children: Elaine Kathryn Napp, Geraldine Lynn Bodley. B.S., U. Wis., 1957, M.A. in Arts, 1975, M.F.A., 1977; student, U. Notre Dame Art Workshop, 1976. vis. artist, lectr. univs. and seminars in U.S., Korea and Japan; artist studio in Tokyo, 1983, 84, studio in Paris, 1987, 88. Exhibitor one-person shows: U. Wis.-Madison, 1975, 77, Source Gallery, San Francisco, 1977, Cin. Acad. Art, 1977, Galeria Kin, Mexico City, 1979, Loyola U.-Chgo., 1979, Getler-Pall Gallery, N.Y.C., 1980, 82, Evanston (Ill.) Art Ctr, 1980, Fendrick Gallery, Washington, 1981, Carleton Coll., Northfield, Minn., 1982, American Ctr., Tokyo, 1983, Ina Gallery, Tokyo, 1984, Nagoya Jr. Coll., Japan, 1984, Squibb Gallery, Princeton, N.J., 1984, Sakura Gallery, Nagoya, 1985; group shows include: Nat. Collection Fine Arts, Washington, 1977, Pratt Graphics Ctr., N.Y.C., 1978, Detroit Inst. Arts, 1979, Visual Arts Ctr., Beer-Sheva, Israel, 1979, Seibu Mus Art, Toyko, 1979, Alice Simsar Gallery, Ann Arbor, Mich., 1979, Rockland Ctr. for Arts, West Nyack, N.Y., 1980, New Eng. Found. Arts touring exhbn., 1980-81, Printmaking Council N.J. touring exhbn., 1981, Centre International de la Tapisserie Ancienne et Modern Lausanne (Switzerland), 1981, Mus. Applied Arts, Belgrade, Yugoslavia, 1981, New American Paperworks internat. travelling exhbn., 1982-86, Am. Craft Mus., N.Y.C., 1982, Arts Council Gt. Britain touring exhbn., 1982, Australian Nat. Gallery, Canberra, 1982, Fine Arts Mus. L.I., Hempstead, 1982-83, Eve Mannes Gallery, Atlanta, 1983, Gallery Beni, Kyoto, Japan, 1983, Bibliotheque Publiqued' Information, Centre Georges Pompidou, Paris, 1985, Nat. Mus. Am. Art, Washington, 1985, Cleve. Mus. Art, 1986, Leopold-Hoesch Mus., Fed. Republic Germany, 1986, Livres d'Artistes traveling exhbn. Aubes 3935 Gallery, Montreal, Ctr. for Book Arts, N.Y.C., and Galerie Caroline Corre, Paris, 1987, Palais de Justice, Aix en Provence, France, 1988, Leopold-Hoesch Mus., Fed. Republic Germany, 1988, Phila. Mus. Art, 1988, INAX Gallery, Tokyo, 1990, Textile Art Internat., Inc., Mpls., 1992, Salle des Fetes de la Mairie de Gentilly, Paris, 1992, Studio Galleria, Budapest, Hungary, 1992, Documenta Galeria de Arte, Sao Paulo, Brazil, 1994; represented in permanent collections: Art Inst. Chgo., Australian Nat. Gallery, Elvehjem Mus. Art, U. Wis.-Madison, Indpls. Mus. Art, Jessie Besser Mus., Alpena, Mich., Madison Art Ctr., Mpls. Inst. Arts, Mus. Modern Arts, N.Y.C., Phila. Mus. Art, EPA, San Francisco, Bibliotheque National, Paris, Library of Congress, Washington, Nat. Mus. Am. Art, Washington, Wesleyan U., Middletown. Conn. Grantee Nat. Endowment Arts, 1983; Am. Ctr. Paris residency, 1987-88. Address: 3400 Cross St Madison WI 53711-1715*

GREENWALD, PATRICIA B., advertising executive; b. N.Y.C., Sept. 9, 1940; d. Charles and Rose (Nathanson) Braunstein; m. James L. Greenwald, Dec. 18, 1962; 1 child, Thomas Adam. BS, Case Western Res. U., 1961; MA, Columbia U., 1962. Assoc. rsch. dir. Marschalk Co., N.Y.C., 1962-63; dir. creative rsch. McCann Erickson, N.Y.C., 1963-65; assoc. research dir. J. Tinker & Ptnrs., N.Y.C., 1965-70; exec. v.p. deGarmo Inc. Advt., N.Y.C., 1970-80; sr. v.p. D'Arcy, McManus & Masius, N.Y.C., 1980-83; pres. P. Greenwald Rsch., N.Y.C., 1983-86, Cox & Greenwald Inc. Advt., N.Y.C., 1986-88; ptnr. Barham & Ptnrs. Advt., N.Y.C., 1989-90; prin., part owner Daynet Radio Broadcasting Inc., 1991-94; lectr. Grad. Sch. Bus. NYU, Grad. Sch. Communications Simmons Coll., Boston, Dennison U., Ohio. Trustee, chmn. Light Opera Manhattan, 1987—. Named Woman Achiever Yr. YWCA, 1980. Mem. Market Rsch. Coun., Am. Mktg. Assn., Internat. Radio and TV Soc., Comms. Rsch. Coun., Am. Assn. Pub. Opinion Rsch., N.Y. Women's Agenda. Home: 830 Park Ave New York NY 10021-2757

GREENWALT, JANET ANN, city clerk; b. St. Paul, Nebr., Nov. 15, 1941; d. Clement and Elma L. (Alexander) O'Neill; m. Alvin A Greenwalt, July 7, 1962; children: Russ, David, Rebecca, Christopher. Cert. in cosmetology, Grand Isalnd Beauty Sch., 1960. Cert. mcpl. clk. Cosmetologist Maison Lorenzo-Brandies, Omaha, 1961-65, SarRob, Grand Island, Nebr., 1965-67; mgr. Bel Air Motel, St. Paul, 1967-74; asst. mgr. Johnson Steakmaster, Dannebrog, Nebr., 1974-84; city clk. City of St. Paul, 1984—. Sec. Howard County 911 Bd., St. Paul, 1992-94. Mem. Nebr. Mcpl. Clk. Assn. (bd. dirs. 1990-93, sec.-treas. 1993), Heartland Clks. Assn. (pres. 1989-90). Roman Catholic. Office: City of St Paul 522 Howard Saint Paul NE 68873

GREENWALT, MARY SUSAN, counselor; b. St. Louis, Dec. 26, 1946; d. LeGrand West and Susan Frances (Frier) Wheeler; m. Allen Duane Greenwalt, Apr. 11, 1992; stepchildren: Scott Harrison, Emily Megan. BS, So. Ill. U., 1968, MS, 1972; MBA, St. Louis U., 1982. Tchr. Lindbergh Sch. Dist., St. Louis, 1968-79, counselor, 1979—. Stage mgr. V-P Fair, St. Louis, 1984-93; vol. St. Louis Nursery Found. Book Fair, 1985-93. Recipient Tuition grant for women MBA students IBM, 1977. Mem. NEA, Mo. Edn. Assn., Lindbergh Edn. Assn. (pres. 1982-83), Am. Counseling Assn., Mo. Sch. Counselors Assn., St. Louis Suburban Sch. Counselors Assn. (Elem. Counselor of Yr. 1993), Jr. League St. Louis, Alpha Gamma Delta (St. Louis Alumnae Club). Republican. Methodist. Home: 14 Girard Dr Saint Louis MO 63119-4802 Office: Crestwood Elem Sch 1020 S Sappington Rd Saint Louis MO 63126-1005

GREENWOOD, HARRIET LOIS, environmental banker, researcher; b. Detroit, Oct. 4, 1950; d. Samuel H. and Elizabeth Ann (Bode) G.; m. Michael E. Carlson, Aug. 23, 1981 (div. Sept. 1986); m. Eric J. Halbeisen, Sept. 5, 1987; 1 child, Robin Faith. BA in Biology, Antioch Coll., 1972; MS in Teaching, Antioch Coll. of New Eng., 1975; postgrad. U. Mich., 1985-87. Dir. environ. studies Swanson Environ., Southfield, Mich., 1978-80; project mgr. ESEI, Ecol. Scis., Detroit, 1981-82; pres. Greenwood & Assocs., Detroit, 1982-83; mgr. environ. studies Environ. Rsch. Group, Ann Arbor, Mich., 1983-85; environ. policy specialist Clayton Environ., Southfield, 1985-91; pres. Environ. Tng. Svcs., Detroit, 1991-93; personal trust officer Comerica Bank, 1993—. part-time instr. Wayne State U., 1992—; rec. clk. Detroit Friends Meeting, 1985-88; bd. dirs. Friends Sch. Detroit, 1987-89. U. Mich. fellow, 1985-86. Mem. East Mich. Environ. Acton Coun., Mich. Assn. Environ. Profls., Nat. Assn. Environ. Profls. (ASTM com. E-50 on environ. assessment S.W. Detroit environ. vision project); Mich. Air and Waste Mgmt. Assn. Quaker. Avocations: English country dancing, rapper sword dancing, cross country skiing. Office: Comerica Bank Trust Real Estate-3228 PO Box 75000 Detroit MI 48275-3228

GREENWOOD, JANET KAE DALY, psychologist, educational administrator; b. Goldsboro, N.C., Dec. 9, 1943; d. Fulton Benton and Kelminy Ethel Esther (Ball) Daly; 1 child, Gerald Thompson. AA, Peace Coll., 1963; BS in English and Psychology, East Carolina U., 1965, EdM in Counseling, 1967; postgrad., N.C. State U., 1967-69, U. London, 1969; PhD in Counseling and Higher Ednl. Adminstrn., Fla. State U., 1972. Tchr. English Kinston (N.C.) City Schs., 1965-66, Goldsboro City Schs., 1966-67; counselor and psychometrist primary and secondary schs. County of Wake, N.C., 1967-69; coord. Am. Inst. for Fgn. Study, 1969; supr. student tours in Eng., France, Switzerland, Italy, and Capri, 1969; counselor Fla. State U., Tallahassee, 1969-72; asst. dir. counseling Rutgers U., New Brunswick, N.J., 1972-73; cons. to v.p. for student svcs. Rutgers U., New Brunswick, 1973-74, lectr. in counseling psychology, 1972-74; coord. and assoc. prof. counselor edn. U. Cin., 1974-77, adviser to grad. students, 1974-77, vice provost student affairs, 1977-81; cons. guidance South Plainfield Pub. Schs., 1973-76; adviser Parents Without Ptnrs., 1976; pres. Longwood Coll., Farmville, Va., 1981-87, U. Bridgeport, Conn., 1987-92; cons. Heidrick & Struggles, Washington D.C., 1992—, bd. dirs. The Hydraulic Co., Gov.'s Partnership to Prevent Substance Abuse in the Workforce, audit com. and community, govt. rels. com. Contbr. articles to profl. jours. Mem. Gov.'s Ad Hoc Edn. Com. on Tchr. Edn. and Counselor Edn., State of Ohio, 1975; mem. state planning commn. Nat. Identification of Women Project; chair Twin Rivers Tenants Rights Assn., 1972-74; bd. dirs. Bridgeport Hosp., Bridgeport Bus. Coun.; mem. adv. com. Bridgeport Pub. Edn. Fund; bd. dirs. Conn. Ballet Theatre, chair South End streeting com; mem. mgmt. adv. com. City of Bridgeport; mem. adv. com. United Way Tri-State; chair South End Partnership Com; mem. The Schiavone Steering Com./Downtown Bridgeport Project, YWCA Bd., Champion/United Way, United Way Community Human Svcs. Planning Coun., Bridgeport Symphony Bd., Bridgeport Opera Bd., Bridgeport Area Coll./Univ. Consortium, Conn. Conf. Ind. Colls., The Newcomen Soc. of U.S., The United Way Ea. Fairfield County; mem. adv. bd. Sacred Heart/St. Anthony Sch., Roosevelt Sch; mem. ct. com. Regional Plan Assn. Fairfield 2000; bd. dirs. Conn. Ballet Theatre; chair The Bridgeport Regional Bus. Coun. Brass Ring Task Force on Leadership; bd. govs. Fairfield County Study; mem. hon. bd. dirs. Conn. Earth Day 20, Inc.; chair L.I. Sound Western Regional Coun.; mem. L.I. Sound Assembly; mem. membership com., campus partnership subcom. Drugs Don't Work program, 1989—. Recipient Spl. award Black Arts Festival, Meritorious Svc. award Am. Assn. State Colls. and Univs. Mem. AAUP, Am. Coll. Pers. Assn. (editor and chair media bd. 1975—), Am. Pers. and Guidance Assn., Cin. Pers. and Guidance Assn., Ohio Psychol. Assn., Cin. Psychol. Assn., Organizational Behavior Assn., Am. Sch. Counselors Assn., Ohio Sch. Counselors Assn., Assn. for Women Faculty, Ohio Counselor Edn. and Supervision Assn., Kappa Delta Pi. Office: Heidrick & Struggles 1301 K St NW Ste 500E Washington DC 20005

GREENWOOD, JANET KINGHAM, sanitarian, county official; b. Houston, Sept. 29, 1939; d. Harold Lloyd and Angelina (Mann) Kingham; m. James Richard Greenwood, June 13, 1959; children: Cynthia Anne, Patricia Greenwood Hardcastle. BA in Sociology cum laude, U. Houston, 1975. Registered sanitarian, Tex. Sanitarian-in-tng. Galveston County Health Dist., LaMarque, Tex., 1975-76, sanitarian II, 1976-79, sanitarian III, 1979-81, sr. sanitarian, 1981-88, sanitarian supr., 1988-90, chief sanitarian, 1990-93, dir. environ. and consumer health, 1993—; mem. Sanitarian's adv. Com., Austin, Tex., 1984, vice chmn., 1985. Vol. St. Joseph's Hosp., Houston, 1951-53; mem. recycling com. City of Galveston, 1990—. Fellow Tex. Pub. Health Assn. (governing council, 1980-81, legis. com. 1981-83, scholarship com. 1988-90, exhibit procurement com. 1992-93, chair exhibit procurement com. 1993—, benefits com. 1991—, sect. chmn. 1980-81, President's award 1985, 90, edn. and tng. grantee 1978, fund raising com. 1992—, 2d vice pres. 1994, pub. health mus. com. 1992—); mem. Nat. Environ. Health Assn. (governing coun. 1988-89, merit award 1988), Internat. Milk, Food and Environ. Sanitarians, Tex. Environ. Health Assn. (pres. 1987-89), Gulf Coast Tex. Environ. Health Assn. (pres. 1981, President's award 1986), Tex. Assn. Mcpl. Health Ofcls. (charter), La Marque Rotary. Democrat. Roman Catholic. Office: Galveston County Health Dis 1205 Oak St La Marque TX 77568-5925

GREENWOOD, JOEN ELIZABETH, economist, consultant; b. Mineral Point, Wis., Aug. 29, 1934; d. John Edward and Lillian Laile (Rohr) G. BS, MA, U. Wis., 1956, 57; postgrad., Newnham Coll. Cambridge U., Eng., 1961-62; diploma in advanced mgmt. program, Harvard Bus. Sch., 1983. Instr. econs. Wellesley (Mass.) Coll., 1962-68; sr. assoc. Charles River Assocs., Boston, 1968-79, v.p., 1979—; mem. bd. editors Energy Jour., 1979-83. Co-author: Folded, Spindled and Mutilated: Economic Analysis and U.S. v. IBM, 1983; contbr. to profl. publs. Mem. Commonwealth of Mass. Pub. Health Coun., Boston, 1973-79. Earhart fellow U. Calif.-Berkeley, 1960-61; Fulbright scholar U.K., 1961-62. Mem. Internat. Assn. Energy Economists (v.p. 1978-84, exec. v.p. 1981-84), Nat. Coal Coun., U. Wis. Alumni Assn. (bd. dirs. 1987-93), Wis. Alumni Assn. Greater Boston (pres. 1987-89), Boston Club, Harvard Club, Phi Beta Kappa. Home: 108 Chestnut St Cambridge MA 02139-4704 Office: Charles River Assocs 200 Clarendon St Boston MA 02116-5092

GREENWOOD, LOIS J., association executive; b. Doty, Wis.; d. Thomas Ryall and Bessie Louise (Baker) G. BA, U. Oreg., 1934; MA, Columbia U., 1940. Field sec. youth divsn. Nat. Episcopal Ch., N.Y.C., 1940-42; exec. student dept. Met. YWCA, Chgo., 1942-44; exec. YWCA U. Oreg., Eugene, 1944-51; adminstrv. asst. Annie Wright Sch., Tacoma, Wash., 1952-54; exec. YWCA, Olympia, Wash., 1954-57; councillor student affairs, YWCA exec. U. Oreg., Eugene, 1958-63; acting field sec. N.W. area-student divsn. YWCA, Portland, Oreg., 1957-58; exec. ea. region nat. student divsn YWCA, Cambridge, Mass., 1963-71; program dir., acting exec. YWCA, Boston, 1971-75; acting exec. YWCA, Lowell, Mass., 1975—. Docent Mus. Sci., Boston, 1981-84; dir. altar guild Christ Ch. Episcopal, 1972-94, coord. thrift shop. Mem. Nat. Resources Def. Fund, CARE, Amnesty Internat.

GREENWOOD, VIRGINIA MAXINE MCLEOD, real estate executive, broker; b. Ballinger, Tex., Mar. 3, 1930; d. Vernie L. and Alma (Simpson) McLeod; m. Lester Greenwood, Apr. 21, 1951 (div. May 1985), children: Virginia Leslie Pattison, Randal Lester, Sheree Lou Stiles. Student, Draughn's Bus. Sch., Wichita Falls, 1948-49; completed real estate courses, Grad. Realtors Inst., 1972. Cert. Residential Specialist, 1979. Real estate agt. C. V. Perry Co., Columbus, Ohio, 1967-69, Montague, Miller and Co., Charlottesville, Va., 1970-74; sales mgr. Great Eastern Mgmt. Corp., Charlottesville, 1974-75; real estate broker Greenwood Realty Ltd., Charlottesville, 1975-93; sr. assoc. broker Coldwell Banker-Bailey Realty Co., 1993—. Mem. Monticello Area Cmty. Action Agy. adv. bd., 1988-92, Albemarle (Va.) County Rep. com., 1974-76; Albemarle County Housing adv. com., 1991-92, 94—, Thomas Jefferson Planning Dist. Housing adv. com., 1991-92. Mem. Nat. Assn. Realtors, Va. Assn. Realtors (bd. dirs. 1985-92), Charlottesville Area Assn. of Realtors (sec. 1983-84, bd. dirs. 1983-91, 2d v.p. 1988, 1st v.p. 1989, pres. 1990), Albemarle Housing Coalition. Office: Coldwell Banker Bailey Realty Co 1455 E Rio Rd PO Box 6700 Charlottesville VA 22906

GREER, MARSHA ADAIR, health facility administrator; b. Nowata, Okla., Aug. 12, 1940; 1 child, Joe Tom Adair. ADN, Odessa Coll., 1990. Cert. gerontol. nurse. Psychiat. nurse Glenwood Hosp., 1990-92; dir. nurses Long Term Care Avalon, Odessa, 1989-90; dir. nurses, owner West Tex. Nursing Affiliation and Health Care Enterprises, Odessa, 1990—; instr. nursing Odessa Coll., 1991-93; instr. Am. Red Cross, 1994; RN cons. Sr. Life Care, 1993; instr. ARC, 1994; insvc. coord. Monahans Care Ctr., 1994. Mem. ANA, Tex. Nurses Assn. Office: W Tex Nursing Affiliation 2817 Jb Sheppard Odessa TX 79764

GREER, MARY ELLEN, nutritionist; b. Buffalo, June 12, 1959; d. Billy Pat Sr. and Lila Mae (Cole) G. BS in Dietetics, Howard U., 1981; MPA, U. D.C., 1993. Lic. nutritionist. Nutritionist Washington Women, Infant Children Supplemental Program (WIC), 1993—. Mem. Am. Soc. Pub. Adminstrs. Home: 3200 16th St NW Apt 714 Washington DC 20010-3345

GREGG, MARIE BYRD, retired farmer; b. Mount Olive, N.C., Jan. 12, 1930; d. Arnold Wesley and Martha (Reaves) Byrd; m. Robert Allen Gregg, July 11, 1953; children: Martha Susan, Kathryn Elizabeth, Kenneth Allen. BA in Elem. Edn., Furman U., 1951. 3rd grade tchr. Greenville (S.C.) City Schs., 1951-53; med. social worker Cen. Carolina Rehab. Hosp., Greensboro, N.C., 1959-61; window display designer Kerr Rexall Drugs, Durham, N.C., 1960's; antiques shop owner Something Else Antiques, Lima, Ohio, 1979-81; farm owner Mt. Olive, 1978-92. Democrat. Methodist. Home and Office: 212 Baucom Park Dr Greer SC 29650

GREGG, REGINA CAROL, administrator; b. Glenroy, Ohio, Nov. 11, 1943; d. Warren G. and Dora Marcella (Deck) Young; m. John W. Gregg Jr., June 28, 1964; children: John W. III, Andrea Michele. ADN, Sinclair Coll., 1976; BS in Health Care Adminstrn., St. Joseph's Coll., 1987; MS in Health Care Adminstrn., St. Joseph's Hosp., 1994. Cert. nurse adminstr. Charge nurse Riverside Meth. Hosp., Columbus, Ohio, 1976-77; head nurse Robinson Meml. Hosp., Ravenna, Ohio, 1978-80, nursing coord., 1980-85, dir. critical care nursing, 1985-87; clin. nurse supr. St. Joseph's Hosp., Lowell, Mass., 1988-89; nurse mgr. Cath. Med. Ctr., Manchester, N.H., 1989-94; dir. inpatient svcs. Parkland Med. Ctr., Derry, N.H., 1994—. Mem. ANA, N.H. Nurses Assn., Sigma Theta Tau (fin. com. 1992—). Home: 6 Dublin Rd Windham NH 03087 Office: Parkland Med Ctr 1 Parkland Dr Derry NH 03038

GREGGS, ELIZABETH MAY BUSHNELL (MRS. RAYMOND JOHN GREGGS), retired librarian; b. Delta, Colo., Nov. 7, 1925; d. Joseph Perkins and Ruby May (Stanford) Bushnell; m. Raymond John Greggs, Aug. 16, 1952; children: David M., Geoffrey B., Timothy C., Daniel R. BA, U. Denver, 1948. Children's librarian Grand Junction (Colo.) Pub. Library, 1944-46, Chelan County Library, 1948, Wenatchee (Wash.) Pub. Library, 1948-52, Seattle Pub. Library, 1952-53; children's librarian Renton (Wash.) Pub. Library, 1957-61, dir., 1962, br. supr. and children's services supr., 1963-67; area children's supr. King County Library, Seattle, 1968-78, asst. coordinator children's services, 1978-86; head librarian Valley View Library of King County Library System, Seattle, 1986-90; cons., organizer Tutor Ctr. Library, Seattle South Community Coll., 1969-72; mem. Puget Sound (Wash.) Council for Reviewing Children's Media, 1974—, chmn., 1974-76; cons. to children's TV programs. Editor: Cayas Newsletter, 1971-74; cons. to Children's Catalog, Children's Index to Poetry. Chmn. dist. advancement com. Kloshee dist. Boy Scouts Am., 1975-78; mem. Bond Issue Citizens Group to build new Renton Library, 1958, 59; mem. exec. bd. Family Edn. and Counseling Ctr. on Deafness, 1991—. Recipient Hon. Service to Youth award Cedar River dist. Boy Scouts Am., 1971, Award of Merit Kloshee dist., 1977, winner King County Block Grant, 1990. Mem. ALA (Newbery-Caldecott medal com. 1978-79, com. chmn. 1983-84; membership com. 1978-80, Boy Scouts com. children's svcs. div. 1973-78, chmn. 1976-78, exec. bd. dirs. Assn. for Libr. Svc. to Children 1979-81, mem. coun. 1985-92, chmn. nominating com. 1986-87, councillor 1989-92, exec. bd. 1989-92, exec. com. 1989-92, coun. orientation com. 1987-89), Wash. Libr. Assn. (exec. bd. children's and young adult svcs. div. 1970-78, chmn. membership com. 1983-90, publs. com. 1988-92, emeritus 1991, mem. elections com.), King County Right to Read Coun. (co-chmn. 1973-77), Pierce-King County Reading Coun., Wash. State Literacy Coun. (exec. bd. 1971-77), Wash. Libr. Media Assn. (jr. high levels com. 1980-84), Pacific N.W. Libr. Assn. (young readers' choice com. 1981-83, chmn. div. 1983-85, exec. bd. 1983-85). Methodist. Home: Unit 49 20 1 Union Ave SE Renton WA 98059

GREGOIRE, CHRISTINE O., state attorney general; b. Auburn, Wash.; m. Michael Gregoire; 2 children. BA, U. Wash.; JD cum laude, Gonzaga U., 1977. Clerk, typist Wash. State Adult Probation/ Parole Office, Seattle, 1969; caseworker Wash. Dept. Social and Health Scis., Everett, 1974; asst. atty. gen. City of Spokane, Wash., 1977-81, sr. asst. atty. gen., 1981-82; dep. atty. gen. City of Olympia, Wash., 1982-88, atty. gen., 1993—; dir. Wash. State Dept. Ecology, 1988-92. chair Puget Sound Water Quality Authority, 1990-92, Nat. Com. State Environ. Dirs., 1991-92, States/B.C. Oil Spill Task Force, 1989-92. Mem. Nat. Assn. Attys. Gen. (consumer protection and environment com., energy com., children and the law subcom.). Office: PO Box 40100 905 Plum St SE Bldg 3 Olympia WA 98501-1529*

GREGOR, DOROTHY DEBORAH, librarian; b. Dobbs Ferry, N.Y., Aug. 15, 1939; d. Richard Garrett Heckman and Marion Allen (Richmond) Stewart; m. A. James Gregor, June 22, 1963 (div. 1974). BA, Occidental Coll., 1961; MA, U. Hawaii, 1963; MLS, U. Tex., 1968; cert. in Library Mgmt., U. Calif., Berkeley, 1976. Reference libr. U. Calif., San Francisco, 1968-69; dept. libr. Pub. Health Libr. U. Calif., Berkeley, 1969-71, tech. services libr., 1973-76; reference libr. Hamilton Libr., Honolulu, 1971-72; head serials dept. U. Calif., Berkeley, 1976-80, assoc. univ. libr. tech. svcs.

dept., 1980-84, univ. libr., 1992-94; ret., 1994; chief Shared Cataloging div. Libr. of Congress, Washington, 1984-85; univ. libr. U. Calif.-San Diego, La Jolla, 1985-92, OCLC asst. to pres. for acad. and rsch. libr. rels., 1995—; instr. sch. libr. and info. studies U. Calif., Berkeley, 1975, 76, 83; cons. Nat. Libr. of Medicine, Bethesda, Md., 1985, Ohio Bd. Regents, Columbus, 1987; trustee Online Computer Libr. Ctr., asst. to pres. for acad. and rsch. libr. rels., 1995—. Mem. ALA, Libr. Info. Tech. Assn., Program Com. Ctr. for Rsch. Librs. (bd. chair 1992-93, Hugh Atkinson award 1994).

GREGOR, MARLENE PIERCE, primary educator, elementary science consultant; b. Oak Park, Ill., Apr. 22, 1932; d. Kenneth Bryant and Dorothy (Bloeser) Pierce; m. G. Ray Timmons, Aug. 1, 1953 (div. 1972); children: Gregg R., Todd P., Wendy S. McGuire; m. Harold Laurence Gregor, May 30, 1987. BS in Elem. Edn., U. Ill., 1953; MS in Elem. Edn., Ill. State U., 1974, postgrad., 1975—. Tchr. 2d grade Wethersfield Community Unit Schs., Kewanee, Ill., 1953-54; primary tchr. Fairbury (Ill.) Cropsey Schs., 1965-84, Prairie-Cen. Community Unit #8 Schs., Fairbury, 1984-91; ret. Prairie-Ctr. Community Unit # 8 Schs., Fairbury, 1991; item writer Stanford Achievement Test Psychol. Corp., San Antonio, 1989, sci. assessment Ill. State Bd. Edn., Springfield, 1987-88; grant reader Ctr. Sci. Literacy, Springfield, 1991-93; textbook reviewer The Wheetley Co., Wilmette, Ill., 1994-95. Author: (with others) Horizons Plus Science Stories-Grade 2, 1992, Toys That Teach Science, 1993, Celebrating Science, 1990, Award Winning Nutrition Education Lessons and Units, 1994; mem. sci. tchrs. writing team Ill. State U., 1992; contbr. articles and stories to various publs. Bd. dirs. Friends of the Arts Ill. State U., Normal, 1980-86, 92-94, v.p., 1994-96; mem. Bloomington (Ill.) Mayoral Downtown Devel. Commn., 1993—; mem. adv. bd. Kid's Crossing Childrens Mus., 1993—; mem. steering com. Downtown Hist. Festival, Bloomington, 1995, Ill. State U. Jesse Fell Arboretum, 1994—. Named Outstanding Tchr. Sci. NSF-Ill. State U., 1985, Honors Sci. Tchr. Ill. State U., 1985, 86, 87; Chpt. II Mini grantee Edn. Svc. Ctr. #13, 1985-90; recipient Creative Nutrition award Nutrition and Edn. Tng. Ctr., 1989. Mem. ASCD, NEA, Nat. Sci. Tchrs. Assn. (presenter conv. 1985, 87), Coun. for Elem. Sci. Internat., Ill. Edn. Assn. (Tchr. Excellence award 1989), Ill. Ctr. Sci. Literacy (adv. mem. 1991-93), Ill. Sci. Tchrs. Assn. (sec. 1989-93, Presdl. Excellence Sci. Teaching award 1991, state finalist), Delta Kappa Gamma (v.p. chpt. 1990-92). Presbyterian. Home: 107 W Market St Bloomington IL 61701-3917

GREGOR, MARY JEANNE, educator; b. Portland, Oreg., Jan. 1, 1928; d. John Logan and Pauline (Hudson) Irish; m. Richard Gregor, May, 1953 (div. 1982); 1 child, Ian Nicholas. BA, Creighton U., 1949; MA, St. Louis U., 1952; PhD, U. Toronto, 1957. Fellow St. Louis U., 1949-50; lectr. overseas program U. Md., various countries, 1959-62; lectr. York U., Toronto, 1967-82; assoc. prof. San Diego State U., 1982-86, prof., 1986-92, prof. emeritus, 1992—. Editor, referee, cons. various philos. jours. including U. Chgo. Press, Princeton U. Press, Cambridge U. Press; author: Laws of Freedom, 1963; contbr. numerous articles on ethics, legal philosophy and aesthetics to profl. jours. Vol. various orgns., Toronto, San Diego. Susan Stebbing fellow, 1958-59, Margaret Snell fellow, 1959-60; named Henri Renard Lectr. Creighton U., 1984, Matchette Found. Lectr., 1981. Mem. Metaphys. Soc. Am., North Am. Kant Soc. (adv. bd. 1986—). Republican. Roman Catholic. Home: 5708 Baltimore Dr Apt 410 La Mesa CA 91942-4232 Office: San Diego State U Dept Philosophy San Diego CA 92182

GREGORICH, PENNY DENISE, production procurement analyst; b. Newark, Ohio, May 27, 1968; d. William Raymond and Ethel Faye (Wineman) G. AS in Office Adminstrn., Ctrl. Ohio Tech. Coll., 1989, AS in Bus. Mgmt., 1991; student, Otterbein Coll., 1991—. Sec./clk. Rockwell Internat., Newark, 1985-86, accounts receivable coll. co-op., 1987-89, inventory control specialist, 1989-90, purchasing buyer/analyst, 1990-92, material procurement analyst, 1992—; bookkeeper's asst. Spenley Newspapers/Fostoria Times Rev., Newark, 1986-87. Licking County Joint Vocat.-Tech. Sch./Coop. Office Edn. historian, 1985-86; driver participant Miss Ohio Parade, Mansfield, 1990. Mem. NAFE, Assoc. Humane Soc., Capital Area Humane Soc., Licking County Humane Soc., Ctrl. Ohio Tech. Coll. Alumni Assn., Phi Theta Kappa. Office: Rockwell Internat Rt 79 Heath OH 43056-1440

GREGORIUS, BEVERLY JUNE, retired obstetrician-gynecologist; b. Ottawa, Ill., June 21, 1915; d. Henry Godfrey and Arline (Barry) Pruette; m. Hans Harvey Gregorius, Apr. 6, 1939 (dec.); 1 child, Joan Gregorius Jones. BS, Madison (Tenn.) Coll., 1935; MD, Loma Linda (Calif.) U., 1946, postgrad, 1947-48, MS, 1953. Intern, Los Angeles County Gen. Hosp., 1946-47; resident in ob-gyn, White Meml. Hosp., Los Angeles, 1949-52; practice medicine specializing in ob-gyn, Burbank, Calif., 1953-77; assoc. clin. prof. Loma Linda U. Med. Sch., also U. So. Calif. Med. Sch., 1956-94; clin. prof. ob-gyn U. So. Calif. Med. Sch., 1985-94, emeritus clin. prof., 1994—; program dir. ob-gyn residency program Glendale (Calif.) Adventist Med. Ctr., 1976-82, chmn. dept. ob-gyn, 1981-83, cons., 1983—. Bd. dirs. Arroyo Vista Family Health Ctr.; adminstrv. bd. dirs. Glendale Adventist Ctr., 1985—; mem. bd. councilors Loma Linda U., 1991— (Honored Alumnus 1991). Diplomate Am. Bd. Ob-Gyn. Fellow Am. Coll. Ob-Gyn, ACS, Internat. Coll. Surgeons; mem. AMA, CMA, Assn. Profs. Ob-Gyn., Los County Med. Assn., Los Angeles Ob-Gyn Soc. (coun. 1979-86, pres. 1984-85). Home: 10635 Landale St North Hollywood CA 91602-2316

GREGORY, ANN YOUNG, editor, publisher; b. Lexington, Ky., Apr. 28, 1935; d. David Marion and Pauline (Adams) Young; m. Allen Gregory, Jan. 29, 1957; children: David Young, Mary Peyton. BA with high distinction, U. Ky., 1956. Sec. Ky. edit. TV Guide, Louisville, summer 1956; traffic mgr. Sta. WVLK, Lexington, 1956-61; part time tchr. adult basic edn. Wise County (Va.) Sch. Bd., St. Paul, 1966-72; adminstrv. asst. Appalachian Field Services, Children's TV Workshop, St. Paul, 1971-74; editor, co-pub. Clinch Valley Times, 1974—; pres. Clinch Valley Pub. Co., Inc., St. Paul, 1974—; mem. mktg. com. Mountain Empire TechPrep Consortium, 1993—. Editor, text writer: The Flood of '77 in the St. Paul Area, 1977; weekly newspaper columnist Of Shoes...and Ships...and Sealing Wax, 1974—. V.p. St. Paul PTA, 1970-73; trustee Lonesome Pine Regional Library Bd., 1972-80, chmn., 1978-80; chmn. com. to establish br. library in St. Paul, opened 1975; mem. adv. bd. Pro-Art, Wise County chpt. Va. Mus. Fine Arts, 1979-86; co-leader Brownie troop Girl Scouts U.S.A., 1971-76, bd. dirs. Appalachian council, 1983—, 1st v.p. Appalachian Coun., 1985-91; mem. adv. bd. Wise County YMCA, 1977-80; mem. Wise County Bd. Edn., 1975—, vice chmn., 1981—; pres. So. Region Sch. Bds. Assn., 1987-88; mem. Va. Edn. Block Grants Adv. Com., 1981-86, Region I State Literacy Coun., 1989-91; mem. Local Vocat. Adv. Coun., 1980—, chmn., 1981—; mem. statewide planning coun. Va. Dept. Edn.; mem. Va. Coun. on Vocat. Edn., 1987-95, chmn., 1989-91; mem. exec. com. Va. High Sch. League, 1984-88; past pres. Wise County Humane Soc., Inc.; bd. dirs. Va. Sch. Bds. Assn., 1979-89, pres., 1985-86; bd. dirs. Va. Literacy Found., 1987-89, Appalachia Ednl. Lab., 1995—; sec., treas. S.W. Va. Pub. Edn. Found. Bd., 1993—; mem. Mountain Empire C.C. Found. Bd., 1994—; mem. adv. com. Va. State Supt. Pub. Instrn.; mem. devel. and cmty. rels. com. Clinch Valley Coll.; mem. adv. bd. Wise Appalachian Regional Hosp. Named Outstanding Clubwoman of Yr., St. Paul Jr. Women's Club, 1964, 66, Outstanding Citizen, S.W. Va. dist. Va. Fedn. Women's Clubs, 1968, Woman of Yr. Wise County/ Norton Dem. Women's Club, 1986; recipient Rufus Beamer award Va. Poly. Inst., 1989, William P Kanto Meml. award for contbns. to edn. Clinch Valley Coll., Mountain Empire C.C. and Wise County and Norton Pub. Schs., 1990; Ky. Broadcasters Assn. scholar, 1956; named Citizen of Yr. Wise County C. of C., 1990. Mem. Va. Press Assn. (1st place award for editorial writing 1976), Nat. Press Women, Va. Press Women, Nat. Newspaper Assn., Women in Communications, Nat. Sch. Bds. Assn. (pub. relations com., nominating com. 1987), Mortar Bd., Delta Kappa Gamma (hon. mem. Alpha Psi chpt.), Phi Beta Kappa, Alpha Delta Pi. Democrat. Methodist. Home: PO Box 303 Saint Paul VA 24283-0303 Office: PO Box 817 Saint Paul VA 24283-0817

GREGORY, BETTINA LOUISE, journalist; b. N.Y.C., June 4, 1946; d. George Alexander and V. Elizabeth Friedman; m. John P. Flannery, II, 1981; 1 child, Diana Elizabeth. Student, Smith Coll., 1964-65; diploma in acting, Webber-Douglas Sch. Dramatic Art, London, 1968; BA in Psychology, Pierce Coll., Athens, Greece, 1972; LittD (hon.), Susquehanna U., 1988, St. Thomas Aquinas U., 1992; LLD (hon.), Wilmington Coll., 1989; D in Journalism (hon.), U. Findlay, 1990. Reporter Sta. WVBR-FM, Ithaca, N.Y., 1972-73, Sta. WCIC-TV, Ithaca, 1972; reporter, anchorwoman Sta. WGBB, Freeport, N.Y., 1973, Sta. WCBS, N.Y.; freelance reporter, writer AP, N.Y.C., 1973-74; freelance reporter N.Y. Times, 1973-74; with ABC News, 1974—; corr. ABC News, Washington, 1977-79; White House corr. ABC News, 1979—, sr. gen. assignment corr., 1980—; elected rep. for corr.'s ABC News Women's Adv. Bd. Reporter TV spl. Flaws in the Shield, 1989 (1st pl. Headliner award), A&E's Biography of Hillary Rodham Clinton, 1994 (Best Documentary ACE award 1994). Recipient 1st Place award Nat. Feature News, Odyssey Inst., N.Y., 1978, Clarion award Women in Communications, Inc., 1979, hon. mention Nat. Commn. on Working Women, 1979, Media award for Am. Agenda segment on homeless World Hunger Found., 1990, Cable Ace Best Documentary award, 1995; named one of top 10 investigative reporters, TV Guide, 1983. Mem. Radio TV Corrs. Assn., White House Corrs. Assn. Clubs: Newswomen's N.Y. (recipient Front Page award 1976); Nat. Press; Washington Press. Office: ABC News Washington Bur 1717 Desales St NW Washington DC 20036-4407

GREGORY, HOLLY WANDA JANUSZKIEWICZ, lawyer; b. Rutland, Vt., May 14, 1956; d. Tadeusz and Marjorie Beatty (Martinson) Januszkiewicz; m. Robert Stephen Gregory, Aug. 23, 1987; 1 child, Thaddeus Robert. BA with honors, SUNY, Purchase, 1979; JD summa cum laude, N.Y. Law Sch., 1986. Bar: N.Y. 1987. Law clk. U.S. Ct. Appeals (2d cir.), Albany, N.Y. and N.Y.C., 1986-87; assoc. Weil, Gotshal & Manges, N.Y.C., 1987—; counsel WestFest, Inc., N.Y.C., 1988-91. Editor: Journal of Proprietary Rights, 1989-91; exec. editor: N.Y. Law Sch. Law Rev., 1985-86. Frederick C. Scholem scholar N.Y. Law Sch., 1983-86. Mem. ABA (antitrust sect.). Soc. of Friends. Office: Weil Gotshal & Manges 767 5th Ave New York NY 10022

GREGORY, JACKIE SUE, critical care nurse; b. Amarillo Potter County, Tex., Nov. 26, 1946; d. Albert Ray and Rosa Inez (Bryson) Horner; children: Larry, Paula, Justin. BSN, West Tex. State U., Canyon, 1989. RN, Tex., Okla. Staff nurse vascular ICU Baylor U. Med. Ctr., Dallas, 1991-93; adminstr. Assocs. Home Health Inc., Jacksonville, Tex., 1994—; part-time clin. instr. Cameron U., Lawton, Okla., 1990-93. Vol. hospice program Vis. Nurse Assn., 1989-90. USPHS scholar, 1989. Mem. AACN, ANA, Okla. Nurses Assn., Sigma Theta Tau.

GREGORY, JANET FAYE, principal, educator; b. Olney, Ill., July 1, 1949; d. Donald Dale and Norva Pearl (Riggs) Daubs; m. Dennis Keith Gregory, Aug. 5, 1972; children: Heidi Michelle, Darren Keith, Justin Lee. BS, So. Ill. U., 1971. Cert. tchr. Tchr. Rockford (Ill.) Christian Elem. Sch., 1981-86; prin., tchr. West County Christian Sch., St. Louis, 1986—. Mem. Assn. Christian Schs. Internat. Home: 5830 Mayberry Dr Imperial MO 63052-2138

GREGORY, JEAN WINFREY, ecologist, educator; b. Richmond, Va., Feb. 13, 1947; d. Thomas Edloe and Kathryn (McFarlane) Winfrey; m. Ronald Alfred Gregory, Dec. 13, 1973. BS in Biology, Mary Washington Coll., 1969; MS in Biology, Va. Commonwealth U., 1975, postgrad. in pub. adminstrn., 1982-90; MA in Environ. Sci., U. Va., 1983. Cert. fisheries sci. Lab. specialist A Cardiovascular Div. Med. Coll. Va., Richmond, 1969-70; pollution specialist State Water Control Bd. (now Dept. Environ. Quality), Richmond, 1970-77, pollution control specialist B, 1977-81, ecologist, 1981-85, ecology programs supr., 1985-88, environ. program mgr., 1988-93; mgr. environ. program Va. Dept. Environ. Quality, Richmond, 1993—; adj. faculty Va. Commonwealth U., Richmond, 1978-93. Contbr. articles to profl. jours., 1972-88. Named One of Outstanding Young Women of Am., 1974; EPA fellow, Va., 1974-76. Mem. Am. Soc. Limnology and Oceanography, N.Am. Lake Mgmt. Soc., N.Am. Benthological Soc., Ecol. Soc. Am., Romance Writers Am., Sisters in Crime. Democrat. Methodist. Office: Office Environ Rsch & Quality Water Divsn PO Box 11143 Richmond VA 23240-0007

GREGORY, LESLIE FINLAYSON, tax accountant, financial consultant, realtor; b. Halifax, N.S., Can., Nov. 18, 1956; d. F. Douglas and Beverley Jeanne (Adams) Finlayson; m. Michael R. Gregory, May 15, 1981 (div. 1982); children from previous marriage: Jarrell (Geno) Hurley II, Jason Douglas Hurley. AA magna cum laude, Diablo Valley Coll., Pleasant Hill, Calif.; BS in Fin., Mktg. and Bus. Adminstrn. Mgmt., Calif. State U., Hayward, 1990. Lic. tax acct.; lic. real estate agt. Investment analyst Camilto Mgmt. Co., Lafayette, Calif., 1980-82; office mgr. Gilbert Constrn., Martinez, Calif., 1982-84; acctg. mgr. Richmond (Calif.) Drydock; A/P mgr. Sassoon-Sherman, Oakland, Calif.; tax acct. Beneficial Tax, Pleasant Hill, 1985-88; realtor Mason-McDuffie Real Estate, Clayton, Calif., 1990—; fin. cons., tax acct. Gregory & Assocs., Clyde, Calif., 1983—; tax/audit. rep., Concord, Calif. Mem. NAFE, Nat. Assn. Realtors, Calif. Assn. Realtors, Contra Costa Bd. Realtors (participant canned food dr. Walnut Creek, Calif. 1990—), Moose, BAM, R.E. Fin. Planners. Republican. Office: Mason McDuffie Real Estate 5400 B 1 Ygnacio Valley Rd Concord CA 94520

GREGORY, MARTHA ANN, librarian; b. Springfield, Mo., July 8, 1942; d. Ralph Winfred and Ruth (Clement) Pogue; m. Benjamin Ralph Gregory, Nov. 16, 1963; 1 child, Sarah. BS, U. Tulsa, 1972; MS, Okla. State U., 1989. Interlibrary loan libr. Tulsa City-County Libr. System, 1970-71, libr. asst., 1972-79, information II libr., 1979-86, econ. devel. information ctr. libr., 1986—; mem. Information and Rsch. Com., Met. Tulsa Econ. Devel. Found., 1988—; chmn. Okla. Online Users Group, Tulsa, 1980-86. Author: Tulsa Data Book, 1988. Mem. Special Librs. Assn. (program chmn. Okla. chpt. 1983-84), Am. Sociol. Assn., Southwestern Social Sci. Assn., Alpha Kappa Delta, Bus. and Profl. Women's Club (legis. chmn. 1985). Office: Tulsa City-County Library 400 Civic Ctr Tulsa OK 74103-3830

GREGORY, MYRA MAY, educator, religious organization administrator; b. N.Y.C., Sept. 21, 1912; d. Thomas and Anna (Collins) G. Diploma, Maxwell Tchrs. Tng. Sch., Bklyn., 1933; BS in Edn., Bklyn. Coll., 1940, MA in History, 1952. Cert. music tchr. Tchr. N.Y.C. Bd. Edn., Bklyn., 1943-75; social worker Berean Bapt. Ch., Bklyn., 1932-48, supr., 1932-94, fin. sec. Sunday sch., 1935-94; bd. dirs. Berean-Vacation Bible Sch., Bklyn.; tchr. Protestant Coun., N.Y.C., 1940-81; bd. dirs. Recreation Bedford-Stuyvesant Area Project, Bklyn.; dir. seminar Christian Teaching, Bklyn., 1974-86, 1990—. Bd. mgrs. Bklyn. Sunday Sch. Union, 1974—; pres. Coun. of Chs. of the City of N.Y., Bklyn., 1984-86; bd. dirs. Bklyn. Div. Coun. of Chs., 1984—. Recipient Ecumenism citation Borough Pres.'s Office, Bklyn., 1985, Religious Educator citation Bklyn. Ch. Women United, Inc., 1993, Cmty. Svc. award Mayor's Office, N.Y.C., 1993, Ecumenical Svc/Educator Honors Office of the Coun. of City of N.Y., 1994; named Tchr. of Yr. Cmty. Sch. Bd. Dist. 14, Bklyn., 1973, Outstanding Tchr., Stuyvesant divsn., Bklyn. Sunday Sch. Union, 1977, Educator/Leader Berean Bapt. Ch., 1977. Mem. ASCD, Am. String Tchrs. Assn., Am. Viola Soc., Assn. Childhood Edn. Internat., Orgn. Am. Historians, Ctr. Study of Presidency. Democrat.

GREGORY, SUSAN B., lawyer; b. Terre Haute, Ind., Apr. 30, 1965; d. Robert Leroy and Patricia Mary (French) Eddleman; m. Kevin L. Gregory, Aug. 13, 1988. BS, BA, Purdue U., 1987; JD, U. Ill., 1991. Assoc. Baker & Daniels, Indpls., 1991-93; corp. atty. USA Group, Inc., Fishers, Ind., 1993—. Sec./treas. Marion County 4-H Clubs, Inc., Indpls., 1991—; charter mem. Beacon Soc. in Support of Meth. Hosp., Indpls., 1993—. Mem. Purdue U. Sch. Consumer and Family Scis. Alumni Assn. (pres.-elect 1994—), Indpls. Zoo Guild, Order of Coif, Order of Barristers, Phi Beta Kappa, Phi Kappa Phi, Omicron Delta Kappa, Omicron Nu. Home: 123 Morningside Dr Brownsburg IN 46112

GREGUS, LINDA ANNA, government official; b. Hartford, Conn., Mar. 24, 1956; d. Steven and Sylvia Christine (Ramunno) G. AB, Bowdoin Coll., 1978; MA in Law and Diplomacy, Tufts U., 1985. Vol. VISTA, Phoenix, 1978-79; research asst. Econ. Research Assocs., Boston, 1979; ops adminstr. CRT Inc., Hartford, Conn., 1980-82; program officer U.S. Dept. of State, Washington, 1986-90; intelligence officer CIA, Washington, 1990—. Recipient Milo Peck Scholarship Town of Windsor, Conn., 1984. Republican. Home: 1904 Wilson Ln Mc Lean VA 22102-1958

GREIG, EDNA VIRGINIA, finance manager; b. Paterson, N.J., Nov. 28, 1956; d. James O. and Edna V. (Strother) G. BS in Acctg. summa cum laude, Fairleigh Dickinson U., 1980. CPA. Auditor Price Waterhouse, Hackensack, N.J., 1980-82; staff mgr. fin. AT&T, Bridgewater, N.J., 1982-87; mgr. fin. analysis Volvo Penta Am., Chesapeake, Va., 1987-92; cons. AGS Info. Svcs., Clark, N.J., 1992-93; fin. mgr. Becton Dickinson and Co., Franklin Lakes, N.J., 1993—. Mem. N.J. Soc. CPA.

GREILING, MARION GAIL (MINDY GREILING), state legislator; b. Rochester, Minn., Feb. 28, 1948; d. Robert Columbus and Jeanette Ruth (Sleeper) Rittenhouse; m. Roger Morrison Greiling, Dec. 26, 1970; children: Angela Dawn, James Brian. BA, Gustavus Adolphus Coll., 1970; MA, U. Minn., 1974. Tchr. St. Paul Pub. Schs., 1970-75; rsch. interviewer U. Minn., Mpls., 1985-92; mem. Minn. Legislature, St. Paul, 1993—. Hon. chair Am. Cancer Soc. Jail and Bail, 1987; bd. dirs. Minn. Friends of Pub. Edn., 1986-87, N.W. Suburban Youth and Family Svcs., 1987-92; mem. sex equity adv. com. Minn. Dept. Edn., 1985-86, chair All-Am. com., 1985-86; mem. pub. access adv. com North Suburban Cable Corp., 1986-87; mem. Roseville Bicentennial of the Constn. Com., 1987-88; mem. pay equity com. Commn. on Econ. Status of Women, 1987-88; bd. dirs. Assn. Met. Sch. Dists., 1987-92; troop leader Girl Scouts Am., 1984—; mem. state adv. bd. 4-H; bd. dirs., mem. exec. com. North Ctrl. Regional Ednl. Lab., 1993—; active PTA. Recipient Outstanding Leadership award North Suburban Gavel Assn., 1985, Friend of Edn. award Minn. Coalition for Pub. Edn., 1987, Outstanding Leader award Girl Scouts Am., 1988, Individual Sch. Bd. Mem. Recognition award Minn. Sch. Bds. Assn. 1990. Mem. LWV of Minn. (Rose award 1981, v.p., legis. chair 1986-87), Minn. Women Elected Officials, Citizens League, Ramsey County Friends of the Libr., Roseville Hist. Soc., Parents Comm. Network (charter). Democrat. Methodist. Home: 2495 Marion St Roseville MN 55113-3645 Office: Minn State Legislature 559 State Office Bldg Saint Paul MN 55155

GREIMAN, APRIL, graphic designer; b. Rockville, N.Y., Mar. 22, 1948. BFA, Kansas City (Mo.) Art Inst., 1970; studied design with, Armin Hoffmann and Wolfgang Weingart, Allgemeine Kunstgewerbeschule, Basel, Switzerland, 1970-71. Free-lance designer N.Y.C., 1971-75; asst. prof. Phila. Coll. Art, 1971-75; cons. MOMA, N.Y.C., 1975-76; founder April Greiman Inc., L.A., 1976; dir. design program Calif. Inst. Arts., L.A., 1982-84. One woman shows include Arc en Reve, Ctr. d'Architecture, Bordeaux, France, 1994; exhibited in group shows at Albright Knox Gallery, Buffalo, 1979, Cooper Hewitt Mus., Walker Art Ctr., Mpls., Mus. Modern Art, Smithsonian. Nat. Endowment for Arts grantee, 1987; winner The Modern Poster MOMA, 1989. Mem. Am. Inst. Graphic Arts (past nat. bd. dirs., past pres. L.A. chpt.), Alliance Graphique Internat. (mem. exec. com. 1991-93). Office: April Greiman Inc 620 Moulton Ave #211 Los Angeles CA 90031-3288*

GREINER, BETTY ANN, patient educator; b. Fort Smith, Ark., Apr. 22, 1932; m. Verlin P. Greiner, Feb. 14, 1950 (div. 1977); children: Lee, Tom, Cathy Rennie, Sarah Boorstein; m. Jackie Blackwell, Nov. 29, 1991. LPN, Mid Am. VoTech, 1977; AD, Rose State Coll., 1988. RN, Okla. Coronary care unit Norman (Okla.) Regional Hosp., 1977-91, cardiac educator, 1991—, ACLS instr., 1988—, CPR instr., 1988—; speaker in field; advisor Moore-Norman Vo Tech Sch., 1988-91. Worksite chmn. Am. Heart Assn., Norman, 1990-92, bd. dirs., 1988—. Named Nurse of Yr., Moore Norman Vo Tech Class # 22, 1983, Class # 25, 1948; recipient Nursing Excellence award Norman Regional Hosp., 1989, 93. Home: 704 N Fifth Noble OK 73068 Office: Norman Regional Hosp 901 N Porter Norman OK 73070

GREIST, MARILYN LEE, advertising agency executive; b. Phila., May 21, 1945; d. David and Florence Gertrude (Wolfe) Vernik; m. Lewis Charles Greist, May 21, 1972. Student, Temple U., 1966; cert., HB Studios, N.Y.C., 1979. Media buyer Brownstein Advt., Phila., 1969-71, media dir., 1971-73, account exec., 1973-75; media cons. Marilyn Greist Media, Phila., 1975-77; dir. advt. Cottman Transmissions, Ft. Washington, Pa., 1977-79; research analyst Katz Communications, Inc., N.Y.C., 1979-83; media dir., account exec. Gregory & Clyburne, Inc., Stamford, Conn., 1983-85; v.p. and sr. account exec. Gregory & Clyburne, Inc., Stamford, 1985-88; v.p., media dir. Dickison & Rakaseder, Inc., Stamford, 1988—. Mem. Westport Community Theater, 1982-83; mem. North Park Civic Assn., Bridgeport, Conn., 1985-87; mem. ch. choir, Bridgeport. Mem. Ad Club of Fairfield County (v.p. 1985-86, Matty awards 1984, 85, 86), Women in Communications (Fairfield County chpt.). Republican. Home: 578 Cleveland Ave Bridgeport CT 06604-1603 Office: Dickison & Rakaseder Inc 205 Main St Westport CT 06880-3206

GRENFELL, GLORIA ROSS, freelance journalist; b. Redwood City, Calif., Nov. 14, 1926; d. Edward William and Blanch (Ross) G.; m. June 19, 1948 (div. Nov. 15, 1983); children: Jane, Barbara, Robert, Mary. BS, U. Oreg., 1948, postgrad., 1983-85. Coll. bd., retail sales Meier & Frank Co., Portland, Oreg., 1945; book sales retailer J.K. Gill & Co., Portland, Oreg., 1948-50; advisor Mt. Hood Meadows Women's Ski Program, Oreg., 1968-78; corp. v.p. OK Delivery System, Inc., Oreg., 1977-82; ski instr. Willamette Pass, Oreg., 1983-85, Mt. Shasta, 1986; Campfire girls leader Portland, 1958-72; freelance journalist Marina, Calif., 1986—. Mem. Assn. Jr. League Internat., 1957-87; mem. Rep. Nat. Com., 1991—; mem. Monterey County Mental Health Adv. Commn., 1994—; mem. No. Mariposa County History Ctr., Calif. Recipient Golden Poles award Mt. Hood Meadows, 1975. Mem. Soc. Profl. Journalists, Profl. Ski Instrs. Am., U.S. Ski Coaches Assn., Calif. State Sheriffs' Assn. (assoc.), Monterey History and Art Assn., Yosemite Assn., Friends of Sea Otter, Mariposa County C. of C., Monterey Bay Area Nat. Alumnae Panhellenic, Order Ea. Star, Mortar Bd., Kappa Alpha Theta. Republican. Episcopalian. Home and Office: 3128 Crescent Ave Space 9 Marina CA 93933

GRENIER, MICHÈLE FLEUR, environmental scientist; b. Burlington, Vt., May 4, 1956; d. Gordon Louis and Joan Helen (Brown) G. BA in Secondary Edn., BS in Biology, SUNY, Cortland, 1979; MA in English summa cum laude, Cornell U., 1981; postgrad., l'Universite de la Suisse, Neuchetâl, Switzerland, 1981. Tchr. biology, English Whitney Point (N.Y.) High Sch., 1981-86; edn. coord. Mass. Soc. Prevention Cruelty Animals, Boston, 1986-88; biologist, aquatic entomologist Springborn Labs., Inc., Wareham, Mass., 1988-94; environ. scientist Rizzo Assocs., Inc., Natick, Mass., 1994—; biologist, marine mammal rsch. cons. cetacean rsch. Web of Life Sci. Ctr., Carver, Mass., 1988-91. Chairwoman Middleborough (Mass.) Bd. Selectman; bd. dirs. Middleborough Pub. Libr. Recycling grantee Dept. Environ. Protection, 1991. Mem. Nat. Assn. Environ. Profls., N.Am. Benthological Soc., Assn. Mass. Wetland Scientists, Soc. Environ. Toxicology and Chemistry, Soc. Wetland Scientist, Women's Transp. Seminar. Home: PO Box 586 Middleboro MA 02346-0586 Office: Rizzo Assocs Inc 235 W Central St Natick MA 01760

GRENZ, LINDA L., Episcopal priest; b. Eureka, S.D., Apr. 9, 1950; d. Milbert A. and Frieda (Junker) G.; m. Delbert C. Glover, Dec. 27, 1992. BA, Westmar Coll., 1972; M Theol. Studies, Harvard U., 1974; MDiv, Episcopal Div. Sch., 1977. Rector St. Paul's Episcopal Ch., Camden, Del., 1977-83; mgmt. and tng. cons. Wilmington, Del., 1983-89; assoc. dir. overseas devel. Episcopal Ch. Ctr., N.Y.C., 1990-92, coord. adult edn. and leadership devel., 1992-94; pres. LeaderResources, Wilmington, 1994—. Author: (tng. manuals) Discipleship Groups, 1994, (booklet) Covenant of Trust, 1994; editor, contbr. In Dialogue With Scripture, 1992 (Polly Bond award 1992), Ministry in Daily Life, 1994. Office: LeaderResources 1116 W 8th St Wilmington DE 19806

GRESHAM, ANN ELIZABETH, retailer, horticulturist executive, consultant; b. Richmond, Va., Oct. 11, 1933; d. Allwin Stagg and Ruby Scott (Faber) Gresham. Student, Peace Coll., Raleigh, N.C., 1950-52, East Carolina U., 1952-53, Penland Sch., N.C., 1953-54, Va. Commonwealth U., 1960-64. Owner, prin. Ann Gresham's Gift Shop, Richmond, 1953-56; pres., treas. Gresham's Garden Ctr., Inc., Richmond, 1955-79; v.p. Gresham's Nursery, Inc., Richmond, 1959-73, pres., treas., 1973-84; pres., treas. Gresham's Country Store, Richmond, 1964—; tchr., 1982—. Bd. dirs. Bainbridge Community Ministry, 1979, Handworkshop, 1984-89; class agt. Peace Coll., Raleigh, 1987-88, mem. alumnae council, 1987, 88—, bd. visitors, 1987-93; focus group mem. Hand Workshop, Richmond, 1983, bd. dirs., 1984-87. Mem. Midlothian Antique Dealers (treas. 1975-79), Richmond Quilt Guild (chpt. v.p. 1983-84), Nat. Needlework Assn., Quilt Inst., Am. Hort. Soc. Episcopalian. Clubs: Chesmond Women's (v.p. 1979-80), James River Woman's (Richmond) (tres. 1990-92). Home and Office: Gresham's Inc 2324 Logan St Richmond VA 23235-3462

GRESHAM, SUZANNE LEE, mental health center executive; b. Pontiac, Mich., Sept. 7, 1939; d. Orlando Bert and Anne Mae (Borst) Craft; m. Julian Rochelle Gresham, Oct. 6, 1973. BA, Wayne State U., 1961, MA, 1968, PhD, 1972. Cert. cons. psychologist, Mich. Chief psychologist Livingston County Community Mental Health Ctr., Howell, Mich., 1968-69, Downriver Guidance Ctr., Lincoln Park, Mich., 1969-74; unit coord. N.E. Guidance Ctr., Detroit, 1974-76, asst. dir., 1976-78; pres., CEO Comprehensive Mental Health Svc., Muncie, Ind., 1979—. Chmn. bd. Delaware County Community Corrections, Muncie, 1992-94; v.p. bd. dirs. Delaware United Way, Muncie, 1991. Named Women of Achievement, Women in Comms., Inc., Muncie, 1988. Mem. Ind. Coun. of Community Mental Health ctrs. (pres. 1985-86), Am. Psychol. Assn., Muncie-Delaware C. of C. (treas. of bd. 1990), Altrusa Club of Muncie, Inc. (pres. 1988-89), Phi Beta Kappa. Office: Comprehensive Mental Health Svcs Inc 240 N Tillotson Ave Muncie IN 47304

GRESSER, CAROL A., school system administrator. Pres. N.Y.C. Bd. Edn., Bklyn. Office: NYC Bd Edn 110 Livingston St Brooklyn NY 11201-5065

GREW, KIMBERLY ANN, social service administrator; b. Saginaw, Mich., Nov. 25, 1962; d. Chester Joseph and Ruth Irene (Kemmerling) G. AA, Delta Coll., University Center, Mich., 1981; BA, Saginaw Valley State U., 1983, MA, 1987; Cert. Paralegal Studies with distinction, Am. Inst. Paralegal Studies, Detroit, 1988. Lead tchr. Child & Family Svcs., Bay City, Mich., 1986-87; legal advocate/counselor Saginaw County (Mich.) Sexual Assault Ctr., 1987-88; specialized foster care worker Family & Children's Svc. Midland, Mich., 1989-90; asst. payments V Saginaw County Dept. Social Svcs., 1990-92, welfare svcs. specialist-foster care, 1992—. Editor/chmn. cookbook: Edible, Palatable, Delights, 1985. Mem. Child Abuse and Neglect Coun. Saginaw, Midland Art Coun.; membership com., nominations com. Saginaw Social Svc. Club, 1988, sec., 1989-90, nominations com. 1991-92; vol. Bay City (Mich.) YWCA, Saginaw Vet. Hosp.; bd. dirs. Bay City Crime Stoppers, 1987—, treas., 1989—; mem. Midland Ctr. for Arts, 1990—. Mem. NAFE, AAUW (v.p. 1986-88, pres. 1988-90), Am. Soc. Criminology, Am. Criminal Justice Soc., Legal Assts. Assn. Mich., Mil. Order Purple Heart Aux. (v.p. 1987—), Saginaw Valley State U. Alumni Bd. (rec. sec. 1993—), Altrusa, Phi Alpha Delta, Sigma Beta Phi (rec. sec. Xi Beta Delta chpt. 1990-92, Pledge of Yr. 1990, Perceptor 1993—). Democrat. Baptist. Home: 3329 W Douglas Dr Bay City MI 48706-1223

GREWELL, JUDITH LYNN, consultant; b. New Orleans, Aug. 27, 1945; d. Raymond Walter and Dorothy Marie (Reymann) Potratz; m. John Nolting Grewell, Aug. 28, 1964; children: Patricia Lynn, Amy Elizabeth. BA with honors, Wayne State U., 1972; MA with honors, Oakland U., 1976. Cert. prodn. and inventory mgmt. Supr. mfg. Chevrolet-Pontiac-GM of Can. div., Pontiac, Mich., 1978-80, purchasing agt., 1980-82, trainer, organizational cons., 1982-84; supr. systems tng. Electronic Data Systems Div., Troy, Mich., 1985-86, supr. tech. tng. devel., 1986-88, supr. tng. and communications, 1988-89, prin. sr. cons. divsn., 1989—; head trainer UAW-GM Nat. Workshop, Black Lake, Mich., 1983. Contbg. editor Univ. Assocs. Handbook of Structured Experiences, 1985. Mem. Am. Prodn. and Inventory Control Soc., Pi Lambda, Phi Upsilon Omicron. Republican. Presbyterian. Home: 27085 Winchester Ct Farmington Hl MI 48331-3686 Office: 26533 Evergreen Southfield MI 48086

GREY, DEBORAH CLELAND, Canadian government official; b. Vancouver, B.C., Can., July 1, 1952; d. Mansell Caverhill Grey and Lilian Joyce (Russell) Levy; m. Lewis Larson, Aug. 7, 1993. BA, U. Alta., Edmonton, Can., 1978, B of Edn., 1979. Tchr. Frog Lake (Alta.) Indian Res., 1979-80, Dewberry (Alta.) Sch., 1980-89; M.P. Ho. of Commons, Ottawa, Ont., Can., 1989—. Caucus chmn. Reform Party, 1993—. Recipient Can. 125 medal, 1992. Home: Box 69, Heinsburg, AB Canada T0A 1X0 Office: Ho of Commons, Parliament Bldgs, Ottawa, AB Canada K1A 0A6

GREY, ELIZABETH K., critical care nurse; b. Lansdowne, Pa., Feb. 18, 1951; d. Charles Knight and Marian Swope (Wing) Morgan; m. James Tracy Grey III, Dec. 27, 1980; children: Michael, James Tracy IV, Joshua. AA, Elmira (N.Y.) Coll., 1976; grad., Upper Bucks Voc-Tech, Perkasie, Pa., 1979; AA in Nursing, Bucks County Community Coll., Newtown, Pa., 1989; student, LaSalle U., 1992—. Cert. health profl. paramedic, Pa.; cert. CPR, ACLS, TNCC. Paramedic Warminster (Pa.) Ambulance; staff practical nurse Warminster Gen. Hosp.; ICU/CCU staff nurse Nazareth Hosp., Phila.; mem. Warrington Ambulance Corps. Mem. AACN.

GREY, JENNIFER, actress; b. N.Y., Mar. 26, 1960; d. Joel and Jo (Wilder) G. appearances include: (stage) Album, 1980, The Twilight of the Golds, 1993, (film) Reckless, 1984, Red Dawn, 1984, The Cotton Club, 1984, American Flyers, 1985, Ferris Beuller's Day Off, 1986, Dirty Dancing, 1987 (Golden Globe award nom. for best actress 1988), (voice) Light Years, 1988, Bloodhounds of Broadway, 1989, Wind, 1992, (T.V. movies) Murder in Mississippi, 1990, Criminal Justice, 1990, Eyes of a Witness, 1991, A Case for Murder, 1993. Office: c/o Creative Artists Agy Inc 9830 Wilshire Blvd Beverly Hills CA 90212-1804*

GREY, RUTHANN E., pharmaceutical company executive; b. Buffalo, N.Y., May 13, 1945; d. Wilson Campbell and Rosalie (Briggs) Evege; m. Daine A. Grey, Aug. 25, 1990; children: Daine, Jr., Keenan, Nichole. BS, SUNY, Buffalo, 1966, MS, 1970, PhD, 1980; postgrad., Harvard U., 1988. Tchr. Bennett High Sch., Buffalo, 1966-69; prof. Erie C.C., Buffalo, 1970-73; adminstr. No. Va. Community Coll., Annandale, 1975-76, Wayne State U., Detroit, 1978-80; dir. pub. affairs Burroughs Corp., Detroit, 1981-86; exec. asst. to chmn. bd. dirs. The Equitable, N.Y.C., 1986-89; mgr. pub. affairs N.Y. Times, N.Y.C., 1989-90; mgr. divsn. corp. rels. Pub. Svc. Corp. Colo., Denver, 1990-93; v.p. comm. and pub. affairs Hoechst Celanese, Bridgewater, N.J., 1993—; cons. A+ For Kids, Newark, 1989-90, Rockefeller Found., N.Y.C., 1989-90. Bd. dirs. Citizens Scholarship Found., Minn., 1990-94. Mem. Pub. Rels. Seminar, Arthur Page Soc., The Wisemen, Pub. Rels. Rsch. Found. Home: 28 Stonegate Dr Watchung NJ 07060 Office: Hoechst Celanese Rt 202-206 PO Box 2500 Somerville NJ 08876-1258

GREYTAK, SHARON ANN, film director, writer, producer; b. Bridgeport, Conn., May 13, 1958; d. Joseph and Anna Dorothy (Niznik) G. BFA magna cum laude, U. Hartford, 1980; MFA, Calif. Inst. Arts, 1982. Film maker, N.Y.C., 1982—. Writer, prodr., dir. (documentary) Weirded Out and Blown Away, 1986, (dramatic feature films) Hearing Voices, 1990, The Love Lesson, 1994; films shown at Margaret Mead Film Festival, 1986, Joseph Papp's Pub. Theatre, 1986, Sta. WNET-13, 1986, 90, (all N.Y.C.), Florence (Italy) Film Festival, 1989, Houston Internat. Film Festival, 1990, L.A. Internat. Film Festival, 1990, Films de Femmes Internat. Fest Women Dirs., Creteil, France, 1990; represented in permanent collections Mus. Modern Art, N.Y.C.; one woman shows at Mus. Modern Art 1983, 86, 90, Mus. Fine Arts, Boston, 1990, Wadsworth Arboretum, Hartford, 1995. Mem. exec. bd. Leo Dratfield Endowment, v.p., 1988-90; mem. exec. bd. MacDowell Colony Exec. Fellows Com., 1993-96. Honored by Ms. Found. for Women, 1994; film fellow N.Y. Found. for Arts, 1987, 93, N.Y. State Coun. on Arts, 1993, Jerome Found., St. Paul, 1993; MacDowell Colony fellow, 1987, 89, 91, 94, Annette Kade collaborative works fellow Arts Internat., N.Y.c., 1993; Yaddo fellow, 1988; Am. Film Inst. fellow, 1994. Democrat. Address: 85 8th Ave Apt 2K New York NY 10011

GRICIUS, RAMONA MARIA, accountant; b. L.A., June 4, 1958; d. Vytautas and Donna (Rusteika) Alseika. BSBA, U. So. Calif., 1981, M in Taxation, 1989. CPA, Calif. Tax mgr. Peat, Marwick, Mitchell & Co., L.A., 1981-86, Dole Food Co., Inc., Westlake Village, Calif., 1986—. Former student Tamara Maximova Sch. Dance; mem. staff L.A. Olympic Organizing Com., 1984. Mem. AICPA, Calif. Soc. CPAs, Tax Execs. Inst., Beta Gamma Sigma.

GRICOSKI, ALICE ANN, general surgeon; b. Pottsville, Pa., Apr. 4, 1955; d. Leonard Edward and Helen Elizabeth (Kolet) G. BS, Chestnut Hill Coll., Phila., 1977; MD, Washington U., St. Louis, 1981. Diplomate Am. Bd. Surgery. Intern U. Cin. Med. Ctr., 1981-82, resident in surgery, 1982-86; gen. surgeon Holzer Clinic, Gallipolis, Ohio, 1986—, bd. dirs., 1991—. Coeditor: Mont Reid Surgery Handbook, 1986. Fellow ACS; mem. AMA, Ohio State Med. Assn., Gallia County Med. Soc. (v.p. 1987, pres. 1988), Assn. Women Surgeons, Pembroke Lit. Club. Roman Catholic. Office: Holzer Clinic Dept Surgery 90 Jackson Pike Gallipolis OH 45631

GRIEB, ELIZABETH, lawyer; b. Chestertown, Md., Nov. 14, 1950; d. Henry Norman and Lillian (Ballard) Grieb; m. George Stewart Webb, Aug. 18, 1979 (div. 1990); children: Timothy Stewart, Margaret Elizabeth. BA English, Wells Coll., 1972; JD cum laude, U. Balt., 1977. Bar: Md. 1977. Assoc. Piper & Marbury, Balt., 1977-84, ptnr., 1984—. Adv. bd. U. Md. Sys. Downtown Ctr., Balt., 1990-92; bd. dirs., sec. Choice Jobs Inc., Balt., 1991-93; pres. U. Balt. Alumni Assn., 1994—; bd. dirs. Balt. Zoo, 1995—. Mem. Md. State Bar Assn. (chair securities laws com. 1990-92), Ho. of Ruth (bd. dirs. 1994—), Ctr. Club. Episcopal. Office: Piper & Marbury 36 S Charles St Baltimore MD 21201-3020

GRIECO, HELEN LORETTA, self-defense educator, author; b. Mineola, N.Y., Mar. 28, 1954; d. Oscar Benjamin Grieco and Gwendolyn Patricia Belisto. BA in Women's Studies, San Francisco State U., 1985; MA in Clin. Psychology, Antioch U., 1991. Lectr. women's studies dept. San Francisco State U., 1990-91; co-founder, instr. Defending Ourselves Self-Defense Sch., San Francisco, 1991—. Author: Guide to the Relationship Galaxy, 1994; producer documentary We Won't Go Back, 1992. Mem. R.A.P.E. task force San Francisco Commn. on Status of Women, 1986; mem. Commn. for Responsive Democracy, San Francisco, 1991. Mem. NOW (pres. 1984-86, exec. dir. San Francisco orgn. 1986-91, pub. rels. coord. Calif. state 1993—, Beyond the Call of Duty award 1986, pres. edn. fund 1986-94). Office: Defending Ourselves 1101 Clement St San Francisco CA 94118-2114

GRIER, BARBARA G. (GENE DAMON), editor, lecturer, author; b. Cin., Nov. 4, 1933; d. Phillip Strang and Dorothy Vernon (Black) Grier; grad. high sch. Author: The Lesbian in Literature, 1967, (with others) 2d edit., 1975, 3d edit., 1981, 4th edit.; The Least of These (in Sisterhood is Powerful), 1970; The Index, 1974; Lesbiana, 1976; The Lesbian Home Jour., 1976; The Lavender Herring, 1976; Lesbian Lives, 1976, The Mysterious Naiad, 1994, The First Time Ever, 1995; editor: (with Katherine V. Forrest) The Erotic Naiad, 1992, The Romantic Naiad, 1993; pub. The Ladder mag., 1970-72, fiction and poetry editor, 1966-67, editor, 1968-72; dir. promotion Naiad Press, Reno, Nev., 1973—, treas., 1976—, v.p., gen. mgr., Tallahassee, Fla., 1980—, chief exec. officer, 1987—. Democrat. Home: RR 1 Box 3319 Havana FL 32333-9737 Office: Naiad Press Inc PO Box 10543 Tallahassee FL 32302-2543

GRIER, RUTH, provincial legislator; b. Dublin, Ireland, Oct. 2, 1936; arrived in Can., 1956; d. Alexander Earls and Gertrude (Sykes) Dowds; m. Terence Wyly Grier, Dec. 5, 1958; children: David, Timothy, Patrick. Diploma in pub. adminstrn., Trinity Coll., Dublin, 1956; BA in Polit. Sci., Econs. with honors, U. Toronto, Ont., Can., 1958. Min. of the environment Toronto, 1990-93, min. of health, 1993—. Alderman City of Etobicoke, Ont., 1970-85; mem. provincial parliament Etobicoke-Lakeshore, 1985—. Anglican. Home: 74 Arcadian Circle, Toronto, ON Canada M8W 2Y9 Office: Ministry of Health, 80 Grosvenor St, Toronto, ON Canada M7A 2C4

GRIEST, GUINEVERE LINDLEY, government official; b. Chgo., Jan. 14, 1924; d. Euclid Eugene and Marianna (Lindley) Griest; A.B., Cornell U., 1944; A.M., U. Chgo., 1947, Ph.D., 1961; postgrad. (Fulbright fellow) Cambridge (Eng.) U., 1953-55. Instr., U. Ill., Chgo., 1947-61, asst. prof., 1961-66, assoc. prof. English, 1966-72; program officer div. of fellowships and seminars Nat. Endowment for Humanities, Washington, 1969-73, dep. dir. div. of fellowships, 1973-85, acting dir., 1985-86, dir., 1986-91, dir. divsn. rsch. programs, 1991—. Mem. MLA, Phi Beta Kappa, Phi Kappa Phi. Episcopalian. Author: Mudie's Circulating Library and the Victorian Novel (MLA scholars' library award 1971), 1971; contbr. articles to profl. jours. Office: NEH Divsn Rsch Programs 1100 Pennsylvania Ave NW Washington DC 20506-0001

GRIFFEY, LINDA BOYD, lawyer; b. Keokuk, Iowa, Aug. 6, 1949; d. Marshall Coulter and Geraldine Vivian (White) Boyd; m. John Jay Griffey, June 24, 1972. BS in Pharmacy, U. Iowa, 1972; JD, Duke U., 1980. Bar: Calif. 1980; lic. pharmacist, Iowa, N.C. Pharmacist Davenport (Iowa) Osteo. Hosp., 1972-75, Wagner Pharmacy, Clinton, Iowa, 1975-77, Durham (N.C.) County Gen. Hosp., 1977-80; assoc. O'Melveny & Myers, L.A., 1980-88, ptnr., 1988—; speaker, writer in field. Active Applause for the Music Ctr., Met. Assocs., Pasadena, Calif., L.A. Philharm. Bus. & Profl. Assn. Mem. ABA (employee benefits com. tax sect.), Am. Law Inst., L.A. County Bar Assn. (chair employee benefits com. 1994-95), L.A. Duke Bar Assn. (pres. 1987-90, 91-92), Rotary (com. chair L.A. club). Office: O'Melveny & Myers 400 S Hope St Los Angeles CA 90071

GRIFFIN, ANITA JANE, elementary education educator; b. East Chicago, Ind., Dec. 16, 1945; d. John Tatu and Alfreda (Kaspick) Granger; m. Joseph Raymond Griffin, June 14, 1969; children: Jason David, Jennifer Sue. BA, Purdue U., Hammond, Ind., 1969, MS, 1972. Tchr. 2d grade Dist. 158, Lansing, Ill., 1969-73; tchr. 6th grade sci. Lake Cen. Sch. Corp., St. John, Ind., 1983, tchr. 6th grade English, 1984, tchr. 5th grade, 1985—; advisor, coach Sci. Club, 1992-94; mem. core team Integrated Learning System Computer Tech., 1992—; faculty advisor Star Lab. Program, 1988—; coord. Artist in Residency Program, 1993; mem. Peifer Sch. Parent's Adv. Com., 1991-94, prin.'s selection com., 1993, performance bd. accreditation team, 1993-94; advt. mgr. Lake Ctrl. Hockey Club, 1991-92. Editor newspaper on staff devel. Success Connection, 1988—. Mem. pastoral adminstrv. bd. Meth. Ch., Dyer, Ind., 1988-90. Mem. AAUW, NEA, ASCD (conv. presenter 1988), Ind. Tchrs. Assn., Peifer Home and Sch. Assn. (treas. 1990-91), Kappa Kappa Kappa (chpt. pres. 1990-91). Office: Lake Cen Sch Corp Peifer Sch 1824 Cline Ave Schererville IN 46375-2260

GRIFFIN, CHRISTINE MARIE-INGRID, elementary school educator; b. Innsbruck, Austria, Aug. 27, 1946; came to U.S., 1952; d. Michael Alexander and Regina (Zwicknagel) Subbotin; m. Vincent A. Griffin, July 8, 1967; children: Christine A., Vincent, Michael C. Student, Marymount Coll., 1965-67; BS, U. of Bridgeport, 1979; MA, Fairfield Coll., 1986; postgrad., St. Joseph Coll., 1987. Tchr. elem. grades Stratford (Conn.) Bd. Edn., 1979—. Pres., v.p. PTA, Strattford, 1977, tchr. rep., 1982-91; guide Protect Your Environment, Great Salt Meadow Marsh, 1980—; bd. dirs. Our Lady of Peace Coun., 1987-91. Mem. Phi Delta Kappa (v.p. 1991-92). Republican. Roman Catholic. Home: 62 Laurel St Stratford CT 06497-7901 Office: Lordship Elem Sch 254 Crown St Stratford CT 06497-7511

GRIFFIN, DIANE EDMUND, research physician, virologist, educator; b. Iowa City, Ia., May 12, 1940; d. Rudolph William and Doris Irene (Swanson) Edmund; m. John Wesley Griffin, June 13, 1965; children: Christopher Todd, Erik Edmund. BA, Augustana Coll., Rock Island, Ill., 1962; MD, Stanford U., 1968, PhD, 1970. Diplomate Am. Bd. Internal Medicine, Am. Bd. Infectious Diseases. Resident in medicine Stanford (Calif.) U. Hosp., 1968-70; fellow Johns Hopkins U. Sch. Medicine, Balt., 1970-73, asst. prof., 1973-79, assoc. prof., 1979-86, prof., 1986—; prof., chair molecular microbiol. immunology Johns Hopkins U. Sch. Pub. Health; investigator Howard Hughes Med. Inst., Balt., 1973-79; mem. virology study sect. NIH, 1982-86; mem. adv. com. Nat. Multiple Sclerosis Soc., 1986-92; mem. microbiology and infectious diseases rsch. adv. com. NIH, 1989-92, chair, 1992-94. Author films and tapes; contbr. chpts. to books, articles to profl. jours. Grantee NIH, 1983—, Nat. Multiple Sclerosis Soc., 1986—. Fellow Infectious Diseases Soc. Am.; mem. Am. Soc. for Clin. Investigation, Am. Soc. for Virology (council 1987-89), Interurban Clin. Club. Democrat. Lutheran. Office: Johns Hopkins Sch Medicine 600 N Wolfe St Baltimore MD 21205

GRIFFIN, GLADYS BOGUES, critical care nurse, educator; b. Elizabeth City, N.C., July 18, 1937; d. Matthew Boques and Lucy Griffin Boques Eason; m. Oct. 21, 1957 (div.); children: Terry, Lucy, Misty, Derrick. AAS, Nassau (N.Y.) Community Coll., 1972. RN, N.C.; cert. ACLS. Nurse Long Beach (N.Y.) Meml. Hosp., 1968-70, staff nurse team leader, 1972-75, head nurse, 1975-76; staff nurse Critical Care Unit Albemarle Hosp., Elizabeth City, 1976-78, staff nurse Surg. Intensive Care Unit then coord., 1978—; BLS instr., head nurse surg. intensive care —, 1981-87; pub. speaker health related topics, Long Beach and Elizabeth City. Featurered Life Styles of Elizabeth City. Named one of Disting. Women N.C., 1989. Mem. AACN, NAFE, ARC Nurses, Critical Care Nurses, Soc. Notary Pub., N.Y. Nurses Assn. Democrat. Home: 616 Crooked Run Rd Elizabeth City NC 27909-7538

GRIFFIN, GLORIA JEAN, elementary school educator; b. Emmett, Idaho, Sept. 10, 1946; d. Archie and Marguerite (Johnson) G. AA, Boise (Idaho) Jr. Coll., 1966; BA, Boise Coll., 1968; MA in Elem. Curriculum, Boise State U., 1975. Cert. advanced elem. tchr., Idaho. Tchr. music, tutor, Boise; sec. Edward A. Johnson, atty., Boise; tchr. Head Start, Boise; elem. tchr. Meridian (Idaho) Sch. Dist., 1968—; developer multi-modality individualized spelling program; co-developer program for adapting curriculum to student's individual differences. Author: The Culture and Customs of the Argentine People As Applied to a Sixth Grade Social Studies Unit. Sec. PTA. Named Tchr. of Yr., Meridian Sch. Dist., 1981. Mem. NEA, Internat. Reading Assn., Idaho Edn. Assn., Meridian Edn. Assn. (bldg. rep.), Idaho Reading Coun., Orton Dyslexia Soc., Horizons Reading Coun., Alpha Delta Kappa (rec. sec.). Office: Silver Sage Elem Sch 7700 Snohomish St Boise ID 83709-5975

GRIFFIN, (ALVA) JEAN, entertainer; b. Detroit, June 1, 1931; d. Henry Bethel White and Ruth Madelyn (Gowen) Durham; m. Francis Jay Griffin, July 8, 1958 (dec.); stepchildren: Patra, Rodney; 1 adopted child, Donald; children: Rhonda Jean, Sherree Lee. Student, Anderson Coll., 1952-53; DD (hon.), Ministry of Salvation, Chula Vista, Calif., 1990, Ministry of Salvation, 1990. Ordained minister, 1990. Supr. Woolworth's, Detroit, 1945-46; operator, supr. Atlantic Bell Telephone Co., Detroit, 1947-5l, Anderson, Ind., 1952-56; sec. to div. mgr. Food Basket-Lucky Stores, San Diego, 1957-58; owner, mgr. Jay's Country Boy Markets, Riverside, Calif., 1962-87; entertainer, producer, dir., singer Mae West & Co., 1980—; owner The Final Touch, Colorado Springs; tchr. art Grant Sch., Riverside, 1964-65; tchr., adviser Mental Retarded Sch., Riverside, 1976-77; instr. Touch for Health Found., Pasadena, Calif., 1975-79; cons., hypnotist, nutritionist, Riversaide, 1976-79; mem., tchr. Psi field parapsychology. Mem. Rep. Presdl. Task Force, 1983. Recipient svc. award Rep. Presdl. Task Force, 1986. Mem. Parapsychology Assn. Riverside (pres. 198l-82). Mem. Ch. of Religious Science New Thought. Home: 201 Chapel Rd Sedona AZ 86336

GRIFFIN, KAY MCLEAN, librarian; b. Quanah, Tex., Oct. 12, 1930; d. Harvey Samuel and Willie Kavanaugh (Simpson) McLean; m. James Carl Pengelly, Mar. 6, 1951 (dec. Sept. 1964); children: James William, Katherine Elizabeth; m. John Lidstone Woolford, Apr. 2, 1970 (dec. Apr. 1979). BS in Edn., Tex. Ctrl. U., 1951; MLS, Ea. Tex. State U., 1969. Tchr. Quanah (Tex.) High Sch., 1951-52, Am. Sch., Pachuca, Mexico, 1953, Fannin, Corpus Christi, Tex., 1962-64, Woodlawn Sch., Corpus Christi, 1965-67; libr. Hamlin Jr. High Sch., Corpus Christi, 1967—. Mem. DAR, Women's Investment Network (pres. 1986-87, 92-93), CCCTA, AFT, ATPE, TLA. Republican. Episcopalian. Home: 1010 Miramar Pl Corpus Christi TX 78411-2130 Office: Hamlin Mid Sch 3900 Hamlin Dr Corpus Christi TX 78411-2237

GRIFFIN, KELLY ANN, public relations executive, consultant; b. Buffalo, May 20, 1964; d. Michael Gerald and Patricia Frances (Lippert) G.; m. Thomas Richard Kleinberger, Oct. 11, 1992. B in Polit. Sci., SUNY, Geneseo, 1986; postgrad., CUNY, Bklyn., 1994—. Legis. asst. to N.Y. State Assembly Spkrs. Stanley Fink and Mel Miller Buffalo, 1986-87; acct. exec. Griffin Media Group, N.Y.C., 1987-88, acct. supr., v.p., 1988-90, pres., CEO, 1990-94; pub. rels. cons. N.Y.C., 1994—; assoc. dir. N.Y. State Funeral Dirs. Assn., N.Y.C., 1992-94, Met. Funeral Dirs. Assn., N.Y.C., 1992-94, Nat. Coun. Elected County Execs., N.Y.C., 1993—; instr. remedial reading Cornell U. Sch. Industry/Lab. Rels., Buffalo, 1987. Editor N.Y. State AFL-CIO Unity, 1988-90, Nat. Coun. Elected County Execs. News, 1993—, N.Y. State Funeral Dirs. Assn./Met. Funeral Dirs. Assn. News, 1992-94, Amalgamated Transit Union News, 1988-90. cons. Interfaith Assembly on Homelessness, N.Y.C., 1994—, Voter Assistance Commn., N.Y.C., 1990-92; participant, cons. Erie County Dem. Party, Buffalo, 1985-87; mem. assocs. steering com. Children's Health Fund, N.Y.C., 1991—. Recipient Acad. award DAR, 1978. Mem. Pub. Rels. Soc. N.Y.C. Roman Catholic. Home: 505 Court St Apt 5M Brooklyn NY 11231 Office: Griffin Media Group PO Box 203 New York NY 10009

GRIFFIN, LAURA M., retired educator; b. Woodland, Calif., Aug. 14, 1925; d. George Everette Ramsey and Bertha (Storz) Ramsey Lowe; m. Roy J. Griffin, Nov. 19, 1944; children: Robert Eugene, Dennis Charles, Kathleen Ann. AA in Social Sci., Sacramento City Coll., 1969; BA in Geography, Calif. State U., Sacramento, 1972. Cert. elem. and secondary tchr., Calif.; Master Gardener. Sec. Alameda Naval Air, Alameda, Calif., 1944-45, Cal-Western Life Ins., Sacramento, 1945-47, Pacific Sch. Dist., Sacramento, 1956-57; substitute tchr. Sacramento Unified Sch. Dist., 1974-75; tchr. Mt. Diablo Unified Sch. Dist., Concord, Calif., 1976-91; ret., 1991; dir. Heather Farm Garden Ctr., Walnut Creek, Calif., 1985-86, edn. chmn., 1986-87, pres., 1987-88, fin. sec., 1993-94; sec. investment group AAUW, Walnut Creek, 1978-79. Guardian Jobs Daus.-Bethel 325, Walnut Creek, 1978-79; leader Girl Scouts Am., Sacramento, 1971-72; den mother Boy Scouts Am., Sacramento, 1957-60; publicity chmn. membership Northgate Music Boosters, Walnut Creek, 1976-77. Mem. Heather Farm Garden Ctr. (pres. 1987-88), Walnut Creek Garden Club (pres. 1983-84, civic projec chmn. 1994-95), Order of Eastern Star. Republican.

GRIFFIN, LINDA GILLAN, fashion editor; b. Dallas, Sept. 19, 1942; d. Arthur William Riedel and Cora Lillian Dumas; m. Tom Carpenter Gillan, Sept. 1, 1962 (div. 1976); m. Bobby Juel Griffin, July 19, 1985; children: Thomas Gregory Gillan, Christopher Carpenter Gillan, Stuart Riedel Gillan; stepchildren: Bobby J., Diann Griffin Warren, Mark Liles. BA in Sociology, U. Houston, 1965, postgrad., 1965-66. Freelance writer, 1976—; Houston bur. rschr., reporter L.A. Times, 1976-79; bus. writer Houston Chronicle, 1979-80, energy writer, 1980-81, fashion writer, 1986-89, columnist, 1988-93, fashion editor, 1989—; editor Offshore Intelex Offshore Data Svcs., Inc., 1981-84; v.p. mktg. Everest Geotech, Inc. and Peak Energy, 1984-86. Recipient Best Article in Major Newspaper award Aviation/Spacewriters Assn., 1979, Outstanding Columns and Feature Story Atrium award, 1988, 89, 91, Outstanding Fashion Market Coverage Atrium award, 1990, Nat. Headliners award, 1991, Best Feature Photograph of Yr. award, 1989. Mem. Houston Press Club Forum (co-founder). Office: Houston Chronicle Pub Co 801 Texas St Houston TX 77002-2906

GRIFFIN, LINDA L., English language and speech educator; b. Yale, Mich., Dec. 23, 1942; d. Benjamin and Ruth (Steenbergh) Hinton; m. James Griffin, Nov. 23, 1980. BA, U. Mich., 1965, MA, 1967; postgrad., Bowling Green (Ohio) State U., 1975, U. N.C., 1985; ABD, U. South Fla. Tchr. English and speech Sandusky (Mich.) High Sch.; instr. Jackson (Mich.) Community Coll., Terra Tech. Coll., Fremont, Ohio, Edison Community Coll., Naples, Fla.; frequent speaker and presenter, including harp lecture programs; mem. NEH Shakespeare Seminar, 1985; keynote speaker Collier County Tchrs. Assn. Conf., 1987. Mem. MLA, South Atlantic MLA, SE Medieval Assn., Medieval Inst., S.C. Renaissance Assn., Nat. Coun. Tchrs. English, Folger Shakespeare Libr., So. States Communication Assn., Fla. Communicaiton Assn. (pres. 1989-90), Phi Kappa Phi. Home: 9781 Bobwhite Ln Bonita Springs FL 33923-4416 Office: 7007 Lely Cultural Pky Naples FL 33962-8976

GRIFFIN, LINNER WARD, social work educator; b. Charlotte, N.C., Apr. 24, 1942; d. Yorke Anthony and Minnie Lee (Mitchell) Ward; m. Bobby G. Griffin, July 24, 1964; children: Jannifer Lynne, Jeffrey Franklin. BA, U. N.C., Greensboro, 1964; MSW, U. N.C., 1969; EdD, U. Houston, 1985. Intake/adult svcs. Guilford County Dept. Social Svcs., Greensboro, 1965-69; family counselor Family Svc. Phila., 1969-72, Cath. Welfare Bur., Trenton, N.J., 1972-74; supportive svcs. supr. Lehigh County Area Agy. on Aging., Allentown, Pa., 1974-77; project. mgr. Phila. Geriatric Ctr., 1977-80; NIMH project mgr./dir. Inst. on Aging, Temple U., Phila., 1980-82; dir. adult day care Western Mass. Hosp., Westfield, 1985-87; asst. prof. W.Va. U., Morgantown, 1987-90, East Carolina U., Greenville, N.C., 1990—; cons. Pa. Dept. Welfare/Aging, Harrisburg, 1977-82; cons. in field, 1982-85. Author, editor: (resource books) A Guide for Adult Protective Services, 10 vols., 1988-90; sr. author: Mental Health and Aging, 1983; contbr. articles and book revs. to profl. jours., chpts. to books. Bd. dirs. InTouch and Concerned, Morgantown, 1987-89; mem. Pitt County Infant Mortality Task Force, Greenville, 1990—, Ea. N.C. Poverty Com., Greenville, 1991—, Mediation Ctr. Ea. N.C., 1992—. W.Va. Adult Protective Svc. Tgn. grantee W.Va. Dept. Health and Human Resources, 1988-90. Mem. NASW, Acad. Cert. Social Workers (cert.), Am. Soc. on Aging, Assn. for Gerontology in Higher Edn., So. Gerontol. Soc. (continuing edn. tng. adv. com.). Presbyterian. Office: East Carolina U Sch Social Work 112 Ragsdale Greenville NC 27858-3918

GRIFFIN, LOIS ANN, mathematics educator; b. Cin., Jan. 29, 1938; d. Ronald A. and Lilian (Gradel) Ebel; m. Norman L. Griffin, Jan. 30, 1960; children: Catherine, Michael, Christopher, Timothy. BS, Wilmington (Ohio) Coll., 1960; MA, Ea. Mich. U., 1988. Recreation leader Middletown (Ohio) Pks. and Recreation, 1954-60; tchr. W. Middletown (Ohio) High Sch., 1960-62, Eastmoor High Sch., Columbus, 1962-63, Bel Air (Md.) High Sch., 1963-65; child care provider Flushing, Mich., 1965-81; account exec. Profl. Assocs., Flint, Mich., 1981-82;, 1985-89; tchr. Powers Cath. High Sch., Flint, 1985; tchr., cons. UAW/GM, Flint, 1985-87; instr. math. Mott Community Coll., Flint, 1989—, acad. advisor, 1990—; math. tchr. Carman/Ainsworth Bendle Adult High Sch., Flint, 1982—; upward bound math. instr. Mott Community Coll., Flint, 1990—, math. instr., acad. advisor literacy project, 1991—. Author learning modules for UAW/GM. Mem. AAUW (pres. 1984-86). Methodist. Home: 428 Bellewood Dr Flushing MI 48433-1847

GRIFFIN, MARIBETH, administrator; b. Warren, Ohio, Aug. 20, 1960; d. Robert Sydney G. and Alberta Louise (Likens) Morales. BA, Bowling Green State U., 1983; MA, Western Conn. State U., 1986. Instr. Youngstown (Ohio) State U., 1987-88; asst. to dir., resident dir. Western Conn. State U., Danbury, 1988-93, assoc. dir. housing, 1993—. Editor: In Our Own Words, 1992, Revisioning Our Future, 1993; newsletter editor Conn. Coll. Personnel Assn., 1989-90. Mem. Feminist Reading Group, Danbury, 1993-94. Named Danbury Area Women's History Project Woman of Yr., 1993. Mem. Northeast Assn. Coll. & Univ. Housing Officers (co-chair legal issues com. 1993-94, co-chair women's issues com. 1990-93, sec. 1994—). Office: Western Conn State U 181 White St Danbury CT 06810

GRIFFIN, MARIE KNIGHT, educational administrator; b. Charleston, S.C., Oct. 8, 1943; d. Shields E. Knight and Ruby B. Barwick; m. John F. Griffin, Jan. 11, 1963; children: Sherri, Parrish, Tina, Andrew, Angelia, Mike. BA, U. Md., 1969; MA, Ball State U., 1974; postgrad., Clemson U., 1977; EdD, U. S.C., 1987. Cert. tchr. elem. edn., psychology, S.C., cert. prin. elem. and h.s. edn., S.C., cert. supt., supr., S.C. Tchr. elem. schs. U.S. and abroad, 1967-77; asst. prin. Pickens (S.C.) Elem. Sch., 1977-78; prin. Morrison Elem. Sch., Clemson, S.C., 1978-82, AR Lewis Elem. Sch., Pickens, 1982-87; asst. supr. instrn. Union (S.C.) County Schs., 1987-90; asst. supr. instrn., K-12 Greenwood (S.C.) Sch. Dist. 50, 1990—; supr. programs Before and After Sch. Care, Head Start; supr. Early Childhood At-Risk Programs; asst. developer Drug Edn. Grant, Reading Recovery Program, After Sch. Devel. Program; mem. Dist.-Wide At-Risk Student Program, Middle Sch. Devel. Program; cons. in field, Greenwood, 1990—; pub. speaker various orgns. Chair Coun. on Ministries Main St. United Meth. Ch., Greenwood; lay speaker United Meth. Ch.; bd. visitors Piedmont Tech. Coll., Edn. Enrichment Found. Recipient S.C. Ho. of Reps. Resolution for Outstanding Achievement award, 1980, 81, 89, Gov.'s award for Sch./Comty. Involvement, 1982. Mem. ASCD, S.C. Assn. Sch. Adminstrs., S.C. Assn. Elem. Sch. prins., S.C. Assn. Sch. Supts., Phi Delta Kappa. Home: 138 Gatewood Dr Greenwood SC 29646 Office: Greenwood Sch Dist 50 PO Box 248 1855 Calhoun Rd Greenwood SC 29648

GRIFFIN, MARY ANN, library director; b. Hazleton, Pa., Mar. 6, 1946; d. John and Mary (Kudlick) Timko; m. Joseph Griffin, Dec. 30, 1967. BS, Pa. State U., 1967, MA, 1970; MS, Simmons Coll., 1974, DA, 1980. Libr. asst. Pa. State U., State College, 1970-73; libr. dept. head Tufts U., Medford, Mass., 1974-77; libr. dir. Xavier U., Cin., 1979-84, Villanova (Pa.) U., 1984—; mem. exec. bd. Tri-State Coll. Libr. Coop., Rosemont, Pa., 1988-92; pres., mem. exec. bd. Greater Cin. Libr. Consortium, 1979-84; trustee PALINET, 1992—, exec. com., 1992—; presenter profl. confs. Editor (alumni assn. newsletter) Simmons Libr., 1978-81; contbr. articles to profl. jours. ALA, AAUP, Assn. Coll. and Rsch. Librs. (pres., mem. exec. bd. Delaware Valley chpt. 1985-92, ACRL membership com. 1991-95). Home: 92 Covered Bridge Rd Oley PA 19547-9336 Office: Villanova U Office of Libr Lancaster & Ithan Aves Villanova PA 19085

GRIFFIN, MARY FRANCES, retired library media consultant; b. Cross Hill, Laurens County, S.C., Aug. 24, 1925; d. James and Rosa Lee (Carter) G. BA, Benedict Coll., 1947; postgrad., S.C. State Coll., 1948-51, Atlanta U., 1953, Va. State Coll., 1961; MLS, Ind. U., 1957. Tchr.-librarian Johnston (S.C.) Tng. Sch., Edgefield County Sch. Dist., 1947-51; librarian Lee County Sch. Dist., Dennis High, Bishopville, S.C., 1951-52, Greenville County (S.C.) Sch. Dist., 1952-66; library cons. S.C. Dept. Edn., Columbia, 1966-87; vis. tchr. U. S.C., 1977; bd. dirs. Greater Columbia Lit. Coun.; mem. Richland County unit Assault on Illiteracy. Recipient Cert. of Living the Legacy award Nat. Council Negro Women, 1980. Mem. ALA, Assn. Ednl. Communications and Tech. S.C., Assn. Curriculum Devel., AAUW (pres. Columbia br. 1978-80), Southeastern Library Assn. (sec. 1978-80), S.C. Library Assn. (sec. 1979), S.C. Assn. Sch. Librarians, Nat. Assn. State Ednl. and Media Personnel. Baptist. Home: PO Box 1652 Columbia SC 29202-1652 also: 1100 Skyland Dr Columbia SC 29210-8127

GRIFFIN, MELANIE HUNT, accounting firm executive; b. Corpus Christi, Tex., Oct. 25, 1949; d. Roy Albert and Ola Emma (Hunt) G.; m. Robert Thompson; children: Maurice Dale, Donald Dwight, Merideth Thompson, Laura Thompson. BBA summa cum laude, Corpus Christi State U., 1977; MBA, Tex. A&M U., 1994. CPA, Tex.; cert. fin. planner. Sec.-treas. Roy Hunt, Inc., Corpus Christi, 1970-78, dir., 1970-82; v.p. White, Sluyter & Co., Corpus Christi, 1978-80; pres. Whittington & Griffin, Corpus Christi, 1980-82, also dir.; sec.-treas., dir. Sand Express, Inc., Corpus Christi, 1975-82; prin. Melanie Hunt Griffin & Assocs., CPAs, Corpus Christi, 1982-84; v.p. Fields, Nemec & Co., P.C., Corpus Christi, 1984—; mem. edn. and tng. task force White Ho. Conf. Small Bus., 1993. Contbr. articles to profl. jours. Devel. chair Am. Heart Assn., chmn. bd. 1989-90, Leadership Corpus Christi Alumni, 1982—; mem. adv. coun. Tex. A&M U., Corpus Christi. Recipient Women in Careers award YWCA, 1989, Outstanding Svc. award Corpus Christi chpt. CPA's, 1990-93. Mem. AICPA (personal fin. planning dir. small bus. taxation com. 1990-93), Tex. Soc. CPAs (bd. dirs. 1987—, v.p. 1988-89, 93-94, 95—, pres. Corpus Christi chpt. 1987-88, chmn. devel. new legis. leaders 1990-93, vice chair CPAs Helping Schs. 1994—, Outstanding Svc. award 1990-91, Presdl. citation), Corpus Christi State U. Alumni Assn. (bd. dirs. 1987-90), Tex. State CPAs Ednl. Found. (trustee 1990-93), Exec. Women Internat. (chmn. philanthropy com. 1986-87), Corpus Christi Rotary. Home: 10817 Stonewall Blvd Corpus Christi TX 78410-2429 Office: Fields Nemec & Co PC 501 S Tancahua PO Box 23067 Corpus Christi TX 78403

GRIFFIN, NANCY RENAY, legal secretary; b. Phila., Feb. 27, 1962; d. Dominick Patrick and Anna Marie (Bunting) Griffin. AA, Peicre Jr. Coll., Phila., 1982; student, New Hampshire Coll., Brunswick, Maine, 1983-84, LaSalle U., 1992-93, Holy Family Coll., 1994. notary public. Legal sec. Matty & Ferroni, Phila., 1981, Hepburn, Willcox, Hamilton, Phila., 1982; radioman U.S. Navy, Naples, Italy, 1982-86, USNR, Phila., 1986-90; supr. legal sec. Toolan & Yanni, Phila., 1987-94; legal sec. Sheller, Ludwig & Badey, Phila., 1994—. With USNR, 1994—. Recipient good conduct medal U.S. Navy, 1986, meritorious svc. medal, 1990. Mem. NAFE, Phila. Legal Secs. Assn. (corr. sec. 1991-92), Phi Theta Kappa. Office: Sheller Ludwig & Badey 3d Fl 1528 Walnut St Philadelphia PA 19102

GRIFFIN, SHEILA MB, marketing executive; b. Chgo., June 17, 1951; d. George Michael and Frances Josephine (Sheehan) Spielman; m. Woodson Jack Griffin, Dec. 30, 1972; children: Woodson Jack, II, Kelly Sheehan. BS, U. Ill., 1975, MBA, 1979. Personal banking rep. Am. Express Banking, Boeblingen, Fed. Republic Germany, 1973-74; market rsch.analyst Market Facts, Chgo., 1975-77; mgr. strategic rsch. Motorola, Inc., Schaumburg, Ill., 1977-83, mgr. mktg. resource, 1985-88, mgr. spl. projects Corp. Strategy Office, 1988-89, dir. corp. advt. worldwide, 1989-93, dir. bus. assessment corp. strategy office, 1993-94, dir. multimedia strategy office; gen. mgr. mktg. rsch. and info. Ameritech Mobile Communications, Inc., Schaumburg, 1983-85. Trustee (founding), Ill. Math. and Sci. Acad., 1985—. Mem. U. Ill. Chgo. MBA Alumni Assn. (founder, pres. 1984-86), U. Ill. Alumni Assn. (bd. dirs. 1984-86, Disting. Alumni 1985, Constituent Leadership award 1989). Home: 53 Highgate Course Saint Charles IL 60174-1422 Office: Motorola Inc 1303 E Algonquin Rd Schaumburg IL 60196

GRIFFIN, SYLVIA GAIL, reading specialist; b. Portland, Oreg., Dec. 13, 1935; d. Archie and Marguerite (Johnson) G. AA, Boise Jr. Coll., 1955; BS, Brigham Young U., 1957, MEd, 1967. Cert. advanced teaching, Idaho. Classroom tchr. Boise (Idaho) Pub. Schs., 1957-59, 61-66, 67-69, reading specialist, 1969-90, 91—, early childhood specialist, 1990-91; tchr. evening Spanish classes for adults, 1987-88; lectr. in field; mem. cons. pool U.S. Office Juvenile Justice and Delinquency Prevention, 1991—. Author: Procedures Used by First Grade Teachers for Teaching Experience Readiness for Reading Comprehension, The Short Story of Vowels, A Note Worthy Way to Teach Reading. Advisor in developing a program for dyslexics Scottish Rite Masons of Idaho, Boise. Mem. NEA, AAUW, Internat. Reading Assn., Orton Dyslexia Soc., Horizon Internat. Reading Assn., Idaho Edn. Assn. (pub. rels. dir. 1970-72), Boise Edn. Assn. (pub. rels. dir. 1969-72, bd. dirs. ednl. polit. involvement com. 1983-89), Alpha Delta Kappa. Office: 5007 Franklin Rd Boise ID 83705-1106

GRIFFIN-HOLST, (BARBARA) JEAN, marketing professional; b. Pasadena, Calif., May 20, 1943; d. DeWitt James and Jean Marie (Donald) Griffin; m. Rodney C. Holst, Mar. 22, 1969 (div. May 1975); 1 child, Justin D. Griffin-Holst. BA cum laude, San Jose State U., 1967. Designer integrated cir. mask Fairchild Semicondr., Mountain View, Calif., 1967-69; sr. custom integrated cir. mask designer Nat. Semicondr., Santa Clara, Calif., 1969-71; sr. specialist Advanced Micro Devices, Sunnyvale, Calif., 1971-75; mgr. mask design and computer-aided design groups Precision Monolithics, Santa Clara, 1975-76; mgr. analog mask design and graphic services Signetics Corp., Sunnyvale, 1976-82; dist. mgr. tech. mktg. Computervision Corp., Santa Clara, 1982-84, dist. mgr. sales, 1984-85, mgr. distbr. sales, 1985-87; dir. U.S. field mktg. Sun Microsystems Inc., Mountain View, 1987—; bd. dirs. U.S. Thin Film Products, Inc., Campbell, Calif. Mem. NAFE, AAUW, Navy League U.S., San Francisco Mus. Modern Art, St. Francis Yacht Club (San Francisco), Commonwealth Club of San Francisco. Republican. Office: Sun Microsystems Inc 2550 Garcia Ave Mountain View CA 94043-1100

GRIFFITH, ANNE EUGENIA, school system administrator; b. New Haven, Conn., Jan. 27, 1943; d. Angelo Mario and Jeanette (Ferrucci) Marcarelli; m. William Whitney Griffith, Apr. 24, 1965; children: Rebecca Anne, Graham Whitney, William Tucker. AB, Mt. Holyoke Coll., 1964; MEd, Worcester State Coll., 1979. Cert. supr. attendance, Mass. Personnel planning and placement specialist Aetna Ins. Co., Hartford, Conn., 1964-65; math. tchr. Rosemary Hall, Greenwich, Conn., 1965-69; supr. attendance, transp. coord. Shrewsbury (Mass.) Pub. Schs., 1981—. Elected rep. Shrewsbury Town Meeting, 1978—; dir. Shrewsbury Cmty. Svcs., 1985-93; deacon Shrewsbury Congl. Ch., 1992—; mem. Shrewsbury LWV, past coord.; mem. United Ch. of Christ. Mem. Mass. Assn. Pupil Transp. (dir. 1993—). Office: Shrewsbury Pub Schs 100 Maple Ave Shrewsbury MA 01545-5398

GRIFFITH, BARBARA E., social worker, political activist; b. Bklyn., Feb. 17, 1943; d. Carl and Ruth (Cramer) Horowitz; m. Richard Michael Griffith, Feb. 12, 1942; children: Kim Griffith McFadden, David Wark. BSW, Ohio State U., 1965; postgrad., Adelphi U., 1965-66. Social worker Columbus Home for Mentally Disturbed Children, Columbus, Ohio, 1965; case worker Nassau County Social Svcs., L.I., N.Y., 1965-66, Red Bank (N.J.) Dept. Social Svcs., 1966-67, Dept. Social Svcs. Honolulu, 1967-69; asst. dir. nursery sch. Cleve., 1975-78; advt. mgr. mags. Toronto, Ont., Can., 1979-84; substitute tchr. West Windsor (N.J.) Plainsboro H.S., 1987-90; polit. activist Bus. & Profl. Women's Assn., N.J., 1989-93; owner R.M.G. Assocs., Inc., Princeton Junction, N.J.; real estate devel. cons., 1991—. Counselor for homeless people; campaign worker Clinton Presdl. Campaign, N.J., Hughes Congl. Campaign for U.S. Congress, 1992, N.J.; local town councilwoman, Can., 1982; participant Lobby Day, Washington, 1990-94. Recipient Honor award Thornhill Month Mag. Pub., 1985. Mem. NOW, LWV (Princeton chpt. 1988—), N.J. Bus. & Profl. Women Assn. (chmn. N.J. legis. chpt. 1992-93), Women's Agenda (com. mem. N.J. law sect.). Home: 14 Zeloof Dr Lawrenceville NJ 08648

GRIFFITH, JENNIFER LYNN, environmental engineer; b. Glen Ridge, N.J., Feb. 10, 1962; d. Ralph Warren and Jane B. Griffith. BS in Environ. Engring., U. Vt., 1984; MS in Tech. and Policy, MIT, 1993, MS in Civil and Environ. Engring., 1993. Registered profl. engr., Vt. Staff engr. Wehran Engrs. and Scientists, Methuen, Mass., 1985-88; project mgr. ENSR Cons. and Engring., Acton, Mass., 1988-91; rsch. engr. MIT, Cambridge, 1993—. Coord. Tuesday Meals Program, Harvard Square, Cambridge, 1992—, Monday Supper, Maynard, Mass., 1989—; treas. Paine Social Svcs., Cambridge, 1994—. Rabinowitz fellow, 1991. Mem. ASCE, Chi Epsilon, Tau Beta Pi. Office: MIT 1-179 Cambridge MA 02139

GRIFFITH, LEAH MARIE, librarian; b. Astoria, Oreg., Mar. 4, 1956; d. Frank Howard and Patricia (Kemmerer) G. BS in Social Scis., So. Oreg. State Coll., Ashland, 1978; MLS, Clarion (Pa.) U., 1987. Clk. libr. Multnomah County Libr., Portland, Oreg., 1979-83; libr. asst. Hillsboro (Oreg.) Pub. Libr., 1983; libr. dir. Cornelius (Oreg.) Pub. Libr., 1983-89; extension libr. Ohio Valley Area Librs., Wellston, Ohio, 1989-92; libr. dir. Newberg (Oreg.) Pub. Libr., 1992—. Mem. ALA, Ohio Libr. Assn., Oreg. Libr. Assn. (chair pub. rels. com. 1985-86, founder small librs. round table, chair pub. libr. divsn., 1994-95). Democrat. Office: Newberg Pub Libr 503 E Hancock St Newberg OR 97132

GRIFFITH, MADLYNNE VEIL, controller; b. Johnstown, Pa., Jan. 2, 1951; d. J. Donald and Mary Jane (Veil) G.; 1 child, Philip Bryce. BA, St. Mary's Coll., 1973; MBA, U. Notre Dame, 1975; doctoral candidate, Pa. State U., 1985—. Cost and budget analyst U. Mich., Ann Arbor, 1980-81; acct. U. N.C., Wilmington, 1981, Johnstown Med. Devel. Corp., 1982-83; controller Mt. Aloysius Coll., Cresson, Pa., 1983—. Republican. Roman Catholic. Office: Mt Aloysius Coll Cresson PA 16630

GRIFFITH, MARY L. KILPATRICK (MRS. EMLYN I. GRIFFITH), civic leader; b. Gadsden, Ala., Mar. 22, 1926; d. Lewis A. and Willie (Reid) Kilpatrick; m. Emlyn I. Griffith, Aug. 13, 1946; children: William L., James R. AB, Huntingdon Coll., 1947. Pres. Evergreen Twig, Rome, N.Y., 1966-67, Rome Home, 1973-75, Rome Coll. Found., 1990-93, Ctrl. Assn. Blind and Visually Impaired, 1992—; mem. Bd. Edn. Rome City Sch. Dist., 1967-77; del. U.S.-China Joint Session on Trade and Law, Beijing, 1987, Soviet-Am. Conf. on Comparative Edn., Moscow, 1988, Gov.'s Conf. on Librs., 1990. Bd. dirs. Utica Coll. Found., 1974-80, George Jr. Republic, 1974-88, Pub. Broadcasting Coun. Ctrl. N.Y., 1977-83, Rome Art and Community Ctr., 1978-84, 1st Presbyn. Ch., Rome, 1979-85, Ctrl. N.Y. Libr. Resources Coun., 1992—, Kirkland Coll. Coun., 1967-75, Rome chpt. Am. Field Svc., 1969-77, Utica Symphony Orch., 1989—, Utica Found., 1992—. Recipient Rose for Living award Rotary Club, 1973, Civic award for conspicuous pub. service Colgate U., 1978. Mem. AAUW, PEO (pres. 1965-66), Wednesday Morning Club (pres. 1968-70). Home: Golf Course Rd Rome NY 13440

GRIFFITH, MELANIE, actress; b. N.Y.C., Aug. 9, 1957; d. Tippi Hedren; m. Steven Bauer (div.); 1 child, Alexander; m. Don Johnson, 1989; 1 child, Dakota. Student, Hollywood Profl. Sch., 1981; studied acting with, Stella Adler. Acting debut in Night Moves, 1975, other films include The Drowing Pool, 1975, Smile, 1975, One on One, 1977, Roar, Joyride, 1977, Underground Aces, Body Double, 1984, Fear City, Something Wild, 1986, Cherry 2000, 1988, The Milagro Beanfield War, 1988, Stormy Monday, 1987, Working Girl (Acad. Award nomination), 1988, In the Spirit, The Grifters, Pacific Heights, 1990, Bonfire of the Vanities, Shining Through, Paradise, 1991, A Stranger Among Us, 1992, Born Yesterday, 1993, Milk Money, 1994, Nobody's Fool, 1994; TV appearances include (series) Carter Country, (mini-series) Once an Eagle, (movies) Daddy, I Don't Like This, Steel Cowboy, The Star Marker, (pilots) She's in the Army Now, Golden Gate; guest in Alfred Hitcock Presents. Recipient Golden Globe award, 1989. *

GRIFFITH, PATRICIA KING, journalist; b. San Francisco, Jan. 20, 1934; d. Earl Beardsley and Frankie Mae (Kelly) King; m. Winthrop Gold Griffith, Oct. 4, 1958 (div. Jan. 1986); children: Kevin Winthrop, Christina Suzanne. BA, Stanford U., 1955. Copy asst., reporter Washington Post, 1956-57, 60-64; reporter San Francisco Examiner, 1957-59; Washington bureau chief Monterey Herald and Toledo Blade, Washington, 1979-81; investigative reporter Monterey (Calif.) Peninsula Herald, 1973-79, city editor, 1981-83, mng. editor, 1983-88; Washington bureau chief, White House corr. Toledo Blade and Pitts. Post-Gazette, Washington, 1988—. Bd. dirs. Lyceum of Monterey Peninsula, 1977-79, All Sts. Episcopal Day Sch., Carmel, Calif., 1977-79, Monterey Coll. Law, 1978-79; sr. warden St. Dunstan's Episcopal Ch., Carmel Valley, Calif., 1983-84. Recipient Silver Gavel award ABA, 1978. Mem. Stanford Alumni Assn., Nat. Press Club, Gridiron Club, Stanford Club Washington, Stanford Cap and Gown Soc. Home: 3001 Veazey Ter NW Washington DC 20008 Office: Blade Comm 955 National Press Bldg Washington DC 20045

GRIFFITH, SIMA LYNN, investment banking executive, consultant; b. N.Y.C., Sept. 7, 1960; d. Morris Benjamin and Mary (Buberoglü) Nahum; m. Clark Calvin Griffith, Sept. 13, 1987. BA in English, Amherst Coll., 1982. Account exec. D.F. King & Co., Inc., N.Y.C., 1982-84; asst. v.p. D.F. King & Co., Inc., 1984-86, v.p., 1986-88; v.p. Wells & Miller, Mpls., 1988; with Griffith, Lexi Capital, Inc, Mpls., 1988—; co-chmn. seminars, 1987; bd. advisors Pacer, Inc. Mem. Internat. Assn. Bus. Communicators (bd. govs. 1987-88), Pub. Relations Soc. Am. (bd. govs. investor relations sec. 1987—), Nat. Investor Relations Inst. Office: Griffith Lexi Capital Inc 4830 IDS Ctr 80 S 8th St Minneapolis MN 55402

GRIFFITH FRIES, MARTHA, controller; b. Brockton, Mass., Sept. 9, 1945; d. Ishmael Hayes and Jettie L. (Dudley) Davis; m. Jack C. Griffith, May 29, 1965 (dec. June 1984); Michael S., David M.; m. Dan H. Fries, Nov. 5, 1994. Student, U. Ark., 1962-64; BA, Ball State U., 1967. Prin. Griffith Acctg. Co., Indpls., 1968-70; probate adminstr. Johnson & Weaver, Indpls., 1970-74; personnel adminstr. Hercules Inc., Houston, 1974-76; adminstr. Lapin Totz & Mayer, Houston, 1976-80; bus. mgr. Pasadena (Tex.) Citizen, 1980-84; contr. Houston Community Newspapers, 1984-88, DCI Pub., Alexandria, Va., 1989-90, Telescan Inc., Houston, 1990-93, Advolink, Inc., 1993—. Commr. Houston council Boy Scouts Am., 1983. Recipient Dist. Merit awards Boy Scouts Am., Houston, 1983. Mem. Internat. Newspaper Fin. Execs. (com. mem. 1986-89), Collier Jackson Users Group (moderator 1986-89), Nat. Assn. Female Execs. Democrat. Baptist. Address: 17218 Telegraph Creek Dr Spring TX 77379

GRIFFITH JOYNER, FLORENCE DELOREZ, track and field athlete; b. L.A., Dec. 21, 1959; d. Robert and Florence Griffith; m. Al Joyner; 1 child: Mary Ruth Joyner. Student, Calif. State U., Northridge, UCLA; PhD (hon.), Am. U., Washington, 1994. Co-owner New Co. Nails; Designed line of sportswear, and uniforms for NBA Ind. Pacers. Actress (prin. role film) The Chaser, (recurring role TV drama) Santa Barbara, guest 227 TV situation comedies; host, commentator various sports events; guest numerous talk shows. Co-chairperson Pres. Coun. on Phys. Fitness & Sports, 1993—, founder The Florence Griffith Joyner Youth Found. Winner Silver medal Summer Olympics, L.A., 1984, 3 Gold medals, 1 Silver medal Summer Olympics, Seoul, Republic of Korea, 1988; U.S. Olympic Com. Sports Woman of the Year 1988, TAC Jesse Owens outstanding track and field athlete, 1988, Internat. Jesse Owens award Most Outstanding amateur athlete, 1988, Tass News Agy. Sports Personality of Yr., 1988, Internat. Fedn. Bodybuilders Most Outstanding Physique 1980s, 1988, UPI and AP Sportswoman of the year, 1988; named Athlete of Yr. Track and Field, 1988, recipient of the Harvard Found. award for outstanding contribution to the field of athletics, 1989, Essence Mag's. Sports award Extraordinary Accomplishments in Athletics, 1989, Golden Camera award from German Advt. Industry, 1989, James E. Sullivan Meml. award as most outstanding athlete in Am., 1989. Office: Florence Griffith Joyner Youth Found 30021 Tomas St Ste 300 Rancho Santa Margarita CA 92688

GRIFFITHS, JOSÉ-MARIE, information science educator; b. Middlesex County, England; m. Donald W. King; 1 child, Rhiannon Joyce. BSc in Physics with honours, London U., England, 1973, PhD in Info. Sci., 1977. Rsch. fellow Univ. Coll., London U., Teddington, England, 1974-76; lectr. Sch. Libr., Archive and Info. Studies, Univ. Coll., London U., 1972-79; dir. computing lab. Imperial Cancer Rsch. Fund Labs., London, 1978-79; head edn. and tng. ctr. Marconi Avionics, Hertfordshire, Eng., 1979-80; v.p., bd. dirs. King Rsch., Inc., Rockville, Md., 1980-89; prof., collaborating scientist in info. sci., dir. U. Tenn. Sch. Info. Scis., Knoxville, England, 1989—; dir. Ctr. Info. Studies U. Tenn. Sch. Info. Scis., Knoxville, Md., 1989—; prof. U. Tenn. Sch. Info. Scis., Knoxville, Tenn., 1989—, 1994—, acting vice chancellor computing and telecomms., 1994—; vis. lectr. dept. libr. and info. studies Queen's U., Belfast, No. Ireland, 1976-77; vis. prof. U. Calif. Sch. Libr. and Info. Studies, U. Calif., Berkeley, 1979-80; cons. dept. librarianship U. Ibadan, Nigeria, 1984; instr. Cath. U. Washington, 1986-89; tech. advisor divsn. gen. infor programme UNESCO, Paris, 1978; also others. Author: (with Donald W. King) Special Libraries and Information Services—Increasing the Information Edge, 1993; editor: Perspectives on Information Management series, 1987-90; mem. editl. bd. Microcomputers for Info. Mgmt., 1984-86; contbr. numerous articles to profl. jours. Recipient rsch. award Spl. Librs. Assn., 1992; rsch. studentship Nat. Phys. Labr., 1972, Brit. Libr., 1974-77; rsch. fellow City U., 1976-78, hon. rsch. fellow Univ. Coll., 1977—, rsch. fellow Royal Soc.-Brit. Libr., 1977-79. Mem. Inst. Info. Scientists (rsch. com. 1976-79), Brit. Computer Soc. (info. retrieval specialist group), Am. Libr. and Info. Sci. Educators (awards com. 1994-96), Am. Soc. for Info. Scis. (chmn. professionalism com. 1987-88, nominations com. 1993—, mem. rsch. com. 1982-86, edn. com. 1983-86, networking com. 1981-87, awards and honors com. 1993—, pres.-elect. 1992, pres. 1993, rep. on Nat. Commn. on Softwre Issues in 80's 1982—, on ALISE-ASIS coop. activities com. 1993-95, rsch. award 1990). Office: U Tenn Sch Info Scis 804 Volunteer Blvd Knoxville TN 37996-4330

GRIGG, BARBARA BOEHM, geriatrics services professional; b. LeCenter, Minn., May 23, 1939; m. Robert Grigg; children: Alyssa Ann, Daniel. Diploma, DePaul Hosp., 1966; BSN, U. Pa., Phila., 1968; MSN, Calif. State U., Chico, 1984. RN, Calif.; cert. pub. health nurse. Nursing supr. Hosp. Coromoto, Mariaquibo, Venezuela; respite program coord. Mental Health Assn., Davis, Calif.; medical inspector nursing homes Local Physicians, Yolo County, Calif.; pub. health nurse Health Dept., Mpls.; eldercare program specialist Yolo County Health Svcs. Agy., Woodland, Calif., mental health nurse specialist, older adult program; adv. com. Yolo County Eldercare. Contbr. articles to profl. jours.; producer video and guide Hiring In Home Help, Tips For Seniors and Their Families. Fed. grantee. Mem. ANA, Am. Pub. Assn., Case Mgr. Soc. Am., Sigma Theta Tau.

GRIGGS, BOBBIE JUNE, civic worker; b. Oklahoma City, Feb. 14, 1938; d. Robert Jefferson and Nora May (Green) Fish; m. Peter Harvey Griggs, Apr. 16, 1955; children: Diana (dec.), Terry, James. Grad. high sch., Salina, Kans. Commissary rep. Family Mag., Charleston AFB, S.C., 1976—; rep. Avon Corp., Charleston, S.C., 1976—; freelance demonstrator to USAF and USN orgns. Charleston, 1976—; rep. Salute Mag., Charleston AFB, 1986—; consumer edn. counselor Air Force-Navy exchs. Oster Kitchen Appliances, Charleston, 1987-90. Contbr. World's Largest Poem for Peace, 1991, Selected Works of our Best Poets, 1992, In A Different Light, 1992. Youth advisor, Charleston AFB, 1966-78; vol. doll distbn. program Salvation Army; clinic vol. ARC, Charleston AFB, 1967-75, chmn. family svcs. publicity and spl. projects, 1989; clinic vol. Clara Barton award, 1972; vol. Spoleto Festival, 1989—, Twin Oaks Retirement Ctr., 1992—, Chapel SUMMOM program, 1991—; asst. coord., publicity chmn. Family Svcs., 1967-83, named vol. of quarter, 1970, 72, 74, 76, named vol. of yr., 1970; active various scouting orgns., 1967—; asst. kindergarten Sunday sch. supt. Chapel I, 1966-68; active North Charleston (S.C.) Christian Women's Club, 1988—, hosp. chmn., mem. Charleston AFB Protestant Women's Club., 1965—; tchr. Bible sch., 1984-89; vol. tutor Lambs Elem., 1992, Trident Literacy Assn. (Laubach Literacy Action cert. 1992); coun. rep. Charleston AFB parish coun., 1988—; mem. Rocketeers Actors Group, Goals 2000 com. 1993—, Barnabas Outreach program, 1991—, Clown Ministry Charleston AFB, 1993—; chairperson Helping Hands Charleston AFB, 1991—, Voyagers Sunday Sch. Class Project, Summerville Homeless Shelter Charleston AFB, 1993—, Publicity Protestant Women, 1993—; vol. Lambs

Elem., 1992—, Twin Oaks Retirement Ctr., 1992—, Barnabas Outreach Com., 1991—, Military Retirees, 1994—; counselor Jr. Achievement Program, 1994. Recipient 1,000 Hours award Air Force Times, 1971, 1st Pl. award Designer Craftsman show, 1967-71, Dedicated Svc. award Charleston AFB, 1981, Hurricane Hugo Hero award, 1989, 1st Pl. award Bake-Off Contest YMCA, 1981, Hist. Charleston Trail Hike award Cub Scouts, 1988, Family Svcs. Vol. of Quar. award, 1990, Family Svcs. 6,000 Hour award, 1990, Golden Poet award, 1991, 1992, In a Different Light award Libr. Congress, 1991; named Enlisted Wife of Yr., Charleston AFB, 1974, Family Svcs. Vol. of Quarter Charleston AFB, 1990, Family Svcs. 6000 Hour award, 1991, Outstanding Vol. Svc. award Operation Desert Shield/Storm, 1991, Family Svcs. Spl. Recognition award, 1991, Appreciation acknowledgement Pres. of U.S., 1991, First Lady Barbara Bush, 1992, Pres. of U.S., 1994, First Lady Hillary Clinton, 1994. Mem. Nat. Trust Hist. Preservation, Smithsonian Inst., Charleston AFB Non-Commd. Officers' Wives Club (pres. 1971-73, publicity chmn. 1969-70, wife of month 1967, wife of quarter 1973), Rocketeers Actors Group, Friends of Dock St.-Ushers.

GRIGGS, EMMA, management executive; b. Cleveland, Ark., Feb. 8, 1928; d. James and Frazier (Byers) Wallace; m. Augusta Griggs, Mar. 20, 1954 (dec.); children: Judy A., Terri V. Grad. high sch., Chgo. Pres., CEO Burlington No. Inc., Inglewood, Calif., 1986—. Republican. Home: 2601 W 82nd St Inglewood CA 90305-1428

GRIGGS, RUTH MARIE, retired journalism educator, writer, publications consultant; b. Linton, Ind., Aug. 11, 1911; d. Roy Evans Price and Mary Blanche (Hays) P.; m. Paul Philip Griggs, Aug. 4, 1940. BS, Butler U., 1933; postgrad. U. So. Calif., 1938, Northwestern U., 1939; MA, U. Wyo., 1944. Cert. tchr. journalism, English, speech, bus. edn. Travel writer Indpls. Star, 1927-37; summer reporter Worthington Times, Ind., 1928-33; journalism, speech tchr. Warren Cen. High Sch., Indpls., 1937-37; tchr. bus. edn., journalism Greene Twp. High Sch., South Bend, Ind., 1937-38; tchr. journalism, English, bus. edn. Howe High Sch., Indpls., 1938-46; tchr. journalism Butler U., Indpls., 1946-48, evenings 1972-76; dir. publs. Broad Ripple High Sch., Indpls., 1948-77; summer journalism workshop instr. numerous univs. 1949-80. Author: History of Broad Ripple, 1968; co-author: Handbook for High School Journalism, 1951; Teacher's Guide to High School Journalism, 1965. Dow Jones Newspaper Fund fellow U. Minn., 1967; named Nat. Journalism Tchr. of Yr. Wall Street Jour., 1968, Woman of Achievement Woman's Press Club of Ind., 1984; recipient Rabb award Women's Press Club of Ind., 1988, Disting. Alumni award Butler U. Alumni Bd., 1989. Mem. AAUW, DAR, Journalism Edn. Assn. (v.p., pres. 1963-69, Towley award 1965), Women in Communications (pres. Indpls. 1969-70, Wright award 1969, Kleinhenz award 1978), Nat. Fed. Press Women (youth projects bd. 1979-87, Recognition award 1991), Columbia Scholastic Press Assn. (Gold Key award 1964, Golden Crown 1975, life mem. 1977), Ind. High Sch. Advisers Assn. (pres. 1972, Sengenberger award 1965), Delta Zeta (Ind. Woman of Yr. 1984). Republican. Presbyterian.

GRIGSBY, JANET BURRAGE, psychotherapist; b. Waco, Tex., July 10, 1954; d. John L. Burrage and Edna (Lewis) Burrage Yowell; m. Bill K. Grigsby, Aug. 1, 1981; 1 child, Brett Logan. BA in Psychology, U. Tex., Dallas, 1982; MS in Human Rels. & Bus., Amber U., 1985. Lic. profl. counselor. Media buyer Bozell & Jacobs Advt., Dallas, 1978-82; case mgr. Dallas County MHMR, 1982-86; dir. pub. rels. Green Oaks Psychiatric Hosp., Dallas, 1986-88; pvt. practice psychotherapist Plano, Tex., 1989-91, San Antonio, 1991-94; dir. provider and cmty. rels. Southwestern Mental Health Ctr., San Antonio, 1994—; adj. prof. psychology Collin Coun. C.C., Plano, 1990. Speaker Senate Com. Hearing on Mental Healthcare, San Antonio, 1991. Mem. AACD, Tex. Assn. Counseling and Devel., Tex. Assn. Alcohol and Drug Abuse Counselors, Mental Health Assn. Greater San Antonio, Bexar County Psychol. Assn., Mind Sci. Found. Home: 2207 Deerfield Wood San Antonio TX 78248-1915 Office: 8535 Tom Slick Dr San Antonio TX 78229-3363

GRIGSBY, MARGARET ELIZABETH, physician; b. Prairie View, Tex., Jan. 16, 1923; d. John Richard and Lee (Hankins) G. BS, Prairie View State Coll., 1943; MD, U. Mich., 1948. Diplomate: Nat. Bd. Med. Examiners, Am. Bd. Internal Medicine. Intern Homer G. Phillips Hosp., St. Louis, 1948-49, asst. resident medicine, 1949-50; asst. resident Freedmen's Hosp., Washington, 1950-51, asst. physician, 1952-56, attending physician, 1956; practice medicine specializing in internal medicine Washington, 1953-54; instr. medicine Howard U., Washington, 1952-57, asst. prof., 1957-60, assoc. prof., 1960-66, prof., 1966-93, prof. emerita, 1993—, chief of infectious diseases, 1952-71, lectr. sch. social work, 1955-59, adminstrv. asst. dept. medicine sch. social work, 1961-63; epidemiologist USPHS, Ibadan, Nigeria, 1966-68; hon. vis. prof. preventive and social medicine U. Ibadan, 1967-68; cons. AID, Dept. State, 1970-71; mem. adv. com. anti-infective agents FDA, 1970-72. Contbr. articles to med. jours. Rockefeller Found. fellow Harvard U., 1951-52; research fellow Thorndike Meml. Lab., Boston City Hosp., 1951-52; China Med. Bd. fellow tropical medicine U. P.R., 1956; Commonwealth Fund Fellow U. London, 1962-63. Fellow ACP; mem. Nat. Med. Assn., Med. Soc. D.C., Royal Soc. Tropical Medicine and Hygiene, Am. Soc. Tropical Medicine and Hygiene, Medico-Chirug. Soc. D.C., Assn. Former Interns and Residents Freedman's Hosp., U. Mich. Alumni Assn., Prairie View Alumni Assn., Sigma Xi, Alpha Epsilon Iota, Alpha Kappa Alpha, Alpha Omega Alpha. Office: Howard U Dept Medicine 2041 Georgia Ave NW Washington DC 20060-0002

GRIGSBY-STEPHENS, KLARON, corporate executive; b. East Prairie, Mo., Feb. 15, 1952; d. Claron Grigsby and Sylvia Mae (Grigery) Oliver; m. Richard Earl Stephens, Aug. 13, 1986. Exec. asst. Quasar Petroleum Corp., Ft. Worth, 1974-80; sales mgr. ITT Life Ins. Corp., Ft. Worth, 1980-83; media buyer Boca Blue Star, Boca Raton, Fla., 1983-84; video editor Video Workshop, Pompano Beach, Fla., 1984-85; pres. Stephens Alfa Corp., Pompano Beach, 1985—. Contbr. articles to profl. jours., also numerous poems. Sgt. USAF, 1970-74. Mem. Alfa Romeo Owners Club, Challenger Ctr. (Washington, hon.). Office: 1321 S Dixie Hwy W Pompano Beach FL 33060-8520

GRILLO, MARY ANN ANGELA, communications professional; b. St. Louis, Jan. 8, 1958; d. Vincent and Virginia Susanne (Nicoletti) G. B of Comm., St. Louis U., 1980; postgrad., Washington U., St. Louis. Inventory mgmt. coord. Anheuser-Busch, Inc., Baldwinsville, N.Y., 1982-84; mktg. analyst Anheuser-Busch, Inc., St. Louis, 1984-86, retail mktg. coord., 1986-89, mgr. retail mktg., 1990-92, mgr. retail comm., 1992—. Named to Women of Yr. Bartender mag., Liberty, N.J., 1993, Woman of Achievement, Alliance, St. Louis, 1987; recipient Leadership cert. YWCA, St. Louis, 1988. Mem. Women in Comm., Women in Bus. (asst. coord. 1987-88), NAFE, Odd Lot Investment Club (sec. 1988-89). Office: Anheuser-Busch Inc One Busch Pl Saint Louis MO 63118

GRIM, ELLEN TOWNSEND, artist, retired art educator; b. Boone County, Ind., Nov. 1, 1921; d. Horace Wright and Sibyl Conklin (Lindley) Townsend; m. Robert Little Grim, Apr. 5, 1952; children: Nancy Ellen Grim Davis, Howard Robert. BA in Art, U. Wash., 1946; MA in Art, UCLA, 1950; postgrad., Otis Art Inst., L.A., 1970-71. Cert. secondary tchr., Calif. Art tchr., chairperson secondary Calif. and L.A. Unified Sch. Dist., 1947-82; retired, 1982; artist L.A., 1975—; guest speaker on art TV and cable, L.A., 1993. One-woman shows include Ventura (Calif.) County Mus. Art, 1982, Riverside (Calif.) Mcpl. Mus., 1984, Craft and Folk Art Mus., L.A., 1986, Southwest Mus., L.A., 1987, Santa Monica (Calif.) Heritage Mus., 1991, and others; exhibited in 7 invitational shows, Calif., 1982-93; exhibited in 125 group shows, Calif., 1947-93; contbr. articles to mags. 1st lt. USMC, 1943-45. Recipient Purchase prize Gardena Fine Arts Collection, 1982, Watercolor West award San Diego Watercolor Soc. Internat., 1983, N.Mex. Watercolor Soc. award, San Diego Watercolor Soc. Exhbn., 1989, 1st pl. award Fine Arts Fedn., 1987, 1st pl. award Art Educators L.A., 1988, 89, and others. Mem. Nat. Watercolor Soc. (historian 1989-90, Painting award 1985), Watercolor West (Painting award 1989), Women Painters West (membership chair, mem.-at-large 1983-89, Painting award 1985, 86, 88, 89, 92), L.A. Art Assn. (bd. dirs. 1993-95), Pasadena Soc. Artists (Painting award 1986, 88, 90, 92, 93), Collage Artists Am., Women Marines Assn. and Alliance of Women Vets., Alpha Phi, Pi Lambda Theta.

GRIMBALL, CAROLINE GORDON, sales professional; b. Columbia, S.C., Dec. 21, 1946; d. John and Caroline Grimball. B.A. in Polit. Sci., Converse Coll., 1968; postgrad., S.C. Law Sch., 1968-69. Asst. buyer, buyer Rich's, Inc., Atlanta, 1971-78, spl. events fashion coordinator, Columbia, S.C., 1978-83; gen. mdse. mgr. Rackes, Inc., Columbia, 1983-84, Parasol Boutique, Columbia, 1984-86; retail cons. Retail Mdsg. Service Automation, Columbia, 1986-88; sales rep. Palmetto Promotions, 1989-93; retail mdse. supr. Riverbanks Zoo & Garden, 1993—. Pres. Columbia Action Coun., 1990-92; bd. dirs. Palmetto Leadership Coun., 1991-92, Palmetto State Orch. Assn., Columbia, 1979-89, Women's Symphony Assn., Columbia, 1985; com. chmn. Columbia Action Coun., 1984-85, exec. com., 1989—. Named one of Outstanding Young Women Am., 1979, 80; recipient Community Service award Rich's, Inc., 1981. Mem. Nat. So. Colonial Dames Am., Columbia Jr. League. Democrat. Episcopalian. Club: Columbia Drama. Avocations: bridge, reading, needlepoint, tennis. Home: 4000 Bloomwood Rd Columbia SC 29205-2847

GRIMES, HEILAN YVETTE, publishing executive; b. Hamilton, Ohio, Sept. 16, 1949; d. J and Claudette (Hinkle) G. Grad., New Eng. Sch. Photography, 1987. Founder, pres. Dot & Line Graphics, 1975—, Color Computer Weekly, 1982—, Hollow Earth Pub., 1983—. Author: Norse Mythology, 1984, Legend of Niebelungenlied, 1984, Using QuarkXPress 3.3, The Laxdaela Saga, Beginning Internet, Beginning QuarkXPress, The Newton Source Book; founder (mag.) Byte, 1974, Macpower, 1993. Recipient various photographic awards and grants. Democrat. Office: PO Box 1355 Boston MA 02205-1355

GRIMES, JUDY DAVIS, psychologist; b. Falls, Pa., June 23, 1941; d. Milan and Vera (Fitch) Davis; m. Jorge A. Grimes; children: Mark, Lori, Timothy, Kelly. BS in Rehab. Edn., Pa. State U., 1984, MS in Counselor Edn., 1986, PhD in Ednl. Psychology, 1989. Neuropsychology assoc. Nittany Valley Rehab., State College, Pa., 1986; neuropsychologist New Medico Rehab., Cortland, N.Y., 1988-89; psychologist N.Y.State Office of Mental Retardation, Auburn, N.Y., 1989-91, Elmerest Children's Ctr., Syracuse, N.Y., 1991-93, Psychol. health Svcs., Syracuse, N.Y., 1993—; adj. faculty Divsn. of Health-Related Svcs. and Coll. Nursing, SUNY-Syracuse, 1988—. Mem. APA, N.Y. State Psychol. Assn., Ctrl. N.Y. Psychol. Assn., Phi Lambda Theta, Rho Chi Sigma. Office: Psychol Health Svcs PC 5112 W Taft Rd Liverpool NY 13088-4873

GRIMES, MARGARET WHITEHURST, medievalist, educator; b. New Bern, N.C., Oct. 12, 1917; d. Robert Emmet and Margaret Edna (Ervin) Whitehurst; m. Alan Pendleton Grimes, May 16, 1942; children: Margaret, Alan P. Jr., Katherine E., Peter E. BA, U. N.C., 1938; MA, Mich. State U., 1967, PhD, 1969. Instr. Mich. State U., E. Lansing, 1969-71; asst. prof. humanities asst. prof. humanities, E. Lansing, 1971-75; assoc. prof. Mich. State U., E. Lansing, 1975-80, prof., 1980-86, prof. emeritus, 1986—; chmn., organizer Medieval Studies Consortium, Mich. State U., E. Lansing, 1991—. Contbr. articles to profl. jours.; presenter to medieval studies groups. Mem. Medieval Assn. Midwest, Dante Soc. Am., Medieval Acad. Am., Mich. State U. Dante Soc. (chmn., founder 1985). Democrat. Home: 728 Lantern Hill Dr East Lansing MI 48823-2828 Office: Mich State U Ctr Integrative Studies Linton Hall East Lansing MI 48824

GRIMES, MARTHA, author; b. Pittsburgh, Pa.; d. D.W. and June (Dunnington) G.; div.; 1 s.: Kent Van Holland. BA, MA, U. Md. Formerly instr. English U. Iowa, Iowa City; asst. prof. Frostburg State Coll., Frostburg, Md.; prof. Montgomery Coll., Takoma Park, Md., 1970—. Author: mystery novels The Man With a Load of Mischief, 1981, The Old Fox Deceiv'd, 1982, The Anodyne Necklace, 1983 (Nero Wolfe Award for best mystery of yr.1983), The Dirty Duck, 1984, The Jerusalem Inn, 1984, Help the Poor Struggler, 1985, The Deer Leap, 1985, I Am the Only Running Footman, 1986, The Five Bells and Bladebone, 1987, The Old Silent, 1989, Send Bygraves, 1989, The Old Contemptibles, 1991, End of the Pier, 1992, The Horse You Came In On, 1993. Address: care Alfred A Knopf, Inc. 201 E 50th St New York NY 10022-7703*

GRIMES, PATRICIA STRAHOTA, architect, interior designer; b. Detroit, Sept. 27, 1951; d. Edward John and Teresa (Fodor) S.; m. Eugene Peter Grimes, Sept. 17, 1988. BS in Design, U. Mich., 1973. Registered architect, N.Y. Draftsperson Hoad Engring., Ypsilanti, Mich., 1973; interior designer contract div. J.L. Hudson's, Detroit, 1973-74, John Steven's Assocs., Detroit, 1974, U. Mich., Ann Arbor, 1974-76, Ostgren Assocs., San Francisco, 1976-77; interior designer, architect Gensler & Assocs., San Francisco and N.Y.C., 1977-90; architect Cushman & Wakefield, Inc., N.Y.C., 1990-91, The Phillips Janson Group, N.Y.C., 1991—; guest lectr. N.Y. Sch. Interior Design, N.Y.C., 1984—. Mem. AIA (interiors subcom. 1988—), U. Mich. Alumni Assn. Office: Phillips Janson Group 11 W 42d St New York NY 10036

GRIMES, RUTH ELAINE, city planner; b. Palo Alto, Calif., Mar. 4, 1949; d. Herbert George and Irene (Williams) Baker; m. Charles A. Grimes, July 19, 1969 (div. 1981); 1 child, Michael; m. Roger L. Sharpe, Mar. 20, 1984; 1 child, Teresa. AB summa cum laude, U. Calif., Berkeley, 1970, M in City Planning, 1972. Rsch. and evaluation coord. Ctr. Ind. Living, Berkeley, 1972-74; planner City of Berkeley, 1974-76, sr. planner, 1983—, analyst, 1976-83; bd. dirs. Vets. Asssistance Ctr., Berkeley, pres., 1978-93; bd. dirs. Berkeley Design Advisors, treas., 1987—. Author: Berkeley Downtown Plan, 1988; contbr. numerous articles to profl. jours. and other publs. Bd. dirs. Berkeley-Sakai Sister City Assn., 1994—, Ctr. Ind. Living. Honored by Calif. State Assembly Resolution, 1988; Edwin Frank Kratt scholar, 1966. Mem. ASPA, Am. Inst. Cert. Planners, Am. Planning Assn., Mensa, Lade Merrit Joggers and Striders (sec. 1986-89, pres. 1991-93), Lions Internat. (bd. dirs. Berkeley club 1992—), U. Calif. Coll. Environ. Design Alumni Assn. (bd. dirs., treas. 1994-95). Home: 1330 Bonita Ave Berkeley CA 94709-1925 Office: City of Berkeley 2121 Mckinley Ave Berkeley CA 94703-1584

GRIMES, SUSAN MARIE, financial analyst; b. Seward, Nebr., Dec. 10, 1964; d. Gleason Charles and Patricia Kay (Thompson) G. BSBA, U. Nebr., Kearney, 1987; postgrad., Vanderbilt U. Cert, mgmt. acct. Fin. analyst Electonic Data Systems, Dallas, 1987-88, Warren, Mich., 1989-91; fin. analyst Electonic Data Systems, Nashville, 1992-94, bus. planning specialist, 1994—. Mem. Inst. Mgmt. Accts. Office: Electronic Data Systems 100 Saturn Pkwy Spring Hill TN 37174

GRIMES, TRESMAINE JUDITH RUBAIN, psychology educator; b. N.Y.C., Aug. 3, 1959; d. Judith May (McIntosh) Rubain; m. Clarence Grimes, Jr., Dec. 22, 1984; children: Elena Joanna, Elijah Jeremy. BA, Yale U., 1980; MA, New Sch. for Social Rsch., 1982; MPhil, PhD, Columbia U., 1990. Advanced tchg. fellow Jewish Bd. Family and Childrens Svcs., N.Y.C., 1980-82; tchg./rsch. asst. Tchrs. Coll., Columbia U., N.Y.C., 1983-84; rschr., historian Youth Action Program, N.Y.C., 1984-86; psychologist Hale House for Infants, N.Y.C., 1986-89; asst. rschr. Bank St. Coll., N.Y.C., 1988; addiction program adminstr. Harlem Hosp. Ctr., N.Y.C., 1989-91; asst. prof. psychology S.C. State U., Orangeburg, 1991—; adj. prof. psychology Tchrs. Coll., Columbia U., N.Y.C., 1990-91. Named Outstanding Young Women of Am., 1981. Mem. APA, Southeastern Psychol. Assn., Delta Sigma Theta, Kappa Delta Pi, Psi Chi. Democrat. Office: SC State Univ Box 7003 300 College St NE Orangeburg SC 29117-0001

GRIMES-FARROW, DOROTHEA D., communications executive; b. New Orleans, Feb. 10, 1952; d. Morris and Rosemary (Birch) Grimes. BS in Physics, So. U., Baton Rouge, 1974; EDD, Rutgers U., 1980. Tchr. physics Piscataway (N.J.) Sch. System, 1975-78; tech. asst. AT&T Bell Labs., Murray Hill, N.J., 1978-80; mem. tech. staff. AT&T Bell Labs., Piscataway, 1980-85; tech. supr. small system devel. lab. AT&T Bell Labs., Middletown, N.J., 1985-88; tech. supr. quality system devel. AT&T Bell Labs., Parsippany, N.J., 1988-89; dept. head communications systems devel. lab. AT&T Bell Labs, Middletown, 1989-94; sr. coach, technology planning AT&T Bell Labs, Basking Ridge, N.J., 1994—. Contbr. articles to profl. jours. Mem. YWCA Mgmt. Forum, Summit, N.J., 1988, bd. dirs., 1989-93. Mem. AAAS, IEEE, Assn. Computing Machinery, Am. Ednl. Rsch. Assn., Coalition of 100 Black Women. Office: AT&T Bell Labs 211 Mt Airy Rd Rm 2E110 Basking Ridge NJ 07920

GRIMLEY, CYNTHIA PATRIZI, rehabilitation consultant, special education educator; b. Sharon, Pa., Mar. 29, 1958; d. James Donald and Delores Virginia (Maykowski) Patrizi; m. Kevin Neil Grimley, Apr. 11, 1987; children: Ronald James, Jennifer Rose. BS, Youngstown (Ohio) State U., 1981; MS, Calif. State U., 1986. Lic. multiple subject tchr., spl. edn. and elem. tchr., severely handicapped edn. tchr., Ohio, Pa.; specialist credential, Calif.; cert. rehab. counselor, case mgr. Residential program worker, supr., classroom tchr. Mercer County Assn. for the Retarded, Hermitage, Pa., 1980-82; tchr. spl. edn. Hermitage Sch. Dist., 1982-83; cons. property mgmt. Lorden Mgmt. Co., Covina, Calif., 1983-84; tchr. spl. edn. Fullerton (Calif.) Elem. Sch. Dist., 1984-87; vocat. rehab. cons. Profl. Rehab. Cons., Santa Ana, Calif., 1986-89, Pvt. Sector Rehab., Fullerton, 1989—i. Contbr. curriculum, articles in field. Coach Spl. Olympics, Fullerton, 1982-87; sec. So. Calif. Rehab. Exch., 1989, mem.-at-large, 1990, treas., 1991. Polish Art Club scholar, 1977. Fellow Am. Bd. Vocat. Experts, Am. Acad. Pain Mgmt.; mem. NEA, Nat. Assn. Rehab. Profls. in the Pvt. Sector, Calif. Assn. Rehab. Profls., Assn. Retarded Citizens. Democrat. Roman Catholic. Office: Pvt Sector Rehab 2555 E Chapman Ave Ste 300 Fullerton CA 92631-3656

GRIMM, PAULA, advertising executive, strategic planner; b. Troy, N.Y., Nov. 10, 1950; d. Frederick Henry and Helen Marie (Johnson) G.; m. David K. Mickle; m. David K. Mickle. BA in Am. Studies, Manhattanville Coll., Purchase, N.Y., 1974. Rsch. assoc. Scali McCabe, Sloves, N.Y.C., 1974-79, assoc. rsch. dir., 1981-86; rsch. group head Dancer, Fitzgerald, Sample, N.Y., 1979-81; exec. v.p., dir. strategic planning and rsch. Saatchi & Saatchi DFS/Pacific, Torrance, Calif., 1986—. Mem. Townhall of L.A., 1989-90. Recipient Outstanding Womna of Yr. in Automotive Industry award McCalls, Wards Automotive and Internat. Auto Show. Mem. Am. Mktg. Assn., Western States Advt. Agys., AEF Advt. Ednl. Found., ECO/Advt. Adv. Alliance. Home: 601 N Gardner St Los Angeles CA 90036-5712 Office: Saatchi & Saatchi DFS/Pacific 3501 Sepulveda Blvd Torrance CA 90505-2538

GRIMMER, MARGOT, dancer, choreographer, director; b. Chgo., Apr. 5, 1944; d. Vernon and Ann (Radville) G.; m. Weymouth Kirkland; 1 child, Ashley Samantha Grimmer Kirkland; student Lake Forest; 1963, Northwestern U., 1964-68. Dancer, N.Y.C. Ballet prodn. of Nutcracker Chgo., 1956-57, Kansas City Starlight Theatre, 1958, St. Louis Mcpl. Theatre, 1959, Chgo. TentHouse-Music Theater, 1960-61, Lyric Opera Ballet, Chgo., 1961, 63-66, 68, Ballet Russe de Monte Carlo, N.Y.C., 1962, Ruth Page Internat. Ballet, Chgo., 1965-70; dancer-choreographer Am. Dance Co., Chgo., 1972—, artistic dir., 1972—; dancer, choreographer Bob Hope Show, Milw., 1975, Washington Bicentennial Performance, Kennedy Center, 1976, Woody Guthrie Benefit Concerts, 1976-77, Assyrian Cultural Found., Chgo., 1977-78, Iranian Consulate Performance, Chgo., 1978, Israeli Consulate Concert, Chgo., 1980, Chgo. Council Fine Arts Programs, 1978-87, U.S. Boating Indsl. Show, 1981—; dir.-tchr. Am. Dance Sch., 1971—; tchr. master classes U. Ill, 1975, 83, Anderson Hall, Occidental and Sebastopol Community Ctr., Calif., 1988-90, Park Point Club, Santa Rosa, Calif., 1988-89, Oakland (Calif.) Dance Collective, 1989—; soloist Showcase to Benefit Sebastopol Ctr. For Arts, Calif., 1990, benefit perfomances Chgo. Area Settlement Houses, Lake Forest, Ill., 1991, 92, 93, 94, Milw. Charities, 1992; appeared in TV commls. and indsl. films for Libbys Foods, Sears, Gen. Motors, others, 1963—, also in feature film Risky Business, 1982; soloist in ballet Repertory Workshop, CBS-TV, 1964, dance film Statics (Internat. Film award), 1967; soloist in concert Ravinia, 1973; important works include ballets In-A-Gadda-Da-Vida, 1972, The Waste Land, 1973, Rachmaninoff: Theme and Variations, 1973, Le Baiser de la Fee and Sonata, 1974, Four Quartets, 1974, Am. Export, 1975, Earth, Wind and Fire, 1976, Blood, Sand and Empire, 1977, Disco Fever, 1978, Pax Romana, Xanadu, 1979, Ishmael, 1980, Vertigo, 1982, Eye in the Sky, 1984, Frankie Goes to Hollywood, 1986, Power House Africano, 1987, Cole Porter Tribute, 1994, others; dance critic Mail-Advertiser Publs., 1980-82; host cable TV show Spotlight, 1984-85, Viewpoints, 1987. Ill. Arts Council Grantee, 1972-75, 78; Nat. Endowment Arts grantee, 1973-74. Mem. Actors Equity Assn., Screen Actors Guild, Am. Guild Mus. Artists. Home: 970 Vernon Ave Glencoe IL 60022-1266 Office: 442 Central Ave Highland Park IL 60035-2651

GRINARML, SANDI MOLNAR, elementary education educator; b. Tyrone, Pa., Oct. 18, 1950; d. John Francis and Helen (Chalan) Molnar; m. Robert Grinarml, July 20, 1974; children: Jason, Beth Ann. BS in Art Edn., Edinboro U., 1972, BS in Elem. Edn., 1974. Masters equivalency, 1980. Tchr. elem. art Berwick (Pa.) Schs., 1972-74; subs. tchr. Penncrest Schs., Cambridge Springs, Pa., 1974-75, tchr. 5th grade, 1975—; developer, coord. coach Odyssey of Minds, Cambridge Springs, 1985-90. Leader, program developer Cub Scouts, Cambridge Springs, 1983-88; leader Brownies, Cambridge Springs, 1990-92; chair community beautification project, 1980, repairing Youth Activity Bldgs., 1993; coach Odyssey of the Mind, 1993—. Home: RD 2 Box 189B Cambridge Springs PA 16403

GRINER, DEBRA LEA MILLÈRE, accountant; b. Camden, N.J., Feb. 3, 1961; d. Edmond Simpson and Nancy Saunders (Ris) Millère; m. Steven Worthy Griner, Aug. 23, 1986. Cert., Katharine Gibbs Sch., Boston, 1981; BBA in Fin./Acctg., Mercer U., 1988. Adminstrv. asst. ITO Corp., Boston, 1981-84, FMR Corp., Boston, 1984; staff acct. First South Bank N.A., Macon, Ga., 1989-91; wool procurement acct. Forstmann & Co., Dublin, Ga., 1991-92, accounts receivable mgr., 1992—; acct. Vann Air, Inc., Dublin, 1993. Office: Forstmann & Co 141 Nathaniel Dr Dublin GA 31021-7801

GRINNELL, HELEN DUNN, musicologist and arts administrator; b. N.Y.C., Nov. 22, 1936; d. Kempton and Susan Barret (Gill) D.; children: Taylor, James Bodman; m. Alexander Grinnell, July 6, 1991. New Eng. Conservatory, 1957-60; BMus, San Francisco Conservatory of Music, 1968; MA in Musicology, Am. U., 1982. Dir. Opera and Symphony Previews, San Francisco, 1966-67; instr. piano, music theory, San Francisco, 1969-71, Wilmington, Del., 1973-76; dir. constituent rels. Office of Congressman William Mailliard, Washington, 1973; arts coord. Del. State Arts Coun., 1977-78; music libr. Am. U., Washington, 1981-84; pres. Music Info. Specialists, 1984—, dir. Discovering Music, 1984—; dir. Rsch. Ctr. for Chinese Mus. Iconography, 1984—; cons. Boys Clubs of Am. Young Artists Program. Author: Chinese Musical Iconography: A History of Musical Instruments Depicted in Chinese Art, 1987, Chinese Musical Iconography: A Catalogue, 1988, National Symphony Orchestra Discography, 1988; program annotator Dumbarton Concert Series, Smithsonian Institution, Kennedy Ctr. Stagebill, Handel Festival Orch., Nat. Chamber Orch.; editor: American Women Composers' Forum; steering com. Friends of Music Smithsonian Instn. Bd. dirs. Spring Opera of San Francisco, 1967-71, Wilmington Music Sch., 1973-78, Washington Performing Arts Soc., 1980-90, Nat. Symphony Orch., Washington, 1979-82, Bargemusic Ltd., 1992—, Nat. Orchestral Assn., 1993—, Shelter Island Hist. Soc., 1993—; chmn. acad. policy com., trustee San Francisco Conservatory of Music, 1967-71; bd. overseers New Eng. Conservatory, 1985—; chmn. archl. rev. bd. Village of Dering Harbor, N.Y., 1991—. Mem. Am. Musicol. Soc., Amateur Ski Club N.Y., Shelter Island Yacht Club. Office: 1199 Park Ave Ste 16B New York NY 10128-1774

GRISSOM, PAMELA ANN, sales professional; b. Saginaw, Mich., Nov. 13, 1958; d. Alvin Louis and Margaret (Willey) Thiede; m. Stephen Arnold Grissom, June 23, 1984; children: Joshua Stephen Arnold, Ashley Margaret Ann. Grad. high sch., Dearborn, Mich. With First of Mich. Corp., Detroit, 1978-87; sales sec. First of Mich. Corp., Dearborn, 1987—. Office: First of Mich Corp 23400 Michigan Ave Dearborn MI 48124-1915

GRISSOM, PATSY COLEEN, college administrator, English educator; b. Mt. Pleasant, Tex., Jan. 9, 1934; d. Thomas A. and Cleo (Jones) G. BA, East Tex. State U., 1955; MA, Syracuse U., 1957; PhD, U. Tex., 1966. Student dean, head resident Syracuse (N.Y.) U., 1955-57; head resident, instr. English Hanover (Ind.) Coll., 1957-58, Trinity U., San Antonio, 1958-61; teaching asst., assoc. dean of students U. Tex., Austin, 1961-64; assoc. dean of students, asst. prof. English Trinity U., San Antonio, 1964-72, v.p. student affairs, prof. English, 1972—. Named Outstanding Prof., Trinity U. chpt. Mortar Bd., 1976. Mem. AAUW, Nat. Assn. Student Personnel Adminstrs., Nat. Assn. Women Deans and Counselors. Democrat. Presbyterian. Office: Trinity Univ Box 99 715 Stadium Dr San Antonio TX 78212

GRIZZARD, RICHELLE ALLENE, state official; b. Sioux Falls, S.D., Nov. 6, 1948; d. Charles Richard and Barbara Shirley (Tough) Knudsen; m. John Barry Grizzard; 1 child, John Charles. BA in Polit. Sci. summa cum laude, U. North Fla., 1981, MPA, 1992. Legal sec. George W. Kent, Orange Park, Fla., 1982-84, Maness & Kachergus, Jacksonville, Fla., 1984-87; free-lance legal sec. Orange Park, Jacksonville, 1987-89; legal sec. Adams, Rothstein & Siegel, Jacksonville, 1989; legal asst. Dale & Bald, P.A., Jacksonville, 1989-92; Madison/Mullis fellow Ctr. for Local Govt. Adminstrn., U. North Fla., Jacksonville, 1992; free-lance legal asst. Jacksonville, 1993—; resource devel. specialist Agy. Approval & Devel., Inc., Jacksonville, 1993-94; notary public State of Fla., 1982—. With USN, 1968-70. Mem. Am. Soc. Pub. Adminstrn., Lions (dir. 1992-94, sight chmn. 1993—, Gov.'s Achievement award 1994), Phi Theta Kappa, Pi Alpha Alpha. Democrat. Baptist.

GRMEK, DOROTHY ANTONIA, accountant; b. Cleve., July 7, 1930; d. Louis and Antonia (Korosec) Lipanye; m. M. Charles Stelmach, June 13, 1953 (div. May 1977); children: Monica Doran Meade, Dwayne Alan Stelmach, Dale Richard Stelmach; m. William Edward Grmek, Aug. 18, 1978. BBA in Acctg., Fenn Coll., 1953. Chief acct. Pyromatics, Inc., Willoughby, Ohio, 1975-87; acct., exec. sec. Auctor Assocs., Inc., Cleveland Heights, 1972—; ptnr., tax cons. Diversified Bus. Svc., Rocky River, Ohio, 1980—; contr., human rels. specialist Telefast Industries, Inc., Berea, Ohio, 1988-94; treas., buyer River Toy Box, Inc., Rocky River, 1990—. Mem. Slovene Nat. Benefit Soc. (ins. agt. 1982—, charter mem., fin. sec. lodge 781 1982—, Cleve. Fedn. Lodges rec. sec. 1968-72, fin. sec. 1972-82). Home: 3645 Kings Post Pky Rocky River OH 44116-3816 also: River Toy Box Inc 20130 Center Ridge Rd Rocky River OH 44116-3500 also: Auctor Assocs Inc 3109 Mayfield Rd Cleveland Hts OH 44118

GROAH, LINDA KAY, nursing administrator and educator; b. Cedar Rapids, Iowa, Oct. 5, 1942; d. Joseph David and Irma Josephine (Zitek) Rozek; diploma St. Luke's Sch. Nursing, Cedar Rapids, 1963; student San Francisco City Coll., 1976-77; BA, St. Mary's Coll., Moraga, Calif., 1978; BS in Nursing, Calif. State U.; MS in Nursing, U. Calif.; m. Patrick Andrew Groah, Mar. 20, 1975; 1 child, Kimberly; stepchildren: Nadine, Maureen, Patrick, Marcus. Staff nurse to head nurse U. Iowa, 1963-67; clin. supr., dir. oper. and recovery room Michael Reese Hosp., Chgo., 1967-73; dir. oper. rooms Med. Ctr. Cen. Ga., Macon, 1973-74; dir. oper. and recovery rooms U. Calif. Hosps. and Clinics, San Francisco, 1974-90, asst. dir. hosps. and clinics, 1982-86; divsn. dir. Kaiser Found. Hosp., San Francisco, 1990—; asst. clin. prof. U. Calif. Sch. Nursing, San Francisco, 1975—; cons. to oper. room suprs., to div. ednl. resources and programs Assn. Am. Med. Colls., 1976—; condr. seminars. Mem. Nat. League for Nurses, Am. Nurses Assn. (vice chmn. operating room conf. group 1974-76), Assn. Oper. Room Nurses (com. on nominations 1979-84, treas. 1985-87, 93—, bd. dirs. 1991-93, pres. found., Award for Excellence in Preoperative Nursing 1989), Ctr. for Study Dem. Instns. Author: Perioperative Nursing Practice, 1983, 3d edit., 1995; contbr. articles on operating room techniques to profl. jours. and textbooks; author, producer audio-visual presentations; author computer software. Home: 5 Mateo Dr Belvedere Tiburon CA 94920-1071 Office: 3020 Bridgeway Ste 299 Sausalito CA 94965-2839

GROAT, JENNY HUNTER (LAVIDA JUNE GROAT), painter, artist, choreographer, calligrapher; b. Modesto, Calif., Aug. 30, 1929; d. Leo Hunt and Lola Tuttle (Atwood) Miller; m. Maurice Frederick Groat, Jan. 15, 1955. AA in Music, San Joaquin Delta, 1950. Modern dance tchr. San Dominican Schs., San Rafael, Calif., 1952-54; dance dir., tchr. Reed Coll., Portland, Oreg., 1954-56 summers; co-founder, artistic dir., tchr. various dance coops., San Francisco Bay Area, 1951-61; founder, dir., tchr., soloist, choreographer Dance West: The Jenny Hunter Sch. and Dance Co., San Francisco, 1962-68; invited art tchr. Internat. workshops, 1983—; tchr. art clligraphy Coll. of Marin, Kentfield, Calif., 1980-90; tchr.-mentor art classes Lagunitas, Calif., 1987—; tchr., tng. for creative dance Dancers and Artists, Bay area, 1955—; mast classes, dance Bay area groups, colls. and univs., 1958-68; organizer panel discussions on art Jenny Hunter Sch., Dance West, San Francisco, 1963. One-woman shows include Claudia Chapline Gallery, Stinson Beach, Calif., 1994, 93, Gallery One, Petahuma, 1994, Zon Ctr., San Francisco, 1993, 90, Bechtel Ctr. Stanford U., 1993, Marin County Civic Ctr. Libr., San Rafael, San Geronimo Valley Cultural Ctr., 1990, Detroit Pub. Libr., 1988, Markings Gallery, Berkeley, Calif., 1985, Fairfax (Calif.) Pub. Libr., 1981-82, Lyford Ho., Tiburon, Calif., 1982, Palace Legion of Honor Theatre, 1967, 68, 65; numerous group exhbns. including Klingspor Mus., Germany, 1983, Grand Palais, Paris, 1990; permanent collections include Nat. Mus. Women in Arts, Washington, U. Tex., Austin, Harrison Collection-San Francisco Pub. Libr.; represented in many pvt. collections. Grantor scholarships for child and adult dancers Jenny Hunter Dance West Sch., 1962-68; founder, mentor, tchr. Grass Root Scribes, Marin County, Calif., 1987-89; curator, art exhbns. Coll. of Marin and Kentfield, and Fairfax (Calif.) Libr., 1980-82. Grantee for art work in modern dance City of San Francisco, 1968; recipient Golden Quill award Calligraphic Soc. of Ariz., 1986. Mem. Colo. Calligrapher's Guild (hon.), Friends of Calligraphy, Marin Soc. of Artists (life), Soc. for Calligraphy (L.A.), Marin Arts Coun. Democrat. Buddhist.

GROAT, LINDA NOEL, architectural educator; b. Stamford, Conn., Aug. 18, 1946; d. Everett Linwood and Vivian (Smith) G.; m. Lawrence K. Stern, Apr. 29, 1979; 1 child, Laura Linwood. BA, Conn. Coll., 1968; MA in Teaching, Yale U., 1969; MFA, Calif. Inst. Arts, 1972; MS, U. Surrey, 1979, PhD, 1985. Designer Charles Moore Assocs., New Haven, 1969-70, McCue Boone Tomsick Architects, San Francisco, 1974-77; cons. Kaplan, McLaughlin, Diaz Architects, San Francisco, 1979-80; asst. prof. U. Wis., Milw., 1980-86, assoc. prof., 1986-87; assoc. dean U. Mich. Coll. Architecture and Urban Planning, Ann Arbor, 1987-92, assoc. prof, 1987—. Mem. editorial bd. Jour. Archtl. Edn., Jour. Environ. Psychology, Jour. Archtl. and Planning Rsch. Mem. Nat. Trust for Hist. Preservation, Washington, 1983—, Nat. Mus. Women in the Arts, Washington, 1987—. Recipient Environ. Graphics award Print Casebooks, 1979; design rsch. grantee Nat. Endowment for the Arts, 1982, 92, Graham Found. for Advanced Studies in Fine Arts, 1991. Mem. AIA (assoc.), Internat. Assn. for Study People and Their Phys. Surroundings, Assn. Collegiate Sch. Architecture (east ctrl. regional dir. 1992—), Environ. Design Rsch. Assn., Nat. Assn. for Women in Edn. Office: U Mich Coll Architecture & Urban Planning 2000 Bonisteel Blvd Ann Arbor MI 48109-2069

GROCHOWSKI, MARY ANN, psychotherapist; b. Milw., Oct. 8, 1944; d. Leonard Edward and Mary (Hitti) Rebatzke; m. James Allen Grochowski, Jan. 27, 1968; children: Bradley, Brandon. BA, Marquette U., 1966; MSW, U. Wis., Milw., 1968. Cert. social worker; lic. ind. clin. social worker. Psychotherapist L.A. Child Guidance Clinic, 1968-70, Milw. Children's Hosp., 1970-74; psychotherapist Family Social & Psychotherapy Svcs., Milw., 1972-74, 79-93, clinic dir., 1986-93; psychotherapist Apogee-Winston Clinic, Inc., Milw., 1993—; chair adv. coun. Family Social & Psychotherapy Svcs., Milw., 1987-90; mem. bd. Children's Legal Action Fund, Milw., 1989; active Nat. Clin. Adv. Bd. Apogee, 1994—. Contbr. articles to jours. Mem. NASW, Am. Profl. Soc. on Abuse of Children, Internat. Soc. Study of Dissociation. Roman Catholic. Office: Apogee Winston Clinics Inc 7330 W Layton Ave PO Box 20800 Milwaukee WI 53220-0800

GRODSKY, JAMIE ANNE, lawyer; b. San Francisco; d. Gerold Morton and Kayla Deane (Wolfe) G. BA in Human Biology/Natural Scis. and History with distinction, Stanford U., 1977, JD, 1992; MA in Econ. Geography, U. Calif., Berkeley, 1985. Ednl. dir. Oceanic Soc., San Francisco, 1979-81; rsch. asst. Woods Hole (Mass.) Oceanog. Inst., 1983; analyst Office Tech. Assessment U.S. Congress, Washington, 1984-89; counsel Com. Natural Resources, U.S. Ho. of Reps., Washington, 1993-95. Articles editor Stanford Law Rev.; contbr. articles to profl. jours.

GROENENDAAL, CLAUDETTE I., insurance broker, track and field athlete; b. Torrance, Calif., Nov. 1, 1963; d. Albert Bernard and Irene (Amberg) G. BS, U. Oregon, 1985. Account exec. Johnson & Higgins, L.A., Calif., 1990—. Recipient NCAA Track and Field championship 1500 meters Eugene, Oreg., 1984, 800 meters, Austin, Tex., 1985, U.S. Nat. championship 800 meters Indpls., Eugene, 1985, 86. Home: PO Box 3186 Santa Monica CA 90408-3186

GROESBECK, ELISE DE BRANGES DE BOURICA, artist; b. Versailles, France, Jan. 31, 1936 (parents Am. citizens); d. Vicount Louis de Branges de Bourcia II and Diane (McDonald) de Branges de Bourcia; student Phila. Coll. Art, 1954-55; m. James Richard Groesbeck, Oct. 3, 1958 (div. June 1969); children: Gretchen Atlee, Genevieve de Branges. One-man shows The Agnes Irwin Sch., Rosemont, Pa., 1973, Phila. Cricket Club, Chestnut Hill, Pa., 1973. Recipient prize Rehoboth Beach Art League, 1944; Agnes Allen Art prize Agnes Irwin Sch., 1954. Repubican. Episcopalian. Home: 3204 Leigh Rd Pompano Beach FL 33062-1214 Office: PO Box 58 Pompano Beach FL 33061-0058

GROFF, SUSAN CAROLE, elementary education educator; b. Marshalltown, Iowa, Feb. 16, 1954; d. Ernest Jerome and Alice Marjorie (Harmon) G.; m. Wayne A. Van Arendonk, Aug. 14, 1994. BS, Iowa State U., 1976; MS in Edn., U. Kans., 1981; edn. specialist, U. Iowa, 1984. Resource rm. aide Pinckney Elem., Lawrence, Kans., 1976-77; tchr. spl. edn. Booth Elem., Wichita, Kans., 1977-78; tchr. resource rm. Clinton (Iowa) Community Schs., 1978-80; tchr. spl. edn. Henry Sabin Elem., Clinton, 1980-83; cons. No. Trails Area Edn. Agy., Clear Lake, Iowa, 1984-86; tchr. resource rm. Tomiyasu Yr.-Round Sch., Las Vegas, Nev., 1986-88, 90-92; tchr. elem. edn. Tomiyasu Yr.-Round Sch., Las Vegas, 1988-90, 92-94; cons. Heartland Area Edn. Agy., Johnston, Iowa, 1994—; student tchr. supr. U. Iowa, Iowa City, 1983, grad. asst., 1984. Treas. U.S. Rep., Iowa, 1974-75. Recipient Excellence in Edn. award Clark County Sch. Dist., Las Vegas, 1992. Mem. Iowa State Edn. Assn., Iowa State Cons. Assn., Coun. for Exceptional Children, U. Iowa Alumni Assn. (life), Iowa State U. Alumni Assn. (life), U. Kans. Alumni Assn. Democrat. Congregational. Home: 1104 Johnson St Ames IA 50010

GROGAN, BETTE LOWERY, steel fastener distribution executive; b. Seminole, Okla., Nov. 18, 1931; d. C.J. and Martha C. (Eakin) Lowery; m. Morris Rowell, Feb. 8, 1947 (div. Oct. 1960); children: Ronald Michael, Kathy D. Rowell Burkard; m. John Kenneth Grogan, Oct. 28, 1967. Student Del Mar Coll., 1949-51, So. Meth. U., 1963-65. Sec., office mgr. Carrigan Realty, Orlando, Fla., 1958-61; dist. sec. Tektronics, Inc., Orlando, 1961-63; legal sec. Jenkens, Anson, Spradley & Gilchrist, Dallas, 1963-67; real estate broker, Dallas, 1967-77; v.p. Grogan & Co., Dallas, 1972-77; pres. Fla. Threaded Products Inc., Orlando, 1977—; dir. Women's Bus. Ednl. Council (pres. 1986, chmn. bd. 1987), Inc., Orlando, pres., 1986. Mem. Planning and Zoning Commn., Carrollton, Tex., 1972-74; bd. dirs. Jr. Achievement, Orlando, 1981-83, Healthcare Cost Containment Bd., Fla. Def. Conversion and Transition Commn., 1993—; del. Gov.'s Conf. on Small Bus., 1987, 89, 91, White House Conf. on Small Bus., Fla., 1986; sec.-treas. Cmty. Health Purchasing Alliance, State of Fla., 1993—. Named Cen. Fla. Small Bus. Person of the Yr., SBA-C. of C., 1981. Mem. Women's Bus. Ednl. Confs. Fla. (bd. dirs. 1984-85, exec. v.p. 1985-86, pres. 1986, chmn. bd. dirs. 1987), Nat. Fedn. Ind. Bus. (guardian adv. council), Fastener Assn. (bd. dirs. 1980-84), Central Fla. Leadership Council (bd. dirs. 1984—), Greater Orlando C. of C. (chairperson N.W. regional coun. 1990), Fla. Exec. Women, Better Bus. Bur. Cen. Fla. (mem. exec. com., chmn. 1989, bd. dirs. 1989), Beta Sigma Phi (pres. Orlando 1957-59), Rotary. Republican. Episcopalian. Avocations: tennis, golf, reading. Office: Fla Threaded Products Inc 3060 Clemson Rd Orlando FL 32808-3992

GROGAN, SUZANN JEANETTE-WYMAN, artist; b. L.A., July 6, 1962; d. Frank Adelbert Jr. and Beverly Ann (Burge) Wyman; m. Marvin John Grogan, June 1, 1985. AA, Fullerton Coll., 1984. Drafter Cetec Corp., Southgate, Calif., 1983-85; drafter, illustrator MegaTape Corp., Duarte, Calif., 1985-94; designer drafter Magellan Systems Corp., San Dimas, Calif., 1994—; writer Victorville, Calif., 1988—, artist, 1990—; dir. publishing Mojave Inst. Arts, Apple Valley, Calif., 1994—. Artist (painting) Art of the West mag., 1993. Charter mem. Nat. Mus. Am. Indian, Washington, 1993-94; mem. Nat. Mus. Women in Arts, Washington, 1993-94. Adopted Hon. mem. Wappo Tribe, Sonoma County, Calif., 1994. Mem. Oil Painters Am. (assoc.), Laguna Art-A-Fair Coop. Home and studio: 13840 Galaxy Way Victorville CA 92392-9385

GROH, SUSAN, physician; b. N.Y.C., Apr. 19, 1947; d. Arthur and Angela G.; children: Lisa, Erik, Megan. BS summa cum laude (Ward Melville Validictory award), SUNY, Stony Brook, 1968, MS magna cum laude, Hofstra U., 1971, MD, Downstate Med. Ctr., 1988. Diplomate Am. Bd. Family Practice. Tchr. sci. and math., counselor Bellmore-Merrick Consol. High Sch. Dist., Merrick, N.Y., 1968-71, 75-76, 1979-84, Green St. Elem. Sch., Cazenovia, N.Y., 1971-75; intern internal medicine and pediatrics North Shore U. Hosp., Manhasset, 1988-89; resident in family practice South Nassau Community Hosp., 1989-91; asst. dir. Acad. Affairs Nassau County Health Care Systems, 1992—; primary care physician Holly Patterson Geriatric Ctr, Uniondale, N.Y., 1991—; pvt. practice in family medicine, Merrick, 1993—; attending physician emergency svcs. Franklin Hosp. Med. Ctr., Valley Stream, 1991-93. Author: College Support Services for Learning Disabled, 1st edit., 1980, 2d edit., 1981; Life Skills and Career Education for Secondary Students With Learning Disabilities, 1980. Facilitator, founder Parent Support Group Svcs., Merrick, 1980-82; mem. Ad Hoc Com. for Mt. Sinai Sch. Constrn., 1976-78; 1st v.p. Mothers Ctr. Suffolk County, 1976-79; mem. Com. for Full Time Kindergarten, Long Beach, N.Y., 1982. Recipient A&S Spirited Woman award, 1984, Execellence and Profl. Achievement award A. Holly Patterson Geriatric Ctr., 1994. Mem. AMA, Am. Med. Women's Assn., Am. Acad. Family Physicians, Am. Coll. Physicians, Med. Soc. State of N.Y. Office: 2914 Frankel Blvd Merrick NY 11566

GROLLMAN, SARA NANCY, airline marketing manager; b. St. Louis, Feb. 8, 1955; d. Jerome Winston and Elaine (Braff) G. BA in Psychology cum laude, Brandeis U., 1977; MBA in Mktg., U. Calif., Berkeley, 1987. Sys. analyst Logicon Inc., Lexington, Mass., 1977-78; programmer Millipore Corp., Bedford, Mass., 1979-83; tour rep. Internat. Weekends, The Netherlands, 1984; sys. analyst GWV Travel, Needham, Mass., 1985; analyst mktg. and planning Am. Airlines, Ft. Worth, 1987-88, analyst sales devel., 1988-90, supr. nat. accounts, 1990, temp. mgr. salon, 1992, spl. assignment, 1992-93, mgr. AAir Born Fearless Flyer Program, 1990-94, mgr. reservations, leisure sales, 1994—. Supporter, mem. Komen Found., Nat. Breast Cancer Coalition, Childreach Found. A.L. Simmons grad scholar Am. Soc. Travel Agts., 1986. Mem. NAFE, Phi Beta Kappa. Democrat. Jewish. Home: 3861 N O'Connor Rd Irving TX 75062 Office: Am Airlines MD 2300 PO Box 619616 Dallas TX 75261-9616

GRO MAMBO ANGELA NOVANYON IDIZOL See LEWIS, JOCELYA

GRONAU, CRYSTAL LYNN, accountant; b. Newton, Kans., May 27, 1957; d. Albert Earl and Patricia Ann (Ulmer) G. BA, Tabor Coll., 1977; MBA, Golden Gate U., 1984. CPA, Calif., Kans. Sr. Grant Thornton, Wichita, Kans., 1979-83; mgr. Price Waterhouse, San Jose, Calif., 1984-86, Palo Alto, 1987-88; sr. mgr. Price Waterhouse, Palo Alto, Calif., 1990-92, 94—; Price Waterhouse GmbH, Frankfurt, Germany, 1992-94; mgr. taxation Geothermal Resources Internat., San Mateo, Calif., 1986-87; sr. mgr. Berger Lewis, San Jose, 1988-89. Mem. Calif. Soc. CPAs, Am. Women's Soc. CPAs. Office: Price Waterhouse 525 University Ave Ste 200 Palo Alto CA 94301

GRONBERG, EVELYN VIOLA, jewelry designer, small business owner; b. Cleve., Dec. 5, 1957; d. Joseph Edward and Viola Margaret (Ganger) Lynch; m. Robert John Gronberg, May 26, 1979; children: Sandra Michele, Lauren Kristine. Grad., Katharine Gibbs Sch., Boston, 1977; BSBA in Fin., Northeastern U., Boston, 1994. Legal sec. Nutter, McClennant & Fish, Boston, 1978-80, Sullivan & Worcester, Boston, 1980-81; funding asst. Leasing Svcs., Inc., Boston, 1982, funding mgr., 1983-85; lease documentation specialist Shawmut Bank, Boston, 1985-86; real estate agt. Century 21, Wellesley, Mass., 1990-91; owner Designs by Evelyn, Weston, Mass., 1990—; chairperson Whittemore Fashion Show, Weston, 1990. Creator jewelry Rain Forest, 1992, Aquarius, 1994. Mem. bd. dirs. Weston Cmty. Children's Assn., Weston, 1987—, pres. 1993-94, chairperson fundraising events, Weston, 1990-92; bd. dirs. Countryside Playsch., Weston, 1990-91, Women's Community League Chrysanthamum Scholarship Ball, Weston, 1992, 93; treas. Alphabet Park Com., Weston, 1989-90; mem. women's coun. Spaulding Rehab. Hosp., boston, 1993.; Weston Children's Cmty. Assn. liaison to bd. dirs. Weston PTO, 1990-93; also tchr. Sunday Sch., coach elem. soccer, scout vol. Mem. Weston LWV (bd. dirs. 1989, 90, 92, 93), Women's Community League, Weston Arts and Crafts Assn., Golden Key, Sigma Epsilon Rho. Congregationalist. Home and Office: 91 Viles St Weston MA 02193-1746

GROOMS, SUZANNE SIMMONS, music educator; b. New Orleans, Jan. 9, 1945; d. Claude Arthur and Mary Rachel (Pierce) Simmons; m. Barton Collins Grooms, May 12, 1973; children: David Barton, Michael Claude. BS, U. Tenn., 1966; M Music Edn., So. Ill. U., 1969. Cert. Suzuki tchr. instrumental music. Mem. violin sect. Knoxville (Tenn.) Symphony Orch., 1958-66; violinist St. Louis Philharmonic Orch., 1967-68; instr. Suzuki Inst., U. Wis., Stevens Point, 1970-73; violinist Amarillo (Tex.) Symphony Orch., 1973-77; dir., coordinator Suzuki string program Amarillo Coll., 1977—; violin tchr., co-founder Amarillo Area Youth Symphony. co-author: (Suzuki handbook) How To Make Your Twinkle Brighter, 1985. Bd. dirs. March of Dimes, Amarillo, 1977-79, Greater S.W. Music Festival, 1990—, Amarillo Symphony Youth Orch., Art Force, 1988-92; mem. Amarillo Jr. League, 1977-84; cir. chmn. United Meth. Ch., Amarillo. Grantee Harrington Found., 1981. Mem. Suzuki Assn. Ams., Internat. Suzuki Assn., Symphony Guild. Home: 4908 Erik Ave Amarillo TX 79106-4703 Office: Amarillo Coll PO Box 447 Amarillo TX 79178-0001

GROSE, ELINOR RUTH, retired elementary education educator; b. Honolulu, Apr. 23, 1928; d. Dwight Hatsuichi and Edith (Yamamoto) Uyeno; m. George Benedict Grose, Oct. 19, 1951; children: Heidi Diane Hill, Mary Porter, John Tracy, Nina Evangeline. AA, Briarcliff Jr. Coll., 1948; postgrad., Long Beach State U., 1954-55; BS in Edn., Wheelock Coll., Boston, 1956; MA in Edn., Whittier Coll., 1976. Cert. tchr., Mass., N.Y., Calif. Reading tchr. Cumberland Head Sch., Plattsburgh, N.Y., 1968-70; master tchr. Broadoaks Sch., Whittier (Calif.) Coll., 1971; reading tchr. Phelan/Washington Schs., Whittier, 1971-73; elem. tchr. Christian Sorensen Sch., Whittier, 1978-94, ret., 1994; cons. Nat. Writing Project and Calif. Writing Project, 1987—, South Basin Writing Project, Long Beach, 1987—; team tchr. Young Writers' Camp, Long Beach State U., 1988. First v.p. Women's League of Physicians Hosp., Plattsburgh, 1970; asst. to Christian, Jewish and Muslim pres., v.p.s of Acad. Judaic, Christian and Islamic Studies 6th Assembly World Coun. Chs., Vancouver, 1983. Named Companion of the Order of Abraham, Acad. for Judaic, Christian and Islamic Studies, 1987. Mem. NEA, Calif. Tchrs. Assn., Whittier Elem. Tchrs. Assn., English Coun. of Long Beach. Presbyterian. Home: 6085 E Brighton Ln Anaheim Hills CA 92807-4702

GROSE, MOLLY PICKERING, performing company executive; b. Charleston, W.Va., Oct. 9, 1938; d. Silas Wright II, and Marie Louise (Ohley) Pickering; divorced;. BA, Sweet Briar Coll., 1961. From sch. sec. to registrar The Spence Sch., N.Y.C., 1963—; from stage mgr. to mng. dir. York Theatre co., N.Y.C., 1968—. Active various coms. Ch. Heavenly Rest, N.Y.C., 1965—. Democrat. Episcopalian. Home: 1435 Lexington Ave New York NY 10128-1625 Office: York Theatre Co 2 E 90th St New York NY 10128-0603

GROSHNER, MARIA STAR, nuclear engineer; b. Las Vegas, Nev., Aug. 31, 1961; d. Robert Leroy and Stepheny (Higby) G.; m. Robert Clay Singleterry Jr., May 18, 1984. BS in Nuclear Engring., U. Ariz., 1984. Engr. in tng., Idaho. Reactor operator EG&G Idaho, Inc., Idaho Falls, 1985-89, engr., 1989-90, sr. engr., 1990-91; export control reviewer EG&G Idaho Inc., Idaho Falls, 1990-91; engr. III Westinghouse Idaho Nuclear Co., Idaho Falls, 1991-92, sr. engr. I, 1992-94; sr. engr., safety analyst Lockheed Idaho Techs. Co., Idaho Falls, 1994—. Mem. Citizen Energy Alert Network, Nuclear Energy Inst., Washington, 1987—. Mem. AAAS, AAUW, NAFE, Nat. Soc. Profl. Engrs., Am. Nuclear Soc. (media rels. chmn. Idaho chpt. 1990), Soc. Women Engrs. (chpt. sect. rep. 1990-91, treas. 1993—, v.p. southeastern Idaho chpt. 1989, coord. young women's conf. 1990), Toastmasters Internat. (chpt. pres. 1990, adminstrv. v.p. Jack C. High unit 1989, v.p. pub. rels. 1995 Competent Toastmaster, Able Toastmaster). United Methodist. Home: 365 Carol Ave Idaho Falls ID 83401-3176 Office: Lockheed Idaho Techs Co PO Box 1625 Idaho Falls ID 83415-3210

GROSS, BEATRICE SCHAAP, education educator, consultant, writer; b. N.Y.C., Jan. 23, 1935; married; 2 children. BA in Am. Studies, Syracuse U., 1956; MS in Edn., Bank Street Coll. Edn., N.Y.C., 1958. Cert. pre-sch. and elem. tchr. Adj. faculty NYU, N.Y.C., 1968-81, New Sch. Social Research, N.Y.C., 1983-87; vis. prof. Vassar Coll., 1985; assoc. prof. humanities SUNY, Old Westbury, 1972-76; cons. to govt., industry and founds., 1976—; participant univ. seminars Columbia U.; adj. prof. Queens Coll., 1993—. Author: Radical School Reform, 1970, Will it Grow in a Classroom?, 1974, The Children's Rights Movement, 1977, The New Old, 1978, Teaching Under Pressure, 1979, Towards Improved Compensatory Education, 1982, Independent Scholarship: Promise, Problems and Prospects, 1983, The Great School Debate: Which Way for American Education, 1985; syndicated columnist: The Family Viewpoint, 1979-82; co-editor: Ind. Scholarship newsletter; contbr. articles to profl. jours.; author teaching materials McGraw Hill, Sci. Research Assocs. Program adv. Beacon Coll., 1978-82; assoc. dir. Writers in the Pub. Interest, 1981—; assoc. project dir. Ind. Scholars Project, 1982—; adj. assoc. prof. La Quardia Community Coll., 1992—, CUNY, Queens, 1994—; exec. com. Womanspace, Great Neck, N.J. Recipient Disting. Achievement award Ednl. Press Assn. Am., 1974; Faculty Exchange scholar SUNY, 1975. Mem. Soc. Journalists and Authors. Home: 17 Myrtle Dr Great Neck NY 11021-1807

GROSS, CYNTHIA ANN, foreign exchange systems development executive; b. Somerset, N.J., Apr. 28, 1964; d. Andrew Michael and Elizabeth Marie (Holt) G. BS in Computer Info. Systems, Clemson U., 1986. Mgmt. assoc. trainee, systems planning officer NCNB Corp., Charlotte, N.C., 1986-88; asst. mgr., systems analyst Citibank, London, 1988-90; assoc., fgn. exch. systems Morgan Stanley & Co., N.Y.C., 1990-93; regional product mktg. mgr. for London and Europe Morgan Stanley UK Group, London, 1993—. Mem. benefit com. Trail Blazers, 1991-92, Kids with Kids Shelter, N.Y.C., 1991, The Grosvenor House; mem., performer Theatre Charlotte, 1988. Mem. Am. Mus. Natural History, French Inst., Jr. League N.Y., Jr. League London, Smithsonian Instn., English-Speaking Union, Honey Pot Home Shelter. Office: Morgan Stanley UK Group, 25 Cabot Sq, London E14 4QA, England

GROSS, DOROTHY-ELLEN, library director, dean; b. Buffalo, June 13, 1949; d. William Paul and Elizabeth Grace (Hough) G. BA, Westminster Coll., 1971; MLS, Rosary Grad. Sch. Libr. Sci., 1975; MDiv, McCormick Theol. Sem., 1975. Jr. cataloger McCormick Theol. Sem., Chgo., 1972-75; head tech. svcs. Barat Coll., Lake Forest, Ill., 1975-79, head libr., 1980-82; dir. coll. libr. North Park Coll. and Theol. Sem., Chgo., 1982-87, dir. coll. and sem. libr., 1987—, assoc. dean, 1990—, prof., 1991—; cons. acad. librs.; spkr. various profl. meetings and confs. Contbr. chpts. to books, including: Managing Student Workers in College Libraries, 1986; editor: Libras Handbook and Directory; co-editor North Park Faculty Publs. and Creative Works, 1992, Pvt. Acad. Librs. in Ill. newsletter; contbr. articles to profl. jours. Vol. United Way. Mem. ALA, LIBRAS (pres. 1983-85), Am. Coun. Edn. (participant nat. identification program), Assn. Coll. and Rsch. Librs., Pvt. Acad. Librs. Ill. (pres. 1981-83, 91—), Ctr. for Scandinavian Studies (bd. dirs. 1983-94), Swedish Am. Hist. Soc., Foster Investors (pres. 1990-91). Presbyterian. Office: North Pk Coll and Theol Sem 3225 W Foster Ave Chicago IL 60625

GROSS, FREDYE WRIGHT, fundraising executive; b. Dallas, Jan. 7, 1949; d. William Larry and Fredonia (Robinson) Wright; m. John R. Murphy, Feb. 15, 1981 (div. Feb. 1992); m. Adam Anthony Gross, July 11, 1992. BA, U. Tex., 1971. Pub. info. dir. Aurora Higher Edn. Ctr., Denver, 1973-77; pub. rels. dir. Colo. Hist. Soc., Denver, 1977-78; promotion dir. San Francisco Examiner, 1978-81; exec. dir. Friends of the Balt. Symphony, 1982-84; sales and mktg. assoc. Coldwell Banker Comml. Real Estate, Balt., 1985-89; dir. resource devel. The Enterprise Found., Columbia, Md., 1989—; pres. bd. dirs. Md. Art Place, Balt., 1984—; nat. mem. visual arts adv. bd. Coll. Santa Fe, N.Mex., 1992—. Contbr. photogrphy to newspaper and mags. Trustee Balt. Mus. Art, 1989—, Md. Inst. Coll. Art, Balt., 1984—; mem. capital campaign com. Salvation Army, Balt., 1988; co-chair benefit Assoc. Black Charities, Balt., 1991; mem. comml. real estate com. Greater Balt. Bd. Realtors, 1986-89. Recipient pub. svc. awards; Spl. Events award Assn. Newspaper Promoters, 1980; Photography award Denver Art Mus.,

1975, others. Mem. Parks and People Found., Balt. Country Club. Democrat. Episcopalian. Office: The Enterprise Found 500 American City Bldg Columbia MD 21044

GROSS, HARRIET P. MARCUS, religion and writing educator; b. Pitts., July 15, 1934; d. Joseph William and Rose (Roth) Pincus; children: Sol Benjamin, Devra Lynn. AB magna cum laude, U. Pitts., 1954; cert. in religious teaching, Spertus Coll. of Judaica, Chgo., 1962; MA, U. Tex., Dallas, 1990. Assoc. editor Jewish Criterion of Pitts., 1955-56; publs. writer B'nai B'rith Vocat. Svc., 1956-57; group leader Jewish Community Ctrs. of Met. Chgo., 1958-63; columnist Star Publs., Chicago Heights, Ill., 1964-80; pub. info. specialist Operation ABLE, Chgo., 1980-81; dir. religious sch. Temple Emanu-El, Dallas, 1983-86; freelance writer, 1986—; columnist Dallas Jewish Life Monthly, 1992—; lectr. U. Tex., Dallas, 1994—; tchr. writing Homewood-Flossmoor (Il.) Park Dist., Brookhaven Jr. Coll., Dallas; advisor journalism program Prairie State Coll., Chicago Heights, 1978-80; adv. bd. The Creative Woman quar. publ. Governors State U., Governors Park, Ill., The Mercury U. Tex., Dallas. Bd. dirs., sec. Family Svc. and Mental Health Ctr. of South Cook County, Ill., 1965-71; active Park Forest (Ill.) Commn. on Human Rels., 1969-80, chmn., 1974-76; bd. dirs. Ill. Theatre Ctr., 1977-80, Jewish Family Svc. of Dallas, 1982—; mem. Dallas Jewish Edn. Com., 1992—. Recipient Fellowship for Action Humanitarian Achievements award, 1974; Anti-Defamation League of B'nai B'rith Honor award, 1978; Dr. Charles E. Gavin Found. Community Service award, 1978, 1st Ann. Leadership award Jewish Family Svc., 1990. Mem. Nat. Fedn. Press Women, Tex. Press Women, Ill. Woman's Press Assn. (named Woman of Yr. 1978), Intertel (pres. Gateway Forum of Dallas 1984-85), Nat. Assn. Temple Educators, Mensa, Sigma Delta Chi, Phi Sigma Sigma. Jewish. Developed 1st community newspaper action line column, 1966. Office: 8560 Park Ln Apt 23 Dallas TX 75231-6312

GROSS, KAREN CHARAL, lawyer; b. N.Y.C., Nov. 25, 1940; d. Harry B. and Adele (Hook) Charal; m. Meyer A. Gross, Aug. 16, 1964; children: Dana Leslie, Jennifer P., Pamela A. AB, Barnard Coll., 1962; JD, NYU, 1965. Bar: N.Y. 1965. Atty. Wolder & Gross, N.Y.C., 1965-78, Wolder, Gross & Yavner, N.Y.C., 1978-86; v.p. legal and bus. affairs Good Times Home Video Corp., N.Y.C., 1986—. Editor NYU Law Rev., 1963-65. Parent liaison Ramaz Sch., N.Y.C., 1980-86; del. Dem. County Com., N.Y.C., 1988—; legal mentor to students Barnard Coll., N.Y.C. John Norton Pomeroy scholar NYU, 1963-65. Mem. Copyright Soc. USA. Office: GoodTimes Home Video Corp 16 E 40th St New York NY 10016

GROSS, KATHLEEN FRANCES, parochial school mathematics educator; b. Phila., Nov. 16, 1945; d. John Paul and Margaret Regina (Moore) G. BS in Edn., St. Joseph's U., 1968; postgrad. various instns., 1968-91. Cert. tchr., N.J. Tchr. St. Edmond's Grade Sch., Phila., 1964-68; tchr. math. St. Maria Goretti High Sch., Phila., 1968-71; tchr. math. Holy Spirit High Sch., Absecon, N.J., 1971—, chair dept. math., 1973-86, 91-94; adj. tchr. math. Atlantic C.C., Mays Landing, N.J., 1989—. Coord. Holy Spirit H.S. unit March of Dimes, 1980—. Mem. ASCD, Nat. Coun. Tchrs. Math., Assn. Math. Tchrs. N.J., Nat. Cath. Edn. Assn., South Jersey Cath. Sch. Tchrs. Orgn., Am. Assn. U. Women, Math. Assn. Am. Home: 332 Asbury Ave Ocean City NJ 08226-4022

GROSS, LAURA ANN, marketing and communications professional; b. Kew Gardens, N.Y., July 11, 1948; d. Melvin Fredericks and Harriette (Levy) G. BA, Boston U., 1970; MA, Columbia U., 1974. Staff writer Am. Banker, N.Y.C., 1974-82, assoc. editor, 1982-88; dir. fin. svcs., instns., communications Am. Express Travel/Related Svcs. Co., N.Y.C., 1988-89; dir. sales promotion and pub. rels. Am. Express Travelers Cheque Group/Am. Express Travel Svcs., N.Y.C., 1989-92; dir. strategic bus. comm. Am. Express Travel Related Svcs., N.Y.C., 1992-93; pres. Strategic Comm. Cons., N.Y.C., 1993—. Author, editor consumer surveys and articles; speaker in field. Recipient editorial awards Pannell Kerr Forster, 1984, N.E. Bus. Press Editors, 1986, N.Y. Bus. Press. Editors, 1987, first Boston U. Coll. of Liberal Arts Young Alumni award, 1985. Mem. Bank Mktg. Assn., Promotion Mktg. Assn. (Spire award 1991), Pub. Rels. Soc. Am. (Silver Anvil award 1990, Big Apple award 1992, Creativity in Pub. Rels. award 1993). Home: 14 Horatio St New York NY 10014-1652

GROSS, LESLIE PAMELA, sales executive, consultant; b. N.Y., Aug. 23, 1952; d. Gerald Jay and Pearl (Meltzer) G.; m. Ned T. Ashby. AB, Cornell U., 1976. Ins. agt. Equitable Life, San Francisco, 1976-79; sales assoc. Digital Equipment Corp., San Francisco, 1979-81; from sales rep. to sales exec. Digital Equipment Corp., Santa Clara, Calif., 1981-87; corp. acct. mgr. Digital Equipment Corp., San Francisco, 1987-92; area mgr. WordPerfect Corp., Orem, Utah, 1992-94; sr. account mgr. Novell, Inc., Sunnyvale, Calif., 1994—. Missionary, LDS Ch., Boston, 1973-75; jr. Sunday sch. tchr., Menlo Park, Calif., 1993—; pres. Women's Relief Soc., Stanford, Calif., 1986, counselor, Palo Alto, Calif., 1987-88, counselor, stake pres., Menlo Park, 1991-92; sec. Channing Pl. Homeowners Assn., Palo Alto, 1987-88, 90-91, pres., 1988-90.

GROSS, MARY ELIZABETH, pharmacy manager, educator; b. Chgo., Nov. 20, 1957; d. Henry Thomas and Patricia (Kloska) G. BS in Pharmacy, Drake U., 1980; PharmD, U. Utah, 1982. Lic. pharmacist; cert. in gerontology. Resident in clin. pharmacy U. Utah, Salt Lake City, 1980-82; asst. prof. clin. pharmacy Sch. Pharmacy W.Va. U., Charleston, 1982-84, asst. prof. pharmacology Sch. Medicine, 1982-84; asst. prof. clin. pharmacy, clin. pharmacist Drake U. Coll. Pharmacy & Health Scis./Mercy Hosp. Med. Ctr., Des Moines, 1984-89, assoc. prof. clin. pharmacy, clin. pharmacist, 1989-93; mgr. pharmacy, assoc. prof. clin. pharmacy Mercy Hosp. and Drake U., Des Moines, 1993—; cons. pharmacist Madrid (Iowa) Home for the Aging, 1989-92; faculty assoc. W.Va. U. Gerontology Ctr., Morgantown, 1983; cons. pharmacist Iowa long-term care coordinating unit Case Mgmt. Project for the Frail Elderly, Crossroads of Iowa, 1991—. Author, editor monograph; contbr. articles to profl. jours. Mem. task force Dept. Elder Affairs, Des Moines, 1989—; mem. Healthy Older People Adv. Coun., Des Moines, 1985-86. Recipient State of Iowa Gov.'s Vol. award, 1991, Merck Clin. Pharmacy award U. Utah, 1982; grantee in field. Mem. Am. Assn. Colls. of Pharmacy (profl. affairs com. 1992—), Iowa Soc. Hosp. Pharmacists (chair nominations com. 1990-91, computer com. 1988-89, pres. 1989-90, key mem. 1990-94, Hosp. Pharmacist of Yr. 1988). Office: Mercy Hosp Med Ctr Des Moines IA 50311

GROSS, PRIVA BAIDAFF, art historian, retired educator; b. Wieliczka, Poland, June 19, 1911; came to U.S., 1941, naturalized, 1955; d. Israel and Leopolda (Friedman) Baidaff; Ph.M., Jagellonian U., Cracow, Poland, 1937; postgrad. (N.Y. U. scholar 1945-47), N.Y. U. Inst. Fine Arts, 1945-48; m. Feliks Gross, July 25, 1937; 1 dau., Eva Helena Gross Friedman. Mem. faculty Queensborough Community Coll., CUNY, 1961-81, assoc. prof. art history, 1971-81, ret., 1981, co-chmn. art and music dept., 1966-68, chmn. art dept., 1968-74, dir. coll. gallery, 1968-77. SUNY grantee, 1967. Mem. AAUW (dir. 1972-76, 1980-82), Coll. Art Assn. Am., Soc. Archtl. Historians, Gallery Assn. N.Y. State (dir. 1972-73), N.Y. State Assn. Jr. Colls., AAUP, Polish Inst. Arts and Scis. Am., Council Gallery and Exhbn. Dirs. (dir. 1970-72). Contbr. articles, revs. to profl. publs. Home: 310 W 85th St New York NY 10024-3819

GROSS, RUTH CHAIKEN, educational administrator; b. Irvington, N.J., Mar. 22, 1941; d. Edward and Miriam (Rothman) Chaiken; m. Arnold Gross, July 4, 1960; children: Ira, Allen. BA in Edn., Newark State Coll., 1962; collateral in Judaic studies, Kean Coll. of N.J., 1987. Cert. religious tchr., cert. prin. Tchr. Temple Sinai, Summit, N.J., 1966-76, Temple Emanu-El, Westfield, N.J., 1972-77, Temple Beth-El, Cranford, N.J., 1975-78; dir. high sch. program Temple Beth Ahm, Springfield, N.J., 1975-85; dir. edn. Congregation Beth Israel, 1985—. Co-author: Ulpan for the Afternoon Hebrew School, 1991. Mem. N.J. Region Commn. on Jewish Edn.; founding mem. Project Manna; co-chair Soviet Jewry Action Com. Ctrl. N.J. Fedn.; mem. cmty. svcs. com. Nat. Conf. on Soviet Jewry; mem. Prins. Coop. Exch. Ctrl. N.J. Recipient Chai award Jewish Edn. Assn., 1985. Mem. Coalition for Advancement Jewish Edn. (charter), Coun. for Jewish Edn., Jewish Educator's Assembly, Assn. Jewish Spl. Educators, Hadassah, Women's League for Conservative Judaism. Office: Congregation Beth Israel 1920 Cliffwood St Scotch Plains NJ 07076-2330

GROSS, RUTH TAUBENHAUS, physician; b. Bryan, Tex., June 24, 1920; d. Jacob and Esther (Hirshenson) Taubenhaus; m. Reuben H. Gross, Jr., Aug. 22, 1942; (div. June 1952); 1 son, Gary E. BA, Barnard Coll., 1941; MD, Columbi U., 1944. Intern, Charity Hosp., New Orleans, 1944; resident in pediatrics Tulane U., New Orleans, 1945, Columbia U., N.Y.C., 1946, 47; instr. Radcliffe Infirmary, Oxford, Eng., 1949-50; instr. pediatrics Stanford (Calif.) U., 1950-53, asst. prof., 1953-56, assoc. prof., 1956-60, prof., 1973-92, prof. emerita, 1992; acting exec. pediatrics, 1957-59, assoc. dean student affairs, 1973-75, dir. div. gen. and ambulatory pediatrics, 1975-85, dir. Stanford-Children's Ambulatory Care Ctr., 1980-85, nat. study dir. Infant Health and Devel. Program, 1983-92; assoc. prof. pediatrics, co-dir. div. human genetics Albert Einstein Coll. Medicine, Yeshiva U., N.Y.C., 1960-64, prof. pediatrics, 1964-66; clin. prof. pediatrics U. Calif. Med. Ctr., San Francisco, 1966-73; dir. dept. pediatrics Mt. Zion Hosp. and Med. Ctr., San Francisco, 1966-73. Commonwealth fellow human genetics Instituto de Genetica, Pavia, Italy, 1959-60. Mem. Inst. Medicine, NAS, Am. Fedn. Clin. Rsch., Am. Pediatric Soc., Soc. Pediatric Rsch., Am. Acad. Pediatrics, Ambulatory Pediatric Assn., Soc. Rsch. in Child Devel., Phi Beta Kappa, Alpha Omega Alpha, Sigma Xi. Contbr. articles to profl. jours.

GROSS, SALLY LUCILLE, librarian; b. Cleve., Feb. 17, 1943; d. John Albert and Harriette Frances (Galbraith) Sekerak; m. Douglas Hale Gross, June 17, 1967. BA, Baldwin Wallace Coll., 1965; MSLS, Western Res. U., 1967. Cert. libr., N.Y. Libr. I Denver Pub. Libr., 1967-68, libr. II, 1968-69; libr. grad. sch. internat. studies U. Denver, 1969-70; asst. libr. dept. rare books U. Rochester, N.Y., 1970-75; assoc. libr. DeGolyer Libr. So. Meth. U., Dallas, 1982-86; head spl. collections U. Tex., Arlington, 1988—. Vol. libr. Mayfield State Hosp., Upper St. Clair, Pa., 1977. Mem. ALA, Tex. Libr. Assn. (sec. local history roundtable 1986-87), Tex. State Hist. Assn., Am. Assn. State and Local History, Soc. S.W. Archivists, Phi Alpha Theta, Beta Phi Mu. Home: 4002 Wingren Rd Irving TX 75062-3808 Office: U Tex Arlington Librs PO Box 19497 702 College St Arlington TX 76019-0497

GROSS, SHARON RUTH, psychology educator, researcher; b. L.A., Mar. 21, 1940; d. Louis and Sylvia Marion (Freedman) Lackman; m. Zoltan Gross, Mar. 1969 (div.); 1 child, Andrew Ryan; m. Ira Chroman, June 1994. BA, UCLA, 1983; MA, U. So. Calif., L.A., 1985, PhD, 1991. Tech. Rytron, Van Nuys, Calif., 1958-60; computress on tetrahedral satellite Space Tech. Labs., Redondo Beach, Calif., 1960-62; owner Wayfarer Yacht Corp., Costa Mesa, Calif., 1962-64; electronics draftsperson, designer stroke-writer characters Tasker Industries, Van Nuys, 1964-65; pvt. practice cons. Sherman Oaks, Calif., 1965-75, 77-80; printed circuit bd. designer Systron-Donner, Van Nuys, Calif., 1975-76; design checker, tech. writer Vector Gen., Woodland Hills, CAlif., 1976-77; undergrad. adv. U. So. Calif., L.A., 1987-89, rsch. asst. prof., rsch. assoc. social psychology, 1991—. Contbr. chpts. to books. Mem. ACLU, L.A., 1991. Recipient Haynes Found. Dissertation fellowship U. So. Calif., 1990. Mem. APA (student dissertation rsch. award 1991), AAAS, Computer Graphics Pioneers, Am. Psychol. Soc., Western Psychol. Assn. Democrat. Jewish. Office: U So Calif Dept Psychology Los Angeles CA 90089-1061

GROSS, SHIRLEY MARIE, farm manager, artist; b. Beardstown, Ill., Apr. 4, 1917; d. Robert Lee and Marie Elizabeth (Ellrich) Northcutt; A.A., Stephens Coll., 1936; B.A., Ill. Coll., 1938; m. Carl David Gross, Oct. 4, 1941; children—David Lee, Susan Jean Gross Conner. Med. technologist St. John's Hosp., Springfield, Ill., 1938-41, Schmidt Meml. Hosp., Beardstown, 1957-64; librarian Beardstown Public Library, 1970-76; pvt. practice farm mgmt., Beardstown, 1958—; bd. dirs. First State Bank Beardstown, Heart of Ill. Investment Clubs; exhibitor various art shows, Ill., 1969—. Bd. dirs. Beardstown Hosp., Head Start; trustee First Congregational Ch. Beardstown. Winner art awards various shows. Mem. Am. Soc. Clin. Pathologists (med. technologist), Beardstown Bus. and Profl. Women's Investment Club, Cass County Hist. Soc., Beardstown Restoration Soc. Jacksonville Area Artist League, Beardstown Hosp. Aux., Beardstown Woman's Club, Cass County Coun. for the Arts Club, Beardstown Bus. and Profl. Women's Club (pres. local chpt. 1968-70), Supreme Emblem Club. Democrat. Home: 15 Blvd Rd Beardstown IL 62618

GROSS, SU KWAK, artist, educator; b. Busan, Korea, Sept. 16, 1949; came to U.S., 1973; d. Joseph and Young A. (Oh) Kwak; m. Donald G. Gross, Aug. 30, 1981; 1 child, Lisa. BA, St. Thomas U., Houston, 1977; MFA, U. Chgo., 1979. Lectr. Georgetown U., Washington, 1985—. One-person shows include N.Y. Acad. Scis., N.Y.C., 1991, Gallery Korea, 1992, Humphrey Gallery, 1993. Mem. Coll. Art Assn. Am. Address: 51 MacDougal St # 41 New York NY 10012

GROSS, WENDY S., public relations consultant; b. Cleve., Oct. 6, 1942; d. Alton E. and Jeanne (Schoen) G. BA in English, U. Mich., 1963. Asst. dir. pub. relations Girl Scouts of Chgo., 1964-66; account exec. Beveridge Orgn., Inc., Chgo., 1966-70; free-lance consultant Chgo., 1970-78; acct. exec. Golin/Harris Comm., Chgo., 1978-80, acct. supr., 1980, v.p., 1981-82, sr. v.p., 1982-90; sr. v.p. Ruder Finn, Chgo., 1990-94, Manning, Selvage & Lee, Chgo., 1994—. Mem. Pub. Relations Soc. Am. Club: Publicity of Chgo. (Golden Trumpet award, 1981, 87, 90, 94). Home: 1000 Lake Shore Plz Chicago IL 60611-1129 Office: Manning Selvage & Lee 303 E Wacker Chicago IL 60601

GROSSET, JESSICA ARIANE, computer analyst; b. Paris, Aug. 31, 1952; came to U.S., 1970; d. Raymond Louis and Barbara Ann (Byrne) G.; m. Bruce Edward Kaskubar, May 23, 1986. AA, Berkshire Community Coll., Pittsfield, Mass., 1972; BS, SUNY, Potsdam, 1979; postgrad., Ariz. State U., 1980, U. Minn., 1980-81. Computer programmer Kay-Bee Toy and Hobby Shops, Lee, Mass., 1974-78; computer analyst Mayo Clinic, Rochester, Minn., 1981—. Mem. Nat. Assn. Female Execs. Office: Mayo Clinic 200 1st St SW Rochester MN 55905-0001

GROSSETETE, GINGER LEE, gerontology administrator, consultant; b. Riverside, Calif., Feb. 9, 1936; d. Lee Roy Taylor and Bonita (Beryl) Williams; m. Alec Paul Grossetete, June 8, 1954; children: Elizabeth Gay Blech, Teri Lee Zeni. BA in Recreation cum laude, U. N.Mex., 1974, M in Pub. Adminstrn., 1978. Sr. ctr. supr., Office of Sr. Affairs, City of Albuquerque, 1974-77, asst. dir. Office of Sr. Affairs, 1977—; conf. coord. Nat. Consumers Assn., Albuquerque, 1978-79; region 6 del. Nat. Coun. on Aging, Washington, 1977-84; conf. chmn. Western Gerontol. Soc., Albuquerque, 1983; del. White House Conf. on Aging from N.Mex., 1995. Contbr. articles to mags. Campaign dir. March of Dimes N.Mex., 1966-67; pres. Albuquerque Symphony Women's Assn., 1972; mem. exec. com. Jr. League Albuquerque, 1976; mem. Gov.'s Coun. on Phys. Fitness, 1987-91, chmn. 1990-91. Recipient N.Mex. Disting. Pub. Service award N.Mex. Gov.'s Office, 1983, Disting. Woman on the Move award YWCA, 1986. Fellow Nat. Recreation and Pk. Assn. (bd. dirs. S.W. regional coun. rep., bd. dir. leisure and aging sect., pres. N.Mex. chpt. 1983-84, Outstanding Profl. award 1982); mem. Am. Soc. Pub. Adminstrn. (pres. N.Mex. coun. 1987-88), S.W. Soc. on Aging (pres. 1984-85, bd. dirs., Outstanding Profl. award 1991), U. N.Mex. Alumni Assn. (bd. dirs. 1978-80, Disting. Alumni award 1985), Las Amapolas Garden Club (pres. 1964), Pi Alpha Alpha, Chi Omega (pres. alumni 1959-60), Pi Lambda Theta. Home: 517 La Veta Dr NE Albuquerque NM 87108-1403 Office: Office of Sr Affairs 714 7th St SW Albuquerque NM 87102-3814

GROSSMAN, BARBARA SUSANNE, publisher; b. Phila., Apr. 22, 1951; d. Morris I. and Gladys (Yovel) G.; m. Michael Jon Gross, Dec. 31, 1978; children: Willa Rebecca, Max Lawrence, Gilda Hanna. BA, Bard Coll., 1973; MFA, U. Iowa, 1975. Teaching and writing fellow U. Iowa, Iowa City, 1974-75; editorial asst. Knopf, N.Y.C., 1975-77; asst. editor Harper & Row, N.Y.C., 1977-79; editor, sr. editor Crown, N.Y.C., 1979-88; pub. Scribners, N.Y.C., 1988-94, Viking, N.Y.C., 1994—; trustee Bard Coll. Bd. Trustees, Annandale on Hudson, 1991—. Mem. Women Media Group. Democrat. Jewish. Office: Viking 375 Hudson St New York NY 10014

GROSSMAN, ELIZABETH KORN, nursing administrator, retired college dean; b. S.I., N.Y., May 15, 1923; d. George and Ethel (Elliot) Korn; m. Thomas Grossman, Feb. 23, 1952 (dec. 1987); 1 child, Thomas. BA, Hunter Coll., 1944; MN, Western Res. U., 1947; MS in Nursing Edn., Ind. U., 1960, EdD, 1972. Researcher Columbia Carbon Corp., Bklyn., 1944; staff nurse, asst. head nurse, head nurse, supr. Univ. Hosp., Cleve., 1947-52; Instr. Mt. Sinai Hosp. Sch. Nursing, Cleve., 1952-53; supr. maternity nursing Meth. Hosp., Indpls., 1953-57; instr. maternity nursing, 1957-59; instr. DePauw U., Indpls., 1959-62; asst. prof., then assoc. prof., grad. maternity Ind. U., Indpls., 1959-66, prof., chairperson grad.-undergrad. maternity nursing, 1966-73, dean Sch. Nursing, 1973-88, dean, prof. emeritus, 1988—; civilian nat. cons. emeritus USAF Nurse Corps, 1983-86. Contbr. articles to profl. jours. Elected mem. Hunter Coll. Hall of Fame, 1973. Fellow Am. Acad. Nursing; mem. Am. Nurses Assn., Nat. League Nursing (Nurse of Yr.), Ind. Citizen League for Nursing, Am. Assn. Colls. Nursing (treas. 1981-85), Nurses Assn. of Am. Coll. Ob-Gyn (4th and 7th nat. program meeting com. 1987-88, chair com. on edn. 1980-82), Midwest Alliance Nursing (treas. 1979-81), Sigma Xi, Sigma Theta Tau (Disting. Service award 1977, co-chmn. campaign for Ctr. for Nursing Scholarship), Rotary, Altrusa, Julian Ctr., Delta Kappa Gamma, Alpha Xi Delta (Woman of Distinction 1988). Republican. Roman Catholic. Home: 11201 Westfield Blvd Carmel IN 46032-3551 Office: Ind U Sch Nursing 610 Barnhill Dr Indianapolis IN 46223-0001

GROSSMAN, FRANCES KAPLAN, psychologist; b. Newport News, May 28, 1939; d. Rubin H. and Beatrice (Fischlowitz) Kaplan; m. Henry Grossman, July 26, 1970; children: Jennifer, Benjamin. BA, Oberlin (Ohio) Coll., 1961; MS, PhD, Yale U., 1965. Diplomate Am. Bd. Profl. Psychology. Asst. prof. Yale U., New Haven, 1965-69; asst. prof. Boston U., 1969-71, assoc. prof. psychology, 1971-82, prof. psychology, 1982—. Author: Brothers and Sisters of Retarded Children, 1971, Pregnancy, Birth and Parenthood, 1980. Trustee Oberlin Coll., 1990-92, pres. Alumni Assn., 1979-80. Recipient Cert. of Appreciation Oberlin Coll. Alumni Assn., 1993. Fellow APA (mem. ethics com. 1994—); mem. Mass. Psychol. Assn. (chair ethics com. 1989-91, Career Contbn. award 1991), Oberlin Coll. Alumni Assn., Sigma Xi, Phi Beta Kappa. Jewish. Office: Boston Univ Dept Psychology 64 Cummington St Boston MA 02215-2407

GROSSMAN, JANICE, publisher; b. Montreal, Que., Can., Nov. 3, 1949; m. Daniel Rubinstein, July 11, 1978; 1 child, Lauren Alexandra. MA, NYU, 1970; BA, New Sch. Social Research, 1971. Advt. sr. exec. recruiter Merrill, Lynch, Pierce, Fenner & Smith Inc., N.Y.C., 1976-78; advt. sales rep. Ms. mag., N.Y.C., 1978-80; N.Y. advt. mgr. Ms. Mag., N.Y.C., 1980-82, advt. dir., 1982-84; advt. dir. New Woman Mag., N.Y.C., 1984-86, assoc. pub., 1986-88, became pub., 1989; became pub. In Fashion Mag., N.Y.C., 1988, N.Y. Mag., 1991; pub. Seventeen Mag., 1992—; v.p., group pub. K-III Magazines, 1992—. Mem. Fragrance Found., Fashion Group, Advt. Women N.Y., Cosmetic Exec. Women, Advt. Club N.Y. Home: 12 Colvin Rd Scarsdale NY 10583-1408 Office: Seventeen Mag 850 3rd Ave New York NY 10022-6222

GROSSMAN, JOANNE BARBARA, lawyer; b. Brookline, Mass., Oct. 23, 1949; d. Bernard R. and Beatrice G. (Quint) G.; m. John H. Seesel, Dec. 30, 1973; children: Benjamin P., Rebecca A. AB, Radcliffe Coll., 1971; JD, U. Calif., Berkeley, 1975. Bar: Calif. 1975, D.C. 1976, U.S. Dist. Ct. D.C. 1976, U.S. Ct. Appeals (D.C. cir.) 1976, U.S. Supreme Ct. 1979. Assoc. Covington & Burling, Washington, 1975-83, ptnr., 1983—. Office: Covington & Burling PO Box 7566 1201 Pennsylvania Ave NW Washington DC 20044

GROSSMAN, LISA ROBBIN, clinical psychologist, lawyer; b. Chgo., Jan. 22, 1952; d. Samuel R. and Sarah (Kruger) G. B.A. with highest distinction and departmental honors in Psychology, Northwestern U., 1974, J.D. cum laude, 1979, Ph.D., 1982. Bar: Ill. 1981; registered psychologist, Ill. Jud. intern, U.S. Supreme Ct., Washington, 1975; pre-doctoral psychology intern Michael Reese Hosp. and Med. Center, Chgo., 1979-80; therapist Homes for Children, Chgo., 1980-83; psychologist Psychiat. Inst., Cir. Ct. Cook County, Chgo., 1981-87; pvt. practice, 1984—; invited participant workshop HHS, Rockville, Md., 1981. Contbr. articles to profl. jours. Mem. ABA, Am. Psychol. Assn. (com. on legal issues 1992-95), Ill. Psychol. Assn. (pres.-elect 1994), Chgo. Assn. for Psychoanalytic Psychologists (parliamentarian 1982), Ill. State Bar Assn., Chgo. Bar Assn., Soc. Personality Assessment, Mortar Bd., Phi Beta Kappa, Shi-Ai, Alpha Lambda Delta. Office: 500 N Michigan Ave Ste 1520 Chicago IL 60611-3703

GROTE, JEANNE LYNN, marketing and public relations professional; b. Seattle, Apr. 3, 1944; d. Raymond and Betty Davis (Lee) Galyon; m. Dennis Darrell Grote, June 22, 1963; children: Kimmy Ann, Nicole Elizabeth. AA, Bellevue (Wash.) C.C., 1980; BA, Western U., Bellingham, Wash., 1963; postgrad. in mktg., fundraising, U. Wash., 1993, 94. Stock market mgr. Cargill, Inc., Portland, Oreg., 1964-66; bookkeeper Sunrise Co., Seattle, 1973; student adviser Bellevue C.C., 1978, crisis adviser, 1979, store mgr., bookstore, 1980; bus. mgr. Newcomers, Bellevue, 1981; mem. dir. Conv. Bur., Bellevue, 1982-86; mktg. dir. Crossroads Shopping Ctr., Bellevue, 1987-92, Kirkland Parkplace Shopping Ctr., Wash., 1987—; owner Mktg./Events Unltd., 1992—; v.p. mktg. and pub. rels. State Farmers Assn., Seattle, 1987-89; v.p. mktg. Campfire, Bellevue, 1980-84; festival dir. Kirkland Arts Festival, 1987-93. Editor student newspapers and yearbooks. Student body pres. Bellevue C.C., 1978, v.p. 1977, senate pres. 1979, senator, 1980, others offices; pres. Children's Hosp. Guild, Bellevue, 1975. Mem. Pub. Rels. Soc. Am., Internat. Assn. Bus. Communicators, Nat. Dirs. of Non-Profit Assns., Soroptimists, Lioness, Civitan. Mem. Unity Ch. Home: 4552 152nd Ln SE Bellevue WA 98006-2544

GROTHAUS, PAMELA SUE, marketing professional; b. Alameda, Calif., Mar. 25, 1958; d. Michael James and Patricia Ann (Owsley) Spillers; m. David Michael Grothaus, June 3, 1977; children: Shannon Marie, Matthew David. Student, Webster U., Webster Groves, Mo., 1984-86, Cen. Mo. State U., 1976-77, St. Louis Community Coll., 1981-83. With U.S. Civil Svc., K.I. Sawyer AFB, Mich., 1979-80; adminstrv. asst. Mo. Dept. Consumer Affairs, Jefferson City, Mo., 1980-81; adminstrv. coord. Baur Properties, Inc., St. Louis, 1981-82; account exec. Atkinson Group Inc., St. Louis, 1982-87; advt. coord. Eveready Battery Co., St. Louis, 1987; advt. officer Mercantile Bancorporation, Inc., St. Louis, 1987-88; copywriter, sr. account exec. Wilson Sculley Assoc. Inc., 1989-91; mktg. mgr., copywriter Nehmen-Kodner, Inc., St. Louis, 1991-92; dir. mktg. and creative svcs. AdSell, St. Louis, 1993-94; account supr. Wilson Sculley Assocs., St. Louis, 1994—. Fitness instr. YMCA, Webster Grove, 1988-89. Mem. Direct Mktg. Assn. St. Louis (pres., bd. dirs. 1995). Republican. Roman Catholic. Home: 7872 Big Bend Apt 3 Webster Groves MO 63119

GROTT, GERALDINE, librarian; b. Bklyn., Aug. 6, 1941; d. Francis Geoffrey Jr. and Rita (Miller) Griffith; m. Norman Matthew Grott, Aug. 24, 1972; children: Anne Frances, Joan Marie. Student, Purdue U., 1961, Ball State U., 1963, LaPorte County Leadership Inc., 1987. Mem. staff LaPorte (Ind.) Pub. Libr., 1963-69; children's libr. Michican City (Ind.) Pub. Libr., 1969-75; br. mgr. LaPorte County Pub. Libr., 1977—; bd. dirs. emeritus LaPorte County Leadership, Inc., 1990—. Bd. dirs. South Cen. Community Sch. Corp., Union Mills, Inc., 1988—, LaPorte County Cooperative Extension Svc., LaPorte County Child Abuse Coun.; mem. coun. LaPorte County 4-H, 1989—, leader Hanna-Noble Twp. 4-H Club, Union Mills, 1986—. Mem. Toastmasters, Lions. Roman Catholic. Office: La Porte County Pub Libr 904 Indiana Ave La Porte IN 46350

GROTTA, SANDRA BROWN, interior designer; m. Louis William Grotta. Student U. Mich., 1952-55, N.Y. Sch. Interior Design, 1964. Pres. S.G. Interiors, New Vernon, N.J., 1964—. Mem. Am. Soc. Interior Designers.

GROTTANELLI, PAMALA N., critical care nursing educator; b. Corinth, Miss.; d. William R. and Estelle (Carter) Stewart; m. Richard Grottanelli. AS, MUW, 1975, BSN, 1980; MSN, U. Ala., Birmingham, 1983. CCRN. Asst. dir. staff devel. Golden Triangle Regional Med. Ctr., Columbus, Miss., 1980-81, staff/charge nurse ICU, 1981-82; nursing instr. Auburn U., Montgomery, Ala., 1983-84, La. State U., New Orleans, 1984-85; staff nurse ICU East Jefferson Gen. Hosp., Metairie, La., 1984-85; nursing instr. Itawamba Community Coll., Fulton, Miss., 1985-86, 90-92; varied hourly critical care nurse U. Colo. Health Scis. Ctr., Denver, 1986-87; mgr. nursing systems U. Community Hosp., Tampa, Fla., 1987-89; critical care float Northside Hosp., Atlanta, 1989-90, N.E. Miss. C.C., Corinth, 1992—; malpractice cons. to various law firms, 1978—; speaker Miss. Student Nurses Assn., Biloxi, 1991. Affiliate faculty Am. Heart Assn., Miss., Ala., 1982-86. Mem. AACN, Emergency Nurses Assn., NLN, ANA,

Miss. Nurses Assn., Sigma Theta Tau. Home: RR 1 Box 72 Glen MS 38846-9710 Office: Northeast Miss C C Extension Ctr Corinth MS 38834

GROTZINGER, LAUREL ANN, university librarian; b. Truman, Minn., Apr. 15, 1935; d. Edward F. and Marian Gertrude (Greeley) G. BA, Carleton Coll., 1957; MS, U. Ill., 1958, PhD, 1964. Instr., asst. libr. Ill. State U., 1958-62; asst. prof. Western Mich. U., Kalamazoo, 1964-66; assoc. prof. Western Mich. U., 1966-68, prof., 1968—, asst. dir. Sch. Librarianship, 1965-72, chief rsch. officer, 1979-86, interim dir. Sch. Libr. and Info. Sci., 1982-86, dean grad. coll., 1979-92, prof. univ. libr., 1993—. Author: The Power and the Dignity, 1966; mem. editl. bd. Jour. Edn. for Librarianship, 1973-77, Dictionary Am. Libr. Biography, 1975-77, Mich. Academician, 1990—; contbr. articles to profl. jours. Trustee Kalamazoo Pub. Libr., 1991-93, v.p., 1991-92, pres., 1992-93. Mem. ALA (sec. treas. Libr. History Round Table 1973-74, vice chmn., chmn.-elect 1983-84, chmn. 1984-85, mem.-at-large 1991-93), Assn. Libr. Info. Sci. Edn., Am. Assn. Higher Edn., Mich. Acad. Sci., Arts and Letters (mem.-at-large, exec. com. 1980-86, pres. 1983-85, exec. com. 1990-94, pres. 1991-93), Internat. Assn. Torch Clubs (v.p. Kalamazoo chpt. 1992-93, pres. 1993-94, exec. com. 1989—), Phi Beta Kappa (pres. S.W. Mich. chpt. 1977-78, sec. 1994—), Delta Phi Mu, Pi Delta Epsilon, Alpha Beta Alpha, Delta Kappa Gamma (pres. Alpha Psi chpt. 1988-92), Phi Kappa Phi. Home: 2729 Mockingbird Dr Kalamazoo MI 49008-1626

GROULX, CONNIE LOUISE, accountant; b. Valparaiso, Ind., July 30, 1956; d. Robert Otis Hershman and Helen Jean (Lovely) Thrasher; m. Robert Joseph Groulx, May 25, 1980 (div. Jan. 1987); children: Holly Dawn, Nicholas Scott. A in Small Bus. Mgmt., Ivy Tech, 1981; A in Gen. Studies, Ind. U., 1992; student, Ind. U.-Purdue U., Columbus, Ind., 1989—. Front desk clk. Ramada Inn, Columbus, Ind., 1975, Holiday Inn, Killeen, Tex., 1976-77; front deskmgr. Lees Inns. of Am., Inc., Columbus, Ind., 1977-79, assoc. mgr., 1979-81; acctg. clk. Lees Inns. of Am., Inc., North Vernon, Ind., 1981-86, acctg. mgr., 1986—. Youth sponsor First Bapt. Ch., North Vernon, 1990—. Recipient Acad. Pacesetter award Ky. Christian Coll., Grayson, 1974, 75. Mem. Inst. Mgmt. Accts. (dir. mem. retention 1992-93, dir. mem. attendance, 1991-92, dir. employement 1990-91). Baptist. Office: Lees Inns of America Inc 130 N State St North Vernon IN 47265-1724

GROUSE, JAN ELLEN, physician; b. Seattle, Apr. 14, 1947; d. John Galt and Jean Frances (Shaver) Lindwed; m. Lawrence Douglas Grouse, Oct. 27, 1973; children: Eric, Carrie, Christopher. BS, U. Puget Sound, 1969; MD, U. Wash., 1973. Diplomate Am. Bd. Family Practice. Intern in family practice Meml. Hosp. Med. Ctr., Long Beach, Calif., 1973-74; resident in family practice Franklin Sq. Hosp., Balt., 1974-76; asst. dir. Cmty. Family Practice Residency, LaGrange, Ill., 1979-80; staff physician primary care Student Health, U. Md., College Park, 1977-79; asst. dir. Hinsdale (Ill.) Family Practice Residency, 1980-83, dir. edn., 1983-84; faculty coord. geriatrics Glendale (Calif.) Adventist Family Practice Residency, 1985-88, assoc. dir., 1986-88; columnist med. news Family Cir. mag., N.Y.C., 1988-89; asst./ assoc. dir. St. Joseph Family Practice Residency, Stamford, Conn., 1989-92; v.p. Med. Comm. Resources Inc., Gig Harbor, Mass., 1992—; leader task force on elderly Hinsdale (Ill.) Hosp., 1981-83. Med. editor Women's Health Advocate newsletter, Fairfax, Va., 1994—. Fellow Am. Acad. Family Physicians; mem. Am. Geriatric Soc., Soc. Tchrs. Family Medicine, Wash. Acad. Family Physicians (mem. publs. com. 1993—). Office: Med Comm Resources Inc 8316 86th Ave NW Gig Harbor WA 98332

GROVE, BARBARA A., interior design educator, consultant; b. Atlanta. B of Visual Arts, Ga. State U. Interior designer Rich's, Atlanta, Fran Speer & Assocs., Houston, Foley's, Houston, Suniland, Houston, Conversano Assocs., Oakland, Calif., Hallenbeck, Chamorro Assocs., Alameda, Calif., E.P.R., San Francisco, Wudtke, Watson Assocs., San Francisco, The Shorenstein & Co., San Francisco; instr. interior design Acad. Art Coll., U. Calif. Berkeley Extension, San Francisco; exam. juror Nat. Coun. Interior Design Qualification, 1986, 87, 88. Office: Barbara Grove Interior Design 2159 California St # 1A San Francisco CA 94115-2821

GROVE, MYRNA JEAN, elementary education educator; b. Bryan, Ohio, Oct. 24, 1949; d. Kedric Durward and N. Florence (Stombaugh) G. Student, Bowling Green State U., 1970-71; BA in Edn., Manchester Coll., 1971; postgrad., U. No. Colo., 1974-76, Purdue U., 1977, St. Francis Coll., Ft. Wayne, Ind., 1986, Coll. Mount St. Joseph, Ohio, 1986. Cert. elem. tchr., Ohio. Tchr. elem. sch. Bryan City Schs., 1972—. Editor newspaper column Education Today, 1975-82, newsletter Northwest Ohio Emphasis, 1981-83, (award 1981). Dir., violinist Bryan String Ensemble, 1981—; organist Trinity Episc. Ch., Bryan, 1979-89; active Lancaster Mennonite Hist. Soc., Hans Herr Found., trustee Bryan Area Cultural Assn., 1984-89; Williams County Community Concerts (bd. dirs.). Jennings scholar Martha Holden Jennings Found., Bowling Green State U., 1982-83. Mem. NEA (Ohio del., state contact 1986-87), Nat. Assn. Gifted Children, Am. Booksellers' Assn. (assoc. mem.), Writers Info. Network, Ohio Edn. Assn. (presenter 1984, del. global issues 1986, sec. N.W. Ohio Tchrs. Uniserv. 1975-78), Ohio Assn. Gifted Children, Bus. and Profl. Women Ohio (individual devel. com. 1986-90, speaking skills cert. 1987), N.W. Ohio Manchester Coll. Alumni Assn. (past pres.), Bryan Edn. Assn. (exec. com., pres. 1985-86), P. Buckley Moss Soc., Trees of Life (v.p. 1994—), Alpha Delta Kappa (pres.-elect 1994—), Alpha Mu, Alpha Delta Kappa.

GROVE, VIVIAN LORRAINE, former social service executive consultant; b. Trenton, N.J., June 21, 1923; d. Charles E. and Edythe (Inman) G. BS, N.J. State Coll., 1945; MED, Springfield Coll., 1953; MSS, Bryn Mawr Coll., 1962. Program dir. YWCA, Trenton, N.J., Springfield, Mass.; nat. teenage cons. YWCA of the U.S.A., field cons. cen. and western regions; exec. dir. YWCA Seattle-King County; dir. urban svcs. divsn. Nat. YWCA, exec. human resources divsn.; conv. coord. YWCA, 1993; ret., 1994. Recipient Ambassador award YWCA of the U.S.A., 1993; YWCA scholar 1951-53, 60-61. Mem. Majority Coun., Emily's List. Home: 229 Convent Rd Cranbury NJ 08512-4403

GROVER, ROSALIND REDFERN, oil and gas company executive; b. Midland, Tex., Sept. 5, 1941; d. John Joseph and Rosalind (Kapps) Redfern; m. Arden Roy Grover, Apr. 10, 1982; 1 child, Rosson. BA in Edn. magna cum laude, U. Ariz., 1966, MA in History, 1982; postgrad. in law, So. Meth. U., Dallas. Libr. Gahr High Sch., Cerritos, Calif., 1969; pres. The Redfern Found., Midland, 1982—; ptnr. Redfern & Grover, Midland, 1986—; pres. Redfern Enterprises Inc., Midland, 1989—; chmn. bd. dirs. Flag-Redfern Oil Co., Midland. Sec. park and recreation commn. City of Midland, 1969-71, del. Objectives for Convocation, 1980; mem., past pres. women's aux. Midland Community Theatre, 1970, chmn. challenge grant bldg. fund, 1980, chmn. Tex. Yucca Hist. Landmark Renovation Project, 1983, trustee, 1983-88; chmn. publicity com. Midland Jr. League Midland, Inc., 1972, chmn. edn. com., 1976, corr. sec., 1978; 1st v.p. Midland Symphony Assn., 1975; chmn. Midland Charity Horse Show, 1975-76; mem. Midland Am. Revolution Bicentennial Commn., 1976; trustee Mus. S.W., 1977-80, pres. bd. dirs., 1979-80; co-chmn. Gov. Clements Fin. Com., Midland, 1978; mem. dist. com. State Bd. Law Examiners; trustee Midland Meml. Hosp., 1978-80, Permian Basin Petroleum Mus., Libr. and Hall of Fame, 1989—. Recipient HamHock award Midland Community Theatre, 1978. Mem. Ind. Petroleum Assn. Am., Tex. Ind. Producers and Royalty Owners Assn., Petroleum Club, Racquet Club (Midland), Horseshoe Bay (Tex.) Country Club, Phi Kappa Phi, Pi Lambda Theta. Republican. Home: 1906 Crescent Pl Midland TX 79705-6407 Office: PO Box 2127 Midland TX 79702-2127

GROVES, BONNIE K., state legislator; b. Slocum, Pa., Oct. 16, 1942; married; 3 children. BS, U. N.H.; MA, Boston U. Ret. small bus. owner; mem. N.H. Ho. of Reps.; mem. econ. devel. com. Mem. Winnacunnet Dist. Sch. Bd., 1978-87, chairperson, 1982, 86; bd. dirs. Planned Parenthood No. New England, 1992—, Family Planning Rockingham County, 1989-92. Mem. N.H. State Sch. Bd. Assn. (bd. dirs. 1985-87). Office: NH House of Reps State Capitol Concord NH 03301*

GROVES, SHARON SUE, elementary education educator; b. Springfield, Mo., Apr. 25, 1944; d. William Orin Jr. and Ruth M. (Jones) Hodge; m. Donald L. Groves, July 20, 1963. BA, Drury Coll., 1966, MEd, 1969. Cert. life elem. tchg.; Psychol. Examiners Cert. Adminstrn. Elem. tchr. Springfield Pub. Schs., 1966—; asst. instr. individual testing Drury Coll., Springfield, 1969-76; asst. instr. enhancing math. S.W. Mo. State U., Springfield, 1991-94. Author: Modeling Effective Practices: Geometry and Computation. Active Springfield's Curriculum Coun.; mem. Tchg. Cadre, Strategic Planning Team; hon. life mem. PTA; chmn. adminstrv. coun. Hood United Meth. Ch.; children's coord. math. workshops.; sr. leader Mo. Assessment Project, 1993—. Recipient Extra Mile award, 1989; named Fremont Tchr. of the Yr., 1988, 93. Mem. ASCD, Internat. Reading Assn., Assn. for Childhood Edn., Nat. Coun. Tchrs. Math., Mo. Coun. Tchrs. Math., Mo. State Tchrs. Assn. (pres. S.W. dist., Educator of Yr. 1989, Leader of Yr. 1990), Springfield Edn. Assn. (pres.), Delta Kappa Gamma (1st v.p.). Home: Rte 7 RR 7 Box 374 Springfield MO 65802-9555

GROWDON, MARCIA C. COHN, art historian, computer rental business owner; b. San Francisco, Dec. 17, 1945; d. Arthur C. and Barbara E. (Gardiner) Cohn; m. Charles K. Growdon, Aug. 31, 1968; children: Scott G., Mark A. BA, Stanford U., 1967, PhD, 1976; MA, U. Mich., 1968. Chief curator Nev. Mus. Art, Reno, 1978-87, dir., 1981-87; prin., treas. Bus. Computer Rentals, Reno, 1984—; chmn. C.I.T.Y. 2000 Arts Commn., Reno, 1993—, Nev. Commn. for Cultural Affairs, 1991-95; dep. chmn. Nev. Bd. History and Mus., 1993-95; letter of appointment U. Nev., Reno, 1989—. Author: (catalogs) Computers and the Visual Arts: Harold Cohen, 1979, Artists in the American Desert, 1980, Robert Cole Caples, 1981, (essays) Culture of the Middle Ages, 1978. Chmn. Nev. Commn. for Cultural Affairs, Carson City, 1991—, Nev. Adv. Hist. Preservation and Archaeology, Carson City, 1989-93. Recipient Gov.'s Arts award Nev. State Coun. on Arts, 1992. Mem. Stanford Assocs. (bd. govs.), Art Table, Western Indsl. Nev. Office: Bus Computer Rentals 1004 Forest St Reno NV 89509

GROWE, JOAN ANDERSON, state official; b. Mpls., Sept. 28, 1935; d. Lucille M. (Brown) Johnson; children: Michael, Colleen, David, Patrick. B.S., St. Cloud State U., 1956; cert. in spl. edn., U. Minn., 1964; exec. mgmt. program State and local govt., Harvard U., 1979. Tchr. elem. pub. schs. Bloomington, Minn., 1956-58; tchr. for exceptional children elem. pub. schs. St. Paul, 1964-65; spl. edn. tchr. St. Anthony Pub. Schs., Minn., 1965-66; mem. Minn. Ho. of Reps., 1973-74; sec. of state State of Minn., St. Paul, 1975—; mem. exec. coun. Minn. State Bd. Investment. Mem. Women Execs. in State Govt., Women's Campaign Fund, Women's Polit. Caucus, Minn. Women's Econ. Roundtable; candidate U.S. Senate, 1984; bd. dirs. Greater Mpls. coun. Girl Scouts U.S., Wayside House. Recipient Minn. Sch. Bell award, 1977, YMCA Outstanding Achievement award, 1978, Disting. Alumni award St. Cloud State U., 1979, Charlotte Striebel Long Distance Runner award Minn. NOW, 1985, The Woman Who Makes a Difference award Internat. Women's Forum, 1991, Esther V. Crosby Leadership award Greater Mpls. Girl Scout Coun., 1992. Mem. Nat. Assn. Secs. of State (pres. 1979-80), Minn. Equal Rights Alliance, LWV. Roman Catholic. Office: Sec of State's Office 180 State St Saint Paul MN 55155-0001

GRUBB, PHYLLIS BOWMAN, substance abuse counselor; b. North Tazewell, Va., Aug. 24, 1934; d. Clarence Earl and Russie (White) Bowman; m. James N. Grubb, July 18, 1953 (dir. 1983); 1 child, Phyllis Ann Grubb Brady. AA, Durham Tech. Inst, 1976; BA, Goddard Coll., 1980. Cert. substance abuse counselor, N.C. Sec., comptroller Duke U. Med. Ctr., Durham, N.C., 1963-69; substance abuse counselor Alcoholic Rehab. Ctr., Butner, N.C., 1969—; pres., owner Triangle Employees Assistance Program, Durham, 1990—; mem. faculty, N.C. Sch. Alcohol & Drugs, Wilmington, 1979; pres., owner, South Granville Counseling Svcs., Butner, 1980—, Men/ Women in Crisis Counseling Svcs., Durham, 1981—, Triangle Home Health Care, Inc., Durham, 1986—; pres., PEM Ventures, Durham, 1985—. Collaborator on TV spl., Women and Alcohol, 1977. Appointee women's com. Gov.'s Coun. on Alcohol and Drug Abuse Among Children and Youth, 1990—. Mem. Alcoholism Profls. N.C. (exec. bd. 1970-72, regional v.p. 1984-86), State Employees Assn., N-Vestment Assn. (pres. 1985-87), South Granville Exchange (bd. dirs. 1986—). Democrat. Presbyterian. Home: 1601 Kirkwood Dr Durham NC 27705-2141 Office: Men Women In Crisis Counsel 1318 Broad St Durham NC 27705-3533

GRUBE, ELISABETH FRANCES, bank officer; b. N.Y.C., Nov. 9, 1965; d. Heinrich and Elisabeth Klara (Leitner) M.; m. Patsy Matthew Grube, Aug. 20, 1988. BBA, Western Conn. State U., 1987; MBA, Pace U., 1993. Broker trainee Dean Witter Reynolds, Inc., N.Y.C., 1987; trust acct. Mfrs. Hanover Corp., N.Y.C., 1987-89, trust officer, asst. mgr., 1989-90; investment, mktg. asst. Bayeriche Vereinsbank, AG, Munich, 1991; legal asst. P. Matthew Grube, Poughkeepsie, N.Y., 1991-94; cost analyst People's Bank, Bridgeport, Conn., 1993-95, mgmt. devel. cons., 1994-95. Home: 812 N Iverson St Apt 204 Alexandria VA 22304

GRUBE, ELIZABETH, investment company executive; b. Indpls., 1917; d. Emery Warner and Jessie (Foster) Hanes; m. William F. Grube, Mar. 15, 1937; children: Carol Buck, F. William. Student, Consol. Bus. Coll., 1936, Ind. U.-Purdue U., Indpls., 1984. Pres. Prospect Investment Co.; bd. dirs. Indpls. Water Co., IWC Resources Corp., Indpls. Bd. dirs. Jameson Camp for Children, Indpls., 1981—, Greenwood Village South, Indpls., 1982—; mem. Rep. Senatorial Inner Circle, Washington, 1984. Methodist. Home: 4734 Bluff Rd Indianapolis IN 46217-3475

GRUBER, MARY ELIZABETH, association administrator; b. Bridgeport, Conn., Nov. 15, 1946; d. I. Nevin Palley and Dorothy Ellen (Johnson) Bryant; m. Francis Andre Gruber, Aug. 1, 1970 (div. 1993); children: Andre, Christiane, Floriane. BA magna cum laude, Smith Coll., 1968; postgrad. studies, U. Colo., 1992—. Rsch. analyst GE, Santa Barbara, Calif., 1969-72, Bache & Co., Geneva, Switzerland, 1972-73; tchr. pub. and private schs., Geneva, Switzerland, 1985-89; exec. asst. Prime Internat., Denver, 1991-92; project coord. Justice Mgmt. Inst., Denver, 1993—. Mem. Arapahoe County Dem. Com., 1990, Colo. Dem. Exec. Com., 1992—; campaign coord. Callihan for Colo., 1990, campaign staff, Josie Heath for U.S. Senate, 1990; candidate Colo. State Legis., 1992. Mem. AAUW (pub. policy chmn. local br. 1993), Smith Club of Colo., Grad. Sch. Pub. Affairs Student Assn. (v.p. 1993), Phi Beta Kappa. Office: Justice Mgmt Inst 1301 Pennsylvania St Denver CO 80203

GRUBER, ROSALIND H., counseling psychologist; b. Bronx, N.Y., Feb. 10, 1943; d. Lazarus L. and Beatrice (England) G.; B.A. cum laude, SUNY, New Paltz, 1974; M.A., Suffolk U., 1978. Nat. Cert. Counselor; lic. clin. social worker; lic. marriage and family therapist; lic. Mass. mental health counselor. Sch. registrar Assn. Help Retarded Children, N.Y.C., 1968-70; counselor Neighborhood Youth Corps, Poughkeepsie, N.Y., 1971-73; liaison Govt. Subsidized Housing, Cambridge, Mass., 1975-77; dir., counselor Aradia Counseling, Boston, 1978-91; ptnr.-owner real estate investment co., 1982—; producer C3 TV, South Yarmouth, Mass., 1990—; dir., owner Clearview Counseling, Brookline, Mass., 1991—; student supr. Suffolk U., Lesley Coll., Boston U.; group facilitator Provicetown Aids Support Group, Cape Cod Aids Coun., Women's HIV Support Group; mem. mental health com. Cape Cod Aids Coun. Mem. Nat. Assn. Social Workers, Am. Personnel and Guidance Assn., Assn. Humanistic Edn. and Devel., Am. Assn. for Marriage and Family Therapy, Mass. Mental Health Counselors Assn., Assn. Women in Psychology, U.S. Power Squaron. Home: 41 Babbling Brook Rd Centerville MA 02632-3157 Office: 308A Harvard St Brookline MA 02146-2917 also: 290 A Commercial St Provincetown MA 02657

GRUBER, SHARON DORIS, former secondary educator; b. Buffalo, June 2, 1942; d. Adam Michael and Helen Mary (Donovan) G. BS, SUNY, Geneseo, 1963; MEd in English, Kent State U., 1968; MEd in Adminstrn., Cleve. State U., 1988. Cert. secondary English tchr., Ohio. Tchr. English, John Adams High Sch., Cleve., 1963-65, John F. Kennedy High Sch., Cleve., 1965-93. Democrat. Roman Catholic.

GRUBIN, SHARON E., federal judge; b. Newark, Feb. 9, 1949; d. Harold and Blanche (Dultz) G. AB with honors, Smith Coll., 1970; JD, Boston U., 1973. Litigator White & Case, N.Y.C., 1973-84; judge U.S. Dist. Ct. (so. dist.) N.Y., N.Y.C., 1984—; lectr. N.Y.U. Sch. Law, Brooklyn Law Sch., N.Y. Law Sch. Author: (with others) Advocacy-The Art of Pleading a Cause, 1985, Federal Civil Practice, 1989; speaker seminars in field. Mem. ABA (jud. adminstrn. divsn.), Nat. Assn. Women Judges, Fed. Bar Coun. (v.p., mem. exec. com., com. on 2d cir. cts., long-range planning com., nom. com.), N.Y. State Bar Assn. (exec. com. comml. and fed. litigation sect.), N.Y. State Assn. Women Judges, Assn. of Bar City of N.Y. (exec. com., spl. com. on gender bias in fed. cts., coun. on jud. adminstrn, 1986-90, prof. and jud. ethics com. 1986-89, nom. com. 1984-85, com. on jud. 1982-83, chair, young lawyers com. 1979-81). Office: US Dist Ct US Courthouse 40 Foley Sq Rm 431 New York NY 10007 also: PO Box 174 210 Beale Rd Spencertown NY 12165*

GRUCCIO-THORMAN, LILLIAN JOAN, lawyer; b. Camden, N.J., Jan. 30, 1927; d. Joseph and Millie Gruccio. grad. Steelman Bus. Sch., 1945; AA, Rutgers U., 1947, LLB, 1951, LLD, 1968. Bar: N.J. 1952, U.S. Dist. Ct. N.J. 1952, U.S. Supreme Ct. 1960. Ptnr., Frank C. Propert, Camden, 1952-55; assoc. Lewis & Hutchinson and successors, Camden, 1956-61; with legal dept. Campbell Soup Co., 1955; sole practice Pennsauken, N.J., 1961-73, Medford, N.J., 1973—. Mem. Camden City Juvenile Conf. Com., 1957-62; mem. Burlington County coun. Girl Scouts USA, 1975, chmn. by-laws com., 1975; bd. dirs. Camden County Health and Welfare Coun., 1957-61, YWCA Camden, 1959-67, chmn. adult program com. 1957-67; mem. budget com. United Fund, 1968; recreation sec. Leisure Towne Civic League, mem. by-laws com. 1975. Mem. ABA, N.J. Bar Assn., Burlington County Bar Assn., Camden County Bar Assn., Rutgers U. Law Sch. Alumni Assn. (chancellor South Jersey div. 1962). Republican. Baptist. Lodge: Zonta. Home: 63 Sheffield Pl Southampton NJ 08088-1306 Office: Cedarbrook Bldg Taunton Blvd Medford NJ 08055

GRUEBEL, BARBARA JANE, internist, pulmonologist; b. Honolulu, May 12, 1950; d. Robert William and Elenor Jane (Perry) G.; B.S., Stephen F. Austin State U., 1977; M.D. (Robert Wood Johnson Found. scholar, Coll. Women's Club scholar), Baylor Coll. Medicine, 1974. Intern in internal medicine U. Rochester, 1974-75, resident in internal medicine, 1974-77; pulmonary fellow U. Mich., 1977-79; mem. med. staff Anthony L. Jordan Health Center, Rochester, N.Y., 1976-77, Univ. Health Service, Ann Arbor, Mich., 1978-79; med. dir. progressive respiratory care unit Meth. Med. Ctr., 1979-80; asst. prof. medicine U. Tex. Health Sci. Center, Dallas, 1979-80; cons. in pulmonary disease, Dallas, 1980-93; pvt. practice of pulmonary medicine, 1993—; clin. asst. prof. medicine U. Tex. Health Sci. Center; nat. affiliate faculty Am. Heart Assn. Mem. TEXPAC. Recipient award for gen. excellence in pediatrics, 1974, Stanley W. Olson award for acad. excellence, 1974, John Richard Fox award, 1974, Stuart A. Wallace award in pathology, 1974; Welch Found. grantee, 1970; Am. Lung Assn. tng. fellow, 1977-79. Diplomate Nat. Bd. Med. Examiners. Fellow Am. Coll. Chest Physicians (named Young Pulmonary Physicians of Future 1979); mem. Am. Med. Women's Assn. (scholastic excellence award 1974), Am. Thoracic Soc., Am. Lung Assn., AMA, Am. Coll. Physicians, Dallas County Med. Soc., Tex. Med. Soc., Dallas Internist Assocs., Nat. Assn. Med. Dirs. Respiratory Care, Dallas Acad. Internal Medicine, Am. Cancer Soc., Dallas C. of C., Oak Cliff C. of C., Alpha Omega Alpha, Beta Beta Beta. Office: 221 W Colorado St Ste 310 Dallas TX 75208

GRUENER, JENNIFER LEE, accountant; b. Ft. Worth, Feb. 13, 1967; d. Randall Dean and Judith Lea Wakefield Williams; m. Robert Anton Gruener, Aug. 11, 1990; 1 child, Evan Anthony. BS, S.W. Mo. State U., 1990. Cert. mgmt. acct. Acct. PSC Acctg. and Tax Svc., Springfield, Mo., 1985-88, RMS Co., Springfield, 1989-91, Kirkpatrick, Phillips & Miller, CPAs, Springfield, 1988-89; plant acct. City Utilities of Springfield, 1991—; bd. dirs. Center City Care Corp. Mem. Inst. Mgmt. Accts., Assn. Govt. Accts. (dir. edn. 1993-94). Office: City Utilities of Springfield 301 E Central Springfield MO 65802

GRUENWALD, RENEE, special education educator; b. Bklyn., Oct. 8, 1948; d. Isidor and Monia (Kaczanowska) Oshinsky; m. Laurence David Gruenwald, June 22, 1969; children: Kate, Sara. BA, Brandeis U., 1969; MA, Kean Coll., 1983. Cert. elem., spl. edn., learning disabilities tchr., cons. supervision and adminstrn. Tchr. Marlboro (Mass.) Pub. Schs., 1969-71, Colegio Anglo-Mexicano, Guadalajara, Mex., 1971-73, So. Orange/ Maplewood (N.J.) Pub. Schs., 1980—. Mem. N.J. Edn. Assn. (negotiations cons. 1993—), South Orange-Maplewood Edn. Assn. (v.p. 1984-86, pres. 1986-88, negotiations chair 1991-94, grievance chair 1994—), N.J. Assn. Learning Cons., Kappa Delta Pi. Home: 364 Redmond Rd South Orange NJ 07079-1505 Office: South Orange Middle Sch 70 N Ridgewood Rd South Orange NJ 07079

GRUHL, ANDREA MORRIS, librarian; b. Ponca City, Okla., Dec. 9, 1939; d. Luther Oscar and Hazel Evangeline (Anderson) Morris; m. Werner Mann Gruhl, July 10, 1965; children: Sonja Krista, Diana Krista. BA, Wesleyan Coll., 1961; MLS, U. Md., 1968; postgrad., Johns Hopkins U., 1970-71, U. Md., 1968, 71-73. Tchr. Broward County, Fla., Dept. Def. Montgomery County (Md.), 1961-66; libr. Prince Georges County (Md.) Pub. Libr., 1966-68, 81-83, U. Md., College Park, 1970-72; art. history rschr. Joseph Alsop, Washington, 1972-74; libr. Howard County Pub. Libr., Columbia, Md., 1969-70, 74-79; European exch. staff Libr. of Congress, Washington, 1982-86; cataloger fed. documents GPO, Washington, 1986-93, supervisory libr., 1993—; mem. women's program adv. com., processing dept. rep. Libr. of Congress, 1983-86, mem. ofcl. Libr. of Congress delegation to Internat. Fedn. Libr. Assn. ann. conf., Munich, 1983, Chgo., 1985; state del. White House Conf. on Librs., 1978, 90. Indexer, editor: Learning Vacations, 3d edit., 1980; LCPA Index to Libr. of Congress Info. Bull., 1984; editor Fed. Libr., 1994—. Trustee Howard County (Md.) Community Coll., 1989—, Howard County Pub. Libr., Columbia, Md., 1979-87; publ. chmn. LWV of Howard County, Md., 1974; citizen's rep. for Howard County and exec. bd. Balt. Regional Planning Coun. Libr. Com., 1976-79; Friends of the Libr., Howard County, pres., 1976; vol. Nat. Gallery of Art Libr., Washington, 1978-80. Mem. ALA (mem. trustee assn. 1982-87, cataloging sect. 1988—, govt. documents roundtable 1988—, fed. librs. roundtable 1988—, internat. rels. roundtable 1988—), United Nations Assn. (Nat. Capitol area chpt., mem. membership com., Md. telephone chair, 1992—), Assn. Libr. Collections and Tech. Svcs. of ALA, Art Librs. Soc. N. Am. (coord. mems. publ. exhbn. 1980-82), Libr. Congress Profl. Assn. (coord. ann. staff art show 1982, 83, chmn. libr. sci. group 1985-87), Libr. Congress Am. Fedn. State County and Mcpl. Employees Union 1477 (program chmn. 1984-86), Md. Libr. Assn. (pres. trustee div. 1982-83), Assn. C.C. Trustees, Md. Assn. C.C. Trustees (sec. 1991-92, bd. dirs. 1992-93), Md. Assn. C.C.s (bd. dirs. 1992—). Democrat. Lutheran. Home: 5990 Jacobs Ladder Columbia MD 21045-3817 Office: Govt Printing Office Washington DC 20401

GRUMBACHER, JACQUELINE W., communications executive; b. Tarrytown, N.Y., Apr. 30, 1944; d. Gaspare and Josephine (Galiano) Giuliano; m. Steven Wertime, June 10, 1967 (div. July 1, 1988); 1 child, Gregory Steven; stepchild, Sara Katherine; m. Steven Grumbacher, Apr. 22, 1989. BA, Bryn Mawr Coll., 1966. Editor Harper & Row Pub., Evanston, Ill., 1968-72; freelance writer, editor Washington, 1973-77; comm. dir. ARC Nat. Hdqs., Washington, 1977-88; sr. v.p. comm. Mortgage Bankers Assn. Am., Washington, 1988—; mem. homeownership-2000 task force Dept. Housing & Urban Devel. Active AIDS Edn. Task Force, 1987-88. Mem. Nat. Press Club, Am. Soc. Assn. Execs., Jane Austen Soc. N.Am. Home: 2412 S Queen St Arlington VA 22202 Office: Mortgage Bankers Assoc of Am 1125 15th St NW Washington DC 20005-2766

GRUMET, PRISCILLA HECHT, fashion specialist, consultant, writer; b. Detroit, May 11, 1943; d. Lewis Maxwell and Helen Ruth (Miller) Hecht; m. Ross Frederick Grumet, Feb. 24, 1968; 1 child, Auden Lewis. AA, Stephens Coll., 1963; student, Ga. State Coll., 1983-85. Buyer Rich's Dept. Store, Atlanta, 1963-68; instr. fashion retail Fashion Inst. Am., Atlanta, 1968-71; pres., lectr., cons. Personally Priscilla Personal Shopping Svc., Atlanta, 1971—; retail and customer svc. cons. By Priscilla Grumet, Atlanta, 1989—; instr. Cont. Edn. Program Emory U., Atlanta, 1976—; fashion merch. coord. Park Pl. Shopping Ctr., Atlanta, 1979-83; writer Atlanta Bus. Mag., 1984—; cons., buyer Greers-Regensteins Store, Atlanta, 1986-87; writer Atlanta Mag., 1994—; guest lectr. Fashion Group of Am., Rancho La Puerta Resort, Tecate, Mex., 1985—; bus. cons. Atlanta Apparel Mart, 1992—; adv. bd. Bauder Fashion Col., 1986—, Atlanta Apparel Mart, 1992—; fashion panel judge Weight Watchers Internat., 1981; columnist Marquee mag., Atlanta, 1992—; lectr. on customer svc. Rhodes Furniture, Marriott Corp., So. Bell, Lady Love Cosmetics, Atlanta Retail Stores, others, 1994—. Author: How to Dress Well, 1981; reporter Women's Wear Daily, 1976-90; columnist Atlanta Scene Mag.; contbr. articles to mags. and publs. including Atlanta, Seventeen, Nat. Jeweler's, The Old Farmer's Almanac. Pub. rels. dir., Atlanta Jewish Home Aux., 1986-89; admissions advisor, Stephens Coll.,

1979—. Mem. Fashion Group, Inc., Women in Comm., Nat. Coun. Jewish Women, Atlanta Press Club, Buckhead Bus. Assn., Temple Sisterhood (spkr., spl. events com. 1983—). Home and Office: 2863 Careygate NW Atlanta GA 30305-2821

GRUNBLATT, HILDA RUTH, translator, editor; b. Bklyn., Mar. 20, 1922; d. Samuel and Anna (Robson) Waterman; m. Jacques Grunblatt, Nov. 27, 1947 (dec. Jan. 1989); children: Ellen Miriam, Jesse Elliott, Mark Henry. BA, Bklyn. Coll., 1943. Tchr. N.Y.C. Bd. of Edn., Bklyn., 1946-49; med. asst., bookkeeper Offices of Dr. Jacques Grunblatt, North Creek, N.Y., 1949-75; freelance co-translator and editor North Creek, 1981—; bd. dirs. Johnsburg Pride, North Creek, N.Y., 1993—. Editor, co-translator: Seven Hells, 1990, The Shattered Dream, 1989. Organizer, vol. Town of Johnsburg Headstart, Johnsburg, N.Y., 1962-73; vol. Lit. Vols. Am., Glens Falls, 1990—; bd. dirs. Warren County Planned Parenthood, Glens Falls, 1966-75, Adirondack Ctr. for the Arts, Blue Mountain Lake, N.Y., 1966-75, Warren County Homemaker Svc., Glens Falls, 1967-75; bd. dirs. Glens Falls Warren County Com. on Children and Pub. Welfare, 1960-75, Warren County Mental Health Assn., 1964-70. Recipient Golden Poet award World of Poetry, 1985, 87, Editor's Choice award The Nat. Libr. of Poetry, 1994. Mem. AAUW, Environ. Def. Fund, Amnesty Internat., Natural Resources Def. Coun., Internat. Physicians for Prevention of Nuclear War, So. Poverty Law Ctr., Ctr. for Marine Conservation, Union of Concerned Scientists. Jewish. Home: PO Box 25 North Creek NY 12853

GRUNDBERG, BETTY, state legislator, property manager; b. Woden, Iowa, Feb. 16, 1938; d. Edwin and Eva Ruth Meyer; m. Arnie Grundberg, Dec. 31, 1960; children: Christine, Julie, Michael, Susan. BA, Wartburg Coll., 1959; MA, U. Iowa, 1969; postgrad., Drake U. Cert. tchr. Property mgr. and renovator Des Moines, 1973—; with Des Moines Sch. Bd., 1975-90; legis. State of Iowa, Des Moines, 1993—. Active LWV, Des Moines, 1972—. Republican. Home and Office: 224 Foster Dr Des Moines IA 50312*

GRUNDY, BETTY LOU BOTTOMS, anesthesiology and pharmaceutics educator; b. Dothan, Ala., Jan. 3, 1940; d. Wilmer Rudolph and Marie Belle (Brandon) Bottoms; m. David Mather Grundy, June 3, 1963; children: Jennifer Marie, Thomas Mather. Postgrad., Huntington Coll., Montgomery, Ala., 1956-59; MD, U. Fla., 1963. Rotating intern Gen. Rose Meml. Hosp., 1963-64; gen. med. practice Homestake Gold Mine, Lead, S.D., 1964-65; resident in anesthesiology Peter Bent Brigham Hosp., Boston, 1965-67; pvt. practice, anesthesiology St. Luke's Hosp., Saginaw, Mich., 1967-75; asst. prof. anesthesiology Mich. State U., Saginaw, 1967-75, Case Western Res. U., Cleve., 1975-79, U. Pitts., 1979-82; prof., chmn. of anesthesiology Coll. of Medicine, Oral Roberts U., Tulsa, 1982-84; prof. anesthesiology U. Fla., Gainesville, 1984—; chief anesthesiology svc. VA Med. Ctr., Gainesville, Fla., 1984-92; prof. anesthesiology and pharmaceutics U. Fla., Gainesville, 1992—; assoc. examiner Am. Bd. Anesthesiology, Hartford, Conn.; vol. site visitor Residency Rev. Com. for Anesthesiology, Accreditation Coun. for Grad. Med. Edn., 1982—. Editor: The Quality of Care in Anesthesia, 1982, Evoked Potentials Intraoperative and ICU Monitoring, 1988. Recipient Spl. award for New Investigators in Anesthesiology, NIH, 1979. Mem. Am. Electroencephalographic Soc. (evoked potentials com. 1982-89). Methodist. Home: 504 NW 89th St Gainesville FL 32607-1453 Office: Univ Fla Box J 254 JHMHC Gainesville FL 32610-0254

GRUNNER-TURNER, JOCELYN SARI, broadcast executive; b. N.Y.C., Mar. 15, 1958; d. Bernard and Ruth Rosa (Jaslove) G. BA, CUNY, 1979. Advt. broadcast negotiator Sawdon & Bess Advt., N.Y.C., 1979-80, Marschalk Advt., N.Y.C., 1980-81, Wells, Rich & Green Advt., N.Y.C., 1981-83; broadcast dir. Media Gen. Broadcast, N.Y.C., 1983-86; account exec., broadcast account mgr. Katz Communication, N.Y.C., 1986-89; broadcast account exec. NBC, N.Y.C., 1989—. Mem. Advt. Women of N.Y. Office: NBC 30 Rockefeller Plz New York NY 10112-0001

GRUNNET, MARGARET LOUISE, pathologist; b. Mpls., Feb. 20, 1936; d. Leslie Nels and Grace Harriet (Thomson) Grunnet; m. Irving Noel Einhorn, Mar. 10, 1972; stepchildren: Jeffrey Allan, Franne Ruth, Eric Carl, Stanley Glenn. BA summa cum laude, U. Minn., Mpls., 1958; MD, U. Minn., 1962; MS, Ohio State U., 1969. Resident in psychiatry U. Pa. Sch. Medicine, Phila., 1963-64; resident anatomic pathology Presbyn.-U. Pa. Med. Ctr., Phila., 1965-66; fellow neuropathology Phila. Gen. Hosp., 1967, Ohio State U. Hosp., Columbus, 1968-69; instr. Ohio State U., 1969; asst. prof. U. Utah Sch. Medicine, Salt Lake City, 1970-76, assoc. prof., 1976-80; assoc. prof. pathology U. Conn. Sch. Medicine, Farmington, 1980-90, prof., 1990—. Contbr. articles to profl. jours. Mem. Am. Med. Women's Assn., Internat. Soc. Neuropathology, Conn. Soc. Pathologists, Am. Assn. Neuropathologists, Phi Beta Kappa, Alpha Omega Alpha. Mem. Ch. of Christ. Home: 1550 Asylum Ave West Hartford CT 06117-2805 Office: U Conn Health Ctr Dept Pathology Farmington CT 06032

GRUSH, HELEN BUTLER, educational consultant; b. Winchester, Mass., Aug. 1, 1921; d. Horace and Helen Gretchen (Avery) Butler; m. Willard Parker Grush, Aug. 29, 1942 (dec.); children: Sandra LeFlore Bergmann, Jeffrey Willard, Kimball Warren. BS, Northeastern U., 1970; MEd, Boston U., 1974. Tchr. Smith Sch., Lincoln, Mass., 1962-64; instr., author Mass. Coun. Pub. Schs., Boston, 1963-65; supr. Community Svc. Corps-Migrant, Boston, 1965-66; ednl. dir. Perceptual Edn. Rsch., Wellesley, Mass., 1966-68; asst. prof. Lesley Coll. Grad. Sch., Cambridge, Mass., 1972-80; co-founder LEAD Ednl. Resources, Lexington, Mass., 1972; author, lectr., instr. Logical Encoding and Decoding Program, 1972-85; editorial cons. Logical Encoding and Decoding Program Ednl. Resources, Bridgewater, Conn., 1985—. Mem. founding com. Pilgrim Congl. Ch., Lexington; pres. Florence Crittenden League. Mem. AAUW (bd. dirs.), Laudholm Preserve, Fla. Ctr. for the Arts, Vero Beach ARt Club. Republican. Congregationalist. Home: 200 Greytwig Rd # 111 Vero Beach FL 32963

GRUSKIN, MARY J. (MRS. ALAN D. GRUSKIN), art gallery director emeritus; d. Mauro Bovio and Tina Simone; m. Alan D. Gruskin, July 16, 1940; children—Richard B., Robert A. Student, Cooper Union, Traphagen Sch. Design, Grand Central Art Sch., N.Y. Sch. Design, Art Students League. Designer for china; dress buyer Martin's, Bklyn., 1937-40; ptnr. Midtown Payson Galleries, 1944—, dir., 1970-85, adviser, dir. emeritus, 1985—. Assembled paintings for Art-in-Industry collections; assisted arrangement contemporary Am. artists group for design of print fabrics; illustrated: book jacket and story for book House That Runs Itself. Mem. Trenton, Friends of N.J. State Mus., Trenton. Mem. Nat. Council Women U.S. Office: Midtown Payson Galleries 745 Fifth Ave New York NY 10151-0002

GRUSS, CLAUDIA BETH, physician; b. Norwalk, Conn., July 25, 1952; d. Marvin Israel and Syma (Birnbaum) G.; m. Eric Brandt Einstein, June 12, 1977; 1 child, Joshua Adam Einstein. BA, Brown U., 1974, MD, 1977. Resident in internal medicine R.I. Hosp., Providence, 1977-80, fellow in gastroenterology, 1980-82; pvt. practice Georgetown (Conn.) Med. Assocs., 1982—. Vol. musician Norwalk (Conn.) Symphony Orch., 1982-93; bd. govs. Norwalk Symphony Soc., 1985-93; mem. edn. com. Temple B'Nai Chaim, Georgetown, 1994—; chmn. cmty. resource com. John Read Mid. Sch., Redding, Conn., 1994—. Haffenreffer fellow R.I. Hosp., 1982. Mem. ACP, Am. Gastroenterol. Assn. Office: Georgetown Bus Profl Ctr Georgetown CT 06829

GU, CLAIRE XIANG-GUANG, physicist; came to U.S., 1985; BS, Fudan U., Shanghai, China, 1985; PhD, Calif. Inst. Tech., 1989. Rsch. asst. Calif. Inst. Tech., Pasadena, 1986-89, vis. assoc., 1989-90; mem. tech. staff Rockwell Sci. Ctr., Thousand Oaks, Calif., 1989-92; asst. prof. Pa. State U., 1992—. Author: (with others) Optical Processing and Computing, 1989, An Introduction to Neural and Electronic Network, 1990; contbr. articles to Nature, Jour. Applied Physics, Optics Letters. Recipient Young Investigator award NSF, 1993; Calif. Inst. Tech. fellow, 1985, Fudan U. scholar, 1984, 85. Mem. Optical Soc. Am. Office: Pa State U Dept Elec Engring 121 Elec Engring East University Park PA 16802

GUADAGNO, MARY ANN NOECKER, social scientist, consultant; b. Springville, N.Y., Sept. 21, 1952; d. Francis Casimer and Josephine Lucille (Fricano) Noecker; m. Robert George Guadagno, Aug. 29, 1970 (div. Mar. 1981). BS in Edn. cum laude, SUNY, Buffalo, 1974; MS, Ohio State U., 1977, PhD, 1978. Grad. teaching assoc. Ohio State U., Columbus, 1974-77, grad. rsch. assoc., 1977-78; asst. prof. U. Minn., St. Paul, 1978-83; cons. Nationwide Ins. Co., Columbus, 1982-83, rsch. assoc. Corp. Rsch., 1983-86, product devel. assoc., Office of Mktg., 1986-89; adjunct prof. Coll. Bus. & Pub. Adminstrn. Franklin U., Columbus, Ohio, 1985-89; lectr. Coll. Bus. Adminstrn. and Econ. Ohio Dominican Coll., Columbus, 1986-89; scientist family econ. rsch. group USDA, Washington, 1989-93; survey statistician Nat. Ctr. for Health Stats., HHS, Washington, 1993—; com. mem. fed. women's program USDA, Beltsville, Md., 1991-93, mem. women in sci., 1991-93. Author: Family Inventory of Money Management, 1982, Family Inventory, 1982; contbr. articles to profl. jours., 1978—. Com. mem. United Way, Mkt. Rsch. Info. Exchange, Columbus, Ohio. Recipient Spl. Recognition award Ohio House Reps., 1987, Cert. Grad. award Columbus Area Leadership Program, 1987, Cert. Appreciation award Am. Mktg. Assn., 1987, Cert. Merit award U.S. Dept. Agr., 1991. Mem. Columbus Area Leadership Program, Ohio State U. Coll. Human Ecology Alumni. Republican. Roman Catholic. Home: 3401 Hampton Hollow Dr # M Silver Spring MD 20904-6179 Office: HHS Nat Ctr for Health Stats 6525 Belcrest Rd Rm 915 Hyattsville MD 20782-2003

GUADIANA-BUNTING, PAULA MICHELE, marketing professional, electrical engineer; b. Miami, Ariz., Sept. 25, 1963; d. Michael John and Teresa (Silvain) Guadiana; m. William Everett Bunting III, May 25, 1994. BSEE, No. Ariz. U., 1987. Design engr. Hughes Aircraft Co., L.A., 1987-90; acct. mgr. Sheldahl Inc., L.A., 1990-92; mktg. mgr. Tecnetics, Inc., Boulder, Colo., 1992-93, Nat. Tech. Transfer, Inc., Denver, 1993—; guest spkr. SSI Corp., Denver, 1992-93. Author, co-editor: Hughes Engineering and Handbook, 1990. Vol., supporter Humaine Soc., Boulder, 1992-93; contbr., supporter Safe House through Salvation Army, Boulder, 1993. Mem. NAFE, IEEE, Electronics Rep. Assn. Roman Catholic. Office: Nat Tech Transfer Inc PO Box 4558 Englewood CO 80155-4558

GUARD, MARY BETH, lawyer, small business owner, bank trade executive; b. Carmi, Ill., Aug. 19, 1955; d. William Frank and Jacqueline Lee (Galloway) Sharp; m. Lynndon Michael Guard, May 28, 1978. AA, Kaskaskia Coll., 1975; BS, So. Ill. U., 1977, JD, 1980. Bar: Okla., U.S. Dist. Ct. (we. and no. dists.) Okla., U.S. Ct. Appeals (10th and 5th cirs.). Atty. oil and gas dept. Commrs. Land Office State of Okla., Oklahoma City, 1980-84; gen. counsel Banking Dept. State of Okla., Oklahoma City, 1984-89; exec. v.p., gen. counsel, COO Okla. Bankers Assn., Oklahoma City, 1989—; gen. ptnr. Sweatshirt Chic, Oklahoma City, 1987—, BankGuard Resources, 1993—; lectr. continuing legal edn. courses, Okla., 1981—; magician Oklahoma City, 1985—; presenter of seminars; speaker in field; faculty mem. Jack T. Conn Grad. Sch. of Comm. Banking Oklahoma City U. Editor The Phys. Edge; contbr. articles to profl. jours. Vol. various orgns.; mentor Search Sch. for Gifted Children, Moore, Okla., 1986, 87; bd. dirs., 3d v.p. YWCA, Oklahoma City, 1985-88. Mem. ABA (local com.), Okla. Bar Assn. (com. post 1982-85), Okla. County Bar Assn., Oklahoma City Magic Soc. (v.p. 1985-86), Soc. Am. Magicians, Internat. Brotherhood Magicians, Am. Soc. Assn. Execs., Tex. Assn. Bank Counsel, Bus. and Profl. Women's Club (pres. 1983-84, Outstanding Woman of Yr. 1982, Outstanding Young Careerist 1985), Order of the Barrister, Phi Alpha Delta (justice 1979-80). Democrat. Methodist. Home: 201 NW 33d St Oklahoma City OK 73118 Office: Okla Bankers Assn PO Box 18246 Oklahoma City OK 73154-0246

GUARDALABENE, JEANNINE SUE, marriage and family therapist; b. Walton, N.Y., June 14, 1952; d. James Harby and Ruth Louise (Le Tourneur) Courtney; m. Anthony E. Guardalabene. AA, Citrus Coll., Azusa, Calif., 1972; BA, Azusa Pacific Coll., 1974; MA, N.W. Christian Coll., 1994. Elementary sch. tchr. Azusa Unified Schs., 1974-78; sales rep. Red Carpet Real Estate, Claremont, Calif., 1978-79; owner Statewide Transmissin Svc., Inc., Elmira, Oreg., 1982-94; owner, cons. ReGard, Eugene, Oreg., 1992—; family therapist pvt. practice, Eugene, 1994—. Co-author: (workbook) ReGard: Men and Women Working Together, 1992. Case mgr. United Way, Eugene, 1991-93; crisis phone vol. Women Space, Eugene, 1991-93; vol., contbr. ARC, Oreg., 1994. Mem. AAUW, Women in the Arts, Women's Bus. Network. Republican. Office: Re Gard 350 E 11th St Ste 3 Eugene OR 97401

GUARDO, CAROL J., association executive; b. Hartford, Conn., Apr. 12, 1939; d. C. Fred and Marion (Biase) G. BA, St. Joseph Coll., 1961; MA, U. Detroit, 1963; PhD, U. Denver, 1966. Asst. prof. psychology Eastern Mich. U., Ypsilanti, 1966-68; assoc. prof., staff psychologist U. Denver, 1968-73; assoc. prof., dean coll. Utica Coll. of Syracuse U., Utica, N.Y., 1973-76; prof., dean Coll. Liberal Arts, Drake U., Des Moines, 1976-80; provost, prof. U. Hartford, 1980-85; pres. R.I. Coll., Providence, 1986-90, Great Lakes Colls. Assn., Ann Arbor, Mich., 1990—; mem. Iowa Humanities Bd., 1976-80, pres., 1978-80; bd. dirs. Am. Coun. Edn., People's Bank. Author: The Adolescent As Individual: Issues and Insights, 1975; contbr. articles to profl. jours. Trustee St. Joseph Coll., Monmouth Coll., Colby-Sawyer Coll., Cabrini Coll. NSF fellow, 1964, NIMH fellow, 1964-66. Mem. Am. Assn. Higher Edn., Assn. Am. Colls. (vice chair 1987, chair 1988), Am. Psychol. Assn., Assn. Gen. and Liberal Studies (pres. 1979-81), Soc. Rsch. in Child Devel., Greater Providence C. of C., Phi Beta Kappa. Office: Great Lakes Colls Assn 2929 Plymouth Rd Ste 207 Ann Arbor MI 48105-3206

GUARINO, IRIS COOPER, realtor, appraiser; b. N.Y.C., Feb. 15, 1923; d. Charle Ray and Lillian S. (Yarbrough) Cooper; m. Louis J. Guarino, May 13, 1950; 1 child, Victoria. BSBA cum laude, NYU, 1946. Lic. realtor, N.Y., appraiser, N.Y. Assoc. buyer R.H. Macy, N.Y.C., 1946-50; buyer Frederick Atkins Ctrl. Buying Office, N.Y.C., 1950-54; realtor Flynn Real Estate, Washingtonville, N.Y., 1973-84; mng. realtor, appraiser Joseph Green Real Estate, Washingtonville, N.Y., 1984—. Regional chairperson Girl Scouts Am., Middletown, N.Y., 1961-72; mem. Sierra Club, Saratoga Springs, N.Y., 1994—, Wilderness Soc., Washington, 1994—, Hudson River Clear Water Assn., Beacon, N.Y., 1994—. Recipient scholarship NYU, 1946. Mem. Nat. State and County Bd. Realtors, Orange County C. of C., Blooming Grove C. of C., NYU Stern Sch. Bus. Alumni. Methodist. Home: PO Box 164 Washingtonville NY 10992 Office: Joseph Green Real Estate Rt 208 S Washingtonville NY 10992

GUDANEK, LOIS BASSOLINO, social worker; b. N.Y.C., Jan. 28, 1944; d. Frank and Anna (Scarlata) Bassolino; m. Richard Stanley Gudanek, Sept. 3, 1977. BA in Anthropology and Sociology, Queens Coll., 1973; postgrad., Hunter Coll., 1973-76, JRW Inst. Alcohol Studies, 1988-89; student Eating Disorders Inst., Rollins Coll., Eating Disorders Inst., 1991; MSW, Fordham U., 1994. Credentialled alcoholism counselor, N.Y; cert. social worker, N.Y. Sec. various orgns., N.Y.C., 1962-76; pers. asst. career devel. Equal Employment Opportunity Mobil, N.Y.C., 1976-78; real estate sales agt. N.Y., 1979-81; adminstrv. support rep., field trainer Savin, Valhalla, N.Y., 1981-83; owner The Printwheel, Ossining, N.Y., 1983-89; student intern Arms Acres, Carmel, N.Y., 1988-89; adult therapist Arms Acres, Carmel, 1989-91; vocat. counselor Westchester County Med. Ctr.-Alcoholism Treatment Svcs., Yonkers, 1991-94, Westchester County Med. Ctr.-WEST-PREP, Valhalla, N.Y., 1994—; lectr. JRW Inst. on Alcohol Studies, Yonkers, N.Y., 1991, St. Thomas Aquinas Coll., 1994; presenter in field. Mem. NASW, Internat. Assn. Eating Disorders Profls. (sec. tri-state region 1989-91, vice chmn. 1991—, ednl. coord. 1992—), Nat. Assn. Alcoholism and Drug Abuse Counselors, N.Y. Fedn. Alcoholism and Chem. Dependency Counselors, N.Y. Women's Coalition on Chem. Dependency (treas. 1991-92, bd. dirs. 1994—), Gamma Sigma Sigma (del. to nat. conv. 1971, 1st v.p.- svc. 1972, pres. 1973). Roman Catholic.

GUDINSKY-KREISEL, MARION FAITH, nursing educator, critical care & pediatrics nurse; b. Bklyn., Aug. 18, 1965; d. Philip and Pearl Helen (Postofsky) Gudinsky; m. Leopold David Kreisel, Feb. 3, 1991. BSN, Adelphi U., Garden City, N.Y., 1987; MSN, Ga. So. U., 1995. Cert. BCLS instr., ACLS instr.; cert. CNOR, TNCC, BTLS, EMT; cert. HIV/AIDS educator, counselor. Staff nurse adult ICU NYU Med. Ctr., N.Y.C., 1987-88; staff nurse pediatric ICU Jackson Meml. Hosp., Miami, Fla., 1988-89; oper. room nurse Mercy Hosp., Miami, Fla., 1989-91; emergency room nurse Gillman Hosp., St. Marys, Ga., 1991-93, Baptist Med. Ctr., Jacksonville, Fla., 1991—; instr. nursing Brunswick Coll., 1992-93, Fla. C.C., Jacksonville, 1993-94; adj. prof. nursing USN, 1994—. Scholar Teagle Found., 1986, Peggy A. Burleigh Meml. scholar, 1987. Mem. AACN, Assn. Oper. Rm. Nurse, Emergency Nurses Assn., Fla. Nurses Assn., Sigma Theta Tau.

GUDMUNDSON, BARBARA ROHRKE, ecologist; b. Chgo.; d. Lloyd Ernest and Helen (Bullard) Rohrke; m. Valtyr Emil Gudmundson, June 14, 1951 (dec. Dec. 1982); children: Holly Mekkin, Martha Rannveig. BA, U. Tenn., 1950; MA, Mankato State Coll., 1965; PhD, Iowa State U., 1969. Microbiologist Hektoen Inst. & Ill. Ctr. Hosp., Chgo., 1950-52; immunologist Jackson Meml. Lab., Bar Harbor, Maine, 1952-54; dist. ecologist Corps of Engrs., St. Paul, 1971-72; sr. ecologist North Star Rsch. Inst., Mpls., 1972-76; staff engr. Met. Waste Control Commn., St. Paul, 1976-77; pres., prin. ecologist Ecosystem Rsch. Svc./Upper Midwest, Mpls., 1978—; pvt. practice as cons. ecologist, Des Moines and Mpls., 1968-70; mem. Citizens League Task Force on the Mississippi Riverfront, 1973-74; mem. adv. com. Mpls. Lakes Water Quality, Mpls., 1974-75; field ecologist Mississippi River Canoe Expdn., Coll. of the Atlantic, Bar Harbor, 1979. Author: V. Emil Gudmundson: Icelandic Canadian Unitarian, A Personal Biography, 1991; editor-in-chief The Icelandic Unitarian Connection, 1984; contbr. articles to profl. jours. Mem. from 61st dist. Dem.-Farmer-Labor Cen. Com., Minn. 1978-80; mgr. Minnehaha Creek Watershed Dist., Hennepin & Carver Counties, Minn., 1979-83; mem. Capital Long-Range Improvements com., Mpls., 1981. River Basin Ecology grantee Iowa Acad. Scis., Cedar Falls, 1976, Mississippi River Ecology grantee Freshwater Biol. Rsch. Found., Navarre, Minn., 1979, Fulbright Sr. Rsch. grantee USA/Iceland Fulbright Commns., Washington, Reykjavik, 1986, 92; recipient Anita Hill Courage and Justice award, 1994. Mem. Ecol. Soc. Am. (pres. Minn. chpt. 1971-75), Geol.Soc. Minn. (pres. 1981), Psychol. Soc. Am., Sigma Delta Epsilon (nat. membership com. 1990-93, chair 1991-93), Internat. Assn. Diatom Rsch., Phi Kappa Phi, Sigma Xi. Unitarian Universalist. Home: 5505 28th Ave S Minneapolis MN 55417-1957 Office: Ecosystem Rsch Svc/Upper Midwest PO Box 17102 Minneapolis MN 55417-0102

GUDNITZ, ORA M. COFEY, secondary education educator; b. Crawforddsville, Ark., Jan. 24, 1934; d. Daniel S. and Mary (Oglesby) Cofey; children: Ingrid M. Hunt, Carl Erik, Katrina Beatrice. BA, Lane Coll., Jackson, Tenn., 1955; MEd, Temple U., 1969; student, U. Copenhagen, 1957, U. Pa., 1961. Cert. permanent English, social studies and French tchr., Pa. Tchr. English, chmn. dept. Sayre Jr. High Sch., Phila.; tchr. English, Overbrook High Sch., Phila.; founder, exec. dir. Young Communicators Workshop, Inc.; lectr., Denmark. Contbr. articles to newspapers, poetry to anthologies. Active in Masters of Arts in Theological Studies program for family counseling Ea. Bapt. Theol. Sem., Pa. Recipient award Chapel of Four Chaplains, 1976, Women in Edn. award, 1988; grantee Haas Found., 1977, also others. Mem. Nat. Coun. Tchrs. English, Assn. for Ednl. Communication and Tech., Phi Delta Kappa, Delta Sigma Theta.

GUELZOW, DEBORAH ANNE, librarian; b. Dayton, Ohio, Apr. 16, 1949; d. Clarence William and Gretchen Louise (Swoffer) G. B in Gen. Sci., Rollins Coll., 1976; MLS, Fla. State U., 1979. Tech. svcs. libr. Kennedy Space Ctr. (Fla.) Libr., 1980—. Chmn. bd. dirs. Cocoa Beach (Fla.) Pub. Libr., 1981—, Friends of Libr., 1976—. Mem. Spl. Libr. Assn., Nat. Mgmt. Assn. (chpt. sec. 1994), Libr. Assn. of Brevard. Democrat. Office: NASA/Kennedy Space Ctr Libr A Kennedy Space Center FL 32899

GUENTHER, SHEILA WALSH, sales and promotion executive; b. Hamilton, Mont., Sept. 19, 1933; d. Leo Frederick and Edith Frances (Leonard) W.; James William Guenther, June 29, 1957; children: Kurt Dennis, Kelly David, Gayla Koleen. BA cum laude, Wash. State Coll., 1955. Layout artist The Bon Marche, Spokane, Wash., 1955-56; sales promotion mgr. The Bon Marche (formally The Paris), Great Falls, Mont., 1956-57; faculty staff artist info. & pub. rels. Mont. State Coll., Bozeman, 1958-61; sales promotion mgr. David's House Name Brands, Wichita, Kans., 1961-65; writer, graphic artist Warren Printing, Chamberlain Graphics, Olympia, Wash., 1965-73; writer, graphics freelancer Prescott Co. Advt. Pub. Relation, Olympia, Wash., 1970-77; instr. Clark Coll., Vancouver, Wash., 1979-81; sales promotion dir. Vancouver Furniture, 1974-94; pres. Walsh Guenther & Assocs., Inc., Vancouver, 1982—; Printer's Ink juror. Co-author: Vancouver on the Columbia Business History, 1986. Columbia People in Need Adv. Com., Ellen Goodman Project for YWCA Emergency Shelter, Hands Across Clark County Stop Hunger Campaign; co-founder Swift Charity Auction, 1977. Recipient Silver Microphone award 1984, Spokane and Wichita Newspaper and Television Advertising award winner, Sertoma, Benjamin Franklin Service award, 1984, Woman of Achievement award YWCA, 1988. Wichita Press Women, Advt. Fed., Oregon Women Communications, C. of C, LWV, Spokane Advt. Club, Delta Phi Delta . Democrat. Office: PO Box 61628 Vancouver WA 98666

GUERLAC, SUZANNE, French language educator; b. Ithaca, N.Y., Mar. 20, 1950; d. Henry Edward and Rita (Carey) G.; 1 child, Catherine Lillian. BA in Philosophy magna cum laude, Barnard Coll., 1971; MA in French Lit., Johns Hopkins U., Balt., 1976; PhD in French Lit., Johns Hopkins U., 1984. Vis. asst. prof. U. Va., Charlottesville, 1983-84; asst. prof. Yale U., New Haven, Conn., 1984-86; asst. prof. Johns Hopkins U., Balt., 1986-89, assoc. prof., 1989-90; assoc. prof. Emory U., Atlanta, 1990—. Author: The Impersonal Sublime, 1990, Intimate Mechanics, 1995; assoc. editor: Semiotexte, 1978; mem. editorial bd. Modern Language Notes, 1987-90. Gilman fellow Johns Hopkins U., 1974-76, 79-83; Mellon Jr. scholar U. Va., 1985-87. Mem. MLA, Internat. Assn. Philosophy and Lit. Office: Emory U Dept French Atlanta GA 30033

GUERRANT, HELEN ORZEL, artist; b. Boston, Mar. 19, 1920; d. Staley Orzel and Jo Ann Hite; m. Paul Nelson Horton (div.); m. Robert Shields Guerrant, Mar. 1, 1947; children: Somerset Orzel, David Denison, Daniel Guerin, Emerson Roy. BS, Cornell U., 1942; postgrad., U. Va., Roanoke Coll., Radford Coll., Hollins Coll., Va. Poly. Inst. Asst. geneticist Atlee Burpee Seed Co., Doylestown, Pa.; with diagnostic dept. N.Y. State Health Dept., N.Y.C.; pilot Martha Ann Woodrum Svcs., Woodrum Field, Roanoke, Va.; judge Nat. Coun. Flower Show. One woman shows include Palette Art Gallery, White House Gallery, Roanoke Fine Arts Ctr., Martinsville Fine Arts Ctr., Va. Employment Commn., Olde Eng. Frame; exhibited in group shows Valentine Mus., Richmond, Va., Empire State Bldg., N.Y.C., Reynolds Metal Co., Norfolk (Va.) Mus. Art Svc. and Art Lending, Winston-Salem (N.C.) Gallery Contemporary Art, 20th Century Gallery Contemporary Art, Williamsburg, Va., L.I. Art Show, Lynchburg Area Show, Roanoke Area Artists Show, Roanoke Coll. Ann. Shows, Wesley Found., Dominion Bank, Roanoke, Sovran Bank, United Va. Bank, Richmond, Va. Commonwealth Bankshares, Richmond, Miller and Rhoads Sidewalk Show, AAUW Heironimus Show, Roanoke Fine Arts Ctr., Lynchburg Fine Arts Ctr., Roanoke Area Shows, Lynchburg Area Shows, Radford Coll., Roanoke Coll., Bath County Regional Area Show. Active Docent Guild, Miller and Main Galleries, White House Galleries, New River Arts Coun., Arts Coun. of Blue Ridge. With USN. Recipient Prints Bath County Area Show award, Best Oil Bath County Regional Area Show award, Best in Show award Dogwood Festival, 1st Watercolor award Roanoke Coll. Show, Watercolor award Bath County Regional Art Show, Best in Show award Lynchburg Area Show, Watercolor award Roanoke Coll. Art Show, Watercolor award AAUW Show, Oil award Radford Coll. Show, Drawings and Graphics award Roanoke Coll. Show. Mem. Am. Legion, Va. Watercolor Soc., League of Roanoke Artists, Morning Music Club. Home: 1816 Windsor Ave SW Roanoke VA 24015

GUERRERO-ANDERSON, ESPERANZA, management consultant; b. Managua, Nicaragua, Dec. 22, 1944; came to U.S., 1978; d. Julian Napoleon Guerrero and Gertrudis Mairena. BA in Bus. Adminstrn., Universidad Centro, Nicaragua, 1969; MS in Mgmt. Info. Systems, U. Mpls., 1973; postgrad., Hubert H. Humphrey Inst., 1986-87, Yale U., 1989. Assoc. dir. and prof. of fin. and acctng. Centro de Estudios Superiores, Nicaragua, 1966-69; group head Banco Cent. de Nicaragua, 1970-79; founding ptnr. Consultores Interamericanos, Nicaragua, 1975-79; mgmt. cons. Touche Ross and Co., Atlanta; internat. banking officer First Bank Mpls., 1980-81; pres. chief exec. officer, Chief oper. officer Met. Econ. Devel. Assn., 1981-89; pres., chief exec. officer Milestone Growth Fund, 1990—; adv. U.S. SBA, Mpls.; bd. dirs. Milestone Growth Fund, Mpls., Nat. City Bank. Active Mpls. United Way, Norstar Guarantee, Minn. Internat. Ctr., Walker Art Ctr., Ctr. of Am. Expt. Mem. Nat. Assn. Small Investment Cos., Nat. Assn. Investment Cos.

Roman Catholic. Office: Milestone Growth Fund Plaza VII 45 S 7th St # 2326 Minneapolis MN 55402

GUESS, AUNDREA KAY, accounting educator; b. Seth, W.Va., Feb. 7, 1943; d. Hobert and Inez Elizabeth (Howell) Adams; m. George F. Guess, June 3, 1962; children: Renae, Rhonda. BBA, Baylor U., Waco, Tex., 1988; MBA, Auburn U., 1989; PhD, U. North Tex., 1993. CPA, Ala., Fla. Co-owner Stevenson (Ala.) All-Mart, 1967-94; grad. rsch. asst. Auburn (Ala.) U., 1988-89; teaching fellow U. North Tex., Denton, 1989-90, lectr., 1990-93; prof., dir. acctg. program Samford U., Birmingham, Ala., 1993—, dir. new masters of acctg. degree program; cons. Kay Guess Cons., Birmingham, 1993—, activity based costing Coca-Cola; presenter Southwestern Bus. Adminstrn. Conf., 1994; discussant, 1995 track chair for acctg. and fin. Southwestern Case Rsch. Assn.; owner Kay's Designer Dresses, Stevenson. Contbr. articles to profl. jours. Recipient Fin. Execs. Inst. award, 1987, 89; Rsch. grantee Samford U.Heloise Brown Canter scholar Am. Women's Soc. CPA and Am. Soc. Women Accts., 1992. Mem. AICPA, Am. Acctg. Assn., Am. Soc. Women CPAs (South Birmingham chpt., Laurel scholar 1992, scholar 1989), Fla. Inst. CPAs, Inst. Mgmt. Accts. (bd. dirs. 1994—, dir. tech. meetings 1994—), Acad. Acctg. Historians, Inst. Internal Auditing, Phi Theta Kappa, Alpha Kappa Psi, Beta Alpah Psi (treas. Auburn chpt. 1989), Phi Kappa Phi, Beta Gamma Sigma. Baptist. Home: 5548 Parkview Cir Birmingham AL 35242-3536

GUEST, JUDITH ANN, author; b. Detroit, Mar. 29, 1936; d. Harry Reginald and Marion Aline (Nesbit) G.; children: Larry, John, Richard. BA in Edn., U. Mich., 1958. Elem. tchr. Birmingham (Mich.) Pub. Schs., 1959-60, Royal Oak (Mich.) Pub. Schs., 1969-70; tchr. continuing edn. Troy (Mich.) Pub. Schs., 1974-75. Author: Ordinary People, 1976 (Janet Heidinger Kafka prize Univ. of Rochester 1977), Second Heaven, 1982, Mythic Family, 1988, (with Rebecca Hill) Killing Time in St. Cloud, 1989, (screenplay) Rachel River, 1989. Mem. Detroit Women Writers, Authors Guild, PEN Am. Center. Office: care Viking Press 40 W 23rd St New York NY 10010-5200*

GUFFEY, BARBARA BRADEN, elementary educator; b. Pitts., Aug. 10, 1948; d. James Arthur and Dorothy (Barrett) Braden; 1 child, William Butler Guffey III. BA in Elem. Edn., Westminster Coll., New Wilmington, Pa., 1970; MEd in Elem. Edn., Slippery Rock State Coll., 1973; postgrad., U. Pitts., Duquesne U., Westminster Coll. Cert. tchr., elem. and secondary history and govt. edn, elem. prin. Tchr. Shaler Area Sch. Dist., Glenshaw, Pa., lang. arts area specialist, 1988-91, 92-93, grad. level chmn., 1991-92, mem. instrnl. support team, 1994-95, curriculum support person math/sci., 1995; mem. Shaler Area Strategic Planning Core Team; condr. seminars and workshops in field. Former deacon, mem. nominating com. Cmty. Presbyn. Ch. Ben Avon; mem. alumni coun. Westminster Coll., chmn. homecoming all-alumni luncheon, 1991-93, homecoming chair, 1995; former homeroom mother Burchfield Elem. Sch. PTA. Mem. ASCD, NEA, Children with Attention Deficit Disorders, Pa. Edn. Assn., Shaler Area Edn. Assn. (v.p., negotiator, former rec. sec., bldg. rep., editor newsletter), Western Pa. Geneal Soc. (rec. sec., bd. dirs.), Perry Historians, Indiana County Geneal. and Hist. Soc., Kappa Delta Pi. Office: Burchfield Elem Sch 1500 Burchfield Rd Allison Park PA 15101-4099

GUGENHEIM, ARIELA KATZ, historian; b. Mexico City, Mar. 19, 1960; d. Marcos David and Adina (Kenner) Katz; m. Elie Alain Gugenheim; children Giselle, Batya, Shlomit, Natanel. Lic. in history summa cum laude, U. Iberoamericana, 1981; Jewish history degree, U. Iberoamericana/U. Jerusalem, 1991; grad. student, Bernard Revel Grad. Sch., 1992-95. cons. editor Raices Pub. House, Mexico City, 1992—. Author, transl.: The Jews in Mexico, 1987; co-author: Images of an Encounter, 1992 (Best Book of Yr. Juan Pablos award 1993). Co-founder, bd. dirs. Emuna Elem. and Jr. H.S., Mexico City, 1985—. Jewish. Office: PO Box 60326 # 108 Houston TX 77205-0326

GUGGENHEIMER, ELINOR, civic leader, writer; b. N.Y.C., Apr. 11, 1912; d. Nathan and Lillian (Fox) Coleman; m. Randolph Guggenheimer, June 2, 1932; children: Charles, Randolph Jr. Student, Vassar Coll., 1929-31; BA, Barnard Coll., 1938; DHL (hon.), Marymount-Manhattan Coll., 1987, CUNY Grad. Ctr., 1993. Dir. N.Y.C. Audio-Visual Tng. Office, 1943-44, Day Care Coun. of N.Y., N.Y.C., 1948-60; commr. City Planning, N.Y.C., 1960-67; on-air host, "Straight Talk" WOR-TV, N.Y.C., 1970-73; chmn. Def. Adv. Com. on Women in Svcs., Washington, 1963, 64; commr. N.Y.C. Dept. Consumer Affairs, 1974-78; dir. Coun. Sr. Ctrs. and Svcs., N.Y.C., 1978-83; dir., pres. Nat. Child Care Action Campaign, N.Y.C., 1983-92; lectr. Ctr. for Urban Affairs, New Sch. for Social Rsch., N.Y., 1965-70; tchr. Tchrs. Coll., Columbia U., 1969. Author: Planning for Parks, 1968, The Pleasure of Your Company, 1990; lyricist: Potholes, 1982. Bd. dirs. Community Svc. Soc., 1953—, Jewish Assn. Svcs. to the Aged, 1968—; pres. N.Y. Women's Agenda, 1991—. Recipient Finley award City Coll. Alumni, Spl. award City of N.Y. Human Resource Adminstrn., 1984; named one of 100 Most Important Women in U.S. Ladies Home Jour., 1980, 88, Louise Waterman Wise Woman of Yr. Nat. Coun. Jewish Women, 1974. Mem. Bus. & Profl. Women, Cosmopolitan Club, Women's City Club, City Club of N.Y. (bd. dirs. 1978-85), Lexington Democratic Club, Internat. Women's Forum (bd. dirs., founder, former pres.). Jewish. Office: New York Women's Agenda 218 W 40th St Rm 206 New York NY 10018

GUGLIELMO, ROSANNE, pediatrics nurse, sales executive; b. Sacramento, Jan. 9, 1959; d. Mauro and Maryetta (Englund) G.; m. (dec. June 1987); 1 child, Joseph Mauro Rucker-Guglielmo. AA with honors, Fresno City Coll., 1980, AS, 1984. RN, Calif., lic. vocat. nurse, Calif. Candy striper Bel Haven Convalescent Hosp., Fresno, Calif., 1972-76; nurses aide Hypanna Convalescent Hosp., Fresno, Calif., 1976-79; neonatal ICU staff nurse Valley Childrens Hosp., Fresno, Calif., 1979-90, post anesthesia care unit staff nurse, 1990—; quality assurance chair Valley Childrens Hosp., Fresno, 1991-95, intensive care nurse, 1979-95, risk mgmt. com. mem., safety com. mem., tchr. hosp. orientation program, 1993—; sales rep. Avon, 1981—; lectr. in field. Nursing scholar Valley Med. Ctr. Womens Aux., Fresno, 1978, 82, 83. Mem. Post Anesthesia Nurses Assn. Calif. Home: 878 E Bedford Ave Fresno CA 93720-2505 Office: Valley Childrens Hosp 3151 N Millbrook Ave Fresno CA 93703-1497

GUGLIUZZA, KRISTENE KOONTZ, transplant and general surgery educator; b. Siloam Springs, Ark., May 2, 1956; d. Lloyd Lawson Koontz Jr. and Helen Ruth (Camfield) Smith; m. Joseph Thomas Gugliuzza III, Sept. 3, 1989. AS, Lake Land Coll., Mattoon, Ill., 1977; BS with honors, Ea. Ill. U., Charleston, 1978; MD, U. Ill., Rockford, 1982. Diplomate Am. Bd. Surgery. Intern dept. surgery Tulane U. Med. Sch. and Affiliated Hosps., New Orleans, 1982-83, resident, 1983-87, fellow divsn. transplantation, 1987-89, instr. surgery, rsch. assoc. in surgery and transplantation, 1989-90; asst. prof. U. Tex. Med. Br., Galveston, 1990—; spl. fellow in pancreas transplantation U. Minn., Mpls., 1989; courtesy staff St. Mary's Hosp., Galveston, 1991—; recovery surgeon La. Organ Procurement Agy., New Orleans, 1989-90; presenter in field. Contbr. articles to med. jours. Fellow ACS; mem. AMA, Am. Diabetes Assn., Galveston County Med. Soc., Tex. Med. Assn., Cell Tansplant Soc., Am. Med. Women's Assn., Assn. Women Surgeons, Singleton Surg. Soc., Assn. Acad. Surgery, Transplantation Soc., Tex. Transplant Soc., Tulane Surg. Soc., Southwestern Surg. Conf., N.Y. Acad. Scis., Am. Soc. Gen. Surgeons, Am. Soc. Transplant Physicians. Office: U Tex Med Br Dept Surgery Rt E42 Galveston TX 77555

GUIDA, PAT, information broker, literature chemist; b. Highland Park, Mich., Aug. 30, 1929; d. Wilfred Bernard and Patricia Mary (Kelly) Graham; m. Alexander Herbert Bohr, May 25, 1948 (div. July 1965); m. Edward Silvio Guida, Aug. 29, 1965; children: Niels Graham, Eric Alexander. Student, Regis Coll., 1946-48, Rutgers U., 1952-55; BS cum laude, Fairleigh Dickinson U., 1961. Asst. librarian Warner-Lambert Research Inst., Morris Plains, N.J., 1961-64; librarian Reaction Motors Div. Thiokol, Denville, N.J., 1964-69; mgr., info. ctr. Foster D. Snell Div., Booz Allen & Hamilton Inc., Florham Park, N.J., 1969-80; pres. Pat Guida Assocs., Fairfield, N.J.; mem. Sci. Adv. Bd. EPA, Washington, 1978-82, Library Com. Chemists Club, N.Y.C., 1983-89. Editor: Chemical Digest, 1971-74. Pres. PTA, Sparta, N.J., 1959-60. Mem. AAAS, Am. Chem. Soc., N.Y. Acad. of Sci., Assn. Ind. Info. Profls., Chemists Club, Inst. Food Technologists (profl.). Office: 24 Spielman Rd Fairfield NJ 07004-3412

GUILDOO, KAREN LEWELLEN, guidance counselor; b. Hannibal, Mo., Apr. 27, 1956; d. Norris Vernon and Melva Nadine (Head) Lewellen; m. Denis Verne Guildoo, Apr. 23, 1978; 1 child, Crystal Brook. BSW, BA in Psychology, Columbia Coll., 1978, BA in Edn., 1980; postgrad., U. Mo. Cert. elem. tchr., secondary social studies tchr., Mo. Intercollegiate softball coach Columbia (Mo.) Coll., 1978-80; field rep. Am. Cancer Soc., Hannibal, 1980-81; elem. tchr. Marion County R-II Sch., Phila., Mo., 1981-85; elem. tchr. North Shelby Sch., Shelbyville, Mo., 1985-91, guidance counselor, 1991—; varsity girls basketball coach Marion County R-II Sch., 1981-82; community rep. divsn. family svcs. Permanency Planning Com., Shelbyville, 1992-93. Incentive for Sch. Excellence grantee Mo. Dept. Edn., 1989-90. Mem. North Shelby County Tchrs. Assn. (pres. 1989-90, v.p. 1988-89, treas. 1986-87), Mo. State Tchrs. Assn. Office: North Shelby Sch RR 2 Box 142 Hwy 15 N Shelbyville MO 63469-9659

GUILL, MARGARET FRANK, pediatrics educator, medical researcher; b. Atlanta, Jan. 18, 1948; d. Vernon Rhinehart and Margaret N. (Tichenor) Frank; m. Marshall Anderson Guill III, July 6, 1974; children: Daniel Marshall, Laura Elizabeth. BA, Agnes Scott Coll., 1969; MD, Med. Coll. Ga., 1972. Diplomate Am. Bd. Pediatrics, Am. Bd. Pediatrics subbd. pulmonology, Am. Bd. Allergy and Immunology, Nat. Bd. Med. Examiners. Resident in pediatrics Kaiser Found. Hosp., San Francisco, 1976-78, fellow in allergy, 1978-79; staff physician Waipahu (Hawaii) Clinic, 1973-76; intern in internal medicine Med. Coll. Ga., Augusta, 1973, resident in pediatrics, 1974, fellow in allergy and immunology, 1979-80, from asst. prof. to prof. pediatrics, 1981—; also chief sect. pediatric pulmonology and dir. Asthma Ctr. Med Coll. Ga., Augusta, dir. Cystic Fibrosis Ctr., 1990—; spkr. in field. Host Healthwatch weekly program WJBF-TV, 1982-83; contbr. articles to profl. jours. Active Reid Meml. Presbyn. Ch.; vol. tchr. Episcopal Day Sch., 1982-85; career day participant Acad. Richmond County, 1982, 83; med. advisor Augusta Area Allergy and Asthma Support Group, 1984-86; adv. bd. East Cen. br. Am. Lung Assn. Ga., 1985—, program of work com., 1987—, bd. dirs., 1987—, program coordinating com., 1990-91, exec. bd. 1989-91, adv. bd. Asthma Ski Mates Am., 1990; med. staff Camp Breathe Easy, 1985—. Recipient Mosby Book award, 1973; rsch. grantee BRSG, 1981-86, Del Labs., 1982, Merrell-Dow, 1983, 84, Elan Pharms., 1986, Am. Lung Assn. Ga., 1986, 87, Hollister-Stier, 1986, Fisons Corp., 1989, 91, 92, 93, 95, Med. Coll. ga., 1989, Am. Heart Assn., 1991, Gerentech, 1991-94, Miles, 1992. Fellow Am. Acad. Pediatrics, Am. Coll. Chest Physicians, Am. Acad. Allergy and Immunology, Am. Coll. Allergy, Am. Assn. Cert. Allergists; mem. AMA, Med. Assn. Ga., Richmond County Med. Soc., Allergy and Immunology soc. Ga., S.E. Allergy Assn. (Hal Davison award 1985), Am. Assn. Clin. Immunologists and Allergists, Ga. Thoracic Soc., Am. Thoracic Soc., Assn. for Care of Asthma, Alpha Omega Alpha. Home: 2247 Pickens Rd Augusta GA 30904-4462 Office: Med Coll Ga Dept Pediatrics Augusta GA 30912

GUILLEMETTE, GLORIA VIVIAN, dressmaker, designer; b. North Attleboro, Mass., June 27, 1929; d. Wilfred Anthony Roy and Sylviana (Bonnoyer) King; student Nat. Sch. Dress Design, 1976; m. Thomas William Guillemette, Mar. 24, 1963; children: Sylvia Marie, Katherine Anne, John Thomas. Machine operator dress mfg. cos., 1945-60; asst. to dressmaker and designer, Windsor, Conn., 1960-63; owner Mrs. G's Studio, Enfield, Conn., 1963-87; dir. Fashion Show, 1973, 76. Cub Scout commr. Boy Scouts Am., 1979-85; mem. Enfield Fair Rent Commn., 1979-87; justice of peace Conn., 1979—; mem. Republican Town Com., 1976-91; sec. United Meth. Women, 1977-82; mem. Enfield Fair Rent Commn., 1979-87, Presdl. Task Force, 1982-83. Club: Republican Women.

GUILLERMO, LINDA SUE, clinical social worker; b. Chgo., July 4, 1951; d. Triponio Pascua and Helen Elizabeth (Moskal) G.; B.A., U. Ill., Chgo., 1973, M.S.W., 1975, postgrad., 1980; postgrad. Jane Addams Coll. Social Work, 1980-82; Diplomate in clin. social work, 1987. Mktg. research interviewer Rabin Research Co., Chgo., 1970-73; mktg. research interviewer, coder Marcor Mktg. Research, Inc., Chgo., 1973-75; social work intern Child and Family Services, Chgo., 1973-74, Chgo. Bd. Edn., 1974-75; social worker, therapist child abuse and neglect, case investigator, case planning cons., social service program planner Ill. Dept. Children and Family Services, Chgo., 1975-78, social service program planner, contract negotiator, monitoring agt. Central Resources Contracts and Grants, 1978-79; real estate sales person Sentry Realty, Chgo., 1976—; social worker, therapist, program coordinator, casework supr. of child abuse assessment and intervention program, proposal writer Casa Central, Chgo., 1979-82, casework cons. of child abuse assessment and intervention program, proposal writer, program dir. and casework supr. of early intervention program, 1979-85; social worker, clin. supr. Chgo. Bd. Edn., 1985—; tng. specialist City Coll. of Chgo., 1980; adj. asso. researcher Asher Feren Law Office, Chgo., 1980-81. Treas. Greenleaf Condominium Assn., Chgo., 1980-81, sec., 1987-88, interim pres. 1988, regional rep. North Ill. Assn. of Sch. Social Workers, 1986-87, Lic. real estate salesperson, Ill. Mem. Nat. Assn. Social Workers (register clin. social workers), Acad. Cert. Social Workers, Ill. Cert. Lic. Social Workers, North Side Real Estate Bd. Home: 3550 S Lake St # 402 Chicago IL 60624-1906

GUILMET, GLENDA JEAN, artist; b. Tacoma, Wash., Mar. 28, 1957; d. Cody Calvin Black and Maria Isabel Rivera; m. George Michael Guilmet, May 24, 1980; children: Michelle Rene, Douglas James. Student, Clover Park Vocat. Tech. Inst., 1982-83; BA in Bus. Adminstrn., U. Puget Sound, 1981, BA in Art, 1989. Freelance photographer Tacoma, 1976—; women's sports photographer U. Puget Sound, Tacoma, 1977-78, asst. photographer, 1978-79; visual artist Tacoma, 1982—; photographic cons. Puyallup Tribe of Indians, Tacoma, 1984; on-call photographer Puyallup Tribal Health Authority, Tacoma, 1984-86; represented by Sacred Circle Gallery Am. Indian Art, Seattle, Mahler Fine Arts, Seattle, Instituto de Cultura Puertorriquena, Jayuya, Puerto Rico; instr. sculpture Tacoma Arts Commn., 1989; guest lectr. U. Puget Sound, 1990, 94; grants juror Artist Trust, Seattle, 1990; video festival juror Tacoma Mcpl. TV, 1990. Contbr. photographs to various publs.; one woman shows include Stage Door Gallery, Tacoma Little Theatre, 1993, Seattle U. Women's Ctr., 1994, Instituto de Cultura Puertorriquena, Jayuya, P.R., 1994; exhibited in group shows at Nat. Mus. of Women in the Arts, Washington, D.C., 1989-90, U. Puget Sound, Tacoma, 1989, Windhorse Gallery, Seattle, 1990, Chase Gallery, Spokane City Hall, 1990 Hanforth Gallery, Tacoma, 1990, 91, Washington State Capital Mus., Olympia, Washington, 1990, Foyer of the Okean Theater, Vladivostok, Russia, 1992, First Night Gallery, Tacoma, 1992, Sacred Cir. Gallery of Am. Indian Art, Seattle, 1993, Cunningham Gallery, U. Wash., 1993, Western Gallery, Western Wash. U., Bellingham, 1993, Seattle Art Mus., 1993, Bibliotheque Nationale de France, 1994, others; represented in permanent collections at Steilacoom (Wash.) Tribal Mus., Bibliotheque Nat. de France, also corp. collections. Recipient 1st Place Photography award, Crosscurrents Art Contest, 1988. Mem. Artist Trust, En Foco, Atlatl. Home and Studio: 1211 S Tyler Tacoma WA 98405

GUINN, JANET MARTIN, psychologist, consultant; b. Rapid City, S.D., Aug. 16, 1942; d. Verne Oliver and Carolyn Yetta (Clark) Martin; m. David Lee Guinn, Oct. 27, 1962 (div. June 1988); children: Cynthia Gail, Kevin Scott, Garrett Lee. BS in Psychology, U. Alaska, 1980, MS in Counseling Psychology, 1983; PhD in Clin. Psychology, Calif. Sch. Profl. Psychology, 1988. Lic. psychologist, Alaska, Nev. Pvt. practice Anchorage, 1988-93, Carson City and Reno, Nev., 1993—; clinician Behavior Medicine Cons., 1983-84; pvt. practice clinician, 1983-84; supr. Southcentral Counseling Ctr., Anchorage, 1984-85; cons. City/Borough of Juneau, Alaska, 1988; psychologist youth treatment program Alaska Psychiat. Inst., Anchorage, 1989-90; psychologist Nev. Mental Health Inst., Sparks, 1994—; cons. in field; cons. Alaska Small Bus. Coalition, Anchorage, 1990-92; reviewer Blors Corp. Contbr. articles to profl. jours. Active in politics. Mem. APA, Nev. Psychol. Assn., Internat. Neuropsychol. Soc., Rotary, Psi Chi. Republican. Office: 2470 Wrondel Way #111 Reno NV 89502

GUINNESS, KATHLEEN PELLEGRINO, counselor; b. Granville, N.Y., Aug. 2, 1949; d. John and Kathleen (Ryan) Pellegrino; divorced; children: Aubin, Brennan. BA with distinction, U. Wis., 1971; MEd, U. Vt., 1978; postgrad., Andover-Newton Theol. Sem., 1992. Lic. sch. counselor. Group supr. Elizabeth Lund Home, Burlington, Vt., 1972-73; tchr., house parent Hampshire Country Sch., Rindge, N.H., 1973-75; adminstrv. asst. Vt. Dental Care Program, Burlington, 1975-76; grad. teaching asst. U. Vt., Burlington, 1976-78; guidance counselor Telstar Regional High Sch., Bethel, Maine, 1978-80; elem. sch. counselor Rutland S.W. Sup. Union, Poultney, Vt., 1985—, coord. drug-free schs., 1993—, facilitator active parenting, 1993-94; adj. psychology faculty St. Joseph the Provider, Rutland, Vt., 1981, Gr. Mt. Coll., Poultney, 1982, C.C. of Vt., Rutland, 1984. chair program com. Rutland Unitarian U.-Fellowship, 1989—, mem. peace and social action com., 1989—. Grad. fellow U. Vt., 1976-78. Mem. NEA, Vt. Counselor's Assn. Democrat. Office: Poultney Elem Sch Allen Ter Poultney VT 05764

GUINTHER, CHRISTINE LOUISE, special education educator, staff development facilitator; b. Chgo., Oct. 27, 1949; d. William Joseph and Olga (Sandul) Bacha; m. Paul H. Demper, July 22, 1972 (div. 1987); m. William Robert Guinther, June 25, 1988. BS in Edn., Ill. State U., 1971; MA in Exceptional Child Edn., Ohio State U., 1974. Cert. tchr., Mo. Resource tchr. for learning disabled students Palatine (Ill.) Community Consol. Sch. Dist. #15, 1971-72, Scioto-Darby City Schs., Hilliard, Ohio, 1972-76, Francis Howell Sch. Dist., St. Charles, Mo., 1976—. Mem. NEA (human rels. com. 1983—, bd. dirs. 1993—), ACLU, ASCD, Mo. NEA (bd. dirs. 1985-91, human rels. com. 1983—, exec. com. 1993—), Coun. Exceptional Children (divsn. learning disabilities), Nat. Staff Devel. Coun., Francis Howell Edn. Assn. (pres. 1981-82), Delta Kappa Gamma. Methodist. Home: 161 Castlewood Rd Ballwin MO 63021-7217

GUION, LIDA RODMAN, educator; b. Greenville, S.C., Sept. 28, 1951; d. Thomas Hyman and Mary Carter (Whitehurst) G. AA, Durham County C.C., 1979; BA, U. N.C., 1973; MA, San Francisco State U., 1994. Registered respiratory therapist. Staff therapist U. N.C. Meml. Hosp., Chapel Hill, 1979-80; edn. dir., clin. coord. St. Luke's Hosp., San Francisco, 1981—; faculty respiratory therapy dept. Skyline Coll., San Bruno, Calif., 1987—; mem. adv. bd. Skyline Coll. Respiratory Therapy, 1992—. Mem. Am. Assn. Respiratory Care, Am. Soc. Aging, Calif. Pulmonary Rehab. Home: 143 Stillings Ave San Francisco CA 94131 Office: St Lukes Hosp Respiratory Care 3555 Army St San Francisco CA 94110

GUIRL, W. SUE, prison warden; b. Paris, Tex., Dec. 8, 1943; d. Robert E. and Elizabeth (Schrimsher) Tingle; m. Jimmy McGill, Apr. 17, 1959 (div. 1980); m. Russ Guirl, Apr. 7, 1987; children: Laurie Klindgest, Jim McGill Jr. BBA, Memphis State U., 1975, MS, 1984. Lic. profl. counselor. Supr. Salvation Army Halfway House, Memphis, 1982-85; counselor Juvenile Ct. Shelby County, Memphis, 1985-87; work release supr. women's unit Ark. Dept. Corrections, Pine Bluff, 1987-93; warden Mississippi County Work Release Ctr. Ark. Dept. Corrections, Luxura, 1993—. Scholar Alpha Beta Psi, 1973. Mem. Am. Correction Assn., So. States Corrections Assn. Mem. Calvary Bapt. Ch. Office: Ark Dept Corrections MSCW/R PO Box 10 Luxora AR 72358-0010

GUISEWITE, CATHY LEE, cartoonist; b. Dayton, Ohio, Sept. 5, 1950; d. William Lee and Anne (Duly) G. BA in English, U. Mich., 1972; LHD (hon.), R.I. Coll., 1979, Eastern Mich. U., 1981. Writer Campbell-Ewald Advt., Detroit, 1972-73; writer Norman Prady, Ltd., Detroit, 1973-74, W.B. Doner & Co., Advt., Southfield, Mich., 1974-75; group supr. W.B. Doner & Co., Advt., 1975-76, v.p., 1976-77; creator, writer, artist Cathy comic strip Universal Press Syndicate, Mission, Kans., 1976—. Author, artist: The Cathy Chronicles, 1978, What Do You Mean, I Still Don't Have Equal Rights??!!, 1980, What's a Nice Single Girl Doing with a Double Bed?!!, 1981, I Think I'm Having a Relationship with a Blueberry Pie!, 1981, It Must Be Love, My Face Is Breaking Out, 1982, Another Saturday Night of Wild and Reckless Abandon, 1982, Cathy's Valentine's Day Survival Book, How to Live through Another February 14, 1982, How to Get Rich, Fall in Love, Lose Weight, and Solve all Your Problems by Saying "NO", 1983, Eat Your Way to a Better Relationship, 1983, A Mouthful of Breath Mints and No One to Kiss, 1983, Climb Every Mountain, Bounce Every Check, 1983, Men Should Come with Instruction Booklets, 1984, Wake Me Up When I'm a Size 5, 1985, Thin Thighs in Thirty Years, 1986, A Hand to Hold, An Opinion to Reject, 1987, Why Do the Right Words Always Come Out of the Wrong Mouth?, 1988, My Granddaughter Has Fleas, 1989, $14 in the Bank and a $200 Face in My Purse, 1990, Reflections (A Fifteenth Anniversary Collection), 1991, Only Love can Break a Heart, but a Shoe Sale Can Come Close, 1992, Revelations From a 45-Pound Purse, 1993; TV work includes 3 animated Cathy spls. (Emmy award 1987). Recipient Reuben award Nat. Cartoonists Soc., 1992. Office: Universal Press Syndicate 4900 Main St Kansas City MO 64112-2644

GULBRANDSEN, NATALIE WEBBER, religious association administrator; b. Beverly, Mass., July 7, 1919; d. Arthur Hammond and Kathryn Mary (Doherty) Webber; m. Melvin H. Gulbrandsen, June 19, 1943 (dec. Feb. 1991); children: Karen Ann Bean, Linda Jean Goldsmith, Eric Christian, Ellen Dale Williams, Kristin Jane Morgan. BA, Bates Coll., 1942; HDL, Meadville/Lombard Theol. Sch., Chgo., 1991. Social worker Bur. Child Welfare, Bangor, Maine; moderator Unitarian Universalist Assn., Boston, 1985-93. Exec. dir. Girl Scouts U.S., Belmont, Mass., 1943-45, leader 1941-44, 52-65, leadership trainer 1946-63, bd. dirs., Wellesley, Mass., 1950-63, pres. 1960-63; mem. permanent sch. accomodations com., Wellesley, 1970-76, Wellesley Youth Commn., 1968-70, Wellesley town meeting, 1967-91; trustee Wellesley Human Relations Service, 1964-76, pres. 1973-76; bd. dirs. Newton Wellesley Weston Needham Area Mental Health Assn., 1975-78, Am. Field Service, 1964-70; co-chair METCO Program of Wellesley, 1965-69; trustee Unitarian Universalist Women's Fedn., 1971-81, pres. 1977-81. Recipient Wellesley Ctr. Community award, 1981. Mem. Boston Bates Alumnae Assn. (pres. 1966-69), Internat. Assn. Religious Freedom (mem. council 1981-90, v.p. 1990-93, pres. 1993-96). Lodge: Sons of Norway. Home: 35 Riverdale Rd Wellesley MA 02181-1625 Office: Internat Assn for Religious Freedom, 2 Market St, Oxford 0X1 3EF, England

GULICK, DEBORAH JEAN, elementary education educator; b. Edenton, N.C., Oct. 21, 1953; d. Lyman Mark and Rena (Bakker) G. AA, Centenary Coll., Hackettstown, N.J., 1974; BA, Oral Roberts U., 1976; MA, Fairleigh Dickinson U., 1981. Cert. elem. and mid. sch. tchr., K-12 supr., N.J. Tchr. Mt. Olive Twp. Bd. Edn., Budd Lake, N.J., 1976—. Editor (newsletter) Mountain View News, 1986—. Mem. Chancel Choir, United Presbyn. Ch., Flanders, N.J., 1988-92, Sr. Choir, Hacketts-Town, N.J., 1993—. Recipient Gov.'s Tchr. Recognition award State of N.J., 1991. Mem. Edn. Assn. Mt. Olive (treas. 1986-88), Morris County Coun. Edn. Assn. (rep. 1987-93). Home: 25A Rockport Rd Hackettstown NJ 07840 Office: Mountain View Sch Cloverhill Dr Flanders NJ 07836

GULICK, DONNA MARIE, accountant; b. N.Y.C., Jan. 25, 1956; d. H.R. and M.G. Gulick. MBA, Fairleigh Dickinson U., 1981, MS, 1986. Programmer Wash. State U., Pullman, 1983; acctg. analyst IBM, Tarrytown, N.Y., 1983-89, program mgr., 1989-91; program mgr. long-term disability plan IBM, Purchase, N.Y., 1991-92; staff acctg. analyst labor charges IBM, Tarrytown, N.Y., 1992-94; project mgr. IBM, Somers, N.Y., 1994—. Mem. Assn. MBA Execs., ACM, Inst. of IEEE, Nat. Assn. Unknown Players, Delta Mu Delta. Roman Catholic. Home: 395 Hwy 28 Bridgewater NJ 08807 Office: IBM Rt 100 Somers NY 10589

GULLACE, MARLENE FRANCES, systems analyst, programmer, consultant; b. Ft. Belvoir, Va., Jan. 12, 1952; d. Amerigo Francis and Martha Arlene (Wise) Guy; m. Gerald Lynn Tolley, June 26, 1970 (div. Nov. 1974); 1 child, Gerald Lynn Tolley Jr.; m. Salvatore Gullace, Nov. 19, 1976 (div. Apr. 1991). AA in Pre-Law, Cochise Coll., 1979; BA in Polit. Sci., U. Ariz., 1982; AA in Computer Sci., Bus., Chaparral Coll., 1985. Realtor, entrepreneur, inventor Sierra Vista, Ariz., 1977-84; ADP instr. Chaparral Coll., Tucson, 1985; model Barbizon, Tucson, 1986-87; clk. HUD/FHA, Tucson, 1987-88; computer programmer DOD Inspector Gen., Arlington, 1988-89; programmer analyst U.S. Army Corps of Engrs., USAF, Washington, 1989-91, Calibre Systems Inc., Falls Church, Va., 1991; cons., systems analyst/programmer EDP, Vienna, Va., 1991-93; info. engr. Ogden Govt. Svcs., Vienna, 1993—; owner Second Wind Art Studio and Gallery. Patented toy, registered trademark. Realtor assoc. Cochise County Bd. Realtors, 1977-84. Mem. Assn. for Computing Machinery, IEEE, NAFE, IPA, Inst. Noetic Scis., Fed. Women's Program at SBA (sec. 1976). Methodist. Home: 3327 Piney Ridge Ct Herndon VA 22071

GULLATT, JANE, state legislator; b. Phenix City, Ala., Oct. 6, 1932; d. Claude Bertram Jr. and Julia (Hornsby) G. AB, U. Ala., Tuscaloosa, 1954.

News reporter The Tuscaloosa News, 1954-58, The Pensacola (Fla.) News, 1958-60, The Columbus (Ga.) Enquirer, 1960-66; editor, pub. The Phenix Citizen, Phenix City, Ala., 1966-74; at large counciler Phenix City Coun., 1977-80; mayor City of Phenix City, 1981-89; mem. Ala. Ho. of Reps., Montgomery, 1989-94, mem. joint hwy. com., legis coun., chmn. local govt. com., 1989-94. Recipient Best Column award Ala. Press Assn., Tuscaloosa, 1968; named Woman of Achievement Concharty coun. Girl Scouts U.S.A., Columbus, 1988, Citizen of Yr., Kiwanis Club, Phenix City, 1989. Mem. Rotary Club. Democrat. Methodist.

GULLEDGE, KAREN STONE, educator, administrator; b. Fayetteville, N.C., Feb. 3, 1941; d. Malcolm Clarence and Clara (Davis) Stone; m. Parker Lee Gulledge Jr, Oct. 17, 1964. BA, St. Andrews Presbyn. Coll., Laurinburg, N.C., 1963; MA, East Carolina U., 1979; EdD, Nova U., 1986. Social worker Lee County, Sanford, N.C., 1963-64; tchr. Asheboro (N.C.) City Schs., 1964-67, Winston-Salem (N.C.)/Forsyth County Schs., 1967-70; research analyst N.C. Dept. Pub. Instrn., Raleigh, 1971-76, sch. planning cons., 1976-89, dir. sch. planning, 1989—; chmn. N.C. Elem. Commn. of So. Assn. Colls. and Schs., 1989-95; leader profl. seminars; spkr. in field. Trustee St. Andrews Coll. Recipient Outstanding Educator award, 1992. Mem. Coun. Ednl. Facility Planners (pres. 1995), Delta Kappa Gamma. Democrat. Home: 7405 Fiesta Way Raleigh NC 27615-3325 Office: Divsn Sch Planning Edn Bldg 301 N Wilmington St Raleigh NC 27601-2825

GULLETTE, ETHEL MAE BISHOP (ETHEL MAE BISHOP), pianist; b. St. Paul, Mar. 29, 1908; d. Clarence Eugene and Alma (Beckman) Bishop; m. William Brandon Gullette, Sept. 5, 1936; children: Ethel Mae, Charlene Ann. MusB, MacPhail Sch. Music, Mpls., 1928; BA, U. Minn., 1931; diploma, Juilliard Sch. Music, 1936; pvt. study piano with Donald N. Ferguson, James Friskin. Pianist and accompanist in concerts and radio appearances, Midwest U.S., 1925-33; voice accompanist Juilliard Sch. Music, also pvt. piano tchr., N.Y.C., 1933-47; duo-pianist, accompanist Fairfield County, Conn., 1951-89, also Hartford, Conn., N.J. and N.Y.C., 1967-89; concert pianist, Ea. U.S., 1953-89; 30 concerts Fairfield Hills Hosp., New Town, Conn., 1957-71; concerts, Savannah, Ga., Hilton Head Island and Beaufort, S.C., 1972; accompanist Darien Troupers, 1968, 69; New Canaan High Sch. Summer Theater, 1972-73; concert appearances include Dallas, 1983, Scottsdale, Ariz., 1985, Lebanon, Bridgeport, Greenwich, New Canaan, Norwalk and Darien, Conn., 1980-89; mem. New Canaan Piano Quartet, 1960-68, New Canaan Town Players, 1952-88, accompanist, 1958-63, 73; mem.; accompanist Nutmeg Music Theatre, 1957-61, Westport, Ct.; Demi-Opera Co., Brookfield Summer Theatre, Conn., 1961, many others. Bd. govs., rehearsal pianist Norwalk Symphony Orch., 1955-62; mem. New Canaan Community Concerts Assn., 1954-88, membership chmn., 1967-69, bd. dirs. 1961-69, 84-88; active fund drives charitable orgns.; co-pres. New Canaan High Sch. Parent's Coun., 1964-65; active New Canaan Congregational Ch., also mem. music com., 1994. Recipient Hon. Golden Eaglet award Southwestern Coun. Girl Scouts U.S.A., 1985; also citations for work in Am. Cancer Soc. and ARC drives. Mem. N.Y. Singing Tchrs. Assn., New Canaan Hist. Soc. (photographer gown exhibits 1968-86), Darien Community Assn. (bd. dirs. 1962-64, chmn. duo piano group 1962-64, 82-84, sec. duo piano group 1984-86), New Canaan Libr., New Canaan Audubon Soc., Norwalk Symphony Orch. Women's Assn. (mem. bd. 1976-82, life mem.), Am. Shakespeare Guild, AAUW (charter 1970—, named Outstanding Mem. Conn. chpt. 1980, life mem., nat. named Gift fellowship 1988), Friends N.Y. Philharm. Orch. (New Canaan chmn. 1968-71), Fairfield County Panhellenic Coun., Juilliard Alumni Assn., U. Minn. Alumni Assn. (past dir. N.Y.), New Canaan Community Concerts Assn. (hon. life, Membership and Svc. award 1974, citation for 25 yrs. outstanding achievements 1979), Mu Phi Epsilon (recognition as 50 yr. mem. 1977), Delta Zeta (alumni charter; pres. local alumnae chpt. 1961-63, treas. 1982-84; named Outstanding New Eng. Alumna 1980, Nat. Woman of Yr. 1982; recipient Golden Rose 50 yr. mem. award 1981, New Eng. Cert. Achievement, 1989, Very Spl. Delta Zeta Alumna award, 1990; ann. alumna svc. award established in her name by Fairfield County chpt. 1983). Clubs: Schubert (St. Paul); Atlantic Beach (L.I., N.Y.); Schubert of Fairfield County (duo piano group sec. 1980-82 life mem.). Home: 225 Essex Mdws Essex CT 06426-1524

GULLETTE, RHONDA YUVONNE, logistic management specialist; b. Dayton, Ohio, Nov. 25, 1962; d. Peter M. and Helen L. (Baker) G. BS, Central State U., Wilberforce, Ohio, 1986. Cert. in acquisition logistics, program mgr.; lic. real estate salesperson. Logistics mgmt. specialist Wright-Patterson AFB, Ohio, 1986—; beauty cons. Mary Kay Cosmetics, 1993; realtor Century 21, 1990. Named one of Outstanding Young Women in Am., 1991; recipient 3rd runner up prize Jocelyns Modeling Contest, 1st runner up Miss Hemisphere, Top Ten Miss Heart of Ohio; participant in beauty contests. Mem. Blacks in Govt., Federally Employed Women, Nat. Bd. Realtors, Ohio Bd. Realtors, Dayton Bd. Realtors, Kappa Alpha Psi, Delta Sigma Theta (Alpha Psi scholarship). Democrat. Baptist. Home: PO Box 33763 Dayton OH 45433-0763

GULLEY, JOAN LONG, banker; b. Balt., Sept. 10, 1947; d. Thomas F. and Florence (Waldron) Long; m. Philip Gordon Gulley, aug. 2, 1969; 1 child, Colin Jason. BA, U. Rochester, 1969; postgrad., Harvard U., 1985. Analyst U.S. Dept. Commerce, Washington, 1969-70, Fed. Res. Bd., Washington, 1970-74; sr. analyst 5, Washington, 1979-81; asst. v.p. Fed. Res. Bank Boston, 1975-79, v.p., 1981-83; sr. v.p. 5, 1983-86; exec. v.p. The Mass. Co., Boston, 1986-94, pres., CEO, 1994—, also bd. dirs. Bd. dirs. YMCA Greater Boston. Mem. Algonquin Club, Phi Beta Kappa. Office: The Mass Co 125 High St Boston MA 02110

GULLIKSON, ANGELA KATHLEEN, quality management analyst; b. Aberdeen, S.D., Nov. 30, 1936; d. Albert H. and Winifred K. (Smith) G. Nursing diploma, Presentation Sch. Nursing, Aberdeen, 1957; student, SUNY, Albany, 1984—, U. Wis., 1984—. Cert. healthcare quality profl. Healthcare Quality Cert. Bd. Staff nurse Gettysburg (S.D.) Hosp., 1957-58, Mercy Hosp., Toledo, 1959-61; staff nurse William S. Middleton Meml. Vets. Hosp., Madison, 1961-69, head nurse, 1969-87, quality mgmt. analyst, 1987—. Mem. Nat. Assn. for Healthcare Quality, Wis. Assn. for Healthcare Quality, City-Wide Quality Assurance Assn. (chairperson 1990-91). Home: 722 Sauk Ridge Trl Madison WI 53705-1157 Office: Wm S Middleton Meml Vets Hosp 2500 Overlook Ter Madison WI 53705-2286

GULYA, AINA JULIANNA, neurotologist, surgeon, educator; b. Syracuse, N.Y., Feb. 3, 1953; d. Aladar and Sylvia E. Gulya; m. William R. Wilson, May 21, 1983. AB cum laude, Yale Coll., 1974; MD with distinction, U. Rochester, 1978. Intern, jr. resident in gen. surgery Beth Israel Hosp., Boston, 1978-80; resident in otolaryngology Mass. Eye & Ear Infirmary, Boston, 1980-83; fellow in otology/neurotology Bapt. Hosp., Nashville, 1983-84; asst. prof. surgery George Washington U., Washington, 1984-87; fellow otology/neurotology Ear Found., Nashville, 1983-84, assoc. prof. surgery, 1987-90; assoc. prof. otolaryngology and head and neck surgery Georgetown U., Washington, 1990-94, prof. otolaryngology and head and neck surgery, 1994—. Co-author: Anatomy of the Temporal Bone With Surgical Implications, 1986, 95; assoc. editor Am. Jour. Otology, 1989—. Recipient Libr. award Rochester Acad. Medicine, 1975, Honor award Am. Acad. Otolaryngology-Head and Neck Surgery, 1991. Mem. Am. Otological Soc. (coun. 1993—), Am. Neurotology Soc. (coord. for continuing med. edn. 1990—), Washington Hearing and Speech Soc. (bd. dirs. 1988—). Office: Dept Otolaryngology-Head & Neck Surgery 3800 Reservoir Rd NW Washington DC 20007

GULYA, BRIGITTA RIANNA, federal government official; b. Rochester, N.Y., May 17, 1965; d. Aladar and Sylvia (Elerts) G. BA magna cum laude, Harvard U., 1986; JD, U. Chgo., 1989; LLM, Georgetown U., 1994. Bar: Ill. 1989, D.C. 1990, U.S. Tax Ct., U.S. Ct. Appeals (Fed. cir.), U.S. Ct. Internat. Trade, U.S. Supreme Ct. Assoc. Fried, Frank, Harris, Shriver & Jacobson, Washington, 1989-90, Dewey Ballantine, Washington, 1990-94; tax counsel U.S. Senate Fin. Com., Washington, 1994—; bd. dirs. Tax Coalition. Mem. Harvard Club of Washington (bd. dirs.). Home: 1530 N Key Blvd # 1132 Arlington VA 22209 Office: US Senate Fin Com 219 Dirksen Senate Office Bldg Washington DC 20510

GUMM, JANET MARGARET, accountant, lawyer; b. Indpls., May 1, 1942; d. Rudolph and Catherine Margaret (Cleary) Stumpp; m. William H. Gumm, Jan. 9, 1965; children: William, Mary, James. BA in Philosophy, Marian Coll., 1964, BS in Acctg., 1976; JD with honors, IIT, 1992. Bar: Ill. 1992; CPA, Ind.; CMA. Acct. Boyd, Dehmel & Lucas, Indpls., 1978-83; acct. state income tax Ind. Bell, Indpls., 1983-85; acct. state & local tax Ameritech, Chgo., 1985-93, acct. state and fed. income tax, 1993-95; mgr. state and local taxes WMX Techs., Inc., Oak Brook, Ill., 1995—; spkr. in field. Exec. editor Chgo. Kent Law Rev., 1989-91. Mem. ABA, AICPAs, Ind. CPA Soc., Am. Soc. Women in Acctg., Ill. Bar Assn., Chgo. Bar Assn., Mensa. Office: WMX Techs Inc 3003 Butterfield Rd Oak Brook IL 60521

GUMMELT, JUDY PINGO CHANG, psychologist; b. Tainan, Taiwan, Jan. 10, 1955; came to U.S., 1958; d. Joseph Jui-fu and Mary Hsueh-Mei (Yang) Chang; m. Michael Harold Gummelt, June 19, 1976 (div. May 2, 1989); children: Michael Chang Gummelt, Holly Chang Gummelt. BA in Psychology, U. Vt., 1976; grad., NYU, 1984, D of Psychology, 1990. Cert. sch. psychologist, N.Y.; lic. psychologist, N.Y. state. Psychotherapy trainee N.Y.C., 1984-85; psychologist in tng. P.S. 163 Bd. of Edn., N.Y.C., 1984-85, Chips Warm Line, N.Y.C., 1984-86, Forest Glen Sch., Bloomfield, N.J., 1985-86, Elizabeth (N.J.) Gen. Med. Ctr., 1986-87; psychology intern dept. child psychiatry St. Luke's/Roosevelt Hosp., N.Y.C., 1987-88, psychology intern second yr., 1988-89, psychologist CAPA program, 1989-92; psychologist, cons. Freedom Inst., N.Y.C., 1990—; psychologist pvt. practice N.Y.C., 1992—. Contbr. scholarly papers to profl. publs. Mem. APA, Nat. Assn. Sch. Psychologists. Home: 508 E 79th St Apt 5B New York NY 10021-1525 Office: 16 E 79th St # 41 New York NY 10021-0150

GUMPPERT, KARELLA ANN, federal government official; b. N.Y.C., Oct. 16, 1942; d. Leonard Lewis and Florence M. Gumppert. AB in Polit. Sci., George Washington U., 1963, postgrad., 1963-65. Lic. in realty sales, Md. Editor to bd. govs. Fed. Res. Sys., Washington, 1966-67; editorial asst. Jour. of Maritime Law and Commerce, N.Y.C., 1969-71; adminstr. NYU Law Sch., N.Y.C., 1968-73; law asst. White & Case and other firms, N.Y.C., Boston, Hartford, 1974-80; vol. asst. U.S. Presdl. Inaugural Com., Washington, 1981; confidential asst. The White House Staff, Washington, 1981; publs. asst. Congressional Budget Office, Washington, 1982-84; credit summarizer Xerox Corp., Arlington, Va., 1985-86; asst. in govtl. affairs Mut. Omaha, Washngton, 1988; land law adjudicator U.S. Dept. Interior, Anchorage, 1991—. Author, illustrator: (children's book) An Adventure, 1949; founding editor lit. mag. Springboard, 1959; mem. editorial bd. newspaper Amicus Curiae, 1964-65. Charity asst. Girl Scouts U.S.A., N.Y.C., 1952-54, Christian Assn., N.Y.C., 1959-61, Wesley Found., Washington, 1962-63; vol. asst. N.Y. Rep. County Com., 1959-62, Conn. Reps. State Com., Hartford, 1979-80. Recipient numerous scholarships, 1957-60. Mem. NAFE, Nat. Trust for Hist. Preservation, Nat. Audubon Soc., Women's Nat. Rep. Club, Subscribers of Anchorage Symphony Orch.

GUNDERSEN, ALLISON MAUREEN, massage therapist, intercultural consultant; b. Syracuse, N.Y., Oct. 14, 1959; d. Jerrold Paul and Rosemarie Noël (Harvey) G. AB, Cornell U., 1981; postgrad., NYU, 1982-83, Swedish Inst., 1991, Lesley Coll., 1994—. Assoc. Morgan Stanley & Co., N.Y.C., 1981-84, sr. assoc., 1985-86; project mgr. Morgan Stanley Internat., Tokyo, 1987-88; cons. Computech Cons. Svcs., Winchester, N.J., 1989-90; pres. Woman About Globe, Ltd., N.Y.C., 1990-93; assoc. Cambridge (Mass.) Myotherapy, 1992—; cons. Nomura Rsch. Inst. Am., N.Y.C., 1989-90. Mem. NAFE, NOW (dir. membership processing N.Y.C. 1990), Internat. Feminists Japan (coord. 1987-88), Am. Massage Therapists Assn., Soc. Intercultural Educators, Trainers and Rschrs. Democrat.

GUNDERSON, JUDITH KEEFER, golf association executive; b. Charleroi, Pa., May 25, 1939; d. John R. and Irene G. (Gaskill) Keefer; student public schs., Uniontown, Pa.; m. Jerry L. Gunderson, Mar. 19, 1971; children: Jamie L., Jeff S.; stepchildren: Todd G. (dec.), Marc W., Bookkeeper, Fayette Nat. Bank, 1957-59, gen. ledger bookkeeper, 1960-63; head bookkeeper First Nat. Bank Broward, 1963-64; bookkeeper Ruthenberg Homes, Inc., 1966-69; bookkeeper, asst. sec./treas. Pennisular Properties, Inc. subs. Investors Diversified Svcs. Properties, Mpls., 1969-72; comptr., pres. Am. Golf Fla., Inc., dba Golf and Tennis World, Deerfield Beach, 1972-89, stockholder, 1992—; sales assoc. Realty Brokers Internat., Inc., 1990; former sec., treas. Internat. Golf, Inc., now stockholder; dir. Mary Kay Cosmetics, county committeewoman, Broward County, Fla., 1965-66; ind. agt. personal and family devel. seminars Slight Edge Enterprises, Inc.; active Performing Arts Ctr. Energetic Resourceful Supporters. Mem. NAFE, Internat. Platform Assn., Nat. Golf Found., C. of C., Beta Sigma Phi.

GUNDY, DOLORES ELAINE, artists representative; b. Reading, Pa., July 20, 1949; d. James Franklin and Mildred Emma (Moore) Miller; m. Gregory Samuel Gundy, Feb. 21, 1970 (div. 1992); 1 child, Derek Lee. Student, West Chester State Coll., 1970. Picture framer Soule Glass Industries, Rockland, Maine, 1977-79; owner Huston-Tuttle and Gallery One, Rockland, 1979-92; artists' rep. Lori Enterprises, Belgrade, Maine, 1993—; mem. coun. of advisors Farnsworth Art Mus., Rockland, 1991-94. Daffodil Days promoter Am. Cancer Soc., Rockland, 1985-90; chmn. Penobscot Bay chpt. ARC, Rockland, 1990-92. Home: Grandview Dr Belgrade ME 04917-0060

GUNDY, FRANCES DARNELL, librarian, healthcare manager; b. Muskegon, Mich., Aug. 19, 1947; d. Joseph Leo and Olaverne (Mathis) Merle; m. Russell Norman Gundy, Sept. 18, 1965 (div. 1985); 1 child, Raymond Joseph. AS, Aquinas Coll., 1988, BA, 1991; MLS, Wayne State U., 1993. Owner, pres. Helpmates, Inc., Muskegon, 1992—. Active Mich. Strategic Planning Com., Muskegon Cmty. Health Project. Mem. ALA (nat. chair grassroots com., Specialized Svcs. Coordination com.), AAUW, Nat. Assn. for Self-Employed, Am. Bus. Club, Network Small Bus. Owners, Intellectual Freedom Roundtable, Libr. Info. and Tech. Assn., Assn. Libr. Collections and Tech. Svcs., Mich. Libr. Assn., Pub. Libr. Assn. Home: 3755 Henry St Muskegon MI 49441-4752

GUNKEL, KATHY TREIBLE, women's health nurse; b. Cherry Point, N.C., Oct. 22, 1955; d. Herbert Robert and Nancy Lou (Tomkins) Treible; m. Robert F. Gunkel Jr., May 19, 1978; 1 child, Robert F. III. AAS, Brookdale Commun. Coll., Lincroft, N.J., 1982; postgrad., U. Pa., 1987. Cert. ob-gyn. nurse practitioner. Staff nurse Riverview Hosp., Red Bank, N.J., 1982-83; asst. dir. client svcs. Planned Parenthood, Shrewsbury, N.J., 1983-86, dir. client svcs., 1986-93, assoc. dir., 1993—; advisor N.J. Bd. Nursing, Newark, 1991; speaker in field. Mem. NAACOG, N.J. State Nurses Assn., Assn. Reproductive Health Profls., Nat. Assn. Nurse Practitioners in Reproductive Health, Family Planning Assn. N.J. (regulatory affairs com. 1990—). Home: 78 Kings Hwy Middletown NJ 07748-2027 Office: Planned Parenthood PO Box 95 69 Newman Springs Rd E Shrewsbury NJ 07702-4038

GUNN, CHRISTY HOWARD, actuary; b. Evanston, Ill., Oct. 6, 1954; d. Coydel Sandford and Ethel Marie (Franklin) Howard; children: Raymond Christopher, Justin Howard. BA, Oberlin Coll., 1976; MS in Stats., Carnegie Mellon U., 1979, MS in Pub. Policy and Mgmt., 1979. Analyst CNA, Chgo., 1979-83, mgr. comml. property pricing, 1983-85, mgr. profl. liability res. and ops. analysis, 1985-92, asst. v.p. splty. lines reserving and ops. analysis, 1993—. Trustee Prairie State Coll. Fellow Casualty Actuarial Soc.; mem. Am. Acad. Actuaries. Office: CNA CNA Plaza Chicago IL 60685

GUNN, MARY ELIZABETH, retired English language educator; b. Great Bend, Kans., July 21, 1914; d. Ernest E. and Elisabeth (Wesley) Eppstein; m. Charles Leonard Gunn, Sept. 13, 1936 (dec. Apr. 1985); 1 child, Charles Douglas. AB, Ft. Hays State U., 1935, BS in Edn., 1936, MA, 1967. Tchr. English Unified Sch. Dist. 428, Great Bend, 1963-80; tchr. English Barton County C.C., Great Bend, 1977-84, tchr. adult edn., 1985-87, tchr. ESL, 1988-94; ret., 1994. Named Fellow Conf. on Am. Studies, De Pauw U., 1969. Mem. AAUW (Outstanding Mem. 1991), NEA, Bus. and Profl. Women (Woman of Yr. 1974), Kans. Adult Edn. Assn. (Master Adult Educator 1986), Kans. Assn. Tchrs. English, PEO, Delta Kappa Gamma, Alpha Sigma Alpha. Democrat. Mem. United Ch. of Christ. Home: 3009 16th St Great Bend KS 67530-3705

GUNN, SANDRA JOYCE, musician and church lay leader; b. Allentown, Pa., Oct. 30, 1951; d. Hilbert Guy and Joyce Marie (Mantz) Snyder; m. Bruce Myron Gunn, Oct. 17, 1981. BS in Music Edn., Lebanon Valley Coll, 1973. Cert. instrumental and vocal music tchr. Handbell dir. Calvary Presbyn. Ch., Riverton, N.J., 1983-87; dir. music (choir and instruments) Broad St. United Meth. Ch., Burlington, N.J., 1987—; part-time bookkeeper Lippincott Fuel Co., Delanco, N.J., 1985-92; ch. auditor Calvary Presbyn. Ch., Riverton, 1988, 91; chmn. Christian edn., elder Calvary Presbyn. Ch., Riverton, 1979-82; youth advisor Broad St. United Meth. Ch., 1987, chmn. Ann. Choir Festival, 1990—; chmn. worship com. Broad St. United Meth. Ch., Burlington, 1991—, coord. youth Sunday and Christmas Eve svcs., 1989—; asst. dir. N.J. Meth. Chorale for Gr. Britain concert tour, 1991. Treas. Porch Club, Riverton, 1983-85; sec. Riverton Rep. Club, 1985-86; mem. Riverton Improvement Com., 1989: pres. N.J. Women's Clubs, Riverton, 1985-90, dir. chorus, 1992—: instr. music appreciation course Burlington County Continuing Edn. Program, 1991. Home: 808 Main St Riverton NJ 08077-1707 Office: Broad St United Meth Ch 36 E Broad St Burlington NJ 08016-1631

GUNN, SUSAN KATHIE GOETZ, cable, public relations, publishing company executive; b. Yonkers, N.Y., Apr. 22, 1943; d. Philip A. and Eleanor L. (Meyer) Goetz; m. Steven I. Gunn, May 22, 1965 (div. June 1983); children: Carolyn L., William T. BS in Journalism, U. Colo., 1985. V.p. Colo. Coun. on Econ. Devel., Boulder, 1985-86; pres sec., comm. dir. Colo. State Rep. Party, Denver, 1986-87; v.p. corp. comms. Xpress Info Svcs., Denver, 1987-89; pres., CEO Cable TV Svcs., Inc., Boulder, 1989—. Campaign mgr. state and nat. campaigns for legislature and congress, 1972-83. Mem. Nat. Cable TV Assn., Women in Cable, Cable TV Adminstrn. Soc., Cable TV Pub. Affairs Assn., Soc. Profl. Journalists. Republican. Mem. Christian Ch. Home: 960 55th St Boulder CO 80303

GUNNOE, NANCY LAVENIA, food executive, artist; b. Southside, Tenn., Jan. 7, 1921; d. Edgar Hatton and Clara Sharp (McCurdy) Thompson; m. Raymond Glen Gunnoe, Dec. 6, 1941; children: Lynn Thompson Gunnoe Sheets, Paul Randall (dec.), Joy Virginia Gunnoe Woodrum. Student, Austin Peay Coll., 1939, U. Charleston, 1973-87, 91. Cashier Kroger Co., Charleston, W.V., 1939-40; with Superior Laundry & Cleaning, Charleston, 1940-41; file clk. Hancock Oil Co., Oakland, Calif., 1942; office clk. Office Price Adminstrn., Stockton, Calif., 1943; sec.-treas. R.G. Gunnoe Farms Inc., Charleston, 1947—. Exhibited at local orgns. Mem. Presdl. Task Force. Mem. Nat. League Am. Pen Women, Inc., Allied Artists W.Va., Women Builders U. Charleston, Kanawha Valley Hist. and Preservation Soc., Charleston Woman's Club, Sunrise Mus. Republican. Home: 2040 Oakridge Dr Charleston WV 25311-1112 Office: 2115 Oakridge Dr Charleston WV 25311

GUNTER, AVIS BETH, county official; b. Warsaw, Ind., Jan. 7, 1928; d. Avery B. and Lucy M. (Leckrone) Kimes; m. Everett R. Gunter, May 25, 1946; children: Hal J., Ava E. Gunter Gore. Grad., Claypool (Ind.) High Sch., 1946. Level II cert. Ind. assessor-appraiser. 2nd dep. County Assessor Office, Warsaw, 1964-70, chief dep., 1970-74, assessor, 1974—. Commr. Kosciusko County, 1994—; mem. Gov.'s Adv. Coun., Ind., 1988—; past pres. Kosciuko County Rep. Women's Club, Warsaw; sec. Crime Stoppers, Warsaw; mem. exec. com. Kosciusko County Found., Warsaw. Named to Fall of Fame Woman of Yr., Kosciusko County Rep. Ctrl. Com., 1982; named Outstanding County Assessor Assn. of Ind. Counties, Inc., 1985. Mem. Ind. County Assessor's Assn. (pres. 1985-86), Assn. of Ind. Counties (pres. 1992), Warsaw Bus. and Profl. Women's Club (past pres.), Warsaw Businesswomen's Club, Lamplighter's Club (past pres.). Methodist. Home: 829 W 600 S Claypool IN 46510-8923 Office: Kosciusko County Commr Courthouse 100 W Center St Warsaw IN 46580-2847

GUNTER, DEVONA ELIZABETH, special education educator; b. Jonesboro, Ark., Jan. 25, 1933; d. Coy W. and DeVona Bethel (Rogers) Hiett; m. Norman Lee Gunter, Sept. 26, 1952; children: Carolyn Sue, Ronald Lee, Rickey Lynn. BEd, S.W. Mo. State U., 1972, MEd in Learning Disabilities, 1979, specialist degree in adminstrn., 1985. Cert. elem., spl. edn. tchr., prin., supt., Mo. Kindergarten, 6th grade tchr., tchr. of learning disabled Oregon-Howell R-3 Sch. Dist., Koshkonong, Mo., dir. spl. svcs., tchr.; coord. spl. svcs., tchr. Fair View R-XI Sch. Dist., West Plains, Mo., elem. prin.; sec., treas., bd. dirs., co-founder tng. ctr. for handicapped adults. Contbr. articles to profl. publs. Mem. ASCD, Assn. Spl. Citizens (bd. dirs., sec.-treas.), Missouri State Tchrs. Assn., Koshkonong Tchrs. Assn. (pres.). Home: 3869 County Rd 6340 West Plains MO 65775

GUNTER, EMILY DIANE, communications executive, marketing professional; b. Atlantic City, N.J., Apr. 5, 1948; d. Fay Gaffney and Verlee (Wright) G.; children: Saliha, Kadir, Amin, Shedia. BA in Math. Stats., Am. U., 1970, postgrad. computer sci., 1971; postgrad. mktg., San Diego C.C., 1986. Traffic engr. C&P Bell, Washington, 1970-71; market analyst Market Towers Inc., Atlantic City, N.J., 1978-79; outside plant engr. N.J. Bell, Atlantic City, 1979-81; market analyst Empcor Group, Atlantic City, 1981-83; outside plant engr. Pacific Bell, San Diego, 1983-91, account exec., 1991-93; exec. v.p. Black Am. of Achievement, Inc., San Diego, 1994—; lectr. women and minorities in engring. and math. Princeton (N.J.) U., 1979-81, Atlantic C.C., Atlantic City, 1979-81; customer coord. Pacific Bell-Telsam, San Diego, 1983-85; prof. math. Grossmont Coll., 1992—, instr. super learning skills seminar, 1992—. Author: Superlearning 2000: The New Technologies of Self-Empowerment, 1993, Supermath 2000: How to Learn Math Without Fear, 1993, Achieve Goals 2000: A Personal Handbook for the Lifelong Learner, 1995. Bd. dirs. Lead, San Diego, Atlantic City Transp. Authority, 1981-82, San Diego Urban Math. Collaborative; trustee Reuben H. Fleet Sci. Found., 1989, San Diego Sci. Found., 1989—, 1990 class Leadership Edn. Awareness Devel., San Diego; mem. steering com. United Negro Coll. Fund, San Diego; mem. Atlantic City Urban Area Transp. Commn., 1982-83; mem. Am. Humanics Bd. U. San Diego, 1991—; pres. bd. dirs. World Beat Cultural Ctr., Balboa Park, Calif., 1992—. Mem. African Am. Womens Conf. Democrat. Islamic. Home: PO Box 152121 San Diego CA 92195-2121 also: Gunter Devel Enterprises PO Box 152121 San Diego CA 92195-2121

GUNTER, JO ELLEN, educational administrator; b. Franklin, Ky., June 13, 1939; d. James Howard and Nina Marie (Stringer) Hall; m. James William Fagg, Dec. 3, 1959 (div. 1981); children: Sandra Jo F. Dunn, Philip Neal Fagg; m. Ferrill Ray Gunter, June 12, 1983. BA in English, Tenn. Tech. U., 1978, MA in English, 1982, grad. with high distinction, 1985; postgrad., U. Tenn. Inst. Leadership Effectiveness in Higher Edn., 1991. Sec. The Lenk Co., Frankling, Ky., 1957-62; adminstrv. asst. Monument Record Corp., Hendersonville, Tenn., 1966-71; legal sec. Val Sanford, Nashville, 1971-72; exec. sec. office of pres. Tenn. Tech. U., Cookeville, 1980-85; exec. asst. to exec. dir. Tenn. Higher Edn. Commn., Nashville, 1985-92, pers. officer, 1986-92; part-time instr. dept. English Tenn. Tech. U., 1978, 84, Western Ky. U., Bowling Green, 1988-89; state facilitator, chair Tenn. state planning com. Am. Coun. Edn. Nat. Identification Program for Advancement of Women Adminstrs. in Higher Edn., 1992-94. Organist Ctrl. Emanuel Bapt. Ch., Cookeville, 1972-85. Recipient June Anderson award, 1990. Mem. Bus. and Profl. Women (local chair CHOICES program 1991-94, state chair CHOICES program 1992-93, pres.-elect Franklin chpt. 1990, pres. Franklin chpt. 1991, Woman of Yr. Franklin chpt. 1988, Woman of Achievement Franklin chpt. 1989), Women in Higher Edn. in Tenn. (sec. 1989-90, pres.-elect 1990-91, pres. 1991-92), Phi Kappa Phi (past. treas. Tenn. Tech. chpt., mem. Western Ky. U. chpt.), Sigma Tau Delta (past v.o, Tenn. Tech. chpt.). Home: 1041 Temperence Rd Franklin KY 42134-7282

GUNTER, KAREN JOHNSON, government official; b. Pensacola, Fla., Jan. 7, 1948; d. Erskine DeWitt and Grace (Crutchfield) Johnson; m. Thomas A. Gunter, Aug. 25, 1975 (div. Dec. 1981). BS, U. So. Miss., 1970; MS, Fla. State U., 1976. Social svc. worker Fla. Bur. Blind Svcs., Pensacola, 1970-74; supervising counselor Fla. Bur. Blind Svcs., Tallahassee, West Palm, 1974-75; M.D. examiner Office Disability Determinations, Social Security Adminstrn., Tallahassee, 1976-80, M.D. rev. examiner, 1980-81, M.D. hearing examiner, 1981-82, M.D. examiner supr., 1982-86, area office program adminstr., 1986—; govt. official, Jafra; skin care cons. Vol. ARC. Recipient Director's citation Social Security Adminstrn., 1978, Commr.'s citation, 1988, Profl. Supr. of Quarter award Office Disability Determination, 1987. Mem. Nat. Assn. Disability Examiners (treas. 1982-85, pres. 1988-89, pres. S.E. region 1985-86, 91-92, S.E. regional dir. 1993—), Fla. Assn. Disability Examiners (pres. 1982, Examiner of Yr. 1984). Democrat. Baptist. Home: 812

Voncile Ave Tallahassee FL 32303-4683 Office: PO Box 7417 Tallahassee FL 32314-7417

GUNTHER, CATHRYN ELIZABETH, sales executive; b. Boston, Apr. 11, 1958; d. Robert James and Harriett Ruth (Berube) G.; m. Benjamin Snow Mosher, Sept. 12, 1987; 1 child, Graham Gunther Mosher. BS in Biology, U. Conn., 1980. Tchr. Amity Jr. High Sch., Woodbridge, Conn., 1980-81; sales rep. Merck Sharp & Dohme, New Britain, Conn., 1982-86; hosp. sales rep. Merck Sharp and Co. Inc., Boston, 1986, health sci. assoc., 1987; sr. trainer Merck Sharp and Co. Inc., West Point, Pa., 1987-88; state dist. mgr. Merck Sharp and Co. Inc., Conn., 1988-92; dir. sales Astra Merck Group of Merck & Co. Inc., N.Y.C., 1992—; EMT Hartford (Conn.) Hosp., 1986-88. Tutor disturbed student program Amity High Sch., Woodbridge, 1981; recruiter ARC, West Point, 1988. Mem. Appalachian Mountain Club. Office: Astra Merck Group/Merck Co 101 Merritt 7 Fl 5 Norwalk CT 06851-1059

GUNZBURGER, SUZANNE NATHAN, city commissioner, social worker; b. Buffalo, July 12, 1939; d. Lawrence Emil and Ruth Lucille (Wohl) Nathan; m. Gerard Josef Gunzburger, Apr. 10, 1960; children: Ronald Marc, Cynthia Anne, Judith Lynn. BS in Edn., Wayne State U., 1959; MSW, Barry U., 1974. Tchr. pub. schs. Detroit, 1959-63, Trumbull, Conn., 1963-66, North Miami Beach, Fla., 1967-68, Broward County, Fla., 1968-72; pvt. practice clin. social work Hollywood, Fla., 1975—; vice mayor City of Hollywood, 1983-84, 85-87, city commr., 1982-92; commr. Broward County, 1992—, chair, 1994—. Bd. dirs. Environ. Coalition Broward County, 1982-89; chmn. Met. Planning Org., Broward County, 1984-87, 89, Statewide Human Rights Adv. Com., 1988-89; pres. Broward County Mental Health Bd., 1984; active on Broward County Commn. Status Women, 1978-82, White House Conf. Families, Balt., 1980; del. Broward County League Cities, 1988-92; mem. adv. bd. Broward Homebound, 1991—; mem. Broward Children's Svc. Bd., 1988-92; mem. bd. dirs. Fla. League of Counties, 1992—; mem. Broward County Water Adv., 1992—; mem. Broward County Community Redevel. Agy., 1992—; mem. bd. dirs. Broward County Econ. Devel. Agy., 1992—; mem. South Fla. Regional Planning Coun., 1992-94. Named Broward County Woman of Yr., 1990, Humanitarian of the Yr. David Posnack Jewish Community Ctr., 1994, Environmentalist of the Yr. Broward County Environ. Coalition, 1994; recipient Disting. Achievement award Am. Jewish Congress, 1990. Mem. Nat. Assn. Social Workers (diplomate clin. social work), Internat. Acad. Behavioral Med., Counseling and Psychotherapy (diplomate profl. psychotherapy), Am. Acad. Behavioral Med. (clin. mem.), Women in Communications (Woman of Yr. in Govt. 1983), Nat. Coun. Jewish Women (pres. 1980-82, Hannah G. Solomon award 1989), Hollywood C. of C. (leadership devel. 1990—), Kiwanis. Democrat. Office: Office Bd County Commrs Govtl Ctr Rm 421 115 S Andrews Ave Fort Lauderdale FL 33301

GUPTON, NORMA JENEANE, technical writer; b. Asheville, N.C., Nov. 28, 1943; d. Melvin P. and Ruby L. (Swearingen) Rogers; m. Philip W. Williams, Aug. 30, 1964 (div. Mar. 1982); children: Shane, Valerie; m. Milton C. Gupton, Nov. 30, 1985. BA in Gen. Sci., Ft. Hays State U., 1965; MS in Adult Edn., Okla. State U., 1983. Math. and sci. tchr. Graham Park Jr. High Sch., Triangle, Va., 1967-68; tech. writer Amoco Prodn. Co., Tulsa, 1968-73, 82-84; social worker Okla. Dept. Social and Rehab. Svcs., Tulsa, 1973-75; print shop supr. St. Francis Hosp., Tulsa, 1979-82; cons., tech. writer Tulsa, Dallas, 1984-88; v.p. publs. Skilldex, Inc., Dallas, 1988-90; performance support specialist Automatic Data Processing, Dallas, 1990—. Mem. NAFE, AAUW, Soc. for Tech. Comm. (sr.), Women's Golf Assn., Rolling Hills Country Club. Methodist. Home: 1902 Moody Ct Arlington TX 76012 Office: Automatic Data Processing 2300 Valley View Ste 900 Irving TX 75062

GURHOLT-WIESE, VICTORIA JEAN (VICKI WIESE), special needs educator; b. Sheboygan, Wis.; d. Victor Eugene and Francis Blanche (Lynch) Gurholt; m. Steven John Wiese, Oct. 14, 1978; 1 child, Brett Harvey Wiese. BS in Spl. Edn./Elem. Edn., Silver Lake Coll., 1985; M in Transitional Spl. Needs, U. Wis., Whitewater, 1991. Cert. spl. edn. learning/emotional disabilities tchr., tech. coll. system spl. needs and goal instr., Wis. Parent involvement/social svc. coord. Head Start, Sheboygan, 1980-84; relief house parent Hearthside Group Home for Girls, Sheboygan, 1984-85; spl. edn. tchr. of emotionally disturbed Port Washington (Wis.) Mid. Sch., 1985-86; spl. edn. tchr. of emotionally disturbed Sheboygan Pub. Schs., 1986-89, program support tchr. for emotionally disturbed, 1989; spl. needs instrnl. support/affirmative action 504 coord. Lakeshore Tech. Coll., Cleve., Wis., 1989-94. Mem. Internat. League of Peace/Freedom, Sheboygan, 1987—. Mem. Am. Vocat. Assn., Nat. Assn. Vocat. Assessment in Edn., Wis. Coun. Exceptional Children (pres. profl. devel. 1992%), Phi Delta Kappa (tech. prep. Lakeshore Dist. co-chair 1992-93, tech. prep. spl. populations chair 1992—). Home: 6279 S 18th St Sheboygan WI 53081 Office: Lakeshore Tech Coll 1290 North Ave Cleveland WI 53015

GURIN, MEG, dancer; b. LaGrange, Ohio. Scholarship student, The Joffrey Ballet Sch., 1981, 82, Robert Joffrey Workshop, 1983. Dancer Joffrey II Dancers, N.Y.C., 1985-86, The Joffrey Ballet, N.Y.C., 1987—. Silver medalist Internat. Dance Competition of Americas, 1983; winner Princess Grace Found. award, 1987. Office: The Joffrey Ballet 130 W 56th St New York NY 10019-3818*

GURKE, SHARON MCCUE, naval officer; b. Bklyn., Apr. 4, 1949; d. James Ambrose and Marion Denise (Coombs) McCue; B.A., Molloy Cath. Coll., 1970; M.S. in Systems Mgmt., U. So. Calif., 1977; m. Lee Samuel Gurke, Apr. 16, 1977; children: Marion Dawn, Leigh Elizabeth. Commd. ensign U.S. Navy, 1970; advanced through grades to capt., 1991; aircraft maintenance duty officer Orgn.-Intermediate Maintenance Officer, Comdr. Naval Air Force U.S. Pacific Fleet, Naval Air Sta., North Island, San Diego, 1974-77; head quality assurance div. Intermediate Maintenance Dept. Supporting Aircraft, Naval Air Sta., Miramar, San Diego, 1977-78, avionics div. officer, 1978-80; officer in charge Naval Aviation Engring. Service Unit Pacific Naval Air Sta., North Island, 1980-82; aircraft Intermediate Maintenance officer Naval Air Sta., Alameda, Calif., 1982-84; aircraft Intermediate Maintenance officer Naval Sta., Rota, Spain, 1984-86, Naval Air Systems Command Aviation Maintenance Policy Br., 1986-88, asst. program mgr. NACOLMIS, 1987-88; dir. ops. Naval Aviation Depot, North Island, 1988-90, Dept. of Navy OP-514C, 1990-92; exec. officer Naval Aviation Depot, Pensacola, Fla., 1992-94; commdg. officer Naval Avistion Depot, Pensacola, Fla., 1994—. Interviewed by S.D. TV for Success Story. Decorated 2 Naval Commendation medals, 3 Meritorious Svc. medals. Lic. pilot; first female naval officer selected for aero. engring. tng.; recipient Capt. Winifred Q. Collins award USN, 1980. Mem. Ninety Nines, San Diego Naval Women Officers Network (chmn.).

GURNEY, PAMELA KAY, social services official; b. Joliet, Ill., Sept. 25, 1948; d. Wayne Franklin and Charlotte Marie (Geissler) G. BA, Coll. St. Francis, 1971. Tchr. Joliet Pub. Schs., 1971-73; field dir. Trailways coun. Girl Scouts U.S., Joliet, 1973-76; dir. adult devel. Mich. Waterways coun. Girl Scouts U.S., Port Huron, 1976-80; dir. adult devel. Irish Hills coun. Girl Scouts U.S., Jackson, Mich., 1980-88; planning specialist for community svc. Northeastern Ill. AAOA (formerly Region Two Area Agy. on Aging), Kankakee, 1989—; bd. dirs. Kankakee chpt. Alzheimer's Disease and Related Disorders. Trainer Trailways coun. Girl Scouts U.S.; chairperson child care bd., former tchr. Sunday sch., former leader youth group Asbury United Meth. Ct., Kankakee; mem. svc. team Kankakee Girl Scouts. Mem. Nat. Assn. Nutrition and Aging Svcs. Programs, Zonta. Home: 1090 S Nelson Ave # 8 Kankakee IL 60901-5675 Office: Northeastern Ill AAOA PO Box 809 Kankakee IL 60901-0809

GURNSEY, KATHLEEN WALLACE, state legislator; b. Donnelly, Idaho; d. Robert G. and Thelma (Halferty) Wallace; m. Vern L. Gurnsey, May 7, 1950; children: Kristina Johnson, Steve, Scott. BA in Bus. Adminstn., Boise State U., 1976. Mem. Idaho Ho. of Reps., Boise, 1974—. Bd. dirs. YMCA, Boise; elder, pres. Women's Assn. First Presbyn. Ch.; bd. dirs. Fundsy, St. Luke's Aux.; mem. Def. Adv. Com. Women in the Svc., Dept. Def., 1982-84. Named Disting. Citizen Idaho Statesman, Woman of Yr. Soroptimist, Woman Achievment Altrusa Club, Outstanding Alumna Boise State U., 1991. Mem. AAUW (Outstanding Community Svcs. award 1991), Bus. and Profl. Women, Jobs Daus. (Bethel guardian honored quenn). Republican. Presbyterian. Home: 1111 W Highland View Dr Boise ID 83702-1319

GURVICH, SUSAN ELLEN, marriage and family therapist; b. N.Y.C., Feb. 28, 1955; d. Philip Bernard and Bernice M. (Hornstein) G.; m. Paul Porter, Oct. 9, 1993. B Music Therapy, Mich. State U., East Lansing, 1978; M Music Therapy, So. Meth. U., 1982; PhD in Marriage and Family Therapy, Tex. Woman's U., 1991. Lic. profl. counselor, marriage and family therapist. Music therapist Oakdale Ctr. Devel. Disabilities, Lapeer, Mich., 1978-80; dir. music therapy CPC Millwood Hosp., Arlington, Tex., 1982-85; family therapist Family Guidance Ctr., Dallas, 1987-88; primary therapist psychiat. hosp. Mesquite (Tex.) Physician's Hosp., 1988-90; supr., tng. dir. Galaxy Ctr. Counseling Svc., Garland, Tex., 1990—; pvt. practice therapist Garland Psychol. Ctr., 1993—; cons. Delta Omega, Dallas, 1990—, Boulton & Park Soc., San Antonio, 1990—, Help Me Accept Me, Dallas, 1990—. Author: Music Therapy for Speech and Language Impaired, 1980. Mem. ACA, Am. Assn. Marriage and Family Therapy (clin.). Office: Garland Psychol Ctr 2301 Forest Ln Ste 101 Garland TX 75042-7925

GURWITZ-HALL, BARBARA ANN, artist; b. Ayer, Mass., July 7, 1942; d. Jack and Rose (Baritz) Gurwitz; m. James M. Marshall III, Mar. 12, 1966 (div. 1973); m. William D. Hall, May 3, 1991. Student, Boston U., 1960-61, Katherine Gibbs Sch., Boston, 1961-63. Represented by Karin Newby Gallery, Tubac, Ariz.; represented by Wilde-Meyer Gallery, Scottsdale, Ariz.; Artist-in-residence Desert House of Prayer, Tucson, 1989-91; oblate mem. Benedictine Sisters Perpetual Adoration, 1986—. One-artist shows: YWCA, Bklyn., 1977, Henry Hicks Gallery, Bklyn., 1978, Misty-Mountain Gallery, Tubac, Ariz., 1987, Karin Newby Gallery, Tubac, 1989; exhibited in group shows: Becket (Mass.) Art Ctr., 1978, Winter Gallery, Tucson, 1980, Johnson Gallery, Bisbee, Ariz., Hilltop Gallery, Nogales, Ariz., 1981, Scharf Gallery, Sante Fe, 1982, Data Mus., Ein Hod, Israel, 1985, C.G. Rein Gallery, Santa Fe, 1986, New West Views Tubac Ctr. for Arts, 1985, Mesquite Gallery, Patagonia, Ariz., 1986, Beth O'Donnell Gallery, Tucson, 1989, Karin Newby Gallery, 1989—, Wilde-Meyer Gallery, Scottsdale, Ariz., 1991—, ArtWest, Art Collector's Gallery, Tulsa, 1992, Ann. Juried Festival Show, 1989, 90, 91, 92, 93, 94, Mountain Oyster Club Ann. Western Art Show, Tucson, 1994, Phoenix Mus. League, 1994; represented in permanent collections: Diocese of Tucson, N.J. Sambul & Co., N.Y.C., Goldman Sachs & Co., N.Y.C., Data Mus., Israel, Desert House of Prayer, Tucson, Ethical Culture Soc., Bklyn., St. Andrews Episcopal Ch., Nogales, Tubac Elem. Sch., numerous private collections U.S., Eur. Mem. Tubac Village Coun., 1979-86; bd. dirs. Pimeria Alta Hist. Soc., Nogales, Ariz., 1982-84; creator Children's Art Walk, Tubac Sch. System and Village Coun., 1980; set designer, choreographer ann. De Anza Ann. Pageant, Tubac Ctr. Arts, 1982—; pastoral asst. St. Ann's Parish, Tubac, 1986-89. Mem. Santa Cruz Valley Art Assn. (honorable mention ann. juried show 1989-94, Best of Show award 1989, award for excellence 1992), Assn. Contemplative Sisters.

GUST, JOYCE JANE, artist; b. Milw., June 5, 1952; d. Walter F. and Jane A. (Klappa) Stoelzel; m. Wayne C. Fitzner, Feb. 13, 1971 (div. 1979); 1 child, Mark Wayne; m. Melvin. R. Gust, June 24, 1983. BS, Marquette U., 1981; postgrad., U. Wis., Oshkosh, 1985-90. Registered med. technolgosit. One woman shows include Pinecotheca Gallery, Waupun, Wis., 1993, Blatz Gallery, Milw., 1994, Lazarro Signature Galley Fine Art, Stoughton, Wis., 1994; two person shows include Capitol Civic Ctr., Manitowoc, Wis., 1992; represented in group shows at Signature Gallery, Stoughton, Wis., 1989, 91, Allen Priebe Art Gallery, Oshkosh, Wis., 1990, Jura Silverman Gallery, Spring Green, Wis., 1990, Cudahy Gallery, Milw., 1990, 91, Chimerical Gregg Art Gallery, La Puente, Calif., 1990, Peltz Gallery, Milw., 1991-92, Ariel Gallery, N.Y., 1990, Neville Mus., Green Bay, Wis., 1992, others; represented in permanent collections Carroll Coll. Art Mus., Waukesha, Very Special Arts Wis. Permananet Wis. Artists Collection, Madison, John Michael Kohler Art Ctr., Sheboygan, Wis., 1993, Neville Pub. Mus., Green Bay, others; featured artist Artworks Gallery, Green Bay, Wis., 1993. Recipient Jurors award 1st Ann. Wis. Artists Exhbn., 1992, purchase awards Parkside Nat. Print Exhbn., 1993, Galex Nat., Galesburg, Ill., 1993. Very Spl. Arts Wis. Purchase award, 1993. Mem. Wis. Painters and Sculptors (Jurors award 1992), Wis. Women in The Arts. Home and Studio: 7064 Jacobson Dr Winneconne WI 54986-9764

GUSTAF, EVA MAE, school counselor; b. Petersburg, Nebr., Apr. 4, 1925; d. Peter James and Elizabeth Gertrude (Kroeker) Esau; m. John Vincent Gustaf (dec. Sept. 1985); children: Timothy, Peter, Cynthia, Mark, Scott, Christopher. AS, Dakota State U., 1983, BS, 1984; MEd, S.D. State U., 1985. Cert. counselor, S.D. Guidance counselor Lake Ctrl.-Howard Schs., Madison and Howard, S.D., 1986-89; guidance counselor, alcohol and drug coord. Howard Sch. Dist. 48-3, 1989—. Pres. Miner County Child Protection Team, Howard, 1992-94; sec. Lake County Kinship Bd., Madison, S.D., 1991-94. Recipient Esther Solberg scholarship S.D. State U., 1985. Mem. NEA, S.D. Educators Assn., Howard Educators Assn., S.D. Sch. Counselor Assn., Delta Kappa Gamma, Phi Kappa Phi. Methodist. Home: 1005 NE 4th Apt 6 Madison SD 57042

GUSTAFSON, SANDRA LYNNE, educator; b. Phila., Mar. 8, 1948; d. William Henry Gustafson and Ruth Blossom (Berger) Watson. BS in Edn., Temple U., 1969. Tchr. Lincoln H.S., Phila., 1969-78, 85-88, Germantown H.S., Phila., 1978-85; tchr. Germantown-Lankenau Motivation H.S., Phila., 1988—, coord. freshman orientation program, 1993, dean of discipline, 1994—; asst. to vice prin. Lincoln H.S., Phila., 1970-78; sponsor Nat. Honor Soc., Phila., 1989-92, 93—, Peer Counselors and Peer Tutors, Phila., 1989—; chaperone on choir's trip to Europe, Lincoln H.S., 1973, coord. Freshman Orientation Program, Phila., 1993—. Sponsor Big Brother/Big Sister Program, 1994—. Mem. Phila. Fedn. Tchrs. (del. to state conv. 1973, del. to nat. conv. 1973, 74), Phila. Area Spanish Educators, MLA, Sigma Delta Pi, Kappa Delta Epsilon. Democrat. Jewish. Office: Germantown Lankenau Motivation HS 201 Spring Ln Philadelphia PA 19128

GUSTIN, ANN WINIFRED, psychologist; b. Winchester, Mass., 1941; d. Bertram Pettingill and Ruth Lillian (Weller) G.; B.A. with honors in Psychology, U. Mass., 1963; M.S. (USPHS fellow), Syracuse U., 1966, Ph.D., 1969. Registered psychologist, Sask.; lic. psychologist, Ga.; Diplomate Am. Bd. Med. Psychotherapists. Research asst., psychology trainee U. Mass., Tufts U., Harvard U., Syracuse U., 1961-66; psychology intern VA, Canandaigua, N.Y., 1967-68; asst. prof. psychology U. Regina (Sask., Can.), 1969-74, assoc. prof. psychology, dir. counseling services, head clin. tng., 1974-78; pvt. practice psychology, Carrollton, Ga., 1978—, Atlanta, 1980—; staff tng. cons. Frobisher Bay Dept. Social Services, N.W. Territories, Can., 1979-80; cons. staff Tanner Hosp.; ancillary staff West Paces Ferry Hosp.; psychiat. cons. Social Security Adminstrn., Ga. Dept. Human Resources, 1980—. Membership chmn. Carroll County Mental Health Assn., 1979-81; mem. nat. mental health disaster response team ARC. Fellow Ga. Psychol Assn. (exec. divsn. lic. psychologists 1986-91, 92—, Nat. Red Cross disaster mental health team 1991—); mem. Am. Psychol. Assn., Can. Psychol. Assn., Sask. Psychol. Assn. (mem. exec. council 1971-72, registrar 1972-73), Nat. Assn. Disability Examiners, Ga. Assn. Disability Examiners. Office: 107 College St Carrollton GA 30117-3136 also: One Decatur Town Ctr 150 E Ponce De Leon Ave Ste 46 Decatur GA 30030-2526

GUSTITUS, LINDA, lawyer, legislative aide; b. Rockford, Ill., Dec. 29, 1947; d. Joseph Jerome and Helen Victoria (Danielson) G.;p m. Robert Oswald Johnsen, Oct. 2, 1971: children: Robert Joseph Johnsen, Sandra Satre Johnsen. BA, Oberlin Coll., 1969; JD, Wayne State U., 1975. Bar: Ill. Staff atty. Ill. Fair Employment Practices Commn., Chgo., 1975-76; asst. state's atty. Cook County State's Atty. Office, Chgo., 1976-77; trial atty. U.S. Dept. Justice, Washington, 1977-79; staff dir., chief counsel subcom. oversight of govt. mgmt. U.S. Senate, Washington, 1979—; adj. prof. George Washington U., 1993-94. Democrat. Unitarian. Office: US Senate Oversight Com 442 Hart Senate Office Bldg Washington DC 20510

GUST-JENSON, CINDY, administrator; b. Sale Lake City, Sept. 2, 1959; d. Ernest and Kathryn Ruth (Leonard) G.; m. Cory J. Jenson, Jan. 23, 1982; children: Amanda, Kevin. Student, U. Utah, 1977-80; BSBA, U. Phoenix, 1988. Rsch. analyst Salt Lake City Mayor's Office, 1978-83; dir. pub. rels. & edn. Utah Health Care Assn., Salt Lake City, 1983-88; coord. community rels. Salt Lake City Coun. Office, 1988-89, exec. dir., 1989—. Contbr. articles to profl. jours. Com. mem. Utah AIDS Found., 1992—; press sec. Ted Wilson for U.S. Senate, Salt Lake City, 1982; campaign mgr. John Hiskey for County Commr., Salt Lake City, 1980; vice chair Salt Lake City Dem. Party, 1981. Home: 1061 Windsor St Salt Lake City UT 84105-1309

GUTENTAG, PATRICIA RICHMAND, social worker, family counselor, occupational therapist; b. Newark, Apr. 10, 1954; d. Joseph and Joan (Miller) Leflein; m. Herbert Norman Gutentag; children: Steven, Jesse. BS in Occupational Therapy, Tufts U., 1976; MSW, Boston Coll., 1979. Lic. family and marriage counselor, lic. clin. social worker, N.J.; diplomate Am. Bd. Examiners in Clin. Social Work; registered occupational therapist, N.J. Social worker Jewish Family Svc., Salem, Mass., 1979-82; pvt. practice family and marriage counselor Westfield and Red Bank, N.J., 1982—; cons. high stress, Westfield and Red Bank, 1982—. Fellow N.J. Soc. for Clin. Social Work; mem. NASW, Am. Occupational Therapists Assn., Registered Occupational Therapists Assn., Soc. for Advancement Family Therapy in N.J., Am. Anorexia-Bulimia Assn., Am. Assn. Marriage and Family Therapy. Office: 200 Maple Ave Red Bank NJ 07701-1732

GUTH, JAMIE ANN, video producer; b. Sturgeon Bay, Wis., Aug. 30, 1955; d. Gerald Raymond and Mary Lou (Paul) G.; m. Paul Robert Bilgen, Nov. 22, 1980; children: Galen Bilgen, Brendan Bilgen. BS, No. Mich. U., 1977; M of Arts and Liberal Studies, Dartmouth, 1992. News reporter Sta. WLUC-TV, Marquette, Mich., 1977-82; prodr. mag. show First Monday, Marquette, 1980-82; prodr., co-host daily show Upper Michigan Today, Marquette, 1982-84; reporter med. show The Doctor Is In Dartmouth-Hitchcock Med. Ctr., Hanover, N.H., 1985-89, prodr., host The Doctor Is In, 1989—. Author: (screenplay) Camera Running, 1992. Recipient award for excellence in med. edn. Am. Assn. Med. Colls., 1988, 90, 92, Broadcast Edn. award Nat. Multiple Sclerosis Soc., 1988, 89, award of video pub. excellence Am. Med. Writers Assn., 1992, 93. Mem. Health Scis. Comms. Assn. (editor med. prodrs. newsletter 1992-94, workshop leader on video tng. 1990—, 3d place video award 1993). Home: RR 1 Box 653 Hartland Hill Rd Woodstock VT 05091 Office: Dartmouth-Hitchcock Med Ctr One Medical Center Dr Lebanon NH 03756

GUTH, MARY ANNE, business communications service company executive; b. Oil City, Pa., Feb. 28, 1954; d. Ralph Joseph and Helen Louise (Hinds) G.; m. Thomas Charles Fulton, Oct. 5, 1985. BA, Holy Cross Coll., 1976. Tech. writer, supr. Travelers Cos., Hartford, Conn., 1977-83; tech. writer, mgr. Coleco Industries, West Hartford, Conn., 1983-85; sr. cons. Courseware Developers, Manchester, Conn., 1985-88; pres. Mentor Comm., Ellington, Conn., 1989-94, exec. dir, 1995—; mem. Hartford Area Trainers, 1989-90, exec. bd. dirs., 1990-92. Author: Adamcalc User Manual, 1984; contbr. articles to profl. jours. Named Woman to Watch Hartford Woman Newspaper, 1990. Mem. Soc. Tech. Communication (treas. Cen. Conn. chpt. 1982-83, v.p. 1981-82, pres. 1983-86, membership mgr. 1987-94, exec. bd., newsletter editor 1994—, Disting. Svc. award 1988, Merit award 1991).

GUTHORN, AMANDA MAY, public safety professional; b. Neptune, N.J., Feb. 21, 1961; d. Peter Jay and Katherine (Tappen) G. BS in Criminal Justice, Northeastern U., 1984, MS in Criminal Justice, 1990. Cert. crime prevention officer, rape investigator, Mass. Police officer Northeastern U., Boston, 1984-90, police cpl., 1990, crime prevention coord., 1990-92; chief pub. safety Newbury Coll., Brookline, Mass., 1992-94; dir. security Pine Manor Coll., Chestnut Hill, Mass., 1994—; chair Northeastern U. Sexual Assault and Acquaintance Rape Coalition, Boston, 1991-92. Mem. Am. Soc. Indsl. Security, Internat. Assn. Campus Law Enforcement Adminstrs., Mass. Crime Prevention Officers Assn., Northeastern Univ. Criminal Justice Alumni Assn. (sec. 1988-90, v.p. 1990-91, pres. 1992-94). Home: 199 Canton St Westwood MA 02090-2248 Office: Pine Manor Coll 400 Heath St Chestnut Hill MA 02167

GUTHRIE, DIANA FERN, nursing educator; b. N.Y.C., May 7, 1934; d. Floyd George and A. May (Moler) Worthington; m. Richard Alan Guthrie, Aug. 18, 1957; children: Laura, Joyce, Tammy. AA, Graceland Coll., 1953; RN, Independence (Mo.) Sanitarium, 1956; BS in Nursing, U. Mo., 1957, MS in Pub. Health, 1969; EdS, Wichita State U., 1982; PhD, Walden U., 1985. Cert. profl. counselor, Kans.; cert. in stress mgmt. edn. and clin. hypnosis; cert. clin. hypnotherapy; cert. holistic nursing. Instr. red cross U.S. Naval Sta., Sangley Point, Philippines, 1961-63; acting head nurse newborn nursery U. Mo., Columbia, 1963-64, birth defect nurse dept. pediatrics, 1964-65, nursing dir. clin. research ctr., 1965-67, research asst., 1967-73; asst. then assoc. prof. sch. medicine U. Kans., Wichita, 1974-86, diabetes nurse specialist Sch. Medicine, 1973—; joint appointment prof. Sch. Nursing U. Kans., 1982—; adj. prof. dept. nursing Wichita State U., 1986—; prof. dept. pediatrics and psychiatry Sch. Medicine U. Kans., 1983—; nurse cons. diabetes Mo. Regional Med. Program, Columbia, 1970-73; nat. advisor Humana Diabetes Ctr. for Excellence, Lexington, Ky., 1982-90, Phoenix, 1983-92, Charlottesville, Ky., 1990—. Author: Nursing Management of Diabetes, 3d edit. 1991, The Diabetes Source Book, 1990; contbr. articles to profl. jours. Health adv. bd. Mid-Am. All Indian Ctr., Wichita, 1978-80; bd. dirs. Wichita Urban Indian Health Clinic, 1980-82. Fellow Am. Acad. Nursing; mem. ANA, APHA, Am. Diabetes Assn. (affiliate bd. dirs. 1979-83, pres. Kans. affiliate 1980-81, 90-91, Outstanding Educator award 1979), Am. Assn. Diabetes Educators (cert. 1988, Disting. Svc. award 1984), Am. Assn. Med. Psychotherapists (profl. adv. bd. 1985—), Am. Assn. Biofeedback Clinicians. Democrat. Mem. Reorganized LDS Ch.

GUTHRIE, GLENDA EVANS, educational consultant; b. De Funiak Springs, Fla., Aug. 10, 1945; d. Owen Clement and Vera Mae (Adams) Evans; m. Theron Asbury Guthrie Jr., June 10, 1967; children: Michael Patrick, Jennifer Leigh. BS in Elem. Edn., Samford U., 1967; MA in Elem. Edn., U. Ala., 1983; EdS in Ednl. Leadership, U. Fla., 1990. Tchr. grades 8-9 Warrington Jr. High, Pensacola, Fla., 1967; tchr. grades 4-5 Birmingham (Ala.) City Schs., 1967-69; tchr. grade 5 Faith Christian Sch., Bessemer, Ala., 1969-70; tchr. grade 4 Fairfield Highlands Christian Sch., Birmingham, 1973-74, First Bapt. Sch., Pleasant Grove, Ala., 1974-83; tchr. grade 5 Ctrl. Park Christian Sch., Birmingham, 1983-84, elem. dir., 1984-86; tchr. grades 5-6 Duval County Sch., Jacksonville, Fla., 1986-90; ednl. cons. Jostens Learning Corp., Phoenix, 1990-92; sr. ednl. cons., 1993—; co-founder Success Unlimited Learning Ctr., Birmingham, 1985-86; judge Sci. Fair, Jacksonville, 1988-90; seminar/workshop leader; mem. elem. textbook com. Duval County Schs., 1988-89. Active Clearview Bapt. Ch. Named Tchr. of Yr. Livingston Sch., Jacksonville, 1989, Ednl. Cons. of Yr., 1991-92. Mem. ASCD, Internat. Reading Assn., Nat. Coun. Tchrs. Math., Kappa Delta Pi. Republican. Baptist. Home: 838 Mckays Ct Brentwood TN 37027-2989

GUTHRIE, HELEN A., nutrition educator, consultant; b. Sarnia, Ont., Can., Sept. 25, 1925; d. David and Helen (Sweet) Andrews; m. George Guthrie, June 4, 1949; children: Barbara, Jane, James. B.A., U. Western Ont., 1946, D.Sc. (hon.), 1982; M.S., Mich. State U., 1948; Ph.D., U. Hawaii, 1968. Registered dietetian, Pa. From instr. to prof. Pa. State U., University Park, 1949-73, endowed prof. nutrition, dept. chair, 1989-91, prof. emerita, 1992—; v.p. Heinz Nutrition Sci. Inst., 1993—; nutrition cons. to industry, govt. and academia. Chmn. Bd. of Health, State College, Pa., 1977-82. Recipient Borden award Am. Home Econs. Assn., 1976, W.O. Atwater award USDA, 1989, Pacemaker award Pa. Nutrition Coun., 1994. Fellow Am. Inst. Nutrition (councillor 1982—, pres. 1987—, Elvehjhem award for pub. svc. 1989), Soc. Nutrition Edn. (pres. 1978-79); mem. Internat. Life Sci. Inst.-Nutrition Found. (trustee 1979-92, v.p. nutrition 1986-89, editor Nutrition Today 1987—). Home: 1316 S Garner St State College PA 16801-6328 Office: Pa State U S-125 S Human Devel Univ Park PA 16802

GUTHRIE, JANET, professional race car driver; b. Iowa City, Mar. 7, 1938; d. William Lain and Jean Ruth (Midkiff) G. B.S. in Physics, U. Mich., 1960. Comml. pilot and flight instr., 1958-61; research and devel. engr. Republic Aviation Corp., Farmingdale, N.Y., 1960-67; publs. engr. Sperry Systems, Sperry Corp., Great Neck, N.Y., 1968-73; racing driver Sports Car Club Am. and Internat. Motor Sports Assn., 1963-86; profl. racing driver U.S. Auto Club and Nat. Assn. for Stock Car Racing, 1976-80; pres. Janet Guthrie Racing Enterprises Inc., 1978—; highway safety cons. Met. Ins. Co., 1980-87. Recipient Curtis Turner award Nat. Assn. for Stock Car Racing-Charlotte World 600, 1976; First in Class, Sebring 12-hour, 1970; North Atlantic Road Racing champion, 1973; named to Women's Sports Hall of Fame, 1980. Mem. Madison Ave. Sports Car Driving and Chowder Soc., Women's Sports Found., Les Dames d'Aspen, Internat. Wine and Food Soc.

GUTHRIE, JANET PETERSON, insurance claims examiner; b. Louisville, Miss., Nov. 6, 1960; d. Jerry Dale and Addie Will (Rhodes) Peterson; m. William Albert Guthrie, July 12, 1984. Grad. high sch., Birmingham, Ala. Cert. workers compensation laws and med. terminology, Ala. Workers compensation claims examiner Gen. Adjustment Bur. Bus. Svcs., Birmingham, 1982—; sec. Workers Compensation Claims Assn., Birmingham, 1991-92, treas., 1992-93, 2d v.p., 1993-94, 1st v.p., 1994-95. Home: 800 8th St Midfield AL 35228-2907

GUTHRIE, JUDITH K., federal judge; b. Chgo., July 13, 1948; d. David Curtis and Kathleen McAfee G.; m. John H. Hannah, Jr., May 9, 1992. Student, Ariz. State U., 1966-68; BA, St. Mary's U., 1971; JD cum laude, U. Houston, 1980; postgrad., Harvard U., 1990. Bar: Tex. 1981, U.S. Dist. Ct. (ea. dist.) Tex. 1982, U.S. Ct. Appeals (5th cir.) 1982, U.S. Dist. Ct. (no. dist.) Tex. 1983, U.S. Dist. Ct. (we. dist.) Tex. 1984. Editor Am. Coun. Edn., Washington, 1972-73; exec. asst. Tex. Ho. Reps., Austin, 1973-75; lobbyist Bracewell & Patterson, Austin, 1975-80; assoc. Bracewell & Patterson, Houston, 1980-81; briefing atty. Tex. Ct. Appeals, Tyler, 1981-82; ptnr. Hannah & Guthrie, Tyler, Tex., 1982-86; magistrate judge U.S. Dist. Ct. (ea. dist.) Tex., Tyler, 1986—; instr. legal asst. program, Tyler Jr. Coll., 1986-87; apptd. Tex. Judicial Coun., 1991—, gender bias task force, 1991—; lectr. in field. Contbr. articles to profl. jours. Bd dirs. Found. Women's Resources, Leadership Am., Leadership Tex.; adv. bd. Main St. Project; former Dem. chmn. Smith County; legal asst. adv. bd. Tyler Jr. Coll., 1986—; mem. Citizens Commn. Tex. Judicial System, 1992—. Mem. ABA (fed. trial judges leg. com. 1991—), Am. Judges Assn., Assn. U.S. Magistrates, 5th Cir. Bar Assn., State Bar Tex. (dist. 2A grievance com. 1990—, coun. mem. women & law sect., 1981-84, bd. dirs. lawyers' credit union, 1983-84, citizens & law focused edn. com. 1984-85), Smith County Bar Assn. (chmn. law libr. com. 1985—). Office: US District Court 300 Federal Bldg & US Ct House 211 W Ferguson St Tyler TX 75702-7222

GUTIERREZ, HELEN SALYERS, social worker, antique appraiser and dealer; b. Wayne, W.Va., Aug. 3, 1942; d. Homer Burton and Ella Marie (Phillips) Salyer; m. Laurence Arthur Gilles, Jr., Nov. 19, 1960 (div. May 28, 1974); children: Cheryl Anne, Laura Carole, Mark Evan; m. David M. Gutierrez, July 2, 1974; 1 stepchild, David Michael. A.Journalism, Marshall U., Huntington, W.Va., 1965, BSN, 1969; MSW, Ball State U., 1989. Cert. in recreational therapy, social svc., Ind. Reporter Herald Advertiser, Huntington, 1966-67; practical nurse St. Mary's Hosp., Huntington, 1969-71; owner Dawn's Donuts, Kenova, W.Va., 1971-74; mgr. and resident dir. Saul Cohen Mgmt. Corp., Gary, Ind., 1975; co-owner G&S Rooting, Gary, 1976—; owner Attic Antiques and Appraisals, Portage, Ind.; stage singer/band leader 25 yrs. Singer: (recording) Anthem, 1979. N.W. Ind. dir. Women Helped Out of Poverty; vol. advocate child abuse; ct. advocate spokesperson. Mem. NOW, ACLU, LWV, NARL, Ind. Health Care Assn., Mensa. Democrat. Home: 139 Coral Ave Portage IN 46368-2503 Office: Attic Antiques/Appraisals 156 Coral Ave Portage IN 46368-2503

GUTIERREZ, PAMELA JEAN HOLBROOK, nurse, clinical perfusionist; b. Maryville, Mo., Jan. 13, 1956; d. John Peter and Doris Ladene (Allen) Curry; m. Mark Lee Gutierrez, Dec. 9, 1978. Student, U. Nebr., 1973-93, Nebr. Meth. Sch. Nursing, 1976; BSN, U. State N.Y., 1989; grad. Clin. Perfusionist, U. Nebr., 1992-94. RN, cert. perfusion scis. Charge nurse ICU St. Joseph's Hosp., Omaha, 1976-80, staff nurse emergency dept., 1980-81, flight nurse Life Flight, 1981-91, charge and staff nurse emergency dept., 1991-94; project nurse, rsch. asst. dept. surgery Creighton U., 1978-79; mem. PACU staff, nurse/clin. profl. Immanuel Med. Ctr., Omaha, 1994—; trauma nurse core course instr. emergency dept. Nurse's Assn., Neonatal Advanced Cardiac Life Support, 1990, Am. Heart Assn.; pediatric advanced life support instr.; advanced cardiac life support instr. Am. Heart Assn., 1985—; paramedic cert., pre-hosp. trauma life support instr. Nat. Assn. Emergency Med. Technicians and Paramedics, 1982. Contbr. articles to profl. jours. Mem. AACN, Nat. Flight Nurses Assn., Nat. Emergency Med. Svcs. Pilots Assn., Emergency Nurses Assn. Roman Catholic. Home: 4207 Woolworth Ave Omaha NE 68105-1752

GUTIN, MYRA GAIL, communications educator; b. Paterson, N.J., Aug. 13, 1948; d. Stanley and Lillian (Edelstein) Greenberg; m. David Gutin, Sept. 5, 1971; children: Laura, Sarah, Andrew. BA, Emerson Coll., 1970, MA, 1971; PhD, U. Mich., 1983. Asst. prof. communications Cumberland County Coll., Vineland, N.J., 1972-80, Rider U., Lawrenceville, N.J., 1981-88; assoc. prof. Rider Coll., Lawrenceville, N.J., 1989—; adj. instr. Essex County Coll., Newark, 1971-72, Nassau C.C., Garden City, N.Y., 1972, Trenton (N.J.) State Coll., 1981-84; adj. asst. prof. Rider U., 1981-85; lectr. in field. Author: The President's Partner The First Lady in the 20th Century, 1989; contbr. articles to profl. jours. Mem. Emerson Coll. Nat. Alumni Bd., 1994—. Recipient Alumni Achievement award Emerson Coll., Boston, 1991. Mem. Ctr. for Study of the Presidency, Speech Comm. Assn., Ea. Comm. Assn., Internat. Platform Assn. Home: 119 Greenvale Ct Cherry Hill NJ 08034-1701

GUTMAN, GRETCHEN KAY, financial analyst; b. Ft. Wayne, Ind., Oct. 3, 1961; d. Phillip Edward and Carolyn (Prickett) G. BA, Ind. U., 1986, MPA, 1987, postgrad. Fiscal and info. officer Allen County Commrs., Ft. Wayne, 1988-89; rsch. assoc. Ind. Fiscal Policy Inst., Indpls., 1989-92; majority fiscal analyst Ind. Senate, Indpls., 1992—. Bd. dirs. Sch. Pub. and Environ. Affairs Alumni, Ind. U., Bloomington, 1991—; mem. Jr. League, Indpls., 1985-93, Festival 500 Assn., Indpls., 1991—. Mem. ASPA (v.p. Ind. chpt. 1992-93), Assn. for Pub. Policy Analysis and Mgmt., Nat. Conf. for State Legislators. Republican. Methodist. Home: 700 N Alabama St Apt 1602 Indianapolis IN 46204-1358 Office: Ind Senate 200 W Washington St Indianapolis IN 46204-2728

GUTMAN, LUCY TONI, school social worker, educator, counselor; b. Phila., July 13, 1936; d. Milton R. and Clarissa (Silverman) G.; divorced; children: James, Laurie. BA, Wellesley Coll., 1958; MSW, Bryn Mawr Coll., 1963; MA in History, U. Ariz., 1978; MEd, Northwestern State U., 1991, MA in English, 1992; postgrad., U. So. Miss., 1992—. Cert. secondary tchr., La., qualified clin. social worker; cert. La. Bd. social worker, profl. counselor. Social worker Phila. Gen. Hosp., 1963-65; sr. social worker Irving Schwartz Inst. Children and Youth, 1965-66; sr. psychiat. social worker Child Study Ctr. Phila., 1966-68; chief social worker Framingham (Mass.) Ct. Clinic Juvenile Offenders, 1968-72; cons. Nashua (N.H.) Community Coun., 1969-72; dir. clinic, supr. social work Tucson East Community Mental Health Ctr., 1972-74; coord. spl. adoptions program Cath. Social Svcs. So. Ariz., Tucson, 1974-75; social worker Met. Ministry, 1983; supr. social work Leesville (La.) Mental Health Clinic, 1984; sch. social worker Vernon Parish Sch. Bd., Leesville, 1984—; adj. instr. English, sociology, Am. and European history Northwestern State U., Ft. Polk, La., 1984—; part-time counselor River North Psychol. Svcs., Leesville, 1989-92; presenter ann. conf. NASW, 1987, 88, La. Sch. Social Workers Conf., 1986, 87, La. Spl. Edn. Conf., 1988, La. Conf. Tchrs. English, 1991, 94, So. Assn. women Historians, 1994. Nat. Soc. Colonial Dames scholar, 1978-79; fellow Pa. State, 1961-62, NIMH, 1962-63. Mem. NASW, AACD, MLA, LWV, Am. Coll. Pers. Assn., Acad. Cert. Social Workers (diplomate), Bus. and Profl. Women Assn., Am. Legion Aux., So. Hist. Assn., So. Assn. Women Historians, Gamma Beta Phi, Phi Alpha Theta. Home: 2004 Allison St Leesville LA 71446 Office: Vernon Parish Sch Bd Leesville LA 71446

GUTTERMAN, JUNE KAREN, rehabilitation services administrator; b. Kingston, Pa., June 6, 1949; d. Louis Jr. and Lillian S. (Jackier) G. BA in European History, NYU, 1971; MA in Rehab. Counseling, U. Cin., 1975, cert. advanced study rehab. adminstrn., 1981, EdD in Spl. Edn./Adminstrn., 1982. Work adjustment counselor Springfield (Mass.) Goodwill Industries, 1975-76; program dir. Living Arrangements for Developmentally Disabled, Cin., 1977-78; project cons. instrnl. resource ctr. project Ctrl. Ohio Spl. Regional Resource Ctr., Columbus, 1981-83; supt. Pickaway County Bd. Mental Retardation/Develop. Disabilities, Circleville, Ohio, 1983-88; dir. Ohio bur. svcs. for visually impaired Ohio Rehab. Svcs. Commn., Columbus, 1988, dir. Ohio bur. vocat. rehab., 1988—; adj. faculty Coll. Edn., Ohio State U., Columbus, 1991—; mem. governing bd. Ctrl. Ohio Spl. Edn. Regional Resources Ctr., 1983-89; mem. Ohio's Mental Retardation and Developmentally Disabilities Prevention Coalition, 1986-88. Co-author: The Transition of Severely Handicapped Adolescents from Education to Rehabilitation: A Needs Assessment Process and Conference Report, 1982, A Resource Guide for the Referral of Severely Handicapped Students from Education to Rehabilitation, 1982, Developing a Referral-Based Local Level Linkage System: A Facilitator's Guide, 1982, (manual) Ohio Rehabilitation Services Commission and Orient Developmental Ctr., 1980. Trustee Columbus AIDS Task Force, pres., 1992-93. Recipient award of Merit, Ctrl. Ohio Parent Adv. Coun., 1987, Advocacy award Epilepsy Found. Am., 1992—; Univ. grad. scholar U. Cin., 1974, 78-80. Mem. Nat. Rehab. Assn., Am. Assn. Mental Retardation (Ohio exec. com. 1987-88), Ohio Rehab. Assn., Ohio Assn. County Bds. of Mental Retardation/Devel. Disabilities (trustee 1984-88, task force on strategic planning 1984-86, task force on devel. disabilities definition 1985-87), Ohio Supts. Assn. County Bds. Mental Retardation/Devel. Disabilities (sec. 1984-88), Ohio Fedn. Coun. for Exceptional Children (exec. com., pres. divsn. mental retardation 1983, sec. divsn. career devel. 1982-84, divsn. early childhood), Coun. State Adminstrs. for Vocat. Rehab. (client svcs. com.). Office: Ohio Rehab Svcs Commn 400 E Campus View Blvd Columbus OH 43235-4685

GUTTMAN, GILDA RAE, writer, humanities and theatre arts educator; b. N.Y.C., Jan. 5, 1951; d. Morris Hiram and Louise (Wasserman) Dobrin; m. Bruce Guttman, July 5, 1971. BSEd, NYU, 1971, PhD, 1982; MSEd, Long Island U., 1973; postgrad., Shakespeare Inst., Stratford-on-Avon, 1975. High sch. tchr. drama N.Y.C. Bd. Edn., 1972-80; free lance dir., designer of lighting and sets, 1980-85; arts and entertainment editor Derry (N.H.) News, 1985-90; adj. prof. humanities N.H. Coll., Salem, 1986—; adj. prof. puppetry and ednl. theatre Hesser coll., Manchester, N.H., 1990—; adj. prof. theatre Plymouth State Coll., 1992—; adj. women's history and puppetry Mt. Ida Coll., Newton, Mass., 1990—; lighting designer Bklyn. Arts and Cultural Assn., 1982; historian Am. Community Theatre Assn., 1984-86; community TV coord. CTV-20, Londonderry, N.H., 1986-88, producer, 1984-87; guest speaker opera Music Masters, Londonderry, 1989-90; creative cons. for multi media presentations. Writer, photographer Manchester mag.; photographer Harcourt, Brace & Jovanovich, 1988, N.H. Gateways, Nashua C. of C., 1990—; founder, mem. NYU Creative Arts Team, 1975-80; dir., artistic dir. Mus. and Drama Co., 1985-88; feature writer, editor N.H. Assn. Realtors Newsletter, 1989, Highnotes, Nashua Symphony Assn. Newsletter, 1991—, Higgins Herald, N.H. Coll. Newsletter; contbr. hundreds revs., articles to popular mags., newspapers. Pres. N.H. Community Theater Assn., Concord, 1986-88; mem. Animal Rescue League N.H., 1990—; bd. dirs. N.H. Friendship Chorus, 1988—, trustee, 1988—; trustee Nashua Symphony Assn., 1990—. Recipient Bicentennial Medal U.S. Bicentennial Com., 1988. Mem. N.H. Press Assn. (bd. dirs., chair better newspaper contest, editor NHPA Handbook), Federated Arts (communications com., newsletter and calendar editor 1990—), New Eng. Press Assn. (conv. com.), New Eng. Collegiate Press Assn. (founder, exec. dir. 1992—), Women in Communication, Inc. (v.p. fin. 1987-88), U.S. Inst. Theatre Tech., Alpha Psi Omega. Jewish. Home: 12 Dan Hill Rd Londonderry NH 03053-3130

GUTTMAN, HELENE NATHAN, research science executive; b. N.Y.C., July 21, 1930; d. Arthur and Mollie (Bergovoy) Nathan. BA, Bklyn. Coll., 1951; AM, Harvard U., 1956; MA, Columbia U., 1958; PhD, Rutgers U., 1960. Chartered chemist Royal Soc. Chemistry; registered profl. animal scientist, profl. past-life regression therapist; cert. nutrition specialist; bd. cert. and registered hypnotherapist. Rsch. technician Pub. Health Rsch. Inst., N.Y.C., 1951-52; control bacteriologist Burroughs-Wellcome, Inc., Tuckahoe, N.Y., 1952-53; vol. researcher Haskins Labs., N.Y.C., 1952-53; rsch. asst. Haskins Labs., 1953-56, rsch. assoc., 1956-60, staff microbiologist, 1960-64; lectr. dept. biology Queens Coll., N.Y.C., 1956-57; rsch. collaborator Brookhaven Nat. Labs., Upton, L.I., N.Y., 1958; guest investigator Botanisches Institut der Technisches Hochschule, Darmstadt, Germany, 1960; rsch. assoc. dept. biol. scis. Goucher Coll., Towson, Md., 1960-62; vis. asst. rsch. prof. dept. medicine Med. Coll. Va. Richmond, 1960-62; asst. prof., then assoc. prof. dept. biology NYU, 1962-67; from assoc. prof. to prof. dept. biol. scis. U. Ill.-Chgo., 1967-75, prof., 1969-75; prof. dept. microbiology U. Ill. Med. Sch., 1969-75; assoc. dir. for rsch. Urban Systems Lab. U. Ill., 1975; expert Office of Dir. Nat. Heart, Lung and Blood Inst., NIH, Bethesda, Md., 1975-77; coordinator rsch. resources Office Program Planning and Evaluation Nat. Heart, Lung and Blood Inst., NIH, 1977-79; dep. dir. Sci. Adv. Bd., Office of Adminstr., EPA, 1979-80; program coordinator, post-harvest tech., food safety and human nutrition, sci. and edn. adminstrn. USDA, 1980-83, assoc. dir. Beltsville Human Nutrition Rsch. Ctr., Agrl. Rsch. Svc., 1983-89; pres. HNG Assocs., 1983—; nat. animal care coord. Nat. Program Staff Agr. Rsch. Svc./USDA, Beltsville, Md., 1989—. Sr. author: Experiments in Cellular Biodynamics, 1972; co-editor (procs.) First Joint USA-USSR Joint Symposium on Blood Transfusion, Moscow, 1976, DHEW Publ. No. (NIH) 78-1246, 1978; editorial bd. Jour. Protozoology, 1972-75, Jour. Am. Med. Women's Assn., 1978-81, Methods in Cell Science, 1994—; sr. editor: Science and Animals: Addressing Contemporary Issues, 1989; editor: Guidelines for Well-being of Rodents in Research, 1990, Rodents and Rabbits: Current Research Issues, 1994; (with others) Rodents and Rabbits: Addressing Current Issues, 1994; contbr. articles profl. jours. Mem. edn. com. Ill. Commn. on Status Women, 1974-75; cons. EPA, sci. adv. bd., 1974-79; bd. dirs. Du Page County Comprehensive Health Care Agy., 1974-75. Andelot fellow Harvard U., 1956, Rutgers scholar Rutgers U., 1960; recipient Thomas Jefferson Murray prize Theobald Smith Soc., 1959; spl. award for work in Germany Deutscher Forschungs Gemeinschaft, 1960; Fellow Dazian Found., 1956; research grantee. Fellow AAAS, Am. Inst. Chemists (com. chmn.), Am. Acad. Microbiology, N.Y. Acad. Scis.; mem. Soc. Am. Bacteriologists (pres.'s fellow 1957), Internat. Soc. for the Study of Subtle Energies and Energy Medicine, Soc. for In Vitro Biology (chair constitution and by laws com 1994—), Tissue Culture Assn. (com. chmn. Nat. Capital Area br. 1988-90), Am. Soc. Neurochemistry, Am. Soc. Biol. Chemistry and Molecular Biology, Neuroscis. Soc., Am. Soc. Microbiologists, Am. Soc. Cell Biology (past com. chmn.), Am. Soc. Clin. Nutrition, Soc. Protozoology (past mem. exec. com., past jour. editorial bd.), Assn. Women in Sci. (past mem. exec. bd., past com. chmn.), Fed. Orgn. Profl. Women (past task force chmn., past pres.), Univ. and Coll. Women Ill. (past v.p.), Am. Running and Fitness Assn. (bd. dirs., mem. editorial bd., mem. bd. advisors 1993—), Assn. Past Life Rsch. and Therapy, Sigma Xi, Sigma Delta Epsilon (past coord. regional ctrs.). Home: 5607 Mclean Dr Bethesda MD 20814-1021 Office: Nat Program Staff Agrl Rsch SVC USDA BARC Rm 327 Beltsville MD 20705

GUY, L(EONA) RUTH, educator; b. Kemp, Tex., Mar. 17, 1913; d. Henry Luther and Minnie Elizabeth (Murphy) G. AB, Baylor U., 1934, MS, 1949; PhD, Stanford (Calif.) U., 1953. Rsch. fellow NOOO Stanford U., 1951-53, teaching asst., 1951; with U. Tex. Southwestern Med. Sch., Dallas, 1962-82, prof., 1977-82, prof. emeritus, 1982—; assoc. dir. Parkland Meml. Hosp. Blood Bank, Dallas, 1953-78; cons. VA Hosp., Dallas, 1960-80, Temple, 1964-80; vis. prof. to Far East, China Med. Bd. of N.Y., N.Y.C., 1969-70. Author: (with others) Modern Blood Banking and Transfusion Practices, 1982; editor: Technical Manual, 1966; contbr. numerous articles to profl. jours. Bd. dirs. Dallas Repertory Theater, Dallas, 1983-89. Named Disting. Alumnus Baylor U., 1994; inducted into Tex. Women's Hall of Fame, Gov.'s Commn. for Women, 1989. Fellow Am. Soc. Clin. Pathologists (hon., assoc., Disting. Svc. award 1989); mem. Bus. and Profl. Women's Club Dallas (pres. 1970-71), Baylor Women's Coun. (Woman of Distinction award 1988), Baylor Heritage Club (pres. Dallas chpt. 1991-92), Zonta (pres. Dallas chpt. 1961-62, Spirit of Zonta award 1994). Baptist. Home: 5455 La Sierra Dr Dallas TX 75231-4178

GUY, SHARON KAYE, state agency executive; b. Nashville, Apr. 5, 1958; d. Dallas Hearold and Elizabeth Jean (Towns) Gregory; 1 child, Anthony Lee. Grad. high sch., Chgo. Clk. Pub. Health dept. State of Tenn., Nashville, 1979-84, office mgr. Health Facilities commn., 1984-92; asst. Legis. Svcs., Nashville, 1992—; acct. Bryant Guy Constrn., Nashville, 1984—. Blood drive coord. ARC, Nashville, 1984—; campaign vol. United Way, Nashville, 1984—; vol. State Community Coll., 1990—, Nashville Tech., 1991—. Baptist. Home: PO Box 582 Goodlettsville TN 37070 Home: PO Box 582 Goodlettsville TN 37070 Office: Legis Svcs 204 War Meml Bldg Nashville TN 37210-2748

GUY, TERESA ANN, aerospace engineer; b. Dayton, Ohio, Apr. 12, 1961; d. John Joseph and Charlotte Jean (Ninneman) Sollars; m. James Kevan Guy, June 10, 1989; 1 child, James Cameron. BSME, U. Wash., 1983; MSAA, MIT, 1991. Registered profl. engr., Calif. With NASA Johnson Space Ctr., Houston, 1980-81; assoc. engr. Gen. Dynamics Space Systems Div., San Diego, 1983, engr., 1984-87, sr. engr., 1988-91; tech. specialist McDonnell Douglas Technologies, Inc., San Diego, 1991-94, prin. tech. specialist, 1994—; conf. presenter in field. Contbr. articles to profl. jours. Mem. USA Track and Field Assn., San Diego, 1991—; coach track high sch./coll., Seattle, San Diego, Cambridge, 1982—. Recipient First Shuttle Flight Achievement award NASA, JSC, 1981. Mem. ASME (assoc., Structures and Materials award 1988), Sigma Xi (assoc.). Office: McDonnell Douglas Tech Inc 16761 Via Del Campo Ct San Diego CA 92127

GUYONNEAU, CHRISTINE HUGUETTE, librarian; b. St. Etienne, France, Jan. 20, 1948; d. Maurice Daniel and Helene Marcelle (Bossoutrot) G.; m. Thomas A. Mason, Aug. 11, 1984; 1 child, Charlotte. Lic., U. St. Etienne, 1973; MA in French Lit., U. Va., 1983; MS in Libr. and Info. Sci., U. Ill., 1984. Libr. asst. U. Va. Libr., Charlottesville, 1975-78, bibliographer, 1978-87; dir. reference svcs. U. Indpls. Libr., 1987-94, dir. pub. svc., 1994—; pres. U. Ill. Libr. Sch. Alumni Assn., Urbana, 1993—. Author book revs.; contbr. articles to profl. jours. Pres. Ameri-France, Indpls., 1993—. Rsch. grantee Woodson Inst., 1986. Mem. ALA, Assn. Coll. and Rsch. Librs. (officer 1991-93), Ctrl. Ind. Area Libr. Svc. Authority, Ind. Online Libr. User Group, African Lit. Assn., Ind. Libr. Fedn. Office: U Indpls Libr 1400 E Hanna Library Indianapolis IN 46227

GUZE, SANDRA LEE, secondary education educator; b. Hartford, Conn., Feb. 24, 1956; d. Michael and Jennie J. (Gidzinski) G.; children: Sara Coleman, Sean Coleman. Student, Hartford (Conn.) Art Sch., 1974-75; BS, Ctrl. Conn. State Coll., 1980; MA in Liberal Studies, Wesleyan U., Middletown, Conn., 1994. Cert. profl. educator, Conn. Art instr., dept. head Bolton (Conn.) High Sch., 1985-91; art instr. Conard High Sch., West Hartford, Conn., 1991-92; visual arts mentor, instr. Ctr. for Creative Youth Wesleyan U., Middletown, Conn., 1993—; art instr. Farmington (Conn.) H.S., 1994—. Exhibited in shows at Conard Gallery, West Hartford, Conn., 1992, Wintonbury Art League, Bloomfield, Conn., 1992, Wesleyan U., Middletown, 1993, Artspace, New Haven, 1993, 94, Pump House Gallery, Hartford, 1993, Artworks Gallery, Hartford, 1993, 94, Discovery Mus., Bridgeport, Conn., 1994, Guilford (Conn.) Handcrafts Ctr., 1994. Recipient 1st Pl. award Artworks Gallery, 1993. Mem. Conn. Art Edn. Assn., Artworks Gallery.

GUZMAN, ANNA MARIA, court officer; b. Phoenix, Ariz., Jan. 13, 1957; d. Manuel and Margaret (Magdaleno) Miranda; married, July 2, 1983; children: Gabriel Alexander, Nicholas Alexander, Alexander Xavier, Adam Alexander. BA, Holy Names Coll., Oakland, Calif., 1979. Ltd. duty dep. San Diego Sheriff's Dept., 1979-80; recreation therapist Mental Health Svcs., San Diego, 1980-85; pretrial svcs. officer Superior Ct., San Diego, 1989—. Active Mex.-Am. Polit. Action Com., San Diego, 1992. Mem. Am. Assn. Undergrad. Women, Calif. Assn. Pretrial Svcs. Roman Catholic. Office: Superior Ct 220 W Broadway San Diego CA 92101

GUZY, MARGUERITA LINNES, educator; b. Santa Monica, Calif., Nov. 19, 1938; d. Paul William Robert and Margarete (Rodowski) Linnes; m. Stephen Paul Guzy, Aug. 25, 1962 (div. 1968); 1 child, David Paul. AA, Santa Monica Coll., 1959; student, U. Mex., 1959-60; BA, UCLA, 1966, MA, 1973; postgrad. in psychology, Pepperdine U., 1988-92; cert. bilingual competence, Calif., 1994. Cert. secondary tchr., quality review team ednl. programs, bilingual, Calif. Tchr. Inglewood (Calif.) Unified Sch. Dist., 1967—, chmn. dept., 1972-82, mentor, tchr., 1985-88; clin. instr. series Clin. Supervision Levels I, II, Ingelwood, 1986-87; clin. intern Chem. Dependency Ctr., St. John's Hosp., Santa Monica, 1988-92; lectr. chem. and codependency St. John's Hosp., Santa Monica, 1992—; tchr. Santa Monica Coll., 1975-76; cons. bilingual edn. Inglewood Unified Sch. Dist., 1975—, lead tchr. new hope program at-risk students, 1992; cons. tchr. credentialing fgn. lang. State of Calif., 1994; sch. rep. restructuring edn. for state proposal, 1991—; mem. Program Quality Rev. Team Pub. Edn., Calif., 1993; mem. Supt.'s Com. for Discrimination Resolution, 1994-95. Author: Elementary Education: "Pygmalian in the Classroom", 1975, English Mechanics Workbook, 1986. Recipient Teaching Excellence cert. State of Calif., 1986; named Tchr. of Yr., 1973, 88. Mem. NEA, Calif. Tchrs. Assn., Inglewood Tchrs. Assn. (local rep. 1971-72, tchr edn. and profl. services com. 1972-78), UCLA Alumnae Assn. (life), Prytanean Alumnae Assn. Republican. Club: Westside Alano (Los Angeles)(bd. dirs., treas. 1982-83). Lodge: Masons. Office: Monroe Jr High Sch 10711 S 10th Ave Inglewood CA 90303-2015

GWIN, JAMIE, librarian; b. Pine Bluff, Ark., Dec. 12, 1942; d. James Walter and Annette (Bryant) Boast; m. Aaron Gwin, Aug. 15, 1964; children: Marc, Quanta. BSE, U. Ctrl. Ark., 1963; postgrad., Ark. State U., 1986, U. Ark. Little Rock, 1986. Libr. Holly Grove (Ark.) Schs., 1963-64, Monticello (Ark.) Schs., 1964-66, 69-71, U.S. Army, APO 09069, 1967-68, Warren (Ark.) Schs., 1973-75, Woodlawn Sch., Rison, Ark., 1976-79, Wilmar (Ark.) Sch., 1980-87, Crawfordville (Ark.) Sch., 1987-89, West Memphis (Ark.) Sch., 1989—. Mem. Sec. Boy Scout Dist., S.E., Ark., 1980-84; mem. Crittenden County Rep., West Memphis, 1992—. Mem. NEA, Ark. Edn. Assn., Wilmar Edn. Assn. (pres. 1984-85). Republican. Baptist. Home: 511 N Roselawn W Memphis AR 72301 Office: Wedlock Sch PO Box 445 Edmondson AR 72332

GWINN, MARY ANN, newspaper reporter; b. Forrest City, Ark., Dec. 29, 1951; d. Lawrence Baird and Frances Evelyn (Jones) G.; m. Richard A. King, June 3, 1973 (div. 1981); m. Stephen E. Dunnington, June 10, 1990. BA in Psychology, Hendrix Coll., 1973; MEd in Spl. Edn., Ga. State U., 1975; MA in Journalism, U. Mo., 1979. Tchrs. aide DeKalb County Schs., Decatur, Ga., 1973-74, tchr., 1975-78; reporter Columbia (Mo.) Daily Tribune, 1979-83; reporter Seattle Times, 1983—, now natural resources and maritime reporter; instr. extension div. U. Wash., Seattle, 1990. Recipient Charles Stewart Mott Found. award for edn. reporting, 1980, C.B. Blethen award for enterprise reporting Blethen Family, Seattle, 1989, Pulitzer Prize for national reporting, 1990. Mem. Newspaper Guild. Office: Seattle Times PO Box 70 1120 John St Seattle WA 98111*

GWINN, NANCY ELIZABETH, library administrator; b. Sheridan, Wyo., Aug. 19, 1945; d. George Stillwagon and Elizabeth (Waddle) G.; m. John Y. Cole Jr., Apr. 23, 1973. BA, U. Wyo., 1967; MA in Libr. Sci., U. Mich., 1969. Spl. recruit Libr. of Congress, Washington, 1969-70, sr. reference libr., 1970-72, libr. Cong. Reference Ctrs., 1972-75; info. officer Coun. Libr. Resources, Inc., Washington, 1975-78, program officer, 1978-80; assoc. dir., program coord. Rsch. Librs. Group, Mountain View, Calif., 1980-83; asst. dir. collections mgmt. Smithsonian Instn. Librs., Washington, 1984—; cons. Assn. Rsch. Librs., Washington, 1984, Assn. Southeastern Rsch. Librs., Atlanta, 1989, Rsch. Librs. Group, Mountain View, Calif., 1989, U.S. Agr. Info. Network, 1992. Editor: Preservation Microfilming, 1987 (Waldo Gifford Leland prize 1988), (with Robert Rydell) Fair Representations, 1994; contbr. articles to profl. jours. Membership trustee Greater Wash. Ednl. TV Assn., 1986-91; leadership com. 2691 Club, 1985-93. U.S. Dept. Edn. fellow U. Mich., 1968, Fulbright Commn. scholar, U.K., 1967, UCLA sr. fellow, 1987; recipient Disting. Alumni award U. Mich., 1971. Mem. ALA, AAUW, PEO Sisterhood (Scholar award 1993-94), Am. Studies Assn., D.C. Libr. Assn. (pres. 1979-80), U. Mich. Sch. Info. and Libr. Studies Alumni Soc. (pres. 1993-94). Office: Smithsonian Instn Librs NHB 24 Mail Stop 154 Washington DC 20560

GWOZDZ, KIM ELIZABETH, interior designer; b. Spokane, Wash., June 10, 1958; d. Myron Marcus and Marilyn Kay (Alsterlund) Westerkamp; m. Edwin Eugene Gwozdz, June 14, 1981; children: Ryan Marcus, Lauren Taylor. Student, U. Florence, Italy, 1979; BFA in Graphic Design, Illustration and Art History, U. Ariz., 1980. Design asst. Morse Studio, Scottsdale, Ariz., 1982; interior designer Pat Bacon & Assocs., Scottsdale, Ariz., 1983-88; prin., interior designer Provenance, Inc., Scottsdale, Ariz., 1988-90; dir. residential design Cox, James & Assocs., Phoenix, Ariz., 1990; prin, interior designer Kim E. Gwozdz/Provenance, Phoenix, Ariz., 1991, 1993—; interior designer Brady's Interior Design and Florist, Scottsdale, 1991-93. Contbr. articles to profl. jours. Nursery dir. infant and toddler care Mt. Cavalry Luth. Ch., Phoenix, 1985, mem. youth bd., 1984-89, trustee, 1993—; mem. Jr. League of Phoenix, 1989—, Orpheum Theater com., 1989—, vice chmn., 1990-91, chmn., 1992-94, Gift Mart com. Design Decorations, 1991-92, chmn., 1991, exec. com., bd. dirs. Orpheum Theatre Found., 1992—; active annual gala com. Am. Cancer Soc., 1993-94, 94—; design affiliate Nat. Trust for Hist. Preservation, 1986—. Recipient First Place award Annual Wool Rug Design Competition, Edward Fields, Inc., 1989, Second Place award,

1990, Third Place award, 1991. Mem. Am. Soc. Interior Designers (assoc. Ariz. North chpt., significant interiors survery com. 1975-91, chmn. 1990-91, Phoenix Home and Garden com. 1989-90, Herberger Theatre com. 1989-91, awards com. 1989, 91, chmn. 1990, competitions com. 1991, chmn. 1989-90, Rosson House Christmas chmn. 1986-91, hist. preservation chmn. 1988-91, directory chmn. Designers Market 1991; mem. nominating com. 1991-92, Third Place award Ariz. North 1987, Second Place award 1987, 88, 92, First Place award Nat. 1989, 94). Republican. Lutheran. Home: 529 W Palm Ln Phoenix AZ 85003 Office: Kim E Gwozdz/Provenance 2425 E Camelback Rd # 450 Phoenix AZ 85016

GYLSETH, DORIS (LILLIAN) HANSON, librarian; b. Helena, Mont., May 26, 1934; d. Richard E. and Lillie (Paula) Hanson; m. Arlie Albeck, Dec. 26, 1955 (div. Apr. 1964); m. Hermann M. Gylseth, Apr. 29, 1983 (dec. Aug. 1985). BS in Edn., Western Mont. Coll. Edn., 1958; MLS, U. Wash., 1961. Tchr. Helena Sch. Dist., 1955-56, Dillon (Mont.) Elem. Sch., 1957-59, Eltopia (Wash.) Unified Sch. Dist., 1959-60; sch. libr. Shoreline Sch. Dist., Seattle, 1960-64, Dept. of Def., Chateauroux, France, Hanau, Fed. Republic Germany, Tachikawa, Japan, 1964-68, Long Beach (Calif.) Unified Sch. Dist., 1968-70; br. libr. Long Beach Pub. Libr., 1970-74, coord. children's svcs., 1974-85; libr. Long Beach (Calif.) Unified Sch. Dist., 1986-94; realtor Century 21, All Pacific, 1994—. Bd. dirs. Children's Svcs. divsn. Calif. Libr. Assn., 1985, Literary Guild of Orange County, 1993—; co-chmn. Long Beach Authors Festival, 1978-86; mem. planning coun. Third Pacific Rim Conf. on Children's Lit., UCLA, 1986. Mem. So. Calif. Coun. on Lit. for Children and Young Poeple (bd. dirs. 1974-88, pres. 1982-84), Helen Fuller Cultural Carrousel (bd. dirs. 1985—), Friends of Long Beach Pub. Libr. (bd. dirs. 1988—), Zonta (pres. 1978-80). Home: 5131 Kingscross Rd Westminster CA 92683-4832

GYORKY, SUSAN MEINIG, medical/surgical nurse; b. Reading, Pa., June 11, 1947; d. Hans Richard and Elsie Marian (Miller) Meinig; m. Attila Istvan Gyorky, Aug. 22, 1970; 1 child, Robert Stephan. Student, East Stroudsburg State Coll., 1965-67; diploma, Reading Hosp. Sch. Nursing, 1970. RN, Pa.; CNOR; cert. laser safety officer Rockwell Inst. Evening charge nurse Monroe County Hosp., East Stroudsburg, Pa., 1970-71, Community Gen. Hosp., Reading, Pa., 1973-74; oper. rm. staff nurse Reading Hosp. and Med. Ctr., 1971-73, 74-77, head nurse oper. rm., 1977-88, head nurse laser surgery, 1986-89, asst. supr. ambulatory surgery, 1988-94, supr., head dept. ambulatory surgery, 1994—; presenter at profl. confs. Bd. dirs. Reading Hosp. and Med. Ctr. Fed. Credit Union, 1974-88; mem. CAP, Reading, 1990-91. Mem. Assn. Oper. Rm. Nurses (cert., pres. Tri-County chpt. 1983-87, bd. dirs. 1987-89, workshop chmn. 1987). Lutheran. Home: 7432 Brimway Ln Reading PA 19606 Office: Reading Hosp and Med Ctr 6th and Spruce Sts West Reading PA 19612

GYPE, MARY, clerk of courts; b. Wauseon, Ohio, Feb. 6, 1928; d. Ralph and Lillie (Vonier) Thierry; m. James A. Gype, Mar. 21, 1948; children: Jeffry A., Jana L. Gype Rupp. Grad. H.S., Wauseon. Office acct. Wauseon, 1947-56; with auto title dept. Clk. of Cts. Office, Wauseon, 1974-77; clk. of cts. Wauseon County Govt., 1977—. Pres. Wauseon Bd. Edn., 1976-77; mem. civil svc. com. City of Wauseon, 1985-86; v.p. Fulton County Rep. Women, 1992-93. Recipient Rep. Women Mamie Eisenhower award, 1991, Citizen of Yr. award City of Wauseon, 1988. Mem. Ohio Clk. of Cts. Assn. (exec. com. 1988, 92-93, sec. 1988-90, co-chmn. edn. com. 1987, title manual com. 1987, legis. com. 1983-85, 87, 93-94, Edn. cert. award 1985-91, 93, 94), Bus. and Profl. Women (pres. 1991-92, pres.-elect 1990-91), Internat. Assn. of Clks., Recorders, Election Ofcls. and Treas. Office: Courthouse Rm 203 Wauseon OH 43567

HAAB, REGINA ANN, data communications executive; b. Teaneck, N.J., June 20, 1948; d. Herman G. and Anastatia B. (Hanley) H. BS cum laude, St. Thomas Aquinas Coll., Sparkill, N.Y., 1991; postgrad., Iona Coll., 1991—. Mgr./adminstr. N.J. Bell, Paramus, 1966-79; dir. order svcs. ASCOM Timeplex, Woodcliff, N.J., 1980—. Bd. dirs., comm. com. St. Anselms, 1990, mem. parish coun., mem. fin. adv. bd. Mem. Tribute to Women in Industry (mgmt. forum), Alpha Sigma Lambda. Republican. Roman Catholic. Home: 15 Santa Fe Ct Asbury Park NJ 07712-3173 Office: ASCOM Timeplex 100 Commerce Way Hackensack NJ 07601

HAAG, CAROL ANN GUNDERSON, marketing professional, consultant; b. Mpls.; d. Glenn Alvin and Genevieve Esther (Knudson) Gunderson; m. Lawrence S. Haag, Aug. 30, 1969; 1 child, Maren Anne. BJ, U. Mo., 1969; postgrad., Roosevelt U., Chgo., 1975—. Pub. relations writer, advt. copywriter Am. Hosp. Supply Corp., Evanston, Ill., 1969-70; asst. dir. pub. relations Rush-Presbyn. St. Luke's Med. Ctr., Chgo., 1970-71; asst. mgr. pub. and employee communications Quaker Oats Co., Chgo., 1971-72, mgr. editorial communications, 1972-74, mgr. employee communications programs, 1974-77; dir. pub. relations Shaklee Corp., San Francisco, 1978-82; pres. CH & Assocs., San Francisco, 1982-84; dir corp. communications BRAE Corp., San Francisco, 1984; dir. mktg. St. Francis Meml. Hosp., San Francisco, 1985-89, dir. mktg. and planning svcs., 1989-91; ptnr. Haag & Rohan, San Francisco, San Diego, 1991—; cons. in field. Bd. dirs. Calif. League Handicapped; mem. adv. bd. San Francisco Spl. Olympics; mem. pub. relations com. San Francisco Recreation and Parks Dept., San Francisco Vol. Bur. Recipient 1st place cert. Printing Industry Am., 1972, 74, 1st place spl. comm. award Internat. Assn. Bus. Communicators, 1974, 1st place citation Chgo. Assn. Bus. Communicators, 1974, gold award Healthcare Mktg. Reports, 1989, 90. Mem. NATAS, Indsl. Com. Coun., Pub. Rels. Soc. Am., San Francisco C. of C. (grad. leadership program 1991, bd. dirs. leadership coun.), San Francisco Press Club. Home and Office: 133 Fernwood Dr Moraga CA 94556-2315

HAARMANN, DIANE CHRISTINE, guidance director; b. Albany, N.Y., Oct. 28, 1948; d. Levi Moak and Joyce Anne (Ingraham) Moak Roe; m. Carl R. Haarmann, Aug. 27, 1972. BA in English, Russell Sage Coll., Troy, N.Y., 1970; MA in Marital and Family Therapy, Assumption Coll., Worcester, Mass., 1977. Cert. secondary tchr. and prin. Tchr. English Nashoba Regional H.S., Bolton, Mass., 1970-78, guidance counselor, 1978-92, dir. guidance and coll. counseling, 1992—; cons. Haarmann Ednl. Assocs., West Boylston, Mass., 1990—. Named to USA Today Nat. Faculty, 1994. Mem. NEA, Mass. Tchrs. Assn., New Eng. Assn. Coll. Admissions Counselors, Mass. Guidance Assn. Methodist. Office: Nashoba Regional HS 12 Green Rd Bolton MA 01740-1027

HAAS, CAROLYN BUHAI, publisher, writer, consultant; b. Chgo., Jan. 1, 1926; d. Michael and Tillie (Weiss) Buhai; m. Robert Green Haas, June 29, 1947 (dec. June 30, 1984); children—Andrew Robert, Mari Beth, Thomas Michael, Betsy Ann, Karen Sue. B.Ed., Smith Coll., Northampton, Mass., 1947; postgrad. Nat. Coll. Edn., Evanston, Ill., 1956-59; Art Inst. Chgo., 1958-59. Tchr., Francis W. Parker Sch., Chgo., 1947-49; tchr. art Glencoe Pub. Schs., Ill., 1967-68, substitute tchr., 1964-72; co-founder PAR Leadership Tng. Found., Northfield, Ill., 1969-81; pres., editor CBH Pub., Inc., Northfield, 1979-92; cons., writer, adv. bd. The Learning Line; cons. presch. sci. program Mus. Sci. and Industry, Chgo.; adv. bd. My Own Mag.; cons. in field. Author: (with Ann Cole and Betty Weinberger) I Saw a Purple Cow, 1972, A Pumpkin In A Pear Tree, 1974, Children Are Children Are Children, 1976, Backyard Vacation, 1978, Purple Cow to the Rescue, 1982, Recipes for Fun and Learning, 1982, (with A.C. Friedman) My Own Fun, 1990, The Big Book of Recipes for Fun, 1979, Look At Me: Activities for Babies and Toddlers, 1985; co-editor: Know Your Town/East Hampton League Women Voters of the Hamptons, 1993; contbr. articles to profl. jours. Pres., West Sch. PTA, Glencoe; pres. Jr. Bd. Scholarship and Guidance, Chgo.; bd. dirs. Family Counseling Service of Glencoe, Glencoe Human Relations Com.; pres., sec., bd. dirs. Glencoe Pub. Library; pres. Friends of Glencoe Pub. Library; co-founder Glencoe Patriotic Days Com.; co-chmn. Frank Lloyd Wright Bridge Com., Glencoe; pres., bd. dirs. Chgo. League Smith Coll.; mem. women's bd. Northwestern U.; bd. dirs. Chgo. chpt. Am. Jewish Com., LWV of the Hamptons; mem. women's com. Chgo. Symphony Orch. Clubs; bd. dirs. Art Resources in Teaching; vol. Parish Art Mus., The Retreat. Mem. AAUW, Internat. Reading Assn., Soc. Children's Bookwriters, Children's Reading Roundtable, Nat. Assn. Edn. Young Children, Assn. Childhood Edn. Internat., NEA, Jimmy Ernst Artists Alliance (bd. dirs.), Phi Delta Kappa. Democrat. Jewish. Avocations: art, reading, sports, travel.

HAAS, ELLEN, federal agency administrator; b. N.Y.C., July 25, 1939. BA in History, U. Mich., 1961. Am. history and govt. tchr. Oklahoma City Pub. Schs., 1961-63; dir. consumer edn. County of Montgomery, Md., 1973-74; acting exec. dir. Nat. Consumers League, 1975-76; exec. dir. Pub. Voice for Food and Health Policy, Washington, 1982-93; asst. sec. agriculture food and consumer svcs. USDA, Washington, 1993—. Office: USDA Food & Consumer Svcs 14th & Independence Ave SW Washington DC 20250-0002

HAAS, JACQUELINE CRAWFORD, lawyer; b. St. Louis, Nov. 9, 1935; d. Ernest Augustus and Nora (Fullard) Crawford; m. Karl Alan Haas, Jan. 27, 1962 (dec. Mar. 1986); children: James Andrew, Susan Jennifer, David Reid, Peter Crawford. AB, Cornell U., 1957; LLB, Harvard U., 1961. Bar: N.Y. 1962, U.S. Dist. Ct. (so. dist.) N.Y. 1963, U.S. Ct. Appeals (2d cir.) 1968, Mass. 1972. Assoc. Lord, Day & Lord, N.Y.C., 1961-63; atty. family ct. div. Legal Aid Soc., Bklyn., 1964-66; exam. atty. N.Y.C. Dept. of Investigation, 1966-68, exec. asst. to commr., 1969-71; pvt. practice Weston, Mass., 1971—; mem. Greater Boston com. Harvard U. Law Sch. Fund, Cambridge, Mass., 1976—. Del. Mass. Dem. Issues Conv., 1983, 85, 87, 89, 92, 93, Mass. Dem. Nominating Conv., 1984, 86, 94; mem. Mass. Dem. Party Platform Com., 1993; mem. Dem. Town Com., Weston, 1984—, vice chmn., 1984-86; chmn. bd. Roxbury-Weston Programs, Inc., 1982-84; mem. family com. METCO, 1973-75, cmty. coord. coun., 1982-85; mem. Weston Housing Needs Com., 1991-93. Mem. ABA (civil practice and procedure of the antitrust sect.), Mass. Bar Assn., Assn. of Bar of N.Y.C., Harvard Law Sch. Assn. Mass. (v.p. 1991—). Democrat. Episcopalian. Office: 42 Partridge Hill Rd Weston MA 02193-1750

HAAS, JUNE F., special education educator, consultant; b. Burien, Wash., June 5, 1934; d. Carl Edwin and Mary Rebecca (Best) Flodquist; m. Frank M. Haas, June 21, 1958; children: Michael Edward, Katherine June Haas Dunning. BA in Elem. Edn., Psychology, U. Wash., 1956; MS in Early Childhood Edn., Oreg. Coll. Edn., 1975. Tchr. Haines (Alaska) Borough Sch. Dist., 1956-76, spl. edn. tchr., 1976-86, gifted, talented coord., 1978-87, migrant edn. tchr., 1986-87; instr. U. Alaska, Haines, 1984-85; cons. Ednl. Cons. Svcs., Haines, 1987—; instr. World Conf. Gifted/Talented Children, Hamburg, Germany, 1985, Sydney, Australia, 1989, 2d Gifted Asian Conf. on Giftedness, Taipei, Taiwan, 1992, World Conf. Gifted/Talented Children, Toronto, Can., 1993 ; coach Alaska Future Problem Solving Program, 1982-87; del. Citizen Ambassador Program Russia, Siberia, Hungary, 1991; del./presentor U.S./Russia Joint Conf. Edn., Moscow, 1994. Pres. Bus. and Profl. Women's Clubs, Alaska, 1973-74, Am. Legion Aux., Alaska, 1990-91, nat. exec. com., 1991-92, mem. nat. edn. com., 1991-92; bd. dir. Am. Cancer Soc., Alaska, 1976—; chmn. we divsn. Nat. Edn. Com., 1992-93. Mem. World Coun. Gifted/Talented Children, Coun. Exceptional Children, Bus. and Profl. Women's Club (v.p. 1972-73, Woman of Yr. 1972), Am. Legion Aux. (nat. jr. activities com., western divsn. chmn. 1993-94, mem. citizens flag alliance 1994-95), Lynn Canal Community Players (nat. drama festival com. 1983), Haines Women's Club (pres. 1988-90), Pioneers of Alaska (pres. 1990-91). Methodist. Home and Office: Ednl Cons Svcs PO Box 97 Haines AK 99827-0097

HAAS, KELLEY WEYFORTH, marketing and communications company executive; b. St. Louis, July 27, 1964; d. Francis Griffin Jr. and Mara (Kelley) Weyforth; m. Timothy John Haas, June 27, 1987. BSBA, U. Kans., 1986. Bookkeeper Mktg. Resources, Inc., Overland Park, Kans., 1983-84, prodn./traffic asst., 1984-85, media buyer, planner, 1985-86, coord. tng. programs, 1986-87, traffic mgr., 1987-89; sr. account. exec. Mktg. Resources Am., Inc., Overland Park, 1989-91, account supr., 1991-92, v.p., account supr., 1992-93, v.p. mktg. svcs., 1993-94, sr. v.p. mktg. svcs., 1994—, also bd. dirs., mem. exec. com. Mem. Advt. Club Kansas City. Office: Mktg Resources Am Inc 10551 Barkley Overland Park KS 66212

HAASE, KAREN MARGARET, wildlife rehabilitation center administrator; b. Newport News, Va., Dec. 31, 1969; d. Harold William Jr. and nancy Alice (Phillips) H. BA in Biology, Cedar Crest Coll., Allentown, Pa., 1992. Conservation biologist Mote Marine Lab., Sarasota, Fla., 1990; teaching asst., lab. asst. Cedar Crest Coll., 1990-92; animal caretaker Trexler Game Preserve, Schnecksville, Pa., 1991; naturalist Pool Wildlife Sanctuary, Emmaus, Pa., 1992—; vet. technician Emmaus Animal Hosp., 1992—; wildlife rehab. asst. Aark Found., Newtown, Pa., 1992—; exec. dir. Wachter Wildlife Rehab. Ctr., Emmaus, 1994—. Mem. Internat. Wildlife Rehab. Coun., Nat. Wildlife Rehab. Coun., Nat. Audubon Soc., Beta Beta Beta, Phi Alpha Theta, Kappa Mu Epsilon.

HABEEB, VIRGINIA THABET, magazine editor; b. Charleston, W.Va.; d. Mitchell Joseph and Rose M. (Couri) Thabet; m. Mitchell H. Habeeb. B.A. in Home Econs., Marshall U., 1946. Home service adviser Appalachian Electric Power Co., Abingdon, Va., 1946-49; with Crosley div. Avco Mfg. Corp., Cin., 1949-54; staff mem. field home econs. program, regional home economist, dir. nat. home econs. tng. program; women's editor daily show WCHS-TV, Charleston, 1954-55; assoc. home equipment editor Am. Home mag., N.Y.C., 1955-58; home equipment editor Am. Home mag., 1958-62, food and equipment editor, 1962-69, mng. editor, 1969-70; dir. Editorial Services, N.Y.C., 1970-84; media liaison Assn. Home Appliance Mfrs., 1984—; contbg. editor Ladies Home Jour., 1972—, Modern Bride mag., 1972—, Girl Talk mag., 1972-75, Family Health Mag., 1975-78, Home Mag., 1983—, 1,001 Home Ideas, 1983—, Working Mother mag., 1986—. Author: The Little Chef's Book, 1953; editor: Handbook of Household Equipment Terminology, 1956-60; Editor: American Home All-Purpose Cook Book, 1966; author: Ladies Home Journal Art of Homemaking, 1973, Macap's Handbook for the Informed Consumer, 1973, Thousands of Creative Kitchen Ideas, 1976, The Complete Blender Cookbook, 1978, Remodeling Your Kitchen, 1980, Pita, the Great, 1986. Former mem. home com. Greater N.Y. Safety Council; mem. home conf. com. Nat. Safety Council; bd. dirs. Talbot-Perkins Children's Services, 1976—. Recipient Disting. Alumna award Dept. Home Econs. Marshall U., 1981, Disting. Alumna award Marshall U. Alumni Assn., 1982. Mem. Am. Home Econs. Assn., Elec. Women's Round Table (chmn. N.Y. chpt. 1962-63), nat. dir. elec. women, nat. v.p. (1964-66), Advt. Women N.Y. (dir. 1971-72), Home Economists in Bus. (nat. chmn. housing and household equipment com. 1959-60), Maj. Appliance Consumer Action Panel (chmn. 1975-79), Assn. Home Appliance Mfrs. (hon. life). Home and Office: 200 E 62nd St New York NY 10021-8209 also: 200 E 62nd St # 6-b New York NY 10021-8209

HABEGGER, CYNTHIA A., geriatrics nursing educator; b. Van Wert County, Ohio, Dec. 14, 1953; d. Palmer Paul and Donna Jean (Hertel) Johnson; m. Alan Duane Habegger, Oct. 13, 1979; children: Duane Alan, Rebekkah Ann. ADN, Purdue U., Ft. Wayne, 1985, AD in Supervision, 1991; BSN, Luth. Coll. Health Profls., Ft. Wayne, 1994. RN, Ind.; lic. supr. Staff nurse Swiss Village, Berne, Ind., 1985-87; staff nurse med.-surg. unit Caylor Nickel Clinic, Bluffton, Ind., 1987-88; DON geriatric Decatur (Ind.) Community Care, 1988; charge nurse Cooper Community Care Corp., Bluffton, 1988; psychiat. staff nurse and charge nurse Caylor Nickel Clinic, Bluffton, 1988-92; ADON Meadowvale Nursing Home, Bluffton, 1992-93; intermittent RN Vis. Nurse Svc. and Hospice, Fort Wayne, Ind., 1993-94; instr. nursing Ivy Tech., Ind.'s Tech. Coll., 1994—. Home: 665 High St Berne IN 46711-1320

HABEGGER, LISA LYNN, artist, librarian, art administrator; b. Indpls., Dec. 27, 1959; d. Robert Malcolm and Ruth Jane (Hartley) Lynch; m. Dean Brian Habegger, Aug. 24, 1980. BA, Ind. U., 1983; postgrad., Sch. Art Inst. Chgo., 1986-87; MFA, U. Colo., 1990. Libr., head circulation Ryerson Slide Libr., Art Inst. Chgo., 1985-87; dir. Univ. Meml. Ctr. Fine Arts Gallery, U. Colo., Boulder, 1987-90; preparator design dept. Denver Art Mus., 1991; libr. adult svcs. Standley Lake Libr., Arvada, Colo., 1991—; mng. dir. Alternative Arts Alliance, Denver, 1991-94; preparator art galleries Arvada Ctr. for Arts and Humanities, 1992—. One-woman shows include CORE New Art Space, Denver, 1991, 92, 94, Auraria Libr. Gallery, Denver, 1991; group exhbns. include Lincoln Ctr. Galleries, Ft. Collins, Colo., 1988, 92, Ec-lec-tic Art Gallery, Denver, 1990, Blackhart Gallery, Denver, 1992, Gallery of Contemporary Art, Colorado Springs, 1993, Emmanuel Gallery, Denver, 1993, Arvada Ctr. for Arts and Humanities, 1993, 94, Roby Mill Gallery, Colorado Springs, 1993, Permanent Profs. Gallery, USAF Acad., 1994, MAX ART Gallery, Colorado Springs, 1994; represented by CORE New Art Space, Denver, Zaks Gallery, Chgo., Ruschman Gallery, Indpls., MAX ART Gallery, Colorado Springs, Colo. Recipient mdse. award 27th Poudre Valley Art League Regional, Ft. Collins, Colo., 1988; grantee U. Colo., 1990. Mem. Nat. Woman's Caucus for Art (v.p. Colo. chpt. 1991-92, pres. 1992-93), Colo. Libr. Assn., CORE New Art Space, Alt. Arts Alliance. Home: 4936 Quitman St Denver CO 80212

HABERER, MARY HELEN, draftsperson; b. Highland, Ill., Mar. 18, 1963; m. Jim G. Haberer, Oct. 7, 1988; 2 children. BFA in Indsl. Design, U. Ill., 1985. Draftsperson Wicks Organ Co., Highland, Ill., 1985—, advt. mgr., 1986—; freelance design worker, Highland, Ill., 1994—. Eucharistic minister, 1990-92, ch. host minister, 1994—. Recipient Chamber Person of the Yr. award Highland C. of C., 1994, Cmty. Svc. award, 1994. Mem. Highland C. of C. (treas. 1989, sec. 1990, v.p. 1991, pres. 1992-93), Highland Mfrs. Assn. (sec.-treas. 1989, pres. 1991). Roman Catholic. Office: Wicks Organ Co 1100 5th St PO Box 129 Highland IL 62249

HABERL, VALERIE ELIZABETH, educator, company executive; b. N.Y.C., July 6, 1947; d. William Anthony and Rose Mary (Hoholecek) H. BS, So. Conn. State U., 1969, postgrad., 1979. Cert. elem. tchr., Conn. Tchr. phys. edn. West Haven (Conn.) Bd. Edn., 1969—; supr. West Haven Parks and Recreation, 1980—; pres. Creative Studio, 1992—. Mem. Conn. Assn. Health, Phys. Edn., Recreation and Dance. Republican. Roman Catholic.

HABERLAND, SUSAN ROBERTA, chemical company executive; b. Cleve., Oct. 29, 1946; d. Frederick C. and Mildred E. Haberland. BS in Chem. Engring., Carnegie-Mellon U., 1968; MBA, Harvard U., 1973. Chem. engr. Polaroid Corp., Waltham, Mass., 1968-71; internal cons. Squibb Iran S.A., Tehran, 1974-75; prin. cons. Khadamat Modiryat Sanaye, Tehran, 1976-78; mgr. bus. planning Union Carbide, N.Y.C., 1978-80, mkt. mgr., 1981-83; bus. mgr. Union Carbide now Rhone-Poulenc Inc., N.Y.C., 1984-87; mgr. info. systems strategic plan project Rhone-Poulenc Inc., Cranbury, N.J., 1988-89, dir. strategic planning Specialty Chems. Group, 1989-90, dir. strategic planning and new bus. deve. Surfactants, 1991, dir. bus. devel. Latex & Specialty Polymers Group, 1992-93, dir. strategic planning Specialty Chems. divsn., 1993-94. Home: 840 Highland Ave Morrisville PA 19067-1070

HABERMAN, LOUISE SHELLY, consulting company executive; b. N.Y.C.; d. Harry Martin and Rebecca (Binstock) H.; m. Gordon Joel Schochet. BA, Cornell U., 1971; PhD, Princeton (N.J.) U., 1984. Mem. faculty numerous colls. and univs.], 1975-84; researcher pub. policy U.S. Dept. Commerce, 1976; prin. investigator pub. policy study State of N.J., Trenton, 1979-80; pvt. practice cons. Highland Park, N.J., 1984-86; head regional bank svcs. Multinational Strategies, Inc., N.Y.C., 1986-90; pres. Haberman Assocs., Inc., Edison, N.J., 1990—. Author: (monograph) Regional Banks: International Strategies for the Future, 1987; editor: (with Paul Sacks) Ann. Rev. of Nations, 1988; contbr. articles to profl. jours. Issues advisor selected polit. candidates and civil liberties causes. Office: Haberman Assocs Inc 315 N 8th Ave Edison NJ 08817-2914

HABERMANN, HELEN MARGARET, plant physiologist, educator; b. Bklyn., Sept. 13, 1927. AB, SUNY, Albany, 1949; MS, U. Conn., 1951; PhD, U. Minn., 1956. Asst. botanist U. Conn., Storrs, 1949-51; asst. U. Minn., Mpls., 1951-53, asst. plant physiologist, 1953-55, head residence counselor, 1955-56; rsch. assoc. U. Chgo., 1956-57; rsch. fellow Hopkins Marine Sta. Stanford (Calif.) U., 1957-58; from asst. prof. to assoc. prof. biol. scis. Goucher Coll., Towson, 1958-70, chmn. dept. biology, 1963-66, 68, 78-79, prof., 1970-92, Lilian Welsh prof. biol. scis., 1982-92; prof. emeritus, 1992—. Co-author Biology: A Full Spectrum, 1973, Mainstreams of Biology, 1977. NIH spl. rsch. fellow Rsch. Inst. Advanced Study, Balt., 1966-67. Fellow AAAS; mem. Phytochem. Soc. N.Am. (sec. 1987-93), Am. Soc. Plant Physiologists, Am. Soc. Hort. Sci., Soc. Devel. Biology, Am. Soc. Photobiology, Am. Inst. Biol. Scis., Scandinavian Soc. Plant Physiology, Internat. Soc. Plant Molecular Biology, Japanese Soc. Plant Physiology, Soc. Exptl. Biology and Medicine, Am. Camellia Soc., Pioneer Camellia Soc. (pres. 1994-96), Am. Hort. Soc., Sigma Xi. Office: Goucher College Dept Biol Scis 1021 Dulaney Valley Rd Baltimore MD 21204-2794

HABICHT, PATRICIA T., lawyer; d. Frank H. and Jeanne (Patrick) H. BS in Math., Purdue U., 1971; JD, Northwestern U., 1974. Sr. v.p., assoc. gen. counsel The 1st Nat. Bank Chgo., 1974—. Mem. ABA, Am. Coll. Real Estate Lawyers, Chgo. Bar Assn. Office: The 1st Nat Bank Chgo Ste 0801 1 First National Plz Chicago IL 60670

HABLUTZEL, NANCY ZIMMERMAN, lawyer, educator; b. Chgo., Mar. 16, 1940; d. Arnold Fred Zimmerman and Maxine (Lewison) Zimmerman Goodman; m. Philip Norman Hablutzel, July 1, 1980; children: Margo Lynn, Robert Paul. BS, Northwestern U., 1960; MA, Northeastern Ill. U., 1972; JD, Ill. Inst. Tech. Chgo.-Kent Coll. Law, 1980; PhD, Loyola U., Chgo., 1983. Bar: Ill. 1980, U.S. Dist. Ct. (no. dist.) Ill. 1980. Speech therapist various pub. schs. and hosps., Chgo. and St. Louis, 1960-63, 65-72; audiologist U. Chgo. Hosps., 1963-65; instr. spl. edn. Chgo. State U., 1972-76; asst. prof. Loyola U., Chgo., 1981-87; adj. prof. Ill. Inst. Tech. Chgo.-Kent Coll. Law, 1982—, Lewis U., 1990-92; lectr. Loyola U., Chgo., 1990—; legal dir. Legal Clinic for Disabled, Chgo., 1984-85, exec. dir., 1985-87; of counsel Whitted & Spain P.C., 1987-89; prin. Hablutzel & Assocs., Chgo., 1989-94; hearing officer Circuit Ct. of Cook County, 1994—. Mem. Ill. Gov.'s Com. on Handicapped, 1972-75; mem. Coun. for Exceptional Children, faculty moderator student div., 1982-87, Ill. Atty. Gen. adv. com. for disabled, 1985—; mem. adv. com. Scouting for People With Disabilities, Chgo. Area Boy Scouts Am., 1988-92. Loyola-Mellon Found. grantee, 1983. Author: (with B. McMahon) Americans With Disabilities Act: Access and Accomodations, 1992; contbg. editor Nat. Disability Law Reporter, 1991-92. Fellow Chgo. Bar Found. (life), Ill. Bar Found. (sec. fellows 1992, vice-chair fellows 1993, chair 1994); mem. ABA, Ill. Bar Assn. (assoc., standing com. on juvenile justice, sec. 1986-87, vice chmn. 1987-88, chmn. 1988-89, Inst. Pub. Affairs 1985—, legis. com. 1991—, mem. juvenile justice sect. coun. 1994—), Chgo. Bar Assn. (corp. law com., exec. com. 1984—, chmn. Div. IV 1988-91, sec. 1991-92, vice chair 1992-93, chair 1993-94), Chgo. Hearing Soc. (Marion Goldman award 1988, bd. dirs. 1992-94). Republican. Avocations: sailing, travel, swimming, cooking.

HACKENBERG, BARBARA JEAN COLLAR, advertising and public relations executive; b. Venango County, Pa., Apr. 15, 1927; d. Guy Lamont and Marion Leona (Kingsley) Collar; m. George Richardson, June 13, 1953; children: Kurt Edward, Kim Ellen, Caroline Kingsley. BA, Grove City (Pa.) Coll., 1948; ML, U. Pitts., 1949. Advt. dir. The Halle Bros. Co., Erie, Pa., 1950-52, advt. and sales promotion dir., 1952-54; exec. dir. Wyomissing (Pa.) Inst. Fine Arts, 1970-74; dir. and community liason Freedman Gallery, Albright Coll., Reading, Pa., 1976-78; selling supr. Pomeroy's Children's Dept., Wyomissing, Pa., 1981-83; pub. relations account exec. Wentworth Assocs., Lancaster, Pa., 1983-84; exec. dir. World Affairs Coun., Reading, 1987—; owner The WRITE Place, Reading, 1979—. V.p. Harrisburg (Pa.) Foreign Policy Assn., 1964-67; various fund-raising activities, 1954-70; pub. relations chmn. Erie World Affairs Ctr., 1957-60. Mem. Women in Communications, Inc. (pub. relations chmn. cen. Pa. chpt., 1984-87, sec. cen. Pa. chpt., 1986-87).,. Methodist. Home and Office: 1334 Welsh Rd Reading PA 19607

HACKER, CAROLYN CARLISLE, child development program administrator; b. Dallas, Jan. 11, 1957; d. Thomas Wayne Sr. and Patricia Louise (Barron) Carlisle; m. Zachary E. Wright, July 18, 1981 (div. Oct. 1991); 1 child, Zachary Edward Jr.; m. Joseph Granville Hacker II, Nov. 20, 1992; children: Joseph G. III, Megan Rebecca. BS in Recreation Adminstrn., Tex. A & M U., 1979, MS in Ednl. Psychology, 1994. Dir. pks. and recreation City of Galena Park, Tex., 1980; recreation coord. Tulsa (Okla.) County Pk. Dept., 1981-83, City of Corpus Christi, Tex., 1985-88; child devel. program adminstr. USN, Corpus Christi, 1988—; bd. dirs., chmn. children's svcs. com., children's adv. Child Abuse Prevention Coun., Corpus Christi, 1991—; bd. dirs., children's adv. Children's Adv. Ctr., Corpus Christi, 1992—. Children's adv. Directions for Children, Corpus Christi, 1993. Recipient Community Svc. award Child Abuse Prevention Coun., Corpus Christi, 1992. Mem. Nat. Assn. for the Edn. Young Children. Republican. Baptist. Office: USN Child Devel Code 22 Bldg 39 Corpus Christi TX 78419

HACKER, SHEILA RENEE, media specialist; b. Ellinwood, Kans., Dec. 15, 1963. BS in Biology, S.W. Bapt. U., 1986. Cert. tchr., Mo. Media specialist, libr., tchr. Fair Play (Mo.) R-II Sch., 1988—. Recipient State award IBM Tech. and Learning Tchr. of Yr., 1992, Fair Play R-II Sch. Tchr. of the Yr., 1991-92; grantee Mo. Dept. Edn., 1991-92. Mem. Mo. Assn. Sch. Librs., S.W. Regional Assn. Sch. Librs., P.E.O. (officer 1992—). Baptist. Home: Rt 3 Box 155 Bolivar MO 65613 Office: Fair Play R-II Sch Rt 1 Box 1020 Fair Play MO 65649

HACKETT, BARBARA (KLOKA), federal judge; b. 1928. B of Philosophy, U. Detroit, 1948, JD, 1950. Bar: Mich. 1951, U.S. Dist. Ct. (ea. dist.) Mich. 1951, U.S. Ct. Appeals (6th cir.) 1951, U.S. Supreme Ct. 1957. Law clk. U.S. Dist. Ct. (ea. dist.) Mich., 1951-52; chief law clk. U.S. Ct. Appeals, Mich., 1965-66; asst. pros. atty. Wayne County, Mich., 1967-72; pvt. practice law Detroit, 1952-53, 72-73, Frasco, Hackett & Mills, 1984-86; U.S. magistrate U.S. Dist. Ct. (ea. dist.) Mich., Detroit, 1973-84, judge, 1986—; mem. Interstate Commerce Commn., 1964. Trustee U. Detroit, 1983-89, Mercy High Sch., Farmington Hills, Mich. 1984-86, Detroit Symphony Orch., Orch. Hall Assocs., Detroit Sci. Ctr., United Community Svcs. Recipient Pres.'s Cabinet award U. Detroit Mercy, 1991. Mem. ABA (spl. ct. judge discovery abuse com. 1978-79, com. on cts. in community 1979-84), Am. Judicature Soc., Fed. Bar Assn. (sec. 1981-82), Fed. Judges Assn., Nat. Assn. Women Judges (Nat. Conf. program com. 1981), Nat. Assn. Women Lawyers, Nat. Dist. Attys. Assn., Nat. Assn. R.R. Trial Counsel, State Bar of Mich., Women Lawyers Assn. of Mich., Pros. Attys. Assn. of Mich. Disting. Svc. award 1971), Oakland County Bar Assn., Detroit Bar assn., (program com. 1965-75), U. Detroit Law Alumni Assn. (officer 1970-75, pres. 1975-77, Alumni Tower award 1976), Women's Econ. Club (bd. dirs. 1975-80, pres. 1980-81, named One Detroit's Dynamic Women 1992), Econ. Club of Detroit (bd. dirs. 1979-84, 88—), Phi Gamma Nu. Office: US Dist Ct 718 US Courthouse 231 W Lafayette Blvd Detroit MI 48226-2719

HACKETT, CAROL ANN HEDDEN, physician; b. Valdese, N.C., Dec. 18, 1939; d. Thomas Barnett and Zada Loray (Pope) Hedden; BA, Duke, 1961; MD, U. N.C., 1966; m. John Peter Hackett, July 27, 1968; children: John Hedden, Elizabeth Bentley, Susanne Rochet. Intern. Georgetown U. Hosp., Washington, 1966-67, resident, 1967-69; clinic physician DePaul Hosp., Norfolk, Va., 1969-71; chief spl. health services Arlington County Dept. Human Resources, Arlington, Va., 1971-72; gen. med. officer USPHS Hosp., Balt., 1974-75; pvt. practice family medicine, Seattle, 1975—; mem. staff, chmn. dept. family practice Overlake Hosp. Med. Ctr., 1985-86; clin. asst. prof. Sch. Medicine U. Wash. Bd. dirs. Mercer Island (Wash.) Preschool Assn., 1977-78; coordinator 13th and 20th Ann. Inter-profl. Women's Dinner, 1978, 86; trustee Northwest Chamber Orch., 1984-85. Mem. AAUW, Am. Acad. Family Practice (trustee 1993-94), King County Acad. Family Practice, King County Med. Soc. (chmn. com. TV violence), Wash. Med. Soc., DAR, Bellevue C. of C., NW Women Physicians (v.p. 1978), Seattle Symphony League, Eastside Women Physicians (founder, pres.), Sigma Kappa, Wash. Athletic Club, Lakes Club, Seattle Yacht Club. Episcopalian. Home: 4304 E Mercer Way Mercer Island WA 98040-3826 Office: 1414 116th Ave NE Bellevue WA 98004

HACKETT, LOUISE, personnel services company executive, consultant; b. Sheridan, Mont., Nov. 11, 1933; d. Paul Duncan and Freda A. (Dudley) Johnson; m. Lewis Edward Hackett, June 24, 1962; 1 child, Dell Paul. Student U. Oreg., 1959-61; BA, Calif. State U.-Sacramento, 1971. Legal sec. Samuel R. Friedman, Yreka, Calif., 1952-58, Barber & Cottrell, Eugene, Oreg., 1958-59; paralegal Elmer Sahlstrom, Eugene, 1959-62; legis. aide Calif. Legislature, Sacramento, 1962-72; owner Legal Personnel Services, Sacramento, 1973-78, corp. pres., 1979—; pres. Legalstaff, Inc., 1987—; curriculum adv. dept. bus. Am. River Coll., Sacramento, 1974-79; founder, adminstr. Pacific Coll. Legal Careers, Sacramento, 1973-84; cons. legal edn. Barclay Schs., Sacramento, 1984; active Sacramento Employees Adv. Coun. Designer, pub. Sacramento/Yolo Attys. Directory, 1974—. Author operations manual and franchise training textbook; contbr. articles to profl. jours. Adv. bd. San Juan Sch. Dist., 1975-84. Mem. Calif. Assn. Personnel Cons., Sacramento Council Pvt. Edn. (pres. 1976-77), Pi Omega Pi. Clubs: Sierra Sail and Trail, Soroptimist Internat. Lodge: Order of Rainbow. Avocations: skiing, sailing, gardening, horseback riding. Office: Legal Personnel Svcs 1415 21st St Sacramento CA 95814-5208 also: 433 California St # 904 San Francisco CA 94104 also: 2107 Landings Dr Mountain View CA 94043-0839 also: 111 N Market St Ste 404 San Jose CA 95113-1101

HACKLER, JANET ANTHONY, public relations generalist; b. Piedmont, Calif., July 13, 1938. BA in Polit. Sci., U. Calif., Berkeley, 1961, MA in Edn., 1968; postgrad. in bus. adminstrn., Fordham U., N.Y.C. Tchr. English Orinda Union Sch. Dist., Calif., 1962-68; coordinator ednl. research, edn. counselor Hill & Knowlton Inc., N.Y.C., 1968-70; cons., writer Ednl. Systems & Designs, Westport, Conn., 1974; writer, producer Producers Row Inc., N.Y.C., 1975; v.p. public rels. V & J Tax Co., 1993—. Mem. championship synchronized swimming team; appearances include Australian Olympics, Brussels World Fair, Ed Sullivan Show. Recipient Helms award, 1963 (All-American 1956-61).

HACKNEY, VIRGINIA HOWITZ, lawyer; b. Phila., Jan. 11, 1945; d. Charles Rawlings and Edith Wren (Pope) Howitz, m. Barry Albert Hackney, Feb. 15, 1969; children: Ashby Rawlings, Roby Howison, Trevor Pope. BA in Econs., Hollins Coll., 1967; JD, U. Richmond, 1970. Bar: Va. 1970. Assoc. Hunton & Williams, Richmond, Va., 1970-77, ptnr., 1977—; pres. Am. Acad. Hosp. Attys. Chgo., 1992-93. Mem. agy. evaluation com. United Way of Greater Richmond, 1981-86; sustainer Jr. League of Richmond. Named Outstanding Woman in field of law, YWCA, Richmond, 1981. Mem. ABA (bus. law sect. 1984—, forum com. on health law 1982—), Am. Acad. Hosp. Attys. (bd. dirs. 1988-94, pres. 1992-93), Va. State Bar (long range planning com. 1985-90, chmn. standing com. lawyer discipline 1986-90, exec. com. 1988-90). Office: Hunton & Williams Riverfront Plz East Tower 951 E Byrd St Richmond VA 23219-4074

HACKNEY-SIMMONS, MARY ALICE, nurse; b. Middletown, Ohio, Mar. 7, 1955; d. Byron Allen and Joan Elaine (Meeker) H.; m. Roy Leslie Brown, Sept. 12, 1974 (dec. Nov. 1979); m. Randolph Anthony Hackney-Simmons, July 26, 1980 (div. Nov. 1992). AAS in Nursing, Miami U., 1975; BSN, U. Hawaii, 1991, postgrad., 1993—. CNOR. Staff nurse Shriners' Burn Inst., Cin., 1975-76, Cin. Gen. Hosp., 1976-77, Middletown (Ohio) Hosp., 1977-80; pub. health nurse Middletown Bureau Pub. Health Nursing, 1980-81; staff nurse Ambulatory Care Ctr., Centerville, Ohio, 1981-82, St. Francis Med. Ctr., Honolulu, 1982-84; mgr. Hawaiian Eye Surgictr., Wahaiwa, 1984-85; coord. operating rm. quality assurance and edn. St. Francis Med. Ctr., Honolulu, 1985-87; nurse mgr., patient care coord., surgery The Queen's Med. Ctr., Honolulu, 1987-88, staff nurse, 1988-91; clin. nurse III surgery Queen's Med. Ctr., Honolulu, 1991—; negotiator St. Francis Med. Ctr., 1983, 85, Queen's Med. Ctr., 1993. Mem. So. Poverty Law Ctr., 1990. Recipient Nat. Collegiate Nursing award, U.S. Achievement Acad., Lexington, Ky., 1990. Mem. NOW, ANA, Assn. Oper. Rm. Nurses (sec. 1987-89, pres. 1989-91), Hawaii Nurses Assn. and Collective Bargaining Assn. (bd. dirs. 1991—, chairperson 1994-95, Hawaii rep. ANA Inst. Collective Bargaining (vice chair 1994-95), Golden Key (charter), Sigma Theta Tau-Gamma Psi (scholar). Buddhist. Home: 3071 Pualei Cir Apt 308 Honolulu HI 96815-4927

HACKWOOD, MARY-JEAN, administrator retirement system; b. Turlock, Calif., Nov. 7, 1935; d. Arthur Wellesley and Gertrude Chandler (Stimson) H. BA, U. Nev., 1959. Adminstr. State Tchrs. Retirement System, Alaska, 1959-72, Pub. Employees Retirement System, Alaska, 1959-72, Police and Fire Retirement System, Alaska, 1959-72, Jud. Retirement System, Alaska, 1959-72, Hughes Air West Retirement System, Calif., 1959-72, Missouri State Employees Retirement System, Mo., 1959-72, Orange County Employees Retirement System, 1987—. Named to 25 Top Pension Officers, Investing Mag., 1991. Mem. I.F. Employee Benefit Plan, Am. Indsl. Ptnrs. (adv. bd.), NASRA (v.p. western region, v.p. midwestern region). Office: Orange County Retirement Sy 2942 Daimler St Santa Ana CA 92705-5824

HACKWOOD, SUSAN, electrical and computer engineering educator; b. Liverpool, Eng., May 23, 1955; came to U.S., 1980; d. Alan and Margaret Hackwood. BS with honors, DeMonfort U., Eng., 1976; PhD in Solid State Ionics, DeMontfort U., Eng., 1979; PhD (hon.), Worcester Poly. Inst., 1993; DSc (hon.), DeMontfort U., 1993. Rsch. fellow DeMonfort U., Leicester, Eng., 1976-79; postdoctoral rsch. fellow AT&T Bell Labs., Homdel, N.J., 1980-81; mem. tech. staff AT&T Bell Labs., Homdel, 1981-83, supr. robotics tech., 1983-84, dept. head robotics tech., 1984-85; prof. elec. and computer engring. U. Calif., Santa Barbara, 1985-89, dir. Ctr. Robotic Systems in Microelectronics, 1985-89; dean Bourns Coll. Engring. U. Calif., Riverside, 1990—. Editor Jour. Robotic Systems, 1983, Recent Advances in Rototics, 1985; contbr. over 100 articles to tech. jours.; 7 patents in field. Mem. IEEE (sr.). Office: U Calif Coll Engring Riverside CA 92521

HADAR, MARY ELLEN, newspaper editor; b. Bklyn., Mar. 23, 1945; d. Martin H. and Fay (Himmelstein) Selman; m. Yosef Hadar, Mar. 16, 1971 (div. 1987); children—Doron, Yaniv. B.A., U. Pa., 1965; M.S. in Journalism, Columbia U., 1966. Copy editor Balt. Sun, 1966-69; fgn. editor Jerusalem Post, 1969-77; night editor Washington Post, 1977-81, dep. editor Style, 1981-83, asst. mng. editor, 1983—. Recipient Penney-Mo. award Best Feature sect. 1985, 86, 87, 91. Office: The Washington Post 1150 15th St NW Washington DC 20071-0001

HADAS, ELIZABETH CHAMBERLAYNE, publisher; b. Washington, May 12, 1946; d. Moses and Elizabeth (Chamberlayne) H.; m. Jeremy W. Heist, Jan. 25, 1970 (div. 1976); m. Peter Eller, Mar. 21, 1984. A.B., Radcliffe Coll., 1967; postgrad. Rutgers U., 1967-68; M.A., Washington U., St. Louis, 1971. Editor U. N.Mex. Press, Albuquerque, 1971-85; dir., 1985—. Mem. Assn. Am. Univ. Presses (pres. 1992-93). Democrat. Home: 2900 10th St NW Albuquerque NM 87107-1111 Office: U NMex Press 1720 Lomas Blvd NE Albuquerque NM 87131-1591

HADAS, JULIA ANN, social services administrator; b. Rome, Ga., May 23, 1947; d. Robert Franklin and Myrtle Julia (Patrick) Richmond; m. John R. Hadas, Apr. 22, 1967 (div.); children: Kevin, Brian. BS magna cum laude, No. Mich. U., 1972, MA, 1977. Cert. social worker; lic. profl. counselor. Placement worker adult community Mich. Dept. Social Svcs., Marquette, 1976-80, supr. vol. svcs., 1980-86, supr. children svcs., 1986-93; dir. Marquette Local Office, 1993—. Chair Parent Adv. Coun. Marquette Area Pub. Schs., 1984-85, Upper Peninsula Children's Coalition, 1993—; adv. bd. Student Vol. Orgn. No. Mich. U., 1984-85; sec., pers. com. Women's Ctr. Named one of Outstanding Young Women in Am., 1982. Mem. Childbirth Edn. Assn. (pres. 1975-76), Mich. Assn. Vol. Adminstrs., Zonta (pres. Marquette chpt. 1982-83). Episcopalian.

HADDA, JANET RUTH, Yiddish language educator, lay psychoanalyst; b. Bradford, Eng., Dec. 23, 1945; came to U.S., 1948; d. George Manfred and Annemarie (Kohn) H.; m. Allan Joshua Tobin, Mar. 22, 1981; stepchildren—David, Adam. B.S. in Edn., U. Vt., 1966; M.A., Cornell U., 1969; Ph.D., Columbia U., 1975. Prof. Yiddish UCLA; research psychoanalyst So. Calif. Psychoanalytic Inst., Los Angeles, 1988—. Author: Yankev Glatshteyn, 1980, Passionate Women, Passive Men: Suicide in Yiddish Literature, 1988; editorial bd. Prooftexts, Yivo Ann.; contbr. articles to profl. jours. Mem. Assn. Jewish Studies, MLA, Am. Psychoanalytic Assn. (assoc.), Inst. Contemporary Psychoanalysis, Phi Beta Kappa. Office: UCLA Dept Germanic Langs 310 Royce Hall Los Angeles CA 90024

HADDOX, ARDEN RUTH STEWART, automotive aftermarket manufacturing executive; b. Wheeling, W.Va., Sept. 29, 1930; d. Oliver Shaw and Helen (Neitzel) Stewart; children: Mark, Todd. BA, Baldwin Wallace Coll., 1952. Trainee GM, Cleve., 1952-57; tchr. Elyria (Ohio) City Bd. Edn., 1967-85; pres., CEO AAR, Inc., Cleve., 1984—, also chmn. bd. dirs. Pres. Elyria schs. PTA, 1967; treas. Homeowners Assn., North Ridgeville, Ohio, 1988-89. Recipient Weatherhead 100 award Case Western REs. U., 1990, 91, 92, 93, 94. Republican. Episcopalian. Home: 32889 Brownstone Ln N Ridgeville OH 44039-2503 Office: AAR Inc 34999 Mills Rd North Ridgeville OH 44039

HADIARIS, MARIE ELLEN, special education educator; b. N.Y.C., July 16, 1944; d. Regis Henri and Mary (Cullen) Courtemanche; m. Daniel P. Hadiaris, May 27, 1972; 1 child, Regis. BA, Molloy Coll., 1966; MS, Canisius Coll., 1968. Cert. deaf educator, N.Y., Mich. Tchr. of hearing impaired Cath. Charities Sch. for Deaf, Westbury, N.Y., 1967-68, Mill Neck (N.Y.) Manor Sch. for Deaf, 1968-69, Grand Rapids (Mich.) Pub. Schs., 1969-72; tchr. cons. for physically impaired Muskegon (Mich.) Pub. Schs., 1972-79, tchr. of hearing impaired, 1979—; presenter Nat. Symposium on Use of Tech. in Edn. of Deaf Nat. Tech. Inst. for Deaf Rochester (N.Y.) Inst. Tech., 1992; coord. Theater of the Deaf program Rochester Inst. Tech. Nat. Tech. Inst., Muskegon Pub. Schs., 1978-91; introduction AT&T Learning Network Computer Program, Muskegon Pub. Schs., 1990—; presenter AT&T Learning Network Program West Shore Spotlight, 1993. Contbr. articles to newspapers. Grantee Mich. Dept. Edn., 1990, 92. Mem. Conv. of Am. Instrs. of Deaf. Home: 962 Hampden Rd Muskegon MI 49441-4121 Office: Marquette Sch 480 Bennett St Muskegon MI 49442-2199

HADLEY, CAROLYN BETH, physician, educator; b. Dallas, Nov. 22, 1945; d. Charles Franklin and Sadie Beth (Humphreys) Hadley; m. Richard G. Suchan, Dec. 28, 1985; children: Richard C., Stephen G. BA with honors in Microbiology, U. Kans., 1968; MS in Clin. Microbiology, Columbia U. Coll. Physicians and Surgeons, 1974; MD, U. Pa., 1981. Diplomate Am. Coll. Med. Examiners., Am. Bd. Ob-Gyn. Maternal-Fetal Medicine. Lab technologist St. Joseph Mercy Hosp., Ann Arbor, Mich., 1968-70; sr. technologist, diagnostic microbiology svc. Columbia Presbyn. Med. Ctr., N.Y.C., 1970-73, sr. asst. supr., 1973-75; asst. microbiologist Hosp. of U. Pa., Phila., 1975-77, resident in ob-gyn., 1981-85, fellow in maternal fetal medicine, 1985-87; teaching asst. in microbiology U. Kans., 1968; teaching fellow microbiology U. Mich. Med. Sch., 1969; asst. prof. Med. Coll. Pa., 1987-91, assoc. prof., 1991-93, dir. obstetrics, 1992, asst. prof. anesthesiology, 1993. Recipient Undergrad. Rsch. award U. Kans., 1967; Phillip Williams prize in obstetrics, 1984; S. Leon Israel prize in obstetrics, 1985; Henrietta Ottinger/Huston MacFarlane scholar Med. Coll. Pa., 1978-93. Fellow Am. Coll. Ob-Gyn.; mem. AMA, Am. Soc. Microbiology (specialist in microbiology), Am. Soc. Clin. Pathologists (specialist microbiologist), Phila. Perinatal Soc., Soc. for Perinatal Obstetricians, DAR, U. Kans. Alumni Assn., Phila. Obstet. Soc., Phi Beta Kappa. Office: Med Coll Pa Dept Ob-Gyn 3300 Henry Ave Philadelphia PA 19129-1121

HADLEY, ELIZABETH HARRISON, lawyer, health policy analyst; b. Lawrence, Mass., May 20, 1955. BA, Yale U., 1977, MPH, 1989; JD, U. Calif., Berkeley, 1981. Asst. atty. gen. State of Conn. Office of the Atty Gen., Hartford, 1984-87; atty.-advisor U.S. Dept. Health & Human Svcs., Washington, 1989-93, policy coord., 1993; sr. policy fellow ANA, Washington, 1994; sr. policy analyst U.S. Congress, Office Tech. Assessment, Washington, 1994—. Bd. dirs. Guilford (Conn.) Land Conservation Trust, 1984-88, Washington Com. for the Frontier Nursing Svcs., 1990—, trustee, 1992-94, bd. govs., 1994—. Mem. Phi Beta Kappa. Office: Office of Tech Assessment US Congress Washington DC 20510-8025

HADLEY, JANE BYINGTON, psychotherapist; b. N.Y.C., Apr. 24, 1929; d. David and Ruth (Johnson) Millar; m. Arthur Twining Hadley, Feb. 24, 1979; children: Elisabeth Jane Hadley Wheeler, Caroline Anne Hadley Thies. BA, U. Va., 1951; MA, Columbia U., 1967; analytic tng., Met. Ctr. for Mental Health, 1970-73. Intern Queens Coll., 1969; pvt. practice psychotherapy N.Y.C., 1971—. Coun. mem. Planned Parenthood of N.Y.; bd. dirs. UN Plz. Mem. APA, Cosmopolitan Club, Century Assn. Democrat. Episcopalian.

HADLEY, LEILA ELIOTT-BURTON (MRS. HENRY LUCE, III), author; b. N.Y.C., Sept. 22, 1925; d. Frank Vincent and Beatrice Boswell (Eliott) Burton; m. Arthur T. Hadley, II, Mar. 2, 1944 (div. Aug. 1946); 1 child, Arthur T. III; m. Yvor H. Smitter, Jan. 24, 1953 (div. Oct. 1969); children: Victoria C. Van D. Smitter Barlow, Matthew Smitter Eliott, Caroline Allison F.S. Nicholson; m. William C. Musham, May 1976 (div. July 1979); m. Henry Luce III, Jan. 1990. MD, St. Timothy's Sch., 1943. mem. bd. advisors Tricyle, The Buddhist Rev., 1991—; bd. dirs. Wings Trust, Inc. Author: Give Me the World, 1958, How to Travel with Children in Europe, 1963, Manners for Children, 1967, Fielding's Guide to Traveling with Children in Europe, 1972, rev., 1974, 84, Traveling with Children in the U.S.A., 1974, Tibet-20 Years After the Chinese Takeover, 1979, (with Theodore B. Van Itallie) The Best Spas: Where to Go for Weight Loss, Fitness Programs and Pure Pleasure in the U.S. and Around the World, 1988, rev., 1989; assoc. editor: Diplomat mag., N.Y.C., 1964-65, Saturday Evening Post, N.Y.C., 1965-67; editorial cons. TWYCH, N.Y.C., 1985-87; book reviewer Palm Beach Life, Fla., 1967-72; contbg. editor Spa Vacations mag., 1989—; contbr. articles to various newspapers, mags. Mem. Soc. Woman Geographers (exec. council 1984—), Authors Guild, Nat. Writers Union, Nat. Press Club, Explorers Club. Republican. Presbyterian. Home: 4 Sutton Pl New York NY 10022-3056 Office: Sterling Lord Literistic One Madison Ave New York NY 10010

HADLEY-BANAHENE, SARA SINGLETARY, educator; b. Lake City, S.C., Feb. 26, 1956; d. Charles Carr Jr. and Dorothy Belle (Singletary) Williams; m. Eugene L. Hadley Jr., Dec. 12, 1981 (div. June 1984); 1 child, Brandon Alexander; m. Rockson O. Banahene, Apr. 11, 1988; 1 child, Aryelle Evian. BA cum laude, CCNY, 1978, MS magna cum laude, 1983; postgrad., N.Y. Law Sch., 1978-79; profl. diploma adminstrn., St. John's U., Jamaica, N.Y., 1995. Tchr. N.Y.C. Bd. Edn., Bklyn., 1981—. Mem. United Fedn. Tchrs., N.Y. Librs. Assn., N.Y. State United Tchrs. Democrat. Baptist.

HAEBERLE, ROSAMOND PAULINE, retired educator; b. Clearwater, Kans., Oct. 23, 1914; d. Albert Paul and Ella (Lough) H. BS in Music Edn., Kans. State U., 1936; MusM, Northwestern U., 1948; postgrad., Wayne State U., 1965, 65, 66. Profl. registered parliamentarian. Tchr. sch. dist., Plevna, Kans., 1936-37, Esbon, Kans., 1937-41, Frankfort, Kans., 1941-43, Garden City, Kans., 1943-44; music supr. sch. dist., Waterford Twp., Mich., 1944-47; tchr. sch. dist., Pontiac, Mich., 1947-80; ret. sch. dist., Pontiac, 1980. Bd. dirs., ho. chmn. Pontiace-Oakland Symphony); adv. coun. Waterford Sr. Citizens.; pres. Oakland County Pioneer and Hist. Soc., 1992-94. Recipient Tchrs. Day award Mich. State Fair, 1963. Mem. Mich. Fedn. of Music Clubs (state pres. 1993-95, tuesday musicale of pontiac), Mich. Fedn. Bus. & Profl. Women's Club (Woman of Achievement award dist. IX 1994), Mich. Assn. Ret. Pers. (Disting. Svc. award 1994), Mich. DARS (state parliamentarian), DAR (Gen. Richardson chpt., libr. and parliamentarian), AAUW (Pontiac br., founds. chmn.), Waterford-Clarkston Bus. and Profl. Women's Club (bylaws and parliamentarian, contbr. monthly newsletter), Pontiac Area Retired Sch. Pers. (paliamentarian), Detroit Coll. Women's Club, Mich. Registered Parliamentarians, Eastern Star, Zeta Tau Alpha, Mu Phi Epsilon, Beta Sigma Phi (life). Republican. Methodist.

HAECK, CHRISTEL, provincial legislator; b. Stuttgart, Germany, Mar. 9, 1948; came to Can., 1952; d. Rudolf Karl and Gertrud Frieda (Fuhrer) H.; m. Dennis Lawrence Gannon, Oct. 21, 1989. BA, Trent U., 1970; MLS, SUNY, Buffalo, 1977. Libr. asst. Ft. Erie (Ont., Can.) Pub. Libr., 1974-77; libr. St. Catharines (Ont., Can.) Pub. Libr., 1977-90; mem. Ont. Legislature, Toronto, 1990—. Exec. mem. St. Catharines-Brock NDP Riding Assn., 1987. Mem. Ont. Libr. Assn. New Democratic Party. Anglican. Office: Ont Legis Assembly, Legis Bldg, Toronto, ON Canada M7A 1A5 also: 125 Queenston St, Saint Catharines, ON Canada L2R 2Z6

HAEHL, MARGARET ROSE, pharmacist; b. Shelbyville, Ind., July 26, 1949; d. Carey Dennis and Annabelle (Miller) H. BS, Purdue U., 1972. Pharmacist mgr. Hook's Drugs, Shelbyville, Ind., 1973-82; CSA adminstr. Hook's Drugs, Indpls., 1982-83, pharmacist mgr., 1983-84; pharmacist mgr. Peoples Drugs, Indpls., 1984-86, Wal-Mart Pharmacy, Shelbyville, 1986—. Bd. dirs. Shelby County Hospice, Shelbyville, 1994; active St. Joseph Ch., 1978—. Mem. Am. Pharm. Assn., Ind. Pharm. Assn., Shelby County Cancer Assn. (bd. dir.), Purdue Alumni Assn. Democrat. Roman Catholic. Home: 1633 S Riley Hwy Shelbyville IN 46176 Office: Wal-Mart Pharmacy 884 1800 E St Rd 44 Shelbyville IN 46176

HAEMMERLIE, FRANCES MONTGOMERY, psychology educator, consultant; b. Gainsville, Fla., Feb. 2, 1948; d. Henry John and Ruth Elizabeth (Collins) H.; Robert L. Montgomery, June 16, 1979. BA, U. Fla., 1972; MS, Fla. State U., 1976, PhD, 1978. Prof. U. Mo., Rolla, 1978—; rsch. fellow Ctr. for Applied Engring., U. Mo., Rolla, 1984-87. Contbr. articles to profl. jours, chpts. to books. Sec. Rolla Jr. High Parent-Student-Tchr. Assn., 1989-90. Recipient Teaching awards U. Mo., 1980-85, 87-94, Disting. Tchg. award, 1995, Amoco Teaching award, 1981-82, Faculty Excellence award, 1986-89, Reade Beard Faculty Excellence award, 1989-90, John Stafford Brown, 1991-92, 92-93, 93-94. Mem. APA (membership chmn. div. 12 sect. IV 1990—), Southwestern Psychol. Assn. (placement chmn. 1986, program chmn. 1988-89, coun. rep. 1994—), Psi Chi (Outstanding Advisor award 1980, 86, Profl. Svc. award 1983). Home: 12341 Williams Pl Rolla MO 65401 Office: U Mo Dept Psychology 110 Hss Rolla MO 65401

HAENSLY, PATRICIA A., psychology educator; b. Kronenwetter, Wis., Dec. 4, 1928; d. Paul Frank and Valeria (Woyak) Banach; m. William E. Haensly, 1954; children: Paul, Robert, Thomas, James, John, David, Mary, Katherine. BS, Lawrence U., 1950; MS in Genetics, Iowa State U., 1953; PhD in Ednl. & Devel. Psychology, Tex. A&M U., 1982. Histo technique specialist dept. vet. pathology Iowa State U., Ames, 1958-63; asst. prof. dept. ednl. psychology Tex. A&M U., College Station, 1982—; instr. Blinn Jr. Coll., College Station; assoc. dir. programs Inst. for Gifted and Talented Tex. A&M U., College Station, dir. summer presch. program Minds Alive, 1987—. Contbr. articles to profl. publs., chpts. to books on mentoring creativity and giftedness. Recipient Outstanding Woman award AAUW, 1980, Govt. Rsch. Javits grant, 1993—, Hon. Mention Hollingworth award Intertel Found., 1993. Mem. Tex. Assn. for Gifted and Talented (1st v.p. 1988, 89, editor news mag. 1988, 89), Nat. Assn. Gifted Children (co-chmn. rsch. and evaluation com. 1985-87, John Curtis Gowan Rsch. award 1981), World Coun. for Gifted and Talented Children, Inc., Southwestern Ednl. Rsch. Assn., Soc. for Rsch. in Child Devel., Coun. for Exceptional Children, Nat. Assn. Edn. of Young Children, Phi Kappa Phi. Home: 1015 Walton Dr College Station TX 77840-2310

HAERING, SUSAN DONALDSON, newspaper publisher; b. Boston, June 21, 1962; d. John Cecil and Marilyn Jean (Smith) Donaldson, Jr.; m. James Michael Haering, June 10, 1989. AB, Princeton U., 1984; MBA, Columbia U., 1986. Sr. fin. analyst Time Warner Inc., N.Y.C., 1986-87; fin. mgr. Time Inc., N.Y.C., 1987-88, account exec., 1988-89; bus. mgr. Harvard Bus. Rev., Boston, 1989-92; pub. dir. World Monitor, The Christian Sci. Pub. Soc., Boston, 1992-93; dir. pub. devel. Christian Sci. Monitor, Boston, 1993-94, pub. dir., 1994—; prin. Haering Cons., Boxford, Mass., 1991—; mem. mktg. com. Parents & Children's Svcs. Inc., Boston. Chair community project Jr. League of Boston, Inc., 1992—, vice chair, 1991-92. Mem. Advt. Club Greater Boston, New Eng. Direct Mktg. Assn. Republican. Christian Scientist. Home: 6 Baren Ln Boxford MA 01921 Office: Christian Sci Monitor One Norway St P200 Boston MA 02115

HAFFNER, MARLENE ELISABETH, internist, health care administrator; b. Cumberland, Md., Mar. 22, 1941. Student Western Res. U., 1958-61; MD, George Washington U., 1965; MPH, Johns Hopkins U., 1991. Intern, George Washington U. Hosp., Washington, 1965-66; fellow in dermatology Columbia-Presbyn. Med. Ctr., N.Y.C., 1966-67; resident in internal medicine St. Luke's Hosp., N.Y.C., 1967-69; fellow in hematology. Albert Einstein Coll. Medicine, Bronx, 1969-71, asst. clin. prof. medicine, 1971-73; vis. asst. attending Bronx Mcpl. Hosp. Ctr. (N.Y.), 1969-71; clin. assoc. in family, community and emergency medicine U. N.Mex. Sch. Medicine, Albuquerque, 1974-83, clin. assoc. dept. medicine, 1974-83; acting clin. dir. Gallup Indian Med. Ctr. (N.Mex.), 1973-74, chief adult outpatient dept., 1971-74, chief dept. internal medicine, 1971-74; dir. Navajo Area Indian Health Service, Indian Health Service, Window Rock, Ariz., 1974-81; assoc. dir. for health affairs Bur. Med. Devices, FDA, Rockville, 1981-82, dir. Office Health Affairs, Ctr. for Devices and Radiol. Health, 1982-87; dir. office of orphan products devel. FDA, 1987—; MPH Johns Hopkins Sch. Hygiene and Pub. Health, 1991; asst. clin. prof. dept. medicine Uniformed Services Univ. of Health Scis., Bethesda, Md.; asst. surg. gen., rear admiral USPHS. Home and Office: Orphan Products Devel FDA HF 35 5600 Fishers Ln Rockville MD 20857-0001

HAFFORD, PATRICIA ANN, electronic company executive; b. Springfield, Mass., Feb. 11, 1947; d. Arthur Charles and Sophie Louise (Piesyk) Rood;

m. Jerry William Hafford, May 1, 1971 (div. Apr. 1993); children: Mark Dutton, Lauren Melynn. BA in Liberal Arts and Scis., U. Conn., 1968. Elem. tchr. East Granby (Conn.) Schs., 1968-69; presch. tchr. RCA-Discovery Ctr., East Hartford, Conn., 1969-70; tng. specialist Travelers Ins. Co., Hartford, 1970-73; scriptwriter ednl. TV Ednl. Satellite Tech. Demonstration Fedn. of Rocky Mt. States, Denver, 1973; with computer documentation dept., tech. writer Hewlett-Packard Corp., Ft. Collins, Colo., 1973-77, documentation mgr., 1977-82, market devel. engr., 1982-83, product mgr., 1983-92, sales devel. mgr., 1993, product mgr., 1994—. Editor: Writing and Designing Operator Manuals. Vol. Mountain Prairie Coun. Girl Scouts U.S.A., 1991-93. Mem. Soc. for Tech. Comm. (v.p. Rocky Mountain chpt. 1979-81, chmn. Art and Writing Competition 1980-81, chmn. Art and Writing Competition 1980-81, dir.-sponsor on bd. dirs. Region 8 1981-84), Ft. Collins Jr. League. Republican. Methodist. Office: Hewlett-Packard 3404 E Harmony Rd Fort Collins CO 80525-9599

HAFT, GAIL K., pediatrician; b. N.Y.C., Mar. 5, 1938; d. Herbert and Pearl (Mittleman) Klein; m. Jacob I. Haft, Mar. 27, 1964; children: Bethanne, Ian. AB in Chemistry, Vassar Coll., 1959; MD, U. Rochester, 1963. Diplomate Nat. Bd. Med. Examiners, Am. Bd. Pediatrics. Intern Albert Einstein Coll. Medicine, N.Y.C., 1963-64, resident, 1964-65; resident Mt. Sinai Hosp., N.Y.C., 1967-68; pediatrician Dept. Health, Staten Island, N.Y., 1965-67, Head Start, Englewood, N.Y., 1969-71, Dept. Health, Hackensack, N.J., 1970-71; utilization rev. physician Hosp. Corp., N.Y.C., 1973-76; pediatrician Westchester County Health Dept., N.Y., 1974-76; sch. physician Bd. Edn., Yonkers, N.Y., 1974-76; bus. mgr. Heartronics, Newark, 1980-94; chief med. officer Bergen County Spl. Svcs., Paramus, N.J., 1984—; physician Tenafly (N.J.) Sch. Bd. Edn., 1990-94. Mem. Tenafly Bd. Edn., 1983-89, pres., 1986-88.

HAFT, MARILYN GEISLER, lawyer; b. N.Y.C, Aug. 1, 1943; d. Frank and Sarah (Engelsohn) Geisler; m. Kenneth W. Bowser; 1 child, Samantha Danielle. BA, Bklyn. Coll., 1965; JD, NYU, 1968. Bar: N.Y. 1969, U.S. Supreme Ct. 1973, D.C. 1978. Staff counsel ACLU Nat. Office, N.Y.C., 1970-76; dep. counsel govt. ops. com. U.S. Congress, Washington, 1976-77; assoc. dir. office of pub. liaison The White House, Washington, 1977-78, dep. counsel to v.p. Walter Mondale, 1978-79; N.Y. Primary campaign dir. Re-election for Carter/Mondale, N.Y.C., 1979-80; U.S. rep. Mission to the U.N., N.Y.C., 1980-81; sole practice entertainment law N.Y.C., 1981-89; of counsel Summit, Rovins & Feldesman, N.Y.C., 1989-90; ptnr. Fischbein, Badillo & Wagner, N.Y.C., 1990-93, Tanner, Propp & Farber, N.Y.C., 1993—; film prodr. Barking Dog Prodns., N.Y.C., 1987—. Author: Time Without Work, 1984; author, editor: Prisoner's Rights Sourcebook, 1972, Rights of Gay People, 1973; prodr.: (film) In a Shallow Grave, 1988, Preston Sturges: The Rise and Fall of an American Dreamer, 1990. Democrat. Jewish. Home: 111 E 10th St New York NY 10003-7514 Office: Tanner Propp & Farber 99 Park Ave New York NY 10016-1503

HAGA, JUDITH ANN, volunteer; b. Eureka, Kans., Oct. 5, 1939; d. Francis Clayborne and Audre Elaine (Vancleve) Basham; m. Raymond D. Haga, Feb. 15, 1961; 1 child, Shelly Raye. Student, U. Mich., 1957, Sorbonne U., Paris, 1959; BS in Elem. Edn., Kans. State U., 1960. Tchr. Green Bay Sch., North Chicago, Ill., 1964-65, Forrestal Sch., Great Lakes, Ill., 1965-66, Lake Forrest (Ill.) Country Day, 1967-71. Jr. cadette Brownies Lakeview Scout Coun., North Chicago, Grayslake, Ill.; scholarship chmn. DAR, Waukegan, Ill., 1964-75, vice-regent, regent, 1975-85; libr. liaison Grayslake Libr., Grayslake Woman's Club; art sponsor Grayslake Community High Sch.; v.p. Haga's Amoco Food Shop, Lake Villa, Ill.; cultural found. bd. Coll. of Lake County. Mem. Grayslake Woman's Club (art chairperson, v.p., yearbook chair, art scholarships), AAUW (chair community rep.), Questor Antique Group (sec.), Alpha Chi Omega. Republican. Home: 357 S Slusser St Grayslake IL 60030-2430

HAGANS, TERESA ROSE, industrial engineer; b. Dayton, Ohio, Dec. 30, 1961; d. James Clayton and Rosa (Bowling) Pennington; m. Timothy James Hagans, Sept. 4, 1982; children: Maxwell Penn, Cori Rose. BS in Indsl. & Systems Engring., Ohio State U., 1984; postgrad., Capital U., 1994. Engr. trainee Defense Constrn. Supply Ctr., Columbus, Ohio, 1982; spl. tech. asst. AT&T Network Systems, Columbus, Ohio, 1984; indsl. engr. Aerospace Guidance and Metrology Ctr., Heath, Ohio, 1985—; elected exec. AGMC Employee Buyout Assn., Heath, 1994—; ptnr. TNT Reconditioning, Reynoldsburg, Ohio, 1990—. Chmn. Parents Adv. Group, Heath, 1992. Mem. Inst. Indsl. Engrs. (mem. fed. women's program com.), Reynoldsburg PTA. Home: 7308 Broadwyn Dr Reynoldsburg OH 43068-2542

HAGBERG, VIOLA WILGUS, lawyer; b. Salisbury, Md., July 3, 1952; d. William E. and Jean Shelton (Barlow) Wilgus; m. Chris Eric Hagberg, Feb. 19, 1978. BA, Furman U., Greenville, S.C., 1974; JD, U. S.C., 1978, U. Tulsa, 1978; DOD Army Logistics Sch. honor grad. basic mgmt. def. acquisition, def. small purchase, advanced fed. acquisition regulation, Fort Lee, Va., 1981-82. Bar: Okla. 1978, Va. 1979, U.S. Ct. Appeals (4th cir.) 1979. With Lawyers Com. for Civil Rights, Washington, 1979; pub. utility specialist Fed. Energy Regulatory Commn., Washington, 1979-80; contract specialist U.S. Army, C.E., Ft. Shafter, Hawaii, 1980-81; contract officer/supervisory contract specialist Tripler Army Med. Ctr., Hawaii 1981-83; supervisory procurement analyst and chief policy Procurement Div. USCG, Washington, 1983; contracts officer and chief Avionics Engring Contracting Br., 1984; procurement analyst office of sec. Dept. Transp., 1984-85; contracting officer Naval Regional Contracting Ctr., Long Beach, Calif., 1985-87; chief acquisition rev. and policy, Hdqrs. Def. Mapping Agy., Washington, 1987-92, dir. acquisitions, Fairfax, Va., 1992-93, dir. acquisition policy, 1994—. Mem. ABA (law student div. liaison 1977-78), Nat. Contract Mgmt. Assn., Va. State Bar Assn., Okla. Bar Assn., Phi Alpha Delta, Kappa Delta Epsilon. Home: 9810 Meadow Valley Dr Vienna VA 22181-3215 Office: Def Mapping Agy (AQ) 8613 Lee Hwy Fairfax VA 22030

HAGEMANN, DOLORES ANN, water company official; b. Parkston, S.D., June 5, 1935; d. Jacob George and Margaret Marie (Mayer) Schumacher; m. Norbert Bernard Hagemann, June 8, 1954; children: Douglas, Pamela, Susan. AS, Des Moines Community Coll., 1984. Cert. notary pub., Iowa. Sales rep. Stanley Home Products, Westfield, Mass., 1970-76; owner, mgr. Hagemann Gen. Store, Lidderdale, Iowa, 1974-77; motor rt. carrier Des Moines Register, 1977-82; accounts receivable clk. City Water Dept., Lidderdale, 1981—; owner, designer Dolores' Silk Flower Shop, Lidderdale, 1986—; bd. dirs. Lidderdale Apts., Inc., sec., 1974-91. Author: (with other) The Official Carroll County Democrat Cookbook, 1984. Com. person Carroll County Dems., 1970—, sec., 1985-86, 2d vice chair, 1989-90, 1st vice chair, 1990-92, chair, 1992—, chmn. chairs and vice chairs assn. 5th Congl. Dist. Iowa, 1990-92, chmn. county affirmative action com., 1994—; mem. affirmative action com. 5th Congl. Dist.; mem. Iowa Dem. Party Election Rev. Com., 1991—; hospice mem. Community Hospice of Stewart Meml. Community Hosp., 1988—; counselor Carroll Help Line, 1982-87; mem. adv. bd. We. Iowa Transit, 1990—; mem. Carroll County steering com. Child Support Pub. Awareness Project, 1992—. Mem. Am. Assn. Ret. Persons, Holy Family Parish Guild (chair person 1976), Des Moines Community Coll. Alumni, Stewart Meml. Community Hosp. Aux. Democrat. Roman Catholic. Home: PO Box 68 Lidderdale IA 51452-0068

HAGEN, EDNA MAE, medical nurse; b. Jasper, Ark., Nov. 30, 1932; d. Eugene and Dovie (Combs) Keef; m. Harry Hagen, Jan. 4, 1952; children: Catherine, Harry, Jr. ADN, Santa Barbara Coll., 1973. RN, Calif. Staff nurse Cottage Hosp., Santa Barbara, Calif., 1970-74; head nurse to pvt. physician L.A. Price, M.D., Inc., Santa Barbara, 1974—. Mem. U.S. Army Med. Corps, 1951-52. Mem. ANA, CNA.

HAGEN, IONE CAROLYN, religion educator; b. Spring Grove, Minn., Nov. 19, 1924; d. Peter Norris and Ida Bertina (Kittelson) Wennes; m. Dean LeRoy Hagen, Oct. 16, 1954; children: Steven Dean, David Lee, Deone Marie, Susan Ilene, Daniel Paul. BA, Luther Coll., 1947. Cert. music tchr., Minn. Parish worker Glenwood (Minn.) Luth. Ch., 1947-53, Trinity Luth. Ch., LaCrosse, Wis., 1953-55; sec. Nat. ELC Hdqrs. Higher Edn., Mpls., 1955; instr. Bethel series Zion Luth., Buffalo, Minn., 1966-67; supr. Christian Sch. Rivercrest, Monticello, Minn., 1979-81, Christian Sch. New Life, Buffalo, Minn., 1981-82; adminstr. Community Christian Sch., Buffalo, 1982—. Del. State Rep. Conv., Rochester, 1988; clarinetist Assembly ofGod Orch., Buffalo, 1974—; choir mem. Assembly of God Choir, Buffalo, 1990-91. Mem. Nat. Parish Workers Assn. (pres. 1951-53), Internat. Choral Union (sec. 1951-55). Republican. Home: 409 Sigrid Dr Buffalo MN 55313-1259 Office: Community Christian Sch 206 2nd Ave NE Buffalo MN 55313

HAGEN, UTA THYRA, actress; b. Göttingen, Germany, June 12, 1919; came to U.S., 1926; d. Oskar F. L. and Thyra A. (Leisner) H.; m. Herbert Berghof, Jan. 25, 1957 (dec. Nov. 1990); 1 child, Leticia. DFA (hon.), Smith Coll., 1978; LHD (hon.), De Paul U., 1981, Wooster Coll., 1982; DFA (hon.). Tchr. acting Herbert Berghof Studio, N.Y.C., 1947—. Appeared as Ophelia, Dennis, Mass., 1937, as Nina in Sea Gull, N.Y.C., 1938, Key Largo, 1939, Vicki, 1942, Othello, 1943-45, Masterbuilder, 1947, Faust, 1947, Angel Street, 1948, Street Car Named Desire, 1948, 50, Country Girl, 1950, G.B. Shaw's Saint Joan, 1951-52, Tovarich, City Center, 1952, In Any Language, 1952, The Deep Blue Sea, 1953, The Magic and the Loss, 1954, The Island of Goats, 1955, A Month in the Country, 1956, Good Woman of Setzuan, 1957, Who's Afraid of Virginia Woolf, 1962-64, The Cherry Orchard, 1968, Charlotte, 1980; also univ. tour 1981-82, Mrs. Warren's Profession, Roundabout Theatre, N.Y.C., 1985—, You Never Can Tell, Circle in the Square, 1986—; (films) The Other, 1972, The Boys from Brazil, 1978, Reversal of Fortunes, 1990; TV appearances include A Month in the Country, 1956, Out of Dust, 1959; appeared in numerous TV spls. and guest star appearances including Lou Grant, 1982, A Doctor's Story, 1984, PBS Am. Playhouse prodn. The Sunset Gang, 1991; author: Respect for Acting, 1973, Love for Cooking, 1976, Sources, a Memoire, 1983, A Challenge For The Actor, 1991; appearances include numerous roles with H.B. Playwrights Found., 1965-95. Chmn. bd. HB Playwrights Found., 1991—. Recipient Antoinette Perry award, 1951, 63, N.Y. Drama Critics award, 1951, 63, Donaldson award for best actress, 1951, London Critics award for best actress 1963-64 season, Outer Cir. award, Mayor's Liberty medal, 1986, Living Legacy award Women's Internat. Ctr., 1994; named to Theatre Hall of Fame, 1981. Office: Herbert Berghof Studio 120 Bank St New York NY 10014-5999

HAGENBRUCH, HARRIET ANN, educational librarian; b. N.Y.C.; d. Abraham and Augusta (Kiel) Cohen); m. Arthur Hagenbruch; children: Arthur, Michael, Lee-Ann, Eric, Carl. BA, Hunter Coll.; MLS, L.I. Univ. Cert. pub. libr. Paraprofl. libr. East Meadow (N.Y.) Sch. Dist., 1982-86, sch. media specialist, 1986-88; edn. libr. Curriculum Materials Ctr. Hofstra U., Hempstead, N.Y., 1988—. Mem. ALA, Nassau Country Libr. Assn. (v.p. acad. and spl. librs. divsn. 1992, pres. 1993), Assn. Coll. Rsch. Librs. (exec. bd. dirs. N.Y. chpt. 1990—, symposium planning com., chmn. edn.-curriculum materials ctr. librs. group 1990—; vice chmn., chmn.-elect L.I. sect. 1994—, chairperson 1994-95). Home: 545 Pontiac Rd East Meadow NY 11554-5418 Office: Hofstra U Axinn Libr 123 Hofstra University Hempstead NY 11550-1090

HAGER, BARBARA LYNN, health educator; b. Meadville, Pa., Sept. 29, 1954; d. Walter Richard and Margaret Jean (Ketchum) Hager; m. Jess Lloyd Berman, Sept. 9, 1979 (div. July 1985); children: Melanie Sandra, David Jeffrey. BS, East Carolina U., 1976; MPH, U. N.C., 1983. Cert. health edn. specialist. Lead health educator Dist. Health Dept., Elizabeth City, N.C., 1977-79; health edn. coord. East Carolina U. Sch. Medicine, Greenville, N.C., 1980-83; health edn. cons. N.C. State Health Dept., Raleigh, 1983-90; health edn. dir. Ark. Dept. Health, Little Rock, 1990—; lectr. U. Ark., Little Rock, 1992—; cons. Nat. Heart Lung & Blood Inst., Bethesda, Md., 1993—. Mem. Ark. Gov.'s Coun. on Phys. Fitness and Sports, Ark. Divsn. Cancer Soc., Little Rock, 1990—. Recipient Ark. Sophe Disting. Fellow award, 1994. Fellow Soc. for Pub. Health Edn.; mem. Ark. Soc. for Pub. Health Edn., Phi Kappa Delta. Democrat. Jewish. Office: Ark Dept Health 4815 W Markham St # 36 Little Rock AR 72205-3866

HAGER, ELIZABETH SEARS, state legislator; b. Washington, Oct. 31, 1944; d. Hess Thatcher and Elizabeth Grace (Harper) Sears; m. Dennis Sterling Hager, Sept. 3, 1966; children: Annie Elizabeth, Lucie Caroline. BA, Wellesley Coll., 1966; MPA, U. N.H., 1979. Prin. Philbrook Ctr., Concord, N.H., 1970-71; rep. N.H. Gen. Ct., Concord, 1973-76, 85-94; del. N.H. Constitutional Conv., Concord, 1974, 84; campaign coord. Anderson for Pres. Rep. Primary, N.H., 1980; mem. Concord City Coun., 1982-90; mayor City of Concord, 1988-90; bd. dirs. Chubb Investment Funds, Concord, Cheshire Fin. Corp. Commr. N.H. Commn. on the Status of Women; pres. Greater Concord United Way, 1980-81; campaign chair United Way of Merrimack County, Concord, 1986. Republican. Episcopalian. Home and Office: 5 Auburn St Concord NH 03301-3002

HAGERDON, KATHY ANN (KAY HAGERDON), financial analyst, educator; b. Fremont, Ohio, Mar. 20, 1956; d. Willis Harold and Lillian Mae (Bahnsen) Lehmann; m. Michael Lee Hagerdon, Apr. 21, 1979; children: Patrick Michael, Robert Joseph, Andrew Richard. BSBA, Ohio State U., 1978; MBA, Ashland U., 1991. Budget analyst Small Motors divsn. Westing House, Bellefontaine, Ohio, 1978-80; fin. analyst Aerospace Elec. divsn. Westing House, Lima, Ohio, 1980-82, fin. cost analyst, 1982-85; sr. fin. analyst Elec. Sys. divsn. Westing House, Lima, 1985-91, lead profl., 1991-92; sr. fin. analyst Sund Strand Electric Power Sys., Lima, 1992—; chmn. supervisory com. Westing House Credit Union, 1991-94; part-time prof. Tiffin U., Lima, 1994—, Northwestern Bus. Coll., Lima, 1994—. Mem. Inst. Mgmt. Accts. (v.p. membership 1991—), Toastmasters Internat. (pres. 1993—, Com. award 1991). Roman Catholic. Home: 1340 W State St Lima OH 45805

HAGERTY, POLLY MARTIEL, financial analyst, construction executive; b. Joliet, Ill., Aug. 17, 1946; d. George Albert and Gene Alice (Roush) Jerabek; m. Theodore John Hagerty, Feb. 12, 1972. BS in Elem. Edn., Midland Luth. Coll., 1968; MEd in Early Childhood Edn., U. Ill., 1977; MBA in Fin., U. Tex., 1986. Elem. tchr. Madison Heights (Mich.) Sch. Dist., 1968-70, Taft Sch. Dist., Lockport, Ill., 1970-72; systems clerk U.S. Army, The Pentagon, Washington, 1972-74; psychology aide Psychology Clinic U. Ill., Urbana, 1974-75; elem. tchr. Champaign (Ill.) Sch. Dist., 1975-77; with recruitment Standard Oil of Ohio, Cleve., 1977-78; v.p. NCNB Texas-Houston, 1981-88, Citibank, Tucson, 1988-92; substitute tchr. Austin (Tex.) Ind. Sch. Dist., 1993-94; fin. analyst MK Devel. Inc., Austin, 1994—; co-owner Hagerty Constrn. Co., Austin, 1994—. Pres. Christus Victor Luth. Ch., League City, Tex., 1985-88, Luth. Ch. of the Foothills, Tucson, 1990-92. Recipient Golden Circle Sales and Svc. award, 1991. Mem. NAFE, AAUW, U. Ill. Alumni Club, Longhorn Assn. Republican. Lutheran. Home: 7403 Callbram Ln Austin TX 78736 Office: 7200 N Mopac # 400 Austin TX 78731

HAGEY, ERIN OWEN, city treasurer; b. Ft. Worth, Tex., June 8, 1961; d. David Benton Owen and Jane Clary Owen Strange; m. David Dulaney Hagey, Jr., June 1, 1985; 1 child, Tara Elizabeth. BBA in Fin., Tex. Tech. U., 1983. Chartered fin. analyst (CFA). Registered rep. First Investors Corp., Hurst, Tex., 1983-84; investment analyst Electronic Data Systems, Dallas, 1984-86; portfolio asst. Ross Perot Family, Dallas, 1986-87; treas. City of Carrollton, Tex., 1987—; lectr. in field; conductor seminars in field. Mem. Neighborhood Co-op Assn., Plano, Tex., 1993—. Mem. NAFE, Govt. Treas. Orgn. of Tex. (past pres., adv. bd. 1994), Mcpl. Treas. Assn. U.S. and Can., Assn. for Investment Mgmt. and Rsch., Tex. Tech. Alumnae Assn., Alpha Delta Pi Alumnae Assn. Republican. Christian Ch. (Disciples of Christ). Office: City of Carrollton PO Box 110535 Carrollton TX 75011-0535

HAGGARD, VICTORIA MARIE, elementary education educator, secondary education educator; b. Denver, Nov. 7, 1951; d. Donald Eugene and Elaine Marie (Geisert) Russell; m. Robert Michael Haggard, Dec. 22, 1973; 1 child, Robert Donald. BS in Edn., Concordia Tchrs. Coll., 1973; postgrad., U. Tex., 1993. Cert. tchr., Colo., Okla., Tex.; cert. Dantes test specialist, gifted and talented endorsement. Elem. tchr. Bethlehem Luth Sch., Lakewood, Colo., 1973-85; idea instr., testing coord. USAF Vance AFB, Enid, Okla., 1985-87; elem. tchr. St. Thomas Moore Cath. Sch., San Antonio, 1987-89; secondary English tchr. Kirby Jr. High Judson Ind. Sch. Dist., San Antonio, 1989-94, coord. gifted and talented program, 1992—, gifted and talented elective tchr., 1992—, chair English dept., 1994—; mem. Coll. Bd. for Acad. Excellence, San Antonio, 1992-93; presenter in field. Named Outstanding Tchr. Bethlehem Luth. Sch., 1983-85, Outstanding IDEA instr. USAF, 1985-87, Clearly Outstanding Tchr. Kirby Jr. High., 1990-94, Dr. Helen Rook Gifted/Talented Educator Judson Ind. Sch. Dist., 1992-93, Class Act Tchr. Hispanic Univs. and Colls., 1993. Mem. San Antonio Area Coun. Tchrs. English, Delta Kappa Gamma (sec. Epsilon Beta chpt. 1993, rec. sec. 1994-96). Republican. Methodist. Home: 7827 Sun Forest San Antonio TX 78239

HAGGERTY, ELIZABETH LOPEZ, psychologist; b. West Islip, N.Y., Aug. 3, 1966; d. Donald James Lopez and Barbara Louise (Tory) Marks; m. Sean Barry Haggerty, Aug. 10, 1991. BA, Cornell U., 1988; MA, Hofstra U., 1990, PhD, 1994. Consulting psychologist Nassau County Dept. Drug and Alcohol Addiction, N.Y., 1990-93; sch. psychologist Island Trees Sch. Dist., Levittown, N.Y., 1992-93, Levittown Sch. Dist., 1993—.

HAGGERTY, GRETCHEN R., petroleum industry executive V.p., treas. USX Corp., Pitts. Office: USX Corp 600 Grant St Pittsburgh PA 15219*

HAGGERTY, MARY ANN, social services professional; b. Orange, N.J., Dec. 23, 1945; d. Francis Anthony and Grace Mary (Cullen) H. BA, St. Joseph Coll., Emmitsburg, Md., 1967. Exec. dir. Child Advs. of Calif., San Luis Obispo, 1986-87; case mgr. Wiley House, Allentown, Pa., 1987-89; spl. projects adminstr. KidsPeace, Inc., Orefield Pa., 1989—. Mem. NAFE, Nat. Mus. Women in Arts (assoc.), Nature Conservancy. Address: 6668 Chestnut Hill Church Coopersburg PA 18036

HAGGERTY, MARY ELIZABETH, educator; b. Little Falls, N.Y., Jan. 15, 1948; d. Edward C. and Margaret (Dise) H. BA, Utica Coll., 1969; MS, Syracuse U., 1971. Cert. elem. tchr., N.Y. Tchr. Little Falls City Schs., Little Falls, 1969—. Active Foothills Girl Scout Coun., Utica, ARC, Herkimer, N.Y.; bd. dirs. Greater Little Falls Community Ch., 1976—, Women's Christian Assn., Little Falls, 1984—. Mem. DAR (registrar 1980—), Little Falls Tchr.'s Assn. (treas. 1976—). Roman Catholic. Office: Monore St Sch 156 W Monroe St Little Falls NY 13365

HAGGERTY, PATRICIA LOUISE, chemist; b. Upland, Pa., Jan. 5, 1958; d. Albert Patrick and Kathryn Carol (Baldwin) H. BA, Grinnell Coll., 1980; MS, Cornell U., 1985. Rodent control rsch. and ext. officer U.S. Peace Corps, Western Samoa, 1981-82; chemist Carderock divsn. Naval Surface Warfare Ctr. USN, Phila., 1987—. Tutor Alternatives for Exceptional Women, Phila., 1978, Project GIVE, Phila., 1989, Delaware County Adult Literacy Coun., Chester, Pa., 1989-90. Fellow Cornell U., 1983. Mem. ASTM (com. D-15 on engine coolant), Phi Beta Kappa. Office: CDNSWC code 6243 Phila Naval Base Philadelphia PA 19112

HAGGERTY, SUZANNE, information systems executive; b. Cape May Courthouse, N.J., Aug. 21, 1963; d. Joseph Nicholas Haggerty and Mary Ann (Mead) Campbell. BA in Mathematics, Oberlin Coll., 1988; summer student, Am. Coll. Switzerland; student, Aberdeen U., Scotland. Coord. Cleve. Collaborative for Math. Edn., 1987-88; computer systems cons. R & J Contractors, Rio Grande, N.J., 1989; info. systems mgr. The Zacker Group, Avalon, N.J., 1989—; tutor math. Oberlin (Ohio) High Sch., 1986-87; substitute tchr. math. and computer sci. Wildwood Cath. High Sch., North Wildwood, N.J., 1988-89; curriculum cons. for evening sch. home constrn. and improvement course, 1992-94. Layout editor: Annscript. Vol. Mid-Atlantic Ctr. for the Arts, Cape May, N.J. Mem. AAUW, Mensa, Yacht Club Stone Harbor. Home: 701 Whildane Ave North Cape May NJ 08204-3161 Office: The Zacker Group Ste 6 2123 Dune Dr Avalon NJ 08202

HAGLUND, BERNICE MARION, elementary education educator; b. Negaunee, Mich.; d. Paul and Bernice Cody; m. Charles Haglund; children: Christopher C., Mary. BA, No. Mich. U., 1971, MA, 1978. Tchr. Arnold Elem. Sch., Mich. Center Schs., Mich.; social sec., v.p., pres. Mich. Ctr. Jr. Child Study Group, 1979-83, com. mem. sci. com., dept. head to curriculum counsel, 1993—. V.p., treas., social sec. Commonwealth Wives, Jackson, 1971-82. Mich. State grantee U.S. Optical Soc., 1993, Optical Soc., 1993. Mem. AAUW (sec. social edn. area), ASCD, Bus. and Profl. Women (sec. 1969-71, coord. study group 1972—, sec., social, contact edn. chair, woemn's issues), Orton Soc. (workshop trainer), Mich. Dyslexia Inst., Mich. Sci. Tchrs. Assn., Nat. Sci. Tchrs., Phi Delta Kappa. Roman Catholic. Home: 1840 N Noon Jackson MI 49201

HAGOOD, ANNABEL DUNHAM, speech communication educator, communication consultant; b. Hattiesburg, Miss., Feb. 7, 1924; d. John H. and Isabella (Smith) Dunham; m. William Knox Hagood, June 6, 1950 (div. Sept. 1969). A.B., Southwestern La. Inst., 1944; M.A., U. Wis., 1946; postgrad., 1947-49. Asst. dir. debate and drama Southwestern La. Inst., 1944-45; asst. counselor U. Wis., 1945-46; instr. U. Ala., Tuscaloosa, 1946-49; asst. prof. speech U. Ala., 1949-57, assoc. prof., 1957-63, prof., 1963-87, prof. emeritus, 1987-94, dir. forensics, 1946-77, chmn. area rhetoric and speech communication, 1973-76, chmn. dept. speech communication and theatre, 1976-79, chmn. dept. speech communication, 1979-87, chmn. student acad. affairs Coll. Arts and Scis., 1969-71; chmn. arts and scis. faculty senate (U. Ala.), 1972-73; pres. faculty senate U. Ala., 1975-77; pres. Annabel Hagood and Assocs., communication cons., Biloxi, Miss., 1989—; Mem. adv. com. contests and awards Alexander Hamilton Bicentennial Comm., 1956-57; trustee Nat. Debate Tournament Com., 1967-77, chmn., 1968-69, 74-76, treas., 1972-73. Editor: The Register, 1956, 57; Contbr. chpts. to books, articles to profl. jours. Designer Fla. Endowment for Humanities; trustee, chmn. bd. trustees Delta Sigma Rho-Tau Kappa Alpha, 1980-93, mem. long-range fin. com. Nat. Debate Tournament com., 1979-83; participant 1st Presdl. Librs. Conf. on Pub. and Pub. Policy, Gerald Ford Presdl. Libr., 1983. Recipient Outstanding Commitment to Teaching award U. Ala. Nat. Alumni Assn., 1986, Disting. Service award U. Ala. Faculty Senate, 1986, Service award U. Ala. Sch. Communication, 1987, Leadership award U. Ala. Sch. Communication, 1987. Mem. Am. Forensic Assn. (past nat. pres., 1st recipient Disting. Svc. award 1979), Speech Comm. Assn. (chmn. com. internat. discussion and debate 1953-55), Assn. Comm. Adminstrn. (exec. com. 1982-84), Ala. Speech Assn., Phi Kappa Phi, Pi Kappa Delta, Delta Sigma Rho, Tau Kappa Alpha (past nat. pres., bd. of trustees, chmn. bd. 1980-95). Home and Office: Annabel Hagood and Assocs Communication Cons 1324 Beach Blvd Biloxi MS 39530-3527

HAGOOD, SUSAN STEWART HAHN, clinical dietitian; b. Balt., May 31, 1953; d. Paul Gilbert and Phyllis Jeanette (Mann) Hahn; m. Thomas Richard Hagood, Jr., Nov. 25, 1978; 1 child, Margaret Foster. BS, Western Ky. U., 1975; MS, Ga. State U., 1992. Registered and lic. dietitian. Dietetic trainee U. Hosp., Jacksonville, Fla., 1975-76; clin. dietitian VA Med. Ctr., Lake City, Fla., 1976-80; in-service and staff devel. dietitian VA Med. Ctr., Lake City, 1980-85; clin. specialist Clayton Gen. Hosp., Riverdale, Ga., 1985-88; grad. teaching asst. Ga. State U., 1991; ambulatory care dietitian VA Med. Ctr., Atlanta, 1992—. Pres. Lake City (Fla.) Hist. Preservation Bd., 1982-83; chmn. youth adv. com. Columbia County 4-H, Lake City, 1981-84; vol. instr. Tech. Assistance Health Resource Group, Lake City, 1982-84; co-chmn. Com. for Restoration Columbia County Hist. Mus., 1983-84; bd. dirs. Clayton County unit Am. Heart Assn., 1987-88; mem. Dekalb unit nutrition and cancer work group Am. Cancer Soc., 1993—; leader Avondale-Decatur svc. unit Girl Scouts U.S.A., 1993—. Mem. Am. Dietetic Assn., Atlanta Dist. Dietetic Assn., Atlanta English Speaking Union, DAR, Colonial Dames Am., Colonial Dames XVII Century, Phi Upsilon Omicron, Alpha Xi Delta. Republican. Presbyterian. Home: PO Box 982 Decatur GA 30031-0982

HAGOPIAN, FRANCES, political science educator; b. Milford, Mass., Dec. 27, 1953; d. Leo Francis and Elizabeth (Bilazarian) H.; m. Anthony Mark Messina, July 26, 1980; 1 child: Michael David Messina. BA magna cum laude, Brandeis U., 1975; PhD, Mass. Inst. Tech., Cambridge, 1986. Asst. prof. U. Notre Dame, South Bend, Ind., 1986; asst. prof. govt. and social studies Harvard U., Cambridge, 1987-91; asst. prof. polit. sci. Tufts U., Medford, Mass., 1991-92; assoc. prof. Tufts U., Arlington, Mass., 1992—; vis. assoc. prof. MIT, 1993; referee L.Am. Rsch. Rev., Comparative Politics, Am. Polit. Sci. Rev., Jour. Inter-Am. Studies and World Affairs, Comparative Polit. Studies, Polit. Rsch. Quar.; assoc. Ctr. for Internat. Affairs, Harvard U., 1991, chair seminar on L.Am., Com. on L.Am. and Iberian Studies, 1988-91. Fulbright-Hays rsch. grantee, 1991-92, Ctr. for Latin Am. Studies and Howard Heinz Endowment grantee, 1991-92, numerous others. Mem. Am. Polit. Sci. Assn. (Gabriel Almond award 1987), Phi Beta Kappa, Social Sci. Rsch. Coun. (screening panel internat predissertation fellowship program, 1992-94), Latin Am. Studies Assn., New Eng. Coun. Latin Am. Studies (exec. coun. 1989-91). Office: Tufts U Medford MA 02155

HAGY, TERESA JANE, elementary educator; b. Bristol, Va., Nov. 1, 1950; d. Don Houston and Mary Garnett (Yeatts) Hagy. AA in Pre-Edn., Va. Intermont Coll., 1970, BA in Elem. Edn., 1972; MEd, U. Va., 1976, post-grad.; postgrad., Radford U. Cert. tchr., Va., Tenn. Tchr. 1st and 4th grades St. Anne's Demonstration Sch., Bristol, Va., 1972-75; tchr. 1st, 3d, 4th, 5th and 6th grades Washington Lee Elem. Sch., Bristol, 1975—; clin. instr. edn. Va. Intermont Coll., Bristol, 1972-75; coordinator gifted and talented program Bristol Schs., 1980-82; condr. workshops; developer tests to evaluate reading progress. Pres. women's circle Cen. Christian Ch., Bristol, Tenn., also v.p. women's fellowship, libr. chmn., mem. ch. choir, dir. music for Bible Sch., Sunday sch. tchr. 3d and 4th grades, 1979—. Recipient numerous edn. awards; named Tchr. of Yr., S.W. Va. Reading Coun., 1994, Tchr. of Quarter, Bible Sch., 1992. Mem. NEA, AAUW (sec. 1976-79, v.p. 1981-86), Va. Edn. Assn., Bristol Edn. Assn. (sec. 1978-80, chmn. Am. Edn. Week 1993, v.p.-membership chair 1994—), Va. State Reading Assn., U. Va. Alumnae Assn., Va. Intermont Coll. Alumni Assn. (nat. pres. 1987-89), U. Va. Alumni Assn., Delta Kappa Gamma (chpt. v.p. 1986-88, pres. 1988-90, coordinating coun. chmn. 1990-92), Nat. Trust for Hist. Preservation, Phi Theta Kappa. Republican. Home: 820 Virginia Ave Bristol TN 37620-3935 Office: Washington Lee Elem Sch Washington Lee Dr Bristol VA 24201

HAHN, BESSIE KING, library administrator, lecturer; b. Shanghai, People's Republic of China, May 14, 1939; came to U.S., 1959; d. Jen Fong and Wei (Lok) King; m. Roger Carl Hahn, 1962 (div. 1983); children: Angela Yee-mei, Michael King-yau, Belinda Shee-wei; m. David Ware Duhme, 1989. B.A., Mt. Marty Coll., Yankton, S.D., 1961; M.S.L.S., Syracuse U., 1972. Librarian Carrier Corp., Syracuse, N.Y., 1972; life sci. bibliographer Syracuse U. Libraries, 1973-75, head sci. and tech., 1975-78; asst. dir. reader services Johns Hopkins U. Library, Balt., 1978-81; dir. libraries Brandeis U., Waltham, Mass., 1981—; cons. Shanghai Jiao Tong U. Library, Shanghai, 1983—, hon. prof., 1984. Editor Jour. Ednl. Media and Library Scis., 1983—; contbr. articles to profl. jours. Bd. govs. Abraham Lincoln Brigade Archives, 1989—; commr. New England Assoc. Schs. and Colls., Inc., 1991—. Recipient Golden Cup award Johns Hopkins U. Class of 1980, 1980. Mem. ALA, Chinese-Am. Librarians Assn. (pres. 1982-83), Brandeis U. Nat. Women's Com. (hon. benefactor 1986, hon. life 1990—). Home: 148 Sudbury Rd Weston MA 02193-1351 Office: Brandeis U Libr 415 South St Waltham MA 02254-9110

HAHN, CATHY ANN CLIFFORD, sales executive; b. Celina, Ohio, June 6, 1947; d. William Eugene and Kathleen (McNally) Clifford; m. John Hahn (div.). BS, U. Dayton, 1969. Sales rep. J.T. Baker Instruments, Bridgeport, Conn., 1972-76, E.I. duPont de Nemours & Co., Dallas, 1976-81; new bus. developer E.I. duPont de Nemours & Co., Wilmington, Del., 1981-83, sr. tng. designer, 1983-84, sales tng. mgr., 1984-85; ter. mgr., trainer E.I. duPont de Nemours & Co., Dallas, 1985-94; v.p. Planet Cadillac Clothing Co., 1994—. Vol. Am. Cancer Soc., Dallas, 1986—. Home and Office: 5217 Old Shepard Pl Plano TX 75093-5002

HAHN, CYNTHIA LEIGH, training and marketing consultant; b. Harrisburg, Pa., Mar. 2, 1950; d. Arthur John Jr. and Fern Elizabeth (Exner) Hack; m. Gary S. Hahn, Apr. 24, 1988. Student, U. East Anglia, Norwich, Eng., 1970-71; BA in Liberal Arts, Hollins Coll., 1972. Programmer/analyst Spectra-Physics, San Jose, Calif., 1980-83; customer support mgr. Multidata Corp., San Jose, 1983-85; installation/tng. mgr. Gill Mgmt. Services, San Jose, 1985; dir. client support Jostens Learning Corp., San Diego, 1985-89; dir. sales tng. Jostens Learning Corp. (subsidiary Jostens Inc.), San Diego, 1989—; pres. Hahn Comm., Cardiff by the Sea, Calif., 1993—. Mem. ASTD (bd. dirs. 1995), Computer and Electronics Mktg. Assn. Office: Hahn Comm PO Box 1300 Cardiff By The Sea CA 92007

HAHN, HELENE B., motion picture company executive; b. N.Y.C.. BA, Hofstra U.; JD, Loyola U., Calif., 1975. Bar: Calif. 1975. V.p. bus. affairs Paramount Pictures Corp., L.A., sr. v.p. bus. affairs, 1983-84; sr. v.p. bus. and legal Walt Disney Studios, Burbank, Calif., 1984-87, exec. v.p., 1987-94; with Dreamworks, 1994—. Recipient Frontrunner award in bus. Sara Lee Corp., 1991, Big Sisters Achievement award, 1992, Clairol Mentor award, 1993.

HAHN, JOAN CHRISTENSEN, drama educator, travel agent; b. Kemmerer, Wyo., May 9, 1933; d. Roy and Bernice (Pringle) Wainwright; m. Milton Angus Christensen, Dec. 29, 1952 (div. Oct. 1, 1971); children: Randall M., Carla J. Christensen Teasdale; m. Charles Henry Hahn, Nov. 15, 1972. BS, Brigham Young U., 1965. Profl. ballroom dancer, 1951-59; travel dir. E.T. World Travel, Salt Lake City, 1969—; tchr. drama Payson High Sch., Utah, 1965-71, Cottonwood High Sch., Salt Lake City, 1971—; dir. Performing European Tours, Salt Lake City, 1969-76; dir. Broadway theater tours, 1976—. Bd. dirs. Salem City Salem Days, Utah, 1965-75; regional dir. dance Latter-day Saints Ch., 1954-72. Named Best Dir. High Sch. Musicals, Green Sheet Newspapers, 1977, 82, 84, 90, Utah's Speech Educator of Yr., 1990, 91, named to Nat. Hall of Fame Ednl. Theatre Assn., 1991; recipient 1st place award Utah State Drama Tournament, 1974, 77, 78, 89, 90, 91, 94, Tchr. of Yr. award Cottonwood High Sch., 1989-90, Limelight award, 1982, Exemplary Performance in teaching theater arts Granite Sch. Dist., Salt Lake City, 1982; named to the Nat. Hall of Fame, Ednl. Theatre Assn., 1991. Mem. Internat. Thespian Soc. (sponsor 1968—, internat. dir. 1982-84, trustee 1978-84), Utah Speech Arts Assn. (pres. 1976-78, 88-90), NEA, Utah Edn. Assn., Granite Edn. Assn., Profl. Travel Agts. Assn., Utah High Sch. Activities Assn. (drama rep. 1972-76), AAUW (pres. 1972-74). Republican. Mormon. Avocations: reading; travel; dancing. Home: 685 S 1st E PO Box 36 Salem UT 84653-0036 Office: Cottonwood High Sch 5715 S 1300 E Salt Lake City UT 84121-1099

HAHN, LITHIA B., finance executive; b. Troy, N.C., Nov. 2, 1951; d. Tom Stewart and Anne Grace (Ward) Brooks; 1 child, Leslie Grace Hahn. AS in Bus. Adminstrn. Acctg., Wingate U., 1972. Cert. govtl. acctg. and fin. reporting, county adminstrn., acctg. and fiscal control, budgeting and fin. planning, effective mgmt.; cert. local govtl. fin. officer. Dir. fiscal ops. Brunswick County, Bolivia, N.C.; fin. officer Stanly County, Albemarle, N.C., 1994—. Participant conf. Nat. Assn. Counties, Anaheim, Calif., 1988-89, Miami, Fla., 1990-91, legis. conf. NACO, Washington, 1987-88, DGFOA Nat. Conf., Orlando, Fla., 1992-93. Named N.C. Outstanding Fin. Officer, 1991-92. Mem. Govt. Fin. Officers Assn., N.C. Assn. County Finance Officers (sec.-treas. 1988-89, 2nd v.p. 1989-90, 1st v.p. 1990-91, pres. 1991-92, chmn. legis. com. 1992-93, mem. nom. com. 1994—), N.C. Cash Mgmt. Trust (chmn., adv. bd. 1987-88), NAFE, Nat. Assn. County Finance Officers and Treasurers, Carolinas Assn. Govt. Purchasers. Home: PO Box 249 Bolivia NC 28422-0249

HAHN, LUCILLE DENISE, paper company executive; b. Stony Point, N.Y., Oct. 8, 1940; d. Raymond and Catherine (Nobert) Hoyt. Lab. asst. Champion Internat. (formerly St. Regis Paper Co.), West Nyack, N.Y., 1972-74, technician, 1974-77, tech. asst., 1977-79, rsch. asst., 1979-82, technologist, 1982-84, sr. technologist, 1984-86, assoc. testing coord., 1986-89, testing engr., 1989—. Author: Testing Guidebook, 1990, (videos) Testing the Strength Properties of Paper, 1991, Testing the Strength Properties of Board, 1991. Mem. NAFE, TAPPI (sec. process and product quality divsn. 1987-88, vice chair 1989-90, chmn. 1991-92, bd. dirs. 1993—). Office: Champion Internat West Nyack Rd West Nyack NY 10994

HAHN, MARY DOWNING, author; b. Washington, Dec. 9, 1937; d. Kenneth Ernest and Anna Elisabeth (Sherwood) Downing; m. William Edward Hahn, Oct. 7, 1961 (div. 1977); children: Katherine Sherwood, Margaret Elizabeth; m. Norman Pearce Jacob, Apr. 24, 1982. BA in Fine Arts and English, U. Md., 1960, MA in English, 1969. Asst. libr. children's sect. Prince George's County Meml. Libr. System, Laurel, Md., 1975-91; instr. English U. Md., College Park, 1970-74; free-lance illustrator PBS/WETA, Arlington, Va., 1973-75. Author: The Sara Summer, 1979, The Time of the Witch, 1982, Daphne's Book, 1983 (William Allen White Children's Choice award 1985-86), The Jellyfish Season, 1985, Wait Till Helen Comes: A Ghost Story, 1986 (11 children's choice awards), Tallahassee Higgins, 1987, Following the Mystery Man, 1988, December Stillness, 1988 (Book award Child Study Assn. 1989, Honor Book award Jane Addams Peace Assn. 1989, Calif. Young Readers' medal 1990-91), The Doll in the Garden, 1989 (Md. Children's Book award 1990-91, 7 childrens choice awards), The Dead Man in Indian Creek, 1990 (4 childrens choice awards), The Spanish Kidnapping Disaster, 1991, Stepping on the Cracks, 1991 (Scott O'Dell Hist. Fiction award 1992, ALA notable 1991, Joan G. Sugarman award, Hedda Seisler Mason award, Children's Choice awards), The Wind Blows Backward, 1993 (ALA Best Books for Young Adults), Time For Andrew, 1994, Look for Me by Moonlight, 1995. Recipient Scott O'Dell award for hist. fiction, 1992. Mem. PEN, Soc. Children's Book Writers, Washington Children's Book Guild, Authors Guild.

HAHN, MONICA LUISE, marketing professional; b. St. Joseph, Mich., Oct. 23, 1961; d. Roland D. and Margarete (Keil) H. BSBA in Mgmt. Sci. and Ops. Rsch., Mich. Tech. U., 1983; MBA in Mktg., West Mich. U., 1987. MIS trainee Whirlpool Corp., Benton Harbor, Mich., 1983; assoc. ops. rsch. analyst Whirlpool Corp., Benton Harbor, 1984, ops. rsch. analyst, 1986-87, decision support analyst, 1988-89; systems analyst Burger King Corp., Miami, 1989-90, mgr. sales and bus. analysis, 1990-93; field sales and promotion mgr. Burger King Corp., Chgo., 1993—. Mem. Am. Mktg. Assn., Amnesty Internat., Sierra Club, NOW. Office: Burger King Corp 1400 Opus Pl Ste 600 Downers Grove IL 60515-5706

HAHN, SHARON LEE, city official; b. Kenosha, Wis., Sept. 22, 1939; d. Vincent B. and Mary Lee (Vaux) McCloskey; 1 child, John V. Calhoun. Student Kent State U., 1983. Cert. mcpl. clk., notary pub., Ohio. Sec., Simmons Bedding Co., Columbus, Ohio, 1960-61; exec. sec. Westinghouse, Columbus, 1962-68; legal sec. Bricker Law Firm, Columbus, 1969-70; asst. to prosecutor Whiteleather Law Firm, Columbia City, Ind., 1970-77; legal sec. Metz, Bailey & Spicer, Westerville, Ohio, 1977-80; clk. of coun., sec. to city mgr. City of Westerville, 1981-87; clk. of coun., records mgr. City of Westerville, 1981—. Deputy Registrar, Franklin Bd. of Elections; pres. Meadowlake Assn., 1991—. Mem. Ohio Mcpl. Clks. Assn. (bd. dirs. 1984-86, 91-94, asst. treas. 1994-95), Internat. Inst. Mcpl. Clks. (CMC award 1984, records mgmt. com. 1986-94), Am. Assn. Records Mgrs. and Adminstrs., Nat. Assn. Govt. Archives and Records Adminstrs. Presbyterian. Avocations: golf, organ, crocheting. Home: 356 Macintosh Way Westerville OH 43081-3595 Office: City of Westerville 21 S State St Westerville OH 43081

HAI, CAROL SUE, interior designer; b. Ithaca, N.Y., Sept. 16, 1938; d. Norman Charles and Edna (Voronoff) Epstein; m. Richard B. Hai, June 18, 1961 (div. Apr. 1984); children: Jill Ilene, Paul Bradley. BS, Cornell U., 1960, postgrad., 1960-61. Showroom asst. Jack Lenor Larsen, N.Y.C., 1960; teaching asst. Cornell U., 1960-61; sportswear sales mgr. Davison-Paxon Co., Columbus, Ga., 1962-63; owner, interior designer Carol Sue Hai Interiors, N.Y.C., Rochester, N.Y., 1964—; mem. adj. faculty Monroe C.C., Rochester; mem. dept. design and environ. analysis adv. coun. Cornell U. Trustee Soc. Preservation Landmarks Western N.Y., 1971-85, Temple B'rith Kodesh; bd. dirs. Opera Theatre Rochester, Girl Scouts Genesee Valley; mem. Cornell U. Coun.; mem. Women's Coun. Meml. Art Gallery, U. Rochester. Recipient Helen Bull Vandervort Alumni Achievement award Cornell U., 1987. Mem. Interior Design Soc. (profl.), Am. Soc. Interior Design (allied), Nat. Assn. Women Bus. Owners. Home and Office: 172 Allens Creek Rd Rochester NY 14618-3230

HAIFLEY, SHARON VIRGINIA, administrative secretary; b. Fairfield, Iowa, July 13, 1951; d. John Junior and Ruth Esther (Green) H. BA in Bus. Adminstrn., Mid-Am. Nazarene Coll., 1973. Asst. libr. Fairfield Pub. Libr., 1974-78; ins. sec. Loudens, Fairfield, 1978-79; bookkeeper Anderson Welding Co., Richland, Iowa, 1979-80; adminstrv. sec. Iowa Dept. Human Svcs., Fairfield, 1980—. Sec. Fairfield Child Abuse Coun., 1983-85, Human Svc. Planning Coun., Fairfield, 1984-88, Jefferson County Mental Health, Mental Retardation, Devel. Disabilities Adv. Coun., Fairfield, 1984-93, Fairfield Multidisciplinary Child Abuse Team, 1989-93; sec. bd. dirs. Crisis Line, 1986-92; mem. edn. com. Ch. of the Nazarene, 1992—; mem. disaster com. Jefferson County, 1993—. Mem. AAUW (past sec.-treas.), DAR (vice regent Log Cabin chpt. 1988—, sec. 1986-88). Republican. Mem. Ch. of Nazarene. Home: PO Box 516 Fairfield IA 52556-0516 Office: Iowa Dept Human Svcs PO Box 987 51 W Hempstead Fairfield IA 52556-0987

HAIGH, CINDY LOU, private/parochial school physical education educator; b. Uniontown, Pa., Apr. 12, 1962; d. Benjamin Francis and Linda Karen (Amos) H. BS in Edn., Indiana U. of Pa., 1984, MS in Sport Sci., 1992. Cert. tchr., Pa. Substitute tchr. Indiana County (Pa.) Pub. Schs., 1984-85; grad. asst. softball coach Indiana U. of Pa., 1984-86; health, phys. edn. tchr. Purchase Line (Pa.) Sch. Dist., 1985-87, Diocese of Greensburg (Pa.), 1987—; demonstration site tchr. phys. edn. Learning Is for Everyone Demonstration Sch., 1989—; asst. basketball coach Purchase Line Sch. Dist., 1985-87, Greensburg Cen. Cath. High Sch., 1987-90; head basketball coach Greensburg Cath. Mid. Sch., 1989-91; softball umpire Amateur Softball Assn., Pa., 1985—. Named Outstanding Tchr. of Yr., St. Paul Sch. Bd., 1989, 90, Phsy. Edn. Tchr. of Yr., Pa. State Assn., 1993, Alumni Amb., Coll. of Health and Human Svcs. Ind. U. Pa., 1994. Mem. AAHPERD, Pa. State Assn. Health, Phys. Edn., Recreation and Dance (Tchr. of Yr. 1993), Pa. Sch. Health Assn., Amateur Softball Assn. Roman Catholic. Home: PO Box 253 Crabtree PA 15624 Office: St Paul Sch 820 Carbon Rd Greensburg PA 15601

HAIGH, NANCY, set decorator. Films include: Checking Out, 1988. Field of Dreams, 1989, Earth Girls Are Easy, 1989, The Grifters, 1990 (also set designer), Miller's Crossing, 1990, Guilty By Suspicion, 1991, Bugsy, 1991, Barton Fink, 1991, Hero, 1992, The Hudsucker Proxy, 1994, Forrest Gump, 1994 (Acad. award nom., Best Art Direction). Office: IATSE Local 847 Penthouse B 14724 Ventura Blvd Sherman Oaks CA 91403-3501*

HAIGHT, CAROL BARBARA, lawyer; b. Buffalo, May 3, 1945; d. Robert H. Johnson and Betty R. (Walker) Hawkes; m. H. Granville Haight, May 28, 1978 (dec. Nov. 1983); children: David Michael, Kathleen Marie. BSW summa cum laude, Widener U., Chester, Pa., 1980, BA in Psychology summa cum laude, 1980; JD cum laude, Widener U., Wilmington, Del., 1984. Assoc. Pepper, Hamilton & Scheetz, Phila., 1985-88, Hodgson, Russ, Andrews, Woods & Goodyear, Buffalo, 1988-90; pvt. practice Boca Raton, Fla., 1990—; arbitrator Am. Arbitration Assn., 1988—, mediator, 1989—, mediation instr.; founding dir. Mediation Ednl. Svc.: Coun. for Marriage Preservation and Divorce Resolution, Inc., 1992. Contbr. article to profl. jours. Mem. ABA (com. on adr), Pa. Bar Assn., Fla. Bar Assn., Phi Kappa Phi, Phi Alpha Delta, Phi Gamma Mu. Republican. Episcopalian. Home: Braemar Isle Townhouse 9 4744 S Ocean Blvd Highland Bch FL 33487 Office: 370 Camino Gardens Blvd Ste 300 Boca Raton FL 33432-5826

HAIKEN, LEATRICE BROWN, periodical editor; b. Morristown, N.J., Mar. 27, 1934; d. Ellen (Liss) Schwartz; m. Martin Leslie Haiken, June 24, 1956; children: Matthew Scott, Susan Beth. Student, Douglass Coll., 1951-54; BA, Upsala Coll., 1955; postgrad., China Inst., 1960, Art of Baking, 1962, Cordon Bleu Sch. Cooking, 1974, NYU, 1976-77. Mkt. rep. Allied Stores Corp., N.Y.C., 1956-66; dir. showroom Philmaid Lingerie, N.Y.C., 1966-76; editor food and equipment div. Weight Watchers Mag., N.Y.C., 1976-85, editor in chief, 1985—; editorial dir. Weight Watchers Pub. Group, 1991—, v.p., 1992—; founder, dir. North Shore Cooking Sch., Port Washington, 1970; owner North Shore Caterers, Port Washington, 1970-76; instr. Youth Employment Services, Great Neck, N.Y., 1973, community enrichment program, 1974-75, Port Washington Adult Edn., 1982-84. Contbg. editor: Great Meals in Minutes, 1985. Nutrition cons. Port Washington community action council, 1977-87. Mem. Roundtable Women in Food Svc., Women in Comm., Am. Soc. Mag. Editors, Am. Inst. Wine and Food, Les Amis du Vin, N.Y. Hort. Soc., Hort. Alliance of the Hamptons, Oldways Preservation and Exch. Trust, Newswomen's Club, Knickerbocker Yacht Club, Chandon Club. Office: Weight Watchers Magazine WW 21st Corp 360 Lexington Ave New York NY 10017-6502

HAINES, BETH ANN, psychologist; b. Milw., Mar. 20, 1957; d. William Oscar and Mary Donna (Bussard) H.; 1 child, Tyler William Haines. BS, U. Wis., 1978, MS, 1983, PhD, 1988. Asst. prof. DePauw U., Greencastle, Ind., 1988-92, Lawrence U., Appleton, Wis., 1992—. Contbg. author: The Growth of Proportional Reasoning, 1987, Formal Models of Cognitive Development, 1987. Mem. Soc. Rsch. in Child Devel., MIdwestern Psychol. Assn., Phi Beta Kappa, Psi Chi, Sigma Epsilon Sigma, Phi Eta Sigma. Home: 770 N Lake St Neenah WI 54956 Office: Lawrence U PO Box 599 Appleton WI 54912

HAINES, BONNIE LEE, elementary school counselor; b. Mitchell, S.D., July 24, 1956; d. Orville Lain and Darlene Elinor (Glissendorf) Haines. BA, Dakota Wesleyan U., 1978; MEd, S.D. State U., 1982; cert. in religious studies, N.Am. Baptist Sem., 1983-85. High sch. bus., phys. edn. tchr. Watertown (S.D.) Sch. Dist., 1978-79; high sch. bus. tchr. Huron (S.D.) Sch. Dist., 1979-83; counselor Behavioral Medicine, Sioux Falls, S.D., 1984-85; instr. Sinte Gleska U., Rosebud, S.D., 1990-91; elem. counselor Todd County Sch. Dist., Mission, S.D., 1986—; coord. drug-free schs. program Todd County Sch. Dist., Mission, 1992—, coord. counseling dept., 1992—, prevention coord., 1994—. Mem. ACA, NEA, Am. Sch. Counselors Assn., Assn. Play Therapy, S.D. Counseling Assn., S.D. Sch. Counselors Assn., S.D. Edn. Assn., Todd County Edn. Assn. (pres. Ctrl. chpt. 1994-95). Republican. Baptist. Home: 214D Ave D PO Box 926 Mission SD 57555-0926 Office: Todd County Sch Dist PO Box 308 Mission SD 57555-0308

HAINES, JACQUELINE IRENE, institute director; b. Denver, June 26, 1933; d. Carl James and Elsie Irene (Hurt) H. Bachelor's degree, U. No. Colo., 1955. Tchr. Aurora (Colo.) Pub. Schs., 1955-67, guidance counselor, 1967-69; rsch. asst. Gesell Inst., New Haven, 1969-75, coord. clin. svc., 1975-80, dir. clin. svc., 1980-86, lectr., dir., 1978—, dir. devel. dept., 1980-88, sr. devel. specialist, 1988-90. Co-author: School Readiness, 1978, The Child From 1 to 6, 1979, Gesell Pre-school Assessment test manual, 1980. Active Women's Internat. League Peace and Freedom, New Haven, 1982—. Recipient Outstanding Tchr. of Yr. award Univ. No. Colo., Greeley, 1980. Mem. NEA, Nat. Assn. Edn. Young Children, Assn. Childhood Edn. Internat., Delta Kappa Gamma. Office: Gesell Inst 310 Prospect St New Haven CT 06511-2188

HAINES, VIRGINIA E., assemblywoman; b. Lakewood, N.J., June 6, 1946. Student, Ocean County C.C. Clk. N.J. Gen. Assembly, 1987-90; asst. dir. Ocean County Securities Dept., 1990-91; mem. Dover Twp. Mcpl. Utilities Authority, 1987—, chmn., 1991—; N.J. state assemblywoman 10th Legis. Dist., Brick, N.J., 1991—; N.J. state del. Rep. Nat. Conv., 1992; Rep. state committeewoman, Ocean County, 1985—; vice-chmn. labor com. Nat. Coun. State Legislatures; mem. Assembly Labor Com., Assembly State Govt. Com. Hon. bd. dirs. Lyons-Sambora Charity Ski Series; mem. Monmouth-Ocean Devel. Coun., Alice Paul Centennial Found., Inc.; mem. adv. bd. Ctr. for Kids and Family at Comty. Med. Ctr.; alt. mem. Regional Perinatal Consortium of Monmouth and Ocean County; bd. dirs. Ocean County Girl Scouts, Big Bros./Big Sisters of Ocean County; chmn. Ocean County Family Planning Ctr.; bd. dirs., past chmn. Local Adv. Coun. Alcohol and Drug Abuse, bd. dirs., past pres. Ocean County chpt. Am. Heart Assn. Named Citizen of Yr., Nat. Coun. Drug and Alcohol Abuse, 1990. Mem. Nat. Rep. Legislators Assn., Nat. Orgn. Women Legislators, N.J. Rep. Coalition for Choice, N.J. Rep. Women of 90s (vice chmn.), Women in the Senate and House, N.J. Assn. for Elected Women Ofcls., Women's Polit. Action Com. of N.J., Monmouth County Fedn. Rep. Women. Home: 497 Batchelor St Toms River NJ 08753-6702 Office: 10th Legis Dist 852 Route 70 Brick NJ 08724-2951

HAINING, JEANE, psychologist; b. Camden, N.J., May 2, 1952; d. Lester Edward and Adina (Rahn) H. BA, Calif. State U., 1975; MA, Pepperdine U., 1979; MS, Calif. State U., 1982; PhD, Calif. Sch. Profl. Psychology, 1985. Lic. clin. psychologist 1987, lic. ednl. psychologist 1982. Intern recreation therapist UCLA Neuropsychiatric Inst., L.A., 1975-76; intern sch. psychologist Los Nietos (Calif.) Sch. Dist., 1977-79; sch. psychologist Rialto (Calif.) Unified Sch. Dist., 1979-82; clin. psychologist field work San Joaquin County Dept. Mental Health, Stockton, Calif., 1982-83; intern clinical psychologist Fuller Theol. Sem. Psychology Ctr., Pasadena, Calif., 1984-85; clin. psychologist U.S. Dept. Justice, Terminal Island, Calif., 1985-86; psychologist community mental health L.A. County Dept. Mental Health, 1987-89; clin. psychologist Calif. Dept. Corrections, Parole Outpatient Clinic, L.A., 1990—, Mary Magdeline Project, Commerce, Calif., 1992—; mem. psychiatric-psychol. panel adult and juvenile Superior Ct., L.A., 1992—; mem. psychiatric panel U.S. Dist. Ct. (ctrl. dist.) Calif., L.A., 1989—. Examiner Lic. Ednl. Psychologist Oral Examinations, Calif. Bd. Behavioral Sci. Examines, Sacramento, 1985. Recipient award Outstanding Achievement Western Psychology Conf., Calif., 1974. Mem. Am. Psychol. Assn., Calif. Psychol. Assn., L.A. Psychol. Assn., Forensic Mental Health Assn. (con. planning com. 1993). Democrat. Lutheran.

HAIR, KITTIE ELLEN, secondary educator; b. Denver, June 12, 1948; d. William Edward and Jacqueline Jean (Holt) H. BA, Brigham Young U., 1971; MA in Social History, U. Nev., Las Vegas, 1987. cert. tchr., Nev. Health educator Peace Corps, Totota, Liberia, 1971-72; tchr. Clark County Sch. Dist., Las Vegas, Nev., 1972-77, 1979—; chair dept. social studies Clark County Sch. Dist., Las Vegas, 1993—; missionary Ch. Jesus Christ Latter-Day Saints, Alta., Can., 1977-79. Recipient Outstanding Faculty award U. Nev./Southland Corp., Las Vegas, 1991. Mem. NEA, Nat. Coun. for Social Scis., Clark County Tchrs. Assn., Phi Kappa Phi, Phi Alpha Theta, Delta Kappa Gamma. Democrat. Office: Eldorado High Sch 1139 Linn Ln Las Vegas NV 89110-2628

HAIR, MARCIA ELIZABETH, corporate art consultant; b. Miami, Fla., Oct. 16, 1948; d. James Ralph Hair and Marie Louise (Shonter) Yorra; m. Keith Terence Kelley, Jan. 10, 1970 (div. Oct. 1975); children: Patrick Shonter Kelley, Benjamin James Kelley; m. Ronald Elias Hickman, Mar. 15, 1986. Student, U. Ga., 1966-70; BA, Ga. State U., 1981, MA, 1994. Cert. civil and divorce mediator, Ga. Asst. dir. Apple Tree Sch., Atlanta, 1971-74; dir. Mini Sch., Atlanta, 1974-76, Kinder Care, Atlanta, 1976-77, A Learning Place, Decatur, Ga., 1977-78; with sales/design div. Frameworks Gallery, Marietta, Ga., 1978—, corp. cons., 1985—. Contbr. articles to profl. jours. Bd. dirs. Cobb County YWCA; chairperson Art to Heart Auction, Friends of Kenya Internat. Inc.; founder Deer Atlanta Task Force, Atlanta's Table; founder, auction host, com. chmn. Cobb County Humane Soc.; fundraiser Ga. Coun. on Child Abuse. Mem. NAFE, Atlanta Track Club, The Circle for Tallulah Falls Sch. Democrat. Roman Catholic. Home: 3350 Bryant Ln Marietta GA 30066-4610 Office: Frameworks Gallery 26 Mill St Marietta GA 30060-1967

HAIRALD, MARY PAYNE, vocational education educator, coordinator; b. Tupelo, Miss., Feb. 25, 1936; d. Will Burney and Ivey Lee (Berryhill) Payne; m. Leroy Utley Hairald, May 31, 1958; 1 child, Burney LeShawn. BS in Commerce, U. Miss., 1957, M in Bus. Edn., 1963; postgrad., Miss. Coll., 1964, Miss. State U., 1970, U. So. Miss., 1986-88, 90. Bus. edn. tchr. John Rundle High Sch., Grenada, Miss., 1957-59; youth recreation leader City of Nettleton, Miss., summers 1960-61; tchr. social studies Nettleton Jr. High Sch., 1959-70; tchr.-coord. coop. vocat. edn. program Nettleton High Sch., 1970—; area mgr. World Book, Inc., Chgo., 1972-84; local coord. Am. Inst. for Fgn. Study, Greenwich, Conn., 1988—; instr. bus. Itawamba C.C., Tupelo, 1975-80; sponsor Coop. Vocat. Edn. Club, Nettleton, 1970—; advisor DECA, Nettleton, 1985—. Editor advisor State DECA Newsletter, 1987-92; contbr. articles on coop. edn. to newspapers. Co-organizer Nettleton Youth Recreation Booster Club; fundraiser Muscular Dystrophy Assn.; Sunday sch. tchr. coll. and career class Nettleton United Meth. Ch. Named Star Tchr., 1995, Miss. Econ. Coun., 1978, Dist. II DECA Advisor of Yr., Miss. Assn. DECA, 1990, 93; recipient 1st place nat. newsletter award Nat. DECA, 1988, 89, 90, 92. Mem. AAUW (charter), Am. Vocat. Assn. (Region IV Coop. Vocat. Edn. Educator of Yr. 1985, Region IV Mktg. Edn. Educator of Yr. 1988), Coop. Work Experience Edn. Assn., Miss. Assn. Vocat. Educators (dist. sec.), Miss. Assn. Coop. Vocat. Edn. Tchrs. (v.p. 1980-83, pres. 1983-84, Miss. Tchr. of Yr. 1984, 87), Miss. Assn. Mktg. Educators (Dist. II Tchr. of Yr. 1993, 94), Mktg. Edn. Assn., Nettleton Ladies Civitan Club (charter). Democrat. Methodist. Home: PO Box 166 Nettleton MS 38858-0166

HAIRE, BARBARA GAIL, counselor, speech-language pathologist, educational diagnostician; b. Littlefield, Tex., June 26, 1954; d. Lloyd Frederick and Martha Vera (Smith) H. BA in Honors Studies, Tex. Tech. U., 1975, MBA, 1981; MEd, Hardin-Simmons U., 1988. Lic. profl. counselor, marriage and family therapist, speech lang. pathologist; cert. spl. edn. counselor, high sch. bus. adminstrn., high sch. psychology, ednl. diagnostician, speech and hearing therapy, Tex.; registered profl. ednl. diagnostician. Speech-lang. pathologist Lamesa (Tex.) Ind. Sch. Dist., 1976-78, Gorman (Tex.) East-End Edn. Co-Op, 1978-79; teaching/rsch. asst. Tex. Tech. U., Lubbock, 1979-81; copy editor Amarillo (Tex.) Globe News, 1981, Lubbock Avalanche-Jour., 1981-85; assoc. dir. Haire Speech, Lang. and Learning Ctr., Abilene, Tex., 1985—; adj. instr. Hardin-Simmons U., Abilene, 1987—; program presenter Dyess Attention-Deficit Disorder Support Group, Abilene, 1988, Big Country Head Injury Assn., Abilene, 1987. Vol. Hospice of Big Country, Abilene, 1993—. Mem. Am. Counseling Assn., Tex. Counseling Assn., Soc. for Creative Anachronism (newsletter editor 1982-92, arts and scis. officer 1993—, Star of Merit 1992). Baptist. Office: Haire Speech Lang Learning 1925 Hospital Pl Abilene TX 79606

HAISCHER, LISA KERSCHENSTEINER, accounting manager; b. Corning, N.Y., May 15, 1966; d. Alfred Christian and Susan Elizabeth (Kapral) Kerschensteiner; m. Thomas J. Haischer, July 22, 1991 (div. July 1993). BS cum laude in Acctg., Elmira Coll., 1988. Cost supr. Simpson Paper Co., Kalamazoo, Mich., 1988-90; mgr. gen. acctg. svcs. Dresser Rand, Painted Post, N.Y., 1990—. Mem. fin. planning com. Corning-Painted Post Hist. Soc. Mem. Inst. Mgmt. Accts. (dir. mtgs. Elmira/Corning, N.Y. chpt. 1990—), Women's Ctr. Roman Catholic. Office: Dresser Rand 100 Chemung St Painted Post NY 14870

HAJDAJ, KATHY YVONNE, speech language pathologist; b. Washington, Nov. 1, 1946; d. Earl Maxwell and Virginia Neff (Bathgate) Cain; m. James Wingfield Williamson, Apr. 17, 1972 (div. Sept., 1972); 1 child, Jonathan Blair; m. Eugene Hajdaj, Apr. 3, 1976 (div. Sept., 1993); 1 child, Ryan Nicholas. BA in Speech Pathology, Fla. State U., 1968; BA in Elem. Edn., U. Ctrl. Fla., 1987, M in Speech Lang. Pathology, 1993. Provisional lic. speech lang. pathologist, Fla. Singing waitress (summers) Farm House Inn, Blowing Rock, N.C., 1965, 66, 67; flight attendant Pan Am. World Airways, N.Y.C., 1969-70; madrigal singer Walt Disney World, Lake Buena Vista, Fla., 1971-72; speech lang. pathologist Putnam County, Crescent City, Fla., 1987-88, Brevard County, Titusville, Fla., 1988-94, Harborside Rehab. Ctr., 1994—; spelling bee sponsor Coquina Elem. Sch., Titusville, Fla., 1991-94, yearbook com. mem., 1993-94. Mem. Fla. Right to Life, Orlando, 1994. Mem. Am. Speech, Hearing Assn., Fla. Speech, Hearing Assn. Republican. Home: 6385 Stillwater Ave Cocoa FL 32927-3306 Office: Harborside Rehab Ctr 1775 Huntington Ln Rockledge FL 32955

HALAS, CYNTHIA ANN, systems support analyst; b. Norristown, Pa., July 24, 1961; d. George and Maria (Mitrik) H. Student, Temple U., 1979-80; AS in Bus. Adminstrn., Montgomery County Coll., Blue Bell, Pa., 1993; student, Springhouse Computer Sch., Exton, Pa., 1994—. Columnist, corr. The Recorder, Conshohocken, Pa., 1980-81; claims supr. Liberty Mut. Ins. Co., Blue Bell, 1980-84; claims svc. rep. Met. Property & Liability Ins. Co., Wayne, Pa., 1984-87; model Frank James Assocs., Phila., 1986-87; auditor/tng. coord. Coresource, Inc., Wayne, 1987-94; sys. support analyst Del. Valley Fin. Svcs., Inc., Berwyn, Pa., 1994—. Active Nat. Arbor Day Found. Mem. NAFE, U.S. Fencing Assn. Byzantine Catholic. Office: Del Valley Fin Svcs Inc 300 Berwyn Park PO Box 3031 Berwyn PA 19312-0031

HALASZ, MARILYNN JEAN, information services manager; b. Chgo., Nov. 12, 1937; d. Frank John and Vera Josephine (Staab) Macku; m. John Ernest Halasz, May 21, 1981. B.A., Rosary Coll., 1959; M.A.L.S., 1977; student foreign study, Univ. Coll., Oxford, Eng., 1971; M.A., DePaul U., 1972. Tchr. elem., secondary, and collegiate levels in English, sci. and math., 1959-77; cons. resource manual Ill. State Bd. Edn., Triton Coll., River Grove, Ill., 1975-76; sci. librarian John Crerar Library, Chgo., 1977-78; assoc. librarian Portland Cement Assn., Skokie, Ill., 1978, librarian, 1978-80, mgr. info. services sect., 1980-85; supr. Tech. Info. Ctr., Inst. Gas Tech., 1988-89; sr. info. specialist, Corn Products CPC Internat., 1989— cons. in field. Contbr. articles to profl. jours. Recipient grad. asst. award Dale Carnegie & Assocs., 1984. Mem. Spl. Libraries Assn. Roman Catholic. Club: Am. Assn. Univ. Women, Lyric Opera. Home: 157 Pheasant Hollow Dr Burr Ridge IL 60521 Office: Corn Products 6500 S Archer Rd Box 345 Summit Argo IL 60501-1944

HALBERT, MARVA ANN, bank executive; b. Rolla, Mo., Oct. 7, 1959; d. Marvin Jay and Birdie Lou (Scott) H. BS, S.W. Mo. State U., 1982; JD, U. Mo., Kansas City, 1985. Assoc. Howard S. Levitan, P.C., Prairie Village, Kans., 1985-86; constrn./sales mgr. Golden Hills Resort, Pocatello, Idaho, 1986; comml. loan officer Landmark Bank St. Louis, St. Charles, Mo., 1986-89; asst. v.p. comml. loans Boatmen's Nat. Bank St. Louis, 1989-93; v.p. comml. lending First Bank, St. Louis, 1993—. Editor Urban Lawyer, 1984-85. Mem. blue ribbon com. United Svcs., St. Peter, Mo., 1992—; big sister Big Bros. Big Sisters, St. Louis, 1992-93. Mem. St. Peters C. of C. (chair govt. concerns com. 1993—). Home: 11270 Pineside Dr Saint Louis MO 63146 Office: First Bank 10900 Manchester Kirkwood MO 63122

HALE, BRENDA L., medical/surgical nurse; b. Roanoke, Va., Dec. 22, 1945; d. Daniel Monroe Sr. and Ruth Roberta (Watson) H. LPN, U.S. Army Fitzsimmons Gen. Hosp., 1967; AAS, Va. Western Community Coll., Roanoke, 1989. Nurse VA Med. Ctr., Salem, Va.; staff nurse VA Med. Ctr., Salem. With U.S. Army, 1965-78. Home: 3595 Parkwood Dr Roanoke VA 24018-4439

HALE, CHARLOTTE, author, publishing executive; b. Jacksonville, Fla., Jan. 6, 1928; d. Anthony W. and Eleanor (Cunningham) Hale; m. Norris TeBeau Pindar III, May 23, 1986; 1 child by previous marriage, Stanley R. Smith Jr. Student, Armstrong Jr. Coll., 1947-48. Copy writer Sta. WSAV, Savannah, Ga., 1948-49, copy dir., 1949-51; copy dir. Sta. WSAV-TV, 1955-57; with advt. dept. Savannah News-Press, 1957-59; staff writer Sunday mag. Atlanta Jour.-Constn., 1960-70; free-lance writer, 1969—; founder, owner Charlotte Hale Communiqué; founder, pres. Epiphany Press, Savannah; cons. U.S. CSC, 1976-79; guest speaker various colls., schs., chs., clubs, 1969—; founder Time of Your Life mgmt. seminar, 1978, Facing Forward motivational seminar and workshop on aging, 1982, Going First Class seminar, 1984; speech writer state polit. candidates, 1959-68; news writer U.S. Army, Ft. Stewart, Ga., 1951. Author: Full-Time Living, 1978, (with Layona Glenn) I Remember, I Remember, 1968; editor and writer various books by Anita Bryant and Bob Green, 1970-77, A New Day, 1992, Atlanta's Source Guide, 1991; editor: The Super Years, 1984; contbr. book revs. to newspapers. Vol. Savannah Symphony, 1955-59; bd. dirs. Savannah Mental Health Assn., 1957-59, Citizens Crime Commn., Ga. Women's Bus. Initiative; trustee Ga. Conservancy, Inc., 1968-70. Mem. Nat. Speakers Assn., Chatham Commerce CLub (chmn. 1991-92). Home and Office: 629 E 55th St Savannah GA 31405-3617

HALE, DONNA LAURIE, aeronautical engineer; b. Pequannock Township, N.J., Aug. 31, 1962; d. Donald L. and Mildred M. Post.; m. John A. Hale. BS, Rutgers U., 1984; MS, Calif. Inst. Tech., 1985. Registered profl. engr., Idaho. Sr. mem. tech. staff TRW Inc., San Bernardino, Calif., 1985-91; sr. engr. Sci. Applications Internat. Corp., Albuquerque, 1991-93; engring. specialist Idaho Nat. Engring. Lab., Idaho Falls, Idaho, 1993—. Home: 1955 Midway Ave Idaho Falls ID 83406

HALE, KAYCEE, research marketing professional; b. Mount Hope, W.Va., July 18, 1947; d. Bernard McFadden and Virginia Lucille (Mosley) H. AA, Compton Coll., 1965; BS, Calif. State U., Dominguez Hills, 1981. Fashion model O'Bryant Talent Agy., L.A., 1967-77; faculty mem. L.A. Trade-Tech. Coll., 1969-71, Fashion Inst., L.A., 1969-77, 1975—; pres. The Fashion Co., L.A., 1970-75; co-host The Fashion Game TV Show, L.A., 1982-87; exec. dir. Fashion Inst. Design and Merchandising Resource & Rsch. Ctr., L.A., 1975—, Fashion Inst. Design and Merchandising Mus. and Libr., L.A., 1977—; lectr. in field, internat., 1969—. Author: (brochure) What's Your I.Q. (Image Quotient)?; (tape) Image Builders; contbg. editor Library Management in Review; columnist The Public Image, 1990; contbr. Bowker Annual 1990-91, (newsletter) Northeast Library System, 1991. Adv. bd. Calif. State U., Long Beach, 1988-91. Mem. ALA, Spl. Librs. Assn. (pres. elect 1986—, pres. 1987-88, bd. dirs. So. Calif. chpt. 1985—), Spl. Librs. Adv. Coun. (pub. rels. com. 1987-89), SLA Libr. Mgmt. Div. (chmn.-elect 1987-88, chmn. 1988-89, pres.'s task force on image of libr./info. profl.), Textile Assn. L.A. (bd. dirs. 1985-87), Calif. Media and Libr. Educators Assn., Am. Mktg. Assn., Western Mus. Conf., Am. Mus. Assn., Costume Soc. Am. Office: Fashion Inst Design & Merchandising 919 S Grand Ave Los Angeles CA 90015-1421

HALE, MARCIA L., federal official. B in Polit. Sci., U. S.C., MPA. Asst. county planner Aiken County (S.C.) Planning Commn.; legis. asst. to U.S. rep. Butler Derrick of S.C. Washington; Washington dir. State of S.C.; dir. scheduling Hollings for Pres. campaign, 1984; dir. of advance Rep. Geraldine Ferraro's v.p. campaign Rep. Geraldine Ferraro's Vice Presdl. Campaign; field dir. Dem. Congl. Campaign Com.; southern field dir., conv. mgr., pre-election transition planning Dukakis Presl. Campaign; cons. Greenberg-Lake, Washington, Dem. Senatorial Campaign Com., 1990; polit. dir. Dem. Congl. Campaign Com.; asst. to Pres., dir. scheduling and advance White House, Washington, 1992-93; asst. to Pres., dir. intergovtl. affairs, 1993—. Office: The White House Office Intergovtl Affairs 1600 Pennsylvania Ave NW Washington DC 20500-0001

HALE, MARIE STONER, artistic director; b. Greenwood, Miss.. Student in Piano, U. Miss., Hattiesburg; studied with Richard Ellis, Christine du Boulay, Jo-Anna Kneeland, David Howard. Tchr. Ellis/du Boulay Sch., Chgo., Jo-Anna Kneeland Imperial Studios, Palm Beach County, Fla.; co-founder Ballet Arts Found., West Palm Beach, Fla., 1973-86; co-founder, artistic dir. Ballet Fla., West Palm Beach, 1986—. Office: Ballet Fla 500 Fern St West Palm Beach FL 33401

HALES, LINDA, newspaper editor; b. Kansas City, Mo., Nov. 30, 1949; d. Samuel Dale and Erika Anne (Sitte) Hales; m. George Edward Gudauskas Jr. BA in French and Polit. Sci., U. Kans., 1971, BSJ, 1974. Copy editor Chgo. Today, 1974, Chgo. Tribune, 1974-78; asst. nat. editor Washington Star, 1978-79; news editor U.S. News and World Report, 1979-82; spl. reports editor Internat. Herald Tribune, Paris, 1983-88; sr. editor Health sect. Washington Post, 1988-89, editor Washington Home sect., 1990—. Recipient J.C. Penney Journalism award U. Mo., 1991. Office: The Washington Post 1150 15th St NW Washington DC 20071-0001

HALEY, JOHNETTA RANDOLPH, musician, educator, university administrator; b. Alton, Ill., Mar. 19; d. John A. and Willye E. (Smith) Randolph; children from previous marriage: Karen, Michael. MusB in Edn., Lincoln U., 1945; MusM, So. Ill. U., 1972. Vocal and gen. music tchr. Lincoln High Sch., E. St. Louis, Ill., 1945-48; vocal music tchr., choral dir. Turner Sch., Kirkwood, Mo., 1950-55; vocal and gen. music tchr. Nipher Jr. High Sch., Kirkwood, 1955-71; prof. music Sch. Fine Arts, So. Ill. U., Edwardsville, 1972—, dir. East St. Louis Campus, 1982—; adjudicator music festivals; area music cons. Ill. Office Edn., 1977-78; program specialist St. Louis Human Devel. Corp., 1968; interim exec. dir. St. Louis Council Black People, summer 1970. Bd. dirs. YWCA, 1975-80, Artist Presentation Soc., St. Louis, 1975, United Negro Coll. Fund, 1976-78; bd. curators Lincoln U., Jefferson City, Mo., 1974-82, pres., 1978-82; chairperson Ill. Com. on Black Concerns in Higher Edn.; mem. Nat. Ministry on Urban Edn., Luth. Ch.-Mo. Synod, 1975-80; bd. dirs. Council Luth. Chs., Assn. of Governing Bds. of Univs. and Colls.; mem. adv. council Danforth Found. St. Louis Leadership Program, nat. chmn. Cleve. Job Corps, 1974-78; trustee Stillman Coll; pres. congregation St. Philips Luth. Ch.; bd. dirs. Target 2000; mem. Ill. Aux. Bd., United Way, v.p. East St. Louis Community Fund, Inc. Named Woman of Achievement in Edn. award Elks, 1987, Disting. Citizen St. Louis Argus Newspaper, 1970; recipient Cotillion de Leon award for Outstanding Community Service, 1977, Woman of Achievement award Suburban Newspaper of Greater St. Louis and Sta. KMOX Radio, 1988; Disting. Alumnae award Lincoln U., 1977; Disting. Service award United Negro Coll. Fund, 1979, SCLC, 1981; Community Service award St. Louis Drifters, 1979; Disting. Service to Arts award Sigma Gamma Rho, Fred L. McDowell award, 1986, Nat. Negro Musicians award, 1981, Sci. Awareness award, 1984-85, Tri Del Federated award, 1985, Bus. and Profl. Women's Club award, 1985-86, vol. yr. Inroad's Inc., 1986, Love award Greeley Community Ctr.; named Duchess of Paducah, 1973; Sammy Davies Jr. award in Edn., 1990; received Key to City, Gary, Ind., 1973; recipient Yes I Can award in Edn., 1990, Merit award Urban League, 1994. Mem. Council Luth. Chs., AAUP, Coll. Music Soc., Music Educators Nat. Conf., Ill. Music Educators Assn., Nat. Choral Dirs. Assn., Assn. Tchr. Educators, Midwest Kodaly Music Educators, Nat. Assn. Negro Musicians, Jack and Jill Inc., Women of Achievement in Edn., Friends of St. Louis Art Mus., The Links, Inc., Las Amigas Social Club, Alpha Kappa Alpha (internat. parliamentarian), Mu Phi Epsilon, Pi Kappa Lambda. Lutheran. Home: 230 S Brentwood Blvd Clayton MO 63105 Office: So Ill U PO Box 1200 Edwardsville IL 62026-1500

HALEY, RUTH NANCY, social services administrator; b. Mahanoy City, Pa., July 14, 1938; d. Edward James and Alice Rachel (Snyder) H. BA, D'Youville Coll., 1960; MSW, St. Louis U., 1962. Lic. social worker, Pa. Case worker Children's Svcs., St. Louis, 1960-65; social worker Northampton County Children's Bur., Easton, Pa., 1965-68; exec. dir., adminstr. Children, Youth and Families Northampton County Dept. Human Svcs., Easton, Pa., 1968—. Mem. steering com. Project Child of Lehigh Valley, Allentown, Pa., 1993—; bd. dirs. Project of Easton, Inc., 1978—; mem. Allentown Pa. Art Mus.; mem. women's coun. St. Bernard's Ch. Recipient Colleague of Yr. award Am. Bus. Women's Assn., 1986. Mem. NASW (cert., Social Worker of Yr. 1986), Am. Pub. Welfare Assn., Child Welfare Adminstrs., Pa. Children and Youth Adminstrs. (exec. bd. dirs. 1968-86). Democrat. Roman Catholic. Home: 509 Parsons St Easton PA 18042-1700 Office: Northampton County Children Youth and Families 45 N 2nd St Easton PA 18042-3637

HALFORD, SHARON LEE, crime victim services administrator, victimologist, educator; b. Clifton, Colo., July 22, 1946; d. Robert Lee and Florence V. (Kubly) Eighmy; m. Allen A. Dreher, Jan. 29, 1967 (div. Jan. 1979); children: Heidi Ann, Gretchen Christine, Kirsten Beth; m. Donald Gary Halford, May 23, 1986. BS in Edn., U. Colo., 1969; postgrad., U. Denver, 1981-83; M in Criminal Justice, U. Colo., 1987. Legal asst. 1st Jud. Dist. Atty., Golden, Colo., 1979-81, legal rschr., 1981-83; victim witness coord. 18th Jud. Dist. Atty., Englewood, Colo., 1983-92; mem. faculty Aurora (Colo.) C.C. Criminal Justice Dept., 1989—, Colo. Faculty Adv. Coun., 1993—. Contbg. author, editor: Colorado Crime Victims Rights Contitutional Amendment Outreach Manual and Implementation Manual, 1992-93. Mem. Domestic Violence Task Force, Douglas County, Colo., 1985-92, Arapahoe County, Colo., 1985-94; trainer Rape Assistance and Awareness Program, Denver, 1985-91, MADD, 1990-92, Colo. Victim Witness Coord. Coalition, 1991; mem. 18th Judicial Dist. Child Advocacy Ctr. Com., 1990—, Gov.'s Victims' Compensation and Assistance Coord. Com., 1991—, Colo. Victim Asst. and Law Enforcement Bd., 1991—, Criminal Justice Educators Task Force, 1992—, Colo. Corrections Consortium, 1992—, Colo. Crime Victim Rights Constl. Ammendment Com., 1990—; sec. Colo. Faculty Adv. Coun., 1993—; com. chair Colo. PACT Project, 1993—. Fellow Nat. Orgn. for Victim Assistance, Nat. Victim Ctr.; mem. Colo. Orgn. for Victim Assistance (pres.), S.W. Criminal Justice Educators Assn., Nat. Criminal Justice Educators Assn., Nat. Criminal Justice Assn., Am. Criminal Justice Assn., Internat. Platform Speakers Assn. Democrat. Methodist. Office: CC Aurora 16000 E Centretech Pky Aurora CO 80011-9036

HALFVARSON, LUCILLE ROBERTSON, music educator; b. Petersburg, Ill., May 17, 1919; d. Harris Morton and Lucille (Fox) Robertson; m. Sten Gustaf Halfvarson, Aug. 8, 1946; children: Laura, Eric, Linnea, Mary. BA, Knox Coll., 1941; MusM, Am. Conservatory, 1969. Cert. tchr., Ill. Tchr. Music & Speech Freeman Elem. Sch., Aurora, Ill., 1941-44; choral dir. Galesburg (Ill.) Sr. High Sch., 1944-46; dir. of music Our Savior Luth. Ch., Aurora, Ill., 1950-63; oratorio soloist, 1952-67; dir. of music Westminster Presbyn. Ch., Aurora, 1963-84; vocal instr. Merit Music Program, Chgo., 1982-93; ret., 1993; choir dir. 1st Meth. Ch., Galesburg, Ill., 1944-46; choral-vocal instr. Waubonsee Community Coll. Sugar Grove, Ill., 1967-79; organizer Jr. Coll. Music Fest. Waubonsee Coll., Sugar Grove, 1972-73; pvt. practice vocal instr., Aurora, 1979—. Conductor Messiah Concert Waubonsee Coll., Paramount Arts Ctr., 1968—, 25th Concert, 1992. Co-chair Citizens Adv. Com. Paramount Arts Ctr., Aurora, 1977-78; founder, pres. United Arts Bd. Fox Valley, 1977-82, chair Paramount Celebration Arts, 1985-86; residency dir. Met. Life Affiliate Artist, Aurora, 1982-83; bd. dirs. YWCA, 1984—, chair corp. awards com., 1994—. Recipient Disting. Svc. award Cosmopolitan Club, Aurora, Ill., 1983; named Woman of Year YWCA, Aurora, 1976, Disting. Alumni Knox Coll., Galesburg, Ill., 1984. Mem. AAUW, DAR, PEO, Music Educators Nat. Conf., Am. Choral Dirs. Assn., Aurora C. of C. (Image Maker 1992), Phi Beta Kappa. Home: 1105 W Downer Pl Aurora IL 60506-4821

HALL, ADRIENNE ANN, international marketing executive; b. Los Angeles; d. Arthur E. and Adelina P. Kosches; m. Maurice Hall; children: Adam, Todd, Stefanie, Victoria. B.A., UCLA. Founding ptnr. Hall & Levine Advt., L.A., 1965-80; vice chmn. bd. Eisaman, Johns & Laws Advt. Inc., L.A., Houston, Chgo., N.Y.C., 1980-94; pres., CEO The Hall Group, Beverly Hills, Calif., 1994—; founder, ptnr. Women, Inc.; chmn. Eric Bovy Inc., 196-89, Hall Partnership; bd. dirs. Calif. Mfrs. Assn. Svc. Corp., Inc. Trustee UCLA; bd. regents Loyola-Marymount U., Los Angeles; mem. The Founders of Music Ctr., Pres. Circle, L. A. County Comsnr. Mus. Art, Calif. Gov.'s Commn. on Econ. Devel., task force Rebuild L.A.; bd. dirs. United Way, ARC, Exec. Svc. Corps, The 2000 Zoo Regional Ptnrship., Shelter Ptnrship, Nat. Health Found., Am. Women in Econ. Devel.; mem. adv. council Girl's Clubs Am.; mem. adv. bd. Girl Scouts U.S., Asian Pacific Women's Adv., Coalition of 100 Black Women, Nat. Network of Hispanic Women, Downtown Women's Ctr. and Residence, Leadership Am., Washington, L.A. Food Bank; mem. exec. bd. Greater Los Angeles Partnership for Homeless, Los Angeles Shelter Partnership Bd. Recipient Nat. Headliner award Women in Comm., 1982, Profl. Achievement award UCLA Alumi, 1979, award for cmty. svc., 1994, Asian Pacific Network Woman Warrior award, 1994, Woman of Yr. award Am. Advt. Fedn., 1973, Ad Person of West award Mktg. and Media Decisions, 1982, Bus. Woman of Yr. award Boy Scouts Am., 1983, Women Helping Women award Soroptimists Internat., 1984, 1st ann. portfolio award for exec. women, 1985, Communicator of Yr. award Ad Women, 1986, leader award YWCA, 1986;. Mem. Internat. Women's Forum (bd. dirs., Woman Who Made a Difference award 1987), Am. Assn. Advt. Agys. (bd. dirs. 1980, chmn. bd. govs. western region), Western States Advt. Agys. Assn. (pres. 1975), Hollywood Radio and TV Soc. (dir.), Nat. Advt. Rev. Bd., Overseas Edn. Fund, Com. 200 (western chmn.), Women in Communications, Orgn. Women Execs., Calif. Women's Forum (founder, chmn. The Trusteeship), Rotary (L.A. 5 chpt.), Internat. Bus. Fellows (mem. adv. bd.), Women's Econ. Alliance, Nat. Assn. Women Bus. Owners (adv. bd.), Am. Heart Assn. (adv. bd.). Clubs: Calif. Yacht; Stock Exchange, Los Angeles Advt. (pres.) (Los Angeles). Lodge: Rotary.

HALL, ALEX SMITH, psychotherapist, educator and researcher; b. Lafayette, Ind., Sept. 15, 1955; d. Wilbur Lee and Joann (Hughes) H.; m. Terry L. Thompson, May 15, 1979 (div.); 1 child, Jonathan James; m. Kevin R. Kelly, Sept. 16, 1989; 1 child, Megan L. BA in Religion and Philosophy, Hope Coll., 1977; MS in Counseling and Personnel, Purdue U., 1983, PhD in Counseling, 1989. Staff counselor Purdue U., 1983-85, grad. teaching asst., 1986-87, rsch. asst. dept. voct. edn., 1987-89, grad. instr. dept. edn., 1988-89, adj. faculty dept. supervision tech., 1988-89; vis. asst. prof. psychology, acting dir. counseling ctr. Wabash Coll., 1989-90; assoc. prof. psychology, chair dept. psychology St. Joseph's Coll., Rensselaer, Ind., 1990—; indsl. rsch. cons. A.E. Staley Co., Decatur, Ill., 1986; speaker in field. Contbr. articles to profl. jours.; guest co-editor: Jour. Mental Health Counseling, mem. editorial bd., 1993—. Mem. Am. Assn. Marriage and Family Therapy, Am. Psychol. Assn., Am. Counseling Assn. Home: 208 Forest Hill Dr West Lafayette IN 47906-2402 Office: Saint Josephs Coll PO Box 905 Rensselaer IN 47978-0905

HALL, ALICE AVERETTE, college administrator, counselor; b. Gastonia, N.C., June 13, 1957; d. Richard Glenn and Juanita Wanda (Watkins) Averette; m. Kenneth Eldridge Hall, June 16, 1979; children: Aryn Leigh, Lindsey Ann, Lauren Ashley. BA in Psychology & Music, Coll. of William and Mary, 1979; MEd in Counselor Edn., Auburn U., 1981; postgrad., Va. Poly. Inst., 1986—. Counselor II Mt. Rogers Mental Health Clinic, Marion, Va., 1983-85, acting clinic dir., 1984-85; asst. prof., support svcs. counselor Wytheville (Va.) C.C., 1985-91; dir. student devel. ctr. Western Wyo. C.C., Rock Springs, 1991—; presenter various workshops, seminars at state, regional & nat. confs. Bd. dirs. Family Resource Ctr., Wytheville, 1982-85, Task Force on Sexual Assault, Sweetwater County, Wyo., 1992. Named Woman of Yr. Bus. & Profl. Women, Rock Springs, 1992. Mem. ACA, Am. Coll. Pers. Assn., Am. Coll. Counseling Assn., Nat. Career Devel. Assn., Wyo. Counseling Assn., Phi Kappa Phi. Methodist. Office: Western Wyoming CC 2500 College Dr Rock Springs WY 82901

HALL, ANNA CHRISTENE, government official; b. Tyler, Tex., Dec. 18, 1946; d. Willie B. and Mary Christene (Wood) H. BA in Polit. Sci., So. Meth. U., 1969. Clk.-stenographer Employment and Tng. Adminstrn., U.S. Dept. Labor, Dallas, 1970, fed. rep., 1970-80; program analyst U.S. Dept. Labor, Washington, 1980-84, div. chief, 1984-87, exec. asst., 1987-88; office dir. U.S. Dept. Labor, Dallas, 1988—. Recipient Outstanding Performance award U.S. Dept. Labor, 1972, 73, 74, 79, Meritorious Achievement award, 1986. Mem. Partnership for Employment and Tng., Nat. Honor Soc. Democrat. Presbyterian. Home: 2304 Hunters Run Dr Dallas TX 75232-4146 Office: US Dept Lab ETA 525 Griffin St Rm 315 Dallas TX 75202

HALL, BEVERLY ADELE, nursing educator; b. Houston, Aug. 19, 1935; d. Leslie Leo and Lois Mae (Pesnell) H. BS, Tex. Christian U., 1957; MA, NYU, 1961; PhD, U. Colo., 1974. RN, Tex., N.Y. With Ft. Worth (Tex.) Dept. Health, 1957-59; asst. prof. U. Mass., Amhurst, 1961-65; chief nurse N.Y.C. Med. Coll., 1965-67; asst. prof. U. Colo., Denver, 1967-70; assoc. prof. U. Washington, Seattle, 1974-80; prof., chmn. dept. U. Calif., San Francisco, 1980-84; Denton Cooley prof. nursing U. Tex., Austin, 1984—; mem. grad. faculty Sch. Biomed. Sci. U. Tex., Galveston; pres. med. svcs. Bd. Dir. Project Transitions. Author: Mental Health and the Elderly, 1985 (Book of Yr.); mem. editl. rev. bd. Advances in Nursing, Archives Psychiat. Nursing, Qualitative Health Rsch., Rsch. in Nursing and Health, Nursing Outlook, Jour. Profl. Nursing, Jour. of the Am. Psychiat. Nurses Assn.; contbr. articles to profl. jours., chpts. to books. Served to capt. U.S. Army, 1962-66. Recipient Tex. Excellence Teaching award U. Tex. Ex-Students Assn., 1994. Fellow Am. Acad. Nursing (governing bd.), Am. Coll. Mental Health Adminstrn.; mem. Council Nurse Researchers, Am. Inst. Life Threatening Illness and Loss, So. Nursing Rsch. Soc., Am. Nursing Assn. (div. gerontological practice). Home: 8401 Mesa Doble Ln Austin TX 78759-8028 Office: U Tex 1700 Red River St Austin TX 78701-1499

HALL, CAROL LYNN, purchasing agent; b. Evansville, Ind., Dec. 10, 1947; d. Lynn Elder and Mildred K. (Wulf) H. BA in Bus. Edn., U. Evansville, 1969. Tchr. high sch. bus. North Montgomery Sch. Corp., Linden, Ind., 1969-70; purchasing agt. Brown & Hubert, Inc., 1971—. Chairperson pastor-parish com. Wesley United Meth. Ch., Evansville, 1987-94; sec.-treas. Priscilla Circle, sec. bd. trustees, 1989—. Office: Brown & Hubert div Lensing Wholesale 306 N 7th Ave Evansville IN 47710-1024

HALL, CAROLYN, association executive; b. Sturgis, Mich., Sept. 25, 1946; d. Frederic William and Margaret Frances Thiele; m. Kenneth Arthur Hall, June 28, 1969; children: Elizabeth Anne, Stephanie Marie. AS, Ferris State Coll., 1966, BS in Commerce magna cum laude, 1968. Pers. mgmt. officer USAR, Kalamazoo, Mich., 1970-77; instr. USAR, Macon, Ga., 1977-86; fitness instr. YWCA of Brunswick, Ga., 1978-80, exec. dir., 1981—; mem. liaison com. Commn. on Children and Youth, Brunswick, 1990-93. Co-Chair Leadership Glynn, Brunswick, 1989-90; dir. basketball Glynn Acad. Booster Club, Brunswick, 1991-93. 1st lt. U.S. Army, 1967-70. Mem. Nat. Assn. YWCA Execs. Roman Catholic. Office: YWCA of Brunswick 144 Scranton Connector Blvd Brunswick GA 31525-0516

HALL, CARRIE (CAROLYN JO ANNE HALL), fashion consultant, association executive, speaker; b. Dubuque, Iowa, Sept. 7, 1936; d. Raeburn Grey Miller and Opal Louise Dellinger; m. Joseph De Witt Hall, June 28, 1958; children: Elizabeth Louise, Patrick Grey De Witt. Student, Am. U., 1957-58; BA, Simpson Coll., 1958. Food mgmt. supr. U. Iowa, Iowa City, 1958-62; urban ministry assoc. United Meth. Ch., Des Moines, 1968-70; fashion cons. Tanner Corp., Des Moines, 1985-94; cons., trainer Tanner Corp., Rutherfordton, N.C., 1989-94; fashion adv. bd. Doncaster, N.Y.C., 1993-94. founding mem. HOME Inc., Des Moines, 1968; steering com. Pub. Schs. Desegregation Plan, Des Moines, 1974; chair Urban Coalition Desegregation, Des Moines, 1970-74; coun. mem. Mayor's Task Force, Des Moines, 1990-93; bd. dirs. YWCA Greater Des Moines, 1979-82 (pres., v.p., Women Reaching Out award 1989), YWCA USA, 1989-93, Hospice Ctrl. Iowa Found., 1993-94; active Children's Families Iowa Planned Giving,

1990-93. Recipient Outstanding Svc. award Des Moines Symphony, 1979, Key to City award, Des Moines City Coun., 1980, Vol. Svc. award United Way, Des Moines, 1981, Vol. Svcs. award Children's Families Iowa, 1990. Democrat. Presbyterian. Home: 2323 Park Ave Des Moines IA 50321-1505

HALL, CATHY E., sales professional; b. Ridley Park, Pa., Jan. 10, 1959; d. John Edward and Lois Joyce (Croasdale) H.; m. Daniel William O'Connell, June 5, 1982 (div. Sept. 1985). Student, Trinity Coll., Washington. Beverage mgr. Easton's Inn Corp., Newport, R.I., 1979-82; banquet and beverage mgr., bartender Maison Blanche/White House Connection, Washington, 1982-86; beverage mgr., bartender Fourways Inn, Washington, 1982-86; mgr., sommelier Oliver Carr Co./Occidental Restaurant, Washington, 1986-90; sales mgr. wine divsn. Forman Bros., Inc., Washington, 1990-95; N.E. regional sales mgr. Chalone Wine Group, Calif., 1995—; lectr. L'Academie de Cuisine Culinary Sch., Bethesda, Md., 1989-91;. Chmn. charity event Tuberous Sclerosis, Washington, 1987; bd. dirs. charity events March of Dimes, Washington, 1989-90. Recipient award of Excellence for wine list Wine Spectator mag., 1990. Mem. Women for WineSense (chmn. D.C. chpt. 1990—), Les Dames d'Escoffier, Sommelier Soc. (bd. dirs. 1989-91), Brotherhood of Knights of the Vine (Master Lady 1988—), Amicale Culinaire, Young and Decadent Club. Democrat. Home and Office: 2603-B South Walter Reed Dr Arlington VA 22206

HALL, CHARLOTTE HAUCH, publishing executive; b. Washington, Sept. 30, 1945; d. Charles Christian and Ruthadele Bertha (LaTourrette) H.; m. Robert Lindsay Hall, June 8, 1968; 1 child, Benjamin H. BA, Kalamazoo Co., 1966; MA, U. Chgo., 1967. Reporter, news editor The Ridgewood (N.J.) Newspapers, 1971-74; copy editor, news editor The Record, Hackensack, N.J., 1975-76; asst. mng. editor The Boston Herald Am., 1977-78; dep. met. editor The Washington Star, 1979-80; news editor, Nassau County editor, Washington news editor Newsday, Melville, N.Y., 1981-87, asst. mng. editor, 1988-94; mktg. dir. L.I. Newsday Inc., Melville, 1994—. Mem. Soc. Profl. Journalists, Phi Beta Kappa. Office: Newsday Inc 235 Pinelawn Rd Melville NY 11747-4226

HALL, CHERYL FARRIS, accountant, educator; b. Lexington, Ky., Mar. 17, 1966; d. David Elbert Jr. and Martha Anna (Edwards) Farris; m. James F. Hall, July 2, 1988. BS in Acctg., U. Ky., 1990, MS in Acctg., 1992. Acct. Island Creek Corp., Lexington, 1987-93; acct. adminstrv. acctg. res. R.R. Donnelley & Sons, Danville, Ky., 1993—; instr. Ky. Coll. Bus., Lexington, 1993-94, Fugazzi Coll., Lexington, 1993-94, Ky. Coll. Bus., Danville, 1994. Tchr., dir. Sunday sch. Edgewood Bapt. Ch., Nicholasville, Ky., 1985—; fin. advisor Alpha Xi Delta, Lexington, 1992—. Recipient Master of Accountancy award Peat Marwick Main & Co., 1988. Mem. Inst. Mgmt. Accts., Jessamine County Beef Cattle Assn., Lena Madesin Phillips Bus. & Profl. Women's Club (sec. 1993-94, treas. 1994—). Home: 1554 Groggins Ferry Rd Nicholasville KY 40356-9439

HALL, CYNTHIA HOLCOMB, federal judge; b. Los Angeles, Feb. 19, 1929; d. Harold Romeyn and Mildred Gould (Kuck) Holcomb; m. John Harris Hall, June 6, 1970 (dec. Oct. 1980);. A.B., Stanford U., 1951, J.D., 1954; LL.M., NYU, 1960. Bar: Ariz. 1954, Calif. 1956. Law clk. to judge U.S. Ct. Appeals 9th Circuit, 1954-55; trial atty. tax div. Dept. Justice, 1960-64; atty.-adviser Office Tax Legis. Counsel, Treasury Dept., 1964-66; mem. firm Brawerman & Holcomb, Beverly Hills, Calif., 1966-72; judge U.S. Tax Ct., Washington, 1972-81, U.S. Dist. Ct. for central dist. Calif., Los Angeles, 1981-84; cir. judge U.S. Ct. Appeals (9th cir.), Pasadena, Calif., 1984—. Served to lt. (j.g.) USNR, 1951-53. Office: US Ct Appeals 9th Cir 125 S Grand Ave Pasadena CA 91105

HALL, DOLORES ANN, systems analyst; b. Empress, Alta., Can., Feb. 6, 1952; d. Donald Jennings and Catherine (Miller) H. BS in Math., Lamar U., 1974; MS in Mgmt., Computing and Systems, Houston Bapt. U., 1988. Assoc. engr. McDonald Douglas Aerospace, Houston, 1974-75; systems analyst Exxon Co. USA, Houston, 1975-78; EDP auditor, programmer Am. Gen., Houston, 1978-79; systems analyst Conoco, Houston, 1979-80; systems specialist Union Tex. Petroleum, Houston, 1980-91; sr. systems staff analyst Exxon Prodn. Rsch., Houston, 1991—. Mem. Soc. Petroleum Engrs., Sierra Club, Nature Conservancy.

HALL, ELEANOR WILLIAMS, public relations executive; b. Boston; d. James Murray and Julia Eleanor (Williams) H. A.B. cum laude, Radcliffe Coll., 1945. Exec. sec. Am. Express Co., N.Y.C., 1950-62, adminstrv. asst. corp. mktg., 1963-65, mgr. corp. mktg., 1965-69, mgr. corp. pub. relations, 1969-71; mgr. mktg. services Am. Express Internat. Banking Corp., N.Y.C., 1971-72, asst. treas. advt. and pub. relations, 1972-76, asst. v.p. advt. and pub. relations, 1976-82; pres. Eleanor Hall Assocs., Inc., 1982-90. Mem. Harvard Radcliffe Club. Home: 3206 E Lexington Way Apt 223 Mercer Island WA 98040

HALL, ELLA TAYLOR, clinical psychologist; b. Macon, Miss., Nov. 30, 1948; d. Essex and Mamie (Roland) Taylor; children: Banyikaai Monique (dec.), Motiqua Shante. BA, Fisk U., 1971, MA, 1973; PhD, George Peabody Coll., 1978. Mental health specialist behavioral sci. div. Meharry Med. Coll., Nashville, 1976-77; assoc. psychologist Bronx (N.Y.) Psychiat. Ctr., 1979; clin. psychologist Wiltwyck Residential Treatment Ctr., Ossining, N.Y., 1979-81; clin. cons. Abbott House, Irvington, N.Y., 1982-85; asst. school psychologist Abbott Union Free Sch. Dist., 1985—; cons. psychologist Youth Theater Interactions, Inc., N.Y.; rschr in the field. Author: (poetry) Double Twister, Somebody, Clinging Tears, 1994, In My Mind, 1995, (poetry) Maple Tree at Dawn, Down My Three Roses. Lay reader Episcopal Ch. Mem. Yonkers schs. PTA; mem. Com. on Spl. Edn., YWCA. NIMH tng. grantee, Kendall grantee; Crusade fellow. Mem. Nat. Assn. Sch. Psychologists, Schomburg Ctr. for Rsch., N.Y. State Psychol. Assn., Coun. Exceptional Children, Delta Sigma Theta. Avocation: photography.

HALL, GEORGIANNA LEE, special education educator; b. Greeley, Colo., Apr. 2, 1947; d. John Russell and Lois Louise (Urich) Martin; m. William James Bailey, 1970 (div. June 1972); m. Rex Henry Hall, Dec. 22, 1984; 1 stepchild, Jorri Colleen. AA, Fullerton (Calif.) Jr. Coll., 1967; BA, Calif. State U., Fullerton, 1969, elem. edn. credential, 1971, learning handicapped credential, 1976. Cert. resource specialist, lang. devel. specialist. Tutor Edn. Project for Disadvantaged Youth Savanna Sch. Dist., Stanton, Calif., 1965-69; math. tchr. Norwalk (Calif.)-LaMirada Sch. Dist., 1971-72; tchr. Cypress (Calif.) Sch. Dist., 1972-74, tchr. learning disability, 1974-80, tchr. learning handicapped, 1976, tchr. communicatively handicapped, 1981—, resource specialist, 1981—, dist. mentor tchr. for spl. edn., 1993—; dist. spl. edn. rep. for writing of Original Greater Anaheim Consortium Plan for Spl. Edn., 1980; dist. interview team for tchrs., prins. and aides, Cypress, 1985—; compliance program quality reviewer dist. leadership team rep. State Calif., Orange County, 1991—; Cypress dist. rep. for drug free schs. Cypress Sch. Dist./U. Calif., Irvine, 1992—; King sch. rep. dist. drug alcohol tobacco edn.; leadership team King Elem. Sch., Cypress, 1989—; lead tchr. for conflict mgt. training, 1993—; coord. sch. intervention team, 1989—; coord. activities Svcs. for At-Risk Students, King Elem. Sch., 1990—; dist. coord. CCR, 1994—; mem. Dist. Coord. Curriculum Com., 1994—; mem. dist. adv. com. Medi-Cal, 1994—; mem. Dist. Testing and Assessment Com., 1994—. Neighborhood rep. Muscular Dystrophy Assn., Huntington Beach, Calif., 1988—, Coun. for Paralyzed vets., Huntington Beach, 1989—; vol. reading tutor PLUS, Huntington Beach, 1992; publicity chmn. King Sch. PTA, 1992-93, 93-94; coord. resources needy families, King elem. sch. Recipient Hon. Svc. award PTA King Sch., Cypress, 1982; named Spl. Edn. Tchr. of Yr. Resource Specialists Calif., 1989. Mem. NEA, Calif. Tchrs. Assn., Assn. Cypress Tchrs. (sch. rep. 1974-76, 79-82, sec. 1976-77, 2d v.p. 1978-79, 1st v.p. 1979-80), Calif. Assn. Resource Specialists, Children with Attention Deficit Disorder, Learning Disability Assn., Calif. Assn. for Supervision and Curriculum Devel. Office: King Elem Sch 8710 Moody St Cypress CA 90630-2220

HALL, GERRI LYNN, legislative staff member; b. Aberdeen, S.D., Apr. 6, 1954; d. Randall H. and Helen Elizabeth (Mallett) H.; m. David Koehler Nickels, May 20, 1989. BS in Govt., U. S.D., 1975; MPA, U. Winnipeg, Man., Can., 1982; postgrad., Harvard U., 1992. Legis. asst. U.S. Senator Larry Pressler, Washington, 1976-79; rsch. cons. Man. Dept. No. Affairs, Winnipeg, 1981; policy analyst, program planner No. Devel. Can. Dept. Indian Affairs, Winnipeg, 1982-83; program analyst, auditor Employment Svcs. Man. Dept. Labour, Winnipeg, 1983-84; policy analyst Man. Provincial Cabinet, Winnipeg, 1984-85; sr. profl. staff mem. U.S. Senate Com. Commerce, Sci. and Transp., Washington, 1986—. Mem. a capella group Nat. Singers. Mem. Women's Tranp. Sem., Can. Club. Washington. Republican. Presbyterian. Home: 4217 Puller Dr Kensington MD 20895 Office: Senate Com Commerce Sci & Transp 516 Dirken Senate Office Bldg Washington DC 20510

HALL, GRACE ROSALIE, physicist, educator, literary scholar; b. Meriden, Conn., July 15, 1921; d. George John and Grace Cleora (Gleason) White; m. Eldon Conrad Hall, July 2, 1948; children: Brent Channing, Pamela Rosalie, Craig Gleason, Gordon Timothy. BS in Chemistry, Eastern Nazarene Coll., 1946; MA in Physics, Boston U., 1946, doctoral studies in physics, 1946-53; MA in English, Simmons Coll., 1975. Bookkeeper Cherry & Webb Co., Providence, 1939-42; sec. to registrar Eastern Nazarene Coll., Quincy, Mass., 1942-44, instr. physics, chemistry, 1945-46; teaching fellow physics Boston U., 1946-49; instr. physics lab. Northeastern U., Boston, 1956-57; instr. physics Simmons Coll., 1949; asst. prof. physics Eastern Nazarene Coll., Quincy, 1957-61, asst. prof. chemistry, 1969, asst. prof. phys. sci., 1974; instr. Shakespeare Barrington (R.I.) Coll., 1984; tchr. Westwood (Mass.) Sem., 1975; ch. sch. dir. 1st Parish, Westwood, 1977-81; chair sem. U. Louisville, 1988. Author: (chpt. in book) Webs & Wardrobes, 1987; contbr. articles to profl. jours. Dir. South County Norfolk Assn. for Retarded Citizens, 1978-79; judge H.S. Sci. Fairs, North Quincy, Mass., 1960-64, 69-76, Regional Sci. Fairs, Bridgewater, Mass., 1960-62. Recipient Faculty scholarship Eastern Nazarene Coll., 1943-45, Libr. Family of Yr. award City of Quincy, 1960; named to R.I. Honor Soc. Mem. MLA (session participant 1978, 84), Shakespeare Assn. Am. (seminar participant 1988—), Christianity and Lit. Assn., MIT Women's League (editor activities guide and newsletter 1989—), New Eng. Hist. Geneal. Soc., Internat. Soc. Poets, Munro So., Pres.' Soc., Inc.

HALL, JANE ANNA, writer, model; b. New London, Conn., Apr. 4, 1959; d. John Leslie Jr. and Jane Dezzie (Green) H. Grad. model, Barbizon Sch., 1976. Model Barbizon Agy., New Haven, 1977; employed by dir. of career planning Wesleyan U., Middletown, Conn., 1985-86; free lance writer, poet, 1986—; poetry contest judge Saybrook 25th Anniversary Celebration, Acton Pub. Libr., 1992. Author: Cedar and Lace, 1986, Satin and Pinstripe, 1987, Fireworks and Diamonds, 1988, Stars and Daffodils, 1989, Sunrises and Stone Walls, 1990, Mountains and Meadow, 1991, Moonlight and Water Lilies, 1992, Sunsets and Beaches, 1993, New and Selected Poems 1986-94, 1994, Under Par Recipes, 1994, New and Selected Poems for Children, 1986-94, 1995; founder, editor Poetry in Your Mailbox newsletter, 1989—; one-woman shows include Westbrook (Conn.) Pub. Libr., 1989-94. Sunday sch. tchr. 1st Congl. Ch., Westbrook, 1977-90, asst. supt., dir. Christian edn., 1979-84; poetry reader Congl. Ch., Broad Brook, Conn., 1988; group poetry reader and displayer Westbrook Pub. Libr., 1989, 91, reader Night of Thousand Stars readathon, 1990; group poetry displayer Acton Pub. Libr., Old Saybrook, Conn.,1990, judge poetry contest 25th anniversary celebration, 1992. Recipient 2d prize Conn. Poetry Soc., 1983, 86, Cert. of Merit for disting. svc. to community, 1989, Cert. World Leadership, 1989. Mem. Internat. Platform Assn., Romance Writers Am. (book cover bd. designer Conn. chpt. 1991-93), Conn. Poetry Soc. (pres. Old Saybrook chpt. 1989-91, world poetry chmn. 1989; poetry reader 20th anniversary Russell Libr. Middletown, Conn. 1994). Home and Office: PO Box 629 Westbrook CT 06498-0629

HALL, JANIS HELEN, architect, environmental artist, landscape designer; b. Glen Ellyn, Ill., Dec. 15, 1952; d. Norman Bell and Helen Grace (Tillis) H. Student, Dartmouth Coll., 1973-74; BA magna cum laude, Mt. Holyoke Coll., 1975; postgrad., Cambridge U., Eng., 1975-76; MArch, Harvard U., 1981. Registered architect. Apprentice to Isamu Noguchi, N.Y.C., 1975; design assoc. A.E. Bye Assocs., Greenwich, Conn., 1984-88; prin. Janis Hall, N.Y.C., 1986—; ptnr. A.E. Bye and Janis Hall, N.Y., Ridgefield, Conn., 1988—; design critic The Cooper Union, N.Y.C., 1990—; adj. prof. archtl. and environ. design dept. Parsons Sch. of Design, N.Y.C., 1991—; artist/designer various environ. artworks and landscapes, 1985—. Mem. Parks Coun. Mem. Archtl. League N.Y. (Young Architects Forum Competition winner 1991), Mcpl. Art Soc., Phi Beta Kappa. Office: 158 Danbury Rd Ridgefield CT 06877

HALL, JOANNE MARIE, nursing educator; b. Dubuque, Iowa, Mar. 4, 1953. BSN, BS in Psychology, U. Dubuque, 1977; MA in Nursing, U. Iowa, 1986; PhD in Nursing, U. Calif., San Francisco, 1992, postgrad., 1992-94. RN, Iowa, Calif., Wis. Nursing instr. Finley Hosp. Sch. of Nursing, Dubuque, 1979-80, Clark Coll., Dubuque, 1982-84; staff nurse Mercy Health Ctr., Dubuque, 1977-79, 80-82; primary nurse San Francisco Gen. Hosp., 1986-89; rsch. cons. Lyon-Martin Women's Health Svcs., San Francisco, 1992-94; postdoctoral fellow U. Calif., San Francisco, 1992-94; asst. prof. U. Wis., Milw., 1994—; coord. internat. women's health conf. Internat. Kellogg Found., 1990; rsch. cons. Am. Found. for AIDS Rsch., San Francisco, 1992-94; lectr. in field. Contbr. articles to profl. jours., chpts. to books; author papers in field; mem. editorial rev. bd. Advances in Nursing Sci., 1994—, Western Jour. Nursing Rsch., 1994—. Co-founder Cath. Worker House Shelter for Homeless Women and Children, Dubuque, 1977-83. Recipient Nat. Rsch. Svc. award predoctoral fellow NIH, 1989-92, Nat. Rsch. Svc. postdoctoral fellow NIH, 1992-94, U. Calif. Chancellor's Grad. Rsch. fellow, 1991-92. Mem. ANA (coun. nurse rschrs.), APHA, Am. Orthopsychiat. Assn., Am. Assn. Physicians for Human Rights (nat. adv. bd.), Sigma Theta Tau. Office: U Wis Sch Nursing Cunningham Bldg PO Box 413 Milwaukee WI 53201

HALL, JUDITH ANN, artist, printmaker; b. Cape Giradeau, Mo., July 30, 1940; d. Earl Wayne and Frances Ione (Bryan) H.; m. Marvin Eugene Cloves, Oct. 7, 1972 (div. Aug. 1982); m. Leslie Ray Manzer, Apr. 23, 1988; stepchildren: Michael Leslie, David Walter, Barbara Elizabeth Manzer. Student, Wesleyan Coll., 1958-59, U. Tenn., Memphis, 1961-62. Owner, gallery dir. Hall Galleries, St. Simons Island, Ga., 1970-82; artist, printmaker Judith Hall Etchings, St. Simons Island, Ga., Gainesville, 1978—. Art editor: Islander Newspaper, St. Simons Island, 1973-80; represented in permanent collections at U. Miss., Oxford, Brenau, Gainesville, Walt Disney Enterprises, Calif. Sponsor Christian Children's Fund, 1981—. Mem. Nat. Wildlife Fedn., Quinlan Art Assn., Coastal Art Alliance, Coastal Ctr. for Arts, Audubon Soc., World Wildlife Fund. Home: 2958 Glen Haven Dr Gainesville GA 30504-5510 also: 1912 Demere Rd Saint Simons Is GA 31522-2805

HALL, JULIE JANE, community health nurse, administrator; b. Berkeley, Calif., Jan. 14, 1951; d. Dale Oliver and Patricia Martha (Krone) Hall; m. Norman Charles Weinstein, Mar. 22, 1986. ADN, Boise State U., 1980, BS, 1983. Cert. community health nurse. Staff nurse St. Luke's Regional Med. Ctr., Boise, Idaho; hospice nurse Mountain States Tumor Insts., Boise; staff devel. coord. Hillcrest Care Ctr., Boise; asst. mgr. St. Alphonsus Home Health, Boise; dir. St. Alphonsus Home Health, Boise; dir. prevention and cmty. care St. Alphonsus Regional Med. Ctr., Boise. Mem. APHA, Idaho Nurses Assn., Idaho Orgn. of Nurse Execs., Sigma Theta Tau.

HALL, KATHRYN EVANGELINE, author, lecturer; b. Biltmore, N.C.; d. Hugh Canada and Evangeline Haddon (Jenkins) Hall; B.A., U. N.C., M.A.; diploma Adams Sch. Music, Montreat, N.C.; postgrad. Yale, U. London, Fla. Atlantic U. Author: The Papal Tiara, History of the Episcopal Church of Bethesda-By-The-Sea, 1964, The Architecture and Times of Robert Adam, 1969, The Pictorial History of the Episcopal Church of Bethesda-By-The-Sea, 1970-71, 86, Joseph Wright of Derby, A Painter of Science, Industry, and Romanticism, 1974, A History of English Architecture, 1976-82; Sir John Vanbrugh's Palaces and the Drama of Baroque Architecture, 1982-84, History of the Episcopal Church of Bethesda-by-the Sea 1889-1989, The First One Hundred Years and Into the Second Century, 1990-93; lectr. history, art and architecture, U.S., Eng. and Scotland, 1961—. Vice pres. The Jr. Patronesses, Palm Beach, Fla., 1964. Mem. Nat. League Am. Pen Women (Owl award 1972, 76, 77, pres. Palm Beach chpt. 1975-80, 2d v.p. 1994—), Palm Beach Quills (historian), Palm Beach County Hist. Soc. (gov.), Internat. Platform Assn., Nat. Soc. Arts and Letters, Soc. Four Arts, Cum Laude Soc., Palm Beach Civic Assn. Episcopalian. Clubs: Everglades (Palm Beach); English Speaking Union (Palm Beach and London). Home: Acadie PO Box 648 Palm Beach FL 33480-0648

HALL, KATHRYN O'NEIL, photographic company official; b. St. Joseph, Mo., Apr. 16, 1952; d. Monte Virgil O'Neil and Ardyce Marie (Hartman) Couch; m. Bruce Edwin Hall, June 8, 1974; children: Nathan Estes, Patrick O'Neil. BSBA, U. Denver, 1974. Master scheduler Colo. div. Kodak, Windsor, 1974-79, adminstrv. mgr., 1979-81, prodn. mgr., 1982-84, materials mgr., 1985—. Mem. sch. bd. St. Vrain Valley Sch. Dist., Longmont, Colo. Mem. Am. Prodn. and Inventory Control Soc. (cert. in prodn. and inventory mgmt., program chmn. 1988-89), AAUW (publicity chmn. 1993-94). Home: 502 Collyer St Longmont CO 80501-5543

HALL, LEE, artist, educator; b. Lexington, N.C., Dec. 15, 1934; d. Robert Lee and Florence (Fitzgerald) H. BFA, U. N.C., 1955; MA, N.Y. U., 1959, PhD, 1965; postgrad., Warburg Inst. U. London, 1965; DFA (hon.), U. N.C.-Greensboro, 1976. Asst. prof. N.Y. State U. Coll., Potsdam, 1958-60; assoc. prof., chmn. art dept. Keuka Coll., 1960-62; assoc. prof. art Winthrop Coll., 1962-65; asst. prof., chmn. art dept. Drew U., Madison, N.J., 1965-67; assoc. prof., chmn. art dept. Drew U., 1967-70, prof., chmn. art dept., 1970-74; dean visual arts State U. N.Y. Coll. at Purchase, 1974-75; pres. R.I. Sch. Design, Providence, 1975-83; sr. v.p., dir. div. arts and communications Acad. for Ednl. Devel., N.Y.C., 1984-92; dir. rsch. on Pres. Kennedy's image in recent art, John F. Kennedy Meml. Library; panelist NEH, 1972-80. Exhibited in group shows in London, N.Y.C., Winston-Salem, Eugene, Oreg., others; author: Wallace Herndon Smith: Paintings, 1987, Ale Ajay, 1989, Betty Parsons: Artist, Dealer, Collector, 1991; Common Threads: A Parade of American Clothing, 1992; Elaine and Bill (de Kooning), 1993; contbr. articles to profl. jours. Recipient research grant Am. Philos. Soc., 1965, 68; Childe Hassam Purchase award Am. Acad. Arts and Letters, 1977; RISD Athena medal, 1983. Mem. PEN, Cosmopolitan Club, Nat. Arts Club. Home: 14 Silverwood Terr South Hadley MA 01075

HALL, LOIS RIGGS, former state senator, former symphony orchestra administrator; b. Beeville, Tex., May 22, 1930; d. Ira Franklin and Pearl Ophelia (McCoy) Riggs; m. Walter William Hall, Dec. 28, 1950 (dec.); children: Robert Macfarlane, Elaine Denise, Judith Lea. Student, Tex. Women's U., 1947-49, U. Tex., Austin, 1949-50. Exec. sec. N.Mex. Symphony Orch., Albuquerque, 1975-93; mem. N.Mex. Senate, 1980-85. Active Boy Scouts Am., Girl Scouts U.S.A., Officers Wives Clubs; 2d v.p. Albuquerque Symphony Women's Assn.; bd. dirs. Friends of Music, 1986-88; treas., publicity dir. N.Mex. Aviation Assn. Republican. Home: 620 Ortiz NE Albuquerque NM 87108

HALL, MADELON CAROL SYVERSON, elementary education educator; b. Kerkhoven, Minn., Dec. 27, 1937; d. Reuben C. and Hattie C. (Anderson) Syverson; m. Lewis D. Hall, June 13, 1959 (dec. 1984); children: Warren L., Charmaine D. BA, Trinity Bible Coll., Chgo., 1959; MEd, U.Cin., 1973. Cert. tchr., Ohio. Dir. admissions, asst. registrar Trinity Bible Coll., 1959-62; supr. elem. music edn. Dist. 80 Cook County Schs., Norridge, Ill., 1962-65; tchr. Rockford (Ill.) City Schs., 1966-67; tchr. music elem. grades Boone County Pub. Schs., Florence, Ky., 1970-72; tchr. music elem. grades Oak Hills Local Sch. Dist., Cin., 1972—, also bldg. career coord., safety patrol sponsor. Composer: Seven Ways to Grow for Children's Mus., 1991. dir. Summer Safety Village Program, 1987-91, Cin. May Festival Chorus. Recipient Spl. Projects award Great Oaks Career Devel., 1992; named Tchr. of Yr. Oak Hills Sch. Dist, 1990-91. Mem. NEA, Ohio Edn. Assn., Music Educators Nat. Conf., Career Edn. Assn. (Tchr. of Yr. Ohio unit 1989-90), World Future Soc., The Hunger Project, Just Say No Club. Methodist. Home: 456 Happy Dr Cincinnati OH 45238-5254

HALL, MARCIA JOY, non-profit organization administrator; b. Long Beach, Calif., June 24, 1947; d. Royal Waltz and Norine (Parker) Stanton; m. Stephen Christopher Hall, March 29, 1969; children: Geoffrey Michael, Christopher Stanton. AA, Foothill Coll., 1967; student, U. Oreg., 1967-68; BA, U. Washington, Seattle, 1969. Instr. aide Glen Yermo Sch., Mission Viejo, Calif., 1979-80; market rsch. interviewer Rsch. Data, Framingham, Mass., 1982-83; adult edn. instr. Community Sch. Use Program, Milford, Mass., 1982-83; career info. ctr. coord. Milford High Sch., 1983-86; corp. rels. dir. Sch. Vols. for Milford, Inc., 1985-86; NE area coord. YWCA of Annapolis and Anne Arundel County, Severna Park, Md, 1987-89; exec. dir. West Anne Arundel County C. of C., Odenton, Md., 1989—. Pres. PTO, Mission Viejo, 1979-80, Milford, 1981-84; consumer assistance vol., Calif. Pub. Interest Rsch. Group, 1977-78. Mem. ABWA, Internat. Platform Assn., Toastmasters (treas. 1988—, pres. 1989—). Home: 507 Devonshire Ln Severna Park MD 21146-1017

HALL, MARIAN ELLA See ROBERTSON, MARIAN ELLA

HALL, MARILYN M., occupational health nurse; b. Bay City, Mich., Mar. 1, 1941; d. Oscar and Esther (Kolb) Pfannes; m. Harold D. Hall, June 5, 1965; children: Veronica Hall Henley, Gregory H. Diploma in nursing, Saginaw (Mich.) Gen. Hosp., 1962. RN, Ala., S.C.; cert. occupational health nurse; cert. in pulmonary function testing, audiometrics. Occupational health nurse GM, Athens, Ala., MeMC Materials Inc., Spartanburg, S.C. Mem. Patnership for Nursing, S.C., 1990-92. Mem. Am. Assn. Occupational Health Nurses, S.C. Assn. Occupational Health Nurses, Saginaw Gen. Hosp. Sch. Nursing Alumni Assn. Home: 201 Hunters Woods Dr Simpsonville SC 29681-6737

HALL, MARY JANE STEVENS, counselor; b. Dallas, Feb. 7, 1944; d. Artie Thomas and Fay Lee (Talley) Stevens; children: Melanie Hollyn Hall Fowler, Melissa Heather Hall. BS in Edn., North Tex. State U., 1967, MEd in Counseling, 1979. Cert. profl. sch. counselor; lic. profl. counselor; lic. marriage and family therapist. Tchr. Dallas Ind. Sch. Dist., 1967-79, counselor, 1979-90, instructional specialist, 1990-92, counselor, 1992—; nat. trainer Quest Internat., 1990-92. Mem. Tex. Counseling Assn., Dallas Metro Counseling Assn. (pres. 1992-93). Office: Arthur Kramer Sch 7131 Midbury Dr Dallas TX 75230-3168

HALL, MARY TAUSSIG, volunteer; b. St. Louis, Feb. 21, 1911; d. Frederick Joseph and Florence (Gottschalk) Taussig; m. Louis Benoist Tompkins, June 17, 1941 (dec. Oct. 1950); children: Frederick Kingsbury Tompkins, Mary Waterman Tompkins (Mrs. Neil Houghton); m. Thomas Steele Hall, Oct. 21, 1952 (dec. 1990). BA, Bryn Mawr Coll., 1933; MSW, Washington U., St. Louis, 1938; LHD (hon.), Lindenwood Coll., 1979. Cert. social worker. Caseworker New England Home for Little Wanderers, Boston, 1938-39. Editor: Stones for Bread, 1940. Pres., Mo. Assn. Social Welfare, 1942-44, bd. dirs., 1942-48; bd. dirs., chair industry com. Urban League Greater St. Louis, 1943-52; bd. dirs. Family and Children's Svcs., St. Louis, 1944-57; apptd. by gov. state commr. Children's Code Commn., 1945, Bd. Children's Guardians, 1946-55; apptd. by mayor bd. dirs. City Hosp. # 2 during racial integration; founding bd. dirs. Washington U. Med. Ctr. Child Guidance Clinic, St. Louis, 1948-52; chmn. bd. Divsn. Children's Svcs., St. Louis, 1955-66; nat. com. policy Child Welfare League Am., 1955-57; nat. coun. Internat. Social Svc., 1968-88; mem. world coun. YWCA, N.Y.C., 1963—; pres. St. Louis chpt. bd. UN Assn., 1977-80, nat. steering com. coun. chpt. pres., 1979-82, nat. bd. govs. UN Assn. USA, 1980-90; mem. nat. coun. UN Assn. USA, 1991—. Rcipient alumni award Washington U., 1956, Woman of Achievement award for Social Concern, City of St. Louis, 1979, Arnold Goodman Nat. Leadership award UN Assn. U.S.A., 1994. Mem. Cosmopolitan Club (N.Y.C.). Home: 4969 Pershing Pl Saint Louis MO 63108-1220

HALL, MAUREEN THERESE, restaurant executive; b. San Francisco, Feb. 9, 1963; d. Stanley Gene and Catherine Jean (Phelan) H. Student, U. Ibero Americana, Mexico City, 1983; BA in Spanish, U. Mo., 1985, BJ in Mag., 1985. Pub. rels. asst. Moberly (Mo.) Regional Med. Ctr., 1986; dir. communications Kans. affiliate Am. Heart Assn., Topeka, 1986-88; exec. asst., editor Kans. Coop. Coun., Topeka, 1988-89; mktg. asst. SW Pub., Topeka, 1989; advt. cons. Sta. KMAJ-FM, Topeka, 1990; asst. mgr. Taco Tico, Inc., Topeka, 1990-93, mgr., 1993—. Vol. Cornerstone of Topeka, 1987, 89-91; mem. program planning com. YWCA, Topeka, 1989—; mem. promotions com. Everywoman's Resource Ctr., 1991—. Mem. Women in Comm. (bd. dirs. 1989-90), Nat. Women's Hall of Fame. Roman Catholic. Home: 1106 SW Taylor St Topeka KS 66612

HALL, MINNA WILSON, educator; b. Washington, Oct. 16, 1939; d. Charles Richard and Minna Rozetta (Cannon) Wilson; m. William Harvey Hall, June 22, 1963; children: Michael Wilson, Scott Praeger, Sarah Emily. BA, Westhampton Coll., 1961; MEd summa cum laude, U. Ctrl. Okla., 1991. Cert. sch. psychometrist, Okla. English tchr. McLean (Va.) H.S., 1961-63; ednl. cons.-pub. rels. C & P Telephone Co., Balt., 1963-65; ednl. cons.-pers. Bell Telephone Co. of Pa., Phila., 1965-66; pvt. piano tchr. Oklahoma City, 1978-89; sch. counselor, psychometrist Westminster Day Sch., Oklahoma City, 1988-94; sch. psychologist Western Heights Sch. Dist., Oklahoma City, 1994—. Pres. Oklahoma City Orch. League, Inc., 1991-92, v.p. edn., 1982-84; pres. Ladies Music Club, Oklahoma City, 1983-85, Faculty Women's Club, Oklahoma City, 1979-80; v.p. pub. rels. Civic Music Assn., Oklahoma City, 1988-89. Mem. Okla. Sch. Psychol. Assn. Republican. Episcopalian. Home: 1710 Huntington Ave Oklahoma City OK 73116

HALL, NANCY CHRISTENSEN, publishing company executive, author, editor; b. N.Y.C., Nov. 14, 1946; d. Henry Norman and Elvira (Dugan) Christensen; m. John R. Hall Jr., June 12, 1968; children: Jonathan Scott, Kirsten Marie. B.A., Manhattanville Coll., 1968; postgrad., Old Dominion U., 1970-71. Sr. assoc. editor Cahners Pub. Co., N.Y.C., 1972-74; freelance editor N.Y.C., 1974-78; sr. editor Grosset and Dunlap, N.Y.C., 1978-81; exec. editor, asst. v.p. Macmillan Pub. Co., N.Y.C., 1981-84; assoc. pub., v.p. Simon & Schuster Pub. Co., N.Y.C., 1984-85; founder, prin. Nancy Hall, Inc., juvenile book devel co., N.Y.C., 1986—. Author: Monsters: Creatures of Mystery, 1980, Macmillan Fairy Tale Alphabet Book 1983; editor: Platt and Munk Treasury of Stories for Children, 1981, Favorite Tales from Hans Christian Andersen, 1988; prodr. series: Macmillan Jumbo Seasonal Patterns, Macmillan Manipulatives, Sesame Street Early Learning Games, Mickey's Young Readers Libr., Disney's Small World Libr., My First Hello Readers, A Better World, My First Readers, Friends Everywhere. Home: 86 Woodbury St Providence RI 02906-3510 Office: Nancy Hall Inc 435 E 14th St New York NY 10009-2709

HALL, NANCY ESTELLE, software educator; b. Washington, Nov. 2, 1959; d. Donald Everett and Gretta Ann (Kaiser) H. B of Vocat. and Bus. Edn., Auburn U., 1982. Customer svc. rep. 1st Nat. Bank Atlanta, 1982-83; tchr. bus. edn. Fulton County Bd. Edn., Atlanta, 1983, tchr. vocat. bus. edn., 1984, tchr. computer bus. edn., 1985-87; instr. Unisys Corp., Atlanta, 1987-89; instr. Oracle Corp., Atlanta, 1989-91, mgr. S.E. regional edn., 1991-93, nat. edn. mgr., 1993-94, dir. core techs. edn. divsn., 1994—. Mem. aux. staff Northside Hosp., Atlanta, 1988, 89. Republican. Methodist. Office: Oracle Corp 1100 Abernathy Rd NE Ste 1500 Atlanta GA 30328-5643

HALL, PAMELA ELIZABETH, psychologist; b. Jacksonville, Fla., Sept. 10, 1957; d. Gary Curtiss and Ollie (Banko) H. BA, Rutgers U., 1979; MS in Edn., Pace U., 1981, D in Psychology, 1984. Lic. psychologist, N.Y., N.J., Calif. Psychology extern St. Vincent's Med. Ctr., N.Y.C., 1981-82; intern in clin. psychology Elizabeth (N.J.) Gen. Med. Ctr., 1982-83, staff psychologist, 1983-85; staff psychologist J.F.K. Med. Ctr., Edison, N.J., 1985-87; pvt. practice Summit and Perth Amboy, N.J., 1985—; sr. supervising psychologist Muhlenberg Med. Ctr., Summit, N.J., 1987-90; rsch. affiliate, internat. lectr. affiliate NIMH field trials on assessment of dissociative disorders Yale U., New Haven, 1990—. Mem. Mayor's Com. on Substance Abuse, Perth Amboy, 1987. Named Henry Rutgers scholar, 1979. Mem. Am. Soc. Clin. Hypnosis, Internat. Soc. for Study of Dissociation (founder, pres. N.J. chpt. 1988—), Pace U. Alumni Assn., Rutgers U. Alumni Assn., Psi Chi. Home: PO Box 1820 Perth Amboy NJ 08862-1820

HALL, PAMELA S., environmental consulting firm executive; b. Hartford, Conn., Sept. 4, 1944; d. LeRoy Warren and Frances May (Murray) Sheely; m. Stuart R. Hall, July 21, 1967. BA in Zoology, U. Conn., 1966; MS in Zoology, U. N.H., 1969, BS summa cum laude, Whittemore Sch. Bus. and Econs., U. N.H., 1982; student spl. grad. studies program, Tufts U., 1986-90. Curatorial asst. U. Conn., Storrs, 1966; rsch. asst. Field Mus. Natural History, Chgo., 1966-67; teaching asst. U. N.H., Durham, 1967-70; program mgr. Normandeau Assocs. Inc., Portsmouth, N.H., 1971-79, marine lab. dir., 1979-81, programs and ops. mgr., Bedford, N.H., 1981-83, v.p., 1983-85, sr. v.p., 1986-87, pres., 1987—. Mem. Conservation Commn., Portsmouth, 1977-90, Wells, Estuarine Rsch. Res. Review Commn., 1986-88, Great Bay (N.H.) Estuarine Rsch. Res. Tech. Working Group, 1987-89; trustee Trust for N.H. Lands, 1990-93; trustee, vice chmn. N.H. chpt. Nature Conservancy, 1991—; incorporator N.H. Charitable Fund, 1991—; bd. advisors Vivamos Mejor, USA, 1990—. Graham Found. fellow, 1966; NDEA fellow, 1970-71. Mem. ASTM, Am. Mgmt. Assn., Water Pollution Control Fedn., Nat. Assn. Environ. Profls., Sigma Xi. Home: 4 Pleasant Point Dr Portsmouth NH 03801-5275 Office: Normandeau Assocs Inc 25 Nashua Rd Bedford NH 03110-5500

HALL, PHOEBE POULTERER, lawyer, judge; b. Watertown, N.Y., Dec. 4, 1941; d. William Taylor, Jr., and Betty (Bennett) Poulterer; m. Franklin P. Hall, July 26, 1969; children—Kimberly Ann, Franklin P. B.A., U. Del.-Wilmington, 1963; J.D., Georgetown U., 1969. Bar: Va. Assoc., Hall & Hall, Richmond, Va., 1969—; substitute judge Gen. Dist. Cts., City of Richmond, 1983—, commr. in chancery, circuit cts., 1981—; founding dir., Cardinal Savs. & Loan Assn., Richmond, 1978—. Bd. trustees, Va. Mus. Fine Arts, 1983—; commr. Human Relations Commn., Richmond, 1972-73; dir. Family and Children's Services, Richmond, 1976-78; mem. worship com. 1st Presbyterian Ch., Richmond, 1983—; mem. state central com. Democratic Party, Va., 1974-80; pres. Women's Health Adv. Bd. Med. Coll. Va., 1989—; mem. adv. bd. Make Women Count, 1994—; trustee Presbytery of the James, 1989—. Recipient Outstanding Citizenship award Urban League, Richmond, 1983; first woman pub. defender, City of Richmond, 1970; designer, instr. first course for paralegals, Va. State Bar, 1974. Mem. ABA, Richmond Bar Assn., Met. Richmond Women's Bar (founding 1971—), Va. Trial Lawyers Assn., Assn. Trial Lawyers Am., Bus. and Profl. Women's Assn., Am. Bus. Women's Assn. Lodge Soroptimists. Home: 9006 Cherokee Rd Richmond VA 23235-1414 Office: Hall & Hall BonAir Profl Bldg 2800 Buford Rd Ste 202 Richmond VA 23235-2453

HALL, PHYLLIS CHARLENE, therapist, counselor; b. L.A., Mar. 18, 1957; d. Clellan James Jr. and Yvonne Rayedith (Ralls) H. BA, Whittier Coll., 1979; MS in Phys. Edn., Calif. State U., Fullerton, 1985, MS in Counseling, 1988; postgrad., U.S. Internat. U., 1990—. Coach varsity girls basketball, softball Calif. High Sch., Whittier, 1979-80; counselor Rio Hondo Coll., Whittier, 1980-88; coach asst. girls varsity basketball Long Beach (Calif.) Wilson High Sch., 1985-88; therapist intern Turning Point Counseling, Garden Grove, Calif., 1988-89; counselor Long Beach City Coll., 1988—, girls acad. advisor, 1989-94, asst. coach girls basketball, 1993-94; psychologist asst./intern Family Svcs. Long Beach, 1994—; bd. dirs. Long Beach City Coll. Author: Liberators from Planet Liberx, 1985. Co-sponsor African Am. in Unity Long Beach City Coll., 1990-92; com. mem. 1st Annual African Am. Achievement Conf., San Deigo, 1994. Mem. Calif. Tchrs. Assn., Long Beach City Coll. Counselors Assn., Women in Arts. Office: Long Beach City Coll 1305 E Pch Long Beach CA 90806

HALL, SARAH FUTCH, nursing educator; b. Homerville, Ga., May 16, 1947; d. Seward Smith and Verna Lee (Stalvey) Futch; m. Enoch Combs Hall III, Mar. 29, 1969; 1 child, Elisabeth Melinda. ADN, Lake City Community Coll., Fla., 1967; B in Psychology, Ea. Ky. U., 1976, B in Nursing, 1977; M in Psychiatry/Mental Health Nursing, Vanderbilt U., 1978. RN, Ky.; cert. clin. specialist in adult mental health nursing. Staff nurse, ast. supr. CCU Lake Shore Hosp., Lake City, 1967-70; staff nurse oper. rm. Tallahassee Meml. Hosp., 1970-71; staff nurse, supr. night shift Pattie A. Clay Hosp., Richmond, Ky., 1972-77; staff nurse psychiatry unit VA Hosp., Lexington, Ky., 1978-83; nurse mgr. staff edn. Charter Ridge Hosp., Lexington, Ky., 1983-84; staff nurse Charter Ridge Hosp., lexington, 1987—; educator psychiatric nursing So. Hills. Hosp., Portsmith, Ohio, 1984; mgr. nursing care St. Joseph Hops. Ctr. for Chem. Dependency, Lexington, 1984-85; asst. prof. Ea. Ky. U., Richmon, 1985—; treatment team mem. Nurses Assisting Nurses, Lexington, 1984-93, vol. faculty U. Ky., Lexington, 1988-93; cons. VA Med. Ctr. Leestown, Lexington, 1988-93; bd. dirs. Family Renewal Ctr., Lexington; facilitator Parents of Children with Tourette's Syndrome Support Group, 1994—; presenter of workshops on co-dependency, Ky., Ind., W.Va., Kans. Sec. Breckinridge Elem. PTA. Mem. ANA, Ky. Nurses Assn. (nominating com. dist. 2 1991, 93-94), Sigma Theta Tau (archivist Delta Psi chpt. 1989-90). Democrat. Mem. Christian Ch. (Disciples of Christ). Home: 2429 Windwood Ct Lexington KY 40509-1013 Office: Ea Ky U 223 Rowlett Bldg Richmond KY 40475

HALL, SUSAN LIDDELL, elementary education educator; b. Logansport, Ind., July 5, 1951; d. Robert William and Marjorie Evelyn (Barnes) Bulmer; m. Harold Michael Hall, Sept. 4, 1971. BS in Edn. summa cum laude, Ind. U., New Albany, 1991. Cert. tchr. K-6, Ind. Corp. officer Citizen's Fidelity Bank & Trust, Louisville, 1975-80; tchr. N.Harrison Elem. Sch., Ramsey, Ind., 1991-92, Morgan Elem. Sch., Palmyra, Ind., 1992—; math., sci. tutor Floyd Cen. High Sch., Floyds Knobs, Ind., 1988—. Named to Hon. Order Ky. Cols.; Ind. U. Found. travel scholar to Egypt, 1992. Mem. Pi Lmabda Theta (v.p. 1989—, Disting. Nat. Scholar award 1991), Kappa Delta Pi (pres. 1992), Kappa Kappa Kappa, Phi Delta Kappa, Alpha Chi (Ind. U. Southeast Alumni Spotlight 1993). Home: 8504 N Valley View Dr Greenville IN 47124 Office: Morgan Elem Sch Palmyra IN 47164

HALL, TELKA MOWERY ELIUM, educational administrator; b. Salisbury, N.C., July 22, 1936; d. James Lewis and Malissa (Fielder) Mowery; m. James Richard Elium III, June 20, 1954 (div. 1961); 1 child, W. Denise Elium Carr; m. Allen Sanders Hall, Apr. 15, 1967 (div. 1977). Student, Am. Inst. Banking, 1955-57, Mary-Hardin Baylor Coll., Waco, Tex., 1957; BA, Catawba Coll., Salisbury, 1967; MEd, Miss. U. for Women, Columbus, 1973; EdS, Appalachian State U., 1975; postgrad., U. N.C., Greensboro, 1977; EdD, U. N.C., Chapel Hill, 1990. Cert. early childhood, intermediate lang. arts and social studies tchr., curriculum specialist, adminstr., supr., supt., N.C.; notary pub., N.C. Bookkeeper, teller Citizens & So. Bank, Spartanburg, S.C., 1955-56; bookkeeper 1st Nat. Bank, Killeen, Tex., 1956-58; bookkeeper, savs. teller Exchange Bank & Trust Co., Dallas, 1958-61; acct. Catawba Coll., 1961-65; floater teller bookkeeping and proof depts. Security Bank & Trust Co., Salisbury, 1965-68, 71; tchr. Rowan County Sch. System, Salisbury, 1967-70, 71-72, 1973-82; asst. prin. North Rowan Elem. Sch., Spencer, N.C., 1982-94, Rockwell (N.C.) Elem. and China Grove Elem. Schs., 1994—; receptionist H & R Block, Salisbury, 1979-83; Chpt. I reading tchr. Nazareth Children's Home, Rockwell, N.C., 1979-81. Author: The Effect of Second Language Training in Kindergarten on the Development of Listening Skills. Mem. Salisbury Community Chorus, 1951-52, Historic Salisbury Found., Inc., Salisbury Concert Choir, 1981-83; foreperson Rowan County Grand Jury, 1991; pianist Franklin Presbyn. Ch., Salisbury, 1952-55, choir dir., 1975-87; past pres. Women of Ch., Sunday Sch. tchr., sec., 1979-80, deacon, 1980-83, elder, 1991-92, clk. of session, 1992, choir mem.; cons. Dial HELP, Salisbury, 1981-83; charter mem. bd. dirs. Old North Salisbury Assn., 1980—. Civitan Music scholar, 1954, Kiwanis Acad. scholar, 1966, Catawba Coll. Acad. scholar, 1965-67, Mary Morrow Ednl. scholar N.C. Assn. Educators, 1966. Mem. AAUW (v.p. 1985-87, 91—), ASCD, N.C. Assn. Sch. Adminstrs., N.C. Assn. Educators, Tarheel Assn. Prins. and Asst. Prins., U. N.C. Gen. Alumni Assn., Rowan County Prins. Assn., Sci. Alliance (Rowan County, charter), Salisbury Hist. Assn., Kappa Delta Pi, Theta Phi (pres. 1992-93). Home: 1626 N Main St Salisbury NC 28144-2928 Office: Rockwell Elem Sch 114 Link St Rockwell NC 28138

HALL, TENNIEBEE M., editor; b. Bakersfield, Calif., May 21, 1940; d. William Elmer and Lillian May (Otis) Hall; m. Harold Robert Hall, Feb. 20, 1965. BA in Edn., Fresno State Coll., 1962; AA, Bakersfield Coll., 1960. Cert. tchr., Calif. Tchr. Edison (Calif.) Sch. Dist., 1962-65; substitute tchr. Marin and Oakland Counties (Calif.), Berkeley, 1965-66; engring. asst. Pacific Coil Co., Inc., Bakersfield, 1974-81; editor United Ostomy Assn., Inc., Irvine, Calif., 1986-91. Co-author: Treating IBD, 1989, Current Therapy in Gastroenterology, 1989; author, designer: Volunteer Leadership Training Manuals, 1982-84; contbr. articles to Ostomy Quar., 1973—. Mem. Pacific Beach Town Coun., San Diego, 1977—; campaign worker Maureen O'Connor (1st woman mayor of city), San Diego, 1986; mem. Nat. Digestive Diseases Adv. Bd., NIH, Washington, 1986-91; mem. planning and devel. bd. Scripps Clinic and Rsch. Found. Inflammatory Bowel Disease Ctr., San Diego, 1993—; various vol. activities, 1966-74, 81-86. Recipient Outstanding Svc. award VA Vol. Svc., Bur. of Vets. Affairs, Washington, 1990. Mem. Nat. Assn. Parliamentarians, United Ostomy Assn. Inc. (regional program dir. 1980-84, pres. 1984-86, Sam Dubin award 1983, Industry Adv. award 1987), Crohn's and Colitis Found. Am. (nat. trustee 1986—, nat. v.p. 1987-92). Home and Office: 5284 Dawes St San Diego CA 92109-1231

HALL, TERRY LEE, accountant; b. Champaign, Ill., Dec. 10, 1949; d. Albert L. and Catherine A. (Comstock) Hall; m. Thomas F. Johnston, Sept. 27, 1971 (div. Jan. 1979); 1 child, Daniel K. Johnston. BA, Barat Coll., Lake Forest, Ill., 1984. CPA, Ill., Wis. Acct. Terry Hall, CPA, Waukegan, 1985—; bd. dirs. Lake Forest (Ill.) Profl. Women's Round Table. Bd. dirs. YWCA of Lake County, Waukegan, Ill., 1987-89; bd. dirs. Women in Dir.'s Chair, Chgo., 1989—, Stage Two Theater Co., 1991—; mem. alumni coun. Lake Forest Acad., 1986—. Mem. AICPA, ABA (assoc.), Nat. Assn. Tax Preparers, Ill. Soc. CPAs (mem. faculty, mem. state litigation com. 1988—), Wis. Inst. CPAs (state litigation com. 1989-92), Chgo. Soc. Women CPAs, Lake County Estate Planning Coun., Women's Fin. Network, Am. Woman's Soc. CPAs, CPAs for the Pub. Interest (Outstanding Vol. 1991).

HALL, WANDA JEAN, mental health professional, consultant; b. Miami, Okla., July 3, 1943; d. Max Calvin Kinnaman and Dorothy D. (Peck) Fadler; m. James Marvin Hall, Apr. 10, 1964 (div. Feb. 1965); m. George Edward Hall, Mar. 21, 1973; children: Heather Renata, Samuel. AA, Stephens Coll., Columbia, Mo., 1963; BS, Kans. U., Pittsburg, 1965; MS, New Sch. for Social Rsch., N.Y.C., 1991. Asst. psychologist Parsons (Kans.) State Hosp., 1966-67; hosp. care investigator N.Y. Dept. Social Work, N.Y.C., 1968-70; social worker Drug Abuse Program, Amsterdam, The Netherlands, 1970-74; dir. Washington Park Co-op Presch., N.Y.C., 1974-75; project dir. Manhattan Devel. Ctr., N.Y.C., 1975-77; pvt. practice as human devel. specialist, N.Y.C., 1978-81; community rels. coord. Orange County Dept. Mental Health, Goshen, N.Y., 1981—; parenting cons. Teens Exploring Parenting, Inc., Middletown, N.Y., 1990-94; instr. Orange County C.C., Middletown, 1990—, Mt. St. Mary Coll., Newburgh, N.Y., 1993—. Producer, host radio talk show Conversation on Epilepsy, Radio Sta. WGNY, 1981; dir, narrator mental health skits Forum Players, 1980; producer, host 6 TV series Love from the 26, 000 Club, 1983. Bd. dirs. Orange County Coalition for Choice, Warwick, N.Y., 1981—, Orange County Task Force on Child Abuse/Neglect, 1984-89, Ct. Apptd. Spl. Assts., 1987—; bd. dirs. Bandwagon Community Ctr., chair pers., 1990-95; mem. Planned Parenthood, Orange County, N.Y., 1989—, Safe Homes, Orange County, 1987—; co-founder Orange County Parenting Coalition, 1990—; mem. Middletown Coun. Community Agys., 1980; mem. Interagy. Coun. Child Sexual Abuse. Recipient DWI Alcohol Safety award N.Y. State Alcohol Bur., Albany, 1986, Community Svc. award Youth Bur., Goshen, 1987, ZONTA scholar award , 1989, Community Svc. award Otisville (N.Y.) State Correction. 1989, NAt. Assn. Counties award Confident Parenting Program, 1993, Hospice Orange Vol. award, 1993. Mem. NAACP. Methodist. Office: Orange County Dept Mental Health Drawer 471 Harriman Dr Goshen NY 10924

HALL, YVONNE WILSON, educational administrator, educator, consultant; b. Foules, La., Nov. 3; d. Annie and Barbara (Bell) Wilson; m. James Weathersby Hall, Nov. 23, 1974; children: Jonquil Renee, Jason Ryan. BS in English and Bus. Edn., Grambling (La.) State U., 1965; MA in Guidance and Counseling, Ea. Mich. U., 1973, postgrad., 1991-94; postgrad., U. Mich., 1985. Lic. profl. counselor, Mich. Rsch. sect. Frosting Ctr. Ednl. Therapy, L.A., 1965-67; tchr. Flint (Mich.) Cmty. Schs., 1967-74, counselor, 1974-91; asst. prin. Mott Mid. Coll., Genesee Intermediate Sch. Dist., Flint, 1991—; adj. prof. Ctrl. Mich. U., Mt. Pleasant, 1990—; mem. Mich. Bd. Counseling, 1989-93; mem. personal and career devel. curriculum team Ferris State U. and Mich. Dept. Edn., 1990-91; presenter in field; mem. H.S. counselor adv. bd. U. Mich., Flint, 1986—. Mem. edn. com. Urban League, Flint, 1985-93; mem. adv. bd. Hurley Sch. Nursing, Flint, 1985—; bd. dirs. Big Bros. and Big Sisters, Flint, 1986—; tutor Vols. for Adult Literacy, 1987. Mem. ACA, ASCD, Am. Sch. Counselors Assn. (ethics com. 1988-89), Mich. Counseling Assn., Mich. Sch. Counselors Assn. (chmn. pub. rels. com. 1985-87, pres.-elect 1987-88, pres. 1988-89), Genesee Area Assn. for Counseling and Devel. (pres. 1984-85, Counselor of Yr. award 1988), Mich. Assn. Coll. Admissions Counselors (human rels. com. 1983-84, chair, planning com. 1987-88), Nat. Assn. Secondary Sch. Prins., Mich. Assn. Secondary Sch. Prins., Phi Delta Kappa, Delta Sigma Theta (life, chpt. pres.). Democrat. Roman Catholic. Home: 3313 Mackin Rd Flint MI 48504-3288 Office: Mott Mid Coll 1401 E Court St Flint MI 48503

HALLADAY, LAURIE ANN, public relations consultant, former franchise executive; b. Monroe, Mich., Aug. 18, 1945; d. Alvin John and Florence (Lowrey) Kohler; m. Edward L. Howell, Aug. 27, 1966; m. 2d Fredric R. Halladay, May 24, 1980. BJ, U. Mo., 1967. Reporter, staff writer Copley Newspapers, L.A., 1967-69; account exec. Furman Assocs., L.A., 1969-71, v.p., 1971-74; account supr. Bob Thomas & Assocs., L.A., 1974-76, v.p., 1976-78; v.p., sr. ptnr. Fleishman-Hillard, Inc., St. Louis, 1980-84; owner, operator McDonald's, Portland, Oreg., 1984-87, McDonald's McStop of Mid.-Mo., Kingdom City, 1988-92; chmn. press ops. for Budweiser/G.I. Joe's Portland 200 Indy Car Race, 1984-87; mem. advt., promotions com. Hollywood Boosters, 1986. Bd. dirs. Waterman Place Assn., St. Louis, 1983; mem. pub. rels. com. Winston Churchill Meml., Fulton, 1988-92. Recipient Merit award Calif. Press Women, 1969, Lulu award Los Angeles Women's Ad Club, 1976, McDonald's Outstanding Store award, 1985, 86, 89, 90, 91. Mem. Pub. Rels. Soc. Am. (Prism award 1977), Soc. Am. travel Writers (assoc. 1981-84), Women in Comm. (dir. St. Louis 1980-82), Nat. tour Assn., Mo. Travel Coun., Delta Delta Delta (alumna adviser 1989, 90, v.p., Delta Xi House Corp. 1991, collegiate dist. officer 1991, 94, regional program chmn., 1994). Home: 2071 Tocobaga Ln Nokomis FL 34275-5310

HALLAGAN, PAMELA COHEN, management consultant; b. Cleve., June 7, 1963; d. Michael Edward and Joan (Neuman) Cohen; m. David Salo Hallagan, Aug. 28, 1993. AB, Dartmouth Coll., 1985; MEd, Harvard U., 1990, MBA, 1992. Loan officer Bank of Boston, 1985-87; assoc. dir. Harvard Coll. Fund, Harvard U., Cambridge, Mass., 1987-90; mgmt. cons. CSC Index, Cambridge, 1992—. Mem. steering com. City Yr., Boston, 1987—. Mwm. NAFE, Harvard Bus. Sch. Alumni Assn. Boston, Harvard Bus. Sch. Network Women Alumnae. Home: 150 Walnut St Brookline MA 02146 Office: CSC Index 5 Cambridge Ctr Cambridge MA 02142

HALLANAN, ELIZABETH V., federal judge; b. Charleston, W.Va., Jan. 10, 1925; d. Walter Simms and Imogene (Burns) H. U. Charleston, 1946; JD, W.Va. U., 1951; postgrad, U. Mich., 1964. Atty. Crichton & Hallanan, Charleston, 1952-59; mem. W.Va. State Bd. Edn., Charleston, 1955-57, Ho. of Dels., W.Va. Legis., Charleston, 1957-58; asst. commr. pub. instns. Charleston, 1958-59; mem., chmn. W.Va. Pub. Service Commn., Charleston, 1969-75; atty. Lopinsky, Bland, Hallanan, Dodson, Deutsch & Hallanan, Charleston, 1975-84; judge U.S. Dist Ct. (so. dist.) W.Va., 1983—. Mem. ABA, W.Va. Bar Assn. Office: US Dist Ct PO Box 5009 Beckley WV 25801-7509

HALLAWELL, ANN LUCILLE, management trainer, educator; b. Seymour, Ind., Dec. 31, 1953; d. Charles Edward and Marjorie Jeanne (Adams) H.; m. Dean Thomas Brown, Oct. 25, 1982 (div.); 1 child, Rexford Hallawell Brown; m. William Roy Sumner, Mar. 30, 1991. BA, Western Mich. U., 1976, MA, 1979. Tchr. Pt. Huron (Mich.) Pub. Schs., 1977-78; rsch. assoc. Western Mich. U., Kalamazoo, 1979-81; mem. faculty Va. Poly. Inst. and State U., Herndon, 1981—, George Mason U., Fairfax, Va., 1988; cons. Abel, Datt & Earley, Alexandria, Va., 1989-92; trainer, cons. Mgmt. Concepts, Inc., Vienna, Va., 1989—, Falmouth Inst., Fairfax, 1990—; pres. Ender York, Inc., Herndon, 1993—; cons. Am. Soc. Extracorporeal Tech., Reston, Va., 1991-92. Club treas. Civitan Internat., 1989-90, club edn. mgr., 1990-91, club pres.-elect, 1993-94, dist. chaplain, dist. jr. chair Chesapeake dist., 1992-93; pres.-elect Fairfax Civitan Club, 1993. Named Outstanding Chair, Chesapeake dist. Civitans, 1993.

HALLBAUER, ROSALIE CARLOTTA, business educator; b. Chgo., Dec. 8, 1939; d. Ernest Ludwig and Kathryn Marquerite (Ramm) H. BS, Rollins Coll., 1961; MBA, U. Chgo., 1963; PhD, U. Fla., 1973. CPA, Ill.; cert. mgmt. acct., cost analyst, profl. estimater. Assoc. prof. acctg. Fla. Internat. U., Miami, 1972—. Mem. Am. Acctg. Assn., Am. Woman's Soc. CPAs, Ill. Soc. CPAs, Inst. Mgmt. Accts., Acctg. Historians Soc., Beta Alpha Psi, Pi Gamma Mu. Office: Fla Internat Univ N Miami Campus 3000 NE 145th St North Miami FL 33181

HALLBERG, CLAUDIA SKYE, marketing executive, consultant; b. Huntington Park, Calif., May 6, 1951; d. Ted Ulf and Lynn (Hansen) H. Student U. London, 1971-72; B.A., Scripps Coll., 1973. Brand mgr. Procter & Gamble Co., Cin., 1973-76; account exec., account supr. Needham, Harper & Steers Advt., Chgo., 1976-78; account supr., mgmt. supr. Tracy Locke Advt., Dallas, 1978-80; mgmt. supr. Young & Rubicam, San Francisco, 1980-82; exec. v.p. worldwide dir., 1982-87; pres. Hallberg, Schireson & Co., San Francisco, 1987—. Mem. Older Women's League, Confrérie des Chevaliers du Tastevin, Phi Beta Kappa. Office: Hallberg Schireson & Co 2044 Union St San Francisco CA 94123

HALLE, LISA ELLEN, advertising executive; b. Balt., Sept. 28, 1959; d. David Herman and Barbara Mary (Kann) H. BA in Psychology, Trinity Coll., 1981. Media planner Benton & Bowles, N.Y.C., 1981-83; acct. exec. Foote, Cone & Belding, N.Y.C., 1983-85; acct. supr. Saatchi & Saatchi Compton, N.Y.C., 1985-87, McCann-Erickson, N.Y.C., 1987-90; mgmt. dir. Buckley DeCerchio Cavalier, N.Y.C., 1990-91; mktg. dir. The Finals, N.Y.C., 1991-92; sr. v.p., group mgmt. supr. Publicis/Bloom, N.Y.C., 1992—. Home: 400 E 55th St Apt 12B New York NY 10022 Office: Publicis/Bloom 304 E 45th St New York NY 10017

HALLER, HAYDEN ABNEY, research analyst government affairs; b. Oklahoma, Dec. 2, 1950; d. William Charles and Jean (Lowry) Abney; 1 child, Aryn Andrew. BA in Psychology, U. Okla., 1976. Health planner W. Contra Costa Community Health Care Corp., Richmond, Calif., 1977-79; prin. planner, analyst W. Contra Costa Community Health Care, Richmond, 1979-80; cons. rsch. grant writer Cosmetic Surgeon, Oklahoma City, 1980-81; mktg. rep. The Prudential, Oklahoma City, 1981-83, administrv. mgr., 1983-86, govt. rels. specialist, 1986-90; govt. affairs rsch. analyst Sierra Health Svcs., Las Vegas, Nev., 1991—. Mem. Okla. Health Planning Adv. Coun., Oklahoma City, 1987-90; pres. bd. dirs. Community Health Ctr., 1988-89, v.p. bd. dirs., 1987-88; pres. Okla. HMO Assn., 1988-89, v.p., 1988; legis. advocate Sex Edn. and Info. Coun. Recipient Okla. Debutante award Beaux Arts Soc. Okla., 1969-70. Mem. Soc. for Sci. Study of Sex, Kappa alpha Theta. Home: Apt 1016 4607 Connecticut Ave NW Washington DC 20008-5743

HALLER, IRMA TOGNOLA, secondary social studies educator; b. Bainbridge, N.Y., Aug. 25, 1937; d. Tullio and Margaretha (Fuchs) Tognola; m. Hans R. Haller, July 11, 1964. BA, SUNY, Albany, 1959; MEd in Teaching of Social Studies, Boston U., 1962. Tchr. social studies Chenango Valley Jr.-Sr. High Sch., Binghamton, N.Y., 1959-64; tchr. social studies and English Sidney (N.Y.) High Sch., 1964—, chair dept. social studies, 1986—; mem. tchr. edn. adv. bd. SUNY, Oneonta, chair, 1985-88, 93-94. Active local sch. improvement coms. N.Y. State Electric and Gas Corp. grantee, 1985; Catskill Regional Tchr. Ctr. grantee, 1985, 87, 89. Mem. Catskill Area Social Studies Coun. (newsletter editor 1989-90), N.Y. State Social Studies Coun., Nat. Coun. Social Studies, N.Y. State United Tchrs., Sidney Tchrs. Assn., Phi Delta Kappa. Office: Sidney H S 95 W Main St Sidney NY 13838

HALLER, JEANINE MARIE, petroleum landman; b. Waukegan, Ill., Feb. 15, 1963; d. Gary Francis Haller Sr. and Peggy Dale (Carmon) Brown. BS in Bus. Adminstrn., U. Southwestern La., 1985. Ind. petroleum landman Lafayette, La., 1985-88; land negotiator Amoco Prodn. Co., Houston, 1988—; mem. project rev. com. Dept. Energy, 1994—. Vol. Houston Food Bank, 1990—, Spl. Pals, Houston, 1991-92; vol., membership drive Mus. Fine Arts, Houston, 1992—; vol., campaigner United Way, Houston, 1989-93. Named Woman to Watch, Houston Women Mag., 1992. Mem. Houston Assn. Profl. Landmen (dir. 1991-93, 3d v.p. 1994—, sec. 1993-94), Am. Assn. Profl. Landmen (cert., trustee, co-chair landman's scholarship trust com. 1994—), Mich. Oil and Gas Assn. (mem. oil and gas leasing com. 1993—). Office: Amoco Prodn Co 501 Westlake Park Blvd Houston TX 77079

HALLER, SONJA MARIA, lawyer; b. Columbus, Ind., Aug. 22, 1958; d. Roland and Renate (Dusswald) H. BA cum laude, Ohio State U., 1980, JD, 1983. Bar: Ohio. Assoc. Schwartz, Kilm, Warren & Rubenstein, Columbus,

1983-88; corporate counsel, sr. corporate counsel The B.F. Goodrich Co., Akron, Ohio, 1988—. Vol., allocations panelist United Way of Summit County, Akron, Ohio, 1992-93. Mem. Ohio State Bar Assn., Phi Beta Kappa. Roman Catholic. Home: 2343 Fixler Rd Medina OH 44256 Office: BF Goodrich Co 3925 Embassy Pkwy Akron OH 44333

HALLERAN, DONNA MARIE DVORAK, accountant; b. Newport, R.I., May 12, 1956; d. Dewaine Damien and Jean Margaret (Fallon) Dvorak; m. Scott Francis Halleran, Aug. 21, 1982; children: Nina Michelle, Trevor Michael. BA in Econs., U. Wis., 1982, MA in Mgmt., 1984. CPA, Wis. Internal audtior U. Wis., Madison, 1984-87, asst. dir. acctg. svcs., 1987—. Sec. fin. commn. St. Bernards Ch., Middleton, Wis., 1993-94. Mem. Assn. Govt. Accts. (treas. so. Wis. chpt. 1991-93, Disting. Svc. award 1993). Office: U Wis 750 University Ave Rm 316 Madison WI 53706-1490

HALLIDAY, JOYCE RUTH WILLIS, geriatrics nurse, educator; b. Jackson, Mich., Jan. 16, 1929; d. Archibald James Morris and Anne (Hughes) Willis; m. William D. Halliday, June 30, 1956; children: William Andrew, Mary Margaret, Elizabeth Michel, John Paul, Joyce Anne, Sandra Eileen. Diploma, W.A. Foote Meml. Sch. Nursing, 1950; BSN, Incarnate Word Coll., San Antonio, 1955; MEd, U. Tex., El Paso, 1970; postgrad., U. Tex., 1994—. RN, Tex. Staff nurse W.A. Foote Meml. Hosp., Jackson, Mich., 1950, Meth. Hosp., Bklyn., 1951; instr. Norwegian Hosp., Bklyn., 1956-57; instr. Sch. of Nursing, staff nurse Breckinridge Hosp., Austin, Tex., 1958-62; relief nurse Ellis Fiscel Cancer Hosp., Columbia, Mo., 1962-64; staff nurse Sun Tower Hosp., El Paso, 1965; tchr. sci. El Paso County Ind. Sch. Dist., El Paso, 1967-82; instr., staff nurse Seabury Nursing Ctr., Odessa, Tex., 1982-92; instr. nurse aide Odessa Coll., 1990-92; instr. Hotel Dieu Sch. Nursing, El Paso, 1966-67, hosp. staff nurse, 1967; tchr. sci. Ector County Ind. Sch. Dist., Odessa, Tex., 1982-90; relief nurse Hill Haven Nursing Home, El Paso, 1975-77. Capt. Nurse Corps USAFR, 1951-56. Mem. ANA, NG/NA, Tex. State Nurses Assn., Phi Delta Kappa. Episcopalian.

HALLIGAN, FREDRICA ROSE, clinical psychologist; b. Greenwich, Conn., Sept. 21, 1938; d. Wilmer Herman and Eunice Rose (Wixon) Greul; m. John Francis Halligan, Apr. 8, 1961 (dec. Apr. 1987); children: Patricia Ann Schumacher, Michael Edward, Stephen Frederick. BA in Math. summa cum laude, Hollins Coll., 1959; MA in Counseling and Psychology, Fairfield U., 1975, cert. advanced studies, 1980; PhD in Clin. Psychology, Fordham U., 1985. Cons. Yale U. Med. Sch., New Haven, Conn., 1976-77; counselor, dir. guidance Sacred Heart Acad., 1977-78; counselor Fairfield (Conn.) U., 1978-80; psychology intern VA Med. Ctr., Northport, N.Y., 1984-85; lectr. Rehab. Inst. Chgo. Northwestern U. Med. Sch., 1985-86; cons. Albert Einstein Coll. Medicine, N.Y.C., 1982-88; pvt. practice Riverside, Conn., 1987—; assoc dir. Counseling Ctr. Fordham U., Bronx, N.Y., 1986—; adj. faculty Fairfield U., Coll. New Rochelle, Mercy Coll., Northwestern U. Med. Sch; co-host Cafh Found. Spirt Seminars, N.Y.C., 1991—; co-tchr. Cape Cod Inst., Albert Einstein Coll. Medicine, Wellfleet, Mass., 1991-93; tchr. C.G. Jung Inst., N.Y.C., 1992. Co-editor: The Fires of Desire: Erotic Energies and the Spiritual Quest, 1992; contbr. chpts. to books, numerous articles to profl. jours., papers to profl. confs. Active in civic and ch. programs. Recipient Rotary Club scholarship, Schering-Plough fellowship, 1985. Mem. APA, Am. Bd. Med. Psychotherapists, Conn. Psychol. Assn., New Eng. Assn. Specialists in Group Work, Sigma Xi, Phi Kappa Phi, Pi Epsilon Mu. Office: Fordham Univ Counseling Ctr Bronx NY 10458

HALLIGAN, MARY ANN, aerospace company manager; b. Monterey Park, Calif., May 18, 1954; d. T. Glenn and Ursula Irene (O'Brien) H. BA, U. Redlands, 1976; MPA, U. So. Calif., L.A., 1979. Contract specialist NASA Dryden Flight Rsch. Ctr., Edwards, Calif., 1979-81; contract adminstr. Air Force Flight Test Ctr., Edwards, 1981-84; contract analyst Space Shuttle Divsn. Rockwell, Downey, Calif., 1984-85, sr. contract analyst, 1985-87; mgr. contracts and pricing Space Sta. Rocketdyne, Canoga Park, Calif., 1987-92; mgr. contracts, pricing and data Rockwell Space Ops. Co., Houston, 1992—. Recipient Ray Whitmus Young Alumni award U. Redlands, 1986. Mem. Nat. Contract Mgmt. Assn. (program chair 1992-94). Office: Rockwell Space Ops Co 600 Gemini Ave Houston TX 77058

HALLINAN, MAUREEN THERESA, sociologist. BA, Marymount Coll., 1961; MS, U. Notre Dame, 1968; PhD, U. Chgo., 1972. Prof. U. Wis., Madison, 1980-84; with U. Notre Dame, 1984—, now William P. and Hazel B. White prof. arts and letters, dept. sociology. Assoc. editor: (jours.) Social Forces, 1977-80, Sociology of Edn., 1979-81, editor, 1981-86, session organizer, 1980, 84, 89, 92; author: The Structure of Positive Sentiment, 1974; editor: The Social Orgn. of Schs.: New Conceptualizations of the Learning Process, 1987, Restructuring Schs.: Promising Policies and Practices, 1995; co-editor: The Social Context of Instrn.: Group Orgn. and Group Processes, 1983, Change in Societal Institutions, 1990; contbr. articles to profl. jours. *. Mem. Am. Sociol. Assn. (pres. sociology of edn. sect. 1993-94, sec.-treas. 1988-90, chairperson 1991-92, pres. 1995-96), Phi Beta Kappa. Office: U Notre Dame Dept Of Sociology Notre Dame IN 46556

HALLOCK-BANNIGAN, SUZY, counselor, consultant, counselor educator; b. Moline, Ill., Mar. 26, 1942; d. Warren Arthur Hallock and Norma Anita (Ames) Nytes; m. Timothy Butterworth, June 26, 1966 (div. May 1976); children: Elizabeth Brook, Benjamin Clark. AB, Mount Holyoke Coll., 1964; MEd, Lesley Coll., 1978; Cert. Advanced Grad. Studies, U. Vt., 1988. Lic. counselor, Vt.; cert. reality therapist. English tchr. MacDuffie Sch., Springfield, Mass., 1964-66; 2d grade tchr. Horton Pub. Sch., Pittsboro, N.C., 1966-67, Elm Hill Sch., Springfield, Vt., 1967-68; tchr. adult basic edn. Bellows Falls (Vt.) High Sch., 1969-75; admissions counselor Hartford (Conn.) Coll. for Women, 1973-76; writer, reporter Keene (N.H.) Sentinel, Brattleboro (Vt.) Reformer, 1975; counselor Woodstock (Vt.) Union High Sch., 1976—; pvt. practice counselor Norwich & South Pomfret, Vt., 1978—; dir. Dept. Counseling and Health, Woodstock, Student Peer Counselor Program, Woodstock; sr. faculty assoc. Inst. Reality Therapy, L.A., 1985—, practicum supr., faculty assoc., 1978—; instr. Inst. Reality Therapy in Ireland, Dublin, Cork, Waterford. Case author: What Are You Doing?, 1980, Control Theory in the Practice of Reality Therapy, 1989; contbr. articles to profl. jours. Mem. Woodstock Child Protection Team, 1990-95; negotiator Woodstock Union Tchrs. Assn., 1986-91; mem. Local Stds. Bd., 1992-94; writer Vt.'s Common Core, SocialScis. Commn., 1993-94. Named Educator of Yr., Woodstock Community and Sch. Assn., 1983. Mem. NEA, Am. Assn. Sch. Counselors, Vt. Assn. Sch. Counselors, Vt. Assn. Counseling & Devel. (Guzetta award 1991, pres. 1993-94), Vt. Edn. Assn., New Eng. Assn. Coll. Admissions Counselors (outstanding counselor 1986). Democrat. Home: Donegal On The Stage Rd South Pomfret VT 05067 Office: Woodstock High Sch Woodstock VT 05091

HALLOCK-MULLER, PAMELA, oceanography educator, biogeologist, researcher; b. Pierre, S.D., June 2, 1948; d. Graydon B. and Marjorie L. (Millard) H.; m. Robert Glenn Muller, Aug. 22, 1969. BA in Zoology, U. Mont., 1969; MSc in Oceanography, U. Hawaii, 1972, PhD in Oceanography, 1977. Asst. prof. earth scis. U. Tex. of Permian Basin, Odessa, 1978-83; assoc. prof. marine sci. U. South Fla., St. Petersburg, 1983-88, prof., 1988—. Assoc. editor Jour. Foraminiferal Rsch., Washington, 1985—; mem. editorial bd. Marine Micropaleontology jour., 1990—; tech. editor field trip guidebooks, 1982, 83; contbr. articles to sci. jours., chpts. to books. Vol. speaker Pinellas County (Fla.) Schs. Speaker Bur., 1984—, U. South Fla.-St. Petersburg Speakers Bur., 1989—; judge local, regional, and state sci. fairs, Fla., 1989-94; vol. Pinellas County Dems., St. Petersburg, 1988, 92. Deutscher Akademischer Austanschdienst rsch. fellow, Kiel, Germany, 1978; summer faculty fellow NASA Goddard Space Flight Ctr., 1986; NSF rsch. grantee, 1981, 85, 87, 89, 92. Fellow Cushman Found. for Foraminiferal Rsch. (bd. dirs. 1989—, v.p. 1992, 94), Geol. Soc. Am.; mem. Paleontol. Soc., Assn. Women Geoscientists, Soc. Sedimentary Geology (v.p. Permian Basin sect. 1982-83), Am. Littoral Soc. (sci. advisor Coral Reefs 1988—), N.Am. Micropaleontol. Soc., Am. Acad. Underwater Scis. Democrat. Office: U South Fla Dept Marine Sci 140 7th Ave S Saint Petersburg FL 33701-5001

HALLSTRAND, SARAH LAYMON, denomination executive; b. Nashville, Oct. 25, 1944; d. Charles Martin and Lillian Christina (Stenberg) Laymon; m. John Peter Hallstrand, July 6, 1974; 1 child, Lillian Johanna. BA cum laude, Fla. So. Coll., 1966; ThM, Boston U., 1971; D of Ministry, McCormick Theol. Sem., 1985; grad., Coll. for Fin. Planning, Denver, 1990. Ordained Am. Baptist Ch., 1976. Dir. Christian edn. Trinity United Meth. Ch., Bradenton, Fla., 1968-70, Univ. United Meth. Ch., Syracuse, N.Y., 1971-73; assoc. min. First Bapt. Ch., Syracuse, 1973-78; pastor Oneida (N.Y.) Bapt. Ch., 1978-80; midwest rep. Mins. and Missionaries Benefit Bd., Am. Bapt. Chs., Oak Park, Ill., 1981—; leader retirement planning seminars Am. Bapt. Assembly, Green Lake, Wis., 1985—; mem. rep. Midwest Commn. on the Ministry, Valley Forge, Pa., 1985—; adj. prof., pastoral care McCormick Theol. Sem., Chgo., 1986—; adj. prof. retirement planning The Divinity Sch., Rochester, N.Y., 1994—; vis. scholar Am. Bapt. Bd. Ednl. Ministries, Valley Forge, 1986-87; bd. dirs. Midwest Career Devel. Svc., Chgo., 1987—, chair, 1993—; bd. dirs. The Gathering Place Retreat Ctr., Gosport, Ind., 1988—; mem. program com. and women in ministry rep. Roger Williams Fellowship, 1988—; mem. nat. continuing edn. team Am. Bapt. Chs., Valley Forge, Pa., 1991—; speaker in field. Contbg. author: Songs of Miriam: A Women's Book of Devotions, 1994; contbr. articles to profl. jours. Mem. Am. Bapt. Chs. Mins. Coun., Inst. Cert. Fin. Planners (cert.), Internat. Soc. Retirement Planners, Alpha Gamma Delta. Democrat. Office: Mins and Missionaries Benefit Bd PO Box 549 Oak Park IL 60303-0549

HALL-STRAUSS, CHRISTINA LYN, artist; b. Tucson, Sept. 17, 1947; d. Robert L. and Dorothy H. Hall; m. Ronald H. Strauss, Dec. 21, 1986. BFA in Painting, U. Ariz., 1970; studied with, Hazel Archer, Santa Fe, 1978-80. Drawing instr. U. Ariz. Student Union, Tucson; instr. Tucson Mus. Art Sch., 1971-76; pvt. art tchr. Santa Fe, 1976-78; dir. art, art tchr. New Sch. of Santa Fe, 1976-80; vis. guest artist Rancho Linda Vista, Oracle, Ariz., 1985. One /two person shows include Tucson Mus. Art Sch., 1975, Banquest 1st Nat. Bank, Santa Fe, 1987, Davis Gallery, Tucson, 1987, Ohori's, Santa Fe, 1987, 88, 89, The Artist's Gallery, Santa Fe, 1988, 89, 91, CAFE, Albuquerque, 1991, 92-93; exhibited in group shows at Tucson Mus. Art Sch., 1973-76, Scharf Gallery, Santa Fe, 1982, Armory for the Arts, Sante Fe, 1984, Davis Gallery, Tucson, 1986, Fenix Gallery, Taos, N.Mex., 1990-91, Baker Gallery, Loveland, Colo., 1992; represented in numerous pub. and pvt. collections. Mem. AAUW. Democrat. Home: 30-C Old Arroyo Chamiso Santa Fe NM 87505

HALM, NANCYE STUDD, foundation executive; b. Jamestown, N.Y., Mar. 26, 1932; d. Thomas Howerton and Margaret Hazel (LeRoy) Neathery; m. David Philip Mack, Aug. 25, 1951 (div. 1972); children: Margaret, Jennifer, Geoffrey, Peter; m. Loris L. Studd, July 6, 1974; m. James Richard Halm, Aug. 30, 1991. BS in Edn., SUNY, Fredonia, 1954, postgrad.; postgrad., St. Bonaventure U. Tchr. Morning Sun (Iowa) Consolidated Schs., 1956-57, Panama (N.Y.) Cen. Schs., 1958-65, Jamestown (N.Y.) Pub. Schs., 1967-69, Olean (N.Y.) Pub. Schs., 1969-72, Jamestown Pub. Schs., 1972-73; pers. mgr. F.W. Woolworth Co., Lakewood, N.Y., 1972-79; dir. Nat. Conf. Christians & Jews, Jamestown, 1979-86; counselor N.Y. State Div. for Youth, Jamestown, 1979-89; exec. rep. Am. Bapt. Found., Valley Forge, Pa., 1989-94; ret., 1994. Nat. bd. dirs. Am. Bapt. Chs. U.S.A., Valley Forge, Pa., 1988-89; v.p. Chautauqua County Am. Bapt. Women, 1981-90; pres. Falconer Bapt. women, 1986-90; love gifft chmn. Pitts. Bapt. Assn., 1990-91. Recipient Cert. of Merit Cassadaga Job Corp, 1984. Mem. Rebekah. Republican. Home: 1702 W Washington St New Castle PA 16101

HALPENNY, DIANA DORIS, lawyer; b. San Francisco, Jan. 18, 1951; d. William Frederick and Doris E. Halpenny; m. Gregory D. Prowell, Aug. 28, 1982. BA, Calif. State Coll., 1973; JD, Univ. Pacific, 1980. Bar: Calif. 1980. Bookkeeper/sales clerk Farmers Empire Drugs, Santa Rosa, Calif., 1971-73; activity dir. Beverly Manor Convalescent Hosp., Anaheim, Calif., 1973-74; instructional aide Los Angeles County Supt. Schs., Downey, Calif., 1974-76, sub. tchr., 1976-77; assoc. Littler, Mendelson, Fastiff & Tichy, San Jose, Calif., 1980-82, Walters & Shelburne, Sacramento, Calif., 1982-84, Kronick Moskovitz Tiedemann & Girard, Sacramento, 1984-85; legal advisor Pub. Employment Rels. Bd., 1985-87; gen. counsel San Juan Unified Sch. Dist., 1987—. Founding mem. In-house Sch. Attys No. Calif.; past pres. no. sect. Sch. Law Study Sect. County Counsels Assn., 1991-92; mem. legal coun. com. Calif. Sch. Bd. Assn. Legal Alliance; mem. exec. bd. Calif. Edn. Mandated Cost Network, 1987—. Mem. ABA, Calif. Bar Assn., Calif. Coun. Sch. Attys. (v.p. programs 1993, pres.-elect 1994, pres. 1995), Sacramento County Bar Assn., Trayner Honor Soc., Order of Coif. Republican. Lutheran. Office: San Juan Unified Sch Dist 3738 Walnut Ave Carmichael CA 95608-3099

HALPERIN, ESTHER WAITZ, clothing company executive; b. Allentown, Pa., Aug. 17, 1925; d. Abraham and Sadie (Ostrow) Waitz; m. Marvin Goldberg, 1947 (div. 1957); m. Bernard Halperin, June 15, 1963 (dec. 1964); children—Richard Goldberg, Jonathan Halperin; m. Abe Krantz, June 19, 1974 (div. dec. 1985). B.A., Moravian coll., 1948; M.S., Temple U., 1962. Pre-sch. tchr. Jewish Community Ctr., Allentown, 1955-63, summer camp tchr. 1955-63; kindergarten tchr. Jewish Day Sch., Allentown, 1962; pres. Halsen Products, Inc., Slatington, Pa., 1964—. Chmn. Allentown United Way, 1966-81; subscriber Met. Opera, N.Y.C., 1974—. Mem. Atlantic Apparel Assn., Lehigh Valley Needle Trades (bd. dirs. 1964-80, chmn. Pa. apparel week 1969), Pi Delta Epsilon. Republican. Clubs: Hadassah, ORT (Allentown). Lodge: Shriners. Avocations: opera; ballet; dancing; travel. Home: 3717 W Congress St Allentown PA 18104-2645 Office: Halsen Products Inc 216 Cherry St Slatington PA 18080-2004

HALPIN, ANNA MARIE, architect; b. Murphysboro, Ill., July 24, 1923; d. John William and Anna Christina (Weilmuenster) H. B.S. in Architecture, U. Ill., 1948. Designer, project architect various firms,, San Francisco, Rome, N.Y.C., 1948-67; editorial dir. Sweet's div. McGraw-Hill, Inc., N.Y.C., 1967-88; ret. Sweet's div. McGraw-Hill, Inc.; freelance cons., 1988—; rep. to Constrn. Industries Coordination Com., Am. Nat. Metric Council, 1974-80. Mem. AIA (treas., dir. N.Y. chpt. 1974-78, coll. fellows 1976, nat. dir. 1977-79, nat. v.p. 1980, dir. Found. 1980, Richard Upjohn fellow 1991), Women's Equity Action League (pres. N.Y. state orgn. 1976-77), Constrn. Specifications Inst., Alliance Women in Architecture, City Club N.Y. Home: 519 E 86th St New York NY 10028

HALPIN, MARY ELIZABETH, psychologist; b. Oak Park, ILl., June 4, 1951; d. Thomas Joseph and Rita Helen (Foley) H. BA, Marquette U., 1973, MEd, 1975, PhD, 1983. Lic. psychologist, Ill., Calif. Staff psychologist Milw. Children's Hosp., 1975-83; postdoctoral intern El Dorado County Mental Health Ctr., Placerville, Calif., 1983-84; psychologist Inst. for Motivational Devel., Lombard, Ill., 1985-88; psychologist, founder, gen. ptnr. Assocs. for Adolescent Achievement, Deerfield, Ill., 1989—. Chmn., mem. peer rev. com. Charter Barclay Hosp., Chgo., 1991—. Mem. APA, AAUW, Internat. Platform Assn., Ill. Psychol. Assn. (standing hearing panel ethics com. 1993, pub. rels. com. 1994). Democrat. Roman Catholic. Office: 420 Lake Cook Rd # 109 Deerfield IL 60015-4914

HALPRIN, ROBIN CLAIRE, psychologist; b. New Brunswick, N.J., Apr. 5, 1952; d. Jerome Joshua and Violet Ann Louise (Rulewich) H.; m. Patricia Dinnen Hawkins, Apr. 24, 1993. AB in Psychology cum laude with honors, Smith Coll., Northampton, Mass., 1974; MA, Am. U., Washington, 1981, PhD, 1985. Lic. psychologist, Md., D.C. Program psychologist So. Md. Community Counseling & Drug Abuse Program, California, Md., 1977-82; predoctoral intern Crownsville (Md.) Hosp. Ctr., 1982-83; pvt. practice Bay Psychology Group, D.C., Md., 1983—; dir. psychology treatment svcs. U.S. Soldiers' & Airmen's Home, Washington, 1986-87; clin. psychologist St. Luke's Inst., Suitland, Md., 1987-88, St. Elizabeths Hosp., Washington, 1989—, Devel. Psychol. Svcs. Assocs., Ft. Washington, Md., 1991-94; Psyche Systems, 1994—. Mem. Calver County (Md.) Mental Health Adv. Com., 1984-87, chair., 1987-89; chair women's issues com. Whitman-Walker Clinic, Washington, 1989-90, mem. pers. com., 1989-90, program evaluation and tech. asst. com., 1992—. Sloam Found. grantee, 1973, 74. Mem. APA, Sigma Xi (assoc.). Home: 2982 Mourning Dove Pl # G Waldorf MD 20603 Office: Psyche Systems 10905 Ft Washington Rd Ste 202 Fort Washington MD 20744

HALSBAND, FRANCES, architect; b. N.Y.C., Oct. 30, 1943; d. Samuel and Ruth H.; m. Robert Michael Kliment, May 1, 1971; 1 child, Alexander H. B.A., Swarthmore Coll., 1965; M.Arch., Columbia U., 1968; Registered architect, N.Y., N.J., Mass., Conn., Ohio, Va., N.H., Cert. Nat. Coun. Archtl. reg. bds.; Architect Mitchell/Giurgola Architects, N.Y.C., 1968-72; ptnr. R.M. Kliment & Frances Halsband Architects, N.Y.C., 1972—; vis. critic archtl. design Columbia U., 1975-78, N.C. State U., 1978, Rice U., 1979, U. Va., 1980, Harvard U., 1981, U. Pa., 1981, Columbia U., 1987; dean, Sch. of Architecture, Pratt Inst., 1991-94; mem. N.Y.C. Landmarks Preservation Commn., 1984-87; lectr. U. So. Calif., U. Va., Temple U., Washington U., Tulane U., Harvard U., U. Oreg., U. Washington Projects include: Computer Sci. Bldg., Columbia U. (AIA Nat. Honor award 1987), Gilmer Hall addition U. Va., Town Hall, Salisbury Conn., Computer Sci. Bldg., Princeton U. (AIA Nat. Honor award 1994), Case Western Reserve Adelbert Hall restoration (AIA Nat. Honor award 1994), Alvin Ailey Am. Dance Theater Found., N.Y.C. hdqs. Marsh & McLennan Co, Ind. Bank Hdqs., Bklyn. Coll. Master Plan, Entrance Pavillion L.I. Rail Rd. Penn. Sta.; works exhibited in Cooper-Hewitt Mus., Bklyn. Mus., Nat. Acad. Design, Deutsches Architekturmuseum, Frankfurt; author: Annotated Bibliography of Technical Resources for Small Museums, 1983. Trustee Nat. Inst. Archtl. Edn., 1988-93; mem. archtl. rev. panel Fed. Res. System, 1993—. Fellow AIA (exec. bd. N.Y.C. chpt. 1979, pres. N.Y.C. chpt., 1991-92), Century Assn.; mem. Archtl. League N.Y. (exec. bd. 1975—, v.p. arch. 1981-85, pres. 1985-89), Assn. Collegiate Schs. Architecture (northeast regional dir. 1993—). Office: R M Kliment & Frances Halsband 255 W 26th St New York NY 10001-8000

HALSEY, EUGENIA GRIFFIN, health correspondent; b. Richmond, Va., May 17, 1956; d. John Selden and Judith Cary (Burnett) H.; m. David Kent Jenkins Jr., May 14, 1988. BA in English, U. Va., 1978. Anchor, reporter Va. Network WINA Radio, Charlottesville, Va., 1977-78, WRVA Radio, Richmond, Va., 1978-79; reporter WDBJ-TV, Roanoke, Va., 1979-82; state capitol corr. WDBJ-TV, Richmond, Va., 1982-85; corr. CNN, Chgo., 1985-87; freelance corr. CNN, Washington, 1987-94, corr., 1994—. Recipient Spot News TV award UPI, Va., 1980, MS Pub. Edn. award Nat. Multiple Sclerosis Soc., Washington, 1993. Office: CNN Bldg Health Unit 820 1st St NE Washington DC 20002

HALSEY, MARGARET BROWN, art history educator, painter, writer; b. Baylor County, Tex., Jan. 28, 1932; d. John E. Brown and Faye (Chambless) Bartos; m. John E. Halsey, Aug. 24, 1963 (div.). BS, Tex. Women's U., 1953; MA, NYU, 1963, PhD, 1968; student, Art Student's League, N.Y.C., 1960, 62, 74; summer program, N.Y. Sch. Interior Design, N.Y.C., 1970; program in Chinese painting, China Inst., N.Y.C., 1983; program in N.Y.C. photography, Internat. Ctr. Photography, N.Y.C., 1980, 84. Tchr. art Schenectady (N.Y.) Schs., 1958-59; tchr. N.Y. Elem. Schs., N.Y.C., 1960-62; tchr. art N.Y. High Schs., N.Y.C., 1963-68; asst. prof. Coll. of Mt. St. Vincent, Riverdale, N.Y., 1969-70; from asst prof. to assoc. prof. N.Y.C. Tech. Coll. CUNY, Bklyn., 1970-89, prof., 1989-92, prof. emeritus, 1992—; lectr. in field. One-women shows include Grace Gallery, Bklyn., 1977, Donnell Libr. Ctr., N.Y.C., 1988; author (art report) Ency. American's Ann., 1990-94. Fellow N.Y. City Tech. Coll., 1981-82, 89-90, CUNY, 1985-86, Andrew W. Mellon Found., 1988. Home: 50 E 89th St New York NY 10128-1225

HALSTED, JUDITH ANN WYNN, educational consultant; b. Adrian, Mich., June 12, 1940; d. George Howard and Ruth Marian (Shriver) Wynn; m. David Wright Halsted, June 24, 1961; children: David George, Mark Jonathan. Student, Ohio Wesleyan U., 1958-60; BA, Mich. State U., 1962; MSLS, U. Ill., 1970. Cataloger Episcopal Sem. So. Austin, Tex., 1970-74; libr. Jr. High, Traverse City, Mich., 1975-77; libr. Pathfinder Sch., Traverse City, Mich., 1974-86, tchr. Latin, 1976-84, gifted program dir., 1977-82; tchr. external edn. N.W. Mich. Coll., Traverse City, Mich., 1985—; prin. Halsted Acad. Advisors, Traverse City, Mich., 1985—; cons. in field. Author: Guiding Gifted Readers, 1988, Some of My Best Friends Are Books, 1994; contbr. articles to profl. jours. Pres. Unitarian Universalist Fellowhip, Traverse City, 1987-88, chair bldg. com., 1990-92; bd. dirs. LVW, 1988-91, chair libr. action. com., 1989—; bd. dirs. AuSable River Property Owners Assn., 1992—, pres., 1994—. Mem. ACA, Mich. Alliance for Gifted Edn., Mich. Assn. Coll. Admission Counselors, Nat. Assn. for Gifted Children, Nat. Assn. Coll. Admission Counselors. Unitarian. Office: Halsted Academic Advisors 934 E 8th St Traverse City MI 49686

HALTER, LAURINE MAE, educational consultant; b. LeMars, Iowa, Nov. 17, 1946; d. Paul C. and Lowene E. (Rutherford) Hasselmann; m. John Ernest Halter, Nov. 29, 1968; children: Lisa Rachelle, Robert Christopher, Daniel Patrick Paul. BA in Sci. Edn., Augustana Coll., 1968; postgrad., U. S.D., 1975-80, Black Hills State U., 1987-94. Cert. nat. trainer Operation Smart, K-12 sci. educator. Libr. media dir. various pub. schs., 1968—; instr. single parents and homemakers Black Hills Spl. Svcs., Sturgis, S.D., 1987-90, coord. single parents and homemakers program, 1990-91; K-12 prevention coord. Hill City (S.D.) Schs., 1990—; project dir. Operation SMART, Rapid City, S.D., 1992-93, trainer/specialist/cons., 1993—; ednl. equity cons., Girl's, Inc., Rapid City, S.D., 1993—; active student assistance programs, others. Lector/youth tchr. local ch., Hill City, 1980—; presenter S.D. Lung Assn. Mem. Nat. Coalition for Equity in Edn., Nat. Sci. Tchr.'s Assn., S.D. Women in Ednl. Leadership, ASCD. Roman Catholic.

HALTERMAN, MARTHA LEE, social services administrator, counselor; b. Poole, Ky., Feb. 4, 1940; d. Byron Lee and Mary Helen (Reinhardt) Melton; m. John David Halterman Jr., Apr. 26, 1968; 1 child, Rebecca Marie. B in Psychology and Sociology, Henderson (Ky.) Community Coll., 1975; postgrad., Brescia Coll., 1977; M in Psychology, U. Evansville, Ind., 1980; cert. in mgmt., U. So. Ind., 1990. Cert. intervention tng. I and II, Am. Mgmt. Assn.; cert. dir. Rainbow for All Children. Office cashier J. J. Newberry Co., Henderson, 1958-63; regional trainer, office cashier C.I.T. Fin. Corp., Henderson, 1965-74; intern Redbanks Nursing Home, Henderson, 1975; dir. counseling and family svcs. Cath. Charities Bur., 1978—; supr. family & children svcs. Cath. Charities Bur. Family Life Diocese of Evansville, 1985-94; counseling and family svcs. dir., 1994—; coord. family life Cath. Charities Bur. Family Life Diocese of Evansville, 1987-94, coord. total svcs., 1993—. Diocesan rep. Ind. Pro-Life Task Force, Indpls., 1987—; sec. Domestic Violence Task Force, Evansville, 1980-88; v.p., bd. dirs. Birthright, Evansville, 1983—; mem. Green River Regional Mental Health and Mental Retardation Bd., Inc., Owensboro, 1990—. Mem. Evansville Psychol. Assn. Roman Catholic. Home: 117 N Bobolink Run Henderson KY 42420-4701 Office: Cath Charities 123 NW 4th St Ste 603 Evansville IN 47708-1725

HALTOM, CRISTEN EDDY, psychologist; b. Albion, N.Y., Oct. 22, 1948; d. Arthur Benedict and Susan (Cooper) Eddy; m. Maurice Haltom Jr., Apr. 5, 1980; children: Jhakeem, Ajemo, Rebecca. BA, Albion Coll., 1970; MS, Cornell U., 1974, PhD, 1978. Lic. psychologist, N.Y. Instr. Eisenhower Coll., Seneca Falls, N.Y., 1976, Elmira (N.Y.) Coll., 1976-77, Cornell U., Ithaca, N.Y., 1977-78; clin. psychology intern Benjamin Rush Ctr. Mental Health and Mental Retardation, Phila., 1978-79; assoc. psychologist Elmira Psychiat. Ctr., 1979-84; pvt. practice Ithaca, 1984—. Co-editor: Women and Problem Drinking, 1980; contbr. articles to profl. jours. Panelist Cable Channel 7 TV, Ithaca, 1988, arts & scis. career ctr. Cornell U., 1994. Mem. APA, Ctrl. N.Y. Psychol. Assn., World Fedn. Mental Health, Internat. Assn. Eating Disorders Profls., Christian Assn. Psychologists. Office: 215 N Geneva St Ithaca NY 14850

HALTOM, KATHERINE ANNE, oral and maxillofacial surgeon; b. Nashville, June 28, 1952; d. Thomas Branson and Martha Anne (O'Connor) Haltom. AB cum laude, Hollins Coll., 1974; DMD, Boston U., 1979, cert., 1982. Bd. cert. Am. Bd. Oral and Maxillofacial Surgeons. Dir. oral surgery clinic Boston U. Sch. Grad. Dentistry, Boston, 1982-86; oral and maxillofacial surgeon Oral Surg. Assoc., Framingham, Mass., 1982-90, Oral and Maxillofacial Surg. Ctr., Framingham, 1990—; mem. sci. com. Yankee Dental Congress, Boston, 1994. Contbr. book chpt.: Textbook of Primary Care, 1986. Bd. dirs. Framingham Edn. Found., 1990—; mem. spl. events com. YMCA, Framingham, 1992-93. Fellow Am. Assn. Oral and Maxillofacial Surgery; mem. ADA, Am. Coll. Oral and Maxillofacial Surgeons, Am. Dental Soc. Anesthesiology, Internat. Congress Oral Implantologists, Mass. Soc. Oral and Maxillofacial Surgeons (evaluator/office emergency 1990—), Mass. Dental Soc., (alt. del. 1993), Met. Dist. Dental Soc. (exec. com., chair emergency com. 1990—), West Metro Study Club (v.p. 1993-94, pres. 94-95). Office: Oral/Maxillofacial Surg Ctr 223 Walnut St Framingham MA 01701

HALUSKA, BONNIE FRATI, rehabilitation nurse; b. Taylor, Pa., Sept. 4, 1950; d. Emilio and Ann (Anselmi) Frati; m. John Andrew Haluska, May

20, 1972. RN, Mercy Hosp. Sch. Nursing, 1971. Cert. rehab. nurse. Charge nurse Mercy Hosp., Scranton, Pa., 1971-72; staff nurse Allied Svcs. Rehab. Hosp., Scranton, Pa., 1972-79, asst. dir. nursing, 1979-89, dir. nursing, 1989—; coord. Spinal Cord Injury Ctr., 1988—; mem. nursing community adv. bd. U. Scranton, 1992—. Recipient Florence Nightingale Recognition award Hosp. Assn. Pa., 1990, 91, 92. Mem. Assn. Rehab. Nurses (bd. dirs. Montage chpt. 1992), Pa. Orgn. Nurse Execs., Alpha Sigma Lambda.

HALVORSON, JUDITH ANNE (JUDITH ANNE DEVAUD), elementary education educator; b. Bethesda, Md., Apr. 28, 1943; d. Henri J. and Mary L. (Baumgart) Devaud; m. Peter L. Halvorson, Feb. 4, 1964; 1 child, Peter Chase. BS in Edn., U. Cin., 1965; MA in Edn., U. Conn., 1974, Cert. Advanced Grad. Study in Edn., 1980. Tchr. Greenhills-Forest Park (Ohio) City Schs., 1965-67, Weld County Schs., Greeley, Colo., 1969-70, Chaplin (Conn.) Elem. Sch., 1970—; mentor Beginning Educator Support program State of Conn. and Chaplin Elem. Sch., 1988—; supr. student tchrs. East Conn. State U., U. Conn., U. No. Colo., 1969—. Vice-chmn., past chmn., past sec. Coventry (Conn.) Bd. Edn., 1981—; chmn. Coventry Sch. Bldg. com., 1981-92, Coventry Parks and Recreation Com., 1980-82, chmn., 1982; mem. Dem. Town Com. Coventry, 1973—. Grantee Nat. Sci. Edn. project, 1977-78; named Outstanding Elem. Tchr. Am., 1974; recipient Citation for Cmty. Leadership Nat. Women's History Month, 1991; recognized for svc. to pub. edn. in Conn., Conn. Assn. Bds. Edn., 1993, 94, for contbns. to Conn. Beginning Educator Support and Tng. Program, Conn. State Dept. Edn., 1991-93, for svc. to cooperating tchr. programs Ea. Conn. State U., 1993. Mem. NEA, Conn. Edn. Assn., Chaplin Edn. Assn. (past pres., v.p., chmn. negotiations 1970—), Pi Lambda Theta (past pres., v.p., chmn. membership Beta Sigma chpt. 1974—), Phi Delta Kappa. Episcopalian. Home: 90 David Dr Coventry CT 06238-1320

HALVORSON, MARY ELLEN, educator; b. Salem, Ohio, Apr. 23, 1950; d. Robert J. and Betty June (Bear) Batzli; m. Thomas Henry Halvorson, June 10, 1972; children: Christine Lynn, Matthew Thomas, Rebecca Lynn. BS in Edn. with distinction, No. Ariz. U., 1972, postgrad., 1973-92; postgrad., U. Ariz., 1974-76, Ariz. State U., 1975-76, U. Phoenix, 1989-90. Cert. elem. tchr., libr., Ariz. Tchr. Prescott (Ariz.) Unified Schs., 1972-77, dir. community nature ctr., 1978, reading tutor, 1985-88, family math. tchr., 1989-90, part-time libr., 1991-92; dir. Prescott Study Ctr., 1987-90; writer ednl. materials Herald House, Independence, Mo., 1994—; instr. Yavapai C.C., 1994—; guest speaker Abia Judd Young Authors, Prescott, 1992; math. enthusiast instr. Ariz. Dept. Edn., Prescott, 1989-92; asst. instr. outdoor edn. Ariz. State U., Prescott, 1977-78; tutor English grammar No. Ariz. U., Flagstaff, 1971-72. Co-author: Arizona Bicentenial Resource Manual, 1975; contbr. book rev. column to Prescott Courier, 1993, also articles to profl. publs. Cert. adult instr. Temple Sch., Independence, Mo., 1985—; sec., bd. dirs. Whispering Pines, Prescott, 1989-93; music docent Prescott Symphony Guild, 1982-85; state Christian edn. dir. Reorganized Ch. Jesus Christ of Latter Day Sts., Ariz., 1977-82, elder, counselor to pastor, 1993—; spokesperson Franklin Heights Homeowners, Prescott, 1985; leader Prescott Pioneers 4-H Club, 1989—, Christian Youth Group, 1985—; fundraiser Graceland Coll., 1993; craft demonstrator Sharlott Hall Mus. Named Outstanding Young Educator, Prescott Jaycees, 1976; named to Outstanding Young Women of Am., 1985. Mem. Phi Kappa Phi, Kappa Delta Pi, Sigma Epsilon Sigma. Home: 2965 Pleasant Valley Dr Prescott AZ 86301

HAM, STEPHANIE ANN, interior architect; b. Elgin, Ill., Oct. 29, 1950; d. Erwin Joseph and Adele Lou (Wagner) Seyk; m. Arthur Daniel Vermeire, Aug. 14, 1970 (div. 1978); 1 child, Holly Ann Vermeire; m. Jay Todd Ham, Jan. 1, 1987. BS in Interior Architecture, Ariz. State U., 1987. Interior designer United Bank, Phoenix, 1987-88, Architecture One, Phoenix, 1988-89, CBS Property Svcs. Inc., Phoenix, 1989-93; interior designer, sr. planner McCarthy Nordburg, Ltd., Phoenix, 1993-94; facilities project planner City of Phoenix, 1994—. Mentor Ariz. Womens' Found., Phoenix, 1990. Recipient First Place Elderly Care Housing award Del Webb Corp., 1986. Mem. NAFE. Republican. Roman Catholic. Office: City of Phoenix 200 W Washington 14th Flr Phoenix AZ 85003

HAMANN, LINDA RAE, psychologist, pastor; b. Estelline, S.D., Mar. 4, 1952; d. Marvin Arthur and Darlen Helen (Boone) H. BS in Home Econs./Dietetics, S.D. State U., 1974; MDiv, Wartburg Theol. Sem., 1980; MS in Clin. Counseling, N.D. State U., 1992. Ordained pastor Luth. Ch., 1980; lic. psychologist, Minn. Consulting dietitian Nutrition Mgmt. Assocs. Ltd., Grand Forks, N.D., 1975-76; parish pastor Evangelical Lutheran Ch. of Am., New Salem Center, N.D., 1980-88; asst. to bishop Western N.D. ELCA, Bismark, N.D., 1988-89; human svcs. counselor Luth. Social Svcs. of Minn., Moorhead, Minn., 1991-94, mental health coord., 1993—. High Edn. scholar N.D. State U., 1990. Mem. NAFE, Phi Upsilon Omicron, Mortar Bd., Phi Kappa Phi. Democrat. Office: Luth Social Svcs of Minn 715 11th St N Ste 401 Moorhead MN 56560

HAMBLEN, L. JANE, lawyer; b. Edna, Tex., June 16, 1949; d. William Herbert and Lillian Gertrude (Hotman) H. BA, Rice U., 1971; JD, U. Tex., 1976; LLB, Cambridge (Eng.) U., 1977. Assoc. Davis Polk & Wardwell, N.Y.C., 1977-84; assoc. O'Melveny & Myers, N.Y.C., 1984-86, ptnr., 1987—. Mem. devel. com. Planned Parenthood N.Y., 1990—; alumni dist. dir. U. Tex. Law Sch., N.Y., 1991-94, dir. alumni bd., 1994—. Office: O'Melveny & Myers Citicorp Ctr 153 E 53rd St 54th Fl New York NY 10022-4611

HAMBRICK, ERNESTINE, colon and rectal surgeon; b. Griffin, Ga., Mar. 31, 1941; d. Jack Daniel and Nannie (Harper) Hambrick Rubens. BS, U. Md., 1963; MD, U. Ill., 1967. Diplomate Am. Bd. Colon and Rectal Surgery, Am. Bd. Surgery. Intern surgery Cook County Hosp., Chgo., 1967-68, resident gen. surgery, 1968-72, colon and rectal surgery fellow, 1972-73, attending surgeon, 1973-74, part-time attending surgeon, 1974-80; pvt. practice colon and rectal surgery Chgo., 1974—; chief of surgery Michael Reese Hosp., Chgo., 1993—. Contbr. articles to profl. jours. Trustee Rsch. & Edn. Found., Michael Reese Med. Staff, Chgo., 1994—. Mem. Am. Coll. Surgeons, Am. Soc. Colon and Rectal Surgeons (v.p. 1992-93, trustee rsch. found. 1992—), Am. Coll. Gastroenterology. Office: 30 N Michigan Ave # 1118 Chicago IL 60602

HAMBRICK, PATRICIA, state legislator; b. Dayton, Ohio, June 4, 1947; d. Leonard Burns and Lucille (Kidd) Tanksley; m. John Wilmer Hambrick, June 14, 1969; children: Kristen, Brian, Bradley. BA in Psychology, U. Cin., 1976; Grad., Inst. for Paralegal Tng., 1976. House mother, resident counselor New Life for Girls, Inc., Cin., 1972-74; paralegal real estate Lerner, Sampson & Rothfuss, Cin., 1977; paralegal civil litigation Stuart, Smith, Messina, Harris & Rieders, Williamsport, Pa., 1978; with dept. purchasing, inventory control Avco Internat. Svcs. Div., Riyadh, Saudi Arabia, 1980-81; dir. religious edn. Northwoods Unitarian Ch., Woodlands, Tex., 1984-87; state rep. State of N.H., Durham, Lee, Madbury, 1990—; ptnr., dir. devel. Victims, Inc., Rochester, N.H., 1991—. Leader Girls Scouts U.S.A., Lee, Tucson, 1987-91, 93—; bd. dirs. Children's Workshop Presch., Barrington, N.H., 1988; treas. Dem. Party, Strafford County, 1988—; coach, judge Odyssey of the Mind, Lee, 1991—. Mem. N.E. Network Progressive Legislators, Rochester C. of C. Home: 33 Wednesday Hill Rd Durham NH 03824 Office: Victims Inc PO Box 455 Rochester NH 03867

HAMBURG, BEATRIX ANN, medical educator, researcher; b. Jacksonville, Fla., Oct. 19, 1923; d. Francis Minor and Beatrix McCleary; married, May 25, 1951; children: Eric N., Margaret A. A.B., Vassar Coll., 1944; M.D., Yale U., 1948; DHL (hon.), Northwestern U., 1994. Diplomate: Nat. Bd. Med. Examiners. Intern Grace-New Haven Hosp., 1948-49; resident Yale Psychiat. Inst., New Haven, 1949-50; resident in pediatrics Children's Hosp., Cin., 1950-51; resident in psychiatry Inst. Juvenile Research, 1951-53; research assoc. Stanford U. Med. Sch. (Calif.), 1961-71, assoc. prof. psychiatry, 1976-80; assoc. prof. Harvard Med. Sch., Boston, 1980-83; exec. dir. Div. Health Policy Research, 1981-83; prof. psychiatry and pediatrics Mt. Sinai Med. Sch., N.Y.C., 1983—, dir. div. child and adolescent psychiatry, 1988-92; pres. William T Grant Found, NYC, 1992—; assoc. dir. Lab. of Stress and Conflict, Stanford U. Med. Sch., 1974-76; sr. research psychiatrist NIMH, Bethesda, Md., 1978-80; dir. studies Pres.'s Commn. Mental Health, 1977-78; mem. vis. com. Sch. Pub. Health, Harvard U., 1977-80, commn. on behavior and soc., Nat. Acad. Scis., 1983—. Author: Behavioral and Psychosocial Issues in Diabetes, 1980, School Age Pregnancy and Parenthood, 1986; contbr. numerous sci. articles to profl. jours. Trustee W.T. Grant Found., 1978—; bd. dirs. New World Found., 1978-83, Bush Found., Revson Found., Greenwall Found., 1986—; mem. Pub. Health Coun. State of N.Y., 1978-80. Vis. scholar Ctr. Advanced Study Behavioral Scis., 1967-68; recipient Outstanding Achievement award Alcohol, Drug Abuse and Mental Health Adminstrn., 1980. Fellow Am. Acad. Child Psychiatry; mem. AAAS (bd. dirs. 1987-91), NIMH (nat. adv. mental health coun.), Inst. of Medicine of NAS, Soc. Profs. Child Psychiatry (program com. 1972-74), Am. Acad. Child Psychiatry (adolescent com. 1977-81), Soc. Adolescent Medicine, APHA (adolescent com. 1978-80), Soc. Study of Social Biology, Acad. Rsch. in Behavioral Medicine (exec. coun. 1980), N.Y. Acad. Medicine (bd. trustees 1992), Century Club, Phi Beta Kappa. Office: William T Grant Found 515 Madison Ave New York NY 10022-5403

HAMBURG, MARGARET ANN (PEGGY HAMBURG), city commissioner; b. Chgo., July 12, 1955; d. David Alan and Beatrix Ann (Mc Cleary) H.; m. Peter Fitzhugh Brown, May 23, 1992; 1 child, Rachel Ann Hamburg Brown. BA magna cum laude, Harvard/Radcliffe Coll., 1978; MD, Harvard, 1983. Diplomate Am. Bd. Internal Medicine, Nat. Bd. Med. Examiners. Intern, resident in internal medicine The N.Y. Hosp., Cornell Med. Coll., N.Y.C., 1983-86; spl. asst. to the dir., office of disease prevention and health promotion, office of the asst. sec. for health U.S. Dept. Health and Human Svcs., Washington, 1986-88; spl. asst. to the dir. Nat. Inst. Allergy and Infectious Diseases, NIH, Bethesda, Md., 1988-89, asst. dir., 1989-90; deputy commr. Family Health Svcs., N.Y.C. Dept. Health, N.Y.C., 1990-91; commr. of health N.Y.C. Dept. Health, N.Y.C., 1991—; guest investigator The Rockefeller U., N.Y.C., 1985-86; clin. instr. dept. medicine Georgetown U. Sch. Medicine, Washington, 1986-90; asst. prof. clin. pub. health Columbia U. Sch. Pub. Health, N.Y.C., 1991—; adj. asst. prof. medicine Cornell U. Med. Coll., N.Y.C., 1991—; scholar Pub. Health Leadership Inst. Ctr. for Disease Control U. Calif., 1992; bd. dirs. N.Y.C. Health Systems Agy., Med. and Health Rsch. Assn., Health Hosps. Corp, Nat. Coun. on Women's Health, Primary Care Devel. Corp.; steering com. women and aids NIH, 1991; bd. govs. Greater N.Y. Hosp. Assn., 1991—; mem. bd. sci. advisors. Nat. Pub. Radio, 1992—; com. mem. on substance abuse mental health issues in aides rsch., 1993—; advisory bd. mem. Medunsa Trust, Inc., Med. U. So. Africa, 1993—; mem. defense sci. bd. task force on Gulf War Syndrome U.S. Dept. Defense, 1993—; bd. mem. sci. counselors Nat. Ctr. Infectious Diseases, U.S. Ctrs. for Disease, 1994—; rschr. in the field. Editorial bd. mem. Jour. N.Y. Acad. Sci., 1992—, The Bull. of N.Y. Acad. Medicine, 1992—, Current Reviews in Pub. Health, 1993—; contbr. to numerous profl. jours. Vol. attending physician The Washington Free Clinic, Washington, 1988-90. Recipient commendation Pub. Health Svc., 1988, 90, Spl. Recognition award Pub. Health Svc., 1990, cert. of Honor The Women's Club of N.Y., 1993, N.Y. Rotary Club award, 1993, Robert F. Wagner Pub. Svc. award NYU, 1993. Mem. AAAS (med. scis. section com. 1989—), ACP, APHA, Am. Med. Women's Assn., Coun. on Fgn. Rels., Health Care Exec. Forum, N.Y. Acad. Medicine, Pub. Health Assn. N.Y.C., Inst. Medicine, Soc. Social Biology, Women in Health Mgmt. Office: NYC Dept Health 125 Worth St New York NY 10013

HAMBURGER, MARY ANN, medical management consultant; b. Newark, Aug. 25, 1939; d. Herman and Sylvia (Strauss) Marcus; div. June 1966; children: Bruce David, Marc Laurence. AA, U. Bridgeport (Conn.), 1960. Office mgr. Millburn, N.J., 1970-84; propr., mgr. Mary Ann Hamburger, Assocs., med. mgmt. cons. co., Maplewood, N.J., 1984-; tchr. adult edn. South Orange Maplewood Bd. Edn., 1975-83; cons. Wellcare of N.Y.; profl. physician recruiter, N.Y., N.J.; broker med. practices. Mem. NAFE. Democrat. Jewish. Home and Office: 74 Hudson Ave Maplewood NJ 07040-1403

HAMBY, JEANNETTE, state legislator; b. Virginia, Minn., Mar. 15, 1933; d. John W. and Lydia M. (Soderholm) Johnson; m. Eugene Hamby, 1957; children—Taryn Rene, Tenya Ramine. BS, U. Minn., 1956; MS, U. Oreg., 1968, PhD, 1976. Vice chmn. Hillsboro High Sch. Dist. Bd., 1973-81; mem. Washington County Juvenile Services Com., 1980—; mem. suggested legis. com. Council State Govts., 1981—, Oreg. state rep., 1981-83; mem. Oreg. State Senate from 5th dist., 1983—. Mem. Oreg. Mental Health Assn., Am. Nurses Assn., Oreg. Nurses Assn., Am. Vocat. Assn., Oreg. Vocat. Assn., Oreg. Vocat./Career Adminstrs., Phi Kappa Phi, Phi Delta Kappa. Lutheran. Republican. Home: 952 NE Jackson School Rd Hillsboro OR 97124-2314 Office: Oreg State Senate State Capital Salem OR 97310*

HAMEISTER, LAVON LOUETTA, farm manager, social worker; b. Blairstown, Iowa, Nov. 27, 1922; d. George Frederick and Bertha (Anderson) Hameister; B.A., U. Iowa, 1944; postgrad. N.Y. Sch. Social Work, Columbia, 1945-46, U. Minn. Sch. Social Work, summer 1952; M.A., U. Chgo., 1959. Child welfare practitioner Fayette County Dept. Social Welfare, West Union, Iowa, 1946-56; dist. cons. services in child welfare and pub. assistance Iowa Dept. Social Welfare, Des Moines, 1956-58, dist. field rep., 1959-64, regional supr., 1964-65, supr., specialist supervision, adminstrn. Bur. Staff Devel., 1965-66, chief Bur. Staff Devel., 1966-68; chief div. staff devel. and tng. Office Dep. Commr., Iowa Dept. Social Services, 1968-72, asst. dir. Office Staff Devel., 1972-79, coordinator continuing edn., 1979-86; now mgr. Hameister Farm, Blairstown, Iowa. Active in drive to remodel, enlarge Oelwein (Iowa) Mercy Hosp., 1952; active in devel. mental health ctrs. in N.E. Iowa in 1950's. Mem. Bus. and Profl. Women's Club (chpt. sec. 1950-52), Am. Assn. U. Women, Nat. Assn. Social Workers (chpt. sec.-elect 1958-59), Am. Pub. Welfare Assn., Iowa Welfare Assn., Acad. Cert. Social Workers. Lutheran.

HAMEL, ELIZABETH CECIL, volunteer, educator; b. Altoona, Pa., June 13, 1918; d. Francis Anthony and Charlotte Margaret (Devine) Murphy; m. William Rogers Hamel, Mar. 2, 1943; children: Michele Ferencsik, Deirdre, Anthony, Cecily Charlyn Houston. BArt, Villa Maria Coll., 1939; MA, Pa. State U., 1940; cert. approval, U. Cambridge, Eng., summer 1986. Tchr. English, head Spanish dept. East High Sch., Erie, Pa., 1940-43; prof. lit. Vernon Ct. Jr. Coll., Newport, R.I., 1966-69. Mem. Francestown (N.H.) Improvement Assn., 1958—, Peterborough (N.H.) Hist. Soc., 1987—, Art and Hist. Soc. East Martello Tower Mus., Key West, Fla., 1987—, Founders' Soc. Tennessee Williams Fine Arts Ctr., Key West, 1986—; bd. dirs. Old Island Restoration Found., Key West, 1990—; bd. dirs. Friends of Libr., 1985-86, 93—, sec., 1986-87, 92—; mem. White House Vol. Group, Washington, 1972-74; trustee Newport County Preservation Soc. Mem. Gen. Fedn. Women's Club (bd. dirs. Key West chpt. 1986—), Key West Woman's Club (bd. dirs., parliamentarian 1986—, del. state con. 1988—), Peterborough Woman's Club, Garden Club, Greenfield Woman's Club (pres. 1979-80). Republican. Roman Catholic. Home: Blacksmith Shop Main St Francestown NH 03043

HAMILL, JUDITH ELLEN, municipal government administrator; b. Chgo., Mar. 8, 1953; d. William Patrick and Dolores Jean (Lhamon) H.; m. Thomas A. Jaconetty, Aug. 3, 1991; 1 child, Nicole Alicia Jaconetty. MusB, Roosevelt U., 1975; M of Urban Planning and Policy, U. Ill., Chgo., 1979; M of Pub. Adminstrn., Harvard U., 1982. Staff asst. Thomas H. Miner & Assocs., Chgo., 1972-75; project dir. Chgo. Council on Fine Arts, 1977-78; project planning dept. planning City of Chgo. Dept. Planning, Ill., 1978-81; research staff Stevenson/Stern for Ill., Chgo., 1982; ind. cons. Chgo., 1982-86; city planner Dept. Aviation, Chgo., 1986-87; dir. noise abatement office Dept. of Aviation, Chgo., 1987-95; program dir. first dep. comm. officer O'Hare Internat. Airport, Chgo., 1995—. Vice chairperson Ill. Women's Polit. Caucus, Chgo., 1975-82; active Women in Govt. Rels., Chgo., 1977-82, Ill. Dem. Women, Springfield, Ill., 1981—, Cook County Dem. Women, Chgo., 1982—; mem. jr. gov. bd. Chgo. Symphony Orch., 1981-89; mem. Bus. and Profl. Assn. Chgo. Symphony Orch., 1990—; bd. dirs. Rogers Park Cmty. Coun., 1990-93. Recipient Community Svc. award S.W. Parish and Neighborhood Fedn., 1993; Harvard U. scholar, Cambridge, Mass., 1981-82. Club: Harvard of Chgo. Home: 4801 N Harlem Ave Chicago IL 60656-3505

HAMILTON, BEATRICE, psychotherapist, counseling administrator; b. Macon, Miss., Dec. 2, 1947; d. Walter Henley and Tiller (Cotton) Henley. BS, Miles Coll., 1972; MA, Atlanta U., 1974; EdD, Vanderbilt U., 1986. Nat. cert. counselor; cert. profl. counselor. Researcher Iowa State U.; dir., asst. prof. counseling ctr. U. Md. Eastern Shore, Salisbury; pvt. practice counseling Salisbury; lectr. Salisbury State U.; mgr. budgeting and planning Collins Svcs., Huntsville, Ala.; dir. residence Ala. A&M Univ., Huntsville. Contbr. articles to profl. jours. V.p. PTA. Recipient Human Rels. award, 1986. Mem. NAPW (chair evaluation com.), ACPA (adminstrv. leadership com.). Home: RR 6 Box 854 Salisbury MD 21801-9088

HAMILTON, BETH ALLEMAN, information scientist, editor; b. Stewartstown, W.Va., Apr. 3, 1927; d. Hubert Charles and Gay Elizabeth (Zearley) Alleman; m. Rex Hamilton, Apr. 17, 1949 (dec. 1993); children: Shelley Hamilton Hutter, Meredith L., Eric R., Elizabeth Hamilton Gruhn, John Z. BS, W.Va. U., 1948; MA, Rosary Coll., 1969; Cert. Advanced Studies in Library and Info. Sci., U. Chgo., 1977. Chemist Standard Pharmacal, Chgo., 1948-49; tech. libr. Am. Meat Inst. Found., Chgo., 1949-51; rsch. libr. Glidden Co., Chgo., 1952-53; owner, ptnr. Hamilton Truck Leasing, Elk Grove Village, Ill., 1957-63; editor, bus. analyst Internat. Minerals & Chem. Corp., Skokie, Ill., 1964-69; sci. libr., assoc. prof. U. Ill., Chgo., 1969-72, adj. assoc. prof., 1972-79; sr. info. scientist Triodyne Inc. Cons. Engrs. and Scientists, Niles, Ill., 1979-91; editor Triodyne Safety Brief, 1991—; cons. Libr. Systems Devel., 1991—; exec. dir. Ill. Regional Library Council, Chgo., 1972-79; vis. lectr. Rosary Coll., 1970-71; vis. asst. prof. U. Ill. Grad Sch. Library Sci., Urbana, 1977-79. Editor: Libraries and Infomation Centers in the Chicago Metropolitan Area, 1973; Union List of Serial Holdings in Illinois Special Libraries, 1976, 77, Multitype Library Cooperation, 1977; (with others) As Much to Learn as to Teach: Essays in Honor of Lester Asheim, 1979, Chemical Engineering Data Sources: AIChE Symposium Series, 1986; contbr. articles to profl. jours. Mem. Arlington Heights (Ill.) Bd. Edn., 1966-70, Burr Ridge (Ill.) Bicentennial Commn., 1975-76; exec. v.p. Rep. Women's Club of Lyons Twp., Ill., 1975-76; librarian, tchr. First Presby. Ch. of Arlington Heights, 1960-69. Mem. ALA, DAR (Lady Houston chpt.), Am. Chem. Soc., Spl. Librs. Assn. (joint task force with Nat. Commn. on Librs. and Info. Sci. on role of the spl. libr.), Beta Phi Mu. Home: 2406 Mills Creek Dr Kingwood TX 77339-3092

HAMILTON, CONSTANCE BETTE, real estate broker, property manager; b. Northampton, Mass, May 7, 1933; d. Roy A. and Loretta Gracie (Short) H. BM in nursing, Syracuse U., 1960, MS, 1962; postgrad., Long Beach City Coll., Calif., 1977-81, present. Head nurse emergency room, clin. instr., supr. various hosps., Mass., N.Y., Calif.; grad. asst.sch. edn., dept. Philosophy Syracuse U., 1960-62; instr. nursing Los Angeles County, U. So. Calif. Med. Ctr. Sch. Nursing, 1962-64; project coordinator Develop. Diploma programs, Calif., 1964-67, master tchr., 1964-67; guest faculty, staff mem., cons. death dying and crisis Research and Training Ctr. Research Methods Course, Calif., 1967-75; research review, critique U.S. Pub. Health Service, Nursing Research div., Nursing Review and patient Care Com., 1967-70; nursing research assoc. Los Angeles County, Rancho Los Anigos Hosp., Calif., 1967-70; assoc. dir. patient care, comunity services Martin Luter King Jr. Gen. Hosp., Los Angeles, 1970-72; nurse cons. Staff Builders Assn., James Evans Assocs., 1972-73; dir. health services Comprenetics, Beverly Hills, Calif., 1972—; assoc. dir. nursing, critical care Meml. Hosp. Med. Ctr., Long Beach, Calif., 1973-78; real estate seminar coordinator Women Investing Now, 1975; real estate assoc. Pacific Shore Realty, Long Beach, Calif., 1977-82; real estate broker Park Terrace, Long Beach, Calif., 1982-85, H&L Properties, Long Beach, Calif., 1985—; nursing rep. research subcom. phys. therapy, occupational therapy Rancho Los Anigos Hosp., 1967-79; nurse cons. Am. Coll. Surgeons and Trauma, U. Ala., 1972.; cons. WICHE Conf. Nursing Research-Patient Quality Care, 1972-73; faculty Annual Con. Clin. Application Hyperbaric Oxygen; cons. VA Hosp., Wadsworth, Calif., 1976-77, VA Nursing Service Dept., Wadsworths, Va., 1977-78. Active Community Nursing Adv. Council, Watts-Willowbrook, Calif.; mem. United Way (adv. com., region IV). Nat. Assn. Realtors, Calif. Assn. Realtors, Long Beach Dist. Bd. Realtor, Health Manpower Com. Comprehensive Health Planning Assn. Los Angeles County, Am. Hosp. Assn. Am. Bus. Woman's Assn., Calif. Nurses' Assn., Long Beach Dist. Bd. Realtors Equal Opportunity Com. (chmn.), Long Beach Dist. Bd. Reators, Sigma Theta Tau, Pi Lambda Theta. Republican. Episcopalian. lodges: Zonta, Zonta Internat. Office: H&L Properties 355 Redondo Ave Long Beach CA 90814-2656

HAMILTON, DAGMAR STRANDBERG, lawyer, educator; b. Phila., Jan. 10, 1932; d. Eric Wilhelm and Anna Elizabeth (Sjöström) Strandberg; A.B., Swarthmore Coll., 1953; J.D., U. Chgo. Law Sch., 1956; J.D., Am. U., 1961; m. Robert W. Hamilton, June 26, 1953; children: Eric Clark, Robert Andrew Hale, Meredith Hope. Admitted to Tex. bar, 1972; atty., civil rights div. U.S. Dept. Justice, Washington, 1965-66; asst. instr. govt. U. Tex.-Austin, 1966-71; lectr. Law Sch. U. Ariz., Tucson, 1971-72; editor, researcher Assoc. Justice William O. Douglas, U.S. Supreme Ct., 1962-73, 75-76; editor, research Douglas autobiography Random House Co., 1972-73; staff counsel Judiciary Com., U.S. Ho. of Reps., 1973-74; asst. prof. L.B. Johnson Sch. Pub. Affairs, U. Tex., Austin, 1974-77, assoc. prof., 1977-83, prof., 1983—, assoc. dean, 1983-87; vis. prof. Washington U. Law Sch., St. Louis, 1982; vis. fellow Univ. London, 1987-88, vis. prof. U. Maine Portland, 1992. Mem. Tex. Bar Assn., Am. Law Inst., Assn. Pub. Policy Analysis and Mgmt., Kappa Beta Phi (hon.), Phi Kappa Phi (hon.). Democrat. Quaker. Contbr. to various publs. Home: 403 Allegro Ln Austin TX 78746-4301 Office: U Tex LBJ Sch Pub Affairs Austin TX 78712

HAMILTON, ILA JOHNSON, general contractor, interior designer, real estate broker; b. Norfolk, Va., Dec. 14; d. Verlee Hope; m. Donald G. Hamilton, July 9, 1966; children: David, Brian. BS, U. Pacific, 1968; life teaching credential, Claremont Grad. Sch., 1971; postgrad., Woodbury U., L.A., 1974. In-house interior designer Lewis Homes Calif., Upland, 1977-81; pvt. practice interior design, Claremont, 1975—, gen. contractor,, 1981—; real estate broker, contractor, designer Triple Crown Devel., Claremont, 1993—; instr. U. Calif., Riverside, 1988; dir. interior design John Robert Powers, Riverside, 1984. Commr. Cmty. Svcs. Dept., Claremont, 1981-84. Mem. Am. Soc. Interior Designers (profl. mem., cert. interior designer), Claremont C. of C. (amb. 1988), Chamber Chino Valley (event coord. 1993-94, interior designer Ethan Allen Montclair Interiors 1994—), Claremont Heritage, Rotary (event planner Claremont 1988-92). Methodist. Home and Office: 2239 La Paz Claremont CA 91711

HAMILTON, JACQUELINE, art consultant; b. Tulsa, Mar. 28, 1942; d. James Merton and Nina Faye (Andrews) H.; m. Richard Sanford Piper, Jan. 2, 1968 (div. June 1976). BA, Tex. Christian U., 1965; grad., Stockholm U., 1967; postgrad., Harvard U., 1972-73, Tufts U., 1971, Rice U., 1982-83, Houston C.C., 1986-87. Pvt. practice art cons. Houston, 1979—. Contbr. articles to profl. publs. Active Cultural Arts Council of Houston. Mem. Assn. Corp. Art Curators, Nat. Assn. Corp. Art Mgmt., Rice Design Alliance, Tex. Arts Alliance, The Houstonian Club, The Forum Club, L'Alliance Francaise, Swedish Club. Presbyterian. Office: PO Box 1483 Houston TX 77251-1483

HAMILTON, JEAN ANN, physician, psychologist, educator; b. Oklahoma City, Apr. 13, 1950; d. Richard Earl Hamilton and N. Joan Burk May; m. Henry H. Holcomb, Aug. 1972 (div. Apr. 1979); m. J. Lynn Dolkart, June 25, 1981; 1 child, Jennifer Scher. BA, Rice U., 1972; postgrad., U. Chgo., 1972-73; MD, U. Tex., San Antonio, 1977. Lic. physician Tex., Washington, N.C. Postdoctoral rsch. fellow U. Chgo./Michael Reese Hosp., Chgo., 1977-78; intern and resident in psychiatry U. N.C., Chapel Hill, 1978-80; postdoctoral rsch. fellow in neuropharmacology NIMH, Bethesda, Md., 1980-83; head biology of depression rsch. unit NIMH, Rockville, Md., 1983-84; dir. Inst. for Rsch. on Women's Health, Washington, 1984-90; assoc. prof. psychiatry U. Tex. Med. Sch., Dallas, 1990-92; prof. psychology, women's studies and psychiatry Duke U., Durham, N.C., 1990—; panelist Inst. of Medicine, Washington, 1991; lectr. in field; expert adv. panel NIMH Rsch. Agenda on Women's Mental Health, 1985-86; funding reviewer Psychobiology of Depression Network, MacArthur Found., Chgo.; rsch. adv. group Vets. Affairs, 1991-92; expert cons. NIMH, 1983, 85, 88, 89, 90, NICHD, 1983, 84, NIDA, 1985, USPHS, 1984, numerous instns. and orgns. Contbr. over 80 articles to profl. jours.; editorial bd. Jour. Women's Health, Women's Health Forum, Social Pharmacology; ad hoc reviewer Jour. Nervous and Mental Disease, Psychosomatic Medicine, Psychology of Women Quar., Women and Health, Violence and Victims, Jour. of AMA, Psychosomatics, Am. Jour. Psychiatry, Jour. Psychiatry Rsch., Contemporary Psychiatry, Integrative Psychiatry, Contemporary Psychology, Am. Psychologist. Grantee Arts and Scis. Rsch. Coun., 1993-94, Nat. Heart,

Lund and Blood Inst., 1991, NIH, 1992-94, Inst. for Rsch. on Women's Health, 1987—, Spencer Found., 1988, Uniformed Svcs. U. of Health Scis., 1985-89, NIMH, 1981-83, many others. Office: Duke University Dept Psychology PO Box 90085 Durham NC 27708-0085

HAMILTON, JEAN CONSTANCE, judge; b. St. Louis, Nov. 12, 1945; d. Aubrey Bertrand and Rosemary (Crocker) H. A.B., Wellesley Coll., 1968; J.D., Washington U., St. Louis, 1971; LL.M., Yale U., 1982. Bar: Mo. 1971. Atty. Dept. of Justice, Washington, 1971-73, asst. U.S. atty., St. Louis, 1973-78; atty. Southwestern Bell Telephone Co., St. Louis, 1978-81; judge 22d Jud. Circuit, State of Mo., St. Louis, 1982-88; judge Mo. Ct. Appeals (ea. dist.), 1988-90; U.S. dist. judge U.S. Dist. Ct. (ea. dist.) Mo., 1990—. Mem. ABA, Bar Assn. Met. St. Louis, Women Lawyers Assn. Met. St. Louis, Nat. Assn. Women Judges, Am. Law Inst. Episcopalian. Office: US Court and Custom House 1114 Market St Fl #1 Saint Louis MO 63101-2043

HAMILTON, JUDITH ANN, human resources professional; b. Humboldt, Nebr., Nov. 19, 1946; d. Donald Leonard and Betty June (Warner) Stalder; m. Rodney Gene Hamilton, Mar. 23, 1973; 1 child, Russell Allen. BBA, U. Denver, 1990; cert. mgmt. devel., U. Colo., 1984. Cert. sr. profl. in human resources. V.p. adminstrn. Particle Measuring Systems Inc., Boulder, Colo., 1979-85; dir. human resources Access Graphics, Inc., Boulder, 1990-93; prin. Solutions Resource Group, Santa Fe, 1994—; speaker Colo. Bus. Educators Conf., Denver, 1991; event judge Future Bus. Leaders Am., Colo., 1991. Chairperson Bus. Adv. Com., Adams County Sch. Dist. 12, Colo. Named Bus. Person of Yr., Future Bus. Leaders Am., 1991. Mem. Soc. Human Resource Mgmt., Colo. Human Resource Assn., No. N.Mex. Human Resource Assn. (basic reading tutor Santa Fe literacy program), Boulder Area Human Resource Assn. (dir. 1992, 93). Office: 2801 W Rodeo Rd Ste B435 Santa Fe NM 87505-6503

HAMILTON, JUDITH HALL, computer company executive; b. Washington, June 15, 1944; d. George Woods and Jane Fromm (Brogger) Hall; m. David Hamilton, Oct. 2, 1970 (div. 1980); m. Stephen T. McClellan, Oct. 29, 1988. BA, Ind. U., 1966; postgrad., Boston U., 1966-68; postgrad. Exec. Sch. Mgmt., UCLA, 1980-81. Programmer System Devel. Corp., Santa Monica, Calif., 1968-69, dir. programming, 1975-80; systems analyst Daylin, Inc., Beverly Hills, Calif., 1969-71; systems mgr. Audio Magnetics, Gardena, Calif., 1971-73; pres. Databasics, Inc., Santa Monica, 1973-75; v.p. Computer Scis. Corp., El Segundo, Calif., 1980-87; ptnr. Ernst & Young, L.A., 1987-89, Manhattan, N.Y., 1989-91; sr. v.p., gen. mgr. Locus Computing Corp., L.A., 1991-92; pres., CEO, Dataquest, Inc., a Dun & Bradstreet Corp., San Jose, Calif., 1992—; bd. dirs. The Application Group, Com. Econ. Devel.; bd. advisors Perot Systems. Active World Affairs Coun. L.A.; mem. bus. bd. N.Y. Zool. Soc.; San Jose bd. dirs. World Forum. Mem. Assn. Data Processing Svc. Orgns. (bd. dirs., chmn.), Information Tech. Assn. Am., Orgn. Women Execs., Calif. C. of C. (bd. dirs. 1994—, Dept. of Commerce Dist. Export Coun. No. Calif.), Kappa Alpha Theta. Office: Dataquest 1290 Ridder Park Dr San Jose CA 95131-2398

HAMILTON, LINDA, actress; b. Salisbury, Md., Sept. 26, 1956; m. Bruce Abbott (div.). Appeared in plays Looice, 1975, Richard III, 1977; films include T.A.G.: The Assassination Game, 1982, Children of the Corn, 1984, The Stone Boy, 1984, The Terminator, 1984, Black Moon Rising, 1986, King Kong Lives!, 1986, Mr. Destiny, 1990, Terminator 2: Judgment Day, 1991, Silent Fall, 1994; TV series include The Secrets of Midland Heights, 1980-81, King's Crossing, 1982, Beauty and the Beast, 1987-90 (Golden Globe award nomination 1988, 89); TV movies include Reunion, 1980, Rape and Marriage - The Rideout Case, 1980, Country Gold, 1982, Secrets of a Mother and Daughter, 1983, Secret Weapons, 1985, Club Med, 1986, Go Toward the Light, 1988. Office: Internat Creative Mgmt 8942 Wilshire Blvd Beverly Hills CA 90211*

HAMILTON, LINDA HELEN, clinical psychologist; b. N.Y.C., Dec. 2, 1952; d. Peter and Helen (Casey) Homek; m. Terrence White, Aug. 10, 1974 (div. 1983); m. William Garnett Hamilton, Dec. 29, 1984. BA summa cum laude, Fordham U., 1984; MA, Adelphi U., 1986, PhD, 1989. Lic. psychologist, N.Y. Dancer N.Y.C. Ballet, 1969-88; clin. psychologist Fair Oaks Hosp., Summit, N.J., 1989-90, Miller Inst. for Performing Artists, N.Y.C., 1989—; pvt. practice N.Y.C., 1991—; rsch. assoc. Miller Inst. Performing Artists, N.Y.C., 1987—; chair dance com. MedArt U.S.A., N.Y.C., 1990-92; cons. psychologist Sch. Am. Ballet, N.Y.C., 1991—; advice columnist Dance Mag., 1992—; co-leader Performing Arts Medicine Delegation to Russia and Ea. Europe, 1992. Contbr. articles to profl. jours. Miller Inst. Performing Artists grantee, 1987. Mem. APA (Daniel E. Berlyne award 1993, mem.-at-large psychology and the arts divsn.), Ea. Psychol. Assn., Soc. for Exploration and Psychotherapy Integration. Office: 30 W 60th St New York NY 10023-7902

HAMILTON, LORRAINE REBEKAH, adult education consultant; b. York, Pa., Jan. 17, 1960; d. Robert Stephen Sheely and Emma Estella (Taylor) Ford; m. Ronald Dana Hamilton, Apr. 14, 1990. Diploma in Drafting and Design Tech., Cumberland-Perry Tech. Sch., Mechanicsburg, Pa., 1978; BS in Psychology, U. Houston, 1992, MA in Gen. Behavioral Scis., 1994. Drafter aluminum products Capitol Products, Camp Hill, Pa., 1978-81; drafter oil field equipment Continental Emsco, Houston, 1981-82; coll. prof. Coll. of the Mainland, Texas City, Tex., 1983-87; contract drafter/piping Astech Svcs., Houston, 1985-86; computer specialist Amoco Oil Co., Texas City, 1986-92; ind. cons. Sage Learning Method, 1994—; owner Synergy Systems, 1994—. Convenor Women's Studies Student Assn., Houston, 1994; treas., forum rep. NOW, Houston, 1992; vol. Landmark Edn. Corp., Houston, 1992-94. Mem. Omicron Delta Kappa. Home: PO Box 625 La Marque TX 77568

HAMILTON, MARY LUCIA KERR, retired banker, lawyer; b. Denver, Aug. 3, 1926; d. Henry Hamilton and Helen (Clancy) Kerr; m. William A. Hamilton, June 15, 1957 (dec. Feb. 1989); children: Lucia M., Henry K., John A., Peter D. BS, Simmons Coll., Boston, 1948; JD, U. Toledo, 1958. Bar: Ohio 1958, U.S. Dist. Ct. (no. dist.) Ohio 1959. Sec. United Airlines, Toledo, 1953-55; exec. dir. Toledo Bar Assn., 1955-58; staff atty. Legal Aid Soc., Toledo, 1958-60; assoc. Cobourn, Yager, Smith & Beck, Toledo, 1960-69; trust officer, v.p. Toledo Trust Co., 1969-79; v.p., trust officer First Nat. Bank Toledo, 1979-89, Fifth Third Bank Toledo, N.A. (formerly First Nat. Bank Toledo), 1989-91; retired, 1991. Bd. dirs. United Way of Toledo, 1987-90, Sight Ctr., 1987-88; trustee Ohio Bar Found., 1982-87; treas. Maumee Valley Coun. Girl Scouts U.S., 1991-93; bd. dirs. Sunset House, 1992—. Fellow Ohio Bar Assn. (exec. com. 1987-90), ABA (ho. of dels. 1990-94); mem. Toledo Bar Assn. (pres. 1977-78), Toledo Auto Club (bd. dirs. 1982—, vice chmn. bd. 1991-92, chmn. 1992-94), Zonta (pres. Toledo club 1986-87), Toledo Club. Roman Catholic.

HAMILTON, NANCY BETH, data processing administrator; b. Lakewood, Ohio, July 22, 1948; d. Edward Douglas and Gloria Jean (Blessing) Famila; m. Thomas Woolman Hamilton, June 10, 1970; children: Susan Elizabeth, Catherine Anne. BA, Denison U., 1970. Cert. secondary edn. tchr., Fla. Tchr. Orange County (Fla.) Bd. Edn., 1970-71; registrar Jones Coll., Orlando, Fla., 1971-72; mgr. service dept. Am. Lawyers Co., Cleve., 1972-79, mgr. data processing dept., 1980—. Mem. bd. editors Comml. Law Jour., 1991—. Trustee, treas. Westshore Montessori Assn., Rocky River, Ohio, 1984-88; bd. dirs. Holly Ln. PTA, Westlake, Ohio, 1988-94, treas., 1992-94; bd. dirs. Parkside PTA, Westlake, 1991—, treas., 1994—. Mem. Comml. Law League Am. (chmn. com. 1989-94, membership chmn. 1994—), Alpha Phi (pres. Cleve. Westshore chpt. alumnae 1986-88). Republican. Methodist. Clubs: Westwood Country, Cleve. Yachting (Rocky River). Office: Am Lawyers Co 853 Westpoint Pky Ste 710 Cleveland OH 44145-1532

HAMILTON, PHYLLIS JEAN, judge; b. Jacksonville, June 12, 1952. BA, Stanford Univ., 1973; JD cum laude, Univ. of Santa Clara Sch. of Law, 1976. Bar: Calif. 1976. Dep. state pub. defender San Francisco, Calif., 1976-80; adminstrv. judge U.S. Merit Systems Protection Bd., San Francisco, Calif., 1980-85; court commr. Oakland Mcpl. Ct., Oakland, Calif., 1985-91; magistrate judge U.S. Dist. Ct. (Calif. no. dist.), 9th circuit, San Francisco, 1991—. Mem. Nat. Assn. of Women Judges, Calif. Women Lawyers Assn., Women Lawyers of Alameda County, Charles Houston Bar Assn., Alameda County Bar Assn. Office: US Courthouse PO Box 36105 450 Golden Gate Ave Rm 15-5408 San Francisco CA 94102*

HAMILTON, RHODA LILLIAN ROSEN, educator, consultant; b. Chgo., May 8, 1915; d. Reinhold August and Olga (Peterson) Rosen; grad. Moser Coll., Chgo., 1932-33; B.S. in Edn., U. Wis., 1953, postgrad., 1976; M.A.T., Rollins Coll., 1967; postgrad. Ohio State U., 1959-60; postgrad. in clin. psychology Mich. State U., 1971, 76, 79, 80; postgrad. Yale U., 1972, Loma Linda U., 1972; postgrad. in computer mgmt. systems U. Okla., 1976; postgrad. in edn. U. Calif., Berkeley, 1980; m. Douglas Edward Hamilton, Jan. 23, 1936 (div. Feb. 1952); children: Perry Douglas, John Richard. Exec. sec. to pres. Ansul Chem. Co., Marinette, Wis., 1934-36; personnel counselor Burneice Larson's Med. Bur., Chgo., 1954-56 adminstrv. asst. to Ernst C. Schmidt, Lake Geneva, Wis., 1956-58; asso. prof. fin. aid Ohio State U., 1958-60; tchr. English to speakers of other langs., Istanbul, Turkey, 1960-65; counselor Groveland (Fla.) High Sch., 1965-68; guidance counselor and psychol. cons. early childhood edn. Dept. Def. Overseas Dependents Sch., Okinawa, 1968-85; pres. Hamilton Assocs., Groveland, Fla., 1985—; vis. lectr. Okla. State U., 1980; co-owner plumbing, heating bus., Marinette, 1943-49; journalist Rockford (Ill.) Morning Star, 1956-58, Istanbul AP, 1960; lectr. Lake Sumter Community Coll., 1989—. Vol. instr. U.S. citizenship classes, Okinawa, 1971-72. Mem. Fla. Retired Educators, Am. Fedn. Govt. Employees, Phi Delta Gamma. Episcopalian. Clubs: Order Eastern Star (organist Shuri chpt. 1 Japan, life mem. Trillium No. 208 Wis.), Marinette Woman's Club (Wis., pres. 1949-51), Groveland Woman's Club (Fla.). Author poetry on Middle East, 1959-64; Career Awareness, 1978. Office: Hamilton Assocs Cons 255 E Waldo St Groveland FL 34736 also: 2408 Ellsworth Way 1A Frederick MD 21702-3104

HAMILTON, RUTH HELLMANN, design company owner; b. Millboro, S.D., Oct. 15; d. Walter Otto and Laura Ethel (King) Hellmann; m. Gordon Eugene Hamilton, June 11, 1950; children: Kristin Goodnight, Bret Hamilton, Lori O'Toole, Lynnelle Anderson. AB, Nebr. Wesleyan U., Lincoln, 1948; MEd and Humanities, So. Meth. U., 1952. Owner, chief exec. officer Sonoran Desert Designs, Tucson, 1976-91; lectr. Ariz. Desert Mus., Tucson, 1985-86, Tohono Chul Mus., Tucson, 1986, 93, Prescott Coll., Tucson, 1987, Tucson Bot. Gardens, 1985-91, Elderhostel, 1991; tchr. design student classes. Exhibited displays for Old Pueblo Mus. at Foothills Mall, 1987-90; demonstrations of desert designs Ariz. State Conv. Garden Clubs N.Mex., 1987, 89; one-woman shows at Tucson Garden Club, 1988, 90; original designs published by Nat. Coun. Garden Clubs Calendars, 1984, 87, 89, 95. Mem. pub. svcs. bd. KVOA-TV, 1969-74. Mem. Los Cerros Garden Club (pres. 1984-85, 94-95). Home: 7720 N Sendero De Juana Tucson AZ 85718-7517

HAMILTON, SHIRLEY SIEKMANN, arts administrator; b. South Bend, Ind., Aug. 31, 1928; d. George F. and Clarice B. (Rapp) Burdick; m. Max R. Siekmann, June 23, 1951; children: Sheryl, Pamela, David; m. Keith L. Hamilton, Sept. 3, 1983. Student St. Mary's Coll., 1946-47; BA, DePauw U., 1950; postgrad. Ind. U., South Bend. Tchr. public schs., St. Joseph County, Ind., 1950-51, Greencastle, Ind., 1951-52, Ft. Lauderdale, Fla., 1952-53; exec. dir. Michiana Arts and Scis. Council, Inc., South Bend, Ind., 1973-86; tech. asst. cons., adv. panelist Ind. Arts Commn.; treas. Ind. Alliance Arts Councils, 1982. Mem. St. Joseph County Parks and Recreation Bd., 1971-81, park found. bd., 1988—; pres. Mental Health Assn. of St. Joseph County, 1972; St. Joseph County Scholarship Found., 1977-82; Community Found. of St. Joseph County, 1979— (bd. dirs. and grant chmn.); pres., bd. dirs. United Way St. Joseph County, 1981-82; bd. dirs. Meml. Hosp. Found., 1990—, South Bend Regional Mus. Art, 1988—, Friends of Snite Mus. Art, Notre Dame Ind., 1989—, Logan Ctr. Found., 1990—. Recipient Community Service award Michiana Arts and Scis. Council, 1968, Arts award, 1987, Arts Service award, Ind. Assembly of Local Arts Agys., 1987. Mem. Ind. Arts Advs., Ind. Alliance Arts Councils, Nat. Assn. Arts Councils. Club: Jr. League South Bend (pres.). Producer 13 week TV series: Inside Our Schools (Jr. League of South Bend Outstanding Community Service award 1964).

HAMILTON, SUSAN OWENS, transportation company executive, lawyer; b. Birmingham, Ala., Aug. 7, 1951; d. William Lewis and Vonnette (Wilson) Owens; m. M. Raymond Hamilton, June 8, 1974. BA, Auburn U., 1973; JD, Samford U., 1977. Bar: Ala., Fla. Claim agt. Seaboard System R.R. and predecessor cos., Birmingham, Ala., 1977-78; atty. Seaboard System R.R. and predecessor cos., Louisville, 1978-80, claims atty., 1980-81; asst. gen. atty. Seaboard System R.R. and predecessor cos., Jacksonville, Fla., 1981-83, asst. gen. solicitor, 1983-84, gen. mgr. freight claim services, 1984-85; asst. v.p. casualty prevention Chessie System R.R.'s, Balt. and Jacksonville, 1985-86; asst. v.p. freight damage prevention and claims CSX Transp., Jacksonville, 1986-87, asst. v.p. adminstrv. svcs., 1987-90, sr. asst. v.p. adminstrv. svcs., 1990—. Mem. allocations com. United Way, vice chair fund distbn. com., 1991-93, chmn., 1993-94, mem. exec. com., 1992—; mem. Gator Bowl Com., 1993—. Mem. ABA, Jacksonville Bar Assn., Bus. and Profl. Women (pres. Jacksonville chpt. 1984-85), Fla. Bus. and Profl. Women (Outstanding Young Career Woman 1982), Uptown Civitan (bd. dirs. Jacksonville club 1982-84, v.p., pres. elect. 1993, pres. 1993-94). Methodist. Home: 12154 Hidden Hills Dr Jacksonville FL 32225-3653 Office: 500 Water St Jacksonville FL 32202-4422

HAMILTON, VIRGINIA (MRS. ARNOLD ADOFF), author; b. Yellow Springs, Ohio, Mar. 12, 1936; d. Kenneth James and Etta Belle (Perry) H.; m. Arnold Adoff, Mar. 19, 1960; children: Leigh Hamilton, Jaime Levi. Student, Antioch Coll., 1952-55, Ohio State U., 1957-58, New Sch. for Social Research. May Hill Arbuthnot honor lectr., 1992. Author: children's novels Zeely, 1967 (Nancy Block Meml. award Downtown Community Sch. Awards Com.), The House of Dies Drear, 1968 (Edgar Allan Poe award for best juvenile mystery 1969), The Time-Ago Tales of Jadhu, 1969, Planet of Junior Brown, 1971; W.E.B. Dubois: A Biography, 1972; children's novels Time-Ago Lost: More Tales of Jahdu, 1973, M.C. Higgins the Great (John Newbery medal 1974), 1974 (Nat. Book award 1975), Paul Robeson: The Life and Times of a Free Black Man, 1974, Arilla Sun Down, 1976, Illusion and Reality, 1976, The Justice Cycle: Justice and Her Brothers, 1978, Dustland, 1980, Gathering, 1980, Jahdu, 1980, Sweet Whispers, Brother Rush, 1982 (Boston Globe/Horn Book award 1983), The Magical Adventures of Pretty Pearl, 1984, A Little Love, 1984, Junius Over Far, 1985, The People Could Fly, 1985, The Mystery of Drear House, 1987, A White Romance, 1987; editor: Writings of W.E.B. Dubois, 1975, In the Beginning: Creation Stories from Around the World, 1988 (Newbery Honor Book award 1988), Anthony Burns: The Defeat and Triumph of a Fugitive Slave, 1988 (Boston Globe Horn Book award 1988), The Bells of Christmas, 1989, The Darkway: Stories From the Spirit World, 1990, The All Jahdu Storybook, 1991, Drylongso, 1992, Many Thousands Gone: African-Americans from Slavery to Freedom, 1993, Plain City, 1993. Recipient Ohiana Lit. award, 1969, 84, Ohiana Lit. award for body of work, 1981, Coretta Scott King award for fiction, 1980, 85, Regina medal for body of work, 1989, Internat. Hans Christian Anderson Prose award; U.S. nominee for prose Internat. Hans Christian Anderson award, 1992. Address: care Arnold Adoff Agy PO Box 293 Yellow Springs OH 45387-0293

HAMLER, MARY COWLES, school principal; b. N.Y.C., Feb. 25, 1950; d. Stuart Cushman and Miriam Willis (Hoxie) Cowles; m. Frank Richard, July 31, 1981. BS in Edn., Southwest Mo. State U., 1972; MEd, U. Mo., Kansas City, 1975; EdS in Reading, U. Mo., 1981, EdS in Adminstrn., 1991. Cert. dist. level adminstr., Kans. Reading specialist New Haven (Mo.) Pub. Schs., 1972-75, Grandview (Mo.) Pub. Schs., 1975-77; tchr. grade three, reading specialist Sallisaw (Okla.) Pub. Schs., 1977-79; reading specialist Spring Hill (Kans.) Pub. Schs., 1981-89, elem. prin., 1990—; dir. curriculum Spring Hill Pub. Schs., 1992-93. Mem. Kansas City Pub. TV, Kansas City, Mo., KKFI Community Radio Sta., Kansas City, Mo., fundraiser, Am. Heart Assn., Spring Hill, 1993; vol. carpenter for wheel chair ramp. MS Soc., 1994. Mem. Internat. Reading Assn., Nat. Assn. Elem. Sch. Prins., Kans. Assn. Elem. Sch. Prins., ASCD, Kans. Assn. Supervision and Curriculum Devel., Phi Delta Kappa.

HAMLIN, LOUISE ELIZABETH, artist, educator; b. Litchfield, Conn., June 26, 1949; d. Elbert B. and Barbara (Batchelor) H.; m. Gary Lenhart; 1 child, Katherine. BFA, U. Pa., 1972; Student, L'Universite d'Aix-en-Provence, France, 1972-73, N.Y. Studio Sch., Paris and N.Y.C., 1972, 74-75, Skowhegan Sch. for Sculpture, and Painting, Maine, 1977. Various art instr. positions to Vassar Coll., N.Y., 1984-86; art instr. Queens Coll., CUNY, 1986, N.Y. Studio Sch., 1987, Hartwick Coll., N.Y., 1987, Union Coll., N.Y., 1987-89, SUNY, Purchase, 1989-90, Dartmouth Coll., Hanover, N.H., 1990—. One-woman shows include Carleton Coll., St. Paul, Minn., 1994, Blue Mountain Gallery, N.Y.C., 1984, 86, 89, 92, Klein Gallery, Pittsfield, Mass., 1986, 92, River City Arts, White River Junction, Vt., 1992, Washington Art Assn., Conn., 1987, Taft Gallery, Watertown, Conn., 1976, Loomis Gallery, Windsor, Conn., 1975, New Milford Pub. Libr., Conn., 1974; numerous group exhbns. including Dartmouth Coll., 1993, Trenton City Mus., Trenton, N.J., 1993, Bowery Gallery, N.Y.C., others. N.Y. Found. for Arts fellow, 1986, Jr. Faculty fellow Dartmouth Coll., 1994; grantee Ingram Merrill Found., 1985, Mellon Found., 1987; recipient Djerassi Found. Residency award, 1987, Vermont Coun. on Arts Individual award, 1994. Office: Dartmouth Coll Dept Studio Art Hinman Box 6081 Hanover NH 03755

HAMLIN, SONYA B., communications specialist; b. N.Y.C.; d. Julius and Sarah (Saltzman) Borenstein; m. Bruce Hamlin (dec. 1977); children: Ross, Mark (dec. 1992), David. BS, MA, N.Y.U.; HLD (hon.), Notre Dame Coll., 1970. Host arts program Sta. WHDH-TV, Boston, 1963-65; host, producer, writer (syndicated program) Meet the Arts Sta. WGBH-TV, Boston, 1965-68; cultural reporter Sta. WBZ-TV, Boston, 1968-71, TV host, producer The Sonya Hamlin Show, 1970-75; host, producer Sunday Open House program Sta. WCVB-TV, Boston, 1976-80; host, producer, writer Speak Up and Listen program Lifetime Cable Network, N.Y.C., 1982-84; pres. Sonya Hamlin Communications, Boston and N.Y.C., 1977—, Different Drummer Prodns., N.Y.C., 1982-86; pvt. comm. cons., U.S., Can., and Europe, 1977—; adj. lectr. Harvard Grad. Sch., Edn., Cambridge, Mass., 1974-76, Harvard Law Sch., 1977-81, Kennedy Sch. Govt., Harvard U., 1978-79; adj. asst. prof. Boston U. Med. Sch., 1977-80; mem. faculty Nat. Inst. Trial Advocacy, South Bend, Ind., 1977—, U.S. Dept. Justice, Washington, 1979-87, ABA, Chgo., 1979—; chmn. Law/Video Co., N.Y.C. and Waltham, Mass., 1987-92. Author: What Makes Juries Listen, 1985, How to Talk So People Listen, 1988; prodr, dir., writer (films) China: A Different Path, 1979 (Emmy nominee), Paul Revere: What Makes a Hero, 1976, others; contbr. articles to numerous profl. jours. Active Gov. Commn. Status of Women, Mass., 1973-83; campaign co-chair Mass. ERA Campaign, 1975-76; cons. Gov. Michael Dukakis, 1978, Dem. Nat. Party, Washington, 1979; bbd. dirs. mem. nat. vol. action com. United Way, Washington, 1986-91; bd. dirs. Taubman Ctr. Kennedy Sch. Harvard U., 1989—. Recipient Best Program award for Meet the Arts Internat. Ednl. TV Assn., Tokyo, 1969, Ohio State Cultural Reporting award, 1970; named Outstanding Broadcaster New Eng. Broadcasters, Boston, 1973; Sonya Hamlin Day named in her honor Mayor of Boston, 1974.; archive of her works established Boston U. Library, 1983. Mem. Am. Fedn. TV and Radio Artists, Nat. Acad. TV Arts and Scis. (two Emmy nominations).

HAMMACK, GLADYS LORENE MANN, reading specialist, educator; b. Corsicana, Tex., Nov. 15, 1923; d. John Elisha and Maude (Kelly) Mann; m. Charles Joseph Hammack; Sept. 4, 1949;children: Charles Randall, Cynthia Lorain, Kelly Joseph. B in Journalism, U. Tex., 1953; elem. tchr. cert., U. Houston, 1970, MEd, 1974, cert. reading specialist, 1974. Cert. profl. reading specialist, Tex. Tchr. Zion Luth. Sch., Pasadena, Tex., 1964-68, Housman Elem. Sch., Houston, 1970-74, Pine Shadows Elem. Sch., Houston, 1975-76; reading lab. tchr. Spring Br. High Sch., Houston, 1976-82; tchr. St. Mark Luth. Sch., Houston, 1982-88, pvt. tutor and homework study hall tchr., 1988—; mem. Spring Br. Ind. Sch. Dist. Textbook Selection Com., Houston, 1973; field rep. to. student tchrs., U. Houston, 1974; presenter reading workshop, U. Tex., Austin, 1983. Author: (guide) Evaluation of Textbooks, 1974. Del. Tex. Dem. Conv., Austin, 1960. Recipient scholarship, U. Tex. Sports Assn., Austin, 1947. Mem. Tex. State Tchrs. Assn., Tex. Ret. Tchrs. Assn. Lutheran. Home: 8926 Theysen Dr Houston TX 77080

HAMMAN, NANCY ANN, health center executive; b. Toledo, Nov. 16, 1929; d. Raphael Lawrence and Helen Mary (Close) Nusbaum; m. Keith LaVern Hamman, Aug. 12, 1950; children—Kathleen, Robert, Lucina, Karen, Daniel, Edith, Eileen. RN, Mercy Hosp., 1950; BE, U. Toledo, 1981. Pvt. duty nurse Ofcl. Nurses's Registry, Toledo, 1950-52; charge nurse Flower Hosp., Toledo, 1952-55, St. Vincent Hosp., Toledo, 1956-70; supr. health services Bedford Sch., Temperance, Mich., 1970-80; exec. dir. Citizens Health Council, Temperance, 1980—; task force on family planning Mich. Dept. Health, Lansing., 1984; dir. First Am. Bank, Deerfield, Mich. Adv. bd. Sr. Nutrition Program, Monroe, Mich., 1975, Ret. Sr. Vol. Program, Temperance, 1980—, Bedford and Mason Nurses Aid Program, Temperance, 1975-80, Bedford Bus. Voc. Edn., 1980. Mercy Hosp. nursing scholar, 1947-50; recipient Service award Bedford Lions, 1978; Community Service award, Bedford Twp., 1979. Mem. Mich. Primary Care Assn. (bd. dirs. 1980—), Bedford Bus. Assn. (trustee 1983-85), Bus. and Profl. Women's Club (v.p. 1978-80), Ladies Christian Benevolent Assn. (trustee 1955-60). Democrat. Roman Catholic. Club: Bedford Lioness (dir. 1983-85). Home: 955 Dempster St Temperance MI 48182-9275 Office: Citizens Health Coun 8765 Lewis Ave Temperance MI 48182

HAMMATT KAVALOSKI, JANE FAYE, school social worker; b. Dayton, Ohio, Dec. 8, 1941; d. Stanley A. and Louise E. (Potterf) Hanawalt; m. William F. Hammatt, June 26, 1965 (dec. Dec. 1974); children: Amanda, Matthew; m. Vincent C. Kavaloski, June 4, 1978; stepchildren: Joshua, Alainya. BA, Blackburn Coll., 1964; MSW, U. Wis., Milw., 1968. Vol. Peace Corps, Morocco, 1964-66; sch. social worker Madison (Wis.) Met. Sch. Dist., 1974—; tchr. Internat. People's Coll., Denmark, 1989, Poland, Czechoslovakia, UNESCO, Cezch. Tech. U., 1984-85, 91. Co-editor Metanoia Quar., 1984—; contbr. articles to profl. jours. Co-dir. Wis. Ecumenical Partnership for Peace and Justice, 1984—; foster parent Cath. Social Svsc., Madison, 1971-74, Briar Patch Runaway Ctr., Madison, 1971-74, Dane County Social Svcs., Madison, 1971-74; mem. nat. coun. Fellowship of Reconcilation, Nyack, N.Y., 1988-94, Iowa County coord., Dodgeville, 1981—; coord. cmty. edn. project Marquette Neighborhood Assn., Madison, 1979-81; state coord. Pledge of Resistance, Wis., 1986-89; coord., mem. peace dels. to Israel/Occupied Territories, 1989, 90, El Salvador, 1984, 91; coord. environ. stewardship dels. and rainforests of Belize and Panama, 1993, 94. Mem. NASW (Midwest Sch. Social Worker of Yr. 1983), Wis. Sch. Social Workers Assn. (Sch. Social Worker of Yr. 1983). Mem. Soc. of Friends. Home: Rt 3 Box 228E Dodgeville WI 53533

HAMMER, DEBORAH MARIE, librarian; b. Bronx, N.Y., Nov. 16, 1947; d. Ben and Helen (Lorenz) Halprin; m. Mark Stewart Hammer, May 30, 1976; 1 child, Joshua Robert. BA, CCNY, 1968; MLS, Rutgers U., 1969. Cert. libr. N.Y. Gen. asst. info., tel. ref. div. Queens Borough Pub. Libr., 1969-71, gen. asst. popular libr., 1972-80; asst. div. head history, travel & biography Queens Borough Pub. Libr., Jamaica, N.Y., 1972-81; div. head history, travel & biography Queens Borough Pub. Libr., 1981-92, div. mgr. social scis., 1992—. Libr. Temple Emanuel, New Hyde Park, N.Y., 1987. Democrat. Office: Queens Borough Pub Libr 89-11 Merrick Blvd Jamaica NY 11432

HAMMER, SUSAN W., mayor; b. Monrovia, Calif., Dec. 21, 1938; d. James Nathan and Katrine (Krutzsch) Walker; m. Philip Hammer, Sept. 4, 1960; children: Philip, Hali, Matthew. BA in History, U. Calif., Berkeley, 1960. Svc. rep. Pacific Telephone Co., Berkeley, 1960-61; staff asst. Peace Corps, Washington, 1962-63; councilwoman City of San Jose, Calif., 1980-81, 83-90, spl. asst. to mayor, 1981-82, vice mayor, 1985-87, mayor, 1991—. Bd. dirs. San Jose Mus. Art, 1971-90,, pres., 1978-80; mem. governing bd. NCCJ, 1978—; mem. adv. bd. Community Found. Santa Clara County, 1978—; mem. Santa Clara County Transp. Com., 1976-77, Santa Clara County Juvenile Justice Commn., 1974-80, San Jose Fine Arts Comm., 1980, Victim-Witness Adv. Bd., 1977—, Children's Health Coun. San Jose, 1981-89, Santa Clara Valley Leadership Program, 1986—, Childrens Shelter Project, 1991—, Am. Leadership Forum, 1992—; past chmn. parents adv. com. Trace Sch. Recipient Rosalie M. Stern Community Svc. award U. Calif., 1975, Disting. Citizen of San Jose award Exch. Club, 1979, Investment in Leadership award Coro Found., 1985, Tzedek award for honor, compassion and community svc. Temple Emanu-El, 1987, Recognition award YWCA, Santa Clara County, 1989, resolution of commendation Assn. for Responsible Alcohol Control, 1990, Woman of Achievement award The Women's Fund, 1990, Dox Quixote award Nat. Hispanic U., 1991, Friends of Bay Area Mcpl. Elections Com. award, 1991. Democrat. Office: Office of Mayor 801 N 1st St Rm 600 San Jose CA 95110*

HAMMERSTROM, BEVERLY SWOISH, state representative; b. Mineral Wells, Tex., Mar. 28, 1944; d. William Graham and Marjorie Wirth (Lillis) Swoish; m. Don Preston Hammerstrom, June 25, 1966 (div. Oct. 1976); children: Todd Preston, Rory Scott. BA, Adrian Coll., 1966; MPA, U. Toledo, 1994. Cert. mcpl. clk. Tchr. Geneva (N.Y.) Pub. Schs., 1966-69; substitute tchr. Darien (Wis.) Pub. Schs., 1970-71; tchr. Bedford Coop. Nursery Sch., Lambertville, Mich., 1975; retail mgr., buyer Gallerie, Toledo, 1975-78, Personal Touch, Toledo, 1978-80; clk. Bedford Township, Temperance, Mich., 1980-92; state rep. State of Mich., Lansing, 1993—; bd. dirs. Family Med. Ctr., Temperance; emergency mgmt. bd. Washtenaw County, Ypsilanti, Mich., 1993—, Monroe (Mich.) County, 1993—. Mem. Mich. Assn. Clks. (life, pres. 1990-91). Republican. Roman Catholic. Home: 1183 Oakmont Dr Temperance MI 48182 Office: Mich Ho Rep PO Box 30014 Lansing MI 48909

HAMMERT, DOROTHY SAVAGE, investment company executive; b. Hartshorne, Okla.; d. Eugene Bertrand and Lillian Vivian (Graves) Savage; m. Walter Scott Hammert Jr., Sept. 2, 1972; children: Diane Welker, Cindy Heinze, Warren, June. BA in English, U. Okla., 1951. Cert. profl. sec. Sr. sec. Stanolind Oil and Gas Co., Oklahoma City, Okla., 1951-58, Pan Am. Petroleum Corp., Oklahoma City, Okla., 1963-67; exec. sec. to chmn. of bd., chief exec. officer Benham-Blair and Affiliates, Oklahoma City, Okla., 1967-81; dist. mgr., area ednl. cons. World Book Ednl. Products, Oklahoma City, Okla., 1987—; owner Practical Publishing Co., Oklahoma City, Okla., 1991—. Author: Rights are Responsibilities, 1991. V.p. Oklahoma City chpt. Freedoms Found. at Valley Forge, 1991-92. Named Sec. of Yr. Nat. Secs. Assn., 1979, Okla. Mother's Assn. Mother of Yr., 1994. Mem. ABWA (yearbook chmn. 1991), Synergy Bus. Group (pres. 1987-88, 94), Women's Bus. Network (mem. chmn. 1991), Psi Psi Psi (pres. 1979-80, 93-94), Alpha Chi Omega (sect. chmn. 1987-88), Joi de Vie Club (pres. 1993-94). Republican. Episcopalian. Home: 1616 Westminster Pl Oklahoma City OK 73120-1230 Office: Practical Pub Co 1616 Westminster Pl Oklahoma City OK 73120-1230

HAMMES, TERRY MARIE, advertising, public relations and marketing executive; b. Chgo., Mar. 27, 1955; d. Howard John and Lorna Marie (Jeans) H. BFA with honors, U. Miami, Coral Gables, Fla., 1976; MBA in Internat. Bus., St. Thomas U., Miami, 1992. Lic. real estate broker, Fla. Pres. Hammes Advt. Agy., Coral Gables, Fla., 1978—; pres., broker Hammes Realty Mgmt. Corp., Coral Gables, 1986—; pres. Pro-Motion Media, Inc., Coral Gables, 1990-92; external bank dir. 1st Fla. Savings, FSB, 1990-93; v.p. Ponce de Leon Devel. Assn., Coral Gables, 1990-91, bd. dirs. One-woman show includes U. Miami, Fla., 1975; juried art show Lowe Art Mus., 1976, Internat. Erotic Art Show, Miami Beach, 1995. Bd. dirs. Young Dems., Dade County, 1982-86; trustee Miami Youth Mus., 1990—; mem. Leadership Miami, 1988—, mem. exec. com., co-chair comms., 1990—, chair pub. rels. and comms. com., 1991-93; bd. dirs. Crime Stoppers, 1992—. Named Miss Minn. Coun. of State Socs., 1975, Valley Forge Freedom Found. scholar, 1971; recipient Fla. award for mktg. excellence in best print campaign Best Corp. Campaign, Best Print Ad, Best Spl. Event, Best Collateral, 1989, 1991 Up and Comer award for advt. Price Waterhouse/South Fla. Mag., 1991. Mem. Nat. Assn. Women Bus. Owners (pub. rels. chmn. 1985-89), Builders Assn. South Fla. (editor, publisher 1986-87), Advt. Fedn. Greater Miami, Coral Gables C. of C., Greater Miami C. of C., Orange Key, Alpha Lambda Delta. Democrat. Home: 460 Hardee Rd Coral Gables FL 33146-3555 Office: Hammes Advt Inc 896 S Dixie Hwy Coral Gables FL 33146-2604

HAMMOCK, NANCY ANN, realtor; b. Chgo., June 5, 1955; d. Sidney and Mary (Coscino) Feldner; m. Harold Gene Hammock, June 24, 1973; children: Julie Ann, Melissa Mary, Christopher Michael. Grad., Real Estate Inst., 1990. Cert. residential specialist. Realtor assoc. Century 21 Hallmark, Lyons, Ill., 1985-89; broker assoc. Re/Max Ptnrs., Berwyn, Ill., 1989—. Mem. Women's Coun. Realtors (sec. 1991, pres.-elect 1992, pres. 1993). Home: 6507 Quincy Dr Willowbrook IL 60521 Office: Re/Max Ptnrs 6420 W Cermak Rd Berwyn IL 60402

HAMMON, ELIZABETH FARMER, small business owner, nurse; b. Epes, Ala., Mar. 7, 1936; d. Sidney and Ollie Bea (Brassfield) Farmer; m. Ernest Austin, Mar. 27, 1959 (div. 1986); children: Ernest Jr., Edward B., Erin E.; m. Colin Paul Hammon, Dec. 27, 1986. BA in Nursing, U. S.C., 1955. RN, S.C. Nurse Columbia (S.C.) Hosp., 1955-56; evening supv. McHarry Med. Sch., Nashville, 1956-57; recovery rm. nurse Freidman Hosp., Washington, 1957-60; antique gift shop owner Alexandria, Va., 1978-80; mall owner Alexandria, 1980-85, Antique Emporium, Annandale, Va., 1985—. Fund raiser The Urban League, Washington, 1960-65, Dems. for Pres. Johnson, Washington, 1964; active NAACP. Roman Catholic. Home: 2590 Golden Pleasant Pl Catlett VA 22019

HAMMON, KATY JO, research scientist; b. Dallas, May 29, 1938; d. James Haskell and Irma La Dell (Belcher) Coyle; m. Neal Clifton Miller, Dec. 20, 1961 (dec. Aug. 1969); 1 child, Bobbie Jean; m. William Stanley Hammon Jr., Aug. 15, 1974; children: Rebecca Diane, William Stanley III. BA, North Tex. State Coll., 1961; MA, North Tex. State U., 1963; postgrad., Baylor U., 1963-65, U. Calif., Berkeley, 1966, U. Tex. Southwestern Med. Sch., 1967-69. Libr. Southwestern Med. Sch., Dallas, 1963, rsch. technician, 1965-75; diagnostic bacteriologist Wadley Rsch. Inst., Dallas, 1963-65; instr. Ctrl. Tex. Coll., Kileen, 1975; rsch. assoc., rsch. scientist U. Tex. Health Sci. Ctr., Dallas, 1975—. Contbr. articles to profl. jours. Coun. coord. Girl Scouts USA, 1985—; explorer advisor Boy Scouts Am., 1991—. Mem. Electron Microscopy Soc. Am., Tex. Soc. for Electron Microscopy, Am. Soc. for Cell Biology, Sigma Xi. Methodist. Home: 4525 Ancilla Garland TX 75042 Office: U Tex Southwestern Med Sch 5323 Harry Hines Blvd Dallas TX 75235

HAMMOND, ALICE FAY, military officer; b. Alexandria, La., Apr. 10, 1949; d. James and Annie Mae (Edwards) H.; 1 child, Noland James. Student, Southern U., 1967-68; AA, Spokane Falls Community Coll., 1975; BA in Human Services, Ft. Wright Coll., 1977; MEd, Whitworth Coll., 1977; PhD in Law (hon.), PhD in Humanities (hon.). Enlisted USAF, 1973, advanced through grades to capt., 1983, retired, 1993; dir. La. Parish Civil Svc. and Personnel, Alexandria, 1993—. Supporter St. Jude Children's Research Hosp. 1986—, sponsor Korean Ophanage, Osan 1983; bd. dirs. Am. Heart Assn., 1981-82, also supporter 1981—, Am. Cancer Soc., 1980-82, also telephon chmn. 1981.; Named Outstanding Young Woman Am., 1984, Woman of Yr., Colo., 1984. Mem. NAFE, NAACP, Nat. Coun. Negro Women, Panama City (Fla.) Jr. Women's Club, Daus. of Isis, Order Ea. Star, La. Wildlife Assn., Biog. Inst. Am., La. Ctrl. C. of C., Delta Sigma Theta (hon.). Democrat. Methodist. Home: PO Box 8552 Alexandria LA 71306-1552

HAMMOND, CAROL ELAINE, real estate agent; b. Decatur, Ind., Mar. 2, 1948; d. Clifford Milton and Elizabeth Marie (Imler) Hoverman; m. David Lee Hammond, Jan. 6, 1968; children: Michael, Mark. BSEd summa cum laude, Ind. U.-Purdue, 1984, MSEdn., 1987. Cert. sch. counselor, Ind. Tchr. Ft. Wayne (Ind.) Christian Sch., 1984-86; adminstrv. asst. Summit Christian Coll., Ft. Wayne, 1987-88; sch. counselor Luth. Social Svcs., Ft. Wayne, 1988-89, East Allen County Schs., New Haven, Ind., 1989-90; real estate agent Sullivan Assocs Realtors, Ft. Wayne, 1993-94; real estate agent and new constrn. rep. Realty World, Kees, Ft. Wayne, 1994—. Mem. Ft. Wayne Realtors, Ind. Realtors. Republican. Office: Realty World Kees 619 Broadway New Haven IN 46774

HAMMOND, DEANNA LINDBERG, linguist; b. Calgary, Alta., Can., May 31, 1942; d. Albin William and Emma Lou (Thompson) Lindberg; m. Jerome J. Hammond, 1968 (div. 1980). B.A., Wash. State U., 1964; M.A., Ohio U., 1968; Ph.D., Georgetown U., 1977; student summer sch., U. Ariz., Guadalajara, Portland State U. With Peace Corps., Colombia, 1964-66; prof. English Universidad Industrial, Bucaramanga, Colombia, 1966-67; tchr. English, Spanish Pullman High Sch., Wash., 1969-74; lectr. Georgetown U., Washington, 1974-77; dir. summer sch. program Georgetown U., Quito, Ecuador, 1977; head lang. services Congl. Research Services Library of Congress, Washington, 1977—; part-time faculty George Mason U.; mem. adv. bd. traduction, terminologie, redaction U. Que., Can.; pres. Interlingua Inst., Westchester, N.Y. Translator: Psychological Operations in Guerrilla Warfare. Active Friends of Colombia. Recipient Community Service award Sec. Califano, 1978. Mem. Am. Translators Assn. (guest editor ATA Scholarly Monograph series 1994, Gode medal 1992, past pres.), Nat. Coun. Returned Peace Corps Vols. Washington, Libr. Congress Profl. Assn., Nat. Peace Corps. Assn., Libr. Congress Profl. Assn., Libr. Congress Hispanic Cultural Soc., Assn. for Machine Translation in Ams. (bylaws com., edn. com.), Am. Assn. Tchrs. Spanish and Portuguese, Mid-Am. Translators Assn. (life, chmn. nominating com. 1994), Zonta Internat. (pres. Alexandria club, mem. scholarship com., internat. rels. com., bd. dirs., del. internat. conv. Detroit 1994), Carolina Assn. of Translators and Intrepreters, Phi Beta Kappa. Democrat. Home: 3560 S George Mason Dr Alexandria VA 22302-1034 Office: Libr of Congress Congl Rsch Lang Svcs Washington DC 20540

HAMMOND, DEBORAH LYNN, lay worker; b. Olney, Md., Feb. 12, 1958; d. Cornelius Dennis Sr. and Beverly Laura (Dunn) H. AA in Gen. Studies, Catonsville C.C. Sec. Mt. Zion United Meth. Ch., Ellicott City, Md., 1980—; with Balt. Gas Electric Co., Pasadena, Md. Home: 3668B Mt Ida Dr Ellicott City MD 21043-4530 Office: Mt Zion United Meth Ch 8565 Main St # 81 Ellicott City MD 21043-4309

HAMMOND, DORIS BLERSCH, school counselor, educator, therapist, author; b. Cin., Jan. 27, 1933; d. Ernest Morris and Dorothy (Robisch) Blersch; m. H. Ted Hammond, May 30, 1953; children: Kim, Darcy, Lauri. BS in Edn., U. Cin., 1954; MA in Counseling, Marshall U., 1975; PhD in Counseling, U. Ga., 1979. Cert. tchr., profl. counselor, guidance counselor, sex counselor, gerontologist. Tchr. various states, 1954-77; guidance counselor Buffalo Pub. Schs., 1979-80; assoc. prof. psychology D'Youville Coll., Buffalo, 1980-87; dir. Sr. Vols. in the Schs., Buffalo, 1981-86; dir. MS in gerontology D'Youville Coll., Buffalo, 1985-87; counselor Aiken (S.C.) County Schs., 1987-93; pvt. practice as therapist; cons. ctr. for study of aging SUNY, Buffalo, 1980-81; adj. prof. U. S.C., Aiken. Author: My Parents Never Had Sex, 1987; co-author two books; contbr. articles to profl. jours.; developer Wise Outrageous Women. Dir. Sr. Vols. in the Schs., Buffalo, 1980-87; cons. ARC, Buffalo, 1986-87; bd. dirs., pres. Mental Health Assn. Aiken County, Aiken, 1988-94; adv. com. Salvation Army, Buffalo, 1981-82; v.p. mgmt. com. YWCA, Buffalo, 1984-86, bd. dirs., Flint, Mich., 1967; pres. Newcomers' Club, Flint, 1966. Recipient Intergenerational award Nat. Sch. Vol. Program Inc., Alexandria, Va.,1983, Achievement award Vol. Action Ctr., Buffalo, 1984. Mem. AAUW, Bus. and Profl. Women, Am. Assn. for Counseling & Devel., S.C. Counselors' Assn., Understanding Aging Inc., Nat. Sch. Vol. Program Inc. Home: 611 Medinah Dr Aiken SC 29803-5948 Office: 1310 Pine Log Rd Aiken SC 29803

HAMMOND, JUDITH ANNE, family nurse practitioner; b. Newburgh, N.Y., Jan. 2, 1945; d. Barney and Violet (Cervoni) Carfarone; m. Richard R. Hammond; children: Michael, Teresa. Diploma, St. Francis Hosp. Sch. Nursing, Poughkeepsie, N.Y., 1966; BSN cum laude, Mt. St. Mary Coll., Newburgh, 1982; MS in Family Primary Care, Pace U., 1990. RN, cert. nurse practitioner in family health, sch. nurse-tchr. Staff nurse St. Luke's Hosp., Newburgh, 1966-69; pvt. duty nursing, 1974-75; sch. health nurse Mt. St. Mary Coll., Newburgh, 1976-79; occupational health nurse IBM Corp., Poughkeepsie, 1984-85, 87-88; nurse practitioner, sch. nurse-tchr. Newburgh Enlarged City Sch. Dist., 1989—; adj. instr. Dutchess Community Coll., Poughkeepsie, 1988-89, coord. nursing/health-related program, 1989. Mem. ANA, N.Y. State Nurses Assn., Nat. Assn. Sch. Nurses, N.Y. State Coalition of Nurse Practitioners, Am. Acad. Nurse Practitioners, Sigma Theta Tau Internat. (Mu Epsilon chpt., Zeta Omega chpt.).

HAMMOND, JUDITH HAWKINS, high school counselor; b. Fort Payne, Ala., Feb. 11, 1943; d. R. Gladstone and Nell M. (O'Shields) Hawkins; m. Al M. Hammond, Mar. 29, 1963; 1 child, R. Matt. BS, Troy State U., 1967; MS, Jacksonville State U., 1975. Cert. sch. psychometrist, Ala. Sci. tchr. Eufaula (Ala.) High Sch., 1967-68, Talladega (Ala.) High Sch., 1968-70; counselor Valley Head (Ala.) High Sch., 1975-80; psychometrist DeKalb County Schs., Fort Payne, Ala., 1980-85; counselor Fort Payne (Ala.) High Sch., 1985—. Sun. sch. tchr. First Bapt. Ch., Fort Payne, 1993-94. Mem. NEA, Ala. Edn. Assn., Fort Payne Tchrs. Assn., Ala. Counselor Assn., Alpha Delta Kappa Ednl. Sorority (ACT State Adv. Coun. sec.). Baptist. Office: Fort Payne High Sch 201 45th St NE Fort Payne AL 35967-4011

HAMMOND, KAREN SMITH, marketing professional, paralegal; b. Baton Rouge, Dec. 20, 1954; d. James Wilbur Smith and Carolyn (May) Carper; m. Ralph Edwin Hammond, Dec. 17, 1985. Student, La. State U., 1973-75, Colo. Women's Coll., 1976; BJ, U. Colo., 1978; cert. paralegal, U. Tex., 1981. Newspaper reporter Lakewood (Colo.) Sentinel, 1978; paralegal Office U.S. Atty. No. Dist. Tex.; sales rep. Arlington Citizen Jour. newspaper, 1979-80; legal asst. Oscar H. Mauzy Atty.-at-Law, Dallas, 1981; editor Ennis (Tex.) Press, 1981-82; sales rep. VEU Subscription TV, Dallas, 1983-84; comml. account rep. U.S. Telecom, Dallas, 1984; with The Movie Channel/Showtime, 1985; mktg. rep. Allnet Comm., Dallas, 1985-87, ChemLawn Svcs. Inc., Plano, Tex., 1992, Accuroof, 1994, Diversified Info. Svcs., Plano, 1994, Elite Roofing, Plano, 1994—; owner Smith, Hammond & Assocs., Dallas, 1986—; advt. sales rep. Legal Asst. Today Mag., 1987; sales rep. Telecable Inc., Richardson, Tex., 1988-91; account exec. Brewer Comm., Carrollton, Tex., 1988-89, Plano (Tex.) Cellular, 1989-90; triex agt. Pkwy. Pontiac, Dallas, 1983-86; free lance writer Dallas Metro mag., 1991—. Bus. writer Mid-Cities Daily News, 1981. Campaign mgr. Mark Bielamowicz for Mayor, Cedar Hill, Tex., 1979; active campaigns Martin Frost for U.S. Congress, Dallas, 1978, Jimmy Carter for Pres., Ft. Worth, 1980, Ann Richards for Gov., Tex., 1990. Mem. NAFE, Women in Communications (fin. com. 1979), Dallas Assn. Legal Assts., Soc. Profl. Journalist, Dallas C. of C., Plano C. of C. Democrat. Home: 3500 Hillridge Dr Apt 118 Plano TX 75074-4367 Office: Elife Roofing 555 Republic Dr Plano TX 75074

HAMMOND, LINDA, artist; b. Dallas, Jan. 11, 1938; d. Rorie Emmitt and Mary Jane (Alexander) Cowden; m. Weldon Woolf Hammond, Aug. 3, 1963; children: Weldon Woolf III, Rory Cowden. BA magna cum laude, So. Meth. U., 1960. Exhibited in one-woman shows in San Antonio, 1984, 86, 93; group shows include Rocky Mountain Nat. Watercolor Soc., Golden, Colo., 1989, We. Fedn. Watercolor Socs., Corpus Christi, 1991, Sun City (Ariz.) Art Mus., 1994; Soc. Layerists in Multi-Media shows, San Antonio, 1992, Nat. Watercolor Soc., Fullerton, Calif., 1994—, Bee County Coll., Beeville, Tex., 1994, Bradford Coll., Mass., 1994, U. Ark. Fayetteville, 1994; represented in permanent collection at San Antonio Art League. Docent emeritus McNay Mus. Art, San Antonio, 1984—; active San Antonio Art League. Recipient Onderdonk award, 1991, Contbrs. award, 1993, Betty Maddux award, 1994. Mem. Nat. Watercolor Soc. (signature mem.), Tex. Watercolor Soc. (signature mem., pres. 1990-92, purchase prize 1992), San Antonio Watercolor Group (bd. dirs., membership chmn., bronze medal 1992, silver medal 1993), Soc. of layerists in Multi-Media, San Antonio Symphony Assn., San Antonio Art League, Tex. Fine Arts Assn., Hill Country Arts Found., S.W. craft Ctr., Club Giraud, Zeta Tau Alpha. Home: 4 Lazy Ln San Antonio TX 78209

HAMMOND, LOU RENA CHARLOTTE, public relations executive; b. Muenster, Tex., Sept. 3, 1939; d. Louis Martin and Regina L. (Schoech) Wolf; m. Christopher Weymouth Hammond, Sept. 6, 1964; 1 child, Stephen. BA, U. Houston, 1962. Rep. pub. rels. Pan Am. Airways, N.Y.C., 1966-76, mgr. pub. rels., 1977-79, dir. pub. rels., 1980-81, dir. pub. affairs, 1981; pres., ptnr. Taylor and Hammond, N.Y.C., 1981-84; prin., pres. Lou Hammond and Assocs., N.Y.C., 1984—. Editor: (calendar) Avenue mag., 1976-79. Mem. Women's Bd. of Madison Sq. Boys and Girls Club, N.Y.C. Opera Guild; corp. adv. bd. Longwood Coll. Recipient Matrix award in pub. rels., 1992, Winthrop W. Grice award Hotel Sales and Mktg. Assoc. Internat., 1992, Inside PR Mag.'s All-Star award, 1992. Mem. Soc. Am. Travel Writers, Fashion Group, Assn. Better N.Y., Les DAmes de Escoffier, Women's Forum, Women Execs. in Pub. Rels., Doubles Club. Roman Catholic. Office: Lou Hammond & Assocs Inc 39 E 51st St New York NY 10022-5916

HAMMOND, PATRICIA FLOOD, lawyer; b. Racine, Wis., Aug. 29, 1948; d. Francis James Flood and Shirley (Osterholt) Erickson; children: Bradley D. Mortensen, Erin N. Mortensen. Student, Wis. State U., Oshkosh, 1966-69, Alverno Coll., West Allis, 1973-74. Bar: Va.1985, U.S. Dist. Ct. (ea. dist.) Va. 1988. Br. dir. Am. Heart Assn., Manassas, Va., 1977-85; attorney Manassas, Va., 1985--; ptnr. Smith, Hudson, Hammond and Alston, Manassas, Va.; mem. VBA-VSB joint com. on alternative dispute resolution. Contbr. articles to newspapers. Mem. ABA, ACLU, ATLA, Nat. Abortion and Reproductive Rights Action League, Va. State Bar Assn., Prince William County Bar Assn. (treas., pres. 1991). Democrat. Episcopalian. Office: Smith Hudson Hammond Alston 9403 Grant Ave Manassas VA 22110-5509

HAMMOND-KOMINSKY, CYNTHIA CECELIA, optometrist; b. Dearborn, Mich., Sept. 1, 1957; d. Andrew and Angeline (Laorno) Kominsky; m. Theodore Glen Hammond, Sept. 21, 1985. Student Oakland U., Rochester, Mich., 1976-77; OD magna cum laude, Ferris Coll. Optometry, 1981. Lic. optometrist, Mich. Intern, Optometric Inst. and Clinic of Detroit, 1980, Ferris State Coll., Big Rapids, Mich., 1980, Jackson Prison (Mich.), 1981; assoc. in pvt. practice, Warren, Mich., 1981-82; optometrist Pearle Vision Ctr., Sterling Heights, Mich., 1982-87, K-Mart Optical Ctr., Sterling Heights, 1982-87, Royal Optical, Sterling Heights, 1988—; provided eye care to nursing homes, Mt. Clemens, Mich. Inventer binocular low vision aid device. Avocations: music, sports, clogging, gardening, antique crystal. Home: 47626 Cheryl Ct Shelby Township MI 48315-4708 Office: Royal Optical Lakeside Mall 14300 Lakeside Circle Sterling Heights MI 48313

HAMNER, SUZANNE LEATH, history educator; b. Ft. Worth, Feb. 29, 1940; d. Roland Martin and Mabel Lois (Hall) Leath; m. W. Easley Hamner, June 18, 1961; children: Janine Suzanne, Michael Edward. BA summa cum laude, Meredith Coll., Raleigh, N.C., 1961; MA, Tulane U., New Orleans, 1964. Teaching asst. Tulane U., New Orleans, 1963-64, 65-66; instr. history Coll. Liberal Arts Northeastern U., Boston, 1966-71, lectr. history Univ. Coll., 1972-73, 74-75; lectr. history Coll. Arts and Scis. and Univ. Coll. Coll. Arts and Scis., Boston, 1985—; sr. lectr. U. Coll., 1985—. Contbg. editor Reclaiming Our Global Heritage, Vol. I and Vol. II, 1990. Mem. adv. com. Follow Through Program, Cambridge (Mass.) Sch. Dept., 1977-79; treas., v.p. adv. bd. Buckingham Browne & Nichols Sch., Cambridge, 1980-86; clk., bd. dirs., adv. bd. Cambridge Civic Assn., 1976—; treas. Alice Wolf Election Com., City Coun., Cambridge, 1979—; overseer Handel & Haydn Soc., Boston, 1989—; trustee Chorus pro Musica, 1993—; mem. adv. com. Meml. Ch., Harvard U., 1992—. Woodrow Wilson Found. fellow, Princeton, N.J., 1961-62; Tulane U. scholar, 1962-64. Mem. Am. Hist. Assn., New Eng. Hist. Assn., Phi Alpha Theta. Democrat. Home: 3 Ellery Sq Cambridge MA 02138-4227 Office: Northeastern U History Dept 360 Huntington Ave Boston MA 02115-5096

HAMOR, KATHY VIRGINIA, consultant; b. Port Jervis, N.Y., Aug. 2, 1957; d. John Barry and Grace Marion (Carpenter) H. BA, Elmira Coll., 1979; MPA, U. S.C., 1983. Paralegal Bergson, Borkland, Margolis & Adler, Washington, 1979-81; presdl. mgmt. intern U.S. Customs Svc., Washington, 1983-85, project mgr., 1986-88, pub. affairs officer, 1989-90, chief press ops. br., 1991-92; cons., lobbyist Mehl & Pickens Assocs., Inc., Washington, 1992-94; pres. Capital Concepts, Washington, 1994—. Home: 4535 28th Rd S # A Arlington VA 22206-3372

HAMPL, MARY NOTERMANN, materials agent; b. Mpls., Feb. 3, 1945; d. Joseph and Fern Irene (Ladwig) Little; m. Richard L. Notermann, Aug. 2, 1968 (div. July 1981); children: Jennifer Anne, Jason Richard; m. Werner Heinz Hampl, July 6, 1986; stepchildren: Matthew H., Carrie Elizabeth. BA, U. Minn., 1974. Caseworker Outreach Ctr. Retarded Citizens, Mpls., 1974-75; exec. dir. South Side Svc. Retarded Citizens, Mpls., 1975-79; material control adminstr. Honeywell, Inc., Mpls., 1979-81; sr. buyer, planner NBI, Inc., Boulder, Colo., 1981-85; materials mgr. Zymacom, Inc., Westford, Mass., 1985-88; materials purchasing Roll Systems, Inc., Burlington, Mass., 1989-91; purchasing mgr. Medisense, Inc., Waltham, Mass., 1991—; sec. Reubin Lindh Day Care Ctr., Mpls., 1977-79. Mem. LWV, Am. Assn. Purchasing Mgmt., Am. Prodn. & Inventory Control Soc. (cert.), Mensa. Home: 17 Arborwood Dr Burlington MA 01803-3816 Office: Medisense Inc 266 2nd Ave Waltham MA 02154-1102

HAMPSON, MARY JOAN, microbiologist; b. Buffalo, Apr. 18, 1947; d. Allan James and Marian Anita (Tripodi) Williams; children: Augustus, Rebecca. BS, Quinnipiac Coll., Hamden, Conn., 1972; MBA, U. New Haven, 1993. With Miles Inc., West Haven, Conn., 1976-93; mgr. quality assurance standards Miles Inc., 1984-93; dir. quality assurance Schein Pharm., Carmel, N.Y., 1993—; cons. in field. Bd. dirs. Friends of Orch. New England, New Haven, 1985-86, treas., 1986-90. Mem. Am. Soc. Microbiology, Soc. Indsl. Microbiology, Perenteral Drug Assn., Artspace (bd. dirs., v.p. fin., pres. 1988-94), Jr. League, Yale Figure Skating Club (pres., treas., bd. dirs. 1984-90), New Haven Symphony Orch. (bd. dirs. 1991-93). Republican. Roman Catholic. Office: Schein Pharm 1033 Stoneleigh Rd Carmel NY 10512

HAMPTON, ANNA CHODER, psychologist; b. Rovno, Poland, July 6, 1940; came to U.S., 1963; d. David and Klara (Silberberg) Choder; m. Kenneth Robert Hampton, June 14, 1966; children: Ruth Joan, Rachel Claire. BA, Hebrew U., Jerusalem, Israel, 1963; PhD in Clin. Psychology, U. Minn., 1969. Psychometrist, interviewer Psychol. Assessment Unit Israeli Armed Forces, 1958-60, regional head, 1959-60; rsch. psychologist St. Louis Park (Minn.) Pub. Schs., 1967-68; clin. psychologist Student Health Svc. U. Minn., 1968-69; clin. psychologist Hamm Meml. Psychiat. Clinic, 1969-81, sr. psychologist, 1981-84, coord. cognitive behavior therapy program and staff tng., 1979-84; postdoctoral tng. in cognitive behavior therapy Hamm Clinic/U. Minn., 1979-82, postdoctoral tng. in psychoanalytic therapy, 1983-84; dir. psychol. svcs. Obesity and Eating Disorders program Hennepin County Med. Ctr., Mpls., 1991-92; pvt. practice clin. psychology Mpls., 1981—; instr. dept. psychology U. Minn., 1965-66, clin. asst. prof., 1975-84; co-founder, mem. faculty Psychotherapy Tng. Inst., Inc., 1984—; mem. community faculty, dept. human svcs. Met. State U., 1984—; mem. edn. com. Midwest Health Network, 1987-88; cons. in field. Sgt. Israeli Def. Forces, 1958-60. Recipient Awards for Acad. Excellence, Hebrew U.; John Cowles fellow U. Minn., 1965, Fgn. Students Tuition scholar, 1964-65. Mem. APA, Assn. for Advancement of Behavior Therapy, Soc. for Exploration of Psychotherapy Integration, Am. Group Psychotherapy Assn., Minn. Psychol. Assn. (edn. and tng. com. 1987-92, exec. coun. 1990-92), Minn. Women Psychologists (founding steering com. 1977-78), , Minn. Psychologists in Pvt. Practice, Minn. Group Psychotherapy Soc. Office: 69 Arthur Ave SE Minneapolis MN 55414-3440

HAMPTON, CAROL MCDONALD, religious organization administrator, educator, historian; b. Oklahoma City, Sept. 18, 1935; d. Denzil Vincent and Mildred Juanita (Cussen) McDonald; m. James Wilburn Hampton, Feb. 22, 1958; children: Jaime, Clayton, Diana, Neal. BA, U. Okla., 1957, MA, 1973, PhD, 1984. Teaching asst. U. Okla., Norman, 1976-81; instr. U. of Sci. and Arts of Okla., Chickasha, 1981-84; coord. Consortium for Grad. Opportunities for Am. Indians, U. Calif., Berkeley, 1985-86; trustee Ctr. of Am. Indian, Oklahoma City, 1981—; vice chmn. Nat. Com. on Indian Work, Episc. Ch., 1986; field officer Native Am. Ministry, 1986-94, field officer for congl. ministries, 1994—; mem. nat. coun. Chs. Racial Justice Working Group, 1990—, co-convenor, 1991-93, convenor, 1993—. Contbr. articles to profl. jours. Trustee Western History Collections, U. Okla., Okla. Found. for the Humanities, 1983-86; mem. bd. regents U. Sci. and Arts Okla., 1989—; bd. dirs. Okla. State Regents for Higher Edn., mem. adv. com. on social justice; mem. World Coun. of Chs. Program to Combat Racism, Geneva, 1985-91; bd. dirs. Caddo Tribal Coun., Okla., 1976-82. Recipient Okla. State Human Rights award, 1987; Francis C. Allen fellow, Ctr. for the History of Am. Indian, 1983. Mem. Western History Assn., Western Social Sci. Assn., Orgn. of Am. Historians, Am. Hist. Assn., Okla. Hist. Soc., Assn. Am. Indian Historians (founding mem. 1981—). Democrat. Episcopalian. Club: Jr. League (Oklahoma City). Avocation: travel. Home: 1414 N Hudson Ave Oklahoma City OK 73103-3721 Office: Episcopal Ch Congl Ministry 924 N Robinson Ave Oklahoma City OK 73102-5814

HAMPTON, JOAN MARSHELLE, insurance claims adjuster; b. Jacksonville, Fla., Aug. 15, 1958; d. Raymond Howard and Elizabeth (Heinke) H.; m. Irvine Keith Furman, Feb. 14, 1990 (div. Apr. 1993). Student, Fla. State U., 1976-77; cert. in gen. ins., Ins. Inst. Am., Phila., 1990; ed. resdl. bldg. damage estimation, Vale Nat. Tng. Ctr., Mechanicsburg, Pa., 1992. Lic. co. employer adjuster, Fla. Ind. multi-line claims adjuster Ins. Svcs. and Investigations, Jacksonville, 1979-82; claims examiner Fla. Ins. Guaranty Assn., Jacksonville, 1982-83; sr. claims adjuster Hanover Ins. Co., Jacksonville, 1983-86; resident claims adjuster Auto Owners Ins. Co., Ocala, Fla., 1986—; participant Casualty Tng. Program, Wurster, Mass., 1984, Advanced

Casualty Tng. Program, Wurster, 1985. 2nd v.p. Country Garden Club, Middleburg, Fla., 1990—. Recipient Fla. Master Gardener award U. Fla. Extension Agy., Gainesville, 1992. Mem. Jacksonville Claims Assn. (various offices 1980—). Republican. Methodist. Home and Office: 3887 Darlene Rd Middleburg FL 32068-7216

HAMPTON, JUDY ANNE, librarian; b. Harvey, Ill., Aug. 4, 1946; d. Winfield Irvin and Hazel Christina (Schmadeke) Nash; m. Albert Hampton, June 24, 1972; 1 child, Marshall. BS in Edn., Ea. Ill. U., 1968; MS in Edn., Purdue U., 1972. Cert. tchr., Ill. Libr. South Stickney Sch. Dist., Burbank, Ill., 1968-72, Granite City (Ill.) Sch. Dist. # 9, 1972—. Past. treas. Ladies Civic Improvement Assn., Chautauqua, Ill., 1989-91; v.p. Parkridge Condo Assn., Belleville, 1992, 93. Mem. Ill. Sch. Libr. Media Assn. (pres. 1986-87, 93-94, 94-95, presenter conv. 1991), Belleville Jr. Woman's Club (pres. 1986-87, 93-94), 22d Jr. Dist.-Ill. Federated Woman's Club (treas. 1987-88, dist. dir. 1988-89), Phi Delta Kappa. Lutheran. Office: Coolidge Jr High Sch 3231 Nameoki Rd Granite City IL 62040

HAMPTON, MARGARET FRANCES, securities dealer, direct marketing professional; b. Gainesville, Fla., May 12, 1947; d. William Wade and Carol Dorothy (Maples) H.; m. Kenneth Lee Kauffman (dec.); 1 child, Robert Lee. BA in French summa cum laude, Fla. State U., 1969; postgrad. U. Nice (France), summer 1969; MBA in Fin. (Alcoa Found. fellow), Columbia U., 1974. Fin. analyst, economist Bd. of Govs. of Fed. Res. System, Washington, 1974-75; v.p. corp. fin. Mfrs. Hanover Trust Co., N.Y.C., 1975-76; v.p., dir. corp. planning and fin., asset and liability mgmt. and strategic planning coms. Nat. Bank of Ga., Atlanta, 1976-81; sr. v.p. corp. planning and devel. Bank South Corp., Atlanta, 1981-85; mng. ptnr. Hampton Mgmt. Cons., Atlanta, 1985—; pres., bd. dirs. Accent Enterprises, Inc., Atlanta, 1993—; pres., CEO Accent Global Mktg., Inc., Atlanta, 1993—; registered rep. Rockwell Investments, Inc., Evergreen, Colo., 1994—. Nat. trustee Leukemia Soc. Am., 1986-90; trustee Ga. chpt. Leukemia Soc., 1980-94, treas., 1981-82, 1st v.p., 1982-84, sec., 1991-92, hon. bd. dirs.; dir. Combined Health Appeal Ga., 1991—, sec., 1992—. Named Trustee of Yr., Leukemia Soc., 1982, 85; recipient Gold Key, Fla. State U. Hall of Fame. Mem. Planning Execs. Inst., Atlanta Venture Forum, Am. Inst. Banking, Inst. of Fin. Edn., Am. Fin. Assn., Downtown Atlanta C. of C., (govt. affairs subcom. 1976-77) Atlanta C. of C. (high tech. task force 1982-83), Ga. Women's Forum (sec./treas., bd. dirs. 1985-86), Ga. Exec. Women's Network (sec. 1982-83, dir. 1982-84), Bus. and Tech. Alliance, Mortar Bd., Alliance Française, Kappa Sigma Little Sisters (pres., treas., sweetheart), Phi Beta Kappa, Beta Gamma Sigma, Phi Kappa Phi, Alpha Lambda Delta, Pi Delta Phi, Alpha Delta Pi. Episcopalian. Clubs: Women's Commerce (charter mem., steering com. 1985-86), Northside Athletic.

HAMPTON, SHELLEY LYNN, hearing impaired educator; b. Muskegon, Mich., Nov. 27, 1951; d. Donald Henry and Ruth Marie (Heinanen) Tamblyn; m. John Pershing Hampton Jr., Aug. 10, 1985; 1 child, Sarah Elizabeth. BA, Mich. State U., 1973, MA, 1978. Cert. tchr., Wash., Mich., N.Y. Tchr. presch. thru 3d grade N.Y. State Sch. for Deaf, Rome, 1973-78; cons. Ingham Intermediate Sch. Dist., Lansing, Mich., 1978-81; hearing impaired coord. Shoreline Sch. Dist., Seattle, 1981—; N.W. rep. Bur. of Edn. Handicapped, N.Y.C., 1978; N.Y. del. Humanities in Edn., 1977; adv. bd. State Libr. for the Blind, Lansing, 1980-81; adj. prof. Mich. State U., 1979-81, Seattle Pacific U., 1984-86; participant World Cong. Edn. and Tech., Vancouver, B.C., 1986; computer resource technician Spl. Programs, 1988-92, collegial team leader, 1992—; rep. Site-Based Mgmt. Coun., Seattle, 1992—. Writer: Social/Emotional Aspects of Deafness, 1983-84. Del. N.Y. State Assn. for Edn. of Deaf, N.Y.C., 1974-78; N.Y. del. Humanities in Edn., 1977; mem. bd. Plymouth Congl. Ch., Seattle, 1983-87. Recipient Gov.'s Plaque of Commendable Svc., State of Mich., 1981; grantee State of Wash., 1979, 82, Very Spl. Arts Festival, 1979-81; recipient Outstanding Svc. award Mich. Sch. for the Blind, 1980. Mem. NEA, Wash. State Edn. Assn., Shoreline Edn. Assn., Alexander Graham Bell Assn., Regional Hearing Impaired Coop. for Edn., Internat. Orgn. Educators of the Hearing Impaired, U.S. Pub. Sch. Caucus, Conf. Ednl. Adminstrs. Serving the Deaf. Home: 14723 62nd Dr SE Everett WA 98208-9383 Office: Shoreline Hearing Program 16516 10th Ave NE Seattle WA 98155-5904

HAMREN, NANCY VAN BRASCH, bookkeeper; b. L.A., Feb. 2, 1947; d. Milton Carl and Winifred (Taylor) Van Brasch; m. Jerome Arthur Hamren, Feb. 14, 1981; children: Emily Allison, Meredith Ann. Student, Pasadena City Coll., 1964-65, San Francisco State Coll., 1966-67, U. Oreg., 1975-79. Bookkeeper Springfield Creamery, Eugene, Oreg., 1969—, also bd. dirs.; originator Nancy's Yogurt, Nancy's Cultured Dairy Products; bd. dirs. B.R.I.N.G. Active mem. Oreg. Shakespearean Festival, Ashland, 1986, Oreg. Nat. Abortion Rights Action League, Sta. KLCC-PBS Radio; bd. dirs. BRING Recycling. Mem. Audubon Soc., N.Am. Truffling Soc., The Wilderness Soc., Oreg. Pub. Broadcasting, Buhl (Idaho) Arts Coun., Conservation Internat. Democrat. Unitarian. Home: 1315 Ravenswood Dr Eugene OR 97401-1912 Office: Springfield Creamery 29440 Airport Rd Eugene OR 97402-9537

HAMRICK, MARGUERITE DARNELL, association executive; b. Louisville, June 7, 1920; d. Daniel and Nelle Margaret (MacEwen) Darnell; m. Charles Fullerton Hamrick, Apr. 20, 1940; children: Elaine Hamrick Shields, Pamela Hamrick Huber. Student, Hochaday, Dallas, Corroll Sch., Mexico City, Alliance Francaise, Paris. Pres. Blue Ridge Sch. Aux., N.Y.C., 1960-64; exec. v.p., bd. dirs. pediatric sect. Bellevue Hosp., N.Y.C., 1960-66; mem. women's bd. St. Lukes-Roosevelt Hosp., N.Y.C., 1958-86; dir. Oxridge Charity House Shows, Darien, Conn., 1960-86; mem. world svc. coun. YWCA, N.Y.C., 1972-94, ret., 1994. Chmn. Brick Ch. Fair, N.Y.C., 1972-73. Mem. Colony Club, Winged Foot Golf Club, Country Club of Fla., Biltmore Forest Golf Club, Coral Beach Club. Republican. Presbyterian. Home: 2000 S Ocean Blvd # 704 Delray Beach FL 33483

HANAUER, ELLEN SOME, sculptor; b. Newark, Jan. 26, 1957; d. Richard Martin and Phyllis (Shulman) Some; m. Ronald I. Hanauer, Nov. 29, 1980; children: Leslie, Jacqueline, Scott. BFA, Syracuse U., 1981. Art dir. McCann Erickson Worldwide, N.Y., 1981-83, United Jewish Ctrs., West Orange, N.J., 1984-86; dir. advt. promotion Group Travel Incentives, East Hanover, N.J., 1986-92; sculptor, 1992—. Illustrator: (books) Mother's Writes, 1983, Art Director Illustrator, Catalog, Summer Scoops, 1985. Mem. Mothers of Multiples, Amit Women. Home: 2 Surrey Ln Livingston NJ 07039-1912

HANBACK, HAZEL MARIE SMALLWOOD, management consultant; b. Washington, Sept. 19, 1918; d. Archibald Carlisle and Mary Louise (Mayhugh) Smallwood; m. William B. Hanback, Sept. 26, 1942; 1 child, Christopher Brecht. AB, George Washington U., 1940; MPA, Am. U., 1968. Archivist, U.S. Office Housing Expediter, 1948-50; mgmt. engr. U.S. Archives, 1950-51; spl. asst.-indsl. specialist Sec. Def., 1951-53; dir. documentation div. Naval Facilities Engring., Alexandria, Va., 1953-81; mgmt. cons., 1981—. Author: Military Color Book, 1960—, Status of Women in a Cybernetically Oriented Soc., 1968—, (newsletter) Worms Eye View, 1982—, The Military Industrial Complex, 1982—. Pres., West End Citizens Assn., Washington, 1956-58; trustee George Washington U., 1979—. Nominee Rockefeller Pub. Service award, 1969, Fed. Woman's award, 1969; recipient cert. of merit Dep. Def., 1965. Mem. Mortar Bd., Phi Delta Gamma, Sigma Kappa. Democrat. Episcopalian. Clubs: George Washington U. (chmn. bd. 1971-75), Columbian Women (pres. George Washington U. Club 1967-69), Order Ea. Star. Home: 2152 F St NW Washington DC 20037-2712

HANCOCK, DORIS COLLEEN, critical care nurse; b. Kansas City, Kans., Nov. 9, 1948; d. Joseph C. and Shirley Mavis (Darling) Stephens; m. Shaun W. Kelly, June 15, 1974 (div. 1983); children: Colleen, Casandra, Shannon; m. DeVerre Hancock, Feb. 14, 1994. AA, Kansas City Community Jr. Coll, 1968; BSN, Kans. U., 1973; Nurse Practitioner, Wichita State U., 1980; postgrad., Kans. U., 1988-89, Hays U., 1991. Cert. cardiovascular technologist. Nurse ICU Kans. U. Med. Ctr., Kansas City, Kans., 1970-73; urology CCU nurse Wadsworth VA Hosp., Leavenworth, Kans., 1973-75; charge supr. and ICU LaBette County Hosp., Parsons, Kans., 1976-79; med. surg. instr. LaBette County Community Jr. Coll., Parsons, Kans., 1975-76; adult care nurse practitioner Dr. D. Pauls, Parsons, Kans., 1977-82; home health nurse Upjohn Home Health, Topeka, 1984-85; nurse ICU telemetry Meml. Hosp., Topeka, 1981, 84-85; nurse ICU emergency Meml. Hosp., Manhattan, Kans., 1984-85; nurse ICU, CCU, cardiac care lab, emergency room St. Francis Hosp., Topeka, 1981-90; nurse ICU Colmery O'Neil VA Hosp., Topeka, 1990-95; nurse in spl. procedures, cardiac catheterization lab. Lawrence (Kans.) Meml. Hosp., 1994—; nurse cardiac catheterization lab. Lawrence Meml. Hosp., 1994—; mem. infection control com. Elm Haven Nursing Home, Parsons, 1981-82; bd. dirs. Nursing Home, Parsons, 1981-82; founder, advisor Diabetes Assn., Parsons, 1980-83; instr. in field. Mem. Jaycees, Parsons, 1980-82. Recipient Scholarship, Kans. Heart Assn., 1966, Outstanding Young Woman of Am. award, 1981. Mem. AACN (cert.), Am. Heart Assn. Democrat. Home: 2626 SE Tidewater Topeka KS 66605

HANCOCK, JOAN HERRIN, search company executive; b. Indpls., Apr. 16, 1930; d. Roy Silvey and Glenna Olive (Metsker) Herrin; widowed; children: Glenna Jill Hancock Smith, Jeri Lee Hancock Moore, John Norman. BA, Butler U., 1953. Cert. Profl. Cons. Career counselor Career Cons. Inc., Indpls., 1974-82; counselor, corp. officer Unique Alternatives Inc., Indpls., 1982-84, Alternatives Plus Inc., Indpls., 1984-92; pres. Herrin & Assocs., 1992—. Precinct Committeeperson Dem. Com., Indpls, 1960-67, 86—; pres. Sch. # 59 PTA, 1964, CWF, 1957-59, bd. dirs., 1957—, chair centennial com.; past group leader Camp Fire Girls; past mem. of chmn.'s club Marion County Dem. Cen. Com.; active Buller U. 1953 Reunion Com., Allisonville Christian Ch. Mem. State Assn. Pers. Cons., Am. Mgmt. Assn. (bd. dir. membership 1986, v.p. membership & human rels. 1990), Indpls. C. of C. (mem. community affairs group 1989—, mem. three to five percent club 1988—), Blue Ridge Garden Club (v.p.), Kappa Kappa Gamma (pres. Indpls. Assn. 1967-69; province dir. chpts. 1970-74, Mu club 1958-59, Betty Miller Brown award 1982). Club: Hoosier 500 Toastmistress (pres. 1963) (Indpls.). Home and Office: 4127 Timber Ct Indianapolis IN 46250-2279

HANCOCK, NANNETTE BEATRICE FINLEY, educator, mental health consultant; b. Birmingham, Ala., Aug. 24, 1937; d. James L. and Minnie (Mason) Finley; m. Frank J. Hancock Jr., Dec. 27, 1958 (div. May 1976); children: Andria Denise, Frank J. III, Cheryl René. BSN, Dillard U., 1958; MPH in Pub. Health, U. Calif., Berkeley, 1970; PhD in Psychology, Western Colo. U., 1977; MA in Clin. Psychology, John F. Kennedy U., 1991. 2d lt. staff nurse U.S. Army Nurse's Corp, Denver, 1958-59; staff nurse, head nurse St. Francis Hosp., Evanston, Ill., 1960-64, Richmond (Calif.) Hosp., 1964-65; sch. nurse Richmond Unified Sch. Dist., 1965-69; prof. Contra Costa Coll., San Pablo, Calif., 1970—; pvt. practice mental health cons. Richmond, 1977—; founder, owner Nannette's Beauty and Figure Salon, 1982-86; marriage and family therapist AIDS Minority Health Initiative, Oakland, Calif., 1990—. Mem. Social Heritage Group, 1964—, human rels. com., 1966-70, Easter Hill Meth. Ch., 1964—. Col. Army Nurse's Corp. USAR, 1978—. Mem. Calif. Assn. Marriage and Family Therapy, Calif. Nurse's Assn., Bay Area Assn. Black Psychologists, Res. Officer's Assn. Home: 4801 Reece Ct Richmond CA 94804-3444 Office: Contra Costa Coll 2600 Mission Bell Dr San Pablo CA 94806-3195

HANCOCK, SANDRA OLIVIA, secondary school educator; b. Jackson, Tenn., Oct. 22, 1947; d. Carthel Leon and Thelma (Thompson) Smith; m. Jerome Hancock, Aug. 1, 1969; children: Casey Colman, Mandy Maria. BS, U. Tenn., 1969, MS, 1973; grad. safety seminar, Universal Cheerleaders Assn., 1989. Cert. educator. Educator Lexington (Tenn.) High Sch., 1969-70, Clarksburg (Tenn.) High Sch., 1970-78, 83-90, Dresden (Tenn.) Jr. H.S., 1994-95. Contbr. poetry to various publs. Cub scout leader Boy Scouts Am., Clarksburg, 1982-84; assoc. mem. St. Labre Indian Sch. and Home Arrow Club, Ashland, Mont., 1988-89; former vol. March of Dimes; vol. Leukemia Soc. Am.; mem. fund raising com. Project Graduation, Huntingdon H.S., 1992-95; dir. presch. 1st United Meth. Ch., Huntingdon, 1992—; art edn. asst. Huntingdon Spl. Sch. Dist., 1993-94. Mem. U.S. Olympic Assn., Nat. Cheerleaders Assn. (Superior Advisor Performance award 1988), Am. Assn. Cheerleading Coaches and Advisors, Jackson Writer Group (recording sec. 1992-93), Poetry Soc. Tenn. (recording sec. 1993-94), Phi Delta Kappa (N.W. Tenn. chpt. sec. 1993-94). Mem. U.S. Olympic Assn., Nat. Cheerleaders Assn. (Superior Advisor Performace award 1988), Am. Assn. Cheerleading Coaches and Advisors, Jackson Writer's Group (rec. sec. 1993-94), Poetry Soc. Tenn. (rec. sec. 1993-94), Haiku Soc. Am., Phi Delta Kappa. Republican. Home and Office: 435 Timber Ln Huntingdon TN 38344-1625 also: Dresden Jr HS N Wilson St Dresden TN 38225

HANCOCK, VICKI ELAINE, technology educator, consultant; b. Silver Spring, Md., May 14, 1956; d. Floyd Ellsworth and Gladys Georgetta (Moyer) H.; m. Justin F. Baer, Aug. 9, 1978 (div. July 1989). BA in English, Secondary Edn., Towson State U., 1978; MA in Reading, Hood Coll., 1982; PhD in Edn. Comm., U. Md., 1986. Tchr. English, reading Wash. County Schs., Hagerstown, Md., 1978-85, chair dept. English, reading, 1982-85, computer lab. adminstr., staff developer, 1985-87; dir. Learning Resource Ctr. N.Mex. State U., Las Cruces, 1987-89, asst. prof. curriculum and instrn., 1987-89; asst. dir. Edn. and Tech. Resources Ctr. ASCD, Alexandria, Va., 1989-94, dir. Edn. and Tech. Resources Ctr., 1995—; ednl. instrnl. specialist IBM, Atlanta, 1989-91. Editor Curriculum/Technology Quarterly, 1991-93 (Effie award 1992); contbr. articles to profl. jours. Mem. Nat. Forum for Info. Literacy (charter, co-chair 1991—), Assn. Edn. Comm. & Tech., Internat. Soc. Tech. & Edn., Internat. Coun. Tech. & Edn., Nat. Coord. Coun. Tech. Edn. and Tng., Soc. Applied Learning Tech., Lambda Iota Tau, Phi Delta Kappa. Office: ASCD 1250 N Pitt St Alexandria VA 22314-1453

HANDELMAN, ALICE ROBERTA, public relations professional, freelance writer; b. Bklyn., Mar. 17, 1943; d. Ned Harlan and Margaret (Isaacs) Samuels; m. Howard Talbot Handelman, Aug. 29, 1965; children: Karen Handelman Hirshman, Patricia Gail Handelman Bloom, Marjorie Lynn. BJ, U. Mo., 1965. Intern reporter Miami (Fla.) News, summer 1964; staff feature writer St. Louis Blues, 1968-77; freelance writer, St. Louis, 1967—; also community rels. assoc. Jewish Ctr. for Aged of Greater St. Louis, Chesterfield, Mo., 1981-85, dir. community rels., 1985—; instr. hockey for women Meramec C.C., St. Louis, 1976-77; pub. rels. cons. Jewish Family and Children's Svc., St. Louis, 1983, 89; adv. com. vis. prof. program JCA Assocs., 1981-83, Gerontol. Inst., St. Louis, 1981-83. Author, photographer: LaSalle Street--A History of the St. Louis Wholesale Flower Market, 1987; freelance writer, contbr. to St. Louis Globe-Dem., St. Louis Post-Dispatch, St. Louis Jewish Light, Hockey News, Hockey World, Ladue News, Sporting News, Hockey Pictorial, Suburban Jour. Newspapers; writer copy for Knight's Catalogue, 1983. Pub. rels. chmn. Nat. Coun. Jewish Women, 1981-83, publicity chmn. fashion sale, 1985; pres. Weber Sch. PTA, Creve Coeur, Mo., 1982; mem. Women's Am. ORT, 1965—; life mem. Jewish Hosp. Aux., 1965—, Jewish Ctr. for Aged Aux., 1986—; pres. Young Women's Coun. on Edn. of Jewish Fedn. St. Louis, 1969; mem. cen. advancement team Pkwy. Central High Sch., 1985-89; photographer Tour de Cure bicycle ride to benefit Am. Diabetes Assn., 1992, 93. Recipient William Randolph Hearst award Hearst Found., Columbia, Mo., 1965, United Way Graphic Design award, 1986, United Way Photography award, 1987, Star Communicator Photography award, 1987, 89, 2d place award Guide to Jewish Life in St. Louis photo contest, 1989, 2d place award Jewish Hosp. St. Louis Generations of Women photo contest, 1989, Star Communicator comm. program award United Way Greater St. Louis, 1990; Besse Marks Meml. scholar, 1964-65. Mem. Nat. Fedn. Press Women (1st place award comm. contest, 3rd place photo feature 1989, 3rd place award advt. photography 1993) , Jewish Ctr. for Aged Aux., Fellows of Jewish Hosp., Mo. Press Women (1st place corp. newsletter category state feature writing comm. contest, 1988, 93, 1st place advt. photography, 2nd place feature article, 3 1st place awards, 1994, 1st place not for profit newsletter, 1994), Mo. Assn. Homes for the Aging (publicity com., Outstanding 1st Place Newsletter award), Nat Fedn. Press Women (1st place feature photo 1994), Mo. Press Women (pub. chmn. 1994), Women in Communications (Ruth Philpott Collins award 1984, Best in the Midwest, 2d place feature writing, 1992), Meadowbrook Country Club (Ballwin, Mo.). Jewish. Home: 12 Terry Hill Ln Saint Louis MO 63131-2422 Office: Jewish Ctr for Aged of Greater St Louis 13190 S Outer 40 Rd Chesterfield MO 63017

HANDLER, DELORES ANNE, artist; b. Chicago Heights, Ill., Aug. 23, 1947; d. Ivan John and Marie (Engbard) Frank; adoptive parents Anton J. Petroski and Carrie L. Engbard; m. Adrian L. Shipley, Oct. 30, 1965 (div. Oct. 1975); m. Mark J. Handler, Feb. 25, 1989; children: Anne Marie, Anthony Adrian. BA, Bellevue Coll., 1982; Degree in Comml. Art, North Light Art Sch., Cin., 1989; Degree in Floral Design, Lifetime Career Sch., Bellevue, Nebr., 1992. Portrait artist, wall muralist, calligrapher, illustrator Omaha, Nebr., 1975—; artist crafts Miami, Fla., 1992; display mgr. Sears/ Homestead (Fla.) Plaza; dir. Aardvark and Calico Cat Galleries, Sumter, Council Bluffs, Iowa. Author, illustrator: (book) The Great Nebraska Fly, 1990, There Are All Kinds of Grandmas, 1993; exhibitor Women in the Arts gallery, Washington, so. Fla. region including the Fla. Keys, Homestead AFB, Miami, others; commissioned portraiture and wall murals Omaha, Nebr. and Council Bluffs; regional art work thoughout N. Dakota, S. Dakota, Kans., Ill., Iowa and Nebr. Mem. Am. Soc. Portrait Artists, Women in the Arts (charter), Oil Pastel Assn. Republican. Roman Catholic. Home: 603 Scuffletown Rd Simpsonville SC 29681 Office/Studio: 603 Scuffletown Rd Simpsonville SC 29681

HANDLER, ENID IRENE, health care administrator, consultant; b. N.Y.C., Oct. 17, 1932; d. Solomon and Fran S. (Bernstein) Ostrov; m. Murry Raymond Handler, Nov. 22, 1952; children: Lowell S., Lillian Handler Koch, Evan Elliott. BS, Queens Coll., 1968; MS in Adminstrv. Medicine, Columbia U., 1973. Adminstrv. dir. Phelps Mental Health Ctr., North Tarrytown, N.Y., 1973-85; ind. cons. E. Handler Assoc., Cortlandt Manor, N.Y., 1986-92; mgmt. cons. Durham County (N.C.) Mental Health/Devel. Disabilities Svc., 1993-94; presenter to profl. orgns. Contbr. articles and book revs. to profl. jours. Mem. adv. bd. Marymount Coll., North Tarrytown, 1983, Iona Coll., New Rochelle, N.Y., 1983; mem. adv. bd. Search for Change, Inc., White Plains, 1987-90; bd. dirs. Keon Sch., Montrose, N.Y., 1986-88; chair North Westchester County Mental Health Coun., 1974-80; pres. Westchester Assn. Vol. Agys., 1981-82; mem. Westchester County Community Svcs. Bd., 1980-86. NIH fellow Columbia U., N.Y.C., 1971-72. Fellow Am. Orthopsychiat. Assn.; mem. NAFE, Columbia U. Alumni Assn. Home and Office: Enid Handler Cons 9318 Laurel Springs Dr Chapel Hill NC 27516-5649

HANDLER, JANICE, lawyer; b. Newark, July 9, 1945; d. Lester Robert and Rose Mildred (Reider) Handler; m. Norman Harry Ilowite, June 4, 1978. BA, Douglass Coll., 1967; JD, Rutgers Law Sch., 1970; LLM, NYU, 1980. Bar: N.Y. Law clk. to presiding justice U.S. Dist. Ct. (so. dist.), N.Y.C., 1970-71; assoc. Fried, Frank, Harris, Shriver & Jacoboon, N.Y.C., 1971-72; atty. SEC, N.Y.C., 1972-74; counsel Thomas J. Lipton, Englewood Cliffs, N.J., 1974-77; mktg. counsel Lever Brothers Co., N.Y.C., 1977-83, asst. gen. counsel, 1983-87; sr. counsel Chesebrough-Ponds, Inc., Greenwich, Conn., 1987-90; gen. counsel Elizabeth Arden Co., N.Y.C., 1990—. Reviewer N.Y. Law Jour., N.Y.C., 1982—. Bd. dirs. Douglass Coll. Assoc. Alumnae, 1972-74. Mem. ABA (sect. on litigation's com. on corp. counsel), N.Y. State Bar Assn. (Corp. Counsel Sect.), Assn. Bar City N.Y. (advt. industry subcom. 1982—).*

HANDLER, MIMI, editor, writer; b. Boston, Sept. 16, 1934; d. Eli and Josephine (Bronstein) Richman; m. Jack G. Handler, June 11, 1956 (div. 1981); children—Jessica, Susannah, Sarah. B.A., Brandeis U., 1956. Staff corr. Ladies' Home Jour., Phila., 1956-59; sec. law jour. Emory U., Atlanta, 1970-71; free-lance ct. reporter Atlanta, 1971-73; projects editor Early Am. Life, Harrisburg, Pa., 1979-80, mng. editor, 1980-88, sr. editor, 1988-90; editor New England, 1990-93; editor in chief Early Am. Life, Harrisburg, Pa., 1993—; speaker Old Sturbridge Village conf., 1986, 87, Strawbery Banke Antiques Symposium, 1992. Democrat. Jewish. Office: Early American Life PO Box 8200 Harrisburg PA 17105-8200

HANDLEY, ELEANOR LUCRISTOR, eyewear and accessories executive; b. Detroit, Feb. 24, 1950; d. Anna Lowery Toliva; m. Ramond Lenory Handley, Dec. 17, 1990; children: Sophia, Candace, Christopher, Ramond. Student, Mary Grove Coll., 1990—. Pvt. nurse Suburban Nurses Registry, St. Clair Shores, Mich., 1978-84; make up and color cons. Vaunda Cosmetics, Detroit, 1980-83; founder, owner Peeping Tom Ltd., Warren, Mich., 1985—; high fashion dress cons. Women's Empowerment, Detroit, 1989-90; fashion sponsor Full & Fabulous. Author: (book) Business At Home, 1989; contbr. poetry to books. Mem. NAACP, Jewelry Bd. Trade. Democrat.

HANDLEY, MARGIE LEE, business executive; b. Bakersfield, Calif., Sept. 29, 1939; d. Robert E. and Jayne A. (Knoblock) Harrah; children: Steven Daniel Lovell, David Robert Lovell, Ronald Eugene Lovell; m. Leon C. Handley, Sr., Oct. 28, 1975. Grad. high sch., Willits, Calif. Lic. gen. engring. contractor. Owner, operator Shasta Pallet Co., Montague, 1969-70; owner, operator Lovell's Tack 'n Togs, Yreka, Calif., 1970-73; v.p. Microphor, Inc., Willits, 1974-81; pres. Harrah Industries, Inc., Willits, 1981—, Hot Rocks, Inc., Willits, 1983-89; gen. ptnr. Madrone Profl. Group, Willits, 1982—; bd. dirs. SAFE-BIDCO, Nat. Bank of the Redwoods, NBR Mortgage Co., Howard Found.; active State of Calif. Employment Tng. Panel, 1993—, coord. State Calif. Timber Transition, 1994—. Sec. Willits Community Scholarships, Inc., 1962; trustee Montague Methodist Ch., 1966-73; sec. Montague PTA, 1969; clk. bd. trustees Montague Sch. Dist., 1970-73; del. Calif. State Conf. Small Bus., 1984; alt. del. Rep. Nat. Conv., Kansas City, Detroit, 1976, 80; 3d dist. chmn. Mendocino County Rep. Central Com., 1978-84; mem. Calif. State Rep. Central Com., 1985, 86, 87; Rep. nominee for State Senate Calif. 2nd Senate Dist., 1990, 93; mem. Rep. Congl. Leadership Council, 1980-82; Mendocino County chmn. Reagan/Bush, 1980, 84; Mendocino County co-chmn. Deukmejian for Gov., 1982; mem. Region IX Small Bus. Adminstrn. Adv. Council, 1982-93; mem. Gov.'s Adv. Council, 1983-90; del., asst. sgt. of arms Rep. Nat. Conv., Dallas, 1984, del., New Orleans, 1988; vice chmn. Mendocino County Rep. Central Com., 1985; mem. Willits C. of C. (hon.), Calif. Transp. Commn., 1986-90; state dir. North Bay Dist. Hwy. Grading and Heavy Engring. div. 1986; dir. Lit. Vols. Am. Named Mendocino 12th Dist. Fair Woman of the Year, 1987. Mem. No. Coast Builders Exch., Soroptimist Internat. Home: PO Box 1329 Willits CA 95490-1309 Office: Harrah Industries Inc 42 Madrone St Willits CA 95490-4249

HANDLEY, SUE ANN, professional quiltmaker, educator; b. Decatur, Ill., Feb. 22, 1955; d. Max Bail and Virginia Ellen (Paul) Handley; m. Gregory Alan Poteat, June 28, 1975 (div. 1992); children: Brian, Zachary. Student, Antelope Valley Jr. Coll., Lancaster, Calif., 1983-85. Tchr. quilting Sr. Citizen Ctr., Lancaster, 1984-85, House of Fabrics, Palmdale, Calif., 1984-88; lectr. quilting Palmdale Sch. Dist., 1984-88; vol. St. Andrew's Priory, Valyermo, Calif., 1983—; quiltmaker MGM Studios, Hollywood, Calif., 1990; banner maker So. Calif. Renewal Communities, Anaheim, 1986; lectr. First Presbyn. Ch., Palmdale, 1991, Palmdale Elks Lodge, 1991, othrs. Completed more than 400 quilts; contbr. to Quilter's Newsletter. Recipient 1st place award Inland Empire Quilt Guild, Riverside, Calif., 1990, 3d place award Smoky Mountain Quilt Competition, 1982, Best of Show award Antelope Valley Fair, Lancaster, 1978; Calif. State champion Calif. State Fair Bd., Sacramento, 1979. Mem. Am. Quilters Soc. (included in calendar 1994). Democrat. Roman Catholic. Home: 38563 Jacklin Ave Palmdale CA 93550-4019 Office: Sue's Custom Quilting 38563 Jacklin Ave Palmdale CA 93550-4019

HAND WRIGHT, LAURA BELLA, broadcast executive; b. Petersburg, Va., Jan. 25, 1950; d. Clifton Earl and Libera Elisa Hand; m. Ronald H. Wright, May 26, 1979; children: Kyle Randall, Carinne Alissa. BA, Syracuse U., 1971. Newscaster Sta. WFBL, Syracuse, N.Y., 1970-72; reporter Sta. WSYR, Syracuse, N.Y., 1972-76; cmty. rels. dir., anchor/prodr. Sta. WSTM, Syracuse, N.Y., 1976—; columnist Community Newspapers, Manlius, N.Y., 1990-93; adj. instr. colls. and univs., 1979-82. Adv. bd. Syracuse Salvation Army, 1986—, Am. Lung Assn. Ctrl. N.Y., 1994—. Named Woman of the Yr. Syracuse AAUW, 1985, Syracuse U. Alumna of the Yr., 1992; recipient numerous media awards. Mem. Syracuse Press Club (bd. dirs. 1986-88, 1990—), Syracuse Univ. Alumni Assn. (bd. dirs. 1989—), Newhouse Alumni Assn., Sedgwick Farm Tennis Club, Chi Omega. Office: WSTM-TV 1030 James St Syracuse NY 13203

HANDY, ALICE WARNER, state agency administrator; b. Wilmington, Del., Apr. 17, 1948; d. Carleton Thomas and Ruth Francis (Lees) H.; m. Peter A. Stoudt; children: Nicholas Lyon Gerow, Jennifer Lees Gerow, Abigail Hurst Gerow. BA, Conn. Coll., 1970; postgrad., U. Va., 1975-78. Asst. investment officer Travelers Ins. Co., Hartford, Conn., 1970-74; investment officer U. Va., Charlottesville, 1974-81, asst. v.p., investment officer, 1981-88, univ. treas., 1988, 90—; treas. Commonwealth of Va., Richmond, 1988-90; chmn. state coun. on local debt, state treasury bd.; commr. Va. Agrl. Devel.

Authority, Va. Port Authority; treas. Va. Coll. Bldg. Authority; mem. Va. Edn. Loan Authority, Va. Resources Authority, Va. Small Bus. Financing Authority; sec.-treas. Va. Pub. Bldg. Authority, Va. Pub. Sch. Authority, all 1988-90; cons. various U. Va. founds., 1985—; mem. investment adv. com. Va. Retirement System, 1994—. Trustee Va. Outdoors Found., 1988-90, Va. Hist. Preservation Found., 1989-90; troop leader Girl Scouts U.S., Charlottesville, 1985-88; bd. dirs. Va. Discovery Mus., Charlottesville, 1988, Conn. Mut. Property Mgmt., 1991—, Investment Fund for Founds., 1991—, Charlottesville chpt. Am. Heart Assn., 1992-93; mem. fin. com. Thomas Jefferson Ch., Charlottesville, 1987—; treas. Preservation Alliance, 1990-93, U. Va. Real Estate Found., 1991—; mem. Mcpl. Securities Rulemaking Bd., 1993—. Mem. Nat. Assn. Coll. and Univ. Bus. Officers (chair fin. mgmt. and higher edn. coms.). Democrat. Unitarian. Office: U Va PO Box 9012 Charlottesville VA 22906-9012

HANDY, DRUCILLA, public relations executive; b. Lynchburg, Va., Aug. 21, 1924; d. John Bryant and Allen (Steele) H.; m. Robert M. Redinger, Oct. 30, 1954. Student, Swarthmore Coll., 1941-43. Publicist Metro-Goldwyn-Mayer, Washington, 1943-45; editor house organ Du Pont, Richmond, Va., 1945-47; account exec. Rosemary Sheehan Publicity, N.Y.C., 1947-50; pub. rels. dir. Helene Curtis Industries, Inc., Chgo., 1950-54; account supr. Gardner & Jones (name now Hill & Knowlton), Chgo., 1954-56; pres. Drucilla Handy Co. div. L.C. Williams & Assocs., Inc., Chgo., 1956—. Bd. dirs. various civic and cultural orgns., Chgo. Mem. NAFE, Nat. Assn. Women Bus. Owners, Pub. Rels. Soc. Am. (accredited), Counselors Acad., Chgo. Network, Arts Club Chgo., Execs. Club Chgo.

HANFT, RUTH S. SAMUELS (MRS. HERBERT HANFT), health care consultant, educator, economist; b. N.Y.C., July 12, 1929; d. Max Joseph and Ethel (Schechter) Samuels; m. Herbert Hanft, June 17, 1951; children: Marjorie Jane, Jonathan Mark. BS, Cornell U., 1949; MA, Hunter Coll., 1963; PhD, George Washington U., 1989; ScD (hon.), U. Osteo. Med & Health Scis., 1993. Cons. Urban Med. Econs. Project, Hunter Coll., N.Y.C. and D.C. Dept. Health, 1962-63; health economist Office of Rsch. and Stats., Social Security Adminstrn., Washington, 1964-66; chief grants mgmt. health div. Office Econ. Opportunity, Washington, 1966-68; sr. health analyst Office of Asst. Sec. Planning and Evaluation HEW, Washington, 1968-71, spl. asst., asst. sec. health, 1971-72; dep. asst. sec. for health policy, rsch. and stats. Office of Asst. Sec. for Health HEW, 1977-79, dep. asst. sec. for health rsch., stats. and tech., 1979-81; health care cons., 1981-88; cons., rsch. prof. dept. health svcs. mgmt. and policy George Washington U., Washington, 1988-91, prof., 1991—; vis. prof. Dartmouth Med. Sch., 1976—; sr. rsch. assoc. Inst. Medicine-NAS, Washington, 1972-76. Contbr. articles to profl. jours. Mem. Med. Assistance Svc. Bd. Commonwealth Va., 1984-89, Meharry Med. Coll. Bd. Trustees, 1989-94. Fellow Hastings Ctr.; mem. Inst. of Medicine, Nat. Acad. Sci. Jewish. Home: 3609 Cameron Mills Rd Alexandria VA 22305-1107 Office: 1001 22d St NW Washington DC 20037

HANKINS, BARBARA LEE, auditor; b. Bklyn., May 28, 1933; d. William John and Helen Elizabeth (Christensen) Schickler; m. Philip Charles Hankins, May 8, 1955; children: Susan E. Hankins Witcraft, Patricia L., Evelyn C. BS, Cornell U., 1954; MBA, Boston U., 1959; MPA, U. Tex., 1986. Acct. Charter Info. Corp., Austin, Tex., 1968—; auditor/audit mgr. Tex. State Auditors Office, Austin, 1986—. Commr. City of Austin Planning Commn., 1988-91; selectman/chair Town of Winchester (Mass.) Bd. of Selectman, 1975-80, mem., chair fin. com., 1972-75. Home: 1801 Lavaca St Apt 14J Austin TX 78701-1332

HANKINS, MARY DENMAN, elementary school educator; b. Roane County, Tenn., Jan. 31, 1930; d. Elmer Hoyle and Lela Emiline (Cox) Denman; m. Charles Russell Hankins, Mar. 23, 1951; children: Jennifer, Susan, Charles Thomas, Amy. BS, Montreat (N.C.) Coll., 1950; postgrad., East Tenn. State U., Tusculum Coll., Greeneville, Tenn. Cert. elem. tchr., Tex., Tenn. Tchr. elem. Greene County (Tenn.) Schs., 1955-87; tchr. adult basic edn. Greeneville (Tenn.) Schs., 1978-85; elem. tchr. Cedar Hill (Tex.) Ind. Sch. Dist., 1987—. Contbg. author of sci. and math. home activities for children for textbook cos. Mem. NEA, Tex. Tchrs. Assn., Tenn. Edn. Assn., Tenn. Tchrs. Study Coun., Greene County Edn. Assn. (past editor newsletter), Delta Kappa Gamma.

HANKINSON, HARRIETTE FOSTER, amusement company executive; b. Atlanta, Feb. 25, 1942; d. Walter Price and Harriette Louise (Moore) Foster; m. Donald Dean Hankinson, Dec. 2, 1966; children: Donald Dean Jr., Philip Scott, Andrea Elaine. B in Liberal Arts in Journalism, U. Ga., 1963; postgrad., Clayton State Coll., 1994. Advt. copywriter Rich's Dept. Stores, Atlanta, 1963-65; rsch. asst. indsl. devel. dept. Atlanta C. of C., 1965-67; rsch. assoc. Atlanta Region Met. Planning Commn., 1967-69; v.p., sec. Phoenix Amusements, Inc., Riverdale, Ga., 1982—. Mem. Profl. Secs. Internat., Nat. Soc. DAR (state regent 1990-92, NSDAR speakers staff 1989-90, 92-95, state vice regent 1988-90, state 2nd vice regent 1986-88, state chaplain 1984-86, state treas. 1982-84, state corr. sec. 1976-78, state outstanding jr. 1978), Jamestown Soc., Nat. Soc. Descendants Early Quakers, Nat. Soc. Descendants Ancient Planters, Daus. of Am. Colonists, Daus. Colonial Wars State Ga., U.S. Daus. 1812, United Daus. Confederacy, Dames Ct. of Honor (hon. life pres. Ga. 1990, state pres. 1988-90), Freedoms Found. at Valley Forge (rec. sec. Atlanta chpt. 1981-83), Continental Soc. Daus. Indian Wars, First Families Ga., Ga. Fedn. Women's Clubs, Magna Charta Dames, Colonial Order of Crown, Descendants Order of Garter, Plantagent Soc., United Daus. of Confederacy, Order Descendants of Ancient Planters, Descendants of Early Quakers. Episcopalian. Home: 170 Dix Leeon Dr Fairburn GA 30213-3606

HANLEY, SUSAN BELL, humanities educator, editor; b. Mpls., June 11, 1939; d. Franklin Bell and Frances Alden (Haskins) H.; m. Kozo Yamamura, June 1, 1969. AB, Radcliffe Coll., 1961; MA, Yale U., 1964, PhD, 1970. Vis. asst. prof. U. Wash., Seattle, 1971, 72-74, asst. prof., 1974-77, assoc. prof., 1977-86, prof., 1986—; rsch. assoc. East-West Ctr., Honolulu, 1971-72. Author: Economic and Demographic Change in Preindustrial Japan, 1977, The Tokugawa Legacy, 1990, (Joseph Roggendorf prize 1990); co-editor: Family and Population in East Asian History, 1985; Mng. editor Jour. Japanese Studies, 1974-86, editor, 1986—. Fellow NDEA, 1962, 63, 66, 67, Ford Found., 1964; grantee Social Sci. Rsch. Coun., Japan, 1968, 79, 86, NIH, 1973. Mem. Assn. for Asian Studies (Disting. Lectr. award 1990-91). Office: U Wash Thomson Hall Dr # 05 Seattle WA 98195

HANN, VICTORIA ANN, human resources executive; b. Phila., Feb. 18, 1946; d. Victor Adams and Jean (Harpster) H. BA in Psychology, Roanoke Coll., 1968; MEd in Counseling and Pers. Adminstrn., Pa. State U., 1970. Residence hall dir. Pa. State U., College Park, 1968-70, SUNY, Oswego, 1970-74; corp. trainer, maitre d' Charley's Crab, Chuck Muer Corp., Troy, Mich., 1977-80; dir. mgmt. devel. Thompson Food Enterprises, Birmingham, Mich., 1980-82; dir. human resources, then asst. gen. mgr. Ramada Hotel, Oxon Hill, Md., 1985-89; human resources cons. to pres. Waterford Devel., Inc., Reston, Va., 1989-90; dir. human resources Internat. Loan Network, Lanham, Md., 1989-90; pres. Nat. Resource Tng. Ctr., Inter-Continental Trade Assocs., Lanham, Md., 1991—. Fellow ABI (Woman of Yr. 1993, dep. gov.); mem. NAFE, Soc. for Human Resource Mgmt., Prince George's C. of C. Home: 14564 London Ln Bowie MD 20715 Office: Nat Resource Tng Ctr 9470 Annapolis Rd Ste 226 Lanham Seabrook MD 20706-3019

HANNA, EMMA HARMON, architectural designer, business owner, official; b. Sharpsville, Pa., Apr. 29, 1939; d. James McKarney Supplee and Anne (Woods) Thompson; m. William Hayes Harmon, Sept. 1, 1962 (div. 1984); 1 child, James McKarney Harmon; m. Hugh Allen Hanna, Mar. 21, 1992. BArch, Kent (Ohio) State U., 1962. Drafter W.H. Harmon Architects, Orlando, Fla., 1970-73; pres., owner The Plan Shop, Inc., Orlando and Palm Bay, Fla., 1973-87, The Plan Place, Inc., Palm Bay, 1987—; pres. Engrng. & Design Concepts, Palm Bay, 1986—; vice chmn. substance abuse program Broken Glass, Valkaria, Fla. Mem. coun. City of Palm Bay, 1989-91, dep. mayor, 1991-92; treas. League of Cities, Brevard County, Fla., 1989-92, East Cen. Fla. Planning Coun., Orlando, 1989-90; mem. Federated Rep. Women, South Brevard County, 1989—; exec. com. Brevard County Reps.; mem. Panther Athletic Assn. Bd. Fla. Inst. Tech., 1990—, open campus adv. coun. Brevard Community Coll., Holmes Regional Hosp. Devel. Coun., 1991—. Mem. Home Builders and Contractors Brevard County (assoc., Assoc. of Month 1989, bd. dirs. 1993—, 2d v.p. 1994), Bldg. Ofcls. Assn. Brevard County (assoc., Assoc. of Yr. 1989), Drafter's Guild (organizer), Palm Bay C. of C., Greater South Brevard C. of C. (govt. affairs com., bd. dirs. 1991-93), Exch. Club (chpt. pres., charter pres., charter pres. Yellow Umbrella child abuse prevention program South Brevard 1988-89), Palm Bay Utility Corp. (vice chmn. 1992—). Home: 1482 Meadowbrook Rd NE Palm Bay FL 32905-5007 Office: The Plan Place 1398 Palm Bay Rd NE Palm Bay FL 32905-3837

HANNA, KATHRYN LURA, university administrator; b. Fairmont, Minn., Jan. 23, 1947; d. Russell George and Dorothy Jane (Buchner) Hanna; m. Jeffrey R. Hoelmer, June 10, 1968 (div. Dec. 1980). BA, Hamline U., 1969; MA, Mankato State U., 1971. Instr. biology U. Minn., Waseca, 1971-77, asst. prof., 1977-86, assoc. prof., 1986—, dir. arts & scis., 1990, vice chancellor acad. affairs, 1990-93; asst. dean Coll. Biol. Scis. U. Minn., St. Paul, 1993—; v.p. membership Grad. Women in Sci., Mpls., 1988-93; mem. Commn. on Women, U. Minn., Mpls., 1988—. Author: The New Bio Book, 1984; co-author: The Bio Book Too, 1984. Bd. dirs. Mpls. Coll. of Art & Design Assocs., 1991—. Recipient Svc. award Sigma Delta Epsilon, 1989; named Outstanding Educator Adminstr. South Cen. Edn. Assn., 1991. Mem. Grad. Women in Sci., Minn. Soc. Optical Micriscopists, Henrici Soc., Minn. Women in Higher Edn. (regional dir. 1983-93), Assn. for Study of Higher Edn., Univ. Edn. Assn. (contract adminstr. 1983-93), Soc. Coll. and Univ. Planning. Home: 5643 Green Circle Dr Apt 312 Hopkins MN 55343-9655 Office: U Minn Coll Biol Scis 123 Synder Hall 1475 Gortner Ave Saint Paul MN 55108

HANNA, NOREEN ANELDA, adult education administrator, consultant; b. Napa, Calif., Nov. 28, 1939; d. Thomas James and Eileen Anelda (Jordan) H.; m. Leon O'bine Gotcher, Aug. 14, 1971 (div. Nov. 1980); children: John Allen, Tamara Kay. BA, San Francisco State U., 1963; postgrad., Sonoma State U., 1974-81, Ctr. for Leadership Devel., 1982-83; MA, U. San Francisco, 1989. Cert. gen. elem., specialist in reading, gen. adminstrv. svcs. Classroom tchr. Ullom Elem. Sch., Las Vegas, Nev., 1963; classroom tchr. J. L. Shearer Elem. Sch., Napa, 1963-78, reading resource tchr., 1978-80; asst. prin. Napa Valley Adult Sch., Napa, 1980-81, acting prin., 1981-82; prin. El Centro Elem. Sch., Napa, 1982-83; adminstr. J.T.P.A./Gain Programs, Napa, 1983-90; prin. Napa Valley Adult Sch., Napa, 1983—; commn. mem. Calif. Post Secondary Edn., 1987-89; cons. Calif. Dept. Edn., Sacramento, 1988—; adv. bd. dir. Ctr. for Adult Edn., San Francisco (Calif.) State U., 1988—; adv. bd. mem. Immigration Reform & Control Act, Sacramento, 1989-92; presenter and cons. in field. Exec. bd. dirs. Leadership Napa Valley, 1985—; sec. Leadership Napa Valley Found., 1988—. State Edn. scholar Calif. PTA, 1976, Grad. Edn. scholar Delta Kappa Gamma, Napa, 1977; recipient Cmty. Leadership award Napa Valley Unified Sch. Dist., 1988, Assn. Calif. Adminstrs. Adult Edn. Adminstr. of yr. award, 1992, George C. Mann Discing. Svc. award Calif. Coun. for Adult Edn., 1994. Mem. ASCD, Am. Assn. for Adult and Continuing Edn., Assn. Calif. Sch. Adminstrs. (chair to state adult edn. com. 1988-89, state rep. assembly del. 1989-92, state adult edn. com. chairperson 1989-92, others), Calif. Coun. for Adult Edn. (North Coast chpt. bd. dirs. 1988—), Napa C. of C. (bd. dirs. 1985-88, edn./bus. com. 1985—, others), Correctional Educators Assn., Soroptimist Internat. of Napa, Phi Delta Kappa, Delta Kappa Gamma. Republican. Roman Catholic. Office: Napa Valley Adult Edn 2425 Jefferson St Napa CA 94558-4931

HANNA, SUZANNE LOUISE, nurse; b. Mankato, Minn., Aug. 31, 1953; d. Frank Edward and Phyllis Ruth (Moeller) Wilkins; m. Thomas Ray Hanna, Sept. 15, 1973; children: Elizabeth Amy, Joseph Ryan, Thomas Wilkins. Diploma in nursing with highest honors, Iowa Western C.C., Council Bluffs, 1991. RN, Iowa; cert. provider ACLS, Am. Heart Assn. Exec. sec. First Nat. Bank, Mpls., 1971-72, Nat. Bank of Am., Salina, Kans., 1972; receptionist The Evening Sentinel, Shenandoah, Iowa, 1972-73; ins. sec. Wilson Ins. Agy., Shenandoah, 1973-79; med./surg. staff nurse Shenandoah Meml. Hosp., 1980-81; office nurse Dr. Floyd A. Jones, Shenandoah, 1983-91; med./surg. staff nurse Shenandoah Meml. Hosp., 1991—, emergency rm. nurse, 1992—; bd. dirs. Ag-Pro Corp., Shenandoah; co-chairperson family life com., 1989-90. Alt., Rep. Page County Convs., 1988, 92, active Ladies Guild St. Mary Ch., Shenandoah, 1986—; mem. parish coun. bd., pres. parish coun., 1989-92, instr. religious edn., 1988-90, mem. choir, 1991—, organist, song leader, 1992—; mem. local Am. Legion Aux., 1994—. Mem. Beta Sigma Phi (pres. 1979-80). Roman Catholic. Home: 1302 Johnson Dr Shenandoah IA 51601-2606 Office: 300 Park Ave Shenandoah IA 51601-2351 also: 300 Pershing Ave Shenandoah IA 51601-2355

HANNAFAN, KAY H. PIERCE, lawyer; b. Wilmington, Del., Nov. 6, 1952; d. Clifton and Monica Harvey; m. Christopher J. Hannafan, Aug. 21, 1993; children: John Harvey Pierce, Stephen Harvey Pierce. BS in Engring., U. Tenn., 1974, JD, 1979. Patent agt. Union Carbide Corp., Oak Ridge, Tenn., 1974-77; patent atty. Gould Inc., Rolling Meadows, Ill., 1980-85; corp. atty. Baxter Healthcare Corp., Deerfield, Ill., 1985—. Pro bono atty. Lake County, Ill. Vol. Lawyers Program, 1993-94. Office: Baxter Healthcare Corp 1435 Lake Cook Rd Deerfield IL 60015

HANNAH, BARBARA ANN, nurse, educator; b. Pawnee, Okla., Sept. 25, 1943; d. Harold Ray and Betty Jean (Newport) Norris; m. Charles Bush Hannah, Mar. 25, 1971; children: Charles Douglas, Harry William. AS, Rogers State Coll., Claremore, Okla., 1974; BS in nursing, Tulsa U., 1976; MS, Okla U., 1985; postgrad., Okla. State U., 1989. RN, Okla.; cert. BLS, ACLS, PALS. Nurse St. Francis Hosp., Tulsa, 1968-77, edn. specialist, 1986-90, clin. mgr. post-anesthesia care unit, 1991—; dir. clin. prodn. CSI Prodns. for Medcom Inc., Tulsa, 1977-86; asst. adminstr. nursing Cleveland (Okla.) Area Hosp., 1990-91; cons. St. Anthony Hosp., Oklahoma City, 1985; mem. affiliate faculty, chmn. emergency cardiac care com. Am. Heart Assn., 1986, mem. nat. faculty, 1990—; bd. dirs. Citizen CPR, 1986-91, chmn. comprehensive monitoring com., 1990-91. Producer audio-visual programs for nursing edn., 1977-86. Mem. Food & Refreshment Com. Channel 8 fund raising drive, Tulsa, 1985, 86. Recipient spl. awards and honors All Heart Vol., 1988. Mem. NAFE, Acute Care Nurses Assn. (Tulsa Greater area chpt. seminar dir., treas.), Okla. Nurses Assn. (dist. #2 com. on profl. practice), Am. Heart Assn. (v.p. program com. 1990—, chmn. faculty BLS task force Woman of Yr., Okla. affiliate 1993, chmn. elect Okla. affiliate 1993, chmn. 1994), Am. Soc. Post Anesthesia Nurses (1st pl. poster award Nat. Ann. Conf. 1993, alt. del. from Okla. 1994), Okla. Soc. Post Anesthesia Nurses (pres. Tulsa chpt. 1993), Sigma Theta Tau. Home: PO Box 112 Skiatook OK 74070-0112 Office: Saint Francis Hosp 6161 S Yale Ave Tulsa OK 74136-1992

HANNAH, DARYL, actress; b. Chgo., 1960; d. Don and Sue Hannah. Student, U. So. Calif., Goodman Theater Co., Chgo. Ind. actress, 1978—. Films include The Fury, 1978, The Final Terror, 1981, Hard Country, 1981, Summer Lovers, 1982, Blade Runner, 1982, Reckless, 1984, Splash, 1984, The Pope of Greenwich Village, 1984, The Clan of the Cave Bear, 1986, Legal Eagles, 1986, Roxanne, 1987, Wall Street, 1988, High Spirits, 1988, Steel Magnolias, 1989, Crimes and Misdemeanors, 1989, Crazy People, 1990, At Play in the Fields of the Lord, 1991, Memoirs of an Invisible Man, 1992, Grumpy Old Men, 1993; TV film Paper Dolls, 1982, Attack of the 50 Foot Woman, 1993. Office: ICM 8942 Wilshire Blvd Beverly Hills CA 90211*

HANNAKA, SHERRY LYNN, psychotherapist; b. Denville, N.J., Aug. 7, 1958; d. Floyd and Guilda (Niper) H. AA, Broward C.C., Coconut Creek, Fla., 1979; BS, Nova U., 1982, MS, 1984. Counselor Ctr. for Effective Living, Deerfield Beach, Fla., 1986-88; pvt. practice psychotherapy, Lighthouse Point, Fla., 1988—; counselor Women in Distress, Ft. Lauderdale, Fla., 1984. Bd. dirs. Outreach Broward, Ft. Lauderdale; vol. Jr. League, Ft. Lauderdale, Covenant House, Ft. Lauderdale. Mem. Am. Counseling Assn., Fla. Counselors Assn., Fla. Mental Health Counselors Assn., Assn. Adult Devel. and Aging. Office: 3170 N Federal Hwy Ste 114 Lighthouse Point FL 33064-6721

HANNAN, BRADLEY, educational publishing consultant and executive; b. Rochester, N.Y., Apr. 24, 1935; d. Jack Seymour MacArthur and Alice E. (Knapp) Staley; m. William J. Hannan, Jr., June 15, 1957 (div. 1977); children: Megan Lee, Timothy, Patrick, Moira. BA, Ariz. State U., 1957. Tchr. various sch. dists. Ariz., 1957-62; English language cons. Evanston (Ill.) Twp. High Sch., 1963-65; editor, then sr. editor Harper & Row Pubs., Evanston, 1965-75; sr. reading text editor Scott, Foresman & Co., Glenview, Ill., 1975-78, sr. editor lang. arts, 1982-87; dir. reading McDougal Littell & Co., Evanston, 1978-81; project dir. spelling Ednl. Challenges, Alexandria, Va., 1981-82; dir. curriculum and product mgmt. for reading and lang. arts texts Open Court Pub. Co., Chgo. and Peru, Ill., 1987-88; cons., project dir. lang. arts texts Harcourt, Brace, Jovanovich, Orlando, Fla., 1988-89; sr. mng. editor reading, lang. arts, social studies Sci. Rsch. Assocs., Chgo., 1989; cons. ednl. pub. Chgo., 1989-90; dir. reading, lang. arts, social studies Proof Positive/Farrowlyne Assocs., Chicago, 1990—; speaker Internat. Reading Assn., New Orleans, 1981, Chgo. Women in Publishing, 1981, Childrens' Reading Roundtable, Chgo., 1985; developer reading textbook series. Mem. Internat. Reading Assn., Nat. Council Tchrs. English, Chgo. Book Clinic. Home: 800 Judson Ave Apt 301 Evanston IL 60202-2451 Office: 1620 Central St Evanston IL 60201-1506

HANNAWAY, PATRICIA HINMAN, art scholar, historian; b. Mpls., Jan. 25, 1929; d. Ira Perry and Florence Elizabeth (Montgomery) Hinman; m. Glenn H. Altland, June 12, 1948 (div. 1968); children: David Lee, Roger Dean, Stanley William (dec.), Glenn H. III (dec.); m. Walter F. Hannaway, Feb. 7, 1972 (dec. 1985). Grad. high sch., Mpls., 1947. Freelance writer Mpls., 1953-59; advt. copywriter Boutell's Inc., Mpls., 1958-59, Colle McVoy, Mpls., 1959, Knox-Reeves Advt., Mpls., 1960-62; woman's page editor Key West (Fla.) Citizen, 1963-65; creative dir. Grant Advt., Miami, 1967-68; info. specialist Fla. Dept. Commerce, Tallahassee, 1968-69; creative dir. Daniels Rainey Advt., Clearwater, Fla., 1970-72, Profl. Bus. Assocs., Lutz, Fla., 1988-90; freelance researcher/author. Author: Winslow Homer in the Tropics, 1974. Pres. Friends of Library, Clearwater, 1975-76, Friends of Tampa Hills Library; adv. bd. mem. Pasco Library System, 1991-93; active Tampa Bay Poetry Coun., 1994-95. Democrat. Lutheran. Office: Agape Unlimited PO Box 7112 Wesley Chapel FL 33543

HANNEMAN, ELAINE ESTHER, salesperson; b. Waupaca, Wis., Aug. 28, 1928; d. Martin Fred Strey and Laura Rucks; m. Alfred Adam Hanneman, Feb. 14, 1948; children: Karen, Dale, Sally, Sandra. High sch. grad., 1946. Acct. AAL Life Ins. Co., Appleton, Wis., 1946-48; sales Artex Paint, Milw., 1960-74, Car Ins. and Memberships (AAA), Appleton, Wis., 1974-78, Am. Family Life, Columbus, Ga., 1979—. Mem. Gold Century Club, Pres. Club, Am. Family Life. Lutheran. Home: PO Box 244 103 W St Weyauwega WI 54983-0244 also: 1842 Edgewater Dr Amherst WI 54407

HANNER, DAWNA MELANSON, medical/surgical nurse, analyst; b. Boston, June 4, 1947; d. Frank O. and Patricia C. (Sears) Melanson; m. David M. Hanner, Sept. 1984; children: Daniel Thompson, Scott Thompson. RN Sch. Nursing, Cooley-Dickinson Hosp., Northampton, Mass., 1968. RN, Tex., Mass., N.Y. Staff nurse Columbia Presbyn. Hosp., N.Y.C., St. Elizabeth's Hosp., Boston; triage nurse Children's Med. Ctr., Austin, Tex.; pediatrics charge nurse S.W. Tex. Med. Ctr. Hosp., San Antonio; pediatrics office nurse Dr. Robert A. Wymer, M.D., San Antonio; internat. med. triage supr./mgr. Southboro (Mass.) Med. Group; unit coord. insvc. implementation, nurse mgr. HMO unit Austin Regional Clinic, 1983-84; nurse auditor cost containment svcs. TSSF, Austin, Tex., 1985-88; nurse IV analyst Recipient Utilization Control Tex. Dept. Human Svcs., Austin, 1988—. Mem. NAFE, Tex. Med. Auditors Assn., Exec. Women Tex. Govt. Home: 1004 Alegria Rd Austin TX 78757-3404 Office: Tex Dept of Human Svcs PO Box 149030 # 923 Austin TX 78727

HANNI, GERALDINE MARIE, therapist; b. Salt Lake City, Nov. 14, 1930; d. John Henry and Theresa Justine (Keirce) Gold; m. Kenneth J. Hanni, Mar. 14, 1951; children: Debra, Valerie, Kathleen, Cynthia, Kristine. BS, U. Utah, 1951, MSW, 1983. Lic. clin. social worker. Tchr. Hillside Jr. High Sch., Salt Lake City, 1970-73; intern Davis County Schs., Farmington, Utah, 1981-82, Westside Mental Health, Salt Lake City, 1982-83; group leader LDS Social Services, Salt Lake City, 1985; therapist ISAT, Salt Lake City, 1983-90, clin. dir., 1987-90; clin. instr. U. Utah, Salt Lake City, 1986-90; pvt. practice, 1990—; mem. bd. Salt Lake County Sexual Abuse Task Force, Salt Lake City; cons. LDS Social Services, Salt Lake City, 1984-86. Contbg. author: Abuse and Religion, Confronting Abuse—an LDS Perspective. Sect. dir. Mortar Bd. Honor Soc., western U.S., 1970; pres. Highland High PTA, Salt Lake City, 1980; chairperson Highland High Community Sch. Orgn., Salt Lake City, 1981. Mem. Nat. Assn. Social Workers (Utah chpt.). Democrat. Mormon.

HANNINGTON, MARY LEE, production company executive; b. Detroit, July 18, 1960; d. Ian and Bernice (Sumiec) H. BFA, Mich. State U., 1982. Database program design and tng. profl. Bus. Computer, Southfield, Mich., 1983-86; animator, producer Geoffrey & Jeffrey, Farmington, Mich., 1987-89; exec. producer The Big Picture, Farmington, 1989-91; owner, creative dir. Rivet Films, Inc., Detroit, 1991—. Exec. prodr. (TV) Litter Pigs, 1988 (BDA Bronze award); exec. prodr., animator (TV) Jacobson's, 1990 (Silver Caddy); animator on computer (video for Chevy) Milton (N.Y. Film Festival Bronze); illustrator: Don't Stand Too Close to a Naked Man (by Tim Allen), 1994. Mem. Founders Soc. D.I.A., Detroit, 1990—, Nat. Mus. of Women in Art, Washington, 1991—. Mem. Detroit Producers Assn., Nat. Audubon Soc. Office: Rivet Films Inc 230 E Grand River 6th Fl Detroit MI 48226

HANO, E. GAIL, mayor; b. Bklyn., May 8, 1938; d. Jesse and Elvira M. (Fischetti) Eastman; m. Saizo Hano, June 7, 1957; children: Kim D., Dorian L. Mem. planning commn. City of Encinitas, Calif., 1987-88, mem. city coun., 1988—, mayor, 1990-91, 93—. Home: 730 Piedras Oro Calle Encinitas CA 92024 Office: City of Encinitas 505 S Vulcan Ave Encinitas CA 92024

HANRAHAN, JOYCE YANCEY, educational administrator; b. Fyffe, Ala., Sept. 29, 1933; d. Wallace Odell and Nellie Lee (Raughton) Yancey; m. Edward John Hanrahan, Nov. 12, 1960. BA, U. Ala., University, 1955; MEd, U. N.H., 1964, 68; postgrad., Boston U., U. Calif., Boston U., Harvard. Cert. tchr., prin., N.H., N.J., Maine, Wis. Tchr. pub. schs., Madison, Wis., Durham, N.H., 1960-68; prin. Little Harbour Sch., Portsmouth, N.H., 1969-72, York (Maine) Elem. Sch., 1978-84; ednl. field agt. New Eng. Program in Tchr. Edn., Durham, 1972-75; exec. dir. Community Day Care Ctr., Portsmouth, 1975-76; cons. N.H. Child and Family Svcs., Concord, N.H., 1976-78; headmistress lower sch. Internat. Sch., Brussels, 1984-87; head lower sch. Shady Side Acad., Pitts., 1987-89; asst. head, prin. The Pingry Sch., Short Hills, N.J., 1989—; mem. accrediting com. European Coun. Internat. Schs., 1984-87; cons. on early childhood edn. and child care related issues, New Eng., 1970-84; participant numerous TV panels on edn. related issues, 1970-84; ptnr. J & J Hanrahan, rare books. Author: Works of Maurice Sendak: 1947-1994, 1995; writer, dir. TV program on child care as polit. issue. Mem. Portsmouth City Coun., 1972-76, C. of C., N.H. Gov.'s Task Force on Mental Health of Children, 1976-80, N.H. Early Childhood Task Force, Concord, 1972-80; bd. dirs. N.H. Charitable Trust, Concord, 1974-84, United Fund, Children's Mus., SPNEA, AAA-NH, numerous others. Fellow U.S. Govt., U. N.H., 1968-69, NEH, Ga. Inst. Tech., 1980, Prin.'s Ctr., Harvard U. Sch. Edn., 1984, Aspen Inst., 1990. Mem. ASCD, Nat. Assn. Ind. Schs., Harvard Prin.'s Ctr., Antiquarian Booksellers Assn. AM., Nat. Assn. Edn. Young Children. Home: 320 White Oak Ridge Rd Short Hills NJ 07078-1158

HANRATH, LINDA CAROL, librarian, archivist; b. Chgo., Aug. 22, 1949; d. John Stanley and Victoria (Fraint) Grzesiakowski; m. Richard Alan Hanrath, Nov. 1, 1980; 1 child, Emily. BA in History, Rosary Coll., 1971, MA in Library Sci., 1974. Tchr. social studies Notre Dame High Sch., Chgo., 1971-75; outreach libr. Indian Trails Pub. Libr., Wheeling, Ill., 1975-76, Arlington Heights (Ill.) Meml. Libr., 1976-78; corp. libr. William Wrigley Jr. Co., Chgo., 1978—. Mem. Spl. Librs. Assn. (chmn. libr. jobline com. 1981-83, 86-87, food agrl. and nutrition divsn. 1988-89, sec. Ill. chpt. 1984-86, pres.-elect 1993-94, pres. Ill. chpt. 1994-95), Assn. Records Mgrs. and Adminstrs., Soc. Am. Archivists, Midwest Archives Conf., Beta Phi Mu. Home: 715 E Devon Ave Roselle IL 60172-1461 Office: William Wrigley Jr Co 410 N Michigan Ave Chicago IL 60611

HANRATTY, CARIN GALE, pediatric nurse practitioner; b. Dec. 31, 1953; d. Burton and Lillian Aleskowitz; m. Michael Patrick Hanratty, May 22, 1983; 1 child, Tyler James. BSN, Russell Sage Coll., 1975; postgrad., U. Calif., San Diego, 1980. Cert. CPR instr.; cert. NALS; cert. specialist ANA. PNP day surgery unit Children's Med. Ctr., Dallas, 1981-85; clin. mgr.

pediatrics Trinity Med. Ctr., Carrollton, Tex., 1985-86; pediatric drug coord. perinatal intervention team for substance abusing women and babies Parkland Meml. Hosp., Dallas, 1990—. Guest talk show Morning Coffee, Sta. KPLX-FM, various TV programs. Rep. United Way, 1988; blood donor chair Parkland Hosp., 1990—, chair March of Dimes, 1992; bd. mem., med. cons. Kidnet Found. Mem. ARC (profl., life), Nat. Assn. PNPs (v.p. Dallas chpt. 1982-83), Tex. Nurses Assn. Office: Parkland Meml Hosp care Pediatric Nurse Practitioners 5201 Harry Hines Blvd Dallas TX 75235

HANSEN, BARBARA CALEEN, physiology educator, scientist; b. Boston, Nov. 24, 1941; d. Reynold L. and Dorothy (Richardson) Caleen; m. Kenneth Dale Hansen, Oct. 8, 1976; 1 son, David Scott. B.S., UCLA, 1964, M.S., 1965; Ph.D., U. Wash., 1971. Asst. prof. then assoc. prof. U. Wash., Seattle, 1971-76; prof., assoc. dean U. Mich., Ann Arbor, 1977-82; assoc. v.p. acad. affairs and research, dean grad. sch. So. Ill. U., Carbondale, 1982-85; v.p. for grad. studies and research U. Md., Balt. and Baltimore County, 1985-90; prof. physiology, dir. obesity and diabetes rsch. ctr. U. Md., 1990—; mem. adv. com. to dir. NIH, Washington, 1979-83; mem. joint health policy com. Assn. Am. Univs., Nat. Assn. State Univs. and Land-Grant Colls., Am. Coun. on Edn., Washington, 1982-86; mem. nutrition study sect. NIH, 1979-83; mem. program com. Inst. Medicine-NAS, Washington, 1982-84; mem. Armed Forces Epidemiology Bd., 1991—, Bd. Sci. Counselors, Nat. Toxicology Bd., NIEHS, NIH, 1992-94; mem. search com. Office of Rsch. Integrity, NIH, 1992-93. Contbr. articles to profl. jours.; editor: Controversies in Obesity, 1983; chpts. on physiology. Mem. adv. com. Am. Bur. Med. Advancement China, N.Y.C., 1982-85, Robert Wood Johnson Found., Princeton, N.J., 1982-91; mem. adv. bd. African-Am. Inst. 1987-91. U. Pa. Inst. Neuroscis. fellow, 1966-68; Arthur Patch McKinley scholar of Phi Beta Kappa, 1964. Mem. Am. Physiol. Soc., Inst. Medicine of NAS, Am. Inst. Nutrition, Am. Soc. for Clin. Nutrition (v.p., pres.-elect 1994—), Internat. Assn. for Study of Obesity (pres. 1986-90), N.Am. Assn. for Study of Obesity (pres. 1984-85, 86—), Nat. Assn. State Univs. and Land Grant Colls. (chairperson coun. on rsch. policy and grad. edn. 1986-87), Phi Beta Kappa. Republican. Presbyterian. Office: U Md Sch Medicine MSTF6-00 10 S Pine St Baltimore MD 21201-1192

HANSEN, CORAL JUNE, nurse practitioner, respiratory therapist; b. Seattle, June 5, 1950; d. Raymond Leland and Rosalie (Van Deman) H. Cert. in respiratory therapy, Seattle Cen. Coll., 1975; BS in Nursing summa cum laude, Seattle U., 1987; M in Psychosocial Nursing magna cum laude, U. Wash., 1990. Registered respiratory therapist, nurse, Wash.; advanced registered nurse practitioner; cert. clin. specialist in adult mental health/psychiat. nursing. Respiratory therapist Cura-Care Inc., Modesto, Calif., 1975-84, Northwest Hosp., Seattle, 1984-88; critical care and rehab. nurse University Hosp., Seattle, 1986-87; psychiat. nurse jail psychiat. health Seattle Dept. Pub. Health, 1991; psychiat. nurse Minerth-Meier Psychiat. Unit, Seattle, 1991—; pvt. practice psychotherapy/counseling adult mental health Seattle, 1991—. Contbr. letters to profl. jours. Profl. Nurse Traineeship grantee NIH, 1988-89. Mem. ANA, Assn. Advanced Practice Psychiat. Nurses, DAR, Sigma Theta Tau. Home: PO Box 75193 Seattle WA 98125 Office: PO Box 75193 Seattle WA 98125

HANSEN, DONNA LAUREE, court reporting educator; b. Concordia, Kans., Dec. 25, 1939; d. Peter August and Lynda Bernice (Carlson) H. BA, Bethany Coll., 1961; MS, Kans. State U., 1986. Cert. tchr., Kans., notary pub., Kans. Tchr. Munden (Kans.) High Sch., 1961-64; instr. typing Brown Mackie Coll., Salina, Kans., 1964-74, instr. ct. reporting, 1974-77, chairperson ct. reporting, 1977-88, cons., instr., 1989—; instr. shorthand workshop Pittsburg (Kans.) State U., 1978, Emporia (Kans.) State U., 1978; adminstr. social work spl. project City of Camden, N.J., summers 1962, 63. Compiler (books) Court Reporting Procedures, 1981, Court Reporting Theory Review Books 1, 2, 3, 1983, Court Reporting Advanced Theory Review, Vols. I, II, III, 1984. Bd. dirs. YWCA, Salina, 1991-93, membership chair, 1992-93; mem. alumni bd. Bethany Coll., Lindsborg, Kans., 1979-81. Mem. AAUW (numerous offices, Outstanding Mem. 1980), Kans. Bus. Tchrs. Assn., Nat. Bus. Tchrs. Assn., Kans. Shorthand Reporters Assn., Nat. Shorthand Reporters, Delta Kappa Gamma (numerous offices). Republican. Lutheran. Office: Brown Mackie Coll 126 S Santa Fe Ave Salina KS 67401-2810

HANSEN, ELISA MARIE, art historian; b. Sarasota, Fla., July 14, 1952; d. Gotfred and Barbara (Ham) Hansen; m. Flemming Sogaard, 1987; children: Inga Marie, Anna Sofia. BA in Art History, Fla. State U., 1974; MA in Art History, So. Meth. U., 1982; MA, U. So. Fla., 1984. Edn. specialist Pinellas County Art Coun., Clearwater, Fla., 1977-78; curator of edn. Mus. Fine Arts, St. Petersburg, Fla., 1978-80; asst. prof. Eckerd Coll., St. Petersburg, 1985-88, adj. prof., 1988—; dir. adult and acad. programs, acting curator The John & Mable Ringling Mus. Art, Sarasota, 1989—; adj. instr. Ringling Sch. Art and Design, 1992—. Contbr. articles and book reviews to profl. jours. Mem. Am. Assn. Mus., Coll. Art Assn. Republican. Lutheran. Office: The John & Mable Ringling Mus Art 5401 Bay Shore Rd Sarasota FL 34243-2161

HANSEN, HEIDI NEUMANN, advertising executive; b. N.Y.C., Feb. 2, 1955; d. Roy G. and Carolyn (Holmes) Neumann; m. Bruce Alan Hansen, Sept. 1, 1985. Student MIT, 1975-76; A.B., Colby Coll., Waterville, Maine, 1977. Benefits adminstr. Gen. Host Corp., Stamford, Conn., 1977-78; pres. Letterworks Internat., Portland, Maine, 1981—; bd. dir. SALT Ctr. Documentary Studies, Ingraham; bd. advisors Docktrap River Fish Farm, 1992—. Editor Indsl. Report MIT, 1975. Dir., Maine Handicapped Skiing, Portland, 1984-92; vol. Maine Med. Ctr., Portland, 1982—; bd. dir. Portland Concert Assn., 1992—; trustee Portland Mus. Art, 1993—; corporator Maine Med. Ctr., 1993—. Mem. Maine Audubon Soc, Nature Conservancy, Ad Club of Greater Portland (dir. 1983-85, v.p. 1985-87, pres. 1987-88), Portland C. of C. (bd. dir. 1990-92). Avocations: travel, hiking, sailing. Home: 313 Fowler Rd Cape Elizabeth ME 04107-2501 Office: Letterworks Internat 18 Ashmont St Portland ME 04103-4468

HANSEN, JEAN MARIE, math and computer educator; b. Detroit, Mar. 8, 1937; d. Harvey Francis and Ida Marie (Hay) Chapman; m. Donald Edward Hansen, Aug. 29, 1968; children: Jennifer Lynn, John Francis. BA, U. Mich., 1959, MA, 1960. Cert. Secondary Sch. Tchr. Tchr. Detroit Pub. Schs., 1959-60, Newark (Calif.) Sch. Dist., 1960-65, Dept. Def., Zweibruken, Germany, 1965-67, Livonia (Mich.) Pub. Schs., 1967-69; instr. Ford Livonia Transmission Plant, 1990—; trustee/pres. Northville (Mich.) Bd. Edn., 1981—. Author: California People and Their Government, 1965, Voices of Government, 1969-70. Named Disting. Bd. Mem., Mich. Assn. Sch. Bds., 1991, Citizen of Yr., Northville C. of C., 1991. Mem. AAUW (v.p. Northville bd. 1982-86, pres. 1987-89, Mich. chpt. Agt. of Change award, edn. area 1985), LWV, Kiwanis, Northville Women's Club. Republican. Home: 229 Linden St Northville MI 48167-1426

HANSEN, JO-IDA CHARLOTTE, psychology educator, researcher; b. Washington, Oct. 2, 1947; d. Gordon Henry and Charlotte Lorraine (Helgeson) H.; m. John Paul Campbell. BA, U. Minn., 1969, MA, 1971, PhD, 1974. Asst. prof. psychology U. Minn., Mpls., 1974-78, assoc. prof., 1978-84, prof., 1984—, dir. Ctr. for Interest Measurement Rsch., 1974—, dir. counseling psychology program, 1987—. Author: User's Guide for the SII, 1984, 2d edit., 1992, Manual for the SII, 1985; contbr. numerous articles to profl. jours., chpts. to books. Recipient early career award U. Minn., 1982, E.K. Strong, Jr. gold medal Strong Exec. Bd., 1984. Fellow APA (coun. reps. 1990-93, pres. divsn. counselor psychology 1993-94, chmn. joint com. testing practices 1989-93, com. to revise APA/AERA.NCME testing standards 1993—), Am. Psychol. Soc.; mem. ACA(extended rsch. award 1990), Assn. for Measurement and Evaluation (pres. 1988-89, Exemplary Practice award 1987, 90). Office: U Minn Dept Psychology Ctr Interest Measurement 75 E River Rd Minneapolis MN 55455-0280

HANSEN, KAREN THORNLEY, accountant; b. Chgo., June 1, 1945; d. Charles Bruce and Arlene Ann (McHale) Thornley; m. Terry Lee Hansen, Aug. 17, 1968; 1 child, Charles Scott. BA, Marycrest Coll., Davenport, Iowa, 1967. CPA, N.Y.; cert. M.T. Med. staff tech. Mercy Hosp., Davenport, Iowa, 1967-68, St. Joseph Hosp., Chgo., 1968, Spl. Hematology, Wilford Hall, USAF Hosp., Lackland AFB, Tex., 1973-78; staff acct. Lewittes & Co., Poughkeepsie, N.Y., 1980-81; sr. acct. Urbach, Kahn & Werlin, Poughkeepsie, 1981-82; ptnr. Hansen & Dunn, CPA's, Poughkeepsie, 1982—. Bd. dirs., sec. bd. United Way Dutchess County, Poughkeepsie, 1988—; bd. dirs. YMCA Dutchess County, Girl Scouts U.S.A., 1983-87; bbd. dirs. Mid-Hudson Civic Ctr., Inc., 1993-95; mem. Jr. League Poughkeepsie, 1979—; mem. membership com. and econ. devel. com. Poughkeepsie Partnership, Inc.; trustee St. Martin de Porres Ch., 1990-94; bd. dirs. Civic Properties, Inc., 1992. Mem. AICPA, N.Y. State Soc. CPAs, Greater Poughkeepsie Area C. of C. (bd. dirs. 1986—, sec. exec. com. 1991, v.p. exec. com. 1993—), Amrita Club (bd. dirs. 1982-92, pres. 1990), Poughkeepsie Tennis Club. Republican. Roman Catholic. Office: Hansen & Dunn 309 Main Mall Poughkeepsie NY 12601-3116

HANSEN, KATHRYN GERTRUDE, former state official, association editor; b. Gardner, Ill., May 24, 1912; d. Harry J. and Marguerite (Gaston) Hansen; BS with honors, U. Ill., 1934, MS, 1936. Sec., U. N.C., 1936-37; sec., U. High Sch., U. Ill., 1937-44; Personnel asst. U. Ill., Urbana, 1944-46, supr. tng. and activities, 1946-47, personnel officer, instr. psychology, 1947-52, exec. sec. U. Civil Service System Ill., also sec. for merit bd., 1952-61, adminstrv. officer, sec. merit bd., 1961-68, dir. system, 1968-72; lay asst. firm Webber, Balbach, Theis and Follmer, P.C., Urbana, Ill., 1972-74. Bd. dirs. U. YWCA, 1952-55, chmn., 1954-55; bd. dirs. Champaign-Urbana Symphony, 1978-81; sec. Presbyn. Women 1st Presbyn. Ch., Champaign, 1986-90, mem. coordinating team, 1986-91. Mem. Coll. and Univ. Personnel Assn. (hon., life mem., editor jour. 1955-73, newsletter, internat. pres. 1967-68, nat. publs. award named in her honor 1987), Annuitants Assn. State Univs. Retirement System Ill. (state sec.-treas. 1974-75), Pres.'s Council U. Ill. (life), U. Ill. Alumni Assn. (life), Friends of the Library (bd. dirs. 1987-91), U. Ill. Found., Nat. League Am. Pen Women, AAUW (state 1st v.p. 1958-60, hon., life), Champaign-Urbana Symphony Guild, Secretariat U. Ill. (life, named scholarship 1972—), Grundy County Hist. Soc. (life), Delta Kappa Gamma (state pres. 1961-63), Phi Mu (life), Kappa Delta Pi, Kappa Tau Alpha. Presbyterian. Clubs: Fortnightly (Champaign-Urbana), Bus. and Profl. Women's, U. Ill. Women's Club, Evening Etude-Mozart Club (hon.). Lodge: Order Eastern Star. Author: (with others) A Plan of Position Classification for Colleges and Universities; A Classification Plan for Staff Positions at Colleges and Universities, 1968; Grundy-Corners, 1982; Sarah, A Documentary of Her Life and Times, 1984, Ninety Years with Fortnightly, Vols. I and II, an historical compilation, 1986, Whispers of Yesterday, 1989, Through the Years with the Champaign-Urbana Business and Professional Women's Club, 1912-1993, 1993; editor: The Illini Worker, 1946-52; Campus Pathways, 1952-61; This is Your Civil Service Handbook, 1960-67; author, cons., editor publs. on personnel practices. Home: 1004 E Harding Dr Apt 307 Urbana IL 61801-6346

HANSEN, LISA YOUNG, municipal agency administrator; b. Rexburg, Idaho, Apr. 28, 1957; d. Rulon Squires and Lucille Cole (Young) McCarrey; m. Darrel Chancy Hansen, Mar. 23, 1984. A, Ricks Coll., 1977; student, Harvard U., summers 1977, 78, Brigham Young U., 1980-82. Geneal. clk. Stevensons Geneal. Ctr., Provo, Utah, 1977; typesetter, news clk. Valley News, Rexburg, Idaho, 1977-78; credit clk. Credit Bur. Idaho Falls, 1982-83; adminstrv. asst. Bonneville County Civil Defense, Idaho Falls, 1983—; speaker in field; radiol. defense officer State of Idaho, Bureau of Disaster Services, 1984—; sec. Bonneville Tricentennial Commn., 1983—, Bonneville Flood Control Coordinatig com., 1983—, Bonneville Bicentennial of the Constn. com., 1983—. Editor: Bonneville Tricentennial Commn. Newsletter; contbr. articles to profl. jours. Rep. United Way, Idaho Falls, 1986; vote clerk Bonneville County Elections Dept., Idaho Falls, 1980, 81; mem. Bonneville County Centennial Com., Nat. Coordinating Coun. Emergency Mgmt. Mem. Am. Civil Def. Assn. (co-resolutions chmn. 1985-87), Idaho Civil Def. Assn., Bonneville County Employees Assn. (pres. 1989), Bonneville County Humane Soc., Humane Soc. of U.S., Am. Soc. for Prevention of Cruelty to Animals, People for the Ethical Treatment of Animals, Doris Day Animal League, Nat. Wildlife Fedn., Nat. Coordinating Coun. on Emergency Mgmt., Lambda Delta Sigma. Republican. Mormon. Home: 874 Goldie St Idaho Falls ID 83402-4727 Office: Bonneville County Civil Def 605 N Capital Ave Idaho Falls ID 83402-3582

HANSEN, LORRAINE SUNNY SUNDAL (SUNNY HANSEN), counselor, educator; b. Albert Lea, Minn.; d. Rasmus O. and Cora B. Sundal; m. Tor Kjaerstad Hansen, Dec. 15, 1962; children: Sonja, Tor S. BS, U. Minn., 1951, MA, 1957, PhD, 1962; postgrad., U. Oslo, Norway, 1959-60. Nat. cert. counselor; cert. career counselor. English tchr. St. Louis Park, Minn., 1951-53, Lab. Sch. U. Chgo., 1953-54; tchr. English and journalism Univ. High Sch., U. Minn., Mpls., 1954-57, counselor, dir. counseling, 1957-70; asst. prof., assoc. prof., prof. ednl. psychology U. Minn., Mpls., 1962—, dir. project BORN FREE; founder, dir. project BORN FREE; cons. schs. and colls.; lectr. throughout U.S. and 16 countries; dir. workshops on career devel. and career counseling, new age and integrative life planning; co-dir. Internat. Counseling Inst., 1989, 91, 93. Author: Career Guidance Practices in School and Community, 1970, An Examination of Concepts and Definitions of Career Education, 1976, Integrative Life Planning, 1987, (with others) Educating for Career Development, 1975, 80, Career Development and Planning, 1982, Eliminating Sex Stereotyping in Schools, 1984; editor: Career Development and Counseling of Women, 1978, Career Patterns of Selected Women Leaders, 1987, Integrative Career Planning, 1994; mem. editorial bd. Internat. Jour. Advancement Counseling, 1980—, Minn. Jour. for Counseling and Human Devel., 1984—. Fulbright scholar U. Oslo, 1959-60; named Outstanding Leader in Edn. Mpls. YWCA, 1984; recipient Career Devel. Profl. Award S.E. Minn. chpt. ASTD, 1986. Fellow APA; mem. AAUW, AACD (pres.-elect 1988-89, pres. 1989-90, past pres. 1990-91), Minn. Psychol. Assn., Minn. Assn. for Counseling and Devel. (recipient cert. recognition 1976, Nat. Disting. Achievement award 1990), Am. Sch. Counselors Assn., Am. Coll. Pers. Assn., Am. Coll. Counselors Assn., Assn. for Counselor Edn. and Supervision (Nat. Disting. Mentor award 1985), Nat. Career Devel. Assn. (pres.-elect 1984-85, pres. 1985-86, past pres. 1986-87, Eminent Career award 1990), Minn. Career Devel. Assn. (pres. 1982-83, Rsch. award 1980, Outstanding Achievement award 1986), Internat. Assn. Ednl.-Vocat. Guidance, Internat. Round Table for Advancement of Counseling (exec. coun., v.p. 1986-88), Assn. for Multicultural Counseling and Devel., Assn. for Adult Devel. & Aging, Minn. Women's Consortium, Upper Midwest Norwegian-Am. C. of C. (v.p., pres., bd. dirs. 1988—), Phi Delta Kappa, Chi Sigma Iota. Democrat. Congregationalist. Office: U Minn Dept Ednl Psychology 139 Burton Hall 178 Pillsbury Dr SE Minneapolis MN 55455-0296

HANSEN, MARION JOYCE, nursing administrator; b. Wadena, Minn., Oct. 20, 1951; d. Charles R. and Dorothy M. (Hennen) Hillig; m. Keith Hansen, June 2, 1979; children: Adam, Angela, John James, Jason. Diploma, St. Luke's Hosp. Sch. Nursing, Duluth, Minn., 1972; BS, Moorhead State U., 1991. Staff RN ICCU Tri-County Hosp., Wadena, 1972-74, house supr. ICCU, staff RN, edn. dir., ICCU coor., 1974-89, asst. adminstr.; dir. of nursing Elders' Home, Inc., New York Mills, Minn., 1989—; claims coord. workers compensation; chair nursing program adv. com., Northwest Tech. Coll. Mem. Nat. Assn. Dirs. Nursing Assn. Long Term Care, Minn. Dirs. Nursing Assn. Long Term Care, Am. Cancer Soc. (comms. chair, past pres.). Home: RR 1 Box 144F Sebeka MN 56477-9735

HANSEN, MARY ANN MELLOR, education administrator; b. Manchester, Conn., June 20, 1952; d. Edward Gunther and Mildred Theresa (Mellor) H. BA, Syracuse U., 1974, MS, 1976, PhD, 1983. Cert. French tchr., sch. adminstr. Tchr. of French Syracuse (N.Y.) Schs., 1978-79; researcher Conn. Gen. Assembly, Hartford, 1985-86; staff assoc. for spl. projects Conn. Dept. Higher Edn., Hartford, 1986-87; edn. cons. Conn. Dept. Edn., Hartford, 1987—; state rep. New Eng. Articulation and Achievement Project: The Challenge of the 1990s in Fgn. Lang. Edn., 1992—. Mem. Coventry (Conn.) Conservation Commn., 1987-92. Edn. policy fellow Inst. for Ednl. Leadership, Washington, 1990; grantee USIA, Washington, 1993, 94, Nat. Endowment for Democracy, 1993; recipient citation for Outstanding Svc., Conn. Gen. Assembly, Hartford, 1986. Mem. Nat. Assn. State Suprs. of Fgn. Langs., Conn. Coun. Lang. Tchrs. (bd. dirs. 1992—), New Eng. Acad. Alliance (steering com. 1992—), Am. Coun. on Tchng. of Fgn. Lang. Office: Conn Dept Edn PO Box 2219 Hartford CT 06145

HANSEN, ROBYN L., lawyer; b. Terre Haute, Ind., Dec. 2, 1949; d. Robert Louis and Shirley (Nagel) Wieman; m. Gary Hansen, Aug. 21, 1971 (div. 1985); children: Nathan Ross Hansen, Brian Michael Hansen; m. John Marley Clarey, Jan. 1, 1986. BA, Gustavus Adolphus, 1971; JD cum laude, William Mitchell Coll. Law, 1977. Bar: Minn. 1977, U.S. Dist. Ct. Minn. 1977. Atty. Briggs and Morgan P.A., St. Paul, 1977-93, Leonard Street & Deinard, Mpls., 1993—. Trustee Actors Theatre St. Paul, 1980-88; bd. dirs. St. Paul Downtown Coun., 1985-93, Met. State U. Found., 1993—; exec. dir. Minn. Inst. Pub. Fin., 1987-93, bd. dirs., 1993—, pres., 1995—. Mem. ABA, Minn. Bar Assn., Ramsey County Bar Assn., Nat. Assn. Bond Lawyers. Office: Leonard Street & Deinard 1414 Landmark Tower Saint Paul MN 55102

HANSEN, SHARON M., state agency administrator, policy analyst; b. Point Angeles, Wash., Sept. 28, 1935; d. Herbert Milton and Caryl (Heslin) McGee; m. Janis T. Hansen, Sept. 2, 1956; children: Andrew John, Matthew Thomas. BA, U. Wash., 1957, cert. in Mgmt., 1988. Planner Office of Cmty. Devel., State Wash., Olympia, Wash., 1974-75; exec. dir. Pierce County Assn. for Retarded Citizens, Tacoma, 1975-80; resource mgr. Dept. Social and Health Svcs., State Wash., Tacoma, 1980-82; planner Dept. Social and Health Svcs., State Wash., Olympia, Wash., 1982-84; exec. dir. Developmental Disabilities Planning Coun., State Wash., Olympia, Wash., 1984-91; analyst Family Policy Coun., State Wash., Olympia, Wash., 1992-94; dir. Tacoma Pierce County Commn. on Children, Youtrh and Families, Tacoma, 1994—; bd. dirs. Nat. Assn. Developmental Disabilities Coun., Washington, D.C., 1985-90, v.p. 1990-91; cons. Westside Regional Ctr., Calif., 1987, N.J. Developmental Disabilities Coun., 1991, Govt. India Ministry of Welfare, 1991. Contbd. articles to profl. jours. Fulbright Hayes lectureship, 1991. Home: 714 N Stadium Way Tacoma WA 98403 Office: Tacoma Pierce County Commn Children 3629 South D Street Tacoma WA 98408

HANSEN-KYLE, LINDA L., managed health care nurse; b. Selma, Calif., Aug. 24, 1947; d. Ernest L. and Mary (Terzian) Hansen; m. Kenton L. Kyle, Feb. 16, 1974. BA in Psychology, Humboldt State, 1969, MA in History summa cum laude, 1972; ASN, Saddleback Coll., 1976; MS in Human Resources and Mgmt. Devel., Chapman U., 1993. RN, Calif. Mgr. ops. for Conservco Travelers Inc., San Diego; asst. dir. nursing Maric Coll., San Diego; ICU nurse supr. Scripps Clinic and Rsch., San Diego. Mem. ASTD, ACCN, AAUW, Soroptomist Club of Poway.

HANSEY, RENEE JEANNE, retired communications executive; b. Tacoma, Apr. 24, 1927; d. Francis J. and Genevieve (Hewitt) Payette; m. James Burpee, Mar. 13, 1947 (dec. 1950); children: James, Victoria; m. Orville D. Hansey (div. 1987); children; Dan, Terri, John, Bill; m. Ralph Edward Lecky Sr., June 26, 1989 (div. Dec. 1993); stepchildren: Ralph Edward Jr., Brent. Student in Layout and Design, Art Inst. Chgo., 1943; BS in Psychology, St. John's U., 1988; MS in Psychology, St John's U., 1991; postgrad. in Graphics, U. Alaska, 1985. Copy writer Sta. KIT, Yakima, Wash., 1942-44; program mgr. Sta. KING, Seattle, 1945-47; advt. mgr. Sequim (Wash.) Press, 1967-70, editor, 1970-76; TV producer Municipality of Anchorage, 1976-86; pub. Voice, Port Angeles, Wash., 1986-89; cons. on media rels. and sr. citizens; coord. Lifeline Olympic Meml. Hosp., Pt. Angeles, Wash., 1994—; founder Widowed Persons Svc., Anchorage, 1983-85; owner Frontier Pub., Anchorage, 1983-85; dir. Far North Network, Anchorage, 1982-86. Author: Go to the Source, 1977, One Way to the Funny Farm, 1978; producer (TV show) Opportunities for Seniors, 1981-86 (TV Prodn. award, 1982-85). Sec. Dem. Cen. Com. Clallam County, Wash., 1965-76; founder Olympic Women's Resource Ctr., Port Angeles, 1966-75; councilwoman City Sequim, 1973-76; active Affirmative Action Clallam County, Wash., 1974, Sr. Companions, Elder Abuse Task Force; bd. dirs. Port Angeles Sr. Ctr. With WAC, 1944. Mem. AAUW, Alaska Press Women (pres. 1981-82, 85-86), Nat. Fedn. Press Women, Alaska Press Club. Roman Catholic. Home: 235 N Sunnyside Ave Sequim WA 98382-3479

HANSKNECHT, LISA MARIE, legislative policy analyst; b. Detroit, May 15, 1966; d. Joseph Leo and Mary Elizabeth (Beckwith) H. BA, Mich. State U., 1988. Constituent svc. rep., immigration specialist U.S. Senator Carl Levin's Office, Detroit, 1988-89; legis. and com. aide Rep. Curtis Hertel, Mich. Ho. of Reps., Lansing, 1989-93; legis. policy analyst house Dems. Speaker Curtis Hertel, Mich. Ho. of Reps., Lansing, 1993-95, legis. policy analyst, 1995—. Campaign vol. Mich. Dem. Party, Lansing, 1988—; fundraising planner Rep. Curtis Hertel, Lansing, 1989-92; phone bank coord. Senator Tsongas-Presdl. Primary, Detroit, 1992. State of Mich. Competetive scholar, 1984. Democrat. Roman Catholic. Office: Office of Ho Dem Leader Ho Dem Policy PO Box 30014 Lansing MI 48909-7514

HANSON, ANNE COFFIN, art historian; b. Kinston, N.C., Dec. 12, 1921; d. Francis Joseph Howells and Annie Roulhac (Coffin) Coffin; m. Bernard Alan Hanson, June 27, 1961; children by previous marriage: James Warfield Garson, Robert Coffin Garson, Ann Blaine Garson. B.F.A., U. So. Calif., 1943; M.A. in Creative Arts, U. N.C., 1951; Ph.D., Bryn Mawr Coll., 1962. Instr. Albright Art Sch., U. Buffalo, 1955-58; vis. asso. prof. art Cornell U., 1963; asst. prof. Swarthmore Coll., 1963-64, Bryn Mawr Coll., 1964-68; dir. Internat. Study Center, Mus. Modern Art, N.Y.C., 1968-69; adj. assoc. prof. NYU, 1969-70; prof. history art Yale U., New Haven, 1970-92; chmn. dept. Yale U., 1974-78, acting dir. Art Gallery,, 1985-87, John Hay Whitney prof. emeritus, 1992—; vis. Clark prof. Clark Art Inst., Williams Coll., fall 1990; Samuel H. Kress prof. (hon.) Ctr. Advanced Study Visual Arts Nat. Gallery Art, Washington, 1992-93. Author: Jacopo della Quercia's Fonte Gaia, 1965, Edouard Manet, 1966, Manet and the Modern Tradition, 1977, The Futurist Imagination, 1983; also articles in profl. jours; mem. editorial bd. The Art Bull., 1971-91; editor monograph series Coll. Art Assn., 1968-70; mem. governing bd. Yale U. Press, 1977-90; mem. editorial com. Art Jour., 1979-83. Mem. governing bd., v.p. Hillstead Mus., Farmington, Conn., 1989-92, v.p., 1991-92; adv. bd. Swann Found. for Cartoon and Caricature, N.Y.C., 1988-93. NEH fellow, 1967-68; Am. Coun. Learned Socs. grantee, summer 1963, fellow, 1983-84; resident Am. Acad. Rome, spring, 1974; fellow Inst. Advanced Study, fall, 1983. Mem. Coll. Art Assn. Am. (pres. 1972-74), Comité Internationale de l'histoire de l'Art (nat. mem. 1975-92). Office: Yale U Dept History Art PO Box 208272 New Haven CT 06520-8272

HANSON, ANNE MARIE LALONDE, speech and theatre educator; b. Avon, Ohio, Jan. 18, 1955; d. Robert James and Marjory Verl (Eckstein) LaL.; m. Bruce Arden Hanson, June 4, 1985; 1 child, Eric Loren. BA, Baldwin-Wallace Coll., 1977; MA, Ariz. State U., 1983; postgrad., U. Kans., 1989-91. Tech. dir. Phoenix Ctr. Performing Arts, 1978-79; grad. teaching asst. Schiller Coll., Strasbourg, France, 1977, Ariz. State U., Tempe, 1978-79; asst. prof. theatre and English Benedictine Coll., Atchison, Kans., 1979-84; instr. theatre and speech Northeastern State U., Tahlequah, Okla., 1984-89; grad. teaching asst. U. Kans., Lawrence, 1989-91; instr. speech Haskell Indian Nations U., Lawrence, 1991—. Tech. dir., costume and scene designer Benedictine Coll. Theatre, 1979-84; costume/scenic designer River City Players Summer Theatre, 1985-90. Summer fellow Grad. Coll. U. Kans., Lawrence, 1990. Mem. AAUW, Speech Comm. Assn., U.S. Inst. Theatre Tech. Home: 1436 S Olive St Ottawa KS 66067-3447 Office: Haskell Indian Nations U 155 Indian Ave Lawrence KS 66046-4817

HANSON, CATHERINE IRENE, lawyer; b. Oakland, Calif., Apr. 18, 1955; d. Hobart and Adele Frances (Brooks) H.; m. Theodore E. Lobman, Sept. 6, 1981; 1 child, Alexander Theodore. BA, U. Calif., Berkeley, 1978, JD, 1982. Assoc. Hassard Bonnington, San Francisco, 1982-86; chief atty. Calif. Med. Assn., San Francisco, 1986-94, v.p., gen. counsel, 1992—. Co-author: Peer Review Law, 1991, 93, California Physicians Legal Handbook, 1990, 95. Mem. ABA, Am. Soc. Law and Medicine, Am. Soc. Med. Assn. (past pres. 1994—), Nat. Health Lawyers Assn., Calif. Soc. Health Care Attys. (past pres. 1994—). Office: Calif Med Assn PO Box 7690 221 Main St San Francisco CA 94120-7690

HANSON, DIANE CHARSKE, management consultant; b. Cleve., May 15, 1946; d. Howard Carl and Emma Katherine (Lange) Charske; m. William James Hanson, June 30, 1973. BS, Cornell U., 1968; MS, U. Pa., 1989. Home service rep. Rochester Gas and Electric, N.Y., 1968-70; home economist U. Conn., Storrs, 1970-72; job analyst personnel dept. State of Conn., Hartford, 1972-73; sales rep. Ayerst Labs., Waterbury, Conn., 1973-80, sales trainer, 1979-80; dist. sales mgr. Phila., 1980-87; pres. Creative Resource Devel., W. Chester, Pa., 1986—; developer, pres. Womens Referral Network, West Chester, 1987-89. Vice-pres., bd. dirs., aux. pres. Chester County Soc. for Prevention Cruelty to Animals, 1986-91, pres. bd. dirs.,

1992-94, mem. exec. com., 1994—. Mem. ASTD (v.p. comm. 1991-92), Nat. Soc. Performance and Instrn. (v.p. programs Great Valley chpt. 1993-94, pres.-elect 1995), Pa. State Tech. Devel. Ctr. (bd. dirs. 1991-92), Assn. Quality and Participation, Phila. Area Coun. Excellence, Phila. Soc. for Human Resources, Phila. Human Resources Planning Group, Phila. Orgn. Devel. Network, Chester County Human Resources Assn. (program chmn. 1991-92). Home and Office: 824 W Strasburg Rd West Chester PA 19382-1927

HANSON, EILEEN, principal; b. Camden, N.J., Mar. 3, 1948; d. Thomas Edward and Rita Theresa (Madison) Bannan; m. Kenneth Wesley Hanson, Mar. 22, 1975; 1 child, Michelle Eileen. BA, San Diego State U., 1970; teaching cert., Calif. State U., Dominguez Hills, 1974, cert. adminstr., 1976. Prin. St. Anthony Sch., El Segundo, Calif., 1976-80; dir. St. Charles Catechetical Program, San Diego, 1980-87; prin. Holy Family Sch., San Diego, 1987-92, St. Pius X Sch., Chula Vista, Calif., 1992—; grant project coord. for Cath. Schs. San Diego, 1992-94. Mem. ASCD, Nat. Cath. Educators Assn., Greater Math. Assn., San Diego Child Care and Devel. Com., San Diego Alcohol and Tobacco Edn. Assn., Western Assn. Schs. Colls. (accreditation chair). Home: 942 Grove Ave Imperial Beach CA 91932-3347 Office: 37 E Emerson St Chula Vista CA 91911-3507

HANSON, ELIZABETH CRUMP, political science educator; b. Memphis, Dec. 11, 1934; d. Brooks Athey and Elizabeth (Kelly) Crump; m. Kenneth Ralph Hanson, June 13, 1958; children: Patrick Stuart, Gaelen Elizabeth. BA, So. Meth. U., 1956; MA, Columbia U., 1960, PhD, 1966. Rsch. asst. Yale U., New Haven, Conn., 1970-74, lectr., 1973-76; from asst. to assoc. prof. U. Conn., Storrs, 1976-90, prof., 1990—; rsch. assoc. Conf. Bd., N.Y.C., 1975-76. Co-author: Interest and Ideology, 1975, Multinationals in Contention, 1978, Science, Politics, and International Conference, 1989. Mem. ethics bd. dirs. Town of Orange, Conn., 1988—; trustee Conn. Pub. Broadcasting, 1980-86. Fulbright scholar, 1986, 91. Fellow Inter-Univ. Consortium for Armed Forces and Soc.; mem. Am. Polit. Sci. Assn., Internat. Studies Assn. (v.p. 1982-83), Internat. Polit. Sci. Assn. (chair polit. rsch. com. 1982-94, chair polit. comm. sect. 1992-93), Assn. for Asian Studies, Internat. Communication Assn. Democrat. Office: U Conn 341 Mansfield Rd Storrs CT 06268

HANSON, HEIDI ELIZABETH, lawyer; b. Portsmouth, Ohio, Nov. 13, 1954. BS, U. Ill., 1975, JD, 1978. Bar: Ill. 1978, U.S. Dist. Ct. (no. dist.) Ill., U.S. Ct. Appeals (7th cir.). Atty. water, air and land pollution divs. Ill. EPA, Springfield, Ill., 1978-85; atty. water pollution div. Ill. EPA, Maywood, Ill., 1985-86; assoc. Ross & Hardies, Chgo., 1987-89, ptnr., 1990-94; founder H.E. Hanson Law Offices, Western Springs, Ill., 1994—. Mem. ABA, Ill. State Bar Assn., Chgo. Bar Assn., Air and Waste Mgmt. Assn., Indsl. Water, Waste and Sewer Group. Office: 4721 Franklin Ave Ste 1500 Western Springs IL 60558-1720

HANSON, KAREN, philosopher, educator; b. Lincoln, Nebr., Apr. 11, 1947; d. Lester Eugene and Gladys (Diessner) H.; m. Dennis Michael Senchuk, Aug. 22, 1970; children: Tia Elizabeth, Chloe Miranda. BA summa cum laude, U. Minn., 1970; MA, Harvard U., 1980, PhD, 1980. Lectr. to assoc. prof. Ind. U., Bloomington, 1976-91, prof. philosophy, 1991—, adj. prof. Am. studies, women's studies and comparative lit., 1991—; mem. governing bd. Ind. U. Inst. for Advanced Study, Bloomington; mem. editorial bd. Peirce Edition Project, Indpls., 1982-89, 90—. Author: The Self Imagined, 1986; co-editor: Romantic Revolutions, 1990; assoc. editor Jour. Social Philosophy, 1982-86; edtl. bd. Philosophy of Music Edn. Review, 1992—; edtl. cons. Am. Philos. Quarterly, 1995—; contbr. articles to profl. jours. Del. Am. Coun. Learned Socs., 1993— (exec. com., 1994—); officer John Dewey Found., 1989—. Mem. Am. Philos. Assn. (exec. officer 1986-91, program com. 1984-91, nominating com. 1993-94), Am. Soc. for Aesthetics (program com. 1989-90), Soc. for Women in Philosophy, Phi Beta Kappa (exec. com. Gamma of Ind. chpt. 1993—, officer, 1995—). Home: 1606 S Woodruff Ln Bloomington IN 47401-4448 Office: Ind U Dept of Philosophy Sycamore 026 Bloomington IN 47405

HANSON, MARGARET, social worker; b. Liverpool, Eng., July 6, 1933; d. Joseph and Catherine Agnes (Bergin) H. BA, Coll. of St. Rose, 1956; MA, Cath. U., 1967; MSW, Marywood Sch. Social Work, 1977. Cert. social worker, N.Y.; diplomate Am. Bd. Examiners in Clin. Social Work. Tchr. Latin and English h.s. Cath. Schs. of Diocese of Syracuse, Binghamton and Rome, N.Y., 1957-69; clin. social worker Cath. Social Svcs., Binghamton, 1969-75, Alch. Ctr. Broome City, Binghamton, 1975-78, PROBE, Inc., Binghamton, 1978-79, Binghamton Psychiat. Clinic, 1979-81, Binghamton Gen. Hosp., 1981—; bd. dirs., pres. PROBE, Inc., Binghamton. Bd. dirs. Ladies of Charity of USA, St. Louis, 1993—, mem., Binghamton, 1969—. Roman Catholic.

HANSON, MARIAN W., state legislator; b. Santa Maria, Calif., Jan. 17, 1933; m. Darrel Hanson; 4 children. Rancher; mem. Mont. Ho. of Reps., 1983—, spkr. of the ho. pro tempore, 1993; county mem. Local Govt. Study Commn. Republican. Home: PO Box 237 Ashland MT 59003-0237 Office: Mont Ho of Reps State Capitol Helen MT 59620*

HANSON, PATTI LYNN, human resources director; b. Kennewick, Wash., Apr. 21, 1953; d. Lyle Harry and Ellene Lavonne (McGrath) Morgan; m. Dale R. Hanson, Jan. 18, 1995. AS, El Paso C.C., Colorado Springs, Colo., 1972; BS, Regis Coll., 1982; M in Human Resources Devel., Webster U., 1994. Sec. Adams County Sch. Dist., Thornton, Colo., 1972-73; sec. Montgomery Ward & Co., Denver, 1973-77, computer operator, 1977-79, sec., 1979-83, pers. supr., 1983-84; pers. mgr. Montgomery Ward & Co., Shawnee Mission, Kans., 1984-86; govt. funds coord. Montgomery Ward & Co., Kansas City, Mo., 1986; div. tng. mgr. Montgomery Ward & Co., Kansas City, 1986-88; regional human resource mgr. KFC Nat. Mgmt. Co., Irving, Tex., 1988-90; human resources dir. Businessland, Inc./JWP, Lenexa, Kans., 1990-91; dir. Entex Info. Svcs. (formerly JWP), Lenexa, Kans., 1992—. Active Big Sisters Am., Denver, 1984. Mem. Am. Soc. Quality Control, Human Resource Mgmt. Assn. Republican. Home: 11978 Connell Overland Park IL 66213 Office: Entex 10509 W 84th Ter Lenexa KS 66214-1643

HANSON, PAULA E., state legislator; b. Jan. 21, 1944; m. Jim Hanson; 3 children. Mem. Minn. State Senate, 1992—, mem. various coms. Democrat. Home: 2428 Bunker Lake Blvd NE Ham Lake MN 55304 Office: Minn State Senate State Capitol Saint Paul MN 55155*

HANSON, TAMARA SHIELDS, accountant; b. Lewiston, Idaho, Oct. 23, 1948; d. Brooks E. and Dona J. (Rogers) O'Kelley; m. Thomas J. Hanson Jr., 1 son Stewart Alan. BBA cum laude, North Tex. State U., 1976; Securities lic., Insurance lic. Staff acct. James C. Beach CPA, Carrollton, Tex., 1972-76, Deloitte, Haskins & Sells, CPA, 1976-77; chief fin. officer Communications Systems, Inc. (name changed to Scott Cable Communications 1983), Irving, Tex., 1977-84; pvt. practice acctg., Dallas, 1984—; treas. and v.p. FTS Life Insurance Agy., Inc., 1993—. lectr. in field. Bd. trustees local charity; active St. Andrews United Meth. Ch. Mem. AICPA, Tex. Soc. CPAs (former Dallas chpt. ethics com.), Beta Alpha Psi.

HANSON, WENDY KAREN, chemical engineer; b. Mpls., May 29, 1954; d. Curtis Harley Hanson and Patricia Lou (Vogler) Schweiger. BS, U. Minn., 1976; BA, U. Colo., Denver, 1984; postgrad., U. Calif., La Jolla, 1984-87. Chem. technician Shasta Beverages, Mpls., 1977-78, Conwed, Roseville, Minn., 1978-80; geologist Century Geophys. Corp., Grand Junction, Colo., 1980, Tooke Engring., Grand Junction, 1980-82; sr. scientist Sci. Ventures, San Diego, 1987—. Patentee magnesium separation from dolomite phosphate by sulfuric acid leaching. Judge San Diego (Calif.) Sci. and Engring. Fair, 1987—; leader, publs. editor San Diego (Calif.) Wilderness Assn., 1989—. Mem. Am. Chem. Soc. Office: Sci Ventures Ste E 8909 Complex Dr San Diego CA 92123

HANTMAN, SARAH ANN, health professional; b. Wyandotte, Mich., Oct. 19, 1952; d. Paul Reginald and Betty Elaine (Wilson) Longfield; m. Barry Mark Hantman, Dec. 27, 1970; 1 child, Bryan Jonathan. BA in Journalism, Rider U., 1975. Bur. chief United Artists-Columbia CATV-NJ, Oakland, N.J., 1976-77; offset and sr. offset machine operator N.J. Dept. Labor, Trenton, 1980-88; tng. technician div. of AIDS prevention and control N.J. Dept. Health, Trenton, 1988-90, clearinghouse coord. div. of AIDS prevention and control, 1990-91, health profl. divsn. family health svc. WIC program, 1991-92, health profl., div. mgmt. and adminstrn., 1992—; co-owner Sabar Internat., West Trenton, N.J., 1984—. Community activist Grand Ave. Hist. Assn., West Trenton, 1989—. Recipient Letter and Plaque designating her house as hist. Ewing Twp. Hist. Commn. and Zoning Bd., West Trenton, 1989. Mem. NAFE, Nat. Trust and Hist. Preservation (preservation forum 1976—), Nat. Geog. Soc., The Wilderness Soc., Nat. Parks and Conservation Assn., Environ. Def. Fund, World Wildlife Fund. Presbyterian. Office: NJ Dept Health CN 350 John Fitch Plz Trenton NJ 08625-0360

HANTON, SHARON ELEANOR, social worker; b. Superior, Wis., Mar. 23, 1939; d. Earl Richards and Eleanor Dungan; m. John P. Hanton, June 12, 1970; children: Marjorie (dec.), Katherine, Patricia. BA in Social Work, Coll. St. Catherine, 1961; MSW, Cath. U., 1976. Program dir. Urban Life Inst., San Francisco, 1967-70; instr. U. San Francisco, 1967-70, Mont. State U., Bozeman, 1971-81; exec. dir. Mont. Chpt. NASW, Bozeman, 1981—, Galnatin Coun. on Health & Drugs, Bozeman, Mont., 1981-82; social worker pvt. practice, Bozeman, Mont., 1983—; cons. Mount View Care Ctr., Bozeman, Mont., 1990-91, Mt. View Nursing Home, White Sulphur Springs, Mont., 1986—, Wheatland Meml. Nursing Home, Harlowton, Mont., 1990—; founder, dir. One Family Assessment Program, 1994—; tchr. in field. Contbr. articles to profl. jours. Founder Daycare Ctr. U. Mont., Bozeman, Mont., 1975, Rural Generalist Soc. Work Office, gardiner, Mont., 1976, Career Transition Program For Women, 1981; lobbyist Licensing of Social Workers/Vendorship for Social Workers, 1983-85. Recipient Social Workers of Yr. award Nat. Assn. Soc. Workers Mont. chpt., 1992. Mem. NASW, Am. Bd. Examiner in Clin. Social Work. Democrat. Roman Catholic. Home: 9440 Hodgeman Canyon Dr Bozeman MT 59715-8322 Office: 13 S Willson Ave Bozeman MT 59715-4610

HANTZ, ANNA BARBARA, lawyer, political consultant; b. York, Pa., Feb. 12, 1956; d. Benjamin Franklin and Virginia Louise (Stauffer) H. BA, U. N.H., 1977; JD, Ill. Inst. Tech., 1992. Bar: Maine 1992, N.H. 1992, Mass. 1993. Dorm parent, resident asst. Austine Sch. for Deaf, Brattleboro, Vt., 1977-78; intern N.H. Rep. State Com., Concord, 1978; field staff Reagan for Pres., N.H., 1979-80; field coord. Clay Shaw for Congress, Ft. Lauderdale, Fla., 1980; adminstrv. asst. State Senator John Stabile, Nashua, N.H., 1980-82; exec. dir. N.H. Rep. State Cty, Concord, 1982-85; devel. coord. H.J. Stabile and Son, Inc., Nashua, 1985-89; law clk. Maine Supreme Jud. Ct., Portland, 1992-93; atty. Sheehan Phinney Bass & Green, Manchester, N.H., 1993—; polit. cons. Scamman for Congress, Manchester, 1991, Donovan for Mayor, Nashua, 1988; bd. dirs. Nashua Childrens Assn. Nat. Rep. del. Dupont for Pres., N.H., 1988. Recipient Lowell Thomas scholarship Ill. Inst. Tech., 1989-92, Kent Legal scholarship, 1989-92, Student Bar Assn. award, 1992. Mem. N.H. Bar Assn., Maine Bar Assn., Mass. Bar Assn. Home: 36 Doggett Ln Nashua NH 03060-1181 Office: Sheehan Phinney Bass Green PO Box 3701 1000 Elm St Manchester NH 03101-3701

HANZAK, JANICE CHRISMAN, accountant; b. Cleve., Mar. 20, 1944; d. William Patrick and Helen (Mulvich) Chrisman; m. Henry Stanley Hanzak, July 18, 1964; 1 child, Kevin. BBA, Ursuline Coll., 1979. CPA, CFP; cert. mgmt. Clk. Prudential Ins. Co., East Cleveland, Ohio, 1962-63; bookkeeper White Motor Co., Cleve., 1963-68; CPA, tax mgr. Heiser & Assocs., Willoughby, Ohio, 1974-85; CPA, tax supr. Bond Sippola & DeJoy, Willoughby, 1985-91; CPA, pres. J.C. Hanzak & Co., Willoughby Hills, Ohio, 1991—; tax cons. Lake County Realtors Assn., Mentor, Ohio, 1992; speaker seminars in field. Treas. Highland Heights (Ohio) Mayoral Com., 1983; mem. Highland Heights Legis. Com., 1982, St. Paschal Bull. Com., Highland Heights, 1978; charter mem. Willoughby Hills Bus. Assn., 1992; founding pres. Network Profls. of Lake County, 1993; pres. Lake County Estate Planning Coun., Mentor, 1990-92; v.p. Women Bus. Owners of Western Res., Mentor, 1990-92; exec. bd. Ursuline Coll., Pepper Pike, Ohio. Recipient scholarship Bus. and Profl. Women's Assn., Washington, 1973. Mem. AICPA, Ohio Soc. CPAs, Am. Women's Soc. CPAs, Tax Club of Cleve., Internat. Bd. CFPs, Wildwood Yacht Club. Roman Catholic. Office: JC Hanzak & Co 2860 Bishop Rd Willoughby Hills OH 44092

HANZALEK, ASTRID TEICHER, public policy consultant; b. N.Y.C., Jan. 6, 1928; d. Arthur Albin and Luise Gertrude (Funke) Teicher; m. Frederick J. Hanzalek, Nov. 11, 1955. A, Concordia Coll., 1947; BA, U. Pa., 1949. Cons. Suffield, Conn., 1960—; state rep. Conn. Gen. Assembly, Hartford, 1970-80, asst. majority leader, 1973-74, asst. minority leader, 1975-80; corporator Newington (Conn.) Children's Hosp., 1986—; bd. dirs. Conn. Water Co., Clinton. Contbr. articles to profl. jours.; comment features Sta. WSFB-TV and Sta. CP-TV,Hartford, 1975—. Trustee Priscilla Maxwell Ednicott Scholarship Fund, 1972—; chmn. Conn. Energy Found., Hartford, 1986—; vice-chmn. Bradley Internat. Airport Commn., 1972—, Greater Hartford chpt. ARC, 1975-82; mem. Conn. Inter Agy. Libr. Planning Com., Hartford, 1975-85, Conn. State Coun. Environ. Quality, Hartford, 1980-93; chmn. Conn. River Watershed Coun., Easthampton, Mass., 1980-92; pres. Conn. Sr. Intern Program, Bridgeport, 1980-90; chmn. Conn. State Ethics Commn., Hartford, 1985-93; sec. Conn. Humanities Coun., Middletown, 1980-92; commr. New England Interstate Water Pollution Control Commn., 1993—; mem. Conn. Greenways Commn., 1992—. Recipient Man of Yr. award Conn. Jaycees, 1972, Panelist of Yr., Auto. Consumer Action Panel, 1975-85. Mem. Antiquarian and Landmarks Soc. (v.p. 1974—), Conn. Forest and Park Assn. (bd. dirs. 1975—), Conn. Coun. Environ. Quality, Suffield Land Conservancy (bd. dirs. 1965—, founder), Nat. Order Woman Legislators. Republican. Lutheran. Home: 155 S Main St Suffield CT 06078-2238

HAOLE, JANET LANI, accountant; b. Sacramento, Jan. 19, 1956; d. Edwin A. Sr. and Josephine M. (Madeira) Vincent; 1 child, Jeanine Kuualohaokapuaonaona. AA, Honolulu Bus Coll., 1974; AS, Kapiolani Community Coll., 1980. Gen. mgr. Joe Brown Enterprises, Honolulu, 1979-83; pres., chief exec. officer Triple Check Income Tax and Acctg. Svc., Honolulu, 1981—; treas. Women in Bus. com. of the Small Bus. Adminstrn., Honolulu, 1989—; organizer profl. confs. Recipient U.S. SBA Acct. Adv. of Yr. award State of Hawaii and Island of Oahu, 1992. Mem. Nat. Assn. Tax Practitioners (bd. dirs.), Nat. Soc. Pub. Accts., Am. Inst. Profl. Bookkeepers, Am. Mktg. Assn. (treas.), Profl. Women's Network, Honolulu C. of C. (bd. dirs. small bus. coun.), Small Bus. Assn. Hawaii (dist. coord. women's bus. ownership program SCORE/SBA). Republican. Unity. Office: Triple Check Income Tax and Acctg Svc # 203 1750 Kalakaua Ave Honolulu HI 96826-3756

HAPNER-ROCKHILL, ELIZABETH, lawyer, writer; b. Cleve., May 15, 1957; d. William Ralph Hapner and Anita F. (Thomas) Gillen; m. Paul William Rockhill, June 13, 1987; 1 child, Kyle William. BA in English, U. Fla., 1978, JD, 1980. Bar: Fla. 1981, U.S. Dist. Ct. (mid. dist.) Fla. 1986. Atty. Pub. Defender's Office, Bartow, Fla., 1981, State Atty.'s Office, Tampa, 1981-86; prin./pres. Elizabeth L. Hapner, P.A., Tampa, 1986—; dir. DUI Counterattack Sch., Tampa, 1985—, Prevention, Rehab., Edn. Program, Inc., Tampa, 1990—; adv. Children's Bd Task Force for Judiciary, Tampa, 1991-93. Author: Texas Probate Manual, 1983, Georgia Probate, 1985, Virginia Probate, 1987, Florida Juvenile, 1986, Florida Civil Procedure, 1990. Mem. Hillsborough County Democratic Adv. Coun., 1988—; trustee Carrollwood Recreation Dist., 1989-91; chair sr. pastor nom. com., Forest Hills Presbyn. Ch., 1989-91, 93-94. active mem. Jr. League of Tampa, Inc. Named Victim's Voice, Hillsborough County Victim Assistance Coun., 1991; recipient Pro Bono Svc. award Guardian Ad Litem's Office, Tampa, 1989-93. Mem. ABA, Fed. Bar Assn., Nat. Assn. Female Execs., Internat. Platform Assn., Fla. Bar Assn. (juvenile ct. rules com. 1991—, chair 1994—, family law special needs of children com. 1992—, bar fee arbitration com., 1989—, family law juvenile com.), Fla. Acad. Trial Lawyers, Hillsborough County Bar Assn., Mensa. Democrat. Presbyterian. Home: PO Box 272998 Tampa FL 33688-2998 Office: 101 S Franklin St Ste 100 Tampa FL 33602-5327

HAQUE, MALIKA HAKIM, pediatrician; b. Madras, India; came to U.S., 1967; d. Syed Abdul and Rahimunisa (Hussain) Hakim; MBBS, Madras Med. Coll., 1967; m. C. Azeez Haque, Feb. 5, 1967; children: Kifizeba, Masarath Nashr, Asim Zayd. Diplomate Am. Bd. Pediatrics. Rotating intern Miriam Hosp., Brown U., Providence, 1967-68; resident in pediatrics Children's Hosp., N.J. Coll. Medicine, 1968-70; fellow in devel. disabilities Ohio State U., 1970-71; acting chief pediatrics Nisonger Ctr., 1973-74; staff pediatrician Children and Youth Project, Children's Hosp., Columbus, Ohio, also clin. asst. prof. pediatrics Ohio State U., 1974-80; clin. assoc. prof. pediatrics Ohio State U., 1981—, clin. assoc. prof. dept. internat. health Coll. Medicine, 1993—; pediatrician in charge community pediatrics and adolescent svcs. clinics, Columbus Children's Hosp., 1982—, dir. pediatric acad. assoc., Columbus Children's Hosp., Ohio State U., 1992—; cons. Central Ohio Head Start Program, 1974-79; med. cons. Bur. Rehab. and Devel. Disabilities for State of Ohio, 1990—; v.p. A.M. Haque Internat., Columbus. Contbr. articles to profl. jours. and newspapers. Charter mem. Rep. Presdl. Task Force, 1982—, Nat. Rep. Senatorial Com., 1985—, U.S. Senatorial Club; charter founder Ronald Reagan Rep. Ctr.; trustee Asian Am. Health Alliance Network, Columbus, 1994—. Recipient Physician Recognition award AMA, 1971-86, 88-91, 92—, Gold medals in surgery, radiology, pediatrics and ob/gyn; Presdl. medal of Merit, 1982. Fellow Am. Acad. Pediatrics; mem. Ambulatory Pediatric Assn., Cen. Ohio Pediatric Soc. Muslim. Research on enuresis. Home: 5995 Forestview Dr Columbus OH 43213-2114 Office: 700 Childrens Dr Columbus OH 43205-2666

HARADA, ARLETTE SHISAE OKIMOTO, lawyer; b. Honolulu, June 18, 1958; d. Howard M. and Chisato L. Harada; m. Gordon S. Okimoto. BA, Wellesley Coll., 1980; JD, U. So. Calif., 1983. Bar: Hawaii, 1984, Calif. 1985. Assoc. Gill, Park, Park & Kim, Honolulu, 1984-88, Dinman Nakamura Elisha Nakatani & Neeley, Honolulu, 1988-89, Dinman, Nakamura, Elisha & Nakatani, Honolulu, 1989-91; ptnr. Dinman Nakamura Elisha & Lahne, Honolulu, 1991-94; ptnr. Elisha Ekimoto & Harada, Honolulu, 1994—, also treas., bd. dirs., 1994—; arbitrator Ct. Annexed Arbitration Program, Honolulu; del. State Jud. Conf., Honolulu, 1992—. Area coord. Neighborhood Security Watch, Honolulu, 1993—. Mem. Hawaii State Bar Assn., Calif. Bar Assn., Fed. Bar Assn., Hawaii Women Lawyers, Wellesley Club of Hawaii (alumnae admissions rep. 1984-94). Office: Elisha Ekimoto & Harada 707 Richards St PH-1 Honolulu HI 96813

HARA-ISA, NANCY JEANNE, graphic designer; b. San Francisco, May 14, 1961; d. Toshiro and Masaye (Nakahira) Hara; m. Stanley Takeo Isa, June 15, 1985. Student, UCLA, 1979-82; BA in Art and Design, Calif. State U., L.A., 1985. Salesperson May Co., L.A., 1981; svc. rep. Hallmark Cards Co., L.A., 1981-83; prodn. artist Calif. State U., L.A., 1983, Audio-Stats Internat. Inc., L.A., 1983; prodn. asst. Auto-Graphics Inc., Pomona, Calif., 1984-85, lead supr., 1985-86; art dir., contbg. staff writer CFW Enterprises, Burbank, Calif., 1987-88; graphic designer, prodn. mgr. Bonny Jularbal Graphics, Las Vegas, Nev., 1988-90; graphic designer Weddle Caldwell Advt., Las Vegas, 1990-92; owner Nancy Hara-Isa Designs, 1992—; graphic artist Regional Transp. Commn. of Clark County, Las Vegas, 1993—; freelance designer Caesar's Palace. Writer Action Pursuit Games mag. Parade asst., mem. carnival staff Nisei Week, L.A., 1980-84; asst., mem. Summit Orgn., L.A., 1987—. Mem. NAFE, Women in Profl. Graphic Svcs. (acting 1st v.p. 1990, 2d v.p. 1991), Women in Comms. Republican. Presbyterian. Home: 367 Cavos Way Henderson NV 89014-3555

HARALSON, LINDA JANE, communications executive; b. St. Louis, Mar. 24, 1959; d. James Benjamin and Betty Jane (Myers) N.; married. BA summa cum laude William Woods Coll., 1981; MA, Webster U., 1982. Radio intern Stas.-KFAL/KKCA, Fulton, Mo., 1981; paralegal Herzog, Kral, Burroughs & Specter, St. Louis, 1981-82; staffing coordinator, then mktg. coordinator Spectrum Emergency Care, St. Louis, 1982-85, mktg. mgr., 1985-87; dir. mktg. and recruitment Carondelet Rehab. Ctrs. Am., Culver City, Calif., 1987—; mktg. dir. outpatient and corp. services Calif. Med. Ctr., Los Angeles, 1987-88; mktg. dir. Valley Meml. Hosp., Livermore, Calif., 1988-89; account exec. Laurel Communications, Medford, Oreg., 1989-91; community rels. dir. Rogue Valley Med. Ctr., Medford, 1991—. Party chmn. Heart Assn., St. Louis, 1982—; bd. dirs. Am. Lung Assn. Oreg. Recipient Flair award Advt. Fedn. St. Louis, 1984, Hosps. award Hagen Mktg. Research and Hospitals mag., 1984; presdl. acad. scholar William Woods Coll., Fulton, 1977-81. Mem. IABC, NAFE, Am. Mktg. Assn., So. Oreg. Advt. Profls., Britt Music Festivals, Alpha Phi Alumnae Assn. (pres. chpt. 1985-87). Republican. Presbyterian. Avocations: running, travel, sports, French, needlepoint. Office: Laurel Communications 1322 E Mcandrews Rd Ste 202 Medford OR 97504-6177

HARASTA, CATHY ANN, journalist; b. Glens Falls, N.Y., July 1, 1952; d. Guy J. and Margaret C. (Daly) Luciano; m. Joe P. Harasta, Aug. 24, 1974; children: Lindsey Anne, Valerie M. BA in English, SUNY, Oswego, 1974; MA in English, SUNY, Binghamton, 1977. Cert. secondary tchr., N.Y. Ref. libr. asst. Dallas Times Herald, 1976-78, asst. ref. editor, 1978-81; sports copy editor Dallas Morning News, 1981-83, sports media columnist, 1983-85, sports writer, reporter, 1985-90, sports columnist, 1990—. Recipient Charles E. Green Journalism award, Headliners Found. Tex., 1994, 2d pl. award for column writing, Tex. Assoc. Press Mng. Editors Assn., 1993. Mem. Assn. Women in Sports Media. Office: Dallas Morning News Communications Ctr Dallas TX 75265

HARAYDA, JANICE, newspaper book editor, author; b. New Brunswick, N.J., July 31, 1949; d. John and Marel (Boyer) H. BA cum laude, U. N.H., 1970. Editorial asst. Mademoiselle mag., N.Y.C., 1970; asst. to travel editor Saturday Rev., N.Y.C., 1971; sr. editor, contbg. editor Glamour mag., N.Y.C., 1971-78; editorial dir. Boston mag., 1978-81; freelance writer, Boston, 1981-87; book editor Plain Dealer, Cleve., 1987—; lectr. Radcliffe Pub., Cambridge, Mass., 1979, 80, Cath Conf., among others; instr. writing Marymount Coll., N.Y.C., 1977; instr. journalism Boston U. Sch. Pub. Comm., 1979; freelance writer for numerous nat. mags., newspapers, including N.Y. Times, Wall Street Jour., Washington Post. Author: The Joy of Being Single, 1986; contbg. author: Rooms with No View, 1974, Titters, 1979, Women: A Book for Men, 1979. Mem. adminstrv. bd. Park Ave. United Meth. Ch., N.Y.C., 1975-78, active civic, corp. and religious groups, 1988—. Recipient award for Excellence in Journalism Cleve. Press. Club, 1994; named guest editor Mademoiselle mag., 1970. Mem. Am. Soc. Journalists and Authors, Nat. Book Critics Cir., Royal Scottish Country Dance Soc., English Speaking Union, Clan Donald USA, Cleve. City Club. Office: The Cleve Plain Dealer 1801 Superior Ave Cleveland OH 44114

HARBIN, DENISE DELL, advertising executive; b. Akron, Ohio, Nov. 18, 1950; d. Dell Howard and Nester Lillian (Nelson) H. BA, Miami U., 1972; postgrad., Sch. Visual Arts, N.Y.C., 1972-76, Parsons Sch. Design, N.Y.C., 1977-78. Art dir. Warwick Advt., N.Y.C., 1972-76; sr. art dir. J. Patrick Moore Advt., Mpls., 1976-78; exec. v.p., creative dir. BH&W Advt., Westport, Conn., 1978-80; pres. Harbin Communications, N.Y.C., 1980-88; exec. dir. Advt. Club N.Y., N.Y.C., 1988-90, The Internat. Andy Awards, N.Y.C., 1988-90; sr. art dir. Saatchi & Saatchi Advt., N.Y.C., 1990-92; pres., creative dir. Robison & Harbin Advt., N.Y.C., 1992-94; dir. creative svcs. Donnelly Marketing/Carol Wright Sales, Stamford, Conn., 1994—; advisor St. John's U. Sch. for Advt. Rsch., Queens, N.Y., 1988; lectr. travel and tourism NYU. Pub. Tipps Dir., N.Y.C., 1986. Com. for spring gala Parrish Art Mus., Southhampton, N.Y., 1989. Recipient Andy award, 1981-82. Mem. Advt. Club N.Y., Advt. Women of N.Y. Republican. Presbyterian. Office: Donnelly Mktg Co 70 Seaview Ave Stamford CT 06902

HARBISON, MARIE EMMA, organization executive; b. Phila., July 13, 1927; d. John and Marie Louisa (Kunkele) Grimmie; m. Norman Harbison, Aug. 24, 1944; children: Kathleen Norma, Kenneth Norman. Student pub. schs., Phila. Founder Liberty Bell Matchcover Club, Phila., 1982—. Lutheran. Home: 6048 N Water St Philadelphia PA 19120-2015

HARBISON, PAULA KAY, podiatric physician; b. Long Beach, Calif., Apr. 27, 1955; d. Arthur Edward and Leona Maxine (Smith) H.; m. James Francis Cook, Sept. 10, 1983; children: James Arthur Cook, Alyssa Noel Cook. BS in Biol. Scis., U. Calif., Irvine, 1977; BS in Med. Scis., Calif. Coll. Podiatric Medicine, 1980, D Podiatric Medicine, 1982. Resident in podiatric medicine and surgery Detroit, Mich., 1982-83; pvt. practice Fullerton, Calif., 1983-88; staff podiatric Kaiser Permanente Med. Group, Anaheim, Calif., 1988—, dir. podiatric residency program, 1991—.

HARCUM, LOUISE MARY DAVIS, retired elementary education educator; b. Salisbury, Md., May 1, 1927; d. E. Linwood and Dora Ellen (Shockley) Davis; m. W. Blan Harcum, Sr., Sept. 5, 1944; children: W. Blan,

Jr., Angie E., Lee P., R. Linwood. BS, Salisbury State U., 1962, MEd, 1969. Cert. tchr., Md. Tchr. Wicomico County Bd. Edn., Salisbury, Md., 1962-93; columnist Daily Times, 1985—; tchr. cons. Eastern Shore Md. Writing Project. Co-author: Wicomico County History, 1981; author: Behavior Modification, 1989-92. Co-coord. Rep. Party Campaign, Wicomico County, Md., 1992; vice chmn. Zoning Appeals Bd.; pres. Wicomico County Farm Bur. Women, 1993, leader Olympians-Mardela 4-H Club. Mem. AAUW (pres. 1968-70, 74-75), Third Time Around, Eastern Shore Writers Assn., Wicomico County Rep. Women (edn. chair), Wicomico Rep. Club (4th v.p.), Sweet Adelines (Ocean Bay chpt.). Republican. Methodist. Home: 10720 Snethen Church Rd Mardela Springs MD 21837

HARDAGE, PAGE TAYLOR, health care administrator; b. Richmond, Va., June 27, 1944; d. George Peterson and Gladys Odell (Gordon) Taylor; m. Thomas Brantley, July 6, 1968; 1 child, Taylor Brantley. AA, Va. Intermont Coll., Bristol, 1964; BS, Richmond Profl. Inst., 1966; MPA, Va. Commonwealth U., Richmond, 1982. Cert. tchr. Competent toastmaster, dir. play therapy svcs. Med. Coll. Va. Hosps., Va. Commonwealth U., Richmond, 1970-90; dir. Inst. Women's Issues, Va. Commonwealth U., U. Va., Richmond, 1986-91; adminstr. Childhood Lang. Ctr. at Richmond, Inc., 1991—; bd. dirs. Math. and Sci. Ctr. Found., Richmond, Emergency Med. Svcs. Adv. Bd., Richmond. Treas. Richmond Black Student Found., 1989-90, Leadership Metro Richmond Alumni Assn.; bd. dirs. Richmond YWCA, 1989-91; group chmn. United Way Greater Richmond, 1987; bd. dirs. Capital Area Health Adv. Coun.; commr. Mayors Commn. of Concerns of Women, City of Richmond. Mem. NAFE, ASPA, Adminstrv. Mgmt. Soc., Internat. Mgmt. Coun. (exec. com.), Va. Recreation and Park Soc. (bd. dirs.), Va. Assn. Fund Raising Execs., Rotary Club of Richmond. Unitarian. Office: Childhood Lang Ctr at Richmond Inc 4202 Hermitage Rd Richmond VA 23227-3755

HARDEGREE, GLORIA JEAN FORE, health services administrator; b. Atlanta, July 18, 1940; d. Lee Harrison and Corine Joan (Atkinson) Fore; m. Guy H. Hardegree Jr., Jan. 23, 1960; children: Pamela Jean Reas, Sherie Etta Drew. Diploma in nursing, Crawford W. Long Hosp., 1971; BS, Coll. St. Francis, 1982; postgrad., Liberty U. RN, Ga.; cert. occupational health nurse; cert. case mgr. Occupational health nurse Dobbs House Inc., Dallas, 1974-75, AT&T, Atlanta, 1974; occupational health nurse Ga. Power Co., Atlanta, 1976—, coord. Wellness Program. Recipient Schering award, 1987, Nurse of Yr. award, Med. Products S.E., 1991. Mem. Ga. Assn. Occupational Health Nurses (recording sec., Nurse Yr. award, 1987), Atlanta Assn. Occupational Health Nurses. Office: Ga Power Co PO Box 4545 Atlanta GA 30302-4545

HARDEMAN, LYNDA JO, telecommunications company executive; b. Anniston, Ala., Mar. 13, 1946; d. Ralph Jonah and Sybil Minnie (Walker) Howell; m. Danny Lee McCraw, June 15, 1968 (div. Sept. 1977); m. William P. Hardeman, Jan. 14, 1978 (dec. Jan. 1993); children: Danny Lee, Britt Ashton. BS in Math./English, U. Ala., Tuscaloosa, 1968; postgrad., U. S.C., 1970, Tarrant County Jr. Coll., Ft. Worth, Tex., 1978, U. Tex., Arlington, 1979-80. Tchr. geometry Jefferson County Bd. Edn., Homewood, Ala., 1968-70; tchr. AlgebraIII/trig Lower Richland Bd. Edn., Columbia, S.C., 1970-73; sales rep. U.S. C. of C., Arlington, Tex., 1977; tchr. math. Grand Prairie (Tex.) Ind. Sch. Dist., 1977-79, Duncanville (Tex.) Ind. Sch. Dist., 1979-80; assoc. analyst/programmer Enserch Exploration, Inc., Dallas, 1980-84, analyst programmer, 1980-83, sr. analyst programmer, 1983-85, project leader, 1985-89; from staff adminstr. to mgr. SysProv GTE Telephone Ops., Irving, Tex., 1989—; vice chair computer sci. curriculumTelecomm. Industry Forum, 1980, electronics commerce, 1994; lectr. in field. Recipient Quality award Sprint/GTE, 1991. Data Processing Mgmt. Assn. Home: 935 Wellington Duncanville TX 75137 Office: 700 Hidden Ridge Irving TX 75038-3888

HARDEN, ALICE V., state legislator; b. Magnolia, Miss., Apr. 17, 1948; m. Dennis Labert Harden. Student, Jackson State U. Tchr.; mem. Miss. State Senate; mem. Hinds County Dem. Women. Mem. NAACP, various ednl. assns. Baptist. Home: 3247 Copperfield St Jackson MS 39209-6706 Address: Senate House New Capitol Jackson MS 39205*

HARDEN, OLETA ELIZABETH, English educator, university administrator; b. Jamestown, Ky., Nov. 22, 1935; d. Stanley Virgil and Myrtie Alice (Stearns) McWhorter; m. Dennis Clarence Harden, July 23, 1966. BA, Western Ky. U., 1956; MA in English, U. Ark., 1958, PhD, 1965. Teaching asst. U. Ark., Fayetteville, 1956-57, 58-59, 61-63; instr. S.W. Mo. State Coll., Springfield, 1957-58, Murray (Ky.) U., 1959-61; asst. prof. English Northeastern State Coll., Tahlequah, Okla., 1963-65; asst. prof. Wichita (Kans.) State U., 1965-66; asst. prof. English Wright State U., Dayton, Ohio, 1966-68, assoc. prof., 1968-72, prof., 1972—, asst. chmn. English dept., 1967-70, asst. dean, 1971-73, assoc. dean, 1973-74, exec. dir. gen. univ. services, 1974-76, pres. of faculty, 1984-85. Author: Maria Edgeworth's Art of Prose Fiction, 1971, Maria Edgeworth, 1984. Wright State U. rsch. and devel. grantee, 1969, 78, Ford Found. grantee, 1971, Wright State U. sabbatical grantee Oxford U., Eng., 1978-79, 86-87; recipient Presdl. award for Outstanding Svc. Wright State U., 1986, Alumni Teaching Excellence award, 1993. Mem. MLA, Coll. English Assn., AAUP, Women's Caucus for Modern Langs., Am. Com. Irish Studies. Home: 2618 Big Woods Trl Fairborn OH 45324-1704 Office: Wright State U Dept English 7751 Colonel Glenn Hwy Dayton OH 45431-1674

HARDEN, VICTORIA ANGELA, historian, curator; b. Savannah, Ga., Jan. 10, 1944; d. William Charles and Florence (Hembree) H.; m. Charles Durward McDonell Jr., May 14, 1966 (div. 1975); children: Charles Durward III, Emily Victoria; m. Robert Lewis Berger, May 23, 1981. BA, Emory U., 1966, PhD, 1983; MA, U. Fla., 1968. Instr. Huston-Tillotson Coll., Austin, Tex., 1968-72; part-time instr. Howard Coll. Big Spring, Tex., 1972-74; tchr. Dixie County High Sch., Cross City, Fla., 1974-75, Marietta (Ga.) High Sch., 1975-79; historian Nat. Inst. Allergy and Infectious Diseases, Bethesda, Md., 1984-86; historian, curator NIH, Bethesda, Md., 1986—, dir. DeWitt Stetten Jr. Mus. Med. Rsch., 1986—. Author: Inventing the NIH, 1986, Rocky Mountain Spotted Fever, 1990 (Henry Adams award 1991). Mem. Am. Assn. of the History of Medicine (co-chair AIDS history group 1988—, coun. 1989-92), Am. Hist. Assn., Am. Assn. Mus., History of Sci. Soc., Soc. for History in the Fed. Govt. (Powell award 1988, Adams award 1991), Orgn. Am. Historians, Washington Soc. for the History of Medicine (v.p. 1992-93, pres. 1993-94), Sigma Xi. Office: NIH Bldg 31 Rm 2B09 Bethesda MD 20892

HARDER, WENDY WETZEL, communications executive; b. Oceanside, Calif., Feb. 14, 1951; d. Burt Louis and Marjorie Jean (Evans) W.; m. Peter N. Harder, Dec. 1, 1984; 1 child, Jonathan Russell. AA, Palomar Coll., 1971; BA in Communications, U. So. Calif., 1973; MBA, Pepperdine U., 1988. Pub. rels. dir. Orange County Community Devel. Coun., Santa Ana, Calif., 1975-76; assoc. producer Sta. KOCE-TV, Huntington Beach, Calif., 1976-77, reporter, 1977-79, anchor, assoc. producer, 1979-82; sr. adminstr. communications Mission Viejo (Calif.) Co., 1983-84, mgr. corp. affairs, 1984-85, dir. corp. affairs, 1985-91, v.p. corp. affairs, 1991-93, v.p. mktg. and corp. comm., 1993—. 1st v.p. Aliso Viejo (Calif.) Community Found., 1988-93, pres., 1993—, Saddleback Coll. Found., Mission Viejo, 1989-94; co-chmn. The Ctr. on Tour-Schs. Com., Orange County, Calif., 1989—; bd. dirs. Dunaj Internat. Dance Ensemble, Orange County, 1985—. Recipient Golden Mike award Radio & TV News Assn., 1981; co-recipient Best Spl. Event award, Pub. Rels. Soc. Am., 1986, Golden Mike award Radio & TV News Assn., 1979. Mem. Orange County Press Club (Best Feature Release award 1983), Royal Scottish Country Dance Assn., Orange County Folk Dancers. Republican. Lutheran. Office: Mission Viejo Co 26137 La Paz Rd San Juan Capistrano CA 92691-5387

HARDIMAN, THERESE ANNE, lawyer; b. Chestnut Hill, Pa., Mar. 2, 1956; d. Edward Joseph and Grace Joan (Shaw) Hardiman; m. David J.P. Malecki, Feb. 3, 1990; 1 child, Christine Mary; BA in History, BA in Psychology, Mt. St. Mary's Coll., 1978; JD, Thomas M. Cooley Law Sch., 1983. Bar: Pa. 1983. U.S. Dist. Ct. (ea. dist.) Pa. 1983, U.S. Ct. Appeals (3d cir.) 1984, U.S. Dist. Ct. (mid. dist.) Pa. 1989. Staff rsch. asst. Internat. Brotherhood of Teamsters, Washington, 1978-79; law clk. Richard R. Rashid, Atty. at Law, Lansing, Mich., 1981-82; law clk. Pearlstine, Salkin, Hardiman & Robinson, Landsdale, Pa., 1981; staff asst. Employment Rels. Bd., Mich. Dept. Civil Svc., Lansing, 1982; mem. Pearlstine, Salkin, Hardiman & Robinson, Landsdale, 1983-86; v.p. Edward J. Hardiman & Assocs. P.C., 1986—. Editor-in-chief Pridwin, 1978, layout editor, 1977. Recipient Golden Key award, Delta Theta Phi, 1981; Outstanding Student award Student Bar Assn., Thomas M. Cooley Law Sch., 1982. Mem. ABA, Assn. Trial Lawyers Am., Pa. Assn. Trial Lawyers, Pa. Bar Assn., Monroe County Bar Assn., Montgomery County Bar Assn., Delta Theta Phi. Republican. Roman Catholic. Office: PO Box 850 Pocono Pines PA 18350

HARDIN, CONNIE BLACKWELL, state budget director; b. Clarksville, Tenn., Mar. 2, 1955; d. Charles R. and Anita (Shepherd) Blackwell; m. William A. Hardin, Jan. 1, 1988. BS in Bus. Edn. with honors, Austin Peay State U., 1977. Program evaluator comptroller of treasury State of Tenn., Nashville, 1979-83, budget analyst fin. and adminstrn., 1983-87, budget coord. fin. and adminstrn., 1987-90, asst. budget dir. fin. and adminstrn., 1990-92, budget dir. fin. and adminstrn., 1992—. Vol. Room-in-the-Inn Homeless program, Nashville, 1992, 93. Mem. Nat. Assn. State Budget Officers (S.E. regional dir. 1993-94, mem. exec. com. 1993-95), Tenn. Govt. Exec. Inst. (steering com. 1993-94, cert. of attainment 1990), Tenn. NG Aux. (bd. dirs. 1993-95). Office: Budget Divsn Fin & Adminstrn Ste 200 John Sevier State Office Bd Nashville TN 37243-0286

HARDIN, ELIZABETH ANN, manufacturing consultant; b. Charlotte, N.C., Nov. 21, 1959; d. William Gregg and Ann (Astin) H. BBA magna cum laude, U. Ga., 1981; MBA, Harvard U., 1985. Spl. project coord. NCNB Corp., Charlotte, 1981-82, investment officer, 1982-83; cons. Booz, Allen & Hamilton, Atlanta, 1985-86; asst. placement dir. Harvard U. Bus. Sch., Boston, 1986-87, dir. MBA program adminstrn., 1987-89, acting placement dir., 1988-89; mgr. employment Sara Lee Hosiery, Winston-Salem, N.C., 1990-92, mfg. mgr., 1992-93; dir. product devel. Sara Lee Hosiery, Winston-Salem, 1993-94; mng. cons. Info. Sci. Assocs., Charlotte, N.C., 1994—; cons., developer adminstrv. policy guide Chelsea (Mass.) Pub. Schs., 1989-90. Mem. adv. bd. Harvard Non-Profit Fellowship, 1986—; chmn. Harvard Non-Profit Mgmt. Fellowship, 1989—; active AIDS Action Com. Mass., Holy Comforter, Charlotte; mem. total quality edn. task force N.C. Bus. Com. on Edn., 1992-93; troop leader Girl Scouts U.S.A. Fellow State Farm Co. Found., 1980, Delta Gamma Found., 1983. Mem. Assn. for Corp. Growth, Harvard Bus. Sch. Assn., Phi Kappa Phi, Delta Gamma (pres. alumnae Charlotte 1982-83). Republican. Office: Info Sci Assocs 3910 Chevington Rd Charlotte NC 28226

HARDIN, LESLIE, financial analyst; b. Seoul, Korea, Feb. 13, 1959; came to U.S., 1960; d. Emory Coleman Jr. and Dorothy D. (Wilkins) H. BBA, Abilene Christian U., 1980; MBA, U. Tex., 1991. CPA, Tex. Internal audit mgr. Fidelity Union Life, Dallas, 1984-86; dir. MIS, corp. risk mgr. Alliance of Am. Corp., Dallas, 1986-91; fin. acct. specialist, dir. fixed-income rels. AMR Corp., Dallas, Ft. Worth Airport, 1991-93; v.p. BT Securities Corp., N.Y.C., 1993—. Mem. AICPAs, Tex. Soc. CPAs (ins. trust ins. com. 1991-93), N.Y. Soc. Airline Analysts (sec.). Office: Bankers Trust 130 Liberty St Fl 10 New York NY 10006-1105

HARDIN, MARTHA LOVE WOOD, civic leader; b. Muncie, Ind., Aug. 13, 1918; d. Lawrence Anselm and Bonny Blossom (Williams) Wood; m. Clifford Morris Hardin, June 28, 1939; children: Susan Hardin Wood, Clifford Wood, Cynthia Hardin Milligan, Nancy Hardin Rogers, James Alvin. Librarian U. Chgo., 1939-40. Co-author Genealogy: Ancestors of Lawrence Anselm Wood, Genealogy Ancestors of Bonny Williams Wood; contbr. articles to profl. jours. Chmn. Nebr. Heart Fund, 1967; vol. worker Lincoln Gen. Hosp., 1965, Clarkson Hosp., 1966; hon. chmn. Symphony Ball, Washington, 1970; mem. met. bd. YWCA, Washington, 1969-71, St. Louis, 1973—; mem. Women's Com. of Pres.'s Com. on Employment of Handicapped, 1970-91, permanent mem. bd., 1970—; bd. dirs. St. Louis Speech and Hearing Clinic, St. Louis Met. YWCA, Cen. Inst. Deaf, St. Louis, 1986-92; co-chmn. nat. fund-raising campaign U. Nebr. Found., 1977-80. Mem. DAR, PEO, St. Louis Geneal. Soc., Mortar Bd., Old Warson Country Club, St. Louis Club, Wednesday Club, Phi Beta Kappa, Pi Beta Phi.

HARDIN, SHERYL DAWN, primary school educator; b. Austin, Tex., Sept. 12, 1963; d. James West and Emma Heaner (Larison) Shelton; 1 child, Matthew Doyle. BS in Edn., U. Tex., 1986. Cert. tchr., Tex. Primary tchr. Austin (Tex.) Ind. Sch. Dist., 1987—; facilitator Early Literacy Insvc. Course, 1994—. Mem. NEA, Internat. Reading Assn., Nat. Coun. Tchrs. English, Whole Lang. Umbrella, Ctrl. Tex. Whole Lang. Network (membership dir. 1992—). Home: 3412 A Willow Springs Austin TX 78704 Office: Linder Elem Sch 2800 Metcalf Rd Austin TX 78741

HARDING, CAROL GIBB, psychologist, educator; b. Mercer, Pa., July 2, 1943; d. Raymond E. and Edith Elizabeth (Martin) Gibb; m. L. Arthur Safer; children: Julie, Chris, Alan, Elizabeth, Mark. BS Edn., Indiana U. Pa., 1965, MS, 1966; PhD, U. Del., 1981. Tchr. pub. schs. Pa., N.Y., Del., 1965-80; prof. Loyola U., Chgo., 1980—, dir. Rsch. Ctr. for Children & Families, 1987—. Editor: Moral Dilemmas, 1987; contbr. articles to profl. jours. Office: Loyola U 820 N Michigan Ave Chicago IL 60611

HARDING, ETHEL M., state legislator; b. Fishtail, Mont., Oct. 19, 1927; m. Warren Harding; 2 children. Student, Heald's Bus. Coll. Clk., recorder Lake County, Mont., 1967-84; owner, operator Mission Valley Concrete, 1967-84; rep. State of Mont., 1985-86, senator, 1987—. Republican. Mem. Ch. of Nazarene. Office: PO Box 251 Polson MT 59860-0251 also: Mt State Senate State Capitol Helena MT 59620*

HARDING, JESSICA ROSE, public affairs specialist, journalist; b. Provincetown, Mass., Jan. 10, 1942; d. Joseph Anthony and Jessica Henrietta (Grace) Lema; m. Jan. 7, 1960 (dec. Sept. 1990); children: Victoria Lee Harding Johnston, H. William, David Charles. Student, U. Md., 1979—. Legal asst., paralegal Dept. Energy, Washington, 1977-82; aide to asst. dir. Automated Sys. Office, Libr. of Congress, Washington, 1982-84; spl. asst. for internat. security Office of Sec. Def., Washington, 1984-85; pub. affairs officer Army Chief Chaplains, Washington, 1985-88; pub. affairs specialist Navy Drug and Alcohol Program, Washington, 1988—; weekly columnist From a Woman's Point of View, Enterprise and Inner Harbor News, Balt.; freelance writer; founder The Write Angle; tech. advisor, writer for videotape prodns. for drug and alcohol program edn. and tng. br. USN, 1992—. Mem. chorus Annapolis (Md.) chpt. Sweet Adelines, 1975-85; group facilitator Single Again, Crofton, Md., 1988-92. Mem. NAFE, Soc. for Applied Learning Tech. Roman Catholic.

HARDING, MARGARET TYREE, minister; b. Lynchburg, Va., May 28, 1951; d. Aubrey Nathaniel and Audrey (Riley) Tyree; m. William R. Harding, Sep. 11, 1993. BA, Averett Coll., 1978; MDiv, Southeastern Bapt. Theol. Sem., Wake Forest, N.C., 1981. Ordained to ministry So. Bapt. Conv., 1982. Min. youth Moffett Meml. Bapt. Ch., Danville, Va., 1976-78, West Main Bapt. Ch., Danville, 1979-81; min. edn. and youth North Run Bapt. Ch., Richmond, Va., 1981-84; min. edn., youth and adminstrn. Grandin Ct. Bapt. Ch., Roanoke, Va., 1984—. Contbr. articles to profl. jours. Devotional officer Jr. Women's Club, Madison Heights, Va., 1971-75; alumni rep. Averett Coll., Danville, 1984—, mem. mins. adv. com., 1991; usher Mill Mountain Theater, Roanoke, Va., 1990—. Mem. Religious Edn. Assn. U.S. and Can. (bd. dirs. 1991), Va. Bapt. Gen. Assn. (gen. bd. 1989—), Va. Bapt. Religious Assn. (pres. 1989), So. Bapt. Religious Edn. Assn. (asst. sec. 1994-95), Roanoke Area Religious Edn. Assn. (pres. 1991). Home: 7977 Williamson Rd Roanoke VA 29019 Office: Grandin Ct Bapt Ch 2660 Brambleton Ave SW Roanoke VA 24015-4306

HARDING, MARIE, finance executive; b. Glen Cove, N.Y., Nov. 13, 1941; d. Charles Lewis and Marie Brinkerhoff (Parish) H.; m. John P. Allen (div.); 1 child, Eden Appleton. BA, Sarah Lawrence Coll., 1964; postgrad., Arts Students League, N.Y.C., 1965, New Sch. for Social Rsch., N.Y.C., 1965. Vol. Swallows, Madras, India, 1964, Project Concern, Hong Kong, 1964-65; founder, owner Synergia Ranch, N.Mex., 1969; founding mem., dir. Inst. Ecotechnics, London, 1974; dir., treas. Synopco Corp., N.Mex., 1974-81; capt. R V Heraclitus, Oakland, Calif., 1975; artist, founder, trustee October Gallery trust, London, 1979; chairperson, dir. EcoWorld Inc., N.Mex., 1982; exec. dir. Caravan of Dreams Prodns., Ft. Worth, 1985-87; chairperson, CEO Oceans Expeditions Inc., 1986-92; dir., v.p. fin. Space Biospheres Ventures, 1988—; bd. dirs. Hotel Vajra, Kathmandu, Savannah Systems Pty Ltd., Outback Station Pty. Ltd., Caravan of Dreams Performing Arts Ctr., Ft. Worth, Synergetic Press, London, Ariz., Space Biospheres Ventures, Biosphere 2; sec. Planetary Coral Reef Found., 1993—. Exhibitions include San Francisco, London, Ft. Worth, Santa Fe, Biosphere 2; project dir., artist History of Jazz, Dance, Theater, Ft. Worth, 1982-83. Mem. Ariz. Friends of Tibet, N.Mex. Friends of Tibet. Home and Office: PO Box 689 Oracle AZ 85623-0689

HARDMAN, JANE MCWILLIAMS, pathologist; b. Huntington, W.Va., Aug. 30, 1946; d. Robert White and Eleanor Ogden (Hardman) McWilliams; m. Andrew Hale Hardman, Jan. 24, 1975; children: Jennifer, Rebecca, Maryann. BS in Biology, Rensselaer Polytech. Inst., 1968; MD, Washington U., St. Louis, 1972; student naval flight surgeon sch., Naval Aerospace Med. Inst., Pensacola, Fla., 1973. Diplomate Am. Bd. Pathology, Am. Bd. Anatomic and Clin. Pathology, Am. Bd. Forensic Pathology, Am. Bd. Hematology. Intern in internal medicine SUNY, Syracuse, N.Y., 1972-73; commd. lt. med. corps USN, 1973, advanced through grades to capt., 1987, ret., 1993; resident pathologist Nat. Naval Med. Ctr., Bethesda, Md., 1978-82, fellow in hematopathology, 1984-85, assoc. and acting head hematopathology, 1985-86, head hematopathology, 1986-87; staff pathologist dept. forensic pathology Armed Forces Inst. Pathology, Washington, 1982-84, staff pathologist dept. hematologic and lymphatic pathology, 1990-92, staff pathologist dept. gynecology/brest pathology, 1992-93; head lab. dept., dir. ancillary svcs. Naval Hosp., Roosevelt Roads, P.R., 1987-90; asst. lab. dir. Oneida (N.Y.) City Hosp., 1993—; adj. asst. prof. dept. pathology Uniformed Svcs. U. of Health Scis., 1986-87, 92-93; presenter in field. Contbr. articles to profl. jours. Fellow Coll. Am. Pathologists. Office: Oneida City Hosp Lab Dept 321 Genesee St Oneida NY 13421

HARDRICK, MARIA DARSHELL, government official, accountant; b. Milw., Feb. 5, 1966; d. Dorotha G. Hardrick. BS, Wilberforce U., 1988. CPA, Ohio. Revenue agt. IRS, Cleve., 1988—. Vol. Project Friendship. Mem. Nat. Assn. Black Accts., Black Profl. Assn. Baptist. Home: 5382 Lee Rd Apt 203 Cleveland OH 44137-2569 Office: IRS 6400 Rockside Rd Independence OH 44131

HARDWICK, ELIZABETH, author; b. Lexington, Ky., July 27, 1916; d. Eugene Allen and Mary (Ramsey) H.; m. Robert Lowell, July 28, 1949 (div. Oct. 1972); 1 child, Harriet. A.B., U. Ky., 1938, M.A., 1939; postgrad., Columbia U., 1939-41. Adj. assoc. prof. Barnard Coll. Author: novels The Ghostly Lover, 1945, The Simple Truth, 1955, Sleepless Nights, 1979; essays A View of My Own, 1962; Seduction and Betrayal, 1974; Bartleby in Manhattan, 1983. Editor: The Selected Letters of William James, 1960; adv. editor: N.Y. Rev. Books. Recipient George Jean Nathan award for dramatic criticism, 1966, gold medal for criticism Am. Acad. Arts and Letters, 1993; Guggenheim fellow, 1947. Mem. Am. Acad. and Inst. Arts and Letters. Home: 15 W 67th St New York NY 10023-6226

HARDWICK, (MARTHA) JEAN, school psychologist, consultant; b. Hamilton, Ala., Aug. 20, 1941; d. Clebston B. and Stella (Dyar) Kelly; m. Jack Carroll Hardwick, Aug. 1, 1970; children: Cara Hillmeyer, James Hardwick, Kathy Hardwick. BS in Vocat. Home Econs., U. N. Ala., 1965, MA in Secondary Edn. and Sci., 1967, EdS in Secondary Edn., 1975; ABD, U. Ala., 1981-91. Lic. profl. counselor, Ala., Ga.; nat. cert. counselor, sch. psycholotgist, home economist. Tchr. career edn. resource Memphis (Ala.) City Schs., 1972-73; tchr., counselor Florence (Ala.) City Schs., 1965-72, psychometrist, 1973-85, coord. student referrals, 1983-85; dir. career ctr., counselor Waycross (Ga.) Coll., 1986; tchr. biology and phys. sci. Waycross High Sch., 1986-87; therapist Marc Eaton, PhD, Waycross, 1988; dir., counselor displaced homemakers and gender equity N.W. Shoals C.C., Phil Campbell, Ala., 1989—; dir. edn. talent search N.W. C.C., Phil Campbell, Ala., 1991—; pvt. practice Florence, 1988—; cons. Even Start Franklin County, Russellville, Ala., 1993—, Hospice N.W. Ala., Winfield, 1993—; sch. psychometrist, psychologist various communities, Ala., 1989—. Chairperson bd. dirs. Hospice N.W. Ala., Winfield, 1993—. Displaced and Homemakers grantee, Gender Equity grantee Postsecondary State Dept Edn., 1990—, Displaced and Homemaker's Supplemental grantee, 1993, High-Risk Youth grantee Gov.'s Drug Task Force, Marion and Winston Counties, 1992—. Mem. AAUW, NEA, ACA, Ala. Counseling Assn., Ala. Edn. Assn., Nat. Assn. Sch. Psychologists, Ala. Assn. Sch. Psychologists, Phi Delta Kappa, Kappa Delta Phi, Upsilon Nu Allpha chpt. Chi Sigma Iota. Democrat. Baptist. Home: 534 W Cumberland St Florence AL 35630 Office: NW Shoals CC Rt 3 Box 77 Phil Campbell AL 35581

HARDY, BETH BENITA, nurse; b. Vallejo, Calif., Sept. 11, 1964; d. Agre Abaloc Sanchez and Benita (Licopit) Ionin; m. Troy Allen Hardy, Dec. 16, 1983; children: Tylina Marie, Darryl Allen. AA in Vocat. Nursing, Merced Coll., 1991, ASN, 1993; postgrad., Eastern N.Mex. U., 1995—. LVN, Calif.; RN. Staff RN Clovis (N.Mex.) Vets. Primary Care Clinic, 1994—, Plains Regional Med. Ctr., Clovis, 1993-95; staff LVN Chowchilla (Calif.) Dist. Meml. Hosp., 1991-92, Anberry Health Care, Atwater, Calif., 1991; float pool LVN Mercy Hosp., Merced, Calif., 1991. Asst. troop leader Girl Scouts U.S., Atwater, 1990-92, troop leader, Clovis, 1994-95. With USAF, 1982-86. Mem. ANA, Nat. League of Nursing, N.Mex. Nurses Assn., Sigma Veta Ni (pres. 1989-90).

HARDY, DONNA DEE, music educator; b. McKeesport, Pa., Aug. 5, 1941; d. Daniel Hale and Maryland Virginia (Brant) H. MusB, U. Mich., 1964, MusM, 1971, postgrad.; MA, U. Pitts., 1989. Tchr. music Wayne (Mich.) Area Sch. Dist., 1964-66; music cons. Livonia (Mich.) Area Sch. Dist., 1966-68; choral dir. L'Anse (Mich.) Area Sch. Dist., 1968-71; Orff supr. Copper County Intermediate Sch. Dist., Hancock, Mich., 1971-74; music instr. Union Coll., Lincoln, Nebr., 1979-80; mem. adj. faculty Pa. State U., McKeesport, 1980-84; instr. music Shippensburg (Pa.) U., 1984-92, asst. prof. music, 1992—; owner Donna Dee's Dolls, 1994—; vis. prof. Colegio Adventista de Etudie Superiores, Alajuela, Costa Rica, 1980; cons. music edn. various orgns. in Pa., Mich.; dir. Cumbelaires Shippensburg U. at White House, Washington, 1985, 92, also in Taiwan, London, Seville, Spain, U.S. Pavillion, 1992; owner Donna Dee's Dolls, 1993—. Author: Music Mixtures, 1977; performer White House, 1992; contbr. papers to profl. publs. Mem. AAUW, Women's Consortium State System Higher Edn., Pa. Music Educators Assn., Music Educators Nat. Coun. Republican. Seventh-day Adventist. Home: 2510 Grandview Ave Mc Keesport PA 15132 Office: Shippensburg Univ Dept Music Shippensburg PA 17257

HARDY, DORCAS RUTH, government relations and public policy consultant; b. Newark, N.J., July 18, 1946; d. Colburn and Ruth (Hart) H. B.A., Conn. Coll., 1964-68; M.B.A., Pepperdine U., 1976. Legis. rsch. asst. U.S. Senator Clifford P. Case, Washington, 1970; spl. asst. White House Conf. Children and Youth, Washington, 1970-71; exec. dir. Health Svcs. Industry Commn., Cost of Living Coun., Washington, 1971-73; asst. sec. Calif. Dept. Health, Sacramento, 1973-74; assoc. dir. U. So. Calif. Ctr. Health Svcs. Rsch., 1974-81; asst. sec. human devel. svcs. HHS, Washington, 1981-86; commr. Social Security HHS, Washington, DC, 1986-89; pres. Dorcas R. Hardy & Assocs., Spotsylvania, Va., 1989—. Author: Social Insecurity: The Crisis in America's Social Security System and How to Plan Now for Your Own Financial Survival, 1992. Mem. Girl Scouts USA; bd. dirs. Wolf Trap Found. for Performing Arts, Com. on Developing Am. Capitalism; former chmn. Pres.'s Task Force on Legal Equity for Women. Mem. Nat. Fedn. Rep. Women, Exec. Women in Govt. Office: Washington Metro Office 11407 Stonewall Jackson Dr Spotsylvania VA 22553

HARDY, FRANCES ANNE, artist; b. Chgo., Jan. 19, 1953; d. George Fiske and Sarah (Harris) H.; m. Robert Burton Demboski, Aug. 1, 1986. BS, Kutztown (Pa.) U., 1974; MEd, Temple U., 1976; postgrad., Sch. of Visual Arts, Parsons Sch. of Design. In permanent collection of Dunnegan Gallery of Art. Recipient Patron Purchase award Springfield Art Mus., 1989, Women in Watercolor, Transco Gallery, 1988. Mem. Women's Caucus for the Arts, Nat. Mus. for Women in the Arts, Carnegie Mus. Home and Studio: 63 Wilson Rd Marianna PA 15345

HARDY, JACQUELINE ANNE, resource specialist; b. Brentwood, N.Y., June 10, 1961; d. Edward Joseph and Joanne Barbara (Tomer) Murphy; m. Chris Hardy, June 24, 1989; 1 child, Megan Nichole. BS in Edn., U.

Springfield, 1983; M in Spl. Edn., Calif. State U., Bakersfield, 1993. Resource specialist Kernville Union Sch. Dist., Lake Isabella, Calif., 1984—. Home: 1539 N China Lake Blvd # 122 Ridgecrest CA 93555-2606 Office: Kernville Union Sch Dist PO Box 3077 Lake Isabella CA 93240-3077

HARDY, JANE ELIZABETH, communications educator; b. Fenelon Falls, Ont., Can., Mar. 27, 1930; came to U.S., 1956, naturalized, 1976; d. Charles Edward and Augusta Miriam (Lang) Little; m. Ernest E. Hardy, Sept. 3, 1955; children: Edward Harold, Robert Ernest. BS with distinction, Cornell U., 1953. Garden editor and writer Can. Homes Mag., Maclean-Hunter Pub. Co., Ltd., Toronto, Ont., 1954-55, 56-62; contbg. editor Can. Homes, Southam Pub. Co., Toronto, Ont., 1962-66; instr. Cornell U., 1966-73, sr. lectr. in communication, 1979—; mem. Cornell U. Provost's Adv. Com. on Status of Women, 1977-81; lectr., condr. workshops on writing. Contbr. numerous articles to mags.; author numerous other publs., including brochures, slide set scripts; editor pro tem Cornell Plantations Quar., 1981-82. Mem. Women in Communications, Inc. (faculty advisor Cornell chpt. 1977—, liaison 1986-94, chair, adv. mem. 1988-90), Royal Hort. Soc., Ithaca Garden Club, Ithaca Women's Club, Pi Alpha Xi, Phi Kappa Phi, Alpha Omicron Pi. Home: 215 Enfield Falls Rd Ithaca NY 14850-8797 Office: Cornell U Dept Communication 328 Kennedy Hall Ithaca NY 14853-4203

HARDY, LINDA LEA STERLOCK, secondary school educator; b. Balt., Aug. 15, 1947; d. George Allen and Dorothy Lea (Briggs) Sterlock; m. John Edward Hardy III, Apr. 25, 1970; 1 child, Roger Wayne. BA in History, N.C. Wesleyan Coll., 1969; MEd in History, East Carolina U., 1972, MLS, 1990. Cert. tchr., N.C. History tchr. Halifax (N.C.) County Schs., 1972-83, learning lab tchr., 1983-91, computer lab tchr., 1990—; part-time history instr. Nash C.C., 1993. Mem. AAUW (pres. Rocky Mount br. 1993-95, named gift award 1987), Bus. and Profl. Women (pres. Rocky Mount chpt. 1986-87, 90-91, treas. 1992-94, sec.-treas. Dist. X 1989-90, state election chmn. 1989-90, 93-94, Girl Friday award 1981, Woman of Yr. award 1986), Nat. Assn. Educators, N.C. Assn. Educators, Halifax County Assn. Educators, Halifax County Assn. Educators (faculty rep. 1989-92, 94—), Phi Delta Kappa, Pi Gamma Mu. Republican. Methodist. Office: Halifax County Schs SE Haifax High Sch RR 1 Box 206 Halifax NC 27839-9701

HARDY, LOIS LYNN, educational seminar training company executive; b. Seattle, Aug. 20, 1928; d. Stanley Milton and Helen Berniece (Conner) Croonquist; m. John Weston Hardy, July 29, 1951 (div. 1974); children: Sarah Lynn, Laura Lynn; m. Joseph Freeman Smith, Jr., Apr. 18, 1981; stepchildren: Nancy Smith Willis, Martha Smith Dahlquist. BA, Stanford U., 1950, MA, 1952; postgrad., U. Calif., Berkeley, 1957-78, U. San Francisco, 1978-81. Cert. life secondary tchr., life counselor, adminstr., Calif.; lic. career and ednl. counselor, Calif. Tchr., counselor Eastside Union High Sch. Dist., San Jose, Calif., 1951-55; dir. Lois Lynn Hardy Music Studio, Danville, Calif., 1955-69; high sch. tchr. San Ramon Unified Sch. Dist., Danville, 1969-71, counselor, 1971-83; dir. Growth Dynamics Inst., Alamo, Calif., 1976—; instr. Fresno (Calif.) Pacific Coll., 1976-79, Dominican Coll., San Rafael, Calif., 1979—; cons., trainer Personal Dynamics Inst., Mpls., 1976—, Performax Internat., Mpls., 1979—, San Jose Unified Sch. Dist., 1986-86, Novato (Calif.) Unified Sch. Dist., 1985-86, IBM, San Francisco, 1984, corp. and ednl. cons., 1951—. Author: How To Study in High School, 1952, 3d edit., 1973; (with B. Santa) How To Use the Library, 1954; How To Learn Faster and Succeed: A How to Study Workbook For Grades 1-14, 1982, rev., 1985; author various seminars; contbr. numerous articles to profl. jours. Choir dir., organist Community Presbyn. Ch., Danville, 1966-68, elder, 1974-75; speaker to numerous orgns., 1955—. Named Musician of Yr., Contra Costa County, 1978, Counselor of Yr., No. Calif. Personnel and Guidance Assn., 1980; Olive S. Lathrop scholar, 1948, AAUW scholar, 1950; recipient Colonial Dames prize in Am. History, 1950. Mem. Am. Assn. Counseling and Devel., Calif. Assn. Counseling and Devel., Calif. Tchrs. Assn., Calif. Career Guidance Assn., Nat. Speakers Assn., Am. Guild Organists, Stanford U. Alumni Assn., Calif. Assn. for the Gifted, Delta Zeta. Democrat. Presbyterian. Office: Growth Dynamics Inst PO Box 1053 Alamo CA 94507-7053

HARDY, NANCY VISSER, small business owner; b. Syracuse, N.Y., Apr. 18, 1943; d. Henry John and Loata Mae (Benedict) Visser; m. David R. Fitzgibbons, July 8, 1963 (div. 1973); children: David, Kevin, Michael; m. Robert Appleby Hardy, Aug. 24, 1974; children: Paul, Kim, Steve, Scott, Jeff. AA, Rider Coll., 1963. Exec. sec. Stratton Mountain (Vt.) Sch., 1976-81; broker Trask & Waite, Bondville, Vt., 1982-84; prin., pres. Stratton Country Properties, Bondville, Vt., 1984—. Trustee Stratton Mountain Sch., 1976-81; chmn. Town of Stratton Sch. Bd., 1981-84; planning commn. Town of Stratton, 1986-93; bd. dirs. Stratton Civic Assn., 1982—. Recipient Excellence award, World Cup Commn., 1978. Mem. U.S. Ski Assn. (nat. race sec. 1980), Eastern Ski Assn. (excellence award 1979), South Cen. Bd. Realtors, Stratton Country Club, Melrose Club (S.C.). Republican. Office: Stratton Country Properties PO Box 8 Bondville VT 05340

HARDY, VICTORIA ELIZABETH, management educator; b. Marion, N.C., Feb. 26, 1947; d. Milton Victor Roth and Bertha Jean (Norris) R.; m. Michael Carrington Hardy, June 19, 1983 (div. 1993); 1 child, Christopher. BS in Edn., U. Mo., 1970; postgrad., So. Ill. U., 1974-75; postgrad. Mgmt. Devel. Program, Stanford U., 1980-81. Pub. sch. tchr. English and Theater, 1970-75; gen. mgr. Miss. River Festival, Edwardsville, Ill., 1975-77; dir. events and svcs. Stanford (Calif.) U., 1977-83; exec. dir. Meadowlands Ctr. for the Arts, Rutherford, N.J., 1983-87; pres., chief exec. officer Music Hall Ctr. for the Arts, Detroit, 1987-89; prin. AMS Planning & Rsch., Conn., 1989-94; prof. facility mgmt. Ferris State U., Big Rapids, Mich., 1994—; mem. faculty CUNY, 1986-88. Pres., bd. dirs. New Performance Gallery, San Francisco, 1977-83; mem. Wingspread Conf. Johnson Found., Milw., 1983; mem. USICA study team People's Republic of China, 1981; state bd. dirs. Arts Found., Mich., 1987—, Arts Action Alliance. Recipient Gold medal for Community Programs Coun. for Advancement and Support of Edn., Stanford, 1985; named in Creativity in Business Doubleday, 1986. Mem. League of Hist. Am. Theaters (pres. bd. dirs. 1987-89), Nat. Trust for Hist. Preservation, Assn. of Coll. Univ. and Community Arts Adminstrs. (exec. bd. dirs. 1977-83), Internat. Facility Mgmt. Assn. (bd. dirs.). Democrat. Office: Ferris State Univ Coll of Tech Swan 312 915 Campus Dr Big Rapids MI 49307-2291

HARE, ELEANOR O'MEARA, computer science educator; b. Charlottesville, Va., Apr. 6, 1936; d. Edward King and Eleanor Worthing (Selden) O'Meara; m. John Leonard Ging, Feb. 4, 1961 (div. 1972); 1 child, Catherine Eleanor Ging Huddle; m. William Ray Hare, Jr., May 24, 1973. BA, Hollins Coll., 1958; MS, Clemson U., 1973, PhD, 1989. Rsch. asst. cancer rsch. U. Va. Hosp., Charlottesville, 1957-58; rsch. specialist rsch. labs. engring. sci. U. Va., Charlottesville, 1959-64; tchr. Pendelton (S.C.) High Sch., 1964-65; vis. instr. dept. math. Clemson (S.C.) U., 1974-79, instr. dept. computer sci., 1979-83, lectr. dept. computer sci., 1983-90, asst. prof. dept. computer sci., 1990—. Contbr. articles to profl. jours. Bd. dirs. LWV of the Clemson Area, 1988—; chmn. nursing home study LWV of S.C., 1988-92; oboe and English horn player Anderson (S.C.) Symphony, 1980—. Fellow Inst. Combinatories and its Applications; mem. AAUP, Assn. for Computing Machinery. Office: Clemson U Dept Computer Sci Clemson SC 29634-1906

HARE, SANDRA FLORENCE, internist, public health consultant; b. Phila., Oct. 23, 1952; d. John Dalrymple Hare and Hortense Cecelia (Daniels) Morris; divorced; 1 child, Meredith Tilse. BA, Clark U., 1974; postgrad. in medicine, Loyola U., Chgo., 1974-75; MPH, U. Ill., Chgo., 1978; MD, Chgo. Med. Sch., 1983. Diplomate Am. Bd. Internal Medicine, Nat. Bd. Med. Examiners. Tchr. chemistry and physics Wyoming Sem., Kingston, Pa., 1975-76; rsch. asst., assoc. U. Ill. Sch. Pub. Health, 1976-78, occupational medicine cons., 1983-84; preceptor Western Ala. Health Svcs., Eutaw, 1980; cons. Carnow, Conibear & Assocs., Chgo., 1983-84; resident in internal medicine Mercy Hosp. and Med. Ctr., Chgo., 1984-87; attending staff physician Nat. Health Svc. Corps Pub. Health Svc., Chgo., 1987-92; attending physician Cook County Hosp., Chgo., 1987-92; pvt. practice, North Suburban Clinic Ltd., Skokie, Ill., 1994—; clin. asst. in medicine U. Ill. Med. Ctr., Chgo., 1985-87. Chmn. Big Bro.-Big Sister Program, Worcester, Mass., 1972-74; bd. dirs. Sheridan Square Condominium Assn., Evanston, Ill., 1987-89. 1st lt. USPHS, 1978-79. AAUW scholar, 1970, Jonas Clark scholar, 1970-74, USPHS scholar, 1979-83. Mem. AMA (physician recognition award 1987), ACP, Ill. Med. Soc., Chgo. Med. Soc. Democrat. Unitarian. Office: 4801 Church St Skokie IL 60077

HARF, PATRICIA JEAN KOLE, syndicated columnist, educational consultant, lecturer; b. Berea, Ohio, Oct. 14, 1937; d. Paul Frederic and Mena (Labordes) Kole; m. Fredric Henry Harf, June 21, 1969. BS in Edn., Baldwin-Wallace Coll., Berea, Ohio, 1959; MS in Edn., Akron U., 1966; Dr. in Edn., Ariz. State U., 1972. Rsch. Ednl. Rsch. Coun. Am., 1967-69; tchr. Berea City Schs., Cleve. and Parma, Ohio, 1969-73; asst. prof. Cleve. State U., 1975—; corr., columnist, freelance writer, syndicated columnist Chronicle-Telegram, Elyria, Ohio, 1986-89; owner, mgr. Harf's Comms. Inc., Berea, Ohio, 1993—; ednl. cons. State of Ohio; syndicated columnist Universal Press, Cleve. Plain Dealer; diagnostician of reading difficulties; cons. learning disabilities; guest lectr.; TV guest appearances. Author teaching materials and tchr. and children's texts; contbr. articles to profl. jours. ; also advisor to book pubs. and magazines. Pres. Berea Hist. Soc.; mem. Cleve. Orch. Women's Com.; advisor Cleve. Radio and TV Coun.; tutor Project Learn, Cleve; mem. Berea Rep. Precinct Com. Recipient Women's Inner Circle of Achievement, 1991, Internat. Order of Merit award, 1993; named Ohio State Outstanding Educator Assoc. Prof., C.C.C., 1968, Women of Today, 1992, Internat. Woman of Yr., 1990, 92, 93, World Intellect, 1993, Woman of Yr., 1994. Mem. NOW, Soc. Profl. Journalists (Excellence in Journalism award 1990), Berea C. of C. (Outstanding Citizen 1965), Berea Hist. Soc., Berea Bus. and Profl. Women, Nat. Edn. Assn., Internat. Reading Assn. (cons. and writer for reading tchrs.), Ohio Edn. Assn. (Woman of the Yr. in Comms. 1991), Kiwanis (sec., v.p.), Berea Rep. Club (Mayoral Volunteerism award 1987), Press Club of Cleve., Internat. Platform Assn., World Found. of Successful Women. Republican. Methodist. Home: 323 Westbridge Dr Berea OH 44017-1562

HARGIS, PATRICIA LEA, law librarian; b. Richmond, Va., Mar. 26, 1956; d. Richard Corbett and Helen Louise (Herthel) H. BA, Randolph-Macon Woman's Coll., 1978; MLS, U. Ky., 1979. Law libr. Warren County, Lebanon, Ohio, 1979-81, U.S. Ct. Appeals 4th Cir., Balt., 1981—; mem. benchmark com. for new salary plan Adminstrv. Office of U.S. Cts., Washington, 1992-93. Co-coord. Woodlawn Beautification Project, Balt., 1989—. Mem. Am. Assn. Law Librs., Md. Assn. Law Librs. Democrat. Roman Catholic. Office: US Cts Libr 101 W Lombard St Baltimore MD 21201

HARGRAVE, CATHERINE DELP, marketing consultant; b. New Orleans, Nov. 18, 1960; d. Ivan David and Jeanne Elizabeth (Favalora) Delp; m. Alexander W. Hargrave, May 23, 1992. BFA, Loyola U., New Orleans, 1982; MBA, Golden Gate U., 1989. Acct. exec. Olsten Corp., San Francisco, 1984-86; sr. acad. program asst. Golden Gate U., San Francisco, 1986-90; acct. supr. DIMAC Direct, San Francisco, 1990-93; prin. Mktg. Solutions, Larkspur, Calif., 1993—. Active San Francisco Jr. League. Mem. NAFE, Direct Mktg. Assn., Alpha Sigma Nu. Home and Office: 74 Diane Ln Larkspur CA 94939

HARGRAVE, SARAH QUESENBERRY, marketing, public relations company executive; b. Mt. Airy, N.C., Dec. 11, 1944; d. Teddie W. and Lois Knight (Slusher) Quesenberry. Student, Radford Coll., 1963-64, Va. Poly. Inst. and State U., 1964-67. Mgmt. trainee Thalhimer Bros. Dept. Store, Richmond, Va., 1967-68; Cen. Va. fashion and publicity dir. Sears Roebuck & Co., Richmond, 1968-73; nat. decorating sch. coord. Sears Roebuck & Co., Chgo., 1973-74, nat. dir. bus. and profl. women's programs, 1974-76; v.p., treas., program dir. Sears-Roebuck Found., Chgo., 1976-87, program mgr. corp. contbns. and memberships, 1981-84, dir. corp. mktg. and pub. affairs, 1984-87; v.p. personal fin. svcs. and mktg. Northern Trust Co., Chgo., 1987-89, Hargrave Consulting, 1989—. Bd. dirs. Am. Assembly Collegiate Schs. Bus., 1979-82, mem. vis. com., 1979-82, mem. fin. and audit com., 1980-82, mem. task force on doctoral supply and demand, 1980-82; mem. Com. for Equal Opportunity for Women, 1976-81; chmn., 1978-79, 80-81; mem. bus. adv. coun. Walter E. Heller Coll. Bus. Adminstrn., Roosevelt U., 1979-89; co-dir. Ill. Internat. Women's Yr. Ctr., 1975. Named Outstanding Young Women of Yr. Ill., 1976; named Women of Achievement State Street Bus. and Profl. Woman's Club, 1978. Mem. Eddystone Condominium Assn. (v.p. 1978-86), Am. Mktg. Assn., Profl. Women's Network. Home and Office: 34 Fairlawn Ave Daly City CA 94015-3425

HARGROVE, GAIL ANNETTE, educational administrator; b. Washington, Oct. 30, 1940; d. Benny Hill Hargrove and Allie Lee Lovelady; m. Joseph Gayle Henderson, May 12, 1962 (div.); children: Monica Lee, Stanley James, Molly Marie. BS, La. State U., 1962, Masters degree, 1970. Cert. tchr., Level A Evaluator. Tchr. East Baton Rouge Parish, 1967-70; dir., ESEA, Chpt. 1 Dept. Corrections, Baton Rouge, 1970—; mem. adv. coun. Spl. Sch. Dist. #1, Baton Rouge, 1994. Evaluator Libr. Power Vols. in Pub. Schs., Baton Rouge, 1993-94; mem. com. United Way of Greater Baton Rouge, 1993. Mem. Am. Correctional Assn., Correctional Ednl. Assn., La. Assn. Sch. Adminstrs. of Federally Assisted Programs. Office: Dept Pub Safety & Corrections 504 Mayflower St Baton Rouge LA 70802

HARING, ELLEN STONE (MRS. E. S. HARING), philosophy educator; b. L.A., 1921; d. Earl E. and Eleanor (Pritchard) Stone; m. Philip S. Haring, Dec. 1942 (div. June 1951). BA, Bryn Mawr Coll., 1942; MA, Radcliffe Coll., 1943, PhD (AAUW fellow), 1959. Adminstrv. worker ARC, Boston, 1943; mem. faculty Wheaton Coll., Norton, Mass., 1944-45; mem. faculty Wellesley Coll., 1945-72, assoc. prof., 1958-64, prof. philosophy, 1964-72; prof. philosophy U. Fla., Gainesville, 1972-93, prof. emerita, 1993—; chmn. dept. U. Fla., 1972-80. Mem. Am. Philos. Assn., Metaphys. Soc. Am. Office: U Fla Griffin-Floyd 330 Gainesville FL 32611-8545

HARING, MARILYN JOAN, academic dean; b. Jerome, Ariz., Aug. 29, 1941; d. Earl Austin and Genevieve Teresa (Defilippi) S. BA in Edn., Ariz. State U., 1963, MA in Edn., 1966, PhD, 1978. Vis. asst. prof. Ariz. State U., Tempe, 1978-80, asst. prof., 1980-84; assoc. dean for edn. U. N.C., Greensboro, 1984-88; dean Sch. Edn. U. Mass., Amherst, 1988-91, Purdue U., West Lafayette, Ind., 1991—; sr. rsch. assoc. Ctr. for Evaluation and Rsch., Greensboro, 1985-88; dir. Commonwealth Acad. for Mentoring, Amherst, 1989-91. Contbr. articles to profl. jours., book chpts. Carnegie Corp. grantee, 1989-90. Mem. Am. Ednl. Rsch. Assn., Am. Psychol. Assn., Women Educators (nat. coord. 1987-89), Am. Coun. on Edn. (state coord. nat. identification project 1987-88). Office: Purdue U Sch Edn 1440 LAEB West Lafayette IN 47907-1440

HARIRI, GISUE, architect, educator; b. Abadan, Iran, May 16, 1956; came to U.S., 1974; d. Karim Hariri and Behjat (Isphahani) Saboonchi. BArch, Cornell U., 1980. Apprentice Jennings and Stout, San Francisco, 1980-82; Paolo Soleri, Arcosanti, Ariz., 1982-83; apprentice Paul Segal Assocs. Architects, N.Y.C., 1983-85; ptnr. Hariri & Hariri, N.Y.C., 1986—; lighting and furniture designer, 1993—; participant in Urban Housing Festival, The Hague, The Netherlands, 1991; lectr. in field. Work exhibited in Storefront for Art and Architecture, N.Y.C., 1988, Parson Sch. Design, N.Y.C., 1988, Princeton (N.J.) U., 1988, Archtl. League N.Y., 1990, Kent (Ohio) State U., 1991, Richard Anderson Gallery, N.Y.C., 1993, Cornell U., Ithaca, N.Y., 1993, Contemporary Arts Ctr., Cin., 1993, others, also in various profl. publs. Recipient Young Architects Forum award Archtl. League N.Y., 1990. Office: Hariri & Hariri 18 E 12th St New York NY 10003

HARKER, NORRENE, banker; b. Holyoke, Colo., Jan. 22, 1927; d. Wilbur J. and Mildred Mae (Baldwin) Summers; m. John Eugene Harker, July 15, 1945 (dec. 1989); children: Joan Y. Todd, Jean N. Andersen. Student, Colo. U., Boulder, 1944-45. Chairwoman Nat. Bank Burlington, Colo., 1989—; bd. dirs. Kit Carson State Bank, Kit Carson Agy., 1st Burlington Agy., Harker Land & Cattle Co., Burlington; pres. Hi-Plains Ag Credit Assn., Burlington, 1991—. Mem. Am. Cancer Soc. (county chairperson fund raising 1959, 90, Community Leadership and Svc. award 1975-76), Colo. 4-H Leadership Devel. (mem.-at-large, bd.dirs. 1977-79), United Meth. Women (dist. v.p. 1968-69, del. nat. conv. 1969), Women's Cancer Detection Clinic (organizor 1976), 4-H (leader, sponsor 1965), Epsilon Sigma Alpha. Republican. Methodist. Home: 48522 Snead Dr Burlington CO 80807-9036

HARKIN, RUTH R., federal agency administrator, lawyer; b. Vesta, Minn.; d. Walter Herman and Virginia (Coull) Raduenz; m. Tom Harkin, July 6, 1968; children: Amy, Jenny. BA in English, U. Minn., 1966; JD, Cath. U., 1972. With Dept. Army, Korea, 1966-67, Polk County Social Svcs., Des Moines, 1968; clk. Lawyers Com. Civil Rights under Law; elected county atty. Story County, Iowa, 1972-76; spl. prosecutor Polk County, 1977-78; dep. gen. counsel Dept. Agriculture, Washington, 1979-81; of counsel Akin, Gump, Strauss, Hauer & Feld, LLP, Washington, 1983-93; pres., chief exec. officer Overseas Pvt. Investment Corp., Washington, 1993—. Polit. advisor, strategist numerous presdl., senatorial campaigns. Mem. Iowa Bar Assn., D.C. Bar Assn. Democrat. Lutheran. Office: Internat Devel Cooperation Agy Office of the President 1100 New York Ave NW Washington DC 20527-0003*

HARKINS, ANN ELIZABETH, broadcast executive, management information specialist; b. N.Y.C., Sept. 24, 1952; d. James Aloysius and Mary Patricia (Mohan) Harkins; m. Michael Kromer, Nov. 8, 1986. BS, St. Bonaventure U., 1974. Programmer, analyst N.Y. Life Ins., N.Y.C., 1974-76; systems analyst CBS TV Network, N.Y.C., 1976-78, assoc. dir., 1978-82, dir. resources and planning, 1982-86, dir. fin. systems, 1986-88, dir. mgmt. infor. systems, 1988-89; mng. dir. bus. systems analysis CBS Inc., N.Y.C., 1989-93, v.p. sales svcs., 1993—. Mem. Internat. Radio and TV Soc., Am. Mgmt. Assn. Office: CBS Inc 51 W 52nd St New York NY 10019

HARKINS, LIDA E., state legislator, educator; b. Jersey City, Jan. 24, 1944; d. Paul Vincent and Lida Cecelia (Higgins) McMahon; children: Michael, Julie, Joseph. BA, Regis Coll., 1966; cert. in pub. policy mgmt., Boston Coll., 1986. Tchr. Mass. Pub. Schs., 1966-68; dir. sch. bus. tng. partnership The Edn. Co-op., Wellesley, Mass., 1988-89; state legislator 13th Norfolk Dist., Needham, Dover and Medfield, Mass., 1989—; bd. dirs. Charles River Workshop for Retarded Citizens, Needham, 1989. Mem. com. Needham Sch., 1976-82, chmn., 1979-80; mem. Needham Town Meeting, 1976—; chmn. Needham Dem. Town Com., 1983-85; bd. dirs. Needham area Boy Scouts Am., 1989. Recipient Alumnae Achievement award Boston Coll., 1989, Golden Donkey award Rendon Report Annual Polit. awards, 1989. Mem. Women Dems. of Dover and Needham. Roman Catholic. Home: 14 Hancock Rd Needham MA 02192-1926 Office: Mass Ho of Reps State Capitol Boston MA 02133*

HARKINS, ROSEANN HILDEBRANDT, real estate broker; b. Phila., July 20, 1941; d. Oscar L. and Anna Rose (Hepp) Hildebrandt; m. Dennis J. Vensel, Jan. 18, 1964 (dec. 1980); children: Heidi Rose, Amy Leigh; m. Ignatius J. Harkins III, Nov. 2, 1981 (dec. 1990). BS, Pa. State U., 1963. Cert. tchr., Pa., N.Y., Conn. Tchr. Conn. Sch. System, Hartford, 1963-68; real estate sales rep. Fossett Co., Rising Sun, Md., 1972-76; real estate broker, builder Harkins Real Estate, Chestnut Hill Bldg., Inc., Newark, Del., 1976—; pres. Home Owners Warranty Del., Wilmington, 1988-90, mem. quality com., 1991—, bd. dirs. Bd. dirs. Home Econs. Assn. Md., College Park, 1972-74, LWV Md., Annapolis, 1976-82, Humane Soc. Del., Wilmington, 1992-94, Housing and Cmty. Devel. Coun. of Del., 1994-95. Recipient Life Mem. award PTA Md., 1980; named Builder of Month Builder-Architect Mag., 1992. Mem. Nat. Assn. Home Builders, Nat. Assn. Realtors, Home Builders Assn. Del., New Castle County Bd. Realtors, Cecil County Bd. Realtors. Office: Harkins Realty 248 E Chestnut Hill Rd Newark DE 19713

HARKLEROAD, JO-ANN DECKER, special education educator; b. Wilkes-Barre, Pa., Oct. 22, 1936; d. Leon Joseph Sr. and Beatrice Catherine (Wright) Decker; m. A. Dwayne Harkleroad; 1 child, Leon Wade. AS, George Washington U., 1960, BS in Health, Phys. Edn. and Recreation, 1968, MA in Spl. Edn. and Ednl. Diagnosis and Prescription, 1969, also postgrad. Recipient Appreciation cert. Fairfax County (Va.) Police Dept., 1987, Meritorious Svc. medal Pres. Com. on Employment of People with Disabilities, 1988. Instr. Cath. U. Am., Washington, 1960-61; tchr. Bush Hill Day Sch., Franconia, Va., 1961-63; ednl. diagnostician Prince William County Schs., Manassas, Va., 1969-71, supr. title I, 1971-72; writer, editor Sta. WNVT-TV, Fairfax, Va., 1980-82; dir. spl. edn. Highland County Schs., Monterey, Va., 1987-90. Author: (novel) Horse Thief Trail, 1981, 83, 86; columnist op-ed page The Recorder; radio broadcaster Sta. WVMR, Frost, W.Va. Elder Presbyn. Ch., McDowell, Va., Clifton, Va.; former mem. comm. com. Shenandoah Presbytery; dir. McDowell Presbyn. Ch. Choir; rotating dir. Highland County Cmty. Choir; pres. Highland County Pub. Libr. Bd. Home: Windy Ridge Farm HRC 33 Box 60 Mc Dowell VA 24458

HARKNESS, MABEL GLEASON, retired librarian; b. Oil City, Pa., Jan. 20, 1913; d. Charles Wilcox and Mabel Amy (Fulton) Gleason; m. Benjamin Olney, Mar. 23, 1946 (dec. 1963); m. Bernard Emerson Harkness, Sept. 5, 1964 (dec. 1980). AB, U. Rochester, 1935, MA, 1962. Cert. libr., N.Y. Libr. Stromberg-Carlson Co., Rochester, N.Y., 1942-51, Garden Ctr. Rochester, 1953-67, Monroe County (N.Y.) Bookmobile, 1952-53; now ret.; vol. cataloger Geneva (N.Y.) Hist. Soc.; editor Gleam mag., Rochester Poetry Soc., 1945, Engr.'s Notebook, Stromberg-Carlson Co., 1946-50, Garden Ctr. Bull., 1955-67; co-founder, past pres. Western N.Y. chpt. Spl. Librs. Assn., 1945. Compiler: Harkness Seedlist Handbook 1986 (Worth award for bot./hort. writing Am. Rock Garden Soc.), 2d edit., 1993; contbr. articles on horticulture and local history to various publs. Trustee Keuka Coll., Keuka Park, N.Y., 1971-80, now emeritus. Mem. AAUW (life), Am. Rock Garden Soc. (life), Alpine Garden Soc. (Eng.), Scottish Rock Garden Club (life). Republican. Episcopalian. Home: 5169 Pre Emption Rd Geneva NY 14456-9736

HARKNESS, MARY LOU, librarian; b. Denby, S.D., Aug. 19, 1925; d. Raleigh Everette and Mary Jane (Boyd) Barker; m. Donald R. Harkness, Sept. 2, 1967. B.A., Nebr. Wesleyan U., 1947; A.B. in L.S, U. Mich., 1948; M.S., Columbia U., 1958. Jr. cataloger U. Mich. Law Library, 1948-50; asst. cataloger Calif. Poly. Coll., 1950-52; asst. cataloger, then head cataloger Ga. Inst. Tech., 1952-57; head cataloger U. S.Fla., Tampa, 1958-67; dir. libraries U. S.Fla., 1967-87, dir. emeritus, 1987—; cons. Nat. Library Nigeria, 1962-63. Bd. dirs. Southeastern Library Network, 1977-80. Recipient Alumni Achievement award Nebr. Wesleyan U., 1972. Mem. Am., S.E., Fla. library assns., Fla. Women's Alliance, Athena Soc. Democrat. Mem. United Ch. Christ. Home: 13511 Palmwood Ln Tampa FL 33624-4409

HARKNESS, SARAH PILLSBURY, architect; b. Swampscott, Mass., July 8, 1914; d. Samuel Hale and Helen (Watters) Pillsbury; m. John C. Harkness, June 14, 1941; children: Sara, Joan, Nell, Timothy, Alice, Frederick, John P. M.Arch., Smith Coll., 1940; M.F.A. (hon.), Bates Coll., 1974. Registered architect, Mass. Prin. The Architects Collaborative, Cambridge, Mass., 1945-87; profl. adviser ecol. architecture Oberlin Coll., 1993; participant "Design-In" Coll. of the Atlantic, 1991; vis. critic U. Ariz. Sch. Architecture, 1990, MIT Sch. Architecture, 1986, 87; adv. bd. U. Tenn., 1982-85, Princeton U. Sch. Architecture, 1976-84; faculty rep. Boston Architecture Ctr., 1989; rev. com. in architecture La. Bd. Regents, 1978; selection com. U. Va. Sch. Architecture Thomas Jefferson Meml. Found., 1975-76; juries AIA design awards; lectr. schs. architecture AIA chpts. Author: (with James N. Groom, Jr.) Building Without Barriers, 1976, The Architects Collaborative Encyclopedia of Architecture, 1986; editor: Sustainable Design for Two Maine Islands, 1985, Visions of Sustainability, 1991, and others. Recipient honor award for Bates Coll. Library AIA-ALA, 1976, Louis I. Kahn citation for Olin Arts Ctr., Bates Coll., 1987, AIA honor award for Chase Learning Ctr., Eaglebrook Sch., 1967, Am. Assn. Sch. Adminstrs. award Fox Lane Middle Sch., Bedford, N.Y., 1961. Fellow AIA (bd. dirs. 1972-75, v.p. 1978); mem. Boston Soc. Architects (bd. dirs. 1979-80, pres. 1985, award of honor 1991, Honor award in edn. and rsch. 1994). Address: 34 Moon Hill Rd Lexington MA 02173-6113

HARKRADER, MARY ELLEN, county clerk; b. Pontiac, Ill., May 8, 1934; d. Lawrence Arthur and C. Marcella (Jacobson) Wheeler' m. Alan D. Harkrader Jr., July 17, 1954; children: Alan D. III, Mark E. Diploma, St. Francis Hosp. Sch. Nursing. Cert. pub. official Nat. Assn. County Recs. and Clks., Washngton, 1990. County clk. Peoria (Ill.) County, 1982—. Corp. sec. Forest Park Found., Peoria, 1990—; mem. NAACP; treas. Dem. Women Peoria, 1984—; mem. YWCA, Peoria Old Settlers. Named Woman of Achievement Women in Mgmt., Peoria, 1988, YWCA Woman in Govt., Peoria, 1978; recipient cert. Appreciation State Comptroller, 1990, 93. Mem. Nat. Assn. Recorders and Clks. (cert. pub. ofcl. 1990, 2d v.p. 1993-94, pres. 1994—), Ill. Assn. County Clks. (legis. 1986—), State Bd. Elections (adv. bd. 1985-91), Heart of Ill. Sierra Club (chair, pres.), Heart of Ill. ASPA (program chair 1994—). Roman Catholic. Home: 1712 E Shady Oak Dr Peoria IL 61614-7906

HARLAN, KATHLEEN T. (KAY HARLAN), business consultant, professional speaker and seminar leader; b. Bremerton, Wash., June 9, 1934; d. Floyd K. and Rosemary (Parkhurst) Troy; m. John L. Harlan, Feb. 16, 1952 (div. 1975); children: Pamela Kay, Kenneth Lynwood, Lianna Sue; m. Stuart Friedman, Nov. 10, 1991. Chair Kitsap-North Mason United Way, 1968-70; owner, operator Safeguard N.W. Systems, Tacoma, 1969-79; devel., mgr. Poulsbo (Wash.) Profl. Bldg., 1969-75; pres. Greenapple Graphics, Inc., Tacoma, 1976-79; owner, mgr. Iskrem Hus Restaurant, Poulsbo, 1972-75; pres. Bus. Seminars, Tacoma, 1977-82; owner, mgr. Safeguard Computer Ctr., Tacoma, 1982-91; owner Total Systems Ctr., Tacoma, 1983-88; mem. Orgnl. Renewal, Inc., Tacoma, 1983-88; assoc. mem. Effectiveness Resource Group, Inc., Tacoma, 1979-80; pres. New Image Confs., Tacoma, 1979-82; speaker on mgmt. and survival in small bus.; CEO Manage Ability, Inc., profl. mgmt. firm, 1991—; bus. mgr. Another Door to Learning, 1993—. Contbg. author: Here is Genius!, 1980; author small bus. manuals. Mem. Wash. State Br. Boundary Rev. for Kitsap County, 1970-76, Selective Svc. Bd. 19, 1969-76; co-chair Wash. State Small Bus. Improvement Coun., 1986; del. White House Conf. on Small Bus., 1986; chair Wash. State Conf. on Small Bus., 1987; mem. exec. bd. Am. Leadership Forum, 1988—; dir. Bus. Leadership Week, Wash. State, 1990—; chair Pro-Tech Pierce County, 1992—; chair Allenmore Hosp., 1993—. Recipient Nellie Cashman award; named Woman Entrepreneur of Yr. for Wash. State, 1986, 87. Mem. Tacoma-Pierce County C. of C. (lifetime exec. bd. 1985—, chair spl. task force on small bus. for Pierce County 1986-89, treas. 1987-88, chair-elect 1988-90, chair 1990-91).

HARLAN, MARY RUTH, health service officer; b. Des Moines, Nov. 17, 1938; d. Ellis and Julia Elizabeth (Blount) H.; m. Harris Hardin Schultz, Dec. 30, 1967 (div. May 1983); children: Mark Harlan, Paul Larkin, David Stephen. BA, Drake U., 1961; MA, Vanderbilt U., 1967; MS, So. Ill. U., 1981. Program planner Iowa Dept. Pub. Health, Des Moines, 1990—. Bd. dirs. Wood River (Ill.) Twp. Hosp., 1981-84. Named Outstanding Profl., Iowa Head Injury Assn., 1993. Mem. AAUW, ASPA, Older Women's League (pres. mid. Iowa chpt. 1992-94), Toastmasters, Phi Sigma Iota. Democrat. Congregationalist. Home: 2509 35th St Des Moines IA 50310 Office: Iowa Dept Pub Health 321 E 12th St Des Moines IA 50319

HARLAN, NANCY MARGARET, lawyer; b. Santa Monica, Calif., Sept. 10, 1946; d. William Galland and Betty M. (Miles) Plett; B.S. magna cum laude, Calif. State U., Hayward, 1972; J.D., U. Calif., Berkeley, 1975; m. John Hammack, Dec. 1, 1979; children—Laryssa Maria Rebello, Leea Elyce Harlan. Admitted to Calif. bar, 1975, Fed. bar, U.S. Dist. Ct. for Central Dist., 9th Circuit, 1976; assoc. firm Poindexter & Doutré, Los Angeles, 1975-80; residential counsel Coldwell Banker Residential Brokerage Co., Fountain Valley, Calif., 1980-81; sr. counsel for real estate subs. law dept. Pacific Lighting Corp., Santa Ana, Calif., 1981-87; sr. v.p., gen. counsel The Presley Cos., 1987—. Exec. v.p. student body U. Calif., Berkeley, 1974-75; bd. dirs. La Casa. Mem. State Bar Calif., Am. Bar Assn., Los Angeles County Bar Assn., Orange County Bar Assn. (dir. corp. counsel sect. 1982—), Calif. Women Lawyers Assn., Orange County Women Lawyers Assn., Los Angeles Women Lawyers Assn., Nat. Assn. Female Execs., Bus. and Profl. Women. Office: The Presley Cos 19 Corporate Plaza Dr Newport Beach CA 92660-7920

HARLASS, SHERRY ELLEN POOL, writer, aquatics instructor; b. Bourne, Mass., Jan. 2, 1961; d. Sydney Smith and Shirley Ruth (Fisher) Pool; m. Mark Paul Harlass, July 17, 1982; children: Rachel Miranda, Mark Daniel. Student, S.W. Tex. State U., 1979-80; BA in Journalism, Midwestern State U., Wichita Falls, Tex., 1982. Reporter Wichita Falls Record News, 1980-82, Wichita Falls Times, 1982-83; staff writer Branch-Smith, Inc., Ft. Worth, 1984-85, prodn. editor, 1986-88, mng. editor, 1988-91; freelance writer, editor, photographer Arlington, Tex., 1991-94, Hurst, Tex., 1994—; instr. aquatic fitness, 1993—, arthritis aquatic, 1994—. Contbr. articles to newspapers and mags. Named one of the Notable Women of Tex., 1983. Mem. Women in Comms. Inc. (v.p. membership Ft. Worth chpt. 1994-95), Nat. Fedn. Press Women, Tex. Press Women, Nat. Assn. Women in Horticulture, Mary/Martha Soc. (sec. 1986-88, pres. 1992-94), Tex. Rangers Women's Club (sec. 1986-88), Mothers of Little Lambs (MOLLIES), Aquatic Exercise Assn. Lutheran. Home and Office: 852 Park Forest Dr Hurst TX 76053

HARLEM, SUSAN LYNN, librarian; b. L.A., Oct. 1, 1950; d. Frank Joseph and Esther Frances (Bomell) H.; m. Anthony Stephen Hacsi, Aug. 31, 1990. BA, UCLA, 1972, MLS, 1976. Libr. U. Md., College Park, 1976-79, U.S. Dept. Edn., Washington, 1979-82, GSA, Washington, 1982-87, NLRB, Washington, 1988—. Co-author: Washington on Foot, 1984. Office: NLRB Libr 1099 14th St NW Washington DC 20570-0002

HARLEMAN, ANN, English language educator. BA in English, Douglass Coll., 1967; PhD in Linguistics, Princeton U., 1972; MFA in Creative Writing, Brown U., 1988. Asst. prof. dept. English Rutgers U., New Brunswick, N.J., 1973-74; asst. prof. dept. English U. Wash., Seattle, 1974-79, assoc. prof. dept. English, 1979-84; vis. assoc. prof., research affiliate Writing Program MIT, Cambridge, 1984-86; vis. scholar Program in Am. Civilization Brown U., Providence, 1986—; Cole Disting. prof. Wheaton (Ill.) Coll., 1992-93; prof. English RISD, Providence, 1994—. Author: Graphic Representation of Models in Linguistic Theory, 1976, (with Bruce A. Rosenberg) Ian Fleming: A Critical Biography, 1989, Happiness, 1994; translator: Mute Phone Calls, 1992; contbr. 20 scholarly articles, translations and revs., poems and short stories to lit. mags. Guggenheim fellow, 1976-77, Huntington Libr. fellow, 1979-80, MacDowell Colony fellow, 1988, ACLS fellow, 1992, Fulbright-Hays lectr., 1980-81, R.I. State Coun. Arts, 1989—; ACLS/IREX sr. scholar, 1976-77; recipient grant Rockefeller Found., 1989, Raymond Carver prize, 1986, Nelson Algren runner-up award Chgo. Tribune, 1987, 3d prize Judith Siegal Pearson award, 1988, Chris O'Malley Fiction prize Madison Rev., 1990, NEH grant, 1988, Wurlitzer Found. fellowship, 1992, Judith Siegal Pearson award, 1991, Syndicated Fiction award PEN, 1991, John Simmons Short Fiction award, 1993. Mem. MLA (chair exec. com. Gen Linguistics), Linguistic Soc. Am., Poets and Writers, Inc., Am Lit. Translators Assn. Home: 55 Summit Ave Providence RI 02906-2709 Office: Brown U Program In Am Civilization Providence RI 02912

HARLEY, ELLEN A., state legislator; b. Nashville, Dec. 31, 1946; m. Edwin Westbrook Harley; children: Beth, Greg. BA in English, Monmouth Coll.; MA in City and Regional Planning, U. Pa. NASD/SEC lic.; lic. real estate agt. Rep. Pa. Ho. of Reps., Harrisburg; cons. U. Pa., Phila. Author: Study of Preservation of Open Space and Growth Management Through the Use of Performance Standards; co-author: Study on Affordable Housing in Montgomery County. Elder First Presbyn. Ch., Lower Merion, Pa.; commn. mem. Pa. Pub. TV Network, Harrisburg, Pa.; coun. mem. Pa. Coun. on the Arts, Harrisburg. Mem. LWV, Am. Planning Assn., Urban Land Inst. Republican. Presbyterian. Office: Pa Ho fo Reps State Capitol Harrisburg PA 17120*

HARLEY, RUTH, artist, educator; b. Phila., July 24, 1923; children: Peter Wells Bressler, Tori Angela. Student, Pa. State U., 1941; BFA, Phila. Coll. Art, 1945; postgrad., U. N.H., 1971, Hampshire Coll., 1970. Former instr. Phila. Mus. Art, 1946-59; former art supt. Ventnor (N.J.) City Bd. Edn., 1959-61; art tchr. The Print Club, Phila., Allens Lane Art Ctr., Phila., Suburban Ctr. Arts, Lower Merion, Pa., Radner (Pa.) Twp. Adult Ctr., 1949-59, Atlantic City Adult Ctr., 1959-60. One woman shows include Dubin-Lush Galleries, Phila., 1956, Greenhill Galleries, Phila., 1974, Phila. Civic Ctr., 1978, Natal Rio Grande du Norte, Brazil, 1979, Galerie Novel Esprit, Tampa, Fla., 1992, 93, 94, The Mind's Eye Gallery, St. Petersburg, Fla., 1993; exhibited in various group shows including Group 55, Phila., 1955, The Print Club, Phila., 1955, Phila. Civic Ctr. Mus., 1975, Galerie Nouvel Esprit Assemblage Russe, 1992, The Mind's Eye Gallery, St. Petersburg, Fla., 1993, Polk Mus. Art, Lakeland, Fla., 1993, Don Roll Gallery, Sarasota, Fla. 1994, Las Vegas Internat. Art Expo, 1994; commns. include City of Phila., 1973; represented in permanent collections at U. Villanova (Pa.) Mus., Temple U. Law Sch., Pa. Address: PO Box 433 Melrose FL 32666-0433

HARLIN, MARILYN MILER, marine botany educator, researcher, consultant; b. Oakland, Calif., May 30, 1934; d. George T. and Gertrude (Turula) Miler; m. John E. Harlin II, Oct. 25, 1955 (dec. Feb. 1966); children: John E. III, Andrea M. Harlin Cilento. AB, Stanford U., 1955, MA, 1956; PhD, U. Wash., 1971. Instr. Am. Coll. Switzerland and Leysin, 1964-66; asst. prof. Pacific Marine Sta., Dillon Beach, Calif., 1969; asst. prof. marine biology U. R.I., Kingston, 1971-75, assoc. prof., 1975-83, prof., 1983—, chair botany dept.; guest scientist Atlantic Regional Lab., Halifax, N.S., Can., 1973-78; hon. vis.prof. LaTrobe U., Bundoora, Victoria, Australia, 1984; resource person R.I. Coastal Resource Mgmt. Coun., 1980—, R.I. Dept. Environ. Mgmt., 1980; cons. Applied Sci. Assocs., Narragansett, R.I., 1988—, Western Australia Water Authority, Perth, 1994; rsch. assoc. U. Calif., Santa Cruz, 1993. Co-editor: Marine Ecology, 1976, Freshwater and Marine Plants of Rhode Island, 1988. Bd. dirs. Westminster Unitarian Ch., East Greenwich, R.I., 1987; bd. govs. Women's Ctr., Kingston, 1989-90. Grantee NOAA, 1975-81, Dept. Environ. Mgmt./EPA, 1989-91, U.S. Fish and Wildlife, 1995. Mem. Internat. Phycological Soc., Phycological Soc. Am. (editor newsletter 1982-84, editorial bd. 1988-90), N.E. Algal Soc. (exec. com.), Sigma Xi (pres., sec. 1979-82). Office: U RI Dept Botany Kingston RI 02881

HARLOW, KAY UPTON, industrial engineer; b. Gadsden, Ala., Oct. 30, 1958; d. Hugh Max and Juanita Merle (Parr) Upton; m. Herbert Lloyd Cleveland, Jr., Aug. 23, 1980 (div. 1990); children: Rachel, Allison; m. Chris Harlow, Nov. 25, 1993; children: Ted, John. BSIE, Auburn U., 1981. Registered engr., Ala. Jr. engr. Ala. Power Co., Birmingham, 1981-83, asst. engr., 1983-87, engr., analyst, 1987-91; assoc. dir. Ala. Resource Ctr., Montgomery, 1991—. Sponsor Explorer-Boy Scouts, Montgomery, Ala., 1993-94. Mem. Nat. Mgmt. Assn. (sec. 1993-94), So. Indsl. Devel. Coun., Econ. Devel. Assn. Ala., Urban & Regional Info. Sys. Assn. (pres. 1991-92, treas. 1992-94). Office: Ala Resource Ctr PO Box 160 Montgomery AL 36101-0160

HARMAN, BARBARA SUE, business owner; b. Sturgis, Mich., Nov. 6, 1943; d. Hugh Edgar and Myrna Irene (Auten) Fry; m. Thomas Russell Harman, Sept. 24, 1966; children: Michael Hugh, Scott Thomas, James Gregory. Freelance writer, photographer South Bend (Ind.) Tribune, 1977-86; commr. Cass County Bd. Commrs., Cassopolis, Mich., 1986-92; supr. Mason Twp. Cass County, Edwardsburg, Mich., 1992-96; owner Merle Norman Studio, Elkhart, Ind., 1987—. Cons. hist. project Mason Twp., 1987-88; cons. Mich. Hist. Commn., 1987-92, also campaign promotions; mem. Mich. Women's Commn. Bicentennial, Lansing, 1987-89; coord. Cass County Bicentennial, Cassopolis, 1987-88. Presbyterian. Office: Merle Norman Studio 1515 Cassopolis St Elkhart IN 46514

HARMAN, JANE FRANK, congresswoman, lawyer; b. N.Y.C., June 28, 1945; d. A. N. and Lucille (Geier) Lakes; m. Sidney Harman, Aug. 30, 1980; children: Brian Lakes, Hilary Lakes, Daniel Geier, Justine Leigh. BA, Smith Coll., 1966; JD, Harvard U., 1969. Bar: D.C. 1969, U.S. Ct. Appeals (D.C. cir.) 1972, U.S. Supreme Ct. 1975. Spl. asst. Commn. of Chs. on Internat. Affairs, Geneva, Switzerland, 1969-70; assoc. Surrey & Morse, Washington, 1970-72; chief legis. asst. Senator John V. Tunney, Washington, 1972-73; chief counsel, staff dir. Subcom. on Rep. Citizen Interests, Com. on Judiciary, Washington, 1973-75; adj. prof. Georgetown Law Ctr., Washington, 1974-75; chief counsel, staff dir. Subcom. on Constl. Rights, Com. on Judiciary, Washington, 1975-77; dep. sec. to cabinet The White House, Washington, 1977-78; spl. counsel Dept. Def., Washington, 1979; ptnr. Manatt, Phelps, Rothenberg & Tunney, Washington, 1979-82, Surrey & Morse, Washington, 1982-86; of counsel Jones, Day, Reavis & Pogue, Washington, 1987-92; mem. 103rd Congress from 36th Calif. dist., 1992—; mem. vis. coms. Harvard Law Sch., 1976-82, Kennedy Sch. Govt., 1990—. Counsel Dem. Platform Com., Washington, 1984; vice-chmn. Ctr. for Nat. Policy, Washington, 1981-90; chmn. Dem. Nat. Com. Nat. Lawyers' Coun., Washington, 1986-90. Mem. Phi Beta Kappa. Democrat. Office: US House Reps 325 Cannon House Office Bldg Washington DC 20515-0536 also: 5200 W Century Blvd Ste 960 Los Angeles CA 90045 also: 3031 Torrance Blvd Torrance CA 90503-5015

HARMEL, HILDA HERTA See PIERCE, HILDA

HARMENING, DENISE M., academic administrator, educator; b. Balt., Jan. 24, 1952; d. George and Catherine (Leimbach) H. BS in Med. Tech., U. Md., Balt., 1974, MS in Medicine and Med. Tech., 1976, PhD in Clin. Pathology, 1981. Clin. asst. prof. Georgetown U. Sch. Medicine, Washington, 1983-87; clin. assoc. prof. program in med. tech. Cath. U. Am., Washington, 1986-87; prof., chmn. dept. lab. sci. Thomas Jefferson U., Phila., 1987-90; asst. prof., asst. dir. program in med. tech. U. Md. Sch. Medicine, Balt., 1984-85, dir. continuing edn. program in med. tech., 1984-85, assoc. prof. dept. path., 1986-87, prof., chmn. dept. med. and rsch. tech., 1990—; dir. ednl. svcs. Am. Assn. Blood Banks, Washington, 1982-84, insp. accrediation program, 1985-88. Author: Clinical Hematology and Fundamentals, 1987, (with I. Isbister) Clinical Hematology, 1988, Modern Blood Banking, 1994; patentee cellular preservation field. Recipient teaching award Pathology Bds. Study Group, Inc., 1984; Clay Adams rsch. grantee, 1979; fellow Wallace Internat.-RMIT, Melbourne, Australia, 1988. Mem. Am. Assn. Blood Banks, Am. Soc. Clin. Pathologists (cert. med. technologist), Am. Soc. Hematology, Am. Soc. Med. Tech. (chmn. hematology-hemostasis-sci. sect. region II 1985, 87, 89, editor-in-chief CLS jour. 1987-89, editorial adv. bd. Lab. Med. 1993—, outstanding svc. award 1988), Md. Soc. Med. Technologists (pres. 1987-88), Internat. Soc. Blood Transfusion, Internat. Soc. Thrombosis and Hemostasis, Phi Kappa Phi, Omicron Sigma. Office: U Med Dept Med and Rsch Tech 32 S Greene St Baltimore MD 21201-1544

HARMON, ADRIENNE SECCIA, anthropologist; b. N.Y.C., Oct. 30, 1947; d. Thomas G. Seccia and Anne L. (Scionti) Smith; m. George Jay Harmon, Mar. 30, 1985. AA, Miami-Dade Jr. Coll., 1972; BA in Anthropology and Sociology, Fla. Internat. U., 1974; MA in Cultural Anthropology, U. Ga., 1978; PhD in Social and Cultural Anthropology, U. Ill., 1993. Grad. teaching asst. dept. anthropology U. Ga., Athens, 1974-78; grad. asst. Social Sci. Quantitative Lab., U. Ill., Champaign, 1982-83, grad. teaching asst. in charge anthropology reading room, 1983-84, 84, grad. teaching asst. dept. anthropology, 1985, grad. rsch. asst. to resource libr. Transition Rsch. Inst., 1985-93, vis. postdoctoral rsch. assoc., 1993—; presenter in field at profl. meetings. Author: (with Lynda N. Leach) Annotated Bibliography on Transition from School to Work, Vols. 1-6, 1986-91, (with Leach) Annotated Bibliography on Secondary Special Education and Transitional Services, Vols. 7-9, 1992-94, (with T.E. Grayson, Leach, B.F. Wallace and Hui-Ju Huang) Compendium of Transition Model Programs, 1993, (with B.F. Wallace, T.E. Grayson, and L.N. Leach) Compendium of Transition Model Demonstration Programs, 1994, (with J. P. Decoteau and Leach) Handbook for Project Directors, 1986; compiler: Master Index to Volumes 1-6: Annotated Bibliography on Transition from School to Work, 1991. Mem. Am. Anthrop. Assn., Am. Ethnol. Soc., Soc. for Med. Anthropology, Nat. Assn. for Practice Anthropology. Office: U Ill Transition Rsch Inst 113 Children's Rsch Ctr 51 Gerty Dr Champaign IL 61820

HARMON, ARTICE WARD, occupational therapist; b. Hughes, Ark., Oct. 2, 1940; d. William Oscar and Alice Williams (Turner) Ward; BS, Ind. U., 1973; MPH, U. Ill., 1975; m. Luther Harmon, Dec. 5, 1959. Occupational therapy intern St. Elizabeth's Hosp., Washington, 1973, Helen Hayes Rehab. Hosp., W. Haverstraw, N.Y., 1973; staff occupational therapist Mercy Hosp. and Med. Center, Chgo., 1973-76; dir. occupational therapy program Westside Parents Ctr., of Retarded Children United, Chgo., 1976-77; head occupational therapy dept. Americana Health Care Ctr., Champaign, Ill., 1977-81; dir. occupational therapy program Chgo. State U., 1981-89, acting dean Coll. Allied Health, 1985-86, 89, program devel. specialist, 1986-90, weekend coll. coord., 1991-92, spl. asst. to provost, 1992—; guest lectr. allied health curriculum U. Ill., Champaign, 1975, grad. teaching assoc. occupational therapy curriculum Coll. Assoc. Health Professions, 1978-80, instr., 1980-81; chmn. steering com. Ill. Coun. Occupational Therapy Edn.; coord. statewide internship program Ill. Bd. Govs. State Colls. and Univs., Springfield, Ill., 1986-87; cons. in field. Mem. 1st congl. dist. of Ill. Congl. Health Adv. Task Force, 1988—. Mem. Am. Occupational Therapy Assn. (accreditation evaluator 1989—), Ill. Occupational Therapy Assn., Am. Pub. Health Assn., Am. Vocat. Assn., Ill. Vocat. Assn., Am. Vocat. Ednl. Rsch. Assn., Am. Soc. Allied Health Professions, People United to Save Humanity, Phi Delta Kappa, Kappa Delta Pi. Roman Catholic. Home: 5020 S Lake Shore Dr # 806N Chicago IL 60615-3201 Office: Chgo State U Coll Allied Health 95th St at King Dr Chicago IL 60628

HARMON, GAIL MCGREEVY, lawyer; b. Kansas City, Kans., Mar. 15, 1943; d. Milton and Barbara (James) McGreevy; m. John W. Harmon, June 11, 1966; children: James, Eve. BA cum laude, Radcliffe Coll., 1965; JD cum laude, Columbia U., 1969. Bar: Mass. 1970, D.C. 1976, U.S. Dist. Ct. D.C. Assoc. Gaston Snow & Ely Bartlett, Boston, 1970-75, Steptoe & Johnson, Washington, 1975-76, Roisman, Kessler & Cashdan, Washington, 1976-77; ptnr. Harmon, Curran & Tousley, Washington, 1977-90, Harmon, Curran, Gallagher & Spielberg, Washington, 1990—. Pres. Women's Legal Def. Fund, 1982-84; mem. steering com. Emily's List, 1985—. Democrat. Episcopalian.

HARMON, JANE ELLEN, occupational therapist; b. Muskegon, Mich.; d. Robert Junior and Edith (Boven) H. BS in Occupational Therapy, Western Mich. U., 1974. Registered occupational therapist; licensed occupational therapist, Tex.; cert. CPR/BCLS instr.-trainer. From vol. to staff therapist Hackley Hosp., Muskegon, 1972-75; head occupational therapy dept. Mercy Hosp., Muskegon, 1975-79; pvt. practice, 1976-79; with Mary Free Bed Hosp. & Rehab. Ctr., Grand Rapids, 1979; free-lance writer, 1979—; cons. Tri-City Health Ctr./Hosp., Dallas, 1993. Contbr. articles to profl. jours.; contbg. editor, cons. Occupational Therapy Forum, 1993—. Active Arthritis Vol. Action Com., 1975-79; founder Vols. Against Multiple Sclerosis Mich. chpt. Nat. Multiple Sclerosis Soc., 1973 (recipient Individual Vol. of the Yr. award, 1994), mem. profl. adv. com. North Tex. chpt., mem. patient svc. com.; mem. HIV/AIDS Com. Bethel Ch., Dallas, 1992—, prayer chain coord., 1990—, editor Bethel News, 1989-90; editor, cage bird cons. pet-facilitated therapy program Baylor Inst. for Rehab., Dallas, 1992-93; founder, dir. Project HAVEN Dallas Cage Bird Soc., 1991-93; vol. Dallas Ctr. for Ind. Living, 1990—; liaison Classis Pella Com. on Disability Concerns; founder, dir. Ecology Ministries, 1987—; rep. com. disability concerns Classics Pella, Christian Reformed Ch. N.Am., 1994—. Mem. Tex. Occupational Therapy Assn., Environ. Health Assn. Dallas, Am. Occupational Therapy Assn., Write Shop Writer's Assn. Office: 14232 Marsh Ln Ste 320 Dallas TX 75234-3899

HARMON, MARIAN SANDERS, writer, sculptor; b. Detroit, Jan. 16, 1916; d. Joseph and Anne (Stern) Sanders; m. Edward Stein, Jan. 15, 1950 (dec. 1960); m. Leonard Byron Harmon, 1963. BA, U. Mich., 1937. Dir. radio and TV Simons Michelson, Detroit, 1948-60; editor Table Talk Bridge Newspaper, 1954-62; writer ABC-TV, N.Y.C., 1960-65; organizer, pres. Visual Arts Forum, 1981-93. Author: (poems) The Hourglass, 1982; editor AAUW, East Hampton, 1984-87, various newspapers, 1945-65; first editor Northwest Detroiter, 1947; freelance writer for newspapers and mags. Recipient Best Sculpture in Show award Guild Hall East Hampton, 1989. Home: PO Box 1547 East Hampton NY 11937-0795

HARMON, MEGAN ELIZABETH, lawyer; b. Pitts., May 17, 1960; d. Patrick Joseph and Grace Lillian (Butler) H.; m. Robert S. Simon, Sept. 26, 1992 (div.). BA in Polit. Sci., Ind. U. Pa., 1983; JD, Duquesne U., 1985. Assoc. Berkman, Ruslander, Pohl, Lieber & Engel, Pitts., 1985-88, Thorp, Reed, & Armstrong, Pitts., 1988-90; dep. gen. counsel Chambers Devel. Co., Pitts., 1990—. Mem. ABA, Nat. Assn. Bond Lawyers, Pa. Bar Assn., Allegheny County Bar Assn. Office: Chambers Development Co 10700 Frankstown Rd Pittsburgh PA 15235

HARMON, MELINDA FURCHE, federal judge; b. Port Arthur, Tex., Nov. 1, 1946; d. Frank Cantrell and Wilma (Parish) Furche; m. Frank G. Harmon III, Oct. 16, 1976; children: Mary Elizabeth, Phelps, Francis. AB, Harvard U., 1969; JD, U. Tex., 1972. Bar: Tex. 1973, U.S. Dist. Ct. (so. dist.) Tex. 1974, U.S. Dist. Ct. (no. dist.) Tex. 1975, U.S. Dist. Ct. (ea. dist.) Tex. 1978, U.S. Ct. Appeals (5th and 11th cirs.) 1981, U.S. Supreme Ct. 1982, U.S. Ct. Claims 1987. Law clk. to presiding judge U.S. Dist. Ct. (so. dist.) Tex., Houston, 1973-75; atty. Exxon Co., Houston, 1975-88; judge 280th Jud. Dist. Ct. Tex. State Trial Ct., ctrl. jurisdiction, 1988-89; judge U.S. Dist. Ct. (so. dist.) Tex., Houston, 1989—. Mem. Tex. Bar Assn., Houston Bar Assn., Harvard Radcliffe Club. Roman Catholic. Office: US Dist Ct US Courthouse 515 Rusk Ave Rm 9535 Houston TX 77002*

HARMON, MELVA JANE, lawyer; b. Terrell, Tex., Dec. 23, 1947; d. Hillard M. and Josephine (Carper) H.; m. Stanley K. Kozinsky, May 1, 1973 (div. 1980). BA, Stephen F. Austin State U., 1970; JD, U. Tex., 1976. Bar: Ark. 1976, U.S. Dist Ct. (ea., we. dists.) Ark. 1976, U.S. Ct. Appeals (8th cir.) 1979, U.S. Supreme Ct. 1980. Assoc. Law Offices John T. Lavey, Little Rock, 1976-81; ptnr. Lavey, Harmon & Burnett, Little Rock, 1981-91, Youngdahl, Trotter, McGowen & Harmon, Little Rock, 1991-92; pvt. practice Little Rock, 1992—; bd. dirs., officer Cen. Ark. Legal Svcs., Little Rock, 1981-91; mem. Fed. Practice Com. East. Dist. Ark., 1992-94, co-chair, 1993. Author: (withothers) How Arbitration Works, 1987, 2d edit., 1989, Supplement to How Arbitration Works, 1990. Mem. Ark. Tchr. Career Devel. Commn., Little Rock, 1985-87. Recipient Spl. Citation Merit Nat. Fedn. Blind of Ark., 1981. Mem. ABA (com. labor law and law collective bargaining agreement), Ark. Bar Assn. (pres. labar law sect. 1990-91, chmn. legal aid com. 1984-85), Ark. Trial Lawyers Assn. Home: 2901 Reservoir Rd Little Rock AR 72207-3233 Office: Law Office Melva Harmon 111 Center St Ste 1434 Little Rock AR 72201-4416

HARMON, NANCY JEAN, elementary school educator; b. Rockford, Ill., Apr. 21, 1946; d. Wayne Walter and Cecilia Marie (Wasileski) Crotzer; m. John Edmund Harmon, June 13, 1970. BA, Monmouth Coll., 1968; cert., Nat. Coll. Edn., 1974; MA, Roosevelt U., 1985. Tchr. 4th grade Sch. Dist. #54, Schaumburg, Ill., 1968—. Leader Girl Scouts Am., Schaumburg, 1968-70; chmn. Crusade of Mercy, Schaumburg, 1980-92. Recipient Outstanding Educator award Schaumburg Jaycees, 1972; named Tchr. of Yr., Aldrin Sch. PTA, 1993. Mem. NEA, Coun. for Exceptional Children, Schaumburg Ednl. Assn., Delta Kappa Gamma. Home: 496 Sheridan Ln Schaumburg IL 60193-2928 Office: Sch Dist 54 524 E Schaumburg Rd Schaumburg IL 60194-3597

HARMON, SYLVIA ESTHER, nurse, artist; b. Sharon, Pa., Feb. 21, 1926; d. Ira Guy and Martha Gladys (Irving) Camp; m. George William Harmon, Sept. 6, 1952 (dec.); children: David, Valerie. Diploma, Freedmen's Hosp. Sch. Nursing, Washington, 1948. RN, D.C. Pvt. duty nurse Washington, 1948-53; staff nurse Cooper Hosp., Camden, N.J., 1953-94; pub. health nurse Camden City Dept. Pub. Health, 1958-65; adj. freelance artist painter Nice, France, 1967-74, U.S., 1974—; vis. nurse Falmouth (Mass.) VNA, 1974-76. Columnist: Diary of an Artist, Atlanta Daily World, 1979-80; artist: one person exhbns. include: Casino of Monte Carlo, Monaco, 1969, 70, David's Gallery, Roswell, New Mex., 1973, Francis Aronson's Gallery Ltd., Buckhead Atlanta, 1979, Howard U. Alumni, Balt., 1992. Mem. Howard U. Nurses Alumni, Monumenatal City Med. Soc., Aux. Episcopalian. Home and Office: 211 W Lanvale St Baltimore MD 21217

HARMON BROWN, VALARIE JEAN, hospital laboratory director, information systems executive; b. Peoria, Ill., June 21, 1948; d. Donald Joseph and Frances Elizabeth (Classen) Harmon; m. James Roger Brown, Aug. 21, 1982 (dec. May 1994). BSMT, Northwestern U., Chgo., 1970. Med. tech. Evanston (Ill.) Hosp., 1970-71, chief tech., 1971-75; med. tech. II M.D. Anderson Hosp., Houston, 1975-76; dir. lab. Physicians Ref. Lab., Houston, 1978-81, Med. Ctr. Hosp., Conroe, Tex., 1981-91, Palo Pinto Gen. Hosp., Mineral Wells, Tex., 1993-94; sales mgr. Long Beach (Calif.) Meml. Med. Ctr., 1995—; lab. cons. Texaco Chem. Wellness Program, Conroe, 1989; health career sponsor Willis Ind. Sch. Dist., Tex., 1989, 90; mem. adv. bd. Med. Lab. Technician program Weatherford Coll., 1994. Coord. blood drive Gulf Coast Region Blood Ctr., 1986-91; sponsor colon cancer screening Montgomery County Health Fair, 1986; sponsor Camp Sunshine/Lions Club, 1988; sponsor cholesterol screening Med. Ctr. Hosp. Health Fair, 1989. Mem. NAFE, Am. Soc. Clin. Pathologists, Am. Soc. Med. Technologists, Clin. Lab. Mgmt. Assn. Republican. Roman Catholic. Home: Apt 306 30001 Golden Lantern Laguna Niguel CA 92677 Office: Long Beach Meml Med Ctr 2801 Atlantic Ave Long Beach CA 90801-1428

HARMS, DEBORAH GAYLE, psychologist; b. Ft. Worth, Aug. 12, 1950; d. Raymond O. Smith and Billie (Allen) Greenwade; m. Joel Randall Harms; children: J. Christopher, Ryan R., Catherine R. BA with honors with high distinction, Wayne State U., 1977; MA in Clin. Psychology, U. Detroit, 1979, PhD in Clin. Psychology, 1984. Lic. psychologist. Trainee in psychology Henry Ford Hosp., Troy, Mich., 1978-79; intern in psychology Detroit Psychiat. Inst., 1979-82; staff psychologist Eastwood Clinic, Harper Woods, Mich., 1983-86; pvt. practice Harms and Harms, PC, Birmingham, Mich., 1985—; staff psychologist Dominican Consultation Ctr., Detroit, 1986-89; sr. psychologist Oakland County Probate Ct., Pontiac, Mich., 1990. Teaching fellow U. Detroit, 1978-79. Mem. APA, Nat. Register Health Care Providers in Psychology, Mich. Psychol. Assn., Mich. Women Psychologists, Mensa, Phi Beta Kappa. Home: 21783 Corsaut Ln Beverly Hills MI 48025 Office: Harms and Harms PC 31815 Southfield Rd Ste 31 Franklin MI 48025-5471

HARMSEN, LYDIA, classical dancer; b. The Hague, The Netherlands, Nov. 16, 1968; came to the U.S., 1987; d. Johannes Cornelis and Elena Reina (Carmona) H. BA, Royal Conservatory, The Hague, 1987. With corps de ballet N.Y.C. Ballet, 1988—; featured in two dance documentaries by Marjke Jongbloed, 1982, 92. Performed in Ballet Capsule, Tokyo, 1991, Kiyumizudera Tempel, Kyoto, 1992, Dansers Fonds Gala, Amsterdam, 1991. Recipient Prix de Lausanne Bourse scholarship for sch. Am. Ballet, 1986, DanserFonds prize, Amsterdam, 1991. Office: NYC Ballet New York State Theater New York NY 10023

HARNETT, LILA, publisher; b. Bklyn., Oct. 4, 1926; d. Milton Samuel and Claire S. (Merahn) Mogan; m. Joel William Harnett. BA, CUNY, 1946; postgrad., New Sch. for Social Rsch., 1950. Pers. exec. Walter Lowen Agy., N.Y.C., 1947-52; pub. Bus. Atomics Report, N.Y.C., 1953-63; weekly columnist N.Y. State Newspapers, 1964-74; fine arts editor Cue Mag., N.Y., 1975-80; founder, contbg. editor Phoenix Home & Garden mag., 1980—, assoc. pub., 1988—; pub. Scottsdale (Ariz.) Scene mag., 1992—. Home: 4523 E Clearwater Pky Paradise Valley AZ 85253-2815 Office: Phoenix Home & Garden 4041 N Central Ave Phoenix AZ 85012-3330

HARNEY, DEBRA ANN, publishing executive; b. Mineola, N.Y., Aug. 20, 1962; d. Edward Patrick and Arline Frances (Duffy) H. BA, SUNY, Albany, 1984. Tchr. A.G. Berner High Sch., Massapequa, N.Y., 1984-85; mktg. asst. Instl. Investor, N.Y.C., 1985; domestic sales Bankers Trust Co., N.Y.C., 1985-87; assoc. pub. Investing, N.Y.C., 1987—; v.p. DMA Communications, Inc., N.Y.C., 1987—. Office: DMA Communications Inc 280 Park Ave S Apt 13B New York NY 10010-6130

HARNEY, JOYCE ANN, nursing educator, administrator; b. Columbus, Ind., Apr. 2, 1952; d. John B. and Joan G. (Meredith) Redmon; m. Eugene Harney, Aug. 17, 1979; 1 child, Timothy Eugene. Degree in practical nursing, Bartholomew County Sch., 1971; BSN, Ind. U., Indpls., 1987, MS in Nursing, 1992. RN, Ind.; BLS, BLS instr., ACLS. Practical nurse Bartholomew County Hosp., Columbus, 1971-87; critical care nurse Richard Roudebush VA Hosp., Indpls., 1987-90; nursing instr. Ind. Tech. Coll., Columbus, 1988—; dir. nursing dept. practical nursing Ind. Tech. Coll., 1992; dir. nursing dept. practical nursing Ind. Tech. Coll., Columbus, 1992-95, dir. health and human svcs., 1995—. Item writer Nat. Coun. State Bds. of Nursing, 1993, 94. Vol. ARC, Columbus, 1987—, Ind. AIDS Task Force, Ind. Dept. Health, 1991, 92, AIDS Support Group Bartholomew County Health Dept. Mem. ANA, Sigma Theta Tau. Home: 2589 N Talley Rd Columbus IN 47203-9169 Office: Ind Vocat Tech Coll 4475 Central Ave Columbus IN 47203-1868

HARNSBERGER, THERESE COSCARELLI, librarian; b. Muskegon, Mich.; d. Charles and Julia (Borrell) Coscarelli; B.A. cum laude, Marymount Coll., 1952; M.L.S., U. So. Calif., 1953; postgrad. Rosary Coll., River Forest, Ill., 1955-56, U. Calif., Los Angeles Extension, 1960-61; m. Frederick Owen Harnsberger, Dec. 24, 1962; 1 son, Lindsey Carleton. Free-lance writer, 1950—; librarian San Marino (Calif.) High Sch., 1953-56; cataloger, cons. San Marino Hall, South Pasadena, Calif., 1956-61; librarian Los Angeles State Coll., 1956-59; librarian dist. library Covina-Valley Unified Sch. Dist., Covina, Calif., 1959-67; librarian Los Angeles Trade Tech. Coll., 1972—; med. librarian, tumor registrar Alhambra (Calif.) Community Hosp., 1975-79; tumor registrar Huntington Meml. Hosp., 1979—; pres., dir. Research Unltd., 1980—; free lance reporter Los Angeles' Best Bargains, 1981—; med. library cons., 1979—; reviewer various cookbooks, 1991—. Author numerous poems. Chmn. spiritual values com. Covina Coordinating Council, 1964-66; chmn. Neighborhood Watch, 1976—. Winner poetry contest Pasadena Star News, 1993. Mem. ALA, Internat. Women's Writing Guild, Calif. Assn. Sch. Librarians (chmn. legis. com.), Covina Tchrs. Assn., AAUW (historian 1972-73), U. So. Calif. Grad. Sch. Libr. Sci. (life), Am. Nutrition Soc. (chpt. Newsletter chmn.), Nat. Tumor Registrars Assn., So. Calif. Tumor Registrars Assn., Med. Libr. Assn., So. Calif. Libr. Assn., So. Calif. Assn. Law Libr., Book Publicists So. Calif., Am. Fedn. Tchrs. (exec. bd. part-timers 1994, alt. exec. bd. local # 1521 coll. guild 1994—), Coll. Guild, Calif. Libr. Assn., Assn. Poetry Bibliographers, Faculty Assn. Calif. Community Colls., Immaculate Heart Coll. Alumnae Assn., Assistance League Pasadena, Loyola Marymount Alumnae Assn. (coord. 1986), Pi Lambda Theta. Author: (poetry) The Journal, 1982, To Julia: in Memoriam; contbr. articles to profl. jours., poems to newspapers. Office: 2809 W Hellman Ave Alhambra CA 91803-2737

HARP, TONI N., state legislator; b. San Francisco. BA, Roosevelt U.; MEd, Yale U. Mem. New Haven Bd. Aldermen, 1988-92, Commn. Affirmative Action, 1990-92; Conn. state senator, 1993—; project coord. health svcs. Democrat. Address: 26 Lynwood Pl New Haven CT 06511-4713 Office: Conn State Senate State Capitol Hartford CT 06106*

HARPER, BRENDA KAY, nurse; b. Grayson, Ky., Oct. 26, 1956; d. Emird Jr. and Anna Gale (Mayo) Damron; m. Ronald Duncan, June 1, 1974 (div. Oct. 1984); 1 child, Derek L.; m. Jacky Ray Harper, June 6, 1986 (dec. 1993). AAS in Nursing, Ashland (Ky.) Community Coll., 1979; student, Morehead State U., 1994—. CEN, ACLS. Med.-surg. charge nurse Kings Daus. Hosp. (now Med. Ctr.), Ashland, 1979, labor and delivery-postpartum charge nurse, 1982, charge nurse emergency dept., 1983-87; team leader maternity and gynecology units Cabell Huntington (W.Va.) Hosp., 1980; charge nurse Carter County Primary Care Ctr., Grayson, 1981; mental health therapist, rape crisis adv. Pathways Inc., Grayson, 1987-90; home health nurse Our Lady of Bellefonte Hosp., Russell, Ky., 1990; nurse Carter County Med. Clinic St. Claire Med. Ctr., Olive Hill, Ky., 1991-92; nurse West Carter Health Ctr., Olive Hill, 1992-94; sch. nurse East Carter Jr. High Health Ctr., 1994—; adv. com. Yough Svc. Ctr., 1994—, bd. dirs. 1994—; mem. site based coun. com. East Carter Hr. H.S., 1993—. Vol. bloodmobile ARC, Grayson, 1976—; den leader, asst. cubmaster Cub Scouts Am., Grayson, 1989—; homeroom mother PTA, Grayson, 1986—; mem. Prichard Boosters Club, Grayson, 1986—; vol. Grayson Area Little League, 1987—. Recipient appreciation award Pathways Inc., 1990, Extended Campus scholarship Morehead State U., 1994, Nellie E. Ellis State Homemakers scholarship, 1994, Carter County Homemakers scholarship Displaced Homemaker, 1994. Mem. Grayson Jaycees (award of merit 1988), Grayson Homemakers, Grayson Bowling Ctr. Womens League. Mem. Ch. of Christ. Home: PO Box 563 Grayson KY 41143-0563 Office: East Carter Jr/Sr Health Ctr PO Box 1133 Grayson KY 41143

HARPER, CARMELA ROSE, direct marketing company executive; b. N.Y.C.; d. Antonio and Assunta (Grenci) Vergara; m. Rondel H. Harper, May 8, 1947 (dec.). Student Coll. New Rochelle, 1936-38. Auditor, Liberty Mut. Ins. Co., N.Y.C., 1947-50; pres., chief exec. officer The Kleid Co. Inc., N.Y.C., 1950—. Author: Mailing List Strategies, 1986; contbr. articles to profl. jours. Named to Direct Mktg. Hall of Fame, 1985. Mem. Direct Mktg. Assn. (bd. dirs., chmn. 1981-82). Roman Catholic. Avocations: investments, animals, children, old people's and edn1. causes, swimming. Office: The Kleid Co Inc 530 5th Ave New York NY 10036-5101

HARPER, CYNTHIA LYNN, art educator; b. Burbank, Calif., Jan. 4, 1966; d. Robert Stephen H. and Kathleen DeLena (Schweppee) Sheetz. BFA, Otis Art Inst., 1987; MFA, Calif. Coll. Arts & Crafts, 1990. Adj. faculty U. Nebr., Omaha, 1992—, Met. C.C., Omaha, 1992—; co-coord. Save Outdoor Sculpture!, NE, 1994. Calif. State Grad. fellow, 1989, 90; NEH Summer Seminar grantee, 1993; Nebr. Arts Coun. Individual Artist fellow, 1994, Mid-Am. Arts Alliance fellow, 1994. Mem. Women's Caucus for Art (mem.-at-large 1993—), Coll. Art Assn. Office: Livestock Exch Bldg #616 29th & O'Plaza Omaha NE 68107

HARPER, DELPHINE BERNICE, health administrator; b. Boston, Sept. 6, 1947; d. James Albert and Bernice (Bell) Garnett; m. John Henry Redd III, Dec. 31, 1966 (div. May 1972); 1 child, John; m. Morris Harper, Aug. 18, 1975; children: Michele, Kimberly. Cert. acctg., Boston Sch. Bus., 1966; BS, Northeastern U., 1973; postgrad., L.I. U., 1975-76. Lic. real estate agt., D.C., Md. Asst. Admissions Office Northeastern U., Boston, 1968-71; adminstrv. asst. to dir. Assn. for Better Housing, Boston, 1971; community organizer Roxbury Multi Svc. Ctr., Boston, 1971-72; unit mgr. Peter Bent Brigham Hosp., Boston, 1972-74; mgmt. analyst State of Mass., Boston, 1974-75; proprietor Kimele's Wine & Cheese, Cambridge, Mass., 1978-79; real estate agt. Bd. Realtors, D.C., Md., 1983-86; program officer, asst. dir. resident svcs. Dept. Housing, 1986-88; v.p. ops., mgmt. officer Health Care Systems Corp., Silver Spring, Md., 1988—. Bd. dirs. Dem. Nat. Com., Washington, 1988; mem. Kennedy Ctr., 1989—. John F. Kennedy scholar Northeastern U., Boston, 1971-73, Martin Luther King scholar, 1970-71. Mem. Am. Mgmt. Assn., Greater Washington Edn. Telecommunication Assn., Women in Arts, Smithsonian Assocs., Nat. Trust for Hist. Preservation, Nat. Geog. Soc., Nat. Assn. Investors Corp., N.Y. Met. Opera Guild, Archaeol. Inst. Am., N.Y. Mus. Natural History, Phi Beta Kappa.

HARPER, GLADYS COFFEY, health services adviser; b. Pitts.; d. Clarence William and India Anna (James) Jackson; B.A., U. Pitts., 1970, M.P.A., 1972, M.S.H., 1973; m. Thomas A. Harper, Jan. 21, 1968. With Allegheny County (Pa.) Health Dept., 1958—, chief office tng. and edn. adminstr., 1975-76, adv. curriculum devel. and health adminstrn., 1976—; health technician specialist office health affairs OEO, Washington, 1965; vis. lectr. Grad. Sch. Public and Internat. Affairs, U. Pitts., 1970—; bd. dirs. Heritage Nat. Bank, 1988—; panelist Sta. WQED-TV White House Conf. Food, Nutrition and Health; trustee Mayview State Hosp., 1975—, v.p. bd. trustees, 1978, trustee clin. pastoral edn. program, 1979-80; bd. dirs. United Mental Health, Inc. Co-producer documentary: What's Buggin' The Blacks?, Sta. KDKA-TV, 1968; host Weekly News Notes, Sta. KDKA-Radio, 1989—. Program chmn. Law Day, Allegheny County Assn. Lawyers' Wives, 1980; program chmn. Pa. Bar Assn. Wives Program, 1978; trustee Louis Little Meml. Fund, Allegheny County Bar Assn., 1979; founder Judge Thomas A. Harper Meml. Scholarship, Howard U. Sch. Law, 1984. Active Allegheny County Bicentennial Com., 1987, Afro-Am. Heritage Day Parade Com., 1987; exec. v.p. Afro-Am. Heritage Parade Assn., chmn. judging com., 1988; v.p. Hist. Soc. of Western Pa., 1988; pres. Tri-Rivers African Am. Archives, Inc., 1991. Named Woman of Yr., Greyhound Corp., 1967, 1 of 25 Outstanding Pittsburghers, Wayfarer Mag., Chrysler Corp., 1967; recipient Health Services award Pitts, Club United, 1970, Harold B. Gardner award-Md. Citizen Health award, Allegheny County Med. Soc., 1973, Drug Edn. recognition Pitts. Press, 1971, citation for environ. health curriculum devel. and supervision Chatham Coll., 1976, award African Meth. Episcopal Zion Ch., 1984, Trailblazer award Renaissance Publs, 1992, Outstanding Citizen award Hand in Hand, 1992, Black History Month citation Bur. Surface Mining, U.S. Dept. Interior, 1992; crowned Bahamas Princess Christmas Queen, Freeport, 1976. Mem. APHA, Royal Soc. Health, Am. Soc. Pub. Adminstrn., Conf. Minority Pub. Adminstrs., Legis. Council Western Pa. (dir., v.p. elect 1982), Western Pa. Genealogy Soc. (pres. 1983), Legis. Council Western Pa. (pres. 1983), League Community Health Workers, AAUW, NAACP (Isabel Strickland Youth Advisor award 1967, Daisy E. Lampkin Human Rights award 1969), Hist. Soc. Western Pa. (trustee 1984, v.p. bd. trustees 1988), U. Pitts. Alumnae Assn. (Bicentennial scholarship com.), Program to Aid Citizen Enterprises (commr., treas. 1968-76). Home: 5260 Centre Ave Pittsburgh PA 15232-1315

HARPER, GLORIA JANET, artist, educator; children: Dan Conyers, Jan Shriver. Student, Famous Artists Sch., 1967-69, 69-71; BA in Comml. Art, Portland C.c., 1981; postgrad., Valley View Art Sch., 1982-89, Carrizzo Art Sch., 1983-88, Holdens Portrait Sch., 1989; studied with Daniel Greene, 1989, postgrad. in paralegal studies. Cert. art educator. Artist, art instr. Art By Gloria, Pendleton, Oreg., 1980—; owner Art By Gloria Art Sch. and Gallery, Pendleton, 1991—; lectr., workshop presenter in field, 1980—. Paintings and prints included in various mags. Mem. NAFE, Water Color Soc. Am., Nat. Mus. Women in Arts, So. Career Inst. Profl. Legal Assts. (area rep.), Profl. Legal Assts., Pendleton C. of C. Home: PO Box 1734 Pendleton OR 97801-0570 Office: Art By Gloria 133 S Main St Pendleton OR 97801-2214

HARPER, JANE, critical care nurse, educator; b. Ironton, Ohio, Sept. 10, 1951; d. Ralph Lee and Martha Ann (Cooper) Hicks. BSN, Wright State U., 1982; MS, U. Calif., San Francisco, 1987; postgrad., U. Calif., 1991—. RN; CCRN; cert. pub. health nurse, BLS, ACLS instr., coronary care nurse. Staff nurse Kaiser Permanente Med. Ctr., San Fransisco, 1982-84, Herrick Hosp. and Health Ctr., Berkeley, Calif., 1984-86; staff nurse critical care Med. Pers. Pool, Walnut Creek, Calif., 1984-87; critical care clin. nurse specialist San Joaquin Gen. Hosp., Stockton, Calif., 1987-89; staff nurse critical care Nurse's Network, San Jose, Calif., 1989—; lectr. dept. nursing Sch. Applied Arts and Scis., San Jose State U., 1990—. Contbr. articles to profl. jours. Recipient Regent's fellowship U. Calif., San Francisco, 1991. Mem. ANA (coun. clin. nurse specialists), AACN (chpt. bd. dirs. 1985-86), Nat. League Nursing, Am. Heart Assn., Soc. Critical Care Medicine, Calif. Nurses Assn., Sigma Theta Tau.

HARPER, JANET SUTHERLIN LANE, educational administrator, writer; b. La Grange, Ga., Apr. 2, 1940; d. Clarence Wilner and Imogene (Thompson); m. William Sterling Lane, June 28, 1964, (div. Jan. 1981); children: David Alan, Jennifer Ruth; m. John F. Harper, June 9, 1990. BA in English and Applied Music, LaGrange Coll., 1961; postgrad., Auburn U., 1963; MA in Journalism, U. Ga., Athens, 1979. Music and drama critic The Brunswick News, Brunswick, Ga., 1979—; info. asst. Glynn County Schs., Brunswick, 1979-82; adj. prof. Brunswick Coll., Ga., 1981-87; dir. pub. info. and publs. Glynn County Schs., Brunswick, 1982—; media relations Ga. Assn. of Ednl. Leaders, 1983—. Contbg. editor Ga. Jour., 1981-84; editor, writer GAEL Conf. Jours., 1987-89. Organist St. Simons United Meth. Ch., 1981—; pres. Jekyll Island Music Theater Bd., 1994—. Recipient award of excellence in sch. and community rels. Ga. Bd. Edn., 1984, 92, Edn. Leadership award, Ga., 1989. Mem. Nat. Sch. Pub. Rels. Assn. (Golden Achievement award 1985, 2 awards 1988, 90, 3 awards 1991, 92, 94), Ga. Sch. Pub. Rels. Assn. (Disting. Svc. award 1991), Brunswick Press-Advt. Club (award of excellence in pub. rels. 1992), Brunswick Golden Isles C. of C., Mozart Soc., Phi Delta Kappa, Phi Kappa Phi, Sigma Delta Chi. Office: Glynn County Schs 1313 Egmont St Brunswick GA 31520-7244

HARPER, JUDITH BEAVERS, artist; b. Brookhaven, Miss., May 26, 1944; d. John William and Neva Newman (Beavers) H. MEd, U. South Ala., 1993. Artist, tech. illustrator, computer animator. Exhibited in group show at U. South Ala. Recipient Best of Show award U. South Ala., 1991. Mem. Mobile Art Assn., Contemporary Arts Ctr., New Orleans Mus. Art, Phi Kappa Phi, Kappa Delta Pi.

HARPER, MARY SADLER, banker; b. Farmville, Va., June 15, 1941; d. Edward Henry and Vivien Morris (Garrett) Sadler; m. Joseph Taylor Harper, Dec. 21, 1968; children by previous marriage: James E. Hatch III, Mary Ann Hatch Czajka. Cert. Fla. Trust Sch., U. Fla., 1976. Registered securities rep., Fla. Dep. clk. Polk County Cts., Bartow, Fla., 1964-67; rep. Allen & Co., Lakeland, Fla., 1967-71; with First Nat. Bank, Palm Beach, Fla., 1971-89, sr. v.p., 1984-86, sr. v.p. S.E. Bank N.A., Palm Beach, 1986-89; pres., CEO Palm Beach Capital Svcs., Inc., 1986-88, mng. dir. Investment Svcs., Palm Beach Capital Svcs. Div., 1988; v.p. investments, trustee J.M. Rubin Found., Palm Beach, 1983—; sr. v.p. investment div. Island Nat. Bank of Palm Beach, 1989—; dir., pres. CEO Island Investment Svcs., Inc., Palm Beach, 1989—, also bd. dirs.; mem. adv. coun. Nuveen, 1987-94. Mem. adv. panel Palm Beach County YWCA, 1984—; Jupiter Hosp. Found.; life mem. June Beach Civic Assn. Mem. YWCA (adv. panel 1985, endowment com. 1990-93), Nat. Assn. Securities Dealers (registered dist. com. mem. 1995—), Fin. Women Internat., Fla. Securities Dealers Assn., Exec. Women of Palm Beaches (mem. fin. com. 1985-92), Internat. Soc. Palm Beach (treas., trustee 1986—), Jupiter Hosp. Med. Assn. (pres.'s club 1989—), Loxahatchee Hist. Soc. (bd. dirs. 1991-93, chmn. devel. com. 1992-93), Sebring, Fla. Hist. Soc. (life), Jupiter/Tequesta C. of C. (assoc.), United Daus. of Confederacy, Gov.'s Club, Pub. Securities Assn. (exec. rep.), Jonathans Golf Club, Rotary (Palm Beach found. com. 1990—, bd. dirs. 1992, 93-94), Lighthouse Gallery Art (life), Norton Gallery Art (patron). Democrat. Baptist. Avocations: reading, history. Home: 630 Ocean Dr Apt 103 Juno Beach FL 33408-1916 Office: Island Investment Svcs Inc Island Nat Bank Palm Beach 180 Royal Palm Way Palm Beach FL 33480-4254

HARPER, NORMA IRENE, academic administrative assistant; b. Painseville, W.Va., Sept. 26; d. Fred Nelson and Pearl (Vance) Green; divorced; children: Vicki, Jimmie, Paul, Debra. Grad. high sch., Johnstown, Monroe. PBX operator, receptionist Ohio State U., Columbus, 1965, clk. typist, sec., 1965-78, adminstrv. asst. 1, 1978—. Trustee and vol. Ronald McDonald House coms.; mem. Rosemont Ctr. Sustaining Bd.; vol., mentor Big Bros./Big Sister Assn.; mem. Ohio State U. Med. Ctr. svc. bd. Mem. Nat. Assn. Hosp. Hospitality Houses (bd. dirs., cmty. dir.), Nat. Assn. Working Women 9 to 5 (v.p., cardinal chpt.), Profl. Secs. Internat. (mem. coms.), Whestone Folk Dancers Group (v.p.), Vaudvillities (hon. mem.). Home: 49 W Hudson St Columbus OH 43202-2501 Office: Ohio State U 590 Woody Hayes Dr Columbus OH 43210-1057

HARPER, PAMELA SOLVITH, management consultant; b. Cleve., May 18, 1953; d. Marvin and Jean M. (Charney) Solvith; m. D. Scott Harper, May 8, 1976; children: Jason, Rebecca. Student, U. Mich., 1976-78; PhB, Northwestern U., 1982. Cert. sr. profl. human resources, Soc. for Human Resource Mgmt. Pers. asst. Films Inc., Wilmette, Ill., 1983-84; asst. mgr. human resources Infolink Corp., Northbrook, Ill., 1984-85; recruiting coord. Timeplex Inc., Woodcliff Lake, N.J., 1985-86; employment mgr. Simon & Schuster Inc., Englewood Cliffs, N.J., 1987-89; mgr. staffing ABB Power Generation Inc., North Brunswick, N.J., 1989-91; ptnr. Paradigm Assocs. TQ, Glen Rock, N.J., 1991-93; pres. Bus. Advancement Inc., Glen Rock, N.J., 1994—; instr. divsn. continuing edn. Bergen C.C., Paramus, N.J., 1993—, SUNY/Westchester C.C., Valhalla, N.Y., 1994—; spkr. in field. Columnist/panelist The Record N.J., 1993. Mem. Assn. Quality and Participation, Total Quality Inst. (charter), Soc. Human Resource Mgmt., Alpha Sigma Lambda. Office: Bus Advancement Inc 178 Sycamore Ter Glen Rock NJ 07452-1907

HARPER, PATRICIA M., state legislator; b. Cresco, Dec. 4, 1932; d. Patrick Mullaney and Martha Gossman; 1 child, Susan. BA, U. No. Iowa, MA. Tchr. secondary math. and sci., 1955-86; mem. Iowa Ho. of Reps. Bd. dirs. Independence Haven. Mem. AAUW, LWV, Waterloo Edn. Assn., Alliance for Mentally Ill. Democrat. Home: 3336 Santa Maria Dr Waterloo IA 50702-5334 Office: Iowa Ho of Reps State Capitol Des Moines IA 50319*

HARPER, PATRICIA NELSEN, psychiatrist; b. Omaha, July 25, 1944; d. Eddie R. and Marjorie L. (Williams) Nelsen. BS, Antioch Coll., Yellow Springs, Ohio, 1966; MD, U. Nebr., 1975. Cert. psychiatrist. Psychiatric residency Karl Menninger Sch. of Psychiatry, Topeka, 1975-78; staff psychiatrist The Menninger Clinic, Topeka, 1978--; faculty mem. Karl Menninger Sch. of Psychiatry, Topeka, 1982--, candiate Topeka Inst. for Psychoanalysis, 1982--. Program dir. Alcohol and Drug Abuse Recovery Program C.F. Menninger Meml. Hosp., Topeka, 1987--. Mem. Am. Psychiatric Assn., Am. Med Women Assn., Am. Psychoanalytic Assn. Office: The Menninger Clinic PO Box 829 Topeka KS 66601-0829

HARPER, PATSY ELAINE, educational specialist, counselor; b. Hempstead, Tex., Feb. 2, 1939; d. Whittie Benjamin Whitfield Reese and Ruby (Hammock) Nelson; m. Jerry Davidson Harper, June 1, 1957; 1 child, Rhonda Kim Harper Rigby. BA in Elem. Edn., Sam Houston State U., 1972, MEd in Edn. and Psychology, 1975. Lic. profl. counselor, Tex.; spl. edn. cert., elem. edn. cert., early childhood endorsement. Tchr. 1st grade Rockport-Fulton Consol. Ind. Sch. Dist., 1970-72; tchr. spl. edn., early childhood edn. Madisonville Consol. Ind. Sch. Dist., 1972-75, counselor, 1975-87; ednl. specialist Edn. Svc. Ctr. Region VI, Huntsville, Tex., 1987—. Recipient Outstanding Achievement award field of tchr. edn. Sam Houston State U., 1986; named Woman of Distinction by Bluebonnet Coun. Girls Scouts Am., 1994, Woman of Yr. by Madison County C. of C., 1987. em. Am. Counselors Assn., Am. Sch. Counselors Assn., Tex. Counselors Assn., Tex. Sch. Counselors Assn., Brazos Valley Counselors Assn. (Outstanding Svc. award 1989, past officer), Tex. State Tchrs. Assn. (life), Sam Houston State Alumni Assn. (bd. dirs. 1990-92, adv. bd. 1993-94), Sam Houston State U. Ex-Students Assn. (sec. 1993-94), Sam Houston State Parent's Assn. (Cert. Outstanding Svc. 1989, charter, life), Phi Delta Kappa (editor newsletter 1992—, pres. 1991-92), Alpha Delta Kappa (charter, pres. 1982-84), Alpha Chi, Yellow Rose Lions Club (charter, past pres., sec.-treas. 1994—), Madisonville C. of C. (participant Harvest of Love 1991, 92), Homemakers of Am. (hon. life). Baptist. Home: 301 Heath Ave Madisonville TX 77864-1719 Office: Edn Svc Ctr Region VI 3332 Montgomery Rd Huntsville TX 77340-6417

HARPER, PAULA, art history educator, writer; b. Boston, Nov. 17, 1938; d. Clarence Everett and Maura (Lee) Fish. BA in Art History magna cum laude, Hunter Coll., 1966, MA in Art History, 1968; postgrad., U. N.Mex., 1968-69; PhD in Art History, Stanford U., 1976. Dancer Munt-Brooks Modern Dance Co., N.Y.C., 1963-65; teaching fellow U. N.Mex., 1968-69; asst. prof. Calif. Inst. Arts, Valencia, 1971-72; dir. Hunter Arts Gallery CUNY, 1977-78; vis. asst. prof. Mills Coll., Oakland, Calif., spring 1979, 80-81, Stanford (Calif.) U., 1979-80; assoc. prof. art history U. Miami, Coral Gables, Fla., 1982—; art critic Miami News, 1982—; frequent lectr. mus., art galleries and univs.; project advisor TV series on Camille Pissarro, PBS Channel 10, St. Thomas, V.I., 1992—. Author: (with R.E. Shikes) Pissarro: His Life and Work, 1980 (transl. into French, German, and Romanian), Daumier's Clowns, 1981; author (catalogues) "Powerplay" Paintings by Judy Chicago, 1986, Contemporary Sculpture from the Martin Z. Margulies Collection, 1986, Visions from Brazil-The Drawings of Paolo Gomes Garcez, 1993; contbr. articles to profl. jours., books, exhbn. catalogues. Bd. trustees Ctr. for Fine Arts, Miami, 1990-93; mem. Art in Pub. Places Com., Miami Beach, 1991—. Recipient Film Inst. fellowship CUNY, 1966, Tuition fellowship Hunter Coll., 1966-67, Ford Found. grant Stanford U., 1969-73, Rsch. grant French govt., 1973-74, Rockefeller Found. grant, 1991, Ailsa Mellon Bruce Vis. Sr. fellowship Nat. Gallery of Art, 1990-91. Mem. Coll. Art Assn. (founder Women's Caucus for Art 1972, pres. N.Y. chpt. 1977-78, nat. adv. bd. 1977-80), Internat. Assn. Art Critics, Soc. Mayflower Descs., Foundlings Club, Art Table. Home and Office: 11 Island Ave Ph 7 Miami Beach FL 33139-1303

HARPER, REBECCA COLEMAN, accountant; b. Dothan, Ala., Feb. 20, 1959; d. Floyd D. Sr. and Anne (Harrelson) Coleman; m. Richard A. Smith, June 10, 1976 (div. 1983); 1 child, Jennifer Smith; m. William L. Harper, June 2, 1988 (div. July 1994); 1 child, Mack. AA, George C. Wallace C.C., Dothan, 1987; BS magna cum laude, Troy State U., 1989. CPA, Ala. Staff acct. Terry B. Ray, CPA, Dothan, 1989, Coates McCullar & Biggers, Dothan, 1989-90; advanced staff acct. McDaniel & Assocs., Dothan, 1990-91, sr. acct., 1991—. Bd. dirs. Houston County Jr. Miss, Dothan, 1992—. Mem. AICPAs, Ala. Soc. CPAs, Ga. Soc. CPAs, Ala. Soc. Enrolled Agents (cert.), Nat. Soc. Tax Profls., Inst. Mgmt. Accts. (bd. dirs. 1992-93), SE Ala. CPAs Soc. Baptist. Office: McDaniel & Assocs PC 4 Northside Exec Park Dothan AL 36303

HARPER, SANDRA STECHER, university dean; b. Dallas, Sept. 21, 1952; d. Lee Roy and Carmen (Crespo) Stecher; m. Dave Harper, July 6, 1974; children: Justin, Jonathan. BS in Edn., Tex. Tech. U., 1974; MS, U. N. Tex., 1979, PhD, 1985. Speech/reading tchr. Nazareth (Tex.) High Sch., 1974-75; speech/English tchr. Collinsville (Tex.) High Sch., 1975-77, Pottsboro (Tex.) High Sch., 1977-79; communication instr. Austin Coll., Sherman, Tex., 1980-82; rsch. asst. U. N. Tex., Denton, 1982-84; vis. instr. communication Austin Coll., Sherman, 1985; asst. prof. communication McMurry Coll., Abilene, Tex., 1985-89; assoc. prof. communication McMurry U., Abilene, Tex., 1989—, dean Coll. Arts and Scis., 1990—, asst. dir. NEH univ. core curriculum project; critic judge Univ. Interscholastic League, Austin, 1980-93; mem. adv. bd. Univ. Rsch. Consortium, Abilene, 1990—. Contbr. articles to profl. jours.; author: To Serve the Present Age, 1990; co-author U.S. Dept. Edn. Title III Grant. Planner TEAM Abilene, 1991; del. Tex. Commn. for

Libr. and Info. Svcs., Austin, 1991; chair Abilene Children Today: Life and Cmty. Skills Task Force, 1994-95. Named Outstanding Faculty Mem., McMurry U., 1988, Outstanding Adminstrv., 1993; Media Rsch. scholar, Ctr. for Population Options, 1989. Mem. Internat. Communication Assn., Speech Communication Assn., So. Speech Communication Assn., Film and Video Assn., Council Coll. of Arts and Sciences. Democrat. Roman Catholic. Home: 5058 Oaklawn Dr Abilene TX 79606-3535 Office: McMurry U PO Box 57 Abilene TX 79604-0057

HARPER, SHIRLEY FAY, nutritionist, educator, consultant; b. Auburn, Ky., Apr. 23, 1943; d. Charles Henry and Annabelle (Gregory) Belcher; m. Robert Vance Harper, May 19, 1973; children: Glenda, Debra, Teresa, Suzanna, Cynthia. BS, Western Ky. U., 1966, MS, 1982. Cert. nutritionist and lic. dietitian, Ky. Dir. dietetics Logan County Hosp., Russellville, Ky., 1965-80; cons. Western State Hosp., Hopkinsville, Ky., 1983-84, instnl. dietetic adminstr., 1984-88; dietitian Rivendell Children's Psychiat. Hosp., Bowling Green, Ky., 1988-90; instr. nutrition Western Ky. U., Bowling Green, 1990-92; cons. Auburn (Ky.) Nursing Ctr., 1976—, Belle Meade Home, Greenville, Ky., 1980—, Brookfield Manor, Hopkinsville, Ky., 1983—, Sparks Nursing Ctr., Central City, Ky., 1983—, Muhlenberg Cmty. Hosp., Greenville, 1989—, Russellville (Ky.) Health Care Manor, 1978-83, 92—, Westlake Cumberland Hosp., Columbia, Ky., 1993—, Franklin-Simpson Meml. Hosp., Franklin, Ky., 1993—. Mem. regional bd. dirs. ARC of Ky., Frankfort, 1990—; vice chair ARC of Logan County, 1992-93, chmn., 1993—; co-chair adv. coun. devel. disabilities Lifeskills, 1992-93; chair Let's Build our Future Campaign; nutrition del. Citizen Am. Program to USSR, 1990; adv. chair for vocat. edn., Russellville; mem. Adv. Coun. for Home Econs. and Family Living, We. Ky. U., 1990-93. Recipient Outstanding Svc. award Am. Dietetic Assn. Found., 1993, Outstanding Svc. award Barren River Mental Health-Mental Retardation Bd., 1987, Svc. Appreciation award Logan-Russellville Assn. for Retarded Citizens, 1987; named Ky. Col., 1961. Mem. Am. Dietetic Assn., Nat. Nutrition Network, Ky. Dietetic Assn. (pres. Western dist. 1976-77, Outstanding Dietitian award 1984), Bowling Green-Warren County Nutrition Coun., Nat. Ctr. for Nutrition and Dietetics (charter), Ky. Nutrition Coun., Logan County Home Economist Club (sec. 1994—), Internat. Biog. Assn., ADA Nationwide Nutrition Network, Gerontol. Nutritionist, Oncology Nutrition, Diabetes Care and Edn., Dietitians in Nutrition Support, Dietitians in Gen. Clin. Practice, Cons. Dietitians in Health Care, Dietetic Educators of Practice Nutrition, Edn. of Health Profls. and Nutrition Rsch. Practice Groups, Phi Upsilon Omicron (pres. Beta Delta alumni chpt. 1994—). Home and Office: 443 Hopkinsville Rd Russellville KY 42276-1286

HARPER, THELMA, state legislator; b. Williamson County, Tenn., Dec. 2, 1940; d. William and Clara (Thomas) Claybrooks; m. Paul Wilson Harper, 1957; children: Dylan Wayne, Linda Gail. Grad., Tenn. State U., 1978. Former commr. Davidson County, Tenn.; former councilwoman City of Nashville; entrepreneur Paul Harper's Convenience Markets, 1972—; mem. Tenn. State Senate, 1991—; foreman Grand Jury Tenn. (5th cir.), 1977-79. Mem. YMCA, Nat. Hook-Up of Black Women, Davidson County Dem. Women's Club, Nashville Women's Pol. Caucus. Democrat. Mem. Church of Christ. Address: PO Box 934 Union City TN 38261 Home: 714 Ringgold Dr Nashville TN 37207 Office: Senate House State Capitol Nashville TN 37219*

HARPER, VALERIE, actress; b. Suffern, N.Y., Aug. 22, 1940; d. Howard and Iva (McConnell) H.; m. Richard Schaal, 1964 (div. 1978); m. Tony Cacciotti, 1987; 1 child, Cristina. Student, Hunter Coll., New Sch. Social Research. Dancer corps de ballet, Radio City Music Hall, N.Y.C., 1956-57, actress Second City, Chgo., 1964-69; appeared in Broadway prodns. Lil Abner, 1958, Take Me Along, 1959, Wildcat, 1960, Subways Are For Sleeping, 1961, Something Different, 1968, Story Theatre, 1970-71, Metamorphoses, 1971, also regional theatre Seattle Repertory Co.; mem. touring co. Agnes of God; appeared on Mary Tyler Moore Show, CBS-TV, 1970-74, Rhoda, CBS-TV, 1974-78, Valerie, NBC, 1986-87, City, CBS, 1990, The Office, CBS, 1994; film appearances in Freebie and the Bean, 1974, Chapter Two, 1979, Last Married Couple in America, 1979, Blame it on Rio, 1984; TV films include Thursdays Game, 1974, Night Terror, 1977, Fun and Games, 1980, The Shadow Box, 1980, The Day the Loving Stopped, 1981, Farrell for The People, 1982, Don't Go to Sleep, 1982, An Invasion of Privacy, 1983, The Execution, 1985, Drop Out Mother, CBS, 1987, Strange Voices, NBC, 1987, The People Across the Lake, NBC, 1988, Stolen: One Husband, 1989, A Friend to Die For, 1994. Co-founder LIFE (Love Is Feeding Everyone) project. Recipient Emmy awards, Nat. Acad. TV Arts and Scis., 1971, 72, 73, 75, Golden Globe award for best actress, 1975, Photoplay Gold Medal award, Presdl. End Hunger award, 1987; named Hasty Pudding Woman of Yr. Harvard Hasty Pudding Soc., 1975. Address: PO Box 7187 Beverly Hills CA 90212-7187

HARR, LUCY LORAINE, association executive; b. Sparta, Wis., Dec. 2, 1951; d. Ernest Donald Harr and Dorothy Catherine (Heintz) Harr Vetter. B.S., U. Wis.-Madison, 1976, M.S., 1978. Lectr. U. Wis., Madison, 1977-82; asst. editor Everybody's Money Credit Union Nat. Assn., Madison, 1979-80, assoc. editor Everybody's Money, 1980-82, editor Everybody's Money, 1982-84, mgr. ann. report, 1984-92, v.p. pub. relations, 1984-93, sr. v.p. credit union devel., 1993—; dir. consumer appeals bd. Ford Motor Co., Milw., 1983-87. Bd. dirs. Madison Area Crimestoppers, 1982-84. Recipient Clarion award, 1982. Mem. Women in Communications (pres. Madison profl. chpt. 1982-83, nat. v.p. programs 1986-87), Internat. Assn. Bus. Communicators (program chmn. dist. meeting 1981), Am. Soc. Assn. Execs. (Gold Circle award 1984). Home: 514 Westmorland Blvd Madison WI 53711-1639 Office: Credit Union Nat Assn Inc 5710 Mineral Point Rd Madison WI 53705-4454

HARRELL, CONSTANCE LORESS, elementary education educator; b. N.Y.C., Aug. 27, 1949; d. Clearance Carter and Dorethea (Branch) Thomas; m. Robert Harrell, Sr., Oct. 25, 1969; children: Robert Jr., Terrance, Justin. BA, William Paterson Coll., 1972; MA, Montclair State U., 1985. Cert. elem. edn., tchr. handicapped, learning disabilitites tchr. cons. Tchr. elem. Pub. Sch. No. 25, Paterson, N.J., 1972-80, basic skills instr., 1980-84; supplementary instr. Pub. Sch. No. 2, 9, 12, 24 and Rosa Parks, Paterson, N.J., 1984-88; tchr. cons. learning disabilities Eastside High Sch., Paterson, N.J., 1988—; learning cons. Dept. of Corrections, N.J., 1991—. Pers. chairperson YWCA, Paterson, 1990—; sec. 4-Ward Alliance, Paterson, 1991—; bd. dirs. TLP Performing Arts Ctr., Gilmore Meml. Learning Ctr. Mem. ASCD, N.J. Assn. Learning Cons., Orton Dyslexia Soc., PTA of Rosa Parks (treas. 1989-91). Home: 560 Broadway Paterson NJ 07514-2518 Office: Eastside High Sch 150 Park Ave Paterson NJ 07501-2355

HARRELL, DEBORAH STRICKLAND, nursing educator, pediatrics nurse; b. Rocky Mount, N.C., Mar. 14, 1952; d. Clifford Stanley and Edith Hines (Gossett) Strickland; m. Donald Lee Joyner, May 28, 1972 (div. 1985); children: Bradford Lee, Matthew Ryan; m. Maynard Alex Harrell Jr., Aug. 2, 1986; 1 stepchild, Maynard Alex III. BSN, Atlantic Christian Coll., Wilson, N.C., 1981; MSN, East Carolina U., Greenville, N.C., 1992; postgrad., Duke U. Pediatric staff nurse Nash Gen. Hosp., Rocky Mount, 1981-86; staff, lead nurse Roanoke Home Ctr., Plymouth, Williamston, N.C., 1986-88; clin. instr. Beaufort County C.C., Washington, N.C., 1988; grad. tchr. asst. Sch. Nursing, East Carolina U., Greenville, 1989-92; clin. instr. East Carolina Univ., Greenville, 1992—; mem. Washington County Infant Mortality Reduction Com., 1991-94; mem. Washington County Health and Drug Adv. Coun., Plymouth, 1992—; co-dir. Washington County State of Child Conf., 1991. Bd. dirs. Roanoke home Care Adv. Bd., Plymouth, 1990-93, Washington County Bd. Edn., 1992—; v.p. Options to Domestic Violence and Sexual Abuse, Washington County, 1991-93; N.C. Sch. Health Adv. Com., 1994—. Mem. ANA (cert. sch. nurse, pediatric nurse), N.C. Nurses Assn., Nat. Assn. of Pediatric Nurse Assocs., Nat. Assn. of Sch. Nurses, Sigma Theta Tau. Democrat. Baptist. Home: 301 Conaby Dr Plymouth NC 27962-1603 Office: East Carolina U Sch Nursing Greenville NC 27858

HARRELL, INA PERRY, maternal women's and medical/surgical nurse; b. Gates County, N.C., Dec. 26, 1930; d. Willie Lee and Willa Maris (Tinkham) Perry; m. Reuben Brooks Harrell, Dec. 19, 1954; children: Brooks Lee, David Austin. Diploma in nursing, Norfolk Gen. Hosp., 1952; diploma in obstetrics, Providence Lying-In Hosp., 1953. RN, N.C., Va.; cert. obstet. labor and delivery nurse, in CPR, admissions assessment nurse. Office nurse Dr. Bruce J. Franz, Asheville, N.C.; head nurse labor and delivery room and obstetrics unit Meml. Mission Hosp., Asheville; staff nurse obstetrics unit, labor and delivery room Norfolk (Va.) Gen. Hosp.; staff nurse St. Joseph's Hosp., Asheville. Mem. Nat. Bapt. Nurses Fellowship, N.C. Nurses Assn., Norfolk Gen. Hosp. Alumni Assn.

HARRIETT, JUDY ANNE, medical equipment company executive; b. Walterboro, S.C., July 22, 1960; d. Billy Lee and Loretta (Rahn) H. BS in Agrl. Bus./Econs., Clemson U., 1982. Sales rep. III Monsanto Corp., Atlanta, 1982-85; surg. stapling rep. Ethicon, Inc., Johnson & Johnson Corp., Somerville, N.J., 1985-87; dist. sales mgr. Imed Corp., San Diego, 1987—, regional tng. coord., 1992-93; mem. pres. adv. panel, 1991, 92, mem. pres. club, 1993. Author: Time and Territory Management, 1984. Com. mem. Multiple Sclerosis Fund Raising Benefit, Knoxville, Tenn., 1988, 89, Women's Ctr. Benefit, Knoxville, 1990. Mem. NAFE. Republican. Home: 21620 Mayhew Rd Mooresville NC 28115-8661 Office: Imed Corp 9775 Business Park Ave San Diego CA 92131

HARRIGAN, LAURA G., newspaper editor; b. Newark, Nov. 29, 1953; d. Michael Charles and Sarah Ellen (Hutchinson) Guarino;. BA, Wagner Coll., 1975. Reporter/columnist S.I. (N.Y.) Advance, 1975-79, Sunday editor, 1979-84; asst. news editor Courier-News, Bridgewater, N.J., 1984-85, news editor, 1985-86, spl. projects editor, 1986-87, exec. news editor, 1987-90, asst. mng. editor, 1990-91, mng. editor, 1991—. Recipient hon. mention Charles Stewart Mott nat. edn. writing award, 1978, EDI award Nat. Easter Seals, 1994. Mem. AAUW, AP Mng. Editors Assn. (pres. N.J. chpt. 1992-94). Office: The Courier-News PO Box 6600 1201 Route 22 Bridgewater NJ 08807

HARRILL, LAUREL WOOD, interior designer; b. N.Y.C., Dec. 8, 1954; d. John Henry and Grace Ann (Ermish) Wood; m. Willis Jackson, Oct. 9, 1981 (div. 1987); m. James Edward Harrill, Aug. 14, 1987. AAS, Fashion Inst. Tech., N.Y.C., 1974. Pres., interior designer Interior Motives, Knoxville, Tenn., 1982-86; interior designer Law's Interiors, Maryville, Tenn., 1986-88, Beverly Hall Galleries, Atlanta, 1988-91; pres., interior designer Atlanta Design Group, Ltd., 1991—; designer Christmas at Callonwoide, Atlanta, 1993, Atlanta Symphony Decorator Showhouse, 1989, 92, 94, Street of Dreams, Atlanta, 1988 (Pres.'s Choice award). Major projects include Trust Co. Bank, Stockbridge & McDonough Georgia brs., Columbia Theol. Sem., Decatur, Ga., Holston Hills C.C., Knoxville, Cardiovascular Medicine Surgeon's offices, Marietta, Peachtree Presbyn. Ch., Atlanta, Bike Athletic Corp. Hdqrs., Knoxville, Law Offices of Weinstein, Rosenthal, Tobin and Caldwell, P.C., Blackburn Farms Restaurant, Gatlinburg, Tenn. Bd. dirs. Open Gate, Marietta, Ga., 1993—, Metro Atlanta Christian Women's Club, Marietta; mem. Showhouse bd. Atlanta Symphony League Jr. Com., 1993, Atlanta Women's Network, 1992-93, Atlanta High Mus., 1993, Atlanta Visitors and Conv. Bur., 1991-92. Recipient Restoration award United Fedn. Women's Clubs, Knoxville, 1985; winner design competition March of Dimes, Knoxville, 1986. Home and Office: Atlanta Design Group 2279 Glenridge Dr Marietta GA 30062-1878

HARRIMAN, CONSTANCE BASTINE, federal official; b. Palo Alto, Calif., Oct. 10, 1948; d. John Howland and Barbara (Brunmark) H.; m. W. Edward Whitfield, Sept. 22, 1990. BA cum laude, Stanford U., 1970, MA, 1973; JD, UCLA, 1980. Bar: Calif. 1980, D.C. 1985, U.S. Dist. Ct. (no., ctrl. and ea. dists.) Calif. 1980, U.S. Ct. Appeals (9th cir.) 1983. Assoc. Sheppard, Mullin, Richter & Hampton, 1980-85; atty. advisor Office Legal Policy, Dept. Justice, Washington, 1982; spl. asst. to solicitor Dept. Interior, Washington, 1985-86, assoc. solicitor for energy and resources, 1986-87, asst. sec. for fish, wildlife and parks, 1989-91; assoc. Steptoe & Johnson, Washington, 1987-89; dir. Export-Import Bank of U.S., Washington, 1991-94. Mem. UCLA Law Rev. Apptd. commr. Gt. Lakes Fishery Commn., 1989; mem. Adv. Coun. Hist. Preservation. Mem. Phi Beta Kappa.

HARRIMAN, PAMELA DIGBY CHURCHILL, diplomat, philanthropist; b. Farnborough, Eng., Mar. 20, 1920; came to U.S., 1959, naturalized, 1971; d. Edward Kenelm and Constance Pamela Alice (Bruce) Digby; m. Randolph Churchill, 1939; 1 son, Winston Spencer; m. Leland Hayward, May 4, 1960; m. W. Averell Harriman, Sept. 27, 1971. B in Domestic Sci.-Economy, Downham (Eng.) Sch., 1937; postgrad. Sorbonne, Paris, 1937-38. With Ministry of Supply, London, 1942-43; with Churchill Club for Am. Servicemen, 1943-46; journalist Beaverbrook Press, Europe, 1946-49; amb. to France, Paris, 1993—; chmn., founder Democrats for the 80s, 1980-90 and Democrats for the 90s, 1991; nat. co-chair Clinton-Gore Presdl. Campaign, 1992; bd. dirs. Commn. on Presdl. Debates, 1987-93; mem. Nat. Com. Dem. Party, 1989-93; past hon. trustee, past hon. mem. exec. com. Brookings Instn.; mem. Council on Fgn. Rels.; past trustee Rockefeller U., Coun. Nat. Gallery Art, Winston Churchill Found. U.S.; past adv. council W. Averell Harriman Inst. for Russian Studies; past mem. bd. friends Kennan Inst. for Advanced Russian Studies; past vice chmn. Atlantic Council, past bd. dirs. Mary W. Harriman Found., also various philanthropic founds. Named Dem. Woman of Yr., Woman's Nat. Dem. Club 1980. Office: American Embassy Paris PSC 116 APO AE 09777

HARRINGTON, CAROL A., lawyer; b. Geneva, Ill., Feb. 13, 1953; d. Eugene P. and M. Ruth (Bowersox) Kloubec; m. Warren J. Harrington, Aug. 19, 1972; children: Jennifer Ruth, Carrie Anne. BS summa cum laude, U. Ill., 1974, JD magna cum laude, 1977. Bar: Ill. 1977, U.S. Dist. Ct. (no. dist.) Ill. 1977, U.S. Tax Ct. 1979. Assoc. Winston & Strawn, Chgo., 1977-84, ptnr., 1984-88; ptnr. McDermott, Will & Emery, 1988—; speaker in field. Co-author: Generation Skipping Tax BNA Management, 1991, The New Generation Skipping Tax, 1986; contbr. articles to profl. jours., Trusts and Estates mag. Fellow Am. Coll. Trusts and Estate Coun.; mem. ABA (chmn. B-1 generation skipping transfer com. 1987-92, coun. real property, probate and trust law sect. 1992—), Ill. State Bar Assn., Chgo. Bar Assn. (trust law com. divsn. 1), Chgo. Estate Planning Coun. Office: McDermott Will & Emery 227 W Monroe St Chicago IL 60606-5016

HARRINGTON, DIANA RAE, finance educator, consultant, author; b. Phila., Mar. 25, 1940; d. George J. and Violet Van de Erve Becker; m. William C. Harrington, Oct. 14, 1967; 1 child, Maya Anna. BA, Coll. William and Mary, 1962; MS in Bus. Adminstrn., Boston U., 1969; D Bus. Adminstrn., U. Va., 1978. Field dir. Greater Hartford (Conn.) coun. Girl Scouts U.S.A., 1962-68; field advisor Logansport (Ind.) State Hosp., 1970-71; fiscal dir. Terre Haute (Ind.) Mental Health Ctr., 1971-72; coord. S.W. Va. Community Devel. Found., Roanoke, 1972-73; asst. prof. U. No. Iowa, Cedar Falls, 1974-75, Iowa State U., Ames, 1975-78; from asst. prof. to prof. U. Va., Charlottesville, 1978-93; disting. prof. fin., divsn. chair Babson Coll., Babson Park, Mass., 1993—; bd. dirs., trustee Land Mark Fund, N.Y.C. and Grand Caymans; vis. prof. fin. Kellogg Sch., Northwestern U., 1992-93. Author: Modern Portfolio: The Capital Asset Pricing Model and Arbitrage Pricing Theory, 1983, 3d edit. 1986, Corporate Financial Analysis: Decisions in the Global Environment, 1984, 4th edit. 1993, Case Studies in Financial Decision Making, 1986, 3d edit., 1993, The New Stock Market, 1991; contbg. author: Handbook of Finance, 1990, 2d edit., 1993. Bd. dirs. Hospice—The Piedmont, Charlottesville, 1990-92, Shelter for Help in Emergency, Charlottesville, 1990-92. Mem. Fin. Mgmt. Assn. (bd. dirs. 1993-94, v.p. awards 1993-94), Ea. Fin. Assn. (trustee, v.p. program, pres.), So. Fin. Assn. (bd. dirs. 1989-90). Office: Babson Coll Dept Fin Babson Park MA 02157

HARRINGTON, DIANE GAIL, retail executive; b. Miami, Fla., Aug. 5, 1963; d. James Thomas and Eva Mae (Stephens) H. BBA, U. Miami, 1985, MBA, 1987. Mktg. rep. John Hancock Mut. Life Ins. Co., Boston, 1985-86; pres. Fla. Gold Seal Inc., Miami, 1986—; ext. agt., entrepreneurial educator USDA, Washington, 1994—; adj. prof. entrepreneurial edn., small bus. devel. U. Fla., 1994—. Counselor New Testament Bapt. Ch., Hialeah, Fla., 1983. Mem. NAFE, Nat. Assn. Life Underwriters, Internat. Platform Assn. Nat. C. of C., Ctr. Fine Arts, Nat. Assn. Hist. Preservation, Smithsonian Inst., Am. Inst. Researchers. Republican. Baptist. Home: 2620 NW 111th St Miami FL 33167-3400

HARRINGTON, ELIZABETH ANN, psychologist, consultant; b. Springfield, Mass., Dec. 24, 1954; d. James Joseph and Janet Elizabeth (Brisbois) H. AB in English and Philosophy, Emmanuel Coll., 1976; PhD in Clin. Psychology, Boston U., 1984. Lic. psychologist, Mass. Staff psychologist West Ros Park Mental Health Ctr., Boston, 1982-86; staff psychologist Charles River Hosp., Wellesley, Mass., 1985-86, team psychologist, 1986-89, dir. group psychotherapy, 1987-92, dir. women's program, 1989-92; pvt. practice Newton Highlands, Mass., 1986—; consulting psychologist Stone Ctr., Wellesley (Mass.) Coll., 1991—; dir. group psychotherapy Westwood (Mass.) Lodge, 1993—; clin. instr. psychiatry Sch. Medicine, Boston U., 1985—. Mem. APA, Am. Group Psychotherapy Assn., Mass. Psychol. Assn., Northeastern Soc. Group Psychotherapy. Office: 4-6 Hartford St Newton MA 02161

HARRINGTON, JOAN KATHRYN, counselor; b. Harvey, Ill., Dec. 21, 1934; d. Roy W. and Thelma (Hedlund) H. BA, Gordon-Barrington Coll., 1967; MPS, Alliance Theol. Sem., 1984; MEd, William Paterson State U., 1986; postgrad., So Calif. Grad. Sch. Theology. Cert. counselor; ordained Bapt. min. Rural Bible tchr. New Eng. Fellowship Evangs., Boston, 1960-62; co-dir. Children's Haven Inc., East Douglas, Mass., 1962-78; dir. edn. Calvary Gospel Ch., Newark, 1975-80; min. edn. Northside Community Chapel, Paterson, N.J., 1980-85; dir. guidance Eastern Christian High Sch., North Haledon, N.J., 1985-87; counselor Passaic County C.C., Paterson, 1987-89; counselor activities, social svcs. Palm Shores Retirement: The Colonnade, St. Petersburg, Fla., 1989-91; mental health therapist sr. support svcs. Suncoast Ctr. for Cmty. Mental Health, St. Petersburg, Fla., 1990-93; prof., asst. dean students St. Petersburg Theol. Sem., 1992—; urban coord. Africa Inland Mission, Newark, Paterson, 1975-82; vis. prof. Alliance Theol. Sem., Nyack, N.Y., 1986-88; min. parish witness First Bapt. Ch., Paterson, 1987-89; min. counseling Am. Bapt. Ch. of Beatitudes, St. Petersburg, 1990—; clin. dir. Life Mgmt. Counseling Svcs., 1994—. Author: (poetry) Deep Rivers, 1981; script writer, producer Haven Radio Club, 1962-78. Family Selection com. Habitat for Humanity, Paterson, 1985; bd. dirs. Urban Ministries of A.I.M., Newark, Children's Haven, Inc. (clk. 1962-77); mem. Paterson Clergy Assn., Paterson, 1980-85. Mem. ACA, Am. Assn. Christian Counselors, Assn. Specialists in Group Work, Am. Mental Health Counselor's Assn., Assn. for Spiritual, Ethical and Religious Values in Counseling, Nat. Assn. Alcoholism and Drug Abuse Counselors, Christian Assn. Psychol. Studies, Pi Lambda Theta. Democrat. Home: 5220 Brittany Dr S Apt 801 Saint Petersburg FL 33715-1537 Office: Am Bapt Ch Beatitudes 2812 8th St N Saint Petersburg FL 33704-2007 also: 300 Duncan Ave S Ste 295 Clearwater FL 34615

HARRINGTON, LAMAR, curator, museum director; b. Guthrie Center, Iowa, Nov. 2, 1917; d. Arthur Sylvester and Anna Mary (Landkamer) Hannes; m. Stanley John Harrington, 1938 (div. 1972); 1 dau., Linda Harrington Chace. Student music, Cornish Sch. Fine Arts, Seattle, 1945-50; B.A. in History of Art, U. Wash., 1979. Mem. staff Henry Art Gallery, U. Wash., Seattle, 1957-75; assoc. dir. Henry Art Gallery, U. Wash., 1969-75; curator, research assoc. Archives Northwest Art, U. Wash. Libraries, 1975-77; dir., chief curator Bellevue Art Mus., Wash., 1985-90; cons. in arts, 1977—; mem. panel visual arts div. Nat. Endowment Arts, 1976-78; juror fellowships Western States Arts Fedn., 1989; pres. Western Assn. Art Museums, 1973-75; trustee Pacific Northwest Arts Center, 1971-74; exec. com. Pacific Northwest Arts Council of Seattle Art Mus., 1976, mem. steering com. photography council, 1977-78; v.p. Pottery Northwest, 1977-78; participant 1st Symposium on Scholarship and Lang., Nat. Endowments for Humanities and Arts, 1981; mem. adv. com. N.W. Oral History Project, Archives Am. Art, 1981; mem. Pilchuck Adv. Coun., 1992—; trustee, chmn. archives Pilchuck Glass Sch., 1981-87, Internat. Council, 1987-92; trustee Seattle bd. Santa Fe Chamber Music Festival, 1981-87, adv. bd. Santa Fe, 1985-89; trustee Puget Sound Chamber Music Soc., 1987-88; lectr. in field, organizer exhbns., leader seminars, mem. art juries, appearances on TV, 1963-73. Author: Ceramics in the Pacific Northwest: A History, 1979, Washington Craft Forms: an Historical Perspective, 1981; founder: Archives of Northwest Art, U. Wash., 1969, Index of Art in Pacific Northwest, U. Wash. Press, 1970; curator Third Wyoming Biennial Exhbn., 1988-89, James W. Washington Jr.: The Spirit in the Stone Bellevue Art Mus., 1989; resident curator, mgr. Frank Lloyd Wright: In the Realm of Ideas Bellevue Art Mus., 1989; curator: Between Night and Morning: The Work of Guy Anderson, 1990, Eternal Laughter: A Sixty-Yr. Retrospective of George Tsutakawa Bellevue Art Mus., 1990. Recipient Friends of Crafts award Seattle, 1972, Woman of Achievement award Women in Communications, 1974, Gov. Writer's award, 1980, Arts Svc. award King County Arts Commn., 1987, Gov. Wash. Art award, 1988, Bellevue Art Commn. Arts award, 1989, Community Svc. award Am. Inst. Interior Designers, 1990, Pyramid award Corp. Coun. for Arts, 1990; establishment of LaMar Harrington endowment Bellevue Art Mus., 1991. Fellow Am. Crafts Coun. (hon.); mem. AIA (hon.), Am. Assn. Mus., Pacific Northwest Arts and Crafts Assn. (pres. 1957-59), Allied Arts Seattle (trustee 1962-81), Japan-Am. Soc. Wash. (trustee 1986-88), U. Washington Retirement Assn. (exec. com. 1992—). Home: PO Box 1996 Port Townsend WA 98368-0079

HARRINGTON, LUCIA MARIE, elementary educator; b. Marquette, Mich., May 19, 1947; d. Eugene Elmer and Saima (Bentti) Latvala; m. Warren Henry Harrington, June 21, 1969; children: Robert Joseph, Christen Marie. BS with high honors, No. Mich. U., 1969. Cert. tchr., Mich. Tchr. Marquette Area Pub. Schs., 1969-70, 71-73, 75-76, 82-93, Ysleta Ind. Schs., El Paso, Tex., 1970-71; substitute tchr. Schaumburg (Ill.) and Clear Lake (Iowa) Schs., 1973-75; tchr. 2d grade Whitman Elem. Sch., Marquette, 1995—; instr. aerobic dance Aerobic Dancing, Inc., Marquette, 1980-82; participant Gessell Sch. Readiness and Devel. Placement, 1985, Mich. Model Comprehensive Sch. Health Edn., 1987—, Essential Elements of Effective Instrn., 1988, Lions/Quest Skills for Growing, 1990, Dyslexia Outreach Program Seminar, 1992; supr. student tchrs., 1988—; mem. Marquette-Alger Reading Coun.; presenter, trainer at writing workshops. Named Elem. Tchr. of Yr., Kiwanis, 1991, Marquette Area Pub. Schs. Outstanding Educator, 1994. Mem. ASCD, Mich. Coun. Tchrs. Math., Upper Peninsula Reading Assn. (hospitality chair 1990-92, 90-94), Mich. Edn. Assn. (cert. of Merit), Marquette City Edn. Assn., Melaf Project, Phi Delta Kappa. Lutheran. Home: 1705 West Ave Marquette MI 49855 Office: Marquette Area Pub Schs Whitman Elem Sch 1400 Norway Ave Marquette MI 49855

HARRINGTON, MARGUERITE ANN, health care executive; b. Phila., Mar. 31, 1949; d. S. Thomas F. and Marguerite Ann (Haggerty) H. Academic Dip., Gwymedd-Mercy Academy, PA, 1967; BA in English Lit., Immaculata Coll., PA, 1971; MBA in Health Care Mgmt., Wharton Sch., Phila., 1976; MS in Social Admin., London Sch. of Econ. Univ. Lon, England, 1977. Field rep. Bureau of Labor Statistics, Phila., 1972-74; ast. dir., graduate health care program Wharton-Univ. Pa., Phila., 1977-79; asst. secretary Hartford (Conn.) Insurance Group, 1979-86; asst. v.p. Lincoln National Life Ins. Co., Fort Wayne, Ind., 1986-88; 2d v.p. Lincoln Nat. Life Ins. Co., Fort Wayne, Ind., 1988-90; v.p. planning Mercy Health Corp., Bala Cynwyd, Pa., 1991—; chair Gwynedd Mercy Acad. Adv. Bd., 1994; bd. dirs. Health Care Alumni Assn., Phila., 1979—, NCC HMO, Hartford, 1980-83, Kaiser Found.; found. dir. Wharton Allumni Club Hartford, 1980-86; chair adv. coun. Kaiser Found. Health Plan Conn., 1983-86; founding mem. Bus. Coalition for Health, Hartford, 1983-85; chmn., bd. dirs., exec. com. Wharton Alumni Assn., Phila., 1989-91. Chmn. adv. bd. Gwynedd Mercy Acad., 1994—.

HARRINGTON, MARY EVELINA PAULSON (POLLY HARRINGTON), religious journalist, writer, educator; b. Chgo.; d. Henry Thomas and Evelina (Belden) Paulson; m. Gordon Keith Harrington, Sept. 7, 1957; children: Jonathan Henry, Charles Scranton. BA, Oberlin Coll., 1946; postgrad., Northwestern U., Evanston, Ill., Chgo., 1946-49, Weber State U., Ogden, Utah, 1970s, 80s; MA, U. Chgo.-Chgo. Theol. Sem., 1956. Publicist Nat. Coun. Chs., N.Y.C., 1950-51; mem. press staff 2d assembly World Coun. Chs., Evanston, Chgo., 1954; mgr. Midwest Office Communication, United Ch. of Christ, Chgo., 1955-59; staff writer United Ch. Herald, N.Y.C., St. Louis, 1959-61; affiliate missionary to Asia, United Ch. Bd. for World Ministries, N.Y.C., 1978-79; freelance writer and lectr., 1961—; corr. Religious News Svc., 1962—; prin. lectr. Women & Family Life in Asia series to numerous librs., Utah, 1981, 81-82; pub. rels. coord. Utah Energy Conservation/Energy Mgmt. Program, 1984-85; tchr. writing Ogden Community Schs., 1985-89; adj. instr. writing for publs. Weber State U., 1986—; instr. Acad. Lifelong Learning, Ogden, 1992—, Eccles Community Art Ctr., Ogden, 1993—; dir. communication Shared Ministry, Salt Lake City, 1983—; chmn. communication Intermountain Conf., Rocky Mountain Conf., Utah Assn. United Ch. of Christ, 1970-78, 82—, Ind. Coun. Chs., 1960-63; chmn.

communication Ch. Women United Utah, 1974-78, Ogden rep., 1980—. Contbr. numerous articles and essays to religious and other publs. Pres. T.O. Smith Sch. PTA, 1976-78, Ogden City Coun. PTA, 83-85; assoc. dir. Region II, Utah PTA, Salt Lake City, 1981-83, mem. State Edn. Commn., 1982-87; chmn. state internat. hospitality and aid Utah Fedn. Women's Clubs, 1982-86, v.p. Ogden dist., 1990-92, pres. Ogden dist., 1992—; trustee Family Counseling Svc. No. Utah, Ogden, 1983—; Utah rep. to nat. bd. Challenger Films, Inc., 1986—; state pres. Rocky Mountain Conf. Women in Mission, United Ch. of Christ, 1974-77, sec., 1981-84, vice moderator Utah Assn., 1992-94. Recipient Ecumenical Svc. citation Ind. Coun. Chs., 1962, Outstanding Local Pres. award Utah PTA, 1978, Outstanding Latchkey Child Project award, 1985, Cmty. Svc. award City of Ogden, 1980, 81, 82, Celebration of Gifts of Lay Woman Nat. award United Ch. of Christ, 1987, Excellence in the Arts in Art Edn. award Ogden City Arts Commn., 1993, Spirit of Am. Woman in Arts and Humanities award Your Cmty. Connection, Ogden, 1994; Utah Endowment for Humanities grantee, 1981, 81-82. Mem. Nat. League Am. Penwomen (chmn. Utah conv. 1973, 10 awards for articles and essays 1987-94), League Utah Writers (2d pl. award 1991, 1st pl. news award 1992), AAUW (state edn. rep. 1982-86). Democrat. Home and Office: 722 Boughton St Ogden UT 84403-1152

HARRINGTON, MICHAELE MARY, watermedia artist, graphic designer, consultant; b. Boston, June 27, 1946; d. William Gerard and Jadwiga (Jerasonek) H.; m. Jeffrey Fancher Nicoll, Sept. 12, 1970; children: Heather Anne, James Craig William. BFA cum laude, Mass. Coll. Art, 1968. Prodn. mgr. R.H. Stearns Co., Boston, 1968-69; layout artist Grossman's, Braintree, 1971-72, Bradlee's, Braintree, 1973; asst. art dir. Canton (Mass.) Advt. Agy., 1973-78; watermedia and collage artist, graphic designer, illustrator Hyattsville and Darnestown, Hyattsville & Darnestown, Md., 1978—; mem. faculty Rockville Arts Place, 1990-92; demonstrator, studio and workshop tchr., 1988—; design cons. KBL Group, Silver Spring, Md., 1986-92; book illustrator Denlinger Publs., Ltd., Fairfax, Va., 1986. Exhibited in group shows So. Watercolor Soc., Pensacola, Fla., 1982, Am. Watercolor Soc., N.Y.C., 1983, 90, Catherine Lorillard Wolfe Arts Club, N.Y.C., 1983, 84, Midwest Watercolor Soc., Davenport, Iowa, 1983, Mid-Atlantic Regional, Balt., 1983, 84, 86, 87, 89, 91, New Orleans Art Assn., 1984, Dundalk Coll., Md., 1985, San Diego Watercolor Soc., 1990, North Coast Collage Soc., Pitts., Watercolor Soc., Rocky Mountain Nat., 1991, Rock Creek Gallery, Washington, 1993, The Art Barn, 1993, Ariz. Aqueous IX, Tubac, 1994 (Merit award), Three Rivers Art Festival, Pitts., 1994; one-person shows Montpelier Cultural Arts Ctr., Laurel, Md., 1982, Friendship Gallery, Chevy Chase, Md., 1990, Artshowcase Gallery, Balt., 1991, 92, Rockville Civic Ctr. Mansion Galleries, 1992; represented in permanent collections including Washington Health Ctr., Coast Guard Art Collection of Smithsonian Instn., Washington. Juror art in pub. places program Md.-Nat. Capital Parks and Planning Commn., Hyattsville, Md., 1980-91, also assorted Washington area art assns.' regional exhbns., 1990—. Recipient Jurors Choice award Md. Fedn. Art, 1982, 2d Place award New Orleans Art Assn., Gold medal Catherine Lorillard Wolfe Arts Club, 1984, Abstract award Md. Nat. Found., 1989, Zeber Exptl. award North Coast Collage Soc., 1991, award of merit Ariz. Aqueous IX, 1994. Mem. The Art League (Grumbacher Gold Medal 1991), Balt. Watercolor Soc. (award 1989), Potomac Valley Watercolorists (juried), Coast Guard Artists Program.

HARRINGTON, PAMELA ANN, grant writer; b. Washington, Nov. 7, 1944; d. Herbert Allen Harrington and Mary Hilda Fagan; m. Mark N. Brown, Aug. 9, 1973 (div. Aug. 1987); children: Amanda Harrington Brown, Jonathan Harrington Brown; m. Christopher W. McMahan, Aug. 15, 1987. BA, Wheaton Coll., 1971; MA, U. Pitts., 1974, PhD, 1982. Teaching fellow English dept. U. Pitts., 1972-78; with Fleet Bank, R.I., 1990-92; grant writer Providence, 1994—; mem. part-time faculty English dept. R.I. Sch. Design, 1982-90. Vol. Wheaton Coll., RISD Mus. Art, Gordon Sch., Providence Atheneum. Home: 97 Transit St Providence RI 02906

HARRINGTON, PATRICIA BATES, artist; b. Saginaw, Mich., May 21, 1924; d. Gerald David and Henrietta Fay (Parker) Bates; m. Donald W. Harrington, July 26, 1945; children: Gregory David, Michael Bates, Stephen Clark, Douglas Minor. Student, Ctrl. Mich. U., 1942-45, Randolph Macon Woman's Coll., 1976. One-woman shows include Lynchburg (Va.) Art Club, 1969, 79, Lynchburg Fine Arts Ctr., 1973, 83, Va. Poly. Inst. U., Blacksburg, 1972, Washington and Lee U., Lexington, Va., 1974, Ga. State Botanical Gardens, Athens, 1993, Lynchburg Coll., 1989, 93, Twentieth Century Gallery, Williamsburg, Va., 1994; represented in permanent collections Va. Poly. Inst. U., Lynchburg Coll., Sweet Briar (Va.) Coll., Longwood Coll., Farmville, Va., Philip Morris, Richmond, Va., Roanoke Mus., Fidelity Banks, Lynchburg, Bedford, Va., Farmville, Wintergreen, Va., Altavista, Va. Bd. dirs., officer Lynchburg Fine Arts Ctr., 1970-75. Recipient gold medal award Allied Artists, 1977, Water Media gold medal, 1992, Ida Wells Stroud Meml. award Am. Watercolor Soc., 1993. Mem. Nat. League Am. Pen Women (bd. dirs.), Va. Watercolor Soc. (pres.), Balt. Watercolor Soc., Lynchburg Art Club (bd. dirs. and officer 1975-80). Home and Studio: Trents Ferry Rd Rt 4 Box 314 Lynchburg VA 24503

HARRINGTON, PATRICIA JOY WALTER, educational researcher; b. Troy, N.Y., June 14, 1959; d. John Arthur and Joyce Ellen (Fraedrich) Walter; m. Mark Randal Harrington, June 26, 1982; children: Cara Elizabeth, Dana Kathryn. BS, Duke U., 1981. Rschr. Duke Med. Ctr., Durham, N.C., 1981-85; dir. of vols. and svc. to mil. Cape Fear ARC, Wilmington, N.C., 1985-88; rschr. Oreg. Social Learning Ctr., Eugene, 1988—; cons. Oreg. Rsch. Inst., Eugene, 1992-94, Internat. Instrument Lab., Durham, 1985-88. Vol. com. mem. ARC, Eugene, 1992-93; vol. Tibetan Refuge Relief, Eugene, 1989—; parent adv. com. YMCA, Eugene, 1989-92. Office: Oregon Social Learning Ctr 207 E 5th Ave Eugene OR 97401-2762

HARRINGTON, PATSY ANN, geriatrics nurse; b. Jackson, Tenn., Sept. 1, 1948; d. Tommy Andrew and Hattie Mae (Moody) Mullins; m. Joseph Randall Harrington, June 3, 1966; children: Gina C. Harrington Parham, Pamela Gail Harrington. ADN, U. Tenn., Martin, 1983; cert., U. Tenn., Knoxville, 1991. Cert. CEN, ACLS, PALS, BLS instr. Am. Heart Assn.; cert. CPR and First Aid instr. ARC. Nurse CCU and emergency rm. Bapt. Meml. Hosp., Huntingdon, Tenn., 1983-84, emergency rm., CCU nurse, 1988-91; emergency rm., recovery rm. and shift supr. Benton County Hosp., Camden, Tenn., 1984-87; tchr. LPN class Benton County Vocat. Sch., Camden, 1987-91; emergency rm. nurse Henry County Med. Ctr., Paris, Tenn., 1991; DON Hillhaven Convalescent Ctr., Huntingdon, 1991—. Med. team leader Disaster Team, Hollow Rock, Tenn., 1990-92; girl scout leader Girl Scouts Am., Hollow Rock, 1976-81; softball coach Little League, Hollow Rock, 1980-81; pres. PTA, Hollow Rock, 1979; chmn. Cystic Fibrosis Fundraising, Hollow Rock, 1979-81. Mem. ANA (bd. dirs. 1989-91), Tenn. Nurses Assn., Emergency Nurse Assn., Am. Cancer Assn., Tenn. Health Care Assn. Democrat. Baptist. Home: Massey Dr PO Box 414 Hollow Rock TN 38342-0414 Ofifce: Hillhaven Convalescent Ctr 635 High St Huntingdon TN 38344

HARRINGTON, SANDRA SERENA, biology educator; b. Washington, May 30, 1960; d. Wallace Erwin and Anna Ingeborg (Anderson) Seidel; m. Thomas John Harrington, June 10, 1989. BS in Biology, Coll. of William and Mary, 1981; ME in Biomed. Engring., U. Va., 1985, PhD in Biomed. Engring., 1989. Polysomnographic technologist Stanford (Calif) U. Sleep Disorders Clinic, 1981-83; rsch. assoc. gastroenterology U. Va. Med. Ctr., Charlottesville, 1989-90; asst. prof. radiology Med. Coll. of Wis., Milw., 1990-92; asst. prof. biology Carthage Coll., Kenosha, Wis., 1992—; adj. instr. U. Wis. Parkside, Kenosha, 1991-92, Marquette U., Milw., 1991. Bd. dirs. Kinship of Kenosha, 1991—; patron Kenosha Symphony Orch., 1992—. Mem. Biomed. Engring. Soc., Sigma Xi. Office: Carthage Coll 2001 Alford Park Dr Kenosha WI 53140-1900

HARRINGTON, TERRI ANN, elementary school educator; b. Watsonville, Calif., Aug. 15, 1947; d. Theodore Norville and Mary Nell (Crippen) Prather; m. James Leo Harrington Jr., Apr. 4, 1971; children: Matthew Lee, Andrew James. BA in Sociology with honors, U. Calif., Santa Barbara, 1969. Cert. elem. tchr., Calif. Tchr. Evergreen Sch. Dist., San Jose, Calif., 1970-74, Bethany Presbyn. Kindergarten, Grants Pass, Oreg., 1978-85, Grants Pass Sch. Dist., 1985—. Chairperson Children's Festival, Grants Pass, 1983-84. AAUW Ednl. Found. Named Gift honoree, 1987-88. Mem. AAUW. Democrat. Methodist.

HARRIOTT, ESTHER, writer, editor; b. London, Ont., Can.; d. Isidore and Anna (Nathanson) Goldstick; children: Ellen Miriam, William Mark. MA, SUNY, Buffalo, 1971, PhD, 1983; diploma arts adminstrn., Harvard U., 1973. Dir. cultural affairs SUNY, Buffalo, 1971-85, lectr. English and theater, 1972-76, arts editor, 1972-76; TV producer/host Conversations in the Arts Internat. Cable, Buffalo, 1976-85; columnist The Buffalo News, 1978-85; lectr. theatre NYU, 1988-89; book reviewer New York Newsday, N.Y.C., 1988—; writer, editor The N.Y. Pub. Libr., 1985—; founding dir. Poets-in-the-Schs., Buffalo, 1971-75; mem., chair lit. panel N.Y. State Coun. on the Arts, N.Y.C., 1981-84, cons. lit. program, cons. arts-in-edn., 1985-86; cons. NYU Sch. Continuing Edn., 1986-87. Author: American Voices: Five Contemporary Playwrights in Essays and Interviews, 1988, (with others) Drama Criticism, 1994. Mem. cultural subcom. Mayor's Adv. Coun., Buffalo, 1978-81; mem. Bd. Young Audiences, Buffalo, 1981, Theatre Dist. Com., Buffalo, 1982; cons. Puerto Rican Cultural Ctr., Buffalo, 1982. Grantee SUNY, 1973, N.Y. Pub. Libr., 1990. Office: NY Pub Libr Fifth Ave # 42nd St New York NY 10018

HARRIS, ANN BIRGITTA SUTHERLAND, art historian; b. Cambridge, Eng., Nov. 4, 1937; came to U.S., 1965; d. Gordon B.B.M. and Gunborg Elizabeth (Wahlström) Sutherland; m. William Vernon Harris, July 13, 1965; 1 son, Neil William Orlando Sutherland. B.A. with 1st class honours, Courtauld Inst., U. London, 1961, Ph.D., 1965. Asst. lectr. U. Leeds, 1964-65; asst. prof. art history Columbia U., N.Y.C., 1965-71, Hunter Coll., N.Y.C., 1971-73; asso. prof. SUNY, Albany, 1973-77; chmn. for acad. affairs Met. Mus. Art, N.Y.C., 1977-80; part-time faculty Juilliard Sch., N.Y.C., 1978-84; prof. U. Pitts., 1984—; a founder, 1st pres. Women's Caucus for Art, 1973-76; disting. vis. prof. U. Tex.-Arlington, fall 1982; Mellon prof. history of art U. Pitts., spring 1984; vis. prof. history of art So. Meth. U., Dallas, fall 1993. Author: Andrea Sacchi, 1977, Selected Drawings of Gian Lorenzo Bernini, 1977; co-author: Die Zeichnungen von Andrea Sacchi und Carlo Maratta, 1967, Women Artists: 1550-1950; exhbn. catalogue, 1977. Fellow Guggenheim Found., 1971, Ford Found., 1975-76, NEH, 1981-82, rsch. fellow Getty Mus. Art, 1988. Mem. Coll. Art Assn., Women's Caucus for Art. Address: 1315 Denniston Ave Pittsburgh PA 15217-1330

HARRIS, ANN MARIE, mining executive; b. Trenton, N.J., Dec. 7, 1946; d. William and Thelma Marie (Bryan) Staub; m. Richard W. Harris, Jan. 07, 1983; children: Victoria Marie, Elizabeth Audrey. BA in Geology, Rutgers U., 1970; MS in Geology, U. Utah, 1975; postgrad., U. Nevada, 1993—. Curator, instr. U. Utah, Salt Lake City, 1970-73; rsch. geologist Kennecott Exploration Svc., Salt Lake City, 1973-74; project geologist Kearns-Tribune Corp., Salt Lake City, 1974; exploration geologist U.S. Steel Corp., Salt Lake City, 1975-76; mineral specialist U.S. Bur. of Land Mgmt., Salt Lake City, 1976-77; exploration geologist U.S. Steel Corp., Salt Lake City, 1977-79; sr. geologist Pathfinder Mines Corp., Reno, 1979-80; CEO Comstock Mining Svcs., Reno, 1980—; hybridizer Highland Roses, Reno, 1989—; commd. abstractor State Nev., Carson City, 1981—. Author: Environmental Assessment Report on the Adelaide Crown Mine, 1988. Patron, fund raiser Nev. Women's Fund, Reno, 1983—; special events comm. U. Nev., Reno, 1989-93, arboretum bd., 1992—; hort. judge Am. Rose Soc., 1994. Mem. AIME (Nev. sect. asst. sec. 1991—), Am. Acad. Advancement Sci., Nev. Landmen's Assn. (founder, pres. 1982, 88), Am. Inst. Mining Engrs., Geol. Soc. Nevada, Geol. Soc. Am., Am. Water Resource Assn., Am. Hort. Soc., No. Nev. Native Plant Soc., Sierra Garden Club, Heritage Rose Assn., Am. Rose Soc. (cons. rosarian 1991—, NCNH conf. chmn. 1994), Reno Rose Soc. (pres. 1991, 94, sec. 1993, editor 1992—), Sacramento Rose Soc., Santa Clara Rose Soc., Tidewater Rose Soc., Austin Rose Soc., East Hawaii Rose Soc., Tintseltown Rose Soc., Las Vegas Valley Rose Soc., L.A. Rose Soc., Gold Country Rose Soc. Office: Comstock Mining Svcs Ste 260 6121 Lakeside Dr Reno NV 89511-8527

HARRIS, ANN S., editor; b. N.Y.C.; d. Harry T. and Alice R. Schakne; m. Cyril Manton Harris; children: Nicholas Bennett, Katherine Anne. B.A., Hunter Coll.; M.A., Radcliffe Coll. Asst. and assoc. editor Harper & Row, N.Y.C., 1950-70, sr. editor, 1970-82; spl. projects coordinator dept. geriatrics Mt. Sinai Med. Ctr., N.Y.C., 1982-84; editor-in-chief Arbor House Pub. Co., N.Y.C., 1984-86; sr. editor Bantam Books, N.Y.C., 1987—. Mem. Phi Beta Kappa. Office: Bantam Books 1540 Broadway New York NY 10036

HARRIS, ARLENE, lawyer; b. Buffalo, Dec. 29, 1944; d. Yetta (Kerner) Cramer; m. Ira S. Harris, Dec. 25, 1971; children: Elliot, David, Sara. BA cum laude, Bklyn. Coll., 1965; JD, NYU, 1968. Bar: N.Y. 1969. Assoc. trusts and estates dept. Paul, Weiss, Rifkind, Wharton & Garrison, 1968-75; asst. atty. gen. N.Y. State Dept. Law, 1975-76; law asst.-referee N.Y. County Surrogate's Ct., 1976-78, chief law asst., 1978-90; ptnr. trusts and estates dept. Shea & Gould, N.Y.C., 1990-93; of counsel dept. wills and estates Kaye, Scholer, Fierman, Hays & Handler, N.Y.C., 1993—; mem. Internat. Acad. of Estate and Trust Law, Estate's Discussion Groups; bd. dirs. Estate Planning Coun.; adj. prof. law St. John's U. Sch. Law, 1984-92; instr. NYU Sch. Continuing Edn., 1991—; lectr. on estate planning, trusts and estates ABA Nat. Inst., World Trade Inst., N.Y. County Lawyer's Assn., Acad. Trial Lawyers, United Jewish Appeal Ann. Estates Conf., Practising Law Inst. Contbr. chpt. to book, articles to legal publs. and procs. Bd. dirs. East Bay Civic Assn., Inc., 1974-87. John Norton Pomeroy scholar NYU, 1968. Mem. Am. Coll. Trusts and Estate Counsel, N.Y. State Bar Assn. (chmn. legislation com., former mem.-at-large trusts and estates sect., lectr. trusts and estates law sect.), Assn. of Bar of City of N.Y. (mem. trusts, estates and surrogate's cts. com. 1979-81), Order of Coif. Office: Kaye Scholer Fierman Hays & Handler 425 Park Ave New York NY 10022-3598

HARRIS, BARBARA HULL (MRS. F. CHANDLER HARRIS), social agency administrator; b. L.A., Nov. 1, 1921; d. Hamilton and Marion (Eimers) Baird; m. F. Chandler Harris, Aug. 10, 1946; children: Victoria, Randolph Boyd. Pres., Victoria Originals, 1955-62. Student, UCLA, 1939-41, 45-47. Ptnr.J.B. Assocs., cons., 1971-73; statewide dir. vols. Children's Home Soc. Calif., 1971-75. L.A. County Heart Sunday chmn. L.A. County Heart Assn., 1965, bd. dirs., 1966-69; mem. exec. com. Hollywood Bowl Vols., 1966-84, chmn. vols., 1971, 75; chmn. Coll. Alumni of Assistance League, 1962; mem. exec. com. Assistance League So. Calif., 1964-71, 72-80, 83-89, pres., 1976-80; bd. dirs. Nat. Charity League, L.A., 1965-69, 75, sec., 1967, 3d v.p., 1968; ways and means chmn., dir. L.A. Am. Horse Show, 1969; dir. Coronet Debutante Ball, 1968, ball bd. chmn., 1969-70, 75, 84, mem. ball bd., 1969—; pres. Hollywood Bowl Patroness com., 1976; v.p. Irving Walker aux. Travelers Aid, 1976, 79, pres., 1988-89; pres. So. Calif. alumni council Alpha Phi, 1961, fin. adviser to chpts. U. So. Calif., 1961-72, UCLA, 1965-72; benefit chmn. Gold Shield, 1969, 1st v.p., 1970-72; chmn. Golden Thimble III Needlework Exhbn., Hosp. of Good Samaritan, 1975; bd. dirs. UCLA Affiliates, 1976-78, KCET Women's Council, 1979-83, Region V United Way, 1980-83; pres. Jr. Philharmonic Com., 1981-82; bd. dirs. L.A. Founder chpt. Achievement Rewards for Coll. Scientists, 1980-91, pres., 1984-85; pres. L.A. County chpt. Freedom Found. of Valley Forge. Recipient Outstanding Svc. award L.A. County Heart Assn., 1965, Outstanding Alumna Ivy award Alpha Phi, 1969, Outstanding Alumni award for community service UCLA, 1978, Mannequin's Eve award, 1980, Outstanding Bd. Mem. of Yr. award Assistance League of So. Calif., 1989-90. Mem. Hollywood C. of C. (dir. 1980-81). Home: 7774 Skyhill Dr Los Angeles CA 90068-1232

HARRIS, BERNICE ELLEN, data processing executive; b. South Plainfield, N.J., June 5, 1957; d. James Austin and Sarah (Garrett) H. Bus. Mgmt. Cert., Middlesex County Coll., 1975-76, 81-83, student, 1986-87; student, Barbizon Sch. Modeling, 1977, Rutgers U., 1992. Lab. asst. Engelhard Corp., Edison, N.J., 1978-80, lab. technician II, 1980-84, sr. lab. technician, 1984-89, data processing coord., 1989—; sales assoc. Lane Bryant, Woodbridge, N.J., 1980-82; cons. Community Resource Specialist for N.Y., Highland, 1988-90, Laval's Finest, New Orleans, 1990—. Patron Crossroads Theatre Co., 1981—, Negro Ensemble Co., 1992, Jane Voohees Zimmerill Art Mus., 1991—; appointed to rsch. bd. advisor Am. Bio. Inst., 1991—; mem. area coord. Edison Beach, NAACP; mem. N.W. Bergen Craft Guild, 1991; regent Nat. Fedn. Rep. Women, 1987-89; mem. N.J. Fedn. Rep. Women, 1987—, minority outreach chairperson, 1987-88. Mem. NAFE, Am. Chem. Soc. Baptist. Home: 409 Pitt St South Plainfield NJ 07080 Office: Englehard Corp CN 23 Menlo Pk Edison NJ 08818

HARRIS, CAROL REJEAN, sales professional; b. West Point, Miss., June 12, 1952; d. Booker Lynwood and Arcola (Grays) H. BA, Cornell Coll., 1976; MBA, Keller Grad. Sch., 1978. Sales rep. ADT Security Systems, Elmhurst, Ill., 1977-91, sales mgr., 1991—. Treas. Young Execs. in Politics, Chgo., 1986-90, v.p., 1991. Names Young Exec. in Politics of Yr., 1986; names one of Outstanding Young Women in Am., 1984. Mem. Nat. Black MBA Assn., Chgo. Urban League. Office: ADT Security Systems 455 W Lake St Elmhurst IL 60126-1400

HARRIS, CAROLE WOODS, county official; b. Omaha, Mar. 17, 1940; d. James Sr. and Frances M. (Paris) Anders; m. Vernon J. Woods, Feb. 4, 1961 (div. 1980); children: Vernon R., Michael D. Woods, Kimberly Weaver; m. Wayne F. Harris, July 31, 1987. Student, Coll. of St. Mary. Dir. U S West Comms., Omaha, 1960-90; commr. Douglas County, Omaha, 1993—; vice chair Bd. County Commrs., 1994, 95. Bd. dirs. Omaha 100, Inc., 1993—, The Food Bank, Omaha, 1993—; vice chair steering com. Omaha Cmty. Found.'s Women's Fund, 1991—; sec. bd. dirs. Planned Parenthood, Omaha, 1988-94; mem. jud. nominating commn. County Ct. of 4th Dist., Omaha, 1993—. Recipient Cmty. Role Model award Girls, Inc., 1991, Tribute to Women, YWCA, 1993, Influence Alumni award ICAN, 1994. Mem. NCCJ (bd. dirs. 1993—), Nat. Assn. Black County Ofcls., Nt. Assn. County Ofcls. (health steering com.), Nebr. Assn. County Ofcls. Bd., Omaha Leadership Roundtable, Omaha Chpt. Links, Inc. Democrat. Methodist. Office: Douglas County 1819 Farnam St LC2 Omaha NE 68183

HARRIS, CHARNEY ANITA, painter; b. Chgo.. Student, Phila. Coll. Art, Phila. Mus. Art, 1964-68, New Sch. Social Rsch., N.Y.C., 1970-73. One-woman shows Phila. Art Alliance, 1973, Kling Gallery, Phila., 1976, Samuel S. Fleisher Art Meml., 1979, A.J. Wood Galleries, Phila., 1979, 80, Carneige-Mellon U., 1980, Allentown (Pa.) Art Mus., 1981, Gallery K, Washington, 1984, Hudson River Mus., N.Y., 1985, Mangel Gallery, Phila., 1982, 91, 93; exhibited in numerous group shows, including Phila. Mus. Art, 1982, West/Art and the Law, 1985, 86, Cleve. Ctr. for Contemporary Art, 1985, 86, Woodmere Art Mus., Phila., 1989, Soho Gallery, N.Y.C., 1992, Nicholas Alexander Gallery, 1994; represented in permanent collections Phila. Mus. Art, Allentown Art Mus., also corp., univ., coll. and pvt. collections. Recipient painting prize Pa. Gallery Fine Arts, New Sch. Social Rsch., 1970, Pa. Acad. Fine Arts, 1964. Mem. Am. Artists Equity Assn. Home: 2 Sunnyside Ln Yardley PA 19067-2616 also: Nicholas Alexander Gallery 155 Spring St New York NY 10012

HARRIS, CHERYL DENISE, market research executive; b. Gassaway, W.Va., Mar. 30, 1961; d. Charles David and Kathryn Marie Harris. BA in Mktg., Ohio State U., 1982, MA in Photography, Film, 1984; PhD in Mass. Comm., U. Mass., 1992. Ptnr., sr. rsch. dir. Harris-Midkiff Advt., Austin, Tex., 1984-86; exchange participant BBC Spl. Projects, London, 1985; project dir. Rsch. Communications Ltd., Chestnut Hill, Mass., 1986-87; study dir. Market Facts, Inc., Wellesley, Mass., 1987-90; exec. dir. Media Rsch. Ctr., Carlsbad, Calif., 1990—; instr. Ohio State U., Columbus, 1982-84, Austin C.C., 1985-86, U. Mass., 1988-89; prof. Calif. State U., San Bernardino, 1990—. Author: Point of View, 1983, Theorizing Fandom: Fans, Subculture and Identity, 1994, An Internet Education, 1995; asst. dir. Together Cairo Egypt, 1983; translator (book) Oriental Decorative Arts, 1984. Mem. Broadcast Edn. Assn., Am. Mktg. Assn., Adv. Club. San Diego. Home: 1334 Cynthia Ln Carlsbad CA 92008 Office: Media Rsch Ctr PO Box 1828 Carlsbad CA 92018

HARRIS, CYNTHIA COOLIDGE MEAD, executive editor; b. Yonkers, N.Y., Feb. 23, 1937; d. Rolan J. and Rachel C. (Knight) Mead; m. Jerome S. Harris, Dec. 29, 1962 (dec. Aug. 1966). BA, Beaver Coll., 1959. News editor Soc. Automotive Engrs. Jour., N.Y.C., 1959-61; advt. asst. Graver Water Conditioning Co., N.Y.C., 1961-63; copy editor, copy editing supr. Reinhold Publishing Corp., N.Y.C., 1963-65, 65-67; chief copy editor Meredith Press, N.Y.C., 1967-69; copy editing supr. Random House, N.Y.C., 1969-71; freelance editor, copy editor, 1971-76; prodn. editor Greenwood Press, Westport, Conn., 1976-77, 77—, editor reference books, 1986, 86-90, acquisitions editor, exec. editor, 1990—. Democrat. Congregationalist. Office: Greenwood Pub Group Inc Box 5007 88 Post Rd W Westport CT 06880-4208

HARRIS, DALE HUTTER, judge, lecturer; b. Lynchburg, Va., July 10, 1932; d. Quintus and Agnes (Adams) Hutter; m. Edward Richmond Harris Jr., July 24, 1954; children—Mary Fontaine, Frances Harris Russell, Jennifer Harris Haynie, Timothy Edward. BA, Sweet Briar Coll., 1953; MEd in Counseling and Guidance, Lynchburg Coll., 1970; JD, U. Va., 1978; LLD (hon.), Wilson Coll., 1988. Bar: Va. 1978, U.S. Dist. Ct. (we. dist.) Va. 1978, U.S. Ct. Appeals (4th cir.) 1978. Admissions asst. Sweet Briar Coll. (Va.), 1953-54; caseworker Winchester/Frederick Dept. Welfare, Va., 1954-55; vis. lectr. Lynchburg Coll. (Va.), 1971; assoc. Davies & Peters, Lynchburg, 1978-82; substitute judge 24th Dist. Gen. Dist. and Juvenile and Domestic Relations Dist. Cts. Va., 1980-82; judge Juvenile and Domestic Relations Dist. Ct., Lynchburg, 1982—; lectr. law U. Va. Law Sch., 1986—; pres. VA Coun. of Juvenile and Family Ct. Judges, 1995—; panel of experts, adv. com. Child Protection and Custody Resource Ctr., 1994—; mem. commn. on Future Va's. Jud. system, 1987-89; adv. bd. mem. Hilton project on model state laws about family violence. Vice chmn. bd. dirs. Sweet Briar Coll., 1976-86; vol. coordinator vols. in probation with Juvenile and Domestic Ct., 1971-73; chmn. steering com. for establishment Youth Service Bur., Lynchburg, 1972-73; chmn. bd. dirs. Lynchburg Youth Services, 1973-75; mem. adv. bd. Juvenile Ct., 1957-60, 62-68, sec., 1966-68; bd. dirs. Family Service Lynchburg, 1967-69; Lynchburg Fine Arts Ctr., 1965-67, Seven Hills Sch., 1966-73, Greater Lynchburg United Fund, 1963-65, Lynchburg Assn. Mental Health, 1960-61, Miller Home, 1980-82, Lynchburg Gen.-Marshall Lodge Hosps., Inc., 1980-82; v.p. Lynchburg Mental Health Study Commn., 1966; bd. dirs. Lynchburg Sheltered Workshop for Mentally Retarded Young Adults, 1965-69; bd. dirs. Lynchburg Guidance Ctr., 1959-61, v.p., 1970, pres., 1961; bd. dirs. Hist. Rev. Bd. Lynchburg, 1978-82. Mem. Nat. Council Juvenile and Family Ct. Judges, ABA, Va. State Bar (bd. govs. criminal law sect. 1988—, bd. govs. family law section 1989—), Va. Trial Lawyers Assn., Va. Bar Assn., Lynchburg Bar Assn., Phi Beta Kappa. Office: Juvenile and Domestic Relations Dist Ct PO Box 757 Lynchburg VA 24505-0757

HARRIS, DEBRA LYNNE, jewelry sales company executive; b. Columbus, Ohio, Oct. 26, 1956; d. Conrad London and Ruth Evelyn (Bergglas) H. B.S. in Bus., Ind. U., 1978. Founder, owner Conrad London Jewels Ltd., 1978—. Mem. Jewelers Bd. of Trade, Jewelers of Am.

HARRIS, DEIDRE EILENE, computer specialist; b. Tallahassee, Fla., Sept. 19, 1959; d. Dugger and Phyllis (Eppes) H. BS, Monmouth Coll., West Long Branch, N.J., 1989, MBA, 1994. ADP intern U.S. Army Dept. Def., Ft. Monmouth, N.J., 1984-86, computer system programmer, 1986-89, supervisory computer specialist, 1989-92, info. system security officer Directorate of Info. Mgmt., 1992—. Mem. Blacks In Govt. (bd. dirs. Mentors Chpt. 1990—). Democrat. Methodist.

HARRIS, DIANA KOFFMAN, sociologist, educator; b. Memphis, Aug. 11, 1929; d. David Nathan and Helen Ethel (Rotter) Koffman; student U. Miami, 1947-48; BS, U. Wis., 1951; postgrad. Tulane U., New Orleans, 1951-52; MA, U. Tenn., 1967; postgrad. U. Oxford (Eng.), 1968-69; m. Lawrence A. Harris, June 24, 1951; children: Marla, Jennifer. Advt. and sales promotion mgr. Wallace Johnston Distbg. Co., Memphis, 1952-54; welfare worker Tenn. Dept. Pub. Welfare, Knoxville, 1954-56; instr. sociology Maryville (Tenn.) Coll., 1972-75; instr. sociology Fort Sanders Sch. Nursing, Knoxville, 1971-78; instr. sociology U. Tenn., Knoxville, 1967—; series editor Garland Pub., Inc. 1989—. Chmn. U. Tenn. Coun. on Aging, 1979—; organizer Knoxville chpt. Gray Panthers, 1978; mem. Gov's. Task Force on Preretirement Programs for State Employers, 1973; mem. White House Conf. on Aging, 1981; bd. mem. Knoxville-Knox County Council on Aging, 1976, Sr. Citizens Info. and Referral, 1979, Sr. Citizens Home-Aide Svc., 1977; del. E. Tenn. Coun. on Aging, 1977. Recipient Meritorious award Nat. U. Continuing Edn. Assn., 1982, Pub. Svc. award Nat. Alumni Assn., 1992, Nat. Alumni Assn. Pub. Svc. award, 1992, Appreciation award Assn. Gerontology in Higher Edn., 1994. Mem. Am. Sociol. Assn., AAAS, Gerontol. Soc. Am., Popular Culture Assn., So. Sociol. Soc., So. Gerontol. Soc. (Pres.'s award 1984), N. Central Sociol. Assn. Clubs: London Competitor's, Nat.

Contest Assn., Knoxville Kontestars. Author: Readings in Social Gerontology, 1975, (with Cole) The Elderly in America, 1977, The Sociology of Aging, 1980, 2d edit., 1990; co-author: Sociology, 1984, Annotated Bibliography and Sourcebook: Sociology of Aging, 1985, Dictionary of Gerontology, 1988, Teaching Sociology of Aging, 3d edit., 1991; aging series editor Garland Pub., Inc., 1989—; contbr. articles to profl. jours. Home: PO Box 50546 Knoxville TN 37950-0546 Office: U Tenn Dept Sociology PO Box 50546 Knoxville TN 37950-0546

HARRIS, DIANE CAROL, health care and optics products executive; b. Rockville Centre, N.Y., Dec. 25, 1942; d. Daniel Christopher and Laura Louise (Schmitt) Quigley; m. Wayne Manley Harris, Sept. 30, 1978. BA, Cath. U. Am., 1964; MS, Rensselaer Poly. Inst., 1967. With Bausch & Lomb, Rochester, N.Y., 1967—, dir. applications lab., 1972-74, dir. tech. mktg. analytical systems div., 1974-76, bus. line mgr., 1976-77, v.p. planning and bus. programs, 1977-78, v.p. planning and bus. devel. Soflens div., 1978-80, corp. dir. planning, 1980-81, v.p. corp. devel., 1981—; v.p. RID-N.Y. State, 1980-83; mem. adv. bd. Merger Mgmt. Report, 1986-92; internat. bd. dirs. Assn. Corp. Growth, v.p. corp. mem. affairs, 1993—; bd. dirs. Delta Labs., Inc., Duriron Co. Contbr. articles to profl. jours. Pres. Rochester Against Intoxicated Driving, 1979-83, chmn. polit. action com., 1983, 86; bd. dirs., chmn. long-range planning com. Rochester area Nat. Council on Alcoholism, 1980-84; bd. dirs. Rochester Rehab. Ctr., 1982-84, Friends of Bristol Valley Playhouse Found., 1983-87; mem. Stop DWI Adv. panel to Monroe County Legislature, 1982-87, N.Y. State Coalition for Safety Belt Use, 1984-85; mem. key exec. group Rensselaer Poly. Inst., 1993—; mem. Com. 200, 1993—. Recipient Disting. Citizen's award Monroe County, 1979, Tribute to Women in Industry and Service award YWCA, 1983; NSF grantee, 1963; selected as one of 50 Women to Watch in Corp. Am., Bus. Week mag., 1987, 92, one of 100 Women To Watch, Duns Bus. Rev., 1988. Mem. Am. Mgmt. Assn., Fin. Execs. Inst., Assn. Corp. Growth, C. of C. (pub. safety com. Rochester Area chpt., task force on hwy. safety and legis. 1981-86, high tech. Rochester adv. panel 1989—), Phi Beta Kappa, Sigma Xi, Delta Epsilon Sigma. Home: 60 Mendon Center Rd Honeoye Falls NY 14472-9363 Office: Bausch & Lomb Inc 1 Lincoln First Sq PO Box 54 Rochester NY 14601-0054

HARRIS, DIANNE KAREN, medical technologist; b. Oak Park, Ill., Jan. 19, 1961; d. Robert Michael and Hilda Caroline (Filipczak) Dalton; m. John Benjamin Harris, Apr. 15, 1955. A in Applied Sci., Oakton C.C., Des Plaines, Ill., 1983; BS, U. Health Scis./Chgo. Med. Sch., North Chgo., 1988. Electrocardiographic technician Martha Washington Hosp., Chgo., 1978-83; med. lab. technologist MetPath Ref. Lab., Des Plaines, 1983-86; flow cytometry/lab. technologist Chgo. Med. Sch., North Chgo., 1986-91; flow cytometry tech. cons. Coulter Electronics, Kendall, Fla., 1991—. Med. Tech. Faculty and Alumni scholar U. Health Scis./Chgo. Med. Sch., 1987. Mem. Am. Soc. Clin. Pathologists (cert. med. tech.), Internat. Soc. for Analytical Cytology. Home and Office: 1784 Sycamor Ln Gurnee IL 60031

HARRIS, DORIS ANN, nurse; b. Sayre, Pa., Mar. 5, 1947; d. Allan N. and Ruth E. (Stafford) H. Student, RPH Sch. Nursing, Sayre, 1968; BSPA, St. Joseph's Coll., Windham, Maine. RN, Conn. Staff nurse Conn. Hospice, Inc., Branford, 1980-88; spl. procedures nurse Yale Gynecology-Oncology Clinic, New Haven, 1988-90; nurse oncology unit Middlesex Hosp., Middletown, Conn., 1990-94; staff nurse The Madison (Conn.) House, 1994—. Mem. Soc. Gynecologic Nurse Oncologists, Nat. League for Nursing, Oncology Nursing Soc., Ind. Assn. Hospice Caregivers (co-founder, co-dir. 1987—). Home: 131 Liberty St Clinton CT 06413-1739

HARRIS, EMMA EARL, nursing home executive; b. Viper, Ky., Nov. 6, 1936; d. Andrew Jackson and Zola (Hall) S.; m. Ret Haney Marten Henis Harris, June 5, 1981; children: Debra, Joseph, Wynona, Robert Walsh. Grad. St. Joseph Sch. Practical Nursing. Staff nurse St. Joseph Hosp., Bangor, Maine, 1973-75; office nurse Dr. Eugene Brown, Bangor, 1975-77; dir. nurses Fairborn Nursing Home, Ohio, 1977-78; staff nurse Hillhaven Hospice, Tucson, 1979-80; asst. head nurse, 1980. Author: Thoughts on Life, 1988. Vol. Heart Assn., Bangor, 1965-70, Cancer Assn., Bangor, 1965-70. Mem. NAFE. Democrat. Avocations: theatre, opera. Home: 530 E Flores Dr Tucson AZ 85705-3567

HARRIS, EMMYLOU, singer; b. Birmingham, Ala., Apr. 2, 1947; children: Hallie, Meghann. Student, U.N.C.-Greensboro. Country music performer, singer, 1967—; assisted Gram Parsons on albums GP, Grievous Angel, 1973; toured with Fallen Angel Band, performed across Europe and U.S.; rec. artist on albums Reprise Records, Warner Bros. Records, ASYLUM Records; appeared in rock documentary The Last Waltz, 1978; albums include Gliding Bird, 1969, Pieces of the Sky, 1975, Elite Hotel, 1976 (Grammy award 1976), Luxury Liner, 1977, Quarter Moon in a Ten-Cent Town, 1978, Profile: Best of Emmylou Harris, 1978, Blue Kentucky Girl, 1979, Light of the Stable, 1979, Evangeline, 1981, Cimarron, 1981, Last Date, 1982, White Shoes, 1983, Profile II: Best of Emmylou Harris, 1984, Ballad of Sally Rose, 1985, Thirteen, 1986, Trio (with Dolly Parton, Linda Ronstadt) 1987 (Grammy award 1987), Angel Band, 1987, Bluebird, 1988, Duets, 1990, Brand New Dance, 1990, (with Nash Ramblers) At the Ryman, 1992 (live recording, Grammy award 1992), Cowgirl's Prayer, 1993; co-writer, co-prodr.: (with Paul Kennerley) Ballad of Sally Rose, 1985; composer songs. Pres. Country Music Found., 1983—. Recipient Grammy awards, 1979, 80, 81, 84, 87, 92, (with Dolly Parton and Linda Ronstadt) Album of Yr. award Acad. Country Music, 1987; named Female Vocalist of Yr., Country Music Assn., 1980. Office: M Hitchcock Mgmt Box 159007 Nashville TN 37215

HARRIS, FRANCES ALVORD (MRS. HUGH W. HARRIS), consultant, retired radio and television broadcaster; b. Detroit, Apr. 19, 1909; d. William Roy and Edith (Vosburgh) Alvord; m. Hugh William Harris, Sept. 24, 1932; children: Patricia Anne (Mrs. Floyd A. Metz), Hugh William, Robert Alvord. AB, Grinnell Coll., 1929; LHD (hon.), Ferris State Coll., 1980. With advt. dept. Himelhoch Bros. & Co., Detroit, 1929-31; broadcaster as Julia Hayes Robert P. Gust Co., 1931-34; tng. and pers. dept. Ernst Kern Co., 1935-36; broadcaster as Nancy Dixon Young & Rubicam, Inc., 1939-42; women's editor Sta. WWJ, Detroit, 1943-64, Sta. WWJ-TV, 1947-64; spl. features coord. Sta. WWJ-TV-AM-FM, 1964-74; treas. I.C. Harris & Co., Detroit, 1963-82, pres., chief exec. officer, 1982-84, chmn. bd., 1984-85; creator 1st ct. show Traffic Ct., 1949. Author, editor: Focus: Michigan Women, 1977. Mem. exec. bd. Wayne County chpt. Mich. Soc. for Mental Health, 1953-63; chmn. Mental Health Week, 1958-59; mem. Wayne County Commn. on Aging, 1975-85, chmn., 1976-77; publicity com. YWCA, 1945, 2d v.p., 1963; mem. publicity com. Tri-County League for Nursing, 1956-61; publicity chmn. Met. Detroit YWCA Bd. Dirs., 1961-66, exec. com., 1962-67; campaign dist. chmn. United Found., 1959, unit chmn., 1960-61, chmn. speakers bur., 1974; exec. bd. United Found. Women's Orgn., 1962-64; governing bd. United Community Svcs. Women's Com., 1961-66; bd. dirs. United Community Svcs., 1964-67; bd. dirs. Homemaker Svc. Met. Detroit, pres., 1969-70, co-founder, 1965; bd. dirs. Vis. Nurse Assn., pres., 1974-76; bd. dirs. Camp Fire Girls of Detroit, mem. nat. coun., 1967-72, mem. nat. bd., exec. com., 1970-72, pres., 1978-80; bd. dirs. Well Being Svc. Aging, 1969-74, Sr. Ctr., 1971-76, Friends Detroit Pub. Libr., 1972—, Friends Children's Museum, 1972-74, 83—; trustee Detroit Com. Alcoholism, 1961-64; mem. Mayor's Com. for Freedom Festival, 1959, chmn. women's activities, 1965; mem. Mayor's Com. for UN Week, 1959; mem. Gov.'s. Commn. Status of Women, 1962-69, Mich. State Women's Commn., 1969-77; mem. nat. coun. Homemaker Svc., 1970-73; mem. adv. com. to trustees Grinnell Coll.; mem. bd. control Ferris State Coll., 1968-78; mem. def. adv. com. Women in the Svcs., 1970-73, chmn., 1973; program chmn. Met. Detroit YMCA, 1973-75; sec.-treas. Mich. Assn. Governing Bds. State Colls. and Univs., 1975, v.p., 1976-77, pres., 1977-78; bd. dirs. United Community Svcs., Detroit, 1973-75, mem. assembly, 1984-90; mem. communications com. local congregation and Episc. Diocese of Mich., 1965-66. Recipient Grinnell Coll. Alumni award, 1959, Mental Health Soc. Mich. award, 1958, Theta Sigma Phi Headliner award for Mich., 1951, nat., 1952, Heart of Gold award, 1976, Women's Advt. Club of Detroit Civic award, 1957, Mich. Gov. award NATAS, 1987; named Advt. Woman of Year, Detroit, 1958, 73, Soroptimist Woman of Yr., 1965, Fran Harris Day in her honor, Detroit, 1960, Vol. State of Mich., 1975; inducted into the Mich. Jouralism Hall Fame, 1986, Mich. Women's Hall of Fame, 1988; commendation service award Mich. Assn. Bus. Owners; 1st woman comml. newscaster, Detroit, 1943. Mem. Am. Women in Radio and TV (pres. Detroit chpt. 1957-58, gen. chmn. nat. conv. 1966, Outstanding Community Svc. award 1972, Life Achievement award 1991), Women's Advt. Club of Detroit (pres. 1959-60, mem. bd. 1974-77), UN Assn. U.S.A. (dir. Detroit chpt. 1962-65, Mich. div. bd. 1963-65), Advt. Fedn. (nat. v.p. women's activities 1964-67), Nat. Fedn. Press Women (hon.), 1973, Women in Communications (pres. Detroit 1950-51; del. to Asian-Am. Women in Broadcasting Conf. 1966, nat. 1st v.p. 1968-71, nat. pres. 1971-73, chmn. Communications Conf. Ams., 1968, del. III World Congress Women Journalists 1973), Women's Econ. Club (charter mem., dir. 1975-82, membership chmn. 1975, program chmn. 1976, pub. rels. co-chmn. 1977, treas. 1978, sec. 1979, 1st v.p. 1980, pres. 1981), Pi Epsilon Delta. Home: 34601 Elmwood St Apt 241 Westland MI 48185-3079

HARRIS, GLENDA STANGE, medical transcriptionist, writer; b. Jacksonville, Fla., Jan. 11, 1954; d. Robert Lee and Wynelle (Jowers) S.; m. David Michael Harris Sr., Aug. 11, 1973; children: David Michael Jr., Mason Andrew. AA, Fla. Jr. Coll., Jacksonville, 1980. Asst. adminstr. Primary Health Care Ctr., Orange Park, Fla., 1980-83; med. transcriptionist, exec. sec. Ctr. for Plastic and Reconstructive Surgery, Orlando, Fla., 1984-90; med. transcriptionist Fayette Med. Clinic, Fayetteville, Ga., 1991—. Author: (newspaper column) Grand Slam News, 1991-94. Republican. Methodist. Home: 135 Mark Ln Fayetteville GA 30214-7202 Office: Fayette Med Clinic 101 Yorktown Dr Fayetteville GA 30214-1585

HARRIS, GLORIA JAMES, accountant; b. Waterproof, La., June 10, 1950; d. Ernest James and Camille (Johnson) Savage; m. Horace Harris Jr., Aug. 15, 1982. BS, So. U., New Orleans, 1974. Tax cons. H & R Block, Metairie, La., 1980—; property acctg. supr. Cytec Industries, Westwego, La., 1978—. Mem. Am. Soc. Women Accts., Inst. Mgmt. Accts. (v.p. New Orleans chpt.). Democrat. Baptist. Home: 8423 Plum St New Orleans LA 70118

HARRIS, HARRIETT SMITHERMAN, elementary school educator; b. Centreville, Ala., Apr. 28, 1932; d. Burl Herbert and Adelaide Helen (Parker) Smitherman; m. Winton Walter Harris, June 3, 1955. BS, U. Chattanooga, 1956; postgrad., Cumberland U., Lebanon, Tenn., 1990. Profl. career ladder III cert., Tenn. Tchr. 5th grade Eastdale/Woodmore Elem. Sch., Hamilton County, Tenn., 1954-56; tchr. 4th and 5th grades Spring Creek Elem. Sch., Hamilton County, Tenn., 1956-59, Anna B. Lacey Elem. Sch., Hamilton County, Tenn., 1959-85, East Ridge Elem. Sch., Chattanooga, 1985—; homework hotline tchr. Hamilton County Bd. Edn., 1988—; chmn. Sci. and Health Textbook Adoptionk, Chattanooga, 1991, Hamilton County Zone Spelling Bee, 1991; coord. for sch. Acad. Olympics, Chattanooga State Tech. C.C., 1991-93; mentor Gov.'s Sch. for Prospective Tchrs., U. Tenn. Chattanooga Campus, 1992; mentor Pub. Edn. Found., 1992-94; mem. Site-Based Decision Making Coun., 1992-94, adv. coun. PACE, 1992—; judge Tenn. Dept. Edn. Mini-Grants, 1993. Co-author: Write On, Hamilton County, 1986. Membership v.p. Freedoms Found., Chattanooga, 1990—, pres. Chattanooga chpt., 1992-94. AAUW grantee, 1976; recipient Master Tchr. award East Ridge Elem Sch, 1990; named Tchr. of Yr. (grades. 5-8), Hamilton County Sch. System, 1991, S.E. Dist. Tchr. of the Yr., Tenn. Dept. Edn., 1991, Tenn. Tchr. of Yr., 1992, Hamilton County Edn. Assn. (bd. dirs. 1992); nominee Walt Disney Am. Tchr. awards, 1992. Mem. NEA, PTA (life), AAUW (corres. sec. Tenn. div. 1988-89), Tenn. Edn. Assn., Hamilton County Edn. Assn. (chmn. 1990—), Tenn. Middle Schs. Assn., Internat. Speakers Platform Assn., Delta Kappa Gamma (membership chmn. Alpha XI chpt. 1990-91), Phi Mu (v.p. local chpt. 1953-54). Baptist. Home: 4101 Wiley Ave Chattanooga TN 37412-2635 Office: East Ridge Elem Sch 1014 John Ross Rd Chattanooga TN 37412-1620

HARRIS, HELAINE ZITOFSKY, marriage, family and child therapist; b. Bklyn., May 28, 1942; d. Benjamin Nathan and Rose (Zelinsky) Z.; m. Allen Yale Harris, Aug. 9, 1964 (div. July, 1975); children: Tamara, Janine. BA with honors, UCLA, 1963; MA in Counseling, Calif. State U., Norhridge, 1975. Cert. tchr. life, marriage, family and child counselor, hypnotherapist. Tchr. Chase Elem. Sch., Panorama City, Calif., 1972-82; workshop asst. Bindrim Inst., Hollywood, Calif., 1976-79; dir. profl. tng. Bindrim Inst., Hollywood, 1980-84; counselor Ctr. for Study of Drug Abuse, Reseda, Calif., 1977-78; tchr. O'Melveny Elem. Sch., San Fernando, Calif., 1982-84; founder, dir. Helaine Harris Psychotherapy and Tng. Svcs., Van Nuys, Calif., 1984—; dir., trainer Psychoshamanism, Van Nuys, 1990—; lectr., workshop leader, Calif. State U., Northridge, 1991-93, Assn. for Past Life Rsch. and Therapise, Riverside, Calif., 1992—, Brain Mind Symposium, Venice, Calif., 1992-93. Author: (cassette tapes) The Feminine Warrior, 1989, The Relationship Dance, 1991. Mem. Assn. for Humanistic Psychology, Calif. Assn. Marriage and Family Therapists (chairperson 1984—), Assn. for Transpersonal Psychology, Am. Assn. for Marriage and Family Therapy, Am. Assn. Marriage and Family Therapists. Office: Helaine Harris MA MFCC PO Box 18722 Encino CA 91416-8722

HARRIS, JEAN ANGELLO, training specialist; b. Kingston, Jamaica; m. Joseph R. Harris, July 14, 1992; children: Joseph Jr., Keith, Allison. AB, Chestnut Hill Coll., 1957; MA, Fordham U., 1962; cert. in copy editing and proofreading, CUNY, 1988. Tchr. Alpha Acad., Kingston, 1959-62; tutor Nat. Tutoring Ctrs., N.Y.C., 1969-72; adj. lectr. La Guardia C.C., Long Island City, N.Y., 1971-72; adj. instr. Middlesex County Coll., Edison, N.J., 1977-78, tng. instr., 1978-88; ind. cons. Harris Assocs., Plainfield, N.J., 1988—; tng. specialist World of Difference program Anti-Defamation League, 1993—. Editor: (with others) Educational Policy Seminar Papers on Mathematics and Science, 1986; editor Career Connections, 1988-94. Mem. adv. coun. Union County Coll., Plainfield, 1986-93; mem. sub-com. edn. girl child UNICEF, 1992; bd. dirs. YWCA, Plainfield, North Plainfield, Fanwood, 1988-94, treas., 1990-92, pres. bd. trustees, 1992-94. Scholar Chestnut Hill Coll., 1953-57; fellow Fordham U., 1957-59. Mem. ASTD (met. chpt.), LWV (Plainfield chpt., editor fin. sect. This is Plainfield), Internat. Listening Assn. Roman Catholic. Address: 1015 Kenyon Ave Plainfield NJ 07060-2805

HARRIS, JEAN LANEY, state legislator; b. Cheraw, S.C., Oct. 29, 1932; d. Campbell Plyler and Grace (Baskin) L.; m. C. Anthony Harris, 1955; children: Lorraine Harris Knight, Anthony, Mary Margaret, Frederick. Student, U. S.C., 1950-53. Mem. S.C. Ho. of Reps. from dist. 53, 1979—; bd. dirs. S.C. Nat. Bank. Mem. Chesterfield County Hist. Soc., United Fund, Girl Scout Coun. Mem. Chi Omega. Democrat. Methodist. Home: 317 Market St Cheraw SC 29520-2634 Office: SC House of Reps Office of House Mems Columbia SC 29211*

HARRIS, JEAN LOUISE, physician; b. Richmond, Va., Nov. 24, 1931; d. Vernon Joseph and Jean Louise (Pace) H.; m. Leslie John Ellis Jr., Sept. 24, 1955; children: Karen Denise, Pamela Diane, Cynthia Suzanne. BS, Va. Union U., 1951; MD, Med. Coll. Va., 1955; ScD (hon.), U. Richmond, 1981. Intern Med. Coll. Va., Richmond, 1955-56, resident internal medicine, 1956-58, fellow, 1958-60; fellow Strong Meml. Hosp.-U. Rochester (N.Y.) Sch. Medicine, 1958-60; rsch. assoc. Walter Reed Army Inst. Rsch., Washington, 1960-63; pvt. practice medicine specializing in internal medicine allergy Washington, 1964-71; instr. medicine Howard U. Coll. Medicine, Washington, 1960-68, asst. prof. dept. community health practice, 1969-72; prof. family practice Med. Coll. Va., Va. Commonwealth U., 1973-78; also dir. Center Community Health, 1973-78; sec. Human Resources Commonwealth of Va., 1978-82; v.p. state mktg. programs Control Data Corp., 1982-84, v.p. state govt. affairs, 1984-86, v.p. bus. devel., 1986-88; pres., chief exec. officer Ramsey Found., 1988-92; sr. assoc. dir., dir. med. affairs U. Minn. Hosp. and Clinic, Mpls., 1992—; lectr. dept. med. care and hosps. Johns Hopkins, Balt., 1971-73; asst. clin. prof. dept. community medicine Charles R. Drew Postgrad. Med. Sch., L.A., 1970-73; adj. asst. prof. dept. preventive and social medicine UCLA, 1970-72; chief bur. resources devel. D.C. Dept. Health, 1967-69; exec. dir. Nat. Med. Assn. Found., Washington, 1969-72; Cons. div. health manpower intelligence HEW, 1969; mem. recombinant DNA adv. com. HEW USPHS-NIH, 1979-82; vice chmn. Nat. Commn. on Alcoholism and Alcohol Related Diseases, 1980-81; mem. Pres.'s Pvt. Sctor Initiatives Task Force, 1981-82, Def. Adv. Com. on Women in the Service, 1985-88, Eden Prairie City Council, 1987—. Trustee U. Richmond, 1982-90; bd. dirs. United Way St. Paul; mem. Greater Mpls. coun. Girl Scouts U.S. Recipient award East End Civic Assn. Richmond, Va., 1955, 1st Ann. Serwa award Va. Commonwealth chpt. Nat. Coalition of 100 Black Women, 1989, Leadership award S.W. Suburban Twin Cities chpt. NAACP, 1989; named one of Top 100 Black Bus. and Profl. Women, Dollars and Sense mag., 1985. Mem. Nat. Med. Assn., Inst. Medicine of NAS, Am. Coll. Physician Execs., NAACP, Women's Econ. Roundtable, Rotary, Sigma Xi, Beta Kappa Chi, Alpha Kappa Mu, Delta Sigma Theta. Home: 10860 Forestview Cir Eden Prairie MN 55347-2022 Office: U Minn Hosp and Clinic Harvard St at E River Rd Minneapolis MN 55455

HARRIS, JOAN BERNSTEIN, writer, editor, producer; b. N.Y.C.; d. Leo and Hope (North) Bernstein; m. Thomas A. Harris. BA summa cum laude, U. Rochester, 1976. Host, interviewer, producer Warner Cable TV, Somerville, Mass., 1977-78; researcher, writer Sta. WBZ-TV, Boston, 1978; newscaster, writer, reporter Sta. WERS-FM, Boston, 1979; news anchor, producer, reporter Sta. WLBZ-TV, Bangor, Maine, 1979, Sta. WCSH-TV, Portland, Maine, 1979; newscaster, producer, editor, reporter Sta. WGSM/WCTO, L.I., N.Y., 1980-83; stringer reporter The Associated Press, N.Y.C., 1981-83; newswriter, editor, producer, reporter Capital Cities/ABC, Inc., N.Y.C., 1983—; actress, singer Springfield St. Dinner Theater, Cambridge, Mass., 1978; narrator, radio commls. , Huntington, N.Y., 1981-82; narrator, actress Vanderbilt Planetarium Centerport, N.Y., 1982-83, Hayden Planetarium, N.Y.C., 1984; tchr. English The Internat. Ctr. N.Y., Inc., 1986-88. Mem. Writers Guild Am., AFTRA, Phi Beta Kappa. Office: ABC Radio News 125 W End Ave New York NY 10023-6345

HARRIS, JOAN WHITE, television producer, foundation officer, arts administrator; b. New Haven, Mar. 9, 1931; d. Louis and Martha (Rahm) White; m. Gerald Baumann Frank, Feb. 12, 1953 (div. 1974); children: Daniel Bruce, Jonathan White, Louise Blanche; m. Irving Brooks Harris, June 19, 1974. BA, Smith Coll., 1952. Editorial asst. Oxford U. Press, N.Y.C., 1952-53, Ency. Brit., Chgo., 1953-54; TV producer, Chgo., 1976, 78, 80; pres. Chgo. Opera Theater, 1977-84, chair, 1984-87, bd. dirs., 1975-80; panelist, cons. Nat. Endowment for the Arts, 1980—; chair nat. bd. Aspen Music Festival, Colo., 1984-85, trustee, 1990—; mem. adv. bd. U.S.-China Arts Exchange, 1985-93. Pres. Harris Found., Chgo., 1976—; bd. dirs./trustee Mus. Contemporary Art, Chgo., 1976—, vice chmn., 1989—, Hampshire Coll., Amherst, Mass., 1977-84, Chgo. Symphony Orch., 1978—, Nat. Inst. Music Theater, Washington, 1982-87, Ind. Sector, Washington, 1983-89; pres. Ill. Art Alliance, 1990—; pres. Chgo. Music and Dance Theater, 1993—; trustee Columbia Coll., 1994—; bd. dirs. Ill. Ctr. for the Book, 1990-94, Northwestern Program for Performing Artists, 1986—, Am. coun. for the Arts, 1990-94, Nat. Cultural Alliance, 1991—, Sculpture Chgo., 1991—, Chgo. Inst. Architecture & Urbanism, 1992-94; commr. cultural affairs City of Chgo., 1987-89; pres. Ill. Arts Alliance, 1990—. Clubs: Arts, Saddle and Cycle, Lake Shore, Standard (Chgo.), Lotos (N.Y.C.). Home: 2 N LaSalle St Ste 605 Chicago IL 60611-1307 Office: Harris Found 2 N La Salle St Chicago IL 60602-3702

HARRIS, JOLIE MARIE, nursing administrator, educator; b. Jefferson, La., Oct. 2, 1958; d. Donald James and June (Triche) Estopinal; m. Rodney Joseph Harris, Apr. 14, 1984; children: Brian, Gregory, Rachel. BSN, La. State U., 1981, M in Nursing, 1990. Cert. provider, instr. ACLS. Relief supr., charge nurse Lakeside Hosp., Metairie, La., 1981-84; head dept. med.-surg. oncology Doctor's Hosp., Metairie, 1984-88; dir. med.-surg. divsn. So. Bapt. Hosp., New Orleans, 1988-93, Mercy-Bapt. Hosp., New Orleans, 1993—; adj. faculty William Carey Coll., Metairie, 1984-88. Mem. NAFE, Oncology Nurses Soc. (nat. and New Orleans chpts.), La. Assn. Homes and Svcs. for Aging, Acad. Med.-Surg. Nurses, New Orleans Assn. Nurse Execs. Roman Catholic.

HARRIS, JUDITH ANN WHITE, health occupations vocational educator, nurse; b. Springfield, Ohio, Mar. 6, 1939; d. Willis and Tennessee Belle (Poole) Martin; m. Allen G. Harris, Mar. 21, 1986; 1 child by previous marriage, Denise Marian Kauffman. Student, U. South Fla., 1978-85. RN, Fla.; cert. tchr., Fla. Nurse Dr. Robert Tapogna, Springfield, Ohio, 1960-62, Springfield City Hosp., 1962-65, Dr. Robert Beam, Springfield, 1965-75; ednl. coord., instr. med. assisting Sarasota Vocat. Ctr., Fla., 1977-82, instr. med. assisting program, chmn. dept., 1982-84, 89-91, instr. health svc. occupations, placement coord. health occupations, 1985-88, dept. chmn, Allied Health, 1989—; bd. dirs. Fla. Bd., Inc. Contbr. articles to profl. jours. Vol. Children's Breath Clinic, Sarasota, 1977-79, Kidney Found., Sarasota, 1982; vol. ARC, Sarasota, 1976-88, dir. Spl. Care unit, 1984-88; v.p. Sons of Norway, 1993-95. Named Outstanding Vocat. Tchr. Sarasota County Sch. Bd., 1985; choir soloist Beneva Christian Ch., 1989—, deaconess, 1993—; asst. state dir. Fla. Good Sons, 1993-94; bd. dirs. Fla. Bd. Camping Assn., Inc; chmn. FVA Leadership Forum, 1992-95; parish nurse and chmn. health svcs. dept. Beneva Christian Ch., 1995—. Mem. Am. Vocat. Assn. (Outstanding Vocat. Tchr. region II 1985, Vocat. Tchr. Yr., 1987), Health Occupations Educators (vice chmn. policy com. 1985-86), Nat. Assn. Health Occupations Tchrs. (v.p. region II 1984-86, pres. elect. 1988, pres. 1989-91), Fla. Vocat. Assn. (bd. dirs. 1983-85, pres. 1987-88, Pres. award 1984, Outstanding Vocat. Educator region 23 award 1982, Sarasota Mayors award 1984, Gov.'s Proclamation for Outstanding Teaching 1987, chmn. leadership forum 1993—), Health Occupations Educators Assn. Fla. (pres. 1983-84, chmn. legis. com. 1985-93, Outstanding Tchr. 1983), Sarasota County Vocat. and Adult Edn. Assn. (pres. 1978-80, editor newsletter, 1978-83), Am. Assn. Med. Assts., Good Sams Inc. Fla. (asst. state dir. dist. 12 1993—), Sons Norway (asst. social dir.), Delta Kappa Gamma, Phi Kappa Phi. Republican. Avocations: swimming, camping, knitting, sewing, biking. Home: 3846 Malec Cir Sarasota FL 34233-2132 Office: Sarasota Vocat Ctr 4748 Beneva Rd Sarasota FL 34233

HARRIS, JULIA ALICE, career and occupational information consultant; b. Stamford, Conn., Nov. 28, 1957; 1 child, William. BA, U. Conn., 1979; MS, Simmons Coll., 1984. Dir. resource ctr. Mass. Office Tng. and Employment Policy, Boston, 1984-88; project mgr. Mass. Occupational Info. Coord. Com., Boston, 1988-93; cons. HCC Assocs., Auburndale, Mass., 1993—, Stamford, Conn., 1993—. Author: Building a Career Information Resource Center, 1991; editor: Directory of Licensed Occupations, 1988, Who to Call Directory, 1989. Home and office: PO Box 4834 Springdale CT 06907-0834

HARRIS, JULIE (ANN), actress; b. Grosse Pointe Park, Mich., Dec. 2, 1925; d. William Pickett and Elsie (Smith) H.; m. Jay I. Julien, Aug. 12, 1946 (div. 1954); m. Manning Gurian, Oct. 21, 1954 (div. 1967); 1 child, Peter; m. Erwin Carroll, Apr. 1977, (div. 1982). Student, Perry Mansfield Theatre Work Shop,, 1941-43, Yale Drama Sch.,, 1944-45. Theater debut in It's a Gift, N.Y.C., 1945; appeared in plays Playboy of the Western World, 1946, Oedipus, 1946, Henry IV-Part II, 1946, Alice in Wonderland, 1947, We Love A Lassie, 1947, Macbeth, 1948, Sundown Beach, 1948 (Theatre World award 1949), The Young and Fair, 1948-49, Magnolia Alley, 1949, Montserrat, 1949, The Member of the Wedding, 1950-51 (Donaldson award 1950), I Am a Camera, 1951-52 (Tony award 1952, Donaldson award 1952, Variety-N.Y. Drama Critics Poll 1952), Mademoiselle Colombe, 1954, The Lark, 1955 (Tony award 1956), The Country Wife, 1957, The Warm Peninsula, 1959, Little Moon of Alban, 1960, Romeo and Juliet, 1960, King John, 1960, A Shot in the Dark, 1961, Marathon 33, 1964 (Tony nomination 1964), Hamlet, 1964, Ready When You Are, C.B, 1964, The Hostage, 1965, Skyscraper, 1965 (Tony nomination 1969), A Streetcar Named Desire, 1967, Forty Carats, 1968 (Tony award 1969), The Women, 1970, And Miss Reardon Drinks A Little, 1971-72, Voices, 1972, The Last of Mrs. Lincoln, 1972 (Tonyaward 1973), The Au Pair Man, 1973 (Tony nomination 1974), In Praise of Love, 1974, Break a Leg, 1979, On Golden Pond, 1980, Mixed Couples, 1980, Under the Ilex, 1983, Tusitala, 1988, (nat. co.) Driving Miss Daisy, Love Letters, 1989; one-woman theater presentations include The Belle of Amherst, 1977 (Grammy award 1977, Tony award 1977), Currer Bell, Lucifer's Child, 1991, Glass Menagerie, 1994; film debut in The Member of the Wedding, 1952 (Acad. award nomination); other films include The East of Eden, 1955, I Am A Camera, 1955, The Truth About Women, 1958, Poacher's Daughter, 1960, Requiem for a Heavyweight, 1962, The Haunting, 1963, The Moving Target, 1966, You're a Big Boy Now, 1966, Reflections in a Golden Eye, 1967, The Split, 1968, Journey into Midnight, 1968, The People Next Door, 1970, The Hiding Place, 1975, Voyage of the Damned, 1976, The Bell Jar, 1979, The Prostitute, 1980, The Nutcraker: The Motion Picture, 1986, Gorillas in the Mist, 1988, Housesitter, 1992, The Dark Half, 1993; TV series include Thicker Than Water, 1973, The Family Holvak, 1975, Knots Landing, 1979-87; TV movies include Wind From the South, 1955, The Good Fairy, 1956, The Lark, 1957,

Johnny Belinda, 1968, Little Moon of Alban, 1958 (Emmy award 1959), A Doll's House, 1959, Victoria Regina, 1961 (Emmy award 1962), The Power and the Glory, 1961, Pygmalian, 1964, Hamlet, 1964, The Holy Terror, 1965, Anastasia, 1967, The House on Green Apple Road, 1970, How Awful About Alan, 1970, Home for the Holidays, 1972, The Greatest Gift, 1974, Backstairs at the White House, 1979, The Gift, 1979, The Christmas Wife, 1979, Too Good To Be True, 1988, Single Women, Married Men, 1989; author: (with Barry Tarshis) Julie Harris Talks to Young Actors, 1971. Recipient Antoinette Perry award for best actress in Forty Carats, 1969, The Last of Mrs. Lincoln, 1973; Nat. Medal of the Arts, 1994. Office: William Morris Agy 1350 6th Ave New York NY 10019-4701*

HARRIS, KATHERINE SAFFORD, speech and hearing educator; b. Lowell, Mass., Sept. 3, 1925; d. Truman Henry and Katherine (Wardwell) Safford; m. George Harris, Oct. 2, 1952; children: Maud White, Louise. BA, Radcliffe Coll., 1947; PhD, Harvard U., 1954. Rsch. assoc. Haskins Labs., New Haven, 1952-85, v.p., 1985—; prof. speech and hearing CUNY, N.Y.C., 1970—, Disting. prof., 1982—; active U.S./Israeli Speech Program Littauer Found., N.Y.C., 1986. Author: (with Borden) Speech Science Primer, 1980, (with Raphael) 3d edit., 1994, (with Baer and Sasaki) Phonatory Control, 1986. Nat. Inst. Neurol. Diseases and Stroke grantee. Fellow AAAS, Acoustical Soc. Am., Am. Speech Hearing Assn., N.Y. Acad. Scis. Office: CUNY Grad Sch 33 W 42nd St New York NY 10036-8003

HARRIS, KATHRYN MARIE, librarian; b. Carbondale, Ill., Dec. 5, 1947; d. William Richard and Eurma Cordella (Jones) Hayes; m. Al C. Harris, Oct. 28, 1972; 1 child, Kori Lynette Hayes. BS in Edn., So. Ill. U., 1969; MS in Libr. Sci., U. Ill., 1971. Reference libr. Lincoln Libr., Springfield, Ill., 1971-72; instrnl. svcs. profl. Sangamon State U., Springfield, 1972-74; circulation libr. Fla. Internat. U., Miami, 1974-79; ext./reference libr. Sch. Medicine Libr. So. Ill. U., Springfield, 1979-84; head reference sect. Ill. State Libr., Springfield, 1984-90; head reference/tech. svcs. Ill. State Hist. Libr., Springfield, 1990—; del. White House Conf. on Libr. and Info. Svc., Washington, 1991. Editor: (booklet) MHSLN Hosp. Adminstrv. Packet, 1983; contbr. articles to profl. jours. Mem. curriculum coun. Dist. # 186 Sch. Bd., Springfield, 1992—; bd. dirs. Planned Parenthood, bd. sec., 1983-93, bd. pres. 1993—. Recipient Disting. Svc. award Planned Parenthood, Springfield, 1992. Mem. AAUW, Ill. Libr. Assn. African Methodist Episcopalian. Home: 1315 E Adams St Springfield IL 62703-1032 Office: Ill State Hist Libr Old State Capitol Springfield IL 62701

HARRIS, LENORE ZOBEL, school nurse; b. Shoemaker, Calif., Nov. 1, 1944; d. Jerome Fremont and Louise Maxine (Purwin) Zobel; m. Robert Thomas Harris, June 19, 1966; children: Rebecca Louise, Grant Thomas. BSN, Stanford U., 1967; postgrad., Calif. State U., San Diego, 1969-72; MA, Stanford U., Northridge, 1993; postgrad., Calif. State U.-Stanislaus, Turlock, 1990—. RN, Calif. Staff nurse Stanford (Calif.) Univ. Hosp., 1967-68; pediatric nurse to pvt. practice physician San Diego, 1968-73; sch. nurse Oak Park Unified Sch. Dist., Agoura, Calif., 1978-79, Simi Valley (Calif.) Unified Sch. Dist., 1975-85; camp nurse Kennolyn Camps, Aptos, Calif., 1982, 83, 84; sch. nurse Ventura (Calif.) Unified Sch. Dist., 1984-87; coord. health svcs., Lincoln Unified Sch. Dist., Stockton, Calif., 1987—; originator, chmn. Disaster Preparedness Com., 1985-87; chmn. health advc. com. Lincoln Unified Sch. Dist., 1987—, family life edn. adv. com., 1988—, trainer S.J. County teen advs., 1992-94; organizer, adviser Mid. sch. "Just Say No" Club, 1988-91; speaker on health issues to sch. nurses and educators. Writer Calif. Office of AIDS Manual; contbr. articles to profl. jours. Troop leader San Diego and Ventura area Girl Scouts U.S., 1963, 78-81; officer Ventura Parent Coop. Nursery Sch., 1976-81; pres. Poinsettia PTA, Ventura, 1985-87; officer Pacific Middle Sch. PTSA, Stockton, 1988-90, Lincoln High Sch. PTSA, Stockton, 1990-94. Mem. AAUW, Nat. Assn. Sch. Nurses, San Joaquin County Sch. Nurse Orgn. (chmn. 1990-92), Calif. Sch. Nurse Orgn. (nominating com. 1991-92), San Joaquin County Health Edn. Com. (speaker on health issues). Office: Lincoln Unified Sch Dist 2010 W Swain Rd Stockton CA 95207-4055

HARRIS, MADELINE JOYCE, art gallery owner; b. Spangler, Pa., Sept. 16, 1924; d. Michael and Mary (Sidwar) Salamanchuk; m. Peter Fetko, Aug. 31, 1942 9div. 1963); m. Vernon Emerson Harris, June 19, 1970. Student, Pitts. Inst. Art, J. Kelly Art Sch., N.Y.C. Bookkeeper Western Electric, Newark, Princess Form, Orange, N.J.; office mgr. Calavo Growers Calif., N.Y.C.; owner, operator Continental Art Ctr.-Gallery, Orange. Exhibited paintings in one-person shows in Pa., N.J., N.Y.; group shows include Nat. Acad. Galleries, N.Y., Temple Emanuel, N.J., Continental Art Ctr., N.J., Nat. Acad. Design, Greenwick, N.Y.C.; paintings represented in permanent collections including N.J. Rehab. Hosp., Continental Art Ctr., numerous pvt. collections. Office: Continental Art Ctr 474 Valley Rd West Orange NJ 07052

HARRIS, MARCELITE JORDAN, air force officer; b. Houston, Jan. 16, 1943; d. Cecil Oneal and Marcelite Elizabeth (Terrell) Jordan; m. Maurice Anthony Harris, Nov. 29, 1980; children: Steven Eric, Tenecia Marcelite. BA, Spelman Coll., 1964; postgrad., Ctrl. Mich. U., 1976-78, Chapman Coll., 1979-80; BS, U. Md., Okinawa, Japan, 1986. Tchr. Head Start, Houston, 1964-65; commd. 2d lt. USAF, 1965, advanced through grades to brig. gen., 1965—; student Squadron officers Sch., 1975; with Hdqrs. USAF, Pentagon, 1975; comdr. 39 Cadet Squadron, USAF Acad., Colorado Springs, Colo., 1978, Air Refueling Wing, McConnell AFB, Kans., 1980, Avionics Maintenance Squadron, McConnell AFB, 1981, Field Maintenance Squadron, McConnell AFB, 1982; dir. maintenance Pacific Air Forces Logistics Support Ctr., Kadena Air Base, Japan, 1982; student Air War Coll., 1983; dep. chief maintenance Tech. Tng. Ctr., Keesler AFB, Miss., 1986, wing comdr., 1988; student Harvard U.Sr. Officers Course, 1988, Capstone Flag and Gen. Officers Course, 1990; vice comdr. Oklahoma City Air Logistics Ctr., Tinker AFB, 1990—; dir. tech. tng. USAF, Randolph AFB, Tex., 1993—. Cabinet mem. United Way, Oklahoma City, 1991; mem. adv. bd. Salvation Army, Oklahoma City, 1991—; bd. dirs. U.S. Automobile Assn., 1993—, 5 Who Care, 1992, Urban League. Decorated Bronze star, 1972; named one of Top 100 Afro-Am. Bus. and Profl. Women, Dollars and $ense Mag., 1989, named Most Prestigious Individual, 1991. Mem. Fed. Mgrs. Assn., Nat. Contract Mgmt. Assn., Tinker Mgmt. Assn., Air Force Assn.

HARRIS, MARGARET, pianist, conductor, composer; b. Chgo., 1943; d. William and Clara Harris. BS, Juilliard Sch. Music, 1964, MS, 1965. Am. mus. specialist, cons. Porgy and Bess Bolshoi Theater of Opera and Ballet, Uzbekistan, 1995; adj. lectr. and prof. Bronx Community Coll. of CUNY, 1991—; adjudicator, lectr. Unisys Symposium for African-Am. Composers Detroit Symphony Orch., 1993. Debut as pianist at age 3; toured as child prodigy; debut with Chgo. Symphony Orch., 1953; condr., pianist Black New World ballet prodn.; toured Europe twice as mus. dir. Black New World and Negro Ensemble Co. N.Y.; debut Town Hall, 1970; pianist, condr. prodn. Hair; musical dir., condr. Two Gentlemen of Verona, Guys and Dolls; made debut as symphonic condr. with Grant Park and Chgo. Symphonies, 1971; soloist original piano concerto L.A. Philharmonic, 1972, 73; condr. St. Louis, Minn., San Diego, Detroit symphonies, L.A. Philharmonic, Wolf Trap Park, Opera Ebony, N.Y.C., 1977, Winston-Salem, N.C. Symphony, 1988; mus. dir. One More Time, Israel, Europe, N.Y.; mus. dir./pianist I Love New York, Europe, 1984; mus. dir. Amen Corner, Broadway, 1984; artist-in-residence Hillsborough Coll., Tampa, Fla., 1984; mus. dir., condr. nat. TV spls.; mus. dir., condr. Raisin on Broadway and nat. tour; exec./music dir. Newark Boys Chorus; panelist Nat. Endowment Arts, Nat. Opera Inst. Affiliate Artists, N.Y.C., Dame Knights of Malta; composer of musical (with Ruby Dee), 1988; former artistic dir., condr. N.Y. Boys Choir; vis. disting. prof. U. West Fla., 1989—; pres. Margaret R. Harris Enterprises; condr. Dayton Philharm., 1991; apptd. permanent artistic and music dir. Olympus Music Soc., N.Y.C., 1994; pianist European Concert tour, Germany, 1994; guest condr. Bklyn. Philharmonic, 1994; other compositions include David, Cycle of Psalms, Spiritual Suite, Stabat mater, Mass in A, the Lord's Prayer, We are D.C.'s Future, Christ is Alive Here, 1994; European concept tour as pianist, 1994; Am. cultural specialist for U.S.I.A., Porgy & Bess in Russian, 1995; numerous commissioned compositions for chorus, orch., voice and piano, 1994.

HARRIS, MARILYN, retired academic administrator; b. N.Y.C.; d. Bernard and Rose (Block) Hochberg; m. Seymour J. Harris; children: Randall (dec.), April. AB summa cum laude, Hunter Coll., 1945; MS, Iowa State U., 1947. Faculty dept. math and stats. Hunter Coll., N.Y.C., 1946-48; systems analyst, statistician market research services Gen. Electric Co., N.Y.C., 1962-67; biostatistician comprehensive child care project Einstein Med. Sch., N.Y.C., 1967-69; asst. to dean, acting dir. computer ctr. Baruch Coll. CUNY, 1969-72; dir. data collection and evaluation office univ. mgmt. data Cen. Office, CUNY, 1972-74; dir. mgmt. info. systems Bklyn. Coll., CUNY, 1974-79, dir. personnel services, 1979-85, asst. v.p. human resources and adminstrv. services, 1985-89, bd. dirs. Bklyn. Ctr. Performing Arts, 1982-89, chair seat campaign, 1984-86. Bd. dirs. Project Greenhope, 1988-93; vol. mgmt. cons. Women in Need, 1988—, bd. dirs., 1989-92, sec. exec. com., 1990-92; bd. dirs. Women's City Club, 1990—, active homeless project, 1989-91, mem. emergency task force, 1992-93, v.p. ops., 1993-94; active Womanspace of Gt. Neck, 1989, mem. exec. com.-at-large, 1990-94, mem. adv. bd., 1994—; adv. bd. Omsbudservice of Nassau County, 1991—. Named to Hunter Coll. Hall of Fame, 1990. Mem. Phi Beta Kappa, Phi Kappa Phi, Pi Mu Epsilon. Home: 9 Knightsbridge Rd Great Neck NY 11021-4569

HARRIS, MARION HOPKINS, college educator; b. Washington, July 27, 1938; d. Dennis Cason and Georgia (Greenleaf) Hopkins; m. Charles E. Harris, July 1957 (div. 1964); 1 child, Alan E. MPA, U. Pitts., 1971; M in Mgmt. Systems, U. So. Calif., 1984, DPA, 1985. Dir. program planning Rochester Urban Renewal Agy., N.Y., 1971-72; exec. dir. Fairfax County Redevel. and Housing Authority, Fairfax, Va., 1972-73; dep. dir. housing mgmt. HUD, Detroit, 1973-75; pres., prof. dept. bus. and pub. adminstrn. Bowie State U., Md.; mng. auditor GAO, Washington, 1979-80; sr. field officer for housing, Washington, 1979-89, dir. evaluation div. adminstrn., 1989-91. Bd. dirs. S.W. Neighborhood Assembly, Washington, 1979-80; commr. S.W. Adv. Neighborhood Commn., Washington, 1986; mem. pub. adv. com. Washington Council Govts., 1985-87; Wash. Suburban Sanitary Commn.; mem. consumer adv. bd. Wash. Suburban Sanitary Com., 1989—; bd. dirs. Bowie State U. Found., 1991—; mem. transition team Gov. State of Md., 1995. Maj. USAMC. Recipient Outstanding Performance award HUD, 1984; Carnegie-Mellon mid-career fellow, 1970; Ford Found. travel-study awardee, 1970. Mem. Am. Acad. Soc. and Polit. Sci., U. So. Calif. Doctoral Assn., LWV (exec. bd. Washington 1983-84). Roman Catholic. Avocations: cross-country skiing; foreign travel; swimming. Home: 12306 Sea Pearl Ct Laurel MD 20708-2848

HARRIS, MELVA J., management consultant, writer, professional speaker; b. Montgomery, Ala., Dec. 25, 1944; d. Clisby Harris and Flore (Smith) Poole. BBA, Baruch Coll., 1980; MA, N.Y. Inst. Tech., N.Y.C., 1991. Supr. ops. AT&T, N.Y.C., 1967-83; pres. Harris Devel. Cons., East Windsor, N.J., 1984—; cons. Mercer County Coll. Small Bus. Devel. Ctr., Trenton, N.J., 1988—. Bd. chmn. Mercer County Pvt. Industry Coun., Trenton, 1990-92; bd. trustee Mill Hill Child and Family Devel. Ctr., Trenton. With USAF, 1963-67. Recipient Officer Outstanding Svc. award Mercer County Pvt. Industry Coun., 1991; named Outstanding Bus. and Profl. Woman, N.Y. Dist. Bus. and Profl. Women's Orgn., 1986. Mem. N.Y. Met. Am. Soc. Tng. and Devel., Nat. Speakers Assn., Princeton Area C. of C. (bd. dirs.), N.Y. Speakers Assn. Home and Office: Harris Devel Cons 834 Jamestown Rd Hightstown NJ 08520-5604

HARRIS, MICALYN SHAFER, lawyer; b. Chgo., Oct. 31, 1941; d. Erwin and Dorothy (Sampson) Shafer. AB, Wellesley Coll., 1963; JD, U. Chgo., 1966. Bar: Ill. 1966, Mo. 1967, U.S. Dist. Ct. (ea. dist.) Mo. 1967, U.S. Supreme Ct. 1972, U.S. Ct. Appeals (8th cir.) 1974, N.Y. 1981, N.J. 1988, U.S. Dist. Ct. N.J., U.S. Ct. Appeals (3rd cir.) 1993. Law clk. U.S. Dist. Ct., St. Louis, 1966-68; atty. The May Dept. Stores, St. Louis, 1968-70, Ralston-Purina Co., St. Louis, 1970-72; atty., asst. sec. Chromalloy Am. Corp., St. Louis, 1972-76; pvt. practice, St. Louis, 1976-78; internat. atty. CPC Internat., Inc., 1978-80; div. counsel CPC N.Am., 1980-84; asst. sec. CPC Internat., Englewood Cliffs, N.J., 1981-88; gen. counsel S.B. Thomas, Inc., 1983-87; corp. counsel, CPC Internat. Englewood Cliffs, N.J. 1984-88; assoc. counsel Weil, Gotshal & Manges, N.Y.C., 1988-90; pvt. practice, 1991; v.p., sec., gen. counsel Xian Corp., 1991—; arbitrator Am. Arbitration Assn., NYSE, NASD, The Aspen Ctr. for Conflict Mgmt. Mem. ABA (chair corp. counsel com., past chair subcom. counseling the mktg. function, securities law com., tender offers and proxy statements subcom., task force on computer software contracting, task force on bus. ethics of lawyers, task force on conflicts of interest), Ill. Bar Assn., N.Y. State Bar Assn. (securities regulation com. computer law com., task force on shrink-wrap licensing, sablaw), Bar Assn. Met. St. Louis (past chmn. TV com.), Mo. Bar Assn. (past chmn. internat. law com.), Am. Corp. Counsel Assn. N.J. (past bd. dirs. and chmn. bus. law com.), Am. Corp. Counsel Assn. N.Y. (mergers and acquisitions com., corp. law com.), N.J. Bar Assn., Computer Law Assn. Address: 625 N Monroe Ridgewood NJ 07450

HARRIS, NATHOLYN DALTON, food science educator, researcher; b. Calvary, Ga., Feb. 26, 1939; d. Martin Luther and Elvie (Clinard) Dalton; m. Ronald A. Harris, June 15, 1967; children: Rhonda Lynn, Scott Eaton. BS, Berry Coll., Mt. Berry, Ga., 1961; MS, Ohio State U., 1962; PhD, U. Wis., 1967. Instr. Berry Coll., 1962-63; rsch. asst. U. Wis., Madison, 1963-66, lectr., 1966-71; asst. prof. food sci. Fla. State U., Tallahassee, 1971-74, assoc. prof., 1975-86, prof., 1986—. Co-author: Meal Management, 1984; contbr. rsch. articles to profl. jours. Named an Outstanding Young Woman Am., 1961; Helena Chamberlain fellow Ohio State U., 1961. Mem. Inst. Food Technologists, So. Assn. Agrl. Scientists (exec. bd. 1974-83), Fla. Assn. Milk, Food and Environ. Scientists (exec. bd. 1988—), Southeastern Tchrs. Food and Nutrition (pres. 1983-84), Springtime Tallahassee, Sigma Xi (pres local chpt. 1985-86), Alpha Chi. Democrat. Baptist. Office: Fla State U 413 Sandels Bldg Tallahassee FL 32306

HARRIS, PAMELA MAIZE, journalism educator; b. Topeka, Aug. 14, 1952; d. Oliver Loren and Patricia (Kuhnke) Maize; m. Allen Dortch Harris, May 30, 1976. BA, So. Coll., 1975; MLS, Vanderbilt U., 1979; PhD, U. Tenn., 1994. English, speech and journalism tchr. Madison Acad., Nashville, 1975-79; English tchr., pub. info. officer Forest Lake Acad., Orlando, Fla., 1979-83; asst. editor Classic Chevy World Mag., 1983-84; mng. editor E. Tex. Farm and Ranch News, 1984; editor, corp. comm. Blue Cross and Blue Shield of Tenn., Chattanooga, 1986-88; assoc. prof. journalism So. Coll. of SDA, Collegedale, Tenn., 1989—; chair journalism and comm. dept. So. Coll. of SDA, Collegedale, 1994. Recipient East Tex. Addy and Praddy award, 1985, Award of Merit, Associated Ch. Press, 1991, Parternship Rsch. award Coun. for Advancement Support Edn., 1992, Mark Excellence award Soc. Profl. Journalist Dist. III, 1992, Grad. Rsch. award U. Tenn. Coll. Comm., 1992-93. Mem. Am. Soc. Info. Scientists, Assn. Educators Journalism and Mass Comm. (newspaper divsn. McDougal award 1993), Soc. Profl. Journalists, Pub. Rels. Soc. Am., Internat. Assn. Bus. Communicators, Beta Phi Mu, Phi Kappa Phi, Kappa Tau Alpha. Home: 5613 Landrum Dr Ooltewah TN 37363-8765

HARRIS, PATRICIA, architect, academic administrator; b. Springfield, Ohio, July 10, 1952; d. Albert Edward and Ople (Davis) H. BA, Wittenberg U., 1974; MArch, MIT, 1986. Cert. vocat. rehab. counselor, Ohio. Program dir. and coord., vocat. counselor Opportunities Industrialization Ctr., Springfield, Ohio, 1976-78; ednl. planner Montgomery County Bd. Edn., Dayton, Ohio, 1979-81; teaching asst. MIT, Cambridge, 1982-86; planner, intern in city mgmt. Town of Acton, Mass., 1986-87; designer Interact Inc., Acton, 1987-89; project mgr. Freelon Group, Inc., Triangle Park, N.C., 1990-93; coord. African-Am., dir. design camp N.C. State U., Raleigh, 1993—; owner PEH Architecture and Planning, Durham, N.C., 1994—; freelance designer and builder, N.C., Ohi, Mass., Calif., 1976—. Mem. Durham Planning Commn., 1992—. Recipient Presdl. award Pres. J. Carter, 1979; MIT faculty scholar, 1982-86, John P. Sprecher scholar, 1970-74. Mem. AIA, NAFE, Nat. Orgn. Minority Architects, Nat. Assn. Women in Edn., N.C. Sch. Sci. and Math Mentorship Program, Theta Alpha Phi. Office: NC State U Sch Design PO Box 7701 Raleigh NC 27695 also: PEH Architecture and Planning 1111 Virginia Ave Durham NC 27705

HARRIS, PATRICIA LYNN, accountant; b. Duarte, Calif., Mar. 17, 1967; d. Raymond Miles and Dolores Kathleen (Selan) McManaman; m. William Edmund Harris, Jr., Oct. 7, 1989. AS, Citrus Coll., Glendora, Calif., 1987; BS in Acctg., Calif. State Poly. U., 1993. Cert. mgmt. acct. Video dir. Wherehouse Entertainment, Glendora, 1985-87; sales assoc. May Co., West Covina, Calif., 1987-88; bookkeeper/acct. Carpet Town/Carpet City, West Covina, 1987-88, 92; acct. Soc. for the Advancement of Material and Process Engrng., West Covina, 1988, Aaron P. Sharma & Assocs., West Covina, 1988-89; acctg. mgr. Justice Bros., Inc., Duarte, Calif., 1989-91; rsch./teaching asst. Anwar Salimi, PhD, Pomona, Calif., 1993; owner W.E. Harris Acctg. Svc. Co., Glendora, 1990—. Writer, reporter news articles. Mem. Inst. Mgmt. Accts. (dir. membership acquisition Greater San Gabriel Valley chpt.). Republican. Roman Catholic.

HARRIS, PATRICIA SHEFFIELD, counselor; b. Donaldsville, Ga., Aug. 14, 1947; d. Robert Felton and Toy Irene (Smith) Sheffield; m. Leonard Moyer Harris, May 25, 1969; 1 child, Jeffrey Michael. BS, Northwestern State U., 1969. Lic. profl. counselor. Counselor Ctrl. La. State Hosp., Pineville, 1970-86, Rapides Chem. Dependency Svcs., Alexandria, La., 1986-92; case mgr. Rapides Indsl. Medicine, Alexandria, 1992-94; counselor Alexandria, 1992—; counselor Vernon Cmty. Action Coun., Leesville, La., 1992-94; program coord., counselor Avoyelles Outpatient Counseling Svc., 1994—. Bd. dirs. Crimestoppers, Inc., Alexandria, 1991-94, YWCA, Alexandria, 1994; mem. Women in Forum, Alexandria, 1993-94. Named Woman of Yr. Quota Club, 1974-75. Mem. ACA, La. Counseling Assn. (govt. rels. com., Svc. award 1991), La. Found. Against Sexual Assault, Substance Abuse Counselor Orgn. (pres. 1990-91), Exchangettes (pres. 1990-91, Woman of Yr. 1990-91). Republican. Episcopalian. Home: 6200 Mil Mar Blvd Alexandria LA 71302-2541

HARRIS, PEGGY BROWER, not-for-profit foundation administrator; b. Hamlet, N.C., Mar. 27, 1951; d. Glenwood Jr. and Elizabeth (Sledge) Brown; m. Cordell D. Harris, Dec. 28, 1974; 1 child, Candice Lyn. Cert. French lang., U. Paris-Sorbonne, 1972; BA in English, Va. State U., 1973; MPA, U. Pitts., 1978. Position classification specialist FBI, Washington, 1973-74; job analyst Carnegie-Mellon U., Pitts., 1975-76, mgr. compensation, 1976-78; tech. writer H.B. Maynard & Co., Pitts., 1978-83; dir. fin. mgmt. svc. Community Tech. Assistance Ctr., Pitts., 1983-94; COO Alternative Program Assocs., Pitts., 1994—. Treas. Miryam's Women's Shelter, 1987-93, pres., 1993—; v.p. YWCA Greater Pitts., 1991-93; mem. adv. coun. Pa. Human Rels. Commn., 1991—; pres. Jack and Jill of Am., Pitts., 1993—; treas. Alternative Program Assocs., 1993—; v.p. Oakland Cath. High Sch. Parent Tchr. Coun., 1993—. Democrat. Home: 1846 Atkinson Pl Pittsburgh PA 15235-2750

HARRIS, ROBERTA LUCAS, social worker; b. St. Louis, Nov. 13, 1916; d. Robert Joseph and Clara Louise (Mellor) Lucas; A.B., St. Louis U., 1955, M.S.W., 1964; m. William F. Sprengnether Jr., Aug. 21, 1937 (dec. 1951); children: Robert Lucas, Madelon Sprengnether Littlejohn, Ronald John; m. Victor B. Harris, Sept. 13, 1955 (dec. June 1960). Field instr. Sch. Social Work St. Louis U., 1967-70; chief of domestic rels. City of St. Louis, 1966-86. Dir., Citizens' Housing Coun., 1956-60; del. to Community Family Life Clinic, 1957; dir. Landmarks Assn., 1957-63; pres. Compton Heights Improvement Assn., 1973. NIMH grantee. Mem. Nat., Mo. assns. social workers, Assn. Family Conciliation Cts. (dir. 1968-86), Greater St. Louis Probation and Parole Assn. (sec. 1976), St. Louis U. Sch. Social Svc. Alumni Assn. (sec. 1973), LWV (dir. 1956-61), Wednesday Club. Methodist. Home: 3137 Longfellow Blvd Saint Louis MO 63104-1609

HARRIS, ROSALIE, psychotherapist, clinical counselor, Spanish language professional and multi-linguist, English as second language educator; b. N.Y.C., Dec. 9, 1937; d. Herman and Lilly (Hyman) H.; children: Attila, Steven. BA in Psychology, Hunter Coll., 1967, MA in ESL, 1973; MS in Community Mental Health, L.I. U., 1990. Advanced cert. in marriage and family counseling, Queens Coll. Adminstr., supr. N.Y.C. Bd. Edn., 1967-79, tchr., 1967-88; social worker Bur. Child Welfare, N.Y.C., 1967-69; lectr. Queens Coll., Flushing, N.Y., 1979-86; mental health counselor Copay, Great Neck, N.Y., 1989-90; marriage and family counselor Aspects, Ozone Park, N.Y., 1990—; bilingual counselor Copay, Great Neck, 1989-90; multi-lingual specialist, 1967—. Mem. Am. Assn. Marriage and Family Therapy (clin.), N.Y. State Assn. Marriage and Family Therapy (L.I. chpt.), N.Y. State Assn. Counseling and Devel., N.Y. State Assn. Tchrs., ESL, L.I. Mental Helath Counselors Assn., Kappa Delta Pi. Home and Office: 67 Bayview Ave Great Neck NY 11021-1731

HARRIS, ROSEMARY ANN, actress; b. Ashby, Eng., Sept. 19, 1930; d. Stafford Berkley and Enid (Campion) H.; m. Ellis Rabb, Dec. 4, 1959 (div. 1967); m. John Ehle, Oct. 21, 1967; 1 child, Jennifer. Student, Royal Acad. Dramatic Art, 1951-52; hon. doctorate, Smith Coll., 1969, Wake Forest U., 1978. Theater debut in Winter Sunshine, Bognar Regis, Eng., 1948; Broadway debut in Climate of Eden, N.Y.C., 1952; other theatrical appearances include Seven Year Itch, London, 1953, various Shakespearean and other roles, Bristol Old Vic, 1954-55, London Old Vic, 1955-56, 1963, 1964, Interlock, N.Y.C., 1957, The Disenchanted, N.Y.C., 1958; with Group 20 Players, Wellesley, Mass., in Pygmalion, Much Ado About Nothing, Man and Superman, Peter Pan, 1958-59; The Tumbler, N.Y.C., 1960; Assn. Producing Artists Repertory Company, U. Mich., 1962-63, 1964, N.Y.C., 1964-67; Chichester (Eng.) Festival, 1963, 64; A Streetcar Named Desire, Merchant of Venice, N.Y.C., 1973, The Royal Family, N.Y.C., 1975, The New York Idea (Obie award), Three Sisters, 1977; The Seagull, N.Y. Shakespeare Festival, 1981; All My Sons, London, 1981; Heartbreak House, London, 1982, N.Y.C., 1983; A Pack of Lies, 1984; Hay Fever, Broadway, 1985-86, ; film appearances include Beau Brummell, 1954, The Shiralle, 1956, A Flea in Her Ear, 1967, Camelot, The Boys from Brazil, 1978, The Ploughman's Lunch, 1983; To the Lighthouse (Locarno Film Festival award 1983), Crossing Delancy, 1988, Tom and Viv, 1994 (Acad. award nominee for Best Supporting Actress 1995); TV appearances include series the Chisholms, 1979-80, Holocaust, 1978 (Golden Globe award), Profiles in Courage, A Dickens Chronicle, Athens Where The Theater Began, Blithe Spirit, Strange Interlude, 1988, Great Appearances: Old Reliable, 1988. Recipient Antoinette Perry award, 1966, for A Lion in Winter, 1984, for A Pack of Lies; Vernon Rice award, 1962; Theatre World award, 1953; Delia Austrian Drama League award, 1967; Obie award, 1961, 65; Whitbread award, 1965-67; London Evening Standard award, 1969; Outer Circle Critics award, 1972; Drama Desk award, 1971, 72, 76; Emmy award, 1976; Golden Globe award, 1978. Mem. Actors Equity Assn., AFTRA, Screen Actors Guild. Address: care Paul Martino Internat Creative Mgmt 40 W 57th St New York NY 10019-4001*

HARRIS, ROXANNA MARIE, emergency room nurse; b. Kansas City, Kans., July 16, 1950; d. Alvin Thomas Harris and Emilia Frances (Scigliano) Harris-Douthat. Lic. paramedic, Med. Ctr., Independence, Mo., 1985; ADN, Fort Scott (Kans.) C.C., 1991. RN, Kans.; cert. ACLS, Pediatric Advanced Life Support instr. Paramedic Sac-Osage Hosp., Osceolo, Mo., 1988-91, Mercy Hosp., Fort Scott, 1991-92; nurse Am. Home Health, O.P., Kans., 1992-93; travel emergency rm. nurse St. Thomas, V.I., 1994; travel emergency rm. nurse Yukon Kuskokwin Delta Regional Hosp., Bethal, Alaska, 1993-94, emergency rm. and trauma flight bush nurse, 1994—; trauma flight bush nurse St. Thomas Hosp., Bush Hosp.; instr. pediat. advanced life support. CPR instr. Am. Heart Assn., Fort Scott, Kansas City, 1985-92. Mem. Emergency Rm. Nurses Assn.

HARRIS, RUBY LEE, realtor; b. Booneville, Miss., Mar. 5, 1939; d. Carl Jackson and Gladys (Downs) Hill; m. Lee Kelly Harris, Apr. 21, 1962; children: Lee Kelly Jr., Bradford William. Student, N.E. Miss. Jr. Coll., Booneville, 1957-58, U. Ala., Tuscaloosa, 1958-59. Lic. real estate agt., Calif. Agt. Forest E. Olson, El Toro, Calif., 1974-76, Coldwell Banker, Mission Viejo, Calif., 1976-78, Associated Realtors, Mission Viejo, 1978—. Mem. Children's Home Soc. Calif., Mission Viejo, 1985—, Boys and Girls Club Am., San Clemente, Calif., 1989-91, Capistrano, 1994—; mem. election com. Orange County, Mission Viejo, 1974—. Mem. Nat. Assn. Realtors, Calif. Assn. Realtors, Saddleback Valley Bd. Realtors (bd. dirs. 1989). Republican. Office: Associated Realtors 25350 Marguerite Pky Mission Viejo CA 92692-2908

HARRIS, RUTH ELLEN BEALL, nursing researcher, educator; b. Hamilton, Ohio, Jan. 6, 1947; d. F. Wayne and Edythe Edna (Gerlach) Beall; m. Philip Edwin Harris, Sept. 12, 1970; children: Philip Michael, Robert Scott, Mark Edward, Lauren Elizabeth. Diploma, Fairview Park Hosp. Sch. Nsg., 1968; BA, BS, Baldwin-Wallace Coll., 1970; BS, MS in Nursing, U. Colo., Denver, 1973, 75; PhD, NYU, 1985. RN, N.Y., N.J. Critical care nurse various hosps., N.Y. and N.J.; asst. clin. prof. nursing UCLA, 1976-78;

asst. prof. nursing Adelphi U., 1978-85; malpractice cons., 1976—; assoc. prof. Seton Hall U. Coll. Nursing, South Orange, N.J., 1986—; vis. prof. Sch. Nursing Boston U., 1986; staff nurse various nursing registries; rsch. asst. VA Hosp., L.A., 1980-81; mem. coun. on dialysis and transplantation Nat. Kidney Found., 1979-89; cons., presenter, rschr., speaker in field. Co-editor Scholarly Inquiry for Nursing Practice: An Internat. Jour.; contbr. articles to profl. publs. Probation counselor Jefferson County Ct., Denver, 1974-767; vol. inoculation program ARC, L.A., 1976; group counselor Sherman Oaks Luth. Ch., 1976-78; tchr. CPR classes Am. Heart Assn., 1976-79. Grantee HEW, 1974-75, Adelphi U., 1980, 81, 84, Am. Heart Assn., 1983, F.A. Davis/Nat. League Nursing, 1983, Seton Hall U., 1992, 93; rsch. fellow Jersey Shore Heart Inst., 1990-92. Mem. ANA (coun. nurse researchers 1979), N.J. State Nurses Assn., AACN (bd. dirs. N.Y.C. chpt. 1979-85, mem. various coms.), Am. Herat Assn. (sci. coun. on nursing 1988—, coun. on nursing practice N.Y.C. chpt. 1979-91, merit award 1978, 83), Sigma Theta Tau, Alpha Tau Delta (faculty advisor Gamma Tau chpt. 1978-79, Excellence in Rsch. award 1994). Home: 1236 Oak Rd Manasquan NJ 08736-2010

HARRIS, SHELLEY FOLLANSBEE, contracts administrator; b. Quantico, Va., Oct. 20; d. Lawrence Peyton and June Maynard (Trout) H. BS in Fine Arts, Towson State U., 1973. Surgeon's asst. Drs. Bennett, Johnson & Eaton, P.A., Balt., 1979-82; pers. adminstr., human resources specialist Legent Assocs., Vienna, Va., 1983-88; pers. cons. Snelling & Snelling, Vienna, 1988-89; acct. exec. Forbes Assocs., Inc., Annandale, Va., 1989-90; spl. projects adminstr. for dep. gen. counsel, contracts and legal divsn. Electronic Data Systems Corp., Herndon, Va., 1991—. Vol. EDS Mentor Program, In Touch-EDS Friends of Viet Nam Vets; team capt. Walk for Wealth; cmty. rels. ambassador Bowl for Bus. Jr. Achievement; active Holiday LINCS family project, Holiday 1994. Recipient regional awards for paintings, regional and nat. awards for sales and mktg., also awards for community contbns. Mem. Artist's Equity. Episcopalian. Home: 851 Dogwood Ct Herndon VA 22070-5446

HARRIS, STACY, print and broadcast journalist; b. Mpls.; d. LLoyd and Francine H. Student, Coll. of Emporia, Kans., 1969, Vanderbilt U., 1972; BA, U. Md., 1973. Regular contbr. Country Song Roundup, Derby, Conn., 1976-92; interim Nashville editor Country Song Roundup, Derby, 1978-79, Newsweek mag., N.Y.C., 1983—; writer Sta. ABC Radio News, N.Y.C., 1986—, SDX Gridiron Show, Nashville, 1990—. Author: (children's books) Comedians of Country Music, 1978, The Carter Family, 1978, The Best of Country, 1993; editor Country Spirit 1990—; contbg. author, rschr. Country Music Stars and the Supernatural, 1978-79; contbg. editor Inside Country Music, 1981-83; columnist Stacy on Line, for Country on Line, Internet, 1995—; contbr. articles to Nashville Banner, US, New Woman, Entertainment Weekly and other publs. Arbitrator Better Bus. Bur., Nashville, 1988. Recipient Voice of Democracy award VFW, 1969, Outstanding Teenager award, 1970. Mem. Nat. Entertainment Jounalists Assn. (pres. 1989), Country Music Assn., Soc. Profl. Journalists, Nat. Press Club, Music Country PC Users Group, Williamson County Human Assn. (now Animaland) (vol. 1988—), Am. Mensa Ltd. Home and Office: The Windsor Tower 4215 Harding Rd Nashville TN 37205-2017

HARRIS, SUSAN, television producer; b. Mt. Vernon, N.Y.; m. Paul Junger Witt. Dir. various episodes Soap, All in the Family, Then Came Bronson; creator, writer, co-exec. producer The Golden Girls, 1985-92 (Emmy awards for best comedy series, Acad. Television Arts and Scis, 1986, 1987), Good and Evil, 1991, Nurses, 1991-94, Golden Palace, 1992-93; prodn. asst. (film) Heart and Souls, 1993. Office: Witt/Thomas/Harris Prodns Bldg 35 4th Fl 1438 N Gower St Los Angeles CA 90028*

HARRIS, SUSAN FOX, legal assistant; b. Uniontown, Pa., June 17, 1955; d. James Ira Sr. and Elizabeth Ann (Kirk) Fox; m. William Wayne Harris, Mar. 7, 1987. BS in Journ., W.Va. U., 1977; Cert. Completion, Nat. Ctr. for Paralegal Tng., Atlanta, 1977. Legal asst. Jackson, Kelly, Holt & O'Farrell, Charleston, W.Va., 1978-79, Dennis, Corry, Webb & Carlock, Atlanta, 1979-84, Dennis, Corry, Porter & Thornton, Atlanta, 1984-89, Ga.-Pacific Corp., Atlanta, 1989—. Bd. dirs. Met. Atlanta Coun. on Alcohol and Drugs, 1991-92, treas., 1992-93, pres., 1993-94; bd. dirs. DeKalb Rape Crisis Ctr., 1994—; chmn., mem. devel. Jr. League of DeKalb County, Decatur, Ga., 1989-90, cmty. rsch. chmn., 1990-91, corres. sec., 1991-92, pres.-elect, 1994—. Mem. Ga. Assn. Legal Assts. (newsletter asst. 1980-81, mem. chmn. 1981-82), Embroiderers Guild of Am., Atlanta Needlepoint Guild (sec. 1992-93, chmn. cmty. projects), Atlanta Jaguar Soc., High Mus. of Art. Republican. Presbyterian. Home: 210 Woodcliff Dr Dunwoody GA 30350-3158 Office: Georgia-Pacific Corp 133 Peachtree St Atlanta GA 30303

HARRIS, SUSAN LOUISE, financial services company executive. AB, UCLA, 1978; JD, U. So. Calif., 1981. Bar: Calif. 1981. Assoc. Lillick, McHose & Charles, 1981-85; v.p., assoc. gen. counsel, sec. SunAmerica, Inc., L.A., 1985—. Office: SunAmerica Inc 1 SunAmerica Ctr Los Angeles CA 90067-6022

HARRIS, SISTER TERESA L., state nursing administrator; b. Newark, Aug. 29, 1923; d. Carl Alvin and Agnes (Herring) H. Grad. RN, St. Mary's Hosp. Sch. Nursing, Passaic, N.J., 1944; BSN, Seton Hall U., 1958; MS, St. Louis U., 1963. V.p. nursing Hackensack (N.J.) Med. Ctr.; v.p. nursing, dir. Sch. of Nursing St. Elizabeth (N.J.) Hosp.; exec. dir. Bd. of Nursing, State of N.J., Newark. Mem. ANA, N.J. State Nurses Assn. (practice com. chair, treas.), Nat. League for Nursing, Nat. Coun. State Bds. Nursing (nurse practice and edn. com., dir. Area IV), Sigma Theta Tau. Office: NJ Bd Nursing 124 Halsey St Elizabeth NJ 07202

HARRIS, TERRY LYNN, finance director; b. San Diego, Oct. 8, 1961; d. Robert Anthony Freeman and Patricia Gail (Gibson) Savoroski; m. Robert Martin Harris, June 6, 1981 (div. 1987). BBA, San Diego State U., 1992. Fin. analyst Coca-Cola Bottling Co., San Diego, 1981-85; dir. fin. Mesa Distbn. Co., Inc., San Diego, 1985—. Republican.

HARRIS, VALERIE COLEMAN, office assistant; b. King William, Va., June 5, 1957; d. James Edward Sr. and Maude Ellen (Taylor) Coleman; m. Ronald Stevenson Harris Sr., Aug. 1, 1981; 1 child, Ronald Steven Harris Jr. Student, Va. Commonwealth U., 1982-88, J. Sargeant Rey Coll., 1978-86. Adminstr. Med. Coll. Va., Richmond, 1981-90; office asst. CSX Corp., Richmond, 1991—. Mem. NAFE. Home: 3404 Hollow Ridge Ct Chesterfield VA 23832-8560

HARRIS, VERA EVELYN, personnel recruiting and search firm executive; b. Watson, Sask., Can., Jan. 11, 1932; came to U.S., 1957; d. Timothy and Margaret (Popoff) H.; student U. B.C. (Can.), Vancouver; children—Colin Clifford Graham, Barbara Cusimano Page. Office mgr. Keglers, Inc., Morgan City, La., 1964-67; office mgr., acct. John L. Hopper & Assos., New Orleans, 1967-71; office mgr. Elite Homes, Inc., Metairie, La., 1971-73; comptroller Le Pavillon Hotel, New Orleans, 1973-74; controller Waguespack-Pratt, Inc., New Orleans, 1974-76; adminstrv. controller Sizzler Family Steak Houses of So. La., Inc., Metairie, 1976-79; dir. adminstrn. Sunbelt, Inc., New Orleans, 1979-82, sec., dir., 1980—; exec. v.p. Corp. Cons., Inc., 1980-83, pres., 1984-86; pres. Harris Personnel Resources, Arlington, Tex., 1986—, Harris Enterprises, Arlington, 1986—, Harris Personnel Resources Health Staff, Arlington, 1990—; exec. dir. Nat. Sizzler Franchise Assn., 1976-79. Mem. NAFE, Am. Bus. Women's Assn., La. Assn. Personnel Consultants (treas. 1985-86). Home: 3110 Waterside Dr Arlington TX 76012-2123 Office: Harris Personnel Resources 2201 N Collins St Ste 260 Arlington TX 76011-2653

HARRIS-OFFUTT, ROSALYN MARIE, psychotherapist, counselor, nurse anesthetist, educator; b. Memphis; d. Roscoe Henry and Irene Elnora (Blake) Harris; 1 child, Christopher Joseph. R.N., St. Joseph Catholic Sch. Nursing, Flint, Mich., 1965; B.S. in Wholistic Health Scis., Columbia-Pacific U., 1984, postgrad., 1985—. RN; cert. nurse in anesthesia; nat. cert. counselor; cert. psychiat. nursing Kalamazoo State Hosp.; lic practicing counselor, N.C. Staff nurse anesthetist, clin. instr. Cleve. Clinic Found., 1981-82; pvt. practice psychiat. nursing and counseling; Assoc. Counselor in Human Services, Shaker Heights, Ohio, 1982-84; ind. contractor anesthesia Paul Scott & Assocs., Cleve., 1984, Via Triad Anesthesia Assocs., Thomasville, N.C., 1984-85; sec. Cons., Psychology and Counseling, P.A., pvt. practice psychiat. nursing and counseling, Greensboro, N.C., 1984-86, pvt. practice psychiat. nursing, counseling and psychotherapy UNA Psychol. Assocs., 1986—, staff cons. Charter Hills Psychiat. Hosp., 1991—; cons. Am. Assn. Nursing Anesthetist Peer Adv. Group on Addictive Disease. Co-sponsor adolescent group Jack and Jills of Am., Inc., Bloomfield Hills, Mich., 1975; co-sponsor Youth of Unity Ctr., Cleveland Heights, Ohio, 1982-84; vol. chmn. hospitality Old Greensboro Preservation Soc., 1985; bd. dirs. Urban League, Pontiac, Mich., 1972; apptd. mem. gov's. coun. on alcohol and other drug abuse State of N.C., 1989—, gov's. coun. women's issues of addiction, 1991—; apptd. advisor to assoc. clin., med. dir. Ctr. for Substance Abuse Prevention, Dept. Health and Human Svcs. U.S., 1991—, nat. speakers bureau, 1991—, cons.; apptd. legis. com., mental health study commn. on child and adolescent substance abuse State of N.C., 1992—; lay min. United Meth. Ch.; mem. Triad United Meth. Native Am. Mission in Christ. Columbia-Pacific U. scholar, 1983. Contbr. chpt. to book, also articles and columns in health field. Fellow Soc. Preventitive Nutritionists; mem. Am. Assn. Profl. Hypnotherapists (registered profl. hypnotherapists, adv. bd.), Am. Assn. Nurse Anesthetists (cert.), Am. Assn. Counseling and Devel., Am. Assn. Clin. Hypnotists, Am. Assn. Wholistic Practitioners, Am. Nurse Hypnotherapy Assn. (state pres. 1992—), Am. Nurse Assn., Negro Bus. and Profl. Women Inc. (v.p., parliamentarian 1961-83), Oakland County Council Black Nurses (v.p. 1970-74), Zeta Phi Beta (Nu Xi Zeta chpt. 2d antibasilevs 1992-93). Republican. Avocations: music; nature; reading; Egyptian history; metaphysics. Office: UNA Psychol Assocs Ste 371 620 S Elm St Greensboro NC 27406

HARRISON, ANNA JANE, chemist, educator; b. Benton City, Mo., Dec. 23, 1912; d. Albert S.J. and Mary (Jones) H. Student, Lindenwood Coll., 1929-31, L.H.D. (hon.), 1977; A.B., U. Mo., 1933, B.S., 1935, M.A., 1937, Ph.D., 1940, D.Sc. (hon.), 1983; D.Sc. (hon.), Tulane U., 1975, Smith Coll., 1975, Williams Coll., 1978, Am. Internat. Coll., 1978, Vincennes U., 1978, Lehigh U., 1979, Hood Coll., 1979, Hartford U., 1979, Worcester Poly. Inst., 1979, Suffolk U., 1979, Eastern Mich. U., 1983, Russell Sage Coll., 1984, Mt. Holyoke Coll., 1984, Mills Coll., 1985; L.H.D. (hon.), Emmanuel Coll., 1983; D.H.L., St. Joseph Coll., 1985, Elms Coll., 1985, R.I. Coll., 1990. Instr. chemistry Newcomb Coll., 1940-42, asst. prof., 1942-45; asst. prof. chemistry Mt. Holyoke Coll., 1945-47, asso. prof., 1947-50, prof., 1950-76, prof. emeritus, 1979—, chmn. dept., 1960-66, William R. Kenan, Jr. prof., 1976-79; Mem. Nat. Sci. Bd., 1972-78; Disting. Vis. prof. U.S. Naval Acad., 1980. Author: (textbook with Edwin S. Weaver) Chemistry: A Search to Understand, 1989; contbr. articles to profl. jours. Recipient Frank Forrest award Am. Ceramic Soc., 1949; James Flack Norris award in chem. edn. Northeastern sect. Am. Chem. Soc., 1977; AAUW Sarah Berliner fellow Cambridge U., Eng., 1952-53; Am. Chem. Soc. Petroleum Research Fund Internat. fellow NRC Can., 1959-60; recipient Coll. Chemistry Tchr. award Mfg. Chemists Assn., 1969. Mem. AAAS (dir. 1979-85, pres. 1983, chmn. bd. 1984-85), Am. Chem. Soc. (chmn. divsn. chem. edn. 1971, pres. 1978, dir. 1976-79, award in chem. edn. 1982), Internat. Union Pure and Applied Chemistry (U.S. nat. com. 1978-81), Vols. in Tech. Assistance (bd. dirs. 1990-94), Sigma Xi (bd. dirs. 1988-91). Address: 14 Ashfield Ln South Hadley MA 01075-1321

HARRISON, BETTY CAROLYN COOK, vocational educator, administrator; b. Cale, Ark., Jan. 11, 1939; d. Denver G. and Minnie (Haddox) Cook; m. David B. Harrison, Dec. 31, 1956; children: Jerry David, Phyllis Lynley. BSE, Henderson State Tchrs. Coll., Arkadelphia, Ark., 1961; MS, U. Ark., 1971; PhD, Tex. Agrl. and Mech. U., 1975. Tchr. secondary schs., McCrory, Ark., 1962-64, Taylor, Ark., 1964-69, Shongaloo, La., 1969-73, Minden, La., 1974-76, 77-80; adminstrv. intern La. Dept. Edn., 1974; cooperating tchr., supr. student tchrs. Grambling (La.) State U., 1974-76, La. Tech. U., Ruston, 1974-76, 78-80; asst. prof. vocat. edn. Va. Poly. Inst. and State U., Blacksburg, 1976-77; asst. prof. vocat. edn. Coll. Agr., La. State U., Baton Rouge, 1980-85, assoc. prof. Sch. Vocat. Edn., 1985-90, prof. vocat. edn., 1990—, sect. leader home econs. edn., 1982-85, head dept. home econs. edn. and bus. edn., 1985-87, dir. La. Job Link Ctr., 1988-91; dir. Sch. of Vocat. Edn., 1993-94, grants U.S. Office of Edn., La. Dept. of Edn., U.S. Dept. of Labor-Job Tng. Ptnrship. Act, La. Dept. of Employment and Tng., Va. Dept. of Edn.; mem. La. State U. Grad. Coun., 1990—, courses and curriculum sch. and coll., 1989-92. Contbr. articles to profl. jours. HEW fellow, 1973; grantee Future Homemakers Am., 1956, Coll. Acads., 1956, Ark. Edn. Assn., 1966-69, Internat. Paper Co., 1966-68, La. Dept. Edn., 1972. Mem. Assn. Tng. Devel. (v.p. communication 1991-92, sec. 1993-94), Am. Vocat. Assn. (regional pub. rels. voting del.), Nat. Assn. Vocat. Spl. Needs Personnel, Am. Vocat. Edn. Rsch. Assn., Am. Home Econs. Assn., La. Home Econs. Assn. (bd. dirs., pres.-elect), La. Vocat. Assn. (bd. dirs.), La. Assn. Vocat. Home Econs. Tchrs. (pres.), Nat. Assn. Vocat. Home Econs. Tchrs., Nat. Assn. Vocat. Home Econs. Tchr. Educators (newsletter editor), Home Econs. Edn. Assn. (regional dir., nat. v.p., editor and chair publs. 1987-93), NEA (nat. assembly del.), Family Relations Council La. (edn. chmn. officer), Phi Delta Kappa, Delta Kappa Gamma (chpt. v.p., rsch. chair 1978-86), Gamma Sigma Delta (historian, sec., treas. 1984-93). Democrat. Baptist. Home: 2100 College Dr 157 Baton Rouge LA 70808-1810 Office: La State U Sch Vocat Edn Baton Rouge LA 70803

HARRISON, CANDACE J., physician assistant; b. Reno, June 19, 1949; d. Robert George and Gleva T. (Trevenen) H. BA, Ind. U., 1971; M in Health Sys. Leadership, U. San Francisco, 1989. Cert. physician asst. Physician asst. Stanislaus County Family Practice Residency, Modesto, Calif., 1978-81, Merced (Calif.) County, 1981-92; clinic coord., physician asst. John C. Fremont Med. Clinic, Mariposa, Calif., 1992—; advisor Area Health Edn. Com., Modesto, 1980-85, Mariposa (Calif.) Peri-natal Coun., 1992—. Bd. dirs. New Directions for Women, Modesto, 1979-81; pres., bd. dirs. YMCA Rehab. Com., Modesto, 1980-81. Recipient Women Helping Women award Soroptimist Internat., 1994. Fellow Am. Acad. Physician Asst., Calif. Assn. Physician Asst. Office: John C Fremont Med Clinic 5186 Hospital Rd Mariposa CA 95338-9524

HARRISON, CAROLE ALBERTA, museum curator, restaurateur, civic worker; b. Dayton, Ohio, Jan. 16, 1942; d. Chester Arthur and Mildred Irene (Focke) Shaw; student U. Dayton, 1959-60, U. Colo., 1960-61; children: Amelia Holmes, Ann Elizabeth, Abigail Shaw. With Council for Pub. TV, Channel 6, Inc., Denver, 1972-78, Hist. Denver, Inc., 1973-93; owner Harrison Enterprises, Inc., 1982—; general mgr. The Denver Club, The Denver Club; dir. devel. Sewall Rehab. Center, Denver, 1979-80; exec. v.p. Marilyn Van Derbur Motivational Inst., Inc., 1980-82. Bd. dirs. Center for Public Issues, Denver, 1979-82, Passages, 1982-88, Hall of Life, 1981-83, Historic Denver, 1982-84, Denver Firefighters Mus., 1979—; bd. dirs. KRMA-TV Vols., 1970—, pres., 1973-74; founder Com. for Support of Arts, Denver, 1978-79; chmn. Graland Country Day Sch. Auction, 1979, 80, Channel 6 Auction, 1971, 72, Colo. Acad. Auction, 1980, The Hundred Most Interesting Women in Denver, 1988; mem. Denver Mayor's Task Force on Infrastructure Fin., 1988-90; bd. dirs. Met. Denver and Colo. Conv. and Visitors Bur. Named Outstanding Bus. Woman of the Yr. Colo. Woman's C. of C., 1991. Mem. Leadership Denver Alumni Assn. (dir. 1980-82), Colo. Restaurant Assn., Denver C. of C. (govt. relations com. 1983-87, state local affairs council 1987-88, urban affairs), Women's Forum. Home: 2450 E 5th Ave Denver CO 80206-4245 Office: 55 17th St Ste 3700 Denver CO 80202

HARRISON, CHRISTINE DELANE, educational administrator; b. Dearborn, Mich., July 22, 1947; d. Walter Frederick and Marguerite Elaine (Champagne) Hancock; m. Charles Richard Bashawaty, Aug. 31, 1968 (div. 1972); 1 child, Brett Charles; m. Andrew David Harrison, June 14, 1980; 1 child, Andrew David, II. BS, Ea. Mich. U., 1969. Cert. early elem. tchr., Mich. Tchr. Westland Schs., Mich., 1969-71, Dept. Army, Ansbach, Germany, 1971-72; prin. sec. chemistry dept. U. Mich., Ann Arbor, 1973-78; word processing mgr. Great Copy Co., Ann Arbor, 1978-79; dir., v.p. Great Lakes Sch., Madison Heights, Mich., 1979-92; bd. dirs., pub. rels. dir., Good Herbs, Inc., 1992—. Editor: Thorne's Guide to Herbal Extracts, 1992, A Practical Guide to Herbal Extracts, 1995; editorial asst. Herbal Extracts, 1984; Bull. of Thermodynamics and Thermochemistry, 1973-78. Bd. dirs. Perry Nursery Sch., Ann Arbor, 1976-77. Recipient Prodn. award and Dedication award Los Feliz Apple Sch. Mem. Mich. Assn. for Supervision and Curriculum Devel., Nat. Trust for Hist. Preservation, Clawson C. of C., Greenpeace, Sierra Club. Avocations: reading, bicycling, aerobics, sailing. Office: Good Herbs Inc 1875 Woodslee Troy MI 48083

HARRISON, DENISE LEE, editor; b. Washington, Aug. 3, 1960; d. David Ellis and Marlene Ann (Robertson) Lee; m. Charles Robert Harrison Jr., June 29, 1985. BA, U. Md., 1983; postgrad., Johns Hopkins U., 1990—. Editor Johns Hopkins U., Balt., 1986—, sr. publs. editor, 1990-94; writing intern TRAC, Washington, 1983; writing intern adviser Inst. Internat. Programs, Sch. Hygiene and Pub. Health Johns Hopkins U., 1986-94, internat. visitor and workship coord. Book reviewer The Daily Record Newspaper, 1986. English tutor U. Md., Catonsville, 1980-83; newsletter editor Kensington Improvement Assn., Balt., 1991—. Mem. Johns Hopkins Women's Forum, Omicron Delta Kappa (sec. 1981), Sigma Pi Tau (sec. 1982). Office: Johns Hopkins U Ctr Human Nutrition Sch Hygiene & Pub Health 615 N Wolfe St Baltimore MD 21205-2179

HARRISON, DOROTHY GORDY, infosystems specialist; b. Pittsfield, Mass., Jan. 1, 1939. B.A. in Chemistry, U. N.C., Greensboro, 1960; Cert. Info. Sci., Ga. Inst. Tech., 1962, MS in Info./Computer Sci., Indsl. Mgmt. and Engring., 1965; Cert. Physics, Math., Wake Forest U., 1964; MLn in Adminstrn., Emory U., 1973. With tech. library and info. services Cone Mills Research and Devel., Greensboro, N.C., 1960-63; chmn. dept. physics Pittsfield High Sch., Mass., 1964; with sci. div. Pittsfield, Pub. Schs., 1964; research asst. Price Gilbert Meml. Library Ga. Inst. Tech., Atlanta, 1964-66, Engring. Expt. Sta., 1965-66; research assoc. Sch. Info. and Computer Sci., 1967; info. scientist and projects dir. Office Computing Activities, U. Ga., Athens, 1971-73; cons. info./computer sci. and adminstrn., 1962—; dir. computer info. services Clarke County, Ga., 1983-93, project dir., 1993—; bd. dirs. Ga. Govt. Mgmt. Info. Scis., State Archives Athens Vocat.-Tech. Sch., Ga., pres. bd. dirs. Internat. Govt. Mgmt. Info. Scis. NSF scholar, 1965-66; NSF fellow 1964-65; NSF grantee 1964; recipient citation Recording for the Blind, 1968-70, Young Info./Computer Scientist award, 1969, Outstanding Tchr. award, 1964; named Young Woman Engr. of Yr., 1964. Mem. Beta Phi Mu.

HARRISON, ELLEN KROLL, lawyer; b. East Orange, N.J., Mar. 2, 1946; d. William and Harriet (Herman) Kroll; m. Donald Harrison, 1970; children: Matthew, Margaret. BA, U. Mich., 1968; JD, Harvard U., 1971. Bar: D.C., 1973, U.S. Tax Ct., 1981, U.S. Supreme Ct. Ptnr. Morgan, Lewis & Bockius, Washington; adj. prof. Georgetown Law Sch., Washington, 1987—. Mem. ABA (subcom. chair), ACTEC, D.C. Estate Planning Coun., Phi Beta Kappa. Democrat. Home: 5205 Portsmouth Rd Bethesda MD 20816-2928 Office: Morgan Lewis & Bockius 1800 M St NW Washington DC 20036-5869

HARRISON, FAYE VENETIA, anthropologist, educator; b. Norfolk, Va., Nov. 25, 1951; d. James and Odelia Blount (Harper) H.; m. William Louis Conwill, May 17, 1980; children: Giles, L. Mondlane, Justin. AB, Brown U., 1974; MA, Stanford U., 1977, PhD, 1982. Asst. prof. U. Louisville, 1983-89; assoc. prof. U. Tenn., Knoxville, 1989—. Assoc. editor Urban Anthropology, 1992—; cons. editor Women and Aging, 1990—, Identities: Global Studies of Culture and Power, 1992—; editor: Decolonizing Anthropology, 1991, Black Folks in Cities Here and There, 1988; contbr. articles to profl. jours. Organizer Ky. Rainbow Coalition, Louisville, 1988-89; mem. Black Women Organized for Power, Louisville, 1984-86, Alliance Against Women's Oppression, Louisville, 1988-89. Recipient Cert. of Merit, Phi Beta Kappa, 1993; Ford Found. fellow, 1987-88. Mem. Assn. Black Anthropologists (pres. 1989-91), Internat. Union Anthrop. and Ethnol. Scis. (co-chair commn. on women 1993—0. Office: U Tenn Dept Anthropology South Stadium Hall Knoxville TN 37996-0720

HARRISON, JAN, artist; b. West Palm Beach, Fla., Dec. 18, 1944; d. Oskar Roy Harrison and Dorothy (Wilson) Oliphant. BFA, U. Ga., 1967; MA in Art, San Jose State U., 1976. Visiting asst. prof. painting Antioch Coll., Yellow Springs, Ohio, 1986-87; membership dir. Women's Studio Workshop, Rosendale, N.Y., 1992-93; leader workshops, lectr. on painting various univs., own studio, Women's Studio Workshop, N.Y., 1992—; asst. dir. for design SUNY, New Paltz, 1993—. Solo exhbns. include Emerging Talent, Wright State U., Dayton, Ohio, 1982, A Perilous Eden, Chidlaw Gallery Art Acad. Cin., 1988, Jan Harrison, Sunnen Gallery, N.Y.C., 1992, Animal Tongues, Women's Studio Workshop, Rosendale, N.Y., 1993; group exhbns. include Cin. Art Mus., 1984, Chgo. Internat. Art Expo., Navy Pier, 1988-90, The Definitive Am. Contemporary Quilt, travelling exhbn. through 14 states Bernice Steinbaum Gallery, N.Y.C., 1990-94; over 100 exhbns. in all. Mem. artists' adv. bd. Contemporary Arts Ctr., Cin., 1987-88; panel mem. for selection of art fellowships Ohio Arts Coun., 1991; activist for animal rights various orgns., 1984—. Recipient Art fellowship Ohio Arts Coun., Columbus, 1983, 85, 88; grantee: Ohio Arts Coun., 1986, Summerfair, 1988. Mem. Women's Studio Workshop (membership dir. 1992-93), United Univ. Profls. Democrat. Studio: 34 Hunter St Kingston NY 12401

HARRISON, JEANETTE KEMCHICK, business executive; b. Point Pleasant, N.J., Sept. 2, 1954; d. Patrick John and Gloria E. (Stensland) Kemchick; m. Roger Anthony Piantadosi, Aug. 4, 1975 (div. Mar. 1982); m. John G. Harrison, Mar. 1989. BA in Sociology magna cum laude, Am. U., 1977, MEd, 1979; postgrad., Va. Poly. Inst. and State U., 1980, George Washington U., 1981, UCLA Extension, 1983; D in Pub. Adminstrn. U. So. Calif., 1994. Dir. fin. aid Am. U., Washington, 1977-81; Revson fellow to Rep. Patricia Schroeder, Washington, 1981-82; dir. fed. and state rels. Systems Rsch., Inc., Washington, 1981-84; v.p. mktg. Sigma Systems, Inc., L.A., 1982-84; v.p. The Wyndgate Group, Sacramento, 1984-89; v.p. adminstrn. Noel/Levitz Ctrs., Inc., Coralville, Iowa, 1989-90; ind. cons., 1990-91; coord. projects Iowa Program Assistive Tech., 1991-93; dir. strategic planning and bus. devel. Info. Tech. divsn. Nat. Computer Sys., 1992-93, v.p. edn. strategic planning and bus. sys., 1993—. Recipient Meritorious Svc. award Am. U., 1977, 80; Gen. U. scholar, 1975-76, Mathas scholar, 1975-77; Charles Revson fellow, 1981-82. Mem. Nat. Assn. Women Deans, Adminstrs. and Counselors (chmn. div. govt./agy. spl. programs 1984). Democrat. Roman Catholic. Home: 5345 E McLellan Rd #35 Mesa AZ 85205

HARRISON, JUDY BAKER, physician; b. Albertville, Ala., Mar. 27, 1951; d. Leonard Glenn and Edna Lenora (Marlin) Baker; m. Jeffrey Harrison, July 28, 1974; children: Josh William, Jason Douglas. BS, U. Ala., 1973; MD, U. Fla., 1977. Diplomate Am. Bd. Family Practice, Am. Bd. Emergency Medicine. Intern and resident in family medicine Naval Hosp., Jax, Fla., 1977-80, staff physician emergency medicine, ambulatory care dept., 1980-82, staff physician emergency dept., 1994—; mem. staff emergency dept. St. Augustine (Fla.) Gen. Hosp., 1982-85; staff physician Family Practice Assocs., Orange Park, Fla., 1985-89, 94—; dir. emergency dept. Naval Hosp., Lemoore, Calif., 1989-91; staff physician emergency dept. Coronado (Calif.) Hosp., 1991-94, Paradise Valley Hosp., National City, Calif., 1991-94, Scripps Hosp. East County, San Diego, 1991-94. Lt. comdr. USNR, 1977-82. Fellow Am. Acad. Family Physicians; mem. AMA, Am. Coll. Emergency Physicians, Am. Assn. Physician Specialists. Republican. Methodist. Office: Family Practice Assocs 1594 Kingsley Ave Orange Park FL 32073

HARRISON, LEISA DIONE, systems administrator; b. L.A., June 16, 1962; d. Alphonse Manfred and Willie Mae (Mickels) H. BS in Computer Sci., Calif. State U., Northridge, 1986; cert. vocat. tng., UCLA, Long Beach, 1987; postgrad., El Camino Coll., Torrance, Calif, 1988. CAD application engr. Xerox Corp., El Segundo, Calif., 1986-89; CAD system adminstr., staff engr. Hughes Aircraft Co., El Segundo, 1989—; CAD cons. CDM and Assocs., Fox Hills, Calif., 1988-90; instr. basic programming L.A. Coun. Black Profl. Engrs., Inglewood, Calif., 1986-89. Mem. NAFE, L.A. Coun. Black Profl. Engrs. (v.p. programs 1989-90, chmn. computer lab. 1987-89). Democrat. Home: 415 Tamarack Ave # 1 Inglewood CA 90301 Office: Hughes Aircraft Co PO Box 92919 Los Angeles CA 90009-2919

HARRISON, LOIS SMITH, hospital executive, educator; b. Frederick, Md., May 13, 1924; d. Richard Paul and Henrietta Foust (Menges) S.; m. Richard Lee Harrison, June 23, 1951; children: Elizabeth Lee Boyce, Margaret Louise Wade, Richard Paul. BA, Hood Coll., 1945, DHL (hon.), 1993; HHd (hon.), Columbia U., 1946; LHD (hon.), Hood Coll., 1993. Counselor CCNY, 1945-46; founding adminstr., counselor, instr. psychology and sociology Hagerstown (Md.) Jr. Coll., 1946-51, registrar, 1946-51, 53-54, instr. psychology and orienta, 1954-56; registrar, instr. psychology, Balt. Jr. Coll., 1951-54; bus. mgr., acct. for pvt. med. practice Hagerstown, 1953—;

trustee Washington County Hosp., Hagerstown, 1975—; chmn. bd. Washington County Hosp., 1986—; bd. dirs. Home Fed. Savs. Bank, Hagerstown, 1983—; speaker ednl. panels, convs. hosp. panels and seminars. Author: The Church Woman, 1960-65. Trustee Hood Coll., Frederick, 1972—, chmn. bd., 1979—; mem. Md. Gov.'s Commn. to Study Structure and Ednl. Devel. Commn., 1971-75; pres. Washington County Coun. Ch. Women, 1970-72; appointee Econ. Devel. Commn., County Impact Study Commn. Bd.; bd. dirs. Md. Hosp. Assn., Md. Chs. United, 1975—; chmn. bd. dirs. Md. Hosp. Edn. Inst., 1988—; pres. Ch. Consistory. Recipient Alumnae Achievement award Hood Coll., 1975, Washington County Woman of Yr. award, AAUW, 1984, Md. Woman of Yr. award, 1984, Md. Woman of Yr. award Francis Scott Key Commn. for Md.'s 350th Aniversary, 1984; named one of top 10 women Tri-State area, Herald-Mail Tri-State newspaper, 1990, Zonta Internat. Woman of Yr., 1994. Mem. Hagerstown C. of C. Republican. Home: 12835 Fountain Head Rd Hagerstown MD 21742-2748 Office: Washington County Hosp Hagerstown MD 21740

HARRISON, MARY ANNE, lawyer; b. Syracuse, N.Y., Apr. 15, 1944; d. James Robertson and Ruth (O'Connor) Urquhart. BA, U. So. Calif., 1966; JD, U. Calif., Berkeley, 1969. Bar: Calif. 1970. Dep. atty. gen. State of Calif., 1970-73; sr. atty. Pacific Lighting Corp., 1973-76; v.p., sec., gen. counsel Buena Vista Distbg. Co., Inc., Burbank, Calif., 1976-85; sr. v.p., asst. gen. counsel Fox, Inc., Beverly Hills, Calif., 1985—. Bd. dirs. ofcl. salaries authority City of L.A., 1979-80. Mem. ABA, State Bar Calif., L.A. County Bar Assn., Calif. Women Lawyers, Women Lawyers Assn. L.A. Office: Fox Inc PO Box 900 Beverly Hills CA 90213-0900*

HARRISON, ROSALIE THORNTON (MRS. PORTER HARMON HARRISON), retired educator; b. Birmingham, Ala., Jan. 24, 1917; d. John William and Zora (Whetstone) Thornton; m. Porter Harmon Harrison, Apr. 12, 1941; 1 child, Porter Harmon. AB, Samford U., 1937; MA, U. Ala., 1945; postgrad., Tchrs. Coll., Columbia U., 1945-46, 53, Cath. U. Am., 1956, 63-64, George Washington U., 1957-58, 59, Am. U., 1962, U. Md., 1964-65, U. D.C., 1967-69, 70. Tchr. Pinson (Ala.). Elem. Sch., 1937-41; tchr. Children's Sch., U. Ala., summers 1939-41; tchr., asst. prin. Avondale Estates (Ga.) Elem. Sch., 1941-45; asst. tchr. Horace Mann-Lincoln Sch. of Tchrs. Coll., Columbia U., 1946; instr. English, Samford U., 1948; tchr. Lakeview Elem. Sch., Birmingham, 1948-49, Hazelwood Elem. Sch., Louisville, 1950-51, McFerran Elem. Sch., Louisville, 1952-53; with pub. schs. of Dist. of Columbia, Washington, D.C., 1956-82: tchr. Congress Heights Elem. Sch., Washington, 1956-63; guidance counselor Barnard Elem. Sch., Washington, 1963-82; adminstr. D.C. Project Head Start, summers 1966-69, coord. parent program, summers 1968-69; prin. Congress Heights-Savoy Elem. Summer Sch., Washington, 1971, Blow-Bowen Elem. Summer Sch., Washington, 1972. Del. Congress of Bapt. World Alliance, Rio de Janeiro, Brazil, 1960, Miami, Fla., 1965; dir. D.C. Bapt. Conv. Summer Mission Camp Girls Aux., 1955, assembly officer Dept. Bapt. Women, 1967-71, 73-77; dir. Bapt. Tng. Union, Riverside Bapt. Ch., Washington, 1954-65, also mem. choir, council, mem. numerous coms., officer, 1953—; past pres. Ministers Wives, D.C. Bapt. Conv. Ky. Col. Mem. NEA (life), Am. Counseling Assn., D.C. Counseling Assn. , Am. Sch. Counselor Assn., D.C. Sch. Counselor Assn., D.C. Elem. Sch. Counselor Assn. (past v.p.), D.C. Career Devel. Assn. (past pres.), Nat. Career Devel. Assn., Assn. for Multicultural Counseling and Devel., D.C. Assn. for Multicultural Counseling and Devel., Assn. Specialists in Group Work, D.C. Assn. Specialists in Group Work (charter), Am. Mental Health Counselors Assn., D.C. Mental Health Counselors Assn.; also Internat. Platform Assn., Council for Exceptional Children, Nat. Trust Hist. Preservation, D.C. Ret. Tchrs. Assn., The Columbian Women of the George Washington U. (past 1st v.p.), Smithsonian Nat. Assocs., U.S. Capitol Hist. Soc., Concerned Citizens Council Washington (past pres.), Washington City Bible Soc. (bd. dirs.), Alpha Delta Kappa (past state pres. Washington, past pres. Gamma chpt.). Home: 3828 17th Place NE Washington DC 20018-2314

HARRISON, SHAWN LESLIE, marketing professional; b. Caldwell, Idaho, Nov. 21, 1964; d. Alvin Wesley and Susanna Malinda (Page) Hancock; m. George Brent Harrison, Oct. 18, 1986; children: Trent James, Brady Warren. BBA, Coll. Idaho, 1987. Asst. to dir. grad. studies Coll. Idaho, Caldwell, 1983-87; legal clk. Canyon County Prosecuting Atty., Caldwell, 1985-87; legal asst. Opton, Galton & Rosenthal, Portland, Oreg., 1987-88; sec. I R & D J. R. Simplot Co., Caldwell, 1988-89; mktg. asst. fruit & vegetable divsn. J. R. Simplot Co., Boise, Idaho, 1989-90; asst. product mgr. fruit & vegetable divsn. J. R. Simplot Co., Boise, 1990-91, mktg. analyst FVD, 1991, sales assoc. indsl., 1991-94, product mgr. food svc., 1994, zone mktg. mgr. Mid South, 1994—. Office: J R Simplot Co PO Box 9386 Boise ID 83707-3386

HARRISON, TERI G., human resources director; b. Norfolk, Va., Jan. 4, 1947; d. Fleetwood Lee and Geraldine (Webb) Gardner; m. Wilson Scott Harrison, Nov. 29, 1969; 1 child, Gwen R. BA in English/History, Old Dominion U., 1969; MA in Guidance and Counseling, Ea. Mich. U., 1974. Cert. compensation profl., Am. Compensation Assn. Various human resources positions Bendix Rsch. Labs. & Bendix Advanced Products, Farmington and Southfield, Mich., 1971-73; sr. pers. adminstr. Bendix Rsch. Labs., Southfield, 1973-75; human resources adminstr. Bendix Exec. Offices, Southfield, 1975-79; mgr. compensation and benefits Bendix Advanced Tech., Columbia, Md. and Southfield, 1979-83; mgr. employee rels. Allied-Signal Aerospace Tech., Columbia, 1983-90; dir. human resources Allied-Signal Microelectronics and Tech. Ctr., Columbia, 1990—. Bd. dirs. Columbia Med. Plan, 1983—, The Columbia Found., 1985-93, Howard County Leadership, Columbia, 1992, Fgn. Born Info. & Referral Network, Columbia, 1993-94, John Hopkins U.-Columbia Ctr., 1993—. Mem. Howard County C. of C. Home: 5301 Night Shade Ct Columbia MD 21045 Office: 9140 Old Annapolis Rd Columbia MD 21045

HARRISON, VIRGINIA M., federal government agency employee; b. Cheverly, Md., Oct. 14, 1954; d. John Emory and Josephine (Holiday) H. AA in Bus. Mgmt., Prince George's C.C., Largo, Md., 1986; BRE, Washington Saturday Coll., 1992, MRE, 1993. Ordained minister. Corr. clk. typist Passport Office Dept. of State, Washington, 1972-75; passport/visa clk. typist US Army Svc. Ctr. for Armed Forces Dept. of Army, Washington, 1975-77, passport agt./adminstrv. asst. Nat. Def. U., 1977-79, tng. coord. Automation Support Detachment, 1979-81; mgmt. asst. Mil. Pers. Command Dept. of Army, Alexandria, Va., 1981-82; mgmt. analyst Adj. Gen. Ctr. Dept. of Army, Washington, 1982-84, mgmt. analyst Cmty. and Family Support Ctr., 1984-89; mgmt. analyst Bur. Naval Pers. Dept. of Navy, Washington, 1989—; speaker Seminars, Retreats, Radio Talk Program. Author: Wedding Vows for Christians, 1933, 1994. Named Outstanding Club Pres., Toastmasters Internat., 1991. Mem. Toastmasters Internat. (Disting. toastmaster). Democrat. Home: 11006 Penny Ave Clinton MD 20735

HARRISON, WENDY JANE MERRILL, medical management consultant; b. Waterbury, Conn., Dec. 4, 1961; d. David Kenneth and Jane Joy (Nevius) Merrill; m. Aidan T. Harrison. BA in Journalism, George Washington U., Washington, 1981; MBA in mgmt., Cornell U., 1992. Intern in edn. HEW, Washington, summer 1978, writer, summer 1979; rsch. asst. dep. health svcs. adminstrn. George Washington U., Washington, 1979-81; sec. Nat. Assn. Beverage Importers, Washington, 1981; account exec. Staff Design, Washington, 1982; adminstrv. aide Internat. Food Policy Rsch. Inst., Washington, 1983-86; program assoc. Acad. for Ednl. Devel., Washington, 1986-87; pvt. practice cons. Washington, 1987-88; adminstrv. mgr. food and nutrition policy program Cornell U., Ithaca, 1988-92; cons. in mgmt. of med. practices Med. Bus. Mgmt., Ithaca, 1994—; cons., editor George Washington U., 1986; cons., rapporteur Internat. Food Policy Restaurant Inst., Washington and Copenhagen, Denmark, 1987; cons., adminstr. Hansell & Post, Washington, 1987-88, Cornell U., Washington and Ithaca, 1988. Sponsor Worldvision, Tanzania, 1988-91. George Washington U. scholar, 1979-81. Mem. NAFE, Bus. and Profl. Women's Club, Sigma Delta Xi (scholar 1980). Democrat. Episcopalian. Home: 25 Woodcrest Ave Ithaca NY 14850-6242

HARRISON-JONES, LOIS, school system administrator; b. Westmoreland County, Va., Apr. 30, 1934; widowed. BS in Elem. Edn., Va. State Coll., 1954; MS in Reading, Temple U., 1962; postgrad., Columbia U., 1964; postgrad. in adminstrn. and supervision, U. Va., 1967-68; EdD, Va. Tech., 1982; LLD (hon.), Mt. Ida Coll., 1992, New England Sch. of Law, 1994. Cert. elem. and middle sch. tchr., elem. supr., gen. supr., dir. instrn., asst. supt. instrn., Va., supt., Va., Mass. Tchr. Woodville Elem. Sch., 1954-59; consulting tchr. Richmond (Va.) Pub. Schs., 1959-61; asst. prin. Baker Elem. Sch., Richmond (Va.) Pub. Schs., 1961-67, prin., 1967-70; coord. student teaching and summer programs Richmond (Va.) Pub. Schs., 1970-73, dir. area II, 1973-76, asst. supt. elem. edn., 1976-81, asst. supt. elem. and secondary edn., 1981-83, asst. supt. elem. edn., 1983-85, supt., 1985-88; assoc. supt. ednl. svcs. Dallas Ind. Sch. Dist., 1988-90, dep. supt., 1990-91; supt. Boston Pub. Schs., 1991—; assoc. prof. grad. sch. edn. Harvard U., Cambridge, 1991—; mem. adjunct faculty U. Mass., Boston. Contbr. articles to profl. jours. Former chair bd. dirs. Math & Sci. Ctr., Richmond; former mem. Polit. Congress African-Am. Women, Dallas, Coalition of 100 Black Women, Richmond, Alpha Bettes, Richmond, Urban League, Richmond; former bd. dirs. YWCA, Richmond, United Way Greater Richmond, chmn. pers. com., Communities in Schs., Dallas, St. John Missionary Bapt. Ch., Dallas; past chmn. city/county govt. divsn. United Way Richmond, Henrico, Chesterfield, Hanover; former trustee Va. State U.; past chairperson bd. trustees Ebenezer Bapt. Ch., Richmond; alumna Dallas Opportunity; trustee Mus. Fine Arts, Boston; overseer Boston Sci. Mus. Recipient citation Newton (Mass.) Rotary Club, 1991, Proclamation award Tex. State Senate, 1991, Support citation Sarah Gorham Women's Missionary Soc. Charles St. AME Ch., 1991, Boston City Coun. Resolution, 1991, Ofcl. citation Senate Commonwealth Mass., 1991, Ofcl. citation Ho. Reps. Commonwealth Mass., award Congress Exemplary Supts., 1992, Disting. Women Leader Lecture Series award Greater Dallas C. of C., 1992, Pres. citation Alpha Kappa Alpha Sorority, 1992, ciation Mt. Zion Lodge, 1992, Appreciation award Project 2000 Boston Coll., 1992, citation Italian-Am. Com. Mass. Quincentennial Commn., 1992, cert. recognition Fed. Exec. Bd. Women's Opportunity Com., 1992, award Parent's and Children's Svcs., 1992, award Exec. Club Greater Boston C. of C., 1993, Outstanding Black Women of Yr. award Big Sister Assn. Greater Mass., 1993, Women of Courage and Conviction award Nat. Coun. Negro Women, 1993, citation Boston Urban Bankers Forum, 1993, Truth award Nat. Sojourner, 1993, Dr. Martin Luther King, Jr. Leadership award, citation for commitment to Engring. Workforce for Future, 1993; named Woman of Yr. Boston Network for Women in Politics and Govt., 1993. Mem. ASCD (former bd. dirs., former pubs. com., urban edn. adv. bd. critical issues com.), NAACP (former exec. com. Dallas and Richmond brs., Disting. Svc. award 1992), Va. Assn. Supervision and Curriculum Devel. (past pres.), Am. Assn. Sch. Adminstrs., Nat. Alliance Black Sch. Adminstrs. (pres. supts. commn.), Coun. Great City Schs., Mass. Assn. Sch. Supts., Mass. Assn. Law Enforcement Officers (hon.), Richnond Travelers Aid Soc. (past pres., bd. dirs.), Continental Socs., Inc (past pres.), Alpha Kappa (Alpha Xi Omega chpt.). Office: Boston Public Schools Office of Superintendent 26 Court St Boston MA 02108-2505

HARRISS, MARGARET WEEMS, data processing company executive; b. Canton, Miss., Dec. 11, 1948; d. Robert Edward Lee and Alice (Siefke) Weems; children: Liz, Scott, Chris. BA in Math. cum laude, Millsaps Coll., 1972; MS in Math., Jackson State U., 1977. Cert. data processer. Asst. prof. Hinds Jr. Coll., Raymond, Miss., 1978-81; human rels. specialist Jackson (Miss.) Pub. Schs., 1973-78; software devel. mgr. Miss. State Tax Commn., Jackson, 1978-82; software analyst TRUSCO Data Systems, Atlanta, 1982-83; supr. Metro. Atlanta Rapid Transit Authority, Atlanta, 1983; analyst J. Riggins, Atlanta, 1983-84; dir. Am. Software, Inc., Atlanta, 1984-92; CEO Solution Scientists, Inc., Atlanta, 1992—; cons. Miss. Ednl. TV Math Series, Jackson, 1979-80, N.E. Ga. Girl Scout Program Devel., Atlanta, 1990-91. Author: On the Reverse Spelling of a Point Universal Word, 1979. Fundraiser N.E. Ga. Girl Scouts Am., Atlanta, 1988-92; mem. Am. Diabetes Assn., Atlanta, 1992—; v.p. Ch. Womens Group, Atlanta, 1987-88. Named one of Outstanding Young Women of Am., 1982. Mem. MENSA, Data Processing Mgmt. Assn. (bd. dirs. 1989-90), Assn. Women Entrepreneurs. Office: Solution Scientists Inc 2768 Arldowne Dr Tucker GA 30084-2513

HARROLD, MERRY ELLENOR, secondary education educator; b. New Phila., Ohio, Oct. 27, 1937; d. Paul Davis and Ellenor Adella (Close) Geis; m. Richard Max Harrold, Aug. 29, 1958; 1 child, Lee Ellen Harrold Hollingsworth. BS in Math., Chemistry, Music, Ctrl. Mich. U., 1959, MA in Math., 1963. Cert. secondary permanent credential, Mich., gen. secondary credential, Calif., adminstrv. svc. credential, Calif. Tchr. math., chair dept. Pinconning (Mich.) H.S., 1959-61; tchr. math., physics, music Rapid River (Mich.) H.S., 1961-62; tchr. math., chair dept. Gladwin (Mich.) H.S., 1962-63, Escalon (Calif.) H.S., 1963-67; tchr. math. Modesto (Calif.) H.S., 1967-74, Fred C. Beyer H.S., Modesto, 1974-76; tchr. math., chair dept. THomas Downey H.S., Modesto, 1976—; dir. Ctrl. Calif. Math Project Calif. State U., Stanislaus, Turlock, 1983-84; cons. Calif. State Dept. Edn., Sacramento, 1976-92. Mem. NEA, Nat. Coun. Tchrs. Math. (del. 1957-94), Calif. Math. Coun. (life, editor newsletter Communicator 1982-85, Polya award 1993), Stanislaus Math. Coun. (v.p., pres., treas.), Calif. Tchrs. Assn., Modesto Tchrs. Assn., Calif. Math. Coun. (ctrl. v.p., sec., life). Republican. Presbyterian. Home: 1121 Spring Creek Dr PO Box 476 Ripon CA 95366-0476 Office: Thomas Downey High Sch 1000 Coffee Rd Modesto CA 95355

HARROP, DIANE GLASER, shop owner, mayor; b. Lafayette, Ind., June 2, 1953; d. Donald Anthony and Mary Ophelia (Rohner) G.; m. Randolph Allen Harrop, Aug. 7, 1976; children: William Donald, Steven Randolph. BE, U. Kans., 1975. Researcher U. Kans. Speech Dept., Lawrence, 1973-75; clk., book designer Pruett Pub. Co., Boulder, Colo., 1975; debate coach, English tchr. Olathe (Kans.) High Sch., 1975-76; cash items teller Converse County Bank, Douglas, Wyo., 1976-79; owner, mgr. R-D Pharmacy & Books, Douglas, 1979—; mayor City of Douglas, 1989-91, councilmember, 1991-93; columnist Casper Star Tribune, 1993—; weekly columnist Douglas Budget Newspaper, 1994; appt. Wyo. Econ. Devel. and Stabilization Bd., 1991—. Creator original jewelry (silverwork 1st prize winner Wyo. State Fair 1978). First woman councilmember City of Douglas, 1987-89; gov's. appointee, 1st chmn. State Adv. Coun. on Innovative Edn., Wyo., 1991; charter pres. Converse County Hosp. Aux., 1985; sec.-treas. Converse County Joint Powers Bd., 1987; bd. dirs. Nicolaysen Art Mus., 1987; mem. Wyo. Mcpl. League Legis. Com. (chmn. 1988—); mem., exhibitor Firearms Engravers Guild of Am., 1988, 89; moderator Congl. Ch.; Douglas chpt. pres. Wyo. Jaycee Women, 1984-85; mem. P.E.O. Sisterhood Chpt. N, 1983-84, Zonta Internat. (treas. 1982-83); pres. Friends of Wyoming State Fair, 1990—; bd. dirs. Ea. Wyoming Mental Health, 1991, Converse County United Way, 1993—; Wyo. adv. com. Dwight D. Eisenhower Math. and Sci. Grant, 1992; mem. parents adv. coun. Douglas H.S., 1994—. Recipient Celebrate Literacy award Internat. Reading Assn. Wyo., 1988, Outstanding Community Svc. award Douglas C. of C., 1991, Apple for Edn. award Gov. Mike Sullivan, 1992, Kellogg Found. scholarship to Heartland Ctr. for Leadership Devel. Seminars, 1993; named one of Outstanding Young Women in Am., 1983-86. Mem. Mountains and Plains Booksellers (bd. dirs. 1992—), Douglas C. of C., Am. Booksellers Assn., Nat. Fedn. Ind. Businesses, Kiwanis (sec. 1994—). Republican. Office: R-D Pharmacy & Books 206 Center St Douglas WY 82633-2543

HARROP, SHIRLEY ANN, retired secretary; b. Moberly, Mo., Mar. 10, 1923; d. Jasper Franklin and Georgia Yates Jacobs; m. Clayton Keith Harrop, Dec. 24, 1944; children: Judith Ann, Joyce Elaine, Janice Louise. AA in Commerce, Moberly (Mo.) Jr. Coll., 1943. Sec. So. Bapt. Sem., Louisville, 1950-51, Ctrl. Travel Agy., Oakland, Calif., 1955-66, Talbot of Tiburon Travel, Mill Valley, Calif., 1966-68; mgr. bookstore Golden Gate Bapt. Sem., Mill Valley, 1968-73; sec. Bank of Am., San Francisco, 1973-80, Mill Valley, 1980-85. Usher Marion County Civic Ctr., San Rafael, Calif., 1985-94; vol. Habitat for Humanity, Mill Valley, 1992-94. Mem. AARP (pres. chpt. # 4139 1986-88, Outstanding Svc. to Cmty. 1990), Am. Bus. Women's Assn. (pres. 1963-65, Woman of Yr. 1986). Democrat. So. Baptist. Home: 16 Platt Ct Mill Valley CA 94941

HARRS, CAROLYN MARY, accountant; b. Queens, N.Y., May 7, 1960; d. Robert Francis and Mary Terese (Brady) H. BS in Acctg., SUNY, Binghamton, 1982; MBA in Mgmt., NYU, 1994. CPA, N.Y. Staff acct. Athur Young & Co., N.Y.C., 1982-85; mgr. acctg. Nynex Credit Co., N.Y.C., 1985-92; dir. acctg. Nynex Telesector Resources Corp., N.Y.C., 1992—. Mem. NAFE. Home: 69-10 Yellowstone Blvd # 618 Forest Hills NY 11375

HARRY, DEBORAH ANN, singer; b. Miami, Fla., July 11, 1945; d. Richard Smith and Catherine (Peters) H. A.A., Centenary Coll., 1965. Singer, songwriter rock group Blondie, 1975-83. Albums include Blondie, 1976, Plastic Letters, 1977, Parallel Lines, 1978, Eat to the Beat, 1979, Autoamerican, 1979, The Best of Blondie, 1981, The Hunter, 1982, (solo) Koo Koo, 1981, Rockbird, 1981, Def, Dumb & Blond, 1989, Debravation, 1993, The Platinum Collection, 1994; songs include Heart of Glass, 1978 (ASCAP award), Call Me, Tide is High, Rapture, 1980; film appearances include Union City Blues, 1980, Videodrome, Roadie, 1980, Hairspray, 1988, Tales From the Darkside: The Movie, 1990; TV appearances include Saturday Night Live, The Muppet Show, Tales from the Darkside, Wiseguy; appeared on Broadway Teaneck Tanzi, The Venus Flytrap, 1983; (movie) Satisfaction. Recipient Gold, Silver and Platinum records. Mem. ASCAP, AFTRA, Screen Actors Guild, Equity. Office: care Creative Artists Agy Inc 1816 Holmby Ave Los Angeles CA 90025-4902 also: care Press Relations Chrysalis Records 645 Madison Ave New York NY 10022-1010 also: care Gary Kurfirst Overland 1775 Broadway New York NY 10019-1903*

HARSNEY, JOHANNA MARIE OFFNER, nurse; b. Youngstown, Ohio, Oct. 15, 1914; d. Michael and Elizabeth (Untch) Offner; m. Theodore Harsney, Aug. 11, 1941; 1 child, Karl Michael. Grad. Youngstown Hosp. Sch. Nursing, 1939; BA in Fgn. Langs., Youngstown U., 1972. Staff nurse Youngstown Hosp., 1939-40; pvt. duty nurse Youngstown Profl. Nurse's Registry, Youngstown, 1940-92, sec., 1991-93. Vol. Red Cross Nurses. Mem. Am. Nurses Assn., Ohio Nurses Assn. (pres. pvt. duty sect. 1979-84), Profl. Nurses Registry Greater Youngstown (sec. 1993), Am. Bus. Women Assn. (v.p. Gold Torch chpt. 1978, Nurse of Yr. Dist. 3, 1983), Phi Lambda Pi (sec. Kappa chpt. 1973-74, v.p. 1973-74, pres. 1975). Home: 2204 Cranbrook Dr Youngstown OH 44511-1236 Office: Profl Nurses Registry 3119 Market St Ste 224 Youngstown OH 44507-1823

HART, BETSY CANFIELD, political commentator; b. Arlington Heights, Ill., Apr. 25, 1963; d. Lee Briggs and Eloise Ann (Rinne) Canfield; m. Benjamin John Hart, Oct. 10, 1987; 1 child, Jeffrey Peter. BA in Russian Studies, U. Ill., 1985. Staff asst., comm. coord. White House Conf. on Small Bus., Washington, 1985-86; staff, press spokeswoman for Pres. Ronald Reagan White House Office of Media Rels., Washington, 1986-88; press sec. Ho. Rep. Policy Com., Washington, 1989; dir. lectrs. and seminars The Heritage Found., Washington, 1989-92; columnist Scripps Howard News Svc., 1992—; commentator, host American Family, Nat. Empowerment Television, 1992—; frequent guest on CNN and Company, CNN TV, Fox Morning News, Oprah Winfrey Show. Office: Nat Empowerment TV Am Family 717 2nd St NE Washington DC 20002

HART, BRENDA GUTH, school counselor; b. Bloomington, Ill., June 13, 1952; d. Duane Eldon and Alice Janette (Shive) Guth; m. Stephen Edward Hart, June 11, 1983. MA, Ill. State U., 1975; BA, U. Ill., 1973. Profl. sch. counselor. Counselor K-6 Lincoln (Ill.) Elem. Sch., 1975-76; counselor high sch. Pontiac (Ill.) High Sch., 1976-80; counselor 7-9 Aurora (Ill.) East Pub. Schs., 1980-84; counselor 6-8 Newport News (Va.) Pub. Schs., 1984—. Mem. Peninsula Counselors Assn. (pres. 1989-90, chpt. mem. of yr. 1990), Va. Sch. Counselors Assn. (middle sch. v.p. 1991-93, sec. 1993—), Am. Counselors Assn., Am. Sch. Counselors Assn., Kappa Delta Pi. Home: 361 Deputy Ln Apt F Newport News VA 23602-4603 Office: Newport News Pub Schs 3700 Chestnut Ave Newport News VA 23607-3239

HART, DONNA A., accounting executive; b. Rochester, N.Y., Apr. 29, 1953; d. Donald C. and Constance M. (Pidgeon) Durbin; children: Brian W., Abigail L. BA in Math., Nazareth Coll. Rochester, 1975; MBA, Rochester Inst. Tech., 1979. Acct. Itek Leasing Co., Rochester, 1975-77, lease adminstr., 1977-79; ops. analyst H.L. Yoh Co., Rochester, 1979-80; consolidation acct. Gannett Co. Inc., Rochester, 1980-82, property acct./analyst, 1982-84, fin. systems analyst, 1984-85; acct. Smartware Inc., Rochester, 1988; sr. fin. analyst Praxis Biologics Inc., Rochester, 1988-90; mgr. acctg. and budgets Lederle-Praxis Biols. divsn. Am. Cyanamid, Rochester, 1990—; auditor cons. St. Lukes Ch., Fairport, N.Y., 1993. EMT Perinton Vol. Ambulance Corps, Fairport, 1986—, treas., 1986-89, bd. dirs., 1988-91, v.p. fin., 1991; troop leader Genesee Valley coun. Girl Scouts U.S., Fairport, 1991—, troop cons., Rochester, 1994. Mem. Inst. Mgmt. Accts. (assoc. dir. mem. activities 1993). Republican. Episcopalian. Office: Lederle Praxis Biols 211 Bailey Rd West Henrietta NY 14586

HART, ELSIE FAYE, elementary education educator; b. Shelbyville, Ill., Oct. 15, 1920; d. James Ray and Maude May (Allison) Cain; m. Harold Delbert Bible, June 15, 1941 (div. Apr. 1948); children: Gary H., Rex. E. (dec.); m. Frederick Christopher Hart, July 28, 1950 (dec. Dec. 1994); children: Susan Hart Eichman, Pamela L. Elem. teaching cert., Ea. Ill. U., 1942; BS in Edn., No. Ill. U., 1968; postgrad., Rockford Coll., 1972-73. Cert. elem. tchr., Ill. Tchr. Findlay (Ill.) Elem. Sch., 1942-47; tchr. Winnebago County Schs., Rockford, Ill., 1948-52, Rockford Parochial Schs., 1957-63; tchr. Rockford Pub. Schs., 1964-82, substitute tchr., 1982—. Author: The On and the Under Dog, 1992; contbr. articles to profl. jours. Pres. Assn. for Childhood Edn. Internat., Rockford, 1968-76; sec.-treas. Ill. Assn. for Supervision & Curriculum Devel., Rockford, 1970-80; mem. NEA, Ill. Edn. Assn., Rockford Edn. Assn., 1964-82; mem. Rockford Art Assn., 1968, Beta Sigma Phi, Rockford, 1950, Rockford Creative Dramatics Assn., 1968, Mauh-Nah-Tee See Country Club, Rockford, 1982; vol. tchr. Rockford Parochial schs. Recipient Cert. of Commendation in recognition of meritorious svc. Ill. Supt. Pub. Instrn., 1974; nominated Ill. Retired Tchrs. Hall of Fame. Mem. AAUW (historian Rockford chpt. 1970—), Ill. Ret. Tchrs. Assn., Winnebago/Boone Ret. Tchrs. Assn., Women of the Moose, Holy Family Women's Guild, Rockford Woman's Club (sec. 1970, publicity com. 1971, membership com. 1972, way/means com. 1988-91, bd. dirs. 1993-94, long-range planning com. 1994—, program com. 1994-95), Nat. Women's Hall of Fame. Republican. Roman Catholic. Home: 1507 Al Crest Rd Rockford IL 61107-2125

HART, JEAN HARDY, information systems specialist, consultant; b. Cleve., Jan. 19, 1942; d. Gilbert Elliott and Jessie (Peterson) Brown; m. Richard Pierpont Thomas, June 16, 1962 (div. Sept. 1974); children: Perry Glenn, Geb Weller, Hans Richard; m. Howard Phillips Hart, Jan. 19, 1988; stepsons: Colin, Guy. BA, Goddard Coll., 1973. Tech. communications specialist The Mitre Corp., Boston, 1973-75; site adminstr., tech. communications expert The Mitre Corp., Madrid, 1975-77; mgr. internat. programs Honeywell Info. Systems, Newton, Mass., 1977-78; account mgr. sales and contracts Honeywell Info. Systems, 1978-79, tech. analyst, 1979-81; dist. mgr. Europe Honeywell Info Systems, 1981-84; mgr. third party svc. Honeywell Info. Systems, Boston, 1984-85, 85-86; resident mgr. Honeywell Info. Systems, Beijing, 1985; dir. fed. accounts Honeywell Info. Systems, McLean, Va., 1986-88; bus. advisor CIA, McLean, Va., 1989-90; dir. Hartwell Mgmt., Ltd. Internat. Strategic Info. Group, London and, Va., 1991—; internat. bus. cons. U.S. Govt., Washington, 1991—; info. profl. various cos., Washington, 1991—; lectr. numerous worldwide colls. and govt. orgns., 1968—; strategy cons. to provost Coll. Integrated Sci. and Tech., James Madison U., Harrisonburg, Va., 1992; cons. internat. bus. ops. Author, producer: (videotape) Chief Justice Warren Burger, 1987; exec. producer: (videotape) Exec. V.p. Reynolds Metals, 1993; contbr. articles to profl. jours. Mem. NAFE, AAUW, Am. Assn. Info. Profls., Am. Mgmt. Assn. Episcopalian. Home and Office: Hart Consultancy HCR-1 Box 131B Free Union VA 22940

HART, JOY, communications executive, writer; b. Tucson, Aug. 4, 1948; d. John R. and Margaret (Jackson) H.; m. Gerald R. Hunter, July, 1974; children: Mary Elizabeth Hart Hunter, James Gerald Hunter. Student, McMurry Coll., 1965-67; BA with honors, U. N.Mex., 1969; MS, Kans. State U., 1971; postgrad., U. Dallas, 1981-83. Writer Odessa (Tex.) Am., 1969, St. Petersburg (Fla.) Times, 1971-73; instr. U. Tulsa, 1973-74; writer for local and nat. publs., 1973—; writer Tulsa Tribune, 1974-75, Dallas Times Herald, 1976-78; editor, writer Liquid Paper Corp., Dallas, 1978-80, Exxon Co., U.S.A., Dallas, 1980-83; prin. Hart/Hunter Comms., Dallas, 1983—. Leader Girl Scouts Am.; tchr. Sunday sch. Mem. Internat. Assn. Bus. Communicators (found. liaison dist. 5 1991—, Dallas found. liaison 1990-92, mem. internat. task force 1989, dist. 5 dir., 1st asst. dir., 2d asst. dir., coord. profl. devel., sec., chpt. grant coord., sr.del., Dallas pres., v.p. comms., v.p. profl. devel., Gold Quill award of merit), Women in Comms.,

Soc. Profl. Journalists. Methodist. Office: Hart/Hunter Comms Box 741262 Dallas TX 75374

HART, KITTY CARLISLE, arts administrator; b. New Orleans, Sept. 3, 1917; d. Joseph and Hortence (Holtzman) Conn; m. Moss Hart, Aug. 10, 1946 (dec. 1961); children: Christopher, Cathy. Ed., London Sch. Econs., Royal Acad. Dramatic Arts; DFA (hon.), Coll. New Rochelle; DHL (hon.), Hartwick Coll.; LHD (hon.), Manhattan Coll., Amherst Coll. Chmn. N.Y. State Council on the Arts. Former panelist: TV show To Tell the Truth; actress on stage and in films including The Marx Brothers A Night at the Opera, 1936; Broadway theatre appearance in On Your Toes, 1983-84; singer, Met. Opera, TV moderator and interviewer; author: (autobiography) Kitty, 1988; contbr. book revs. to jours. Assoc. fellow Timothy Dwight Coll. of Yale U.; bd. dirs. Empire State Coll.; formerly spl. cons. to N.Y. Gov. on women's opportunities; mem. vis. com. for the arts MIT. Recipient Nat. medal of Arts from Pres. Bush, 1991. Office: Arts Coun 915 Broadway 8th Fl New York NY 10010-7108*

HART, LAUREN L., marketing executive; b. Providence, Jan. 30, 1952; d. Giovanni and Ruth Elsie (Schultheis) Luongo. BS, U. R.I., 1975, MS, 1981. Mktg. asst. Agawam Creative Mktg., Rowley, Mass., 1977-79; asst. sales & mktg. Ocean State Jobbers Inc., North Kingstown, R.I., 1979-81; rsch. assoc. U. R.I., Kingston, 1979-81; mktg. rep. lab supply & chem. sales Ea. Scientific Co., Providence, 1981-82; mktg. mgr., v.p. mktg., v.p. corp., ops. officer Alan's Bus. Machines Inc., Barre, Vt., 1983-89; chief exec. officer Continental Resource Group, Ltd., Barre, Vt., 1989—. Mem. NAFE, Women Bus. Owners Vt., Nat. Women Bus. Owners, AAUW (nat. and local), Inst. Food Technologists (Z John Ordahl award 1981), Advt./Image/Mktg. Assn. (pres. 1985-86, 92—), Ptnrs. of the Cornell Fine Arts Mus. (founding mem., chmn. pub. rels. 1990-91, pres. 1991-92),. Home: 1326 E 60th St 4N Tulsa OK 74105

HART, MARIAN GRIFFITH, retired educator; b. Bates City, Mo., Feb. 5, 1929; d. George Thomas Leon and Beulah Winiferd (Hackley) Griffith; m. Ashley Bruce Hart, Dec. 23, 1951; children: Ashley Bruce Hart II, Pamela Cherie Hart Gates. BS, Cen. Mo. State Coll., 1951; MA, No. Ariz. U., 1976. Title I-Chpt. I reading dir. Page (Ariz.) Sch. Dist.; Title I dir. Johnson O'Malley Preschool, Page Sch. Dist.; dist. reading dir. Page Sch. Dist. Contbr. articles to profl. jours. and children's mags. Vol., organizer, mgr., instr. Page Community Adult Lit. Program; lifetime mem. Friends of Page Pub. Libr., sec. bd., 1990-91. Mem. Lake Powell Inst. (bd. dirs., sec. 1993—, Page Main St. Vol. of Yr. 1992), Delta Kappa Gamma (pres. chpt. 1986-90, historian 1990-92, Omicron state coms., scholarship 1988-89, nominations 1991), Beta Sigma Phi (pres. chpt., v.p. chpt.). Home and Office: 66 S Navajo Dr PO Box 763 Page AZ 86040

HART, MARILYN JEAN, commercial insurance underwriter; b. Indpls., May 26, 1958; d. Daniel Clement Owen and Marlene Ann (Moller) Lanman; m. Ronald Lee Hart, June 21, 1986; step children: Carrie Lynn, Brian Allen. Student, Ind. U./Purdue U., Indpls., 1977-78. Profl. assoc. in underwriting; cert. profl. ins. woman. Salesperson Hot Sam, Indpls., 1975-77, L.S. Ayres, Indpls., 1975-81, Rug Crafters, Indpls., 1980-81; microfiche records clk. Am. States Ins. Co., Indpls., 1980-82, property rater, 1982-83, multiline rater, 1983-85, asst. underwriter, 1985-86, underwriter comml., 1986—; quality commitment facilitator Am. States Ins. Co., Indpls., 1992—. Mem. Indpls. Assn. Ins. Women (bd. dirs. 1991-94, v.p. 1994—). Republican. Home: 153 N Windswept Rd Greenfield IN 46140 Office: Am States Ins 500 N Meridian Indianapolis IN 46204

HART, MARY, television talk show host; b. Sioux Falls, S.D., Nov. 8, 1951; m. Burt Sugarman, Apr. 8, 1989; 1 child. BA, Augustana College, 1972. Co-host, prodr. Danny's Day, Oklahoma City, Iowa; co-host PM Mag., L.A., 1978, The Regis Philbin Show, N.Y.C., 1981-92, Entertainment Tonight, Hollywood, 1982—; co-owner Customer's Last Stand. host Tournament of Roses Parade, Macy's Thankgiving Day Parade; other TV appearences include (miniseries) Hollywood Wives, 1985, Circus of the Stars, Good Morning America, Blossom, Coach; exec. prodr., host Mary Hart Presents: Love in the Public Eye, 1990, Mary hart Presents: Power in the Public Eye, 1990; musical debut Dolly, ABC-TV; headliner, dancer, singer, Las Vegas debut Golden Nugget, 1988, Resorts Internat., Atlantic City; videos include: Shape Up with Mary Hart, 1989, Mary Hart: Fit and Firm, 1990. Address: Paramount TV 5555 Melrose Ave Los Angeles CA 90038-3149*

HART, MELISSA A., state legislator; b. Pitts., Apr. 4, 1962; d. Donald P. and Albina Simone Hart. BA, Washington and Jefferson Coll., 1984; JD, U. Pitts., 1987. Pa. state senator, atty. Mem. Pa. Bar Assn., Allegheny County Bar Assn., Women's Bar Assn. Western Pa., North Suburban Builders Assn. Republican. Office: Pa State Senate State Capitol Harrisburg PA 17120*

HART, MILDRED, counselor; b. Ever, Ky., Apr. 7, 1937; d. Dewey Otis and Malta Virginia (Adams) Cooper; m. Joseph Paul Surace, Oct. 26, 1956 (dec. Jan. 1966); children: Marisa Surace Craig, Vincent, Angela, Stephen. BS in Edn., Ohio State U., 1974, MA in Guidance-Counseling, 1976. Cert. elem. and secondary tchr., secondary prin., supr., Ohio; lic. profl. counselor, Ohio. Sec. H.G. Snyder & Assocs., accts., Columubus, Ohio, 1958-63; tchr. Columbus Pub. Schs., 1974-79, counselor, 1977—, chmn. student svcs. dept., 1985—; adjustor Bancohio Nat. Bank, Columbus, 1985-93. Author: (booklet) College Handbook for Independence High School Students, 1988. Leader Girl Scouts U.S., Columbus, 1969-73. Mem. NEA, Ohio State U. Alumni Assn., Nat. Honor Soc., Pi Lambda Theta (sec. Cen. Ohio chpt. 1985—), Phi Kappa Phi. Democrat. Roman Catholic. Home: 2328 Sedgwick Dr Columbus OH 43220-5431 Office: Independence High Sch 5175 Refugee Rd Columbus OH 43232-5352

HART, PAMELA HEIM, banker; b. Chgo., July 14, 1946; d. Gordon Theodore and Leah Almira (Gardner) Heim; m. William Richard Hart, July 8, 1972 (div. 1979); 1 child, Elizabeth Alyson. BA, DePauw U., 1968; MA in Teaching, Washington U., St. Louis, 1970; M in Mgmt., Purdue U., 1982. Chartered bank auditor; cert. bank compliance officer. Tchr. history University City (Mo.) High Sch., 1969-74; teaching asst. Purdue U., Hammond, Ind., 1980-82, guest faculty, 1983-84; auditor Continental Bank NA, Chgo., 1984-86, legal and regulatory compliance specialist, 1986-88, asst. auditor, 1988-92, sr. portfolio risk analyst, 1992-94; with securitized products group Bank of Am. (formerly Continental Bank NA), Chgo., 1994—; v.p. Capital Raising Products, 1994—. Trustee Forest Ridge Acad., Schererville, Ind., 1987-88; mem. vestry St. Paul Episc. Ch., Munster, Ind., 1982-92; active LWV. Mem. Chartered Bank Auditors Assn., Chicagoland Compliance Assn. (bd. dirs., treas. 1987-88), Cert. Bank Compliance Officer Assn. (exam. com. mem. 1992—), P.E.O. Home: 8936 Southmoor Ave Hammond IN 46322-1808 Office: Bank of Am 231 S La Salle St Chicago IL 60697-0001

HART, TRACY LYNNE, environmental consultant, artist, art gallery owner; b. Amesburg, Mass., Sept. 29, 1962; d. William Livingston and Shirley (Jones) H. AA, Mesa Coll., BS, 1985; postgrad., Calif. State U., San Bernardino, 1987-88; MS, Colo. State U., 1991. Forestry technician USDA Forest Svc., Montrose, Colo., 1986, 88; naturalist Los Angelos County Dept. Edn., Wrightwood, Calif., 1986-87; substitute tchr. San Bernardino County Dept. Edn., Victorville, Calif., 1987-88; park ranger Larimer County Parks Dept., Ft. Collins, Colo., 1989, 90; minerals adminstr. USDA Forest Svc., Austin, Nev., 1990-91; range mgmt. specialist USDA Forest Svc., Yampa, Colo., 1991-94; aerobic instr. Colo. Northwest C.C., Oak Creek, 1992—; artist, owner Timberline Gift and Gallery, Oak Creek; environ. cons. Oak Creek. Mem. Soc. Range Mgmt. Home: PO Box 823 107 Grant Oak Creek CO 80467 Office: Timberline Gift and Gallery PO Box 855 116 W Main Oak Creek CO 80467

HARTE, REBECCA ELIZABETH, computer scientist, consultant; b. Camp LeJeune, N.C., Jan. 28, 1967; d. Franklin James and Rebecca Irene (Adams) H. BA in Maths., Hollins Coll., 1989; MS in Info. Mgmt., George Washington U., 1994. Math. asst. Hollins Coll., Roanoke, Va., 1987-89; chief information officer BRTRC, Vienna, Va., 1989—. Mem. AAAS, IEEE, Math. Assn. Am., Am. Math. Soc., Assn. for Computing Machinery, Phi Beta Kappa, Sigma Xi. Home: 5200 Olley Ln Burke VA 22015-1747 Office: BRTRC Ste 800 8260 Willow Oaks Corporate Dr Fairfax VA 22031-4513

HARTER, CAROL CLANCEY, university president, English language educator; m. Michael T. Harter, June 24, 1961; children: Michael R., Sean P. AB, SUNY, Binghamton, 1964, MA, 1967, PhD, 1970; LHD, Ohio U., 1989. Instr. SUNY, Binghamton, 1969-70; asst. prof. Ohio U., Athens, 1970-74, ombudsman, 1974-76, v.p., dean students, 1976-82, v.p. for adminstrn., assoc. prof., 1982-89; pres., and prof. English SUNY, Geneseo, 1989—. Co-author: (with James R. Thompson) John Irving, 1986, E.L. Doctorow, 1990; author dozens of presentations and news columns; contbr. articles to profl. jours. Office: SUNY Office of President Erwin Hall Geneseo NY 14454

HARTER, VICTORIA KATHLEEN, customer service executive; b. Mpls., Feb. 18, 1951; d. Roger Raymond and Kathleen Florence (Schuster) Warrington; m. Alan Lee Cimbura, June 29, 1970 (div. 1973); 1 child, Elias; m. William Wayne Harter, July 5, 1984; children: Kathryn, Joseph. AA, Mpls. Community Coll., 1982; BA, Bethel Coll., 1992. Customer svc./fin./clin. profl. Medtronic Inc., Fridley, Minn., 1976-85, 89—; sch. bus. driver Ryder Student Transp., Arden Hills, Minn., 1985-91; profl. Medtronic tour guide Medtronic World Wide Head Quarters, Mpls., 1980—; chair career devel. Medtronic Women's Coun., Mpls., 1991. Mem. Sch. Dist. 621 study adv. com.; troup leader Girl Scouts U.S., Mpls., 1990—. Mem. New Brighton Hist. Soc. Office: Medtronic Inc 7000 Central Ave NE Minneapolis MN 55432

HARTFORD, ANN MARIE, accountant, controller; b. Methuen, Mass., Mar. 7, 1961; d. John Michael and Stephanie Mary (Bajor) Kaminski; m. Allen Edward Hartford Jr., Sept. 17, 1989; 1 child, Meredith Lynne. BS in Acctg., Bentley Coll., 1982, MS in Taxation, 1990. CPA, Mass. Staff acct. James, Turonis & McLeod, PC, Lawrence, Mass., 1982-85; sr. acct. Martin D. Braver & Co., Chestnut Hill, Mass., 1985-87; acct. Tofias, Fleishman, Shapiro, Cambridge, Mass., 1987-89; contr. CJ McCarthy Ins. Agy., Wilmington, Mass., 1989—; acct. Hartford Assocs., Tewksbury, Mass., 1992—; student mentor Bentley Coll. Career Devel., 1992—. Scholar Bentley Coll., 1979, 80, 81. Fellow Nat. Assn. Accts. (dir. community responsibility 1983-86), Mass. Assn. Pub. Accts. Republican. Roman Catholic. Office: CJ McCarthy Ins Agy Inc 229 Andover St Wilmington MA 01887-1088

HARTFORD, MARGARET ELIZABETH (BETTY HARTFORD), social work educator, gerontologist; b. Cleve., Dec. 12, 1917; d. William A. and Inez (Logan) H. BA, Ohio U., 1940; MS, U. Pitts., 1944; PhD, U. Chgo., 1962. Dir. youth svc. YWCA, Canton, Ohio, 1940-42; program cons. Intercultural Rels. Am. Svc. Inst., Pitts., 1943-48, exec. dir., 1948-50; prof. social work Case Western Res. U., Cleve., 1950-75; founding dir. Sch. Gerontology U. So. Calif., L.A., 1975-77, prof. gerontology, social work, 1977-83, prof. emeritus, 1983—; instr. Claremont (Calif.) Adult Sch. Dist., 1983—, mentor/tchr. adult edn., 1990—; instr. retirement Pasadena (Calif.) City Coll., 1983-84, Mt. San Antonio Coll., 1988-90; cons. pre-retirement, retirement planning to corps. and ednl. systems, various cities, 1980—; freelance writer, cons., lectr. 1970—. Author: Groups in Social Word, 1973, (workbook) Making the Best of the Rest of Your Life, 1982, Leaders Guide to Making the Best of the Rest of Your Life, 1986; contbr. monthly column on successful aging Pomona Valley Cmty. Svcs. on Aging Newsletter, monthly column on transitions to Tempo mag.; contbr. numerous articles to profl. publs. Commr. human svcs. City of Clairmont, 1986-89, city coun. observer LWV, 1994-95; trustee Mt. San Antonio Gardens Retirement Com., 1985-92, sec., 1988-91; v.p. Mt. San Antonio Gardens Club Coun. Residents Orgn., 1991—, area chmn., 1994—, trustee Corp. Pilgrim Pl. Ret. Cmty., chmn. health and svcs. com., 1987-94; bd. dirs., trustee Vol. Assn. Rancho Santa Ana Bot. Gardens, 1991-92; chmn. vol. pers. com. St. Ambrose Episcopal Ch., Claremont, 1988—. Named Outstanding Contbn. to Social Work, Alumni Assn. Schs. Social Work U. So. Calif., 1984, Outstanding Contbr. Social Group Work, Com. Advancement of Group Work, Toronto, Ont., Can., 1985, Woman of Yr., Trojan Women U. So. Calif., 1976, Woman of Yr., YWCA of Pomona Valley, 1989, Vol. of Yr., L.A. County Coun. on Aging, 1990; recipient Dart award for Innovative Teaching, U. So. Calif., 1974, 1st pl. award at juried show Am. Assn. Chinese Brush Painting, 1987, 2nd pl. short story Sedona Writers Contest, Hon. Mention non fiction, 1989, County Commnr. Citation State of Calif. Ho. of Reps., Outstanding Contbn. award Mt. San Antonio Gardens Retirement Cmty., 1994, Contbn. to Srs. award Pomona Valley Cmty. Svcs., 1994. Fellow Gerontol. Soc. Am.; mem. AAUW, Nat. Assn. Social Workers (cert., nat. chmn. 1962-64, group work sect., chmn. Cleve. chpt. 1969-72), Am. Soc. Aging (chmn. program com. 1983-85, City of Claremont com. on aging, chmmn. 1991, program chair 1985-94), Delta Kappa Gamma, Alpha Xi Delta. Episcopalian. Home: 918 W Harrison Claremont CA 91711

HARTIGAN, GRACE, artist; b. Newark, Mar. 28, 1922; d. Matthew A. and Grace (Orvis) H.; m. Robert L. Jachens, May 1941 (div. 1948); 1 son, Jeffrey A.; m. Robert Keene, Dec. 14, 1959 (div. 1960); m. Winston H. Price, Dec. 24, 1960 (dec. 1981). Student pvt. art classes. Dir. Md. Inst. Grad. Sch. Painting, 1965—. One-woman shows Tibor de Nagy Gallery, N.Y.C., 1951-55, 57-59, Vassar Coll. Art Gallery, 1954, Martha Jackson Gallery, N.Y.C., 1962, 64, 67, 70, U. Chgo., 1967, Gertrude Kasle Gallery, Detroit, 1968, 70, 72, 74, Robert Keene Gallery, Southampton, N.Y., 1957-59, Gres Gallery, Washington, 1960, U. Minn., 1963, William Zierler Gallery, N.Y.C., 1975—, C. Grimaldis Gallery, Balt., 1979, 81, 82, 84, 86, 87, 89, 90, 93, Hamilton Gallery, N.Y.C., 1981, Gruenebaum Gallery, N.Y.C., 1984, 86, 88, Kouros Gallery, N.Y.C., 1989, ACA Gallery, N.Y.C., 1991, 92, 94; exhibited in numerous group shows including Modern Art in U.S., 1955-56, 3d Internat. Contemporary Art Exhbn., 1957, 4th Internat. Art Exhbn., Japan, 1957, IV Biennial, Sao Paulo, 1957, New Am. Painting Show, Europe, 1958-59, World's Fair, Brussels, 1958, The Figure Since Picasso, Mus. Ghent, Belgium, Moca in Moca Chicago, Hand Painted Pop Moca L.A., Whitney Mus. Am. Art, N.Y.C., 1992-93; represented in permanent collections Mus. Modern Art, Walker Art Center, Whitney Mus. Am. Art, Art Inst. Chgo., Met. Mus. Art, Raleigh Mus., Providence Mus., Bklyn. Mus., Mpls. Mus., Albright-Knox Gallery, Buffalo, numerous others. Recipient Merit award for art Mademoiselle Mag., 1957, Nat. Inst. Arts and Letters purchase award, 1974. Address: 1701 1/2 Eastern Ave Baltimore MD 21231-2420

HARTIGAN, KARELISA DOROTHY, classics educator; b. Stillwater, Okla., Mar. 5, 1943; d. Charles Henry and Elsie Florence Voelker; m. Barry Hartigan, Apr. 21, 1966 (div. Feb. 1978); 1 child, Timothy Lawrence; m. Kevin Michael McCarthy, Dec. 22, 1992. BA in Classics, Coll. of Wooster, 1965; AM in Classics, U. Chgo., 1966, PhD in Classics, 1970. Asst. prof. St. Olaf Coll., Northfield, Minn., 1969-73; asst. prof., assoc. prof. Greek studies U. Fla., Gainesville, from 1973, prof., 1991—, co-dir. Ctr. for Greek Studies, 1980—, assoc. dir. honors program, 1989—. Author: The Poets and the Cities, 1979, Ambiguity and Self-Deception, 1991, Greek Tragedy on the American Stage, 1995; editor Text and Presentation jour., 1983-94; editor spl. issues Classical and Modern Lit.; Classical Reflections, 1980. Recipient Excellence in Tchg. award Am. Philol. Assn., 1985; Disting. Alumni Prof. award U. Fla., 1987-89, Univ.-Wide Tchg. award, 1990, Tchg. award, 1994. Mem. Modern Greek Studies Assn. (sec. 1983-3386), Classical Assn. Mid. West and South (pres. so. sect. 1986-88, nat. pres. 1992-93). Office: University of Florida Ctr Greek Studies 3-C Dauer Hall Gainesville FL 32611

HARTLAND, NANCI JEAN, communications executive, educator; b. Passaic, N.J., Feb. 3, 1944; d. Irvin Correll and Maureen Victory (Elmer) H.; m. Frederick Emerson Gilbert, May 30, 1962 (div. June 1968); children: Jacqueline Jean, Juré Noel, Frederick Thomas II. BS in Psychology, U. Maine, Orono, 1978; BA in Art, U. Maine, 1978. Human resources profl. Woolco Dept. Stores, Bangor, Maine, 1968-72; asst. to pres. Fransway Realty, Bangor, Maine, 1972-78; pres. Mgmt. Pro-Tem, Bangor, Maine, 1978-82, LifeTracks, San Diego, 1982—; trainer, developer Leap of Faith Global Leaders, San Diego, 1992-93, Ethnics & Ethics, San Diego, 1992-93. Author: My Spirit Speaks, 1985, Future Perfect, 1991, Some Places I Will Kiss You, 1992; contbr. articles to profl. jours. Vol. Consumers of Maine Bringing Action, Bangor, 1978-82, Maine Nuclear Referendum, Bangor, 1978-82, Global Energy Network Internat., San Diego, 1989-93. Mem. Optimist Club (v.p. 1990-93), Liason League. Democrat. Home: 7347 Almaden Ln Carlsbad CA 92009-6902 Office: LifeTracks 5169 Chelsea St La Jolla CA 92037

HARTLEY, ELDA EMILY, film producer; b. Brownwood, Tex., Mar. 6, 1911; d. Leonidas Carl and Emily Avis (Lockwood) Voelkel; m. William Keighley, Aug. 16, 1930 (div. 1936); m. Charles Irving Hartley, Oct. 18, 1940; children: Keith, Monty, Donn, David. BEd, UCLA, 1936; MA, Columbia U. Actress Paramount and 20th Century Fox, Hollywood, Calif., 1929-32; supr. visual edn. State of N.C., 1940; film prodr. Hartley Prodns., N.Y.C., 1940-78, Hartley Film Found., Cos Cob, Conn., 1978—; prodr. video: Voices of the New Age, 1989. Prodr., writer, dir. films: The Mood of Zen, 1967 (Blue Ribbon 1967), Requiem for a Faith, 1968 (Cine Gold Eagle 1968), Evolution of a Yogi, 1970 (Blue Ribbon), Islamic Mysticism: The Sufi Way, 1971 (Red Ribbon), Hinduism and the Song of God, 1974 (Cine Gold Eagle), Christian Mysticism, 1976 (Cine Gold Eagle), Holistic Health: The New Medicine, 1978 (1st place NFPW), India and the Infinite, 1979 (Cine Gold Eagle), Green winter, 1986 (Cine Gold Eagle), In Search of a Holy Man, 1987. Hon. trustee Wainwright Ho., 1993—. Recipient citation as pioneer in film making Wainwright House, Rye, N.Y., 1979, Bravo award Greenwich YWCA, 1980, Woman of Achievement award Conn. Press Women, 1980, Founders award Alpha Logics, 1982. Mem. Temple of Understanding (bd. dirs. 1967-93), Inst. Noetic Scis. (bd. dirs. 1990—), Spiritual Frontiers Fellowship (bd. dirs. 1991-92), Phenix Soc. (bd. dirs. 1991-92). Home: Cat Rock Rd Cos Cob CT 06807 Office: Hartley Film Found Cos Cob CT 06807

HARTLEY, ELISE MOORE, theatrical milliner, costume designer; b. Salt Lake City, Mar. 11, 1953; d. Paul Caine and Elaine Mary (Harvey) Moore; m. Edward A. Hartley, Feb. 14, 1986. BFA in Theatre, Design, U. Utah, 1976. Protégée Patricia Zipprodt, N.Y.C., 1976; costumeiere Equity Libr. Theatre, N.Y.C., 1977-78; costumer, milliner Triad Amphitheatre, Salt Lake City, 1986; milliner Utah Opera, Salt Lake City, 1986—; fashion design asst. Shari Alexander Design Firm, N.Y.C., 1978; design cons. First Presbyn. Ch. 202nd Gen. Assembly, Salt Lake City, 1990—; dir. Children's Camp Ministry and Program, Wasatch Acad., Mt. Pleasant, 1994. Milliner, costume designer for numerous prodns. including Eddnymion, 1976, Music Man, 1986, West Side Story, 1986; set designer Ceilidh, Ann Scottish Festival, Salt Lake City, 1989, 90, milliner Utah Opera prodns. including La Traviata, 1986, La Boheme, 1987, The Magic Flute, 1987, The Marriage of Figaro, 1988, Die Fledermaus, 1988, Rigoletto, 1989, Don Giovanni, 1989, The Tales of Hoffman, 1990; dresser Les Misérables, 1993. Deacon, Sun. sch. tchr., Bethel series 1990-, mission bull. bd. artist and designer, First Presbyn. Ch., Salt Lake City, 1989-91, mem. Evangelism Com., 1990, 92, staff Small Group Coord., 1993—. Theatre Guild scholar U. Utah, 1974. Home: 446 Wall St Salt Lake City UT 84103-1751

HARTLEY, KAREN JEANETTE, lawyer, mediator; b. Oakland, Calif., Aug. 2, 1950; d. Samuel Louis and Jean Iris (Beven) Ostrow; m. Terry Van Hook, Aug. 29, 1970 (div. Mar. 1976); m. William Headley, Jan. 22, 1977 (div. Mar. 1988). BA in Psychology with highest honors, UCLA, 1972; DMin, Sch. of Theology, Claremont, Calif., 1976; JD cum laude, U. San Diego, 1982. Bar: Calif. 1982, U.S. Dist. Ct. (9th cir.), 1983, Hawaii 1991; ordained to ministry, Meth. Ch., 1973. From intern to asst. United Meth. Ch., 1969-71; asst. minister St. Paul's United Meth. Ch., San Bernardino, Calif., 1973-74; assoc. minister Claremont United Meth. Ch., 1974-76; sr. minister Santee (Calif.) United Meth. Ch., 1977-79; clk. Calif. Supreme Ct., San Francisco, 1981; cons. Regional Dept. Edn., San Diego, 1979-81; assoc. atty. Duke, Gerstel, Shearer & Bregante, San Diego, 1983-84, Finley, Kumble, Wagner et al, San Diego, 1984-87; prin. atty. Hartley & Assocs., San Diego, 1987—; prin., AV-rated, owner Resolution, A Mediation Svc., San Diego, 1991—; mediator San Diego Mediation Ctr., 1990—. Mem. ABA, Calif. Bar Assn., San Diego Bar Assn., Lawyer's Club. Democrat. Office: Hartley & Assocs 4194 Stephens St San Diego CA 92103

HARTLEY, MARIETTE (MARIETTE HARTLEY BOYRIVEN), actress; b. N.Y.C., June 21, 1940; d. Paul Hembree and Mary Ickes (Watson) H.; m. Patrick Francois Boyriven, Aug. 13, 1976; children: Sean Paul, Justine Emilia. Student, Carnegie Tech. Inst., 1956-57; studied with Eva Le Gallienne. Co-host Today Show, June 9-27, 1980. Appearences include (theatre) Measure for Measure, 1958-59, Winter's Tale, 1959-60, A Midsummer Night Dream, 1959-60, The Merchant of Venice, Antigone, 1961-62, The Miser, 1968, Put Them All Together, 1978, Detective Story, 1984, (films) Ride the High Country, 1962, Marooned, 1969, Barquero, 1970, Skyjacked, 1972, Nightmare at Forty Third Hillcrest, 1974, Improper Channels, 1979, O'Hara's Wife, 1969, 1988, Encino Man, 1992, (TV) Incredible Hulk (Emmy award for best actress 1979), M*A*S*H, Star Trek, (TV series) Peyton Place, 1965, The Hero, 1966-67, Goodnight, Beantown, 1983-84, The Morning Program, 1987, WIOU, 1990, (TV films) Earth II, 1971, Sandcastles, 1972, Genesis II, 1973, The Killer Who Wouldn't Die, 1976, Last Hurrah, 1977, The Secret War of Jackie's Girls, 1980, The Love Tapes, 1980, No Place to Hide, 1981, Drop Out Father, 1982, M.A.D.D.: Mothers Against Drunk Driving, 1982, Silence of the Heart, 1984, My Two Loves, 1986, One Terrific Guy, 1986, To Love, Honor and Arrest, 1986, Passion and Paradise, 1989, Murder C.O.D., 1990, Diagnosis of Murder, 1992, The House on Sycamore Street, 1992, Child of Rage, Calloway's Climb, The Halloween That Almost Wasn't, The Second Time Around, African Queen; author: (with Anne Commire) Breaking the Silence, 1990. Recipient Clio award (for series of Polaroid TV commercials with James Garner), 1979, 80, 81, Golden Apple award Hollywood Women's Press Club, 1979. Mem. Acad. Motion Picture Arts and Scis. Office: Innovative Artists Talent & Literary Agy Ste 2850 1999 Avenue Of The Stars Los Angeles CA 90067

HARTLEY-LINSE, BONNIE JEAN, nurse; b. Chgo., July 26, 1923; d. Frank and Anna Kathleen (Koutecky) Kadlec; m. Robert William Hartley, June 23, 1949 (div. Feb. 1961); children: Robert Greig, Franklin James; m. Howard Albert Linse, June 10, 1978 (dec. Nov. 1985); stepchildren: Michael Howard, Janet Stokes. BS in Nursing, St. Xavier Coll., Chgo., 1945; cert. edn. Portland State Coll., 1965; MS in Nursing Edn., U. Oreg., 1972; cert. coll. health nurse practitioner program Brigham Young U., 1976. R.N., Oreg. Mem. faculty nursing St. Xavier Coll., 1945-47; head nurse U. Chgo. Clinics, 1947-48; nurse research newborn neurology U. Oreg. Med. Sch., Portland, summer 1961; coordinator dental assistant program, instr. biology Portland Pub. Schs., Oreg., 1965-67; health service clinician, adminstr. Clackamas Community Coll., Oregon City, Oreg., 1970-84; cons. Health Services Community Colls. of Oreg., 1972-84; pres. Coll. Health Nurses, State of Oreg., 1976-78. Vol. Task Force for Medically Needy of Clackamas County, Oreg.; mem. svc. vol. environ. learning ctr., Clackamas Community Coll. Mem. N.W. Oreg. Health Systems, Clackamas County Sub-Area Council, Oregon City, 1980-86. Recipient Recognition for Outstanding Service award Clackamas Community Coll., 1984; USPHS grantee, 1968. Mem. Am. Nurses Assn., Oreg. Nurses Assn. (Clackamas County unit 26, planning com. nat. day of the nurse awards celebration 1992), Pacific Coast Coll. Health Assn. (ann. conf. program coordinator 1980), Oreg. Coll. Health Dirs. Assn., Oreg. Health Decisions. Avocations: travel, piano, choral singing, swimming. Home: 9700 SW Marjorie Ln # 3 Beaverton OR 97005-6556

HARTMAN, ARLEEN, artist; b. Cleve., Jan. 17, 1954; d. Raymond Joseph and Margaret (Schuman) H. BA, Cleve. State U., 1981; MFA, U. Cin., 1984. Tchr. Deer Elem. Sch., Banchang, Thailand, 1973-74; artist Cleve., 1979—; asst. prof. art Bowling Green State U., Huron, Ohio, 1993-94; vis. artist various schs., Ohio, 1970-94; lectr. art CCC/CSU/UC, Cleve. and Cin., 1983-90, CSU Gov. Inst. Gifted & Talented, Cleve., 1987-92; lectr. Cleve. State U., 1987-89, vis. asst. prof., 1989-92; gallery dir. BGSU-Firelands Coll., Huron, 1993-94; radio host pub. affairs WCSB-FM, Cleve., 1991-92. One-woman shows include Out Art: A Purgative Event, 1992, Urban Life, 1992, Possession of Women, 1992, Dia de Los Muertos Celebration, 1993, Feminism Spanning the Americas: The Scream Continues, 1994, Women Rage: Men Listen, 1994, Land Sculptures, 1994, World War Four, 1995, Calling the Question, 1995; lectr. in field. Coord. Celebrating Women's Sexualities, Cleve., 1987, Shadow Project, Cleve., 1985. Home: 3033 Lorain Ave Cleveland OH 44113

HARTMAN, JENNIFER WEAVER, community college administrator; b. Decatur, Ga., Mar. 10, 1947; d. John R. and Bette (Farmer) Weaver; m. Gary E. Hartman, June 15, 1968; children: Bradley Harris, Brooke Morgan. BS, Pa. State U., 1969; MEd, Pa. State U., Harrisburg, 1994. Asst. buyer Woodward & Lothrop, Washington, 1971-72; exec. dir. YWCA, Gettysburg, Pa., 1975-77, program dir., 1978-84, exec. dir., 1984-89; dir. Gettysburg Ctr.-Harrisburg Area C.C., 1990—; sec. Adams County Coun. Cmty. Svcs., Gettysburg, 1986-87; v.p., founder Survivors, Inc., Gettysburg,

1981—; mem. steering com. YWCA Capital Campaign, 1978-81; bd. dirs. Adams County Nat. Bank. Area coordinator Adams County United Way, 1973; v.p. Friends of the Library, 1974-76; mem. Martin Luther King Celebration Com., 1981-87. Recipient Outstanding Alumni award Pa. State, 1989. Mem. AAUW (Women Making a Difference award 1984). Democrat. Lutheran. Home: 70 Park Ave Gettysburg PA 17325-8473 Office: Gettysburg Ctr Harrisburg Area C C 22 Liberty St Gettysburg PA 17325

HARTMAN, JOAN EDNA, English educator; b. Bklyn., N.Y.C., Oct. 5, 1930; d. H. Graham and Edna (Kuebler) H. Student, Mt. Holyoke Coll., 1951; postgrad., Duke U., Durham, 1952, Oxford U., 1958-59; PhD, Radcliffe Coll., Cambridge, 1960. Instr. Washington Coll., Chestertown, Md., 1952-54; instr. Wellesley Coll., 1959-62, asst. prof., 1962-63; asst. prof. Conn. Coll., New London, 1963-66, CUNY-Queens Coll., Flushing, 1967-70; asst. prof. CUNY-S.I. C.C., 1970-72, assoc. prof., 1972-76; prof. CUNY-Coll. S.I., 1976—, acting dean humanities and social scis., 1995—. Editor: Women in Print I, II, 1982 (En)Gendering Knowledge, 1991, The Norton Reader, 1992, Concerns; contbr. articles to profl. jours. Fellow, AAUW, NEH, Mellon Found., Folger Shakespeare Libr. Mem. MLA, Nat. Coun. Tchrs. English, Soc. for the Study of Women in the Renaissance, Women's Caucus for the Modern Langs., Nat. Arts Club. Office: Coll Staten Island 2800 Victory Blvd Staten Island NY 10314

HARTMAN, JOAN EVANS, educational supervisor; b. Gibson, Tenn., Sept. 30, 1935; d. William Slaton and Helen (Mann) Evans; children: John Scott, Edwin Evans, Mary Lane Hartman McKinney. BA, Lambuth U., Jackson, Tenn., 1957; MA, Vanderbilt U., 1958; EdD, Memphis State U., 1991. Tchr. Davidson County Schs., Nashville, 1958-60, pvt. kindergartens, Memphis and Ripley, Tenn., 1971-74; tchr. Lauderdale County Schs., Ripley, 1982-90, supr. fed. projects, 1990—; mem. evaluation teams So. Assn. Coll. and Schs., Memphis, 1985-88. Recipient Grad. Rsch. Symposium award Memphis State U., 1989, Career Ladder III Tenn. State Dept. Edn., Nashville, 1988—. Mem. Western Tenn. Edn. Assn. (v.p. 1985-88), Tenn. Edn. Assn., NEA, ASCD, Tenn. Assn. for Supervision and Curriculum Devel., Kappa Delta Pi. Methodist. Home: 169 Lake Dr Ripley TN 38063-1139 Office: Lauderdale Dept Edn 402 S Washington St Ripley TN 38063-2048

HARTMAN, LEE ANN WALRAFF, educator; b. Milw., Apr. 21, 1945; d. Emil Adolph and Mabelle Carolyn (Goetter) Walraff; m. Patrick James Hartman, Oct. 5, 1968; children: Elizabeth Marie, Suzanne Carolyn. BS, U. Wis., 1967; postgrad., U. R.I., 1972-73, Johns Hopkins U., 1990. Cert. tchr., Wis., Md. Educator Port Wash. Bd. Edn., Wis., 1967-68; instr. ballet YWCA, Wilmington, Del., 1977-78; tutor Md. Study Skills Inst., Columbia, 1984-86; tchr. Howard County Bd. Edn., Columbia, 1985—. Contbr. articles to profl. jours. Bd. dirs. Columbia United Christian Ch., 1980-83; mem. Gifted and Talented Com., Columbia, 1980-90, Lang. Arts Com., 1985—, USCG Officers Wives Club, 1970-72, Hosp. Aux. Bay St. Louis, 1970-72; troop leader Girl Scouts U.S., Columbia, 1980-91, Hospice; mem. exec. bd. PTA, 1990—. Recipient World Life Achievement award Internat. Biog. Ctr., 1994, Woman of Yr. award Am. Biog. Inst., 1994. Mem. AAUW (exec. bd. 1985—), NAFE, Home Hosp. Tchrs. Assn. Md. (chair pub. rels., sec.), Internat. Platform Assn. Home: 5070 Durham Rd W Columbia MD 21044-1445 Office: Howard County Bd Edn Rte 108 Columbia MD 21044

HARTMAN, LENORE ANNE, physical therapist; b. Cleve., May 27, 1938; d. Howard Andrew and Emma Elizabeth (Beck) H. BS in Agriculture, Ohio State U., 1960, MS in Agriculture, 1963; postgrad., Kans. State U., 1963-67; cert. in phys. therapy, U. Kans., 1968. Staff phys. therapist R.J. Delano Sch. for the Handicapped, Kansas City, Mo., 1969-74; chief phys. therapist Children's Mercy Hosp., Kansas City, 1974-78; relief staff Mass Gen. Hosp., Boston, 1969-70; staff phys. therapist Menorah Med. Ctr., Kansas City, 1979-87; clin. instr. phys. therapy St. Louis U., 1974-78, U. Ky., 1974-78, U. Mo., Columbia, 1973-78, U. Kans. Med. Ctr., Kansas City, 1974-87; mem. med. adv. com. Hospice Care of Mid Am., Kansas City, 1984-87; staff phys. therapist S.W. Gen. Hosp., 1992—; phys. therapy cons. Rocky River Riding Therapeutic Riding Program, 1994—; chapel organist St. Luke's Hosp., Kansas City, 1978-87. Ohio del. Internat. Farm Youth Exch., Brazil, 1962. Mem. Internat. Farm Youth Exhcange Assn. (life), Am. Physical Therapy Assn. (del. to nat. 1975-76), Mo. Physical Therapy Assn. (chmn. northwest dist. 1974-76), Am. Guild of Organists (chmn. profl. concerns com. Greater Kansas City chpt. 1983), Japan Am. Soc., Ohio State U. Alumni Assn. (life mem.), Ohio Physical Therapy Assn., Cleve. All-Breed Tng. Club, Western Reserve Kennel Club, Pembroke Welsh Corgi Club of Western Reserve, Am. Morgan Horse Assn., Am. Hippotherapy Assn., N.Am. Riding Assn. for Handicapped, U.S. Dressage Fedn., Omicron Delta Epsilon, Phi Delta Gamma (contbr. articles to jour.). Office: Southwest Gen Hosp Middleburg Heights OH 44130

HARTMAN, MARY S., historian; b. Mpls., June 25, 1941; married. BA, Swarthmore Coll., 1963; MA, Columbia U., 1964, PhD, 1970. Instr. to asst. prof. Rutgers U., 1968-75; assoc. prof. to prof. history Douglass Coll., Rutgers U., 1975—; dean Douglass Coll. Rutgers U., 1982—. Author: Clio's Consciousness Raised, 1974, Victorian Murderesses, 1978. Office: Rutgers U Douglass Coll Office of the Dean New Brunswick NJ 08903

HARTMAN, NANCY LEE, physician; b. Philipsburg, Pa., July 29, 1951; d. Richard Lee and Ann Hartman. Grad. Barbizon Sch. Modeling, 1970; AA, Harcum Jr. Coll., 1969-71; BA, Lycoming Coll., 1974; MS, L.I. U., 1977; MD, Am. U. of Caribbean in Plymouth, Montserrat, W.I., 1981. Med. technologist Lock Haven (Pa.) Hosp., 1971-72, Williamsport (Pa.) Hosp., 1972-73, Renovo (Pa.) Hosp., 1974; microbiologist and med. technologist Jersey Shore (Pa.) Hosp., 1974; microbiologist N.Y. Hosp. and Cornell Med. Center, N.Y.C., 1974-75, Drekter and Heisler Labs., N.Y.C., 1975, North Shore Labs., Inc., Syosset, N.Y., 1976-78; lab. technician North Shore Hosp., Manhasset, N.Y., 1981-82, Nat. Health Labs. Inc., Bethpage, N.Y., 1982; resident internal medicine program Interfaith Med. Ctr., Bklyn., 1983-84; med. cons. Shapiro & Baines, Mineola, N.Y., 1985-88; resident pathology program Lenox Hill Hosp., N.Y.C., 1986-87; resident clin. pathology Beth Israel Med. Ctr., N.Y.C., 1988-89; resident internal medicine, Lenox Hill Hosp., 1990; med. specialist, pres. Advt. Ltd., Glenwood Landing, N.Y., 1990-92; med. cons. Reichenbaum and Silberstein, Great Neck, N.Y., 1990-92, Leader Mfg., Inc., Que., Can., 1988-89, Meiselman, Boland, Reilly and Pittoni, Mineola, 1988-92, Law Offices of Sybil Shainwald, N.Y.C., 1989-91, Audio Visual Med. Mktg., Inc., N.Y.C., 1990-92, Law Office of Peter D. Kolbrener, Westbury, N.Y., 1990-92, Siben & Siben, Bayshore, N.Y., 1990-92, Whiteman & Gorray, Uniondale, N.Y., 1990-92, Law Offices of Jed Neil Kirsch, Mineola, 1990-92, Gandin, Schotsky, & Rappaport, Melville, N.Y., 1990-92, Doniger, Garland & Engstrand, N.Y.C., 1991-92, Law Offices of Steven Miller, Mineola, 1991-92, Law Offices of Harry Organek, Westbury, 1991-92, Law Offices of Micheal Flomenhaft, N.Y.C., 1991-92, Damashek, Godosky & Gentile, N.Y.C., 1991-92, Easton & Clark, Levittown, N.Y., 1991-92. Author: The Pocket Handbook of Infectious Agents and Their Treatments, 1987; also articles. Mem. Rep. Presdl. Task Force. Recipient Allied Health Professions Traineeship grant, 1975-77. Mem. AMA, Am. Women's Med. Assn., Am. Soc. Clin. Pathologists (registered med. technologist), Internat. Platform Assn., Am. Soc. Microbiology. Home: PO Box 492 Wynnewood PA 19096-0492

HARTMAN, RUTH ANN, educator; b. Galion, Ohio, Aug. 18, 1938; d. Richard Lewis and Florence Evelyn (Ireland) Campbell; m. Richard Louis Hartman, Jan. 14, 1956; children: Jeffery Lee, Marsha Elaine, Jerry Steven. BS, Ohio State U., 1970; MEd, U. LaVerne, 1976, postgrad., 1985—; postgrad., U. Akron, 1977-85. cert. tchr., Ohio. Tchr. Willard (Ohio) City Schs., 1964-65; educator Mansfield (Ohio) City Schs., 1966—, home tutor, 1971-81, educator, 1977—, faculty advisory com., 1990-92, young authors coord., 1991-92, co-coord. career edn., 1991-92; cons. Ohio State U., Ashland (Ohio) Coll., Mt. Vernon (Ohio) Nazarene Coll., 1976—. Co-author: Handbook for Student Teachers, 1983; contbr. to Norde News. Mem NEA, Ohio Edn. Assn., North Cen. Ohio Tchrs. Assn., Mansfield Edn. Assn. Republican. Methodist. Home: RR 1 Plymouth OH 44865-9801 Office: Mansfield City Schs 1138 Springmill St Mansfield OH 44906-1525

HARTMAN, RUTH GAYLE, rancher; b. San Francisco, Apr. 17, 1948; d. William James and Doris June (Reinhold) Nixon; m. Marcus Max Hartman, Dec. 14, 1968; children: William Marcus Hartman, Alicia Marlene Hartman. Grad. high sch., Sunnyvale, Calif. Cert. cosmetologist. Cosmetologist Palo Alto, Calif., 1966-68; engring. clk. Pacific Telephone, San Francisco, 1968-69, traffic data clk., 1969-76; owner, mgr. Coffee Creek (Calif.) Ranch Inc., 1976—. Appointed parent mem. Act Testing Secondary Adv. Bd., Sacramento, 1988-90; mem. Trinity High Sch. Curriculum Com., Weaverville, Calif., 1984, 85. Mem. Dude Ranch Assn., Trinity County C. of C., U.S. C. of C., Calif. Hotel and Motel Assn. (bd. dirs. 1992—, mem. ednl. com., mem. govtl. affairs com.), Internat. Platform Assn. Episcopalian. Home and Office: HC2 Box 4940 Trinity Center CA 96091

HARTMAN-ABRAMSON, ILENE, adult education educator; b. Detroit, Mich., Nov. 8, 1950; d. Stuart Lester and Freda Vivian (Nash) Hartman; m. Victor Nikolai Abramson, Oct. 24, 1941. BA, U. Mich., 1972; MED, Wayne State U., 1980, PhD in Higher Edn., 1990. Mich. Secondary Continuing Teaching Cert. Program developer and instr. William Beaumont Hosp., Royal Oak, Mich., 1972-74; vocational counselor for emigres Jewish Vocational Service and Community Workshop, Detroit, Mich., 1974-81; program developer and cons. Detroit Psychiat. Inst., Detroit, Mich., 1982; instr. for foreign students Oakland Community Coll., Farmington Hills, Mich., 1983—; mem. adv. bd. Mich. Dept. Edn., Detroit, 1981; lectr. Internat. Conf. Tchrs. English to Speakers of Other Langs., 1981; guest presenter Wayne State U., Lawrence Tech. U., 1991, U. Mich. Anxiety Disorders Program, 1993; presenter rsch. presentations Nat. Coalition for Sex Equity in Edn., Ann Arbor, Mich. Contbr. articles to prof. jours. Am. Arabic and Jewish Friends, Detroit, 1988—, Orgn. for Rehabilitation Through Training, 1986—, Wayne State U., Alumni Assn., 1980—. Mem. Am. Anthropol. Assn., Am. Mensa Ltd., Math. Assn. Am., Nat. Assn. Fgn. Student Affairs, Mich. Coun. on Learning for Adults, Assn. for Women in Math., Tchrs. of English to Speakers of Other Langs. Jewish. Office: Oakland Community Coll 27055 Orchard Lake Rd Farmington Hills MI 48334-4579

HARTMAN-IRWIN, MARY FRANCES, retired language professional; b. Portland, Oreg., Oct. 18, 1925; d. Curtiss Henry Sabisch and Gladys Frances (Giles) Strand; m. Harry Elmer Hartman, Sept. 6, 1946 (div. June 1970); children: Evelyn Frances, Laura Elyce, Andrea Candace; m. Thomas Floyd Irwin, Apr. 11, 1971. BA, U. Wash., 1964-68; postgrad., Seattle Pacific, 1977-79, Antioch U., Seattle, Wash., 1987, Heritage Inst., Seattle, Wash., 1987. Lang. educator Kennewick (Wash.) Dist. # 17, 1970-88; guide Summer Study Tours of Europe, 1971-88. Sec. Bahai Faith, 1971-94, libr., Pasco, Washington, 1985-88; trustee Mid. Columbia Coun. Girl Scouts USA; mem. Literacy Coun. Fulbright summer scholar, 1968. Mem. NEA, Wash. Edn. Assn., Kennewick Edn. Assn., Nat. Fgn. Lang. Assn., Wash. Fgn. Lang. Assn., Literacy Coun. Home: 1119 W Margaret St Pasco WA 99301-4134

HARTMANN, RUTH ANNEMARIE, health care education specialist; b. Naumburg, Saale, Germany, Mar. 16, 1936; came to U.S., 1957; d. Kurt and Anna (Jöesch) H.; m. Karl-Heinz Falatyk (div. 1983); children: Ulrich, Ute; m. Franklin J. Herzberg, 1987. Diploma in nursing, Medizinische Fachschule, Potsdam, German Dem. Republic, 1956; BA in German summa cum laude, U. Wis., Milw., 1978, MLS, 1979; EdD in Adult Edn., Nova U., 1987. Info. specialist Fluid Power Assn., Milw., 1980-81; asst. librarian Miller Brewing Co., Milw., 1979-82; patient edn. librarian VA Med. Ctr., Milw., 1982-85, health care edn. specialist, 1986—; adj. prof. (part-time) grad. health-care scis. Cardinal Stritch Coll. Mem. editorial bd. Jour. Healthcare Edn. and Tng.; contbr. articles to profl. jours. Bd. dirs. Concord Chamber Orch., Milw., 1982-91; vol. Cancer Soc., Milw., 1985—; reviewing bd. for program certification Am. Diabetes Assn., 1990—; chairperson pub. edn. com. Am. Cancer Soc., mem. exec. bd. dirs., editorial bd. Jour. Healthcare Edn. and Tng. Mem. Am. Assn. Adult Continuing Edn., Am. Soc. Healthcare Edn. and Tng., Spl. Libr. Assn. (treas. 1981-83), Libr. Community Milw., Area Coun. Health Educators (chairperson 1986-88), Nat. Wellness Coun., U. Wis. Alumni Assn., Phi Kappa Phi. Office: Clement J Zablocki VA Med Ctr Milwaukee WI 53295

HARTNESS, SANDRA JEAN, venture capitalist; b. Jacksonville Fla., Aug. 19, 1944; d. Harold H. and Viola M. (House) H. AB, Ga. So. Coll., 1969; postgrad., San Francisco State Coll., 1970-71. Researcher Savannah (Ga.) Planning Commn., 1969, Environ. Analysis Group, San Francisco, 1970-71; dir. Mission Inn, Riverside, Calif., 1971-75; developer Hartness Assocs., Laguna Beach, Calif., 1976—; ptnr. Western Neuro-Care Ctr., Tustin Calif., 1983-89; pres. Asset Svcs., Inc., 1981—. V.p., mem. bd. dirs. Evergreen Homes, Inc. Recipient numerous awards for community svc. Democrat. Office: Hartness Assocs 32612 Adriatic Dr Monarch Beach CA 92629-3510

HARTNETT, ELIZABETH A., trade association executive; b. Metuchen, N.J., June 28, 1952; d. John J. and Rita (Hackett) Kirwan; m. Raymond T. Hartnett, July 16, 1977; children: Kathleen E., John T. BS, Wheeling Coll., 1974. CPA, Pa. Jr. acct. Deloitte Haskins & Sells, Pitts., 1974-76; sr. acct. Deloitte Haskins & Sells, Washington, 1976-81, mgr., 1981-84; contr. Electronic Industries Assn., Washington, 1984-86, v.p. fin., 1986—; treas. Electronic Industries Found., Washington, 1984—. Mem. Am. Soc. Assn. Execs., Greater Washington Soc. Assn. Execs., Pa. Inst. CPA's, D.C. Inst. CPA's. Republican. Roman Catholic. Office: Electronic Industries Assn 2500 Wilson Blvd Arlington VA 22201-3834

HARTSE, DENISE YVONNE, society editor; b. Miles City, Mont., Nov. 5, 1951; d. Wayne Edwin and Lola Marion (Shipman) Durfee; m. Marcus R. Hartse, June 16, 1979. AA, Miles C.C., 1972; BA, U. Mont., 1975. Typesetter H & T Quality Printing, Miles City, Mont., 1975-76, 79-81; layout Larson Publs., Miles City, Mont., 1976-78, Sagebrush Publs., Miles City, Mont., 1978-79; soc. editor Miles City Star, Miles City, Mont., 1981—. Precinct committeewoman Dem. Party, Custer County, Mont., 1970-72; asst. Bills Coord., Mont. State Ho. of Reps., 1975; Mont. Dem. Exec. Bd., pres. New Dem. Coalition; mem. Miles City Concert Assn. Bd.; sec./treas. Miles City Arts, Cultural and Hist. Preservation Commn., 1991—. Mem. AAUW, Nat. Fedn. Press Women, Mont. Press Women (past pres.), Barn Players, Inc., Rainbow Girls (bd. dirs. 1981-94), Miles City Centennial Quilters (pres. 1987-90, 92-93), Custer County Art Ctr., Quilters Art Guild No. Rockies (bd. dirs. 1992—). Presbyterian. Home: 615 Yellowstone Ave Miles City MT 59301-4230 Office: Miles City Star PO Box 1216 Miles City MT 59301-1216

HARTSELL, MICHELLE LAWRENCE, materials engineer, researcher; b. Lynwood, Calif., Nov. 25, 1963; d. Claudis Frank and Marilyn Geraldine (Vigue) Lawrence; m. Benjamin Edward Hartsell, Dec. 16, 1989. AAS, Carteret Tech. Coll., 1984; BS, N.C. State U., 1989, MS, 1991. Rsch. assoc. Kobe Steel USA Inc., Research Triangle Park, N.C., 1991—. Mem. Product Devel. and Mgmt. Assn., Japan Soc. N.C. Office: Kobe Steel USA Inc PO Box 13608 79 TW Alexander Dr 4401 Bldg Research Triangle Park NC 27709

HARTSHORN, TERRY O., health facility administrator; b. 1944. Adminstrv. sec. Centinela Valley Hosp., Inglewood, Calif., 1965-68, adminstrv. asst., 1969; adminstr., cons. Community Health Svc., USPHS, L.A., 1969-71; adminstr. Luth. Hosp. Soc. So. Calif., L.A., 1971-73, Moore-White Med. Clinic, L.A., 1973-76; chmn. Pacificare Health Systems, Inc., Cypress, Calif., 1977—; chmn., pres., CEO Pacificare Health Systems, Inc., Burbank, Calif., 1993—; chmn. bd., pres., CEO UniHealth Am., Inc., Burbank, 1993—. Office: Unihealth Am 4100 W Alameda 4th Fl Burbank CA 91505*

HARTSOCK, JANE MARIE, nurse, educator; b. Rock Island, Ill., Nov. 19, 1948; d. George Vincent and Patricia Anna (Holland) Woeber; m. Donald Lee Hartsock, Jan. 16, 1971; children: Cara Elizabeth, David Vincent. B.S. in Nursing, Marycrest Coll., 1977; M.A., U. Iowa, 1982. Cert. oncology nurse. Head nurse U.S. Naval Hosp., Great Lakes, Ill., 1970-71; staff nurse Moline Pub. Hosp. (Ill.), 1971-72, instr. Sch. Nursing, 1977-87; nurse bone marrow transplant unit, U. Minn., 1987-92; instr. Mpls. Community Coll., 1988-92; instr., staff nurse oncology Trinity Med. Ctr., 1992—. Contbr. chpt. in book. Song leader Blue Grass Ch., 1977-87. With USN 1970-72, capt. Nurse Corps USAR. Mem. AAUW, Am. Nurses Assn., Nurse Educators Assn. (pres. 1984-85), Oncology Nursing Soc, Pioneer Club (Blue Grass, Iowa, sec. 1983-87), Sigma Theta Tau (pres. elect). Home: 2035 43rd St Rock Island IL 61201-4913

HARTSOUGH, KAREN MARIE, elementary education educator, artist; b. Somers Point, N.J., Dec. 7, 1959; d. Benjamin Lee and Elvera Marie (Pullo) New; m. Stephen Charles Hartsough, May 6, 1980; children: Mikel Brandon, Christian Vail, Nathaniel Dalton. BA, Stockton State Coll., 1985; postgrad. in real estate, South Jersey Sch. Real Estate, 1986; postgrad. in Edn., Rider Coll., 1992. Realtor French Real Estate, Ocean City, N.J., 1986; substitute tchr. Ocean City Pub. Schs., 1986; freelance comml. artist Image Cons., Ocean City, 1985—, Print Art, Pleasantville, N.J., 1985—, D&B Printing, Ocean City, 1985-90; instr. Ocean City Cultural Arts Ctr., 1987-92; tchr. St. Augustine's, Ocean City, 1990-94; pvt. tutor, Ocean City, 1991-94; instr., substitute Galloway (N.J) Twp. Sch. Consortium, 1994. Works include painted photographs Images of Rythm, 1990. grantee N.J. Divsn. for Arts, 1989. Mem. Am. Bus. Women Assn. (historian 1986—), N.J. Edn. Assn., Beach Babies Mother's Club (co-founder, bd. dirs. 1989—). Republican. Roman Catholic.

HARTUNG, MARY, state legislator; m. Morris Hartung; children: Elizabeth, Susan, David. Retailer; former rep. from dist. 9 Idaho Ho. of Reps.; state senator Idaho Senate, 1990—. Bd. dirs. Payette Libr. Named Outstanding County Chmn., Idaho Rep. Party, 1982-83; named to Idaho Rep. Hall of Fame. Mem. Payette C. of C. Home: PO Box 147 Payette ID 83661-0147 Office: Idaho State Sen State Capitol Boise ID 83720*

HARTUNG, MARY JO, nurse; b. Clear Lake, S.D., Jan. 20, 1954; d. Ronald Harold and Alice Fay (Barr) H. BS, Nebr. Wesleyan U., 1976; BA, Dakota Wesleyan U., 1981; BSN, McNeese State U., 1993. RN, La. Nurse aid, ward clk. Trinity Med. Ctr., Minot, N.D., 1982-84; nurse aid Bienville Gen. Hosp., Arcadia, La., 1984-87; tchg. parent VOA Group Home for Adolescent Boys, Pineville, La., 1988-90; mental health technician Recovery Ctr., Lake Charles (La.) Meml. Hosp., 1990-92; nurse technician West Cal-Cameron Hosp., Sulphur, La., 1990-93, ICU staff R.N., 1993—. Mem. ANA, LWV, AAUW, Am. Assn. Critical Care Nurses, Sigma Theta Tau. Democrat. Methodist.

HARTUNG, PATRICIA MCENTEE, therapist; b. Syracuse, N.Y.; d. James Henry and Frances Julia (Yehle) McEntee; m. Duane James Hartung, July 30, 1960; children: James Joseph, Tamara Ann, John Patrick, Jennifer Lynn. BS, LeMoyne Coll., 1957; MSW, Boston U., 1959. Lic. social worker; bd. cert. diplomate in social work. Social worker Dept. of Pub. Welfare/Child Welfare Div., Bay Shore, N.Y., 1959-60, Dept. Pub. Welfare/Alcohol Rehab. Prog., Omaha, 1961; cons./social worker Carnegie Gardens Nursing Home, Melbourne, Fla., 1970-72; parent educator Brevard Community Coll., Cocoa, Fla., 1968-74; therapist Circles of Care, Rockledge, Fla., 1974-81;, 1981-93; therapist Circles of Care, Rockledge, Fla., 1974-81; program dir. Circles of Care, Titusville, 1981-93, therapist, 1981—; adv. com. When Entering New Directions I, Cocoa, 1988-93; mem. Family Svc. Planning Team, Titusville, 1991-93. Mem. NASW, AAUW (Ctrl. Brevard chpt., v.p. membership 1991-93, pres. 1993—), Fla. Alcohol and Drug Assn., Acad. Cert. Social Workers. Democrat. Roman Catholic. Office: Circles of Care 6700 S US # 1 Titusville FL 32780

HARTUNG, THERESE CLAIRE, veterinarian; b. Omaha, Oct. 9, 1962; d. Thomas Joseph and Virginia Claire (Usher) Hartung; m. Myron L. Bultman, June 25, 1994. BS, U. Notre Dame, 1984; DVM, Okla. State U., 1988. Veterinarian Westwood Vet. Hosp., Norman, Okla., 1988—; admissions com. Okla. State U., Stillwater, 1994—; spkr. in field. Rabies prevention veterinarian Norman (Okla.) Animal Shelter, 1994—. Salsbury scholar, 1987; U. Tex. Health Sci. Ctr. fellow, 1985. Mem. NOW, Am. Animal Hosp. Assn., Am. Vet. Med. Assn., Am. Rabbit Breeder's Assn., Rotary (Norman club, com. chair 1993-94), Phi Beta Kappa, Phi Zeta. Democrat. Roman Catholic.

HARTWELL, ERIN, Olympic athlete, cycling. Olympic cyclist Barcelona, Spain, 1992. Recipient Bronze medal cycling 1km time trial, Olympics, Barcelona, 1992. Office: US Cycling Fedn One Olympic Plz Colorado Springs CO 80909

HARTY, SHEILA THERESE, theologian, writer, editor; b. Nurnberg, Germany, Jan. 24, 1948; came to U.S., 1951; d. Gerald Aloysius and Rosella Therese Harty. BA in Theology, U. South Fla., 1970; MA in Theology, Fla. State U., 1973. Lectr., counselor in drug sci. and drug edn. U.S. Army, Nurnberg, Fed. Republic Germany, 1974-75; personal adminstr. to campaign mgr. Ramsey Clark Senate Race, N.Y.C., 1976-77; personal adminstr. to Ralph Nader Ctr. for Study of Responsive Law, Washington, 1977-84; lectr. bus. ethics Faculty of Commerce Univ. Coll. Cork, Ireland, 1982-83; dir. corp. initiatives div. Nat. Wildlife Fedn., Washington, 1984-86; free lance writer, editor Washington, 1986-89; editor Congl. Budget Office, Washington, 1989-91; communication dir. Project 2061 AAAS, Washington, 1991-93; sr. editor, project mgr. Fed. Program Directories Carroll Pub. Co., 1993—; cons. Internat. Orgn. Consumers Unions, Hague, Netherlands, 1982-88. Author: Hucksters in the Classroom, 1979 (George Orwell award 1980); Consumer Initiatives, 1983; The Corporate Pied Piper, 1984; contbr. articles to profl. jours. Mem. Nat. Writers Union. Democrat. Roman Catholic. Home and Office: 2032 Belmont Rd NW Washington DC 20009-5426

HARTY, SHIRLEY COX, executive search consultant; b. Fredericksburg, Va., Feb. 14, 1952; d. William Cephas and Roberta Gladys (Henderson) Cox; 1 child, Scott Ashby. BS in Commerce, U. Va., 1981. Asst. v.p. 1st Nat. Bank of Atlanta, 1981-85; sr. assoc. Korn/Ferry Internat., Washington, 1985-91; recruitment mgr. Holiday Inn Worldwide, Atlanta, 1991-93; cons. Paul Ray Berndtson, Atlanta, 1993—. Runner races for charity; bowler Cystic Fibrosis. Home: 2440 Peachtree Rd NW # 7 Atlanta GA 30305

HARTZ, LUETTA BERTHA, insurance agent; b. Stevens Point, Wis., Sept. 29, 1947; d. Alfred Bernard Carl and Bertha Martha (Stauffer) Janz; student Madison (Wis.) Bus. Coll., 1965-66; m. James Patrick Hartz, Dec. 31, 1975. With Employers Ins. of Wausau (Wis.), 1966-68; casualty rater Sentry Ins. Co., Stevens Point, Wis., 1968-70, casualty supr., 1970-71, casualty trainor, 1971-72, customer service corr., 1972-74, bur. technician, 1974-75, customer service and acctg. mgr., Concord, Mass., 1975-79, personal lines property processing mgr., 1979-81, personal lines casualty processing mgr., 1981-83, comml. lines underwriting services mgr., 1983-85, comml. lines ops. mgr., 1985-87; agent Lewis P. Bither Ins. Agy., Inc., Tewksbury and Tyngsboro, Mass., 1988-90; acct. rep. Brewer & Lord, Acton, Mass., 1990—. Campaign treas. Reps., county clk. candidate, Portage County, Wis., 1972. Mem. U.S. Golf Assn. (asso.), Nat. Assn. Ins. Women, Mass. Assn. Ins. Women. (Middlesex chpt.). Lutheran. Clubs: Emblem (1st asst. marshall 1980-81, treas. 1981-83). (Concord, Mass.); Maynard Country (bd. govs. 1984-86) (Mass.). Home: 40 Drummer Rd Acton MA 01720-5202

HARTZ, RENEE SEMO, cardiothoracic surgeon; b. Bessemer Twp., Mich., Dec. 7, 1946; d. Rita Ann Semo; children: Tyler Joseph, Colin Wilson. BA, Western Mich. U., 1969; MD, Northwestern U., 1974. Diplomate Am. Bd. Surgery, Am. Bd. Thoracic Surgery. Intern pediatrics Children's Meml. Hosp., Chgo., 1974-75; intern gen. surgery Northwestern Meml. Hosp., Chgo., 1975-76, resident gen. surgery, 1976-79; chief resident cardiothoracic surgery Northwestern Meml. Hosp., 1979-81; instr. dept. surgery Northwestern U. Med. Sch., Chgo., 1978-81, assoc. in surgery, 1981-85; asst. prof. surgery med. sch. Northwestern U., Chgo., 1985-87, assoc. prof. surgery med. sch., 1987-92; prof. surgery, chief div. cardiothoracic surgery U. Ill. Hosp. & Clinics, Chgo., 1992—; apptd. to Northwestern Meml. Hosp., Chgo., Children's Meml. Hosp., Chgo., VA Lakeside Hosp., Chgo., Evanston (Ill.) Hosp., Columbus Hosp., Chgo.; laser researcher Northwestern U. Med. Sch., 1984—, U. of Ill. Hosp., West Suburban Hosp., Ill. Masonic Hosp. Contbr. articles to profl. jours.; contbr. chpts. to Perioperative Cardiac Dysfunction II, 1985, General Thoracic Surgery, 1989, New Technology in Vascular Surgery, 1988. Mem. Am. Coll. Chest Physicians, Am. Coll. Surgeons, Am. Heart Assn., Am. Women's Med. Assn., Assn. for Acad. Surgery, Chgo. Heart Assn., Chgo. Surg. Soc., Ill. Surg. Soc., Laser Inst. Am., Soc. Thoracic Surgeons, Soc. Univ. Surgeons, Am. Thoracic Surgeons, Sigma Xi. Office: U Ill Chgo 1740 W Taylor St # C 959 Chicago IL 60612-7232

HARTZELL, IRENE JANOFSKY, psychologist; b. L.A. Vor-Diplom, U. Munich, 1961; BA, U. Calif., Berkeley, 1963, MA, 1965; PhD, U. Oreg., 1970. Lic. psychologist, Calif., Wash., Ariz. Psychologist Lake Washington Sch. Dist., Kirkland, Wash., 1971-72; staff psychologist VA Med. Ctr., Seattle, 1970-71, Long Beach, Calif., 1973-74; dir. parent edn. Children's Hosp., Orange, Calif., 1975-78; clin. psychologist Kaiser Permanente, Woodland Hills, Calif., 1979-94; pvt. practice; clin. instr. dept. pediatrics U. Calif. Irvine Coll. Medicine, 1975-78. Author: The Study Skills Advantage, 1986; contbr. articles to profl. jours. Intern Oreg. Legislature, 1974-75. U.S. Vocat. Rehab. Adminstrn. fellow U. Oreg., 1966-67, 69. Mem. APA, Western Psychol. Assn., Pi Lambda Theta.

HARVARD, BEVERLY JOYCE BAILEY, chief of police; b. Macon, Ga., Dec. 22, 1950; d. Arcelious and Irene (Perkins) Bailey; m. Jimmy C. Harvard, 1972; 1 child: Christa. BA, Morris Brown Coll., 1972; MS, Ga. State U., 1980. Cert. FBI Nat. Acad. Police officer Police Bur. City of Atlanta, crime analysis officer Police Bur., exec. protection officer Police Bur., dep. chief of police, spl. asst. to commr. dept. pub. safety, dir. pub. affairs dept. pub. safety, chief of police, 1994—; commr. Commn. Accreditation for Law Enforcement Agys., 1991; bd. dirs. Met. Atlanta ARC, 1991, Coun. on Battered Women, 1991; trustee Leadership Atlanta, 1991; adv. bd. dir. Big Bros./Big Sisters, 1986—, Atlanta Victim/Witness Assistance Program, 1985—. Named Outstanding Atlantan, 1983, Alumna Yr., Morris Brown Coll., 1985, Bronze Woman Yr., Iota Phi Lambda, 1986, Woman Achiever Atlanta YWCA; recipient Trailblazer award for Law Enforcement City of Atlanta. Mem. Internat. Assn. Chiefs Police (tng. com. Ga. chpt.), Nat. Orgn. Black Law Enforcement (chmn. program), Bus. System Planning Team, Ga. State U. Alumni Assn. (bd. dirs. Atlanta chpt.), Delta Sigma Theta (parliamentarian). Office: Police Svcs City Hall 9th Fl 675 Ponce de Leon Ave NE Atlanta GA 30308*

HARVEY, BESS KOSSOUDJI, writer; b. Dayton, Ohio, Oct. 21, 1933; d. Demetrius and Athena (Tepelides) Kossoudji; m. Sept. 13, 1953 (div. Sept. 24, 1984); children: Ann Marie, James, Gregory. Student, Montgomery County Joint Vocat. Sch., 1980-81, Sinclair C.C., Dayton, Ohio, 1985-86. Onwer, operator Springview Day Care Ctr., Union, Ohio, 1964-69; realtor Timbercreek Realtors, Englewood, Ohio, 1980-84; telemktg. rep. AT&T-L.M. Berry, Kettering, Ohio, 1984-85; writer, pub., mktg. Golden Light Press, Englewood, 1989—; founder Golden Light Press, Englewood, Ohio; speaker numerous orgns. Author, pub.: MS, Lupus and Me (And That's Not All!), 1992. Mem. Am. Bus. Women's Assn., Eagles Aux., Kiser High Sch. Alumni Assn. (charter mem.). Greek Orthodox. Office: Golden Light Press PO Box 415 Englewood OH 45322-0415

HARVEY, CYNTHIA, ballet dancer; b. San Rafael, Calif.. Studied with Christine Walton, The Novato Sch. Ballet; student, San Francisco Ballet Sch., Marin Ballet Sch., Sch. Am. Ballet Theatre, N.Y.C., Am. Ballet Theatre Sch., N.Y.C., Nat. Ballet Sch. Can., Toronto. With Am. Ballet Theatre, N.Y.C., 1974, soloist, 1978-82, prin. dancer, 1982-86, 1988—; prin. dancer Royal Ballet, London, 1986-88; Guest artist, The Royal ballet, The Birmingham Royal Ballet. Creator: role of Gamzatti in La Bayadere; appeared in Swan Lake, Don Quixote, Sleeping Beauty, Giselle, Raymonda, Ballet Imperial, Coppelia, Etudes, Manon, Romeo and Juliet, La Sylphide, Les Sylphides, Symphony Concertante, Symphonic variations, Theme and Variations. Recipient John Anthony Bitson award, 1973. Office: care Am Ballet Theatre 890 Broadway New York NY 10003-1211 also: 133 W 71st St New York NY 10023-3834*

HARVEY, DORIS CANNON, trust company executive, citrus grower; b. Lake Wales, Fla., Mar. 13, 1930; d. Charles Bertal and Sarah (Holbrook) Cannon; m. O.J. Harvey (dec.); children: Barbara Kay Ryals, Nancy Jean Mynard. Pres. O.J. Harvey Inc., Tampa; v.p. Elfers Citrus Growers Assn., Palm Harbor, Fla.; personal rep. Estate of O.J. Harvey, Tampa; trustee O.J. Harvey Trust, Tampa; trustee Elfers Citrus Liquidating Trust, Palm Harbor. Bd. dirs. Tampa Home Assn., 1982-84, Alpha House, Inc., 1992—; trustee Doris C. Harvey Marital Trust, Tampa, 1984—; trustee, mem. fin. com. Palma Ceia United Meth. Ch., Tampa. Mem. Centre Club, Tampa Woman's Club, Tampa Yacht and Country Club, Sword of Hope Club, Rose Circle Club, Hearts of Gold Club, The Chiselers, Inc. Republican. Methodist. Home and Office: 1114 Culbreath Isles Dr Tampa FL 33629-4807

HARVEY, ELAINE LOUISE, artist, educator; b. Riverside, Calif., Mar. 1, 1936; d. Edgar Arthur and Emma Louise (Shull) Siervogel; m. Stuart Herbert Harvey, June 16, 1957; children: Kathleen Robin, Laurel Lynn, Mark Stuart. BA with highest honors, with distinction, San Diego State U., 1957. Cert. gen. elem. tchr., Calif. Tchr. Cajon Valley Schs., El Cajon, Calif., 1957, 58; free-lance artist El Cajon, 1975—; tchr. Athenaeum Sch. Music & Art, 1990—; juror various art exhbns., Calif., 1983—; lectr., 1984—; tchr. painting seminars, 1987—. Editor: Palette to Palate, 1986; contbr. The Artists Mag., 1987, 94, The New Spirit Watercolor, 1989, Calif. Art Rev., 1989, The Artists So. Calif., 1989, Splash, 1990, Splash II, 1992, Watercolor Techniques for Releasing the Creative Spirit, 1992, Collage Techniques, 1994, The Artistic Touch, 1994. Trustee San Diego Mus. Art, 1985, 86; leader El Cajon Coun. Girl Scouts of U.S., 1968; vol. art tchr., San Diego area pub. schs., 1973-76; choral dir. Chapel of Valley United Meth., 1991—. Recipient Merit award La. Watercolor Soc., 1984, Arches Canson Rives award Midwest Watercolor Soc./Tweed Mus., Greenbay, Wis., 1984, Winsor Newton award Midwest Watercolor Soc./Neville Mus., Duluth, Minn., 1985, McKinnon award Am. Watercolor Soc. 1985, Creative Connection award Rocky Mountain Nat. Exhbn., 1986, 1st Juror's award San Diego Internat. Watercolor Exhbn., 1986, Dassler Mochs award Adirondacks Exhbn. of Am. Art, 1988, Arjomari/Arches/Rives award Watercolor West, Brea Cultural Ctr., 1990. Mem. Nat. Watercolor Soc. (bd. dirs. 1987-88, elected juror 1989), Watercolor West (bd. dirs. 1986-88, 94), West Coast Watercolor Soc. (pres. 1992—), San Diego Watercolor Soc. (pres. 1979-80, chmn. internat. exhbn. 1980-81, Silver Recognition award 1986), San Diego Mus. Art Artists Guild (pres. 1985-86, bd. dirs. 1986-87, 90—) Western Fedn. Watercolor Socs. (del. 1983-91), Rocky Mountain Nat. Watermedia Soc., Allied Artists Am., Grossmont Garden Club (Elson Creativity Trophy 1977, 79). Home and Studio: 1602 Sunburst Dr El Cajon CA 92021

HARVEY, ELINOR B., child psychiatrist; b. Boston, Jan. 11, 1912; d. William and Florence (Maysles) H.; m. Donald K. Freedman, July 2, 1936; children: Peter, F. Kenneth. BS cum laude, Jackson Coll., 1933; MD, Tufts U., 1936. Diplomate Am. Bd. Psychiatry and Neurology, Nat. Bd. Med. Examiners. Intern New Eng. Hosp. Women and Children, Roxbury, Mass., 1936-37; resident Sea View Hosp., Staten Island, N.Y., 1937-39; adminstrv. and indsl. physician Assoc. Hosp. Svc. N.Y., 1939-41; house physician, resident Henry St. Settlement House, N.Y.C., 1939-41; pvt. practice Arlington, Va., 1941-43; pvt. practice as pediatrician Newport News, Va., 1943-46; clinician Westchester County Health Dept., White Plains, N.Y., 1947; pediatrician Arrowhead Clinic, Duluth, Minn., 1947-48; resident in psychiatry VA Hosp., Palo Alto, Calif., 1949-52; resident in child psychiatry child guidance clinic Children's Hosp. San Francisco, 1952-53, fellow in child psychiatry, 1953-54; pvt. practice as child and family psychiatrist Berkeley, Calif., 1954-68, Juneau, Alaska, 1968-77; instr. Am. U., Washington, 1941-43; clinician prenatal clinics Arlington County Health Dept., Arlington, 1941-43; clinician Planned Parenthood, Washington, 1941-43; mem. adv. com. emergency maternal and infant care program Children's Bur., Washington, 1942-48; instr. pediatrics schs. nursing Buxton and Riverside Hosps., 1943-46; consulting pediatrician Cmty. Hosp. & Clinic, Two Harbors, Minn., 1947-48; mem. courtesy staff Herrick Hosp., Berkeley, Calif., 1955-68, Bartlett Meml. Hosp., Juneau, 1968-77; cons. U.S. Bur. Indian Affairs Dept. Edn., Alaska, 1968-76, S.E. Regional Mental Health Clinic, Juneau, 1975-77, Mars & Kline Psychiat. Clinic and Hosp., Port-Au-Prince, Haiti, 1977-78, Navajo Area Indian Health Svc., Gallup, N.Mex., 1980—, Brookside Hosp., San Pablo, Calif., 1984—; instr. mental health and mental illness Alaska Homemaker-Home Health Aide Svcs., Juneau C.C., 1968-77; coord. State of Alaska Program Continuing Edn. Mental Health, 1974-76; clin. assoc. prof. dept. psychiatry and behavioral scis. U. Wash., Seattle, 1976-77; vol. child and family psychiatrist Bapt. Mission, Fermathe, Haiti, 1977-79; instr. child devel. Mars & Kline Psychiat. Clinic and Hosp., 1977-78; mem. hosp. staff Gallup (N.Mex.) Indian Med. Ctr., 1980—; cons. Brazelton neonatal behavioral assessment Navajo Area Indian Health Svc., 1982—, infant-parent program Brookside Hosp., 1984—; demonstrator, trainer Brazelton neonatal behavioral assessment scale Ctr. de Recursos Educatius per a Deficients Visuals a Catalunya, Barcelona, Spain, 1992; active Child Protection Agy., Juneau; mem. planning bd. Coordinated Child Care Ctr., Juneau; mem. grant writing com. of planning bd. Cmty. Mental Health Ctr., Juneau; presenter in field. Author: (with others) Annual Progress in Child Psychiatry and Child Development, 10th ann. edit., 1977, Expanding Mental Health Intervention in Schools, Vol. I, 1985, Psychiatric House Calls, 1988, The Indian Health Service Primary Care Provider, 1991; contbr. articles to profl. jours. Mem. comprehensive health planning coun. City and Borough of Juneau. Grantee NIMH, 1958-63. Fellow Am. Psychiat. Assn. (life), Am. Acad. Child and Adolescent Psychiatry (life, mem. task force Am. Indian children); mem. No. Calif. Psychiat. Assn., Internat. Assn. Child Psychiatry, World Fedn. Mental Health, Internat. Assn. Circumpolar Health, Soc. Reproductive and Infant Psychology. Home and Office: 1547 Buckeye Ct Pinole CA 94564

HARVEY, JANE R., investment company executive; b. Tarrytown, N.Y., Oct. 13, 1945; d. Fred W. and Margaret (White) Rosenbauer. Student, U. Ariz., Iona Coll., Coll. Fin. Planning; grad., Pace U. Lic. ins. counselor; registered fin. cons. Registered rep. KMS Fin. Svcs., Inc., Tucson, acct. exec., 1994—. Contbr. articles to profl. jours. Active Resources for Women. Mem. NAFE, Internat. Assn. Fin. Planning (past bd. dirs., v.p. membership So. Ariz. chpt., pres. 1994—), Internat. Assn. Registered Fin. Planners (bd. govs., speaker conv.), Internat. Assn. Registered Financial Cons. (bd. dirs. 1995—), Am. Bus. Womens Assn., Am. Assn. Individual Investors, Tucson C. of C. Office: 2311 E Broadway Blvd Tucson AZ 85719-6085

HARVEY, JUDITH GOOTKIN, elementary education educator, real estate agent; b. Boston, May 29, 1944; d. Myer and Ruth Augusta (Goldstein) Gootkin; m. Robert Gordon Harvey, Aug. 3, 1968; children: Jonathan Michael, Alexander Shaw. BS in Edn., Lesley Coll., Cambridge, Mass., 1966; MS in Edn., Nazareth Coll., Rochester, N.Y., 1987. Kindergarten tchr. Williams Sch., Chelsea, Mass., 1966-69; owner, tchr. Island Presch., Eleuthera, Bahamas, 1969-70; substitute tchr. Brighton Cen. Schs., Rochester, N.Y., 1985—; agt. The Prudential R.J. Russell, Realtors, Pittsford, N.Y. Author, dir.: (play) The Parrot Perch, 1991. Bd. dirs. in charge pub. rels. George Eastman House Coun., mem. award steering com honoring Lauren Bacall, 1990, chmn. gala celebration honoring Audrey Hepburn, 1992; mem. art in bloom steering com. for fashion show Meml. Art Gallery, 1994; co-chmn. Fashionata, Rochester Philharm. Orch., 1990; mem. steering com. of realtors Ambs. to Arts. Mem. Chatterbox Club, Genesee Valley Club. Home: 14 Whitestone Ln Rochester NY 14618-4118 Office: The Prudential RJ Russell 8 N Main St Pittsford NY 14534

HARVEY, KATHERINE ABLER, civic worker; b. Chgo., May 17, 1946; d. Julius and Elizabeth (Engelman) Abler; student La Sorbonne, Paris, 1965-66; AAS, Bennett Coll., 1968; m. Julian Whitcomb Harvey, Sept. 7, 1974. Asst. librarian McDermott, Will & Emery, Chgo., 1969-70; librarian Chapman & Cutler, Chgo., 1970-73, Coudert Freres, Paris, 1973-74; adviser, organizer library Lincoln Park Zool. Soc. and Zoo, Chgo., 1977-79, mem. soc.'s women's bd., 1976—, chmn. library com., 1977-79, sec., 1979-81, mem. exec. com., 1977-81; mem. jr. bd. Alliance Francaise de Chgo., 1970-76, treas., mem. exec. com., 1971-73, 75-76, mem. women's bd., 1977-80; mem. Fred Harvey Fine Arts Found., 1976-78; hon. life mem. Chgo. Symphony Soc., 1975—; mem. Phillips Acad. Alumni Coun., Andover, Mass., 1977-81, mem. acad.'s bicentennial celebration com. class celebration leader, 1978, co-chmn. for Chgo. acad.'s bicentennial campaign, 1977-79, mem. student affairs and admissions com., 1980-81; mem. aux. bd. Art Inst. Chgo., 1978-88; mem. Know Your Chgo. com. U. Chgo. Extension, 1981-84; mem. guild Chgo. Hist. Soc., 1978—, bd. dirs., 1993—; mem. women's bd. Lyric Opera Chgo., 1979—, chmn. edn. com., 1980, mem. exec. com., 1980-84, 88—, treas. women's bd., 1983-84, 1st v.p. 1988-90; mem. women's bd. Northwestern Meml. Hosp., 1979—, treas., chmn. fin. com., 1981-84, 92—, mem. exec. com., 1981-88; bd. dirs. Found. Art Scholarships, 1982-83; bd. dirs. Glen Ellyn (Ill.) Children's Chorus, 1983-90, founding chmn. pres.'s com., 1983-90; mem. women's bd. Chgo. City Ballet, 1983-84; trustee Chgo. Acad. Scis., 1986-88; adv. coun. med. program for performing artists Northwestern Meml. Hosp., 1986-94, mem. exec. com., 1992—, bd. treas., 1992—; pres., bd. dirs. William Ferris Chorale, 1988-89; chmn. pres. com. Chgo. Children's Choir, 1991-93. Mem. Antiquarian Soc. of Art Inst. Chgo. (life); bd. dirs. Grant Park Concerts Soc., 1986-92, Guild of the Chgo. Historical Soc., 1993—, Antiquarian Soc. Art Inst. Chgo., 1994—. Mem. Arts Club of Chgo., Friday Club (corr. sec. 1981-83), Casino Club (gov. 1982-88, sec. 1984-85, 1987-88, 1st v.p. 1985-86, 2d v.p. 1986-87), Cliff Dwellers CLub. Home: 1209 N Astor St Chicago IL 60610-2300

HARVEY, LYNNE COOPER, broadcasting executive, civic worker; b. nr. St. Louis; d. William A. and Mattie (Kehr) Cooper; A.B., Washington U., St. Louis, 1939, M.A., 1940; m. Paul Harvey, June 4, 1940; 1 son, Paul Harvey Aurandt. Broadcaster ednl. program KXOK, St. Louis, 1940; broadcaster-writer women's news WAC Variety Show, Fort Custer, Mich., 1941-43; gen. mgr. Paul Harvey News, ABC, 1944—; pres. Paulynne Prodns., Ltd., Chgo., 1968—, exec. producer Paul Harvey Comments, 1968—; pres. Trots Corp., 1989—; editor, compiler The Rest of the Story. Pres. woman's bd. Mental Health Assn. Greater Chgo., 1967-71, v.p. bd. dirs., 1966—; pres. woman's aux. Infant Welfare Soc. Chgo., 1969-71, bd. dirs., 1969—; mem. Salvation Army Woman's Adv. Bd., 1967; reception chmn. Community Lectures; Woman's com. Chgo. Symphony, 1972—; pres. Mothers Council, River Forest, 1961-62; charter bd. mem. Gottlieb Meml. Hosp., Melrose Park, Ill.; mem. adv. bd. Nat. Christian Heritage Found., 1964—; mem. USO woman's bd., 1983, woman's bd. Ravinia Festival, 1972—; trustee John Brown U., 1980—; bd. dirs. Mus. Broadcast Communications, 1987—mem. adv. coun. Charitable Trusts, 1989—. Recipient Religious Heritage of Am. award, 1974, Little City Spirit of Love award, 1987, Salvation Army Others award, 1989. Mem. Phi Beta Kappa, Kappa Delta Pi, Phi Sigma Iota, Eta Sigma Phi. Clubs: Chicago Golf, Woman's Athletic, Nineteenth Century Woman's, Press (Chgo.); Oak Park Country. Home: 1035 Park Ave River Forest IL 60305-1307 Office: PO Box 77 Oak Park IL 60303-0077

HARVEY, MICHELLE MAUTHE, foundation administrator; b. Bethesda, Md., Dec. 29, 1954; d. Benjamin Camille and Lelia Anne (Webre) Mauthe; m. Don Warren Harvey, Mar. 31, 1979; children: Elise Brandner, Benjamin Casimir. BS in Forestry, U. South, 1976; MBA, Duke U., 1989. Forester Internat. Paper Co. Inc., Natchez and Brandon, Miss., 1976-80; framer, mgr. Frame Workshop, Lexington, Ky., 1981-83; mgr., dir. Country Stitchery Frameshop, Raleigh, N.C., 1984; dir. found. rels., placement and internship Sch. Forestry & Environ. Studies Duke U., Durham, N.C., 1984-90; dir. Am. Forest Found., Washington, 1990-92; mgr. planning and devel. Am. Forest Coun., 1990-92; dir. Environ. Partnership Initiative-MEB, Washington, 1993; v.p. programs Nat. Environ. Edn. and Tng. Found., Washington, 1994—; mem. N.Am. Waterfowl Mgmt. Plan Implementation Bd., 1990-92; chair Animal Inn Nat. Partnership, 1992. Mem., dir. devel. Humane Soc. Greater Louisville, 1980; bd. dirs. Raleigh Civic Ballet, 1989-90, Wake County Literacy Coun., Raleigh, 1984-88, Soc. Preservation Hist. Oakwood City Lights Ball, 1988; fundraiser N.C. Symphony, Raleigh, 1985-86; bd. dirs. Ctr. Children's Environ. Literature, 1994—. Mem. Soc. Internat. Practical Tng. (regional com. 1985-90), Soc. Am. Foresters (nat. task force on forestry edn. 1991-93, sec. human resources working group rep. social scis. to Forest Sci. and Tech. Bd. 1995—, chair-elect nat. capitol chpt.1995, 1993-94, nat. leadership conf. steering com. 1990-93, nat. com. on women and minorities 1984-88), Assn. Found. Group (co-chair program planning 1991-93, dean tng. workshops 1991-93), Washington Ethical Soc. (steering com. nat. helping hands craft sale 1992, teen youth leader 1993—). Democrat. Office: NEETF 915 15th St NW Washington DC 20005

HARVEY, ROSE MARIE, stockbroker; b. Bellefonte, Pa., July 23, 1924; d. Charles Joseph and Frances (Bruno) Nelo; m. Norman Richard Harvey, Mar. 31, 1948; children: Michael David, Patricia Arlana Harvey Johnson, Stephen Wayne, Joseph Walter II, Daniel Thomas. A, Pa. State U., 1945; Degree in Spl. Corr., N.Y. Inst. Fin., 1965. Registered all U.S. exchanges; lic. life ins., Pa. Sec. Cerro Metal Products, Bellefonte, 1942-60, Green Ellis and Anderson, State College, Pa., 1960-64, Clark Dodge & Co., State College, 1964; registered rep. Josephthal & Co., State College, 1965-82, Prudential Bache, State College, 1982-84, Shearson Lehman, State College, 1984-90, Investment Mgmt. and Rsch., Inc., State College, 1990-93; ret., 1993; treas., bd. dirs. GHM & Assocs., Inc., State College, 1990—; bd. dirs., v.p. sales Art Alliance Cen. Pa., Lemont, 1992. Precinct chmn. Centre County Rep. Com., Bellefonte, 1960—; mem. Shade Tree Commn., Bellefonte Borough, 1980-91, Med. Commn., 1980—. Roman Catholic. Home: 207 W Linn St Bellefonte PA 16823-1519

HARVEY, VIRGINIA MARIE, nurse, administrator; b. Bronx, N.Y., Dec. 6, 1959; d. John Robert and Adrienne (Bennett) Erd; m. William S. Harvey, Oct. 1, 1983. AAS, Rockland C.C., 1979; BS, Mercy Coll., 1982. RN, N.Y., N.J. Staff nurse Englewood (N.J.) Hosp., 1979-81; charge nurse Rockland Psychiat. Ctr., Orangeburg, N.Y., 1983-86, nurse adminstr., 1986—. Mem. ANA (cert. mental health and psychiat. nurse). Home: 26 Sand St Garnerville NY 10923-1423 Office: Rockland Psychiat Ctr Orangeburg NY 10962

HARVILLE SMITH, MARTHA LOUISE, special education educator; b. Detroit, Sept. 28, 1958; d. Henry and Emma Jean (Campbell) H.; m. Russell Smith, May 1, 1993. BA in Edn., Queens Coll., 1981, MS in Edn., 1986; postgrad., Columbia U., 1992. Cert. tchr. spl. edn., elem. tchr. N-6, sch. dist. adminstr., N.Y. Caseworker Bur. of Child Welfare, Jamaica, N.Y., 1981-82; tchr. spl. edn. Pub. Sch. 46Q, Bayside Queens, N.Y., 1982-83, Pub. Sch. 213Q, Bayside Queens, N.Y., 1983-85; Pub. Sch. 153, Maspeth, 1986; gen. indsl. arts tchr. Ind. Sch. 227Q/Louis Armstrong East, Elmhurst, N.Y., 1985-89; spl. edn. tchr. Pub. Sch. 153, Bayside Queens, 1986; tchr. technology Ind. Sch. 227Q/Louis Armstrong East, Elmhurst, N.Y., 1990-91, 93-94; staff devel. specialist Cen. Bd. Edn., Bklyn., 1989-90; rsch. asst. Columbia U. Tchr.'s Coll., N.Y.C., 1991—; rsch. asst., intern Ctr. If Adaptive Tech., N.Y.C., 1991—; tech. cons. CSTIP project Tchrs. Coll. Columbia U. IUME Ctr.; computer tchr. Bd. Edn. Dist. 26, Bayside Queens, 1983-85; software evaluator, Bd. Edn., Bklyn., 1988-89; yearbook adv. Ind. Sch. 227Q, 1986-89; adj. lectr. Big Buddy Program at Queens Coll., Flushing, N.Y., 1989-90. Inventor in field; contbr. articles to profl. jours. Exec. bd. Reach for Cultural Heights, 1992—; mem. Lincoln Ctr. Inst., 1984—; del. Early Childhood Math. Readiness Del. Team, Citizen Amb. Program in China, 1995. Recipient Svc. award Girl Scouts US., Jamaica, 1980. Mem. Coun. Exceptional Children, Queens Coll. Alumni, Edn. Adminstrn. Orgn. Columbia U., Queens Coll. Grad. Student Assn. (pres. 1988), Kappa Delta Pi.

HARVITT, ADRIANNE STANLEY, lawyer; b. Chgo., May 15, 1954; d. Stanley and Maryln (Loye) H.; m. Donald Martin Heinrich, Aug. 27, 1977; children: Patrick Loye, Christina Marie. AB, U. Chgo., 1975, MBA, 1976; JD with honors, Ill. Inst. Tech., 1980. Bar: Ill. 1980, U.S. Dist. Ct. (no. dist.) Ill. 1980, U.S. Ct. Appeals (7th cir.) 1985, (9th cir.) 1988, U.S. Supreme Ct. 1985, Wis. 1993. Fin. analyst Bell & Howell Co., Chgo., 1976-77; trial atty. U.S. Commodity Futures Trading Commn., Chgo., 1980-83; assoc. Hannafan & Handler, Chgo., 1983-85; ptnr. Harvitt & Gekas, Ltd., Chgo., 1985—. Mem. Law Rev. Chgo.-Kent Coll. Law, 1979-80. Mem. ABA, Ill. Bar Assn. (article hon. mention 1982), Chgo. Bar Assn., U. Chgo. Women's Bus. Group (v.p. 1988-90), U. Chgo. Women's Bd., Art Inst. Chgo. Office: Harvitt & Gekas Ltd 135 S La Salle St Ste 2600 Chicago IL 60603-4501

HARWARD, VALERIE PIERCE, property consultant; b. Brigham City, Utah, 1928; d. Julian M. Pierce and Bonnie B. (Jeppesen) Jurgensmeier; m. Thomas O. Harward, Jan. 14, 1986; children: George, Allison, Russell, Laura, Lisa, Rachel, Mick, David. Degree, Long Beach (Calif.) City Coll., 1959, postgrad., 1959; postgrad., Utah State U., 1985. Adminstrv. asst. Med. Ctr., Long Beach, 1958-60; pres. Creative Cons., Orange County, Calif., 1970-73; real estate agy. Cache Enterprises and Realty, Logan, Utah, 1980-85; residential sales mgr. Bus. Capital Inc., Logan, 1986; real estate sales agent Preferred Real Estate Investments, Logan, 1986; real estate and bus. cons. McKinley Inst., Orem, Utah, 1986-89; owner Assoc. Property Cons., Murray, Utah, Denver, and Nev., 1986—, Color Me Beautiful. Active Mormon Ch., Long Beach, 1957-71, PTA, Pleasant Grove, Utah; precinct capt. Rep. Central Com., Long Beach, 1959-60; chmn. Nat. Save Children Air Lift, Virginia Beach, Va., 1976. Recipient Svc. award ARC, 1975. Mem. Logan Bd. Realtors (chmn. multiple listing svc. 1985, svc. award 1985, chmn. polit. action com. 1984-86), Utah County Bd. Realtors, Salt Lake County Bd. R ty Taxation, Cypress C. of C. (chmn. 1971), Cypress Jr. Women's Club (chmn. 1970). Home and Office: Assoc Property Cons 4253 Sumac Ct Pleasant Grove UT 84062-9456

HARWAY, MICHELE, psychology educator and researcher; b. Takoma Park, Md, Sept. 13, 1947; d. Maxwell and Georgette (Volcovici-Nadelar) H.; m. Bruce Eric Antman, Dec. 23, 1979; children: Sasha Antman, Alissa Antman. BS, Tufts U., 1969; MA, U. Maryland, 1971; PhD, U. Md., 1974. Asst. dean U. Calif., Irvine, 1974; rsch. psychologist Higher Edn. Rsch. Inst., UCLA, 1974-77; asst. rsch. prof. psychology U. So. Calif., L.A., 1978-81; assoc. prof. Calif. Grad. Inst., L.A.; prof., dir. rsch. Calif. Family Study Ctr., North Hollywood, Calif., 1987--; mem. rsch. faculty Fielding Inst., Calif., 1986—; cons. various orgns. including Hughes Aircraft, Met. Water Dist., U.S. Dept. State, others, 1978-87; mem. part-time faculty UCLA, Mt. St. Mary's Coll., Wright Inst., Calif. Sch. Profl. Psychology, Calif. State U., 1978-86. Editor: Handbook of Longitudinal Research, vol. 1 and vol. 2, 1984, Battering and Family Therapy: A Feminist Perspective, 1977, Sex Discrimination in Career Counseling and Education, 1977, Assessing and Tracking Battered Women, Batterers, and Their Children, 1994. Fellow APA. Home: PO Box 241865 Los Angeles CA 90024-9665

HARWELL, FRANCES OLIVIA, parochial school administrator; b. Phila., Jan. 13, 1960; d. Clarence T. Jr. and Olivia Elizabeth (Lee) H.; 1 child, Sherrell Olivia. BA, Montclair State Coll., 1982; MEd, U. N. Tex., 1988. Cert. elem. tchr., Tex., mid-mgmt. adminstr., instrnl. leadership trainer, Tex. tchr. appraiser, CPR and first aid. Primary tchr. Zion Demonstration Primary Sch., Phila., 1983-84; adminstr. Oak Cliff Bible Fellowship Acad., Dallas, 1988—; tchr. appraiser Dallas schs., 1991—. Founder, dir. summer feeding program, community tutoring program, Deptford (N.J.) Twp. Bd. Edn., 1982; judge oratorical contest H.S. Thompson Sch., Dallas, 1989—; coord. community fair day, coach with basketball camp, Dallas, 1989—; mem. PTA, Dallas, 1987—; mem. Dallas Ind. Sch. Dist. Religious and Character Edn. Task Forces, 1989—. Recipient Black Alumni Recognition award, Minority Recognition award Montclair State Coll. Alumni, 1982; named Tchr. of Yr., Bayles Elem. Sch., Dallas, 1987. Mem. Assn. Christian Schs. Internat. (mem. sch. accreditation team 1989—), Internat. Fellowship Christian Sch. Adminstrs., Phi Delta Kappa. Office: Fellowship Christian Acad 1808 W Camp Wisdom Rd Dallas TX 75232-3332

HARWICK, BETTY CORINNE BURNS, sociology educator; b. L.A., Jan. 22, 1926; d. Henry Wayne Burns and Dorothy Elizabeth (Menzies) Routhier; m. Burton Thomas Harwick, June 20, 1947; children: Wayne Thomas, Burton Terence, Bonnie Christine Foster, Beverly Anne Carroll. Student, Biola, 1942-45, Summer Inst. Linguistics, 1945, U. Calif., Berkeley, 1945-52; BA, Calif. State U., Northridge, 1961, MA, 1965; postgrad., MIT, 1991. Prof. sociology Pierce Coll., Woodland Hills, Calif., 1966—, pres. acad. senate, 1976-77, pres. faculty assn., 1990-91, chair dept. for philosophy and sociology, 1990—; co-founder, faculty advisor interdisciplinary religious studies program Pierce Coll., Woodland Hills, 1988—, creator courses in religious studies in philosophy and sociology depts., Pierce Coll. Author: (with others) Introducing Sociology, 1977; author: Workbook for Introducing Sociology, 1978. faculty rep. Calif. Community Coll. Assn., 1977-80. Alt. fellow NEH, 1978. Mem. Am. Acad. Religion, Soc. Bibl. Lit., Am. Sociol. Assn. Presbyterian. Home: 19044 Superior St Northridge CA 91324-1845 Office: LA Pierce Coll 6201 Winnetka Ave Woodland Hills CA 91371-0002

HARWOOD, BERNICE BAUMEL, artist, community volunteer; b. Bklyn., Mar. 6, 1923; d. Max and Mildred (Weinberger) Baumel; m. Daniel J. Harwood, Aug. 23, 1947; children: René Gordon, Felice Spodick. BS in Art Edn., Hofstra U., 1973, MA in Spl. Edn., 1975; student, Ruth Leaf Studio, Douglaston, N.Y., 1980-87, Studio Camitzer, Valdottavo, Italy, 1983. Artist in residence Syossett (N.Y.) Sch. Dist., 1986; pres. Graphic Eye Gallery, 1986-87. Exhibited in one-woman shows at Calkins Gallery, Hofstra U., 1985, Graphic Eye Gallery, Port Washington, N.Y., 1989; exhibited in group shows at Norton Gallery Art, Artists Guild, West Palm Beach, Fla., Hutchins Gallery, C.W. Post U., Greenvale, N.Y., 1982, Albrecht Mus., St. Joseph, Mo., 1986, Monmouth (N.J.) Mus. Art, 1986, Foxhall Gallery,

Washington, 1987, Elaine Benson Gallery, Bridghampton, N.Y., 1989, Daruma Gallery, Cedar Hurst, N.Y., 1991, others; works included in pvt. collections including IBM, Bethlehem, Pa., Am. Stock Exchange, N.Y.C., Chase Manhattan (N.Y.) Bank; illustrator: Five Towns, 1962. Chairperson LWV, Woodmere, N.Y., 1957-61; v.p. Nat. Coun. Jewish Women, Lawrence, N.Y., 1976-81; committeewoman Dem. Party, Woodmere, 1962-84; mem. bd. advisors Nassau County Mus. Fine Art, 1981-88. With WAVES, 1944-46. Recipient art awards including Sally Carson award Norton Gallery of Art, 1993, 2d prize Emily Lowe Gallery, Hofstra U., 1984, award of excellence Long Beach (N.Y.) Art League, 1987. Mem. Nat. Assn. Women Artists (juror 1988-90, Leila Sawyer award 1983,2d v.p., 1995), N.Y. Artists Equity, Long Beach Art League, Prints Etcetera. Democrat. Jewish. Home: 835 Fiske St Woodmere NY 11598-2429 also: 41 Windsor Ln Boynton Beach FL 33436

HARWOOD, ELEANOR CASH, librarian; b. Buckfield, Me., May 29, 1921; d. Leon Eugene and Ruth (Chick) Cash; B.A., Am. Internat. Coll., 1943; B.S., New Haven State Tchrs. Coll., 1955; m. Burton H. Harwood, Jr., June 21, 1944 (div. 1953); children—Ruth (Mrs. William R. Cline), Eleanor, James Burton. Librarian, Rathbun Meml. Library, East Haddam, Conn., 1955-56; asst. librarian Kent (Conn.) Sch., 1956-63; cons. to Chester (Conn.) Pub. Library, 1965-71. Author: (essay) Growing Up in Chester, 1993. Served from ensign to lt. (j.g.) USNR, 1944-46. Mem. Am., Conn. library assns., Chester Hist. Soc. (trustee 1970-72), D.A.V., Am. Legion Aux., Soc. Mayflower Descs. Mem. United Ch. Author: (with John G. Park) The Independent School Library and the Gifted Child, 1956, The Age of Samuel Johnson, (essay) Remember When, 1987. Recipient The Commemorative medal of Honor Am. Biog. Inst., 1987; biog. tribute Dr. Katie Wilcox, 1975. Home: 10 Maple St Box 255 Chester CT 06412-0255

HARWOOD, VIRGINIA ANN, retired nursing educator; b. Lawrenceville, Ohio, Nov. 5, 1925; d. Warren Leslie and Ruth Ann (Wilson) H.; m. Kenneth Dale Juillerat, Dec. 21, 1946 (div. 1972); children: Rozanne Augsburger, Vicki Sue Terry, Carol Mann, Karen Juillerat. RN, City Hosp. Sch. Nursing, Springfield, Ohio, 1946; BSN, Ind. U., 1968; MS in Edn., Purdue U., 1973, PhD, 1982. cert. psychiat/mental health nurse. Staff nurse various hosps., 1946-60; pub. health nursing supr. Whitley County Health Dept., Columbia City, Ind., 1960-65; nursing supr., coordinator staff devel. Ft. Wayne (Ind.) State Hosp., 1965-69; faculty sch. nursing Parkview Hosp., Ft. Wayne, 1969-74; faculty dept. nursing Ball State U., Muncie, Ind., 1974-77; dir. nursing program Thomas More Coll., Ft. Mitchell, Ky., 1977-79; faculty sch. nursing Purdue U., West Lafayette, Ind., 1979-80; dean sch. nursing Ashland (Ohio) Coll., 1980-83; retired, 1983-86; charge nurse admission psychiat. unit VA Med. Ctr., Marion, Ind., 1986-93, ret., 1994—; cons. to nursing program Franklin U., Columbus, Ohio, 1981-82. Bd. dirs. Opera d'Lafayette, 1979-80, Am. Cancer Soc., Ashland, 1980-83, Kno-Ho-Ko Community Action Agy., Ashland, 1982-83; active Rep. Nat. Com., 1978—, U.S. Senatorial Club, 1984—, Rep. Pres. Task Force, 1982—; stewardship com. mem. Trinity Luth. Ch., Ashland, 1982-83; worship com. mem. St. John Luth. Ch., Marion, 1988-92; sec. ch. coun. Grace Luth. Ch., Gas City, Ind., 1993—. Fellow Acad. Psychiat. Nurse Specialists; mem. Am. Nurses Assn., Ky. Nurses Assn. (by-laws com.), Ohio Nurses Assn. (pres. Mohican dist. 1981-83), Ind. State Nurses Assn. (legis. com. 1979-80, program chmn. dist. 1 1970-71), Am. Nurses Found., Nat. League for Nursing (coun. baccalaureate and higher degree programs 1974-83), Ind. League for Nursing (chair edn. coun. 1972-73), Mensa (participant U.S.-Can. rondevous 1988, Cambridge, Eng. 1980, 90) Intertel, Sigma Theta Tau. Home: 115 E 50th St Marion IN 46953-5362

HASELTINE, FLORENCE PAT, research administrator, obstetrician, gynecologist; b. Phila., Aug. 17, 1942; d. William R. and Jean Adele Haseltine; m. Frederick Cahn, Mar. 12, 1964 (div. 1969); m. Alan Chodos, Apr. 18, 1970; children: Anna, Elizabeth. BA in Biophysics, U. Calif., Berkeley, 1964; PhD in Biophysics, MIT, 1964-69; MD, Albert Einstein Coll. of Medicine, 1972. Diplomate Am. Bd. Ob-Gyn, Am. Bd. Reproductive Endocrinology. Asst. prof. dept. ob-gyn. and pediatrics Yale U., New Haven, 1976-82, assoc. prof. dept. ob-gyn. and pediatrics, 1982-85; dir. Ctr. for Population Research, Nat. Inst. Child Health and Human Devel. NIH, Bethesda, Md., 1985—; Chmn. Woman's Council of the Am. Fertility Soc. Co-author: Woman Doctor, 1976, Magnetic Resonance of the Reproductive System, 1987; co-editor 25 books on reproductive scis. Fellow Am. Coll. Ob-Gyn; mem. Inst. of Medicine, AAAS (bd. dirs.), Am. Fertility Soc., Soc. Gynecol. Investigation, Soc. Study of Reproduction, Endocrine Soc., Soc. Reproductive Endocrinologists, Soc. for Advancement Women's Health Rsch. (founder, pres. bd. dirs.), Soc. Cell Biology. Office: NIH/NICHD Ctr Population Rsch 9000 Rockville Pike 6100/8B07 Executive Blvd Bethesda MD 20892

HASEN-SINZ, SUSAN KATHERINE, actress, political organization worker; b. LaGrange Park, Ill., Jan. 30, 1965; d. Hans and June Catherine (Huml) H. BA in Polit. Sci., Spanish, U. Ill., 1987; postgrad., Loyola U., Chgo. Actress Springfield (Ill.) Theatre Ctr., 1987—; mem. mgmt. staff Ill. Dept. Driver Svcs., Chgo., Gov.'s Office, Ill. Dept. Pub. Aid; speaker various youth groups, 1985—; dance instr. YMCA, Springfield, 1987, counselor Miss Ill./USA Pageant, Arlington Heights, Ill., 1987; fellow adminstrv. hearings under Sec. of State Jim Edgar, Springfield, 1987—. Lead actress A Day in Hollywood-A Night in the Ukraine, 1987 (Best of Springfield award), 42d St., Ill., 1991—; actress Manny, nat. tour A Christmas Carol, 1989, Joseph and the Amazing Technicolor Dreamcoat, Ill.; backup singer Kenny Rogers Christmas Tour, Ill.; actress, singer, dancer Jesus Christ Superstar, 1992; singer Miss Ill./USA Pageant, 1987; understudy Puttin on the Ritz, Ill., West Side Story, Ill.; lead actress The Dance Factory, Chgo, A... My Name is Still Alice, Chgo. Active in drama ministry Hope Ch., Springfield; soloist Christ Ch. of Oak Brook, Ill., 1983—, also leader youth group Koinonia; student del. Internat. Strategic Affairs Conf., N.Y.C., 1987—; mem. campaign staff Jim Edgar for Gov. Ill., 1991; judge Miss Teen Ill./U.S.A. Pageant; staff asst. Congressman Harris Fawell's OFfice; rep. for 13th dist. Ill. Recipient Miss Amity award Miss. I.../U.S.A., 1986; scholarship winner Miss Illini contest. Mem. U. Ill. Alumni Assn. (named one of 100 top srs. at Champaign-Urbana campus 1986, named outstanding student 1986-87), Kappa Alpha Theta, Kappa Alpha Theta Alumni Assn. (chaplain, pres. standards com. 1986-87, songleader 1986-87). Home: 1447 Bannock Ct Bartlett IL 60103-2978 Office: 624 S Michigan Ave Fl 4 Chicago IL 60605-1904

HASHIM, ELINOR MARIE, librarian; b. Pittsfield, Mass., Dec. 13, 1933. B.A., U. Vt., 1955; M.S., So. Conn. State U., 1970. Engring. asst. United Techs. Research Ctr., East Hartford, Conn., 1956-58, tech. research asst., 1958-63, supr. engring. aides and assts., 1963-68; head reference dept. Mary Cheney Library, Manchester, Conn., 1968-71; head circulation dept. New Britain (Conn.) Pub. Library, 1971-72, head bus., sci. and tech. depts., 1972-73, head reference dept., 1973-75; dir. Welles-Turner Meml. Library, Glastonbury, Conn., 1975-81; supr. reference and tech. services Perkin-Elmer Corp., Norwalk, Conn., 1981-85; program dir. spl. libraries Online Computer Library Ctr., Dublin, Ohio, 1985-90, govt. rels. officer, 1990-93, legis. analyst, 1993—; mem., chmn. Nat. Commn. on Libraries and Info. Sci., Washington, 1982-86, chmn. emeritus, 1986—; apptd. Conn. State Library Bd., 1974, chmn., 1976-82. Recipient Disting. Alumni award So. Conn. State U., 1982. Mem. ALA (pub. library assn. membership com. 1979-80, councilor Conn. chpt. 1980-82, councilor-at-large 1987-88, com. on legis. 1987-89, resolutions com. 1989-91, standards com. 1991-95), Conn. Library Assn. (chmn. legis. com. 1971-73, chmn. nominations com. 1975-76, rep. to ALA 1980-82, Librarian of Yr. award 1982), Spl. Libraries Assn. (fellows designation 1987, gov. rels. com. 1987-91), New Eng. Libr. Assn. (pres. 1977-78, Emerson Greenaway award 1989). Home: 2001 N Adams St Arlington VA 22201-3751 Office: Online Computer Libr Ctr Ste 350 1320 Old Chain Bridge Rd Mc Lean VA 22101-3930

HASHIMOTO, CHRISTINE L., physician; b. Chgo., June 29, 1947; d. Shigeru and Kiyo (Sato) H. BA, Oberlin Coll., 1968; MD, Med. Coll. of Pa., 1973. Clin. instr. internal medicine, emergency medicine Med. Coll. and Hosp. of Pa., Phila., 1976-77; asst. prof. medicine Health Service Ctr. U. Colo., Denver, 1977-80, clin. asst. prof. medicine, 1980-87; staff physician emergency dept. St. Joseph Hosp., Denver, 1980-88, Rose Med. Ctr., Denver, 1988-91; physician Luth. Med. Ctr., Wheatridge, Colo., 1991—. Mem. Colo. Med. Soc., Denver Med. Soc., Am. Coll. Emergency Physicians. Home: 5112 S Perry Pk Rd Sedalia CO 80135 Office: Luth Med Ctr 8300 W 38th Ave Wheat Ridge CO 80033

HASKELL, MOLLY, author; b. Charlotte, N.C., Sept. 29, 1939; d. John Haskell and Mary Clark; m. Andrew Sarris, May 31, 1969. BA, Sweet Briar Coll.; student, U. London, England, Sorbonne, Paris. Pub. rels. assoc. Sperry Rand; writer, editor French Film Office, New York; film critic Village Voice, Viva, New York Magazine, Vogue; film reviewer "Special Edition" Pub. TV; film reviewer "All Things Considered" Nat. Pub. Radio; assoc. prof. Barnard Coll., New York, 1989; writer; artistic dir. Sarasota French Film Festival. Author: From Reverence to Rape: The Treatment of Women in the Movies, 1973, rev. edit., 1987, Love and Other Infectious Diseases: A Memoir, 1990; (plays) The Last Anniversary, 1990; contbr. articles and essays to jours. Recipient Nat. Bd. Review of Motion Pictures award, 1989, Chevalier de l'Ordre des Artes et des Lettres, 1989. Mem. Nat Soc. of Film Critics, N.Y. Film Critics Circle, N.Y. Film Festival Selection Com., Phi Beta Kappa. Office: care William Morrow & Co Inc Adults Book Dept 1350 Ave of the Americas New York NY 10019

HASKIN, LUCILLE ARLEPHA, religion educator; b. Dixon, Nebr., Nov. 12, 1926; d. John Edward and Adeline (Harvey) McDaniel; m. Jimmie O. Haskin, Dec. 18, 1948; children: Bonnie, Betty, Dick. Grad. high sch., Creighton, Nebr. Tchr. pub. schs., 1945-49; tchr. Sunday Sch. United Meth. Ch., Royal, Nebr., 1986-94; pres. United Meth. Women, 1991-94; owner Haskin Draperies, Royal, 1977-92; bible study leader, 1988-94; treas. United Meth. Ch., Royal, 1986-91; lay person ann. conf. 1990-92. Counselor, nurse Christian Ch. Camp, 1992, 93, 94, art dir., 1994. Home: PO Box 95 Royal NE 68773-0095

HASKINS, BRENDA RAE, cartographer; b. Madison, Wis., June 27, 1963; d. Bernard Frank and Marcia Rae (Rossi) H. BA, U. Wis., 1985, MS, 1991. Cartographer Wis. Geol. Survey, Madison, 1984-90; analyst Wis. State Assembly, Madison, 1990-93; analyst/cartographer Wis. State Senate, Madison, 1993—. Contbr. articles to profl. jours. Bd. dirs. Dem. Party of Wis., Dane County, 1985-92. Recipient Planning Achievement award Am. Inst. Cert. Planners, 1991. Mem. Am. Planning Assn., Am. Congress on Surveying & Mapping, Wis. Land Info. Assn. (treas. 1989—, Pres.'s award 1994). Democrat. Home: 843 Williamson St Madison WI 53703

HASKINS, MARIAN MCKEEN, nursing administrator; b. N.Y.C., Jan. 27, 1954; d. Sean and Margaret (Hegarty) McKeen; m. Thomas Creed Haskins, Sept. 27, 1981. BS in Nursing, Hunter Coll., N.Y.C.; MA in Marriage, Family and Child Counseling, Calif. Family Study Ctr., Burbank. Lic. marriage, family and child counselor. Critical care registry nurse Critical Care Svcs., Inc., L.A., 1978-79; staff devel. cons.-instr. Profl. Med. Educators, Northridge, Calif., 1979; clin. nurse III respiratory intensive care unit UCLA, 1979-81; counselor marriage, family and child svcs. Encino, Calif., 1989-94; critical care edn. coord. Daniel Freeman Meml. Hosp., Inglewood, Calif., 1981-89, profl. nurse, case mgr., 1990—. Recipient Outstanding Nurse award UCLA, 1980; Named one of Top Ten Nurses in State of Calif., 1993. Mem. Calif. Assn. Marriage and Family Therapists, Am. Assn. Marriage and Family Therapists. Home: 22566 Cardiff Dr Santa Clarita CA 91350-3028 Office: Daniel Freeman Meml Hosp Nursing Adminstrn 333 N Prairie Ave Inglewood CA 90301-4514

HASKINS-JASLOVSKY, BONITA M., commercial real estate broker; b. N.Y.C., Dec. 9, 1937; d. Denzil Haskins and Josephine Mary (Bell) Lashure; m. Harold Lee Lashure, Jan. 13, 1954 (div. July 1974); children: Geraldine, Joseph, H. Peter, Suzanne; m. John T. Jaslovsky, Apr. 5, 1980. AAS in Bus. Mgmt., Brookdale C.C., 1993. Lic. real estate broker N.J., N.Y. Telephone oper. N.Y. Telephone Co., Belle Harbor, 1954-56; switchbd. oper. VA Hosp., Buffalo, 1956-57; v.p. Lashure Crown, Inc., Lawrence, N.Y., 1959-74; asst. mgr. JAck Lalanne Health Spa's, Rockville Center, N.Y., 1974-80; real estate broker Cross & Brown Co., Springfield, N.J., 1981-90; owner, real estate broker The Haskins Co., Shrewsbury, N.J., 1991—. Vice pres. Tinton Woods Homeowners Assn., Eatontown, N.J., 1993—, sec.-treas., 1986-87. Republican. Office: The Haskins Co 41 Riordan Pl Shrewsbury NJ 07702-4305

HASLER DOGGETT, STACY LYNN, mental health facility administrator; b. Jefferson City, Mo., Aug. 23, 1966; d. William Edward and Linda Kay (Linsenbardt) Hasler; m. Michael Joseph Doggett, Sept. 18, 1993. BS in Psychology, Lincoln U. of Mo., 1988, MEd in Guidance Counseling, 1990. Lic. profl. counselor; cert. nat. counselor. Title III program asst. Lincoln U. of Mo., Jefferson City, 1989-91; community support specialist Family Mental Health Ctr., Jefferson City, 1991-92; community support worker Ctr. for Psychiat. Rehab., Columbia, Mo., 1992-93, dir., 1993—; mgr. Hasler's Stables, Jefferson City, 1992—; guest speaker TV program, Jefferson City, 1992. Mem. Citizen Adv. Bd., Cole, Monteau and Osage Counties, 1992—; pres. Margaret cir., St. Paul's Evangelical Luth. Ch., 1994—, mem. choir, 1992—, mem. WELCA coun., 1994—. Mem. ACA, Assn. Humanistic Edn. and Devel., Am. Quarter Horse Assn. Office: Ctr for Psychiat Rehab Ste 110 1000 W Nifong Bldg 3 Columbia MO 65203

HASSED, SUSAN JANE, genetic counselor; b. Greeley, Colo., Nov. 23, 1954; d. James David and Judith Anne (Helfrich) H. Student, Cornell Coll., 1972-73; BA in Biology, U. Colo., Colorado Springs, 1986; MS in Genetics, U. Colo., Denver, 1989. From file clk. to systems analyst William Gruer-erwald & Assocs., Inc., Colorado Springs, Colo., 1974-89; data processing mgr. Canyon Colo. Equid, Wagon Mound, N.Mex., 1984-89; cytogenetic lab. asst. U. Colo. Health Scis. Ctr., Denver, 1987-89; genetic counselor U. South Fla., Tampa, 1989-90, Ark. Children's Hosp. and U. Ark. for Med. Sci., Little Rock, 1990—. Editor: Computerized Studbook Studies of Grevy's Zebra, Hartmann Zebra, Asian and African Wild Asses, Przewalski Horses, 1985-90, North American Regional Studbook-Wild Asses, 1990; newsletter editor Gt. Plains Genetic Svcs. Network, 1993—. Tech. dir. Colorado Springs Music Theatre, 1975-83 (Annual Recognition award 1977); child sponsor World Vision, Pasadena, Calif., 1977—. Mem. Am. Soc. Human Genetics, Am. Bd. Genetic Counseling, Nat. Soc. Genetic Counselors, Gt. Plains Clin. Genetics Soc. (v.p. 1994, pres. 1995). Office: Ark Genetics 800 Marshall St Little Rock AR 72202

HASSEL, TERESA ANN, bank officer; b. Evansville, Ind., Dec. 27, 1952; d. Milton Pete and Virginia (Nunnelly) Zinn; m. Frank Kenneth Hassel, Apr. 2, 1978 (div. Aug. 1981); 1 child, Peter Jacob. BA in Econs. and French magna cum laude, U. Evansville, 1974, postgrad., 1981, 87. Sr. acct. Old Nat. Bank, Evansville, 1981-90, time mgmt. analyst, 1990-92, supr., mgr., 1992—, bd. govs., 1985-86. Tutor Community Action Program Evansville, 1974-79; adviser Jr. Achievement, Evansville, 1988; auction vol. Sta. WNIN-TV, pub. TV, Evansfille; bd. dirs. Parents Helping Parents, sec., 1979-81. Scholar AAUW, 1970, Hoosier scholar, 1970. Mem. Bank Adminstrn. Inst. Methodist. Home: 7300 E Gum St Evansville IN 47715-4347 Office: Old Nat Bank 420 Main St Evansville IN 47708-1500

HASSELBALCH, MARILYN JEAN, state official; b. Omaha, Jan. 2, 1930; d. Paul William and Helga Esther (Nodgaard) Campfield; m. Hal Burke Hasselbalch, June 13, 1954 (div. 1973); children: Kurt Campfield, Eric Burke, Peter Nels, Ane Catherine. BA with high distinction, U. Nebr., 1951. Cert. secondary tchr., Nebr. Pub. sch. tchr. Omaha and Long Beach, Calif., 1951-55; staff asst. U.S. Congressman Charles Thone, Lincoln, Nebr., 1973-78, Gov. of Nebr., Lincoln, 1978-82; exec. asst. Nebr. State Treas., Lincoln, 1983-86; sr. asst. Nebr. Gov. Kay A. Orr, Lincoln, 1987-91; exec. dir. Nebr. Appraiser Licensing Bd., Lincoln, 1991—. Mem. camp bd. dirs. YMCA, Nebr., 1969-70; mem. Nebr. Edn. Policies Commn., 1982; state convention del. Rep. Party Nebr., 1986, 88; gov.'s rep. Nebr. State Hist. Soc., Lincoln, 1987-89; del. Edn. Commn. on States, Balt., 1988; participant strategic leadership for gubernatorial execs.; sec. Mission Bd. Christ Luth. Ch., 1993—; treas. Danish Sisterhood # 90, 1995—. Named to Outstanding Young Women Am., 1961. Mem. Nat. Fedn. Rep. Women, Lancaster Couny Rep. Women (exec. bd. 1988), Am. Legion Auxiliary, Danish Sisterhood Am., Phi Beta Kappa, Theta Sigma Phi, Kappa Tau Alpha. Lutheran. Home: 4705 South St Lincoln NE 68506-1257 Office: Real Estate Appraiser Bd Nebr State Office Bldg Lincoln NE 68509

HASSELL, SANDRA KAY, academic counselor; b. San Angelo, Tex., Sept. 11, 1943; d. Ralph Holmes Jr. and Syble Aileene (Lucas) Benge; m. Gary Leon Hassell, Aug. 22, 1964; children: Chad, Dana. BA, West Tex. State U., 1966, MEd, 1971, cert. in counseling and diagnostician, 1973. Lic. profl. counselor, Tex. Sec. West Tex. State U., Canyon, 1962-64; trchr. 4th and 5th grades Amarillo (Tex.) Ind. Sch. Dist., 1966-67, tchr. 5th grade, 1970-71, counselor, diagnostician, 1971-78, counselor, 1978—; tchr. 5th grade El Paso (Tex.) Ind. Sch. Dist., 1967-68, Happy (Tex.) Ind. Sch. Dist., 1968-69. Mem. ACA, NEA, Am. Sch. Counselors Assn., Tex. Sch. Counselors Assn. (v.p. 1991—), Tex. Counseling Assn. (senator 1994—), Tex. Tchrs. Assn. (legis. coms. 1986-91), Amarillo Classroom Tchrs. Assn. (chairperson 1987-93, v.p., sec.), Amarillo Sch. Guidance Assn., High Plains Counseling Assn. (past pres., v.p., sec.), Benevolent Patriotic Order of Does. Home: 5014 Westway Trl Amarillo TX 79109-6348

HASSELL, TERESA JONES, telecommunications executive; b. Nashville, Jan. 19, 1954; d. Josiaha (Joe) Turner and Daisy Virginia (Stokes) Jones; m. James Rainey Hassell, June 18, 1972 (div. Oct. 1985); children: Amanda Michelle, Clint Austin. Student, Nashville State Tech. Inst., 1982-84. Processing clk. South Ctrl. Bell Telephone Co., Brentwood, 1971-73, stenographic clk. acctg., 1973-75, stenographer, 1975-77, sec. stenographer, 1977-78, sec. divsn. mgr., 1978-81, adminstrv. asst., 1981-87, asst. staff mgr., 1987; supr. engring. South Ctrl. Bell Telephone Co., Nashville, 1987—. Campaign coord. United Way, Brentwood and Nashville, 1978-91; blood-mobile coord. ARC, Brentwood and Nashville, 1978-88; chmn. Williamson County Community Rels. Team, Brentwood, 1988-89, sec., 1986-87, vice chmn., 1987-88; mem. Tenn. Leadership, 1993. Recipient Coord. of Yr. award ARC, Nashville, 1987, Donor Motivator of Yr., 1984, 85, 86, Svc. award Grassland Mis. Sch. for Coordination Just Say No to Drugs program, 1989. Mem. Bus. and Profl. Women's Orgn. (area 26 coord. Davidson County 1989-90, pres. 1987-88, 1st v.p. 1985-86, 1st v.p., pres-elect 1986-87, Outstanding Young Careerist chmn. 1990-91), Telephone Pioneers Am. (chmn. fund raising, social, ednl. opportunities, Just Say No to Drug program 1978-91), Nashville C. of C. (mem. retention com. 1991-92, new mem. ptnr. com. 1992—). Home: 1124 Brookside Dr Franklin TN 37064-4601 Office: South Ctrl Bell Telephone Rm A200 2002 Richard Jones Rd Ste A200 Nashville TN 37215-2809

HASSENBOEHLER, DONALYN, principal. Prin. McMain Magnet Secondary Sch.; evaluator FIRST grants U.S. Dept. Edn. Recipient U.S. Dept. Edn. Blue Ribbon award, 1990-91. Office: McMain Magnet Secondary Sch 5712 S Claiborne Ave New Orleans LA 70125

HASSERT, ELIZABETH ANNE, transportation executive; b. Joliet, Ill., July 28, 1956; d. Wilbur Clarence and Frances Romayne (McLaughlin) H. BA, St. Mary's Coll., Notre Dame, Ind., 1978. Dept. mgr. Lord & Taylor, Aurora, Ill., 1978-79, Oak Brook, Ill., 1979-80; account exec. Cast (N.Am.) Ltd., Rolling Meadows, Ill., 1980-82; sales mgr. Cast (UK) Ltd., London, 1982-83, Sofati Container (UK), Birmingham, Eng., 1983-84; account exec. Sea-Land Svc., Inc., Rolling Meadows, 1984-88, sales mgr., 1988-90, sales exec., 1990—; recognition sponsor Quality Mgmt. Sea-Land Svc., Inc., 1989-92. Recipient of CSX award of Excellence, 1993. Mem. Ocean Freight Agts., World Trade Club, Midwest Fgn. Freight Club, Hinsdale Jr. Women's Club, Cin. World Trade Assn., Cleve. World Trade Assn., Detroit Ocean Freight Agy., St. Mary's Coll. Alumnae Assn. Republican. Roman Catholic. Home: 625 N County Line Rd Hinsdale IL 60521-2406 Office: Sea-Land Svc Inc 3501 W Algonquin Rd Ste 600 Rolling Meadows IL 60008-3142

HASSFURDER, LESLIE JEAN, principal; b. Bedford, Ind., June 26, 1943; d. Don Bernell and Rose E. (Bridwell) Armstrong; m. M. Duane Wilson, June 17, 1965 (dec. Aug. 1986); children: Douglas Troy, Marisa Lynn; m. Steven Wayne Hassfurder, Mar. 19, 1988; step-children: Holly Renee, Lorrie Leigh. BS, Ind. U., 1965, MS, 1971; EdS, Ind.-Purdue U., Indpls., 1984. Cert. tchr. and prin., Ind. Elem. tchr. Fontana, Calif., 1965-67, Churubusco, Ind., 1967-69; dir. presch., Goshen, Ind., 1977-80; prin. Pittsboro Elem. Sch. (Ind.), 1980—; dir. summer library. Co-author: Energy Play, 1982, operettas for local schs. Mem. Internat. Reading Assn., Mortar Bd., Enomone, Pleiades, Phi Delta Kappa, Alpha Delta Kappa. Republican. Mem. Christian Ch. (Disciples of Christ). Office: Pittsboro Elem Sch North Meridian Pittsboro IN 46167

HASTINGS, DEBORAH, bass guitarist; b. Evansville, Ind., May 11, 1959; d. Mortimer Winthrop Hastings and Margaret Hooper (Smith) Zimmerman. Student music, U. Wis. Bass guitarist N.Y.C. and Madison, Wis., 1975—; freelance photographer Madison, 1976-81; band leader Bo Diddley, 1992—; performed Inauguration Pres. George Bush, 1989; performed with Billy Preston, Dr. John, Koko Taylor, Willie Dixon, Albert Collins, Joe Cocker, Carla Thomas, Eddie Floyd, Ron Wood, Steve Cropper (Blues Brothers), Bo Diddley, Jerry Lee Lewis, George Gobel, Chuck Berry, Joe Louis Walker, Ben E. King, Sarah Dash, Little Anthony and the Imperials, Sam Moore, Chuck Jackson, John Lee Hooker, Mick Fleetwood, Al Kooper, Hewy Lewis, James Cotton; TV shows include Legends of Rock and Roll live from Rome performed with Bo Diddley, BB King, James Brown, Little Richard, Ray Charles, Fats Domino, others. Author: Photographers Market, 1981; bass player TV shows Joan Rivers, 1987, Classsics of Rock and Roll, 1988, Gunslingers tour Live from the Ritz with Ron Wood & Bo Diddley, 1988, Live from the Ritz, 1989, Legends of Rock and Roll (live from Australia), Legends of Guitar from Seville, Spain, 1991, Showtime at the Apollo, 1992, N.Y. at Night, 1992; performed Into The Night, 1991 (TV show) Nashville Now, 1991, American Musicshop, 1991, Greece, Johnny Carson Show, 1990, Pat Sajak Show, 1990, Carla Thomas, 1991, Arts & Entertainment Revue, 1990, (Madison Sq. Garden) Tribute to John Lee Hooker, 1990, Richard Nader's 25th Anniversary Show, 1994; 89 tours in Europe, Australia and Japan. Fundraiser, bassist polit. campaigns, Madison; bass player Pres. Bush inauguration, 1989. Recipient numerous awards for pottery, award Arts Coun., Madison, Arts Coun., Ann Arbor, Mich. Mem. Musicians Union (local 802). Democrat. Office: Talent Cons Internat Ste 1308 1560 Broadway New York NY 10036

HASTINGS, EVELYN GRACE, retired elementary school educator; b. Seguin, Tex., May 25, 1938; d. Ed Howard Coleman and Mae Stella (King) Haywood; m. Marvin Hastings, Oct. 9, 1982. BS, Tex. Luth. Coll., 1960; MA, U. Tex., San Antonio, 1985. Cert. tchr., Tex. Tchr. Seguin (Tex.) Ind. Sch. Dist., 1962-94, Vogel Elem. Sch., Seguin, 1991-94, retired, 1994; sec. Guadalupe County Tchr.'s Meeting, Seguin, 1962-65, Juan Seguin Sch. PTA, 1969. Historian, corr. sec. Tex. Women's Conv. Ch. of our Lord Jesus Christ, 1961-69, internat. treas. IFAE; treas. Tex. Armor Bears Young Peoples Union, 1960-63, pres., 1963-65, 68-70; sec. Tex. Sunday Sch. Assn., 1960-63, asst. supt., 1968-70, state supt., 1970-74; local missionary pres., fin. sec. Rufuge Ch.; state supr. Tex. Jr. Conv., 1970—; Sunday supr. Lighthouse Ch., 1975—; state missionary v.p. Tex.-Okla. Conv. Ch. of Our Lord Jesus Christ of Apostolic Faith. Recipient Cert. of Outstanding Svc. Nat. Youth Congress Ch. of Our Lord Jesus Christ, 1968, Cert. of Appreciation, Tex.-Okla. Conv. of the Ch. of Our Lord Jesus Christ of The Apostolic Faith, 1989, Outstanding Svc. Plaque, 1981, Tchr. of Yr. Plaque Seguin-Guadalupe County C. of C., 1990; inducted into The Internat. Sunday Sch. Hall of Fame of the Ch. of Our Lord Jesus Christ of the Apostolic Faith, 1990. Mem. AAUW (sec. 1968-70), NEA, Tex. State Tchrs. Assn. (minority del. 1982) Seguin Educators Assn. Democrat. Home: 950 Elsik St Seguin TX 78155-6756

HASTINGS, L(OIS) JANE, architect, educator; b. Seattle, Mar. 3, 1928; d. Harry and Camille (Pugh) H.; m. Norman John Johnston, Nov. 22, 1969. B.Arch., U. Wash., Seattle, 1952, postgrad. in Urban Planning, 1958. Architect Boeing Airplane Co., Seattle, 1951-54; recreational dir. Germany, 1954-56; architect (various firms), Seattle, 1956-59, pvt. practice architecture, 1959-74; instr. archtl. drafting Seattle Community Coll., part-time 1969-80; owner/founder The Hastings Group Architects, Seattle, 1974—; lectr. design Coll. Architecture, U. Wash., 1975; incorporating mem. Architecta (P.S.), Seattle, 1980; pres. Architecta (P.S.), from 1980; mem. adv. bd. U. Wash. YWCA, 1967-69; mem. Mayor's Com. on Archtl. Barriers for Handicapped, 1974-75; chmn. regional public adv. panel on archtl. and engring. services GSA, 1976; mem. citizens adv. com. Seattle Land Use Adminstrn. Task Force, from 1979; AWIU guest of Soviet Women's Con., 1983; speaker Pacific Rim Forum, Hong Kong, 1987; guest China Internat. Conf. Ctr. for

Sci. and Tech. of the China Assn. for Sci. and Tech., 1989; mem. adv. com. Coll. architecture and urban planning U. Wash., 1993; mem. accreditation team U. Oreg. Coll. Architecture, 1991, N.J. Inst. Tech. Sch. Architecture, 1992. Design juror for nat. and local competitions, including Red Cedar Shingle/AIA awards, 1977, Current Use Honor awards, AIA, 1980, Exhibit of Sch. Architecture award, 1981; Contbr. to: also spl. features newspapers, articles in profl. jours. Sunset mag. Mem. bd. Am. Women for Internat. Understanding, del. to, Egypt, Israel, USSR, 1971, Japan and Korea, 1979, USSR, 1983; mem. Landmarks Preservation Bd. City of Seattle, 1981-83; mem. Design Constrn. Rev. Bd. Seattle Sch. Dist., 1985-87; mem. mus. con. Mus. History and Industry, 1987—; leader People to People del. women architects to China, 1990. Recipient AIA/The Seattle Times Home of Month Ann. award, 1968; Exhbn. award Seattle chpt. AIA, 1970; Environ. award Seattle-King County Bd. Realtors, 1970, 77,; AIA/House and Home/ The American Home Merit award, 1971, Sp. Honor award Wash. Aggregates and Concrete Assn., 1993, Prize bridge Am. Inst. Steel Contrn., 1993; Honor award Seattle chpt. AIA, 1977, 83; Women Achievement award Past Pres. Assembly, 1983, Washington Women and Trading Cards, 1983; Nat. Endowment for Arts grantee, 1977; others; named to West Seattle High Sch. Hall of Fame, 1989, Woman of Achievement Matrix Table, 1994; named Woman of Distinction, Columbia River Girl Scout Coun., 1994. Fellow AIA (pres. Seattle chpt. 1975, pres. sr. council 1980, state exec. bd. 1975, NW regional dir. 1982-84, 86, Seattle chpt. found. bd. 1985-87, Bursar Coll. Fellows, 1989-90, internat. rels. com. 1988-92, vice chancellor, 1991, chancellor 1992); Internat. Union Women Architects (v.p. 1969-79, sec. gen. 1985-89, del. UIA Congress, Montreal 1990), Am. Arbitration Assn. (arbitrator 1981—), Council of Design Professions, Assoc. Woman Contractors, Suppliers and Design Cons.'s, Allied Arts Seattle, Fashion Group, Tau Sigma Delta, Alpha Rho Chi (medal). Office: The Hastings Group-Architects 1516 E Olive Way Seattle WA 98122-2130

HASTINGS, SUSAN NANCY, health information consultant; b. Barre, Vt., June 20, 1952; d. Ernest Lemon and Velma Martin (Ewen) Ironside; m. David A. Hastings, June 16, 1992. Accredited record technician, Am. Med. Record Assn., Chgo., 1974; diploma contemporary legal asst., McGraw-Hill Continuing Edn., Washington, 1991. Med. sec. Ctrl. Vt. Hosp., Berlin, 1970-79; dir. med. records Gifford Meml. Hosp., Randolph, Vt., 1979-84; pvt. companion Montpelier, Vt., 1984-85; adminstrv. sec. Mayo Nursing Home, Northfield, Vt., 1986-92; owner, cons. Health Info. Ctr., Corinth, Vt., 1975—; adminstrv. dir., fin. mgr. Vt. Drs. Care, Barre, 1993-94. Mem. Am. Health Info. Mgrs. Assn. (long term care nominating com. sect. 1992-93), Am. Cons. League, Vt. Health Info. Mgrs. Assn., Nat. Notary Pub. Assn., Nat. Computer Security Assn. Home and Office: Health Info Ctr HC 82 Box 100 Corinth VT 05039-7901

HASTINGS-CASEL, MARY LYNN, real estate broker; b. Carthage, N.Y., Jan. 16, 1943; d. Floyd Albert and Mary Frances (Schack) Neuroth; m. Ronald Anthony Casel, Nov. 28, 1963 (div. Nov. 1977); children: Mark, Steven, Glen; m. Charles F. Hastings, Apr. 27, 1991. Grad. Harper Method, Rochester, N.Y., 1961. Lic. real estate broker. Owner M. L. Salon, Rochester, N.Y., 1962-72; specialty tchrs.-aide Broward County, Ft. Lauderdale, Fla., 1973-77; office mgr. Broward County Voter Registration, Margate, Fla., 1977-82; real estate salesperson Pelican Bay, Daytona Beach, Fla., 1982-84, broker, 1984—, broker; owner Mary Lynn Realty, 1989—. Mem. adv. bd. Dem. Club, Margate, Fla., 1977-82. Mem. Nat. Assn. Realtors, Fla. Home Builders Assn., Nat. Home Builders Assn., Daytona Beach Home Builders Assn., Daytona Beach Bd. Realtors, Ft. Lauderdale Bd. Realtors, Nat. Assn. Women in Constrn. (v.p. 1988-89, pres.-elect 1989—, pres. 1990—), NAFE, Sales and Mktg. Council. Avocations: travel, dancing, theater, real estate investments. Democrat. Roman Catholic. Home: 112 Marsh Wren Ct Daytona Beach FL 32119-8752 Office: Mary Lynn Realty 112 Marsh Wren Ct Daytona Beach FL 32119-8710

HATCH, KELLEY MARIE, journalist, television news anchor; b. Balt., June 16, 1958; d. Roland W. and Ava Marie (Jackson) Marsh; m. James R. Johnson II (div.); children: Jeremiah Shawn, Joshua Adam; m. Brett Wilder Hatch, Feb. 22, 1992. Student, Lincoln Meml. U., 1976-77, U. Mich., Flint, 1987-88, N.Mex. State U., 1989. Mktg.cons. Sta. KPSA, Alamogordo, N.Mex., 1989-90; dir. mktg. Temporarily Yours, Inc., Farmington, N.Mex., 1991; account exec. Sta. KOBF-TV, Farmington, 1991-92, news anchor, 1992—. Pres. Am. Heart Assn., 1994, bd. dirs., sec., 1991-92; bd. dirs. Childhaven, 1992—, San Juan Stage Co., 1991—; bd. dirs., fin. devel. com. ARC, 1992—. Recipient Best Investigative News award, AP, 1993. Mem. Am. Bus. Women's Assn. (pres. 1991). Republican. Office: Sta KOBF-TV 825 W Broadway Farmington NM 87401

HATCH, MARY MAGDALENE, architect; b. Dallas, Oct. 21, 1953; d. David Arthur and Magdalene (Kondracsek) Roberts; m. Gregory James Hatch, May 18, 1974 (separated); children: Danielle Marie, Kristyn Diane. BS in Architecture, U. Tex., Arlington, 1975. Registered arch., Tex., interior designer. Arch. Hatch/Hatch & Assocs., Richardson, Tex., 1987-93, Terry F. Brewer & Assocs., Irving, Tex., 1993, Perrin & Assocs., Dallas, 1994—. Active Dallas Mus. Art, 500 Inc. Home: 912 Wedgewood Way Richardson TX 75080 Office: Perrin & Assocs 12225 Greenville Ave Ste 532 Dallas TX 75243

HATCH, MARY WENDELL VANDER POEL, non-profit organization executive, interior; b. N.Y.C., Feb. 6, 1919; d. William Halsted and Blanche Pauline (Billings) Vander Poel; m. George Montagu Miller, Apr. 5, 1940 (div. 1974); children: Wendell Miller Steavenson, Gretchen Miller Elkus; m. Sinclair Hatch, May 14, 1977 (dec. July 1989). Pres. Miller Richard, Inc., Interior Decorators, Glen Head, N.Y., 1972—; bd. dirs. Eye Bank Sight Restoration, N.Y.C., 1975—, pres., 1980-88, hon. chair, 1988—; bd. dirs. Manhattan Eye Ear and Throat Hosp., N.Y.C., 1966-92, v.p., 1978-90; sec. Cold Spring Harbor Lab., N.Y., 1985-89, 92—, bd. dirs., 1985-90; chair DNA Learning Ctr., 1991—; bd. dirs. Cold Spring Harbor Lab, 1991—, sec., 1992—. V.p. North Country Garden Club, Nassau County, N.Y., 1979-81, 1983-85; dir. Planned Parenthood Nassau County, Mineola, N.Y., 1982-84, Hutton House C.W.Post Coll.,Greenvale, N.Y., 1982—; chair Hutton House, 1992-94. Recipient Disting. Trustee award United Hosp. Fund, 1992. Mem. Colony Club (N.Y.C.), Church Club (N.Y.C.), Piping Rock Club (Long Island), Order St. John Jerusalem (N.Y.C.). Republican. Episcopalian. Home: Mill River Rd # 330 Oyster Bay NY 11771-2712

HATCH, WILDA GENE, broadcast company executive; b. Ogden, Utah, Nov. 28, 1917; d. Abraham Lincoln and Edris Alida (Toombs) Glasmann; m. George Clinton Hatch, Dec. 24, 1940; children: Michael Zbar, Diane G. Orr, Jeffrey B., Randall C., Deepika Avanti. BA, Stanford U., 1939; HHD (hon.), Weber State U., 1981. V.p. The Standard Corp., Ogden, 1955-93, Sta. KUTV, Inc., Salt Lake City, 1956—. Pres. Women's State Legis. Coun., Salt Lake City, 1967-69; active LWV, Salt Lake City, 1965—. Democrat. Home: 1537 Chandler Dr Salt Lake City UT 84103 Office: Sta KUTV Inc 2185 S 3600 W Salt Lake City UT 84119

HATCHER, BIRNELL MITCHELL, marketing agent, airline executive; b. Cairo, Ga., Sept. 5, 1945; d. Joseph Charles and Ada (Butler) Mitchell; div.; 1 child, Ronald A. Taylor. BS, Savannah State Coll., 1966; postgrad. studies, U. Ga., 1970, Clayton State Coll., 1991. Cert. tchr., Ga. Teacher Coffee County Bd. of Edn., Douglas, Ga., 1967-69, Meriweather County Bd. of Edn., Woodbury, Ga., 1969-71, Atlanta Pub. Schs., 1971-72; acct. United Bd. Coll. Devel., 1972-80; acct. Delta Air Lines, Inc., 1980-91, mktg. agt., 1991—. Fin. sec. Pilgrim Travelers Bapt. Ch. , 1985—; mem. Atlanta Urban League, 1985. Recipient Svc. award Pilgrim Travelers Bapt. Ch., 1989. Mem. NAACP, Nat. Coun. Bus. Women, Savannah State Coll. Alumni Assn. (treas. Atlanta chpt. 1986-90, pres. 1990-94, newsletter editor 1993-94, Atlanta scholarship award 1984-86, Tiger award 1988-89, Nat. Alumnus of Yr. 1991), S. Atlanta Met. Bridge Club (treas. 1980—). Democrat. Home: 2917 Briarwood Blvd East Point GA 30344

HATCHER, MARILYN ANN, realtor, educator; b. Newark, Sept. 27, 1950; d. Charles George and Ann (Hencoski) K.; m. Creel David, Aug. 10, 1974; children: Deborah Ann, David Michael. BA in Bus. Edn., Montclair State Coll., 1972; MBA in Mgmt., Fairleigh Dickinson U., 1980. Cert. tchr. N.J.; lic. realtor, N.J. Instr. Ocean Twp. Adult Even Sch., Oakhurst, N.J., 1969; instr., counselor Katharine Gibbs Sch., N.Y.C., 1972-75; instr. The Berkeley Sch., Ridgewood, N.J., 1977, No. N.J. Civil Svc. Tng. Ctr., Newark, N.J., 1978-80, Middlesex County Coll., Edison, N.J., 1980-83, Brookdale Community Coll., Lincroft, N.J., 1980-84; realtor-assoc. Schlott Realtors, Matawan, N.J., 1987—; tchr. St. John Vianney High Sch., Holmdel, N.J.; tech. sec. A.L. Straubing & Assocs., South Orange, N.J. Counselor day camp YMCA, YWCA; active local PTO, 1988-89; mem. legis. com., strategic planning com. Monmouth County Bd. Realtors, Middletown, N.J., 1988, strategic planning com. Mem. Assn. MBA Execs., N.J. Assn. Realtors, N.J. Bd. Realtors (mem. Million Dollar Sales club 1988), Monmouth County Bd. Realtors, Nat. Assn. Realtors, Residential Coun., Hazlet (N.J.) Thunderetts (bd. dirs. 1987). Home: 220 Randolph Rd Freehold NJ 07728-1535 Office: Schlott Realtors 132 State Route 34 Matawan NJ 07747

HATCHER, PATRICIA LOUISE, technical writer; b. Omaha, Feb. 10, 1949; d. William L. and Margaret (Gregg) Law; 1 child, Kelly Todd. BS in Math., U. Tex., 1972. Author People Talk Assn., Plano, Tex., 1984-87; contract tech. writer Dallas, 1987—; lectr. Dallas Geneal. Soc. Symposium, 1988—, Nat. Geneal. Soc. conf., 1992, 94, Fedn. Geneal. Soc. conf., 1993, 94, Geneal. Inst. Tex., 1993, 94. Author: (4 vol. book) Abstract of Graves of Revolutionary Patriots, 1988; contbr. articles to profl. jours. Coun. mem. Casa View United Meth. Ch., Dallas, 1985-94; mem. LWV, Dallas, 1986-94, Dallas Women's Found., 1989-94.

HATFIELD, JULIE STOCKWELL, journalist, newspaper editor; b. Detroit, Mar. 22, 1940; d. William Hume and Ruth Reed (Palmer) Stockwell; m. Philip Mitchell Hatfield, Aug. 1, 1964 (div. 1979); children—Christian Andrew, Juliana, Jason David; m. Timothy Leland, Nov. 23, 1984; stepchildren—Christian Bourso, London Chamberlain. B.A., U. Mich, 1962. Staff reporter Women's Wear Daily, NYC, 1962-64; freelance feature writer Bath-Brunswick Times, Wis. State Jour., 1964-68, Quincy Patriot Ledger, Mass., 1968-77; freelance music critic, fashion editor Boston Herald, 1977-79; fashion editor Boston Globe, 1979—, living/arts writer, 1995—. Author: (with others) Guide to the Thrift Shops of New England, 1982. Recipient Lulu award Men's Fashion Assn., 1985, Atrium award for Outstanding Writing on Fashion U. Ga., 1987, 92, Lifestyle Writer award Boston Globe, 1995; Nat. Endowment Arts grantee, 1973. Episcopalian. Office: Boston Globe Newspaper 135 Morrissey Blvd Dorchester MA 02125

HATHAWAY, ANNA MARIA, accountant; b. Saugus, Mass., Aug. 5, 1961; d. Stanislaus R. and Krystyna (Adaczak) Cisto; m. David Edward Hathaway, June 18, 1983; 1 child, David Edward Jr. BS in Bus. Adminstrn., Salem State Coll., 1983; MS in Taxation, Bentley Coll., 1989. CPA, Mass. Staff acct. William T. Appleyard CPA-PC, Malden, Mass., 1983-86; sr. acct. Baker & Co. P.C., Lynnfield, Mass., 1986-89; supervisory mgr. Baker & Co. P.C., Lynnfield, 1989—; notary pub. Commonwealth of Mass., 1987—. Recipient GTE Sylvnia scholarship, Danvers, Mass., 1983. Mem. AICPA, Mass Soc. CPAs (2 student awards 1982, 83), Inst. Mgmt. Accts. Home: 251 Linwood St Lynn MA 01905

HATHAWAY, LOLINE, zoo and botanic park curator; b. Whittier, Calif., June 27, 1937; d. Richard Franklin and F. Nadine (Applegate) H.; 1 child, Patrick Paul Kundtz. BA, Reed Coll., Portland, Oreg., 1959; PhD, Washington U., St. Louis, 1969. Instr. St. Louis U., 1966-68; curator of edn. Chgo. Zool. Soc., Brookfield, Ill., 1968-71; cons. on terrestrial biology Ryckman, Edgerly, Tomlinson & Assocs., St. Louis, 1972-75; marina mgr. Lake Piru (Calif.) Recreation Area, 1976-77; curator, dir. Navajo Nation Zool. and Botanical Park, Window Rock, Ariz., 1983—. Vice chmn., chmn. City of Santa Fe Springs (Calif.) Traffic Commn., 1979-83; mem. Navajo Estates Vol. Fire Dept., Yah-ta-hey, N.Mex., 1984-85; bd. dirs. Hathaway Ranch Mus., Santa Fe Springs, 1986-93, Gallup Cmty. Concerts Assn., 1994—; leader 4-H Club, 1989—. Mem. AAAS (vice chmn. S.W.-Rocky Mountain div. sci. edn. sect. 1983-84, chmn. 1984-85), AAUW (scholarship com. Gallup 1992—), Am. Assn. Zool. Parks and Aquariums, Am. Assn. Bot. Gardens and Arboretums, Assn. Living. Hist. Farms and Agr. Mus., Am. Inst. Biol. Scis., Sierra Club (Ozarks chpt. founder, bd. dirs., sec. Gt. Lakes chpt. 1963-72). Democrat. Home: 27 S LaChee PO Box 4172 Yah-ta-hey NM 87375 Office: Navajo Nat Zool and Bot Pk PO Box 9000 Window Rock AZ 86515-9000

HATHAWAY, LYNN MCDONALD, education advocate, administrator; b. N.Y.C., Mar. 28, 1939; d. William Douglas IV and Dorothy Edna (Homan) McDonald; m. Earl Burton Hathaway II, July 7, 1962; children: Earl Burton III, Amanda McDonald. BA, Bryn Mawr Coll., 1960. Editorial asst. Mademoiselle mag., N.Y.C., 1960-61; adminstrv. asst. Peace Corps office Nat. Coun. Chs., N.Y.C., 1961-62; vice chmn. community rsch. N.Y. Jr. League, 1969-70; editor, chmn. N.Y. Entertains cookbook, 1973-74; edn. chair London Svc. League, 1979-80; pres., dir. London Svc. League, Jr. League, 1980-82; ind. writer, editor London, 1983. Bd. dirs. Friends of Ferguson Libr., Stamford, Conn., 1988, mem., rec. sec., v.p., pres., 1988—; trustee, exec. com., student life com. chair Conn. State U. System, 1991—. Mem. Bryn Mawr Alumnae Assn. (pres. London 1983-86, internat. councillor 1988-90). Episcopalian. Home: 50 Old North Stamford Rd Stamford CT 06905-3961

HATHCOCK, YVONNE SHIRLEY, graphic arts administrator; b. Elkhorn, Wis., Mar. 21, 1935; d. Edward and Tina (Huisman) Vanden Berg; m. George Calvin Hathcock, Oct. 4, 1952 (dec. Sept. 17, 1969); children: Ronald Charles, Patricia Jan, Thomas Edward (dec.), Russell Calvin. BS in English Edn., U. Ark., Pine Bluff, 1976; MA, Ark. State U., Jonesboro, 1982. Asst. dir. publs. office of pub. rels. U. Ark., Pine Bluff, 1977-79; industry supr. graphic arts Ark Correctional Industries Ark. Dept. Correction, Pine Bluff, 1980—. Vol. ARC, Pine Bluff, 1979-81; mem. sanctuary choir First Bapt. Ch., Pine Bluff, 1991—, also mem. women's ensemble; hon. life mem. UAPB Vesper Choir. Recipient Spl. Lady award Women's Unit Jaycees, 1982, Appreciation award Grass Roots Campaign R. Carter, 1979, Gov.'s Quality award State of Ark., 1992. Mem. So. States Correctional Assn., Correctional Industries Assn., Am. Assn. Retired Persons, S.E. Ark. Kennel Club, VFW Aux., Internat. Soc. Poets, Sigma Iota Tau. Democrat. Home: 5711 W Jones St Pine Bluff AR 71602-4411 Office: Wrightsville Unit Graphic Arts PO Box 1000 Wrightsville AR 72183

HATHORNE, SUSAN KING, insurance agent; b. Bangor, Maine, Jan. 17, 1947; d. Harry G. and Dorothy E. (Sawtelle) King; m. James C. Hathorne, Nov. 29, 1969; children: Lori, Rebecca. Grad. high sch., Brewer, Maine. Customer svc. rep. Liberty Mut., Bangor, 1965-71, State Farm Ins., Bangor, 1978-86; sr. personal account specialist The Dunlap Corp., Bangor, 1986—. Mem. Nat. Assn. Ins. Women (state pub. rels. com. 1991-92, asst. state bd. dirs. 1992-93, state bd. dirs. 1993-94, mem. nat. nominating com. 1994, Maine Ins. Woman of Yr. award 1993), Ins. Women Ea. Maine (pres. 1991-92, Local Ins. Woman of Yr. award 1992), Altrusa. Republican. Methodist. Home: 66 Washington St Brewer ME 04412 Office: The Dunlap Corp 260 Harlow St Bangor ME 04401

HATHY, LOUISE AGNES, veterans service counselor; b. McKeesport, Pa., Apr. 14, 1932; d. Joseph and Emma (Sabo) Hegyi; m. Samuel Hathy Jr., Nov. 21, 1953 (dec. Aug. 1993); children: Samuel III, Daniel, Michael, Susan, Larry, Gary. Grad. high sch., Conneautville, Pa. Exec. sec. Community Action Agy., Palatka, Fla., 1969-74; vets. svc. counselor Putnam County Bd. County Commrs., Vets. Svc. Office, Palatka, Fla., 1974—. Mem. Nat. County Vets. Sec. Officers Assn., County Vets. Svc. Officers Assn. Presbyterian. Office: Putnam County Vets Svc Office 515 Reid St Palatka FL 32177-3641

HATLER, PATRICIA RUTH, lawyer; b. Las Vegas, Nev., Aug. 4, 1954; d. Houston Eugene and Laurie (Danforth) Hatler; m. Howard A. Coffin II; children: Sloan H. D. Coffin, Laurie H. M. Coffin. BS, Duke U., 1976; JD, U. Va., 1980. Bar: Pa. 1980. Assoc. Dechert, Price & Rhoads, Phila., 1980-83; assoc. counsel Independence Blue Cross, Phila., 1983-86, sr. v.p., gen. counsel, corp. sec., 1987—. Home: 116 Mill Creek Rd Ardmore PA 19003 Office: Independence Blue Cross 1901 Market St Philadelphia PA 19103-1400

HATLEY, AMY BELL, elementary education educator, broadcast journalist; b. Concord, N.C., May 5, 1940; d. Austin H. and Frances Louise (Norris) Bell; m. Wayne Douglas Hatley, Aug. 27, 1961; 1 child, Adam Douglas. BA, Meredith Coll., 1962; MEd, Converse Coll., 1986. Cert. tchr. N.C., S.C. Tchr. grades 1-3 Thomasboro Elem., Charlotte, N.C., 1962-67; tchr. grade 3 Thomasboro Elem., Charlotte, 1968-71; tchr. grade 2 Allenbrook Elem., Charlotte, 1966-67, Charlotte (N.C.) Latin, 1971-72, Carmel Acad., Charlotte, 1972-75, Spartanburg (S.C.) Day Sch., 1977—; broadcast journalist WSPA AM-FM Radio, CBS Affiliate, Spartanburg, 1984—. Author, producer: (broadcast documentary series) The Unraveling of the American Teacher, 1989 (1st pl. award AP 1989), Standardized Testing: Has It Failed the Grade?, 1990 (1st pl. award AP 1990), Illiteracy: S.C.'s Abiding Legacy, 1991 (1st pl. award AP 1991). Com. chmn. Bd. Spartanburg (S.C.) Little Theater, 1990; mem. pub. rels. com. United Way of the Piedmont, Spartanburg, 1991-94; bd. regents Leadership Spartanburg, 1992-94; bd. dirs. Spartanburg County Literacy Orgn.; edn. com. Spartanburg CCounty Consensus Project, 1991-94; strategy com. Spartanburg County Am. 2000 Project, 1992-94. Mem. Nat. Press Fedn., Palmetto Assn. Ind. Schs., Spartanburg Speakers Bur., S.C. Media Women. Methodist. Home: 2581 Moore Duncan Hwy Moore SC 29369-9453 Office: Spartanburg Day Sch 1701 Skylyn Dr Spartanburg SC 29302

HATMAKER, A. LYDIA, medical/surgical and orthopedics nurse; b. Anderson County, Tenn., Feb. 2, 1935; d. Virgel and Lucinda (Daugherty) Armes; m. Robert L. Hatmaker, Apr. 7, 1952; 4 children. ADN, AS, Lincoln Meml. U., Harrogate, Tenn., 1982; lic. practical nurse, Jackboro (Tenn.) Vocat. Sch., 1978; student, St. Joseph's U. Lic. practical nurse, Tenn.; RN, Tenn. Aide Lake City (Tenn.) Nursing Home; practical nurse Lake City Hosp.; staff nurse med.-surg.-orthopedic floor Meth. Med. Ctr. Oak Ridge, Tenn.

HATTAN, SUSAN K., legislative staff member; b. Lincoln, Nebr., Jan. 11, 1951; d. Hurbert Curtis and Margaret Marie H. BA summa cum laude, Washburn U., 1973; MA with distinction, Am. U., 1977. Legis. aide to Senator Robert J. Dole, Washington, 1973-77; policy analyst, special asst. Adminstrn. of Food Safety and Quality Svc., Dept. Agrl., Washington, 1977-78; legis. dir. to Senator Nancy L. Kassebaum, Washington, 1978-89; minority staff dir., sub-committee on edn., arts and humanities Senate Com. on Labor and Human Resources, Washington, 1989-92, minority staff dir., 1993—. Mem. Phi Kappa Phi., Zeta Tau Alpha. Office: Labor & Human Resources Rm 835 Senate Hart Office Bldg Washington DC 20510*

HATTON, PATRICIA LEANORE, administrative assistant; b. Chgo., Nov. 27, 1942; d. Stephan Frank and Eleanor Clara (Moudry) Uhlarik; m. Olin Kent Van Liew, Jan. 8, 1966 (div. Aug. 1971); children: Nicole Marie, Brett Kenneth; m. Horace Bromiley Hatton, June 19, 1982. Cert. real estate broker, Ill., Ind. Broker, asst. mgr. Coldwell Banker Real Estate, Schaumburg, Ill., 1977-82; owner, dir. Chicagoland Referral Network, Oak Brook, Ill., 1987-90; exec. asst. Nat. Material Co.-Tang Industries, Elk Grove Village, Ill., 1990-93; office adminstr. Thomson Newspapers, Des Plaines, Ill., 1993-94; adminstrv. asst. Brokers Risk Placement Svc., Inc., Chgo., 1994—. Office: Brokers Risk Placement Svc Inc 525 W Monroe St Ste 2400 Chicago IL 60661

HAU, MARILYN LEE, community health nurse, occupational health nurse; b. Pitts., Jan. 25, 1948; d. Merwyn and Ruth Ruella (Gibson) Swank; m. Robert George Hau, Jan. 19, 1980. Diploma, Presbyn.-U. Hosp., 1968; BSN, U. State N.Y., 1989; MS, Western States U., 1992. RN, Ohio; cert. occupational health nurse, community health nurse, EMT instr. Indsl. nurse Ferro Corp., Cleve., 1977-81; occupational health nurse Foseco Inc., Cleve., 1981-83; nurse clinician Parkside Health Mgmt. Corp., Toledo, 1983-86, UCAR Carbon Co./Union Carbide, Parma, 1986-91; pres. M.L. Hau & Assocs., Inc., 1991—; cons., trainer in field; assoc. cons. Nat. Safety Coun., 1992—. Author: In Control Freedom From Smoking Program Group Leaders Guide, 1990, In Control Weight Loss and Maintenance Group Leader's Guide, 1992, While Help Is On The Way, 1994; contbr. articles to profl. jours. Vol. paramedic, firefighter Catawba Island VFD. Capt. USAR. Recipient Community Svc. award Union Carbide, Cert. Appreciation Lions Club, Port Clinton Power Squadron. Mem. ANA (cert. cmty. health nurse), Northwestern Ohio Assn. Occupational Health Nurses, Am. Heart Assn. (northeast Ohio affiliate worksite adv. com.). Home: 4385 E Ledge Rd Port Clinton OH 43452-9760 Office: PO Box 429 3345 1/2 NW Catawba Rd Port Clinton OH 43452

HAUBERT, ALAINE, ballet dancer. Student, Sch. Am. Ballet, San Francisco Ballet Sch. Dancer Pacific Ballet; soloist, prin. dancer Am. Ballet Theatre, N.Y.C., 1965-69, ballet mistress, 1993—; prin. dancer The Joffrey Ballet, N.Y.C., 1969-79; ballet mistress N.J. Ballet, Ballet Hispanico, Ballet Concierto de San Juan; mem. dance faculty U. Hawaii; dance tchr. in N.Y., Europe, P.R.. Performed in dances including The Green Table, The Moor's Pavane, The Three-Cornered Hat, Le Beau Danube, The Dream. Office: Am Ballet Theatre 890 Broadway New York NY 10003*

HAUCK-FUGITT, CHRISTINE CLAIRE KRAUS, insurance executive; b. McKeesport, Pa., May 22, 1951; d. Lawrence Elmer and Anne Mae (Seinar) Kraus; m. David T. Hauck, Feb. 6, 1971 (div. Apr. 1986); children: Benjamin David, Christopher Thomas, Andrew Lawrence; m. Jonathan Fugitt, 1988. Student, Duquesne U., 1969-71, U. Pitts., 1972-78, U. Charleston, 1978-81; BA, Ohio State U., 1984. Cert. ins. counselor. Claims asst. John Hancock Ins., Pitts., 1971-73; underwriter Chubb Ins. Group, Pitts., 1973-76; account rep., ins. agt. Frank B. Hall, Columbus, Ohio, 1982-85; customer svc. rep., agt. Andrew Ins. Assoc., Columbus, 1986-88, sr. customer svc. rep., 1988-90; spl. accounts mgr., account exec. Willis Corroon Corp. Ohio, Inc., 1990-94; pres., sec. Positively Successful, Columbus, 1988—; comml. underwriter McElroy Minister Co., Columbus, 1994—. Author poetry. Active Welcome Wagon, Upper Arlington, Ohio, 1981-84, Barrington Sch. Assn., Upper Arlington, 1982-87, Tremont Sch. Assn., Upper Arlington, 1987-93, Upper Arlington Civic Assn., 1986-95; instr. St. Agatha Dept. Religious Edn., Upper Arlington, 1983-87; foster parent, 1975—; active Jones Sch. Assn., 1988-95, Upper Arlington H.S. Assn., 1991-95; registered leader Boy Scouts Am., 1991-95, advancement chmn. troop 417, 1994—; mem. St. Agatha Folk Group, 1992—. Recipient Bridgebuilder award Boy Scouts Am., 1992. Mem. NAFE, Steps to Greatness, Internat. Platform Assn., Phi Kappa Phi. Democrat. Roman Catholic. Home: 2121 Jervis Rd Columbus OH 43221-2727 Office: Positively Successful 2121 Jervis Rd Columbus OH 43221-2727

HAUEISEN, KATHRYN MARIE, clergywoman; b. Akron, Ohio, July 17, 1946; d. Henry C. and Elizabeth J. (Ross) Hieber; m. James P. Haueisen, Sept. 6, 1969; children: Carol Haueisen Flores, Karen M. Haueisen Mahaffey. Student, Miami U., Oxford, Ohio, 1964-66; BA, Bowling Green State U., 1968; postgrad., Trinity Luth. Sem., Columbus, Ohio, 1981; MDiv, Wartburg Theol. Sem., Dubuque, Iowa, 1985. Ordained to ministry Evang. Luth. Ch. in Am., 1986. Editorial asst. The Defiance (Ohio) Coll., 1968-70, News Svc. Office Bowling Green (Ohio) State U., 1970; asst. editor Ohio Dept. Natural Resources, Columbus, 1977-78; pub. rels. dir. Outdoor Drama, New Phila., Ohio, 1979-80; assoc. pastor Living Word Luth. Ch., Grapevine, Tex., 1986-90; program dir. Luth. Outdoor Ministry, Dallas, Ft. Worth, 1990-92; assoc. pastor Zion Luth. Ch., Wooster, Ohio, 1992—; mem. corp. bd. Tex. Luth. Coll., Seguin, 1988-92; bd. dirs. Wooster (Ohio) Clergy Acad., 1992—, Wayne United Ministries, Wooster, 1992—; v.p., bd. dirs. Camp Mowana, Mansfield, Ohio, 1994—; presenter workshops on family, marriage and living. Author: (book) Married and Mobile, 1982; contbr. articles to a variety of pubs.; creator of curriculum for Augsburg Fortress, 1970—. Cons. GRACE (emergency relief agy.) Grapevine, 1988-92; vol. chaplain Wooster Cmty. Hosp., 1991. Office: Zion Luth Ch 301 N Market Wooster OH 44691

HAUFRECHT, MARCIA, playwright, actress; b. N.Y.C., Jan. 3, 1937; d. Herbert Haufrecht and Judith Denis. Student, Shakespeare Acad., 1956-57. Founder, artistic dir. The Common Basis Theater, N.Y.C., 1989—; tchr. Lee Strasberg Theatre Inst.; workshop leader Kultur Imm Gugg, Braunau, Australia, 1994, U. Perth, Australia, 1994, Melbourne, Australia, 1989, 91, 94; mem. Actors Studio, N.Y.C., 1963—, Ensemble Studio Theatre, N.Y.C., 1977—. Playwright: Welfare, 1981, Knitting, 1991, Eve, 1991, Flat Tire, 1992, Lucky Star, 1992, An Exchange, 1992, Full Moon and High Tide in the Ladies Room, 1993, Promethea Bound & Sysiphus Too, 1994; actress (films) Prince of the City, Dog Day Afternoon, (TV) No Place Like Home, Supervision, (Broadway prodns.) Mert & Phil, The Three Sisters, Can-Can, also off-Broadway and repertory prodns.; dir.: (plays) Knitting, Eve, An

Exchange, On Bliss Street in Sunnyside, others. Democrat. Home: 484 W 43d St New York NY 10036

HAUGAN, GERTRUDE M., clinical psychologist; b. New Richland, Minn.; d. Henry Albert and Ella Pauline (Gardson) H. BA, George Washington U., 1952, MA, 1956; PhD, U. Md., 1970. Lic. psychologist, D.C., Md. Research psychologist New Eng. Med. Ctr., Boston, 1959-62; intern clin. psychology Hall Psychiat. Inst., Columbia, S.C., 1968-69; fellow in pediatrics Sch. Medicine Johns Hopkins U., Balt., 1970-71; clin. psychologist adloescent program Devel. Services Ctr., Washington, 1971-72, chief children's unit, 1972-85; chief Devel Services Ctr., Washington, 1986-94; cons. in psychology Ea. Shore State Hosp., Cambridge, Md., 1969-71, in child psychology Ctr. for Spl. Edn., Annapolis, Md., 1972-76; instr. in child psychology Montgomery Coll., Rockville, Md., 1977-78. Contbr. articles to profl. jours. Mem. profl. adv. council Easter Seal Soc. for Disabled Children and Adults, Washinton, 1987. Mem. APA, D.C. Psychol. Assn., Am. Assn. on Mental Retardation, Phi Beta Kappa. Home: 4720 S Chelsea Ln Bethesda MD 20814-3720

HAUGEN, MARY MARGARET, state legislator; b. Camano Island, Wash., Jan. 14, 1941; d. Melvin Harry and Alma Cora (Huntington) Olsen; m. Basil Badley; children: Mary Beth Fisher, Katherine Heitt, Richard, James. Mem. Wash. Ho. Reps., Olympia, 1982-1992, past mem. natural resources com., transp. com., mem. joint legis. com. on criminal justice system; mem. Wash. Senate, Olympia, 1993—; chmn. govt. ops. com., transp. com., natural resource com., law and justice com. Wash. State Senate. Mem. Camano Homeowners Assn.; mem. United Meth. Ch. Mem. LWV, Stanwood Camano Soroptomists. Democrat. Lodge: Order Ea. Star. Home: 1268 N Olsen Rd Camano Island WA 98292-8708 Office: Wash State Legislature JAC Wac # 414 Olympia WA 98504

HAUGER, ELEANOR PRAPION KALLEJIAN, pianist, singer; b. Fresno, Calif., July 15, 1920; d. Robert Muggerdich and Prapion R. (Barsamian) Kallejian; m. Harry Hoyt Hauger, Jr., Apr. 17, 1943 (dec. July 1975); children: Philip Hoyt, Steven Harry. Student, UCLA, 1939-41; BA in Music, San Fernando State Coll., 1964. pvt. piano tchr., L.A., Dayton, Ohio. Debut San Fernando State Coll., Northridge, Calif., 1964; performed for symphonies and orchs., chs., L.A., Dayton, Ohio. Mem. AAUW, Westshore Musicians, Phi Beta. Congregationalist.

HAUGLAND, BRYNHILD, retired state legislator, farmer; b. Ward County, N.D., July 28, 1905; d. Nels and Sigurda (Ringoen) H.; BA, Minot State Coll., 1956; LLD (hon.), N.D. State U., 1984. Mem. N.D. Ho. of Reps., 1938-90, chmn. com. social services and vets. affairs, mem. com. industry, bus. and labor. Mem. Def. Adv. Com. Women in Services, 1955-58. Vice chmn. N.D. Gov.'s State Health Planning Com., 1944-75; past mem. Ward County Zoning Commn., Minot City Planning Commn., N.D. Bicentennial Commn. Bd. dirs. Internat. Peace Garden, 1953—, Minot State Coll. Found., Minot Commn. on Aging; mem. N.D. Legislature, 1938-90; mem. adv. com. Women in Svcs. Nat. Defense, Washington, 1953-56; past mem. adv. coun. N.D. Employment Security Bur., Ward County Zonin Commn., Minot Planning Commn., N.D. Bicentennial Commn., 1976—. Named Outstanding Legislator, Nat. Assembly Govt. Employees, 1979; recipient Golden award for Outstanding Service, Minot State Coll. Alumni, 1968, Genie award Minot C. of C., 1973, award Nat. Coun. Advancement and Support Edn., 1988 ; Hon. Mem. Uniformed Fire Fighters N.D., 1976; recipient Milky Way award Dairy Industry N.D., 1977, Disting. Service award Western N.D. Health Systems Agy., 1977-78, N.D. Water Wheel N.D. Water Users Assn./N.D. Water Mgmt. Dists. Assn., 1981, Service to Mankind award Sertoma Clubs, 1983, Merit award Pub. Health Assn. N.D., 1983, Liberty Bell award State Bar Assn., 1983, Disting. Service award Mental Health Assn. N.D., 1983, award Minot Assn. Home Builders, 1984, Good Citizen Scouting award, 1984, Disting. Service award Am. Protestant Health Assn., 1985; recognized state conv. Rep. Party for Half Century of Dedicated Pub. Service, longest serving legislator in nation on date of retirement, elected 26 terms-52 yrs., Woman of Distinction award Minot YWCA, 1993; numerous others; inducted into Scandinavian Hall of Fame, 1984; com. rm. named for her N.D. State Capital Bldg., Bismarck, 1987; Paul Harris fellow Rotary, 1993. Mem. Bus. and Profl. Women's Club (named Woman of Yr. 1956, 71, 89), Am. Assn. Ret. Persons, Nat. Ret. Tchrs. Assn., Farmers Union and Farm Bur., Minot State Coll. Alumni Assn. (dir., award for 50 yrs. svc. bd. dirs. 1993), Eureka Homemakers Club, Quota Club, Delta Kappa Gamma. Lutheran. Home: PO Box 1684 Minot ND 58702-1684

HAUK, JEANETTE FEENEY, accountant; b. Pasadena, Calif., Dec. 23, 1962; d. Joseph Leland and Maria Teresa (Guiteras) Feeney; m. Patrick Fabian Hauk, Apr. 5, 1986; children: Catharine Regina, Patrick Ryan, Jeanine Maria, Carolyn Antoinette. BS in Acctg., Loyola Marymount U., L.A., 1986. Staff acct. Price Waterhouse, L.A., 1986-87; cost acct. Iolab Corp., Claremont, Calif., 1987-89; sr. acct. Pharmacia Inc. Ophthalmics, Monrovia, Calif., 1989—. Mem. Foothill Jaycees, Monrovia, 1993. Mem. Inst. Mgmt. Accts. Office: Pharmacia Ophthalmics Inc 605 E Huntington Dr Monrovia CA 91016-3636

HAUPT, ANDREA MOORE, psychologist, therapist; b. Princeton, N.J., Aug. 1, 1943; d. Frank Leslie and Lucille M. (Kipp) Moore; m. Raymond E. Haupt, Aug. 19, 1978. BA in Liberal Arts and Chemistry, SUNY, Binghamton, 1965; ABD in Biochemistry, U. Pa., 1967; MEd in Ednl. Psychology, Temple U., 1972, PhD in Counseling Psychology, 1990. Lic. psychologist. Caseworker Dept. Pub. Assistance, Phila., 1967-69; mental health worker Phila. State Hosp., 1969-72; counselor Horizon House, Phila., 1972-74; psychologist Jefferson Cmty. Mental Health Ctr., Phila., 1974-84; pvt. practice Phila., 1984—; consulting psychologist Grad. Hosp. Dept. Psychiatry, Phila., 1990—; consulting psychol. examiner City of Phila., 1990—; bd. dirs. Women Therapist's Network, 1993—. Juried mem. Phila. Watercolor Soc., 1982—. NIH fellow U. Pa., 1965-67, Univ. fellow Temple U., 1984-86. Mem. APA (assoc.), Pa. Psychol. Assn., Am. Anorexia and Bulimia Assn. Home: 639 W Ellet St Philadelphia PA 19119-3428 Office: 301 S 19th St Fl 1 Philadelphia PA 19103-6621

HAUPT, CAROL MAGDALENE, elementary education educator; b. New Britain, Conn., Aug. 3, 1945; d. Richard Henry and Alfrieda (Sitz) Haupt. BS in Edn., Wagner Coll., Staten Island, N.Y., 1967, MS, 1969; EdD, Rutgers U., 1984. Elem. sch. tchr. N.Y.C. Bd. Edn., 1969—. Mem. edn. com. S.I. Hist. Soc.; mem. PTA of P.S. 69R (Tchr. Recognition Day award N.Y.C. Bd. Edn. 1981). Recipient Alumni Svc. award Wagner Coll., 1982, Cert. of Commendation, N.Y. Alliance for Pub. Schs., 1988; named to Outstanding Young Women of Am., 1972. Mem. AAUW (life, pres. S.I. chpt. 1985-87, past membership chair, past v.p.), S.I. Reading Assn. (pres. 1992-94), Archaeology Soc. S.I. (pres. 1987—, past treas., sec., v.p., membership chmn.), Wagner Coll. Alumni Assn. (treas., v.p. S.I. chpt. 1988—), Delta Kappa Gamma (world fellowship chair 1992-93, personal growth chair 1993-94, legis. chair 1994-95), Zeta Tau Alpha (life). Republican. Lutheran. Home: 66 Seneca Ave Staten Island NY 10301-4224

HAUPTLI, BARBARA BEATRICE, environmental specialist; b. Glenwood Springs, Colo., Sept. 20, 1953; d. Frederick James and Evelyn June (Rood) H.; m. Curtis Scott Bostian, July 4, 1992. BBA, Western State Coll., 1975. Contract specialist USA-TACOM, Warren, Mich., 1981-86; contract buyer Martin Marietta Orlando (Fla.) Aerospace, 1986; purchasing expediter Moog, Inc., Clearwater, Fla., 1986-89; subcontract adminstr. Olin Ordnance, St. Petersburg, Fla., 1989-91; sr. subcontract adminstr. Olin Ordnance, 1991-93; reimbursement specialist Tod. K. Allen, Inc., 1993—. Mem. Nat. Contract Mgmt. Assn.

HAUPTMAN, MARJORIE ANNE LEAHY, communications executive; b. Jackson, Tenn., Aug. 31, 1938; d. John Solinsky and Marjorie Elizabeth (Aylor) Solinsky; m. Edward J. Leahy, July 2, 1960 (div. Mar. 19, 1991); children: James Peter, Laura Marjorie, John Edward; m. John Andrew Hauptman, Sept. 18, 1991; stepchildren: Skye, Tara, Kyle. BS, Syracuse U., 1960. TV editor, reporter Rome (N.Y.) Daily Sentinel, 1961-62; freelancer Croton-on-Hudson, N.Y., 1966-74; editor The Navigator, Poughkeepsie, N.Y., 1974-76; staff writer Gannett Westchester Newspapers, Tarrytown, N.Y., 1978-81; pres. Five String Prodns., Croton-on-Hudson, 1981-89, Corp. Editions, Inc., Bellport, N.Y., 1989—; cons. in field. Mem. Water Control Commn., Croton-on-Hudson, 1989-90, Conservation Adv. Coun., Croton-on-Hudson, 1978-90; environ. instr. Westchester County Pks., White Plains, N.Y., 1988-91; coord. Clearwater Hudson River Revival, Poughkeepsie, N.Y., 1978—. Mem. Women in Comms. (v.p. pub. rels. 1982-84), Nat. Writers Union (Westchester Fairfield chpt., workshop speaker writers' conf. 1990, 94). Office: Corporate Editions Inc PO Box 14 Bellport NY 11713-0014

HAUSE, EDITH COLLINS, college administrator; b. Rock Hill, S.C., Dec. 11, 1933; d. Ernest O. and Violet (Smith) Collins; m. James Luke Hause, Sept. 3, 1955; children—Stephen Mark, Felicia Gaye Hause Friesen. B.A., Columbia Coll., S.C., 1956; postgrad. U. N.C.-Greensboro, 1967, U. S.C., 1971-75. Tchr. Richland Dist. II, Columbia, 1971-74; dir. alumnae affairs Columbia Coll., 1974-82, v.p. alumnae affairs, 1982-84, v.p. devel., 1984-89, v.p. alumnae rels., 1989—. Named Outstanding Tchr. of Yr., Richland Dist. II, 1974. Mem. Columbia Network for Female Execs., Council for Advancement and Support Edn., Nat. Soc. Fund Raising Execs. Republican. Methodist. Home: RR 4 Box 760 Prosperity SC 29127-9804 Office: Columbia Coll Alumnae Office Columbia SC 29203

HAUSELT, DENISE ANN, lawyer; b. Wellsville, N.Y., Oct. 12, 1956; d. John Donald and Maureen (Whelan) H. BS, Cornell U., 1979, JD, 1983. Bar: N.Y. 1984, Ill. 1984, U.S. Dist. Ct. (we. dist.) N.Y. 1984, U.S. Bankruptcy Ct. 1984. Summer assoc. Wildman, Harrold, Allen & Dixon, Chgo., 1982; assoc. Nixon Hargrave Devans & Doyle, Rochester, N.Y., 1983-86; asst. counsel Corning (N.Y.) Inc., 1986—; Bd. dirs. So. Tier Legal Svcs., Bath, N.Y., 1986-89, Home Health Svcs., Inc., Corning, 1986—. Recipient Am. Jurisprudence Constl. Law prize, Cornell U., 1981, others. Mem. ABA, N.Y. State Bar Assn., Cornell Law Assn., Keuka Yacht Club. Republican. Home: 164 Delevan Ave Corning NY 14830-3224 Office: Corning Inc Riverfront Plz MP-HQ-E2 Corning NY 14831

HAUSER, MARLENE LEA (CODY), writer, qualitative analyst, management consultant; b. Falls Church, Va., Feb. 9, 1955; d. Harry Francis and Mary Elizabeth (Cody) H. BA in English, U. Ark., 1978; MFA in Creative Writing, Columbia U., 1982. Pres. Cody Comm. Corp., N.Y.C., 1982-92; cons. Marlene Cody Hauser, Westport, Conn., 1990—; cons. Deloitte and Touche, Wilton, Conn., 1993-94, Champion Internat., Stamford, Conn., 1992-94, World Environ. Ctr., N.Y.C., 1994, and others. Editor: The Writer's NYC Source Book, 1982; dir. program devel. (documentary) Project 2nd Chance, 1986; assoc. prodr. (film) Under the Influence, 1986 (Top 10 Film award TV Digest 1986). Recipient Kansai Gaidai fellow U. Ark., 1977. Office: PO Box 2102 Westport CT 06880

HAUSER, RITA ELEANORE ABRAMS, lawyer; b. N.Y.C., July 12, 1934; d. Nathan and Frieda (Litt) Abrams; m. Gustave M. Hauser, June 10, 1956; children: Glenvil Aubrey, Ana Patricia. A.B. magna cum laude, Hunter Coll., 1954; Dr. Polit. Economy with highest honors (Fulbright grantee), U. Strasbourg, France, 1955; Licence en Droit, U. Paris, 1958; student law sch., Harvard U., 1955-56; L.L.B. with honors, NYU, 1959; LL.D. (hon.), Seton Hall U., 1969, Finch Coll., 1969, U. Miami, Fla., 1971. Bar: D.C. 1959, N.Y. 1961, U.S. Supreme Ct. 1967. Atty. U.S. Dept. Justice, 1959-61; sole practice N.Y.C., 1961-67; ptnr. Moldover, Hauser, Strauss & Volin, 1968-72; sr. ptnr. Stroock & Stroock & Lavan, N.Y.C., 1972-92, of counsel, 1992—; pres. The Hauser Found., N.Y.C., 1990—; Handmaker lectr., Louis Brandeis Lecture Series, U. Ky. Law Sch.; lectr. on internat. law Naval War Coll. and Army War Coll.; Mitchell lectr. in law SUNY, Buffalo; USIA lectr. constl. law Egypt, India, Australia, New Zealand; bd. dirs. The Eisenhower World Affairs Inst.; U.S. chmn. Internat. Ctr. for Peace in Middle East, 1984-92; bd. dirs. Internat. Peace Acad., 1990—, chair 1993—; U.S. pub. del. to Vienna follow-up meeting of Conf. on Security and Cooperation in Europe, 1986-88; mem. adv. panel in internat. law U.S. Dept. State, 1986-92. Contbr. articles on internat. law to profl. jours. U.S. rep. to UN Commn. on Human Rights, 1969-72; mem. U.S. del. to Gen. Assembly UN, 1969; vice chmn. U.S. Adv. Com. on Internat. and Cultural Affairs, 1973-77; mem. N.Y.C. Bd. Higher Edn., 1974-76, Stanton Panel on internat. info., edn., cultural rels. to reorganize USIA and Voice of Am., 1974-75, Mid. East Study Group Brookings Inst., 1975, 87-88, U.S. del. World Conf. Internat. Women's Yr., Mexico City, 1975; co-chair Com. for Re-election Pres., 1972, Presdl. Debates project LWV, 1976, Coalition for Reagan/Bush; adv. bd. Nat. News Coun., 1977-79; bd. dirs. Bd. for Internat. Broadcasting, 1977-80, Catalyst, Internat. Peace Acad., Salzburg Seminar, The Aspen Inst., Italy, U.S. Coun. Germany; trustee, exec. com. N.Y. Philharm. Soc.; adv. bd. Ctr. for Law and Nat. Security, U. Va. Law Sch/. 1978-84; vis. com. Ctr. Internat. Affairs Harvard U., 1975-81, John F. Kennedy Sch. Govt., Harvard U., 1992—; mem. bd. advisors Middle East Inst., Harvard U.; bd. of visitors Georgetown Sch. Fgn. Svc., 1989-94; chmn. adv. panel Internat. Parliamentary Group for Human Rights in Soviet Union, 1984-86; mem. spl. refugee adv. panel Dept. State, 1981; bd. fellows Claremont U. Ctr. & Grad. Sch.; former trustee Internat. Legal Ctr., Legal Aid Soc. N.Y., Freedom House. Intellectual Exchange fellow, Japan Soc. Fellow ABA (life, standing coms. on law and nat. security, 1979-85, on world order under law 1969-78, on judicial selection, tenure, compensation, 1977-79, coun. sect. on ind. rights and responsibilities, 1970-73, adv., bd. jour., 1973-78); mem. Assn. of Bar of City of N.Y., Am. Soc. Internat. Law (v.p. 1988—, exec. com. 1971-76), Am. Fgn. Law Assn. (dir.), Am. Arbitration Assn. (past dir.), Ams. Soc. (bd. dirs. 1988—), Coun. on Fgn. Rels. (bd. dirs.), Harvard Law Sch. Assn. N.Y.C. (trustee), Friends of The Hague Acad. Internat. Law (bd. dirs.), N.Y. Philharm. Symphony Soc. (bd. dirs., mem. exec. com.), Catalyst (bd. dirs. 1989—). Republican. Office: Stroock & Stroock & Lavan 7 Hanover Sq New York NY 10004-2616 also: The Hauser Found 712 Fifth Ave New York NY 10019

HAUSER-CRAM, PENNY, developmental psychologist; b. Detroit, Mar. 29, 1947; d. John Eugene and Dorothy Jane Hauser; m. Bestor Cram, June 14, 1969; children: Slater Ernesto, Lacey Barbara. BS, Denison U., 1968; MA, Tufts U., 1976; EdD, Harvard U., 1983. Asst. prof. Wellesley Coll., Wellesley, Mass., 1982-84; dir. Eliot-Pearson Children's Sch., Tufts Univ., Medford, Mass., 1984-87; assoc. prof. Boston Coll., Chestnut Hill, Mass., 1990—. Author: Essays on Educational Research, 1983, Early Education in the Public Schools, 1991. Recipient Excellence in Rsch. award Boston Inst. for the Devel. of Infants and Parents, Mass, 1992. Office: Boston College Campion Hall Chestnut Hill MA 02167

HAUSS, DEBORAH, marketing communications consultant, magazine writer; b. Elizabeth, N.J., Sept. 5, 1955; d. Henry and Beatrice Susan (Manasse) H.; m. David B. Baron, June 19, 1994. BA in Journalism and English Lit., U. Del., 1977; postgrad., U. Oreg., 1976. Local news reporter Wilmington (Del.) News-Jour., 1976; advt. prodn. asst. Ladies Home Jour., N.Y.C., 1977-78; asst. editor Gralla Publs., N.Y.C., 1978-79, assoc. editor, 1979-80, sr. assoc. editor, 1980, mng. editor, 1980-84, editor-in-chief, 1984-87, assoc. pub., 1987-89; editor-in-chief, assoc. pub. Premium/Incentive Bus., 1984-89; pres. In-Hauss Strategies, Inc., Hillside, N.J., 1989—. Editor: Incentive Travel Case Study Book, 1990. Reading tutor Lit. Vol. Am., Newark, 1993—. Mem. Soc. Incentive Travel Execs. (past bd. dirs. 1988-90), Premium Merchandising Club N.Y. (past bd. dirs. 1989-93). Democrat. Jewish. Home: 26 Carter Rd West Orange NJ 07052 Office: In-Hauss Strategies Inc 100 Central Ave Hillside NJ 07205

HAUSWALD, JEANANNE KAY, consumer products company executive; b. Sycamore, Ill., May 23, 1944; d. Walter E. and Amalia (Nemec) H.; m. William B. Harris, June 2, 1979; 1 child, Alexandra. BS, Iowa State U., 1967; MBA, NYU, 1971. Internal fin. cons. Shell Oil Co., N.Y.C., 1967-70; dir. cash mgmt. Internat. Paper Co., N.Y.C., 1970-72; banking officer Morgan Guarantee Trust Co., N.Y.C., 1972-74; asst. treas. Celanese Corp., N.Y.C., 1974-87; treas. Seagram Co. Ltd., Montreal, Que., Canada, 1987-90, Joseph E. Seagram & Sons, Inc., N.Y.C., 1987-90; v.p. human resources Joseph E. Seagram & Sons, Inc., Seagram Co. Ltd., N.Y.C., 1990-93; v.p., treas. Seagram Co., Ltd., N.Y.C., 1993—, Joseph and Seagram & Sons, Inc., N.Y.C.; bd. dirs. Thomas & Betts Corp., Memphis.

HAVEMAN, JACQUELINE RUTH, library specialist; b. Cedar Rapids, Iowa, May 5, 1948; d. Jake and Wilma Ruth (Nihlen) H. BA in English, Coe Coll., 1971. Cert. tchr., Iowa; cert. librarian, Iowa. Elem. tchr., music tchr. St. Patrick's Sch., Perry, 1971-73; libr. reader svc. specialist I, extension dept. Cedar Rapids Pub. Libr., 1973—. Soloist St. Paul's United Meth. Ch. choir, 1980—; vol. lobby pianist Mercy Hosp., Cedar Rapids, mem. Mercy Aux., 1986—. Mem. AAUW (mem. bd. 1989-90), Iowa Libr. Assn., Am. Legion, Beta Sigma Phi. Republican. Methodist.

HAVEN, MONICA, financial and tax planner, investment counselor; b. Pasadena, Calif., Feb. 18, 1958; d. Walter J. and Annette P. (Schneider) Lehmann; m. Byron Haven, May 27, 1983 (div.). BS in Small Bus. Adminstrn./New Ventures, Calif. State U., Hayward, 1985. Lic. tax practitioner, Calif.; realtor assoc. Calif. Dept. Real Estate; life, disability and variable annuity agt., Calif.; lic. security dealer series 7. Lab. technician Xerox Corp., Pomona, Calif., 1978-80; rsch. assoc. Chevron Rsch. Co., Richmond, Calif., 1980-85; investment exec. Baraban Securities, Long Beach, Calif., 1985-92; sole propr. fin. svcs. firm, Thousand Oaks, Calif., 1989—; contract instr. Securities Tng. Corp., N.Y.C., 1992-93; fin. svcs. specialist Aegon USA Securities Inc., Cedar Rapids, Iowa, 1992—; contract instr. Investment Tng. Inst., Inc., Tucker, Ga., 1995—. Membership dir. League Women Voters, Mt. Diablo chpt. Mem. Internat. Soc. Fin. Planners, Nat. Soc. Pub. Accts. Home: 48 Cantera St Thousand Oaks CA 91360-2611 Office: 1534 Edris Dr Los Angeles CA 90035-2915

HAVENS, CANDACE JEAN, planning consultant; b. Rochester, Minn., Sept. 13, 1952; d. Fred Z. and Barbara Jean (Stephenson) H.; m. Bruce Curtis Mercier, Feb. 22, 1975 (div. Apr. 1982); 1 child, Rachel; m. James Arthur Renning, Oct. 26, 1986; children: Kelsey, Sarah. Student, U. Calif., San Diego, Darmouth Coll., Am. U., Beirut, 1973-74; BA in Sociology, U. Calif., Riverside, 1977; MPA, Harvard U., 1994. Project coord. social svc. orgn. Grass Roots II, San Luis Obispo, Calif., 1976-77; planning enforcement technician City San Luis Obispo, 1977-81, asst. planner, 1981-83; assoc. planner City of San Luis Obispo, 1983-86, coord. parking program, 1986-88, spl. asst. to city adminstr., mgr. constr. libr. and parking structures, 1989, planning cons., 1991—. Past pres. Nat. Charity League, Riverside; mem. San Luis Obispo Med. Aux., 1986—, San Luis Obispo Arts coun., 1986—; pres. bd. dirs. San Luis Obispo Children's Mus., 1990-91, pres. 1990-91, CFO, 1993. Mem. AAUW, San Luis Obispo Med. Aux., Toastmasters (sec. 1986-87, v.p. 1987-88, pres. 1989-90, treas. 1991-92). Office: PO Box 1395 San Luis Obispo CA 93406-1395

HAVENS, CAROLYN CLARICE, librarian; b. Nashville, Sept. 11, 1953; d. Charles Buford and Iris Mae (Anderson) H.; m. Hilton Harris Huey, June 9, 1990; children: Heather Louise, Quentin Harris. AA, Sue Bennett Coll., 1973; BA in English, U. West Fla., 1974; MLS, U. Ky., 1981. Tchr. Escambia High Sch., Pensacola, Fla., 1974-75; salesperson Univ. Mall, Pensacola, 1975-77; libr. tech. U. Ky., Lexington, 1978-82; libr. Auburn (Ala.) U., 1982—. Contbr. articles to profl. jours. and newspapers; editorial bd.: A Dynamic Tradition, 1991. Bd. dirs. Nat. Kidney Found. Ala., Opelika, 1986-89; active Conscientious Alliance for Peace, Auburn, 1989—. Clergy and Laity Concerned, Atlanta, 1991—. Mem. ALA, Southeastern Libr. Assn., Ala. Libr. Assn., North Am. Serials Interest Group, Ala. Assn. Coll. and Rsch. Librs., Studio 218. Democrat. Methodist. Office: Auburn U Ralph Draughon Libr Auburn AL 36849-5606

HAVENS, PAMELA ANN, college official; b. Plattsburgh, N.Y., Nov. 30, 1956; d. Thomas L. and MaryAnn (Zalen) Romeo; m. Stephen L. Havens, Aug. 9, 1986. BA, Eisenhower Coll., 1978; MA summa cum laude, SUNY, Plattsburgh, 1987. VISTA vol. Retired Sr. Vol. Program, Plattsburgh, 1978-79; copywriter, newsperson Stas. WEAV-AM/WGFB-FM, Plattsburgh, 1979-83; traffic clk. Sta. WCFE-TV, Plattsburgh, 1983-84, pub. info. coord., 1984-85; coll. rels. officer Clinton Community Coll., Plattsburgh, 1985-89; dir. publs. and communications Cayuga Community Coll., Auburn, N.Y., 1989—. Bd. dirs. Auburn Players Cmty. Theatre, 1991-93. Named Young Careerist Alternate Bus. and Profl. Women's Club, 1986. Mem. NAFE, AAUW, Eisenhower Coll. Alumni Assn. (bd. dirs. 1990-97, chmn. bd. 1992-95), Auburn Kiwanis Club. Office: Cayuga Community Coll 197 Franklin St Auburn NY 13021-3099

HAVILAND, CAMILLA KLEIN, lawyer; b. Dodge City, Kans., Sept. 13, 1926; d. Robert Godfrey and Lelah (Luther) Klein; m. John Bodman Haviland, Sept. 7, 1957. A.A., Monticello Coll., 1946; B.A., Radcliffe Coll., 1948; J.D., Kans. U., 1955. Bar: Kans. 1955. Assoc. Calver & White, Wichita, Kans., 1955-56; sole practice, Dodge City, 1956—; probate, county and juvenile judge Ford County (Kans.), 1957-77; mem. Jud. Coun. Com. on Probate and Juvenile Law. Mem. adv. bd. Salvation Army, U. Kans. Sch. Religion. Recipient Nathan Burkan award ASCAP, 1955. Mem. Ford County Bar Assn. (pres. 1980), S.W. Kans. Bar Assn. (pres. 1968), Kans. Bar Assn., ABA, C. of C., Order of Coif, PEO, Phi Delta Delta. Democrat. Episcopalian. Clubs: Prairie Dunes Country (Hutchinson, Kans.); Soroptimists. Contbr. articles to profl. jours. Home: 2006 E Lane Ave Dodge City KS 67801-2828 Office: PO Box 17 203 W Spruce St Dodge City KS 67801-4426

HAVILAND, KAY LYNN (KADE HAVILAND), English language educator; b. Deer Lodge, Mont., July 16, 1952; d. Jackson C. and Juanita Maxine (Voekel) Price; children: Jesse Jean, Kelsey Ann, Molly Claire. MA in Guidance and Counseling, Adams State Coll., 1994. Counselor Creative Resource Ctr., Alamasa, Colo., 1991; mental health counselor, intern victims of abuse Tu Casa, Inc., Alamasa, 1992; biofeedback technician Adams State Coll., Alamasa, 1992-93; profl. vol., intern Seattle Mental Health Ctr., 1993-94; with Arapahoe House, Thornton, Colo., 1994—. Author, editor: (mag.) Human Interest, 1987-88 (1st place award 1989); contbr. articles to profl. jours. Mem. APA, Colo. Counselors Assn.

HAVILAND, MARLITA CHRISTINE, elementary school educator; b. Moses Lake, Wash., Sept. 4, 1952; d. Marvin Curtis and Delita F. (Grout) McCully; m. James A Haviland, June 18, 1971. BS in Edn., So. Nazarene U., Bethany, Okla., 1973; MA in Edn., No. Ariz. U., 1987. Cert. elem. tchr., Ariz., Colo., ESL tchr., c.c., Ariz., early childhood edn., Colo,. Elem. tchr. St. Paul (Ark.) Pu. Sch., Twin Wells Indian Sch., Sun Valley, Ariz., Navajo Gospel Mission, Kykotsmovi, Ariz., Shonto (Ariz.) Boarding Sch.; instr. Northland Pioneer Coll.; coord. Sch. Wide Book Fair. Mem. Nat. Fedn. Fed. Employees (local sec., treas.), Ariz. CADRE, Alpha Nu, Phi Kappa Phi. Home: Shonto Boarding Sch Shonto AZ 86054

HAWKE, BARBARA ANN, municipal official; b. Midland, Mich., Nov. 9, 1954; d. Richard and Marilyn (Lutz) H. BA in Advt., Mich. State U., 1976; student, Saginaw Valley State U., 1977; MBA, Grand Valley State Coll., 1986. Coord. housing asst. program City of Grand Rapids, Mich., 1981-84, event coord., 1984-87, mgr. citizen ctr., 1987-91, adminstrv. analyst, 1991—. Bd. dirs. Urban Inst. Contemporary Arts, Grand Rapids, 1987-93; vol. Grand Rapids Art Mus., Habitat for Humanity. Mem. ASPA (bd. dirs. 1992-94). Office: City of Grand Rapids 300 Monroe NW Grand Rapids MI 49503

HAWKEN, PATTY LYNN, nursing educator, dean of faculty; b. Wheaton, Ill., July 13, 1932; d. Leonard William and Betty (Stock) H. BSN, U. Mich., 1956; MSN, Case Western Res. U., 1962, PhD, 1970. Instr. U. Mich., Ann Arbor, 1956-57, Highland Hosp., Oakland, Calif., 1957-59; instr. Case Western Res. U., Cleve., 1960-63, asst. prof., 1963-67, assoc. prof., 1967-69, assoc. prof., assoc. in adminstrn., 1969-71; assoc. prof. Emory U., Atlanta, 1971-72, prof., dir., 1972-74; dean, prof. U. Tex. Health Sci. Ctr. Sch. Nursing, San Antonio, 1974—. Contbr. articles to nursing jours. Bd. dirs. Wesley Community Ctr., San Antonio, 1986, 89; mem. United Way Allocation Com., San Antonio, 1987; mem. adv. com. Trinity U. Health Care Adminstrn., San Antonio, 1984—, VA Dean's Com., San Antonio, 1982—. Recipient Nurse of Yr. award Tex. Nursing Assn., San Antonio chpt., 1985, Disting. Alumni award Case Western Res. U., 1991; named to Women's Hall of Fame, Mayor's Commn. on Women, San Antonio, 1986. Mem. ANA (cabinet on edn. 1986-88), Nat. League for Nursing (pres. 1989-91, Disting. Svc. award 1991), Am. Assn. Colls. of Nursing (com. on edn. 1986-88), Commns. Grads. Fgn. Nursing Schs. (trustee, pres. 1983-85), Am. Acad. Nursing (bd. govs. 1994—), San Antonio 100 Club, Internat. Women's Forum (San Francisco). Home: 1826 Fallow Run San Antonio TX 78248-2000 Office: U Tex Health Sci Ctr 7703 Floyd Curl Dr San Antonio TX 78284-6200

HAWKES, ELIZABETH LAWRENCE (BONNIE HAWKES), health facility administrator; b. Bryn Mawr, Pa., May 28, 1944; d. Edward Bettle and Anna Correy (Keen) Scull; m. Geoffrey Neale Hawkes, Aug. 12, 1972. BA in Chemistry, Hood Coll., 1966; cert. in occupational therapy, U. Pa., 1968; cert. in health care mgmt., B.C. Inst. Tech., Can., 1981; MS in Health Care Mgmt., U. B.C., 1988. Therapist Mary Bridge Children's Hosp., Tacoma, 1968-72; staff occupational therapist Pearson Hosp., Vancouver, B.C., 1972-74; staff occupational therapist Lions Gate Hosp., North Vancouver, B.C., 1974-76, sr. occupational therapist, 1976-78, supr. occupational therapy, 1978-82; rschr. med. engring. dept. surgery U. B.C., Vancouver, 1983-84, lectr., 1981-86, clin. instr., 1981-93; cons. health services North Vancouver, 1983—; adminstrv. dir. clin. practice unit Vancouver Gen. Hosp., 1992-93; coord. quality improvement Vancouver Hosp. and Health Scis. Ctr., 1993—; bd. dirs. Lions Gate Med. Rsch. Found., 1988-89. Contbr. articles to profl. jours. Bd. dirs. First Aid Ski Patrol, (coordinator 1977-79) (patrol 1973-80); first aid instr. St. John Ambulance, 1977-80, CPR instr. 1978. Mem. B.C. Soc. Occupational Therapists, Can. Coun. Health Svcs. Execs. Home: # 14-3634 Garibaldi Dr, North Vancouver, BC Canada V7H 2X5 Office: Vancouver Hosp Health Sci Ctr Quality Improvement Team, 855 W 12th Ave, Vancouver, BC Canada V5Z1M9

HAWKINS, DEBORAH CRAUN, community health nurse; b. Atlanta, Feb. 13, 1941; d. Adolph F. and Suzanne (Catchings) Spear; m. Hugh M. Hawkins Jr.; children: Kimberley Ann, Susan Elizabeth. BSN, U. Va., 1962, MS in Nursing, 1981. Cert. in nursing adminstrn., advanced. Pub. health nurse supr. Va. Dept. Health, Charlottesville, 1975-85; pub. health nurse mgr. Va. Dept. Health, Culpeper, 1985—. With Nurse Corps, USN, 1961-63, lt. comdr. USNR. Mem. Va. Nurses Assn., Va. Pub. Health Assn., Sigma Theta Tau. Home: 2312 Banbury St Charlottesville VA 22901-1823 Office: 640 Laurel St Culpeper VA 22701-3910

HAWKINS, DENISE SUSAN, accountant, auditor; b. Mt. Kisco, N.Y., May 13, 1969; d. Donald Mark and Carol E. (Roy) Andrus. BS in Acctg., SUNY, New Paltz, 1990. CMA. Acctg. asst., then acct. SUNY, New Paltz, 1990-91; staff acct. Alex. D. Goldfarb, CPA PC, Kingston, N.Y., 1991-92; staff acct. Video Aid Svc. Corp., Middletown, N.Y., 1992-94, internal auditor, 1994—. Home: RD1 24A Goshen Turnpike Circleville NY 10919

HAWKINS, ELINOR DIXON (MRS. CARROLL WOODARD HAWKINS), retired librarian; b. Masontown, W.Va., Sept. 25, 1927; d. Thomas Fitchie and Susan (Reed) Dixon; AB, Fairmont State Coll., 1949; BS in Libr. Sci., U. N.C., 1950; m. Carroll Woodard Hawkins, June 24, 1951; 1 child, John Carroll. Children's librarian Enoch Pratt Free Library, Balt., 1950-51; head circulation dept. Greensboro (N.C.) Pub. Library, 1951-56; librarian Craven-Pamlico Library Service, New Bern, N.C., 1958-62; dir. Craven-Pamlico-Carteret Regional Library, 1962-92; storyteller children's TV program Tele-Story Time, 1952-58, 63—; bd. dirs. Triangle East Bank of New Bern. Mem. New Bern Hist. Soc., 1973—, Tryon Palace Commn., 1974—; mem. adv. bd. Salvation Army. Authority. Mem. N.C. Assn. Retarded Children, Pilot Club (pres. 1957-58, v.p. 1962-63). Baptist. Home: PO Box 57 Cove City NC 28523-0057

HAWKINS, IDA FAYE, educator; b. Ft. Worth, Dec. 28, 1928; d. Christopher Columbus and Nannie Idella (Hughes) Hall; m. Gene Hamilton Hawkins, Dec. 22, 1952; children: Gene Agner, Jane Hall. Student Midwestern U., 1946-48; BS, N. Tex. State U., 1951; student Lamar U., 1968-70; MS, McNeese State U., 1973.Tchr. DeQueen Elem. Sch., Port Arthur, Tex., 1950-54, Tyrrell Elem. Sch., Port Arthur, 1955-56, Roy Hatton Elem. Sch., Bridge City, Tex., 1967-68, Oak Forest Elem. Sch., Vidor, Tex., 1968-91, ret. 2d v.p. Travis Elem. PTA, 1965-66, 1st v.p., 1966-67; corr. sec. Port Arthur City coun. PTA, 1966-67; Sunday sch. tchr. Presbyn. Ch., 1951-53, 60-66. Named Tchr. of Yr., Oak Forest Elem., 1984-85. Mem. NEA, Tex. State Tchrs. Assn., Am. Psychol. Assn. Home: 6315 Central City Blvd #619 Galveston TX 77551-3807

HAWKINS, JACQUELYN, elementary and secondary education educator; b. Russell Springs, Ky., Apr. 30, 1943; d. J.T. Hawkins and Maudie Bell Crew. BS, Andrews U., 1969; MEd, Xavier U., 1976. Cert. elem. tchr., Ohio, reading tchr. elem. and high sch., Ohio. Tchr. Cin. Pub. Schs., 1969—, Cummins Sch., Cin., 1971-81; tchr. Windsor Sch., Cin., 1982-83; tchr. Windsor Sch., 1983-89, acting contact tchr. chpt. 1 reading program, 1989—; rep. Cin. Coun. Educators, 1986-89, 91-92, 92-93, mem. book com.; mem. sch. improvement program Windsor Sch., 1982-84; mem. Sch. Improvement Program Cin. Chairperson United Way at Windsor Sch. Cin., 1986-89, 90-92, United Negro Coll. Fund Cin., 1986-89, ARC, Windsor Sch., Cin., 1986-89, 90-92; rep. Fine Arts Fund Cin., 1986-88; co-leader 4-H Club, Cin., 1987-88; leader Girl Scouts U.S., Cin., 1988-93; tutor Tabernacle Bapt. Ch., 1989; co-chairperson Windsor ARC, 1991-92. Recipient Cert. Achievement Cummins Sch. Cin., 1978. Democrat.

HAWKINS, JO ANNE WALKER, library administrator; b. El Paso, Tex., Nov. 28, 1938; d. Alfred Hewlett and Jonell J. (Seargeant) Walker; m. Daniel Fleming Hawkins, Apr. 2, 1961; children: Laura, Frederick, Wendy. BS in Art, U. Tex., 1960, MLS cum laude, 1966, MPA, 1987. Graphic designer univ. publs. U. Tex., Austin, 1962-64, reference libr., 1967-69, head libr. inter-libr. borrowing, 1969-73, head libr. inter-libr. svc., 1973-75, head libr. circulation svcs. dept., 1975-86, head libr. Perry-Castaneda Libr., 1986-87, asst. dir. for pub. svcs. gen. librs., 1986-93, assoc. dir., 1993—. Recipient Libr. Excellence award gen. librs. U. Tex., 1983, Disting. Grad. award Grad. Sch. Libr. and Info. Sci., 1983. Mem. ALA, Tex. Libr. Assn. (chmn. publs. com. 1985-86, dist. III 1988-89, coll. and univ. librs. div. 1989-90), Tex. Assn. Coll. Tchrs. (pres. U. Tex. chpt. 1981-82, state sec.-treas. 1981-85), St. Vincent de Paul Soc. Home: 315 N Tumbleweed Trail Austin TX 78733 Office: U Tex Gen Librs Austin TX 78713

HAWKINS, JOELLEN MARGARET BECK, nursing educator; b. Harvey, N.D., Dec. 15, 1941; d. Charles Joel and Gertrude Adelaide (Waits) Beck; m. Charles Albert Watson, June 27, 1964 (div. 1978); children: John Charles, Andrew Bruce; m. David Gene Hawkins, Oct. 4, 1978. Student, Oberlin Coll., 1959-61; Diploma, Chgo. Wesley Meml. Hosp., Sch. of Nursing, 1964; BS in Nursing, Northwestern U., Chgo., 1964; MS, Boston Coll., 1969, PhD, 1977. Cert. obstetric/gynecol. nurse practitioner. Staff nurse Sheboygan (Wis.) Meml. Hosp., 1964-65; instr., staff Boston Lying in Hosp., 1965-66, 68-69; staff nurse Brookline (Mass.) Vis. Nurse Assn., 1968, Guy's Hosp., London, 1968; campus nurse Roger Williams Coll., Bristol, R.I., 1969-70; instr. Salve Regina Coll., Newport, R.I., 1970-74; mem. faculty Roger Williams Coll., Bristol, 1974-75; prof. U. Conn., Storrs, 1978-83; assoc. prof. Boston Coll., Chestnut Hill, Mass., 1975-78, prof., 1983—. Author, coauthor 26 books; editor: Linking Nursing Education and Practice, 1987 (Book of Yr. award Am. Jour. Nursing 1988), Dictionary of American Nursing Biography, 1988; contbr. numerous articles to profl. jours. Recipient Disting. Alumni award North H.S., 1989. Fellow ANA (March of Dimes Nurse of Yr. 1992), Am. Acad. Nursing; mem. Mass. Nurses Assn. (Disting. Nurse Rsch. award 1984, Lucy Lincoln Drown Nursing History award 1994), Internat. Coun. Women's Health, Am. Assn. for History Nursing (nominating chmn. 1989), Assn. Women's Health, Obstetric, and Neonatal Nurses, Sigma Theta Tau (Elizabeth Russell Belford Founder's award for excellence in edn. 1993). Democrat. Unitarian. Home: 151 Stanton Ave Auburndale MA 02166-3005 Office: Boston Coll Chestnut Hill MA 02167

HAWKINS, KATHERINE ANN, hematologist, educator; b. Teaneck, N.J., Oct. 25, 1947; d. Howard Robert and Helen Ann (Foley) Hawkins; m. Paul Jonathan Chrzanowski, June 29, 1974; children: Eric, Brian. AB, Manhattanville Coll., Purchase, N.Y., 1969; MD, Columbia U., 1973. Intern Presbyn. Hosp., N.Y.C., 1973; intern Roosevelt Hosp., N.Y.C., 1974-75, resident, 1975-77; fellow NYU, 1977-79; attending hematologist Sickle Cell Ctr. St. Luke's Hosp., N.Y.C., 1985-87; assoc. attending physician St. Luke's - Roosevelt Hosp. Ctr., N.Y.C., 1989; asst. prof. clin. medicine Columbia U., N.Y.C., 1987-94, assoc. clin. prof., 1994—; asst. dir. dept. medicine, dir. med. edn. St. Luke's Hosp., N.Y.C., 1991—; mem. attending staff Beth Israel Hosp., N.Y.C., Calvary Hosp., N.Y.C., 1991. Contbr. articles to profl. jours. Fellow ACP; mem. AMA, Am. Soc. Hematology. Roman Catholic. Office: 200 W 86th St New York NY 10024

HAWKINS, LINDA PARROTT, school system administrator; b. Florence, S.C., June 23, 1947; d. Obie Lindberg Parrott and Mary Francis (Lee) Evans; m. Larry Eugene Hawkins, Jan. 5, 1946; 1 child, Heather Nichole. BS, U. S.C., 1969; MS, Francis Marion Coll., 1978; EdS in Adminstrn., U. S.C., 1994. Tchr. J.C. Lynch High Sch., Coward, S.C., 1973-80; tchr. Lake City (S.C.) High Sch., 1980-89, coord. alternative program, 1989-90, asst. prin., 1990-94; assoc. prin. Lake City H.S., 1994—; chair dept. Lake City H.S., 1980-89; mem. Williamsburg Tech. Adv. Coun., Kingstree, S.C., 1985-90; mem. adv. coun. Florence-Darlington (S.C.) Tech., 1981-87, co-chmn. allied health adv. com., 1990-93; speaker, presenter leadership workshops. Editor: Parliamentary Procedure Made Easy, 1983; contbr. articles to profl. jours. State advisor Future Bus. Leaders of Am., Columbia, S.C., 1978-86; treas. S.C. State Women's Aux., 1983-93; sec.-treas. J.C. Lynch Elem. Sch. PTO. Named Outstanding Advisor S.C. Future Bus. Leaders of Am., 1985, Tchr. of Yr., S.C. Bus. Edn. Assn., 1988-89, Secondary Tchr. of Yr., Nat. Bus. Edn. Assn., 1989-90, Educator of Yr. S.C. Trade & Indsl. Edn. Assn., 1993, S.C. Asst. Prin. of Yr., 1995. Mem. Profl. Secs. Internat., Nat. Bus. Assn. (S.C. chpt. membership dir. 1986-89, so. region membership dir. 1989-92, secondary program dept. dir. 1991-92), S.C. Bus. Edn. Assn. (jour. editor 1985-86, v.p. for membership 1986-87, treas. 1987-88, pres. elect 1988-89, pres. 1989-90), Am. Vocat. Assn., S.C. Vocat. Assn. (parliamentarian 1985-86, v.p. 1989-90, treas. 1991-92), Internat. Soc. Bus. Educators, Lake City C. of C. Democrat. Baptist. Office: Lake City High Sch PO Box 1157 Lake City SC 29560-1157

HAWKINS, MARY ELLEN HIGGINS (MARY ELLEN HIGGINS), former state legislator, public relations consultant; b. Birmingham, Ala.; student U. Ala., Tuscaloosa, 1945-47; m. James H. Hawkins, Feb. 13, 1960 (div., 1971); children: Andrew Higgins, Elizabeth, Peter Hixon. Congl. aide to several mems. U.S. Ho. Reps., 1950-60; art instr. Sumter County Schs., Americus, Ga., 1971-72; staff writer Naples (Fla.) Daily News, 1972-74; prin. Daniels-Hawkins, Naples, 1982-84; mem. Fla. Ho. of Reps., Tallahassee, 1974-94; vice chmn. BancFlorida Fin. Corp., Naples, 1979-91, chmn., 1991-93, pres., CEO, 1991-92, also bd. dirs. Columnist, contbr. articles to local newspapers. V.p. Naples Philharmonic, 1984-91; numerous offices Rep. Party of Ga., Americus, 1965-71. Recipient numerous awards for work in Fla. Legislature. Mem. Zonta Internat. Avocation: painting.

HAWKINS, NAOMI RUTH, nurse; b. Ft. Smith, Ark., Mar. 8, 1947; d. William Oscar and Sallie Inez (Reynolds) H. BS in Nursing, U. Cen. Ark., 1974. RN, Ark.; cert. pediatric nurse practitioner, Ark. Nurse practitioner Booneville (Ark.) Med. Clinic, 1975-78; lic. practical nurse Greenhurst Nursing Home, Charleston, Ark., 1967-73, nurse, 1973-75; nurse practitioner Ark. Dept. Health, Paris, Ark., 1978-80; pediatric nurse practitioner Ark. Dept. Health, Paris, 1980—. Fellow Nat. Assn. Pediatric Nurse Assocs. and Practitioners; mem. ANA, Ark. Assn. Pediatric Nurse Assocs. and Practitioners, Ark. State Nurses Assn., Am. Assn. Christian Counselors, Pub. Health Nurses Assn. Ark., Ark. State Employees Assn. Democrat. Baptist. Home: RR 2 Box 93 Charleston AR 72933-9418 Office: 102 E Academy St Paris AR 72855-4432

HAWKINS, PAULA, federal official, former senator; b. Salt Lake City; m. Walter Eugene Hawkins; children: Genean, Kevin Brent, Kelley Ann. Student, Utah State U., 1944-47, HHD (hon.), 1982; PhD (hon.), Nova U., St. Thomas Villa Nova, Bethune-Cookman, 1986, Rollins Coll., 1990. Dir. Southeast First Nat. Bank, Maitland, Fla., 1972-76; del. Rep. Nat. Conv., Miami, 1968, 72, 76, 80, 84, 88, 92; mem. rules com. Rep. Nat. Conv., 1972, co-chmn. rules com., 1980, co-chmn. platform com., 1984; bd. dirs. Fla. Fedn. Rep. Women, 1968—; elected mem. Fla. Pub. Svc. Commn., Tallahasee, 1972-79, chmn., 1977-79; mem. Rep. Nat. Com. for Fla., 1968-87, mem. rule 29 com., 1973-75; U.S. senator from Fla., 1981-87; mem. labor and human resources com., agrl. com., banking com., fgn. rels. com., drug free sch. com. U. S. Senate, chmn. subcom. on drug abuse, chmn. family and children subcom., 1982-86, chmn. drug enforcement caucus, 1981-87; apptd. permanent subcom. on narcotics control and terrorism OAS, 1981—; apptd. chmn. Nat. Commn. on Responsibilities for Financing Post Secondary, 1990-92; pres. Paula Hawkins and Assocs., Winter Park, Fla., 1988—; v.p. Air Fla., 1979-80; bd. dirs. Philip Crosby Assocs., Alexander Proudfoot; del. UN Narcotic Conv., Austria, 1987, Spain, 1993, N.Y.C., 1994. Author: Children at Risk, 1986. Charter mem. bd. dirs. Fla. Americans Constl. Action Com. of 100, 1966-68, sec.-treas., 1966-68; mem. Fla. Gov.'s Commn. Status Women, 1968-71; mem. Pres.'s Commn. White House Fellowships, 1975; bd. dirs. Freedom Found., 1981—; del. UN Narcotic Conv., Seville, Spain, 1993; U.S. del. UN Conv., N.Y.C., 1994—. Recipient citation for service Fla. Rep. Party, 1966-67, award for legis. work Child Fund Inc, 1982, Israel Peace medal, 1983, Tree of Life award Jewish Nat. Found, 1985, Nat. Mother of Yr. award, 1984, Grandmother of Yr.award, 1985, Albert Einstein Good Govt. award, 1986, Good Govt. award Maitland Jaycees, 1976, Outstanding award Am. Acad. Pediatricians, 1986; named Guardian of Small Bus. Nat. Fedn. Ind. Bus., 1982, 83, 84, 86, Rep. Woman of Yr. N.Y. Women's Nat. Rep. Club, 1981, Outstanding Woman of Utah, 1985, Outstanding Woman of Yr. in Govt. Orlando C. of C., 1977, Woman of Yr., KC, 1973. Mem. Maitland C. of C. (chmn. congl. action com. 1967). Mem. Ch. Jesus Christ of Latter-day Saints (pres. Relief Soc., Orlando Stake 1960-64. Club: Capitol Hill (Washington), Interlaken Country (Winter Pk.). Office: PO Box 193 Winter Park FL 32790-0193

HAWKINS, SUE S., insurance adjustor; b. Benton, Ill., May 22, 1932; d. Curtis E. and Beryl O'Rear (Bassett) Smith; m. Frank Lewis Hawkins, June 26, 1956 (div. 1983); 1 child, Leslie Susan Hawkins Eschete. BS, So. Ill. U., 1953. Lic. ins. adjustor. Co-owner, gen. mgr., comptr. Holiday Inns of Mobile, Ala., 1958-83; catastrophe ins. adjustor Charleston, S.C., 1989-90, L.A., 1992, Miami, Fla., 1992-93; catastrophe ins. adjustor Internat. Catastrophe Inc., Arcadia, Calif., 1994—. Propsmistress Mobile Opera, 1976-87; actress Joe Jefferson Players, Mobile, 1982-94, Mobile Theatre Guild, 1982-94, South of the Saltline Players, Mobile, 1982-94; active Arts Patrons League, Freedoms Found. at Valley Forge, Sister Cities Orgns. Mem. Alpha Gamma Delta (alumnae). Episcopal. Home: 1852 Springhill Ave Mobile AL 36607 Office: Internat Catastrophe Inc 933 Arcadia Ave Arcadia CA 91006

HAWKINS, TRACY DENISE, buyer; b. McKinney, Tex., Dec. 17, 1968; d. Donald Ray and Dixie Carroll (Read) H. AS, Cooke County Coll., 1989; BBA, U. North Tex., 1991. Accts. payable clk. Denton (Tex.) Regional Med. Ctr., 1989-91; buyer Nat. Chemsearch, Irving, Tex., 1992—. Baptist. Office: 2727 Chemsearch Blvd Irving TX 75062-6454

HAWKS, CAROL PITTS, librarian; b. New Orleans, Mar. 8, 1958; d. Leland Bascom and Mae Nell (Harper) Pitts. BA, Baylor U., 1980; M of Libr. and Info. Sci., U. Tex., 1981. Serials cataloger U. Houston Librs., 1981-82, head acquisition dept., 1982-87; head acquisition dept. Ohio State U. Librs., Columbus, 1987—. Mem. editorial bd. Libr. Acquisitions: Practice & Theory, 1989-90, editor-in-chief, 1990—; contbr. articles to profl. jours. Chair acquisitions serial control com. OhioLink, asst. dir. for policy devel., 1991-92. Mem. ALA (chairperson discussion group, com. mem., sec. mem.-at-large, chmn. sect., Esther J. Piercy award 1991), N.Am. Serials Interest Group, INNOVATIVE Users' Group (com. mem.). Office: Ohio State U Librs 1858 Neil Ave Columbus OH 43210-1286

HAWKS, KATHERINE A., special education educator; b. Vancouver, Wash., May 25, 1943; d. Kenneth Charles and Mary Elizabeth (Rumbaugh) H. BS in Edn., U. Idaho, 1965; MA, Mich. State U., 1970. Cert. in spl. edn. and phys. edn., Wash., Tex., South Africa. Phys. edn. tchr. Schoenbar Jr. High Sch., Ketchikan, Alaska, 1965-66, Wapato (Wash.) Jr. High Sch., 1966-68, Port Wheel Jr. High Sch. (with Dept. Def.), Okinawa, Japan, 1968-69, Queenstown (South Africa) Girls' High Sch., 1971, Roosevelt Elem. Sch., Granger, Wash., 1972-73; adapted phys. edn. Browns for Cerebral Palsied, Pinetown, South Africa, 1971-74, Bill Buchanan/Aged, Durban, South Africa, 1985; lectr. phys. edn., adapted phys. edn. U. Durban, Westville, South Africa, 1975-76; adapted phys. edn. tchr., supr. Denton (Tex.) State Sch., 1977-80; spl. edn. tchr. Congress Jr. High Sch., Denton, Tex., 1980-81, Fulton Sch. Deaf, Durban, South Africa, 1986-87, Evergreen Elem. Sch., Tacoma, Wash., 1988—; adapted phys. edn. cons. Child Guidance Clinic, U. Durban, 1975-76, Tex. Women's U., Denton, Tex., 1977; speaker Nat. Conf. on Perceptual Motor Phys. Edn. for Cerebral Palsied Children, South Africa. 1974, Nat. Conf. for Health, Phys. Edn. and Recreation, Phys. Edn. for Cerebral Palsied Children, South Africa, 1975. Coached Spl. Olympics, Denton, Tex., 1977-81; mem. Amnesty Internat., 1973-76; treas. Rainbow Landowners Cooperative, Denton, 1983. Mem. NEA, Wash. Edn. Assn. Democrat. Office: Clover Park Sch Dist 10020 Gravelly Lake Dr SW Tacoma WA 98499

HAWLEY, ANNE, museum director; b. Iowa City, Iowa, Nov. 3, 1943; d. Marshall Newton and Leone Ardith (Wilson) Hawley; m. Bruce Ivor McPherson, Sept. 4, 1977; 1 child, Katherine Black. BA, U. Iowa, 1966; MA, George Washington U., 1969; LHD (hon.), Lesley Coll, 1987; LHD (hon.), Williams Coll., 1989, Babson Coll., 1990, sr. exec. prog., Kennedy Sch. Govt, Harvard Univ., Intern in edn., Washington, 1967-69; research assoc. Nat. Urban League, Washington, 1969-71, Ford Found. Study Leadership in Pub. Edn., Washington, 1971-73; exec. dir. Cultural Edn. Collaborative, Boston, 1974-77, Mass. Council Arts/Humanities, Boston, 1977-89; mus. dir. Isabella Stewart Gardner Mus., Boston, 1989—; resident Nat. Hist. Soc. 1993—; adv. com. Nat. Trust of Historic Preservation, 1993—; vis. com. Fitchburg Art Mus., 1992-94. Bd. dirs. New Eng. Found. for Arts, 1978-89, Nat. Assembly/State Arts Agencies, Washington, 1981-83, Greater Boston Arts Fund, 1984-89, Boston Archtl. Found., Nat. Art Stabilization Fund, Boston Fenway Program. Trustee, Old Sturbridge Village, Inst. Contemporary Art, Boston, 1990—, vis. comm. Sch. Mus. Fine Arts, Boston, 1989—, adv. bd. Mass. Coll. Art, 1979-81. Fulbright scholar, 1986; recipient Design Travel Grant, Women's Travel Club, Boston, Mass., 1982, Polaroid travel grant, 1987, Fund for Mutual Understanding travel grant to USSR, 1988, Art award Mass. Coll. Art, 1987, Lyman Ziegler award Commonwealth of Mass., 1988. Mem. Nat. Endowment for Arts (mus. panel 1978-81, task force on trng. and devel. of artists and art edu., 1978, dance panel 1982-84, design panel 1978-81, 88—, Pres. Clinton's transition team for arts and humanities, 1992-93), Boston Soc. Architecture (hon. mem. 1989); Radcliffe Alumnae Career Svcs. (adv. comm. 1974). Office: Isabella Stewart Gardner Mus 2 Palace Rd Boston MA 02115-5897

HAWLEY, LINDA DONOVAN, advertising executive; b. Bryn Mawr, Pa., Nov. 1, 1946; d. John Donovan and Ann (Durnall) H.; diploma in advt. Charles Morris Price Sch. Advt., Phila., 1965. Sr. writer The Bulletin Co., Phila., 1968-72, The Advt. People, Inc., Bala Cynwyd, Pa., 1973-75, Elkman Advt. Co., Inc., Bala Cynwyd, 1975-77; sr. copywriter Mel Richman Inc., Bala Cynwyd, 1977-80; pres., creative dir. Hawley & Matthews Inc., Valley Forge, Pa., 1980—; instr. Charles Morris Price Sch., Pa. State U. Recipient various advt. awards including Neographics award, 1970, Addy award, 1976, Addy awards 2d Dist., 1980, Phila., 1981, 89; Charles Morris Price Sch. Disting. Alumni Award, 1977; TRAC award, 1983, 84, Billy award, 1985, Addy award, 1993. V.p. bd. Pa. Lupus Found., pres. 1993-94; mem. adv. bd. Joseph J. Peters Inst., 1991-93. Mem. Phila. Club Advt. Women (pres. 1978-80), Phila. Women's Network (pres. 1983-84, dir. 1984-85), Am. Advt. Fedn. (Pa. lt. gov. 1979-84, 87-88, lt. gov. 1990—, 2d dist. sec. 1981-82, Crystal Prism award), TV and Radio Advt. Club, Phila. Advt. Club (bd. dirs.). Roman Catholic. Office: Hawley & Matthews Inc PO Box 905 Davis Rd and Oakwood Ln Valley Forge PA 19482

HAWLEY, NANCI ELIZABETH, public relations and communications professional; b. Detroit, Mar. 18, 1942; d. Arthur Theodore and Elizabeth Agnes (Fylling) Smisek; m. Joseph Michael Hawley, Aug. 28, 1958; children: Michael, Ronald, Patrick (dec.), Julie Anne. Pres. Tempo 21 Nursing Svcs., Inc., Covina, Calif., 1973-75; v.p. Profl. Nurses Bur., Inc., L.A., 1975-83; cons. Hawley & Assocs., Covina, 1983-87; exec. v.p. Glendora (Calif.) C. of C., 1984-85; dir. membership West Covina (Calif.) C. of C., 1985-87; exec. dir. San Dimas (Calif.) C. of C., 1987-88; mgr. pub. rels. Soc. for Advancement of Material and Process Engrs., Covina, 1988-92; small bus. rep. South Coast Air Quality Mgmt. Dist., 1992-94; bus. counselor Commerce and Trade Agy., Small Bus. Devel. Ctr., 1994; exec. v.p. Ont. (Calif.) C. of C., 1994—. V.p. Sangabriel valley chpt. Women in Mgmt. Recipient Youth Motivation award Foothill Edn. Com., Glendora, 1987. Mem. NAFE, Pub. Rels. Soc. Am., Soc. Nat. Assn. Publs., Am. Soc. Assn. execs., Nat. Assn. Membership Dirs., Profl. Communicators Assn. So. Calif., Kiwanis Internat. (sec. 1989-90, pres. West Covina 1990-91, Kiwanian of Yr. 1989), Rotary Internat. Office: Ontario C of C 121 West B St Ontario CA 91762

HAWLEY, SANDRA SUE, electrical engineer; b. Spirit Lake, Iowa, May 7, 1948; d. Byrnard Leroy and Dorothy Virginia (Fischbeck) Smith; m. Michael John Hawley, June 7, 1970; 1 child, Alexander Tristin. BSEE, U. Dayton, 1981; BS in Math. and Stats., Iowa State U., 1970; MS in Stats., U. Del., 1975. Rsch. analyst State of Wis., Madison, 1970-71; rsch. asst. Del. State Coll., Dover, 1972-73; asst. prof. math. and statis. Wesley Coll., Dover, 1974-81, chmn. dept. math. and computer sci., 1978-80; elec. engr. Control Data Corp., Bloomington, Minn., 1982-85; sr. elec. engr. Custom Integrated Circuits, 1985-89; sr. lead engr. Cardiac Pacemakers, Inc., 1989-90; mgr. Tech. Rosemount Inc., 1990-94; prin. cons. Tri-Ess, Mpls., 1994—. Contbr. articles to profl. jours. Elder Presbyn. Ch. U.S.A., 1975—, mem. session Oak Grove Presbyn. Ch., Bloomington, 1985-88; vice moderator Presbtery of Twin Cities Area, 1995—, mem. Presbytery Coun. on United Action, 1989-92, adminstrv. comm., 1989-91, commr. to Synod of Lakes & Prairies, 1990, commr. Gen. Assembly Coun., 1992—, com. on coun., 1992, chair Presbytery Coun., 1994. NSF scholar U. Dayton, 1981. Mem. IEEE, Soc. Women Engrs. Office: Tri-Ess 7724 W 85th St Minneapolis MN 55438-1311

HAWN, GOLDIE, actress; b. Washington, Nov. 21, 1945; d. Edward Rutledge and Laura (Steinhoff) H.; m. Gus Trinkonis, May 16, 1969 (div.); m. Bill Hudson (div.); children: Oliver, Kate Garry, Wyatt Russell. Student, Am. U. Profl. dancer, 1965; profl. acting debut in Good Morning, World, 1967-68; mem. company TV series Laugh-In, 1968-70; appeared in TV spl. Pure Goldie, 1971; films include: The One and Only Genuine Original Family Band, 1968, Cactus Flower, 1969 (Acad. award best supporting actress 1969), There's A Girl In My Soup, 1970, Dollars, 1971, Butterflies Are Free, 1971, The Sugarland Express, 1974, The Girl from Petrovka, 1974, Shampoo, 1975, The Duchess and the Dirtwater Fox, 1976, Foul Play, 1978, Seems Like Old Times, 1980, Lovers and Liars, 1981, Best Friends, 1982, Swingshift, 1984, Overboard, 1987, Bird on a Wire, 1989, Deceived, 1991, Housesitter, 1992, Death Becomes Her, 1992, Crisscross, 1992; exec. producer and star films Private Benjamin, 1980, Protocol, 1984, Wildcats, 1986, My Blue Heaven (co-exec. prodr.), 1990; host TV spl. Pure Goldie, 1970, Goldie Hawn Special, 1978, Goldie and Liza Together, 1980, Goldie and Kids: Listen to Us!, 1982. Office: care Creative Artists Agy 9830 Wilshire Blvd Beverly Hills CA 90212*

HAWRYLUK, CHRISTINE JOANNE, school nurse; b. Balt., June 19, 1964; d. John and Alexandra S. (Skoblak) H. BSN, Rutgers U., Camden, N.J., 1986; sch. nurse cert., Trenton (N.J.) State Coll., 1990, MEd in Health Edn., 1994. Cert. EMT, CPR instr. Emergency dept. technician Meml. Hosp. of Burlington County, Mt. Holly, N.J., 1985-86; emergency rm. nurse Zurbrugg Meml. Hosp., Riverside, N.J., 1986-93; sch. nurse Cinnaminson Mid. Sch., 1991—; part time freelance photographer. Contbr. articles to profl. jours. Mem. Am. Sch. Health Assn., N.J. State Sch. Nurses Assn., N.J. Edn. Assn., Burlington County Sch. Nurses Assn., Cinnaminson Edn. Assn., Palmyra Ambulance Assn. (publicity chmn. 1986—, 2d lt. 1990-93, bd. trustees 1994—).

HAY, BETTY JO, civic worker; b. McAlester, Okla., June 6, 1931; d. Duncan and Kathryn Myrtle (Albert) Peacock; m. Jess Thomas Hay, Aug. 3, 1951; children: Deborah Hay Spradley, Patricia Lynn Daibert. BA, So. Meth. U., 1952. Bd. dirs. White House Preservation Fund, 1980-87, Nat. Parents as Tchrs., 1991-94; bd. dirs. Nat. Mental Health Assn., 1978-87, pres., 1986, mem. fin. com. and child adolescent com., 1978-79, mem. resource devel. com., 1980-83; v.p. fundraising Mental Health Assn. Tex., 1980, bd. dirs., 1974-90, pres., 1983-84; bd. dirs. Mental Health Assn., Dallas County, 1972-88, pres., 1981-82; bd. dirs. United Way Met. Dallas, 1983-94, treas., 1989; bd. dirs. Assn. Higher Edn. North Tex., 1980-82, vice chmn., 1982-83, chmn., 1984-85; mem. adv. bd. Sch. Social Work, U. Tex., Arlington, 1983-94; mem. Nat. Commn. on Children, 1989-92, Dallas Coun. on World Affairs, Woman's Div., March of Dimes Aux., 1982—; bd. dirs. Baylor Coll. Dentistry, 1987-94. mem. exec. com., 1989, vice chmn., 1992; mem. Tex. Commn. on Children and Youth, 1994-95; pres. Tex. Mental Health Found., 1982—; many past involvements in charitable orgns. Address: 7236 Lupton Cir Dallas TX 75225-1737

HAY, ELIZABETH DEXTER, embryology researcher, educator; b. St. Augustine, Fla., Apr. 2, 1927; d. Isaac Morris and Lucille (Lynn) H. AB, Smith Coll., 1948; MA (hon.), Harvard U., 1964; ScD (hon.), Smith Coll., 1973, Trinity Coll., 1989; MD, Johns Hopkins U., 1952, LHD (hon.), 1990. Intern in internal medicine Johns Hopkins Hosp., Balt., 1952-53; instr. anatomy Johns Hopkins U. Med. Sch., Balt., 1953-56, asst. prof., 1956-57; asst. prof. Cornell U. Med. Sch., N.Y.C., 1957-60; asst. prof. Harvard Med. Sch., Boston, 1960-64, Louise Foote Pfeiffer assoc. prof., 1964-69, Louise Foote Pfeiffer prof. embryology, 1969—, chmn. dept. anatomy and cellular biology, 1975-93; prof. dept. cell biology, 1993—; cons. cell biology sect. NIH, 1965-69; mem. adv. coun. Nat. Inst. Gen. Med. Sci., NIH, 1978-81; mem. sci. adv. bd. Whitney Marine Lab., U. Fla., 1982-86; mem. adv. coun. Johns Hopkins Sch. Medicine, 1982—; chairperson bd. sci. counselors Nat. Inst. Dental Rsch., NIH, 1984-86; mem. bd. sci. counselors Nat. Inst. Environ. Health Sci., NIH, 1990-93. Author: Regeneration, 1966; (with J.P. Revel) Fine Structure of the Developing Avian Cornea, 1969; editor: Cell Biology of Extracellular Matrix, 1981, 2d edit., 1991; editor-in-chief Developmental Biology Jour., 1971-75; contbr. articles to profl. jours. Mem. Scientists Task Force of Congressman Barney Frank, Massach, 1982-92. Recipient Disting. Achievement award N.Y. Hosp.-Cornell Med. Ctr. Alumni Council, 1985, award for vision research Alcon, 1988. Mem. Soc. Devel. Biology (pres. 1973-74), Am. Soc. Cell Biology (pres. 1976-77, legis. alert com. 1982—, E.B. Wilson award 1989), Am. Assn. Anatomists (pres. 1981-82, legis. alert com. 1982—, Centennial award 1987, Henry Gray award 1992), Am. Acad. Arts and Scis., Johns Hopkins Soc. Scholars, Nat. Acad. Sci., Inst. Medicine, Internat. Soc. Devel. Biologists (exec. bd. 1977), Boston Mycol. Club. Home: 14 Aberdeen Rd Weston MA 02193-1733 Office: Harvard Med Sch Dept Cell Biology 220 Longwood Ave Boston MA 02115-5717

HAY, ELOISE KNAPP, English language educator; b. Chgo., Nov. 19, 1926; d. G. Prather and Lucy (Norvell) Knapp; m. Stephen Northup Hay; June 11, 1954; children: Catherine, Edward. BA, Elmira Coll., 1948; PhD, Radcliffe Coll., 1961; DLitt (hon.), Elmira Coll., 1994. Tchg. fellow Harvard U., Cambridge, Mass., 1950-54; asst. prof. English U. Ill., Chgo., 1961-64; lectr. dept. English U. Calif., Santa Barbara, 1967-70, acting assoc. prof., religious studies, 1975-77, asst. prof. English, 1977-80, assoc. prof. English, 1980-82, prof., 1982—; prof. English U. Delhi, India, 1970-71; mem. English lit. adv. com. Coun. for Internat. Exch. of Scholars, Washington, 1983-85, 88. Author: The Political Novels of Joseph Conrad, 1963, 2d edit., 1981, T.S. Eliot's Negative Way, 1982; contbr. articles on other lit. subjects including Hawthorne, Dickens, James, Kipling, Forster, and Proust. Mem. U. Calif. Santa Barbara Sr. Women's Coun. Radcliffe (Bunting) Inst. fellow, 1964-66; sr. fellow NEH, 1974-75; recipient Disting. Teaching award U. Calif.-Santa Barbara Alumni, 1981. Mem. MLA Am. (mem. exec. com. on late 19th-early 20th-century lit. 1979-84, chmn. com. 1984), Phi Bet Kappa. Democrat. Roman Catholic. Home: 3310 Los Pinos Dr Santa Barbara CA 93105-2630 Office: U Calif Dept English Santa Barbara CA 93106

HAYASHIDA, NAOKO VICKY, securities trader; b. Iizuka, Fukuoka, Japan, Oct. 22, 1965; came to U.S., 1985; d. Hiroshi and Masano (Abe) H. BA in Econ., U. Utah, 1989. Asst. sales mgr. Fendi-Aoi, Osaka, Japan, 1984-85; euro deposits broker Tradition Berisford N.Am., L.A., 1989-90; sr. broker Tradition Fin. Svcs., N.Y.C., 1990—. Office: Tradition Financial Svcs 180 Maiden Ln 20th Fl New York NY 10038

HAYDEN, KATHLEEN BERNADETTE, nursing administrator; b. LaSalle, Ill., Aug. 18, 1948; d. George Jeffery and Bernadette I. (Zandecki) H. Diploma in nursing, Oak Park Hosp. Sch. Nursing, 1969; BSN, Colo. Women's Coll., 1975. RN, Ill., Colo., Calif. Staff nurse Children's Meml. Hosp., Chgo., 1969-70, Presbyn. Med. Ctr., Denver, 1970-75; head nurse plastic surgery svc. U. Calif., San Francisco, 1975-78; scrub nurse pvt. practice med. office, Modesto, Calif., 1978-84; asst. dept. mgr., oper. rm. bus. mgr. Dr.'s Med. Ctr., Modesto, 1984—; item writer Nat. Cert. Bd.-Perioperative Nursing Inc., Denver, 1992. Co-author: Post Graduate Course in Perioperative Nursing, 1989. Vol. ARC, San Francisco, 1989. Mem. Assn. Oper. Rm. Nurses (bd. dirs., chair membership Ctrl. Valley chpt. 1991-93), Oper. Rm. Nursing Coun. Calif. (program chair 1991-92, v.p./treas. 1993—). Roman Catholic. Office: Dr's Med Ctr 1441 Florida Ave PO Box 4138 Modesto CA 95352

HAYDEN, MARTHA NESSLER, artist, educator; b. Evanston, Ill., Jan. 7, 1936; d. Aldo Edward and Minerva Elizabeth (Kraft) Nessler; m. Robert Eugene Hayden, Nov. 30, 1957 (div. 1987); children: Edward, Mary, Bridget, Brian, Martha, Stephan, Sarah, David, John. Student, Bradley U., 1953-55; BFA, Sch. of the Art Inst. Chgo., 1961; postgrad., Schule des Sehens, Salzburg, Austria, 1962. One-woman show Gertrude Herbert Inst. Art, Augusta, Ga., Charles A. Wustum Mus., Racine, Wis., Bradley Galleries, Milw., Chgo. Pub. Libr., Mt. Mary Coll., Milw., Beloit (Wis.) Coll., West Bend (Wis.) Art Mus.; 6 by 92 foot mural executed Beloit Mcpl. Bldg., 1985; represented in permanent collections Art Inst. Chgo., City Mus. Salzburg, Mus. Modern Art, Sao Paulo, Brazil, Okla. Mus. Art, Oklahoma City, Smithsonian Instn., Burpee Mus. Art, Rockford, Ill., Wustum Mus., Freeport Art Mus., corp. Recipient Oskar Kokoschka award City of Salzburg; Bryron Lathrop fgn. travel fellow Art Inst. Chgo., 1961. Home and Studio: 143 Prairie St Sharon WI 53585-9781

HAYDEN, MELISSA BETH, special education educator, consultant; b. Boston, May 23, 1953; d. John Wood and Mary Phyllis (Briddell) H. BA in Psychology and Edn., Luther Coll., Decorah, Iowa, 1975; MS in Spl. Edn., U. Oreg., 1979, PhD in Spl. Edn., 1988; MEd in Computers in Edn., St. Martin's Coll., Lacey, Wash., 1985. Cert. spl. edn. tchr., Wash. Elem. tchr. Spring Grove (Minn.) Pub. Schs., 1975-78; rsch. asst. Direct Instrn. Follow Through Project U. Oreg., Eugene, 1978-79, grad. teaching fellow dept. spl. edn., 1978-79, rsch. asst. dept. spl. edn., 1985-88; elem. tchr. spl. edn. Groner Pub. Schs., Hillsboro, Oreg., 1979-80; secondary tchr. spl. edn. Olympia (Wash.) Pub. Schs., 1981-85; rsch. assoc. Edn. Rsch. and Svc. Ctr., Dekalb, Ill., 1989-90; asst. prof. spl. edn. Saginaw Valley State U., University Center, Mich., 1990—; tng. cons. for Direct Instrn. Programs SRA, Chgo., 1992—; ednl. cons. Consortium for Internat. Earth Sci. Info. Network, University Center, 1992-94. Contbr. articles to profl. jours. Vestrywoman St. John's Episcopal Ch., Saginaw, Mich., 1993—. Rsch. grantee Saginaw Valley State U. Found., 1991, 92, 93. Mem. ASCD, Am. Ednl. Rsch. Assn., Assn. for Direct Instrn., Coun. for Exceptional Children, Learning Disabilities Assn. Am., Midwest Rsch. Assn., Soc. for Applied Learning Tech., AAUW. Office: Saginaw Valley State U 7400 Bay Rd University Center MI 48710

HAYEK, CAROLYN JEAN, retired judge; b. Portland, Oreg., Aug. 17, 1948; d. Robert A. and Marion L. (DeKoning) H.; m. Steven M. Rosen, July 21, 1974; children: Jonathan David, Laura Elizabeth. BA in Psychology, Carleton Coll., 1970; JD, U. Chgo., 1973. Bar: Wash. 1973. Assoc. firm Jones, Grey & Bayley, Seattle, 1973-77; sole practice law, Federal Way, Wash., 1977-82; judge Federal Way Dist. Ct., 1982-95; ret., 1995. Task force mem. Alternatives for Wash., 1973-75; mem. Wash. State Ecol. Commn., 1975-77; bd. dirs. 1st Unitarian Ch. Seattle, 1986-89, vice chair 1987-88, pres., 1988-89; den leader Cub Scouts Mt. Rainier coun. Boy Scouts Am., 1987-88, scouting coord., 1988-89; bd. dirs. Twin Lakes Elem. Sch. PTA. Recipient Women Helping Women award Federal Way Soroptimist, 1991, Martin Luther King Day Humanitarian award King County, 1993, Recognition cert. City of Federal Way Diversity Commn., 1995. Mem. AAUW (br. pres. 1978-80, 90-92, chmn. state level conf. com. 1986-87, mem. diversity com. 1991—), ABA, Wash. Women Lawyers, Wash. State Bar Assn., King County Dist. Ct. Judges Assn. (treas., exec. com. 1990-91, 92-93, com. chmn., chair and rules com. 1990-91, 92-94), Elected Wash. Women (dir. 1983-87), Nat. Assn. Women Judges (nat. bd. dirs., dist. bd. dirs. 1984-86, chmn. rules com. 1988-89, chmn. bylaws com. 1990-91), Fed. Way Women's Network (bd. dirs. 1984-87, 88-91, 95—, pres. 1985, program co-chair 1989-91, co-editor newsletter), Greater Fed. Way C. of C. (dir. 1978-82, sec. 1980-81, v.p. 1981-82), Sunrise Rotary (com. svc. chair, bd. dirs., membership com., Federal Way chpt. 1991—). Republican. Address: PO Box 24494 Federal Way WA 98093

HAYES, ALBERTA PHYLLIS WILDRICK, retired health service executive; b. Blakeslee, Pa., May 31, 1918; d. William and Maude (Robbins) Wildrick; diploma Wilkes Barre Gen. Hosp. Sch. Nursing, 1938-41; student Wilkes Coll., 1953-54, Pa. State U., 1969—; m. Glenmore Burton Hayes, Oct. 9, 1942; children: Glenmore Rolland, William Bruce. Nurse, Monroe County Gen. Hosp., East Stroudsburg, Pa., 1941-44; pvt. duty nurse, 1944-56; with White Haven (Pa.) Center, 1956-82, dir. residential services, 1966-82, ret., 1982. Pres. Tobyhanna Twp. Sch. PTA, 1948-49, Top-o-Pocono Women of Rotary, 1975-76; nurse ARC, 1955; adv. council Luzerne County Foster Grandparent Program, 1977—, Health Services Keystone Job Corps, Drums, Pa., 1977—; active Tobyhanna Twp. Zoning Hearing Bd., Pocono Pines, Pa.; coord. Pocono Mountain Chpt. Choral Group, 1993—; chmn. bd. trustees Blakeslee United Meth. Ch. Mem. Am. Assn. Mental Deficiency, Am. Legion Aux. (unit pres. 1946-47), Ea. Star (Lehigh chpt.). Club: Pocono Mountains Women's (Blakeslee, sec. 1993, pres. 1994—). Home: PO Box 11 Blakeslee PA 18610-0011

HAYES, ALICE BOURKE, university official, biology educator; b. Chgo., Dec. 31, 1937; d. William Joseph and Mary Alice (Cawley) Bourke; m. John J. Hayes, Sept. 2, 1961 (dec. July 1981). B.S., Mundelein Coll., Chgo., 1959; M.S., U. Ill., 1960; Ph.D., Northwestern U., 1972; DSc (honoris causa), Loyola U., Chgo., 1994. Researcher Mcpl. Tb San., Chgo., 1960-62; faculty Loyola U., Chgo., 1962—, chmn. dept., 1968-77, dean natural scis. div., 1977-80, asso. acad. v.p., 1980-87, v.p. acad. affairs, 1987-89; provost, exec. v.p. St. Louis U., 1989—; mem. space biology program NASA, 1980-86; mem. adv. panel NSF, 1977-81, Parmly Hearing Inst., 1986-89; del. Bot. Del. to South Africa, 1984, to People's Republic China, 1988, to USSR, 1990; reviewer Coll. Bd. and Mellon Found. Nat. Hispanic Scholar Awards, 1985-86; bd. dirs. Pulitzer Pub. Co. Co-author books; contbr. articles to profl. publs. Campaign mem. Mental Health Assn. Ill., Chgo., 1973-89; trustee Chgo.-No. Ill. div. Nat. Multiple Sclerosis Soc., 1981-89, bd. dirs., 1980-88, com. chmn., sec. to bd. dirs., vice chmn. bd. dirs.; trustee Regina Dominican Acad., 1984-89, Civitas Dei Found., 1987-92, Rockhurst Coll.; trustee St. Ignatius Coll. Prep. Sch., bd. dirs., 1984-89, sec., vice chmn.; bd. dirs. Urban League Met. St. Louis, St. Louis Sci. Ctr., 1991—, Cath. Charities St. Louis, 1992—, St. Louis County Hist. Soc., 1992—. Named to Teachers' Hall of Fame Blue Key Soc.; fellow in botany U. Ill., 1959-60; fellow in botany NSF, 1969-71; grantee Am. Orchid Soc., 1967; grantee HEW, 1969, 76; grantee NSF, 1975; grantee NASA, 1980-85. Mem. AAAS, AAUP (corp. rep. 1980—), Am. Assn. for Higher Edn., Am. Assn. Univ. Adminstrs. (mem. program com. nat. meeting 1988), Am. Soc. Gravitational and Space Biology, Assn. Midwest Coll. Biology Teachers, Am. Soc. Plant Physiology, Bot. Soc. Am., Am. Inst. Biol. Scis. Acad., Chgo. Network, Soc. Ill. Microbiologists (edn. com. 1969-70, Pasteur award com. 1975, pub. rels. com. 1974, chair speakers' bur. 1974-79), Chgo. Assn. Tech. Socs. (acad. liaison 1982-85, awards com. 1984—), Am. Council on Edn. (corp. rep. higher edn. panel), Ctr. Rsch. Librs. (nominating com. 1986), North Cen. Assn. Colls. and Schs. (cons., evaluator Commn. on Higher Edn., 1984—, commr.-at-large, 1988—), Mo. Women's Forum Club, Sigma Xi, Delta Sigma Rho, Sigma Delta Epsilon, Phi Beta Kappa, Alpha Sigma Nu. Democrat. Roman Catholic. Office: St Louis Univ 221 N Grand Blvd Saint Louis MO 63103-2006

HAYES, ALLENE VALERIE FARMER, government executive; b. Washington, Sept. 23, 1958; d. Thomas Jonathan and Allena V. (Joyner) Farmer; m. Thomas Gary Hayes; 1 child, Tommia Chanel. Student, Richmond Coll., London, 1980; BA, Clark U., 1980; cert., U. Oxford, Eng., 1981; M.L.S., U. Md., 1986. Libr. asst. NUS Corp., Gaithersburg, Md., 1981-82; cataloger Libr. of Congress, Washington, 1982-84, copyright specialist, 1984-85; congl. fellow Ho. of Reps. Com. on D.C., Washington, 1985—; English tutor, writer Natural Motion, Washington, 1983-84; intern, archivist Howard U., Washington, 1985; intern Libr. Congress Intern Program, 1991-92. Compiler: Single Mother's Resource Directory, 1984. Compiler, editor: Policy Research, 1985. Author booklet: D.C. Statehood Issue, 1986. Mem. U. Md. College Park Black Women's Coun., 1984, NAACP; vol. Congl. Black Caucus Found., Washington, 1985. Recipient Fgn. Study award Am. Inst. for Fgn. Study, 1981; Congl. Black Caucus fellow, 1985. Mem. ALA, Libr. of Congress Profls. Assn., Daniel A.P. Murray Afro-Am. Culture Assn. of Libr. of Congress (mem. exec. bd., newsletter editor, pres. 1994—), Delta Sigma Theta (tutor 1986). Avocations: travel; writing; dance; drama; tennis. Home: 1120 K St NE Washington DC 20002-7110 Office: Libr of Congress 101 Independence Ave SE Washington DC 20540-0001

HAYES, ANN LOUISE, English educator, consultant, poet; b. Los Angeles, May 13, 1924; d. George Henry and Bernice (Derby) Bowman; m. Frank A. Hayes, Oct. 29, 1943 (dec. Oct. 1968). B.A. summa cum laude, Stanford U., 1948, M.A., 1950. Instr. Stanford U., Calif., 1950; teaching assoc. Ind. U., Bloomington, 1953-55; instr. Coe Coll, Cedar Rapids, Iowa, 1955-57; instr. English Carnegie-Mellon U., Pitts., 1957-60, asst. prof., 1960-65, assoc. prof., 1965-74, prof., 1974—; cons. Coll. Bd., N.Y.C., 1964—. Author: The Dancer's Step, 1973, The Living and the Dead, 1975, Witness: How All Occasions, 1977, Progress, Dancing, 1986, Circle of the Earth, 1990; contbr. poems and essays to mags. Recipient Borestone Mountain Poetry award, 1969, Elliott Dunlap Smith prize Carnegie-Mellon U., 1991. Mem. Phi Beta Kappa. Democrat. Office: Carnegie-Mellon Univ Dept English Pittsburgh PA 15213

HAYES, BERNARDINE FRANCES, computer systems analyst; b. Boston, June 29, 1939; d. Robert Emmett and Mary Agnes (Tague) H. BA in Edn., St. Joseph Coll., 1967; MA in Urban Affairs and Pub. Policy, U. Del., 1973, PhD in Pub. Policy, 1978. Elem. tchr. St. Dominick Sch., Balt., 1960-63; tchr. sci., math. and art St. Mary's Sch., Troy, N.Y., 1963-65, Our Lady Queen of Peace Sch., Washington, 1965-68, St. Patrick Sch., Richmond, Va., 1968-69, St. Peter Cathedral Sch., Wilmington, Del., 1969-71; planner health and social svcs. Model Cities Program, Wilmington, 1971-72; dir. rsch. Del. State Dept. Mental Health, Wilmington, 1972-75; dir. planning and evaluation Mental Health, Mental Retardation Svcs., West Chester, Pa., 1976-78; instr. Boston U., 1978; div. dir. Systems Architects, Inc., Randolph, Mass., 1979-81; group mgr. Unisys Corp., Cambridge, Mass., 1981—; cons. in field; pres., founder Hayes Assocs., a communication firm, 1989—; developed Project Helplink, 1990-92; instr. Radcliffe Seminars, Cambridge, 1994—. Contbr. numerous articles to profl. jours. Bd. sec. Model Cities, 1969-70; chairperson bd. State Service Ctr., Wilmington, 1972-75; mem. Human Rels. Commn., Washington, 1965-68; co-chmn. State-wide Coalition for Human Svcs., Del., 1972-74; activist Vietnam protest, Del., 1970-74, Civil Rights Movement, 1965—, numerous polit. campaigns, 1972—; alt. del. Mass. Dem. Conv., 1985; bd. v.p. Women's Action for Nuclear Disarmament, Arlington, Mass., 1982-91, fin. com. chmn., 1983-85, 88-90, treas., 1988-90, chmn. polit. action com., 1983-84, dir. nat. voter registration campaign, 1984.; active Mondale for Pres., 1984, John Kerry for Senator campaign, Mass., 1984, Clinton for Pres., 1992, Studds for Congress, 1992; del. Com. for an Enduring Peace, Soviet Peace Commn., Moscow, 1987; bd. trustees Mass. Assn. for the Blind, 1989—, Children's Justice Ctrs., Tulsa, 1994—. Fellow NSF, 1966. Mem. NAACP, NOW, Women's Inst. Housing and Econ. Devel. (bd. dirs. 1985-88), Boston Computer Soc., Boston Mus. Fine Arts. Roman Catholic. Home: 49 Crane Rd Quincy MA 02169-2621

HAYES, BREE AUDREY, educator, consultant, author; b. Newark, Apr. 27, 1945; d. Harvey and Gerry (Soroka) Botkin; m. Robert M. Levin, Sept. 5, 1965 (div. June 1977); children: Jon M., Ali; m. Richard Lee Hayes, Aug. 18, 1977; 1 child, Gillian Rachael. BS, Boston U., 1967, MEd, 1973, EdD, 1987. Lic. sch. psychologist, N.Y.; cert. tchr., N.Y. Tchr. English Zama (Japan) Machi High Sch., 1968-70; counselor Wayland (Mass.) High Sch., 1973-74, The High Sch., Brookline, Mass., 1974-75; psychologist Hamilton (N.Y.) Cen. Sch., 1977-79; lectr. in edn. Colgate U., Hamilton, 1979, vis. instr., 1980; dir. consultation and edn. Human Svc. Ctr., Peoria, Ill., 1980-83; pres. Resource Mgmt. Svcs., Inc., Peoria, 1983-88; asst. prof. U. Ga., Athens, 1988-90; pres. The Hayes Group, Athens, 1990-93; cons. RHR Internat., 1993—. Author: Counseling Women Over the Life Span, 1992. Mem. com. Greater Peoria C. of C., 1983-88; bd. dirs. Parents Anonymous, Peoria, 1980-83. Recipient Pres.'s award Assn. for Specialists in Group Work, 1989. Mem. ACA, APA, Nat. Bd. Cert. Counselors (bd. dirs., sec., treas. 1990-92), Assn. Specialists in Group Work (pres. 1994-95), Assn. for Humanistic Edn. and Devel. (v.p. for rsch. 1990-91), Phi Delta Kappa, Pi Lambda Theta. Office: RHR Internat 1355 Peachtree St Atlanta GA 30309

HAYES, BRENDA SUE NELSON, artist; b. Rockford, Ill., May 26, 1941; d. Reuben Hartvick and Mary Jane (Pinkston) Nelson; m. John Michael Hayes, Jan. 26, 1964; 1 child, Amy Anne. BFA in Graphic Design, U. Ill., 1964. Exec. officer JMH Corp., Indpls., 1971—. Exhibited at Art Source L.A., Ariel Gallery, Atlanta, Art Source, Bethesda, Md., The Corp. Collection, Kansas City, Mo., The Hang Up Gallery, Sarasota, Fla., Susan Musleh/Art By Design, Inc., Indpls., Swan Coach House Gallery, Atlanta, Arnot Art Mus., Elmira, N.Y., Indpls. Mus. Art, Pindar Gallery, Soho, N.Y; represented in permanent collections at Holy Family Hosp., Des Plaines, Ill., Lilly Endowment, DowElanco Venture Centre Internat. Hdqs., Kimble Internat., Hardee's Hdqrs., Deloitte, Haskins & Sells, IBM, AT&T, U.S. Sprint, Eli Lilly Corp. Offices, Hewlett-Packard, Trammell Crow, Dow Consumer Products, Melvin Simon & Assocs., Dow Elanco Corp. Hdqs., Copyrite Nat., Support Net, NBD Banking Processing Ctr. Lobby, Indpls., Cellular One, Regional Offices, others. Bd. dirs. Contemporary Art Soc. for Indpls. Mus. Art, 1993—, sec., 1992-94; charter mem. Nat. Mus. Women in Arts. Lydia Bates scholar U. Ill., 1961-63, Ill. Found. of Study scholar, 1963-64, resident schoar, 1960-64; recipient Panhellenic award for Study U. Ill., 1963-64, Gallery Exhbn. awards. Mem. Nat. Mus. Women in the Arts (charter), Gamma Alpha Chi (Outstanding Woman in Journalism 1964). Home: 157 E 71st St Indianapolis IN 46220 Studio: 921 E 66th St Indianapolis IN 46220

HAYES, CONSTANCE J., pediatric cardiologist; b. Cortland, N.Y., July 16, 1937; d. John Burns and Anna Marie (McGuire) H.; m. Edward William Lewison, Nov. 8, 1980. RN, BS, Coll. St. Rose, 1959; MD, Loyola U., Chgo., 1965. Diplomate Am. Bd. Pediatrics, Am. Bd. Pediatric Cardiology, Nat. Bd. Med. Examiners. Resident in pediatrics St. Vincent's Hosp., N.Y.C., 1965-68; fellow in pediatric cardiology Columbia U., N.Y.C., 1968-71, assoc. pediatrics coll. p. & s., 1971-72, asst. prof. clin. pediatrics, 1972-80, assoc. clin. prof. pediatrics, 1980—. Contbr. articles to profl. jours. Fellow Am. Acad. Pediatrics, Am. Coll. Cardiology; mem. Am. Heart Assn., N.Y. Heart Assn., Pediatric Cardiology Soc. Greater N.Y. (pres. 1987-88). Office: Columbia Presbyn Med Ctr 3959 Broadway New York NY 10032

HAYES, GLADYS LUCILLE ALLEN, community care official, poet, writer; b. Havelock, Nebr., Nov. 29, 1913; d. Harry Arthur and Louise (Vogel) Allen; m. James Franklin Hayes, Oct. 5, 1943; children: J. Allen, Warren Andrew. Secretarial diploma, Lincoln (Nebr.) Sch. Commerce, 1932; student, Santa Clara U., 1950-60; BS in Media Studies, Sacred Heart U., Fairfield, Conn., 1989, exec. MBA, 1991. Cert. profl. religion tchr. Archdiocese of San Francisco. Exec. tech. sec. McCormick-Selph div. Teledyne Corp., Hollister, Calif., 1960-65; adminstrv. asst. to v.p. Greater Bridgeport Regional Narcotics Program, Inc., Bridgeport, Conn., 1979-81; adminstrv. asst. to scientists and engrs. CBS Lab. div. CBS Inc., Stamford, Conn., 1968-76; sec. to Nobel laureate and physicist Dennis Gabor, Dsc, FRS U. London, U.S.; corp. sec. Automated Power Systems, Inc., Bridgeport, 1976-90; owner, mgr. GA Secretarial Svc., Stratford, Conn., 1980-91; secretarial asst. Conn. Community Care, Inc., Stratford, Conn., 1986-91; sec., environ. resources U.S. Army Corps Engrs., Elmendorf AFB, Anchorage, Alaska, 1992-93; substitute tchr. Anchorage Sch. Dist., 1992-93; cmty. svc. rep. Alaska Dept. Corrections, Juneau, 1994—; radio broadcaster Fairfield U., 1985-90. Former residential fund raising chmn. ARC, Gilroy, Calif.; former motion picture chmn. St. Mary's Sch., Gilroy, also past pres. Mothers' Guild, former mem. Edn. Commn.; former fundraiser March of Dimes; mem. various choirs and choral groups, Calif., Conn., Alaska; mem. Nat. Coun. on Aging; tchr. religion Archdiocese of San Francisco, Diocese of Lincoln, 1933-67, Archdiocese of Bridgeport, 1968-72. Recipient Excellence in Aging award Conn. Community Care, Inc., 1989, prize for photograph City of Bridgeport, 1987, Pope Pius X Medal of Honor, 1959. Mem. Nat. Honor Soc. Republican. Roman Catholic.

HAYES, GRACE, pharmacist; b. Houston, Jan. 21, 1963; d. Daniel E. and Carol (Strong) Hayes; m. Manuel O. Romero, Jr. AS, Cuesta C.C., San Luis Obispo, Calif., 1983; Dr. Pharmacy, U. So. Calif., L.A., 1988. Pharmacy resident Dept. Vets. Affairs, L.A., 1988-89; pharmacist Economy Drug, San Luis Obispo, 1989—; clin. pharmacist Atascadero (Calif.) State Hosp., 1990—; adj. asst. prof. pharmacy practice U. So. Calif., L.A., 1992—; adj. asst. clin. prof. pharmacy U. Calif., San Francisco, 1991—; neuropsychopharmacy rsch. cons. Dept. vets. Affairs, Outpatient Clinic, L.A., 1989—. Contbr. articles to profl. jours.; mng. editor Atascadero State Hosp. Pharmacy Bull., 1990—; coord. editor Acad. Update, Calif. Pharmacist, 1993; peer reviewer jour. articles Am. Jour. Hosp. Pharmacy, 1993, Annals of Pharmacotherapy, 1993-94. Vice pres. Cuesta Coll. Found., San Luis Obispo, 1993-94; participant in leadership San Luis Obispo, 1993; mem. Friends of the Estuary, Morro Bay, Calif., 1990—. Named Alumna of the Yr. Cuesta C.C., 1991. Mem. Am. Pharm. Assn., Calif. Pharmacists Assn. (dist. 7 trustee 1994—, vice-speaker 1993, Pharmacy Student of the Yr. 1988), Ctrl. Coast Pharmacist Assn. (pres. 1991-93), Am. Inst. Parlimentarians, Phi Lambda Sigma (chpt. pres. 1988), Alpha Gamma Sigma. Office: Atascadero State Hosp PO Box 7001 Atascadero CA 93423

HAYES, JANET GRAY, retired business manager, former mayor; b. Rushville, Ind., July 12, 1926; d. John Paul and Lucile (Gray) Frazee; A.B., Ind. U., 1948; M.A. magna cum laude, U. Chgo., 1950; m. Kenneth Hayes, Mar. 20, 1950; children: Lindy, John, Katherine, Megan. Psychiat. caseworker Jewish Family Service Agy., Chgo., 1950-52; vol. Denver Crippled Children's Service, 1954-55; vol. Adult and Child Guidance Clinic, San Jose, 1958-59; mem. San Jose (Calif.) City Council, 1971-75, vice-mayor, 1973-75, mayor, 1975-82; co-chmn. com. urban econs. U.S. Conf. Mayors, 1976-78, co-chmn. task force on aging, mem. sci. and tech. task force, 1976-80, trustee, 1979-82; bd. dirs. League Calif. Cities, 1976-82, mem. property tax reform task force, 1976-82; chmn. State of Calif. Urban Devel. Adv. Com., 1976-77; mem. Calif. Commn. Fair Jud. Practices, 1976-82, client-community relations dir. Q. Tech., Santa Clara, Calif., 1983-85, bus. mgr. Kenneth Hayes MD, Inc., 1985-88; pres. bd. trustees San Jose Mus. Art, 1987-89; founder, adv. bd. Calif. Bus. Bank, 1982-85. Mem. Dem. nat. campaign com., 1976; mem. Calif. Dem. Commn. Nat. Platform and Policy, 1976; del. Dem. Nat. Conv., 1980; bd. dirs. South San Francisco Bay Dischargers Authority; chmn. Santa Clara County Sanitation Dist.; mem. San Jose/Santa Clara Treatment Plant Adv. Bd.; chmn. Santa Clara Valley Employment and Tng. Bd. (CETA); past mem. EPA Aircraft/Airport Noise Task Group; bd. dirs. Calif. Center Rsch. and Edn. in Govt., Alexian Bros. Hosp., 1983-92; bd. dirs., chmn. adv. council Public Tech. Inc.; mem. bd. League to Save Lake Tahoe, 1984—. AAUW Edn. Found. grantee. Mem. Assn. Bay Area Govts. (exec. com. 1971-74, regional housing subcom. 1973-74, regional housing subcom. 1973-74), LWV (pres. San Francisco Bay Area chpt. 1968-70, pres. local 1966-67), Mortar Bd., Phi Beta Kappa, Kappa Alpha Theta.

HAYES, KARLA RENE, special education educator; b. Columbus, Ohio, Nov. 22, 1967; d. Carl Glenn and Linda Lou (Diamond) H. BS, Ohio State U., 1990. Cert. spl. edn. tchr. grades K-12, Ohio. Preschool tchr. Little Sch. in the Prairie, Columbus, summer 1987; spl. edn. vol. J. W. Reason Elem. Sch., Hilliard, Ohio, 1987-90; spl. edn. tchr. Madison-Plains Middle Sch., London, Ohio, 1990-93, Grandview Heights Mid. Sch., Columbus, Ohio, 1993—. Vol. Spl. Olympics, Columbus, 1989-91; leader, co-dir. Fellowship of Christian Students, 1991-92. Named Best Christian Athlete, Heritage Christian Sch., 1986. Mem. Coun. for Exceptional Children. Republican. Baptist. Home: 1520 Cole Rd Columbus OH 43228-9706

HAYES, LAURA JOANNA, psychologist; b. Winnebeau, N.C., Mar. 26, 1943; d. Victor Wilson and Pansy Lorraine (Springsteen) Hayes; m. Jerry Allen Gladson, June 20, 1965 (div. Mar. 1992); children: Joanna Kaye, Paula Rae. BA, So. Coll., 1965; MEd, U. Tenn., Chattanooga, 1977; EdD, Vanderbilt U., 1985. Lic. psychologist, Ga. Psychol. intern Lakeshore Mental Health Inst., Knoxville, Tenn., 1985-86; counselor, psychologist Tara Heights Enterprises, Atlanta, 1986—; psychologist, owner Assoc. Psychol. Svcs., Inc., Ringgold, Ga., 1990—. Mem. APA, Christian Assn. for Psychol. Studies, Ga. Psychol. Assn. Democrat. Home: 327 Homestead Cir Kennesaw GA 30144 Office: Assoc Psychol Svcs Inc 3640 Battlefield Pkwy PO Box 133 Ringgold GA 30736

HAYES, LAURIE SCHULTZ, speech communication educator, academic administrator; b. Detroit, Jan. 22, 1945; d. Bernard Walter and Mildred Katherine (Schneider) Schultz; m. James Todd Hayes, Aug.21, 1969; children: Eric Edwin, Katherine Grace. BS in Speech & Theatre Arts Edn., U. Minn., 1966, BA in Speech summa cum laude, 1966; MA in Speech, U.Wis., 1968, PhD in Comm. Arts, 1980. Instr. speech U. Wis., Madison, 1968-69; vis. instr. speech comm. U. Minn., Mpls., 1972-74, asst. to dir. honors program Coll. Liberal Arts, 1974-76, asst. prof. rhetoric, 1981-84, acting asst. dean acad. and student affairs Coll. Agr., 1988-90, interim assoc. v.p. student affairs, 1990-91; assoc. prof. rhetoric U. Minn., St. Paul, 1984—, assoc. dean curricular and student affairs Coll. Agr., 1992—; asst. prof. speech Gustavus Adolphus Coll., St. Peter, Minn., 1977-81; workshop leader Minn. Ext. Svc., 1983—, Soc. Tech. Comm., 1986, 89, 90, Nat. Acad. Advising Assn., 1989, 93, King Abdulaziz U., Jeddah, Saudi Arabia, 1994—. Co-author: The Communicative Experience, 1976; editor: In Touch With Students, 1988, Proceedings of the Council for Programs in Technical and Scientific Communication, 1988, 89. Co-chair, del. Dem. Farmer Labor party, Minn., 1982—; active St. Anthony Park Luth. Ch., St. Paul, 1986—, St. Anthony Park Cmty. Chorus, St. Paul, 1986-92, Roseville (Minn.) Area High Sch. PTA, 1986-89, 93—. Recipient Morse-Minn. Alumni Assn. award for outstanding contbn. to undergrad. edn. U. Minn., 1990, Hon. State FFA degree, 1994. Mem. Coun. for Programs in Sci. and Tech. Comm. (treas. 1990—), Nat. Confs. Undergrad. Rsch. (bd. govs. 1990—), Speech Comm. Assn., Soc. Tech. Comm. (sr. mem.), Luth. Campus Ministry Coun., Mortar Bd., Phi Beta Kappa, Phi Kappa Phi. Home: 2280 Folwell Falcon Heights MN 55108 Office: U Minn Coll Agr 277 Coffey Hall 1420 Eckles Ave Saint Paul MN 55108

HAYES, MARILYN KAY, elementary school administrator; b. Mooreland, Okla., Dec. 5, 1951; d. Fred Ray and Vera Marie (Zinn) Ownbey; m. Terry Clarence Hayes, Dec. 30, 1983; children: Brett, Regina, Daron, Teresa. BA in English and Speech, Madonna U., 1974; MEd in Reading Edn., U. Okla., 1977. Elem. educator Plymouth (Mich.) Schs., 1974; early childhood educator Hillcrest Presbyn. Sch., Oklahoma City, 1974-75; elem. educator Oklahoma City Schs., 1976-82, elem. adminstr., 1983-87; elem. educator Lone Grove (Okla.) Schs., 1988, elem. adminstr., 1988—; co-presenter, presenter workshops in field. Tchr. Bible sch. Fobb-Willis Ch. of Christ, Willis, Okla., 1993; tchr. Sunday sch. Powell (Okla.) Ch. of Christ, 1994. Mem. Okla. Assn. Elem. Sch. Prins. (Dist. Adminstr. of Yr. 1990), Am. Fedn. Sch. Prins. Office: Lone Grove Schs PO Box 1330 Lone Grove OK 73443-1330

HAYES, MARY ESHBAUGH, newspaper editor; b. Rochester, N.Y., Sept. 27, 1928; d. William Paul and Eleanor Maude (Seivert) Eshbaugh; B.A. in English and Journalism, Syracuse (N.Y.) U., 1950; m. James Leon Hayes, Apr. 18, 1953; children—Pauli, Eli, Lauri Le June, Clayton, Merri Jess Bates. With Livingston County Republican, Geneseo, N.Y., summers, 1947-50, mng. editor, 1949-50; reporter Aurora (Colo.) Advocate, 1950-52; reporter-photographer Aspen (Colo.) Times, 1952-53, columnist, 1956—, reporter, 1972-77, assoc. editor, 1977-89, editor in chief, 1989-92, contbg. editor, 1992—; contbg. editor Destinations Mag., 1994—. tchr. Colo. Mountain Coll., 1979. Mem. Nat. Fedn. Press Women (1st prizes in writing and editing 1976-80), Colo. Press Women's Assn. (writing award 1974, 75, 78-85, sweepstakes award for writing 1977, 78, 84, 85, 91, 92, 93, also 2d place award 1976, 79, 82, 83, Woman of Achievement 1986). Mem. Aspen Community Ch. Photographer, editor: Aspen Potpourri, 1968, rev. edit., 1990. Home: PO Box 497 Aspen CO 81612-0497 Office: Box e Aspen CO 81612

HAYES, MARY JOANNE, special education educator; b. Bloomington, Ind., Feb. 3, 1944; d. John and Marie (Van Buskirk) Reeves; m. Jack Lee Hayes, June 25, 1983. BA, Olivet U., Kankakee, Ill., 1968; MA, Ind. U., 1972; postgrad., Ind. U., South Bend, 1987, Ind. State U., 1989. Lic. tchr., Ind. Tchr. 3rd grade Saulk View Sch., Steger, Ind., 1968-69; tchr. 1st grade Break-O-Day Sch., New Whiteland, Ind., 1969-83; tchr. emotionally handicapped David Turnham Edn. Ctr., Dale, Ind., 1987—. Mem. Coun. Exceptional Children, Coun. Behavorial Disorders, Ind. Reading Coun. Home: PO Box 191 Dale IN 47523-0191 Office: David Turnham Ednl Ctr Dale IN 47523

HAYES, MARY PHYLLIS, savings and loan association executive; b. New Castle, Ind., Apr. 30, 1921; d. Clarence Edward and Edna Gertrude (Burgess) Scott; m. John Clifford Hayes, Jan. 1, 1942 (div. Oct. 1952); 1 child, R. Scott. Student, Ball State U., 1957-64, Ind. U. East, Richmond, 1963; diploma, Inst. Fin. Edn., 1956, 72, 76. Teller Henry County Savs. and Loan, New Castle, 1939-41, loan officer, teller, 1950-62, asst. sec., treas., 1962-69, sec., treas., 1969-73, corp. sec., 1973-84; v.p., sec. Ameriana Savs. Bank (formerly Henry County Savs. and Loan), New Castle, 1984-91; exec. sec. Am. Nat. Bank, Nashville, 1943-44; corp. sec. Ameriana Fin. Svcs., 1984-91. Treas. Henry County Chpt. Am. Heart Assn., New Castle, 1965-67, 76-87, vol. Indpls. chpt. 1980—; membership sec. Henry County Hist. Soc., New Castle, 1975-90; sec. Henry County chpt. ARC, New Castle, 1976-91; elected mem. Found. Inst. Fin. Edn., 1991—; mem. Internat. Platform Assn., 1974—, Woman's Club 1992—; vol. Ind. Basketball Hall of Fame, 1993—. Mem. Inst. Fin. Edn. (sec.-treas. East Ctrl. Ind. chpt. 1973-91), Ind. League Savs. Insts. (25 Yrs. award 1975, 40 Yrs. Cert. award 1988), Internat. Platform Assn., Henry County Hist. Soc. (membership sec.), Altrusa (past officer, bd. dirs. New Castle chpt.), PEO (past chaplain, sec.), Woman's Club, Psi Iota Xi (past sec.-treas.). Mem. Christian Ch.

HAYES, MARY REGINA, hand therapist, administrator; b. Dorchester, Mass., Mar. 27, 1959; d. John Stephen and Nora Joan (Johnston) Hayes. BA in Psychology, St. Anselms Coll., Manchester, N.H., 1982; MS in Occupational Therapy, Boston U., 1987. Registered occupational therapist; cert. hand therapist. Behavior tng. specialist South Shore Mental Health Ctr., Quincy, Mass., 1982-84; staff occupational therapist Walter Reed Army Med. Ctr., Washington, 1986-87, Brooke Army Med. Ctr., San Antonio, 1987-88; asst. chief occupational therapy U.S. Army Inst. Surg. Rsch., San Antonio, 1988-89; clin. supr. rehab. Brigham and Women's Hosp., Boston, 1989—; cons. in devel. of computerized therapeutic equipment EXOS, Burlington, Mass., 1992. Group leader, organizer group to establish a commn. on handicapped affairs, Quincy, 1983. 1st lt. USAR, 1986-89; capt. Res. Mem. Am. Soc. Hand Therapists, Am. Occupational Therapy Assn., Mass. Occupational Therapy Assn. Roman Catholic. Home: 45 Harvard St North Quincy MA 02171 Office: Brigham and Women's Hosp 45 Francis St Boston MA 02171

HAYES, MICHELE THELMA, insurance professional; b. Hartford, Conn., June 24, 1948; d. Henry William and Harriet Frances (Gordon) H.; m. LeRoy M. Ganges, May 28, 1983 (div. Oct. 1987). BA, U. Conn., 1970. Field exec. Girl Scouts Am., Hartford, 1970-71; claim rep. Aetna Life and Casualty, Chgo., Boston, 1971-73, Crum & Forster, Atlanta, 1973-75; work measurement adv. The Hartford, 1975; claim rep., claim supr. INA, Chgo., 1975-78; claim rep. Fireman's Fund Ins., Milw., Parsippany, Phila., 1978-89; litigation specialist Zurich Ins., Marlton, N.J., 1989-94; team mgr. Zurich Ins., Parsippany, N.J., 1994—. Bd. dirs. Amistad House, Hartford, 1970. Mem. Nat. Ins. Industry Assn. Baptist. Home: Apt U-501 46 Center Grove Rd Dover NJ 07869 Office: Zurich Am Ins Co 140 Littleton Rd Parsippany NJ 07054

HAYES, PATRICIA ANN, university president; b. Binghamton, N.Y., Jan. 14, 1944; d. Robert L. and Gertrude (Congdon) H. BA in English, Coll. of St. Rose, 1968; PhD in Philosophy, Georgetown U., 1974. Tchr. Cardinal McCloskey High Sch., Albany, N.Y., 1966-68; teaching asst. Georgetown U., Washington, 1968-71; instr. philosophy Coll. of St. Rose, Albany, 1973-75, instr. bus., spring 1981, adminstrv. intern to acad. v.p., 1973-74, dir. admissions, 1974-78, dir. adminstrn. and planning, 1978-81, v.p. adminstrn. and fin., treas., 1981-84; pres. St. Edward's U., Austin, Tex., 1984—. Bd. dirs. Sta. KLRU Pub. TV, United Way, Seton Med. Ctr. for Battered Women. Mem. Ind. Colls. and Univs. Tex., So. Assn. Colls. and Schs. (commn. on colls.), Tex. C. of C. (bd. dirs.). Roman Catholic. Office: St Edwards U Office of the President 3001 S Congress Ave Austin TX 78704-6425

HAYES, REBECCA ANNE, communications professional; b. Princeton, Ky., June 3, 1950; d. James Luther and Margaret Anne (Sparks) H. AA, Midway Coll., 1970; AB, U. Ky., 1972; MEd, U. Louisville, 1974. Educator Jefferson County Bd. Edn., Louisville, 1972-78; mgmt. asst. S. Cen. Bell, Louisville, 1978-80, engr., 1980-82; engr. AT&T, Tucker, Ga., 1983-84, asst. staff mgr., 1984-87, systems cons. bus. markets group, 1987-88; staff mgr. hdqrs. BSD sales ops. AT&T, Bridgewater, N.J., 1988-90; staff mgr. BC Systems AT&T, San Francisco, 1990-91; CFO Global Bus. Comms. Systems AT&T, Columbia, S.C., 1991—. Advisor Career Explorers S. Cen. Bell, Louisville, 1979-80. Mem. Nat. Assn. Female Execs., Ky. Hist. Soc., U. Ky. Alumni Assn. (life), High Mus. Art (Atlanta), Phi Theta Kappa. Democrat. Roman Catholic. Office: AT&T 1201 Main St Columbia SC 29201-3200

HAYES, SHIRLEY MARIE ROSE, credit manager, accountant; b. Barridge, Ky., Aug. 16, 1937; d. Ira and Birtha (Thomas) R.; divorced; children: Robert A., Mathew H. Student in Acctg., Middletown Bus. Coll., 1956-58. Bookkeeper Sears Roebuck & Co., Middletown, Ohio, 1959-67; credit collector Sears Roebuck & Co., Dayton, Ohio, 1967-72; credit investigator Montgomery Wards Co., Middletown, 1972-77; credit mgr. Halsey-Myers Inc., Middletown, 1977-94. Mem. AARP, Nat. Assn. Credit Mgmt., Carlisle Hist. Soc. (sec. 1989-89), Sigma Phi Gamma (chmn. ways and means 1979-87). Home: 3750 Sarah St Franklin OH 45005 Office: Halsey-Myers Inc 2890 S Main St Middletown OH 45044

HAYLETT, MARGARET WENDY, television director, engineer; b. Ravenna, Ohio, Jan. 11, 1953; d. James Edward and Edith Marie (Campbell) H. Tech. cert., WIXY Sch. Broadcasting, Cleve., 1973; student, Empire State Coll., 1988—. FCC 1st class/gen. radio telephone lic. Engr. Sta. WJKW-TV, Cleve., 1973-81; engr. Sta. WOKR-TV, Rochester, N.Y., 1981-87, dir., 1987—. Home: 26 Harvest Rd Fairport NY 14450-2849

HAYMAKER, STEPHANIE ELISE, psychologist; b. Phila., Feb. 21, 1960; d. Martin Robert and Marcia Evelyn (Weinerman) Brody; m. Douglas James Haymaker, Apr. 4, 1987. BS, NYU, 1982; PhD, U. Fla., 1988. Staff psychologist Elizabeth (N.J.) Gen. Med. Ctr., 1987-88; psychologist, managed care resources Medicine and Dentistry of N.J., Piscataway, 1988-93, sr. psychologist, 1993—. Mem. Am. Psychol. Assn., Phi Beta Kappa. Office: U Medicine & Dentistry NJ 671 Hoes Ln Piscataway NJ 08854-5633

HAYNE, HARRIET ANN, state legislator, rancher; b. Puget Island, Washington, Sept. 11, 1922; d. Albert Greger and Angeline Marie (Benjaminsen) Danielsen; m. Jack McVicar Hayne, Apr. 3, 1946; children: Mary Joan, John David, Alice Sue, Nancy Ann. Student, Healds Bus. Coll., San Francisco, 1941-42, Wash. State U., 1946-47. Rep. Mont. Legis. Assembly, 1979-80, 84—. Precinct, then state committeewoman, vice-chmn., active various campaigns Mont. Reps., Pondera County, 1964. Served as staff sgt. USMC, 1943-45. Mem. Am. Nat. Cattlewomen, Nat. Order Women Legislators, Am. Farm Bur., Am. Legion Aux., Am. Legion, Women Marines Assn., Nat. Fedn. Rep. Women. Lutheran.

HAYNER, JEANNETTE CLARE, state legislator; b. Jan. 22, 1919; m. Herman H. Hayner, 1942; children: Stephen A., James K., Judith A. BA, U. Oreg., 1940, JD, 1942, PhD (hon), Whitman Coll., 1992. Atty. Bonneville Power Co., Portland, Oreg., 1943-47; mem. Wash. Ho. of Reps., 1972-76, Wash. Senate from Dist. 16, 1977-92, minority leader, 1979-80, 83-86, majority leader, 1981-82, 87-92; dist. chmn. White House Conf. on Children and Youth, 1970; dir. Standard Ins. Co. Portland, 1974-90. Mem. Walla Walla Dist. 140 Sch. Bd., 1956-63, chmn. bd., 1959-61; mem. adv. bd. Walla Walla Youth and Family Svc. Assn., 1968-72; active YWCA, 1968-72; chmn. Walla Walla County Mental Health Bd., 1970-72; former mem. Wash. Coun. on Crime and Delinquency, Nuclear Energy Coun., Bonneville Power Regional Adv. Coun., State Wash. Organized Crime Intelligence Adv. Bd.; mem. Coun. State Govts. Governing Bd.; former asst. whip Republican Caucus. Mem. Wash. State Centennial Commn. Recipient Merit award Walla Walla C. of C., Pres's. award Pacific Luth. Univ., 1982, Pioneer award U. Oreg., 1988, Lifetime Achievement award Wash. State Ind. Colls., 1991, Washington Inst. Columbia, 1991; named Legislator of Yr. Nat. Rep. Legislators' Assn., 1986, Chairman's award, 1989, Wash. Young Rep. Citizen of Yr., 1987, Legislator of Yr. Nat. Rep. Legislators Assn., 1989. Mem. Oreg. Bar Assn., Delta Kappa Gamma (hon.), Kappa Kappa Gamma. Lutheran. Home: 1508 Ironwood Dr PO Box 454 Walla Walla WA 99362

HAYNES, CAROLINE HOPPER, preschool administrator; b. Cheyenne, Wyo., May 28, 1959; d. George William and Sally (Hunter) Hopper; m. Mark F. Haynes, Aug. 24, 1985. BA in Econs. and Polit. Sci. cum laude, U. of South, 1981; MBA in Internat. Bus., George Washington U., 1987. Legis. aide to Senator Alan K. Simpson, U.S. Senate, Washington, 1982-83, legis. asst., 1983-87; legis. mgr. legis. affairs U.S. Treasury Dept., Washington, 1987-88, sr. legis. mgr., 1988-89, dep. asst. sec. for legis. affairs, 1989-91, prin. dep. asst. sec. for legis. affairs, 1991-92; v.p. Arlington Unitarian Coop. Pre-sch., Arlington, 1993-94, pres., 1994—. Office: Arlington Unitarian Coop Pre-sch Arlington VA 22203

HAYNES, CHERYL ETTORA, army non-commissioned officer; b. Washington, Oct. 13, 1948; d. Joseph Harvey Jr. and Rosalie Elizabeth (Brown) F.; m. Leon Haynes Jr., Feb. 15, 1988 (dec. Feb. 1989); 1 child, Aisha Nia Ruffin-Haynes. BS, Wayland Bapt., 1991; MA, Webster U., 1993. Clk. typist Dept. Def., Battle Creek, Mich., 1971-76, USDA, Howell, Mich., 1976-78; acctg. tech. dept. mgmt. and budget State of Mich., Lansing, 1978-80; enlisted U.S. Army, 1980; served as med. lab. tech. Walter Reed Army Med. Ctr., Washington, 1981-84; student adv. lab. Acad. Health Scis., St. Sam Houston, Tex., 1984-85; med. lab. non-commd. officer dept. pathology Brooke Army Med. Ctr., Ft. Sam Houston, 1985-87, 89-91; med. lab. non-commd. officer 121st Evacuation Hosp., Seoul, Republic of Korea, 1987-88, 41st Combat Support Hosp., Ft. Sam Houston, 1988-89; mgr. Supply Ctr. Logistics div., Ft. Sam Houston, 1991-94. Mem. Nat. Coun. Negro Women, Washington, 1966-70, Bapt. Tng. Union, Washington, 1975-70. Mem. Am. Coll. Healthcare Execs., Nat. Assn. Health Svc. Execs. Home: 6868 Columbia Rdg Converse TX 78109-3419 Office: Brooke Army Med Ctr Logistics Divsn Ft Sam Houston San Antonio TX 78234

HAYNES, DEBORAH GENE, physician; b. York, Neb., Feb. 18, 1954; d. Gene Eldridge and Margaret Lucille (Manchester) Haynes; m. Russell Larry Beamer, Mar. 3, 1979; children: Staci E. Beamer, Lindsay M. Beamer, Stephanie L. Beamer. BA in Biology cum laude, Wichita State U., 1976; MD, U. Kans., Wichita, 1979. Diplomate Am. Bd. Family Practice; cert. Added Qualifications-Geriatrics. Resident St. Joseph Hosp., Wichita, 1979-82; instr. dept. family and community medicine St. Joseph Family Practice Residency, U. Kans., Wichita, 1982-84, asst. prof. dept. family and community medicine, 1984-85; pvt. family practice Northeast Family Physicians, Wichita, 1985—; clin. asst. prof. U. Kans. Sch. Medicine, Witchita, 1985—; bd. dirs. Kans. Acad. Family Physicians, 1985—. Mem. adv. com. Blue Cross/Blue Shield of Kans., Topeka, 1990-94; bd. trustees Wichita Collegiate Sch., 1993—, chair com. on trusteeship, 1995; vis com. Wichita State U., Coll. Health Profls., Wichita, 1988-92; mem. campaign for students Wichita State U., 1993-95. Recipient P.G. Czarlinsky award for Disting. Clin. Svc., U. Kans., 1979. Fellow Am. Acad. Family Physicians (del. 1991—, commn. on edn. 1991—, task force on procedures, Mead Johnson award 1990-91, chair COD credential com. 1994), Kans. Acad. Family Physicians (pres. elect 1988-89, pres. 1989-90), Kans. Med. Soc., Med. Soc. Sedgwick County (del. 1990-91, chair profl. investigation com. 1993-95), Alpha Omega Alpha. Presbyterian. Home: 1015 N Linden Cir Wichita KS 67206-4075 Office: 8100 E 22nd St N Bldg 2200 Wichita KS 67226-2301

HAYNES, JEAN REED, lawyer; b. Miami, Fla., Apr. 6, 1949; d. Oswald Birnam and Arleen (Wiedman) Dow. AB with honors, Pembroke Coll., 1971; MA, Brown U., 1971; JD, U. Chgo., 1981. Bar: Ill. 191, U.S. Ct. Appeals (7th cir.) 1982, U.S. Dist. Ct. (no. dist.) Ill. 1983, N.Y. 1991, U.S. Dist. Ct. (so. dist.) N.Y. 1991, U.S. Dist. Ct. (no. and ea. dists.) N.Y. 1992, U.S. Ct. Appeals (10th cir.) 1993. Tchr. grades 1-4 Abbie Tuller Sch., Providence, 1971-72; tchr./facilitator St. Mary's Acad., Riverside, R.I., 1972-74; tchr./head lower sch. St. Francis Sch., Goshen, Ky., 1974-78; law clk. U.S. Ct. Appeals (7th cir.), Chgo., 1981-83; assoc. Kirkland & Ellis, Chgo., 1983-87, ptnr., 1987—. Governing mem. Art Inst. Chgo., 1982-90, mem. aux. bd., 1986-90, membership com. aux. bd., 1987-90, v.p. for devel., 1988-90; vis. com. U. Chgo. Law Sch., 1990-92. Mem. ABA (com. on affordable justice litigation sect. 1988—), Ill. Bar Assn. (life), Chgo. Bar Assn., Assn. Bar City N.Y., Internat. Bar Assn., Am. Judicature Soc. (life, chmn. membership com. 1991—, v.p. 1994—, mem. exec. com. 1992—, bd. dirs. 1991—), Law Club Chgo., Mid-Am. Club. Office: Kirkland & Ellis Citicorp Ctr 153 E 53rd St New York NY 10022-4611

HAYNES, MARILYN MAE, accountant, educator; b. Fond du Lac, Wis., Apr. 30, 1933; d. Clinton Charles and Addie May (Pavey) Ehrhardt; m. Ivan R. Haynes, Aug. 13, 1960. Jr. Acctg. diploma, Madison Bus. Coll., 1952; BE, Wis. State U., Whitewater, 1959; postgrad., U. Wis., 1975-77. Bookkeeper Gas Mags., Inc., Madison, Wis., 1952-55; various positions Wis., summers 1956-60; bus. edn. tchr. Sheboygan (Wis.) Sch. Vocat. and Adult Edn., 1959-60, Edgerton (Wis.) High Sch., 1960-61; acct. Graber Mfg. Co., Middleton, Wis., 1961-71; bookkeeper Alexander Grant and Co., Madison, 1971-79; night sch. bus. edn. instr. Stoughton (Wis.) Vocat.-Adult Ctr., 1961-82, Madison Area Tech. Coll., 1961—; acct. Dane County Housing Authority, Madison, 1979—. Pres., v.p. Campus Coed Club, U. Wis., Whitewater, 1956-59; chmn. ch. coun. United Meth. Ch., Stoughton, 1970-72, com. chmn., 1972-76, officer ch. cir., 1970-72, handbell ringer, choir mem., Monona, Wis., 1983—. Mem. Inst. Mgmt. Accts., Order of Ea. Star. Office: Dane County Housing Authority 2825 University Ave Madison WI 53705-3643

HAYNES, NANCY ELLEN BARTLETT, marketing professional; b. Melrose, Mass., July 4, 1959; d. William Robinson and Beatrice Jane (Cady) H. BS, Northeastern U., 1983. Market specialist Wang Labs, Lowell, Mass., 1984-86, market coord., 1986-89; market rsch. specialist Thomson & Thomson, North Quincy, Mass., 1989-91, mktg. mgr., 1991—. Mem. com. Trinitarian Congl. Ch., Concord, Mass., 1991—; mem. records and archives coms. Town of Concord, 1992—. Mem. DAR (treas. Concord chpt. 1987—), NAFE, Am. Mktg. Assn., Ad Club of Boston, Northeastern U. Alumni Assn. (gov. bd. 1993—, pres. 1990-92), Concord-Carlisle High Sch. Alumni Assn. (bd. dirs. 1989—). Office: Thomson & Thomson 500 Victory Rd Quincy MA 02171-3132

HAYNES, OLIVE DURHAM, clergywoman, artist; b. Balt., Oct. 2, 1930; d. John Mills and Mary Matilda (Durham) H. BA in Broadcasting, Ohio State U., 1952, MA in Broadcasting, 1954; MDiv, Princeton Theol. Sem., 1973; DMin, Louisville Presbyn. Theol. Sem, 1980. Ordained to ministry, Presbyn. Ch., 1973. Asst. libr. Columbus (Ohio) Libr. System, 1948-58; continuity writer, artist Cy Landy Advt., Columbus, 1958-59; writer, producer, on-air talent WOSU Radio, TV, Columbus, 1959-70; pastor First Presbyn. Ch., St. Marys, Ohio, 1973-80, Spenceville (Ohio) Presbyn. Ch., 1973-80, Prebyn. Ch., Marion, Ill., 1980=88; assoc. pastor missions and outreach Solano Beach (Calif.) Presbyn. Ch., 1988—; trustee Med. Benevolence Found. Presbyn. Ch. U.S.a., 1981-86; v.p. ministerial alliance, Merion, Ill., 1981; moderator Maumee Valley Presbytery, St. Mary, Ohio, 1987-88, team leader Med. Mission team to Africa, 1990; writer, presenter AIDS paper Chinese Med. Assn., People to People Project, Beijing, 1990. Artist: creator of note cards now being sold locally, makes and sells woodcraft, doll houses, etc. Initiator, developer Agape Pantry, N.w. Ohio, Latchkey children program, Marion, literacy program, Marion; co-founder Rainbow House home and resource ctr. for children and women with HIV and AIDS; instrumental in initiation of Church Trucking Ministry to feed the hungry and respond to crisis situations across the nation. Recipient Ohio Ho. Reps. award, 1979, State of Ill. award, 1983, CDC award, 1982, Quality of Life cert. Ill. Hospice, 1983, Disting. Alumni award Louisville Presbyn. Theol. Sem., 1993; Named Woman of Yr. St. Mary's Bus. and Profl. Women's Club, 1979, Regional Woman of Distinction, Women's Hist. Week, Carbondale, Ill., 1986. Mem. Presbyn. AIDS Network: Health, Edn., Welfare (S.W. rep. 1992—), Presbyn. Mission Pastors Network (S.W. rep.), Urban Ministries Com. Presbytery of San Diego. Office: Solano Beach Presbyn Ch 120 Stevens Ave Solana Beach CA 92075-2039

HAYNOR, PATRICIA MANZI, nurse, hospital administrator; children: Kelly Christine, Craig; m. Donald C. Maaswinkel. Diploma in nursing, Grasslands Hosp., Valhalla, N.Y.; BSN, Fairleigh Dickinsn U., 1967; MSN in Nursing Adminstrn., U. Pa., 1969; D Nursing Sci., Widener U., 1989. RN, Pa., N.J., N.Y. Asst. dir. surg. nursing Thomas Jefferson U. Hosp., Phila., 1972-74; asst. dir. nursing care depts. Our Lady of Lourdes Hosp., Camden, N.J., 1974-76; assoc. dir. nursing West Jersey Hosp., Camden, 1976-79; dir. nursing West Jersey Health System, Camden, 1979-8l, corp. dir. nursing, 1981-82; v.p. nursing Crozer-Chester (Pa.) Med. Ctr., 1982-85; coord. nursing adminstrn. program, asst. prof. Widener U., Chester, 1985-87; v.p. for nursing St. Francis Med. Ctr., Trenton, N.J., 1987-90; asst. prof. U. Del. Coll. Nursing, 1990-92; assoc. prof. Villanova (Pa.) U. Coll. Nursing, Phila., 1992—; cons. Nurse Assocs., Haddonfield, N.J., 1985—; spkr. in field; abstractor Am. Orgn. Nurse Execs. Leadership Perspectives. Contbr. articles to profl. publs. Mem. adv. bd. Camden County unit Am. Cancer Soc. Mem. AAUP, Am. Orgn. Nurse Execs., Acad. Nursing Svc. Adminstrs., S.E. Pa. Orgn. Nurse Leaders (bd. dirs., chair by-laws). Home: 201 9th Ave Haddon Heights NJ 08035-1632 Office: Villanova U Coll Nursing Villanova PA 19085

HAYS, BONNIE LINN, county official; b. Silverton, Oreg., Aug. 21, 1950; d. Lacy Emmett and Ethel Marie (Hunt) Bowlsby; m. Robert Verne Hays, Mar. 21, 1972 (dec. Aug. 1976); m. Arthur J. Lewis, Aug. 22, 1981. BS, Oreg. State U., 1972; postgrad. Portland State U., 1973-74, Rocky Mt. Inst., 1982, Sch. Pub. Adminstrn. Lewis & Clark Coll., Northwestern Sch. Law, 1985-87. Cert. tchr. secondary edn., Oreg. Tchr. high sch. Astoria Sch. Dist., Oreg., 1972-75; ins. agt. Equitable Life Assurance Co., Portland, Oreg., 1975-77; br. mgr. Transamerica Title Ins. Co., Beaverton, Oreg., 1977-82; county commr. Washington County, Hillsboro, Oreg., 1981—; advisor Washington County Community Corrections, Hillsboro, 1983-93, elected chmn., bd. commrs., 1987—; candidate exec. officer Metro Gen. Election, 1994; dir. State Job Tng. Coordinating Council, Salem, Oreg., 1985-88, Multnomah-Washington Pvt. Industry Council, Portland, 1983-87; project dir. Washington County Driving Under the Influence of Intoxicants Act Com., Hillsboro. Mem. Commn. on Accreditation for Corrections, 1985-92; pres. Washington County Visitors Assn., 1989-90; bd. dirs. Un Lugar para Niños, Hillsboro, 1984-94; bd. mgmt., chmn. YMCA of Washington County, Beaverton, 1983-89; corp. bd. dirs. YMCA of Columbia-Williamette, 1987-89; bd. dirs. Tualatin Valley Econ. Devel. Corp., 1987—, Washington County Roundtable for Youth, 1988-93, El Centro Cutural, 1989—, Washington County Hist. Soc., Hillsboro, 1985-89, pres., 1986-88; mem. Young Reps. of Oreg., Salem, 1984-89; mem. Oreg. Episc. Sch. Wetlands Adv. Com., 1986; head of delegation Dalsuh (Korea) Tech. Exch. Team Mcpl. Govts., 1991. Named One of Washington County's 10 Most Influential People, Valley Times Newspaper Poll, 1985, Woman of Distinction, Environ. Columbia River Girl Scout coun., 1992. Mem. Am. Corrections Assn., Assn. Oreg. Counties (com. pub. safety and human resources 1982-90, vice chmn. 1982, chmn. 1986-90, 1st v.p. 1990, pres. 1990-91), Nat. Assn. Counties (justice and pub. safety steering com. 1987-92, energy & environ. steering com. 1994), Multnomah Athletic Club. Republican. Roman Catholic. Avocation: gourmet cooking. Home: 5469 NW Deerfield Way Portland OR 97229-1757 Office: Washington County Courthouse 155 N 1st Ave Hillsboro OR 97124-3072

HAYS, DIANA JOYCE WATKINS, consumer products company executive; b. Riverside, Calif., Aug. 29, 1945; d. Donald Richard and Evelyn Christine (Kolvoord) Watkins; m. Gerald N. Hays, Jan 30, 1964 (div. Jan. 1970), 1 child, Tad Damon. BA, U. Minn., 1975, MBA, 1982. Dir. environ./phys. sci. Sci. Mus. Minn., St. Paul, 1972-76; dir. mktg. rsch. No. Natural Gas Co., Omaha, 1977-78; mktg. asst., asst. product mgr. Gen. Mills, Inc., Mpls., 1978-81; product mgr. ortho pharms. Consumer Products div. Johnson & Johnson, Raritan, N.J., 1981-82, product dir. home diagnostics, 1982-86; mktg. dir. new market devel. Consumer Products div. Becton Dickinson & Co., Franklin Lakes, N.J., 1986-90; dir. home diagnostics worldwide program Becton Dickinson Advanced Diagnostics Div. Becton Dickinson & Co., Balt., 1990-93; founder, pres. Exec. Computing Solutions, Inc., Vista, Calif., 1991—; product mktg. mgr. Jostens Learning Corp., San Diego, 1994—; chmn. energy exhibit com. Assn. Sci.-Tech. Ctrs., Washington, 1974-75. Producer Ecologenie, 1975. Recipient Tribute to Women and Industry award YWCA, 1989. Mem. Am. Mktg. Assn., NAFE, Twin Mgmt. Forum, Am. Assn. of Health Svcs. Mktg., Capital PC User Group, Beta Gamma Sigma (life). Republican. Roman Catholic. Office: Jostens Learning Corp 9920 Pacific Heights Blvd San Diego CA 92121

HAYS, FELECIA ANN, television news producer; b. Dallas, June 6, 1959; d. James Kenneth Sr. and Hilda Lee (Shamburger) Hays; m. Christopher Gerard Abel, July 20, 1985; children: Alise, Austin, Alannah. BA in Radio-TV, U. Tex., Arlington, 1981; MLA, So. Meth. U., 1989. Tv prodn. asst. KXAS-TV, Ft. Worth, 1980-81; tv news prodr. WFTV-TV, Orlando, Fla., 1981-84, WXFL-TV, Tampa, Fla., 1984-85, KXAS-TV, Ft. Worth, 1985-87; freelance prodr. St. Louis, 1987-88; tv news writer WFAA-TV, Dallas, 1990-

91; tv news prodr. KDFW-TV, Dallas, 1991—. Recipient Best Newscast in Tex., UPI, Austin, 1985, 86, AP, 1985, 86. Mem. Am. Assn. Female Execs., Leadership Arlington. Democrat. Methodist. Home: 3812 Yacht Club Dr Arlington TX 76016

HAYS, HOLLY MARY, editor, freelance photojournalist; b. L.A., Nov. 28, 1952; d. Herschel Martin and Mary Catherine (Miller) H. Cert. art history, Fla. State U., 1971; cert. computer sci., Fla. Atlantic U., 1979; BS in Journalism, U. Fla., 1974. Layout editor Ind. Fla. Alligator, Gainesville, 1974; reporter Gainesville Sun, 1974; computer specialist Gilbert Law Printing, Gardena, Calif., 1975; copy editor Hartford (Conn.) Courant, 1976-78; mech. artist CRC Press, Inc., Boca Raton, Fla., 1980-85; asst. editor Fla. Living mag., Gainesville, 1986-92, mng. editor, 1993-94, editor-in-chief, 1994—; asst. editor Ga. Living mag., Gainesville, 1989-91; writer Womans World Mag., Englewood, N.J., 1987-89; writer, photographer Fla. Sportsman Mag., Miami, 1988. Vol. Marjorie K. Rawlings State Hist. Site, Cross Creek, Fla., 1987—. Mem. Outdoor Writers Am., Internat. Group for Hist. Aircraft Recovery (expedition mem.). Republican. Home: PO Box 96 Lochloosa FL 32662-0096 Office: North Florida Pub 102 NE 10th Ave Ste 6 Gainesville FL 32601

HAYS, MARY KATHERINE JACKSON (MRS. DONALD OSBORNE HAYS), civic worker; b. Flora, Miss.; d. Rufus Lafayette and Ada (Collum) Jackson; student U. Miss., 1925-26, Millsaps Coll., 1926-27, 43-44; grad. Clark Bus. Sch., 1934; student Columbia U., 1935, Strayer Bus. Coll., 1951; m. Halbert Puffer Oliver, Aug. 9, 1927 (dec. 1934); m. 2d, Donald Osborne Hays, Aug. 30, 1937. Sec. to pres. McCullough Box and Crate Co., Pharr, Tex., 1934-36; sec. to field supr. Miss. Unemployment Compensatio Commn., 1936-37; rep. Homes of Tomorrow, 1940 N.Y. World's Fair; sec. to head interior design Lord & Taylor, N.Y.C., 1940; sales dept. Knabe Piano Co., N.Y.C., 1941-43. Active, Little Theatre, Wilkes Barre, Pa., 1937-39; charter mem. and incorporator Conf. State Socs., Washington, 1952; vol. worker Am. Cancer Soc., Washington, 1957; mem. Center City Residents Assn., Phila., 1956; mem. women's com. Nat. Symphony Assn., vol. worker USO, 1945-48, symphony sustaining com. drives, 1957; mem. women's com. Corcoran Gallery Art, Washington, 1957-62; mem. Pierce-Warwick Adoption Assn. of Washington Home for Foundlings; vol. Washington Heart Assn., 1959-66; mem. Nat. Capital Area chpt. United Ch. Women, 1957-72; mem. D.C. Episcopal Home for Children, 1961-86, D.C. Salvation Army Aux., 1962—. Mem. Miss. State Soc. D.C. (sec. 1950-53), Miss. Women's Club D.C., DAR (vice regent chpt. 1970-72, regent chpt. 1972-74, vice chmn. D.C. com. celebration Washington's birthday 1972-76, state librarian 1974-76, state officers club 1976—), chpt. chmn. DAR Service for Vet. Patients Com., 1986-88, 90-92, UDC (chpt. historian 1982-84, 86—, chaplain 1984-86), Johnstone Clan Am. (exec. coun. 1976-81, nat. chmn. membership com. 1976-81), First Families of Miss. Episcopalian. Club: The Washington. Home: 4000 Massachusetts Ave NW Washington DC 20016-5105

HAYS, RUTH, lawyer; b. Fukuoka, Japan, Sept. 20, 1950; d. George Howard and Helen Jincy (Mathis) H. AB, Grinnell Coll., 1972; JD, Washington U., 1978. Bar: Mo. 1978. Law clk. U.S. Ct. Appeals (8th cir.), St. Louis, 1978-80; assoc. Husch & Eppenberger, St. Louis, 1980-87, ptnr., 1987—. Articles editor Urban Law Annual, 1977-78. Bd. dirs. Childhaven, St. Louis, 1982-93, pres. 1987-88. Olin fellow Monticello Coll. Found., St. Louis, 1975-78; recipient Spl. Svc. award Legal Svs. Ea. Mo., 1993. Mem. ABA, Mo. Bar Assn., Bar Assn. Met. St. Louis, Employee Benefits Assn. (pres. 1995), Working in Employee Benefits, Order of Coif, Phi Beta Kappa. Office: Husch & Eppenberger 100 N Broadway Ste 1300 Saint Louis MO 63102

HAYS, WILMA RUBY, health agency executive; b. Pleasant Hill, Mo., Apr. 25, 1923; d. Floyd George and Ruby Margaret (Overton) Shurtleff; student Okla. State U. Tech., 1978-80; m. Thomas Richard McCullagh, Dec. 29, 1943; children—Patricia Ann McCullagh, Claudia Kay McCullagh; m. Thomas Marshall Hays, Oct. 29, 1954; children—Mary Margaret, Cecilia Marie. Exec. sec. Armed Forces Induction Sta., Tulsa, 1941-43; sec. Guaranty Abstract Co., Tulsa, 1943-49, Earlougher Engring. Co., Tulsa, 1949-51, Bethlehem Supply Co., Tulsa, 1951-54; exec. dir. Kidney Found. of Okla., Oklahoma City, 1969-86; treas. Nat. Health Agys., Okla., state chmn., 1981-83; ret. 1986. Mem. NAFE (dir. 1984-86), Profl. Staff Assn. of Nat. Kidney Found., Okla. Soc. Assn. Execs., Am. Mgmt. Assn., LaPetite Seur Book Rev. Club, LWV. Republican. Roman Catholic. Clubs: Bus. and Profl. Women's (rec. sec. 1978, pres. 1980) (Oklahoma City); Zonta Internat., Christian Women's of Okla. Avocations: gardening, piano, spending time with grandchildren. Home: 4040 NW 61st St Oklahoma City OK 73112-1418

HAYWARD, KAREN GUNDERSON, psychologist, researcher, psychotherapist; b. Patterson, N.J., June 16, 1944; d. Victor Charles and Louise Josephine (Torgerson) Gunderson; m. Robert Wilson Madry Jr., June 18, 1966 (div. July 1980); children: Lisa Katherine, Robert Wilson III, Eric Charles; m. Warren Chase Hayward, Mar. 7, 1994. BS, U. N.C., 1966; MA, Corpus Christi State U., 1981; PhD, U. Tex., 1991. Lic. profl. counselor, Tex.; lic. chemical dependency counselor, Tex. Pediatrics staff nurse N.C. Meml. Hosp., Chapel Hill, 1966-67; pub. health nurse DeKalb County Health Dept., Atlanta and Decatur, Ga., 1967-68; pediatrics staff nurse Sacred Heart Hosp., Pensacola, Fla., 1975-76; nurse Corpus Christi (Tex.) State U., 1980-81; treatment coord. Southside Community Hosp., Corpus Christi, 1981-86; teaching asst. U. Tex., Austin, 1987, rsch. asst., 1987-90, assoc. instr., 1988-89; rsch. analyst Tex. Commn. on Alcohol-Drug Abuse, Austin, 1990—. Contbr. articles to profl. jours. Mem. APA, NOW, AAUW, Exec. Women in Govt., Soc. for Rsch. in Child Devel., Nat. Assn. for Perinatal Addiction Rsch. and Edn. (mem. adv. bd.), Soc. for Rsch. in Addiction Medicine, Phi Kappa Phi, Sigma Theta Tau. Home: 16201 Westview Tr Austin TX 78737 Office: Tex Com Alcohol Drug Abuse 710 Brazos Austin TX 78701

HAYWARD, TERESA CALCAGNO, foreign language educator; b. N.Y.C., Jan. 28, 1907; d. Vito and Rosalie (Amato) Calcagno; m. Peter Hayward, Feb. 6, 1932; children: Nancy, Peter. BA, Hunter Coll., 1929; MA, Columbia U., 1931. Tchr. romance langs. Jr. High Sch. 164, N.Y.C., 1936-57, Jr. High Sch. 141, Riverdale, N.Y., 1957-71; tchr. English to Japanese women Nichibei Fujinkai, Riverdale, 1972—, chmn. Riverdale chpt., 1976-92, Manhattan, 1992—. Bd. dirs. Riverdale chpt. UN Assn., 1973—; mem. Hunger and Social Outreach com. Christ Ch., Riverdale. Democrat. Episcopalian. Avocations: concerts, piano, art lectures, travel.

HAYWARD-JONES, SANDRA, elementary education educator, musician; b. New Orleans, Oct. 9, 1956; d. Paul Rudolph, Sr. and Audrey Mae (Norman) Hayward; m. Charles Edward Jones, Aug. 4, 1979 (dec. June 1993); children: Michael, Maria. BA in Elem. Edn., Xavier U., 1978. Cert. elem. and middle sch. tchr., Va. Tchr. Orleans Parish Schs., New Orleans, 1978-80, Richmond (Va.) Pub. Schs., 1989—. Youth achiever, mentor North Richmond YMCA, Richmond, 1990. Mem. Jack & Jill Am. (Richmond chpt.), Alpha Kappa Alpha (chaplain 1989). Home: 1808 Leslie Ln Richmond VA 23228

HAYWOOD, ANNE MOWBRAY, pediatrics, virology, and biochemistry educator; b. Balt., Feb. 5, 1935; d. Richard Mansfield and Margaret (Mowbray) H. BA in Chemistry, Bryn Mawr Coll., 1955; MD, Harvard U., 1959. Cert. Am. Bd. Pediatrics. Intern pediatrics U. Calif. Med. Ctr., San Francisco, 1959-60; postdoctoral fellow biochemistry dept. Columbia U., N.Y.C., 1961-62; postdoctoral fellow div. biology Calif. Inst. Tech., Pasadena, 1960-61, 62-64; asst. prof. microbiology, microbiology dept. Northwestern U. Med. Sch., Chgo., 1964-66, Yale U. Med. Sch., New Haven, 1966-73; resident pediatrics U. Wash., Seattle, 1974-75, pediatric infectious disease fellow, 1975-76; pediatric infectious disease fellow Vanderbilt U., Nashville, 1976-77; assoc. prof. pediatrics and microbiology U. Rochester, N.Y., 1977—; vis. asst. prof. Rockefeller U., N.Y.C., 1971-72; vis. scientist biophysics unit Agrl. Rsch. Coun., Cambridge, Eng., 1972-74, Inst. for Immunology and Virology, U. Zürich (Switzerland), 1987; vis. assoc. prof. dept. zoology U. Calif., Davis, 1986. Co-author: Practice of Pediatrics, 1977, Infections in Children, 1982, Liposome Letters, 1983, Practice of Pediatrics, 1987, Molecular Mechanisms of Membrane Fusion, 1988, Membrane Fusion, 1991, Encyclopedia of Human Biology, 1991, Cell and Model Membrane Interactions, 1991. Fogarty Internat. Ctr. Sr. fellow NIH, 1987, European Molecular Biology Orgn. fellow, 1973-74, NIH Spl. fellow, 1971-73, Am. Cancer Soc. Postdoctoral fellow, 1960-62; Harvard Med. Sch. scholar, 1955-59, Harriet Judd Sartain scholar, 1955-59, N.Y. Alumnae scholar Bryn Mawr Coll., 1951-55. Mem. Biophys. Soc., Am. Soc. for Biochem. and Molecular Biology, Infectious Diseases Soc. Am. Democrat. Office: U Rochester Med Ctr PO Box 777 Rochester NY 14642

HAYWOOD, B(ETTY) J(EAN), anesthesiologist; b. Boston, June 1, 1942; d. Oliver Garfield and Helen Elizabeth (Salisbury) H.; m. Lynn Brandt Moon, Aug. 29, 1969 (div. Aug. 1986); children: Kaylin, Kris Lee, Kelly, Kasy R. BSc, Tufts U., 1964; MD, U. Colo., 1968; MBA, Oklahoma City U., 1994. Intern Wilford Hall AFB, San Antonio, Tex., 1968-69; resident in pediatrics U. Ariz., Tucson, 1971-72, resident in anesthesiology, 1972-74; dir. anesthesia dept. Pima County Hosp., Tucson, 1975-76; staff anesthesiologist South Community Hosp., Oklahoma City, 1977—; staff anesthesiologist Moore (Okla.) Mcpl. Hosp., 1981-94, chief of anesthesia, 1990-94; staff anesthesiologist St. Anthony Hosp., Oklahoma City, 1982—. Bd. dirs. N.Am. South Devin Asns., Lynnville, Iowa, 1978-86; mem. med. com. Planned Parenthood Okla., 1992—. Maj. USAFR, 1968—. Mem. AMA, World South Devon Assn. (U.S. rep. 1985, 88—), Tufts U. Alumni Assn. (rep.), Chi Omega (treas. 1963-64). Republican. Presbyterian. Home: 6433 Brandywine Ln Oklahoma City OK 73116-3519

HAZAN, LYNN, executive recruiter; b. Montreal, Apr. 16, 1955; came to U.S., 1978; d. Elie Gabriel and Eddie (Pardo) H. BA with honors, McGill U., Montreal, 1977; MA, Brandeis U., 1980. Program coordinator Golden Age Assn., Montreal, 1977-78; dir. Hillel/Cays, Chgo., 1980-84; assoc. Plaza, Inc., Chgo., 1985-92; assoc. Beverly von Winckler & Assocs., Chgo., 1992—, now v.p. Author: A Taste of Honey, A Taste for Love, in Chosen Tales by Jewish Storytellers. Profl. storyteller Greater Chgo. Jewish Folk Arts Festival, 1990, 92, 94, Spertus Mus., Chgo., 1991; A World of Difference facilitator Anti Defamation League, 1990-93; tchr., artist-in-residence North Shore Congregation Israel, Glencoe, Ill., 1993—; tchr. Lakeside Congregation, Highland Park, Ill., 1990-93; presenter Project Kesher First Internat. Conf. Jewish Women, Kiev, Ukraine, 1994; storyteller, presenter Rancho La Puerta Tecate, Mexico, Heartland Spa, Gilman, Ill., Oman in Beyachad, 1993, 95. Mem. Women's Direct Response Group (programming com. 1986-89, chair 1988-89, bd. dirs. 1988-90, sec. 1989-90, Wesley award), Chgo. Direct Mktg. Assn., Ad-Net Chgo. (founder, bd. dirs., co-chmn. programming com. 1986, chair 1988-89, membership chair 1988-90 v.p. 1989-90), Prodn. Orgn. for Cultural Events and Theatre (exec. com. 1985—), Brandeis U. Roundtables (bd. dirs. 1988-90), Brandeis U. Alumni Assn., Jewish Storytellers Network, Nat. Assn. Preservation and Perpetuation of Storytelling, Coalition for Advancement in Jewish Edn. (presenter 1991—), Etz Hayim. Jewish. Office: Beverly von Winckler Assocs 123 W Madison Ste 1105 Chicago IL 60660

HAZAN, MARCELLA MADDALENA, author, educator, consultant; b. Cesenatico, Italy, Apr. 15, 1924; d. Giuseppe and Maria (Leonelli) Polini; m. Victor Hazan, Feb. 24, 1955; 1 child, Giuliano. Dr. in Natural Scis., U. Ferrara, 1952, Dr. in Biology, 1954. Researcher Guggenheim Inst., 1955-58; prof. math. and biology Italian State schs., 1963-66; founder Sch. of Italian Cooking, N.Y.C., 1969-94, Marcella Hazan Sch. of Classic Italian Cooking, Bologna, Italy, 1976-94, Master Classes in Classic Italian Cooking, Venice, Italy, 1986—; pres. Hazan Classic Enterprises, Inc., 1978—. Author: The Classic Italian Cookbook, 1973, More Classic Italian Cooking, 1978, Marcella's Italian Kitchen, 1986, Essentials of Classic Italian Cooking, 1992. Roman Catholic. Address: PO Box 285 Circleville NY 10919-0285

HAZEEM, KATHRYN A., legislative counsel; b. Pitts., Sept. 10, 1959. BA, Oral Roberts U., 1982; JD, Cath. U. Am., 1985. Dir. legal affairs Coalition Religious Freedom, 1985-87; assoc. Coale, Kananack & Murgatroyd, 1987-89; minority counsel Subcom. Civil and Constl. Rights Com. Judiciary, 1989—. Office: Subcom Civil & Constl Rights Rayburn House Office Bldg Rm B-351C Washington DC 20515*

HAZEL, JOANIE BEVERLY, elementary educator; b. Medford, Oreg., Jan. 20, 1946; d. Ralph Ray Lenderman and Vivian Thelma (Holtane) Spencer; m. Larry Aydon Hazel, Dec. 28, 1969. BS in Edn., So. Oreg. Coll., Ashland, 1969; MS in Edn., Portland State U., 1972; postgrad., U. Va., 1985. Elem. tchr. Beaverton (Oreg.) Schs., 1972-76, Internat. Sch. Svcs., Isfahan, Iran, 1976-78; ESL instr. Lang. Svcs., Tucker, Ga., 1983-84; tchr. Fairfax (Va.) Schs., 1985-86; elem. tchr. Beaverton (Oreg.) Schs., 1990—. Mem. AAAS, U.S. Hist. Soc., Platform Soc., Smithsonian Instn., Am. Mus. Natural History, Nat. Mus. Women in Arts, U.S. Hist. Soc., The United Nations, The Colonial Williamsburg Found., Wilson Ctr., N.Y. Acad. Scis. Home: 9247 SW Martha St Portland OR 97224-5577

HAZELTINE, JOYCE, state official; b. Pierre, S.D.; m. Dave Hazeltine; children: Derek, Tara, Kirk. Student, Huron (S.D.) Coll., No. State Coll.; Aberdeen, S.D., Black Hills State Coll., Spearfish, S.D. Former asst. chief clk. S.D. Ho. of Reps.; former sec. S.D. State Senate; sec. of state State of S.D., Pierre, 1987—. Adminstrv. asst. Pres. Ford Campaign, S.D.; Rep. county chmn. Hughes County S.D. Mem. Nat. Assn. Secs. of State (mem. exec. bd., pres. elect). Office: Sec of State's Office 500 E Capitol Ave Pierre SD 57501-5070

HAZELTON, PENNY ANN, law librarian, educator; b. Yakima, Wash., Sept. 24, 1947; d. Fred Robert and Margaret (McLeod) Pease; m. Norris J. Hazelton, Sept. 12, 1971; 1 dau., Victoria MacLeod. BA cum laude, Linfield Coll., 1969; JD, Lewis and Clark Law Sch., 1975; M in Law Librarianship, U. Wash., 1976. Admissions counselor Linfield Coll., 1969-71; serials librarian Lewis and Clark Law Sch. Law Library, Lewis and Clark Coll., 1972-75; admitted to Wash. bar, 1976; assoc. law librarian, assoc. prof. U. Maine, 1976-78, law librarian, assoc. prof., 1978-81; asst. librarian for research services U.S. Supreme Ct., Washington, 1981-85, law librarian U. Wash., Seattle, 1985—, prof. law, 1985—; tchr. legal research, law librarianship, Indian law; cons. Maine Adv. Com. on County Law Libraries, Nat. U. Sch. Law, San Diego, 1985-88, Lawyers Cooperative Pub., 1993-94. Contbr. articles to Environ. Law, Legal Reference Svcs. Quar. Mem. Law Librs. New Eng. (sec. 1977-79, pres. 1979-81), Am. Assn. Law Libraries (cert.; program chmn. ann. meeting 1984, exec. bd. 1984-87, v.p., pres.-elect 1989-90, pres. 1990-91), Law Librs' Soc. Washington (exec. bd. 1983-84, v.p., pres.-elect 1984-85), Law Librs. Puget Sound, Wash. State Bar Assn. (chair editl. adv. bd. 1990-91), Wash. Adv. Coun. on Librs., Am. Bar Assn. Westpac. Office: U Wash Marian Gould Gallagher Law Libr 1100 NE Campus Pky # JB-20 Seattle WA 98105-6617

HAZELTON, VINA JANE, retired claims representative, artist; b. Toppenish, Wash., Mar. 18, 1931; d. Dow Lefield and Ruth Gladys (Jenks) Ashford; m. Melbourne Eugene Jenks, Dec. 25, 1952 (dec. Nov. 1987); 1 child, William Randall; m. Byron W. Hazelton, May 1991. Student, Chemeketa C.C., 1978—. With ID bur. Oreg. State Police Dept., Salem, 1949-55, supr. clerical dept., 1953-55, clk. typist patrol office, 1956-59; sec. pers. dept. Boeing Airplane Co., Seattle, 1952-53; lithographer Moore Bus. Forms, Salem, 1959-65; clk. Marion County Dist. Ct., Salem, 1965; with Social Security Adminstrn., 1965-91; telephone svc. rep. Social Security Adminstrn., San Diego, 1976-77; claims rep. Social Security Adminstrn., Salem and Albany, Oreg., 1978-91; ret., self employed artist, author, 1991—. With USNR, 1950-54. Mem. Am. Fedn. Govt. Employees (union rep.). Democrat. Methodist. Home and Office: 3792 Augusta National Dr S Salem OR 97302-9716

HAZEN, ELIZABETH FRANCES, retired special education educator; b. Lamar, Colo., May 27, 1925; d. Otis Garfield and Cora B. (Baker) McDowell; children: H. Ray, Bobby D., Anita K. Iezza, Gloria G. Gill. AA, Lamar Jr. Coll., 1946; BS in Edn., Southwestern Okla. U., 1967, MS in Edn., 1969; postgrad., Ea. Ky. U., 1983. Cert. speech-hearing therapist, reading specialist, learning and behavior disorders, Ky. Elem. tchr. Granada (Colo.) Sch., 1946-51, South Ctrl. Elem. Sch., Lamar, Colo., 1951-52; lead tchr. Tom Thumb Pre-Sch., Ellsworth AFB, S.D., 1961-62; math. and sci. tchr. Elk City (Okla.) Elem. Sch., 1966-67; beginning speech tchr. Sayer Jr. Coll., Okla., 1967-68; speech and hearing therapist Maconaquah Sch. Corp., Bunker Hill, Ind., 1969-72, Burns Flat (Okla.) Schs.; reading specialist Myers Mid. Sch., Louisville, Ky., 1972-76; tchr. Core Westport Jr. H.S., Louisville, 1977-79, chmn. Core dept., 1978-79; learning disabled resource tchr. Jeffersontown H.S., Louisville, 1979-80, Waggoner Mid. Sch., Louisville, 1980-81, Westport Mid. Sch., Louisville, 1981-94; ret., 1994; chmn. exceptional children's edn. dept. Westport Mid. Sch., Louisville, 1983-91; speech and hearing therapist Burns Flat (Okla.) Bd. Edn., 1967-69. Bd. dirs. Westport Middle Schs. PTA/Student Assn., 1989-90. Named Outstanding Tchr. of Disadvantaged, State of Okla., 1969. Mem. NEA, Ky. Mid. Sch. Assn., Ky. Edn. Assn., Jefferson County Tchrs. Assn. Home: 3130 Hewitt Ave Louisville KY 40220-2226

HAZLETT, PEGGI, small business owner; b. Covina, Calif., Aug. 5, 1964; d. Paul Weidinger and Patricia Ann (McKenna) Emerson; m. Dennis Edward Hazlett, June 10, 1984; children: Falicia Noël, Tanis Christine. Student, Chaffey Coll., 1983-84. Profl. waiter Red Lion Inn, Ontario, Calif., 1982-87; owner Checkers Pizza, San Bernardino, Calif., 1987-95; tutor/adminstr. Dikalos Christian Acad., San Bernardino, 1993—. Pres. PTA North Verdemont Sch., San Bernardino, 1993-94; troop leader Girl Scouts Am., San Bernardino, 1994—; sponsor, instr. 4-H Calif. Focus, Sacramento, 1994; mem. Soroptimist, San Bernardino, 1994. Republican. Office: Dikalos Christian Acad 166 E 45th St San Bernardino CA 92404

HAZLEWOOD, JUDITH EVANS, librarian; b. McKenzie, Tenn., Mar. 30, 1930; d. Henry Bascom and Bertie (Harvey) Evans; m. Bob J. Hazlewood, June 11, 1955; children: Jeffrey E., Amy H. McAtee. BS in English, Memphis State U., 1952; MA in English, Vanderbilt U., 1954; MA in Libr. Sci., George Peabody Coll., 1959. Sec. bus. office Memphis State U., 1951-53; tchr. English and home econs. Messick High Sch., Memphis, 1954-57; statis. clk. office v.p. U. Fla., 1957-58; English tchr. Hume-Fogg High Sch., Nashville, 1958-59; cataloger Nashville Pub. Libr., 1962-63; acquisitions libr. Lambuth U., Jackson, Tenn., 1964-74, libr. dir., 1974—; part-time English instr. Bethel Coll., McKenzie, 1960-62. Mem. Tenn. Libr. Assn. (sec. for educators, nominating com., chair honors awards com., chair staff devel./recruitment com., membership com.), West Tenn. Libr. Assn., West Tenn. Acad. Libr. Consortium, Tenn. Archivists, Delta Kappa Gamma, Kappa Delta Pi. Methodist. Office: Lambuth U 705 Lambuth Blvd Jackson TN 38301-5280

HAZZARD, JEAN S., insurance processing specialist; b. Bklyn., Mar. 18, 1946; d. Benjamin and Mabel (Harris) Allston; m. Linwood Simon, Nov. 20, 1966 (div. Mar. 1972); m. Alfred Otis Hazzard Sr., June 27, 1987; 1 stepchild, Alfred Otis Hazzard, Jr. Assoc. office mgr. Prudential Ins., Flushing, N.Y.; office mgr. Prudential Ins., Woodhaven, N.Y.; assoc. office mgr. Prudential Ins., College Park, Ga.; office mgr. Prudential Ins., Decatur, Ga.; processing ctr. specialist Prudential Ins., Fayetteville, Ga.; ret. Prudential Ins. Mem. St. Paul's Ambassadors (treas. 1974-82). Episcopalian. Home: 2794 Narron Ct Atlanta GA 30331

HAZZARD, SHIRLEY, author; b. Sydney, Australia, Jan. 30, 1931; d. Reginald and Catherine (Stein) H.; m. Francis Steegmuller, Dec. 22, 1963 (dec. Oct. 1994). Ed., Queenwood Sch., Sydney, to 1946. With Combined Services Intelligence, Hong Kong, 1947-48, U.K. High Commr.'s Office, Wellington, N.Z., 1949-50, UN (Gen. Service Category), N.Y.C., 1952-62; Boyer lectr., Australia, 1984, 88. Author: Cliffs of Fall and Other Stories, 1963; novel The Evening of the Holiday, 1966; fiction People in Glass Houses, 1967; novel The Bay of Noon, 1970; History Defeat of an Ideal: A Study of the Self-Destruction of the United Nations, 1973; novel The Transit of Venus, 1980, History Countenance of Truth, 1990; contbr. short stories to New Yorker mag. Trustee N.Y. Soc. Library. Recipient 1st prize O. Henry Short Story awards, 1976, Lit. award Nat. Inst. Arts and Letters, 1966; Guggenheim fellow, 1974; recipient Nat. Book Critics Circle award for Fiction, 1981. Mem. Nat. Acad. Arts and Letters. Address: 200 E 66th St New York NY 10021-6728

HEACOCK, ROSALIE GRACE VILMURE, literary agent; b. Girard, Kans., Dec. 28, 1927; d. August Walter and Ethel Marie (Knight) Vilmure; m. James Bendernagel Heacock, Aug. 29, 1947; 1 child, Mark James. AA, Antelope Valley Coll., 1965; BA in Fine Art and English cum laude, Calif. State U., Northridge, 1971; MA in Humanities magna cum laude, Calif. State U., Dominguez Hills, Calif., 1991. Editor Green Hut Press, Valencia, Calif., 1970-75; pres. Shelley Muir Literary Agy., Venice, Calif., 1975-78; v.p., corp. sec. Heacock Literary Agy., Inc., Santa Monica, Calif., 1978—; exec. editor Kids & Co., Pubs., L.A., 1980-83. Illustrator: Thought Has Wings, 1969, Linnets and Pomegranites, 1970; author: In Nature's Presence, 1991. Guest spkr. Women Writers West, L.A., 1983, Am. Assn. Women Writers, L.A., 1993, Santa Barbara (Calif.) Writers' Conf., 1994; keynote spkr. Soc. Children's Writers, Orange, 1994. Mem. Assn. Authors' Reps., Assn. Talent Agts., Plein Air Artists of Santa Monica Mountains/Seashore (founding mem.). Republican. Methodist. Office: Heacock Literary Agy Inc Ste 14 1523 6th St Santa Monica CA 90401

HEAD, ELIZABETH, lawyer; b. Rochester, Minn., Dec. 17, 1930; d. Walter Elias and Ruth Winnogene (Evesmith) Bonner; m. C.J. Head, Dec. 30, 1950; 1 child, Alison Elizabeth. BA, U. Chgo., 1949, JD, 1952. Bar: Ill. 1952, Calif. 1955, N.Y. 1958, U.S. Supreme Ct. 1963, D.C. 1978. Atty. Nat. Labor Rels. Bd., Washington, 1953-54; assoc. Johnston & Johnston, San Francisco, 1954-56; atty. Aminoil Inc., San Francisco, 1956-57; teaching assoc. Law Sch. Columbia U., N.Y., 1957-58; assoc. Skadden Arps, N.Y., 1958-60; atty. The Coca-Cola Corp., N.Y., 1961-65; assoc. Kaye Scholer, N.Y., 1965-72, ptnr., 1972-82; ptnr. Hall & Estill, Tulsa, 1983-87; vis. fellow antitrust analysis Fed. Energy Regulatory Commn., Washington, 1987-89; gen. counsel Columbia U., N.Y.C., 1989—. Trustee Philbrook Mus., Tulsa, 1983-87, Mary Baldwin Coll., Staunton, Va., 1983-87. Mem. ABA (standing com. on dispute resolution 1983-90), Assn. of Bar of City of N.Y. (non-profit orgns. com. 1989-90, chair 1992-95), Century Assn., Order of Coif, Phi Beta Kappa. Office: Columbia U Office Gen Counsel 110 Low Memorial Libr New York NY 10027

HEAD, ELIZABETH SPOOR, retired medical technologist; b. Galveston, Tex., July 10, 1928; d. Robert Newcomb and Bernice Lillian (Lumley) Spoor; m. Foy Paul Head, Feb. 23, 1952; children: Robert Paul, Phillip Lee, Elisabeth Anne. Student, North Tex. State U., 1945-47, U. Tex. Med. Br., Galveston, 1947-48; BS in Health Care Scis. with high honors, U. Tex., Galveston, 1984. Cert. med. technologist. Med. technologist, lab dir. dept. dermatology U. Tex. Med. Br., Galveston, 1948-91; ret., 1991. Contbr. articles to profl. jours., chpts. to books. Mem. Altar Guild, Trinity Episcopal Ch., Galveston. Mem. Am. Soc. Med. Technologists, Galveston Dist. Soc. Med. Technologists (pres. 1976-77), Internat. Oleander Soc. (pres. 1978-82, corr. sec. 1985—, editor newsletter Nerium News 1986—), Galveston Hist. Found., Friends of Moody Gardens (pres., chmn. bd. 1990-92), Wednesday Lit. Club (pres. 1976-77, 92-93). Home: 4610 R 1/2 Galveston TX 77550 Office: U Tex Med Br Dept Dermatology Galveston TX 77555

HEADDEN, SUSAN M., editor. Formerly reporter Indianapolis Star, Indianapolis; now assoc. editor U.S. News & World Report, Washington. Recipient Pulitzer Prize for investigative reporting, 1991. Office: US News and World Report 2400 N St NW Washington DC 20037-1196*

HEADDING, LILLIAN SUSAN (SALLY HEADDING), writer, forensic clairvoyant; b. Milw., Jan. 1, 1944; d. David Morton and Mary Davis (Berry) Coleman; m. James K. Hill (div. 1976); children: Amy Denise; m. John Murray Headding (div. 1987). BA, U. Nev., 1975; MA, U. Pacific, 1976. With Gimbels, Milw., 1963-65; spl. assignment U.S. Womens Army Corp., 1963; retail mgr. Frandisco Corp., N.Y.C., 1965-66; dist. mgr. Anita Shops, Los Angeles, 1966-68; store mgr. Clothes Closet, Sunnyvale, Calif., 1969-70; owner Lillian Headding Interiors & Comml. Design, Pittsburg, Calif., 1976-88; mfrs. rep. and assoc. J.G. West, San Francisco, 1989-91; Karate instr. Sch. of the Tiger, Pleasant Hill, Calif., 1988-94, 1st degree black belt, 1973; clairvoyant, physic cons. on numerous crime and missing persons cases, U.S., Can., Eng. and France, 1972—. Author: (as Sally Davis): When Gods Fall; author short stories, poetry. Bd. dirs. and co-founder Community Action Against Rape, Las Vegas, 1972-75; self-def. expert Las Vegas Met. Police Dept., 1972-75, North Las Vegas (Nev.) Police Dept.; co. supr. Family & Children's Svcs., Contra Costa County, Calif., 1985-86. With U.S. Army, 1962-63. Mem. AAUW, People for Ethical Treatment of Animals, Walnut Creek Writers Group (pres.), Berkeley Women's Writer Group, Philippine Hawaiian Black Belters Assn. Democrat. Jewish. Office: # 33 5333 Park Highlands Blvd Concord CA 94521-3718

HEADINGTON, BONNIE JAY, psychologist; b. Alameda, Calif., Sept. 22, 1940; d. Jerome Willard and Beth Arlene (Dye) Headington; children: Christopher James, Tai Sirima. BA, San Francisco State, 1961; MEd, Ohio U., 1967, PhD, 1969. Lic. psychologist, Calif., Tex., Pa. Prof. psychology Humboldt State U., Arcata, Calif., 1972-86; psychologist, dir. North Coast Mental Health Clinic, McKinleyville, Calif., 1975-84; psychologist Counseling Services, Arcata, Calif., 1984-87, Nev. Dept. of Prisons Indian Springs, Las Vegas, 1987-89, Spring Ind. Sch. Dist., Houston, 1989—; cons. West Coast Cancer Found., Calif., 1978-80, U.S. Forest Service, 1982-83, Humboldt County Welfare Dept., 1982-84. Author: (book) Communication in Counseling Relationship, 1979, (monograph) Cancer consulting for health care professionals, 1980; contbr. articles to profl. jours. Mem. Am. Psychological Assn., Am. Assn. Counseling Devel. (editor newsletter 1979-83), Phi Kappa Phi. Democrat. Roman Catholic. Home: PO Box 90004 Houston TX 77290-0004

HEADLEY, ANNE RENOUF, technology commercialization financier; b. N.Y.C., Apr. 3, 1937. Diploma, Emma Willard Sch., 1954; student, Inst. World Affairs, 1957; AB magna cum laude, honors in Anthropology, Columbia U., 1959; MA, Yale U., 1962, PhD, 1966; JD with honors, Am. U., 1978; postgrad., Duke U. Sch. Law. Asst. prof. U. N.C., Chapel Hill, 1966-71; sr. profl. cons. U.S. Govt., Washington, 1972-75; pvt. practice fin. cons. Washington, 1976—; vis. assoc. prof. George Washington U. Sch. Bus. Adminstrn., Washington, 1983-84; gen. ptnr., v.p. Tech. Mgmt. Corp., Montgomeryville, Pa., 1986-88; chmn. Pivot, Inc., 1988—; founding prin. SaraTech Fin. Inc., 1990-92; sr. v.p., head internat. bus. Hectron Inc., Washington, 1992-93; corp. dir.; dir. fin. devel. Ctr. for Space and Advanced Tech., 1990; cons. The Brookings Instn., Washington, 1966, U.S. Dept. State, Washington, 1967, World Bank, 1992—; mem. Pres.'s Commn. Grad. Edn., 1967-68, Nat. Chamber Found. Task Force on Space Commercialization, Washington, 1983-86; vis. scholar Carnegie Endowment for Internat. Peace, N.Y.C., 1968-69; fellow U.S. Dept. State, EUR/RPE, 1967; bd. dirs. Advanced Tech. Orgn. of Md., 1985-88; northeastern dir. Va. Advanced Tech. Assn., 1984-88; fin. and tech. speaker. Contbr. articles on tech. commercialization and fin. to profl. jours. co-chair, charter mem. U.S./China Capital Cities Coun., Washington, 1985—; advisor Greater Washington D.C. Bd. Trade, 1985-86, Internat. Red Cross, 1987-90; mem. Mayor's Adv. Coun. on Trade and Investment, 1987-91; mem. adv. coun. Ctr. for Internat. Bus. Edn. U. Alaska, Fairbanks, 1990-91, co-chmn. World Trade Day, 1989; bd. dirs. Nat. Symphony Orch., 1990—, Greater Washington Met. Boys and Girls Clubs, 1992—. Woodrow Wilson fellow, 1958, Bushnell fellow, Yale U., 1964, Hon. Officer-Faculty fellow U.S. Dept. State, 1967; recipient citation Washington D.C. Mayor's Office, 1986. Fellow Washington Acad. Scis.; mem. Am. Soc. Internat. Law, Internat. Forum U.S. C. of C., Internat. Energy Seminar-Johns Hopkins Sch. for Advanced Internat. Study, Corcoran Gallery of Art (nat. coun.), Washington Internat. Trade Assn., Assn. for Corp. Growth, Phi Beta Kappa.

HEADLEY, KATHRYN WILMA, secondary education educator; b. Grand Rapids, Mich., Mar. 10, 1940; d. William L. and Kathryn (Mekkes) H. BA, Hope Coll., 1967; MEd, Grand Valley Univ., 1981. Cert. tchr., Mich. Missionary, Reformed Ch. in Am., N.Y.C., summers, 1959-64; various ch. positions Ottawa Reformed Ch., West Olive, Mich., 1956—, Bible day camp dir., 1979-92; tchr. English Jenison Pub. Schs. (Mich.), 1967—, head coach girls basketball, volleyball, 1967-78, head coach girls track, softball, 1967-73, head coach girls bowling, 1973-78, class advisor, 1983-90, numerous other sch. activities. coach girls soccer, basketball, Borculo Christian Sch., Mich., 1981-88. Bd. dirs. Ottawa County Tchrs. Credit Union, Grand Haven, Mich., 1978-90, 94—, v.p., 1984-88. Mem. Mich. Edn. Assn. (rep.), NEA, Jenison Edn. Assn. (rep.), Mich. High Sch. Athletic Assn. (ofcl.), Hope Coll. Alumni Assn., Mich. Christian Endeavor Bd., Delta Kappa Gamma. Mem. Reformed Ch. in Am. Home: 9111 96th Ave RR 1 Zeeland MI 49464 Office: Jenison Pub Schs 2140 Bauer Rd Jenison MI 49428-9539

HEADLEY, LUNETTA FORSYTH, retired librarian; b. Conshohocken, Pa., Apr. 15, 1925; d. William Robinson and Olive Augusta (Zug) Forsyth; m. William Kenneth Headley, June 26, 1948; 1 child, Lisa Jane Headley Guglielmino. BA, Wilson Coll., 1947; MS of Libr. Scis., Villanova U., 1975. Cert. sch. librarian K-12, Pa., cert. jr. and sr. high sch. English and history, Pa. Tchr. Souderton (Pa.) Jr.-Sr. High Sch., 1947-48; circulation libr. Haverford (Pa.) Coll., 1948-54; dir. curriculum lab. Eastern Coll., St. Davids, Pa., 1970-77; coord. edn. Resource Ctr. Rosemont (Pa.) Coll., 1977-82; asst. med. libr. Bryn Mawr (Pa.) Hosp., 1983-93. Mem. AAUW (v.p. 1981-83, ednl. found. gift honoree Valley Forge br. 1975), Wilson Coll. Alumnae Assn. (bd. dirs. 1971-73), Wilson Coll. Club of Phila. (pres. 1968-70).

HEADLY, GLENNE AIMÉE, actress; b. New London, Conn., Mar. 13, 1958. Mem. of ensemble Steppenwolf Theatre. Appeared on stage Curse of Starving Class, Balm in Gilead, Arms in the Men; films: Making Mr. Right, 1987, Nadine, 1987, Dirty Rotten Scoundrels, 1988, Paperhouse, 1989, Dick Tracy, 1990, Mortal Thoughts, 1991 ; TV mini-series: Lonesome Dove, 1989 (Emmy nomination for best supporting actress); TV films include Seize the Day, 1986, And The Band Played On, 1994. Recipient three Joseph Jefferson awards for best supporting actress, Chgo.; named Best Newcomer Theatre World Award Com., N.Y. Office: Internat Creative Mgmt 8942 Wilshire Blvd Beverly Hills CA 90211

HEAGY, LORRAINE MARY, office manager; b. Lancaster, Pa., Aug. 19, 1935; d. Ralph Long and Ella Ruth Shreiner; m. John Franklin Heagy, Oct. 15, 1960 (dec. 1979); children: John Franklin III, Loralie Leslie, Michael David. Grad. high sch., Lititz, Pa. Clk. typist Woodstream Corp., Lititz, 1953-54, Lititz Mut. Ins. Co., 1955-56; sec. Warner Lambert Co., Lititz, 1956-61; adminstrv. asst. Elam G. Stoltzfus, Jr., Lancaster, Pa., 1973-84; mgr. office support dept. Lancaster Labs., 1984—. Democrat. Office: Lancaster Labs 2425 New Holland Pike Lancaster PA 17601-5946

HEALD, KALA DONNA LUCKADO, real estate broker and appraiser, business owner; b. Roanoke, Va., June 24, 1943; d. Cecil Liggon and Dorothy Hazel (Hambrick) Luckado; m. Ralph David Jones, Apr. 13, 1963 (div. Dec. 1980); children: Ralph David Jr., Jacqualine Joy, Colleen Michelle, Ramonia Darlene, Jason Jay; m. Ovide Alan Heald, June 27, 1981. Grad. high sch., Roanoke. Cert. real estate appraiser, Fla. Grocery clk. Kroger Co., Roanoke, 1971-81; owner The Rose Petal Florist, Roanoke, 1976-86, The Squeeze Inn Resturant, Jacksonville, Fla., 1982-85, Cornerstone Realty Svcs., Neptune Beach, Fla., 1983-86, Heald & Assocs. R.E. Appraisal Svcs., Neptune Beach, 1986—, E-Z Parking Lot, Atlantic Beach, Fla., 1986-90; real estate broker/sales Century 21 & Henry Crews, Jacksonville, 1983-86. Inventor specialty doll. Mem. Nat. Assn. of Realtors, Nat. Assn. of Real Estate Appraisers (sec. southeast chpt.), Jacksonville Beach Bd. of Realtors, Fla. Assn. of State Cert. Real Estate Appraisers, Nat. Assn. of Master Appraisers, Soc. Real Estate Appraisers (candidate mem.), Women of Moose, Am. Legion Aux. Republican. Southern Baptist. Home: 1820 Sherwood Ln Jacksonville FL 32266-3632 Office: Cornerstone Realty Svcs 929 N 3d St Jacksonville Beach FL 32250

HEALEY, ANN RUSTON, diaconate program director; b. Havana, Cuba, Dec. 29, 1939; d. Homer Max and Elizabeth Dillon (Rea) H. BA in Spanish, French, Ohio Wesleyan U., 1961; MA in Religious Studies, Mundelein Coll., 1975; cert. pastoral leadership, St. Louis U., 1982; MDiv, Assn. for Clin. Pastoral Edn., Atlanta, 1983; PhD, Columbia Pacific U., 1991. Cert. social worker, Ill. Mental health social worker Dept. Mental Health, Chgo., 1964-68; hosp. social worker St. Joseph Hosp., Chgo., 1968-73; social work progam dir. Sr. Ctrs. Met. Chgo., 1973-75; retreat and spiritual dir. Cenacle Retreat House, Chgo., 1975-80; hosp. chaplain Barnes Hosp., St. Louis, 1981-82, Mercy Med. Ctr., Bakersfield, Calif., 1982-83; chaplain tng. supr. Immanuel Med. Ctr., Omaha, 1983-84; program dir. permanent deacon formation program Catholic Diocese Ft. Worth, 1984—; resident in clin. pastoral edn. Assn. for Clin. Pastoral Edn., Atlanta, 1981-82, 83-84; exec. bd. dirs. S.W. Career Devel. Ctr., Arlington, Tex., v.p. 1990-93, pres. 1993-95, chair search com., 1993-95; mem. adj. faculty Inst. for Pastoral Life, Kansas City, Kans., 1988-92, Inst. for Religious and Pastoral Studies, U. Dallas, 1989-90; chmn. 2d Ecumenical Consultation on Deacons and Diaconate, Nat. Coun. Chs., Ft. Worth, 1988; mem. exec. bd. Tarrant Area Community Chs., 1991-93; retreat and spiritual dir., 1982—; dir. Twelve Step Journey to Wholeness Workshop, 1986-92; mem. Bishop's Task Force on Women's Concerns, 1987-93; mem. Tex. Cath. Conf. Task Force for Priest Shortage, 1984-85. Mem. Nat. Assn. Permanent Diaconate Dirs. (sec. 1987-89, region X rep. 1990-92, exec. bd. 1992-95, pres.-elect 1992-93, pres. 1993-94, past pres. 1994-95), Nat. Assn. Cath. Chaplains (cert.), Assn. for Clin. Pastoral Edn. (clin.), Spiritual Dirs. Internat., Coll. Chaplains (assoc.), Am. Assn. Pastoral Counselors (profl. affiliate 1990—), Charles A. Lindbergh N-X-211 Collectors' Soc. (curator 1988-90, archivist 1990—, charter mem.). Democrat. Home: 210 Mountainview Dr Hurst TX 76054-3068 Office: The Catholic Center 800 W Loop 820 S Fort Worth TX 76108-2936

HEALEY, KERRY MURPHY, policy consultant; b. Omaha, Apr. 30, 1960; d. Edward Morris and Shirley (Cumming) M.; m. Sean Michael Healey, Dec. 28, 1985; children: Alexander Edward, Averill Adair. AB in Govt., Harvard Coll., 1982; PhD in Law and Polit. Sci., Trinity Coll., Dublin, Ireland, 1991. Proctor freshman dean's office, vis. reseacher Law Sch. Harvard U., Cambridge, Mass., 1985-86; legal policy analyst ABT Assocs., Inc., Cambridge, 1986-87; pub. policy cons. Bklyn., 1990—. Author: State and Local Experience with Drug Paraphernalia Laws, 1987; co-author: Compendium of Federal Justice Statistics, 1989, Handbook of Drug Control in the United States, 1990, Prosecutorial Response to Heavy Drug Case Loads, 1993. Fundraiser Civitas, N.Y.C., 1987—; bd. dirs. YWCA, N.Y.C., 1992—; mem. nat. bd. task force on internat. leadership exch. and devel. YWCA of the U.S.A., 1987—, mem. World Svc. Coun., 1992—. Grad. fellow Rotary Internat., 1983-84; rsch. grantee Mark DeWolfe Howe Fund of Harvard Law Sch., 1986. Mem. Harvard Club N.Y.C. (mem. schs. com. 1987—), City Women's Club, N.Y. Jr. League (rep. N.Y.C. ednl. priorities panel 1992—).

HEALEY, LYNNE KOVER, editor, broadcaster, writer, educator; b. L.I., N.Y.; d. Richard Frederick Bascom and Margaret Harriet (Fuchs); div.; children: Christine Josepha, Lauren Teresa. AA in Journalism and Psychology, Middlesex County Coll., 1979; BA in Comm., Rutgers U., 1983; MA in English, Drew U., 1987. Editor A.M. Best Co., Oldwick, N.J., 1985-91; mktg. communications cons. MetLife Ins. Co., 1992—; free-lance cons. Sea-Land Corp., Menlo Park, N.J., 1984-85; free-lance writer, 1977—; adj. prof. English Middlesex County Coll., Edison, N.J. Mem. Meeting Planners Internat. (bd. dirs. N.J. chpt., co-chairperson com. for Give Kids the World project), Rutgers U. Alumni Assn. (exec. com.), Alpha Sigma Lambda (grad. sch. scholar 1986, bd. dirs. Rutgers chpt.). Office: MetLife Bridgewater NJ 08807

HEALY, ALICE FENVESSY, psychology educator, researcher; b. Chgo., June 26, 1946; d. Stanley John and Doris (Goodman) Fenvessy; m. James Bruce Healy, May 9, 1970; 1 dau., Charlotte Alexandra. AB summa cum laude, Vassar Coll., 1968; PhD, Rockefeller U., 1973. Asst. prof. psychology Yale U., New Haven, 1973-78, assoc. prof. psychology, 1978-81; assoc. prof. psychology U. Colo., Boulder, 1981-84, prof. psychology, 1984—; rsch. assoc. Haskins Labs., New Haven, 1976-80; mem. com. NIMH, Washington, 1979-81; co-investigator rsch. contract USAF, U. Colo., 1985-86; prin. investigator rsch. contract U.S. Army Rsch. Inst., U. Colo., 1986—, Naval Tng. Systems Ctr., 1993-94. Co-author: Cognitive Processes, 2d edit., 1986; editor Memory and Cognition, 1986-89, (with S.M. Kosslyn and R.M. Shiffrin) From Learning Theory to Connectionist Theory: Essays in Honor of William K. Estes, Vol. II, 1992, (with L.E. Bourne, Jr.) Learning and Memory of Knowledge and Skills: Durability and Specificity, 1995; assoc. editor Jour. Exptl. Psychology, 1982-84; contbr. over 90 articles to profl. jours., chpts. to books. Recipient Sabbatical award James McKeen Cattell Fund, 1987-88; NSF Rsch. grantee, 1977-86, Spencer Found. Rsch. grantee, 1978-80. Fellow APA (exec. com. divsn. 3 1989-92, chair membership com. 1992-93), AAAS (nominating com. 1988-91, chair 1991, chair-elect psychology sect. 1994, chair psychology sect. 1995—); mem. Psychonomic Soc. (governing bd. 1987-92, publs. com. 1989-93), Soc. Math. Psychology, Rocky Mountain Psychology Assn. (pres.-elect 1993-94, pres. 1994—), Cognitive Sci. Soc., Univ. Club, Phi Beta Kappa, Sigma Xi. Home: 840 Cypress Dr Boulder CO 80303-2820 Office: U Colo Dept Psychology Campus Box 345 Boulder CO 80309-0345

HEALY, BARBARA MARY, public health nurse; b. Sydney, Australia; came to U.S., 1965; d. Leo Joseph and Doreen Elizabeth (Maunsel) H. BSN in Pub. Health Nursing, Calif. State U., Carson, 1988; grad., U.S. Army Command and Staff Gen. Coll., 1987; postgrad., Calif. State U., San Jose, 1988—; M in Mil. and Polit. Sci., Command & Staff Gen. Coll., Leavenworth, Kans., 1989. RN; cert. critical care infection control practitioner, advanced cardiac life support instr., advanced life support burn instr. Critical care and pediatric staff nurse Toronto (Can.) Gen. Hosp. and Hosp. Sick Children, 1961-65; asst. head nurse ICU Stanford (Calif.) U. Med. Ctr., 1965-68; nurse CCU U.S. Army, Tacoma, 1968-70; nurse ICU and M.U.S.T. unit Lai Khi U.S. Army, Vietnam, 1968-70; clin. instr. CCU Sydney Hosp., U. Sydney, 1971-74; nurse spl. procedure lab. Kaiser Hosp., Santa Clara, Calif., 1974-89; primary care case mgr. HomeMed of Am. Inc., 1989—; chief nursing edn. and devel. USAR Gen. Hosp., Sunny Vale, Calif., 1974—; instr. tng. course Assn. for Practitioners in Infection Control Inc., 1989. Basic life support instr. ARC, 1989; advanced burn life support provider/instr. Am. Burn Assn., 1988; advanced trauma life support tng. Am. Coll. Surgeons, 1988; advanced cardiac life support, mem. Am. Heart Assn., 1988. Lt. col. USAR, 1974—. Decorated Army Commendation medal with oak leaf cluster. Mem. Am. Nurses Assn., Diagnostic Med. Sonographers Assn., Gastroenterologist Assns., C.P.R., Infection Control Practitioner. Home: 85 Baringa Rd, 2063 Northbridge New South Wales, Australia

HEALY, CAROLYN B., counselor, alcohol/drug abuse services professional, consultant; b. Chgo., Mar. 15, 1948; m. David A. Healy, 1970; children: Benjamin, Katherine. BA in English, U. Ill., 1969, MEd in Counseling, 1970, postgrad., 1970-72. Cert. NCACII, sr. alcohol and drug counselor, employee assistance profl. Cons. social svcs. Americana Health Ctr., Joliet, Ill., 1973-80; mental health counselor Will County Mental Health Divsn., Joliet, 1973-76, with outpatient alcoholism treatment Alcohol Counseling Ctr., 1976-79; coord., trainer alcoholism prevention project various schs., orgns., 1980-81; pres., dir. Healy & Assocs., Joliet, 1981—; Mem., former chair Will-Grundy-Kanakakee Coalition for Treatment and Prevention of Alcohol Abuse, 1979—; vice chair adv. bd. Groundwork Shelter for Victims of Domestic Violence, 1983-89; adv. bd. addiction counselor tng. program Coll. St. Francis, Joliet, 1987—; adj. clin. prof. alcohol and drug abuse scis. Coll. Health Professions Govs. State U.; bd. dirs., organizer Will County Rape Crisis Ctr. Bd. dirs. Sheltering Arms Halfway House for Women, 1977-88; chair adv. bd. Rialto Theatre, 1987. Mem. Am. Assn. Counseling Devel., Ill. Alcoholism and Drug Dependence Assn., Employee Assistance Profls. Assn. (assoc.), Rotary (co-chair charity raffle). Office: Healy & Assocs 121 Springfield Ave Joliet IL 60435

HEALY, DEBORAH PERRY, counselor; b. Utica, N.Y., Feb. 23, 1955; d. Edward Joseph and Mary Ann (DeCotis) Perry; m. Timothy James Healy, Nov. 29, 1986; 1 child, James Austin. BS summa cum laude, Syracuse U., 1975; MS magna cum laude, SUNY, Albany, 1978; counseling cert., State U. of Tex., 1992; postgrad., Our Lady of the Lake U., 1995—. Cert. reading specialist, English tchr., elem. tchr.; lic. profl. counselor. English tchr. New Hartford (N.Y.) Ctrl. Schs., 1978-80, Sauquoit (N.Y.) Ctrl. Schs., 1980-86; reading specialist Northside Ind. Sch. Dist., San Antonio, 1986-93, guidance counselor, 1993—. Co-author: Death Out of the Closet, 1976. Vol. St. Matthew's Cath. Ch., San Antonio, 1990-93. Recipient Svc. award Nat. Jr. Honor Soc., 1991; named Educator of Yr. Sauquoit Valley Optimist Club, 1986. Mem. ACA, Tex. Counseling Assn., South Tex. Counseling Assn. (scholar 1994), Northside Counseling Assn. Roman Catholic. Home: 3602 Pinebluff Dr San Antonio TX 78230 Office: Jack C Jordan Middle Sch 1725 Richland Hills Dr San Antonio TX 78251

HEALY, JANE ELIZABETH, newspaper editor; b. Washington, May 9, 1949; d. Paul Francis and Connie (Maas) H.; children: Randall, Kevin. BS, U. Md., 1971. Copy clk. N.Y. Daily News, Washington, 1971-73; met. reporter Orlando (Fla.) Sentinel, 1973-81, editorial writer, 1981-83, chief editorial writer, 1983-85, assoc. editor, 1985-92; mng. editor, 1993—. Recipient Pulitzer Prize, Columbia U., 1988, Sigma Delta Chi Disting. Service award, 1988. Mem. Am. Soc. Newspaper Editors (bd. dirs.), Nat. Conf. Editorial Writers. Office: Orlando Sentinel 633 N Orange Ave Orlando FL 32801

HEALY, JANET, graphics expert, producer. BA in History, U. Calif., Santa Barbara. Set producer, assoc. producer Sam Peckinpah, Hal Ashby, Stanley Kramer, others; from asst. prodn. supr. to effects producer Indsl. Light & Magic, San Rafael, Calif., 1986-90, sr. effects producer, 1990—. Credits include asst prodn. supr. (films) Star Trek: The Next Generation, 1987, Empire of the Sun, 1987, Witches of Eastwick, 1987, Batteries Not Included, 1987, Innerspace, 1987, Who Framed Roger Rabbit, 1988; effects producer (films) Willow, 1988, Ghostbusters II, 1989; sr. effects producer (films) Joe Vs. the Volcano, 1990, Total Recall, 1990; cons. with Steven Spielberg Close Encounters of the Third Kind, "1941". Office: Indsl Light & Magic PO Box 2459 San Rafael CA 94912-2459*

HEALY, JUDITH ANN, school social worker; b. Nov. 4, 1942; d. Howard and Elenora (Hutchison) Crothers; children: Eric David, Mark Daniel. AAS, Moraine Valley Community Coll., Palos Hills, Ill., 1979; BS, Nat. Coll. Edn., 1980; postgrad., George Williams Coll., 1983-86; MSW, Loyola U., Chgo., 1987. Cert. sch. social worker, Ill.; lic. clin. social worker. Counselor Community Resources for Youth, Palos Park, Ill., 1977-79; case mgr., weekend coord. Proviso Assn. for Retarded Citizens, Hillside, Ill., 1979-87; sch. social worker Arbor Park Sch. Dist. 145, Oak Forest, Ill., 1987—; therapist Midwest Resources, 1994—; social worker cons. Village Inn, Intermediate Care Facility for Developmentally Disabled Adults, Dixon, Ill., 1987-89. Vol. Cmty. Response, Oak Park, Ill., 1991—; youth leader Morgan Park Bapt. Ch., Chgo. Mem. NASW, Ill. Assn. Sch. Social Workers, Assn. Individual Devel. Home: 8148 W 111th St # 2A Palos Hills IL 60465

HEALY, MARGARET MARY, retail marketing executive; b. Bklyn., Dec. 31, 1938; d. Nicholas Joseph and Margaret Marie (Ferry) H.; m. Robert L. Parker, 1979 (div. 1988); 1 child, Nicole Parker. BA, Manhattanville Coll., 1961; cert., NYU, 1967, Columbia U., 1971. Account exec. Geer, DuBois & Co., Inc., N.Y.C., 1965-71; dir. mktg. comm. Dry Dock Savs. Bank, N.Y.C., 1971-72; operating v.p. Bloomingdales, N.Y.C., 1972-79; owner, pres. Healy & Pratts, Inc., N.Y.C., 1979-88, PH Network, Dallas, 1992—; mgr. corporate pub. rels. J.C. Penney Co., Dallas, 1988-92; bd. dirs. North Side Savs. Bank, Floral Park, N.Y. Co-author: Salute to Italy Celebrity Cookbook, 1984, Salute to America Celebrity Cookbook, 1986. Bd. dirs. Dallas Children's Theatre, 1989—. Recipient Cmty. Svc. award VFW, 1978. Roman Catholic. Home: 5435 Mercedes Ave Dallas TX 75206 Office: P N Network 2811 McKinney Ste 222 Dallas TX 75204

HEALY, MARY (MRS. PETER LIND HAYES), singer, actress; b. New Orleans, Apr. 14, 1918; d. John Joseph and Viola (Armbruster) H.; m. Peter Lind Hayes, Dec. 19, 1940; children: Peter Michael, Cathy Lind. Student parochial schs., New Orleans; hon. degree, St. Bonaventure U. With 20th Century Fox, Hollywood, Cal. Author: Twenty-five Minutes from Broadway, 1961; pictures and others, 1937-40; Broadway prodns. Around the World, 1943-46; (with husband) TV series Inside U.S.A, 1949, Peter and Mary Show, Star of the Family, 1952, Peter Lind Hayes Radio show, CBS, 1954-57; Broadway prodn. Who Was That Lady, 1957-58, Peter Lind Hayes show, ABC-TV, 1958-59, Peter and Mary, ABC-Radio, 1959—, Peter and Mary in Las Vegas; TV-film; Star (with husband) WOR radio show, 6 yrs; TV film series Fin. Planning for Women; (with husband) Film The 5000 Fingers of Dr. T, 1953; Appeared in: (with husband) Film Peter Loves Mary, 1960, When Television Was Live, 1975; films: You Ruined My Life, 1986, Looking To Get Out with Jon Voight, 1985. Roman Catholic. Club: Pelham Country. Home: 3538 Pueblo Way Las Vegas NV 89109-3339

HEALY, PATRICIA, management consultant, educator; b. N.Y.C., Apr. 20, 1951; d. Raymond and Patricia (Manning) H.; m. Michael Hanahoe, Dec. 2, 1972; children: Colin, Terance, Evan. BA, NYU, 1972, postgrad., 1988—; MBA, Rutgers U., 1974. CPA, N.Y. Staff acct. Coopers & Lybrand, White Plains, N.Y., 1975-76; lectr. acctg. Mercy Coll., Dobbs Ferry, N.Y., 1976; lectr. Herbert H. Lehman Coll., Bronx, 1976; asst. chairperson, assoc. prof. Pace U., Pleasantville, N.Y., 1976; pres. H.H. Cons., Peekskill, N.Y., 1980—; assoc. prof., chair acctg. Pace U., Pleasantville, N.Y.; cons. ednl. tng. IBM, Armonk, N.Y. 1983—, Corning Glass Works, 1989—, Readers Digest, 1991. Author: Internal Reporting, 1986, Integrating Critical Thinking and Communication Skills, 1990, Satellite Education, 1990, Uses of Computers in Accounting Education, 1990, Responding to the Profession's Needs--An Accounting Prospective, 1991, Computer Applications for Today's Accounting Curriculum, 1993, Integrating Computer Technology into the Accounting Curriculum to Enhance Communication Skills, 1994; (videos) Job Order and Process Costing, 1991, An Empirical Investigation of the Current State of Management Accounting, 1991, Diversity in Accounting, 1995. Active Continental Village Property Owners Assn., Peekskill, N.Y., 1978—; mem. Van Cortlandville Sch. Bd., Peekskill, 1981—, legis. adv. com. State of N.Y., Albany, 1982—. Named Prof. of Yr., 1987, Tchr. of Yr., 1992; Deloitte Haskins and Sells fellow, N.Y.C., 1979, faculty fellow Coopers & Lybrand, N.Y.C., 1983. Mem. AICPA, Am. Soc. Women Accts., Am. Acctg. Assn., Nat. Assn. Accts., Delta Pi Epsilon. Democrat. Episcopalian. Home: 8 Apple Hill Dr Cortland Manor NY 10566 Office: Pace U Bedford Rd Pleasantville NY 10570

HEALY, PHYLLIS M. CORDASCO, school social worker; b. Newark, Oct. 2, 1939; d. Carl and Mae (Seritella) Cordasco; married, Dec. 22, 1966. BA, Caldwell Coll., 1978; MS, Columbia U. Sch. Social Work, 1981; MA, Fairleigh Dickinson U., 1989. Cert. social worker, N.Y.; sch. social work specialist; diplomate in clin. social work; qualified clin. social worker; lic. clin. social worker, N.J. Social worker United Cerebral Palsy of North N.J., East Orange, 1982-84, Cerebral Palsy Assn. Middlesex County, Edison, N.J., 1984-85; social worker, coord. presch. handicapped program Newark Bd. Edn., 1985-92, social svcs. coord., 1992—; cons. in field. Founding mem. sr. citizen ctr. Borough of Caldwell; chair rent review bd. Recipient Alumna of Yr. award Caldwell Coll., 1985-86, Marion award, 1991. Mem. AAUW (legis. chair 1982-84), Acad. Cert. Social Workers, Coun. for Exceptional Children (N.J. divsn. early childhood pres. 1992-94, regional coord. 1994—), Caldwell Coll. Alumni Assn. (scholar chair 1982-87), Columbia U. Alumni Assn. Home: Westover House 519 Bloomfield Ave Caldwell NJ 07006 Office: Newark Bd Edn 2 Cedar St Newark NJ 07102

HEALY, VIRGINIA PERKINS, management consultant; b. New Haven, June 17, 1941; d. Edward Francis and Olive Virginia (Zott) Perkins; m. Gerald J. Healy, Sept. 19, 1964; children: Jonathan Edward, Kimberly Ann. AS in Fgn. Trade, Fisher Jr. Coll., Boston, 1961. Office mgr., adminstrv. asst. Calif. Regional Teaching Community, Burbank, 1973-76; adminstrv. asst. Nat. Spiritual Assembly of the Bahais of the U.S., Wilmette, Ill., 1976-78; owner Talisman Mgmt. Svcs., Cafdiff by the Sea, Calif., 1978—. Mem. UN Assn. (San Diego chpt. treas. 1989-93, treas. Internat. Gift Shop 1992—), Bahais of Encinitas (sec. 1983—). Home: 2068 Bulrush Ln Cardiff by the Sea CA 92007 Office: Talisman Mgmt Svcs PO Box 44 Cardiff CA 92007

HEANUE, ANNE ALLEN, librarian; b. Ft. Oglethorpe, Ga., Feb. 7, 1940; d. James Edward and Mary (Dennean) Allen; m. Kevin E. Heanue, July 20, 1963; children: Mary, Brian, Patricia. BA cum laude, Dunbarton Coll., 1962; MA, Georgetown U., 1966; MS in Libr. Sci., Cath. U. Am., 1976. Libr. Deloitte Haskins and Sells, Washington, 1977-79; asst. to dir. Am. Libr. Assn., Washington, 1979-81, asst. dir., 1981-84, assoc. dir., 1984—. Bd. dirs. Alexandria (Va.) LWV, 1967-78; chmn. Alexandria Spl. Edn. adv. com., 1978-79; mem. Alexandria Gypsy Moth Control Commn., 1991—. Mem. ALA, Am. Soc. Access Profls., Am. Soc. Assn. Execs. D.C. Libr. Assn., Beta Phi Mu, Pi Gamma Mu. Roman Catholic. Home: 610 Pullman Pl Alexandria VA 22305-1226 Office: ALA 110 Maryland Ave NE Washington DC 20002-5626

HEAP, SYLVIA STUBER, civic worker; b. Clifton Springs, N.Y., Sept. 25, 1929; d. Stanley Irving and Helen (Hill) Stuber; BA cum laude, Bates Coll., 1950; postgrad. U. Conn. Sch. Social Work, 1952-54, Boston U. Sch. Social Work, 1953-54, SUNY, Brockport, 1979, SUNY-Potsdam, 1980, MS in Adult Edn., Syracuse U., 1989; m. Walker Ratcliffe Heap, June 9, 1951; children: Heidi Anne, Cynthia Joan, Walker Ratcliffe III. Dir. Y-Teens, YWCA, Holyoke, Mass., 1950-51; social group worker West Haven (Conn.) Community House, 1951-54; program dir. YWCA, Ann Arbor, 1954-55, part-time, 1955-59; mem. adv. bd. div. continuing edn. Jefferson Community Coll., 1965—, chmn. adv. bd., 1968—; pres. Jefferson County Med. Soc.

Aux., 1971-72; bd. dirs. St. Lawrence Valley Ednl. TV, 1973-83, sec., 1976-80, treas., 1980-82; v.p., 1982-83, dir. Chem. People Project, 1983; bd. dirs. Watertown Lyric Theatre, 1973-83; bd. dirs. N.Y. State Med. Soc. Aux., 1974-85, 2d v.p. bd., 1979-80; fitness instr. Jefferson Community Coll., Watertown, 1977-86; chmn. health projects N.Y. State Med. Soc. Aux., 1981-85. Named Citizen of Yr. Greater Watertown C. of C., 1975, Friend of Community Colls. N.Y. State Bd. Trustees, 1988. Mem. AAUW, Friends of Pub. TV, Coll. Women's Club Jefferson County, Phi Beta Kappa. Unitarian Universalist. (UN office envoy 1978—, St. Lawrence dist. envoy 1992—).

HEARN, JOYCE CAMP, retired educator, state legislator; b. Cedartown, Ga., d. J.C. and Carolyn (Carter) Camp; m. Thomas Harry Hearn (dec.); children: Theresa Hearn Potts Bailey, Kimberly Ann Johnson, Carolyn Lee Becker. Student, U. Ga.; BA, Ohio State U., 1957; postgrad, U. S.C. Former high sch. tchr.; dist. mgr. U.S. Census, 2d Congl. Dist., 1970; mem. S.C. Ho. of Reps., 1975-89, asst. minority leader, 1976-78, 86-89; chmn. commn. alcohol beverage control, 1989—. Mem. Richland County Planning Commn., 1974-76; bd. dirs. Meml. Youth Ctr. and Stage South; chmn. Nat. Adv. Com. on Occupational Safety and Health, 1982—; chmn. Sexual Assault Awareness Week; vice chmn. Dist. Republican Com., 1968; Rep. chmn. 2d Congl. Dist., 1969; Rep. chmn. Richland County, 1972; del., platform com. Rep. Nat. Conv., 1980, 84; moderator Kathwood Bapt. Ch., 1979-80, former asst. Sunday Sch. tchr.; bd. dirs. Small Bus. Devel. Ctr. S.C., Columbia Coll. Bd. Vis., Columbia Urban League, Fedn. of Blind; trustee Columbia Mus. Art; apptd. to Alcohol Beverage Control Bd., 1989, apptd. chmn. commn., 1990-92, commr., 1991—; bd. dirs. Lupus Found., 1990—; chair nat. adv. com. Occupational Safety and Health, 1980-88. Recipient Outstanding Citizen award Columbia Rape Coalition, 1977, Disting. Service award Claims Mgmt. Assn. S.C., 1977, Nat. Fedn. Blind S.C., 1978, Columbia Urban League, 1983, MADD, 1985, Outstanding Legislator of Yr. award Alcohol and Drug Abuse Assn., 1980, Retarded Citizens Assn., 1982, S.C. Rehab. Assn., 1984, S.C. Assn. of Deaf, 1987, Legislator of Yr., Fedn. of Blind, 1988, Disting. Legislator, DAV, 1989; Honoree, Easter Seals, 1989; numerous other awards. Mem. Nat. Order of Women Legislators (v.p., pres.), Order of the Palmetto, S.C. Women's Club, Columbia Women's Club (bd. dirs.), Larkspar Garden Club.

HEARN, KATHLEEN K. (KATHLEEN KLOTZ CROSHAL), lawyer; b. Sandusky, Ohio, Mar. 21, 1947; d. Earl A. and Mary W. (Donahue) Klotz; m. Dane P. Winters, Nov. 14, 1964 (div. Feb. 1972); children: Lisa C. Winters, Timothy D. Winters; m. Bruce L. Hearn, Apr. 18, 1981 (div. Dec. 1986); 1 child: Cassandra; m. James M. Croshal, May 3, 1987. BA Communications and Theatre, U. Colo., 1973, JD, 1979. Gen. mgr. Goldenrod Showboat, St. Louis, 1975; asst. mgr. box office, adminstrv. asst. Heritage Sq. Opera House, Golden, Colo., 1974-75, box office mgr., bus. mgr., 1976, bookkeeper, adminstrv. asst., 1975-76; bookkeeper Internat. Sports Distbrs., Boulder, Colo., 1978-79; student atty. Legal Aid and Defender Program, 1977-78; dep. dist. atty. 10th Jud. Ct., Pueblo, Colo., 1979-81; assoc. J.E. Losavio Jr., Pueblo, 1981; pvt. practice Pueblo, 1981-87; asst. to county atty. Pueblo County Dept. Social Svcs., 1982-88; assoc. Petersen & Fonda, P.C., Pueblo, Colo., 1987-91; ptnr. Petersen & Fonda, P.C., Pueblo, 1992—. Mem. ABA, Colo. Bar Assn. (bd. govs. 1994—), Pueblo County Bar Assn. (exec. com., v.p., pres. elect 1992-93, pres. 1993—), Colo. Trial Lawyers Assn., Pueblo C. of C., Kiwanis Internat. Club, Phi Delta Phi (outstanding grad. region X), others. Office: Petersen & Fonda P C 650 Thatcher Bldg Pueblo CO 81003

HEARN, ROSEMARY, English language educator; b. Indpls., May 1, 1929; d. Oscar Thomas and Mabel Lee (Ward) H. BA, Howard U., 1951; MA, Ind. U., 1958, PhD, 1973. Mem. dept. English Lincoln U., Jefferson City, Mo., 1958-62, prof. English, 1962-64; dir. hon. program Lincoln U., Jefferson City, 1968-72, exec. dean acad. affairs, 1982-85, exec. asst. to pres., 1985-87, dean Coll. Arts and Scis., 1989—; cons. HEW, Washington, 1977-78, Nat. Endowment for Humanities, Washington, 1980-81; mem. adv. bd. Am. Coun. on Edn. Mem. adv. bd. Sta. KBIA Nat. Pub. Radio, Columbia, Mo., 1979-82, Mo. State Planning Commn., Nat. Identification Program for Women, Am. Coun. on Edn., Mo. Coun. Arts. Recipient Community Svc. award Jefferson City United Way, 1983—, Second Bapt. Ch. Mem. AAUW, Consortium of Doctors, Nat. Coun. Tchrs. English, Coll. Lang. Assn., Am. Coun. Edn. Home: 811 E Dunklin St Jefferson City MO 65101-3350 Office: Lincoln U Jefferson City MO 65101

HEARN, SHARON SKLAMBA, lawyer; b. New Orleans, Aug. 15, 1956; d. Carl John and Marjorie C. (Wimberly) Sklamba; m. Curtis R. Hearn. BA magna cum laude, Loyola U., New Orleans, 1977; JD cum laude, Tulane U., 1980. Bar: La. 1980, Tex. 1982; cert. tax specialist. Law clk. to presiding judge U.S. Ct. Appeals Fed. Cir., Washington, 1980-81; assoc. Johnson & Swanson, Dallas, 1981-84, Kullman Inman Bee & Downing, New Orleans, 1984—. Recipient Am. Legion award, 1970. Mem. ABA, La. State Bar Assn., Tex. State Bar Assn., Dallas Women Lawyers Assn. Democrat. Roman Catholic. Home: 44 Swallow St New Orleans LA 70124-4404 Office: Kullman Inman Bee & Downing 615 Howard Ave New Orleans LA 70130-3917

HEARNE, CAROLYN FOX, art and history educator, artist; b. Brownwood, Tex., June 15, 1945; d. Marshal D. and Lena May (Parson) Fox; m. Roy Nicholas Hearne, Apr. 14, 1968; children: Jason Nicholas, Angela Della. BA in Spanish, Art, So. Meth. U., 1967; MA in Fine Arts, U. Tex., Tyler, 1985. Astrology lady, commls. K-BUY Radio, Ft. Worth, 1970-71; decorator, exec. dir. Holiday Inns, Inc., Houston, 1971-73; exec./bilingual sec. Kennecott Copper Corp., Houston, 1973-74; owner Fox-Hearne Studio, Kilgore, Tex., 1977-92; art/music, history tchr. LeTournear U., Longview, Tex., 1988—; chmn. LeTourneau Fine Arts Week, Longview, 1992; demonstrator, lectr. mus. and art groups, Longview and Tyler, 1979—; judge East Tex. art groups, Longview, Kilgore, and Henderson, 1990—; invited participant Master Artists Workshop, L.I. U., 1990. Prin. works include book cover, Gory Days, 1987, bronze sculpture, Frontier Spirit, 1983 (Citation 1983), sculpture for dedication, Gussie Nell Davis, 1983, commnd. A Race Against Time, 1978 (Spl. award 1978), model for catalogue, TV commls. for Strictly Petites, 1987—; exhbns. incl. Tex. Art Gallery, 1990-92. Bd. dirs. Kilgore Hist. Preservation Found., Kilgore, 1989—, past sec., now pres.; chmn. art fest Kilgore Improvement and Beautification Assn., 1981-86; chmn. Kilgore Civic Ball, 1980; decorator Jr. League Charity Ball, Longview, 1992; pres. Kilgore Garden Club, 1982-83; chmn. Theatre Restoration, Kilgore, 1989-92; life mem. Tex. PTA, 1978—; bd. dirs. Longview Art Mus., 1994—. Recipient 5 Citation awards East Tex. Classics, 1981, Outstanding Achievement award Artitudes mag., 1989. Mem. East Tex. Fine Arts Assn. (pres. 1981-83, Top Citation award 1984), Tex. Fine Arts Assn., LeTourneau Faculty Orgn., Coterie Club (pres. 1990). Republican. Presbyterian. Home: 8 Briar Ln Kilgore TX 75662 Office: LeTourneau Univ Mobberly Ave PO Box 7001 Longview TX 75607-7001

HEARNS, PATRICIA A., nurse pracitioner; b. Paw Paw, Mich., Dec. 2, 1947; d. Dwayne Russell and Marion G. (Meyer) Guiter; divorced; children: William Arthur, Jennifer Lynn. Diploma, Butterworth Hosp., Grand Rapids, Mich., 1969; BS, Western Mich. U., 1982; MSN, Mich. State U., 1986. Cert. family nurse practitioner, ANCC, case mgr. Staff nurse Bronson Meth. Hosp., Kalamazoo, Mich., 1971-79, instr., 1979-81, supr., 1981-84, clin. nurse specialist, 1985-88; nurse practitioner Portage (Mich.) Med. Group, 1984-85, Cardiology Assocs., Kalamazoo, 1985; clin. nurse specialist Butterworth Hosp., Grand Rapids, 1988-91, Battle Creek (Mich.) Health System, 1992-93; mgr. CCU Borgess Med. ctr., Kalamazoo, 1993—; adj. faculty U. Mich., Ann Arbor, 1994—; adj. faculty Grand Valley State U., Allendale, Mich., 1987-93, Ferris State U., Big Rapids, Mich., 1988-89; cons. Genentech, Inc., South San Francisco, 1987—, Cardiology Assocs., Kalamazoo, 1991-93; researcher Butterworth Hsop., Grand Rapids, 1988-91; cons. Dimensions of Critical Care Nursing, Lakewood. Vol. March of Dimes, Vicksburg, Mich., 1991-92; alt. del. State Rep. Conv., Detroit, 1972. Grad. fellow Mich. State U., 1984, 85. Mem. ANA, AACN (hosp. liaison west Mich. chpt. 1990), Am. Heart Assn. (cert. BLS, ALS, sec. Kalamazoo chpt. 1987-88), Sigma Theta Tau (Alpha Psi chpt.). Republican. Methodist. Home: 312 S Michigan Vicksburg MI 49097 Office: Borgess Med Ctr 1521 Gull Rd Kalamazoo MI 49007

HEARNSBERGER, NELDA JEAN, counselor, educator; b. Silsbee, Tex., July 7, 1941; d. Knox E. and Ora Lee (Woodson) Dixon; m. Walter L. Hearnsberger, June 1, 1962; children: Lea Roxanne, Jeffrey Lee. BS, Stephen F. Austin State U., Nacogdoches, Tex., 1964, MEd, 1985; MEd, Tex. A&M U., 1975. Lic. profl. counselor, Tex. Tchr. home econs. Brookeland (Tex.) Ind. Sch. Dist., 1964-65; tchr., supr. Corrigan (Tex.)-Camden Ind. Sch. Dist., 1969-76, dir. curriculum, 1976-78, counselor, 1978-83; counselor Huntington (Tex.) Ind. Sch. Dist., 1983-85; tchr. home econs., counselor West Sabine Ind. Sch. Dist., Pineland, Tex., 1985-88; elem. tchr. San Augustine (Tex.) Ind. Sch. Dist., 1988-90, counselor, 1990—; presenter seminars on women's issues and interests, 1978—; tchr., presenter parenting classes, 1990—. Mem. San Augustine Women's Svc. League, 1985—. Mem. ACA, Assn. Tex. Profl. Educators (treas. 1989-91), Am. Assn. Christian Counselors, San Augustine C. of C., Delta Kappa Gamma. Southern Baptist. Home: 801 Cartwright Dr San Augustine TX 75972-0562

HEARST, BELLA RACHAEL, physician, researcher, artist; b. Pitts.; d. Aba and Bertha (Alpern) H. B.M., Chgo. Med. Sch., 1949, M.D., 1950; postgrad., Johns Hopkins U., 1952-53, Art Inst. Chgo., 1958-68. Rotating intern Norwegian Am. Hosp., Chgo., 1949-50; jr. asst. pathologist Cook County Hosp, Chgo., 1950-52; fellow med. legal pathology U. Md., 1953-54; sr. pathology resident Charity Hosp., New Orleans, 1955-56; spl. cardiac researcher Armed Forces Inst. Pathology, Washington, 1956-57; dir., coordinator pathology dept Hosp. O'Horan Menda Yucatan, Mexico, 1957-58; founder Bertha Hearts Found., Inc., 1958, exec. dir., 1958-63; founder Diabetic Inst. Am., Inc., Chgo., 1959, exec. dir., 1959-63; founder Internat. Diabetic Inst., Inc., Chgo., 1963, exec. dir, 1963—; dist. med. dir. compensation U.S. Dept. Labor, Chgo., 1968—; with Chgo. Dept. Health, 1977—, Uptown Neighborhood Health Ctr., 1977-78, Copernicus Multipurpose Ctr., 1978-79, Lakeview Neighborhood Health Ctr., Chgo., 1979—; research dir. Fed. Safety and Fire Council, Chgo.; research assoc. microbiology Stritch Sch. Medicine, Loyola U., Chgo.; staff physician Western Ill. U., 1971-72, assoc. prof., 1971-72. Author: Diabetes and Juvenile Delinquency, 1964, Diabetes and Fitness, 1964, Diabetic Statistical Research Survey, 1961-65, Diabetes and Blood Groups, 1965, Diabetes and Aging, 1965, Diabetes and Newborns; contbr. articles to various publs., art exhibit, Shuster Art Gallery, N.Y., 1966, Internat. Dermatology Congress, Munich, 1967. Recipient 3d prize AMA Conv., Chgo., 1962; recipient testimonial plaque for work sr. citizens Chelsea House, Chgo. Fellow Am. Coll. Angiology, Internat. Coll. Angiology, Am. Geriatric Soc., Royal Soc. Pub. Health; mem. Internat. Acad. Pathology, Am. Women's Med. Assn., Am. Soc. Microbiology, Am. Assn. for Study Neoplastic Diseases, Reticuloendothelial Soc. Home: 514 W Jefferson Macomb IL 61455 also: PO Box 373 Macomb IL 61455 Office: 8 S Michigan Ave Chicago IL 60603-3302

HEATH, MARIWYN DWYER, legislative issues consultant; b. Chgo., May 1, 1935; d. Thomas Leo and Winifred (Brennan) Dwyer; m. Eugene R. Heath, Sept. 3, 1956; children: Philip Clayton, Jeffrey Thomas. BJ, U. Mo., 1956. Mng. editor Chemung Valley Reporter, Horseheads, N.Y., 1956-57; self-employed freelance writer, platform speaker, editor Tech. Transls., Dayton, Ohio, 1966—; cons. Internat. Women's Commn., 1975-76; ERA coord. Nat. Fedn. Bus. and Profl. Women's Clubs, 1974-82; mem. polit. and mgmt. coms. ERAmerica, 1976-82, exec. dir., 1982-88; pres. Miami Valley Regional Transit Authority, 1986-88, bd. dirs. 1984-91; chair Regional Transit Coalition, 1991-94. Author: 75 Years and Beyond-BPW/USA, 1994. Mem. Gov. Ohio Task Force Credit for Women, 1973; mem. Midwest regional adv. com. SBA, 1976-82; mem. Ohio Women's Commn., 1990—, vice chair, 1993—; pres. Dayton Pres.'s Club, 1973-74; chmn. Ohio Coalition ERA Implementation, 1974-75; appt. joint civilian orientation conf., U.S. Dept. Def., 1988. Recipient Legion of Honor award Dayton Pres.'s Club, 1987, Keeper of Flame award Ohio Sec. of State, 1990; named One of 10 Outstanding Women of World Soroptimist Internat., 1982; named to Ohio Women's Hall of Fame. Mem. AAUW (dir. Dayton 1965-72, Woman of Year award Dayton 1974), Nat. Fedn. Bus. and Profl. Women's Clubs (pres. Dayton 1967-69, Ohio 1976-77, nat. polit. action com. 1985—, chmn. 1988—), Miami Valley Mil. Affairs Assn. (bd. dirs.), Ohio Women (v.p. 1983-86, bd. dirs. 1977-89), Assn. Women Execs., Women in Communications. Republican. Roman Catholic. Address: 10 Wisteria Dr Dayton OH 45419-3451

HEATH, MARY ANNE, management consultant; b. Vincennes, Ind., Jan. 20, 1949; d. John Blaine and Betty Louise (Warner) Hoffner; m. Charles Samuel Heath, Sept. 16, 1979 (div. Apr. 1982). BA, Ind. U., 1981. With mktg., customer services depts. Fla. Power and Light Co., Ft. Myers, 1978-86, supr. mktg., 1986-88, mgr., 1988-92; mgmt. cons. Qualtec Quality Svcs., N. Palm Beach, Fla., 1992—; mem. nat. com. older women and energy cons. Am. Assn. Retired Persons, Washington, Ft. Myers, 1985-86; motivational spkr., 1989—; mem. conf. steering coms Women Winning in the 90's, 1992—. Playwright, 1979—. Mem. adv. com. tech. studies Edison Community Coll., Ft. Myers, 1983-92; mem. adv. council career edn. Lee County Sch. Bd., Ft. Myers, 1985-92; bd. dirs. Concerned Citizens for Sexually Abused Children, Ft. Myers, 1985-90, Am. Cancer Soc., Ft. Myers, 1986-90, Area Agy. on Aging Dist. 8, 1989-92; mem. adv. bd. Sarasota Palms Partial Hosp., 1990-92; mem. adv. com. Congressman Porter Gross, 1989-92. Mem. Met. Ft. Myers C. of C. (ch-chaire Challenge '87), Christian Women in Bus. (steering com. Ft. Myers chpt.). Republican. Baptist. Home: 2385 Tall Oak Ct Sarasota FL 34232-6843 Office: 11760 US Hwy 1 Ste 500 North Palm Beach FL 33408

HEATHERLEY, MELODY ANN, nursing administrator; b. Dallas, Apr. 15, 1957; d. Harold Ray and Barbara Ann (Roebuck) Jones; m. James Lawrence Heatherley, July 21, 1982. BSN, U. Tex., Arlington, 1979. RN, Tex., Fla. Surg. nurse St. Paul Hosp., Dallas, 1979, Mesquite (Tex.) Meml. Hosp., 1979-80; charge nurse All Saints Hosp.-Main, Ft. Worth, 1980-87; house supr., charge nurse All Saints Cityview Hosp., Ft. Worth, 1987-88; staff nurse ICU, critical care coord. Hosp. Corp. Am. Med. Plz. Hosp., Ft. Worth, 1986-89; staff nurse ICU, CCU Harris Meth. Hurst, Euless, Bedford, Bedford, Tex., 1989-91; staff nurse rehab. unit Harris Meth. HEB, Bedford, 1991; charge nurse surg. ICU, cardiovascular recovery Humana Hosp.-Lucerne, Orlando, Fla., 1991-93, relief house supr., 1991-93; divsn. supr. nursing adminstrn. St. Paul Med. Ctr., Dallas, 1993-94; adminstrv. supr Baylor Med. Ctr. Ellis County, Waxahachie, Tex., 1994—. Mem. AACN, ANA, NAFE, Assn. Rehab. Nurses, Tex. Orgn. Nurse Execs., Tex. Nurses Assn. Episcopalian. Office: Baylor Med Ctr Ellis County Waxahachie Campus 1405 W Jefferson Waxahachie TX 75165

HEATLEY, CONNIE FRANCES, association executive; b. Bronx, N.Y., Oct. 10, 1942; d. Salvatore Charles and Mary Moscatiello LaMotta; children: Raphael, Peter, David. BA, SUNY, Albany, 1969; postgrad., Fordham U., 1974. Activities coord. San Diego Assn. for the Retarded, 1970-72; edn. program dir. Edn. Ctrs. of Newark Archdiocese, 1973-79; dir. communications tng. Riverside Eating Disorder Clinic, Secaucus, N.J., 1979-84; communications coord. Sun Chem. Corp., N.Y.C., 1984-86; pub. relations dir. Nat. Coffee Assn., N.Y.C., 1986-87; v.p. pub. rels. Direct Mktg. Assn., N.Y.C., 1987-94, sr. v.p. pub. rels., 1988—. Mem. Pub. Rels. Soc. Am., Women in Communications, Am. Soc. Assn. Execs. (assoc.). Episcopalian. Office: Direct Mktg Assn 1120 Ave of the Americas New York NY 10036-6700

HEATON, JEAN, early childhood educator, retired; b. Equality, Ill., Feb. 27, 1933; d. Lytle and Loretta (Drone) Mossman; m. Fred T. Heaton, June 10, 1954 (div. Dec. 1979); children: Fred T., Laura, Sheri; m. Michael Marticorena, Mar. 14, 1987; children: Michael, Maria. BS in Home Econs., Southern Ill. U., 1955, MS in Edn., 1958; PhD in Child Devel., Early Childhood Edn, Fla. State U., 1971. Cert. secondary educator Ill., Fla., Calif. Tchr. Corham (Ill.) High Sch., 1955-57; rsch. asst. Southern Ill. U., Carbondale, 1957-58; tchr. Jefferson High Sch., Tampa, Fla., 1958-60, Hamilton Jr. High Sch., Oakland, Calif., 1960-61; prof. San Francisco State U., 1961-94, prof. emeritus, 1994—; prof. emeritus, 1994—; ednl. cons. Dept. Home and Cmty. Devel., U. Monrovia, Liberia, 1982, Calif. State Dept. Edn., 1974-76; mem. adv. bd. Skyline Coll., 1973—; coord. Study Tours; presenter at profl. confs. Contbr. articles to profl. jours. and newsletters. Recipient Meritorious Performance award SFSU, 1986 and 1989. Mem. Infant/Toddler Consortium San Francisco Bay Area (exec. com. 1988-93), San Francisco/San Mateo Child Care Consortium (exec. com. 1987-93), Calif. Coun. on Children and Youth (exec. com. Region II 1982-90), San Francisco Assn. for Edn. Young Children (pres. 1990-92), AAUW (exec. com. San Mateo br. 1981-83), Pi Lambda Theta, Omicron Nu.

HEATON, KATHRYN, freight company executive; b. Levittown, N.Y., Jan. 19, 1961; d. William and Olga Heaton. Import agt. Hudson Gen. Corp., Jamaica, N.Y., 1984-86; cargo agt. Weber Internat. Freight Inc., Inwood, N.Y., 1986-90; export mgr. PBL Aircargo Ltd., Jamaica, 1990-94; pres. Blue Line Forwarding, Inc., Jamaica, 1994—. Republican. Home: 5 Block Blvd Massapequa Park NY 11762

HEAVEN, VENITA DORINE WATERMAN, elementary school educator, administrator; b. Bklyn.; d. George H. and Viola D. (Braithwaite) Waterman; m. Everett F. Heaven, Aug. 16, 1986; children: Taariq, Jabari. BS, York Coll., 1976; MS, Queens Coll., 1983, postgrad., 1984-86. Cert. tchr. early childhood elem., spl. edn., N.Y. (life), Ga. (permanent). Early childhood tchr. Alph Kappa Alpha Child Care Ctr., S. Oxone Park, N.Y., 1977-82; elem., spl. edn. tchr. N.Y.C. Bd. Edn., Laurelton, N.Y., 1982-88; tchr. Fulton Count Bd. Edn., Atlanta, 1988-89; program coord. exec. dir. Atlanta Prep. Pre-sch., East Point, Ga., 1989-90; exec. dir., founder, chmn. bd. Arise Acad., Atlanta, 1991—, program coord., dir. Extended Day Program, 1993—, program dir., exec. dir. Summer Learning Explosion, 1993—. Editor, founder (newsletter) Arise, 1992. Recipient scholarship Emerald Debutante Cotillion, St. Albans, N.Y., 1972. Mem. ASCD, Save the Children. Lutheran. Home: 3915 Thaxton Rd Atlanta GA 30331 Office: Arise Acad Inc PO Box 43721 Atlanta GA 30336

HEBENSTREIT, JEAN ESTILL STARK, religion educator, practitioner; d. Charles Dickey and Blanche (Hervey) Stark; student Conservatory of Music, U. Mo. at Kansas City, 1933-34; AB, U. Kans., 1936; m. William J. Hebenstreit, Sept. 4, 1942; children: James B., Mark W. Authorized C.S. practitioner, Kansas City, 1955—; bd. dir. 3d Ch., Kansas City, 1952-55, chmn. bd. 1955, reader, 1959-62; authorized C.S. tchr., C.S.B., 1964—; bd. dirs. First Ch. of Christ Scientist, Boston, 1977-83, chmn. bd., 1981-82; mem. Christian Sci. Bd. of Lectureship, Christian Sci. Bd. Edn. Bd. trustees The Christian Sci. Pub. Soc. Mem. Art of Assembly Parliamentarians (charter, 1st pres.), Internat. Platform Assn., Pi Epsilon Delta, Alpha Chi Omega (past pres.), Carriage Club. Contbr. articles to C.S. lit. Home and Office: 310 W 49th St Ste A-2 Kansas City MO 64112-2425

HEBER, RUTH R., psychologist, consultant; b. Lodz, Poland, June 27, 1935; came to U.S., 1957; d. Moses Zwi and Ryna (Glucklich) Borenstein; m. Jacob Heber, 1955 (div. 1982); children: Ron, Sheldon, Lorraine; m. Lawrence Walter Kullman, 1987. BA in Psychology, CUNY, 1972; MS in Ednl. Psychology and Guidance, Yeshiva U., 1974, PhD in Devel. Psychology, 1979. Lic. psychologist, N.Y. Adj. instr. Jersey City State Coll., N.Y., 1976-77; instr. psychology Pace U., N.Y., 1980-81; rsch. assoc. New Careers Tng. Labs. Grad. Sch. and Univ. Ctr. N.Y., 1978-80; staff psychotherapist North Suffolk Mental Health Ctr., N.Y., 1980-82; supervising psychologist, clinic and program coord. Creedmoor Psychiat. Ctr., N.Y., 1982-88; dir. East Side Consultation Ctr., N.Y.C., 1988—; adj. asst. prof. psychology Queens Coll., CUNY, 1981-83, adj. asst. prof. dept. edn. and community svcs., 1987; cons., lectr. Humanistic Psychology Ctr., N.Y., 1983-93; East Coast conf. coord. Assn. for Transpersonal Psychology, 1983-86; lectr. psychiatry Mt. Sinai Sch. Medicine, CUNY, 1990—; supr. psychiat. residents Mt. Sinai Med. Ctr., N.Y.C., 1989—; adj. prof. The Union Inst. Grad. Sch. Cin., 1991—; participant, supr. Holocaust Survivors Treatment Program, 1993—; active Hidden Children Speakers Bur., 1994—; pvt. practice; presenter, guest speaker, workshop leader. Mem. APA (pres. proposed divsn. transpersonal psychology 1987-88, program chmn. humanistic psychology divsn. 1988-89, treas. 1989-92, pres. 1993-94), Am. Acad. Psychotherapists, Internat. Coun. Psychologists, Internat. Assn. Applied Psychology, Internat. Assn. Cross-Cultural Psychology, Am. Group Psychotherapy Assn., Ea. Group Psychotherapy Assn., N.Y. State Psychological Assn. (disaster/crisis response network 1993—, colleague assistance program com. 1992—), Assoc. Alumni Mt. Sinai Med. Ctr., Phi Beta Kappa, Psi Chi, Kappa Delta Pi, Delta Phi Alpha. Office: 200 E 33rd St Apt 4I New York NY 10016-4826

HEBERT, MARY ELIZABETH LEBLANC, secondary school counselor, educator; b. Donaldsonville, La., Nov. 21, 1940; d. Jean Batiste and Gladys (Berniard) LeBlanc; m. Leroy Joseph Hebert, June 23, 1962; children: Leroy Joseph Jr., Mary Francis, Christopher, William IV, Andrew. BS in Edn., Nicholls State U., 1962, MEd in Math. and Guidance, 1969. Lic. profl. counselor, La. Tchr. Lafourche Parish Sch. Bd., Thibodaux, La., 1963-77, guidance counselor, 1977—; health educator Thibodaux Hosp. and Health Ctr., 1991—. Home: 319 Melrose Dr Thibodaux LA 70301-2920

HEBERT, MARY OLIVIA, retired librarian; b. St. Louis, Nov. 11, 1921; d. Arthur Frederick and Clara Marie (Golden) Meyer; certificate librarianship, Washington U., St. Louis, 1972; m. N. Hal Hebert, Sept. 9, 1943 (dec. Mar. 1969); children—Olivia, Stephen (dec.), Christina, Deborah, Beth, John, James. Secretarial positions in advt., 1942-43; v.p. Hebert Advt. Co., 1955-66; adminstrv. asst. communications Blue Cross, St. Louis, 1966-69, librarian, 1969-91, ret., 1991. Mem. Spl. Libraries Assn. (pres. St. Louis Metro chpt. 1984), St. Louis Med. Librs., St. Louis Regional Libr. Network (coun. 1986-89). Roman Catholic.

HECETA, ESTHERBELLE AGUILAR, anesthesiologist; b. Cebu City, Philippines, Jan. 1, 1935; came to U.S., 1962, naturalized, 1981; d. Serafin Aquilar and Elsie (Nichols) Aguilar; m. Wilmer G., Heceta, Apr. 5, 1962; children: W. Cristina, W. Elgine, Wuela E. BS Chemistry cum laude, Silliman U., Dumaguete City, Philippines, 1955, BS cum laude, 1956; MD cum laude, U. East Ramon Magsaysay Meml. Med. Center, Quezon City, Philippines, 1961. Diplomate Am. Bd. Anesthesiology, Philippine Bd. Anesthesiology. Intern, Youngstown (Ohio) Hosp. Assocs., 1962-63, resident in anesthesiology, 1963-66; anesthesiologist Salem (Ohio) City Hosp., 1967, St. Joseph's Hosp., Manapla, Philippines, 1967-72; instr. dept. anesthesiology U. Tenn., Memphis, 1972-74; staff anesthesiologist Ohio Valley Med. Ctr., Wheeling, W.Va., 1974—; anesthesiologist Bellaire (Ohio) City Hosp., 1975—; staff anesthesiologist East Ohio Regional Hosp., Martins Ferry, Ohio, 1989—; Joint Conf. Comm. for Profl Affairs, Ohio Valley Med. Ctr., 1992—, mem. exec. comm., sec.-treas. med. dental staff, 1992—, pres.-elect, 1993-94, pres. med. dental staff, 1994-95, physician reviewer Anesthesiology W. Va. Med. Inst., 1992—, mem. Claims Review Panel W. Va. Med. Assn., 1990—; Vol. med.-surg. mission to Philippines, 1982-90. Fellow Am. Coll. Anesthesiology; mem. AMA, Am. Soc. Anesthesiologists, Ohio Valley Philipine Med. Assn. (pres. 1988-90), Tri-State Phillipine-Am. Assn. (pres. 1991-92), Assn. Philippine Physicians in Am., Philippine Soc. Anesthesiologists in Am., W.Va. Soc. Anesthesiologists, Internat. Anesthesia Research Soc., Am. Med. Women's Assn. (organizer, pres. 1983, regional gov. Region IV 1987-89), W.Va. Med. Soc., Ohio County Med. Soc. Presbyterian. Home: 15 Holly Rd Wheeling WV 26003-5656 Office: Ohio Valley Med Ctr Dept Anesthesiology 2000 Eoff St Wheeling WV 26003-3870

HECHENBERGER, NAN BELL, academic administrator; b. Phila., Nov. 29, 1932. RN, St. Joseph Hosp. Sch. Nursing, Phila., 1953; BSN, Villanova U., 1956; MSN, Cath. U. Am., 1959, PhD, 1974; hon. degree, Hahnemann U. Sch. Health Scis. and Humanities, 1990. Staff nurse St. Joseph Hosp., Phila., 1953-54, instr. Sch. Nursing, 1955-57; supr. Kensington Hosp., Phila., 1954-55; instr. med. and surg. nursing, Sch. Nursing Cath. U. Am., Washington, 1959-61, dir. undergrad. divsn. Sch. Nursing, 1961-62, lectr. nursing edn. Sch. Nursing, 1963, asst. dean of women, 1967-69, assoc. dean of students, 1969-70, grad. teaching asst., Sch. Edn., 1970-71; assoc. prof. Dept. Career Devel. U. Md. Sch. Nursing, Balt., 1972-77, prof. Dept. Career Devel., 1977-78, dean, prof., 1978-89; pres. Neumann Coll., Aston, Pa., 1989—; presenter workshops on nursing, 1958-80; cons. Potomac Found. for Mental Health, Bethesda, Md., 1974-75, numerous orgns. in health field; lectr. Internat. Nurses' Edn. Program, Johns Hopkins U., Balt., 1977-78; rschr. in field. Contbr. articles to jours. in field. Bd. visitors U. Pitts. Sch. Nursing, 1984-87; mem. strategic planning com., trustee Franciscan Health System, 1989—; mem. higher edn. com. ARC, 1989-90; mem. visiting com. Coll. Health and Human Devel., Pa. State U., 1990—. Recipient Alumni Achievement award Cath. U. Am., 1980, Alumni medal Villanova U. Coll. Nursing, 1982; HEW grantee, 1958; doctoral study fellow Cath. U. Am., 1970. Mem. Md. Hosp. Assn. (task force on nursing issues 1979-80), Md. Cath. Health Care Consortium (task force on manpower needs 1979-80), Am. Assn. Colls. Nursing (com. on continuing edn. for deans 1979-80, chair 1980-81, task force on Medicare reimbursement for nursing edn. 1984, instnl. rep. 1978-89, pres. elect 1988-89, bd. dirs. 1988-89, hon. mem. 1989), Nat.

League for Nursing (Mary Adelaide Nutting award 1991), Am. Assn. for Higher Edn., Nat. Assn. Ind. Colls. and Univs., Pa. Assn. Colls. and Univs., Middle State Assn. Colls. and Schs., Alpha Sigma Lambda, Sigma Theta Tau, Sigma Epsilon Phi, Phi Kappa Phi, Sigma Theta Tau (excellence in nursing award 1988, bd. dirs. Friends of the Internat. Nursing Libr., 1991—). Office: Neumann Coll Office of the President Aston PA 19014*

HECHT, MARIE BERGENFELD, educator, author; b. N.Y.C., Oct. 21, 1918; d. Frank Falle and Marie (Trommer) Bergenfeld; B.A., Goucher Coll., 1939; M.A., New Sch. for Social Research, 1971; m. Morton Hecht, Jr., Dec. 17, 1937 (div.); children—Ann (Mrs. David Bloomfield), Margaret, Laurence, Andrew. Tchr. Am. history Mineola High Sch., Garden City Park, N.Y., 1960-80. Mem. Am. Hist. Assn., Orgn. Am. Historians. Author (with Herbert S. Parmet): Aaron Burr: Portrait of an Ambitious Man, 1967; Never Again: A President Runs for a Third Term, 1968; John Quincy Adams: A Personal History of An Independent Man, 1972; The Women, Yes, 1973; Beyond the Presidency: The Residues of Power, 1976; Odd Destiny: The Life of Alexander Hamilton, 1982, The Church on the Hill, 1987. Address: 5 Hewlett Pl Great Neck NY 11024

HECHT, MARJORIE MAZEL, editor; b. Cambridge, Mass., Dec. 21, 1942; d. Mark and Theresa (Shuman) Mazel; m. Laurence Michael Hecht, July 2, 1972. B.A. cum laude, Smith Coll., 1964; postgrad., London Sch. Econs., 1964-65; M.S.W, Columbia U., 1967. Dir. Forest Neighborhood Service Ctr., N.Y.C., 1967-70, Wiltwyck Sch. for Boys, Bronx Center, N.Y., 1970-73; mng. editor Fusion Mag., Washington, 1977-87, 21st Century Sci. & Technol. Mag., Washington, 1987—. Co-author: Beam Defense: An Alternative to Nuclear Destruction, 1983 (Aviation and Space Writers award 1983); editor: Colonize Space! Open the Age of Reason, 1985, The Holes in the Ozone Scare: The Scientific Evidence That the Sky Isn't Falling, 1992. Press rep. LaRouche Campaign, N.Y.C., 1984. Democrat. Jewish. Office: 21st Century Sci & Technol Mag PO Box 16285 Washington DC 20041-6285

HECKART, EILEEN, actress; b. Columbus, Ohio, Mar. 29, 1919; d. Leo Herbert and Esther (Stark) Purcell; m. John Harrison Yankee Jr., June 26, 1943; children: Mark Kelly, Philip Craig, Luke Brian. BA, Ohio State U., 1942, LHD (hon.), 1981; postgrad., Am. Theatre Wing, 1944-48; LLD, Sacred Heart U., Bridgeport, Conn., 1973; DFA (hon.), Niagara U., 1981. Broadway plays include Voice of the Turtle, 1944, Brighten the Corner, 1946, They Knew What They Wanted, 1948, Stars Weep, 1949, The Traitor, 1950, Hilda Crane, 1951, In Any Language, 1953, Picnic, 1953, Bad Seed, 1955, A View From the Bridge, 1956, Dark at the Top of the Stairs, 1958, Invitation to a March, 1960, Everybody Loves Opal, 1961, Family Affair, 1962, Too True To Be Good, 1963, And Things That Go Bump in the Night, 1965, Barefoot in the Park, 1965-66, You Know I Can't Hear You When the Water's Running, 1967, The Mother Lover, 1968, Butterflies Are Free, 1969, Veronica's Room, 1973, The Effect of Gamma Rays on Man-in-the-Moon Marigolds, 1971, Remember Me, 1975, Mother Courage and Her Children, 1975, Mrs. Gibbs in Our Town, 1976; one-woman shows Eleanor, 1976, Ladies at the Alamo, 1977, Margaret Sanger-Unfinished Business, 1989, The Cemetery Club, 1990, Love Letters, 1991, Driving Miss Daisy, 1991; movies include Miracle in the Rain, Bad Seed (Oscar nomination), Bus Stop, Hot Spell, Daily Citation, 1956 (Oscar nomination, Drama Critics award), My Six Loves, 1962, Up the Down Staircase, 1966, Save Me a Place at Forest Lawn, 1967 (Emmy award), No Way To Treat A Lady, 1968, Butterflies Are Free, 1972 (Acad. award, Straw Hat award, 1973, 75, 77), Zandy's Bride, 1974, The Hiding Place, 1975, Burnt Offerings, 1975, Wedding Band, 1975 (Emmy nomination), Heartbreak Ridge, 1986, Eleemosynary, 1989, The Cemetery Club, 1990, Love Letters, 1990, Driving Miss Daisy, 1991; TV movies, 1947—; TV series Trauma Center, Annie McGuire, 1988-89, Partners in Crime, Mary Tyler Moore Show, 1976, 77 (2 Emmy nominations), Back Stairs at the White House, 1979 (Emmy nomination), FDR's Last Year, 1987, The Cosby Show, 1987 (Emmy nomination), (daytime show) One Life to Live, 1987 (Emmy nomination), Love and War (Emmy award, Guest Actress - Comedy Series, 1994), The Five Mrs. Buchanans, 1994. Recipient Outer Circle award, 1953, Daniel Blum award, 1953, Sylvania TV award, 1954, Donaldson award, 1955, Hollywood Fgn. Press award, 1956, March Dimes award, 1970, Aegis award, 1970, Ohio State U. Centennial award, 1970, Gov.'s award of Ohio, 1977, Ohiana Libr. award, 1978, Emmy award 1994, Lichtenberg award Pi Beta Phi, 1994; named to Theatre Hall of Fame, 1995. Mem. Pi Beta Phi.

HECKERLING, AMY, film director; b. Bronx, May 7, 1954; m. Neal Israel. Grad., NYU, 1975; fellow, Am. Film Inst. directing program, 1975. Dir. films including (short film) High Finance, Getting It Over With, Fast Times at Ridgemont High, 1982, Johnny Dangerously, 1984, National Lampoon's European Vacation, 1985, Look Who's Talking Too, 1990; screenwriter, dir. Look Who's Talking, 1989; co-exec. prodr., dir. Look Who's Talking Now, 1993; dir. (TV) Twilight Zone, 1986, (series) Fast Times at Ridgemont High; film appearance in Into the Night, 1985; author: (with Pamela Pettler) The No-Sex Handbook, 1990. Office: CAA 9830 Wilshire Blvd Los Angeles CA 90028*

HECKMAN, CAROL A., biology educator; b. East Stroudsburg, Pa., Oct. 18, 1944; d. Wilbur Thomas and Doris (Betts) H. BA, Beloit (Wis.) Coll., 1966; PhD, U. Mass., Amherst, 1972. Rsch. assoc. Yale U. Sch. Medicine, New Haven, 1973-75; staff mem. Oak Ridge (Tenn.) Nat. Lab., 1975-82; adj. assoc. prof. U. Tenn.-Oak Ridge Biomed. Grad. Sch., 1980-82; assoc. prof. Bowling Green (Ohio) State U., 1982-86, prof. biology, 1986—; cons. NSF, Washington, 1977-80; dir. EM facility Bowling Green State U., 1982—; NSF trainee, Amherst, 1967-70. Contbr. articles to profl. jours., chpts. to books. Internat. Cancer Rsch. Tech. fellow Internat. Union Against Cancer, 1980, Heritage Found. fellow, 1982, guest rsch. fellow, Uppsala, Sweden, 1989-90; grantee NSF, 1981-84, 90-92, NIH, 1987-88. Mem. AAAS, Am. Soc. Cell Biology, Microscopy Soc. Am., N.W. Ohio Microscopy (sec.-treas. 1986-90, pres. 1990-94), Tissue Culture Assn., Ohio Drug Devel. (pres. 1993—), Ohio Acad. Sci., Sigma Xi. Episcopalian. Home: 861 Ferndale Ct Bowling Green OH 43402-1609 Office: Bowling Green State U Dept Biol Scis Bowling Green OH 43403

HECKMAN, CAROL E., judge; b. Clinton, Iowa, Oct. 18, 1952; children: Tyler, Ethan. BA magna cum laude, Lawrence Univ., Wis., 1974; JD magna cum laude, Cornell Law Sch., 1977. Bar: N.Y., U.S. Supreme Ct., U.S. Tax Ct., U.S. Dist. Ct. (we. dist.) N.Y. Law clk. to Chief Judge John T. Curtin U.S. Dist. Ct. (we. dist.) N.Y., Buffalo, 1977-79, asst. U.S. atty., 1981-85, magistrate judge, 1992—; trial atty. Dept. of Justice, Civil Rights Div., D.C., 1979-81; assoc. Albrecht, Maguire, Heffern & Gregg, P.C., Buffalo, 1985-86, ptnr., 1986-89; ptnr. Lippes, Kaminsky, Silverstein, Mathias & Wexler, Buffalo, 1989-92. Recipient Farley prize in philosophy Lawrence Univ., Fraser prize for outstanding scholarship and character Cornell Law Review, Achievement award N.Y. State Women's Bar Assn., 1992. Mem. Cornell Law Sch. Advisory Coun., Nat. Assn. of Women Judges, Fed. Magistrate Judges Assn., Erie County Bar Assn., Women's Bar Assn. of the State of N.Y., Women Lawyers of We. N.Y., N.Y. State Bar Assn., Am. Lung Assn. of We. N.Y., Nat. Assn. of Women Judges. Office: US Courthouse 68 Court St Rm 418 Buffalo NY 14202*

HECK-RABI, LOUISE EVELYN, writer; b. Detroit; d. Andrew Martin and Mary (Varga) Heck; m. Gerald E. Naughton, Feb. 1, 1958 (div. 1965); m. Imre Rabi, Aug. 1, 1975 (dec. 1989). MA in Libr. Sci., U. Mich., 1960; MA, Wayne State U., 1971, PhD, 1976. With Wayne County Libr. Fedn., Detroit, 1954-62, Bacon Meml. Pub. Libr., Wyandotte, Mich., 1962-66, Soc. Mfg. Engrs., Dearborn, Mich., 1967-70; asst. prof. Wayne State U., Detroit, 1971-79; freelance writer Lincoln Park, Mich., 1980—. Author: (plays) Hier Ist Tobytown, 1971, The People Pound, 1980, (book) Women Filmmakers: A Critical Reception, 1984. Mem., various bd. positions Coop. Svcs., Inc., Oak Park, Mich., 1949—. Recipient Mich. Coun. of the Arts Creative Writing grant, Detroit, 1982. Mem. NOW (libr. Downriver br. 1979—, Woman Who Has made History award 1992), ALA, AAUW, Mich. Women's Studies Assn., Poetry Soc. Mich., Detroit Women Writers, Dramatists Guild (assoc., N.Y.). Democrat. Home: 1459 Philomene Blvd Lincoln Park MI 48146-2396

HEDDEN, HEATHER BEHN, information specialist; b. Concord, Mass., June 29, 1965; d. Prescott and Gertrud Magdalena (Blum) Behn; m. Thomas D. Hedden, Nov. 28, 1992. BA, Cornell U., 1987; MA, Princeton U., 1990. Project coord. Am. Translators Internat., Palo Alto, Calif., 1990-91; sr. writer Mid. East Times, Cairo, Egypt, 1991-92; abstractor Info. Access Co., Foster City, Calif., 1993-94, abstractor-editor, 1994, editl. analyst, 1995—; assoc. editor Multilingual Computing mag., 1994—; free lance Arabic translator. Contbr. to Internat. Directory of Company Histories, Annual Obituary, Ency. of Bus., Ency. of Am. Industries; contbr. articles to mags. Mem. Am. Translators Assn., Am. Soc. Indexers, Mid. East Studies Assn., Phi Beta Kappa. Home: 555 Forest Ave # 11 Palo Alto CA 94301

HEDGE, JEANNE COLLEEN, health physicist; b. Scottsburg, Ind., May 30, 1960; d. Paul Russell and Barbara Jean (Belshaw) H. BS in Environ. Health, Purdue U., 1983. Chemistry and health physics technician Marble Hill Nuclear Generating Sta., Pub. Svc. Ind., Madison, 1983-84; radiation protection asst. Pub. Svc. Electric and Gas Co., Hancock's Bridge, N.J., 1984-85, radiation protection technician, 1985-89, engr., 1989-90, lead engr., 1990-91, sr. staff engr., 1991—; mem. People to People Internat. Citizen Amb. Exch., People's Republic of China, 1988; del. Internat. Environ. Conf., Moscow, 1994. Mem. NOW, Am. Nuclear Soc., Health Physics Soc.

HEDGES, KAMLA KING, library director; b. Covington, Va.; d. John Wilton and Rhoda Alice (Loughrie) K.; m. Harry George Hedges, July 24, 1988. AB, Coll. of William and Mary, 1968; MLS, Vanderbilt U., 1969. Law and legis. reference libr. Conn. State Libr., Hartford, 1969-74; dep. law libr. Steptoe and Johnson, Washington, 1974-78; law libr. Wilkinson, Cragun and Barker, Washington, 1978-83; dir. libr. rels., corp. libr., libr. mgr. The Bur. of Nat. Affairs, Inc., Washington, 1983-94, dir. libr. rels., 1995—. Compiler: (directories) BNA's Directory of State and Federal Courts, Judges, Clerks, 1994, BNA's State Administrative Codes and Registers, 1993; contbr. chpt. to law manual. Mem. Am. Assn. Law Librs. (exec. bd. dirs. 1984-87), Spl. Libr. Assn. Episcopalian. Home: 4331 Embassy Park Dr NW Washington DC 20016 Office: Bur Nat Affairs Inc 1231 25th St NW Washington DC 20037

HEDIEN, COLETTE JOHNSTON, lawyer; b. Chgo.; d. George A. and Catherine (Bugan) Johnston; m. Wayne E. Hedien; 3 children. BS with honors, U. Wis., 1960; JD, DePaul U., 1981. Bar: Ill. 1981. Tchr. Sch. Dist. 39, Wilmette, Ill., 1960-63, Tustin Pub. Schs. (Calif.), 1964-66; extern law clk. to judge, Chgo., 1980, U.S. Atty.'s Office, Chgo., 1980; pvt. practice, Northbrook, Ill., 1981—; atty. Chgo. Vol. Legal Svcs.; mem. Chgo. Appellate Law Com., 1982-83, chmn., 1987-88; chmn. Northbrook Planning Commn., 1984-89; founder Am. Women of Surrey (Eng.), 1975-77; founding dir. U. Irvine Friends of Libr., 1965-66; guidance vol. Glenbrook High Sch., 1984-89; trustee Village of Northbrook, 1989—; mem. Women's Bd. Field Mus. NSF scholar, 1962. Mem. ABA (com. on real property), Chgo. Bar Assn., Ill. Bar Assn., North Shore Panhellenic Assn. (rep. 1989—), Phi Kappa Phi, Kappa Alpha Theta (bd. dirs.).

HEDLESTON, SALLY FAUNTLEROY, career counselor, educator, small business owner; b. Richmond, Va., Mar. 8, 1938; d. Henry Temple and Ada Virginia (Ring) Fauntleroy; m. Martin Reese Mitchell Jr., Oct. 8, 1956 (dec. 1976); children: Martin Reese Mitchell III, Catherine Ann Mitchell; m. Boyd Brister Hedleston Jr., Mar. 31, 1979. BA, Va. Commonwealth U., 1990, MEd, 1993. Telephone operator Am. Airlines, Washington, 1961-62; receptionist U.S. Steel, Washington, 1962-64; sec. AFL-CIO, Washington, 1964-69; adminstrv. asst. Scottish Rite Hosp., Dallas, 1970-71; salesperson Gen. Binding Co., Dallas, Atlanta, 1971-75; co-owner Baby Tenda of Va., Richmond, Va., 1979-94; career counselor Women's Resource Ctr. U. Richmond, 1994—. Author, editor: Bargain Shopper's Handbook, 1977, 78. Mem. ACA, Nat. Employment Counselors Assn., Nat. Career Devel. Assn., Nat. Soc. Arts and Letters (Richmond chpt., 2nd v.p. 1994—), Ginter Park Women's Club, Phi Kappa Phi. Home: 306 Tuckahoe Blvd Richmond VA 23226 Office: U Richmond Women's Resource Ctr Richmond VA 23173

HEDLUND, KAREN JEAN, lawyer; b. Chgo., Oct. 27, 1948; d. Reuben E. and Jane C. (Scarborough) H.; m. Barry M. Schneider; children—Erik, Alexander. A.B., Harvard U., 1970; J.D., Georgetown U., 1974. Bar: Ill. 1974, U.S. Dist. Ct. (no. dist.) Ill. 1974, Calif. 1989. Assoc. Mayer, Brown & Platt, Chgo., 1974-80, ptnr., 1980-84; ptnr. Skadden, Arps, Slate, Meagher & Flom, Chgo., L.A., 1984-93, Sun America Inc., 1993-94. Advisor debt com. Govt. Fin. Officer's Assn. Mem. ABA (mem. Tax sect. tax exempt fin. com. 1983—), Nat. Assn. Bond Lawyers, Assn. for Govtl. Leasing and Fin., Univ. Club, Banking Club. Office: SunAmerica Inc 1 SunAmerica Ctr Los Angeles CA 90067-6022

HEDMAN, JANICE LEE, business executive; b. Elmhurst, Ill., Feb. 7, 1938; d. George Marion Hickman and Vera Beryl (Olsen) Sample; m. Daryl F. Hedman, Aug. 29, 1971 (div. Aug. 1983); children: Kevin G., Gregory Scott, Danny L., Shelly L. Wolanski. Student, U. Puget Sound, 1970, Tacoma (Wash.) Community Coll., 1980. Head teller Puget Sound Nat. Bank, Tacoma, 1970-75; real estate agt. Shorewood Realty, Gig Harbor, Wash., 1975-80; mktg. rep. Western Fin. Planning, Inc., Tacoma, 1981-83; co-owner Schatz Avant Garde, Gig Harbor, 1984-86; asst. mgr. Classic Restaurant, Gig Harbor, 1984; co-owner Hedman Enterprises, Gig Harbor, 1976-93; owner, property mgr. Hedman Enterprises, 1993—; v.p. adminstrn. Teardrop Am., Inc., Wenatchee, Wash., 1986-90; pres. Teardrop N.W. Inc., Wenatchee, 1988-90; co-owner J&R Mktg., Wenatchee, 1989-90; mktg. specialist John L. Scott, Inc., Gig Harbor, 1991—. Asst., Women's Task Force, Tacoma, 1980-81; asst. in fund raising events Am. Cancer Soc., 1992—. Mem. Epsilon Sigma Alpha (pres. 1980-81, v.p. 1981-82). Home: 5109 Point Fosdick Dr NW 235E Gig Harbor WA 98335-1774 Office: John L Scott Inc 5500 Olympic Dr Apt H-106 Gig Harbor WA 98335-1491

HEDRICK, DARLA DEANE, communications developer; b. Parsons, Kans., May 6, 1956; d. Raymond L. and Mary E. (Montgomery) H. BS in Math and Computer Sci., Pitts. State U., 1977; MBA, Washington U., St. Louis, 1994. Systems devel. Southwestern Bell Telephone Co., St. Louis, 1977-80, systems mgr., 1980-88, systems planning, 1988-90, product mgr. mktg., 1990-93, product developer network svcs., 1993—; educator Washington U., 1981-82. Vol. helpline Contact-St. Louis, 1986-91, bd. dirs., 1987-91, pres. bd., 1990-91; fin. sec. St. John's United Meth. Ch., St. Louis, 1986-91; vol. Support Dogs, St. Louis, 1993-94. Mem. Profl. Women Southwestern Bell (chair charity golf tournament 1991, 92, 94). Democrat. Presbyterian. Home: 5575 Waterman Unit D Saint Louis MO 63112

HEDRICK, JANET LEE, fundraising executive; b. Birmingham, Ala., Aug. 15, 1951; d. Clarence Berkley and Louise Bennett (Osborne) H. BS in Math., Mary Wash. Coll., 1973; MEd, U. Va., 1976. Secondary sch. tchr. Buena Vista (Va.) City Pub. Schs., 1973-77; dir. ann. funds Longwood Coll., Farmville, Va., 1977-79; dir. devel. Hood Coll., Frederick, Md., 1979-83, Johns Hopkins Children's Ctr., Balt., 1983-86; asst. adminstr. for devel. St. Christopher's Hosp. for Children, Phila., 1986-93; v.p. Millard Fillmore Health System, Buffalo, 1993—; tchr. U. Pa., 1989, Villanova U., 1990-93, Del. Valley Assn. Dirs. Vol. Programs, 1992, Assn. for Care of Children's Health, Cleve., 1988, Delaware Valley, 1987, San Francisco, 1986, Boston, 1984, Nat. Assn. for Hosp. Devel., 1986. Bd. dirs. Phila. Concerned About Housing, 1987-90, chairperson devel. and pub. rels. com.; lay del. Southeastern Pa. Ann. conf. First United Meth. Ch. Germantown, Phila., 1987-93, chairperson coun. of ministries, chairperson commn. on the status and role of women; del. to ann. conf. Balt. Conf., United Meth. Ch., 1983, 84, 86, mem. conf. young adult coun., chairperson, 1985-86, mem. conf. coun. of ministries, 1985-86, mem. conf. episcopacy com., 1984-85. Mem. Nat. Soc. Fund Raising Execs. (presenter 1993, 94, tchr. 1993—, nat. assembly 1991-94, nat. minority outreach com. 1991-92, nat. nominations com. 1994—, bd. dirs. Greater Phila. chpt. 1990-93, chair 1993-94, pres. 1991-92, chair nat. philanthropy day 1990, Frannkin forum com. chair logistics 1990, chair program 1991), Assn. Healthcare Philanthropy, Coun. Advancement and Support of Edn., Mary Washington Coll. Alumni Assn. (bd. dirs. 1992-93, chair budget and fin. com. 1982), Phi Beta Kappa. Democrat. Methodist. Office: Millard Fillmore Health Edn & Rsch Found 1231 Delaware Ave Buffalo NY 14209

HEDRICK, JOANN M., legislative staff member; b. Madison, Wis., Feb. 25, 1943; d. Joseph R. and Jessica I. (Cunningham) Ponti; m. Edward S. Hendrick, Aug. 4, 1962; children: Ronald, Robert, Christina, Mary Catherine. Med. sec. St. Francis Hosp., Wilmington, Del., 1962-64; self-employed med. sec., 1964-79; sec., caucus asst. Del. Ho. of Reps., Dover, 1979-83; legal sec., receptionist Walsh & Monzack, P.A., Wilmington, 1983-84; chief clk. of ho. Del. Ho. of Reps., Dover, 1984—. Rep. dist. chairperson 21st Rep. Dist., Wilmington, Newark, Del., 1984-92; treas. Newark Region Reps., 1992—. Mem. Am. Soc. Legis. Clks. & Secs. (exec. com. 1991, 92), Nat. Conf. State Legis. (legis. mgmt. com. assembly on legis. 1985—, reapportionment task force 1986—). Roman Catholic. Home: 13 Gristmill Ln Newark DE 19711-8003 Office: Del Ho Reps Legis Hall # 109 Dover DE 19903

HEDRICK, LOIS JEAN, retired investment company executive, state official; b. Topeka, Kans., Jan. 25, 1927; d. Arthur Lenard and Nellie Cecelia (Johnson) Lungstrum; m. Clayton Newton Hedrick, Apr. 26, 1949; 1 dau., Carol Beth. Cert., Strickler's Bus. Coll., 1947; student Washburn U., Topeka, 1980-83. Staff sec. Kans. State Senate, Topeka, 1946-65; co-owner Hedrick's Market, Topeka, 1953-67; exec. sec. to sr. legal counsel Security Benefit Life Ins. Co., Topeka, 1963-73; asst. corp. sec. Security Mgmt. Co., Topeka, 1973-92, Security Distbrs. Inc., SBL Planning Inc., SBL Fund, Security Action Fund, Security Equity Fund, Security Investment Fund, Security Ultra Fund, Security Bond Fund, Security Cash Fund, Security OmniFund, Security Tax-Exempt Fund, Security Benefit Group, Ins., Security Mgmt. Co.; ; mem. Kans. Adv. Coun. on Aging, 1990-93; mgmt. cons. United Way of Greater Topeka, 1981-89 , mem. pub. relations staff, 1982—, rep. precinct woman. Organizer, chmn. Topeka Crime Blockers, 1976—; vol. fundraiser Am. Heart Assn., Stormont-Vail Hosp. Expansion, 1976-77; chmn. Plant a Tree for Century III, 1976; mem. Greater Topeka Career Edn. Com., 1981—; staff sec., fundraiser Christian Rural Overseas Program, 1951, staff sec. USAF Supply Depot, 1951-53; vol. community and various hosps. Named Woman of Year, Am. Bus. Women's Assn., 1970, Sec. of Yr., Profl. Secs. Inc., 1975. Mem. Greater Topeka C. of C. (chmn. edn. com. 1981—, ambassador chmn. high sch. honors banquet, 1982—), Adminstrv. Mgmt. Soc. (dir., pres. 1976—). Republican. Home: 1556 SW 24th St Topeka KS 66611-1329

HEERE, KAREN R., astrophysicist; b. Teaneck, N.J., Apr. 9, 1944; d. Peter N. and Alice E. (Hall) H. BA, U. Pa., 1965; MA, U. Calif., Berkeley, 1968; PhD, U. Calif., Santa Cruz, 1976. Rsch. assoc. NRC NASA Ames Rsch. Ctr., Moffett Field, Calif., 1977-79; rsch. astronomer U. Calif., Santa Cruz/NASA Ames Rsch. Ctr., 1979-86; assoc. prof. San Francisco State U., 1986-87; scientist Sci. Applications Internat. Corp., Los Altos, Calif., 1987-93; rsch. specialist Sterling Software, Palo Alto, Calif., 1993—; vis. scientist TATA Inst. for Fundamental Rsch., Bombay, India, 1984; adj. prof. San Francisco State U., 1987—. Author numerous articles in field. Mem. Am. Astron. Soc. Home: PO Box 2427 El Granada CA 94018-2427

HEFFERAN, COLIEN JOAN, economist; b. Mpls., May 13, 1949; d. Bernard and Rosemary Arnsdorf; m. Hollis Spurgeon Summers, Oct. 14, 1987; 1 child, Margaret Vimont Summers. BS, U. Ariz., 1971; MS, U. Ill., 1974, PhD, 1976. Asst. prof. Pa. State U., University Park, 1975-79; econ., rsch. leader Agrl. Rsch. Svc., USDA, Hyattsville, Md., 1979-88; dep. adminstr. Coopertive State Rsch. Svc., USDA, Washington, 1988—; adj. prof. U. Md., University Park, 1982-88; chmn. Ctr. for Family, Washington, 1985-87; vis. fellow Australian Nat. U., Canberra, NSW, 1989-91. Mem. editl. bd. Jours.-Family Econ. Issues, 1987—. Recipient Outstanding Citizen award U. Ariz., 1985, Outstanding Alumni award U. Ill., 1986. Mem. Am. Econ. Assn., Am. Coun. on Consumer Interests. Democrat. Roman Catholic.

HEFFERNAN, PATRICIA CONNER, management consultant; b. N.Y.C., Oct. 11, 1946; d. Arthur S. and Catherine (Center) Conner; B.A., U. Va., 1968; M.B.A., Suffolk U., 1980; m. John Joseph Heffernan, Sept. 13, 1969. Cert. mgmt. cons. office mgr. Wobbly Barn, Killington, Vt., 1968-72; bus. mgr. Woodstock Country Sch., Vt., 1972-74; assoc. dean Vt. Law Sch., Royalton, Vt., 1974-83; mgmt. cons. Heffernan & Assocs., Killington, 1982-87; mgmt. cons., v.p. Sandage Inc., Burlington, Vt., 1987-92; mgmt. cons., ptnr. Mktg. Ptnrs., Inc., Burlington, 1992—. Vt. del. White House Conf. on Small Bus.; mem. region 1 adv. coun. U.S. Small Bus. Adminstrn.; mem. Gov.'s Commn. on Women; bd. dirs. Rutland div. Chittenden Bank, 1975-92, Rutland Regional Med. Ctr., 1986-91, New England Bus. for Social Responsibility, 1990-93. Trustee, pres. Killington Mountain Sch., 1978-85; mem. Killington Planning Commn., 1975-87; mem. Killington Zoning Bd., 1979-84, Vt. Epilepsy Assn., 1977—, Vt. Telecommunications Commn., Vt. Econ. Devel. Adv. Coun.; mem. Vt. steering com. for ACE Nat. Identification Program for Women in Higher Edn., 1978-83. Named Outstanding Leader Vt. YWCA, 1985, Woman of Yr. Vt. Bus. and Profl. Women Found., 1986, Women in Bus. Adv. Small Bus. Adminstrn., 1993. Mem. Inst. Mgmt. Cons. (v.p. New Eng. region, nat. dir. 1991-93), Vt. Bus. Assn. for Social Responsibility (dir., pres. 1991—), Women Bus. Owners Vt. (dir. 1983—, founder, pres. 1984-86), Nat. Assn. Women Bus. Owners. Office: Mktg Ptnrs Inc 176 Battery St Burlington VT 05401

HEFFERON, LAUREN JEANINE, tour operator, business owner; b. Lawrence, Mass., May 24, 1961. BA in Anthropology, Cornell U., 1983. Owner, founder Ciclismo Classico-Italian walking and biking vacations, Arlington, Mass., 1988—. Author: (book) Cycle Food, 1983. Named Rotary scholar Rotary Found., 1983; recipient Gen. Excellence Entrepreneurial Prize Home Office Computing Mag., 1994. Office: Ciclismo Classico 13 Marathon St Arlington MA 02174-6940

HEFNER, CHRISTIE ANN, international media and marketing executive; b. Chgo., Nov. 8, 1952; d. Hugh Marston and Mildred Marie (Williams) H. BA summa cum laude in English and Am. Lit., Brandeis U., 1974. Freelance journalist, Boston, 1974-75; spl. asst. to chmn. Playboy Enterprises, Inc., Chgo., 1975-78, v.p., 1978-82, bd. dirs., 1979—, vice chmn., 1986-88, pres. 1982-88, chief oper. officer, 1984-88, chmn., chief exec. officer, 1988—; bd. dirs. Playboy Found.-Playboy Enterprises, Inc., Ill. chpt. ACLU, Mag. Pubs. Assn., Sealy Corp. Bd. dirs. Nat. Coalition on Crime and Delinquency, Goodman Theatre, Chgo., Brandeis U., Rush-Presbyn.-St. Lukes Med. Ctr. Recipient Agness Underwood award L.A. chpt. Women in Communications, 1984, Founders award Midwest Women's Ctr., 1986, Human Rights award Am. Jewish Com., 1987, Harry Kalven Freedom of Expression award ACLU, Ill., 1987, Spirit of Life award City of Hope, 1988, Eleanor Roosevelt award Internat. Platform Assn., 1990, Will Rogers Meml. award Beverly Hills C. of C. and Civic Assn., 1993. Mem. Brandeis Nat. Women's Com. (life), Com. of 200, Young. Pres. Orgn., Chgo. Network, Voters for Choice, Phi Beta Kappa. Democrat. Office: Playboy Enterprises Inc 680 N Lake Shore Dr Chicago IL 60611-3057*

HEFNER, TERRY THOMAS, soil conservationist; b. Magnolia, Ark., Aug. 1, 1949; d. Sam Terrell and Ann (Keese) Thomas; m. Joe B. Hefner, Aug. 14, 1982; children: Thomas Carroll, Joseph Terrell. BS, So. Ark. U., 1972. Clk.-typist USDA, Denton, Tex., 1970; soil conservationist USDA, Waco, Tex., 1978-80, Ballinger, Tex., 1980-83; soil conservationist USDA, Snyder, Tex., 1983-87, dist. conservationist, 1987—; mil. personnel clk. Hdqrs. 3rd ROTC Region, Ft. Riley Kans. at So. Ark. U., Magnolia, Ark., 1972-78; clk.-typist Hdqrs. III Corp., Ft. Hood, Tex., 1978; charter com. mem. Fed. Women's Program, Temple, Tex., 1986-90. Recipient Cert. Merit USDA, 1981, 83, 88. Mem. Soil and Water Soc. Am. (bd. dirs. 1983-84, pres.-elect 1992, pres. 1993), Nat. Assn. conservation Dists., Orgn. of Profl. Employees of Dept. Agr., Am. Quarter Horse Assn., Am. Bus. Women's Assn. Methodist. Home: PO Box 1295 Snyder TX 79550-1295 Office: USDA Soil Conservation Svc 5309 Big Springs Hwy Snyder TX 79549-6347

HEGARTY, MARY FRANCES, lawyer; b. Chgo., Dec. 19, 1950; d. James E. and Frances M. (King) H. BA, DePaul U., 1972, JD, 1975. Bar: Ill. 1975, U.S. Dist. Ct. (no. dist.) Ill. 1976, U.S. Supreme Ct. 1980. Ptnr. Lannon & Hegarty, Park Ridge, Ill., 1975-80; pvt. practice, Park Ridge, 1980—; dir. Legal Assistance Found. Chgo., 1983—. Mem. revenue study com. Chgo. City Coun. Fin. Com., 1983; mem. Sole Source Rev. Panel, City of Chgo., 1984; pres. Hist. Pullman Found., Inc., 1984-85; apptd. Park Ridge Zoning Bd., 1993-94. Mem. Ill. State Bar Assn. (real estate coun. 1980-84), Chgo. Bar Assn., Women's Bar Assn. Ill. (pres. 1983-84), NW Suburban Bar Assn., Park Ridge Women Entrepreneurs, Chgo. Athletic Assn. (pres. 1992-93). Democrat. Roman Catholic. Office: 301 W Touhy Ave Park Ridge IL 60068-4204

HEGE, LINDA, financial executive, accountant; b. L.A., Feb. 3, 1947; d. Walter Dale Runyan and Phyllis Naomi (Perkins) Thomas; m. Joseph H.

Kwan, June 12, 1965 (div. 1972); children: Katherine Elizabeth, Sandra Helen Kwan Wilde; m. Raymond Elder Hege, Feb. 18, 1978. BS in Bus., SUNY, Albany, 1986. CPA. Pub. acct. Katz & Co., L.A., 1980-82; CFO Hege, Gregor & Assocs., Venice, Calif., 1983-91; CFO George Elkins Co., Beverly Hills, Calif., 1991-93, CEO, 1993—. Vol. fund raiser Boy Scouts Am., L.A., 1993. Recipient Disting. Woman of Yr. award Boy Scouts Am., 1993. Office: George Elkins Co 499 N Canon Dr Beverly Hills CA 90210

HEGEL, CAROLYN MARIE, farmer, farm bureau executive; b. Lagro, Ind., Apr. 19, 1940; d. Ralph H. and Mary Lucile (Rudig) Lynn; m. Tom Lee Hegel, June 3, 1962. Student pub. schs., Columbia City, Ind. Bookkeeper Huntington County Farm Bur. Co-op, Inc. (Ind.), 1959-67; office mgr., 1967-70; twp. woman leader Wabash County Farm Bur., Inc. (Ind.), 1970-73, county woman leader, 1973-76; dist. woman leader Ind. Farm Bur., Inc., Indpls., 1976-80, 2d v.p., bd. dirs., 1980—, chmn. women's com., 1980—, exec. com. 1988—; farmer, Andrews, Ind., 1962—; dir. Farm Bur. Ins. Co., Indpls., 1980—, exec. com., 1988; mem. rural task force Great Lakes States Econ. Devel. Commn., 1987-88, Ind. Farm Bur. Svc. Co., 1980—, bd. dirs. Ind. Farm Bur. Found., Indpls., 1980—, Ind. Inst. Agr., Food and Nutrition, Indpls., 1982—, Ind. 4-H Found., Lafayette, 1983-86; mem. Ind. Rurual Health Adv. Coun., 1993—; com. mem. Hoosier Homestead Award Cert. Com., Indpls., 1980—; speaker in field. Women in the Field columnist Hoosier Farmer mag., 1980—. Named one of Outstanding Farm Woman of Yr. Country Woman Mag., 1987. Organizer farm div. Wabash County Am. Cancer Soc. Fund Dr. (Ind.), 1974; Sunday sch. tchr., bd. dir. childrens' activities Bethel United Meth. Ch., 1965—, pres. Bethel United Methodist Women, Lagro, 1975-81; bd. dirs. N.E. Ind. Kidney Found., 1984—, Nat. Kidney Found. of Ind., 1985-89, v.p., 1986—; active Leadership Am. Program, 1988. Recipient State 4-H Home Econs. ward Ind. 4-H, 1960; named Farm Woman of 1987 Country Woman mags. Mem. Women in Comm., Inc., Ind. Agrl. Mktg. Assn. (bd. dirs. 1980-94), Producers Mktg. Assn. (bd. dirs. 1980—), Am. Farm Bur. Fedn. (midwest rep. to women's com. 1986-93). Republican. Home: 3330 N 650 E Andrews IN 46702-9616 Office: Ind Farm Bur Inc PO Box 1290 225 S East St Indianapolis IN 46202-4042

HEGEL, PAMELA RENE, elementary school educator; b. Fargo, N.D., July 9, 1958; d. James and Delores (Fisher) Booke; m. Darwin George Hegel, Aug. 3, 1984. BA, Dickinson (N.D.) State U., 1989. Office mgr. Farmers Ins. Group, Dickinson, N.D., 1974-77, Kukowski Land Co., Dickinson, 1981-88; real estate agt. Joe LaDuke Real Estate, Dickinson, 1977-81; tchr. Banning (Calif.) Unified Schs., 1988-94, Palm Springs (Calif.) Sch. Dist., 1994—. Recipient cert. of appreciation Ednl. Testing Svc., 1991. Mem. Calif. Tchrs. Assn.

HEGENDERFER, JONITA SUSAN, public relations executive; b. Chgo., Mar. 18, 1944; d. Clifford Lincoln and Cornelia Anna (Larson) Hazzard; m. Gary William Hegenderfer, Mar. 12, 1971 (dec. 1978). BA, Purdue U., 1965; postgrad. Calif. State U.-Long Beach, 1966-67, Northwestern U., 1969-70. Tchr. English, Long Beach schs., Calif., 1965-68; editorial asst. Playboy Mag., Chgo., 1968-70; communications specialist Am. Med. Assn., Chgo., 1970-72; v.p. Home Data, Hinsdale, Ill., 1972-75; mktg. mgr. Olympic Savs. & Loan, Berwyn, Ill., 1975-79; sr. v.p. Golin/Harris Communications, Chgo., 1979-89; pres. JSH & A, Chgo., 1989—; bd. dirs. Chgo. Internat. Film Festival, 1989, 90. Editor directory, Fin. Info. Nat. Directory, 1972; author: Slim Guide to Spas, 1984, (video) PR Guide for Chgo. LSCs, 1991; contbr. articles to profl. jours. Co-chmn. pub. rels. com. Am. Cancer Soc., Chgo., 1984; com. mem. March of Dimes, Chgo., 1986; mem. pub. rels. com. Girl Scouts Chgo., 1989-90, mem. bd. dirs. 1994-95; bd. dirs. Greater DuPage Women's Bus. Coun., 1992-93, Girl Scouts Am. DuPage County, 1994-95; vol. ctr. adv. com. United Way, Chgo., 1990-93, mem. community svc. com. Publicity Club Chgo., 1990—. Recipient 5 Golden Trumpet awards Publicity Club Chgo., 1983, 86, 94, Silver Trumpet awards, 1984, 86, 88, Spectra awards Internat. Assn. Bus. Communicators, 1984, 85, 87, Gold Quill award, 1985, Bronze Anvil award Pub. Rels. Soc. Am., 1985. Mem. Am. Mktg. Assn., Publicity Club of Chgo., Pub. Rels. Soc. Am., Chgo. Women in Pub. Clubs: Council on Fgn. Relations, Metropilitan Womens Forum, Cinema Chgo. (bd. dirs. 1988-89). Avocations: travel, photography. Office: JSH & A Comms 1311 Butterfield Rd Ste 312 Downers Grove IL 60515-5605

HEGWOOD, ZELMA RUTH, librarian; b. Bearden, Ark., Feb. 7, 1949; d. Otis and Roberta (Throwes) Parham; m. Jerry Wayne Hegwood, Aug. 19, 1972; 1 child, Jerri Ruth. BS, So. State Coll., Magnolia, Ark., 1972. Cert. tchr. social scis., Ark. Social worker Smackover (Ark.) Sch. Dist., 1974-82, libr., 1977—. Active Girl Scouts U.S., Smackover, 1991. Democrat. Baptist. Home: PO Box 9 Smackover AR 71762-0009 Office: Smackover Elem Sch 303 W 7th St Smackover AR 71762-1703

HEIDELBERGER, KATHLEEN PATRICIA, physician; b. Bklyn., Apr. 13, 1939; d. William Cyprian and Margaret Bernadette (Hughes) H.; m. Charles William Davenport, Oct. 8, 1977. B.S. cum laude, Coll. Misericordia, 1961; M.D. cum laude, Woman's Med. Coll. Pa., 1965. Intern Mary Hitchcock Hosp., Hanover, N.H., 1965-66, resident in pathology, 1966-70; mem. faculty U. Mich., Ann Arbor, 1970—, assoc. prof. pathology, 1976-79, prof., 1979—. Mem. Am. Soc. Clin. Pathologists, U.S.-Can. Acad. Pathology, Soc. for Pediatric Pathology, Coll. Am. Pathologists. Office: U Mich Box 0054 Dept of Pathology UH 2G/332 Ann Arbor MI 48109

HEIDEMANN, MARY ANN, community planner; b. Detroit, Feb. 17, 1950; d. O.K. and Mary Elizabeth (Berry) Rodewald; m. Karl Werner, June 19, 1982; children: Heather Lisa, Karl Kristoffer. BA in Archtl. History, Reed Coll., Portland, Oreg., 1970; postgrad., U. Pa., Phila., 1972-75; MA in Pub. Adminstrn., U. Wis., 1985, PhD in Land Resources, 1989. Profl. cmty. planner, Mich. Apprentice Paolo Soleri, Architect, Scottsdale, Ariz., 1970-71; staff planner Jack McCormick & Assocs., Devon, Pa., 1972-74; natural resource planner Brown County Planning Commn., Green Bay, Wis., 1976-78; planning cons. Champ, Parish, Raasch, De Pere, Wis., 1978-80; policy analyst U.S. EPA, Chgo., 1980-81; cmty. svc. specialist Wis. Dept. Natural Resources, Madison, 1981-85; chief environ. analysis Wis. Dept. Transp., Madison, 1985-86; project mgr. Wade-Trim/Impact, Taylor, Mich., 1987-88; owner, prin. planner Mary Ann Heidemann & Assocs., Rogers City, Mich., 1988—; lectr. U. Wis., Green Bay, 1977-78; asst. prof. Kans. State U., Manhattan, 1975-76; exec. dir. East Mich. Environ. Action, West Bloomfield, 1986-87; adj. prof. Lake Superior State U., Sault Ste. Marie, 1988—; mem. planner lic. bd. Gov. State Mich., Lansing, 1990-94. Founding mem. Bay Renaissance, Green Bay, 1979-80; mem. Orion Twp. Planning Commn., Mich., 1986-87; county commr. Presque Isle County Bd., Rogers City, Mich., 1992-93; bd. dirs. Presque Isle Harbor Assocs., 1993—. Dean Webster Meml. scholar Reed Coll., Portland, Oreg., 1968-69; fellow NEH, San Diego, 1978. Mem. Am. Inst. Cert. Planners (planning exam. com. 1992), Am. Planning Assn. (lic. com.), Mich. Soc. Planning Ofcls., Harmony Choraleers, Mich. Historic Preservation Network, Presque Isle Lighthouse Assocs. Democrat. Presbyterian. Office: Mary Ann Heidemann & Assocs 150 S 3rd St Rogers City MI 49779

HEIDEN, LAURA KAY, personnel administrator; b. Sioux Falls, S.D., Dec. 18, 1967; d. Daniel Luther and Ruby Delores (Jahr) H. BS, Moorhead State U., 1990. Pers. generalist Total Bedroom, Mpls., 1991—; sales rep. JBL Trading, Inc., Prior Lake, Minn., 1992—. Vol. tchr. English and Spanish Chicanos Latinos Unidades En Sevicios, St. Paul, 1992. Home: 3533 Idaho Ave N Minneapolis MN 55427

HEIDEN, SUSAN JANE, elementary education educator; b. La Porte, Ind., Mar. 8, 1942; d. Benno Henry and Helen Frances (Rollins) Bargholz; m. Ronald William Heiden, Sept. 28, 1963; children: Gregory Scott, David Patrick, Katrina Jane. BS in EEdn., Ind. U., Bloomington, 1964; MS in Edn., Purdue U., Westville, Ind., 1976; postgrad., Ind. U., South Bend, 1989-90. lic. in real estate, Ind. Elem. tchr. La Porte Community Sch. Corp., 1964-95, parenting trainer, 1986; elem. tchr. Michigan City (Ind.) Area Schs., 1964—; bd. dirs. La Porte Fed. Credit Union, Michigan City, 1989-95, La Porte County Literacy Coalition, 1994; owner, operator pvt. tutoring svc., 1993—. Mem. adv. com. 4-H Club, La Porte, 1980-85; scholarship chair PTA. Mem. Am. Fedn. Tchrs. (ednl. rsch. and dissemination linker 1986-95), Ind. U. Alumni Assn. (Write-on Hoosiers Writing award 1994), Purdue U. Alumni Assn., Purdue North Ctrl. Alumni Assn. Home: 2065 N 100 W La Porte IN 46350-8707 Office: Hailmann Elem Sch 1001 Ohio St La Porte IN 46350-4301

HEIDIG, ELIZABETH ANNE, lawyer; b. Grand Rapids, Mich., Apr. 25, 1959; d. Eugene Michael and Betty Jane (Tobin) Skazinski; m. Edward G. Heidig II, Aug. 13, 1988. BA, Grand Valley State Coll., Allendale, Mich., 1981; JD, Thomas Cooley Law Sch., 1984. Bar: Calif. 1986, U.S. Dist. Ct. (cen. dist.) Calif. 1988. Assoc. Berris & Seton, Century City, Calif., 1985-86, Law Offices of Michael J. Rand, Encino, Calif., 1986-89; officer Sacramento Ct. Appointed Spl. Advocates, 1992—. Fellow Nat. Trust for Hist. Preservation, 1990; appointee Calif. Commn. Tchr. Credentialing. Mem. ABA. Roman Catholic.

HEIDISH, LOUISE ORIDGE-SCHWALLIE, transportation specialist, marketing professional; b. Cin., May 21, 1938; d. Leslie Jacob and Louise (Oridge) Schwallie; m. William Edward Heidish, Sept. 2, 1961; children: Sara Louise, Amy Jean. BA in History, Denison U., 1960; MA in History, Miami U., Oxford, Ohio, 1962; MS in Urban Studies, Ala. A&M U., 1994. Secondary tchr. Fox Chapel Sch. Dist., Pitts., 1962-69; part-time instr. U. Ala., Huntsville, 1976-78; substitute history tchr. City of Huntsville Schs., 1977-79; dir. comm. svcs. Heidish Enterprises, Huntsville, 1979-83; transp. specialist City of Huntsville, 1981—; regional 5 state coord. AAUW and NEH, Huntsville, 1981-83. Author: Biography: Alexander Long 1816-86, 1962, Marketing Ride Sharing, 1994. Mem., project chair Huntsville Symphony Orch. Guild, 1974—; pres., v.p., bd. dirs. Huntsville-Mad. Co. Sr. Ctr., 1980-86; pres., bd. dirs. Huntsville High Sch. PTA, 1983-88; com. chmn. Panoply of the Arts Festival, Huntsville, 1985-87. Mem. AAUW (local pres., v.p., state v.p. 1970—), Pub. Rels. Coun. No. Ala. (newsletter editor 1989—), Assn. for Commuter Transp. (conf. chair 1987—), Kappa Kappa Gamma (alumnae officer, local pres., regional officer 1958—). Presbyterian. Office: Pub Transp City Huntsville 100 Church St Huntsville AL 35801

HEIDLAGE, KATHARINE SANDERSON, lawyer; b. Geneva, N.Y., Mar. 16, 1951; d. Francis Thayer and Adele Julie (Owens) Sanderson; m. Richard Clemens Heidlage, May 31, 1975; children: Benjamin Frederick, Charles Jackson, William Richard. AB, Smith Coll., 1973; JD, Boston U., 1978, LLM in Taxation, 1983. Bar: Mass. 1978, U.S. Dist. Ct. (1st cir.) 1979, U.S. Tax Ct. 1979, U.S. Ct. Appeals (1st cir.) 1979. Assoc. Gaston & Snow and predecessor firms, Boston, 1978-82, Peabody & Brown, Boston, 1982-85; gen. counsel, mng. dir., v.p. New England Funds L.P., Boston, 1982-92, 1988—. Bd. dirs. Underwood After Sch. Program, Inc., 1990-94. Mem. ABA, Mass. Bar Assn., Boston Bar Assn., Mass. Women's Bar Assn. Democrat. Episcopalian. Office: New England Funds L P 399 Boylston St Boston MA 02116-3305

HEIDLER, CECILE E., public health nurse; b. Cleve.; d. James Joseph and Anna (Novak) H. Diploma, Mercy Coll., Detroit, 1944; BSN, Western Res. U., 1951; MSN, Wayne U., 1955; MPH, U. Mich., 1961. RN, Fla., Ohio. Dir. nursing Maria Manor Health Care, St. Petersburg, Fla.; coll. nurse, instr., counselor St. John Coll., Cleve.; staff instr., supr. Div. Health City of Cleve.; staff nurse Little Sisters of the Poor, Cleve.; ret.; prefect, lay consultor Secular Franciscan Order. Bd. dirs., mem. coms. ARC; mem. Five Towns Women's Club, Gt. Lakes Club, Choristers, Sr. Care and Seniority orgns.; hospice vol. Fed. Nurse Traineeship U. Mich. Mem. Am. Assn. Ret. Persons, Ohio Nurses Assn. (Greater Cleve. dist.), Cleve. Diocesan Coun. Cath. Nurses (pres.), Wayne State U. Nurse Scholars Soc., Holy Cross Cath. Women's Club.

HEIDT-DUNWELL, DEBRA SUE, vocational education educator; b. Liberty, N.Y., Oct. 28, 1952; d. Charles William and Lillian Lorraine (Ball) H. AA, Sullivan County Community Coll., Lock Sheldrake, N.Y., 1972; BS, SUNY, Oneonta, 1974, MS in Edn., 1979. Cert. permanent math. tchr., provisional elem. tchr., N.Y. High sch. tchr. math. Downsville (N.Y.) Cen. Sch., Oneonta Cen. Sch.; tutor Sullivan County Community Coll.; cons. tchr. related skills for vocat. programs Sullivan County Vocat.-Tech. Ctr., Liberty; conf. presenter in field; rschr. Hudson Valley Faculty Portfolio Assessment. Contbr. poetry to various publs. Recipient Golden Poet award World of Poetry Press, 1986-91. Mem. ASCD, AAUW, AMTNYS, AMS, SSMA, Sullivan Reading Coun., Nat. Coun. Tchrs. Math., Am. Vocat. Assn., Nat. Coun. Tchrs. English, Internat. Reading Assn., Am. Poetry Assn. (Poet of Merit award 1989), Kappa Delta Pi., Delta Kappa Gamma (Tau chpt).

HEIFETZ, SONIA, retired pharmacist; b. Rowne, Poland; came to U.S., 1929, naturalized, 1934; d. Zise and Toiba (Ehrlich) Heifetz. PhG, Temple U., 1933. Asst. chief pharmacist Grad. Hosp. U. Pa., Phila., 1937-49, dir. pharmacy svcs., 1949-77; formerly pharmacist-mgr. Rite-Aide Corp., now ret. Cert. tchr. of Russian, Phila. Bd. of Edn. div. sch. extension; asst. dir. pharmacy Eastern State Sch. and Hosp., Trevose, Pa., 1982—. Mem. AAUW, Am. Soc. Hosp. Pharmacists, Del. Soc. Hosp. Pharmacists (hon.), Pa. Soc. Hosp. Pharmacists (hon.), Phila. Guild Hosp. Pharmacists (v.p. 1966, treas. 1967-77). Home: 2665 Willits Rd Apt 324 Philadelphia PA 19114-3470

HEIGHT, DOROTHY EPHRATES, insurance company executive; b. Albion, Mich., Feb. 23, 1950; d. Woodrow and Lillie Bell (Simpson) Wilson; m. Elbert L. Gibson, Aug. 6, 1968 (div. 1984); children: Illya, Erika; m. Jim F. Height. AA, Kellog's Community Coll., 1982; BA, Eastern Mich. U., 1985; MBA, Nazareth Coll., 1992. Sr. agy. adminstrn. specialist IV State Farm Ins. Co., Marshall, Mich., 1971-84, supr. II, 1984-88, supr. III, sr. agy. adminstrn. specialist, 1988—. Speaker Call Someone Concern, Inc., Albion, 1985-86; chmn. State Farm campaign United Way, 1988, active bd. of Greater Battle Creek; vol. Black History program Albion Pub. Schs., 1987; chmn. hospitality com. Albion Community Theater, 1981-84; mem. Table for Black Women, Battle Creek, Mich., 1985; grad. Project Blueprint, 1989; active Mid County Consortium Exec. Bd.; bd. dirs. Family & Children Svc., 1992—, Battle Creek Focus Group, 1991—. Scholar Am. Bus. Women Assn., 1984, Miller Found., 1982, Eastern Star, 1982; recipient Nat. Stephen Buffon award Am. Bus. Women Assn., 1985, Ambassador award YWCA, 1993. Mem. NAACP (bd. dirs. 1985-86, post v.p.), NAFE, Sch. Social Work Assn., Nat. Mgmt. Assn. (bd. dirs. 1988), Urban League (bd. dirs. 1990-91, trustee 1991-92). Democrat. Baptist.

HEIGHT, DOROTHY I., association executive. Mem. nat. staff YWCA of the U.S.A., 33 yrs. Pres. Nat. Coun. Negro Women, 1957—; hon. mem. nat. bd. dirs. YWCA of the U.S.A. Recipient Ambassador award YWCA of the U.S.A., 1993. Home: 10 Waterside Plz New York NY 10010-2602

HEIL, MARY RUTH, former counselor; b. Westerville, Ohio, June 8, 1921; d. George Walter and Bertha Ellen (Shrodes) H. BS in Edn., Ohio State U., 1944; MEd, Wayne State U., 1956; cert. advanced study, Western Carolina U., 1987; cert. theol. edn., U. South, 1987. Cert. counselor, tchr., Ohio, Ky., Mich., Fla., N.C. Tchr. 7th grade Cheshire (Ohio) Sch., 1942-43; tchr. biology, English Ohio Soldiers' and Sailors' Orphans' Home, Xenia, 1943-47; tchr. 7th grade Lakeview High Schs., Winter Garden, Fla., 1947-48; tchr. English, journalism Pine Mountain (Ky.) Settlement Sch., 1948-49; field and established camp dir. Columbus (Ohio) and Franklin County Girl Scouts, 1949-50; tchr. Mary Lyon Jr. High Sch., Royal Oak, Mich., 1950-56, 57-62, Coston Secondary Modern Girls' Sch., Greenford, Middlesex, Eng., 1956-57; tchr. English West Henderson High Sch., Hendersonville, N.C., 1962-65, guidance counselor, 1965-86. Chmn. Mayor's Com. Employment of Handicapped, Hendersonville, 1972-74; v.p. Mountain Ramparts Health Planning Bd., Asheville, N.C., 1972-76, Western Carolina Health Systems Agy. Bd., Morganton, N.C., 1976-82; bd. dirs., sec., com. chmn., Henderson County Disput Settlement Bd., 1989—; exec. com., bd. dirs. Western Carolina Presbyn. Retirement Com., 1987—; active Henderson County Coun. Women, Hendersonville, 1994—, treas.; mem.-at-large Pisgah coun. Girl Scouts U.S., 1994—. Named Civitan Citizen of Yr. Civitan Club, Hendersonville, 1986, Woman of Achievement Hendersonville, Bus. and Profl. Women's Club, 1978; recipient award Galludet U., Washington, 1986; named to Hon., Order Ky. Cols., 1988. Mem. NEA, ACA, Royal Oak Edn. Assn. (pres. 1954-56), N.C. Assn. Educators (pres. dist. 1970-72), Henderson County Mental Health Assn. (bd. dirs. 1965-74), Alpha Delta Kappa (N.C. 1st v.p. 1978-80, state pres. 1980-82, S.E. region grand v.p. 1987-89). Democrat. Episcopalian. Home: RR 6 Box 137 Hendersonville NC 28792-9428

HEILBRUN, CAROLYN GOLD, English literature educator; b. East Orange, N.J., Jan. 13, 1926; d. Archibald and Estelle (Roemer) Gold; m. James Heilbrun, Feb. 20, 1945; children: Emily, Margaret, Robert. B.A., Wellesley Coll., 1947; M.A., Columbia U., 1951, Ph.D., 1959; D.H.L. (hon.), U. Pa., 1984, Bucknell U., 1985, Russell Sage Coll., 1987, Smith Coll., 1989, Berea Coll., 1991, New Sch. for Social Rsch., 1993, Lewis & Clark Coll., 1993; D.F.A. (hon.), Rivier Coll., 1986; DHL, Lewis and Clark U., 1993; DFA, U. St. Thomas, 1994. Instr. Bklyn. Coll., 1959-60; instr. Columbia U., N.Y.C., 1960-62, asst. prof., 1962-67, assoc. prof., 1967-72, prof. English lit., 1972—; Avalon Found. prof. humanities Columbia U., 1986-93; prof. emerita Columbia U., N.Y.C., 1986-93; vis. prof. U. Calif., Santa Cruz, 1979, Princeton U., N.J., 1981, Yale Law Sch., 1989. Author: The Garnett Family, 1961, Christopher Isherwood, 1970, Towards Androggyny, 1973, Reinventing Womanhood, 1979, Writing a Woman's Life, 1988, Hamlet's Mother and Other Women, 1990, The Education of a Woman: The Life & Times of Gloria Steinem, 1995; 11 novels as Amanda Cross, 1964 (recipient Nero Wolfe award 1981—. Guggenheim fellow, 1966; Rockefeller fellow, 1976; Sr. Rsch. fellow NEH, 1983; recipient Alumnae Achievement award Wellesley Coll., 1984, award of excellence Grad. Faculty of Columbia Alumni, 1984. Mem. MLA (pres. 1984), Mystery Writers Am. (exec. bd. 1982-84), Phi Beta Kappa.

HEILEMAN, SANDRA MARIE, oncological nurse, educator; b. Chgo., Jan. 28, 1959; d. Stanley Vincent and Angeline Sajkiewicz; m. Robert James Heileman. BS, Rush U., 1988, MS, 1989; postgrad., U. Ill., Chgo., 1992—. RN, Ill.; cert. BLS instr. Am. Heart Assn.; cert. oncology nurse. Acct., comptr. McKinsey Steel Co., Inc., Forest Park, Ill., 1976-79; exec. dir. Adolescent Youth Svcs., Village of Stone Park, Ill., 1979-81; coord. Midwest Therapeutic Assocs., Morton Grove, Ill., 1981-83, adminstr., 1983-86; in-outpatient oncology nurse Rush North Shore Med. Ctr., Skokie, Ill., 1988-89; oncology resource nurse West Suburban Hosp. Med. Ctr., Oak Park, Ill., 1989-90; oncology clin. nurse specialist Holy Family Hosp., Des Plaines, Ill., 1990-92; oncology clin. specialist, dir. autologous transplant program N.W. Oncology, Hematology S. C., Elk Grove Village, Ill., 1992—; asst. prof. Wright Coll., Chgo., 1990—; mem. profl. adv. bd. Rainbow Hospice, Park Ridge, Ill., 1990-93; profl. educator Ill. Cancer Pain Initiative, N.W. Suburban Cook County, Ill., 1991—. Author: (ednl. program) AIDS-Facts & Myth, 1988, (audio cassettes-patient edn.) Chemo-Induced Sequelae, 1989. Bd. dirs. Am. Cancer Soc. Unit 113, 1992—. Rush U. scholar, 1987-88; recipient Luther Christman award and scholarship Rush U./Rush Presbyn. St. Lukes Med. Ctr., 1988, Excellence in Gerontol Nursing award, 1988, Spl. Project award, 1988. Mem. Oncology Nursing Soc., Am. Cancer Soc. (mem. nurses ednl. com. 1990—, profl. educator 1990—, Grad. scholar 1988-89, bd. dirs. unit 113 1992—), Soc. Otolaryngology and Head-Neck Nurses (treas. 1990-93, legis com. 1991, editor newsletter 1991), Gamma Phi chpt. Sigma Theta Tau. Republican. Roman Catholic. Home: 267 Butternut Ln Streamwood IL 60107 Office: N W Oncology Hematology S C N Pavillion Ste 120 820 Biesterfield Rd Elk Grove Village IL 60007

HEILIGER, BETTY YVONNE, school system administrator; b. Kearney, Nebr., Mar. 30, 1940; d. Merl Edward Sheldon and Margaret Irma Sheldon Campbell; m. Duane Phillip Heiliger, Sept. 6, 1959; children: David Duane, Randall Kent. BA in Elem. Edn., Kearney State Coll., 1973, MA in Elem. Edn., 1983; MA in Edn. Adminstrn., Kearney State U. (formerly Coll.), 1986. Elem. tchr. Kearney Pub. Sch., 1973-88, elem. prin., 1988-90, dir. personnel, 1990-93, supr. nurses, ADA coord., 1990—. Recipient Christa McAuliffe prize 1986, Scottish Rite Masons award 1987; Pratt-Heinz scholar Pratt-Heinz Found. Meml., 1987. Mem. NEA, Am. Assn. Sch. Personnel Adminstrs., Nebr. State Edn. Assn., Kearney Edn. Assn. Republican. Lutheran. Home: 911 W 33rd St Kearney NE 68847-3362 Office: Kearney Pub Sch 310 W 24th St Kearney NE 68847-5355

HEIM, KATHRYN MARIE, geropsychiatric nurse, author; b. Milw., Sept. 29, 1952; d. Lester Sheldon Wilcox and Laura Dora (Corpie) Wilcox Sears; m. Vincent Robert Gouthro, June 30, 1970 (div. 1976); 1 child, Robert Vincent; m. George John Heim, Sept. 17, 1977 (div. 1988). AS in Nursing, Milw. Area Tech. Coll., 1983; BS in Nursing, NYU, 1986; MS in Mgmt., Cardinal Stritch Coll., 1988; postgrad., Newport U., 1989—. Cert. psychiatric and mental health nurse, AMA. Staff geriatric nurse Clement Manor, Greenfield, Wis., 1983; nurse, health educator Milw. Boys Club, 1983-84; nurse mgr. Milw. County Mental Health Complex, Milw., 1984—, mem. gero-psychiat. inpatient adv. com., 1986-87; RN Psychiat. Acute Care Day Hosp., 1992—; mem. nursing rsch. com. Milwaukee County Mental Health Complex, 1986—; research on loneliness as it relates to mental health, 1989-92. Mem. wellness task force Milw. County Mental Health Complex, 1988-89, chairperson sensory deficit com. Geropsychiatry, 1989-90; active Boy Scouts Am., Milw., 1978-80. Mem. ANA (cert. gerontol. nurse), NAFE (network dir. Milw. chpt. 1982-92), Wis. Nurses Assn., NYU Alumni Assn., Cardinal Stritch Alumni Assn. (class rep. 1986-88), Milw. Area Tech. Coll. Alumni Assn. Home: 351 N 62d St Milwaukee WI 53213 Office: Milw County Mental Health 9455 W Watertown Plank Rd Milwaukee WI 53226-4805

HEIM, MARCY LYNN SCHULTZ, foundation executive; b. Theresa, Wis., Nov. 15, 1957; d. Robert Julius and Irene Laura (Wecker) Schultz; m. Kenneth J. Heim; stepchildren: Carly, Elliott; 1 child, Robert James. BS in Natural Scis. with distinction, U. Wis., 1979. Exec. asst. Wis. Phys. Therapy Svcs., Madison, 1975-80; dir. pub. rels. Wis. DHI Coop., Madison, 1980-83; dir. devel. U. Wis. Found., Madison, 1983—; lead singer Marcy & The Highlights, 1980—; cons. Marks Entertainment and Pub. Rels., 1985—. Vol. United Way of Dane County, 1987, Salvation Army, 1990—. Mem. Nat. Agriculture Alumni and Devel. Assn. (bd. dirs. 1994—, mem. edn. com. 1992-94, chair edn. com. 1994-95), Nat. Agriculture Mktg. Assn., Pub. Rels. Soc. Am., Assn. Women Bus. Coalition (bd. dirs. 1988-91), Women in Comm. Inc. (bd. dirs. 1988-91, pres. Madison chpt. 1990-91), Downtown Madison Kiwanis (chairperson/co-chairperson agriculture conservation and environ. com. 1991—), Alpha Zeta. Republican. Lutheran. Home: 471 Presidential Ln Madison WI 53711-1129 Office: U Wis Found 1848 University Ave PO Box 8860 Madison WI 53708-8860

HEIM, TONYA SUE, nurse, small business owner; b. Huntingburg, Ind., Nov. 9, 1948; d. Harold William and Marjorie Elouise (Buse) Rothert; m. James Frederick Heim, Sept. 6, 1969; children: Brian Christopher, Andrea Christine. Diploma, Deaconness Sch. Nursing, Evansville, Ind., 1969. RN, Ind. Oper. rm. staff nurse St. Joseph's Hosp., Huntingburg, 1969-71, emergency rm. staff nurse, 1969-71, staff nurse obstetrics dept., 1971-73, supr. obstetrics dept., 1973-85, dir. obstetrics oper. rm., 1985-88, dir. nursing, 1988-89, dir. obstetrics, oper. rm., infection control sterilizing, 1989—; owner, operator Holland (Ind.) Toning and Tanning Ctr., 1987—; co-owner Heim Hardware, 1989—. Instr., trainer ARC So. Ind., 1970—; chmn. health profl. adv. com., mem. exec. com. So. Ind./Ill. chpt. March of Dimes, 1978—; v.p., chmn. program com., bd. dirs. So. Hills Counseling Ctr., Jasper, Ind., 1988—; event coord. Hoosiers for Safety Belts, Dale, Ind., 1987; troop co-leader Girl Scouts Am., Holland, 1986-88; active Southridge Band Boosters, Huntingburg, 1986-91; mem. AIDS coun. S.W. Dubois County Sch. Corp., 1988—; mem. adv. coun. Prenatal Substance Use Prevention Program, 1989-93; mem. HIV prevention community planning com., Ind. State Dept. Health, 1994—; chmn. schs. com., chmn. Midwest AIDS Tng. and Edn. Ctr. com., founding co-chmn. Dubois County AIDS Community Action Group, Huntingburg, 1991—; mem. S.W. Dubois County Sch. Bd., 1992—, pres., 1995; active March of Dimes, 1978-90. Mem. ANA (bd. dirs.), NAACOG, Ind. Coun. Nurse Mgrs., Assn. for Practitioners in Infection Control (Amelia K. Sloan lectureship Ind. 1992), Assn. Oper. Rm. Nurses, Huntingburg C. of C., Beta Sigma Phi (v.p.). Republican. Lutheran. Home: PO Box 88 403 2nd Ave Holland IN 47541-9757 Office: St Josephs Hosp 1204 E 6th St Huntingburg IN 47542-9375

HEIMAN, DEBORAH REID, medical legal consultant, rehabilitation consultant; b. Sharon, Pa., June 25, 1950; d. Harold and Jo Anne (Offie) Reid; m. Ronald T. Heiman, July 24, 1994. Student, Youngstown (Ohio) State U., 1969, Edinboro (Pa.) State U., 1974; diploma, Jameson Meml. Hosp., New Castle, Pa., 1981; BSN, Pa. State U., 1990. Cert. in med.-legal issues. Coord. ambulatory surgery Shenango Valley Med. Ctr., Farrell, Pa., 1981-90; owner, mgr. Med. Legal Cons., 1989—.

HEIMANN, JANET BARBARA, trail consultant; b. Santa Cruz, Calif., Dec. 18, 1931; d. John Louis and Charlotte Lucina (Burns) Grinnell; m. Richard Frank Gustav, July 10, 1953; children: David Robert, Gary Alan, Kathleen Janet. BS, U. Calif., Berkeley, 1954. Vol. trail rschr. Monterey County Pks. Dept.; appointee Carmel Valley Trail Adv. Com., 1993—. Pres. Folsom Freedom Trails, Placer County, Calif., 1980-83; chmn. Adopt-a-Trail, Folsom Lake Trail Patrol, Placer County, 1986-88; bd. dirs. Loomis Basin Horseman Assn., Placer County, 186-87. Mem. AAUW. Republican. Home and Office: 11565 Mccarthy Rd Carmel Valley CA 93924-9239

HEIMANN-HAST, SYBIL DOROTHEA, language arts and literature educator; b. Shanghai, People's Republic of China, May 8, 1924; came to U.S., 1941; d. Paul Heinrich and Elisabeth (Halle) Heimann; m. David G. Hast, Jan. 11, 1948 (div. 1959); children: Thomas David Hast, Dorothea Elizabeth Hast-Scott. BA in French, Smith Coll., 1946; MA in French Lang. and Lit., U. Pitts., 1963; MA in German Lang. and Lit., UCLA, 1966; diploma in Spanish, U. Barcelona, Spain, 1972. Cert. German, French and Spanish tchr., Calif. Assoc. in German lang. UCLA, 1966-70; asst. prof. German Calif. State U., L.A., 1970-71; lectr. German Mt. St, Mary's Coll., Brentwood, Calif., 1974-75; instr. French and German, diction coach Calif. Inst. of Arts, Valencia, 1977-78; coach lang. and diction UCLA Opera Theater, 1973-93, emeritus, 1993—, lectr. dept. music, 1980-93; interviewer, researcher oral history program UCLA, 1986-93; dir., founder ISTMO, Santa Monica, Calif., 1975—; cons. interpreter/translator L.A. Music Ctr., U.S. Supreme Ct., L.A., J. Paul Getty Mus., Malibu, Calif., Warner New Media, Panorama Internat. Prodn., Sony Records, 1986—; voice-over artist; founder, dir. Westside Opera Workshop, Santa Monica, Calif., 1987—. Author of poems. UCLA grantee, 1990-91. Mem. AAUP, AFTRA, MLA, SAG, Sunset Succulent Soc. (v.p., bd. dirs., reporter, annual show chmn.), German Am. C. of C., L.A. Home and Office: 1022 17th St Apt 7 Santa Monica CA 90403-4339

HEIMBOLD, MARGARET BYRNE, publisher, educator, consultant; b. Tullamore, Ireland, June 24; came to U.S., 1966, naturalized, 1973; d. John Christopher and Anne (Troy) Byrne; m. Arthur Heimbold, Feb. 26, 1984; 1 child, Eric Thomas Gordon. BA, Queens Coll. Recipient cert. Dale Carnegie, 1977, Psychol. Corp. Am., 1981, Wharton Sch., 1983, Stanford U., 1989. Group advt. mgr. N.Y. Times, N.Y.C., 1978-85; pub. Am. Film, Washington, 1985-86, v.p., pub. Nat. Trust for Hist. Preservation, Washington, 1986-90; pres. Summerville Press, Inc., Washington, 1990—; pub. Metro Golf, 1992—; advisor Mag. Pubs. Bd. dirs. Anchor Ctrs. Ireland; bd. trustees Nat. Mus. Women in Arts. Mem. NAFE, Am. Soc. Assn. Execs., Women's Econ. Alliance, Soc. Nat. Assn. Publs. (chmn. editl. com., bd. dirs.), D.C. Preservation League. Avocations: golf, writing, volunteering.

HEIMBURGER, ELIZABETH MORGAN, psychiatrist; b. Atlanta, Apr. 23, 1932; d. Henry Durand and Lillian Elizabeth (Palmour) Morgan; div.; children: Elizabeth Morgan Whitaker, Homer Aggie Whitaker III, Margaret Diane Heimburger, Richard Ames Heimburger Jr., Katherine Durand Heimburger. BS, Ga. State U., 1963; MD, Med. Coll. Ga., 1967. Diplomate Am. Bd. Psychiatry and Neurology. Intern in internal medicine Med. Coll. Ga., Augusta, 1967-68, resident in gen. psychiatry, 1968-70; fellow in child and adolescent psychiatry U. Tex., Galveston, 1970-72; asst. prof. dept. psychiatry U. Tex. Med. Br., Galveston, 1972-73, assoc. prof., dir. residency tng., 1980-87; asst. prof., assoc. prof., dir. psychosomatic svcs. U. Mo. Sch. Medicine, Columbia, 1973-80, clin. assoc. prof. dept. psychiatry, 1987—; pvt. practice specializing in adolescent psychiatry Columbia, 1987—; examiner Am. Bd. Psychiatry and Neurology, Chgo., 1977—; specialist, site visitor residency rev. Coun. Grad. Med. Edn., Washington, 1983—; exec. bd. Am. Assn. Dirs. Psychiat. Residency Tng., 1982-90; exec. coun. Tex. Psychiat. Soc., Austin, 1983-86; dir. confs., workshops on orgnl. and group dynamics. Editorial cons. bd. Am. Psychiat. Assn. Press., Inc., Washington,1 987-90; contbr. articles, scholarly papers to profl. publs. Bd. dirs. Mental Health Assn., Galveston, 1984-87, YMCA, Columbia, 1987-89. Grantee NIMH, 1978-80, 80-83. Fellow Am. Psychiat. Assn.; mem. Am. Soc. Adolescent Psychiatry, Am. Assn. Child and Adolescent Psychiatry (com. mem.), A.K. Rice Inst. (bd. dirs. 1979-85, pres. Cen. States Ctr. 1979-88, bd. dirs. 1979—), Am. Horticulture Soc., Am. Orchid Assn. Episcopalian. Home: 814 Hulen Dr Columbia MO 65203-1472 Office: 814 Hulen Dr Columbia MO 65203-1472

HEIN, KAREN KRAMER, pediatrician, epidemiologist; b. N.Y.C., Feb. 2, 1944; d. Irving W. and Ruth (Eisenberg) Kramer: m. Ralph Deil, Aug. 28, 1983; children: Ethan, Molly. BA, U. Wis., 1966; B of Med. Sci., Dartmouth Med. Sch., 1968; MD, Columbia U., 1970. Intern Bronx Mcpl. Hosp., Bronx (N.Y.) Mcpl. Hosp. Ctr., 1970; resident Bronx (N.Y.) Mcpl. Hosp. Ctr., Bronx, 1971-73; dir. adolescent AIDS program Montefiore Med. Ctr., N.Y.C., 1987-94; prof. pediatrics Albert Einstein Coll. Medicine, N.Y.C., 1991—, prof. epidemiology and social medicine, 1993—; exec. officer Inst. of Medicine, Nat. Acad. of Scis., Washington, 1995—; cons. N.Y.C. Dept. Health, 1980-85, N.Y.C. Bd. Edn., 1987-93; bd. dirs. Dartmouth Med. Sch., Hanover, N.Y. Author: AIDS: Trading Fears for Facts Consumer Reports Books, 1989; contbr. articles to profl. jours. Named Outstanding Physician, Dept. Health and Human Svcs., 1989, Adminstrs. Citation award, 1993. Fellow Am. Bd. Pediatrics; mem. Am. Pediatric Soc., Soc. for Pediatric Rsch., Am. Acad. Pediatrics, Soc. for Adolescent Medicine (pres. 1992-93). Office: Inst Medicine Nat Acad Sci 2101 Constitution Ave NW Washington DC 20418

HEINE, MARISA ANN, financial communications consultant; b. Caracas, Venezuela, July 10, 1965; d. David Lee Heine and Lowelle Lou (Trexler) Schaefer. BA in History, Coll. of Charleston, 1987; postgrad., NYU, 1993. Sales and mktg. assoc. Prudential Securities, Inc., N.Y.C., 1987-89; media rels. asst. Kidder, Peabody & Co., N.Y.C., 1989-90; v.p. D.F. King & Co., Inc., N.Y.C., 1990—. Vol. Children's Aid Soc., N.Y.C., 1988-90, United Meth. Ch.-Homeless Feeding Program, N.Y.C., 1992, God's Love We Deliver, 1994. Mem. Nat. Investor Rels. Inst., Pub. Rels. Soc. Am. Episcopalian. Office: DK King & Co Inc 77 Water St Fl 20 New York NY 10005-4401

HEINEMANN, KATHERINE (KAKI HEINEMANN), author; b. St. Louis; d. Herbert N. and Elsa S. (Straus) Arnstein; BS, Washington U., St. Louis, 1950, MA (Arts and Scis. Faculty award 1950), 1956; m. Morton D. May, 1937; children: David A., Philip F.; m. Sol Heinemann, July 8, 1950; 1 child, Kate Heinemann Taucher. Freelance writer, poet, 1960—; prof. English, U. Tex., El Paso, 1968-74; condr. poetry readings, workshops, 1968—; mem. El Paso Art Resources Dept. Bd., 1980-81; author: Brandings, 1968; Some Inhuman Familiars, 1983; taping for Poetry Collection of Library of Congress, 1982. Mem. PEN, Nat. Soc. Arts and Letters. Clubs: Coronado Country, El Paso Tennis, Sunset Heights Garden. Home: 4252 Ridgecrest Dr El Paso TX 79902-1381

HEINES, MOLLY KATHLEEN, lawyer; b. Bklyn., July 29, 1953; d. William Joseph and Muriel Rita (Brown) H.; m. Thomas Joseph Moloney, Dec. 26, 1976. BA, Barnard Coll., 1975; JD, Columbia U., 1978. Bar: N.Y. 1979, U.S. Dist. Ct. (so. and ea. dists.) N.Y. 1979. Assoc. Simpson, Thacher & Bartlett, N.Y.C., 1978-83; assoc. counsel The Equitable Life Assurance Soc. of U.S., N.Y.C., 1983-85, asst. gen. counsel, 1985-88, v.p. and counsel, 1988-90; sec. The Equitable Cos. Inc., N.Y.C., 1991—, v.p., 1992—. Democrat. Roman Catholic. Office: The Equitable Cos Inc 787 7th Ave # 37N New York NY 10019-6018

HEINRICH, BONNIE, state legislator; m. Willis Heinrich; 1 child. Student, Valley City (N.D.) State Coll. Writer, polit. cons.; mem. N.D. State Senate. Chmn. Dem. Com. dist. 32, N.D. Office: Senate House State Capitol Bismarck ND 58505*

HEINRICHS, MARY ANN, former dean; b. Toledo, Mar. 28, 1930; m. Paul Warren Heinrichs, Jan. 26, 1952; children: Paul, John, Nancy, James. PhD, U. Toledo, 1973. Prof. English, U. Toledo, Ohio, 1965-77, dean, 1977-93; prof. emeritus Coll. Edn. Contbr. articles to profl. jours. Mem. Community Planning Coun. Rsch. Project Employed Women, Ohio, 1982-84; mem. Coun. Family Violence, Toledo, 1981—; com. chmn. St. Joseph Sch. Bd., Toledo, 1976-79. Recipient Outstanding Scholarship award U. Toledo, 1965; AAUW scholar, 1984, Humanities scholar, 1987—; named One of Foremost Women 20th Century, 1987, Outstanding Woman U. Toledo, 1991; inducted into Notre Dame Acad. Hall of Fame, 1991. Mem. AAUW (corp. rep. 1978-84), Internat. Tech. Communications Soc. (chmn. 1979-80), Zonta, Pi Lambda Theta (chpt. pres. and del. 1974-76), Phi Kappa Phi (chpt. pres. and del. 1969). Roman Catholic. Avocations: hiking, travel, music. Office: U Toledo 2801 W Bancroft St Toledo OH 43606-3328

HEINTZ, CAROLINEA CABANISS, retired home economics educator; b. Roanoke, Va., Jan. 19, 1920; d. Luther Bertie and Emblyn Bird (Jennings) Cabaniss; m. Howard Elmer Smith, Dec. 19, 1942 (div. Aug. 1975); children: Emblyn Davis, Cynthia Shannon, Cheryl Peterson, Melyssa Sexton; m. Raymond Walter Heintz, May 21, 1977; 1 stepchild, James. BS in Home Econ. Edn., U. Ala., Tuscaloosa, 1941; vocat. home econ. degree, Montevallo Coll., 1941. Cert. vocat. home econs. tchr. Swimming instr. Camp Mudjekeewis, Centerlovel, Maine, summer 1940; home econs. tchr. Roanoke Pub. Schs., 1941-43; dietitian U. Va., Charlottesville, 1943; nutrition edn. specialist Liberty Health Ctr. Svcs., Liberty Center, Ohio, 1974-80; home economist Dayton Hudson Dept. Store, Toledo, 1980-84; splty . food instr., continuing edn. U. Toledo, 1984-85; pres., mem. Greater Toledo Nutrition Coun., 1966-92, 94-95. Speaker United Way, Toledo, 1965-90; founder, pres. Mobile Meals Toledo, Inc., 1968-71, mem. adv. bd., 1988-94, 95; affiliate mem. Arts Commn., Toledo, 1976-77; chmn. Sapphire Ball, Toledo Symphony Orch., Toledo Opera, 1978; adminstrv. coord. feed Your Neighbor program Met. Chs. United, Toledo, 1979-86; deacon Collingwood Presbyn. Ch., 1969-71, elder, 1972-74, 77-79, trustee, 1984-86, elder, clk. of session, 1991-94; mem. steering com. Interfaith Hospitality Network, 1992-94, bd. dirs., 1993-94; alt. del. Gen. Assembly Presbyn. Ch. U.S.A., 1993, del.-commr., 1994. Recipient Woman of Toledo award St. Vincent Hosp. and Med. Ctr. Guild, 1967, 80, Outstanding Community Svc. award United Way, 1987. Mem. AAUW (bd. dirs. 1974-76, 94-95, chmn. mem. gourmet group 1972-80, 92-95, edn. found. chmn. 1994-95, book sale chmn.), Ohio Med. Aux. (1st v.p. 1973-74), Aux. Acad. Medicine (pres. 1967-68, chmn. med. gourmet group 1966, 92-94, 95, Health Care award 1974), Sigma Kappa (various alumni offices). Republican. Home: 3407 Bentley Blvd Toledo OH 43606-2860

HEINTZ, SUSAN JANE, government official; b. Kalamazoo, Oct. 30, 1947; d. Bert and Wilma (Koets) Vande Vusse; divorced; children: Julie, Jim. Degree in polit. sci., U. Mich., 1980. Clk. Northville (Mich.) Twp., 1980-84, supr., 1984-87; commr. Wayne County, 1987-91; dir. gov.'s S.E. Mich. office State of Mich., Detroit, 1991—; exec. dir. Conf. Western Wayne County, Mich., 1982-84; ex-officio Southwestern Mich. Coun. Govt., Detroit, 1984—. Vol. Mich. Reps., Lansing, 1973—; mem. Rep. Women's Forum, Oakland County, 1986—; mem. alumni bd. dirs. U. Mich., Dearborn, 1993-96. Recipient Young Polit. Leader of Yr. award Gov. State of Mich., 1987. Mem. Detroit Econ. Club, Detroit Women's Econ. Club, U. Mich. Club. Presbyterian. Office: State of Mich Office Gov 1200 6th St 20th Fl Detroit MI 48226

HEISE, MARILYN BEARDSLEY, public relations company executive; b. Cedar Rapids, Iowa, Feb. 26, 1935; d. Lee Roy and Angeline Myrtle (Knudson) Beardsley; m. John W. Heise, July 9, 1960; children: William Earnshaw, Steven James, Kathryn Kay Heise Benninghoff. BA, Drake U., 1957. Account exec. The Beveridge Orgn., Chgo., 1958-60; editor, pub. The Working Craftsman mag., Northbrook, Ill., 1971-78; columnist Chgo. Sun-Times, 1973-78; pres. Craft Books, Inc., Northbrook, 1978-84; v.p. Sheila King Pub. Rels., Chgo., 1984-87, Aaron D. Cushman, Inc., Chgo., 1987-88; pres. Creative Cons. Assocs., Inc., Glencoe, Ill., 1989—, Charity Cards, 1991—; mem. adv. panel Nat. Crafts Project, Ft. Collins, Colo., 1977; mem. adv. panel and com. Nat. Endowment for Arts, Washington, 1977; mem. adv. bd. The Crafts Report, Seattle, 1978-86. Recipient achievement award Women in Mgmt., 1978. Mem. Pub. Rels. Soc. Am. (accredited). Office: Creative Cons Assocs Inc 854 Grove St Glencoe IL 60022

HEISEN, JOANN HEFFERNAN, health care company executive; b. Silver Spring, Md., Jan. 25, 1950; d. Milton F. and Jeanne (Berger) Heffernan; m. Richard F. Heisen, June 7, 1980; children: Douglas, Gregory, Cynthia, Courtney. BA, Syracuse U., 1972; MBA in Fin., NYU, 1978. Comml. lending officer Chase Manhattan Bank, N.Y.C., 1972-77; chief fin. officer Kenmill Textile Corp., N.Y.C., 1977-82; v.p. corp. affairs Primerica Corp., Greenwich, Conn., 1982-89; asst. treas. Johnson & Johnson, New Brunswick, N.J., 1989-90, v.p., mem. corp. staff, 1990-91, treas., corp. office, 1991—. Bd. dirs., v.p., corp. adv. chmn. Abbott House, Westchester, N.Y., 1983-91; bd. dirs. Women's Rsch. and Edn. Inst., Washington, 1990—, Rec. for Blind, Princeton, N.J., 1990—. Recipient Women Achiever award YWCA N.Y., 1983, TWIN award Nat. YMCA, 1987. Mem. Fin. Women's Assn. (pres. 1980-81), Nat. Investor Rels. Inst. (bd. dirs. N.J. chpt. 1991—), Pharm. Mfg. Treas. Group, N.Y. Treas. Group, Econ. Club N.Y. Office: Johnson & Johnson One Johnson & Johnson Pla New Brunswick NJ 08933*

HEISS, MARY WYNNE, artist; b. Martinsville, Va., May 14, 1954; d. Robert Wayne and Ruth Elizabeth (Midkiff) H. AA, Montgomery Coll., 1975; BA, U. Md., 1978; MFA, George Washington U., 1984. Prodn. asst. Pyramid Atlantic, Riverdale, Md., 1992; represented by David Adamson Gallery, Washington; demonstration artist ann. Discover Graphics Day, Nat. Mus. Am. Art, Smithsonian Instn., 1978. One and two woman shows at Prince George's C.C., Largo, Md., 1987, C. Alden Phelps Gallery, Reisterstown, Md., 1989, Clin. Ctr. Galleries, NIH, Bethesda, Md., 1991, Arnold and Porter Law Firm, Washington, 1992; exhibited in group shows at Rose Art Mus., Brandeis U., Waltham, Mass., 1985, Trenton (N.J.) State Coll., 1988, Internat. Monetary Fund Art Soc. Gallery, Washington, 1989, Minot (N.Dak.) State U., 1989, Rockland Art Ctr., Ellicott City, Md., 1989, Somerstown Gallery, Somers, N.Y., 1990, Queensborough C.C., Bayside, N.Y., 1991, Museu de Gravura Citade De Curitiba, Rio de Janeiro, 1991, Acad. Arts, Easton, Md., 1992, Soc. Am. Graphic Artists, N.Y.C., 1993; represented in permanent collections including Trenton State Coll., Freddie Mac Corp., Vienna, Va., Nassau C.C., Garden City, N.Y., The State Dept., Washington, So. Utah U., Cedar City, Alexandria (La.) Mus. Art. Recipient Purchase award Nassau C.C., 1989, 1st place and Purchase award Riverwalk Art Festival and Juried Exhbn., York, Pa., 1989, 90, 3d Place and Cash award Clary-Miner Gallery, 1991, Hon. Mention award Stockton (Calif.) Nat. Print and Drawing Exhbn., 1990, Cash award San Bernardo County Mus., Redlands, Calif., 1989. Mem. L.A. Printmaking Soc. (Purchase award 1990), Md. Printmakers.

HEIST, KAREN GARTLAND, elementary education educator; b. Pennsacola, Fla., Apr. 11, 1950; d. Frithiof N. and Anne (Monihan) Sagerholm; m. J. Donald Gartland III, Sept. 12, 1970 (dec.); children: J. Donald IV, G. Taylor; m. Thomas H. Heist III, Oct. 17, 1987; stepchildren: Thomas, Amanda, Kristina, John. AA, Briarcliffe Coll., 1970; BA, Beaver Coll., 1972. 2nd grade tchr. Pennsbury Sch. Dist., Fallsington, Pa., 1972-74; 1st grade tchr. Delran (N.J.) Sch. Dist., 1974-78; dist. sales mgr. C.R. Jolly Couture Sales, Edgefield, S.C., 1982-85; mgr. Crossings Motor Inn, Ocean City, N.J., 1985-88; salesperson Monihan Realty, Ocean City, 1988-90; substitute tchr. Ocean City Sch. Dist., 1989-90, basic skills instr., 1990-91, 1992, 3rd grade tchr., 1993—. Bd. dirs. Ocean City Humane Soc., Atlantic City Med. Ctr. Aux., Found. Spina Bifida; mem. Miss Am. Hostess Com.; youth activities chairperson Ocean City Yacht Club; soccer coach Ocean City Recreation Ctr. Named Outstanding Young Woman of Am., 1980, Role Model, Sun Newspaper, 1989. Mem. Ruth Newman Shapiro Cancer Soc., Ocean City Yacht Club (bd. dirs.). Republican. Episcopalian. Home: 501 Waverly Blvd Ocean City NJ 08226-4749 Office: Ocean City Primary Sch 5th St and West Ave Ocean City NJ 08226

HEITKAMP, HEIDI, state attorney general; b. Breckenridge, Minn.; m. Darwin Lange; children: Alethea, Nathan. BA, U. N.D., 1977; JD, Lewis and Clark Coll., 1980. Intern asst. Environ. Study Conf., Washington, 1976; legis. intern N.D. Legis. Coun., Bismarck, 1977; exec. dir. Northwestern Environ. Def. Ctr., Portland, 1978-79; rsch. asst. Nat. Resources Law Inst., Portland, 1979; atty. enforcement divsn. EPA, Washington, 1980-81; asst. atty. gen. Office of N.D. State Tax Commr., Bismarck, 1981-85, adminstrv. counsel, 1985-86; tax commr. Office of N.D. State Tax Commr., Bismark, 1986-93; atty. gen. State of N.D., 1993—; del. Am. Coun. Young Polit. Leaders, UK Internat. Def. Conf., 1988; trustee Fedn. Tax Adminstrs., 1991. N.D. State Crusade chmn. Am. Cancer Soc., 1988—; bd. dirs. Mo. Slope United Way, 1992—. Recipient Young Achiever award Nat. Coun. Women, 1987; named One of 20 Young Lawyers Making a Difference, ABA Barrister mag., 1990; Toll fellow Coun. State Govts., 1986. Mem. Nat. Assn. Atty. Gen. (vice chair multistate tax com. 1987, chmn. 1988-89, mem. exec. com. 1990). Office: Attorney General 600 E Boulevard Ave Bismarck ND 58505

HEIZER, IDA ANN, real estate broker; b. Oxford, Colo., Mar. 14, 1919; d. Albert Henry and Ella (Engbrook) Ordener; m. Donald Heizer, Apr. 7, 1947; children—Robert John. Diploma, Brown's Bus. Coll., 1939; student Otero Jr. Coll., 1946-47, U. So. Colo., 1962; grad. Realtors Inst., Nat. Assn. Real Estate Bds., 1972. Cert. closer real estate, cert. residential specialist. Clk., Montgomery Ward Co., LaJunta, Colo., 1935-37; bookkeeper Colo. Bank & Trust Co., LaJunta, 1937-38; cashier/bookkeeper Fox Theatre, LaJunta, 1939-40; clk. Civil Service, LaJunta, 1940-45; stenoabstractor Deaf Smith Abstract Office, Hereford, Tex., 1948-50; sec. Otero County Agt. Office, Rocky Ford, Colo., 1953-55; real estate broker Pueblo Realty & Service Co., Inc., Colo., 1958-86; ret., 1988. Mem. Pueblo Bd. Realtors, Nat. Assn. Real Estate Appraisers, Nat. Assn. Realtors, Colo. Assn. Realtors, Women's Council Realtors, Daus. of the Republic Tex., Beta Sigma Phi. Lodge: Quota Internat. Home and Office: 331 Van Buren St Pueblo CO 81004-1807

HEIZER, RUTH BRADFUTE, philosophy educator; b. Knoxville, Tenn., Oct. 8, 1933; d. George Archibald and Margaret Eleanor (Smith) Bradfute; m. James Lee Heizer, Aug. 3, 1956; children: John Philip, Mark Russell, Virginia Ruth. BA, Baylor U., 1954; MRE, So. Baptist Theol. Sem., 1957; MA, U. Ky., 1965; PhD, Ind. U., 1971; postgrad., Oxford (Eng.) U., 1980-81, 89. Tchr. Jefferson County Pub. Schs., Louisville, 1956-58; secondary tchr. Gallatin County Pub. Schs., Warsaw, Ky., 1959-60, 61; teaching assoc. dept. philosophy Ind. U., Bloomington, 1965-67; from instr. to assoc. prof. Georgetown (Ky.) Coll., 1967-83, prof., 1983—, chair dept. of philosophy, 1981—; vis. prof. philosophy Baylor U., Waco, Tex., 1979, 84; tchr. oral English Jiangnan U., Wuxi, China, summers 1990, 91. Author: Bradfute Beginnings, 1988; co-author: Women, Philosophy, & Sport, 1983, Contemporary Essays on Greek Ideas, 1987. Deacon Faith Bapt. Ch., Georgetown. Recipient NEH summer stipend, 1973. Mem. AAUW, Am. Philos. Assn., So. Soc. Philosophy and Psychology, Ky. Philos. Assn. (pres. 1973-74), Bapt. Assn. Philosophy Tchrs. (pres. 1988-89), Omicron Delta Kappa (Baylor Woman of Merit award 1980). Republican. Office: Georgetown Coll 400 E College St Georgetown KY 40324-1696

HELBERG, SHIRLEY ADELAIDE HOLDEN, artist, educator; b. Solvay, N.Y., Mar. 9; d. Isaac Edgar and Gladys Evelyn (Tucker) Holden; student Syracuse U.; m. Burton Edward Helberg; children: Keir Holm Helberg, Kristin Vaughan Helberg, Kecia Tucker Lau, Kandace Holden Mead, Kraig Brownlee Helberg. BE, Johns Hopkins U., 1969; MFA, Md. Inst. Art, 1975. Tchr. various schs. in N.J. and Pa.; tchr. Manchester (Pa.) Pub. Schs., 1965-84, Balt. City Schs., 1988-92. One-woman art show U. Va., Charlottesville, 1974, Cayuga Mus. Art and History, Auburn, N.Y., 1974, Hist. Soc. York Mus., Pa., 1977, York Coll., 1984, Country Club of York. Bd. dirs. York (Pa.) Arts Coun., 1964-66. Mem. NEA, Nat. League Am. Pen Women (Pa. State art chmn. 1972-74, pres. Pa. orgn. 1974-76, nat. scholarship chair 1976-94, registrar 1986-88, 5th v.p. 1988-90, chmn. nat. sch. com. 1992-94, Disting. Svc. award 1978, 80, 82, 84, 86, 88, 90, 92. Disting. Achievement award 1988, 1994), NEA, Pa. State Edn. Assn., Internat. Platform Assn., Harrisburg and York Art Assns., Pa. Watercolor Soc., Johns Hopkins Faculty Club. Republican. Methodist. Home: RR 4 Spring Grove PA 17362-9804 also: 727 S Ann St Baltimore MD 21231

HELBRAUN, CAROL, interior designer; m. Fred R. Helbraun, Dec. 9, 1974; children: Robin, Michael, Neil. BA, Roosevelt U., 1965. Interior deisgner pvt. practice, Chgo., 1976—. Interior designer ann. gourmet gala March of Dimes, Chgo., 1989-93. Mem. Am. Soc. Interior Designers (bd. dirs.). Home: 2916 SUmmit Highland Park IL 60035

HELD, LILA M., art appraiser; b. Cleve., Oct. 5, 1925; d. Mark and Edythe H. (Dobrin) Bloomberg; m. Jacob Herzfeld, Oct. 20, 1946 (div. 1964); children: Garson, Michael; m. Merle Donald Held, Feb. 19, 1966; children: Joanne, Barbara. Student, Coll. William and Mary, 1945-46, Ohio State U., 1943-44, Case Western Res. U., 1944-45; postgrad., Case Western Res. U., 1962-66; student, Akron U., 1960-61; BS in Art Edn., Kent State U., 1961-62; M in Valuation Sci., Lindenwood Coll., 1989. Instr. art Canton (Ohio) YMCA, 1965, Beachwood (Ohio) Bd. Recreation, 1967-68; substitute tchr. art, art history Cleveland Heights, Ohio, 1967-68; freelance artist, writer, researcher, 1940—; art cons., appraiser Art Consultants Assocs., Englewood, Colo., 1985—; curatorial aid Denver Art Mus., 1985-89; fine arts appraiser, Cleve. Works exhibited in museums and galleries in Cleve., Akron, Richmond, Va., St. Louis; speaker in field; judge at numerous art shows. Bd. dirs. Cleve. Artists Found.; mem. Akron (Ohio) Art Mus., Butler Inst. of Am. Art, Cleve. Mus. Natural History, Western Res. Hist. Soc., Toledo Mus. of Art; sec. Coun. of Cleve. Ctr. of Contemporary Art; active Continuing Edn. Assn. Case-Western Res. U., Allen Meml. Art Mus. Mem. Am. Soc. Appraisers (sr. mem., cert. in fine arts), Cleve. Mus. Art, Cleve. Ctr. for Contemporary Art (vol.), Cleve. Soc. for Contemporary Art, Nat. Coun. Jewish Women, Ohio Contemporary Glass Alliance, Art Alliance for Contemporary Glass, Temple Mus., Mus. of Am. Folk Art, Allbright-Knox Mus. (Buffalo, N.Y.). Home and Office: 13800 Shaker Blvd Apt 804 Shaker Hts OH 44120-1574

HELD, NANCY B., perinatal nurse, lactation consultant; b. Winchester, Mass., Sept. 4, 1957; d. Ann and Laurence Babine; m. Lew Held, May 22, 1976; children: David, Jessica. BSN, NYU, 1979; MS, U. Calif., San Francisco, 1992. Cert. lactation and childbirth educator, Am. Soc. Psychoprophylaxis Obstetrics. Labor/delivery nurse Pascack Valley Hosp., Westwood, N.J., 1979-83; obstetrics educator Drs. Pinski, Wiener & Grasso, Westwood, N.J., 1982-85; ob/gyn office nurse Drs. Power Hagbom Holter & Clark, San Francisco, 1986-87; asst. to dir. maternity svcs. Women's Health Assn., Greenbrae, Calif., 1987-89; perinatal edn. and lactation ctr. coord. Calif. Pacific Med. Ctr., San Francisco, 1989—; owner North Bay Lamaze, 1988—; spkr. in field. Mem. AWHONN nat. rsch. utilization team, 1993—, spkr. nat. conf., 1993. Recipient Founders Day award, NYU. Fellow: Am. Coll. Childbirth Educators; mem. Am. Soc. Psychoprophylaxis (chpt. copres.), Nurses Assn. of Am. Coll. Ob/Gyn, Internat. Childbirth Educators Assn., Internat. Lactation Cons. Assn., Sigma Theta Tau.

HELD, SHEILA ANNE, artist; b. Niles, Mich., July 20, 1946; d. Charles Jacob anb Olive Helen (Jevna) Dillman; m. HArvey Held, Sept. 13, 1968; 1 child, Maya Anjori. BA in COmparative Religions, Western Mich. U., 1968. Exhibited in group shows at The Arts Ctr., Iowa CIty, Iowa, 1984, Mussavi Gallery, N.Y.C., 1985, Adams Meml. Gallery, Dunkirk, N.Y., 1987, Chautauqua (N.Y.) Art Assn. Galleries, 1988, West Bend (Wis.) Gallery, 1990, Milw. Art Mus., 1992, John Michael Kohler Arts Ctr., Sheboygan, Wis., 1993, Pitts. Ctr. Arts, 1993, State of the Art Gallery, Ithaca, N.Y., 1993, Art Ctr. Gallery, Warrensburg, Mo., 1994. Wis. Arts Bd. Individual Artist's fellow, 1994. Home: 2762 Mayfair Ct Wauwatosa WI 53222-4105

HELD, VIRGINIA, philosophy educator; b. Mendham, N.J., Oct. 28, 1929; d. John Howard Nott and Margaretta (Wood) Potter; m. Hans W. Held, Sept. 1950 (div. 1981); children: Julia, Philip. A.B., Barnard Coll., 1950; Ph.D., Columbia U., 1968. Mem. staff Reporter mag., 1954-65; lectr. philosophy Barnard Coll., 1964-66; mem. faculty Hunter Coll., CUNY, 1965—, prof. philosophy CUNY Grad. Sch., 1977—; vis. lectr. Yale U., 1972; dir. NEH summer seminar, Stanford U. Law Sch., 1981; vis. scholar Harvard U. Law Sch., 1981-82; vis. prof. Dartmouth Coll., 1984, UCLA, 1986; Truax vis. prof. Hamilton Coll., 1989. Author: The Public Interest and Individual Interests, 1970, Rights and Goods. Justifying Social Action, 1984, 89, Feminist Morality: Transforming Culture, Society and Politics, 1993; also over 70 articles; editor: Property, Profits and Economic Justice, 1980; co-author: Women's Realities, Women's Choices, 1983; co-editor: Philosophy and Political Action, 1972, Philosophy, Morality and International Affairs, 1974; mem. editorial bd.: Am. Philos. Quarterly, Ethics, 1982-91, Hypatia, Philosophy and Phenomenological Research, Polit. Theory, Pub. Affairs Quar., Social Theory and Practice. Fulbright fellow, 1950; Rockefeller Found. fellow, 1975-76; fellow Ctr. for Advanced Study in Behavioral Scis., 1984-85. Mem. Am. Philos. Assn. (exec. com. Eastern divsn. 1979-81, Eastern divsn. rep. 1992—), Columbia U. Seminars (Assoc.), Conf. Methods (exec. com. 1971—), Internat. Assn. Philosophy Law and Social Philosophy (pres. Am. sect. 1981-83), Soc. Philosophy and Pub. Affairs (chmn. 1972), Soc. Women in Philosophy. Office: CUNY Grad Sch Dept Philosophy 33 W 42nd St New York NY 10036-8003

HELDRICH, ELEANOR MAAR, publisher; b. Hagerstown, Md, Nov. 4, 1929; d. Richard and Sara (Mish) Maar; m. Frederich Joseph Heldrich; children: Sarah, Susan, Frederick, Philip. Grad. high sch., Balt. Editor Federated Garden Clubs of Md., Balt., 1975—; pub., founder Prospect Hill Press, Balt., 1981—. Pres. Beautiful Balt., Inc., 1985-87. Recipient of Publication Award Nat. Council of State Garden Clubs, 1984, 86. Mem. Pub. Mktg. Assn., Balt. Pubs. Assn., Internat. Assn. Ind. Pub. (Com. Small Mag. Editors and Pubs.). Office: Prospect Hill Press 216 Wendover Rd Baltimore MD 21218-1895

HELFRECHT, KAREN ANN, chemical engineer; b. Madison, Wis., May 12, 1964; d. Donald John and Carol Elaine (Hoveland) H. BSChemE, U. Wis., 1986. Engr. II Kraft, Inc., Glenview, Ill., 1987-90; rsch. engr. Kraft Gen. Foods, Glenview, 1990-92, sr. rsch. engr. I, 1992—. Tutor, instr. Adopt-A-Sch., Chgo., 1988-91. Mem. Am. Inst. Chem. Engrs., Tau Beta Pi. Lutheran. Office: Kraft Gen Foods 801 Waukegan Rd Glenview IL 60025

HELGENBERGER, MARG, actress; m. Alan Roseberg; 1 child, Hugh. Appeared in TV series Ryan's Hope, 1984-86, The Shell Game, 1987, China Beach, 1988-91 (Emmy award; named Primetime Programming Individual Outstanding Supporting Actress in Drama Series, 1990, 91); co-host of New Year's Rockin' Eve, 1988, Home, 1989, (TV movies) Blind Vengence, 1990, Death Dreams, 1991, In Sickness and In Health, 1992, Through the Eyes of a Killer, 1992, When Love Kills: The Seduction of John Hearn, 1993, Stephen King's The Tommyknockers, 1993, Where Are My Children?, 1994, Lie Down with Lions, 1994, Partners, 1994; appeared in films Always, 1989, After Midnight, 1989, Crooked Hearts, 1991, Desperate Motive, 1993, The Cowboy Way, 1994. Office: c/o The Gersh Agency Inc 232 N Canon Dr Beverly Hills CA 90210-5302*

HELGESON, EUNICE MAY, machine tool distribution executive; b. Tracy, Minn., Oct. 21, 1947; d. Oscar J. and Louella A. (Rialson) H. BA in Bus. Adminstrn. magna cum laude, Augsburg Coll., 1969; cert. credit and fin. mgmt. with high distinction, U. Minn., 1977. Cert. mgmt. acct., credit exec. Sec. Tracy (Minn.) Luth. Ch., 1964-65; bookkeeper Milton Granquist Co., Mpls., 1965-68, office mgr., 1968-70, sec., treas., 1970—. Author: Helleson Family History, 1983, Helgeson Family History, 1984. Bd. dirs., treas. Boundary Creek 6th Homeowners Assn., Maple Grove, Minn., 1979-83; coun. mem. Advent Luth. Ch., Maple Grove, 1982-88, treas. 1984-85, v.p., 1986. Fellow Nat. Assn. Credit Mgmt. (bd. dirs. N. Cen. chpt., pres. 1984-85, assoc. award with distinction 1972, fellow award with distinction 1977, credit master designation 1987, cert. credit exec.); mem. Credit Womens Group (pres. 1976-77), Am. Soc. Women Accts. (pres. Mpls.-St. Paul chpt. 68, 1974-75), Sons of Norway (pres. Syttende Mai Lodge 1-517 1987-88). Home: 10943 105th Ave N Osseo MN 55369-2837 Office: Milton Granquist Co 3515 48th Ave N Minneapolis MN 55429-3932

HELKE, CINDA JANE, pharmacology and neuroscience educator, researcher; b. Waterloo, Iowa, Feb. 27, 1951; d. Gerald and Lorna (Smith) Pieres; m. Joel Edward Helke, Aug. 10, 1974. BS in Pharmacy, Creighton U., 1974; PhD, Georgetown U., 1978. Staff fellow NIH, Bethesda, Md., 1978-80; asst. prof. dept. pharmacology Uniformed Svcs. Univ. of the Health Scis., Bethesda, 1980-85, assoc. prof. dept. pharmacology, 1985-88; prof. dept. pharmacology Uniformed Svcs. Univ. Health Scis., Bethesda, 1988—, prof. neurosci. program, 1991—, dir. neurosci. program, 1993—; mem. adv. panel Am. Heart Assn., 1984-87, NIH, Bethesda, 1987-91; mem. oversight rev. panel NSF, 1986, pharmacology test com. Nat. Bd. Med. Examiners, 1992-94. Author chpts. in books; mem. editl. bd. Synapse, Pharmacology, Jour. Comparative Neurology; contbr. numerous articles to profl. jours. NIH grantee, 1981—. Mem. AAAS, Am. Soc. Pharmacology and Exptl. Therapeutics, Soc. for Neurosci. Women in Sci., Women in Neurosci., Soc. for Neurosci. (sec., treas. Washington chpt. 1985-87). Office: Uniformed Svcs U Health Sci 4301 Jones Bridge Rd Bethesda MD 20814-4712

HELLER, DOROTHY, artist; b. N.Y.C., June 15, 1926; d. Samuel and Rebecca (Cohn) H. Studied with, Hans Hofman, N.Y.C., 1942. lectr. in field. One-person shows include Betty Parsons Gallery, N.Y.C., 1972, 76, 78, U. Pa., 1976, Cathedral St. John the Divine, N.Y.C., 1976, East Hampton Gallery, N.Y.C., 1963, Galerie Facchetti, Paris, 1955, Tibor De Nagy, N.Y.C., 1953, Poindexter Gallery, 1956, 57; exhibited in group shows at Denver Art Mus., 1953, Whitney Mus. Ann., 1957, Mus. Modern Art Traveling Show, 1963, Betty Parsons Gallery, 1972-81, U. Calif. Art Mus., 1974, Met. Mus. Art, N.Y.C., 1979, Otis Art Inst., 1979, Bklyn. Coll. Art Gallery, 1990; represented in permanent collections Met. Mus. Art, N.Y.C., U. Calif. Art Mus., Berkeley, Cornell U. Johnson Mus., Ithaca, N.Y., Wadsworth Atheneum, Hartford, Conn., Smithsonian Instn. Archives, Washington, Zimmerli Mus., New Brunswick, N.J., Alexandria (La.) Mus., Auburn (Ala.) U., Whitney Communications, N.Y.C., Chase Manhattan Bank, N.Y.C., many others. Recipient Internat. Woman of Yr. award, 1976.

HELLER, LOIS JANE, physiologist, educator, researcher; b. Detroit, Jan. 4, 1942; d. John and Lona Elizabeth (Stockmeyer) Skagerberg; m. Robert Eugene Heller, May 21, 1966; children: John Robert, Suzanne Elizabeth. BA, Albion Coll., 1964; MS, U. Mich., 1966; PhD, U. Ill., Chgo., 1970. Instr. med ctr. U. Ill., Chgo., 1969-70, asst. prof., 1970-71; asst. prof. U. Minn., Duluth, 1972-77, assoc. prof., 1977-89, prof., 1989—. Author: Cardiovascular Physiology, 3d edition, 1989; contbr. numerous articles to profl. jours. Mem. Am. Physiol. Soc., Am. Heart Assn., Soc. Exptl. Biology and Medicine, Sigma Xi. Home: 311 Halsey St Duluth MN 55803-2535 Office: Univ Minn Sch of Medicine Duluth MN 55812

HELLER, MARY BERNITA, psychotherapist; b. Roland, Iowa, Feb. 11, 1934; d. Casper and Blanche (Hanson) Stenberg; m. John R. Heller, June 7, 1958; children: Kristen, Jonathan, Kathryn. BA, St. Olaf Coll., 1956; MSW, Fordham U., 1970. Cert. social worker, N.Y.; bd. cert. diplomate in social work. Psychiatric social worker Beloit Children's Home, Ames, Iowa, 1957-58; caseworker Luth. Community Svcs., N.Y.C., 1958-59, Soc. Seamen's Children, Staten Island, N.Y., 1971-75; psychiatric social worker Staten Island Mental Health, 1971-75; psychotherapist Mid-Hudson Cons. Ctr., Wappinger Falls, N.Y., 1976-94; pvt. practice Poughkeepsie, N.Y., 1977—; psychotherapist Windsor Counseling Group, New Windsor, N.Y., 1989—; supr. Luth. Community Svcs., N.Y.C., 1987—. Bd. dirs. Children;s Home of Poughkeepsie, 1983-88, Seafarers and Internat. House, N.Y.C., 1990—; mem. candidacy com. Met. N.Y. Synod, N.Y.C., 1986-94, v.p., 1992—; mem. coun. Hudson Valley Philharm., Poughkeepsie, 1983-88. Fellow Am. Orthopsychiat. Assn.; mem. NASW, Acad. Cert. Social Workers. Democrat. Lutheran. Home: 45 Kingston Ave Poughkeepsie NY 12603-3418 Office: 55 Wilbur Blvd Poughkeepsie NY 12603-3424

HELLER, PATRICIA ELLEN, domestic violence counselor; b. Torrance, Calif., Mar. 15, 1943; d. Robert Henry and Elizabeth (Hughes) H.; children: Marci Lyn Andis, Leslie Ann Brush, Geri Liane Kenfield. Student, Calif. State U., 1986-87, 92-93, San Jose State U., 1989—. Bookkeeper Eastgate Oil, Missoula, Mont., 1980; credit mgr. Pierce Flooring Inc., Missoula, Mont., 1983-85; with Bemiss-Jason Corp., Newark, Calif., 1986-88, supr. accts. payable, 1988; counselor Miramur-Headway, San Jose, Calif., 1989, Gray's Group Home, San Jose, Calif., 1989; domestic violence counselor A Safe Place, Oakland, Calif., 1990—. Mem. AAUW (student affiliate), Am. Psychol. Assn. (student affiliate), Calif. Assn. Marriage & Family Therapists (prelic. mem.), Golden Key Honor Soc. (life), Psi Chi.

HELLERSTEIN, NINA SALANT, French literature and language educator; b. N.Y.C., Mar. 29, 1946; d. Allan and Martha (Cantor) Salant; m. Walter Hellerstein, Aug. 31, 1970; children: Michael, Margaret. BA, Brown U., 1968; MA, U. Chgo., 1969, PhD, 1974. Adj. asst. prof. Baruch Coll. CUNY, N.Y.C., 1974-75; vis. asst. prof. Vassar Coll., Poughkeepsie, N.Y., 1975-76; instr. Rosary Coll., River Forest, Ill., 1976-78, Roosevelt U., Chgo., 1976-78; asst. prof. U. Ga., Athens, 1978-83, assoc. prof. French literature and language, 1983-92, prof., 1992—, acting head dept. Romance langs., 1992-3. Author: Mythe et Structure Dans Les 'Cing Grandes Odes', 1990; mem. editorial bd. South Atlantic Rev., 1990-93; contbr. articles to profl. jours. Grantee Ford Found., 1968-72, U. Ga., 1982, 91. mem. MLA, MADD, Am. Assn. Tchrs. French, Paul Claudel Soc. (v.p. 1978-79, sec.-treas. 1979-80, pres. 1981-82), Handgun Control, Inc., Societe Paul Claudel, Assn. des Amis de la Fondation St. John Perse. Jewish. Office: U Ga Dept Romance Langs Athens GA 30602

HELLHAKE, GERRI ANN, critical care nurse, cardiology nurse; b. Lincoln, Ill., Aug. 29, 1960; d. Ronald Bruce and Bonnie Jean (Eager) Hellhake. LPN, John Wood Community Coll., Quincy, Ill., 1981; ADN, Southea. C.C., Keokuk, Iowa, 1987; BSN, Hannibal-LaGrange Coll., Hannibal, Mo., 1994. RN, Ill.; cert. ACLS provider and instr. Am. Heart Assn. Staff nurse cardiology Quincy Physician's and Surgeon's Clinic, 1988-91; staff nurse ICU St. Mary Hosp., Quincy, 1991-92; staff nurse critical care Blessing Hosp., Quincy, 1987-88, staff nurse renal dialysis, 1991-93, staff nurse cardiology dept., 1993—. Mem. AACN (CCRN), Am. Nephrology Nurses Assn. Home: 937 Jackson Quincy IL 62301-4541 Office: Blessing Hosp Dept Cardiology Quincy IL 62301

HELLINGER, PAMELA L., accountant; b. Nashville, June 19, 1966; d. Bobby Lee and Ann Belle (Mitchell) Hazelwood; m. Mark Robert Hellinger, Oct. 27, 1990. Bachelor's degree, Vanderbilt U., 1988. Fin. asst. Gordon Bailey & Assocs., Inc., Atlanta, 1989-91, staff acct., 1991-93, mgr. agency acctg., 1993—. Mem. Inst. Mgmt. Accts. Office: Gordon Bailey & Assocs 675 Village Sq Dr Stone Mountain GA 30083

HELLMAN, MARCIA JOAN, organizational development consultant; b. Berwick, Pa., Nov. 28, 1935; s. Albert Sherman and Jeanne Sherman; children: Jeffrey, Deborah. BA, Syracuse U., 1957; MEd, Harvard U., 1981. Tchr., Minoa pub. schs. (N.Y.), 1957-59, Needham High Sch. (Mass.), 1959-60, East Haven pub. schs. (Conn.), 1960-61; polit. reporter Newton Times (Mass.), 1979-81; asst. dir. housing Northeastern U., Boston, 1981-83; tng. coord. Assn. Jr. Leagues N.Y., N.Y.C., 1983-89; orgnl. devel. cons., Michael Reese Hosp., Chgo., 1989-90; organizational devel./tng. cons. U. Chgo., 1990—; bd. dirs. Chgo's. Vis. Nurses Assn., 1988—, Ounce of Prevention Fund, 1989—; tng. cons. U. Chgo. Asst. editor The Common 1973-74. Mem. Newton Democratic City Com., 1968-83; mem. PTA, Newton, 1968-81; bd. dirs. Brigham and Women's Hosp. Aux., Boston, 1968-83; mem. Branford LWV (Conn.), 1959-68. Mem. Assn. Counseling and Devel. Am., Mass. Assn. Women Deans, Adminstrs. and Counselors, Am. Soc. Tng. and Devel., Nat. Soc. Performance and Instrn., Harvard Club. Home: 4950 S Chicago Beach Dr # 21B Chicago IL 60615-3204 Office: U Chgo Dept Human Resources 956 E 58th St Chicago IL 60637-1432

HELLMAN, RICCI ANN, counselor; b. Kennett, Mo.. BA in Sociology-Anthropology cum laude, Rhodes Coll., Memphis, 1988; MS in Counseling and Student Pers. Svcs., Memphis State U., 1989—, postgrad., 1989—, EdD in Counseling/Student Pers. Svcs., 1994. Lic. profl. counselor, Tenn.; nat. cert. counselor. Career and acad. counselor Ednl. Opportunity Ctr., Memphis, 1989; coord. advisement and placement East Ark. C.C., Forrest City, 1989-90; counselor evening regular programs State Tech. Inst. at Memphis, 1991; sexual assault counselor Memphis Secual Assault Resource Ctr., 1990-94; asst. dir. of counseling Rhodes Coll., Memphis, 1994—; sexual assault cons. for Rape: Cries from the Heartland, HBO, 1991; presenter in field. Intake and mediation counselor Shelby County Pretrial Svcs., 1988-89; vol. Memphis-Shelby County AIDS Coalition, 1992. Mem. ACA, Am. Coll. Pers. Assn., Tenn. Coalition Against Sexual Assault. Office: Rhodes Coll Resource Ctr 2000 N Parkway Memphis TN 38112

HELLSTRÖM, INGEGERD, business executive; b. Stockholm; came to U.S., 1966; m. Karl Erik Hellström. MD, Karolinska Inst. Med. Sch., Stockholm, 1964, PhD, 1966, docent in tumor biology. Rsch. assoc. Karolinska Inst. Med. Sch., 1959-66, asst. prof. dept. tumor biology, 1966; asst. prof. microbiology U. Wash., Seattle, 1966—, rsch. assoc. prof. microbiology, 1969-72; sr. scientist Oncogen, Seattle, 1983-84, lab. dir., 1984-86; prof. microbiology, immunology U. Wash., Seattle, 1972-83; v.p. Oncogen/Bristol-Myers Squibb, Seattle, 1986-90; v.p. immunological diseases Bristol-Myers Squibb Pharm. Rsch. Inst., Seattle, 1990—; adj. prof. pathology U. Wash., 1972—. Patentee in field. Recipient Lucy Wortham James award, 1971, Matric Table award, 1972, Pap award Outstanding Contbn. Cancer Rsch., 1973, Am. Cancer Soc. Nat. award 1974, Humboldt award, 1980. Mem. AMA, Am. Assn. Immunologists, Am. Fedn. Clin. Rsch., Am. Assn. Cancer Rsch., Soc. Biol. Therapy. Office: Bristol-Myers Squibb Pharmaceutical Rsch Inst 3005 1st Ave Seattle WA 98121-1035

HELLSTROM, PAMELA DONWORTH, corporate executive, writer; b. Bangor, Maine, Apr. 4, 1948; d. Clarence Arlowe and Margaret Mary (Donworth) Small; m. Michael Willard Hellstrom, Oct. 12, 1978; 1 child, Kirsten Elyse. BA in English Edn., Merrimack Coll., 1970. Lic. vocat. educator, Wash. Asst. dir. pub. relations, employment counselor Meals-On-Wheels, Seattle, 1970-72; social services asst. Madigan Army Med. Ctr., Tacoma, 1972-73, social work asst., 1974-81; chief counselor drug and alcohol treatment ctr. Am. Lake VA Health Ctr., Tacoma, 1973-74; trainer, cons. alt. chief examiner Gen. Equivalency Diploma program L.H. Bates Vocat. Tech. Inst., Tacoma, 1983-84; founder, pres. Growth Techs., Inc., Tacoma, 1984—, dir. trainer edn. program and ednl. rsch. project; founder Omni-Ed, 501C, 1988—; founder, pres. Hellstrom & Dahl, Ltd., 1992—; pub. The Starboard Watch newsletter, 1994—. Democrat. Roman Catholic.

HELLYER, CONSTANCE ANNE, communications executive, writer; b. Puyallup, Wash., Apr. 22, 1937; d. David Tirrell and Constance (Hopkins) H.; m. Peter A. Corning, Dec. 30, 1963 (div. 1977); children: Anne Arundel, Stephanie Deak; m. Don W. Conway, Oct. 12, 1980. BA with honors, Mills Coll., 1959. Grader, researcher Harvard U., Cambridge, Mass., 1959-60; researcher Newsweek mag., N.Y.C., 1960-63; author's asst. Theodore H. White and others, N.Y.C., 1964-69; freelance writer, editor Colo., Calif., 1969-75; writer, editor Stanford (Calif.) U. Med. Ctr., 1975-79; communications dir. No. Calif. Cancer Program, Palo Alto, 1979-82; comm. dir. Stanford Law Sch., Palo Alto, 1982—. Founding editor (newsletters) Insight, 1978-80, Synergy, 1980-82, Stanford Law Alum, 1992—; editor (mag.) Stanford Lawyer, 1982—; contbr. articles to profl. jours. and mags. Recipient silver medal Coun. for Advancement and Support Edn., 1985, 89, award of distinction dist. VII, 1994. Mem. No. Calif. Sci. Writers Assn. (cofounder, bd. dirs. 1979-93), Phi Beta Kappa. Democrat. Home: 2080 Louis Rd Palo Alto CA 94303-3451 Office: Stanford Law Sch Stanford CA 94305-8610

HELM, DEBORAH KATHRYN, educator; b. Corpus Christi, Tex., Oct. 21, 1950; d. John Calvin Pope and Betty (Zimmerman) Haas; m. Malcolm Latta Helm, June 20, 1981. Student, Del Mar Coll., 1968-70; B. Music Edn., Ea. N.Mex. U., 1972, MA, 1973. Cert. tchr. (choral dir.). Choral dir. Edison Freshman & Alamo Jr. High, Midland, Tex., 1973-77, Lake Highlands High Sch., Richardson, Tex., 1977-80, Brandenburg Mid. Sch., Garland, Tex., 1980-91, Hudson Mid. Sch., Garland, Tex., 1992-93; South Garland H.S., 1993—. Mem. Jr. League, Garland, Highland Park Presbyn. Ch. Mem. Tex. Music Educators Assn. (sec. region III 1983-85, jr. high vocal chmn. region III 1985-86, mem. honor choir 1986, 89), Tex. Choral Dirs. Assn. (sec.-treas. 1985-87, v.p. 1989-91, pres.-elect 1992-93, pres. 1993—), Am. Choral Dirs. Assn. (nat. conv. performing choir 1991), Tex. Music Adjudicators Assn. Republican.

HELM, JUNE, anthropologist, educator; b. Twin Falls, Idaho, Sept. 13, 1924; d. William Jennings and Julia Frances (Dixon) H.; m. Pierce Erwin King, Aug. 15, 1967. Ph.B., U. Chgo., 1944, A.M., 1950, Ph.D., 1958. Lectr. Carleton U., Ottawa, Ont., Can., 1949-59; asst. prof. anthropology U. Iowa, Iowa City, 1960-63, assoc. prof., 1963-66, prof., 1966—; adviser Indian Brotherhood for N.W.T. Can. 1974; cons. Mackenzie Valley Pipeline Inquiry, Govt. of Can., 1975-76. Author: The Lynx Point People: The Dynamics of a Northern Athapaskan Band, 1961, Indians of the Subarctic, 1976; editor: Subarctic: Vol. VI Handbook of North American Indians, 1981, Social Contexts of American Ethnology, 1840-1984, 1985; contbr. numerous articles to profl. jours. Fellow Am. Acad. Arts and Scis. (chmn. sect. H 1978), Am. Anthropol. Assn. (pres. 1985-87); mem. Am. Ethnol. Soc. (pres. 1982-83, editor publs. 1964-68), Ctrl. States Anthrop. Soc. (pres. 1970-71). Office: U Iowa Iowa City IA 52242

HELM, SHELLI LYNN, clinical psychologist; b. Omaha, July 10, 1956; d. Sidney Rubin and Sharon L. Swartzman; married, Oct. 1, 1988; 2 children. BA, U. Tex., 1978; PhD, U. Tex. Southwestern Med. Ctr., 1987. Lic. psychologist, Tex.; registered health care provider, nat. and Tex. Staff psychologist P.R.I.D.E., Dallas, 1985-89; asst. prof. psychology U. Tex. Southwestern Med. Sch., Dallas, 1987-89; pvt. practice clin. psychology Dallas, 1989—. Presenter to civic and profl. orgns., 1989—. Recipient Excellence in Rsch. award Psi Chi, 1976. Mem. APA, Dallas Psychol. Assn., Sigma Xi. Office: 5956 Sherry Ln Ste 715 Dallas TX 75225-8018

HELMER, CAROL A., psychologist, school psychologist; b. Newport News, Apr. 24, 1946; d. Frederick Otto and Phyllis Amelia (Calve) Helmer; 1 child, Shannon Helmer Ducey. BA, Roanoke Coll., Salem, Va., 1967; MS, Radford U., Va., 1968; PhD, Hofstra U., 1985. Lic. psychologist, N.Y. Tchr. math. Brentwood (N.Y.) pub. schs., 1968-70, psychologist, 1970-72; psychotherapist Bi-County Cons. Ctr., Amityville, N.Y., 1970-78; psychologist BOLES II, Patchogue, N.Y., 1972-73, Middle Country Schs., Centereach, N.Y., 1973—; psychotherapist North Shore Cons., Smithtown, N.Y., 1978-82; pvt. practice psychology Coram, N.Y., 1986—; supr. interns, Hofstra U., 1980—, Adelphi U., 1985-86, Queens Coll., 1986-87, St. John's U., 1987-88. Bd. dirs. Community House, Centreach, 1986-87. Redford U. grad. assistantship, 1967-68. Mem. APA, N.Y. State Psychol. Assn. (pres. sch. divsn. 1994), Suffolk County Psychol. Assn. (sch. psychology com. chmn., exec. bd. mem. 1990-94), Rotary. Office: 1 Freemont Ln Coram NY 11727-3234

HELMER, M. CHRISTIE, lawyer; b. Portland, Oreg., Oct. 8, 1949; d. Marvin Curtis and Inez Bahl (Corwin) H.; m. Joe D. Bailey, June 23, 1979; children: Tim Bailey, Bill Bailey, Kim Easton. BA in English magna cum laude, Wash. State U., 1970; JD cum laude, Lewis & Clark, 1974. Bar: Oreg. 1974, U.S. Supreme Ct. 1975, U.S. Ct. Appeals (9th cir.) 1975. Assoc. Miller, Nash, Wiener, Hager & Carlsen, Portland, 1974-81, ptnr., 1981—; mem. Oreg. Bd. Bar Examiners, Portland, 1978-81; del. 9th Cir. Jud. Conf., 1984-87, mem. exec. com., 1987-90. Author: Arrest of Ships, 1985. Mem. ABA, FBA (bd. dirs. 1994), Oreg. Bar (bd. govs. 1981-84, treas. 1983-84), Oreg. Law Found. (bd. dirs. 1991-92), Maritime Law Assn., Founder's Club (v.p., bd. dirs., sec. 1986-92), Multnomah Athletic Club, Phi Beta Kappa. Office: Miller Nash Wiener Hager & Carlsen 111 SW 5th Ave Ste 3600 Portland OR 97204

HELMERICH, PEGGY VARNADOW, actress; b. Columbia, Miss., Mar. 18, 1928; d. Leon A. and Minnie Lee (Roper) Varnadow; m. Walter H. Helmerich III, Nov. 24, 1951; children: Walter H. IV, Dow Zachary, Matthew Galloway, Hans Christian, Jonathan David. BA, Northwestern U., 1948. Actress: (radio) WWL, New Orleans, 1948-49; (films) Woman in Hiding, , 1949, Undertow, 1949, Sleeping City, 1949, Reunion in Reno, 1950, You Never Can Tell, 1950, Bright Victory, 1951, I Want You, 1951, Harvey, 1951; (Screen Dirs. Playhouse) One Way Passage, 1950. Trustee Tulsa County Libr. Commn., 1975—, Okla. State Arts. Coun., 1989—; bd. dirs. Pro America, 1975—, Philbrook Art Ctr., 1980—, Gilcrease Mus., 1982-88, Tulsa Ballet Theatre, 1984-87, Woman's Bd. Northwestern U., 1986—, Okla. Found. for Excellence, 1986—, Tulsa Garden Ctr., 1988—. Recipient Am. Libr. Assn.'s Trustee citation, Tulsa, 1985, Citizen's Recognition award, Okla. Libr. Assn., 1985, Medici award, Tulsa Ballet Theatre, 1985; named Outstanding Philanthropist, Nat. Soc. Fund Raising Execs., 1985, Tulsa Headliner, Tulsa Press Club, 1987. Republican. Methodist. Home: 2121 S Yorktown Ave Tulsa OK 74114-1417

HELMOND, KATHERINE, actress; b. Galveston, Tex., July 5, 1934; d. Patrick Joseph and Thelma Louise (Malone) H.; m. David Christian, Dec., 1968. Pres. Taur Can Prodns., Hollywood, Calif., 1979—. Appeared as Jessica Tate in TV series Soap, 1978-81 (Emmy award best actress, 1978, 79, 80, 81, Golden Globe award 1980); co-star TV series Who's The Boss?, 1984-92; guest star appearances in TV series and in TV movies including Dr. Max, 1974, Larry, 1974, Locusts, 1974, The Autobiography of Miss Jane Pittman, 1974, The Legend of Lizzie Borden, 1975, The Family Nobody Wanted, 1975, Cage Without a Key, 1975, The First 36 Hours of Dr. Durant, 1975, James Dean, 1976, Wanted: The Sundance Woman, 1976, Little Ladies of the Night, 1977, Getting Married, 1978, miniseries Pearl, 1978, Diary of a Teenage Hitchhiker, 1979, Scout's Honor, 1980, miniseries World War III, 1982, For Lovers Only, 1982, Rosie: The Rosemary Clooney Story, 1982, When Will I Be Loved, 1990, The Perfect Tribute, 1991, Deception: A Mother's Secret, 1991, Grass Roots, 1992; film appearances include: The Hospital, 1971, The Hindenberg, 1975, Baby Blue Marine, 1976, Family Plot, 1976, Time Bandits, 1981, Brazil, 1986, Shadey, Overboard, 1987, Lady in White, 1988, Inside Monkey Zetterland, 1993; stage appearences include House of Blue Leaves, 1971 (N.Y. Drama Critics Variety award 1971, Clarence Derwent award 1971, L.A. Drama Critics award 1972), Great God Brown, 1973, Quartermaine's Terms, 1984, Mixed Emotions, 1993; appeared with numerous repertory theatres including Associated Producing Artists, N.Y.C., Trinity Sq. Repertory Co., R.I., Hartford Stage, Phoenix Repertory, N.Y.C. Mem. Screen Actors Guild, AFTRA. Roman Catholic. Office: William Morris Agy 151 S El Camino Dr Beverly Hills CA 90212-2704*

HELMS, LISA MARIE, nurse, military officer; b. Sioux City, Iowa, Nov. 24, 1962; d. Dean Edward and Betty Lou Victora (Guenther) H. BA in Nursing, Carroll Coll., Helena, Mont., 1986; postgrad., Calif. State U., Sacramento, 1990-92, Incarnate Word Coll., 1993—. RN, Tex. Enlisted U.S. Army, 1981, advanced through grades to capt., 1990; nurse U.S. Army, San Francisco, 1986-90, Calif. Nat. Guard, San Francisco, 1990-92, Rio Linda (Calif.) Union Sch. Dist., 1990-92; enlisted USAF, 1992; mem. A.F. Nurse Corps Wilford Hall Med Ctr., Lackland AFB, Tex., 1992—. Vol. Big sister/Big brother program United Way. Decorated Humanitarian Svc. medal, Army Commendation medal. Mem. Am. Assn. Critical Care Nurses. Roman Catholic.

HELMS, MARY ANN, critical care nurse, consultant; b. Compton, Calif., Jan. 7, 1935; d. Raymond Whitfield and Amanda Zelpha (Hancock) Spencer; m. Willard Ford Helms, Mar. 15, 1958; children: Michael Steven, Steven Allen. AA in Nursing, El Camino Coll., 1971; BSN, Calif. State U., L.A., 1976; MA in Mgmt., St. Mary's Coll., 1978; MSN, Ariz. State U., 1985; PhD in Health Svc. Adminstrn., Columbia Pacific U., 1993. RN; cert. clin. specialist, critical care nurse, health care quality, CCRN. Med. sec., bookkeeper Palm Springs (Calif.) Med. Clinic, 1956-61; office mgr. William R. Stevens Ins. Agy., Santa Ana, Calif., 1961-63, I.J. Weinrot & Son Ins. Agy., L.A., 1963-67; staff nurse Veteran's Adminstrn. Hosp., 1971; staff nurse Kaiser Found. Hosp., Harbor City, Calif., 1971-76; supr., coord. pediatrics Maricopa County Gen. Hosp., Phoenix, 1976-80; critical care nurse Phoenix Baptist Hosp., 1980-81, critical care mgr., 1981-89, clin. nurse specialist, 1989—, critical care cons., 1986—. Mem. ANA, AAAS, Nat. Assn. Healthcare Quality, Am. Cons's. League, Am. Statis. Assn., N.Y. Acad. Sci., Am. Soc. Women Accts., Natural History Mus., Met. Mus. Art, Smithsonian Instn., Phoenix Zoo, Phoenix Art Mus., Cousteau Soc., Calif. State U. Alumni Assn., KAET Public Broadcasting System, Ariz. Nurses Assn., Am. Assn. Legal Nurse Cons., Ariz. State U. Alumni Assn., Phi Kappa Phi, Alpha Gamma Sigma, Sigma Theta Tau. Mem. Episcopal Ch. Research on effects of noise pollution on physical and mental health of citizenry, phenylketonuria testing in Los Angeles, measurement of attitudes toward children in pediatric nurses, nursing practice, physiological changes with back massage, incidence of prolonged Q-T interval in critically ill patients, assessment of artierial circulation in vascular surgery patients; use of autotransfusion in hip and knee surgery patients; use of pulse oximetry in pre and post operative patients; side effects of patient-controlled analgesia; conf. medication histories in hospitalized patients; correlation of patient medication histories to nurses and physicians. Home: 1007 E Michelle Dr Phoenix AZ 85022-6048 Office: 2601 E 20th Ave Phoenix AZ 85015

HELMS, NANCY EDDINS, mental health counselor, educator, consultant; b. Rockingham, N.C., Feb. 12, 1937; d. Edward B. and Hettie Pearl (Smith) Eddins; m. Bill C. Helms, Dec. 25, 1956; children: Kyle Edward, Kendell Craig. AB, Coll. of William & Mary, 1959, MA, 1972, CAS, 1980, EdD, 1982. Lic. profl. counselor. Tchr. social studies Warwick Jr. and Warwick High Schs., Newport News, Va., 1959-64; elem. tchr. South Morrison Elem. Sch., Newport News, Va., 1964-72; counselor, civics tchr. Denbigh High Sch., Newport News, Va., 1972-73; counselor, dir. guidance Dozier Intermediate Sch., Newport News, Va., 1973-80; dir. guidance Warwick High

Sch., Newport News, Va., 1980-83; dir. guidance and testing Hampton (Va.) Pub. Schs., 1983-91; ednl. cons. advisor-advisee program Va. Beach and York County Pub. Schs., 1991-92; counselor Oyster Point Psychol. Practice, Newport News, 1993-94; pvt. practice mental health counseling, 1994—; adj. faculty The Coll. of William and Mary, 1984—, Old Dominion U., Master's Field Program and Mil. Transition Program, 1992—, U. Va., 1991-92; cons. Va. Beach City Schs., 1991-92, Green County Schs., Charlottesville, Va., 1991-92, York County Schs., Yorktown, Va., 1992, Newport News Schs., 1992. Contbr. articles to profl. jours. Mem. Hampton Rds. Exch. Club, 1983-91, York County Hist. Com., Yorktown, 1993—, Colonial Svc. Bd., Yorktown, 1993—, Dem. Com., Yorktown, 1990—. Recipient Counselor of Yr. award Peninsula Counselors Assn., 1988, Va. Counselors Assn., 1988, Career Svc. award Va. Counselors Assn., 1991, Post Secondary Counselor of Yr. award Am. Sch. Counselor Assn., 1992. Mem. Am. Counseling Assn., Am. Sch. Counselors Assn. (state del. and rep. to Nat. Assn. Secondary Sch. Prins. 1984—), Va. Counselors Assn. (sec., pre.-elect, pres., chairperson of ACA awards, rep. to Va. Ednl. Leadership Congress, chairperson Challenge Fund), Va. Assn. for Specialists in Group Work, Va. Assn. Counselor Educators and Suprs., Va. Sch. Counselors Assn. (pres., chairperson nominations and elections com. 1984—), Peninsula Counselors Assn. (sec., v.p., pres., ethics chairperson).

HELMS-VANSTONE, MARY WALLACE, anthropology educator; b. Allentown, Pa., Apr. 15, 1938; d. Samuel Leidich and Mary (Wallace) Helms; divorced. BA, Pa. State U., State College, 1960; MA, U. Mich., 1962, PhD, 1967. Instr. Wayne State U., Detroit, 1965-67; asst. prof. Syracuse (N.Y.) U., 1967-68; lectr. Northwestern U., Evanston and Chgo., Ill., 1969-79; prof. U. N.C., Greensboro, 1979—, head dept. anthropology, 1979-85. Author: Asang: A Miskito Community, 1971, Middle America, 1975, Ancient Panama, 1979, Ulysses' Sail, 1988, Craft and the Kingly Idea, 1993; contbr. articles to profl. jours. Fellow Am. Anthrop. Assn.; mem. Am. Soc. Ethnohistory (pres. 1976), Am. Ethnological Soc., So. Anthrop. Soc. (pres. 1980-81, proceedings editor 1982-94). Office: Univ NC Dept Anthropology Greensboro NC 27412

HELOISE, columnist, lecturer, broadcaster, author; b. Waco, Tex., Apr. 15, 1951; d. Marshal H. and Heloise K. (Bowles) Cruse; m. David L. Evans, Feb. 13, 1981. B.S. in Math. and Bus, S.W. Tex. State U., 1974. Owner, pres. Heloise, Inc. Asst. to columnist mother, Heloise, 1974-77, upon her death took over internationally syndicated column, 1977; author: Hints from Heloise, 1980, Help from Heloise, 1981, Heloise's Beauty Book, 1985, All-New Hints from Heloise, 1989, Heloise: Hints for a Healthy Planet, 1990, Heloise from A to Z, 1992, Household Hints for Singles, 1993, Hints for All Occasions, 1995; contbg. editor Good Housekeeping mag., 1981, Speaker for the House; co-founder, 1st co-pilot Mile Pie in the Sky Balloon Club. Mem. Good Neighbor Coun. Tex.-Mex.; sponsor Nat. Smile Week. Recipient Mental Health Mission award Nat. Mental Health Assn., 1990, The Carnegians Good Human Rels. award, 1994. Mem. AFTRA, SAG, Women in Comm. (Headliner 1994), Tex. Press Women, Internat. Women's Forum, Women in Radio and TV, Confrerie de la Chaine des Rotisseurs (bailli San Antonio chpt.), Ordre Mondial des Gourmets De'Gustateurd de U.S.A., Death Valley Yacht and Racket Club, Zonta. Home: PO Box 795000 San Antonio TX 78279-5000 Office: care King Features Syndicate 235 E 45th St New York NY 10017-3305

HELPERT-NUNEZ, RUTH ANNE, clinical social worker, psychotherapist; b. Rosebud, Tex., Jan. 7, 1956; d. Otto Henry and Lorene Margaret (Hoelscher) Helpert; m. J.W. Will Nunez. BS with high honors in Social Work, U. Tex., Austin, 1978, MS in Social Work, 1981. Lic. master social worker-advanced clin. practitioner; lic. marriage and family therapist, Tex. Student intern Child Protective Svcs. Tex. Dept. Human Svcs., Austin, 1978; child protective svcs. specialist Tex. Dept. Human Svcs., Killeen and Belton, 1979-80; grad. student intern Austin Child Guidance Ctr., 1981; caseworker Heart of Tex. Region Mental Health Mental Retardation, Waco, Tex., 1981-83; child protective svcs. specialist Tex. Dept. Human Svcs., Austin, 1983-84; caseworker DayGlo Family Treatment program Austin-Travis County Mental Health Mental Retardation Ctr., 1984-88; therapist, clin. social worker Anthony W. Arden, Ph.D & Assocs., Bryan, Tex., 1989-90, Thomas Edwards, Ph.D., P.C., Bryan, 1990—. Bd. dirs. Toy Libr., College Station, Tex., 1989. Mem. NASW (qualified clin. social worker, bd. diplomate; chair Brazos Valley unit 1990-94, bd. dirs. Tex. chpt. 1990-94, exec. com. 1993-94, chair profl. stds. com. 1993-94), Child Advocacy Resource and Edn. Coalition (v.p. 1991, spkrs. bur.), Acad. Cert. Social Workers, Phi Kappa Phi, Phi Theta Kappa. Democrat. Office: Thomas H Edwards PhD PC 3705 S College Ave Bryan TX 77801-4494

HELTERBRAND, PEARL JANE, special programs adminstrator, educator; b. Dayton, Ohio, July 19, 1943; d. Forest Omar Humphreys and Nora Pauline (Glaze) Williams; m. James Glenn Helterbrand, Sept. 9, 1972 (div.); 1 child, Glenda Gail. BS in Elem. Edn., U. Tampa, 1965; MEd, Ohio U., 1990; postgrad., U. Dayton, 1992—. 4th grade tchr. Hillsborough County Schs., Tampa, 1965-68, Dept. Def. Sch., Mannheim, Germany, 1968-70; 3rd grade tchr. Dept. Def. Sch., Fuchu, Japan, 1970-72; chpt. I tchr. Lynchburg (Ohio)-Clay Local, 1974-76; elem. tchr. Western Local Schs., Piketon, Ohio, 1976-92, spl. program supr., 1992—. Contact person Early Childhood Edn. Western Local Schs., Piketon, Ohio, 1992—, SEARCH collaborative, Waverly, 1992—; mem. Effective Sch. Leadership, Piketon, 1990-93; assoc. mem. Leesburg Brush and Palette Guild, 1991—; emergency med. technician Brushcreek Life Squad, Sinking Spring, Ohio, 1977-83. Scholar Martha Holden Jennings, 1988-89. Mem. ASCD, Ohio Assn. Elem. Sch. Adminstrs., Ohio Assn. Adminstrs. Fed. Program. Home: 1100 Northview Dr 15E Hillsboro OH 45133 Office: Western Local Schs 12599 State Rt 124 Piketon OH 45661

HELTON, LUCILLE HENRY HANRATTIE, academic administrator; b. Ft. Worth, Mar. 2, 1942; d. P.D. and Virginia (Clark) Henry; m. Wayne Hanrattie, June 26, 1965 (div. Apr. 1986); children: Clark, Chris; m. William M. Helton, Jr., Mar. 19, 1988. BA, So. Meth. U., 1964; MEd, U. Pitts., 1968; cert. in adminstrn., William Paterson Coll., 1984; cert. in mid-mgmt., Tex. Christian U., 1987. Cert. elem. tchr. N.J., Pa., Tex. Nat. field sec. Kappa Kappa Gamma Sorority, Columbus, Ohio, 1964-65; elem. tchr. Pitts. Bd. Edn., 1965-69; co-dir, chmn. dept. maths. Assn. Children with Learning Disabilities Sch., Pitts., 1969-72; tchr. elem., secondary, gifted and remedial and home instrn. programs West Milford (N.J.) Bd. Edn., 1976-84; prin., exec. dir. Hill Sch., Ft. Worth, 1984—. Mem. Coun. of Ministries of 1st Meth. Ch., 1986-87; adminstrv. bd. 1st United Meth. Ch. Ft. Worth. Mem. DAR, ASCD, Tex. Ind. Sch. Consortium, Assn. for Children with Learning Disabilities, Leadership Tex., Coalition for Spl. Needs Students, Orton Dyslexia Soc., Forum Ft. Worth, Rotary. Democrat. Methodist. Office: Hill Sch 4817 Odessa Ave Fort Worth TX 76133-1640

HELTON, SANDRA LYNN, finance executive; b. Paintsville, Ky., Dec. 9, 1949; d. Paul Edward and Ella Rae (Van Hoose) H.; m. Norman M. Edelson, Apr. 15, 1978. BS, U. Ky., 1971; MBA, MIT, 1977. Capital budget adminstr. Corning (N.Y.) Glass Works, 1978-79, fixed assets mgr., 1979-80, contr. electronics divsn., 1980-82, mgr. customer fin. svcs., 1982-84, dir. fin. svcs., 1984-86, asst. treas., 1986-91, v.p., treas., 1991-94, sr. v.p., treas., 1994—. Vol. Mass. Gen. Hosp., Boston, 1976; asst. treas. Corning Mus. of Glass; treas., pres. bd. dirs. Chemung Valley Arts Coun., Corning, 1981-87; bd. dirs. Corning Summer Theatre, 1987-91, Arnot Hosp. Found., 1988—; mem. fin. com. Clemens Performing Arts Ctr., Elmira, N.Y., 1985-92; mem. adv. bd. Chase Lincoln, 1988-91; mem. bus. com. Met. Mus. Art, 1992—; pres. bd. dirs. Rockwell Mus., 1992—; mem. Regional Cultural Adv. Com., 1992—.

HELVIK, MAY LOIS, accountant; b. Clear Lake, Iowa, Nov. 9, 1941; d. Harry Harrison and Esther Elnora (BeenKen) Holmes; m. Lawrence Ray Hansen, Sept. 22, 1965 (div. 1983); children: Lorna May Hansen Smith, Daniel Lawrence, Sarah Elnora; m. Kelvin Arthur Helvik, Apr. 6, 1985. Grad. high sch., Clear Lake, 1959. Sch. bd. sec., asst. bus. mgr. Clear Lake Community Schs., 1959-85; acctg. supr. Fort Dodge (Iowa) Community Schs., 1986—; bd. dirs. Frontier Credit Union, Fort Dodge. Mem. Iowa Assn. Sch. Bus. Ofcls., Am. Payroll Assn. Lutheran. Office: Fort Dodge Community Schs 104 S 17th St Fort Dodge IA 50501

HELWICK, CHRISTINE, lawyer; b. Orange, Calif., Jan. 6, 1947; d. Edward Everett and Ruth Evelyn (Seymour) Hailwood; m. Robert C. Helwick, May 27, 1972; children: Ted C., Dana J. BA, Stanford U., 1968; MA, Northwestern U., 1969; JD, U. Calif., San Francisco, 1973. Bar: Calif., U.S. Supreme Ct. U. S. Ct. Appeals (9th cir.), U.S. Dist. Ct. (no., ctrl., so. and ea. dist.) Calif. Tchr. history New Trier Twp. High Sch., Winnetka, Ill., 1968-69; sec. to the producer Flip Wilson Show, Oakland, 1970; rsch. assoc. Bingham, Summers, Welsh & Spilman, Indpls., 1973; assoc. Crosby, Heafey, Roach & May, Oakland, Calif., 1973-78; asst. counsel litigation U. Calif., Oakland, 1978-84, mng. univ. counsel, 1984-94, counsel Berkeley campus, 1989-94; interim gen. counsel Calif. State Univ. System, 1994—; lectr. in field. Mem. instnl. review bd. Devel. Studies Ctr., Oakland, 1990—; DECIDE project instr. Wildwood Elem. Sch., Peidmont, Calif., 1989-91; cub scout leader Piedmont, 1988-91; leader Camp Fire Girls Club, Piedmont, 1990-93; bd. dirs. Wildwood Sch. Parents' Club, 1987—, col. coord., 1987-89, parent edn., 1989-90, membership com., 1990-91, bd. edn. rep., 1991-94. Mem. Nat. Assn. Coll. and Univ. Attys. (publs. com. 1993-94, arrangements coms. 1992-93, annual cong. program com. 1992-94), State Bar Calif. (exec. com. 1980-83), Alameda County Bar Assn. (exec. com. trial practice sect. 1994, minority access program com. 1989, bd. dirs. 1977), Alameda County Bar Found. (adv. trustee 1988-90, bd. dirs. 1991), Alameda County Fee Arbitration Panel, Order of Coif. Episcopalian. Office: Calif State U 400 Golden Shore Long Beach CA 90802

HEMBROUGH, DORIS KAY, artist; b. Jacksonville, Ill., Feb. 25, 1951; d. Gerald Lavon and Wilma Lucille (Menge) H.; m. Alex A. Sokovich, March 5, 1972 (div. 1980); 1 child, Emily Noreen. Student, Western Ill. U., 1969-70; BBA, U. Wis., 1982. Buyer, mgr. S.A. Barker, Springfield, Ill., 1974-77; prin. D.K. Gallery, Cassville, Wis., 1986—. One-woman shows include Dubuque (Iowa) Mus., 1989, Plains Gallery, Portland, Maine, 1989, Gallaway Gallery, Rochester, Minn., 1990, Lands' End Gallery, Dodgeville, Wis., 1992, Internos Gallery, Milw., 1994, others; group shows include Gallery Ten, Rockford, Ill., 1986, Whitefish Bay Farm Gallery, Door County, Wis., 1985-94, U. Wis., La Crosse, 1990; represented in collections at Brainerd (Minn.) Regional Ctr., Wis. Sch. Music, Madison, Kohler-Clarke Gallery, Milw., others. Address: 202 Durtschi Dr Mount Horeb WI 53572

HEMINGWAY, BETH ROWLETT, author, columnist, lecturer; b. Richmond, Va., May 6, 1913; d. Robert Archer and Evelyn Lucille (Doggett) Rowlett; B.Mus., Hollins Coll., 1934; m. Harold Hemingway, Apr. 2, 1938; children—Ruth Hartley, Martha Scott. Writer, Richmond-Lifestyle mag.; columnist Artistry in Bloom, Richmond Times-Dispatch; author: A Second Treasury of Christmas Decorations, 1961; Flower Arrangement with Antiques, 1965; Christmas Decorations Say Welcome, 1972; Antiques Accented by Flowers, 1975; Beth Hemingway's No Kin to Ernest, 1980; Holidays with Hemingway, 1985; lectr. numerous states, also Australia, 1966, Eng., 1977. Vol., Hermitage Meth. Home, 1977-79. Mem. Nat. League Am. Pen Women, Va. Writers Club, Richmond Hort. Assn., Va. Fedn. Garden Clubs (book rev. chmn.), Richmond Council Garden Clubs (flower arrangement chmn.), Clay Spring Garden Club (pres. 1953-55), Barton Garden Club (pres. 1959-61, 74). Republican. Methodist. Home: Apt E-103 1900 Lauderdale Dr Richmond VA 23233

HEMINGWAY, MARIEL, actress; b. Mill Valley, Calif., Nov. 21, 1961; d. John Hadley and Byra Louise (Whittlesey) H.; m. Steven Douglas Crisman, Dec. 9, 1984; children: Dree, Langley. Studies with Harold Guskin. Owner, sec. Clear Water Pictures, 1986; co-owner Sam's Cafe Restaurant, N.Y. Actress: (stage prodns.) The Palace of Amateurs, California Dog Flight, 1985, (feature films) Lipstick, 1976, Manhattan, 1979 (Acad. award nomination 1979), Personal Best, 1982, Star '80, 1983, Creator, 1985, The Mean Season, 1985, Superman IV: The Quest for Peace, 1987, Sunset, 1988, The Suicide Club, 1988, Delirious, 1991, Falling From Grace, 1992, (TV movies) I Want to Keep My Baby, 1977, Amerika, 1987, Into the Bad Lands, 1991, Desperate Rescue: The Cathy Mahone Story, 1993, (TV series) Civil Wars. Office: care ICM 8942 Wilshire Blvd Beverly Hills CA 90211*

HEMLOW, JOYCE, language and literature educator, author; b. Liscomb, N.S., Can., July 30, 1906; d. William and Rosalinda (Redmond) H. B.A., Queen's U., Kingston, Can., 1941, M.A., 1942; A.M., Harvard U., 1944; Ph.D., Radcliffe Coll., 1948; LL.D., Queen's, 1967, Dalhousie U., 1972. Mem. faculty McGill U., 1945—, Greenshields prof. English lit. and lang., 1965—, prof. emerita, 1975—. Author: The History of Fanny Burney, 1958 (James Tait Black Meml. book prize for best biography in U.K., also Gov. Gen. Can. medal for academic non-fiction 1958, Rose Mary Crawshay prize Brit. Acad. 1960); editor: Journals and Letters Fanny Burney (Madame d'Arblay), 12 vols., Fanny Burney: Selected Letters and Journals, 1986, 87. Guggenheim fellow, 1951-52, 66-67; recipient Disting. Achievement award Radcliffe Coll., 1969. Fellow Royal Soc. Can.; mem. Johnsonians, Internat. Assn. Univ. Profs. English, Phi Beta Kappa. Home: Liscomb, NS Canada B0J 2A0

HEMMER, JANE REYNOLDS, state senator, real estate executive; b. Gainesville, Ga., Mar. 23, 1947; d. Minor Garland Reynolds Sr. and Julia Mae Rochester; m. John Lee Hemmer, Jr., Aug. 31, 1968; children: John Lee III, Mary Reynolds. BS, Med. Coll. Ga.; postgrad., U. Ga., Brenau Coll. Pres. White Sulphur Properties, Inc., Gainesville; senator State of Ga., Atlanta; chair senate storm water pollution study com., 1993-94; mem. seamless edn. study com., 1993-94, joint comms. com. for senate and house, 1993-94; vice chair senate natural resources com., 1993-94; mem. appropriations com., 1993-94. Mem. Ga. Environ. Adv. Coun., 1991-92, Ga. Local Governance Commn., 1991-92, trustee trustee North Ga. Coll., 1988—, Lakeview Acad., 1988—; trustee Gainesville Coll., 1983-86, treas. bd. trustees, 1985-86; trustee Lanier Tech. Sch., 1981-86, vice-chair bd. trustees, 1984, chairperson, 1985; chair Lanier Clean Lakes Task Force, 1993—; mem. Gainesville/Hall County Bd. Health, 1989-92, vice-chair, 1991-92; chair Hall County Citizens Adv. Com. on Solid Waste, 1989—; Fanning fellow Leadership Ga. Class of 1990, 1990, bd. trustees, 1992-94. Recipient Ed Dodd Svc. award Elachee Nature Sci. Ctr., 1990, Legislator of Yr. award 9th Dist. Ga. Mcpl. Assn., 1993, 94, ACCG Legis. award, 1994. Mem. Nat. Assn. Counties (bd. dirs. 1991—, mem. resolutions com. 1991—, vice chair growth mgmt. subcom. 1991—, other coms.), Rotary. Democrat. Episcopalian. Home: 3645 White Sulphur Rd Gainesville GA 30507-7617 Office: PO Box 907306 Gainesville GA 30501-0906

HEMMI, LYNN MARIE, financial executive; b. Livonia, Mich., Aug. 9, 1967; d. Robert William and Barbara Jean (West) H. BBA, U. Mich., 1988, M Acctg., 1990. CPA, Conn., Md. Fin. analyst Chesebrough Ponds U.S.A., Greenwich, Conn., 1990-91, fin. mgr., 1992-94; internal auditor Unilever U.S., N.Y.C., 1991-92; comml. mgr. sales & trade mktg. Van den Bergh Foods, Trumbull, Conn., 1994—. Office: Van den Bergh Foods 75 Merritt Blvd Trumbull CT 06611

HEMMING, CAROL, make-up artist. films include: Heat and Dust, 1983, The Bostonians, 1984, Castaway, 1986, Maurice, 1987, Howard's End, 1992, The Remains of the Day, 1993, Mary Shelley's Frankenstein, 1994 (Acad. award nom., Best Make-up). *

HEMMINGER, PAMELA LYNN, lawyer; b. Chgo., June 29, 1949; d. Paul Willis and Lenore Adelaide (Hennig) H.; m. Robert Alan Miller, May 14, 1979; 1 child, Kimberly Anne. BA, Pomona Coll., 1971; JD, Pepperdine U., 1976. Tchr. Etiwanda (Calif.) Sch. dist., 1971-74; law clerk Gibson Dunn & Crutcher, Newport Beach, Calif., 1974-76; assoc. Gibson Dunn & Crutcher, L.A., 1976-84, ptnr., 1985—. Contbg. author Sexual Harassment, 1992, Employment Discrimination Law, 1993; contbr. articles to profl. jours. Mem. comparable worth task force Calif., Sacramento, 1984, Pepperdine U. Sch. of Law Bd. Visitors, 1990—. Mem. L.A. County Bar Assn. (treas., labor and employment sect. 1994-95), Calif. C. of C. (employment rels. com. 1984—). Republican. Lutheran. Office: Gibson Dunn & Crutcher 333 S Grand Ave Los Angeles CA 90071-1504

HEMMINGSEN, BARBARA BRUFF, microbiology educator; b. Whittier, Calif., Mar. 25, 1941; d. Stephen Cartland and Susanna Jane (Alexander) Bruff; m. Edward Alfred Hemmingsen, Aug. 5, 1967; 1 child, Grete. BA, U. Calif., Berkeley, 1962, MA, 1964; PhD, U. Calif., San Diego, 1971. Lectr. San Diego State U., 1973-77, asst. prof., 1977-81, assoc. prof., 1981-88, prof., 1988—; vis. asst. prof. Aarhus U. Denmark, 1971-72; cons. AMBIS, Inc., San Diego, 1984-85, Woodward-Clyde Cons., 1985, 87-91. Author: (with others) Microbial Ecology, 1972; contbr. articles to profl. jours. Mem. Planned Parenthood, San Diego. Mem. AAAS, Am. Soc. Microbiology, Am. Women in Sci., Sigma Xi, Phi Beta Kappa (pres. Nu chpt. 1986-88, historian 1990-94, corr. sec. 1994—). Democrat. Office: San Diego State U Dept Biology San Diego CA 92182-4614

HEMMY, MARY LOUISE, social work administrator; b. Mpls., Nov. 14, 1914; d. Albert H. and Mary (Scott) H. BS, U. Minn., 1936, MA in Social Wk., 1941. Caseworker Washington U. Med. Ctr., St. Louis, 1937-40, Ill. Svcs. for Crippled Children, Springfield, 1941-42; instr., asst. prof. Sch. Social Wk., Washington U., 1942-45; dir. social wk. dept. Washington U. Med. Ctr., 1945-52; assoc. prof., dir. social wk. Coll. Medicine, U. Ill., Chgo., 1952-53; exec. dir. Am. Assn. Med. Social Workers, Washington, 1953-55; prof. sch. medicine sch. social work U. Pitts., 1956-59; exec. dir. Benjamin Rose Inst., Cleve., 1959-77; mem. spl. med. adv. group VA, 1963-68; mem. Ohio Bd. Examiners Nursing Home Adminstrs., 1973-77. Mem. Nat. Assn. Social Workers (bd. dirs. 1961-63), Am. Assn. Homes for Aging (bd. dirs. 1963-70). Home: 13505 SE River Rd Portland OR 97222-8038

HEMPFLING, LINDA LEE, nurse; b. Indpls., July 28, 1947; d. Paul Roy and Myrtle Pearl (Ward) H. Diploma Meth. Hosp. Ind. Sch. Nursing, 1968; postgrad. St. Joseph's Coll. Charge nurse Meth. Hosp., Indpl., 1968; staff nurse operating room Silver Cross Hosp., Joliet, Ill., 1969; charge nurse operating room Huntington (N.Y.) Hosp., 1969-73; night supr. oper. rm., post anesthesia care unit Hermann Hosp., Houston, 1973-76; unit. mgr., purchasing coord. oper. rms., 1976-83; RN med. auditor, quality improvement and tng. coord. Nat. Healthcare Rev., Inc., Houston, 1984—. Future Nurses Am. scholar, 1965, Nat. Merit scholar, 1965. Mem. Nat. League Nursing, Am. Nurses Assn., Assn. Oper. Rm. Nurses, Tex. Med. Auditors Assn. Office: 1130 Earle St Houston TX 77030-5008

HEMPHILL, NORMA JO, special event planning and tour company executive; b. Enid, Okla., Nov. 25, 1930; d. Wyatt Warren and Wanda Markes (Parker) Stout; m. Benjamin Robert Hemphill, June 21, 1952; children: Susan Colleen, Robert Gary. Student, Okla. State U.; BA, U. Calif., Berkeley, 1955. Former acct. Better Bus. Bookkeeping, Lafayette, Calif.; tchr., Head Start tchr. Chino (Calif.) Elem. Sch., 1966-68; pres., founder Calif. Carousel and Carousel Tours, Lafayette, 1972—; mem. adv. com. The William Penn Mott, Jr. Vis. Ctr., San Francisco, 1995—; speaker in field; cons., dir. various orgns. Past bd. dirs. PTA, Moraga, Calif., Lafayette; bd. dirs. Children's Home Soc., Upland, Calif., 1965-69; past demonstation tchr. Presbytery of Bay Area, San Francisco; past supt. 1st Presbyn. Ch., Oakland, Calif., elder, 1977—, trustee, 1980; mem. hon. adv. com. Festival of Lake, Oakland, 1982; bd. govs. Goodwill Industries, 1978-79; founder, chmn. Joint Svc. Clubs Foster Children's Ann. Christmas Party; mem. adv. com. for William Penn Mott Jr. Visitors Ctr., Presidio of San Francisco Nat. Park, 1995—. Named Person of Yr. award Advt.-Mktg. Assn. East Bay, 1978; co-recipient Event of Yr. award, Am. Pub. Rels. Assn., 1984. Mem. Lake Merritt Breakfast Club (Oakland, spl. events com., bd. govs., named Citizen of Community 1992), Lake Merritt Inst. (hon.), Soroptimist (very important women honor roll Diablo Valley 1990, keynote speaker 1991), Pi Beta Phi (bd. dirs., spl. events com. Contra Costa County chpt., Founder's Day speaker at U. Calif.-Berkeley, 1993). Office: Calif Carousel & Carousel Tours PO Box 537 Lafayette CA 94549-0537

HEMSING, JOSEPHINE CLAUDIA, public relations professional for performing arts; b. Paris, France, June 5, 1953; d. Albert E. and Esther (Davidson) H.; m. Daniel F. Cameron, Sept. 22, 1990. Student, Sorbonne U. de Paris, 1972-73; BA, Sarah Lawrence Coll., 1974; postgrad., CUNY, 1982—. Dep. dir. distbn. ASCAP, N.Y.C., 1975-81; assoc. dramaturg and festival coordinator Städtische Bühnen Freiburg, Fed. Republic Germany, 1981-82; publicity asst. Audrey Michaels Pub. Relations, N.Y.C., 1983; publicity assoc. N.Y. Philharmonic, N.Y.C., 1984-85; publicist The Carson Office, N.Y.C., 1985-89; founder, dir. Hemsing Assocs., N.Y.C., 1989—. Mem. prodn. staff for New Russian Chamber Orch., N.Y.C., 1976-79, Encompass Music Theatre, N.Y.C., 1978-79, Wallgraben Theater on Tour, U.S.,A., 1980, Rodger Hess Prodns., N.Y.C., 1982, John Hart Assoc., N.Y.C., 1982, Peter Witt Players Prodns., N.Y.C., 1982-83, numerous Broadway and off-Broadway shows including How I Got That Story, 1982, Twice Around the Park, 1983, Diary of a Madman, 1989; NBC-TV documentary Missiles Go Home, 1981; numerous published translations. Democrat. Home: Apt 29K 401 E 80th St New York NY 10021 Office: Apt 14H 401 E 80th St New York NY 10021-0654

HENARD, ELIZABETH ANN, controller; b. Providence, Oct. 9, 1947; d. Anthony Joseph and Grace Johanna (Lokay) Zorbach; m. Patrick Edward Mann, Dec. 18, 1970 (div. July 1972); m. John Bruce Henard Jr., Oct. 19, 1974; children: Scott Michael, Christopher Andrew. Student, Jacksonville (Fla.) U., 1966. Sec. So. Bell Tel.&Tel., Jacksonville, 1964-69; office mgr. Gunther F. Reis Assocs., Tampa, Fla., 1969-71; exec. sec. Ernst & Ernst, Tampa, 1971-72; exec. sec. to pres. Lamalie Assocs., Tampa, 1972-74; exec. sec. Arthur Young & Co., Chgo., 1975; adminstrv. asst. Irving J. Markin, Chgo., 1975; contr., v.p., corp. sec. Henard Assocs., Inc., Dallas, 1983-92. Mem. Dallas Investors Group (treas. 1986-91), Tampa Palms Country Club. Republican. Roman Catholic. Home: 15705 Mifflin Ct Tampa FL 33647-1120

HENCH, COLLEEN DENA, artist; b. Palo Alto, Calif., Feb. 23, 1953; d. Robert Con Hench and Betty (Aldrin) Bentley; m. Robert Colescott, 1986 (div. 1992); 1 child, Cooper Robert. BA, Chico State U., 1975; postgrad., San Francisco Art Inst., 1976. Graphic designer Addison-Wesley Pub., Menlo Park, Calif., 1978-82, Ketchum Comm. Vicom Advt. Design Vectors, 1982-84, Busse & Cummins, San Francisco, 1984-85, Am. West Mag., Tucson, 1985-86; prodr., dir. Video Art Prodns., Tucson, 1987-93; freelance graphic design Tucson, 1988-91; graphic designer Types, Tucson, 1991-93. One-woman shows include Rancho Linda Vista Gallery, Oracle, Ariz., 1988, Tucson (Ariz.) Community Cable Corp. Gallery, 1992, Phoenix (Ariz.) Ctr. Visual Arts Gallery, 1993; exhibited in group shows including Mo David Gallery, N.Y.C., 1985, Yuma (Ariz.) Art Ctr., 1988, Del Rio Coun. for the Arts, S.W. Art Exhbn., Tex., 1992; prodr., dir.: (art videos) In The Studio with Robert Colescott, 1989 (2d place BBest Arts Program 1989), Desert Ballet, 1989 (2d place Best Arts Program 1989), Rodeo (first place). Recipient Visual Art fellowship in two dimensional media Ariz. Commn. on the Arts, 1992. Home: 3525 E Elida St Tucson AZ 85716

HENDERSHOT, CAROL MILLER, physical therapist; b. Lancaster, Pa., July 24, 1959; d. Richard Horace and Joan Marie (Nonnenmocher) Miller; m. Richard A. Hendershot, Dec. 29, 1989; 1 child, Scott Michael. BS in Physical Therapy, Quinnipiac Coll., 1981. Staff phys. therapist Easter Seal Rehab. Ctr., Lancaster, 1981-85, phys. therapy dept. head, 1986-89; staff phys. therapist Community Hosp. of Lancaster, 1985-86, Guilds' Sch. & Neuromuscular Ctr., 1990—. Dir. publicity and pub. rels. Lancaster Dist. United Meth. Women, 1988-89; vice chmn. coun. on ministries Covenant United Meth. Ch., Lancaster, 1988-89, chmn. ch. and soc. com., 1987, 88, mem. chancel choir, 1981-89, mem. adminstrv. bd., 1975-88; trustee Audubon Pk. United Meth. Ch., 1990-93, mem. chancel choir, 1990-92, mem. staff parish rels. com. 1993—, mem. Jubilee Bell Choir, 1990—; dir. Bethlehem and Joy Bells Handbell Choirs, 1994—. Mem. Neuro-Devel. Treatment Assn., Visiting Nurse Assn. (profl. adv. com. 1987-89), Beta Beta Beta. Democrat. Methodist. Home: W 6007 Hopi Ct Spokane WA 99208

HENDERSHOTT LOVE, ARLES JUNE, television news director; b. Rockford, Ill., Oct. 22, 1956; d. Eugene Bourden and Rose Marie (Erickson) Hendershott; m. Joseph William Love, Sept. 20, 1986. BS with high honors, Ill. State U., 1979. Reporter Sta. WTVO-TV, Rockford, 1979-82, news producer, 1982-83; news assignment editor Sta. WIFR-TV, Rockford, 1983-86, news dir., 1986—; speaker Rockford Pub. Schs., 1980-83. Producer news story Pee Wee Explosion, 1985 (AP award 1986). Bd. dirs. Rockford Airshow, 1994-95; mem. com. YWCA, Rockford, 1987, Westminister Presbyn. Ch., Rockford, also tchr. Sunday Sch.; bd. dirs. No. Ill. chpt. March of Dimes, 1980-84, NW Ill. chpt. Spl. Olympics, Rockford, 1986—, Discovery Ctr. Mus., Rockford, 1987—, N.W. Ill. Alzheimer & Related Disorder Assn., 1991, Rockford CrimeStoppers, 1992—; active YMCA Luncheon Coun., 1992-93, leader Lunch Coun., 1994-95. Recipient Leadership award Ken-Rock Community Ctr., Rockford, 1980, Presidential award of honor

Rockford Jaycees, 1986, Dist. award Zonta Pub. Rels. Campaign, 1990, Leader Luncheon award YWCA, 1991. Mem. AAUW (bd. dirs. 1982-84), NAFE, Radio-TV News Dirs. Assn. (TV state coord. for Ill. 1989—), Ill. News Broadcasters Assn., Soc. Profl. Journalists, Am. Mgmt. Assn., Archeology Inst. Am., Rockford C. of C. (pres. club 1993), Univ. Chgo. Oriental Inst., Ill. Assoc. Press (exec. com. 1989—, pres.-elect 1990, pres. 1991), Lens & Shutter Club (pres. 1983-85, others), Zonta. Office: Sta WIFR-TV 2523 Meridian Rd Rockford IL 61102

HENDERSON, ANGELA ANITA, media specialist; b. N.Y.C.; d. Walter Alexander and Anita Rae (Marshall) H. BA, CCNY, 1978; MA, Howard U., 1985. Reporter The Black Am., N.Y.C., 1977-78, The Oakland Press, Pontiac, Mich., 1978-79; pub. info. officer Sta. WTVS-TV, Detroit, 1979-83; tchg. asst. Howard U., Washington, 1983-84; pub. info. asst. NSF, Washington, 1984-87; editl. asst. AAAS, Washington, 1987-88; publicity and media rels. coord. Sta WHMM-TV, Washington, 1988—. Vol. Smithsonian Inst., Washington, 1992—; active Nat. Hook-up of Black Women, Washington, 1988-93. Recipient advt. and promotion award PBS, 1980, 90, 91, 92, 93. Mem. Capital Press Club. Office: Sta WHMM-TV 2222 4th St NW Washington DC 20059

HENDERSON, ANNE MARIE, internal revenue agent; b. Camden, N.J., Oct. 18, 1964; d. John Joseph and Elizabeth Marjorie (Gibbons) McCormick; m. Joseph Eugene Henderson, Sept. 24, 1988. BSBA, Drexel U., 1988. Internal revenue agt. IRS, Phila., 1985-94, spl. agt., 1994—. Trustee libr. bd. Oaklyn (N.J.) Meml. Libr., 1991—. Mem. Inst. Mgmt. Accts. (So. N.J. chpt. dir. community svc. 1989-91, v.p. community svc. 1991-92, pres. 1992-93). Office: IRS PO Box 12060 6th and Arch Sts Philadelphia PA 19105

HENDERSON, ARIA DALE, owner; b. Denton, Tex., Oct. 7, 1933; d. Roy Franklin and Maxyne Lee Edsall; m. George Dan Lowe, May 11, 1950 (div. 1953); children: George Arthur Lowe, Alicia Faye Lowe Harms; m. Raymond Peril Henderson, June 24, 1968. Student, Howard Payne Coll., 1967-68. Owner Lil Ole Fish Bowl, Brownwood, Tex., 1968-85; co-owner Henderson Mobile Home Transport Inc., Brownwood, 1971—. Various positions Ext. Homemaker Club, Brownwood, 1977—. Republican. Baptist. Home and Office: Rte 4 Box 106H Brownwood TX 76801

HENDERSON, CAROL MORNER, nurse, educator; b. Milw., Oct. 12, 1941; d. Lester A. and Mildred M. (Ford) Kindschi; children from previous marriage: Alicia, Angela, Shannon. BSN, U. Ala., 1963; MA, U. So. Ala., 1970, MSN, 1987; EdD, Nova U., 1983. Staff nurse Providence Hosp., Mobile, Ala., 1964-65; instr., coord. Mastin Sch. Nursing, Mobile, 1966-73; asst. prof. Coordiate Coll. for Health Professions U. South Ala., Mobile, 1973-74, asst. to dir. Sch. Nursing, 1974-76, assoc. dean Coll. Nursing, 1981-89, asst. mem. grad. faculty Coll. Nursing, 1982, prof. Coll. Nursing, 1983-95, dir. grad. studies Coll. Nursing, 1987-88; mem. grad. faculty, Coll. Nursing U. South Ala., 1993-95; dir., chair divsn nursing Spring Hill Coll., 1995—. Mem. ANA, Nat. League Nursing, Nat. Wellness Assn., Sigma Theta Tau, Phi Kappa Phi (past pres.). Office: U South Ala Coll Nursing Mobile AL 36688

HENDERSON, GERALDINE THOMAS, retired social security official, educator; b. Luling, Tex., Jan. 7, 1924; d. Cornelius Thomas and Maggie (Keyes) Thomas; m. James E. Henderson, Feb. 9, 1942 (dec. Apr. 1978); children—Geraldine, Jessica, Jennifer. BS, Fayetteville State U., 1967. Tchr. Cumberland County Schs., Fayetteville, N.C., 1966-67, Fayetteville City Schs., 1967-68; with Social Security Adminstrn., Fayetteville, 1968-87; substitute tchr. Cumberland County Sch. System, 1987—; claims rep. Pres. Fayetteville State U. Found., 1981-82; pres. NAACP, Fayetteville br., 1983-86. DeaconColl. Heights Presbyn. Ch., 1965-79, ruling elder, 1980-91; bd. dirs. Fayetteville Art Coun., 1984—, Cumberland County United Way, 1983—, chmn. div. corp. mission Fayetteville Presbytery, 1986, mem. personnel review bd. City of Fayetteville, 1987—; inductee Nat. Black Coll. Alumni Hall of Fame, 1988; bd. dirs. Habitat for Humanity, Fayetteville, N.C., 1989, Share, Heart of the Carolinas, 1991; moderator Presbytery of Coastal Carolina, 1989; vice chair Cape Fear Food Bank, 1991. Mem. LWV, Nat. Assn. Equal Opportunity in Higher Edn. (disting. alumni 1989), Legion Aux. (treas. 1981-83), Zeta Phi Zeta (Woman of Yr. 1984), Omega Psi Phi (Citizen of Yr. 1985). Democrat. Presbyterian. Avocations: creative dress design; gardening; travel.

HENDERSON, HARRIET, librarian; b. Pampa, Tex., Nov. 19, 1949; d. Ervin Leon and Hannah Elizabeth (Yoe) H. AB, Baker U., 1971; MLS, U. Tex., 1973. Sch. libr. Pub. Sch. System, Pampa, Tex., 1971-72; city libr. City of Tyler, Tex., 1973-80, City of Newport News, Va., 1980-84; dir. librs. and info. svcs. City of Newport News, 1984-90; dir. Louisville Free Pub. Libr.; del. White House Conf. Librs. and Info. Svcs.; bd. mem. Tex. Libr. Systems Act Adv. Bd., 1979-80. Budget panel chmn. Peninsula United Way, Hampton, Va., 1984-85; mem. bd. Peninsula coun. Boy Scouts Am., 1982-84, Peninsula Womens Network, Newport News, 1983-85; mem. Leadership Louisville, 1991—, Alliant Health System Adult Oper. Bd., 1991—; mem. adv. com. dept. edn. Spalding U., 1991—; diaconate Hidenwood Presbyterian Ch., Newport News, 1983-85; del. White House Conf. Librs. and Info. Svcs., 1991. Recipient Tribute to Women in Bus. and Industry, Peninsula YWCA, Newport News, 1984. Mem. ALA, Ky. Libr. Assn. (vice chair pub. libr. sect. 1994), Va. Libr. Assn. (chmn. legis. com. 1981-84, v.p. 1985, pres. 1986), Rotary Club Louisville (chair youth svc. com. 1994—), Jr. League Louisville. Office: Louisville Free Pub Libr Office of Dir 301 York St Louisville KY 40203-2257

HENDERSON, JANA L., federal agency administrator, infosystems specialist; b. Anamosa, Iowa, Feb. 19, 1944; d. H. Dean and Rosetta I. (Lyon) H.; m. Steven J. Reinking, June 18, 1966 (div. June 1971). BA cum laude, U. Iowa, 1966, MBA, 1975. Cert. secondary edn. tchr., math. Systems analyst Iowa Nat. Mut. Ins. Co., Cedar Rapids, 1966-73; sr. systems analyst Westinghouse Learning Corp. div. Westinghouse Corp., Iowa City, Iowa, 1973-77, sr. computer specialist, 1977-88; sr. program mgr. U.S. Dept. Edn., Washington, 1988—, also cons., 1976. Mem. NAFE, Beta Gamma Sigma. Methodist. Lodge: Order Eastern Star. Office: US Dept Edn ROB3 # 4642 400 Maryland Ave SW Washington DC 20202-0001

HENDERSON, JANET KAREN, English language educator; b. Matherville, Ill., Apr. 25, 1943; d. Clare C. and Lillian O. Henderson; m. Edward Conde, Aug. 18, 1990. BS in Edn., Western Ill. U., 1965, MA, 1966; MS, Ill. State U., 1971; EdD, Rutgers U., 1982. Teaching asst. Western Ill. U., Macomb, 1965-66; English tchr. Ill. State U., Normal, 1966-71; counselor Bergen C.C., Paramus, N.J., 1971-86, English tchr., 1987—; N.J. faculty exch. fellow Rutgers U., New Brunswick, 1994—. CIRD grantee, 1976, 78, 91; Mid Career fellow Princeton U., 1991. Mem. Nat. Coun. Tchrs. English, N.E. Regional Assn. Tchrs. English in Two Yr. Coll. Composition and Comm. Home: 39 E Walnut St Teaneck NJ 07666-3926

HENDERSON, JOHNNIE MAE, nursing educator; b. McDonald, Ga., Feb. 6, 1926; d. Johnny Kyle and Ollie Mae (Thompson) Hardeman; m. Lorenza Henderson, Aug. 21, 1945; children: Lorenza II, Johnny Kenneth. BS in Nursing, BA in Sociology, Case Western Res. U., 1970, MS, 1973; EdD, Nova U., 1979. Staff nurse Univ. Hosp., Cleve., 1966-67, charge nurse, 1967-69; instr. nursing Cuyahoga C.C., Cleve., 1970-74, asst. prof., 1974-77, assoc. prof., 1977-80, prof., 1980-90, assoc. dean nursing, 1984-90; ret., 1990; case mgr. April Care Health Svcs., 1994—. Bd. dirs. Cleve. Coun. Black Nurses, 1982—, rsch. dir., 1991, Friends of Nardonia Libr., 1991; bd. trustees Madonna Nursing Home & Ctrl. Sch. Practical Nursing, 1993—; active NAACP. Mem. Nat. League for Nursing, Sigma Theta Tau, Alpha Kappa Alpha. Baptist.

HENDERSON, JONI LYNNE, cultural organization administrator; b. Glendale, Calif., May 1, 1968; d. Glenn Donald and Jeanette Ann (Johnson) H. BS, U. Redlands, 1990; MS, Drexel U., 1992. Substitute tchr., coach volleyball Burbank (Calif.) Unified Sch. Dist., 1990-91; intern in edn. pub. affairs Phila. Mus. Art, 1991-92; devel. assoc. Meridian Internat. Ctr., Washington, 1992-93; corp. assoc. Smithsonian Inst., Washington, 1993—. Vol. fund raising cons. for vaious non-profit orgns. Mem. Women of Washington, Jr. League. Home: 1201 S Scott St # 519 Arlington VA 22204 Office: Smithsonian Instn 1481 Arts & Industries Washington DC 20560

HENDERSON, KAREN LECRAFT, federal judge; b. 1944. BA, Duke U., 1966; JD, U. N.C., 1969. Ptnr. Wright & Henderson, Chapel Hill, N.C., 1969-70, Sinkler, Gibbs & Simons, P.A., Columbia, S.C., 1983-86; asst. atty. gen. Columbia, 1973-78; sr. asst. atty. gen., dir. of spl. litigation sect., 1978-82, deputy atty. gen., dir. of criminal div., 1982; judge U.S. Dist. Ct. S.C., Columbia, 1986-90, U.S. Ct. Appeals (D.C. cir.), Washington, 1990—. Apptd. Dist. Ct. Adv. Com. Mem. ABA (litigation sect. and urban, state and local government law sect.), N.C. Bar Assn., S.C. Bar (government law sect., trial and appellate practice sect., fed. judges assn.). Office: US Ct Appeals DC Cir US Courthouse 3rd & Constitution Ave NW Washington DC 20001*

HENDERSON, KATHRYN LUTHER, library science educator; b. Champaign, Ill.; d. Carl F. and Ida (Lietz) Luther; m. William T. Henderson, Aug. 22, 1953. AB, U. Ill., 1944, BS, 1948, MS, 1951. Clerical asst. U. Ill. Library, Urbana, 1944-46; asst. Grad. Sch. Library Sci. U. Ill., Urbana, 1947-50; serial cataloger U. Ill., Urbana, 1950-53; circulation libr. McCormick Theol. Sem., Chgo., 1953-56, head cataloger, 1956-65; instr. Grad. Sch. Library Sci., U. Ill., Urbana, 1965-67, asst. prof., 1967-71; assoc. prof. Grad. Sch. Library and Info. Sci., U. Ill., Urbana, 1971-85, prof., 1985—; cons. to various profl. insts. and orgns.; presenter in field. Mem. editorial bd. Cataloging and Classification Quar., 1984—; editor: Major Classification Systems, 1977, MARC II Records and Their Uses, 1971, Trends in American Publishing, 1968; co-editor: (with William T. Henderson) Conserving and Preserving Library Materials, 1983, Conserving and Preserving Nonbook Materials, 1991; contbr. articles to profl. jours. Recipient Disting. Alumnus award Grad. Sch. of Libr. & Info. Sci. Alumni Assn. U. Ill. at Urbana-Champaign, 1993. Mem. ALA (mem. coms., Beta Phi Mu award for Outstanding Svc. to Edn. in Librarianship 1993), Ill. Libr. Assn. (chair resources and tech. svc. sect.), AAUP, Am. Theol. Libr. Assn. (mem. coms.), Assn. for Libr. and Info. Sci. Edn. (Teaching Excellence award 1995), Am. Soc. for Info. Sci., Beta Phi Mu, Kappa Delta Phi. Mem. United Ch. of Christ. Home: 1107 E Silver St Urbana IL 61801-6807 Office: University of Illinois Grad Sch Libr & Info Sci 501 E Daniel Champaign IL 61820

HENDERSON, LINDA KAY, state legislator. BA, MA, Ind. U. Mem. Ind. Ho. of Reps. from dist. 65, 1992—; mem. aged and aging com., edn. com., fin. instns. com., vice chair roads and transp. com.; svc. coord. Res-Care Cmtys., Inc. Active Leadership Lawrence County; mem., former bd. dirs. Lawrence County Red Cross. Mem. Farm Bur. Democrat. Home: 628A Riley Blvd Bedford IN 47421-9600 Office: Ind Ho of Reps State Capitol Indianapolis IN 46204*

HENDERSON, MARSHA ROSLYN THAW, clinical social worker; b. San Antonio, Dec. 31, 1946; d. Eugene and Ann (Pokloff) Thaw; m. Thomas Jay Henderson, July 14, 1976; 1 child, Ashley Erin. BA, U. Houston, 1968, MSW, 1973. Lic. clin. social worker, Calif.; diplomate Am. Bd. Examiners in Clin. Social Work. Intake worker St. Joseph's Mid Houston Community Mental Health Ctr., 1968-69; caseworker II, Tex. Rsch. Inst. Mental Scis., Houston, 1969-71; pvt. practice, Houston, 1971-73; psychiat. social worker Intercommunity Child Guidance Ctr., Hawaiian Gardens, Calif., 1974-75; clin. social worker Family Guidance Ctr., Buena Park, Calif., 1975-77; pvt. practice, Huntington Beach and Mission Viejo, Calif., 1976—; presenter at high schs. on adoption as alternative, 1986—; condr. art therapy workshops Calif. State U., L.A., 1977, U. Calif., Irvine, 1980. Mem. NASW, Acad. Cert. Social Workers, Calif. Soc. for Clin. Social Worker, Am. Adoption Congress, Calif. Forensic Mental Health Assn., Child Sexual Abuse Network. Office: 26932 Oso Pky Ste 200 Mission Viejo CA 92691 also: 8071 Slater Ste 230 Huntington Beach CA 92649

HENDERSON, MARY LOUISE, civic worker; b. Windsor, Ont., Can., Apr. 24, 1928; came to U.S., 1932; d. Kenneth Charles and Florence McGie (Morton) Campbell; m. Ernest Flagg Henderson III, Dec. 31, 1953; children: Ernest Flagg IV, Roberta C. BA, Bard Coll., 1950. V.p. Ruse & Urban, Inc., advt., Detroit, 1950-53; v.p., bd. dirs. Henderson House Am., Sudbury, Mass., 1969—. Pres. Wellesley (Mass.) Friendly Aid Assn., 1970-75, Newton (Mass.) Wellesley Hosp. Aid, 1980-82, 88-89; co-founder Wellesley Community Ctr., 1972, pres., 1983-85; bd. dirs., mem. exec. com. Norumbega Coun. Boy Scouts Am., 1974—, pres., 1989-91; trustee Newton-Wellesley Hosp., 1982—, mem. exec. com., 1990—; bd. dirs., mem. Greater Boston adv. bd. Salvation Army, 1985—, Sch. for Officers Tng. Salvation Army, 1994—; mem. nat. adv. bd. Officers Tng. Sch. Salvation Army, 1994—; bd. dirs. Newton-Wellesley Vis. Nurse Assn., 1974—; corporator Boston Bio-Med. Inst., 1990—; also others. Mem. Mensa, Am. Needlepoint Guild (founder, pres. Mass. chpt. 1974-77, bd. dirs. 1974—, nat. historian 1989—). Republican. Episcopalian. Home: 171 Edmunds Rd Wellesley MA 02181-1331

HENDERSON, MAUREEN MCGRATH, medical educator; b. Tynemouth, Eng., May 11, 1926; came to U.S., 1960; d. Leo E. and Helen (McGrath) H. MB BS, U. Durham, Eng., 1949, DPH, 1956. Prof. preventive medicine U. Md. Med. Sch., 1968-75, chmn. dept. social and preventive medicine, 1971-75; assoc. epidemiology Johns Hopkins U. Sch. Hygiene and Pub. Health, 1970-75; prof. epidemiology and medicine U. Wash. Med. Sch., 1975—, asst. v.p. and assoc. v.p. health scis., 1975-81, head cancer prevention rsch. program Fred Hutchinson Cancer Rsch. Ctr., 1983-94; mem. Nat. Inst. Environ. Health Scis. Coun., 1994—; chmn. epidemiology and disease control study sect. NIH, 1969-82; chmn. clin. trial rev. com. Nat. Heart Lung and Blood Inst., 1975-79; mem. Nat. Cancer Adv. Bd., 1979-84; mem. bd. Robert Wood Johnson Health Policy Fellowship, 1989-93; bd. on radiation effects rsch. NRC, 1991—. Assoc. editor jour. Cancer Rsch., 1987-88; mem. editorial bd. Jour. Nat. Cancer Inst., 1988—; mem. editorial adv. bd. Cancer Detection and Prevention, 1992—. Recipient John Snow award Am. Pub. Health Assn., 1990; Luke-Armstrong scholar, 1956-57; John and Mary Markle scholar acad. medicine, 1963-68. Mem. Inst. medicine of NAS (coun. 1981-85), Am. Coll. Epidemiology, Assn. Tchrs. Prevention Medicine (pres. 1972-73), Soc. Epidemiol. Rsch. (chmn. 1969-70), Internat. Epidemiol. Assn. (exec. officer 1971-76), Internat. Coun. Cancer Rsch. (sci. adv. bd. 1989—), Am. Epidemiol. Soc. (pres. 1990-91). Home: 5309 NE 85th St Seattle WA 98115-3915 Office: Fred Hutchinson Cancer Ctr Cancer Prevention Rsch Program 1124 Columbia St Seattle WA 98104-2092

HENDERSON, MAXINE OLIVE BOOK (MRS. WILLIAM HENDERSON, III), association executive; b. Rush, Colo., Apr. 22, 1924; d. Jesse Frank and Olive (Booth) Book; B.A., U. Colo., 1945; m. William Henderson III, Apr. 10, 1948 (dec. May 1983); children—William IV, Meredith. Personnel adminstr. Gen. Electric Co., Schenectady and N.Y.C., 1945-54; asst. dir. placement Katherine Gibbs Sch., N.Y.C., 1967-70; v.p., dir. William Henderson Cons., Inc., N.Y.C., 1969-83, pres., dir., 1983-86; dir. recruitment Girl Scouts U.S.A., N.Y.C., 1973-78, dir. human resources, 1978-82, dir. career devel., 1982-91, adminstr. human resources 1991-93; pres., adminstr. World Found., 1993—. Pres., Goddard-Riverside-Trinity Sch. Thrift Shop, N.Y.C., 1964-65, Trinity Sch. Mothers' Orgn., N.Y.C., 1965-66; treas. Brearley Sch. Parents Assn., N.Y.C., 1966-67; mem. The Museums at Stoney Brook, Smithtown Arts Coun., Mus. Modern Art. Mem. Am. Portuguese Soc., 1983—. Episcopalian. Clubs: North Suffolk Garden, Nissequoque Beach, Nissequoque Platform Tennis Assn. (St. James, L.I., N.Y.). Home: 606 W 116th St New York NY 10027-7011 also: Nissequogue River Rd Saint James NY 11780 Office: 420 Fifth Ave New York NY 10018-2702

HENDERSON, NANCY ELLEN, student services director; b. Scottsbluff, Nebr.. BA in Polit. Sci., U. Denver, 1981, MA in Philosophy, 1983; MA in Edn., Calif. Polytech. State U., 1990. Asst. to dir. Tchr. Edn. Inst. Calif. Polytech. State U., San Luis Obispo, 1987-91, cons. tchr. diversity project, 1989-90; assoc. dir. student svcs. U. Wis.-Wash. County, West Bend, 1991-93, dir. student svcs., 1993—; tutor Laubach Literacy Chpt., San Luis Obispo, 1986-91. V.p. comms. ACLU of San Luis Obispo County, 1989-91; leadership candidate West Bend Area C. of C., 1994—. Kaplan grantee, 1993-94. Mem. Am. Coll. Pers. Assn., Wis. Coll. Pers. Assn. Democrat. Office: U Wis-Wash County 400 University Dr West Bend WI 53095

HENDERSON, NANCY GRACE, marketing and systems executive; b. Berkeley, Calif., Oct. 23, 1947; d. John Harry and Lorraine Ruth (Johnson) H. BA, U. Calif., Santa Barbara, 1969; MBA, U. Houston, 1985; teaching credential, U. Calif., L.A., 1971. Chartered Fin. Analyst. Tchr. Keppel Union Sch. Dist., Littlerock, Calif., 1969-72, Internat. Sch. Prague, Czechoslovakia, 1972-74, Sunland Luth. Sch., Freeport, Bahamas, 1974-75; tchr., dept. head Internat. Sch. Assn., Bangkok, Thailand, 1975-79; exec. search Diversified Human Resources Group, Houston, Tex., 1979-82; data processing analyst Am. Gen. Corp., Houston, 1982-83, personnel and benefits dept., 1983-85, investment analyst, 1985-86, equity security analyst/quantitative portfolio analyst, 1986-87; dir. mktg. and communications Vestek Systems Inc., San Francisco, 1987—; tchr. English as Second Language program Houston Metro. Ministries, 1980-81. Pres., bd. dirs. Home Owners Assn., Walnut Creek, Calif., 1988-90; tchr. English to refugees Houston Metro Ministries, 1982; exec. dir. Internat. Child Abuse Prevention Found., 1989; ch. choir, coun., fundraising and com. chmn. Presbyn. Ch.; active Crisis Hotline, 1978-79, 92-93; dir. project Working in Networks for Good Shelter, 1993—. Named a Notable Woman of Tex., 1984-85. Mem. Assn. for Investment Mgmt. and Rsch., Toastmasters (pres. Houston chpt. 1983, v.p. 1982-83). Office: Vestek Systems 388 Market St Ste 700 San Francisco CA 94111-5347

HENDERSON, PAMELA MASON, elementary education educator; b. Fullerton, Calif., Feb. 26, 1947; d. Joseph Harold and Marilyn (Rogers) Mason; m. Martin D. Kobaly, June 1, 1968 (div. 1981); children: Michael Drew Kobaly, Christopher Scott Kobaly; m. Eldon Leroy Henderson, Aug. 7, 1982. AA, Coll. of the Desert, 1966; BA, Whittier Coll., 1968; MA, Pepperdine U., 1976. Tchr. Shelley (Idaho) Sch. Dist., 1969-70, Fontana (Calif.) United Sch. Dist., 1974-82; tchr. Mariposa (Calif.) County Unified Sch. Dist., 1983—, mentor, tchr. aerospace tech., 1988-89. Historian, sec. No. Mariposa County Hist. Mus., Coulterville, Calif., 1982-84. Mem. Calif. Tchrs. Assn. (rep. 1983-92), Mariposa Tchrs. Assn. (pres. 1992-94). Home: 2295 Golfito Way La Grange CA 95329-9625 Office: Coulterville-Greeley Sch 10326 Fiske Rd Coulterville CA 95311-9502

HENDERSON, PEGGY, psychotherapist; b. Ogden, Utah, Nov. 25, 1946; d. Reed Howey and Marjorie Weaver) H.; m. Lynn M. Sargent, Apr. 14, 1966 (div. July 16, 1989); children: Myke Sargent, Lyndee Sargent, Phillip Sargent. BS, Met. State U., 1989; MA, U. Colo., Denver, 1993. Nat. cert. counselor. Secretarial svcs. Payne Enterprises, Midwest City, Okla., 1971-79; real estate salesperson Blue Ribbon Real Estate, Mountain Green, Utah, 1977-79; ins. salesperson Met. Ins., Aurora, Colo., 1982-87; therapist Excelsior Youth Ctr., Aurora, Colo., 1989—; com. mem. Life Underwriters Assn., Denver, 1986-88; seminar leader Children, Adolescent Family Assn. of Colo., 1992. Various positions Boy Scouts of Am., Utah, Colo., 1968-88; precinct chair, various positions Dem. Party, Utah, Colo., 1975-87; active 4-H, Girl Scouts, Aurora Girls Softball Assn. Recipient scholarship Weber St. Coll., 1966, Ogden Bd. Realtors, 1978. Mem. Am. Counselor Assn., Am. Assn. Marriage and Family Therapy, Alpha Omega Honor Soc. Democrat. LSD. Home: 14303F E Dickinson Dr Aurora CO 80014-2321 Office: Excelsior Youth Ctr 15001 E Oxford Ave Aurora CO 80014-4186

HENDERSON, RITA RENEE, public administrator; b. Richmond, Va., Feb. 2, 1959; d. Arnold Reginald and Florence Evelyn (Bailey) H. BA, Hampton U., 1981; MS, Va. State U., 1983; cert., Va. Exec. Inst., 1993, Duke U., 1993. Grad. teaching asst. Va. State U., Petersburg, 1981-83; rsch. asst. NIH/Med. Coll. Va., Richmond, 1982; rschr. NIH/Va. State U., Petersburg, 1982-83; health educator Med. Coll. Va., Richmond, 1984-88, info. officer, 1988-90; program mgr. Va. Dept. Health, 1990-91; dep. adminstrn. Va. Dept. Alcoholic Beverage Control, Richmond, 1991—; leig. lobbyist, intern Va. Gen. Assembly/Va. Retail Merchants Assn., Commonwealth Va., 1983; mem. adv. bd. Intergovtl. Tech. Conf., 1994—, Coun. on Info. Mgmt., 1993—. 2d vice chmn. bd. dirs. Urban League Greater Richmond, Va., 1989—; bd. trustees Sci. Mus. Va., Commonwealth Va., 1990—; exec. com. Va. Black Caucus, Commonwealth Va., 1993—. Mem. Am. Soc. Pub. Adminstrs., Quality Control Richmond.

HENDERSON, ROBBYE ROBINSON, library director; b. Morton, Miss., Nov. 10, 1937; d. Robert and Aljuria (Myers) R.; 1 child, Robreka Aljuria. BA in Lang. Arts, Tougaloo Coll., 1960; MSLS, Atlanta U., 1968; PhD in Ednl. Leadership, So. Ill. U., 1976. Librarian Patton Lane High Sch., Basteville, Miss., 1960-66, Utica (Miss.) Jr. Coll., 1966-67, Miss. Indsl. Coll., Hollysprings, 1967-68; acquisition librarian Miss. Valley State U., Itta Bena, 1968-72, acting librarian, 1972-73, dir. James Herbert White Library, 1973—; cons. Office of Health Resources Opportunity, Washington, 1977-79, Miss. Assn. of Colls., Jackson, 1970-79. Vol. Teen Parenting Project State of Miss., 1987. Mem. Miss. Library Assn., Alpha Kappa Alpha (pres. Kappa Alpha Omega chpt. 1984-86, coordinator 1987, Baseilus award 1985). Home: MVSU Box 42 14000 Hwy 82 W Itta Bena MS 38941-0042 Office: Mississippi Valley State U James Herbert White Libr Itta Bena MS 38941

HENDERSON, ROBERTA MARIE, librarian, educator; b. Mosinee, Wis., July 27, 1929; d. Roy H. and Marie Helena (Dittman) H. BS, Cen. State Tchrs. Coll., Stevens Point, Wis., 1951; MS, U. Wis., 1958; MA, No. Mich. U., 1975; Cert. of Adv. Studies, U. Denver, 1980. Librarian Wiesbaden (Ger.) Am. High Sch., 1954-55, Ashland (Wis.) High Sch., 1955-56; tchr./librarian Clark AFB, Philippines, 1956-57; librarian Prescott (Ariz.) Jr. High Sch., 1958-59, Frankfurt (Ger.) Am. High Sch., 1959-63; tchr./librarian Zama Am. High Sch., Camp Zama, Japan, 1963-66; librarian Ankara (Turkey) Am. High Sch., 1966-68; tutor Nkozi Tchr. Tng. Coll., Mpigi, Uganda, 1968-70; ref. librarian/prof. No. Mich. U., Marquette, 1971-93; retired, 1993; cons. No. Mich. U. and Pub. Librs., 1993—; coord. faculty workshops No. Mich. U., 1986-88; cons. Escanaba (Mich.) Pub. Libr., 1987, 90, 92. Author slide/tape: Locating Materials in Periodicals and Documents, 1977, Library Materials for Literature Students, 1979. Mem. libr. com. Marquette County Hist. Soc., 1981—; mem. Upper Peninsula Environ. Coalition, Houghton, 1985—; host Marquette-Japan Sister Coalition City Program, 1988. Title II-B fellow, U. Denver, 1979-80; Human Resources Dept., No. Mich. U. grantee, 1986, 87; recipient Disting Faculty award No. Mich. U., 1988. Mem. ALA, AAUP, Libr. Instrn. Roundtable, Phi Kappa Phi (chpt. treas. 1987-91). Home: 515 E Ridge St Marquette MI 49855-4216

HENDLER, ROSEMARY NIELSEN, business owner; b. Sydney, Australia, Oct. 18, 1946; came to U.S., 1954, naturalized, 1970; d. Robert Stanley McFarlane and Joyce Elizabeth (Annetts) Nielsen; m. Joel Arnold Hendler, June 1, 1977; 1 child, Stewart Maxwell. BA, U. Calif., Berkeley, 1968; postgrad., Acad. Art San Francisco, 1974-76, UCLA, 1985-87. Buyer linens Breuners Home Furnishings, Oakland, Calif., 1969-71; buyer textiles Liberty House, San Francisco, 1971-73, Bullock's, Palo Alto, 1973-75; graphic artist Montclarion Pubs., Oakland, 1975-77; pres., owner Cordeaux River Trading Co., L.A., 1986-93. Advisor (CD-ROM) Visionary Stampede. Bd. dirs. docent coun. Los Angeles County Mus. Art, 1981—; VIP hostess Olympic Games, L.A., 1984; bd. dirs. Young Audiences, L.A., 1985-87; exec. bd. Orinda Arts Coun., 1991—, pres., 1993-94; mem. Calligraphers Forum, 1991—; mem. art guild Oakland Mus., 1991—; youth commr. Orinda Community Ch., 1991—; mem. task force Arts and Cultural Coun. of Contra Costa County, 1994—. Recipient Design award Levi Strauss, 1975. Mem. NAFE, Nat. Assn. Local Arts Agys., Calif. Assn. Local Arts Agys., Jr. League L.A., Costume Coun., Los Angeles County Mus. Art, Town Hall, Orinda C. of C. Republican. Office: 16 El Verano Orinda CA 94563-1912

HENDLEY, EDITH DI PASQUALE, physiology and neuroscience educator; b. N.Y.C., Sept. 5, 1927; d. Michael and Rose (Parillo) Di Pasquale; m. Daniel Dees Hendley, Apr. 21, 1952; children: Jane Alice, Joyce Louise, Paul Daniel. AB, Hunter Coll. City N.Y., 1948; MS, Ohio State U., 1950; PhD, U. Ill., Chgo., 1954. Instr. U. Chgo., 1954-56; asst. lectr. U. Sheffield (Eng.), 1956-57; instr., rsch. assoc. Johns Hopkins U. Sch. Medicine, Balt., 1963-72; sr. investigator Friends Med. Sci. Rsch. Ctr., Balt., 1972-73; assoc. prof. U. Vt. Coll. Medicine, Burlington, 1973-83, prof., 1983-94; prof. emeritus, 1994—. Co-author 6 books; contbr. over 60 articles to profl. jours. Rsch. grantee NIH, 1974—, NSF, 1986-89, Vt. affiliate Am. Heart Assn., 1982-83, The Sugar Assn. Inc., 1984-85. Mem. AAAS, Am. Physiol. Soc., Am. Soc. Pharmacology and Exptl. Therapeutics, Soc. for Neurosci. (exec. com., treas. Vt. chpt. 1978—), Assn. for Women in Sci. (treas. 1972-74, exec. com., long-range planning com. 1974-76). Home: 10 Highland Ter S

Burlington VT 05403-7601 Office: U Vt Coll Medicine Dept Molecular Phys Bi Burlington VT 05405

HENDRA, BARBARA JANE, public relations executive; b. Watertown, N.Y., July 14, 1938; d. Frederick R. and Irene J. (Rotundo) H. BA, Vassar Coll., 1960. Publicity dir. Fawcett World Library, N.Y.C., 1961-69; v.p., dir. publicity and pub. relation Pocket Books-Simon & Schuster, N.Y.C., 1969-77; corp. dir. publicity and pub. relations Putnam Pub. Group, N.Y.C., 1977-79; pres. Barbara J. Hendra Assocs., Inc., N.Y.C., 1979-91, The Hendra Agy. Inc, Bklyn., 1991—; adj. prof. NYU, 1981. Contbg. author: Trade Book Marketing, 1983, The Encyclopedia of Publishing, 1995. Mem. Pubs. Publicity Assn. (bd. dirs. 1977-81, pres. 1979-81), Vassar Club, Regency Whist Club. Home: 140 Sterling Pl Brooklyn NY 11217-3307 Office: The Hendra Agy Inc 142 Sterling Pl Brooklyn NY 11217

HENDREN, DEBRA MAE, critical care nurse; b. Belle Fourche, S.D., Apr. 27, 1959; d. Clyde Leslie and Kathryn Ann (Daughters) F.; m. Anthony Ray Martinez, May 21, 1983 (div.); m. Cecil B. Hendren, Nov. 21, 1992. AD, Casper Coll., 1987, cert. EMT, 1990. RN, Colo., Wyo.; CCRN. Nurse Wyo. Med. Ctr., Casper, North Suburban Med. Ctr. (formerly Humana Hosp. Mountain View), Thornton, Colo.; nurse Swedish Med. Ctr., Englewood, Colo., charge nurse ICU, 1993—. Mem. Wyo. Nurses Assn., Colo. Nurses Assn., AACN. Home: 5168 E 126th Ct Thornton CO 80241

HENDREN, MERLYN CHURCHILL, investment company executive; b. Gooding, Idaho, Oct. 16, 1926; d. Herbert Winston and Annie Averett Churchill; student U. Idaho, 1944-47; B.A. with honors, Coll. of Idaho, 1986. m. Robert Lee Hendren, June 14, 1947; children—Robert Lee, Anne Aleen. With Hendren's Furniture Co., Boise, 1947-69; co-owner, v.p. Hendren's Inc., Boise, 1969-87, pres. 1987—. Bd. dirs. Idaho Law Found., 1978-84; chmn. Coll. of Idaho Symposium, 1977-78, mem. adv. bd., 1981—; bd. dirs. SW Idaho Pvt. Industry Council, 1984-87; pres. Boise Council on Aging, 1959-60, mem. adv. bd., 1986—; mem. Gov.'s Commn. on Aging, 1960, Idaho del. to White House Conf. Aging, 1961; trustee St. Luke's Regional Hosp., 1981-92; mem. adv. bd. dirs. Boise Philharm. Assn., Inc., 1981—, Ballet Idaho; bd. dirs. Children's Home Soc. Idaho, 1988; founding pres. Idaho Congl. Award Program, 1993—; sustaining mem. Boise Jr. League. Mem. Boise C. of C. (bd. dirs. 1984-87), Gamma Phi Beta. Episcopalian. Home: 3504 Hillcrest Dr Boise ID 83705-4503 Office: 1109 Main St Ste 230 PO Box 9077 Boise ID 83702

HENDRICKER, SARA LYNN AGUE, mayor; b. Coffeyville, Kans., June 21, 1941; d. Paul Stewart and Elizabeth Ellen (Slaughter) Ague; m. David George Hendricker, June 19, 1965; children: Alan David, Ellen Paige. BA in Chemistry cum laude, Austin Coll., 1962; BA in Russian summa cum laude, Ohio U., 1979, MA in Polit. Sci., 1985. Rsch. chemist Nat. Cancer Inst., 1964-65; mem. city coun. City of Athens, Ohio, 1979-84, chmn. fin. com., 1980-84, personnel/budget adminstr., 1984-85, mayor, 1988—; coord. pub. adminstrn. programs Inst. for Local Govt. Adminstrn. and Rural Devel. Ohio U., Athens, 1986-87; part-time instr. Russian Ohio U., 1979-81, part-time instr. polit. sci., 1985-86. Author: Public Budgeting in Ohio: A Handbook for Local Government Officials, 1986, Public Sector Collective Bargaining: A Handbook for Local Government Officials in Ohio, 1986, 88, The Municipal Legislature in Action: A Handbook for Village and City Councils, 1987. Active Appalachian Task Force, Community Improvement Corp., ILGARD Adv. Bd., Gov.'s Commn. on Hazardous Materials, MORPC/ODNR Urban Forestry Task Force, dist. 18 exec. com. Ohio Pub. Works Commn., adv. bd. Salvation Army; past pres. bd. trustees Southeastern Ohio Emergency Med. Svc.; past chairwoman AHGJMV Solid Waste Mgmt. Dist. Sr. fellow Hemisphere Inst. for Pub. Svc. Mem. Am. Soc. for Pub. Adminstrn., Internat. City Mgmt. Assn., Am. Polit. Sci. Assn., Nat. League Cities (fin., adminstrn. and intergovtl. rels. policy com.), Am. Planning Assn., Govt. Fin. Officers Assn., Ohio Mayors' Assn. (trustee), Ohio Mcpl. League (trustee), Athens Found. (trustee), Southeastern Ohio Regional Coun., Athens C. of C. (econ. devel. com.), Rotary, Civitan (Disting. Pres. Athens chpt., Honor Key), Alpha Chi, Phi Kappa Phi, Phi Beta Kappa, Blue Key. Home: 13 Roxbury Dr Athens OH 45701-3307

HENDRICKS, FANNY-DELL See FANNY-DELL

HENDRICKS, IDA ELIZABETH, mathematics educator; b. Roanoke, Va., Aug. 13, 1941; d. Samual Jarboe and Nannie Virginia (Needy) Hodges; m. William Hampton Hendricks, Aug. 10, 1963; 1 child, William Hodges. BS in Math. & BA in Secondary Edn., Shepherd Coll., 1963; Ma in Devel. Studies & Higher Edn., Appalachian State U., 1992, cert. devel. edn. specialist, 1988. Faculty Harpers Ferry (W.Va.) High Sch., 1963-72, Jefferson High Sch., Shanandoah Junction, W.Va., 1972-78; mem. math. faculty, devel. math. specialist, adminstr. Shepherd Coll., Shepherdstown, W.Va., 1981-94; ret., 1994; creator, implementor devel. math. program Shepherd Coll.; tutor. Contbr. articles to profl. jours. Elder, organist, mem. Christ Reformed Ch., Shepherdstown, 1950—; organist Shepherdstown Presbyn. Ch., 1957—. Mem. AAUW (past treas.), Nat. Assn. Devel. Edn., W.Va. Assn. Devel. Edn. (sec. 1993—), W.Va. Coun. Tchrs. Math., Shepherdstown Hist. Soc. Home: PO Box 123 Shepherdstown WV 25443

HENDRICKS, MINNIE MARIE, secondary education teacher; b. St. Charles, Va., Dec. 30, 1933; d. James and Mary Minnie (Robbins) Poe; m. George Hendricks, Nov. 19, 1955; children: Phyllis, Elizabeth. BA and BS in Edn., Union Coll., 1955; MS in Biology, Marshall U., 1970. Tchr. jr. high sci. Big Walnut Local, Sunbury, Ohio, 1955; tchr. third grade Beaver (Ohio) Bd. Edn., 1958-59; tchr. biology, chemistry and earth sci. Ea. Local Sch. Bd., Beaver, 1964—. Mem. choir Beaver Emmanuel United Meth. Ch., mem. sec., lay delegate, Sunday Sch. tchr. Recipient tuition/stipend NSF, Capital U., 1966, Marshall U., 1967, Ohio U., 1969, Ohio Bd. Regents, Miami U., 1992. Mem. Nat. Sci. Tchrs. Assn., NEA, Ohio Edn. Assn., S.E. Ohio Edn. Assn. (mem. exec. com. 1976—), Ea. Local Classroom Tchrs. Assn. (pres. 1981—). Home: 291 Van Fossan Rd Beaver OH 45613 Office: Ea High Sch 1170 Tile Mill Rd Beaver OH 45613

HENDRICKS, SUSAN SPANGLER, public relations consultant, lobbyist; b. Macon, Ga., Nov. 30, 1943; d. James Christian and Martha Ann (Lamon) Spangler; m. Lloyd Inman Hendricks, Sept. 3, 1966; children: Lloyd Inman, Jr., James Christian. AA, St. Mary's Coll., Raleigh, N.C., 1964; BA in Sociology, U. S.C., 1966. Registered lobbyist, S.C. Youth counselor S.C. Employment Security Commn., 1966-68; tchr. sociology and civics Dentsville High Sch., 1968-69; Britannica assoc. Encyclopaedia Britannica Ednl. Corp., 1974-81; exec. dir. State Mus. Campaign, 1982-84; exec. dir., lobbyist Safety Belts for S.C., 1985-92; pres. Hendricks & Co., Mktg., Pub. & Govt. Rels., Columbia, S.C., 1985—. Publisher, editor: (ann. directory) S.C. Guide to Media/Legislature, 1990—. Past pres., mem. Legal Aux., Columbia, 1974—; past treas., mem. Palmetto Cabinet, S.C., 1976—; bd. dirs. Friends of Library, Columbia, 1976-80, Crime Stoppers, Columbia, 1994—. Recipient State Recreation award, 1980, Best of the Best award Write One, 1993, Best Newsletter award Appraisal Inst., 1992, 93; named to Order of Palmetto, 1983, Assns. Advance Am. Honor Role, 1992. Mem. Am. Soc. Assn. Execs., Pub. Rels. Soc. Am. (Mercury award 1990, 91, Silver Wing award 1993), S.C. Soc. Assn. Execs.(Best in Bus. award 1990, 92, 93), Mortgage Bankers Assn. Columbia, Columbia Rotary Club (bulletin chair 1993—). Office: Hendricks & Co PO Box 7773 Columbia SC 29202

HENDRICKS, TRACY LEE, secondary education educator; b. Tulsa, Oct. 2, 1955; d. Joe Emil and Joella (Carson) H. BA, Northeastern Okla. State U., 1977, MA, 1978. Cert. tchr., Okla. High sch. tchr. Claremore (Okla.) High Sch., 1977—; head math. dept. Claremore (Okla.) High Sch., 1992—. Mem. NEA, Okla. Edn. Assn., Claremore Classroom Tchr. Assn. Republican. Baptist. Office: Claremore High Sch 1910 N Florence Ave Claremore OK 74017-3100

HENDRICKSON, BARBARA CONSUELO, artist, retired educator; b. Columbus, Ohio, Mar. 26, 1932; d. Gallia George and Lena Margaret (Vellani) DeNucci; m. Gilbert L. Hofacker, June 14, 1952 (div. 1967); children: Rachel Alison, Gilbert L. Jr.; m. Christopher P. Hendrickson, Dec. 12, 1969. BA in English, Miami U., Oxford, Ohio, 1954; MA in English, Calif. State U., Hayward, 1966, postgrad., 1966-75; MA in Art, San Jose State U., 1982. life standard teaching credential with specialization in jr. coll. teaching, life lang. arts tchr., life C.C. supr. credential, life C.C. instrn. credential in fine and applied arts and related techs., Calif. Instr. English, Calif. State U., 1966-67, lectr., 1972, 73, 80; prof. English and women's studies Ohlone Coll., Fremont, Calif., 1967-89, prof. emeritus, 1989—, chmn. dept. English, 1970-72, supr. writing lab., 1978-81, mem. faculty senate, 1967-87, v.p. senate, 1971; master tchr. Ohlone Coll. in relationship with Calif. State U. and San Jose State U., 1969-80. Exhibited in group shows at Hayward Area Artists, 1978, 80, Livermore (Calif.) Art Festival, 1980, Ohlone Coll. Art Gallery, 1981, 85, Vida Gallery, San Francisco, 1983, Richmond (Calif.) Art Ctr., 1983, Sun Gallery, Hayward, 1983, 84, 85, Hayward Area Forum Arts, 1986, Bedford Gallery, Walnut Creek, Calif., 1992, Pacific Art League Palo Alto, Calif., 1992, 94, Berkeley (Calif.) Art Ctr., 1993, others, 1978—. Mem. NOW, Women's Caucus for Art. Democrat. Home and Studio: 25201 2nd St Hayward CA 94541-5614

HENDRICKSON, LOUISE, retired association executive, retired social worker; b. Lansdowne, Pa., Sept. 14, 1916; d. Norman and Gertrude (Powers) H. AA, Long Beach Jr. Coll., 1936; BA, U. Calif., Berkeley, 1938, gen. secondary tchr.'s cert., 1939; MS in Social Work, Columbia U., 1952. Cert. secondary tchr., Calif.; registered social worker. Dir. young adult program YWCA, Oakland, Calif., 1944-48; dir. group work and informal edn. svcs. YWCA, Bklyn., 1948-53; exec. dir. YWCA, Spokane, Wash., 1953-58; field cons. Nat. Bd. YWCA, Chgo., 1958-63; assoc. exec. community divsn. Nat. Bd. YWCA, N.Y.C., 1963-66, exec. community divsn., 1966-71, dir. orgn. devel., 1971-74, dep. exec. dir., 1974-82, ret., 1982. Contbr. articles to profl. jours. Pres. Community Welfare Coun., Spokane, 1956-57; majority coun. Emily's List, Washington, 1994. Mem. NASW (charter 1958-82). Democrat.

HENDRICKSON-GREAVES, JOANNE MARIE, private school educator; b. LaPorte, Ind., May 21, 1947; d. Frank Carl and Elizabeth Marie (Okrzesik) Chlupacek; m. James Earl Hendrickson, Aug. 24, 1968 (div. May 1987); m. Phillip Sheridan Greaves, July 24, 1993 (div. 1994); children: Joseph, Janice. BS, Ball State U., 1968; MS, Purdue U., 1973. Cert. elem. tchr. Elem. tchr. LaPorte (Ind.) Cmty. Schs., 1968-72; dir., tchr. Bldg. Blocks Day Nursery, LaPorte, 1975-76; elem. tchr. St. Joseph's Sch., LaPorte, 1979-88, St. Mary's Sch., Michigan City, Ind., 1988—. Mem. AAUW, NSTA, Nat. Coun. Tchrs. Math., Ind. Coun. Tchrs. Math., Hoosier Assn. Sci. Tchrs. Office: Saint Mary's Sch 321 W 11th St Michigan City IN 46360

HENDRIE, ELAINE, public relations executive; b. Bklyn., d. David and Pearl Kostell; m. Joseph Mallam Hendrie; children: Susan, Barbara. Asst. account exec. Benjamin Sonnenberg Public Relations firm, N.Y.C., 1953-57; pub. relations cons., writer, editor, dir. pub. relations and media Religious Heritage of Am., Washington, 1973-75; producer, interviewer radio program, sta. WRIV and stas. WALK-AM and -FM, L.I., N.J., Westchester County, N.Y., Conn., 1974-77; exec. dir. Women in New Directions, Inc., Suffolk County, N.Y., 1974-77; nat. media coordinator NOW, Washington, 1978; media dir. Am. Speech-Lang.-Hearing Assn., Washington, 1979-80; pub. info. officer, head media and mktg. Dept. Navy, Washington, 1980-81; pres. Hendrie & Pendzick, 1982-92, Elaine Hendrie Pub. Rels., 1992—; resource person for media Nat. Commn. on Observance of Internat. Women's Yr., 1977; cons. Multi-Media Prodns. Inc., N.Y.C., 1978—, Women in New Directions, Inc., 1981—. Mem. adv. bd. Women's Edn. and Counseling Ctr., SUNY-Farmingdale. Home: 50 Bellport Ln Bellport NY 11713-2736

HENDRIX, BONNIE ELIZABETH LUELLEN, elementary school educator; b. Corry, Pa., July 21, 1942; d. Francis Wilson and Frances (Welch) Luellen; m. E. Lindsey Hendrix, Aug. 24, 1963; children: Lance Adair, Djuana Sue, Shane René. BEd, Anderson Coll., 1965; MEd, Berry Coll., 1986. 1st grade tchr. Madison County Bd. Edn., Anderson, Ind.; kindergarten tchr. Walker County Bd. Edn., LaFayette, Ga.; pvt. practice piano tchr. Active community and ch. orgns. Mem. NEA, ASCD, PAGE, Ga. Assn. Edn., Walker Assn. Edn. Home: 76 Old Trion Rd La Fayette GA 30728-9802

HENDRIX, SUSAN CLELIA DERRICK, civic worker; b. McClellanville, S.C., Jan. 19, 1920; d. Theodore Elbridge and Susan Regina (Bauknight) Derrick; m. Henry Gardner Hendrix, June 5, 1943; children: Susan Hendrix Redmond, Marilyn Hendrix Shedlock. BA, Columbia Coll., 1941; MA, Furman U., 1961; EdD (hon.) Columbia Coll., 1985. Cert. tchr., S.C. Tchr. Whitmire Pub. Schs., 1941-43, Greenville Pub. Schs., S.C., 1944-46, 58-63, dir. Reading clinic, 1965-68; counselor Greenville Pub. Schs., 1963-65; supr. Greenville County Sch. Dist., S.C., 1965-68, dir. pub. rels., 1968-83; grad. instr. Furman U., 1967-69; cons. Nat. Seminar on Desegregation, 1973. Author: (with James P. Mahaffey) Teaching Secondary Reading, 1966; Communicating With the Community, 1979; editor: Communique, 1968-83; contbr. articles to profl. jours. and mags. Chmn. bd. trustees Columbia Coll., 1969-70; chmn. Greenville County Rehab. Bd., S.C., 1974-76; vice chmn. bd. Jr. Achievement, Greenville, 1978-79; chmn. S.C. Commn. on Women, Columbia, 1982-88; pres. United Meth. Women, Buncombe St. Ch., Greenville, 1956-57; mem. adminstrv. bd. Buncombe St. Ch., 1968—, bd. trustees, 1980-88, lay del. to S.C. Ann. Conf., 1986—; mem. United Meth. Ch. Southeastern Jurisdictional Coun. on Ministries, 1984-88; chmn. S.C. Conf. Coun. on Ministries United Meth. Ch., 1980-88, del. gen. conf., 1980, 84, 88, 92; mem. Bd. Global Ministries United Meth. Ch., 1972-80, mem. commn. study of ministry, 1984-92, mem. gen. ch. coun. ministries, 1988—, mem. gen. conf. agys. staff and site location com., 1988—, rschr. missions project, West Africa, 1986, chmn. com. legis., 1992—, chmn. com. on interagency legis, 1992—, mission agy. site location com., 1993—, structure com., 1992—. Recipient Medallion Columbia Coll., 1980, Alumnae Disting. Svc. award Columbia Coll., 1983, Disting. Achievement award Women's History Week, Greenville, 1984, S.C. Woman of Achievement award, 1988. Mem. S.C. PTA (life), Columbia Coll. Alumnae Assn. (life), Democratic Women, S.C. Women in Govt. (bd. dirs. 1985-87), Alpha Delta Kappa (pres. 1970-72, 90-91). Home and Office: 309 Arundel Rd Greenville SC 29615-1303

HENDRIX-WARD, NANCY KATHERINE, environmental energy professional; b. Russellville, Ala., Nov. 28, 1944; d. Raymond Clyde and Mattye Lou (Kimbrough) Smith; m. Adrian Dale Hendrix, Jan. 8, 1963 (div. Mar. 1982); children: David Wayne, Amy Kathleen, Susan Gayle; m. Robert Lawrence, Feb. 22, 1986. AA, Draughon's Bus. Coll., Jackson, Miss., 1963; student, East Miss. Jr. Coll., Scoobe, 1978-79; AA, Anchorage Community Coll., 1981; BBA, U. Alaska, 1982-84. Dir. Retired Sr. Vol. Program, Big Springs, Tex., 1974-76; adminstr. USAF, Adana, Turkey, 1977-79; environ. specialist Minerals Mgmt. Svc. Dept. of Interior, Anchorage, 1980-85; tech. editor Intelligence and Threat Analysis Ctr. U.S. Army, Washington, 1985-87; editor Inst. Def. Analyses, Alexandria, Va., 1987-88; writer, editor minerals mgmt. svc. U.S. Dept. Interior, Herndon, Va., 1988-89; environ. protection specialist, program mgr. U.S. Dept. Energy, Oak Ridge, Tenn., 1989—; coordinator Equal Opportunity com., Anchorage, 1983-85. Vol. counselor The Women's Ctr., Vienna, Va., 1987, Parent's Aid, Child Advocacy com., Anchorage, 1981-85; counselor Suicide Prevention Ctr., Anchorage, 1982-85. Mem. NAFE, LWV, Soc. for Tech. Communication, Federally Employed Women.

HENDRY, ANNA MARIE, customer service administrator; b. Reading, Pa., Jan. 12, 1944; d. Karl and Marie (Hamilton) Link; m. Gary Paul Hendry, Aug. 28, 1965; children: Brian, Chris, Rene'. Student, Auburn U., 1962-65. Visual mdse. coord. O'Neil's Dept. Store, Coshocton, Ohio, 1982-83, spl. events coord., 1983-84; pvt. practice as pub. rels. cons. Atlanta, 1985-87; sales Zachry, Atlanta, 1987-90; compliance coord. Ga. Soc. CPAs, Inc., Atlanta, 1990—. Author: Around Ohio Magazine, 1983, Metro South Magazine, 1985; editor: Metro South Magazine, 1986. V.p. LWV, Fayette County, Ga., 1989-90; bd. dirs. South Fulton C. of C., Atlanta, 1989-90; pres. Women Ga. Power, Atlanta, 1991-92; active Leadership South Fulton, 1991-93. Named Outstanding Young Woman of Am., 1972; recipient Mamie K. Taylor award Women Ga. Power, Atlanta, 1993. Mem. Kappa Kappa Gamma. Presbyterian.

HENG, SIANG GEK, communications executive; b. Singapore, Singapore, Dec. 4, 1960; came to U.S., 1984.; m. G.J. Sturgis, 1991. BSEE with honors, Nat. U. Singapore, 1983; MSEE in Computer Engring., U. So. Calif., 1985; MS in Engring. Mgmt., Nat. Technol. U., 1993. Rsch. engr. Nat. Univ. Singapore, 1983-84; systems mgr. LinCom Corp., L.A., 1985-87; fin. planner N.Y. Life Ins. Co., L.A., 1987-88; systems engr. Bell Labs. AT&T, N.J., 1988—; freelance computer and comm. cons., N.J., 1987-94. Contbr. articles to profl. jours. Office: AT&T Bell Labs Rm 2M-617 101 Crawfords Corner Rd Holmdel NJ 07733-1900

HENKE, ANA MARI, secondary education educator; b. Albuquerque, Apr. 21, 1954; d. David Ernest and Mary Anne (Gallegos) Sanchez; m. Michael John Henke, Aug. 14, 1976; children: Kristin Mari, Michelle Lee. BA in Spl. Edn., U. N.Mex., 1976, MA in Spl. Edn., 1983. Cert. elem. and secondary spl. edn. tchr., N.Mex.; cert. elem. and secondary phys. edn. tchr., N.Mex.; cert. elem. and secondary behavior disorder tchr., N.Mex. Tchr., supr. Perceptual Motor Learning Sch. U. N.Mex., Albuquerque, 1976, 82, tchr. phys. edn., 1980-82; tchr. phys. edn. Nat. Youth Sports Program, Albuquerque and San Diego, 1976-82; tchr. multihandicapped Chula Vista (Calif.) Pub. Schs., 1976-77; tchr. adaptive phys. edn. San Diego City Schs., 1977-78; lab. asst. Presbyn. Hosp., Albuquerque, 1979-80; tchr. Hermosa Jr. High Sch., Farmington, N.Mex., 1983-85, Heights Jr. High Sch., Farmington, 1985—; mem. Leadership & Risk-Taking, Nat. Summit for Hispanic Women, Albuquerque, 1989; in-svc. exercise therapist Four Corners Reg. Ednl. Conf., Farmington, 1985-86; supr. parents workshop Intervention/Awareness for Substance Abuse, Heights Jr. High Sch., 1985-86; instr. workshop Farmington Schs., 1986; active nat. youth sports prog. Leaders Are in Demand, NCAA-U. N.Mex., 1989; active progs. Bldg. Self Esteem by Taking Risks-AWAREL, 1989, Leadership/Self-Esteem Multicultural Settings workshop, dir. new tchr. tng, Wellness & Prevention, Four Corners Retirement Assn., Body Talk, Presbyn. Med. Svcs. Coord. New Educator Support Program, 1989, 90; mem. Leadership San Juan, 1990-91; commr. N.Mex. Bd. Edn., 1992—, N.Mex. State Standards, 1992—. Named Young Career Woman of San Juan County Nat. Fedn. Bus. & Profl. Women, 1988-89, Leadership award, 1990. Mem. Hispanic Women's Leadership Inst., Phi Delta Kappa (sec. 1987—, v.p. 1988-89). Republican. Roman Catholic. Home: 981 Callecita Jicarilla Santa Fe NM 87505

HENKE, JANICE CARINE, educational software developer and marketer; b. Hunter, N.D., Jan. 28, 1938; d. John Leonard and Adeline (Hagen) Hanson; children: Toni L., Tom L., Tracy L. BS, U. Minn., 1965; postgrad., misc. schs., 1969—. Cert. elem. tchr., Minn., Iowa. Tchr. dance, 1953-56; tchr. kindergarten Des Moines Pub. Schs., 1964-65; tchr. elem. Ind. Sch. Dist. 284, Wayzata, Minn., 1969-93; pvt. bus. history Wayzata, 1978—; marketer, promoter health enhancement Jeri Jacobus Cosmetics Aloe Pro, Am. Choice Nutrition, Multiway, KM Matol, Wayzata, 1978—; developer ednl. software, marketer of software Computer Aided Teaching Concepts, Excelsior, Minn., 1983—; authorized rep. Minn. Edn. Assn. with Midwest Benefit Advisers, Excelsior, Minn., 1993—; developer, author drug edn. curriculum, Wayzata, 1970-71; mem. programs com. Health and Wellness, Wayzata, 1988-93; chmn. Wayzata Edn. Assn. Ins. Com., 1991-93; mem. Staff Devel. Adv. Bd., Wayzata, 1988-93; coach Odyssey of the Mind, 1989-93. Author, developer computer software; contbr. articles to newspapers. Fundraiser Ind. Reps. Wayzata, 1976-79; mem. pub. rels. com. Lake Minnetonka (Minn.) Dist. Ind. Reps., 1979-81, fundraising chmn., 1981-82; chmn. Wayzata Ind. Reps., 1981-82; sec. PTO, Wayzata, 1981-82. Mem. NEA, Minn. Edn. Assn., Wayzata Edn. Assn. (bd. mem., ins. chairperson). Lutheran. Office: Computer Aided Teaching 20380 Excelsior Blvd Excelsior MN 55331-8733

HENKE, SHAUNA NICOLE, family service worker, small business owner; b. San Bernardino, Calif., Oct. 25, 1966; d. Gary Duane and Pamela Denyne (Duke) H. BA, U. San Francisco, 1988. Cert. police officer std. and tng. dispatcher, Calif. Pub. rels. dir. Sta. KUSF Radio, San Francisco, 1986; theater and recreational asst. Hamilton Field Recreation, Novato, Calif., 1986-89; morning asst., newswriter Sta. KTID Radio, San Rafael, Calif., 1987-88; dispatcher Warren Security, San Rafael, Calif., 1988-89; pub. safety dispatcher Twin Cities Police Dept., Larkspur/Corte Madera, Calif., 1989-94; family svc. worker Head Start, Bogalusa, La., 1994—; co-owner Time After Time Designs. Named Outstanding Young Woman, Outstanding Young Women of Am., 1987. Mem. Marin Emergency Dispatchers Assn. (hon. bd. dirs.). Office: Bogalusa Head Start 1202 Erie Ave Bogalusa LA 70427

HENKEL, CATHY, newspaper sports editor. Office: The Seattle Times Fairview Ave N & John St PO Box 70 Seattle WA 98111-0070

HENKEL, KATHERINE L., systems analyst, lawyer; b. Germany, Dec. 19, 1958; came to U.S., 1959; d. James Thomas and Katherine (Lavelle) Drew; m. Henry Joseph Henkel, Dec. 29, 1990. BS in Math. and Econs., Coll. Mt. St. Vincent, 1980; MS in Computer Sci., Baruch Coll., 1988; JD, Fordham Law Sch., 1992; postgrad. in tax law, Georgetown U. Bar: N.Y. 1993, D.C. 1993, Va. 1993. Programmer analyst George B. Buck Cons., N.Y.C., 1980-84; sr. systems analyst Met Life, N.Y.C., 1984-91; assoc. Brown, Raysman & Millstein, N.Y.C., 1991; programmer analyst NRECA, Washington, 1993; systems analyst NME, Fairfax, Va., 1993-95. Mem. St. Vincent de Paul Soc. Roman Catholic. Home: 8201 Lone Oak Ct Manassas VA 22111

HENLE, MARY, retired psychology educator; b. Cleve., July 14, 1913; d. Leo and Pearl (Hahn) H. A.B., Smith Coll., 1934, A.M., 1935; Ph.D., Bryn Mawr Coll., 1939; L.H.D. (hon.), New Sch. Social Research, 1983. Research assoc. Swarthmore Coll., Pa., 1939-41; instr. U. Del., Newark, 1941-42, Bryn Mawr Coll., Pa., 1942-44; mem. faculty Sarah Lawrence Coll., Bronxville, N.Y., 1944-46; from asst. prof. to assoc. prof. psychology New Sch. Social Research, N.Y.C., 1946-54, prof., 1954-83, prof. emeritus, 1983—; cons. Ednl. Services, Cambridge, Mass., 1965-67. Author: 1879 and All That, 1986; also articles, chpts. Editor books, including: Documents of Gestalt Psychology, 1961; Selected Papers of W. Köhler, 1971. J.S. Guggenheim Meml. Found. fellow, 1951-52, 60-61; research fellow Harvard U., Cambridge, 1963-64; sr. scholar Ednl. Services, Cambridge, 1964-65; vis. prof. Cornell U., fall 1981. Fellow Am. Psychol. Assn. (pres. div. 26 1971-72, pres. div. 24, 1974-75), AAAS; mem. EA. Psychol. Assn. (pres. 1981-82). Democrat. Avocations: old houses; reading. Home: 3300 Darby Rd Apt 5212 Haverford PA 19041-1072

HENLEY, BETH, playwright, actress; b. Jackson, Miss., May 8, 1952; d. Charles and Elizabeth Josephine (Becker) H. BFA, So. Meth. U., 1974, U. Ill., 1975-76. Performed with Dallas Minority Repertory Theater, pageant Gt. American People Show, New Salem State Park, Ill., 1976; author plays: Morgan's Daughters (script for t.v. pilot), 1979, Crimes of the Heart (Broadway), 1981, The Wake of Jamey Foster (Broadway), 1982, Am I Blue, 1982, The Miss Firecracker Contest (off Broadway), 1984, The Debutante Ball (world premiere South Coast Repertory Theatre), 1985, Survival Guides (television script with Budge Threlkeld), 1985, The Lucky Spot (produced Manhattan Theatre Club), 1987, Abundance (world premiere South Coast Repertory Theatre), 1989, The Debutante Ball, 1991, Beth Henley: Monologues For Women, 1992, Control Freaks, Met. Theater, L.A., 1993, (N.Y. stage, film) Revelers, 1994, Signatures, 1990; co-screenwriter: True Stories, 1986; screenwriter: Nobody's Fool, 1986, Crimes of the Heart, 1986, Miss Firecracker, 1989. Recipient awards for Crimes of the Heart including Pulitzer prize for drama, 1981, N.Y. Drama Critics Circle Best Play award, 1981, Guggenheim Award from Newsday, 1981, Tony Award Nomination for Best Play, 1981, Acad. Award Nomination for best Adapted screenplay, 1986. Office: care Gilbert Parker William Morris Agy 1350 Avenue Of The Americas New York NY 10019-4701

HENLEY, LILA MARY, retired state official; b. Hinsdale, N.H., May 21, 1926; d. Arthur Paul and Delia Emmaline (Stewart) Bouchie; m. Nicholas John Rompon, May 3, 1945 (div. 1959); children: Sylvia Evelyn McDevitt, Donald Barry, John Stewart; m. Robert Wright Henley, Dec. 19, 1962; children: Robert Edward, Edith Elizabeth, Melinda Fell. AB, Bixby Bus. Coll., St. Petersburg, Fla., 1963; B in Ind. Studies, U. South Fla., 1988. Registered lobbyist. Office mgr. Rompon & Assoc. Surveyors, Clearwater, Fla., 1946-53; investigative aide Pinellas County Constable, Clearwater, 1963; aide Pinellas County Legis. Del., Clearwater, 1963-69; legis. aide Fla. Ho. of Reps., Clearwater and Tallahassee, 1969-78, legis. aide IV, 1978-91; registered lobbyist, 1991—; mem. Gov.'s Commn. Status of Women-State of Fla., 1969-72; dir. Total Profl. Health Care, Clearwater, 1982—; mem. adv. com. Day Care and Early Childhood Devel.-Juvenile Welfare Bd., 1982-87, Joint Com. on Reapportionment, 1982, Joint Task Force on Howard Frankland Bridge, 1984-85, Joint Legis. Commn. on Blood Supplies, 1978, Spl. Com. on

Child Day Care Facilites and Licensing, 1976, Gov.'s Task Force on Edn., 1972-73. Sec. bd. dirs. Pinellas Emergency Mental Health Svcs., Clearwater, 1988—; mem. Nat. Rep. Com., 1963—. Named Woman of Yr., Largo Bus. and Profl. Women, 1985, Outstanding Citizen of Pinellas County, President's Point of Light Com., 1992; recipient Pinellas County Vol. award of Yr., 1993. Mem. NOW, Fla. Sheriffs Assn., Pinellas County Hist. Soc., Pinellas County Sch. Food Svc. Assn. (life), Tiger Bay Club, Beta Sigma Phi.

HENN, CATHERINE E. C., lawyer; b. St. Louis, May 13, 1942; d. Alexander and Rachel (Davis) C.; m. John H. Henn, Nov. 1, 1969; 1 child, Jameson. BA, Wellesley Coll., 1964; student, Yale U., 1964-65; JD cum laude, Harvard U., 1969. Bar: Mass. 1969. Law clk. Mass. Supreme Jud. Ct., Boston, 1969-70; assoc. Bingham, Dana & Gould, Boston, 1970-80; v.p., corp. counsel Affiliated Pubs., Inc., Boston, 1980—. Office: Affiliated Pubs Inc PO Box 2378 135 Morrissey Blvd Boston MA 02107-2378*

HENN, SHIRLEY EMILY, retired librarian; b. Cleve., May 26, 1919; d. Albert Edwin and Florence Ely (Miller) H.; AB, Hollins Coll., 1941; MS, U. N.C., 1966; m. John Van Bruggen, July 14, 1944 (div. May 1947); 1 child, Peter Albert (dec.). Libr. asst. Hollins (Va.) Coll., 1943-44, 61-64, reference libr., 1965-84, ret., 1984; advt. mgr. R.M. Kellogg Co., Three Rivers, Mich., 1946-47; exec. sec. Hollins Coll. Alumnae Assn., 1947-55; real estate salesman Fowlkes & Kefauver, Roanoke, Va., 1955-61. Pres. Soc. for Prevention Cruelty to Animals, 1959-61, 69-72, bd. dirs., 1972-81; donor Mary Williamson award in Humanities Hollins Coll., 1947—; endowed fund for purchase books children's lit. collection Fishburn Libr. Hollins Coll., 1986-93; donor, patron Women's Ctr. Hollins Coll., 1993—, Scholarship Aids, 1994, Children's Lit. Masters Program, 1993—; active Nat. Trust for Historic Preservation, 1994—, Roanoke Valley Hist. Soc., 1984—, Roanoke Valley Hist. Mus., Roanoke Valley Sci. Mus., Cystic Fibrosis Found., 1995—, Nat. Audubon Soc., 1995—, MADD, 1995—; donor Va. Tech. Found. for restoration Hotel Roanoke, 1992—; ptnr. Spl. Olympics, 1995—. Recipient Rath award, 1984. Donated in name Children's Lit. Master Program Scholarship, 1993, 94. Mem. ALA, Am. Alumni Council (dir. 1952-54, dir. women's activities 1952-54), Va. Libr. Assn., Nat. DAR (libr. Nancy Christian Fleming chpt. Roanoke 1977-84, regent 1984-88, chair Good Citizenship award 1990-92, Am. Essay awards 1991—), Poetry Soc. Va. Clubs: Quota Internat. (chpt. pres. 1958-60) (Roanoke), Antique Automobile Club Am., Roanoke Valley Antique Auto Club, Roanoke Valley Mopar Club, Children's Lit. Assn., Am. Mus. Nat. History, Blue Ridge Zool. Soc. Author, illustrator: Adventures of Hooty Owl and His Friends, 1953; editor: Hollins Alumnae Bull., 1947-56. Avocations: collecting teddy bears, antique French and English plates, bells, pewter. Home: 6915 Tinkerdale Rd Roanoke VA 24019-1530

HENNECY, BOBBIE BOBO, English language educator; b. Tignall, Ga., Aug. 11, 1922; d. John Ebb and Lois Helen (Gulledge) Bobo; student, Wesleyan Conservatory, 1943-44; AB summa cum laude, Mercer U., Macon, Ga., 1950; postgrad. Oxford (Eng.) U. English-Speaking Union Scholar, 1961; MA, Emory U., 1962; postgrad. Cambridge U., Eng., 1987; m. James Howell Hennecy, Dec. 28, 1963; 1 child, Erin. Sec. Tattnall Sq. Bapt. Ch., 1943-48; sec., adminstrv. asst. to pres., instr. Mercer U., 1950-61, instr. English, 1961-76, asst. prof., 1976-89, emeritus assoc. prof. and adj. prof., 1989—; founder Tattnall Sq. Acad., Macon, 1968, sec. acad. corp., 1968-73, dir., 1968-78; Bobbie Bobo Hennecy scholarship named in her hon. Tattnall Sq. Acad., Mercer U.; NDEA fellow Emory U., 1962. Mem. AAUW (chpt. v.p. 1959, pres. 1964), AAUP, MLA, S. Atlantic MLA, So. Comparative Lit. Assn., Am. Comparative Lit. Assn., Internat. Comparative Lit. Assn., Nat. Assn. Tchrs. English, Ga. Assn. Tchrs. English, English Speaking Union, LWV, Collegiate Press (adv. bd.), Am. Acad. Poets, Pres. Club of Mercer U., YWCA (life), Mid. Ga. Art Assn., Hereditary Register, Soc. Genealogists London, Nat. Soc. So. Dames, Nat. Soc. Magna Charta, DAR (registrar 1980-82), Daus. of 1812, Descendants, Colonial Clergy, Daus. of Am. Colonists, Jamestowne Soc., UDC (pres. 1994—), Colonial Dames XVII Century (chpt. 1st v.p. 1988-91), Huguenot Soc. England and Ireland, Colonial Order of the Crown (descendants of Charlemagne), Ams. of Royal Descent, Mid. Ga. Hist. Soc., Coosa County Ala. Hist. Soc., Cardinal Key, Sigma Tau Delta, Sigma Mu (pres., v.p., sec.-treas.), Phi Delta (advisor), Phi Kappa Phi, Alpha Psi Omega, Chi Omega (alumnae advisor). Baptist. Home: 1347B Adams St Macon GA 31201-1515

HENNER, MARILU, actress; b. Chgo., Apr. 6, 1952; m. Frederic Forest, 1980 (div.); m. Rob Lieberman, 1990. Attended, U. Chgo. Appearances include (TV series) Taxi, ABC, 1978-82, NBC, 1982-83, Evening Shade, CBS, 1990-94, (TV movies) Dream House, 1981, Stark, 1985, Love With A Perfect Stranger, 1986, Ladykillers, 1988, Chains of Gold, (films) Between the Lines, 1977, Blood Brothers, 1978, Hammett, 1983, The Man Who Loved Women, 1983, Johnny Dangerously, 1984, Cannonball Run II, 1984, Perfect, 1985, Rustler's Rhapsody, 1985, L.A. Story, 1991, Noises Off, 1992; Broadway debut in Over Here; other Broadway prodns. include Pal Joey, Social Security; stage performances include Grease (nat. co.), Carnal Knowledge, Grown-Ups, Super Sunday.

HENNESSEY, AUDREY KATHLEEN, educator; b. Fairbanks, Apr. 4, 1936; d. Lawrence Christopher and Olga Virginia (Strandberg) Doheny; m. Gerard Hennessey, Mar. 10, 1963; children: Brian, Kate. BA, Stanford U., 1957; HSA, U. Toronto, Ont., Can., 1968; PhD, U. Lancaster, Eng., 1982. Asst. dir. European sales Univ. Soc., Heidelberg, Fed. Republic Germany, 1959-61; landman's asst. Union Oil Co. Calif., Anchorage, 1962-63; adminstr. group pension Mfgs. Life Ins., Toronto, 1963-65; instr. office systems Adult Edn. Ctr., Toronto, 1965-68; lectr. office systems Salford Coll. Tech., Lancashire, Eng., 1968-70; sr. lectr. data processing Manchester (Eng.) Polytechnic, 1970-79; lectr. computation U. Manchester, Eng., 1979-82; assoc. prof. computer sci. Tex. Tech. U., Lubbock, 1982-86, assoc. prof. info. systems, 1987-94, prof. info. systems, 1994—, dir. ISOA bus. adminstrn., 1987-94, prof., 1994—; pres. ISOA Inc., 1994—; vis. instr. Fed. Law Enforcement Tng. Ctr., Glynco, Ga., 1984-88; adj. prof. West Tex. A&M U., Canyon, 1994—, U. Alaska, Anchorage, 1995—. Author: Computer Applications Project, 1982; editor procs.: Office Document Architecture Internat. Symposium, English version, 1991; contbr. articles to profl. jours.; inventor in field; 5 patents pending. Organizer Explorer Scouts Computer Applications, Lubbock, 1983-85. Recipient various awards Tex. Instruments, 1982-86, 94-95, Xerox Corp., 1985, Halliburton, 1986, Systems Exploration, 1987, State of Tex., 1988-93, Knowledge-Based Image Analysis award USN Space Systems, 1991—, Immunization Tracking System award Robert Wood Johnson Found., 1993, Leica, 1994, Sematech ADC award, 1994. Mem. IEEE, Soc. Mfg. Engrs., Assn. Computing Machinery, Data Processing Mgmt. Assn. (pres. chpt. 1989, Disting. Info. Sci. award 1992). Office: ISOA-Tex Tech U Ms # 2101 Lubbock TX 79409

HENNESSY, ELLEN ANNE, lawyer, educator; b. Auburn, N.Y., Mar. 3, 1949; d. Charles Francis and Mary Anne (Roan) H.; m. Frank Daspit, Aug. 27, 1974. BA, Mich. State U., 1971; JD, Cath. U., 1978; LLM in Taxation, Georgetown U., 1984. Bar: D.C. 1978, U.S. Ct. Appeals (D.C. cir.) 1978, U.S. Supreme Ct. 1984. Various positions NEH, Washington, 1971-74; atty. office chief counsel IRS, Washington, 1978-80; atty.-advisor Pension Benefit Guaranty Corp., Washington, 1980-82; assoc. Stroock & Stroock & Lavan, Washington, 1982-85; assoc. Willkie Farr & Gallager, Washington, 1985-86, ptnr., 1987-93; dep. exec. dir. and chief negotiator Pension Benefit Guaranty Corp., Washington, 1993—; adj. prof. law Georgetown U., Washington, 1985—. Mem. ABA (supervising editor taxation sect. newsletter 1984-87, mem. standing com. on continuing edn. 1990-94, chairperson joint com. on employee benefits 1991-92, mem. ABA-ALI com. on continuing profl. edn. 1994—, ALI-ABA standing com. 1994—), Women in Employee Benefits (pres. 1987-88), D.C. Bar Assn. (mem. steering com. tax sect. 1988-93, chairperson continuing legal edn. com. 1991—). Democrat. Home: 1926 Lawrence St NE Washington DC 20018-2734 Office: Pension Benefit Guaranty Corp 1200 K St NW Ste 210 Washington DC 20005

HENNESSY, MARGARET BARRETT, health care executive; b. Oak Park, Ill., Apr. 16, 1952; d. Bernard Leo and Frances (Madigan) H. BA in Sociology and Psychology, St. Norbert Coll., DePere, Wis., 1974; MS, Rush U., Chgo. Communications specialist Ill. Cancer Coun., Chgo., 1983-84; adminstrv. asst. Rush-Presbyn./St. Luke's Med. Ctr., Chgo., 1984-85; adminstrv. intern Cook County Hosp., Chgo., 1985-86; fin. analyst Loyola U. Med. Ctr., Maywood, Ill., 1986-89; operating officer Howard Brown Meml. Clinic, Chgo., 1989-93; hematology-oncology adminstr. Loyola U. Med. Ctr., Maywood, Ill., 1993—; guest lectr. Loyola U. Law Sch., 1989-90. Contbr. articles to profl. jours. Tchr. English as a second lang. World Relief Orgn., Chgo., 1989; cons. United Charities Camps, Chgo., 1989. Recipient Foster G. McGaw scholar, Am. Coll. health Care Execs., 1985. Mem. Rush U. Alumni Assn. (pres.), Chgo. Health Execs. Forum, Am. Coll. Healthcare Execs., Assn. Ambulatory Care Adminstrs. Office: Loyola U Med Ctr Hematology Oncology Div 2160 S 1st Ave Bldg 54 Maywood IL 60153-3304

HENNINGER, POLLY, neuropsychologist, researcher; b. Pasadena, Calif., Apr. 1, 1946; d. Paul Bennett and Mary (MacNair) Johnson; m. Richard Henninger Jr., 1966 (div. 1983); children: Marguerite, Nathan; m. Clyde Pechstedt, 1985 (div. 1992). BA, Ind. U., 1967, Pomona Coll., 1977; MA, U. Toronto, 1969, PhD, 1982. Registered psychologist, Ont., Can. Postdoctoral fellow Calif. Inst. Tech., Pasadena, 1982-84; asst. prof. Pitzer Coll., Claremont, Calif., 1984-87, Brock U., St. Catharines, Ont., 1987-91; vis. assoc. divsn. biology Calif. Inst. Tech., Pasadena, 1984-94; asst. dir. neuropsychol. svcs. Ctr. for Aging Resources, Fuller Theol. Sem., Pasadena, 1991-92; psychology intern Boston VA Med. Ctr. and New Eng. Med. Ctr., 1994—. Contbr. chpts. to books, articles to profl. jours. Recipient fellowships and grants. Mem. APA (div. 40 chair rsch. selection 1986-89), Can. Psychol. Assn., Internat. Neuropsychol. Soc. Democrat. Episcopalian. Home: 126 S San Marino Ave Pasadena CA 91107-4039 Office: VA Med Ctr Psychology Svc 116B 150 S Huntington Dr Boston MA 02130

HENNION, CAROLYN LAIRD (LYN HENNION), investment executive; b. Orange, Calif., July 27, 1943; d. George James and Jane (Porter) Laird; m. Reeve L. Hennion, Sept. 12, 1964; children: Jeffrey Reeve, Douglas Laird. BA, Stanford U., 1965; grad. Securities Industry Inst., U. Pa., 1992. Cert. fin. planner, fund specialist; lic. ins. agt.; registered gen. securities prin. Portfolio analyst Schwabacher & Co., San Francisco, 1965-66; adminstrv. coordinator Bicentennial Commn., San Mateo County Calif., 1972-73; dir. devel. Crystal Springs Uplands Sch., Hillsborough, Calif., 1973-84; tax preparer Household Fin. Corp., Foster City, Calif., 1982, freelance, 1983-87; sales promotion mgr. Franklin Distbrs., Inc., San Mateo, 1984-86, v.p. and regional sales mgr. of N.W., 1986-91, Mid-Atlantic, 1991-94; v.p. Viatech, Inc., 1986-92; v.p. Keypoint Svcs. Internat., 1992—; pres. Brock Rd. Corp., 1993—; v.p. Strand, Atkinson, Williams & York, Medford, Oreg., 1994—. Editor: Lest We Forget, 1975. Pres. South Hillsborough Sch. Parents' Group, Calif., 1974-75; sec. Vol. Bur. of San Mateo County, Burlingame, Calif., 1975; chmn. Community Info. Com., Town of Hillsborough, 1984-86; mem. coun. Buncom., Oreg., 1990—; mem., subcom. chmn. fin. adv. com., Town of Hillsborough, 1984-86. Recipient awards Coun. for Advancement and Support of Edn., 1981, Exemplary Direct Mail Appeals Fund Raising Inst., 1982, Wholesaler of Yr. Shearson Lehman Hutton N.W Region, 1989, Golden Mic award Frederic Gilbert Assocs., 1993. Mem. Securities Industry Assn. (chmn. state membership 1989-91), Internat. Assn. Fin. Planners (sec. Oreg. chpt. 1988-89, bd. dirs.), Inst. Cert. Fin. Planners, Bond Club Phila., Buncom Hist. Soc., Ashland Shakespeare Festival, Jr. League. Republican. Home: 3232 Little Applegate Rd Jacksonville OR 97530 Office: Strand Atkinson Williams & York # 1 North Holly Medford OR 97501

HENRIKSEN MACLEAN, EVA HANSINE, former anesthesiology educator; b. Petaluma, Calif., Jan. 1, 1929; d. Peder Henrik Boas and Karen (Nielsen) Henriksen; m. Daniel Edward MacLean, Aug. 25, 1957 (dec. Dec. 1981); children: Elizabeth, Mary Ann. AA, U. Calif., Berkeley, 1948, BA, 1950; MD, Yale U., 1954. Diplomate Am. Bd. Anesthesiology. Intern, resident Los Angeles County Hosp., L.A., 1954-57; from instr. to asst. prof. anesthesia Loma Linda U. (formerly Coll. Med. Evangelists), L.A., 1957-68; from instr. to assoc. prof. surgery anesthesiology Sch. Medicine U. So. Calif., L.A., 1957-94, assoc. prof. anesthesiology emeritus, 1994—; anesthesia cons. L.A. Coroner's Office, 1992-94. Mem. governing coun. Angelica Luth. Ch., 1994. Democrat. Home: 957 Arapahoe St Los Angeles CA 90006

HENRIKSON, LOIS ELIZABETH, photojournalist; b. Lytton, Iowa, Nov. 10, 1921; d. Daniel Raymond and Cora Elizabeth (Thomson) Wessling; m. Arthur Allen Henrikson, July 3, 1943; children: Diane Elizabeth, Janet Christine, Michele Charlene Henrikson Smetana. BS, Northwestern U., 1943. Adminstrv. asst. to v.p., dir. ops. bus. communications div. ITT Telecommunications Corp., Des Plaines, Ill., 1980-82; adminstrv. asst. to exec. v.p. Wholesale Stationers' Assn., Des Plaines, 1982-84, membership svcs. coord., editor membership roster, 1984-88; field editor Office World News, BUS Publ. Group, Jericho, N.Y., 1988-92. Contbg. editor: Home World Bus. ICD Publs., Today's Office, FM Bus. Publs., Inc., Office Tech. Mgmt., Bus. Tech. Comms. Inc.; project editor: Dyna Search, Inc., Wallace Offutt Cons. Chair safety com. Cumberland Sch. PTA, Des Plaines, 1957-58, publicity 1960-61; bd. dirs. Maine West High Sch. Music Boosters, Des Plaines, 1967-69; capt. fin. dr. YMCA, Des Plaines, 1964; mem. diaconate bd., visitation coord., growth and membership bd. 1st Congl. Ch., Des Plaines; mem. Art Inst. Chgo., Peal Ctr. for Christian Living. Mem. NAFE, AAUW (chair social com. 1983-84, editor newsletter 1984-85, 88-94, newsletter 1st pl. award 1993, membership com. 1988-94, N.W. Suburban Ill. br. Ednl. found. contbn. made in honor 1992), DAR, Am. Soc. Assn. Execs. (cert. membership mktg. 1986), Am. Soc. Profl. Exec. Women, Am. Assn. Editorial Cartoonists, Aux. Chgo. Soc. Assn. Execs. (registrar 1984-85), Soc. Profl. Journalists, Soc. Am. Bus. Editors and Writers, Nat. Soc. Magna Charta Dames, Am. of Royal Descent, Alpha Gamma Delta. Home and Office: 27 N Meyer Ct Des Plaines IL 60016-2243

HENRIQUEZ-FREEMAN, HILDA JOSEFINA, fashion design executive; b. Palmarito de Cauto, Oriente, Cuba, June 18, 1938; came to U.S., 1960; d. Matias and Isabel Beatrice (Freeman) Henriquez. BA, Bethune-Cookman Coll., 1963; postgrad., Tchrs. Coll., 1965-66, Roosevelt U., 1966, Northwestern U., 1969-70; cert., No. Ill. U., 1975; postgrad., Loop Coll., 1972-84. Modiste/couturier Fina Modas, Habana, Cuba, 1952-59; instr. English Habana Pub. Sch., Cuba, 1956-58; ct. reporter Govt. La Cabana, Habana, Cuba, 1959-60; language instr. Ft. Lauderdale Sch. Dist., Fla., 1963-64; custom design Freeman's Fashion Atelier, Chgo., 1965-68; pres. dir. Acad. for Fashion Art Design, Chgo., 1968—; head designer Eur-Am. Creations, Chgo., 1978-81; cons. Freeman's Enterprise, Chgo., 1982—. Mentor Spanish coalition, Youth Career Awareness Program, Chgo., 1987. Mem. Cuban C. of C., Cuban Liceo, Ill. Assn. Trade and Tech. Schs., NAFE. Office: Acad for Fashion Art Design 410 S Michigan Ave Chicago IL 60605-1302

HENRY, ANN RAINWATER, education educator; b. Okla., Nov. 2, 1939; d. George Andrew and Opal Norma (Cohea) Rainwater; m. Morriss M. Henry, Aug. 1, 1964; children: Paul, Katherine, Mark. BA, U. Ark., 1961, MA, 1964, JD, 1971. Bar: Ark. 1971. Pvt. practice law Fayetteville, Ark., 1971-72; instr. Coll. Bus. Adminstrn. U. Ark., Fayetteville, 1976-78, asst. prof., 1978-84, assoc. prof., 1984—, asst. dean, 1984-86, assoc. dean, 1986-89, faculty chair, 1989-91. Bd. dirs. City of Fayetteville, 1977-83, 91-92, McIlroy Bd., Fayetteville, 1986—; chmn. cert. com. Ark. Tchrs. Evaluation, 1984-85; mem. Ark. Local Svcs. Adv. Bd., 1980-88, Ark. Gifted and Talented, 1989—, Ark. State Bd. Edn., 1985-86. Mem. Ark. Alumni Assn. (bd. dirs., asst. treas. 1989-93), Fayetteville C. of C. (bd. dirs. 1983-85), Ark. Bar Assn. (chmn. ethics com. 1986-87). Democrat. Methodist. Home: 2465 Township Common Dr Fayetteville AR 72703-3568 Office: U Ark BA 204 Fayetteville AR 72701

HENRY, CLAUDETTE, state official; b. Oklahoma City, Okla., Mar. 13, 1947; d. William Ray and Janette (Edwards) Craig; m. Jack Henry. Student, Rose State U., U. Okla. With U.S. Dept. Treasury, Oklahoma City, Okla., 1986-88; state rep. Okla. Ho. of Reps., Oklahoma City, 1986-88; treas. State of Okla., Oklahoma City, 1991-95. Mem. Kirkpatrick Ctr. Bd. Cons., Oklahoma City, 1991—, v.p. So. Region Nat. Assn. State Treasury, 1993. Mem. Nat. Assn. State Treas., Nat. Assn. State Auditors, Comptroller and Treas., Nat. Fedn. Rep. Women, Oklahoma City Rep. Women, First Ladies Okla. (assoc.), YWCA Inst. Pub. Leadership, Nat. Assn. Women Bus. Owners. Republican. Mem. LDS Ch. Office: Office of Treas 217 Capitol Bldg 2300 N Lincoln Blvd Oklahoma City OK 73105

HENRY, DEBORAH JANE, construction executive; b. Lake Village, Ark., June 17, 1952; d. Jack Ladd Henry and Dorothy Geneva (Wyatt) Cate; m. Karl Joseph Kenkel, Aug. 21, 1971 (div. July, 1978); children: Lori Ann, Scott Joseph. BS in History and Polit. Sci., Washington U., St. Louis, 1993. Mgmt. asst. Linclay Corp., St. Louis, 1973-78; adminstrv. asst. Turco Devel. Corp., St. Louis, 1978-79; asst. contractor adminstr. Tarlton Corp., St. Louis, 1979-81; project engr. McCarthy Constr. Co., St. Louis, 1981-86; project mgr. Wefelmeyer Constr. Co., St. Louis, 1986-87; constr. mgr. Paragon Group, Inc., 1987-90; constrn. mgr. Tricorp Constrn. Inc., Bridgeton, Mo., 1991-92; tchg. asst. U. Mo., St. Louis, 1994—. Mem. Greater Mo. Focus on Leadership, 1993, Metro St. Louis Tradeswomen Commn., Pride Study Commn. Edn. Mem. LWV, Nat. Assn. Women in Constrn. Home: 636 Pearl Ave Saint Louis MO 63122-2722

HENRY, FRANCES ANN, journalist, educator; b. Denver, July 23, 1939; d. Lewis Byford and Betsy Mae (Lancaster) Patten; m. Charles Larry, June 28, 1963 (div. May 1981); children: Charles Kevin, Tracy Diane. BA in English, Carleton Coll., 1960; MA in Social Sci., U. Colo., Denver, 1988; MA in Journalism, Memphis State U., 1989. Cert. tchr. Lang. arts tchr. Rolla (Mo.) Pub. Schs., 1963-66; journalism tchr. Douglas County Pub. Schs., Castle Rock, Colo., 1976—, chmn. English dept., 1993—; mng. editor Douglas County News-Press, Castle Rock, 1986-87; editor Fourth World Bulletin, 1988; exec. editor Daily Helmsman Memphis State U., 1988-89, gen. mgr. Daily Helmsman, 1991-92. Contbr. articles to profl. jours. Mem. ACLU, Colo. H.S. Press Assn. (sec. 1981-83, pres. 1983-91, bd. dirs., named Colo. Journalism Tchr. of Yr. 1985), Assn. for Edn. in Journalism and Mass Comm., Mensa, Kappa Tau Alpha. Democrat. Episcopalian. Office: Douglas County High Sch 2842 Front St Castle Rock CO 80104

HENRY, KAREN HAWLEY, lawyer; b. Whittier, Calif., Nov. 5, 1943; d. Ralph Hawley and Dorothy Ellen (Carr) Hawley; m. John Dunlap, 1968; m. Charles Gibbons Henry, Mar. 15, 1975; children: Scott, Alexander, Joshua; m. Don H. Phemister, June 21, 1991; children: Justin Phemister, Jonathan Phemister, Keith Phemister. BS in Social Scis., So. Oreg. Coll., 1965; MS in Labor Econs., Iowa State U., 1967; JD, U. Calif., 1976. Instr., Medford (Oreg.) Sch. Dist., 1965-66; rsch. asst. dept. econs. Iowa State U., Ames, 1966-67; dir. rsch. program Calif. Nurses Assn., San Francisco, 1967-72; labor rels. coord. Affiliated Hosps. of San Francisco, 1972-79; ptnr. Littler, Mendelson, Fastiff & Tichy, San Francisco, 1979-86; mng. ptnr. labor and employment law Weissburg and Aronson, Inc., San Francisco, 1986-90; prin. Karen H. Henry, Inc., Sacramento, 1991—. Author: Health Care Supervisor's Legal Guide, 1984, Nursing Administration Law Manual, 1986, ADA: Ten Steps to Compliance, 1992, 2nd edit., 1994; edit. bd. Health Care Supervisor; contbr. articles on employment law issues to profl. jours. Mem. Calif. Soc. Healthcare Attys. (bd. dirs. 1986-87, pres. 1987-88), Am. Hosp. Assn. (ad hoc labor atty. com.), State Bar of Calif., Sacramento Bar Assn., Thurston Soc., Order of Coif. (law jour.). Office: Karen H Henry Inc Senator Hotel Office Bldg 1121 L St Ste 1000 Sacramento CA 95814-3926

HENRY, MARGUERITE, author; b. Milw.; d. Louis and Anna (Kaurup) Breithaupt; m. Sidney Crocker Henry. Author: Auno and Tauno: A Story of Finland, 1940, Dilly Dally Sally, 1940, Birds at Home, 1942, Geraldine Belinda, 1942, (with Barbara True) Their First Igloo on Baffin Island, 1943, A Boy and a Dog, 1944, Little Fellow, 1945, Justin Morgan Had a Horse, 1945 (Newbery Honor award 1948, Jr. Scholastic Gold Seal award 1948, Friends of Lit. award 1948), Robert Fulton: Boy Craftsman, 1945, Misty of Chincoteague, 1947 (Boys' Club of Am. award, Lewis Carroll Shelf award, Newbery Honor award), Benjamin West and His Cat, Grimalkin, 1947, Always Reddy, 1947, King of the Wind, 1948 (John Newbery medal 1949), Sea Star: Orphan of Chintoteague, 1949, Little-or-Nothing from Nottingham, 1949, Born to Trot, 1950, Album of Horses, 1951, Portfolio of Horses, 1952, Brighty of the Grand Canyon, 1953 (William Allen White award 1956), Wagging Tails: An Album of Dogs, 1955, Cinnabar: The One O'Clock Fox, 1956, Black Gold, 1957 (Sequoyah Children's Book award 1959), Muley-Ears, Nobody's Dog, 1959, Gaudenzia: Pride of the Palio, 1960 (Clara Ingram Judson award Soc. Midland Authors 1961), Misty, the Wonder Pony, by Misty, Herself, 1961, All About Horses, 1962, Five O'Clock Charlie, 1962, Stormy, Misty's Foal, 1963, White Stallion of Lipizza, 1964, Portfolio of Horse Paintings, 1964, Mustang, Wild Spirit of the West, 1966 (Western Heritage award Nat. Cowboy Hall of Fame 1967, Sequoyah Children's Book award 1969), Dear Readers and Riders, 1969, Album of Dogs, 1970, San Domingo: The Medicine Hat Stallion, 1972 (Clara Ingram Judson award Soc. Midland Authors 1973), Stories From Around the World, 1974, Pictorial Life Story of Misty, 1976, One Man's Horse, 1977, The Illustrated Marguerite Henry, 1980, Marguerite Henry's Misty Treasury, 1982, Our First Pony, 1984, Misty's Twilight, 1992, (pop-up book) Marguerite Henry's Album of Horses, 1993; "pictured geographies" series Alaska, 1941, Argentina, 1941, Brazil, 1941, Canada, 1941, Chile, 1941, Mexico, 1941, Panama, 1941, West Indies, 1941, Australia, 1946, Bahamas, 1946, Bermuda, 1946, British Honduras, 1946, Dominican Republic, 1946, Hawaii, 1946, New Zealand, 1946, Virgin Islands, 1946; films: Brighty, 1967, Justin Morgan Had a Horse, 1971, Peter Lundy and the Medicine Hat Stallion, 1977, King ofthe Wind, 1990; documentary: The Story of a Book, 1979. Recipient Lit. for Children award So. Calif. Coun., 1973, Kerlan award Univ. of Minn., 1975; named Author of Diamond Jubilee Yr. Ill. Assn. of Tchrs. of English, 1982. Office: care Macmillan Pub Co 866 3d Ave New York NY 10022*

HENRY, PATRICIA ANN, broadcast executive; b. Columbia, S.C.; d. Willis Wendell and Lauretta M. (Gorby) H. BA in Elem. Edn., U. S.C., 1973, M of Mass Communication, 1981. News intern Sta. WIS-TV, Columbia, 1981; endowment intern Sta. S.C. ETV Network, Columbia, 1981; producer, dir. Sta. S.C. ETV Network, Columbia, S.C., 1989—; videographer Sta. WRJA-TV, Sumter, S.C., 1981-82; producer, dir. Sta. KAMU-TV, College Station, Tex., 1982-83, Sta. WSPA-TV, Spartanburg, S.C., 1983-84; program prodn. mgr. Sta. WRET-TV, Spartanburg, 1985-89; producer, dir. S.C. ETV Network, Columbia, 1989—; freelance football camera operator, College Station, 1982-83; instr. journalism Tex. A&M U., College Station, 1982-83. Writer, producer (TV show) That's What Friends Are For, 1987 (Mothers Against Drunk Divers award, S.C. Drug and Alcohol Abuse Commn. award). Del. Rep. S.C. conv., Lexington, 1970. Recipient Ann. Commercial Media award dir., editor Spina Bifida Assn. Am., Cine Golden Eagle award dir., editor, Gold award editor Worldfest Charleston, Local, State, Regional, Internat. award editor, dir., co-prodr. Rotary Internat. Clubs; finalist video award, Worldfest in Charleston and Houston. Mem. Am. Lung Assn. (publicity chmn. 1987), Horseman's Coun. S.C., Pets, Inc. Methodist. Office: SC ETV Network 2712 Millwood Ave # L Columbia SC 29205-1221

HENRY, PAULA LOUISE (PAULA LOUISE HENRY COOVER), association executive; b. White Plains, N.Y., Mar. 5, 1947; d. Raymond Francis and Carolyn Louise (Landis) Henry; m. John David Coover, Nov. 18, 1967 (div. Jan. 1992); children: Jeffrey Darren, Robert Benson, Jennifer Danielle (dec.). AA in Psychology, Monmouth Coll., 1967; student, Pace U., 1972-76; BA in Psychology, Monmouth Coll., 1993. Chair gifted and talented com., then pres. Hunterdon County (N.J.) Coun. PTAs, 1980-86; chmn. county pres. group, nat. conv. del., gen. conv. chmn. N.J. Congress Parents & Tchrs., Trenton, 1985-87, field svc. chmn., 1985-89, pres., 1989-91, immediate past pres., 1991-93, hon. v.p., 1991—. Mem. sch. bd. Union Twp. Bd. Edn., Hampton, N.J., 1983-86, assembly del., 1984-86, legis. chmn. 1984-86, policy chmn. 1986, edn. chmn. 1984-85; trustee Jennie M. Haver Scholarship Fund, 1984-89; mem. Hunterdon County Edn. Coalition, 1984-88, Child Abuse and Missing Children Com., Hunterdon, 1987—, Hunterdon County Youth Svcs. Commn., Flemington, 1987—, N.J. Gov.'s Commn. on Quality Edn., 1991-93; treas. Fannie B. Abbott Student Loan Found., 1985-90, trustee, 1985—; v.p. Hunterdon County Child Assault Protection Program, 1986-90; mem. strategic planning com. United Way of Essex and West Hudson, 1994—. Republican. Methodist. Home: PO Box 5228 Clinton NJ 08809-0228 Office: NJ Congress Parents Tchrs 900 Berkeley Ave Trenton NJ 08618-5322

HENRY, SHERRON LYNNE, nursing consultant; b. New Castle, Pa., May 22, 1951; d. Eugene Emil and Shirley June (Kehna) Scotia; m. William Kenneth Henry, Dec. 27, 1971; 1 child, Megan. Diploma, St. Joseph's Hosp. Sch. Nursing, Pitts., 1971. RN, Pa., Ohio; cert. ACLS, Beaver C.C. Charge nurse in critical care unit Bashline Osteo. Hosp., Grove City, Pa., 1971-72, Grove City Hosp., Grove City, 1972-73; staff/charge nurse in ICU and critical care unit St. Francis Hosp., New Castle, 1973-76, charge nurse in post anesthesic recovery, 1976-79; rehab. coord. Rehab. Coords., Inc., Pitts., 1979-80; rehab. specialist M & M Rehab. Svcs., Pitts., 1980-83; pvt. practice Sherron Henry RN & Assocs., New Castle, 1983-88; program dir. Med/Aid, New Castle, 1988-90; pvt. practice Proactive Case Mgmt., New Castle, 1990—; cons. Jameson Health Systems, New Castle, 1991, Greenville Regional Hosp., Greenville, Pa., 1991-92, Keystone Rsch., Greenville, 1991—. Pres. Hickory Vol. Firemans Aux., New Castle, 1985-89, 93-94; pres. Laurel Elem. PTO, 1993-94. Mem. Assn. of Rehab. Nurses, Certification of Ins. Rehab. Specialists Commn. (cert. CIRS), Individual Case Mgmt. Assn., Greater New Castle C. of C., Bowlmorettes. Democrat. Presbyterian. Office: Proactive Case Mgmt 137 Lakewood Rd New Castle PA 16101-2731

HENRY, SYLVIA CROCKER, rehabilitation specialist, artist; b. Smithfield, N.C., May 24, 1953; d. Richard Hampton and Willa Nell (Thompson) Crocker; m. Samuel Gray Henry, July 24, 1976; children: Ashley Nell, Gray Hamilton. BS in Art Edn., East Carolina U., 1980, MS in Rehab. Studies, 1990. Cert. vocat. evaluator; cert. rehab. counselor. Sales assoc. Clark Gallery, Greenville, N.C., 1980-90; art tchr. Pitt County Schs., Greenville, 1980-81; coop. edn. coord. East Carolina U., Greenville, 1989-90; evaluation program mgr. Tri County Industries, Rocky Mount, N.C., 1990; vocat. evaluator Dept. Vocat. Rehab., Washington, N.C., 1990-91; rehab. specialist Intracorp, Raleigh, N.C., 1991—. Exhibited in various shows. Cultural arts chairperson Wilson Mills PTA, Wilson Mills (N.C.) Sch., 1992-93. Mem. Vocat. Evaluation and the Work Adjustment Assn. (pres. elect 1994—), N.C. Rehab. Assn. (chpt. rep. 1993-94), Wake Visual Artists Assn., River Dell Chase Homeowners Assn. (v.p. 1993-94), Rho Chi Sigma. Democrat. Home: 1696 Jordon Narron Rd Selma NC 27576-8714 Office: Intracorp 3101 Poplarwood Ct Ste 113 Raleigh NC 27604-1045

HENRY-THIEL, LOIS HOLLENDER, human resources executive; b. Phila., Jan. 19, 1941; d. Edward Hubert and Frances Lois (Nesler) Hollender; m. Charles L. Henry, Oct. 24, 1964 (div. 1971); children: Deborah Lee, Randell Huitt, Andrew Edward; m. Brian L. Thiel, Jan. 1, 1989. BA, Thomas A. Edison Coll., 1979; MSW, Fordham U., 1981; PhD in Psychology, City U. L.A., 1992. Cert. social worker, Ariz., N.Y., N.J.; lic. svc. profl., career counselor, Ariz. Personnel asst., sec. IBM, Paterson, N.J. and St. Louis, 1964-66; minister's asst. Grace Luth. Ch., St. Cloud, Fla., 1966-68; adminstr./tchr. Fla. Finishing Acad., St. Cloud, 1968-70; adminstrv. asst. Newark Book Ctr., 1972-77; intern, med. social worker Jersey City Med. Ctr., 1979-80; intern, psychiatric/med. social worker VA Med. Ctr., Lyons, N.J., 1980-81; sch. social worker Lakeview Learning Ctr., Budd Lake, N.J., 1981-82; mgr. human resources Terak Corp., Scottsdale, Ariz., 1982-85; v.p. counseling and bus. devel. Murro & Assocs., Phoenix, 1985-88, exec. v.p. cons., 1988-91; prin. career cons. Henry & Assocs., Scottsdale, 1982—; career cons., individual/family counselor/psychotherapist, speaker, Henry & Assocs., Scottsdale, 1982—; adj. prof. Ottawa U.; mem. employers com. Ariz. Dept. Econ. Security; cons. in field. Coordinator-vol. Job-A-Thon, Phoenix, 1983. Fellow Am. Orthopsychiat. Assn.; mem. Internat. Assn. Outplacement Profls. (treas. Ariz. region 1992—), Nat. Assn. Social Workers, Soc. Human Resource Mgmt., Soc. Study of Neuronal Regulation, Am. Assn. Psychophysiology. Office: Henry and Assocs 6900 E Camelback Rd Scottsdale AZ 85251-2431

HENSEL, KAREN ASTRID, museum director; b. N.Y.C., Dec. 18, 1944; d. John J. and Dorothy (Buhr) H. BS, Oneonta (N.Y.) State Tchrs. Coll., 1966; MA, Columbia U., 1982; MEd, 1983, EdD, 1987. Tchr., N.Y.C. Pub. Schs., 1966-67, Virgin Islands schs., 1967-70; curator edn. N.Y. Zool. Soc.-N.Y. Aquarium, 1970-87; program dir. The Maritime Ctr. at Norwalk, Conn., 1987-88; dir. East Hampton Hist. Soc. Mus., 1988—; cons. in field. Bd. dirs.The Hampton Day Sch., Animal Rescue Fund, East Hampton. Contbr. articles to profl. jours. NDEA fellow, 1967; Virgin Islands Council on Arts grantee, 1967-68. Mem. Nat. Marine Edn. Assn. (founder 1976, dir. 1976-78), N.Y. State Marine Edn. Assn. (founder 1974, bd. dir. 1974-78), Am. Assn. Mus., Am. Assn. Zool. Parks and Aquariums (chmn. pub. edn. com. 1974-78, Outstanding Svc. award 1978), Kappa Delta Pi, Phi Delta Kappa. Office: East Hampton Hist Soc 101 Main St East Hampton NY 11937-2714

HENSEL, KATHERINE RUTH, investment strategist; b. Summit, N.J., Nov. 24, 1959; d. John Charles and Carolyn (Bahle) H. AB, Harvard U., 1981, MBA, 1985. Securities analyst Donaldson Lufkin & Jenrette, N.Y.C., 1981-83; investment banker Paine Webber, N.Y.C., 1985; investment banker Shearson Lehman Bros., N.Y.C., 1986, sr. v.p., securities analyst, 1987-91; mng. dir., chief investment strategist, 1992—; chief investment strategist Shearson Lehman Bros., N.Y.C., 1993—. Contbr. articles to profl. jours. Named Instl. Investor All Am. Rsch. Team, 1989-93. Named Instl. Investor All Am. Rsch. Team, 1989-92. Mem. Harvard Club N.Y.C. Office: Shearson Lehman Bros World Financial Ctr New York NY 10285

HENSELER, SUZANNE MARIE, legislator, social studies educator, majority whip; b. Brookline, Mass., Dec. 7, 1942; d. Paul R. and Evelyn (Warren) McGoldrick; m. John L. Henseler, June 26, 1965; children: Sean Patrick, Warren Paul, Timothy Brian. BS in History Edn., Boston Coll., 1964. Tchr. Pilgrim High Sch., Warwick, 1964-66; clk. house labor com. R.I. Ho. Reps., Providence, 1977-82; tchr. St. Rocco Sch., Johnston, R.I., 1984—; mem. R.I. Ho. of Reps., Providence, majority whip, 1992—. Former mem., bd. mem. North Kingstown Soccer Assn., 1974-89; mem. North Kingstown (R.I.) Dem. Town Com., 1974—; mem. sch. com., Kingstown, 1978-82; chmn. R.I. Mobile Home Commn., 1988—; chmn. Legis. Commn. to Study the Solid Waste Mgmt. Corp. Named Outstanding Young Women of Yr., North Kingstown Jaycees, 1977, Nat. Environ. award 1993. Mem. Nat. Orgn. Women Legislators, Women in Govt. Home: 210 Edmond Dr North Kingstown RI 02852-2416 Office: Majority Whip State House # 303 Providence RI 02903

HENSELMEIER, SANDRA NADINE, training and development consulting firm executive; b. Indpls., Nov. 20, 1937; d. Frederick Rost Henselmeier and Beatrice Nadine (Barnes) Henselmeier Enright; m. David Albert Funk, Oct. 2, 1976; children: William H. Stolz, Jr., Harry Phillip Stolz II, Sandra Ann Stolz. AB, Purdue U., 1971; MAT, Ind. U., 1975. Exec. sec. to dean Ind. U. Sch. Law, Indpls., 1977-78; adminstrv. asst. Ind. U.-Purdue U., Indpls., 1978-80, assoc. archivist, 1980-81; program and communication coordinator Midwest Alliance in Nursing, Indpls., 1981-82; tng. coordinator Coll./Univ. Cos., Indpls., 1982-83; pres. Better Bus. Communications, Indpls., 1983—; adj. lectr. Ind. U.-Purdue U. at Indpls., 1971—, U. Indpls. Center Continuing. Mgmt. Devel. and Edn., Indpls., 1984—. Author: Successful Customer Service Writing, Winning with Effective Business Grammar, Successful Telephone Communication and Etiquette, Management Writing; contbr. articles to profl. jours. Bus. adv. com. computer programmer tng. Crossroads Rehab. Ctr. Mem. ASTD, Assn. Bus. Communication, Soc. Tech. Communications, Indpls. C. of C., Assn. Profl. Writing Cons., Economic Club Indpls. Republican. Presbyterian. Avocations: traveling, walking, reading, learning new ideas. Office: Better Bus Communications PO Box 20309 Indianapolis IN 46220

HENSHAW, BEVERLY ANN HARSH, women's health nurse, consultant; b. Jasper, Mich., Aug. 26, 1937; d. Arthur Estol and Doris Ione (Lindsay) Harsh; m. Kenneth P. Wilkinson, Apr. 8, 1978; children: Kit, Jeff, Kim, Brad, Brian, David. BSN, U. Mich., 1960; cert. ob-gyn. nurse practitioner, Johns Hopkin's U., 1973; MSN, Pa. State U., 1983. RN, Pa.; cert. nurse practitioner. Instr. Sch. Nursing Pa. State U., University Park, NP women's health; NP, clinic mgr. Family Health Svcs., Inc., State College, Pa.; pvt. practice cons. 5. Mem. NAACOG, ANA, NANPRH, Jacobs Inst. of Women's Health. Home: PO Box 340 RD 1 Port Matilda PA 16870-9246

HENSLEY, ANNE LUND, counselor; b. St. Louis, Aug. 16, 1945; d. Shirley Martin and Lucia Tuttle (Chamberlain) Lund; m. John C. Hensley, Aug. 12, 1970 (div. June 1993); children: Scott Martin, Emille Margaret. BSEd, U. Idaho, 1967; MAEd in Counseling, Washington U., St. Louis, 1975. Nat. cert. career counselor, nat. cert. counselor; lic. prof. counselor, Mo. Jr. high tchr. Shoreline Schs., Seattle, Wash., 1967-70, Ladue Schs., St. Louis, Mo., 1970-73; asst. mgr. beauty shop Saks Fifth Ave., St. Louis, 1973-75; high sch. counselor Webster Schs., St. Louis, 1975-80; career counselor Career Planning Ctrs. of Am., St. Louis, 1985-89, St. Louis, 1991—; salesperson Ken Miesner Flower Shop, St. Louis, 1991—. Chair Warson Woods Community Assn., St. Louis, 1985-89. Mem. ACA, PEO, Nat. Assn. Law Placement, St. Louis Counseling Assn. (pres. 1975—), Jr. League of St. Louis (chair numerous coms. 1973-92), Mo. Counseling Assn. (bd. dirs. 1975—). Home: 2 Winnetka Ln Saint Louis MO 63122-3252

HENSLEY, SHARON LEE, controller; b. Lexington, Ky., Apr. 12, 1949; d. Lee R. and Anne L. (White) H. Student, Augustana Coll., 1975. Dir. sales Circa '21 Dinner Playhouse, Rock Island, Ill., 1977-78; asst. subscription mgr. The Goodman Theatre, Chgo., 1978-80; gen. mgr. Maven Prodns., Chgo., 1980-82; pres., owner Arts Mgmt. Group, Inc., Chgo., 1983-86; mng. dir. New Am. Theater, Rockford, Ill., 1986-89, 90-92; stockbroker Blunt Ellis & Loewi, Rockford, 1989-90; contr. Candlelight Dinner Playhouse, Summit, Ill., 1992—. Commr. svc. com. United Way, Rockford, 1989; bd. dirs. Rockford Area Arts Coun., Rockford, 1989-91; mem. steering com. First Night Rockford, 1991.

HENSON, (BETTY) ANN, media specialist, educator; b. Tampa, Fla., Dec. 20, 1944; d. James (Jim) and Beth (Tabb) H. BA, U. South Fla., 1966; MEd, U. Fla., 1980, EdS, 1985. Cert. tchr., Fla. English tchr. Hillsborough County Schs., Tampa, 1967-68; drama tchr. Cultural Enrichment Ctr., Gainesville, Fla., 1969-70, Title II Grant, Gainesville, 1970-72; lang. arts tchr. Alachua County Schs., Gainesville, 1972-74; team leader humanities ESAA Grant Alachua County, Gainesville, 1975-82; media specialist Alachua County Schs., Gainesville, 1982—; adj. faculty Nova U., Gainesville, 1988-91. Presenter in field; slide show prodr. (Fla. ctr. for children and youth award 1984). Recipient First Liberty Inst. award Ams. United Rsch. Found., Washington, 1991; grantee in field. Mem. Nat. Coun. for the Social Studies, Profl. Assn. Libr. and Media Specialists (sec. 1991-92), Fla. Assn. Media in Edn., Alpha Delta Pi. Home: 203 SW 41st St Gainesville FL 32607-2778 Office: Westwood Middle Sch 3215 NW 15th Ave Gainesville FL 32605

HENSON, ANNA MIRIAM, otolaryngology researcher, medical educator; b. Springfield, Mo., Nov. 7, 1935; d. Bert Emerson and Esther Miriam (Crank) Morgan; m. O'Dell Williams Henson, Aug. 1, 1964; children: Phillip, William. BA, Park Coll., Parkville, Mo., 1957; MA, Smith Coll., 1959; PhD, Yale U., 1967. Instr. Smith Coll., Northampton, Mass., 1960-61; rsch. assoc. Yale U., New Haven, 1967-74; instr. U. N.C., Chapel Hill, 1975-78, rsch. asst. prof., 1978-83, rsch. assoc. prof., 1983-86, rsch. prof. dept. surgery Sch. Medicine, 1986—; mem. study sect. on hearing rsch. NIH, Bethesda, Md., 1990-93. Contbr. articles to profl. jours. Fulbright scholar, Australia, 1959-60; NIH grantee, 1975—. Mem. Assn. for Rsch. in Otolaryngology, Sigma Xi. Office: U NC Cb 7090 Taylor Hall Chapel Hill NC 27599

HENSON, GENE ETHRIDGE, retired legal administrator; b. Lawrenceville, Ga., Sept. 26, 1924; d. Fred Golden and Cora Jewell (Smith) Ethridge; student public schs., Lawrenceville; m. James Arthur Henson, May 2, 1948 (dec.); diploma Interior Design Gwinnett Tech. Inst., 1991. 1 child, Gena Arlene. With Smith, Currie & Hancock, Atlanta, 1959-90, adminstr., 1965-90; chair fashion & design adv. com. Gwinnett Tech. Inst., 1992-93; owner Gene Henson Interiors. Ofcl. hostess for State of Ga., So. Gov.'s Conf., Atlanta, 1971; past adult tchr. First Bapt. Ch., Lawrenceville; mem. adv. council Center for Profl. Edn., Ga. State U., 1980-84; bd. dirs., v.p. County Seat Players Theatre Group, actress Steel Magnolias prodn.; bd. dirs. Gwinnett Coun. for the Arts, Vines Botanical Gardens. Mem. Assn. Legal Adminstrs. (nat. v.p. 1979—, dir. 1979-83), Internat. Interior Design Assn., Atlanta Assn. Legal Execs. (1st pres. 1975), Assn. Legal Adminstrs. (v.p. Atlanta chpt., pres.-elect 1986-87, pres. 1987-88, life mem. 1991). Home and Office: 74 Scenic Hwy Lawrenceville GA 30245-5729

HENSON, GLENDA MARIA, newspaper writer; b. Marion, N.C., June 17, 1960; d. Douglas Bradley and Glenda June (Crouch) H. BA in English cum laude, Wake Forest U., 1982. Reporter Ark. Dem., Little Rock, 1982-84; bur. reporter Tampa Tribune, Crystal River, Fla., 1984; statehouse reporter Ark. Gazette, Little Rock, 1984-87; bur. chief Ark. Gazette, Washington, 1987-89; editorial writer Lexington (Ky.) Herald-Leader, 1989-94; editorial writer, columnist The Charlotte (N.C.) Observer, 1994—. Mem. Wake Forest Presdl. Scholarship Com., Ky., 1992, Pulitzer Prize juror, 1994, 95. Arthur F. Burns fellow Ctr. for Fgn. Journalists, 1992; Nieman fellow Harvard U., 1993-94; recipient Pulitzer prize Columbia U., 1992, Walker Stone award Scripps Howard Found., 1992, Ky. Press Assn. award, 1992; named Wake Forest Woman of Yr., 1992. Mem. Soc. Profl. Journalists (Sigma Delta Chi award 1991, Green Eyeshade award Atlanta chpt. 1992), Nat. Conf. Editorial Writers, Omicron Delta Kappa. Home: 1527-B Cleveland Ave Charlotte NC 28203 Office: The Charlotte Observer PO Box 32188 Charlotte NC 28232

HENSON, MICHELE, state legislator; b. Boston, Aug. 29, 1946; m. Doug Henson. AA, LaSalle U., 1966; BA, U. Miami. Adminstr. Metro Dental Svcs., 1985—; mem. Ga. Ho. of Reps. from dist. 57, 1990-92, Ga. Ho. of Reps. from dist. 65, 1993—; mem. health and ecology com., defense and vet. affairs com., industry com., sec. ins. com. Democrat. Jewish. Office: Ga House of Reps State Capitol Atlanta GA 30334*

HENTON, M. LOIS SMITH, English language arts educator; b. Archer, Fla., June 26, 1947; d. Chris Smith and Cora Lee Smith (Clayton) Kennon. AA with honors, Housatonic Community Coll., Bridgeport, Conn.; BS with honors, So. Conn. State U., New Haven; MA, U. South Fla., Tampa; postgrad., U. South Fla. Counselor, fin. aid specialist and CHOICES coord. Pasco-Hernando Community Coll., Brooksville, Fla., instr. lang. arts, 1978—; mem. staff devel. com., learning lab. com. Pasco-Hernando Community Coll., Brooksville, 1991—, minority adv. bd. dirs., 1986—, vice-chairperson ednl. support com. SACS; mem. adv. and planning com. for devel. of student internship program Southwest Fla. Water Mgmt. Dist.; mem. dist. adv. coun. Hernando County, Fla. Speaker, program developer Save Moton Sch.; organizer coord., dir. 1st Dr. Martin Luther King, Jr. Community March, Brooksville, 1989; mem. Bethlehem Progressive Bapt. Ch., Brooksville; tchr. Sunday Sch., chairperson, coord. Women's Day Program, 1985, 87, 88, 90, 91, mem. pastor's Aide Club and Benevolent Bd. Named Woman of Distinction Hernando County and State of Fla. Suncoast Girl Scout Coun. of Am., 1992. Mem. NAACP (v.p. 1988, 89 Brooksville chpt., acting v.p. 1990, 2nd v.p. 1991, life), Nat. Devel. Edn. Assn., Fla. Devel. Edn. Assn., Fla. Adult Edn. Assn., Brotherhood Orgn. of Hernando County (award 1989), Black Educators Caucus (Appreciation award). Home: 941 Twigg St Brooksville FL 34601

HEPBURN, KATHARINE HOUGHTON, actress; b. Hartford, Conn., May 12, 1907; d. Thomas N. and Katharine (Houghton) H.; m. Ludlow Ogden Smith (div.). Grad., Bryn Mawr Coll, 1928; LHD (hon.), Columbia U., 1992. Actress: (films) A Bill of Divorcement, 1932, Christopher Strong, 1933, Morning Glory, 1933 (Acad. award for best performance by actress 1934), Little Women, 1933, Spitfire, 1934, The Little Minister, 1934, Alice Adams, 1935, Break of Hearts, 1935, Sylvia Scarlett, 1936, Mary of Scotland, 1936, A Woman Rebels, 1936, Quality Street, 1937, Stage Door, 1937, Bringing up Baby, 1938, Holiday, 1938, The Philadelphia Story, 1940 (N.Y. Critic's award 1940), Woman of the Year, 1941, Keeper of the Flame, 1942, Stage Door Canteen, 1943, Dragon Seed, 1944, Undercurrent, 1946, Sea of Grass, 1946, Song of Love, 1947, State of the Union, 1948, Adam's Rib, 1949, The African Queen, 1951, Pat and Mike, 1952, Summertime, 1955, The Rainmaker, 1956, The Iron Petticoat, 1956, The Desk Set, 1957, Suddenly Last Summer, 1959, Long Day's Journey into Night, 1962 (Best Actress, Cannes Internat. Film Festival), Guess Who's Coming to Dinner, 1967, (Acad. award for best actress 1968),The Lion in Winter, 1968 (Acad. award for best actress 1969), Madwoman of Chaillot, 1969, Trojan Women, 1971, A Delicate Balance, 1973, Rooster Cogburn, 1975, Olly, Olly, Oxen Free, 1978, On Golden Pond, 1981 (Acad. award for best actress 1981), The Ultimate Solution of Grace Quigley, 1985, Love Affair, 1994; (plays) The Czarina, 1928, The Big Pond, 1928, Night Hostess, 1928, These Days, 1928, Death Takes a Holiday, 1929, A Month in the Country, 1930, Art and Mrs. Bottle, 1930, The Warrior's Husband, 1932, Lysistrata, 1932, The Lake, 1933, Jane Eyre, 1937, The Philadelphia Story, 1939, Without Love, 1942, As You Like It, 1950, The Millionairess, Eng. and U.S.A., 1952, The Taming of the Shrew, The Merchant of Venice, Measure for Measure,, Eng. and Australia, 1955, Merchant of Venice, Much Ado about Nothing, Am. Shakespeare Festival, 1957, toured later, 1958, Twelfth Night, Antony and Cleopatra, Am. Shakespeare Festival, 1960, Coco, 1969-70, toured, 1971, The Taming of the Shrew, 1970, A Matter of Gravity, 1976-78, West Side Waltz, 1981, (TV movies) The Glass Menagerie, 1973, Love among the Ruins, 1975, The Corn Is Green, 1979, Mrs. Delafield Wants to Marry, 1986; Laura Lansing Slept Here, 1988, This Can't Be Love, 1994, One Christmas, 1994; narrator, co-writer documentary Katharine Hepburn: All About Me, 1993; author: The Making of the African Queen, 1987, (autobiography) Me, 1991. Recipient gold medal as world's best motion picture actress Internat. Motion Picture Expn., Venice, Italy, 1934, ann. award Shakespeare Club, N.Y.C., 1950, award Whistler Soc., 1957, Woman of Yr. award Hasty Pudding Club, 1958, outstanding achievement award for fostering finest ideals of acting profession, 1980, lifetime achievement award Coun. Fashion Designers Am., 1986, award Kennedy Ctr. Awards, 1990. Address: William Morris Agy 151 El Camino Beverly Hills CA 90212*

HEPP, LYNN CARSON, marketing professional; b. Phila., Aug. 28, 1957; d. John Salom and Patricia Ann (Teetsell) Carson; m. Timothy John Hepp, Apr. 23, 1988; 1 child, Julie Maria. BS in Consumer Electronics, U. Del., 1979; MBA, Villanova U., 1986. Sales promotion coord. Econ. Resources Assocs., Inc., King of Prussia, Pa., 1979-82; mktg. rsch. analyst The Franklin Mint, Franklin Ctr., Pa., 1982-83; assoc. project mgr. Beneficial Nat. Bank USA, Wilmington, Del., 1984-86; mktg. project mgr. Donnelley Directory, King of Prussia, 1986-88; asst. v.p., product mgr. Philadelphia Savs. Fund Soc., Phila., 1988-91; sr. mktg. cons. Control Group Ltd., Wilmington, 1991—. Vol. Big Bros./Big Sisters of Chester County, Pa., 1984-88, Interfaith Hospitality Network, Ardmore, Pa., 1992—, Greater Phila. Food Bank, 1992—. Office: Control Group Ltd 1401 Silverside Rd Wilmington DE 19810

HEPPE, KAROL VIRGINIA, lawyer, educator; b. Vinton, Iowa, Mar. 14, 1958; d. Robert Henry and Audry Virginia (Harper) H. BA in Law and Society, U. Calif., Santa Barbara, 1982; JD, People's Coll. of Law, 1989. Community organizer Oreg. Fair Share, Eugene, 1983; law clk. Legal Aid Found. L.A., summer 1986; devel. dir. Ctrl. Am. Refugee Ctr., L.A., 1987-89; exec. dir. Police Watch-The Police Misconduct Lawyer Referral Svc., L.A., 1989-94; prof. law People's Coll. of Law, L.A., 1992-94; dir. alternative sentencing project Ctr. Juvenile and Criminal Justice, 1994—; vol. law clk. Legal Aid Found. L.A., 1984-86, Lane County Legal Aid Svc., Eugene, 1983. Editor newsletter Ctrl. Am. Refugee Ctr., 1987-89. Bd. dirs. People's Coll. of Law, 1985-90, Law Student Civil Rights Rsch. Coun., N.Y.C., 1986; bd. dirs., law student organizer Nat. Lawyers' Guild, L.A., 1984-87; mem. Coalition for Human Immigrants Rights, 1991-92, So. Calif. Civil Rights Coalition, 1991-92. Scholar Kramer Found., 1984-88, Law Students' Civil Rights Rsch. Coun., 1986, Davis-Putter Found., 1988, Assn. for Community Based Edn. Prudential, 1988.

HEPPLER, ROBIN LEE, project manager; b. Detroit, Aug. 12, 1953; d. Warren G. and Maurida (Tillie) H. Student, Glendale Community Coll., 1971-74, 82, Ariz. State U., 1975, 81, U. Wis., 1981. Various positions Valley Nat. Bank, Phoenix, Ariz., 1971-78; project bus. regional dir. Jr. Achievement, Inc., Phoenix, San Jose, Atlanta, 1978-81; asst. v.p., ctr. mgr. 1st Tenn. Bank, Memphis, 1981-83; customer svc. mgr., ops. analyst Wells Fargo Credit Corp., Phoenix, 1983-84; officer Citibank, Ariz., Phoenix, 1984-85; ops. mgr., asst. v.p. MeraBank, Phoenix, 1985-89; lending officer, policy analyst 1st Interstate Bank, Phoenix, 1989; project mgr. Colo. Nat. Bank, 1991-93; project mgr. Ctr. of Excellence for Project Mgmt. US West Techs., Denver, 1993—. Precinct bd. Maricopa County Election Dept., Phoenix, 1990; fundraiser Fiesta Bowl Com., Tempe, Ariz., 1990-92; bd. sec. Ariz. Easter Seal Soc., Phoenix, 1989-90; bd. dirs. Cen. Ariz. Arthritis Found., Phoenix, 1989-90, chmn. jingle bell run, 1989, active Fiesta Bowl Parade Com., 1983-92; chmn. jail-athon Am. Cancer Soc., 1989; coord. Andre House Diocese of Phoenix, 1987-90; sec. bd. dirs. Human Svcs. Inc., Denver, 1991-95; chmn. Festival of Kites, Denver, 1992, champagne and chocolate black tie silent auction, 1994, Denver Jr. League, 1994-95. Named one of Outstanding Young Women Am., 1979; recipient award for outstanding contbn. Arthritis Found., 1990, award for outstanding achievement Am. Cancer Soc., Phoenix, 1989. Mem. Fin. Women Internat. (bd. dirs. 1988-90), Soc. Tech. Communicators. Home: 3635 S Carr St Denver CO 80235-1801

HEPPNER, GLORIA HILL, science administrator; b. Gt. Falls, Mont., May 30, 1940; d. Eugene Merrill and Georgia M. (Swanson) Hill; m. Frank Henry Heppner, June 6, 1964 (div. 1975); 1 child, Michael Berkeley. BA, U. Calif., Berkeley, 1962, MA, 1964, PhD, 1967. Damon Runyon postdoctoral fellow U. Wash., Seattle, 1967-69; asst. and assoc. prof. Brown U., Providence, 1969-79, Herbert Fanger meml. lectr., 1988; chmn. dept. immunology, dir. labs., sr. v.p. Mich. Cancer Found., Detroit, 1979-91; dir. breast cancer program Meyer L. Prentis Comprehensive Cancer Ctr., 1991—; assoc. chairperson for rsch. dept. internal medicine Wayne State U. Sch. Medicine, Detroit, 1991—; dep. dir. Mich. Cancer Found./Prentis Comprehensive Cancer Ctr., 1994—; mem. external adv. com. basic sci. program M.D. Anderson Hosp. and Tumor Clinic, Houston, 1984-94; mem. external adv. com. Case Western Res. U. Cancer Ctr., Cleve., 1988—, Roswell Park Meml. Inst., Buffalo, 1991—; Sarah Stewart meml. lectr. Georgetown U., Washington, 1988. Editor: Macrophages and Cancer, 1988; mem. editorial bd. Cancer Rsch., 1989-93, Jour. Nat. Cancer Inst., 1988, Sci., 1988-92; contbr. over 200 articles to sci. jours. Recipient Mich. Sci. Trail-Blazer award State of Mich., 1987; fellow Damon Runyon-Walter Winchell Found., 1967-69. Mem. AAAS, Am. Assn. for Cancer Rsch. (bd. dirs. 1983-86, chmn. long-range planning com. 1989-91), Am. Assn. Immunologists, Metastasis Rsch. Soc. (bd. dirs. 1985-89), Women in Cancer Rsch. (nat. pres.), Internat. Differentiation Soc. (v.p. 1990-92, pres. 1992-94), LWV (bd. dirs. Grosse Pointe, Mich. 1989—). Democrat. Office: Mich Cancer Found 110 E Warren Ave Detroit MI 48201-1312 Office: John R Harper Hosp Dept Internal Medicine Detroit MI 48201

HEPTINSTALL, DEBRA LOU, newspaper executive; b. Tacoma, Mar. 5, 1952; d. Fred Bernard and June Isabella (Carter) H.; m. Michael Emory Smith, Sept. 26, 1980. Cert. Ctrl. Va. C.C., 1970, AAS cum laude, 1973; student Longwood Coll., 1971-72. Advt. mgr. Times Record/Roane County Reporter, Spencer, W.Va., 1976-78; advt. clk., sales asst. The Washington Post, 1978-79, advt. mgr. The Reston (Va.) Times, 1979-80; ind. sales contractor, The Washington Post, 1980-81, advt. sales rep., 1981-85, mktg. analyst (pricing), 1985-87; advt. mgr. The Springfield (Va.) Connection Newspaper, 1988; mktg. promotional mgr. Def. News, Springfield, 1988; asst. rsch. dir. The Times Jour. Co., Springfield, 1988-91; mktg. analyst B&W Nuclear Environ. Svcs., Inc., Lynchburg, Va., 1993-94; adminstr., receptionist Indsl. Products Co., Lynchburg, Va., 1994—. Methodist. Avocation: playing classical piano, Tae Kwon Do karate. Home: 102 Forest Park Dr # B Forest VA 24551-1213

HERALD, CHERRY LOU, research educator, research director; b. Beeville, Tex., Dec. 23, 1940; d. Edwin Sherley and Margaret Lucille (Caron) Bell; m. Delbert Leon Herald, Jr., July 31, 1964; children: Heather Amanda, Delbert Leon, III. BS, Ariz. State U., 1962, MS, 1965, PhD, 1968. Faculty rsch. assoc. Cancer Rsch. Inst. Ariz. State U., Tempe, 1973-74, sr. rsch. chemist Cancer Rsch. Inst., 1974-77, asst. to dir. and sr. rsch. chemist Cancer Rsch. Inst., 1977-83, asst. dir., assoc. rsch. prof. Cancer Rsch. Inst., 1984-88, assoc. dir., rsch. prof. Cancer Rsch. Inst., 1988—. Co-author: Biosynthetic Products for Cancer Chemotherapy, vols. 4, 5, & 6, 1984, 85, 87, sci. jours. Mem. Am. Soc. Pharmacognosy, Am. Chem. Soc. Office: Ariz State U Cancer Rsch Institute Tempe AZ 85287

HERBEL, PATRICIA FRANCES, elementary education administrator; b. Grafton, N.D., Sept. 20, 1936; d. Fred D. Kerian and Henrietta M. Osowski; m. Donald Herbel, Aug. 20, 1957; children: Denise, Bryon, Jo, Julie, Keri, Donna. Student, Mayville State Coll., 1956, BS, 1965; MS, No. State U., Aberdeen, S.D., 1985. Credentialed prin.; cert. elem. edn., N.D., libr. media dir., N.D. Tchr. 5th grade Eveleth (Minn.) Pub. Sch., 1956-57; tchr. 5th, 6th grade Bisbee (N.D.) Pub. Sch., 1957-58; libr. K-12, 3-5 Rocklake (N.D.) Pub. Sch., 1961-70; tchr. 6th grade Turtle Mountain Elem. Sch., Belcourt, N.D., 1970-71; libr. K-12 Hebron (N.D.) Pub. Sch., 1971-76; libr.-ednl. coord. Dept. Pub. Instrn., Bismarck, N.D., 1977-80; facilitator curriculum-NDN Nat. Diffusion Network, Bismarck, N.D., 1980-86; dir. elem. edn. Dept. Pub. Instrn., Bismarck, N.D., 1986—. Mem. Assn. Mid Level Edn. in N.D. (exec. bd. 1993—), N.D. Assn. Elem. Prins. (exec. bd. 1986—, Golden Apple award 1988), N.D. Libr. Media Assn. (Pres.'s award 1984), North Ctrl. Assn. (dep. dir. 1986—), N.D. Joint Com. Sch. Improvement (co-dir.

1986—), Delta Kappa Gamma (chair chpt. rsch. 1991-93). Roman Catholic. Office: ND Dept Pub Instrn 600 E Boulevard Bismarck ND 58505-0440

HERBER, PAMELA LYNN, public relations executive; b. Ocean Side, Calif., Feb. 27, 1957; d. John A. and Patricia C. (Sparling) H.; m. Anthony P. Peccolo Jr., Sept. 10, 1988; children: Isabella Corinne, Giovanna Sophia. BA in Journalism, U. Wash., 1980, postgrad., 1981, 82. Pub. rels. rep. U.S. Army Corps of Engrs., Seattle, 1979-80; mktg. coord. Wright Schuchart Harbor Co., Seattle, 1981-84, pub. rels. mgr., 1985-86; account exec. Color and Design Exhibits, Seattle, 1987; pub. rels. account exec. Ehrig and Assocs., Seattle, 1987-88; corp. comm. dir. Optical Data Corp., Warren, N.J., 1988-92; pres. Herber-Peccolo Comm., Redmond, Wash., 1992-93; dir. Kaufer Miller Comm., Bellevue, Wash., 1993—. Editor (corp. newsletter) Optical Data News, 1988-92; contbr. articles to mags. Mem. AAAS, ASCD, Bus. and Profl. Advt. Assn. (sec. N.J. chpt. 1991-92, cert. bus. communicator, publicity chairperson Puget Sound chpt. 1987-88), Nat. Sci. Tchrs. Assn., Pub. Rels. Soc. Am. Presbyterian. Office: 1750 112th Ave NE Bellevue WA 98004-3727

HERBERT, AMANDA KATHRYN, special education educator; b. Cleve., Apr. 10, 1948; d. Ralph Earle and Nina Kathryn (Burkey) Herbert; m. John Davis Reeves, June 26, 1971 (div. 1978). Student, Coll. of Wooster, Ohio, 1966-68; BA, Defiance Coll., 1971; MEd, Lynchburg Coll., 1982. Cert. tchr., Va. Elem. tchr. Napoleon (Ohio) City Schs., 1970-72; substitute tchr. Juvenile Boys Correction Ctr., Maumee, Ohio, 1972-73; Title I reading tchr. Defiance City Schs., 1973-76, tchr. 4th grade, 1976-78; tchr. 4th to 6th grades Platte Valley Schs. RE3, Ovid, Colo., 1978-81; tchr. elem. and secondary spl. edn. Amherst County (Va.) Schs., 1982—; tchr. Camp Little Indian, Defiance, 1967-77. Contbr. to book. Deacon, elder First Presbyn. Ch., Defiance, 1973-78; singer Defiance Community Choir, 1972-77; actor, singer Fine Arts Ctr., Lynchburg, Va., 1983—; mem. choir Parkland United Meth. Ch., Lynchburg, 1982—. Mem. NEA, Coun. for Exceptional Children (div. learning disabilities), Va. Edn. Assn., People to People Citizen Ambassador Program to Peoples' Rep. China, Amherst Edn. Assn., Alpha Chi. Methodist. Office: Amherst County High Sch Old Rt 29 Amherst VA 24521

HERBERT, CAROL SELLERS, farming executive, lawyer; b. Durham, N.C., Mar. 2, 1943; d. George Grover and Mae (Savage) Sellers; m. James Keller Herbert, Nov. 13, 1980; children: John, Katherine, Paul, Barry. BA, Duke U., 1964; JD cum laude, Whittier Coll., 1976. Bar: Calif. 1976, U.S. Dist. Ct. (cen. dist.) Calif. 1976. Tchr. h.s. Wasatch Sch. Dist., Heber, Utah, 1964-67; dir., tchr. Pinedale (Mont.) Sch. Dist., 1967-71; adminstr. Whittier Law Sch., L.A., 1971-76; lawyer Katz Granof Palarz, Beverly Hills, Calif., 1976-79; exec. dir. MBJ Legal and Profl. Pub., Inc., L.A., 1979-83; dean San Joaquin Coll. Law, Fresno, Calif., 1981-85; pres., co-founder Barrister Project, L.A., 1985-90, Herbert Found., Fresno and Lindsay, Calif., 1990—; dir., CFO HerCal Corp., Lindsay, Calif.; trustee Domus Mitus Found., Fresno, 1994—; founder Beverly Hills Bar Assn. Com. on Women and Law, 1977. Mem. ABA, Calif. State Bar Assn.

HERBERT, KATHY LYNNE, lawyer; b. Great Neck, N.Y., Mar. 18, 1959; d. Victor Daniel Herbert and Jacqueline Lois (Lubin) Edelstein. BA in Psychology, Brandeis U., 1980; JD, Columbia U., 1983. Bar: N.Y. 1984, Conn. 1995. Assoc. Simpson Thacher & Bartlett, N.Y.C., 1983-88; sr. v.p./gen. counsel Creditanstalt-Bankverein, N.Y.C., 1988—; mem. Internat. Bank Regulatory Compliance Com., 1994. Mem. ABA, Inst. Internat. Bankers (lawyers divsn. 1988—), N.Y. State Bar Assn. (vol. elderly project lifetime planning 1992—), Bar City N.Y. (com. Ea. Europe 1992-94, Robert McKay community outreach program 1993, 94). Office: Creditanstalt-Bankverein 245 Park Ave 27th Flr New York NY 10167

HERBERT, MADELINE ANN, administrative assistant; b. Bklyn., June 5, 1947; d. Anthony James and Vincenza Jean (Proce) Zabatta; m. John Richard Herbert, Aug. 13, 1967 (div.); children: Jennifer Ann, Dana Lynn. AA, Rockland Community Coll., 1993. Sec. Meadowbrook Bank, N.Y.C., 1965-67, Hillside Hosp., Long Island Jewish Hosp., New Hyde Park, N.Y., 1967-69; clk. Becton Dickinson, Orangeburg, N.Y., 1975-76; payroll clk. Dairylea Coop., Pearl River, N.Y., 1976-78; adminstrv. asst. Pear River Sch. Dist., 1983—. Fundraising chair Pearl River Jr. Women's Club, 1980-91, sec., 1981-82, pres., 1982-83, active, 1975-92; fundraising vol. Rockland County Girl Scout Coun., 1979-82. Mem. Pearl River Clerical Assn. (negotiations team mem. 1993—). Roman Catholic. Home: 311 Holt Dr Pearl River NY 10965

HERBERT, MARY KATHERINE ATWELL, free-lance writer; b. Grove City, Pa., Dec. 9, 1945; d. Stewart and Luella Irene (Brown) Atwell; m. Roland Marcus Herbert; children: Stephen Todd, Amy Elizabeth, Jill Anne. BA, Ariz. State U., 1968, MA, 1973; film cert., U. So. Calif., 1978. Film writer Scottsdale Daily Progress, 1976-79; dir. pub. relations Phoenix Theatre, 1980-85; script analyst, 1985-86; exec. asst. to v.p. prodn. De-Laurentiis Entertainment Group, 1986; producer's assoc. film TRAXX, 1986-87; devel. dir. Devin/DeVore Prodns., 1988-89; free-lance script analyst and writer Glendale, Calif., 1989—. Script writer: (TV shows) Trial By Jury, Dick Clark Prodn., Dry Heat, Blind Desire, others; author: Writing Scripts Hollywood Will Love, 1994. Mem. Encanto Homeowners Assn., Phoenix, 1976-80; bd. mgrs. Hollywood-Wilshire YMCA. Mem. Women in Comms., Artists Rights Found., Kappa Delta Pi, Pi Lambda Theta.

HERBERT, TERI LYNN, librarian; b. Cedar Falls, Iowa, May 31, 1948; d. Richard Morris and Helene Kathryn (Zarecky) H. BS, Memphis State U., 1970; MS, U. N.C., 1975, MLS, 1978. Chem. technician marine lab. Duke U., Beaufort, N.C., 1972-75, sr. rsch. technician in biopaleontology marine lab., 1975-76, biomed. rsch. technician, info. specialist biomed. lab., 1978-83; rsch. technician in marine mycology U. N.C., Morehead City, 1975-77; food technologist asst. N.C. State U., Morehead City, 1976-77; dir. libr. Skidaway Inst. Oceanography, Savannah, Ga., 1983-85; reference libr., info. specialist Med. U. S.C., Charleston, 1985—. Home: 1726 Brantley Dr Charleston SC 29412-3503 Office: Library of Med U SC 171 Ashley Ave Charleston SC 29425-0001

HERBIN, REECE A., psychotherapist; b. Greensboro, N.C., Oct. 27, 1946; d. Howard and Mary Louise (Headen) H. BA, U. D.C., 1973; MS, Nova U., 1982. Cert. LSWA. Soc. worker D.C. Pub. Defender Svc., Washington, 1972-76; social worker Yadkin-Surry County Mental Health, Yadkinville, N.C., 1982-83; psychotherapist Washington Assessment and Therapy Svcs., 1986-89; contract psychotherapist Focus/Home Intervention Program, Washington, 1986-88, Change Inc., Washington, 1989-90, Beal & Assocs., Atlanta, 1990-91; dir., psychotherapist Washington Psychotherapy Svcs., 1990-91; dir. Herbin's Therapeutic Svc., Fort Washington, Md., 1991—. Mem. NAFE, DC Mental Health Assn., Am. Assn. for Counseling and Devel., Am. Mental Health Counselor Assn. Mem. A.M.E. Ch. Home and Office: 2306 Old Gate Ct Fort Washington MD 20744-2660

HERBOLSHEIMER, HENRIETTA, physician, consultant; b. Peru, Ill., Feb. 10, 1913; d. George Leonard III and Catherine Carolyn (Neureuther) H. SB, U. Chgo., 1936, MD, 1938; MPH, Johns Hopkins U., 1948. Diplomate Am. Bd. Preventive Medicine. Maternal and child health physician Ill. Dept. Pub. Health, Springfield, 1941-44, dir. Hill Bureton Hosp. Program, 1044-48, dir. maternal and child health, 1945-48, med. adminstrv. asst. to dir., 1948-51, dir. civil def. program-med. aspects, 1950-51; mem. faculty of medicine U. Chgo., 1951-80, assoc. prof. medicine emeritus, 1980—; dir. adult health/occ. medicine City of Chgo., Dept. Pub. Health, 1981-83; physician cons. Ill. Dept. Pub. Aid, Springfield, 1984—. Contbr. numerous articles to profl. jours. Bd. dirs. Vis. Nurse Assn., Chgo., 1960-74; mem. vis. com. Oriental Inst. U. Chgo., 1994—. Recipient Alumni award medicine U. Chgo., 1994. Fellow Am. Coll. Preventive Medicine; mem. AMA (del. 1977-92, Benjamin Rush award 1985), Am. Pub. Health Assn., Ill. State Med. Soc. (trustee 1975-84), Chgo. Med. Soc. (councillor 1977—), Am. Inst., Phi Beta Kappa, Alpha Omega Alpha, Sigma Xi. Home: 1700 E 56th St Apt 3507 Chicago IL 60637

HERBST, MARIE ANTOINETTE, former state senator; m. Paul Herbst. BA, Albany State Tchr.'s Coll.; Masters, Columbia U.; postgrad. secondary sch. adminstrn., U. Conn. Pub. sch. tchr. East Windsor, Conn.; mem., asst. majority leader Conn. State Senate from 35th Dist.; 7th-9th grade tchr. E.W. H.S.; chmn. pub. safety com.; asst. minority leader, 1989-92; mem. fin., revenue, bonding com., 1989; mem. edn. com. Lector Sacred Heart Ch.; past chmn. H.S. DDC; past mem. Ladies of Sacred Heart; past mem. Tri-Town Disabled Com., Vernon Town Coun., 1975-79; past mem. Vernon Bd. Edn.; mem. Adult Edn. Adv. Commn., 1985; treas. Capitol Region Coun. Govts., 1985; active New Rockville Youth Studies, 1994—; activities corporator Rockville Ctrl. Hosp., 1994—; bd. dirs. Tolland Health Inc. Mem. Internat. Edn. Assn., Nat. Edn. Assn., Conn. Edn. Assn., Phi Delta Kappa, Gamma Kappa Rho. Democrat. Roman Catholic. Home: 245 Brandy Hill Rd Vernon Rockville CT 06066-5609

HERBSTREITH, YVONNE MAE, primary education educator; b. Wayne County, Ill., Aug. 18, 1942; d. Daniel Kirby and Rizpah Esther (Harvey) Smith; m. Bobbie L. Cates, Oct. 18, 1964 (div. 1969); 1 child, Shawn L.; m. Jerry Carrol Herbstreith, Sept. 15, 1979. BS, So. Ill. U., 1964. Cert. elem. tchr., Ill. Kindergarten tchr. Beardstown (Ill.) Elem., 1964-65, Pekin (Ill.) Pub. Schs. # 108, 1966-94. V.p. Pekin Friends of 47, 1986-91, pres., 1991-93; pres. Rebecca-Sarah cir. 1st United Meth. Ch., Pekin, 1988—; trustee Sta. WTVP-TV, Peoria, Ill., 1990-92; active PTA, 1965-94, treas., 1992-93. Mem. NEA (life), AAUW, IEA, Pekin Edn. Assn., Pekin Friends of Libr., Alpha Delta Kappa, Alpha Theta (chpt. pres. 1986-88, state sgt. at arms 1990-92, state chaplain 1992-94, state pres.-elect 1994—). Democrat. Methodist. Home: 1922 Quail Hollow Rd Pekin IL 61554-6351

HERD, CHARMIAN JUNE, educator, singer, actress; b. Waterville, Maine, June 1, 1930; d. Samuel Braid and Jennie May (Lang) Herd; B.A., Colby Coll., 1950; postgrad. Boston U., 1951, EdM, U. Maine, 1965; edn. cert. No. Conservatory, Bangor, Maine, 1954; also study voice with Roger A. Nye. Dir. music State Sch. for Girls, Hallowell, Maine, 1950-51; head English, French, dramatics depts. St. George High Sch., Tenants Harbor, 1951-52; dir. music pub. schs. Albion and Unity, 1952-54, Troy, Freedom, Maine, 1953-54; dir. music pub. sch. system Belgrade, Maine, Waterville Jr. High Sch., 1954-55; dir. vocal music Waterville Jr. and Sr. high schs., 1954-58; head English and dramatics depts. Besse High Sch., Albion, 1959-62; tchr. French, Skowhegan Jr. High Sch., 1962-63; tchr. French, English, Skowhegan Sr. High Sch., 1963-69; tchr. French, Lawrence Sr. High Sch., Fairfield, Maine, 1969-71, chmn. drama and speech dept., 1972-79; instr. dramatics U. Maine, Farmington, 1969-70; tchr. conversational French, Skowhegan Adult Edn. Sch., 1963-69, drama instr., 1965-69; dance asst. Plaza Studio; producer, appeared in role of Vera, Mame, Waterville; soloist various churches, Maine, 1951—; mus. dir. children's sect., performing mem. Theater at Monmouth, Maine, 1970—, mem. exec. bd., 1976—, sec. bd. trustees, 1977—; performing mem. Augusta Players, Camden Civic Theatre, Portland Lyric Theatre, Waterville Players, Titipu Choral Soc., Waterville Community Ballet, Choral Arts Soc., Portland, Maine, 1980—, Treasure Coast Opera Soc., Ft. Pierce, Fla., 1986—, Riverside Theatre Co., Vero Beach, Indian River Ctr. for Arts; theatre chmn. ann. Maine Festival Arts, Bowdoin Coll., 1978—; soloist Vero Beach Chorale Soc., 1986—, numerous club, ch., conv., coll. concerts, oratorios; performing mem. Vero Beach Solo Gates, Encore Alley Theatre, 1987-91, Esprit des Amis, Vero Beach, Ft. Pierce City Ballet, Fla.; treas. Coast Opera Co., Ft. Pierce, Fla., 1986—; hostess, prodr. TV show Lively Arts of the Treasure Coast with Charmian Herd, Ft. Pierce, Fla., 1994—. Bd. dirs. Opera New Eng., 1980—, Portland Lyric Theatre, 1982—Mem. Waterville Friends Music, DAR, Waterville Theatre Guild (charter mem., pres. 1967—), Vero Beach Theatre Guild (Fla.), Encore Alley Theatre, Vero Beach, Waterville Bus. and Profl. Women's Club (program chmn. 1957-58, v.p. 1958-59, pres. 1959-61, chmn. drama dept. 1961, drama and music chmn. 1961—), Fla. Profl. Theatre Assn., Ednl. Speech and Theatre Assn. Maine (mem. exec. bd., pres. 1972-74), Maine Profl.-Community Theatre Assn. (mem. organizing com.), Actors Equity Assn., Albion-Burnham Tchrs. Club (sec. 1960-61), NEA, Maine Tchrs. Assn., New Eng. Theatre Conf. (exec. bd. 1976—, 1st v.p. 1976-77, conf. chmn. 1977), Theatre Assn. Maine (membership chmn. 1972-73, 2d v.p. 1973-74, exec. bd. 1972—, exec. sec. 1975—, state pres. 1976—), Internat. Platform Assn., Nat. Assn. Tchrs. of Singing (sec. Maine chpt. 1980—), Pine Tree Post Card Club (exec. bd., Spring show chmn. 1979-80, pres. 1982-84), Maine Hist. Soc., Bay State Post Card Club, R.I. Post Card Club. Club: Cecilia (Augusta, Maine). Composer sacred music: Babylon, 1959, The Greatest of These is Love, 1961, Pan; Keep Not Thy Silence, O God, Remember Now Thy Creator, Slow, Slow, Fresh Fount, A Witch's Charm, Hymn to God the Father. Avocations: acting, singing, oil painting, collecting opera and operetta scores. Home and Office: 601 Seaway Dr E-2 Fort Pierce FL 34949

HERGENHAN, JOYCE, public relations executive; b. Mt. Kisco, N.Y., Dec. 30, 1941; d. John Christopher and Goldie (Wago) H. B.A., Syracuse U., 1963; M.B.A., Columbia U., 1978. Reporter White Plains Reporter Dispatch, 1963-64; asst. to Rep. Ogden R. Reid Washington, 1964-68; reporter Gannett Newspapers, 1968-72; with Consol. Edison Co. of N.Y., Inc., N.Y.C., 1972-82, v.p., 1977-79, sr. v.p. pub. affairs, 1979-82; v.p. corp. pub. relations General Electric Co., Fairfield, Conn., 1982—. Office: GE 3135 Easton Tpke Fairfield CT 06431-0001

HERING, DORIS MINNIE, dance critic; b. N.Y.C., Apr. 11, 1920; d. Harry and Anna Elizabeth (Schwenk) H. B.A. cum laude, Hunter Coll., 1941; M.A., Fordham U., 1985. Freelance dance writer, 1946-52; assoc. editor, prin. critic Dance mag., N.Y.C., 1952-72; exec. dir. Nat. Assn. for Regional Ballet, N.Y.C., 1972-87; adj. assoc. prof. dance history NYU, 1968-78; freelance dance writer, lectr., cons., 1987—; mem. dance panel NEA, 1972-75, cons., 1991—; mem. dance panel N.Y. State Coun. Arts, 1992—; bd. dirs. Walnut Hill Sch., 1975—, Internat. Ballet Competition, 1981—; hon. bd. dirs. Phila. Dance Alliance, 1980—; cons. Regional Dance Am.; adj. assoc. prof. dance history NYU Grad. Sch. Edn. Author: 25 Years of American Dance, 1950, Dance in America, 1951, Wild Grass, 1965, Giselle and Albrecht, 1981; sr. editor Dance mag., 1989—. Howard D. Rothschild Rsch. fellow Harvard U., 1992; recipient 33d ann. Capezio Dance Found. award for lifetime svc., 1985, award of distinction Dance mag., 1987, Sage Cowles Land Grant chair in dance U. Minn., 1993; named to Hunter Coll. Alumni Hall of Fame, 1986. Mem. Dance Critics Assn., Assn. Dance History Scholars, Phi Beta Kappa, Chi Tau Epsilon (hon.).

HERING, LU ANN PAULINE, state official; b. Manhattan, N.Y., Nov. 29, 1955; d. Lucille M. Castelluccio; m. Richard S. Hering, Nov. 11, 1978. AAS, SUNY, Loch Sheldrake; BSW, SUNY, Stony Brook. Legal sec., office adminstr. Law Offices of David Cohen, Liberty, N.Y., 1978-89, Law Offices of Michael Altman, South Fallsburg, N.Y., 1989-90; chief clk. N.Y. State Surrogate's Ct., Sullivan County, Monticello, 1990—. Past pres. Liberty Group Cornell Coop. Ext. Home Econs. Divsn., 1987—. Mem. Chief Clks. of Surrogate's Cts. N.Y. State, 1990—, Surrogate's Law Assn. Democrat. Roman Catholic. Office: NY State Surrogates Ct Govt Ctr 100 North St Monticello NY 12701

HERKNER, BERNADETTE KAY, occupational health nurse; b. East Liverpool, Ohio, Apr. 29, 1947; d. Charles R. and Anna G. (Parr) Geon. Diploma in nursing, East Liverpool City Hosp., 1973; BS in Applied Sci., Youngstown (Ohio) State U., 1976. RN, Ohio, Mich., Fla; cert. in audiometrics, sipromety, ICD-9-CM; cert. case mgr. Charge nurse emergency room East Liverpool City Hosp.; sr. occupational health nurse Mich. div. Dow Chem. USA, Midland, 1978—. Active Vol. Action Ctr. Midland County. Recipient Best Bedside Nurse, Centennial award for svc. to humanity, 1973, Ctrl. Mich. Outstanding Occupational Health Nurse of the Yr. award, 1993; named Miss Hope Columbiana County unit Am. Cancer Soc., 1977. Mem. ANA, Am. Assn. Occupl. Health Nurses (cert.), Mich. Assn. Occupl. Health Nurses (bd. dirs.), Emergency Nurses Assn., Mich. Nurses Assn., Ctrl. Mich. Assn. Occupl. Health Nurses (bd. dirs., corr. sec. 1986-90, rec. sec. 1990-91, pres. 1991-95, legis. chmn. 1995—), East Ctrl. Mich. Emergency Nurses, Ohio Emergency Nurses Assn. (membership sec.), Individual Case Mgrs. Assn.

HERLIHY, MAURA ANN, psychology technician; b. Yokohama, Japan, July 13, 1953; d. Joseph Brendan and Margaret Cecilia (Corrigan) H. AA in Liberal Arts, Middlesex Community Coll., 1973; BA in Elem. Edn., Rivier Coll., 1975, MA in Counseling, 1986. Sub. tchr. Bedford (Mass.) Pub. Schs., 1975-76; sec. Instrumentation Labs., Lexington, Mass., 1976-77, Electronized Chems. Corp., Burlington, Mass., 1977-78, Digital Equipment Corp., Bedford, Mass., 1978-80; sales clk. Lord and Taylor, Burlington, 1979-81; sec. Dept. VA, Bedford, 1980-89, psychology technician, 1989—. Mem. DAV Aux. Roman Catholic. Home: 5 Springs Rd Bedford MA 01730-1654 Office: Dept Vet Affairs 200 Springs Rd Bedford MA 01730-1114

HERMAN, ALEXIS M., federal official; b. Mobile, Ala.. Grad., Xavier U. Founder, CEO A.M. Herman & Assocs., Washington; nat. dir. Minority Women's Employment Program, Washington, until 1977; dir. Women's Bur. Dept. Labor, Washington, 1977-81; chief staff, then dep. chair Dem. Nat. Conv. Com., Washington, until 1991, CEO, 1991-92; dep. dir. Clinton-Gore Presdl. Transition Office, Washington, 1992-93; asst. to President U.S., Pub. Liason dir. White House, Washington, 1993—. Mem. Nat. Coun. Negro Women, Delta Sigma Theta. Office: White House Office Pub Liaison 1600 Pennsylvania Ave NW Washington DC 20500

HERMAN, ANDREA MAXINE, newspaper editor; b. Chgo., Oct. 22, 1938; d. Maurice H. and Mae (Baron) H.; m. Joseph Schmidt, Oct. 28, 1962. BJ, U. Mo., 1960. Feature writer Chgo.'s Am., 1960-63; daily columnist News Am., Balt., 1963-67; feature writer Mainichi Daily News, Tokyo, 1967-69; columnist Iowa City Press-Citizen, 1969-76; music and dance critic San Diego Tribune, 1976-84; asst. mng. editor features UPI, Washington, 1984-86, asst. mng. editor news devel., 1986-87; mng. editor features L.A. Herald Examiner, 1987-91; editor/culture We/Mbl Newspaper, Washington, 1991—. Recipient 1st and 2d prizes for features in arts James S. Copley Ring of Truth Awards, 1982, 1st prize for journalism Press Club San Diego, 1983. Mem. Soc. Profl. Journalists, Am. Soc. Newspaper Editors, AP Mng. Editors, Women in Communications. Office: We/Mbl Newspaper 1350 Connecticut Ave NW Ste 1020 Washington DC 20036

HERMAN, BARBARA ROSE, interior decorator; b. Worcester, Mass., Feb. 14, 1938; d. Albert H. and Mary Margaret (Convery) Garnache; children: Diane G. Herman Johnson, Mary E. Herman Thurston, Tracy A., Barry J. Cert., N.Y. Sch. Interior Design, N.Y.C., 1972, RISD, Providence, 1974. Owner Decorating Barn, Auburn, Pa., 1970-79, Barbara Herman Ineriors, Worcester, Mass., 1979—; tchr. Worcester Night Life Continuing Edn., Worcester, 1970-89, Becker Jr. Coll., Worcester, 1982; lectr. in field. Work appeared in Womens Day Mag., 1987, Condo Media Cover, 1989, Condo Media Cover, 1992. Mem. Worcester Exec. Assn. (pres. 1984). Roman Catholic. Home: 73 Pointe Rok Dr Worcester MA 01604-1466 Office: Barbara Herman Interiors 104 June St Worcester MA 01602-2950

HERMAN, ELIZABETH MULLEE, elementary educator; b. N.Y.C., May 1, 1939; d. Raymond Garrett and Theresa (Lang) Mullee; m. Paul Herman, Feb. 10, 1962; children: Susan, Christina, Andrew, Marianne Schell, Jane (dec.). BA, Manhattanville Coll., Purchase, N.Y., 1960; MA, Columbia U., 1962; Cert. Advanced Study, Sacred Heart U., Fairfield, Conn. Tchr. Birch Wathen Sch., N.Y.C., 1960-61, Madison Jr. High Sch., Trumbull, Conn., 1978-79, Holy Rosary Sch., Bridgeport, Conn., 1979-82, St. Teresa Sch., Trumbull, 1982-88, Roosevelt Sch., Bridgeport, 1988-94, Maplewood Annex Sch., Bridgeport, 1994—. Baptism tchr. St. Theresa Ch., Trumbull, 1980—, reader, 1980—; mem. Secular Order Franciscans. Chase Bank mini grantee, 1993, Bridgeport Bus. Coun. mini grantee, 1994; Pimms scholar, 1993; mem. Italian Cmty. Club. Mem. NEA, APA, Bridgeport Edn. Assn., Conn. Edn. Assn., Candlewood Lake Club. Roman Catholic. Home: 144 Plymouth Ave Trumbull CT 06611-4152 Office: Roosevelt School 680 Park Ave Bridgeport CT 06604-4698

HERMAN, FELICIA GAIL, librarian; b. Phila., Dec. 4, 1955; d. Ken Maynard and Irene (Sofian) H.; m. Joel Rosenberg, June 3, 1979; children: Judith Eleanor Rosenberg, Rachel Hannah Rosenberg. MusB, U. Conn., 1978; MLS, So. Conn. State U., 1986. Reference libr. Russell Libr., Middletown, Conn., 1986-87; exec. v.p. JR Enterprises, Mpls., 1986—; MIS resource libr. Dayton Hudson Corp. Dept. Store Div., Mpls., 1989—. Editor: The Source, 1989—. Mem. Spl. Libr. Assn. Tech. Libr. User Group. Office: Dayton Hudson Corp 700 Nicollet Mall Box 1060 Minneapolis MN 55402

HERMAN, JEAN HULL, poetry magazine editor, writer; b. Wilmington, Del., Sept. 25, 1944; d. Donald Robert and Blanche (Williams) Hull; m. Charles William Herman, July 27, 1975. BA in English, Allegheny Coll., Meadville, Pa., 1966. Cert. tchr. Tchr. English Seaford (Del.) High Sch., 1968-70; tchr. GED courses Del. Tech. C.C., Wilmington, 1971-73; mgr. Ins. Co. N.Am., Detroit, 1974-81, 81-89; editor Mobius, The Poetry Mag., St. Clair Shores, Mich., 1990—. Mem. AAUW (bd. dirs., cultural rep.). Home: 23027 Gary Ln Saint Clair Shores MI 48080-2715 Office: Mobius Publs PO Box 674 Saint Clair Shores MI 48080-0674

HERMAN, LETA GWEN, marketing professional; b. Sommerville, N.J., Apr. 26, 1967; d. Stephen Jay and Gail (Neary) H.; m. Neal Stuart Parks. BA, Smith Coll., 1989. Vol. U.S. Peace Corps, Kiffa, Mauritania, 1990; corp. cons. Hybridon, Worcester, Mass., 1991; comms. dir. Complete Bus. Solutions, Inc., Farmington Hills, Mich., 1991-93; mktg. dir. Software Alliance Corp., Berkeley, Calif., 1993—. Sara Williston scholar Mt. Holyoke Coll., 1987. Mem. NOW, NAFE, Nat. Orgn. Returned Peace Corps Vols., Phi Beta Kappa. Democrat. Home: 2439 Russell St Berkeley CA 94705 Office: Software Alliance Corp 2150 Shattuck Ave 11th Fl Berkeley CA 94704

HERMAN, MAJA See HERMAN-SEKULICH, MAYA B.

HERMAN, MARY MARGARET, pathologist; b. Plymouth, Wis., July 26, 1935; d. Elmer Fredolein and Esther Lydia (Bross) H.; m. Lucien Jules Rubinstein, Jan. 31, 1969. BS in Med. Sci., U. Wis., 1957, MD, 1960. Diplomate Nat. Bd. Med. Examiners, Am. Bd. Anatomic Pathology, Am. Bd. Neuropathology. Rotating intern Mary Hitchcock Meml. Hosp., Hanover, N.H., 1960-61; resident in neurology U. Wis. Hosps., 1961-62; intern in pathology Yale U., New Haven, 1962-63, asst. resident in pathology, 1963-64, fellow neuropathology, 1964-65, rsch. assoc. pathology, 1967-68; fellow neuropathology Stanford U., Palo Alto, Calif., 1965-66, fellow, acting instr. neuropathology, 1966-67, asst. prof. pathology, 1967-74, assoc. prof., 1974-81; prof., co-dir. div. neuropathology U. Va. Sch. Medicine, Charlottesville, 1981-91, prof. div. clin. pathology, 1991-92; spl. expert neuropathology in clin. brain disorders br. NIMH, Washington, 1992—; NIMH Brain Bank; neuropathologist Stanley Fund Brain Bank, 1993—; vis. asst. prof. Albert Einstein Coll. Medicine, Bronx, N.Y., 1971-72; mem. program project rev. com. Nat. Inst. Neurol. and Communicative Diseases, NIH, 1973-77; cons. lab. svc. VA Hosp., Salem, Va., Ctrl. Va. Tng. Ctr., Lynchburg, 1982-92, ad hoc mem. pathology A study sect., 1986-91; cons. neuropathologist D.C. Med. Examiner's Office, Washington, 1992—, D.C. Gen. Hosp., 1992—. Mem. editorial bd. Jour. Neuropathology and Exptl. Neurology, 1989-93; contbr. over 125 articles to profl. jours. Recipient Rsch. Career Devel. award NIH, 1967-72, Faculty Devel. award Merck Found., 1969. Mem. AAAS, Am. Assn. Neuropathologists (Weil award 1974), Am. Soc. for Investigative Pathology, Soc. for Devel. Biology, Internat. Soc. Neuropathology, Am. Soc. Cell Biology (rsch. fellowship program, mentor scientist summer tchr. 1994), Internat. Acad. Pathology, Am. Tissue Culture Assn. Home: Oakwood Apts Apt J501 125 S Reynolds St Alexandria VA 22304 Office: NIMH Neurosci Ctr at St Elizabeths Clin Brain Disorders Brg Washington DC 20032

HERMAN, SHIRLEY YVONNE, accountant; b. Jersey City, Nov. 22, 1941; d. Otto and Mary (Erde) H. BA, CCNY, 1963. IRS enrolled agt. Pvt. practice N.Y.C., 1984—. Mem. Nat. Assn. Pub. Accts., Nat. Assn. Tax Practioners, Nat. Assn. Enrolled Agts, Am. Assn. Women Accts. Office: 853 Broadway Ste 1101 New York NY 10003-4703

HERMAN, SUSAN N., legal educator; b. Bklyn., Feb. 16, 1947; d. Nathan H. and Frances (Pickus) H.; m. Paul A. Gangsei, June 16, 1978; 1 child, Erica Herman Gangsei. AB, Barnard Coll., 1968; JD, NYU, 1974. Bar: N.Y. 1975, U.S. Dist. Ct. (so., ea., we. and no. dists.) N.Y. 1975, U.S. Ct. Appeals (2d cir.) 1975. Law clk. to presiding justice U.S. Ct. Appeals (2d cir.), N.Y.C., 1974-76; assoc. dir. Prisoners' Legal Services N.Y., N.Y.C., 1976-80; from asst. prof. to prof. Bklyn. Law Sch., 1980—; reporter, criminal procedure com. U.S. Dist. Ct. (ea. dist.) N.Y., Bklyn., 1986—, coord. tng. program civil litigation fund, 1984. Contbr. articles to profl. jours. Mem.

due process com. ACLU, 1982—, chmn., 1985—. Mem. ABA, N.Y.C. Bar Assn., ACLU (nat. bd. dirs. 1988—), Order of Coif. Office: Bklyn Law Sch 250 Joralemon St Brooklyn NY 11201-3798

HERMANN, MARGARET GLADDEN, political science educator; b. Rogersville, Pa., July 11, 1938; d. James W. and Cynthia E. (Hales) Gladden; m. Charles F. Hermann, June 4, 1960 (div. June 1994); children: Chris, Karen. BA, DePauw U., 1960; MA, Northwestern U., Evanston, Ill., 1963, PhD, 1965. Postdoctoral fellow Ednl. Testing Svc., Princeton, N.J., 1965-67; rsch. assoc. Mershon Ctr. Ohio State U., Columbus, 1970-86, rsch. scientist Mershon Ctr., 1986—, assoc. prof. polit. sci., 1988-90, prof. polit. sci., co-dir. summer inst. polit. psychology, 1990—; dir. NSF Rsch. Tng. Group Polit. Psychology, 1991-96; cons. various govt. agys., 1973—, Worthington (Ohio) Pub. Schs., 1983-86. Editor: A Psychological Examination of Political Leaders, 1977, Political Psychology, 1986; co-author: Foreign Policy Behavior, 1982; editor Polit. Psychology jour., 1980-82, Mershon Internat. Studies Rev., 1994—; contbr. articles to profl. jours. Trustee, treas. Columbus Met. Women's Ctr., 1980-83; adv. com. Ctr. for Leadership and Change, Urban League, Columbus, 1980-86, Ohio Displaced Homemaker Network, 1986; co-dir. Leadership for the 90s, Columbus, 1988-92. Recipient Woodrow Wilson fellowship, 1960-62, NIMH postdoctoral fellowship Edn. Testing Svc., 1965-67, award AAUW, 1985. Mem. Internat. Studies Assn. (v.p., chmn. publs. com. 1982, 89-91, Outstanding Scholar award 1994), Internat. Soc. Polit. Psychology (pres. 1987-88, Outstanding Svc. award 1990), Am. Polit. Sci. Assn. (several coms.), Am. Psychol. Soc. Home: 7035 Rieber St Columbus OH 43085-2209 Office: Mershon Ctr/Ohio State Univ 1501 Neil Ave Columbus OH 43201-2399

HERMANN, NAOMI BASEL, librarian, interior decorator; b. N.Y.C., Feb. 12, 1918; d. Alexander and Rebecca (Deinard) Basel; m. Henry I. Almour, June 26, 1938 (dec.); 1 child, Jay Alexander; m. Stanford Leland Hermann, Dec. 20, 1951. BS in Edn., NYU, 1937, MS in Psychology, 1939; MLS, Columbia U., 1963; postgrad., Vassar Coll., Cornell U., Hunter Coll. Newspaper reporter Times Picayune, New Orleans, 1935; tchr. gifted children N.Y.C. Schs., 1946-58; libr. supr. 22 elem., jr. and sr. high schs., N.Y.C., 1958-72; libr. Brandeis High Sch., 1972-75; interior decorator, pvt. practice, N.Y.C., 1946—; instr. Children's Literature, N.Y.C. Bd. Edn., 1969-73; libr. examiner, N.Y.C. Bd. of Edn., 1967-72. Pres. Hadassah, N.Y.C., 1939-41, life mem.; life mem. Coun. Jewish Women, 1974—; charter mem. Eleanor Roosevelt Fund for Women and Girls; established adult library Temple Beth El, Boca Raton, Fla. Mem. AAUW (pres. Boca Raton chpt. 1987-89), Boca Raton Noontime Ladies Club (pres.). Home: 550 S Ocean Blvd Boca Raton FL 33432-6264

HERMAN-SEKULICH, MAYA B. (MAJA HERMAN), poet, essayist, editor; b. Belgrade, Serbia, Yugoslavia, Feb. 17, 1959; came to U.S., 1980, naturalized, 1992; d. Bogomir Herman and Lily (Strauss) Tišma; m. Milosh Sekulich. MA, Belgrade U., 1977; PhD in Comparative Lit., Princeton U., 1986. Fulbright lectr. Rutgers U., New Brunswick, N.J., 1982-84; cons. Novo Arts, N.Y.C., 1988-90; vis. lectr. Princeton (N.J.) U., 1985, 88; lectr., reader in field. Author: (poems) Camerography, 1990, Cartography, 1992, Sketches for Portraits, 1992, (essays) Literature of Transgression, 1986, rev. edit., 1994, The Jade Window: Images from Southeast Asia, 1994; editor/translator: Anxiety of Influence (Harold Bloom), 1981, Cathedral (Raymond Carver), 1991, Myth and Structure (Northrop Frye), 1991, Poems of Our Climate (Wallace Stevens), 1995; contbg. editor Night, 1990-91; edited and translated intros. to 10 books; contbr. to scholarly jours. Princeton U. fellow, 1980-85, Fulbright fellow, 1982-84. Fellow AAUW; mem. PEN (Am. chpt., Serbian chpt.), Poetry Soc. Am. Home: 250 W 16th St Apt 2G New York NY 10011

HERMES, MARJORY RUTH, machine embroidery and arts educator; b. Caldwell, Kans., June 28, 1931; d. Truman Homer and Olive Ruth (Ridings) Brown; m. Ogden S. Jones, Jr., Dec. 17, 1949 (div. Aug. 1956); m. Richard Lawrence Hermes, July 18, 1963; children: Penelope, Peter, Deborah, Patricia, Pamela, Kristin. Student, U. Kans., 1949-50, Arkansas City Jr. Coll., 1953-54. Sec. Maurer-Neuer Corp., Arkansas City, Kans., 1954-56, Lesh, Bradley & Barrand, Lawrence, Kans., 1959-60; exec. sec. Houston Corp., Wichita, Kans., 1956-57; mgr. Ind. Ins. Co., Landstuhl, Fed. Republic Germany, 1960-62; sec. U. Kans., Lawrence, 1962-63; photograph restorer Herb's Studio, Lawrence, 1977-78; ptnr., agt. Hayes-Richardson-Santee Inc., Lawrence, 1978-83; instr. sewing and machine embroidery Self & Bob's Bernina, Lawrence, 1985—; mem. Lawrence Ins. Bd., 1980-83. Bd. dirs. United Way, Lawrence, 1981-83; host Am. Indian Athletic Hall of Fame, 1980-82; treas. local polit. campaigns, 1984, 88; leader Therapeutic Horse Riding Instrn., Lawrence. Mem. Nat. Machine Embroidery Instrs. Assn. (bd. dirs. for N.D., S.D., Nebr., Iowa, Mo., Minn. and Kans. 1987-90), Am. Sewing Guild, Am. Bus. Women's Assn. (v.p. Lawrence 1980-81, pres. 1981-82, Inner Circle award 1982, Woman of Yr. award 1984), Lawrence C. of C. (envoy 1978-83). Republican. Home: 2513 W 24th Ter Lawrence KS 66047-2818

HERNANDEZ, ANTONIA, lawyer; b. Torreon, Coahuila, Mexico, May 30, 1948; came to U.S., 1956; d. Manuel and Nicolasa (Martinez) H.; m. Michael Stern, Oct. 8, 1977; children: Benjamin, Marisa, Michael. BA, UCLA, 1971, JD, 1974. Bar: Calif. 1974, D.C. 1979. Staff atty. Los Angeles Ctr. Law and Justice, 1974-77; directing atty. Legal Aid Found., Lincoln Heights, Calif., 1977-78; staff counsel U.S. Senate Com. on the Judiciary, Washington, 1979-80; assoc. counsel Mexican Am. Legal Def. Ednl. Fund, Washington, 1981-83, employment program dir., 1983-84; exec. v.p., dep. gen. counsel Mexican Am. Legal Def. Ednl. Fund, Los Angeles, 1984-85, pres., gen. counsel, 1985—; bd. dirs. Fed. Immigration Law Reporter, Washington, Oxfam Am., Boston, The Alan Guttmacher Inst., N.Y.C. Contbr. articles to profl. jours. Co-chmn. enriching diversity com. Los Angeles 2000; mem. Nat. Competition on the Constn., Hon. Com. on 75th Anniversary Dept. Labor, Quality Edn. for Minorities (QEM) Network; active Inter-Am. Dialogue Aspen Inst., Learn Working Group, Nat. Com. Innovations in State and Local Govt., Nat. Endowment for Democracy, Nat. Hispanic Leadership Agenda, Pres.'s Commn. White House Fellowships; bd. dirs. Ramona Convent Secondary Sch., Skirball Inst. Am. Values; chair Latino Mus. Mus. History, Art & Culture,. AAUW fellow, 1973-74. Fellow AAUW; mem. ABA, State Bar Calif., Washington D.C. Bar Assn., Mexican-Am. Bar Assn., L.A. County Bar Assn., 9th Cir. Jud. Conf. Roman Catholic. Office: Mexican Am Legal Def Fund 634 S Spring St Fl 11 Los Angeles CA 90014-3921

HERNANDEZ, CHRISTINE, educator; b. San Antonio, July 23, 1951; d. Joe and Aurora (Zapata) H. BA, Our Lady of the Lake Coll., 1973; MA, U. Tex., 1981. Cert. elem. tchr. Tchr. San Antonio Ind. Sch. Dist., 1973-83; pres. San Antonio Fedn. of Tchrs., 1983-86; ednl. cons. Bexar County Fedn. Tchrs., San Antonio, 1986-90. Mem. Dist. 124 Tex. Ho. of Reps., 1991—, mem. legis. budget bd., 1994—, mem. appropriations com., 1993—, mem. pub. edn. com., 1993—; bd. edn. San Antonio Ind. Sch. Dist., 1986-91; pub. mem. bd. dirs. State Bar Tex., 1989-92; bd. dirs. So. Regional Coun., 1990—, Target '90 Goals for San Antonio, 1987-91, Providence High Sch., 1987-90; bd. dirs. Tex. Lyceum, sec., 1991-93, v.p. 1993-94; exec. com. San Antonio River Corridor com. 1987-89, Govs. Commn. for Women, 1985-87, Tex. Task Force on Indigent Health Care, 1983-84; bd. mgrs. Bexar County Hosp. Dist., 1982-84; bd. review Hist. Dists. and Landmarks, 1981-82; task force Southland Corps. Coll. Program, 1985; mem. San Antonio Commn. on Literacy, 1987-89; trustee United Way, 1988—. Named Hispanic Woman of Yr., 1984, Young Woman of Promise, Good Housekeeping Mag., 1985, Sunday's Woman, S.A. Light, 1985, Alumnus of Yr., U. Tex., San Antonio, 1993, Friend of Bus., Tex. C. of C., 1993; recipient Outstanding Leadership award YWCA, 1989, others. Mem. Tex. Assn. Sch. Bds. (bd. trustees 1989-90), Leadership Am. Alumnae Assn., Hispanic Women's Network of Tex. (bd. dirs.), Leadership San Antonio Alumni Assn., Tex. Women's Forum (v.p.), Any Baby Can Alliance, Leadership Tex. Alumnae Assn., San Antonio 100 (charter), Labor Coun. for Latin Am. Advancement (nat. exec. bd.), San Antonio AFL-CIO Coun., Am. Fedn. Tchrs. (v.p. 1978-81, treas. 1981-83, pres. 1983-86). Democrat. Roman Catholic. Office: 301 S Frio St #152 San Antonio TX 78207-4414

HERNANDEZ, IRENE CANTINI, software engineer; b. Galveston, Tex., Mar. 18, 1954; d. Clarence Claude and Angela Marie (Giuliani) Cantini; m. Robert Paul Head, Aug. 19, 1973 (div. Feb. 15, 1989); 1 child, Cara Leah; m. Raymond Hernandez, May 30, 1991. BA, Sam Houston State U., 1975. Tchr. math. Clear Creek Ind. Sch. Dist., League City, Tex., 1975-80; computer software programmer Jefferson Assocs., Inc., Houston, 1982-84; computer software analyst Lockheed Corp., Houston, 1984-86; sr. software engr. Unisys Corp., Houston, 1986-89; systems specialist Rockwell Space Ops. Co., Houston, 1989-92, project engr., 1992—. Editor Flight Design and Dynamics Newsletter, 1989-91. Named Woman of the Yr. YMCA, Houston, 1988. Mem. NAFE. Home: 911 Lake Country Dr Taylor Lk Vlg TX 77586-4507 Office: Rockwell Space Ops Co 600 Gemini St Houston TX 77058-2754

HERNANDEZ, JO FARB, museum and curatorial consultant; b. Chgo., Nov. 20, 1952. BA in Polit. Sci. & French with honors, U. Wis., 1974; MA in Folklore and mythology, UCLA, 1975; postgrad., U. Calif., Davis, 1978, U. Calif., Berkeley, 1978-79, 81. Registration Mus. Cultural History UCLA, 1974-75; Rockefeller fellow Dallas Mus. Fine Arts, 1976-77; asst. to dir. Triton Mus. Art, Santa Clara, Calif., 1977-78, dir., 1978-85; adj. prof. mus. studies John F. Kennedy U., San Francisco, 1978; grad. advisor arts administrn. San Jose (Calif.) State U., 1979-80; dir. Monterey (Calif.) Peninsula Mus. Art, 1985-93, cons. curator, 1994—; prin. Curatorial and Mus. Mgmt. Svcs., Watsonville, Calif., 1993—; lectr., panelist, juror, panelist in field USIA, Calif. Arts Coun., others; vis. lectr. Am. Cultural Ctr., Jerusalem, 1989, Binat. Ctr., Lima, Peru, 1988, Daytona Beach Mus. Art, 1983, Israel Mus., 1989, U. Chgo., 1981, others; guest on various TV and radio programs. Contbr. articles to profl. publs.; author: (museum catalogs) The Quiet Eye: Pottery of Shoji Homada and Bernard Leach, 1990, Alan Sheppard: The Language of Stone, 1991, Wonderful Colors: The Paintings of August Francois Gay, 1993, Jeannette Maxfield Lewis: A Centennial Celebration, 1994, Armin Hansen, 1994, among others. Bd. dirs. Bobbie Wynn and Co. of San Jose, 1981-85, Santa Clara Arts and Hist. Consortium, 1985; bd. dirs. Non-Profit Gallery Assn., 1979-83, v.p., 1979-80. Recipient Golden Eagle award CINE, 1992, Leader of the Decade award Arts Leadership Monterey Peninsula, 1992. Mem. Am. Assn. Mus. (mus. assessment program surveyor 1990, 94, lectr. 1986, nat. program com. 1992-93), Calif. Assn. Mus. (chair ann. meeting 1990, chair nominating com. 1988, 90, 93, bd. dirs. 1985-94, v.p. 1987-91, pres. 1991-92), Artable, Am. Folklore Soc., Western Mus. Conf. (bd. dirs., exec. com. 1989-91, program chair 1990), Nat. Coun. for Edn. in Ceramic Arts, Phi Beta Kappa. Office: Curatorial and Mus Mgmt Svcs 345 White Rd Watsonville CA 95076

HERNANDEZ, LILLIAN A., health facility administrator; b. Inglewood, Calif., May 12, 1959; d. John Erling and Lillian Alice (Hastings) Johnson; m. David Robert Hernandez, Aug. 11, 1979; children: Linda Marie, Amber Michelle, Christine Lee. AA, Cerritos Jr. Coll., 1981; BS in Bus., Calif. State U., Long Beach, 1986. Cert. quality circle facilitator. Note teller Bank of Am., Bellflower, Calif., 1978-79; computer operator Piping Products West, Vernon, Calif., 1981; counselor/asst. mgr. Zoe Employment Agy., Los Alamitos, Calif., 1981-82; pers. asst./quality circle facilitator Hazel of Calif. Inc., Santa Fe Springs, 1982-86; employment coord. PARTNERS Nat. Health Plans, San Bernardino, Calif., 1987-89; owner Cream Whippeeze, Riverside, Calif., 1989-91; Riverside County media coord. William Dannemeyer for U.S. Senate, 1991-92; human resources dir. Manor Care Nursing Ctr., Hemet, Calif., 1993—; Interview panalist City of Riverside, Calif., 1990. Chmn. Citizens' Adv. Affirmative Action Com., Riverside, Calif., 1990; founding mem. Riverside Citizens for Responsible Behavior, 1990—; bd. dirs. Greater Riverside Hispanic Chamber, 1989-91; mem. Community Rels. Commn., 87-94; chmn. recreation and culture, 1989-90, parliamentarian, 1988-90; assoc. mem. Calif. Rep. State Cen. Com., 1989-92; mem. Calif. Rep. State Com., Riverside County Ctrl. Com.; vice-chair 2d supervisoral dist.; adv. com. law enforcement policy, Calif. Rep. State Party, 1989-92, del., 1992—; founding mem. v.p. Riverside Citizens for Responsible Behavior, 1990—; mem. Cmty Rels. Commn., 1987-89. Mem. Personnel and Indsl. Rels. Assn. Republican. Office: Manor Care Nursing Ctr Manor Care Nursing Ctr 1717 W Stetson Ave Hemet CA 92545

HERNANDEZ-FRANCIS, HAYDEE PAMELA, lawyer; b. N.Y.C., Aug. 6, 1931; d. Juano and Haydee (Bello) Hernandez; m. Amadeo I.D. Francis, Mar. 7, 1958 (div. June 1971); children: Lloyd D., Lorraine D. B of Social Scis., U. P.R., San Juan, 1949, JD, 1963. Bar: P.R. 1962, N.Y. 1981. Lawyer dept. commerce Govt. P.R., San Juan, 1963-68; pvt. practice law San Juan, 1968-71, Francis & Simmons P.C., N.Y.C., 1971—. Office: Francis & Simmons PC 139 Fulton St Ste 715 New York NY 10038-2594

HERNÁNDEZ TORRES, ZAIDA, state legislator; b. Bayamon, P.R., Aug. 30, 1953; d. Enrique Hernádez Rivera and Felicita Torres Burgos. B of Social Studies, U. P.R., 1973; JD, Interam. U., Rio Piedras, P.R., 1976; M in Gen. Law, Cath. U. P.R., 1989. Asst. state's atty. Arecibo, P.R.; counsel Gov.'s Office of Assistance to Citizens; rep.-at-large New Progressive Party, 1984—; mem. P.R. Ho. of Reps., 1984—, speaker, 1992; 1st vice chmn. New Progressive Party. Office: PR House of Reps Box 2228 San Juan PR 00903

HERNDON, ALICE PATTERSON LATHAM, public health nurse; b. Macon, Ga.; d. Frank Waters and Ruby (Dews) Patterson; m. William Joseph Latham, July 21, 1940 (dec. Apr. 1981); children: Jo Alice Latham Miller, Marynette Latham Stephens, Lauruby Cathleen Beach; 1 adopted child, Courtney Marie Herndon; m. Sidney Dumas Herndon, Apr. 26, 1985. diploma, Charity Hosp. Sch. Nursing, New Orleans, 1937; student George Peabody Coll. Tchrs., 1938-39; BS in Pub. Health Nursing, U. N.C., 1954; MPH, Johns Hopkins U., 1966. Staff pub. health nurse assigned spl. venereal disease study USPHS, Darien, Ga., 1939-40; county pub. health nurse Bacon County, Alma, Ga., 1940-41; USPHS spl. venereal disease project, Glynn County, Brunswick, 1943-47; county pub. health nurse Glynn County, 1949-51, Ware County, Waycross, 1951-52; pub. health nurse supr. Wayne-Long-Brantley-Liberty Counties, Jesup, 1954-56 dist. dir. pub. health nursing Wayne-Long-Appling-Bacon-Pierce Counties, Jesup, 1956-70; dist. chief nursing S.E. Ga. Health Dist., 1970-79, organizer mobile health services, 1973—. Exec. dir. Wayne County Home Health Agy., 1968-80; exec. dir. Ware County Home Health Agy., 1970-79, mem. exec. com., 1978-85; mem. governing bd. S.E. Ga. Health Systems Agy., 1975-82; mem. governing bd. Health Dept. Home Health Agy., 1978—, also author numerous grant proposals. Bd. dirs. Wayne County Mental Health Assn., 1959, 60, 61, 81, 82, Wayne County Tb Assn., 1958-62; a non-alcoholic organizer Jesup group Alcoholics Anonymous, 1962-63; mem. adv. coun. Ware Meml. Hosp. Sch. Practical Nursing, Waycross, Ga., 1958; mem. Altar Guild, St. Paul's Episc. Ch., 1979-86, vestrywoman, 1981-82. Recipient recognition Gen. Service Bd., Alcoholics Anonymous, Inc. Fellow APHA; mem. ANA, 8th Dist. (pres. 1954-58, sec. 1958-60, dir. 1960-62, 1st v.p. 1962), Ga. Nurses Assn. (exec. bd. 1954-58, program rev. continuing edn. com. 1980-86, Dist. 21 Excellence in Nursing award 1994), Ga. Pub. Health Assn. (chmn. nursing sect. 1956-57), Ga. Assn. Dist. Chiefs Nursing (pres. 1976). Contbr. to state nursing manuals, cons. to Home Health Svc. Agys. Home: 192 Bluff Dr Brunswick GA 31525-9110

HERNDON, ANNE HARKNESS, sales executive; b. Knoxville, Tenn., July 21, 1951; d. Alexander Jones and Mary Belle (Lothrop) Harkness; m. David S. Egerton, Apr. 21, 1972 (div. 1979); children: David, Mary; m. Morris Herndon, Nov. 26, 1993. Student, Agnes Scott Coll., Decatur, Ga., 1969-71, U. Tenn., 1971-73. Mktg., advt. mgr. Volunteer Realty, Knoxville, 1975-77; adminstrv. asst. nat. sales Creative Displays, Knoxville, 1977-81; salesperson Sta. WJXB Radio, Knoxville, 1981-86, sales mgr., 1988—; sales and mktg. mgr. Cellular One, Knoxville, 1986-87; cons. nat. ourdoor advt. Berkline Corp., Morristown, Tenn., 1978-81, Knoxville C. of C.; speaker nat. convs. Contbr. articles to profl. jours. Bd. dirs. Knoxville Polit. Action Com., Knosville Arts Coun., Knoxville Beautification Bd., Boy Scouts Fin. Com.; com. mem. Dogwood Arts Festival, United Way. Recipient Pres.'s award South Ctrl. Comm. Corp., 1991, 92, 93. Mem. Ad Club. Republican. Presbyterian. Home: 605 Westborough Rd Knoxville TN 37909-2132 Office: WJXB 825 N Central St Knoxville TN 37917-7122

HERNDON, BETTY LARUE, medical educator; b. Monett, Mo., Nov. 10, 1936; d. Edward Franklin and Anna Lola (Higgins) LaRue; m. Richard Sanders Herndon, Sept. 7, 1958. BS, Cen. Mo. State U., 1958; MS, U. Mo., Kansas City, 1963, PhD, 1974. Asst., assoc., sr. physiologist Midwest Rsch. Inst., Kansas City, 1963-81; staff Dept. Health & Human Svcs., Kansas City, 1982-85; assoc. rsch. prof. U. Mo., Kansas City, 1986—. Contbr. articles to profl. jours. Dir.. Centennial Celebration, St. Mary's Episcopal Ch., Kansas City; bd. dirs. U. Mo. Kansas City Civic Orch. Grantee: U. Mo. Kansas City Sarah Morrison Fund, 1990—, Am. Heart Assn., 1991-94. Mem. Am. Assn. Immunologists, Soc. for Exptl. Biology and Medicine, Soc. Leukocyte Biology, Am. Soc. Microbiologists, Sigma Xi. Episcopalian. Office: U Mo 2411 Holmes St Kansas City MO 64108-2741

HERNDON, DONNA RUTH GROGAN, educational administrator; b. Murray, Ky., Aug. 14, 1942; d. E. Leon and Virgil (Childress) Grogan; m. Clarence W. Herndon Jr., Jan. 31, 1963; children: Melissa Herndon Graves, Roger Allan (dec.). BS summa cum laude, Murray State U., 1960; MA, Western Ky. U., 1975. Tchr. biology Calloway County High Sch., Murray, 1964-66, dir. project COPE, 1978-81; coord. of vols. Army Community Svc., Berlin, Fed. Republic of Germany, 1972; vol. supr. Army Community Svc., Ft. Knox, Ky., 1974-75; mayor Van Voorhis Community, Ft. Knox, Ky., 1975-76; plant mgr. Lin-Val Garden Ctr., Penn Hills, Pa., 1977; admissions rep. Art Inst. Pitts., 1978; dir. alumni affairs Murray (Ky.) State U., 1981-92; coord. Family Resource Ctr., Calloway County Schs., Murray, 1992—. Bd. dirs., co-founder CHAMP, Murray, 1986-93; rep. edn. Ky. Juvenile Justice Commn., 1982-92; mem. adv. coun., mem. social work dept. adv. bd. Murray State U. Coll. Industry and Tech.; mem. rural health adv. bd. U. Ky.; bd. dirs. Murray United Way. Recipient Recognition award Murray State U. Black Alumni, 1989, Humanitarian of Yr. award Murray Rotary Club, 1994; named Vol. of Yr., United Way of Ky., 1993; Donna Herndon scholarship established Murray State U. Student Alumni Assn., 1988. Mem. Ky. Alliance for Exploited and Missing Children (bd. dirs. 1982-92), Ky. Ctr. Pub. Issues (bd. dirs. 1990-92), Nat. Coun. for Advancement and Support Edn. (achievement award 1984, bronze award 1987, Dist. III Outstanding Advisor award 1992), Nat. Assn. Parents and Tchrs. (hon. life), Leadership Ky. (bd. dirs. 1990—), Leadership Ky. Alumni Assn. (trustee 1989—), Murray Woman's Club. Mem. Ch. of Christ. Office: Calloway County Schs Family Resource Ctr RR 6 Box 57 Aa Murray KY 42071-9104

HERNDON, KATHERINE ROSE, administrator; b. Brighton, Mass., Feb. 1, 1955; d. Daniel Arthur and Jeanne Therese (LaMair) Huntoon; m. David Earl Johnson, Jan. 9, 1983 (div. Sept. 1992); 1 child, Dixie Rose. Student, Calif. State U., Long Beach, 1976, U. Ariz., 1977-78; BFA, Old Dominion U., 1983. Dir. display Basil Collier Fine Art, L.A., 1979-80; office asst., slide libr. Old Dominion U. Art Dept., Norfolk, Va., 1982-84; office mgr. Va. Tidewater Consortium Higher Edn., Norfolk, Va., 1984-85; asst. dir. Old Dominion U. Gallery, Norfolk, Va., 1982-88; mgr. Main Art Frame Shop, Richmond, Va., 1989-90; instr. art Virginia Beach (Va.) Ctr. ARt, 1990; artist, coord. ArtWorks Gallery, Norfolk, 1991-92; adminstrv. dir. Delta Axis Contemporary Arts Ctr., Memphis, 1992—; juror Dark Humor Show ArtWorkers Union, Memphis, 1994. Exhibited in numersou group and one-woman shows including Plan B Gallery, Memphis, 1994, Peninsula Fine Arts Ctr., Newport News, Va., 1989, Virginia Beach (Va.) Ctr. for Arts, 1988, Old Dominion U. Gallery, Norfolk, Va., 1987, Alternative Art Gallery, Norfolk, 1986, others. Vol. Memphis May Festival, 1993, Va. Mus. Fine Art Children's Art Resource, Richmond, Va., 1989, Children's Mus., Richmond, 1989, 1708 Coop. Gallery, Richmond, 1989. Mem. Nat. Campaign Freedom Expression, Am. Folk Art Soc. Office: Delta Axis Contemporary Arts Ctr PO Box 3025 Memphis TN 38173-0025

HERNDON, NANCY RUTH, writer; b. St. Louis, May 29, 1934; d. Robert Stanley and Ruth Edna (Tutein) Fairbanks; m. William Cecil Herndon, Dec. 27, 1956; children: William Robert, Matthew. BA in English, U. Mo., 1956, B of Journalism in Advt., 1956; Ma in English, Rice U., 1958. Advt. writer, proofreader Foley's Dept. Store, Houston, 1957; advt. proofreader Darcy Advt. Co., N.Y.C., 1958; advt. copuwriter Howlands Dept. Store, Bridgeport, Conn., 1959; lectr. English NYU, N.Y.C., 1959-61, U. Miss., Oxford, 1962-63, Fla. Atlantic U., Boca Raton, 1965-66, U. Tex., El Paso, 1976-81; freelance writer El Paso, 1989—. Author: (as Elizabeth Chadwick) Wanton Angel, 1989, Widow's Fire, 1990, Virgin Fire, 1991, Bride Fire, 1992, Reluctant Lovers, 1993, The Fourth Gift in Wilderness Christmas, 1993, Elusive Lovers, 1994, Acid Bath, 1995, Widow's Watch, 1995. Rice U. Fellow, 1956-58, NYU fellow, 1961-62. Mem. NOW, Southwest Writers Workshop, Sisters in Crime, U. Womens Club El Paso, Nat. Trust Hist. Preservation, Smithsonian Assocs., Planned Parenthood, Phi Beta Kappa (mem. Mortar Bd. 1955). Democrat. Home and Office: 6504 Pino Real Dr El Paso TX 79912-2928

HERNING-SWAIM, SHIRLEY RUTH, general earthworks and utilites contractor; b. Fairbanks, Alaska, Jan. 31, 1954; d. Carl Roland and Mattie Lee (Clay) Herning; m. John Edward Brainerd, Aug. 28, 1972 (div. Sept. 1979); m. Kelvin Eugene Swaim, Apr. 15, 1989; children: Stephanie Michelle, Veronica Renee. AA in Gen. Sci., U. Alaska, Fairbanks, 1975, BS in Home Econs., 1975; cert. in adminstrv. law/fair hearing, Nat. Jud. Coll., Reno, Nev., 1983, 88. Substitute tchr. North Star Borough Sch. Dist., Fairbanks, 1976; driver lic. examiner State of Alaska, Dept. Motor Vehicles, Fairbanks, 1976; postal rt. carrier U.S. Govt. Contract, Fairbanks, 1976-77; employment security specialist State of Alaska Dept. Labor, Fairbanks, 1977-82; hearing officer employment security divsn. State of Alaska Dept. Labor, Anchorage, 1982-83, Fairbanks, 1985-92; investigator State of Alaska, Dept. Revenue, Alcohol Beverage Control Bd., Fairbanks, 1983-84, State of Alaska, Health & Social Svcs., Fraud Unit, Fairbanks, 1984-85; gen. contractor ptnr. Swaim Enterprises, Fairbanks, 1992—; northern regional negotiator Alaska Pub. Employees Assn., Juneau, 1979-81, employee rep., 1977-7. Judge, author: Employment Security Divsn. Unemployment Ins., Appeal Tribunal Case Decisions, 1985-92. Nutrition instr. North Star Coun. on Aging, Fairbanks, 1974. Recipient Appreciation award Alaska Pub. Employee Assn., Fairbanks, 1982, Silent Svc. award Community Svc. Vol. Assn., Fairbanks, 1993. Mem. Alaska Peace Officers Assn., Nat. Assn. Adminstrv. Law Judges. Democrat. Baptist. Home: 2279 Franklin St Fairbanks AK 99709-6236 Office: Swaim Enterprises 2279 Franklin St Fairbanks AK 99709-6236

HERNLY, SHARON KELLEY, geriatric nurse practitioner, consultant, educator; b. Wolfeboro, N.H., Mar. 27, 1947; d. Charles William and Dorothy (Brown) Kelley; m. Thomas Knight Hernly, June 25, 1967; children: Thomas Knight II, Gregory, Sharon Marie. Diploma, Flushing (N.Y.) Hosp., 1968; BSN, Western Conn. State U., 1985; MSN, Columbia U., 1989. RN, Conn., N.Y.; cert. geriatric nurse practitioner ANA. Staff nurse Flushing Hosp., 1968, St. Lukes, N.Y.C., 1968-69; supr. long term care Danbury (Conn.) Pavilion, 1977-82; substitute sch. nurse Danbury Edn. Dept., 1981-82; psychiat. nurse Danbury Hosp., 1982-85, asst. dir. nursing, 1985-87, nurse mgr. geriatrics, 1987-89, geriatric nurse practitioner, 1989-90; geriatric nurse practitioner New Rochelle (N.Y.) Hosp., 1991—; program developer satellite clinics and geriatric med. home visit program, urinary incontenence, sexual dysfunction in elderly, geriatric gynecology; mem. adv. bd. Westchester Office of Aging, White Plains, N.Y., 1991—; cons. long term care; instr. case mgmt. to hosps.; adj. faculty Columbia U., Pace U., NYU, N.Y. Med. Ctr. Contbr. articles to profl. jours.; poster presenter GSA, Am. Geriatrics Soc. and Coalition Nurse Practitioners. Mem. ANA, Gerontol. Soc. Am., Coalition Nurse Practitioners N.Y., Am. Geriatrics Soc., Nat. Conf. Gerontol. Nurse Practitioners, Conn. Nurses Assn., Am. Soc. on Aging, Conn. Nurse Practitioners, Sigma Theta Tau. Home: 20 Fox Den Rd Danbury CT 06811-3424 Office: New Rochelle Hosp 16 Guion Pl New Rochelle NY 10801-5503

HERNS, JULIA ALICE, sales executive; b. Atlanta, July 26, 1956; d. Charles Kenneth and Jeane (Amos) H.; m. Brian Charles McGinnis, Sept. 16, 1972 (div. Jan. 1991). Student, Clemson U., 1969-72; BS in Human Resources, Ctrl. Wesleyan Coll., 1989. Math. and sci. tchr. Our Lady of the Rosary, Greenville, S.C., 1973-78; sales rep. Am. Home Products Corp., N.Y.C., 1978-85; terr. sales mgr. Abbott Labs., Chgo., 1985-91; dir. mktg. Quality Assurance Labs., Greenville, 1991-92; area sales mgr. United Industries Corp., St. Louis, 1992—. Bd. dirs. Grocery Mfrs. Rep. Assn., Greenville, 1984-89; bd. dirs. Harbour Towne Assn., 1978-83, pres. 1980). Mem. Canebrake Homeowners Assn. (bd. dirs. 1994—), Mossland Partnership (bd. dirs. 1990—, pres. 1994), Catalina 22, Fleet # 56 (capt. 1980-90, Boat of Yr. 1982). Roman Catholic. Home: 116 Ticonderoga Dr Greer SC 29650 Office: United Industries Corp 8825 Page Blvd Saint Louis MO 63114

HERON, CAROL ELLEN, lawyer; b. Stamford, Conn., June 19, 1949; d. James Peter and Eleanor Eugenia (Krugelis) H. BA, U. Chgo., 1972; MLS, SUNY, 1975, MA, 1979; JD, Whittier Coll., 1987. Cataloging librarian Sch. Law Whittier Coll., L.A., 1983-85; law clk. Legal Aid Found., L.A., 1985; technical librarian Pasadena (Calif.) City Coll., 1985-86; law clk. San Fernando Neighborhood Legal Services, Pacoima, Calif., 1986; asst. librarian Calif. State U., Northridge, 1986-87; assoc. Law Offices of L. Rob Werner, Canyon Country, Calif., 1988-89, Jacoby & Meyers, L.A., 1989-91, Law Offices of Leslie Klein & Assocs., Sherman Oaks, Calif., 1991-95; prin. Carol E. Heron & Assocs., PLC, 1995—. Am. Jurisprudence scholar, 1984; N.Y. State Assembly fellow, 1978. Mem. NAFE, State Bar Calif., Calif. Trial Lawyers Am., San Fernando Valley Bar Assn., L.A. County Bar Assn. Home: 17937 San Fernando Mission Blvd Granada Hills CA 91344-4063

HERRERA, CAROLINA, fashion designer; b. Caracas, Venezuela, Jan. 8, 1939. Founder, head designer Carolina Herrera, 1981—, introduced CH line, 1986—. Office: 501 7th Ave Fl 17 New York NY 10018-5902*

HERRERA, MARY CARDENAS, education educator, music minister; b. Sugar Land, Tex., Feb. 21, 1938; d. Jose Chavez and Juanita (Lira) Cardenas; m. Saragosa Martin Herrera, Sept. 20, 1960 (dec.); children: Michael (dec.), Patricia Ann, Aaron Martin, Katherine Ann. Grad., Patricia Stevens Bus. Sch., 1960; student, Houston C.C., 1991, 92. Sec. William Penn Hotel, Houston, 1959-66; payroll clk. Peakload, Inc., Houston, 1967-69; acctg. clk. Am. Gen., Inc., Houston, 1970-73; nurse asst. Ft. Bend Ind. Sch. Dist., Stafford, Tex., 1973-88; tchr.'s asst. Ft. Bend Ind. Sch. Dist., Sugarland, Tex., 1988—; numerous offices Holy Family Cath. Ch., Missouri City, Tex., 1981-90, Hispanic choir dir., 1981-89; Hispanic choir dir. Notre Dame Cath. Ch., 1990-91; Hispanic del. Galveston-Houston Diocese, 1987-89; regional del. Encuetro Diocesceno Conf., San Antonio, 1983, 84, 85; dir., coord. Diocesan Hispanic Choir, 1982-86, music workshops, 1982-88. Songwriter in field. Mem., tchr. PTO, 1973—; mem. Holy Family Hispanic Com.; mem. choir Iglesia del Pueblo, Pasadena, Tex., 1991, 92, asst. Sunday sch. tchr., 1992-93, coord. monthly Women's Praise Gathering, 1994—; music minister local prayer groups Houston area, 1990—. Mem. Women's Aglow (praise and worship music minister Pasadena chpt. 1988-90), Nat. Assn. Pastoral Musicians, Iglesia del Pueblo. Democrat. Home and Office: 4506 Ludwig Ln Stafford TX 77477-5219

HERRERA, PALOMA, dancer; b. Buenos Aires, Dec. 21, 1975; d. Alberto Oscar and Diana Lia (Rube) H. Attended, Olga Ferri Studio, 1982, Ballet Sch. of Minsk, 1987, English Nat. Ballet, London, 1990, Sch. Am. Ballet, N.Y.C., 1991; diploma, Inst. Superior Art at The Colon Theatre, Buenos Aires, 1991. Soloist Am. Ballet Theatre, N.Y.C., 1992—. Dancer (ballets) Don Quixote, 1987, 88; soloist La Bayadere, The Sleeping Beauty, Don Quixote, Met. Opera, N.Y.C., 1992, Etudes, The Sleeping Beauty, Swan Lake, Symphonie Concertante, Voluntaries, 1993, prin. Symphonie Concertante, Symphonic Variations, 1993; prin. Giselle, Colon Theatre, Buenos Aires, 1992, La Bayadere, 1993; prin. Don Quixote, soloist Etudes, Voluntaries, Theme and Variations, Kennedy Ctr., Washington, 1993; prin. The Nutcracker, Dorothy Chandler Pavilion, L.A., 1993, Palace Theatre, Stamford, Conn., 1993; guest artist Ballet Gala, Toronto, 1993, Colon Theatre, Buenos Aires, 1993, Gala Ballet of Aix-En-Provence, France, 1993. Recipient First prize Latino Am. Ballet Contest, Lima, Peru, 1985, Coca-Cola Contest of Arts and Scis., 1986, Finalist diploma XIV Varna (Bulgaria) Internat. Competition of Ballet, 1990; scholar Colon Theatre Found., 1989; Dance scholar Antorchas Found., 1991. Home: One Lincoln Plz 20 W 64th St Apt F New York NY 10023-7129 also: Billinghurst 2553 1o Piso Dto, CP 1425 Buenos Aires Argentina Office: American Ballet Theatre 890 Broadway Fl 3 New York NY 10003-1211

HERRERA, SANDRA JOHNSON, school system administrator; b. Riverside, Calif., June 21, 1944; d. William Emory Johnson and Mildred Alice (Alford) Wimer; m. Wynn Neal Huffman, Feb. 19, 1962 (div. May 1967); 1 child, Kristen Lee; m. Steven Jack Herrera, June 21, 1985. AA in Purchasing Mgmt., Fullerton Coll., 1983; BSBA, U. Redlands, 1985, MA in Mgmt., 1988. Sr. purchasing clk Fullerton (Calif.) Union High Sch. Dist., 1969-77, buyer, 1977-79, coord. budgets and fiscal affairs, 1979-83; asst. dir. fin. svcs. Downey (Calif.) Unified Sch. Dist., 1983-85; dir. acctg. Whittier (Calif.) Union High Sch. Dist., 1985-89; asst. supt. bus. Whittier City Sch. Dist., 1989-91, Oxnard Elem. Sch. Dist., 1991—; cons. Heritage Dental Lab., El Toro, Calif, 1981—. Spl. dep. sheriff Santa Barbara (Calif.) County Sheriff's Mounted Posse, 1986-90; spl. dep. marshal U.S. Marshals Posse, Los Angeles, 1987-95. Mem. Calif. Assn. Sch. Bus. Ofcls. (treas. S.E. sect. 1985, mem. acct. R & D com. 1983-89, mem. chief bus. officials com. 1989—), So. Calif. Paraders Assn. (exec. sec. 1976—), Calif. State Horsemens Assn. (regional v.p. 1986-87, sec. 1988), Alpha Gamma Sigma. Home: 5688 La Cumbre Rd Somis CA 93066-9719 Office: Oxnard Elem Sch Dist 1051 S A St Oxnard CA 93030-7442

HERRERA, SHIRLEY MAE, personnel and security executive; b. Lynn, Mass., Apr. 5, 1942; d. John Baptiste and Edith Mae Lagasse; m. Christian Yanez Herrera, Apr. 30, 1975; children: Karen, Gary, Ivan, Iwonne. AS in Bus., Burdette Bus. Coll., Lynn, 1960; student, Wright State U., 1975-78. Cert. facility security officer, med. asst. in pediatrics. Med. asst. Christian Y. Herrera, M.D., Stoneham, Mass., 1972-74; human resource adminstr. MTL Systems, Inc., Dayton, Ohio, 1976-79; dir. pers. and security Tracor GIE, Inc., Provo, Utah, 1979—; cons. on family dynamics family enrichment program Hill AFB, Utah, 1980-82; cons. on health care memt. Guam 7th Day Adventist Clinic, 1983; cons. on basic life support and CPR, Projecto Corazon, Monterrey, Mex., 1987—; faculty mem. Inst. for Reality Therapy, 1991—. Contbg. editor Inside Tractor, 1991—. Chmn. women's aux. YMCA Counselling Svcs., Woburn, Mass., 1970; chmn. youth vols. ARC, Wright-Patterson AFB, Dayton, 1974-76; trustee Quail Valley Homeowner's Assn., Provo, 1988-89; rep. A Spl. Wish Found., Provo, 1989. Recipient James S. Cogswell award Def. Investigative Svc., Dept. Def., 1987. Mem. Soc. for Human Resource Mgmt., Inst. for Realty Therapy (cert.), Pers. Assn. Ctrl. Utah, Women in Mgmt. (coun. mem. 1991—), Nat. Classification Mgmt. Soc. (chairperson Intermountain chpt. 1992-94), Provo/Orem C. of C. (gov. rev. coun.). Republican. Home: 3824 Little Rock Dr Provo UT 84604-5234

HERRERIAS, CARLA TREVETTE, epidemiologist; b. Chgo., Apr. 8, 1964; d. Ludvik Frank and Carlotta Trevette (Walker) Koci; m. Jesus Herrerias, Feb. 25, 1989; 1 child, Elena Mikele. BS in Med.Tech., Ea. Mich. U., 1987; MPH in Molecular and Hosp. Epidemiology, U. Mich., 1991. Med. clk. hydramatic divsn. GM, Ypsilanti, Mich., 1983-86; researcher, staff dept. human genetics U. Mich., Ann Arbor, 1987-91; program mgr. Am. Acad. Pediatrics, Elk Grove Village, Ill., 1991—. Project mgr., contbr.: Clinical Practice Guideline: Otitis Media with Effusion in Young Children, 1994. Mem. APHA, Ill. Pub. Health Assn., U. Mich. Alumni Soc., U. Mich. Club Chgo. Office: Am Acad Pediatrics 141 Northwest Point Blvd Elk Grove Village IL 60007

HERRICK, KATHLEEN MAGARA, social worker; b. Mpls., Oct. 18, 1943; d. William Frank and Mary Genevieve (Gill) Magara; m. John Middlemist Herrick, Feb. 5, 1966; children: Elizabeth Jane, Kathryn Mary. BA in Social Work and French, Coll. St. Benedict, St. Joseph, Minn., 1965; MSW (Mildred B. Erickson fellow 1975), Mich. State U., E. Lansing, 1976. Social worker II, Carver County Social Services, Chaska, Minn., 1965-70; therapist St. Lawrence Community Mental Health Center, Lansing, Mich., 1974-75; sch. social worker Ingham Intermediate Sch. Dist., Mason, Mich., 1975-76; home/sch. coordinator Eaton Intermediate Sch. Dist., Charlotte, Mich., 1976-81, sch. social worker, 1994—; caseworker St. Vincent Home for Children, Lansing, 1979-80; tchr. cons. for severely emotionally impaired, 1981-83; behavior disorder cons., 1983-85; sch. social work cons., 1985-87. Chairperson bd. dirs. Eaton County Child Abuse and Neglect Prevention Council, 1986—; Democratic precinct del.; bd. dirs. Catholic Social Services, Lansing; specialist substance abuse prevention region XIII SAPE, 1987-94. Mem. NEA, Nat. Platform Assn., Mich. Edn. Assn., Nat. Assn. Social Workers, Nat. Assn. Retarded Citizens, Am. Orthopsychiat. Assn., Mich. Assn. Sch. Social Workers, Mich. Assn. Emotionally Disturbed Children, Eaton County Assn. Retarded Citizens, Nat. Platform Assn., NOW, Nat. Women's Health Network, Amnesty Internat., Mich. Assn. Suicidology, Phi Kappa Phi, Phi Alpha. Democrat. Roman Catholic. Home: 2113 Long Leaf Trail Okemos MI 48864-3210 Office: 1790 E Packard Hwy Charlotte MI 48813

HERRICK, SYLVIA A., health service administrator; b. Minot, N.D., Oct. 5, 1945; d. Sylvester P. and Ethelina (Harren) Theis; m. Michael M. Herrick, Nov. 8, 1989; children: Leo J., Mark A. BSN, U. N.D., 1967; MS in Pub. Health Nursing, U. Colo., Denver, 1970; sch. nurse credential, San Jose State U., 1991; postgrad., Golden Gate U. RN, Calif.; cert. pub. health nursing, health svc. Pub. health nurse Dept. Pub. Health City of Mpls.; instr. nursing San Francisco State U.; cons. exec. search Med-Power Resources, Alameda; coord. health svcs. Alameda Unified Sch. Dist.; team mgr., program devel. coord. home care nursing Vis. Nurse Assn. and Hospice of No. Calif.; speaker Bay Area Scoliosis Assn., 1990. Mem. Nat. Nurses Bus. Assn., Calif. Sch. Nurses Orgn. (bd. dirs., chair edn Bay Coast sect.), Delta Kappa Gamma. Home: 1711 Encinal Ave Alameda CA 94501-4020

HERRIN, FRANCES SUDOMIER, retired volunteer social worker; b. Hamtramck, Mich., Dec. 1, 1914; d. Wesley Valentine and Anna Theresa (Langowski) Sudomier; widowed. Grad., high sch., 1933. Sec. Parke Davis & Co., Detroit, 1946-47; assembler Gen. Motors, Detroit, 1947, Chrysler Corp., Hamtramck, 1950-57; mem. adv. coun. Detroit Area Agy. on The Aging, Detroit, 1981-92; speaker St. Theresa Guild, 1980-92, Golden Agers, 1982-92, Polish-Am. Sr. Citizens, 1981-90; prescision-tool tested parts of B-29 bomber planes in World War II, Henry Ford Aircarft Bldg., River Rouge Plant. Active in Dem. and Rep. election campaigns; mem. St. Florian's Hist. Commn., Hamtramck, 1985—; sr. citizen activist several Sr. Orgs., Washington; mem. ret. sr. vol. program Catholic Socal Svcs., Wayne County, 1986-87; mem. Presdl. Task Force for Pres. Reagan. Recipient Medal of Merit from Pres. Reagan. Mem. St. Theresa's Guild. Roman Catholic.

HERRIN, MARY LU, artist; b. Beckley, W.Va., Feb. 22, 1944; d. Seymour Bruce and Zella Faye (Cottle) Shelton; 1 child, Kimberly Michelle. AA, Beckley Coll., 1962; MA, Jacksonville (Fla.) U., 1964. Asst. pub. rels. mgr. Sunkist Growers, L.A., 1965-70; art dir. Graphics & Other Things, Newport Beach, Calif., 1970-80; pub. Dollarsaver Publs., Paris, Tex., 1980-85; owner, mgr. Image Communications, Rancho Mirage, Calif., 1985—. Author: Of Pros and Cons, 1985. Mem. Palm Springs Writers Guild, Calif. Assn. Advt. Artists, Women's Network, Palm Springs Press Club. Libertarian. Home: 4420 N Varsity Ave Apt 1107 San Bernardino CA 92407-4638 Office: Image Communications 8491 Orange St Alta Loma CA 91701-3239

HERRING, SUSAN WELLER, anatomist; b. Pitts., Mar. 25, 1947; d. Sol W. and Miriam (Damick) Weller; m. Stephen E. Herring, Nov. 18, 1967 (div. Oct. 1983). BS in Zoology, U. Chgo., 1967, PhD in Anatomy, 1971. NIH postdoctoral fellow U. Ill., Chgo., 1971-72, from asst. prof. to prof. oral anatomy and anatomy, 1972-90; prof. orthodontics U. Wash., Seattle, 1990—; vis. assoc. prof. biol. sci. U. Mich., Ann Arbor, 1981; cons. NIH study sect., Washington, D.C., 1987-89; sci. gov. Chgo. Acad. Sci., 1982-90; mem. pub. bd. Growth Pub. Inc., Bar Harbor, Maine, 1982—. Mem. editorial bd. Acta Anatomica, 1989—; contbr. articles to profl. jours. Woodrow Wilson fellow, 1967, NSF predoctoral fellow, 1967-71, AAAS fellow, 1993; rsch. grantee NIH, 1975-78, 81—, Muscular Dystrophy Found., 1981-82, NSF, 1990-92, 94-95. Mem. Internat. Assn. Dental Rsch. (dir. craniofacial biol. group 1994—), Am. Soc. Zoologists (chmn. vertebrate zoology 1983-84, exec. com. 1986-88), Am. Soc. Biomechanics, Am. Assn. Anatomists (chmn. Basmajian com. 1988-90), Soc. Vertebrate Paleontology, Am. Soc. Mammalogists, Internat. Soc. Vertebrate Morphology (convenor 4th congress 1994, pres. 1994—), Sigma Xi. Office: U Wash Dept Orthodontics Sm # 46 Seattle WA 98195

HERRINGTON, BARBARA ANN, educational administrator; b. Kenedy, Tex., Mar. 6, 1936; d. Arch Charles and Anna Loretta (James) Nobles; m. John Earl Herrington, June 30, 1956; children: Beverly Ann Herrington Cheney, Richard Earl. BS in Edn., S.W. Tex. State U., 1971; MEd, Our Lady of Lake U., San Antonio, 1975; EdD, Nova U., 1984. Cert. supt., counselor, adminstr., tchr., Tex. Clk.-typist U.S. Army, Ft. Sam Houston, Tex., 1954-56; acct. Chiles Drilling Co., Alice, Tex., 1956-62, Harkins & Co., Alice, 1962-65; tchr. Jourdanton (Tex.) Ind. Sch. Dist., 1971-76, asst. prin. elem. sch., 1976-80, prin. high sch., 1980-83, bus. mgr., dir. curriculum, 1983-85; dir. instrn. S.W. Ind. Sch. Dist., San Antonio, 1985-91; asst. supr. Nixon (Tex.)-Smiley Consol. Ind. Sch. Dist., 1991—. Pres. Jourdanton C. of C., 1966-67. Mem. Tex. Tchrs. Assn. (pres. Atascosa-McMullen County chpt. 1975). Methodist.

HERRINGTON, DALE ELIZABETH, lay worker; b. Logansport, La., Feb. 1, 1913; d. Charles Ross and Ola Delnorte (Tillery) Currie; m. Cecil Doyle Herrington, June 25, 1939; 1 child, Jo Earle Herrington Hartt. BS, Stephen F. Austin Univ., 1932, MA, 1948, MEd, 1948. Cert. tchr., Tex. Min. edn. First Bapt. Ch., Garrison, Tex., 1947-81, organist, 1947—, lay worker, 1947—, tchr. Sunday sch. Bible, 1947—, woman's missionary union dir., 1990-92; tchr. Garrison Pub. Schs., 1940-76; dir./asst. dir. Vacation Bible Sch., Garrison, 1950-92; vol. local newspaper, nursing home and sch. Named Mother of Yr., First Bapt. ch., Garrison, 1988, Citizen of Yr., Garrison, 1992. Mem. Nat. Ret. Tchrs. Assn., Tex. Ret. Tchrs. Assn. (life), Stephen F. Austin Alumni Assn. (life), Lions (Sweetheart), Heritage Club, Genealogy Soc., Order Eastern Star (past Matron, organist), Delta Kappa Gamma. Home: 319 N Avenue A Garrison TX 75946

HERRINGTON-BORRE, FRANCES JUNE, sign language school director; b. Austin, Tex., June 14, 1935; d. George Wilmas Neill and Mildred Lucille (Alexander) Williamson; m. Harold M. Herrington, June 6, 1953 (dec. Dec. 1978); children: Harold M. (dec.), Cheryl Anne Herrington; m. Thomas Raymond Borre, Apr. 5, 1985. Student, U. Tex., 1967-71. With Tex. Dept. Human Services, Austin, 1961-90, adminstrv. technician, 1967-71, field rep., 1971-81, asst. personnel dir., 1981-88, labor relations dir., 1988-89, judge adminstrv. law, 1989-90; free-lance profl. interpreter for deaf, 1964—; dir. Austin Sign Lang. Sch., 1964—; legis. liaison symposium Deaf and Hard-of-Hearing Texans, 1991—; cons. in field; project dir. Gov.'s Office, 1980. Gov.'s appointee Joint Adv. Com. on Ednl. Services to Deaf, Austin, 1976-78; chmn. Tex. Commn. for Deaf Bd. Eval. of Interpreters, 1981-84; chmn. Tex. State Agy. Liaisons to Gov.'s Commn. for Women, 1985. Recipient Tex. Rehab. Commn. Merit award, 1977, Gov.'s citation, 1978; co-recipient Lydon B. Johnson award Tex. Assn. for the Deaf and the Gallaudet U. Regional Ctr., 1992; named An Outstanding Woman Central Tex., AAUW, 1982, Significant and Meritorious Service to Mankind award Capitol Sertoma Club, 1976, Disting. Service as Adv. and Interpreter award Dal-Tar Lions Club, 1977. Mem. Nat. Assn. of Deaf (Golden Hand award 1987), Tex. Assn. of Deaf (Service citation 1967, Vol. Service award 1971, Interpreter of Decade award 1981, Prsdl. citation for Outstanding Svc. to symposium on deafness 1989, Frendship award, 1994), Nat. Registry Interpreters for Deaf, Tex. Soc. Interpreters for Deaf (pres. 1969-70), Austin Interpreters for Deaf. Mem. Ch. of Christ. Home: 2404 Laramie Trail Austin TX 78745-2844

HERRIOTT, KATHLEEN HELEN, science educator; b. L.A., May 26, 1954; d. William Keller and Betty Ann (Colburn) H.; 1 child, Joleen Michelle. AS, Cuesta Coll., 1979; BS, Calif. Poly. State U., San Luis Obispo, 1988; postgrad., Calif. State U., Bakersfield, 1991; multiple subject teaching credential, Chapman U., 1993. Owner, operator Home Day Care Program, Los Osos, Calif., 1983-84; spl. project intern Calif. Poly. State U. Calif. Conservation Corps, San Luis Obispo, 1985; conservation awareness program asst. San Luis Obispo Ctr. Calif. Conservation Corps, 1986; curriculum asst. Calif. Conservation Corps Acad., San Luis Obispo, 1987; environ. interpreter for supt. of schs. Rancho El Chorro Environ. Ednl. Ctr., San Luis Obispo, 1987-88; substitute biology tchr. Santa Maria-Bonita/Santa Maria Joint Union High Sch. Dists., Santa Maria, Calif., 1989-90; recreation tchr. Peach Factory Day Care program Desert Christian Sch., Lancaster, Calif., 1990-93; substitute tchr. Antelope Valley Sch. Dists., Lancaster, 1990-93; drama tchr. Young People's Inst. of Arts, Lancaster, 1992; tchr. sci. Park View Jr. High Sch., Lancaster, 1994—; workshop facilitator Project Learning Tree, Calif. Dept. Forestry and Fire Protection, Sacramento, 1990—; ednl. cons. Lancaster City's Ptnr.'s Program, 1992-93; directory chair edn. ad hoc com. City of Lancaster, 1993-94. Fundraiser coord. Sci. Camp and local natural disaster relief account Antelope Valley, 1993-94. Recipient Outstanding Contbn. Recognition award Lancaster City Coun., 1993; scholar San Luis Obispo Bus. Women, 1986, William Randolf Hearst Found., 1987. Mem. Soil and Water Conservation Soc. (hon. mem. Calif. chpt., coord. conservation edn. 1989-94, Cert. Appreciation 1989, Chpt. Merit award 1993), Assn. Environ. Profls. (Calif. Poly. chpt., sec. 1986, activity coor. 1987-88), Lancaster Edn. Found. (edn. ptnr. 1993-94), Forestry Inst. Tchrs. Republican. Home: 2005 Westwood Ct Apt 103 Lancaster CA 93536-7229 Office: Park View Intermediate Sch 808 W Avenue J Lancaster CA 93534

HERRMANN, CAROL, university adminstrator; b. Mt. Kisco, N.Y., Dec. 23, 1944; d. Eugene C. and Anne M. McGuire; m. Robert O. Herrmann; children: John Martin II, Nell Elizabeth. AB, Bucknell U., 1966; MA, Pa. State U., 1970. Bus. editor, writer Centre Daily Times Newspaper, State College, Pa., 1980-82; with Pa. State U., University Park, 1982—, exec. asst. to pres. for adminstrn., 1986-88, v.p. for adminstrn., 1988-94, sr. v.p. for adminstrn., 1994—; mem. ctrl. region bd. Mellon Bank, 1994—; bd. dirs. Woolrich, Inc. Bd. trustees Pa. Coll. Tech., 1989—; mem. Centre Regional Planning Commn., State Coll., 1973-80, chmn., 1974-76, borough planning commn., 1973-80; media coord. Common Cause 23d Congl. Dist., 1977-80; bd. dirs. United Way, Centre County, Pa., 1989-91. Mem. AAUW, Women in Communications, Kappa Tau Alpha, Phi Delta Kappa. Home: 568 Ridge Ave State College PA 16803-3441 Office: Pa State U Old Main # 205 Univ Park PA 16802-1571

HERRON, CAROL CHRISTINE, financial planner, home economist; b. Lebanon, Oreg., Dec. 17, 1944; d. Ralph Elwood and Mary Mabel (Morris) H. BS, Oreg. State U., 1967, MS, 1971. Cert. home economist; CFP. Home economist W.F. West High Sch., Chehalis, Wash., 1968-69; extension agt. Wash. State U., Bellingham, 1971; extension specialist Wash. State U., Pullman, 1972-74; coord., instr. Portland (Oreg.) Community Coll., 1974-83; energy cons. Energy Counselors, Beaverton, Oreg., 1983-86; dir. devel. Coll. Home Econs. Oreg. State U., Corvallis, 1986-88; registered rep. Waddell and Reed Fin. Svcs., Beaverton, Oreg., 1988—. Mem. fin. coun. St. Anthony's Ch., 1994—. Mem. Internat. Assn. for Fin. Planning, Home Economists in Bus. (nominating com. 1988-90, certification chair 1992—, saving fair facilities chair 1990, 92, 94, ex-officio fin. com. 1993—), Am. Home Econs. Assn., Oreg. Home Econs. Assn. (bd. dirs., pres. 1986-89), Oreg. State U. Coll. Home Econs. Alumni Assn. (bd. dirs. 1984-87). Democrat. Roman Catholic. Office: Waddell and Reed Fin Svcs 8625 SW Cascade Ave Ste 290 Beaverton OR 97008-7100

HERRON, CAROLIVIA, novelist, English educator; b. Washington, July 22, 1947; d. Oscar Smith and Georgia Carol (Johnson) H. AB in English Lit., Ea. Bapt. Coll., 1969; MA in English Lit., Viallanova (Pa.) U., 1973; MA, PhD, U. Pa., 1985; student, MIT, 1995. Asst. prof. Afro-Am. studies and comparative lit. Harvard U., Cambridge, Mass., 1986-90; assoc. prof. English Mt. Holyoke Coll., South Hadley, Mass., 1990-92; bd. dirs. curriculum devel. program NEH, Cambridge, Study Group in Afro-Asiatic Roots of Classical Civilization, Cambridge; vis. fellow Folger Shakespeare Libr., Washington, 1989—; Benedict vis. prof. Carleton Coll., Northfield, Minn., 1989-90; dir. Epicenter for the Study of Epic Lit.; vis. scholar Hebrew Coll., Mass., 1991-95, Harvard Divinity Sch., 1995. Author: (novels) Thereafer Johnnie, 1991, Asenath, 1994, (scholarly books) Selected Works of Angelina Weld Grimke, 1991, Early African American Poetry, 1994, (juvenile) Nappy Hair, 1994; contbr. articles to profl. jours. Fulbright scholar, 1985-86; Bunting fellow Radcliffe Coll., 1988—. Mem. Classical Assn. New Eng. Home: 25 Duval St Brighton MA 02135

HERRON, ELLEN PATRICIA, retired judge; b. Auburn, N.Y., July 30, 1927; d. David Martin and Grace Josephine (Berner) Herron; A.B. Trinity Coll., 1949; M.A., Cath. U. Am., 1954; J.D., U. Calif.-Berkeley, 1964. Asst. dean Cath. U. Am., 1952-54; instr. East High Sch., Auburn, 1955-57; asst. dean Wells Coll., Aurora, N.Y., 1957-58; instr. psychology and history Contra Costa Coll., 1958-60; dir. row Stanford, 1960-61; assoc. Knox & Kretzmer, Richmond, Calif., 1964-65. Bar: Calif., 1965. Ptnr. Knox & Herron, 1965-74, Knox, Herron and Masterson, 1974-77 (both Richmond, Calif.); judge Superior Ct. State of Calif., 1977-87; pvt. judge, 1987-90; pvt. judge Jud. Arbitration and Mediation Svc., Inc. (JAMS- Endispute), 1990—; ptnr. Real Estate Syndicates, Calif., 1967-77; owner, mgr. The Barricia Vineyards, 1978—. Active numerous civic orgns. Democrat. Home: 51 Western Dr Richmond CA 94801-4011

HERRON, PATRICIA FAY, entrepreneur; b. Richmond, Ind., Nov. 27, 1950; d. William Gordon and Golden Ruth (Ely) Shinliver; m. Dannie Herron, Sept. 17, 1974 (div. Nov. 1978); 1 child, Jennifer Lee. Grad., Wayne High Sch., Chgo., 1968. Pharmacy technician Mac's Pharmacy, Richmond, 1968-75; office mgr. Dr. J.D. Hernly, Richmond, 1979-86; ptnr. Clown Connection Balloon Boutique, Richmond, 1986-90; owner Clown Connection Balloon Dispatch, Richmond, 1990—. Bd. dirs., dispatch and instr. Wayne County Emergency Mgmt. Tornado-Severe Storm Spotter Program, Richmond, 1975—; mem. React Internat., Inc., 1975—, pres. Wayne County React, Inc., 1975—; mem. Civil Emergency Radio Team, 1975—. Mem. Eagles. Office: PO Box 2541 Richmond IN 47375-2541

HERRANS-PEREZ, LAURA LETICIA, psychology educator, research consultant; b. Vega Baja, P.R., June 16, 1935; d. Juan B. and María T. (Pérez)) Herrans. BA, U. P.R., 1955; MA, Cath. U. Am., 1957, PhD, 1969. Lic. psychologist, P.R. Psychologist I, Dept. Health, San Juan, P.R., 1957-60, rsch. cons. mental health secretariat, 1983—; prin. investigator WISC-R rsch. project U. P.R., Rio Piedras, 1960-63, instr. psychology, 1963-69, assoc. prof., 1969-77, prof., 1977—; prin. investigator, WISC-R rsch. project U. P.R., San Juan, P.R., 1987-92. Author: Psicologia y Medición, 1985; co-author: Dos Modelos Psicometricos para el Diagnostico Diferencial, 1989. Mem. APA, Assn. Psychologists P.R. (pres. 1970-71), Assn. Univ. Profs. Roman Catholic. Office: ICPE de PR Inc Ste 107 Med Ophthalmic Pla Hnas Davila Bayamon PR 00959

HERSCHER, SUSAN KAY, English language educator; b. Wisconsin Rapids, Wis., Nov. 11, 1949; d. Martin Joseph and Marian Margie (Hentz) Arnold; m. Walter Ray Herscher, June 12, 1976; children: Anne, Brian. BS in Edn., U. Wis., Stevens Point, 1971; MS in Reading Edn., U. Wis., Oshkosh, 1983. Elem. tchr. Wausaukee (Wis.) Pub. Schs., 1971-73; elem. tchr., unit leader Hortonville (Wis.) Pub. Schs., 1974-82; adult basic edn. instr. Fox Valley Tech. Coll., Appleton, Wis., 1983—; master tchr., facilitator for Wis. Adult Basic Edn./English as a Second Lang. Summer Inst., 1993; presenter in field. Recipient Quality Improvement award Fox Valley Tech. Coll., 1994. Mem. Tchrs. of English to Speakers of Other Langs., Wis. Tchrs. of English to Speakers of Other Langs., Wis. East Cen. Assn. for Vocat. Edn., Wis. Edn. Assn., NEA. Home: 1341 W Cloverdale Dr Appleton WI 54914 Office: Fox Valley Tech Coll PO Box 2277 1825 N Bluemound Dr Appleton WI 54913-2277

HERSEY, MARILYN ELAINE, performing company executive; b. N.Y.C., June 28, 1943; d. Charles Kenneth Hersey and Ella Margaret (Morgan) Decker; m. David William Orange, Nov. 17, 1972 (div. Dec. 1984); 1 child, Kristin Eleanor. BA, SUNY, Binghamton, 1965. Mng. dir. Boston Post Rd. Stage Co. (dba Fairfield County Stage Co.), Westport, Conn., 1985-93; exec. dir. Westport Arts Ctr., 1994—. Actress-singer, 1965-72; freelance writer, 1972-84. Named to Dean's List Harpur Coll., 1961-65. Mem. Am. Fedn. Television & Radio Artists, Actors' Equity Assn., Black Rock Yacht Club. Independent. Office: Westport Arts Ctr 17 Morningside Dr S Westport CT 06880

HERSHEY, BARBARA (BARBARA HERZSTEIN), actress; b. Hollywood, Calif., Feb. 5, 1948; d. William H. Herzstein; 1 child, Tom; m. Stephen Douglas, Aug. 8, 1992. Student pub. schs., Hollywood. Appearences include (TV series) The Monroes, 1966-67, From Here to Eternity, 1979, (mini-series) A Man Called Intrepid, 1979, Return to Lonesome Dove, 1993, Abraham, 1994; other TV appearances include Gidget, 1965, The Invaders, 1967, Daniel Boone, 1967, Love Story, 1973, Bob Hope Chrysler Theatre, 1967, High Chaparral, 1967, Kung Fu, 1973, CBS Playhouse, 1967, (TV movies) Flood, 1976, In the Glitter Palace, 1977, Just a Little Inconvenience, 1977, Sunshine Christmas, 1977, Angel on My Shoulder, 1980, The Nightingale, 1985, My Wicked, Wicked Ways... The Legend of Errol Flynn, 1985, Passion Flower, 1986, Killing in a Small Town, 1990 (Emmy award 1990, Golden Globe award 1991), Paris Trout, 1991 (Emmy award nomination), Stay the Night, 1992, (films) With Six You Get Egg Roll, 1968, Last Summer, 1969, Heaven with a Gun, 1969, The Liberation of L.B. Jones, 1970, The Baby Maker, 1970, The Pursuit of Happiness, 1971, Dealing, 1971, Boxcar Bertha, 1972, Angela (Love Comes Quietly), 1974, The Crazy World of Julius Vrooder, 1974, Diamonds, 1975, You and Me, 1975, Dirty Night's Work, 1976, The Stunt Man, 1980, Take This Job and Shove It, 1981, The Entity, 1982, The Right Stuff, 1983, Americana, 1983, The Natural, 1984, Hoosiers, 1986, Hannah and Her Sisters, 1986, Tin Men, 1987, Shy People, 1987 (Best Actress Cannes Film Festival, 1987), A World

Apart, 1988 (Best Actress Cannes Film Festival, 1988), The Last Temptation of Christ, 1988, Beaches, 1988, Tune in Tomorrow, 1989, Defenseless, 1991, The Public Eye, 1992, Falling Down, 1993, Swing Kids, 1993, Splitting Heirs, 1993, A Dangerous Woman, 1993, (theatre, Broadway) Einstein and the Polar Bear, 1981. Recipient Golden Palm award for best actress Cannes Film Festival, 1987, 1988. Office: care Creative Artists Agy 9830 Wilshire Blvd Beverly Hills CA 90212-1825*

HERSHMAN, JUDITH, advertising executive; b. Boston, Sept. 16, 1949; d. Max and Mollie (Cohen) H. BFA, Boston U., 1971. Pres., owner Hershman Advt. & Design, Foxboro, Mass., 1979—. Executed mural Kenmore Subway Sta., Boston, 1970. Adv. com. Tri-County Vocational Tech. High Sch. Mem. Women's Success Network. Home and Office: 41 Mechanic St Foxboro MA 02035-2027

HERSON, ARLENE RITA, television program host; b. N.Y.C.; d. Sam and Mollie (Friedman) Hornreich; m. Milton Herson, June 16, 1963; children: Michael, Karen. Student, Queens Coll., 1957, New Sch. for Social Rsch., N.Y.C., 1960. Exec. sec. Tex McCrary, Inc., N.Y.C., 1958-60; asst. to William L. Safire Safire Pub. Rels., N.Y.C., 1960-62; columnist The Advisor, Inc., Middletown, N.J., 1974-78; prodr., host The Arlene Herson Show, N.Y.C., 1978—; syndicated nationally on Tempo TV, 1988, Channel Am., 1989-93; spokesperson Storer Cable TV, Monmouth County, 1989-91, Nutri/Systems, Monmouth and Ocean Counties, 1989-90, 92d St. Y Benefit Com., Variety-The Children Charity; mem. Women's Project and Prodns., 1992; news anchor Nostalgia Cable TV Network at Rep. Nat. Conv., 1993; cons., talent coord. Super Annunities, 1993-94. Columnist The Washington/Hampton Connection Dan's Papers, 1993—; contbg. writer The Hill Newspaper, 1994. Bd. dirs. women's activities campaign for Sen. Jacob J. Javits, N.Y.C., 1968, Monmouth (N.J.) Mus., 1982-86, Will Rogers Inst., 1992—, Washington Symphony Orch., 1994—, v.p., 1994; com. mem. Children's Psychiat. Ctr., 1971-90, Monmouth Park Charity Fund, 1980-90; mem. corp. exec. bd. Family and Children's Svcs., 1985-90; active Monmouth Ocean Devel. Coun., 1981-90, Ctrl. Park Conservancy, Women of Washington, also mentor program, Women's Econ. Devel. Coun.; life mem. N.Y. chpt. Brandeis U. Libr. Fund.; mem. dir.'s resource coun. Nat. Women's Econ. Alliance; mem. social com. Westbridge Condominium; fin. chmn. Mike Herson for Congress, 1994; mem. profl. women's coun. Nat. Mus. of Women in the Arts, 1994. Recipient CAPE award for best talk show on Cable TV Network, 1984-93, Woman of Achievement in Comm. award Adv. Commn. on Status of Women, 1986, Pub. and Leased Access award for best talk show Paragon Cable TV, N.Y.C., 1988, spl. resolution N.J. Assembly, 1988, Willie award for outstanding svc. Will Rogers Inst., 1992; nominee Cable ACE award for best talk show series nationwide. Mem. NAFE, NATAS, Nat. Acad. Cable Programming, Nat. Assn. Profl. Women, Women in Comm., Women in Cable, Women in Film and Video, Am. Women in Radio and TV, Internat. Radio and TV Soc., Internat. Newswomen's Assn., Nat. Press Club, East River Tennis Club, Friars Club, Bethesda Country Club.

HERSZKOWICZ, ROZALIA, pediatrician; b. Chelm, Poland, Sept. 15, 1921; came to U.S., 1968; d. Chaim and Szandla (Gordon) Pofelis; m. Izrael Herszkowicz, Dec. 31, 1949; children: Julia, Yzena, Ana. MD, Med. Inst. Frunze, USSR, 1944. Diplomate Am. Bd. Pediatrics. Surgeon Mil. Hosp., Diviepropietrowsk, USSR, 1944-46; MD laryngology Outpatient Clinic, Diviepropietrowsk, 1946-47, Wroclaw, Poland, 1947-49; from resident to chief resident Med. Acad. Pediatrics, Wroclaw, 1950-53; head pediatric dept. State Hosp., Wroclaw, 1953-68; resident in pediatrics Jewish Meml. Hosp., N.Y.C., 1969-70, attending pediatrician, 1971-78; fellow in pediatrics Downstate Med. Ctr., N.Y.C., 1970-71; pvt. practice N.Y.C., 1971—; lectr. in pediatrics Inst. Poofgzaduak Educatieu, Wroclaw, 1959-68. Capt. USSR Mil., 1944-46. Recipient Excellence in Pediatrics award Ministry Health, 1966. Fellow Am. Acad. Pediatrics.

HERTE, MARY CHARLOTTE, plastic surgeon; b. Milw., May 31, 1951; chief of surgery Humana Sunrise, Las Vegas, 1989-92; chief of plastic surgery Humana Children's Hosp., Las Vegas, 1990—. BS, Mt. Mary Coll., Milw., 1973; MD, U. Wis., 1977. Diplomate Am. Bd. Plastic Surgery. Research fellow in plastic surgery Grad. Sch. Medicine Ea. Va. U., Norfolk, 1978; resident in gen. surgery Univ. Hosps., Madison, Wis., 1978-81, resident in plastic surgery, 1981-83; practice medicine specializing in plastic surgery Las Vegas, Nev., 1983—; chief of surgery Humana Sunrise, Las Vegas, 1989-92; chief of plastic surgery Sunrise Children's Hosp., Las Vegas, 1990—. Recipient Woman of Promise award Good Housekeeping Mag., 1985. Fellow ACS, Am. Acad. Pediatrics; mem. Am. Cleft Palate Assn., Assn. Women Surgeons, Am. Med. Women's Assn., Am. Soc. Plastic and Reconstructive Surgeons, Nev. State Med. Soc. (del. 1986-88), Clark County Med. Soc. (trustee 1986-88), Nev. Soc. Women Physicians (v.p. 1991-93, pres. 1994—), Soroptimist Internat. (treas., fin. sec. Greater Las Vegas chpt. 1985-87). Office: 3006 S Maryland Pky Ste 415 Las Vegas NV 89109-2235

HERTEL, SUZANNE MARIE, personnel administrator; b. Hastings, Neb., Aug. 8, 1937; d. Louis C. Hertel and W. Lenore (Cross) Budd. BA, Doane Coll., Crete, Neb., 1959; MSM, Union Theol. Sem., 1961; postgrad., U. Hartford, 1966, U. Conn., 1975; MA, Merrill Palmer Inst., 1977; EdD, Boston U., 1982. Music tchr. Pub. Sch., Wethersfield, Conn., 1962-63; serials libr. Hartford (Conn.)Sem. Found., 1963-64; elem. tchr. Pub. Sch., Glastonbury, Conn., 1965-79; asst. prof. Univ. Northern Iowa, Cedar Falls, Iowa, 1979-81; training mgr. Focus Research Systems Inc., W. Hartford, Conn., 1982-89; pers. adminstr. City of Hartford, 1989—; mem. Human Resource Mgmt. Delegation, Russia and Estonia, 1992. Recipient Maria Miller Stewart award, 1992. Mem. Am. Soc. Training and Devel., Am. Guild Organists. Democrat. Office: City of Hartford Mcpl Bldg Main St Hartford CT 06103

HERTENSTEIN, MYRNA LYNN, publishing executive; b. Detroit, July 19, 1937; d. Bernard Franklin and Alice Agnes (Stewart) Aller; m. George Ronald Hertenstein, June 21, 1958 (div. July 1979); children: Dale Ronald, Robert Mark. AS in Bus., Wayne State U., 1957; student, Huntingdon Coll., 1980-84. Departmental sec. Sch. of Bus. Wayne State U., Detroit, 1957-59; county and vol. coord. Montgomery (Ala.) Area Coun. on Aging, 1977-80; admissions counselor Coastal Tng. Inst., Montgomery, 1981-83; rural volunteerism coord. State of Ala., Montgomery, 1983-84; account exec. Ala. Bus. Rev., Montgomery, 1984-85, Sta. WRJM-FM, Montgomery, 1985-86; asst. local sales mgr. Sta. WCOV-TV Fox Affiliate, Montgomery, 1986-90; owner, assoc. pub. TRAVELHOST of Cen. Ala., Montgomery, 1990—; mem. Dirs. of Vols. in Agys., Montgomery, 1978-82, Montgomery County Health Coun., 1979-81, Area Agy. on Aging Adv. Coun., Montgomery, 1981-83, Pres.' Coun. Montgomery, 1983, 84; asst. to instr. Dale Carnegie & Assocs., Montgomery, 1978-83. Editor (newsletter) Montgomery Area Coun. on Aging, 1978-80; dir., writer (commls.) Sta. WCOV-TV, 1986-90; writer (commls.) Sta.WRJM-FM, 1985-86. Mem. adminstrv. coun. Whitfield United Meth. Ch., Montgomery, 1977, coord. Meals-on-Wheels, 1978-86; mem. pub. rels. coun. First United Meth. Ch., Montgomery, 1992-94; den leader coach Boy Scouts Am., Bellevue, Nebr., 1969-71; editor Capitol Jr. Woman's Club, Montgomery, 1975-82; pres. Parents Without Ptnrs., 1983-85; bd. dirs., v.p. Arthritis Found., 1992—. Recipient Emerging 30 award Montgomery Area C. of C., 1992, small business of yr. award, 1994, corp. vol. of yr. award Voluntary Action Ctr., Montgomery, 1992, award Montgomery Com. for Arts, 1993. Mem. Pub. Rels. Coun. Ala., Ala. Travel Coun., Montgomery Restaurant Assn., Montgomery Hotel/Motel Assn. (bd. dirs. 1993—), Sales and Mktg. Execs., Montgomery Assn. Bus. Communicators, Montgomery Advt. Fedn. (bd. dirs. 1985-92), Montgomery C. of C. (vice chmn. ambs. 1992, chmn. ambs. 1993, chmn. advt. promotions and publs. 1994, hospitality devel. and mktg. task force 1995), Montgomery Civitans. Home: 3005 Baldwin Brook Dr Montgomery AL 36116-3803 Office: Travelhost of Cen Ala PO Box 20666 Montgomery AL 36120-0666

HERTHER, NANCY K., library consultant; b. St. Paul, Minn., Jan. 19, 1951; d. Norman R. and Gladys E. H. BA, U. Minn., 1973, MA, 1977. Asst. prof., head libr. Northwest Coll. Chiropractic, Bloomington, Minn., 1978-79; libr. Mpls. Pub. Libr., 1978-88; search coord. univ. librs. U. Minn., Mpls., 1985—; rsch. cons. Yamaha Motor Corp., Coon Rapids, Minn., 1979-81; con. in field, 1979—; bus. mgr. Minn. Spl. Librs. Assn. /Am. Soc. Info. Sci. Newsletter, Mpls., 1981-82; pres. High Tech. Ventures, Inc., 1993—. Editor (book): Intellectual Freedom in Minnesota, 1979; (jour.) Laserdisk Professional (name change to CD-ROM Profl. 1990), 1988-94; columnist: ONLINE, 1986-92, Database, 1986-92; contbr. articles to profl. jours. Mem. Minn. Libr. Assn. (chmn. Intellectual Freedom com., 1978-79), ALA, Am. Soc. for Info. Sci., Minn. Chpt. Assn. for Computing Machinery, Minn. Assn. for Continuing Adult Edn. (pub. rels. chmn. 1982-84). Mem. Soc. of Friends. Office: 407 Kingston Ave Saint Paul MN 55117-2424 also: U Minn-Wilson 309 19th Ave S Minneapolis MN 55455-0438

HERTOG, MARY KAY, career officer; b. Bossier City, La., July 9, 1956; d. Donald Edward and Mary (Skocich) Reeves; m. Herman Mark Hertog III, July 14, 1979. BA in Sociology, Miami U., Oxford, Ohio, 1978; MA in Human Rels., Webster U., 1985; postgrad., Air Command and Staff Coll., 1990-91. Commd. 2d lt. USAF, 1978, advanced through grades to lt. col., 1994; security police shift comdr. 1608 Security Police Squadron, Kirtland AFB, Albuquerque, N.Mex., 1979-81; security police ops. officer 63d Security Police Squadron, Norton AFB, San Bernardino, Calif., 1981-83; security police exec. officer HQ Mil. Airlift Command, Scott AFB, Belleville, Ill., 1983-84; security police ops. officer 554 Security Support Squadron, Nellis AFB, Las Vegas, Nev., 1984-86; security police comdr. 554 Security Support Squadron, Nellis AFB, Las Vegas, 1986-87; security police staff officer HQ Pacific Air Forces, Hickam AFB, Honolulu, 1987-90; staff officer HQ USAF/Security Police, Pentagon, Washington, 1991—. Mem. Air Force Security Police Assn. (charter mem.), Air Force Assn., Miami Tribe. Roman Catholic. Home: 1501 Crystal Dr Apt 724 Arlington VA 22202-4124 Office: HQ USAF/Security Police Pentagon Washington DC 20330-5100

HERTWECK, ALMA LOUISE, sociology and child development educator; b. Moline, Ill., Feb. 6, 1937; d. Jacob Ray and Sylvia Ethel (Whitt) Street; m. E. Romayne Hertweck, Dec. 16, 1955; 1 child, William Scott. A.A., Mira Costa Coll., 1969; B.A. in Sociology summa cum laude, U. Calif.-San Diego, 1975, M.A., 1977, Ph.D., 1982. Cert. sociology instr., multiple subjects teaching credential grades kindergarten-12, Calif. Staff research assoc. U. Calif.-San Diego, 1978-81; instr. sociology Chapman Coll., Orange, Calif., 1982-87; instr. child devel. MiraCosta Coll., Oceanside, Calif., 1983-87, 88-89; instr. sociology U.S. Internat. U., San Diego, 1985-88 ; exec. dir., v.p. El Camino Preschools, Inc., Oceanside, 1985—. Author: Constructing the Truth and Consequences: Educators' Attributions of Perceived Failure in School, 1982; co-author: Handicapping the Handicapped, 1985. Mem. Am. Sociol. Assn., Am. Ednl. Research Assn., Nat. Council Family Relations, Nat. Assn. Edn. Young Children, Alpha Gamma Sigma (life). Avocations: foreign travel; sailing; bicycling. Home: 2024 Oceanview Rd Oceanside CA 92056-3104 Office: El Camino Preschs Inc 2002 California St Oceanside CA 92054-5673

HERTZ, LARA BETH, human resources specialist; b. Pa., July 2, 1969; d. Jerome J. and Sheila R. (Rosenthal) H. BA, U. Ga., 1991; MS, Radford U., 1992. Cons., pers. Community Human Resource Ctr., Radford, Va., 1992; mgr. pers. practices Hertz & Link, Atlanta, 1992-94; v.p., adminstr. Drs. Blum, Newman, Blackstock and Assocs., Roanoke, Va., 1994—; job analysis cons. Sub Sta. II, Greenville, S.C., 1992. Mem. Soc. Human Resource Mgmt., Sigma Delta Tau (scholastic award 1988-89), Psi Chi. Office: 2840-D Hershberger Rd NW Roanoke VA 24017

HERTZOG, ARDITH ELYSE, federal agency administrator; b. Washington, Aug. 26, 1964; d. Robert Leon and Ardith Elspeth (Hay) Beadles; m. Scott Lisle Hertzog, Oct. 12, 1991. BSChE, N.C. State U., 1987, postgrad., 1987-88; postgrad., George Mason U., 1991, 92. Acting asst. dept. head sales La Vogue, Durham, N.C., 1981-82; sales assoc. Collections, Durham, 1983; co-op student chem engring. E.I. duPont de Nemours & Co., Wilmington, N.C., 1985-86; rsch. asst. in astrophysics N.C. State U., Raleigh, 1987; sales assoc. Leather 'N' Wood, Raleigh, 1988-89; patent examiner chem. group U.S. Patent & Trademark Office, Washington, 1989-91, 93—. NSF fellow, 1987.

HERUM, JANE LENTZ, psychology educator, consultant; b. Flushing, N.Y., Oct. 13, 1927; d. Henry Druben and Anne (Lupinek) Druben Moore; m. Frank P. Lentz, June 25, 1949 (dec. Oct. 1979); children: Paul, Kathy Lentz Minchew, Eric; m. Jorgen E. Herum, Feb. 27, 1981. AA, Elgin (Ill.) C.C., 1965; BA, No. Ill. U., 1969, MA, 1973, EdD, 1980. Cert. sch. pers. counselor, Ill. Sch. psychologist St. Charles (Ill.) Community Schs., 1972-76; dir. Hanover Learning Ctr., Bartlett, Ill., 1976-77; mem. faculty No. Ill. U., DeKalb, 1979-80; dir. psychol. svcs. Gulf Coast Ctr., Ft. Myers, Fla., 1981-84; pvt. practice Punta Gorda, Fla., 1981—; adj. faculty Elgin (Ill.) C.C., 1980-81, Edison C.C., Punta Gorda, 1981—; psychol. Cons. Sunrise, Cape Coral, Fla., 1982-86; exec. dir. J. Herum & Assocs., Elgin and Punta Gorda, 1978-92; dir., cons. Rsch. Assocs., Elgin, 1977-81. Student editor APA Jour., 1972. Area rep. Punta Gorda Isles Civic Assn., 1991—; bd. dirs. Family Svc. Assn., Elgin, 1981; charter mem. Hanover Twp. Youth Commn., Bartlett, Ill., 1979. Recipient cert. Fla. State Dept. Health and Rehab. Svcs., 1983. Mem. AAUW (bd. dirs. coll. and univ. liaison 1992-94, dir. fin. 1991-93, local scholarship chair 1991-94, mem. chair 1994—), APA, Nat. Assn. Sch. Psychologists, Psi Chi. Office: PO Box 1238 Punta Gorda FL 33951

HERWOOD, MARY CAROL, school administrator; b. Buffalo, May 23, 1931; d. Henry John and Anna Marie (Duffy) Kelleher; m. Ernest A. Herwood, May 26, 1962 (dec. Nov. 1982); children: Kelly Reilly, Patrick, Sheila. BS, D'Youville Coll., 1952; MEd, SUNY, Buffalo, 1970, PhD, 1980. Cert. sch. adminstr. and supr. Exec. sec. to v.p., gen. mgr. Loblaw, Inc., Buffalo, 1960-65; grad. asst. to v.p. acad. affairs SUNY, Buffalo, 1975-76; bus. tchr. Buffalo Pub. Schs., 1971-80, supr. of evaluation, 1980-85, supr. adminstrv. svcs., 1985—; bd. dirs. N.Y. Assn. Local Govt. Records Officers, 1990-91; pres. Ctrl. Office Educators Assn., 1991-92, 92-93; lectr. bus. and philosophy Trocaire Coll. Trustee St. Mary of the Lake Cath. Ch., Hamburg, N.Y., 1990—, mem. parish coun., 1990—, eucharistic min., 1985—, lector, 1988—; chmn. adv. com. Sisters Hosp. Sch. Nursing, Buffalo. Mem. Brierwood Country Club. Democrat. Home: 17 Pinegrove Pk Hamburg NY 14075 Office: Buffalo Pub Schs 708 City Hall Buffalo NY 14202

HERZBERG, SYDELLE SHULMAN, lawyer, accountant; b. N.Y.C., July 24, 1933; d. Hyman and Rose (Green) S.; m. Norman Joseph Herzberg, June 23, 1962; 1 child, Gilbert. BS, NYU, 1955; JD, Bklyn. Law Sch., 1957. Bar: N.Y. 1958; CPA, N.Y. Pub. acct. M. Sharlach & Co, N.Y.C., 1955-62; pvt. practice acctg. and law New Rochelle, N.Y., 1962—. Mem. bd. edn. Solomon Schechter Sch. of Westchester, White Plains, N.Y., 1975-78, bd. dirs. PTA, 1975-78; pres. PTA bd. Westchester Hebrew High Sch., Mamaroneck, N.Y., 1980-82; mem. budget adv. bd. City of New Rochelle, N.Y., 1975. Mem. ABA, AICPA, N.Y. State Soc. CPA, N.Y. State Bar Assn., Huguenot-Thomas Paine Hist. Assn. (treas. 1987—, trustee 1987—), LWV (pres. New Rochelle chpt. 1983-85, treas. Westchester chpt. 1989—, budget chair N.Y. 1989-91, treas. N.Y. state 1991—). Jewish. Home: 46 Longvue Ave New Rochelle NY 10804-4119 Office: 519 Main St New Rochelle NY 10801-6334

HERZECA, LOIS FRIEDMAN, lawyer; b. N.Y.C., July 7, 1954; d. Martin and Elaine Shirley (Rapoport) Friedman; m. Christian S. Herzeca, Aug. 15, 1980; children: Jane Leslie, Nicholas Cameron. BA, SUNY-Binghamton, 1976; JD, Boston U., 1979. Bar: N.Y. 1980, U.S. Dist. Ct. (so. and ea. dist.) N.Y. 1980. Atty. antitrust div. U.S. Dept. Justice, Washington, 1979-80; assoc. Fried, Frank, Harris, Shriver & Jacobson, N.Y.C., 1980-86, ptnr., 1986—. Editor Am. Jour. Law and Medicine, 1978-79. Mem. ABA, N.Y.C. Bar Assn. Office: Fried Frank Harris Shriver Jacobson 1 New York Plz New York NY 10004

HERZENBERG, CAROLINE STUART LITTLEJOHN, physicist; b. East Orange, N.J., Mar. 25, 1932; d. Charles Frederick and Caroline Dorothea (Schulze) L.; m. Leonardo Herzenberg, July 29, 1961; children: Karen Ann, Catherine Stuart. SB, MIT, 1953; SM, U. Chgo., 1955, PhD, 1958; DSc (hon.), SUNY, Plattsburgh, 1991. Asst. prof. Ill. Inst. Tech., Chgo., 1961-66, research physicist ITT Research Inst., 1967-70, sr. physicist, 1970-71; lectr. Calif. State U., Fresno, 1975-76; physicist Argonne (Ill.) Nat. Lab., Ill., 1977—; prin. investigator NASA Apollo Returned Lunar Sample Analysis Program, 1967-71; producer and host TV sci. series Camera on Sci., 1992; disting. vis. prof. SUNY, Plattsburgh, 1991; mem. final selection com. 1993 Bower Award and Prize for Achievement in Sci.; bd. adv. The Bower award and Prize for Achievement in Sci.; mem. nat. panel of advisors PBS/Disney TV sci. series Bill Nye the Sci. Guy. Author: Women Scientists from Antiquity to the Present: An Index, 1986. Contbr. articles to profl. jours. Candidate for alderman, Freeport, Ill., 1975; past chmn. NOW chpt., Freeport. Am. Phys. Soc. Congl. Scientist fellow finalist, 1976-77; recipient award in sci. Chgo. Women's Hall of Fame, 1989. Fellow AAAS, Am. Phys. Soc. (past chmn. com., sec.-treas. Forum on Physics and Soc., exec. bd. Forum on the History of Physics); mem. Assn. Women in Sci. (nat. sec. 1982-84, pres. 1988-90), Sigma Xi. Home: 1700 E 56th St Apt 2707 Chicago IL 60637 Office: Argonne Nat Lab Argonne IL 60439

HERZIG, JULIE ESTHER, architect; b. N.Y.C., Jan. 23, 1951; d. Philip R. and Helene J. (Phillips) H.; m. Robert J. Desnick, Oct. 23, 1988; 1 child, Jonathan Phillips. BA, Mt. Holyoke Coll., 1973; BArch with honors, Pratt Inst., 1983. With Red Roof Design, N.Y.C., 1977-80, Phillips Janson Group, N.Y.C., 1983-84, Herzig, Knechtel Assocs., N.Y.C., 1984-85, Herzig Design, N.Y.C., 1985—. Mt. Holyoke Coll. grantee, 1972. Mem. AIA (assoc.), Mt. Holyoke Club.

HESKY, LUCY ANNE, nurse; b. L.A., Dec. 16, 1950; d. Alfred and Susan (Weil) H. B in Nursing, Mt. St. Mary Coll. RN, Calif. Owner Geri-Care Med. Supplies; cons. Mepassit, Palm Harbor, Fla. Democrat. Jewish. Office: Geri Care Med Supplies 4024 Coolidge Ave Los Angeles CA 90066-5412

HESLIN, CATHLEEN JANE, artist, designer, entrepreneur; b. Bklyn., Feb. 24, 1929; d. Charles Jenkins and Katherine (Bauer) Hunter; AA, Packer Collegiate Inst., Bklyn., 1950; postgrad. Duke U., Pratt Inst.; m. John Thomas Heslin, June 24, 1950. Sr. artist, designer Klopman Mills, Rockleigh, N.J., 1966-72; free-lance designer, 1972-90; propr. Quilters Corner, Tappan, N.Y., 1978-90. Councilwoman Borough of Rockleigh (N.J.), 1973-85, 90-92, pres. coun., 1983-85, historian, 1973-90, chmn. environ. com., 1974, chmn. bicentennial com., 1974-76, chmn. shade tree commn., 1975, chmn. fin. com., 1977-78, chmn. bldg. com., 1983-85; chmn. Historic Adv. Com., 1977-86—, Hist. Preservation Commn., 1987-90; mem. Rockleigh Planning Bd., 1973, 87-89; del. 114th Episcopal Conv., 1988; Rep. mayoral nominee Borough of Rockleigh, 1990; founder Cathleen Heslin Found., 1990; trustee Abram Demaree Homestead, 1982-84; established Rockleigh Wildlife Sanctuary and Land Preserve. Recipient various certs. of appreciation. Mem. Tappantown Hist. Soc. (dir.), Soc. Archtl. Historians, Am. Soc. Planning Ofcls., Bergen County Hist. Soc. (trustee 1984—), Historic Homes Assn. N.J. Author: History of Rockleigh, N.J., 1648-1973, 1973, Old Order Amish-The People and Their Quilts, 1988; inventor Quilters Quarter, measuring device. Obtained Nat. Historic Dist. status for Borough of Rockleigh, 1976, established Wildlife Sanctuary and Land Preserve. Republican. Home: Haring Farm 5 Piermont Rd Rockleigh NJ 07647-2715 Office: Old Haring Farm Rockleigh NJ 07647

HESS, ANN MARIE, systems specialist, electronic data processing specialist; b. Grants Pass, Oreg., Mar. 29, 1944; d. Wilbur Lill and Esther Elaine Groner; m. William Charles Hess, July 25, 1969; children: David William, William Albert. BSEE, BS in Math., Oregon State U., 1968. Engr. Lawrence Livermore Lab., Livermore, Calif., 1968-69; mgr., owner RBR Scales, Inc., Anaheim, Calif., 1969-84; lead engr. Rockwell Internat., Seal Beach, Calif., 1984-86, '87-88; software engr. Hughes Aircraft Co., Fullerton, Calif., 1986-87; sr. engr. Logican Eagle Tech., Inc., Eatontown, N.J., 1988-91; owner Holistic Eclectic Software Svc., Orange, Calif., 1991-93; database adminstr. Jacobs Engring Group, 1993—. Active Calif. Master Chorale, Santa Ana, 1990-92. Mem. IEEE, Am. Soc. Quality Control, Phi Kappa Phi, Eta Kappa Nu, Tau Beta Pi. Lutheran. Office: JEG/PEP 251 S Lake Ave Pasadena CA 91101

HESS, EVELYN VICTORINE (MRS. MICHAEL HOWETT), medical educator; b. Dublin, Ireland, Nov. 8, 1926; came to U.S., 1960, naturalized, 1965; d. Ernest Joseph and Mary (Hawkins) H.; m. Michael Howett, Apr. 27, 1954. MB, BChir BA in Obstetrics, U. Coll., Dublin, 1949; MD, 1980. Intern West Middlesex Hosp., London, Eng., 1950; resident Clare Hall Hosp., London, 1951-53, Royal Free Hosp. and Med. Sch., London, 1954-57; rsch. fellow in epidemiology of Tb Royal Free Med. Sch., London, 1955; asst. prof. internal medicine U. Tex. Southwestern Med. Sch., 1960-64; assoc. prof. dept. medicine U. Cin. Coll. Medicine, 1964-69, McDonald prof. medicine, 1969—, dir. div. immunology, 1964—; sr. investigator Arthritis and Rheumatism Found., 1963-68; attending physician Univ. Hosp., chief clinician Arthritis Clinic, 1965—; attending physician VA Hosp.; cons. Children's Hosp., Cin., 1967—, Jewish Hosp., Cin., 1968—; mem. various coms., mem. nat. adv. coun. NIH; mem. various coms. FDA, Cin. Bd. Health. Contbr. articles on immunology, rheumatic diseases to jours., chpts. to books. Active Nat. Pks. Assn., Smithsonian Instn., others. Recipient Arthritis Found., 1973, 78, 83, Am. Lupus Soc., 1979, Am. Acad. Family Practice, 1980, award for AIDS work State of Ohio, 1989, Spirit of Am. Women award, 1989; travel fellow Royal Free Med. Sch., Scandinavia, 1956, Empire Rheumatism Coun., 1958-59. Fellow ACP, Am. Acad. Allergy, Royal Soc. Medicine; mem. Heberden Soc., Am. Coll. Rheumatology (master), Pan-Am. League Assns. for Rheumatology, Ctrl. Soc. Clin. Rsch., Am. Fedn. Clin. Rsch., Am. Assn. Immunologists, Am. Soc. Nephrology, Am. Soc. Clin. Pharmacology and Therapeutics, Transplantation Soc., Reticuloendothelial Soc., N.Y. Acad. Scis., Soc. Exptl. Biology and Medicine, Rheumatological Soc. Colombia (hon.), Rheumatological Soc. Peru (hon.), Rheumatological Soc. Italy (hon.), Clin. Immunol. Soc. Japan (hon.), Alpha Omega Alpha. Home: 2916 Grandin Rd Cincinnati OH 45208-3418 Office: U Cin Med Ctr Cincinnati OH 45267

HESS, IRMA, academic program director, translator; b. Frankfurt, Germany, Feb. 5, 1939; came to U.S., 1957, naturalized, 1960; d. Frederick and Martha (Mahlert) Alban; 1 child, Harold Alban Hess. B.A., New Sch. for Social Research, 1977; B.S., SUNY-Albany, 1976; M.A., NYU, 1979, M.P.A., 1984, advanced profl. cert., grad. of bus., 1986. Asst. to spl. psychol. testing Bd. Edn., Mt. Vernon, N.Y., 1959-65, health chmn., 1959-66; ind. practice bookkeeping, 1959-65; translator N.Y.C. cts. and agys., 1959—, interpreter, 1959-77; counselor Family Ct., Criminal Ct. Youth Div., N.Y.C., 1976-78; tchr. New Rochell Bd. Edn., 1976-78; adminstr. NYU, N.Y.C., 1978—. Vice pres. PTA, Mt. Vernon, 1968-70; chmn. Mt. Vernon Community Chest, 1971-73; sec. N.Y.C. br. ARC, 1975-77. Recipient Mayor of N.Y. accomplishment cert., 1978; scholar State of N.Y., 1976, NYU, 1978. Mem. Am. Soc. Pub. Adminstrs., U.S. Exec. Women, Am. Translators Assn., Am. Pub. Health Adminstrs., Am. Polit. Sci. Assn., N.Y. Acad. Scis., New Sch. for Social Research Alumni Assn., NYU Alumni Assn. Avocations: golf; ballet; tennis; folk music. Office: NYU D'Agostino Hall 110 W 3rd St New York NY 10012-1012

HESS, JANET LINDLEY, geologist; b. Houston, Jan. 23, 1956; d. Gene Ray and Sally (Hackney) Lindley; m. D. Edward Hess, Nov. 17, 1979; children: Sarah Marie, Emily Adrienne. B.S. in Geology, U. Tex.-Austin, 1978; postgrad. U. Aberdeen, Scotland. Geologist, Union of Calif., Lafayette, La., 1978-81, Aminoil, U.S.A., Lafayette, La., 1981-82, Union Tex. Petroleum, Houston, 1982-89, Royal Dutch/Shell Group (HOCOL), Colombia, 1989-92. Mem. Am. Assn. Petroleum Geologists, Phi Beta Kappa. Avocations: camping; reading; music. Home: PO Box 19583 Houston TX 77224-9583

HESS, MARCIA WANDA, educational assistant; b. Cin., Mar. 15, 1934; d. Edward Frederick Lipka and Rose (Wirtle) Lipka Stanley; m. Edward Emanuel Grenier, Aug. 9, 1952 (div.); m. Thomas Benton Hess, Mar. 25, 1960; children: Kathleen Ann, Cynthia Jean, Thomas Allen. Grad. high sch., Cin. Instr. asst. Cin. Pub. Schs., 1970—, also mem. staff desegregation workshop and unified K-12 reading communication arts program staff tng. com. Contbr. tchr.-instr. asst. handbook, instr. asst. tng. film. Mem. Winton Place Vets of World War II Women's Aux. (pres. 1982-84, bd. dirs. 1982-86, 89-91). Republican. Roman Catholic. Home: 765 Derby Ave Cincinnati OH 45232-1836

HESS, MARGARET JOHNSTON, religious writer, educator; b. Ames, Iowa, Feb. 22, 1915; d. Howard Wright and Jane Edith (Stevenson) Johnston; B.A., Coe Coll., 1937; m. Bartlett Leonard Hess, July 31, 1937; children—Daniel, Deborah, John, Janet. Bible tchr. Community Bible Classes Ward Presbyn. Ch., Livonia, Mich., 1959—, Christ Ch. Cranbrook (Episcopalian), Bloomfield Hills, Mich., 1980-93, Lutheran Ch. of the Redeemer, Birmingham, Mich., 1993—. Co-author: (with B.L. Hess) How to Have a

Giving Church, 1974, The Power of a Loving Church, 1977, How Does Your Marriage Grow?, 1983, Never Say Old, 1984; author: Love Knows No Barriers, 1979; Esther: Courage in Crisis, 1980; Unconventional Women, 1981, The Triumph of Love, 1987; contbr. articles to religious jours. Home: 16845 Riverside Dr Livonia MI 48154-2428

HESS, MARILYN ANN, state legislator; m. Dennis J. Hess; children: Christine, Craig. AA, NYU, 1977; BBA in Mgmt. cum laude, Pace U., 1980. Assoc. Merrill Lynch, N.Y.C., 1972-77; home improvement contractor Conn., 1982-90; mem. Conn. Ho. of Reps., 1993—; state rep. 150th Assembly Dist., Conn., 1993—; mem. Rep. Roundtable of Greenwich, 1993—, Amb. and Roundtable, 1994—, Conn. Reps. for Choice, 1992—; dir. Rep. Town Com., 1989—. Organizer pack 516 Boy Scouts Am., N.Y.C., 1976; fund raiser, chmn. Lewisboro Neighbor's Club, South Salem, 1979; sec. Ridgefield HIst. Dist. Commn., 1984-85, Greenwich Hist. Dist. Commn., 1988-90, Friends of the Byram Shubert Libr. Bd., 1989-93; del. Parents Together, 1980; underwriting com. Bruce Mus. Ball, 1990-91; alternate Greenwich Planning and Zoning Commn., 1990-93; founding trustee Byram Scholarship fund, 1991—. Named Mother of Yr. Town and Village Newspaper, 1974. Home: 61 Byram Shore Rd Greenwich CT 06830 Office: Ho of Reps State Capitol Hartford CT 06106

HESS, SUSAN B., federal agency administrator. Asst. to the dep. chief for rsch. Forest Svc., Dept. Agrl., Washington. Mem. Pub. Rels. Soc. Am., Nat. Assn. Govt. Comm., Soc. of Am. Foresters. Office: Forest Svcs Dept of Agrl 201 14th St SW Rm 4NW Washington DC 20090*

HESSE, CAROLYN SUE, lawyer; b. Belleville, Ill., Jan. 12, 1949; d. Ralph H. Hesse and Marilyn J. (Midgley) Hesse Dierkes; m. William H. Hallenbeck. B.S., U. Ill., 1971, M.S., U. Ill.-Chgo., 1977; J.D., DePaul U., 1983. Bar: Ill. 1983, U.S. Dist. Ct. (no. dist.) Ill. 1983. Research assoc. U. Ill., Chgo., 1974-77; tech. adviser Ill. Pollution Control Bd., Chgo., 1977-80; environ. scientist U.S. EPA, Chgo., 1980-84; assoc. Pretzel & Stouffer, Chartered, Chgo., 1984-87, Coffield Ungaretti Harris & Assocs., Chgo., 1987-88, ptnr. McDermott, Will & Emery, 1988—. Contbr. articles on environ. sci. to profl. jours. Mem. ABA, Chgo. Bar Assn. Office: McDermott Will & Emery 227 W Monroe St Chicago IL 60606-5016

HESSE, MARTHA O., natural gas company executive; b. Hattiesburg, Miss., Aug. 14, 1942; d. John William and Geraldine Elaine (Ossian) H. B.S., U. Iowa, 1964; postgrad., Northwestern U., 1972-76; M.B.A., U. Chgo., 1979. Research analyst Blue Shield, 1964-66; dir. div. data mgmt. Am. Hosp. Assn., 1966-69; dir., chief operating officer SEI Info. Tech., Chgo., 1969-80; assoc. dep. sec. Dept. of Commerce, Washington, 1981-82; exec. dir. Pres.' Task Force on Mgmt. Reform, 1982; asst. sec. mgmt. and adminstrn. Dept. of Energy, Washington, 1982-86; chmn. FERC, Washington, 1986-89; sr. v.p. 1st Chgo. Corp., 1990; now pres. Hesse Gas, Houston; bd. dirs. Am. Nat. Resources Co. Subs. Coastal Corp., Pinnacle West Capital Corp., Ariz. Pub. Svc. Co., Sithe Energies, Inc., Health-Funding. Bd. dirs. grad. sch. bus. exec. program U. Chgo., 1990-91. Office: 2323 Voss Rd # 425 Houston TX 77057

HESSE, NANCY JANE, treasurer; b. Quincy, Ill., Nov. 2, 1948; d. John William and Geraldine Elaine (Ossian) H. BA, U. Ill., 1970; MEd, Memphis State U., 1971; MBA, Northwestern U., 1980; postgrad., Loyola U. Program dir. Memphis State U., 1970-75; regional mgr. SEI Info. Tech., Chgo., 1975-80, mgr. cons. ops. sect., 1980-83, mgr. devel. projects, 1983-85, mgr. adminstrn. and fin., 1985-87; dir. adminstrn. Laventhol & Horwath, Chgo., 1987-91; treas. Hesse Gas Co., Houston, 1991—. Bd. dirs. YWCA Met. Chgo., 1983-91. Office: Hesse Gas Co Ste 425 2323 Voss Rd Houston TX 77057

HESSEL, DEBORAH ELLEN, consultant; b. New Haven, May 11, 1960; d. Mark Lewis and Carolyn Messing (Starman) H. BA, Brandeis U., 1982; MBA, Union Coll., Schenectady, 1984. Supr. Empire Blue Cross Blue Shield, N.Y.C., 1984-85, dept. head, 1985-86, mgr., 1986-87, project mgr., 1987-88; assoc. cons. Coopers & Lybrand, N.Y.C., 1988-89, cons., 1989-90, sr. cons., mgr., 1991—, mgr., 1993—. Mem. NAFE, Women in Health Mgmt. Home: 9-20 166th St Apt 2B Whitestone NY 11357 Office: Coopers & Lybrand 1301 Ave of Americas New York NY 10019

HESSELBEIN, FRANCES RICHARDS, foundation executive, consultant; b. South Fork, Pa.; d. Burgess Harmon and Anne Luke (Wicks) Richards; widowed, 1978; 1 child, John Richards. DHL (hon.), Buena Vista Coll., 1987, Juniata Coll., 1990, Hood Coll., 1991; D Mgmt. (hon.), GM Inst., 1990; LLD (hon.), Wilson Coll., 1991; LHD (hon.), Marymount-Tarrytown Coll., 1993; DHL (hon.), Boston Coll., 1994, U. Nebr., Kearney, 1994. CEO Talus Rock Girl Scout Coun., Johnstown, 1970-74, Penn Laurel Girl Scout Coun., York, Pa., 1974-76, Girl Scouts U.S., N.Y.C., 1976-90; pres., CEO Peter F. Drucker Found. Nonprofit Mgmt., N.Y.C., 1990—; bd. dirs. Mut. of Am. Ins. Co., N.Y.C.; mem. nat. bd. visitors Peter F. Drucker Grad. Mgmt. Ctr., Claremont (Calif.) Grad. Sch., 1987—; chmn. bd. govs. Josephson Ethics Inst.; mem. adv. com. to bd. dirs. N.Y. Stock Exch., 1988-91; bd. govs. Ctr. for Creative Leadership, Greensboro, N.C., 1992—. Mem. edit. adv. bd. Nonprofit Mgmt. and Leadership. Dir. Youth for Understanding, Washington, 1984—; trustee Juniata Coll., Huntingdon, Pa., 1988—, Allentown (Pa.) Coll., 1988—; mem. Pres.'s Adv. Com. on Points of Light Initiative Found., 1989; bd. dirs. Nat. Exec. Svc. Corps., N.Y., Roger Tory Peterson Inst.; bd. dirs. Commn. on Nat. and Cmty. Svc., 1991-94; adv. bd. The Leadership Inst., U. So. Calif., 1991; mem. Kellogg Found. Nat. Task Group on African-Am. Men and Boys. Recipient Outstanding Achievement award Inter-Service Club Council, Johnstown, 1976, Entrepreneurial Woman award Women Bus. Owners of N.Y., 1984, Nat. Leadership award United Way of Am., Washington, 1985, Disting. Community Service award Mut. of Am. Ins. Co., 1985, Dir.'s Choice award Nat. Women's Econ. Alliance, 1988, Excellence in Leadership award Nat. Women's Econ. Alliance, 1989, Pa. Soc. Disting. Citizen award, 1991, Wilbur M. McFeely award Internat. Mgmt. Coun. YMCA, 1993; named Outstanding Exec., Savvy Mag., 1985; on cover BusinessWeek, 1990. Mem. Sky Club, Pa. Soc. Club, Marco Polo Club. Office: Peter F Drucker Found Nonprofit Mgmt 666 Fifth Ave 10th Fl New York NY 10103-0012

HESSLER, CATHERINE FOX, telecommunications company executive; b. Balt., Nov. 14, 1950; d. Lay Martin and Jean Pauline (Selby) Fox; m. George William Hessler Jr., Mar. 15, 1987; 1 child, Melanie D. AA in Bus., Montgomery Coll., 1976; BA in Bus. Mgmt., U. Md., 1980. Bus. sales, market planner AT&T Info. Systems Sales, Vienna, Va., 1980-84; dist. mgr. exec. communications AT&T Gen. Bus. Systems, Parsippany, N.J., 1984-86; corp. industry affairs dir. AT&T Fed. Govt. Affairs, Basking Ridge, N.J., 1986-91; dir. regulatory and legis. govt. affairs AT&T Law & Govt. Affairs Orgn., Austin, Tex., 1991—; bd. dirs. NATA, Washington, 1986-91, TIA, Washington, 1986-91. Chmn. bd. Jr. Achievement of Ctrl. Tex., 1994-95. Recipient Outstanding Achievement award White Ho. Conf. on Small Bus., 1986. Mem. Leadership Tex. Alumnae Assn., Austin Club, Phi Kappa Phi. Office: AT&T 8911 N Capital Of Texas Hwy Austin TX 78759-7203

HESTAD, MARSHA ANNE, educational administrator; b. Evanston, Ill., Apr. 25, 1950; d. Bjorn Mark and Florence Anne (Ragusi) H. BS, U. Ill., 1972; MEd, Nat. Coll. Edn., Evanston, Ill., 1978; postgrad., Purdue U., 1985; PhD, Loyola U., Chgo., 1991. Cert. in elem. edn., spl. reading, gifted edn., gen. adminstrn., Ill., Ind. Tchr. 5th grade Deerfield (Ill.) Sch. Dist. 109, 1972-78; head tchr. North Aegean Acad., Kavala, Greece, 1978-81; gifted resource tchr. Alief Ind. Sch. Dist., Houston, 1983-84, TeKoppel, Evansville, Ind., 1984-85; field supr. Purdue U., West Lafayette, Ind., 1987; gifted coord. MSD Mt. Vernon, Ind., 1985-88; gifted resource Libertyville (Ill.) Sch. Dist. 70, 1988-91; instr. Coll. Lake County, Grayslake, Ill., 1991; clin. prof. Loyola U., Chgo., 1991; prof. Ind. State U., Terre Haute, 1992-93; tchr. lang. arts/lit. 7th grade, co-dir./prin. summer sch. Libertyville (Ill.) Sch. Dist. 70, 1993-94; prin. Chippewa Sch., Bensenville (Ill.) Dist. 2, 1994—; bd. dirs. Odyssey of the Mind, Ind. and Ill., 1985-95; cons. in field. Contbr. articles to profl. jours. Mem. ASCD, Am. Ednl. Rsch. Assn., Nat. Coun. Staff Devel., Midwest Ednl. Rsch. Assn., Phi Delta Kappa. Home: 850 Happ Rd Northfield IL 60093

HESTENES, ROBERTA RAE, college president, minister; b. Huntington Park, Calif., Aug. 5, 1939; d. Robert James and Besse Rae (Nipp) Louis; m. John D. Hestenes; children: Joan Hestenes Lehnen, Eric Magnus, Stephen Eastvold. BA, U. Calif., Santa Barbara; M in Divinity, Fuller Theol. Sem., 1979, D.Min., 1983; DHL (hon.), Houghton Coll.; DD (hon.), Seattle Pacific U. Ordained to ministry Presbyn. Ch., 1979. Dir. adult edn. and small group ministries United Presbyn. Ch., Seattle, 1967-74; assoc. in ministry LaCanada (Calif.) Presbyn. Ch., 1974-84; assoc. prof., dir. Christian Formation and Discipleship program Fuller Theol. Sem., Pasadena, Calif., 1975-87; bd. dirs., chmn. strategic planning com. World Vision U.S., 1980—; bd. dirs. World Vision Internat., 1982—, chmn. bd. dirs., 1985—; pres., prof. Christian spirituality Eastern Coll., St. Davids, Pa., 1987—; assoc. Wayne (Pa.) Presbyn. Ch., 1991—; cons. numerous Presbyn. orgns.; minister Kenya, Australia, South Africa, Singapore, Hong Kong, South Korea, Philippines, Cen. am. Author: (books) Using the Bible in Groups, 1985, 92, Discovering II Corinthians/Galatians, 1986, Turning Committees Into Communities, 1991, Mastering Teaching, 1991, Growing The Church Through Small Groups, 1993; author: (with Earl Palmer) Mastering the Art of Teaching, 1992; (taped courses) Building Christian Communicty Through Small Groups, 1985, Helping Christians Grow: Adult Formation and Discipleship in the Local Church, 1987; co-editor: Women and the Ministries of Christ, 1979; contbr. articles to profl. jours.;. Fellow Case Methods Inst.; mem. Am. Acad. Religion, Religious Edn. Assn., Nat. Assn. of Profs. of Christian Edn. Office: Ea Coll Office of the President 10 Fairview Dr Saint Davids PA 19087-3619

HESTER, LINDA HUNT, university dean, counselor; b. Winston-Salem, N.C., June 16, 1938; d. Hanselle Lindsay and Jennie Sarepta (Hunt) H. BS with honors, U. Wis., 1960, MS, 1964; PhD, Mich. State U., 1971. Lic. ednl. counselor, Wis. Instr. health and phys. edn. for women U. Tex., Austin, 1960-62; asst. dean women U. Ill., Urbana, 1964-66; dean of women, asst. prof. sociology and phys. edn. Tex. Woman's U., Denton, 1971-73; rsch. assoc. bur. higher edn. Mich. Dept. Edn., Lansing, 1969-70; counselor Dallas Challenge and Dallas Ind. Sch. Dist., 1989-90. Bd. dirs. Dallas Opera, 1986—; Stradivarious mem. Dallas Symphony, 1991—; assoc. mem. Dallas Mus. Art, 1991—. Fellow coll. edn. Mich. State U., 1968. Mem. Am. Counseling Assn., Am. Coll. Pers. Assn., Nat. Assn. Women in Edn., Brookhaven Country Club, Delta Kappa Gamma, Alpha Lambda Delta. Republican. Presbyterian. Home and Office: 7606 Wellcrest Dr Dallas TX 75230-4857

HESTER, NANCY ELIZABETH, county government administrator; b. Miami, Fla., Jan. 20, 1950; d. George Temple and Lorraine Patricia (Cluney) Hester; B.A., Bucknell U., 1972; M.I.A., Columbia U., 1974; M.B.A., Fla. Internat. U., 1979. Treasury rep. Westinghouse Elec. Co., N.Y.C., 1974-76; adminstrv. officer serving in bldg. and zoning, gen. services, and corrections and rehab. depts. Metro Dade County, Fla., 1979—, bur. comdr. corrections and rehab. dept., 1990—; adj. prof. Fla. Internat. U., Miami, 1980-83. Bd. dirs. YWCA Greater Miami, 1988-92, LWV, 1993—, pres. bd. dirs., pres. bd. trustees edn. fund, 1994—. Mem. Zool. Soc. Fla., Miami City Ballet Guild.

HESTON, BEVERLY ANN, food scientist; b. Providence, May 29, 1958; d. Richard K. and J. Helen (Sangiuliano) H.; m. Jeff Prince, Apr. 18, 1994. BS in Food Sci., U. Calif., Davis, 1986. Quality control auditor Hunt-Wesson, Sacramento, 1985; intern rsch. & devel. Foster Farms Poultry, Turlock, Calif., 1986; product devel. specialist Tony's Pizza Svc., Salina, Kans., 1986-90; project mgr. rsch. & devel. Design Foods, Inc., Ft. Worth, 1990-93; sr. food technologist Chgo. Bros., Inc., San Diego, 1994—. Mem. So. Calif. Inst. Food Technologists, Inst. Food Technologists, Cal Aggie Alumni Assn. Office: Chgo Bros Inc 7696 Formula Pl San Diego CA 92121

HESTON, NANCY BAUER, interior designer; b. Feb. 8, 1948; m. James R. Heston; children: Karen, Colin. BS in Art Edn. & Design, Butler U., 1974. Interior designer Kittle's, Indpls., 1970-74; dir. mktg. & promotions World Team Tennis, Indpls., 1975; sr. designer Marshall Field & Co., Oak Brook, Ill., 1975-78; interior designer Nancy Heston Interiors, Great Falls, Va., 1978—. Mem. Am. Soc. Interior Designers (profl. mem.), Nat. Hist. Soc., Nat. Mus. Women in Arts, Jr. League Washington. Republican. Office: 9807 Thunderhill Ct Great Falls VA 22066-2613

HETFELD, ELIZABETH ANN, industrial engineer; b. Oshkosh, Wis., Feb. 28, 1954; d. Frederick Damler and Connie Steiger Dempsey; children: Hunter H. Student, U. Autonima, Guadalajara, Mex., 1974; BA in Architecture, U. N.Mex., 1979. Project mgr. drafting Hutchinson, Brown & Ptnrs., Architects, Albuquerque, 1978-80; engr. facilities constrn. mgmt. divsn. Albuquerque Ops. Office, 1982-90, engr. quality engring. divsn., 1982-90, engr. budget and resources mgmt., 1982-90, site mgr. uranium mill tailings remedial action project, 1982-90; sect. chief indsl. tech. Bonneville Power Adminstrn., Portland, Oreg., 1990—; mem. employee support sounding bd. Bonneville Power Adminstrn., Portland, 1990-91, mem. women's resource group, 1990-93. Mem. City Club Portland, 1990-91. Home: 6214 SE 36th Ave Portland OR 97202

HETH, DIANA SUE, therapist; b. Robinson, Ill., Sept. 25, 1948; d. Quentin Wilson and Marguerite (Byrd) Abraham; m. Kenneth Lewis Greider, Aug. 16, 1970 (div. Mar. 1985); children: Kathryn Elizabeth, Susan Nicole, Jonathan Abraham; m. Harold Eugene Heth; children: Joseph Brockwell, Kiley Joy, Mark Quentin. BSE, Eastern Ill. U., 1970; MSW, U. Ill., 1992. Lic. clin. social worker. Exec. dir. Nat. Assn. Downs Syndrome, Chgo., 1976-77, Heartland Hospice, Effingham, Ill., 1983-88; office adminstr. Am. Family Life Assurance, Effingham, Ill., 1988-90; sec. design engring. dept. Fedders N.Am., Effingham, Ill., 1990; co-owner H&S Vending, 1990—; therapist sexual abuse Heartland Human Svcs., Effingham, Ill., 1992-94; child welfare specialist II Ill. Dept. of Children and Family Svcs., Olney, 1994—; mem. Profl. Adv. Com. for Hospice Lincolnland. Author: One Gift to the Next, 1983, Sundance Lady, 1990. Vol. Belleville (Ill.) Hospice, 1981-83; co-chmn. svc. and rehab. com. Am. Cancer Soc. Mem. NASW, Ill. State Hospice Orgn. (bd. dirs. 1985-86), Ill. Pub. Health Assn., County Orgn. SVc. Providers, Newcomers Club (pres. 1984-85), Compassionate Friends Club (bd. dirs. 1985-86), Topnotcher's 4-H Club (leader). Republican. Methodist. Home: RR 1 Box 63 Shumway IL 62461-9722 Office: Olney Field Office Ill Dept Child/Family Svcs 1102A S West St Olney IL 62450

HETRICK, MARY JO, fragrance company executive; b. Noblesville, Ind., Nov. 12, 1954; d. Joseph R. and Mary P. (Clark) Couden; m. Chet Hetrick, Dec. 11, 1976; 1 child, Joel. Founder, pres., CEO Good Scents Ltd., Princeton, Ill., 1989—; cons. in field. Recipient Recognition award Ind. 4-H Alumni, 1981. Mem. Princeton Alliance Lady Mgr. (founder, chair 1991—), Princeton Mcht. Assn. (founding mem., sec. 1992-93, pres. 1993-94), Bus. and Profl. Women (networking specialist, membership com. 1988, Outstanding Working Woman award 1989). Home: RR 4 Princeton IL 61356-9804 Office: Good Scents Ltd 504 S Main St Princeton IL 61356-2007

HETZLER, SUSAN ELIZABETH SAVAGE, educational administrator; b. Monticello, Iowa, Mar. 18, 1947; d. Robert Engelbert and Josephine May (Ricklefs) Savage; children: Stephanie, Michael. BS in Edn., Rockford (Ill.) Coll., 1971; 2MS in Edn., No. Ill. U., 1978, cert. advanced study, 1984; PhD, Walden U., Mpls., 1989. Cert. elem. tchr., adminstr., Ill., Iowa; supr., sociology tchr., Ill. Elem. tchr. Freeport (Ill.) Sch. Dist., 1971-86; prof. elem. edn. Iowa State U., Ames, 1986-90; dir. of practitioner preparation and devel. Iowa Dept. Edn., Des Moines, 1990—; curriculum cons. Ames Sch. Dist., 1985-90, Des Moines Sch. Dist., 1985-90; mem. ISU adv. bd., Ames, 1991—. Author: Elementary Education Practicum Teaching, 1988, Learning Centers, 1989. Comsnr. Drug and Alcohol Prevention Project, Freeport, 1976-85; chairperson Stephenson County (Ill.) Cancer Soc., 1976-78, small bus. dvsn. United Way, Freeport, 1980-85; vol. BSA and GSA, Freeport, 1974-85. Recipient Excellence in Teaching award Iowa State U., 1989-90, Outstanding Elem. Tchrs. Am. Ill., 1974, 81. Mem. AAUP, ASCD, NEA, Iowa ASCD, Am. Assn. Colls. of Tchr. Edn., Iowa Assn. Colls. of Tchr. Edn., Iowa Ednl. Rsch. and Eval. Assn., Assn. Tchr. Educators, Delta Kappa Gamma, Phi Delta Kappa. Protestant. Home: 713 NE Brook Haven Dr Ankeny IA 50021 Office: Iowa Dept Edn Grimes State Office Bldg Des Moines IA 50319-0146

HEUER, MARGARET B., retired microcomputer laboratory coordinator; b. Juneau, Alaska, Sept. 12, 1935; d. William George and Flora (Rusk) Allen; m. Joseph Louis Heuer; children: Leilani, Joseph, Daniel, Suzanne, Karen, Mark, Jerina. AA, San Bernardino Valley Coll., 1980. Cert. data processing, computer repair and maintenance, microcomputer support specialist. Coord. microcomputers lab. Oakton Community Coll., Skokie, Ill., 1981-93; ret., 1993.

HEULER, ELIZABETH ANNE, family nurse practitioner; b. Indpls., Aug. 9, 1955; d. Francis and Julia Magdelene (Grube) H. BSN, U. Southwestern La., 1978; MSN, Sonoma State U., 1987. Nurse tchg. hosp. So. Bapt. Hosp., New Orleans, 1978-85; nurse Sequoia Nat. Park, Kings Canyon Nat. Park, Giant Forest, Calif., 1985; FNP detox ctr. BAART, San Francisco, 1987-88; FNP in health maintenance Kaiser Permanente, Santa Rosa, Calif., 1987-90; FNP Navcare Primary Care, Oakland, Calif., 1988-90; pvt. practice Tallahassee, Fla., 1990-92; gen. med., urgent care nurse Fla. State U., Tallahassee, 1992—. Mem. Jefferson Performing Arts Soc., New Orleans, 1981-82. Mem. ANA, NOW, Fla. Nurses Assn., Sierra Club. Democrat. Home: 1601 Carolewood # 1 Tallahassee FL 32308

HEUMAN, DONNA RENA, lawyer; b. Seattle, May 27, 1949; d. Russell George and Edna Inez (Armstrong) H. BA in Psychology, UCLA, 1972; JD, U. Calif., San Francisco, 1985. Cert. shorthand reporter, 1978—; owner, Heuman & Assocs., San Francisco, 1978-86; real estate broker, Calif., 1990—. Mem. Hastings Internat. and Comparative Law Rev., 1984-85; bd. dirs. Saddleback, 1987-89. Jessup Internat. Moot Ct. Competition, 1985, N. Fair Oaks Mcpl. Adv. Coun., 1993—, vice chair, 1993—. Mem. ABA, NAFE, Nat. Shorthand Reporters Assn., Women Entrepreneurs, Calif. Shorthand Reporters Assn., Calif. State Bar Assn., Nat. Mus. of Women in the Arts, Calif. Lawyers for the Arts, San Francisco Bar Assn., Assn. Trial Lawyers Am., Commonwealth Club, World Affairs Council, Zonta (bd. dirs.). Home: 750 18th Ave Menlo Park CA 94025-2018 Office: Superior Ct Calif Hall Of Justice Redwood City CA 94063

HEUMANN, JANICE, recreational therapist; b. St. Louis, Mar. 26, 1957; d. Paul Henry and Lorraine Theresa (Justi) H.; children: Abby J. Dunne, Corey C. Dunne. BS in Recreation and Park Adminstrn., U. Mo., Columbia, 1979, MA in Ednl. and Counseling Psychology, 1993. Cert. therapeutic recreation specialist. Recreation therapist St. Louis Devel. Disabilities Treatment Ctr., 1979-81; program dir. Burrell Ctr., Springfield, Mo., 1982-85; dir. tng. Project LIFE U. Mo., Columbia, 1985—; activity cons. Katy Manor Nursing Home, Pilot Grove, Mo., 1990-91; recreation therapy instr. U. Mo., Columbia, 1993—; recreation cons. Family Oriented Counseling Svcs., Rolla, Mo., 1994. Co-author, editor 8 book series: Project LIFE Programming, 1986-90; contbr. chpt. to book: Leisure and Mental Health, 1994; creator games. Coach various youth softball orgns., Columbia, 1992-93; bd. dirs. Univ. YMCA, Columbia, 1994. Mem. Am. Therapeutic Recreation Assn., Mo. Assn. Psychosocial Rehab. Svcs. (conf. com. co-chair 1990—). Office: Project LIFE 621 Clark Hall Columbia MO 65211

HEUPLE, RHONDA CLARK, retail accounting administrator; b. Berkeley Springs, W.Va., Apr. 18, 1958; d. Raymond C. and Margie R. (Widmyer) Clark; m. Robert W. Nicholson, Apr. 4, 1981 (div. June 1992); children: Brian Robert, Katrina Marie; m. Clifford Scott Heuple, Sept. 26, 1992; 1 child, Kevin Scott. BS, Va. Tech. Inst., 1980. Acct. Commonwealth Gas, Richmond, Va., 1981-82; budget analyst Bank of Va., Richmond, 1983-84; budget analyst Circuit City, Richmond, 1984-87, mgr., 1987-90, group mgr., 1990—. Neighborhood rep. Woodridge Elem. Sch., Midlothian, Va., 1993; mem. Woodlake Woman's Club, Midlothian, 1993. Mem. Inst. Mgmt. Accts. (bd. dirs. 1984-86, sec. 1987). Republican. Office: Circuit City 9950 Mayland Dr Richmond VA 23233

HEUSCHELE, SHARON JO, university program director; b. Toledo, Ohio, July 12, 1936; 1 child, Brent Philip. BE, U. Toledo, 1965, MEd, 1969, PhD, 1973. Cert. elem., secondary tchr., Ohio. Asst. prof. Ohio Dominican Coll., Columbus, 1970-73, St. Cloud U., Minn., 1973-74; assoc. prof. Ohio State U., Columbus, 1974-79; dean instl. planning Lourdes Coll., Sylvania, Ohio, 1980—, chmn. sociology, econs. and polit. sci. dept.; cons. U. Hawaii, 1979, others. Bd. dirs. Trinity-St. Paul Inner City Program, Toledo, 1968; cons. Ohio Civil Rights Commn., 1972; active Dem. campaigns. U. Toledo fellow, 1967-69; recipient Citation, U. Toledo, 1979, Journalistic Excellence award Columbia Press Assn., N.Y.C., 1954. Mem. Am. Council Edn., Ohio Conf. Coll. and Univ. Planning, Soc. Coll. and Univ. Planning (com. 1984-85), Phi Theta Kappa, Phi Kappa Phi (Citation 1973), U. Toledo Alumni Assn., U.S. Coast Guard Aux. Lutheran. Avocations: fossil and mineral collecting, poetry, novel writing, horseback riding. Office: Lourdes Coll 6832 Convent Blvd Sylvania OH 43560-2891

HEWITT, CYNTHIA A., financial consultant, stockbroker; b. Chattanooga, May 29, 1951; d. Carl D. and Evelyn M. (Byrd) H.; m. C. Daniel Holloway, Dec. 21, 1974; 1 child, William Hewitt. BS, Vanderbilt U., 1973. Tchr. Tchr. Corp., Nashville, 1973-74; sales rep. Litton Industries, Wilmington, Del., 1974-76; fin. cons. Merrill Lynch, Wilmington, 1976—, tax investment specialist, 1982-84, adv. coun. to mgmt., 1989-91. Bd. dirs. Del. Guidance Svc., Wilmington, 1983-90; mem. Forum for Exec. Women, Wilmington, 1992—. Republican. Episcopalian. Home: PO Box 171 Yorklyn DE 19736 Office: Merrill Lynch 1201 Market St Ste 2000 Wilmington DE 19898

HEWITT, FRANKIE LEA, theater producer; b. Roger Mills Cty, Okla., June 17, 1931; d. Frank David and Mary Lou (Wood) Teague; m. Alonzo Robert Childers, Dec. 10, 1951 (div. 1955); m. Don S. Hewitt, June 8, 1963 (div. 1974); children: Jilian, Lisa. Grad., Napa (Calif.) High Sch., 1949. Women's editor Napa Daily Register, 1949-51; asst. advt. dir. Rose Marie Reid Swim Suits, L.A., 1951-52; writer Calif. Inst. Social Welfare, L.A., 1954-55; writer, legis. aide Nat. Inst. Social Welfare, Washington, 1956-58; staff dir. U.S. Senate Subcom. to Investigate Juvenile Deliquency, Washington, 1959-61; pub. affairs advisor U.S. Mission to UN, N.Y.C., 1961-63; founder, producing dir. Ford's Theatre Soc., Washington, 1967—. Recipient Congl. Arts Caucus award, 1993; named Washingtonian of Yr., Washingtonian Mag., 1978, Woman of Yr., Women's Equity Action League, 1981, YWCA, 1986. Office: Ford's Theatre 511 10th St NW Washington DC 20004-1499

HEWITT, MARIANNE SPERANDEO, business executive; b. Pitts., Sept. 21, 1951; d. Joseph Frank and Rosemary Margaret (Lodato) S.; m. David George Hewitt, June 20, 1984; children: Kristen Mary, Kelly Lynn. BS in Bus. magna cum laude, Robert Morris Coll., 1977; MBA, U. Pa., 1992. Statistical analyst Aluminum Co. Am., Pitts., 1977, systems analyst, programmer, 1977-78; EDP auditor Westinghouse Corp., Pitts., 1978-80; sr. EDP auditor Giant Food, Inc., Landover, Md., 1980-81; sr. tech. cons. Cullinet Software, Inc., Falls Church, Va., 1981-83; pres. The Wyndhurst Group, Columbia, Md., 1983-93; dir. strategic alliances Legent Corp., Herndon, Va., 1993; dir. strategy and planning Legent Corp., Herndon, 1993; asst. v.p. U.S. Fidelity & Guarantee Co., Balt., 1994—; chmn. exec. speaker com. Wharton Exec. MBA Program, Phila., 1990-92, exec. symposium Nat. IDMS Users Assn., Chgo., 1988-89. Chairperson planned giving Glenelg (Md.) Country Sch. Ann. Fund Com., 1993-94. Mem. Mid-Atlantic Planning Assn., The Wharton Club of Balt. Home: 10429 Kingsbridge Rd Ellicott City MD 21042 Office: US Fidelity & Guaranty Co 5801 Smith Ave Baltimore MD 21209

HEWITT, MAUREEN GILGORE, college textbook publishing executive; b. Waukegan, Ill., July 16, 1943; d. Rolland Robert Gilgore and Marguerite Annabelle Terrien McHale; m. Terry Ned Trobec, June 8, 1968 (div. Oct. 1983); children: Kerry Morgan Trobec, Justin John Trobec; m. John Douglas Hewitt, July 28, 1985. BA, Lake Forest (Ill.) Coll., 1966; MA, La. State U., 1971. Test adminstr. Abbott Labs., North Chicago, Ill., 1966-67; editor Rand McNally, Lincolnwood, Ill., 1967-69, La. State U. Press, Baton Rouge, 1969-72; freelance editor Libertyville, Ill., 1972-75; devel. editor AHM Pub. Co., Arlington Heights, Ill., 1975-78; mng. editor Harlan Davidson, Inc., Arlington Heights, Ill., 1978-84; editor-in-chief Harlan Davidson, Ic., Arlington Heights, Ill., 1984-86; v.p., editor-in-chief Harlan Davidson, Inc., Wheeling, Ill., 1986—; also bd. dirs. Harlan Davidson, Inc. Mem. mktg. com. Lake County LEARNS, Libertyville, 1992—. Mem. NOW (pres. Baton Rouge chpt. 1970, pres. Lake County chpt. 1972), women in Comms., Inc. (pres.-elect 1994-95, programming cons. North Shore chpt. 1993-94),

Chgo. Women in Pub. (chair mgr.'s roundtable, mem. bd. dirs. 1989-91, mem. exec. adv. bd. 1994—), Chgo. Book Clinic. Unitarian Universalist. Office: Harlan Davidson Inc 773 Glenn Ave Wheeling IL 60090

HEWITT, VIVIAN ANN DAVIDSON (MRS. JOHN HAMILTON HEWITT, JR.), librarian; b. New Castle, Pa.; d. Arthur Robert and Lela Luvada (Mauney) Davidson; m. John Hamilton Hewitt, Jr., Dec. 26, 1949; 1 son, John Hamilton III. AB with honors, Geneva Coll., 1943, LHD, 1978; BSLS, Carnegie Mellon U., 1944; postgrad., U. Pitts., 1947-48. Sr. asst. libr. Carnegie Libr., Pitts., 1944-49; instr., libr. Sch. Libr. Sci. Atlanta U., Atlanta U., 1949-52; with Readers Reference Svc., Crowell-Collier Pub. Co., N.Y.C., 1953-55; libr. Rockefeller Found., N.Y.C., 1955-63; librarian Carnegie Endowment Internat. Peace, N.Y.C., 1963-83; librarian Mexican Agrl. Program, Rockefeller Found., summer 1958; dir. libr. and info. svcs. Katherine Gibbs Sch., N.Y.C., 1984-86; reference asst. Coun. on Fgn. Rels., 1986-89; lectr. spl. librarianship at grad. schs. of L.S. and info. throughout U.S. and Can., 1968—; condr. profl. seminars Am. Mgmt. Assn., 1968-69, UN Inst. Tng. and Rsch., 1973, 74, Grad. Sci. Libr. and Info. Sci., Rutgers U., 1986; SLA rep. to Internat. Fedn. Libr. Assns., 1970-73, 73-75, 75-77; mem. nat. adv. com. Ctr. for the Book, Libr. of Congress, 1979-84. Contbr. chpt. to: The Black Librarian in America, 1970, What Black Librarians Are Saying, 1972, New Dimensions for Academic Library Service, 1975, A Century of Service, 1976, Handbook of Black Librarianship, 1977, The Black Librarian in America Revisited, 1994. Bd. dirs. Graham-Windham, 1967, sec., 1980-87; bd. dirs. Laymen's Club, Cathedral Ch. of St.John the Divine, 1975—, sec., 1986-93. Recipient Outstanding Cmty. Svc. awards United Fund N.Y., 1965-77, Disting. Alumna award U. Pitts.-Carnegie Libr. Schs. Alumni Assn., 1978, Merit award Carnegie Mellon U. Alumni Assn., 1979. Mem. ALA (Disting. Svc. to Librarianship award Black Caucus 1978, Leadership in Profession award Black Caucus 1992), Spl. Librs. Assn. (pres. N.Y. chpt. 1970-71, nat. pres. 1978-79, named to Hall of Fame, condr. seminar 1969, rep. to Pacem In Terris Convocation 1965, rep. to White House Conf. Internat. Cooperation Yr. 1965), Jack and Jill Am., Inc. (ea. regional dir. 1967-69), Alpha Kappa Alpha. Democrat. Episcopalian. Home: 862 W End Ave New York NY 10025-4959

HEWSON, MARY MCDONALD, civic volunteer; b. Larned, Kans., Nov. 5, 1922; d. William Michael and Bernice Ulata (Gregory) McDonald; m. Kenneth Dean Hewson, June 21, 1946; children: Rebecca Hewson Lewis, Roberta Hewson Grogan, Margaret Hewson Smith. BS in Edn. cum laude, Kans. State U., 1948, BS in Psychology, 1948. Cert. secondary edn. tchr. Freshman counselor Kans. State U., 1948-49; substitute tchr. Larned Unified Sch. Dist., 1958—, tchr. gifted program, 1988; at home tutor, 1938—. Trustee Kans. State U. Found., Manhattan, 1980—; mem. Kans. Farmers Union, McPherson, 1982—, Help Eliminate Abuse Locally, Larned, Kans., 1982—, Mental Health Assn., Larned, 1982—; spokesperson 8 counties Pawnee County Health Resource, Kans., 1992—, Ctrl. Kans. Environ. Resource Planning Group, 1992—. Recipient Medallion award Kans. State U., 1986, Nat. Vol. of Yr. award Coun. for Advancement and Support of Edn., 1983. Mem. AAUW (charter), DAR (officer), Kans. Press Women (life mem., patron ednl. support 1988), YMCA (bd. dirs.), Philanthropic Ednl. Orng., Kans. State U. Alumni Assn. (strategic planning com., student rels. com.), Phi Alpha Mu. Home: PO Box 102 Larned KS 67550

HEWSTON, MARY ANN, municipal official; b. Phila., Mar. 11, 1951; d. Lutell and Doshia Louise (Ford) Clark; children: Clinton Gregory Johnson, Tonya Nicole Hewston. AA, C.C. Balt., 1977; BBA, Temple U., 1982. Pers. analyst City of Phila., 1983-94, safety officer, 1994—. Treas. Norris Tenant Adv. Coun., Phila., 1982-86; mem. Neighborhood Watch Group, Phila., 1990-91. Mem. Internat. Pers. Mgmt. Assn. (chair program com. Phila. chpt. 1991-92, 94—, chair bus. adv. com. 1990-92, H.S. liaison for pers. dept. 1993-94). Democrat. Home: 6109 W Oxford St Philadelphia PA 19151-4541 Office: City of Philadelphia 1600 Arch St Flr 6 Philadelphia PA 19103-2028

HEXNER, LILA MAE, business consultant; b. Appleton, Wis., May 14; d. Harold George and Florence Esther (McCabe) Fird; m. Peter E. Hexner (div. 1986); children: Michael T., Holly A., Thomas S. BS in Edn., U. Wis., Madison; M.Phil.Ed., Boston Coll. (formerly Newton Coll. Sacred Heart); founder, dir. Women's adv., mem. adminstrn. Middlesex Community Coll., 1971-78, women's center, 1971-75, Widening Opportunity Research Center, 1975-78, founder, Div. Community Svcs., 1978; founder, Edn. for Commercialization div. No. Energy Corp., N.E. Regional Solar Energy Center Edn. Dept., Boston, 1978-82; owner The Cons. Exchange, Inc., 1982—; bd. dir. Video Research, Inc., Boston. mem. adv. com. Internat. Solar Renewable Energy Conf., 1981; chmn. Bus. Resource Ctr., Small Bus. Assn.; cons. in field. Mem. Mass. Adv. Council on Vocat. Tech. Edn., 1972-79; mem. Mass. Gov.'s Spl. Commn. on Youth Unemployment, 1978—; mem. exec. com. Mass. coordinating com. Internat. Women's Yr., 1978; patient advocate Brigham & Women's Hosp., Boston, 1990—; ombudsman Elder Svcs., Cambridge, Sommerville, Mass., 1990—. Recipient Disting. Service award Middlesex Community Coll., 1973; grants include Fund for Improvement Postsecondary Edn., 1976-78. Mem. Women in Solar Energy (nat. adv. bd. 1980-82), Boston Computer Soc., Small Bus. Assn. New Eng. (chmn. first bus. conf., bd. dirs. 1987-90), Research Mgmt. Assn. (bd. govs.), Profl. Coun. Avocations: theater, art. Home and Office: 105-1 Trowbridge Cambridge MA 02138

HEXT, KATHLEEN FLORENCE, regulatory compliance consultant; b. Bellingham, Wash., Oct. 7, 1941; d. Benjamin Byron and Sarah Debell (Youngquist) Gross.; m. George Ronald Hext, June 13, 1964 (div. 1972); m. William H. Lewis, Nov. 14, 1992. BA magna cum laude, Lewis & Clark Coll., Portland, Oreg., 1963; MA, Stanford U., 1964; MBA, UCLA, 1979. CPA; chartered bank auditor; cert. info. systems auditor. Chief exec. officer Internat. Lang. Ctr., Rome, 1970-77; sr. auditor Peat, Marwick, Mitchell & Co., L.A., 1979-81; mgr. fin. audit Lloyds Bank, L.A., 1981-83, mgr. EDP audit, 1983-85; dir. corp. audit First Interstate Bancorp, L.A., 1985-89, sr. v.p., gen. auditor, 1989-91, sr. v.p., chief compliance officer, 1991-94; compliance cons. Proactive, Inc., 1993—; treas., Arcadia H.O. Assoc., El Monte, Calif., 1982-84, 86-88, pres., 1985. Recipient Edward W. Carter award UCLA, 1979. Mem. AICPA, Calif. Soc. CPA. Republican. Avocations: photography, microcomputers, reading. Home and Office: Proactive Inc 1226 Upland Hills Dr S Upland CA 91786-9173

HEY, NANCY HENSON, educational administrator; b. Cleve., Apr. 1, 1935; d. Henry Brumback Henson and Isabelle (Smock) Selverstone; m. Robert Pierpont Hey, July 4, 1959; 1 child, Julie Dean. AB, Bates Coll., 1957; MS in Edn., Bank St. Coll. of Edn., 1961. Cert. advanced profl. in early childhood nursery thru grade 3, Md. 1st grade tchr. Concord (Mass.) Pub. Schs., 1958-59; tchr. The Potomac Sch., McLean, Va., 1959-60, Galloway Sch., Atlanta, 1968-69; head tchr. Beauvoir Sch. Nursery Dept., Washington, 1969-70; supr. student tchrs. U. Md. Coll. of Edn., College Park, 1973-76, Tufts U., Medford, Mass., 1978-79; head tchr. Newton Ctr. (Mass.) Day Care Ctr., 1980-81, Community Child Devel. Ctr., Peabody, Mass., 1981-82; dir. Greater Lawrence (Mass.) YWCA Children's Ctr., 1982-86; tchr. Prince George's County (Md.) Pub. Schs., 1986-88; dir. Child Devel. Ctr., Fed. Trade Commn., Washington, 1988-92, Chevy Chase Plaza Children's Ctr., Washington, 1992-93; specialist/adminstr. in early childhood Ctr. for Young Children, U. Md., 1994—; supr. student tchrs. Simmons Coll., Boston, 1965-67; teaching asst. to head of lower sch.Shady Hill Sch., Cambridge, Mass., 1960-61; mem. task force com. Region III Dept. of Social Svcs., Middleton, Mass., 1984-86; bd. dirs. Greater Lawrence Coun. for Children, 1984-86. Mem. Nat. Assn. for Edn. of Young Children, World Org. Early Childhood Edn., Congl. and Fed. Child Care Dirs. Assn. (sec. 1990-92), Dirs. Exch. Home: 10908 Candlelight Ln Potomac MD 20854 Office: U Md Ctr for Young Children Valley Dr College Park MD 20742

HEYCK, GERTRUDE PAINE DALY, social club administrator; b. Houston, Nov. 30, 1910; d. David and Gertrude (Paine) Daly; m. Theodore R. Heyck, May 1, 1935; children: Jane Peel (Mrs. Donald H. Gaucher), Theodore Daly. Student, Wellesley Coll., 1929; BA, Brown U., 1934. Bd. dirs. Union Stock Yards, San Antonio, 1961-64. Mem. Jr. League. Clubs: Wellesley, Brown-Pembroke (v.p. 1950-60), Brown (Houston); Brown Faculty (Providence). Home: 1907 Bolsover St Houston TX 77005-1613

HEYDE, MARTHA BENNETT (MRS. ERNEST R. HEYDE), psychologist; b. New Bern, N.C., Jan. 31, 1920; d. George Spotswood and Katherine (McIntosh) Bennett; AB, Barnard Coll., 1941; MA, Columbia, 1949, PhD, 1959; m. Ernest R. Heyde, Aug. 17, 1946. Instr. psychol. founds. and services Tchrs. Coll., Columbia U., N.Y.C., 1953-60, research asst., career pattern study Horace Mann-Lincoln Inst., Tchrs. Coll. Columbia U., 1957-59, research assoc., 1960-70, cons., 1970-73. Mem. Barnard Coll. Alumnae Council, 1956-61, 69—, pres. class, 1956-61. Trustee, Barnard Coll., 1974-78, hon. vice-chmn. Barnard Coll. Centennial, 1987-89. Mem. Am. Psychol. Assn., Am. Personnel and Guidance Assn., Sigma Xi, Kappa Delta Pi, Pi Lambda Theta. Contbr. to research monograph The Vocational Maturity of Ninth Grade Boys, 1960, Floundering and Trial After High Sch, 1967; coauthor: Vocational Maturity During the High School Years, 1979. Home: 530 E 23rd St Apt 8E New York NY 10010-5030

HEYDE, NORMA LEE, singer, music educator; b. Herrin, Ill., Dec. 31, 1927; d. Charles LaRue and Callie (Logan) Swinney; m. John Bradley Heyde, Aug. 24, 1947. MusB, U. Mich., 1949, MusM, 1950; grad. cert. in lieder and oratorio, Mozarteum, Salzburg, Austria, 1956. Mem. voice faculty U. Mich. Sch. Music, Ann Arbor, 1950-54, Eastern Mich. U., Ypsilanti, 1954-57, York Coll. Pa., 1969; artist and tchr. in residence Transylvania Music Camp, Brevard, N.C., 1950-54; assoc. prof. music Salisbury (Md.) State U., 1971-87; dir. music 1st Presbyn. Ch., Milford, Del., 1958-66; artist, tchr. Franklin and Marshall Coll., Lancaster, Pa., 1988—; soprano artist various orchs. and choral socs. Nat. Gallery of Art, Washington, 1950-88. Benefit recitalist Meml. Hosp., Civic Ctr., Marion, Ill., Milford Libr., York Symphony Assn., 1960-90, Habitat for Humanity Project, York, Pa., 1993. Oliver Ditson scholar U. Mich., 1946-50, James L. Babcock scholar, 1946-50. Mem. Nat. Assn. Tchrs. Singing, Music Tchrs. Nat. Assn. (adjudicator music competitions), Music Educators Nat. Conf., AAUP, PEO, Phi Kappa Phi (emeritus life), Pi Kappa Lambda, Mu Phi Epsilon. Home: 940 Clubhouse Rd PO Box 2365 York PA 17405

HEYEN, BEATRICE J., psychotherapist; b. Chgo., June 23, 1925; d. Carl Edwin and Anna W. (Carlson) Lund; m. Robert D. Heyen, June 16, 1950 (dec. Feb. 1981); children: Robin, Jefferson, Neil; m. Robert Christiansen, Nov. 24, 1984. BS, U. Chgo., 1949. Instr. Boone (Iowa) Jr. Coll., 1959-64, Rochester (Minn.) Jr. Coll., 1967-68, Winona (Minn.) State Coll., 1965-68; dir. social svc. State Clinic, Kirksville, Mo., 1968-71; supr., dir. Family Counseling Agy., Joliet, Ill., 1971-85; pvt. practice Muskegon, Mich., 1985—; cons. Homes for Aged, Programs for Aged, Winona, 1965-68, Spl. Programs and Individuals in Psychotherapy, Muskegon, 1984—; dir. Christiansen Fine Art Gallery, North Muskegon. Mem. Gov.'s Com. on Status of Women, Iowa, 1957-62, Gov.'s Com. on Aging, Minn., 1966-68. Grantee for Pilot Projects in Svc. to Women 1971-84. Mem. NASW, Acad. Cert. Social Workers, C.G. Jung Inst. (Chgo.). Methodist. Home: 1610 N Weber Rd Muskegon MI 49445-9629

HEYER, ANNA HARRIET, retired music librarian; b. Little Rock, Aug. 30, 1909; d. Arthur Wesley and Harriet Anna (Gage) H. A.B., B.Mus., Tex. Christian U., 1930; B.S. in L.S., U. Ill., 1933; M.S. in L.S., Columbia U., 1939; M.Mus. in Musicology, U. Mich., 1943. Elem. sch. music tchr. Ft. Worth Pub. Schs., 1931-32; high sch. librarian, 1934-38; cataloguer library, U. Tex.-Austin, 1939-40; music librarian, asst. prof. L.S., N. Tex. State U. (name now U. N. Tex.), Denton, 1940-65, librarian emeritus, 1976; cons. music library materials Tex. Christian U., Ft. Worth, 1965-79; ret., 1979. Author: A Check-List of Publications of Music, 1944; A Bibliography of Contemporary Music in the Music Library, North Texas State College, 1955; Historical Sets, Collected Editions and Monuments of Music: A Guide to Their Contents, 1957, 2d edit., 1969, 3d rev. edit., 1980; contbr. articles to profl. publs. Recipient citations for contbn. to music librarianship Music Library Assn., 1980, to music librarianship in Tex., 1983. Mem. ALA, Tex. Library Assn., Music Library Assn., AAUW, DAR. Mem. Disciples of Christ Ch. Clubs: Altrusa, Woman's Club Ft. Worth, Colonial Country. Home: 5334 Premier Ct Fort Worth TX 76132-4016

HEYLIGER, JOYCE THOMAS, nursing administrator; b. St. Thomas, V.I., July 23, 1942; d. Edward Nathaniel and Jennie Belsina (Rabsatt) Thomas; m. Anselmo R. Heyliger, Sept. 16, 1967; children: Riva Jeannette, Anselmo R. Jr. Diploma, St. Luke's Episcopal Sch., Ponce, P.R., 1962; BS in Nursing, Mich. State U., East Lansing, 1967; MS in Nursing, Boston U., 1975; MPH, San Diego State U., 1989. Cert. nurse adminstr. Staff and pub. health nurse V.I. Dept. Health, St. Croix, 1962-67, nurse supr., 1967-78, nurse cons., 1978-80, assoc. dir. nursing, 1980-90, chmn. nursing, 1990—, rsch. nurse, 1991—; cons., policy bd. mem. Head Start Program; clin. isntr. U. V.I. Recipient Pub. Health Nurse Leadership award, 1989; grantee Maternal-Child Health Implement Program. Mem. ANA, Am. Nurses Credientialing Ctr. (nursing adminstrn. test devel. com.), Fed. Health Cons., V.I. Nurses Assn., Beta Sigma Nu. Home: PO Box 272 Frederiksted Saint Croix VI 00841

HEYMAN, INA HELENE, writer; b. N.Y.C., Oct. 22, 1932; d. William Howard and Mary (Schwartz) Friedelson; m. Edward Irvin Heyman, Nov. 25, 1970. BA, Hunter Coll., 1953. Adminstrv. asst. Office of the Mayor, N.Y.C., 1954-59; pub. rels. Tex McCrary Inc., N.Y.C., 1959-61; freelance pub. rels. N.Y.C., Boston, 1961-63; pub. rels. AFSCME, N.Y.C., Wash., 1963-65; pub. info. officer U.S. Dept. Health & Human Svcs., Wash., 1966-94; freelance writer, editor, 1994—; project officer Nat. Ctr. Edn. in Maternal and Child Health, Alexandria, Va., 1988-93; planning com. Child Health Day, Wash., 1988-93. Editor: Infant Care, 1989, Health Diary, 1993; contbr. chpts. to books. Recipient spl. award Nat. Healthy Mothers, Healthy Babies Coalition, Wash., 1993. Home and Office: 2712 Bel Pre Rd Silver Spring MD 20906-2314

HEYMOSS, JENNIFER MARIE, librarian; b. Detroit, Apr. 14, 1958; d. John Joseph and Virginia Marie (Kern) H. BA in English and German, Wayne State U., 1980, MS in Libr. Sci., 1981. Libr. asst. Wayne State U. Librs., Detroit, 1982-83; asst. libr. Plunkett & Cooney, Detroit, 1983-86, Henry Ford Mus. & Greenfield Village Rsch. Ctr., Dearborn, Mich., 1986-90; libr. Henry Ford Mus. & Greenfield Village Rsch. Ctr., Dearborn, 1990-92; asst. head tch. svcs. Flint (Mich.) Pub. Libr., 1992—. Literacy vol., 1987—. Mem. ALA, Spl. Librs. Assn. (various coms. 1988—), Mich. Libr. Assn., Pub. Librs. Assn., Phi Beta Kappa, Beta Phi Mu. Democrat. Methodist. Office: Flint Pub Libr 1026 E Kearsley Flint MI 48502

HEYN, ELA FREDERICA, executive assistant; b. Bloomington, Ind., May 12, 1966; d. Udo Eberhard Gunnar and Ela (Tkacz) H. BBA, James Madison U., 1990; postgrad., U. Phoenix, San Francisco, 1993-95. Mktg. rschr. Smithsonian Mag., N.Y.C., 1990-91; asst. to v.p. Guest Informant, N.Y.C., 1991-92, The Conf. Bd., N.Y.C., 1992—. Author, reviewer PCM Mag., 1991—. With U.S. Army, 1984-87. Mem. Mensa. Republican. Roman Catholic. Office: The Conference Board 845 3rd Ave New York NY 10022-6601

HEYNE, GRACE LORRAINE, financial consultant; b. San Marino, Calif., Nov. 12, 1931; d. Wilber Cover and Grace Bertha (Hadley) Thomas; divorced; children: David Richard Baker, Joanne Lorraine Baker Deal, Carolyn Jean Baker; m. Milton William Heyne, July 22, 1982; stepchildren: Katie Heyne Caulk, James, Linda, Rebecca Heyne Pfeiffer, John. BS, UCLA, 1953, cert. in personal fin. planning, 1984; MS, U. So. Calif., 1963. Cert. fin. planner; chartered fin. cons.; CLU; lic. stockbroker, real estate broker, ins. agt., notary pub.; enrolled agent IRS; registered fin. cons. Pres. Grace Heyne Fin. Group, San Pedro, Calif., 1987-89, Fin. Design Adv. Svcs., San Pedro, 1987-89; broker/dealer First Fin. Planners, Inc., Torrance, Calif., 1993—. Mem. San Pedro Bay Hist. Soc., 1984—, rec. sec., 1988-90; mem. Las Angelenas Vol. Corps to City Govt., L.A., 1983—. Mem. Am. Bus. Women's Assn. (sec. Peninsula chpt. 1985-88), Am. Soc. CLUs and Chartered Fin. Cons. (mem. chmn. Harbor chpt. 1990—, program chmn. 1991—), Internat. Assn. Registered Fin. Cons., Inc., Bus. and Profl. Women (rec. sec. San Pedro chpt. 1982—, Woman of Achievement award 1988, pres. 1992-93), Nat. Assistance League (profl. mem. San Pedro-Palos Verdes chpt. 1993—), Women's Guild San Pedro-Peninsula Hosp., Exch. Club (Torrance chpt. sec. 1988-90), Delta Kappa Gamma (pres. Alpha Beta chpt. 1986-88), Pi Lambda Theta (v.p. local chpt., treas., corr. sec. 1983—, mem. nat. investment com. 1986-92), Sigma Kappa (South Bay alumnae chpt. 1984—). Republican. Lutheran. Office: First Financial Planners Ste 101 3868 Carson St Torrance CA 90503

HEYREND, PATRICIA MAY, marriage and family therapist; b. N.Y.C., Aug. 27, 1940; d. Arthur Owen and Violet Agnes (Colvin) Williams; m. Leonard Gerald Rightmeier Jr., Aug. 27, 1962 (div. Jan. 1975); children: Larry Brent, Mona Rochelle; m. F. LaMarr Heyrend, June 30, 1979. BSW, U. Kans., 1962; MSW, U. Utah, 1977. Cert. social worker. Caseworker Dept. Pub. Assistance, Payette, Idaho, 1965-71; developer, operator Group Home and Shelter Home, 1971-75; social work cons. child protection-youth rehab. units Region IV, Dept. Health and Welfare, 1977-81; pvt. practice social work Boise, Idaho, 1986—; staff coord. Parents United, 1983-86; instr. Boise State U. Sch. Social Work, 1985, 87-88; supr. child protection and adoption svcs. Region IV, Idaho Dept. Health and Welfare, 1981-86; pvt. practice part-time, Boise, 1977-86. Mem. Ada County Med. Soc. Aux., Boise, 1990—. Recipient Outstanding Leadership award HHS, Idaho, 1985. Mem. NASW (Social Worker of Yr. Idaho Central chpt. 1985). Office: 321 Allumbaugh St Boise ID 83704-9208

HIAPO, PATRICIA KAMAKA, lay worker; b. Honolulu, May 18, 1943; d. Ward Charles and Violet Kaopua (Nicholas) McKeown; m. Bernard Joseph Hiapo, July 9, 1960; children: Bernard Jr., Beatrice, Jacqueline, Mary-Louise. Grad. high sch., Honolulu. Cert. catechist, 1988. Area del. St. John Apostle and Evangelist, Mililani, Hawaii, 1981-84; eucharistic min. St. John Apostle and Evangelist, Mililani, 1981-88; hospice and bereavement ministry St. Francis Hosp., Honolulu, 1983, eucharistic min., 1983-88; religious edn. coord. Resurrection of The Lord, Waipahu, Hawaii, 1984-88; dir. religious edn. St. Jude, Ewa Beach, Hawaii, 1988-91; home visitor Hana Like, Honolulu, 1990—; mem. marriage encounter team Cath. Ch., Honolulu, 1981-83. Recipient award Our Lady of Peace, 1991. Office: St Jude 92-104 Leipapa Way Ewa Beach HI 96707-1342 also: Parents and Children Together-Hana Like 45-955 Kamehameha Hwy Ste 404 Kaneohe HI 96744-3222

HIATT, JANE CRATER, arts agency administrator; b. Winston-Salem, N.C., May 26, 1944; d. Howard Rondthaler Jr. and Irene (Sides) Crater; m. K.W. Everhart Jr. (div. June 1973); m. Wood Coleman Hiatt, May, 1978; 1 child, Jonathan David. BA, U. N.C., 1966; MA, Wake Forest U., 1972. Eng. tchr. Winston-Salem (N.C.)/Forsyth County Schs., 1966-70; exec. dir. Tenn. Com. for the Humanities, Nashville, 1973-77; cons. various ednl. and cultural agys. Ocean Springs, Miss., 1978-80; asst. dir. Miss. Humanities Coun., Jackson, Miss., 1981-85; exec. dir. Arts Alliance of Jackson and Hinds County, Miss., 1985-89, Miss. Arts Commn., Jackson, 1989—; participant Arts Leadership Inst. of Humphrey Inst. for Pub. Affairs, Mpls., 1986, Leadership, Jackson, 1987. Co-editor Peoples of the South, 1976; exec. producer (TV series) The South with John Siegenthaler, 1976; host, reporter Miss. Ednl. TV, Jackson, 1981-87. Mem. Miss. Econ. Coun., 1986-87, Miss. R & D Coun., 1984-88; pres. Mental Health Assn. of Hinds County, Jackson, 1986; treas. Miss. Inst. for Ednl. Broadcasting, 1987, 88, 89, Premier Class Leadership, Jackson, 1987, 88. Recipient Heritage award City of Biloxi, 1984. Mem. Nat. Assembly of Local Arts Agys., Nat. Coun. on Arts, Nat. Assembly State Arts Agys. (bd. dirs. 1992-95), So. Arts Fedn. (bd. dirs. 1989—), Jackson C. of C., Phi Beta Kappa. Home: 507 Roses Bluff Dr Madison MS 39110 Office: Miss Arts Commn 239 N Lamar St Ste 207 Jackson MS 39201-1311

HIATT, MARJORIE MCCULLOUGH, service organization executive; b. Cin., July 12, 1923; d. Robert Stedman and Mildred (Rogers) McCullough; m. Homer E. Lunken, Apr. 15, 1944 (dec. 1970); children: Karen (dec. 1948), Kathryn Lunken Summers, Margo Lunken Yesner; m. William McLeod Ittmann, Mar. 17, 1972 (dec. 1982); m. Harold Hiatt, Apr. 14, 1984. Student, U. Cin., 1941-43. Active Girl Scouts U.S., 1962—, chmn. conv. com., 1972, del. world convs., 1969, 72, 75, 78, 81, 84, 87, 93, chmn. pub. relations com., 1963-66, mem. nat. exec. com., 1963-75, mem. nat. bd., 1962—, 4th v.p., 1966-69, 1st v.p., 1969-72, nat. pres., 1972-75, chmn. nat. adv. council, 1975-82, mem. birthplace adv. com., 1980—; vice chmn. world conf., Orleans, France, 1981; mem. world com. World Assn. Girl Guides and Girl Scouts, 1978-87, vice chmn., 1984-87. Regional dir. Assn. Jr. Leagues Am., 1958-60, nat. pres., 1960-62; mem. br. Jr. League Cin., 1944-58, Nat. Tng. Labs., 1963-66, Nat. Assembly for Social Policy and Devel., 1968-71; mem. exec. com. Council Nat. Orgns. for Children and Youth, 1960-62, 68-72; bd. dirs. United Way Am., 1962-67, sec., 1965-66, v.p., 1966-67, 1989—; mem. policy com. Center Vol. Soc., 1971-72; bd. dirs. Coll. Prep. Sch., Cin., 1962-69, pres., 1964-69; bd. dirs. Cin. Speech and Hearing Center, 1955-66, v.p., 1958-62, pres., 1963-66, trustee emeritus, 1966—; mem. bd. Children's Theatre, Cin., 1948-58, pres., 1948-50; bd. dirs. Community Health and Welfare Council Cin., 1957-63, Hamilton County (Ohio) Research Found., 1963-65, Cancer Family Care, Cin., 1971-72, Boys Clubs Greater Cin., Marjorie P. Lee Home for Aged, Music Hall Assn., Cin. Symphony Orch.; bd. dirs. Beechwood Home for Incurables, 1975-87; bd. dirs. St. Margaret Hall, 1991—, Cin. Civic Garden Ctr., 1992—; mem. Ohio Citizens Council, 1956-58; mem. bd. 7th Presbyterian Ch., 1967-74, 85—, ruling elder, 1976-78, 95—, chmn. bd. trustees, 1992-94; sr. warden St. Martin's in the Field, Biddeford Pool, Maine; bd. dirs. Greater Cin. Found., 1979-87; bd. dirs. U. Cin. Found., 1979—, pres. 1986-88, vice chmn. 1988—, trustee emeritus, 1993—; pres. Garden Club Cin., 1984-86, co-chmn. zone X meeting, 1989, zone X chmn. pub.; bd. dirs. Friends Cin. Parks, 1987—, corr. sec., 1989-92; trustee Cin. Assn. Performing Arts, Inc.; founding bd. dirs. Emery Soc. Children's Hosp; mem. Cin. Parks Found., 1995—. Mem. Olive Baden Powell soc. (v.p. 1991-93, pres. 1993—), World Found. for Girl Guides and Girl Scouts (v.p. 1989—), Garden Club Am. (vice chmn. founder's fund 1991-92), Am. Psychiat. Assn. Aux. (bd. dirs., recording sec. 1991-92). Home: 2353 Bedford Ave Cincinnati OH 45208-2656

HIATT, NANCY ELIZABETH, auditor; b. Boston, Apr. 25, 1963; d. Robert Mark and Alice Theresa (Walsh) Hiatt. BS in Mgmt., U. Mass., 1985; MBA cum laude, Babson Coll., 1994. Cert. mgmt. acct., acquisition profl. Fin. auditor medicaid divsn. Dept. Pub. Welfare, Boston, 1986; sr. auditor Def. Contract Audit Agy., Lexington, Mass., 1986—. Mem. Am. Compensation Assn., Inst. Mgmt. Accts. Office: Def Contract Audit Agy 83 Hartwell Ave Lexington MA 02173

HIBBEN, BARBARA ANN PANDZIK, museum administrator, foreign service officer; b. North Island, Calif., Sept. 22, 1943; d. George Richard and Marguerite Elizabeth (Holzenberg) Pandzik; m. Stuart Galloway Hibben, May 29, 1994; children by previous marriage: Jessica Marguerite Hadley, Amanda Marie, Cara Elizabeth. BA, U. Nebr., 1965; postgrad., Yale U., 1966-67; MFA in Painting, George Washington U., 1980. Asst. to dir. The Phillips Collection, Washington, 1983-86, exec. asst. to dir., 1986-93; fgn. svc. officer U.S. Dept. State, Washington, 1993—. Artist paintings and drawings in numerous pvt. collections. Birdwatcher Md. Ornithol. Soc., Bethesda, 1990-93. Woodrow Wilson fellow, 1965-66. Mem. Diplomatic and Consular Officers Retired (assoc.), Phi Beta Kappa. Home: Rt 1 Box 711-I Accokeek MD 20607 Office: Am Embassy Cairo Unit 64900 Box 7 APO AE 09839-4900

HICKERSON, MELINDA KAY, dietitian; b. Enid, Okla., Sept. 26, 1949; d. Walter Don and Virginia Louise (Shepherd) Martin; m. Willie Wayne Hickerson, Apr. 24, 1981 (div. May 1985); 1 child, Hayley Martin. BA, Washburn U., 1974; MS, Kans. State U., 1989; cert. team leadership and quality mgmt., Kans. U., 1991. Registered dietitian Commn. on Dietetic Registration, Am. Dietetic Assn.; lic. dietitian Kans. Health Occupation Credentialing. Dietary technician/supr. Dr.'s Hosp., Little Rock, 1975-76; dir. dept. dietetics Rebsamen Regional Med. Ctr., Jacksonville, Ark., 1977-85, Coffeyville (Kans.) Regional Med. Ctr., 1989-90, Lawrence (Kans.) Meml. Hosp., 1990—; team leader continuous quality improvement nursing function study Lawrence Meml. Hosp., 1991—; counselor/cons. nutrition Family Med. Clinic, Cabot, Ark., 1980-85, Weber Med. Clinic, Jacksonville, 1979-85; sec. continuous quality improvement dirs. com. Lawrence Meml. Hosp., 1991-92; compiler physician's diet manual Rebsamen Regional Med. Ctr., 1980. Recipient Good Citizenship award U.S. Census Bur., Manhattan, Kans., 1987. Mem. Am. Dietetic Assn., Kans. Dietetic Assn., Delta Gamma Alumnae. Republican. Methodist. Office: Lawrence Meml Hosp 325 Maine St Lawrence KS 66044-1393

HICKERSON, PATRICIA PARSONS, military officer; b. Louisville, Sept. 15, 1942; d. John Millard and Rose (Brill) Parsons; m. Dennis Fogarty, Dec. 18, 1974. MusB, Converse Coll., 1964, MusM, 1966; student, Women's Army Corps Officer Basic Course, 1968, Infantry Officer Advanced Course, 1973, U.S. Army Command and General Staff Coll., 1978, Nat. War Coll., 1986-87; D of Pub. Svc., Converse Coll., 1989. 1st lt. U.S. Army, 1968, advanced through grades to Brig. Gen., 1991; asst. manpower control officer to manpower control officer Manpower Control Divsn., Military Dist. Washington, 1968-69; comdr., 14th Army Band U.S. Women's Army Corps. Ctr., Ft. McClellan, Ala., 1970-72; br. advisor Combat Svc. Support Br., Readiness Group Atlanta, Ft. Gillem, Ga., 1973-75; admissions officer U.S. Military Acad., West Point, N.Y., 1975-77; personnel mgmt. officer U.S. Army Military Personnel Ctr., 8th U.S. Army, Korea, 1978-79; deputy G-1 (personnel) 2d infantry divsn. Korea, 1979-80; pers. staff officer, assignment procedures office U.S. Army Mil. Pers. Ctr., Alexandria, Va., 1980-82; mil. asst. Office of Asst. Sec. of Army for Manpower & Res. Affairs, Washington, 1982-83; chief pers. actions div. VII Corps-U.S. Army, Europe, 1984; commdr. 38th Pers. and Adminstrn. Battalion, VII Corps-U.S. Army, Europe, 1984-86; adminstrv. asst. to chmn. of joint chiefs of staff Office of the Joint Chiefs of Staff, Washington, 1987-89; commdr. ctrl. sector U.S. Mil. Entrance Processing Command, North Chicago, Ill., 1989-91; adj. gen. U.S. Total Army Pers. Command, Alexandria, 1991—; commdr. U.S. Army Phys. Disability Agy., Alexandria, 1991—; dir. Pentagon Fed. Credit Union, 1992-94. Decorated Def. Superior Svc. medal with one oak leaf cluster, Legion of Merit, Meritorious Svc. medal with four oak leaf clusters, Army Commendation medal, Joint Chief of Staff Identification badge, Army Gen. Staff Identification badge, Order of the Horatio Gates Gold medal. Mem. Andrews Air Force Golf Club. Home: 9052 Gavelwood Ct Springfield VA 22153-1125 Office: Office of the Adjutant Gen Dept of the Army Hoffman I Bldg 1 Alexandria VA 22331-0001

HICKEY, DELINA ROSE, educator; b. N.Y.C., Mar. 25, 1941; d. Robert Joseph and Marie (Ripa) H.; m. David Andrews, 1 child by previous marriage, Jon Robert. B.S. in Edn., SUNY, Oneonta, 1963; M.A., Manhattan Coll., 1967; Ed.D. in Counselor Edn. and Psychology, U. Idaho, 1971. Elem. sch. tchr., counselor, Westchester, N.Y., 1963-68; part-time instr. psychology St. Thomas Aquinas Coll., Sparkhill, N.Y., 1971-72; asst. prof. edn. Nathaniel Hawthorne Coll., Antrim, N.H., 1972-75; prof. faculty Keene (N.H.) State Coll., 1975—, assoc. prof. edn., 1978—, prof. edn., coordinator faculty, 1987—; interim dean profl. studies 1987; mem. N.H. Legislature from 13th Dist., 1981-85; mem. adv. council Title IV, 1979-82; fellow Nat. Ctr. Research in Vocat. Edn., 1984-85; assoc. in edn. Harvard U., 1984-85; interim v.p. student affairs Keene State U., 1990, apptd. v.p. student affairs, 1991. Trustee, Big Bros./Big Sisters, Keene, 1978-80, Family Planning Services S.W. N.H., 1976-85, Monadnock Hospice, 1994—; mem. N.H. Juvenile Conf. Com., 1976-81; pres. bd. dirs. CHESCO. Mem. Nat. Assn. Student Pers. Adminstrs. (adv. com. region I), N.H. Order Women Legislators, New Eng. Research Orgn., Am. Vocat. Assn., N.H. Pers. and Guidance Assn., New Eng. Assn. of Tchrs. and Educators. Democrat. Author articles in edns. Office: Hale Bldg Keene NH 03431

HICKEY, EILEEN MCKENNA, state legislator; b. Poughkeepsie, N.Y., July 7, 1945; d. Ruth and Peter McKenna; m. Dan Hickey, 1966; 1 child, Dan, Jr. Grad., White Plains Hosp. Sch. Nursing, 1966. RN, N.Y. Owner, operator Bagel Bin, Poughkeepsie, 1979-86; mem. 1 term Dutchess County Legislature; dir. Hudson Valley regional office speaker Mel Miller, 1982; mem. N.Y. State Assembly. Creator Mid-Hudson Vietnam Vets. Outreach Ctr.; active vets. self-help project Greenhaven Correctional Facility; vol. Am. Cancer Soc., Am. Heart Assn., Ralph R. Smith Elem., Hyde Park Rowing Assn., Jr. League, Our Lady Mt. Carmel Ch.; past pres. LWV; co-founder Dutchess County Coun. for Women. Co-recipient Pres.' award Marist Coll., 1989. Office: NY State Assembly State Capitol Albany NY 12224*

HICKEY, KATE DONNELLY, college library director; b. Durham, N.C., Dec. 29, 1943; d. Frederick Stockham Jr. and Margaret Frances (Dougherty) Donnelly; m. Robert James Hickey Jr., Dec. 21, 1963; children: Robert James III, Marian Margaret. BA, Swarthmore Coll., 1966; MS Libr. Sci., Clarion U., 1982. Children's libr. Green Free Libr., Wellsboro, Pa., 1973-76; libr. U.S. Fish & Wildlife Svc., Wellsboro, 1976-83; reference libr. Williamsport (Pa.) Area Community Coll., 1983-84; dir. of the coll. libr. Pa. Coll. Tech. (formerly Williamsport Area Community Coll.), Williamsport, 1984—; elected sec. Interlibr. Delivery Svc. of Pa. Bd., State College, Pa., 1990—; chair, sec.-treas. Susquehanna Libr. Coop., Williamsport, 1986-90. Contbr. articles and book revs. to profl. publs. Pres., bd. dirs. Mansfield (Pa.) Coop. Nursery Sch., 1969-73, Twin Tiers Regional Sci. Fair, Inc., Wellsboro, 1981-84. Mem. ALA, Pa. Libr. Assn. (sec. coll. and rsch. librs. bd. dirs. 1988-91), Coun. Pa. Libr. Networks (chairperson 1991-93), Beta Phi Mu. Home: 403 W 8th Ave Williamsport PA 17701-7536 Office: Pa Coll Tech 1 College Ave Williamsport PA 17701-5799

HICKEY, WINIFRED E(SPY), former state senator, social worker; b. Rawlins, Wyo.; d. David P. and Eugenia (Blake) Espy; children: John David, Paul Joseph. BA, Loretto Heights Coll., 1933; postgrad. U. Utah, 1934, Sch. Social Service, U. Chgo., 1936; LLD (hon.) U. Wyo., 1991. Dir. Carbon County Welfare Dept., 1935-36; field rep. Wyo. Dept. Welfare, 1937-38; dir. Red Cross Club, Europe, 1942-45; commr. Laramie County, Wyo., 1973-80; mem. Wyo. Senate, 1980-90; dir. United Savs. & Loan, Cheyenne; active Joint Powers Bd. Laramie County and City of Cheyenne. Pub. Where the Deer and the Antelope Play, 1967. Pres., bd. dirs. U. Wyo. Found., 1986-87; pres. Meml. Hosp. of Laramie County, 1986-88, Wyo. Transp. Mus., 1990-92; chmn. adv. council div. community programs Wyo. Dept. Health and Social Services; pres. county and state mental health assn., 1959-63; trustee, U. Wyo., 1967-71, St. Mary's Cathedral, 1986—; active Nat. Council Cath. Women, Gov. Residence Found., 1991—, Wyo. Transp. Mus., 1993—; chair Am. Heritage Assocs. of U. Wyo., 1992—. Named Outstanding Alumna, Loretto Heights Coll., 1959, Woman of Yr. Commn. for Women, 1988, Legislator of Yr. Wyo. Psychologists Assn., 1988. Mem. Altrusa Club (Cheyenne).

HICKMAN, ELIZABETH PODESTA, retired counselor, educator; b. Livingston, Ill., Sept. 30, 1922; d. Louis and Della (Martin) Podesta; BE summa cum laude, Eastern Ill. State U.; MA, George Washington U., 1966; postgrad. U. Chgo., 1945, U. Va., 1964-66, (fellow) Northeastern U., 1967-68; EdD (Exxon Found. grantee, Raskob Found. grantee), George Washington U., 1979; m. Franklin Jay Hickman, Mar. 17, 1944 (dec.); children—Virginia Hickman Hellstern, Franklin. Tchr. public schs., Ill., Ohio, Va., Naples, Italy, 1944-64; dir. coll. transfer guidance Marymount Coll. of Va., Arlington, 1964-67, dir. Counseling Center, 1974-81, assoc. dean counseling and residence life, 1981-84; community counselor div. Mass. Employment Security, Newton, 1968-69; tchr. English conversation, Fuchu, Japan, 1969-73; placement dir., career counselor Coll. Great Falls (Mont.), 1973-74; assoc. researcher George Washington U., 1986; lectr. Far East di v. U. Md., Fuchu, 1971-73; spl. adv. Internat. Ranger Camps, Denmark and Switzerland, 1974-81; spl. cons. Internat. Quaker Sch., Wekhoven, Netherlands, 1959-63; mem. steering com. Pres.'s Com. on Employment of Handicapped, 1975—. Vol., ARC, 1967-78, Family Services, 1954-75, White House Agy. Liaison, 1986—, Kennedy Ctr. Adminstrn., Washington, 1984—. Served with WAVES, 1943-44. Recipient Disting. Alumnus award Eastern Ill. U., 1984. Lic. counselor, Va. Mem. Am. Personnel and Guidance Assn., Nat. Assn. Women Deans, Adminstrs. and Counselors (liaison to president's com.), Nat. Vocat. Guidance Assn., Am. Coll. Personnel Assn., No. Va. Counselors Assn., Delta Epsilon Sigma, Pi Lambda Theta. Roman Catholic. Home: 4708 38th Pl N Arlington VA 22207-2915

HICKMAN, JOLENE KAY, banker; b. Omaha, Sept. 5, 1954; d. Thomas Earl and Bernice Leona (McCoy) H. B.A., Otterbein Coll., 1977. Teller Bancohio Nat. Bank, Columbus, Ohio, 1976-77, auditor, 1977-81; audit supr. Huntington Nat. Bank, Columbus, 1981-85, asst. v.p., mgr., 1985-87, mem. conversion team, 1986-87, mgr. quality assurance, 1987-92, v.p. quality assurance, 1992-94, v.p.-mgr. stock transfer ops., 1994—. Mem. Am. Inst. Banking (instr. 1989), Victorian Village Soc., Columbus, 1983, Up Downtowners, Columbus, 1986; vol. Columbus Aids Task Force, chair Art for Life auction, 1994. Mem. Nat. Assn. Bank Women (chmn. edn. and tng. 1986-87, Ohio state conf., chmn. Looking at Leadership series 1985-86), Nat. Inst. Auditors. Republican. Methodist. Avocations: softball. Home: 358 Blenheim Rd Columbus OH 43214-3220 Office: Huntington Trust Co NA 41 S High St Fl 10 Columbus OH 43287

HICKMAN, MARGARET CAPELLINI, advertising agency executive; b. Hartford, Conn., Sept. 21, 1949; d. Anthony Serafino Capellini and Mary Magdelan (Budash) Zanardi; m. Richard Lonnie Hickman, Nov. 6, 1982; children: Wilder A., Langdon B. B.A., U. Conn., 1971. Mktg. asst. Advo Systems, Inc., Hartford, 1971-72, mktg. analyst, 1972-75; mktg. asst. Cinamon Assocs. Inc., Brookline, Mass., 1975-77, prodn. supr., 1977-81, v.p. prodn., 1981-84, v.p. client services, 1984-85; dir. client services Bozell, Jacobs, Kenyon & Eckhardt, Boston, 1985-86, v.p. client services Cinamon Assocs., 1986; ptnr. Hickman & Hickman, Merritt Island, Fla., 1987; production mgr. The Direct Mktg. Agy., Stamford, Conn., 1988-90; v.p. prodn. The Stenrich Group, Inc., Glen Allen, Va., 1990—. Mem. Direct Mktg. Assn. (past sec., treas., v.p.), Cape Ann Child devel. Programs (past dir.), Central Fla. Direct Mktg. Assn. (past mem.), Am. Legion Aux. Democrat. Roman Catholic. Home: 10717 Wellington St Fredericksburg VA 22407-1272

HICKMAN, MAXINE VIOLA, social services administrator; b. Louisville, Miss., Dec. 24, 1943; d. Everett and Ozella (Eichelberger) H.; m. William L. Malone, Sept. 5, 1965 (div. 1969); 1 child, Gwendolyn. BA, San Francisco State U., 1966; MS, Nova U., 1991; postgrad., Calif. Coast U., 1991—. Lic. State of Calif. Dept. Social Svcs. IBM profl. mechanic operator Wells Fargo Bank, San Francisco, 1961-65; dept. mgr. Sears Roebuck & Co., San Bruno, Calif., 1966-77; adminstr. Pine St. Guest House, San Francisco, 1969-88; fin. planner John Hancock Fin. Svcs., San Mateo, Calif., 1977-81; chief exec. officer Hickman Homes, Inc., San Francisco, 1981—; cons. BeeBe Meml. Endowment Found., Oakland, Calif., 1990—, Calif. Assn. Children's Home-Mems., Sacramento, 1989—. Mem. NAACP, San Francisco. Named Foster Mother of Yr., Children's Home Soc. Calif., 1985, Woman of Yr., Gamma Nu chpt. Iota Phi Lambda, 1991. Mem. Foster Parents United, Calif. Assn. Children's Homes, Nat. Bus. League, Order of Ea. Star, Masons (worthy matron), Alpha Kappa Alpha. Democrat. Baptist. Office: Hickman Homes Inc 67 Harold Ave San Francisco CA 94112-2331

HICKMAN, RUTH VIRGINIA, Bible educator; b. Sac City, Iowa, Oct. 15, 1931; d. Ronald Minor and Ida E. (Willcutt) Wilson; m. Charles Ray Hickman, Aug. 25, 1962; children: Ronald Everett, Lisa Michelle. BS in Home Econs., Morningside Coll., 1953. Ordained to ministry Christian Ch., 1985. Instr. Nat. Ednl. TV, 1964-76; staff coord., tchr. Life for Layman, Denver, 1974-77; founder, tchr. Abundant Word Ministries, Lakewood, Colo., 1980—; tchr. Bible Calvary Temple, Denver, 1980—; sales/trainer Hillestad Internat., San Jose, Calif., 1978—; bd. dirs. Morningstar Counseling, Lakewood; women's com. Billy Graham Assn., Denver, 1986-87. Author: (book) Hope for Hurting People, 1987; speaker, instr. audio and video tape series, 1980—. Mem. Rocky Mountain Fellowship Christian Leaders. Republican. Home: 3043 S Holly Pl Denver CO 80222-7010 Office: Abundant Word Ministries 6900 W Alameda Ave Ste 106 Lakewood CO 80226-3312

HICKMAN, TERRIE TAYLOR, administrator; b. Rapid City, S.D., Dec. 2, 1962; d. William Adrian and Carolyn Gene (Habben) T. BS, Okla. State U., 1985; MEd, Cen. State U., 1988. Mktg. dir. Tealridge Manor, Edmond, Okla., 1989-90; owner Oxford Pointe Jazzercize, Edmond, Okla., 1989-90; adminstr. Retirement Inn at Quail Ridge, Oklahoma City, Okla., 1991-92, Country Club Square, Edmond, 1992-93; planner Areawide Aging Agency, Oklahoma City, 1992—; presenter in field; adv. coun., sr. companion planning com. State of Okla. Conf. on Aging. Contbr. articles to various pubs. Co-chmn. media hosting party Olympic Festival, Norman, Okla., 1989; co-coord. jazzercize for hope Benefit for Hope Ctr., Edmond, The McGruff Safe House Program, Stillwater, Okla.; com. chmn. Coalition for Elderly Concerns, Oklahoma City; vol. Stillwater Domestic Violence Shelter, Payne County Employment Svcs., Stillwater; mem. renter's adv. bd. Okla. State U. Student Senate. Mem. Women in Bus., Edmond Area C. of C., Okla. Bus. and Aging Leadership Coalition, Phi Kappa Delta, Alpha Gamma Delta, Sigma Phi Omega. Republican. Lutheran.

HICKMAN, TRAPHENE PARRAMORE, library director, storyteller, library and library building consultant; b. Dallas, Jan. 31, 1933; d. Redden Travis and Stella (Moore) P.; m. John Robert Hickman, June 9, 1950; children—Lynn Kleifgen, Laurie Ward. A.A., Mountain View Community Coll.; B.A., U. Tex-Arlington; M.L.S., U. North Tex. Cert. librarian, Tex. Librarian Cedar Hill Pub. Library, Tex., 1959-77; dir. Dallas County Library System, Dallas, 1977-93; libr. cons. Dallas County, 1993—. Editor: History and Directory of Cedar Hill, 1976; editor News and Views newsletter Dallas county Employees, 1986-92. Chmn. Bicentennial Com., Cedar Hill, 1976; del. Dem. Nat. Conv. 9th Senate Dist., Tex., 1976; chmn. Sesquicentennial Com., Cedar Hill, 1984-86; Dallas County Dem. Forum; mem. Electoral Coll., 1988; chairperson Women's Bd. Northwood Inst., Cedar Hill. Recipient Newsmaker of Yr. award Cedar Hill Chronicle, 1976; named Ambassador of Goodwill, State of Tex., 1976. Mem. ALA, Tex. Libr. Assn. (legis. com. 1984-95, councillor 1982-83, trustee com. 1987—, pub. info. com. 1987—), Pub. Libr. Adminstrs. of North Tex. (sec., v.p., pres. 1980, 87), Dallas County Libr. Assn., N.E. Tex. Libr. Systems (legis. commn. 1978-95, Libr. of Yr. 1987), U. North Tex. Sch. Libr. and Info. Scis. Alumni Assn. (pres. 1987-88), Cedar Hill C. of C., Cedar Summit Book Club (officer). Democrat. Methodist. Home and Office: 421 Lee St Cedar Hill TX 75104-2697

HICKS, BETHANY GRIBBEN, lawyer, magistrate; b. N.Y., Sept. 8, 1951; d. Robert and DeSales Gribben; m. William A. Hicks III, May 21, 1982; children: Alexandra Elizabeth, Samantha Katherine. AB, Vassar Coll., 1973; MEd, Boston U., 1975; JD, Ariz. State U., 1984. Bar: Ariz. 1984. Pvt. practice Scottsdale and Paradise Valley, Ariz., 1984-91; law clk. to Hon. Kenneth L. Fields Maricopa County Superior Ct. (S.E. dist.), Mesa, 1991-93, judge pro tem, 1993—, commr., 1994—; magistrate Town of Paradise Valley, Ariz., 1993—. Mem. Jr. League of Phoenix, 1984-91; bd. dirs. Phoenix Children's Theatre, 1988-90; parliamentarian Girls Club of Scottsdale, Ariz., 1985-87, 89-90, bd. dirs., 1988-91; mem. exec. bd., sec. All Saints' Episcopal Day Sch. Parents Assn., 1991-92, pres., 1993-94. Mem. ABA, State Bar Ariz., Maricopa County Bar Assn. Republican. Episcopalian. Club: Paradise Valley Country.

HICKS, DOROTHY JANE, obstetrician/gynecologist, educator; b. Cleve., Apr. 18, 1919; d. Arnell R. and Marvel M. (Hale) H. AB, Case Western Reserve U., 1941; MD, Temple U., 1944. Diplomate Am. Bd. Obstetrics and Gynecology. Asst. prof. dept. ob-gyn. U. Miami, 1967-85, prof., 1985—; bd. dirs. rape treatment ctr. Jackson Meml. Hosp., Miami, med. dir., 1974-93, cons., 1993—; dir. pedigyn clinic Jackson Meml. Hosp. Contbr. articles to profl. jours. Fellow Am. Coll. Ob-Gyn., N.Am. Soc. Pediatric and Adolescent Gynecology, South Atlantic Ob-Gyn. Soc., Fla. Soc. Ob/Gyn, Miami Ob/Gyn Soc. Office: U Miami Sch Medicine Dept Ob-Gyn PO Box 016960 Miami FL 33101

HICKS, GRACE ROBERSON, writer, artist; b. Covington, Tex., May 7, 1923; d. John Edgar and Edith Grace (Wallace) Roberson; m. James Marion Hicks, Oct. 20, 1945 (dec. Sept. 1980); children: Bruce Michael, Karen Hicks Ashcraft. Grad. high sch., Covington, Tex., 1939. Freelance writer, dept. mgr. Montgomery Ward, San Antonio, 1965-67, Japan, 1954-57, Hawaii, 1957-59; artist, tchr. Sunrise Beach, Tex., 1980-87; artist Kingsland (Tex.) House of Arts & Crafts, 1976-81, Buchanan Gallery, Buchanan Dam, Tex., 1982-86, Higland Arts Guild, Marble Falls, Tex., 1980-87. Author: (children's books) The Critters of Gazink, 1991, The Most Mannerly Cow and The Rude Cowbird, 1992; contbr. articles and poetry to mags. and newspapers. Republican. Home: 301 N Miracle Dr Apt 126 Corsicana TX 75110-3810

HICKS, JUDITH EILEEN, nursing administrator; b. Chgo., Jan. 1, 1947; d. John Patrick and Mary Ann (Clifford) Rohan; m. Laurence Joseph Hicks, Nov. 22, 1969; children—Colleen Driscoll, Patrick Kevin. B.S. in Nursing, St. Xavier Coll., Chgo., 1969; M.S. in Nursing, U. Ill.-Chgo., 1975. Staff nurse Mercy Hosp., Chgo., 1969-70, nursing supr., 1970-73; cons. continuing edn. Ill. Nurses Assn., Chgo., 1974-75; dir. obstetrics and gynecology nursing Northwestern Meml. Hosp., Chgo., 1975-81; v.p. nursing Children's Meml. Hosp., Chgo., 1981-86; pres. Children's Meml. Home Health, Inc., 1986—, Children's Meml. Nursing Services, 1986—; pres. Allied & Children's Home Health and Nursing Services, 1988, CM Healthcare Resources, Inc., 1988—, The Pediatric Place, Inc., 1994—; dir. Near North Health Corp., Chgo., 1982-85; pres. Pediatric Excellence Program Svc.; bd. dirs. Infant Welfare Soc. Chgo. Mem. Ill. Hosp. Assn. (chmn. Council on Nursing 1982-83), Inst. Medicine, Am. Soc. Nursing Adminstrs., Women's Health Exec. Network (pres. 1984-85). Roman Catholic. Home: 2206 Beechwood Ave Wilmette IL 60091-1508 Office: CM Health Care Resources 1181 Lake Cook Rd Deerfield IL 60015

HICKS, LUCILE P., state legislator; b. Greenwood, Miss., May 11, 1938; m. William Hicks, 1960. BS, Millsaps Coll. High sch. sch. tchr.; mem. Mass. Ho. of Reps., until 1990, Mass. Senate, 1990—; mem. Wayland Rep. Town Com. Mem. LWV, Jr. League Boston, Kappa Delta Epsilon. Home: 5 Wildwood Rd Wayland MA 01778-2121 Office: State House State Capitol Boston MA 02133*

HICKS, MARILYN SUE, lay worker; b. Clarksville, Tenn., Mar. 21, 1949; d. Roy Davis and Ada La Una (Powers) Wright; m. James Ray Hicks, July 5, 1970; children: Jason, Susan, Stephen. Student, Trevecca Nazarene Coll., Nashville, Ind. U., 1991—. Dir. children's ministries Grace Ch. of Nazarene, Nashville, 1971-72, Bloomington 1st Ch. of the Nazarene, 1995—; youth dir. 1st Ch. of Nazarene, Bloomington, Ind., 1988—, sec., del., 1989—. Author: (songs) I Want to Be More Like You, 1990; The Land That I Love, 1992; I Just Want To Be, 1992; contbr. articles to profl. jours. Mem. Nazarene World Mission Soc. (treas. S.W. Ind. Dist. 1990—). Home: 1105 E Allendale Dr Bloomington IN 47401-8708 Office: 1st Ch of Nazarene 700 W Howe St Bloomington IN 47403-2275

HICKS, MARYELLEN WHITLOCK, lawyer, judge; b. Odessa, Tex., Mar. 10, 1949; d. Albert Gannett Whitlock and Kathleen (Durham) Butler; m. Arvid Hicks, Oct., 1945 (dec. 1974); 1 child, Kathleen. BA, Tex. Woman's U., 1970, postgrad., 1971; JD, Tex. Tech. U., 1974. Bar: Tex. 1974. Assoc. Mitchell and Bonner, Ft. Worth, 1974-75; ptnr. Bonner and Hicks, Ft. Worth, 1975-77; judge mcpl. ct. City of Ft. Worth, 1977-78, chief judge, 1978-82; dist. judge 231st Dist. Ct., Ft. Worth, 1983-93; justice 2nd Ct. Appeals, Ft. Worth, 1993—. Vice chmn. Sojourner Truth Theater, Ft. Worth, 1987-88. Nat. Acad. Arts and Scis. grantee Golden State Law Sch., 1979; recipient Heritage of Odessa award, 1994; named Woman of Yr. Ft. Worth Star Telegram, 1993. Fellow Tex. Bar Found., Coll. State Bar Tex.; mem. Nat Bar Assn., Tex. State Bar Assn., Tarrant County Bar Assn., Ft. Worth Black Bar Assn. (pres. 1987-88), Black Women Lawyers Tarrant County (co-founder), Tarrant County Family Ct. Bar Assn., Rotary, Delta Sigma Theta. Democrat. Roman Catholic. Office: 2d Ct Appeals 100 Weatherford Fort Worth TX 76102

HICKS, ROBIN W., nurse; b. Ft. Oglethorpe, Ga., Jan. 16, 1955; d. Marvine Eugene and Opal Evelyn (Edmonds) Wells; m. Dennis Ray Hicks, Nov. 19, 1976 (div. 1994); 1 child, Amy Nicole. Diploma in nursing, J.F. Drake Tech., 1974; degree in nursing, John C. Calhoun, Decatur, Ala., 1979. RN, Ala.; ACLS. Office nurse Cromeans Clinic, Scottsboro, Ala., 1974-76; charge nurse Huntsville (Ala.) Nursing Home, 1976-78; operating rm. nurse Huntsville Hosp., 1980-81, Jackson County Hosp., Scottsboro, 1981-85; hemodialysis charge nurse BMA Dialysis, Scottsboro, 1985-90; asst. dir. blood svc. No. Ala. ARC, Huntsville, 1991—; part-time charge nurse Jackson County Nursing Home, Scottsboro, 1978-80. Vol. Madison chpt. ARC, Huntsville, EMT, Woodville, Ala. Democrat. Home: 1202 Birchwood Dr Scottsboro AL 35768

HICKS, SHIRLEY LUCAS, accountant; b. Amory, Miss., Aug. 22, 1964; d. Billy Ray L. and Mary Ann Lucas Jones; m. Charles Anthony Hicks, June 29, 1985; children: Charles Andrew, Macy Ann. BS in Acctg., Miss. U. for Women, 1985. Cert. emergency med. responder. Asst. Thomas Kerby & Brown, Columbus, Miss., 1982-85; acctg. clk. Miss. U. for Women, Columbus, Miss., 1985, mgr. bookstore, 1986; acct. II Kerr-McGee Chem. Corp., Hamilton, Miss., 1986-89, supr. plant acctg., 1989—; participant Dale Carnegie, 1990; cert. quality facilitator Kerr-McGee Corp., Oklahoma City, 1993-94; chmn. supervisory com. Ampot Fed. Credit Union, Hamilton, 1989—. Participant Leadership Tomorrow Program Lowndes C. of C., Columbus, 1992; co. advisor Free Enterprise Village Miss. U. for Women, 1988-94. Mem. Nat. Assn. Accts. (Extraordinary Achievement award 1993). Office: Kerr-McGee Chem Corp PO Box 180 Hamilton MS 39746

HICKS, SUSAN LYNN BOWMAN, small business owner; b. Flint, Mich., Mar. 24, 1952; d. Richard and Carol Joanne (Haney) Bowman; m. Duane James Hicks, Aug. 6, 1977. BA, U. Mich., Flint, 1975; MA, Cen. Mich. U., 1981. Med. social worker Flint Osteo. Hosp., 1974-77; dir. med. social work and patient rels. Crittenton Hosp., Rochester, Mich., 1978-89; coord. geriatric social work Flint (Mich.) Osteopathic Hosp., 1990—; owner, Susan Hicks Enterprises, 1988—; mgmt. tng. and devel. cons. Buick, Oldsmobile, Cadillac div. GM, Grand Blanc, Mich., 1985. Bd. dirs., chmn. com. Rochester Area Youth Guidance, Mich., 1986, chmn., 1988; bd. dirs. E. ctrl. Mich. chpt. Alzheimer's Assn., 1994. Mem. Soc. for Hosp. Social Work Dirs. (Recognition award 1984, 85, pres.-elect 1985-86, pres. 1986-87, chmn. polit. and social action com. 1988—), Nat. Assn. Social Workers, NAFE, Soc. Patient Representatives. Methodist. Avocations: tap dancing, writing. Home and Office: 8201 Sawgrass Trl Grand Blanc MI 48439-1874

HICKS, VICKI JEAN, lawyer; b. Woodward, Okla., Dec. 30, 1955; d. Morris E. and Betty J. (Hicks) H. BS, Phillips U., 1978; JD, U. Okla., 1981. Bar: Okla. 1981, D.C. 1982, U.S. Dist. Ct. D.C. 1982. Assoc. Balsamo & Dominquez, Washington, 1983-84; internat. cons. Nebr. Wheat Bd., Washington, 1984; policy analyst Office Antiboycott Compliance Internat. Trade Adminstrn., Washington, 1984-87; legis. counsel Sen. Quentin N. Burdick, Washington, 1987—. Pres., Georgetown North Unit Owner's Assn., 1986. Recipient scholarship U. Okla., 1980. Mem. D.C. Bar, Okla. Bar Assn., Women Govt. Rels.

HICKSON, JOYCE FAYE, counseling educator; b. Birmingham, Ala.; d. Jesse Guy and Hazel Lonette (Streetman) Horton. BS, Troy (Ala.) State U., 1965; MA, Auburn U., 1965; EdD, Miss. State U., 1976. Instr. dept. comm. Auburn (Ala.) U., 1965-68; dir. Tyler Ednl. Ctr., Carbondale, Ill., 1968-70; head tchr., coord. Fairfax County Pub. Sch. System, Fairfax, Va., 1972-74; asst. prof. dept. counselor edn. Miss. State U., Starkville, 1976-85; grad. coord. dept. specialized edn. U. Witwatersrand, Johannesburg, South Africa, 1985-91; prof., chmn. dept. counseling and clin. programs Columbus (Ga.) Coll., 1991—, mem. adv. bd. internat. studies program, 1993—; cons. to sch. dists., Ill., 1968-70, Miss., 1976-85, Ga., 1991—. Author: Multicultural Counseling in a Divided and Traumatized Society, 1994; contbr. articles to profl. jours. Mem. ACA, Am. Sch. Counselors Assn. (so. regional rep. 1992), Ga. Sch. Counselors Assn. (at-large), Internat. Assn. for Spl. Edn. (editorial bd. 1992), AAUW. Democrat. Home: 7803 Edgewater Dr Columbus GA 31904 Office: Columbus Coll Sch Edn Dept Counseling-Clin Progs Columbus GA 31993-0001

HIDER, MARJORIE RENÉ, mental health counselor, nurse educator; b. Toledo, Ohio, Aug. 16, 1948; d. Pryor James and Alice Jane (Frankhart) Wood; m. C. William Hider, Apr. 17, 1976; 1 child, Michael. RN, St. Vincent Hosp. Sch. Nursing, Toledo, 1969; BSN, Fla. So. Coll., Lakeland, 1984; MA in Counseling, Rollins Coll., 1991. Staff nurse St. Vincents Hosp. Med. Ctr., Toledo, 1969-74; asst. head nurse Med. Coll. Ohio, Toledo, 1974-76; charge nurse Humana Lucerne, Orlando, Fla., 1976-77; staff nurse in critical care Fla. Hosp. Med. Ctr., Orlando, 1978-82, critical care educator, 1993—; ptnr. Inner Change Facilitators, Orlando, 1994—; lectr. and cons. in field. Mem. AACCN, Fla. Nurses Assn., Am. Counselors Assn., Fla. Counselors Assn., Fla. Mental Health Counselors Assn. Office: Inner Change Facilitators 2718-B N Orange Ave Orlando FL 32804

HIEATT, CONSTANCE BARTLETT, English language educator; b. Boston, Feb. 11, 1928; d. Arthur Charles and Eleonora (Very) Bartlett; m. Allen Kent Hieatt, Oct. 25, 1958. Student, Smith Coll., 1945-47; AB, Hunter Coll., 1953, AM, 1957; PhD, Yale U., 1959. Lectr. City Coll., CUNY, 1959-60; from asst. prof. to assoc. prof. English Queensborough Community Coll., CUNY, 1960-65; assoc. prof., then prof. St. John's U., Jamaica, N.Y., 1965-69; prof. English U. Western Ont., London, Can., 1969-

93; prof. emeritus U. Western Ont., London, 1993—. Author: (with A.K. Hieatt) The Canterbury Tales of Geoffrey Chaucer, 1964, The Realism of Dream Visions, 1967, Beowulf and Other Old English Poems, 1967, rev. edit., 1983, Essentials of Old English, 1968, The Miller's Tale by Geoffrey Chaucer, 1970, Spenser: Selected Poetry, 1970, (with Sharon Butler) Pleyn Delit: Medieval Cookery for Modern Cooks, 1976, rev. edit., 1979, Karlamagnus Saga, Vols. I and II, 1975, 1975, Vol. III, 1980, (with Sharon Butler) Curye on Inglysch, 1985, An Ordinance of Pottage, 1988, (with Robin F. Jones) La Novele Cirurgerie, 1990, (with Minnette Gaudet) Guillaume de Machaut's Tale of the Alerion, 1994, (with Brian Shaw and Duncan Macrae-Gibson) Beginning Old English, 1994; also children's books: (with A.K. Hieatt) The Canterbury Tales of Geoffrey Chaucer, 1961, rev. edit., 1981, Sir Gawain and the Green Knight, 1967, The Knight of the Lion, 1968, The Knight of the Cart, 1969, The Joy of the Court, 1971, The Sword and the Grail, 1972, The Castle of Ladies, 1973, The Minstrel Knight, 1974. Yale U. fellow, and Lewis-Farmington fellow, 1957-59; Can. Council and Social Sci. and Humanities Rsch. Coun. grantee; Yale U. vis. fellow, 1985-86, 89-93. Fellow Royal Soc. Can.; mem. MLA, Medieval Acad. Am., Early English Text Soc., Internat. Saga Assn., Internat. Soc. Anglo-Saxonists, Soc. Advancement Scandinavian Studies, Assn. Can. Univ. Tchrs. English, New Chaucer Soc., Anglo-Norman Text Soc. Episcopalian. Home: 304 River Rd Deep River CT 06417-2120

HIERONYMUS, CLARA BOOTH WIGGINS, journalist; b. Drew, Miss., July 25, 1913; d. Bruce Charles and Maude (Watson) Wiggins; m. Senator Cleo Hieronymus, Apr. 24, 1937; children—Bruce Lee, Jane (Mrs. David Piller). B.A. cum laude, U. Tulsa, 1932; M.S.W., U. Okla., 1936; D.F.A (hon.), R.I. Coll., 1984. Employment sec. and counselor YWCA, Tulsa, 1936-38; labor market analyst Okla. Employment Service, also instr. sociology U. Tulsa, 1938-50; free-lance writer Nashville, Tennessean, 1951-56; art and drama critic, 1956-90, drama critic, 1990—, home furnishings editor, 1956-83; mem. rotating faculty Nat. Critics Inst., 1975—; adj. instr. theatre criticism Belmont Coll., 1989-90; book review radio sta. KFMJ, Tulsa, 1938-45; speaker before groups, 1950—; arts clinician Tenn. Arts Acad. of Tenn. Dept. Edn., 1993. Author: (with Barbara Izard) Requiem for a Nun: On Stage and Off, Scholar's Catalog for Retrospective Exhibit of Lee and Pup McCarty, potters and designers, 1991; editor City of Forest Hills quarterly newsletter, 1992—. Mem. panel jurors for selection Am. Children's Theaters to perform at Internat. Conf. U.S.A., 1972; bd. dirs. Samaritans, Inc., 1967-76, pres., 1967-69; bd. dirs. Middle Tenn. chpt. Nat. Arthritis Found., 1967-70; charter mem. bd. Middle Tenn. Historic Sites Fedn., 1968-70; mem. Tenn. Fine Arts Ctr. and Bot. Gardens, 1959—; mem. adv. bd. O'More Coll. Design, 1970-91, bd. dirs., 1991-94; adv. bd. Nashville Ballet Soc., 1977-79; founder, life mem. O'More Design Guild, 1970—. Recipient Dorothy Dawe award Am. Furniture Mart, 1960, 63, 66, 69, Dallas Market Ctr. award, 1965, Disting. Achievement in Arts awards Tenn. Art League, 1987, 89, Gov.'s award in arts, 1980, Humanitarian award Fisk U., 1983, Disting. Achievement award Tenn. Theater Assn., 1987; named Woman of Year in Communications, Bus. and Profl. Women's Club, Nashville, 1966; named to Mayor's Com. Community Excellence, 1982; honored by Links, Inc., 1982; honored by Tenn. State U. for disting. svc. in art for students, 1986, 89, honored in "Accolade to Clara" Tenn. Performing Arts Ctr., 1986, 87, honored by O'More Coll. Design, 1990, Intermus. Coun. Nashville for disting. svc., 1990; named Pride of Tenn., 1982, Disting. Alumna U. Tulsa, 1988; named among 10 best and most rep. women in critical professions today in Women in Am. Theater, 1981; Metro Arts Commn. honoree, 1991, Botanical Gardens and Fine Arts Ctr. honoree, 1990; award from Stages monthly theater review publ. for lifetime achievement in theater, 1991. Mem. Am. Soc. Interior Designers (press asso.), Nashville Children's Theatre, Assn. Internationale du Theatre pour L'Enfance et Jeunesse, Am. Theater Critics Assn. (founding mem., governing bd. 1974—, nat. chmn. 1980-84, exec. sec. 1984—). Democrat. Methodist. Clubs: Centennial (Nashville), Le Petit Salon (Nashville). Home: 2200 Hemingway Dr Nashville TN 37215-4112 Office: The Tennessean Am Theatre Critics Assn 1100 Broad St Nashville TN 37203

HIESTAND, TINA DUPES, corporate administrator, accountant; b. Harrisburg, Pa., Apr. 6, 1957; d. John Franklin and Frances M. (Walker) Dupes; m. Burnell L. Hiestand, July 9, 1977. BS in Acctg., Elizabethtown Coll., 1986; MBA, Loyola Coll., Balt., 1992. Cert. mgmt. acct. Acct. York (Pa.) Tape & Label Co., 1981-87; sr. acct. High Industries, Inc., Lancaster, 1987-91; asset mgr. High Assocs., Ltd., Lancaster, 1991-93; v.p. corp. adminstrn. Pinnacle Mortgage Investment Co., Lancaster, 1993-94; v.p. bus. devel. Hiestand Supply Co., Marietta, Pa., 1994—; bd. dirs. UN Com. for Habitat, N.Y.C.; task force mem. Enterprise Cmty. Strategic Planning Sessions, Lancaster, 1993—. Treas. Samaritan Ctr. of Lancaster, 1990-93; com. chair Sertoma, Lancaster, 1993—; bd. dirs. Rockford Found., Lancaster, 1994—; safe schs./safe cmtys. com. mem. Youth Violence Coun., Lancaster, 1994; campaign coord. Open Sesame Lancaster County Libr. Mem. Inst. Mgmt. Accts., Mortgage Bankers Assn. Home: 247 Willow Valley Dr Lancaster PA 17602-4788 Office: Hiestand Supply Co 650 Stackstown Rd Marietta PA 17547

HIGBEE, ANN G., public relations executive, consultant; b. Newark, May 6, 1942; d. Roger Herald German and Charlotte May (Ryan) Wentzell; m. James Lyman Higbee, June 25, 1965; 1 child, Travis James. BS, U. Md., 1964. Field rep. Am. Field Svc., N.Y.C., 1964-65; from acct. exec. to v.p. Rath Orgn., Syracuse, N.Y., 1965-71, T.A. Best Co., Skaneateles, N.Y., 1971-75; dir. devel. Manlius Pebble Hill Sch., Jamesville, N.Y., 1975-79; dir. pub. rels., mng. ptnr. Eric Mower and Assocs., Syracuse, 1980—. Chair Pub. Broadcasting Coun./CNY, Syracuse, 1977-84; dir. Crouse Levine Meml. Hosp., Syracuse, 1983—; trustee Coll. Environ. Sci. and Forestry Found., Syracuse, 1991—; regent Lemoyne Coll., Syracuse, 1992—. Named Women of Achievement by Post-Standard, Syracuse, 1973, Outstanding Young Woman by Jaycees, Syracuse. Mem. Pub. Rels. Soc. Am. (accredited, chair accreditations/CNY, counselors sect.), Am. Assn. Advt. Agys. (pub. rels. com.). Office: Eric Mower & Assocs 500 Plum St Syracuse NY 13204

HIGDON, BARBARA J., college president; b. Independence, Mo., May 18, 1930; m. 1950; 3 children. B.A., U. Mo., 1951, M.A., 1952, Ph.D. in Speech, 1961. Assoc. prof. English, speech, Tex. So. U., 1958-62; prof. Graceland Coll., Lamoni, Iowa, 1962-75, pres., 1984-91, pres. emerita, 1992—; dean, v.p. acad. affairs Park Coll., 1975-84; bd. SS. Cyril and Methodius Found., Bulgaria 1992—; chair Iowa Peace Inst., 1992. Office: Graceland Coll Office of the President Lamoni IA 50140

HIGDON, BERNICE COWAN, retired educator; b. Sylva, N.C., Feb. 26, 1918; d. Royston Duffield and Margaret Cordelia (Hall) Cowan; m. Roscoe John Higdon, Aug. 12, 1945; children: Ronald Keith, Rodrick Knox, Krista Dean. BS, Western Carolina U., 1941; cert. tchr., So. Oreg. Coll., 1967; student, Chapman Coll., 1971. Cert. tchr., Calif. Prin., tchr. Dorsey Sch., Bryson City, N.C., 1941-42; expeditor Glenn L. Martin Aircraft Co., Balt., 1942-45; tchr. elem. sch. Seneca, S.C., 1945-46, Piedmont, S.C., 1946-47; tchr. elem. sch. Columbia, S.C., 1950-51, Manteca, Calif., 1967-68; kindergarten tchr. 1st Bapt. Ch., Medford, Oreg., 1965-67; tchr. elem. sch. Marysville (Calif.) Unified Sch. Dist., 1968-83; tchr. Headstart, Manteca, 1968. Past counselor Youth Svc. Bur., Yuba City, Calif.; troop leader Girl Scouts U.S.A., Medford, 1962-63; past Sunday sch. tchr. 1st Bapt. Ch., Medford; bd. dirs. Christian Assistance Network, Yuba City, 1984-85; aux. vol. Fremont Med. Ctr., Yuba City, 1984—; deaconess Evang. Free Ch., Yuba City, 1991-93; vol. Fremont Med. Ctr., 1984-94. Recipient cert. of appreciation Marysville Unified Sch. Dist., 1983, Christian Assistance Network, 1985; cert. of recognition Ella Elem. Sch., Marysville, 1983. Mem. Calif. Ret. Tchrs. Assn., Nat. Ret. Tchrs. Assn., Sutter Hist. Soc., AAUW, Am. Assn. Ret. Persons. Home: 1264 Charlotte Ave Yuba City CA 95991-2804

HIGDON, POLLY SUSANNE, federal judge; b. Goodland, Kans., May 1, 1942; d. William and Pauline Higdon; m. John P. Wilhardt (div. May 1988); 1 child, Liesl. BA, Vassar Coll., 1964; postgrad., Cornell U., 1967; JD, Washburn U., 1975; LLM, NYU, 1980. Bar: Kans. 1975, Oreg. 1980. Assoc. Corley & Assocs., Garden City, Kans., 1975-79, Kendrick M. Mercer Law Offices, Eugene, Oreg., 1980-82; pvt. practice law Eugene, 1983; judge U.S. Bankruptcy Ct., Eugene, 1983—. Active U.S. Peace Corps, Tanzania, East Africa, 1965-66. Mem. Am. Bankruptcy Inst., Nat. Conf. Bankruptcy Judges, Nat. Assn. Women Judges. Office: US Bankruptcy Ct PO Box 1335 211 E 7th Rm 404 Eugene OR 97440*

HIGGINBOTHAM, BARBRA BUCKNER, librarian; b. Dallas, Apr. 12, 1946; d. Zeak Monroe and Myra Mozelle (Wilson) Buckner; m. Hal Ford Higginbotham, Jr., Dec. 27, 1970. BA, Centenary Coll., 1968; MLS, Columbia U., 1969, DLS, 1988. Children's libr. Chgo. Pub. Libr., 1969-70; cataloger R.I. Coll., Providence, 1971-73; libr. U.S. Dept. Transportation, Washington, 1973-75, U.S. Customs Svc., Washington, 1975-77; asst. head cataloging Columbia U., N.Y.C., 1977-79, head of cataloging, 1979-83, access svcs. libr., 1983-85; head libr. Bklyn. Coll., 1985-94, chief libr., exec. dir. acad. info. techs., 1994—; trustee N.Y. Met. Reference and Rsch. Libr. Agy., 1993—. Author: Our Past Preserved, 1990, Access versus Assets, 1993; editor: Advances in Preservation and Access, 1992. Recipient Alumni Bd. Svc. award, 1992. Mem. Am. Libr. Assn., Library and Info. Tech. Assn. (bd. dirs. 1994—, chair program com. 1992—), Assn. Coll. and Rsch. Librs., Archons of Colophon, Golden Key. Home: 303 Mercer St New York NY 10003-6706 Office: Bklyn Coll 2900 Bedford Ave Brooklyn NY 11210-2889

HIGGINBOTHAM, EDITH ARLEANE, radiologist, researcher; b. New Orleans, Sept. 14, 1946; d. Luther Aldrich and Ruby (Clark) H.; m. Terry Lawrence Andrews (div. 1979); m. Donald Temple Ford (div. 1989). BS, Howard U., 1967, MS, 1970, MD, 1974. Diplomate Am. Bd. Radiology, Am. Bd. Nuclear Medicine. Intern St. Vincent's Hosp., N.Y.C., 1974-75, resident in diagnostic radiology, 1975-78, resident in nuclear radiology, 1978-79; asst. prof. radiology, chief nuclear Medicine Howard U., Howard U. Hosp., Washington, 1979-82; assoc. prof. clin. radiology, dir. nuclear medicine U. Medicine and Dentistry N.J., Newark, 1982-90; locum tenems radiologist Sterling Med. Assocs., Cin., 1991-94, Med. Nat., San Antonio, 1991-94; diagnostic radiologist Diagnostic Health Imaging Systems, Lanham, Md., 1994—; cons. Biotech. Rsch. Inst., Rockville, Md., 1989—; profl. assoc. Ctr. for Molecular Medicine and Immunology, Newark, 1984-90; asst. prof. radiology George Washington U., Washington, 1990; presenter in field. Contbr. articles and abstracts to med. jours. Named Outstanding Working Woman, Glamour mag., 1981, Hon. Dep. Atty. Gen., State of La., 1982. Mem. Am. Coll. Radiology, Radiol. Soc. N.Am., Soc. Nuclear Medicine, Sigma Xi, Phi Delta Epsilon. Roman Catholic. Home: 1021 Paper Mill Ct NW Washington DC 20007-3619

HIGGINBOTHAM, WENDY JACOBSON, legislative staff member; b. Salt Lake City, Oct. 23, 1947; d. Alfred Thurl and Virginia Lorraine (LaCom) Jacobson; m. Keith Higginbotham, July 12, 1969; children: Ann Elizabeth, Ryan Keith, Laura Carol. Student, Occidental Coll., 1965-66, U. Grenoble, France, 1967; BA cum laude with highest honors, Brigham Young U., 1969. Teaching instr. Brigham Young U., Provo, Utah, 1969-70, editor univ. press, 1970-71; freelance editor Camarillo, Calif., 1971-78; freelance newspaper writer Vienna, Va., 1983-85; mem. profl. staff U.S. Senate Labor Com., Washington, 1985-86; exec. asst. U.S. Senator Orrin G. Hatch, Washington, 1986-88, legis. dir., 1988-91, chief of staff/adminstrv. asst., 1991—. Pres. Parent-Tchr. Assn., Vienna, 1981-82. Mem. Profl. Rep. Women, Phi Kappa Phi. Mormon. Home: 2022 Willow Branch Ct Vienna VA 22181 Office: US Senate Washington DC 20510

HIGGINBOTHAM JOHNSON, WANDA FAYE, waste disposal company executive; b. Houston, June 23, 1959; d. Wesley J. and Lillie (Jackson) J. Student Houston pub. schs. Sales mgr. Johnson & Sons Disposal Svcs., Houston, 1970-85; pres. Johnson's Disposal Svcs., Houston, 1985—. Mem. NAACP (Houston chpt.), Houston Apt. Assn., Buy Freedom, Houston Restaurant Assn., Greater C. of C. of Houston, Houston Urban League, LWV (Houston chpt.). Home and Office: PO Box 450093 Houston TX 77245-0093

HIGGINS, DOROTHY MARIE, academic dean; b. Lawrence, Mass., May 1, 1930; d. John Daniel and Mary Jane (Herbertson) H. AB, Emmanuel Coll., 1951; MS, Cath. U., 1961; PhD, Boston Coll., 1966. Assoc. prof. chemistry Emmanuel Coll., Boston, 1966-88, chair chemistry dept., 1974-85; div. chair math., sci., tech. Roxbury Community Coll., Roxbury Crossing, Mass., 1988-90; dean arts and scis. Teikyo-Post U., Waterbury, Conn., 1990—; grant cons. N.E. coll. Optometry, Boston, 1986; faculty cons. Zymark Corp., Hopkinton, Mass., 1982; rsch. assoc. U. Mass., Boston, 1975-84. Editor: (workbook) Geometry: Development Students, 1989; editor sci. newsletter, 1989; editorial adv. bd. Jour. Coll. Sci. Teaching, 1984-88. Instrumentation grantee NSF, 1985, Chautauqua grantee NSF, 1981-82, Instrumentation grantee George Alden Trust, 1985, Boston Globe Found., 1985, Extramural Assoc. grantee NIH, 1984. Mem. Am. Chem. Soc., Nat. Sci. Tchrs. Assn., New Eng. Chem. Tchrs., Soc. Coll. Sci. Teaching, Am. Assn. Higer Edn., Sigma Xi. Democrat. Roman Catholic. Office: Teikyo Post U 800 Country Club Rd Waterbury CT 06708-3200

HIGGINS, ISABELLE JEANETTE, librarian; b. Evanston, Ill., Dec. 13, 1919; d. Frank LeRoy and Ada Louise (Wilcox) Heck; m. George Alfred Higgins, Jan. 23, 1945 (dec. Sept. 1994); children: Alfred Clinton, Donald Quentin, Heather Higgins Aanes, Laura Higgins Palmer, Carol Higgins Hutchinson. BS, Northwestern U., 1940; MLS, U. Md., 1971. Cert. libr., Md. With Liebermann Waelchli Co., Tokyo, 1940-41, Shanghai Evening Post, 1941-42; editorial asst. Newsweek mag., N.Y.C., 1944; wire editor FBIS/FCC, Washington, 1944-46; rsch. and analysis China desk CIA, Washington, 1946-49; supr. library vols. Westbrook Sch., Bethesda, Md., 1965-69; reference librarian Montgomery County Pub. Libraries, Bethesda, 1969-83; librarian Brooks Inst. Photography, Santa Barbara, Calif., 1984—; treas. Friends of Santa Barbara Pub. Library, 1987-88. Mem. AAUW (bd. dirs. Santa Barbara br. 1988-94, del. nat. conv. 1989), Spl. Librs. Assn., Calif. Libr. Assn., Santa Barbara Little Gardens Club (pres. 1987-89), Floriade Garden Club (pres. 1990-91). Congregationalist. Home: 1128 Garcia Rd Santa Barbara CA 93103-2128 Office: Brooks Inst Photography 801 Alston Rd Santa Barbara CA 93108-2399

HIGGINS, JOAN MARIE, freelance writer, producer; b. Shamokin, Pa.; d. Leon Francis and Anna (Kiewlak) H. Student, Middlesex County Coll., Edison, N.J., 1971-73, The New Sch. for Social Rsch., N.Y.C. Mem. staff Eyewitness News/ABC-TV, N.Y.C., 1972-86; planning unit editor, field producer Eyewitness News/ABC-TV, 1985-86; freelance producer, writer, publicist N.Y.C., 1986-87, Children's Television Workshop, N.Y.C., 1986-87, Dino DeLaurentis Entertainment Co., N.Y.C., 1987; publicist Zarem Pub. Rels., N.Y.C., 1987; producer, publicist Self Mag., 1986-87; sr. publicist Avon Books/The Hearst Corp., N.Y.C., 1987-89; freelance writer, publicist Dances with Wolves TIG/Orion Pictures, NBC-TV, Universal TV, 1990-91; freelance writer, publicist St. Martin's Press, 1992—. Recipient Emmy award cert. of recognition for rsch. on TV spl., NATAS, 1981. Mem. Writers Guild Am. Home: 301 St James Ave Woodbridge NJ 07095-1609

HIGGINS, JULIANNE MCKENNA, lawyer; b. N.Y.C., Apr. 8, 1959; d. James Joseph and Sheila Patricia (O'Reilly) McKenna; m. Leonard James Higgins, Dec. 28, 1985; children: Caroline McKenna, Sean Michael. BSBA, Manhattan Coll., 1981; JD, Fordham U., 1986. Bar: N.J., N.Y. Assoc. Shanley & Fisher, P.C., Morristown, N.J., 1986-87; asst. counsel The Mennen Co., Morristown, 1987-92; trademark and copyright counsel Colgate-Palmolive, N.Y.C., 1992—. Notes editor Fordham Internat. Law Jour., 1985-86. Mem. ABA, Bar State of N.Y., Bar Assn. State of N.J. Office: Colgate-Palmolive Co 300 Park Ave New York NY 10022

HIGGINS, KATHRYN O'LEARY, government official; b. Sioux City, Iowa, Oct. 11, 1947; d. Paul C. and Mary Kathryn (Callaghan) O'Leary; widowed; children: Liam James, Kevan Paul. BS, U. Nebr., 1969. Manpower specialist U.S. Dept. Labor, Washington, 1969-78; asst. dir. employment policy White House Domestic Policy, Washington, 1978-81; staff dir. minority U.S. Senate Labor & Human Resources Com., Washington, 1981-86; chief of staff U.S. Representative Sander Levin, Washington, 1986-93, Sec. of Labor Robert Reich, Washington, 1993—. Vol. Gonzaga Mother's Club, Washington, 1988—; vol., host parent Project Children, Washington, 1987—. Democrat. Roman Catholic. Home: 6915 Ridgewood Ave Chevy Chase MD 20815 Office: Office of the Sec Dept of Labor 200 Constitution Ave NW Rm 52018 Washington DC 20210

HIGGINS, LINDA WESTAPAL, nursing educator; b. Pitts., Oct. 22, 1960; d. Lois Jean (Laird) Westapal; m. Colin Mark Higgins, Oct. 27, 1984; children: Maura C., Kyle D. BSN, Duquesne U., 1982; MSN, U. Pitts., 1987, doctoral student, 1987—. RN, Pa. Staff nurse trauma unit Allegheny Gen. Hosp., Pitts., 1982-84; triage nurse Health Am., Pitts., 1984-86; teaching asst. U. Pitts., 1986-87; staff nurse ICU St. Clair Hosp., Pitts., 1987-88; nursing educator Carlow Coll., Pitts., 1988—; participated in blood pressure screening and blood sugar testing Medicine Shoppe, Pitts., 1986—. Contbr.: A New Approach to NCLEX-RN, 1989. Mem. Grad. Student Nurses Assn. U. Pitts., Sigma Theta Tau. Episcopalian. Office: Carlow Coll 3333 5th Ave Pittsburgh PA 15213-3165

HIGGINS, MARIKA O'BAIJRE, nursing educator, writer, entrepreneur; b. Manila, Oct. 3, 1947; d. Gerald John and Giovanna (BelForti) Barry; m. Dean. J. P. Higgins, July 1, 1978; children: Matthew, Alexei, Rita, Dean Patrick. Diploma, Ellis Hosp. Sch. Nursing; student, U. Conn., 1964-65, Russell Sage Coll., to 1993; BS, Russell Sage Coll., 1980, postgrad.; postgrad., SUNY, Albany. Team leader, staff RN Samaritan Hosp. Acute Psychiatry, Troy, N.Y.; staff RN, pediatric ICU Albany (N.Y.) Med. Ctr.; rsch. RN Commn. on Quality Care for Mentally Disabled, Albany; staff RN Columbia-Greene Med. Ctr., Catskill, N.Y.; night charge nurse Conifer Park, Scotia, N.Y.; nursing educator St. Clare's Hosp., Schenectady, N.Y.; owner, pres, entrepreneur Future Design & Co.; English tchr. Lang. Inst., Taipei, Taiwan. Novelist, publ. poet, lit. writer; comml. artist Echo Mag. Vol. curriculum designer in gifted and talented programs. Mem. N.Y. State Nurses Assn., Soc. for Applied Learning Tech., Internat. Women Writers Guild, Childreach Plan Internat. Home: 166 Lincoln Ave Saratoga Springs NY 12866-4629

HIGGINS, NANCY BRANSCOME, management and counseling educator; b. New Castle, Pa.; d. Otis and Ola May (Vaughn) Branscome; m. Bernard F. Higgins, Nov. 15, 1969; 1 child, Bernard F. II. BBA, Westminster Coll., 1967, MEd, 1970; MA, Pepperdine U., 1979; EdD, Vanderbilt U., 1990. Cert. counselor; full life cmty. coll. cert. in bus. mgmt. and indsl. human resources mgmt., psychology, office svcs. and related technologies. Counselor U. Md., College Pk., 1976-77; prof. part-time Hartnell Coll., Salinas, Calif., 1977-80; prof. mgmt. Monterey (Calif.) Peninsula Coll., 1977-80; coord., adminstr. Pepperdine U., Ft. Ord, Calif., 1977-80; prof. part-time Park Coll., Ft. Myer, Va., 1980-82, No. Va. C.C., Annandale, 1980-82, Prince George's Coll., Largo, Md., 1980-82; prof. mgmt. and mktg., coord. Montgomery Coll., Rockville, Md., 1982—, chairperson, 1993—; mem. Faculty Congress, Montgomery Coll., 1985-87, diversity com., 1994—, advising com. student devel., 1994—, critical literacy com. mem., 1994—, mgmt. adv. com., tech. prep com., 1994; mem. task force Nat. Coun. for Occupational Edn., 1994. Vol. ARC, Washington, Lakeside Hosp., Cleve., 1990; mem. WETA-Edn. TV, Fairfax, Va. Recipient Student Devel. award Montgomery Coll., 1982, Svc. award, 1982; grantee Montgomery Coll., 1990. Mem. AAUW, ASTD (membership com. and career devel. 1994—), Soc. Human Resources Mgmt., Nat. Soc. Exptl. Edn., Am. Assn. Women in C.C.'s, Pepperdine U. Alumni Assn., Vanderbilt U. Alumni Assn., Westminster Coll. Alumni Assn., Chi Omega (rush chairperson 1994—). Home: 7764 Heatherton Ln Potomac MD 20854-3212

HIGGINS, SISTER THERESE, English educator, former college president; b. Winthrop, Mass., Sept. 29, 1925; d. James C. and Margaret M. (Lennon) H. AB cum laude, Regis Coll., 1947; MA, Boston Coll., DHL, 1993; PhD, U. Wis., 1063; DHL, Emmanuel Coll., 1977, Lesley Coll., 1991; postgrad. in lit. and theology, Harvard U., 1965-66; LLD (hon.), Northeastern U., 1982, Bentley Coll., 1992, Regis Coll., 1994. Joined Congregation of Sisters of St. Joseph, Roman Cath. Ch., 1947; asst. prof. English, Regis Coll., Weston, Mass., 1963-65, asst. prof., 1965-67, assoc. prof. English lit., 1968—, pres., 1974-92, also trustee; book reviewer Boston Globe, 1965—. Trustee Waltham (Mass.) Hosp., 1978-85, Cardinal Spellman Philatelic Mus., 1976-92; mem. Mass. Gov.'s Comm. on Status Women, 1977-79, Nat. Com. Ecclesial Role Women, Archdiocesan Fin. Coun., 1991—. U. Wis. research grantee Eng. Mem. Nat. Cath. Ednl. Assn., AAUW, MLA, AAUP, Assn. Ind. Colls. and Univs. Mass. (exec. com.), New Eng. Colls. Fund, NEASC (commn.). Office: Regis Coll 235 Wellesley St Weston MA 02193-1571

HIGHBARGER, JODI JANELLE, medical/surgical and critical care nurse; b. Wichita, Oct. 20, 1956; d. William David and Norma Dee (Sexton) H. AA, Butler County Community Coll., El Dorado, Kans., 1976; BA in Edn., Wichita State U., 1978, BSN, 1982, postgrad., 1988—. ACLS. Nurse asst. Susan B. Allen Meml. Hosp., El Dorado, 1975-82; staff nurse St. Joseph Med. Ctr., Wichita, 1982-85, Susan B. Allen Meml. Hosp., El Dorado, 1985—. Mem. AACN, Kappa Delta Pi, Pi Omega Pi. Home: 2857 W 4th Ave El Dorado KS 67042-3063

HIGHLAND, MARTHA ELLEN, retired education educator, consultant; b. Lexington, Ky., June 3, 1934; d. William Thomas and Lyda Bruce (Wilson) H.; foster children: Barbara O. Noe, Teresa O. McKenzie, Debby O. Hodges, Joseph Owens. AA, Cumberland Jr. Coll., 1955; BA in Edn., U. Ky., 1958; MA in Edn., U. Louisville, 1981. Cert. tchr., Ky. Tchr. Jefferson County Bd. Edn., Louisville, 1958-59, Ft. Knox (Ky.) Dependent Schs., 1959-65; tchr. Louisville City Schs., 1965-66, reading specialist, 1966-75; reading specialist Jefferson County Sch. System, Louisville, 1975-89, remedial specialist in reading and math., 1989-91; ret., 1991; substitute tchr., vol. Jefferson County Bd. Edn., Louisville, 1991—; faculty rep. Jefferson County Tchrs. Assn., 1981-91. Nominated Disney Tchr. of Yr., 1989. Mem. ASCD, Am. Bus. Women's Assn. (sec. 1989-92, v.p. 1988-89, 92-93, Woman of Yr. 1990). Home: 126 Stevenson Ave Louisville KY 40206

HIGHSMITH, ANNA BIZZELL, executive secretary; b. Richmond, Va., May 31, 1947; d. John Lee and Jacquelyn Frances (Miller) Bizzell; m. Jack Francis Starkey, Jan. 25, 1970 (div. Apr. 1972); 1 child, Mary Cathereine; m. Lemuel Martin Highsmith, May 25, 1974; 1 child, Lemuel Tayloe. Student, N. Fla. Jr. Coll., 1965-66, Armstrong State Coll., 1966-71. Sec. Seaboard Coastline RR, Savannah, Ga., 1966-76; sec., bookkeeper Highsmith Enterprises, Savannah, 1976—. Pres., chmn. of bd. Ballet South, Inc., Savannah, 1982-89, bd. dirs., advisor to pres., 1989—. Mem. Nat. Assn. Women in Constrn. (bd. dirs. 1982-87, 90-92, v.p. 1987-88, pres. 1989-90, 90-91, 94—), Savannah Golf Club, Rinky Dink Sailing Club (sec., editor newsletter 1990-93, liaison 1989-93, prin. race officer 1993, cert. club race officer 1994), Geechee Sailing Club (editor newsletter 1990-91, sec. 1993), Savannah Yacht Club. Republican. Episcopalian. Home: 519-A Whitfield Ave Savannah GA 31406-8207 Office: Highsmith Enterprises 615 Stiles Ave Savannah GA 31401-5322

HIGHSMITH, WANDA LAW, retired association executive; b. Cleveland, Mo., Oct. 25, 1928; d. Lloyd B. and Nan (Sisk) Law; student U. Mo., 1954-56; 1 child, Holly. Legal sec., firms in Mo. and D.C., until 1960; various staff positions Am. Coll. Osteopathic Surgeons, 1960-72, asst. exec. dir., conv. mgr., Alexandria, Va., 1974-94; ret., 1994. Mem. NAFE, Profl. Conv. Mgmt. Assn., Washington Soc. Assn. Execs., Am. Soc. Assn. Execs. Republican. Methodist. Home: 4835 Martin St Alexandria VA 22312-1838

HIGHT, CYNTHIA BOAZMAN, accountant; b. Greenwood, S.C., May 10, 1958; d. Milton Grant and Gladys Emajane (Miner) B.; m. Richard Lamar Hight, July 31, 1982. BS in Bus., Coll. of Charleston, 1980; postgrad., Clemson U., 1993—. Dance instr. Marianna's Dance Studio, Spartanburg, S.C., 1973-77; sr. acct. Fruehauf Corp., Greer, S.C., 1983-88; mgmt. acct. Bommer Industries, Inc., Landrum, S.C., 1988—; computer cons. Spartanburg Devel. Assn., 1992-93. Choreographer of works including Oliver, 1993, Grease, 1992. Notary pub. Spartanburg County, S.C., 1983—. Mem. Inst. Mgmt. Accts., Timberlake Assn. (treas. 1989-90), Spartanburg Little Theatre (pres. 1992-94, sec. 1991-92, dir. 1990-91), Ballet Guild of Spartanburg, Zeta Tau Alpha-Eta Lamda Chpt. (v.p. 1978-79). Republican. Lutheran. Home: 149 Timberlake Cir Inman SC 29349-9659

HIGHTOWER, JEANNE JACKSON, nursing administrator; b. Saratoga Springs, N.Y., Feb. 27, 1949; d. Billy G. and Jeanne Lois (Sickles) Jackson; m. Paul Dudley Hightower, July 6, 1971; children: Bradley, Brandon. BA in English, Mass Comm., Western Ky. U., 1971, ADN, 1973. RN, Ind., Ky. DON Holly Hill Health Care Facility, Brazil, Ind., 1983, Sisters Providence, St. Mary-of-the-Woods, Ind., 1984; staff nurse open heart surgery Terre Haute (Ind.) Regional Hosp., 1985, head nurse surgery, 1988, dir. surg. svcs., 1988-90, asst. DON, 1990-91, DON skilled transitional care unit, 1991-92, dir. special svcs., 1991-94, dir. med. svcs., 1995. Active troop com. Boy Scouts Am., Terre Haute, 1993, 94. Mem. Ind. State Nurse's Assn., Sigma Theta Tau. Republican. Mormon. Office: Terre Haute Regional Hosp 3901 S 7th St Terre Haute IN 47802-5709

HIGMAN, SALLY LEE, company executive; b. Hinsdale, Ill., Sept. 12, 1945; d. Lee Fulton and Freda Margaret (Doehle) H. AB in Social Scis., Shimer Coll., Mt. Carroll, Ill., 1967; MA in Govt., Claremont (Calif.) Grad. Sch., 1969; M of Planning, U. So. Calif., 1973; Cert. in Higher Studies in Ekistics, Athens Tech. Orgn., Athens Ctr. of Ekistics, 1970. Cons. Doxiadis Assocs., Athens, Greece, 1971; rsch. asst. U. So. Calif., 1971-72; cons. Republic of Ecuador, Quito, 1973-75, UN Devel. Prog., Quito, 1975-76; environ. analyst Tetra Tech Inc., Pasadena, Calif., 1976-78; sr. environ. planner Nus Corp., Sherman Oaks, Calif., 1978-81; project mgr. ACT, Inc., Westminster, Calif., 1981-87; owner Higman Doehle Environ. Cons., L.A., 1987-88; pres. Higman Doehle Inc., L.A., 1988—. Contbr. articles to profl. jours. Ford Found. scholar U. So. Calif., 1971-73, jr. rsch. fellow Athens Ctr. of Ekistics, 1969-71; intern Social Sci. Rsch. Coun., Ford Found., 1973-75. Mem. Shimer Coll. Scholastic Soc. Democrat. Episcopalian.

HILBERT, VIRGINIA LOIS, computer consultant and training executive; b. Detroit, June 4, 1935; d. Howard G. and Lois (Garner) Swaggerty; m. James R. Hilbert, Nov. 24, 1958; children: James Jr., Jennifer, Douglas, Alexandra. BA with honors, U. Mich., 1957. Govt. analyst personnel dept. City of Detroit, 1957-60; owner, dir. Profl./Tech. Devel., Inc. dba Lansing (Mich.) Computer Assn. and Lansing Computer Inst., 1978—. Contbd. articles to profl. jours. Sec. Tennis Patrons Bd., Lansing, 1984-89, Pro Symphony, 1984—; active Lansing Art Gallery, 1978-84; tech. bd. mem. Capital Region Cmty. Found. Mem. ASTD, ASCD, Nat. Fedn. Ind. Bus. (guardian), CEO Network, Women Bus. Owners Assn., Mich. Tech. Coun., Nat. Bus. Edn. Assn., Gov.'s Small Bus. Conf. (del. gov.'s work group), Mich. Opportunity Card, Nat. Assn. Trade and Tech. Sch. (key 1989—), Accrediting Commn. of Career Schs. and Colls. of Tech., Bus. Edn. Alliance for Progress, Capital Area Sci. and Math. Challenge Grant Adv. Com., Lansing C. of C. (small bus. coun., co-chair info. and seminar S.B.E., Rotary, Zonta, Alpha Phi (pres. heart equip. fund bd. 1975-86, alumnae pres.). Episcopalian. Home: 938 Wildwood Dr East Lansing MI 48823-3050 Office: Lansing Computer Inst 501 N Marshall St Lansing MI 48912-2306

HILDEBRAND, CAROL ILENE, librarian; b. Presho, S.D., Feb. 15, 1943; d. Arnum Vance and Ethel Grace (Cole) Stoops; m. Duane D. Hildebrand, Mar. 21, 1970. BA, Dakota Wesleyan U., Mitchell, S.D., 1965; M in Librarianship, U. Wash., 1968. Tchr. Watertown (S.D.) H.S., 1965-67; libr. dir. Chippewa County Libr., Montevideo, Minn., 1968-70, The Dalles (Oreg.)-Wasco County Libr., 1970-72; libr. Salem (Oreg.) Pub. Libr., 1972-73; libr. dir. Lake Oswego (Oreg.) Pub. Libr., 1973-82; asst. city libr. Eugene (Oreg.) Pub. Libr., 1982-91, acting city libr., 1991-92, libr. dir., 1993—; cons., condr. workshops in field. Vice chmn. LWV, Lane County, 1987; bd. dirs. People for Oreg. Librs. Polit. Action Com., 1986—; sec. Citizens for Lane County Libr., 1985-88. Mem. ALA (chpt. councilor 1990-94), AAUW (bd. dirs. 1986), Pacific N.W. Libr. Assn. (pres. 1989—), Oreg. Libr. Assn. (pres. 1976-77), Rotary, Phi Kappa Phi. Methodist. Office: Eugene Public Library 100 W 13th Ave Eugene OR 97401-3484

HILDEBRAND, MARGUERITE ANN, nurse; b. Balt., Oct. 8; d. Harry Lingan and Emily Lucille (Koch) Caples; m. Nov. 9, 1963; children: Charles Bradley, Catherine Elaine. Diploma in nursing, Union Meml. Hosp., 1961. RN, Ind. Operating rm. asst. head nurse Union Meml. Hosp., Balt., 1961-62, Crawford Long Hosp., Atlanta, 1962-63; operating rm. nurse, pvt. duty nurse Craven County Hosp., New Bern, N.C., 1963-64; operating rm. head nurse Bloomington (Ind.) Hosp., 1964-65; operating rm. head nurse Cmty. Hosp. Indpls., 1965-68, surg. nurse, 1968-88, laser coord., 1988—. Contbr. articles to profl. jours. Mem. Assn. Operating Rm. Nurses (bd. dirs., sec., pres. 1965-94), Am. Soc. for Lasers in Medicine and Surgery. Democrat. Methodist. Home: Cmty Hosps Indpls 1500 N Ritter Ave Southport IN 46227 Office: Cmty Hosps Indpls 1500 N Ritter Ave Indianapolis IN 46219

HILDEBRAND, SHARON ELIZABETH, artist; b. Medina, Ohio, Aug. 20, 1947; d. Steve and Julia (Farkas) Fodor; children: Keith Richard Hoover, Christopher Alan Hoover; m. James Karl Hildebrand, Sept. 21, 1990. BS in Art, Bowling Green State U., 1969. Cert. tchr. art edn., Ohio. Art instr. Greater Columbus Arts Coun., 1989—; freelance artist for greeting cards Renaissance Card Co., 1988—; leader various art workshops, 1988—. One woman shows include Athletic Club of Columbus, Ohio, 1989, Bushness Gallery, Mansfield, Ohio, 1989, Benjamin Marcus Gallery, Columbus, Ohio, 1989, Mid-Ohio Regional Planning Commn. Columbus, Ohio, 1990, Trumbull Art Gallery, Warren, Ohio, 1990, Room at the Top Gallery, Columbus, 1989, Garrett Gallery, Lancaster, Ohio, 1991, Red Roof Inns Corp. Ctr., Columbus, Ohio, 1992, Ohio State U. Faculty Club, Columbus, 1993, Wile-Kovach Gallery, Columbus, 1993; Group exhibitions include Columbus Art League, Ohio, 1989, N.Am. Open, Boston, 1990, Nat. Art League Open, N.Y., 1990, Bunte Gallery Franklin U., Ohio, 1991, George Walter Vincent Smith Art Mus., Mass., 1991, Canton Art Inst., Ohio, 1991, Ohio Watercolor Soc., 1991, 92, Columbus Art League, 1991, Schumacher Gallery, 1991, 93, 94, Ctrl. Ohio Watercolor Soc., 1991, Worthington Arts Coun, Ohio, 1992, Kussmaul Gallery, Ohio, 1992, Carillon Gallery, Tex., Mus. Fine Arts, Mass., Springfield Mus. Art, Ohio, 1992, The Great Southern Hotel, Ohio, 1992, Salmagundi Club, N.Y., 1993, Broden Gallerry, Wis., 1993, Tubac Ctr. for the Arts, Ariz., 1993, 94, 95, Sidney Rothman The Gallery, N.J., 1993, Sch. of Art Gallery Bowling Green U., Ohio, 1993, Brea Cultural Arts Ctr., Calif., 1993, Worthington Arts Coun., Ohio, 1993, Middletown Fine Arts Ctr., Ohio, 1994, Gallery V, Ohio, 1994, 95; Represented in permanent collections Columbus Metropolitan Library, Bronson Place. Recipient Ctrl. Ohio Watercolor Soc. award 1988, 91, 92, 94, Ohio Watercolor Soc. award 1992, 93, 94, Foothills Arts Festival award 1992, 93, Soc. Watercolor Artists award 1993, Nat. Watercolor Soc. award 1993. Mem. Nat. Watercolor Soc. (Past Pres. award 1993), Ohio Watercolor Soc. (Distinction award 1992, Bronze medal 1994), Ctrl. Ohio Watercolor Soc. (Am. Artist Mag. award 1988). Home and Studio: 5959 Saint Fillans Ct W Dublin OH 43017

HILDEBRANDT-WILLARD, CLAUDIA JOAN, banker; b. Inglewood, Calif., Feb. 12, 1942; d. Charles Samual and Clara Claudia (Palumbo) H.; m. I. LeRoy Willard, Nov. 5, 1993. BBA, U. Colo. Head teller First Colo. Bank & Trust, Denver, 1969-70; asst. cashier First Nat. Bank, Englewood, Colo., 1975-79, asst. v.p., 1979-83, v.p., 1983-92; owner CJH Enterprises, Inc., Breckenridge, Colo., 1980—, Garden Tea Shop, Georgetown, Colo., Laudiac, Inc., Breckenridge, 1993—. Mem. Nat. Assn. Bank Women, Fin. Women Internat. (pres. elect. 1989-92), Am. Soc. for Pers. Adminstrn., Am. Inst. Banking, Mile High Group. Roman Catholic. Home: PO Box 5714 Breckenridge CO 80424 also: PO Box 665 Georgetown CO 80444 Office: 612 A 6th St Georgetown CO 80444

HILDERBRAND, KAREN LYNN, production company owner; b. Lakewood, Ohio, July 16, 1962; d. Andrew and Beatrice (Skowronski) Mitzo; m. Gregg Wesley Hilderbrand, Apr. 14, 1989; 1 child, Tyler. BS in Indsl. Engring., Purdue U., 1985. Indsl. engr. Moore Bus. Forms, Chgo., 1985-87, Martin Brower, Chgo., 1987; project engr. Sedlak Mgmt. Cons., Cleve., 1987-88, Alvey, Inc., St. Louis, 1988-90; logistics engr. Airborne Express, Bartlett, Ill., 1990-93; CEO Twin Sisters Prodns., Akron, Ohio, 1987—. Author: (book and musical video) Rap with the Facts Series, 1988 (Best Product award NSSEA 1991), Rhythm, Rhyme's Read Series, 1990, Colors & Shapes (Parent's Ctr. award 1993), Letters & Numbers, 1993 (Parent's Ctr. award 1993). Mem. NAFE, NOW, NARAS (award judge), Am. Booksellers Assn., Am. Booksellers Children's Product, Ednl. Dealers and Suppliers Assn., Nat. Sch. Suppliers Equipment Assn., Nat. Assn. Ind. Record Distbrs. (award judge). Home: 211 Gatewood Ln Bartlett IL 60103 Office: Twin Sisters Prodns 1340 Home Ave Ste D Akron OH 44310

HILDRETH, CAROLYN JUNE, student health service administrator; b. Grinnell, Iowa, Oct. 12, 1940; d. Glenn Andrew and Almira Anna (Nieman) McDonough; m. Thomas Gerald Hildreth, Sept. 1, 1962; children: Paul Thomas, Charles Thomas, Heather Susan. Student, Grandview Coll., 1959-60; diploma, Iowa Luth. Hosp. Sch. Nursing, 1962. Occupational health nurse John Deere, Ankeny, Iowa, 1971-85; campus nurse Des Moines Area Community Coll., Ankeny, 1985-86, coord. student health svcs., 1986—; bd. dirs. Ankeny Counseling Svcs., 1986-89. Republican. Lutheran. Office: Des Moines Community Coll 2006 S Ankeny Blvd Ankeny IA 50021-8995

HILDRETH, PATRICIA ANNE, software engineer; b. Morristown, N.J., Dec. 10, 1939; d. James Christopher and Dorothy Leonar (Stewart) Lawless; m. Douglas George Hildreth, Oct. 21, 71; children: Emily Louise, Jennifer Edna. BS in Chemistry, Fairleigh-Dickinson U., 1962. Biomed. technician Brookhaven Nat. Labs., Upton, N.Y., 1962-63; libr. asst. Allied Chem. Corp., Parsippany, N.J., 1964-67; tech. abstractor H.W. Wilson Co., Bronx, 1968; computer programmer Polytec Inst. of Bklyn., 1968-69, Dunn & Bradstreet, N.Y.C., 1969-72, Mfrs. Hanover Bank, N.Y.C., 1973, Joint Computer Ctr., Mineola, N.Y., 1984, Nat. West Bank, Melville, N.Y., 1985—. Founder Huntington After Sch. Care, 1981, bd. dirs., 1981—. Mem. Computer Measurement Group. Democrat. Home: 175 Southdown Rd Huntington NY 11743-2505 Office: Nat West Bank 3 Huntington Quad Melville NY 11747-4601

HILDRETH, PATRICIA YVONNE, accounting executive; b. Clinton, Ind., Mar. 15, 1934; d. Leonard Adam and Wilma Vivian (Scifres) Prulhiere; m. James A. Hildreth, Jan. 20, 1954; children: John Alan, Patti Virginia, David Michael, Brian Spencer. Student Jackson Community Coll., 1974-80, Eastern Mich. U., 1980-81. Sales clk. Yeager Co., Akron, Ohio, 1951-52; acctg. clk. B.F. Goodrich Co., Akron, 1952-54; owner bookkeeping firm P.Y. Hildreth, Akron, 1965-72; owner Jackson Small Bus. Service (Mich.), 1972—; cons. in field. Millage campaign chmn. Jackson Pub. Sch., 1977, mem. various coms., 1972-81; active Girl Scouts U.S.A., Akron and Jackson; pres. PTA, Akron, 1968-70; treas. Jackson Med. Ctr. Inc., 1980-82, Jackson Interfaith Shelter, 1985—. Mem. Ind. Accts. Assn. of Mich. (edn. com. 1983-84, chmn. chpt. V 1991—). Republican. Mem. Ch. of Christ. Lodge: Civitan (treas. Jackson club 1981-85, mem. various coms.). Office: Jackson Small Bus Svc 1602 W Washington Ave Jackson MI 49203-1437

HILDRETH, PHYLLIS DRENNON KING, lawyer; b. Berkeley, Calif., Sept. 2, 1957; d. Marshon Phillip and Araminta Eileen (Williams) King; m. James Earl Hildreth, July 12, 1980; children: Sophia Louise, James Earl II. AB in Biology, Harvard U., 1979; JD, U. Md., 1988. Bar: Md. 1988. Med. rsch. asst. Oxford (Eng.) U., 1980-82, Johns Hopkins U., Balt., 1983-84; mem. staff Office of Pub. Defender, State of Md., Towson, Md., 1988-90; chief counsel, adminstr. Offic of Pub. Defender, State of Md., Balt., 1990—. Youth ministries advisor Oak St. African Meth. Episcopal Ch., Balt., 1990—; mem. Juvenile Justice Adv. Coun., 1991—. Mem. Nat. Bar Assn., Nat. Legal Aid and Defender Assn. (defender coun. 1991-93). Office: State of Md Office of Pub Defender 201 Saint Paul Pl Baltimore MD 21202-2001

HILER, MONICA JEAN, reading and sociology educator; b. Dallas, Sept. 3, 1929; d. James Absalom and Monica Constance (Farrar) Longino; m. Robert Joseph Hiler, Nov. 1, 1952; children: Robert, Deborah, Michael, Douglas, Frederick. BA, Agnes Scott Coll., Decatur, Ga., 1951; MEd, U. Ga., Athens, 1968, EdS, 1972, EdD, 1974. Social worker Atlanta Family and Children's Services, 1962-63; tchr. Hall County pub. schs., Ga., 1965-67; mem. faculty Gainesville Jr. Coll., Ga., 1968-87, prof. reading and sociology 1975-87, chmn. devel. studies program, 1973-85, acting chmn. div. social scis., 1986-87, prof. emeritus reading and sociology, 1987—; cons. So. Regional Edn. Bd., 1975-83, Gainesville Coll., 1987—; apptd. spl. advocate Juvenile Ct. Union County, Ga., 1994—. Mem. Internat. Reading Assn., Ga. Sociol. Assn., Assn. Supervision and Curriculum Devel., Gainesville Music Club, Phi Beta Kappa, Phi Delta Kappa, Phi Kappa Phi. Avocations: piano, painting, sewing.

HILFSTEIN, ERNA, science historian, educator; b. Krakow, Poland; came to U.S., 1949, naturalized, 1954; d. Leon and Anna (Schornstein) Kluger; B.A., CCNY, 1967, M.A., 1971, Ph.D., City U. N.Y., 1978; m. Max Hilfstein; children: Leon, Simone Juliana. Tchr. secondary schs., N.Y.C., 1968-84, 86-92; collaborator Polish Acad. Scis., 1968-85; vis. prof. Queens Coll., 1973; affiliate Grad. Sch./Univ. Center, City U. N.Y. NEH grantee, 1984-85; recipient Rector's medal U. N. Copernicus, Torun, 1989, Order of Merit Silver medal Republic of Poland, 1991. Mem. History Sci. Soc., Polish Inst. Arts and Scis. in Am., CUNY Acad. for the Humanities and Scis., N.Y. Acad. Scis., Kościuszko Found., United Fedn. of Tchrs. (chpt. chmn. 1978-84, 86-92, del. 1980-92), N.Y. Acad. Scis., Am. Mus. Nat. History, Internat. Platform Assn. Democrat. Jewish. Author: Starowolski's Biographies of Copernicus, 1980; collaborator English version of Nicholas Copernicus Complete Works, vol. 1, 1972, vol. 2, 1978, vol. 3, 1985, vols. 2 & 3, 2d edit., 1992; contbr. articles and revs. to profl. jours. Editor: Science and History, 1978, Copernicus and His Successors, 1995. Home: 1523 Dwight Pl Bronx NY 10465-1121

HILGARTNER, MARGARET WEHR, pediatric hematologist, educator; b. Balt., Nov. 6, 1924; d. Andrew Henry and Margaret Elizabeth (Wehr) H.;m. Albert Milton Arky; children: George, Elizabeth, John. AB, Bryn Mawr Coll., 1946; MA, Duke U., 1951, MD, 1955. Diplomate Am. Bd. Pediatrics, Am. Bd. Pediatric Hematology/Oncology. Intern Bellevue Hosp., N.Y., 1955-56; resident in pediatrics N.Y. Hosp.-Cornell Med. Ctr., 1956-58, fellow in hematology/oncology, 1958-61, instr. in pediatrics, 1961-67, physician-in-charge pediatric coagulation, 1965—, asst. prof., 1967-73, dir. hemophilia comprehensive treatment, 1970—, assoc. prof., assoc. attending pediatrician outpatient dept., 1973-78, prof., dir. pediatric hematology/oncology div., attending pediatrician, 1978—, Harold Weill prof. pediatric hematology, 1988; dir. hemophilia clinic N.Y. Hosp., 1970—, assoc. attending pediatrician, 1974—; adj. attending physician Sloan-Kettering Cancer Ctr., N.Y., 1979—; bd. dirs., mem. exec. com. N.Y. Blood Ctr.; cons. Bur. Handicapped Children, N.Y., 1971, Factor VIII Inhibitor Study Group, 1974, Ho. Reps. Ways and Means Com., 1977, Senate and Ho. Reps. Health Subcom. on Health, 1978-80, Fgn. and Interstate Commerce Com.-Ho. Reps. Subcom. on Pub. Health and Environment, 1979, N.Y. State Com. on Transfusion, 1979—, Ad Hoc Com. Rev. Rsch. in Edn., 1981-82; cons. in medicine Englewood (N.J.) Hosp., 1974—, in pediatric hematology, 1982—; lectr.-in-medicine Mt. Sinai Hosp., N.Y., 1979—; vis. prof. Rochester (Minn.) Hemophilia Ctr. 1979, 1980, Marshfield (Wis.) Clinic, 1979, Oakland Children's Hosp., 1981, Hangchow, Beijing, Kian, Peoples Republic of China, 1981, Johns Hopkins U. 1982, Rochester Strong Meml., 1985, Duke U., 1985.; chmn. Gov.'s adv. coun. to N.J. Dept. Health Hemophilia Program, 1973-80; mem. task force Factor VIII-Inhibitors Nat. Heart Lung Inst., 1975-80; mem. adv. com. publ. health #94-63 Health Svcs. Adminstrn., 1976lblood disease and resources Nat. Heart Lung Inst. NIH, 1985-89; chmn. Feiba Study Com., U.S. chpt., 1981—, pediatric working group World Fedn. Hemophilia, 1982; mem. ad hoc AIDS adv. com. Nat. Heart Lung Blood Inst. NIH, 1985—;. Mem. profl. adv. bd. mag. Baby Talk, 1987—; contbr. numerous articles to profl. jours. Mem. Am. Acad. Pediatrics (chmn. sect. program oncology/hematology), Am. Heart Assn. Am. Med. Women's Assn., Am. Pediatric Soc., Am. Soc. Hematology, Assn. Women in Sci. (treas. 1974-76), Harvey Soc., Internat. Soc. Blood Transfusion, Internat. Soc. Thrombosis and Hemostasis, Nat. Hemophilia Found. (bd. dirs. met. chpt. 1965—, trustee 1968-88, med. dir. met. chpt. 1970—, mem. med. and sci. bd. 1973—, v.p. 1979-84, mem. edn. resources project 1979—), N.Y. Acad. Sci., N.Y. Soc. Study Blood, World Fedn. Hemophilia (chmn. child care com. 1990), Am. Soc. Pediatric Hematology/Oncology, Children's Blood Found. (med. dir. 1978—, bd. dirs. 1987—), Cooley's Anemia Found. (bd. dirs 1987—). Office: Cornell U Med Coll Dept of Pediatrics 525 E 68th St New York NY 10021-4873

HILGEMANN, CAROL LEE, art educator; b. Aberdeen, S.D., Aug. 27, 1947; d. Edwin and Wilma (Wunner) H. BS in Edn., No. State U., Aberdeen, S.D., 1969. Cert. tchr., Alaska. Tchr. art Taylor Jr. High Sch., Eielson AFB, Alaska, 1969-75, Ben Eielson Jr. High Sch., Eielson AFB, Alaska, 1976-83, Ben Eielson Sr. High Sch., Eielson AFB, Alaska, 1983—. Named Woman of the Yr. Am. biog. Inst., 1992. Mem. Nat. Art Edn. Assn., Nat. Coun. on Edn. in Ceramic Arts, Alaska Art Edn. Assn. (v.p. 1989, pres. 1990, treas. 1993, Alaska Art Educator of Yr. 1990, Disting. Svc. award Within the Profession 1992), Fairbanks Art Assn. (past bd. dirs., edn. com.). Republican. Lutheran. Office: Ben Eielson Jr/Sr High Sch Bldg 5271 Industrial Ave Eielson AFB AK 99702

HILGENBERG, EVE BRANTLY HANDY, government official; b. Balt., Mar. 3, 1942; d. Sydney Speiden and Evelyn Harned (Crady) Handy; m. Thomas Rodney Twells, June 21, 1963 (div. Mar. 1971); 1 child, Thomas Rodney; m. John Christian Hilgenberg, Apr. 3, 1971; 1 child, Elizabeth Crady. BA, Goucher Coll., 1963. U.S. sr. exec. svc., assoc. commr. Social Security Adminstrn., Balt., 1986—. Recipient Superior Achievement award Dept. Human Svcs., 1978, Commr.'s award for Exceptional and Innovative Leadership, 1992, Govt. Computer News award for Excellence in the Application of Info. Tech. to Improve Svcs. Delivery, 1992. Episcopalian. Home: 38 Warrenton Rd Baltimore MD 21210-2925

HILKEMEYER, RENILDA ESTELLA, nurse; b. Martinsburg, Mo., July 29, 1915; d. Henry Gerard and Anna Marie (Bertels) Hilkemeyer. Diploma in nursing, St. Mary's Hosp., St. Louis U., 1936; B.S. in Nursing Edn., George Peabody Coll. for Tchrs., Nashville, 1947; postgrad., U. Minn., 1950, U. Tex. Sch. Nursing, 1981; D of Pub. Svc. (hon.), St. Louis U., 1988. Staff nurse oper. rm. St. Mary's Hosp., Jefferson City, Mo., 1936-37; dist. pub. health nurse Mo. Div. Health, Jefferson City, 1937-40, cons. nursing edn., Mo., 1950-55; asst. dir. nursing Gen. Hosp. No. 1, Kansas City, Mo., 1947-49; asst. exec. sec. Mo. Nurses Assn., Jefferson City, 1949-50; dir. nursing U. Tex. System Cancer Ctr., Houston, 1955-77, asst. to pres. nursing resources, 1977-79, staff asst. to pres., prof. oncology nursing, 1979-84; mem. grant rev. com. NIH Nat. Cancer Inst, 1979-83, program rev. com., 1975-77, cons., 1982—; cons. NIH Nat. Heart, Blood and Lung Inst., 1983—, Worker's Inst. Safety, Health, 1983—; chmn., mem. scholarship and professorship com. Cancer Soc., 1980—, mem. nursing adv. com., 1963-80, 85—, profl. edn. com., 1984—; chmn. nursing adv. com., mem. adminstrv. bd. Renilda Hilkemeyer Child Care Ctr., U. Tex. Med. Ctr., 1969—. Book reviewer Am. Jour. Nursing, 1982; contbr. articles to profl. jours. Pres. Braes Interfaith Ministries, 1991, 94, 95. Recipient Outstanding Profl. Women's award Tex. Fedn. Houston Profl. Women, 1983, outstanding contbns. Award, Nat. Cancer Inst., 1983, Disting. Svc. award Am. Cancer Soc., 1981, Nurse of Yr. Award, Houston Area League Nursing, 1973, Matrix Award, Theta Sigma Phi, Houston, 1963, Disting. Merit award Internat. Soc. Nurses in Cancer Care, 1986; new child care ctr. at U. Tex. Med. Ctr. Houston, named in her honor, 1981 (1st ctr. established 1969); grantee HEW, 1974-77, Am. Cancer Soc., 1974-75, Tex. Fedn. and Profl. Women's Club, 1977-83, Am. Cancer Soc. 1st Nat. Nursing Leadership award, 1989. Achievement: pioneer in cancer nursing. Mem. ANA, Oncology Nursing Soc. (hon. 1991), Tex. Nurses Assn. (pres. 1962-64, bd. dir. 1964-66, 71-75, Nurse of Yr. award 1979, dist. 9 svc. award 1970), Am. Med. Writers Assn. (Houston-Galveston sect. 1983-84), Sigma Theta Tau, Altrusa Club (pres. 1983-84, Houston). Home: 3707 Murworth Dr Houston TX 77025-3531

HILL, ALICE LORRAINE, law researcher, educator; b. Moore, Okla., Jan. 15, 1935; d. Robert Edward and Alma Alice (Fraysher) H.; children: Debra Hrboka, Pamela Spangler, Eric Shiver, Lorraine Smith. Grad., Patricia Stevens Modeling Sch., Orlando, Fla., 1963; student, Draughton Sch. Bus., Oklahoma City, 1968-69, Troy State U., 1970-71, Ventura Coll., 1974; AA in Gen. Edn., Rose Coll., Midwest City, Okla.; BS in Bus. and Acctg., Central State U., 1977; student, U. Okla., 1977-78. Accredited tchr. Calif.; ordained min. Gospel Ministry, 1982; lic. realtor. Former model; with L.A. Unified Sch. Dist., Gravity Drop & Dead Bolt Lock Inc., Oxnard, Calif., 1993, A. Hill & Assocs., Oxnard, Calif., 1993-94; co-founder Law of Moses Common Law Legal Assn., Kingfisher, Okla. Mem. NAFE, NEA, Internat. Platform Assn. Home: 1646 Lime Ave Oxnard CA 93033-6897

HILL, ANITA CARRAWAY, retired state legislator; b. Chatfield, Tex., Aug. 13, 1928; d. Archie Clark and Martha (Butler) Carraway; BA in Journalism, Tex. Woman's U., 1950; m. Harris Hill, Sept. 20, 1952; children: Stephen Victor, Virginia Evelyn. Reporter Garland (Tex.) Daily News, 1950-51; ednl. dir. First Meth. Ch., Garland, 1951-53; chemist Kraft Foods Co., Garland, 1953-56; legis. aide, Tex. Legislature, 1975-77; mem. Tex. Ho. of Reps., 1977-92, mem. mcpl. bond and revenue sharing coms., 1971-74; ret., 1992. Awards chmn. City of Garland Environ. Council; mem. City of Garland Park and Recreation Bd., 1971-77, chmn., 1976-77; life mem. PTA. Named Disting. Alumna, Tex. Woman's U., 1981. Mem. Garland C. of C., Rowlett C. of C., Bus. and Profl. Women's Club (Garland Woman of Year, 1980), AAUW, Tex. Assn. Elected Women. Republican. Methodist.

HILL, ANITA FAYE, law educator; b. 1956. BS in Psychology, Okla. State U., 1977; JD, Yale U., 1980. With Office of Civil Rights, Dept. Edn., Washington, 1981-82, EEOC, Washington, 1982-83; prof. Oral Roberts U., 1983-88, Coll. Law, U. Okla., Norman, 1988—; speaker, lectr. on sexual harassment for colls. and orgns. Baptist. Office: U Okla Coll Law 660 Parrington Oval Norman OK 73019

HILL, ANNA MARIE, manufacturing executive; b. Great Falls, Mont., Nov. 6, 1938; d. Paul Joseph and Alexina Rose (Doyon) Ghekiere. AA, Oakland Jr. Coll., 1959; student, U. Calif., Berkeley, 1960-62. Mgr. ops. OSM, Soquel, Calif., 1963-81; purchasing agt. Arrow Huss, Scotts Valley, Calif., 1981-82; sr. buyer Fairchild Test Systems, San Jose, Calif., 1982-83; materials mgr. Basic Test Systems, San Jose, 1983-86; purchasing mgr. Beta Tech., Santa Cruz, Calif., 1986-87; mgr. purchasing ICON Rev., Carmel, Calif., 1987-88; materials mgr. Integrated Components Test System, Sunnyvale, Calif., 1988-89; mfg. mgr. Forte Comm., Sunnyvale, 1989-94; sr. buyer Cisco Systems, San Jose, Calif., 1994—; cons., No. Calif., 1976—. Counselor Teens Against Drugs, San Jose, 1970, 1/2 Orgn., Santa Cruz, 1975-76. Mem. Am. Prodn. Invention Control, Nat. Assn. Female Execs., Nat. Assn. Purchasing Mgmt., Porsche Club Am., Am. Radio Relay League. Democrat. Club: Young Ladies Radio League. Home: 733 Rosedale Ave # 4 Capitola CA 95010-2248 Office: Cisco Systems 110 W Tasman Dr San Jose CA 95134

HILL, ANNE LYNN, corporate professional; b. Uniontown, Pa., Sept. 3, 1944; d. Robert Benjamin and Katherine Rebecca (Reynolds) Rankin; m. Howard Harry Hill, Aug. 23, 1964 (div. Dec. 1979); children: Jennifer Leigh, Carolyn Jeanne; m. Thomas A. Fessenden, Apr. 29, 1990. BS, U. Md., 1966. Elem. tchr. Prince George's County Bd. Edn., Upper Marlboro, Md., 1966-68; food service mgr. Bloomingdales, White Flint, Md., 1976-78; dist. mgr. ice cream parlors/restaurants Drug Fair, Inc., Alexandria, Va., 1978-80; dir. quality assurance and product devel. Marriott Corp., Washington, 1980-88, corp. procurement dir., 1988-90; sr. v.p., 1990—; bd. dirs. Balt. Internat. Culinary Coll. Mem. NAFE, DAR, SAFSR, Roundtable for Women in Foodservice (Pacesetter award 1986). Republican. Presbyterian. Office: Marriott Internat 1 Marriott Dr # 817.63 Washington DC 20058-0001

HILL, BARBARA ANDERSON, artist, educator; b. Bklyn., Nov. 29, 1941; d. Einar and Martha (Risdal) Anderson; m. John U. Hill, May 28, 1961 (div. Aug. 1989); children: Kevin U., Kristina Hill McDonough, Kenneth Sam. AA in Fine Art, Edison C.C., 1982; BA in Fine Art, U. South Fla., 1984, MFA in Sculpture, 1987. Dir. Stein Gallery, Tampa, Fla., 1987-90; ind. curator Woman's Care Brandon (Fla.) Collection, 1990-91; program coord. City of Tampa, 1990-91; curator, exbhn. collections Fla. Gulf Coast Art Ctr., Belleair, 1991-94; grants and major gifts mgr. The John and Mable Ringling Mus. Art, Sarasota, Fla., 1994—; adj. prof. art U. South Fla., Ft. Myers, 1987, Edison C.C., Ft. Myers, 1985-87; owner, instr. Touch of Clay Sch., Sanibel, Fla., 1978-81; instr. Ceramic League Miami (Fla.), 1974-76. Artist: public collections include: Am. Express, Jacksonville, Nationsbank, Tampa, Barnett Bank, St. Petersburg, (museum collections) U. Fla., Gainesville, U. So. Fla., Tampa. Art advisor City of Tampa Arts in Pub. Places, 1993; panelist Arts Coun. Hillsborough City, Tampa, 1988; mem. arts com. City of Sanibel, Sanibel Island, Fla., 1982-88. SOS grantee, Tampa, 1991. Mem. Am. Assn. Mus., Fla. Assn. Mus., Fla. Ctr. Contemporary Art (bd. dirs., v.p. 1992-94, pres., 1994—), Phi Kappa Phi. Home: 2810 W Sitios St Tampa FL 33629

HILL, BETTY JEAN, academic administator; b. Ishpeming, Mich., Nov. 27, 1937; d. Azarius William and Evelyn (Herring) Parsons; m. Edwin E. Hill, Nov. 27, 1959 (dec. 1979); children: Cheryl, Kenneth; m. Harold Ralph Pawley, June 27, 1981. B in Nursing, No. Mich. U., Marquette, 1972, MEd, 1974; M in Nursing, Wayne State U., 1977, PhD, 1979. RN, Mich. Staff nurse St. Luke's Hosp., Marquette, 1958-60; supr. Meadowbrook Hosp., Bellaire, Mich., 1959-60; head nurse St. Luke's Hosp., Marquette, 1960-62, clin. instr., 1868-70; asst. prof. No. Mich. U., Marquette, 1972-75, assoc. prof., 1978-80, asst. dean, 1980-82, dean, 1982—. Contbr. articles to jours.; author: (with others) Theory Construction, 1981. Fund Chairperson Hospice, Marquette, 1988. Fellow AASCU Acad. Leadership, 1991-93, Harvard Inst. for Ednl. Mgmt., 1992, No. Econ. Initiatives Corp., 1992—. Mem. Mich. and Nat. League for Nursing, Mich. Assn. Colls. of Nursing (treas. 1986-90), Midwest Alliance in Nursing, Am. Assn. State Coll. and Univs., Am. Assn. Colls. and Nursing, Marquette Econ. Club (pres. 1989-90), Rotary Club, Planned Parenthood, Sigma Theta Tau. Methodist. Home: 643

Lakewood Ln Marquette MI 49855-9517 Office: No Mich U Nursing Magers Hall Marquette MI 49855

HILL, BEVERLY ELLEN, health sciences educator; b. Albany, Calif., May 20, 1937; d. Bert E. and Catherine (Doyle) H. BA, Coll. Holy Names, 1960; MS in Edn., Dominican Coll., 1969; EdD, U. So. Calif., 1978. Producer, dir. Health Scis TV U. Calif., Davis, 1966-69, coordinator Health Scis. TV, 1969-73; asst. dir. IMS U. So. Calif., Los Angeles, 1973-76, asst. dir. continuing edn., 1976-80, dir. biocommunications, 1976-80; dir. Med. Ednl. Resources Program Ind. U. Sch. Medicine, Indpls., 1980—; acting asst. dean continuing med. edn. Ind. U. Sch. Medicine, 1991—; Presenter Cath. U. Nijmegen, Netherlands, 1980, 81, European Symposium on Clin. Pharmacy, Brussels, 1982, Barcelona, Spain, 1983. Contbr. articles to profl. jours. Pres. Indpls. Shakespeare Festival, 1982-83; mem. subcom. Ind. Film Commn., Indpls., 1984—. Recipient first place in rehab. category 4th Biannual J. Muir Med. Film Fest., 1980. Mem. Assn. Biomed. Communications (bd. dirs. 1985—), Health Scis. Com. Assn. (bd. dirs. 1976-79, First Place Video Festival, 1979), Assn. for Edn. Communications and Tech. Home: 5249 W 59th St Indianapolis IN 46254-1109 Office: Med Ednl Resources Program 1226 W Michigan St BR 156 Indianapolis IN 46223

HILL, CARLOTTA J. H., physician; b. Chgo., Apr. 8, 1948; d. Clarence Kenneth and Vlasta (Cizek) Hayes; m. Chester James Hill III, June 10, 1967 (div. 1974); m. Carlos Alberto Rotman, July 31, 1980; children: Robin Mercedes. BA magna cum laude, Knox Coll., 1969; MD with honors, U. Ill., 1973. Diplomate Nat. Bd. Med. Examiners, 1974, Am. Bd. Dermatology, 1978. Asst. prof. clin. dermatology Coll. Medicine U. Ill., Chgo., 1978-93, assoc. prof. clin. dermatology Coll. Medicine, 1993—, co-dir. H.D. Clinic, 1980-83, sr. cons. H.D. Clinic, 1983-88; med. dir. Chgo. Regional H.D. Clinic, 1988-93, dir., 1993—; sen. U. Ill. Senate, Chgo., 1986-91; councilor Chgo. Med. Soc., 1990—. Contbr. articles to profl. jours. mem. bd. dirs. Summerfest St. James Cathedral, Chgo., 1986-91, benefit co-chair, 1988; master gardner Chgo. Botanic Garden, Glencoe, Ill., 1994. Recipient Janet Glascow award Am. Women's Med. Assn., 1973. Mem. AMA, Am. Acad. Dermatology, Herb Soc. Am., Ill. State Med. Assn., Ill. State Dermatologic Soc., Chgo. Med. Soc., Chgo. Dermatologic Soc. Episcopalian. Office: Dept Dermatology 808 S Wood Chicago IL 60612

HILL, CLARA EDITH, psychology educator; b. Shivers, Miss., Sept. 13, 1948; d. Fletcher Von and Anna (Teich) H.; m. Jim Gormally, May 25, 1974; children: Kevin, Katherine. BA, So. Ill. U., 1970, MA, 1972, PhD, 1974. Lic. psychologist, Md. Asst. prof. dept. psychology U. Md., College Park, 1974-78, assoc. prof. dept. psychology, 1978-85, prof. dept. psychology, 85—. Author: Therapist Techniques and Client Outcomes, 1989; editor Jour. of Counseling Psychology, 1994—; contbr. articles to profl. jours. Grantee NIMH, 1983-92. Fellow Am. Psychol. Assn.; mem. Soc. Psychotherapy Rsch. (pres. North Am. chpt. 1990, pres. internat. orgn. 1994). Office: U Maryland Dept Psychology College Park MD 20742

HILL, CLAUDIA ADAMS, tax consultant; b. Long Beach, Calif., Oct. 14, 1949; d. Claude T. Adams and Geraldine (Jones) Crosby; m. W. Eugene Hill, Sept. 14, 1968 (div. Oct. 1983); children: Stacia Heather, Jonathan Eugene; m. Larry C. Enoksen, June 4, 1988. BA, Calif. State U., Fullerton, 1972; MBA, San Jose State U., 1978. Systems analyst quality assurance group United Technology Ctr., 1972-73; with Commrs. Adv. Group IRS, 1987; prin., owner Tax Mam, Inc., 1974—; noted lectr. in field of taxation; tax advisor to Rsch. Inst. Am., also pubs., Nev., tax analysts, Va. Contbr. articles to profl. jours. Mem. Nat. Soc. Pub. Accts. (accredited tax advisor, liaison to profl. assns. IRS, Franchist Tax Bd.), Nat. Assn. Enrolled Agts., Calif. Soc. Enrolled Agts. Republican. Office: TAX MAM Inc 10680 S De Anza Blvd Cupertino CA 95014-4446

HILL, DALE STEWART, volunteer; b. Pasadena, Calif., Nov. 13, 1928; d. Frederick Woodward and Dorothy Pierce (Stewart) Walker; m. Robert Hill, Oct. 20, 1951; children: Barry Robert, Allan Stewart, Lorin Frederick. AB, U. Calif., Berkeley, 1949. Registered physical therapist Calif. Staff phys. therapist Orthopedic Hosp., L.A., 1950-51, Alta Bates Hosp., Berkeley, Calif., 1951-53, pvt. practice, Concord, Calif., 1955-61; sec., treas. Hill Rsch. Assocs., Inc., Los Gatos, Calif., 1985—. Chair Charter Rev. Com., Santa Clara County, Calif., 1973-75; foreman Grand Jury, Santa Clara County, 1974-75; planning commr. Town of Los Gatos, 1976-82; bd. dirs. Live Oak Adult Day Svcs., Inc., Los Gatos, 1986—. Recipient Silver Bowl award Jr. League, San Jose, 1991; named Woman of Achievement San Jose Nercury-News, 1976. Mem. LWV (pres. 1971-73, v.p. mgmt. 1981-85, manual series writer 1987-88), AAUW (grantee 1978), Phi Beta Kappa.

HILL, DEBBIE ANNE, architectural designer; b. Palo Alto, Calif., Jan. 6, 1958; d. Stanislaus Joseph and Lea Mary (Antoniolli) Johnston; m. Cy Young Hill, June 5, 1982 (div. May 1993); children: Jessica, Bryce. Archtl. designer Atherton Industries, Menlo Park, Calif., 1976-77, R & B, Santa Clara, Calif., 1977-78, Interland Devel., San Mateo, Calif., 1978-79, Oakley & Assocs., Santa Clara, 1979-87, Thrust IV, Mountain View, 1987—; self-employed archtl. designer, Santa Clara, 1977—. Home: 2073 Kimberlin Pl Santa Clara CA 95051-2247

HILL, DEBBIE LEE, accountant; b. Duluth, Minn., Mar. 13, 1959; d. Arlan P. and Jeanne M. (Paulson) Breitenstein. BSBA in Acctg., U. Ctrl. Fla., 1981. Acct. Simon Mktg. Inc., L.A., 1981-82, First Fed. Savs. & Loan of Martin County, Stuart, Fla., 1982; acctg. officer Naples (Fla.) Fed. Savs. & Loan, 1982-83; acctg. supr. Calif. Fed. Savs. & Loan, Ft. Lauderdale, Fla., 1983-84; asst. v.p., asst. contr. Commonwealth Savs. & Loan Assn., Ft. Lauderdale, 1985-89, Kislak Orgn., Miami, Fla., 1989-94; contr. First Mortgage Network, Inc., Plantation, Fla., 1994—. Mem. Assn. Profl. Mortgage Women, So. Fla. Fin. Network. Home: 4534 NW 94th Way Sunrise FL 33351-5166 Office: First Mortgage Network Inc Ste 500 150 S Pine Island Rd Plantation FL 33324

HILL, DIANE SELDON, corporate psychologist; b. Mpls., Sept. 17, 1943; d. Earl William and Geraldine (Le Veille) Seldon; m. David Reuben Hill, May 14, 1986 (div. Feb. 1988); children: Anna Marion, Jason David. BA, Mt. Holyoke Coll., 1965; MA in Psychology, U. Minn., 1968, PhD in Psychology, 1974; Advanced Mgmt. Program, U. Pa. Wharton Sch., 1992. Lic. psychologist, Colo; diplomate in clin. psychology Am. Bd. Profl. Psychologists. Instr., counselor Student Counseling Bur. U. Minn., Mpls., 1968-70, advisor women's programs, Student Activities Bur., 1970-71; instr. psychology Augsburg Coll., Mpls., 1970-71; counselor, tchr. humanities Emma Willard Sch., Troy, N.Y., 1972-75; dir. counseling and re-engagement Colo. Women's Coll., Denver, 1976-77; clin. field supr., Sch. Profl. Psychology U. Denver, 1977—; asst. clin. prof. psychology U. Colo. Health Scis., Denver, 1981-89, Ctr. for Creative Leadership, Colorado Springs, 1981—; pvt. practice Denver, 1977-89; mgmt. and organizational cons. Somerville and Co., Inc., Denver, 1989—; dir. Profl. Exams. Svc., N.Y.C., 1991—; presenter at profl. meetings; expert witness on psychology ethics; presenter testimony before Colo. legis. hearing coms. and Colo. Ins. Commn.; lobbyist for psychology licensure Parliament of Finland, 1989. Named NDEA IV fellow U. Minn., 1967-68. Fellow Am. Psychol. Assn.; mem. Colo. Psychol. Assn. (bd. dirs. 1979-82, dir. polit. action com.), Am. Assn. State Psychology Bds. (del. 1982-83, mem.-at-large exec. com. 1983, pres. 1988-91), Colo. Bd. Psychologist Examiners (bd. dirs. 198-187, chmn. 1983-88), Women's Forum Colo. (mem. com. 1979—). Episcopalian. Home: 2052 Bellaire St Denver CO 80207-3722 Office: Somerville & Co Inc 1625 Broadway Denver CO 80202-4731

HILL, DONNA MARIE, communications executive; b. Amesbury, Mass., July 25, 1957; d. Robert and Marie Doris (Lucier) Menzigan. BS in Math., U. Lowell, 1979, MBA in Ops., 1983. Material control analyst AVCO Corp., Wilmington, Mass., 1979-81; ops. analyst Blue Cross & Blue Shield, Boston, 1981-83, risk analyst, 1983-84; systems analyst Bell Atlantic Corp., Bethesda, Md., 1984-86; cons. internal Bell Atlantic Corp., Bethesda, 1986-89, project mgr., 1989-91, new tech. strategic planning mgr., 1992—; speaker FUSE Nat. and Regional Confs., 1988, 91. inventor (software) User-assisted Adhoc Reporting, 1988, Natural English Report Access, 1988. Vol. Montgomery County Vol. Assn., Montgomery, Md., 1983—, PALS, Montgomery County, 1984—; chair spl. events New Mem. Svcs. John F. Kennedy Ctr. Performing Arts, Washington, 1985—, mem. vol. adv. com., 1991, 92; chair vol. adv. com. Kennedy Ctr., 1992—; bd. dirs. Sister City Corp., Rockville, 1992—, v.p., 1993-95, pres.-elect, 1994—. Mem. NAFE, Ops. Rsch. Soc., Intelligent Computer Rsch. Inst., Focus User Troup (co-chmn. artificial intelligence group 1989, leader, coord. spl. interest groups for Nat. Com., 1989, nat., regional speaker 1988, 91), Rockville Jr. C. of C. (sec. 1992-93), Md. State Jr. C. of C. (program mgr. internat. involvement 1992-93, dist. dir. 1993-94, cmty. devel. v.p. 1994—), Internat. Speakers Platform. Republican. Roman Catholic. Office: Bell Atlantic 6701 Democracy Blvd Bethesda MD 20817-1563

HILL, EARLENE HOOPER, state legislator; b. Balt., Oct. 22; d. Otis Barnett Hooper and Thelma E. (Richardson) Young; m. Thomas C. Hill Jr., Mar. 9, 1966; 1 child, Charisse E. BA, Norfolk State U., 1967; MSW, Adelphi U., 1976. Mgr. N.Y. State Dept. Social Svcs., N.Y.C., 1979-88; mem. N.Y. State Assembly, 1988—; mem. women's program, shop steward Pub. Employees Fedn., 1980-88, mem. exec. bd. Mem. exec. bd. Jack & Jill of Am., Inc., Nassau County, N.Y., 1985—; mem. Nat. Women's Polit. Caucus, N.Y.C., 1987—. Mem. Negro Bus. and Profl. Women (Cen. Nassau chpt.), Delta Sigma Theta. Democrat. Office: NY State Legislature State Capitol Albany NY 12224*

HILL, ELEANOR JEAN, lawyer; b. Miami Beach, Fla., Dec. 19, 1950; d. Elbert Cray and Florence Louise (Strzycki) Hill; m. Thomas Paul Gross, April 7, 1990; 1 child, Bryan Michael Gross. BS, Fla. State U., 1972, JD, 1974. Bar: Fla. Asst. atty. U.S. Atty's Office, Tampa, Fla., 1975-78; spl. atty. Organized Crime Strike Force, U.S. Dept. Justice, Tampa, Fla., 1978-80; asst. counsel U.S. Senate Permanent Subcommittee on Investigations, Washington, 1980-82, chief counsel to minority, 1982-87, staff dir., chief counsel, 1987—. Mem. Fla. Bar Assn., Phi Beta Kappa, Phi Kappa Phi. Office: Perm Subcom on Investigations Rm SR-100 Russell Senate Office Bldg Washington DC 20510

HILL, ELIZABETH STARR, writer; b. Lynn Haven, Fla., Nov. 4, 1925; d. Raymond King and Gabrielle (Wilson) Cummings; m. Russell Gibson Hill, May 28, 1949; children: Andrea van Waldron, Bradford Wray. Student, Finch Jr. Coll., 1941-42, Columbia U., 1970-73. Freelance writer; past dir. Princeton Creative Ctr.; tchr. writing Princeton Adult Sch. Author: (juvenile books) The Wonderful Visit to Miss Liberty, 1961, The Window Tulip, 1964, Evan's Corner, 1967, 1991 (ALA Notable Book for Children), Master Mike and the Miracle Maid, 1967, Pardon My Fangs, 1969, Bells: A Book to Begin On, 1970, Ever-After Island, 1977, Fangs Aren't Everything, 1985, When Christmas Comes, 1989, The Street Dancers, 1991, Broadway Chances, 1992 (ABA Pick of the Lists), The Banjo Player, 1993; contbr. articles to mags. including Reader's Digest, many others. Mem. Authors Guild Am., Authors League Am., Univ. Club Winter Park. Office: Harold Ober Assn Inc 425 Madison Ave New York NY 10017-1110

HILL, EMITA BRADY, academic administrator; b. Balt., Jan. 31, 1936; d. Leo and Lucy McCormick (Jewett) Brady; children: Julie Beck, Christopher, Madeleine. BA, Cornell U., 1957; MA, Middlebury Coll., 1958; PhD, Harvard U., 1967. Instr. Harvard U., 1961-63; asst. prof. Western Reserve U., 1967-69; from asst. prof. to v.p. Lehman Coll. CUNY, Bronx, N.Y., 1970-91; chancellor, grad. faculty Ind. U., Kokomo, Ind., 1991—. Mem. Am. Assn. Higher Edn., Assn. Am. Coll., Am. Soc. for 18th Century Studies, Am. Assn. State Colls. and Univs., Internat. Assn. Univ. Pres., Internat. Soc. for 18th Century Studies, Phi Beta Kappa. Office: Ind U PO Box 9003 2300 S Washington St Kokomo IN 46902-3557

HILL, FAY GISH, librarian; b. Rensselaer, Ind., Sept. 19, 1944; d. Roy Charles and Vergie (Powell) Gish; m. John Christian Hill, May 20, 1967; 1 child, Christina Gish. BA, Purdue U., 1967; MLS, U. Tex., 1971. Asst. librarian basic reference dept. Tex. A&M U., College Station, 1972, assoc. librarian sci. ref. dept., 1972-74, acting head librarian sci. reference dept., 1975; reference librarian Cen. Iowa Regional Library, Des Moines, 1984—. Troop leader Girl Scouts U.S., Ames, Iowa, 1983-88; bd. dirs. Friends of Fgn. Wives, Ames, 1982-86. Mem. ALA, Iowa Libr. Assn., Iowa Libr. Assn. Found. (bd. dirs. 1990—). Presbyterian. Home: 5604 Thunder Rd Ames IA 50014-9804 Office: Cen Iowa Regional Libr Reference 515 Douglas Ave Ames IA 50010-6215

HILL, GRACE LUCILE GARRISON, education educator, consultant; b. Gastonia, N.C., Sept. 26, 1930; d. William Moffatt and Lillian Tallulah (Tatum) Garrison; m. Leo Howard Hill, July 24, 1954; children: Lillian Lucile, Leo Howard Jr., David Garrison. BA, Erskine Coll., 1952; MA, Furman U., 1966; PhD, U. S.C., 1980. Lic. sch. psychologist, S.C. Tchr. Bible, Clinton (S.C.) Pub. Schs., 1952-53; tchr. English Parker High Sch., Greenville, S.C., 1953-55; elem. tchr. Augusta Circle Sch., Greenville, 1955-57; tchr. homebound children Greenville County Sch. Dist., Greenville, 1961-64, psychologist, 1966-77; adj. prof. grad. studies in edn. Furman U., Greenville, 1977—, U. S.C., Columbia, 1982—; ednl. cons. Ednl. Diagnostic Svcs., Greenville, 1980—; exec. dir. Camperdown Acad., Greenville, 1986-87; cons. learning disability program Erskine Coll., Due West, S.C., 1978—. Contbr. articles to profl. jours. Pres. Lake Forest PTA, Greenville, 1970-71; pres. of Women A.R. Presbyn. Ch., Greenville, 1973-75, adult Bible tchr., 1978—; sec. bd. trustees Erskine Coll., 1982-88; bd. dirs. Children's Bur. S.C., Columbia, 1981-87, YWCA, Greenville, 1984-88; bd. advisors for adoption S.C. Dept. Social Svcs., Columbia, 1987-92. Mem. Am. Edn. Rsch. Assn. (southeastern rep. 1982-84, editor newspaper for SIG group 1982-83), Jean Piaget Soc., Assn. for Supervision and Curriculum Devel., Orton Dyslexia Soc. (pres. Carolinas br. 1984-88), Ea. Ednl. Rsch. Assn., S.C. Psychol. Assn., Order of the Jessamine, Delta Kappa Gamma. Democrat. Home and Office: 28 Montrose Dr Greenville SC 29607-3034

HILL, HULENE DIAN, accountant; b. Salisbury, N.C., Mar. 17, 1948; d. Hulon Clive and Matie Cordelia (Plyler) H.; m. Ed Adkins; 1 child, Daren Steven Starnes. BS in Acctg., U. N.C., Charlotte, 1971. CPA, N.C., S.C. Staff acct. Peat, Marwick Mitchell & Co., Charlotte, 1971-74; sr. tax acct. Arthur Andersen & Co., Charlotte, 1974-76; tax mgr. Ernst & Young (formerly Clarkson, Harden & Gantt), Columbia, 1976-79; ptnr. Deloitte & Touche, Charlotte, 1979-92; v.p. tax Hodge, Steward & Co., P.A., Raleigh, N.C., 1992—. Recipient Hon. Mention as Bus. Woman of Yr. Shearson Lehman and Queens Coll., 1986, 89, 90, 91; named Acct. of Yr. Acad. Women Achievers YWCA, 1985. Mem. AICPA, Women Execs. (pres. 1987-88), Univ. N.C. Charlotte Athletic Found. (v.p. 1986-87), U. N.C. Charlotte Alumni Assn. (pres. 1985-86), Beta Alpha Psi (Acct. of Yr. U. N.C. chpt. 1985). Republican. Roman Catholic. Home: 204 Rosehaven Dr Raleigh NC 27609 Office: Hodge Steward & Co PA PO Box 41168 Raleigh NC 27629

HILL, I. KATHRYN, professional association administrator; b. Phila., Apr. 6, 1950; d. Joseph Anthony and Irma Lorraine (Walther) Piehs; m. John Patrick McElwain, May 17, 1969 (div. Aug. 1979); children: John Charles, Brian Patrick; m. David Terence Hill, Sept. 27, 1980. BA, Widener Coll., 1979; MEd, Temple U., 1982. Cert. secondary tchr., Pa. Translator, transcriber Sci-Tech, Inc., Phila., 1970-77; tchr. West Chester (Pa.) East High Sch., 1978, Garnet Valley Jr.-Sr. High Sch., Concordville, Pa., 1979; asst. to dir. Nat. Bd. Med. Examiners, Phila., 1980-81, evaluation program asst., 1981-82, evaluation program assoc., 1982-84, sr. program assoc., 1984-85; asst. exec. v.p. Fedn. State Med. Bds., Ft. Worth, 1985-86, asst. exec. v.p., exec. dir. of the examination bd., 1986-94, sr. v.p., exec. dir. examination bd., 1995—. Editor: FLEX/SPEX Guidelines, 1985, 87, 90, FLEX/SPEX Info. Bull., 1987-94; co-editor Fedn. Exchange, 1986—; contbr. articles to profl. jours. Mem. Am. Ednl. Rsch. Assn., Nat. Coun. on Measurement in Edn., Assn. of Am. Med. Colls. Republican. Lutheran. Office: Fedn State Med Bds 6000 Western Pl Ste 707 Fort Worth TX 76107-4618

HILL, JAQUI ANN, title company executive, jewelry designer; b. Dallas, Nov. 16, 1955; d. Billy Marvin and Dorothy Ann (Roberts) Faulkenbury. Student, Southeastern Paralegal Inst., Dallas, 1990-91. Legal sec. Hexter-Fair Title Co., Grand Prairie, Tex., 1978-79; escrow officer Hexter-Fair Title Co., DeSoto, Tex., 1979-86; title systems analyst Safeco Title Co., Dallas, 1986-87; asst. v.p., audit dept. mgr. Ticor Title Co., Dallas, 1987-90; escrow officer, mgr. Chgo. Title Co., Dallas, 1990—; owner Joi, Dallas, 1993—. Big sister Big Bro. and Sisters of Met. Dallas. Named Affiliate of Yr. Womens Coun. Realtors, 1984. Mem. Wear Artists Dallas. Home: 7851 Squire Ln Frisco TX 75034-6706 Office: Chicago Title Co 16000 Preston Rd Ste 200 Dallas TX 75248-3566

HILL, JOSEPHINE CARMELA, realtor; b. Tulsa, Feb. 27, 1932; d. Raphael and Jennie (Ferro) C.; m. Billy Gene Hill, Aug. 10, 1957; children: Patricia Ann, Barbara Jo. BEd, Chgo. State U., 1954; postgrad., Southwestern State U., 1957-58, Tulsa U., 1962. Cert. tchr.; lic. real estate broker; cert. residential specialist; cert. in referral and relocation. Clk. typist part-time Glidden Paint Co., Chgo., 1954-57; tchr. Chgo. Pub. Schs., 1954-57, Clinton (Okla.) Pub. Schs., 1958-59; sales rep. and bookkeeper Hill's Drug Shop, Tulsa, 1962-74; realtor assoc. Carriage Co. Realtors, Tulsa, 1974-77; broker assoc. John Hausam Realtors, Tulsa, 1977-87, J. Menger Elite Realtors, Tulsa, 1987—; adv. bd. Tulsa Jr. Coll., 1991—; divsn. v.p. Womens Coun. Realtors Referal and Relocation, 1993. Contbr. articles to profl. jours. Mem. St. Francis Hosp. Aux., Tulsa, 1986—; exec. bd. March of Dimes, 1991-94. Mem. Nat. Assn. of Realtors (realtors active in politics 1990-91, polit. calling network 1988-91, Outstanding award 1990, Svc. award), Women's Coun. of Realtors (regional v.p. 1991, state chpt. pres. 1988, gov. 1989), Okla. Assn. of Realtors (mem. legis. com. 1988—, Okla. State Mem. of Yr. 1990, Mem. of Yr. local chpt. 1990, bd. dirs. 1993-94, edn. com. 1994), Greater Tulsa Assn. of Realtors (vice chair realtors polit. action com. 1991, profl. standards com. 1992, 94, profl. bylaws com. 1992, bd. dirs. 1992-94, treas. 1994, sales assoc. of yr. 1991, chmn. fin. and budget 1994, exec. com. 1993, 94), Women's Coun. of Realtors, Real Estate Sales Assocs., Omega Tau Rho. Roman Catholic. Office: J Menger Elite Realtors 7151 S Braden Tulsa OK 74136

HILL, JUDITH DEEGAN, lawyer; b. Chgo., Dec. 13, 1940; d. William James and Ida May (Scott) Deegan; children: Colette M., Cristina M. BA, Western Mich. U., 1960; JD, Marquette U., 1971; cert. U. Paris, Sorbonne, 1962; postgrad. Harvard U., 1985. Bar: Wis. 1971, Ill. 1973, Nev. 1976, D.C. 1979. Tchr., Kalamazoo (Mich.) Bd. Edn., 1960-62, Maple Heights (Ohio), 1963-64, Shorewood (Wis.) Bd. Edn., 1964-68; corp. atty. Fort Howard Paper Co., Green Bay, Wis., 1971-72; sr. trust adminstr. Continental Ill. Nat. Bank & Trust, Chgo., 1972-76; atty. Morse, Foley & Wadsworth Law Firm, Las Vegas, 1976-77; dep. dist. atty., criminal prosecutor Clark County Atty., Las Vegas, 1977-83; atty. civil and criminal law Edward S. Coleman Profl. Law Corp., Las Vegas, 1983-84; pvt. practice law, 1984-85; atty. criminal div. Office of City Atty., City of Las Vegas, 1985-89, pvt. practice law, 1989—. Bd. dirs. Nev. Legal Services, Carson City, 1980-87, state chmn., 1984-87; bd. dirs. Clark County Legal Services, Las Vegas, 1980-87, Nev. Hist. Preservation Assn.; mem. Star Aux. for Handicapped Children, Las Vegas, 1986—; Greater Las Vegas Women's League, 1987-88; jud. candidate Las Vegas Mcpl. Ct, 1987, Nev. Symphony Guild, Variety Club Internat., Las Vegas Preservation Group. Recipient Scholarship, Auto Specialties, St. Joseph, Mich., 1957-60, St. Thomas More Scholarship, Marquette U. Law Sch., Milw., 1968-69; juvenile law internship grantee Marquette U. Law Sch., 1970. Mem. ABA, Nev. Bar Assn., So. Nev. Assn. Women Attys., Ill. Bar Assn., Washington Bar Assn., Children's Village Club (pres. 1980) (Las Vegas, Nev.). Home: 521 Sweeney Ave Las Vegas NV 89104-1436 Office: 726 S Casino Center Blvd Ste 2 Las Vegas NV 89101-6700

HILL, JUDITH SWIGOST, business analyst, information systems engineer; b. Harvey, Ill., Dec. 31, 1942; d. J.W. and M.J. (Kuczaik) Swigost; m. Wallace H. Hill, May 16, 1982; stepchildren: Scott, Amy, Molly, Elizabeth. BA in English/Theater, U. Ill., 1964; postgrad., Am. U., 1967-69, New Sch. for Social Research, N.Y.C., 1977-82, 83-85. Vol. U.S. Peace Corps, Philippines, 1964-66; recruiter U.S. Peace Corps, Washington, 1966-67; program mgr. U.S. Peace Corps, Micronesia, 1968; dir. corr. U.S. Peace Corps, Washington, 1969; editor, prin. Congl. Monitor, Inc., Washington, 1970-76; legis. analyst Philip Morris, Inc., N.Y.C., 1976-77; tech. analyst, writer Jesco, Inc., N.Y.C., 1978-79; assoc. pub. Thomas Pub. Co., N.Y.C., 1980-84; bus. analyst AGS, Inc. Ind. Cons., N.Y.C., 1984-93; dir. MIS N.Y.C. Sch. Constrn. Authority, 1993-94; ind. cons. in project mgmt. N.Y.C., 1994—; ind. cons. on expert systems design and devel., N.Y.C., 1987—. Contbr. articles to profl. jours. Active Murray Hill Com., N.Y.C., 1986—. Mem. IEEE, ACM, Assn. Systems Mgmt., Am. Assn. for Artificial Intelligence, Spl. Interest Group on Artificial Intelligence, Internat. Assn. Knowledge Engrs., Nat. Assn. Returned Peace Corps Vols., Returned Peace Corps Vols. Greater N.Y. (by-laws com. 1985-86, spkrs. bur. 1987). Jewish. Home and Office: 155 E 34th St Apt 12C New York NY 10016-4726

HILL, JUDY ELLEN, auditor; b. New Castle, Ind., June 8, 1955; d. Edward Nelson and Bercie Ruth (Sloan) H. AS in Bus. Data Processing, Fla. Jr. Coll., 1979; BA in Acctg., U. North Fla., 1994; BS in bus. adminstrn., Jacksonville U., 1994. Computer programmer Am. Heritage Life Ins. Co., Jacksonville, Fla., 1978-79, Peninsular Life Ins. Co., Jacksonville, 1979-80, SAV-A-STOP, Inc. div. Consolidated Foods, Orange Park, Fla., 1980-82; EDP auditor Fla. Nat. Banks, Jacksonville, 1982-83, The Charter Co., Jacksonville, 1983-84, Gulf Life Ins. Co., Jacksonville, 1984-87, First Union Nat. Bank of Fla., Jacksonville, 1987-89, CSX Corp., Jacksonville, 1989—; part-time reservations agt. Delta Air Lines, Jacksonville, 1985-87. Vol. ARC, Rota, Spain, 1975. Mem. Inst. Internal Auditors, Jacksonville Jaycees, Phi Beta Lambda (pres. Fla. Jr. Coll. chpt. 1978). Home: 7098 Beechfern Ln S Jacksonville FL 32244-6020 Office: CSX Audit 500 Water St # 900J Jacksonville FL 32202-4422

HILL, LA JOYCE CARMICHAEL, marketing professional; b. Tifton, Ga., Nov. 14, 1952; d. Ralph Eugene and Vista Eloise (Dooley) Carmichael; m. Bobby Wayne Hill, Jan. 1, 1972. AS, Abraham Baldwin Agrl. Coll., Tifton, 1971. With R.E. Carmichael Co. Inc., 1970-89, sec./treas., 1978-88, pres., chmn. bd., 1988-89; gen. mgr. J & B Power Equipment, Inc., 1989—. Mem. Chula Charge United Meth. Women (sec.-treas. 1986—), Tifton Exch. Club (pres. 1994—). Methodist. Home: PO Box 947 Tifton GA 31793-0947

HILL, LARKIN PAYNE, real estate company data processing executive; b. El Paso, Tex., Oct. 30, 1954; d. Max Lloyd and Jane Olivia (Evatt) H. Student Coll. Charleston, 1972-73, U. N.C., 1973. Lic. real estate broker, N.C. Sec., property mgr. Max L. Hill Co., Inc., Charleston, S.C., 1973-75, sec., data processor, 1979-82, v.p. adminstrn., 1982—; resident mgr. Carolina Apts., Carrboro, N.C., 1975-77; sales assoc., Realtor, Southland Assocs., Chapel Hill, N.C., 1977-78; cons. specifications com. Charleston Trident Multiple Listing Service, 1985. Bd. dirs. Charleston Area Arts Coun., 1992-93. Mem. Royal Oak Found., Scottish Soc. Charleston (bd. dirs. 1989-91), Preservation Soc., Charleston Computer Users Group, N.C. Assn. Realtors, Spoleto Festival USA (chmn. auction catalog com. 1990-92); co-chair Beaux Arts Ball, Sch. Arts. Republican. Methodist. Avocations: reading, crossword puzzles, furniture restoration, T'ai Chi. Home: 7 Riverside Dr Charleston SC 29403-3217 Office: Max L Hill Co Inc 632 St Andrews Blvd Charleston SC 29407-7146

HILL, LAURA CARNES, international credit analyst; b. Jefferson, S.C., Aug 13, 1936; d. John Howard and Lottie Lula (Killough) Carnes; m. John Beasley Benton (dec. 1970); m. Elton Edwin Wolfe Jr., Apr. 2, 1972 (div. 1976); m. John Houston Hill, Oct. 3, 1990. Student, U. S.C., 1955-56. Clk., Sears Roebuck, Florence, S.C., 1954-55; receptionist Am. Textile Mfrs. Inst., Charlotte, N.C., 1961-67, Pilot Life, Charlotte, 1958-60; sec. Chas. T. Main Inc, Charlotte, 1961-67; treas., mgr. Chipper Service, Lancaster, S.C., 1967-68; credit mgr. Buensod Divsn. Aeronca Inc., Pineville, N.C., 1968-72; export internat. credit analyst Scovill Inc., Monroe, N.C., 1972-87; bus. specialist broker, CPI Assocs., Lancaster, 1987-88; internat. credit analyst Homelite Divsn. Deere & Co., Charlotte, 1989—. Pres. Lancaster County Heart Assn., 1981. Mem. Internat. Assn. Execs. in Fin., Credit and Internat. Bus., Nat. Assn. Credit Mgmt., Am. Legion Aux. (Zone 2 v.p.), Lancaster County Coun. Garden Clubs (pres. 1991-92), Evening Garden Club (pres. 1981-83). Democrat. Baptist. Avocations: reading, gardening, travel, swimming. Home: 1122 Hawthorne Rd Lancaster SC 29720-1714

HILL, LOLLIE RUTH, social service administrator, check cashing service executive; b. El Dorado, Ark., July 11, 1930; d. Eddie M. and Effie (Byrd) Ento; m. Grandville Eli Hill, Mar. 16, 1957; children: Deidra J., Lorraine, Terence D. Asst. dir. Walter Brown Hosp., El Dorado; adminstr. Hill Farm Care Home, Vallejo, Calif., 1961—; v.p. Express Check Cashing Co., Vallejo, 1985—. Office: Hill Family Home Care 800 Taper Ave Vallejo CA 94589-2072

HILL, LORIE ELIZABETH, psychotherapist; b. Buffalo, Oct. 21, 1946; d. Graham and Elizabeth Helen (Salm) H. Student, U. Manchester, Eng., 1966-67; BA, Grinnel Coll., 1968; MA, U. Wis., 1970, Calif. State U.,

Sonoma, 1974; PhD, Wright Inst., 1980. Instr. English U. Mo., 1970-71; adminstr., supr. Antioch-West and Ctr. for Ind. Living, San Francisco, Berkeley, 1975-77; dir. tng. Ctr. for Edn. and Mental Health, San Francisco, 1977-80, exec. dir., 1980-81; pvt. practice Berkeley and Oakland, Calif., 1976—; instr. master's program in psychology John F. Kennedy U., Orinda, Calif., 1985, 94; founder group of psychotherapists against racism; speaker on cross-cultural psychology. Organizer against nuclear war; founding mem. Psychotherapists for Social Responsibility; mem. Nat. Abortion Rights League, Sane (anti-nuclear orgn.); psychologist Big Bros. and Big Sisters of the East Bay, 1986-88; vol. instr. City of Oakland Youth Skills Devel. Program; active Rainbow Coalition for Jesse Jackson's Presdl. Campaign, Ron Dellums Re-election Com.; campaigner for Clinton-Gore; founder, chair Psychotherapists against Violence. Democrat-Socialist. Office: 2955 Shattuck Ave Berkeley CA 94705-1808

HILL, MARY BENNETT, functional analyst, military officer; b. Columbus, Ohio, July 28, 1938; d. Thoburn Thomas and Hazel Margarite (Cullins) Bennett; m. Howard Alton Hill, June 25, 1971 (dec.). BS, Ohio State U., 1960. Officer U.S. Army, 1960-82; functional analyst Synoptics Systems Corp., Petersburg, Va., 1987—. Major U.S. Army, 1960-82. Decorated Bronze Star, 1972, Meritorious Svc. medal, 1982. Mem. VFW, Ohio State U. Alumni Assn., Women's Overseas Svc. League, Women's Army Corps. Veterans Assn., Beta Sigma Phi. Mem. Disciples of Christ. Home: 306 Prestige Pl Colonial Heights VA 23834 Office: Synopitc System Corp 325 Brown St Petersburg VA 23803-4247

HILL, MARY LOU, accountant, business consultant; b. Phila., July 8, 1936; d. Norman Findlay and Gladys Louise (Weigand) Tompkins; m. Ernest Clarke Hill Jr., Mar. 15, 1958; children: Sally, Holly, Randy, Chuck, Jim. Student, U. Miami, 1954-55, U. Okla., 1955-57; BBA, Portland State U., 1979, M in Taxation, 1982. CPA, Oreg. Staff acct. Fordham & Fordham, Hillsboro, Oreg., 1982-84; instr. Portland (Oreg.) State U., 1984-85; owner The Bookshelf, Sunriver, Oreg., 1985-88; instr. Cen. Oreg. Community Coll., Bend, 1986, 88-89; small bus. cons., 1988—; staff acct. Richard Rocci CPA, Portland, Oreg., 1990-91, Scribner & Scribner, PC, Portland, 1992-94, Alten & Sakai & Co., Portland, 1994—. Mem. Oreg. Soc. CPAs, Kappa Kappa Gamma. Democrat. Christian Scientist. Home and Office: 9172 SW Wilshire St Portland OR 97225

HILL, NORMA LOUISE, librarian; b. Somerville, Mass., Oct. 27; d. Southern G. and Marguerite M. (Smith) Smallwood; m. George Forris Hill, Dec. 30, 1954; children: Gregory Harrison, Jonathan Smallwood. AB, Wheaton Coll., 1952; MS in Libr. Sci., Our Lady of the Lake Coll., 1975; postgrad., Harvard, U., 1994. Grad. asst. Our Lady of the Lake Coll., San Antonio, 1974-75; libr. Community Guidance Ctr., San Antonio, 1975, 86th Tactical Fighter Wing, Ramstein, Fed. Republic Germany, 1976-79; info. mgmt. specialist Exec. Office of the Pres., Washington, 1980; dept. head Howard County (Md.) Libr., 1980-81, asst. dir., 1981—; del. Gov.'s Conf. on Libr. and Info. Sci., 1991. Mem. Friends of the Howard County Libr., Howard County Literacy Coalition, 1984, Md. Adv. Council on Librs., 1987-88; adv. bd. State Libr. Resource Ctr., 1986-88, network planning and resource sharing task force, 1988-89. Recipient Insp. Gen. Spl. Achievement award USAF, 1977, 78; bd. dirs. Columbia Found., 1992—, sec., 1994—, Howard County Housing Alliance, 1992-93. Mem. Md. Assn. Pub. Libr. Adminstrs., Md. Libr. Assn. (chmn. nominations com. 1984-85, co-chmn. fed. relations subcom. 1985-86, 1st v.p., pres.-elect 1986-87, pres. 1987-88, exec. bd. 1988-89, chair awards com. 1991, award 1993), ALA (pub. libr. div., nominations com. 1989-90), Pub. Libr. Assn., NAFE, Leadership Howard County, Nat. Council of Negro Women, Alpha Kappa Alpha. Democrat. Office: Howard County Libr 6600 Cradlerock Way Columbia MD 21045-2240

HILL, PAMELA, television executive; b. Winchester, Ind., Aug. 18, 1938; d. Paul and Mary Frances (Hollis) Abel; m. Tom Wicker, Mar. 9, 1974; 1 son, Christopher Hill; stepchildren: Cameron Wicker, Grey Wicker, Lisa Freed, Kayce Freed. B.A., Bennington Coll., 1960; postgrad., Universidad Autonoma de Mexico, 1961, U. Glasgow, 1958-59. Fgn. affairs analyst Nelson A. Rockefeller Presdl. Campaign, 1961-64; researcher, assoc. producer, dir., producer NBC News, 1965-73, dir. White Paper series, 1969-72, producer Edwin Newman's Comment, 1972; producer Closeup documentary series ABC News, N.Y.C., 1973-78, exec. producer, 1978-89; v.p. ABC News, 1979-89; v.p., exec. producer CNN Special Assignment, Cable News Network, N.Y.C., 1989—; mem. Coun. on Fgn. Relations. Author: United States Foreign Policy, 1945-65, 1968; Contbr. photographs to Catching Up With America, 1969. Trustee Bennington Coll., Fund for Free Expression, Media and Soc. Columbia U. Recipient (with CNN special assignment staff) 4 Cable Ace awards, 8 CINE awards, 6 Chris awards, 2 Clarion awards, 2 Emmy awards, 4 Headliner awards, 5 Internat. Film & TV Festival of N.Y. awards, 7 Worldfest Houston Film Festival, 8 Unity awards; recipient Joan Sorenstein Barone award, 1993; recipient (with ABC Closeup staff) 24 Emmy awards, 10 DuPont awards, 10 Christopher awards, 19 CINE Golden Eagle awards, 5 Headliner awards, 2 Peabody awards, 10 Am. Film Festival awards, 9 Clarion awards, 3 Gabriel awards, 3 Overseas Press Club awards, Edward R. Murrow prize, 4 Edward R. Murrow Brotherhood awards. Mem. Dirs. Guild (mem. coun. on fgn. rels.), Writers Guild, Nat. Acad. Television Arts and Scis.

HILL, PATRICIA LISPENARD, insurance educator; b. N.Y.C., June 25, 1937; d. George Joseph and Elizabeth (Lispenard) H.; children: George, Christopher, Susan, Daniel, Frederic, Elizabeth. Student Barnard Coll., 1954-55, Pace U., 1972-74, Coll. of Ins., 1980. Lic. ins. broker, 1961—; owner, dir. Hill Sch. of Ins., N.Y.C., 1978—; also ptnr. Hill & Co. Ins. Brokers. Office: 139 Fulton St New York NY 10038-2594

HILL, ROBYN MARCELLA, lawyer; b. Schenectady, Aug. 18, 1951; d. Fred Warren Hill Jr. and Prudence Alberta (Lamper) Shackford; m. Charles A. Boenecke, Jr., Sept. 16, 1977; children: Blake Elizabeth Hill Boenecke, Hayley Alexandra Hill Boenecke. BA with distinction, Simmons Coll., 1973; JD, Rutgers U., Camden, 1976. Bar: N.J. 1977, Pa. 1977, U.S. Dist. Ct. N.J. 1977, U.S. Supreme Ct. 1985. Staff atty. for hearings and regulations N.J. Dept. Pers., Trenton, 1977-79; atty. div. ethics and profl. svcs. Adminstrv. Office Cts., Trenton, 1979-83; dep. ethics counsel Office Atty. Ethics, Supreme Ct. N.J., Trenton, 1983-89, chief counsel disciplinary rev. bd., 1989—, mem. staff N.J. Ethics Commn., 1991—. Mem. ABA, Nat. Orgn. Bar Counsel, N.J. Bar Assn. (profl. responsibility com., lawyers in pub. employment com.), Burlington County Bar Assn. Unitarian. Office: Disciplinary Rev Bd RJ Hughes Justice Complex CN962 Trenton NJ 08625

HILL, RUTH FOELL, language consultant; b. Houston, Sept. 13, 1931; d. Ernest William and Florence Margaret (Kane) Foell; children: Linden Ruth, Andrea Grace. Student, Principia Coll., 1950; BA, U. Calif., Berkeley, 1952; postgrad., San Diego State, 1955, Cen. Piedmont, 1981. Cert. tchr., Calif. Owner, dir. Art Gallery of Chapel Hill (N.C.), 1966-75; ecumenical bd. Campus Ministry, Charlotte; with referral svc. Charlotte (N.C.) Bed and Breakfast Registry, 1980-90; lang. cons. Berlitz Internat., Raleigh, N.C., 1988-91; cert. cons. Performax Internat.; rep. UN Decade for Women Conf., NGO Forum, Nairobi, Kenya, 1985, Women and Global Security Conf., 1986; rep. emerging issues forum N.C. State U., 1987-93; presenter in field. Bd. dirs., chmn. natural resources com. LWV; coord. USIA grant region 6, Internat. Exch. Network; mem. N.C. Leadership Forum, N.C. Citizen's Assembly, 1989; chmn. Week of Edn. Pub. Forum on Energy, Union Concerned Scientists, 1990-93; bd. dirs. Nat. Women's Conf. Commn., 1994—. Named Outstanding Athlete Women's Athletic Assn., Woman of the Yr., Am. Biog. Inst., 1994; Hewlett Found. scholar. Mem. AAUW (v.p. membership com., bd. dirs.), Ams. for Legal Reform (adv. bd.), Am. Farm Land Trust, UN Assn. U.S.A. (chpt. pres. 1991-93, co-chair UN Day Queens Coll. 1992, N.C. divsn. sec. 1993-94), Internat. Platform Assn. (spkrs. seminar 1991), Carolina Coun. on World Affairs, Chapel Hill-Carrboro Sch. Art Guild (pres.), Midwest Acad., World Wide Women in Environment, N.Y. Acad. Sci. Republican. Christian Scientist. Office: PO Box 220802 Charlotte NC 28222-0802

HILL, SUSAN SLOAN, safety engineer; b. Quincy, Mass., June 1, 1952; d. Ralph Arnold and Grace Elenore (Sloan) Crosby; m. William Loyd Hill, Dec. 16, 1973 (div. July 1982); m. William Joseph Graham, Sept. 10, 1983 (div. Feb. 1985). Assoc. Sci. in Gen. Engring., Motlow State C.C., Tullahoma, Tenn., 1976; BS in Indsl. Engring., Tenn. Technol. U., 1978. Intern, safety engr. Intern Tng. Ctr., U.S. Army, Red River Army Depot, Tex., 1978-79, Field Safety Activity, Charlestown, Ind., 1979, system safety engr. Comm.-Electronics Command, Ft. Monmouth, N.J., 1979-84, gen. engr., 1984-85; chief system safety Arnold Air Force Sta., USAF, Tullahoma, 1984; system safety engr. U.S. Army Safety Ctr., Ft. Rucker, Ala., 1985-91; medically retired; ind. cons. system safety, 1991—; founder Fibromyalgia Support Group; leader Arthritis Found. Support Group; active Arthritis Found. Recipient 5 letters of appreciation U.S. Army. Mem. NAFE, Assn. Fed. Safety and Health Profls. (regional v.p. 1980-84), Soc. Women Engrs., Nat. Safety Mgmt. Soc., Am. Soc. Safety Engrs., System Safety Soc., Order Engr. Republican. Episcopalian. Avocations: bowling, needlework, sewing, cooking, golf. Home and Office: PO Box 1075 Tullahoma TN 37388

HILL, SUZANNE MARIE, journalist; b. Carrollton, Ill., Mar. 24, 1958; d. Martin William and Elizabeth Ann (Rawe) Schwab; m. Larry Eugene Hill, July 18, 1981. BA, Ea. Ill. U., 1980; MS, Iowa State U., Ames, 1983. Cert. tchr., Ill. Tchr. Havana (Ill.) Sch. Dist., 1980-81; family living editor Missourian Pub. Co., Washington, 1983—; contest judge Missouri Press Assn., 1990. Contr. articles to profl. jours. Sec. St. Francis Borgia Ch. Liturgy Commn., Washington, Mo., 1989-93. Recipient Best Family Living Sect. award Mo. Press Assn., 1986, Sci. Writers award Mo. Dental Assn., 1990, 3d place award family living sects. Nat. Newspaper Assn., 1991, 2d place award family living sect. Mo. Press Assn., 1992. Mem. AAUW (sec. 1986-88, treas. 1990-94), Am. Legion Aux. (sec. 1982-83), Alpha Phi. Roman Catholic. Home: 25 Buckingham Dr Washington MO 63090-4631 Office: Missourian Pub Co 14 W Main St Washington MO 63090-2518

HILL, TRESA CHERLE, information systems specialist; b. Sioux City, Iowa, 1952; d. Herbert and Laura Hill; m. Don Mayberger, Sept. 1980. BS in Sci. and Humanities with distinction, Iowa State U., 1976. Sr. cons. Arthur Andersen & Co., Kansas City, Mo., 1976-79; sys. mgr., Info. Sys. U. Kans., Lawrence, 1980-84; dir. finance Sprint, Westwood, Kans., 1984—; cons. Penny Lane, Kansas City, Mo., 1980. Organizer Preservation Alliance, Lawrence, Kans., 1981; active Lawrence Bicentennial, 1976, Great Decisions, 1994.

HILL, VALERIE CHARLOTTE, nurse; b. Shaftsbury, Vt., Dec. 2, 1932; d. William Henry Harrison and Angeline Margaret Stella (Fuller) Hill; m. Edward Joseph Klanit (dec. July 1984); 1 child, Joyce Ellen Klanit Artadi. Grad., The Mount Sinai Hosp. Sch. of Nursing, 1955. RN, N.Y. Staff nurse The Jack Martin Respiratory Ctr. of The Mt. Sinai Hosp., N.Y.C., 1955-57; v.p. Chauffeurs Unlimited, Inc., N.Y.C., 1957-77; staff nurse Rusk Inst., N.Y.C., 1957-58, Beth Israel Med. Ctr., N.Y.C., 1978-79; owner, mgr. Powers Fish Market, Inc., N.Y.C., 1977-84; tchr. Techs. for Creating, Albany, N.Y., 1983—; staff nurse Doctors Hosp., N.Y.C., 1984-86; pvt. duty nurse Personal Health Care Services, Albany, N.Y., 1987-88; nurse Albany Med. Ctr. Hosp., 1987—; real estate sales assoc. Century 21-Stanley Major Ltd., West Sand Lake, N.Y., 1988, Century-21 Home Towne Properties, Albany, 1989-92. Author numerous poems. Recipient Outstanding Service to Community award Mayor Koch City of N.Y., 1983. Mem. Alumnae Assn. Mt. Sinai Hosp. Sch. Nursing (bd. dirs. 1968, primary nursing com. 1993-94, 95—). Democrat. Home: 70 2d St Albany NY 12210-2517 Office: Albany Med Ctr Hosp 43 New Scotland Ave Albany NY 12208-3478

HILLARD, CAROLE, state official; b. Deadwood, S.D., Aug. 14, 1936; m. John M. Hillard; children: David, Sue Ellen, Todd, Eddie, Lornell. BA in Edn., Univ. of Ariz., 1957; MA in Edn., S.D. State Univ., 1982; MA in Polit. Sci., Univ. of S.D., 1984. State rep. State of S.D., 34th dist., 1991-95; lt. gov. State of S.D., 1995—; dir. Mich. Nat. Bank., Black Hills Regional Eye Inst., YMCA; mem. exec. bd. Nat. Crime Prevention Coun. Active Rapid City Common Coun., Rapid City C. of C., S.D. Bd. of Charities and Corrections, McGruff Crime Prevention Coun. (exec. bd.), S.D. Corrections Commn., Cmty. Care Ctr., S.D. Children's Home Soc., S.D. Assurance Alliance, Nat. Child Protection Partnership, First United Methodist Ch. (exec. bd.), Rapid City Econ. Devel. Partnership, F.L.A.G.S. Found.; mem. exec. bd. Bog Bros./Big Sisters. Recipient Pub. Svc. award, 1987, Gov.'s Outstanding Citizen award, 1988, George award Rapid City C. of C., 1994; named Outstanding Chirperson, United Way, 1986, S.D. Guardian Small Bus., 1994. Mem. LWV, Women's Network, Mt. Rushmore Soc., Indian-White Coun., Toastmasters, Ninety-niners, Rapid City Fine Arts Coun. Republican. Methodist. Office: Office of Lt Governor State Capitol 500 E Capitol Ave Ste 204 Pierre SD 57501

HILLEGASS, CHRISTINE ANN, psychologist; b. Lancaster, Pa., July 13, 1952; d. Michael and Ann Christine (Wolf) H.; m. E. Cornelius Kocsis, Aug. 6, 1983. BA, Bard Coll., 1975; MA in Forensic Psychol., John Jay Coll. Criminal Justice, 1979; PsyD, Rutgers U., 1993. Staff psychologist Dept. Corrections, Adult Diagnostic Treatment Ctr., Avenel, N.J., 1979-84; dir. Monmouth County Sexual Abuse Treatment and Prevention Program, Ocean, N.J., 1984-87; cons., trainer, therapist various mental health, social svc., correctional and law enforcement agys., 1981—; mem. Monmouth County Sexual Abuse Coalition, 1983—, chair, 1986-87, co-chair, 1987-88; mem. N.J. Statewide Sexual Abuse Network, 1984-89, Monmouth Prosecutor's Task Force on Child Abuse, Freehold, N.J., 1985-86. Recipient Woman of Achievement award Monmouth County Adv. Commn. on Status of Women, 1987. Mem. Am. Psychol. Assn., N.J. Psychol. Assn., Am. Profl. Soc. on Abuse of Children, Am. Assn. of Applied and Preventive Psychol. Office: 500 N Bridge St Bridgewater NJ 08807

HILLER, DEBORAH LEWIS, long term care and retirement facility executive; b. Philipsburg, Pa., Nov. 8, 1947; d. Edward Trumble and Margaret Grace France (Bates) Lewis; m. Alan John Ross, Jan. 20, 1979; 1 child: Edward Simpson Ross. Bar: Ohio. Law clk. to Hon. Robert Krupansky U.S. Dist. Ct., Cleve., 1975-76; trial atty. antitrust divsn. U.S. Dept. Justice, Cleve., 1977-81; ptnr. Calfee, Halter & Griswold, Cleve., 1981-93; pres., CEO The Eliza Jennings Group, Cleve., 1993—. Mem. ABA, Ohio Bar Assn. (chmn. antitrust law sect. 1991-93, bd. govs. 1986-93), Fed. Bar Assn., Cleve. Bar Assn. Democrat. Episcopalian. Home: 427 Bassett Rd Bay Village OH 44140-1815

HILLERS, ELLEN MARSH, film-television production coordinator; b. Syracuse, N.Y., Feb. 19, 1961; d. Robert Stilphen and Eleanor Hunter (Marsh) H. BA, Wells Coll., 1983. Production coord.: (films) Scrooged, Paramount Pictures, N.Y.C., 1987, Reversal of Fortune, Pressman Film, N.Y.C., 1989, Lorenzo's Oil, Universal City Studios, Pitts., 1991, Quiz Show, Disney, N.Y.C., 1993, Little Big League, Castlerock Entertainment, L.A./Mpls., 1993; (TV) Miami Vice, 91; (other) The Super, Funny About Love, A Kiss Before Dying, The Accidental Tourist, Beaches, True Love. Mem. Internat. Alliance Theatrical Stage Employees and Moving Picture Machine Operators of U.S. and Can. Republican. Episcopalian. Home: 124 Rim Rock Dr Durango CO 81301-8603

HILLERT, GLORIA BONNIN, anatomist, educator; b. Brownton, Minn., Jan. 25, 1930; d. Edward Henry and Lydia Magdalene (Luebker) Bonnin; m. Richard Hillert, Aug. 20, 1960; children: Kathryn, Virginia, Jonathan. BS, Valparaiso (Ind.) U., 1953; MA, U. Mich., 1958. Instr. Springfield (Ill.) Jr. Coll., 1953-57; teaching asst. U. Mich., Ann Arbor, 1957-58; instr., dept. head St. John's Coll., Winfield, Kans., 1958-59; asst. prof. Concordia Coll., River Forest, Ill., 1959-63; vis. instr. Wright Jr. Coll., Chgo., 1974-76, Ill. Benedictine Coll., Lisle, 1977-78, Rosary Coll., River Forest, 1976-81; prof. anatomy and physiology Triton Coll., River Grove, 1982-92, prof. emeritus, 1992—; vis. asst. prof. Concordia U., 1993—; vis. instr. Wheaton (Ill.) Coll., 1988; advisor Springfield Jr. Coll. Sci. Club, 1953-57, Concordia Coll. Cultural Group, 1959-62; program dir. Triton Coll. Sci. Lectr. Series, 1983-87; participant Internat. Educators Workshop in Amazonia, 1993. Dem. campaign asst., Maywood, Ill., 1972, 88; vol. Mental Health Orgn., Chgo., 1969-73, Earthwatch., St. Croix, 1987, Costa Rica, 1989. Mem. AAUW, Ill. Assn. Community Coll. Biol. Tchrs., Nat. Assn. Biol. Tchrs. Lutheran. Home: 1620 Clay Ct Melrose Park IL 60160-2419 Office: Triton Coll 2000 N 5th Ave River Grove IL 60171-1907

HILLERY, MARY JANE LARATO, columnist, producer, television host, reserve army officer; b. Boston, Sept. 15, 1931; d. Donato and Porzia (Avellis) Larato; Asso. Sci. (scholar), Northeastern U., 1950; BS, U. Mass. Harvard Extension, 1962; grad. Command and Gen. Staff Coll., 1982; m. Thomas H. Hillery, Feb. 25, 1961; 1 son, Thomas H. Sales agt., linguist Pan Am. Airways, Boston, 1955-61; interpreter Internat. Conf. Fire Chiefs, Boston, 1966; tchr. Spanish, YWCA, Natick, Mass., 1966-67; community rels. cons., adv. bd. dirs., lectr. for migrant edn. project div. Mass. Dept. Community Affairs, Boston, 1967-69; editor-in-chief Sudbury (Mass.) Citizen, 1967-76; assoc. editor The Beacon, 1976-79, contbg. editor, 1979-83; area editorial adviser Beacon Pub. Co., Acton, Mass., 1970-80, editor, 1976-80; columnist Town Crier, 1987—; contbg. editor Towne Talk, 1975-79, Citizens' Forum, 1975-81; editor Spl. Forces Ann. History, 1990; dir. pub. affairs Mass. Dept. Environ. Quality Engring., 1981-83; producer, host TV interview show For the Record. Mem. Bus. Adv. Com., 1972-77, Sudbury Sch. Com., 1976-77; mem. Meml. Day Celebration Com., 1972—, master of ceremonies, 1973-94; chmn. Sudbury WWII Commemorative Community, 1992—; mem. Sudbury Town Report, 1967-72, 85-88, chmn., 1969-72; chmn. Sudbury Vets. Adv. Com., 1986-92; panelist Internat. Women's Year Symposium, 1975, Women in Politics, 1987, Women In Mil., 1987; mem. congl. 5th dist. Mass. nomination bd., apptd. mil. aide-de-camp to Mass. Gov. Wm. Weld, 1992—; Veterans' agent Town of Sudbury, 1992—. Served with USN, 1950-54; lt. col. USAR; Persian Gulf, 1991-92; liaison officer U.S. Mil. Acad. West Point, 1976-89; pub. affairs officer 94th USAR Command, 1982-83, Office of Sec. of Def., The Pentagon, Washington, 1989-93. Editor Hansconian, 1983-85. Decorated Meritorious Svc. medal 1985, Def. Superior Service medal, 1993, Joint Meritorious unit award 1992, Joint Svc. Achievement medal, 1991, Nat. Def. medal-Bronze Stars, 1991, Outstanding Svc. award Sec. Def. Pub. Affairs, 1992; Named Editor of Year, Beacon Pub. Co., 1970; recipient medal of appreciation Internat. Order DeMolay, 1969, certificates of appreciation U.S. Def. Civil Preparedness Agency, 1975, Mass. Bicentennial Commn., 1976, Appreciation award U.S. Mil. Acad., 1976-86, Res. Officers Assn., 1976-86; citations Mass. State Senate, 1979, 82; New-swriting award Media Contest, Air Force Systems Command, 1984, Outstanding Svc. award Sec. Def. Pub. Affairs, 1991. Mem. Nat. Editorial Assn., Nat. Newspaper Assn., Nat. Press Club, Sudbury Rotary Internat. (mem. scholarship com. 1993—, bd. dirs. 1994-95), New Eng. Press Assn., Rotary Internat. (mem. Sudbury chpt. scholarship com. 1993—, bd. dirs. 1994-95), Bus. and Profl. Women's Club (Sudbury 1st v.p. 1973-74, pres. 1974-76, parliamentarian 1978-88, 90-92, legis. chair 1990-92, state bylaws com. 1977-78, 79-81, 1986-88, state legis. chmn. 1979-81, 86-88, state polit. action com. chmn., 1988-89, Woman of Yr. 1979, Woman of Achievement 1982), LWV (dir. 1964-68), Nat. League Am. Pen Women (exec. bd. Boston 1974-76, 78-88, pres. 1976-78, 94—, state exec. bd. 1994—, publicity chmn. 1979-80, chmn. bylaws com. 1979-80, 86-88, parliamentarian 1978-80, 82-88, auditor 1980-82, 84-88, 1st v.p. 1988-92, nat. editor Achievements, The Pen Woman 1992-94), Res. Officers Assn. (life; state sec. 1978-79, state army v.p. 1992—, pres. Boston chpt. 1986-88, army coun. rep. 1989-92, budget com., 1990-91, state publicity chmn. 1988-92, editor Advisor 1991—, Outstanding Svc. award 1978-79), Omega Sigma. Home: 66 Willow Rd Sudbury MA 01776-2663

HILLESHEIM, DAWN ANN, telephone company official; b. Ardmore, Pa., Sept. 22, 1960; d. Anthony A. and Nancy (Grady) H. BA in Psychology, Temple U., 1983; MA in Indsl. Psychology, Fairleigh Dickinson U., 1994. Cert. profl. in human resources. Staff developer, vol. coord. Comprehensive Mental Health Svcs., Independence, Mo., 1992-93; sales specialist AT&T, Wayne, Pa., 1983-88; software specialist, trainer AT&T, Basking Ridge, N.J., 1988-91; force cons. AT&T, Lee's Summit, Mo., 1993-94; prodn. support mgr. AT&T, Dallas, 1994-95. Bd. dirs. Voluntary Action Ctr., Independence, 1993—. Mem. APA (assoc.), ASTD (editor), Toastmasters (ednl. v.p. 1991), Psi Chi. Home: 4551 N O'Connor Blvd Ste 1264 Irving TX 75062 Office: AT&T 6303 Forest Park Rd Dallas TX 75235

HILLGREN, SONJA DOROTHY, journalist; b. Sioux Falls, S.D., May 17, 1948; d. Ralph Oliver and Priscilla Adaline (Mannes) Hillgren; m. Ralph Lee Hill (dec.). BJ, U. Mo., 1970, MA, 1972; postgrad. (Nieman fellow), Harvard U., 1982-83. d. Washington corr. Ohio-Washington News Svc., 1972-73; reporter UPI, Annapolis, Md., 1974-76; reporter/editor UPI, Washington, 1976-78; farm editor UPI, 1978-88; Washington corr. Knight-Ridder, Washington, 1988-90; Washington editor Farm Jour., 1990—. Recipient J.R. Russell award Newspaper Farm Editors Am., 1985, Reuben Brigham award Agrl. Communicators in Edn., 1988; named Old Master, Purdue U., 1992; Woodrow Wilson vis. fellow, 1993—. Mem. Nat. Assn. Agrl. Journalists (pres. 1987-88), Nat. Press Club (bd. govs. 1991—, chair 1993-94, v.p. 1995), Soc. Profl. Journalists, Investigative Reporters and Editors, Coun. on Fgn. Rels., Congl. Country Club, Pi Beta Phi. Episcopalian. Home: 2800 29th Pl NW Washington DC 20008-3501 Office: Farm Jour 941 National Press Bldg Washington DC 20045

HILL-HULSLANDER, JACQUELYNE L., nursing educator and consultant; b. Melrose Park, Ill., Jan. 9, 1940; d. Richard C. and Marian L. (Hamlin) Hill; m. Gale Franklin Hulslander, June 5, 1993; children: Daryl, Gary. Diploma, Evanston (Ill.) Hosp. Assn., 1961; BS, Elmhurst (Ill.) Coll., 1977, BSN, 1981; MS, Nat.-Louis U., Evanston, 1986; PhD, U. Ill., 1990. Cons. in course devel. Ill. Bell Telephone Co., Chgo.; cons. for employee devel. Glen Oaks Med. Ctr., Glendale Hts., Ill.; prof. Triton Coll., River Grove, Ill.; staff nurse OB Evanston (Ill.) Hosp. Assn., 1961-62; staff and charge nurse OB Gottlieb Mem. Hosp., Melrose Park, Ill., 1962-65; faculty OB Proviso Sch. Practical Nursing, Maywood, Ill., 1965-67; charge nurse OB Gottlieb Meml. Hosp., Melrose Park, 1970-75; grad. rsch. asst. dept. vocat. edn. U. Ill., Champaign-Urbana, Ill., 1988-89; faculty prof. basic med. surg. nursing and obstetrics Triton Coll., River Grove, Ill., 1976—; cons. Dawson Tech. Inst., Chgo. City Coll.; cons. Engring. Systems Inc., Aurora, Ill.; presenter in field. Multicompetencies for Practical Nurses grantee, 1986. Mem. Chateau Lorraine Homeowners Assn. (sec., v.p., pres. 1992—), U. Ill. Alumni Assn., Phi Delta Kappa, Phi Kappa Phi. Home: 222 Lorraine Cir Bloomingdale IL 60108-2546 Office: Triton Coll 2000 Fifth Ave River Grove IL 60171

HILLIS, MARGARET, conductor, musician; b. Kokomo, Ind., Oct. 1, 1921; d. Glen R. and Bernice (Haynes) H. MusB, Ind. U., 1947; grad. student choral conducting, Juilliard Sch. Music, 1947-49; D.Mus. (hon.), Temple U., 1967, Ind. U., 1972, Carthage Coll., 1979, Wartburg Coll., 1981; DFA (hon.), St. Mary's Coll., 1977, Lake Forest Coll., 1980, North Park Coll.; DHL (hon.), St. Xavier Coll., 1988; D.Mus. (hon.), Adrian Coll., 1990; LittD (hon.), St. Mary of the Woods Coll., 1990. Dir., Met. Youth Chorale, Bklyn., 1948-51; asst. condr., Collegiate Choral, N.Y.C., 1952-53; mus. dir., condr., Am. Concert Choir, N.Y.C. from 1950, Am. Concert Orch. from 1950; condr., instr., Union Theol. Sem., 1950-60, Juilliard Sch. Music, 1951-53; dir. choral dept., Third St. Music Sch. Settlement, 1953-54; founder, music dir., Am. Choral Found., Inc., from 1954; choral dir., N.Y.C. Opera Co., 1955-56, Chgo. Mus. Coll. of Roosevelt U., 1961-62; condr., choral dir., Santa Fe Opera Co., 1958-59, Chgo. Symphony Chorus, 1957-94; music dir., N.Y. Chamber Soloists, 1956-60; choral condr., Am. Opera Soc., N.Y.C., 1952-68; mus. asst. to music dir., Chgo. Symphony Orch., 1966-68; music dir., condr., Kenosha Symphony Orch., 1961-68; condr., choral dir., Cleve. Orch. Chorus, 1969-71; prof. conducting, dir. choral orgns., Northwestern U. Sch. Music, 1970-77; vis. prof. conducting, Ind. U. from 1978; resident condr. Chgo. Civic Orch., 1967-90; music dir. Choral Inst., 1968-70, 75; mus. dir., condr., Elgin (Ill.) Symphony Orch., 1971-85; condr. Chgo.'s Do-It-Yourself Messiah, 1976—; dir. choral activities San Francisco Symphony Orch., 1982-83; guest condr., Chgo. Symphony, Cleve. Orch., Minn.Orch., Nat. Symphony Orch., others. Artists' adviser Nat. Fedn. Music Clubs Youth Auditions, 1966-70; mem. vis. com. dept. music U. Chgo., 1971—; chmn. choral panel Nat. Endowment for Arts, 1974-82; hon. mem. Roosevelt U. Coun. of 100, 1976—; adv. bd. Cathedral Choral Soc. Washington Cathedral, 1976—; mem. Nat. Coun. Arts, 1985-90. Civilian flight instr. USA CAA, WTS, World War II. Recipient Grammy awards for best choral performances: Verdi's Requiem, 1978, Beethoven's Missa Solemnis, 1979, Brahm's Ein Deutsches Requiem, 1980, Berlioz' La Damnation de Faust, 1983, Haydn's Creation, 1984, Brahm's Ein Deutsches Requiem, 1985, Orff's Carmina Burana, 1987, Bach's B-Minor Mass, 1991, Bartok's Cantata Profana, 1993, Grand Prix du Disque for Berlioz' La Damnation de Faust, 1982, Golden Plate award Am. Acad. Achievement, 1967, Alumnus of Year award Ind. U. Sch. Music Alumni, 1969, Steinway award, 1969, Chgo. YWCA Leader Luncheon I award, 1972, Friends of Lit. award, 1973, SAI Found. Circle of 15 award, 1974, Woman of Yr. in Classical Music award Ladies Home Jour., 1978, Leadership for Freedom award Women's Scholarship Assn. Roosevelt U., 1978, Dushkin award, 1992, Gov.'s award, Chgo.

Chpt. Nat. Acad. Recording Arts Scis., 1992. Mem. Nat. Fedn. Music Clubs (hon., citation for contbns. to musical life of nation 1981), Am. Choral Dirs. Assn., Assn. Choral Condrs., Am. Music Center, P.E.O., Sigma Alpha Iota (hon.), Pi Kappa Lambda (hon.), Kappa Kappa Gamma (Alumni Achievement award 1978), Chorus America (formerly Assn. Profl. Vocal Ensembles), Am. Symphony Orch. League, Nat. Soc. Lit. and Arts. Office: Chgo Symphony Orch 220 S Michigan Ave Chicago IL 60604-2508

HILL-JONES, KATHLEEN LOIS, executive director; b. Denver, Sept. 11, 1955; d. James Jenkins and Elaine (Marcella) Hill; m. Clinton Daniel Jones, Feb. 14, 1982; 1 child, Terrence Drake. BA, Colo. Women's Coll., 1977. Choreographer Fashion Bar TV Comml., Denver, 1981, Pure Gold Cheerleaders USFL, Denver, 1985, Kenny Rodgers Western Wear, Denver, 1990; exec., art dir. Hill Acad. of Dance and Dramatics, Denver, 1976—; bd. dirs. Colo. Dance Alliance, Denver, 1986-89; guest judge I Love Dance, Portland, Oreg., 1991-93. Performer Met. Troupers Charity Entertainers, Colo., 1970-76. Named Young Careerist, Bus. and Profl. Women of Am., 1978; recipient Scholastic scholarships Colo. Women's Coll., 1973-77. Mem. Colo. Dance Alliance (bd. dirs. 1986-89), Colo. Dance Festival, Internat. Tap Assn. Democrat. Roman Catholic. Office: Hill Acad Dance/Dramatics 1338 S Valentia St # 110 Denver CO 80231

HILLMAN, CAROL BARBARA, communications executive; b. N.Y.C., Sept. 6, 1940; d. Joseph Hoppenfeld and Elsa (Spiegel) Hoppenfeld Resika; m. Howard D. Hillman, May 25, 1969. BA with honors, U. Wis., 1961; Fulbright scholar U. Lyon (France), 1961-62; MA, Cornell U., Ithaca, N.Y., 1966. Asst. editor Holt Rinehart & Winston, Pubs., 1965-66; staff assoc. pub. rels. Ea. Airlines, N.Y.C., 1966-74; pub. affairs mgr. Squibb Corp., N.Y.C., 1974-75; asst. dir. corp. pub. rels. Burlington Industries, N.Y.C., 1975-77, dir. corp. pub. rels., 1977-80, v.p. pub. rels., 1980-82; v.p. corp. communications Norton Co., Worcester, Mass., 1982-89, sr. cons. 1989-90; nat. dir. pub. rels. and communications Deloitte & Touche, Wilton, Conn., 1990-91; v.p. Univ. Rels. Boston U., 1991—; mem. Pub. Affairs Coun., Machinery & Allied Products Inst., 1982-89; mem. dep. policy com., agenda com. Mass. Bus. Roundtable, 1982-89; bd. dirs. Mass. Econ. Stabilization Trust, 1987—. Mem. Cornell Coun., Ithaca, 1981-85, pub. rels. com. 1981-88; mem. adv. coun. Coll. Human Ecology, Cornell U., Ithaca, 1982-84; mem. adv. bd. Ct. Apptd. Spl. Advocates, Worcester, 1983-87; voting mem. Wis. Union Trustees, U. Wis., Madison, 1982-90, trustee, 1990—; mem. Clark U. Assocs., Worcester, 1983-89; bd. dirs. Planned Parenthood League Mass., 1986-90; trustee Quinsigamond Community Coll., Worcester, 1987—. Cornell Grad. fellow Cornell U., 1962. Mem. Pub. Rels. Soc. Am., Internat. Women's Forum, Women's Econ. Forum, Arthur Page Soc., The Wisemen, Phi Beta Kappa, Phi Kappa Phi. Home: 299 Belknap Rd Framingham MA 01701-4716 Office: Boston U 143 Bay State Rd Boston MA 02215-1708

HILLMAN, CAROL ELIZABETH, real estate broker; b. Monticello, Ark., July 29, 1947; d. Horace Lavon McManus and Leathel Jeanette (Higgins) Losh; m. William Carlton Hillman, Oct. 21, 1967; 1 child, Carol Lynn. G-rad. high sch., Monticello, 1965. Lic. real estate broker. Exec. sec. Hamburg (Ark.) Shirt Co., 1965-67; office and payroll mgr. Glamorise Founds., Inc., Dermott, Ark., 1967-69; cashier, customer svc. rep. Main Dept. Store, Rolla, Mo., 1975-77; office mgr., chiropractic asst. Dr. J.W. Moffett Chiropractic, Bolivar, Mo., 1977-79; salesperson Sta. KYOO, Bolivar, 1980-83, sales mgr., 1983-91, gen. mgr., 1991-93; real estate broker-salesperson Perkins Realtors, Bolivar, 1993—; bd. dirs. bus. adv. bd. students S.W. Bapt. U., Bolivar, 1992-93. Co-chair entertainment Bolivar Country Days, 1992—. Recipient High Series awards Outreach League, 1991. Mem. Bolivar Bd. Realtors, Ozark Bd. Realtors, Bolivar Area C. of C. (Sta. KYOO rep. 1983-93). Home: RR 3 Box 98 Bolivar MO 65613-9409 Office: Perkins Realtors Hwy 32 W Bolivar MO 65613

HILLMAN, CHARLENE HAMILTON, public relations executive; b. Akron, Ohio; d. Charles Edward and Maeton (Anderson) Hamilton; m. Robert Edward Hillman; 1 child, Robert Edward (dec.). Student, Youngstown Coll., Ind. U. Extension. Mem. Bob Long Assocs., Indpls., 1959-62; pub. relations dir. Paul Lennon Advt. Agy., Indpls., 1962-63, Clowes Meml. Hall, Indpls., 1963-64; owner, pres. Charlene Hillman Pub. Rels. Assocs., Indpls., 1964-75; sr. v.p., dir. pub. rels. Caldwell-van Riper, Inc., Indpls., 1975-90, also dir.; pvt. practice. Editor: Hoosier Ind. quar. mag., 1966—. (Frances Wright award 1984), Pub. Rels. Soc. Am. (pres. Hoosier chpt. 1967, nat. bd. dirs. 1974-75, inducted to coll. fellows, 1992), Ind. Pub. Rels. Soc. (past pres.), Small Bus. Coun. (bd. dirs.), Ind. C. of C. Home and Office: 2216 Oak Run Pl Indianapolis IN 46260-5123

HILLMAN, GRACIA, association administrator; b. Bedford, Mass., Sept. 12, 1949; d. George and Mary Grace H.; m. Robert E. Bates, Jr.; 1 child, Hillman Martin. Student, Univ. of Mass. Coll. of Public and Community Svc., Boston, 1973-78. Adminstr. Mass. Legis. Black Caucus, 1975-77; exec. asst.to commr. Mass. Dept. of Correction, 1977-79; public and govtl. affairs specialist Mass. Port Authority, 1979; project dir. Joint Ctr. for Polit. Studies, 1979-82; exec. dir. Nat. Coalition on Black Voter Participation, 1982-87; program devel. cons. Congl. Black Caucus Found., 1987, interim exec. dir., 1988; sr. advisor congl. affairs Dukakis for Pres. Campaign, 1988; exec. cons. Coun. on Founds., 1989-90; exec. dir. LWV, D.C., 1990—, LWV Edn. Fund, D.C., 1990—; sec. United Front Homes Devel. Corp., New Bedford, 1972-76; pres. United Front Homes Day Care Ctr., New Bedford, 1973-76; pres. ONBOARD Cmty. Action Program, New Bedford, 1974-76; mem. Mass. Post Secondary Edn. Commn., 1975; chmn. Mass. Govt. Svc. Career Program, 1977-78; vice chmn. Ctr. for Youth Svcs., D.C., 1985—. Mem. Nat. Polit. Congress of Black Women. Office: League of Women Voters of the US 1730 M St NW Washington DC 20036-4505*

HILLMAN, JANE E., ceramic designer, artist; b. N.Y.C., Feb. 6, 1952; d. Joel Hillman and Carol Hillman-Berkley; m. Lionel Delevingne, Aug. 29, 1981; children: Lawrence Delevingne, Claire Delevingne. BFA, Alfred U., 1974. Owner, mgr. White Dog Pottery, Easthampton, Mass., 1982—. Office: Box 1092 1 Cottage St Easthampton MA 01027

HILLMAN, JENNIFER ANNE, ambassador, trade negotiator; b. lawyer, Toledo, Jan. 29, 1957; d. Charles Winchell and Anne Sylvia (Mossberg) H.; m. Mitchell Rand Berger, Oct. 20, 1990. BA, Duke U., 1978, MEd, 1979; JD, Harvard U., 1983. Bar: D.C., U.S. Ct. Internat., U.S. Mil. Appeals. Asst. to chancellor Duke U., Durham, N.C., 1979-80; freshman Proctor Harvard U., Cambridge, Mass., 1981-83; assoc. Patton, Boggs & Blow, Washington, 1983-87; legis. asst. Senator Terry Sanford, Washington, 1987-88, legis. dir., 1988-92; dep. cluster coord. for fin. instns. U.S. Presdl. and Vice Presdl. Transition Team, Washington, 1992-93; ambassador, chief textile negotiator Office of U.S. Trade Rep., Exec. Office of Pres., Washington, 1993—; trustee Duke U., 1977-80. Mem. N.C. Dems., Raleigh, 1986—, Georgetown Presbyn. Ch., 1988—; tchr. adult learning Sacred Heart, Washington, 1983-92; adviser Terry Sanford for Senate Campaign, 1986. Mem. Coun. on Women's Studies Duke U., Phi Beta Kappa. Office: US Trade Rep 600 17th St NW Washington DC 20506

HILLMAN, JOYCE, state legislator; b. Deshler, Nebr., June 10, 1936; m. Kenneth Hillman, 1954; children: Janine Hergenreder, Shari Johnston, Terry. Mem. Nebr. Legislature from 48th dist. Bd. dirs. Old West Trail Found., Family Preservation Team. Democrat. Lutheran. Office: Nebr State Legislature State Capitol Lincoln NE 68509*

HILLMAN, PEARL ELIZABETH, minister; b. Lincoln, Kans., Sept. 2, 1907; d. Issiah Marine and Estelle Belle Elizabeth (Masterson) Turner; m. Lester Robert Hillman (dec. July 1973); children: Bernice, Lois, Roberta, Dunward, Donald. BS, Nazarene Bible Coll., 1980; MDiv, Asbury Theol. Sem., 1985. Ordained to ministry Ch. of the Nazarene, 1994. Min. Ch. of Nazarene, Crockett, Tex., 1987—; tchr., bd. dirs. Mt. Hope Ch. of Nazarene, Jacksonville, TEx., 1973-75, steward, del., 1973-79; pres. missionary Kiowa West of Colorado Springs, Colo., 1976-79, tchr. asst. Nicholasville (Ky.) Nazarene, 1982-85. Author: (devotions) Oral Roberts, 1990, Woman Alone mag., 1993, New Horizon, 1993. Mem. Ministerial Assn. Home and Office: Ch of Nazarene 505 S 4th St Crockett TX 75835-2713

HILLMAN, RITA, investor; b. N.Y.C., May 16, 1912; d. Rudolf and Bertha (Goodman) Kanarek; m. Alex L. Hillman, Aug. 23, 1932 (dec. 1968); children: Richard Alan (dec.), Alex L. Student NYU, 1929-32. Mem. Met. Mus. Art (mem. vis. com. 20th century art dept.), Am. Friends Israel Mus. (exec. com.), Bklyn. Acad. Music (vice chmn.), Internat. Ctr. Photography (chmn.), Alex Hillman Family Found. (pres.). Home: 895 Park Ave New York NY 10021-0327 Office: 630 5th Ave New York NY 10111-0001

HILLMER, ROBIN LYNN, critical care, medical/surgical nurse; b. Fairmont, Minn., Jan. 12, 1958; d. Walter Herman and Marilyn Ruth (Hughes) H. BSN, U. Wis., 1981; M. Nursing, U. Wash., 1990, postgrad., 1993-94. Cert. specialist; CCRN, BLS, ACLS. Staff nurse St. Joseph's Hosp., Milw., 1981-87, Harborview Med. Ctr., Seattle, 1987, Providence Med. Ctr., Seattle, 1987-90; clin. faculty Seattle Pacific U., 1990; clin. faculty/lectr. Seattle U., 1990-91; clin. nurse specialist Providence Med. Ctr., Seattle, 1991—. Bd. dirs. Home for Unwed Mothers, Resurrection Luth. Ch., Seattle, 1989-91; sec. Lutherans for Life, Seattle, 1992-94, v.p., 1994—; mem. ch. coun. Resurrection Luth. Ch., 1992—. Recipient Humanitarian award U. Wash. Sch. Nursing, 1990. Mem. AACN (Greater Milw. area chpt. sec. 1984-85, v.p. 1985-86, Puget Sound chpt. sec. 1992-93, edn. coord. 1993—), Sigma Theta Tau, Phi Kappa Phi. Republican. Home: 22020 9th Ave S Des Moines WA 98198 Office: Providence Med Ctr PO Box 34008 Seattle WA 98124-1008

HILL-ROSATO, JANE ELIZABETH, elementary education educator; b. Newton, N.J., Nov. 21, 1958; d. Howard Russell and Gloria Frances (Clark) Hill; m. Nicholas David Rosato, Oct. 14, 1989; 1 stepchild, Domenick Patrick; 1 child, Salvator John. BS, East Stroudsburg U., 1981. Cert. tchr. elem. and early childhood, N.J., Pa. Presch. tchr. Sunrise Learning Ctr., Branchville, N.J., 1981-82; tchr. Knowlton Twp. Elem. Sch., Delaware, N.J., 1982—; tutor pvt. practice, Bangor, Pa., 1984—. Recipient Tchr. Recognition award I N.J. Gov.'s Office, Dept. Edn., Princeton,1989; invitee: Commrs. Symposium for Outstanding N.J. Tchrs., Dept. Edn., Trenton State Coll., 1989, N.J. Rural Schs. Conf. Highlighting Exemplary Programs, Practices and Resources for Rural Educators, N.J. Rural Assistance Coun., 1990. Mem. NEA, N.J. Edn. Assn., Warren County Edn. Assn., Knowlton Twp. Edn. Assn., Warren County Tchrs. Applying Whole Lang. Republican. Methodist. Home: 620 S Main St Bangor PA 18013 Office: Knowlton Twp Elem Sch Rt 46 PO Box 227 Delaware NJ 07833

HILLS, CARLA ANDERSON, lawyer, former federal official; b. Los Angeles, Jan. 3, 1934; d. Carl H. and Edith (Hume) Anderson; m. Roderick Maltman Hills, Sept. 27, 1958; children: Laura Hume, Roderick Maltman, Megan Elizabeth, Alison Macbeth. A.B. cum laude, Stanford U., 1955; student, St. Hilda's Coll., Oxford (Eng.) U., 1954; LL.B., Yale U., 1958; hon. degrees, Pepperdine U., 1975, Washington U., 1977, Mills Coll., 1977, Lake Forest Coll., 1978, Williams Coll., 1981, Notre Dame U., 1993. Bar: Calif. 1959, DC 1974, U.S. Supreme Ct. 1965. Asst. U.S. atty. civil div. Los Angeles, 1958-61; ptnr. Munger, Tolles, Hills & Rickershauser, Los Angeles, 1962-74; asst. atty. gen. civil div. Justice Dept., Washington, 1974-75; sec. HUD, 1975-77; ptnr. Latham, Watkins & Hills, Washington, 1978-86, Weil, Gotshal & Manges, Washington, 1986-88; U.S. trade rep. Exec. Office of the Pres., 1989-93; chmn., CEO Hills & Co., 1993—; bd. dirs. Corning Glass Works, Am. Airlines, Fed. Nat. Mortgage Assn., The Henley Group, Am. Internat. Group, Chevron, AT&T, Time-Warner, Bechtel Inc., Trust Co. of the West, Chevron; adj. prof. Sch. Law, UCLA, 1972; mem. Trilateral Commn., 1977-82, 93—, Am. Com. on East-West Accord, 1977-79, Internat. Found. for Cultural Cooperation and Devel., 1977-89, Fed. Acctg. Standards Adv. Council, 1978-80; mem. corrections task force Los Angeles County Sub-Regional; adv. bd. Calif. Council on Criminal Justice, 1969-71; mem. standing com. discipline U.S. Dist. Ct. for Central Calif., 1970-73; mem. Adminstrv. Conf. U.S., 1972-74; mem. exec. com. law and free soc. State Bar Calif., 1974; bd. councillors U. So. Calif. Law Center, 1972-74; trustee Pomona Coll., 1977-79, Brookings Instn., 1979-84; mem. at large exec. com. Yale Law Sch., 1977-78; mem. com. on Law Sch. Yale Univ. Council; Gordon Grand fellow Yale U., 1978; mem. Sloan Commn. on Govt. and Higher Edn., 1977-79; mem. advisory com. Princeton U., Woodrow Wilson Sch. of Pub. and Internat. Affairs, 1977-80; trustee Am. Productivity and Quality Ctr., 1988—; council mem. Calif. Gov. Coun. Econ. Policy Adv., 1993—, Coun. on Fgn. Affairs, 1993—. Co-author: Federal Civil Practice, 1961; co-author, editor: Antitrust Adviser, 1971, 3d edit., 1985; contbg. editor: Legal Times, 1978-88; mem. editorial bd. Nat. Law Jour., 1978-88. Trustee U. So. Calif., 1977-79, Norton Simon Mus. Art, Pasadena, Calif., 1976-80; trustee Urban Inst., 1978-89, chmn., 1983-89; co-chmn. Alliance to Save Energy, 1977-89; vice chmn. adv. coun. on legal policy Am. Enterprise Inst., 1977-84; bd. visitors, exec. com. Stanford U. Law Sch., 1978-81; bd. dirs. Am. Coun. for Capital Formation, 1978-89, Inst. for Internat. Econs., 1993—; mem. adv. com. MIT-Harvard U. Joint Ctr. for Urban Studies, 1978-82. Fellow Am. Bar Found.; mem. Los Angeles Women Lawyers Assn. (pres. 1964), ABA (chmn. publs. com. antitrust sect. 1972-74, council 1974, 77-84, chmn. 1982-83), Fed. Bar Assn. (pres. Los Angeles chpt. 1963), Los Angeles County Bar Assn. (mem. fed. rules and practice com. 1963-72, chmn. issues and survey 1963-72, chmn. sub-com. revision local rules for fed. cts. 1966-72, mem. jud. qualifications com. 1971-72), Am. Bar Inst. Clubs: Yale of So. Calif. (dir. 1972-74); Yale (Washington). Office: 1200 19th St NW Washington DC 20036-2412

HILLS, LINDA LAUNEY, advisory systems engineer; b. New Orleans, June 21, 1947; d. Edgar Sebastien and Isabel (James) Launey; m. Marvin Allen Hills Sr. Jan. 29, 1977 (div. July 1982); 8 stepchildren. Student, Navy Avionics Schs., Memphis and San Diego, 1979-89; certs. in IBM Tech. Tng., System Mgmt. Schs., Chgo. and Dallas. Cert. disaster recovery planner. Sec. Calhoun and Barnes Inc. Co., New Orleans, 1965; clk. typist Social Security Adminstrn., New Orleans, 1965-67, U.S. Marshal's Office, New Orleans, 1967-69; supr. U.S. Atty.'s Office, New Orleans, 1969; with clk.'s office U.S. Dist. Ct. (ea. dist.) La., New Orleans, 1969-73; steno, sr. sec. Kelly Girl and Norrell Temp Services, New Orleans, 1974; aviation electronic technician, PO2 USN, Memphis and San Diego, 1974-78; customer engr. trainee IBM, Dallas, 1979; customer engr., systems mgmt. specialist IBM, San Diego, 1979-84; system ctr. rep. NSD Washington System Ctr. IBM, Gaithersburg, Md., 1984-87; ops. specialist mktg. dept. IBM, San Diego, 1987—, adv. systems engr., 1988-91; lectr., cons. in field. Author 5 books. Vol. Touro Infirmary, Dialysis Unit, New Orleans, 1965-67, New Orleans Recreation Dept. 1964-68, PALS-Montgomery County Mental Health Orgn., Bethesda, Md., 1984-87, various polit. candidates, 1963—; mem. Calif. Gov.'s Subcom. on Disaster Preparedness. Mem. NAFE, ACP, DAV, Info. System Security Assn., Women Computer Profls. San Diego, Data Processing Mgmt. Assn., San Diego Zoolog. Soc., Assn. System Mgmt., Smithsonian Instn. (resident assoc.), Nat. Trust Hist. Preservation. Office: PO Box 261806 San Diego CA 92196-1806

HILLS, PATRICIA GORTON SCHULZE, curator; b. Baraboo, Wis., Jan. 31, 1936; d. Hartwin A. Schulze and Glennie Gorton Baker; m. Frederic W. Hills, Jan. 17, 1958 (div. Feb. 1974); children: Christina, Bradford; m. Guy Kevin Whitfield, Jan. 3, 1976; 1 child, Andrew. BA, Stanford U., 1957; MA, Hunter Coll., 1968; PhD, NYU, 1973. Curatorial asst. Mus. Modern Art, N.Y.C., 1960-62; guest curator Whitney Mus. Am. Art, 1971-72, assoc. curator 18th and 19th Century art, 1972-74; vis. asst. prof. art dept. Hunter Coll., 1973; adj. assoc. prof. fine arts Inst. Fine Arts NYU, 1973-74; assoc. prof. fine arts and performing arts York Coll. CUNY, 1974-78; assoc. prof. dept. art history Boston U., 1978-88, prof., 1988—; adj. assoc. prof. Grad. Sch. Arts and Scis., Columbia U., 1974-75; adj. curator Whitney Mus. Am. Art, 1974-87. Author: Eastman Johnson, 1972, The American Frontier: Images and Myths, 1973, The Painters' America: Rural and Urban Life, 1810-1910, 1974, Turn-of-Century America: Paintings, Graphics, Photographs, 1890-1910, 1977, Social Concern and Urban Realism: American Painting of the 1930s, 1983, Alice Neel, 1983, John Singer Sargent, 1986, co-author: The Figurative Tradition and the Whitney Mus. Am. Art, 1980, Jacob Lawrence: Thirty Years of Prints: 1963-93. Danforth Found. grad. fellow for women, 1968-72, John Simon Guggenheim Meml. Found. fellow, 1982-83, Charles Warren Ctr. for Studies in Am. History fellow, 1982-83, W.E.B. DuBois Inst. for Afro-Am. Rsch. fellow, Harvard U., 1991-92, NEH fellow, 1995. Mem. Coll. Art Assn., Women's Caucus for Arts, Am. Studies Assn. Home: 238 Putnam Ave Cambridge MA 02139-3767 Office: Boston U Dept Art History Boston MA 02215

HILLS, REGINA J., journalist; b. Sault Sainte Marie, Mich., Dec. 24, 1953; d. Marvin Dan and Ardithanne (Tilly) H.; m. Vincent C. Stricherz, Feb. 25, 1984. B.A., U. Nebr., 1976. Reporter UPI, Lincoln, Nebr., 1976-80, state editor, bur. mgr., 1981-82; state editor, bur. mgr. UPI, New Orleans, 1982-84, Indpls., 1985-87; asst. city editor Seattle Post-Intelligencer, 1987—; panelist TV interview show Face Nebr., 1978-81; vis. lectr. U. Nebr., Lincoln, 1978, 79, 80; columnist weekly feature Capitol News, Nebr. Press Assn., 1981-82. Recipient Outstanding Coverage awards UPI, 1980, 82. Mem. U. Nebr. Alumni Assn., Zeta Tau Alpha. Office: Seattle Post-Intelligencer 101 Elliott Ave W Seattle WA 98119-4226

HILL-WILLIAMS, MONAY FRANCIS, nurse administrator; b. Bklyn., Jan. 28, 1958; d. John Lyen and Elizabeth Turner (Hill) Johnson; m. Stephen Yeates Williams, Sept. 15, 1984; 1 child, Stephen Michael. BSN, U. Pa., 1980. Cert. Critical Care Nurse, ACLS, BCLS instr. Staff nurse Hosp. U. Pa., Phila.; charge nurse adult/pediatric surg. unit St. Mary's Hosp., Phila., 1981-82; advanced staff nurse, asst. nurse mgr., evening coord. Presbyn. Hosp., Phila., 1982-89; nurse mgr. Our Lady of Lourdes, Camden, N.J., 1990-91; nurse Skilled Nursing Inc., 1990—; staff nurse CCU U. Pa. Hosp., 1991-93; weekend nursing supr. Lower Bucks Hosp., Bristol, Pa., 1991-93; guest lectr. U. Pa. Undergrad. Sch. Nursing. Parent chmn. Sch. Governance Coun., Phila. Pub. Schs., Powel Elem. Sch. Mem. Southeastern Pa. Area Black Nurses Assn. (1st v.p.), AACN, Pa. Nurses Assn.. Home: Apt 5P 172-141 133rd Ave Apt10D Jamaica NY 11434

HILSENRATH, LEE BETTY, mathematics educator; b. Bklyn., Dec. 6, 1934; d. Samuel and Gussie (Gelfand) Batch; m. Daniel Wallace Hilsenrath, Dec. 24, 1961; children: Joel Alan, Mark Harris. BA, Bklyn., 1956, MA, 1959. Cert. tchr. Math. tchr. John D. Wells Jr. High Sch., Bklyn., 1956; math. tchr. New Utrecht High Sch., Bklyn., 1956—, ret., 1991; dean of girls New Utrecht High Sch., 1972-85; student activities advisor New Utrecht High Sch., 1959-62; spl. edn. math. cons. New Utrecht High Sch. 1986-88. Mem. exec. bd., pres. Coney Island chpt. Am. Parkinson's Disease Assn. Recipient Outstanding Profl. Svc. Tchr. award Bklyn. High Sch. div. Bd. Edn. N.Y.C., 1988, Bklyn. High Sch. Recognition Day award New Utrecht High Sch., 1989. Democrat. Jewish. Home: 945 E 15th St Brooklyn NY 11230-3703

HILSON, DIANE NIEDLING, nursing administrator; b. Balt., May 28, 1956; d. John William and Marlyn Elaine (Weber) Niedling; m. James Earl Hilson, Sept. 18, 1982 (div.); children: James Ross, Katherine Michelle. BSN, Med. Coll. of Ga. Sch. Nursing, 1977, MSN, 1990. RN, Ga. Staff nurse, RN CCU St. Joseph Hosp., Augusta, Ga.; charge and staff nurse ICU Med. Coll. of Ga. Hosp., Augusta, head nurse med./surg. unit. Recipient Nurses Make a Difference award Am. Hosp. Assn., 1985, Excellence in Nursing award, 1994. Mem. Ga. Nurses Assn., Sigma Theta Tau. Home: 3632 Bermuda Cir # E Augusta GA 30909 Office: Med Coll of Ga 1120 15th St 3 N Augusta GA 30912

HILT, DIANE ELAINE, middle school educator, computer specialist; b. Gadsden, Ala., Jan. 3, 1944; d. William Edward and Adele Helen (Plasman) Frantz; m. James Hines Hilt, Mar. 13, 1968. BS, Jacksonville (Ala.) State U., 1965; MEd, Ga. State U., 1972. Cert. adminstr., supr., tchr. math, Ala., Ga. Actuarial clk. Life Ins. Co. Ala., Gadsden, 1965-66; tchr. Trinity Pvt. Sch., Columbus, Ga., 1968-69, Phenix City (Ala.) Sch. System, 1969-71; tchr. elem. grades Post Dependent Schs., Ft. Benning, Ga., 1970-82, chairperson dept. math., 1973-85, coord. curriculum, 1980-84, instr. staff devel., 1985—, 7th/8th grade math/sci. tchr., 1991—; chairperson negotiation contract com. Post Dependent Schs., Ft. Benning, Ga., 1993—, mediation trainer, 1994; owner computer bus., 1984-85; active Tchr. In Space Program, NASA, 1985; sch. sys. rep. to survey Rand Corp., 1987; pres. Fla. Instructional Computing Conf. for Computer Using Educators, 1988, North Cook Ednl. Svc. Ctr., St. Charles, Ill., 1990, Ga. Tech. Conf., Columbus. Contbr. to curriculum guide, 1969. Sec. PTA, 1979-80, Columbus Community Concerts, 1983; usher Springer Theater, Columbus, 1984. Mem. NEA (del. 1978-79), ACA, Nat. Coun. Tchrs. Math (guest spkr. 1979), Nat. Coun. Tchrs. Math. (guest spkr. 1970), Profl. Assn. Ga. Educators, Benning Edn. Assn. (sec. 1973-77), Rotary (pres. Columbus chpt. 1975-76), Overseas Edn. Assn. Methodist. Home: 3301 Tewson Dr Columbus GA 31909-4742

HILTON, ALICE MARY, cybernetics and computing systems consultant, author, mathematician, art historian; b. London, June 18, 1936; d. Frederick O. and Thea (von Weber) H.; m. Herbert Layton Hayward, Sept. 7, 1957 (dec.); children—Barbara Mary Hilton-Hayward, Kathryn Anne Hilton-Hayward. B.A. with honors; M.A., D.Phil., U. Oxford, Eng.; Ph.D. in Math. and Elec. Engring, U. Calif.; postgrad., Sorbonne, Columbia. Computing systems analyst Electrodata Corp. (name now Burroughs Corp.), Pasadena, Cal., 1951-55; dir. publs. and pub. relations Underwood Corp., N.Y.C., 1955-57; cons. computing-machine applications in industry, sci. research, govt., medicine, art history A.M. Hilton & Assoc., N.Y.C., 1958—; pres. Inst. Cybercultural Research, N.Y.C., 1964—; asso. prof. dept. philosophy Queens Coll., City U. N.Y., N.Y.C., 1970—; computing systems cons., N.Y.C., 1956—; vis. scholar U. Oxford; vis. prof. U. N.C.; pres. A.R.T.S. (Art Registration Terminals System), UNESCO; sr. lectr. Met. Mus. Art, N.Y.C., cons. Cathedral of Lausanne. Author: Computing Machines in Control Systems, 1961, Logic, Computing Machines and Automation, 1963, Human Beings and Their Machines, 1965, The Evolving Society, 1966, Against Pollution and Hunger, 1974, Arts-in-Context: The Logic of Gothic Art, 1979, Arts-in-Context: A Mathematician Looks at Civilisation, Vol. I, The Splendid Twelfth Century, 1983, The Glorious Thirteenth Century, 1984, The Flamboyant Fourteenth Century, 1985, The Fabulous Fifteenth Century, 1986, The Adventurous Sixteenth Century, 1987, The Marvellous Seventeenth Century, 1988, Great Moments in Western Civilisation, 1989, The Elegant Eighteenth Century, 1990, The Prolific Nineteenth Century, 1991, Our Glorious Medieval Heritage, 1992, The Golden Age of Great Cities, Vol. 1-4, 1994; editor: The Cybercultural Review, 1968-90, The Feedback Newsletter, 1964-85, The Age of Cyberculture: The Challenge of Leisure and Abundance; contbr. numerous essays on cybernetics and social change to profl. jours. Recipient A.N. Ribero Sanches award Govt. of Portugal, 1968; Distinguished Achievement award Inst. Cybercultural Research, 1964; Guggenheim fellow. Mem. Am. Math. Soc., Assn. for Computing Machinery, IEEE, Authors League, Fedn. Am. Scientists, Am. Soc. for Cybernetics, Cybernetica, British Computer Soc., Soc. for Social Responsibility in Sci. (past pres.), Internat. Com. on Museums (chmn. Com. Documentation of Fine Arts), Mind Assn. Office: AM Hilton & Assocs 875 5th Ave New York NY 10021-4952

HIME, KIRSTEN BERTELSEN, nursing educator; b. Oakland, Calif., Mar. 23, 1940; d. Elmer V. and Helen E. (Hansen) Bertelsen; children: Colleen Hime Risvold, Sean W., Patrick C. Diploma, Samuel Merritt Coll. Nursing, 1961; BA, U. Redlands, 1982; A in Bus., Advantage-Health Edn., 1992. Pvt. practice cons./stress trainer San Jacinto, Calif.; cons. Calif. State Dept. Edn., Sacramento, 1979—; program dir. nursing asst. program Riverside (Calif.) County Office Edn., 1984—; part-time instr. Mt. San Jacinto (Calif.) Coll., 1989; part-time staff nurse acute psychiat. unit Hemet (Calif.) Med. Ctr.-Behavioral Health; advisor, judge Health Occupation Students Am., 1990—; rater Nurse Asst. Tng. Assessment Program, 1992—. Youth advisor, judge Vocat. Indsl. Clubs Am., 1977-88; instr. ARC, Am. Heart Assn. Recipient Women Helping Women award Soroptimists, 1989. Mem. Calif. Assn. Health Career Educators (pres.-elect 1984-85, pres. 1985-86), Beta Sigma Phi (Order of Rose award). Home: 758 E Washington Ave San Jacinto CA 92583-5432

HIMELSTEIN, SUSAN, psychologist; b. Norwalk, Ohio, Feb. 27, 1951; d. Warren and Frances (Jenkins) Holzhauser. BS, Miami U., Oxford, Ohi, 1973; MA, UCLA, 1981, PhD with honors, 1987. Lic. psychologist, sch. psychologist, counselor, tchr., Calif. Staff psychologist Verdugo Psychotherapy Inst., Glendale, Calif., 1987-88; counselor, psychologist Beverly Hills (Calif.) Unified Schs., 1988—; pvt. practice Santa Monica, Calif., 1989—; psychologist, cons., sr. faculty mem. Reiss-Davis Child Study Ctr., 1987—; adj. prof. Pepperdine U., Culver City, 1989—; supr. interns for various univs.; spkr. UCLA Ext. Confs., 1994—. Acad. scholar Calif. State Fellowship, 1981-83. Mem. APA, L.A. County Psychol. Assn., Calif. Psychol. Assn. Office: 233 Wilshire Blvd Ste 910 Santa Monica CA 90401-1254

HIMES, AMY DIANNE, secondary school educator; b. Butler, Pa., Sept. 9, 1951; d. Thomas Melvin and Dorothy Audene (Heeter) H. BS, Ind. U. of

Pa., 1973, MEd, 1979. Cert. tchr., reading specialist. Mem. retail staff Hills Dept. Store, Indiana, Pa., 1973-75; tchr. Purchase Line Schs., Commodore, Pa., 1974-75, West Forest H.S., Tionesta, Pa., 1975-76; reading specialist Harmony Schs., Westover, Pa., 1976-80; acting asst. prin., educator Sligh Jr. High Sch., Tampa, Fla., 1980-90; mem. guidance staff, educator Greco Jr. H.S., Temple Terrace, Fla., 1990—, track coach, 1991—. Mem. Phi Delta Kappa. Democrat. Methodist.

HIMES, JANE ANN, public relations executive; b. Johnstown, Pa., June 20, 1923; d. Joseph George and Anna (Berg) Dupin; m. William E. Himes, Dec. 29, 1943 (div. Mar. 1977); chidren: Douglas D., Gregory T. Student, Memphis State U., 1977-86. Sec. Nat. Radiator Co., Johnstown, 1940-44; student loan officer 1st Nat. Bank Mercer County, Sharon, Pa., 1970-76; adminstrv. asst. trust div. Nat. Bank Commerce, Memphis, 1976-78; adminstrv. asst. to chmn. bd. Buckman Labs. Internat., Inc., Memphis, 1978-79, dir. pub. rels., 1979—, editor Bu-Lines/By-Lines, 1980—; mem. profl. adv. bd. Sch. Journalism, Memphis State U., 1986—. Mem. adv. bd. Adopt-A-Sch., Memphis, 1983-86, 88—; chmn. bd. dirs. Crime Stoppers Memphis, 1987-88, 89—; mem. adv. bd. arts in schs. Memphis Arts Coun., 1989—; v.p. bd. dirs. Home Health Care Found., Memphis, 1989—; bd. dirs. communications chmn. Tenn. chpt. Am. Heart Assn., Memphis and Nashville; elder Prsbyn. Ch., Memphis; mem. adv. bd. Porter Leath Children's Ctr. Recipient Vol. of Yr. award Am. Heart Assn., Memphis, 1985. Mem. Pub. Rels. Soc. Am. (bd. dirs. Memphis 1985—, pres. 1988, Profl. of Yr. award 1988, nat. presdl. citation 1988), Optimists, Rotary. Republican. Office: Buckman Labs Internat Inc 1256 N McLean Memphis TN 38108

HIMMELBERG, BARBARA TAYLOR, controller; b. Schenectady, N.Y., Aug. 17, 1951; d. Robert Arthur and Maureen (Balhoff) Taylor; m. Jerome Paul Himmelberg Jr., Feb. 14, 1985. BS in Math., U. Mass., 1973. Account rep. GE Info. Svc. Co., Schenectady, 1973-78; fin. mgr. GE, Bridgeport, Conn., 1978-79, Dallas, 1979-80, Rome, Ga., 1980-81, Portland, Oreg., 1982-83; fin. mgr. Tektronix Inc., Portland, 1983-88; chief fin. officer Am. Guarantee Fin. Corp., Portland, 1988-89; contr. Lasco Shipping Co., Portland, 1990—. Treas. Mothers Against Drunk Driving, Portland, Bradley-Angle House Shelter, Portland; bd. dirs. Komen Breast Cancer Found., Portland, Cascase AIDS Project, Portland. Office: Lasco Shipping Co 3200 NW Yeon Ave Portland OR 97210-1524

HIMMS-HAGEN, JEAN MARGARET, biochemist; b. Oxford, Eng., Dec. 18, 1933; d. Frederick Hubert and Margaret Mary (Deadman) Himms; m. Paul Hagen, Sept. 29, 1956; children: Anna, Nina. BSc, U. London, 1955; PhD, Oxford U., 1958. Postdoctoral fellow Harvard U., 1958-59; asst. prof. physiology U. Man., 1959-64; assoc. prof. biochemistry Queen's U., 1964-67; assoc. prof. biochemistry U. Ottawa, 1967-71, prof., 1971—, acting chmn. dept., 1975-77, 87, chmn. dept., 1977-82; mem. coun. Med. Rsch. Coun., 1970-75; mem. Exec. Med. Rsch. Coun., 1970-73, mem. grants coms., 1969-75, chmn. metabolism grants com., 1972-75. Assoc. editor: Can. Jour. Biochemistry, 1967-71, Can. Jour. Physiology and Pharmacology, 1971-75, Am. Jour. Physiology, 1979-89, 92—; mem. editorial bd. proc. Soc. Exptl. Biology and Medicine, 1984-90; contbr. over 100 articles and revs. to sci. jours., chpts. to books. Recipient research grants Med. Research Council, 1960—, career award, 1968-77, Bond award Am. Oil Chemists Soc., 1972. Fellow Royal Soc. Can.; mem. Can. Biochem. Soc. (Ayerst award 1973), Am. Inst. Nutrition, Biochem. Soc. U.K., Soc. for Exptl. Biology and Medicine (coun. 1991—). Home: 233 Tudor Pl, Ottawa, ON Canada K1L 7Y1 Office: U Ottawa Dept Biochemistry, 451 Smyth Rd, Ottawa, ON Canada K1H 8M5

HINCKS, MARCIA LOCKWOOD, retired insurance company executive, lawyer; b. N.Y.C., July 3, 1935; d. John Salem and Dorothy Elinor (Tufts) Lockwood; m. John Winslow Hincks, June 14, 1958; children—Rebecca Towne, Jennifer Winslow, John Morris, Benjamin Lockwood. B.A., Bryn Mawr Coll., 1956; LL.B., Yale U., 1959. Bar: Conn. 1960. Atty. Aetna Life & Casualty, Hartford, Conn., 1961-64, 67-70, counsel, 1970-81, v.p., ins. counsel, 1981-91, sr. counsel litigation, 1991-93. Chmn. United Way Capital Area, Hartford, 1984-85; bd. dirs. Hartford Hosp., 1983—, Conn. Water Co., Clinton, 1983—; trustee Hotchkiss Sch., Lakeville, Conn., 1973-78, Hartford Coll. Women, 1978—. Recipient Community Service award United Way Capital Area, 1982, Alexis de Tocqueville award United Way of Am., 1987. Mem. ABA, Conn. Bar Assn., Assn. Life Ins. Counsel. Democrat. Congregationalist. Club: Hartford Golf.

HINDLE, PAULA ALICE, nursing administrator; b. Cambridge, Mass., Feb. 26, 1952; d. Edward Adam and Geraldine Ann (Donahue) H. BSN, Fitchburg State Coll., 1974; MSN, Duke U., 1980; MBA, Simmons Coll., 1988. Staff nurse Mt. Auburn Hosp., Cambridge, Mass., 1974-75; staff nurse U. Hosp., Boston, 1975-77, head nurse, 1977-79; staff nurse Duke U. Med. Ctr., Durham, N.C., 1979-80, clin. instr., 1980-81, area mgr., 1981; nurse leader, clin. dir. New Eng. Med. Ctr., Boston, 1981-87; cons. Ctr. for Nursing Case Mgmt., Boston, 1984-87; v.p. nursing Faulkner Hosp., Boston, 1987-94; v.p. nursing and support svcs. Alexandria (Va.) Hosp., 1994—; mem. adv. com. Regis Coll. Nursing, 1993-94; mem. planning and resource com. Simmons Coll., 1993-94. Active Am. Heart Assn. Mem. AACN, Am. Orgn. Nurse Execs., Va. Orgn. Nurse Execs., Mass. Orgn. Nurse Execs. (treas. 1991-93), Humane Soc., Simmons Coll. Grad. Sch. Mgmt. Alumni Assn. (bd. dirs. 1991-93, pres. 1992-93), Sigma Theta Tau. Democrat. Roman Catholic. Home: 5908 Munson Ct Falls Church VA 22041-2444 Office: Alexandria Hosp 4320 Seminary Rd Alexandria VA 22304-1500

HINDS, BARBARA MARIE, corporate secretary; b. Lynwood, Calif., Jan. 17, 1949; d. Tildo and Louise Maxine (Duff) Bartoletti; m. Hubert H. Hinds Jr., Apr. 16, 1976 (div. June 1989). Grad. high sch., South Gate, Calif. Various positions Atlantic Richfield Co., L.A., 1969-77, asst. corp. sec., 1977—. Mem. Am. Soc. Corp. Secs. Republican. Office: Atlantic Richfield Co 515 S Flower St Bldg 4589 Los Angeles CA 90071-2247

HINDS, JO ANN, business owner; b. Detroit, Aug. 17, 1950; d. Joseph William and Carmen Gloria (Desbiens) B; m. Donn Stephen Hinds, Aug. 26, 1972 (div. Dec. 1982); 1 child, Kira Ann. BS in Biology, Geology, Cen. Mich. U., 1972, MS in Biology, 1976; MBA, Mich. State U., 1993. Sci. tchr. Walled Lake (Mich.) Schs., 1972-79, Linden (Mich.) Schs., 1979-82; pres.-owner Diamond Die & Mold Co., Mt. Clemens, Mich., 1982—; lectr. Mich. State U., Lansing, 1993—. mem. Nat. Tooling Assn., Detroit Tooling Assn., Audobon Soc., Tri Beta Biol. Assn. Office: Diamond Die & Mold Co 35401 Groesbeck Hwy Clinton Township MI 48035-2518

HINDS, LYN JEAN, artist; b. Orange, N.J., Nov. 9, 1935; d. Carl Ensio and Ruth Elizabeth (Nelson) Hella; m. Harvey Morton Hinds, Mar. 1, 1958; children: Kurt Lawrence, Scott Douglas. BA in English, U. Conn., 1957; BFA in Painting summa cum laude, U. Hartford, 1994. Works have been exhibited in group shows Alexander Gold Farb Student award exhbn., West Hartford, Conn., 1990, 93, West Hartford (Conn.) Open Juried Show, 1994. Named Best in Show, Conn. Women Artists, Inc., 1994. Mem. NOW, West Hartford Art League, Alpha Chi, Kappa Alpha Theta. Home: 14 Sanctuary Dr Bo 722 Simsbury CT 06070

HINE, DARLENE CLARK, history educator, administrator; b. Morley, Mo., Feb. 7, 1947; d. Levester and Lottie May (Thompson) Clark; m. William C. Hine, Aug. 21, 1970 (div. 1975); m. Johnny Earl Brown, July 25, 1981 (div. Aug. 1986); 1 child, Robbie Davine. BA in Am. History, Roosevelt U., 1968; MA, Kent State U., 1970, PhD in Afro-Am. History, 1975. Teaching asst. Kent State U., Ohio, 1968-71; asst. prof. history, coordinator Black studies, S.C. State Coll., Orangeburg, 1972-74; asst. prof. Purdue U., West Lafayette, Ind., 1974-79, assoc. prof., 1980—, interim dir. African Studies and Research Ctr., 1978-79, vice provost, 1981-86; John A. Hannah Prof. History, Mich. State U., East Lansing, 1986—; mem. Ind. Com. for Humanities, 1983-85; invited lectr. colls. and univs. including Harvard U., 1975, U. Ill., Chgo., 1981, Ind. U., 1982, U. Tex., Austin, 1983, So. Meth. U., 1983, Duke U., 1990, U. N.C., Chapel Hill, 1992, Emory U., 1994; grant rev. panelist NEH, 1979-80, Ford Found., NRC, 1980, 81, 82. Author: Black Victory, 1979, When the Truth is Told: A History of Black Women's Culture and Community in Indiana, 1875-1950, 1981, Black Women in the Nursing Profession: A Documentary History, 1984, Black Women in White: Racial Conflict and Cooperation in the Nursing Profession 1890-1950, 1989; editor: Black Women in America: An Historical Encyclopaedia, vol. 2, 1993; contbr. chpts. to books, articles to publs., book revs. to jours. Alumni fellow Kent State U., 1971-72, Nat. Humanities Ctr. fellow, 1986, Am. Council Learned Socs. fellow, 1986; faculty devel. grantee Purdue U., 1978-79; research awardee Rockefeller Archive Ctr., 1978; Rockefeller Found. fellow for minority group scholars, 1980; research grantee Eleanor Roosevelt Inst., 1980-81; project grantee Fund for Improvement of Post-Secondary Edn., 1980-82; NEH grantee, 1982-83; 1st place essay award Degolyer Inst., 1982, Disting. Alumni award Roosevelt U., 1988. Mem. Assn. for Study of Negro Life and History (exec. council 1979, 2d v.p. 1985-88), Orgn. Am. Historians, So. Hist. Assn., So. Assn. Women Historians (v.p. 1983-85, pres. 1985-86), Am. Hist. Assn., Assn. Black Women Historians, Phi Alpha Theta. Democrat. Baptist. Home: 2357 Burcham Dr East Lansing MI 48823-7241 Office: Mich State U Dept History East Lansing MI 48824

HINEMAN, NANCY LEE, protective services official; b. West Chester, Pa., Mar. 23, 1951; d. Leon Joseph and Nancy Josephine (Bruno) Mascaro; 1 child, Marty Hineman. Grad. high sch., Concordville, Pa. Lic. cosmetologist, Del. and Pa.; pvt. detective, Pa.; cert. in sci. crime detection, Pa. Pvt. practice cosmetology Wilmington, Del. and Media, Pa., 1969-74; detective criminal investigation div. Delaware County Dist. Atty., Media, Pa., 1975-78; polygraphist Criminal Investigation div. Delaware County, 1975-78; v.p., co-owner Urella's Detective Bur., Media, 1978—. Recipient Spl. Commendation award U.S. Monetary War Coll., San Diego, 1988. Mem. NAFE, Pa. Polygraph Assn., Nat. Detective Assn. Republican. Roman Catholic. Office: Urella's Detective Bur 160 Paxon Hollow Rd Media PA 19063-1114

HINER, GLADYS WEBBER, psychologist; b. Mt. Park, Okla., Mar. 10, 1907; d. Santford and Erie Emma (Rose) Webber; m. Wayman Hiner, Aug. 11, 1927 (dec. Mar. 1967); children: Waynel Cook, Sandra Homer. BS, U. Okla., 1934, MS, 1955, PhD, 1962; HHD (hon.), Wagon Wheel Found., McCloud, Okla., 1973. Bd. cert. devel. psychologist. Tchr. Okla. City Pub. Schs., 1953-61; dir. Dale Rogers Tng. Ctr., Okla. City, 1962-63; prof. Okla. City U., 1963-72, Rose State Coll., Okla. City, 1972-86; cons. Wagon Wheel Sch. McLoud, Okla., 1962-82, pvt. practice, Okla. City, 1986—. Supr. Sunday Sch. Trinity Baptist Ch., Okla. City, 1940-72; bd. dirs. Okla. State Assn. for Mentally Retarded Children, 1963-67, Youth and Child Coun. Okla. U. Med. Sch., 1966-69, Bridge Builders, Okla. City; Dem. state del., 1986. Fellow Okla. Psychol. Assn., Am. Assn. on Mental Deficiency; mem. The Acad. Ret. Profls., Okla. Hist. Soc., DAR, Colonial Dames, Psi Chi, Phi Theta Kappa. Home: 6452 Brandywine Ln Oklahoma City OK 73116-3520

HINER, MARY ELIZABETH MEAD, graphic designer, illustrator, artist; b. Grand Rapids, Mich., Apr. 12, 1943; d. Robert Gregory and Hazel (Schurman) Mead; m. Richard Gorman Hiner, Nov. 13, 1971; stepchildren: Steven R., Susan Hiner Lamos, Linda Hiner DeWitt. AA, Grand Rapids C.C., 1992; student, Grand Valley State U., 1993—. Studio artist, illustrator, graphic designer Grand Rapids, 1986-90; graphic designer, illustrator Media Svcs., Grand Rapids C.C., 1990—. Graphic designer, illustrator: (newsletter) Michigan Wild, fall 1991, spring 1992 (Paragon award Nat. Coun. Mktg. and Pub. Rels. 1993). Vol. Mich. Amputee Golf Assn., 1979—, Nat. Amputee Golf Assn., 1973-93. Recipient Arthur Andrews award for excellence in scholarship, 1992. Mem. Univ. and Coll. Designers Assn., Delta Pi Alpha. Home: 444 Lakeside Dr NE Grand Rapids MI 49503

HINERFELD, LEE ANN, veterinarian; b. San Francisco, Apr. 24, 1955; d. Norman Martin and Ruth Jean (Gordon) H. BA, Vassar Coll., 1977; DVM, Tufts U., 1986; MS, U. Wyo., 1987. Lic. Conn., Mass. Sr. rsch. technician U. Mass. Med. Ctr., Worcester, 1977-80; small animal clinician, assoc. vet. Mt. Pleasant Hosp. for Animals, Newtown, Conn., 1987, Shakespeare Vet. Hosp., Stratford, Conn., 1988-90, New London (Conn.) Vet. Hosp., 1990—. Mem. Am. Vet. Med. Assn., Conn. Vet. Med. Assn. (Fellow of Acad. 1994), Assn. Women Vets., Defenders of Wildlife, Population Comm. Internat., Common Cause, New Forests Project, Phi Kappa Phi, Beta Beta Beta. Avocations: jogging, skiing, hiking, cooking, photography. Office: New London Vet Hosp 122 Cross Rd Waterford CT 06385

HINERFELD, RUTH J., civic organization executive; b. Boston, Sept. 18, 1930; m. Norman Hinerfeld, children: Lee, Thomas, Joshua. A.B., Vassar Coll., 1951; grad., Program in Bus. Adminstrn., Harvard-Radcliffe Coll., 1952. With LWV, 1954—, UN observer, 1969-72, chairperson internat. relations com., 1972-76, 1st v.p. in charge legis. activities, 1976-78, pres., 1978-82; dir. LWV Overseas Edn. Fund, 1975-76, trustee, 1975-86; chairperson LWV Edn. Fund, 1978-82; mem. White House Adv. Com. for Trade Negotiations, 1975-82; sec. UN Assn. of U.S., 1975-78, vice chmn., 1983—, bd. govs., 1975—, mem. econ. policy coun., 1976-93; vice chair Overseas Devel. Coun.; mem. U.S. del. auspices of Nat. Com. on U.S.-China Rels. and Chinese People's Inst. Fgn. Affairs, 1978. Mem. coun. Nat. Mcpl. League, 1977-80, 83-86. del.-at-large Internat. Women's Year Conf., Houston, 1977; mem. exec. com. Leadership Conf. on Civil Rights, 1978-82; trustee Citizens Research Found., 1978—; mem. Nat. Petroleum Coun., 1979-82; mem. U.S. del. to World Conf. on UN Decade for Women, 1980; mem. adv. com. Nat. Inst. for Citizen Edn. in the Law, 1981-91; mem. North South Roundtable, 1978-88; mem. nat. gov. bd. Common Cause, 1984-90; vice chmn. U.S. com. UNICEF, 1986-90, treas., 1990-91; mem. Nat. Adv. Coun.; mem. vis. com. Harvard U. Bus. Sch., 1984-90; mem. Bretton Woods Com.; bd. dirs. Com. for Modern Cts. Recipient Disting. Citizen award Nat. Mcpl. League, 1978; Outstanding Mother award Nat. Mother's Day Com., 1981; Aspen Inst. Presdl. fellow, 1981. Mem. Council on Fgn. Relations, Phi Beta Kappa. Office: 11 Oak Ln Larchmont NY 10538-3917

HINES, ANNA GROSSNICKLE, author, illustrator; b. Cin., July 13, 1946; d. Earl Stanton and Ruth Marie (Putman) Grossnickle; m. Gary Roger Hines, June 19, 1976; children: Bethany, Sarah, Lassen. Art major, San Fernando Valley St, 1964-67, 72; BA in Human Devel., Pacific Oaks Coll., 1974, MA in Human Devel., 1978. Tchr. L.A. City Day Care Ctrs., 1967-70, Columbia Elem. Sch., Calif., 1975-78. Author: Taste The Raindrops, 1983, Come To The Meadow, 1984, Maybe A Band-Aid Will Help, 1984, Bethany For Real, 1985, All By Myself, 1985, Cassie Bowen Takes Witch Lessons, 1985, Don't Worry I'll Find You, 1986, Daddy Makes The Best Spaghetti, 1986, I'll Tell You What They Say, 1987, Keep Your Old Hat, 1987, It's Just Me, Emily, 1987, Grandma Gets Grumpy, 1988, Boys Are Yucko!, 1989, They Really Like Me, 1989, Sky All Around, 1989, Big Like Me, 1989, Mean Old Uncle Jack, 1990, The Secret Keeper, 1990, Remember The Butterflies, 1991, The Greatest Picnic In The World, 1991, Jackie's Lunch box, 1991, Tell Me Your Best Thing, 1991, Moon's Wish, 1992, Rumble Thumble Boom!, 1992, Moompa, Toby and Bomp, 1993, Gramma's Walk, 1993, Even If I Spill My Milk?, 1994, What Joe Saw, 1994; illustrator: A Ride in the Crummy, 1991, Flying Firefighters, 1993, Day of the High Climber, 1994. Children's Book Coun., 1988. Mem. Soc. of Children's Book Writers and Illustrators, Internat. Reading Assn. Office: care Greenwillow Books 105 Madison Ave New York NY 10016-7418 also: Clarion Books 215 Park Ave S New York NY 10003-1603

HINES, DAISY MARIE, writer; b. Hanna City, Ill., Dec. 31, 1913; d. Frank W. and Edith Earl (Folger) Humphrey; m. Herbert Waldo Hines, Jr., Dec. 20, 1958; children—Grace Consuelo, Ruby Marie. Student Western Ill. U., 1955-57, So. Ill. U., 1956. Mem. staff advt. dept. Macomb Daily Jour. (Ill.), 1943-47; writer, exec., dir., promoter McDonough County Tb Assn., 1949-58; sec. U.S. Dept. Agr., Macomb, 1955-58; researcher, writer 1st Nat. Bank, Springfield, 1963; adminstrv. asst. to state legislator, 1964-69; with Sentinel Printing Co., Illiopolis, Ill., 1965; newspaper columnist, free-lance writer, mem. survey staff Prairie Farmer Pub. Co., Oak Brook, Ill., 1965-79, Successful Farming, Des Moines, 1982; Springfield corr. Automotive News div. Crain Communications, Inc. Active Altar Soc. Blessed Sacrament Cath. Ch., Springfield; freelance writer Springfield Cath. Times newspaper, 1991, Decatur (Ill.) Herald and Review newspaper, 1991; chmn. Illiopolis unit Univ. Ill. Home Extension; pub. relations dir. Springfield chpt. Am. Cancer Soc., 1961-68; 2d v.p. Ill. Conf. Tb Workers, 1952-53; mem. Sangamon County Farm Bur. (women's com., chmn. health and safety), St. John's Hosp. Auxiliary. Mem. Nat. League Am. Pen Women (pres. Springfield chpt. 1972-73, sec. Ill. br. 1974), Western Ill. U. Alumni Council (sec.; Disting. Alumni award 1982; com. mem. Coll. Applied Scis. Agr. rep. Alumni Council), Illiopolis Am. Legion (aux. unit 521), Ill. Press Assn. USAF Air Def. Team (hon. life), Ill. Women for Agr., Civil War Round Table, Sangamon County Hist. Soc. Club: Republican Women's. Address: 2504 S Holmes Ave Springfield IL 62704

HINES, EMMAJEAN ELIZABETH, medical technologist; b. Indpls., Nov. 17, 1933; d. Lee Andrew Jones and Lillian R. (Patton) Woodson; divorced; children: John Thomas, Anthony Charles. AS, Ivy Tech. Coll., Indpls., 1971; BS, Martin U., Indpls., 1987. Registered med. technician. Nursing asst. Vets. Hosp. Inc., Indpls., 1966-71; lab. mgr. Briggs Health Clinic, Indpls., 1971-73, Citizens Health Ctr., Indpls., 1973-75; sr. registered med. technician Community Hosp., Indpls., 1975—; tchr. polit. sci. Martin Center U., Indpls., 1988; lab. mgr. Martin Ctr. Inc., Indpls., 1993. Mem. NAACP, Am. Bus. Women's Assn. (regional sefc. 1985-87, Woman of Yr. 1981, 86), Order Eastern Star (asst. matron 1993, grand queen 1992), Heroines of Jericho. Democrat. Baptist. Home: 4219 N 43d Ct Indianapolis IN 46226

HINES, JANICE SUE, electronics company executive; b. Oklahoma City, Jan. 28, 1954; d. Willard Vernor and Leavie Cordelia (Jenkins) H. BFA, U. Okla., 1978, MBA, 1993. Art, reproduction dept. mgr. Weight Watchers of Okla., Oklahoma City, 1976-77; wireman AT&T Microelectronics (formerly Western Electric Co.), Oklahoma City, 1977-78, quality inspector, 1978-79, mgr. trainee labor rels. and personnel depts., 1979-80, section chief, 1980; section chief parts fabrication AT&T Microelectronics (formerly Western Electric Co.), Richmond, Va., 1980-91; supr. mfg. support AT&T Microelectronics (formerly Western Electric Co.), Richmond, 1993—; cons. Okla State Dept. Commerce, 1993; grad. rsch. and teaching asst. U. Okla. Sch. Bus. Adminstrn. mgmt. div., 1992-93. U.S. Dept. Commerce fellow, U.S.-Japan Mfg. Tech. fellow, 1994-95; named Outstanding Oklahoman, 1978. Mem. Okla. U. Coll. Bus. Adminstrn. Alumni Assn., U.S. Badminton Assn. Office: AT&T Microelectronics 4500 S Laburnum Ave Richmond VA 23231-2422

HINES, MARION LOUISE See DEXHEIMER, MARION LOUISE

HINES, PATRICIA, social worker; b. Watertown, N.Y., Nov. 4, 1947; d. Arthur and Bella (O'Neil) Hines; BS, SUNY, Oswego, 1969; MSW, SUNY, Buffalo, 1975; M in Pub. Adminstrn., Fairleigh Dickinson U., 1982. Supr. social work Ocean County Bd. Social Services, Toms River, N.J., 1973-77, adminstrv. supr. social work, 1977-83, dep. dir., 1983—; social work cons. Ocean County Vis. Homemaker Svc., Inc., Toms River, 1975-80, Community Meml. Hosp., Toms River, 1978-79, Manchester Manor, Lakeview Manor, Bartley Manor Convalescent Ctr., Ocean Convalescent Ctr., Barnegat Nursing Facility, Burnt Tavern Convalescent Ctr., Jackson Health Care Ctr., Logan Manor Medicenter, Whiting Healthcare, Atlantic Coast Rehab., So. Ocean; prin. in Sr. Care Planning Assocs.; instr. social work Georgian Court Coll., Lakewood, 1975—. Chmn. Ocean County Title XX Coalition, 1977-82; bd. dirs. Ocean County Family Planning Program, Toms River, 1969-73, Mental Health Bd., 1983-84; mem. exec. bd. United Way, 1983—; mem. Aging Network Service. Cert., Dr. Thomas Gordon Parent Effectiveness Trainer. Mem. Acad. Cert. Social Workers, Nat. Assn. Social Workers (nat. register clin. social workers, diplomate clin. social work). Home: 13 Bay Harbor Blvd Brick NJ 08723-7303 Office: 1027 Hooper Ave Toms River NJ 08754

HINES, VONCILE, special education educator; b. Detroit, Dec. 1, 1945; d. Raymond and Cleo (Smith) H. AA, Highland Park Community Coll., 1967; BEd, Wayne State U., 1971, MEd, 1975; MA, U. Detroit, 1978. Tchr. primary unit Detroit Bd. Edn., 1971-79, spl. educator, 1979-94; tchr. trainee Feuerstein's Instrumental Enrichment, 1988—; cons. Queen's Community Workers, Detroit, 1977—; evaluator Teen Profl. Parenting Project, New Detroit Inc., 1986-87; guest educator, critic "Express Yourself", Sta. WQBH 1400 AM, 1989. Author: I Chose Planet Earth, 1988; inventor in field. Recipient cert. of merit State of Mich., 1978, 88, cert. of appreciation Queen's Cmty. Workers, 1980, Wayne County Bd. Commrs., 1988, award of recognition Detroit City Coun., 1984, 88. Mem. Assn. for Children and Adults with Learning Disabilities, Assn. Supervision and Curriculum Devel., Nat. Thinking Skills Network, NAFE, Nat. Council Negro Women (presenter 1987), Met. Detroit Alliance of Black Sch. Educators. Democrat.

HINES-MARTIN, VICKI PATRICIA, nursing educator; b. Louisville, Aug. 18, 1951; d. William Adolphus Hines and Mary Iris Bailey; m. Kenneth Wayne Martin, Dec. 30, 1978; 1 child, Michelle Hines Martin. BSN, Spalding Coll., 1975; MA in Edn., Spalding U., 1983; MSN, U. Cin., 1986; PhD, U. Ky., 1994. Cert. clin. specialist in adult psychiat. mental. Asst. chief nursing svcs. VA Med. Ctr., Cin.; nursing instr. Jefferson Community Coll., Louisville; head nurse mgr. VA Med. Ctr., Louisville; asst. prof. nursing Ind. U. S.E., New Albany; bd. dirs. Seven Counties Mental Health Svcs. Contbr. articles to profl. jours. Named to Outstanding Young Women of Am., 1986; recipient Rsch. award Ky. Nurses Found., 1992; Nurses Scholar/Fellow, Lucy Zimmerman sholar, 1982, Estelle MasseyOsborne Meml. scholar, 1983-84, trainee U. Cin., 1983, grad. scholar, 1983, Elizabeth Carnegie scholar, 1991, Am. Nurses Found. scholar, 1992; Fellow U. Ky., 1988, grad. fellow, 1992. Mem. ANA (minority clin. fellow 1991-93), Ky. Nurses Assn. (mental health coun. sec. 1986-88), Kyanna Black Nurses, Inc. (co-founder, past pres.), Nat. Black Nurses Assn., Soc. Edn. and Rsch. Psychiat. Nursing, Sigma Theta Tau. Office: Ind U Southeast 4201 Grant Line Rd New Albany IN 47150

HINKEBEIN, NANCY ELAINE, food service executive; b. Louisville, Jan. 3, 1962; d. Robert B. Jr. and Patricia Fayanne (Walker) H. AA, U. Louisville, 1985. Mgr. in tng. Dominos Pizza, Louisville, 1982-83, mgr., 1983-86; mgr. Dominos Pizza, Memphis, 1986-87; mgr., supervisory cons. Dominos Pizza, Louisville, 1987—; mktg. cons. Dominos Pizza, Louisville, 1983, 87. Contbr. articles to profl. jours. Mem. Camp Horsemanship Assn. Republican. Presbyterian. Home: 11311 Corston Ct Louisville KY 40241 Office: Dominos Pizza 9409 Westport Rd Louisville KY 40242

HINKELMAN, RUTH AMIDON, insurance company executive; b. Streator, Ill., June 4, 1949; d. Olin Arthur and Marjorie Annabeth (Wright) Amidon; m. Allen Joseph Hinkelman, Jr., Oct. 28, 1972; children: Anne Elizabeth, Allen Joseph III. AB in Econs., U. Ill., 1971. Underwriter Kemper Ins. Group, Chgo., 1971-75; acct. exec. Near North Ins. Agy., Chgo., 1975-76; underwriter Gen. Reinsurance Corp., Chgo., 1976-78, asst. sec., 1978-79, asst. v.p., 1979-83, 2nd v.p., 1983-87, v.p., 1987—. Home: 133 Linden Ave Wilmette IL 60091-2838 Office: Gen Reinsurance Corp 300 S Riverside Plz Ste 2000N Chicago IL 60606-6684

HINKLE, BETTY RUTH, educational administrator; b. Atchison Kans., Mar. 18, 1930; d. Arch W. and Ruth (Baker) Hunt; m. Charles L. Hinkle, Dec. 25, 1950 (div.); children: Karl, Eric. B.A., U. Corpus Christi, 1950; M.S., Baylor U., 1956; M.A., U. North Colo., 1972, Ed.D., 1979. Cert. tchr. Tex., 1950, Mass., 1961, Colo., 1966; cert. adminstr., Colo., 1976. Mem. faculty Alice (Tex.) Independent Sch. Dist., 1950, Waco (Tex.) Ind. Sch. Dist., 1951-52, 1953-58; Hawaii Pub. Schs., Oahu, 1952-53, Newton Pub. Schs., Newtonville, Mass., 1962-63; Colorado Springs (Colo.) Pub. Schs., 1966-78; cons., exec. dir. spl. projects unit Colo. State Dept. Edn., Denver, 1978—; exec. dir. Office Fed./State Program Svcs., 1992—; mem. cabinet Colorado Dept. Edn., mem. Quality Coun., fed. liaison rep. to chief state sch. officers, Washington; alt. foreman Denver Grand Jury, 1983. Recipient Dept. of Edn. Specialists award Colo. Assn. Sch. Execs., 1979, Employee Yr. award Colo. Dept. Edn., 1986, Fed. Ednl. Program Adminstrv. Coun. Ann. award for Distinctive Svc. to Colo. Children, 1988. Mem. Am. Assn. School Adminstrs, Colo. Assn. Sch. Execs (coordinating council, 1976-79, v.p. dept. of edn. specialists 1974-75, pres. 1975-76), Assn. for Supervision and Curriculum Devel., Phi Delta Kappa. Republican. Home: 550 E 12th Ave Apt 903 Denver CO 80203-2527 Office: Colo Dept Edn 201 E Colfax Ave Denver CO 80203-1704

HINKLE, JO ANN, English language educator; b. Alton, Ill., Feb. 7, 1961; d. Joe and Dorothy Louise (Stoneburner) Christen; m. Robert Eugene Hinkle, Aug. 19, 1989. BA, So. Ill. U., Edwardsville, 1984; MA, So. Ill. U., 1992. Instr. English, Lewis and Clark Coll., Godfrey, Ill., 1988—. Democrat. Unitarian. Home: 11 Maple RR 1 Dorsey IL 62021

HINKLE, LINDA KAY, psychologist; b. Norfolk, Va., Oct. 18, 1961; d. Robert Loyal and Pauline (Gammichia) Pace; m. Anthony Adam Hinkle, Aug. 2, 1986; 1 child, Clark Anthony. BA, Wheaton Coll., 1982; MS, Purdue U., 1985, PhD, 1989. Lic. psychologist, Ind., Pa.; cert. health svc. provider, marriage and family therapist, Ind. Asst. prof. Edinboro (Pa.) U., 1989-91; psychotherapist Psychology Assocs. Greater Erie, Edinboro, 1989-90; asst. prof. DePauw U., Greencastle, Ind., 1991-92; psychologist Devel. Assocs., Inc., Indpls., 1991—. Contbr. chpt. to book; co-author instructional video, 1992. Recipient NCAA postgrad. scholarship, 1982, Scholastic Honor Soc. grad. scholarship, 1982, Arthur F. Krueger scholarship, 1988. Mem. APA, Eating Disorders Task Force Ind., Assn. Advancement of Behavior Therapy, Ind. Psychol. Assn. Office: Devel Assocs Inc 9002 N Meridian # 200 Indianapolis IN 46260

HINMAN, ROSALIND VIRGINIA, storyteller, drama educator; b. London, May 5, 1938; d. Frederick and Gladys Molly (Seabrook) Ellam; m. Richard Leslie Hinman, Sept. 23, 1967; children: Katherine, Jeremy, Adrian, Isabel. Diploma in Dramatic Art, U. London, 1958; cert. in Edn., Cen. Sch. Speech and Drama, London, 1959. Lectr. Ministere d'Edn. Nat. U. France, Tourcoing, Albi, 1960-63, U. de Caen, France, 1960-63; domestic & overseas exhibit adminstr. The Design Coun., London, 1963-66; artist Boces, Westchester, N.Y., 1968-70, Eugene O'Neill Theater Ctr., Waterford, Conn., 1980—; freelance performer Old Lyme, Conn., 1982—; performing artist Conntours Conn. Commn. on the Arts, Hartford, 1988—; artistic dir. Conn. Student Performing Arts Festival, Middletown, 1988—. Author: Three Hairs From The Devil's Beard and Other Tales, 1990. Sec., bd. mgrs. Old Lyme (Conn.) Pheobe Griffin Noyes Libr., 1987-92, pres., 1992—. Mem. Conn. Storytelling Ctr. Home and Office: 1 Smith Neck Rd Old Lyme CT 06371-2617

HINMAN-SWEENEY, ELAINE MARIE, aerospace engineer; b. Lincoln Park, Mich., Nov. 18, 1960; d. John Edward and Florence Emelie (Langouse) H.; m. Joseph Lee Sweeney, May 24, 1992. BS in Aero. Engring., U. Mich., 1983; MS in Aerospace Engring., U. Tenn., 1989; PhDME, Vanderbilt U., 1993. Engr. Marshall (Ala.) Space Flight Ctr. NASA, 1983-94, Oceaneering Space Sys., Houston, 1995—; mem. Masters of Space studies curriculum planning working group Internat. Space U., 1993. Chmn. Robotics Informal Working Group of Marshall Space Flight Ctr., 1986-87; safety diver Neutral Bouyancy Simulator, Extravehicular Mobility Unit suit, 1987. Recipient performance award NASA, 1987, 90-93, tech. innovation award, 1989, cert. of appreciation, 1988. Mem. AIAA (sr., space ops. support tech. com. 1991—, Outstanding Young Aero. Engr. of Yr. award 1986), Soc. Mfg. Engrs. Robotics Internat. (chmn. chmn. 1989-90, sec. 1987, mem. nat. adv. bd. 1994-96), Outstanding Engr. award 1988), Von Braun Astron. Soc., NOW, North Ala. Sci. Fiction Assn. (bd. dirs. 1985-87). Home: 2703 Shady Ln Webster TX 77598 Office: Oceaneering Space Sys 16665 Space Center Blvd Houston TX 77058

HINNEBURG, PATRICIA ANN, military officer; b. Camden, N.J., May 11, 1937; d. William Rudolph and Helen Martha (Washington) H. BS in Edn., Temple U., 1959; MS in Edn., U. So. Calif., 1969; MS in Logistics Mgmt., Air Force Inst. Tech., 1975; MS in Aviation Mgmt., Emory-Riddle Aeronautical U., 1994. Commd. 2d lt. USAF, 1964, advanced through grades to brig. gen., 1989, ret., 1992, cons. total quality mgmt., 1994—. Mem. Maintenance Officer Assn., Soc. Logistics Engrs. (membership chmn.), 99s, AOPA. Home: 4236 326th Ave Carnation WA 98014

HINNRICHS-DAHMS, HOLLY BETH, middle school educator; b. Milw., Oct. 31, 1945; d. Helmut Ferdinand and Rae W. (Beebe) H.; m. Raymond H. Dahms, June 11, 1983 (dec. Oct. 2, 1983). Student U. Wis., Milw., 1963-64, 66, 79—, Chapman Coll., 1965, 67, Internat. Coll. Copenhagen, summer 1968, Temple U., summer 1970, BA, Alverno Coll., 1971; postgrad. Marylhurst Coll., 1972, Chapman Coll. World Campus Afloat, summers 1973, 74, Inst. Shipboard Edn., 1978, 79, 94. V.p. Hinnrichs Inc., Germantown, Wis., 1964-72; tchr. Germantown Recreation Dept., 1965; coach Milw. Recreation Dept., 1966-67; rep. for Wis., Chapman Coll., Orange, Calif., 1967; clk. Stein Drug Co., Menomonee Falls, Wis., 1967-72; tchr. Milw. area Cath. Schs., 1967-72, 83, 90-91, St. Lawrence Sch., 1991-92; asst. mgr. Original Cookie Co. (Mother Hubbard's) Cookie Store, Northridge Mall, Milw., 1977-84, SAU-U Warehouse Deli, 1984-85, mgr. office, 1985-90; with Pilgrim Message Ctr., 1987—; substitute tchr. cath. schs. Milw. area, 1975-80, 83-89, 90, 92—, St. Rose Sch., 1989-90; tchr. Indian Community Sch., Milw., 1971-72, 88, 94—, Martin Luther King Sch., 1973-74, Crossroads Acad., Milw., 1974-75, Harambee Community Sch., 1980-83; tutor Brookfield (Wis.) Learning Ctr., 1986-87; Midwest rep. World Explorer Cruises, 1978-82. Mem. Wis. Math. Council, Nat. Council Tchrs. Math., Internat. Inst. Milw. Friends of Mus., Alpha Theta Epsilon. Christian Scientist. Lodges: Order Eastern Star, Golden Rule, Miniss Kitigan Drum (Milw. chpt.). Home: N88w15041 Cleveland Ave # 3 Menomonee Falls WI 53051-2239

HINOJOSA, MARIA L., news correspondent; b. Mexico City, July 2, 1961; d. Raul and Berta (Ojeda) H.; m. German E. Perez, July 20, 1991. BA magna cum laude, Barnard Coll., 1984. Reporter Enfoque Nacional, San Diego, 1985, prodr., 1987; asst. prodr. weekend edit. NPR, Washington, 1986; freelance reporter, prodr. NPR, N.Y.C., 1989, correspondent, 1990—; prodr. CBS News Radio, N.Y.C., 1988; asst. prodr. CBS This Morning, N.Y.C., 1988; reporter Sta. WNYC Radio, N.Y.C., 1990; host radio Latino USA, N.Y.C., 1993—; host TV show Visiones Sta. WNBC, N.Y.C., 1993—; lectr. in field. Mem. editl. bd. NACLA, N.Y. Bd. dirs. Pepatian Cultural Orgn., N.Y.C., 1992-94, Columbia U. Coun. on Urban Affairs, N.Y.C., 1994, Parks Coun., N.Y.C., 1994. Recipient Unity award for radio feature Lincoln U., 1992, Cindy award Assn. Visual Communicatoes, 1993, Best Radio Feature award Soc. Profl. Journalists, 1993. Mem. Nat. Assn. Hispanic Journalists (Best Radio Report 1992), Nat. Alliance Third World Journalists, Newswoman's Club of N.Y. Office: Nat Pub Radio 801 2nd Ave New York NY 10017

HINRICHSEN, EVELYN ELIZABETH MERRELL (MRS. WALTER HINRICHSEN), corporate executive; b. Chgo., Nov. 30, 1910; d. Dwight Livingston and Julia (Dodd) Merrell; B.A., Mus.B., Mills Coll., 1938, M.A., 1940; cert. spl. teaching in music, Calif., 1941; m. Walter Hinrichsen, Aug. 2, 1946 (dec. July 1969); children—Martha Eleanor, Henry Hans. Asst. sec. to pres. Mills Coll., Oakland, Calif., 1942-44; sec. to chief asst. and librarian Library of Congress, Washington, 1944-46; v.p., sec. C.F. Peters Corp., N.Y.C., 1948-69, v.p., sec., owner, 1969-70, owner, pres., 1970-78, owner, chmn. bd., 1978—. Mem. AAUW, Met. Mus. Art, Mus. Modern Art, N.Y. Philharmonic, Alumnae Assn. Mills Coll., Sigma Alpha Iota. Home: 431 E 20th St Apt 8C New York NY 10010-7510 Office: 373 Park Ave S New York NY 10016

HINRICHSEN, JULIEANNE LEE, lawyer; b. Carmichael, Calif., May 23, 1964; d. Gary G. Waddell and Donna L. Reed; m. Patrick Lee Hinrichsen, Sept. 1, 1990. BA in Philosophy, U. Calif., Berkeley, 1985; JD, U. of the Pacific, 1990. Bar: Calif. Law clk. child abuse Law Office of Donna L. Reed, Sacramento, 1989-91, lawyer family law and child abuse, 1991—. Mem. multidisiplinary adv. bd. Child Advocates, Sacramento, 1993; asst. PRO-PER Pannel, Sacramento, 1994-95. Mem. ACLU (vice chair Sacramento chpt. 1992-94, bd. dirs. 1990-92, 1st Amendment speaker 1993), Sacramento County Bar Assn. (family law sect., probate sect.). Democrat. Office: Law Office of Donna L Reed 809 8th St Sacramento CA 95814

HINSCH, GERTRUDE WILMA, biology educator; b. Chgo., Oct. 20, 1932; d. Hans Rudolph and Gertrude (Kalb) H. BSEd, No. Ill. U., 1953; MS, Iowa State U., 1955, PhD, 1957. Instr. Mt. Holyoke Coll., South Hadley, Mass., 1957-60; asst. prof., then assoc. prof. Mt. Union Coll., Alliance, Ohio, 1960-67; assoc. prof. U. Miami (Fla.), 1966-74; assoc. prof. U. South Fla., Tampa, 1974-80, prof., 1980—. Office: U S Fla Dept Biology Tampa FL 33620

HINSDALE-KNISEL, ANN L., county extension director; b. Adrian, Mich., Oct. 24, 1950; d. Robert E. and Ardyth L. (Goldsmith) H.; m. William G. Knisel, Dec. 13, 1980; 1 child, Jenna Catherine. BS in Home Econs. Edn., Ea. Mich. U., 1971, MS in Family Life and Child Devel., 1975. Cert. home economist. Tchr. home econs. Dundee (Mich.) High Sch., 1972-76; home economist Mich. State U. Extension, Adrian, 1976-90, extension dir. Lenawee County, 1990—; nat. issues forum faculty Kettering Found., Dayton, 1991-93. Mem. Lenawee County Edn. Found., Adrian, 1993; bd. dirs. United Bank and Trust, Tecumseh, Mich., 1993. Recipient Equal Opportunity award Coop. Extension Svc., 1981-82. Mem. NAACP, Nat. Assn. Ext. Home Economists (1st v.p. 1989-90, Disting. Svc. award 1986, Florence Hall award 1985, Grace Frysinger award 1991, Pub. Policy award 1994), Am. Assn. Family and Consumer Scis., Mich. Assn. Ext. Home Economists (pres. 1982-83, Disting. Svc. award 1982), Mich. Coun. Extension Assns. (pres. 1983-84), Stepfamily Assn. Am., Civitan of Lenawee (chaplain), Epsilon Sigma Phi (Disting. Svc. award 1991). Home: 4404 Livesay Rd Sand Creek MI 49279 Office: Mich State Univ Extension Ste 2020 1040 Winter Adrian MI 49221-3867

HINSHAW, ADA SUE, health facility administrator; b. Arkansas City, Kans., May 20, 1939; d. Oscar A. and Georgia Ruth (Tucker) Cox; children: Cynthia Lynn, Scott Allen Lewis. BS, U. Kans., 1961; MSN, Yale U., 1963; MA, U. Ariz., 1973, PhD, 1975; DSc (hon.), U. Md., 1988, Med. Coll. of Ohio, 1988, Marquette U., 1990, U. Nebr., 1992; D Sci. (hon.), Mount Sinai Med. Ctr. Instr. Sch. Nursing U. Kans., 1963-66; asst. prof. U. Calif., San Francisco, 1966-71; prof. U. Ariz., Tucson, 1975-87; dir. nursing rsch. U. Med. Ctr., Tucson, 1975-87; dir. Nat. Inst. Nursing Rsch. Pub. Health Svc., Dept. Health and Human Svcs., NIH, Washington, 1987—. Contbd. articles to profl. jours. Recipient Kay Schilter award U. Kans., 1961, Lucille Petry Leone award Nat. League for Nursing, 1971, Wolanin Geriatric Nursing Rsch. award U. Ariz., 1978, Alumni of the Yr award Sch. Nursing U. Kans., 1981, Disting. Alumni award Sch. Nursing Yale U., 1981, Alumni Achievement award U. Ariz., 1990, Disting. citation Kans. Alumni Assn., 1992, Health Leader of the Yr. award PHS, 1993, Centennial award Columbia Sch. Nursing, 1993. Mem. ANA (Nurse Scientist of the Yr. award 1985), Coun. on Nursing Rschrs. (Nurse Scientist of the Yr. award 1985), Md. Nurses Assn., Western Soc. for Rsch. in Nursing, Am. Acad. Nursing, Nat. Acad. Practice, Inst. Medicine, Sigma Xi, Sigma Theta Tau (Beta Mu Chpt. award of Excellence in Nursing Edn., 1980, Elizabeth McWilliams Miller award, 1987), Alpha Chi Omega. Office: Nat Inst Nursing Rsch NIH Bldg 31 Rm 5B-03 9000 Rockville Pike Bethesda MD 20892*

HINSON, CATHERINE BREWER, marketing executive; b. High Point, N.C., Aug. 3, 1951; d. Joseph William and Nancy Anne (Greer) Brewer; m. Tampa Bryant Hinson, Aug. 24, 1972; children: William Bryant, Catherine Melissa, Joseph Benjamin, Nancy Paige. BA, High Point (N.C.) Coll., 1973; MEd, U.N.C., Greensboro, 1979; MBA, Century U., 1995, postgrad., 1995—. Tchr. early learning ctr. High Point (N.C.) Coll., 1973-76; ind. distbr. Meadow Fresh Farms Inc., High Point, 1981-83; showroom mgr. The China Lion Collection, High Point, 1983-85; v.p. Market Mgmt. Svc. Assn. Inc., High Point, 1985-89; office mgr., estimator Touch of Beauty Inc., High Point, 1985-88; sales, svc. rep. US Parawood Corp., High Point, 1989-91; sales svc. rep. Bekaert Textiles, USA, Greensboro, N.C., 1992-94; dir. cust. svc. dept. Rapier Cambridge Mills, Inc., 1994—. Sem. and inst. tchr. LDS Ch., High Point. Republican. Home: 1925 Chestnut Dr High Point NC 27262-7151

HINSON, MARVIS THEDORIA, education educator; b. Amsterdam, Ga., Apr. 3, 1950; d. Lawyer and Edna Surlina (Smith) H. BS, Ft. Valley State Coll., 1972; MEd, U. Ga., 1981. Cert. food and beverage exec. Sec. Fayetteville (N.C.) State U., 1972-73; instr. R.W. Groves High Sch., Savannah, Ga., 1973-81; dept. head Savannah Tech. Inst., 1981—. Bd. dirs. Arthritis Found., Savannah, 1993—. Recipie contest winner Athens Phyllo Co., Cleve., 1990. Mem. Savannah Chef's Assn. (sec. 1993—), Am. Culinary Fedn. Office: Savannah Tech Inst 5717 White Bluff Rd Savannah GA 31499

HINSON, SUE ANN, orthopedic nurse; b. Springfield, Ohio, Oct. 27, 1952; d. William H. and Joanna M. (Waits) H. Diploma, Community Hosp., Springfield, 1973. RN, Fla.; cert. in quality mgmt. Staff nurse Cmty. Hosp., Springfield, 1973-78, Mt. Carmel Med. Ctr., Columbus, Ohio, 1978-79, Community Hosp., Springfield, 1979-86; staff nurse orthopedics North Ridge Med. Ctr., Ft. Lauderdale, Fla., 1986-90; nurse Prison Health Svcs., Ft. Lauderdale, Fla., 1990-93; orthopedic nurse Nurse Care, Ft. Lauderdale, Fla., 1993-94, Fla. Med. Ctr., Ft. Lauderdale, Fla., 1994—. Mem. Nat. Assn. Orthopedic Nurses (cert.), Nat. League Nursing.

HINTHORN, MICKY TERZAGIAN, volunteer, retired; b. Jersey City, N.J., July 5, 1924; d. Bedros H. and Aznive (Hynelian) Terzagian; m. Wayne L. Hinthorn, Aug. 11, 1957. BS in Occupational Therapy, U. So. Calif., 1953; MBA, Coll. Notre Dame, Belmont, Calif., 1984. Registered occupational therapist. Gen. office worker Drake Secretarial Coll., Jersey City, 1941-42; sec., expediter Western Electric Co., Kearny, N.J., 1943-45; sec. div. edn. CBS, NYC, 1945-46; sec. to v.p. sales Simon and Schuster, Inc., NYC, 1947-51; gen. office worker in Sch. of Edn. U. So. Calif., L.A., 1951-52; occupational therapist Palo Alto (Calif.) Clinic, 1954-55; chief occupational therapist Children's Health Coun., Palo Alto, 1954-56; sec. to chief mil. engr. Lenkurt Electric Co., San Carlos, Calif., 1956-58; sr. sec. re-entry program Bank of Am., Redwood City, Calif., 1979-80; ret., 1980; organizer occupational therapy dept. Children's Health Coun., Palo Alto, Calif., 1954, chief 1954-56. Author, editor numerous newsletters and orgns.' papers. Charter mem., membership chair U. So. Calif. Pres. Cir., San Francisco, 1978-80; treas. North Peninsula chpt. San Francisco Opera Guild, San Mateo, Calif., 1979; vol. pub. info. chair re-election San Mateo County Supr., Redwood City, Calif., 1978; founder, charter pres. Friends of Belmont (Calif.) Libr., 1974-75; mem. Coastside Fireworks Com., 1989-94, chair corp. sponsorship, 1992-93. Recipient Hon. Mem., Friends of San Francisco Pub. Libr., 1974. Mem. AAUW (pres. San Mateo br. 1976-77; Half Moon Bay br. chair local scholarships 1992, historian 1992-94, name grant honoree Edn. Found. Jodi Gordon Endowment 1991-92), Half Moon Bay Coastside C. of C. (chair bus. edn. scholarships 1992, 93, recognition award 1993), Seton Med. Ctr. Coastside Aux. (assoc.), U. So. Calif. Alumni Assn. (life), Friends of Filoli. Home: PO Box 176 Half Moon Bay CA 94019

HINTON, BARBARA LORRAINE, corporate tax assistant; b. Tuscaloosa, Ala., Jan. 6, 1951; d. Percyville and Irene (Prewitt) Burns; m. Donald Edward Hinton, Feb. 24, 1973; children: Vincent Dwayne, Randall Lamont. BA in Bus. Adminstrn., Stillman Coll., 1973; attended, U. Ala., Birmingham, 1983, U. Ala., Tuscaloosa, 1988. Office mgr. The Selma Project, Tuscaloosa, 1972-73; sec., clerk Gulf States Paper Corp., Tuscaloosa, 1973-78, gen. acct., 1978-94, tax asst., 1994—. grad. mem. Leadership Tuscaloosa, 1987-88; mem. steering com. Leadership Tuscaloosa, 1989, 90; mem. bd. dirs. Big Brothers/Big Sisters, 1991-94. Mem. Leadership Tuscaloosa Alumni Assn., Inst. Mgmt. Accts. (named Mem. of the Yr. 1991-92, Perfect Attendance award 1988-94, v.p. communication 1990-91, v.p. adminstrn. 1991-92, pres. 1992-93, chmn. 1993-94, v.p. mktg. 1994-95). Methodist. Office: Gulf States Paper Corp 1400 River Rd Tuscaloosa AL 35404

HINTON, PAULA WEEMS, lawyer; b. Gadsden, Ala., Dec. 5, 1954; d. James Forrest and Juanita (Weems) H.; m. Steven D. Lawrence, Mar. 31, 1984; 1 child, David Hinton Lawrence. BA, U. Ala., 1976, MPA, 1979, JD, 1979. Bar: Ala. 1979, Tex. 1982, U.S. Dist. Ct. (so. dist.) Ala. 1980, U.S. Dist. Ct. (so. dist.) Tex. 1981, U.S. Dist. Ct. (no. dist.) Tex. 1988, U.S. Dist. Ct. (ea. and we. dists.) Tex. 1989, U.S. Dist. Ct. (no. and mid. dists.) Ala. 1993, U.S. Ct. Appeals (5th and 11th cirs.) 1981. Law clk. to magistrate U.S. Dist. Ct. Ala., Mobile, 1979-80; assoc. Vinson & Elkins, Houston, 1981-88; ptnr. Akin Gump Strauss Hauer & Feld, L.L.P., Houston, 1989—. Rotary fellow U. Sevilla, Spain, 1980-81. Mem. State Bar Tex. (women in the profession com.), Houston Bar Found. (bd. dirs.). Office: Akin Gump Strauss Hauer & Feld 711 Louisiana St Houston TX 77002-2716

HINTON, S(USAN) E(LOISE), author; b. Tulsa, 1948; m. David Inhofe, 1970; 1 child, Nicholas David. BS, U. Tulsa, 1970. Author (teen-age fiction) The Outsiders, 1967 (N.Y. Herald Tribune Best Teenage Book list 1967, Chgo. Tribune Book World Spring Festival Honor Book 1967, Media and Methods Maxi award 1975, Mass. Children's Book award 1979), That Was Then, This Is Now, 1971 (ALA Best Books for Young Adults list 1971, Chgo. Tribune Book World Spring Festival Honor Book 1971, Mass. Children's Book award 1978), Rumble Fish, 1975 (ALA Best Book for Young Adults list 1975, Sch. Libr. Jour. Best Books of Yr. list 1975, Land of Enchantment award N.Mex. Libr. Assn. 1982), Tex, 1979 (ALA Best Books for Young Adults list 1979, Sch. Libr. Jour. Best Books of Yr. list 1979, Am. Book award nominee 1981, Calif. Young Reader medal nominee 1982, Sue Hefly award 1983), Taming the Star Runner, 1988, Big David, Little David, 1994; (screenplay, with Francis Ford Coppola) Rumble Fish, 1983; film appearances Tex, 1982, The Outsiders, 1983. Recipient Golden Archer Award, 1983; Author award ALA Young Adult Svcs. Divsn./Sch. Libr. Jour., 1988. Office: Delacorte Press Press Rels 1540 Broadway # Bdd New York NY 10036-4039*

HINZ, DOROTHY ELIZABETH, writer, editor, international corporate communications and public affairs specialist; b. N.Y.C.. AB, Hunter Coll.; postgrad., Columbia U. Asst. to dir. devel. Columbia U., N.Y.C., 1953-55; mng. editor, econs. rschr.-analyst, writer speeches, position papers W.R. Grace & Co., N.Y.C., 1955-64; staff writer Oil Progress, fgn. news media, speeches, films, internat. petroleum ops., pub. rels. dept. Caltex Petroleum Corp., N.Y.C., 1964-69; fin. editor Merrill Lynch, Pierce, Fenner & Smith, 1969-74; mgr. publs., mgr. speakers' bur., asst. speech writer, mktg. and corp. comm. dept. Mfrs. Hanover Corp., N.Y.C., 1974-88; writer spl. projects on energy, fin., and internat. affairs N.Y.C., 1988—. Contbr. articles on multinat. corps., developing nations, trade and fin. to various publs.; researcher of policy proposals for J.P. Grace's book, It's Not Too Late in Latin America. Mem. N.Y. Press Club, Japan Soc., Americas Soc., Spanish Inst., Bolivarian Soc. Home and Office: 600 W 115th St New York NY 10025-7701

HIRANO, ARLENE AKIKO, neurobiologist, research scientist; b. L.A., Oct. 24, 1962; d. Yasuo and Toyoko (Fujimori) H. BS, U. Calif., Irvine, 1984; PhD, Rockefeller U., 1991. Grad. fellow Rockefeller U., N.Y.C., 1984-91, postdoctoral fellow, 1991; rsch. assoc., postdoctoral fellow Cornell U. Med. Coll., N.Y.C., 1991—. Recipient Nat. Rsch. Svc. award USPHS, 1984-90, Excellence in Rsch. award U. Calif., Irvine, 1984, Postdoctoral Nat. Rsch. Svc. award Nat. Eye Inst., 1993-95; Regents scholar U. Calif., Irvine, 1980-84; Lucille P. Markey Charitable Trust fellow, 1984-90, Rockefeller U. fellow, 1984-91, David Warfield fellow in Ophthalmology, N.Y. Cmty. Trust/N.Y. Acad. Medicine. Mem. AAAS, Soc. for Neuroscience. Office: Cornell Univ Med Coll 1300 York Ave New York NY 10021

HIRASAKI, MARSHA PARRISH, industrial sales company executive; b. Sullivan's Island, S.C., Oct. 27, 1945; d. Louis August Rohde and Ruth Ann (Hynes) Nelson; m. John Kiyoshi Hirasaki, Dec. 29, 1968; children: Kitt Nelson, Parrish Nelson. BSME, Duke U., 1967; MSME, U. Houston, 1971. Aerospace engr. TRW Systems, Houston, 1967-72; design engr. Nat. Maritime Research Ctr., Galveston, Tex., 1972-74; sales mgr. Cooper Valve and Fitting, Inc., LaPorte, Tex., 1974-76; pres., gen. mgr. Eurasia Valve Corp., Houston, 1976-79; gen. mgr. Masoneilan div. McGraw Edison, Houston, 1979-84; gen. mgr. Dresser Valve and Controls, Houston, 1985; pres., gen. mgr. Nelson Controls, Inc., Dickinson, Tex., 1985—; exec. dir. Success Sisters, 1994—. Mem. Task Force 2000, Gulf Coast Quality Consortium, Jr. Achievement Area Com. Named Tech. Adminstr. of Yr. Clear Lake Coun. Tech. Socs., 1989. Mem. Instrument Soc. Am. (pres. chpt. 1982-83, internat. bd. dirs. 1986-88), ISA Svcs. (chmn. bd. dirs. 1986-88), Portrait Artists' Guild (pres. 1985-87), Houston Bus. Coun. (bd. dir. 1995). Home: 931 Shady Oak Ln Dickinson TX 77539-3322

HIRD-KINZLER, SYDELLE DRUCKMAN, interior designer; b. N.Y.C., May 23, 1925; m. M. Hird, 1946 (div. 1961); children: David, Pamela; m. M. Kinzler, 1984. BS, NYU, 1946; cert. N.Y. Sch. Interior Design; student Juilliard Inst. Music, N.Y.C. Designer, Gimbels, Yonkers, N.Y., 1961-65; freelance designer, N.Y.C., 1965-67; space planner-designer Thonet Industries, N.Y.C., 1967-73; chief interior designer MKDA Assocs., N.Y.C., 1973-80; prin. Sydelle D. Hird Ltd., N.Y.C., 1980—; project dir. ASID Design Service Corps, N.Y.C., 1979-80. Designer: Pro Bono Renovation for N.Y.C. Sanitation Dept. Bldg., 1979; Renovation of Pub. Lobby at N.Y. Design Ctr., 1982, Pub. Lounge and Mgmt. Offices, 1984; bd. visitors Found. for Interior Design Edn. Rsch. Fider, 1987—. Bd. dirs. Interior Designers for Licensing in N.Y., 1991—. Mem. Inst. Bus. Designers (pres. N.Y. chpt. 1979-84, nat. bd. dirs. 1984-86), Am. Soc. Interior Design, Internat. Interiors Design Assn. (bd. dirs. 1994—, past pres.).

HIRN, DORIS DREYER, health service administrator; b. N.Y.C., Dec. 3, 1933; d. James Howard and Dorothy Van Nostrand (Young) Dreyer; student Colby Jr. Coll., 1950-51, Hofstra U., 1953-56; m. John D. Hirn, Oct. 27, 1956; children—Deborah Lynn, Robert William. Owner, Dutchlands Farm, Albany, N.Y., 1957-62, Hickory Hill Farm, Galena, Ill., 1965-75; adminstr. Home Health Service, Chgo., 1972-74, exec. dir. Suburban Home Health Service, 1974-87; exec. dir. Home Health Svc. Chgo. North, 1987—; ptnr. Candor Assocs.; dir. Nat. Health Delivery Systems, Serengeti Prodns., Inc.; bd. dirs. Lifeline Pilots, Inc., NAHC, Fin. Mgrs. Forum, Ill. Long Term Task Force, Ill. Homecare Coun., BBH Assocs., Inc.; pres. Caregivers, Inc. Author: Survey Process in Home Health Manual; contbr. nat. seminars on quality assurance, rehab., long term care, reimbursement legislation; also articles to Caring Mag., Elder Svcs. Directory, Jour. Am. Geriatric Soc. Served with WAVES, 1951-52. Recipient Ill. Govs. award for Excellence Home Care Agy., 1989. Mem. ICHA, Nat. Assn. Home Care. Clubs: Chgo. Yacht. Home: 5747 N Sheridan Rd Chicago IL 60660-4755

HIRONO, MAZIE KEIKO, state legislator; b. Fukushima, Japan, Nov. 3, 1947; came to U.S., 1955, naturalized, 1957; d. Laura Chie (Sato) H. B.A., U. Hawaii, 1970; J.D., Georgetown U., 1978. Dep. atty. gen., Honolulu, 1978-80; house counsel INDEVCO, Honolulu, 1982-83; sole practice, Honolulu, 1983-84, Shim, Tam, Kirimitsu & Naito, 1984-88; mem. Hawaii Ho. of Reps., Honolulu, 1980-94; elected lt. gov., 1994. Del., State Democratic Party Conv., Honolulu, 1972-82; bd. dirs. Nuuanu YMCA, Honolulu, 1982-84, Moiliili Community Ctr., Honolulu, 1984, Mem. U.S. Supreme Ct. Bar, Hawaii Bar Assn., Phi Beta Kappa. Democrat. Office: State Capitol Lt Governors Office PO Box 3326 Honolulu HI 96801

HIRSCH, BETTE G(ROSS), college administrator, foreign language educator; b. N.Y.C., May 5, 1942; d. Alfred E. and Gladys (Netburn) Gross; m. Edward Raden Silverblatt, Aug. 16, 1964 (div. Feb. 1975); children: Julia Nadine, Adam Edward; m. Joseph Ira Hirsch, Jan. 21, 1978; stepchildren: Hillary, Michelle, Michael. BA with honors, U. Rochester, 1964; MA, Case Western Res. U., 1967, PhD, 1971. Instr. and head French dept. Cabrillo Coll., Aptos, Calif., 1973-90, div. chair fgn. langs. and communications div., 1990—; mem. steering com. Santa Cruz County Fgn. Lang. Educators Assn., 1981-86; mem. liaison com. fgn. langs. Articulation Coun. Calif., 1982-84, sec., 1983-84, chmn., 1984-85; workshop presenter, 1982—; vis. prof. French Mills Coll., Oakland, Calif., 1983; mem. fgn. lang. model curriculum standards adv. com. State Calif., 1984; instr. San Jose (Calif.) State U., summers 1984, 85; reader Ednl. Testing Svc. Advanced Placement French Examination, 1988, 89; peer reviewer for div. edn. programs, NEH, Washington, 1990, 91, 93; mem. fgn. lang. adv. bd. The Coll. Bd., N.Y.C., 1986-91. Author: The Maxims in the Novels of Duclos, 1973, (with Chantal Thompson) Ensuite, 1989, 93, Moments Litteraires, 1992 (with Chantal Thompson and Elaine Phillips) Mais Oui! Workbook, Lab. Manual, Video Manual; contbr. revs. and articles to profl. jours. Pres. Loma Vista Elem. Sch. PTA, Palo Alto, Calif., 1978-79; bd. dirs. United Way Stanford, Palo Alto, 1985-90, mem. allocations com., 1988. Grantee NEH, 1980-81, USIA, 1992; Govt. of France scholar, 1982. Mem. Am. Coun. on Teaching of Fgn. Langs., Am. Assn. Tchrs. French (exec. coun. No. Calif. chpt. 1980-85), Assn. Calif. Community Coll. Adminstrs., Assn. Depts. Fgn. Langs. (exec. com. 1985-88, pres. 1988). Democrat. Jewish. Home: 4149 Georgia Ave Palo Alto CA 94306 Office: Cabrillo College 6500 Soquel Dr Aptos CA 95003

HIRSCH, DEBORAH JANE, music educator; b. Balt., Aug. 3, 1952; d. Robert Francis and Barbara Anne (Shaw) H. B in Music Edn. and Music Therapy, U. Kans., 1975; MusM, East Tex. State U., 1988. Cert. music tchr., Tex. Recreation therapist Kans. Neurol. Inst., Topeka, 1974-75; band dir. DeSoto (Kans.) High Sch., 1975-78, Beverly Hills Intermediate Sch., Pasadena, Tex., 1978-85, George A. Thompson Intermediate Sch., Pasadena, 1985—; musician 312th Army Res. Band, Lawrence, Kans., 1974-79; dept. chair Thompson Intermediate Sch., 1988—. Mem. choir Bering Meml. Meth. Ch., mem. pastor/parish rels. com. Scholar Delta Kappa Gamma, 1986. Mem. Tex. Music Educators Assn., Tex. Bandmasters Assn., Pasadena Little Theatre (bd. dirs., audience devel. mgr. 1989—), Pasadena

Philharmonic Orch. (violinist). Home: 1627 Kenwick Pasadena TX 77504 Office: Thompson Intermediate Sch 11309 Sagedown Ln Houston TX 77089

HIRSCH, GILAH YELIN, artist, writer; b. Montreal, Quebec, Can., Aug. 24, 1944; came to U.S., 1963; d. Ezra and Shulamis (Borodensky) Y. BA, U. Calif., Berkeley, 1967; MFA, UCLA, 1970. Prof. of art Calif. State U., Dominguez Hills, L.A., 1973—; adj. prof. Internat. Coll., Guild of Tutors, L.A., 1980-87, Union Grad. Sch., Cin., 1990. Founding mem. Santa Monica (Calif.) Art Bank, 1983-85; bd. dirs. Dorland Mountain Colony, Temecula, Calif., 1984-88. Recipient Disting. Artist award Calif. State U., 1985, Found. Rsch. award, 1988-89; grantee Nat. Endowment for the Arts, 1985; MacDowell Colony fellow, N.H., 1987, Banff Ctr. for the Arts fellow, Can., 1985; named artist-in-residence RIM Inst., Payson, Ariz., 1989-90, Tamarind Inst. of Lithography, Albuquerque, 1973, Rockefeller Bellagio Ctr., Italy, 1992, Tyrone Guthrie Ctr. for the Arts, Annamahkerrig, Ireland, 1993. Home: 2412 Oakwood Ave Venice CA 90291-4908 Office: Calif State Univ Dominguez Hills 1000 E Victoria St Carson CA 90747-0001

HIRSCH, IRMA LOU KOLTERMAN, nurse, association administrator; b. Clay Center, Kans., June 11, 1934; d. Arthur Henry and Mildred (Peterson) Kolterman; m. William A. Hirsch, June 8, 1958; children—David William, Brian Duane. BS in Nursing, U. Kans., 1957; M in Nursing, U. Washington, Seattle, 1961. R.N. Mo. Instr. Duke U., Durham, N.C., 1961-64; nurse clinician U. Kans. Med. Ctr., Kansas City, 1968-70; project dir., cons. Mo. Regional Med. Program, Kansas City, 1970-74; project dir., program coordinator Am. Nurses' Assn., Kansas City, 1974-79, policy devel., 1981-92; supr. VA Med. Ctr., Kansas City, 1979-81; dept. dir., 1981-83, policy devel., 1983-92; cons. nursing edn. Joint Commn. on Accreditation of Hosps., Chgo., 1973; cons. for project devel. Am. Nurses Found., Kansas City, 1974; cons. nursing standards Health Standards Directorate, Ottawa, Ont., Can., 1978, Mid-Am. Coalition on Health Care, 1993—. Editor: Guidelines for Review of Nursing Care at the Local Level, 1976, Nursing Quality Assurance Management/Learning System, 1982, Peer Review in Nursing, 1982, Issues in Professional Practice, 1985, Classification Systems for Describing Nursing Practice, 1989. Mem. Friends of Art, Kansas City, 1975—, Internat. Relations Council, Kansas City, 1980—, 2d Presbyn. Ch., Kansas City, elder, deacon, strategic planning chmn.; chpt. pres. Am. Field Services, Kansas City, 1978-79; mem. adv. com. Nancy Whalen Nursing Found., 1992—; mem. evaluation com. Heart Am. United Way, 1993—; trustee Presbyn. Manors Mid-Am., 1979-86, Kansas City Manor, 1992—, Nursing Heritage Found., 1994—. Mem. Am. Nurses Assn. (pres. Mo. dist. 1980-81), Kans. U. Nurses Alumni Assn. (pres. 1964-66), Sigma Theta Tau. Home: 1035 W 57th Ter Kansas City MO 64113-1163

HIRSCH, JUNE SCHAUT, chaplain; b. Green Bay, Wis., Sept. 30, 1925; d. Clifford Charles and Eleanor Josephine (Arts) Schaut; m. Marshall E. Gilette, Jan. 23, 1946 (div. 1974); children: Ronald Leigh, Patrick Allen, Vicki Jeanne Baumann; m. Hubert L. Hirsch, Nov. 7, 1975. Student, St. Mary's Sch. Nursing, Rochester, Minn., 1943-45, U. Wis., Sheboygan, 1974-75. Cert. med. asst., 1966. Med. asst. James W. Faulkner, M.D., Phoenix, 1953-56; med. office mgr. Edward E. Houfek, M.D., Sheboygan, Wis., 1956-75; med. office cons. Profl. Mgmt. Inc., Milw., 1975-77; office mgr., adminstrv. asst. Schroeder & Holt Architects Ltd., Milw., 1977-90; vol. chaplain St. Camillus Health Ctr., Milw., 1991—, Children's Hosp. and Froedent Meml. Hosp., Milw., 1991—; instr. med. asst. program Lake Shore Tech., 1975-76. Mem. Am. Assn. Med. Assts. (nat. trustee 1963-66), Wis. Soc. Med. Assts. (life, exec. bd. 1960-81), Greater Milw. Med. Assts. (life, exec. bd. 1975-89), Lake Shore Med. Assts. (exec. bd. 1959-75). Republican. Roman Catholic. Home: 10200 W Bluemound Rd Apt 918 Milwaukee WI 53226-4372

HIRSCH, LORE, psychiatrist; b. Mannheim, Fed. Republic of Germany, July 8, 1908; came to U.S., 1940; d. Erwin Hirsch and Marie Kiefe; m. Eugene Hesz, Jan. 25, 1958 (div. Oct. 1968). MD, Karl Ruprecht U., Heidelberg, Fed. Republic Germany, 1937. Diplomate Am. Bd. Neurology and Psychiatry. Intern Greenpoint Hosp., Bklyn., 1942-43; resident Bellvue Hosp., N.Y.C., 1943-48; sect. chief VA Hosp., Bronx, N.Y., 1949-54; dir. psychiatry Wayne County Gen. Hosp., Mich., 1954-55; dir. outpatient services Northville (Mich.) Regional Hosp., 1955-58; practice medicine specializing in psychiatry Dearborn, 1958—. Contbr. numerous articles to profl. jours. Fellow Am. Psychiat. Assn. (life); mem. AMA (life), Mich. Med. Soc., Wayne County Med. Soc., Mich. Psychiat. Soc. Unitarian-Universalist. Home: 212 S Melborn St Dearborn MI 48124-1438 Office: 2021 Monroe St Dearborn MI 48124-2926

HIRSCH, ROSEANN CONTE, publisher; b. N.Y.C., Feb. 5, 1941; d. Frank and Anna (Burzycki) Conte; m. Barry Jay Hirsch, Oct. 1, 1967; children: Brian Christopher, Nicholas Benjamin, Jonathan Alexander. Student, Boston U., 1958-61. Editorial asst. Grolier, Inc., 1962-64; editor Ideal Pub. Corp., N.Y.C., 1968-74; editorial dir. Sterling's Mags., Inc., N.Y.C., 1975-78, Hearst Spl. Publs., Hearst Corp., N.Y.C., 1978-84; v.p. Ultra Communications, Inc., N.Y.C., 1984-89; pub., pres. Dream Guys, Inc., N.Y.C., 1986—; pres. Lamppost Press, Inc., N.Y.C., 1989-. Author: Super Working Mom's Handbook, 1986; editor: Young & Married Mag., 1976-77, 100 Greatest American Women, Good Housekeeping's Moms Who Work; contbr. articles to various mags. Home: 1172 Park Ave New York NY 10128-1213 Office: Lamppost Press Inc 1172 Park Ave # 8 B New York NY 10128-1213

HIRSCHFELD, ARLENE F., civic worker, homemaker; b. Denver, Apr. 6, 1944; d. Hyman and Gertrude (Schwartz) Friedman; m. A. Barry Hirschfeld, Dec. 17, 1966; 2 children. Student, U. Mich., 1962-64; BA, U. Denver, 1966. English tchr. Abraham Lincoln High Sch., Denver, 1966-70. Pres. Jr. League of Denver 1986-87, v.p. ways and means, 1985-86, v.p. mktg., 1982-83, chmn. Colo. Cache mktg. com., 1978-79, chair holiday mart 1981, 1985-87, participant in Nat. Jr. League Mktg. Conf.; trustee Graland Country Day Sch., 1988—, bd. sec. 1990—, chmn. edn. com., 1989—, chmn. parent coun. nominating com., 1984-85, pres. parent coun., 1982-83, auction chmn., 1980, 81; bd. dirs. Allied Jewish Fedn., 1988—; co-chmn. collector's choice event Denver Art Mus., 1989, 94; co-chmn. benefit luncheon Pub. Edn. Coalition, 1990, mini grants selection com., 1985-87; mem. bd. Minoru Yasui Community Vol. award, 1986-87; mem. Greater Denver C. of C. Leadership Denver, class of 1987-88; bd. dirs. Women's Found. Colo. 1992—, Anti-Defamation League, 1994—, Colo. Spl. Olympics, 1994—, Disting. Coun Advisors; mem. dean's coun. Harvard Divinity Sch., 1992—; exec. com. Children's Diabetes Found. Denver. Named Humanitarian of Yr. Nat. Jewish Ctr., 1988, named to Colo. Women's Econ. Devel. Coun. by Gov. of Colo., 1989—, Sustainer of Yr. Jr. League, 1992; recipient Nat. Women's Mus. of the Arts. Colo. Chpt. award, 1991, U. Denver Founder's Day Alumni Community Svc. award; recipient Woman of Distinction award Rocky Mtn. News and Hyatt Beaver Creek, 1993, Colo. I Have A Dream Found. award, 1994. Mem. Colo. Women's Forum. Office: 5200 Smith Rd Denver CO 80216-4525

HIRSCHFELD, SUE ELLEN, geological sciences educator; b. Ossining, N.Y., Jan. 12, 1941; d. Ira Bertram and Helen Caroline (Reiner) H. BS, U. Fla., 1963, MS, 1965; PhD, U. Calif., Berkeley, 1971. Prof. Calif. State U., Hayward, 1971—, chair dept. geol. scis., 1988-94. Contbr. articles to profl. jours.; co-author videotapes in field, 1985, 92. Grantee Calif. State U., 1976, 78, 93. Mem. AAAS, Geol. Soc. Am., Paleontol. Soc., Soc. for Sedimentary Geology, Assn. for Women Geoscientists (founder). Office: Calif State U Hayward CA 94542

HIRSCHHORN, ROCHELLE, genetics educator; b. Bklyn., Mar. 19, 1932; d. Hyman and Anna Reibman; m. Kurt Hirschhorn; children: Melanie D., Lisa R., Joel N. BA, Barnard Coll., 1953; MD, NYU, 1957. Intern NYU-Bellevue Med. Divsn., N.Y.C., 1958-59; rsch. fellow, teaching asst. NYU Sch. Medicine, N.Y.C., 1963-65, assoc. rsch. scientist, 1965-66, instr. in medicine, 1966-69, asst. prof. medicine, 1969-74, assoc. prof. medicine, 1974-79, prof. medicine, 1979—, head divsn. med. genetics, 1984—; hon. fellow Galton Lab. Human Genetics & Biometry Univ. Coll., London, 1971-72; assoc. attending physician in medicine Bellevue Hosp., N.Y.C., 1969-80, Univ. Hosp., NYU Sch. Medicine, 1974-81; attending physician Bellevue Hosp., 1980—, Univ. Hosp., 1981—; mem. numerous NIH coms. & study sects., 1973—. Senator NYU Senate, mem. pediatrics search com., 1987-89, human subjects instl. rev. bd., 1989-94, co-dir. second year med. genetics course, 1989-93; trustee AIDS Med. Found./AMFAR; judge Westinghouse Nat. Sci. Talent Search; founding mem. Village Community Sch. Fellow AAAS, Am. Coll. Rheumatology, Am. Coll. Med. Genetics (founder); mem. NAS, Inst. Medicine, Am. Soc. for Clin. Investigation, Assn. Am. Physicians, Am. Assn. Immunologists, Am. Soc. Human Genetics (cert. 1987), Interurban Clin. Club (pres. 1987-88), Peripatetic Soc., Soc. for Inherited Metabolic Diseases, Harvey Soc. (coun. 1989-92), Alpha Omega Alpha (councillor Delta of N.Y. 1982—). Office: NYU Med Ctr 550 1st Ave New York NY 10016-6497

HIRSCHMAN, MARY LYNN, oncology nurse; b. Sioux City, Iowa, Aug. 10, 1947; d. Melvin E. and Mary Viola (Wilson) Tadlock; m. Roger V. Hirschman, Aug. 24, 1968; children: Matthew, Melissa. RN, St. Vincent's Sch. Nursing, 1968; BSN, Bethel Coll., 1992. CNSN, OCN. Staff nurse St. Joseph Mercy Hosp., Sioux City, 1968, Kearney County Hosp., Minden, Nebr., 1968-69, New Western Manor, Billings, Mont., 1969-71, Billings Deaconess Hosp., 1971-76, Bozeman (Mont.) Deaconess Hosp., 1976-77; dir. nursing Bozeman Convalescent Ctr., 1977-79; staff nurse Luth. Hosp., Des Moines, Iowa, 1979-80; edn. coord. Des Moines Gen. Hosp., 1980-87; area clin. coord. Nat. Med. Care, Des Moines, 1987-90; nurse mgr. oncology Mpls. VA Med. Ctr., 1991—; med. advisor United Ostomy Assn., Des Moines, 1980-86; bd. dirs. Polk County div. Am. Cancer Soc., Des Moines, 1986-87; appointee State Coun. on Practice, Bozeman, 1978-79. Contbr. articles to profl. jours. Mem. Mont. Nurses Assn. (del. to conv. 1977, 78, chmn. continuing edn. com. 1977-79), Am. Soc. for Parenteral and Enteral Nutrition (pres.-elect Iowa chpt. 1987), Oncology Nursing Soc. (sec. local unit 1984), Intravenous Nurses Soc. Roman Catholic. Office: Mpls VA Med Ctr 1 Veterans Dr Minneapolis MN 55417-2300

HIRSCHWALD, JUDITH FRANK, social worker; b. Pitts., Nov. 1, 1937; d. Robert Walter and Dorothy (Mulvey) Frank; m. Barry Hirschwald, May 23, 1975 (div. Mar. 1978). BA, Mt. Holyoke Coll., 1959; MSW, U. Pa., 1963. Social worker Magee Rehab. Hosp., Phila., 1963-70, mgr. social work, 1975—; dir. socialsvc. Grad. Hosp. U. Pa., Phila., 1970-75; adj. lectr. U. Pa. Sch. Social Work, Phila., 1973-79; patient systems coord. Regional Spinal Cord Injury Ctr. Delaware Valley, 1979-85; bd. mem. Legal Clinic for Disabled, Phila., 1990—, Resources for Living Independently, Phila., 1979-92; commn. mem. Mayors Commn. for People With Disabilities, Phila., 1986-88. Recipient Regina C. Burger award Resources for Living Independently, Phila., 1989, Kenneth Spaulding Meml. award Disabled in Action, Phila., 1980, Phila. Founder's award Pa. Rehab. Assn., Phila., 1980. Mem. NASW, Soc. for Social Work Adminstrs. in Health Care, Nat. Rehab. Assn., Pa. Coalition Citizens with Disability. Democrat. Office: Magee Rehab Hosp 6 Franklin Plaza Philadelphia PA 19102

HIRSH, CRISTY J., learning specialist, counselor; b. Dallas, Oct. 3, 1952; d. Bernard and Johanna (Cristol) H. BS in Early Childhood and Elem. Edn., Boston U., 1974; MS in Spl. Edn., U. Tex., Dallas, 1978; MEd in Counseling and Student Svcs., U. North Tex., 1991. Nat. cert. counselor; lic. profl. counselor, Tex.; cert. tchr., Tex., Mass. Dir., learning specialist Specialized Learning, Dallas, 1981-93; adj. faculty Richland Coll., Dallas, 1991-92; counselor Eastfield Coll., Mesquite, Tex., 1992—, adj. faculty, 1994—. Mem. Am. Counseling Assn., Coun. for Exceptional Children, Coun. for Learning Disabilities, Pi Lambda Theta, Phi Delta Kappa. Office: Eastfield Coll 3737 Motley Dr Mesquite TX 75150-2099

HIRSH, DEBORAH DRAUGHON, writer; b. Atlanta, Apr. 23, 1949; d. Kerney Lee and Doris Aline (Snyder) Draughon; m. George Douglas Hosea, 1964 (div. 1981); children: Michael Douglas, David George; m. Marvin Charles Hirsh, June 21, 1984. AA in Bus. Adminstrn., Gainesville Coll., 1988; BA in Internat. Affairs cum laude, Kennesaw State Coll., 1991. Freelance writer, 1991—. Mem. Concerned Women for Am., Washington, 1991; instr. Am. Red Cross, Atlanta, 1991. Mem. Internat. Club, Blue Key, Golden Key. Republican. Home: 430 Sanders Rd Cumming GA 30131-5300

HIRSH, JANE, pharmaceutical executive; b. 1942; married; 3 children. Grad., Univ. Conn. Clin. pharmacist Mass. Gen. Hosp., Boston, 1965-72; co-founder, chmn., CEO Copley Pharm., Inc., Canton, 1972—. Office: Copley Pharmaceutical Inc 25 John Rd Canton MA 02021*

HIRSH, SHARON LATCHAW, art history educator; b. Pitts., Apr. 19, 1948; d. Raymond J. and Mary Cassel (Hudock) Latchaw. BA, Rosemont Coll., 1970; MA, U. Pitts., 1971, PhD, 1974. From asst. prof. to prof. Dickinson Coll., Carlisle, Pa., 1974—; guest curator Montreal Mus. Fine Arts, 1989; dir. Trout Gallery, Carlisle, 1992; co-curator Ferdinand Hodler: Views and Visions exhibit Cin. Mus. Art, Nat. Acad. Design, Ontario Art Gallery, Wadsworth Atheneum Mus. Author: Ferdinand Hodler, 1981, Hodler's Symbolist Themes, 1983, (exhbn. catalogue) Fine Art of the Gesture, 1989; guest editor Art Jour., 1985; contbr. articles to profl. jours. Andrew Mellon grantee, 1972, 73. Mem. Coll. Art Assn., Interdisciplinary Nineteenth Century Studies Assn. Office: Dickinson Coll Dept Art History Carlisle PA 17013

HIRSHFIELD, PEARL, artist; b. Chgo., July 5, 1922; d. Louis and Anna (Nissenson) Belly; m. Hyman J. Hirshfield, Dec. 17, 1944; children: Leslie, Laura, Deborah, Jo-Anne. BA, Sch. of Art Inst., Chgo., 1979; AA, Herzl Jr. Coll., 1944; student, Northwestern U. Curator Midwest Artists for Peace, Chgo., 1967; co-curator art works, Peace March, 1982; organizer Midwest Arts Festival, Chgo.; art exhibits include invitation, Internat. Conf. Ctr., Hiroshima, Japan, 1989, Archi-Center Gallery, Chgo., 1989, Peace Mus., Chgo., 1988, Holocaust Meml. Mus., Skokie, Ill., 1988, 11th Ann., Beverly Art Ctr., 1987, Nat. Sculpture Conf./Wks. by Women, Cin., 1987, AIA Hdqrs., San Francisco, 1987, Beverly Art Ctr., 1986, Met. Mus. & Art Ctr., Coral Gables, Fla., Aurora U. Gallery, Ill., 1994, Peace Mus., Chgo., 1993, Arthur Woods Gallery, Embach, Switzerland, 1992, Palais de Congres, Montreaux, Switzerland, 1992, Franklin Furnace Mus., N.Y., 1991, Lafayette Mus. Art, Ind., 1990, others; permanent pub. collections: Mus. Modern Art Book Collection, N.Y., The Peace Mus., Chgo. Author: Conspiracy The Artist as Witness, 1972; film coordinator, Peace Prodns., 1983; creator, organizer Godine Press Art Portfolio, 1972; contbr. articles to jours. and newsletters. Organizer, Peace Ctr., Evanston, 1958, bd. mem., 1958-60; co-chmn., organizer, Peace Walk, 1982; coordinator Peace March, N.Y.C., 1982; mem. planning com., Art for a Nuclear Freeze, Chgo., 1983. Recipient scholarship Columbia Coll., 1940; prize Whirlpool Found. Sculpture Competition, 1986, visual arts award Citizens Alert Bill of Rights, 1991, Task Force Against Police Brutality, 1993; grantee Ill. Arts Council, 1984, grantee tech. assistance Ill. Arts Council, 1983; fellow Ill. Arts Council, 1986. Mem. Nat. Mus. Women in Arts (charter), Chgo. Artists' Coalition, Women's Caucus for Art, Physicians for Social Responsibility, Women's Internat. League for Peace and Freedom, Internat. Soc. Arts, Sci. and Tech. Home and Office: 1333 Ridge Ave Evanston IL 60201-4131

HIRSHMAN, LINDA REDLICK, law educator. BA in Govt. with Honors, Cornell U., 1966; JD, U. Chgo., 1969; postgrad. in philosphy, U. Ill., Chgo., 1990—. Bar: Ill. 1969, U.S. Supreme Ct. 1975. Assoc. Isham, Lincoln & Beale, Chgo., 1969-71; legal specialist Project SAFE, 1971-72; assoc., then ptnr. Jacobs, Burns, Sugarman & Orlove, 1972-82; assoc. prof. Ill. Inst. Tech. Chgo.-Kent Coll. Law, 1983-89, prof., 1989—; organizer Stanford Law review Symposium on Civic Edn. and Legal Edn. 1993; chair appointment com. Kent Coll. Law Ill. Inst. Tech., 1988-89; Lewis scholar Washington and Lee U., Va., 1995; mem. nat. bd. Womens Studies program Brandeis U., Waltham, Mass. Mem. law rev. U. Chgo. 1967-68; contbr. articles to profl. jours. Mem. ABA, Am. Law Inst. Home: 1852 N Burling St Chicago IL 60614-5104 Office: Ill Inst Tech Kent Coll Law 565 W Adams Chicago IL 60661

HIRSON, ESTELLE, retired educator; b. Bayonne, N.J.; d. Morris and Bertha (Rubinstein) Hirson; student UCLA, U. So. Calif., summers 1949-59, San Francisco, summer 1955, U. Hawaii, 1955; B.E., San Francisco State U., 1965. Tchr. High St. Homes Sch., Oakland, Calif., 1949-54, Prescott Sch., 1955-60, Ralph Bunche Sch., 1960-72; owner Puzzle-Gram Co., Los Angeles, 1946-49; pres. Major Automobile Co., 1948-60. Chpt. v.p. City of Hope, San Francisco, 1962-63; bd. dirs. Sinai-Duarte Nat. Med. Center, 1946-50, also parliamentarian, life mem. NEA, Calif., Oakland, Los Angeles tchrs. assns., Sigma Delta Tau. Democrat. Mem. Order Eastern Star; Scottish Rite Women's Assn. (v.p. L.A. 1982, fin. sec. 1989). Rights to ednl. arithmetic game Find the Answer 1948, 51. Home: 8670 Burton Way Apt 328 Los Angeles CA 90048-3953

HIRST, NANCY HAND, retired legislative staff member; b. L.A., Feb. 24, 1926. BA magna cum laude, Stanford U., 1947. Staff dir. Spl. Subcom. on Traffic Safety, Washington, 1957-58; legis. asst., speechwriter Rep. John C. Watts, 1962-71; adminstrv. aide to chmn. Ho. Com. on Edn. and Labor, Washington, 1975-77. Contbr. photographs to Rio Rimac, Ency. Britannica, 1965. Trustee Va. Mus. Fine Arts, Richmond; active Va. Bd. Historic Resources; chmn. Citizens Adv. Coun. on Furnishing and Interpreting the Exec. Mansion, 1988-93; active 175th Anniversary Commn. for Va.'s Exec. Mansion, 1987-88; trustee Am. Friends of Attingham Summer Sch., G.B., 1988-91; chmn. Woodlawn Plantation Coun., 1974-86; trustee, v.p., pres. Woodlawn Found., 1987-88; bd. visitors George Mason U., 1982-90; mem. Stanford in Washington Coun.; vice chair Mid-Atlantic region Stanford Centennial. Home: 1001 Basil Rd Mc Lean VA 22101-1819

HIRST, WILMA ELIZABETH, psychologist; b. Shenandoah, Iowa; d. James H. and Lena (Donahue) Ellis; m. Clyde Henry Hirst (dec. Nov. 1969); 1 child, Donna Jean (Mrs. Alan Robert Goss). AB in Elementary Edn., Colo. State Coll., 1948, EdD in Ednl. Psychology, 1954; MA in Psychology, U. Wyo., 1951. Lic. psychologist, Wyo. Elem. tchr., Cheyenne, Wyo., 1945-49, remedial reading instr., 1949-54; assoc. prof. edn., dir. campus sch. Nebr. State Tchrs. Coll., Kearney, 1954-56; sch. psychologist, head dept. spl. edn. Cheyenne (Wyo.) pub. schs., 1956-57, sch. psychologist, guidance coordinator, 1957-66, dir. rsch. and spl. projects, 1966-76, also pupil personnel, 1973-84; pvt. cons., 1984—; vis. asst. prof. U. So. Calif., summer 1957, Omaha U., summer 1958, U. Okla., summers 1959, 60; vis. assoc. prof. U. Nebr., 1961, U. Wyo., summer 1962, 64, extension divsn., Kabul, Afghanistan, 1970, Cath. U., Goias, Brazil, 1974; investigator HEW, 1965-69; prin. investigator effectiveness of spl. edn., 1983-84; participant seminar Russian Press Women and Am. Fedn. Press Women, Moscow and Leningrad, 1973. Sec.-treas. Laramie County Coun. Community Svcs., 1962; mem. speakers bur., mental health orgn.; active Little Theatre, 1936-60, Girl Scout Leaders Assn., 1943-50; mem. Adv. Coun. on Retardation to Gov.'s Commn.; mem., sec. Wyo. Bd. Psychologist Examiners, 1965-71 vice chmn., 1971-74; chmn. Mayor's Model Cities Program, 1969; mem. Gov.'s Com. Jud. Reform, 1972; adv. council Div. Exceptional Children, Wyo. Dept. Edn., 1974; mem. transit adv. group City of Cheyenne, 1974; bd. dirs. Wyo. Children's Home Soc., 1968, treas., 1978-84; rsch. on women's prisons State of Wyo., 1989; bd. dirs. Goodwill Industries Wyo., chmn., 1981-83; mem. Wyo. exec. com. Partners of Americas, 1970-86; del. Internat. Conv. Ptnrs. of Ams., Jamaica, 1987; del., moderator pers. com. Presbytery of Wyo., 1987-90, mem. mission program com., 1991—, mem. com. spl. gifts, 1994; work opportunities adv. com., bd. trustees AARP, 1992-94; Friendship Force ambassador to Honduras, 1979; chmn. bd. SE Wyo. Mental Health Center, 1969; elder 1st Presbyn. Ch., Cheyenne, 1978—, also bd. deacons; chmn. adv. assessment com. Wyo. State Office Handicapped Children, 1980, 81; mem. spl. gifts com. Wyo. Presbytery, 1994; mem. allocations com. United Way of Laramie County, active People to People Internat., Citizen Amb. Program, Child Welfare Project, 1992; participant People to People Internat. Citizen Amb. Program, child welfare project assist Lithuania, Latvia, Estonia, 1992. Named Woman of Year, Cheyenne Bus. and Profl. Women, 1974. Diplomate Am. Bd. Profl. Psychology. Fellow Am. Acad. Sch. Psychology; mem. APA, ASCD, Internat. Council Psychologists (chmn. Wyo. div. 1980-85), AAUP, Am. Assn. State Psychology Bds. (sec.-treas. 1970-73), Wyo. Psychol. Assn. (pres. 1962-63), Laramie County Mental Health Assn. (bd. mem., corr. sec. 1963-69, pres.), Wyo. Mental Health Assn. (bd. mem.), Internat. Platform Assn., Am. Ednl. Research Assn., Assn. for Gifted (Wyo. pres. 1964-65), Am. Personnel and Guidance Assn., Am. Assn. Sch. Adminstrs., NEA (life, participant seminar to China 1978), AAUW, Cheyenne Assn. Spl. Personnel and Prins. (pres. 1964-65, mem. exec. bd. 1972-76), Nat. Fedn. Press Women (dir. 1979-85), DAR (vice regent Cheyenne chpt. 1975-77), AARP (state coordinator 1988-92, preretirement planning specialist 1986-88, state coord. worker force program, 1992—, leadership coun., state del. nat. conv. 1990, pilot project Wyo. state delivery for retirement planning 1990—, AARP Works, op. project state govt. edn. assn. and AARP work force vols. video for retirement planning statewide 1993, master trainer retirement planning 1993—, employment planning master trainer, 1994—, planning com. Area 8 Conf., leadership meeting 1994), Psi Chi, Kappa Delta Pi, Pi Lambda Theta, Alpha Delta Kappa (pres. Wyo. Alpha 1965-66). Presbyn. Lodge Soc. Colonial Dames XVII Century, Order Eastern Star, Daus. of Nile. Clubs: Wyo. Press Women, Zonta Cheyenne 1965-66, treas. dist. 12 1974). Author: Know Your School Psychologist, 1963; Effective School Psychology for School Administrators, 1980. Home and Office: 3458 Green Valley Rd Cheyenne WY 82001-6124

HISEY, LYDIA VEE, educational administrator; b. Memphis, Tex., July 10, 1951; d. Murray Wayne Latimer and Jane Kathryn (Grimsley) Webster; m. Gregory Lynn Hisey, Oct. 4, 1975; children: Kathryn Elizabeth, Jennifer Kay, Anna Elaine. BS in Edn., Tex. Tech U., 1974, MEd, 1990. Cert. tchr., mid-mgmt., Tex.x. Tchr. phys. edn. Lubbock (Tex.) Ind. Sch. Dist., 1975-79, tchr., 1982-91, asst. prin., 1991—. Vice pres. Alpha Phi Mother's Club, 1989—. Recipient Way-To-Go award Lubbock Ind. Sch. Dist., 1989, Impact II grantee, 1991. Mem. Tex. Elem. Prins. and Suprs. Assn., Delta Kappa Gamma, Phi Delta Kappa. Baptist. Home: 4613 94th St Lubbock TX 79424-5015

HISLE, LORRAINE PEARL, financial executive; b. Rusilip, England, Oct. 16, 1957; d. William L. and Evelyn J. (Klamm) Summers; m. Robert E. Hisle, Nov. 17, 1979; children: Jacqueline K., Jamie L., R. Jason. BBA in Acctg., Cen. Mo. State U., 1979. CPA, Mo. Acct. Andes & Roberts Constrn. Co., Independence, Mo., 1979; jr. acct. to assoc. acct. Panhandle Eastern Pipeline Co., Kansas City, Mo., 1979-81; controller Bio-Pharma, Inc., Kansas City, 1981-83; v.p., controller Mktg. Resources, Inc., Overland Pk., Kans., 1984-87; v.p., chief fin. officer Fletcher, Gampper & Wirth, Inc., Kansas City, 198-91; pvt. practice accounting Kansas City, 1991—; bd. dirs., corp. sec.-treas. Mktg. Resources, Overland Park, 1984-87, Fletcher, Gampper & Wirth, Kansas City. Recipient Mildred M. Lass award Cen. Mo. State U., 1979. Mem. Am. Soc. Women Accts. (chmn. mem. 1989-90, chmn. publicity 1990-91, treas. 1990-91, co-chair pub. rels. 1993-94, Mem. of Yr. 1990-91), Nat. Assn. Tax Preparers. Episcopalian. Home and Office: 21240 Oakleaf Dr Bucyrus KS 66013-9661

HISSONG, BETHANY LUANNE, pharmacist; b. Flint, Mich., May 5, 1960; d. Jerome Richard and Sharon Maxine (Perry) Auger; m. Guy Raymond Hissong, Mar. 26, 1988; stepchildren: Melissa, Chad, Kurtis. Student, Alma Coll., 1978-80; BS in Pharmacy, Ferris State U., 1983. Pharmacist Perry Drug Stores, Flint, 1983-88; asst. pharmacy mgr. Perry Drug Stores, Owosso, Mich., 1989-91; pharmacy mgr. Perry Drug Stores, Swartz Creek, Mich., 1991—. Presbyterian. Home: 5345 Worchester Swartz Creek MI 48473 Office: Perry Drug Store # 140 9110 Miller Rd Swartz Creek MI 48473-1113

HITCHCOCK, KAREN RUTH, biology educator, university dean, academic administrator; b. Mineola, N.Y., Feb. 10, 1943; d. Roy Clinton and Ruth (Wardell) H. BS in Biology, St. Lawrence U., 1964; PhD in Anatomy, U. Rochester, 1969. Postdoctoral fellow in pulmonary cell biology, Webb-Waring Inst. Med. Rsch., 1968-70; asst. prof. dept. anatomy Tufts U. Sch. Medicine, Boston, 1970-75, assoc. prof. dept. anatomy, 1975-80, assoc. prof., acting chmn. dept. anatomy, 1976-78, assoc. prof., chmn. dept. anatomy, 1978-80, prof., chmn. dept. anatomy and cellular biology, 1980-82, George A. Bates prof. histology, chmn. dept. anatomy and cellular biology, 1982-85; prof. dept. cell biology and anatomy Tex. Tech U. Health Scis. Ctr., assoc. dean Tex. Tech U. Sch. Medicine, Lubbock, 1985-87; vice chancellor rsch., dean grad. coll., prof. cell biology, anatomy and biol. scis. U. Ill., Chgo., 1987-91, v.p. acad. affairs, prof. biol. scis. U. at Albany, SUNY, 1991—; mem. nat. adv. rsch. resources coun. NIH, 1992—, Nat. Bd. Med. Examiners, 1983-85. Mem. Am. Assn. Anatomy (chmn., exec. council 1979-81), Am. Assn. Anatomists (exec. com. 1981-85, v.p. 1986-88, pres. 1990-91), Nat. Bd. of Med. Examiners, Nat. Assn. for Biomed. Rsch. (bd. dirs. 1990), Nat. Assn. State Univs. and Land-Grant Colls. (chair coun. acad. affairs com. 1994—), Ill. Soc. Med. Rsch. (pres. 1990). Home: 286 Riverview Rd

Rexford NY 12148-1649 Office: U at Albany VP for Acad Affairs 1400 Washington Ave Albany NY 12222-0001

HITCHCOCK, LILLIAN DOROTHY STAW, educator, actress, artist; b. Detroit, Dec. 19, 1922; d. Charles Stawowczyk And Mary Waligora; m. Richard Elmer Hitchcock, June 28, 1952; children: Charles, Harriet, Roger, Stephen. BA in Edn., Wayne State U., 1946, MA in Interpretative Speech, 1952; postgrad., U. Wis., 1948; cert. in art, Inst. for Am. Univs., Avignon, France, 1981; cert. in French, Cath. U. Paris, 1983; postgrad., Inst. for Am. Univs., Aix-en-Provence, France, 1991. Speech and English tchr. Lakeview High Sch., St. Claire Shores, Mich., 1947-49; speech and journalism tchr. Mercy Coll., Detroit, 1949-52; substitute tchr. in speech and English Birmingham (Mich.) Pub. Schs., 1960-88; speech and English tchr. Bloomfield Hills (Mich.) Pub. Schs., Detroit Pub. Schs., 1960-70; French tchr. Montessori, Bloomfield Hills, 1988—. Performer, dir. Civic Theatre, Wayne U., Cath. Theatre, Detroit, 1943-46; chmn. Detroit Theatre Olympiade for World Community Theatre, 1979; del. to People's Republic of China, People to People-Health Care, 1984; mem. St. Dunstan's Theatre, Bloomfield Hills; docent Cranbrook Mus. Modern Art, Bloomfield Hills, 1988—. Mem. AAUW (bd. dirs. children's theatre Birmingham 1960-80), UN rep. and del. 1970-73), Tuesday Musicale. Mem. Internat. Platform Assn. (1st Place and Silver Bowl award 1994). Roman Catholic. Home: 6140 Westmoor Rd Bloomfield Hills MI 48301-1355

HITE, CATHARINE LEAVEY, orchestra manager; b. Boston, Oct. 1, 1924; d. Edmond Harrison and Ruth Farrington Leavey; m. Robert Atkinson Hite, Aug. 28, 1948; children: Charles Harrison, Patricia Hite Barton, Catharine Hite Dunn. BA, Coll. William and Mary, 1945. Restoration guide Williamsburg Restoration, 1944-45; asst. edn. dept. Honolulu Acad. Arts, 1945-46; sec., tour guide edn. dept. office chief curator Nat. Gallery Art, 1946-48; opera liason/coord. Honolulu Symphony, 1972-73, asst. to gen. mgr., 1973-75, community devel. dir./opera coord., 1975-77, dir. ops./opera prodn. coord., 1977-79, orch. mgr., 1979-84, mem. exec. com., 1965-69, pres. women's assn., 1965-66; com. chmn., opera assn. chmn. Hawaii Opera Theatre, 1966-69. Mem. W. R. Farrington Scholarship Com., 1977-94, chmn., 1982-94; mem. community arts panel State Found. Culture and the Arts, 1982, State Found. Music and Opera, 1984; docent Iolani Palace, 1990—. Active Jr. League, Alliance Français, Hawaii Watercolor Soc. Mem. Phi Beta Kappa. Episcopalian.

HITE, ELINOR KIRKLAND, oil company human resources consultant; b. Abington, Pa., Sept. 28, 1942; d. Bryant Mays and Bernice Eleanor (Tanis) Kirkland; m. Anthony L. Hite, July 7, 1967 (div. 1974); 1 child, Juddson Kirkland. BA in English, Denison U., Granville, Ohio, 1964; MA in Counseling, Princeton Theol. Sem., 1966. Asst. dir. pers. Edwards Bros. Printing Co., Ann Arbor, Mich., 1973-74; asst. dir. career counseling/placement U. Ill., Chgo., 1975-81; human rels. assoc. Amoco Corp., Chgo., 1981-82, sr. human rels. rep., 1982-85, staff human rels. rep., 1985-87, human rels. cons., 1987—; vol. career employment lectr., Chgo., 1985—. Chair clin. mgmt. com. Lorene Replogle Counseling Ctr., Chgo., 1981—; trustee, officer 4th Presbyn. Ch., Chgo., 1985—, elder, officer, 1985-91, chair pers. com., 1989—; mem. adv. bd. Brit. Retirement Home, 1990—; pres. 200 S. Home Condo Assn., Oak Park, Ill., 1982-91, 93—; bd. dirs. Frank Lloyd Wright Mus., 1994—. Presbyterian.

HITE, SHERE D., author, cultural historian; b. St. Joseph, Mo., Nov. 2, 1942; m. Friedrich Hoericke, 1985. B.A. cum laude, U. Fla., 1964, M.A., 1968; postgrad., Columbia U., 1968-69. Dir. feminist sexuality project NOW, N.Y.C., 1972-78; dir. Hite Rsch. Internat., N.Y.C., 1978—; instr. female sexuality NYU, 1977—; lectr. Harvard U., McGill U., Columbia U., Cambridge U. (Eng.), The Sorbonne, Paris, also numerous women's groups, internat. lectr., 1977-90; mem. adv. bd. Am. Found. Gender and Genital Medicine, Johns Hopkins U. Author: The Hite Report: A Nationwide Study of Female Sexuality, 1976, The Hite Report on Male Sexuality, 1981, Women and Love: A Cultural Revolution in Progress, 1987, Fliegen mit Jupiter, 1993, The Hite Report on the Family: Icons of the Heart, 1994, Women as Revolutionary Agents of Change: The Hite Reports and Beyond, 1994, The Divine Comedy of Ariadne and Jupiter, 1994, The Hite Report on the Family: Growing Up Under Patriarchy; co-author: Good Guys, Bad Guys: The Hite Guide to Smart Choices, 1991; cons. editor: Sexual Honesty: By Women for Women, 1974, Jour. Sex Edn. and Therapy, Jour. Sexuality and Disability. Mem. NOW, AAAS, Am. Hist. Assn., Am. Sociol. Assn., Acad. Polit. Sci., Soc. for Women in Philosophy, Internat. Women Writer's Orgn. (v.p.). Office: 2 Soho Sq, London W1V, England*

HIXSON, CLAUDINE MAE, county official; b. Cedar Rapids, Iowa, Mar. 7, 1928; d. Charles B. and Ruth A. (Benda) Kent; m. Harold B. Hixson, Apr. 6, 1947; children: Vicki Sue, Randall Kent, Mark Lee, Marcia Lynn (dec.). Student, Cedar Rapids C.C., 1984-85. Chief dep. auditor Linn County, Cedar Rapids, 1965-83, budget dir., 1983—. State chair lay witness mission United Meth. Ch. Mem. Iowa State Assn. Counties, Quota Club Internat. (chair svcs. 1987—, pres. 1986-87), Govt. Fin. Officers Assn. Home: 257 Alma Dr NW Cedar Rapids IA 52405-4304 Office: Linn County 930 1st St SW Cedar Rapids IA 52404-2164

HIXSON, SHEILA ELLIS, state legislator; b. L'Anse, Mich., Feb. 9, 1933; divorced; children: Denise, Lynn, Andy, Todd. AB, No. Mich. U., 1953. Tchr. Head Start; campaign mgr., aide Congressman William Ford, Mich., 1963-64; adminstrv. aide to state senator, 1965-66, legal aide to sec. of Dem. Nat. Conv., 1966-76; mem. Md. Ho. of Dels., Annapolis, 1976—, mem. ways and means com., environ. matters com., budget and audit com., house rules and exec. nominations com., procurement com., lottery com., others, chair joint com. fed.-state rels.; chair task force on child abuse and neglect; mem. Gov.'s Work Force Investment Bd. Mem. Montgomery County Dem. State Cen. Com. Mem. Nat. Assn. Sunday Sch. Instrs., Nat. Profl. and Bus. Women's Orgn., Women's Polit. Caucus, Plowmen and Fishermen, NOW. Home: 1008 Broadmore Cir Silver Spring MD 20904-3108 Office: Md Ho of Dels Rm 221 Annapolis MD 21401*

HIZER, MARLENE BROWN, library director; b. Shattuck, Okla., Mar. 29, 1940; d. Marvin Ira and Geneva Marie (Wright) Brown; m. Ammon M. Hizer, Mar. 19, 1960; children: Lori Marie Hizer Hunt, Holly Dot Hizer Caldwell. BS in Edn., N.W. Mo. State U., 1962; MS in Edn. emphasizing Libr. Sci., Ctrl. Mo. State U., 1966. Cert. tchr. libr. sci. Stenographer Butler Mfg., Kansas City, 1958-59; tchr., libr. Eastgate Jr. High Sch., Kansas City, 1962-69; dir. Nevada (Mo.) Pub. Libr., 1985—; lit. tutor, Nevada, Mo., 1992—; del. Mo. Gov.'s Conf., Jefferson City, 1990. Editor (newspaper) NEWSMAT, 1962-69, Northwest Missourian, 1958-62. Core communicator Mo. Citizen's Coun., Nev., 1980—; edn. counselor LDS Relief Soc., Nev., 1973-77; Sunday sch. tchr. LDS Ch., 1990—, sem. tchr., 1975-78, pub. affairs dir., 1990—; mem. Friends of Nev. Pub. Libr. Recipient Albert B. Fuson Meml. award for Highest Contbns., 1958, Scholastic award AAUP, 1962, Star award Nat. Scholastic Press Assn., 1962; named one of Outstanding Young Women of Am., 1970; Curator scholar U. Mo., 1958, scholar Bus. and Profl. Women's Assn., 1959. Mem. AAUW (cultural interest com. 1990-91), DAR (vice regent 1991-93), ALA, Mo. Libr. Assn., Pub. Libr. Assn., Pub. Libr. Dirs., Mo. State Libr. Inst., Mo. Pub. Libr. Coun. (recorder 1991-93), Vernon County Hist. Soc., Soroptimist Internat. (chair Internat. Goodwill and Understanding). Democrat. Home: RR 2 Box 158 Nevada MO 64772-9674 Office: Nevada Pub Libr 225 W Austin Blvd Nevada MO 64772-3343

HJORT, LISA DAWN, accountant; b. Worthington, Minn., Nov. 24, 1965; d. David Alan and Linda Kay (Van't Hul) Frey; m. Terry John Hjort, May 5, 1990. BS in Acctg., St. Cloud State U., 1988. Cert. mgmt. acct. Cost analyst Champion Internat., Sartell, Minn., 1988-91; sr. cost analyst Champion Internat., Courtland, Ala., 1991-93, cost acctg. supv., 1994—. Mem. Inst. Mgmt. Accts. Home: 2831 Winthrop Dr SW Decatur AL 35603-1171

HLAWATI, JOYCE F., elementary education educator; b. Pitts., Aug. 23, 1948; d. Kenneth Louis and Frances Meredith (Carson) Hoerner; m. Daniel Richard Hlawati, June 12, 1971; children: Meegan P. L., Adam G. T. BA in English, St. Francis Coll., Loretta, Pa., 1970; cert. in elem. edn., Slippery Rock (Pa.) U., 1988. Cert. elem. edn. tchr., Pa. Tchr. St. Alexis Sch., Wexford, Pa., 1970-73, St. Bonaventure Sch., Huntington Beach, Calif., 1973-74; pre-sch. tchr. Young World, Pitts., 1984-86; retail clk. Sch. Days Supply, Mars, Pa., 1988-89; tchr. McKnight Elem., Pitts., 1989—. Author poems. Vol. Am. Cancer Soc., Pitts., 1976—, Leukemia Soc., Pitts., 1978—, March of Dimes, Pitts., 1979—. Mem. Internat. Reading Assn., North Allegheny Fedn. of Tchrs., Authors and Friends, Three Rivers Reading Coun. Home: 1570 Lenora Dr Pittsburgh PA 15237-1672

HLOZEK, CAROLE DIANE QUAST, financial analyst; b. Dallas, Apr. 17, 1959; d. Robert E. and Bonnie (Wootton) Quast. BS, Tex. A&M U., 1982, BBA, 1982. CPA, Tex. Internal auditor Brown & Root Inc., Houston, 1982-84; asst. contr. Wilson Supply Co., Houston, 1984-86, sr. acctg. supr., Hydro Conduit Corp., Houston, 1986-87; fin. analyst Am. Capital, Houston, 1989-94; dir. adminstrn. CFO Am. Gen. Securities, Inc. 1994—. chmn. bd. dirs. On Our Own Inc. 1987-91. Mem. MENSA, Houston Zool. Soc., Tex. Soc. CPAs, Houston Livestock Show and Rodeo. Lutheran. Home: 15405 Mauna Loa Ln Houston TX 77040-1344 Office: Am Gen Securities Inc 2727 Allen Pkwy Ste 2051 Houston TX 77019

HO, VIVIAN, management consultant; b. Ipoh, Perak, Malaysia, July 21, 1959; d. Herbert J. and Karen Ginn (Chong) H. BA in Econs., Whitman Coll., 1981; MBA, U. Wash., 1986. Sr. fin. analyst world banking divsn. Seattle First Nat. Bank, 1982; loan officer internat. divsn. Chem. Bank, Singapore, 1983; sr. acct. corp. acctg./fin. group Seafirst Bank, Seattle, 1985-87; mgmt. cons. Towers Perrin, Seattle, 1988-91; ptnr. Paradigm Cons. Group, Seattle, 1991-93; mgmt. cons. Queens Health Sys., Honolulu, 1994—. Mem. Wash. Coun. on Internat. Trade, U. Wash. Alumni Assn., Whitman Coll. Alumni Assn.

HO, WEIFAN LEE, merchandise executive; b. N.Y.C., Mar. 11, 1951; d. Ho chee and Kwan Fong Lui. Student, Middlebury Coll.; BA, CCNY, 1972. Buyer Abraham and Straus/Jordan Marsh; mdse. mgr. Conran's-Habitat, N.Y.C.; buyer Bloomingdales, N.Y.C.; sr. buyer Carson Pirie Scott, Chgo.; buyer Gimbels, N.Y.C. Mem. NAFE. Office: Conran's-Habitat 10 Astor Pl New York NY 10003-6935

HOADLEY, DONNA J., school counselor, educator; b. Aurelia, Iowa, Oct. 20, 1951; d. Delaine Lawrence Kolb and Cynthia (Vermeer) Kolb-Kaskey; m. Stephen P. Cosgrove, Aug. 21, 1971 (div. Dec. 1979); children: Kristin, Will, Wade; m. Craig A. Hoadley, July 16, 1994. BA in English, Buena Vista Coll., 1973; MA in Guidance, Counseling and Personnel Svcs., U. S.D., 1985. Permanent profl. cert. in secondary English, speech/drama edn., counseling, Iowa. Secondary English tchr. Aurelia Community Sch., 1973-85; K-12 sch. counselor Marcus (Iowa) Community Sch., 1985-87; 9-12 sch. counselor, K-12 supr. Maurice-Orange City (Iowa) Community Schs., 1987—; N.W. dist. and state speech judge Iowa H.s. Speech Assn., 1974—; therapist Plains Area Mental Health, Cherokee, Iowa, 1984-85; drug free schs. and cmtys. coord. Maurice-Orange City/Floyd Valley Schs., 1990—; adj. faculty Morningside Coll., Sioux City, Iowa, 1991—; speaker N.W. Dist. Counselors' Winter Forum, 1993, 95. Contbr. monthly column Orange City/Floyd Valley Cmty. Sch. Dist. Newsletter, 1987—. Speaker Iowa Dist. West Luth. Ch., 1987; cast mem. Orange City Community Theatre, 1990, 92; area com. mem. Food Pantry, Orange City, 1992—; vol. Hands Around the World Mission Store, Orange City, 1992—. Mem. NEA, Iowa State Edn. Assn., Iowa Counseling Assn. (sec.-treas. 1987-89), Iowa Assn. Counseling and Devel. (chpts. 1 and 12 sec. 1980-81, pres. 1988-89), Maurice-Orange City Edn. Assn. (pres. 1990-91). Office: Maurice-Orange City FV High Sch 615 8th St SE Orange City IA 51041

HOADLEY, IRENE BRADEN (MRS. EDWARD HOADLEY), librarian; b. Hondo, Tex., Sept. 26, 1938; d. Andrew Henry and Theresa Lillian (Lebold) Braden; m. Edward Hoadley, Feb. 21, 1970. BA, U. Tex., 1960; AMLS, U. Mich., 1961, PhD, 1967; MA, Kans. State U., 1965. Cataloger Sam Houston State Tchrs. Coll. Library, Huntsville, Tex., 1961-62; head circulation dept. Kans. State U. Library, Manhattan, 1962-64; grad. asst. U. Mich. Dept. of Library Sci., 1964-66; librarian gen. adminstrn. and research Ohio State U. Libraries, Columbus, 1966-73; asst. dir. libraries adminstrv. services Ohio State U. Libraries, 1973-74; dir. of libraries Tex. A&M U. Library, College Station, Tex., 1974-92; dir. Evans Libr. Capital Campaign, 1993-95; dir. Higher Edn. Act Inst. Quantitative Methods in Librarianship, Ohio State U., summer 1969; instr. inst. U. Calif. at San Diego, 1970, summer; Mem. steering com. Gov's. Conf. on Library and Info. Services, Ohio, 1973-74, joint chairperson, 1974; mem. adv. com. Library Services and Constrn. Act Cuyahoga County Pub. Library, Cleve., 1973. Author: (with others) Physiological Factors Relating to Terrestrial Altitutes: A Bibliography, 1968; Editor: (with Alice S. Clark) Quantitative Methods in Librarianship: Standards, Research, Management, 1972; chair editorial adv. bd. National Forum, 1992—; contbr. (with Alice S. Clark) articles to profl. jours. Co-chair program com. Tex. Conf. Librs. and Info. Svcs., 1989-91. Recipient Scarecrow Press award for libr. lit., 1971, Disting. Alumnus award Sch. Libr. Sci., U. Mich., 1976; named Assn. Coll. and Rsch. Librs. Acad. Rsch. Libr. of Yr. 1994. Mem. ALA (coun. 1990-94, legis. com. 1990-92), Am. Librs. (editorial bd.), Ohio Libr. Assn. (chmn. constn. com. 1967-68, chmn. election tellers com. 1969, asst. gen. chmn. local conf. com. 1969-70, sec. 1970-71, v.p., pres.-elect 1971-72, chmn. budget advisory com. 1971-72, pres. 1972-73, bd. dirs. 1970-75), Tex. Libr. Assn. (com. on White House conf. 1975-77, vice chmn., chmn. coll. and univ. div. 1977-78, exec. bd. 1978-81, legis. com. 1987-89, Tex. Libr. of Yr., chair nominating com. 1994), Assn. Rsch. Librs. (bd. dirs. 1978-81, search com. for exec. dir. 1980, stats. com. 1991-93, Acad. Libr. of Yr. 1994), Midwest Fedn. Libr. Assns. (exec. bd. 1973-74, chairperson program com. 1974), Online Computer Libr. Ctr. (pres. User's Council 1983-84, 84-85, trustee 1984-90, chmn. pers. and compensation com. 1987-89), Tex. Conf. Librs. and Info. Svcs. (co-chair program com.), Coll. and Rsch. Librs. (editorial bd. 1991—), Phi Kappa Phi (chair nat. forum com. 1993—), Phi Alpha Theta, Pi Lambda Theta, Beta Phi Mu, Phi Delta Gamma. Home: 5835 Raymond Stotzer Pky College Station TX 77845

HOAGLAND, JENNIFER HOPE, accountant; b. N.Y.C., Nov. 29, 1955; d. John Joseph and Winifred Adele (Strohmann) Vetter; m. John Grinnell Hoagland, Jr., Jan. 24, 1983; 1 child, John Grinnell III. BS in Acctg., Case We. Res. U., 1977; postgrad., U. Tex., El Paso, 1989—. CPA, Tex.; cert. internal auditor; cert. in mgmt. acctg. Rsch. analyst Predicasts, Inc., Cleve., 1977-79; internal auditor El Paso Electric Co., 1979-80; acct. Exxon Corp., Houston, 1980-81; sr. acct. Colton, Starr, Pena & Co., El Paso, 1981-83, Paul J. Ellenburg Corp., El Paso, 1983-85; chief acct. Life Mgmt. Ctr., El Paso, 1985—. Mem. AICPA, Inst. Mgmt. Accts. Office: Life Mgmt Ctr 8929 Viscount Blvd El Paso TX 79925-5803

HOAR, MARY MARGRETTE, gifted education educator; b. Yonkers, N.Y., Dec. 28, 1948; d. Thomas Aquinas and Margaret Agnes (Delapp) H. BS, Cornell U., 1970; MS, Fordham U., 1973. Cert. tchr. early childhood edn., N.Y., kindergarten, N.Y. Tchr. elem. edn. Sch. # 12, Yonkers, N.Y., 1970-76; tchr. elem. edn. Sch. # 6, Yonkers, N.Y., 1976-81, tchr. gifted and talented edn., 1982-86; tchr. computer King Elem. Summer Sch. King Elem. Summer Sch., Yonkers, 1986—; tchr. early childhood gifted and talented edn. Dr. Martin Luther King Jr. Sch. Computer Sci. and High Tech., Yonkers, 1986—; mem. sch. improvement plan com. Yonkers Bd. Edn., 1987—, United Way rep., 1974-81, mem. tchr.'s interest com., 1972-81, 82—; mem. newspaper staff Yonkers Fedn. Tchrs. Svcs., 1980—, bldg. rep., 1972-81, 87—; trainer Am. Fedn. Tchrs., N.Y. State United Tchrs. Leadership Effectiveness Tng. Workshops, N.Y. State United Tchrs. Officer Yonkers Jay-n-Cees, 1973-83, mem. goals com., golden age com., Outstanding Young Teenager chair; mem. Mayor's Community Rels. Com., 1975—, exec. chair, 1980-82; chair pub. rels. com., exec. com., salute to bus. and industry com., program com.; mem. Westchester exec. bd. No. Metro chpt. March of Dimes, 1974—, walkathon coord. com., reading olympics chair, pub. affairs com.; advisor Mayor's Youth Adv. Com., 1976-79; br. chair Yonkers Red Cross Svc. Ctr., 1975—, chair centennial com., bd. dirs., chair youth svcs.; youth coord. Senator John E. Flynn Sr. Citizens Youth Conf. Day, 1976; bd. dirs. Untermeyer Performing Arts Coun., 1976—, also treas., antique show chairperson, chairperson Art in the Park, chairperson nominating com., chairperson Eileen O'Connor Performing Arts Scholarship, charter mem.; bd. dirs. Family Svc. Yonkers, 1978—, chairperson, 1987—, also mem. exec. com., chairperson ho. com., chairperson homemakers com., mem. vol. com., mem. Nearly New Shop com.; bd. dirs. Enrico Fermi Scholarship Breakfast com., Yonkers Hist. Soc.; mem. steering com. Cornell Women's Club of Westchester, Yonkers Marathon Com. Recipient Janet Hopkins Meml. award for Outstanding Vol. Svc., 1987, Key to City of Yonkers, Mayor Angelo Martinelli, 1977. Mem. Cornell Women's Club of Westchester. Democrat. Roman Catholic. Home: 29 Marshall Rd Yonkers NY 10705-2531 Office: Yonkers Bd Edn 135 Locust Hill Ave Yonkers NY 10701-2917

HOARD, LINDA JANE, lawyer; b. Worcester, Mass., Oct. 8, 1947; d. Edward James and Rose Ann (O'Day) H. AB in English, Boston Coll., 1969, MEd in Reading, 1976, JD, 1981; MA in English, Fordham U., 1971. Bar: Mass. 1981. Assoc. Testa, Hurwitz & Thibeault, Boston, 1981-83; assoc. counsel Bank of Boston, 1983-86; assoc. counsel Mass. Fin. Svcs. Co., Boston, 1986-88, sr. counsel, 1988-92, asst. gen. counsel, v.p., 1992-94; sr. counsel The Shareholder Svcs. Group, 1994—. Contbr. Boston Coll. Law Rev. Roman Catholic. Office: The Shareholders Svcs Group 53 State St Boston MA 02109

HOBAN, CAROLYN J., scientist, researcher; b. Boston, Jan. 24, 1959; d. Allan F. and Frances C. Hoban. BS, Tufts U., 1980; MS, Harvard U., 1985, DSc, 1989. Scientist, postdoctoral fellow MIT Ctr. for Cancer Rsch., Cambridge, Mass., 1989-92; scientist, mem. rsch. staff Cambridge (Mass.) Neurosci., 1992—. Nat. MErit scholar, 1976; Genetics fellow NIH, 1989. Mem. AAAS, Am. Women of Sci., N.Y. Acad. Scis. Office: Cambridge Neurosci One Kendall Sq Bldg 700 Cambridge MA 01239

HOBAN, LILLIAN, author, illustrator; b. Phila., May 18; d. Jules and Fanny (Godwin) Aberman; children: Phoebe, Abron, Esmé, Julia. Student, Phila. Mus. Sch., Hanya Holm Sch. Dance, N.Y.C., Martha Graham Sch. Dance. Author, illustrator: (children's books) I Can Read, Arthur Series, 1972—; illustrator: (children's books) Frances Series, 1964— (Notable Book award), First Grade Series, 1967—, Jim Books, Charlie the Tramp (Christopher award). Mem. PEN, Authors Guild, Soc. Children's Book Writers. Democrat. Jewish.

HOBART, BILLIE, college educator, consultant; b. Pitts., Apr. 19, 1935; d. Harold James Billingsley and Rose Stephanie (Sladack) Green; m. W.C.H. Hobart, July 20, 1957 (div. 1967); 1 child, Rawson W. BA in English, U. Calif., Berkeley, 1967, EdD, 1992; MA in Psychology, Sonoma State U., 1972. Cert. tchr., Calif. Asst. prof. Coll. Marin, Kentfield, Calif., 1969-78; freelance cons., writer, 1969—; asst. prof. Contra Costa Coll., San Pablo, Calif., 1986—. Author: (cookbook) Natural Sweet Tooth, 1974, (non-fiction) Expansion, 1972, Purposeful Self: Coherent Self, 1979; contbr. articles to profl. jours. Served with WAC, 1953-55. Mem. NAFE, Mensa, Phi Delta Kappa, Commonwealth Club San Francisco. Home and Office: PO Box 1542 Sonoma CA 95476-1542

HOBART, MARGERY ANNE, special education educator; b. Fort Dodge, Iowa, Oct. 22, 1942; d. Lawwrence John and Martha Ione (Sanders) Underberg; m. Donald John Hobart, Aug. 1, 1964; children: Patricia Ann, Duane Gilbert, David Lawrence. BS, Briar Cliff Coll., 1964; MS, Iowa State U., 1981. Chemistry and math educator Cedar Valley Community Sch., Somers, Iowa, 1969-79; multicategorical tchr. jr.-sr. high sch. Cedar Valley Community Sch., Farnhamville, Iowa, 1979-88; multicategorical resource room tchr. high sch. Prairie Valley Community Sch., Gowrie, Iowa, 1988—. Bd. trustees J.J. Hands Libr., Lohrville, Iowa, 1990—. Mem. NEA, Iowa Edn. Assn., Coun. for Learning Disabilities, Lioness (pres. Lohrville chpt. 1988), Alpha Delta Kappa. Office: Prairie Valley Comm Sch 1005 Riddle St Gowrie IA 50543

HOBBS, AVANEDA DORENZA, management company executive, minister, singer; b. Charlottesville, Va., July 23, 1955; d. Frederick Douglass and Viola Marie H. BS in Sociology, Va. Wesleyan, 1976; MA in Ednl. Adminstrn., Spirit of Truth Inst., Richmond, Va., 1994, EdD in Ednl. Adminstrn., 1994. Ordained minister, Charismatic Ch., 1990. Lead singer Gospel Equattes, Washington, 1971; vocalist Mighty Clouds of Joy, 1972, various orgns., 1975—; bus. mgr. Rev. Demond Wilson., Washington, 1990-91; CEO World Resource Outreach Co., Forestville, Md., 1991—; bd. dirs. Solid Rock Records, In The Beginning Ministries, Inc., CAPublishing; i nat. dir. pub. rels. Gospelrama conv., 1985-88; internat. comm. and ednl. cons. Idahosa World Outreach, Nigeria, 1990-93. vocalist: popular gospel singer since early 1970's, concert, TV and radio appearances; author: Guide to Black Religious and Supporting Orgns., 1990. Participant in Congl. and White House Briefings as influential religious leader in D.C., 1992. Recipient Outstanding Svc. award Christian Music Conf., 1980, D.C. Mayoral commendation, 1990. Mem. NAFE, Broadcast Music, Inc. (assoc.), Christian Mgmt. Assn., Christian Believers United, Ministerial Fellowship of Christian Believers United, Black Nat. Religious Broadcasters, Christian Mgmt. Assn., Uniformed Code Coun., Traditional Values Coalition. Republican.

HOBOY, SANDRA LOUISE GIBBS, business developer; b. Princeton, Ind., Jan. 1, 1946; d. Eugene and Mary Ailene (Pitman) Gibbs; m. Loren Paul Hoboy, Oct. 11, 1969; children: Shelley Jeanne, Berndt Lance, Garrett Paul. BS in Clin. Biology and English, Ind. State U., 1968; MA, Valparaiso U., 1973. Tchr. Horace Mann High Sch., Garu, Ind., 1968-70; freelance writer/journalist, 1971-76; pub. rels. dir. several non-profit orgns., 1979-80; sp. projects mgr., treas./controller Fluids Engring. Corp., Valparaiso, Ind., 1980-82; purhasing, transp. mgr. Western Refining Corp., 1982-86; mktg., purchasing mgr. Wesfrac, Inc./Westec Inc., Grand Junction, Colo., 1986-89; mktg. and supply dir. Charterhall Refining and Mktg., Inc., Grand Junction, 1989-90; agt. mktg. bus. svcs. United of Omaha, Grand Junction, 1990-91; agt. State St. Investment Trust, Grand Junction, 1991-92; chmn. bd. dirs. Tecnal Resources, Grand Junction, 1989-92; dir. St. Ives Corp., Kent, Wash., 1994—; ptnr. and CFO Enviro25, 1993—; pres., CFO Bio-Marine Technologies, Inc., Seattle. Republican. Lutheran. Home: 4102 Kingsway Anacortes WA 98221-3218 Office: BioMarine Techs Inc 4459 S 134th Pl Tukwila WA 98168-6204

HOCH, PEGGY MARIE, computer scientist; b. Balt., Dec. 2, 1959; d. Stanley Elijah Hoch, Jr. and Nancy Irene (Bishop) Austin; 1 child, Kiana Mariah Shurkin. AA, Catonsville (Md.) Community, Coll., 1982; BS, Towson State U., 1987; MS, Johns Hopkins U., 1989. Lab. technician McCormick & Co., Hunt Valley, Md., 1980-84; computer scientist U.S. Army Concepts Analysis, Bethesda, Md., 1985-88; sr. assoc. programmer IBM Corp., Rockville, Md., 1989-91; computer programmer Nat. Oceanic and Atmospheric Adminstrn., Silver Spring, Md., 1991—. Author: (software) Design CDRLs for IBM/FAA, 1991, Design CDRLs for NOAA, 1994. Recipient Nat. Computer Sci. award U.S. Achievement Acad., 1987, Computer Sci. award Towson (Md.) State U., Chemistry award Catonsville Community Coll., 1980. Mem. AIAA, Am. Assn. Artificial Intelligence, Johns Hopkins U. Alumni Assn. Home: 10551 Twin Rivers Rd Apt D2 Columbia MD 21044-2120 Office: Nat Weather Svc 1325 E West Hwy Silver Spring MD 20910-3233

HOCHBERG, AUDREY G., state legislator; b. Stamford, Conn., June 26, 1933; m. Herbert Hochberg; children: Carol, Brenda, Judith. BA in Econs. magna cum laude, Radcliffe Coll., 1955. Legislator dist # 8 Westchester County, 20 yrs.; mem. N.Y. State Assembly, 1992—; mem. edn., social svcs., energy, local govts., alcoholism and drug abuse, and consumer affairs coms.; minority leader Westchester County Bd. Legislators, 1976-79; chair Westchester County Criminal Justice Coord. Council, 1980-82; mem. Westchester County Task Force on Jail Overcrowding, 1980-92; co-chair Spl. Commns. Additional Revenues and Reducing Expenditures, 1990-92; bd. dirs. Hudson Valley Health Sys. Agy.; mem. task force on Corrections Overcrowding, Westchester Health Planning Coun., Westchester County Bd. of Health; mem. adv. bd. N.Y. State Cmty. Affairs. Bd. dirs. Boy's and Girls' Glub New Rochelle, WESCOP. Recipient Woman of Yr. award NOW, 1973. Mem. Phi Beta Kappa. Office: NY State Assembly State Capitol Albany NY 12224*

HOCHLERIN, DIANE, pediatrician, educator; b. N.Y.C., Feb. 4, 1942; d. William J. and Bertha Hochlerin. BS, Bklyn. Coll., 1958; MD, Med. Coll. Pa., 1962. Diplomate Am. Bd. Pediats. Intern Albert Einstein Hosp., Phila., 1966-67; resident Phila. Gen. Hosp., 1967-69; attending pediatrician St. Luke's Roosevelt Hosp., N.Y.C., 1969—; clin. assoc. prof. pediats. Columbia U., N.Y.C., 1969—; asst. attending physician Cath. Med. Ctr., N.Y.C., 1993—; faculty advisor Adelphi U., N.Y.C., 1994. Fellow Am. Acad. Pediats.; mem. N.Y. State Med. Soc., County Med. Soc. Home and Office: 305 E 86th St Apt 20RW New York NY 10028

HOCHSCHILD, CARROLL SHEPHERD, medical equipment and computer company executive, educator; b. Whittier, Calif., Mar. 31, 1935; d. Vernon Vero and Effie Corinne (Hollingsworth) Shepherd; m. Richard Hochschild, July 25, 1959; children: Christopher Paul, Stephen Shepherd. BA in Internat. Rels., Pomona Coll., 1956; Teaching credential U. Calif., Berkeley, 1957; MBA, Pepperdine U., 1985; cert. in fitness instrn., U. Calif., Irvine, 1988. Cert. elem. tchr., Calif. elem. tchr. Oakland (Calif.) Pub. Schs., 1957-58, San Lorenzo (Calif.) Pub. Schs., 1958-59, Pasadena (Calif.) Pub. Schs., 1959-60, Huntington Beach (Calif.) Pub. Schs., 1961-63, 67-68; adminstrv. asst. Microwave Instruments, Corona del Mar, Calif., 1968-74; co-owner Hoch Co., Corona del Mar, 1978—. Rep. Calif. Tchrs. Assn., Huntington Beach, 1962-63. Mem. AAUW, P.E.O. (projects chmn. 1990-92, corr. sec. 1992-94, chpt. pres. 1994—), Internat. Dance-Exercise Assn., NAFE, ASTD (Orange County chpt.), Assistance League Newport-Mesa. Republican. Presbyterian. Clubs: Toastmistress (corr. sec. 1983), Jr. Ebell (fine arts chmn. Newport Beach 1966-67).

HOCHSTADT, JOY, biomedical research scientist, scientific and research director; b. N.Y.C., May 6, 1939; d. Julius Louis and Edith (Tabatchnick) H.; m. Harvey Leon Ozer, Feb. 3, 1960; 1 child, Juliane Natasha Hochstadt-Ozer. A.B. in Zoology, Barnard Coll., 1960; A.M. in Biologic Scis. (grad. fellow 1961-62), Stanford U., 1963; vis. fellow in tumor biology, Karolinska Inst., Stockholm, 1964-65; research fellow in biol. chemistry, Harvard U., 1965-66; Ph.D. in Microbiology, Georgetown U., 1968; postdoctoral fellow NIH, 1968-70. Diplomate Am. Bd. Clin. Chemistry. Instr. biology Coll. San Mateo, Calif., 1962-63; teaching asst. microbiology Georgetown Med. Sch., 1967-68; established investigator Am. Heart Assn.; lab. biochemistry Nat. Heart and Lung Inst., Bethesda, Md., 1970-72; sr. scientist Worcester Found. Exptl. Biology, Shrewsbury, Mass., 1972-76; adj. prof. biochemistry Central New Eng. Coll., Worcester, Mass., 1974-75; vis. prof. membrane research Weizmann Inst. Sci., Rehovot, Israel, 1976; vis. prof. biochemistry and biophysics U. R.I., Kingston, 1976-77; research prof. microbiology N.Y. Med. Coll., Valhalla, 1977-81; dir. Div. Clin. Biochemistry and Basic Research in Pathology, Cath. Med. Center, Queens, 1981-88; prof. clin. microbiology Cornell U. Med. Sch., 1986—; v.p., scientific dir. Hercon Labs. Corp. subs. Health Chem Corp., N.Y.C., 1988-90; sr. v.p. Biomed. Techs. div. Princeton Polymer Labs., Union, N.J., 1989—; dir. scientific rsch. Maimonides Rsch. and Devel. Found. & Med. Ctr., 1992—; dir. immunopath. Lebanon Hosp. Ctr., 1993—; pres., CEO, chmn. Diagnostic Devel. Team, Ltd., N.Y.C., 1993—; predoctoral trainee USPHS, 1966-67, spl. trainee, 1973; investigator Am. Heart Assn., 1970-75; mem. NSF postdoctoral fellowship evaluation panel in biology NRC, 1975—; mem. postdoctoral fellowship evaluation panel NATO, 1978—; mem. cell biology study sect. NIH, 1979—, mem. biomed. scis. fellowship com., 1979—. Editorial bd. Jour. Bacteriology, 1975-80; contbr. research papers, methods articles and monographs to profl. lit. Mem. nat. policy com. Profl. Women's Caucus, 1970-73; mem. alumnae coun. Barnard Coll., 1975—, v.p. Class of 1960, 1990—; mem. com. revision biochemistry and biotech. subcom., in vitro methods subcom. U.S. Pharmacopeial Conv., 1990—. Cancer Internat. Rsch. Coop. Snell scholar, 1965; fellow USPHS, 1967-70; grantee NIH, 1973, NSF, 1978-80; travel award Am. Soc. Biol. Chemists, Stockholm, 1973, Hamburg, 1976, Am. Soc. Microbiology, Jerusalem, 1973. Fellow Am. Acad. Microbiology, Am. Inst. Chemists (profl. opportunities com., legis. com.), Nat. Acad. Clin. Biochemistry; mem. Am. Heart Assn. (basic sci. council), Am. Soc. Microbiology (status of women com. 1970-73, sec. physiology div. 1972-74, mem. divisional nominating com. 1973), Am. Soc. Biol. Chemists, Am. Assn. Clin. Chemists, AAAS, Am. Soc. Clin. Rsch., Am. Chem. Soc., Genetics Soc. Am., Harvey Soc., Am. Assn. Cancer Rsch., N.Y. Acad. Scis., Fedn. Am. Scientists, Assn. Women in Sci. (affirmative goals and actions com. 1973-75), Tissue Culture Assn. (Northeast planning com. 1986—), Am. Soc. for Cell Biology. Office: Diagnostic Devel Team Ltd 300 Central Park W Ste 2E New York NY 10024-1513 Office: Princeton Polymer Labs 521 Lehigh Ave Union NJ 07083-7928 also: Maimonides Med Ctr 979 48th St Brooklyn NY 11219-2919

HOCKETT, LORNA DEE, elementary education educator; b. Portland, Oreg., Aug. 14, 1954; d. Wallace Loren and Ava Dee (Thomas) Johnson; m. John Bennett, June 15, 1975; children: Tara Dianne, Bryan Nathan, Kevin Loren. BS, Oreg. State U., 1976, MEd, 1986. Cert. elem. tchr., Oreg. Tchr. Waldport Elem. Sch., Waldport, Oreg., 1978—; trainer, ombudsman Drug Edn. Ctr., Charlotte, N.C., 1990-92; trainer developing capable people Sunrise Assocs., Provo, Utah, 1990-92. Mem. NEA (adv. panel profl. libr., mem. task force 1992, diversity tng. cadre 1994—), Oreg. Edn. Assn. (del. 1984-93, chair ins. claims rev. com. 1986-92, bd. dirs. 1993—), Lincoln County Edn. Assn. (Tchr. of Yr. 1991, treas. 1985-92, bargaining team 1992-95), Delta Kappa Gamma. Democrat. Home: PO Box 1388 Waldport OR 97394-1388 Office: Waldport Elem Sch 265 Bay St Waldport OR 97394

HODARA, EDEN, artist; b. Cleve., Oct. 31, 1924; d. Samuel Alexander and Cecelia (Klein) Baruch; m. Henri Hodara, Aug. 1, 1952; 1 child, Paul. Student, Cleve. Sch. Art, Huntington Hartford Art Sch., Cleve.; student of Walter Kuhn, Art Students League, N.Y.C., 1943, 44; student, Acad. Beaux Arts, Paris, Acad. de la Grand Chaumiere, 1952. One-woman show Miami Mus. Modern Art, 1961; exhibited in group shows Galerie Craven, Paris, 1953, Art Inst. Chgo., 1959, 62, Pan Am. Festival, Chgo., 1959, Miami Mus. Modern Art, 1961, Kovler-Heman Gallery, Chgo., 1962, Yamada Art Gallery, Kyoto, Japan, 1962, Long Beach (Calif.) Art Mus., 1966, San Francisco Art Mus., 1966, San Diego Art Mus., 1970, Comsky Gallery, L.A., 1970, L.A. Inst. Contemporary Art, 1975, NAS, Washington, 1987, Nat. Acad. Scis. and Engring., Irvine, Calif., 1991, others; represented in permanent collections Gutai Mus., Osaka, Japan, Insho Damoto Mus. Modern Art, Kyoto, numerous pvt. collections. Home and Studio: 24172 Vista D Oro Dana Point CA 92629-4522

HODENFIELD, CARLA KAY, special education educator, sales specialist; b. Williston, N.D., Feb. 10, 1956; d. Erling Wendell and Charlotte Ann (Johnson) H. BS, Minot State U., 1978. Tchr. Plentywood (Mont.) Pub. Sch., 1978-80, New Eng. (N.D.) Pub. Sch., 1980-84, Westby (Mont.) Pub. Sch., 1984-85; supr. adults HIT, Inc., Mandan, N.D., 1985-86; tchr. Killdeer (N.D.) Pub. Sch., 1986-87, Flaxville (Mont.) Pub. Sch., 1987-89, Ft. Yates (N.D.) Dist. 4, 1989—; salesman World Book/Childcraft, Mandan, 1979—, Princess House Inc., Mandan, 1985—. Editor Taste of Home mag., 1993. Mem. Mandan Art Assn., Homemakers (v.p., treas. 1993-94), Delta Kappa Gamma. Democrat. Lutheran. Home: 1000 Third St NE Mandan ND 58554

HODES, SUZANNE RUTH, artist; b. N.Y.C., May 2, 1939; d. Charles and Helen (Nadell) H.; m. Henry Linschitz, Aug. 28, 1964; 1 child, Joseph Linitz. Student, Radcliffe Coll., 1956-58; BFA, Brandeis U., 1960; MFA, Columbia U., 1962. Artist Impressions Workshop, Boston, 1968-71, Hodes Studio, Waltham, Mass., 1964-80, Artist West Studios, Waltham, 1980—; juror on art panel Tufts Med. Sch., Waltham, 1989-93; tchr. art Francis Cabot Lowell Mill, Waltham, 1990-93; co-founder Artists West Studios, Waltham, 1980, pres., 1985-89; co-founder Artists for Survival, Waltham, 1982. One-woman shows include Revel Gallery, N.Y.C., 1963, Verle Gallery, Hartford, Conn., 1965, Weeden Gallery, Boston, 1968, Radcliffe Inst., 1971, Weizmann Inst., Israel, 1972, Harvard Grad. Sch. Design, 1972-73, Wellesley (Mass.) Coll., 1974, Phoenix Gallery, N.Y.C., 1976, 78, Clark Gallery, Lincoln, Mass., 1978, Allport Assocs. Gallery, San Francisco, 1979, Newton (Mass.) Arts Mus., 1980, Artists West Open House, 1981-91, Zionist House, Boston, 1984, Rockefeller U., N.Y.C., 1984, Julia Saul Gallery, Sudbury, Mass., 1987, Hess Gallery, Pine Manor Coll., Chestnut Hill, Mass., 1989, Common Space Gallery, Artists West, Waltham, Mass., 1990, 92, 93, Eliza Spencer Gallery, Newton, 1991, Beacon Constrn. Co., Boston, 1992, Charles Webb Furniture Showroom, Cambridge, 1993, Tofias Gallery, Reservoir Place, Waltham, 1993, Lightwater Gallery, Wellfleet, Mass., 1994; exhibited in group shows at Boston Pub. Libr., 1986, 94, DeCordova Mus., 1986, Newport (R.I.) Art Mus., 1988, Straus Gallery, N.Y.C., 1990, Boston Printmakers, 1986-94, Copley Soc., 1988, 93; represented in permanent collections at Fogg Mus., Rose Art Mus., Bank of Am., Boston, Cabot Corp., Hale and Dorr, Duxbury Art Complex Mus., DeCordova Mus., Boston Pub. Libr., Rockefeller U., Combined Jewish Philanthropies, also pvt. collections. Mem. Mayor's Commn. for Cultural Affairs, Waltham, 1986-89; mem. exec. com. Internat. Save Life on Earth Project, Cambridge, 1984-88. Fulbright Commn. fellow, Paris, 1963-64, Bunting Inst. fellow Radcliffe Coll., Cambridge, Boston, Israel, 1970-72; recipient award in painting Kokoschka Sch., City of Salzburg, Austria, 1959. Mem. Boston Printmakers, Monotype Guild New England, Copley Soc. Boston, Boston Visual Artists Union, Artists Against Racism and War. Home: 35 Riverside Dr Waltham MA 02154 Office: Artists West Studio 144 Moody St Waltham MA 02154

HODGE, ANN F., environmental company executive; b. Los Angeles, Aug. 17, 1949; d. Harry Carl and Violet (Howard) Calhoun; m. Thomas Michael Sanders (div. Feb. 1971); 1 child, Richard Dean; m. Robert David Hodge, May 15, 1982. B.A., UCLA, 1976. Legal administr. Cossack & Artz, Los Angeles, 1972-80; paralegal Manatt, Phelps, Rothenberg & Tunney, Los Angeles, 1980-82; tech. writer Galler Assocs., Houston, 1982-83; paralegal Mayor, Day & Caldwell, Houston, 1983-85; divisional v.p. ext. affairs Browning-Ferris Industries, Houston, 1985—; cons. non-profit groups, Houston, 1984—. Contbr. articles to profl. jours. Bd. dirs. Odyssey House. Mem. Pub. Affairs Council (bd. dirs.), Leadership Am. (pres.), Leadership Tex. (bd. dirs.). Club: Forum. Lodge: Jobs Daughters (honored queen 1966-67). Avocations: reading, traveling, politics. Office: Browning Ferris Industries 10th fl 580 Westlake Park Blvd Houston TX 77079

HODGE, MARTHA ELIZABETH (BETSY HODGE), executive; b. Phila., Dec. 30, 1950; d. Harry Colvin and Jeannette M. (Hartwell) Taylor; m. Thomas H. Hodge, July 2, 1971; 1 child, Jeannette E. Student, Phila. Coll. of Textiles & Science, Phila., 1990—. Telecommunications mgr. Miller Anderson & Sherrerd, West Conshohocken, Pa., 1985-89; asst. treas./sec., mgr. gen. affairs LTCB-MAS Investment Mgmt., Inc., West Conshohocken, Pa., 1989—. Office: LTCB-MAS Investment Mgmt Inc 1 Tower Brg Ste 1000 West Conshohocken PA 19428

HODGE, MARY GRETCHEN FARNAM, manufacturing company distributor, manager and executive; b. DeFuniak Springs, Fla., Sept. 24, 1943; d. Thomas Dewey and Mary Catherine (Mixon) Farnam; m. Spessard L. Hodge, Apr. 28, 1962; children: Jennifer Robin, Monica Leigh Hodge Schulz, Stephanie Lea. Student, Orlando Coll. Adminstrv. asst. The Cameron and Barkley Co., Orlando, Fla., 1961-68, office mgr. Machine Tool div., 1975-76; mgr. Frazer Machinery and Supply Co., Orlando, 1976—, sec.-treas., 1988—. Pioneered effort to establish parent support groups for gifted edn., Seminole County, 1979; sec. Parent of Gifted Edn., Seminole County, 1980-87; mem. adv. bd. Exceptional Student Edn., Seminole City, Fla., 1980—; chairperson Maitland (Fla.) Centennial Founders Bd., 1985; tour guide Orlando Opera Guild, Winter Park, Fla., 1985; celebrity waitress Leukemia Soc. Am., Orlando, 1986; co-chairperson Project Graduation Lyman High Sch., Seminole County, 1986—; chairperson Alzheimers Resource Auction Dinner, Winter Park, 1987 88; bd. dirs. Maitland Civic Ctr., 1983-86, v.p. bd. dirs. 1987-88, pres., bd. dirs. 1988-89, ex-officio bd. dirs. 1989-90; v.p. bd. dirs. Maitland Civic Club, 1993-94, pres. bd. dirs., 1994—; v.p. Maitland Woman's Ctr., 1994—; mem. Cultural Corridor Adv. Com., Maitland; bd. dirs. non-profit Showcase Group, Maitland. Recipient appreciation plaque Dividends, Seminole City, 1974-75, cert. appreciation Maitland Civic Ctr., 1986, Alzheimer Resource Ctr., Winter Park, 1987, Pres.'s Gavel, 1989. Mem. Am. Machine Tool Distbrs., Soc. Mfg. Engrs., Maitland Woman's Club (several offices 1970—). Democrat. Methodist.

HODGES, ANN, television editor, newspaper columnist; b. McCamey, Tex., Sept. 7, 1928; d. Ernest Cornelius and Margaret Isabel (Wood) Haynes; m. Cecil Ray Hodges, July 2, 1954 (div. Nov. 1974); children—Craig McNeley, Elizabeth Ann. B.J., U. Tex., 1948. Reporter, Houston Chronicle, 1948-51; society editor The News, Mexico City, 1951-52; reporter Houston Chronicle, 1952-54, TV editor, columnist, 1962—; mem. adv. bd. U. Miami TV News Workshop, 1994—. Mem. Critics Consensus (dir. 1965-75), TV Critics Assn. (founder, exec. bd., v.p., pres.). Club: Houston Press (pres. 1967-68). Office: Houston Chronicle Texas And Travis St Houston TX 77002

HODGES, CHERIE SUZANNE, nursing administrator; b. Tulsa, Dec. 6, 1950; d. Donatello Edward Jr. and Ruth Louise (Boyer) Ashby; m. Brian Hodges, July 10, 1971; 1 child, Christopher Evan. BSN, Tex. Christian U., 1980. CCRN. Staff nurse Harris Hosp. Meth., Ft. Worth, 1978-81; staff and charge nurse Wesley Med. Ctr., Wichita, Kans., 1981—; adj. faculty mem., med.-surg. clin. instr. Butler County C.C., 1993—. Recipient Good Sight award Wichita Eye Bank, 1991. Mem. AACN Greater Wichita Chpt., Critical Care Nurses (treas. 1989-92). Office: HCA-Wesley Med Ctr 550 N Hillside St Wichita KS 67214-4910

HODGES, ELIZABETH SWANSON, educator; b. Anoka, Minn., Apr. 7, 1924; d. Henry Otto and Louise Isabel (Holiday) Swanson; m. Allen Hodges, June 27, 1944; children: Nancy Elizabeth, Susan Kathleen, Jane Ellen, Sara Louise. BA cum laude, Regis Coll., Denver, 1966; postgrad., U. No. Colo., 1966-79, Valdosta State U., 1979-81. Cert. secondary edn., hosp./homebound, learning disabilities, Colo., Ga., Ariz. Vol. emergency St. Anthony's Hosp., Denver, 1960-64; v.p., tutor St. Elizabeth's Adult Tutorial, Denver, 1964-69; hosp./homebound tchr. Liberty County Sch. System, Hinesville, Ga., 1979-87; ednl. tutor Colo. River Indian Tribes, Parker, Ariz., 1986-87; vol. Twin Cities Community Hosp., Templeton, Calif., 1987-89, Guardian Ad Litem Cir. Ct. 5th Dist. Fla., 1992—, Munroe Regional Med. Ctr., Ocala, Fla., 1991-92; cons., tutor Sylvan Learning Ctr., Ocala, 1990—. Reporter Trinity Triangle Newsletter, Ocala, 1992—. Mem. AAUW (chmn. internat. affairs 1991-92). Democrat. Roman Catholic. Home: 4544 SE 13th St Ocala FL 34471-3241

HODGES, GAYLA DIANNE, organization development consultant; b. Lyndonville, Vt., Apr. 27, 1950; d. Edgar Francis Field and Velma Phyllis (Brown) F.; m. Timothy Richard Hodges Sr., Dec. 24, 1977; 1 child, Timothy Richard Jr.; stepchildren: Rebekah, Paris. BA in Psychology, Ottawa U., Phoenix, 1989. Dir. mktg. Ariz. Limousines, Phoenix, 1985-87; dir. sales and mktg. Arrangements & Tours, Phoenix, 1987-88; owner, pres. PowerPlay, Phoenix, 1988-91; orgn. devel. cons. Ariz. Pub. Svc. Co., Phoenix, 1990—. Dep. registrar Rep. Party, Phoenix, 1988-92. Recipient Young Careerist award Ariz. State Bus. and Profl. Women, 1977, winner Individual Devel. Program Speakoff, 1989. Mem. ASTD, Ariz. State Bus. and Profl. Women, Ariz. Career Devel. Assn., Ariz. Regional Orgn. Devel. Network, Midtowners Bus. and Profl. Women's Club (pres. 1988-89, Woman of Achievement award 1977, 88-89). Office: Ariz Pub Svc Co PO Box 53999 MS 8328 Phoenix AZ 85072-3999

HODGES, JANET LYNN, administrative services manager; b. Biloxi, Miss., Mar. 14, 1957; d. Jesse Orville and Lois Imogene (Newman) Adcock; m. Roger Wayne Hodges, Jan. 15, 1983; children: Jessica Frances, Sara Elizabeth. BS in Bus. Adminstrn., Miss. State U., 1978, MBA in Bus. Adminstrn., 1980. Cert. Records Mgr. Mktg. analyst Dataplex, Jackson, Miss., 1980-83; sr. records analyst Houston Lighting & Power, Tex., 1983-86; records retention supr. Enron Corp., Houston, 1986-88; records adminstr. Northrop B2 Divsn., Pico Rivera, Calif., 1988-90, records and micrograph mgr., 1990-94, adminstrv. svcs. mgr., 1994—. Mem. Assn. Records Mgrs. and Adminstrs. (v.p. Houston chpt. 1986-88, pub. rels. 1985-87, budget dir. L.A. chpt. 1989-91, pres. 1991-92), Assn. Info. and Image Mgmt. (S.W. chpt. mem. of the yr. 1986, Md. mem. profl. steering com. 1987). Republican. Office: Northrop Grumman B2 Divsn 8900 E Washington Blvd Pico Rivera CA 90660

HODGES, JOYCE E., state legislator; m. Howard Hodges; 4 children. Grad. high sch. Commr. Kingsbury County; mem. S.D. Ho. of Reps., 1993—; mem. agrl. and natural resources com., health and human svcs. com. Republican. Mem. United Ch. of Christ. Home: RR 1 Box 14 Lake Preston SD 57249-9801 Office: SD House of Reps State Capitol Pierre SD 57501*

HODGE-SPENCER, CHERYL ANN, orthodontist; b. Dorchester, Mass., Apr. 1, 1952; d. Herbert Thomas and Edwina Catherine (Morey) Hodge; m. John Lawrence Spencer, June 10, 1978; children: Devin Thomas, Ian Nicholas. BS in Biology cum laude, Boston Coll., 1974; DMD, Tufts Sch. Dental Medicine, 1977; MPH, Harvard U. Sch. Pub. Health, 1981; Cert. in Orthodontics, Harvard Dental Sch., 1983. Orthodontist Brockton/Bridgewater, Mass., 1984—; orthodontic cons. Mass. Hosp. Sch., Canton, Mass., 1990—; vice chmn. Bd. of Investment, Bridgewater Savs. Bank, 1989-92; asst. coach Duxbury Youth Hockey Bantam Team, 1993-94. Lt. Dental Corps USN, 1977-80. Recipient Johnson & Johnson Dentistry award, 1977. Mem. Am. Assn. Orthodontists, Mass. Dental Soc., South Shore Dist. Dental Soc. (sec. 1990-92, peer rev. bd. 1990-92), Northeastern Soc. Orthodontists, Harvard Club Boston, Harvard Soc. Advancement Orthodontics, Metro South C. of C., Rotary (bd. dirs. charitable and ednl. fund 1989-92), Pierre Fouchard Acad., Ma. Amateur Hockey Assn. (intermediate patched hockey coach). Roman Catholic. Office: 572 Pleasant St Brockton MA 02401-2515

HODGES-ROBINSON, CHETTINA M., nursing administrator; b. Roosevelt, N.Y., Mar. 12, 1963; d. Clifford and Janice (Revis) Hodges-Jones; m. Darrell K. Robinson, Mar. 17, 1991. BSN, NYU, 1986. Cert. med.-surg. nurse basic life support and advanced cardiac life support. Cardiothoracic recovery rm. and post-anesthesia nurse, staff nurse Lenox Hill Hosp., N.Y.C.; staff nurse NYU Med. Ctr., N.Y.C., Christ Hosp., Jersey City; asst. nurse mgr. critical care/intensive/coronary care unit Good Samaritan Hosp., West Islip, L.I., N.Y. Mem. Luth. Ch. of the Good Shepherd, Roosevelt, N.Y. Mem. ANA, N.J. Nurses Assn., Black Nurses Assn. (L.I. chpt.), Zeta Alpha Beta. Home: 119 S 28th St Wyandanch NY 11798-2813

HODGESS, ERIN MARIE, statistics educator; b. Pitts., Nov. 12, 1960; d. Edwin E. and Justine J. (Plazak) H. BS in Econs., U. Dayton, 1981; MA in Econs., U. Pitts., 1987; MS in Stats., Temple U., 1989, PhD in Stats., 1995. Econ. rsch. analyst Mellon Bank, NA, Pitts., 1981-85; programmer Techalloy Co., Inc., Rahns, Pa., 1985-86; programmer analyst The Linpro Co., Berwyn, Pa., 1986-87, Jones Apparel Group, Bristol, Pa., 1987-88; programming cons. various cos., Phila., 1988-89; teaching asst. Temple U., Phila., 1990-92, adj. instr., 1992-94, group leader grad. asst. tng. workshop, 1992; asst. prof. U. Houston-Downtown, 1994—; speaker Temple U.-Rutgers U. Stats. Day, Brunswick, N.J., 1988. Fellow Temple U., 1988-90, grantee, 1994. Mem. Am. Statis. Assn., Soc. Indsl. and Applied Math., Intertel Internat., Mensa, Temple Grad. Students in Statistics Assn. (pres. 1991). Democrat. Roman Catholic. Home: 9449 Briar Forest Dr # 3544 Houston TX 77063

HODGSON, JANE ELIZABETH, obstetrician/gynecologist, consultant; b. Crookston, Minn., Jan. 23, 1915; d. Herbert and Adelaide (Marin) H.; m. Frank Walter Quattlebaum, Feb. 22, 1940; children: Gretchen, Nancy. BS, Carleton Coll., 1934, DSc (hon.), 1994; MD, U. Minn., 1939, MS in Ob-Gyn., 1947. Diplomate Am. Bd. Ob.-Gyn. Fellow Mayo Clinic, Rochester, Minn., 1941-44; pvt. practice in ob-gyn. St. Paul, 1947-72; med. dir. Preterm Clinic, Washington, 1972-74; med. dir. fertility control clinic St. Paul Ramsey Med. Ctr., 1974-79; med. dir. Planned Parenthood Minn., St. Paul, 1980-82, Midwest Health Ctr. Women, Mpls., 1981-83, Women's Health Ctr., Duluth, Minn., 1981-84; mem. staff Women's Health Ctr., Duluth, 1986—, also bd. dirs.; ostetrician/gynecologist Project Hope, Grenada, West Indies, 1984; vis. prof. ob-gyn. project hope Zheijiang Med. Sch., Hangzhou, People's Republic of China, 1985-86; clin. assoc. prof. ob-gyn. U. Minn., Mpls., 1986—; vis. med. educator Project Hope, Cairo, 1979-80; vis. prof. dept. ob-gyn. U. Calif., San Francisco, 1983. Editor: Abortion & Sterilization, 1981; contbr. 54 articles to profl. jours. Bd. dirs. Genesis II Women, Mpls., 1988—, Pro Choice Resources, Mpls., 1991—, Wellstone Alliance, Mpls., 1992—. Recipient Ann. Humanitarian award Nat. Abortion Fedn., 1981, Woman Physician of Yr. award Med. Women Minn. Med. Assn., 1983, Ann. Jane Hodgson Reproductive Freedom award Nat. Abortion Rights Action League, 1989, Hanah G. Solomon award Nat. Coun. Jewish Women, 1990. Fellow Am. Coll. Ob-Gyn. (founding); mem. Am. Med. Women's Assn. (E. Blackwell award 1992, Reproductive Health award 1994), Minn. Ob-Gyn. Soc. (pres.), Minn. Med. Assn. (So. Minn. Med. award 1952), Minn. Women's Polit. Caucus (16th Ann. Founding Feminist award 1988), Minn. Civil Liberties Assn. (bd. dirs. 1989—), Mayo Clinic Alumni Assn. Home and Office: 1537 N Fisk St Saint Paul MN 55117-3415

HODSON, NANCY PERRY, real estate agent; b. Kansas City, Mo., Nov. 19, 1932; d. Ralph Edward Perry and Juanita (Youmans) Jackman; m. William K. Hodson, Oct. 4, 1974 (div. Jan. 1985); children: Frank Tyler, Lisa Thompson, Suzanne Desforges, Robert Hodson. Student, Pine Manor Jr. Coll., 1950-51, Finch Coll., 1951-53. Cert. real estate agt., Calif.; cert. interior designer. Owner Nancy Perry Hodson Interior Design, L.A. and Newport Beach, Calif., 1974-82; agt. Grubb and Ellis, Newport Beach, 1990, Turner Assocs., Laguna Beach, Calif., 1990-92. Founder U. of Calif. Arboretum, Irvine, 1987, Opera Pacific, Costa Mesa, Calif., 1987; mem. U. of Calif. Rsch. Assocs., Irvine, 1986; pres. Big Canyon Philharm., Newport Beach, 1990; bd. dirs. Jr. Philharm., L.A., 1975-78. Mem. Big Canyon Country Club, L.A. Blue Ribbon 400 (1975-78), Jr. League Garden Club (pres. 1990-91), Big Canyon Garden Club (pres. 1989-91), Inst. of Logopedics (chmn. 30th Anniversary 1965), Guilds of Performing Arts Ctr. Presbyterian.

HODSON, SHARON LEIGH, display supervisor; b. Tulsa, Mar. 21, 1967; d. Tom Theodore and Delma Jean (Lighty) Birbilis; m. Michael Sonntag Hodson, Aug. 26, 1989; 1 child, Elliot Michael. BFA, Kans. U., 1989. Salesperson Foothill Oriental Rugs, Salt Lake City, 1989-91; asst. mgr. Pacific Linen, Salt Lake City, 1991-92; display supr. R.C. Willey, Salt Lake City, 1992—. Mother's advocate vol. Children's Svc. Soc., Salt Lake City, 1989-92. Mem. NOW, Chi Omega. Democrat. Home: 1943 S 1700 E Salt Lake City UT 84108-3156 Office: RC Willey 861 E 6600 S Salt Lake City UT 84107-7532

HOEFFLIN, MIRIAM ELIZABETH, psychologist; b. Honesdale, Pa., May 24, 1935; d. Lester Albert and Esther Grace (Fleming) Odell; m. Reynold C. Hoefflin, Aug. 6, 1960 (div. Sept. 1981); children: Geoffrey Bradford, Kinmberly Victoria; m. Ralph E. Pippenger, May 16, 1981. BA, Cedar Crest Coll., 1957; MA, Ohio State U., 1959. Lic. psychologist, Ohio. Staff psychologist Ohio Juvenile Diagnostic Ctr., Columbus, 1959-61; exec. dir. Coshocton County (Ohio) Children's Svcs., 1961-62; staff psychologist Green County Guidance Ctr., Xenia, Ohio, 1962-70; pvt. practice psychology Psychol. & Social Svcs. Assocs., Inc., Dayton, Ohio, 1968—. Mem. APA, Ohio Psychol. Assn., Dayton Area Psychol. Assn. Republican. Presbyterian. Home: 2345 Kemp Rd Dayton OH 45431 Office: 1350 Woodman Dr Dayton OH 45432

HOEFLE, BARBARA JEAN, accountant; b. Meridian, Miss., Sept. 15, 1946; d. Elliott Winfield and Marian (Boesiger) Allen; m. James Scott Hill, Jr., May 1, 1966 (div. Aug. 1977); m. Charles Henry Hoefle, Jr., Apr. 25, 1987. AB in Acctg. with honors, U. North Ala., Florence, 1970. CPA, N.C. Jr. staff acct. Thomas Powell, CPA, Atlanta, 1970-72, Sheats, Smith & Garner, CPAs, Atlanta, 1972-75; staff acct. Warren E. James, CPA, Jacksonville, N.C., 1978-85, McCotter, Carter & Williams, CPAs, Jacksonville, 1985-86; auditor Nat. Credit Union Adminstrn., Atlanta, 1986-87; acct. in pvt. practice Swansboro, N.C., 1987—. Vol., Visit Onslow Pines Rest Home, Jacksonville, 1980—. Mem. N.C. Assn. CPAs. Office: PO Box 4393 Emerald Isle NC 28594 also: 638 W Corbett Ave Swansboro NC 28584

HOEFT, MARJORIE CLAIRE, librarian; b. Vancouver, B.C., Can., Feb. 26, 1938; came to U.S., 1947; d. Leonard Neil and Jessie R. R. (McKinnon) Osgood; m. Robert Dean Hoeft, Dec. 19, 1959; children: Melissa Kathryn, Eric Von. BA, U. Oreg., 1960, MA, 1964. Tchr., libr. Creswell (Oreg.) High Sch., 1961; tchr. Agana (Guam) High Sch., 1961-63; cataloging libr. Umatilla County Library, Pendleton, Oreg., 1965, Blue Mountain Community Coll., Pendleton, 1966—. Mem. AAUW (sec. 1990—), Alpha Psi Omega, Phi Beta Kappa. Republican. Home: 1374 SW 37th St Pendleton OR 97801-3650 Office: Blue Mountain C C 2411 NW Carden Ave Pendleton OR 97801-1166

HOEHN, ELIZABETH HILL, sales executive consulting service; b. Minot, N.D., July 18, 1961; d. Curtis Lyle and Marcia Catherine (Fisher) Hill; m. Brooks Dwight Hoehn, Mar. 28, 1987. BS in Bus. Adminstrn., U. Calif., Berkeley, 1983. From account executive to account mgr. Xerox Corp., San Francisco, 1984-87; sales rep. Oracle Corp., Belmont, Calif., 1987-88; corp. sales Tiffany & Co., San Francisco, 1988-89; cons. The Search Firm/Profl. Cons. Network, San Francisco, 1989—. 1st v.p. Children's Garden of Calif. Aux., 1993-94, mem., 1990—; vol. Marin-Humane Soc., 1987-90. Office: Profl Consulting Network 595 Market St Ste 1400 San Francisco CA 94105

HOELTER, MIRIAM ELIZABETH, counselor; b. Monett, Mo., Jan. 28, 1947; d. Walter William and Helen Sophia (Reith) Stuenkel; m. Mark Edward Hoelter, Apr. 12, 1971; children: Peter, Christopher, Micah, Lucas. BA, Concordia Tchrs. Coll., 1970; MS in Edn., U. Kans., 1988. Tchr. Hillcrest Elem. Sch., Lawrence, Kans., 1986-90; counselor elem. sch. Lawrence Sch. Dist., 1988-90, Candy Ln. Elem. Sch., Milw., Oreg., 1990-91, East Gresham (Oreg.) Elem. Sch., 1991—. Mem. LWV, Am. Counseling Assn., Oreg. Counseling Assn., Oreg. Soc. Individual Psychology, Phi Delta Kappa. Democrat. Lutheran. Home: 16452 NE Fargo St Portland OR 97230-5528 Office: East Gresham Elem Sch 900 SE 5th St Gresham OR 97080-8122

HOELTERHOFF, MANUELA VALI, newspaper editor, critic; b. Hamburg, Germany, Apr. 6, 1949; came to U.S., 1957; d. Heinz Alfons and Olga Christine (Goertz) H. B.A., Hofstra U., 1971; M.A., NYU, 1973. Assoc. editor Arete Pub. Co., Princeton, N.J., 1977-80; editor-in-chief Art and Auction Mag., N.Y.C., 1979-81; arts editor Wall Street Jour., N.Y.C., 1981-89, books editor, 1989—; sr. cons. editor Smart Money Mag., N.Y.C., 1989—. Recipient Pulitzer prize Columbia U., 1983; recipient citation for disting. commentary Am. Soc. Newspaper Editors, 1982, 83. Office: Wall St Jour 200 Liberty St New York NY 10281-1099

HOELTZEL, SUSAN SADLER, gallery director, artist; b. Mobile, Ala., Feb. 13, 1949; d. Franklin Dudley and Claire (Passage) S.; m. George Anthony Hoeltzel, Sept. 15, 1969; children: Joshua Sadler, Zoe Tabler. BFA, U. So. Ala., 1970; MA, NYU, 1973. Mus. educator The Met. Mus., N.Y.C., 1977-86; curator of edn. Lehman Coll. Art Gallery, Bronx, N.Y., 1986-89, assoc. dir., 1990-92; dir. Lehman Coll. Art Gallery, Bronx, 1993—. One woman shows include Bertha Urdang Gallery, N.Y.C., 1976, 81, 85, Soho 20, N.Y.C., 1975, 76, Galerie Hecate, Paris, 1975, Off Broadway Gallery, N.Y.C., 1974; exhibited in group shows at Krasdale Gallery, Bronx, N.Y., 1991, 93, Manhattanville Coll. Gallery, Purchase, N.Y., 1990, Conn. Gallery, Danbury, 1990, Lang and O'Hara, N.Y.C., Soho 20, N.Y.C., 1987, Galerie Munro, Hamberg, 1978, Indpls. Mus., 1978, Marianne Deson Gallery, Chgo., 1977, Bertha Urdang Gallery, N.Y.C., 1977, others. Recipient 1st Prize Art of the N.E., Silvermine Guild, 1987, 2d Prize, 1989, 90. Mem. Am. Assn. for Mus. Office: Lehman Coll Art Gallery Bedford Park Blvd W Bronx NY 10468

HOERNLEIN, CAROL ANN, agricultural engineer, musician, freelance writer; b. Teaneck, N.J., Apr. 26, 1965; d. Roger David and Maria Delores (Santucci) H. BS in Agrl. Engring., Food Sci., Rutgers U., 1988. Engr.-in-tng., N.J. Pilot plant asst., lab. technician T.J. Lipton, Englewood Cliffs, N.J., 1986-88; ops. asst. Palisades Interstate Pk. Commn., Alpine, N.J., 1988-89; quality assurance engr. Reckitt and Colman, Inc., Wayne, N.J., 1989-90; process devel. engr. M&M/Mars, Hackettstown, N.J., 1990-92; CEO Binary Records, Inc., Paterson, N.J., 1992-93; freelance writer Pompton Lakes, N.J., 1994—. Singer, co-writer, pub. (compact disc) Molecules Under the Sun, 1992. Mem. Pub. Citizen, Washington, 1993, DCCC, Washington, 1993. Democrat. Roman Catholic.

HOEXTER, CORINNE ROSENFELDER KATZ, author, editor; b. Scranton, Pa., Nov. 3, 1927; d. Edward David and Aimee Helen (Rosenfelder) Katz; BA in English with high honors, Wellesley Coll., 1949; MA, U. Chgo., 1950; m. Rolf Hoexter, Dec. 25, 1955; children: Vivien, Michael Frederic. Promotion asst. Expt. Internat. Living, Putney, Vt., 1950-51; editorial asst. Parents mag., 1951-53; assoc. editor Mag. Mgmt., Inc., 1953-54; asso., then mng. editor Pines Pub. Inc., N.Y.C., 1954-57; picture editor J.J. Little & Ives, N.Y.C., 1957-59; mng. editor Portfolio and Art News Ann., 1959-60; exec. editor Asia mag. of Asia Soc., 1978-84; editor travel sect. N.Y. Times, 1984-85; freelance writer-editor, 1985—; author: From Canton to California, The Epic of Chinese Immigration, 1976; Black Crusader: Frederick Douglass, 1970; co-author: A Nation Conceived and Dedicated, 1970; contbr. to N.Y. Times and other periodicals. Trustee, Flat Rock Book Nature Assn., 1973-78; mem. adv. coun. Chamber Orch. Palisades; active Chinese Am. Arts Coun., Asian Cinevision, Chinese Am. Planning Coun., Sta. WNYC, N.Y.C. Fulbright fellow U. Bologna (Italy), 1953. Mem. LOWV, NOW, Chinese Hist. Soc. Am., Authors Guild, Am. Soc. Journalists and Authors, Assn. Preservation of Cape Cod, N.Y. Zool. Soc., Common Cause, Mass. Audubon Soc., Mus. Modern Art, Met. Mus. Art, Whitney Mus. Am. Art, Friends of N.Y. Pub. Library, Friends of Carnegie Hall, South St. Seaport, Phi Beta Kappa. Clubs: Chatham (Mass.) Yacht; Wellesley of Englewood, Wellesley of N.Y.C. Home and Office: 67 Spring Ln Englewood NJ 07631-3009

HOEY, RITA MARIE, public relations executive; b. Chgo., Nov. 4, 1950; d. Louis D. and Edith M. (Finnemann) Hoey; m. Joseph John Dragonette, Sept. 4, 1982. BA in English and History, No. Ill. U., 1972. Asst. dir. Nat. Assn. Housing and Human Devel., Chgo., 1975; public relations account exec. Weber Cohn & Riley, Chgo., 1975-76; publicity coordinator U.S. Gypsum Co., Chgo., 1976-77; with Daniel J. Edelman, Inc., Chgo., 1977-84, sr. v.p., 1981-84; exec. v.p. Dragonette, Inc., Chgo., 1984-91, pres., 1991—. Mem. Pub. Rels. Soc. Am., Women in Communications. Home: 3416 Cherry Valley Rd Woodstock IL 60098-8173 Office: Dragonette Inc 205 W Wacker Dr Ste 2200 Chicago IL 60606

HOFER, JUDITH K., retail company executive. b. Feb. 16, 1940, Hillsboro, Oreg. d. Frank E. Hofer and Helen K. Cook. BA Oreg. State. U., 1959, BS, Portland State U., 1961. Trainee, buyer, Meier & Frank Dept. Store, Portland, Oreg., 1961-65; v.p., gen. mgr., Clark Jr., Portland, 1966-72; v.p., gen. merchandising mgr. Meier & Frank, Portland, 1972-76; gen. mgr. Emporium-Capwell, San Francisco, 1976-78; exec. v.p. Famous-Barr Stores (subs. The May Co.), 1978-81; pres., chief exec. officer Meier & Frank, Portland, Oreg., 1981-83; pres., chief exec. officer, May Co., L.A., 1983-86, Famous-Barr Co. (div. May Department Stores Co.), St. Louis, 1986-87, Meier & Frank (div. May Department Stores Co.), Portland, 1988—; bd. dirs. Dial Corp., Phoenix, Key Bank of Oreg., Portland. Bd. dirs. Assn. Portland Progress, 1988-931; bd. Trustees Nat. 4-H 1991, Boy Scouts Am., St. Louis, 1986-88, Downtown St. Louis, 1986-88; trustee Nat. Jewish Hosp. & Asthma Ctr., Denver, 1983-87, City of Hope Hosp., Duarte, Calif., 1984-88, Nat. 4-H Coun., 1990—; bd. counselors Sch. Bus. Administrn. U. So. Calif., L.A., 1984-86. Named one of ten Women of Achievement City of St. Louis, 1980; recipient Spirit of LIfe award City of Hope, L.A., 1985. Mem. Nat. Women's Forum, Fashion Group, Com. of 200, Assn. U. Women, Young Pres.' Orgn. Avocation: antique doll collecting. Office: Meier & Frank 621 SW 5th Ave Portland OR 97204-1499

HOFFBERG, JUDITH A., editor, publisher, consultant; b. Hartford, Conn., May 19, 1934; d. George and Miriam (Goldenberg) H. BA cum laude, UCLA, 1956, MA, 1960, MLS, 1964. Cataloger Johns Hopkins U., Bologna Ctr., Italy, 1964-65; intern, cataloger Library of Congress, Washington, 1965-67; fine art librarian U. Pa., Phila., 1967-69; bibliographer art lit. and langs. U. Calif., San Diego, 1969-71; Brand art ctr. librarian Glendale Pub. Library, Calif., 1971-73; exec. sec. Art Libraries Soc. N. Am., 1973-78; editor, pub. Umbrella, 1978—; free-lance archivist, Pasadena, Calif., 1978—. Italian Govt. grantee, 1960-61; Kress Found. grantee, Eng., 1972; Nat. Endowment for Arts grantee, 1979, 80; Fulbright grantee, N.Z., 1984. Mem. ALA, Art Libraries Soc. N.Am. (lifetime mem., chmn., exec. sec.), Soc. Arch. Historians (dir. 1977-80), Coll. Art Assn. (bd. dirs. 1975-79), Internat. Assn. Art Critics (Am. sect.). Home: 1720 Pier Ave Santa Monica CA 90405 Office: PO Box 40100 Pasadena CA 91114-7100

HOFFEE, PATRICIA ANNE, molecular genetics educator; b. Columbiana, Ohio, Oct. 1, 1937; d. Wilbur L. and Alberta H. (Smith) H. BS, U. Pitts., 1959, MS, 1960, PhD, 1963. Asst. prof. molecular biology Albert Einstein Coll. Medicine, Bronx, N.Y., 1966-67; asst. prof. microbiology U. Pitts. Sch. Medicine, 1967-70; vis. prof. U. Parana, Brazil, 1972-73; assoc. prof. microbiology U. Pitts. Sch. Medicine, 1970-78, prof. molecular genetics, 1978—; vis. prof. U. N.C., Chapel Hill, 1982-83; cons. NIH, Bethesda, Md., 1971-76, VA, Washington, 1978-81; co-dir. MD/PhD Program, Pitts., 1985-90. Editor: Purine and Pyrimidine Metabolism, 1978; contbr. articles to profl. jours. Judge, Buhl Sci. Fair, Pitts., 1980-88. Grantee NIH, 1968-1992, ACS, 1976-78. Fellow Nat. Acad. Microbiology; mem. Am. Soc. Microbiology, Am. Soc. Advanced Sci., Am. Soc. Molecular Biology and Biochemistry. Office: U Pitts Sch Medicine Dept Molecular Genetics & Biochemistry Pittsburgh PA 15261

HOFFER, ALMA JEANNE, nursing educator; b. Dalhart, Tex., Sept. 15, 1932; d. James A. and Mildred (Zimlich) Koehler; m. John L. Hoffer, Oct. 7, 1954; children: John Jr., James Leo, Joseph V., Jerome P. BS, Bradley U., 1970; MA, W. Va. Coll. Grad. Study Inst., 1975; EdD, Ball State U., 1981, MA, 1986. Reg. Nurse. Staff nurse St Joseph Hosp., South Bend, Ind., 1958-59, Holy Cross Cen. Sch., St Joseph Hosp., South Bend, 1959-63; sch. nurse South Bend Sch. Corp., 1970-72; faculty staff Morris Harvey Coll., Charleston, W.Va., W.Va. Inst. Tech., Montgomery, 1975-76; asst. prof. Ball State U., Ind., 1976-77, Ind. U.-Purdue U., Ft. Wayne, 1977-81; assoc. prof. U. Akron, Ohio, 1981-83, 91—, asst. dean, grad. edn., 1983-90, assoc. prof., 1991-93; prof., chair Dept. of Nursing St. Francis Coll., Fort Wayne, Ind., 1993—; trustee Akron Child Guidance, 1983-88, 89—, chair planning com., 1988; nursing Blick Clin., Akron, 1988; rsch. cons. St. Joseph Hosp., Ohio, 1989; researcher, presenter in field. Contbg. author: Family Health Promotion Theories and Assessment, 1989, Nursing Connections, 1992. Task force mem. Gov. Celeste's Employee Assistance Program for State U. Campuses, Ohio, 1983-84, del. People to People Citizen Amb. Program to Europe, 1988. Mem. ANA, Nat. League for Nursing, Midwest Nursing Rsch. Soc., Transcultural Nursing Assn., Portage Country Club, Tippecanoe Country Club, Sigma Theta Tau. Republican. Roman Catholic. Office: Saint Francis Coll Dept of Nursing Fort Wayne IN 46808

HOFFER, LOIS GRAYSHAN, nurse, coordinator; b. Passaic, N.J., Feb. 27, 1941; d. Alvin William and Helen Ruth (Jones) Grayshan; m. Richard Stephen Hoffer, Sr., Apr. 11, 1963; children: R. Stephen Jr., Geoffrey A., Timothy J., Matthew P., Michael B. Diploma, Johns Hopkins Hosp. Sch., Nursing, 1962. RN, Md. Staff nurse Johns Hopkins Hosp., Balt., 1962-63, 67-68, Fallston (Md.) Gen. Hosp., 1975-84; staff nurse, coord. unrelated marrow donor program Johns Hopkins Hosp., Balt., 1984—. Treas., den mother Cub Scouts, Edgewood, Md., 1967-80; pres., treas. PTA, Edgewood, 1968-80; treas., fundraiser Boosters Club, Edgewood, 1977-88; elder Presbyn. Ch., Edgewood, 1975-82. Mem. Soc. Hemapheresis Specialists, Johns Hopkins Univ. Nurses Alumni Assn. (bd. dirs. 1989-91, 94—). Office: Johns Hopkins Hosp Hemapheresis Ctr 550 N Broadway Baltimore MD 21205

HOFFER, SHARON MARIE, educator; b. Dallas, Oct. 18, 1941; d. Bates Lowry and Marie E. (Grady) H. BA in Secondary Edn., U. Mo., Kansas City, 1971, MA in Secondary Edn. (Math), 1976; PhD in Adult and Extension Edn., Tex. A&M U., 1986. Tchr. 7th grade St. Peter's Prince Sch., San Antonio, 1962-64, St. Catherine of Siena Sch., Metairie, La., 1964-66; tchr. 7th, 8th grades Holy Trinity Sch., Kansas City, Mo., 1966-69; tchr. math., music, reading Guardian Angels Sch., Kansas City, 1969-70, St. Peter's Sch., Kansas City, 1971-77; dept. chair, tchr. math. St. Mary's High Sch., Independence, Mo., 1977-80; tchr. math. St. Teresa's Acad., Kansas City, Mo., 1980-81; instr. math. Tex. A&M U., College Station, 1982-86; curriculum-grant writer Pan-Ednl. Inst., Independence, 1987; tchr. math. East Environ. and Agribusiness Magnet High Sch., Kansas City, 1987—. Mem. ASCD, Nat. Coun. Tchrs. Math., Mensa. Roman Catholic. Home: 2819 Campbell St Kansas City MO 64109-1125

HOFFERBERT, JULIA MORAN, insurance agency owner; b. Balt., July 10, 1936; d. Leslie Joseph and Thelma (Klecka) Moran; m. Louis T. Hofferbert, Aug. 24, 1957; children: Michele, Stephanie, George, Julie, John. BS, Towson (Md.) U., 1958. CPCU. Tchr. Balt. Sch. System, 1956-57; ins. owner Balt. Hofferbert Ins. Agy., 1973—. Adv. Francis Scott Key Hosp., Balt., 1985-87, Balt. City Fin. Planning, 1982. Mem. CPCUs, Indep. Inst. Agents Md. (pres. 1992, chmn. bd. 1992-93, lobbyist 1985-93), Cert. Profl. Inst. Women. Roman Catholic. Office: Hofferbert Ins Agy 272 S Highland Ave Baltimore MD 21224

HOFF LUPTON, MAUREEN ELIZABETH, nurse, clinical research coordinator; b. Kansas City, Mo., June 23, 1961; d. Albert Alphonsus and Betty Jo (O'Connor) H. BSN cum laude, U. Kans., 1988; BA in Biology, Westminster Coll., 1983. RN, Tex.; cert. critical care. With coronary care unit Baylor Med. Ctr., Dallas; coord. clin. rsch. cardiology sect. Dallas VA Med. Ctr.; supr. nursing Aston Ambulatory Care Ctr. sect. Gen. Internal Medicine U. Tex. Southwestern Med. Ctr., Dallas, 1991—; bd. dirs., East Dallas Health Coalition. Features editor The Columns newspaper. Coord. sch. nursing food drive needy families U. Kans., 1987; mem. vision trips to Africa and South Am. Med. Assistance Program Internat., 1992, 94; mem rsch. and devel. com. Jr. League Dallas, 1992-93, mem. adv. planning com., 1994—; mem. women' s bd. Dallas Opera, 1994—; active Dallas Symphony Orch. Chorus, 1994—; mem. jr. group Dallas Symphony Orch. League; bd. bd. dirs. Dallas County Young Reps. Mem. ACCN, Westminster Women's Assn. (programs com. chmn. 1982-83), Dallas Garden Club (mem. jr. group), Sigma Theta Tau, Beta Beta Beta (v.p. 1982-83).

HOFFMAN, ALICE, writer; b. N.Y.C., Mar. 16, 1952; m. Tom Martin; children: Jake, Zack. BA, Adelphi U., 1973; MA, Stanford U., 1975. Author: Property of, 1977, The Drowning Season, 1979, Angel Landing, 1980, White Horses, 1982, Fortune's Daughter, 1985, Illumination Night, 1987, At Risk, 1988, Seventh Heaven, 1990, Turtle Moon, 1992, Second Nature, 1994, (screenplay) Independence Day, 1983. Mirelles fellow Stanford U., 1975, Breadloaf fellow, 1976. Office: care Putnam Berkley 200 Madison Ave New York NY 10016-3903*

HOFFMAN, ANN FLEISHER, labor union official, lawyer; b. Phila., June 1, 1942; d. Willis Jr. and Mary (Leffler) Fleisher; m. Charles Stuart Hoffman Jr., June 7, 1964 (div. 1979); m. Arnold Perry Rubin, Jan. 1, 1985 (div. 1993). BA, Barnard Coll., 1964; JD, U. Md., 1972. Bar: Md., 1972, N.Y., 1978. Reporter, producer Sta. WBAL-TV, Balt., 1965-68; assignment editor, producer Sta. WJZ-TV, Balt., 1968-69; assoc. Edelman, Levy and Rubenstein, Balt., 1972-77; assoc. gen. counsel Internat. Ladies' Garment Workers Union, N.Y.C., 1977-79, dir. Profl. And Clerical Employees div., 1987-91; asst. dir. legis. dept. Internat. Ladies' Garment Workers Union, Washington, 1991-94, assoc. dir., 1994—; exec. asst. to Atty Gen. U.S. Dept. Justice, Washington, 1979-81; counsel Dist. 1 Communications Workers Am., N.Y.C., 1981-85; adminstrv. asst. to v.p. Communications Workers Am., N.Y.C. and Cranford, N.J., 1985-87; lectr. U. Md. Sch. of Law, Balt., 1972-77; adj. faculty Cornell U. Trade Union Women's Studies Program, N.Y.C., 1979-85; trustee Botto House Am. Labor Mus., Haledon, N.J., 1986-89. Author: (with others) Legal Status of Homemakers in Maryland, 1978, Bargaining for Child Care, 1985, 2d edit., 1991. Founding mem. Women's Law Ctr., Balt., 1971-77; mem. Balt. City Charter Review Commn., 1973-76; bd. dirs. ACLU Md. Chpt., Balt., 1975-77, Campfire Girls Chesapeake Council, Balt., 1976-77; co-chair Sachs for Atty. Gen., Md., 1976-77; pub. mem. N.Y. State Banking Bd., N.Y.C., 1984-85. Mem. ABA, Coalition of Labor Union Women (treas. N.Y.C. chpt. 1981-83), Nat. Network of Women Union Lawyers (founder), Lawyers and Legal Workers for Working Women (founder), Cornell U. Adj. Faculty Fedn., Order of Coif. Home: 2810 Mckinley St NW Washington DC 20015-1216 Office: Internat Ladies Garment Union 815 16th St NW Washington DC 20006-4104

HOFFMAN, ARLENE FAUN, podiatric medicine educator, physiologist; b. N.Y.C., Nov. 23, 1941; d. Abraham S. and Pearl Tootsie (Weiss) H. BS, CUNY, 1962; PhD in Physiology, SUNY, Bklyn., 1966; D of Podiatric Medicine, Calif. Coll. Podiatric Medicine, San Francisco, 1976. Instr. CUNY, N.Y.C., 1964-66; assoc. prof. basic scis. Calif. Coll. Podiatric Medicine, 1967-68, prof., 1969—, asst. dir. basic scis., 1967-69, dir., 1969-75, assoc. dean curricular affairs, 1972-75, assoc. prof. podiatric medicine, 1978-81, prof., chief non-invasive vascular lab., 1981—; postdoctoral fellow immunophysiology Stanford U. Med. Sch., Palo Alto, Calif., 1966-67; mem. physiology sect. Nat. Bd. Podiatry Examiners, 1967-76; mem. tng. grant rev. com., heart and cardiovascular sect. Nat. Heart, Lung and Blood Inst., 1976-77; cons. Vascular Evaluation Cos., 1986—; mem. Bd. Podiatric Medicine, 1985-92; bd. dirs. Am. Bd. Podiatric Orthopedics and Primary Medicine, 1992—. Editor: Yearbook of Podiatric Medicine & Surgery, 1979, Lower Extremity; editor, mem. adv. bd. Jour. Am. Podiatric Med. Edn., 1971-75, editor (adv. bd.) Jour. Am. Podiatric Med. Assn., 1971-92; author: The Podiatry Curriculum, 1970; contbr. articles to profl. jours. Bd. dirs. Lyon-Martin Womens Alternative Med. Svcs., San Francisco, 1980-82, Nat. Ctr. for Lesbian Rights, San Francisco, 1989-93. USPHS fellow, 1962-66. Fellow Am. Assn. Podiatric Dermatology, Am. Soc. Podiatric Medicine, Am. Coll. Foot and Ankle Orthopedics and Primary Podiatric Medicine, Nat. Acad. Practice; mem. Am. Podiatric Med. Assn. (editor jour. 1970—). Office: Calif Coll Podiatric Medicine 1835 Ellis St San Francisco CA 94115

HOFFMAN, BARBARA A., state legislator; b. Balt., Mar. 8, 1940; d. Sidney Wolf and Eve (Simonoff) Marks; m. Donald Edwin Hoffman, 1960; children: Alan Samuel, Michael Stuart, Carolyn Mara. B.S., Towson State U., 1960; M.A., Johns Hopkins U., 1966. Secondary sch. tchr., Balt., 1960-63; supr. student tchrs. Morgan U., Balt., 1968-73; exec. dir. Md. Democratic party, 1979-84; mem. Md. State Senate from 42d Dist., 1983—. Bd. dirs. Kennedy Inst. for Handicapped Children. Co-author: Journeys in English, 1968. Recipient Outstanding Contbns. to Party award Md. Dem. party, 1984. Mem. Md. Assn. Elected Women (exec. bd. 1985), Nat. Order Women Legislators, Balt. Blews Coalition Blacks and Jews, Md. Com. for Children (pres. 1983), Hadassah (group pres. 1980-82). Jewish. Office: Md State Senate State Capitol Annapolis MD 21401 Other: 2905 W Strathmore Ave Baltimore MD 21209-3810*

HOFFMAN, DARLEANE CHRISTIAN, chemistry educator; b. Terril, Iowa, Nov. 8, 1926; d. Carl Benjamin and Elverna (Kuhlman) Christian; m. Marvin Morrison Hoffman, Dec. 26, 1951; children: Maureane R., Daryl K. BS in Chemistry, Iowa State U., 1948, PhD in Nuclear Chemistry, 1951. Chemist Oak Ridge (Tenn.) Nat. Lab., 1952-53; mem. staff radiochemistry group Los Alamos (N.Mex.) Sci. Lab., 1953-71, assoc. leader chemistry-nuclear group, 1971-79, divsn. leader, chem.-nuclear divsn., 1979-82, div. leader isotope and nuclear chem. div., 1982-84; prof. chemistry U. Calif., Berkeley, 1984-91, prof. emerita, 1991-93, prof. grad. sch., 1993—; faculty sr. scientist Lawrence Berkeley (Calif.) Lab., 1984—; dir.'s fellow Los Alamos Nat. Lab., 1990—; dir. G.T. Seaborg Inst. for Transactinium Sci., 1991—; panel leader, speaker Los Alamos Women in Sci., 1975, 79, 82; rschr. Guggenheim Found., 1978-79; mem. subcom. on nuclear and radiochemistry NAS-NRC, 1978-81, chmn. subcom. on nuclear and radiochemistry, 1982-84; titular mem. commn. on radiochem. and nuclear techniques Internat. Union of Pure and Applied Chem., 1983-87, sec., 1985-87, chmn., 1987-91, assoc. mem. 1991-93; mem. com. 2d Internat. Symposium on Nuclear and Radiochemistry, 1988; planning panel Workshop on Tng. Requirements for Chemists in Nuclear Medicine, Nuclear Industry, and Related Fields, 1988, radionuclide migration peer rev. com., Las Vegas, 1986-87, steering com. Advanced Steady State Neutron Source, 1986-90, steering com., panelist Workshop on Opportunities and Challenges in Research with Transplutonium Elements, Washington, 1983; mem. energy rsch. adv. bd. cold fusion panel, Dept. Energy, 1989-90; mem. NAS separations subpanel of separations tech. and transmutation systems panel, 1992-94, NAS-NRC Bd. on Radioactive Waste Mgmt., 1994—; lectr. Japan Soc. Promotion Sci. Contbr. numerous articles in field to profl. jours. Recipient Alumni Citation of Merit Coll. Scis. and Humanities, Iowa State U., 1978, Disting. Achievement award Iowa State U., 1986; Sr. postdoctoral fellow NSF, 1964-65. Fellow Am. Inst. Chemists (pres. N.Mex. chpt. 1976-78), Am. Phys. Soc., AAAS; mem: Am. Chem. Soc. (chmn. nuclear chemistry and technology div. 1978-79, com. in sci. 1986-88, exec. com. div. nuclear chem. and tech. 1987-90, John Dustin Clark award Cen. N.Mex. sect. 1976, Nuclear Chemistry award 1983, Francis P. Garvan-John M. Olin medal 1991), Am. Nuclear Soc. (co-chmn. internat. conf. Methods and Applications of Radioanalytical Chemistry 1987), Norwegian Acad. Arts and Scis, Sigma Xi, Phi Kappa Phi, Iota Sigma Pi (nat. hon.), Pi Mu Epsilon, Sigma Delta Epsilon, Alpha Chi Sigma. Methodist. Home: 2277 Manzanita Dr Oakland CA 94611 Office: Lawrence Berkeley Lab MS70A-3307 NSD Berkeley CA 94720

HOFFMAN, ELIZABETH C., state legislator; b. North Tonawanda, N.Y.; married; 4 children. Real estate broker, 18 yrs.; 1st woman alderman City of North Tonawanda, 2 yrs., 1st woman mayor, 12 yrs.; now mem. N.Y. State Assembly. Trustee YMCA; mem Cardinal O'Hara Adv. Bd.; gen. co-chairperson Mt. St. Mary's 60th ann. fundraising campaign; mem. health edn. adv. coun. North Tonawanda Sch. Dist.; active Grant Sch. PTA, Tonawandas Exchangettes; North Tonawanda and Nigara County campaign dir., chairperson mother's march March of Dimes; elected to state com. March of Dimes; bd. dirs. Niagara County March of Dimes; alt. del. Rep. Nat. Conv., 1984, del., 1988; active Young Reps., North Tonawanda City Rep. Com.; former county committeeman, 8th judicial dist. dir. North Tonawanda. Recipient Mayor of Yr. award Niagara Taxpayers, 1987, Mother of Yr. award March of Dimes. Mem. Zonta Club of the Tonawandas, North Tonawanda Women's Rep. Club, DeGraff Aux., Mt. St. Mary's Alumnae Assn. (past. pres.). Office: NY State Assembly State Capitol Albany NY 12224*

HOFFMAN, GLORIA LEVY, communications executive; b. Norfolk, Va., Feb. 8, 1933; d. Maxwell Lewis and Jessie (Mashbitz) Levy; m. Frank Katz Hoffman (dec.); children: Daniel L., L. Stephen, Victoria Anne, Jonathan M. (dec.). BA in Speech and Radio, U. Wis., 1954. Pres. Creative Concepts in Communications, Ltd., Kansas City, Mo., 1984—, Peoplehood Products, Kansas City, 1987—. Author: I Belong to Me!: A Trip Thru Our Own Feelings, 1984, rev. edit., 1989, (catalog) Peoplehood-by-Mail, 1990; creator: The Super Sluggers, 1989, Captain Slug Slugs Drugs, 1990, Clown Around With Clancy, 1991, Sammy Slugger Slugs Drugs, 1993, rev. edit., 1993, I Slug Drugs apparel and buttons, 1993, Project Play-It-SAFE, 1994. Promotional and pub. relations dir. Menorah Med. Ctr., Trans-Menorahs, Brandeis Books Drives; vol. Nelson Gallery Art, Kansas City Art Inst., Young Woman's Philharmonic, Children's Mercy Hosp. Recipient Commemorative Medal of Honor Hallmark, 1987. Republican. Jewish. Home and Office: 212 E 130th Ter Kansas City MO 64145-1376

HOFFMAN, JANET N., psychic counselor; b. New Somerset, Ohio, Dec. 16, 1936; d. Charles Kennith and Jenny (Douds) Speedy; m. A. William Anderson, May 19, 1956; children: William, Robert, James; m. Sherwin Joseph Hoffman, Nov. 30, 1985. Student, Asbury Coll., 1953-54, Harvard U., 1971. Clk. Higbee Co., Cleve., 1955-56; adminstrv. asst. GE, Cleve., 1956-58, Hardware Mut., Boston, 1958-60; owner, operator Pantry Rest Motel, Toronto, Ohio, 1975-80; pvt. practice psychic counselor Toronto, 1980—; guest talk show Sta. WEIR, Weirton, W.Va., 1980-81, Sta. WLIT, Steubenville, Ohio, 1980-81, Sta. WSTV, 1988-90, 92; lectr. various women's clubs, Steubenville. Home: 1303 N 4th St Toronto OH 43964-1807

HOFFMAN, JEAN, entrepreneur; b. Washington, June 15, 1957; d. Burton and Diane (Thompson) H.; 1 child, Cooper Hoffman Van Vranken. BA, Bowdoin Coll., 1979. Asst. dir./importer svcs. Nat. Coun. for U.S.-China Trade, Washington, 1980-81; mgr. China trade dept. MWM Chem. Corp., N.Y.C., 1982-83; gen. mgr. Far East Zuellig Group N.A., Inc., N.Y.C., 1984-87; pres., CEO and dir. Zeta Pharm., Inc., N.Y.C., 1988-89; prin. Hoffman Pharm. Cons., Brunswick, Maine, 1990-91; pres. Newport Data Assocs., Inc., Brunswick, Maine, 1992—, also dir. Creator/editor software program: DMF Data Search, 1993, Newport DataSearch, 1994, BPD Data Search, 1994. Mem. Richmond (Maine) Comprehensive Planning Com., 1989-91, Richmond Dem. Com., 1989-91; del. Maine Dem. Conv., Presque Isle, 1990. Office: Newport Data Assocs Inc 14 Maine St Ste 207 Brunswick ME 04011-2026

HOFFMAN, JENNIFER ISOBEL, librarian; b. Washington, Sept. 13, 1948; d. Robert Gustavus and Maureen (May) Moll; m. Melvin Jacob Hoffman, Aug. 21, 1971; children: Robert, William. BA in English, SUNY, 1971, MS in Edn., 1973, M in Library Sci., 1978. Librarian Buffalo and Erie County Pub. Libr. Extension Svcs. Br. Libr., 1981-88; librarian Elma Pub. Libr. Buffalo and Erie County Pub. Libr. Contracting Librs., 1988-91; librarian City of Lackawanna Pub. Libr. Buffalo and Erie County Pub. Libr., 1991—. Mem. Am. Library Assn. Democrat. Episcopalian. Office: Lackawanna Pub Libr 560 Ridge Rd Buffalo NY 14218-1320

HOFFMAN, JUDY GREENBLATT, preschool director; b. Chgo., June 12, 1932; d. Edward Abraham and Clara (Morrill) Greenblatt; m. Morton Hoffman, Mar. 16, 1950 (div. Jan. 1983); children: Michael, Alan, Clare. BA summa cum laude, Met. State Coll., Denver, 1972; MA, U. No. Colo., 1976. Cert. tchr., Colo. Pre-sch. dir. B.M.H. Synagogue, Denver, 1968-70, Temple Emanuel, Denver, 1970-85, Congregation Rodef Shalom, Denver, 1985-88; tchr. Denver Pub. Schs., 1988—; bilingual tchr. adults in amnesty edn. Denver Pub. Schs., 1989-90. Author: I Live in Israel, 1979, Joseph and Me, 1980 (Gamoran award), (with others) American Spectrum Single Volume Encyclopedia, 1991. Coordinator Douglas Mountain Therapeutic Riding Ctr. for Handicapped, Golden, Colo., 1985—; dir. Mountain

Ranch Summer Day Camp for Denver Pub. Schs., 1989—. Mem. Nat. Assn. Temple Educators. Democrat.

HOFFMAN, KARLA LEIGH, mathematician; b. Paterson, N.J., Feb. 14, 1948; d. Abe and Bertha (Guthaim) Rakoff; BA, Rutgers, U., 1969; MBA, George Washington U., 1971, DSc in Ops. Research, 1975; m. Allan Stuart Hoffman, Dec. 26, 1971; 1 son, Matthew Douglas. Ops. research analyst IRS, Washington, 1970-72; research asst. George Washington U., 1972-75; asso. professorial lectr., 1978-85; NSF postdoctoral research fellow Nat. Acad. Sci., Washington, 1975-76; mathematician Nat. Bur. Standards, Washington, 1976-84; vis. assoc. prof. ops. research U. Md., spring 1982; assoc. prof. systems engring. dept. George Mason U., 1985-86, assoc. prof. ops. research and applied stats., 1986-89, prof. ops. research, 1990—, disting. prof. 1989; mng. ptnr. Optimization Software Assocs.; cons. to govt. agys., airline, telecom. and def. industries. Recipient Applied Rsch. award Nat. Inst. Stds. and Tech., 1984, Silver medal U.S. Dept. Commerce, 1984. Mem. Ops. Research Soc. Am. (sec.-treas. computer sci. tech. sect. 1979-80, vice chmn. sect. 1981, chmn. sect. 1982, vis. professorial lectr. 1980—, chmn. tech. sect. com. 1983-86, council 1985-88, chmn. Lanchster Prize com. 1989, treas. 1993-94), Inst. Ops. Rsch. and Mgmt. Sci. (treas. 1995—), Math. Programming Soc. (editor newsletter 1979-82, chmn. com. algorithms 1982-85, council 1985-88, exec. com. 1986-88, chmn. mem. com. 1988-89). Contbr. articles to profl. jours.; assoc. editor Internat. Abstracts of Ops. Research, The Math. Programming Jour., Series B, The Ops. Research Soc. Jour. on Computing, Jour. Computational Optimization and Applications. Home: 6921 Clifton Rd Clifton VA 22024-1525

HOFFMAN, KATHERINE ANN, fine arts educator; b. Boston, June 14, 1947; divorced; children: Kristen Gresh, Geoffrey Gresh, Ashley Gresh. BA, Smith Coll., 1969; MA, Bank St. Coll., 1972; PhD, NYU, 1976. Asst. prof. U. S.C., Columbia, 1976-79; from asst. to assoc. prof. Bradford (Mass.) Coll., 1979-90; assoc. prof., chair fine arts St. Anselm Coll., Manchester, N.H., 1990—; trustee Sharon (N.H.) Art Ctr., 1993—. Author: An Enduring Spirit: The Art of Georgia O'Keeffe, 1984, Explorations: The Visual Arts Since 1945, 1991; editor: Collage: Critical Views, 1989. Active Boston Mus. Fine Arts. NEH fellow, 1986, 87. Mem. Coll. Art Assn. Office: St Anselm Coll Fine Arts Dept Box 1708 100 Saint Anselms Dr Manchester NH 03102-1310

HOFFMAN, KATHERINE BALLARD (KOBBY HOFFMAN), planner, distributor; b. Princeton, N.J., July 16, 1954; d. John and June (Crehore) Gulick; m. Michael C. Hoffman, Dec. 27, 1981. BA in Econs., St. Lawrence U., Canton, N.Y., 1972-76; MP in City Planning, U. Va., 1986-88. Acct. TUMAC Industries, Colorado Springs, Colo., 1978-79; office mgr. Mid-States Electric Supply, Colorado Springs, 1980, Abbott Kagan, M.D., P.C., Colorado Springs, 1981-83; acctg. supr. Health Svcs. Found., Charlottesville, Va., 1983-86; project mgr. Republic Capital, Charlottesville, 1987; assoc. Inst. for Environ. Negotiation, U. Va., Charlottesville, 1988-90; sr. planner Thomas Jefferson Planning Dist., Charlottesville, 1990—; pres., treas. Criterion Assocs., Charlottesville, 1989—; pres. Plan & Action Assocs., Charlottesville, 1992—. Rep., mem. adv. coun. to sch. bd. Creative Learning After Sch. and in the Summer, Leadership Charlottesville, Charlottesville-Albemarle C. of C., 1992—. Urban Land Inst. scholar, 1987. Mem. Am. Planning Assn. (Va. Outstanding Student 1988), NOW (treas., v.p., pres. Charlottesville chpt.). Office: Thomas Jefferson Planning Dist 413 E Market St Ste 102 Charlottesville VA 22902

HOFFMAN, LINDA R., social services administrator; b. New Haven, Conn., July 23, 1940; d. Bernard Harry and Sylvia (Paul) Rosenfield; m. Peter A. Hoffman, Sept. 25, 1965; 1 child, Tracie Lee. BA, Russell Sage Coll., 1962; MSW, Columbia U., 1968. Cert. social worker, N.Y. Case worker Conn. Dept. Welfare, New Haven, 1962-63; case worker N.Y.C. Bur. Child Welfare, 1963-65, supr., 1965-66; asst. to commr. program planning N.Y.C. Dept. Social Svcs., 1968-70; spl. asst. to commr. N.Y.C. Spl. Svcs. for Children, 1972-79; pres. N.Y. Found. Sr. Citizens, N.Y.C., 1979—; cons. USIA, Teheran, Iran, summer 1975; adj. prof., mem. dean's adv. coun. Columbia Sch. Social Work. Mem. Cmty. Bd. # 8, N.Y.C., 1981—, legis. com. N.Y.C. Commn. Status of Women, 1981—; mem. exec. com. policy on aging N.Y. Cmty. Trust's Ctr.; mem. pub. programs and policy com. United Jewish Appeal Fedn. N.Y., N.Y.C., 1982—, chmn. subcom. Fed. Govt. Rels., 1994; mem. YWCA/N.Y.C. Acad. Women Achievers, 1994. Recipient Presdl. Recognition award for Community Svc., 1983, East Manhattan C. of C. award for Disting. Civic Svc., 1990. Mem. Nat. Assn. Social Workers (cert.). Office: NY Found Sr Citizens 150 Nassau St Ste 1730 New York NY 10038-1516

HOFFMAN, M. KATHY, graphic designer, packaging designer; b. Sidney, Nebr., Aug. 30, 1956; d. Norman and Irline (Dillon) Barnica; m. Jeffrey W. Hoffman, Apr. 16, 1988. BA, U. Nebr., Kearney, 1978, BFA, 1984, MA, 1987. Product quality assurance Baldwin Filters, Kearney, Nebr., 1978-88, product technician, 1988-90, product devel. technician, 1990-92, product identification coord., 1992—, packaging and graphics designer, 1993—. Mem. Inst. Packaging Profls., Assn. Corel Artists and Designers, Women in Packaging. Office: Baldwin Filters 4400 Highway 30 E Kearney NE 68847-9776

HOFFMAN, MARIANNE MACINA, non-profit organization administrator; b. N.Y.C., Apr. 29, 1951; d. Vito William Jr. and Frances (Florio) Macina; m. Neil Richard Hoffman. BS in Journalism, U. Fla., 1973; postgrad., U. London, 1973; AA in Advt. ARt, Inst. Atlanta, 1975. Writer Clearwater (Fla.) Sun, 1965-69; pub. rels., graphics specialist Hensley-Schmidt Engts., Atlanta, 1975-76; creative dir. Mackey Green & Assocs., Atlanta, 1976; assoc. editor So. Banker Mag., Atlanta, 1977-78; managing editor Pension World Mag., Atlanta, 1978-79; communications writer No. States Power Co., Mpls., 1979-80; advt. dir. Carlton Celebrity Dinner Theater, Bloomington, Minn., 1980-82; coord., mktg. svcs. St. Paul Cos. Inc., 1982-87; regional mgr. We. Ins. Info. Svc., Portland, Oreg., 1987—; bd. dirs. Ins. Edn. Found. Oreg., Portland, 1989—. Exec. prodr.: (consumer videos) Preventing Home Burglary, 1988 (Gold medal 1990), Don't Give a Thief a Free Ride: Preventing Auto Theft, 1990, Bon Voyage: Tips for a Safe Vacation, 1993. Mem. task force Oreg. Juvenile Firesetter Edn., Salem, 1988-92; mem. Oreg. Coun. Against Arson, 1988—, v.p., 1994, 95; mem. exec. bd. Crime Prevention Assn. Oreg., 1992-94, treas., 1995-96; bd. dirs. Oreg. Traffic Safety NOW, 1988-91. Recipient Merit award Ins. Info. Inst., N.Y.C., 1989, Commendation award Oreg. Coun. Against Arson, 1989, Crime Prevention award Crime Prevention Assn. Oreg., 1990, Media award, 1989. Mem. Soc. Chartered Property Casualty Underwriters (Oreg. chpt. bd. dirs. 1990-92, new designee rep. we. region 1989-90, cert.). Republican. Roman Catholic. Office: We Ins Info Svc 11855 SW Ridgecrest Dr # 107 Beaverton OR 97008

HOFFMAN, MARIE THERESE, psychologist; b. Belmar, N.J., Dec. 29, 1953; d. Fred and Rosina (Hasboun) Massabni; m. Lowell William Hoffman, June 14, 1975; children: Robert Lowell, Karissa Marie. BA, Bob Jones U., 1974; MS, Villanova U., 1985; PhD, Union Inst., 1989. Lic. psychologist, Pa. Psychodrama intern Horsham (Pa.) Hosp., 1983-84; psychology intern Lenape Valley Found., Chalfont, Pa., 1984-85, Profl. Counseling Ctr., Allentown, Ft. Washington, Pa., 1985-87; dir. psychodrama Northwestern Inst. Psychiatry, Ft. Washington, 1986-87; psychodrama intern Philhaven Hosp., Lebanon, Pa., 1988-89; psychologist, co-dir. Brookhaven Ctr. for Counseling and Devel., Ft. Washington, 1988—; lectr. Lehigh County Community Coll., 1992. Dems. and Reps. for Continued Good Govt., Weisenberg Twp., Pa., 1989-91. Mem. APA, Pa. Psychol. Assn., Phi Kappa Phi, Kappa Delta Pi. Presbyterian. Home: 8624 Valley Rd Fogelsville PA 18051-2234 Office: Brookhaven Ctr Counseling PO Box 425 Fogelsville PA 18051-0425

HOFFMAN, MARY CATHERINE, nurse anesthetist; b. Winamac, Ind., July 14, 1923; d. Harmon William Whitney and Dessie Maude (Neely) H.; R.N., Methodist Hosp., Indpls., 1945; cert. obstet. analgesia and anesthesia, Johns Hopkins Hosp., 1949, grad. U. Hosp. of Cleve. Sch. Anesthesia, 1952; Staff nurse Meth. Hosp., 1945-49; research asst., then staff anesthetist Johns Hopkins Hosp., 1949-62; staff anesthetist Meth. Hosp., 1962-64, U. Chgo. Hosps., 1964-66; chief nurse anesthetist Paris (Ill.) Community Hosp., 1966-80; staff anesthetist Hendricks County Hosp., Danville, Ind., Ball Meml. Hosp., Muncie, Ind., 1981-86; instr.-trainer CPR, 1975-81; mem. Terr. 08 CPR Coordinating Com., 1975-80. Mem. Am. Assn. Nurse Anesthetists, Am. Heart Assn., Ind. Fedn. Bus. and Profl. Women's Clubs (Ill. dist. chmn. 1977-78, state found. chmn. 1978-79; found. award 1979). Republican. Presbyterian. Home: 1700 N Maddox Dr Muncie IN 47304-2674

HOFFMAN, MERLE HOLLY, political activist, social psychologist, author; b. Phila., Mar. 6, 1946; d. Jack Rheins and Ruth (Dubow) H.; m. Martin Gold, June 30, 1979. BA magna cum laude in Psychology, Queens Coll., 1972; postgrad., CUNY, 1972-75. Founder, pres. Choices Women's Med. Ctr., Forest Hills, N.Y., 1971—; family planning cons. Health Ins. Plan, N.Y.C., 1973—; founder, pres. Ctr. for Comprehensive Breast Svcs., N.Y.C., 1979—, Merle Hoffman Enterprises, N.Y.C., 1986—; speaker, debator on women's rights and polit. issues; founder, pres. Nat. Liberty Com., 1981. Cons. editor Female Health Topics and Diagnostic Reporter, 1979-81; editor, pub. ednl. jour. On The Issues; contbr. articles in field to various publs.; producer documentary film Abortion A Different Light; founder N.Y. Pro-Choice Coalition; host cable TV series MH: On the Issues, 1986. Mem. Nat. Assn. Abortion Facilities (co-founder, pres. 1976-77), Nat. Abortion Fedn. (co-founder, sec. 1977-78), Phi Beta Kappa. Office: Choices Women's Med Ctr Inc 9777 Queens Blvd Flushing NY 11374-3317

HOFFMAN, NANCY YANES, editor, health care consultant, author, lecturer; b. Boston, July 2, 1929; d. William Phillip and Edith Sara (Bernstein) Yanes; m. Marvin J. Hoffman, Feb. 15, 1948; children: William Yanes, Holly Hoffman Brookstein, Jennifer Yanes. Student, Conn. Coll., 1946-48; BS with high distinction, U. Rochester, 1950, MS, 1968. Author, lectr., editor Rochester, 1970—; asst. prof. English St. John Fisher Coll., Rochester, N.Y., 1969-79; assoc. prof. English St. John Fisher Coll., Rochester, 1979-86; dir. Am. Guardian Life Ins. Co., Jenkintown, Pa., 1979-85; pub. relations con. Ochsner Med. Insts., New Orleans, 1978-82; pres. NYH Healthcare Assocs., Rochester, 1985—; Spl. clin. investigator Walter Reed Army Med. Ctr., Washington, 1983-85; vis. prof of med. humanities, U. New England Med. Sch., 1985; mem. breast cancer detection awareness task force Am. Cancer Soc., Syracuse, N.Y., 1986—. Author: Change of Heart: The Bypass Experience, 1985; co-author: Breast Cancer: A Practical Guide to Diagnosis, 1994; columnist Jour. AMA, 1972-85; contbr. numerous articles to profl. and popular jours., 1970—. Named Instr. of Excellence N.Y. State English Council, 1982; recipient scholarship Nat. Endowment for Humanities, 1978. Mem. Am. Med. Writers Assn., Nat. Assn. of Sci. Writers, Am. Soc. Journalists and Authors, Authors Guid, N.Y. Acad. Scis., Am. Diabetes Assn. (profl. sect.), Council of Am. Diabetes, Soc. of Diabetes Educators, AAAS, Soc. for Tech. Communication, Women in Communications, Modern Lang. Assn., Am. Heart Assn., Nat. Council Tchrs. English, Am. Culture Assn. Home and Office: 16 San Rafael Dr Rochester NY 14618-3702

HOFFMAN, PAMELA BETH, geriatrician; b. Grand Forks, N.D., Oct. 31, 1951; d. Glenn Lyle Sr. and Carolyn Elise (Wilson) H. AB, Mt. Holyoke Coll., 1973; MD, U. Va., 1978. Diplomate Am. Bd. Internal Medicine, Am. Bd. Geriatrics. Intern St. Vincent's Med. Ctr., Bridgeport, Conn., 1978-79, resident in internal medicine, 1979-81, med. dir. outreach, 1985—, med. dir. day program, 1987—, chief divsn. geriatrics, 1989—; fellow in geriatric medicine Jewish Inst. for Geriatric Care, New Hyde Park, N.Y., 1981-83, physician-in-charge of med. edn., 1983-85; attending physician Jewish Home for the Elderly, Fairfield, Conn., 1990—; mem. adv. com. S.W. Area Agy. on Aging, Norwalk, Conn., 1994—; bd. dirs. VNS of Conn., Inc., Bridgeport. Trustee Golden Hill United Meth. Ch., Bridgeport, 1989—; mem. profl. adv. bd. MADD, Bridgeport, 1993—, Olsen-Kimberly Quality Care, Bridgeport, 1987—. Recipient Mary Lyon award Mt. Holyoke Coll., 1991, Outstanding Achievement award Conn. Home Care Assn., 1994; NCOA/Travelers geriatrics fellow for med. students, Washington, 1984-92. Mem. ACP, Greater Bridgeport Med. Assn. (sec.-treas. 1993—, Co-Physician of Yr. 1994), Am. Geriatrics Soc., Fairfield County Med. Assn. (com. for geriatric affairs 1990—), Conn. State Med. Soc. (com. on medicine and geriatrics 1992—), Am. Acad. Home Care Physicians (Vincentian award St. Vincent Coll. Nursing 1994). Office: St Vincents Med Ctr Outreach 2800 Main St Bridgeport CT 06606

HOFFMAN, PATRICIA ANN, education educator, consultant; b. Evanston, Ill., May 29, 1952; d. Herman Frank and Evelyn Francis (Lockman) H. BA in Edn., Concordia U., 1976, MA in Edn., 1983; postgrad., U. Wis. Cert. tchr. age 0-grade 8, Wis., cert. tchr. K-8 and 9 social scis., Mich. Tchr. gr. 2, 5 Peace Luth., Saginaw, Mich., 1976-80; tchr. gr. 2, 3 St. John Luth., Mt. Prospect, Ill., 1980-81; tchr. gr. 1, 2, 3 Child of Christ Luth., Hartland, Mich., 1981-86; tchr. gr. 1 Christ Luth., San Pedro, Calif., 1986-87; asst. prof., chair early childhood edn. Concordia U., Wis., 1989-93; asst. prof., dir. early childhood edn. Concordia U., Irvine, Calif., 1993—; curriculum con. Concordia Pub. House, St. Louis, 1990-93; mem. bd. edn. Prince of Peace Ch., Menomonee Falls, Wis., 1991-93; spkr. in field; presenter workshops literacy, reading, 1989-92. Active Child Abuse Task Force, Milw., 1991-93. Mem. Luth. Edn. Assn. (sec./treas. 1985-89, advisor 1989—, convocation planning com. and mgmt. team 1987-93), Nat. Assn. for Edn. of Young Children, Nat. Assn. Early Childhood Tchr. Educators, Internat. Reading Assn. Mem. Lutheran Ch.-Mo. Synod. Home: 77 Foxhollow Irvine CA 92714 Office: Concordia U 1530 Concordia W Irvine CA 92715

HOFFMAN, SHARON LYNN, research editor; b. Chgo.; d. David P. and Florence (Soifer) Seaman; m. Jerry Irwin Hoffman, Aug. 25, 1963; children: Steven Abram, Rachel Irene. BA, Ind. U., 1961; M Adult Edn., Nat. Louis Univ., 1992. High sch. English tchr. Chgo. Pub. Schs., 1961-64; tchr. Dept. of Def. Schs., Braconne, France, 1964-66; tchr. ESL Russian Inst., Garmisch, Fed. Republic Germany, 1966, 67; tchr. adult edn. Monterey Peninsula Unified Schs., Ft. Ord, Calif., 1977-79; tchr. ESL MAECOM, Monmouth County, N.J., 1979-80; lectr., tchr. adult edn. Truman Coll./Temple Shalom, Chgo.; tchr. homebound Fairfax County Pub. Schs., Fairfax, Va., 1976; entry operator Standard Rate & Data, Wilmette, Ill., 1986-87; rsch. editor, spl. projects editor Marquis Who's Who, Wilmette, 1987-92; mem. adj. faculty Nat. Louis U., Evanston, Ill., 1993—; tutor coord., learning specialist Ctr. for Acad. Devel. Nat.-Lewis U., 1993—; pres. Cultural Transitions, Highland Park, Ill., 1992—. Mem. AAUW, LWV, ASTD, TESOL, Nat. Coun. Tchrs. English, Chgo. Drama League. Home and Office: 2270 Highmoor Rd Highland Park IL 60035-1702

HOFFMAN, SUE ELLEN, elementary education educator; b. Dayton, Ohio, Aug. 23, 1945; d. Cyril Vernon and Sarah Ellen (Sherer) Stephan; m. Lawrence Wayne Hoffman, Oct. 28, 1967. BS in Edn., U. Dayton, 1967; postgrad., Loyolla Coll., 1977, Ea. Mich. U., 1980; MEd, Wright State U., 1988. Cert. reading specialist and elem. tchr., Ohio. 5th grade tchr. St. Anthony Sch., Dayton, Ohio, 1967-68, West Huntsville (Ala.) Elem. Sch., 1968-71; 6th grade tchr. Ranchland Hills Pub. Sch., El Paso, Tex., 1973-74; 3rd grade tchr. Emerson Pub. Sch., Westerville, Ohio, 1976, St. Joan of Arc Sch., Aberdeen, Md., 1976-78, Our Lady of Good Counsel, Plymouth, Mich., 1979-80; 5th grade tchr. St. Helen Sch., Dayton, 1980—. Selected for membership Kappa Delta Pi, 1988. Mem. Internat. Reading Assn., Ohio Internat. Reading Assn., Dayton Area Internat. Reading Assn., Nat. Cath. Edn. Assn. Roman Catholic. Home: 2174 Green Springs Dr Kettering OH 45440-1120 Office: St Helen Sch 5086 Burkhardt Rd Dayton OH 45431-2000

HOFFMAN, SUSAN E. SLADEN, medical nurse, case manager; b. Washington, Mar. 3, 1949; d. Burt Deale and Lisette B. (Ridgeway) Sladen; m. Ned Mason Hoffman, June 18, 1973. AA, Montgomery Coll., Takoma Park, Md., 1978; BA, U. Md., 1971; postgrad., Fla. Internat. U., Miami. RN, Fla.; CRRN; cert. rehab. provider, case mgr. Homecare supr., dir. in-svc. edn., dir. health care svcs. Med. Pers. Pool, Miami; rehab. specialist Comprehensive Rehab. Assocs., Inc., Ft. Lauderdale, Fla.; ind. cons. Pompano Beach, Fla. Contbr. articles to newsletter. Mem. Am. Rehab. Nurses Assn., Broward Assn. Rehab. Nurses, Fla. Assn. Rehab. Nurses, Case Mgmt. Assn. (nat./state liaison), U. Md. Alumni Assn., Alpha Omicron Pi. Home: 239 SE 3rd Ter Pompano Beach FL 33060-7130

HOFFMAN, SUSAN PHYLLIS, elementary school educator; b. Shamokin, Pa., July 7, 1952; d. Peter Joseph and Harriet A. (Domaleski) Krull; m. David A. Hoffman, Nov. 22, 1975; 1 child, Elizabeth. BS, Bloomsburg U., 1974, postgrad., 1974-76. Substitute tchr. Shamokin (Pa.) Elem. Ctr., 1974-85; tchr. Queen of Peace Sch., Shamokin, 1985—; tutor-on-call Lock Haven U. pilot program, 1978; tchr. Act 89 Ctr. Susquehanna Intermediate Unit, 1979-80; dir. Learn to Swim program Shamokin/Coal Twp., 1980—; head swim varsity coach Shamokin Area High Sch., 1984—. Sec. Shamokin/Mt. Carmel ARC, 1984—; bd. dirs. YWCA, Shamokin, 1985—. Mem. AAUW (Anthracite chpt.), Delta Kappa Gamma. Republican. Roman Catholic.

HOFFMAN, VALERIE JANE, lawyer; b. Lowville, N.Y., Oct. 27, 1953; d. Russell Francis and Jane Marie (Fowler) H. Student, U. Edinburgh, Scotland, 1973-74; BA summa cum laude, Union Coll., 1975; JD, Boston Coll., 1978. Bar: Ill. 1978, U.S. Dist. Ct. (no. dist.) Ill. 1978, U.S. Ct. Appeals (3rd cir.) 1981, U.S. Ct. Appeals (7th cir.) 1983. Assoc. Seyfarth, Shaw, Fairweather & Geraldson, Chgo., 1978-87, ptnr., 1987—; adj. prof. Columbia Coll., 1985. Contbr. articles to legal publs. Dir. Remains Theatre, Chgo., 1981—, pres., 1991-93, v.p., 1991—; dir. The Nat. Conf., Chgo. Region, 1993—. Mem. ABA, Chgo. Bar Assn., Law Club Chgo., Chgo. Yacht Club, Univ. Club Chgo. (bd. dirs. 1984-87), Phi Beta Kappa. Office: Seyfarth Shaw Et Al 55 E Monroe St Ste 4400 Chicago IL 60603-5803

HOFFMANN, CAROL TOMB, computer systems analyst, real estate developer; b. Balt., Nov. 3, 1952; d. Richard John and Doris Elaine (Shoemaker) Tomb; m. Michael R. Hoffmann, July 29, 1973; children: Kurt M., Kristen E., Kevin R. Student, Drake U., 1972; AS, Harcum Jr. Coll., 1973; cert., Inst. Cert. Fin. Planners, 1988. Various retailing positions N.Y. and Iowa, 1973-76; store opening area supr. Brandeis, Des Moines, 1976-77, Peterson, Harned Von Maur, Des Moines, 1977-78; adminstrv. asst. Clk. Iowa Supreme Ct., Des Moines, 1978-79; pres. Nouveau Riche, Ltd., Des Moines, 1986—, Lake Country Devel., Inc., Des Moines, 1994—. Mem. Blank Park Zoo, Des Moines Art Ctr., Des Moines Sci. Ctr., Friends Iowa Pub. TV. Mem. NRA. Office: Nouveau Riche Ltd Breakwater Bldg 3708 75th St Des Moines IA 50322

HOFFMANN, JOAN CAROL, retired academic dean; b. Cedarburg, Wis., Feb. 20, 1934; d. Frank Ernst and Althea Wilhelmina (Behm) H. Nursing diploma Michael Reese Hosp., 1955; BS in Zoology, U. Wis., Madison, 1959; PhD in Physiology, U. Ill., Chgo., 1965. RN, Wis., Mass., Ariz. Sci. instr. Michael Reese Hosp., Chgo., 1959-62; USPHS trainee U. Ill., Chgo., 1962-64; NSF postdoctoral fellow Coll. de France, Paris, 1964-65; asst. prof. U. Rochester, N.Y., 1965-70; assoc. prof., prof. U. Hawaii, Honolulu, 1970-83; dean of students U. Mass. Med. Sch., Worcester, 1983-94; ret., 1994; chmn. anatomy U. Hawaii, 1973-80. Contbr. articles to sci. jours. NIH rsch. grantee, 1966-75. Mem. Endocrine Soc., Soc. for Study of Reprodn., Am. Physiol. Soc., Am. Assn. Anatomists, Women in Endocrinology (sec. 1978-79, pres. 1987-88), Am. Coun. Edn. (bd.dirs., Mass. chpt., network identification program), Phi Beta Kappa, Sigma Xi. Avocations: gardening, needlework, wood turning, reading. Home: 30 Homestead Rd Sedona AZ 86336-3236

HOFFMANN, KATHRYN ANN, humanities educator; b. Rockville Centre, N.Y., Oct. 26, 1954; d. Manfred and Catherine (Nanko) H.; m. Brook Ellis, Nov. 25, 1987. BA summa cum laude, SUNY Buffalo, 1975; MA, The Johns Hopkins U., 1979, PhD, 1981. Asst. prof. French lit. and lang. U. Wis.-Madison, 1981-88, U. Hawaii-Manoa, Honolulu, 1992—; mng. ptnr. Yuval Design Partnership, Chgo., 1988-92. Assoc. editor Substance, 1982-87; contbr. articles to profl. jours.; designer clothing accessories. Grantee NEH, 1993, 95; fellow Inst. Rsch. in Humanities, 1984-85, Am. Coun. Learned Socs., 1984-85. Mem. MLA, Hawaii Assn. Lang. Tchrs., N.Am. Soc. for 17th Century French Literature, S.E. Am. Soc. for 17th Century Studies, Soc. for Interdisciplinary Study of Social Imagery, Phi Beta Kappa. Home: 2640 Dole St Apt C-6 Honolulu HI 96822-2307 Office: U Hawaii Manoa Dept European Languages & Lit 1890 E West Rd # 483 Honolulu HI 96822-2318

HOFFMANN, MELANE KINNEY, marketing and public relations executive, writer; b. Baton Rouge, Jan. 25, 1956; d. Kenneth Lee and Louise (Walker) Kinney; m. R. Thomas Hoffmann, Oct. 10, 1981; children: Robert James II, Halloran Kinney. BA, Am. U., 1977. Gen. mgr. Dance Project, Inc., Washington, 1979-81; account exec. J. Walter Thompson Advt., Washington, 1981-84; v.p., account supr. Ketchum Advt., Washington, 1984-88, Demaine Vickers Advt., Alexandria, Va., 1988-89; sr. counsel Porter/Novelli Pub. Rels., Washington, 1989—. Dir. Resolve, Washington, 1992-93; bd. dirs. nat. capital area YWCA, Washington, 1980-82. Mem. Am. Mktg. Assn. (mem. program com. 1990-92, co-chair), Ad Club Washington (mem. membership com. 1985-90, Addy award 1987). Presbyterian. Office: Poter/Novelli 1120 Connecticut Ave NW Washington DC 20036

HOFFMANN, NANCY-LORRAINE, state legislator; b. Needham, Mass., Sept. 22, 1947; m. Mark Hoffmann, 1971; children: Eva, Anna, Gustav. B.A., Syracuse U.; M.S., U. Md. Former polit. organizer, Tenn., Miss., city councilor Syracuse, N.Y., 1980-84; mem. N.Y. State Senate from 48th Dist., 1984—, mem. agr., crime and correction, fin., environ. conservation, local govt., tourism, recreation and sports coms. Mem. Gov.'s Council on Fiscal and Econ. Priorities. Democrat. Presbyterian. Home: PO Box 268 Syracuse NY 13214-0268 Office: NY State Senate State Capital Albany NY 12224*

HOFFMEISTER, ANN ELIZABETH, elementary education educator; b. Manitowoc, Wis., Mar. 27, 1957; d. William Anthony and Shirley Mary (Remiker) Gigure; m. Randal Thomas Hoffmeister, Apr. 3, 1982. BS in Spl. Edn., U. Wis., Eau Claire, 1979; MS in Curriculum and Instrn., U. Wis., Madison, 1986, MS in Ednl. Psychology, Gifted Edn., 1992. Cert. tchr., Wis.; lic. reading tchr., reading specialist. Tchr. Verona (Wis.) Area Schs., 1979—, computer coord., 1985-88, learning resource and reading coord., 1990—; whole lang. instr. U. Wis., Platteville, 1992—; Action Rsch. site coord. Verona (Wis.) Area Schs., 1994; cons. Wis. Writing Project, Madison, 1983-90; grad. level cons. U. Wis., Oshkosh, 1993, 94. Co-author: Building Self Esteem Through Writing, 1983. Mem. Verona Jaycees, 1987-92. Grantee Wis. Arts Bd., 1994. Mem. ASCD, Wis. Coun. for Gifted/Talented, Wis. State Reading Assn. (Pat Bricker Meml. Rsch. award 1992, 93, 94), Wis. Edn. Assn., So. Wis. Edn. Insvc. Orgn., Internat. Reading Assn., Verona Edn. Assn. (treas. 1983-86). Office: Sugar Creek Elem Sch 420 Church Ave Verona WI 53593-1800

HOFFMEISTER, JANA MARIE, cardiologist. MD, SUNY Upstate Med. Ctr., Syracuse, 1976. Diplomate Am. Bd. Internal Medicine, Am. Bd. Cardiovascular Diseases. Intern Albany (N.Y.) Med. Ctr., 1976-78, resident, 1978-80, fellow div. cardiology, 1981-83; fellow div. cardiology Emory U., Atlanta, 1984; fellow coronary angioplasty and interventional cardiology Emory U. Hosp., 1985-86; presenter numerous cardiology confs. Contbr. numerous articles to profl. jours. Mem. AMA, Cardiac Soc. Upstate N.Y., N.Y. State Soc. Internal Medicine, Am. Soc. Cardiovascular Intervention, Am. Coll. Physicians. Home: 7 Reddy Ln Albany NY 12211-1697

HOFFNER, MARILYN, university administrator; b. N.Y.C., Nov. 16, 1929; d. Daniel and Elsie (Schulz) H.; m. Albert Greenberg, May 29, 1949; children: Doren Roe, Peter Cooper. BFA, Cooper Union. Art dir. Printers' Ink mag., N.Y.C., 1953-63; art dir. Print mag., N.Y.C., 1960-62; corp. art dir. Vision, Inc., Latin Am., 1963-75; dir. alumni rels. and devel. Cooper Union, 1975—. Bd. dirs. Art Dirs. Club N.Y., 1973-75, 79-82, exec. sec., 1973-75, exec. treas., 1979-82; mem. Citizens Adv. Cultural Arts Com. Dutchess County, 1978-80. Named Alumnus of Yr., Cooper Union, 1968; recipient Gold medal Art Dirs. Club, 1979. Mem. Cooper Union Alumni Assn. (editor-in-chief 1971-74, 1st v.p. 1974-75), Council Advancement and Support of Edn., Type Dirs. Club (numerous awards), Nat. Arts Club (exhbn. com.). Contbg. editor Print mag., 1960-62, Art Direction, 1959-64, Graphis mag., 1959-82; designer mags., advt., books, exhbns. Home: 51 Fifth Ave New York NY 10003-4320 Office: 30 Cooper Sq New York NY 10003-7120

HOFFNUNG, AUDREY SONIA, speech and language pathologist, educator; b. N.Y.C., Mar. 15, 1928; d. Nathan and Gussie (Karp) Smith; BA cum laude, Bklyn. Coll., 1949; MA, Columbia U., 1950; PhD, City U. N.Y., 1974. Cert. and lic. speech pathologist, N.Y.; m. Joseph Hoffnung, Nov. 26, 1950; children: Bonnie Fern, Tami Lynn. Rehab. therapist Ridgewood Cerebral Palsy Center, 1949-50; dir. speech therapy Kingsbrook Med. Center, Bklyn., 1950-55; therapist and cons. Morris J. Solomon Clinic, Bklyn., 1956-58; therapist Speech and Hearing Center Bklyn. Coll., 1958-62, 63-64; pvt. practice speech therapy Hewlett (N.Y.) Med. Center, 1961-63; pvt. practice speech therapy, Oceanside, N.Y., 1964-71; cons. on staff for aphasic patients

Phys. Medicine and Rehab. Center, South Nassau Communities Hosp., 1964-65; part-time lectr. Speech and Hearing Center, Queens (N.Y.) Coll., 1970-72; adj. lectr. dept. speech Bklyn. Coll., 1973-74, asst. prof. speech and lang. pathology, 1974-77; asst. prof. dept. speech communication and theatre St. John's U., Jamaica, N.Y., 1977-80, assoc. prof., 1980-91, prof., 1991—, chair, 1992—; guest lectr. N.Y. Orton Soc., 1979, Brookdale Med. Center, 1978; mem. profl. adv. bd. Vis. Home Health Services of Nassau County, 1973—. Author: (with Valletutti and McKnight) Facilitating communication in young children with handicapping conditions. Mem. Am. Speech-Lang.-Hearing Assn., N.Y.C. Speech, Hearing and Lang. Assn., N.Y. State Speech Lang. and Hearing Assn. (chairperson student activities 1978-79), L.I. Speech, Lang. and Hearing Assn., Nat. Student Speech-Lang.-Hearing Assn. (hon. advisor 1988), Aphasia Study Group of N.Y.C., N.Y. Acad. Scis. Contbr. articles on speech pathology to profl. jours. Home: 3282 Woodward St Oceanside NY 11572-4527 Office: St John's U Dept Speech Comm Scis and Theatre 800 Utopia Pkwy Jamaica NY 11439

HOFMAN, ELAINE D., state legislator; b. Sacramento, Sept. 20, 1937; d. Willard Davis and Venna (Gray) Smart; m. Cornelius Adrianus Hofman, Dec. 14, 1956; children: Catharina, John, Casie, Cornelius. BA, Idaho State U., 1974. Tchr. music edn. Sch. Dist. 25, Pocatello, Idaho, 1977-84; spl. asst. to Gov. Evans State of Idaho, Pocatello, 1984-87; field rep. to Congressman Stallings 2d Dist. Congressional Office, Pocatello, 1987-89; mem. Idaho Ho. of Reps., Pocatello, 1990—. Recipient Elect Lady award Lambda Delta Sigma, 1991; named Idaho Mother of Yr., Am. Mother's Assn., 1992, S.E. Idaho Family of the Yr., 1980. Democrat. Mem. Ch. of Jesus Christ of Latter-day Saints. Home: 216 S 16th Ave Pocatello ID 83201-4003*

HOFMANN, ADELE DELLENBAUGH, pediatrician; b. Boston, Oct. 12, 1926; d. Frederick Samuel and Anne Celestine (Goddard) Dellenbaugh; m. Frederick G. Hofmann, July 26, 1957 (div. 1982); children: Peter, Anne. BA, Smith Coll., 1948; MD, U. Rochester, 1952. Diplomate Am. Bd. Pediatrics. Intern U. Minn. Hosp., Mpls., 1952-53; resident in pediatrics Babies' Hosp., N.Y.C., 1953-55; Nat. Found. fellow Presbyn. Hosp., N.Y.C., 1955-57; chief ambulatory pediatrics St. Luke's Hosp., N.Y.C., 1957-63; assoc. dir. adolescent medicine Beth Israel Hosp., N.Y.C., 1963-70; dir. adolescent medicine NYU Med. Ctr./Bellevue Hosp., N.Y.C., 1970-82; dir. student health UCLA, 1983; med. dir. ambulatory pediatrics Children's Hosp. Orange County, Orange, Calif., 1984-90; dir. adolescent medicine U. Calif.-Irvine, Orange, 1990—, Health Net disting. lectr., 1993; cons. WHO, 1976-84; bd. dirs. Huntington Beach (Calif.) Community Clinic, others; HealthNet Disting. lectr. U. Calif., 1993. Author: The Hospitalized Adolescent, 1976 (Am. Nurses Assn. award 1977), Consent and Confidentiality in Child and Adolescent Health Care, 1984; author, editor: Adolescent Medicine, 1986, 2d edit., 1989 (Am. Coll. Internal Medicine award 1987). Recipient recognition award CAFAM, Bogota, Colombia, 1989, Collegio de Medicos, Venezuela, 1988, others. Fellow Am. Acad. Pediatrics (chair sect. adolescent health 1978-79; sect. award in adolescent health 1984), Soc. Adolescent Medicine (pres. 1976-77; disting. svc. award 1981); mem. Western Soc. Pediatric Rsch., Internat. Soc. Adolescent Medicine. Democrat. Home: 1551 Tahiti Ave Laguna Beach CA 92651 Office: Dept Pediatrics Univ Calif Irvine Med Ctr 101 The City Dr S Orange CA 92668-3298

HOFSTETTER, ELEANORE OTTILIA, librarian; b. Camden, N.J., May 16, 1939; d. George and Anna O. (Kneissl) H. BS, Marywood Coll., 1961; MSLS, Drexel U., 1963; MA, U. Del., 1967. Instr. Trinity Coll., Burlington, Vt., 1961-62; reference libr. U. Del., Newark, 1963-66; assoc. libr. dir. Towson (Md.) State U., 1986—, acting libr. dir., 1989-92. Author: Twentieth Century German Novel, 1989, Newspapers in Maryland Libraries, 1977; contbr. articles to profl. jours. Mem. ALA, Md. Libr. Assn. Office: Towson State U Towson MD 21204

HOFT, LYNNE ANN, educator, remedial specialist, educational consultant; b. Carroll, Iowa, Mar. 1, 1945; d. Norman North and Dorothy Mae (Dean) Hoft; 1 child, Timothy D. Cochran. BA, Briar Cliff Coll., 1971; MA in Spl. Edn., Ariz. State U., 1979; postgrad., U. Minn., 1989-92, U. St. Thomas, 1993—. Cert. elem. and spl. edn. tchr., Ariz., Minn. Tchr. St. Edward Sch., Waterloo, Iowa, 1968-70; tchr. Chino Valley Sch., Ariz., 1971-77, program developer, 1974-76; spl. edn. tchr. Tuba City Pub. Jr. High Sch., Ariz., 1978-82; spl. edn. tchr., dept. chmn. Tuba City High Sch., 1983-86, curriculum developer, 1984-85; remedial specialist Eagles' Nest Mid-Sch., 1986-88; spl. edn. coord. chpt. 1 Epsilon and Nexus programs Hopkins (Minn.) Pub. Schs., Hennepin County Home Sch., 1988—; founder, pres. Unltd. Learning Enterprises, Inc., Tuba City, 1983-85; trainer Developing Capable People, 1990—; invitational cons. Aim for Excellence, Mpls., 1990-91; cons./trainer Keys Programs, 1994—. Probation aide Waterloo Juvenile Ct., 1970-71; vol. instr. Prescott Spl. Olympics 1977-78; local coord. Tuba City Spl. Olympics, 1978-80; cons. in field 1988—. Recipient U.S. Dept Edn. Sec. award, 1991. Mem. NEA, N.Mex. Consortium, Women Against Mil. Madness, Minn. Edn. Assn., Hopkins Edn. Assn., Tuba City Unified Edn. Assn. (pres. 1985-86). Democrat. Avocations: reading, piano, parenting, hiking, writing.

HOGAN, BEVERLY KAY, psychiatric public health nurse specialist; b. Birmingham, Ala., Sept. 20, 1957; d. Thomas and EddieMae (McCormack) H.; m. Andrew A. Kemp, Nov. 13, 1982 (div. Oct. 1993). BSN, U. Ala., 1980, BA in Psychology, 1980, MSN in Cmty. Mental Health Nursing, 1987. cert. in adult psychiatric nursing. Staff RN U. Ala., Birmingham, 1980-88; asst. patient care coord. Bapt. Med. Ctr., Birmingham, 1988, clin. nurse specialist, 1988-90, patient care coord., 1990-91; dir. residential program Jefferson Blount St. Clair Mental Health Authority, Birmingham, 1991-92; pub. health nurse specialist Jefferson County Dept. Health, Birmingham, 1992—; instr. psychiat. nursing U. Ala. Hosp., Birmingham, 1987; spkr. stress mgmt. Bapt. Med. Ctr., 1988-90. Mem. Ala. Assn. Specialists in Psychiat. Nursing, Sigma Theta Tau, Omicron Delta Kappa, Phi Kappa Phi. Home: 1252 Spruce St SE Leeds AL 35094

HOGAN, ILONA MODLY, lawyer; b. Erlangen, Fed. Republic of Germany, Nov. 23, 1947; came to U.S., 1951, naturalized, 1960; d. Stephen Bela and Gunda Pauline (Gastiger) Modly; m. Lawrence J. Hogan, Mar. 16, 1974; children: Matthew Lawrence, Michael Alexander, Patrick Nicholas, Timothy Stefan. Student, Marymount Coll., 1965-67; A.B. in Internat. Affairs, George Washington U., 1969; J.D., Georgetown U., 1974. Bar: D.C. 1975, Md. 1975. Intern and clk. AID, 1965-69; adminstrv. and legis. asst. to mem. Ho. of Reps., 1969-72; editor Legis. Digest, Ho. of Reps., Washington, 1972-73; asso. and law clk. firm Trammell, Rand, Nathan and Lincoln, Washington, 1972-74; mng. ptnr. firm Hogan and Hogan, Washington and Frederick, Md., 1974-93; of counsel Venable, Baetjer, Howard & Civiletti, Washington, 1989-91; pres. Amcom Inc., 1978—; of counsel Salisbury & McLister, Frederick, Md., 1993—. Mem. Prince George's (Md.) Bd. Libr. Trustees, 1976-78, Prince George's County Econ. Devel. Adv. Com., 1979-82; co-chmn. Greater S.E. Community Hosp. Ctr. for Aging, 1979-82; mem. Lawyers Steering Com. for Reagan-Bush, 1980; nat. vice chmn. Assn. Execs. for Reagan-Bush, 1984; mem. bus. and industry adv. com. 50th Am. Presdl. Inaugural, 1985; mem. Md. steering com. Bush for Pres., 1988, Gov.'s Higher Edn. Transition Team, 1988, Presdl. Personnel Adv. Com., 1989; treas., bd. regents U. Md. System, 1988—; v.p. St. John's Sch. Bd., 1987-88, pres., 1989; trustee St. James Sch., 1989-90; pres. St. James Parents Assn., 1989-90; mem. Md. Fed. Jud. Adv. Com., 1989-92; mem. Rep. Presdl. Task Force, 1989-92; mem. Bd. County Commrs., Frederick County, Md., 1994. Mem. ABA, Md. Bar Assn., D.C. Bar, Bar Assn. D.C., Women's Bar Assn. Republican. Roman Catholic. Home: 5614 New Design Rd Frederick MD 21701 Office: Salisbury & McLister 100 W Church St Frederick MD 21701-5411

HOGAN, KATHERINE ANN, entertainment lawyer; b. Denver, Nov. 26, 1951; d. William T. Hogan and Nancy E. (Berry) Trotter; m. Daniel D. Drummond, July 29, 1989. BA, Williams Coll., Williamstown, Mass., 1973; JD, Yale U., 1976. Bar: N.Y. 1977. Assoc. Paul, Weiss, Rifkind, Wharton & Garrison, N.Y.C., 1977-82; sr. v.p., gen. counsel entertainment Viacom Internat., Inc., N.Y.C., 1984—. Office: Viacom Internat Inc 1515 Broadway New York NY 10036-9999*

HOGAN, LAURA WHITAKER, office manager; b. Columbia, S.C., Apr. 21, 1960; d. Andrew J. and Alice (Zingler) Whitaker; m. Lunice Edward Hogan, May 23, 1982. BSBA, The Citadel, 1994. Sales mgr. Prestige Furniture Rentals and Atlantic Document Storage subs. Atlantic Svcs. Group, Charleston, S.C., 1984-94; office mgr. Comml. Bonded Warehouse subs. Atlantic Svcs. Group, Charleston, 1994—. Mem. Assn. Records Mgrs. and Adminstrs. (past v.p., editor newsletter, Mem. of Yr. 1993), Inst. Mgmt. Accts. (bd. dirs., editor newsletter). Methodist. Office: Comml Bonded Warehouse 1002 Trident St North Charleston SC 29406

HOGE, GERALDINE RAJACICH, elementary education educator; b. Eveleth, Minn., Apr. 8, 1937; d. Robert and Dora (Tassi) Rajacich; m. Gregg LeRoy Hoge, Sept. 15, 1963 (div. Feb. 1972); 1 child, Sheryl Maurine. BS, U. Minn., 1959; MA with honors, Pepperdine U. Cert. elem. tchr., Calif. Tchr. Chaska (Minn.) Pub. Schs., 1959-60, Minnetonka (Minn.) Pub. Schs., 1960-62, Norwalk (Calif.) La Mirada Pub. Schs., 1962-64, Culver City (Calif.) Unified Sch. Dist., 1966—. Fellow Culver City Guidance Clinic Guild, 1981-89; mem. Calif. State Rep. Ctrl. Com., Sacramento, 1986-90, 92-94, L.A. County Rep. Ctrl. Com., 1987—; vice chmn. 49th Assembly Dist. Ctrl. Rep. Com., Culver City, 1988—; bd. dirs. Selective Svc. Sys., Culver City, 1993—. Named Tchr. of the Yr. Elks Lodge, 1982; grantee, 1988-89. Fellow Am. Fedn. Tchrs., Calif. Fedn. Tchrs., Culver City Fedn. Tchrs. (v.p. 1978-79), Alpha Delta Pi (historian 1956-59). Republican. Office: Culver City Unified Sch 4034 Irving Pl Culver City CA 90232-2810

HOGENSEN, MARGARET HINER, librarian, consultant; b. Ottawa, Kans., Oct. 11, 1920; d. Hebron Henry and Nellie Evelyn (Godard) Hiner; widowed. BA, U. Wichita, 1942; BS in Library Sci., U. Denver, 1945. Circulation librarian Boise (Idaho) Pub. Library, 1945-49, Pomona (Calif.) Pub. Library, 1950-51; reference librarian WFIL-TV, Phila., 1963-69; rsch. dir. Concept Films, Washington, 1969-72; ind. researcher, cons. Greenbelt, Md., 1973—. Bd. dirs. Greenbelt Homes, Inc., 1977-93, pres., 1983-88; past mem. bd. dis. Greenbelt Consumer Coop., Nat. Coop. Bank, Nat. Coop. Bus. Assn.; mem. Com. to Develop Elderly Housing, Greenbelt, 1987—; pres. Ea. Coop. Housing Orgn., 1992—. Mem. Nat. Assn. Housing Coops (bd. dirs. 1986-87, 1990-94). Democrat. Christian Scientist. Home: PO Box 218 Greenbelt MD 20768-0218

HOGG, JUDITH E., neurologist, educator; b. Binghamton, N.Y.; d. Edwin Charles and Virginia Anne (Pettinato) H. AB, MD, Boston U., 1970. Diplomate Am. Bd. Psychiatry and Neurology. Intern Lenox Hill Hosp., N.Y.C., 1970-71, resident in internal medicine, 1971-72; resident in neurology Mt. Sinai Hosp., N.Y.C., 1972-75; assoc. prof. sch. medicine Tex. Tech. U., Lubbock, 1991—. Mem. Am. Acad. Neurology, Am. Assn. Electrodiagnostic Medicine (assoc.), Phi Beta Kappa.

HOGG, KAREN SUE, telecommunications executive; b. Bay City, Tex., Jan. 12, 1952; d. Ernest Bascom Hogg and Allene (Bishop) Watson; m. Wesley Ray Tucker, Mar. 10, 1989. BS in Indsl. Engring., Tex. Tech. U., 1974; MBA, Washington U., 1982. Profl. engr. Tex. Computer ops. supr. Southwestern Bell, Houston, 1974-75; computer ops. supr. Southwestern Bell, St. Louis, 1975-76, from mgr. installation to staff mgr., 1976-83; prin. cons. AT&T Internat., Basking Ridge, N.J., 1983-85; nat. sales mgr. AT&T Network Systems, Morristown, N.J., 1986; mgr. telecom. Goldman Sachs & Co., N.Y.C., 1986-90, v.p. info. tech., 1990—; mem. indsl. adv. bd. Tex. Tech. U., Lubbock, 1980-86. Judge YWCA Tribute to Women, Knoxville, Tenn., 1992; active Livingston Cmty. Players. Named Disting. Engr., Tex. Tech. U., 1994. Mem. Acad. Indsl. Engring., Inst. Indsl. Engrs., Maplewood Strollers, Maplewood Club, Beta Gamma Sigma, Tau Beta Pi, Phi Kappa Phi, Alpha Pi Mu. Republican. Methodist.

HOGG, REBECCA MASON, computer science educator; b. Valparaiso, Ind., Aug. 9, 1951; d. Donald Dwight and Evelyn Lucille (Wagner) Mason. BS, Ind. State U., 1973; postgrad., We. Piedmont C.C. Elem. tchr. Corpus Christi Sch., Miami, Fla., 1974-76; elem. tchr., dir. learing lab. St. Joseph Sch., Stuart, Fla., 1977-79; elem. tchr. Trinity Sch., Rutherfordton, N.C., 1984-86; cons. in computer sci. Morganton, N.C., 1987—; instr. computer edn. We. Piedmont C.C., Morganton, 1987—; editorial adv. bd. Collegiate Press. Vol. Burke County Arts Coun. Mem. Nat. Bus. Edn. Assn., Computer Instr. Assn., Historic Burke Soc. (vol., donor). Home: 232 N Anderson St Morganton NC 28655

HOGG, ROZALIA CRUISE, genealogist; b. Bluefield, W.Va., Dec. 31, 1931; d. George Mortimer and Beulah Grove (Fleshman) Cruise; m. Edward Welford Hogg, Jr., June 20, 1953 (dec. 1972); children: Gayle Hogg Wells, Alice Ann Hogg Conaty, Nancy Hogg Pingry. Student, Madison Coll., Harrisonburg, Va., 1951-53; BA in History, Mary Baldwin Coll., 1978. Kindergarten tchr. Ft. Meade, Md., 1953-54; tour guide Woodrow Wilson Birthplace, Staunton, Va., 1978-80, P. Buckley Moss Mus., Waynesboro, Va., 1990; genealogist Patrick County, Va., 1985—; bd. advisors Bluefield State Coll. Pres. Women of Ch., 1st Presbyn. Ch., Waynesboro, 1983-85; bd. dirs. Augusta County Hist. Soc., 1987-91, Bluefield State Coll., 1992—; vice chmn. Waynesboro Hist. Commn., 1986-91. Mem. Rosecliff Garden Club (pres. 1973-74), Va. Mus. Fine Arts, Sigma Sigma Sigma, Phi Alpha Theta. Presbyterian. Home: 272 Littletown Quarter Williamsburg VA 23185

HOGUE, BONNIE JEAN, school district transportation coordinator; b. Sharon, Pa., July 7, 1940; d. George P. and Lillian E. (Ramage) Gerber; m. Robert D. Hogue, Sept. 19, 1959; children: Kelly Jean, Tiffany Anne. Cert., Humboldt Airline Sch. Sec. Penn Lakes Girl Scouts, Clark, Pa., 1985-86; day camp dir. Penn Lakes Girl Scouts, Hermitage, Pa., 1985-92; caretaker Penn Lakes Girst Scout Camp, Hermitage, Pa., 1982-87; sec., switchboard Hermitage Sch. Dist., 1986-87, cheerleader advisor, 1985-92, transp. coord., 1987—; sec. IU 4 Transp. Orgn., Grove City, Pa., 1989-91. Mem. Hermitage YMCA; v.p. Penn Lakes Girl Scout Coun., Meadville, Pa. Democrat. Baptist. Home: 1500 French St Hermitage PA 16148-2033 Office: Hermitage Sch Dist 419 N Hermitage Rd Hermitage PA 16148-3316

HOGUE, BONNIE MARIE KIFER GOSCIMINSKI, educator, consultant; b. Niagara Falls, N.Y., May 31, 1947; d. Ralph Henry and Emogene Viola (Severance) Kifer; m. Conrad S. Gosciminski, Aug. 9, 1969; children: Steven, Heidi, Jason; m. William R. Hogue, Nov. 15, 1994. BEd, Mansfield (Pa.) State U., 1969; MS in Human Svcs., Murray (Ky.) State U., 1995. Tchr. Col-Mont Area Vocat. Tech., Bloomsburg, Pa., 1969-70, Coatesville (Pa.) Area Sch. Dist., 1971-72, Bradford (Pa.) Area Schs., 1972-76, Christian County Schs., Hopkinsville, Ky., 1976-82; with supply and pers. depts. U.S. Army Law Enforcement Command, Ft. Campbell, Ky., 1983-87; tng. specialist Blanchfield Army Community Hosp., Ft. Campbell, 1987-91; sch. age latch key specialist Child Devel. Svcs., Ft. Campbell, 1991-92; Family Child Care outreach Child Devel. Svcs., Ft. Richardson, Alaska, 1992—. Officer, bd. dirs. Christian County Assn. for S.P.M.D., Hopkinsville, 1978-92; mem. Hopkinsville Human Rels. Commn., 1989-92; parent advisor Title I com. Christian County High Sch., 1989-90. Recipient Outstanding Performance award Dept. Army, 1983-92, Sustained Performance award, 1989, 93; Vol. of Yr. award Christian County Assn. Dyslexia, 1981. Mem. NAFE, NAYCC, NAEYC, AFCCA, Ky. Coalition for Sch.-Age Child Care. Home: 2200 Grizzly Bear Cir Wasilla AK 99654-2728

HOHL, MARGARET DONLEY, human resources executive; b. St. Louis, Mar. 31, 1958; d. William J. Jr. and Rosemary T. (Hollenbach) Donley; m. Kenneth R. Hohl II, Aug. 22, 1981; children: Christopher N., Michelle L. BSBA, U. Mo., St. Louis, 1980. Front desk clk. Marc's Budgetel Inn, St. Louis, 1979-81; mgr. human resources Clayton Savs. and Loan, St. Louis, 1981-86; v.p. Bridge Info. Systems, St. Louis, 1986—. Scholar Fla. Internat. U. Mem. AAIM Mgmt. Assn. (vice chair human resources roundtable), Am. Mgmt. Assn., Human Resources Mgmt. Assn. Office: Bridge Info Systems Inc 717 Office Pkwy Saint Louis MO 63141-7115

HOHLT, DEBORAH M., insurance company executive; b. Wilmington, Del., Feb. 17, 1956; d. Richard C. and Dorothy A. (Lewis) M. BA in Communications, U. Del., 1978. Dir. fin. Nat. Multiple Sclerosis Soc., Newark, Del., 1979-80; employee communications specialist Delmarva Power Co., Newark, 1980-82; dir. local programs Rep. Nat. Com., Washington, 1982-85, dep. dir. communications, 1988-89, dep. chief of staff, 1989-91; account exec. Daniel J. Edelman, Inc., Washington, 1985-86; account supr. Ruder Finn & Rotman, Washington, 1986-87, Henry J. Kaufman & Assocs., Inc., Washington, 1987-88; dep. asst. sec. HHS, Washington, 1991-94; dir. comms. Blue Cross Blue Shield Nat. Capital Area, Washington, 1994—. Pub. affairs asst. Office of the Gov. Del., Newark, 1978-79; mem. pub. rels. com. Nat. Capitol chpt. March of Dimes, 1992. Home: 209 Princess St Arlington VA 22206 Office: Blue Cross Blue Shield Nat Capital Area 550 12 ST SW Washington DC 20065

HOHNEKE, LINDA LORETTA, clinical director; b. Soap Lake, Wash., May 31, 1950; d. Lyman Leroy and Loretta May (Wilson) Stewart; m. Donald Dale Hohneke, July 26, 1969; children: Valerie Renee, Spring Melissa, Clinton Stewart. Diploma in nursing, Milw. County Gen. Hosp., 1971; BSN magna cum laude, Edgewood Coll., Madison, Wis., 1990; MSN, U. Wis., 1992. RN, Wis.; BALS, NALS, cert. neonatal resuscitation instr. Staff nurse neonatal ICU Milw. County Gen. Hosp., 1971; staff nurse obstetrics Missoula (Mont.) Community Hosp., 1972-74, Meth. Hosp., Madison, Wis., 1975; staff nurse obstetrics Reedsburg (Wis.) Meml. Hosp., 1975-80, head nurse obstetrics, 1980-84, clin. dir. obstetrics, 1984-91, clin. dir. in-patient svcs., 1991-94, dir. acute and critical care svcs., 1994; nurse mgr., acute cre staff nurse Sauk Prairie Meml. Hosp., 1994—; staff nurse obstetrics St. Clare Hosp., 1994—; project coord. differentiated nursing case mgmt. Reedsburg Meml. & Western Wis. Cluster Hosps., 1988—; presenter in field. Tchr. Sunday sch. Bethlehem Ch., Blackhawk, Wis., 1983, family ministry chairperson, 1984-86. Mem. Nurses Assn. of the Am. Ob-Gyn., Wis. Assn. Perinatal Care, Sigma Theta Tau (Beta Eta chpt.). Democrat. Methodist. Home: 1010 Cedar St Plain WI 53577 Office: Reedsburg Area Med Ctr 2000 N Dewey Ave Reedsburg WI 53959-1049

HOITOMT, DEBRA JANE, systems engineer; b. Racine, Wis., July 14, 1953; d. Spencer and Elsie Helen (Pitt) H.; 1 child, Nathaniel Spencer Parrish. BS, U. Wis., 1977; MS, U. Ariz., 1984; PhD, U. Conn., 1990. Mfg. engr. Pratt & Whitney, East Hartford, Conn., 1987-93; staff analyst United Airlines, Chgo., 1993—; asst. prof. U. Conn., Storrs, 1990-93; cons. United Technologies Rsch. Ctr., East Hartford. Contbr. chpt. to book. Mem. IEEE, IEEE Robotics and Automation Soc. (tech. com. chair 1991-94, program com. 1994). Democrat. Lutheran. Office: United Airlines M/S EXOEB Box 66100 Chicago IL 60666

HOKE, JUDY ANN, physical education educator; b. Mesa, Ariz., May 3, 1951; d. Jewell Juett and Margaret Lucille (Gibson) H. BA, Ariz. State U., 1973, MS, 1976. Cert. tchr. Ariz. Tchr., coach womens Tennis Temple Union High Sch. Dist., Tempe, Ariz., 1973—, chmn. Phys. Edn., 1978—; former co-chmn. sch. improvement com.; chmn. East Valley Women's Tennis Region; mem. Nat. Honor Soc. selection com., scholarship com. Mem. First Christian Ch., Phoenix Zoo. Named Outstanding Secondary Phys. Edn. Tchr. Yr. State of Ariz., 1991. Mem. NEA, AAHPERD, Ariz. Alliance Health Phys. Edn. Recreation and Dance, Tempe Secondary Edn. Assn., Women's Internat. Tennis Assn., U.S. Tennis Assn. Republican. Office: Marcos de Niza High Sch 6000 S Lakeshore Dr Tempe AZ 85283

HOKE, S. CANDICE, lawyer, educator; b. Raleigh, N.C., Sept. 5, 1955; m. George H. Taylor. BA in Polit. Philosophy, Hollins Coll., 1977; postgrad., U. Chgo., 1978-79; JD, Yale U., 1983. Bar: Mass. 1984, U.S. Ct. Appeals (1st cir.) 1987. Law clk. to judge U.S. Ct. Appeals (1st cir.), Boston, 1983-85; assoc. Hill and Barlow, Boston, 1985-87; asst. prof. law U. Pitts., 1987-93; vis. assoc. prof. law Case Western Res. U., Cleve., 1993-94, Cleve. State U., 1994—; mem. N.C. Drug Commn., 1973-77. Contbr. to profl. jours. Mem. ABA, ACLU, Equal Rights Advocates, Am. Judicature Soc. Office: Case Western Res Sch Law 11075 East Blvd Cleveland OH 44106-5409

HOLABIRD, KATHERINE, children's book author; b. Cambridge, Mass., Jan. 23, 1948; d. John Augur and Donna (Smith) H.; m. Michael Haggiag, June 15, 1974; children: Tara, Alexandra, Adam. BA in Lit., Bennington Coll., 1969. Asst. editor Bennington (Vt.) Rev., 1969-70; free-lance journalist Rome, 1970-72; nursery sch. tchr. London, 1973-76. Author: The Little Mouse ABC, 1983, Angelina Ballerina, 1984 (Ky. Bluegrass award U. Ky. 1984), Angelina and the Princess, 1984, Angelina at the Fair, 1985, Angelina's Christmas, 1985, Angelina on Stage, 1986, Katie's Feelings, 1987, Alexander and the Dragon, 1988, Angelina and Alice, 1988, Angelina's Birthday Surprise, 1989, Angelina Book and Doll Package, 1989, Alexander and the Magic Boat, 1990, Angelina's Baby Sister, 1991, Christmas with Angelina, 1992, Angelina Dances, 1992, Angelina Ice Skates, 1993. Office: Random House 201 E 50th St New York NY 10022*

HOLADAY, BETH ANNE, pharmacist; b. Kansas City, Mo., June 10, 1965; d. Kenneth Francis and Mary Jo Ann (Wulser) Sulzen; m. Bradley Louis Holaday, June 15, 1990; 1 child, Aubrey Anne. AA, Johnson County Cmty. City Coll., Overland Park, Kans., 1985; BA in Pharmacy magna cum laude, U. Mo., Kansas City, 1992. Registered pharmacist. Chief pharmacist, pharmacy mgr. Biggs Pharmacy (SuperValue), Cin., 1992—; pharm. sales rep. Eli Lilly & Co., Cin., 1993-94. Author: (manual) Laws & Regulations of Nursing Home Facilities, 1992. Program dir. project outreach Kansas City chpt. Say No to Drugs Program, 1991-92. Mem. Am. Pharm. Assn., Ohio Pharmacists Assn., Golden Key Nat. Honor Soc., Rho Chi, Phi Theta Kappa. Roman Catholic. Home: 8969 Hialeah Dr West Chester OH 45069

HOLAN, JERRI-ANN, architect; b. Madison, Wis., May 17, 1959; d. Edward Raymond and Gail J. (Wold) H. BArch with high honors, U. Fla., 1980; MArch with honors, U. Calif., Berkeley, 1983. Lic. architect, Calif. Fellow Arkitekturhøgskolen, Oslo, 1983-84; author Rizzoli Internat. Publs., N.Y.C., 1987—; project mgr. R.H. Lee & Assocs., Larkspur, Calif., 1985-87, Rosekrans & Assocs., San Francisco, 1988; architect Christopherson & Graff, Architects, Berkeley, 1988-91, Abrams & Millikan Assocs., Berkeley, 1991—. Author: Norwegian Wood-A Tradition of Building, 1990. Fulbright grantee, 1983-84, Marshall Fund scholar Marshall Assn., Washington, 1984, Am. Scandinavian fellow Am. Scandinavian Assn., N.Y.C., 1983-84. Mem. AIA (vol. 1987—, photography award, 1990), Fulbright Assn. Alumni, U. Calif.-Berkeley Alumni. Democrat. Home: 833 Carmel Ave Albany CA 94706-1811

HOLBERT, SUE ELISABETH, archivist, writer, consultant; b. Denver, Jan. 24, 1935; d. Roger Dean and Beth Helen (Bryant) Ramey; children: Virginia S., Roger Frederick. BA, U. Nebr., 1956; postgrad., U. Minn., 1975-79. Editor Nebr. Edn. News Nebr. Edn. Assn., Lincoln, 1956-58; advt. asst. Augsburg Pub. House, Mpls., 1961-62; edit. asst. publs. div. Minn. Hist. Soc., St. Paul, 1965-69, asst. curator manuscripts, 1972-75, curator, 1975-76, dep. state archivist, 1976-79, state archivist, 1979-92; grants officer Macalester Coll., St. Paul, 1969-72. Author: (with June D. Holmquist) A History Tour of 50 Twin City Landmarks, 1966, Archives and Manuscripts: Reference and Access, 1977; compiler: (with June D. Holmquist and Dorothy D. Perry) History Along the Highways, 1967; contbr. Women in Minnesota, 1977; contbr. articles to profl. jours. Mem. Women Historians of Midwest, Soc. Am. Archivists (pres. 1988), Midwest Archives Conf., Acad. Cert. Archivists, Assn. of Records Mgrs. and Adminstrs. Democrat. Unitarian. Home: 807 Saint Clair Ave Apt 3 Saint Paul MN 55105-3317

HOLBROOK, BARBARA CARR SAN, advertising agency executive; b. Roanoke, Va.; d. Louis James and Eleanor (Brophy) San; m. John Pinckney Holbrook, May 29, 1956 (dec. 1989); children—David Carr, Priscilla Mann. B.A., U. N.C. Copywriter Doherty, Clifford, Steers, Shenfield, N.Y.C., 1954-56, Doyle, Dane, Bernbach, N.Y.C., 1956-58, Ogilvy & Mather, N.Y.C., 1958-59; copy group head Benton & Bowles, N.Y.C., 1959-70; v.p., assoc. creative dir. Grey Advt. Inc., N.Y.C., 1970-89, creative dir., 1989—. Bd. dirs. Nat. Assn. for Visually Handicapped. Named to Clio Hall of Fame, 1955; recipient Clio award, 1977, Hollywood Internat. Broadcast award, 1970, Andy award, 1970, 83, Grey Advt. Pres.'s award, 1985, 88, 91; Bus. Bldg. award Procter & Gamble, 1989, World Class Advt. award, 1990, Effie award, 1991. Democrat. Episcopalian. Office: Grey Advt Inc 777 3d Ave New York NY 10017

HOLBROOK, NORMA JEANNETTE, nursing educator; b. Napton, Mo., Oct. 26, 1939; d. R. Milton and Thelma M. (Miller) Cochran; m. Ralph E. Holbrook, June 30, 1961; children: Tamara M., Jennifer L. BS in Nursing, Cen. Mo. State U., 1965; M of Nursing, Kans. U., 1982. Staff nurse Menorah Med. Ctr., Kansas City, Mo., 1965-66, head nurse, 1966-67; instr. nursing Met. Community Coll., Kansas City, 1967-68; staff nurse Independence (Mo.) Med. Ctr., 1971-73; staff nurse St. Francis Hosp., Topeka, 1975-80, 84-89, mem. continuing edn. com., 1988—; instr. nursing Washburn

U., Topeka, 1981-85, asst. prof., 1986-89; edn. coord. St. Francis Hosp. and Med. Ctr., 1989-91, 93—, clin. nurse specialist in gerontology, 1991-93; chair nursing rsch. com., 1990—; mem. nursing quality assurance com. Stormont Vail Regional Med. Ctr., Topeka, 1982-83, mem. task force for improved implementation nursing care plans, 1983, mem. nursing svc. stds. com., chair procedures com., mem. std. care plan com., 1989—, mem. editorial bd. Kansas Nurse, 1990-95. Mem. nursing adv. com. ARC, Capital area chpt., Topeka, 1980-90, chmn. 1982-83, 88-89. Presentor ednl. programs on nursing process and care planning, gerontology, stress mgmt. for caregivers, positive communicating with patients with Alzheimer's Disease. Contbr. articles to profl. jours. Mem. ANA (Kansas State Nurses Assn. coun. continuing edn. 1987-89), Nat. Gerontol. Nursing Assn., Alzheimer's Assn. (bd. dirs. Topeka chpt., mem. edn. com. 1994—), Sigma Theta Tau Internat. (pres. Eta Kappa chpt. 1990-92, Excellence in Writing award 1993). Republican. Methodist. Office: St Francis Hosp and Med Ctr 1700 SW 7th St Topeka KS 66606-1690

HOLCOMB, ALICE WILLARD POWER, diversified investments executive; b. Franklin County, Ga., Sept. 11, 1922; d. William McKinley and Flora Sarah (Cash) Cantrell; m. Fleming Mitchell Power, May 6, 1941 (dec. Sept. 1967); children: Susan Cantrell, Fleming Michael; m. George Waymon Holcomb, June 4, 1982. Student, Toccoa (Ga.) Falls Coll., 1939-40; BS, Perry Bus. Sch., 1941. Owner Power Poultry Co., Toccoa, 1950-61, Fleming Mitchell Power Properties, Toccoa and Athens, Ga., 1962—, Power's (retail shops), Athens, 1968-85; ptnr. Power Constrn. Co., Athens, 1972—, Athens Indsl. Electric, Athens, 1973—. Active Ga. Hist. Soc. Mem. DAR. Republican. Baptist. Home and Office: 199 Avalon Dr Athens GA 30606-3234

HOLCOMB, CARAMINE KELLAM, volunteer worker; b. Painter, Va., Jan. 23, 1941; d. Emerson Polk and Amine (Cosby) Kellam; m. Isaac Somers White, Nov. 25, 1961 (div. 1975); children: Kellam White Shaw, Caramine White, Virginia Somers; m. Harry Sherman Holcomb III, May 12, 1979. AA, St. Mary's Coll., Raleigh, 1960; Cert., Richmond Bus. Coll., Va., 1961. Bd. dirs. Kellam Energy, Inc., Belle Haven. Va., 1980—, AUto Plus, Inc., Belle Haven, 1980-89, Shore Stop, Inc., Bele Haven, 1981-89. Contbr. articles to profl. jours. Trustee Northampton-Accomack Meml. Hosp., Nassawadox, Va., 1986—, v.p. aux., 1986-88, pres. aux., 1988-90, sec. bd. trustees, 1989-91, vice chmn. bd. trustees, 1991-94, pres. bd. trustees, 1994—; bd. dirs. Ea. Shore Hist. Soc., Onancock, Va., 1987-92; bd. dirs. Med. Soc. Va. Alliance, Richmond, 1984-94, v.p., 1989-91, pres., 1992-93. Mem. AMA Alliance (ERF com. 1994, AMA-ERF com. chmn. 1994-95), Med. Soc. Va. Trust, Garden Club Ea. Shore (pres. 1973-75, 85-87). Home: PO Box 40 Franktown VA 23354-0040

HOLCOMB, CONSTANCE L., sales and marketing management executive; b. St. Paul, Oct. 28, 1942; d. John E. Holcomb and Lucille A. (Westerdahl) Hope. BS, U. Minn., 1965; MA in Intercultural Edn., U. of the Americas, Puebla, Mex., 1975. Rsch. analyst U.S. Dept. Def., Washington, 1965-66; br. gen. mgr. Berlitz Lang. Schs., Mexico City, 1966-68; pres., gen. mgr. Centro Lingüistico, Puebla, 1968-72; gen. mgr., prof. Lang. Ctr. Am. Sch. Found., Puebla, 1972-74; assoc. prof., dir. lang. programs U. of the Americas, Puebla, 1974-76; prof., dean faculty of langs. Nat. Autonomous U. Mex., Mexico City, 1976-78; dir. sales & mktg. Longman Pub. Co., N.Y.C., 1978-80, dir. internat. sales & mktg., 1980-84; mng. dir. ESL Pub. Div. McGraw-Hill Book Co., N.Y.C., 1984-85; dir. mktg. mgmt. McGraw-Hill Tng. Systems and Book Co., N.Y.C., 1985-86; dir. mktg. electronic bus. McGraw-Hill Book Co., N.Y.C., 1986-87; info. industry mgmt. cons., career mgmt. cons., ind. contractor, N.Y.C., 1987—; v.p. MexTESOL, Mexico City, 1977-78. Editor: English Teaching in Mexico, 1975; contrb. articles to profl. jours. Mem. Assn. Am. Pubs. (com. chmn. internat. div. 1980-84, exec. com. 1980-84), Info. Industry Assn., Nat. Assn. Women Cons., Am. Soc. Profl. and Exec. Women. Office: 3555 Mistletoe Ln Longboat Key FL 34228

HOLCOMB, JUANITA L., printing company executive; b. La Monte, Mo.; d. E. Paul and Grace E. (Scott) Minor; m. Leo D. Holcomb; children: Peggy, Linda, Kathy, Michael, David, Kelli, Joseph. Lic. real estate broker, Tex.; cert. HUB/WBE. Reservation operator, adminstrv. asst. Continental Airlines, Kansas City, Mo., 1968-78; real estate salesperson Red Carpet, Houston, 1978-83; retail salesperson Buffalo Bus. Forms, Houston, 1983-85; wholesale customer svc., sales rep. Gulf Bus. Forms, San Marcos, Tex., 1985-89; wholesale supr. Profl. Bus. Forms, San Antonio, 1989-92; sales rep. Advanced Data Forms, Austin, Tex., 1990-92; owner Holcomb & Assocs., Austin, 1992-94, A-1 Forms and Printing, Austin, 1992—. Mem. ABWA, Greater Austin C. of C. (committeeperson). Office: A-1 Forms and Printing 2000 Burton Dr # 228 Austin TX 78741-4139

HOLDEMAN, HELEN FRANCES, nursing educator; b. Salunga, Pa., June 6, 1925; d. George Washington and Frances Hostetter (Nissley) Cutrell; m. Paul Howard Holdeman, June 27, 1948; children: Bonita Jean, Timothy Cutrell, Mark Alan, Priscilla Frances. BSN, Goshen Coll., 1948. RN, Colo; cert. occupational health nurse. Staff nurse Gates Rubber Co., Denver, 1949-50; instr. nurse aides Gulfport (Miss.) Hosp., 1953-54; staff nurse Denver Gen. Hosp., 1955, Sanford Hosp., Perryton, Tex., 1956-59, Loveland (Colo.) Meml. Hosp., 1959; office mgr. LR Sanford MD, Loveland, Colo., 1960-69; occupational health nurse Hewlett-Packard Co., Loveland, Colo., 1969-82; dir. svcs. Larimer County Hospice, Loveland, Colo., 1982-83; dir. edn. Eu Luth. Good Samaritan, Loveland, Colo., 1983-93; instr. nursing Front Range C.C., Ft. Collins, Colo., 1993—. Mem. hosp. dist. bd. Larimer County, Colo., 1973—; mem. adv. bd. Thompson Valley Hosp. Dist., 1973—, McKea Med. Ctr., 1976-78, Healthy Beginnings, Larimer County, 1991—, Good Samaritan, Loveland, 1993—. Named Profl. Woman of Yr., Loveland, 1965. Mem. Colo. Nurses Assn. (pres., sec. 1972-74, bd. dirs. 92-94), Occupational Health Nurses (pres., sec. 1975-77, bd. dirs.). Democrat. Home: 2815 Waterdale Dr Loveland CO 80538-9723

HOLDEN, ANDREA ROSE, advertising sales executive; b. Detroit, May 27, 1958; d. James Kenneth and Joann (Mularoni) H. BA, Loyola U., Chgo., 1981. Producer, intern Sta. WBBM-TV, CBS, Chgo., 1980; audio-visual prodr. Interand Corp., Chgo., 1981-83; account exec. Pulitzer, Lerner Newpapers, Chgo., 1983-87; nat. account exec. BMT Pubs., Chgo., 1987-88; regional sales dir. Health Facilities Mgmt. Mag. Am. Hosp. Pub. Inc., Chgo., 1988-91; pres. Holden Comm., Ltd., Chgo., 1992—. Fund raiser, Loyola U., Chgo., 1986-88, Civic Opera, Chgo., 1987; mem. Chgo. Maritime Mus., 1990. Mem. Chgo. Advt. Club, Bus. Mktg. Assn., Nat. Assn. Pubs. Reps., Columbia Yacht Club, Lake Shore Ski Club. Roman Catholic.

HOLDEN, CAROL H., state legislator; b. Boston, Nov. 6, 1942; m. Donald B. Holden; 4 children. BA, Trinity Coll., 1964; MAT, Boston Coll., 1965. Intern U.S. Senate, 1963-64; N.H. state senator, vice chair children, youth and juvenile justice com., mem. state-fed. rels. com.; mem. Amherst Ways and Means Commn., 1983-86; tchr., vol. coord. Del. N.H. Constl. Conv., 1984; pres. Amherst Women's Rep. Club, 1986-88; v.p. N.H. Fed. Rep. Women's Club, 1989—; mem. Amherst Sch. Dist. Mod., 1990—; dir. N.H. Ptnrs. in Edn., 1987—, sec., 1989—, vice chair, 1990—, chair, 1992—; mem. Gov.'s Steering Com. on Volunteerism, 1991—; mem. N.H. Alliance for Effective Schs., 1991—; v.p. N.H. Congress Parents and Tchrs., 1984-86, 90—. Mem. Trinity Coll. Alumni Assn. (bd. dirs. 1980-87). Home: PO Box 13 Amherst NH 03031-0013 Office: NH State Senate State Capital Concord NH 03301*

HOLDEN, GRACE MORGAN, counselor; b. New Haven, Aug. 29, 1952; d. Reuben Andrus and Elizabeth (Walker) H.; m. Greg Jon Welsh, June 12, 1993. BA, Pomona Coll., 1975; M in Near Eastern Studies, U. Mich., 1980; M in Community Counseling, George Washington U., 1989. Freelance translator Arabic to English, 1981-84; exec. sec. dept. theater and comm. George Washington U., Washington, 1983-85; patient registration rep. George Washington U. Med. Ctr., Washington, 1986-88; children's svcs. coord. Arlington (Va.) Community Temporary Shelter, 1989-92, case mgr., 1992—. Vol. Emmaus Svcs. for Aging, Washington, 1986-93, My Sister's Place, Washington, 1987-88, F.A.C.T. Hotline, Washington, 1989-90. Mem. Nat. Bd. Cert. Counselors, Phi Beta Kappa. Office: Arlington Cmty Temporary Shelter PO Box 1285 Arlington VA 22210

HOLDEN, LISA ROSE, physical therapist; b. Pitts., Jan. 17, 1962; d. William Thomas and Dorothy Rita (Palombo) H. BA in Human Movementy, Lake Erie Coll., Painesville, Ohio, 1983; AS in Phys. Therapist Asst., C.C. Allegheny County, Monroeville, Pa., 1990; M in Phys. Therapy, Duquesne U., 1994. Lic. phys. therapist, Pa. Mental health and mental retardation specialist Siffrin Assn., Canton, Ohio, 1983-84, Idlewood Ctr., Pitts., 1985-90; phys. therapy aide The Phys. Therapy Ctr., Pitts., 1986-90, phys. therapist asst., 1990-94, phys. therapist, 1994—; instr. N.E. C.C., Canton, 1983-85. Mem. Am. Phys. Therapy Assn., Pa. Phys. Therapy Assn., Phi Theta Kappa.

HOLDEN, MARY (MARY AYACH), museum director, translator, photographer; b. New Haven, Mar. 19, 1959; d. Reuben Andrus and Elizabeth Carter (Walker) H.; m. Jean-Luc Joseph Ayach, Dec. 24, 1984; children: Raphaelle, Nicole. Student, N.C. Sch. of Arts, 1986, Temple U., 1987-89; BA, Warren Wilson Coll., 1990. Freelance photographer Paris, 1983—; translator French/English France Animation & Typhoon & Internat. Droits Divers Holding, Paris, 1986—; founding dir. Black Mountain Coll. Mus. and Arts Ctr., 1993—. Home: 503 Azalea Ave Black Mountain NC 28711-2901 Office: Black Mountain Coll Mus & Arts Ctr PO Box 471 Black Mountain NC 28711

HOLDEN, R(UBY) DARNELL, special education administrator; b. San Angelo, Tex., May 8, 1940; d. Isaac Newton and Hettie Faye (Hamilton) Eubanks; m. Elton Jerry Holden, Dec. 26, 1959; 1 child, Stuart Dean. BS, Sul Ross State U., 1968, MEd, 1971. Lic. profl. counselor, marriage and family therapist, diagnostician. Tchr. Fine Arts Day Sch., Odessa, Tex., 1965-68; tchr. Ind. Sch. Dist., Alpine, Tex., 1970-72, Ballinger, Tex., 1973-74; counselor Spl. Edn. Coop., Ballinger, 1975-76, diagnostician/counselor, 1977-87, program dir., 1988—. Bd. dirs. Concho Resource Ctr., San Angelo, 1991, Chilren's Protective Svcs., Runnels County, Tex., 1987-93; adv. Ct. Apptd. Spl. Advs., Runnels/Tom Green Counties, 1990; mem. LWV, 1988-92; del. Rep. Conv., Dallas, 1986. Mem. Tex. Coun. Adminstrs. Spl. Edn., Coun. for Exceptional Children (presenter internat. conf. 1975), 3 Rivers Counseling Assn., Concho Valley Assn. Supervision and Curriculum Devel. Baptist. Home: 1103 Lakeside Ballinger TX 76821 Office: Coop for Spl Svcs 900 Conda Ave Ballinger TX 76821

HOLDER, ANGELA RODDEY, lawyer, educator; b. Rock Hill, S.C., Mar. 13, 1938; d. John T. and Angela M. (Fisher) Roddey; 1 child, John Thomas Roddey Holder. Student, Radcliffe Coll., 1955-56; B.A., Newcomb Coll., 1958; postgrad., Faculty of Law-King's Coll., London, 1957-58; J.D., Tulane U., 1960; LL.M., Yale U., 1975. Bar: La. 1961, S.C. 1960, Conn. 1981. Counsel Roddey, Sumwalt & Carpenter, Rock Hill, S.C., 1960-91; atty. criminal div. New Orleans Legal Aid Bur., 1961-62; counsel York County Family Ct., S.C., 1962-64; asst. prof. polit. sci. Winthrop Coll., Rock Hill, 1964-74; research assoc. Yale U. Law Sch., 1975-77, exec. dir. program in law, sci. and medicine, 1976-77; lectr. dept. pediatrics Yale U. Sch. Medicine, 1975-77, asst. clin. prof. pediatrics and law, 1977-79, assoc. clin. prof., 1979-83, clin. prof., 1983—; counsel for medicolegal affairs Yale-New Haven Hosp. and Yale Med. Sch., 1977-89. Author: The Meaning of the Constitution, 1968, 2d edit., 1987, Medical Malpractice Law, 1975, 2d edit. 1978, Legal Issues in Pediatrics and Adolescent Medicine, 1977, 2d edit., 1985; contbg. editor: Prism mag.; contbg. editor., AMA; mem. editorial bd.: IRB; Law, Medicine and Health Care, Jour. Philosophy and Medicine; contbr. articles to profl. jours. Mem. Rock Hill Sch. Bd., 1967-68; bd. dirs. Family Planning Clinic, chmn., 1970-73; bd. trustees Ednl. Commn. for Fgn. Med. Grads., 1990—; bd. dirs. Conn. Planned Parenthood, 1993—; mem. lawyers' rev. group Health Care Task Force, The White House, 1993. Mem. S.C. Bar Assn. (medico-legal com. 1973—), La. Bar Assn., New Haven County Bar Assn., Am. Soc. Law and Medicine (treas. 1981-83, sec. 1983-85, pres. 1986-88, bd. dirs. 1977-91). Democrat. Episcopalian. Home: 23 Eld St New Haven CT 06511-3815 Office: Yale U School of Medicine 333 Cedar St New Haven CT 06510-3289

HOLDER, HOLLY IRENE, lawyer; b. Albuquerque, May 16, 1952; d. Howard George and Dorothy Evelyn (Doll) Holzum; m. William B. Holder Jr., June 4, 1974; 1 child, Eric James. BA with honors, U. Colo., 1974; JD with honors, U. Denver, 1980. Bar: Colo. 1980, U.S. Ct. Appeals (10th cir.) 1980. Chemist Indsl. Labs., Denver, 1974-76; law clk. to presiding justice Colo. Supreme Ct., Denver, 1979; assoc. Calkins, Kramer, Grimshaw and Harring, Denver, 1980-82, 84-88, McKenna, Conner & Cuneo, Denver, 1988-90, Saunders, Snyder, Ross & Dickson, Denver, 1990-93; pvt. practice Denver, 1993—. Mem. adv. com. Regional Coun. Govts. Water Resources Mgmt., 1984—; chmn. Chatfield Basin Assn., Denver, 1987, Chatfield Basin Master Plan Task Force, Denver, 1986—. Recipient Disting. Svc. award Denver Regional Coun. Govts., 1987. Mem. Colo. Bar Assn., Denver Bar Assn., Mensa. Republican. Office: Holly I Holder PC 17th St Ste 1500 Denver CO 80202

HOLDER, (WILLIE) JO, psychotherapist; b. Laurel, Miss., Mar. 13, 1932; d. Rufus Daniel and Rita Ruth (Hembree) Myrick; m. Legrande E. Merritte, Jan. 31, 1952 (div. Aug. 1969); 1 child, Timothy Edward; m. Richard McGhee Holder, Aug. 17, 1975. BA, Redlands (Calif.) U., 1981; MA, Internat. U., San Diego, 1990, PhD, 1993. Pers. asst. U.S. Civil Svc. Commn., Pasadena, Calif., 1952-67; pers. staff specialist Office of Pers. Mgmt., Pasadena, 1967-69; pers. officer Navy Dept., L.A., 1969-75; pers. dir. Drug Enforcement Adminstrn., L.A., 1975-82; pers. adminstr. Calif. State U., Carson, Calif., 1983-88; psychotherapist Advanced Behavioral Med. Group, Glendale, Calif., 1994—. With USAF, 1951-52. Mem. APA. Republican. Home: 570 S Orange Grove Blvd Pasadena CA 91105 Office: Advanced Behavioral Med Group 3443 Oceanview Glendale CA 91208

HOLDER, SALLIE LOU, training and meeting management consultant; b. Cin., Jan. 25, 1939; d. David Clifford Austin and Margaret Ruth (Higby) Austin Haver; m. Norman Horace Derwyn Holder, July 14, 1964 (div. Oct. 1975). Student, Duke U., 1957-59; BS in Home Econs. Edn., U. Md, 1962; MA in Human Resource Devel. and Edn., George Washington U., 1982. Tchr. Prince Georges County Schs., Md., 1962-66; home econs. tchr. La Reine Sr. High Sch., Suitland, Md., 1966-68; adult edn. Home econs. tchr. Suitland Sr. High Sch, 1969-73; mgr./asst. area sales mgr. The Fabric Tree, Hyattsville, Md., 1972-75; trainer Woodward & Lothrop, Washington and Prince Georges County, Md., 1975-79; conf. coord., non-credit short course coord. Univ. Coll. U. Md., College Park, 1979-87; analyst SYSCON, Washington, 1987-88; meeting mgmt. and tng. cons. Holder & Assocs., College Park, Md., 1988—; tng. specialist Fed. Deposit Ins. Corp., Washington, 1990; instr. Marymount U., Arlington, Va., 1990, Goucher Coll., Balt., 1991-93; chmn. panelists and promotion Productivity Conf., George Washington U., 1981; facilitator New Beginnings, Takoma Park, Md., 1983-90, chmn. planning com., facilitator co-trainer, bd. dirs., 1983-84, chmn. facilitators, 1985-86; monitor Smithsonian Resident Assocs. Program. Mem. alumni bd. Coll. Human Ecology, U. Md., College Park, 1971-93, pres., 1973-74, 77-80, sec., 1985-86, v.p., 1988-90; bd. dirs. Pastoral Counseling and Consultation Ctrs., 1977-86 mem., cons. lay edn. com., community edn. com.; mem. seminarian com., chmn. retreat com., vestry mem. Ch. of the Nativity, Camp Springs, Md., 1977-82; vestryman St. Andrews Episc. Ch., College Park, 1990-93; usher Arena Stage. Recipient Disting. Svc. award Alumni Bd. of Coll. Human Ecology, U. Md., 1981, Vol. award, 1991. Mem. ASTD (Washington chpt. employer coord. 1984-85, co-chmn. program com. 1986, chmn. meeting arrangements 1987-88, treas. 1989, ASTD day chmn., nat. issues chair 1990, chair scholarship com. 1992, coord. spl. interest group 1993, Spl. Achievement award 1987, 88, 90, Pres.'s award 1993), Soc. Govt. Meeting Planners (program commn. 1987-88, communication com., ann. conf. com. 1988-89, chmn. nominating com. 1990, ann. conf. presenter 1990, 93, 94, bd. dirs. 1991-92, chmn. edn. com. for 1992 ann. conf.), U. Md. Coll. Park Alumni Assn. (bd. govs. 1989-93), Assn. Meeting Profls., Am. Assn. Adult and Continuing Edn., Nat. U. Continuing Edn. Assn., Md. Assn. Adult and Continuing Edn., Coll. Park Bus. and Profl. Women, Bishop Method of Clothing Constrn. Coun. (rec. sec. 1972-73 Washington), Singles on Sailboats Club, Del Marva Depression Glass Club, Washington Met. Glass Club, Prince Georges Hist. Soc. Episcopalian. Home and Office: 9715 48th Pl College Park MD 20740-1404

HOLDER, SUSAN MCCASKILL, computer company executive, small business owner; b. Tulsa, July 8, 1956; d. Allan Murdock McCaskill and Kathryn Irene (Padgett) Dolan; m. Robert Newton Holder, Jr., Nov. 30, 1985; children: Tara Susan, Abigail Megan. BA in Bus. Mgmt., Upsala Coll., East Orange, N.J., 1978; MBA in Fin., Fairleigh Dickinson U., 1985. Comml. underwriter State Farm Ins. Cos., Wayne, N.J., 1978-81, svc. supr., 1981-83; adminstrn. mgr. Digital Equipment Corp., Piscataway, N.J., 1983-85; project mgr. Digital Equipment Corp., Princeton, N.J., 1985-87, area adminstrv. svcs. mgr., 1987-88, area adminstrv. support mgr., 1988-89; bus. analyst U.S. Hdqrs. Digital Equipment Corp., Alpharetta, Ga., 1989-91, Westboro, Mass., 1989-91; project mgr. U.S. Desktop Svcs., Digital Equipment Corp., Alpharetta, 1991-92; co-owner Basket Innovations, Inc., Roswell, Ga., 1992-94; co-owner, corp. officr The Asphodel Assocs., Inc., Roswell, 1994—. Mem. pastor-parish rels. Christ United Meth. Ch., Roswell, Ga., 1990-91, chair pastor-parish rels., 1992, mem. nurture com., tchr. Sunday sch. presch. class, 1990—. Mem. AAUW (br. sec. Point Pleasant, N.J. 1986-89). Home: 1810 Azalea Springs Trail Roswell GA 30075-1857 Office: The Asphodel Assocs Inc Ste 203-231 4651 Woodstock Rd Roswell GA 30075-9999

HOLDRIDGE, BARBARA, book publisher; b. N.Y.C., July 26, 1929; d. Herbert L. and Bertha (Gold) Cohen; m. Lawrence B. Holdridge, Oct. 9, 1959; 2 children. A.B., Hunter Coll., 1950. Asst. editor Liveright Pub. Corp., N.Y.C., 1950-52; co-founder Caedmon Records, Inc., N.Y.C., 1952; partner Caedmon Records, Inc., 1952-60, pres., 1960-62, treas., 1962-70, pres., 1970-75; founder Stemmer House Pubs. Inc., Owings Mills, Md., 1975; pres. Stemmer House Pubs. Inc., 1975—; co-founder, v.p. Shakespeare Rec. So., Inc., N.Y.C., 1960-70, Theatre Rec. Soc., Inc., N.Y.C., 1964-70; founder BEDE Prodns., 1984; co-founder History Rec. Soc., Inc., N.Y.C., 1964, pres., 1964-70; lectr. on Ammi Phillips, 1959; lectr. on book pub., 1992—; adj. prof. writing media Loyola Coll., Balt., 1987-91. Author: Ammi Phillips, 1968, Aubrey Beardsley Designs from the Age of Chivalry, 1983, Chinese Cut-Out Designs of Costumes, 1989; articles on Am. paintings. Recipient Am. Shakespeare Festival award, 1962, N.Y.C. certificate appreciation, 1972; named to Hunter Coll. Hall of Fame, 1972. Mem. Phi Beta Kappa Assocs. Office: 2627 Caves Rd Owings Mills MD 21117

HOLDSWORTH, JANET NOTT, women's health nurse; b. Evanston, Ill., Dec. 25, 1941; d. William Alfred and Elizabeth Inez (Kelly) Nott; children: James William, Kelly Elizabeth, John David. BSN with high distinction, U. Iowa, 1963; M of Nursing, U. Wash., 1966. RN, Colo. Staff nurse U. Colo. Hosp., Denver, 1963-64, Presbyn. Hosp., Denver, 1964-65, Grand Canyon Hosp., Ariz., 1965; asst. prof. U. Colo. Sch. Nursing, Denver, 1966-71; counseling nurse Boulder PolyDrug Treatment Ctr., Boulder, 1971-77; pvt. duty nurse Nurses' Official Registry, Denver, 1973-82; cons. nurse, tchr. parenting and child devel. Teenage Parent Program, Boulder Valley Schs., Boulder, 1980-88; bd. dirs., treas. Nott's Travel, Aurora, Colo., 1980—; instr., nursing coord. ARC, Boulder, 1979-90, instr., nursing tng. specialist, 1980-82. Mem. adv. bd. Boulder County Lamaze Inc., 1980-88 ; mem. adv. com. Child Find and Parent-Family, Boulder, 1981-89; del. Rep. County State Congl. Convs., 1972-94, sec. 17th Dist. Senatorial Com., Boulder, 1982-92; vol. Mile High ARC, 1980; vol. chmn. Mesa Sch. PTO, Boulder, 1982-92, bd. dirs., 1982—, v.p., 1983—; elder Presbyn. ch. Mem. ANA, Colo. Nurses Assn. (bd. dirs. 1975-76, human rights com. 1981-83, dist. pres. 1974-76), Coun. Intracultural Nurses, Sigma Theta Tau, Alpha Lambda Delta. Republican. Home: 1550 Findlay Way Boulder CO 80303-6922 Office: Teenage Parent Program 3740 Martin Dr Boulder CO 80303-5448

HOLEC, ANITA KATHRYN VAN TASSEL, civic worker; b. Rahway, N.J., Nov. 11, 1947; d. Edward T. and Irene Eleanor (Barna) Van Tassel; m. Sidney W. Holec, Oct. 26, 1968. BS, U. Houston, 1969. Stockbroker Drexel Burnham Lambert, Inc., Miami, Fla., 1976-78, Merrill Lynch, Venice, Fla., 1979-80; fin. cons. Shearson Lehman Bros., Venice, 1981-87; owner, mgr. Closet Stretchers, Venice, 1987-89. Bd. dirs. Safe Place and Rape Crisis, Sarasota, 1990—, Womens Resource Ctr., Sarasota, 1990-94, Friends Venice Libr., 1992-94, New Coll. Libr., 1991-94; mem. Leadership Sarasota, 1991-95, Jr. League of Sarasota, 1991, Argus Found., 1982—. Home: 1708 Casey Key Rd Nokomis FL 34275-3370

HOLEN, ARLENE S., federal commissioner; b. N.Y.C., July 5, 1938; m. Sheldon Holen, Sept. 10, 1960; children: Jacqueline, Margaret. Student, Syracuse U., 1956-57; BA with distinction, Columbia U., 1960, MA in Econs., 1963. Economist Bur. Internat. Labor Affairs, 1979-82; economist office of policy Dept. Labor, 1982-83, economist office of mgmt. and budget, 1983-85; sr. staff economist Pres. Coun. Econ. Advisers, 1985-88; assoc. dir. for human resources, vets. and labor Office of Mgmt. and Budget, 1988-90; commr., retiree health benefits Adv. Commn. on United Mine Workers of Am., Dept. Labor, 1990; commr. Fed. Mine Safety and Health Review Commn., Dept Labor, 1990-92; chmn. Fed. Mine Safety and Health Review Commn., Dept Labor, Washington, 1992—. Author: Immigration, Winners and Losers, 1987. Columbia U. fellow, Woodrow Wilson fellow. Mem. Phi Beta Kappa. Office: Fed Mine Safety & Health Commn Rm 604 1730 K St NW Washington DC 20006*

HOLIDAY, EDITH ELIZABETH, former presidential adviser, cabinet secretary; b. Middletown, Ohio, Feb. 14, 1952; d. Harry Jr. and Kethlyn (Watson) H.; m. Terrence B. Adamson, June 8, 1985; children: Kathlyn Holiday Adamson, Elizabeth Holiday Adamson; 1 stepchild, Terrence Morgan Adamson. Student, Miami U., Oxford, Ohio, 1970-71; BS with honors, U. Fla., 1974, JD, 1977. Bar: Fla. 1977, D.C. 1978, Ga. 1984. Assoc. Read Smith Shaw & McClay, Washington, 1977-83, Dow Lohnes & Albertson, Atlanta, 1983-84; exec. dir. Commn. on Exec. Legis. and Jud. Salaries, Washington, 1984-85; spl. counsel polit. action com. Fund for Am. Future, Washington, 1985-87; dir. ops. George Bush for Pres., Inc., Washington, 1987-88; chief counsel, nat. fin. and ops. dir. Bush-Quayle 88, Washington, 1988; with legal svcs. staff George Bush for Pres. Compliance Com., Washington, 1988; asst. sec. for pub. affairs and pub. liaison, counselor to sec. Departmental Offices, U.S. Dept. Treasury, Washington, 1988; gen. counsel U.S. Dept. Treasury, Washington, 1989-90; asst. to U.S. pres., sec. of cabinet Washington, 1990-93; legis. asst. to U.S. Sen. Nicholas F. Brady, Washington, 1982-83; bd. dirs. Amerada Hess Corp., H.J. Heinz Co., Hercules, Inc., Bessemer Trust Co., N.A., Bessemer Trust Co. of N.J. Recipient Alexander Hamilton award Sec. of Treasury, 1991, spl. citation John Marshall Bar Assn. Mem. Phi Delta Phi, Kappa Tau Alpha.

HOLIFIELD, WILMA JEANNETTE (JEAN HOLIFIELD), retired municipal administrator, association executive; b. Hot Springs, Ark., July 8, 1929; d. Sanford Samuel and Wilma (Garrison) Heptinstall; m. Walter Major Holifield, Mar. 25, 1955; 1 child, Deborah Carol Holifield Blakeney. Student, Jones County Jr. Coll., 1947-48, Miss. State U., 1973-76, U. So. Miss., 1987. Stenographer Ellisville (Miss.) State Sch., 1948, Deavours & Hilbun, Laurel, Miss., 1948-50; bookkeeper, stenographer A.B. Martin Nash Motors, Laurel, 1950; acctg. clk., sec. United Gas Corp., Laurel, 1950-55; sec. City of Laurel, 1955-67, dep. city clk., 1967-78, tax assessor, 1978-86. Editor: Laurel Centennial Cookbook 1882-1982, 1982, Evangel. Temple Assembly of God Yearbook, 1983, Mississippi Municipal Clerks, Assessors and Collectors Association Yearbook, 1986. 3d. v.p. YWCA, Laurel, 1991-92, 1st v.p., 1992-93, pres., 1993-95. Recipient Diana award Epsilon Sigma Alpha, 1994. Home: 1104 Crescent Hill Dr Laurel MS 39440-1915

HOLL, ANN C., state legislator; b. Chelsea, Mass., Apr. 25, 1948; married; 3 children. BA, Keene State Coll., 1988; MA, RN, Lawrence Meml. Sch. Nursing, Medford, Mass., 1971. Educator, RN; mem. N.H. Ho. of Reps.; mem. resources, recreation and devel. com.; tchr. adult basic edn. family independence program N.H. Tech. Coll., 1990—. Bd. dirs. Am. Cancer Soc. Sullivan County, 1992—; program and performance coord. Claremont Opera House, 1984-90. Recipient Exceptional Vol. Svc. citation ARC Sullivan County, 1986. Mem. Phi Alpha Theta. Office: NH House of Reps State Capitol Concord NH 03301*

HOLLABAUGH, DONNA JEAN, secondary education educator; b. Ft. Wayne, Ind., May 30, 1946; d. Bobby Owen and Mary Barbara (Huyghe) Black; m. J. Parks Hollabaugh, Feb. 15, 1975; children: Austin Wyatt, Dana Parks. BS in English and Am. History, Ind. U., Ft. Wayne, 1969, MS in Secondary Edn., 1974. Cert. secondary tchr., Ind. Tchr. Leo (Ind.) High Sch., 1970; tchr. Eastside Jr. Sr. High Sch., Butler, Ind., 1970—, lang. arts. dept. chair, 1979—. Mem. NEA, Ind. Tchrs. English, Ind. Tchrs. Assn., Nat. Coun. Tchrs. English, Ea. DeKalb Edn. Assn. (chief negotiator 1975-90), Am. Legion Aux. Lutheran. Home: 7006 State Road 1 Spencerville IN 46788-9401

HOLLADAY, WILHELMINA COLE, interior design and museum executive; b. Elmira, N.Y., Oct. 10, 1922; d. Chauncy E. and Claire Elizabeth (Strong) Cole; m. Wallace Fitzhugh Holladay, Sept. 27, 1946; children: Wallace Fitzhugh, Scott Cole. BA, Elmira Coll., 1944; postgrad. art history, U. Paris, 1953-54, U. Va., 1960-61; PhD (hon.), Moore Coll. Art, 1988, Mt. Vernon Coll., 1988, Elmira Coll., 1989. Exec. sec. Howard Ludington, Rochester, N.Y., 1944-45, Chinese Embassy, Washington, 1945-48; staff Nat. Gallery of Art, Washington, 1957-59; dir. interior design div. Holladay Corp., Washington, 1970—; dir. Holladay-Tyler Printing Corp., 1982-86; dir. Adams Nat. Bank, 1978-86, chmn. 1978-86; founder, pres., bd. dir. Nat. Mus. Women in the Arts, 1982—. Founder archival libr. of periodicals, books, exhbn. catalogs on women's art for rsch. purposes; bd. durs. Am. Field Svc., 1964-80, Internat. Student House, 1973—, Leeds Castle Found.; mem. coun. Friends of Folger shakespeare Libr., 1978-82; mem. world svc. coun. YWCA; trustee Corcoran Gallery of Art, 1980-90; pres. Holladay Found., 1980—; mem. profl. adv. com. interior design Mt. Vernon Coll.; mem. Mayor's Blue Ribbon Com. Recipient Horizon's Theatre award, 1986, Anti-Defamation award, 1987, Thomas Jefferson award Am. Soc. Interior Designers, Disting. Woman's award Northwood Inst., 1987, Disting. Achievement award Nat. League Am. Pen Women, 1988, Women Achievers award Internat. Alliance, 1991, Woman That Makes a Difference award Intenat. Womens Forum, 1991, Women First award YWCA, 1993, Key to City of Kansas City; named Woman of Achievement, Washington Ednl. TV Assn., 1984, Woman of Distinction Coun. Ind. Colls., 1987, Birmingham So. Coll., 1991, Washingtonian of Yr., Washingtonian Mag., 1987, Hon. Citizen by State of Tex. Mem. Am. Assn. Mus., Am. Fedn. Art, Women's Caucus for Arts, Met. Mus. Art, Mus. Modern Art, Art Libraries of N.Am., Archives Am. Art, Arttable, Smithson Soc., Internat. Women's Forum, Nat. Women's Econ. Alliance (bd. dirs. 1984—), Soaring Eagle award 1988), Phillips Gallery Art (patron). Episcopalian. Home: 3215 R St NW Washington DC 20007 Office: Nat Mus Women Arts 1250 New York Ave NW Washington DC 20005

HOLLAND, BETH, actress; b. N.Y.C.; d. Samson and Florence (Liebman) Hollander; m. Louis L. Friedman, Aug. 28, 1953; children: Ellen Lynn, Cathy Jayne. Pvt. studies in acting, voice tng. Arts funding cons. N.Y. State Senate, 1974-89. Appeared in various roles on TV, film and theatre, also comedy video Your Favorite Jokes, 1988. Mem. AFTRA (pres. N.Y. chpt. 1989-91, bd. dirs., trustee Health and Retirement Funds, past treas.), SAG, N.Y. TV Acad. (past bd. dirs.), Actors Equity Assn., Twelfth Night Club (bd. dirs.), Episcopal Actors Guild, Cath. Actors Guild, Players Club, Lambs Club. Home winter: 4300 N Ocean Blvd Fort Lauderdale FL 33308-5944

HOLLAND, DIANNA GWIN, real estate broker; b. Pueblo, Colo., Mar. 9, 1948; d. Everett Paul Gwin and Ava Mariea (Calvert) Johnson. Staff asst. The White House, Washington, 1971-77, exec. asst. to counsel, 1981-89; sales agt. Rand Real Estate, Alexandria, Va., 1977-79, Pagett Real Estate, Alexandria, 1979-81; assoc. broker WJD & Assocs., Alexandria, 1985-93; assoc. broker, asst. mgr. adminstrn. Long & Foster Realtors, 1993—; exec. aide to chmn. Edward Lowe Industries, Inc., 1990-91. Del. Va. Republican Conv., 1981, 82, 84. Roman Catholic. Home: 311 Park Rd Alexandria VA 22301-2737

HOLLAND, GENE GRIGSBY (SCOTTIE HOLLAND), artist; b. Hazard, Ky., June 30, 1928; d. Edward and Virginia Lee (Watson) Grigsby; m. George William Holland, Sept. 22, 1950; 3 children. BA, U. S. Fla., 1968; pupil of Ruth Allison, Talequah, Okla., 1947-48, Ralph Smith, Washington, 1977, Clint Carter, Atlanta, 1977, R. Jordan, Winter Park, Fla., 1979, Cedric Baldwin Egeli Workshop, Charleston, S.C., 1984. Various clerical and secretarial positions, 1948-52; news reporter, photographer Bryan (Tex.) Daily News, 1952; clk. Fogarty Bros. Moving and Transfer, Tampa and Miami, Fla., 1954-57; tchr. elem. Schs., Hillsborough County, Fla., 1968-72; salesperson, assoc. real estate, 1984—; owner, operator antique store, 1982-87. One-woman and group shows include Tampa Woman's Clubhouse, 1973, Cor Jesu, Tampa, 1973, bank, Monks Corner, S.C., 1977, Summerville Artists Guild, 1977-78, Apopka (Fla.) Art and Foliage Festival, 1980, 81, 82, Fla. Fedn. Women's Clubs, 1980, 81, 82; numerous group shows, latest being: Island Gifts, Tampa, 1980-82, Brandon (Fla.) Station, 1980-81, Holland Originals, Orlando, Fla.; represented in permanent collections including Combank, Apopka, also pvt. collections. Vol. ARC, Tampa, 1965-69, United Fund Campaign, 1975-76; pres. Mango (Fla.) Elem. Sch. PTA, 1966-67; pres. Tampa Civic Assn., 1974-75; vol. Easter Seal Fund Campaign, 1962-63; art chmn. Apopka Art & Foliage Festival, 1990; deaconess Ctrl. Christian Ch. of Orlando, 1992-94, chmn. bible study 1993-94. Recipient numerous art awards, 1978-82. Mem. AARP (parlimentarian Apopka chpt.), Internat. Soc. of Artists, Coun. of Arts and Scis. for Cen. Fla., Fedn. Women's Clubs (pres. Hillsborough County 1974-75, v.p. Tampa Civic 1974-75), Meth. Women's Soc. (sec. 1976-77), Nat. Trust Hist. Preservation, Nat. Hist. Soc., Cen. Fla. Geneal. and Hist. Soc., Am. Guild Flower Arrangers, The Nat. Grigsby Family Soc. (mem. SW chpt., assoc. sec. 1991-92, corp. sect. 1992—), Internat. Inner Wheel Club (past chmn. dist. 696, pres. Tampa 1972-73), Musicale Club (1st v.p. bd. incorporators Tampa 1974-75), Apopka Woman's Club (pres. 1981-82, bd. dir. 1983-85, Woman of Yr. 1991, 92), Apopka Tennis Over 50's Group Club (pres. 1988-90). Home: 1001 W Mahoney St Plant City FL 33566-4437 also: PO Box 4043 Plant City FL 33564

HOLLAND, ISABELLE CHRISTIAN, writer; b. Basel, Switzerland, June 16, 1920; d. Philip Edgar and Corabelle (Anderson) H. BA, Tulane U., 1942. Censor U.S. War Dept., New Orleans, 1942-44; corr. sec. Life Mag., N.Y.C., 1944-47; editorial asst. Nat. Coun. Protestant Episcopal Chs., N.Y.C., 1947-48; asst. editor Tomorrow Mag. Creative Age Press, N.Y.C., 1948-49; advt. copywriter Franklin Spier Advt. Agy., N.Y.C., 1949-53; assoc. editor McCall's Mag., N.Y.C., 1953-55; publicity dir. Crown Pubs., Lippincott Co., Delacorte Press, Harper's Mag., G.P. Putnam, Pubs., N.Y.C., 1956-69; writer, 1969—. Author: Cecily, 1967, Amanda's Choice, 1970, The Man Without a Face, 1972, (under name Francesca Hunt) The Mystery of Castle Renaldi, 1972, Heads You Win, Tails I Lose, 1973, Kilgaren, 1974, Journey of Three, 1974, Trelawny, 1976, Moncrieff, 1975, Of Love and Death and Other Journeys, 1975 (nominated Nat. Book award 1976), Darcourt, 1976, Grenelle, 1976, Alan and the Animal Kingdom, 1977, Hitchhike, 1977, The de Maury Papers, 1977, Dinah and the Green Fat Kingdom, 1978, Tower Abbey, 1978, The Marchington Inheritance, 1979, Counterpoint, 1980, Now Is Not Too Late, 1980, Summer of My First Love, 1981, The Lost Madonna, 1981, A Horse Named Peaceable, 1982, Abbie's God Book, 1982, Perdita, 1983, God, Mrs. Musket and Aunt Dot, 1983, The Empty House, 1983, Kevin's Hat, 1984, The Island, 1984 Green Andrew Green, 1984, A Death at St. Anselm's, 1984, Flight of the Archangel, 1985, Jenny Kiss'd Me, 1985, A Lover Scorned, 1986, Henry and Grudge, 1986, Toby the Splendid, 1987, Love and the Genetic Factor, 1987, The Christmas Cat, 1987, Bump in the Night, 1988, A Fatal Advent, 1989, Thief, 1989, The Easter Donkey, 1989, The Unfrightening Dark, 1989, The Journey Home, 1990, The Long Search, 1990, The Search, 1991, The House in the Woods, 1991, Behind the Lines, 1994, Family Trust, 1994. Mem. PEN, Authors Guild, Cosmopolitan Club (N.Y.C.). Address: care Elaine Markson Lit Agy 44 Greenwich Ave New York NY 10011-8347

HOLLAND, KATHIE KUNKEL, university official, educator; b. Lake Worth, Fla., Jan. 4, 1949; d. John Alfred and Annetta (Wellman) K.; m. James Carson Holland, Dec. 15, 1968 (div. Mar. 1987); children: J. Wesley, J. Wyatt. MBA, U. Cen. Fla., 1980, BSBA, 1978. Teller 1st Fed. Savs. and Loan, West Palm Beach, Fla., 1969-70; head teller Tallahassee Fed. Savs. and Loan, 1970-71; br. mgr. Orlando (Fla.) Fed. Savs. and Loan, 1971-75; instr. Orlando Coll., 1982-85; grad. asst. U. Cen. Fla., Orlando, 1978-80, instr., 1986—, asst. dir. Small Bus. Devel. Ctr., 1986—; dir. profl. devel. Fla. Small Bus. Devel. Ctr. Network, Orlando, 1994—; bd. dirs. Profl. Women's Exch., Orlando, Ctr. for Continuing Edn. for Women, Orlando, 1987; cofounder Women Bus. Owners' Network, Orlando, 1988; mgmt. cons., Orlando. Co-author: Starting and Managing a Business in Central Florida, 1989; contbr. articles to profl. jours. Com. mem. Jr. Achievement Ctr., Entrepreneur Task Force, Orlando, 1989; speaker Greater Brevard C. of C., Melbourne, Fla., 1989. Mem. Women's Bus. Ednl. Coun. (bd. dirs. 1987—), Women's Endeavors in Bus., Cen. Fla. Pleasure Divers (coms. 1985—), Greater Orlando C. of C. (com. chmn. 1987), Inst. Mgmt. Cons., Omicron Delta Kappa. Republican. Presbyterian. Office: U Cen Fla Small Bus Devel Ctr Alafaya Trail Orlando FL 32816

HOLLAND, KOREN ALAYNE, chemistry educator; b. South Weymouth, Mass., June 7, 1963; d. Herbert Gerry and Valerie Alayne (Shaw) Lipsett; m. Mitchell Mark Holland, May 14, 1988; children: Alayne Ruth, Harrison Morgan. BA, Skidmore Coll., 1985; PhD, U. Md., 1990. NIH postdoctoral fellow Johns Hopkins U., Balt., 1990-92; asst. prof. chemistry Gettysburg (Pa.) Coll., 1992—. Contbr. articles to profl. jours. Mem. AAAS, Am. Chem. Soc., Nat. Sci. Tchrs. Assn. Unitarian. Office: Gettysburg Coll Dept Chemistry Gettysburg PA 17325

HOLLAND, MERLE SUSAN, psychologist; b. Phila., June 23, 1945; d. Salem Harris and Anne (Goldstein) Lumish; m. Peter M. Holland, May 26, 1968; children: Matthew David, John Michael. BA, U. Pa., 1967; MA, NYU, 1968; EdD, U. Houston, 1985. Lic. psychologist, Tex. Pvt. practice Houston, 1987—; adj. prof. U. St. Thomas, Houston; mem. allied health profl. staff West Oaks Hosp., Houston, 1992—, Devereaux Hosp. Mem. adv. coun. Kesher, Houston, 1988-90. Mem. APA, NASP, Soc. for Personality Assessment, Tex. Psychol. Assn., Houston Psychol. Assn., Orton Dyslexia Soc. (Houston chpt. exec. bd. 1988-93, v.p. 1990-93). Home: 3319 Plumb St Houston TX 77005-2923 Office: 4615 Post Oak Place Dr Ste 201 Houston TX 77027-9730

HOLLAND, ROBIN JEAN, personnel company executive; b. Chgo., June 22, 1942; d. Robert Benjamin and Dolores (Levy) Shaeffer; 1 child, Robert Gene. BA in Pub. Rels. magna cum laude, U. So. Calif., 1977. Account exec., pub. rels. firm, 1977-79, Mgmt. Recruiters, 1979; owner, operator Holland Exec. Search, Marina Del Rey, Calif., 1979—; pres. Bus. Communications, 1983—; cons. on outplacement to bus.; condr. seminars on exec. search; guest lectr. and instr. on exec. recruiting at community colls. Active Ahead with Horses, Audubon Soc., conservation orgns. Recipient numerous local honors. Mem. Am. Coaster Enthusiasts, LK.A. Can., Mensa, Peruvian Paso Horse Owners and Breeders N.Am. Office: Holland Exec Search 4748 Admiralty Way Ste 9774 Marina Del Rey CA 90295

HOLLANDER, GLEE ROSS, clinical psychologist; b. Spokane, Wash., June 1, 1943; d. Floyd Leroy and Gayle Amanda (Bartholomew) Ross; m. Myles Hollander, Aug. 17, 1963; children: Layne, Bart. BA in Psychology magna cum laude, Fla. State U., 1978, MS in Clin. Psychology, 1987, PhD in Clin. Psychology, 1990. Lic. psychologist, Fla. From asst. to assoc. researcher Fla. State U., Tallahassee, 1979-83; sr. psychologist Fla. State Hosp., Chattahoochee, 1990—; therapist Faith Counseling Ctr., Tallahassee, 1991—. Contbr. articles to profl. jours. Mem. APA, Am. Psychol. Soc., Capital Area Psychol. Assn., Am. Assn. Applied and Preventive Psychology, Phi Beta Kappa.

HOLLAR, MARLYS JEAN, oil company executive; b. Hillsboro, Kans., July 25, 1936; d. Walter E. and Evelyn Cleo (Hauser) Rupp; m. Maurice L. Hollar, May 24, 1961; 1 child, Bradley T. BA in Acctg. with honors, Wichita State U., 1958. Acct. Frontier Oil Co., Wichita, 1958-61; head land and legal dept. Frontier Oil Co., Wichita, Kans., 1961—. Mem. Crestview Country Club. Republican. Presbyterian. Home: 561 Turnberry Cir Wichita KS 67230-1522

HOLLATZ, SARAH SCHOALES, rancher, business owner; b. N.Y.C., Sept. 1, 1944; d. Dudley Nevison and Virginia Jocelyn (Vanderlip) Schoales; m. David Earl Hollatz, Jan. 27, 1968 (div. June 1985); children: Melissa Virginia, Peter David. BS, U. Wis., 1966; postgrad., U. So. Calif., L.A., 1966. Copywriter Max W. Becker Advt., Long Beach, Calif., 1966-67; advt. dir. officers news USN, Coronado, Calif., 1968-70; with syndicate dept. Morgan Stanley & Co., N.Y.C., 1970-72; lay-out asst. North Castle News, Armonk, N.Y., 1972-75; performer, writer Candy Band, Pound Ridge, N.Y., 1975-82; owner, mgr. Circle Bar Guest Ranch, Utica, Mont., 1983—; bd. dirs. Park Inn, Lewistown, Mont. Artist, composer: Play Me a Song, 1978, Going Home, 1980; composer: (mus. play) Elsie Piddock, 1979, Secret Garden, 1981, Windows, 1989. Soloist Hobson (Mont.) Meth. Ch., 1983—; founder What the Hay, Utica, 1990—. Mem. Mont. Emergency Med. Assn. (bd. dirs. 1990—), Dude Rancher's Assn. (bd. dirs. 1989—). Episcopalian. Home and Office: Circle Bar Guest Ranch Utica MT 59452

HOLLEB, DORIS B., urban planner, economist; b. N.Y.C., Oct. 26, 1922; m. Marshall M. Holleb, Oct. 15, 1944; children: Alan, Gordon, Paul. BA magna cum laude, Hunter Coll., 1942; MA, Harvard U., 1947; postgrad. U. Chgo., 1959-60, 65-66. Economist Fed. Res. Bd., Washington, 1943-44; freelance journalist, 1945-63; econ. cons. Chgo. Dept. City Planning, 1963-64; rsch. assoc. Ctr. Urban Studies, U. Chgo., 1966-78, sr. rsch. assoc., 1978-88, dir. Met. Inst., 1973—, professorial lectr., 1979—; chmn., Francis W. Parker Sch. Ednl. Coun., 1963-80; cons., 1980-92; mem. adv. coun. Adlai E. Stevenson Inst., 1972-79, Ctr. for the Study Democratic Inst., 1975-79; bd. dirs. Inter. Am. Found., 1980-84, Pacific Basin Inst., 1981—; mem. nat. adv. com. White House Conf. on Balanced Nat. Growth and Econ. Devel., 1978; mem. Northeastern Ill. Planning Commn., 1973-77; mem. Chgo. Met. Area Transp. Coun., 1980-84; mem. adv. coun. to Nat. Ctr. Rsch. on Vocat. Edn., Dept. Edn., 1979-82, Dept. state adv. com. internat. investment, tech. and devel., 1979-81; commnr. Chgo. Plan Commn., 1987—; bd. dirs. Internat. Ctr. for Rsch. on Women, 1985-91. Author: Social and Economic Information for Urban Planning, 1968, Colleges and the Urban Poor, 1972; contbr. articles to profl. jours.; mem. editorial bd. Illinois Issues, 1977—, v.p. 1992—. Mem. Am. Inst. Cert. Planners, Am. Planning Assn., Am. Econ. Assn., Arts Club, Univ. Club, Quadrangle Club, Harvard Club N.Y.C., Phi Beta Kappa (v.p.), Lambda Alpha.

HOLLEIN, HELEN CONWAY, chemical engineer, educator; b. Fort Bragg, N.C., Mar. 21, 1943; d. Arthur Conway and Helen Vann (Parker) Faris; m. Leo Bernard Hollein, Sept. 10, 1966; children: Mary, Kathleen, Michael. BS Chem. Engring., U. S.C., 1965; MS, N.J. Inst. Tech., 1979, D Engring. Sci., 1982. Registered profl. engr., N.J. Process engr. Exxon Rsch. and Engring. Co., Florham Park, N.J., 1965-67; tchr. Livingston (N.J.) High Sch., 1967-69; substitute tchr. Singapore Am. High Sch., 1970-71; teaching asst. N.J. Inst. Tech., Newark, 1977-78, adj. instr., 1978-81; asst. prof. chem. engring. dept. Manhattan Coll., Riverdale, N.Y., 1982-88, assoc. prof., 1988-94; prof., 1994—; head dept. chem. engring. Manhattan Coll., Riverdale, N.Y., 1989—. Contbr. articles to profl. publs., chpt. to book. Recipient Teetor Ednl. award SAE, 1984; NSF grantee, 1983-92. Mem. Soc. Women Engrs. (sr.), Am. Soc. Engring. Edn., Am. Inst. Chem. Engrs., Sigma Xi (pres. Manhattan Coll. chpt. 1989-90). Office: Manhattan Coll Chem Engring Dept Riverdale NY 10471

HOLLEMAN, SANDY LEE, religious organization administrator; b. Celina, Tex., June 6, 1940; d. Guy Lee and Gustine (Kirby-Sheets) Luna; m. Allen Craig Holleman, June 5, 1959. Cert., Eastfield Coll., 1979. Intern Walter Reed Gen. Hosp., Washington, D.C., 1972-73; resident Parkland Meml. Hosp., Dallas, 1973-75; with Annuity Bd. So. Bapt. Conv., Dallas, 1958—, mgr. personnel, 1983-85, dir. human resources, 1985-91, v.p. human resources, 1991—. Mem. Am. Mgmt. Soc. (dir. salary surveys local chpt. 1986—, v.p. chpt. svcs. 1987—), Dallas Soc. Human Resource Mgmt., Soc. Human Resource Mgmt., Diversity Club Dallas (program chmn. 1976, v.p. 1977), Order Ea. Star, Daus. of Nile. Baptist. Home: 4524 Sarazen Dr Mesquite TX 75150-2348 Office: Annuity Bd So Bapt Conv 2401 Cedar Springs Rd Dallas TX 75201-1427

HOLLENBECK, KAREN FERN, foundation executive; b. Snover, Mich., Mar. 30, 1943; d. Glenn Lee and Ada Gertrude (Robinson) Roberts; m. Marvin Allan Hollenbeck, June 18, 1966. AA, Kellogg Community Coll., 1980; BSBA, Nazareth Coll., 1987. Dir. fellowships W.K. Kellogg Found., Battle Creek, Mich., 1979-85, asst. v.p. adminstrn., 1985-88, v.p. adminstrn., 1988—. Bd. dirs. Arc Ministries, Allegan, Mich., 1982—, Vol. Bur., Battle Creek, 1984-86, ARC, Calhoun County, Mich., 1985—. Recipient Outstanding Young Women of Am. award. Mem. NAFE, Am. Mgmt. Assn., Soc. Human Resource Mgmt., Positive Employee Practices Inst. Home: 1713 Bridle Creek St SE Grand Rapids MI 49508-4934 Office: WK Kellogg Found One Michigan Ave East Battle Creek MI 49017-4058

HOLLENBECK, MARYNELL, municipal government official; b. Nashville, May 2, 1939; d. Lee B. and Beulah B. (Bradley) Reifel; children: Braeson, Danelle. BA, Iowa State U., 1976, MS, 1980; PhD, ABD, 1981. Cert. regulatory mgr. EPA, DOT, OSHA regulation. Dir. environ. svcs. Bd. Pub. Utilities, Kansas City, Kans.; prof. Southwest Mo. State U., Springfield, Mo.; instr. Iowa State U., Ames; profl. cons. to Springfield Newspapers, Inc., Victims of Domestic Violence, Springfield Health Dept., 1984-86, Southwest Ctr. for Ind. Living, 1986-88. Contbr. articles to profl. jours. Advisor Gamma Sigma Sigma, 1984-86; mem. Hazardous Materials Ctrl. Rsch. Inst., Kansas City (Kans.) Hazardous Materials Adv. Bd.; mem. Greene County Cen. Dem. Com., 1981-86, Story County Cen. Dem. Com., 1977-81; v.p. bd. dirs. Battered Women's Program, 1985-86. Recipient Bus. and Profl. Women award for Leadership and Service, 1976. Mem. Air & Waste Mgmt. Assn. (dir. midwest sect.), Am. Pub. Power Assn. (chair environ. sect.), Nat. Assn. Hazardous Waste Generators, Gamma Sigma Delta, Phi Kappa Phi, Alpha Kappa Delta, Sigma Xi (E.A. Ross award for sci. rsch. 1977, Von Tungeln award for leadership, rsch. and svc. 1980). Unitarian. Office: 1211 N 8th St Kansas City KS 66101-2192

HOLLERAN, PAULA RIZZO, psychology and counseling educator, researcher, consultant; b. N.Y.C.; d. A.M. and Jean T. Rizzo; m. Brian Patrick Holleran, Aug. 22, 1970; children: Tracy Lynn, Brett Daniel. BA, Bklyn. Coll., 1959; MA, U. Conn., 1963; PhD, U. Mass., 1969. Tchr. Shell Bank Jr. High Sch., Bklyn., 1960-62; instr. psychology SUNY, Oneonta, 1963-67, assoc. prof., 1969-70, prof. psychology and counseling, mem. grad. faculty, women's studies faculty, chair dept., 1970—, spl. asst. to assoc. commr. U.S. Office Edn., Washington, 1967-68; cons., specialist Headstart and Followthrough Projects, 1968-71; v.p. Rainbow Assocs./Cons., Oneonta, 1979—; presenter at nat. and regional confs.; developer several univ. level courses. Contbr. numerous articles to profl. jours.; reviewer ednl. rsch. jour.; co-author Nat. Assessment of Women's Studies Programs in Higher Edn.; co-developer Couples Communication Workshop and Gender Summit Game for Marriage Counselors. Officer Oneonta Taxpayers Assn. 1978-79; bd. dirs. Goodyear Lake Assn., Md., N.Y., 1984—; co-dir. Hillside Homeowner's Assn., 1987—. U.S. Office Edn. fellow HEW, 1967-68, rsch. grantee Commonwealth Mass. Bur. Rsch., 1969-70, Walter B. Ford Faculty grantee, 1988—, PDQ grantee SUNY, 1990, 94. Mem. ACA, Am. Ednl. Rsch. Assn., Assn. for Women in Psychology, New Eng. Ednl. Rsch. Orgn (best paper award 1981, 87), N.E. Ednl. Rsch. Assn. Office: SUNY Dept Psychology and Counseling Oneonta NY 13820

HOLLERN-EICHELBERGER, PATRICA MARIE, critical care nurse, educator; b. Smith Center, Kans., Apr. 28, 1958; d. Lloyd and Donna W. (Roe) H.; m. John Paul Eichelberger, May 25, 1985. AS, Cloud County Community Coll., 1978, Butler County Community Coll., 1987. LPN, RN, Kans. Practical nurse St. Anthony Hosp., Hays, Kans., 1978-85, Wesley Med. Ctr., Wichita, Kans., 1985-86; practical nurse St. Francis Regional Med. Ctr., Wichita, 1986-87, nurse, 1987—; patient educator Cardiac Rehab., 1993—; natural family planning practitioner intern Pope Paul VI Inst., Creighton U., 1994—; pub. spkr. Family of the Americus, Wichita, 1986—, Am. Heart Assn., Wichita, 1993—. Past pres. St. Francis of Assisi Ladies Aux., Wichita, 1989-91; pres. Christian Mothers Orgn., Wichita, 1990—. Named one of Outstanding Young Women of Am. Mem. AACCN, ANA, Kans. Nurses for Life. Republican. Roman Catholic. Home: 1452 Glenhurst Wichita KS 67212 Office: St Francis Regional Med Ctr 925 N Emporia Wichita KS 67212

HOLLEY, SYLVIA A., state legislator; b. Rutland, Vt., Apr. 7, 1942; married; 2 children. Student, Rivier Coll., 1983. Ret. video teleconf. specialist Digital Corp.; mem. N.H. Ho. of Reps.; mem. children, youth and juvenile justice com. Bd. dirs. ARC, Nashua; sec. LWV; cons. Everywoman's Ctr. YWCA, Manchester; gift shop vol. Cath. Med. Ctr. Office: NH Ho of Reps State Capitol Concord NH 03301*

HOLLIDAY, JANICE RUTH SMITH, accountant; b. San Antonio, Apr. 20, 1961; d. Richard Franklin and Nell Jean (Seago) Smith; m. Richard Allen Holliday Jr., Jan. 2, 1981; children: Ashley Lanell, Katy Jane Austell. AA in Bus. Adminstrn., Tarrant County Jr. Coll., 1983; BA in Bus. Adminstrn.-Acctg., U. Tex., Arlington, 1986; MA in Health Svc. Adminstrn., S.W. U., New Orleans, 1994. Diplomate Am. Coll. Healthcare Execs.; CPA, Tex.; cert. healthcare exec., CHE. Staff internal auditor Harris Meth. Health Sys., Ft. Worth, 1986-88, sr. internal auditor, 1988-90, acctg. cons., 1990; asst. adminstr. fin. Walls Regional Hosp., Cleburne, Tex., 1990-94, treas., bd. trustees, 1990-94; acct. in pvt. practice Ft. Worth, 1994—; mem. fin. coun. Harris Meth. Health Sys., Ft. Worth, 1990-94. Active North Benbrook Neighborhood Assn., Ft. Worth, 1986—, Benbrook Bd. Sailing Assn., Ft. Worth, 1986—; asst. treas., mem. coun. Williams Rd. Bapt. Ch., Ft. Worth, 1991—. Mem. AICPA, Healthcare Fin. Mgmt. Assn., Tex. Soc. CPAs. Republican. Home: 4113 Tara Dr Fort Worth TX 76116-7696

HOLLIDAY, PATRICIA RUTH MCKENZIE, evangelist; b. Jacksonville, Fla., Nov. 17, 1935; d. Robert Irving and Leona Adele (Bell) McKenzie; student Massey Bus. Coll., 1969, Luther Rice Sem., 1976; DD, Southeastern Theol. Sem., 1986, ThD, 1989; m. Jan. 20, 1965; children—Connie, Katheryn, Alexander. Sec., Delta Drug Corp., Jacksonville, 1965—; pres. Microfilm Center, Jacksonville, 1974—; pres. Miracle Outreach Ministry, Jacksonville, 1974—; prof. Southeastern Theol. Sem., Jacksonville, Fla., 1992—. Sec.. Four Found., Inc.; Republican candidate for Fla. Ho. of Reps., 1972; mem. Fla. Republican. Com., 1976-80; lobbyist Fla. Legislature, 1978-80; hostess Pat Holliday TV Show, Jacksonville. Clubs: Minutewomen of Fla. (founder), Univ., Women, Ponte Vedra Women's. Author: Holliday for the King, 1978, Be Free, 1979, Only Believe, 1980, Born Anew, 1981, The Walking Dead, 1982, Anointing Power, 1982, Signs, Wonders and Reactions, 1984, Dealing with Heresies, 1986, Marriage Answers, 1992, Solitary Satanist, 1993, Entertaining Angels of Light, 1993, The Plan: Ascended Masters, 1994, The New World Aftershock, 1994; columnist Christian Courier. Home: 9252 San Jose Blvd Apt 2804 Jacksonville FL 32257-9205

HOLLIDAY, POLLY DEAN, actress; b. Jasper, Ala., July 2, 1937; d. Ernest Sullivan and Velma Mabell (Cain) H. B. Music Edn., Ala. State Women's Coll. (now U. Montevallo), 1959; postgrad., Fla. State U., 1960; D.H.L. hon., Mt. St. Mary's Coll., 1982. Tchr. music Sarasota (Fla.) public schs., 1961. Appeared with Asolo Theatre Repertory Co., Sarasota, 1962-72; appeared in Off-Broadway, Wedding Band, 1972; Quarrel of Sparrows, 1993, Broadway shows All Over Town, 1975, Arsenic & Old Lace, 1986-87, Cat on a Hot Tin Roof, 1990, (Tony nomination), Picnic, 1994; appeared in play The Glass Menagerie, Tyrone Guthrie Theatre, Mpls., 1988; appeared as Flo on CBS-TV series Alice, 1976-80, Flo, 1981, appeared in Golden Girls, 1986, Amazing Stories, 1986, Home Improvement, 1993 & 94; appeared in TV movies You Can't Take it With You, 1981, The Shadyhill Kidnapping, 1981, All the Way Home, 1981, Missing Children, 1982, A Gift of Love, 1983; PBS Wonderworks series Konrad, 1985, (TV Movie) Triumph of the Heart, 1991; appeared in feature films All The President's Men, 1975, The One and Only, 1977, Gremlins, 1984, Moon Over Parador, 1987, Mrs. Doubtfire, 1993,. Recipient Golden Globe award for best supporting actress on TV series, 1978, 79. Episcopalian. Office: Lantz Office 888 7th Ave New York NY 10106-0084

HOLLIDAY, TERRY LYNN, artist; b. Corpus Christi, Tex., May 12, 1955; d. David Hezekiah Waldrop and Susie Jane (Etter) Westphal; m. Jay Kenton Holliday, Aug. 16, 1975; children: Lara Dawn, David Glenn. BS, Tex. A&M U., 1977. Cert. tchr., Tex. Tchr. physical sci. Spring High Sch. South, Houston, 1978-79; tchr. sci. Northland Christian Sch., Houston, 1979-80, 81-82. One-woman shows include Brazos Ctr., Bryan, Tex., 1988, MSC Gallery, Tex. A&M U., College Station, Tex., 1989, Arts Coun. Brazos Valley, College Station, 1990, Mus. of the Big Bend Sul Ross State U., Alpine, Tex., 1991; exhibited in group shows at Watercolor Art Soc., Houston, 1985, 86, 88, 91-94, Navasota Art League, 1985-90, (Best of Show award 1985, 89), Watercolor East Tex. Exhbn., 1986, 88, 89, Brazos Valley Art League, 1985, 86, 88, 89, 92, 93 (Best of Show award 1989, Wootan Watercolor award 1986, 89), Woodlands Art League, 1986-90, Lone Star Art Guild, 1987-90, Tex. Watercolor Soc., 1988-89, Aqueous, 1988, Ky. Watercolor Soc. (award), Tex. Artisans, 1990, Pasadena Art League, 1991, Mont. Watercolor Soc., (awards), Okla. Art Workshops, 1992, Bosque County Conservatory Fine Arts, 1993, Boise State U., Idaho, 1994, Taos Nat. Exhbn. Am. Watercolor, 1995; represented in permanent and pvt. collections. Mem. Watercolor Art Soc. Houston (chmn. publicity 1984, exhbn. dir. 1991), Navasota Art League (chmn. show 1987, v.p. 1989), Tex. Watercolor Soc. Mem. Ch. of Christ. Home: Rt 2 Box 2975 Navasota TX 77868

HOLLIEN, PATRICIA ANN, small business owner, scientist; b. N.Y.C., May 11, 1938; d. Leon and Sophia (Biernacki) Milanowski; m. Harry Hollien, Aug. 26, 1969; children: Brian, Stephanie, Christine. AA, Sante Fe Jr. Coll., 1969; ScD (hon), Marian Coll., 1983; student, U. Fla., 1977—. Rsch. asst. Marineland Rsch. Labs., 1965-69; co-owner, exec. v.p. Hollien Assocs., 1969—; owner, dir. Forensic Communication Assocs., Gainesville, Fla., 1981—, The Eden Group, Gainesville, 1995—; vis. assoc. Royal Inst. Spl. Transmission Lab., Stockholm, 1970, Wroclaw Tech. U., Poland, 1974; asst. in research Inst. Advanced Study Communication Scis. U. Fla., 1977-83, assoc. in research, 1983—; adj. asst. prof. Communication Sci. Lab., N.Y., 1982—. Co-author: Current Issues in the Phonetic Sciences, 1979; editor The Phonetician, 1991—; contbr. articles to profl. jours. Bd. dirs. Ann. Retirement Village, Waldo, Fla., 1981-93. Fellow Am. Acad. Forensic Scis.; mem. Internat. Soc. Phonetic Scis. (coun. reps. 1983—), Am. Assn. Phonetic Scis., Acad. Forensic Application of the Comm. Sci., Internat. Assn. Forensic Phonetics (sec. gen. 7th Ann. Congress 1995). Home: 229 SW 43rd Ter Gainesville FL 32607-2270 Office: Forensic Communication Assocs PO Box 12323 Gainesville FL 32604-0323

HOLLIER, JEAN VAN GOSSEN, dietician; b. Alexandria, La., Jan. 19, 1943; d. Ernest Ferdinand and Irma Dale (Greene) Van G.; m. James Paul Hollier, May 10, 1992; children: George Allan, Rhonda Marie, Monica Jean. BS in Dietetics and Institutional Mgmt., Northwestern State U., 1980, MS in Home Econs. Edn., 1984. Registered dietician; lic. dietician, La. Clin./prodn. dietician Rapides Regional Med. Ctr., Alexandria, 1980-83; staff dietician Pinecrest State Sch., Pineville, La., 1983-85, asst. dir. nutrition svcs., 1985-90; dir. nutrition svcs. St. Mary's Residential Tng. Sch., Alexandria, 1990—; cons. Colwell Interest, Inc., Alexandria, 1988—, Wm. Bell, Inc., Colfax, La., 1990—, Our Lady of Sorrows Community Homes, Alexandria, 1991—. Mem. Am. Dietetic Assn., Am. Assn. Mental Retardation, Nutrition Today Soc., La. Dietetic Assn. (bd. dirs. 1986-87), Cenla Dietetic Assn. (pres. 1986-87). Democrat. Roman Catholic. Home: 411 Cloverleaf Blvd Alexandria LA 71303 Office: St Marys Residential Tng Sc Hwy 1 North Alexandria LA 71306

HOLLINGER, PAULA COLODNY, state senator; b. Washington, Dec. 30, 1940; d. Samuel and Ethel (Levy) Colodny; m. Paul Hollinger, Sept. 16, 1962; children: Ilene, Marcy, David. RN, Mt. Sinai Hosp., N.Y.C., 1961. Mem. Md. Ho. of Dels., 1978-86; mem. Md. Ho. of Dels. Md. State Senate, Annapolis, 1987—; vice chair econ. and environ. affairs com.; chmn. health subcom. of econ. and environ. affairs com. Md. State Senate, Annapolis, 1987-92; vice chair econ. and environ. affairs com. Md. Ho. of Dels. Md. State Senate, Annapolis, 1995—; mem. Gov.'s Adv. Coun. on AIDS; senate chair, 1995; mem. joint com. on Health Care Delivery and Financing, 1994—; mem. Joint Com. on Health Care Cost Containment, Gov.'s Task Force to Study Nursing Crisis; vice-chair health com. Nat. Conf. State Legis., 1990, chair, 1992, past chair sci. and resources tech. com., chair health com., 1992. Bd. dirs. Nat. Coun. Jewish Women, Safety First, 1990; past pres. Women Legislators of Md., 1986, 87, 88. Recipient Murry Guggenheim award, 1961, Edith Rosen Strauss award, 1987, Verda Welcome award for outstanding polit. achievements and pub. svc., 1989, Legislator of Yr. award Md. Nurse's Assn., 1984. Mem. B'nai Brith Women, Chi Eta Phi (hon.). Office: Rm 206 Md State Senate Office Bldg Annapolis MD 21401-1991

HOLLINGSHEAD, BONNE LOU, fine art artist; b. Mooreland, Okla., July 17, 1929; d. Floyd Nickolas and Opal Ellena (Lehman) Stoll; m. Gerald Eugene Hollingshead, Nov. 14, 1970; 1 child, Jerry Delmont. Student, Ft. Smith (Ark.) Jr. Coll., 1950s, Okla. A&M Coll., 1950s, Okla U., 1960s, Oklahoma City U., 1960s. Nurse N.W. Community Hosp., Mooreland, 1946-48; spl. nurse Sugg Clinic, Ada, Okla., 1948-50; acct. U.S. Army, Ft. Smith, Ark., 1951-57; nurse Enid (Okla.) Meml. Hosp., 1958-60; acct. Vance AFB, Enid, 1957-60, FAA, Oklahoma City, 1960-76; sec., office mgr. Senate Offices, Oklahoma City, 1979-90; real estate sales assoc. Abide Realtors, Inc., Oklahoma City, 1983-87; with consumer credit div. Atty. Gen., Oklahoma City, 1990; Atty. Gen. Oklahoma City, 1990; sec. to Senate Minority Leader, Okla. State Senate, 1980-82; sec. to Senate Caucus Chmn., 1983-84. Artist, editor: (craft book) Roses in Pink, 1994. Campaign mgr. office Senator John R. McCune, 1990. Mem. Can. Valley Art Guild (sec. 1993-94), Edmond Art Guild, Okla. Art Guild (treas. 1989, 1st v.p. 1994, pres. 1994—, bd. dirs. 1991—), Okla. Watercolor Assn. (treas. 1994—), Ctrl. Arts Assn., Audubon Soc. Home: 12516 Deerwood Dr Oklahoma City OK 73142-5105

HOLLINGSWORTH, MARGARET CAMILLE, financial services administrator, consultant; b. Washington, Feb. 20, 1929; d. Harvey Alvin and Margaret Estelle (Head) Jacob; m. Robert Edgar Hollingsworth, July 14, 1960 (div. July 1980); children: William Lee, Robert Edgar Hollingsworth Jr., Barbara Camille, Bradford Damion. AA, Va. Intermont Coll., 1949. Bookkeeper Fred A. Smith Real Estate, Washington, 1949-53; adminstrv. mgr. Airtronic, Inc., Bethesda, Md., 1953-61; pers. adminstr. Sears Roebuck, Washington, 1973-74; adminstrv. mgr., communication mgr. Garvin GuyButler Corp., San Francisco, 1980-88, exec. sec., pers. mgr., 1989—; assoc. Robert Hollingsworth Nuclear Cons., Walnut Creek, Calif., 1975-79. Mem., bd. dirs. Civic Arts, Walnut Creek, 1975. Recipient Spl. Recognition award AEC, 1974. Mem. Internat. Platform Assn., Commonwealth Club, Beta Sigma Phi (pres. 1954). Democrat. Presbyterian. Home: 1108 Limeridge Dr Concord CA 94518-1923 Office: Garvin GuyButler Corp 456 Montgomery St Ste 1900 San Francisco CA 94104-1252

HOLLINGSWORTH, MARTHA LYNETTE, educator; b. Waco, Tex., Oct. 9, 1951; d. Willie Frederick and Georgia Cuddell (Bryant) J.; m. Roy David Hollingsworth, Dec. 31, 1971; children: Richard Avery, Justin Brian. A.A., McLennan Community Coll., 1972; B.B.A., Baylor U., 1974, MS in Ednl. Administrn., 1992. Tchr., Connally Ind. Sch. Dist., Waco, 1974—; with Adult Edn. Night Sch., 1974-78; chairperson for Area III leadership conf. Vocat. Office Careers Clubs Tex., Waco, 1985—; active Lakeview Little League Booster Club, 1985—. Mem. PTA (hon. life), Vocat. Office Edn. Tchr.'s Assn. Tex., Assn. Tex. Profl. Educators (v.p. local chpt. 1988-90), Future Homemakers Am. Area VIII (hon.), Tex. Future Farmers Am. (hon.), Delta Kappa Gamma. Baptist. Office: Connally Vocat Dept 715 N Rita St Waco TX 76705-1140

HOLLINGSWORTH, MEREDITH BEATON, clinical nurse specialist; b. Danvers, Mass., Oct. 5, 1941; d. Allan Cameron and Arlene Margaret (Jerue) Beaton; m. William Paul Hollingsworth, Nov. 19, 1983; stepchild, Brendon R. Diploma, R.I. Hosp. Sch. Nursing, Providence, 1968; BS in Nursing, U. Ariz., 1976; MS in Human Resource Mgmt., Golden Gate U., 1984; postgrad., U. Tex., 1988, U. N.Mex., 1989—. Cert. enterostomal therapy nurse, health edn. specialist. Commd. ensign USN, 1968, advanced through grades to lt. comdr., 1979; charge nurse USN, USA, PTO, 1968-88; command ostomy nurse, head ostomy clinic Naval Hosp. Portsmouth, Va., 1985-88; pres., chief exec. officer Enterostomal Therapy Nursing Edn. and Tng. Cons. (ETNetc), Rio Rancho, N.Mex., 1989-90; mgr. clin. svcs. we. area Support Systems Internat., Inc., Charleston, S.C., 1990-92; pres., CEO Paumer Assocs. Internat., Inc., Rio Rancho, N.Mex., 1992—; enterstomal therapy nurse, clin. nurse specialist, educator Presbyn. Health Care Svcs., Albuquerque, 1993—. Mem. adminstrv. bd. Baylake United Meth. Ch., Virginia Beach, 1980-83; chmn. bd. deacons St. Paul's United Ch., Rio Rancho; active Am. Cancer Soc. Mem. Wound, Ostomy and Continence Nurses Soc. (nat. govt. affairs com., govt. affairs com. Rocky Mountain region, pub. rels. com., regional pres. 1989-93, nat. sec. 1994-96), United Ostomy Assn., World Coun. Enterstromal Therapists, N.Mex. Soc. Healthcare Edn. and Tng. of Am. Hosp. Assn., N.Mex. Health Care Assn., Care Star Network. Republican. Office: PO Box 44395 Rio Rancho NM 87174-4395

HOLLINGWORTH, BEVERLY A., state senator; b. Haverhill, Mass., Oct. 18, 1935; m. William P. Gilligan, 1978; children: David, Mary Beth. Therese, Kimberly. Student, U. N.H. Formerly rep. dist. 17 State of N.H.; mem. N.H. State Senate, 1991—; owner, mgr. Hollingworth Motor Ct., Hampton Beach, N.H.; chmn. appropriations com.; vice chmn. ins. com.; mem. ways and means com., mem. judiciary com., mem. fin. exec. com., mem. joint adminstrv. peals com. Active United Way, Heart Fund, ARC, Lane Meml. Friends Libr. Mem. Hampton Beach (N.H.) C. of C. Democrat. Roman Catholic. Home: 209 Winnacunnet Rd Hampton NH 03842-2129 Office: NH State Senate State House Concord NH 03301

HOLLINS, LIZ ANNE, physician assistant, surgical technologist; b. Pitts., Oct. 25, 1956; d. William Samuel and Mary Helen (Reagan) H. BS in P.A., St. Francis Coll., 1988, M in Med. Sci., 1994. Cert. physician asst. Surg. technologist West Penn. Hosp., Pitts., 1977-88; physician asst. Shadyside Hosp., Pitts., 1988—; guest lectr. physician asst. program St. Francis Coll., Loretto, Pa., 1990-92, coord. annual musculoskeletal conf.; clin. preceptor physician asst. students, Shadyside Hosp., 1988—. Eucharistic min. St. Joseph Cath. Ch., Pitts., 1980-84. Mem. Am. Acad. Physician Assts. Home: 1426 Morningside Ave Pittsburgh PA 15206

HOLLINSHEAD, ARIEL CAHILL, research oncologist; b. Allentown, Pa., Aug. 24, 1929; d. Earl Darnell and Gertrude Loretta (Cahill) H.; m. Montgomery K. Hyun, Sept. 27, 1958; children: William C., Christopher C. Student, Swarthmore Coll., 1947-48; AB, Ohio U., 1951, DSc (hon.), 1977; MS, George Washington U., 1955, PhD, 1957. Asst. prof., fellow in virology Baylor U. Med. Center, 1958-59; asst. prof. pharmacology George Washington Med. Center, 1959-61, asst. prof. medicine, 1961-64, assoc. prof. medicine, head lab. virus and cancer research, 1964-73, prof. medicine, dir. lab. for virus and cancer research, 1974-89; on sabbatical leave 1990, prof. medicine emeritus, 1991—; pres. HT Virus and Cancer Rsch., 1991—; clin. researcher trials in oncology and virology. Contbr. over 260 articles on active immunotherapy of cancer to profl. jours.; author numerous book chpts. Bd. dirs. Nat. Women's Econ. Alliance, Nat. Bd. Ohio U.; bd. dirs. Nat. Arthritis Fdn., FDA Immunology Commn., Dept. Agriculture Biotech. Rsch. Adv. Commn., NIH Internat. Fellowships Commn., Dept. Agriculture Nat. Fellowships Commn., Nat. Bd. Med. Coll. Pa. Named Med. Woman of Yr. Joint Bd. Am. Med. Colls., 1975-76, one of Outstanding Woman of Am., 1987, Outstanding Alumnus of Yr., Ohio U., 1990; recipient Cert. merit Med. Coll. Pa., 1975-76; decorated Star of Europe, 1980. Fellow Washington Acad. Sci., Am. Acad. Microbiology, AAAS; mem. N.Y. Acad. Sci., Am. Acad. Microbiology, Grad. Women in Sci. (nat. pres. 1985-86, bd. dirs. 1986-92), Internat. Soc. Preventive Oncology, Nat. Soc. Exptl. Biology and Medicine (Disting. Scientist award 1985), Am. Soc. Microbiology, Am. Assn. Cancer Research, Am. Assn. Immunologists, Clin. Immunology Soc., Internat. Soc. Antiviral Research, Am. Soc. Clin. Oncology, Internat. Assn. Study Lung Cancer, Internat. Union Against Cancer, Am. Med. Writers Assn., Phi Beta Kappa (alumnus 1990). Clubs: Kenwood Country, Blue Ridge Mountain Country, Washington Forum (pres. 1987, 91). Home: 3637 Van Ness St NW Washington DC 20008-3130

HOLLINSHEAD, MAY BLOCK, anatomist, educator; b. N.Y.C., Nov. 28, 1913; d. Abraham and Pauline (Markle) Block; m. Merrill Taylor Hollinshead, May 10, 1942; 1 child, Richard Clark. AB, Hunter Coll., 1936; PhD, Columbia U., 1951. Rsch. asst. Vanderbilt U. Sch. Medicine, Nashville, 1942; lab. asst. Stat. Hosp./Army Air Field, Amarillo Shepard Field, Tex., 1943; asst. in anatomy Bowman Gray Sch. Medicine/U. N.C. Med. Sch., Winston-Salem/Chapel Hill, N.C., 1943, U. So. Calif. Sch. Medicine, L.A., 1945, Columbia U. Coll. of Physicians and Surgeons, N.Y.C., 1949-51; instr. in anatomy NYU Coll of Medicine, N.Y.C., 1951-56; asst. prof. anatomy Seton Hall Coll. Medicine and Dentistry, Jersey City, N.J., 1956-61; assoc. prof. anatomy N.J. Coll. Medicine and Dentistry, Jersey City/Newark, 1961-72; prof. anatomy U. of Medicine and Dentistry, N.J. Med. Sch., Newark, 1972-90; retired, 1990. Contbr. articles to profl. jours.; contbg. author to books in field. Recipient grant-in-aid Columbia U., 1941, Curtis Scholarship, 1948; named Woman of the Yr., Am. Med. Womens's Assn. (br. 4, N.J.), 1979. Mem. AAAS, Am. Assn. Anatomists, CAJAL Club, Union of Concerned Scientists, NOW, Nat. Women's Health Network, Gray Panthers of No. N.J. (chair), N.J. Peace Action, Amnesty Internat., Sigma Xi. Home: 2 Winthrop Pl Leonia NJ 07605-1226

HOLLIS, LINDA EARDLEY, urban planning consultant; b. Washington, Feb. 1, 1948; d. Edward Pixton and Margy (Anderson) Eardley; m. Daryl Joseph Hollis, July 18, 1970. BA, Pa. State U., University Park, 1968; M in Regional Planning, U. N.C., 1979. Planning analyst First-Citizens Bank, Raleigh, N.C., 1973-76; research assoc. ctr. for urban regional studies U. N.C., Chapel Hill, 1978-79; research assoc. The Osprey Co., Tallahassee, 1980-81, Patrick H. Hare Planning and Design, Washington, 1982-83; cons. Tischler & Assocs., Inc., Bethesda, Md., Washington and Falls Church, Va., 1983—; analyst dept. fiscal services Md. Gen. Assembly, Annapolis, 1988-89. Contbr. articles to profl. jours. Rep. Mason dist. Fairfax County Commn. on Organ and Tissue Donation and Transplantation, 1995—. NEH grantee, 1980. Mem. Am. Planning Assn. (book reviewer 1980, 93, nat. bd. dirs., regional rep. 1986-88, chmn. nat. state policy coordinating com. 1987-88, chair task force on women and minorities 1987-88), Washington Women in Planning (co-founder), Columbia Pines Citizens Assn. Democrat. Home: 4002 Rose Ln Annandale VA 22003-1943 Office: Tischler & Assocs Inc 4701 Sangamore Rd Ste 210N Bethesda MD 20816-2508

HOLLIS, LOUCILLE, risk control adminstrator, educator; b. Ft. Myers, Fla., Feb. 16, 1949; d. Luke Sr. and Louise (Wilcox) Black; m. Benjamin L. Hollis, Jr., Sept. 26, 1985. BS, N.Y. Inst. Tech., 1982, MBA, 1984. Staff asst. Equitable, N.Y.C., 1977-79, budget analyst, 1979-81, fin. analyst, 1981-85, mgr. operational planning, 1985-87, mgr. expense control, 1987-88; project leader L.I. R.R. Co., Jamaica, N.Y., 1988-91, asst. risk mgr., 1991—; comml. arbitrator Am. Arbitration Assn. Bronx fundraiser Cancer Fund Am., Knoxville, Tenn., 1991, 92; mem. bd. placement project United Way Linkage; literacy vol. Recipient Psychology award N.Y. Inst. Tech., 1981, acad. scholarship Ft. Myers Bd. Edn., 1977; honoree LIRR Women's History Celebration. Mem. NAFE, Nat. Black MBA Assn., Risk and Ins. Mgmt. Soc., RR Ins. Mgmt. Assn., Conf. Minority Transp. Ofcls., Psi Nat. Honor Soc. Democrat. Office: LI RR Co Jamaica Sta Ste 1435 Jamaica NY 11435

HOLLIS, MARY FERN CAUDILL, community health nurse; b. Augusta, Ga., Mar. 13, 1942; d. Robert Paul and Fern (Alderton) Caudill; children: Harry N. III (dec.), Mary Melissa, H. Newcombe IV. B in Music Edn., U. Louisville, 1964; AS in Nursing, Tenn. State U., 1980; postgrad., Nashville Tech. Inst., 1987—. RN, Tenn. Staff nurse oncology and med.-surg. units St. Thomas Hosp., Nashville, 1981-82; staff oncology nurse Alive Hospice, Nashville, 1982-83; scheduling coord. HCA Parkview Med. Ctr., Nashville, 1987-88; nurse, staff relief coord. Partners Home Health, Nashville, 1989-90; nursing supr. Kimberly Quality Care Staffing, Nashville, 1991-92; RN coord. on call MedPartners Nursing Svc. of Mid. Tenn., Nashville, 1994—; profl. vocal soloist; tchr. piano, music edn., music theory, voice. Author: Out of My Suffering: Reflections of a Hospice Nurse, 1984. Mem. Music Tchrs. Nat. Assn. (profl. cert. music edn. and voice), Tenn. Music Tchrs. Assn., Nashville Area Music Tchrs. Assn., Am. Coll. Musicians, Nat. Guild Piano Tchrs., Sigma Alpha Iota, Gamma Phi Beta.

HOLLIS, MARY FRANCES, aerospace educator; b. Indpls., Sept. 18, 1931; d. Lucian Albert and Clara Frances Coleman; divorced; 1 child, Booker Albert Hollis. BS, Butler U., 1952, MS, 1962; postgrad., Stanford U., 1975, San Francisco State U., 1980-81. Cert. elem. tchr., Ind., Calif. Kindergarten tchr. Lockerbie Nursery Sch., Indpls., 1952, Indpls. Pub. Schs., 1952-69; tchr. K-6 San Mateo (Calif.) City Sch. Dist., 1969-91; summer sch. prin. San Mateo City Sch. dist., Foster City, Calif., 1983-91; aerospace educator, 1982—; bd. dirs. Coun. of Math./Sci. Educators of San Mateo County, Belmont, Calif. Editor: San Mateo County Math./Sci. Coun. quarterly newsletter, 1988-90. Bd. dirs. Arts Coun. of San Mateo County, 1986-91, ACLU, San Mateo, 1990-94; office mgr. Roger Winston Campaign for San Mateo Union H.S. Dist. Bd. Trustees, 1993; mem. adv. com. USAF-Pacific Liaison Region-CAP, 1988-94. Recipient Life Down to Earth award NASA, Moffet Field, Mt. View, Calif., 1985-86, Earl Sams Tchr. of Yr. award Calif. Assn. Aerospace Educators, 1989, award of merit Am. Legion, San Bruno, Calif., 1989, citation Air Force Assn., Mountain View, Calif., 1991, Aviation Summer Sch. cert. of appreciation Am. Legion Dept. Calif. Aerospace Commn., 1994. Mem. NEA (life), Am. Bus. Women's Assn. (recording sec. Foster City chpt. 1985), AAUW (bd. dirs. San Carlos chpt. 1993-94). Democrat. Unitarian-Universalist. Office: PO Box 625 Belmont CA 94002-0625

HOLLIS-ALLBRITTON, CHERYL DAWN, retail paper supply store executive; b. Elgin, Ill., Feb. 15, 1959; d. L.T. and Florence (Elder) Saylors; m. Thomas Allbritton, Aug. 10, 1985. BS in Phys. Edn., Brigham Young U., 1981; cosmetologist Sch. Beauty Culture, Berwyn, Ill., 1981. Retail sales clk. Bee Discount, North Riverside, Ill., 1981-82, retail store mgr., Downers Grove, Ill., 1982, Oaklawn, Ill., 1982-83, St. Louis, 1983; retail tng. mgr. Arvey Paper & Supplies, Chgo., 1984, retail store mgr., Columbus, Ohio, 1985—. Mem. Nat. Assn. Female Execs. Republican. Mormon. Avocations: cosmetology, reading, travel. Office: Arvey Paper & Supplies 431 E Livingston Ave Columbus OH 43215-5586

HOLLISTER, JULIET GARRETSON, educator; b. Forest Hills, L.I., N.Y., Oct. 30, 1916; d. James and Dorothy Sewell (Baldwin) Garretson; m. Dickerman Hollister, June 17, 1939; children: Clay, Catharine de Rapalye, Dickerman Jr. Degree in early edn., Froebel League, N.Y.C., 1937; Hon. degree, The New Sem., N.Y.C., 1990. Founder, chmn. bd. dirs. Temple of Understanding, Cathedral of St. John the Divine, N.Y.C., 1960—; co-founder Peace Pyramid Found., Washington, 1993, 94; bd. dirs. Teilhard de Chardin, N.Y.C., Peace Works, Charleston, S.C., Pathways to Peace, Larkspur, Calif., World Peace Prayer Soc., N.Y.C. Recipient Eleanor Roosevelt award Ctr. for Internat. Dialogue, 1994. Mem. Cosmopolitan Club. Home: 661 Steamboat Rd Greenwich CT 06830 Office: Temple of Understanding care Cathedral St John the Divine 1045 Amsterdam Ave New York NY 10025

HOLLISTER, NANCY, state official. Lt. gov. State of Ohio, 1995—. Office: Office of Lt Governor State Office Tower II 30th Fl 77 S High St Columbus OH 43215*

HOLLOWAY, EDNA LARUE, real estate sales agent, administrative assistant; b. Hanover, Pa., July 28, 1942; d. Maurice Edward and Helen Viola (Smith) Wisner; m. Donald LeRoy Holloway, Dec. 29, 1963. BA, Towson State U., 1964, MEd, 1972; cert. in vol. mgmt. U. Colo., 1981. Cert. Grad. Realtors Inst., 1989. Tchr. Balt. County Pub. Schs., Towson, 1964-74; bookkeeping asst. Gen. Bus. Systems, Parkton, Md., 1974-76; bookkeeper sec. Ret. Sr. Vol. Program, Grand Rapids, Mich., 1976-77, dir., 1977-79; vol. resources coord. DeKalb County Health Dept., Decatur, Ga., 1981-87; agt. Northside Realty, Snellville, Ga., 1987-89, Bob Wood Realty, 1989—; adminstrv. asst. status of health project DeKalb County Bd. Health, 1990—; cons., liaison vol. DeKalb, Ga. and Atlanta, 1980-81; cons., trainer First Bapt. Ch. Atlanta, 1983; asst. conv. coord. Balt. Life Ins. Co., 1974-76; sec., receptionist State Farm Ins. Co., 1980-81. Mem. Council Vol. Adminstrs. (bd. dirs. 1982-86), Ret. Sr. Vol. Program (v.p. adv. coun. 1980-86), Assn. Vol. Adminstrn. (regional liaison nat. assn.), Charg II. Republican. Club: Rivermist Women's (Lilburn, Ga.). Avocations: piano, tennis, gardening. Home: 3704 Shawnee Run SW Lilburn GA 30247-2419 Office: DeKalb County Bd Health 440 Winn Way Decatur GA 30030-1715

HOLLOWAY, JULIA BOLTON, retired religion educator; b. London, England, Apr. 14, 1937; Arrived in US Dec. 1953.; d. John Robert Glorney and Sybil Margaret (Rutherford) B.; m. Halbert Harold, (separated 1967); children: Richard, Colin, Jonathan. BA in English, San Jose State, Calif., 1954-57; MA in English, U. Calif., Berkeley, 1966-67; PhD in English, U. Calif., 1974. Asst. tchr. U. Calif., Berkeley, 1967-71; asst. prof. Quincy Coll., Ill., 1971-74; assoc. master Princeton Inn Coll., N.J., 1974-76; asst. prof. Princeton U., 1974-81, U. Colo., Boulder, 1981-87; vis. prof. So. Meth. U., 1987, 91; assoc. prof. U. Colo., Boulder, 1987, 91; acting curator Casa Guidi, Florence, Italy, 1987-88; dir. Medieval Studies U. Colo., Boulder, 1988-92; prof. emerita, 1992—; novice Cmty. of the Holy Family, 1992—. Author: Bibliography of Latini, The Pilgrim and the Book: Dante, Langland, Chaucer, 1986; editor, translator: (book) Latini, Il Tesoretto, 1981, Equally in God's Image: Women in the Middle Ages, 1990, Gregersson, Gascoigne, Life of Saint Birgitta of Sweden, 1991, Saint Bride and Her Book: Birgitta of Sweden's Revelations, 1992, Twice-Told Tales: Brunetto Latino Dance Alighieri, 1992; contbr. articles to profl. jours. Bd. dirs. Colo. Endowment for the Humanities, 1983-86, Rocky Mountain Peace Ctr., 1983-86; mem. Quaker Del. to Heads of State, 1980; vice-chmn. Colo. Women's Agenda, 1988. Recipient Summer Seminar, Summer Stipend awards NEH; AAUW Founders fellow, 1987-88. Mem. Chair Com TEAMS, Early English Text Soc., Medieval Acad., New Chaucer Soc., Bronte Soc., James Joyce Found., Browning Inst., Modern Lang. Assn. Office: Community of the Holy Family, Holmhurst St Mary, Saint Leonards-on-Sea East Sussex, England

HOLLOWAY, NANCY ANNE, artist; b. Stanford, Calif., Jan. 24, 1967; d. Charles Allen and Barbara June (Weise) H. AA, Menlo Coll., 1986; BFA, Pepperdine U., 1989. Artist's apprentice Zuma Studios, Newbury Park, Colo., 1988-89; asst. mgr. Pacific Internat. Art Gallery, Palo Alto, Calif., 1990-91; artist Appletree Press, San Mateo, Calif., 1991—; treas. Portola Valley Art Gallery, 1992—. Visual arts chair Coun. for Arts of Palo Alto, 1992-93; chair Pacific Prints Competition and Exhbn. Pacific Art League of Palo Alto, 1991-92. Home: 875 University Ave # 5 Palo Alto CA 94301-2132

HOLLOWAY, SHARON KAY SOSSAMON, vocational/secondary school educator; b. Ft. Smith, Feb. 26, 1958; d. Floyd Clinton and Ruth Ann (Clemons) Sossamon; m. David Arthur Holloway, Dec. 27, 1985. BS in Bus. Edn., N.E. State U., Tahlequah, Okla., 1980, MS, 1987. Cert. tchr. vocat. bus., Okla. Tchr. vocat. bus. Pawhuska (Okla.) Pub. Schs., 1982—; cons. tchr. Pawhuska Pub. Schs., 1992-93, computer tchr. community edn. program, 1988—. Recipient Tandy Tech. award for Outstanding Tchr., 1994. Mem. Nat. Bus. Assn., Am. Vocat. Assn., Okla. Bus. Assn., Pawhuska Edn. Assn., Delta Zeta Alumnae. Democrat. Baptist. Home: 622 N 12 PO Box 638 Collinsville OK 74021 Office: Pawhuska Pub Schs 1505 Lynn Ave Pawhuska OK 74056-1843

HOLM, AUDREY CHRISTINE, health care organization administrator; b. Spokane, Wash., July 27, 1929; d. A.O. Marcus and Gunda Marie (Myhre) H. BSBA, U. Denver, 1958; MPH, U. Calif., Berkeley, 1966. RN, Calif. Asst. adminstr. Maricopa County Med. Ctr., Phoenix, 1974-78, Tex. Tech Teaching Hosp., Lubbock, 1976-78, Herrick Hosp. and Health Ctr., Berkeley, Calif., 1978-83; assoc. adminstr. Booth Meml. Med. Ctr., Flushing, N.Y., 1983-90, Booth Silvercrest S.N.F., Jamaica, N.Y., 1990-91; adminstr. Salvation Army Retirement Community, Asbury Park, N.J., 1991-94. Commd. officer, Salvation Army, 1948; bd. dirs., officer Soroptimist Internat. Fellow Am. Coll. Healthcare Execs. (examiner); mem. Am. Coll. Healthcare Adminstrs. Office: Salvation Army 222 E Indian Spokane WA 99207

HOLM, CELESTE, actress; b. N.Y.C., Apr. 29, 1919; d. Theodor and Jean (Parke) H.; m. Wesley Addy, May 22, 1966; children: Theodor Holm Nelson, Daniel Schuyler Dunning. Ed., Univ. Sch. for Girls, Chgo., Lycee Victor Durui, Paris, Francis W. Parker Sch., Chgo., Adelphi Acad., Bklyn.; DHL (hon.), Centenary Coll., 1980; AA (hon.), Middle Ga. Coll., 1982; ArtsD (hon.), Ea. Mich. U., 1984; DHL (hon.), Kean Coll. of N.J., 1984, Felician Coll., 1985, Jersey City State Coll., 1986; DFA (hon.), Monmouth Coll., 1987; D Liberal Arts (hon.), Fairleigh Dickinson U., 1988; D Pub. Svc. (hon.), Ea. Ill. U., 1989; DFA (hon.), Seton Hall U., 1990. Appeared in Broadway shows Gloriana, 1938, The Time of Your Life, 1939, Another Sun, 1940, Return of the Vagabond, 1940, Eight O'Clock Tuesday, 1941, My Fair Ladies, 1941, Papa Is All, 1941-42, All the Comforts of Home, 1942, The Damask Cheek, 1942-43, Oklahoma!, 1943-44, 48, Bloomer Girl, 1944-45, She Stoops to Conquer, 1949, Affairs of State, 1950-51, Anna Christie, 1952, The King and I, 1952, Interlock, 1958, Third Best Sport, 1958, Invitation to a March, 1960-61, Mame, 1967, Candida, 1970, Habeas Corpus, 1975-76, The Utter Glory of Morrissey Hall, 1979, I Hate Hamlet, 1991; appeared in films Three Little Girls in Blue, 1946, Gentleman's Agreement, 1947 (Acad. Award for Best Supporting Actress), Carnival in Costa Rica, 1947, The Snake Pit, 1948, Road House, 1948, Chicken Every Sunday, 1948, Come to the Stable, 1949 (Acad. Award nomination for Best Supporting Actress), Everybody Does It, 1949, Champagne for Caesar, 1950, All About Eve, 1950 (Acad. Award nomination for Best Supporting Actress), The Tender Trap, 1955, High Society, 1956, Bachelor Flat, 1961, Doctor, You've Got to be Kidding, 1966, Tom Sawyer, 1972, Three Men and a Baby, 1987; other stage appearances include (tours) Hamlet, 1937, The Women, 1937-38, Back to Methuselah, 1957, Finishing Touches, 1974, Light Up the Sky, 1975, (one-woman show) Paris Was Yesterday, 1978, (other prodns.) A Month in the Country, 1963, Madly in Love, 1964, Night of the Iguana, 1964, Captain Brassbound's Conversion, 1966, Mame, 1967-68 (Sarah Siddons award), Hay

Fever, 1979-83, Lady in the Dark (Eng.), 1981, The Trojan Women, 1985, The Road to Mecca, 1989, Love Letters, 1990, 94, The Cocktail Hour, 1990, 94, Allegro, 1994, 50th Anniversary of The Glass Menagerie, Chgo., 1994; numerous supper club appearances, N.Y.C., Chgo., San Francisco, Washington, L.A., 1943-59; U.S.O. entertainer, ETO, 1945; 21,000 mile tour of U.S. Army bases, 1949; TV appearances include (spls. & TV movies) Cinderella, 1965, The Shady Hill Kidnapping, 1979, Backstairs at the White House, 1979 (Emmy nomination), Nora's Christmas Gift, 1989, Polly, 1989, Polly, One Mo' Time, 1990; regular roles (series) Archie Bunker's Place, 1980-81, Falcon Crest, 1985, Loving, 1986 (Emmy nomination), 91-92, Christine Cromwell, 1989-90, PBS Great Performances Talking With..., 1994; guest starring roles on Trapper John, M.D., The F.B.I., Disney's Wide World of Color, The Streets of San Francisco, Columbo, Medical Center, Captains and the Kings, Spencer For Hire, Magnum P.I., The Underground Man, Fantasy Island, The Love Boat; radio interviewer People at the UN, 1963-65; toured with theatre-in-concert program Interplay, 1963-74; appeared in The Cole Porter 100th Birthday Celebration, Carnegie Hall, 1991. Past mem. gov. bd. U.S. Com. for UNICEF; mem. Nat. Mental Health Assn., 1965—, chmn., 1969-70; v.p. Arts and Bus. Coun.; mem. Nat. Arts Coun., 1982-88; chmn. bd. dirs. N.J. Film Commn., 1983—; bd. dirs. Mayor's Midtown Com., 1975—, Actor's Fund Am., 1988—; pres. bd. Creative Arts Rehab. Ctr., 1978—; mem. nat. vis. coun. for health scis. faculties Columbia U., N.Y.C., 1989—; mem. adv. bd. N.J. Sch. for the Arts, 1989—, adv. coun. UN Assn. of N.Y.C., 1992—; chmn. Stage South Supporting Players, S.C. State Theatre, 1977. Decorated Dame King Olav of Norway, 1979; recipient Brotherhood award Nat. Conf. Christians & 52, Disting. Svc. award United Jewish Appeal, 1953, Award of Merit, 1954, Achievement award Israel Bonds, 1958, Award of Appreciation March of Dimes, 1959, Hadassah, 1960, Nat. Assn. for Retarded Children award, 1961, Disting. Alumni award Francis W. Parker Sch., 1964, U.S. Com. for World Fedn. of Mental Health award, 1965, Performer of Yr. award Variety Clubs Am., 1966, Edward Strecker Meml. Medal for outstanding contbns. to mental health movement, rehab. of mentally disabled, 1971, Woman of Yr. award Anti-Defamation League, 1972, Golden Needle award Am. Home Sewing Coun., 1972, Woman of Yr. award N.Y. Variety Club, 1973, Woman of Yr. nomination Ladies Home Jour., 1975, Spirit of Am. award VFW, 1976, Woman of Yr. award Westchester Fedn. Women's Clubs, 1977, Woman of Yr. award Creative Arts Rehab. Ctr., 1977, Disting. Woman award Northwood Inst., 1977, Golden Scroll award Mayor's Midtown Citizens Com., 1979, Achievement in Arts award Northwood Inst./IASTA, 1979, Actor's Studio award, 1980, Mental Health Assn. Greater Chgo. award, 1982, Zonta Internat. Humanitarian award, 1984, Compostella award, 1984, Town Hall Friend of the Arts award, 1985, Humanitarian award Creative Arts Rehab. Ctr., 1988, Internat. Platform award, 1989, The Coalition of Arts Therapy Assn. Cert. Appreciation, 1990, Edwin Forrest award for Outstanding Contbn. to Theatre, Walnut St. Theatre, Phila., 1991, The Cardinal's Com of Laity Cardinal's award, 1991, The Ellis Island Medal of Honor, 1992, Gold medal Holland Soc. N.Y., 1994; named to The Theatre Hall of Fame, 1992; rsch. scholar in semiotics, Claremont Grad. Sch., Calif., 1988-89.

HOLM, JEANNE MARJORIE, author, consultant, government official, former air force officer; b. Portland, Oreg., June 23, 1921; d. John E. and Marjorie (Hammond) H. B.A., Lewis and Clark Coll., 1956. Commd. 2d lt. U.S. Army, 1943; transferred to USAF, 1948, advanced through grades to maj. gen., 1973; chief manpower and mgmt. Hdqrs. Allied Air Forces So. Europe, Naples, Italy, 1957-61; congl. liaison officer, directorate manpower and orgn. Hdqrs USAF, Washington, 1961-65; dir. Women in the Air Force, 1965-73, Sec. Air Force Personnel Council, Washington, 1973-75; ret., 1975; cons. Def. Manpower Commn., Washington, 1975, undersec. air force, Washington, 1979-81; spl. asst. to Pres., 1976-77; advisor United Services Life Ins. Co., Washington; lectr. on manpower and women in mil., Presideo Press, Novato, Calif. Author: Women in the Military: An Unfinished Revolution, 1982, rev. edit., 1992; contbr. Ency. of the Am. Mil., 1994; contbr. articles to profl. jours. Chmn. adv. com. women vets. VA, Washington, 1986-88; adv. com. USCG Acad., 1983-89; dir. U.S. com. for UN Fund for Women; trustee Air Force Aid Soc.; mem. nat. adv. com. Women in Mil.Svc. Meml. Found.; mem. hon. coun. Vietnam Women's Meml. Project. Decorated D.S.M. with oak leaf cluster, Legion of Merit, medal for Human Action (Berlin Airlift), Nat. Def. Svc. medal with Bronze Star; recipient Disting. Achievement award Alumni Assn. Lewis and Clark Coll., Eugene Zuckert Leadership award Arnold Air Soc., Citation of Honor, Air Force Assn., Living Legacy award Women's Internat. Ctr., 1985; named Woman of Yr. in Govt. and Diplomacy, Ladies Home Jour., 1975; inducted into Women's Hall of Fame, Internat. Women's Forum, 1992. Mem. Air Force Assn., Ret. Officers Assn., Exec. Women in Govt. (founder, 1st chmn.). Home: 2707 Thyme Dr Edgewater MD 21037-1120

HOLM, JOY ALICE, psychology educator, art educator, artist, goldsmith; b. Chgo., May 21, 1929; d. Alvin Herbert and Willette Eugenia (Miller) H. BFA, U. Ill., 1952; MS in Art Edn. Inst. Design, Ill. Inst. Tech., 1956; PhD in Edn., U. Minn., 1967. Tchr. art, Eng. West Chgo. H.S., 1952-54; instr., tchr. art J.S. Morton H.S. & Jr. Coll., Cicero, Ill., 1954-65; asst. prof. art & design Mankato (Minn.) State U., 1965-66; asst. prof. art Ill. State U., Normal, 1966-69; assoc. prof. art & design So. Ill. U., Edwardsville, 1969-71; assoc. prof. art, art edn. Winona (Minn.) State U., 1971-75; assoc. prof., chmn. dept. art St. Mary's Coll. of Notre Dame, Ind., 1975-76; assoc. prof. art & design, secondary, continuing edn. U. Wis., Eau Claire, 1976-78; assoc. prof. art & design Sch. Art & Design Kent (Ohio) State U., 1978-80; lectr. Jungian studies C.G. Jung Inst., Evanston, Ill., 1980-82, U. Calif. Ext., Santa Cruz, 1983—; adj. assoc. prof. art & design U. Ill., Chgo., 1981-82; adj. prof. art edn., design San Jose (Calif.) State U., 1983-84; owner bus. designer-goldsmith Oak Park, Ill., 1980-82, Carmel, Calif., 1982-87; owner bus. designer-goldsmith Atelier XII, Winona, 1988—; curriculum cons. North Ctrl. Assn. Accreditation Team State of Ill., Edwardsville, 1970; regional cons. Supt. Pub. Instrn., Springfield, Ill., 1970; juror exhbns.; panelist, speaker, presenter confs., meetings. One-woman shows: J. Sterling Morton H.S. & Jr. Coll., 1963, Russell Art Gallery, Bloomington, 1968, Owatonna (Minn.) Art Ctr., 1986; exhbns. include La Grange (Ill.) Art League (Best of Show, 1st Place award prints), 1963, 64, Minn. Mus. Art, 1974, 75, Craft & Folk Art Mus., L.A., 1978, The Gallery Kent State U., 1978, 79, Saenger Nat. Small Sculpture and Jewelry Exhibit, 1978, Diamonds Internat., N.Y., 1978, Inst. Design Alumni, 1988, others; contbr. articles to profl. jours. Mem. AAUP, Nat. Art Edn. Assn. (rep. Wis. Women's Caucus Houston Conf. 1978, higher edn. divsn. 1961—), Am. Assn. Higher Edn., Coll. Art Assn., Soc. N.Am. Goldsmiths, Internat. Sculpture Ctr., Gemological Inst. Am., C.G. Jung Inst. (Chgo., San Francisco), Hon. Soc. Illustrators (hon.), Internat. Soc. Study of Subtle Energies and Energy Medicine, Alpha Lambda Delta (hon.), Phi Kappa Phi (hon.). Democrat. Methodist. Home: 168 E Broadway Winona MN 55987 Office: Atelier XII PO Box 183 Winona MN 55987

HOLM, VANJA ADELE, developmental pediatrician, educator; b. Kiruna, Sweden, Oct. 5, 1928; came to U.S, 1955.; d. C.V. Hjalmar and Elma Adele (Nystrom) H.; m. Carl Holm, June 15, 1952; children: Ingrid Adele, Erik Carl Anders. Med. Kand., Karolinska Inst., Stockholm, 1950, MD, 1955. Intern Swedish Hosp., Seattle, 1955-56; resident in pediatrics U. Wash. Sch. Medicine, Seattle, 1956, 62-64, fellow in devel. pediatrics, 1964-65, instr. pediatrics, 1965-69, asst. prof. pediatrics, 1969-81, assoc. prof. pediatrics, 1981—; attending pediatrician Children's Orthopedic Hosp., Univ. Hosp; med. dir. Boyer Children's Clinic and Presch. Editor: Early Intervention: A Team Approach, 1978 (Am. Med. Writers award 1979), The Prader Willi Syndrome, 1981; contbr. some 60 articles to profl. jours. Fellow Am. Acad. Pediatrics, Am. Acad. Cerebral Palsy and Devel. Medicine, Am. Assn. Mental Retardation; mem. Soc. Devel. Pediatrics, Wash. State Med. Assn. (Aesculapius award 1979), Soc. Behavioral Pediatrics. Democrat. Office: U Wash CDMRC WJ10 Seattle WA 98195

HOLMAN, DIANE ROSALIE, lawyer; b. South Bend, Ind., Nov. 5, 1939; d. Raymond Francis and Ann Marie (Batsleer) Paczesny; divorced; children: Paul III, John Adam, Joseph, Felicity. BA, St. Mary's Coll., 1961; MS, St. Francis Coll., 1968; JD, Loyola U., L.A., 1976. Bar: Calif. 1976. Assoc. O'Melveny & Myers, L.A., 1976-81; assoc., ptnr. Manatt, Phelps & Phillips, L.A., 1981-85; of counsel Kindel & Anderson, L.A., 1985-87; dep. city atty. City of El Monte, Calif., 1987-89; sr. legal counsel Family Restaurants, Inc., Irvine, Calif., 1989—. Avocations: feminist theory, reading and writing, Lakers basketball, beach walking. Mem. State Bar Calif., Orange County Bar Assn., Orange County Women Lawyers Assn. Democrat. Home: 31907 Crestwood Pl Laguna Beach CA 92677 Office: Family Restaurants Inc 18831 Von Karman Ave Ste 400 Irvine CA 92715

HOLMES, ANN HITCHCOCK, journalist; b. El Paso, Apr. 25, 1922; d. Frederick E. and Joy (Crutchfield) H. Student, Whitworth Coll., 1940, So. Coll. Fine Arts, 1944. With Houston Chronicle, 1942—, fine arts editor, 1948-89, critic-at-large, 1989—. Author: Presence, The Transco Tower, 1985, Joy Unconfined—Robert Joy in Houston: A Portrait of Fifty Years, 1986, Alley Theater: Four Decades in Three Stages, 1986. Mem. Houston Mcpl. Art Commn., 1965-74; mem. fine arts adv. coun. U. Tex., Austin, 1967—; bd. dirs. Rice Design Alliance, Houston, 1988-91, Alliance Francaise, Houston, 1989-93, Bus. Arts Fund, Houston. Recipient Ogden Reid Found. award for study of arts in Europe, 1953; Guggenheim fellow, 1960-61; recipient Ford Found. award, 1965, John G. Flowers award archtl. writing Tex. Soc. Architects, 1972, 74, 77, 80. Mem. Am. Theater Critics Assn. (exec. com. 1975—, co-chmn. 1987-88). Home: 10807 Beinhorn Rd Houston TX 77024-3008 Office: Houston Chronicle 801 Texas St Houston TX 77002-2996

HOLMES, BARBARA ANN KRAJKOSKI, educator; b. Evansville, Ind., Mar. 21, 1946; d. Frank Joseph and Estella Marie (DeWeese) Krajkoski; m. David Leo Holmes, Aug. 21, 1971; 1 child, Susan Ann Sky. BS, Ind. State U., 1968, MS, 1969, specialist cert., 1976; postgrad. U. Nev., 1976-78. Acad. counselor Ind. State U., 1968-69, halls dir., 1969-73; dir. residence halls U. Utah, 1973-76; sales assoc. Fidelity Realty, Las Vegas, Nev., 1977-82. cert. analyst Nev. Dept. Edn., 1981-82; tchr. Clark County Sch. Dist., 1982-87, computer cons., adminstrv. specialist instructional mgmt. systems, 1987—, chair computer conf., 1990-92, adminstrv. specialist K-6, 1990-93, dean of students summer sch. site adminstr. Eldorado High Sch., 1993—. Named Outstanding Sr. Class Woman, Ind. State U., 1969; recipient Dir's. award U. Utah Residence Halls, 1973, Outstanding Sales Assoc., 1977; Tchr. of Month award, 1983, Dist. Outstanding Tchr. award, 1984, Dist. Excellence in Edn. award, 1984, 86, 87, 88. Mem. Nev. Assn. Realtors, AAUW, Am. Assn. Women Deans, Adminstrs. and Counselors, Am. Personnel and Guidance Assn., Am. Coll. Personnel Assn., Nevadans for Equal Rights Amendment, Alumnae Assn. Chi Omega (treas. Terre Haute chpt. 1971-73, pres., bd. officer Las Vegas 1977-81), Clark County Panhellenic Alumnae Assn. (pres. 1978-79), Computer Using Educators So. Nev. (sec. 1983-86, pres.-elect 1986-87, pres. 1987-88, state chmn. 1988-89, conf. chmn. 1989—), Job's Daus. Club, Order Ea. Star, Phi Delta Kappa (Action award 1990-91, 1991-92, newspaper editor 1992-93). Developed personal awareness program U. Utah, 1973-76. Home: 2531 E Oquendo Rd Las Vegas NV 89120-2413 Office: Eldorado High Sch 1139 N Linn Ln Las Vegas NV 89110-2628

HOLMES, BARBARA CARLILE, oncology nurse, consultant, social psychologist; b. New Orleans, Mar. 14, 1953; d. Frank Joseph and Elvira Felicia (Morantes) Incardona; m. Dennis J. Carlile, May 19, 1974 (div. June 1981); m. Alan D. Holmes, July 29, 1984; 1 child, Matthew Brandon Incardona. BSN, Union Coll., Denver, 1975; MSN, U. Tex. Health Sci. Ctr., San Antonio, 1980; postgrad., U. Tex., 1987—. RN, Tex.; cert. oncology nurse; instr. breast self-examination, CPR. Staff nurse ICU-CCU Porter Meml. Hosp., Denver, 1975; head nurse plastic surgery/adult oncology unit Ft. Worth Children's Hosp., 1975-76; med./surg. patient care coord. Huguley Meml. Med. Ctr., Ft. Worth, 1977; chemotherapy nurse A.J. White, M.D., P.A., San Antonio, 1977-82; from staff nurse to oncology clin. nurse specialist S.W. Tex. Meth. Hosp., San Antonio, 1977-82; health coord. Timberhill Villa Retirement Ctr., San Antonio, 1982-84; nurse therapist in pvt. practice Omni Health Counseling Ctr., San Antonio, 1980-85; oncology clin. nurse specialist med. oncology/hematology Bone Marrow Transplant Ctr., Med. Ctr. Hosp., San Antonio, 1982-87; program dir., oncology clin. nurse specialist OCN program Tex. Nurses Assn./Tex. Nurses Found., Austin, Tex., 1987-90; oncology nursing cons. San Antonio, 1986—; clin. instr. sch. nursing U. Tex. Health Sci. Ctr., San Antonio, 1982-86, clin. asst. prof., 1986-88, oncology clin. nurse specialist div. Gynecological Oncology, Dept. Ob/Gyn., 1982-87; lectr. in field; program cons. Cancer Prevention and Screening Program for Rural Nurses, State of Colo., U.S. Dept. Health and Human Svcs., 1991-93; program dir. Nurse Oncology Edn. Program, Tex. Cancer Coun., State of Tex., 1987-89; instnl. rev. bd. S.W. Tex. Meth. Hosp., San Antonio, 1981-84. Contbr. articles to profl. jours.; reviewer Mosby's Manual of Oncology Nursing, Oncology Nursing, The Human Experience of Pain and Suffering; producer videotape: (with N.J. Sugarek) Doctor-patient Interactions in the Art of Medicine: Observational Skills II, 1986. Nat. Cancer Soc. nursing scholar, 1980; named Vol. of Yr. Am. Cancer Soc., San Antonio 1986, Gibson D. Lewis Award for Excellence in Cancer Control Nursing, Tex. Ho. of Reps., 1988; Oncology Nursing Found. scholar, 1991, Am. Cancer Soc. scholar, 1992-93; ONS/Cetus Rsch. fellow, 1993-94. Mem. Am. Cancer Soc. (bd. dirs. 1984—, pres. 1985-86, dist. 5 lay dir. 1988-90, dir.-at-large 1984—, nat. del. 1991—, treas. 1994—, chair budget com. 1993—, chair nutrition com. 1993—, chair nominating com. 1993—), Oncology Nursing Soc. (San Antonio chpt. bd. dirs. 1981-86, pres. 1981-86, nat. dir.-at-large 1985-87), Oncology Nursing Found. (bd. trustees 1993—, exec. com. 1993—, treas. 1993—), Oncology Nursing Cert. Corp., Am. Nurses Assn. (del. 1983-85), Tex. Nurses Assn. (del. 1983-85, dist. 8 bd. dirs. 1981-85, v.p. 1981-85), Tex. Cancer Coun., APA, Soc. Personality and Social Psychol. Home: 4403 Western Pine Woods St San Antonio TX 78249-1422

HOLMES, CECILE SEARSON, religion editor; b. Columbia, S.C., Jan. 6, 1955; d. James Gadsden and Anne Keene (Searson) Holmes. BA in Journalism magna cum laude, U. S.C., 1977; fellow, U. N.C., 1982; postgrad., U. N.C., Greensboro, 1984-87. Religion writer Greensboro News and Record, 1984-87; religion writer Houston Chronicle, 1987-89, sect. editor, 1989—; mem. faculty summer journalism workshop Houston Chronicle, 1988-92; co-dir. minority journalism workshop News and Record, 1988. Author: Witnesses to the Horror: North Carolinians Remember the Holocaust, 1988; contbr. articles, book revs. to profl. jours. Mem. N.C. Episcopal Diocese Hunger Commn., 1980s; vol. Greensboro Urban Ministry, 1983-86; moderator NCCJ Forum, 1985, Ethics of Humane Care, Greensboro, 1986; mentor Edn. for Ministry, Houston, 1989—; advisor United Way Campaign for Homeless, Houston, 1991. Recipient award Piedmont Bapt. Assn., 1984, Community Journalism award N.C. A&T State U., 1984, Pub. Svc. award N.C. Press Assn., 1985, Wilbur award Religious Pub. Rels. Coun., 1986, others. Mem. Soc. Profl. Journalists (chpt. pres. and v.p., coord. registration nat. conv. 1989), Religion Newswriters Assn. (treas. 1990-92, 2d v.p. 1992-94, 1st v.p. 1994—, 2d place award ann. contest 1989, 92), Houston Press Club, Beta Sigma Phi (past v.p. Greensboro chpt., Woman of Yr. award), Kappa Tau Alpha, Omicron Delta Kappa. Office: Houston Chronicle 801 Texas Ave Houston TX 77002

HOLMES, CHRISTINE MUELLER, accountant; b. Milw., July 10, 1966; d. Joseph Jr. and Kathleen Marjorie (Scherff) Mueller; m. Charles S. Holmes, Feb. 17, 1990. BA in Acctg., N.C. State U., 1988. CPA, N.C. Mgr. Ernst & Young, Raleigh, N.C., 1988-94; mgr. fin. and adminstrn. Quintiles Labs. Ltd., Atlanta, 1994—; instr. Becker CPA Rev. Course, Raleigh, N.C., 1992-93. Treas. Wake Teen Med. Svcs., 1993-94. Mem. Inst. Mgmt. Accts. (bd. dirs. 1992). Home: 1404 Milford Chase Ct Marietta GA 30060-6878 Office: Quintiles Laboratories Ltd 5500 Highlands Pkwy Ste 600 Smyrna GA 30082

HOLMES, CLAIRE COLEMAN, real estate broker; b. Ruston, La., Sept. 14, 1931; d. Eusel Monroe and Mabel Claire (Cahoon) Coleman; m. Major Joe Holmes, Dec. 20, 1951; children: George David, Claire Anne de Noble, William Gray. BA cum laude, U. Ark., 1952. Tchr. Pulaski (Ark.) County Spl. Sch. Dist., 1952-53, Pine Bluff (Ark.) Sch. Dist., 1953-55; real estate salesman Sullivant-Cross Realty, Pine Bluff, 1979-83; legal sec. Joe Holmes, Atty., Pine Bluff, 1985-91; real estate broker C & J, Inc., Pine Bluff, 1985—. Mem. DAR, Soc. Mayflower Descendants, Jr. League, Pine Bluff Duplicate Bridge Club, Am. Contract Bridge League. Home: 22 S Pines Dr Pine Bluff AR 71601 Office: C & J Inc 22 Southern Pines Dr Pine Bluff AR 71603-6934

HOLMES, DOLORIS GRANT, writer, social worker, theater director; b. Manchester, Conn., Feb. 7, 1929; d. George Joseph and Dorothy Josephine (Grant) H.; m. Monte Bliss (wid. 1959); m. Armand Schwerner (div.); children: Adam, Ari. BA, U. Conn., 1952; M of Social Svcs., Boston U., 1957. Social worker S.I. Hosp., 1971-80; med. social worker Maimonides Hosp., Bklyn., 1980-81; dir. youth art NYC Youth Bd., L.I.; dir., performer White Mask Theatre, 1975—; interviewee for Archives of Am. Art, Anais Nin; mem. Barry Harris Jazz Chorus. Dir., writer: (play) Goddess of Red Mud; dir., writer, prodr. and performer: With All the Saints Sing, 1992; active in prodns.: Fish-Joy, Soho 20, 1973, Fish-Joy, White Mask Theatre, 1977, Fish-Joy and Goddess of Red Mud, White Mask Theatre, 1990; contbr. various publs. including Art in America, 1970, Anarchos, 1971, Art Work, No Commercial Value, 1975, American Poetry Review, 1975, Unbuilt America, 1976, Anais Nin, a Woman Speaks, Wellspring, 1986, various jours.; author: The Lady of the Grape Arbor, 1993. Grantee Poets and Writer, N.Y. State Coun. on the Arts, 1977; finalist Louis Comfort Tiffany award, 1969, N.Y.C. Dept. Cultural Affairs, 1974; recipient Golden Poetry award World of Poetry, 1987, 88, Silver Poetry awards, 1986, 89. Grantee Poets and Writer, Poetry Reading of Rochelle Owens, Spencer Holst, Sally Ordway, N.Y. State Coun. on the Arts, 1977, N.Y. State Coun. on the Arts, 1972; finalist Louis Comfort Tiffany award, 1969, N.Y. C. Dept. Cultural Affairs, 1974. Mem. Poets and Writers (N.Y.C.), Women in Limbo (N.Y.C.), Film-makers Cooperative (N.Y.C.), Internat. Women Writers Guild. Office: NYC Bd Edn 400 1st Ave New York NY 10010

HOLMES, EMMA ELIZABETH, education educator; b. Pitts., Mar. 14, 1925; d. John and Louise Eugenia (Michel) Bauman; m. Robert Thomas Holmes, Aug. 20, 1950. BA magna cum laude, Mt. Holyoke Coll., 1947; MA, U. Ill., 1948; PhD, U. Iowa, 1961. Tchr. City Schs., Elmhurst, Ill., 1948-49; instr. Ball State U., Munice, Ind., 1949-54; tchr. City Schs., San Jose, Calif., 1954-55, 60-61; asst. prof. edn. Calif. State U., Fullerton, 1961-65, assoc. prof. edn., 1965-70, prof. edn. and child devel., 1970-90, prof. emeritus, 1990—. Author: Mathematic Instruction for Children, 1968, Children Learning Mathematics: A Cognitive Approach to Teaching, 1985, New Directions in Elementary School Mathematics: Interactive Teaching and Learning, 1995. Named one of Outstanding Educators of Am., 1970. Mem. ASCD, Nat. Coun. Tchrs. Math., Calif. Math. Coun., Phi Kappa Phi (pub. rels. officer 1988-91), Phi Delta Kappa. Home: 5057 Avenida Del Sol Laguna Hills CA 92653-1803 Office: Calif State Univ 800 N State College Blvd Fullerton CA 92634-9480

HOLMES, GENTA HAWKINS, diplomat; b. Anadarko, Okla., Sept. 3, 1940. BA, U. So. Calif., 1962. Jr. officer U.S. Embassy, Abidjan, Ivory Coast, 1964-66; with office spl. assistance to Sec. of State for Refugee Affairs, 1966-68; spl. asst., youth officer U.S. Embassy, Paris, 1968-71; with N.Y. regional office OEO, 1972-73; with office devel. fin., econ. bur. U.S. Dept. State, 1973-74; chief econ. and commercial sect. U.S. Embassy, Bahamas, 1974-77; congl. fellow Am. Polit. Sci. Assn., 1977-78; with bur. congl. rels. U.S. Dept. State, 1978-79; asst. adminstr. legis. affairs AID, 1979-82; mem. 25th Exec. Seminar in Nat. and Internat. Affairs, 1982-83; mem. bd. examiners, 1983-84; dep. chief of mission U.S. Embassy, Lilongwe, Malawi, 1984-86, Port-au-Prince, Haiti, 1986-88, Pretoria, South Africa, 1988-90; U.S. amb. to Namibia, 1990-92; dir. gen. fgn. svc., dir. pers. U.S. Dept. State, Washington, 1992—. Office: Dept of State M/DGP Rm 6218 Washington DC 20520

HOLMES, JACQUELIN ANN, workers compensation administrator; b. Balt., Sept. 5, 1947; d. Paul Chester and Ethel Marie (Parker) Bianchi; m. Larry Lee Lockman, Nov. 29, 1963 (div. Oct. 1972); children: Carole Jean, Gregory Stephen; m. John Stephen Holmes, July 27, 1974 (div. May 1993). AA in Psychology, Community Coll. of Denver, 1975; BBA, Regis Coll., 1988; postgrad., U. Colo., Denver, 1991—. Cert. personnel classification, examinations and rules interpretation, Colo.; lic. claims adjuster. With staff support/counseling div. Community Coll. of Denver North Campus, 1973-74, asst. to dir. community services div., 1974-77; claims adjuster State Compensation Ins. Fund, Denver, 1978-80, 82-84; owner day care ctr. Littleton, Colo., 1980-82; personnel analyst Colo. Dept. Labor & Employment, Denver, 1984-88; adminstr. EEO and affirmative action Colo. Dept. Natural Resources, Denver, 1988-90; adminstr. spl. funds Colo. Div. Labor, Denver, 1990-91; dep. dir. Colo. Div. Workers Compensation, Denver, 1991—. Student govt. rep. Community Coll. of Denver, 1973-74; organizer Classified Employees Council, Denver, 1975; vol. orgn. support Arapahoe County Family Day Care, Littleton, 1981-82; coach Teen Quiz Team (Champions 79-83), Littleton, 1979-83; marriage enrichment cons. Littleton Ch. of the Nazarene, 1986-87; Sunday sch. tchr., 1980-87. Named an Outstanding Employee Gov.'s Office Colo. State Govt., 1986. Mem. Internat. Pers. Mgrs. Assn., Internat. Assn. Accident. Bds. and Commns. (electronic data interchange med. subcom.), Colo. EEO and AFfirmative Action Coalition, Colo. Coun. Mediators Assn., Pilot Club. Home: 1551 Larimer St Apt 2603 Denver CO 80202-1638 Office: Colo Div of Workers Compensation 1120 Lincoln St Ste 1200 Denver CO 80203-2139

HOLMES, JULIA FAYE, librarian; b. Meridian, Miss., May 12, 1950; d. Bilbo and Claudia (Morris) Rodgers; m. William Porter Holmes, Dec. 20, 1969; children: Tanya, Tiffani, Tristan. BS, U. So. Miss., Hattiesburg, 1982, MS in Libr. Sci., 1990; Grad., Leadership Jackson County, 1992. Libr. asst. Jackson-George Regional Libr., Pascagoula, Miss., 1972-74, pub. svcs. asst., 1974-76, serials clk., 1978-80, interlibr. loan clk., 1980-83, reference coord., 1983-86, mgr. reference dept., 1986—. Contbr. articles to libr. jours. Mem. Dem. Exec. Com., Pascagoula, 1988—, 4-H Club Adv. Coun., Pascagoula, 1984—, Foster Care Rev. Bd., Pascagoula, 1985—; pres. East Park Elem. PTA, Moss Point, Miss., 1976-80; mem. NAACP, 1988—; mem. Jackson-George Regional Libr. Sys., Jackson County Civic Action Com., Policy Coun., 1992—; bd. dirs., sec. Jackson County Arts Coun., 1992—; grant review panelist Miss. Arts Commn., 1994—; bd. trustees Moss Point City Libr. Bd., 1985—. Black Pride in Art grantee Miss. Arts Commn., 1991, Black History Program grantee Miss. Arts Commn., 1993, Black So. Voices grantee Miss. Humanities Coun., 1993. Mem. ALA (Black Caucus 1991—), Miss. Libr. Assn. (membership com., scholar com., libr. edn. com., Black Caucus v.p. 1994—), Libr. Instrn. Roundtable (Jackson, sec. 1991-92, v.p. 1992-93, pres. 1993-94), Beta Phi Mu (v.p. chpt. 1993-94, pres. 1994-95), Delta Sigma Theta (sec. 1986-87, 87-88, v.p. 1990-91, pres. 1994-95). Home: 4013 Charles St Moss Point MS 39563-5456 Office: Jackson George Regional Libr 3214 Pascagoula St Pascagoula MS 39567-4217

HOLMES, KATHERINE AMEIL, educator. BS, Chgo. State U., 1972; MS, Memphis State U., 1979; MA in Adminstrn. and Supervision of Edn., Trevecca Nazarene Coll., 1992. Asst. v.p., counselor Lena Park, Boston, 1988-90; dropout prevention counselor Memphis City Schs., 1990-91; tchr. middle sch. Shelby County Schs., Memphis, 1991—; coll. instr. State Tech. Inst. at Memphis, 1985—. Bd. dirs. Project Baby-Boost, Boston. Mem. Bus. and Profl. Women (palimentarian), Alpha Kappa Alpha. Mem. Ch. of Christ. Home: PO Box 34 Union City GA 30291

HOLMES, KATHERINE BARNEY, editor; b. Balt., Aug. 31, 1946; d. William Hadwen and Katherine Louise (Kennedy) Barney; m. William Paul Holmes, Aug. 5, 1972 (div. June 1980); 1 child, Lucinda Ashley. BS, Briarcliff Coll., 1968; MS, U. Pa., 1969; postgrad., Case Western Reserve U., 1977-78. Cert. tchr., N.Y. Tchr. 2d grade Episc. Acad., Merion, Pa., 1969-72; substitute tchr. various pvt. schs., San Francisco, 1972-75; with pub. rels. dept. John Smyth Architect, Newport, R.I., 1983-85; dir. membership Providence C. of C., 1985-86; editor The Diplomat, Greenwich, Conn., 1990—; travel rep. Putnam Travel, Greenwich, 1993-94; pres. Katherine Barney Holmes Stationery, 1986-93. Author: The Best of Newport, 1983. Lay eucharistic min. Christ Ch., Greenwich, 1993—; chmn. lecture-luncheon series Old Westbury Gardens, 1988-92; benefit chmn. Raynham Hall; founder, chmn. champagne concert series Vanderbilt Mus.; region I chmn. English-Speaking Union, 1982-88; docent John Brown House; pres. Newport Coun. for Internat. Visitors; mem. adv. bd. Sta. WPRI-TV; chairwoman, founder John Hay Forum Cleve. Coun. on World Affairs, 1976-82; many other vol. activities. Mem. Jr. League Greenwich, Colonial Dames, Nantucket Yacht Club. Republican. Episcopalian. Home and Office: 31 Orange St Nantucket MA 02554

HOLMES, LORENE BARNES, academic administrator; b. Mineola, Tex., July 27, 1937; d. William Henry and Jessie Mae (Kelly) Barnes; m. Charles Murphy Holmes, Sr., Feb. 9, 1960; children: Charles Murphy, Jr., James Henry, Jessyca Yvette. BS, Jarvis Christian Coll., 1959; M in Bus. Edn., U. North Tex., 1966, EdD, 1970. Dir. fin. aid Jarvis Christian Coll., Hawkins, Tex., 1966-68, asst. prof. bus., 1969-70, acting chair social and behavioral sci. divsn., 1970-71, chair social and behavioral sci. divsn., 1971-75, chair social sci. and bus. divsn., 1975-81, chair bus. adminstrn. divsn., 1981—; nat. treas. Nat. Alumni Assn., Hawkins, 1960. Editorial reviewer Communication in Business, 1989; contbr. articles to profl. jours. Bd. dirs. Hawkins Helping Hands, 1987-93, Allen Meml. Pub. Libr., Hawkins, 1988-94. Recipient Recognition plaque Nat. Urban League, N.Y.C., 1989, T.A. Abbott Teaching award Christian Ch., Indpls., 1988; inductee Pioneer Hall of Fame, Jarvis Christian Coll., 1994. Mem. AAUW, Nat. Bus. Educators Assn., Tex. Bus. Educators Assn. (Bus. Tchr. of Yr. award Dist. 8), Jarvis Christian Coll. Alumni Assn. (Dist. Alumni Educator of Yr. award), Top Ladies of Dist. Inc. (Lady of Yr. award), Hawkins C. of C. (charter), Delta Sigma Theta (v.p., S.W. Gen. Educator of Yr. award 1991), Delta Pi Epsilon. Democrat. Mem. United Methodist Ch. Home: PO Drawer 858 Hawkins TX 75765 Office: Jarvis Christian Coll PO Drawer G Hawkins TX 75765

HOLMES, MARJORIE ROSE, author; b. Storm Lake, Iowa; d. Samuel Arthur and Rosa (Griffith) H.; m. Lynn Mighell, Apr. 9, 1932; children—Marjorie Mighell Croner, Mark, Mallory, Melanie Mighell Dimopoulos; m. George P. Schmieler, July 4, 1981. Student, Buena Vista Coll., 1927-29, D.Litt. (hon.), 1976; B.A., Cornell Coll., 1931. Tchr. writing Cath. U., 1964-65, U. Md., 1967-68; mem. staff Georgetown Writers Conf., 1959-81. Free-lance writer short stories, articles, verse for mags. including McCall's, Redbook, Reader's Digest; bi-weekly columnist: Love and Laughter, Washington Evening Star, 1959-75; monthly columnist: Woman's Day, 1971-77; author: World By the Tail, 1943, Ten O'Clock Scholar, 1946, Saturday Night, 1959, Cherry Blossom Princess, 1960, Follow Your Dream, 1961, Love is a Hopscotch Thing, 1963, Senior Trip, 1962, Love and Laughter, 1967, I've Got to Talk to Somebody, God, 1969, Writing the Creative Article, 1969, Who Am I, God?, 1971, To Treasure Our Days, 1971, Two from Galilee, 1972, Nobody Else Will Listen, 1973, You and I and Yesterday, 1973, As Tall as My Heart, 1974, How Can I Find You God?, 1975, Beauty in Your Own Back Yard, 1976, Hold Me Up a Little Longer, Lord, 1977, Lord, Let Me Love, 1978, God and Vitamins, 1980, To Help You Through the Hurting, 1983, Three from Galilee—The Young Man from Nazareth, 1985, Writing the Creative Article Today, 1986, Marjorie Holmes' Secrets of Health, Energy and Staying Young, 1987, The Messiah, 1987, At Christmas the Heart Goes Home, 1991, The Inspirational Writings of Marjorie Holmes, 1991, Gifts Freely Given, 1992, Writing Articles From the Heart, 1993, Second Wife, Second Life!, 1993; contbg. editor Guideposts, 1977—; bd. dirs. The Writer, 1975—. Bd. dirs. Found. Christian Living, 1975—. Recipient Honor Iowans award Buena Vista Coll., 1966, Alumni Achievement award Cornell Coll., 1963, Woman of Achievement award Nat. Fedn. Press Women, 1972; Celebrity of Yr. award Women in Communications, 1975; Woman of Yr. award McLean Bus. and Profl. Women, 1976; award Freedom Found. at Valley Forge, 1977; gold medal Marymount Coll. Va., 1978. Mem. Am. Newspaper Women's Club, Nat. Fedn. Press Women, Author's Guild, Washington Nat. Press Club. Home: Lake Jackson Hills 8681 Cobb Rd Manassas VA 22111

HOLMES, NANCY ELIZABETH, pediatrician; b. St. Louis, Aug. 3, 1950; d. David Reed and Phyllis Anne (Hunger) Holmes; m. Arthur Erwin Kramer, May 15, 1976; children: Melanie Elizabeth Kramer, Carl Edward Kramer. BA in Psychology, U. Kans., 1972; MD, U. Mo., 1976. Diplomate Am. Acad. Pediatrics. Intern., resident in pediatrics St. Louis Children's Hosp., Washington U., St. Louis, 1976-81; pediatrician Ctrl. Pediatrics, St. Louis, 1981—; sch. physician Sch. Dist. Clayton, Mo., 1985-92; asst. prof. clin. pediatrics Washington U., St. Louis, Mo., 1993—; cons. 1st. Congregational Preschool, Clayton, 1984-86, Jewish Hosp. Daycare Ctr., St. Louis, 1993—, Flynn Park Early Edn. Ctr., Un.iv. City, Mo., 1994—, community outpatient experience Preceptor Hosp., St. Louis Children's Hosp., 1991-93, 94—; mem. med. exec. com. St. Louis Children's Hosp., 1992-94. Elder Trinity Presbyn.Ch., Univ. City, 1989-92; vol. reading tutor Flynn Park Sch., Univ. City, Mo., 1992—; cub scout leader Flynn Park Sch., 1993—. Fellow Am. Acad. Pediatrics; mem. AMA, Mo. State Med. Assn., St. Louis Metro. Med. Soc, St. Louis Pediatric Soc. Presbyterian. Office: Ctrl Pediatrics Inc 8515 Delmar #217 Saint Louis MO 63124

HOLMES, SANDRA EILEEN KILGORE, nurse; b. Florence, Ala., Feb. 23, 1942; d. William Austin and Kathryn Elizabeth (Threet) Kilgore; m. Milton Mapes Holmes, June 16, 1962; 1 child, Kathryn Ann-Elizabeth Holmes Glass. Diploma in Nursing, U. Ala. Hosp. Sch. Nursing, 1963; BSN, Sanford U., 1989. RN, Ala. Head nurse U. Ala. Hosp., Birmingham, 1969-71; staff nurse Bapt. Med. Ctr.-Montclair, Birmingham, 1971-75, coord. patient care, 1975-89, coord. outpatient diabetes edn., 1989-93, internal nurse auditor, 1993—. Mem. Am. Diabetes Assn. (v.p. Jefferson County chpt. 1990-91, pres. 1991-92), Ala. Assn. Diabetes Educators (state v.p. 1990-91, pres. 1991-92), Ala. Med. Auditors Assn. (pres. 1994-95). Republican. Baptist. Home: 612 Tambay Dr Birmingham AL 35217-1035 Office: Montclair Bapt Med Ctr 800 Montclair Rd Birmingham AL 35213

HOLMES, SUSAN G., educator; b. Kansas City, Mo., Mar. 7, 1955; d. Burton E. and Gloria A. (Spencer) H. BA, U. Kans., Lawrence, 1980. Cert. music therapy, education. Tchr. Dade Coutny Schs., Miami, Fla.; entertainment coord. And More Music Corp., Miami, Fla.; music therapist, tchr. ESOL Miami; tchr. ABE Snapper Creek Nursing Home, Sunrise Retirement Community; music therapist Grant Ctr. Psychiat. Hosp.; tchr. ESOL Miami-Palmetto Adult Edn. Ctr. Tchr. ESOL to newly-arrived immigrants. Recipient Honor for TV series CBS News. Mem. Nat. Orgn. for Exec. Women.

HOLMES, VIRGINIA RUTH, school administrator; b. Long Beach, Calif., June 24, 1944; d. John R. and Alice Lucille (Coggins) Newhouse; m. Dick Ray Holmes, June 6, 1964; children: Hayley Jari, Richard Dean. BA, Okla. State U., 1966, adminstrv. cert., 1993; MEd, Northeastern State U., Tahlequah, Okla., 1979. Cert. elem. and secondary prin., superintendency, Okla. Speech pathologist Osage County Spl. Edn. Coop., Pawhuska, Okla., 1966-68; jr. high English tchr. Owasso (Okla.) Pub. Schs., 1968-71, speech pathologist, 1971-80; jr. high counselor Eastwood Sch. System, Tulsa, 1981-82; mid. sch. English tchr. Nowata (Okla.) Pub. Schs., 1982-83, dir. Indian edn., 1983-85, elem. counselor, 1985-89, elem. counselor, spl. edn. dir., 1989-92, dir. spl. programs, 1992—; chair edn. com. Dist. Bd. for Children and Youth, Bartlesville, Okla., 1991-94; regional coord. Build Me a Future Campaign, Sacramento, Calif., 1992-93; presenter in field. Vice chair Nowata County Bd. Health, 1990—; mem. Nowata Child Abuse Prevention Com., 1987-92; mem. task force Nowata County Big Brother Big Sisters, 1992—; rep. from Nowata Schs. to Interdisciplinary Com. for Human Rights, Nowata, 1993—; participant Okla. S.W. AWARE Leadership Conf., Stillwater, 1988. Grantee Okla. State Dept. Edn., 1993—, Nowata Edn. Found., 1993. Mem. Okla. Dirs. of Spl. Svcs. (chair audit com.), Okla. Assn. Sch. Adminstrs., Tulsa Area Dirs. Spl. Svcs., Washington County Assn. Mental Health. Republican. Baptist. Home: RR 2 Box 245-5 Chelsea OK 74016 Office: Nowata Pub Schs 707 W Osage Nowata OK 74048

HOLMGREN, JANET L., academic administrator. BA in English and Linguistics summa cum laude, Oakland U., Rochester, Mich., 1968; MA in Linguistics, Princeton U., 1971, PhD in Linguistics, 1974; degree (hon.), Mt. Vernon Coll., 1992. Asst. prof. English studies Fed. City Coll. (cname changed to U. D.C.), Washington, 1972-76; asst. prof. English, asst. dir. grad. English studies U. Md., College Park, 1976-82, asst. to chancellor, adj. prof. linguistics, 1982; assoc. provost Princeton (N.J.) U., 1988-90, vice-provost, 1990-91; pres. Mills Coll., Oakland, Calif., 1991—; instr., book editor Nat. Childbirth Edn. Assn., Washington, 1980-83; state coord. nat. identification program for women Am. Coun. on Edn./Md. Regional Planning Coun., 1988-89; lectr. Princeton U., 1989, 90, U. Md., 1990, Am. Coun. on Edn., 1990, Ind. U., 1991, Head-Royce Ach., 1991, Wilson Coll., 1992, U.S EPA/Social Security Adminstrn., 1992, Am. Assn. Colls., 1992, AAUW, 1993, 94, Am Assn. Women in Community and Jr. Colls., 1993; mem. extl. adv. bd. dept. English Princeton U. Contbr. articles to profl. jours. Bd. dirs. summer camp St. Columbia's Episc. Ch., 1986-88; vice chair steering com. 20th Anniv. Commemoration Undergrad. Coeducation, Princeton U., 1988-89; chair chaplain's adv. com. Princeton U.; v.p. Proctor Found. for Princeton-Rutgers Episc. Chaplaincies. Fellow Princeton U., 1968-69, 70-72; Trainee fellow NSF, 1969-70; Summer fellow NEH; Summer Study Aid grantee Linguistic Soc. Am./Ohio State U., 1970; Faculty Rsch. grantee U. Md. Mem Nat. Assn. Ind. Colls. and Univs. (bd. dirs.), Am. Coun. on Edn., Assn. Ind. Calif. Colls. and Univs. (vice chair exec. com.), Calif. Acad. Sci. (acad. adv. coun.), Washington Linguistics Club (v.p. 1975-76, pres. 1976-77). Office: Office of Pres Mills Coll Oakland CA 94613*

HOLMSTROM, ANN ELIZABETH, accountant; b. Waterloo, Iowa, May 10, 1958; d. Donald Oscar and Phyllis Esther (Pape) H. BBA, U. Iowa, 1981. Staff acct. Fanny Mae Candy Shops, Inc., Chgo., 1981-82; gen. acct. ARI Industries, Addison, Ill., 1982-84; cost acct. ARI Industries, Addison, 1984-86, Elkay Mfg. Co., Oak Brook, Ill., 1986-91; sr. cost acct. Elkay Mfg. Co., Oak Brook, 1991—. Mem. Inst. Mgmt. Accts. (pres. local chpt. 1994-95), Alpha Chi Omega (treas. local chpt. 1993—). Republican. Lutheran. Office: Elkay Mfg Co 2222 Camden Ct Oak Brook IL 60521-1221

HOLSTON, SHARON SMITH, government official; b. Cleve., Dec. 15, 1945; d. Charles Coolidge and Eva Mae (Hall) Smith; m. Joseph Holston, Jr., Dec. 22, 1973; children: Joseph Ikaweba, Eve Denise. AB, Columbia U., 1967; M in Pub. Adminstrn., Harvard U., 1986. Personnel mgmt. specialist U.S. Commn. Civil Rights, 1967-70, HEW, 1970-72; EEO officer FDA, Rockville, Md., 1972-74, personnel mgmt. specialist, 1975-77, acting exec. officer, 1977-79, spl. asst. to assoc. commr. mgmt. and ops., 1979-80, dep. assoc. commr. mgmt. and ops., 1980-88, acting assoc. commr. mgmt. and ops., 1986-88, assoc. commr. mgt. and ops., 1988-93, assoc. commr. mgt. and sys., 1993—. Recipient Award of Merit, FDA, 1982, 87, also commr.'s spl. citation, 1985-94; Sr. Mgmt. citation HHS, 1988, Presdl. Meritorious Rank award, 1992. Rec. sec., mem. Jack & Jill of Am.; active Mt. Calvary Bapt. Ch. Office: FDA Mgmt and Sys 5600 Fishers Ln Rockville MD 20857-0001

HOLT, BERTHA MERRILL, state legislator; b. Eufaula, Ala., Aug. 16, 1916; d. William Hoadley and Bertha Harden (Moore) Merrill; m. Winfield Clary Holt, Mar. 14, 1942; children: Harriet Wharton Holt Whitley, William Merrill, Winfield Jefferson. AB, Agnes Scott Coll, 1933; LLB, U. Ala., 1941. Bar: Ala., 1941. With Treasury Dept., Washington, 1941-42, Dept. Interior, Washington, 1942-43; mem. N.C. Ho. of Reps. from 22d Dist., 1975-80, 25th Dist., 1980—, chmn. select com. govtl. ethics, 1979-80, chmn. constl. amendments com., 1981, 83, mem. joint commn. govtl. ops., 1982-88, chmn. appropriation com. justice and pub. safety, 1985-88, co-chair House appropriation sub-com. transp., 1991-92, co-chair appropriation sub-com. Justice and Pub. Safety, 1993—. Pres., Democratic Women of Alamance, 1962, chmn. hdqrs., 1964, 68; mem. N.C. Dem. Exec. Com., 1964-75; pres. Episcopal Ch. Women, 1968; mem. coun. N.C. Episcopal Diocese, 1972-74, 84-87, chmn. budget com. 1987; chmn. fin. dept., 1973-75, parish grant com., 1973-80, mem. standing com., 1975-78; chmn. Alamance County Social Svcs. Bd., 1970; mem. N.C. Bd. Sci. and Tech., 1979-83; chair Legis. Women's Caucus, 1991—; past bd. dirs. Hospice N.C.; bd. dirs. State Coun. Social Legis., State Conf. Social Work, N.C. Epilepsy Assn., N.C. Pub. Sch. Forum. 1989, U. N.C. Sch. Pub. Health Adv. Bd., Salvation Army Alamance County, N.C., Nursing Found. 1989, Epilepsy Found., 1989; bd. Alternatives for Status Offenders Burlington, N.C., Sch. Pub. Health Adv. Bd. Recipient Outstanding Alumna award Agnes Scott Coll., 1978, Legis. award for svc. to elderly Non-Profit Rest Home Assn., 1985, health, 1986, ARC, 1987, Faith Active in Pub. Affairs award N.C. Coun. of Chs., 1987, Ellen B. Winston award State Coun. For Social Legis., 1989, Disting. Svc. award Alamance County, 1992, 1st ann. Hallie Ruth Allen Dem. Women award Alamance County, 1992; named One of 5 Distinguished Women of N.C. (Govt.), 1991. Mem. N.C. Women's Forums, Law Alumni Assn. U. N.C. Chapel Hill (bd. dir. 1978-81), N.C. Bar Assn., NOW, English Speaking Union, N.C. Hist. Soc., Les Amis du Vin, AAUW, Pi Beta Phi, Phi Kappa Gamma (hon.), Century Club. Address: PO Box 1111 Burlington NC 27216-1111*

HOLT, CAROLYN JANE, publisher; b. DuPage, Ill., Jan. 12, 1965; d. Richard Burton and Shirley Annette (Dalberg) H. B of English, U. Ill., Chgo., 1991. Beat reporter City News Bur., Chgo., 1987-88; asst. tech. writer The Inst. Elec. Packaging Circuits, Lincolnwood, Ill., 1989; editorial intern Chgo. Mag., 1990-91; publisher Chgo. Flame/Phoenix Press, 1988—, Chgo. Access Corp., 1994—; computer cons. Westmont (Ill.) Ctr., 1993-94. Editorial contbr. Citerari, Chgo., 1992-94; author: (play) Modern Odipius, 1992. Polit. activist Greenpeace, Chgo., 1992. Home: 1133 N Damen Apt 3 Chicago IL 60622 Office: Chgo Flame/Phoenix Press 117 S Morgan St 301 Chicago IL 60607

HOLT, DOROTHY JEAN, critical care nurse; b. Granite City, Ill., Jan. 1, 1959; d. Eugene Marion and Evelyn Marie (DuBish) H. ADN, Belleville Area Coll., 1979; BSN cum laude, St. Louis U., 1983. RN, Mo., Ill. Nurse orthopedics dept. St. Louis U. Med. Ctr., 1979-81, nurse coronary med. ICU, 1981-87, nutrition support nurse, dept. of surgery, 1987-88, clin. nurse specialist, div. cardiology, 1991-92, staff nurse coronary ICU, 1992—; nurse cons./in-svc. coord. Profl. Med. Products, St. Louis Br., Greenwood, S.C., 1987; lectr. in field, 1987-88; rsch. nurse, 1991; study coord. NIH grant, 1988-91. Contbr. articles to profl. jours. Rsch. grantee NIH, 1988-90, 90-91. Home: PO Box 309 Madison IL 62060-0309 Office: St Louis U Med Ctr Intensive Care Unit 9th Fl 3635 Vista at Grand Saint Louis MO 63110-0250

HOLT, ELLEN MARIE, county administrator; b. Jersey City, Nov. 8, 1945; d. William Joseph and Marie Louise (Sorrentino) Lemon; m. John C. Holt, Sept. 8, 1973; children: Amy Marie, Ryan Christopher. BA, Wright State U., 1984, M in Humanities, 1987. Editorial asst. Chgo. Daily News, 1965-68; asst. city editor Asbury Park (N.J.) Press, 1968-71; engring. aide Ocean County, Toms River, N.J., 1971-74; adminstrv. aide dept. engring. City Wichita, Kans., 1977-80; planning aide City Kettering, Ohio, 1986-88; dir. grants Okaloosa County, Shalimar, Fla., 1988-89, county adminstr., 1989-93; exec. dir. Okaloosa Cmty. Devel. Corp., 1993—; chmn. Okaloosa County Environ. Coun., 1988-89, Okaloosa Libr. Planning Bd., 1988-89, Fed. Emergency Mgmt. Agy. Bd., Okaloosa County, 1989—; del. Gov.'s Conf. on Librs., Fla., 1990. Sec. Rep. Club, Beachwood, N.J., 1970-73; mem Econ. Devel. Coun.; pres. Literacy Vols. of Am. Named Vol. of Yr. McConnell AFB, 1977. Mem. AAUW, NAFE, Am. Bus. Women's Assn., Am. Planning Assn., Ft. Walton Beach C. C. Office: Okaloosa Cmty Devel Corp 1170 Martin L King Jr Blvd Fort Walton Beach FL 32549

HOLT, JULIANNE MARIE, public defender; b. Ft. Worth, Sept. 29, 1954; d. Alan D. and Carrie Y. (Reyes) H. AA, Hillsborough C.C., Tampa, Fla., 1974; BA, U. South Fla., 1977; JD, South Tex. Coll. Law, 1980. Bar: Fla. 1981. Pvt. practice Tampa, 1981-92; pub. defender Hillsborough County, Tampa, 1993—; mem. Pub. Safety Coordinating Coun., Tampa, 1993—, Juvenile Justice Coun., Tampa, 1993—. Contbr. articles to profl. jours. Recipient Hispanic Women's award in govt. Tampa Hispanic Heritage, Inc., 1994. Mem. ABA, ATLA, LWV, Fla. Bar Assn., Fla. Assn. Criminal Def. Lawyers, Fla. Assn. Comml. Def. Lawyers (dir.), Hillsborough County Assn. Crim. Def. Lawyers. Democrat. Roman Catholic. Home: 3509 W Palmira Tampa FL 33629 Office: Hillsborough County Pub Defender 801 E Twiggs Tampa FL 33602

HOLT, MARIETTA CLAIR, pediatric nurse practitioner; b. St. Clair, Mich., Jan. 24, 1952; d. Donald B. and Lois A. (Henderson) Fordt; m. Robert K. Holt, Aug. 20, 1977; children: Lindsay, Ashley, Nathaniel, Chelsea. BSN, U. Mich., 1974; MSN, Azusa Pacific U., 1994. Cert. pediatric nurse practitioner. Pediatric nurse Desert Hosp., Palm Springs, Calif., 1976-78; pub. health nurse Riverside County Health Dept., Palm Springs, Calif., 1978-80; pediatric nurse practitioner with pvt. physician Palm Springs, 1980-83; supr. health nurse Riverside County Health Dept., Indio, Calif., 1983-85; mgr. MCH and asst. dir. home health Desert Hosp., Palm Springs, 1985-87, obs. discharge instr., 1990-91, pediatric nurse practitioner, 1991-94; mem. sexual assault investigation team Sch. Medicine U. Nev., Reno, 1994—. Fellow Nat. Assn. Pediatric Nurse Practitioners; mem. Calif. Nurses Assn., Nat. Charity League, Nat. Nurses in Bus. Assn., Med.-Legal Nurse Cons., Coalition of Nurse Practitioners. Home: 1441 Samuel Way Reno NV 89509

HOLT, MARILYN JEAN, business development and management company executive; b. Tacoma, Wash., Oct. 22; d. Maynard Ernest and Mable J. (Walker) H.; m. Clifford Rinko Wind, Aug. 25, 1984. Student, Olympic Jr. Coll., 1968-69; BA in History and English, U. Wash., 1972, MA in English Lit., 1979. Cert. mgmt. cons. Freelance writer Seattle, 1970-81; owner, CEO Holt & Co., Seattle, 1981—; prin. Profit Planners, Inc., Seattle, 1992—; adj. prof. Ctrl. Wash. U., Edmonds, 1983—; lectr. Western Wash. U., Seattle, 1983-84; instr. Seattle C.C., 1983-84; sec., v.p. NW Venture Group, Bellevue, Wash., 1986—, sec., 1986-87, bd. dirs., exec. bd.; Nebul Awards juror Sci. Fiction Writers of Am., 1989-90. Author: Business Planning for One, Venture Capital: When a Small Business Wants to Become Big Business, (with others) Ventura: The Complete Reference, 1989; editor NW Venture Group Newsletter, 1986—. Recipient Achievement award Soc. Tech. Communications, 1985. Democrat.

HOLT, MARJORIE SEWELL, lawyer, retired congresswoman; b. Birmingham, Ala., Sept. 17, 1920; d. Edward Rol and Juanita (Felts) Sewell; m. Duncan McKay Holt, Dec. 26, 1946; children: Rachel Holt Tschantre, Edward Sewell, Victoria Holt Schumaker. Grad., Jacksonville Jr. Coll., 1945; J.D., U. Fla., 1949. Bar: Fla. 1949, Md. 1962. Practiced in Annapolis Md., 1962; clk. Anne Arundel County Circuit Ct., 1966-72; mem. 93d-99th Congresses from 4th Dist. of Md., 1973-86; mem. armed services com.; vice chmn. Office Tech. Assessment, 1977; chmn. Republican Study com., 1975-76; of counsel Smith, Somerville & Case, Balt., 1986-90; supr. elections Anne Arundel County, 1963-65; del. to Rep. Nat. Conv., 1968, 76, 80, 84, 88; mem. Pres.'s Commn. on Arms Control and Disarmament; mem. ind. commn. USAR; bd. dirs. Annapolis Fed. Savs. Bank. Co-author: Case Against The Reckless Congress, 1976, Can You Afford This House, 1978. Bd. dirs. Md. Sch. for the Blind, Hist. Annapolis Found. Recipient: Distinguished Alumna award U. Fla., 1975. Mem. Am., Md., Anne Arundel bar assns., Phi Kappa Phi, Phi Delta Delta. Presbyterian (elder 1959).

HOLT, MILDRED FRANCES, educator; b. Lorain, Ohio, July 30, 1932; d. William Henry and Rachel (Pierce) Daniels; B.S., U. Md., 1962, M.Ed., 1967, Ph.D., 1977; m. Maurice Lee Holt, Sept. 11, 1949 (dec.); children—Claudia, Frances, William, Rudi. Tchr. spl. edn. St. Mary's (Md.) County Public Schs., 1962-64, coordinator Felix Johnson Spl. Edn. Center, 1964-66; demonstration tchr. spl. edn. U. Md., College Park, summer 1970, instr. spl. edn. dept. Coll. Edn., 1969-73; supr. spl. edn. Calvert and St. Mary's (Md.) Counties, 1968-69; asso. prof. spl. edn. W. Liberty (W.Va.) State Coll., 1973-75; asst. prof. Eastern Ill. U., Charleston, 1975-77; supr. spl. edn. Warren County Public Schs., Front Royal, Va., 1977-85; spl. edn. tchr. Dallas Ind. Sch. Dist., 1985—. Mem. NEA, Warren County Edn. Assn., Council Exceptional Children, Assn. for Gifted, Assn. Supervision and Curriculum Devel., Va. Edn. Assn., Va. Council Exceptional Children, Blue Ridge Orgn. Gifted and Talented, Assn. Children with Learning Disabilities, Nat. Assn. Gifted Children, Phi Theta Kappa, Kappa Delta Pi. Contbr. articles to profl. jours.; author: Reach Guidebook, 1979. Home: 2916 Sidney Dr Mesquite TX 75150-2253 Office: Joseph J Rhoads Elem Sch Dallas TX 75260

HOLT, PATRICIA LESTER, book review editor; b. Corona del Mar, Calif., Jan. 18, 1944; d. George William and Leah Beryl (Lester) H. B.A., U. Oreg., 1965. Publicity mgr. Houghton Mifflin Co., N.Y.C. and Boston, 1969-71; sr. editor San Francisco Book Co., San Francisco, 1971-77; western corr. Publishers Weekly, N.Y.C., 1977-82; book rev. editor San Francisco Chronicle, 1982—; originator The Yr. of the Reader, Library of Congress nat. campaign, 1987, The Yr. of the Young Reader, 1989; bd. dirs., v.p. Nat. Book Critics Circle, 1991—. Author: The Bug in the Martini Olive, 1992, reprinted The Good Detective, 1994. Recipient Hilly award No. Calif. Publs. Assn., 1983, Grolier Found. award ALA, 1990; named Woman of Yr. Women's Nat. Book Assn., San Francisco chpt., 1982.

HOLT, SHARON ELIZABETH, sales professional; b. Summit, N.J., Aug. 17, 1964; d. David Bruce and J.G. Louise (Fabro) Fraser; m. Michael Christian Holt, June 30, 1990; 1 child, Michelle Elizabeth. BSEE, Va. Poly. Inst. and State U., 1986. Applications engr. Hewlett-Packard Co., San Jose, Calif., 1986-87; field sales engr. Hewlett-Packard Co., L.A., 1987-91, mgr. distbn. program, 1991-92; mgr. field productivity Hewlett-Packard Co., Mountain View, Calif., 1992-94; dist. sales mgr. Hewlett-Packard Co., Palo Alto, Calif., 1994—. Mem. Redondo Beach (Calif.) City Choir, 1990-92. Mem. Sales Automation Assn., Am. Mgmt. Assn., Delta Delta Delta. Republican. Roman Catholic. Office: Hewlett-Packard Co 1501 Page Mill Rd Palo Alto CA 94304

HOLT, SUSAN LYNNE, mental health counselor; b. Columbus, Ohio, Sept. 28, 1954; d. Robert Charles and Faith Margaret (Hartley) H. Cert. in non-violent crisis intervention. Counselor L.A. Gay and Lesbian Cmty. Svc. Ctr., 1987-89, acting asst. dir. counseling svcs. dept., 1990-91, mental health clinician, 1990—, clin. tng. coord., 1991—; group counselor U. Judaism, L.A., 1986-90, mgr. support group facilitator program, 1988-90; counselor rep., mem. counseling adv. bd. L.A. Gay and Lesbian Cmty. Svc. Ctr., 1988-93, chmn. clin. svcs. and tng., 1990-93, mem. planning and adminstrn. com., 1991-92. Mem. Coun. on Jewish Life, Commn. on Cmty. Outreach, Jewish Fedn. Coun. of L.A., 1985-88, chmn. spkr. bur., 1985-88; presenter on domestic violence Domestic Violence Hearings, Office of Criminal Justice Planning, State of Calif., L.A., 1992; mem. Domestic Violence Task Force, L.A., 1993—. Mem. Am. Counseling Assn., Am. Mental Health Counselors Assn., Assn. for Counselor Edn. and Supervision. Office: 1625 N Schrader Blvd Los Angeles CA 90028

HOLT, TERESA JAN, community health nurse; b. Birmingham, Ala., Dec. 25, 1957; d. Coy Eugene and Elizabeth Jeanette (Vann) Estes; m. Thomas G. Holt, Oct. 7, 1977. AAS in Nursing, Wallace State C.C., Hanceville, Ala., 1986; BBA, Faulkner U., 1994. Staff nurse in surg. ICU Walker Regional Med. Ctr., Jasper, Ala.; staff nurse in cardiovascular intensive care U. Ala. Hosp., Birmingham, circulating RN for cardiovascular oper. rm.; staff devel. coord. with dept. edn. ABC Home Health Svcs., Inc. (name now 1st Am. Home Care, Inc.), Cullman, Ala.; founder, owner Jan Holt and Assocs. With Army N.G., 1982-84.

HOLTE, DEBRA LEAH, investment executive, financial analyst; b. Madison, Wis., July 16, 1952; d. Daniel Kenneth and Marian Anne Reitan. BA, Concordia Coll., Moorhead, Minn., 1973. Cert. CFA. Capital markets specialist 1st Bank Mpls., 1981-83; v.p. Allison-Williams Co., Mpls., 1983-86, Nelson, Benson & Zellmer, Denver, 1986-90; exec. v.p. Hamil & Holte Inc., Denver, 1990-93; pres. Holte & Assocs., Denver, 1993—. Active Denver Jr. League, Western Pension Com., 1986—; bd. dirs. Denver Children's Home, 1987—, treas., 1987-91, chmn. fin. com., 1987-91, v.p., 1990—, chmn. nominating com., 1991—, pres. elect., 1994-95; adv. bd. Luth. Social Svcs., 1987; co-chair U.S. Ski Team Fundraiser; bd. dirs. Minn. Vocat. Edn. Fin., Mpls., 1984-86; bd. dirs. Colo. Ballet, 1988-93, chair nominating com., 1991-93, v.p., 1992-93, chmn. bd., 1993; mem. Fin. Analysis Nat. Task Force in Bondholder Rights, 1988—; bd. dirs. Ctrl. City Opera Guild, 1994—, Western Chamber Ballet, 1994. Mem. Fin. Analysts Fedn. (bd. dirs. 1990—, chair ethics and bylaws com. 1987—, chair edn. com. 1988, chair membership com. 1989, rec. sec. 1990, sec. 1991, treas. 1992, program chair 1993), Denver Soc. Security Analysts (pres. 1994—). Office: Holte & Assocs 191 University Blvd Ste 244 Denver CO 80206-4613

HOLTHAUSEN, MARTHA ANNE, interior designer, painter; b. Columbus, Ohio, Oct. 28, 1934; d. Clyde Aloysius and Olive Letitia (Marlowe) Gloeckner; m. Don Trudeau Allensworth, Aug. 14, 1960 (div. 1976); 1 child, Karen Ayn; m. Ernest Arthur Holthausen, Dec. 9, 1989. BFA cum laude, Ohio State U., 1956; postgrad., Baldwin-Wallace Coll., 1959, Mt. Vernon Coll., Washington, 1980, 81. Fashion illustrator The Marston Co., San Diego, 1956-57, The Higbee Co., Cleve., 1957-58; instr. art Lakewood (Ohio) Pub. Schs., 1958-60; tchr. Princes Georges County (Md.) Pub. Schs., 1960; account exec. Stansbury Design, Inc., Prince Georges County, 1975-76; interior designer Berwin Interiors, Bethesda, Md., 1977-79, W. & J. Sloane, Inc., Washington, 1980-84; pres., interior designer Martha Allensworth Interior Design, Inc., Falls Church, Va., 1984—; guest artist-in-residence Nat. Park Svc., Yosemite Nat. Park, Calif., summer 1988, 89, 91, 95. Watercolor and oil paintings in pvt. collections. Bd. dirs. C. of C. Herndon, Va., 1985-86; v.p. Montgomery County (Md.) Art Assn., 1962-63. Mem. Internat. Furnishings and Design Soc., Vienna (Va.) Arts Soc. Presbyterian. Office: Martha Allensworth Interior Design Inc 7799 Leesburg Pike Ste 900 Falls Church VA 22043-2413

HOLTZ, JAN LESLIE, psychology educator; b. St. Paul, Minn., Feb. 18, 1956; d. H. Arnold and Martha June (Bjur) H. BA, Hamline U., 1978; MA, So. Ill. U., 1981; PhD, U. S.D., 1984. Lic. psychologist, Minn. Asst. prof. Coll. St. Scholastica, Duluth, Minn., 1984-86; assoc. prof. Coll. St. Benedict, St. Joseph, Minn., 1986—, chmn. dept., 1991-94; clin. neuropsychologist VA Hosp., St. Cloud, 1989—; clin. psychologist Sisters of St. Benedict, St. Joseph, Minn., 1991-93; rsch. psychologist VA Hosp, St. Cloud, 1992—.

Author: (manual) Faculty Training on Sexual Violence, 1994. Recipient faculty devel. grantee Coll. St. Benedict, 1987-94. Mem. APA, Midwestern Psychol. Assn. (state rep. 1988-92, 94—), Minn. Psychol. Assn., Ctrl. Minn. Psychol. Assn. (pres. 1989-91). Office: Coll of St Benedict P26 Richarda Hall Saint Joseph MN 56374

HOLTZ, KAREN LYNN, police officer; b. Glendale, Calif., Mar. 10, 1960; d. Denison Lee and Diane Arlyce (Shapiro) Baldwin; m. Steven Henry Holtz, June 1, 1985 (div. Dec. 1992); children: Ashley, Stacey. AS, Coll. of the Desert, 1985; BS, U. Redlands, 1992. Police officer Palm Springs (Calif.) Police Dept., 1982—, explorer advisor, 1985-89, detective, 1989-94, field tng. officer, 1994—. Recipient Medal of Valor, Am. Legion, 1989. Republican. Roman Catholic. Office: Palm Springs Police Dept 200 S Civic Dr Palm Springs CA 92262-7201

HOLTZ, MARGARET B., federal agency administrator; b. Elizabeth City, N.C., Sept. 9, 1943; d. Donald E. and Kathleen (Michie) Bradley; m. Richard E. Holtz Jr., Oct. 28, 1961; children: Richard E. III, Patrick B. AS in Bus., No. Va. C.C., 1983; BS in Bus., George Mason U., 1985; MS in Pub. Rels. Mgmt., Am. U., 1987. Pub. affairs asst., chief of naval tech. tng. Dept. Navy, 1978-80, editor, naval internal rels. activity, 1980-84, pub. affairs officer, naval facilities engrng. command, 1984-88; dir. legis. and pub. affairs, military sealift command Dept. Navy, Washington, 1988—; adj. prof. Am. U. Mem. Pub. Rels. Soc. Am., Nat. Assn. Govt. Communicators, Beta Epsilon Phi, Alpha Chi. Office: Military Sealift Command Dept of the Navy Washington Navy Yard Bldg 210 Washington DC 20398-5100*

HOLTZ, SARA, lawyer; b. L.A., Aug. 7, 1951. BA, Yale U., 1972; JD, Harvard U., 1975. Bar: D.C. 1975, Calif. 1982. Assoc. Brownstein, Zeidman & Schomer, Washington, 1975-77; dep. asst. dir. FTC, Washington, 1977-82; divsn. counsel Clorox Co., Oakland, Calif., 1982-90; v.p., dep. gen. counsel Nestle U.S.A., Inc., San Francisco, 1990-94. Mem. Am. Corp. Counsel Assn. (bd. dirs. 1986—, chmn. 1994-95). Office: 28 Heilmann Ct Nevada City CA 95959

HOLTZ, TOBENETTE, aerospace engineer; b. Rochester, N.Y., June 20, 1930; d. Marcus and Leah (Cohen) H.; m. Joseph Laurinovics, Dec. 25, 1964. BS in Aeronautical Engrng., Wayne State U., 1958; MS in Aero/ Astro Engrng., Ohio State U., 1964; PhD, U. So. Calif., L.A., 1974. Sr. engr. North Am. Aviation, Columbus, Ohio, 1954-59; rsch. assoc. Ohio State U., Columbus, 1959-60; sr. engr. U. So. Calif. Rsch. Found., Pt. Mugu, 1960-62, Northrop Corp., Hawthorne, Calif., 1962-67; engrng. specialist McDonnell Douglas Corp., Huntington Beach, Calif., 1967-75; staff engr. Acurex Corp., Mountain View, Calif., 1975-76; project mgr. Aerospace Corp., El Segundo, Calif., 1976-82; tech. mgr. TRW, Inc., San Bernardino, Calif., 1982—. Contbr. articles to profl. jours. Assoc. fellow AIAA (sect. vice chair 1980-82, 91-92, nat. tech. com. 1991-95, organizer nat. tech. confs. 1979, 86, 88, 94, Disting. Svc. award 1983). Office: TRW Inc PO Box 1310 San Bernardino CA 92402

HOLTZCLAW, DIANE SMITH, educator; b. Buffalo, May 26, 1936; d. John Nelson and Beatrice M. (Salisbury) Smith; m. John Victor Holtzclaw, June 27, 1959; children: Kathryn Diane, John Bryan. BS in Edn. magna cum laude, SUNY, Brockport, 1957, MS with honors, 1961; postgrad., SUNY, Buffalo, 1960-65, Canisus Coll., 1979, Nazareth Coll., 1981-82. Tchr. Greece Cen. Sch., Rochester, N.Y., 1957-60; supr. SUNY, Brockport, 1960-64, assoc. prof. edn., 1960-64; dir. Early Childhood Ctr., Fairport, N.Y., 1968-80; tchr. Fairport Cen. Schs., 1971—; ednl. cons. in field; specialist child devel. Ch. music dir. , Rochester, N.Y., 1983—; pres. bd. dirs. Downtown Day Care Ctr., Rochester, 1974-83; mem. exec. bd. Rochester Theatre Organ Soc., 1988—. Mem. Fairport Edn. Assn. (exec. bd. 1982-83, del. 1983), N.Y. State United Tchrs., AAUW (exec. bd. 1973-74, 77-79, 83-84, pres. Fairport br. 1971-73), Internat. Platform Assn., Kappa Delta Pi. Home: 1455 Ayrault Rd Fairport NY 14450-9301 Office: Fairport Cen Schs 38 W Church St Fairport NY 14450-2130

HOLTZCLAW, SARAH JANE, marketing executive; b. Wheat Ridge, Colo., May 23, 1966; d. Irving Arthur and Elizabeth Jane (Quinby) Lowell; m. Michael Allen Holtzclaw, Sept. 4, 1993. BA, Lewis & Clark Coll., 1988. Mktg. asst. Melvin Simon, Lloyd Ctr., Portland, Oreg., 1989-91; asst. dir. mktg. Escape Enterprises, Inc., Columbus, Ohio, 1991-92, dir. mktg., 1992—. Mem. Am. Mktg. Assn., Columbus Lit. Coun. (vice chmn. com. 1993-94), PEO (treas. Portland chpt. 1990-91). Democrat. Presbyterian.

HOLTZMAN, ELLEN A., foundation executive; b. N.Y.C., Mar. 5, 1952; d. Jerome and Corinne (Weinbaum) H.; m. Michael P. Bloom, June 18, 1978 (div. 1983); m. Robert S. Evans, Aug. 8, 1986. BA in Art History, George Washington U., 1973; MA in Art History, U. Calif., Santa Barbara, 1975. Cert. tchr., Calif. Asst. to dir. Bklyn. Mus., 1980-82, asst. mgr. pub. programs and media, 1983-85; asst. dir. Queens Mus., Flushing, N.Y., 1985-88; mng. dir. New Mus. Contemporary Art, N.Y.C., 1988-92; program dir. for arts Henry Luce Found., Inc., N.Y.C., 1992—; bd. dirs. Gallery Assn. N.Y., 1992—; adj. faculty Bank St. Coll. Edn., N.Y.C., 1990; participant exec. mgmt. workshop NYU, 1986. Exec. com. N.Y.C. Arts Coalition, 1988-92; mem. N.Y. Hist. Soc. Cmty. Adv. Bd., 1994. Mem. Am. Assn. Mus. (surveyor mus. assessment program 1990—), N.Y. Archival Soc. (bd. dirs. 1986—), Art Table, Grantmakers in the Arts. Office: Henry Luce Found Inc 111 W 50th St New York NY 10020-1204

HOLTZMAN, ROBERTA LEE, French and Spanish language educator; b. Detroit, Nov. 24, 1938; d. Paul John and Sophia (Marcus) H. AB cum laude, Wayne State U., 1959, MA, 1961; MA, U. Mich., 1961. Fgn. lang. tchr. Birmingham (Mich.) Sch. Dist., 1959-60, Cass Tech. High Sch., Detroit, 1961-64; from instr. to prof. of French and Spanish Schoolcraft Coll., Livonia, Mich., 1964-84; chair French and Spanish depts. Schoolcraft Coll., 1984—. Trustee Cranbrook Music Guild, Ednl. Community, Bloomfield Hills, Mich., 1976-78. Recipient Fulbright-Hays award, Fulbright Commn., Brazil, 1964. Mem. NEA, Nat. Mus. of Women in Arts (co-founder 1992), Modern Lang. Assn., Am. Assn. Tchrs. of Spanish and Portuguese, Am. Assn. Tchrs. of French, Mich. Edn. Assn. Office: Schoolcraft Coll 18600 Haggerty Rd Livonia MI 48152-2696

HOLYER, ERNA MARIA, adult education educator, writer, artist; b. Weilheim, Bavaria, Germany, Mar. 15, 1925; d. Mathias and Anna Maria (Goldhofer) Schretter; AA, San Jose Evening Coll., 1964; student San Mateo Coll., 1965-67, San Jose State U., 1968-69, San Jose City Coll., 1980-81; DLitt, World U., 1984; DFA (hon.), The London Inst. Applied Rsch., 1992; m. Gene Wallace Holyer, Aug. 24, 1957. Freelance writer under pseudonym Ernie Holyer, 1960—; tchr. creative writing San Jose (Calif.) Met. Adult Edn., 1968—; artist, 1958—. Exhibited in group shows Crown Zellerbach Gallery, San Francisco, 1973, 74, 76, 77; I.B.C. Gallery, San Francisco, 1978 (medal of Congress, 1988, 89, 92, 94, Congress Challenge trophy, 1990), L.A., 1981, Cambridge, Eng., 1992, Cambridge, Mass., 1993, San Jose, Calif., 1993, Edinburgh, Scotland, 1994. Recipient Woman of Achievement Honor cert. San Jose Mercury-News, 1973, 74, 75, Lefoli award for excellence in adult edn. instrn. Adult Edn. Senate, 1972, Women of Achievement awards League of Friends of the Santa Clara County Commn., San Jose Mercury News, 1987, various art awards. Mem. Nat. League Am. Pen Women Inc., Calif. Writers Club, World Univ. Roundtable (doctoral). Author: Rescue at Sunrise, 1965; Steve's Night of Silence, 1966; A Cow for Hansel, 1967; At the Forest's Edge, 1969; Song of Courage, 1970; Lone Brown Gull, 1971; Shoes for Daniel, 1974; The Southern Sea Otter, 1975; Sigi's Fire Helmet, 1975; Reservoir Road Adventure, 1982; Wilderness Journey, 1985. Contbr. articles to various mags., newspapers, and anthologies. Home and Office: 1314 Rimrock Dr San Jose CA 95120-5611

HOLZENDORF, BETTY SMITH, state senator; b. Jacksonville, Fla., Apr. 5, 1939; d. Fannie Holmes; m. King Holzendorf II; children: Kim, King III, Kevin, Kessler. BS in Biology, Edward Waters Coll., Jacksonville, 1965; MS in Biochemistry, Atlanta U., 1971; MEd, U. Fla., 1973; LLD (hon.), Edward Waters Coll., 1994. Tchr. Duval County Sch. Bd., Jacksonville, 1965-70; asst. prof. Edward Waters Coll., Jacksonville, 1971-72, dir. rsch., 1972-74, dir. fin. aid, 1974-75; with affirmative action com. City of Jacksonville, 1975-78; adminstrv. aide Mayor's Office, Jacksonville, 1979-87; field rep. Dept. Transp., Jacksonville, 1987-88; state rep. State of Fla., Jacksonville, 1988-92, state senator, 1992—; chmn., Duval County Legis. Del., 1992-93, Jacksonville C. of C. Outstanding Legislator award, 1994, chairperson, Fla. Conf. of Black State Legislators, 1994. Recipient Outstanding Educator award, 1972, Govtl. Svc. award Jacksonville C. of C., 1989, Pres.'s award Fla. A&M U., 1990, Disting. Svc. award Fla. A&M U., 1990, African Am. Heritage award for support of edn. Fla. A&M U., 1991, Human Svcs. Outstanding Leadership award, Brotherhood award, Appreciation award Nat. Coun. Negro Women, 1988, Governmental award Northwest Coun. Area Community, 1989, Quality Legislative award Fla. League of Cities, 1991, 92, Fraternal Order of Police award, 1992, Putnam County Sch. Bd. Outstanding Legislator award, 1993, Fla. Assocn. Administrators, Raymond B. Stewart Gavel award for work in edn., others. Mem. Nat. Coun. Negro Women (life), Nat. Conf. Black State Legis., Fla. Ins. Commmn., 1993, award for excellence, Alpha Kappa Alpha (life). Democrat. Mem. African Meth. Episcopal Ch. Office: 316 W State St Jacksonville FL 32202-4042*

HOLZER, HELEN D., journalist; b. St. Paul, Apr. 15, 1951; d. Michael and Bertha (Shilkrot) Dorr; m. Charles B. Holzer, Dec. 20, 1970; 1 child, Julie. BA in Journalism, U. Minn., 1972. Reporter Murray Eagle, Salt Lake City, 1972; editor Goleta Valley Sun, Santa Barbara, Calif., 1973; assoc. editor Bell Pub., Denver, 1974-75; reporter, layout artist Sun Newspapers, Kansas City, Kans., 1975-78; layout artist Graphic Assocs., Hapeville, Ga., 1980-81, Associated Grocers Advt., College Park, Ga., 1982-83; mgr. advt. Brownell Electro Inc., Atlanta, 1983-89; editor calendar Atlanta Jour. Constitution, 1990—. Dem. precinct committeewoman, Denver, 1974-75. Mem. Atlanta Press Club. Office: Atlanta Journal Constitution Features Desk 72 Marietta St NW Atlanta GA 30303

HOLZER, TAMERA LEE-PHILLIS, middle school educator; b. Chillicothe, Ohio, Apr. 8, 1961; d. William Lee and Betty Lou (Reeder) Phillis; m. Timothy John Holzer, July 1, 1989; 1 child, Jordyn Elizabeth Lee. AA, Mich. Christian, 1981; BA in Elem. Edn., Harding U., 1983; MA, The Ohio State U., 1989; postgrad., Ga. State U., 1992—. Elem. tchr. Prairie Lincoln Elem. Sch., Columbus, Ohio, 1983-89; tchr. Pinckneyville Middle Sch., Norcross, Ga., 1989-92, tchr. Quest, 1992—; county mem. Tchrs. As Leaders, Norcross, 1990—, OBE Strategic Team, Norcross, 1991—, Tech. Subgroup, Norcross, 1992; chairperson Interdisciplinary Task Force, Norcross, 1991. Upreach leader Campus Ch. of Christ, Norcross, 1991—. Named 1992 Coach of Yr., Gwinnett County. Mem. ASCD, Am. Ednl. Rsch. Assn. Republican. Home: care Kim Eagle 7936 Morris Rd Hilliard OH 43026 Office: Pinckneyville Middle Sch 5440 W Jones Bridge Rd Norcross GA 30092-2021 also: 10 Wallace St, Greenwich Point NSW 2065, Australia

HOLZMAN, ESTHER ROSE, perfume company executive; b. Frankfurt, Germany; d. Fred and Anna Marie (Zell) Wetmore; m. Nicholas J. Holzman; 1 child, Stephanie Maria. M Organic Chemistry, Pvt. Sch. Dr. Binder, Stuttgart, Germany. Exec. asst. Bosch G.M.B.H., Stuttgart; owner, chief exec. officer Holzman & Stephanie Perfumes, Inc., Lake Forest, Ill., 1986—; normal control, pioneering rsch. studies in nuclear medicine under Phillip H. Henneman, M.D., Seton Hall U., Jersey City, N.J.; normal control, diabetes rsch. under Phillip H. Henneman, M.D. Organizer campaign to rescind cutbacks in fed. funding for med. rsch., 1969, 70. Recipient award for historic restoration of residential bldgs., Village of Oak Park, Ill., 1974, 76. Roman Catholic. Office: Holzman & Stephanie Perfumes Inc Box 921 Lake Forest IL 60045

HOMESTEAD, SUSAN, psychotherapist; b. Bklyn., Sept. 20, 1937; d. Cy Simon and Katherine (Haas) Eichelbaum; m. Robert Bruce Randall, 1956 (div. 1960); 1 child, Bruce David; m. George Gilbert Zanetti, Dec. 13, 1962 (div. 1972); m. Ronald Eric Homestead, Jan. 16, 1973 (div. 1980); m. Arthur Elliott Freedlender, April, 1, 1995. BA, U. Miami-Fla., 1960; MSW, Tulane U., 1967. Diplomate Am. Bd. Clin. Social Work; Acad. Cert. Social Workers, 1971, LCSW, Va., Calif. Psychotherapist, cons., Richmond, Va., 1971—, Los Altos, Calif.; pvt. practice, cons. Psychol. Evaluation Rehab. Cons., Inc., Lynchburg, Va., 1994—; cons. Family and Children's Svcs., Richmond, 1981—, Richmond Pain Clinic, 1983-84; Health Internat. Va., P.C., Lynchburg, 1984-86, Franklin St. Psychotherapy & Edn. Ctr, Santa Clara, Calif., 1988-90; pvt. practice, 1971—; cons. Psychol. Evaluation Rehab. Cons., Lynchburg, Va., 1994—; Santa Clara County Children's Svc., 1973-75, 86-88; co-dir. asthma program Va. Lung Assn., Richmond, 1975-79, Loma Prieta Regional Ctr.; chief clin. social worker Med. Coll. Va., Va. Commonwealth U., 1974-79; field supr. 1980 Census, 1981-87. Contbr. articles to profl. jours. Active Peninsula Children's Ctr., Morgan Ctr., Coun. for Community Action Planning, Community Assn. for Retarded, Comprehensive Health Planning Assn. Santa Clara, Mental Health Commn., Children and Adolescent Target Group Calif., Women's Com. Richmond Symphony, Va. Mus. Theatre, mem. fin. com. Robb for Gov.; mem. adv. com. Va. Lung Assn.; mem. steering com. Am. Cancer Soc.(Va. div.), Epilepsy Found., Am. Heart Assn. (Va. div.), Cen. Va. Guild for Infant Survival. Mem. NASW, Va. Soc. Clin. Social Work, Inc. (charter mem., sec. 1975-78), Internat. Soc. Communicative Psychoanalysis & Psychotherapy, Am. Acad. Psychotherapists, Internat. Soc. for the Study of Multiple Personality and Dissociation, Am. Assn. Psychiatric Svcs. for Children.

HOMMEL, FLORA NADINE, educational association administrator, consultant; b. Detroit, Mar. 16, 1928; d. Morris and Rae (Albaum) Suhd; 1 child, Claudia Hommel. BSN cum laude, Wayne State U., 1958; studied psychoprophylactic method of painless childbirth (Lamaze method) with Drs. Lamaze and Vellay. RN, Mich.; cert. tchr. and monitrice (nurse trainer), Paris, 1953. Founder, exec. dir. Childbirth Without Pain Edn. Assn., Detroit, 1958—; montrice, tchr. Lamaze method of painless childbirth, 1958—; cons., lectr., workshop leader for med., nursing, student and lay groups; bd. dirs. Internat. Childbirth Edn. Assn., 1964-68; established biennial confs. Childbirth Without Pain Edn. Assn. in co-sponsorship with Nurses Assn. of Am. Coll. Obstetricians and Gynecologists, presenter workshops and papers, 1964-1984; presenter keynote address NAACOG, 1974, and papers, 1972-82; presenter papers to Congresses of Internat. Soc. for Psychosomatic Obstetrics and Gynecology, Paris, Bogota, Colombia, London, Rome, West Berlin. Contbr. (textbook) A Nursing Perspective (edited by Ann L. Clark and Dyanne D. Affonso), 1976, 2d edit., 1979; contbr. articles to profl. jours. Bd. dirs. Detroit area New Jewish Agenda, 1974-84, treas., 1979-84; bd. dirs. Metro-North Detroit chpt. Gray Panthers, 1988—, covenor, 1991-94, bd. dirs. Gray ptnrs. Project Fund, 1992—; chair Women's Conf. of Concerns Health Task Force, 1988—; presenter paper to com. on Paul Robeson, Mus. African Am. History, 1989. Recipient Key to the City of Detroit, Mayor Coleman A. Young, 1973, Twenty Yr. Gold Logo pendant Childbirth Without Pain Edn. Assn., 1978, Achievement award Women's Conf. of Concerns, 1979, Spirit of Detroit award, 1985, Thirty Yr. award Childbirth Without Pain Edn. Assn., 1988, Thirty-five and Still Going award Childbirth Without Pain Edn. Assn., 1993; selected by Faculty Wives and Social Svc. Dept. of Wayne State U. as one of twelve women making hist. contbns. to Detroit, 1982; inducted into Mich. Women's Hall of Fame, 1994. Mem. Internat. Soc. Psychoprophylaxis in Obstetrics (hon. life), U.S. Peace Coun. (charter mem. 1974, rep. reception Nelson Mandela, 1990), Nat. Alliance Against Racist and Polit. Repression, Universal Health Care Action Network. Office: Childbirth Without Pain Edn Assn 20134 Snowden St Detroit MI 48235-1170

HON, LYNDA BURKE, radiologist; b. Biloxi, Miss., July 22, 1954; d. Harlan Duane and Dorothy Louise (Finch) Burke; m. Jeremy Hon, Apr. 19, 1979; children: Emily Louise, Kevin Duane, Jason Jeremy. BS, Miss. U. for Women, 1975; MD, U. Ala., 1980. Diplomate Am. Bd. Radiology. Resident U. Tex. Health Sci. Ctr., Houston, 1980-83; resident, fellow U. Tex. Health Sci. Ctr., San Antonio, 1983-85; radiologist Radiology Assocs., Huntsville, Ala., 1985-86, Huntsville Radiology Cons., 1986-89; homemaker Huntsville, 1989—. Mem., vol. Randolph Sch. Parents Assn., Huntsville, 1988—; children's tchr. 1st Bapt. Ch., Huntsville, 1990. Recipient Nat. Merit scholarship Miss. U. for Women, Columbus, 1972-75. Mem. Radiology Soc. N. Am., Am. Coll. Radiology, Madison County Med. Soc., Madison County Med. Aux., Du Midi Women's Club, Huntsville Hosp. Angels. Home: 1904 Parkhill Rd SE Huntsville AL 35801

HONNER SUTHERLAND, B. JOAN, advertising executive; b. N.Y.C., Oct. 23, 1952; d. William John and Mary Patricia (Edwards) H.; m. Donald J. Sutherland, Oct. 3, 1987; children: Chelsea Lauren, Whitney Devon. Student, Endicott Coll., 1970-71. Art dir. Kerrigan Studio, Darien, Conn., 1971-73, Foote Cone and Belding, Phoenix, 1973-77; sr. art dir. Foote Cone and Belding, Chgo., 1977-81; v.p., assoc. creative dir. J. Walter Thompson, Chgo., 1982-86; v.p., exec. art dir. BBDO Chgo., 1986-91; creative dir. Knautz & Co., Sarasota, Fla., 1992-93; co-owner X-L Advt., Sarasota, Fla., 1993-94; owner Beyond Design, Sarasota, 1994—; cons. J. Walter Thompson, Toronto and San Francisco, 1983-84; owner Fla. Antiques, Geneva, Ill., 1986-90. Introduced Discover card, 1985. Recipient 1st pla. TV local campaign WGN, 6th dist. Addy, 1980, Kemp. Corp. Addy, 1990; Best Internat. TV campaign Pepsi Clio, 1985. Roman Catholic. Home: 4941 Commonwealth Dr Sarasota FL 34242-1421

HONOR, NOËL EVANS, social services supervisor; b. Indpls., Apr. 11, 1948; d. Frederick Harris and Shirley (Richardson) Evans III; m. Herbert Lincoln Martin, Aug. 18, 1972 (div. Aug. 19, 1982); 1 child, Lisa Rochelle Martin; m. Alan Thompson Honor, Sept. 14, 1990. BA in Psychology, Fisk U., 1970; MSW, Ind. U.-Purdue U., 1972. Cert. social worker; lic. social worker, Ind. Social worker Wis. Dept. Health & Social Svcs., Madison, 1972-75; ct. svcs. social worker Mental Health Ctr. of Dane County, Madison, 1976-85; field practicum supr. in social work U. Wis., Madison, 1983-84; lead group facilitator, social worker Multi Resource Ctr., Inc., Mpls., 1985-86; coord. teen incest program Parental Stress Ctr., Madison, 1986; psychiat. social work case mgr. Goodwill Industries, Madison, 1986-87; outreach therapist BOOST Program of Mental Health Ctr. of Dane County, Madison, 1987-88; outreach social worker St. Elizabeth's, Indpls., 1988-91, supr. social svcs., 1991—; psychiat. social worker, group therapist for incest victims Wishard Hosp. Midtown Mental Health, Indpls., 1988—; field placement instr. Ind. U., Indpls., 1992, 94—. Active Holy Angels Cath. Ch., Indpls., 1988—, ladies aux. Knights of St. Peter Claver, 1993—, Grand Lady, 1994—. Mem. Alpha Kappa Alpha. Democrat. Roman Catholic. Office: Saint Elizabeth's 2500 Churchman Ave Indianapolis IN 46203-4613

HOOD, DENISE PAGE, federal judge; b. 1952. BA, Yale Univ., 1974; JD, Columbia Sch. of Law, 1977. Asst. corp. counsel City of Detroit, Law Dept., 1977-82; judge 36th Dist. Ct., 1983-89, Recorder's Ct. for the City of Detroit, 1989-92, Wayne County Circuit Ct., 1993-94; district judge U.S. Dist. Ct. (Mich. ea. dist.), 6th circuit, 1994—. Recipient Judicial Service award Black Women Lawyers Assn., 1994. Mem. Am. Bar Assn., State Bar of Mich., Detroit Bar Assn. (Chmn. of Yr. award 1988), Assn. of Black Judges of Mich., Mich. Dist. Judges Assn., Am. Inns of Ct., Wolverine Bar Assn. (bd. of dirs.), Women Lawyers Assn. of Mich., Fed. Bar Assn., Nat. Assn. of Women Judges, Nat. Bar Assn. Judicial Coun., Mich. Judicial Inst. Office: US Courthouse 231 W Lafayette Blvd Rm 235 Detroit MI 48226*

HOOD, GLENDA E., mayor; m. Charles M. Hood III; 3 children. BA, Rollins Coll.; postgrad., Harvard U., Ga. State U. Commr. City of Orlando, Fla., 1982-92, mayor, 1992—; pres. Glenda E. Hood & Assocs., Inc. vice chmn. mcpl. planning bd. City of Orlando, mem. nominating bd., chmn. task force bd. and commn. restructure; past chmn., founding mem. bd. dirs. Found. Orange County Pub. Schs.; co-chmn. Orlando Fights Back-Coalition for a Drug-Free Cmty.; bd. dirs. U. Ctrl. Fla. Found., Met. Orlando Urban League; past pres. exec. bd. Ctrl. Fla. Coun. of Boy Scouts; bd. overseers Rollins Coll. Crummer Grad. Sch. of Bus.; mem. adv. bd. Valencia C.C., Fla.- Costa Rica Inst.; past co-chmn. United Negro Coll. Fund; pres. Jr. League Orlando-Winter Park, Vol. Svc. Bur.; mem. Orange County Commn. on Children. Named Mcpl. Leader of Yr., Am. City and County Mag., 1992, one of Ten Outstanding Young Americans, U.S. Jaycees, one of Seven Outstanding Youth Floridians, Fla. Jaycees, Woman of Yr., Downtown Orlando Inc., one of Ten People to Watch, Fla. Trend, one of 100 Young Women of Promise, Good Housekeeping; recipient Willie J. Bruton award for cmty. svc. Met. Orlando Urban League, Summit award Women's Resource Ctr., Svc. to Mankind award Leukemia Soc. Am. Ctrl. Fla. chpt. Mem. Nat. League of Cities (past pres.), Fla. League of Cities (past pres.), Fla. C. of C. (past pres.), Greater Orlando C. of C. (past v.p.). Office: 400 S Orange Ave Orlando FL 32801-3317

HOOD, MARY BRYAN, museum director, painter; b. Central City, Ky., July 5, 1938; d. Irving B. and Mary Louise (Anderson) Cayce; m. Ronnie L. Hood, Oct. 16, 1960. Student Ky. Wesleyan Coll., 1956-59, 68-73. Exec. dir. Owensboro Arts Commn., Ky., 1974-76; founding dir. Owensboro Mus. Fine Art, 1976—. Author/editor exhbn. catalogues. Mem. exec. com. Ky. Citizens for Arts, 1980-86, Owensboro Arts Commn., 1977—, Owensboro Bicentennial Commn., 1990—, Ky. Arts Commn., 1974-76; bd. dirs. Japan/ Am. Soc. Ky., 1987-89, Owensboro Symphony, 1975-76, Owensboro Area Mus., 1970-72, Theatre Workshop Owensboro, 1968-70; chair Owensboro Mayor's Arts Com., 1970-75; me. Cmty. Appearance Planning Bd., 1988-92, Davies County Bicentennial Commn., 1990-92; mem. steering com. Yr. of the Am. Craft, Ky., 1991-93. Mary Bryan Hood Day named in her honor, Owensboro, 1974. Mem. Southeastern Mus. Conf., Am. Assn. Mus., Ky. Assn. Mus. (pres. 1980-82). Office: Owensboro Mus Fine Art 901 Frederica St Owensboro KY 42301-3052

HOOD, OLLIE RUTH, health facilities executive; b. San Francisco, Nov. 26, 1947; d. Rodger Brown and Lucile Brooks (Reid); m. McKinley Hood, Aug. 27, 1969 (div. 1987); children: Antoinette Brown, Kirk Stewart, Seancy Hood. BA, San Francisco State U., 1971. Asst. sec., v.p. Weyerhauser Mortgage Co., L.A., 1971-80; asst. supr. Plaza Mortgage Co., L.A., 1980-84; data entry supr. Western Standard Truck, L.A., 1984-85; mgr. Kaiser Hosp., San Francisco, 1985-92; with St. Joseph Hosp., Atlanta, 1992—. Patentee in field. Mem. Calif. Assn. Hosp. Admitting Mgrs., Nat. Assn. Hosp. Admitting Mgrs., NAFE, Kaiser Permanente Club (2d v.p. 1987), Nat. Assn. Women (v.p. 1989—). Jehovah's Witness. Home: PO Box 87117 College Park GA 30337-0117

HOOD-LARKIN, JOAN CRANDELL, counselor; b. Spokane, Wash., Aug. 4, 1934; d. Millard Allerdice and Gertrude Lydia (Warren) Crandell; m. Wesley Dell Hood, Sept. 2, 1955 (div. Aug. 1971); 1 child, Wesley Dell Jr.; m. Michael E. Larkin, Sept. 29, 1984 (dec.); children: Michael, Karen, Christopher, Laurie. BA in Psychology, Whitworth Coll., 1972; MA, Gonzaga U., 1974. Cert. mental health counselor, Wash.; cert. Nat. Bd. Cert. Counselors, Inc. Various bus. positions Spokane, 1952-72; coord. N.E. Neighborhood Ctr., Spokane, 1973-75; dir. Spokane Neighborhood Ctrs., Spokane, 1975-76; pvt. practice Spokane, 1977—. Mem. gov. bd. dirs. Garland Ave. Alliance Ch., Spokane, 1993, 94, tchr., 1972-74. Mem. Am. Counseling Assn., Am. Mental Health Counselors Assn. Home: 702 E Bismark Ave Spokane WA 99207-3503 Office: PO Box 18859 Ste 4 Spokane WA 99208-0859

HOOK, JANET ANN, journalist; b. Mineola, N.Y., Apr. 25, 1955; d. John D. and Alice Elizabeth (Mays) H.; m. William Blake Patterson, June 17, 1990; children: Luke Samuel Patterson, Nicholas Blake Patterson. BA, Harvard U., 1977; postgrad., London Sch. Econs., 1977-78. Asst. editor Pub. Interest mag., N.Y.C., 1978-79, The Chronicle of Higher Edn., Washington, 1979-83; reporter, sr. writer Congl. Quar., Washington, 1983-95; reporter L.A. Times, Washington, 1995—. Contbr. articles to N.Y. Times Book Rev., Wall St. Jour., The Economist, The New Republic, The Washington Monthly. John S. Knight fellow, Palo Alto, Calif., 1992-93.

HOOK, VIRGINIA MAY, marketing executive; b. Balt., Mar. 11, 1932; d. Arthur M. Monroe McClelland and Margaret (Shipley) McClelland Warfield; m. Donald F. Hook, Aug. 25, 1951 (dec. Dec. 1978); children: Donald F., Jr., Donna J. Hook Kellner. Grad. high sch. Teller, Cen. Savs. Bank, Balt., 1950-68, tng. dir., 1968-71; ops. mgr. Mature Temps, Inc., Balt., 1971-81; pres. VMH Mktg. Ltd., Laurel, Md., 1982—. Mem. adv. coun., sr. aides program D.C. Dept. Labor, 1980-81; active local Democratic party; bd. dirs., asst. sec. Balt./Washington Grocery Mfrs. Retailers. Mem. Bank Pers. Assn. Md. (sec. 1969-71), Pers. Assn. Md. (sec. 1979-80), Exec. Women's Network, Market Rsch. Assn., Am. Mktg. Assn., Nat. Assn. Women Bus. Owners, Nat. Assn. Demonstration Cos. (bd. dirs.). Methodist. Lodge: Order Eastern Star. Home: 3 Southerly Ct Baltimore MD 21286 Office: 8566 Laureldale Dr Laurel MD 20724-2008

HOOK, VIVIAN YUAN-WEN HO, biochemist, neuroscientist; b. Oakland, Calif., Mar. 21, 1953; d. Timothy T. and Cheng-Ping (Wang) Ho; m. Gregory R. Hook, July 9, 1976; children: Lisa, Michelle. AB, U. Calif., Berkeley, 1974; PhD, U. Calif., San Francisco, 1980. From postdoctoral fellow to sr. scientist NIMH, NIH, Bethesda, Md., 1980-85; asst. prof.

Uniformed Svcs. U., Bethesda, 1986-90, assoc. prof., 1991-94; assoc. prof. U. Calif., San Diego, 1994—; biochemistry and neuroscience study sect. Nat. Inst. Drug Abuse, Bethesda, 1989-92. Contbr. articles to profl. jours. NIH grantee, 1987—; Wellcome Sr. Scientist fellow NIH, 1983-86, Pharmacology Rsch. Assoc. fellow, 1980-82. Mem. Soc. for Neurosci., Am. Soc. Biochemistry and Molecular Biology, Endocrinology Soc.

HOOKER, ELAINE NORTON, news executive; b. Rockville Center, N.Y., Dec. 4, 1944; d. Henry Gaither and Ann Lou (Allen) Norton; m. Ronald Wayne Johnson (div.); m. Kennedy Ward Hooker Jr. (div.); children: Alisa, Miranda, Nora, Emily. Student, Wilson Coll., 1962-64, U. Hartford, 1965, Trinity Coll., 1974, Andover Newton Theol. Sch., 1988-89. Reporter, editor The Hartford (Conn.) Courant, 1969-74; newswoman AP, Hartford, 1974-75, Conn. news editor, 1975-79; western Mass. corr. AP, Springfield, Mass., 1979-80; Mass. day news supr. AP, Boston, 1981-84, Mass. news editor, 1984; Conn. bur. chief AP, Hartford, 1984-88; dep. dir. corp. comm. AP, N.Y.C., 1990, gen. exec. newspaper membership, 1991—; spkr. in field. Active various coms. at chs. in Concord, Mass., Harford, Briarcliff, N.Y., Greenwich, Conn., N.Y.C. Recipient Sigma Delta Chi award, 1974. Mem. Soc. Profl. Journalists (mem. Freedom Info. coun. 1984-87), New Eng. Soc. Newspaper Editors (rep. Soviet journalists conf. 1985). Home: 61 Sherwood Pl Greenwich CT 06830 Office: AP 50 Rockefeller Plz New York NY 10020

HOOKER, OLIVIA J., psychologist, educator; b. Muskogee, Okla., Feb. 12, 1915; d. Samuel David and Anita Juliette (Stigger) H. BS, Ohio State U., 1937; MA, Columbia U., 1947; PhD, U. Rochester, N.Y., 1962. Cert. sch. psychologist, N.Y. Elem. tchr. Columbus (Ohio) Pub. Schs., 1937-45; clin. psychologist dept. mental hygiene State of N.Y., Albion, 1948-51, Bedford Hills, 1951-57, Rochester, 1955-57; research psychologist dept. mental hygiene State of N.Y., Letchworth Village, 1957-61; sch. psychologist Bur. Child Guidance, N.Y.C., 1951-52; psychologist Kennedy Child Studies Ctr., N.Y.C., 1961-64, dir. psychol. svcs., 1964-83; assoc. prof. Fordham U., Bronx, N.Y., 1974-85; cons. St. Benedicts's Day Care Ctr., N.Y.C., 1976—, Fred S. Keller Sch., Yonkers, N.Y., 1987—. Trustee Terence Cardinal Cooke Health Svcs. Coun., N.Y.C., 1984-91; mem. adv. bd. Child Life program Westchester County Med. Ctr., Valhalla, N.Y., 1985—; v.p. White Plains NAACP, 1985-87, White Plains Sr. Pers. Employment Coun., 1987—; tutor Literacy Vols. Am., 1987—; bd. dirs. White Plains Child Day Care Assn., 1988-94, Vis. Nurse Assn. Westchester, 1988-94; chmn. adminstrv. bd. Trinity United Meth. Ch., 1985-87. Served with women's res. USCG, 1945-46. U. Rochester fellow, 1955-56; recipient Women's award Women's History Assn., 1986. Fellow APA (div. on devel. disability), Am. Assn. Mental Deficiency (chmn. constn. com.). Office: Fordham U Dept Psychology Bronx NY 10458

HOOKS, LONNA R., state official. Sec. State of N.J. Office: NJ Dept State State Capitol Bldg CN 300 Trenton NJ 08625

HOOKS, LUELLEN CARROLL, school psychologist; b. Dublin, N.C., May 19, 1948; d. Charlie Lee Thomas and Mary Lou (Lewis) Carroll; m. Richard Eugene Hooks Jr., Dec. 20, 1969 (div. Jan. 1986). BS in Speech Pathology and Audiology, East Carolina U., 1969; MEd in Counseling, U. N.C., 1978; PhD in Sch. Psychology, N.C. State U., 1989. Nat. cert. sch. psychologist. Speech pathologist, audiologist Robeson County Schs., Lumberton, N.C., 1970-71, Rowan County Schs., Salisbury, N.C., 1971, Stanly County Schs., Albemarle, N.C., 1971-78; counselor exceptional children, psychologist Montgomery County Schs., Troy, N.C., 1978-81; psychol. asst. Lions Clinic for the Blind N.C. State U., Raleigh, 1981; coord. psychol. svcs. Brunswick County Schs., Southport, N.C., 1981-83; psychology instr. Carteret Community Coll., Morehead City, N.C., 1984; part-time sch. psychologist Carteret County Schs., Beaufort, N.C., 1985-87, sch. psychologist, 1989—; speech pathologist Stanly County Headstart, Albemarle, summers 1971-73, dir., 1973-76, coord. handicapped children programs, summer 1977. Solicitor Cancer Fund Dr., Albemarle, 1977-78; com. mem. N.C. Azalea Festival, Wilmington, 1981—; hostess Hospice-Festival of Trees, Beaufort, 1989; mem. Carteret Residents for Excellence in Edn.; bd. dirs. Carteret County Domestic Violence Program, 1992—, chair fashion show, 1993—, chair fashion show fundraiser, 1993-94, chair edn. com., 1994; mem. Carteret County Child Rev. and Child Protection Teams, 1990—, chair, 1992-93. Mem. NASP, NCSPA. Home: 104 Rattan Ln Brandywine Bay Morehead City NC 28557 Office: Carteret County Bd Edn 107 Safrit Dr PO Box 600 Beaufort NC 28516

HOOKS, VANDALYN LAWRENCE, educator; b. Dyersburg, Tenn., Feb. 26, 1935; d. James Bridges and Mary Lucille (Anderson) Lawrence; m. Floyd Lester Hooks, June 15, 1952; children: Lawrence James, Steven Lester. BA, Ky. Wesleyan U., 1967; MA, Western Ky. U., 1970, Edn. Specialist, 1976; postgrad. U. Tenn., 1975. Tchr., Owensboro Bd. Edn., Ky., 1967-71, adminstr., 1976-85; dir. career experience Western Ky. U., Bowling Green, 1971-73; dir. career edn. Owensboro Daviess County Sch. Dist., elem. tchr., 1967-71, elem. prin. 1974-78, 83-85, adminstr., elem. prin. dir. career experience, 1976-85; curriculum developer Career Experience Voc. Edn., Frankfort, Ky., 1971-76; cons. Motivation Workshop, Bowling Green, 1971-76, Decision and Goal Setting, 1971-76. Editor: Ky. Assn. Elem. Prin. Jour., 1977-81; editor, pub. Ednl. Alert, 1985-90, A Crash Course In Ednl. Reform, 1989, A Dangerous Liaison A Tax Exempt Foundation and Two Teacher Unions, 1990, The Alphabet Books, 1991, Caution! Change Agents at Work, 1992; contbr. articles to profl. jours. Organizer, Ky. Council for Better Edn., Owensboro, 1984; legis. advisor Eagle Forum, leadership forum, Washington, 1985, 86-87, 88-92; Rep. legis. researcher . Recipient Presdl. award, Ky. Wesleyan Coll., 1966. Mem. Concerned Edn. of Am., Nat. Council for Better Edn., Pro Family Forum, Eagle Forum, Plymouth Rock Found., Nat. Council Christian Educators. Republican. Baptist. Address: 1302 Waverly Pl Owensboro KY 42301-3683

HOOPER, ANNE DODGE, pathologist, educator; b. Groton, Mass., July 16, 1926; d. Carroll William and Bertha Sanford (Wiener) Dodge; m. William Dale Hooper, June 17, 1952; children: Elizabeth Anne, Joan Elaine, Caroline Mae. AB, Washington U., St. Louis, 1947, MD, 1952. Diplomate Am. Bd. Pathology, Am. Bd. Pathologic Anatomy, Am. Bd. Forensic Pathology, Am. Bd. Clin. Pathology. Rotating intern Virginia Mason Hosp., Seattle, 1952-53; resident in internal medicine St. Francis Hosp., Hartford, Conn., 1953-54; resident in pathologic anatomy and clin. pathology New Britain (Conn.) Gen. Hosp., 1954-57, Presbyn. Hosp., Phila., 1957-58; resident in forensic pathology Office Med. Examiner, Phila., 1958-60; from pathologist to acting chief lab svc. VA Hosp., Coatesville, Pa., 1960-66, St. Albans (Vt.) Hosp., 1966-69; dir. lab. Kerbs Hosp., St. Albans, 1966-71, Williamson Appalachian Regional Hosp., South Williamson, Ky., 1971-73, Beckley (W.Va.) Appalachian Regional Hosp., 1974-76; asst. prof. pathology W.Va. Sch. Osteo. Medicine, Lewisburg, 1977, assoc. prof. pathology, 1978—; lab. accreditation inspector CAP, 1992, 94. Contbr. articles to profl. jours. Pres. local elem. sch. PTA, St. Albans, 1967-68; pres. Greenbrier unit Am. Cancer Soc., Lewisburg, 1989-93, bd. dirs. W.Va. div., Charleston, 1987-94, profl. edn. com. W.Va. div., 1982-94. Fellow Coll. Am. Pathologists, Am. Acad. Forensic Scis.; mem. AMA, W.Va. Med. Soc., Raleigh County Med. Soc., Am. Soc. Clin. Pathologists, Internat. Acad. Pathologists, Nat. Assn. Med. Examiners, Am. Osteo. Coll. Pathologists (assoc.). Office: WVa Sch Osteo Medicine 400 N Lee St Lewisburg WV 24901-1128

HOOPER, CATHERINE EVELYN, developmental engineering specialist; b. Bklyn., Nov. 10, 1939; d. Frederick Charles Jr. and Catherine Veronica (Heaney) Podeyn; m. Melvyn Robert Lowney, Nov. 30, 1957 (div. 1970); children: Denise Lowney Andrade, Michele Lowney Budris; m. William White Hooper, Sept. 21, 1974. Student, San Jose (Calif.) City Coll., 1969, De Anza Coll., 1980. Insp. Amelco Semiconductor, Mountain View, Calif., 1966-68; lab. technician Fairchild R & D, Palo Alto, Calif., 1968-73; sr. lab. technician Varian Cen. Rsch., Palo Alto, 1973-84; sr. devel. engr. Hughes Rsch. Labs., Malibu, 1984—. Contbr. articles to profl. jours. Pres. Conejo Valley chpt. Nat. Women's Polit. Caucus., 1994—. Mem. Am. Vacuum Soc., Materials Rsch. Soc., Grad. Women in Sci. (L.A. pres. 1990-92), Internat. Soc. Optical Engrs., Sigma Xi (sec. 1987-90, 94). Office: Hughes Rsch Labs 3011 Malibu Canyon Rd Malibu CA 90265-4737

HOOPER, KAY, writer; b. Merced, Calif., Oct. 30, 1957; d. James Henry and Martha Raye (Robbins) H. Author: Lady Thief, 1981, Mask of Passion, 1982, Return Engagement, 1982, Breathless Surrender, 1982, Taken by Storm, 1983, On Wings of Magic, 1983 (Best Ecstasy award Romantic Times Reviewers Choice 1984), Elusive Dawn, 1983, Kissed by Magic, 1983, CJ's Fate, 1984, Moonlight Rhapsody, 1984, Something Different, 1984, Pepper's Way, 1984, If There Be Dragons, 1984 (Bestselling Series Romance Waldenbooks 1985), Illegal Possession, 1985, Eye of the Beholder, 1985, Rebel Waltz, 1986, Belonging to Taylor, 1986, Larger than Life, Time After Time, 1986 (Best Loveswept award Romantic Times Reviewers Choice 1986), The Shamrock Trinity: Rafe, The Maverick, 1986 (Innovative Series award Waldenbooks 1987), On Her Doorstep, 1986, In Serena's Web, 1987, Raven on the Wing, 1987, The Delaneys of Killaroo: Adelaide the Enchantress, 1987, Rafferty's Wife, 1987, Zach's Law, 1987, the Fall of Lucas Kendrick, 1988, Unmasking Kelsey, 1988 (Silver Cert. Affaire de Coeur 1988), Summer of the Unicorn, 1988, Delaney Historicals: Golden Flames, 1988 (Spl. Acheivement award in Hist. Series Romantic Times Reviewers Choice 1988), Outlaw Derek, 1988, Shades of Grey, 1988, Delaney Historicals II: Velvet Lightning, 1988, Captain's Paradise, 1988, It Takes A Theif, 1989, Aces High, 1989, Enemy Mine, 1989, Golden Threads, 1989, The Glass Shoe, 1989, What Dreams May Come, 1990, Through the Looking Glass, 1990, The Lady and the Lion, 1990, Star-Crossed Lovers, 1990, Crime of Passion, 1991 (Contemporary Romantic Mystery award Romantic Times Reviewers Choice 1991), The Matchmaker, 1991, The Haviland Touch, 1991, House of Cards, 1991, Holiday Spirit, 1991, Christmas Future, 1992, The Touch of Max, 1993 (Bestselling Series Romance Paperback award Bookrack 1993, Maggie award Best Short Contemporary catagory Ga. Romance Writers 1993, Best Sales Performance award Barnes & Noble 1993), Hunting the Wolfe, 1993, The Trouble with Jared, 1993, The Wizard of Seattle, 1993 (Bestselling Fantasy award Waldenbooks 1993, Maggie award Best Mainstream catagory Ga. Romance Writers 1993, Best Futuristic award Romantic Times Viewers' Choice 1993), All For Quinn (Bestselling Loveswept award Waldenbooks 1993), Masquerade, 1994, The Haunting of Josie, 1994. Recipient Love and Laughter award Romantic Times, 1984, Most Innovative Series award for Outstanding Contribution to Romance Genre, 1987, Lifetime Achievement award Innovative Series Romance, 1989, Lifetime Achievement award Series Romance, 1990, Career Achievement award Contemporary Romance, 1991. Mem. Romance Writers Am., Am. Crime Writers League, Pvt. Eye Writers Am., Novelists, Inc. Office: PO Box 370 Bostic NC 28018

HOOPER, KELLEY RAE, delivery service executive; b. Tulsa, Aug. 24, 1960; d. Kenneth Roe Sharp and Beverly Jane (Phillips) Jenkins; m. John Patrick Hooper, Apr. 30, 1988 (dec. Oct. 1990). BS, Okla. State U., 1982; postgrad., So. Nazarene U., 1991—. Ter. mgr. Am. Fidelity Ins. Co., Oklahoma City, 1982-87; account exec. United Parcel Svc., Inc., Oklahoma City, 1987-89, customer svc. office supr., 1991, next day air letter ctr. coord., 1990, dist. office mgr., 1991-92, dist. area mgr.; dist. sales mgr. ctrl. Ohio United Parcel Svc., Inc., Columbus. Dist. region grant com. United Parcel Svc. Found., Oklahoma City, 1992; mem., donor Ballet Okla., Oklahoma City, 1992—, Oklahoma City Arts Mus., 1992—. Mem. NAFE, Okla. State U. Alumni Assn., Pi Sigma Alpha. Democrat. Home: 948 S Remington Bexley OH 43209 Office: United Parcel Svc 5101 Trabue Rd Columbus OH 43228

HOOPER, MARCIA SARITA, pediatric critical care nurse; b. Detroit, Dec. 31, 1954; d. Alphonso and Annie M. (Garland) H. BSN, Mercy Coll. Detroit, 1977. RN, Mich.; CCRN; cert. pediatric nurse practitioner, pediatric critical care nurse preceptor; cert. PALS, BCLS instr. Staff nurse Children's Hosp. of Mich., Detroit, 1977-91, preceptor, 1991—. Mem. AACN (cert. critical care nurse), Am. Heart Assn.

HOOPER, SUSAN JEANNE, obstetrician/gynecologist nurse practitioner, midw; b. Rapid City, S.D., Aug. 4, 1950; d. Hugh McNiell and Bertha Regina (Mahlberg) Thomas; m. John D. Lanham, Oct. 6, 1976 (div. Aug. 1979); m. Robert Edward Hooper, Feb. 21, 1981; children: Cassandra, Robert Brian. Diploma, Presbyn. Sch. Nursing, 1971; BS in Psychology, U. Dubuque, 1973; cert. midwife, Frontier Nursing Svc., 1975; MS in Nursing, Vanderbilt U., 1979. RN, Colo., Mo. Staff RN, asst. head nurse Presbyn. Med. Ctr., Denver, 1971-72; dir. student health U. Dubuque, Iowa, 1972-73; dist. RN, preceptor family nurse practitioner clin. inst. Frontier Nursing Svc., Hyden, Ky., 1973-75; staff nurse St. Joseph Hosp., Florence, Colo., 1975-76; home health nurse Custer County Health Dept., Westcliff, Colo., 1975-76; commd. 1st lt. U.S. Army, 1976, advanced through grades to lt. col., 1992; nurse, midwife U.S. Army, Ft. Campbell, Ky., Ft. Hood, Tex., Frankfurt, Fed. Republic Germany, 1976-79, 79-83, 83-86; head nurse mother-baby care unit U.S. Army, Ft. Riley, Kans., 1986-89; head nurse labor and delivery U.S. Army, Ft. Riley, 1989-90; ob-gyn. nurse practitioner, nurse midwife Gen. Leonard Wood Army Community Hosp., Ft. Wood, Mo., 1990-94; chief nurse midwifery svc. Blanchfield Army Cmty. Hosp., Ft. Campbell, Ky., 1994—; pediatric nurse practitioner Custer County Health Dept., Westcliff, Colo., 1975-76. Mem. AWHONN, ANA, Mo. Nurses Assn., Am. Coll. Nurse Midwives. Roman Catholic. Home: 526 Morrison Dr Clarksville TN 37042 Office: Blanchfield Army Cmty Hosp 650 Joel Dr Fort Campbell KY 42223

HOOPER, VIRGINIA FITE, city council member; b. Byhalia, Miss., Sept. 23, 1917; d. Pleasant LaFayette and Nell (Brooks) Fite; m. James F. Hooper III, Jan. 29, 1943 (dec. Sept. 1990); children: Cynthia Hooper Rood, James Fullerton IV, Pleasant Fite Hooper. Student, Rhodes U., 1936-37, U. Miss., 1937-39, U. Ala., 1939-41, U. Ga., 1941-42. Mem. Columbus (Miss.) City Coun., 1985—. Founder, past pres. Columbus City Garden Coun.; nat. del. States Rights Conv., 1948; del. Rep. Nat. Conv., 1960, 64, 68, site com, 1972; Rep. nat. commiteewoman, 1962-76; vice chair Rep. Exec. Com. for Miss., 1960-62; exec. com. Miss. Rep. Party, 1960-76, Nat. Rep. Party, 1968-73, Lowndes County Youth Ct.; mem. Lowndes County Election Commn., 1980-84, Civic Arts Commn.; pres. City Beautification Com., 1972; bd. dirs. Miss. Kidney Found., 1970-80, Prairie Opportunity, R.S.V.P.; mem. adv. bd. So. Debutante Assn., Contact, Today Our Understanding of Cancer is Hope (T.O.U.C.H.); mem. Lady of the Realm com. Cotton Carnival, 1968-77; chmn. Cancermount; mem. community rels. & hospitality coms. Columbus AFB; communicant St. Paul's Episc. Ch. Named Miss. GOP Woman of Yr., 1969, Lowndes County Woman of Yr., 1972. Mem. DAR (regent 1954-56), UDC (pres. 1973), Natchez Pkwy. Assn. (bd. dirs. 1987-89), Lowndes Hist. Soc., Historic Columbus, Lowndes County Chowder & Marching Soc., Lowndes County Heart Assn. (permanent chair meml. gifts 1966—, bd. dirs.), Miss. Heart Assn. (membership com. 1969-70), Lowndes County Cancer Assn. (bd. dirs.), Nat. Assn. Parliamentarians, Lowndes County Voters League (exec. bd.), Nat. Assn. Jr. Auxiliaries (pres. Columbus 1951-52, nat. pres. 1959-60, various nat. offices 1954-59), Order of Daughters of the King (pres. 1981, diocesan founder, pres. Miss. assembly 1980, 82), Espisc. Churchwomen (pres. 1978), Earline Robinson Guild (pres. 1983), Cherokee Garden Club (pres. 1955), Friends and Neighbors Club, Columbus C. of C. (biracial com., community appearance com., chmn. ch. com.), Parents in Support of Pub. Schs., Columbus AFB Officers Club (hon. mem.), Chi Omega Alumnae (pres. Miss. chpt. 1972-73, Most Outstanding Chi Omega Alum 1968). Home: 800 N 8th St Columbus MS 39701

HOOPES, SIDNEY LOU, educational association administrator; b. Monterey, Calif., Oct. 24, 1944; d. Jack Sidney Wayne Combs and Alta Virginia (Lane) Combs-Snow; m. Dan Fredrick Hoopes, Oct. 11, 1969; children: Rachel Virginia, Sarah Elizabeth. BSBA in Mktg., U. Ark., 1964. Market rschr. Procter & Gamble, Cin., 1964-65; asst. press sec. U.S. Senator J. W. Fulbright, Washington, 1966-68; adminstr. regional office Tex. Chapparal Basketball Team, Lubbock, 1970-71; office adminstr., sec. Tex. Tech. U., Lubbock, 1971-72; office adminstr. Hoopes Law Office, Idaho Falls, Idaho, 1973-82; cons. mktg. and advt. Idaho Falls, 1983—; field rep. to Richard H. Stallings U.S. Congressman; exec. dir. Edn. Found., Idaho Falls, 1994—. Environ. educator Sch. Dist. #91, Idaho Falls, 1982-86; treas. Bonneville County Dem. Party, 1975-76, sec., 1988—; chief fund raiser Yellowstone Nat. Park Inst., 1983-84; bd. dirs. Idaho Falls Opera Theatre, 1984—; dist. field. mgr. U.S. Ho. of Reps. in 2d Congl. Dist. of Idaho. Named One of Outstanding Young Women Dems. in Idaho, 1975; proclaimed Sidney Hoopes Appreciation Day, Idaho Falls Opera Theatre, 1989. Mem. Greater Yellowstone Coalition (charter). Episcopalian. Home: 1950 Alan St Idaho Falls ID 83404-5722

HOOSIN, JANICE, social worker; b. Chgo., June 22, 1942; d. Herbert and Ruth Jean (Rubenstein) Lapine; B.A., U. Ill., 1964; M.S.W., Jane Addams Grad. Sch. Social Work, 1966; postgrad. U. Utah, summer, 1977. Cert. mental health adminstr., psychiat. social worker, Ill., lic. clin. social worker. Psychiat. social worker New Trier Twp. High Sch., East Winnetka, Ill., 1966-70; dir. day hosp. St. Vincent's Hosp., N.Y.C., 1970-73; psychotherapist (part-time) New Trier East High Sch., Winnetka, 1973-74; dir. psychiat. day hosp. dept. psychiatry Evanston (Ill.) Hosp., 1974-78, dir. partial hospitalization, 1978-88; pvt. practice, 1988—; clin. assoc., field work supr. U. Chgo. Sch. Social Svc. Adminstrn., 1974—; cons. in field; pvt. practice marital and individual psychotherapy, specializing in co-dependency and chem. dependency, 1975—. NIMH fellow, 1964-66. Mem. Nat. Assn. Social Workers, Assn. Mental Health Adminstrs. Jewish. Home: 2638 N Burling St Chicago IL 60614-1514 Office: 636 Church St Ste 715 Evanston IL 60201-4587

HOOTKIN, PAMELA NAN, apparel company executive; b. N.Y.C., Nov. 14, 1947; d. Louis Arthur and Sally (Perlman) Mash; BA, SUNY, Binghamton, 1968; MA in Econs., Boston U., 1970; m. Stephen Allen, Aug. 2, 1972; 1 dau., Julie Beth. Diversification analyst Champion Internat., N.Y.C., 1971-75; sr. fin. analyst Squibb Corp., N.Y.C., 1975-77, mgr. fin. analyst, 1977-79, dir. fin. planning, 1979-82; asst. controller Charles of The Ritz Group Ltd., N.Y.C., 1982-83, v.p., treas., 1983-87; sr. v.p. fin. Yves St. Laurent Parfums Corp., N.Y.C., 1987-88; v.p., treas., sec. Phillips Van Heusen Corp., N.Y.C., 1988—; lectr. econs. U. York, Heslington, Eng., 1970-71. Mem. Fin. Women's Assn. of N.Y. Office: Phillips Van Heusen Corp 1290 Ave Of The Americas New York NY 10104-0095

HOOTS, PAMELA J., personnel administrator, former mayor; b. Campbellsville, Ky., July 10, 1955; d. Walter G. and Joyce (Loy) Hoots. AA in Pre-Law, Lindsey Wilson Coll.; AA in Comms., Somerset Coll.; B of Bus. Adminstrn., Liberty U. News dir. Sta. WAIN, Columbia, Ky., 1980-84; mayor City of Columbia, 1989-93; pers. adminstr. Imo Industries Inc., Columbia, 1979—. Author: (book of poetry) Fall Gently into My Thoughts. Founder, pres. Columbia Cares Crusade, Inc., 1981-93; chair Am. Heart Assn., Columbia; former v.p. Ky. Young Reps.; former pres. Adair County Rep. Women; former hon. mem. Adair County Rescue Squad; charter mem., former v.p. Pearl Harbor Commemorative Com.; bd. dirs. Columbia Housing Authority; dist. chair State of Ky. Dole for Pres. campaign. Named one of Outstanding Young Women in Am., Adair County Woman of Yr., Young Careerist for Adair County, one of Outstanding Rep. Women of Ky., one of Outstanding Coll. Poets in Am., Silver Poet of Am., Gold Poet of Am. Methodist. Home: PO Box 90 35 Parkview Estates Columbia KY 42728-1826 Office: Imo Industries Inc 476 Industrial Park Rd Columbia KY 42728-9206

HOOVER, BETTY-BRUCE HOWARD, educator; b. Wake County, N.C., Mar. 20, 1939; d. Bruce Ruffin and Mary Elizabeth (Brown) Howard; m. Herbert Charles Marsh Hoover, Sept. 3, 1961; children: David Andrew, Howard Webster, Lorraine VanSiclen. B.A., Wake Forest U., 1961; M.A., U. S. Fla., 1978. Tchr. English, Greensboro Sr. High Sch., N.C., 1961-62, Lindley Jr. High Sch., Greensboro, 1963, Berkeley Prep. Sch., Tampa, Fla., 1976—, chmn. English dept., 1977-85, dir., dean upper div., 1984—, chmn. curriculum com., 1982-86 . Author: Resources in Education, 1992. Pres., Suncoast Midshipmen Parents Club, Tampa Bay Area, 1983-84. Mem. Assn. Supervision Curriculum Devel., Nat. Council Tchrs. English, Sociedad Honoraira Hispanica, The Nat. Coun. States, Wake Forest U. Alumni Assn., DAR, Hillsborough County Bar Aux., Cum Laude Soc. (sec. 1981—), Nat. Honor Soc., Phi Beta Kappa, Phi Sigma Iota, Sigma Tau Delta, Kappa Kappa Gamma. Republican. Episcopalian. Avocations: sewing; gardening. Home: 4504 W Beachway Dr Tampa FL 33609-4234 Office: Berkeley Preparatory Sch 4811 Kelly Rd Tampa FL 33615-5098

HOOVER, DEBORAH, critical care, medical, surgical nurse; b. Bay St. Louis, Miss., Apr. 1, 1958; d. Donald Terence and Mary Mauvereen (Graham) Ball; m. Harold Hoover, Jan. 16, 1982; children: Harold Ryan, Carolyn Mauvereen. BSN, Miss. Coll., Clinton, 1991; LPN, Jones Jr. Coll., Ellisville, Miss., 1980; AA, Jones Jr. Coll., 1982. Pvt. duty nurse Upjohn Health Care, Baton Rouge, 1984; charge nurse Zachary (La.) Manor Nursing Home, 1984; staff nurse Hinds Gen. Hosp., Jackson, Miss., 1982-83, Jones County Community Hosp., Laurel, Miss., 1979-82; 3-11 supr. Clinton (Miss.) Country Manor, 1983-84, 85-86; charge nurse Tracehaven Nursing Home, Vicksburg, Miss., 1986-87; staff nurse Vicksburg (Miss.) Med. Ctr., 1987-91; nurse mgr. ICU Vicksburg Med. Ctr., 1991—, nurse mgr. emergency rm., 1992—, asst. chief nursing officer, critical care coord., 1994. Mem. AACN, Miss. Nurses Assn., Student Nurses Assn., Vicksburg Bus. & Profl. Women's Club, Lions, Alpha Chi. Baptist. Home: 120 Post Oak Ln Vicksburg MS 39180-7686

HOOVER, JESSICA MARY, lawyer; b. Chgo., May 5, 1957; d. W. Carl and Dolores (Foerster) H.; m. John Wesley Campbell III, Sept. 6, 1986; children: John Wesley, Timothy Foerster Campbell. AB in Econs./Polit. Sci. summa cum laude, U. Calif., Berkeley, 1979; JD, Yale U., 1982. Law clk. hon. Robert J. Kelleher U.S. Dist. Ct., L.A., 1982-83; assoc. Brobeck, Phleger & Harrison, San Francisco, 1983-89, ptnr., 1990-94; div. corp. counsel Chiron Corp., Emeryville, Calif., 1994—. Mem. ABA, Calif. Bar Assn., San Francisco Bar Assn., Phi Beta Kappa. Office: Chiron Corp 4650 Horton St Emeryville CA 94608

HOOVER, SHELLEY KAE, physician; b. Council Bluffs, Iowa, Mar. 31, 1955. BS in Biology, Met. State Coll., Denver, 1979; MA in Biology, U. Colo., 1983, PhD in Environ., Population and Organismic Biology, 1985; MD, Med. Coll. Va., 1994. Grad. rsch. immunology dept. environ., population and organismic biology U. Colo., Boulder, 1980-85, teaching asst. microbiology and biology dept. environ., organismic biology, 1980-85; postdoctoral rsch. fellow cellular immunology Med. Coll. Va., Richmond, 1986-90, intern, 1994—. Contbr. articles to profl. jours. class rep. Women in Medicine Exec. Com., 1992-94; coord. Luncheon for 1st Yr. Med. Students, 1991; vol. Women's Prison Facility, Henrico County. Rsch. grantee NIH, 1989-91, seed grantee Am. Cancer Soc., 1987-88; Lewis-Gale scholar, 1990; A.D. Williams summer rsch. fellow, 1991, cancer edn. coun. summer student fellow Am. Cancer Soc., 1991. Mem. AAUW (career devel. grantee 1992-93), AAAS, AMA, Am. Assn. Immunology, Student Family Practice Assn. (treas. 1991-92). Home: 7709 Hudson Dr Richmond VA 23229

HOOVER, THERESSA, association executive; b. Fayetteville, Ark., Sept. 7, 1925; d. James Cortez and Rissie (Vaughn) H. BA, Philander Smith Coll., 1946; MA, NYU, 1962; hon. degree, Bennett Coll., 1990. Assoc. dir. Little Rock Meth. Coun., Ark., 1946-48; mem. field staff Women's Divsn., United Meth. Ch., N.Y.C., 1948-58, staff section Christian soc. rels., 1958-65, exec. edn. program, 1965-68, CEO, 1968-90; retired, 1990. Author: With Unveiled Face, 1983; contbr. to monthly column Response Mag., 1969-90. Bd. mem. Nat. Bd. YWCA of the U.S.A., N.Y.C., 1964-76; bd. mgrs. Ch. Women United, N.Y.C., 1968-90; mem. exec. com. Nat. Coun. Negro Women, N.Y.C./D.C., 1968-88; mem. exec. com., chair, Nat. Coun. Chs., N.Y.C., 1968-72; mem. ctrl. com. World Coun. Chs., Geneva Switzerland, 1969-83. Recipient Quality of Life award Nat. Welfare Rights Orgn., 1973, Bethune Recognition award Nat. Coun. Negro Women, 1974, James A. Harlan award Iowa Wesleyan Coll., 1979. Democrat. Home: 2240 East Oaks Dr Fayetteville AR 72703

HOOVER-MADIGAN, ELEANOR JEAN HOOVER, emergency nurse; b. Pottsville, Pa., Feb. 13, 1964; d. Bruce McKinley and Jean Catherine (Wolfe) Hoover. BSN cum laude, Wilkes Coll. Nursing, 1986. Cert. emergency nurse, health profl. Staff nurse med.-surg. fl. York (Pa.) Hosp., 1986-87, emergency nurse emergency dept./trauma ctr., 1987-91; nurse trauma/surg. ICU Robert Packer Hosp., Sayre, Pa., 1991, emergency nurse emergency dept./trauma ctr., 1991. Mem. Emergency Nurses Assn. Republican. Home: RD 3 Box 122A Towanda PA 18848 Office: Robert Packer Hosp Emergency Dept Sayre PA 18840

HOPE, AMMIE DELORIS, computer programmer, systems analyst; b. Washington, Nov. 28, 1946; d. Amos Alexander and Amanda Irene (Moore) H. BA cum laude, Howard U., 1976; postgrad., Am. U., 1976-84. Police officer Met. Police Dept., Washington, 1972-73, officer, 1972; tchr. St. Benedict the Moor Cath. Sch., Washington, 1979; adminstrv. asst. Coun. of D.C., Washington, 1979-81; computer programmer, systems analyst IRS,

Washington, 1984—. Honoree Civic Assn.; Trustees scholar; Pub. Svc. fellow. Mem. Alpha Kappa Delta. Home: 1904 D St NE Washington DC 20002-6720

HOPE, GERRI DANETTE, telecommunications management executive; b. Sacramento, Feb. 28, 1956; d. Albert Gerald and Beulah Rae (Bane) Hope. AS, Sierra Coll., Calif., 1977; postgrad. Okla. State U., 1977-79. Instructional asst. San Juan Sch. Dist., Carmichael, Calif., 1979-82; telecomm. supr. Delta Dental Svc. of Calif., San Francisco, 1982-85; telecomm. coordinator Farmers Savs. Bank, Davis, Calif., 1985-87; telecomm. officer Sacramento Savs. Bank, 1987-95; owner GDH Enterprises, 1993—; founder Custom Label Designer, Sacramento, Custom Label Designer; mem. telecomm. adv. panel Golden Gate U., Sacramento; lectr. in field. Mem. NAFE, Telecomm. Assn. (v.p. membership com. Sacramento Valley chpt.), Am. Philatelic Soc., Sacramento Philatelic Assn., Errors, Freaks and Oddities Club, Philatelic Collectors. Republican. Avocations: writing, computers, philately, animal behavior, participating in Christian ministry. Home: 3025 U St Antelope CA 95843

HOPE, MARGARET LAUTEM, civic worker; b. N.Y.C.; privately educated; 1 son, Frederick H., III. Mem. ball coms. various charity fund raising events. Mem. Jr. League N.Y.C., Everglades Club, Sailfish Club (Palm Beach), Women's Nat. Rep. Club (N.Y.C.), St. James Club (London). Address: 236 Dunbar Rd Box 601 Palm Beach FL 33480

HOPERMANN, TINA MARIE, sales account executive; b. Pompton Plains, N.J., Aug. 21, 1964; d. Richard Konrad Max and Nlobe Lillian (Nelson) H. BA in Polit. Sci., Psychology, Denison U., 1986. Rsch. asst. political analysis dept. Rep. Nat. Com. Computer Svcs. Div., Washington, 1986-87, asst. to dir., 1987-88; deputy liaison officer office of sec. U.S. Dept. of Labor, Washington, 1988-89; assoc. Elizabeth Veanus and Assocs., N.Y.C., 1989, Linda Levy Grossman and Assocs., Washington, 1989; acct. svc. rep. Metromail Corp., Washington, N.Y.C., 1990, sales asst., 1990-91, acct. exec., 1991-92, acct. exec. fund raising svcs. group, 1992-94; cons. Internat. Very Spl. Arts Festival, WAshington, 1989, Commn. on Bicentenial of U.S. Constitution, Washington, 1987; spl. asst. for pub. affairs, Presdl. Yacht Trust, Washington, 1988; congl. rels. asst. Presdl. Inaugural Com., Washington, 1989. Editor: Republican Almanac, 1987. Vol. Park Ave. Unite Meth. Ch., N.Y.C., 1992, 93, N.A.R.A.L., N.Y.C., 1993, Shakespeare Theatre, Washington, 1987—, Denison Alumni Recruiting Team, 1987, Planned Parenthood, 1989—. Mem. Nat. Soc. Fund Raising Execs., Direct Mail Fundraising Assn., Women's Direct Response Mktg. Group, Kappa Kappa Gamma.

HOPEWELL, MARTHA DAVISON, training consultant; b. Bronxville, N.Y., Feb. 7, 1957; d. Robert Prince and Diana (Davison) H.; children: Seth Nair, Timothy Chase. BA in Econs., Wellesley Coll., 1979; MS in Social Anthropology, London Sch. Econs., 1989. Program assoc. Experiment in Internat. Living, Brattleboro, Vt., 1981-83; vol. Peace Corps, Washington, 1983-85; field dir. Plan Internat., London, 1986-94. Producer: (video) A Letter to Our Foster Parents, 1991, Learning for Life, 1993. Mem. ASTD, Nat. Peace Corps Assn., Nat. Mus. Women in Arts. Home: 22 Payn Ave Chatham NY 12037

HOPKINS, ANN B., bank officer; children: T. Gilbert, Tela, Peter. BS, Hollins Coll., Roanoke; MS in Mathematics, Indiana Univ. Instr. Hollins Coll. Mathematics Dept., Roanoke, Va.; with IBM, Armonk, N.Y.; project mgr. Touche Ross; with Price Waterhouse, N.Y.C.; now sr. budget and policy rev. officer World Bank, Washington, D.C.; ptnr. Price Waterhouse, N.Y.C., 1990—. Office: World Bank 1818 H St NW Washington DC 20433*

HOPKINS, ARLENE MARIE, architect, educator; b. L.A., Aug. 14, 1949; d. Herbert Alexander and Kathleen Teresa (Roach) H. BA in Home Econs., Calif. State U., 1972; MA, San Francisco U., 1982; MA in Architecture, So. Calif. Inst. Architecture, Santa Monica, 1984. Registered architect, Nev., Calif.; single subject teaching credential, Calif. Tchr. various, 1972-82; asst. project mgr. Leviseur Architects, Santa Monica, 1983-85; job capt. People's Housing, Topanga, Calif., 1985-86; asst. project mgr. dept. engring. City of Santa Monica, Calif., 1986; project scheduling analyst State of Calif., Sacramento, 1987; instr. dept. architecture Woodbury U., Burbank, Calif., 1989-91; instr. U. So. Calif., L.A., 1988—; architect Hopkins and Assocs., Santa Monica, 1982—; architect Action Moving, Marina del Rey, Calif., 1986—. Mem. AAUW, Calif. Women in Environ. Design, Constrn. Specifications Inst., Internat. Archive of Women in Architecture (bd. dirs.), Spl. Librs. Assn., Westside Home Economists, Keys to the Les Kelley Family Med. Clinic, Phi Delta Kappa.So. Calif. Inst. Architects Alumni Assn. (bd. dirs.). Office: Hopkins and Assocs 2621 Fifth St Santa Monica CA 90405 also: 442 Buckskin Rd Blacksburg VA 24060

HOPKINS, CECILIA ANN, business educator; b. Havre, Mont., Feb. 17, 1922; d. Kost L. and Mary (Manaras) Sofos; B.S., Mont. State Coll., 1944; M.A., San Francisco State Coll., 1958, M.A., 1967; postgrad. Stanford U.; Ph.D., Calif. Western U., 1977; m. Henry E. Hopkins, Sept. 7, 1944. Bus. tchr. Havre (Mont.) High Sch., Mateo, Calif., 1942-44; sec. George P. Gorham, Realtor, San Mateo, 1944-45; escrow sec. Fox & Cars 1945-50; escrow officer Calif. Pacific Title Ins. Co., 1950-57; bus. tchr. Westmoor High Sch., Daly City, Calif., 1958-59; bus. tchr. Coll. of San Mateo, 1959-63, chmn. real estate-ins. dept., 1963-76, dir. div. bus., 1976-86, coord. real estate dept., 1986-91; cons. to commr. Calif. Div. Real Estate, 1963-91, mem. periodic rev. exam. com.; chmn. C.C. Adv. Com., 1971-72, mem. com., 1975-91; projector direction Calif. State Chancellor's Career Awareness Consortium, mem. endowment fund adv. com., c.c. real estate edn. com., state c.c. adv. com.; mem. No. Calif. adv. bd. to Glendale Fed. Savs. and Loan Assn.; mem. bd. advisors San Mateo County Bd. Suprs., 1981-82; mem. real estate edn. and rsch. com. to Calif. Commr. Real Estate, 1983-90; mem. edn., membership, and profl. exchange coms. Am. chpt. Internat. Real Estate Fedn., 1985-92. Recipient Citizen of Day award KABL, Outstanding Contbns. award Redwood City-San Carlos-Belmont Bd. Realtors, Nat. Real Estate Educators Assn. award emeritus, 1993; named Woman of Achievement, San Mateo-Burlingame br. Soroptimist Internat., 1979. Mem. AAUW, Calif. Assn. Real Estate Tchrs. (state pres. 1964-65, life hon. dir. 1962—, Outstanding Real Estate Educator of Yr. 1978-79), Real Estate Cert. Inst. (Disting. Merit award 1982), Calif. Bus. Edn. Assn. (certificate of commendation 1979), San Francisco State Coll., Guidance and Counseling Alumni, Calif. Real Estate Educators' Assn. (dir. emeritus, hon. dir. 1990), Real Estate Nat. Educators Assn. (award emeritus for outstanding contributions, 1993), San Mateo-Burlingame Bd. Realtors (award emeritus Outstanding Contbrs. to Membership), Alpha Delta, Pi Lambda Theta, Delta Pi Epsilon (nat. dir. interchpt. rels. 1962-65, nat. historian 1966-67, nat. sec. 1968-69), Alpha Gamma Delta. Co-author: California Real Estate Principles; contbr. articles to profl. jours. Home: 504 Colgate Way San Mateo CA 94402-3206

HOPKINS, JAN, journalist, news correspondent; b. Warren, Ohio, May 22, 1947; d. Walter Charles and Lois Auelene (Botroff) Reed; m. Walter Hopkins, June 14, 1969 (div. Nov. 1981); m. Richard Trachtman, Nov. 8, 1986. Dir. news Sta. WTCL, Warren, Ohio, 1973-75; reporter, anchor Sta. WERE, Cleve., 1975-77; reporter Sta. WKBN-TV, Youngstown, Ohio, 1977-80; reporter, anchor Sta. WLWT-TV, Cin., 1980-82; assignment editor CBS News, N.Y.C., 1983; reporter, prodr. ABC News, N.Y.C., 1983-84; anchor bus. news CNN, N.Y.C., 1984—. Author: (chapter) Knight Bagehot Guide to Business Journalism, 1990. Trustee Hiram Coll., 1988-94; adv. bd. Knight Bagehot program jouralism Columbia U., N.Y.C., 1994. Recipient Peabody award U. Ga., 1988, Front Page award N.Y. Newswomen, 1988; Knight Bagehot fellow Columbia U. Sch. Journalism, 1982-83; named to Hall of Excellence Ohio Found. Ind. Colls., 1993. Mem. Econ. Club N.Y. Office: CNN Bus News 20th Fl 5 Penn Plz New York NY 10001

HOPKINS, JEANNETTE ETHEL, book publisher, editor; b. Camden, N.J., Dec. 7, 1922; d. Carleton Roper and Gladys Eugenia (Hull) H. BA, Vassar Coll., 1944; MS, Columbia Sch. Journalism, 1945. Asst. to Sunday editor New Haven Register, 1945-46; reporter Providence Evening Bull., 1946-50, Oklahoma City Times, 1950-51; sr. editor Beacon Press, Boston, 1951-56, Harcourt Brace, N.Y.C., 1956-64, Harper & Row, N.Y.C., 1964-73; v.p. Met. Applied Res. Ctr., N.Y.C., 1970-73, cons. editor, 1973-80, 89—; dir. Wesleyan Univ. Press, Middletown, Conn., 1980-89; adj. prof. English Wesleyan U., 1987-89, U. N.H., 1989; propr. Portsmouth Athenaeum, 1991. Author: Books That Will Not Burn, 1952, 14 Journeys to Unitarianism, 1951, (with K.B. Clark) Relevant War Against Poverty, 1968. Mem. coun. Inst. Religion in an Age of Sci., 1968-72, 80-82, 88-91; mem. bd. Unitarian UN Office, 1977-80; mem. Commn. on Appraisal, Unitarian Universalist Assn., 1976-78; bd. dirs. ACLU, 1970-80, mem. nat. adv. coun., 1986—; bd. govs. Unitarian-Universalist Ch., Portsmouth, 1990-93, lay min., 1991—. Louise Hart Van Loon fellow, Vassar Coll., 1944; recipient Alumni award Columbia Sch. Journalism, 1980. Democrat. Unitarian. Home and Office: 39 Pray St Portsmouth NH 03801-5226

HOPKINS, KAREN MARTIN, cytologist, educator; b. Summerville, S.C., Aug. 29, 1945; d. McLeod Sanchez and Leonell (Knight) Martin; m. Douglas James Hopkins, Feb. 12, 1966; children: Douglas Joel, Elizabeth April, Jonathan Martin. Cert. in cytology, Med. U. S.C., Charleston, 1966; BS, U. Tex. Med. Ctr., 1989; MA, U. Tex., 1992. Instr. cytology Med. U. S.C., Charleston, 1966-67; cytologist, supr. Med. Lab. Svcs., Dallas, 1968-70; cytologist Internat. Clin. Labs., Dallas, 1971-74; sr. cytologist Dallas Pathology Assocs., 1974-87; rsch. fellow U. Tex. S.W. Med. Ctr., Dallas, 1989-90; tng. and devel. coord. Olympus Corp., Dallas, 1991-93; instr., mgmt. and staff devel. Children's Med. Ctr. Dallas, 1993—; cons. Tex. Med. Assn., Austin, 1990. Mem. editl. bd. Jour. Allied Health; contbr. articles to profl. jour. Bd. dirs. Thelma Boston Home for Handicapped Foster Children, Dallas, 1980-82; v.p., program chair Carrollton (Tex.)-Farmers Branch Assn. for Gifted and Talented, 1982-90; pres., v.p., projects chair Children's Found. of Episcopal Diocese of Dallas, 1971-89; neighborhood chair United Way, Dallas., 1989-90. Mem. ASTD (co-chair program com. 1994, v.p. 1995), Am. Coll. Healthcare Execs., Am. Soc. Healthcare, Edn. and Tng. (editl. bd., 25th anniversary com. 1994-95), Tex. Soc. Cytology, Beta Sigma Phi (pres. 1975, 87, v.p. 1974, treas. 1990, Woman of Yr. 1978, 87), Alpha Eta. Republican. Office: Children's Med Ctr Dallas 1935 Motor St Dallas TX 75235

HOPKINS, LEAH CORK, etiquette educator, antique dealer; b. Valdosta, Ga., July 14, 1953; d. Robert Lander and Anne McNeil (Ward) Cork; m. Lewis LeGrand Hopkins Jr., July 12, 1975; children: Catherine Anne, Lewis LeGrand III. BA in English, Stetson U., 1975. Cert. secondary edn. and English tchr., Ga. With mktg. and pub. rels. Trust Co. Bank, Brunswick, Ga., 1975-80; co-publs. editor Sea Island (Ga.) Co., 1981-89; ind. manners instr. Sea Island, 1982—; tchr. English and journalism Glynn Acad., Brunswick, 1989-94; ind. antique dealer St. Simons Island, Ga., 1994—. Editor (newsletter) Staff Lines, 1981-89. Fund raiser chmn. Safe Harbor Aux., Glynn County, Ga., 1991—; active Map Aux., Glynn County, 1991—, Olympic Com., Glynn County, 1992—; fundraiser, vol. Rep. Party, Glynn County, 1992—; bd. dirs. Am. Cancer Soc., Glynn County, 1980-88. Mem. Nat. Coun. Tchrs. English, Magna Charter Dames, Pi Beta Phi. Republican. Presbyterian. Home: 107 Seminole Saint Simons Island GA 31522 Office: Sea Island Co Sea Island GA 31561

HOPKINS, LINDA ANN, school psychologist; b. Bristol, Va., Aug. 23, 1937; d. James Robert and Trula Mae (Mink) Broce; AB, King Coll., 1959; MA, East Tenn. State U., 1977, postgrad., 1977-79; postgrad. Radford U., 1978-79, U. Va., 1980-89; m. James Edwin Hopkins, Oct. 8, 1960; children: James Edwin, David Lawrence. Nat. cert. sch. psychologist. Social worker Washington County Welfare Dept., Abingdon, Va., 1959-61; social worker Bristol (Va.) Welfare Dept., 1963-65, Washington County Welfare Dept., 1965-68, Bristol Meml. Hosp., 1968-72; psychologist Washington County Public Schs., Abingdon, 1978-87; pvt. practice sch. psychology, Abingdon, 1987-91; sch. psychologist Georgetown (S.C.) Dist. Pub. Schs., 1991—; adj. prof. East Tenn. State U., 1989-91. Active Pawleys Island Rescue Squad Midway Fire Dept., Swamp Fox Players Mem. Nat. Assn. Sch. Psychologists, Phi Kappa Phi. Methodist. Home: 402 Osprey Way Georgetown SC 29440-8504 Office: Georgetown County Pub Sch Dist 305 Front St Georgetown SC 29440-3733

HOPKINS, LINDA DENISE, lawyer; b. Columbus, Ga., May 27, 1953; d. Edgar G. and Gussie M. (Newsome) H. BSBA, Bradley U., 1975; JD, Howard U., 1981. Bar: V.I. 1982, D.C. 1991. Law clk. Territorial Ct. V.I., St. Croix, 1981-82; asst. atty. gen. Office of Atty. Gen., St. Croix, 1982-86; asst. prof. U. V.I., St. Croix, 1982-87; chief pub. defender Office of Pub. Defender, St. Croix, 1987-91; sr. atty. Resolution Trust Corp., Washington, 1991—. V.p. Girl Scouts Am., V.I., 1984-90, LWV, V.I., 1989. Mem. ABA, ATLA, Women's Bar Assn., V.I. Bar Assn., D.C. Bar Assn., Women's Coalition of St. Croix. Roman Catholic. Home: 175 Joyceton Ter Upper Marlboro MD 20772

HOPKINS, SHARON PAULETTE, obstetrics nurse, educator; b. Newton, Miss., Mar. 17, 1951; d. Cecil Fair and Jimmie Lee (Castles) Aycock; m. Leonard Clark Hopkins, Aug. 1, 1970; children: Jonathan Scott, David Clark, Joshua Fair. ADN, Meridian Jr. Coll., 1972; BSN, U. So. Miss., 1986; MSN, U. Miss., 1990. RN, Miss.; cert. inpatient ob/gyn nursing. Staff nurse Rush Found. Hosp., Meridian, Miss., 1972-77, ob.-gyn. nurse educator, 1985-89; office nurse Rush Med. Group, Meridian, 1977-85; mem. faculty ADN program Meridian C.C., 1990—. Mem. Assn. Women's Health, Obstet. and Neonatal Nurses, Nat. Orgn. ADN, Miss. Nurses Assn., Sigma Theta Tau, Phi Kappa Phi. Home: 6276 Dunns Fall Rd Enterprise MS 39330

HOPKINS, ZORA CLEMONS, training and development specialist; b. Burleson County, Tex., Nov. 19, 1945; d. Otto and Rubie Lee (Sams) Clemons; children: Thean, Aikia. BA in Elem. Edn., Incarnate Word Coll., San Antonio, 1968; MA in Early Childhood Edn., East Tex. State U., 1974; MEd in Ednl. Adminstrn., Prairie View A&M U., 1979. Tchr. Dallas Ind. Sch. Dist., 1968-88, staff trainer, 1988-89, specialist III, 1989-92, specialist in tng., 1992-94; vice prin. Roger Q. Mills Elem. Sch., Dallas Ind. Sch. Dist., 1994—; curriculum writer Dallas Ind. Sch. Dist., 1987-89, monitor for sch. improvement plan, 1989-92; revision team mem. Texas Assessment Academic Skills Test State of Texas, 1992. Advisor Oratorical Club, Dallas, 1987—; counselor Ch. of Christ Youth Club, Dallas, 1970—, mem. site based decision making team, 1993; vol. tutoring program, Dallas, 1988—; organizer Neighborhood Beautification, Dallas and Cedar Hill, Tex., 1987—; mem. adv. com. infusion multicultural edn. Cedar Hill Ind. Sch. Dist. Mem. ASCD, Internat. Reading Assn., Nat. Assn. for Young Children, Nat. Staff Devel. Coun. Tex. Staff Devel. Coun., Tex. Assn. Adminstrs. and Suprs. of Programs for Young Children, Phi Delta Kappa. Home: 218 N Waterford Oaks Dr Cedar Hills TX 75104 Office: Roger Q Mills Elem Sch 1515 Lynn Haven Dr Dallas TX 75216

HOPKINSON, SHIRLEY LOIS, library science educator; b. Boone, Iowa, Aug 25, 1924; d. Arthur Perry and Zora (Smith) Hopkinson; student Coe Coll., 1942-43; AB cum laude (Phi Beta Kappa scholar 1944), U. Colo., 1945; BLS, U. Calif., 1949; MA (Honnold Honor scholar 1945-46), Claremont Grad. Sch., 1951; EdM, U. Okla., 1952, EdD, 1957 Tchr. pub. sch. Stigler, Okla., 1946-47, Palo Verde High Sch., Jr. Coll., Blythe, Calif., 1947-48; asst. librarian Modesto (Calif.) Jr. Coll., 1949-51; tchr., librarian Fresno, Calif., 1951-52, La Mesa, Cal., 1953-55; asst. prof. librarianship, instructional materials dir. Chaffey Coll., Ontario, Calif., 1955-59; asst. prof. librarian ship, San Jose (Calif.) State Coll., 1959-64; assoc. prof., 1964-69, prof., 1969—; bd. dirs. NDEA Inst. Sch. Librs., summer 1966; mem. Santa Clara County Civil Service Bd. Examiners. Recipient Master Gardner cert. Oreg. State U. Extension Svc. Book reviewer for jours. Mem. ALA, Calif. Library Assn., Audio-Visual Assn. Calif., NEA, AAUP, AAUW (dir. 1957-58), Bus. Profl. Women's Club, Sch. Librs. Assn. Calif. (com. mem., treas. No. sect. 1951-52), San Diego County Sch. Librs. Assn. (sec. 1945-55), Calif. Tchrs. Assn., LWV (bd. dirs. 1950-51, publs. chmn.), Phi Beta Kappa, Alpha Lambda Delta, Alpha Beta Alpha, Kappa Delta Pi, Phi Kappa Phi (disting. acad. achievement award 1981), Delta Kappa Gamma (sec. 1994—). Author: Descriptive Cataloging of Library Materials; Instructional Materials for Teaching the Use of the Library. Contbr. to profl. publs. Editor: Calif. Sch. Libraries, 1963-64; asst. editor: Sch. Library Assn. of Calif. Bull., 1961-63; book reviewer profl. jours. Office: 1340 Pomeroy Ave Apt 408 Santa Clara CA 95051-3658

HOPKO, KATHLEEN M., lawyer; b. Southington, Conn., June 2, 1960; d. Robert S. and Lauretta D. Hopko. BS summa cum laude, Fairfield U., 1982; JD, U. Conn., 1986, MBA, 1988. Atty. Sikorsky Aircraft United Techs. Corp., Stratford, Conn., 1986-89; asst. counsel Pratt & Whitney Group United Techs. Corp., Hartford, Conn., 1989-93, assoc. counsel Pratt & Whitney Group, 1993—. Home: 835 Marion Ave Plantsville CT 06479-1441

HOPP, NANCY SMITH, public relations executive; b. Aurora, Ill., Nov. 1, 1943; d. C. Dudley and Margaret (McWethy) Smith; m. Edward Thompson Reid, July 19, 1963 (div. Feb. 1966); 1 child, Edward Thompson Jr.; m. James C. Hopp, Feb. 4, 1978. Cert., Chgo. Sch. Interior Design, 1965; BA in Social Scis., Aurora U., 1968, MS in Bus. Mgmt., 1982. Dir. pub. rels. Sta. WLXT-TV, Aurora, 1969-70; bookstore mgr. Waubonsee Coll., Sugar Grove, Ill., 1970-79, dir. purchasing, 1979-85, dir. pub. rels., 1984-85; dir. devel. Assn. for Individual Devel., Aurora, 1985-87; dir. pub. rels. Mercy Ctr. Health Care Svc., Aurora, 1988—; active Ninety for the 90s Commn., Ill. Dept. Aging, 1989. Editor: Volunteers Make the Difference, 1982; author Pigeon Woods Cookbook; producer (film) Caring Counts; contbr. articles to profl. jours. Bd. dirs. Family Support Ctr., Aurora, 1984-90, Aurora Area United Way, 1990—, Corridor Group, 1993-94; mem. adv. coun. Mercy Ctr. Health Care, Aurora, 1985-87; moderator New Eng. Congl. Ch., Aurora, 1983; charter mem. bd. dirs. Aurora Cmty. Coordinating Coun., 1985-86; mem. Block Grant Working Com., Aurora, 1987—; bd. dirs., sec. Cities in Schs./Aurora 2000, Inc., 1993-94; active Kane County Health Com., 1994. Recipient citation U.S. Dept. HEW, 1969 ; named Woman of the Day, Sta. WAIT-AM. Chgo., 1974, Optimist of Yr. for Cmty. Svc., 1987, Woman of Distinction, YWCA, 1990. Mem. Women in Mgmt. (bd. dirs., sec., treas., Nat. Charlotte Danstrom Woman of Achievement award 1984), Nat. Soc. Fundraising Execs. (ethics com. Chgo. chpt. 1987), Assn. Coll. Stores (pres. 1976), Nat. Assn. Ednl. Buyers (com. mem. 1984), Exch. Club. Republican. Home: 175 S Western Ave Aurora IL 60506-4617 Office: Mercy Ctr Health Care Svcs 1325 N Highland Ave Aurora IL 60506-1449

HOPPENRATH, KATHY LYNN, school system administrator; b. Peoria, Ill., Apr. 30, 1953; d. Richard Dean and Marylyn Jane (Seitzberg) Schmidt; m. William Carl Hoppenrath, July 27, 1985. BS in Spl. Edn., Ill. State U., 1975, MS in Spl. Edn., 1991. Tchr. Washington (Ill.) High Sch., 1975-77, Manual High Sch., Peoria, Ill., 1977-93; asst. dir. Mid-Illini Ednl. Svc. Ctr., Creve Coeur, Ill., 1993—. Mem. ASCD, Learning Disabilities Assn., Adminstrs. Club, Peoria Fedn. Tchrs. (v.p. 1983-85, 91-93), Timber Lake Club (bd. dirs.). Office: Mid-Illini Ednl Svc Ctr 400 N Highland St Creve Coeur IL 61611-3137

HOPPER, ANITA KLEIN, molecular genetics educator; b. Chgo., Sept. 24, 1945; d. Irving and Rose (Warshawsky) Klein; m. James Ernest Hopper, Jan. 3, 1971; 1 child, Julie Victoria. BS, U. Ill., Chgo., 1967; PhD, U. Ill., 1972. Postdoctoral researcher genetics U. Wash., Seattle, 1971-75; asst. prof. microbiology U. Mass. Med. Sch., Worcester, 1975-78, assoc. prof. microbiology, 1978-79; assoc. prof. biochemistry Hershey Med. Sch., Pa. State U., Hershey, 1979-87, prof. biochemistry, molecular biology, 1987—; genetic biology panel NSF, Washington, 1981-85; mem. genetic study sect. NIH, Bethesda, 1985-89; organizer RNA processing Cold Spring Harbor meetings, 1989, 90; co-chmn. 5th Summer Symposium in Molecular Biology: The Nucleus, Pa. State U., 1986. Editor Molecular & Cellular Biology, 1989—, editl. bd., 1986-90; mem. editl. bd. RNA, 1995—; contbr. articles and symposium papers to profl. jours. Grantee NIH, 1979—, NIH U. Louisville Med. Sch., 1989, NSF, 1988-91; postdoctoral fellow NIH, 1971-73. Fellow Am. Acad. Microbiology; mem. AAAS, Am. Soc. Microbiology (chair-elect genetics & molecular biology div. 1987, chair genetics & molecular biology div. 1988), Am. Assn. Biochemists. Office: Pa State U Med Sch Dept Biochemistry & Molecular Biology Hershey PA 17033

HOPPER, SALLY, state legislator; widowed; children: Nancy, Joan, Caroline, Anne. BA, U. Wyo., 1956. Mem. Colo. Senate, Denver, 1987—; chair Senate Health, Environ., Welfare and Insts. com.; chair Criminal Justice Commn, mem. Judiciary com. Mem. nat. bd. Physically Challenged Access to the Woods; mem., past chair bd. Spalding Rehab. Hosp.; bd. dirs. Bayard Industries. Mem. Kappa Kappa Gamma. Republican. Episcopalian. Home: 21649 Cabrini Blvd Golden CO 80401-9487

HOPPING, JANET MELINDA, principal; b. Washington, Dec. 27, 1943; d. Russell Leroy and Janet L. (Cloud) H. B.S., Tex. Christian U., 1965; M.Ed., Ga. State U., 1977. Edn. cert., Ga. Tchr., Littleton, Colo., 1965-68, East Point, Ga., 1969, Atlanta, 1969-78; Title IVc coordinator Fulton County Schs., Atlanta, 1978-81, middle sch. project coordinator, 1981-82; asst. prin. West Middle Sch., East Point, 1982-83; prin. Holcomb Bridge Middle Sch., Alpharetta, Ga., 1983-91, Crabapple Middle Sch., Roswell, Ga., 1991—; cons., trainer various sch. systems. Mem. ASCD, Am. Soc. Assn. Execs., Nat. Middle Sch. Assn. (bd. trustees 1989-91), Ga. Middle Sch. Assn. (pres. 1984-85, exec. dir. 1991—), Nat. Assn. Secondary Sch. Prins., Prins. Inst. (adv. bd.), Atlanta Hist. Soc., Atlanta Com. for the Olympic Games (edn. task force mem. 1990—, Olympic Day in Schs. steering com. 1989—), Delta Kappa Gamma, Pi Beta Phi. Republican. Roman Catholic. Avocations: golf, tennis. Home: 6877 Glenlake Pky NE Apt G Atlanta GA 30328-3469 Office: 10700 Crabapple Rd Roswell GA 30075-3029

HORAN, MARY ANN THERESA, nurse; b. Denver, July 4, 1936; d. John Paul and Lucille (Somma) Perito; m. Stephen F. Horan, Sr., Dec. 28, 1957; children: Seanna, Dana, Michelle, Annette, Stephen Jr., Christine, David. BSN, Loretto Heights Coll., Denver, 1958; postgrad, Pima Community Coll., 1982. RN, Ala. Staff nurse Med. Ctr. Hosp., Huntsville, Ala., 1978-79, Crestwood Hosp., Huntsville, 1980-81, St. Joseph Hosp. Eye Surgery, Tucson, 1981—; v.p. Success Achievement Ctr., Tucson, 1987—; Amway distbr. Horan and Assocs., 1992—. Contbr. articles to nursing jours. Republican. Roman Catholic. Home: 8311 E 3d St Tucson AZ 85710

HORDEMAN-MARSHALL, AGNES MARIE, real estate professional, investment company executive; b. Phila., May 19, 1929; d. Hector and Victoria (Charais) Hill; m. Walter George Hordeman, Sept. 28, 1947 (dec. Jan. 1990); children: Phyllis, Kim, Henry, Rex, Gary; m. Bernard E. Marshall, Oct. 31, 1992; children: Mona Lisa, Barney, Jeffery, Danny, Kate. BA in Social Sci., Thomas Edison U., 1978; grad., Inst. Children's Lit. Relief dir. New Chgo. Trustee's Office, Hobart Twp., Ind., 1962-64; exec. sec. Real Estate Office, Pine Beach, N.J., 1964-65; office mgr. Crestwood Village, Whiting, N.J., 1965-67; reporter Ocean County Daily Times, Lakewood, 1967-69; real estate agt. De-Bow Agy., Lakewood, 1972-73, Century 21 Sullivan Agy. and Centurion and Rimm Howell, 1973-79; dir. Counteract Agy. for Children, Jackson, N.J., 1974-75; pres. Blue Sky Realty, Jackson, 1989-91; broker assoc. Lutz Snyder Realtors, 1991—; appraiser Garden State Bank, Jackson, 1986-87; pres. Brassica Inc., Jackson, 1986-87. Contbr. articles to profl. jours., writing children's adventure stories. Mem. St. Joseph's Choir, Jacob's Well (widows and widowers); v.p. Legion Mary, New Chgo., 1962-64, Rosary Sodality, Jackson, 1967; mem. com. Jackson Twp. Rep. Orgn., 1964-76; rep. to People's Rep. of China amb. program SBA: active Reading is Fundamental Teaching Program; pres. adopt Harney Sch., homeless shelter programs Altrusa Clark County, 1994—; vol. St. Joseph's Cath. Ch., RIF Program, Women in Action; vol. planning com. for bereaved widowed and div. St. Joseph Cath. Ch.; active Mentoring Program for 5th Grade Girls. Named Woman of Yr. Girl Scouts U.S., 1975. Mem. Nat. Bd. Realtors, Jackson C. of C. (v.p., directory chmn., pres. 1989, map chmn.), Altrusa of Clark County (v.p. 1990, pres. 1994-95, vol. homeless program), Clark County Rep. Women's Club, Inst. Children's Lit. Home: 315 Edwards Ln Vancouver WA 98661-5516

HORELICK, MARY GAIL, physical therapist; b. Westport, Conn., Apr. 27, 1948; d. Michael and Rita (Hermenze) H.; B.S., Ithaca Coll., 1970; M.S., Hartford Grad. Ctr.; student U. Conn. Sch. of Law, 1987—. Staff phys. therapist New Rochelle (N.Y.) Hosp. Med. Ctr., 1971-73, Misericrdia Hosp. Med. Ctr., Bronx, 1974-77, chief phys. therapist/coord. rehab. services, 1977-80; dir. rehab. services Newington (Conn.) Children's Hosp., 1980—. Mem. phys. therapy adv. council U. Conn. Mem. Am. Phys. Therapy Assn. (treas. Conn. chpt. 1986-87), Am. Coll. Sports Medicine, Am. Congress Rehab. Medicine, Conn. Traumatic Brain Injury Assn., Nat. Spinal Cord Injury Assn. Conn. chpt. (v.p. edn. 1981-83). Home: 24 Conestoga Way Glastonbury CT 06033-3304 Office: Newington Children's Hosp 181 E Cedar St Newington CT 06111

HORIUCHI, SOPHIE CHIKA, volunteer services manager; b. San Gabriel, Calif., Sept. 25, 1963; d. Harvey Hiroaki and Akiko Lucy (Shigemoto) H. AB in Psychology, U. Calif., Berkeley, 1985, teaching credential, 1987, MA in Edn., 1988. Resident asst. counselor Project Upward Bound Occidental Coll., L.A., 1984-85; program fellow Internat. House, Berkeley, 1984-85; job counselor summer youth employment & tng. program San Mateo (Calif.) Com. Edn., 1986; tchr. San Lorenzo Unified Sch. Dist., Hayward, Calif., 1987-90; program mgr. UCLA Alumni Assn., L.A., 1990-93; vol. svcs. mgr. City of Sunnyvale, Calif., 1993—. Intern State Assemblyman Johan Klens, San Leandro, Calif., 1989; mem. Leadership Sunnyvale, 1993-94, Santa Clara Valley Leadership Program, 1994; bd. dirs. Family Giving Tree. Recipient Newcomer award Coun. for Advancement and Support of Edn., 1991. Mem. AAUW, Dirs. of Vols. in Agys., Mgrs. of Vols. in Govt., Assn. of Vol. Adminstrs., Vol. Adminstrn. Network. Office: City of Sunnyvale 603 All American Way Sunnyvale CA 95126

HORN, ANN MATHEWS, critical care nurse; b. Nacogdoches, Tex., Dec. 27, 1958; d. Jack B. and Minta (Perry) Mathews; m. P. Richard Horn, Oct. 15, 1983. BA in English, Austin Coll., 1980; BSN, Tex. Christian U., 1983; postgrad., Abilene Christian U. RN, Tex.; cert. critical care. Staff nurse, charge nurse, instr. dept. edn. Hendrick Med. Ctr., Abilene, Tex., 1983—. Founder, mem. adv. bd. Big Country AIDS Support Group; Abilene AIDS Task Force; bd. dirs. Tex. AIDS Network, Austin. Recipient First Decade award Austin Coll., 1988. Mem. AACCN. Home: 1142 S Pioneer Dr Abilene TX 79605-3745

HORN, GWENDOLYN, financial company executive; b. N.J., Nov. 27, 1952; d. Walter W. and Ann (Sherrod) H.; 1 child. AAS, Essex County Coll., 1973; BA, NYU, 1975. Cert. in fed. and state procurement. Audit supr. Inventory Control Systems, East Hanover, N.J., 1975-81; audit mgr. Dairy Stores, Inc., Edison, N.J., 1981-87; owner, mgr. A-G's Convenience, Inc., Union, N.J., 1989—; pres., CEO Profl. Inventory Svcs., Maplewood, N.J., 1984—; pres. Fin. Bus. Connections, Maplewood, N.J., 1992—; owner, pub., writer G&B Publ., Maplewood, 1994. Mem. NAFE, Am. Mgmt. Assn., Nat. Adv. Group, Greater Newark C. of C.

HORN, JANET, physician; b. Oak Ridge, Aug. 10, 1950; d. Harry and Molly (Rich) Horn; m. Alan R. Yuspeh, June 8, 1975. BA magna cum laude, Vanderbilt U., 1972; MS in Physiology and Biophysics, Georgetown U., 1973; MD, George Washington U., 1978. Diplomate Am. Bd. Internal Medicine, also sub-bd. Infectious Diseases; diplomate Am. Bd. Med. Examiners. Intern George Washington U. Hosp., Washington, 1978-79, resident in obstetrics and gynecology, 1979-81; resident in internal medicine Georgetown U., Washington, 1981-83; fellow in infectious diseases Johns Hopkins Hosp., Balt., 1983-85; mem. med. staff Georgetown U. Hosp., also Sibley Meml. Hosp., Washington, 1985-86, Johns Hopkins Hosp., 1986—, Sinai Hosp. of Balt., 1989—, Greater Balt. Med. Ctr., 1990—, St. Joseph's Hosp., 1990—; asst. prof. medicine, div. infectious diseases Johns Hopkins U. Sch. Medicine, 1986—. Mem. editorial bd. Johns Hopkins Med. Grand Rounds, Am. Jour. Gynecologic Health; contbr. articles to profl. jours., chpts. to books. Bd. dirs. Chesapeake AIDS Found., 1989-92; chair AIDS Coordinating and Adv. Coun. to Mayor, Balt., 1988-92. Recipient Pearl M. Stetler Found. rsch. award Johns Hopkins U., 1987, Merck Found. clinician scientist rsch. award Johns Hopkins U., 1988. Mem. AAAS, ACP, Am. Soc. for Microbiology, Infectious Diseases Soc. Am., Johns Hopkins Med. and Surg. Assn., Phi Beta Kappa, Alpha Omega Alpha. Office: 10755 Falls Rd Ste 310 Lutherville MD 21093

HORN, KAREN NICHOLSON, banker; b. Los Angeles, Sept. 21, 1943; d. Aloys and Novella (Hartley) Nicholson; m. John T. Horn, June 5, 1965; 1 child. B.A., Pomona Coll., 1965; Ph.D., Johns Hopkins U., 1971. Economist bd. govs. FRS, Washington, 1969-71; v.p., economist First Nat. Bank, Boston, 1971-78; treas. Bell of Pa., Phila., 1978-82; pres. Fed. Res. Bank, Cleve., 1982-87; chmn. and chief exec. officer Bank One Cleveland NA, Cleve., 1987—; bd. dirs. TRW, Inc., Eli Lilly Co., Rubbermaid, Brit. Petroleum, Coun. Fgn. Rels. Chmn., trustee Case Western Res. U., Cleve.; trustee Rockefeller Found., Cleve. Clinic Found., Cleve. Orch., Cleve. Tomorrow. Office: Bank One Cleve NA 600 Superior Ave Cleveland OH 44114

HORN, MARIAN BLANK, federal judge; b. N.Y.C., June 24, 1943; d. Werner P. and Mady R. Blank; m. Robert Jack Horn; children: Juli Marie, Carrie Charlotte, Rebecca Blank. AB, Barnard Coll., 1962; student, Cornell U., Columbia U., 1965, NYU, 1965-66; JD, Fordham U., 1969. Bar: N.Y. 1970, D.C. 1973, U.S. Supreme Ct. 1973. Asst. dist. atty. Bronx County, N.Y., 1969-72; assoc. Arent, Fox, Kintner, Plotkin & Kahn, 1972-73; project mgr. Am. U. Law Sch. study on alts. to conventional criminal adjudication U.S. Dept. Justice, 1973-75; litigation atty. Fed. Energy Adminstrn., 1975-76; sr. atty. office gen. counsel strategic petroleum res. br. Dept. Energy, 1976-79, dep. asst. gen. counsel for procurement and fin. incentives, 1979-81; dep. assoc. solicitor div. surface mining Dept. Interior, 1981-83, assoc. solicitor div. gen. law, 1983-85, prin. dep. solicitor, acting solicitor, 1985; judge U.S. Ct. of Federal Claims, 1986—; adj. prof. law Washington Coll. Law, Am. U., 1973-76. Office: US Claims Ct 717 Madison Pl NW Washington DC 20005-1011*

HORN, MIRIAM MOLLY, artist; b. Chgo., Oct. 27, 1930; d. Meyer and Sophie (Richter) Millman; m. David M. Wexler, June 7, 1952 (div. Dec. 1972); children: Philip, Larry, Suzan, Pamela; m. Sheldon Horn, June 12, 1973. BA in Psychiatry, Northeastern Ill. U., 1978, MA in Counseling and Guidance, 1980. Cert. mental health generalist therapist. Vocat. counselor Nat. Coun. Jewish Women, Chgo., 1980; artist, 1980—; pers. asst. KW Battery Co., Skokie, Ill., 1981-83, Sargent Welch Sci., Skokie, 1983-85; portraiture artist missing persons program Channel 7, Chgo., 1993. One-woman shows various theatres, librs., restaurants; landscapes and portraits in various pvt. collections. Village clk. candidate Village Lincolnwood Party, 1993. Art Inst. scholar, 1943-47.

HORN, SUSAN ANDREWS, property management company official; b. Boston, May 6, 1946; d. Arthur Wood and Marion (Saunders) Chapman. AA, Colby-Sawyer Coll., 1966; BA, Hiram Coll., 1970. Founder, pres. Gem Island Software, Reading, Mass., 1985-90; dir. Gem Island Software, Carlisle, Mass., 1990-93; property mgr. Finard & Co., Burlington, Mass., 1993—. Class historian Wellesley High Class, 1964; leader, bd. dirs. Camp Fire, Reading, Antiquarian Soc., Reading, 1990-93; mem. steering com., officer Reading 350th Celebration, 1989-94. Mem. Omicron Beta. Office: Finard & Co 3 Burlington Woods Dr Burlington MA 01803

HORN, SUSAN DADAKIS, statistics educator; b. Cleve., Aug. 30, 1943; d. James Sophocles and Demeter (Zessis) Dadakis; m. Roger Alan Horn, July 24, 1965; children: Ceres, Corinne, Howard. BA, Cornell U., 1964; MS, Stanford U., 1966, PhD, 1968. Asst. prof. Johns Hopkins U., Balt., 1968-76, assoc. prof., 1976-86, prof. stats. and health svcs. rsch. methods, 1986-92; sr. scientist Intermountain Health Care, Salt Lake City, 1992—; prof. dept. med. informatics Sch. Medicine U. Utah, Salt Lake City, 1992—. Fellow Am. Statist. Assn.; mem. Am. Pub. Health Assn., Biometric Soc., Assn. for Health Svcs. Research, Sigma Xi, Phi Beta Kappa, Phi Kappa Phi. Presbyterian. Home: 1793 E Ft Douglas Circle Salt Lake City UT 84103 Office: Intermountain Health Care 22d Fl 36 S State St Salt Lake City UT 84111

HORNADAY, ALINE GRANDIER, publisher, independent scholar; b. San Diego, Sept. 14, 1923; d. Frank and Lydia Landon (Weir) Grandier; m. Quinn Hornaday, Oct. 9, 1965. BA, Union of Experimenting Colls., San Diego, 1977; PhD, U. Calif., San Diego, 1984. Pub. San Diego Daily Transcript, 1952-72, columnist, 1972-74; dir. San Diego Ind. Scholars, 1985-87; co-pub. Jour. Unconventional History, Cardiff, Calif., 1989—; vis. scholar U. Calif., San Diego, 1984—; speaker at profl. confs. Co-author: The Hornadays, Root and Branch; contbr. articles to profl. jours. Commr. San Diego City Libr. Commn., 1964-70. Mem. San Diego Ind. Scholars, Nat. Coalition Ind. Scholars, Med. Assn. of Pacific, Am. Hist. Assn., Medieval Acad. Am., Nat. Soc. Colonial Dames of Am., Wed. Club (pres. 1964-65). Home and Office: 6435 Avenida Cresta La Jolla CA 92037-6514

HORNAK, ANNA FRANCES, library administrator; b. College Station, Tex., June 3, 1922; d. Josef and Anna (Drozd) H. B.A., U. Tex., Austin, 1944; B.L.S., U. Ill., Champaign-Urbana, 1945; Ed.M., U. Houston, 1956. Children's librarian Schenectady Pub. Library, N.Y., 1945-47; children's librarian Pasadena Pub. Library, Calif., 1947-49; supr. Juvenile Div. Houston Pub. Library, 1949-57, asst. dir., 1957-89, ret., 1989. Named Outstanding Woman, YWCA of Houston, 1977; Outstanding Houston Profl. Woman, Fed. Houston Profl. Women, 1982. Home: 2217 Woodhead St Houston TX 77019-6820

HORNAK, NANCY JOAN, counseling educator, psychologist; b. Alpena, Mich., July 9, 1943; d. Gregor and Althea (McMaster) Grant; m. James Edward Hornak, June 25, 1966; children: David Grant, Kristin Patrice. BA, Ctrl. Mich. U., 1965, MA, 1967; EdD, U. No. Colo., 1978. Lic. psychologist, profl. counselor, Mich. Tchr. English, Ctrl. High Sch., Bay City, Mich., 1965-66; counselor Bullock Creek H.S., Midland, Mich., 1967-69, counselor, guidance dir., 1970-76; coord. counseling 3 sch. dists., Colo., 1969-70; assoc. prof. counseling, counselor Ctrl. Mich. U., Mt. Pleasant, 1979-85, prof., dir. Human Devel. Clinic, 1986—; cons., counselor Women's Wellness Ctr., Mt. Pleasant, 1987-91, Mt. Pleasant Pub. Schs., 1986-87; cons., lectr. to profl. orgns., Mich., Ga., 1990—; mem. Mich. Bd. Counseling, 1994-97. Co-author: Career Planning and You, 1978; contbg. author: Food Patterns and the Treatment of Eating Disorders, 1987; also articles. Unit solicitor United Way, Mt. Pleasant, 1989-93; mem. nat. com. on ethical relationships Women's Sports Found., 1993-94. Recipient Excellence in Teaching award Ctrl. Mich. U., 1990, Disting. Faculty award Mich. Assn. Governing Bds., 1994; grantee Ctrl. Mich. U., 1993. Mem. APA, ACA, Mich. Counseling Assn. (exec. bd. 1980—), Mich. Coll. Pers. Assn. (past pres.), Mortar Bd. (past v.p.), Phi Kappa Phi. Office: Ctrl Mich U Counseling-Spl Edn Dept 218 Rowe Hall Mount Pleasant MI 48859

HORNBAKER, ALICE JOY, author; b. Cin., Feb. 3, 1927; children: Christopher Albert, Holly Jo, Joseph Bernard III. BA cum laude and honors in Journalism, U. Calif., San Jose, 1949. Asst. woman's editor San Jose Mercury-News, 1949-55; columnist "On Aging" and "Ask Alice" Cin. Post Newspaper, 1993—; free-lance writer Cin.; owner, mgr. Frisch's Big Boy Restaurant, Cin., 1955-68; dir. pub. relations Children's Home Soc. Calif., Santa Clara, 1968-71; asst. dir. pub. relations United Fund Calif., Santa Clara, 1971—; editor Tristate Sunday Enquirer mag., 1986-89, columnist Generations Tristate mag.; editorial dir. Writers Digest Sch., Cin., 1971-75; columnist, critic, mag. writer, reporter, copy editor Tempo sec. Cin. Enquirer, 1975-93, also book editor and critic, columnist for Aging, feature writer Tempo sect.; reporter news segments on aging WKRC-TV; tchr. adult edn. Forest Hills Sch. Dist., Thomas More Coll., 1973—; reporter, specialist on aging for Cin. Enquirer, 1989-93, commentator on aging Sta. WMLX-AM, 1991-93. Author: Preventive Care: Easy Exercise Against Aging, 1974; byline in People, Modern Maturity, St. Anthony Messenger, N.Y. Times Sun. mag., and others; contbr. fiction to Enquirer mag.; freelance mag. writer. Recipient Bronze award in Am. health journalism Am. Chiropractic Assn., 1977, 78, Golden Image award Assn. Ohio Philanthropic Homes, 1989; 1st pl. for feature writing Cin. Editors Assn., 1983, 1st and 3d pl. feature writing awards Ohio Profl. Writers, Inc., 1992, Journalist of Yr. award Ohio chpt. Am. Coll. Health Care Adminstrs., 1993, Journalism award Greater Cin. Joint Coun. on Geraitric Care, 1993. Mem. Blue Pencil of Ohio State U. (pres. 1981-82), Women in Comm., Ohio Newspaper Women's Assn. (v.p. 1981-83, 1st pl. human interest story 1977-85, 2d pl. column award 1979, Tops in Ohio award 1982, M.M. McMullen 2d pl. award, 1982, Recognition award 1985, 4th pl. on aging Nat. Legacies contest 1994), Soc. Profl. Journalists (treas. 1981-82), Ohio Press Women, Inc. (1st and 3d pl. awards for feature writing 1992). Office: CW Post 125 E Court St Cincinnati OH 45202

HORNBY-ANDERSON, SARA ANN, metallurgical engineer, marketing professional; b. Plymouth, Devon, Eng., Apr. 17, 1952; came to U.S., 1986; d. Foster John and Joanna May (Duncan) Hornby; m. John Victor Anderson, Sept. 2, 1978 (div. May 1987). BSc in Metallurgy with honors, Sheffield (Eng.) City Poly., 1973, PhD in Indsl. Metallurgy, 1980. Chartered engr. Metallurgist Joseph Lucas Rsch., Solihull, Eng., 1970, William Lee Maleable, Dronfield, Eng., 1972; tech. sales specialist Applied Rsch. Labs, Luton, Beds, Eng., 1973-74; quality assurance metallurgist Firth Brown Tools, Sheffield, 1974-75, rsch. metallurgist high speed steel, 1975; lectr. Sheffield City Poly., 1975-78; grad. metallurgist, strip devel. metallurgist British Steel Corp., Rotherham, Eng., 1978-80; program mgr. Can. Liquid Air, Montreal, 1980-85; group mktg. mgr. Liquid Air Corp., Countryside, Ill., 1986-90; tech. mgr. Liquid Air Corp., Walnut Creek, Calif., 1990-93; mktg. mgr.-metals Can. Liquid Air, Toronto, Ont., 1993—; bd. dirs., chmn. R & D com., mem. publs. com., chmn. promotions and mktg. com. INvestment Casting Inst., Dallas; presenter to confs. in field. Contbr. articles to profl. jours.; patentee in field of metallurgy. Mem. AIME, Inst. Metals (young metallurgists com. 1974-80), Sheffield Metall. Soc. Inst. Metals (sec. 1978-80), Am. Soc. Metals, Am. Foundry Soc., Powder Metals Soc., Am. Iron & Steel Soc. (steering com. 1987—, chmn. topics com. 1988—, sec. 1992, vice chair 1993, chmn. 1994, bd. dirs.). Mem. Ch. of Eng. Office: Can Liquid Air, 1700 Steeles Ave E, Bramalea, ON Canada L6T 1A6

HORNE, LENA, singer; b. Bklyn., June 30, 1917; d. Gail Lumet Buckley; m. Lennie Hayton, Dec. 1947 (dec. 1971). Dancer, Cotton Club, 1934; toured, recorded with Noble Sissle Orch., 1935-36, Charlie Barnet's Band, 1940-41; became cafe soc. singer; starred in: motion pictures Cabin in the Sky, Stormy Weather, Death of a Gunfighter, Thousands Cheer, I Dood It, Swing Fever, Broadway Rhythm, Two Girls and a Sailor, Ziegfield Follies, Panama Hattie, Till the Clouds Roll By, Words & Music, Duchess of Idaho, Meet Me in Las Vegas, others; singer popular music ; TV appearances include spl. Harry and Lena, 1970, series Cosby Show, Sanford and Son; theatrical appearances in Dance with Your Gods, Blackbird, The Lady & Her Music, 1984; albums: Stormy Weather, The Men in My Life, 1989, Greatest Hits, 1992, At Long Last Lena, 1992, Best of Lena Horne, 1993; author: (with Richard Schickel) Lena, 1965. Recipient Kennedy Ctr. honor for lifetime contributions to the arts, 1984, Paul Robson award Actor's Equity, 1985. Office: care Edward White & Co 5950 Canoga Ave Woodland Hills CA 91367-5011*

HORNE, MARILYN, mezzo-soprano; b. Bradford, Pa., Jan. 16, 1934; d. Bentz and Berneice H.; m. Henry Lewis (div.); 1 child. Ed., U. So. Calif.; MusD (hon.), Rutgers U., 1970, Jersey City State Coll., 1973, Brown U., 1984, Juillard Sch. Music, 1994; DLitt (hon.), St. Peter's Coll.; LHD (hon.), Kean Coll., 1977. Operatic debut as Hata in The Bartered Bride, Los Angeles Guild Opera, 1954; La Scala debut in Oepidus Rex, 1969; Met. Opera debut as Adalgisa in Norma, 1970; other roles include Rosina in Barber of Seville, Cleonte in The Siege of Corinth, Isabella in L'Italiana in Algieri, Carmen at Met. Opera, 1972-73, Laura in Harvest, Chgo. Lyric Opera, Marie in Wozzeck, San Francisco Opera; also appeared in Phigenie en Tauride, Semiramide, Samson et Dalila at Met. Opera, 1987, The Ghost of Versailles, 1991; other appearances include Venice Festival by invitation of Igor Stravinsky, Am. Opera Soc., N.Y.C., for several seasons, Vancouver Opera, Philharm. Hall, N.Y.C., Paris, Dallas, Houston, Covent Garden, London, roles at La Scala, Italy, Rossini Opera Festival, Pesaro, Italy, Met. Opera, 1987; recital debuts in Madrid, Dresden, East Berlin, 1987, performed at inauguration of U.S. President Clinton, 1993; ann. recital at Carnegie Hall, European tour with husband for Dept. State, 1963; rec. artist for London, Columbia, Deutsche Grammaphon and RCA records. Founder Marilyn Horne Found. Recipient Grammy awards, 1964, 81, 83, 94., Handel medallion, 1980, Premio d'Oro, Italian Govt., 1982, Commendatore al merito della Repubblica Italiana, 1983, Gold Merit medal Nat. Soc. Arts and Letters, 1987, Fidelio Gold medal, 1988, George Peabody award, 1989, Silver medal Covent Garden Royal Opera House, 1989, Disting. Dau. of Pa. Silver medal San Francisco Opera, 1990, Nat. Arts medal, 1992; named to Harold C. Schonberg's N.Y. Times' list of 9 All-Time, All-Star Singers in Met. Opera's 100 Years, 1984. Office: care Columbia Artists Mgmt Inc Wilford Div 165 W 57th St New York NY 10019-2201 also: care Met Opera Assoc Lincoln Ctr New York NY 10023 also: BGM Classics/RCA 1540 Broadway New York NY 10036-4098*

HORNER, ALTHEA JANE, psychologist; b. Hartford, Conn., Jan. 13, 1926; d. Louis and Celia (Newmark) Greenwald; children: Martha Horner Hartley, Anne Horner Benck, David, Kenneth. BS in Psychology, U. Chgo., 1952; PhD in Clin. Psychology, U. So. Calif., 1965. Lic. psychologist, N.Y., Calif. Tchr. Pasadena (Calif.) City Coll., 1965-67; from asst. to assoc. prof. Los Angeles Coll. Optometry, 1967-70; supr. Psychology interns Pasadena Child Guidance Clinic, 1969-70; pvt. practice specializing in psychoanalysis and psychoanalytic psychotherapy. N.Y.C., 1970-83; supervising psychologist dept. psychiatry Beth Israel Med. Ctr., N.Y.C., 1972-83, coordinator group therapy tng., 1976-82, clinician in charge Brief Adaptation-Oriented Psychotherapy Research Group, 1982-83; assoc. clin. prof. Mt. Sinai Sch. Medicine, N.Y.C., 1977-91, adj. assoc. prof., 1991—; mem. faculty Nat. Psychol. Assn. for Psychoanalysis, N.Y.C., 1982-83; sr. mem. faculty Wright Inst. Los Angeles Postgrad. Inst., 1983-85; pvt. practice specializing in psychoanalysis and psychoanalytic psychotherapy L.A., 1983—; clin. prof. dept. Psychology UCLA, 1985—. Author: (with others) Treating the Oedipal Patient in Brief Psychotherapy, 1985, Object Relations and the Developing Ego in Therapy, 1979, rev. edit., 1984, Little Big Girl, 1982, Being and Loving, 1978, 3d edit. 1990, Psychology for Living (with G. Forehand), 4th edit., 1977, The Wish for Power and the Fear of Having It, 1989, The Primacy of Structure, 1990, Psychoanalytic Object Relations Therapy, 1991; mem. editorial bd. Jour. of Humanistic Psychology, 1986—, Jour. of the Am. Acad. of Psychoanalysis; contbr. articles to profl. jours. Mem. AAAS, Am. Psychol. Assn., Calif. State Psychol. Assn., Am. Women Sci., Nat. Psychol. Assn. for Psychoanalysis, Am. Acad. Psychoanalysis (sci. assoc.), So. Calif. Psychoanalytic Soc. and Inst. (hon.). Office: 638 W Duarte Rd Arcadia CA 91007-7616

HORNER, MARGO ELIZABETH, municipal official; b. Norfolk, Va., Aug. 14, 1947; d. Samuel Watson II and Elizabeth (O'Connell) H. BA in History, Old Dominion U., 1970, MA in History, 1973; cert. legal asst., Georgetown U., 1974; MS in Mgmt., Nat.-Louis U., 1993. Legis. aide to Del. Warren G. Stambaugh Va. Gen. Assembly, Richmond, 1978; sr. legis. and corp. paralegal Kirkpatrick & Lockhart, Washington, 1974-82; legis. analyst Nat. Fedn. Ind. Bus., Washington, 1982-84; acct. exec. Johnston and Lemon, Washington, 1984-85; editor Bur. Nat. Affairs, Washington, 1986-87; dep. commr. revenue Office the Commr. Revenue, Arlington, Va., 1987—; legal asst. adv. bd. Georgetown U.; writer, cons. in field. Pres. Nat. Capital Paralegal Assn., Washington, 1976-78; bd. dirs. Nat. Fedn. Paralegal Assn., Washington, 1976-78; chmn., vice chmn., sec., ARC, 1978—; chmn. Election Officials Adv. Com., Washington Met. Coun. Govts.; chmn. Arlington Com. 100, 1990-91, Arlington County Dem. Com., 1987-91, 8th Dist. Dem. Com., Va., 1993, Arlington Electoral Bd., 1982-87; mem. Va. Electoral Bd. Assn., 1982-87; aux. com. Status of Women, 1976; exec. com. United Way; mem. steering com. Va. Dem. Party, 1993; active Sheriff's Office Citizen's Advisement Com., Arlington, 1987—; vice-chmn., sec. ARC com. mgmt. Vets. Meml. YMCA, Arlington, 1978—; bd. vis. George Mason U., 1993; com. mem. Va. Gov. Commn. on Campaign Reform, Govt. Accountability and Ethics, 1992; bd. dirs. Sister City Assn., Arlington, 1993, treas. 1995—; dir. Farmington Civic Fed., 1994. Named Outstanding Young Woman of Am., 1979, Outstanding Young Woman of Va., 1979, Outstanding Young Dem., 1981, 84, Arlington (Va.) Outstanding Young Dem., 1991, Outstanding Dem., 1993, Arlington County Govt. Exceptional award, 1994. Mem. AAUW (life), Women in Govt. Rels., '94 Leadership Am., Am. Polit. Items Collectors. Roman Catholic. Home: 3057 S Buchanan St # B-2 Arlington VA 22206-1515 Office: Office the Commr Revenue #1 Courthouse Pla 2100 Clarendon Blvd Rm 200 Arlington VA 22201-5401

HORNER, MATINA SOURETIS, retired college president, corporate executive; b. Boston, July 28, 1939; d. Demetre John and Christine (Antonopoulos) Souretis; m. Joseph L. Horner, June 25, 1961; children: Tia Andrea, John, Christopher. AB cum laude, Bryn Mawr Coll., 1961; MS, U. Mich., 1963, PhD, 1968; LLD (hon.), Dickinson Coll., 1973; LLD, Mt. Holyoke Coll., 1973; LLD (hon.), U. Pa., 1975, Smith Coll., 1979, Wheaton Coll., 1979, U. Mich., 1989; LHD (hon.), U. Mass., 1973, Tufts U., 1976, U. Hartford, 1980, U. New Eng., 1987, Bentley Coll., 1989, New Eng. Coll., 1989, Pine Manor Coll., 1989, Am. Coll. Greece, 1990; DLitt (hon.), Claremont U. Ctr. and Grad Sch., 1988, Hellenic Coll., 1990; LHD (hon.), Colby Sawyer Coll., 1991. Teaching fellow U. Mich., Ann Arbor, 1962-66, lectr. motivation personality, 1968-69; lectr. social relations Harvard U., Cambridge, Mass., 1969-70, asst. prof. clin. psychology, 1970-72, assoc. prof. psychology, 1972-89, cons. univ. health svcs., 1971-89; pres. Radcliffe Coll., Cambridge, 1972-89, pres. emerita, 1989—; exec. v.p. TIAA-CREF, N.Y.C., 1989—; bd. dirs. Neiman Marcus Group, Boston Edison Co. Co-author: The Challenge of Change, 1983; contbr. psychol. articles on motivation to profl. jours. and chpts. to books. Mem. adv. coun. NSF, 1977-87, chair, 1980-86; bd. trustees Twentieth Century Fund, 1973—, Am. Coll. of Greece, 1983-90, Mass. Eye and Ear Infirmary, 1986-90, Com. for Econ. Devel., 1988—, vice-chmn., 1992; bd. trustees Mass. Gen. Hosp., Inst. Health Professions, 1988—, vice chmn., 1994; bd. dirs. Coun. for Fin. Aid to Edn., 1985-89, Beth Israel Hosp., 1989—; bd. dirs. Revson Found., 1986-92, chmn., 1992; bd. dirs. Women's Rsch. and Edn. Inst., 1979—, chair rsch. com., 1982—; mem. Coun. on Fgn. Rels., 1984—; exec. com. ACE Bus. Higher Edn. Forum, 1984-86; exec. com. New Eng. Colls. Fund, 1980—, 2d v.p., 1984-85, 1st v.p., 1985-88, pres., 1988-89; mem. nat. panel to study declining test scores Coll. Entrance Exam. Bd., 1976-77; exec. com., chair task force Pres.'s Commn. for Nat. Agenda for 1980s, 1979-80; adv. com. Women's Leadership Conf. on Nat. Security, 1982—; exec. com. Coun. on Competitiveness, 1986-89; chair task force on health care Challenge to Leadership Conf., 1987-89. Recipient Roger Baldwin award Mass. Civil Liberties Union Found., 1982, citation of merit Northeast Region NCCJ, 1982, Career Contbn. award Mass. Psychol. Assn., 1987, Disting. Bostonian award, 1990, Ellis Island medal, 1990. Mem. NOW (nat. corp. adv. bd. of legal def. and edn. fund 1984—), Nat. Inst. Social Scis. (medal for outstanding svc. 1973), Phi Beta Kappa, Phi Delta Kappa, Phi Kappa Phi.

HORNER, MAXINE EDWYNA CISSEL, state legislator; b. Tulsa, Jan. 17, 1933; d. Earl Henry Sr. and Corrine (Burton) Cissel; m. Donald Montell Horner Sr., 1954; children: Shari, Donald Montell Jr. BS in Pers. Mgmt., Langston U. Personnel adminstr. Tulsa Job Corps Ctr., 1971-75; dir. minority women's employment U.S. Dept. Labor, 1975-81; staff asst. U.S Rep. James Jones, Tulsa, 1984-86; mem. Okla. State Senate, 1986—; vice chmn. human resources com. 1987—; mem. bus. and labor, criminal jurisprudence, fin. coms., 1987—; chmn. govt. ops. & agy. oversight com., 1989—; mem. appropriations com., 1989—. Vol. VIP Read Aloud Program; v.p. North Tulsa Heritage Found., 1984—; pres. adv. bd. North Tulsa YMCA, 1985-86; active Corp. Membership Dr. Okla. Sickle Cell Anemia Found., Gov.'s Task Force on Affirmative Action, Simon Estes Scholarship Found., Health and Human Svcs. Com. for Nat. Conf. State Legislators, Children, Families and Social Svcs. Com., Dem. Nat. Platform Com.; chair Okla. Legis. Black Caucus; co-chair 1988 Nat. Black Caucus State Legislators Conf. Tulsa. Recipient spl. recognition Okla. Say No To Hate Crime Coalition, academic scholarship Wiley Coll., Marshall, Tex., 1951, Outstanding Community Svc. awards Tulsa Urban League, North Tulsa Bus. and Profl. Women, Tulsa Job Corps, Sunray DX Oil Co., Omega Psi Phi, grant Harvard U., MPA Program, Mid-Career Profession. Mem. NAACP, LWV, Nat. Assn. Black Social Workers, Dem. Women Action Group, Delta Sigma Theta. Baptist. Home: 3917 N Elgin Ave Tulsa OK 74106-1515 Office: State Capitol Senate House Oklahoma City OK 73105*

HORNER, WINIFRED BRYAN, educator, researcher, consultant, writer; b. St. Louis, Aug. 31, 1922; d. Walter Edwin and Winifred (Kinealy) Bryan; m. David Alan Horner, June 15, 1943; children: Winifred, Richard, Elizabeth, David. AB, Washington U., St. Louis, 1943; MA, U. Mo., 1961; PhD, U. Mich., 1975. Instr. English U. Mo., Columbia, 1966-75, asst. prof. English, 1975-80, chair lower div. studies, dir. composition program, 1974-80, assoc. prof., 1980-83, prof., 1984-85, prof. emerita, 1985; Radford chair rehetoric and composition, prof. English Tex. Christian U., Ft. Worth, 1985-93, Cecil and Ida Green disting. prof. emerita, 1993—. editor: Historical Rhetoric; An Annotated Bibliography of Selected Sources in English, 1980, The Present State of Scholarship in Historical Rhetoric, 1983, Composition and Literature, Bridging the Gap, 1983; author: Rhetoric in a Classical Mode, 1987, Nineteenth-Century Scottish Rhetoric: The American Connection, 1993. Inst. for the Humanities fellow U. Edinburgh, 1987; NEH grantee, 1976, 87. Mem. Internat. Soc. for History Rhetoric (exec. coun. 1986), Rhetoric Soc. Am. (bd. dirs. 1981, pres. 1987), Nat. Coun. Writing Program Adminstrs. (v.p. 1977-85, pres. 1985-87), Coll. Conf. on Composition and Communication (exec. com.), Modern Lang. Assn. (mem. del. assembly 1981). Office: Tex Christian U English Dept Fort Worth TX 76129

HORNICK, KATHERINE JOYCE KAY, artist, small business owner; b. Chelan, Wa., Jan. 2, 1940; d. Donald Dale and Dorothy Eleanor (Tilton) Shipton; m. Dan Lewis Hornick, Apr. 6, 1959; children: Tod A. and Daniel D. Student, Kinman Bus. U., Spokane, 1957-58, Shoreline Community Coll., Bothell, 1972-74. Owner The Traveling Gallery, Bothell, Wa., 1969-74; juror NW Pastel Soc., Redmond, Wa., 1978; resident artist Qraz Gallery, Seattle, 1968-70; represented by Bainbridge Arts & Crafts, Bainbridge Island, Wash., 1989—, Oceanlake Studio Gallery, Lincoln City, Oreg., 1989-92, Ho. of Wyo. Jade and Art, Casper, 1993, 94; Foothills Gallery Sheridan, Wyo., 1993, 94; Sticks and Stones Gallery, Seattle, 1993-94, The Landing, Bainbridge Island, Wash., 1994; owner, operator Katherine J. Hornick Bus. Svcs., Bainbridge Island, 1990—; condr. Bainbridge Island Studio Tour, 1988-92; lectr. Community Groups & Sch. Puget Sound Area, 1969-92; tchr. Kay Hornick Studios Bothell, 1972-75. Represented by Sticks and Stones Gallery, Pioneer Square, Seattle, 1993-94, Ryan Gallery, Lincoln City, Oreg., 1994. Recipient Hon. Mention Charles & Emma Frye Museum Seattle, 1988. Mem. Nat. League Am. PEN Women (apptd. auditor Seattle 1994), Nat. Mus. Women in Arts (chpt.), Nat. Western Art Assn., Bainbridge Arts and Crafts (bd. dirs. 1989-90).

HOROCHOWSKI, LAURA, artist, art educator; b. Columbia, Mo., Jan. 14, 1963; d. Alejandro and Sara Laura (Ucha) H. BA in Spanish cum laude, U. Mo., 1984, BFA in Art, 1987; MFA in Printmaking, Ind. U., 1993. Intern Echo Press, Bloomington, Ind., 1989; summer intern Ind. Primary Health Care Assn., Indpls., 1990; instr. Indpls. (Ind.) Art Mus., 1990; case worker Ind. Health Ctrs., Kokomo, 1991; asst. instr. Ind. U., Bloomington, 1992-93; instr., asst. Idyllwild (Calif.) Sch. Music and the Arts, 1993; graphics technician Printmasters, Columbia, 1994; gallery dir. Idyllwild Sch. of Music and the Arts, summer 1994. Photographs exhibited North Platte Valley Art Guild Nat. Exhbn., Scotts Bluff, Nebr., 1994, Photo 94 Nat. Exhbn., Cape Girardeau, Mo., 1994, Poudre Valley Art League 33rd Art Exbhn., Ft. Collins, Colo., 1994, Women in the Visual Arts, Erector Sq. Gallery, New Haven, 1994, Counterpoint, Ann. Juried Exhbn., Hill Country Arts Found., Ingram, Tex. Donor ARC, Bloomington. Recipient scholarship Rotary Internat., Ind., 1990, Grant-in-Aid, Ind. U., Bloomington, 1992. Mem. Amnesty Internat., Phi Beta Kappa, Sigma Delta Pi.

HOROSKO, MARIAN, writer; b. Cleve., Aug. 4, 1927; d. Louis Senko and Marian Catherine (Gromand) H. Student, Cleve. Inst. of Music, 1936-43, Juillard Sch. Music, 1944-45, Sch. Am. Ballet, N.Y.C., 1944-51. Performer Ballet Russe de Monte Carlo, 1939, Met. Opera Ballet, 1951-54, N.Y.C. Ballet, 1954-62, (films) Eight By Eight, 1949, Prince Who Was A Thief, 1950, Royal Wedding, 1950, American in Paris, 1950; (Broadway plays), Oklahoma, 1945-47, Along Fifth Avenue, 1948, Dance Me A Song, 1949; (staged classics) Buffalo Ballet; film curator: Dance Collection, Lincoln Ctr., 1960's; television and radio producer Stas. WNET-TV, WNCN-FM, 1961-77; author: Pas De Deux, 1979, Ballet Technique for Male Dancers, 1982, Dancer's Survival Manual, 1987, Martha Graham: Technique and Dance Evolution, 1991, Sleeping Beauty: The Ballet, 1994. Recipient first MEDART spl. recognition award, 1992. Home: 357 W 55th St New York NY 10019-4555 Office: Dance Mag 33 W 60th St New York NY 10023-7905

HOROWITZ, BEVERLY PHYLLIS, occupational therapist; b. N.Y.C., Jan. 10, 1949; d. Abe Joseph and Blanche (Reich) Postman; m. Stuart Daniel Horowitz, July 15, 1973; children: Elizabeth, Sharon, Amy. BA, SUNY, Stony Brook, 1971; MS, Columbia U., 1975; postgrad., Fordham U., 1990—. Lic. occupational therapist, N.Y. Tchr. English, Thomas Alva Edison High Sch., Jamaica, N.Y., 1972-73; occupational therapist St. Charles Hosp., Port Jefferson, N.Y., 1975-79, Vis. Nurse Svc., Northport, N.Y., 1980—, Gurwin Jewish Geriatric Ctr., Commack, N.Y., 1988-90; pvt. practice Huntington Station, 1980—; occupational therapist, cons. Hilaire Farm Nursing Home, Huntington Sta., 1980-94, Muscular Dystrophy Assn., Hauppauge, N.Y., 1980-83, 88-89, Brookhaven Health Care Facility, Patchogue, N.Y., 1988; asst. prof. Touro Coll., Huntington, N.Y., 1990—, mem. occupational therapy adv. bd., 1988—; cons. L.I. Devel. Ctr., Melville, N.Y., 1990-92, Health Svcs. at Home, 1991-93, Multiple Sclerosis Soc., 1994—, HTA, 1994—; presenter workshops on aging Suffolk County Pub. Librs., 1987, 89, N.Y. Occupational Therapy Assn. Conf., 1991, 94, N.Y. State Soc. Aging, 1992; mem. profl. adv. bd. Multiple Sclerosis Soc., 1993—, Lumex Corp., 1994—. Book reviewer Am. Jour. Occupational Therapy, 1981-86; mem. editorial bd. Phys. and Occupational Therapy in Geriatrics, 1993—. Recipient Scholarship Am. Occupational Therapy Found., 1992. Mem. Am. Occupational Therapy Assn., Nat. Coun. on Aging, Gerontol. Soc. Am., N.Y. State Occupational Therapy Assn. (cert. appreciation 1980, 82, 83), N.Y. State Soc. on Aging.

HOROWITZ, FRANCES DEGEN, academic administrator, psychology educator; b. Bronx, N.Y., May 5, 1932; d. Irving and Elaine (Moinester) Degen; m. Floyd Ross Horowitz, June 23, 1953; children: Jason Degen, Benjamin Meyer. BA, Antioch Coll., 1954; EdM, Goucher Coll., 1954; PhD, U. Iowa, 1959. Tchr. elem. sch. Iowa City, 1954-56; grad. rsch. asst. Iowa Child Welfare Sta., U. Iowa, 1956-59; asst. prof. psychology So. Oreg. Coll., Ashland, 1959-61; asst. prof. home econs. U. Kans., Lawrence, 1961-62, USHPS rsch. fellow, 1962-63, assoc. prof. dept. human devel. and family life, 1964-69, prof. dept. human devel. and family life, psychology, 1969—, chmn. dept., 1969-75, rsch. assoc., 1964-75, assoc. dean, 1975-78, vice chancellor rsch., grad. studies and pub. svc., also dean grad. sch., 1978-91, dir. Infant Rsch. Lab., 1964-91; pres. Grad. Sch. and Univ. Ctr. CUNY, 1991—; bd. dirs. Feminist Press, N.Y. Women's Forum, 1995—; guest rsch. assoc. Bur. Child Rsch. U. Kans., and Parsons (Kans.) State Hosp. and Tng. Ctr., summer 1960; vis. prof. dept. psychology Tel Aviv U., 1973-74; guest researcher dept. pediatrics Kaplan Hosp., Rehovot, Israel, 1973-74; vis. lectr. dept. psychology Hebrew U., Jerusalem, 1976, cons. rsch. programs in early edn., 1980—; pres. Ctr. for Rsch., Inc., Lawrence, 1978-91; cons. OAS, 1971, U.S. Office Edn., 1969-73, NIMH, 1979; cons. to early infant stimulation program, Caracas, Venezuela, 1976; lectr. infant devel., day care to local and regional community groups, 1966—; mem. adv. com. Carolina Inst. on Early Edn. of the Handicapped, 1978-83; reviewer NSF, 1978-91; mem. U. Kans. del. to Peoples Republic China, 1980; guest lectr. various profl. groups, univs., 1964—; exch. scholar Chinese Acad. Scis., People's Republic of China, 1982; mem. Office Sci. Integrity Rev. Adv. Com. PHS, 1991-93; nominating com. Weizmann Women in Sci. award Am. Com. Weizmann Inst. Sci., 1994; mem. Nat. Task Force Grad. Edn., 1994—; mem. workforce devel. subcom. N.Y.C. Partnership, 1994—. Co-editor science watch sect. Am. Psychologist, 1993—; mem. editorial bd. Jour. Devel. Psychology, 1969-75, Early Childhood Edn. Quar., 1974—, Devel. Rev., 1981—; contbr. articles to profl. jours. Trustee L.I. Univ., 1992—; bd. dirs. Community Children's Ctr., 1965-68, Douglas County Vis. Nurse Assn., 1968-69. Recipient Trustees award medal Cherry Lawn Sch., Conn., 1971, Outstanding Educator of Am. award, 1973, Disting. Psychologist in Mgmt. award Soc. for Psychologists in Mgmt., 1993; named to Women's Hall of Fame U. Kans., 1974; Ford Found. fellow, 1954, Ctr. for Advanced Studies Behavioral Scis. fellow, Stanford U., 1983-84; OEO grantee, 1965-69. Fellow APA (pres. divsn. devel. psychology 1977-78, chief sci. adviser 1989-93, pres. 1991-94, Centennial award 1992, pres. 1991-94), AAAS; mem. Soc. Rsch. in Child Devel. (editor monographs 1976-83, pres. elect 1995—), Am. Assn. on Mental Deficiency, North Ctrl. Accrediting Assn. (bd. commrs. 1977-80), Am. Psychological Found. (pres. 1991-94), Soc. Rsch. in Child Devel. (pres. elect, 1995—), N.Y. Women's Forum (bd. dir. 1995—), Sigma Xi, Phi Beta Kappa (hon.). Home: 145 Central Park W Apt 4A New York NY 10023-2004 Office: CUNY Grad Sch and U Ctr 33 W 42nd St New York NY 10036-8003

HOROWITZ, MARY CURTIS See CURTIS, MARY ELLEN

HOROWITZ, WINONA LAURA See RYDER, WINONA

HORRELL, KAREN HOLLEY, insurance company executive, lawyer; b. Augusta, Ga., July 10, 1952; d. Dudley Cornelius and Eleanor (Shouppe) Holley; m. Jack E. Horrell, Aug. 14, 1976. B.S., Berry Coll., 1974; J.D., Emory U., 1976. Bar: Ohio 1977, Ga. 1977. Corp. counsel Great Am. Ins. Co., Cin., 1977-80, v.p., gen. counsel, sec., 1981-85; sr. v.p., gen. counsel, sec., bd. dirs. Great Am. Ins. Co., 1985—; counsel Am. Fin. Corp., 1980-81; gen. counsel numerous subsidiaries Great Ins. Co.; sec., asst. sec. numerous other fin. and ins. cos. Trustee Community Chest, 1987-91, Seven Hills Schs., 1991—; mem. cabinet United Appeal, 1984; bd. dirs. YWCA, 1984-90, v.p. fin., 1986-89; mem. Hamilton County Blue Ribbon Task Force on Child Abuse and Neglect Svcs., 1989-91. Mem. ABA, Ohio Bar Assn., Cin. Bar Assn. (admissions com. 1978-91, nominating com. 1987-90), Am. Corp. Counsel Assn. Democrat. Home: 3733 Vineyard Pl Cincinnati OH 45226-1728 Office: Great Am Ins Co 580 Walnut St Cincinnati OH 45202-3108

HORSLEY, PAULA ROSALIE, accountant; b. Smithfield, Nebr., Sept. 7, 1924; d. Karl and Clara Margaret (Busse) Fenske; m. Phillip Carreon (dec.); children—Phillip, James, Robert, David, Richard; m. Norby Lumon, Apr. 5, 1980. Student AIB Bus. Coll., Des Moines, 1942-44, YMCA Coll., Chgo., 1944-47, UCLA Extension, 1974. Acctg. mgr. Montgomery Ward & Co., Denver, 1959-62; acct. Harman & Co., C.P.A.s, Arcadia, Calif., 1962-67; controller, officer G & H Transp., Montebello, Calif., 1967-78; comptroller Frederick Weisman Co., Century City, Calif., 1978-80; chief fin. officer Lutheran Shipping, Madang, Papua, New Guinea, 1980-82; prin. Village Bookkeeper, acctg. cons., Monreno Valley, Calif., 1982—; chief fin. officer Insight Computer Products and Tech., Inc., Carlsbad, 1988—. Vol. crises counselor, supr. and instr. Melodyland Hotline, Anaheim, Calif., 1976-79. Mem. Riverside Tax Cons., Nat. Assn. for Female Execs., Internat. Platform Assn. Republican. Lutheran. Avocations: church activities, reading, cooking, phys. fitness. Home: 1440 Brentwood Way Hemet CA 92545-7774 Office: Insight Computer Products and Techs Inc 4604 Vinyard St Oceanside CA 92057-5127

HORSNELL, MARGARET EILEEN, historian; b. St. Paul, Jan. 3, 1928; d. Kenneth George and Mary Elizabeth (Dowd) H. B.A., U. Minn., 1961, M.A., 1963, Ph.D. (Tozer Found. award 1966), 1967. Instr. history U. Minn., 1966-67; mem. faculty Am. Internat. Coll., Springfield, Mass., 1967—, assoc. prof. history, 1976-84, prof., 1984—, dept. chmn., 1987— . Recipient McKnight Found. award, 1968; alternate fellow AAUW, 1974-75; Am. Internat. Coll. summer grantee, 1970. Mem. Soc. History Edn., Inst. Early Am. History and Culture, So. Hist. Assn., Am. Legal Studies Assn., Phi Alpha Theta. Author: Spencer Roane: Judicial Advocate of Jeffersonian Principles, 1986; mem. editorial bd. This Constn., 1986-88; contbr. Encyclopedia of American Political Parties and Elections. Mem. adv. panel 500 Yrs. of Am. Clothing, 1989-92. Home: 15 Atwood Rd South Hadley MA 01075-1601 Office: Am Internat Coll 24 Lee Hall Springfield MA 01109

HORST, CAROLYN DIANE, accountant; b. Balt., May 20, 1945; d. Norman Kramer and Helen Louise (Gover) Lindner; m. William Earnshaw Horst, Jr., Sept. 7, 1968; children: Michelle L., Cynthia E., Julie A. BS in Acctg. magna cum laude, U. Balt., 1968. Staff acct. J.T. Coughlin, C.P.A., Bel Air, Md., 1968-69; controller GM&W Coal Co., Greencastle, Pa., 1969-77, Crunkleton Elec. Co., Greencastle, 1979-82; acct. pvt. practice, Greencastle, 1982—; assoc. dir. First Nat. Bank, Greencastle, 1984—, pres. assoc.'s bd., 1986. Pres. Greencastle C. of C., 1984. Mem. Nat. Assn. Pub. Accts., Nat. Assn. Tax Practitioners, Jobs Daus. (Bethel guardian, Bethel 26). Mem. Disciples of Christ Ch. Home: 13613 Paradise Church Rd Hagerstown MD 21742-2427 Office: Carolyn Horst Acct 32 E Baltimore St Greencastle PA 17225-1202

HORST, ELISABETH ALBRITTON, psychotherapist; b. Balt., June 11, 1960; d. Sherodd Ray and Margaret Jean (Macneal) Albritton; m. Mark Lewis Horst, June 12, 1982; children: Jesse Lewis, Anna Emily. BA, Yale U., 1982; MA, U. Minn., 1989, PhD, 1992. Psychotherapist Pyramid Mental Health Ctr., Minnetonka, Minn., 1987-88; lectr. U. Minn., Mpls., 1994—; psychotherapist Family and Childrens Svc., Mpls., 1990-92, Meta Resources, St. Paul, 1992—. Contbr. articles to profl. jours. Mem. Am. Psychol. Assn., Minn. Psychol. Assn., Minn. Women Psychologists. Office: Meta Resources 821 Raymond Ave Ste 440 Saint Paul MN 55114-1530

HORST, PAMELA SUE, medical educator, family physician; b. Hershey, Pa., Jan. 23, 1951; d. Ralph H. and Helen (Fry) H.; m. Thomas H. Dennison, Feb. 6, 1982; 1 child, Elizabeth Dennison. BS, Pa. State U., 1972; MD, Pa. State U., Hershey, 1976. Diplomate Am. Bd. Family Practice, Am. Bd. Emergency Medicine. Resident in family practice Shadyside Hosp., Pitts., 1979; family physician North Jefferson Health Svcs., Clayton, N.Y., 1979-82; physician emergency rm. Geisinger Med. Ctr., Philipsburg, Pa., 1982-84; asst. prof. family medicine Albany (N.Y.) Med. Coll., 1984-88; assoc. prof. health sci. ctr. SUNY, Syracuse, 1988—; med. dir. family practice ctr. St. Joseph's Hosp. Health Ctr., Syracuse, 1989—, assoc. residency dir. family practice residency, Syracuse, 1990—. Author: (with others) Ambulatory Medicine, 1993; reviewer Am. Family Physician, Jour. Family Practice. Mem. pub. issues com., bd. dirs. ctrl. N.Y. chpt. Am. Cancer Soc.; mem., past v.p. bd. dirs. Home Aides Ctrl. N.Y., Syracuse. Mem. Am. Acad. Family Physicians (instr. advanced life support in obstetrics 1992—), Soc. Tchrs. Family Medicine. Office: St Joseph's Health Ctr Family Practice Residency 301 Prospect Ave Syracuse NY 13203

HORSTMAN, SUZANNE RUCKER, financial planner; b. Coral Gables, Fla., June 27, 1945; d. Thomas John, Jr. and June Ethel Agusta (Stones) R.; m. James Winter Horstmen, Dec. 28, 1989. BBA, Fla. Atlantic U., 1971, MBA, 1975. CFP; lic. real estate agt. Assoc. dir. Am. Soc. Cons. Pharmacists, 1971-73; chpt. specialist Epilepsy Found. Am., 1973-74; assoc. dir. devel. Fairfax Hosp. Assn. Found., Springfield, Va., 1974-81; dir. devel. Arlington (Va.) Hosp. Found., 1982-86; prin. Suzanne June Rucker, Cert. Fin. Planner, Falls Church, Va., 1986-90; dir. devel. Phoexixville Healthcare Found., 1990-94, Tri-County Tng.-Employment-Cmty., 1994—; instr. George Washington U., Washington; seminar spkr. in field. Bd. dirs. Ronald McDonald House, Wilmington and Washington, Salvation Army Aux. Washington, Rep. Working Women's Forum. Fellow Assn. Health Care Philanthropy. Republican.

HORSTMANN, DOROTHY MILLICENT, physician, educator; b. Spokane, Wash., July 2, 1911; d. Henry J. and Anna (Hunold) H. AB, U. Calif., 1936, MD, 1940; DSc (hon.), Smith Coll., 1961; MA (hon.), Yale, 1961; D Med. Scis. (hon.), Women's Med. Coll. of Pa., 1963. Intern San Francisco City and County Hosp., 1939-40, asst. resident medicine, 1940-41; asst. resident medicine Vanderbilt U. Hosp., 1941-42; Commonwealth Fund fellow, sect. preventive medicine Sch. Medicine, Yale U., New Haven, 1942-43; instr. preventive medicine Sch. Medicine, Yale U., 1943-44, 45-47, asst. prof., 1948-52, assoc. prof., 1952-56, assoc. prof. preventive medicine and pediatrics, 1956-61, prof. epidemiology and pediatrics, 1961-69, John Rodman Paul prof. epidemiology, prof. pediatrics, 1969-82; John Rodman Paul prof. epidemiology, prof. pediatrics emeritus, sr. research scientist Sch. Medicine Yale U., 1982—; instr. medicine U. Calif., San Francisco, 1944-45. Recipient Albert Coll. award, 1953, Gt. Heart award Variety Club Phila., 1968, Modern Medicine award, 1974; James D. Bruce award ACP, 1975, Thorvald Madsen award State Serum Inst. (Denmark), 1977, Maxwell Finland award Infectious Disease Soc.-Am., 1978, Disting. Alumni award U. Calif. Med. Sch., 1979, NIH fellow Nat. Inst. Med. Rsch., London, 1947-48. Master ACP; fellow Am. Acad. Pediatrics (hon.); mem. NAS, Infectious Disease Soc. Am. (pres. 1975), Am. Soc. Clin. Investigation, Am. Epidemiol. Soc. (v.p. 1974-75), Am. Pediatric Soc., Am. Soc. Virology (coun. 1983-84), Soc. Epidemiol. Rsch., Pan-Am. Med. Assn., Internat. Epidemiol. Assn., Royal Soc. Medicine (hon., epidemiology/preventive medicine sect.), Conn. Acad. Sci. and Engring., European Assn. Against Virus Diseases, South African Soc. Pathologists (hon.), Sigma Delta Epsilon (hon.). Home: 11 Autumn St New Haven CT 06511-2220 Office: Yale U Sch Medicine Epidemiology and Pub Health PO Box 208034 New Haven CT 06520-8034

HORTON, ANITA A., financial company executive; b. Colorado City, Tex., Aug. 7, 1952; d. Frederick Ernest and Emma Virginia (Evins) Morris; m. Barry Joe, Apr. 7, 1973; children: Barry Joe Jr., Charles William. Student, Tex. Tech U., 1970-72; MBA (hon.), U. So. Calif., 1981. Typist Friedson Pharmacy, Ft. Worth, 1972-73; sec. traffic control Tex. Farm Products, Nacogdoches, Tex., 1973-75; sec.-treas. Kirby Forest Industries, Inc., Houston, 1975-87; credit mgr. Trussway, Inc., Houston, 1987; regional credit mgr. Bradley-Dixie Co., Houston, 1987—. Designer doll clothes Salvation Army, Houston. Mem. Houston Assn. Credit Mgrs., Nat. Assn. Credit Mgrs., Nat. Notary Assn. Home: 16210 Lakeview Dr Houston TX 77040-2028

HORTON, GWENDOLYN, nursing educator emeritus; b. Moose Jaw, Sask., Can., June 7, 1914; came to U.S., 1919; d. Orville A. and Myrtle (King) H. AA, L.A. City Coll.; BS, Calif. State U., L.A., 1968, MS, 1974. RN; cert. pub. health. Policewoman L.A. Police Dept., 1940-45; prof. nursing L.A. City Coll., Trade Teck Coll., East L.A. Coll., Harbor Coll.; prof. nursing L.A. Pierce Coll., 1972-83, prof. emeritus, 1983—. Mem. Descanso Gardens Guild, LaCanada, Calif., 1953-56, San. Fernando Valley Bd. Realtors, Van Nuys, Calif., 1980-91; bd. dirs. Owners of Subsidized Housing; pres. L.A. Garden Club, 1988-90. Mem. Water and Power Assocs. L.A. (bd. dirs. 1989-94), Apt. Assn. Greater L.A. (v.p. 1990-91, bd. dirs.), Calif. Nurses Assn., L.A. Cinema Club, L.A. Breakfast Club (emergency aid com.), Los Feliz Rep. Women Federated, So. Calif. Rep. Women, Calif. Rep. Women. Home: 2041 N Vermont Ave Los Angeles CA 90027-1952

HORTON, JUNE CAROL, lawyer; b. L.A., June 18, 1957. BA, Mt. Holyoke Coll., 1979; JD, U. So. Calif., 1983. Atty. Metro-Goldwyn-Mayer, Culver City, Calif., 1983-86; v.p. William Morris Agy., Beverly Hills, Calif., 1986—.

HORTON, MADELINE MARY, financial planner, consultant; b. Chgo., Mar. 1, 1939; d. James P. and Priscilla Mary (Caruso) Fiduccia; m. Richard J. Dickman, July 7, 1962 (div. 1981); children: James Earl, Suzanne Dickman Noel; m. Larry B. Horton, June 30, 1984 (dec. 1993). BA in Math. cum laude, Rosary Coll., River Forest, Ill., 1960; MS in Math., U. Miami, Coral Gables, Fla., 1962; postgrad., U. Va., 1974-78. Cert. fin. planner. Instr. in math. U. Miami, Coral Gables, 1962-63, Miami Dade C.C., 1964-65, St. Patrick's High Sch., 1968-69; prin. Dickman Deductions, Charlottesville, Va., 1974-77; instr. devel. math. Piedmont Community Coll., Charlottesville, Va., 1974-78; health affairs planner U. Va. Med. Ctr., Charlottesville, 1978-80; zone mgr. Investors Diversified Svcs., Inc., Charlottesville, 1980-83; fin. cons. Merrill Lynch, Charlottesville, 1983-86; mgr., fin. cons. Prudential-Bache Securities, Inc., Charlottesville, 1986-87; investment broker Wheat First Securities Inc., Charlottesville, 1987; pres., fin. cons., founder Horton Fin. Svcs. Inc., Charlottesville, 1987—. Humor columnist Charlottesville Daily Progress, 1971; featured in article Va. Bus. monthly mag., 1988. Mem. Internat. Mgmt. Coun. (sec. Charlottesville chpt. 1986-88, v.p. 1988-89), Inst. Cert. Fin. Planners, Internat. Platform Assn., Kappa Gamma Pi. Republican. Roman Catholic. Home: 3346 Arbor Ter Charlottesville VA 22901 Office: Horton Fin Svcs Inc 1160 Pepsi Pl Ste 300 Charlottesville VA 22901-0807

HORTON, THELMA WHITE, educational administrator, author; b. Blyesville, Ark., Feb. 7, 1949; d. William Soloman and Corrine (Carrigans) White; m. Charles D. Horton, May 20, 1970 (div. 1991); children: Corrine Daniel, Tiffany Louise, Charles William. BSW, Boise State U., 1975; hon. doctorate degree, World U. Lead tchr. Dade County Elem. Schs., Miami Dade Community Coll., Miami, 1980—; owner, dir. Hi School Day Care and Learning Ctr., Cutler Ridge, Fla., 1981—; lead tchr. gifted Naranja Elem. Sch.; owner Messengers, Fla.; tutor English, Perrine, Fla., 1982—; cons. WESTAT Research, Barr Industries, Perrine, 1981—, The Rand Co., Student Travel Service student placement. Active Boy Scouts U.S., PTSA, ARC; mem. usher bd. Martin Meml. Meth. Ch.; st. capt. Neighborhood Crime Watch. Recipient Equity and Excellence award Magnet Innovative Programs. Mem. The Exec. Female, Children's Advocates (pres. 1975-83), United Tchrs. Dade County, Alumni Assn. Boise State U., Inst. Children's Lit., Miami C. of C., Fla. Assn. for the Gifted, Kappa Delta Pi. Home: 15905 SW 105th Ct Miami FL 33157-1571 Office: Hi School 114 SW 199th St Miami FL 33179-2918

HORVAT, LAURA JEAN, food service executive; b. Saginaw, Mich., May 3, 1947; d. Donald Carl and Rita Lena (Levi) Bielski; m. Robert Frank Horvat, Nov. 9, 1968; children: Melissa Ann, Amy Lynn. Student, Cen. Mich. U., 1965-67. Gen. mgr. Candelite Bowl, Bridgeport, Mich., 1968-75; owner, gen. mgr. Manistee (Mich.) Lanes, 1976-83, Armedo's Restaurant, Manistee, 1976-83; owner, operator Wendy's Old Fashioned Hamburgers, Manistee, 1987—; bd. dirs. Days Inn, Manistee; gen. mgr. D.C. Bielski Real Estate, Manistee, 1971—; v.p. WenCo of Mich., Inc., Manistee, 1987—; pres. No. Mich. Co-op Assn., Manistee, 1987—. Head chmn. Manistee County United Way, 1991—, v.p. bd. dirs., 1992—; bd. dirs. YWCA, Saginaw, 1975-76; active Students Non-Alcoholic Party Supporters, Manistee, 1990—, St. Mary's Ch., Manistee, 1976—; chmn. Downtown Devel. Authority Filer Twp. Mem. Manistee Golf and Country Club. Home: 709 Harbor Dr Manistee MI 49660-1602 Office: WenCo of Mich Inc 1462 Us 31 S Manistee MI 49660-2276

HORVATH, JULIANA, special education educator; b. LaPorte, Ind., Feb. 8, 1948; d. Philip Andrew and Mary Louise (Wozniak) Nowatzke; m. Michael John, Aug. 1, 1970; children: Angela Danielle, Valerie Nicole. BS, Ind. U., 1971, MS, 1973, postgrad., 1974-75; postgrad., Fort Hays State U., 1985-86, Bradley U., 1994-95. Cert. tchr., Ind., Kans., Ill. Tchr. New Prairie United Sch. Corp., New Carlisle, Ind., 1971-74; learning disability cons. Cass County Intermediate Dist., Cassopolis, Mich., 1974-75; tchr. Tucson Unified Dist. # 1, 1975-78; lectr., supr. Marywood Coll., Scranton, Pa., 1978-80; grad. supr. Ind. U., South Bend, 1980-83; tchr. Lourdesmont Sch., Pa., 1982; instr., coord. Fort Hays (Kans.) State U., 1983-84; tchr. LaCrosse, Kans. Coop., McCracken, 1984-86; joint appointment tchr. United Dist., Hays, 1984-89; learning disability tchr. Peoria (Ill.) Pub. Schs., 1989—. Co-author: (research paper), 1984. Mem. Holy Family Parish, Peoria, Ill., St. Nicholas of Myra Parish, Hays, 1984-86, chmn. 1986-87, coord. 1987-88; treas. Fort Hays State U. Faculty Wives, 1984, 87. Mem. NEA, Coun. for Exceptional Children, Phi Delta Kappa, Alpha Delta Kappa (pres. chpt. 1994—). Democrat. Roman Catholic. Home: 6408 N Syler St Peoria IL 61615-2434 Office: Peoria Pub Schs Kingman Elem Sch Peoria IL 61615

HORWITZ, ELEANOR CATHERINE, information and education official; b. N.Y.C., Dec. 21, 1941; d. Fritz and Hedwig E.F. (Kramer) Jahoda; m. Paul Horwitz, Aug. 15, 1964; children: Gregory Douglas, Catherine Helen, Laura Elizabeth. BA, Swarthmore Coll., 1962; MA, NYU, 1967; MS, Cornell U., 1969; postgrad., Oreg. State U., 1969-70. Sci. tchr. New Lincoln Sch., N.Y.C., 1962-67; coordinator outdoor edn. Lane County Int. Edn. Dist., Eugene, Oreg., 1969-70; staff writer Billerica (Mass.) Banner, 1971-72; instr., writer Mass. Audubon Soc., Lincoln, 1972-75; pub. use specialist U.S. Fish and Wildlife Service, Concord, Mass., 1975; staff writer Soc. Am. Foresters, Washington, 1975-76; chief info. and edn. Mass. Div. Fisheries and Wildlife, Westborough, 1977—; mem. Mass. Gov.'s Forestry Rev. Bd., Boston, 1976-77; mem. steering com. Sec.'s Adv. Group on Environ. Edn., 1990—; exec. Office of Environ. Affairs, Commonwealth of Mass., 1988—; bd. dirs. Mass. Wildlife Fedn., 1986—, v.p., 1989—. Author: Clearcutting, A View from the Top, 1974; author, editor: Ways of Wildlife, 1977 (ACI Book award 1978); editor: (mag.) Massachusetts Wildlife, 1977—; contbr. articles to popular mags. Active Concord Natural Resources Commn., 1976-82, chmn. 1979-80; trustee Concord Land Conservation Trust, 1989—, trustee Holbrook Island Trust, 1994—. Recipient R.E. Dimmick award Oreg. Wildlife Soc., 1970, citation Worcester County League Sportsmen's Clubs, 1987, citation Minutemen chpt. Ducks Unltd., 1987, Conservation award Mahar Fish & Game Assn., 1991, Woman of Yr. award N.E. County Quabbin Anglers Assn., 1991. Mem. Outdoor Writers Am., New Eng. Outdoor Writers Assn. (membership sec. 1987-90, sec. 1990-93, v.p. 1993-94, pres. 1994—), Am. Forestry Assn. (life), New Eng. Conservation Info. and Edn. Assn. (chmn. 1986-87, 90-91), Wildlife Soc. (prof. cert., chmn. edn. com. 1974-76, 84-87, nominating com., 1990-91, cert. of recognition 1978), Nashoba Sportsmen's Club, Concord Rod and Gun Club, Maynard Rod and Gun Club (hon.). Mem. United Ch. of Christ. Office: Mass Divsn Fisheries and Wildlife Westborough MA 01581

HORWITZ, KATHRYN BLOCH, molecular biologist; b. Sosua, Dominican Republic, Feb. 20, 1941; came to U.S., 1952; d. Werner Meyerstein and Olga (Schlesinger) Bloch; m. Lawrence David Horwitz, June 14, 1964; children: Phillip Andrew, Carolyn Anita. BA, Barnard Coll., 1962; MS, NYU, 1966; PhD, U. Tex. Southwestern Med. Sch., Dallas, 1975; postdoctoral, U. Tex. Sch. Medicine, San Antonio, 1978. Instr. U. Tex. Sch. Medicine, San Antonio, 1978-79; asst. prof. U. Colo. Med. Sch., Denver, 1979-84, assoc. prof., 1984-89, prof. of medicine, pathology and molecular biology, 1989—; cellular physiology panel NSF, 1985-88; biochem. endocrinology study sect. NIH, 1989-93; scientific adv. bd. Molecular Oncology, Inc., Gaithersburg,

Md., 1990-92; mem. Pres.'s Cancer Panel Spl. Commn. on Breast Cancer, 1992. Author numerous breast cancer research papers, books. Chair, sci. adv. bd. Cancer League of Colo., 1987-91; mem. NOW, ACLU, Common Cause. Recipient Nat. Bd. award Med. Coll. Pa., 1986, Wilson Stone award M.D. Anderson Hosp. and Tumor Inst., 1976, Rsch. Career Devel. award Nat. Cancer Inst., 1981-86, MERIT award NIH, 1992; grantee NSF, Am. Cancer Soc., Nat. Found. Cancer Rsch. Mem. Endocrine Soc. (program com. 1989-91, nominating com. 1989-91, chair 1991, coun. 1992-95), Am. Fedn. Clin. Rsch., Am. Soc. Cell Biology, Am. Assn. Cancer Rsch., Western Soc. Clin. Investigation, AAAS. Democrat. Jewish. Office: U Colo Dept Medicine PO Box B151 Denver CO 80201-0151

HOSACK, ANITA VARGAS, municipal clerk; b. N.Y.C., Mar. 7, 1939; d. Aracelio A. and Ysolina (Vila) Vargas; m. Edgar R. Hosack, Jr., Feb. 1, 1958; children: Karen M. McGraw, Edgar R. III, Theresa A. Banks, M. Kathleen Martin, Richard J. Grad., Blue Ridge C.C., Hendersonville, N.C. Office mgr. Oates Realty Assocs., Inc., Hendersonville, 1982-90; town clk. Town of Laurel Park, N.C., 1991—. Sec. Henderson County Heart Assn., 1993-94. Recipient Svc. award Am. Heart Assn., Hendersonville, 1990. Mem. Internat. Inst. Mcpl. Clks., N.C. Clks. Assn., Nat. Vocat. and Tech. Honor Soc., Phi Theta Kappa. Democrat. Roman Catholic. Home: 18 Ravenwood Ln Horse Shoe NC 28742-9704 Office: Town of Laurel Park PO Box 2529 Hendersonville NC 28793

HOSEK, PATTI JEAN, physical education educator; b. El Paso, Tex., Aug. 26, 1954; d. James Ambrose and Laura Belle (Quebedeaux) Pierce; 1 child, David Ryan Henson. BA in Teaching, Sam Houston State U., 1974; MA in Edn., U. Houston, 1978. cert. aerobics/exercise leader. Instr. physical edn. South Houston H.S., Pasadena, Tex., 1975-76, Clear Lake H.S., Houston, 1976-79, San Jacinto Coll., Pasadena, 1979—; chair exec. bd. Aerobic Fitness-Tex. Style, 1976—. Mem. Tex. Assn. for Health, Phys. Edn., Recreation and Dance (v.p. dance), Tex. Jr. Coll. Tchrs. Assn., Internat. Assn. of Fitness Profls. Home: 1710 Oak Ridge Dr Kemah TX 77565 Office: San Jacinto Coll 8060 Spencer Hwy Pasadena TX 77505

HOSKINS, DEBORAH LEBO, hospital executive; b. Flemington, N.J., Feb. 6, 1960; d. Stephen and Doris Maude (Faulks) L. BS in Acctg., Elizabethtown Coll., 1982; postgrad., Pa. State U., Middletown, 1990. CPA, N.C. Sr. auditor Peat Marwick, Harrisburg, Pa., 1982-86; chief fin. officer Rehab. Hosp. of York (Pa.), 1986-88; v.p. for fin. Community Gen. Hosp., Thomasville, N.C., 1988—. Fellow Healthcare Fin. Mgmt. Assn.; mem. AICPA. Presbyterian. Office: Community Gen Hosp 207 Old Lexington Rd Thomasville NC 27360-3428

HOSKINSON, CAROL ROWE, educator; b. Toledo, Mar. 10, 1947; d. Webster Russell and Alice Mae (Miller) Rowe; m. C. Richard Hoskinson, June 8, 1969; 1 child, Leah Nicole. BS in Edn., Ohio State U., 1968; MEd, Ga. State U., 1972. Tchr. Whitehall City Schs., Columbus, Ohio, 1968-69; tchr. DeKalb County Schs., Decatur, Ga., 1969-74, Mt. Olive (N.J.) Twp. Schs., 1974-75, DeKalb County Schs., Decatur, 1975-79; Fulton County Schs., Atlanta, 1991—; substitute tchr. DeKalb County Schs., Decatur, 1980-91, Fulton County Schs., Atlanta, 1989-91. Pres. Esther Jackson PTA, Roswell, Ga., 1988-89; treas. Women of the Ch., Roswell, 1983-84; chairperson local sch. adv. Esther Jackson, Roswell, 1989-91; del. Women and Constn. Conv., Atlanta, 1988; mem. Supt.'s Adv. Com.; local sch. adv. Holcomb Bridge Mid. Sch.; active Chattahoochee H.S. Booster Club PTA. Named Vol. of Yr. Fulton County Schs., 1988-89. Mem. AAUW (v.p. Atlanta chpt. 1970-89, edn. scholarship honoree 1984, 86), Atlanta Lawn Tennis Assn., Roswell Hist. Soc., Roswell Hist. Preservation Commn., Ga. Sci. Tchrs. Assn., Nat. Mid. Sch. Assn., Zoo Atlanta, High Mus. Art, Ga. PTA, Ohio State Alumni Assn., Ga. State Alumni Assn. Democrat. Presbyterian. Home: 1670 Branch Valley Dr Roswell GA 30076-3007

HOSLER, DORIS KELLER, librarian, educator; b. Berwick, Pa., Feb. 7, 1921; d. Jacob Leroy and Alma Bertha (Howard) Keller; m. Robert Clark Hosler, June 21, 1941. B.S. in Bus. Edn., Bloomsburg U. (Pa.), 1948; M.S. in L.S., Drexel U., Phila., 1967. Tchr. bus. edn. Penn Manor High Sch., Millersville, Pa., 1947-58, librarian, 1958-68; circulation librarian Millersville U., 1968-79, library instruction coordinator, 1979-88, ret. 1988—, faculty emeritus 1988—, assoc. prof., 1977—, chmn. desegregation grievance com., 1980—; chmn. retirement com. Assn. Pa. State Coll. and Univ. Faculties, 1983—. Mem. Millersville Aux. to Lancaster Gen. Hosp., 1975—; Millersville Borough rep. Lancaster Redevelopment Authority Regional Adv. Council, Lancaster, 1979-89, mem. human services, 1980-89; sec. Millersville Boro Planning Commn., 1981—. Grantee in field. Mem. Assn. Pa. State Univ. Faculty, ALA, NEA, Pa. State Edn. Assn., AAUP, Pa. Library Assn., Lancaster Library Assn., Pa. Assn. Higher Edn. (pres. region 1973-76). Democrat. Lutheran. Home: 560 Buttonwood Farm Rd Millersville PA 17551-1104 Office: Millersville Univ Millersville PA 17551

HOSLER, KAREN ARGY, news correspondent; b. Niagra Falls, N.Y., Sept. 23, 1948; d. William Bertram and Phyllis Anne (Reid) Argy; m. Richard Wade Hosler, May 29, 1971 (div. June 1975); m. Alan Richard Friedman, May 15, 1977. BS in Journalism, U. Md., 1971; postgrad. study in pub. fin. theory, U. Balt., 1976; introductory courses in Russian, U.S. Dept. Agr. Grad. Sch., Washington, 1988. County govt. reporter Prince George's County News, Bowie, Md., 1971-74; legis. corres. The Annapolis (Md.) Capital, 1974-77; staff reporter The Balt. Sun, 1977-78, county govt. reporter, 1978-79, state polit. reporter, 1979-83, State House bur. chief, 1981-83, Washington corres., 1983-87, state gen. assignment, 1987-88, White House corres., 1988-93, Congl. corres., 1993—; panelist Fox Morning News, Washington, 1993—, C-Span, 1993—, CNN, 1992; guest panelist MacNeil/Lehrer News Hour, C-Span Reporters Round Table, Md. Ctr. for Pub. Broadcasting Maryland Newswrap. Mem. White House Corres.'s Assn. (pres. 1992-93, v.p. 1991, treas. 1990), State House Corres.'s Assn. (pres. 1982). Office: The Balt Sun 1627 K St NW Washington DC 20006-1702

HOSLEY, MARGUERITE CYRIL, volunteer; b. Houston, July 29, 1946; d. Frederick Willard and Marguerite Estella (Arisman) Collister; m. Richard Allyn Hosley II, July 18, 1968; children: Richard A. III, Sean Frederick, Michelle Cyril. BS in Edn., U. Houston, 1968; postgrad., Tex. A&M U., 1970-71. Cert. tchr., Tex. Tchr. Sharpstown High Sch., Houston, 1968-69, Bryan (Tex.) High Sch., 1969-71; ins. asst. Farmers Ins., Stafford, Tex., 1981-83; adminstrv. asst., fin. asst. Christ United Meth. Ch., Sugarland, Tex., 1984-92. Pres. bd. dirs. Ft. Bend Boys Choir, 1984-85; docent Bayou Bend Collection and Gardens, Houston, 1994, Houston Mus. Fine Arts, 1994—; bd. dirs. Am. Cancer Soc., 1990—; pres. Am. Cancer Soc. League, 1993-94, past pres., 1994—; mem. Lone Star Stomp com. Ft. Bend Mus. Assn., 1991-94; parent vol. Ft. Bend Ind. Schs., 1980-94; raffle chmn. Ft. Bend Drug Alliance Gala, 1989; newsletter chmn. Am. Heart Assn. Guild, 1990-91, v.p., 1992-93. Named Ft. Bend Outstanding Woman, Ft. Bend County, 1992. Mem. Houston Ladies' Tennis Assn. (team capt.), Ft. Bend Mus., Sweetwater Country Club (bd. govs. 1990-93), Aggie Moms Club, Chi Omega Alumnae. Republican. Methodist. Home: 427 W Alkire Lake Dr Sugarland TX 77478

HOSSACK, CATHERINE HAZLETT, volunteer; b. Petersburg, Va., Feb. 16, 1951; d. David Pannill and Jeanne Elizabeth (Snead) Hazlett; m. Robin Ian Francis Fraser-Orr, May 1986 (div. Aug. 1991); 1 child, Kate Hazlett; m. Stephen J. Hossack, Nov. 1992. Student, Univ. Calif., San Francisco, 1990. Asst. to exec. v.p. United Pub. Employees, San Francisco, 1973-92; mem. adv. bd. San Francisco Friends of Dept. Pub. Health; bd. dirs. No. Market Child Devel. Ctr., San Francisco, 1988-91, No. Calif. Labor Heritage Com., 1989-91. Vol. ARC, San Francisco, 1972-73; mem. Women's Leadership for Dianne Feinstein for Gov., San Francisco, 1990; mem. activities sub-com. Friends of Royal Botanic Gardens, Melbourne, Victoria, Australia; mem. Am. Women's Aux. to Royal Children's Hosp., Melbourne. Mem. Commonwealth Club of Calif. Democrat. Home: 398 Montague St, Albert Park 3206 Victoria, Australia

HOSSFELD, CONNIE LYNN, financial analyst; b. Rapelje, Mont., Dec. 31, 1964; d. Dennis Richard and Kathryn Jeanette (Lutgen) H. BA in Polit. Sci., Mont. State U., 1988; M in Mgmt., Willamette U., 1990. Planning and mktg. analyst Legacy Health Sys., Portland, Oreg., 1990-91, fin. analyst, 1991-95, program devel. specialist, 1995—. Mem. Inst. Mgmt. Accts., Healthcare Fin. Mgmt. Assn. Republican. Home: 530 NW 23d Ave # 404 Portland OR 97210

HOSTETLER, ANNE MARIE, psychiatrist; b. Iowa City, Aug. 29, 1958; d. Darrel M. and Marian S. (Brendle) H. BA, Goshen Coll., 1980; MD, Harvard U., 1990. Resident in psychiatry Mass. Gen. Hosp., Boston, 1991-94, chief resident trauma clinic, 1993-94; staff psychiatrist Waltham (Mass.)-Weston Hosp., 1994—; supr. trauma clinic Human Resource Inst., Brookline, Mass., 1994—. Rock Sleyster fellow Harvard Med. Sch., 1989-90. Mem. Am. Psychiat. Assn., Am. Group Psychotherapy Assn. Mem. Mennonite Ch.

HOSTETTER, HENDEY, psychologist; b. Balt., Apr. 10, 1950; d. Robert Davis and Nancy (Fuessenich) H.; 1 child, Suzanne. BS in Psychology, Duke U., 1972, PhD, 1980. Lic. psychologist, N.C. Intern in clin. psychology N.C. Meml. Hosp., Chapel Hill, 1976-77; rsch. asst. dept. psychology Duke U., Durham, N.C., 1972-73; psychol. examiner Granville County Schs., Oxford, N.C., 1975-76; from psychologist to dir. program for children and families Scott Parket Day Treatment Program, Henderson, N.C., 1977-81; clin. assoc. Pines Psychol. Assoc., Hollywood Psychol. Psychiatric Svcs., Pembroke Pines, Hollywood, Fla., 1981-83; clin. assoc. faculty Duke U. Med. Ctr., Durham, 1983-89; pvt. practice Durham, 1987—. Mem. APA, N.C. Psychol. Assn. (bd. dirs. profl. practice div.), Phi Beta Kappa. Office: 1811 Chapel Hill Rd Durham NC 27707-1166

HOTCHKISS, ANDRA RUTH, lawyer; b. Beloit, Wis., Aug. 6, 1946; d. Hilton Delos and Katherine Ruth (Huffer) H.; m. Robert K. Byron, May 31, 1977 (dec. 1978); m. Gerald Thomas Marsischky, Feb. 25, 1990. BA cum laude, Oberlin Coll., 1968; JD, Harvard U., 1971. Bar: Mass. 1971, Calif. 1982, U.S. Dist. Ct. Mass. 1975, U.S. Ct. for Fed. Claims 1987. Dep. gen. counsel Mass. Dept. Pub. Health, Boston, 1971-78; asst. atty. gen. Mass. Dept. Atty. Gen., Boston, 1978-85; assoc. Behar & Kalman, Boston, 1985-88; assoc. Sullivan & Worcester, Boston, 1989-92, ptnr., 1992—; instr. legal writing Harvard U., Cambridge, Mass., summers 1984, 85. Mem. adv. com. Robert K. Byron Pub. Svc. award, 1978—; elected rep. Oberlin Coll. Nat. Alumni Coun., 1973-83, reunion gift com. co-chair, 1992-93; flutist Boston Bar Assn. Orch., 1989—. Mem. ABA, Mass. Bar Assn., Boston Bar Assn., Nat. Health Lawyers Assn., Women's Bar Assn. Mass., Civil Liberties Union Mass. Office: Sullivan & Worcester One Post Office Sq Boston MA 02109

HOTCHKISS, VIVIAN EVELYN, employment agency executive; b. Fulda, Germany, May 5, 1956; came to U.S., 1957; d. Fred Roy and Rosemary (Wehner) Krug. Student, Pierce Coll., 1974-75, Calif. State U., Northridge, 1976, UCLA, 1991-92. Adminstrv. sec. Taurus Fin. Corp., Hollywood, Calif., 1976-79; adminstrv. asst. Peoples Fin. Corp., Encino, Calif., 1979-81, Thor Employment Agy., L.A., 1981-83, Creative Capital Corp., L.A., 1983-85; owner, pres. Bus. Systems Staffing & Assocs., L.A., 1985—; exec. dir. Edn., Counseling & Placement Program, L.A., 1990—. Author: (newsletter) The Leader; contbr. articles to newspaper, 1990. Mem. Execs. Assn. L.A. (membership dir. 1989—, Member of Yr. 1990), Calif. Assn. Pers. Cons., Pers. and Indsl. Rels. Assn. Office: Bus Sys Staffing & Assocs Inc 10680 W Pico Blvd Ste 210 Los Angeles CA 90064-2223

HOTT, PEGGY ANN, banker; b. Flint, Mich., Dec. 15, 1952; d. Aaron Hilman and Alice E. (Fairs) Conger; m. Norman E. Baxter, Mar. 17, 1973 (div. 1986); children: Sarah, Stephanine, Alicia, Adam, Marica; m. Virgil G. Hott Jr., Aug. 27, 1988. Student, Charles Stewart Mott Coll., Flint, Mich., 1973. Pub. rels. rep. and receptionist Turner Elec. Wks., Jacksonville, Fla., 1984-89; personal banking rep. and data entry operator Fla. Nat. Bank and First Union, Jacksonville, 1989; compliance/arbitration rep. First Union Nat. Bank, Jacksonville, 1989-90; customer svc. rep./reconciliation Am. Express Centurion Svcs. Corp., Jacksonville, 1990—. Clio Lions Club scholar, 1971. Mem. NAFE, Am. Soc. Notaries, Nat. Notary Assn., Toastmasters (charter mem. Am. Express chpt.). Republican. Home: 10252 Pine Breeze Rd W Jacksonville FL 32257-7585

HOUCHEN, CONSTANCE ELAINE, nursing administrator; b. Jamaica, W.I., Aug. 25, 1941; d. Leslie Percival and Olive Isabelle Lobban; m. Dave Houchen; children: Trevor, Adrian, Diedre. AAS, N.Y.C. Community Coll., 1968; BSN, CCNY, 1977. Supr. Hollis Park Gardens Nursing Home, Queens, N.Y., 1974—; operating room nurse VA Med. Ctr., Northport, N.Y., 1979-81; operating room nurse VA Med. Ctr., Gainesville, Fla., 1981-85, night supr., 1986—. Mem. F.O.N.E. Home: 4 Lake Ct Ocala FL 34472-2718

HOUCHIN, NANCY JEAN, insurance agent; b. Hammond, Ind., Mar. 28, 1955; d. Vincent A. and Anne J. (Pivarnik) Glennon; m. Jeffrey A. Houchin; children: Dustan A., Amber J. Grad. high sch., Highland, Ind. Pres All Insurors Inc., Griffith, Ind., 1979—. Mem. Ind. Ins. Agts. Democrat. Roman Catholic. Office: All Insurors Inc 237 N Broad St Griffith IN 46319-2220

HOUCK, CHARLEEN MCCLAIN, educator; b. Huntington, Pa., Dec. 1, 1944; d. Charles Lewis and Eunice C. (Keim) McClain; ; children: Michael C., Christopher R. BS in Edn., Secondary Edn., Math., Millersville U., 1968; cert. in mentally and/or physically handicapped, Kutztown U., 1986; postgrad., Allentown Coll., 1990—. Adult edn. supr. secondary math. Orrville (Ohio) City Schs., 1969-74; substitute tchr. math., sci. Hamburg (Pa.) Area Schs., 1974-76; instructional aide SR/TMR, Reading, Pa., 1976-85, Berks County Intermediate Unit; cons. Sci. Rsch. Assocs., Chgo., 1991—; instr. BCIU, Reading, 1989—; tchr. learning support Conrad Weiser High Sch., Robesonia, Pa., 1985—. Contbr. articles to profl. jours. Recipient Sam Kirk award Pa. Assn. for Learning Disabilities, Annie Sullivan award Pa. Assn. Intermediate Units, Salute to Teaching award Pa. Acad. for Profession of Teaching, Outstanding Educator award Berks County Learning Disabilities Assn. Mem. Internat. Soc. Tech. Edn., Pa. Assn. Ednl. Computing & Tech., Coun. Exceptional Children, Assn. Direct Instrn., Assn. Supervision and Curriculum Devel., Order of Eastern Star, VFW Aux., Am. Legion Aux., Women of Moose, Phi Delta Kappa. Avocations: flowers, computer bulletin boards, reading. Office: Conrad Weiser HS 347 E Penn Ave Robesonia PA 19551

HOUGH, JANE RUTH ELDER, soprano; b. Tacoma, May 22, 1923; d. Roger Emerson and Mabel (Bradway) Elder; m. Eldred Wilson Hough, Dec. 28, 1948; children: Christine Elizabeth Hough Smith, Phyllis Jane Hough Wheeler, Roger Eldred, Carl Emerson. BS in Physics, U. Wash., 1945; BA in Music, Occidental Coll., 1946; MLS, U. Maine, 1975; MMEd in Music, Miss. State U., 1982. Mathematician, U.S. Govt. Army Ordnance, L.A., 1946-49; soprano, symphony chorus, L.A., 1946-48, Opera Theater, U. Maine, Orono, 1975, Bangor Community Theater (Maine), 1976; soloist Symphony Chorus, Starkville, Miss., 1976-82; operatic soprano Midland Repertory Players, Alton, Ill., 1983—; profl. entertainer with Bonnie Belles, 1990—; bd. dirs. Carrolton Bank and Trust Co., 1990-91. Mem. AAUW, DAR, PEO Sisterhood (1st pres. chpt. KZ Carbondale, Ill. 1967-69), Nocturne Music Club (pres. 1979-81), Sigma Alpha Iota Alumnae (treas. Tulsa 1951-52, organizer, 1st pres. Austin, Tex. 1959-61, Sword of Honor 1960), Alpha Omicron Pi. Methodist. Home: 4803 Palisade Dr Austin TX 78731-4513

HOUGH, JANET GERDA CAMPBELL, research scientist; b. Glen Ridge, N.J., Dec. 22, 1948; d. Ralph William and Gerda Lydia (Baarck) Campbell; m. John Harrison Hough, Oct. 1, 1966 (div.); 1 child, Laura Leigh. Student Temple U. and Tyler Sch. Art, Phila., 1970-72, Pa. Acad. Fine Arts, 1972, Camden County Coll., Blackwood, N.J., 1973-75; B.S., Thomas Jefferson U., 1977. Lab. animal technician Inst. Med. Rsch., Camden, N.J., 1972-75; rsch. technician dept. biochemistry Thomas Jefferson U., Phila., 1976, phlebotomist, hematology technician, 1976-78, med. technologist spl. hematology, 1978-79, rsch. technician dept. med. genetics, 1979-80; with micromedic systems Rohm & Haas, Horsham, Pa., 1981-85; micromedic Internat. Clin. Nuclear Inc., Costa Mesa, Calif., and Horsham, 1985-91. Collaborator, editor textbook Hematology for Medical Technologists, 1983; poet, illustrator Thought Progressions, 1984. Charter mem. Nat. Rep. Presdl. Task Force, 1984—, Nat. Rep. Senatorial Com., 1984—, Rep. Presdl. Citizen's Adv. Commn., 1989-91, Nat. Rep. Congl. Com., 1992—. Mem. Internat. Soc. Poets, N.J. Hos. Assn., Am. Poetry Assn. (pub. anthologies 1986-90), Nat. Libr. Poetry (pub. anthology 1992). Roman Catholic. Avocations: drawing, painting, long-distance walking.

HOUGH-DUNNETTE, LEAETTA MARIE, industrial organizational psychologist; b. Crookston, Minn., Mar. 26, 1947; d. Mervin Byron and Hazel Viola (Hier) Hough; m. Marvin Dale Dunnette, Feb. 2, 1980. BA summa cum laude, U. Minn., 1970, MA, 1973, PhD, 1981. Adminstrv. fellow U. Minn., Mpls., 1969-70; rsch. asst. Personnel Decisions, Inc., Mpls., 1970-73; teaching asst. U. Minn., Mpls., 1973-74; rsch. psychologist Personnel Decisions Rsch. Inst., Mpls., 1975-80, v.p., 1980-88, exec. v.p., 1988—; editorial asst. Marvin Dunnette, Mpls., 1971-75; adj. prof. U. Minn., Mpls., 1982—. Co-editor: Handbook of Industrial and Organizational Psychology, vol. I., 1990, vol. II, 1991, vol. III, 1992, vol. IV, 1994. Recipient Eva O. Miller fellowship U. Minn., 1974-75. Fellow APA, Am. Psychol. Soc., Soc. for Indsl. and Orgnl. Psychology; mem. U.S. Del. for Friendship Among Women, Phi Beta Kappa, Sigma Epsilon Sigma. Home: 370 Summit Ave Saint Paul MN 55102-2124 Office: Personnel Decisions Rsch 43 Main St SE Ste 405 Minneapolis MN 55414-1048

HOUGHTALING, KAREN SUE, counselor; b. Rome, Ga., Feb. 6, 1952; d. Robert D. and Barbara R. (Johnson) Bishop; m. James D. Houghtaling, Dec. 26, 1990; 1 child, Ramee Amaris. BA, Kennesaw State Coll., 1986; MS, U. South Ala., 1993. Personnel tng. specialist Leath/Maxwell, Charlotte, N.C., 1978-81; mgr. Ky. Fin., Cartersville, Ga., 1981-83; lab. asst. dept. Psychology Kennesaw State Coll., Marietta, Ga., 1985-86; rsch. asst. U. South Ala., Mobile, 1992-93; counselor Strickland Youth Ctr., Mobile, 1993-94, Ga. Highlands Ctr, Dalton, 1994—. Vol. Home of Grace, Eight Mile, Ala., 1993. Mem. Am. Counseling Assn., Assn. for Specialists in Group Work, Phi Kappa Phi, Psi Chi. Republican. Baptist. Home: 748 Old Summerville Rd NW Rome GA 30165-9780

HOUGHTALING, PAMELA ANN, public relations executive; b. Catskill, N.Y., July 8, 1949; d. Stanley Kenneth and Mildred Edythe (Fyfe) H. BA, Princeton U., 1971; cert. Russian Inst., Columbia U., 1976, M in Internat. Affairs, 1974. Internat. rels. analyst Libr. of Congress, Washington, 1974-75, U.S. GAO, Washington, 1976-77; pub. affairs specialist IBM Corp., Washington, 1977-81; sr. external programs analyst IBM World Trade Americas/Far East Corp., North Tarrytown, N.Y., 1981-82; mgr. labor affairs/bus. practices U.S. Coun. Internat. Bus., N.Y.C., 1982-84; communications specialist-advt. IBM Corp., Boca Raton, Fla., 1984-86; staff communications specialist IBM Corp., White Plains, N.Y., 1986-88; communications cons., 1988-90; sr. mktg. specialist Wang Labs., Bethesda, Md., 1990-93; pub. rels. dir. STG Mktg. Comm., 1993-94; mgr. mktg. comm. Cable & Wireless, Inc., Vienna, Va. 1994—. Mem. Am. Mktg. Assn.

HOUGHTON, DAWN LYNN ILNICKI, product research and development manager; b. Detroit, July 21, 1957; d. John R. and Sondra D. (Costantini) Ilnicki; m. Steven B. Houghton, May 5, 1979; children: Adrienne D., Monica L. BSE in Chem. Engring. summa cum laude, U. Mich., 1979. Instrl. asst. U. Mich., Ann Arbor, 1978; process devel. intern Upjohn, Kalamozoo, 1978; product devel. intern Procter & Gamble, Cin., 1977, product devel. engr., 1979-83, product devel. group leader, 1984-87, head product devel. sect., 1988-90, head world strategic opportunities sect., 1990-93; rsch. fellow Kimberly Clark, Neenah, Wis., 1993—. Patentee in field. Mem. PTA, Ohio, Wis., 1988—, com. chair environment, Blue Ash, Ohio, 1991-92; mem. adv. com. Child Care Svcs. YMCA, Blue Ash, 1990-93. Lutheran. Home: 307 E Timberline Dr Appleton WI 54915 Office: Kimberly Clark 2100 Winchester Rd Neenah WI 54956

HOUGHTON, KATHARINE, actress; b. Hartford, Conn., Mar. 10, 1945; d. Ellsworth Strong and Marion Houghton (Hepburn) Grant. BA, Sarah Lawrence Coll., Bronxville, N.Y., 1965. Founding mem. Pilgrim Repertory Co. (Shakespeare touring co. sponsored by Ky. Arts Commn.), 1971-72, S.C. Arts Commn., 1972, Miss. Arts Commn., 1973, Conn. Arts Commn., St. Joseph Coll., 1974. Debut on Broadway stage in A Very Rich Woman, 1965; appeared in stage plays Charley's Aunt, New Orleans Repertory, 1966, The Front Page, Broadway, 1968, Ten O'Clock Scholar, Royal Poinciana Playhouse, Fla., 1969, The Private Ear/The Public Eye, Sullivan, Ill., 1969, Sabrina Fair, Ivoryton Playhouse, 1968, The Miracle Worker, Sullivan, Ill., A Scent of Flowers (Theatre World award), Off Broadway, 1969, Misalliance, Hartford Stage Co., 1970, The Taming of the Shrew, Actors Theatre, Louisville, 1970, Poor Richard, Tartuffe, 1970, Ring Around the Moon, Hartford Stage Co., 1970, Major Barbara, The Glass Menagerie, Actors Theatre of Louisville, 1971, Play It Again Sam, Actors Theatre of Louisville, 1971, Suddenly Last Summer, Ivanhoe, Chgo., 1973, The Prodigal Daughter, Kennedy Center, Washington, 1973, Bell, Book and Candle, Pensacola, Fla., 1974, The Rainmaker, Ind. Repertory Co., 1975, Spiders Web, Atlanta, 1977, Hedda Gabler, Nashville, 1978, Dear Liar, Dayton, Ohio, 1978, 13 Rue de L'Amour, Ind. Repertory Co., 1978, Antigone, Nashville, 1979, Uncle Vanya, Acad. Festival Theatre, Lake Forest, 1979, Forty Carats, Radford U. Theatre, Va., 1979, A Doll's House, St. Edward's U. Theatre, Tex., 1979, The Sea Gull, Pitts. Public Theatre, 1979, The Glass Menagerie, Pa. Stage Co., 1980, Taming of the Shrew, Pa. State Festival, 1980, Terra Nova, Actors Theatre of Louisville, 1980, The Merchant of Venice, South Coast Repertory, Costa Mesa, Calif., 1981, A Touch of the Poet, Yale Repertory Theatre, 1983, To Heaven in a Swing, Am. Place Theatre, N.Y.C., tour various theaters, 1983-85, Sally's Gone She's Left Her Name, Am. Festival Theatre, N.H., 1984-86, Vivat, Vivat Regina, Mad Woman of Chaillot, The Time of Your Life, Children of the Sun, Mirror Repertory Co., N.Y.C., 1985, A Bill of Divorcement, Westport Country Playhouse, Conn., 1985, One Slight Hitch, Charlotte Repertory Co., 1986, To Heaven in a Swing, Amherst Coll., Bowdoin Coll., 1986, and Bronson Alcott Centennial Celebration, 1988, The Hooded Eye, West Bank Downstairs Theatre Bar, 1987, Ivoryton Playhouse, 1987, Murder in the Cathedral, West Point Cadet Chapel, 1987, The Leaves of Vallombrosa, 1988, Our Town, Broadway, 1988-89, Love Letters, Ivoryton Playhouse, 1989, To Kill A Mockingbird, Paper Mill Playhouse, N.J., 1991; motion pictures include Guess Who's Coming to Dinner, 1967, The Gardener, 1972, Eyes of the Amaryllis, 1981, Mr. North, 1987, Billy Bathgate, 1990, Ethan Frome, 1992, The Night We Never Met, 1992, Kalamazoo, 1993, Let It Be You, 1994; TV series The Adams Chronicles, 1975; TV mini-series I'll Take Manhattan, 1986; appeared on TV in Legacy of Fear, 1974, The Color of Friendship, 1981, (daytime serials) One Life to Live, 1989, All My Children, 1992; toured in Sabrina Fair, 1975, The Mousetrap, Arms and the Man, Dear Liar, 1976, The Streets of New York, Westport, Conn., Guildford, N.H., Dennis, Mass., Denver, 1980; appeared in To True to Be Good, Acad. Festival Theatre, Lake Forest, Ill., 1977, Spingold Theatre, Waltham, Mass., 1977, Annenberg Center, Phila., 1977; author: (book) The Marry Month of May, 1988, (stage prodns.) Phone Play, 1988, Good Grief, 1988, Mortal Friends, 1988 (stage prodn. premiere 1988), The Lick Penny Lover, 1988, (screenplays) The Heart of the Matter, 1989, Journey to Glasnost, 1990, Good Grief, 1991, Motherman, 1993, (plays) To Heaven in a Swing, 1982, Merlin, 1984, Buddha, On the Shady Side, The Right Number (3 one-act plays), 1986; co-author: Two Beastly Tales, 1975, (screenplay) Acting in Concert, 1994; editor: MHG: A Biography, 1989. Mem. Dramatists Guild.

HOUGHTON, KATHERINE QUINCY, museum administrator; b. Corning, N.Y., Feb. 19, 1962; d. Amory Jr. and Ruth Frances (West) H.; m. Christopher Scott Bird, Oct. 22, 1994. BA magna cum laude, Harvard U., 1984. Analyst Lazard Bros. & Co. Ltd., London, 1985-86, assoc., 1986-88, sr. assoc., 1988-90; exec. asst. to dir. L.A. County Mus. Art, 1991-94; transition mgr. J. Paul Getty Mus., L.A., 1994—. Mem. pub. affairs com. Planned Parenthood L.A., 1991—; mem. Best Foot Forward com. Lewitzky Dance Co., L.A., 1992—; mem. Radcliffe Coll. 10th Reunion Gift Com., Cambridge, 1993-94. Mem. Am. Assn. Museums.

HOUGLAND, DENA CAROL, insurance underwriter; b. Oklahoma City, Okla., Sept. 24, 1965; d. Raymond Eugene and Carol Lee (Proctor) Wehry; m. Benson Hougland, Sept. 26, 1983; 1 child, Heather Lindsay. Cert. agt. lic., Wall Inst., Salt Lake City, 1991. Auto underwriter S & S Underwriters, Salt Lake City, 1982-83; mortgage processor Credit Bur. Palm Springs, Palm Desert, Calif., 1985-86; personal lines underwriting mgr. Western Colonial Gen. Agy., Salt Lake City, 1986—. Newsletter editor Ins. Women, 1990-93. Named Rookie of Yr., Ins. Women, 1991. Democrat. Methodist. Office: Western Colonial Gen Agy 1225 E Ft Union Blvd # 320 Midvale UT 84047

HOULD-WARD, ANN, theatrical costume designer; b. Glasgow, Mont., Apr. 8, 1955; children: Leah, John. Designed many shows including: (off-Broadway) Cymbeline, On the Verge, Personals; (Broadway) Sunday in the Park with George (Outstanding Costume Design Maharan award), Harrigan and Hart, Into the Woods (L.A. Drama Critics Circle award), Falsettos, St. Joan, 1992, Three Men on a Horse, 1993, Timon of Athens, 1993, Beauty and the Beast, 1994 (Best Costume Design Tony award 1994). Office: Palace Theatre Broadway at 47th St New York NY 10036

HOULE, PAMELA DAVENPORT, school counselor; b. Clearwater, Fla., Feb. 11, 1950; d. James Howard Davenport and Helen J. (Hackman) Davenport-Metcalfe; m. John Houle Jr., 1976 (div. Apr. 1983); children: William John III, Christine Michelle. BS, U. West Fla., 1972; MA, U. South Fla., 1976. Phys. edn. tchr. Azalea Mid. Sch., St. Petersburg, Fla., 1972-76; counselor Oak Grove Mid. Sch., Clearwater, Fla., 1984—. Bd. dirs. Luth. Sch. Bd. of Christian Edn., 1990; treas. Parent Tchr. League, 1985. Mem. NEA, ACA, Fla. Assn. Counseling and Devel., Pinellas County Tchrs. Assn., Clearwater C. of C., Phi Delta Kappa. Office: Oak Grove Mid Sch 1370 S Belcher Rd Clearwater FL 34624-3795

HOULE, RITA C., occupational health nurse practitioner; b. Providence, June 14, 1947; d. Andre Raoul and M.B. Irene (Thibodeau) H. BS in Nursing, Salve Regina Coll., 1978; MS in Nursing, U. R.I., 1987; MSMT, Johnson & Wales U., 1991. RN. Staff nurse R.I. Hosp., Providence, 1968-70, asst. nurse care coord., 1970-75, nursing care coord., 1975-80; clinician R.I. Hosp. Dept. Edn. and Rsch., Providence, 1980-87, clin. specialist, 1987-89, clin. educator, 1989-90; occupational health nurse practitioner Pratt & Whitney, East Hartford, Conn., 1990-92, Berkshire Med. Ctr., Pittsfield, Mass., 1992—; vis. instr. Northeastern U. Coll. Continuing Edn., Boston, 1989-91. Co-author: H.E.L.P., 1986. Mem. NAFE, ANA, Assn. Nursing Profls., R.I. State Nursing Assn., Am. Assn. Occupational Health Nurses, Mass. Nurses Assn., Sigma Theta Tau. Roman Catholic.

HOULIHAN, PATRICIA POWELL, financial planner; b. Emporia, Va., Dec. 16, 1947; d. John Cyrus and Hazel Wright (Hines) Powell; m. Dennis Finley Houlihan, Oct. 13, 1973; children: Sean Finley, Ryan Patrick. BS, U. Richmond, 1969. Cert. and lic. fin. planner. Tchr. math. Fairfax County Schs., McLean, Va., 1970-74; fin. planner Cavill & Co., Washington, 1985—; panelist TV Washington Forum on Fin. Planning, Fairfax, Va., 1987-89, TV Money Watch, Washington, TV the Money Makers, PBS, Video Fin. Planning, The Internat. Found. of Employee Benefit Plans; TV host The Fin. Advisers, PBS, 1991-92; adj. prof. Coll. Fin. Planning, George Washington U. Pres. Homeowners Assn., Oakton, Va., 1984; treas. Navy Elem. PTA, Fairfax, 1984; chmn. Creative Playground Project, Fairfax, 1982. Recipient Disting. Svc. award Va. Congress Parents and Tchrs., 1985. Mem. Internat. Assn. Fin. Planning, Registry Fin. Planning Practitioners (1st place award 1987), Inst. Cert. Fin. Planners, CFP Bd. Stds. (job analysis task force, practice stds. task force, item writing com., elected mem. Bd. Practice Standards, 1995). Methodist. Office: Cavill & Co 3200 Pommel Ct Oakton VA 22124-2316

HOURANI, LAUREL LOCKWOOD, epidemiologist; b. Carmel, Calif., Sept. 10, 1950; d. Eugene Franklin and Katherine Ruth (Miller) Betz; m. Ghazi Fayez Hourani, Feb. 28, 1984; children: Nathan, Danna, Lisa. BA, Chico State U., 1977; MPH, Am. Univ. Beirut, 1983; PhD, U. Pitts., 1990. Prog. evaluator Community Hosp. Monterey Peninsula, Carmel, Calif., 1978-81; instr./researcher Am. Univ. Beirut, 1981-85; predoctoral fellow U. Pitts., 1985-89; researcher, cons. V.A. Med. Ctr., Pitts., 1988-90; dir., tumor registry U. Calif. Irvine Med. Ctr., Orange, 1990-92; researcher Naval Health Rsch. Ctr., San Diego, Calif., 1993—; cons. Nat. Devel. Commn. South Lebanon, 1981-83. Author: No Water, No Peace, 1985; contbr. articles to profl. jours. Bd. dirs. Am. for Justice in Middle East, Beirut, 1982-85, Nat. Devel. Com., South Lebanon, 1983-85. Recipient grant V.A., Pitts., 1989, rsch. grant U. Rsch. Bd., Beirut, 1985. Mem. Am. Psychol. Assn., Am. Pub. Health Assn., Soc. for Epidemiologic Rsch. Office: Naval Health Rsch Ctr Divsn Epidemiology PO Box 85122 San Diego CA 92186-5122

HOUSE, CHARLETTA, librarian; b. Mobile, Ala., July 9, 1937; d. Charlie and Nevada (Travis) H. BS, Ala. State U., 1959; MLS, U.Md., 1973; MEd, Salisbury State U., 1993. Acquisitions asst. libr. Ala. A&M Libr., Normal, Ala., 1963-68; asst. libr. circulation dept. U. Md. Eastern Shore, Princess Anne, 1968-71, head circulation dept., 1972-83; circulation, reference libr. Salisbury (Md.) State U., 1984-86, reference, spl. collection libr., 1986—. Mem. AAUW, Md. Libr. Assn., Nat. Women of Achievemnt, Inc., The Links, Inc., Kappa Delta Pi, Delta Sigma Theta Sorority, Inc. Democrat. Methodist. Office: Salisbury State Univ Blackwell Libr 1101 Camden Ave Salisbury MD 21801-6800

HOUSE, KAREN ELLIOTT, company executive, former editor, reporter; b. Matador, Tex., Dec. 7, 1947; d. Ted and Bailey Elliott; m. Arthur House, Apr. 5, 1975 (div. Sept. 1983); m. Peter Kann, June 4, 1984; children: Hillary, Petra, Jason. B.J., U. Tex., 1970; postgrad. Inst. Politics, Harvard U., 1982. Edn. reporter Dallas Morning News, 1970-71, with Washington bur., 1971-74; regulatory corr. Wall Street Jour., Washington, 1974-75, energy and agr. corr., 1975-78, diplomatic corr., 1978-84; fgn. editor Wall Street Jour., N.Y.C., 1984-89; v.p., Internat. Group Dow Jones & Co., 1989—; dir. German-Am. Coun., 1988—; bd. dirs. Coun. Fgn. Rels.; trustee Boston U.; mem. adv. bd. Ctr. Strategic Internat. Studies; mem. vis. com. Harvard U. Ctr. Internat. Affairs. Recipient Edward Weintal award for Diplomatic Reporting, Georgetown U., 1980-81, Edwin Hood award for Diplomatic Reporting Nat. Press Club, 1982, Disting. Achievement award U. So. Calif., 1984, Pulitzer prize for Internat. Reporting, 1984, Overseas Press Club Bob Considine award, 1984, 88; Harvard fellow, 1982. Fellow Nat. Acad. Arts and Scis. Home: 58 Cleveland Ln Princeton NJ 08540-3077 Office: Dow Jones & Co 200 Liberty St New York NY 10281-1099*

HOUSE, MARTHA ELLEN, artist; b. Decatur, Ind., Oct. 18, 1921; m. Donald Marvin, Oct. 30, 1942. Student, John Harron Sch. Art, St. Francis Coll.; studied with, Edgar Whitney, Phil Austen, Frank Webb, Glenn Bradshaw. Exhibited in one-woman shows and group exhbns. in Ind. and Fla. Recipient art awards Biennial Winners Cir. Show, 1989-93, La. Internat. Show, 1991-93, Panama Art League Show, 1991-93, Venice Art League Show, 1987-89, Art Encounter Show, 1989, 91, 93, Best of Show award Venice Art League Show, 1986, Sarasota Art Assn. Show, 1987-89, Charlotte County Art Guild Show, 1988, 90, 91, 93. Mem. Charlotte County Art Guild (officer), Nat. Watercolor Soc. (award 1991), Fla. Watercolor Soc., Fla. Artist Group. Home and Studio: 962 N Lakeshore Cir Port Charlotte FL 33952

HOUSEMAN, ANN ELIZABETH LORD, educational administrator, state official; b. New Orleans, Mar. 21, 1936; d. Noah Louis and Florence Marguerite (Coyle) Lord; m. Evan Kenny Houseman, June 25, 1960; children: Adrienne Ann, Jeannette Louise, Yvonne Elizabeth. BA, Barnard Coll., 1957; MA, Columbia Univ., 1962; PhD, Univ. Del., 1969. Cert. elem. prin., secondary sch. prin. State supr. reading Dept. Pub. Instrn., Del., 1977-79; prin. M.L. King, Jr. Elem. Sch., Wilmington, Del., 1979-80; adminstr., exec. dir. Del. State Arts Coun., Wilmington, 1980-84; acting dir. Div. Hist. and Cultural Affairs State of Del., Wilmington, 1983-84, prin. P.S. du Pont Intermediate Sch., Wilmington, 1984-91; dir. Mid-Atlantic States Arts Consortium, Balt., 1980-84. Mem. adv. bd. Rockwood Mus., Wilmington, 1981-94; bd. dirs. Opera Del., Inc., Wilmington, 1984-94, pres., 1991-93, dir. devel., 1994—; bd. dirs. Del. Theatre Co., Wilmington, 1984-90. Contbr. articles to profl. jours. Mem. Phi Delta Kappa. Republican. Presbyterian. Office: Opera Del 4 S Poplar St Wilmington DE 19801-5009

HOUSER, BETTY JO, mental health nurse; b. Rocky Ford, Colo., Mar. 13, 1940; d. Otis Willard and Mary Agnes (Hayden) Love; m. Wallace Dan Houser, July 29, 1963; children: Danny, Theresa, Tom. BSN, Loretto Heights Coll., Denver, 1962; MS, U. Wis., 1991. RN, Wis., Colo., Kans. Staff nurse Fort Logan Mental Health Ctr., Denver, 1962, Menninger Clinic, Topeka, Kans., 1963; pvt. duty nurse USAFB Hosp., Tachikawa, Japan, 1964-65; ARC nurse Dep. Sch. Program and Dispensary, Johnson AFB, Japan, 1964-66; staff nurse St. Mary's Hosp. Med. Ctr., Madison, Wis., 1970-75; nurse clinician II Mendota Mental Health Inst., Madison, 1985-90, nurse clinician III, 1990—, clin. specialist child adolescent adult mental healh nursing, 1993—; faculty asst. U. Wis., Madison, 1991, affiliate clin. instr. Sch. Nursing, 1994. Mem. ANA (cert.), Am. Psychiat. Nurses Assn., Sigma Theta Tau. Internat. Home: 5725 Meadowood Dr Madison WI 53711 Office: Mendota Mental Health Inst 301 Troy Dr Madison WI 53711

HOUSER, CONNIE LOU, accounting and computer systems consultant; b. Clinton, Ill., Dec. 7, 1944; d. John W. and Monthell (Meeks) Brennan; children: Kevin D., Debbie S. Wenell. Student, So. Ill. U., Decatur, Ill., 1981-85. Typist State Farm Ins. Co., Bloomington, Ill., 1963; salesperson Montgomery Ward, Waukegan, Ill., 1964; bookkeeper Beneficial Fin., Oakland, Calif., 1964-68, Johnson, Hankins & Brooker, CPAs, Oakland, 1968-71, John W. Brooker & Co., CPA, Oakland, 1974-75; acctg./computer cons. May, Cocagne & King, P.C., Decatur, 1975—; mem. Richland Community Coll. Citizens Computer Adv. Coun. Treas. Decatur Area Women's Network, 1990—; pres. Big Bros./Big Sisters Macon County, Decatur, 1991—; active Noon Women's Network, 1992—. Mem. Ill. Assn. Acctg. Adminstrs. (pres. 1986—), Ace Mem. of Score. Office: May Cocagne & King PC 1353 E Mound Rd Ste 300 Decatur IL 62526

HOUSER, RUTH GERTRUDE, telecommunications company official, certified public accountant, local government official; b. Virginia Beach, Va., Feb. 25, 1953; d. Herbert George and Arlene Fern (Halterman) H.; m. James J. Reddick Jr., May 22, 1982 (div. Nov. 1985). BS in Acctg. cum laude, Wheeling Coll., 1975. CPA, Fla., Ga., W.Va. Sr. acct. Price Waterhouse, Pitts., 1975-79; mgr. internal control Lockheed Space Opers. Co., Cape Canaveral, Fla., 1980-84; mgr. info. systems AT&T, Orlando, Fla., 1984-85; mgr. data systems group AT&T, Morristown, N.J., 1985-86, mgr., CFO systems architecture, 1986-87; fin. dir. France and Italy CTMG AT&T, Paris, 1987-89; mgr. acctg. policy AT&T, Morristown, 1989-90; dir. billing svcs. AT&T, Bridgewater, N.J., 1990-92; controller, Network Wireless Systems AT&T, Morristown, N.J., 1992-93; fin. mgr., leader billing team World Ptnrs./World Source AT&T, Bridgewater, N.J., 1993—; tax cons., Atlanta, 1979-83; fin. cons. Wheeling Coll., 1975; dir. CPA forum AT&T Chief Fin. Orgn., Morristown, 1988-90. Vol. C. Dillon Libr., Bedminster, N.J., 1985, v.p. bd. trustees, 1988-92; sec., trustee Friends of C. Dillon Libr., 1992—; committeewoman Somerset County Reps. Dist. 5, Bedminster, 1993—. Mem. AICPA. Home: PO Box 531 Bedminster NJ 07921-0531 Office: AT&T Global Comm Svcs 55 Corporate Dr Rm 14A82 Bridgewater NJ 08807

HOUSTON, CAROLINE MARGARET, editor; b. Harrogate, Eng., May 8, 1964; came to U.S., 1975; d. William H. and Sylvia (Fineron) H. BA in Internat. Studies and Mid East Studies, George Mason U., 1989, postgrad., 1990—. Cert. fluency in Farsi and French; Gemological Inst. Am. cert. diamontologist and Gemplogist; lic. pvt. pilot. Editor Maxim Techs., Vienna, Va., 1988-89; sec. Am. Near East Refugee Aid, Washington and Israel, 1989-90; asst. sec., treas. World Resources Inst., Washington, 1990-91; asst. dir. client svcs. Britches of Georgetowne, McLean, Va., 1991-92; reference copyright sr. clk., preservation technician Libr. Congress, Washington, 1992—; devel. cons. Legacy Internat., Jerusalem, 1990-91. Violinist with semi-profl. orchs., 1972-84. Mem. NOW, Amnesty Internat.; chmn., treas. Episcopal Ch. of Va., No. Va. Chpt. Holy Land Com. Mem. NAFE, Internat. Studies Assn., Mid. East Inst., Libr. Congress Profl. Assn. (chair membership com., co-chair pub. affairs com.), Atlantic Coun. U.S. Home: 3225 Kenney Dr Falls Church VA 22042-3628

HOUSTON, GERRY ANN, oncologist; b. Baldwyn, Miss., July 16, 1953; d. Jeff Davis and Frances Holland (Agnew) Goodson; m. Terry L. Houston, Dec. 18, 1976 (dec. May 1987); 1 child, Claire Holland; m. Abe John Malouf, July 23, 1988. BA, U. Miss., 1974, MD, 1978. Diplomate Am. Bd. Internal Medicine, Am. Bd. Medical Oncology. Intern U. Med. Ctr., Jackson, Miss., 1978-79, resident, 1979-81, fellow oncology, 1981-83; ptnr. Jackson (Miss.) Oncology Assocs., 1987—; staff physician Miss. Bapt. Med. Ctr., Jackson, 1983—, Meth. Med. Ctr., Jackson, 1983—, St. Dominic Hosp., Jackson, 1983—, River Oaks Hosp., Jackson, 1983—, Univ. Med. Ctr., Jackson, 1983—; med. dir. Hospice of Ctrl. Miss., Jackson, 1989—; mem. exec. com. Baptist Med. Ctr., 1994. Contbr. articles to profl. jours. Chmn. exec. com. Miss. divsn. Am. Cancer Soc., 1993—, pres., bd dirs., 1989-93. Clin. rsch. fellow Am. Cancer Soc. Fellow ACP; mem. AMA, Nat. Hospice Orgn., Acad. Hospice Physicians, So. Assn. Oncology, Am. Soc. Clin. Oncology, Alpha Omega Alpha. Episcopalian. Office: Jackson Oncology Assocs 1190 N State St Ste 501 Jackson MS 39202

HOUSTON, JEAN PHYLLIS, building services executive; b. Dallas, Jan. 8, 1947; d. Joseph Thomas and Mayfair (Shields) Holland; m. Robert Lynn Houston, Dec. 2, 1966; children: Carrie J., Craig R. AAAS, Cedar Valley Coll., 1986; BFA, U. Tex., Arlington, 1992. Sec. Tex. Power & Light, Dallas, 1965-67, Tex. Pacific Oil Co., Dallas, 1967-74; office mgr., v.p. Houston & Houston, Inc., Red Oak, Tex., 1986—. Active mem. Hutchin Bapt. Sch. PTO, Hutchins, Tex., 1993, Dallas Area Am. Eskimo Dog Rescue Program, 1994—. Mem. Orton Dyslexia Soc., U. Tex. Alumni Assn., Alpha Chi.

HOUSTON, MARY LORETTA JONES, humanities educator; b. Ft. Worth, May 25, 1947; d. Jimmie L. and Izora (Cannon) Jones; m. Cecil Hunter Houston; children: Ramona Allaniz, Rhonda Angeline, Cecil Hunter II, Rhesa Aren. BS, Howard Payne U., 1974; MA in Teaching, Tarleton State U., 1980; MSW, U. Tex., Arlington, 1983. Lic. social worker, Tex. Instr. Tarleton State U., Stephenville, Tex., 1986-87; dir. Keen-Beckwith Community Ctr., Ft. Worth, 1987-88; instr. Howard Payne U., Brownwood, Tex., 1988; interim dir. Develop Me Day Care, Sweetwater, Tex., 1988-89; dir. Summer Food Program, Brownwood, 1989; instr. Clark Atlanta U., 1990-92; intern State of Ga. House Rsch., Atlanta, 1992; instr. Eng., Spanish, bus. comm., life mgmt. Life Coll., Marietta, Ga., 1992—; caseworker Tex. Youth Commn., Brownwood, 1978-85. Author: (children's play) Ugly Har Har, 1973. Bd. dirs. Brownwood County Hist. Commn., 1986-90; leader, life mem. Tex. and Ga. Girl Scouts, Brownwood and Atlanta, 1975—; mem. adv. com. Noah Project, Brownwood, 1984-85; coord. homeless program People for Progress, Inc., Sweetwater, 1989; vol. coord. coll. tours, Brownwood, 1988-89. Mem. AAUW (pres. 1986-88, travelship award 1981), Ga. Alliance Black Sch. Educators, Black Social Workers, Atlanta Coalition 100 Black Women. Democrat. African Methodist Episcopalian. Home: 672 Beckwith St SW Apt 6 Atlanta GA 30314-4100

HOUSTON, TRACY ANNE, secondary educator; b. Phila., June 25, 1961; d. Henry Joseph Jr. and Delores Maria (Basmajian) H. BS in Secondary Edn., Pa. State U., 1983; MEd in Curriculum and Instrn., Kutztown U., 1991. Lic. secondary tchr., Pa. Tchr. English Pennridge Sch. Dist., Perkasie, Pa., 1983-85; tng. specialist Commonwealth Fed. Savs. & Loans, Norristown, Pa., 1985-87; tchr. English Quakertown (Pa.) Sch. Dist., 1987—; head field hockey coach Pennridge Sch. Dist., Perkasie, 1984-86; asst. field hockey coach Quakertown Sch. Dist., 1988-90, 9th, 10th grade gifted mentorship program advisor, 1990—. Recipient Pa. Writing Project fellow, 1993. Mem. NEA, Nat. Coun. Tchrs. English, Pa. State Edn. Assn., Quakertown Community Edn. Assn. (union rep. 1990—). Home: Gen Delivery Jim Thorpe PA 18229 Office: Quakertown Sch Dist 600 Park Ave Quakertown PA 18951-1575

HOUSTON, WHITNEY, vocalist, recording artist; b. East Orange, N.J., Aug. 9, 1963; d. John R. and Cissy H.; m. Bobby Brown, July 18, 1992; 1 child, Bobbi Kristina Houston Brown. HHD (hon.), Grambling U. Trained under direction of mother; mem. New Hope Bapt. Jr. Choir, 1974; background vocalist Chaka Khan, 1978, Lou Rawls, 1978, Cissy Houston, 1978, appeared in Cissy Houston night club act; record debut (duet with Teddy Pendergrass) Hold Me, 1984; albums include Whitney Houston, 1985, Whitney, 1986, I'm Your Baby Tonight, 1990; songs include Greatest Love of All, Saving My Love For You, Didn't We Almost Have It All, You're Still My Man, I'm Your Baby Tonight, 1991; appeared in HBO TV spl. Welcome Home, Heroes, With Whitney Houston, 1991; fashion model Glamour Mag., Seventeen mag., 1981; actress (movie) The Bodyguard, 1992. Recipient Grammy award, 7 Am. Music awards, 4 #1 Single Record awards; named Artist of Yr. Billboard mag., 1986. Grammy award for Best Female Pop Performance, 1985, 4 nominations, 1994, 87; Winner Am. Music award, 1985 (2), 1986 (5), 1988 (2). Office: Friedman Inc care Solters Roskin 45 W 34th St New York NY 10001-3008*

HOUSTOUN, MARION F., federal agency administrator; b. Evanston, Ill., Mar. 17, 1937; d. Lyle William and Fannie Rutherford (Dryden) Frank; m. Cornelius D. Scully III, Jun. 30, 1989; child from a previous marriage: Alexandra Taylor. BA, Coll. William and Mary, 1959; MA, U. N.C., 1961; student, Bryn Mawr Coll., 1963-65. Mng. editor Nat. Inst. for Applied Behaviorial Sci., 1972-75; assoc. dir. Ctr. for Labor and Migration Studies, New TransCentury Found., 1975-77; rsch. assoc., project on U.S. immigration Twentieth Century Fund, 1977; editor Congressional Budget Office, 1978; dir. Immigration Policy Group, 1979-87; adminstrn. and planning dir. Office Internat. Orgns., 1988-92; dir. office mgmt., adminstrn. and planning Bur. Internat. Labor Affairs, Dept. Labor, Washington, 1992—. Author: Aliens in a Irregular Status in the United States: A Review of their Numbers, Characteristics and Role in the Labor Market, 1983; Co-author (with David North) The Characteristics and Role of Illegal Aliens in the U.S. Labor Market: An Exploratory Study, 1976, (with Roger Kramer and Joan Barrett) Female Predominance in Immigration to U.S. Since 1930: A First Look, 1984, (with Philip L. Martin) European and American Immigration Policies, 1983, others. Nat. Woodrow Wilson fellow, Bryn Mawr fellow; Bryn Mawr scholar. Mem. Phi Beta Kappa. Office: Bur of Internat Labor Affairs Dept of Labor 200 Constitution Ave NW Rm S-5303 Washington DC 20210*

HOUX, SHIRLEY ANN, personal and business services company executive, consultant, researcher; b. Claremore, Okla., Nov. 1, 1931; d. George Warren and Alta Zena (Starkweather) Pritchard; m. William Dean Munson, June 1, 1951 (div. June 1962); children—Debra Kay, Diana Sue, Donna Lynn; m. Leonard Houx, June 22, 1963 (div. Oct. 1989); 1 child, David Leonard. Student in bus. Okla. State U., 1949-50. Sec. Jack Gordon, P.A., Claremore, Okla., 1947-48; sec., personnel mgr. Gulf Oil Corp., Tulsa, 1950-51; exec. sec. to wing comdr. U.S. Air Force, Cocoa Beach, Fla., 1951-53; exec. sec. to gen. counsel Houston So., P.A., Stillwater, Okla., 1957-60; exec. sec. to exec. v.p. and sr. v.p. Williams Cos., Tulsa, 1962-64; owner, chief exec. officer Hallmark Exchange, Inc., Tulsa, 1981—; cons. small bus., Tulsa, 1981—; mem. small bus. adv. bd. Tulsa Jr. Coll., 1983—. Author: (drama) Wedding Rehearsal for the Bride of Christ, 1985. Contbg. editor The Chronicle, 1984. Co-creator, producer foot health program, 1967 (Am. Podiatry Assn. Outstanding award 1968); creator, advt. campaign for Cystic Fibrosis Found.: I'm One...Be One, 1978. Pres. women's aux. Okla. Podiatry Assn., Tulsa, 1966-82; sec.-treas. Okla. bd. examiners Okla. Podiatry Assn., 1969-76; nat. audio-visual chmn. women's aux. Am. Podiatry Assn., 1976; pres. Tulsa Cerebral Palsy Assn., 1977, Cystic Fibrosis Found. Aux., Tulsa, 1979. Named Miss Claremore, Claremore Bus. and Profl. Women, Okla., 1949; recipient Two-Star award Pure D'Lite Co., 1982. Mem. Nat. Assn. Female Execs. Democrat. Avocations: fashion design; the arts; writing.

HOVDESVEN, HELEN, health facility administration professional; b. Syracuse, N.Y., Apr. 10, 1942; d. Francis J. and Helen G. (Coupe) O'Brien; m. Richard W. Murray, Oct. 16, 1965 (div. Oct. 1987); children: E. O'Brien, Michael, Colleen; m. Arne Hovdesven, Nov. 5, 1988. BA, Barat Coll., 1964; MA, Sarah Lawrence Coll., 1992. Cert. organ donor requestor, HIV pre-post test counselor. Pers. rep. Mgmt. Assistance Inc., N.Y.C., 1964-66; adminstrv. mgr./med. asst. Lawrence J. Severino, M.D., White Plains, N.Y., 1980-89; patient rep. Westchester County Med. Ctr., Valhalla, N.Y., 1992—. Active Jr. League Westchester-on-Hudson, 1969—; mem. postal coun. com. U.S. Postal Svc., Briarcliff, N.Y., 1994—; vol. reach to recovery Am. Cancer Soc., 1994—. Mem. Nat. Soc. Patient Representation & Consumer Affairs (N.Y. chpt.), Sleepy Hollow Country Club. Republican. Roman Catholic. Home: 10 Maple Rd Briarcliff Manor NY 10510 Office: Westchester County Med Ctr Patient Rels Valhalla NY 10595

HOVEL, ESTHER HARRISON, art educator; b. San Antonio, Tex., Jan. 12, 1917; d. Randolph Williamson and Carrie Esther (Clements) Harrison; m. Elliott Logan Hovel, Sept. 30, 1935; children: Richard Elliott, Dorothy Auverne. BA, Incarnate Word Coll., 1935; postgrad., Oxford U., 1979, British Inst. Art, Florence, Italy, 1980. Civil svc. auditor U.S. Govt. Office of Price Adminstrn., San Antonio, 1942-44; interior decorator Parkway Interior Design Studio, El Paso, Tex., 1968-72; instr. stained glass and sculpture El Paso Mus. Art, 1972-78; tchr. sculpture Albuquerque Sr. Ctrs., 1983-85; docent El Paso Mus. Art, 1972-82. Exhibited sculpture Museo De Artes, Juarez, Mexico, 1981 (1st place 1981). Bd. dirs. YMCA, Albuquerque, 1963-64 (plaque 1964); charter mem. and bd. dirs. Contact Lifeline Internat., Albuquerque, 1982-92 (2 plaques 1986, 90); mem. Com. on Bicentennial of U.S. Constitution, Washington and N.M., 1987-89. Recipient 2 medals Exxon Corp., 1986, 89, Medal of Merit Pres. Ronald Reagan, 1987; grantee Exxon Corp., 1986, 90. Mem. Jr. League Internat. (various offices 1948-93), Rotary "Anns" (various offices). Republican. Mem. Christian Ch. Home: 7524 Bear Canyon Rd NE Albuquerque NM 87109

HOVENDEN, JEANNE ELIZABETH, lawyer; b. San Antonio, Mar. 15, 1954; d. Richard Delbert and Mildred Jean (Klecka) H. BS, Tex. A&M U., 1975, MS, 1977, MBA, 1981; JD, U. Va., 1994. Bar: Va., 1994. Strategic analyst Mercantile Nat. Bank, Dallas, 1982-83; project adminstr. Am. Plan. Corp., Plano, Tex., 1983-84; banking officer, fin. analyst Tex. Bank & Trust, Dallas, 1984-87; risk mgmt. analyst/fin. analyst Fed. Savings & Loan Ins. Corp./FDIC, Washington, 1987-91; atty. Krumbein & Assocs., Richmond, Va., 1993—. Mem. ABA, Va. State Bar, Va. Trial Lawyers Am., Am. Orchid Soc., Am. Rabbit Breeders Assn., Lop Rabbit Club of Am., Phi Kappa Phi. Office: Krumbein & Assocs 1650 Willow Lawn Dr Richmond VA 23230

HOVER, LEILA MESSING, medical librarian; b. Bklyn.; d. Herman Messing and Mildred (Klein) Wyte; m. John Gilbert Hover; children: Jeffrey J., Karen L. BS, SUNY, 1977; MLS, Rutgers U., 1978. Dir. libr. svcs. Holy Name Hosp., Teaneck, N.J., 1978-88; corp. libr. Physicians World Communications Group, Secaucus, N.J., 1988-94; dir. clin. info. mgmt. Churchill Comm. N.A., Clifton, N.J., 1994; prin. Hover Assocs., Boonton Twp., N.J., 1995—; cons. libr. planning, 1981—. Mem. Med. Libr. Assn., Spl. Librs. Assn., Health Scis. Libr. Assn. N.J. (chairperson 1983-87, v.p. 1988-89, pres. 1989-90), Bergen-Passaic Health Scis. Libr. Consortium (chairperson 1979-80). Home and Office: 4 Mountain Run Boonton NJ 07005-8710

HOVEY, ANN GARRETT, economics educator; b. Atlanta, Jan. 30, 1957; d. James Richard and Florence E. (Creamer) Garrett; m. Bryan Earl Hovey, May 19, 1979; children: Jason Garrett, Nathaniel Bryan. BA in Internat. Rels. with honors, Lenoir Rhyne Coll., 1979; postgrad., Inst. D'Etudes Francaises, Aix-En-Provence, France, 1979-80; MS in Econs., U. N.C., Charlotte, 1991. Pres. Larch Mountain Country Artists Corp., Corbett, Oreg., 1986-88; lectr. econs. Rowan Cabarrus C.C., Salisbury, N.C., 1991-93; rsch. asst. U. N.C., Charlotte, 1990-92, lectr. econs., 1991—; mgmt. educator Philip Morris Rowan Cabarrus C.C., Concord, N.C., 1992-93. Chan Gordon scholarship Rotary Internat., 1980. Home: 4209 Sapp Rd Concord NC 28025-1563 Office: U NC Dept Econs Friday Bldg Charlotte NC 28223

HOVMAND, BEVERLY ANN, employee assistance professional; b. Lynn, Mass., Nov. 2, 1941; d. Albert Joseph and Mary (Makarowitz) Cocozella; m. Svend Hovmand, Dec. 17, 1966; children: Peter Svend, Lars Michael. BSc, Simmons Coll., 1963; MSW with honors, U. Md., 1985; postgrad., Cambridge U., Eng., 1964-65. Tchr. English Hamilton-Wenham High Sch., Hamilton, Mass., 1963-64, Saugus (Mass.) High Sch., 1965-66, Lakenheath Air Force Base, Eng., 1966-68; employee rels. rep. Westinghouse Def., Balt., 1983-84; counselor Sheppard-Pratt Hosp., Towson, Md., 1984-85; cons. Human Affairs Internat., Rockville, Md., 1986-88; regional mgr. Employee Assistance Svc., Inc., McLean, Va., 1986-94; v.p. devel. EAS, Inc., 1994—. Participant White House Conf. for a Drug-Free Am., 1987; lectr. in field. Mem. NAFE, NASW, Employee Assistance Profls. Assn., McLean Water Action, Phi Kappa Phi.

HOWARD, ANN, transcription services professional; b. Seattle, May 29, 1955; d. Arthur Lee and Phyllis Charlene (Samples) Bolton; m. Albert L. Howard, May 19, 1979; children: Heather Ann, Alexander Lee, Anthony Wayne. BA, San Jose State U., 1982; postgrad., Chapman U., 1994—. Cert. med. transcriptionist. Field svc. publs. editor Memorex Corp., Santa Clara, Calif., 1977-79; scientific publs. editor United Technologies Corp., Sunnyvale, Calif., 1981-83; owner, operator Artis A. Howard Med. Editing and Transcription Svcs., Colorado Springs, 1983—; supv. med. transcription svcs. St. Joseph's Med. Ctr., Albuquerque, 1993—; transcription instr. Denver Tech. Coll., Colorado Springs, 1988-89; co-owner, v.p. The Pine

Studio, Albuquerque, 1993—; transcription instr. St. Joseph Med. Ctr., 1993—. Vol. All Faith's Receiving Home and New Day Runaway House, Albuquerque, 1991-92, St. Joseph Meals-on-Wheels, 1993; vol., group leader St. Joseph Med. Ctr. Adopt-a-Family, 1993, 94. Mem. Am. Assn. for Med. Transcription. Baptist. Home: 37 Sandia Heights Dr NE Albuquerque NM 87122 Office: St Joseph Med Ctr 601 Grand Ave NE Albuquerque NM 87102

HOWARD, AUGHTUM SMITH, retired mathematics educator; b. Almo, Ky., Nov. 10, 1906; d. Leander E. and Anna (Wright) Smith; m. Noel Judson Howard, Jan. 6, 1929; children: Carl Eugene, Robert Alvin. BA, Georgeown Coll., 1926; postgrad., U. Mich., 1927; MS, U. Ky., 1938, PhD, 1942. Lab technician Parke Davis Drug Co., Detroit, 1926-27; tchr. Marshall County High Sch., 1927-29; grad. asst. math. dept. U. Ky., 1936-41, fellow, 1941-42; assoc. prof. math. Ky. Wesleyan Coll., 1942-46, prof., 1946-58; assoc prof. Eastern Ky. State Coll., Richmond, 1958-62, prof., 1962-73; mem. curriculum study com.; commn. on pub. edn., State of Ky., 1961. Tchr. adult Sunday sch. class Richmond 1st Christian Ch., 1971-78, deacon, 1986-87, elder, 1989. Mem. AAUP, Math Assn. Am. (chmn. Ky. sect. 1944-46, lectr. 1953-55, sec.-treas. 1949-51, 69-71, cert. of meritorious svc. 1988), Richmond Women's Club, Sigma Xi. Home: 2351 Egremont Dr Orange Park FL 32073

HOWARD, BARBARA ANN, medical technologist; b. Centralia, Mo., Oct. 7, 1932; d. Samuel Lee and Twila Lynn (Houghton) Harshbarger; m. Edward N. Howard, Oct. 11, 1952 (div. Dec. 1962); children: Ralph Neal (dec.), LeeAnn, David Mark, Donald Edward. Cert. med. technologist, Blessing Hosp., 1958; BA in Biology, Lindenwood Coll., 1966; postgrad., U. Mo., St. Louis, 1979-81. Med. technologist St. Joseph Health Ctr., St. Charles, Mo., 1959-65, 68-77, lab. evening supr. med. technologist, 1977-85; med. technologist supr. Boonslick Med. Group, St. Charles, 1965-76, med. technologist, 1987-94; blood bank med. technologist De Paul Health Ctr., Bridgeton, Mo., 1985-87; rsch. technologist CDIC Monsanto Corp., Chesterfield, Mo., 1987; med. technologist Barnes St. Peters (Mo.) Hosp., 1994—; part-time med. technologist Barnes St. Peters (Mo.) Hosp., 1988-94, Boonslick Med. Group, 1994—. Sunday sch. tchr. 1st Meth. Ch., St. Charles, 1970, 90, 91, mem. worship com., 1992, mem. adminstrv. bd., 1990—, mem. chancel choir, 1970—; co-chmn. Grief Support Group Conf. Ctr., St. Charles, 1987-88; mem. St. Charles Choral Soc., 1970's. PEO grantee, 1977. Mem. AAUW (treas. 1990-92). Home: 719 N 5th St Saint Charles MO 63301

HOWARD, CAROLE MARGARET MUNROE, public relations executive; b. Halifax, N.S., Can., Mar. 5, 1945; came to U.S., 1965; d. Frederick Craig and Dorothy Margaret (Crimes) Munroe; m. Robert William Howard, May 15, 1965. BA, U. Calif., Berkeley, 1967; MS, Pace U., 1978. Reporter Vancouver (Can.) Sun, 1965; editorial assoc. Pacific N.W. Bell, Seattle, 1967-70, employee info. supr., 1970-72, advt. supr., 1972, project mgr. EEO, 1972-73, mktg. mgr., 1973, info. mgr., 1974-75; dist. mgr. media relations AT&T, N.Y.C., 1975-77, dist. mgr. planning, 1977-78, dist. mgr. advt., 1978-80; media relations mgr. Western Electric, N.Y.C., 1980-83; div. mgr. regional pub. relations AT&T Info. Systems, Morristown, N.J., 1983-85; v.p., dir. pub. relations and communications policy The Reader's Digest Assn., Inc., Pleasantville, N.Y., 1985—. Author: (with Wilma Mathews) On Deadline: Managing Media Relations, 1985, 2nd edit., 1994; contbg. author: Communicators' Guide to Marketing, 1987, Experts in Action: Inside Public Relations, 2d edit., 1988, Travel Industry Marketing, 1990; editor newsletters: Wash. State Rep. Cen. Com., 1973-74; contbg. editor Pub. Relations Quar.; pres. The Reader's Digest Found.; adv. bd. Pub. Rels. News and Pub. Rels. Review. Mem. corp. adv. bd. Caramoor Ctr. for Music and the Arts; bd. dirs. The Hundred Club of Westchester, Inc., The Lila Acheson Wallace Fund for Met. Mus. of Art, Madison Square Boy's and Girl's Club of N.Y.C. Mem. Women in Communications (bd. dirs. Wash. state 1973), Internat. Assn. Bus. Communicators, Pub. Relations Soc. Am., Nat. Press Women, Wash. Press Women (bd. dirs. 1972), Issues Mgmt. Assn., Am. Cancer Soc., Arthur Page Soc., Pi Beta Phi. Angelican. Clubs: The Aspen, La Paloma Country. Home: 31 Daniel Ct Ridgewood NJ 07450-5139 Office: Reader's Digest Assn Inc Pleasantville NY 10570

HOWARD, CONSTANCE ADAIR, financial advisor; b. Savannah, Ga., Oct. 2, 1964; d. Frank Roy and Bette Adair (Moore) Hurst; m. Joseph Michael Howard, May 19, 1990; 1 child, Justin Michael. Student, South Coll., Savannah, 1985, Armstrong State Coll., 1988. Cert. fin. advisor series 7, 63 licenses. Office mgr. Millie Lewis Modeling, Savannah, 1983-86; ops. clk. Johnson, Lane, Space, Smith, Savannah, 1986-88; adminstrv. asst. Merrill Lynch, Savannah, 1988-91; fin. advisor Prudential Securities, Savannah, 1991-94; registered rep. A.G. Edwards & Sons, Inc., Savannah, 1994—; fin. instr. Savannah Tech. Inst., 1993—; fin. guest spkr. Sta. WSAV-TV, Savannah, 1993—; find. spkr., instr. to pub. sch. students, Savannah, 1992—; fin. spkr. to local bus. orgns., Savannah, 1992—; stock market report announcer Pub. Radio Sta. 91, Savannah, 1992; co-producer, host women's talk show Money Talks, Cablevision Seven, Savannah, 1994—. Fin. columnist: The Richmond Hill Bryan County News, 1993—, The Ga. Guardian, 1993—, The Savannah Parent, 1993, The Knowledge Exch., 1993. Internship mentor Savannah H.S. Program, 1993. Mem. Am. Bus. Women's Assn., Small Bus. Chamber (bd. dirs., treas. 1993—). Office: AG Edwards & Sons Inc 533 Stephenson Ave Savannah GA 31406

HOWARD, DARCIE SHEILA, special education educator; b. Kingston, Ont., Can., Aug. 20, 1946; came to U.S., 1964; d. Gard Shaw Forrester and Mary Elizabeth (Nunn) Pike; m. Norman D. Howard, Sept. 18, 1966; children: Aaron, Matthew. BA, U. Calif., Berkeley, 1968; edn. credential, Calif. State U., Hayward, 1969; paralegal degree, Rancho Santiago Coll., 1987. Cert. tchr., Calif. Svc. rep. Pacific Bell Telephone Co., Berkeley, 1966; tchr. Oakland (Calif.) Pub. Schs., 1969-73; tchr., tutor Calvary Christian Sch., Santa Ana, Calif., 1980-86; owner ABCaDE Computers, Santa Ana, 1986-93; spl. edn. tchr. Orange (Calif.) Unified Sch. Dist., 1990—; owner Calif. Sweet-Briar, 1991-93. Republican. Home: 1513 E Franzen Ave Santa Ana CA 92701-1641

HOWARD, ELIZABETH, corporate communications and marketing executive; b. Littleton, N.H., Apr. 24, 1950; d. Ellis Woodruff and Elizabeth (Millar) H. BA, Plymouth State Coll., 1972; MS, Pratt Inst., 1985. Dir. corp. pub. rels. Nat. Distillers Chem. Corp, N.Y.C., 1978-85; dir. pub. rels. Transway Internat Corp., White Plains, N.Y., 1985; pres. Corp. Communications Group Millennium Inc., N.Y.C., 1986; pres. Elizabeth Howard & Co., N.Y.C., 1987—; Publ. and editor-in-chief Observations. Contbr. articles to profl. mags. Pres. Katharine Gibbs Sch. Scholarship Found., 1987-88, 94—, bd. dirs.; bd. dirs. Brenda Daniels Dance Com., 1993—, Hamilton-Madison Settlement House, N.Y.C., 1984-89, pres., 1987-89; mem. com. YMCA Greater N.Y., 1993-94. Mem. Global Econ. Action Inst., Women Execs. Pub. Rels. (bd. dirs. 1984-87), Fin. Women's Assn. (bd. dirs. 1994), Carnegie Coun. Home: 152 E 94th St Apt 4H New York NY 10028 Office: 501 Fifth Ave New York NY 10017

HOWARD, FRANCES ESTELLA HUMPHREY, government official; b. Wallace, S.D., Feb. 18, 1914; d. Hubert Horatio and Christine (Sannes) H.; m. Ray Howard, Dec. 7, 1942 (dec. Jan. 1967); children: William, Anne. BA in Sociology, George Washington U., 1937, MA, 1941; HHD (hon.), Lane Coll., 1967; LHD, Seton Hill Coll., 1993, U. Md., Balt., 1993. With U.S. Office Civilian Def., Washington, 1941-43; liaison officer various vol. agys. for fgn. relief, Washington, 1942-60; commd. fgn. service officer Dept. State, Washington, 1960; chief liaison officer vol. agys. AID, Washington, 1960-67; chief spl. project div. Office War Hunger, Washington, 1968; liaison officer vol. health orgns., spl. asst. to assoc. dir. Office Asst. Sec. Health and Sci. Affairs HEW, Washington, 1969-70; spl. asst. to assoc. dir. for extramural programs Nat. Library Medicine, NIH, USPHS, Health and Human Services, Bethesda, Md., 1970—; lectr. to various orgns. Contbr. articles to nat. periodicals. V.p. U.S. Com. for Refugees, 1975-82; bd. dirs. Universalist-Unitarian Service Com., 1975-80, Mus. African Art, Smithsonian Instn., 1962—, Washington Opera, 1977—, Nat. Theatre Corp., 1980—, Capitol area Chpt. CARE, 1980—, Washington Ctr., 1982, Am. Council Nationality Services, 1982—, Capitol Children's Mus., 1982—, Hubert H. Humphrey Inst. Pub. Affairs, U. Minn., 1983—. Recipient Disting. Service award Grand Chpt. Delta Sigma Theta, 1966; Women's Honor award Howard U., 1967; No. Va. service award Altrusa Club, 1967; Emblem of Honor award 6th Ann. Pan Am. Congress Conf. on Social Services, 1968. Mem. AAUW, Am. Polit. Sci. Assn., Bus. and Profl. Women's Assn., Am. Sociol. Assn., Pan Am. Conf. Social Wk., Soc. Internat. Devel., Internat. Coun. on Social Welfare, UN Assn. (dir. 1980-84), AAAS, Cosmos Club. Office: NIH Nat Library of Medicine 8600 Rockville Pike Bethesda MD 20894-0001

HOWARD, GEORGINA RACHEL, women's health and community health nurse; b. N.Y.C., Aug. 18, 1959; d. George and Sylvia (Stanley) H.; m. Gregory Moore, Sept. 5, 1987; children: Nailah Rachel, Mariah Sylvia. BSN, Adelphi U., 1981; MPA, L.I. U., 1986. RN, N.Y.; cert. Am. Soc. Psychoprophylaxis, Lamaze childbirth instr., Am. Coll. Childbirth Educators. Staff nurse Columbia Presbyn. Med. Ctr., N.Y.C., 1981-82, Schneider's Children's Hosp., New Hyde Park, N.Y., 1983, Covenant House, Inc., N.Y.C., 1984; nurse clinician Queens Hosp. Ctr., Jamaica, N.Y., 1985; nursing supr. South Queens Cmty. Health Ctr., Jamaica, N.Y., 1991-94, Charles R. Drew Ctr., 1994—. Mem. ANA (ind. study rev. panelist 1995-96), Assn. Women's Health, Obstetric, and Neonatal Nurses (legis. dist. coord. senatorial dist. 10 Queens, N.Y. chpt.), Am. Soc. for Psychoprophylaxis in Obstet., N.Y. State Nurses Assn.

HOWARD, JANE OSBURN, educator; b. Morris, Ill., Aug. 12, 1926; d. Everett Hooker and Bernice Otilda (Olson) Osburn; B.A., U. Ariz., 1948; M.A., U. N.Mex., 1966, Ph.D., 1969; m. Rollins Stanley Howard, June 5, 1948; children—Ellen Elizabeth, Susan (Mrs. John Karl Nuttall). Instr. U. N.Mex. Sch. Medicine, Albuquerque, 1968-70, mem. staff pediatrics, deaf blind children's program, Albuquerque, 1971-72, asst. dir. N.Mex. programs for deaf blind children, 1972—, instr. psychiatry, instr. pediatrics, coordinator deaf-blind children's program, 1972-76, edn. cons., 1976—, publicity and pub. relations cons., 1983—; Cons. Mountain-Plains Regional Ctr. for Services to Deaf-Blind Children, Denver, 1971-74, Bur. Indian Affairs, 1974. Active Cystic Fibrosis, Mother's March, Heart Fund, Easter Seal-Crippled Children. Recipient fellowships U. N.M., 1965, 66, 66-67, 67-68, U. So. Calif. John Tracy Clinic, 1973. Fellow Royal Soc. Health; mem. Council Exceptional Children, Am. Assn. Mental Deficiency, Nat. Assn. Retarded Children, AAUW, Pi Lambda Theta, Zeta Phi Eta, Alpha Epsilon Rho. Republican. Methodist. Home: 615 Valencia Dr SE Albuquerque NM 87108-3742

HOWARD, JEAN ELLIOTT, physician; b. Pomona, Calif., Apr. 23, 1941; divorced; 1 child, Crystal A. BA in Biochemistry with highest honors, U. Calif., Berkeley, 1962; MS in Biochemistry, Yale U., 1964; MD, U. Calif., San Francisco, 1969. Diplomate Am. Bd. Internal Medicine. Intern Pacific Med. Ctr., San Francisco, 1969-70, resident internal medicine, 1970-73, chief resident, 1972; chief resident Harkness Cmty. Hosp., San Francisco, 1972; fellow hematology U. Calif., San Francisco, 1973-75; rsch. fellow blood banking Irwin Meml. Blood Bank, San Francisco, 1973-74; NIH rsch. fellow ARC Blood Rsch. Lab., Bethesda, Md., 1975-76; project officer divsn. blood diseases and resouces Nat. Heart, Lung, and Blood Inst., NIH, Bethesda, 1976-77; asst. clin. prof. medicine in hematology George Washington U., Washington, 1976-77; asst. med. dir. transfusion svc., asst. clin. prof. pathology Stanford (Calif.) U., 1977-79; pvt. practice internal medicine Burlingame, Calif., 1979-80; hematologist USPHS, San Francisco, 1980-81; hematologist hematology-oncology svc. Fitzsimons Army Med. Ctr., Aurora, Colo., 1981-85; pvt. practice internal medicine, hematology and oncology Yuba City, Calif., 1985-90; med. officer, weight control, profile officer U.S. Army Hosp., Novato, Calif., 1985-91; oncologist, hematologist 9th Strategic Hosp., Beale AFB, Calif., 1987-90; mem. active staff Fremont Med. Ctr. and Rideout Meml. Hosp., Yuba City, 1985-92; oncologist, internist Evans Army Cmty. Hosp., Ft. Carson, Colo., 1990-91; chief profl. svcs. 808th Sta. Hosp., Uniondale, N.Y., 1992-93, 356th Field Hosp., Rocky Point, 1993—; scientist med. dept., staff physician Occupational Medicine Clinic Brookhaven Nat. Lab., Upton, N.Y., 1991—, asst. med. dir. Marshall Island Med. Program, 1991-92, med. dir. Marshall Island Med. Program, 1993—, chief of staff CRC, 1993—; chairperson tumor conf. Fremont Med. Ctr. and Rideout Meml. Hosp. Consortium, 1986-88, pharmacy and therapeutics com. UCMS, 1990, exec. com. med. dept. Brookhaven Nat. Lab., 1993—. Author: (with others) Cryopreservation of Granulocytes in the Granulocyte: Function and Clinical Utilization, 1977; contbr. articles to med. jours. Lt. col. M.C., U.S. Army, 1981-85, 90-91, Pursian Gulf; lt. col. M.C., USAR, 1985—. NSF fellow, 1962-63. Fellow Am. Coll. Physicians; mem. Am. Soc. Hematology, Am. Soc. Clin. Oncology, Am. Coll. Occupational and Environmental Medicine, Assn. Mil. Surgeons U.S., Phi Beta Kappa. Office: Brookhaven Nat Lab Medical Dept Upton NY 11973

HOWARD, JEANINE MARIE, photographer, artist; b. Mt. Kisco, N.Y., Oct. 29, 1966; d. Ernest Eugene and Ursula Ann (Christe) Howard; m. Mark Anthony Birong. BFA in photography, Calif. State U., 1989. Mgr. A&M Enterprises, Long Beach, Calif., 1987-92; photographic asst. Linda Ikeda Productions, Sante Fe Springs, Calif., 1992-93; artist's photographer Long Beach, 1989—; photographer Trend Offset Printing, Los Alamitos, Calif., 1993—. Exhibited in group shows at Univ. Alaska, 1992, The Vault Gallery, 1992, Parkville Fine Arts, 1992, Univ. Art Mus. Calif. State U., 1992, Maude Kerns Art Ctr., 1992, Slocumb Galleries, 1992, The 25th Univ. Del. Biennial Exhibition, 1992, Mad River Post, 1993, Trenton State Coll. Art Gallery, 1993, Lycoming Coll. Art Gallery, 1993, Honolulu Printmaking Workshop, 1993-94; contbr. freelance photography, music and art reviews to local mags. Artist coun. mem. Long Beach Art Mus. Mem. Angels' Gate Cultural Ctr., Long Beach Pub. Corp. Arts. Home: PO Box 30571 Long Beach CA 90853-0571

HOWARD, JO ANN, business owner; b. L.A., Nov. 22, 1937; d. John George and Lucile Anne (Farish) Heinzman; m. William Harold Howard, Dec. 2, 1958; children: Teri Lynn Wilson, Tracey Ann Currie, Randall William, Richard John. Student, Mt. San Antonio Coll., 1957. Escrow officer, mgr. So. Cities Escrow, Hemet, Calif., 1970-75; escrow officer Hemet Escrow, 1975-76; ptnr. Ramona Escrow, Hemet, 1976-79; pres., supr. Howard Escrow, Hemet, 1979—; pres. Recon Enterprises, Inc., Hemet, 1976—; co-owner J & B Mobile Modular Housing, Hemet, 1986—; pres. Chaparral Accomodators, Inc., Hemet, 1990—. Pres. Sorpotimists Internat., San Jacinto-Hemet Valley, Calif., 1979. Named one of Disting. Pres.'s, Soroptimists, 1978-80; recipient Woman of Distinction award Soroptimist Internat. (San Jacinto-Hemet Valley 1990). Mem. Women's Coun. Bd. Realtors (affiliate, treas.), Hemet-San Jacinto Bd. Realtors (affiliate), San Jacinto C. of C., Hemet C. of C., Calif. Escrow Assn. (pres. Calif. chpt. 1991), Riverside County Escrow Assn. (bd. dirs. 1985—), Escrow Inst. of Calif. (bd. dirs. 1992—). Republican. Presbyterian. Office: Howard Escrow 3292 E Florida Ave Ste D Hemet CA 92544-4941

HOWARD, JOAN ALICE, artist; b. N.Y.C., Apr. 28, 1929; d. John Volkman and Mary Alice Devlin; m. Robert Thornton Howard, June 26, 1949; children: Barbara Jo, Robert Thornton Jr., Gregory Lyon, Brian Devlin. Student, Hunter Coll., 1947-48, UCLA, 1967-68, Los Angeles Valley Coll., 1970-71. Dir., choreographer Acad. Dance, Floral Park and Forest Hills, N.Y., 1947-57; dir. dance. Cath. Parochial schs., N.Y.C., Bklyn., and Floral Park, N.Y., 1948-55; chmn. dept. dance Molloy Coll., 1958-67; artist sta. KNBC-TV, Los Angeles, 1967-74, NBC, N.Y.C., 1974-78, sta. WNBC-TV, N.Y.C., 1978-79; artistic dir. Brookville (N.Y.) Sch., 1980-85; dir. dance N.Y.C. YMCA, 1948; founder, dir. Queens-Nassau Regional Dance Theatre, 1950-55; choreographer Molloy Coll. Dance Theatre, 1959-67; cons. prenatal exercise, L.I., N.Y., 1980—; judge art show Westbury (N.Y.) Mural Project, 1979; art cons. Chase Manhattan Bank, Cross River, N.Y., 1993-94. One-woman shows include Dime Savs. Bank, Manhasset, N.Y., 1986-87, Ridgefield (Conn.) Guild Gallery, 1989-90, 91, 92, 93, Nardin Gallery Fine Arts, 1990, Chase Manhattan Bank, 1990-91, 92, 93, 94, Manhasset Libr. Gallery, 1990-91, Hutchinson Gallery L.I. U., 1991, Rose Gallery, Kent, Conn., 1991, 92, 93, 94, Chelsea House, N.Y., 1991, Plandome Gallery, L.I., 1991, Sacco's, Ridgefield, 1991, Great Neck (N.Y.) Libr. Gallery, 1991, N.Y. Inst. Tech., Greenvale, N.Y., 1992, 93, Chase Manhattan Bank, Cross River, N.Y., 1992-93, Hicksville (N.Y.) Gallery, 1993; exhibited in group shows at Valley Ctr. Arts Gallery, L.A., 1968-72, Home Savs. & Loan Art Exhibits, L.A., 1969-70, Westwood Art Gallery, L.A., 1972, Onion Gallery, L.A., 1972, North Ridge Women's Ctr. Gallery, L.A., 1972, Great Neck (N.Y.) Ctr. Gallery, 1976, A&S Gallery, Manhasset, 1976, Gloria Vanderbilt Designers Showcase, 1978, Ridgefield (Conn.) Guild Artists, 1983, Manhasset Libr. Gallery, 1985-89, Great Neck House Gallery, 1986-87, Hutchins Gallery C.W. Post Coll., L.I., 1986-90 (awards 1986, 87, 88, 89, 90), Dime Savs. Bank, Manhasset, N.Y., European Am. Bank, 1988, Nardin Fine Arts, Cross River, N.Y., 1989, Plandome Gallery, N.Y.C., 1990, Aldrich Mus., 1992-93, Hicksville (N.Y.) Gallery, 1993, Ridgefield (Conn.) Guild of Artists Gallery, 1993, Rose Gallery, Hicksville Gallery, 1993, Chase Manhattan Bank, N.Y.C., 1993-94; exhibited in juried shows Nassau County Mus. Fine Arts, Roslyn, N.Y., 1985, Plandome Gallery, 1987-88, Great Neck House Gallery, 1986-89 (hon. mention), East Meadow Libr. Gallery, 1988, Freeport Gallery, 1988, Shelter Rock Gallery, 1989, Ridgefield Gallery Portrait Show, 1989-90, Ridgefield Artists' Guild, 1989, 93, Nardin Gallery, 1989, Hutchins Gallery L.I. U., 1991, Rose Gallery, Kent, Conn., 1991, 92, 94, Chelsea House Mus. Cultural Commn., 1991, Manhasset Gallery, 1990-91, Sacco, Ridgefield, 1991, Great Neck Libr. Gallery, 1991, Chase Manhattan Bank, Cross River, N.Y., 1992-94, Tchrs. Art Yorktown Artists Club, 1994, Aldrich Mus., 1993-94, Ridgefield (Conn.) Art Guild Gallery, 1993, Hicksville (N.Y.) Art Gallery, 1993, Chase Manhattan Bank, N.Y., 1993, 94; choreographer contemporary ballet Crucifixion, 1960, Persephone, 1961, Cubes of Truth, 1962, Somewhere, 1965; appeared on radio show Coast to Coast on a Bus, 1939-47; Broadway prodn. Lady in the Dark, 1940-42; performed ballet in TV show Stars of Tomorrow, 1942, Sleeping Beauty, 1942. Dem. committeewoman, Glen Cove, N.Y., 1954-58. Recipient Del Rey Perpetual Race championship trophy, 1974, Little Sabot Perpetual Race trophy, 1972-74, So. Calif. Women's Sailing Conf. sabot championship, 1972-74, 1st Woman trophy Olympic Regatta, 1973. Mem. Dance Educators Am., Manhasset Art Assn., Women's Sailing Com. of U.S. Yacht Racing Union (fund raiser 1980-81), Am. Women's C. of C. L.A., Tri-County Artists Ridgefield Art Guild. Home and Office: 19 Autumn Ridge Rd South Salem NY 10590-1103

HOWARD, JOANNE FRANCES, research analyst; b. St. Louis, Feb. 5, 1953; d. Frank Henry and Evelyn Julia (Haeckel) Spellazza; m. Claude Lorrain Howard, May 20, 1978; children: Amy Julia, Laura Ann. BA, U. Mo.-St. Louis, 1975; MS, Western Ill. U., 1976. Lic. funeral director. Analyst, Streett Industries, Inc., St. Louis, 1977-78; research analyst Gallup & Robinson Co., Princeton, N.J., 1978-80, Jack Eckerd Corp., Clearwater, Fla., 1980-82, sr. research analyst, 1982-88; mktg. cons. Howard Assocs., 1986—; cons. Anson Lee Rector Inc., Tarpon Springs, Fla., 1982-83, Med-Op Clinics, Tarpon Springs, Fla., 1983-88; funeral dir., extended care coord. Pugh Funeral Home, Golden City, Mo., 1992—; analyst, cons. H.L. Pugh Assocs. Consulting, Golden City, 1992—. Editor monthly newsletter Florida West Coast chpt. Am. Mktg. Assn., 1982-83. Mem. Pinebrook Homeowners Assn., Largo, Fla., 1983-84. Mem. Am. Mktg. Assn. (past sec.-treas.), Mo. Funeral Dirs. Assn., Nat. Funeral Dirs. Assn., Mo. Inst. Funeral Profls. Democrat. Home and Office: 708 SE 70th Ln Golden City MO 64748-9324

HOWARD, JUDITH BALDWIN, investment company executive; b. Vicksburg, Miss., Dec. 28, 1941; d. Leland William and Bernice (Ball) H. Student, Randolph-Macon Woman's Coll., 1959-61; BS in Chemistry, U. Wis., 1963. CFA. Trust investment officer Deposit Guaranty Nat. Bank, Jackson, Miss., 1981-86; dir. investments-fin. Hosp. Corp. Am., Nashville, 1986-89; pres. Howard and McInnes, Inc., Jackson, 1989—. Mem. Miss. Soc. Fin. Analysts. Office: Howard and McInnes Inc 248 E Capitol St Ste 820 Jackson MS 39201-2502

HOWARD, JULIA C., state legislator; b. Salisbury, N.C., Aug. 20, 1944; d. Allen Leary and Ruth Elizabeth (Snider) Craven; m. Abe N. Howard Jr., 1962; children: Amedia Paige, Abe N. III. Grad., Davie H.S., 1962. V.p. Davie Builders Inc.; pres. Howard Realty & Ins. Agy. Inc.; mem. N.C. Ho. of Reps.; chmn. bd. trustees Davie County Hosp., 1978-85. Commr. Town of Macksville, N.C., 1981-88; mem. youth coun. First United Meth. Ch., 1974-84, chmn. coun. of ministries, 1979-81. Mem. Realtors Assn. (pres. Davie County Bd. 1972, state dir. 1973-75), Sertoma Club. Home: 203 Magnolia Ave Mocksville NC 27028 Office: NC Ho of Reps State Capitol Raleigh NC 27611*

HOWARD, JULIE DAY, psychotherapist, social worker; b. Hartford, Conn., Jan. 11, 1949; d. James Leland and Sallie Day (Roberts) H.; m. Angelo John Lewis, June 23, 1985; 1 child, Emmanuel John. M. of Human Svcs., Lincoln U., Oxford, Pa., 1984. Cert. social worker; nat. cert. counselor. Mental health asst. Belchertown (Mass.) State Sch., 1974-76, unit banker, coord. fair labor standards act, 1977-79, occupational therapist asst., 1979-80, rehab. counselor, 1980-81; case adv. Greater Trenton (N.J.) Community Mental Health Ctr., Inc., 1981-82, vocat. counselor, 1982-84, coord. vocat. svcs., 1984—; adj. therapist Family Svc. Princeton, N.J., 1990—; cons. Cath. Charities, Trenton, 1989; workshop presenter 13th ann. conf. Internat. Assn. Psychosocial Rehab. Svcs., Phila., 1988; program developer, group leader Nathan Azrin Job Club model, 1982-85. Author: Multicultural Communication: A Resource Guide for Helping Professionals, 1991. Mem. employment task force Human Svcs. Adv. Coun. Mercer County, Trenton, 1985. Home and Office: 27 Buttonwood St Lambertville NJ 08530-1644

HOWARD, LOU DEAN GRAHAM, elementary education educator; b. Conway, Ark., Aug. 11, 1935; d. Nathan Eldridge and Martha Regina (Sutherland) Graham; m. Robert Hunt Howard, June 4, 1961; 1 child, Kenneth Paul. BSE, U. Cen. Ark., 1957; MA, Vanderbilt U., 1960. Cert. sch. adminstr., prin./supr., curriculum specialist, mentor, grad. elem. Elem. tchr. Hughes (Ark.) Pub. Schs., 1957-59; supervisory tchr. Peabody Demonstration Sch., Nashville, 1959-61; elem. tchr. Orange County Pub. Schs., Orlando, Fla., 1965-68; elem. tchr., K-5 adminstr. Westchester Acad., High Point, N.C., 1968-77; tchr. alternative learning ctr.-mid. sch. Randolph County Pub. Schs., Archdale-Trinity, 1978; elem. tchr. Greensboro (N.C.) Pub. Schs., 1978-93, Guilford County Schs., High Point, N.C., 1993—. Contbr. articles to newspapers and AAUW Bull. Active Stephen Ministry. Mem. ASCD, NEA (sch. rep., instrnl. and profl. devel. com.), AAUW (pres. N.C. state 1982-84, Gift honoree Ednl. Found.), Assn. Childhood Edn. Internat. (past pres.), Ind. Schs. Assn., Peabody Coll. Elem. Coun. (sec.), N.C. Coun. Women's Orgns., Clan Graham Soc. (sec. 1983—, Disting. Svc. award), Internat. Platform Assn., Order of Golden Thistle (charter), Delta Kappa Gamma. Methodist. Home: 1228 Kensington Dr High Point NC 27262-7316 Office: Allen Jay Elem Sch 1311 E Springfield Rd High Point NC 27263

HOWARD, LYN JENNIFER, medical educator; b. Buxton, U.K., Jan. 19, 1938; came to U.S., 1965; naturalized, 1971; d. Peter and Bess (Donnelly) Marsh; m. Burtis Howard, Aug. 13, 1965 (div. 1988); children: Peter Howard, Thia Howard. BA, Oxford U., 1960, MA, BM, BCh, 1964. Diplomate Am. Bd. Internal Medicine. Intern London Hosp., 1964-65; intern Kans. City Med. Ctr., 1965-66, resident, 1966-70; fellow in clin. nutrition and gastroenterology Vanderbilt Hosp., 1971-73; dir. clin. nutrition program Albany (N.Y.) Med. Coll., 1973-80, asst. prof. medicine, pediat., 1973-76, assoc. prof. medicine, pediat., 1977-84, prof. medicine, 1984—, head divsn. clin. nutrition, 1986—; asst. dir. Clin. Studies Ctr., Albany Med. Ctr., 1973-78; attending physician Albany Med. Ctr. Hosp., 1973—; attending physician, cons. clin. nutrition Albany VA Hosp., 1973—; cons. pediat. gastroenterology St. Peter's Hosp., Albany, 1974—; med. dir. Albany Home Health Resources, 1991-92; mem. working group Nat. Commn. Digestive Diseases, 1977; mem. NIH Consensus Devel. Conf., 1978, nutrition rsch. directions, 1979, spl. study sect. clin. nutrition rsch. units, 1980, nutrition study sect., 1989-93; cons. AMA Drug Evaluations, 1982, Medicare, Blue Cross/Blue Shield S.C., 1987—; keynote spkr. Australian Soc. Parenteral and Enteral Nutrition, Perth, 1993, 1st Clin. Nutrition Symposium, Kuala Lumpor, Malaysia, 1994. Contbg. editor Nutrition Reviews, 1981-87, 89; mem. editl. bd. Jour. Drug-Nutrient Interactions, 1984, Contemporary Issues in Clin. Nutrition, 1985, Jour. Am. Soc. Parenteral and Enteral Nutrition, 1987-90; contbr. articles, abstracts to profl. jours., chpts. to books. Exec. dir. Oley Found. for Home Parenteral and Enteral Nutrition, 1983-87, pres., 1987-91, med. dir., 1991; pres. Camphill Found., Pa., 1994. Recipient Clifton C. Thorne Cmty. Svc. award, 1990, Physician of Yr. award Albany chpt. Crohn's Colitis Found. Am., 1991; elected 1st woman mem. Great Lakes Interurban Club, 1990; Major County scholar, 1956; grantee Nutrition Found., 1973-79, U.S. Dept. Agriculture, 1978-81, William F. Donner Found., 1983, Oley Found. for Home Parenteral and Enteral Nutrition Patients, 1983—, Home Health Care of Am., 1983-88, Hosp. for Incurables Found., 1987-88, 91, Schaeffer Found. for Faculty Devel., 1988. Fellow Royal Coll. Physicians, Am. Coll. Physicians, Am. Coll. Nutrition (dir. 1985-88); mem. Am. Bd. Nutrition (dir. 1980, pres. 1982-84), Brit. Med.

Assn., Am. Soc. Parenteral and Enteral Nutrition (abstract selection com. 1980, nutrition support standards com. 1984, future directions com. 1991, OASIS working group 1991-92, award 1992), Am. Soc. Clin. Nutrition (rsch. com. 1978, edn. com. 1979, councilor 1982-85, chair post grad. clin. nutrition tng. com. 1983-88, clin. practice in health and disease 1991), Am. Inst. Nutrition, Am. Gastroent. Assn. (co-organizer post grad. tng. course 1987, tng. and edn. com. 1988-91, abstract selection com. 1989), N.Am. Soc. Pediat. Gastroenterology, Am. Fedn. Clin. Rsch. (abstract selection com. 1986), Alpha Omega Alpha. Office: Albany Med Coll Albany NY 12208

HOWARD, MARY TATUM, psychologist; b. San Francisco; d. Archibald and Mattie (Ross) Tatum; m. Robert M. Howard, Sept. 1951 (div. Sept. 1963). BA, W.Va. State Coll., 1948; MA, U. Mo., Kansas City, 1952; PhD, U. Minn., 1967. Tchr. Bd. of Edn., Kansas City, Kans., 1948-51; faculty Miles Coll., Birmingham, Ala., 1952-57; psychologist and dir. psychol. svc. Kenny Rehab. Inst., Mpls., 1963-68; prof. and dir. counseling ctr. U. D.C., 1968-73; prof. and dean student svcs. Hostos C.C./CUNY, Bronx, 1973-77; dean Kerney campus and union affairs Mercer County C.C., Trenton, N.J., 1977-79; assoc. dir. Commn. on Higher Edn. Middle States Assn., Phila., 1979-80; psychologist and coord. of counseling Vets. Affairs Med. Ctr., St. Cloud, Minn., 1980—; adj. faculty St. Cloud State U., 1983—; asst. prof. Augsburg Coll., Mpls., 1963-68; cons. Washburn Clinic, Mpls., 1993-94. Contbr. articles to profl. jours. Bd. dirs., treas. Minn. Civil Liberties Union, Mpls.; treas. Minn., Dakota Conf., NAACP, 1992—, v.p. St. Cloud br., 1990—; past pres. and mem. St. Cloud Symphony Orch. Bd., 1983—; bd. dirs. Girl Scouts U.S., St. Cloud, 1993—; bd. dirs., sec. Jacob Wetterling Found., St. Cloud, 1991—. Fellow APA (divsn. 17, bd. dirs. 1988-89), Am. Psychol. Soc.; mem. Minn. Psychol. Assn. (past bd. dirs.). Home: 110 32nd Ave N Saint Cloud MN 56303-4140 Office: Veterans Affairs Med Ctr 4801 8th St N Saint Cloud MN 56303-2015

HOWARD, MAUREEN, writer; b. Bridgeport, Conn., June 28, 1930; d. William L. and Loretta (Burns) Kearns; m. Daniel F. Howard, Aug. 28, 1954 (div. 1967); 1 child, Loretta; m. David J. Gordon, April 2, 1968 (div.); m. Mark Probst, 1981. BA, Smith Coll., 1952. Lectr. English and drama U. Calif., Santa Barbara, 1968-69; lectr. English and creative writing New Sch. for Social Rsch., N.Y.C., 1967-68, 70-71, from 1974. Author: (novels) Not a Word About Nightingales, 1961, Bridgeport Bus, 1966, Before My Time, 1975, Grace Abounding, 1982 (PEN/Faulkner award for fiction nomination 1983), Expensive Habits, 1986, (PEN/Faulkner award for fiction nomination 1987), Natural History, 1992; (autobiography) Facts of Life, 1978 (Nat. Book Critics Circle award for gen. non-fiction 1980, Am. Book award for autobiography/biography nomination 1981); editor: Seven American Women Writers of the Twentieth Century, 1977, Contemporary American Essays, 1984. Recipient Literary Lion award N.Y. Pub. Libr., 1993; Guggenheim fellow, 1967-68, Radcliffe Inst. fellow, 1967-68, Ingram Merrill fellow Nat. Endowment Arts, 1988. *

HOWARD-CARTER, THERESA, archaeologist; b. Millbrook, N.Y., May 15, 1929; d. Clarence K. and Ann (Warren) H.; 1 child, Laura Coffin (dec.). AB, Syracuse U., 1950; MA, U. Pa., 1954; PhD in Classical and Near Eastern Archaeology, Bryn Mawr Coll, 1962. Head reprodns. dept. Univ. Mus., Phila., 1950-52; student asst. ethnology dept. Univ. Mus., 1953-55; research asst. Univ. Mus. (Mediterranean sect.), 1960-62, research assoc., 1962-64; dir. Iraq excavations Univ. Mus. (sect. Bibl. archaeology), 1964-66; teaching asst. Bryn Mawr Coll., 1961-62, departmental asst., 1962-63; ann. prof. Am. Sch. Oriental Research, Baghdad, 1965-66; vis. lectr. dept. Near Eastern studies Johns Hopkins U., Balt., 1969-71; asst. prof. Johns Hopkins U., 1971-75; mem. staff U. Pa. Gordion Expdn., Polatli, Turkey, 1955, 57; dir. U. Pa. Phoenician excavations, Lepcis Magna, Homs, Libya, 1960, 61, Cyrenaican Coastal Survey, U. Pa., 1962; asst. dir. Bryn Mawr Coll. excavations Kara Tash, Elmali, Turkey, 1963; co-dir. Tell al-Rimah Expdn., No. Iraq, 1964-66; collaborator for Univ. Mus. with Soprentendenza alle Antichitá di Napoli at Pithecusa, Lacco Ameno, Ischia, 1965; field dir. Sybaris project of U. Pa. in, Calabria, Italy, 1968; dir. Johns Hopkins expdns. to Syrian Euphrates Valley, 1972-74, to Arab-Iranian Gulf, 1972-74; research assoc. Near East sect. Univ. Mus., Phila., 1966-82, cons. scholar for Mesopotamia and Gulf, 1983—; chief adv. to Kuwait Nat. Mus., 1980—; mem. UNESCO Commn. on Rock Art. Contbr. articles to profl. jours. Bd. dirs. Theatre of Living Arts, Phila., 1964-67, chmn. women's com., 1964-65; docent coun. bd. Phila. Zoo, 1993—. Nat. Endowment for Humanities grantee, 1973, 74, 79; recipient Arents Pioneer medal Syracuse U., 1990. Fellow Mid East Studies Assn., Royal Geog. Soc., Archaeol. Inst. Am.; mem. Am. Oriental Soc., Am. Sch. Oriental Rsch., Brit. Sch. Archaeology in Iraq, Middle East Inst. Home: Grubbs Mill 1010 Valley Creek Rd West Chester PA 19380-1980 Office: U Pa Mus 33D And Spruce St Philadelphia PA 19104

HOWARD-ESPARZA, CATHERINE, human resources executive; b. Savannah, Ga., Feb. 23, 1960; d. Francis Xavier and Mary Bertha (Alvarez) Howard; children: Jennifer Gail, Lori Beth, Joseph Alfred. BLS in Sociology, St. Edward's Univ., 1992, MA in Human Resources Adminstrn., 1993—. Specialist Travis County Judge, 1980-86; pers. asst. Travis County Human Resources Mgmt. Dept., 1986-89, pers. analyst, 1989—; team leader Motorola, 1988-89. Leader Girl Scouts; pres. Child Inc., parent policy rep. Mem. Austin Human Resources Mgmt. Assn. (cert. 1992—), U.S. Dept. Aging Soc., Gerontology Club (pres.). Home: 1620 East 10th St Austin TX 78702 Office: City of Austin ECSD Solid Waste Svcs PO Box 1088 Austin TX 78767

HOWARD-PEEBLES, PATRICIA N., clinical cytogeneticist; b. Lawton, Okla., Nov. 24, 1941; d. J. Marion and R. Leona (prestidge) Howard; m. Thomas M. Peebles, Aug. 16, 1975. BSEd, U. Ctrl. Okla., 1963; student, Randolph-Macon Coll. Women, 1964; PhD in Zoology, U. Tex., 1969. Diplomate Am. Bd. Med. Genetics; cert. clin. cytogeneticist, med. geneticist. Sci. and history tchr. Piedmont (Okla.) Pub. Schs., 1963-64; biochem. technician biochemistry sect. biology divsn. Oak Ridge (Tenn.) Nat. Lab., 1964-66; instr. rsch. pediatrics dept. pediatrics, instr. cytotech. U. Okla. Health Scis. Ctr., Oklahoma City, 1971-72; asst. prof., dir. Cytogenetics Lab. U. So. Miss., Hattiesburg, 1973-77, assoc. prof., dir. Cytogenetics Lab., 1977-80; assoc. prof. dept. pub. health, staff Lab. Med. Genetics U. Ala., Birmingham, 1980-81; assoc. prof., dir. Cytogenetics Lab. dept. pathology U. Tex. Health Sci. Ctr., Dallas, 1981-85, prof., dir. Cytogenetics Lab., 1985-87; prof. dept. human genetics Med. Coll. Va., Richmond, 1987—; clin. cytogeneticist, dir. Postnatal Lab. Genetics & IVF Inst., Fairfax, Va., 1987—; Am. Cancer Soc. postdoctoral fellow dept. human genetics U. Mich. Med. Sch., Ann Arbor, 1969-70, dept. human genetics and devel. Coll. Physicians and Surgeons, Columbia U., N.Y.C., 1970-71; genetic cons. Ellisville (Miss.) State Sch., 1973-80; attending staff dept. pathology Parkland Meml. Hosp., Dallas County Hosp. Dist., 1981-87; mem. sci. adv. com. Fragile X Found., 1985—; mem. Internat. Standing Com. on Human Cytogenetic Nomenclature, 1991-2001. Contbr. articles to profl. jours., chpts. to books; reviewer Am. Jour. Human Genetics, Am. Jour. Med. Genetics, Clin. Genetics, Human Genetics. Fellow Am. Coll. Med. Genetics (founding mem.); mem. AAAS, Am. Soc. Human Genetics, Genetics Soc. Am., Assn. Cytogenetic Technologists, Tex. Genetics Soc. (chmn. planning com. ann. meeting 1984), Delta Kappa Gamma, Sigma Xi. Baptist. Office: Genetics & IVF Inst 3020 Javier Rd Fairfax VA 22031-4627

HOWARTH, SUSAN TEER, management executive, consultant, association executive; b. Amityville, N.Y., Mar. 28, 1951; d. Louis Peter and Nettie Sue (Chavers) Teer. BA magna cum laude, Fairfield U., 1973; MA, SUNY, Albany, 1974. Mgr. tng. employment programs non-profit orgs., 1975-80; dir. employment, tng. and tech. assistance Boston YWCA, 1980-84; v.p. Drake Beam Morin Inc., Boston, 1984-87; sr. v.p. Drake Beam Morin Inc., N.Y.C., 1987-90, group v.p., 1990-92; mgmt. cons. San Francisco, 1992—; NGO rep. to the UN; internat. devel. cons. Mem. Nat. Bd. YWCA of the U.S.A., N.Y.C., 1992—. Lehman fellow SUNY. Home: 2210 Jackson St # 701 San Francisco CA 94115

HOWATT, SISTER HELEN CLARE, library director; b. San Francisco, Apr. 5, 1927; d. Edward Bell and Helen Margaret (Kenney) H. BA, Holy Names Coll., 1949; MS in Libr. Sci., U. So. Calif., 1972; cert. advanced studies Our Lady of Lake U., 1966. Joined Order Sisters of the Holy Names, Roman Cath. Ch., 1945. Life teaching credential, life spl. svcs. credential, prin. St. Monica Sch., Santa Monica, Calif., 1957-60, St. Mary Sch., L.A., 1960-63; tchr. jr. high sch. St. Augustine Sch., Oakland, Calif., 1964-69; tchr. jr. high math St. Monica Sch., San Francisco, 1969-71, St. Cecilia Sch., San Francisco, 1971-77; libr. dir. Holy Names Coll., Oakland, Calif., 1977-94; activities dir. Collins Ctr. Sr. Svcs., 1994—. Contbr. math. curriculum San Francisco Unified Sch. Dist., Cum Notis Variorum, publ. Music Libr., U. Calif., Berkeley. Contbr. articles to profl. jours. NSF grantee, 1966, NDEA grantee, 1966. Mem. Cath. Libr. Assn. (chmn. No. Calif. elem. schs. 1971-72), Calif. Libr. Assn., ALA, Assn. Coll. and rsch. Librs. Home and Office: 2550 18th Ave San Francisco CA 94116

HOWE, FLORENCE, English educator, writer, publisher; b. N.Y.C., Mar. 17, 1929; d. Samuel and Frances (Stilly) Rosenfeld. A.B., Hunter Coll., 1950; A.M., Smith Coll., 1951; postgrad., U. Wis., 1951-54; D.H.L. (hon.), New Eng. Coll., 1977, Skidmore Coll., 1979, DePauw U., 1987, SUNY Coll. Old Westbury, 1992. Teaching asst. U. Wis., 1951-54; prof. English City Coll. and the Grad. Sch. CUNY, 1954-57; lectr. English Queens Coll., 1956-57; asst. prof. English Goucher Coll., 1960-71; prof. humanities and Am. studies SUNY-Old Westbury, 1971-87; prof. English City. Coll. and Grad. Sch., CUNY, 1987—; pres., dir. The Feminist Press at CUNY, 1970—; vis. prof. U. Utah, 1973, 75, U. Wash., 1974, John F. Kennedy Inst. Am. Studies Free U. Berlin, 1978, Oberlin Coll., 1978, Denison U., 1979, MLA Summer Inst. U. Ala., 1979, Coll. Wooster, 1980, Grad. Sch. Dept. English CUNY, 1986-87. Author: The Conspiracy of the Young, 1970, Seven Years Later: Women's Studies Programs in 1976, 1977, Myths of Coeducation: Selected Essays, 1964-1984, 1984; editor: (with Ellen Bass) No More Masks! An Anthology of Poems by Women, 1973, Women and the Power to Change, 1975, (with Nancy Hoffman) Women Working: An Anthology of Stories and Poems, 1979, (with Suzanne Howard, Mary Jo Boehm Strauss) Everywoman's Guide to Colleges and Universities, 1982; (with Marsha Saxton) With Wings: An Anthology of Literature by and About Disabled Women, 1987, An Anthology of 20th Century American Women Poets; co-editor: (with John Mack Faragher) Women and Higher Education in American History, 1988; editor: Tradition and the Talents of Women, 1991, No More Masks, 1993; mem. editorial bd. Women's Studies: An Interdisciplinary Jour., 1971—, SIGNS: Women in Culture and Society, 1974-80, Jour. Edn., 1976—, The Correspondence of Lydia Marie Child, 1977-81, Research in the Humanities, 1977—; contbr. essays to profl. jours. Recipient Mina Shaughnessy award Fund for Improvement of Post-Secondary Edn., 1982-83; NEH fellow, 1971-73; Ford Found. fellow, 1974-75; Fullbright fellow, India, 1977; Mellon fellow Wellesley Coll., 1979; U.S. Dept. State grantee, 1983, 93. Office: The Feminist Press at CUNY 311 E 94th St New York NY 10128-5603

HOWE, MAROLYN LOUISE, chemical engineer; b. Memphis, Jan. 17, 1957; d. William Chew and Lucretia Louise (Alldredge) H.; m. Gerald Francis Lenski, Feb. 16, 1985. BS in Chemistry, Christian Brothers Coll., Memphis, 1979; BS in Chem. Engring., Christian Brothers Coll., 1981. Registered profl. engr. in tng., Tex.; cert. asbestos inspector. Lectr. Christian Brothers Coll., Memphis, 1980-81, 93; petroleum engr. Texaco, USA, Midland, Tex., 1981-85; chem. engr. Hess Environ. Svcs., Inc., Hess Environ. Svcs., Inc., 1987-92; environ. project mgr. Fisher & Arnold, Inc., Memphis, 1992—; chem. engr., project mgr. Crittenden County Emergency Response Planning Com., Marion, Ark., 1988—. Vol. Alzheimer Day Care Ctr., Memphis, 1987-90, Crittenden Meml. Hosp., West Memphis, Ark., 1972-73; vol. asst. for waste water permitting City Atty. West Memphis, 1989; spl. adminstrv. asst. Mayor of Crawfordsville, 1990-93; mem. Collierville, Tenn. Design Rev. Commn. and Long Range Planning Steering Com. NSF rsch. fellow, 1974, 78. Mem. Soc. Petroleum Engrs., Nat. Assn. Corrosion Engrs. (cert. corrosion technologist), Am. Soc. Safety Engrs. Methodist. Office: Fisher & Arnold Inc 475 Jack Kramer Dr Memphis TN 38117-4359

HOWE, MARVINE HENRIETTA, newspaper reporter; b. Shanghai, China, Dec. 3, 1928; parents Am. citizens; d. James Lewis and Mary Scott (West) H. BLitt, Rutgers U., 1950. News broadcaster Radio Maroc, Rabat, Morocco, 1951-55; contbr. Brit. Broadcasting Corp., Rabat, 1952-55, McGraw-Hill World News, Morocco, 1958-62; stringer Time-Life, Algiers, Rabat, Lisbon, 1956-65, N.Y. Times, Algiers, Rabat, Lisbon, 1957-71; bur. chief N.Y. Times, Rio de Janeiro, 1972-75; corr. N.Y. Times, Portugal and Angola, 1975-76; bur. chief N.Y. Times, Beirut, Ankara, Athens, 1977-84; reporter Met. staff N.Y. Times, N.Y.C., 1984-94; freelance writer, 1994—; lectr. Lycee, Fez, Morocco, 1950-51, Univ. Ctr., Va., 1959, Rutgers U. Journalism Sch., 1991; del. Internat. Women's Media Conf., Washington, 1986. Author: The Prince and I or One Woman's Morocco, 1956; author travel articles; contbr. to travel guidebooks; contbr. articles to The Monitor, Scholastic, Middle East Jour., The Nation, New Republic, Africa Report, others. Recipient Poetry award Douglass Coll., 1950; Adalaide Zagoren fellow Rutgers U., 1991. Mem. Silurians, U.S.-China People's Friendship Assn. Democrat. Presbyterian. Home: 230 S Jefferson St Lexington VA 24450 Office: Alto Da Barra, Bloco D-4D, 2780 Oeiras Portugal

HOWE, TINA, playwright; b. N.Y.C., Nov. 21, 1937; d. Quincy and Mary (Post) H.; m. Norman L. Levy, Aug. 31, 1961; children: Eben, Dara. BA, Sarah Lawrence Coll., Bronxville, N.Y., 1959; LittD (hon.), Bowdoin Coll., Brunswick, 1988. Adj. prof. playwriting NYU, 1983—; vis. prof. Hunter Coll., N.Y.C., 1990—. Author: (plays) The Nest, 1969, Museum, 1976, Birth and After Birth, 1977, The Art of Dining, 1979, Appearances, 1982, Painting Churches, 1983, Coastal Disturbances, 1986 (Tony award nomination for best play 1987), Aproaching Zanzibar, 1989; publications include Coastal Disturbances: Four Plays by Tina Howe, 1989, Approaching Zanzibar, 1990, One Shoe Off, 1993. Nat. Endowment of the Arts fellow, 1985, Guggenheim fellow, 1990; Rockefeller grantee, 1984; recipient Obie award, 1983, Outer Critic's Circle award, 1983, Academy award in Lit Am. Acad. Arts and Letters, 1993. Fellow PEN, Writers Guild Am.; mem. Dramatists Guild (coun. mem. 1990—). Address: care Flora Robert Inc 157 W 57th St New York NY 10019-2210*

HOWELL, BONNIE HOWARD, hospital administrator; b. Ithaca, N.Y., Dec. 7, 1947; d. Robert Leon and Helen Elizabeth (Ryerson) Howard; children: Carolyn Elizabeth, Kathryn Helene. BS, Cornell U., 1970, MBA, 1972. Planning assoc. Areawide & Local Planning Health Action, Syraucse, N.YL, 1972-74; adminstr. Community Med. Ctr., Aurora, N.Y., 1974-76; asst. adminstr. Tompkins Community Hosp., Ithaca, 1974-79, pres., CEO, 1979—; bd. dirs. Tompkins County Trust Co. Contbr. articles to profl. pubis. Bd. dirs. United Way Tompkins County, Ithaca, 1986-88. Fellow Am. Coll. Healthcare Execs.; mem. Downtown Bus. Women, Rotary. Baptist. Home and Office: Tompkins Community Hosp 101 Dates Dr Ithaca NY 14850-1342

HOWELL, CATHERINE JEANINE, visual arts educator; b. Benton, Ill., Apr. 15, 1935; d. Lloyd William Reed and Lena Pearl (Armstrong) Goodin; m. Charles Lindy Barnfield, Apr. 13, 1950 (div. Apr. 23, 1973); children: Alan Reed, Robert, Timothy Michael; stepchildren: Crystal Lee, Carla Sue. A in Technol., So. Ill. U., 1962, BA, 1968, MS in Edn., 1976, postgrad. specialist, 1986. Cert. educator and supr., Ill. Clk. Kroger, Benton, Ill., 1957-60; elem. tchr. Benton Elem. Sch. Dist. #47, 1968-70; secondary art tchr. Marion (Ill.) Cmty. Unit Sch. Dist. # 2, 1970-94, ret., 1994; art instr. John A. Logan Community Coll., Carterville, Ill., 1975-89, vocat.-edn. art instr., 1992; cons. in field. Prin. work includes Strings of Creation, 1988, Portrait Sketch of Brenda Edgar, 1991. Art judge DuQuoin (Ill.) State Fair, 1990-91; mem. Ill. State Bd. Edn. Leadership conf., 1989-90, 90-91, 92, 93, 94; co-founder Downstate Art Educator's Assn. Recipient Award of Excellence, 1988, Sch. Bell award Williamson Co. ESR, 1988-89, Outstanding Art Educator award Ill. Alliance for Arts Edn., 1988, Ill. Art Educator award, 1989, Nat. Ill. Art Educator award, 1990, Senate REsolution Senator James Rea, 1989, Proclamation Gov. James Thompson, 1990. Mem. AAUW, Ill. Art Edn. Assn. (sec. dir. 1990), So. Ill. U. Alumni Life, Nat. Art Edn., Ill. Edn. Assn., NEA, Delta Kappa Gamma Tchr. Honor Soc., Phi Kappa Phi. Home: 3000 Woodlawn Pl Marion IL 62959-4852

HOWELL, JANET D., state legislator; b. Washington, May 7, 1944; d. Edward Fulton and Elsie (Lightbown) Denison; m. A. Hunt Howell; children: Eric, Brian. BA, Oberlin Coll., 1966; MA, U. Pa., 1968. Tchr. Phila. Pub. Schs., 1968-69; legis. asst. Gen. Assembly, Va., 1989-91; senator Va. State Senate, 1992—. Chair Fairfax County (Va.) Social Svcs. Bd., 1979-82, State Bd. Social Svcs., Va., 1986-91, Reston (Va.) Transp. Com., 1986-91; pres. Reston Community Assn., 1982-85, Citizen of Yr., 1990. Named Restonian of Yr., Reston Times, 1984, Virginian of Yr., Va. Assn. Social Workers, 1991. Democrat. Mem. Unitarian Ch. Office: Va Senate State Capitol Richmond VA 23219

HOWELL, JEANETTE DORIS RATHBURN, elementary education educator; b. Cazenovia, N.Y., July 10, 1936; d. Adelbert Wallace Rathburn and Erna Joan Matilda Reetz; m. Louis A. Howell, Sept. 16, 1963; children: William Henry, Joan Elizabeth Howell Loyd. AB Gen. Home Econs., Brenau Coll. U., 1960; BA in Edn., U. Ga., 1964. Tchr. fourth grade Hall County Bd. Edn., Gainesville, Ga., 1961-62, Oconee County Bd. Edn., Watkinsville, Ga., 1964-65; part-time tchr. Clarke County Bd. Edn., Athens, Ga., 1979—. Mem. Edn. Com. Athens, Ga., 1993-94; active Athens 1996 Olympic Com., 1994— Jeannette Rankin Found., Athens. Mem. AAUW (Am. Fellowship award 1993), LWV, Order Eastern Star (Outstanding Officer award 1993-94), Phi Delta Kappa. Home: 1710 Mars Hill Rd Watkinsville GA 30677-4840

HOWELL, JEFFREY FODEN, educational administrator, financial consultant; b. Middletown, N.Y., Nov. 3, 1952; d. James Arthur and Beverley (Foden) H.; m. William H. Press, Apr. 19, 1991; 1 child, James Alexander Howell. BA, Antioch Coll., 1975; M.Pub. and Pvt. Mgmt., Yale U., 1981. Assoc. emerging bus. Coopers and Lybrand, Boston, 1982-84; store mgr. The Stop and Shop Cos., Boston, 1984-86; assoc. dir. adminstrn. Harvard Coll. Observatory, Cambridge, Mass., 1986-88; asst. dean fin. ops. Harvard U., Cambridge, Mass., 1988-92; exec. search cons. Auerbach Assoc., Boston, 1993—; fin. cons. Numerical Recipes Software, Cambridge, 1991—; founder Howell Cons., Cambridge, 1992—. Fin. com. Shelter, Inc., Cambridge, 1992—; speakers com. Planned Parenthood Mass., Cambridge, 1994—. Mem. Nat. Assn. Women Deans, Nat. Coun. U. Rsch. Adminstrs. Office: Howell Cons 1 Avon Pl Cambridge MA 02140-3606

HOWELL, JOYCE ANN, lawyer; b. Haddonfield, N.J., Dec. 15, 1955; d. Harry O. and Mary Ann (Beaudet) H. BS, Shippensburg U., 1977, MLS, 1980; MA, St. John's Coll., Annapolis, Md., 1983; JD, Rutgers U., 1986. Bar: N.J. 1986, Pa. 1986, D.C. 1988, U.S. Dist. Ct. N.J. 1986, U.S. Dist. Ct. Pa. 1993, U.S. Ct. Appeals (3d cir.) 1987, U.S. Mil. Ct. Appeals 1987. Law clk. to presiding judge N.J. Chancery Ct., Atlantic City, 1986-87; assoc. Riker, Danzig, Scherer, Hyland & Perretti, Morristown, N.J., 1987-92, Levin and Hluchan, Voorhees, N.J., 1992-93; atty. office regional counsel U.S. EPA Region 3, Phila., 1993—. Staff mem. Rutgers Law Jour., 1985-86. NEH fellow, 1981, Roothbert Found. fellow, 1982, 83; Rutgers Law Sch. Alumni grantee, 1985. Mem. N.J. Bar Assn., N.J. Women Lawyers Assn. (v.p. 1989-90, pres. 1990-93). Democrat. Mem. Soc. of Friends.

HOWELL, PAMELA ANN, federal agency professional; b. Pensacola, Fla., Mar. 12, 1957; d. Thomas Pugh and Edith Corinne (McGowan) H.; children: Corinne Elizabeth Howell Meadows. BS, Mississippi Coll., 1978. Benefit authorizer Social Security Adminstrn., Birmingham, Ala., 1979—. H.S. coach Tabernacle Christian Sch., Gardendale, Ala., 1993—. Mem. Am. Fedn. Govt. Employees (v.p.). Republican. Baptist. Home: 712 Cherry Brook Rd Kimberly AL 35091

HOWELL, ROSALIND ROSEMARIE, high school guidance director; b. Gary, Ind., Feb. 14, 1928; d. Ervand and Maran (Murodian) Marjanian; m. Donald Joel Howell, Nov. 5, 1960; children: Marilyn Ann Howell Schenkel, Donald J. Jr. BS, Ind. U., 1953, MS, 1955. Cert. tchr., adminstr., guidance. English tchr. Hobart (Ind.) Jr. H.S., 1953-58, vice prin., 1958-61; English tchr. Hobart H.S., 1963-67, guidance dir., 1967—; mem. adv. com. freshmen Ind. U., Bloomington, 1988—; com. chairperson North Ctrl. Assn. Sch. Evaluation.; com. chairperson Ind. State Pub. Sch. Evaluation. Bd. dirs. local Roman Cath. Ch. Recipient Outstanding Achievement award Football Ofcl.'s Assn., 1993, Family of Yr. award Ind. C. of C., 1983. Mem. NEA, Ind. State Tchrs.' Assn., Hobart Tchrs.' Assn., Ind. Assn. Coll. Admission Counselors, Ind. U. Sch. Edn. Alumni Assn. (life), Ind. U. Alumni Assn., Ind. Restructuring 2000 H.S., Hobart Football Booster Club (bd. dirs., Achievement award 1993), Hobart Exch. Club (hon.). Home: 915 E 8th St Hobart IN 46342

HOWELL, SARAH SMITH, author, artist; b. Birmingham, Ala., Mar. 18, 1929; d. Willie Lofton and Sarah Berta (Masters) Smith; BS in Home Econs., U. Louisville, 1951; MS, U. Tenn., 1967; postgrad. U. Ala., Samford U., David Lipscomb Coll., Arrowmont Sch. Arts and Crafts, U. Tenn. (Nashville); m. A. Crawford Howell, Mar. 18, 1949; 1 child, Cynthia Ann Howell Saunders. Art therapist, tchr. behavior modification Nashville Evaluation Ctr., 1968-69; home economist utilities, 1954-56, 63-64; dietitian Nashville Gen. and Ky. Bapt. hosps., 1951-52, 57-59; regular participant in craft feature Noon Show, TV, 1978; author, artist, Franklin, Tenn., 1969—; activities dir. Belmont Plaza Retirement Ctr., 1980-81; nutritionist Tenn. Dept. Health and Environ., 1983-85, ednl. cons., 1985—; adv. bd. Tenn. Com. Arts for Handicapped, 1985; weaving exhibited Tenn. State Mus. Archives; premier exhibitor Mid. Tenn. Com. Women in the Arts, 1991; one-woman show Botanic Hall Cheekwood Botanical and Fine Art Ctr., Nashville, 1992. Charter mem. Williamson County Heart Assn.; adv. bd. Tenn. Com. Arts for Handicapped; active Nashville Nutrition Coun.; past chair bd. dirs. Very Spl. Arts Tenn., chair, 1990-91; leader HEAR Group. Mem. Nashville Artist Guild (past pres., dir.), Tenn. Artist Craftsmen Assn., Nashville Home Econs. Assn., Tenn. Assn. Craft Artists, Nat. Mus. Women in Arts, U. Louisville Mid. Tenn. Alumni Assn. (treas.), Grossmere Mus. Women in Arts, Nat. Nature Conservancy, Tenn. Nature Conservancy, Williamson County Arts Coun. Baptist. Clubs: Cheekwood Fine Arts Ctr. Author: Creative Crafts for Self-Expression, 1978, Home Cooking in a Hurry, 1985, More Home Cooking in a Hurry, 1986. Home: Rte 14 609 Bois Darc Ln Franklin TN 37064-4763

HOWELLS, MURIEL GURDON SEABURY (MRS. WILLIAM WHITE HOWELLS), volunteer; b. White Plains, N.Y., May 3, 1910; d. William Marston and Katharine Emerson (Hovey) Seabury; student Chapin Sch., 1928; m. William White Howells, June 15, 1929; children: Muriel Gurdon Howells Metz, William Dean. Founder Brit. War Relief Soc., Madison, Wis., 1941, pres., 1941-43; apptd. visitor, dept. decorative arts and sculpture Boston Mus. Fine Arts, 1955-72, dept. Am. decorative arts, 1972—; ladies com. Inst. Contemporary Art, Boston, 1955-68; bd. dirs. Boston br. English-Speaking Union, 1955-80; a founder, trustee Strawbery Banke, Inc., Portsmouth, N.H., 1958-75, overseer, 1975-81, hon. overseer, 1981—; a founder, mem. steering com. Guild, 1959-91; bd. dirs. Garden Club Am., 1959-62, nat. chmn. medal award com., 1962-65, judge flower arrangements; pres. Piscataqua Garden Club, 1952-54; mem. Harvard Solomon Islands Expdn., Malaita, 1968; 1st chmn. Boston chpt. Venice Com., Internat. Fund for Monuments, 1970-71; vice chmn. Boston chpt. Save Venice Inc., 1971-77, mem. exec. com., 1971-89, hon. chmn., 1989—. Recipient King's medal for Service in the Cause of Freedom (Britain), 1946; Historic Preservation award, zone 1 Garden Club Am., 1976. Mem. Nat. Soc. Colonial Dames N.H., Soc. Preservation New Eng. Antiquities (mem. Maine council 1976-78). Clubs: Women's Travel (pres. 1967-69), Chilton (Boston); Colony (N.Y.C.). Home: 11 Lawrence Ln Kittery Point ME 03905-5104 also: 274 Beacon St Boston MA 02116-1240

HOWES, ANN M., artist, cultural organization administrator; b. Boston, Dec. 24, 1937; d. Allen Hunt and Alice Mayhew (Davies) Mathewson; m. Theodore Chapman Howes Jr., Dec. 27, 1958; children: Theodore Chandler, Suzanne Howes Pachico. AA, Centenary Coll. for Women, Hackettstown, N.J., 1957. Adminstr. Upper Marion Cultural Ctr., King of Prussia, Pa., 1970—, instr., 1990-94; freelance fine artist King of Prussia, Pa., 1970—; instr. Greater Norristown (Pa.) Art League, 1985-94, art workshops, Pa., 1993—. Pres., bd. dirs. Rittenhouse Sq. Fine Art Assn., Phila., 1981-90. Recipient Grumbacher award Phila. Sketch Club, 1985, Merit award La. Watercolor Soc., 1993. Mem. Pa. Water Color Soc. (award 1990), Pitts. Water Color Soc. (awards 1987, 93), Knickerbocker Artists USA (Bronze Medallion award 1979), Watercolor West (award 1988), Phila. Water Color Club (bd. dirs., sec. 1989—, award 1990). Home: 383 Hillside Rd King of Prussia PA 19406

HOWES, GLORIA, state legislator. BA, West Tex. U.; MA, U. N.Mex. County mgr. McKinley County, N.Mex., county comr.; mem. N.Mex State Senate from 4th dist. Democrat. Address: 509 Lacima Rd Gallup NM 87301-5738 Office: NM State Senate State Capitol Santa Fe NM 85703*

HOWES, PADDY RUDD (LILIAN B. HOWES), writer, editor; b. Coventry, Eng., May 20, 1909; came to U.S., 1925, naturalized, 1941; d. John Alexander and Mary Elizabeth (Doherty) Rudd; student Liverpool Coll., Huyton, Eng., 1920-25; Oxford U., Sr. Sch. Cert., 1925; student U. Akron, 1934-35, U. Cin., 1941-42, Northwestern U., 1950; m. William R. Howes, Sept. 23, 1946. With Firestone Tire & Rubber Co., Akron, Ohio, 1926-36; sec. Children's Hosp. Research Found., Cin., 1936-42; sr. editor W.B. Saunders Co., Phila., 1942-46; fgn. corre. Country Gentleman Mag., Eng., 1946-48; manuscript editor Jour. Am. Dental Assn., Chgo., 1949-50, news editor, 1950-51; staff writer Survey of Med. Edn., Chgo., 1951-53; free lance writer, editor, publs. cons., Chgo., 1953-56, Phila., 1956-72, Harwich, Mass., 1972—. Bd. dirs. Cape Cod Family and Children's Service, Cape Cod chpt. UN Assn. U.S.A.; corp. mem. bd. dirs. United Way of Cape Cod, 1978-82; mem. Cape Cod Community Council, 1975-82. Mem. Women in Communications (life, Chgo. chpt. pres. 1952-53 pres. Phila. chpt. 1962), Phila. Art Alliance, Asso. Country Women of World (life mem.; exec. com. 1946-48, press officer 1946). Writer-Collaborator Medical Schools in the United States at Mid-Century, 1953. Contbr. articles to mags., newspapers and profl. jours. Address: 328 Bank St Harwich MA 02645-2705

HOWETH, DIANE KATHRYN, mental health nurse; b. Spalding, Nebr., Sept. 22, 1956; d. Joseph J. and Ethel A. (Purdy) Happ; m. Thomas E. Howeth, Sept. 19, 1987; children: Bernadette A., Louis Thomas. ADN, U. Nebr., Omaha, 1977, postgrad., 1993—. Cert. instr. in mng. assaultive patients. Charge nurse Luth. Gen. Hosp., Omaha, 1977-79; charge nurse psychiat. inpatient ICU Richard Young Hosp., Omaha, 1979-88, clin. supr. psychiat inpatient ICU, 1988-92, clin. supr. psychiat. gen. adult programs, 1992-93, staff nurse adult partial program, 1993—. Mem. Omaha Cath. Nurses Assn.

HOWETH, LYNDA CAROL, small business owner; b. Okemah, Okla., Sept. 19, 1949; d. Clyde Leon and Hattie Arlene (Hymer) Williamson; children: Amanda B. Knowles, Harold W., Jennifer M. Student, Okla. State Tech. U., 1969, South Okla. City C.C., 1974. Mgr. five stores European Flower Markets, Oklahoma City, 1972-76; dist. sales rep. Profl. Office Systems, Inc., Oklahoma City, 1976-81; exec., owner Bus. Med. Systems, Inc., Oklahoma City, 1981—. V.p. dist. 41 Sch. Bd. Western Heights, Oklahoma City, 1991-94, pres., 1994—; founding mem. steering com. Okla. Bus. Health Inst., 1994. Mem. Nat. Sch. Bd. Assn., Okla. State Sch. Bd. Assn., Vital Info. Profls. (v.p., treas. 1988-90), Med. Tips Club (v.p., treas. 1990-91). Democrat. Home: 3328 SW 47th St Oklahoma City OK 73119-4325 Office: Bus Med systems Inc Bldg A-200 1601 SW 89th St Oklahoma City OK 73159-6357

HOWIE, FELICIA BARLOWE, blood services director; b. Oxford, N.C., Mar. 19, 1965; d. Felix Russell and Goldie Janet (Hicks) Barlowe; m. Edward Fulton Howie, Sept. 1, 1990. BA, U. N.C., 1987. Dining rm. mgr. Caravelle Resorts, Myrtle Beach, S.C., 1985-86; pub. svc. announcement dir. WRFX Radio Inc., Charlotte, N.C., 1987-88; pre-sch. tchr. Selwyn Ave. Child Care Ctr., Charlotte, N.C., 1988-91; pre-Kindergarten tchr. Matthews (N.C.) Country Day, 1991-92; blood svcs. dir. ARC, Monroe, N.C., 1992—. Mem. Union County Players. Recipient Aubrey Lee Brooks scholarship Aubrey Lee Brooks Found., 1983; named Nat. Merit Scholarship finalist, 1982, Morehead Scholarship finalist, 1982, N.C. Gov.'s Sch. finalist, 1982, N.C. State Champion, Assn. Drug Free Powerlifting, 1993. Mem. NAFE, Gen. Alumni Assn.-U. N.C.-Chapel Hill, Monroe Shag Club. Methodist. Home: 3802 Parkwood School Rd Monroe NC 28112-7546 Office: American Red Cross-Union Co 608 E Franklin St Monroe NC 28112-5702

HOWITT, PAMELA SUSAN, psychologist; b. Guelph, Ont., Can., June 29, 1953; came to U.S., 1978; d. John Edwin and Vera (Jennings) H. BA in Psychology, Brock U., St. Catharines, Ont., 1975; MA in Psychology, U. Windsor, Ont., 1977, PhD in Clin. Psychology, 1984. Lic. psychologist, Mich. Staff psychologist Wayne County Probate Ct. Clinic, Detroit, 1979-84, asst. dir., 1984-89; dir. Oakland County Probate Ct. Clinic, Pontiac, Mich., 1989—; pvt. practice, Livonia, Mich., 1986—; mem. faculty Mich. Jud. Inst., Lansing, 1992-93, 93-94. Contbr. articles to profl. jours. Bd. dirs. Child Abuse and Neglect Coun. Oakland County, Pontiac, 1992—; mem. childrens task force Mich. State Bar, Lansing, 1994. Recipient Gov. Gen.'s medal Brock U., 1975; Rose Horne scholar, 1975, Ont. Govt. scholar, 1975, 76, 77. Mem. APA, Nat. Assn. Ct. Mgrs., Nat. Assn. Juvenile and Family Ct. Judges, Mich. Psychol. Assn., Mich. Assn. Juvenile Ct. Adminstrs., Mich. Soc. for Forensic Psychology. Office: Oakland County Probate Ct Psychol Clinic 1200 N Telegraph Rd Pontiac MI 48341-1032

HOWL, JOANNE HEALEY, veterinarian; b. Mariemont, Ohio, Mar. 16, 1957; d. Joseph Daniel and Claire Helen (Baillargeon) H.; m. Arthur Wesley Howl, May 12, 1990. DVM, U. Tenn., 1987. Groom Salvi Stables, Meadowlands, Pa., 1977-78; weaver Minnewawa Mfg., Knoxville, Tenn., 1979-81; various positions U. Tenn., 1981-83; sr. lab. animal technician Lab Animal Facility, Knoxville, 1983-84; gnotobiology technician U. Tenn., Knoxville, 1984-86; assoc. vet. Mynatt Vet. Clinic, Knoxville, 1987-89; veterinary med. officer U.S. Dept. of Agr. Animal and Plant Health Inspection Svcs., Raleigh, N.C., 1989-90; owner Creature Comfort Veterinary Relief Svc., Laurel, Md., 1991—. Mem. Am. Vet. Med. Assn., Am. Animal Hosp. Assn., Am. Assn. Feline Practitioners. Roman Catholic. Home and Office: 9222 Canterbury Riding Laurel MD 20723-1424

HOWLAND, BETTE, writer; b. Chgo., Jan. 28, 1937; d. Sam and Jessie (Berger) Sotonoff; m. Howard C. Howland (div.); children—Frank, Jacob. B.A., U. Chgo., 1955. Assoc. prof. com. social thought U. Chgo., 1993—. Author: W-3, 1972; Blue in Chicago, 1978 (1st prize Friends of Am. Writers); Things to Come and Go, 1983. Fellow Rockefeller Found., 1969, Guggenheim Found., 1978, Nat. Endowment for the Arts, 1981, MacArthur Found., 1984. Jewish. Address: PO Box 405 Union Pier MI 49129-0405

HOWLAND, JOAN SIDNEY, law librarian, law educator; b. Eureka, Calif., Apr. 9, 1951; d. Robert Sidney and Ruth Mary Howland. BA, U. Calif., Davis, 1971; MA, U. Tex., 1973; MLS, Calif. State U., San Jose, 1975; JD, Santa Clara (Calif.) U., 1983. Assoc. librarian for pub. svcs. Stanford (Calif.) U. Law Library, 1975-83, Harvard U. Law Library, Cambridge, Mass., 1983-86; dep. dir. U. Calif. Law Library, Berkeley, 1986-92; dir. law libr., prof. law U. Minn. Sch. of Law, 1992—. Questions and answers column editor Law Libr. Jour., 1986—; mgmt. column editor Trends in Law Libr. Mgmt. & Tech., 1987-94. Mem. ALA, Am. Assn. Law Librs. (chmn. edn. com. 1987-90), Am. Indian Libr. Assn. (treas. 1992—), Spl. Libr. Assn., Am. Law Inst. Office: U Minn Law Sch 229 19th Ave S Minneapolis MN 55455-0400

HOWLETT, PHYLLIS LOU, athletics conference administrator; b. Indianola, Iowa, Oct. 23, 1932; d. James Clarence and Mabel L. (Fisher) Hickman; m. Jerry H. Howlett, Jan. 2, 1955 (dec.); children: Timothy A., Jane A. Field; m. Ronlin Royer, Dec. 30, 1977. BA, Simpson Coll., 1954. Tchr. Oskaloosa (Iowa) High Sch., 1954-55; psychometrist Drake U., Des Moines, 1956-57, asst. to men's athletics dir., 1974-79; asst. dir. athletics U. Kans., Lawrence, 1979-82; asst. commr. Big Ten Conf., Park Ridge, Ill., 1982—; mem. NCAA football TV com., 1980-87, chmn. com. on women's athletics 1987-94, exec. com., 1990-95, women's golf com., 1983-89, spl. com. women's basketball TV, 1989-90, chair com. for women's corp. mktg., 1990-94, Divsn. I championship com., 1990-95, chair task force on gender equity, 1992-94, exec. dir. search com., NCAA, 1993, spl. com. divsn. I football playoff, adminstrv. com., 1995—, joint policy bd., 1995—; sec., treas. NCAA, 1995—. Chmn. Iowa Commn. Status of Women, 1976-79; pres. Vol. Bur. of Greater Des Moines, 1969-70; chair Arts and Recreation Coun. of Greater Des Moines, 1975; pres. Iowa Children's and Family Svcs., 1973; nat. pres. Assn. Vol. Burs., Inc., 1972-73, svc. award. Inducted into Simpson Coll. Hall of Fame. Mem. Nat. Assn. Dirs. of Collegiate Athletics (exec. com. 1986-90, award for adminstrv. excellence), Coun. Collegiate Women Athletic Adminstrs., Simpson Coll. Alumni (Achievement award 1988). Republican. Office: 1500 Higgins Rd Park Ridge IL 60068-5735

HOWLETT, STEPHANIE ANN, home care equipment sales representative, nurse; b. Kansas City, Kans., Dec. 23, 1957; d. Wayne Stewart and Anna Marie (Barancik) H. AA, Kansas City Community Coll., 1979. RN. Critical care nurse Providence-St. Margarets Health Ctr., Kansas City, Kans., 1979-82; primary pvt. duty nurse Quality Care In, Kansas City, Mo., 1980-81; dir. nursing Profl. Nursing Service, Kansas City, Mo., 1981-86; med. services cons. Crawford Health and Rehab. Services, Kansas City, Mo., 1986; sales rep. HOMEDCO, Lenexa, Kans., 1986-92, mem. presidents adv. coun., 1986-92; mem. adv. bd. Olsten Health Care Svcs., Kansas City, Mo., 1986-92, utilization rev. com., 1986-92, budget com., 1987. Mem. Jr. League, Wyandotte and Johnson County, 1991. Named one of Outstanding Young Women Am., 1987. Mem. NAFE, Nat. Rehab. Assn., Assn. Rehab. Nurses, Support Hospice Oncology Profls., Kansas City Met. Discharge Coords., Kansas City Regional Homecare Assn. (edn. com., infusion therapy com.), Kiwanis Club of Lenexa (bd. dirs.), Nat. Fedn. of the Blind. Republican. Home: 10507 College Ave Kansas City MO 64137-1763

HOWORTH, LUCY SOMERVILLE, lawyer; b. Greenville, Miss., July 1; d. Robert and Nellie (Nugent) Somerville; m. Joseph Marion Howorth, Feb. 16, 1928. A.B., Randolph-Macon Woman's Coll., 1916; postgrad., Columbia U., 1918; J.D. summa cum laude, U. Miss., 1922. Bar: Miss. 1922, U.S. Supreme Ct. 1934. Asst. in psychology Randolph-Macon Woman's Coll., 1916-17; gauge insp. Allied Bur. Air Prodn., N.Y.C., 1918; indsl. research nat. bd. YWCA, 1919-20; gen. practice law Howorth & Howorth, Cleveland, Greenville and Jackson, Miss., 1922-34; U.S. commr. So. Jud. Dist. Miss., 1927-31; assoc. mem. Bd. Vet. Appeals, Washington, 1934-43; legis. atty. VA, 1943-49; v.p., dir. VA Employees Credit Union, 1937-49; assoc. gen. counsel War Claims Commn., 1949-52, dep. gen. counsel, 1952-53, gen. counsel, 1953-54; ptnr. James Somerville & Assocs. (overseas trade and devel.), 1954-55; atty. Commn. on Govt. Security, 1956-57; pvt. practice law Cleveland, Miss., 1958—; mem. nat. bd. cons. Women's Archives, Radcliffe Coll.; mem. lay adv. com. study profl. nursing Carnegie Corp. N.Y., 1947-48; chmn. Miss. State Bd. Law Examiners, 1924-28; mem. Miss. State Legislature, 1932-36, chmn. com. pub. lands, 1932-36; treas. Com. for Econ. Survey Miss., 1928-30; mem. Research Commn. Miss., 1930-34. Editor: Fed. Bar Assn. News, 1944; assoc. editor: Fed. Bar Assn. Jour., 1943-44; editor: (with William M. Cash) My Dear Nellie-Civil War Letters (William L. Nugent), 1977; contbr. articles profl. jours. Keynote speaker White House Conf. on Women in Postwar Policy Making, 1944, at conf. on opening 81st Congress. Recipient Alumnai Achievment award Randolph-Macon Woman's Coll., 1981, Lifetime Achievmenet award Schlesinger Libr. of Radcliffe Coll., 1983; named for her outstanding lifetime achievments by Senate Concurrrent Resolution, adopted by Senate and Ho. of Reps., 1984; recipient Excellence medal Miss. U. for Women, 1989. Mem. AAUW (nat. dir., 2d v.p. 1951-55, mem. found. 1960-63), Nat. Fedn. Bus. and Profl. Women's Clubs (nat. dir.; rep. to internat. 1939, chmn. internat. conf. 1946), Nat. Assn. Women Lawyers, Miss. Library Assn. (life), Miss. Hist. Soc. (dir. 1982—, Merit award 1983), DAR, Daus. Am. Colonists, Am. Legion Aux. (past sec. Miss. dept.), Assembly Women's Orgns. for Nat. Security (chmn. 1951-52), Phi Beta Kappa, Pi Gamma Mu, Phi Alpha Delta, Alpha Omicron Pi (Wyman award 1985), Delta Kappa Gamma, Omicron Delta Kappa, Phi Kappa Phi (hon.). Democrat (del. nat. conv., 1932). Methodist. Club: Soroptimist (Washington). Address: 515 S Victoria Ave Cleveland MS 38732-3738

HOWREY, LINDA MCKAY, medical reimbursement consultant; b. Holden, Mass., Sept. 18, 1953; d. R. Bruce and Jean Elizabeth (Court) McKay; 1 child, Matthew Bruce; m. Gregg E. Howrey, May 5, 1990; stepchildren: Jamie, Amanda. Student, North Adams State Coll., 1971-73; BSA, Coll. St. Mary, Omaha, 1985. Cert. procedural coder. Photographer Ea. Photo Labs., Thomaston, Conn., 1974-76; clin. mgr. Pulmonary Med. Specialists, Omaha, 1980-85; billing supr. Nebr. Meth. Hosp., Omaha, 1985-86; adminstrv. supr. Lincoln Liberty Life Ins., Omaha, 1986-88; mgr., adminstr. Sloan Enterprises, Omaha, 1989-90; reimbursement specialist Profl. Mgmt. MW, Omaha, 1990-92; reimbursement cons., 1992-93; owner, pres. Healthcare Resources, Omaha, 1993—; instr. Met. Tech. Community Coll., Omaha, 1985—; speaker at profl. confs. and meetings. Student adv. bd. Coll. St. Mary, 1983, 84; mem. Nebr. UB-82 com., Lincoln, 1985, 86. Mem. Am. Guild Patient Accts., Bus. Forms Mgmt. Assn. (chpt. pres. 1988-89, nat. chair 1989-90), ABWA, Am. Assn. Med. Assts., Am. Acad. Procedural Coders (nat. adv. bd. 1994, cert. 1993, CEU chmn.). Office: 200 Bank of Nebraska Mall Omaha NE 68105

HOWSE, CAROLE SUZETTE, real estate company official, planning consultant; b. Haines City, Fla., Apr. 18, 1963; d. Barney Edwin and Carole (Sexton) Veal; m. Ronald S. Howse, Dec. 21, 1990. AA, Valencia (Fla.) C.C., 1982; 22BA, Fla. So. Coll., 1984; MA in Urban and Regional Planning, U. Fla., 1986. Assoc. planner North Ctrl. Fla. Regional Planning Coun., Gainesville, 1986-88; sales and mktg. ofcl. Oscola Brokerage Co., Kissimmee, Fla., 1988—; planning cons. Ron Howse, P.A., St. Cloud, Fla., 1989—. Chmn., mem. St. Cloud Planning and Zoning Bd., 1988-91; mem. task force Leadership Oscola, 1988-92; bd. dirs. Jr. Achievement, 1989-91, Osceola Ctr. for Arts, Kissimmee, 1990-92. Mem. Osceola Assn. Realtors, St. Cloud C. of C. (bd. dirs. 1989—, pres. 1990-91). Republican. Home: PO Box 701323 Saint Cloud FL 34770

HOWSE, JENNIFER LOUISE, foundation administrator; b. Glendale, Calif., Jan. 31, 1945; d. Benjamin McCausland and Patricia Louise (Naylor) H. PhD in Linguistics, Fla. State U., 1973; LHD (hon.), SUNY, Bklyn., 1990. Rsch. asst., instr. Inst. Human Devel. Coll. Edn., Fla. State U., Tallahassee, 1967-69; dir. planning and evaluation Wakulla County (Fla.) Sch. System, 1969-72; dir. NARC/HEW Liaison Project Nat. Assn. for Retarded Citizens, Govtl. Affairs Office, Washington, 1972-73; dir. Developmental Disabilities Bur., dir. Bur. Tech. Assistance and Regulation Fla. Dept. Health and Rehab. Svcs., Tallahassee, 1973-75; exec. dir. Willowbrook Rev. Panel, N.Y.C., 1975-78; assoc. commr. N.Y. State Office Mental Retardation and Developmental Disabilities, N.Y.C., 1978-80; state commr. for mental retardation Dept. Pub. Welfare, Harrisburg, Pa., 1980-85; exec. dir. Greater N.Y. chpt. March of Dimes Birth Defects Found., N.Y.C., 1985-89; pres. March of Dimes Birth Defects Found., White Plains, N.Y., 1990—; advisor Ctr. for Family Life in Sunset Park, Bklyn., 1992—. Bd. dirs. Salk Inst., La Jolla, Calif., Nat. Health Coun., Washington, Barrier Island Trust, Tallahassee; mem. Kaiser Commn. on Future of Medicaid, Balt., 1992—. Office: March Dimes Birth Defects Found 1275 Mamaroneck Ave White Plains NY 10605-5201*

HOWZE, LINDER GAIL, school system administrator; b. Cleveland, Miss., Mar. 5, 1958; d. Eligiah and Minnie (Hooper) H. BS, Miss. Valley State U., Itta Bena, 1980; M, Delta State U., 1981, Specialist, 1986. Lic. tchr. secondary edn., adminstrn., supervision, elem. and secondary prin., sch. psychologist, gifted edn. Tchr. spl. edn. Cleveland Pub. Sch., 1980-86; tchr. gifted Mt. Bayou (Miss.) Pub. Schs., 1986-88, sch. psychologist, 1988-89, asst. supt., 1990—; elem. prin. West Point (Miss.) Sch. Dist., 1988-89; cons. Cove Knowledge Found., Charlottesville, Va., 1992—, Psychol. Corp., San Antonio, 1991—. Pub. rels. dir. Internat. Pentecostal Young Peoples Aux., Indpls., 1991-93. Recipient Kapan Nat. Edn. award, 1986, Staff Devel. Leadership award, Cleveland, 1986. Mem. NAACP, Nat. Coun. Exceptional Children, Nat. Assn. Learning Disabled, Nat. Assn. Supervision and Curriculum, Miss. Assn. Sch. Psychologists, Miss. Assn. Staff Devel., Miss. Assn. Asst. Supts. Democrat. Pentecostal Apostolic. Home: 1125 Morgan St Cleveland MS 38732-3513 Office: Mt Bayou Pub Sch PO Box 901 Mount Bayou MS 38762-0901

HOY, MARJORIE ANN, entomology educator, researcher; b. Kansas City, Kans., May 19, 1941; d. Dayton J. and Marjorie Jean (Acker) Wolf; m. James B. Hoy; 1 child, Benjamin Lee. AB, U. Kans., 1963; MS, U. Calif., Berkeley, 1966, PhD, 1972. Asst. entomologist Conn. Agrl. Expt. Sta., New Haven, 1973-75; rsch. entomologist U.S. Forest Svc., Hamden, Conn., 1975-76; asst. prof. entomology U. Calif., Berkeley, 1976-80, assoc. prof. entomology, 1980-82, prof. entomology, 1982-92, prof. emeritus, 1992—; Fischer, Davies and Eckes prof., dept. entomology and nematology U. Fla., Gainesville, 1992—; chairperson Calif. Gypsy Moth Sci. Adv. Panel, 1982—; mem. genetics resources adv. com. USDA, 1992—. Editor or co-editor: Genetics in Relation to Insect Management, 1979, Recent Advances in Knowledge of the Photoseiidae, 1982, Biological Control of Pests by Mites, 1983, Biological Control in Agricultural IPM Systems, 1985, Insect Molecular Genetics, 1994; mem. editl. bd. Exptl. and Applied Acarology, Biol. Control, Biocontrol Sci. and Tech., Jour. Sustainable Agriculture, Internat. Jour. Acarology; contbr. numerous articles to profl. jours. NSF fellow U. Calif., Berkeley, 1963-64. Fellow AAAS, Royal Entomol. Soc. London; mem. Entomol. Soc. Am. (mem. Pacific br. governing bd. 1985, Bussart award 1986, Founder's Meml. award 1992), Am. Genetic Assn., Internat. Orgn. Biol. Control (v.p. 1984-85), Am. Inst. Biol. Scis., Acarological Soc. Am. (governing bd. 1980-84, pres. 1992), Soc. for Study of Evolution, Phi Beta Kappa, Sigma Xi (chpt. sec. 1979-81). Home: 4320 SW 83rd Way Gainesville FL 32608-4131 Office: U Fla Dept Entomology/ Nematology Hull Rd # 970 Gainesville FL 32612

HOYER, PHYLLIS SCARBOROUGH, elementary education educator; b. Salisbury, Md., Oct. 14, 1938; d. Paul Daniel and Norma (Luettinger) Scarborough; m. Lawrence Cogswell Hoyer, July 8, 1961; children: Brian Lawrence, Andrew Scarborough. BS, Hood Coll., 1960; MEd, Towson State U., 1986; post grad., Hood Coll., U. Md. Cert. early childhood edn., home econs., Md. Tchr. Anne Arundel County Bd. Edn., Annapolis, Md., 1960-61, Washington County Bd. Edn., Hagerstown, Md., 1961-64, Frederick County Bd. Edn., Md., 1972—; chairperson communication com., 1984-85; tchr. adv. com., 1977-80, 87-89; team leader, 1989-92; rep. kindergarten class, 1989-92. Instr. frederick County YMCA, 1976-79; participating mem. Earthwatch, Orca Survey, 1989, Fiji Coral Cmtys., 1990, Canary Island Sea Life, 1992, Sierra Wildlife, 1993; vol. ARC, 1993. Recipient Hon. Mention award Nat. Geographic Soc. Photography Contest, 1991. Mem. NEA, Md. State Tchrs. Assn., Frederick County Tchrs. Assn. (tchrs. rep. 1980-83, 94), Nature Conservancy. Republican. Home: 8398 Cub Hunt Ct Walkersville MD 21793-9325 Office: Hillcrest Elem Sch 1285 Hillcrest Dr Frederick MD 21702-1396

HOYLE, KAREN NELSON, author, curator; b. Boston, Jan. 8, 1937; d. Arthur and Ruth (Rasmussen) Nelson. BA in English, St. Olaf Coll., 1958; MLS, U. Calif., Berkeley, 1964; MA in Scandinavian Area Studies, U. Minn., 1970, PhD in Libr. Sci., 1975; doctorate (hon.), U. St. Thomas, 1992. Libr., civil svc. Univ. Librs., 1967-68; libr., instr. Univ. Librs., Mpls., 1968-75; curator, asst. prof. Univ. Librs., 1975-80, assoc. prof., 1980-87, curator, prof., 1987—; adj. faculty Am. Studies, 1983—; grad. sch. faculty examining coms., 1984—; cons. Bloomington Pub. Schs., 1984-85, curriculum materials collection Moorhead State U. Libr., 1982; cons. Five Owls, 1986—. Author: Wanda Gag, 1994; contbr. articles to profl. jours. Cons. Brown County Hist. Soc., 1993, Globe Exhibit, 1994. George C. Marshall fellowship, 1972; scholarship Children's Lit. Assn., 1981; recipient Disting. Alumna award St. Olaf Coll., 1994. Mem. ALA (chmn. Caldecott Award Com. 1985, mem. Caldecott, Newberry, Batchelor Award Coms.), Children's Lit. Assn. (pres. 1993-94), Internat. Rsch. Soc. for Children's Lib. (sec. bd. dirs. 1987-89), Internat. Bd. Books for Young People (Hans Christian Andersen award com. 1988-89, U.S. chmn. reading promotion award nomination com., 1989-92), Minn. Libr. Assn. (Disting. Achievement award 1992). Office: Childrens Lit Rsch Collections U Minn 109 Walter Libr 117 Pleasant St SE Minneapolis MN 55455-0291

HOYT, CHARLEE VAN CLEVE, management executive; b. Bluefield, W.Va., May 21, 1936; d. Charles Ives Van Cleve and Kathryn Margarete (Harden) Perrow; m. Ronald Reiner Hoyt, 1959 (div. 1983); children: Dean Christopher, Jason Allen. BA in Edn., U. Fla., 1959, MEd, 1962, postgrad., 1963-64. Cert. spl. edn. tchr. Tchr. Amherst County Schs., Elon, Va., 1958; tchr. spl. edn. Marion County Schs., Ocala, Fla., 1959-61; counselor Univ. Counseling Ctr., Gainesville, Fla., 1962-63, Sunland Tng. Ctr., Gainesville, 1963; mem. community faculty Minn. Met. State Coll., Mpls., 1972-83; mem. council City of Mpls., 1975-86; ptnr. Van Cleve Assocs., 1980-87, 91—; pres. Van Cleve, Doran & Bruno, Inc. 1987-91; corp. officer BAM Leasing Co., Inc., 1987—; dir. human resources Pascua Yagu Tribe; mem. faculty Govt. Tng. Service, St. Paul, 1978-86, Ariz. Govt. Tng. Services; pres. Minn. Women in City Govt., St. Paul, 1978-79; mem. Met. Land Use Adv. Bd., St. Paul, 1978-83; bd. dirs. Transp. Adv. Bd., St. Paul, 1979-81; mem. conf. faculty League of Minn. Cities, St. Paul, 1979-82; bd. dirs. Met. Council Criminal Justice Adv. Bd., St. Paul, 1979-82; pres. Women in Mcpl. Govt., Nat. League of Cities, Washington, 1980-81, founder minority caucus coalition, 1982, dir., 1982-84; curriculum cons. Nat. Women's Edn. Fund, Washington, trainer, 1982-86; officer JTPA Grantee Orgn. Region IX, 1994—; commr. Pima County/Tuscon Women's Commn. Presenter numerous workshops; contbr. articles to profl. jours. Mem. Women Helping Women YWCA, 1987—; various offices with Republican Party, Minn., 1970-86 ; pres. Burroughs Elem. Sch. PTA, Mpls., 1973-74; panelist White House Conf., 1981; chmn. Senator Durenburger's Task Force on Women's Issues, Mpls., 1981-84; bd. dirs. Nat. Conf. Rep. Mayors and Council Mems., 1984-85; mem. Senator Durenburger's Intergovtl. Relations Adv. Com., Mpls., 1984-86; bd. dirs. Twin Cities Internat. Program, Mpls., 1983-86; participant Women's Dialogue US/USSR, Moscow, 1985; trustee Council Internat. Programs, Cleve., 1985-90; bd. dirs. At the Foot of the Mountain Theater, Mpls., 1985-86, Tucson Ctrs. for Women and Children, 1988-92; bd. dirs. GOP Feminists, Hamline U. Ctr. for Women in Govt.; mem. Nat. Women's Polit. Caucus, Hennepin County Women's Polit. Caucus; mem. Tucson Support for Success Team, 1986-92, Tuscon YWCA Women Helping Women; bd. dirs. Tucson Ctrs. Women and Children. Mem. Am. Soc. Training and Devel., Minn. Women Elected Ofcls. (pres. 1983-85), Izaak Walton League, Tucson C. of C. Methodist. Club: Remington Investment (pres. 1968-70) (Mpls.). Avocations: lapidary, music, handwork, camping, science fiction. Home: 6932 E 2nd St Tucson AZ 85710-1222

HRANIOTIS, JUDITH BERINGER, artist; b. N.Y.C., Jan. 11, 1944; d. Richard Frederick and Barbara Ann (Blight) Beringer; children: Anthony J. Bellantoni, Robert John Bellantoni; m. Peter Hraniotis; stepchildren: Christine Hraniotis, Terry Hraniotis, Helen Finn. Student, Sch. Visual Arts, N.Y.C., 1962, NYU, 1994. Works have appeared at group shows including Hudson Valley Art Assn., White Plains, N.Y., 1990-91, Milford (Conn.) Arts Ctr., 1991, The Am. Artists Profl. League, N.Y.C., 1991, Catharine Lorillard Wolfe Art Club, N.Y.C., 1991-92, Kent (Conn.) Art Assn., 1991, 92, 93, 94, Ridgewood (N.J.) Art Inst., 1992, Mt. St. Mary Coll., Newburgh, N.Y., 1993, Arts Coun. Orange County, Middletown, 1994, Mamaroneck Artist Guild at Westbeth Gallery, N.Y.C., 1994, others. Recipient First Pl. Graphics, Mt. St. Mary Coll., 1994, Newburgh, 1990, 91, Grumbacher Silver medal Mt. St. Mary Coll., Newburgh, 1993, First Pl. Graphics, Annual Open Art Exhibit, Arts Coun. of Orange County, 1994. Mem. Am. Artist Profl. League, Nat. Mus. of Women in the Arts, Kent Art Assn. (bd. dirs., rec. sec. 1993-95, Cert. of Merit 1991), Middletown Art Group (bd. dirs., historian 1993-95), Catharine Lorillard Wolfe Art Club (assoc.), Garrison Art Ctr. Republican. Home: 245 Browns Rd Walden NY 12586

HRITZ, PAMELA LYNNE, accountant; b. Windber, Pa., Apr. 30, 1962; d. John Irvin and Sally Jane (Baldwin) H. AS, Monroe County (Mich.) C.C., 1983; BS in Acctg., U. N.C., Wilmington, 1992. Teller Monroe (Mich.) Bank and Trust Co., N.C., 1983-85; teller, svcs. supr. State Employees Credit Union, Raleigh, N.C., 1985-89; part-time teller State Employees Credit Union, Raleigh, 1989-91, loan officer, 1992, acct. I, 1992—. Leader Young Adult Ministries, Wilmington, N.C., 1992. Mem. Inst. Mgmt. Accts., Inst. of Mgmt. Accts. (v.p. pub. rels. 1991-92). Democrat. Roman Catholic. Office: State Employees Credit Union 1000 Wade Ave Raleigh NC 27603-1607

HSI, DENISE CHUR-YEE TSO, investment consultant; b. San Francisco, Oct. 31, 1958; d. Thompson W.S. and Virginia C.H. (Leung) Tso; m. Edward Yang Hsi, Aug. 3, 1985; 1 child, Edward Yang II. AB in Journalism cum laude, U. So. Calif., 1981; postgrad., Loyola Marymount U., L.A., 1990—. Community rep. L.A. Unified Sch. Dist., 1978-80; exec. dir. student news svc. U. So. Calif., 1979-80; mktg. dir. Pacific Gold Designers, L.A., 1980-81; investment/property mgr. Colyear Devel. Corp., L.A., 1982-85; legal adminstr. O'Connor, Cohn, Dillon & Barr, San Francisco, 1985-86; exec. asst. Gibson, Dunn & Crutcher/WSGP Internat., Inc., L.A., 1986—. Co-founder, editor newspaper Asian Pacific Lifeline, 1980. Pres. Mission Gabriel Homeowners Assn., San Gabriel, Calif., 1984-85; vol. George Bush for Pres., L.A., 1988. Mem. U. So. Calif. Pres.'s Circle, U. So. Calif. Jr. Aux., Alpha Gamma Delta (publicity coord. 1982, sec. 1982-83), Sigma Delta Chi, Alpha Mu Gamma. Republican. Home: 819 S Ridgeside Dr Monterey Park CA 91754-3724 Office: Gibson Dunn & Crutcher 333 S Grand Ave Los Angeles CA 90071

HSIEH, HAZEL TSENG, elementary education educator; b. Beijing, Nov. 4, 1934; came to U.S., 1947; naturalized, 1968; d. Hung-tu and Man-lone (Huang) Tseng; m. Hsueh Ying Hsieh, July 1, 1961; children: Durwynne, Timothy. Student, Adelphi U., 1954-56; BS, Tufts U., 1958; postgrad.,

Harvard U., 1959, U. Hartford, 1962-64; MA, Columbia U., 1977. Cert. tchr., N.Y. Tchr. Parents Nursery Sch., Cambridge, Mass., 1957, Sch. for Young Children, St. Joseph Coll., West Hartford, Conn., 1958-63; dir. Ctr. Nursery Sch., Yorktown Heights, N.Y., 1967-68; tchr. Yorktown Ctrl. Schs., Yorktown Heights, 1968—; substitute Virginia Day Nursery, N.Y.C., sumemr 1953-57; co-chair adv. com. Lakeland-Yorktown BOCES Mass Comm. Project, Yorktown Heights, 1982-87; mem. Internat. Faculty Challenger Ctr. Space Sci. Edn., Alexandria, Va., 1990—. Author: Living in Families, 1991; editor: Honor Society Competition Directory of Nominations, 1985-89. Past mem. Yorktown Schs. Dist. Mission State Com.; active Dist. Acad. Standards Com., 1994—, Mohansic Shared Decision Making Coun., Yorktown Heights, 1992—, Mohansic Literacy, Tech., Sci. Coms., 1992—, Wee Deliver Com., 1993-94, Dem. Party; curriculum coord. Ch. Good Shepherd, Granite Springs, N.Y., 1967-69; organizer Parent Orgn. for Arlington Symphony Orch., 1982-84, Mohansic Space Day, 1993; tchr. rep. PTA, 1977-78; founder Internat. Young Astronaut chpt. 27796, 1990, leader, 1990—; coord. project Marsville, Hudson Valley, 1992-95. Recipient Kohl Internat. Tchg. award, Wilmette, Ill., 1991; Challenger Seven fellow, 1990; grantee NASA, 1989, N.Y. State Electric and Gas Co., 1987, PTA, 1987, No. Westchester Tchr. Ctr., 1988, IBM, 1992. Mem. Am. Fedn. Tchrs., Yorktown Congress Tchrs. (sr. bldg. rep. 1977-78), Sierra Club, Pi Lambda Theta (mem. curriculum innovation award com. 1985—, chairperson com. 1986-89, 1st v.p. 1989-91, 2nd v.p. 1987-89, corr. sec. 1983-87, chairperson region I awards com. 1990—, pres. Westchester area chpt. 1991—, Outstanding chpt. 1991-92, grantee 1991). Home: 22 Mountain Pass Rd Hopewell Junction NY 12533 Office: Mohansic Elem Sch 704 Locksley Rd Yorktown Heights NY 10598

HSIEH-MOY, CATHERINE ELLEN, secondary school educator; b. Hong Kong, June 20, 1950; d. Chen Ping and Jeannie Beverly (Chow) Hsieh. BA in Social Welfare with honors, Calif. State U., Sacramento, 1974; MA in Bilingual Secondary Edn., Seton Hall U., 1978. Cert. bilingual social studies tchr., N.Y. Bilingual social studies tchr. Lower East Side Prep. High Sch., N.Y.C., 1978-85, resource specialist, program coord., 1988-94; sch. trainer Office of Bilingual Edn., N.Y.C., 1979-81; adminstrv. dir. Chinese Gospel Broadcasting Ctr., N.Y.C., 1985-88; bilingual social studies tchr. Galileo H.S., San Francisco, 1994—. Author high sch. curriculum. Mem. Univoice Chorus, N.Y.C., 1986—. Elem. and Secondary Edn. Act nat. fellow in bilingual edn. Mem. No. Calif. Translators Assn.

HSU, MEI-YUNG, chemist; b. Keelung, Taiwan, China, Aug. 31, 1943; d. Huang-Cheng and Yeh-Chin (Chian) Lee; m. Leon Lung-Hsiung Hsu, Sept. 22, 1968; children: Glenn Hsu, Yvonne Hsu. BS in Zoology, Nat. Taiwan U., 1965; PhD in Biochemistry, Northwestern U., Evanston, Ill., 1973. Scientist Worthington Biochemicals, Freehold, N.J., 1972-73; sr. scientist Worthington Diagnostics, Freehold, 1974-80, sr. scientist/group leader, 1980-86; staff scientist Beckman Instruments, Inc., Brea, Calif., 1987-88, project scientist, 1988-90, sr. project scientist, 1990—. Patentee in field; contbr. articles to profl. publs. Mem. Am. Assn. Clin. Chemistry. Home: 20490 Via Sonador Yorba Linda CA 92686 Office: Beckman Instruments Inc 200 S Kraemer Blvd Brea CA 92621-6208

HSU, MING CHEN, federal agency administrator; b. Beijing, China, Sept. 14, 1924; came to U.S., 1944; d. Chin-Men and Mary Sung Yung (Chu) Chen; 1 child, Victoria W. BA summa cum laude, George Washington U., 1949; LLD (hon.), Ramapo Coll., 1988, Kean Coll., 1989. Market rsch. analyst NBC Corp., N.Y.C., 1953-57; mg. market rsch. RCA Internat. Div., N.J., 1957-69; dir. internat. market RCA Corp., N.Y.C., 1969-78, staff v.p. for internat. trade, 1978-82; spl. trade rep. Gov. Tom Kean, Newark, 1982-90; dir. N.J. Div. Internat. Trade, Newark, 1982-90; commr. Fed. Maritime Commn., Washington, 1990—; speaker, lectr. on nat. and internat. affairs on numerous network and local TV programs. Author: American Arbitration Journal, 1956; editor: Suggested Amendments to the United Nations, 1960, Enabling Instruments of the United Nations, 1961; contbr. articles to jours. in field. At-large del to Rep. Nat. Conv., 1984, 88; mem. Def. Adv. Com. on Women in the Svcs., 1989, Nat. Commn. on Observance of Internat. Women's Yr., N.J. Adv. Coun. Channel Thirteen/WNET, U.S. Commn. on Civil Rights, U.S. Sec. Commerce's Adv. Com. on East-West Trade, Sec. Commerce's Export Now Adv. Com., Svc. Policy Adv. Com.; trustee Newark Mus.; bd. dirs. Com. of 100. Recipient Spl. award Women's Equity Action League, 1978, Alumni Achievement award George Washington U., 1983, Woman of Achievement award, N.J. Fedn. Bus. and Profl. Women, 1985, Achievement award Career Women's Achievement Network, 1986, Philbrook award Women's Polit. Caucus, 1989, N.J. Pride award for econ. devel., 1989, Paul L. Troast award, N.J. Bus.and Industry, 1989, Woman on the Move award, Bus. Jour. N.J., 1989; named Woman of Yr., Asian-Am. Profl. Women's Assn., 1983. Mem. Phi Beta Kappa. Office: FMC 800 N Capitol St NW Washington DC 20002-4244

HU, EDNA GERTRUDE FENSKE, pediatrics nurse; b. Arlington, S.D., June 11, 1922; d. Walter O. and Therese (Kautz) Fenske; m. Patrick P.C. Hu, Nov. 26, 1954; children: Lou Anne Hu Yee, Mark C., Lawrence P. BS in Nursing, U. Colo. Sch. Nursing, 1954. RN, Colo. Staff pediatrics nurse Colo. Gen. Hosp., Denver, 1954-63, night nursing supr., 1963-65; staff nurse alcohol withdrawal unit Denver Gen. Hosp., 1971-73; staff surg. nurse Fitzsimons Army Hosp., Denver, 1973-79; staff nurse VA Hosp., Allens Pk., Mich., 1979-81, Drug and Alcohol Withdrawal and Rehab. Ctr., Ft. Dodge, Iowa, 1981-83; researcher Ft. Collins, Colo., 1988—; researcher effects on memory following long term residence in another culture; instr. English, health care, Asia. Recipient Disting. Alumna award Class of 1954. Mem. ANA, Colo. Nurses Assn., Non-practicing and Part-time Nurses Assn. Home: 2518 Timber Ct Fort Collins CO 80521-3120

HU, SUE KING, middle school educator; b. Prince Frederick, Md., Nov. 7, 1938; d. James Elliott and Anna Irene (Hutchins) King; m. Richard Chee Chung Hu, July 2, 1960; children: Stephen Tse Wen, Sharon Yen Mei. BS, Towson (Md.) State U., 1960; MA, Marymount U., Arlington, Va., 1987. Cert. tchr., Va. Elem. tchr. Arlington (Va.) County Pub. Schs., 1977-90, elem. sch. rep., 1986-90, tchr. sci. mid. sch., 1990-94; environ. educator Phoebe Knipling Outdoor Edn. Lab., Broad Run, Va., 1994—; workshop presenter Nat. Wildlife Fedn., Vienna, Va., 1989, 90; ednl. cons. Greenhouse Crisis Found., Washington, 1989-91, Nat. Geog. Soc., Washington, 1988-91; adj. prof. George Mason U., 1991, 94; instr. in environ. sci. Audubon Naturalist Soc., Chevy Chase, Md., 1990—; presenter children's workshops Fairfax County Schs., 1990—. Writer children's newspaper Sci. Weekly, 1990-91. chair edn. com. Fairfax (Va.) Audubon Soc., 1987-92, bd. dirs., 1988-92, v.p. natural history and edn., 1990-92. Recipient Cert. of accomplishment Arlington County Pub. Schs., 1989, Svc. award Fairfax Audubon Soc., 1992; named Notable Woman of Arlington, Arlington Commn. on Status of Women, 1993. Mem. ASCD, Nat. Assn. Biology Tchrs. (elem.-mid. sch. chair 1988-89, presenter conf. 1986-89), Nat. Sci. Tchrs. Assn. (presenter conf. 1988-89), Coun. Elem. Sci. Internat., , Va. Assn. Sci. Tchrs., Delta Epsilon Sigma, Kappa Delta Pi. Democrat. Methodist. Home: 2524 Leeds Rd Oakton VA 22124-9999

HUA, LULIN, technological company executive, research scientist, artist. BS in Chemistry, U. Sci. and Tech. China, Beijing, MS in Chemistry, 1966. Asst. rsch. chemist Inst. Metal Chinese Acad. Sci., 1966-71, Astronomy Observatory Chinese Acad. Sci., 1971-76; rsch. chemist Hong-Xing Chem. Inst. China, 1976-82; vis. scholar Dept. Chemistry U. Md., 1982-84; vis. assoc. prof. Dept. Chemistry U. Ariz., 1984-85; vis. rsch. assoc. Dept. Chemistry Rensselaer Poly. Inst., 1985-86; postdoctoral fellow Dept. Chemistry Georgetown U., 1986-87; rsch. assoc. Dept. Chemistry U. Tenn., 1988-90; v.p. Micro Imaging Systems, Inc., Md., 1990—; owner Lulin Hua Fine Art, Inc., 1991—. Contbr. articles to profl. jours. Recipient numerous sci. awards in China. Mem. Am. Chem. Soc., Analytical Chem. and Applied Spectroscopy Soc., Am. Assn. for the Advancement Sci., Internat. Soc. for the Origin Life. Office: 701 Cornwall St Silver Spring MD 20901

HUANG, ALICE SHIH-HOU, microbiology, molecular genetics educator; b. Nanchang, Kiangsi, China; came to U.S., 1949; d. Quentin K.Y. and Grace Betty (Soong) H.; m. David Baltimore, 1968. Student Wellesley Coll., 1957-59; BA, Johns Hopkins U., 1961, MA in Microbiology, 1963, PhD, 1966; MA (hon.), Harvard U., 1980; DSc (hon.) Wheaton Coll., 1982, Mt. Holyoke Coll., 1988, Med. Coll. Pa., 1991. Postdoctoral fellow Salk Inst. for Biol. Studies, San Diego, 1967; postdoctoral fellow dept. biology MIT, Cambridge, 1968-69, rsch. assoc., 1969-70; asst. prof. microbiology and molecular genetics Harvard U. Med. Sch., Boston, 1971-73, assoc. prof. microbiology and molecular genetics, 1973-78, prof., 1979-91; prof. microbiology in health sci. and tech. Harvard-MIT Program, 1979-91; dean for sci., prof. biology NYU, 1991—; sci. assoc. Channing Lab. and dept. med. microbiology Boston City Hosp., 1971-73; dir. labs. of infectious diseases Children's Hosp., Boston, 1979-89; vis. asst. prof. Academia Sinica, Nat. Taiwan U., Taipei, 1966, lectr., 1970; vis. assoc. prof. virology Rockefeller U., N.Y.C., 1975-76; Wellcome vis. prof. U. Miss., 1980. Assoc. editor Revs. of Infectious Diseases, 1978-89. Mem. editorial bd. Intervirology, 1973-90, Archive of Virology, 1975-78, Jour. Virology, 1976-93, Microbial Pathogenesis, 1985-90. Contbr. numerous articles to profl. jours. Recipient Research Career Devel. award USPHS., 1972-77, Eli Lilly award, 1977, award San Francisco Chinese Hosp., 1989; Alumni citation Nat. Cathedral Sch., Washington, 1978; John Hay Whitney Found. fellow, 1960-61, Burroughs Wellcome traveling fellow, 1979. Fellow Infectious Diseases Soc. Am.; mem. AAAS, Am. Soc. Microbiology (pres. 1988-89), Am. Soc. Biochemists and Molecular Biologists, Am. Soc. Virology, Am. Acad. Microbiology, Academia Sinica (Taiwan), Sigma Xi. Office: NYU 6 Washington Sq N New York NY 10003-6668

HUANG, THERESA C., librarian; b. Nanking, China; m. Theodore S. Huang, Dec. 25, 1959. B.A., Nat. Taiwan U., 1955; M.S. in L.S., Syracuse U., 1958. Cataloger, Harvard U., Cambridge, Mass., 1958-60; with Bklyn. Pub. Library, 1960-78, regional librarian, 1978— . Joint compiler bibliography: Asia: A Guide to Books for Children, 1966; Nuclear Awareness, 1983; The U.S.A. through Children's Books, 1986, 88. Mem. ALA, Assn. Library Service to Children, Pub. Library Assn., Chinese Am. Librarians Assn., Asia Pacific Am. Librarians Assn. Office: Bklyn Pub Libr 1743 86th St Brooklyn NY 11214-3714

HUANG, WENDY WAN-JUOH, lawyer; b. Taipei, Taiwan, Aug. 3, 1966; came to the U.S., 1977; d. Tsung-Chee and Sheree (Shen) H. BA, Cornell U., 1988; JD, Boston U., 1992. Bar: Calif. 1993, D.C. 1994, N.Y. 1994. Intern UN Com. on U.S.-China Rels., N.Y.C., 1986, Internat. Bus. Cons., Washington, 1987; asst. editor P.C. Mag., N.Y.C., 1988-89; law clk. San Diego (Calif.) City Attys., 1990, U.S. Atty.-So. Dist. N.Y., N.Y.C., 1991, L.A. (Calif.) Dist. Attys., 1991; assoc. Law Firm of Kinkle, Rodiger & Spriggs, L.A., 1992-94, Knapp, Marsh, Jones & Doran, L.A., L.A., 1994—; chmn. Pacific Rim bd. govs. Calif. Chinese Bar Assn., L.A., 1993—; arbitrator L.A. County Bar Client Dispute Svcs.; legal cons. Sta. KPFK Radio, Voice of Am. Radio, Chinese Daily News. Exec. editor Grace Pub. Newsletter, 1993; writer, actress Words Across Cultures Theatre Co., L.A., 1993; actress, dancer Bethune Theatre Danse, L.A., 1993; mem. editl. bd. L.A. Lawyer mag. Recipient Westinghouse Nat. Sci. Talent Search scholarship NSF, Washington, 1984. Mem. L.A. County Bar Inns of Ct., Orgn. Chinese Ams. (bd. govs.), Screen Actors Guild. Democrat. Home: 11750 Sunset Blvd # 209 Los Angeles CA 90049 Office: Knapp Marsh Jones & Doran 515 S Figuersa St 14th Flr Los Angeles CA 90071

HUBBARD, BESSIE RENEE, mechanical engineer, mathematician; b. Fayetteville, N.C., Sept. 23, 1961; d. Kenneth Brigman and Ellen Merle H. BSME, N.C. State U., 1983, MME, 1985, BS in Applied Math., 1989, M in Pub. Admin., 1993. Registered profl. engr., N.C. Mech. engr. N.C. State Univ., Raleigh, 1985-94, asst. phys. plant dir. for design svcs., 1994-95; facility mech. engr. N.C. State U., Raleigh, 1995—; spl. engr. cons. United Daughters of Confederacy, Raleigh, 1989—; mem. faculty Indsl. Ventilation Conf., N.C. State U. Author: Marriage and Death Notices, 1991, (with others) NCSU Guidelines for Construction, 1988, 91. Editor Cumberland County Geneal. Soc., Fayetteville, 1991-93. Mem. DAR (sec. 1991—), ASHRAE, NSPE, ASME (chpt. historian 1987-88), N.C. Soc. Engrs. (Order of Engr. 1987), Order of Crown of Charlemagne, Jamestowne Soc., Nat. Soc. Daus. Colonial Wars, Nat. Soc. Daus. Founders and Patriots Am., Nat. Soc. Descs. Colonial Clergy, Tau Beta Pi, Pi Alpha Alpha. Republican. Home: 116 E Ransom St Fuquay Varina NC 27526-2426 Office: NC State U Phys Plant Campus Box 7219 Raleigh NC 27695

HUBBARD, ELIZABETH, actress; b. N.Y.C.; d. Benjamin Alldritt and Elizabeth (Wright) H.; divorced; 1 son, Jeremy Danby Bennett. A.B. cum laude, Radcliffe Coll.; postgrad., Royal Acad. Dramatic Art, London. Leading role: CBS daytime TV serial As the World Turns, 1984— (7 consecutive Emmy nominations for Best Leading Actress), NBC daytime TV serial The Doctors; appeared on Broadway in Present Laughter, Joe Egg, Time for Singing, Look Back in Anger, I Remember Mama (musical), others; appeared in off-Broadway prodn. Boys from Syracuse, Threepenny Opera (musicals); movie appearances include I Never Sang for My Father, The Bell Jar, Ordinary People; frequent guest TV talk shows. Bd. dirs. Women's Commn. for Refugee Women and Children, Found. in Motion, Immigration and Refugee Svcs. of Am. Recipient Clarence Derwent award for The Physicists, 1965; Emmy award for best actress in The Doctors, 1974, Emmy award for best actress in First Ladies Diaries: Edith Bolling Wilson, 1976. Mem. Harvard Club.

HUBBARD, ELIZABETH LOUISE, lawyer; b. Springfield, Ill., Mar. 10, 1949; d. Glenn Wellington and Elizabeth (Frederick) H.; m. A. Jeffrey Seidman, Oct. 27, 1974 (div. May 1982). Student Millikin U., 1967-69; B.A., U. Ky., 1971; J.D. with honors, Ill. Inst. Tech.-Chgo. Kent Coll. Law, 1974. Bar: Ill. 1974, U.S. Dist. Ct. (no. dist.) Ill. 1974, U.S. Ct. Appeals (7th cir.) 1976, U.S. Supreme Ct. 1984. Atty. Wyatt Co., Chgo., 1974-75, Gertz & Giampietro, Chgo., 1975-76, Baum, Sigman, Gold, Chgo., 1976-81, Elizabeth Hubbard, Ltd., Chgo., 1981—; legal counsel NOW, Chgo., 1978—, sec., 1977. Editor Chgo. Kent Law Rev., 1970. Bd. dirs., mem. The Remains Theatre, 1985-94. Mem. Chgo. Bar Assn. (fed. civil procedure com.), Ill. State Bar Assn., Nat. Employment Lawyers Assn. (chair Ill. chpt. 1992—). Democrat. Home: 420 West Grand Unit 4A Chicago IL 60611 Office: 55 E Monroe St Chicago IL 60603

HUBBARD, MARGARET LUANN, counselor; b. Washington, Ind., Oct. 15, 1949; d. Ralph and Evelyn Inez (Allison) Berry; m. William Bryant Hubbard, Jr., Jan. 16, 1976. BS, U. Evansville, 1971; MS, Nova U., 1981; counseling cert., Sam Houston State U., Huntsville, Tex., 1992. Cert. elem. tchr., reading specialist, counselor, Tex. Tchr. Richmond (Ind.) Cmty. Schs., 1971-72, Clayton County Schs., Jonesboro, Ga., 1972-74, Cobb County Schs., Marietta, Ga., 1974-75, St. Charles Parish Schs., Luling, La., 1978-80, Broward County Schs., Ft. Lauderdale, Fla., 1980-82; asst. dir. new store devel. Thrifty Drug Corp., L.A., 1975-78; tchr. Spring Ind. Sch. Dist., Houston, 1982-93, adventure based counseling facilitator, 1992; counselor Klein (Tex.) Ind. Sch. Dist., 1993—; book reviewer Signal mag., 1986-93; presenter Mid. Sch. Conf., Corpus Christi, Tex., 1993, Counseling Conf., Austin, Tex., 1994, Tex. Elem. Counseling Conf. Pres. Champion Pines Homeowners Assn., Spring, Tex., 1988-90. Named Tchr. of Yr., Wells Mid. Sch., Houston, 1986. Mem. NEA, Tex. Counseling Assn., Klein Educators Assn., Sam Houston Play Therapy Assn., Delta Kappa Gamma, Phi Mu. Democrat. Baptist. Office: Eiland Elem Sch 6700 N Klein Circle Dr Houston TX 77068

HUBBARD, Z(ONIA) DIANNE, telephone company official; b. Ypsilanti, Mich., Nov. 26, 1950; d. George Lorenzo and Mattie Lorene (Burton) H. BA, Mich. State U., 1973. Svc. rep. Mich. Bell Tel. Co., Taylor, 1973-77, supr. collections, 1977-79; mgr. collections Mich. Bell Tel. Co., Livonia, 1979-81; mgr. orders Mich. Bell Tel. Co., Allen Park, 1981-84; staff mgr. svc. ctr. ops. Mich. Bell Tel. Co., Southfield, 1984-85; staff mgr. fin. Mich. Bell Telephone Co., Oak Park, 1985-88, staff mgr. comptr. ops., 1989-90, mgr. data ctr. ops., 1990-91; mgr. br. office adminstrn. Ameritech Svcs., Inc., 1991-92; mgr. data ctr. OPRNS Ameritech Network Svcs., 1993—. Bd. dirs. Friendship Manor Nursing Home, Detroit, 1986-93; mem. nominating com. Mich. Metro Girl Scout Coun., Detroit, 1988, chmn. vols. recognition com., mem. fund devel. com., mem. pers. com., bd. dirs., 1989-93; mem. women's com. United Negro Coll. Fund, Detroit, coord. 1988-89, sec. Women's Com. Exec. Coun., 1992-93, vice-chair, 1993—, chair Ebony Fashion Fair, 1994; mem. Detroit Urban League. Mem. NAACP, Detroit Grand Prix Assn., Women's Econ. Club, Zonta (v.p. 1994—), bd. dirs., chair ways and means com., chair pub. rels. com., mem. long-range planning com., corr. sec., chair Inter-City Commn., sec. Dist. XV bd. dirs., del. internat. conv. 1994, chair Dist. XV fall conf. 1995). Democrat. Baptist. Home: 23877 Merrill Ave Southfield MI 48075-3496 Office: Ameritech A230 23500 Northwestern Hwy Southfield MI 48075

HUBBELL, SUSAN LEE, physician; b. Columbus, Mar. 20, 1950; d. John Donald and Norma L. (Miller) H. AB, Miami U., 1972; MD, Ohio State U., 1976, Ohio State U., 1980. Diplomate Am. Bd. Physical Medicine and Rehab. Asst. prof. Ohio State U. Coll. Medicine, Columbus, 1980-86, clin. asst. prof., 1986—; clin. asst. prof. Med Coll. Ohio, Toledo, 1986—; med. dir. physical medicine dept. St. Rita's Med. Ctr., Lima, 1986—; physician pvt. practice, Lima, 1986—; surveyor CARF, Tucson, 1980—. Bd. dirs. YWCA, Lima, 1987-93, Northwest Ohio Easter Seals, Lima, 1988-94. Mem. Am. Assn. Elec. Medicine, Am. Acad. Phys. Medicine and Rehab., Ohio Soc. Phys. Medicine and Rehab. (pres. 1992-94), Acad. Medicine (pres. 1993—), Rotary, Phi Beta Kappa. Office: 658 W Market Ste 106 Lima OH 45801

HUBER, SISTER ALBERTA, college president; b. Rock Island, Ill., Feb. 12, 1917; d. Albert and Lydia (Hofer) H. BA, Coll. St. Catherine, St. Paul, 1939; MA, U. Minn., 1945; PhD, U. Notre Dame, 1954. Mem. faculty Coll. St. Catherine, 1940—, prof. English, 1953—, chmn. dept., 1960-63, acad. dean, 1962-64, pres., 1964-79. Trustee Avila Coll., Kansas City, Mo., St. Joseph's Hosp., St. Paul, 1971-80; pres. UN Assn. Minn., 1980-81; bd. dirs. St. Paul YMCA, 1986-92. Decorated Chevalier, Ordre des Palmes Acad.; recipient Outstanding Achievement award U. Minn. Alumni Assn., 1981. Mem. Phi Beta Kappa, Pi Gamma Mu. Office: 2004 Randolph Ave Saint Paul MN 55105-1750

HUBER, ANN CERVIN, nurse; b. Balt., Dec. 1, 1941; d. John and Rose (Kortus) Cervin; m. Frank H. Huber, Sept. 26, 1964; children: Holly Ann, Joann Františka. Diploma, Union Meml. Hosp. Sch. Nursing, 1963; BSN, U. Md., 1994. RN, Md.; cert. community health nurse. Staff nurse Union Meml. Hosp., Balt., clinical nurse; pub. health nurse Balt. City Health Dept.; community health nurse Harford County Health Dept., Bel Air, Md. Active Czech and Slovak Heritage Assn. Md. Recipient Govs. Citation, 1990. Mem. ANA, Md. Nurses Assn. (chmn. sunshine com.), Md. Classified Employees Assn. (treas. 1986-88), SOKOL (pres. 1986-88, 1994—, v.p. 1991-94, bd. dirs. 1988-90).

HUBER, JOAN ALTHAUS, sociology educator; b. Bluffton, Ohio, Oct. 17, 1925; d. Lawrence Lester and Hallie Moser (Althaus) H.; m. William Form, Feb. 5, 1971; children: Nancy Rytina, Steven Rytina. B.A., Pa. State U., 1945; M.A., Western Mich. U., 1963; Ph.D., Mich. State U., 1967. Asst. prof. sociology U. Notre Dame, Ind., 1967-71; asst. prof. sociology U. Ill., Urbana-Champaign, 1971-73; assoc. prof. U. Ill., 1973-78, prof., 1978-83, head dept., 1979-83; dean Coll. Social and Behavioral Sci., Ohio State U., Columbus, 1984-92; coordinating dean Coll. Arts and Sciences, Ohio State University, Columbus, 1987-92, provost, 1992-93; sr. v.p., provost emeritus prof. Sociology emeritus, 1994. Author: (with William Form) Income and Ideology, 1973, (with Glenna Spitze) Sex Stratification, 1983. Editor: Changing Women in a Changing Society, 1973, (with Paul Chalfant) The Sociology of Poverty, 1974, Macro-Micro Linkages in Sociology, 1991. NSF research awardee, 1978-81. Mem. Am. Sociol. Assn. (v.p. 1981-83, pres. 1987-90), Midwest Sociol. Soc. (pres. 1979-80). Home: 2880 N Star Rd Columbus OH 43221-2959 Office: Ohio State U Dept Sociology 300 Bricker Hall 190 N Oval Mall Columbus OH 43210-1326

HUBER, LYNÉE THERESE, secondary educator; b. Reedsburg, Wis., Sept. 24, 1963; d. Robert Eugene and Donna Mae (Chruchill) Tourdot; m. Mark Ron Huber, Aug. 16, 1985; children: Kara Lynn, Kyle Anthony. BS in Retailing, U. Wis., Madison, 1986; M in Secondary Edn., U. Wis., Platteville, 1992; postgrad., U. Wis. Cert. bus. edn. and math. tchr. Tchr. Union Grove (Wis.) High Sch., 1988-90; tchr., local vocat. edn. coord. Wisconsin Dells High Sch., 1990—. Mem. Nat. Tech Prep Network, Wis. Edn. Assn. Coun., Wis. Assn. Secondary Vocat. Adminstrs. Office: Wisconsin Dells High Sch 520 Race St Wisconsin Dells WI 53965-1824

HUBER, MARY MARTHA, clinical nurse allergy and infectious diseases; b. Pottsville, Pa., Nov. 17, 1935; d. Joseph M. and Mary Wollyung; m. William Huber, 1963 (div. 1978); children: William, David, Mary Beth. Diploma, Sacred Heart Hosp. Nursing Sch, Allentown, Pa., 1956; BSN, Boston Coll., 1963; MA, Trinity Coll., Washington, 1988. RN, Md., Ericksonian Hypnosis Therapist; ordained min. Cmty. Chapel Wholistic Healing. Natural health cons. and office nurse Dr. Frank Varese, Laguna Hills, Calif.; pvt. practice Domel Cons., Albuquerque; assoc. TV producer Natural Health Theme, L.A.; clin. nurse Clin. Ctr. Nat. Health Inst, Bethesda, Md.; instr. creative wellness. Contbr. articles and rsch. to profl. pubs. Treas. Wegeners Found., Inc., 1990—; dir. edn. Cmty. Chapel Wholistic Healing, Reston. Recipient awards for clin. excellence, 1986, '88. Mem. ACA, Md. Nurses Assn., Am. Holistic Nurses Assn., Assn. Nurses in AIDS Care.

HUBER, RITA NORMA, civic worker; b. Cin., July 16, 1931; d. Andrew Elwood and Mary Gertrude (Hille) Stewart; student Cin. Coll. Conservatory Music, 1949-50, Berlitz Sch., Cin., 1951-52; m. Justin G. Huber, July 17, 1954; children: Monica Ann, Sarah Marie, Rachel Miriam. Tchr. Russian lang. for officers' wives Ft. Sill, Okla., 1955-56; bd. dirs. United Community Svcs., Cedar Rapids, Iowa, 1969; founder, chairperson Linn County Consumers League, 1969-70; founder, pub. rels. dir. Cedar Rapids Rape Crisis Svcs., 1974—; owner/operator Huber Janitorial Svcs., 1982-84; chairperson Linn County Dem. Womens Club, 1966-67, Linn County Com., Eugene McCarthy for Pres., 1967-68; campaign mgr. Delores Cortez for Iowa Legislature, 1968, Jan V. Johnson for Iowa Legislature, 1970, Stanley Ginsberg for county supr. Linn County, 1974, E.L. Colton for Cedar Rapids pub. safety commr., 1977; chairperson Linn County Dem. Cen. Com., 1976-77, 88-90; state coord. Jerry Brown for Pres., 1976; chairperson Pat Kane for Linn County Recorder, 1982; chmn. Linn County Bd. Health, 1982-85; supr. Linn County, 1990-95; chairperson Linn County bd. Suprs., 1992; instr. parliamentary procedures Cedar Rapids Women's Community Leadership Inst., 1975-77; lectr. local colls. and svc. orgns.; tchr. conversational Russian, Pierce Elementary Sch., Cedar Rapids, 1976; instr. Russian, Community Edn. div. Kirkwood Community Coll.; mem. care rev. com. Pineview Care Ctr., Cedar Rapids, 1987-90. Named to Iowa Dem. Party DVP Hall of Fame, 1986; recipient Woman of Yr. award Women's Equality Day Cedar Rapids Iowa, 1993. Mem. Am. Inst. Parliamentarians. Roman Catholic (extraordinary minister of Eucharist). Composer: She is Risen, 1973. Home: 2050 Glass Rd NE Cedar Rapids IA 52402-3451

HUCKABEE, PHYLLIS, gas industry professional; b. Andrews, Tex., Aug. 11, 1963; d. Tommie Jack and Sylvia (Wingo) H. BBA in Fin., Tex. Tech U., 1984, MBA, 1986. Clk. loan escrow 1st Fed. Savs. Bank, Lubbock, Tex., 1984; mgmt. trainee El Paso (Tex.) Nat. Gas Co., 1986-87, analyst rate dept., 1987-88, specialist Calif. affairs, 1988-91, rep. Calif. affairs, 1991-92; asst. dir. Cambridge Energy Rsch. Assocs., Oakland, Calif., 1992-93; regulatory rels. mgr. So. Calif. Gas Co., San Francisco, 1994—; mem. adj. faculty No. Calif. campus U. Phoenix, San Francisco, 1994—. Bd. dirs. El Paso Community Concert Assn., 1988, bd. dirs. Performing Arts Workshop, 1991-92, mem. adv. bd., 1992—; vol. Bus. Vols. for Arts, San Francisco, 1989, East Bay Habitat for Humanity, 1993; tutor, fundraiser Project Read, San Francisco, 1990. Mem. Women Energy Assocs. (bd. dirs. 1990—), Berkeley Archtl. Heritage Assn., Pacific Coast Bar Assn. Methodist. Democrat. Home: 1721 Mcgee Ave Berkeley CA 94703-1225 Office: So Calif Gas Co 601 Van Ness Ave Ste 2014 San Francisco CA 94102

HUCKEBA, KAREN KAYE, crafts designer, consultant; b. Decatur, Ind., Aug. 24, 1952; d. Donald Edward and Erma Louise (Morrison) Sliger; m. David Ardie Huckeba, Oct. 17, 1970; children: Scott Alan, Mark Andrew. Grad. high sch., Decatur. Cashier Lerner's Dress Shop, Ft. Wayne, Ind., 1970-71; head cashier Lerner's Dress Shop, Ft. Wayne and Newport News, Va., 1971-75; crafter various locations, 1976-89; pres. Karen's Kreations, Roswell, Ga., 1990-94; cons. wearable art Fruit of the Loom, Bowling Green, Ky., 1993-94; demonstrator Tulip, Ga., 1994. Designer (patriotic clothes line) Habitat, 1990-94, (nautical clothes line) Designer Consignor, 1992-93; clothes displayed at Columbus (Ind.) Heritage Quilt Show, 1993; designer (catalogue) Fruit of the Loom 1995 Activewear Catalogue, 1994; contbr. articles to profl. jours. Pianist Huntingburg (Ind.) Bapt. Ch., 1975-78; children's worship leader Miles Rd. Bapt. Ch., Summerville, S.C., 1981-89; coaching asst. Summerville Soccer Club, 1981-87. Mem. Hobby Industry

Am., Soc. Craft Designers, Assn. Crafts and Creative Industries, Inc. Home and Office: Karen's Kreations 4611 Wickford Circle Roswell GA 30075

HUCKEBY, KAREN MARIE, graphic arts executive; b. San Diego, June 4, 1957; d. Floyd Riley and Georgette Laura (Wegimont) H. Student Coll. of Alameda, 1976; student 3-M dealer tng. program, St. Paul, 1975. Staff Huck's Press Service, Inc., Emeryville, Calif., 1968—, v.p., 1975—. Mem. Rep. Nat. Task Force, 1984—; bd. dirs. CitiArts Benefactors, Concord, Calif., 1990-93, v.p., treas., 1991-93. Recipient service award ARC, 1977. Mem. East Bay Club of Printing House Craftsman (treas. 1977-78), Oakland Mus. Soc., Nat. Trust Historic Preservation, Smithsonian Inst., San Francisco Mus. Soc., Internat. Platform Assn., Am. Film Inst., Commonwealth Club. Home: 1054 Hera Ct Hercules CA 94547 Office: Staff Huck's Press Svc Inc 691 S 31st St Richmond CA 94804-4022

HUCKSTEAD, CHARLOTTE VAN HORN, retired home economist, artist; b. Garwin, Iowa, Jan. 13, 1920; d. George Loren and Esther Olive (Carver) Van Horn; m. Lowell Raine Huckstead (dec.); children: Karen C., Roger H., Martha E., Paul R., Sarah S. BS, U. Wisc., 1942; BFA, Boise (Idaho) State U., 1989. Merchandising Montgomery Ward, Chgo. and Santa Monica, Calif., 1941-42; "Rosie the Riveter" WWII, Chgo. and Beloit, Wis., 1942-46; woman's editor Dairyland News, Milw., 1950-54; interior designer, cons., tchr. South Bend, Marshfield, Wis., Merced, Calif., 1952-69; extenion home economist U. Minn., Rochester, 1973-78; dir. food svcs. Milton (Wisc.) Sch. Dist., 1978-85; artist, 1952—. Painting and sculpture. Bd. dirs. Rock County Hist. Soc., Janesville, Wis., 1979-84, Milton Hist. Soc., 1979-85; vol. Idaho Geneaoclogy Libr., 1994-95; treas. Wis. Food Svc. Assn., 1980-85; leader/mem. Girl Scouts Am., 1934-78. Mem. AAUW, NOW, Idaho Hist. Soc. (vol. 1985-94), Idaho Centennial Art Group (sec. 1991, show chmn. 1992, historian 1993-95), Idaho Water Color Soc., Morrison Ctr. Aux. (vol. 1986-94, bd. dirs. 1992-93), Audubon Soc., Ch. Women United (editor 1985-86), Sierra Club, Boise Art Mus., Wis. Alumni Assn., Friends of Hist. Mus. Boise, Boise Art Alliance. Republican. Protestant. Home: 10507 Irving Ct Boise ID 83704-8054

HUCKSTEP, APRIL YVETTE, chemist; b. Aliquippa, Pa., May 12, 1961; d. Charles Jr. and Geraldine (Wilson) H. Cert., Parkway Tech. Coll., Oakdale, Pa., 1979; BS, Pa. State U., 1984; MS, U. Akron, 1991. Technician Arco Chem. Inc., Newton Square, Pa., 1979-81; technician DiversiTech, Akron, 1986; chemist Goodyear Tire and Rubber, Akron, 1986; intern Lord Corp., Erie, Pa., 1989; chemist, grad. asst. U. Akron, 1988—. U. Akron fellow. Mem. NAACP, Am. Chem. Soc., Soc. Women Engrs., Am. Inst. Chem. Engrs., Nat. Soc. Black Engineers. Democrat. Baptist. Home: 868 Monaca Rd Monaca PA 15061-2831 Office: U Akron Polymer Sci Dept Akron OH 44304

HUDAK, BARBARA MARGARET, securities company executive; b. East Orange, N.J., Aug. 11, 1944; d. Edmond J. and Rosemary B. (Hewett) Kennedy; m. Henry A. Hudak, July 29, 1967 (div. Feb. 1990); children: Margaret, Matthew, Michele, Maureen. BA, St. Joseph Coll., 1966; MLS, Rutgers U., 1982. Library clk. U. Rochester (N.Y.), 1966-67; asst. librarian Mobil Chem. Co., Edison, N.J., 1967-69, 75-82; info. mgr. Morgan Guaranty Trust Co., N.Y.C., 1982-86; v.p. J.P. Morgan Securities, Inc., N.Y.C., 1987—. Mem. Spl. Librs. Assn., Phi Beta Mu. Roman Catholic. Office: JP Morgan Securities 60 Wall St New York NY 10005-2807

HUDDLESTON, MARILYN ANNE, international business financier, educator; b. Fayetteville, N.C., Jan. 28, 1953; d. Allen Paul and Julia Jewel (Hill) Miller; m. Roby Dwayne Huddleston, Sept. 13, 1946; children: Michelle, Christopher, Mathew Anthony, Danyel Paul, Michael David. D in Humanities Law (hon.), Central Tex. U., 1974; diploma Acad. of Coll. of Real Estate, 1977; postgrad. El Paso Community Coll. Owner, fin. cons. Cherokee Fin. Investments, Killeen, Tex., 1983-88; owner, broker All Am. Ins. Agy., Killeen, 1984-88; realtor, assoc. Exec. Fin., Austin, Tex., 1986-88; owner Geodesic Homes of Tex., Killeen, 1984-88; chmn., CFO Wall Street Internat., 1988-90, chmn. bd. dirs., 1988—; tchr. St. Joseph Catholic Sch., Killeen, 1991-92, tchr., adminstr., 1991-94; merchant banker Baytree Investors, Killeen, 1990—; grant writer, adminstrv. asst. to pres. and CEO Advantage Adult Day Care & Health Svcs., Harker Heights, Tex., 1994—. Author: Miracle Baby at Bracken Ridge Hospital, 1979; Financial Consulting Made Easy, 1983. Pres. Mil. Council of Catholic Women, Stuttgart, Fed. Republic Germany, 1980, Non-Commnd. Officers Wives, Stuttgart, 1980-82, Ciudad del Niño Orphanage Assn., Killeen, 1979—; instr. Christian Religion, Killeen, 1976-91, St. Joseph Cath. Sch., Killeen. Recipient Silver Poet award World of poetry Poets, 1989. Mem. Nat. Assn. Female Execs., Internat. Assn. Bus. and Fin. Cons. (hon.), Fort Hood Bd. Realtors, Nat. Assn. Realtors, Tex. Assn. Realtors Soc. Female Execs. (v.p. 1984-86), Internat. Soc. Financiers (cert.). Independent. Roman Catholic. Avocations: singing, writing, tennis, macrame.

HUDECHECK, ROSEMARY ANNE, music director, consultant; b. Phila., Nov. 5, 1949; d. Joseph James and Geraldine Marie (Rooney) H. MusB, Immaculata Coll., 1971; MusM, West Chester U. Pa., 1980; MA in Liturgical Studies, Cath. U. Am., 1989. Cert. music tchr., Pa. Music specialist Chester (Pa.)-Upland Sch. Dist., 1971-82; dir. Archdiocesan Boys Choir, Phila., 1975-87; assoc. dir. Cathedral Choir, Phila., 1975-82; music specialist Visitation Parish Cath. Sch., Norristown, Pa., 1984-87; dir. music and liturgy St. John the Baptist Cath. Community, Silver Spring, Md., 1987—, dir. children's choir, 1990—; music cons. Archdiocese Wilmington, Del., 1991; cantor Archdiocese Washington, 1987—. Vol. Shepherd's Table, Silver Spring, 1989—. Recipient Liturgy/Music award Pa. State Senate, 1985, Pa. Ho. of Reps., 1985. Mem. Nat. Assn. Pastoral Musicians, Dir. Music Ministries, Nat. Music Honor Soc., Pi Kappa Lambda. Democrat. Office: St John Bapt Cath Community 12319 New Hampshire Ave Silver Spring MD 20904-2957

HUDGENS, ANN YOUNG, librarian, counselor; b. Louisville, Ky., Feb. 11, 1931; d. Paul L. and Leona (Pardue) Young; m. Raymond D. Hudgens, July 8, 1949; children: Eric E., Teresa Herndon. BA, Union U., 1964; MA, Peabody Coll., 1970, MLS, 1974; EdD, Tenn. State U., 1989. Cert. psychol. examiner, sch. counselor K-12, tchr. K-8, Tenn. Tchr. Anderson Sch., Brownsville, Tenn., 1964-66, Boyd-Buchanan, Chattanooga, 1966-68; libr., tchr. David Lipscomb U., Nashville, 1968—. Book reviewer Christian Chronicle, 1992. Driver, tchr. Inner City Ministry, Nashville, 1988—. Mem. AASL, ASCD, Tenn. Psychol. Assn., Tenn. Assn. Psychol. Examiners. Republican. Mem. Church of Christ. Office: David Lipscomb Univ 3901 Granny White Pike Nashville TN 37204-3903

HUDGENS, KIMBERLYN NAN, customer service representative; b. Hartwell, Ga., June 18, 1964; d. Kenneth Howard and Nan (Skelton) H.; m. Douglas Howard Abrams, June 30, 1990. BS in Indsl. Engring., Auburn U., 1988; BA in Math., Ogelthorpe U., 1988; postgrad., Mercer U., 1993—. Registered engr. in tng. Field rep. Law Assocs., Inc., Atlanta, 1988-89; assoc. quality engr. ABB Power T&D Co., Athens, Ga., 1989-91; rep. mem. svcs. Atlanta Gas Light Co., 1992—. Democrat. Methodist. Home: 3310 Hart Way Snellville GA 30278-4686

HUDGINS, CATHERINE HARDING, business executive; b. Raleigh, N.C., June 25, 1913; d. William Thomas and Mary Alice (Timberlake) Harding; m. Robert Scott Hudgins IV, Aug. 20, 1938; children: Catherine Harding Adams, Deborah Ghiselin, Robert Scott V. BS, N.C. State U., 1929-33; grad. tchr. N.C. Sch. for Deaf, 1933-34. Tchr. N.C. Sch. for Deaf, Morganton, 1934-36, N.J. Sch. for Deaf, Trenton, 1937-39; sec. Dr. A.S. Oliver, Raleigh, 1937, Robert S. Hudgins Co., Charlotte, N.C., 1949—, v.p., treas., 1960—, also bd. dirs. Mem. Jr. Svc. League, Easton, Pa., 1939; project chmn. ladies aux. Profl. Engrs. N.C., 1954-55, pres., 1956-57; pres. Christian High Sch. PTA, 1963; program chmn. Charlotte Opera Assn., 1959-61, sec., 1961-63; sec. bd. Hezekiah Alexander House Restoration, 1949-52, Hezekiah Alexander House Aux., 1975—, treas., 1983-84, v.p., 1984-85, pres., 1985-89; sec. Hezekiah Alexander Found., 1986—; past chmn. home missions, annuities and relief Women of Presbyn. Ch., past pres. Sunday Sch. class. Named Woman of Yr. Am. Biographical Soc., 1993. Mem. N.C. Hist. Assn., English Speaking Union, Internat. Platform Assn., Mint Mus. Drama Guild (pres. 1967-69), Internat. Biog. Ctr. Eng. (dep. dir. gen.), Daus. Am. Colonists (state chmn. nat. def. 1973-74, corr. sec. Virginia Dare chpt. 1978-79, 84-85, state insignia chmn. 1979-80), DAR (mem. nat. chmn.'s assn., rec. sec. nat. officers club 1990—, chpt. regent 1957-59, chpt. chaplain 1955-57 N.C. program chmn. 1961-63, state chmn. nat. def. 1973-76, state rec. sec. 1977-79, hon. state regent for life, chmn. N.C. Geneal. Register 1982, nat. vice chmn. S.E. region Am. Indians 1989—, rec. sec. Nat. Officers Club 1990-92, v.p. N.C. State Officer's Club 1991-92, pres. 1992-94), Children Am. Revolution (N.C. sr. pres. 1963-66, sr. nat. corr. sec., 1966-68, sr. nat. 1st v.p. 1968-70, sr. nat. pres. 1970-72, hon. sr. nat. pres. life 1972—, 2d v.p. Nat. Officers Club, 1st v.p. 1977-79, pres. 1979-81), Huguenot Soc. N.C., Carmel Country Club (Charlotte), Viewpoint 24 Club, (v.p. 1986, pres. 1987). Home: 1514 S Wendover Rd Charlotte NC 28211-1731 Office: Robert S Hudgins Co PO Box 17217 Charlotte NC 28270-0099

HUDGINS, JANET, company executive; b. Denver, Nov. 19, 1950; d. Charles Edward and Delores Clara (Priller) Barron; m. David Alan Hudgins, May 23, 1970; children: Rebecca Jean, Jonathan Andrew. AAS, Arapahoe C.C., Littleton, Colo., 1989. Owner Denver, 1977-90; design/drafting staff Lerch, Bates & Assocs., Littleton, 1991-93, project asst., 1993-94, project mgr., 1995—; cons. Manville Corp., Denver, 1989-91, Real Property Systems, Denver, 1990-91. Mem. student achievement com. Denver Pub. Schs. CDM Program, 1992. Mem. Profl. Auto CAD Users Group, Phi Theta Kappa. Republican. Office: Lerch Bates & Assocs #300 8089 S Lincoln St Ste 300 Littleton CO 80122-2721

HUDGINS, LOUISE NAN, parochial school educator; b. Ft. Worth; d. Joe Wallace and Lillian Frances (Taylor) H. BA, U. North Tex., 1960, postgrad., 1965. Cert. tchr. art, Tex. Fine arts supr. Dallas Ind. Sch. Dist., 1981-82; tchr. art Lida Hooe Elem. Sch., Dallas, 1966-81, Greiner Arts Acad., Dallas, 1982-86, Hotchkiss Montessori Acad., Dallas, 1986-94, Dealey Montessori Acad., Dallas, 1994—; state textbook com. Tex. Edn. Agy., Austin, 1981-82, com. mem., cons., 1984-85, workshop presenter U. Tex., 1989-91, Montessori Certification Program, Dallas, 1992-93; mem. com. Tex. Art Assessments Study, Richardson, 1993. Co-author: (tchr. textbook) Through Their Eyes, 1989; contbg. author: (student textbooks) Inside Art, 1992. Named Elem. Tchr. of Yr. Oak Cliff C. of C., Dallas, 1980. Mem. ASCD, Nat. Art Edn. Assn., Tex. Art Edn. Assn. (chair elem. divsn. 1983-84, rep. assembly 1987-89, Elem. Art Educator of Yr. 1988), Dallas Art Edn. Assn. (pres. 1988-89). Home: 1451 Winding Brook Cir Dallas TX 75208-2926

HUDGINS, PAULA ELIOSE, psychiatric and substance abuse nurse; b. Oklahoma City, Nov. 24, 1953; d. Robert Winston and Pauline (Hatcher) Winston; m. David A. Hudgins, May 25, 1975; children: Mandi, Jennifer. BSN, Houston Bapt. U., 1976; MS, Tex. Woman's Hosp. U., 1993. RN, Tex. Sch. nurse Needville (Tex.) Ind. Sch. Dist., 1976; insvc. coord. Good Shepherd Med. Ctr., Longview, Tex.; nurse clinician surg. svcs. St. Paul Med. Ctr., Dallas, 1982-88; mgr. children's psychiat. unit Willowbrook Hosp., Waxahachie, Tex., 1988-93; rsch. nurse Southwestern Med. Ctr., U. Tex., Dallas, 1993-94; clin. nurse specialist chem. addictions program Dallas VA Med. Ctr., 1994—. Mem. Am. Psychiat. Nurses Assn. (cert. psychiat. and mental health nurse). Home: 1000 W Main St Waxahachie TX 75165-2910

HUDKINS, CAROL L., state legislator; b. North Platte, Nebr., Feb. 21, 1945; m. Larry Hudkins; children: Janet, Kathy. Mem. Nebr. Senate, 1992—; mem. agr. gen. affairs com.; mem. judiciary com. Republican. Methodist. Home: 8600 NW 112th St Malcolm NE 68402*

HUDSON, BOBBIE BRADSHAW, librarian, media specialist; b. Danville, Va., Dec. 5, 1948; d. Robert Lee and Dora Lee (Jones) Bradshaw; m. Bruce Lynn Hudson, June 19, 1971. AS, Averett Coll., Danville, Va., 1968; BS, Radford U., 1970. Lic. tchr. libr. sci., English, Va. Media specialist Westmoreland and E.A. Gibson mid. schs. Danville Pub. Schs., 1971—; del U.S.-China Conf. on Edn., Beijing, 1992. Mem. Danville City Beautiful, 4th of July Com., Bicentennial Com.; pres. Dan Valley Rep. Women's Club. Mem. VEMA, Pilot Club of Danville, Inc. Republican. Presbyterian. Home: 449 Wimbish Dr Danville VA 24541 Office: E A Gibson Mid Sch Media Ctr 1215 Industrial Ave Danville VA 24541

HUDSON, CAMILLA CAROL, abstracter, examiner; b. Tucumcari, N.Mex., Aug. 30, 1946; d. Henry West and Florence (Curtis) Lindsey; m. Tommy Dewey Hudson, June 5, 1965 (div. Aug. 1993); 1 child, Cecile Sue. BS, Ea. N.Mex. U., 1968. Tchr. secondary edn. El Paso (Tex.) Sch. Sys., 1969-73; abstracter, examiner Stewart Title of Denton, Tex., 1977-84, Lawyers Title of Denton, 1984-87; examiner Graham Abstract Co., Portales, N.Mex., 1988—; escrow officer Stewart Title Co., Denton, 1980-84; title ins. agt. Graham Abstract Co., Portales, 1994. Mem. Soroptomist (chair social com. 1982—). Democrat. Home: PO Box 1295 Portales NM 88130 Office: Graham Abstract Co 107 W 2d St Portales NM 88130

HUDSON, CARLA RUTH, medical/surgical nurse; b. Steubenville, Ohio, May 8, 1962; d. Carl Roger and Ruth Elaine (Casey) H. Diploma, Barnes Hosp. Sch. of Nursing, 1984. RN, N.C., Mo., Ga. Staff nurse neuromedicine unit Barnes Hosp., St. Louis, 1984-86; staff nurse neurosurgery unit Duke U. Med. Ctr., Durham, N.C., 1986-87; staff nurse medicine unit Barnes Hosp., St. Louis, 1987-93; staff relief nurse KQC Staffing, 1993-94; shift supr. Vencor Hosp., St. Louis, 1994—; chairperson staff mgmt. team UBQA, mem. excel com. Barnes Hosp. Mem. ANA, AACN.

HUDSON, CELESTE NUTTING, education educator, reading clinic administrator, consultant; b. Nashville, Sept. 18; d. John Winthrop Chandler and Hilda Bass (Alexander) Nutting; m. Frank Alden Hudson III, Dec. 30, 1948 (dec.); children: Frank Alden IV (dec.), Jo Ann Hudson Algermissen, Celeste Jane Hudson Hayes, John Winthrop Nutting; m. Robert Daniel Quartell, June 3, 1989. BS, Oreg. Coll. Edn., 1952; MS, So. Ill. U., 1963, PhD, 1973. Cert. tchr., Tenn., Oreg., Mo., Iowa. Tchr. pub. schs., Crossville, Tenn., 1949-51, Salem, Oreg., 1952-53, West Walnut Manor and Jennings, Mo., 1953-54, Normandy Sch. Dist., St. Louis County, Mo., 1954-66; reading coord. Sikeston (Mo.) Pub. Schs., 1966-71; traveling cons. Ednl. Devel. Labs., Huntington, N.Y., 1970-71; mem. clin. staff So. Ill. U. Reading Ctr., 1972; asst. prof. edn. St. Ambrose Coll., 1972-75, U. Tenn.-Chattanooga, 1975-76; project dir. Learning Skills Ctr., St. Ambrose Coll. (became St. Ambrose U., 1986), 1976-80, asst. prof. edn., 1976-78, assoc. prof., 1979-86 , dir. elem. edn., 1972-75, 76-94, chmn. dept. edn., 1980-84, div. chmn., 1984-87 prof. edn., 1986-94, prof. emeritus, 1995—, dir. Reading Clinic, 1976-94; faculty vice chair St. Ambrose U., 1989-90, faculty chair, 1990-91; cons. reading; pvt. practice. Mem. Kimberly Village Bd., Davenport, Iowa, 1979-83; chmn. worship comm. Asbury Meth. Ch., 1985-90. Mem. AAUP, ASCD, AAUW, DAR, Assn. Tchrs. Educators, Iowa Assn. Colls. Tchr. Edn. (exec. bd. 1989-92), Internat. Reading Assn. (Scott County council), Am. Assn. Colls. Tchr. Edn., Miss. Bend Coun., Assn. Tchr. Educators, New Eng. Women (pres.-elect 1994—), Orgn. Tchr. Educators Reading, Internat. Platform Assn., Women in Ednl. Adminstrn., United Daus. Confederacy, Women of the Moose, Alpha Delta Kappa (past pres.), Kappa Delta Pi (sponsor), Phi Delta Kappa. Master gardener. Author: Handbook for Remedial Reading, 1967; Cognitive Listening and the Reading of Second Grade Children, 1973, The Effect of Visual Fatigue on Reading, 1990, Longitudinal Study of Children in Clinical Reading, 1994. Address: PO Box E140 Davenport IA 52806

HUDSON, CHERYL YOLUNDA, insurance claim manager; b. Little Rock, Aug. 8, 1960; d. Thomas Lee and Cornelia (Chism) H. BSBA, U. Tenn., 1982. Claims rep. Allstate Ins. Co., Cin., 1984-88; unit claim mgr. Allstate Ins. Co., Centerville, Ohio, 1988-90; casualty unit claim mgr. Allstate Ins. Co., Cin., 1990—; trainer customer focused quality Allstate Ins. Co., Cin. and Dayton, Ohio, 1989—, trainer quality edn., 1990—. Mem. Assn. Minority Enrichment through Networking (treas. 1987-88, Mem. of Yr. 1987), Delta Sigma Theta (treas. 1989-90, 2d v.p. 1990-92, pres. 1992—, Mem. of Yr. 1980). Baptist. Home: 11400 Lyncross Dr Cincinnati OH 45240-2210 Office: Allstate Ins Co 1 Crown Pt Ste 320 Cincinnati OH 45241

HUDSON, DONNA MARIE, medical librarian; b. Dayton, Ohio, Jan. 12, 1948; d. Joe Emory and Virginia Lucile Hudson. BA, Wright State U., 1970; MSLS, Case Western Res. U., 1971; postgrad., Nova U., 1992—. Student asst. libr. resources ctr. Wright State U., Dayton, 1968-70; student asst. sch. medicine libr. Case Western Rev. U., Cleve., 1970-71; tech. svcs. libr. med. ctr. libr. W.Va. U., Morgantown, 1971-73; dir. W.Va. Sch. Osteopathic Medicine Libr., Lewisburg, 1973-87; med. libr. Elmendorf AFB, Alaska, 1988—. Bd. dirs. Greenbrier Valley Theater, pres., treas., chmn. play selection com., chmn. bylaws com. Recipient award in Am. history Woodsmen of the World; God and Community award Girl Scouts Am. Mem. Alaska Health Scis. Libr. Adv. Coun. (bylaws com.), Med. Libr. Assn. (sect. coun. rep., chmn. com to explore sect. status osteopathic libr. group, hosp. sect., Pacific-Northwest chpt. com. info. tech.), Acad. Health Info. Profls. (sr.), W.Va. Libr. Assn. (chmn. spl. librs., chmn. intellectual freedom com.), W.Va. Health Scis. Libr. Assn. (pres., v.p., chmn. bylaws com.), Regional Med. Libr. (region 4 adv. coun., bylaws com., local arrangements 1983 mtg.), Alpha Psi Omega, Order of the Eastern Star. Home: 5300 E 4th Ave Apt 306 Anchorage AK 99508-2574 Office: Med Libr 3d Med Ctr/ CCQL 24800 Hosp Dr Elmendorf AFB AK 99506-3700

HUDSON, ELIZABETH HAMILTON, secondary education educator; b. Bryn Mawr, Pa., Nov. 22, 1945; d. Alexander Moag and Elsie Evelyn (Hamilton) Lyon; m. George Naylor, June 11, 1966 (dec. Jan. 1988); children: Heather Naylor, George Naylor; m. Duncan M. Perry, Sept. 11, 1994. BA, Davis and Elkins Coll., 1967. Cert. gifted and elem. edn. tchr. Mgr. Base Nursery Iraklion Air Sta., Crete, Greece, 1967-69; tchr. Yorktown (Va.) Sch. Dist., 1969-72; tchr., coord. gifted program Smyrna (Del.) Sch. Dist., 1977-87; tchr. gifted children Christina (Del.) Sch. Dist., 1991-94, curriculum facilitator, 1991—, tchr. adult edn. program, 1991-92; office adminstr. Media Rsch. Inst., Prague, Czechoslovakia, 1994—; state dir. Odyssey of the Mind, Del., 1984-87; advisor to class of 1987 Smyrna H.S., 1983-87; Del. MATHCOUNTS coach, 1994; Del. Geography Bee coach, 1994. Chmn. Old Dover (Del.) Days Crafts Display, 1974; mem. Statewide Commn. Gifted Edn.; Del. semifinalist NASA Tchrs. in Space Program, Dover, 1985; v.p. Del. Aerospace Ednl. Found. Recipient Air Force Assn.'s Secondary Educator award, 1992. Mem. AAUW (chairperson marionette show 1974, chairperson women's book sale 1976-77), NEA, Del. Edn. Assn., Del. Talented and Gifted Orgn. (pres.-elect, treas.), Christina Edn. Assn., Macintosh Users Del., Phi Delta Kappa, Phi Mu. Democrat. Presbyterian. Home: PO Box 9261 Newark DE 19714-9261 Office: OMRI, PO Box 268 Kaprova 12, 11001 Prague 1, Czech Republic

HUDSON, JACQUELINE, artist; b. Cambridge, Mass.; d. Eric and Gertrude (Dunton) H.; student Columbia U., Art Students League, Sch. of the Nat. Acad. One-woman shows: Burr Gallery, N.Y.C., Rockport (Mass.) Art Assn., Present Day Club, Princeton, N.J., Maine Art Gallery, Wiscasset, Moulton Union, Bowdoin Coll., 1979; group shows: NAD, Pa. Acad. Fine Arts, Library of Congress, Cin. Mus., Riverside Mus., Portland (Maine) Mus. Art, Dayton Art Inst., Bixler Mus., Colby Coll., Maine Art Gallery, Wiscasset, Bowdoin Coll., Farnsworth Mus., Rockland, Maine, Vallombreuse Gallery, Palm Beach, Fla., Galerie Salammbo, Paris, many others; represented permanent collection Library of Congress; pvt. collections. Recipient Pennell Purchase prize Library of Congress, 1951; Allen Kander Found. award Rockport Art Assn., 1957, Thelma Karr Graphic Prize, 1986; Edith Wengenroth Meml. prize, 1971, 75; Alice Standish Buell Meml. prize Nat. Assn. Women Artists, 1968, Helen Turner Graphic prize, 1974, Donna Miller Meml. prize, 1980; 3d graphic prize Butler Inst. Am. Art, 1983. Mem. Art Students League, Nat. Assn. Women Artists. Rockport Art Assn. (medal of honor 1989, Excellence in Graphics prize, 1992), Monhegan (Maine) Assos. (chmn. mus. com. 1963-67). Home: Monhegan Island ME 04852

HUDSON, JANE DUCLOS, management consultant, writer; b. Great Barrington, Mass., Sept. 23, 1949; d. Edward Warren and Elaine Duclos (Connelly) H.; B.A. magna cum laude, Newton Coll. of Sacred Heart, 1971; postgrad. Syracuse U., 1971-72; M.A., George Washington U., 1975; postgrad. Wesleyan U.; m. Donald Borod, Nov. 11, 1978; children: James Hudson, Catherine Duclos. Cert. mgmt. cons., 1984. Social sci. analyst Fed. Hwy. Adminstrn., Washington, 1972-73; mgmt. intern GSA, Washington, 1973-74, mgmt. analyst, 1974-75; mgmt. analyst Nat. Archives and Records Service, Washington, 1976-78; program analyst Nat. Archives and Records Service, N.Y.C., 1978-80; mgmt. cons. Booz-Allen & Hamilton, N.Y.C., 1980-2, Price Waterhouse, Hartford, Conn., 1982-84; ind. mgmt. cons., writer, 1984—; lectr. public adminstrn. Southeastern U., Washington, 1975. Maxwell fellow Syracuse U., 1971-72; Herbert H. Lehman fellow, 1971-72. Office: Moving Woods PO Box 270360 West Hartford CT 06127

HUDSON, JENNIFER SUE, marketing manager; b. Eugene, Oreg., Sept. 27, 1967; d. John Andrew Hudson and Susan Ann (Jensen) Singer. BS in Biology, Georgetown U., 1989; MBA in Mktg., NYU, 1993. Mgr. investor svcs. EquitiLink USA-First Australia Mut. Funds, N.Y.C., 1989-90; acct. mgr. Jensen & Singer Advt. Agy., N.Y.C., 1991-92; mgr. Am. Express, N.Y.C., 1992—. Recipient Top Mktg. Student award Leonard N. Stern Sch. Bus., 1993, Top Woman Student award, 1993. Office: American Express 200 Vesey St New York NY 10285

HUDSON, KATHERINE RUTH MCCLAIN, elementary school educator; b. Dearborn, Mich., July 29, 1963; d. J.L. and Lorene (Nanney) McClain; m. Robert Wesley Hudson, Aug. 3, 1985; 1 child, Benjamin Robert. BS in Elem. Edn., Liberty U., 1985; MEd in Early Childhood Edn., Lynchburg Coll., 1994. Cert. tchr. Va. Tchr. Amherst (Va.) County Schs., 1987—. Mem. NEA, Va. Edn. Assn., Amherst Edn. Assn. (faculty rep. 1990), Kappa Delta Pi. Republican. Baptist. Home: 1301 Grove Rd Lynchburg VA 24502

HUDSON, KATHLEEN JO, home health care nurse, nursing educator; b. Huntingburg, Ind., July 4, 1964; d. James Edgar and Karen Sue (Coomer) Blemker; m. Ronald Douglas Hudson, Mar. 21, 1987; children: Kayla Ann, Alyssa Lynn. BSN, U. Evansville, 1986, MSN, 1992. RN, Ind. Psychiatric nurse Welborn Bapt. Hosp., Evansville, Ind., 1986-87, critical care nurse, 1987; field nurse Vis. Nurses Assn., Evansville, Ind., 1987-90, quality assurance nurse, 1990-91, clin. educator, 1991-92; instr. nursing Wabash Valley Jr. Coll., Mt. Carmel, Ill., 1993—. Leader 4-H, Gibson County, Ind., 1984—. Mem. Ind. Nurses Assn., Phi Kappa Phi. Methodist. Home: 702 E Evans St Princeton IN 47670-2210

HUDSON, LEE (ARLENE HUDSON), environmental activist; b. Oakland, Calif., Apr. 17, 1936; d. Clyde Edward and Helen Therese (Cerutti) McIrvin; m. James Joseph Coté, Mar. 28, 1958 (div. 1963); 1 child, Steven Michael. BA in Psychology, Calif. State U., Sacramento, 1976, postgrad., 1977-78. Exec. field dir. Dem. State Cen. Com., Sacramento, 1967-68; mem. staff Calif. Legis., Sacramento, 1969-72; founder, chmn., editor newsletter The Group for Alternatives to Spreading Poisons, Nevada City, Calif., 1983—; non-chem. advocate on adv. com. to Calif. Dept. Transp. Roadside Vegetation Mgmt. Com., 1993—. Vol. various state, fed. and local campaigns or initiatives, 1967—; founding mem. Toxics Coordinating Project, San Francisco, 1985-90; co-founder Calif. Coalition for Alternatives to Pesticides, Arcata and Eureka, 1983—, pres., chmn. bd. dirs., 1989—; mem. Com. for Sustainable Agriculture, 1986—, mem. mktg.-order subcom., 1986-89; bd. dirs. NW Coalition for Alternatives to Pesticides, Eugene, 1987-93; mem., chmn. tech. writing com. Nevada County Adv. Com. on Air Pollution, 1988-93; mem. Hazardous Waste Transfer Facility Siting Com. for Nevada County, 1989-90; mem. Nevada County Hazardous Waste Task Force, 1987—, chair tech. sub-com., 1988-90; mem. Cen. Valley Hazardous Waste Minimization Com., 1990-91. Mem. Sierra Club (chmn. toxic subcom. Sierra Nevada group 1985-88), Amnesty Internat. Better World Soc., Cascade Holistic Econ. Cons., Coun. for Livable World, Nat. Peace Inst. Found., People's Med. Soc., Earth First, Nat. Resources Def. Coun., Nevada County C. of C., Greenpeace, Planning and Conservation League, Nevada County Greens Alliance, North Columbia Schoolhouse Cultural Ctr., South Yuba River Citizen's League, Siskiyou Mountains Resource Coun. (life), Rural Def. League. Mem. Universal Life Ch. Home and Office: 10984 Ridge Rd Nevada City CA 95959-8751

HUDSON, LINDA, health care executive; b. Tuscaloosa, Ala., Feb. 12, 1950; d. Elvin and Clara (Duke) Hudson; m. Charles Garrett Kimbrough, May 26, 1984. BS in Edn., U. Ala., 1971; MS in Psychology, U. So. Miss., 1984. Lic. profl. counselor. Recreational therapist West Ala. Rehab. Ctr., Tuscaloosa, 1971-72; flight attendant Delta Air Lines, Miami and New Orleans, 1972-80; pvt. practice psychotherapist Hattiesburg (Miss.) and Atlanta, 1984—; program dir. Eating Disorders Adventist Health System/

Wedst, Atlanta, 1985-88, regional dir./cons., 1986-87, exec. dir. mental health svcs., 1988-89; owner Hudson Cons. Assocs., 1989—, nat. cons., 1986—. Contbr. articles to profl. jours. Mem. Covington Jr. Svc. League, La., 1981-83; co-chmn. St. Tammany Rep. Polit. Action Com., 1980-81; coord. United Way of St. Tammany Parish, 1979-80. Mem. NAFE, Women Healthcare Execs., Atlanta Women's Network, Ga. Mental Health Counselors Assn., Nat. Coun. Sexual Addiction/Compulsivity (bd. dirs.). Democrat. Baptist. Office: 1090 Northchase Pky Ste 238 Marietta GA 30067-6402

HUDSON, MUTSUKO ENDO, Japanese language educator; b. Sapporo, Hokkaido, Japan, Aug. 30, 1949; came to U.S., 1973; d. Kotaro and Toshi (Yamada) Endo; m. Grover Milton Hudson, July 22, 1992. BA, Internat. Christian U., Tokyo, 1973; MA, U. Mich., 1977, PhD, 1989. Cert. Japanese oral proficiency tester. Lectr. U. Mich., Ann Arbor, 1978-87; instr. Middlebury (Vt.) Coll., 1987-89; asst. prof. Mich. State U., East Lansing, 1989—; vis. lectr. DePauw U., Greencastle, Ind., 1973-74, U. Mich., 1974-75, 76-77; vis. asst. prof. workshop for tchrs. of Japanese, Middlebury Coll., 1989, 90, vis. asst. prof. Inst. in Japanese Lang. Pedagogy, Columbia U., N.Y.C., 1991, 92, 94; instr. Japanese Lang. Sch., Middlebury Coll., 1981-83, 87; mem. Mich. Project on Computer-Assisted Instrn., U. Mich., Ann Arbor, 1984-85; interpreter for Gov. James J. Blanchard of Mich., 1984-86; speaker Va. Workshop Japanese Lang., Pedagogy, 1991, Japanese Lang. Cultural seminar Mich. Dept. Edn., 1993, 94; cons. Mich. Japanese Lang. Improvement Project, Mich. Dept. Edn., 1993—. Author: A Practical Guide for Teachers of Elementary Japanese, 1984, Supplementary Grammar Notes to an Introduction to Modern Japanese, part 1, 1986, part 2, 1987, English Grammar for Students of Japanese, 1994; co-author: Shuushoku, 1991; contbr. revs. to profl. jours. Exch. Student scholar Am. Field Svc., 1967-68, Rackham Non-Traditional Student scholar U. Mich., 1983-84, Rackham Dissertation scholar U. Mich., 1989; teaching fellow U. Mich., 1975-76, 77-78, Lilly Endowment Teaching fellow Indpls., 1992-93; Material Devel. grantee Japan Found., 1987, Japanese-Lang. Teaching Materials Donation grantee Japan Found., 1990, 92, Rsch. grantee Japan Forum, 1990-93, Workshop grantee Assn. Asian Studies, 1993. Mem. Am. Coun. on Teaching Fgn. Langs., Assn. Asian Studies, Assn. Tchrs. of Japanese (bd. dirs. 1993—), Linguistic Soc. Am., Mich. Linguistics Soc. Office: Mich State U Dept Linguistics And L East Lansing MI 48824

HUDSON, PHYLLIS JANECKE, librarian; b. Rock Island, Ill., Aug. 16, 1933; d. Clair Gordon and Helen Marie (Caffery) Janecke; m. Paul Alfred Hudson, Apr. 9, 1955; children: Helen Leora, Nancy Jan, Paula Kay, J. Phillip, Danae Claire. BS, U. Ill., 1964; MLS, 1970. Reference librarian Edn. Library U. Ill., Urbana, 1969-71, asst. librarian, 1971-72; head circulation Library U. Cen. Fla., Orlando, 1972-73, cataloger, 1973-74, reference librarian, 1974—. Editor: (column) Florida Libraries, 1978; contbr. articles to profl. jours. Mem. Nat. Commn. for Pay Equity, Washington, 1979—. Mem. ALA, Fla. Library Assn., Spl. Library Assn., Fla. Online Users Group, Fla. Assn. Coll. and Research Libraries (pres. 1982-83), United Faculty of Fla. (pres. U. Cen. Fla. chpt. 1981-83, lobbyist 1981-83, v.p. 1984-86, chief negotiator state univ. system 1984-86), Fla. Teaching Profession Assn. of NEA (bd. dirs. 1987-89), NOW (officer Seminole County chpt. 1980-82). Democrat. Office: U Central Fla 203 Library Orlando FL 32816

HUDSON, SANDRA ROBERTSON, corporate manager; b. Waynesville, N.C., Jan. 16, 1942; d. William Davis and Nettie Mae Robertson; m. Robert Edward Lee, Feb. 1963 (div. Jan. 1967); 1 child, Rebekah Kristine; m. James Frank Hudson, Oct. 1, 1967. Cert., U. N.C., Greensboro, 1961, UCLA, 1991, U. N.Mex., 1992. Div. sec. Sandia Nat. Labs., Albuquerque, 1966-69, dept. sec., 1969-83, staff sec., 1983-85, exec. sec., 1985-91, div. supr., 1991-92, dept. mgr., 1992—; voting mem. Sandia Nat. Labs. Policy Bd., 1991-94, spkr. in field. Registrar Rep. Party, Albuquerque, 1972-79. Presbyterian. Home: 7412 Cielo Grande NE Albuquerque NM 87109 Office: Sandia Nat Labs Operational Systems Dept Albuquerque NM 87185-0575

HUDSON, SARAH LOUISE, elementary school educator; b. San Francisco, June 9, 1966; d. Michael Calvert and Mary (Hahn) H. BA in English, UCLA, 1988, cert. in edn., 1990; postgrad., San Francisco State U., 1994—. Kindergarten tchr. L.A. United Sch. Dist., 1990-91, San Francisco United Sch. Dist., 1992—; master tchr. Sta. KQED Instrl. TV, San Francisco, 1994—. Vol. San Francisco Librs., 1992-93. Democrat.

HUDSON, SUNCERRAY ANN, university administrative assistant, research grants manager; b. San Francisco, Jan. 20, 1960; d. Charles Hudson and Nan Katherine (Coleman) Taylor. BA, U. San Francisco, 1982; student, Southeast Community Coll., San Francisco, 1988. Stock transfer clk. The Bank of Calif., San Francisco, 1983-85; prin. clk. U. Calif., San Francisco, 1985-87, adminstrv. asst. II, 1987-88, adminstrv. asst. III, 1988—; ind. dealer Nat. Safety Assocs., Inc., San Francisco, 1990—; art cons. Artistic Impression, Inc., 1994—. Mem. NAFE, Gamma Phi Delta (Rho chpt. 1990-92, Zeta Nu chpt. 1992—). Office: U Calif Campus Box 0440 521 Parnassus Ave San Francisco CA 94143

HUDSON, W. GAIL, social worker; b. Waxahachie, Tex., Apr. 15, 1953; d. Billy M. and Sarah W. (Bowen) H.; m. Garry H. Gillan, Sept. 7, 1991. BS, S.W. Tex. State U., 1975, MA, 1976; PhD, So. Ill. U., 1979; MSW, U. Tex., Arlington, 1989. Lic. master social worker, advanced clin. practitioner. Asst., assoc. prof. Millikin U., Decatur, Ill., 1978-87; dept. chair communications Millikin U., Decatur, 1984-87; adj. faculty U. Tex., Arlington, 1987-89; social work fellow M.D. Anderson Hosp., Houston, 1988; social work intern U. Houston Counseling, 1989; social worker U. Houston Counseling & Testing, 1989—; rep. AIDS Consortium of Tex., 1991; tng. cons. Caterpillar Tractor Co., Decatur, 1979-81; planning com. Nat. Conf. Against Sexual Assault, 1994; cons. Profl. Devel. Program, Decatur, 1979-81; adj. grad. faculty dept. counseling psychology U. Houston, 1991—. Cons. Houston Area Planning Commn. for Substance Abuse Program, 1990-91; treas. ERA Decatur, 1978-82; vol. Coalition Against Domestic Violence, Decatur, 1979-81. Cons. Houston Area Planning Commn. for Substance Abuse Program, 1990-91; prin. investigator/dir. prevention of substance abuse, U. Houston and Higher Edn. Consortium, Houston/Galveston, 1991-94. Grantee U.S. Dept. Edn. Mem. NASW, NOW, Am. Coll. Personnel Assn. (bd. dirs. 1991, 94), Am. Assn. Counseling and Devel.. Home: 1123 Burning Tree Humble TX 77339 Office: U Houston Counseling 4800 Calhoun Rd Houston TX 77204-0001

HUDSON-EDWARDS, COLETTA ANN, territory manager, veterinary technician; b. Kokomo, Ind., May 10, 1957; d. Robert Eugene Hudson and Gretchen Francis Galvin. AS in Vet. Tech., St. Petersburg Jr. Coll., 1980. Cert. vet. technician. Vet. technician Gainesville (Fla.) Animal Hosp., 1981-88; territory mgr. J.A. Webster, Inc., Gainesville, 1989—.

HUDSON-YOUNG, JANE SMITHER, real estate investor; b. Altavista, Va., July 5, 1937; d. Victor Nelson and Elois Reynolds Smither; A.A.S. summa cum laude in Mgmt., Central Va. Community Coll., 1978; m. J. Lee Hudson, May 15, 1954; 1 child, Michael Edward; m. Gordon M. Young, July 9, 1989. Adminstrv. asst. Altavista (Va.) High Sch., 1954-55; with Lane Co., Inc., Altavista, 1956-89, exec. sec. to chmn. bd., 1976-81, exec. sec. to chmn. exec. com., 1981-84, spl. asst. for pub. rels. communications, 1984-86, acct. exec. nat. accts, 1986, asst. sales mgr. contract div., 1986-87, mktg. adminstr., 1988-89; realtor R. B. Carr & Co., Altavista, 1980-87, assoc. broker, 1985-87; mem. adv. bd. Am. Fed. Savs. and Loan, 1985-89; pres. Hudson-Young Investments, 1989—; dir. Blue Heron Realty, Myrtle Beach, S.C., 1992—. Corr. Lynchburg (Va.) News., 1966-72. Mem. town coun. Town of Altavista, 1980-86; sec. Altavista Community Improvement Coun., 1981-82; mem. bd. deacons First Bapt. Ch., Altavista, 1980-83. Home and Office: 2200 Beverly Hts Altavista VA 24517-2004

HUEBNER, SUZANNE M., insurance company executive; b. Wausau, Wis., Mar. 31, 1958; d. Marvin J. and Janet S. (Reinhold) H. BBA in Risk Mgmt. and Ins., U. Wis., 1980. CLU. Individual life product analyst Wausau (Wis.) Ins. Cos., 1981-82, individual life product coord., 1982-85, dir. individual life products, 1985-87, casualty mktg. specialist, 1987-91, market devel. coord., 1991-94, dir. market R&D, 1994—; instr. Wausau Ins. Cos. and North Cen. Tech. Coll., Wausau, 1989—. Mem. Am. Soc. CLUs, U. Wis. Bus. Alumni, Wausau Country Club (ladies golf chmn. 1992). Office: Wausau Ins Cos 2000 Westwood Dr Wausau WI 54401-7802

HUELSMAN, JOANNE B., state legislator; b. Mar. 21, 1938; married. JD, Marquette U., 1980. Attorney, realtor, businesswoman; former mem. Wis. Ho. Reps. from 31st dist.; mem. Wis. State Senate from 31st dist. Republican. Home: 1924 Stardust Ct Waukesha WI 53186-2845 Office: Wis State Senate State Capital Madison WI 53702*

HUELSMAN, MARY ALICE, human resources professional, recruiter; b. Cin.; d. Henry N. and Barbara C. (Engel) Schmidt; m. J. Barry Huelsman (div.); 1 child, Jared G. BA in Comms., John Carroll U., 1978. Pers. asst. Bowman Distbn., Cleve.; pers. mgr. Craftint Mfg., Cleve.; compensation and benefits specialist TRW Inc., Lyndhurst, Ohio; human resources dir. Agy. Rent-A-Car, Solon, Ohio, 1988-93; v.p. human resources Magill Tech. Group, Solon, 1993—; change mgmt. cons. Magill Tech. Group, Solon, 1993—. Mem. Soc. for Human Resources Mgmt., Human Resources Sys. Profls., Human Resources Planning Soc., Cleve. Compensation Assn., Am. Scandinavian Student Exch. (area rep.). Office: Magill Tech Group PO Box 39188 Solon OH 44139-0188

HUERTA, DOLORES FERNANDEZ, labor union administrator; b. Dawson, N. Mex., Apr. 10, 1930; d. Juan and Alicia Fernandez; children: Celeste, Lori, Fidel, Emilio, Vincent, Alicia, Angela, Juanita, Maria, Elena, Ricky, Camilla. Co-founder, first v.p. United Farm Workers of Am., Keene, Calif., 1962—; co-founder, first v.p., bd. mem. Fund for the Feminist Majority. Recipient Martin Luther King award NAACP, Roger Baldwin award ACLU, Labor award Eugene V. Debs Found., Trumpeters award Consumers Union, Women First award YWCA, 1993; inductee Nat. Women's Hall of Fame, 1993. Office: United Farm Workers Union PO Box 62 La Paz Keene CA 93531*

HUEY, MILDRED SARTOR, school system administrator; b. Spartanburg, S.C., Apr. 24, 1956; d. Curtis and Mildred Flory Ree (Waddell) Sartor; divorced; 1 child, Ashanti Sartor Huey. BA, Converse Coll., 1978, MEd, 1979; EdD, Nova Southeastern U., 1993. Cert. tchr., S.C., Ga., N.C.; cert. supr., supt., prin., S.C., Ga., N.C. Elem. tchr. Spartanburg County Schs., 1978-85; prin. York Sch. Dist. 3, Rock Hill, S.C., 1985-89; dir. elem. edn. York (S.C.) Sch. Dist. 1, 1989—. Mem. S.C. ESEA Adminstrs. (pres. 1993-94), NAFEPA (bd. dirs.), S.C. Coun. Edn. Collaboration (mem. exec. com.), Assn. S.C. Adminstrs., S.C. ASCD (nat. bd. dirs.), Phi Delta Kappa (pres. Piedmont chpt. 1992-93), Sigma Gamma Rho. Office: York Dist One 18 Spruce St York SC 29745

HUF, CAROL ELINOR, tax service company executive; b. Milw., Apr. 21, 1940; d. William Weiss and Florence H. (Melcher) Weiss Lange; m. Walter Franklin Huf, Sept. 9, 1961; children: Mardell Leslie, Walter Albert III. Student Valparaiso U., 1958-60, Waukesha County Tech. Inst., 1968-69. Tax preparer H & R Block, Milw., 1967-84, instr. tax sch., 1969-83; job service interviewer State of Wis., Waukesha, 1984; pres. Personalized Tax Service, Inc., West Allis, Wis., 1984—, div. mgr. Primerica (formerly A.L. Williams), 1986. Vol. worker Girl Scouts US, Waukesha, 1970-80, Boy Scouts Am., Waukesha, 1975-92; swimming referee Wis. Interscholastic Athletic Assn., Milw., 1972-84. Recipient awards Boy Scouts Am. Mem. Nat. Soc. Pub. Accts., Wis. Womens Pub. Links Golf Assn. (past pres., 2d v.p. 1988—, state tournament chairperson 1987, 90, 94), United States Golf Assn. (regional affairs com. 1991—), Nat. Assn. Tax Practitioners (Wisc. bd. dirs. 1989—), Wis. Assn. Accts., Met. Swimming Ofcls., Edgewood Golf Club (pres. Big Bend, Wis. 1984-86). Lutheran. Home: 5508 Bauers Dr West Bend WI 53095-8782 Office: Personalized Tax Service Inc 10533 W National Ave Milwaukee WI 53227-2041

HUFF, CYNTHIA FAE, medical and orthopedic nurse; b. Albany, Ga., Jan. 3, 1950; d. Henry and Mary Catherine (Vannell) Piedmont; m. Michael Brian Shumaker, June 24, 1972 (div. 1979); 1 child, Brian Michael; m. Byron Lee Huff, Apr. 15, 1983. Diploma, Stuart Circle Hosp., Richmond, Va., 1970. RN, Va. Staff nurse St. Mary's Hosp., Richmond, 1970-71, asst. head nurse orthopedics, 1971, staff nurse emergency room, 1971-72, 73-74, head nurse orthopedics, 1972-73; office nurse Richmond, 1978-82; staff nurse Urology Ctr., Richmond, 1983-84; owner Sesroh Farm-Registered Quarterhorses, Powhatan, Va., 1984-89; nurse-technician for veterinarian for large and small animals, Midlothian, VA., 1986-90; staff nurse Amelia (Va.) Nursing Ctr., 1993—. Mem. Nat. Assn. Physicians' Nurses. Republican. Methodist. Home: 3009 Moyer Rd Powhatan VA 23139-7220

HUFF, GAYLE COMPTON, advertising agency executive; b. Washington, Nov. 28, 1956; d. Walter Dale and Jeanne (Parker) C.; m. Lanny Ross Huff, May 22, 1982. B in Gen. Studies, U. Mich., 1978. Mgr. br. merchandising CBS Records, Chgo., 1978; local promotion, mktg. mgr. CBS Records, Indpls., Boston, N.Y.C., 1978-81; spl. projects supr. Pickwick Internat. Musicland Group, Mpls., 1981-82; account exec. Campbell-Mithun Advt., Mpls., 1982-85; mktg. mgr., communications Universal Foods Corp., Milw., 1985-86; nat. advt. mgr. Thorobred Advt. Agy. (Jockey Internat., Inc.), Wis., 1986-88; dir. consumer and trade advt. Thorobred Advt. Agy. (Jockey Internat., Inc.), 1988-89, v.p. advt., 1990-92; dir. mktg./advt. Allen-Edmonds Shoe Co., Port Washington, Wis., 1993—; v.p., sec. Java Masters, Inc., 1992—. Mem. Traffic Audit Bur. for Media Measurement (bd. dirs. 1988-93), Assn. Nat. Advertisers (print adv. com., out of home advt. com. 1989-92). Office: Allen-Edmonds Shoe Corp 201 E 7th Hills Dr Port Washington WI 53074

HUFF, LULA ELEANOR LUNSFORD, controller, accounting educator; b. Columbus, Ga., July 5, 1949; d. Walter Theophilus and Sally Marie (Bryant) Lunsford; m. Charles Efferidge Huff Jr., June 11, 1972; 1 child, Tamara Nicole. BA, Howard U., 1971; MBA, Atlanta U., 1973. CPA, Ga. Acct. Ernst and Young, Columbus, 1973-76; internal auditor First Consol. Gov., Columbus, 1976-84; instr., chair dept. acctg., dir. pers. mgmt. Troy State U., Phenix City, Ala., 1979-89; sr. fin./cost analyst Pratt and Whitney, Columbus, 1984-89; controller Pratt and Whitney, Southington, Conn., 1989-92, Columbus, 1992—; tchr. Troy State U., Phenix City. Mem. fin. bd. Diocese of Savannah; mem. Liberty Theater Historic Preservation Bd., Columbus Housing Authority Bd., Columbus Historic Found. Bd., Columbus Literate Cmty. Program Inc. Bd., Columbus Beyond 2000, 1989-90. Recipient Disting. Black Citizen award Sta. WOKS, 1978, Black Excellence award Nat. Assn. Negro Bus. and Profl. Women's Clubs, Inc., 1977, Outstanding Svc. award St. Benedict Cath. Ch., 1971-76, cert. of merit Congressman Jack Brinkley, 1976, Achievement award Links Inc., 1976, Outstanding Achievement and Svcs. award 1st African Bapt. Ch., 1975, Ga. Jaycees Outstanding Young Woman award, 1989, Leadership Columbus award C. of C., 1983-84, Women on the Move award Spencer Deolettes, 1992; named Outstanding Woman of Yr., Ledger Enquirer Newspaper, 1976, Profl. Woman of Yr., Iota Phi Lambda, 1977, Bus. Woman of Yr., 1979, Columbus Ga. Outstanding Young Woman, Jaycees, 1980, Columbus Young Woman, 1980. Mem. NAACP, Am. Mgmt. Assn., Ga. Soc. CPAs, Howard U. Alumnae Assn., Urban League, Push, Toastmasters Am., Links, Inc. (Achievement award 1976), Delta Sigma Theta (auditor 1991). Roman Catholic. Home: 3630 Willow Bend Run Columbus GA 31907 Office: Pratt and Whitney 8801 Macon Rd M/S 906-32 Columbus GA 31908

HUFF, MARILYN L., federal judge; b. 1951. BA, Calvin Coll., Grand Rapids, Mich., 1972; JD, U. Mich., 1976. Assoc. Gray, Cary, Ames & Frye, 1976-83, ptnr., 1983-91; judge U.S. Dist. Ct. (so. dist.) Calif., San Diego, 1991—. Contbr. articles to profl. jours. Mem. adv. coun. Calif. LWV, 1987—, Am. Lung Assn.; bd. dirs. San Diego and Imperial Counties, 1989—; mem. LaJolla Presbyn. Ch. Named Legal Profl. of Yr. San Diego City Club and Jr. C. of C., 1990; recipient Superior Ct. Valuable Svc. award, 1982. Mem. ABA, San Diego Bar Found., San Diego Bar Assn. (bd. dirs. 1986-88, v.p. 1988, chmn. profl. edn. com. 1990, Svc. award to legal profession, 1989, Lawyer of Yr. 1990), Calif. State Bar Assn., Calif. Women Lawyers, Am. Bd. Trial Advs., Libel Def. Resource Ctr., Am. Inns of Ct. (master 1987—, exec. com. 1989—), Lawyers' Club San Diego (adv. bd. 1989-90, Belva Lockwood Svc. award 1987), Univ. Club, Aardvarks Lt. Office: US Dist Ct US Courthouse 940 Front St San Diego CA 92101-8994*

HUFFMAN, CAROL KOSTER, middle school educator; b. L.I., N.Y., Nov. 4, 1933; d. Harry C. Jr. and Mary M. (Wilchin) Koster; m. William Leslie Huffman. BS, Hofstra U., 1954, MS, 1967. Cert. elem., art, nursery and spl. edn. tchr., N.Y.; cert. advanced Irlen screener I and area coord. Dir. Child's World Sch., New Orleans; in-svc. instr. Half Hollow Hills Schs., Dix Hills, N.Y.; instr. in spl. edn. Hofstra U., Hempstead, N.Y.; resource, self-contained program, art and learning strategies tchr. Half Hollow Hills Schs., Dix Hills, N.Y.; rschr. identification and ednl. accomodations for students with visual disabilities affecting schoolwork; rschr. ednl. accomodations for autistic individuals through visual aids. Editor: The Communicator. Del. N.Y. State Retirement System. Mem. AFT (del.), N.Y. State United Tchrs. (del.), Half Hollow Hills Tchrs. Assn. (exec. bd.), Kappa Pi, Kappa Delta Pi. Home: 6 Ridge Rd Cold Spring Harbor NY 11724-1810

HUFFMAN, NONA GAY, financial consultant, retirement planning specialist; b. Albuquerque, June 22, 1942; d. William Abraham and Opal Irene (Leaton) Crisp; m. Donald Clyde Williams, Oct. 20, 1961; children: Debra Gaylene, James Donald. Student pub. schs. Lawndale, Calif. Lic. ins., securities dealer, N.Mex. Sec. City of L.A., 1960, L.A. City Schs. 1960-62, Aerospace Corp., El Segundo, Calif., 1962-64, Albuquerque Pub. Schs., 1972-73, Pub. Service Co. N.Mex., Albuquerque, 1973; rep., fin. planner Waddell & Reed, Inc., Albuquerque, 1979-84; broker Rauscher Pierce Refsnes, Inc., 1984-85; rep., investment and retirement specialist Fin. Network Investment Corp., 1985-89, John Hancock Fin. Svcs., 1989-90; account exec. Eppler, Guerin & Turner, Inc., 1990-91, Fin. Network Investment Corp., Albuquerque, 1991—; instr. on-site corp. training in fin. strategies for retirement, instr. fin. strategies for successful retirement U. N.Mex. Continuing Edn., instr. employee retirement seminars Fed. Exec. Bd. Mem. Profl. Orgn. Women (co-chmn.), Women in Bus. (Albuquerque chpt.), Internat. Assn. Fin. Planners. Office: Fin Network Investment Corp 8500 Menaul Blvd NE # 195B Albuquerque NM 87112-2298

HUFFMAN, PATRICIA JOAN, accounting coordinator; b. Elmira, N.Y., Mar. 29, 1941; d. F. John and Alice E. (Patterson) Garbay; m. Edward L. Huffman, May 28, 1960; children: Debra L. Palmer, Thomas E., Matthew M. AA in Bus. Adminstrn., Corning C.C., 1984, AA in Data Processing, 1984; BS, Elmira Coll., 1991. Clk. typist Hardinge's Bros., Elmira, N.Y., 1959-62, Gen. Precision Labs., Pleasantville, N.Y., 1965-66; data entry clk. Reader's Digest, Pleasantville, 1966-68, Elmira Data Processing, 1968-69; acctg. clk. Am. LaFrance, Elmira, 1969-73, GE, Elmira, 1973-75, Elmira Star-Gazette, 1975-77; various temporary positions Manpower, Elmira, Corning, N.Y., 1980, 84-85; pers. clk. Atlantic & Pacific Tea Co., Horseheads, N.Y., 1980-82; sales tax clk. Corning, Inc., 1985-88; finished goods inventory clk. Corning, Inc., Big Flats, N.Y., 1988-89; credit & collection clk. Corning, Inc., 1989-94, acctg. coord., 1994—. Author: (poem) Those Black Nights/Where Dreams Begin, 1993 (Editor's Choice award 1993), In Sorrow/Outstanding Poets of 1994 (Editor's Choice award, 1994), Remember the Good Times My Love/Dance on the Horizon, 1994. Sec. Ladies of Charity, Elmira, 1984-86, v.p., 1992—; lector St. Mary Our Mother Ch., Horseheads, N.Y., 1986-90. Mem. Internat. Soc. Poets (adv. panel mem. 1993—, Internat. Poet of Merit award 1993), Inst. Mgmt. Accts. Home: 31 Wolcott Dr Horseheads NY 14845

HUFHAM, BARBARA FRANCES, publishing executive, lawyer; b. Washington, Sept. 23, 1939; d. Ronald Lee and Barbara Adair (Brydon) H.; m. Richard Curtis Wells, Sept. 16, 1972. BA, Hood Coll., 1961; JD, NYU, 1968. Bar: N.Y. 1969. Writer Liberty Mut. Ins. Co., Boston, 1961-64; contracts asst. Macmillan Pub. Co., N.Y.C., 1964-65; mgr. rights and permissions div. Curtis Pub. Co., N.Y.C., 1965-68; asst. gen. counsel Harper & Row Pubs., N.Y.C., 1968-72, sec., asst. gen. counsel, 1972-85, assoc. gen. counsel, 1985-87, v.p., gen. counsel, 1987-89; sr. v.p. and gen. counsel Harper Collins Pubs. (formerly Harper & Row Pubs.), N.Y.C., 1989-94, sr. v.p. human resources, 1994—. Office: Harper Collins Pubs Inc 10 E 53rd St New York NY 10022-5244

HUFNAGEL, LINDA ANN, biology educator, researcher; b. Teaneck, N.J., Nov. 7, 1939; d. Ernest Albert and Frances Marie (Hrbek) H.; m. Dov Jaron, 1969; children: Shulamit, Tamara; m. Robert Van Zackroff, June 1984. BA, U. Vt., 1961, MS, 1963; PhD, U. Pa., 1967. Lectr. U. Pa., Phila., summer 1967; NSF postdoctoral fellow Yale U., New Haven, 1967-69; rsch. assoc. Columbia U., N.Y.C., 1970; asst. prof. Oakland Community Coll., Farmington, Mich., 1970; rsch. assoc. Wayne State U., Detroit, 1971-73; lectr. biology U. R.I., Kingston, 1973-75, asst. prof., 1975-79, assoc. prof., 1979-86, prof., 1986—, dir. cen. electron microscope facility, 1973—. NSF rsch. grantee U. R.I., 1975, Am. Heart Assn. rsch. grantee, 1979; Steps fellow Marine Biol. Lab., Woods Hole, Mass., 1978, 79. Office: U Rhode Island Dept Biochem Microbio & Molecular Gen Kingston RI 02881

HUFSTEDLER, SHIRLEY MOUNT (MRS. SETH M. HUFSTEDLER), lawyer, former federal judge; b. Denver, Aug. 24, 1925; d. Earl Stanley and Eva (Von Behren) Mount; m. Seth Martin Hufstedler, Aug. 16, 1949; 1 son, Steven Mark. BBA, U. N.Mex., 1945, LLD (hon.), 1972; LLB, Stanford U., 1949; LLD (hon.), U. Wyo., 1970, Gonzaga U., 1970, Occidental Coll., 1971, Tufts U., 1974, U. So. Calif., 1976, Georgetown U., 1976, U. Pa., 1976, Columbia U., 1977, U. Mich., 1979, Yale U., 1981, Rutgers U., 1981, Claremont U. Ctr., 1981, Smith Coll., 1982, Syracuse U., 1983, Mt. Holyoke Coll., 1985; PHH (hon.), Hood Coll., 1981, Hebrew Union Coll., 1986, Tulane U., 1988. Bar: Calif. 1950. Mem. firm Beardsley, Hufstedler & Kemble, L.A., 1951-61; practiced in L.A., 1961; judge Superior Ct., County L.A., 1961-66; justice Ct. Appeals 2d dist., 1966-68; circuit judge U.S. Ct. Appeals 9th cir., 1968-79; sec. U.S. Dept. Edn., 1979-81; ptnr. Hufstedler & Kaus, L.A., 1981—; dir. Hewlett Packard Co., US West, Inc., Harman Industries Internat. Mem. staff Stanford Law Rev, 1947-49; articles and book rev. editor, 1948-49. Trustee Calif. Inst. Tech., Occidental Coll., 1972-89, Aspen Inst., Colonial Williamsburg Found., 1976-93, Constl. Rights Found., 1978-80, Nat. Resources Def. Coun., 1983-85, Carnegie Endowment for Internat. Peace, 1983-94; bd. dirs. John T. and Catherine MacArthur Found., 1983—. Named Woman of Yr. Ladies Home Jour., 1976; recipient UCLA medal, 1981. Fellow Am. Acad. Arts and Scis.; mem. ABA, L.A. Bar Assn., Town Hall, Am. Law Inst. (coun. 1974-84), Am. Bar Found., Women Lawyers Assn. (pres. 1957-58), Am. Judicature Soc., Assn. of Bar of City of N.Y., Coun. on Fgn. Relations, Order of Coif. Office: Hufstedler & Kaus 355 S Grand Ave Los Angeles CA 90071-3107

HUGGINS, CHARLOTTE SUSAN HARRISON, secondary education educator, author, travel specialist; b. Rockford, Ill., May 13, 1933; d. Lyle Lux and Alta May (Bowers) H.; student Knox Coll., 1951-52; AB magna cum laude, Harvard U., 1958; MA, Northwestern U., 1960, postgrad., 1971-73; cert. in conversational French Berlitz Lang. Sch.; m. Rollin Charles Huggins, Apr. 26, 1952; children: Cynthia Charlotte Peters, Shirley Ann Cooper, John Charles. Asst. editor Hollister Pubs., Inc., Wilmette, Ill., 1959-65; tchr. advanced placement English New Trier High Sch., Winnetka, Ill., 1965—; master tchr., 1979; leader tchr., 1988; Task Force Commn. on Grading, 1973-74; Sabbatical project 1 yr. world travel History-Lit. Prospectus; cons. Asian Studies New Trier, 1987-88; mem. New Trier Supts. Commn. on Censorship, 1991; instr. critiquing Northwestern U.; cons. McDougall-Littel's Young Writer's Manual, 1985-88; asst. sponsor Echoes, 1981, Trevia, 1982, 83; sponsor New Trier News, 1988—; pres. Harrison Farms, Inc., Lovington, Ill., 1976—; speaker North Suburban Geneal. Soc., 1990; presenter Asian lit. Ill. Humanities Coun., 1992, Nat. Scholastic Press Assn. Conv., 1993; speaker Ill. High Sch. Scholastic Press Assn., No. Ill. Sch. Press Assn., 1992, 93, 94; instr., travel expert New Trier Adult Edn. Keys to the World's Last Mysteries, 1986—. Author: A Sequential Course in Composition Grades 9-12, 1979, A History of New Trier High School, 1982, Passage to Anaheim: An Historical Biography of Pioneer Families, 1984, Cambodia: A Place in Time, 1987; (video tapes) The Glory That Was Greece, 1987, The World of Charles Dickens, 1987. Mem. women's bd. St. Leonard's House, Chgo., 1965-75; Central Sch. PTA Bd., Wilmette, 1960-64; mem. jr. bd. Northwestern U. Settlement, Chgo., 1965-75. Recipient DAR Citizenship award, 1953, Phi Beta Kappa award, 1957, Am. Legion award, 1959, cert. of merit Graphic Arts Competition Printing Industries of Am., 1983, Quill and Scroll George Gallup award, 1990, 1st pl. award Am. Scholastic Press Assn., 1990, cert. of merit Am. Newspaper Pubs. Assn., 1990. Mem. MLA, NEA, ASCD, Ill. Edn. Assn., New Trier Edn. Assn. (sec. 1992, pres.-elect 1994), Nat. Coun. Tchrs. English, Ill. Assn. Tchrs. English, Women Comm., Inc., Northwestern U. Alumni Assn., Jr. Aux. U. Chgo. Cancer Research Bd., Mary Crane League, Nat. Huguenot Soc., Ill. Huguenot Soc., Columbia Scholastic Press Assn. (del 1990, newspaper judge, medalist award), Ill. Journalism Edn. Assn. (awards chmn., bd. dirs. 1992—, sec. 1994), Quill and Scroll (George Gallup award 1990, bd. dirs. 1992-93), Nat. Scholastic Press Assn. (spring convention rep. 1991-92, 92-93, newspaper judge, conv. del. 1991, All-Am. Newspaper award 1990-91, 91-92, Fall and Spring conv. presenter 1993-94, 94—), Women in Comm., Newberry Libr. (assoc.), Art Inst. Chgo. (life), Terra Mus. Chgo. (charter), Lyric Opera (assoc.), Women's Club Wilmette, Mich. Shores Club, Univ. Club Chgo., Knox Coll. Alumni Assn., Radcliffe Coll. Alumnae Assn., Harvard U. Alumni Assn., Pi Beta Phi (North Shore Chgo. alumnae bd., publicity chair). Home: 700 Greenwood Ave Wilmette IL 60091-1748 Office: 385 Winnetka Ave Winnetka IL 60093-4238

HUGGINS, DIANE ROBERTA TURBIN, nursing consultant, publisher, meeting planner; b. Balt., June 18, 1944; d. Irving and Sara (Glatt) Turbin; m. Gene Ender, May 20, 1975 (div. 1978); m. C.T. Huggins, Nov. 11, 1988; children: Melinda Lori Black, Stacey Meryl Black. BSN, Barry Coll., 1967; MS, Tex. Woman's U., 1976. RN, Tex., Fla.; cert. continuing nursing edn. provider. Asst. prof. Tex. Woman's U., Dallas, 1976-80; dir. mktg. and pub. rels. Dallas Rehab. Inst., 1980-88; dir. community rels. Olsten Health Care Svcs., Dallas, 1988-89; mktg. dir., rehab. cons. Response Rehab. Cons., Dallas, 1989-90; program liaison NRI at Brookhaven Hosp., Tulsa, 1990-91; pres., founder Am. Med. Sales Sch., Inc., Dallas, 1991—; cons. in field; pub. USA Med. Directories, 1992-93, 94. Contbg. author: Critical Care Nursing, 1982, 2d edit. 1985. Profl. adv. com. Multiple Sclerosis Soc., Dallas, 1992—; chmn. bd., founder Christ Ch. Dallas, 1993—. Recipient Human Rels. award Dale Carnegie Sales Course, 1991; award for Gt. 100 Nurses in Dallas-Ft. Worth Metroplex, 1992. Mem. Assn. Rehab. Nurses (N.Cen. chpt. bd. dirs.), Tex. and Dallas Head Injury Assn. (founder local chpt. 1982), Dallas/Ft. Worth Continuity of Care Orgn., Rehab. Ins. Nurses Group Dallas, Individual Case Mgmt. Assn., Sigma Theta Tau (Outstanding Mem. of Yr. 1977), Beta Sigma Phi. Home: 4240 Allencrest Ln Dallas TX 75244 Office: 4262 Spring Valley Rd Dallas TX 75244-3616

HUGGINS, ELAINE JACQUELINE, nurse, army officer; b. San Jose, Calif., Mar. 26, 1954; d. William Burt and Edith Gwendolyn (Schindler) Moreland; m. Bruce Carlton Allanach, Oct. 8, 1976, (div. Oct. 1989); stepchildren: Dawn Louise, Christopher Bruce, Jeffrey Scott, Sean Michael; m. Michael Henry Huggins, Dec. 8, 1991; children: Phoebe Marie, Chloe Anne; stepchildren: Abbey Rose, Jamin Michael. BS in Nursing, U.Md., 1976; MS in Nursing, Med. Coll. Ga., 1988; postgrad., Calif. Inst. Integral Studies. RN, Ga., Md., Calif. Commd. 2d lt. Nurse Corps, U.S. Army, 1972, advanced through grades to maj., 1986; staff nurse gen. medicine-oncology Walter Reed Army Med. Ctr., Washington, 1976-78, team leader gen. medicine-oncology, 1978-79, head nurse med. splty. ward, 1979-80; asst. head nurse gynecol. oncology unit Tripler Army Med. Ctr., Honolulu, 1980-81, head nurse med. splty. clinic, 1981-83; staff nurse orthopedics Eisenhower Army Med. Center, Ft. Gordon, Ga., 1983-84, patient edn. coord., 1984-85, head nurse recovery room, 1985-86; head nurse oncology/neurology unit Letterman Army Med. Ctr., Presidio of San Francisco, 1988-89, clin. nurse psychiat. unit, 1989-90, chief nursing adminstrn. E/N, Letterman Army Med. Ctr. Presidio of San Francisco, 1990-92, ret., 1992; casemanager Vis. Nurses Pomona, Claremont, Calif., 1993-94; nursing supr., Vis. Nurses Assn./Hospice of Pomona, San Bernadino, Calif., 1994-95, quality risk resource mgr., 1995—. lectr. in field. Contbr. articles to nursing, mil., and med. publs. Mem. pub. edn. com. Am. Cancer Soc., Honolulu, 1982. Recipient Humanitarian Svc. medal, 1990. Mem. Am. Diabetes Assn., Am. Assn. Diabetic Educators, Grad. Student Nurses Assn. (sec. 1986-87), Am. Nurses Assn., Mensa, Sigma Theta Tau. Avocations: reading, walking, beach combing. Home: 9866 Serrano Ct Rancho Cucamonga CA 91730-2882 Office: Visiting Nurses Assn Pomona Claremont CA 91711

HUGHES, AMBER LYNN, parcel service company administrator; b. L.A., Aug. 27, 1956; d. Raymond Hughes and Darlene Grace (Noe) Preziosi. AA, Golden West Coll., 1976; BA, San Diego State U., 1979. Package car driver United Parcel Svc., Gardena, Calif., 1979-81; human resource supr. United Parcel Svc., Anaheim, Calif., 1981-82; on road supr. United Parcel Svc., Westlake, Gardena, Calif., 1982-85; indsl. engring. supr. United Parcel Svc., Westlake, Ventura, Calif., 1985-86; ctr. mgr. United Parcel Svc., Gardena, Ventura, 1986-90; hub mgr. United Parcel Svc., San Fernando, Calif., 1990-91; div. mgr. United Parcel Svc., Gardena, 1991—; facilitator United Parcel Svc., Kansas City, Mo., 1994, instr., La Miranda, Calif., 1990, Orange, Calif., 1986. Coord. Harvesters, Kansas City, 1994. Recipient Medal of Excellence, Women at Work, 1992. Mem. Brown Betty Club (v.p. 1993—). Democrat. Roman Catholic. Office: United Parcel Svc 17115 Western Ave Gardena CA 90247

HUGHES, ANN, state legislator; b. Ogdensburg, N.Y., Sept. 28, 1943. BA in Biology, Wells Coll., 1965; student, McHenry County C.C., 1982. m. Earl Hughes; 3 children. Sec.-treas. Hughes Seed Farms; mem. Ill. Ho. of Reps., 1993—; mem. com. on counties and twps., mem. appropriations-edn. com., mem. cities and villages com., mem. environ. and energy com., mem. health task force. Home: 407 N Dimmel Rd Woodstock IL 60098-9264 Office: Ill Ho of Reps State Capitol Springfield IL 62706 also: 2114-N Stratton Bldg Springfield IL 62706 also: 5400 W Elm St Ste 212 Mc Henry IL 60050*

HUGHES, ANN FARRELL, business educator; b. Washington, Dec. 14, 1946; d. John Thomas and Elizabeth Ann (Corbly) Farrell; m. Philip Dunn Von Blond; children: George Hughes, Sarah Hughes, Philip Von Blond, Elizabeth Von Blond. BA, Ohio Dominican Coll., 1972; MA, Ohio State U., 1992. Fundraiser Congl. Campaign, Columbus, Ohio, 1972; exec. dir. Ct. Fire Watching Project, Inc., Columbus, 1972-81; regional dir. Youth for Understanding, Internat. Exch., Columbus, 1981-91; cons. Burns, Bertsch & Rainey, Inc., Columbus, 1992-93; tng. rep. Columbus State C.C., Columbus, 1993—; keynote spkr., panelist, workshop leader, trainer and facilitator for wide range of orgns; co-chair Ohio Team Excellence in the Pub. Sector Showcase Com., 1994—. Officer Action for Children, 1976-82, mem. Assisting Bd., Columbus, 1985—; active Columbus Met. Club, 1991—; task force mem. 1992 Commn.'s Host Friendly Project; mem. Cleve. Internat. Vol. Orgns.; diocesan rep. Ohio Coun. of Churches Criminal Justice Commn; mem. Franklin County Alliance for Cooperative Justice; head start program vol. John XXIII Sch.; host family for internat. visitors from Africa, Asia, Europe and Latin Am.; foster parent to unwed, expectant mothers; adv. bd. Ohio Dominican Coll. Criminal Justice Program, 1977-83; edn. program com. Am. Judicature Soc., 1981-83. Mem. World Trade Ctr. Assn., Am. Soc. Pub. Adminstrn., Columbus Area C. of C., Columbus Internat. Ctr. (bd. dirs.), Phi Kappa Phi, Pi Alpha Alpha. Democrat. Roman Catholic.

HUGHES, ANN HIGHTOWER, economist, government official; b. Birmingham, Ala., Nov. 24, 1938; d. Brady Alexander and Juanita (Pope) H. B.A., George Washington U., 1963, M.A., 1969. Asst. U.S. trade rep. Exec. Office of Pres., Washington, 1978-81; dep. asst. sec. trade agreements Dept. Commerce, Washington, 1981-82, dep. asst. sec. Western Hemisphere, 1982—. Recipient meritorious exec. award Pres. of U.S., 1982, 88, disting. exec. award, 1993. Office: Dept Commerce Rm 3826 14th & Constitution Ave NW Washington DC 20230-0002

HUGHES, ANN NOLEN, mental health counselor; b. Ft. Meade, Md.; d. George M. and Georgie T. Nolen; m. Edwin L. Hughes, Oct. 21, 1961; 1 child, Andrew G. BS in Psychology, Rollins Coll., 1985, MA in Counseling, 1986; student in pub. speaking and human rels., Dale Carnegie Inst., 1981; student, Duke U., 1950-52. Lic. mental health counselor; nat. cert. counselor; nat. cert. gerontol. counselor. Supr. top secret control, audio/visual small parts supply U.S. Army, Continental U.S. and Tokyo; adminstrv. sec. System Devel. Corp., Rand Corp., Santa Monica, Calif.; adminstrv. asst., editor, exec. sec., adminstrv. sec. Aerospace Corp., El Segundo, Calif.; staff therapist Circles of Care, Melbourne, Fla.; developer program for leading divorce support groups for Brevard Women's Ctr. Various leadership positions PTA, Pittsford, N.Y., Brookfield, Wis.; mem. Brevard Cmty. Chorus. Various leadership positions PTA, Pittsford, N.Y., Brookfield, Wis., 1968-81; active Brevard Community Chorus. Mem. ACA, Specialists in Group Work, Am. Mental Health Counselors Assn., Assn. for Adult Development and Aging, Space Coast PC User's Group, Nat. Geneal. Soc., Va. Geneal. Soc., Geneal. Soc. South Brevard, Suntree Country Club, Brevard County Alumnae Assn. Kappa Kappa Gamma, Kappa Kappa Gamma. Presbyterian. Home: 447 Pauma Valley Way Melbourne FL 32940-1918

HUGHES, BARBARA ANN, dietitian, public health administrator, nutritionist; b. McMinn County, Tenn., July 22, 1938; d. Cecil Earl and Hannah Ruth (Moss) Farmer; BS cum laude in Home Econs. Carson Newman Coll., Jefferson City, Tenn., 1960; MS in Instl. Mgmt., Ohio State U., Columbus, 1963; MA (Adonarium Judson scholar), So. Bapt. Theol. Sem., 1968; MPH, U. N.C., Chapel Hill, 1972; postgrad. in nutrition U. Iowa, 1974, U. N.C., 1975-85, Case Western Res. U., 1979, Walden U.; PhD 1988; m. Carl Clifford Hughes, Oct. 13, 1962. Registered, lic. nutritionist, dietitian. Instr., clin. dietitian Riverside Meth. Hosp., Riverside Whitecross Sch. Nursing, Columbus, 1963-66; consulting dietitian Mount Holly Nursing Home, Ky. Dept. Mental Health, 1966-68, eastern region N.C. Bd. Health, Raleigh, 1968-73; dir. Nutrition and Dietary Services br., Div. Health Services, N.C. Dept. Human Resources, Raleigh, 1973-89, also dir. Women-Infants-Children Program; pres. B.A. Hughes and Assocs., 1990—; asst. to Rep. Karen Gottovi 14th Dist. N.C. Ho. of Reps., Gen. Assembly N.C., 1994; adj. instr. Case Western Res. U., Cleve., 1988-89; adj. asst. prof. dept. nutrition Sch. Public Health, U. N.C., Chapel Hill, 1975-89; mem. adv. bd. Hospitality Edn. program N.C. Dept. Community Colls., 1974-80, adv. com. Ret. Senior Vol. Program, Raleigh and Wake County, N.C., 1975-79, N.C. Network Coordinating Council for End-Stage Renal Disease, 1975, Nat. Adv. Council on Maternal, Infant, and Fetal Nutrition, Spl. Supplemental Food Program for Women, Infants, and Children, Dept. Agr., 1976-79, adv. com. Nutrition Edn. and Tng. program N.C. Dept. Pub. Instrn., 1978-80; mem.-at-large adv. leadership coun. N.C. Cooperative Ext. Svc., 1994—; advisor com. to Wake County N.C. Cooperative Ext. Svc., 1992—, chair. adv. coun., 1995—; coord. undergrad. program in gen dietetics East Carolina U.; adv. council N.C. Gov.'s Office Citizen Affairs; cons. dietitian Augusta Victoria Hosp. and Jerusalem (Israel) Crippled Childrens Center, 1968; witness U.S. congressional and Senate hearings in field. Active edn. programs Pullen Memorial Bapt. Church, Raleigh, deacon, 1976-80, 94—, area ministry capt., 1977-78, personnel com., 1978-80; bd. dirs. Community Outreach, 1989-92, futuring Com., 1994—; dietitian/dir. food service archeol. expedition to Israel, 1968; bd. dirs. N.C. Literacy Assn. 1978-83, 93—, pres., 1981-83; v.p. Wake County Literacy Council, 1986-87; trustee Gardner-Webb Coll., Boiling Springs, N.C., 1979-82, chmn. curriculum com., 1981-82; chmn. Coalition Pub. Health Nutrition, 1983-85; del. various Democratic Convs., 1981-84, precinct sec.-treas., 1981-83, 1st vice chmn., 1983-85, 2nd vice chmn., 1993—, chair, 1985-87; chmn. adv. bd. dept. home econs. Carson-Newman Coll.; area coord. (N.C.) Pacific Intercultural Exch., 1990—; chair Wake County Affiliate food festival com., 1991-92,chair edn. and community program com., 1992—, Am. Heart Assn., bd. dirs., 1992-94; precinct coord. Ruth Cook for N.C. Senate, Dist. 14, 1994; mem. chronic disease com. Wake County Bd. Health, 1993—; pres. State N.C. Coun. Social Legislation, 1993—. Named Woman of Yr., Wake County, 1975, N.C. Outstanding Dietitian of Yr., 1976, N.C. Outstanding Dietitian, Southeastern Hosp. Conf. for Dietitians, 1978; recipient Disting. Alumna award Carson-Newman Coll., 1983. Fellow N.C. Inst. Polit. Leadership; mem. AAUW (life, pres. Raleigh br. 1971-75, 91-93, pres. N.C. div. 1978-80, coordinator Wake Women Celebrate, 1994, nat. bd. dirs. 1980-82, area rep. 1980-82, nat. edn. found. bd. dirs. 1987-91, ednl. equity roundtable 1992), Am. Dietetic Assn. (del. 1971-74, 87-89, pres. N.C. state assn. 1976-77, N.C. network legis. coordinator 1978-81, 92—, nat. nominating com. 1979-80, nat. chmn. council on practice 1982-83, nat. chair legislation and pub. policy com. 1985-87, nat. area coord. Ho. of Dels. 1989-92, commn. dietetic registration assessment devel. com. for credential of FELLOW program 1994, nat. mem. bylaws com. 1989hair resolutions com. 1990-91), Am. Public Health Assn. (exec. com. So. br. 1977-87, sec.-treas. 1979-80, 1st v.p. 1980-81, Catherine Cowell award 1994), So. Health Assn. (pres. 1982-83, chair nominating com. 1985-86, 91-92, awards com. 1992-93, Spl. Meritorious award 1989), Assn. State and Territorial Pub. Health Nutrition Dirs. (pres. 1977-79, dir. 1981-89, liaison to Assn. Faculties Grad. Program in Pub. Health Nutrition, chair legis. and pub. policy com. 1984-89, Commendation award 1989), N.C. Bds. of Health, N.C. Council Foods and Nutrition (dir. 1976-78, chmn. membership 1975, nominating com. 1979). N.C. Council Women's Orgns. (mem. at large, bd. dirs. 1989-92, leadership com. 1991—, chair nutrition subcom., Wellness in State Employees adv. bd. 1989-91), Am. Acad. Health Adminstrn., Soc. Nutrition Edn., Nutrition Today Soc., N.C. Acad. Public Health, Ohio State U. Alumni Assn. (life), U. N.C. Gen. Alumni Assn. (life), U. N.C. Public Health Alumni Assn. (life), Altrusa Internat. (pres. Raleigh club 1973-74, 93-95, dir. 1976-78, 90—, 1st vice gov. 1978-79, chmn. nomination com. 1980-82, gov. dist. Three, 1979-80, internat. vocat. services chmn. 1977-79, 1st v.p. 1985-87, pres.-elect 1987-89, pres. 1989-91), Altrusa Internat. Found. (1st v.p. 1985-87, chmn.-elect 1990-92, chmn. 1992—, bd. dirs. 1993—), Greater Raleigh C. of C. (mem. west area bus. coun., mem. legis. com., mem. leadership Raleigh 10 1994—), Women's Forum N.C. (young leadership award com. 1989-90, 92—, newsletter editor bd. dirs. 1992—, adminstr. 1995—). Co-author: Diet and Kidney Disease, Assn. for N.C. Regional Med. Program, 1969; contbr. numerous papers, articles to symposia, periodicals in field, vol. areas. Home: 4208 Galax Dr Raleigh NC 27612-3714

HUGHES, BARBARA BRADFORD, nurse; b. Bragg City, Mo., Jan. 21, 1941; d. Lawrence Hurl Bradford and Opal Jewel (Prater) Puttin; m. Robert Howard Hughes, Dec. 9, 1961; children: Kimberly Ann Hayden, Robert Howard II. ASN, St. Louis Community Coll., 1978; student, Webster U., 1980. RN, Mo. Med. surg. nurse Alexian Bros. Hosp., St. Louis, 1979-80; staff nurse Midwest Allergy Cons., St. Louis, 1980; nurse high altitude Aviation Nurse, Ltd., St. Louis, 1980-81; cardiac telemetry staff nurse Jefferson Meml. Hosp., Chrystal City, Mo., 1992—, staff nurse cardiology, 1992-94; pvt. practice real estate mgmt., 1962—. Vol. Luth. Hosp., St. Louis, 1967-70; mem. Mo. Bot. Garden, St. Louis, 1976—, Mo. Hist. Soc., 1993—, St. Louis Zoo Friends Assn., 1986-87, Nat. Trust for Hist. Preservation, 1990—; Channel 9-Ednl. TV, St. Louis; vol. blood drive ARC, St. Louis, 1980; vol. health tchr. Spartan Aluminum Products, Sparta, Ill., 1984. U. Mo. scholar, 1959. Mem. Internat. Flying Nurses Assn. (sec. 1991-92), Mo. Pilots Assn., U.S. Pilots Assn., Tyospaye Club. Republican. Home: 736 Windsor Harbor Rd Imperial MO 63052-2503

HUGHES, GRACE-FLORES, former federal agency administrator, management consulting executive; b. Taft, Tex., June 11, 1946; d. Adan Flores and Catalina San Miguel; m. Harley Arnold Hughes, May 25, 1980. BA, U. D.C., 1977; MPA, Harvard U., 1980. Sec. Dept. Air Force Kelly AFB, San Antonio, 1967-70, Pentagon-Office Sec. of Def., Washington, 1970-72; program asst., social sci. analyst HEW, Washington, 1972-78; social sci. analyst, acting dir. Office Hispanic Ams. HHS, Washington, 1978-81; vis. prof. Nebr. Wesleyan U., Lincoln, 1982-83, U. Nebr., Omaha, 1984; spl. asst. SBA, Washington, 1985-88, assoc. adminstr. for minority small bus., 1988; dir. community rels. Dept. Justice, Washington, 1988-92; pres. Grace, Inc., Alexandria, Va.; spl. asst. Reagan/Bush '84 Campaign, Nebr. and Washington, 1984, 50th Presdl. Inaugural, Washington, 1984-85, Office Pub. Liaison, The White House, 1985. Author: The Bureaucrat, Categorized Workforce, 1992; co-author: New Book of Knowledge, 1980; chair adv. bd. Harvard Jour. Hispanic Policy, 1989—; The Use and Abuse of Diversity Hispanic Mag., 1994. Adv. mem. U.S. Senate Rep. Task Force, Washington, 1988-91; alumni exec. bd. J.F. Kennedy Sch. Govt., Harvard U., Cambridge, Mass., 1989—; mem. Rep. Hispanic Assembly, 1984—; appointed by Gov. Allen of Va. to bd. for Profl. and Occupational Regulations, 1994-98. Recipient Excellence award Nev. Econ. Devel. Corp., 1988, Leadership award Am. GI Forum, Omaha, 1989; named one of 100 Most Influential Hispanics in U.S. Hispanic Bus. Mag., 1988. Mem. Assn. Pub. Adminstrs. (Outstanding Pub. Svc. award 1990), Exec. Women in Govt., Nat. Hispanic Women's Coun., Hispanic Women's Network, Women's Leadership Network, Mexican Am. Women's Nat. Assn., Univ. Club (Washington). Roman Catholic. Home and Office: 5208 Bedlington Ter Alexandria VA 22304-3551

HUGHES, HEIDI, retail executive; b. Orange, N.J., Feb. 23, 1948; d. John Walker and Dorothy Eloise (Walker) H; m. Thomas Michael Valega, Mar. 15, 1988. BS, Skidmore Coll., 1971; MA in Journalism, Am. U., 1983. Curator L.A. Zoo, 1977-78; outdoor recreation planner U.S. Fish and Wildlife Svc., Washington, 1978-80; pub. relations dir. Dept. of Wildlife, Washington, 1981-82; news assignment staff Sta. WRC-TV, Washington, 1984; press sec. to Congressman Don Bonker Ho. of Reps., Washington, 1985; profl. lectr. Am. U., Washington, 1987; pres. News Speak Pub. Relations, Rockville, Md., 1986-88, Am. Wild Bird Co., Rockville, 1988—, Wild Bird Co. Rockville, 1988—; dir. edn. Raccoon Ridge Bird Obs., Layton, N.J., 1976-83; pres. Nat. Backyard Wildlife Ctr., 1994—, Heidi Hughes Enterprises, 1993—; lectr. Smithsonian Assocs., 1990—; cons. in field; lectr. in field. Author: Backyard Bird Feeding, 1989; co-author: The Experts Guide to Backyard Bird Feeding, 1990; editor: Wild Bird Observer, Home for Birds, 1990; author: A Guide to Backyard Birds 1991 Calendar, A Guide to Backyard Birds 1992 Calendar, A Guide to Backyard Birds 1993 Calendar, Feed the Birds!, 1991, Backyard Bird Problems, 1991; publisher: Feed the Birds!, 1994, Put Up A Nest Box!, 1994; contbr. articles to profl. jours.; photographer; author: 1993 Migratory Songbird Conservation. Recipient Merriman award Writers Guild Am., 1983, Image award Nat. Assn. Remodeling Industry, 1986. Mem. Wild Bird Feeding Inst., NATAS (Davis award 1983), Md. Ornithol. Soc., Am. Bat Conservation Soc. (pres. 1991, v.p. 1992), Am. Backyard Bird Soc. (v.p. 1991). Democrat. Pantheist. Home: 802 Cabin John Pky Rockville MD 20852-1025 Office: Wild Bird Co American Wild Bird Co Show 591 Hungerford Dr Rockville MD 20850-1721

HUGHES, JANE COUGHLIN, health education specialist; b. Dayton, Ohio, Mar. 18, 1942; d. Thomas Joseph and Edna Irene (Resh) Coughlin; m. Patrick W. Hughes, May 4, 1963; children: Patrick W. Jr., Jonathan Mark, Suzanne Michelle. ADN, St. Anthony Sch. Nursing, Oklahoma City, 1963; BBA, U. Ctrl. Okla., 1984; MPH, U. Okla., 1989. Cert. health edn. specialist; RN Okla. 1989. Psychiat. nurse St. Anthony Hosp., Oklahoma City, 1963-64; rsch. nurse U. Okla. Sch. Medicine, Oklahoma City, 1965-67; staff nurse Presbyn. Hosp., Oklahoma City, 1969-72; with Okla. State Dept. Mental Health, Oklahoma City, 1983, 86-87; dir. fin. Hospice of Ctrl. Okla., Oklahoma City, 1984-85; staff nurse HealthSouth Rehab., Oklahoma City, 1986-87; med. record abstractor Okla. State Dept. Health, Oklahoma City, 1989; assoc. dir. Emerson Teen Parent Program, Oklahoma City, 1990-91; project dir. Okla. Fetal and Infant Mortality Analysis Program, Oklahoma City, 1992—. Bd. dirs. Visiting Nurses Assn., Oklahoma City, 1980-83, 88-94; treas. AAUW, Oklahoma City, 1984-87, 89-90. Recipient Three Yr. scholarship St. Anthony Sch. Nursing, Oklahoma City, 1960-63, Three Svc. awards Jaycee Jaynes, Oklahoma City, 1964-69, Pres.'s award for vol. svc. Jr. Hospitality Club, Oklahoma City, 1983; named Women of Achievement, AAUW, Oklahoma City, 1992. Mem. Okla. Pub. Health Assn., Teen Pregnancy Coalition Oklahoma City (sec. 1993). Democrat. Roman Catholic. Home: 3101 NW 21st St Oklahoma City OK 73107-3009 Office: Okla Fetal and Infant Mortality Analysis 940 NE 13th St Oklahoma City OK 73107

HUGHES, JANET KATHERINE, artist, educator; b. Balt., Nov. 28, 1944; children: Eric Davidson, Brian Kristopher. BA, Wake Forest U., 1966; MA, Columbia U., 1974; MFA with honors, U. Kans., 1992. Prof. art Ind. State U., Terre Haute, 1992—; creative dir., performance artist W.E. Performance Group, 1991—. Exhibited in group shows Bklyn. Mus., 1974, San Diego Mus. Arts, 1975, U. Western Ont., Can., 1987, Regional Arts Commn., St. Louis, 1987, Imperial Calcasieu Mus., Lake Charles, La., 1988, Smith Art Mus., Springfield, Mass., 1988, Braithwaite Fine Arts Gallery, Cedar City, Utah, 1988, WomanArt XI, Wichita, Kans., 1988, U. Ala., Tuscaloosa, 1993, Jan Weiner Gallery, Kansas City, 1993, Mus. Art and Archaeology, Columbia, Mo., 1993, 94, numerous others. Grantee Indpls. Art League, 1992, Mo. Arts Coun., 1993. Mem. Coll. Art Assn., Kansas City Artists Coalition, Phi Kappa Phi. Home: 2130 Wabash Ave Terre Haute IN 47807-3304 Office: Ind State U Dept Art Terre Haute IN 47809

HUGHES, JANICE DEBORAH, health care administrator; b. Pitts., Mar. 24, 1948; d. James Francis and Margaret Veronica (Wiullmier) H. Diploma in nursing, Columbia Sch. Nursing, Pitts., 1969; BSN, La Roche Coll., 1987; M of Pub. Mgmt., Carnegie-Mellon U., 1988. Cert. nursing adminstr., med. staff coord., profl. in healthcare quality. Staff nurse Forbes Health System, Pitts., 1969-78, head nurse recovery, 1978-79, supr. nursing, 1979-84, clin. asst. to med. dir., 1984-88, dir. med. staff svcs., 1988-90; quality tracking mgr. Humana Inc., Louisville, 1990-91; regional quality mgmt. dir. Gatan Health Care, Inc., Louisville, 1991-92; sr. cons. quality and resource mgmt. Metri Cor, Inc., Louisville, 1992—. Mem. Am. Hosp. Assn., Nat. Assn. Healthcare Quality, Ky. Assn. Quality Assurance Profls., Ky. Soc. Healthcare Risk Mgmt., Nat. Assn. Med. Staff Svcs., Internat. Soc. Quality Assurance, Sigma Theta Tau. Office: Metri Cor Inc 500 W Main St Ste 1900 Louisville KY 40202-2941

HUGHES, JUDY LYNNE, political organization executive; b. San Antonio, Mar. 23, 1939; d. Timothy Endymion Gristy and Clovis Ruth (Mooring) Linville; m. Donald E. LaMora, Nov. 12, 1960 (div. Aug. 1980); children: Grant, Leigh, Eric; m. William J. Hughes, May 11, 1984 (div. 1990). Student, Tex. Tech. U., 1956-60. News reporter Colorado Springs (Colo.) Gazette Telegraph, 1960; vice chair pub. rels. Nat. Fedn. Rep. Women, Washington, 1974-76, mem.-at-large exec. com., 1976-78; 2d v.p. Nat. Fedn. Rep. Women, 1978-82, 1st v.p., 1982-86, pres., 1986-90; western rep. U.S. Dept. Interior, Golden, Colo., 1991-93; polit. edn. specialist Rep. Nat. Com., Washington, 1993-95, chief of staff to co-chmn., 1995—; ofcl. del. U.S. State Dept., El Salvador, 1989; mem. Dept. Interior's Representation on Denver Interagy. Coun. on Homeless, 1990-93; mem. Denver Fed. Exec. Bd. Pub. Rels. Coun., 1990-93. mem. RNC Com. Minority Participation, Washington, 1989; bd. dirs. Colo. Coun. on Econ. Edn., 1991-93. Named Rep. Woman of Yr., Shelby County Rep. Women's Club, 1988. Mem. Pikes Peak Rep. Women's Roundtable (Colorado Springs). Home: 501 Slaters Ln #903 Alexandria VA 22314 Office: Rep Nat Com 310 1st St SE Washington DC 20003

HUGHES, KAREN SUE, geriatrics nurse; b. Wooster, Ohio, Oct. 16, 1955; d. Alvin S. and Pauline Katheryn (Troyer) Yutzy; m. Christopher Charles Marek, Sept. 3, 1977 (div. 1993); m. Raymond H. Hughes, July 20, 1993. LPN, Wayne County Vocat. Sch., 1974; BSN, Akron U., 1994. LPN, RN, Ohio. LPN, GPN, nurse aide Wooster Community Hosp., 1974-76; LPN Apple Creek (Ohio) Devel. Ctr., 1976-77, Smithville Western Care Ctr., Wooster, 1977-78, 78-80; supervisory LPN Gruter Found., Wooster, 1980-87; light indsl. worker Victor Temporary Svcs., Mansfield, Ohio, 1988-89; plant mgr. asst. Detroit Detroit Inc., Wayne, Mich., 1988-89; LPN charge nurse West View Manor, Wooster, 1989, Doylestown (Ohio) Health Care Ctr., 1989-93; charge nurse Manor Care Barberton, Ohio, 1993-94; RN supr., asst. dir. nursing Manor Care of Barberton, Ohio, 1994—. Home: 985 Saxon Ave Akron OH 44314

HUGHES, KATHLEEN BRIDGET, supervisor; b. Shenandoah, Iowa; d. George Patrick and Cecelia Margaret Hughes; children: Keith Patrick, Jacqueline Michele. Student, Creighton U., Coll. St. Mary, 1990—. Prodn. specialist AT&T Network Systems, Omaha, 1962-87, regional account mgr., 1988-92; resource link asst. AT&T Human Resources, Omaha and Chgo., 1992; supr. AT&T Network Systems, Omaha, 1993—. Fellow Nebr. Telephone Assn., Iowa Telephone Assn., Rural Iowa Telephone Assn., Am. Mfg. Excellence, Urban League Greater Omaha.

HUGHES, LAUREL ELLEN, psychologist, educator, writer; b. Seattle, Oct. 30, 1952; d. Morrell Spencer and Eleanore Claire (Strong) Chamberlain; m. William Henry Hughes Jr., Jan. 27, 1973; children: Frank, Ben, Bridie. BA in Psychology, Portland State U., 1980, MS in Psychology, 1986; D in Clin. Psychology, Pacific U., 1988. Lic. psychologist, Oreg. Counselor Beaverton (Oreg.) Free Meth. Ch., 1982-85; psychotherapist Psychol. Svc. Ctr., Portland, Oreg., 1986, Psychol. Svc. Ctr. West, Hillsboro, Oreg., 1987-89; pvt. practice Beaverton, 1990—; adj. mem. faculty Portland C.C., 1990-91, U. Portland,1992—, CU/Seattle. 1993—; vis. asst. prof. U. Portland, 1991-92; psychol. cons. children's weight control group St. Vincent's Hosp., Portland, 1991. Author: How To Raise Good Children, 1988, How To Raise a Healthy Achiever, 1991; contbr. articles to profl. jours. Tchr. Sunday sch. Beaverton Free Meth. Ch., 1983-88; mother helper Walker Elem. Sch., Beaverton, 1988-90, 92-93; foster parent Washington County, Oreg., 1976-77, 79-80; vol. disaster mental health svcs. ARC, 1993—. Mem. APA, Oreg. Psychol. Assn. (bd. dirs. 1990-91, editor jour. 1990-91). Office: 4320 SW 110th Ave Beaverton OR 97005-3009

HUGHES, LAURIE, lawyer; b. Dallas, Oct. 13, 1955; d. Alfred Jay and Suzanne (Clark) H. AB, Smith Coll., 1978; JD, Memphis State U., 1984. Bar: Tenn. 1984, U.S. Dist. Ct. (mid. dist.) Tenn. 1984. Atty. Sesac, Inc., Nashville, 1984-91, gen. counsel, 1991—. Mem. Leadership Music, 1991—. Mem. ABA (forum com. on entertainment), Tenn. Bar Assn., Copyright Soc. South, Copyright Soc. of U.S.A. Office: Sesac Inc 55 Music Sq E Nashville TN 37203-4324

HUGHES, LIBBY, author; b. Pitts., Aug. 11, 1932; d. Lloyd Alfred and Vera Abby (Walker) Pockman; m. R. John Hughes, Aug. 20, 1955 (div.

1988); children: Wendy E., Mark E. BA, U. Ala., 1954; MFA, Boston U., 1955. Profl. actress Kenya, S. Africa, 1955-59; drama critic and feature writer Cape Cod Newspapers, 1977-86, assoc. pubr., 1977-81, pubr., 1981-85; pres. Desert Starfield Prodns., 1994. Author: Bali, 1969, Margaret Thatcher, 1989, Benazir Bhutto, 1990, Nelson Mandela, 1992, Good Manners for Children, 1992, H. Norman Schwarzkopf, 1992, West Point, 1992, Valley Forge, 1992; editor: Ginger Rogers Autobiography, 1989, 91; author 20 plays. Bd. dirs. Wisdom Inst., 1984-86, Cape Cod Mus., 1984-86. Mem. Dramatists Guild, Authors Guild, Ala. Wildlife Rescue Svc. (pres. 1988-89), Nat. Soc. Arts and Letters (chpt. pres. 1984-86, protocol officer 1984-86). Home: PO Box 1000 Orleans MA 02653

HUGHES, LINDA J., newspaper publisher; b. Princeton, B.C., Can., Sept. 27, 1950; d. Edward Rees and Madge Preston (Bryan) H.; m. George Fredrick Ward, Dec. 16, 1978; children: Sean Ward, Kate Ward. BA, U. Victoria (B.C.), 1972. With Edmonton Jour., Alta., Can., 1976—, from reporter to asst. mng. editor, 1984-87, editor, 1987-92, pub., 1992—. Southam fellow U. Toronto, Ont., Can., 1977-78. Office: Edmonton Journal, 10006 101st St PO Box 2421, Edmonton, AB Canada T5J 2S6

HUGHES, LINDA RENATE, lawyer, arbitrator, mediator; b. Hanau, Fed. Republic Germany, Oct. 25, 1947; came to U.S. 1950; d. J.A. and Ilga (Vankins) Eglite. BA magna cum laude, U. Minn., 1968; JD cum laude, Wayne State U., 1980. Bar: Mich. 1980, Ga. 1982, Fla. 1984; cert. mediator, magistrate judge. Human resource mgr. Browning Marine Co., St. Charles, Mich., 1973-76; law clk. to judge U.S. Dist. Ct. (ea. dist.) Mich., 1980-81; asst. county atty. Hillsborough County, Fla., 1985-89; ptnr. Alpert, Josey, & Hughes, P.A., Tampa, 1989—; instr. Valdosta State Coll. (Ga.), 1981; adj. prof. U. Detroit Law Sch., 1982; researcher comparative labor policy, Leigh Creek, Australia, 1983. Editor-in-chief Advocate, Wayne State U. Law Sch., 1979-80, also law rev. With Community Mental Health Intervention, Saginaw, Mich., 1975-76, Ann Arbor, Mich., 1976-78, Clearwater Fla., 1984; dept. registrar Voter Registration, Pinellas County, Fla., 1983-84. Author: Employer's Price for Polygraph, 1986, Section 1983: Who is the Client: Employee or Government, 1988, Hypnosis of Civil Plaintiffs, 1991. Mem. ABA, AAUW (Saginaw chpt. sec. 1974-75), Am. Arbitration Assn. (panel of neutrals), Fed. Bar Assn., State Bar Mich., Ga. State Bar, Fla. State Bar Assn. (chair govt. lawyers sect. 1986-89, mem. mid-yr. com. 1988-89, spl. com. on governance 1988-91, past chair com. on profl. ethics 1989—, mem. all bar conf. 1989—), Hillsborough County Bar Assn. (jud. evaluation com. 1986-90), Fla. Women Lawyers Assn. (officer, bd. dirs.), Tampa Club. Office: PO Box 3270 Tampa FL 33601-3270

HUGHES, LYNN NETTLETON, federal judge; b. Houston, Sept. 9, 1941; m. Olive Allen. BA, U. Ala., 1963; JD, U. Tex., 1968; LLM, U. Va., 1992. Bar: Tex., 1966. Pvt. practice, Houston, 1966-79; judge 165th Dist. Ct. Tex., Houston, 1979-80, 189th Dist. Ct. Tex., Houston, 1981-85; U.S. dist. judge So. Dist. Tex., Houston, 1985—; adj. prof. South Tex. Coll. Law, 1973—, U. Tex., 1990-91; Tex. del. Nat. Conf. State Trial Judges, 1983-85; mem. com. on asbestos case mgmt. Nat. Dist. Ct., 1987-91; cons. Tex. Jud. Budget Bd., 1984; lectr. Tex. Coll. Judiciary, 1983; mem. task force on revision rules of civil procedure Supreme Ct. Tex., 1991-95; cons. on constn. Republic of Moldova, 1993, European Community, 1989. Mem. adv. bd. Houston Jour. Internat. Law, bd. dirs., 1981—, chmn., 1989—. Trustee Rift Valley Rsch. Mission, 1978—; mem. St. Martins Episcopal Ch. Fellow Tex. Bar Found.; mem. ABA, Fed. Bar Assn. (bd. dirs. Houston chpt. 1986-89), Am. Law Inst., Maritime Law Assn., Houston Bar Assn., Tex. Bar Assn. (nominations com. jud. sect. 1983, court cost, delay and efficiency com. 1981-90, vice chmn. 1984-86, selection, compensation and tenure state judges com. 1981-85, vice chmn. 1982-83, liaison with law schs. com. 1987-92, plain lang. com. 1989—), Am. Judicature Soc., Am. Soc. Legal History, Am. Anthrop Assn., Houston Philos. Soc., Am. Inn of Ct. XV (pres. 1986-92), Phi Delta Phi. Office: US Court House 11122 515 Rusk Ave Houston TX 77002-2605

HUGHES, MARIJA MATICH, law librarian; b. Belgrade, Yugoslavia; came to U.S., 1960, naturalized, 1971; d. Zarija and Antonija (Hudowsky) Matich. BA in Music, Mokranjac, Belgrade; BA in English, U. Belgrade and Calif. State U.; MLS, U. Md.; student, McGeorge Sch. Law; MHA in Health Care Adminstrn., George Washington U., 1985, M. in Adminstrv. Scis., 1989. Counselor, gen. mgr. Career Counseling Service, Sacramento, Calif., 1962-64; sec. to mgr. Sacramento State Coll., 1965-66; student librarian High John program U. Md., Fairmont Heights, 1967; reference librarian Calif. State Law Library, Sacramento, 1968; head reference library-faculty liaison librarian Hastings Coll. Law U. Calif., San Francisco, 1969-72; head law librarian AT&T, Washington, 1972-73; chief law librarian Nat. Clearinghouse Library, U.S. Commn. on Civil Rights, Washington, 1973-86; tech. info. specialist U.S. Dept. Labor, OSHA, Tech. Date Ctr., 1988—; owner, pub. Hughes Press. Author, compiler: The Sexual Barrier, Legal and Econ. Aspects of Employment, 1970-73, The Sexual Barriers: Legal, Medical, Economic and Social Aspects of Sex Discrimination, 1977, Computer Health Hazards, 1990, 93; contbr. articles to profl. jours. mem. Am. Assn. Law Librs., Assn. Internat. Law Librs., Washington Ind. Writers, Electromagnetic Radiation Alliance. Home: 2400 Virginia Ave NW Apt C501 Washington DC 20037-2607

HUGHES, MARILYN, psychotherapist; b. Heidleburg, Germany, Apr. 9, 1949; d. Eric Milton and Mary Fay (Oliver) H.; m. John Patrick MacCoon, June 10, 1979 (div. June 1989); 1 child, Margaret Erena MacCoon. BA in English, High Point Coll., 1971; MS in Cmty. Counseling, Ga. State U., 1991. Lic. profl. counselor. Sec. U.S. News & World Report, Washington, 1971-73; asst. dir. Office Spl. Events Smithsonian Instn., Washington, 1973-84; counselor Decatur (Ga.) Hosp., 1991-94, dir. CommonSteps, 1993—; asst. program dir., inpatient coord. Addiction Recovery Resources, 1994—; pvt. practice psychotherapist Decatur, 1993—; dir. Decatur Residential Support Sys., 1992—. Pres. Chattanooga chpt. NOW, 1986; mem. adv. bd. Helpline Ga. Coun. Child Abuse, Atlanta, 1994; mem. Human Rights Campaign Fund, Atlanta, 1994; mem. Fourth Tuesday, Atlanta, 1994. Mem. ACA. Democrat. Office: Decatur Hosp 450 N Candler St Decatur GA 30030

HUGHES, MARY KATHERINE, lawyer; b. Kodiak, Alaska, July 16, 1949; d. John Chamberlain and Marjorie (Anstey) H.; m. Andrew H. Eker, July 7, 1982. BBA cum laude, U. Alaska, 1971; JD, Willamette U., 1974; postgrad. Heriot-Watt U., Edinburgh, Scotland, 1971. Bar: Alaska 1975. Ptnr., Hughes, Thorsness, Gantz, Powell & Brundin, Anchorage, 1974-95, mem. mgmt. com., 1991-92; mcpl. atty. Municipality of Anchorage, 1995—. trustee Alaska Bar Found., pres., 1984—; bd. visitors Willamette U., Salem, Oreg., 1980—; bd. dirs. Alaska Repertory Theatre, 1986-88, pres., 1987-88; commr. Alaska Code Revision Commn., 1987-94; mem. U. Alaska Found., 1985—, trustee, 1990—; bd. dirs. Anchorage Econ. Devel. Corp., 1989-94, chmn. 1994; mem. adv. bd. Providence Hosp., 1993—. Fellow Am. Bar Found.; mem. Alaska Bar Assn. (bd. govs. 1981-84, pres. 1983-84), Anchorage Assn. Women Lawyers (pres. 1976-77), AAUW, Delta Theta Phi. Republican. Roman Catholic. Club: Soroptimists (v.p. 1986-87, pres. 1986-87). Home: 2240 Kissee Ct Anchorage AK 99517-1003 Office: Municipality Anchorage PO Box 196650 Anchorage AK 99519-6650

HUGHES, MICHAELA KELLY, actress, dancer; b. Morristown, N.J., Mar. 31; d. Joseph Francis and Mary Elizabeth (Coughlin) H. Scholarship student, Houston Ballet Acad., 1970-73; part-time scholarship student, Sch. Am. Ballet, 1971. Founder, owner Classic Stocking Co., 1992—. Child actress with Alley Theatre, Houston, 1969, 71, mem. Houston Ballet, 1974, Eliot Feld Ballet, N.Y.C., 1975—, prin. dancer, 1974-79, mem., Am. Ballet Theatre, 1979-81; Broadway appearances include On Your Toes, 1982, as Gloria Upson in Mame, 1983, Raggedy Ann, 1986, as Cassie in A Chorus Line, 1987, Anything Goes, 1988; appeared as Fiona in Another World (serial), Loving, Saturday Night Live, numerous television commls. Mem. AFTRA, SAG, AEA, Am. Guild Mus. Artists.

HUGHES, NORAH ANN O'BRIEN, bank securities executive; b. Taftville, Conn., Aug. 17, 1948; d. William James and Mabel (Gouin) O'Brien; m. Gary Lee Hughes, Sept. 27, 1975. BA, Cushing Coll., Brookline, Mass., 1970; MA, NYU, 1972. V.p. instnl. sales trading Pitfield, Mackay & Co., Inc., N.Y.C., 1972-83; v.p. U.S. Treasury Bond trading Carroll, McEntee & McGinley, N.Y.C., 1983-84; v.p., mgr. U.S. Treasury trading Swiss Bank Corp. Internat. Securities, N.Y.C., 1984-89; 1st v.p., mgr. U.S. Treasury trading and sales Swiss Bank Corp. Govt. Securities Inc., N.Y.C., 1989-91; pres. Sumitomo Bank Securities, Inc., N.Y.C., 1991—. Mem. Women's Fin. Assn., Women's Econ. Round Table, Corp. Bond Club N.Y., Women's Bond Club N.Y. Home: 1 Hickory Tree Rd Far Hills NJ 07931-2300 Office: Sumitomo Bank Securities Inc 277 Park Ave New York NY 10172

HUGHES, ROSEMARIE SCOTTI, counseling educator, university dean; b. Pitts., Nov. 3, 1943; d. Louis Anthony and Carmela Josephine (La Rocca) Scotti; children from previous marriage: James Ray Cook Jr., Christopher G. Cook, Steven L. Cook, Shawn V. Cook; m. Roger N. Hughes, Feb. 16, 1992. BS in Elem. Edn., Duquesne U., 1964; MA in Edn. in Counseling summa cum laude, Regent U., Virginia Beach, Va., 1983; PhD in Urban Svcs., Old Dominion U., 1987. Lic. profl. counselor, Va.; nat. cert. counselor; nat. cert. sch. counselor. Substitute and homebound tchr. pub. schs., Virginia Beach, Key West and Pensacola, Fla., 1964-83; prof. counseling Regent U., 1987—, interim assoc. dean Sch. Counseling and Human Svcs., 1992-93, assoc. dean, 1993-94, dean, 1994—, chmn. faculty assembly, 1991-93, clin. supr. Referral Counseling Ctr., 1987-88, supr. sch. counseling, agy. and counseling ctr. internships, 1987—, cmty. liaison for internships, 1988-91; owner, tchr. Green Run Kindernook Nursery Sch., 1974-76; mental retardation prevention specialist Norfolk (Va.) Cmty. Svcs. Bd., 1983-84; secondary guidance counselor Norfolk Pub. Schs., 1987, cons., 1986-89; mem. adv. com. Va. Bd. Profl. Counselors, 1993-94; mem., chmn. spl. adv. com. Virginia Beach City Pub. Schs., 1983-88; resident Christian Psychotherapy Svcs., 1991-93, psychotherapist, 1993—; conf. and workshop presenter in field; adj. assoc. prof. Old Dominion U., 1986-93; also others. Author: Counseling Families of Children with Disabilities, 1990, Parenting a Child with Special Needs, 1992 (Parents' Choice approval award 1993), S.A.I.L. (Self-Awareness in Language Arts), 1994; contbr. articles to profl. jours., chpts. to books. Virginia Beach rep. Local Human Rights for Disabled Com., 1988—, chmn., 1992-93; bd. dirs. Assn. for Retarded Citizens, 1983-84; retreat coord. Holy Family Ch., Virginia Beach, 1982. Scholar Duquesne U., Diocese of Pitts., 1960-62; doctoral fellow Old Dominion U., 1984-85, 85-86; faculty rsch. grantee Regent U., 1991. Mem. ACA, Am. Assn. Christian Counselors (bd. dirs., ethics com.), Assn. for Counselor Edn. and Supervision, Va. Counselors Assn. (sec.-treas. 1993-94, pres.-elect 1994-95), Hampton Roads Counselors Assn. (bd. dirs. 1991-92), Lic. Profl. Counselors Hampton Roads (ethics com. 1993-94), Nat. Apostolate Mentally Retarded Persons, Va. Assn. Ethical and Religious Values in Counseling (pres.-elect). Office: Regent U Sch Counseling and Human Svcs 1000 Regent University Dr Virginia Beach VA 23464

HUGHES, SALLY PAGE, administrative secretary; b. Elizabeth, N.J.; d. Jeff and Irene (Miller) Page; m. July 31, 1954 (dec. Mar. 6, 1962); 1 child, Edward Joseph. Student, Kean Coll., Union, N.J., 1962-69, Upsala Coll., 1969-75. Sec., stenographer Vis. Nurse Assn., Plainfield, N.J., 1955-60, Kean Coll., Union, N.J., 1962-69; tchr. tng. program Upsala Coll., Urban Edn. Corps, East Orange, N.J., 1969-71; sec. to editor The Daily Jour., Elizabeth, N.J., 1971-75; prin. clk. Schering-Plough Corp., Union, 1976-80; unit sec. Elizabeth Multi-Svc. Ctr. Tng. Unit, Elizabeth, 1980-82; adminstrv. sec. Bd. of Edn., Elizabeth, 1982—. Author: (poetry) New Beginnings, 1991, Inspiration, 1993; composer: (song) On the Winning Side, 1991; co-writer (song) Where Shall I Be, 1991; soloist/poetess Channel 12 and CTN-Gospel Hour Music, TV Nationwide and Internat. Recipient award of Merit, World of Poetry, 1991, Hon. Mention, Watermark Press, 1991, Editor's Choice award Outstanding Achievement in Poetry, Nat. Libr. Poetry, 1993; named Profl. Woman of Yr., Union County Club, Nat. Assn. Negro Bus. and Profl. Women's Club. Mem. NEA, Elizabeth Edn. Assn., N.J. Edn. Assn., Shiloh Bapt. Ch. Choir, Shiloh Bapt. Ch. Missionary Bd., Sun. Sch. Tchrs. Democrat. Baptist.

HUGHES, SARAH GILLETTE, consulting company executive; b. Detroit, Jan. 24, 1947; d. William R. and Virginia M. (Sloan) Gillette; m. Robert Denis Hughes, June 28, 1969. BS in Math., U. Mich., 1969; MBA in Fin., U. Chgo., 1976. Programmer analyst U. Mich., Ann Arbor, 1969-71; mgr. systems and programming Am. Hosp. Assn., Chgo., 1972-82; dir. software devel. SPSS Inc., Chgo., 1982-84; dir. systems devel. InnerLine, Arlington Heights, Ill., 1984-86; dir. product devel. Pansophic Systems, Inc., Lisle, Ill., 1986-90; pres. Gillette Cons., Inc., Chgo., 1991—. Mem. Lakeview Citizens' Council, Chgo. Mem. Inst. Indsl. and Electronics Engrs., Assn. Computing Machinery, Chgo. Software Assn., U. Chgo. Women's Bus. Group (past officer), Beta Gamma Sigma. Office: Gillette Cons Inc 3023 N Clark St Ste 232 Chicago IL 60657-5200

HUGHES, SUE MARGARET, retired librarian; b. Cleburne, Tex.; d. Chastain Wesley and Sue Willis (Payne) H. BBA, U. Tex., Austin, 1949; MLS, Tex. Woman's U., 1960, PhD, 1987. Sec.-treas. pvt. corps. Waco, Tex., 1949-59; asst. in public services Baylor U. Library, Waco, 1960-64; acquisitions librarian Baylor U. Library, 1964-79, acting univ. librarian, summer 1979, dir. Moody Library, 1980-89; interim univ. libr. Baylor U., Waco, 1989-91, spl. materials cons., 1991-92; ret., 1992. Mem. AAUP, ALA, Southwestern Library Assn., Tex. Library Assn., AAUW, Delta Kappa Gamma, Beta Phi Mu, Beta Gamma Sigma. Methodist. Club: Altrusa.

HUGHES, SUSAN KUTSCHER, publishing executive; b. San Antonio, Nov. 24, 1946; d. Willard Frank and Harriet (North) Kutscher; m. Guntis Terauds, Jan. 28, 1970 (div. Nov. 1978); 1 child, Tatjana; m. Jack Bruce Hughes, May 19, 1979. BA in Speech and Drama cum laude, Trinity U., 1967; MLS, U. Tex., 1968; postgrad., U. Tex., San Antonio, 1973-75. Asst. libr. Sch. Nursing Case Western Res. U., Cleve., 1969-70; head fine arts dept. Houston Pub. Libr., 1970-72; rsch. asst. U. Tex., San Antonio, 1973-74; tech. libr. dept. aviation City of Houston, 1975-76; libr. McKinsey & Co., Inc., Dallas, 1977-79; info. resources coord. Mobil Producing Tex. & N.Mex., Houston, 1979-81; pres. Decision Support & Info. Svc., San Antonio, 1981-87; mgr. mktg. communications Datapoint Corp., San Antonio, 1982-90; pres., founder Wordwright Assocs. Environ. and Mktg. Comms., San Antonio, 1990—. Coord. S.W. regional conf. Nat. Audubon Soc., 1993, coord. chpt. newsletter contest, 1994; coord. S.W. regional town meeting U.S. Network for Cairo; asst. coord. legis. agenda Audubon Coun. Tex.; dir. Edwards Underground Water Dist., Dist. 5, 1995—. Mem. Nat. Assn. Profl. Environ. Communicators, Internat. Assn. Bus. Communicators (editor membership dir. 1990-94, Bronze Quill awards Merit and Excellence 1988-90), San Antonio Fedn. Advt. (ADDY award Merit 1988), Women in Communications (Proliner awards Merit 1989-90, Proliner award Excellence 1993), Spl. Librs. Assn. (chair publs. com. 1978-81, pres., exec. bd. Tex. chpt. 1978-84, chair petroleum and energy resources div. 1984), Bexar Audubon Soc. (newsletter editor 1991-94, bd. dirs. 1991-94, pres. 1994—, mem. exec. adv. com. Natural Initiatives 1994—), Bexar County Women's Political Caucus, San Antonio Conservation Soc., King William Assn., Native Plant Soc. Tex., Bexar County Master Gardeners (co-editor San Antonio Gardener 1993-94), Trinity U. Alumni Coun. (San Antonio chpt. com. 1988—).

HUGHES, TERESA P., state legislator; b. N.Y.C., Oct. 3, 1932; m. Frank E. Staggers; children: Vincent, Deidre. BA, Hunter Coll.; MA, NYU; PhD, Claremont Grad. Sch. Prof. edn. Calif. State U., L.A.; social worker; mem. Calif. Senate, 1975—; chair edn. com., mem. pub. employees and retirement com., mem. housing and cmty. devel. and local govt. coms.; bd. trustees L.A. County H.S. for Arts and Edn. Coun. Music Ctr., Calif.; active Mayor Bradley Edn. Com. Founder Aware Women. Mem. Nat. Coalition 100 Black Women, Calif. State Employees Assn., Calif. Tchrs. Assn., Coalition Labor Union Women. Democrat. Home: 1906 W 22 St Los Angeles CA 90007 Office: Calif Senate 4035 State Capitol Sacramento CA 95814 also: One Manchester Blvd Ste 401 Los Angeles CA 90301*

HUGHES, TRUDY SHARON STEWART, educational coordinator; b. Little Rock, Ark., June 9, 1948; d. Samuel T. and Lora E. (Nipps) Stewart; m. Donald A. Hughes, July 17, 1970; 1 child, Joseph A. BSE in Elem. Edn., Henderson State U., 1970; MSE in Spl. Edn., U. Ctrl. Ark., 1977. Cert. GIT. Spl. edn. Hope (Ark.) Pub. Schs., 1970-71; spl. edn., elem. edn., gifted & talented edn. coord., curriculum coord. England (Ark.) Pub. Schs., 1971—; Project Promise coord. for England schs. U. Ark.-Little Rock, 1990—. Mem. Alpha Xi Delta. Baptist. Office: England Pub Schs PO Box 410 Hwy 15 England AR 72046

HUGHES, WAUNELL MCDONALD (MRS. DELBERT E. HUGHES), retired psychiatrist; b. Tyler, Tex., Feb. 6, 1928; d. Conrad Claiborne and Bernice Oletha (Smith) McDonald; B.A., U. Tex. at Austin, 1946; M.D., Baylor U., 1951; m. Delbert Eugene Hughes, Aug. 14, 1948; children—Lark, Mark, Lynn, Michael. Intern VA Hosp., Houston, 1951-52; resident Parkland Hosp., Dallas, 1964-67; practiced gen. medicine in Tyler, Tex., 1952-64; acting chief psychiatry service VA Hosp., Dallas, 1967-68, asst. chief, 1968-73, chief Mental Hygiene Clinic and Day Treatment Center, 1973-82, unit chief acute inpatient psychiatry Med. Center, 1982-88; clin. instr. psychiatry Southwestern Med. Sch., U. Tex. Health Sci. Center, Dallas, 1968-88; psychiat. cons. Dallas Family Guidance Clinics, 1990. Chmn. pre-sch. vision and hearing program Pilot Club, Tyler, 1960-64. Mem. Am. Med. Women's Assn. (pres. Dallas 1980-81), Am. Psychiat. Assn., Am. Group Psychotherapy Assn., (pres. Dallas chpt. 1984-86), North Tex. Soc. Psychiat. Physicians (co-chair Mental Health Mental Retardation pro bono clinic com. Dallas chpt. 1989-91, mem. patient advocacy com. 1992—), Dallas Area Women Psychiatrists (archivist 1985—), Alpha Epsilon Iota (pres. 1950-51). Home: 3428 University Blvd Dallas TX 75205-1834

HUGHES-FULFORD, MILLIE, medical scientist, educator; b. Mineral Wells, Tex., Dec. 21, 1945; d. Charles and Lanore Hughes; m. George A. Fulford; children: Tori, Herzog. PhD in Radiation Chemistry, Tex. Woman's U., 1972. Asst. prof. U. Calif., San Francisco, 1973-82, assoc. prof., 1982—; med. scientist Dept. Vets. Affairs, San Francisco, 1973-94, adj. prof., 1994—; mem. com. on space biology NRC, Washington, 1987-90. Mem. editorial bd. UCSF mag., 1992—; contbr. articles to profl. jours. Trustee Embry-Riddle Aero. U., Fla., 1986-89; mem. admission com. Med. Sch., U. Calif., San Francisco, 1992—. Capt. U.S. Army, 1972-82. Recipient Presdl. award, 1984; NSF fellow, 1965, 68-72, AAUW, 1971-72. Mem. AAAS, Am. Soc. Cell Biology, Am. Physiol. Soc. Office: U Calif VAMC Code 151F 4150 Clement St San Francisco CA 94121-1598*

HUGHS, MARY GERALDINE, accountant, social service specialist; b. Marshalltown, Iowa, Nov. 28, 1929; d. Don Harold, Sr., and Alice Dorothy (Keister) Shaw; A.A., Highline Community Coll., 1970; B.A., U. Wash., 1972; m. Charles G. Hughs, Jan. 31, 1949; children: Mark George, Deborah Kay, Juli Ann, Grant Wesley. Asst. controller Moduline Internat., Inc., Chehalis, Wash., 1972-73; controller Data Recall Corp., El Segundo, Calif., 1973-74; fin. adminstr., acct. Saturn Mfg. Corp., Torrance, Calif., 1974-77; sr. acct., adminstrv. asst. Van Camp Ins., San Pedro, Calif., 1977-78; asst. adminstr. Harbor Regional Ctr., Torrance, Calif., 1979-87; active bookkeeping svc., 1978—; instr. math. and acctg. South Bay Bus. Coll., 1976-77. Sec. Pacific N.W. Mycol. Soc., 1966-67; treas., bd. dirs. Harbor Employees Fed. Credit Union; mem. YMCA Club. Recipient award Am. Mgmt. Assn., 1979. Mem. Beta Alpha Psi. Republican. Methodist. Author: Iowa Auto Dealers Assn. Title System, 1955; Harbor Regional Center Affirmative Action Plan, 1980; Harbor Regional Center - Financial Format, 1978—; Provider Audit System, 1979; Handling Client Funds, 1983. Home and Office: 18405 Haas Ave Torrance CA 90504-5405

HUGLEY, CAROLYN FLEMING, state legislator; m. Isaiah Hugley; children: Isaiah Jr., Kimberly. BA in Polit. Sci. summa cum laude, U. Ark., Pine Bluff, 1979; MPA, Miss. State U., 1980. Sr. analyst, mem. joint com. on performance evaluation Miss. State Legis., mem. state planning and cmty. affairs, edn., industry com., mem. legis. oversight com. for Ga. lottery, mem. Ga. legis. women's coalition, Ga. legis. Black caucus; planner Lower Chattahoochee Area Planning and Devel. Commn.; dir. planning and econ. devel. Lee County Coun. Govts.; ind. contractor, owner agt. State Farm Ins. Mem. choir and mission bd. dirs. Franchise Missionary Bapt. Ch.; mem. Gov.'s Task Force of Welfare Reform, 1992; chairperson Lower Chattahoochee Area Pvt. Industry Coun.; mem. Columbus Olympic Com., Columbus Conv. and Visitors Bur.; mem. local coord. coun. Peach Jobs Program. Mem. Columbus C. of C. (bd. dirs.) Alpha Kappa Alpha (2d v.p. Gamma Tau Omega chpt.). *

HUGO, NANCY, county official, alcohol and drug addiction professional; b. Cedar Rapids, Iowa, May 4, 1944; d. Roger S. and Phyllis Anita (Wenger) Conrad; m. Marshall G. Hugo, Apr. 5, 1968; 1 child, Andrea. BS, Drake U., 1966; MS, Pepperdine U., 1987; adminstrn. credential, U. Calif., Irvine, 1989. Cert. adminstr., middle sch. educator, Calif. Tchr., adminstrv. asst. Ocean View Sch. Dist., Huntington Beach, Calif., 1966-90; coord. alcohol and drug prevention edn., coord. phys. edn., juvenile ct. schs. drug and alcohol programs Orange County Dept. Edn., Costa Mesa, Calif., 1990—. Mem. ASCD, NEA, Assn. Calif. Sch. Adminstrs., Calif. Edn. Assn., Calif. Assn. Health Phys. Edn. Recreation and Dance, Calif. Tchrs. Assn. Home: 4606 Cortland Dr Corona Del Mar CA 92625-2707 Office: Orange County Dept Edn 200 Kalmus Dr Costa Mesa CA 92626-5922

HUGUENIN, NANCY HOFFMAN, psychologist, consultant; b. Franklin, Pa., May 12, 1947. BS in Psychology, U. Pitts., 1969; MA in Psychology, Boston U., 1971, PhD in Psychology, 1978. Rsch. assoc. ednl. rsch. unit Eunice Kennedy Shriver Ctr. for Mental Retardation, Inc., Waltham, Mass., 1977-80; postdoctoral fellow in applied behavior analysis Child Devel. Ctr., R.I. Hosp., Providence, 1978-80; dir. Programmed Instrn. Lab., Grad. Sch. U. Mass., Amherst, 1980-85, staff assoc. U. Computing Ctr., 1980-81, staff assoc. Grad. Sch., 1981-85; behavioral cons. dept. psychology Monson Devel. Ctr., Palmer, Mass., 1981-85; behavioral psychologist mental retardation unit Coast Community Counseling Ctr., Hingham, Mass., 1985-87; behavioral psychologist mental retardation clin. team South Shore Assn. for Retarded Citizens, Inc., Hingham, 1987-89; clin. supr. dept. psychology Walter E. Fernald State Sch., Waltham, 1989-93; pres. Behavior Analysis & Tech., Inc., Groton, Mass., 1993—; grad. teaching fellow exptl. psychology dept. psychology Boston (Mass.) U., 1969-74, instr. psychology dept., 1972; adj. asst. prof. psychology U. Mass., Amherst, 1980-87; behavioral cons. South Shore Collaborative, Hingham, 1986—. Referee: Jour. Behavior Therapy and Exptl. Psychiatry, 1974-78; mem. editorial bd.: Transitions in Mental Retardation, 1984-87; contbr. articles to profl. jours. Mem. AAAS, APA, Ea. Psychol. Assn., Am. Assn. Mental Retardation (chairperson psychology divsn. N.E. region X 1983-86), Assn. for Behavior Analysis, Assn. for Advancement Behavior Therapy, Am. Acad. on Mental Retardation, Phi Beta Kappa, Psi Chi, Quax. Office: Behavior Analysis & Tech Inc PO Box 327 61 Long Hill Rd Groton MA 01450

HUHEEY, MARILYN JANE, ophthalmologist; b. Cin., Aug. 31, 1935; d. George Mercer and Mary Jane (Weaver) H.; B.S. in Math., Ohio U., Athens, 1958; M.S. in Physiology, U. Okla., 1966; M.D., U. Ky., 1970. Tchr. math. James Ford Rhodes High Sch., Cleve., 1956-58; biostatistician Nat. Jewish Hosp., Denver, 1958-60; life sci. engr. Stanley Aviation Corp., Denver, 1960-63, N.Am. Aviation Co., Los Angeles, 1963-67; intern U. Ky. Hosp., 1970-71; emergency room physician Jewish Hosp., Mercy Hosp., Bethesda Hosp. (all Cin.), 1971-72; ship's doctor, 1972; resident in ophthalmology Ohio State U. Hosp., Columbus, 1972-75; practice medicine specializing in ophthalmology, Columbus, 1975—; mem. staff Univ. Hosp., Grant Hosp., St. Anthony Hosp., 1975-79; clin. asst. prof. Ohio State U. Med. Sch., 1976-84, clin. assoc. prof., 1985—, dir. course ophthalmologic receptionist/aides, 1976; mem. Peer Rev. Systems Bd., 1986—, exec. com., 1988—; mem. Ohio Optical Dispensers Bd, 1986—. Dem. candidate for Ohio Senate, 1982. Diplomate Am. Bd. Ophthalmology. Fellow Am. Acad. Ophthalmology; mem. AAUP, Am. Assn. Ophthalmologists, Ohio Ophthalmol. Soc. (bd. govs. 1984-89, del. to Ohio State Med. Assn. 1984-88), Franklin County Acad. Medicine (profl. relations com. 1979-82, legis. com. 1981—, edn. and program com. 1981—, chmn. 1982-85, chmn. community relations com. 1987—, chmn. resolution com. 1987—, mem. fin. com. 1988—), Ohio Soc. Prevent Blindness (chmn. med. adv. bd. 1978-80), Ohio State Med. Assn. (dr.-nurse liaison com. 1983-87), Columbus EENT Soc., Am. Coun. of the Blind (life, bd. dirs.), Life Care Alliance (pres. sustaining bd. 1987-88, United Way planning com. 1992-93), LWV, Columbus Council World Affairs, Columbus Bus. and Profl. Women's Club, Columbus C. of C., Grandview Area Bus. Assn., Federated Dem. Women of Ohio, Columbus Area Women's Polit. Caucus, Phi Mu. Clubs: Columbus Met. (forum com. 1982-85, fundraising com. 1983-84, chmn. 10th anniversary com. 1986), Mercedes Benz (dir. 1981-83), Zonta, (program com. 1984-86, chmn. internat. com. 1983), Herb Soc. Home: 2396 Northwest Blvd Columbus OH 43221-3829 Office: 1335 Dublin Rd Columbus OH 43215-1000

HUIE, MARY ELLEN IVES, continuing education director; b. Phila., Feb. 21, 1940; d. John Bradford and Margaret (Weir) Ives; m. David Lockwood Huie, Oct. 17, 1964; children: Margaret Emma, Janet Lockwood, Arthur Ives, Marion Armstrong. BS, Drexel U., 1961, MS, 1964. Cert. home econs. tchr. Food technologists Tasty Kake, Phila., 1961-65; judge of elections Pa.-Montgomery County, Horsham, 1974-78; home econs. substitute tchr. Hatboro-Horsham Schs., 1978; dir. Hatboro-Horsham Adult Edn., 1980—; owner, dir. Christmas Green's Bus., Horsham, 1979—; dir. adult edn. Am. Cancer Soc., Horsham, 1991—; tutor for math. Hatboro-Horsham Schs., 1983-84; libr. aide H-H Sch. Dist., Horsham, 1974-84. Contbr. articles to profl. jours. Home rm. mother Hatboro-Horsham Schs., 1974-89; active Hatters for Music, Horsham, 1975—. Scholarship Phila. Gas Works, 1957. Mem. Phi Mu. Roman Catholic. Home: 608 Cedar Hill Rd Ambler PA 19002-1504 Office: Hatboro Horsham Adult Sch Keith Valley Mid Sch 227 Meetinghouse Rd Horsham PA 19044

HUISINGA, DIANE JOY, psychology educator; b. Chgo., Dec. 3, 1943; d. Ralph Frederick and Claudia Beth (Renhult) H.; m. Peter Lee Borchelt, Feb. 7, 1970 (div. Nov. 1979); m. G. Kaye Holden, Oct. 1, 1983. BA, So. Ill. U., 1965; MA, Mich. State U., 1970, PhD, 1972. Lic. psychologist, N.J. Social worker Manteno (Ill.) State Hosp., 1965-66; assoc. prof. Jersey City State Coll., 1972—; pvt. practice psychotherapy Jersey City, 1977—; Fulbright lectr. U. Rijeka, Croatia, 1992-93. Co-author: (computer program) The Explorer. Mem. APA. Home: 301 Varick St Jersey City NJ 07302 Office: Jersey City State Coll Jersey City NJ 07305

HUKINS, DANA ANN, community health nurse; b. Raceland, La., Nov. 1, 1964; d. Herman Cecil and Diana Ann (Chiasson) H. BSN, Nicholls State U., Thibodaux, La., 1986. RN, La. Nurse II, staff pediatrics nurse South La. Med. Ctr., Houma, 1986-88; nurse, pub. health nurse III Lafourche Parish Health Unit, Thibodaux, 1988—. Mem. Nicholls State U. Nursing Honor Soc., Sigma Theta Tau.

HULBURT, LUCILLE HALL, artist, educator; b. Portland, Oreg., Oct. 31, 1924; d. Allen Bergen and Agnes Edna (Davis) Hall; m. Frank Theodore Hulburt, Nov. 28, 1943; children: Robert, Carol Davalos, Clarke. Grad. high sch., Whitefish, Mont. Asst. milliner, illustrator Hat Co., N.Y.C., 1944; cafe owner, operator San Diego, 1950-52; profl. artist Vancouver, Wash., 1978—; resident artist Artist's Gallery 21, Vancouver, 1988—; tchr. children and adult art clases, schs. and home studio, Vancouver, 1978—; artist in residence Wash. State Arts Commn., 1987-88; co-founder, coop. Artists Gallery 21, Vancouver, 1988—; cons. nat. Western Art Show and Auction, Trails West, Vancouver; organizer, com. mem. ann. Summer Art at the Ctr., Vancouver, 1986; judge/jurist art exhibits at county fairs, western art shows various locations in Wash. and Oreg., 1980—. Founder, pres. Boundary Assn. Retarded Children, Bonners Ferry, Idaho, 1964-65; com. mem. 1st Bldg. Com., Columbia Arts Ctr., Vancouver, 1980-81; bd. mem. Local Arts Promotion, Vancouver, 1992, 93. Recipient Best of Show award Western Art Show and Auction, Chinook, Mont., 1983, 84, Community Svc. award Arts Coun., Clark County, Wash., 1988, Windsor-Newton award Watercolor 91, 1991. Mem. S.W. Wash. Watercolor Soc. (co-founder, pres. 1979, 80, 84), Soc. Washington Artists (Grumbacher Silver medal 1990), Am. Artists Profl. League, Order Eastern Star (life), N.W. Watercolor Soc. Office: Hulburt Studio 5515 NE 58th St Vancouver WA 98661-2146

HULEN, DEANNA JEAN, physical therapist assistant; b. Amarillo, Tex., Nov. 21, 1965; d. Ronald Dean and Sharon Jean (Woodin) H.; m. Curtis Malone, Aug. 22, 1987 (div. June 1990). AAS, Amarillo Coll., 1987; student, Ctrl. State U., Edmond, Okla., 1989. Lic. phys. therapy asst., Tex., Okla. Phys. therapy asst. St. Mary's Rehab., Lubbock, Tex., 1987-88, Healsouth Rehab., Oklahoma City, 1988-90; phys. therapy asst. Bivins Ctr. Phys. Medicine and Rehab., Amarillo, 1990—, clin. instr. phys. therapist asst. program, 1994—; C.A.R.E. facilitator. Vol. Family Support Svcs., Amarillo; mem. choir Kingswood United Meth. Ch., Amarillo. Democrat. Office: Bivins Ctr for PM&R 1600 Wallace Blvd Amarillo TX 79106

HULING, KENDELL FAYE, sales executive; b. Lynwood, Calif., Nov. 6, 1965; d. Gary Paul and Dulcilee (Danielson) H. AA, Columbia Basin Coll., Pasco, Wash., 1985; BA in History, Whitman Coll., 1987. Sales rep. Sta. KONA, Pasco, 1989; sales mgr. Radio Sta. KORD, Pasco, 1989—. Coach youth basketball program Bethlehem Luth. Sch., Kennewick, Wash., 1983-90. Mem. Women in Communications, Products Indsl. Expn. Home: 3400 W 1st Pl Kennewick WA 99336-4555 Office: KORD Radio 2621 W A St Pasco WA 99301-4702

HULKA, BARBARA SORENSON, epidemiology educator; b. Mpls., Mar. 1, 1931; d. Herbert Fritchof and Mable (Alquist) Sorenson; m. Jaroslav Fabian Hulka, Nov. 13, 1954; children: Carol Ann, Gregory Fabian, Bryan Herbert. BS, Radcliffe Coll., 1952; MS, Juilliard Sch. Music, 1954; MD, Columbia U., 1959, MPH, 1961. Diplomate: Am. Bd. Preventive Medicine; Lic. physician, Pa., N.C. Research asst. prof. U. Pitts., 1966-67; asst. prof. U. N.C., Chapel Hill, 1967-71, assoc. prof., 1972-76, prof., 1977—, chmn. dept. epidemiology, 1983-93, Kenan prof., 1987—; adj. prof. medicine Duke U. Med. Ctr., Durham, N.C., 1982—; chmn. epidemiology and disease study sect. NIH, 1979-83, mem. Endpoint Rev. Safety Monitoring and Adv. Com., Breast Cancer Prevention Trial, Nat. Surg. Adjuvant Breast and Bowel Project, 1992—; bd. sci. counselors Nat. Cancer Inst., 1980—; mem. Inst. of Medicine com. toxic shock syndrome Nat. Acad. Sci., 1981-82; mem. Sci. Rev. and Evaluation Bd. subcom. VA, 1983—; mem. subcom. on long-term effects of short-term exposure to chem. agts. Nat. Acad. Scis., 1985—; mem. preventive medicine and pub. health test com. Nat. Bd. Med. Examiners, 1985—; mem. consensus conf. on smokeless tobacco Nat. Cancer Inst. Panel, 1986; chair WHO steering com. of Task Force on Safety and Efficacy of Fertility Regulating Methods, 1990—; counsellor Internat. Soc. for Environ. Epidemiology, 1990—; mem. Pres.' Cancer Panel Spl. Commn. on Breast Cancer, Nat. Cancer Inst., 1992-93; mem. bd. scientific counselors divsn. cancer etiology, Nat. Cancer Inst., NIH, 1992—; chair WHO steering com. of task force Epidemiologic rsch. in reproductive health, WHO, 1990—. Mem. editorial bd. Postgrad. Medicine, 1985—; contbr. articles to profl. jours., chpts. to books. Bd. dirs. Am. Cancer Soc., 1993—. Recipient Disting. Achievement award Am. Soc. Preventive Oncology, 1991; Health Resources Adminstrn. grantee, 1975-77; tng. grantee in cancer epidemiology Nat. Cancer Inst., 1980—; prostate cancer grantee Nat. Cancer Inst., 1983-85; travel study fellow WHO, 1978. Fellow Royal Soc. Medicine; mem. APHA (governing coun. 1976-78, chmn. epidemiol. sect. 1976-77), NAS (Inst. Medicine, mem. commn. antiprogestins 1992-93, mem. com. passive smoking 1985—), Am. Coll. Epidemiology, Soc. Epidemiol. Rsch. (pres. 1975-76, exec. com. 1973-77), Am. Epidemiol. Soc., N.C. Pub. Health Assn. (award for excellence, stats. and epidemiology sect. 1975), Am. Coll. Preventive Medicine (bd. regents 1986), Delta Omega. Home: 2317 Honeysuckle Dr Chapel Hill NC 27514 Office: U NC Sch Pub Health McGavran-Greenburg Hall CB #7400 Chapel Hill NC 27599

HULL, CONSTANCE MAE (CONNIE HULL), librarian, educator, administrative assistant; b. Pitts., Nov. 29, 1928; d. Lysle Latourelle and Lillian Henriett (Frahm) Gilman; m. Albert Emil Ahrens Jr.; m. Howard Donald Hull (dec. Jan. 1984). B.S. in Elem. Edn., Oreg. State U., 1966, also postgrad.; M.L.S., U. Oreg., 1968, M.S. in Ednl. Media, Oreg. Coll. Edn., 1976, also postgrad. Various teaching and office positions, St. Paul, 1940-57, Missoula, Mont., 1957-61; co-founded library/media program, Sweet Home, Oreg.; dist. adminstrv. asst., dir. Instnl. Materials Ctr., library supr. Sweet Home Sch. Dist. 55, 1961-86 ; tchr. children's lit., media cons.; presenter at state confs. Mem. Oreg. Ednl. Media Assn., Dist. Oreg. Edn. Media Assn., Confedn. Oreg. Sch. Adminstrs., Oreg. Women Ednl. Adminstrn., N.W. Women Ednl. Adminstrn., Am. Assn. Sch. Adminstrs., Assn. Suprs. and Curriculum Dirs., Oreg. Instnl. Media Assn. (co-founder continuing edn. com.), Assn. Ednl. Communication and Tech., AAUW, Delta Kappa Gamma (state media cons.). Republican. Presbyterian. Contbr. to profl. publs. Home: 42899 Green River Rd Sweet Home OR 97386-9723 Office: 1920 Long St Sweet Home OR 97386-2395

HULL, DONNIE FAYE, special education director, educator; b. New Orleans, Apr. 15, 1945; d. Henry Frank and Laura (Mack) H. BA, So. U. A&M Coll., 1966, MEd, 1970; postgrad., La. State U., 1974, Southeastern La. U., 1974. Tchr. East Baton Rouge Sch. System, 1966-77, ednl. strategist, 1977-79, instructional specialist, 1979-81, supr. spl. edn., 1981-84, dir. spl. edn., 1984—; La. rep. to exchange program in Italy, 1991. Mem. exec. bd. March of Dimes, Baton Rouge, 1985—; pres. sr. choir Greater Phila. Bapt. Ch., Sunday sch. tchr., sponsor young adult choir; coord. spl. programs and events Young Women's Christian Auxiliary, sponsor community outreach ministry. Named one of Outstanding Educators, YWCA, 1981, Outstanding Leaders, Greater Phila. Bapt. Ch., 1984, Outstanding Vol. for La. Spl. Olympics, 1994; recipient Outstanding Tchr. award East Baton Rouge Parish Edn. Assn., 1973, Outstanding Leadership in Adminstrn. award 1990, Outstanding Adminstr. of Yr. award So. U., 1990. Mem. Nat. Assn. State Dirs. of Spl. Edn., Coun. for Exceptional Children, Found. for Exceptional Children, La. Assn. State Dirs. of Spl. Edn., La. Assn. Spl. Edn. Adminstrs., La. Sch. Suprs.' Assn., So. U. A&M Coll. Alumni Fedn. (life), La. Assn. Sch. Execs., Phi Delta Kappa (Disting. Svc. award 1990), Zeta Phi Beta (life, Mu Zeta chpt., asst. sec., chaplain, v.p., mem. exec. bd., pres. 1985-88, projects dir. so. region, regional life mem. dir., nat. dir. leadership devel., regional model chpt. coord., Pres. Svc. award 1988). Democrat. Baptist. Home: PO Box 321 Zachary LA 70791-0321

HULL, ELAINE MANGELSDORF, psychology educator; b. Houston, Aug. 15, 1940; d. Paul August and Mary Eleanor (Stephens) Mangelsdorf; m. Richard Thompson Hull, May 30, 1962; 1 child, Geoffrey Alaric (dec.). BA, Austin Coll., Sherman, Tex., 1963; PhD, Ind. U., 1967. Asst. prof. psychology SUNY, Buffalo, 1967-73, assoc. prof., 1973-86, prof., 1986—, dir. biopsychology grad. program, 1986—. Author: Study Guide to Accompany Kalat's Biological Psychology, 1988; contbr. articles to sci. jours. Recipient Chancellor's award for excellence in teaching SUNY, Buffalo, 1975, award for teaching SUNY Students Assn., 1986, N.Y. State Union of Univ. Profls. Excellence award 1990. Mem. AAAS, Soc. for Neurosci., Internat. Soc. for Psychoneuroendocrinology, Ea. Psychol. Assn., N.Y. Acad. Sci. Democrat. Home: 4845 Spaulding Dr Clarence NY 14031-1563 Office: SUNY Park Hall Buffalo NY 14260

HULL, ELIZABETH ANNE, English language educator; b. Upper Darby, Pa., Jan. 10, 1937; d. Frederick Bossart and Elizabeth (Schmik) H.; m. Dean Carlyle Beery, Feb. 5, 1955 (div. 1962); children: Catherine Doria Beery Pizarro, Barbara Phyllis Beery Wintczak; m. Frederik Pohl, July 1984. Student, Ill. State U., 1954-55; AA, Wilbur Wright Jr. Coll., Chgo., 1965; B in Philosophy, Northwestern U., 1968; MA, Loyola U., Chgo., 1970, PhD, 1975. Teaching asst. Loyola U., Chgo., 1968-71; prof. English, coord. honors program William Rainey Harper Coll., Palatine, Ill., 1971—; judge nat. writing competition Nat. Coun. Tchrs. of English, 1975—, John W. Campbell award, 1986—. Co-editor: (with F. Pohl) Tales from the Planet Earth; contbr. articles to profl. jours. Pres. Lexington Green Condominium Assn., Schaumburg, Ill., 1982-84; bd. dirs. Hunting Ridge Homeowner's Assn., Palatine, 1984-86, bd. dirs. Palatine League of Women Voters 1992—. Recipient Northwestern U. Alumni award for Merit, 1995. Mem. MLA, Midwest MLA, Popular Culture Assn., Sci. Fiction Rsch. Assn. (editor 1981-84, sec. 1987-88, pres. 1989-90), Ill. Coll. English Assn. (pres. 1975-77), World Sci. Fiction Assn. (N.Am. sec. 1978—, pres. Honors coun. Ill. region 1992-93), Palatine Area LWV (bd. dirs. 1991—), Am. Assn. for Women in C.C. (v.p. comm., bd. dirs. Harper Coll. chpt. 1993—). Democrat. Home: 855 Harvard Dr Palatine IL 60067-7026 Office: William Rainey Harper Coll 1200 W Algonquin Rd Palatine IL 60067-7398

HULL, GRETCHEN GAEBELEIN, lay worker, writer, lecturer; b. Bklyn., Feb. 5, 1930; d. Frank Ely and Dorothy Laura (Medd) Gaebelein; m. Philip Glasgow Hull, Oct. 24, 1952; children: Jeffrey R., Sanford D., Meredyth Hull Smith. BA magna cum laude, Bryn Mawr Coll., 1950; postgrad., Columbia U., 1950-52. Major presenter Internat. Coun. on Bibl. Inerrancy, Chgo., 1986; guest lectr. London Inst. on Contemporary Christianity, 1988; lectr. at large Christians for Bibl. Equality, St. Paul, 1988—; major presenter Presbyn. Ch. (U.S.A.) Nat. Abortion Dialogue, Kansas City, Mo., 1989; disting. scholar lectr. Thomas F. Staley Found., Stony Brook, N.Y., 1991; elder Presbyn. Ch. (U.S.A.); mem. Madison Ave. Presbyn. Ch., N.Y.C.; vis. prof. Regent Coll., Vancouver, B.C., 1992. Author: Equal to Serve, 1987; (with others) Women, Authority and the Bible, 1986, Applying the Scriptures, 1987; editor Priscilla Papers 1989—; contbg. editor Perspectives, 1992—; mem. editorial bd. Prism, 1994—; contbr. articles to religious mags. Trustee Cold Spring Harbor Village Improvement Soc., 1966-69, Soc. of St. Johnland, Kings Park, N.Y., 1972-75. Mem. Woman's Union Missionary Soc. Am. (bd. dirs. 1954-71), Presbyns. United for Bibl. Concerns (bd. dirs. 1973-75), L.I. Presbytery (gen. coun. 1981-83), Christians for Bibl. Equality (bd. dirs. 1987-94), Latin Am. Mission (trustee 1989—), Evangelicals for Social Action (bd. dirs. 1991—), Network Presbyn. Women in Leadership (steering com. 1994—), Presbyterians for Renewal (mem. bd. dirs. 1994—), Cosmopolitan Club. Home and Office: Oyster Bay Cove 1120 Cove Edge Rd Syosset NY 11791

HULL, JANE DEE, state official, former state legislator; b. Kansas City, Mo., Aug. 8, 1935; d. Justin D. and Mildred (Swenson) Bowersock; m. Terrance Ward Hull, Feb. 12, 1954; children: Jeannette Shipley, Robin Hillebrand, Jeff, Mike. BS, U. Kans., 1957; postgrad., U. Ariz., 1972-78. Spkr. pro tem Ariz. Ho. of Reps., Phoenix, 1993, chmn. ethics com., chmn. econ. devel., 1993, mem. legis. coun., 1993, mem. gov.'s internat. trade and tourism adv. bd., 1993, mem. gov.'s strategic partnership for econ. devel., 1993, mem. gov.'s office of employement implementation task force, 1993, spkr. of house, 1989-93, house majority whip, 1987-88; now secretary of state State of Arizona, Phoenix. Bd. dirs. Morrison Inst. for Pub. Policy, Beatitudes D.O.A.R., 1992, Ariz. Town Hall, Ariz. Econs. Coun.; mem. dean's coun. Ariz. State U., 1989-92; assoc. mem. Heard Mus. Guild, Cactus Wren Rep. Women, ; mem. Maricopa Med. Aux., Ariz. State Med. Aux., Freedom Found., Valley Citizens League, Charter 100, North Phoenix Rep. Women, 1970, Trunk 'N Tusk Legis. Liaison Ariz. Rep. Party, 1993; Rep. candidate sec. of state, 1994. Recipient Econ. Devel. award Ariz. Innovation Network, 1993. Mem. Nat. Orgn. of Women Legislators, Am. Legis. Exch. Coun., Nat. Rep. Legislators Assn. (Nat. Legislator of Yr. award 1989), Soroptimists (hon.). Republican. Roman Catholic. Home: 10458 N 9th St Phoenix AZ 85020-1585

HULL, JANE LAUREL LEEK, retired nurse, administrator; b. Ontario, Calif., July 4, 1923; d. William Abram and Susan Bianca (Pethick) Leek; R.N., Columbia Presbyn. Sch. Nursing, 1944; B.A., Redlands U., 1977; ; m. James B. Hull, Oct. 10, 1944 (dec.); children—James W., William P., Kenneth D. Supr. obstetrics Mid-Valley Hosp., Peckville, Pa., 1945-46; sch. and surg. nurse acute nursing Scranton (Pa.) State Hosp., 1947-52; nurse San Antonio Community Hosp., Upland, Calif., 1953-55; office nurse H.L. Archibald, Upland, 1965; vis. nurse Pomona West End Inc., continuity of care coordinator, Claremont, Calif., 1968-73, exec. dir., 1973-92 (named pres. 1991); tchr. ARC nursing course to high sch. students; cons. Livingston Meml. Vis. Nurse Assn. Ventura, Calif. Recipient Woman Achiever award, Pomona Valley, 1983, Excellence in Edn. award Nat. Assn. Home Care, 1988. Treas. PTA, Pomona, Calif.; vol. exec. dir. Inland Hospice Assn., 1979-80, accreditation commn., 1988-89. Nat. Found. for Hospice/Home Care, 1988. Mem. Am. Assn. Retired Persons (local coord.), Calif. Nurses Assn. (pres. dist. 53 1958), Calif. Assn. for Health Services at Home (dir.), Calif. League Nursing, Nat. Homecaring Council (dir.). Home Care Aide Assn. Am. (chmn.), bd. mem. Nat. Assn. of Home Care. Republican. Club: Zonta (Ontario, Upland, pres., 1976). Organizer Homemaker Dept. in Vis. Nurse Assn., 1972, pres., 1991; developer (with Don Baxter Corp.) plugs for in-dwelling Foley catheters, 1963. Home: 543 W F St Ontario CA 91762-3117

HULL, LOUISE KNOX, retired elementary educator, administrator; b. Springfield, Mo., May 24, 1912; d. William E. and Ruby Joe (Bradshaw) K.; m. Berrien J. Hull, Jan. 1, 1953. BS in Edn., S.W. Mo. State U., 1933; postgrad. Colo. U., 1939, Northwestern U., 1945; MA, NYU, 1952. Cert. elem. and secondary tchr., Mo. Elem. tchr. R12 Sch. Dist., Springfield, 1936-70, supr. tchr., 1956-70, mem. adv. com. to supt., 1955-57. Chmn. Christian edn. com. Westminster Presbyn. Ch., 1953-66, trustee, 1983-86, chmn. bd. trustees, 1986, circle chair, 1986-89, mem. women's adv. bd., 1987-89; pres. Women of Ch., 1970-73, 90-92, pres. bd. trustees, 1983-86; life mem. Wilson Creek Found., Springfield, 1954-67; sec. Greene County Hist. Soc., Springfield, 1960—; mem. Springfield Little Theater Guild, 1970—, Hist. Preservation Soc., Springfield, 1980—; docent Mus. Ozarks, Springfield, 1976-85; chmn. dist. III, John Calvin Presbterial, 1974-76, sec., 1977-80. Mem. Springfield Ret. Tchrs. Assn. (life), Mo. Ret. Tchrs. Assn. (life), Ozarks Genealogy Soc (sec. 1985-87, pub. info. rep. 1987-89), DAR (Rachel Donelson chpt.), Mo. Fedn. Women's Clubs (chmn. home life com. 1986-89), Springfield City Fedn. Women's Clubs (pres. 1990-92), Sorosis Club (Springfield, pres. 1980-92, chmn. hobby dept. 1986-88, 94, chmn. fine arts dept. 1988-90, mem. perpetual endowment com. 1992—, chmn. 1994) Alpha Delta Pi (treas. house corp. 1932-60), Alpha Delta Kappa (sec. 1965-67, corr. sec. Psi chpt. 1990-92).

HULL, MARGARET RUTH, artist, educator, consultant; b. Dallas, Mar. 27, 1921; d. William Haynes and Ora Carroll (Adams) Leatherwood; m. LeRos Ennis Hull, Mar. 29, 1941; children: LeRos Ennis, Jr., James Daniel. BA, So. Meth. U., Dallas, 1952, postgrad., 1960-61; MA, North Tex. State U., 1957, postgrad. R.I. Sch. Design, 1982. Art instr. W.W. Bushman Sch., Dallas Ind. Sch. Dist., 1952-57, Benjamin Franklin Jr. High Sch., Dallas, 1957-58; art instr. Hillcrest High Sch., Dallas, 1958-61, dean, pupil personnel counselor, 1961-70; tchr. children's painting Dallas Mus. Fine Art, 1956-70; designer, coordinator visual art careers cluster Skyline High Sch., Dallas, 1970-71, Skyline Career Devel. Ctr., Dallas, 1971-76, Booker T. Washington Arts Magnet High Sch., Dallas, 1976-82; developer curriculum devel./writing art, 1971-82; artist, ednl. cons., 1982—; mus. reprodns. asst. Dallas Mus. Art, 1984-93. Group shows include Dallas Mus. Fine Arts, 1958, Arts Magnet Faculty Shows, 1978-82, Arts Magnet High Sch., Dallas Art Edn. Assn. Show, 1981, D'Art Membership Show, Dallas, 1982-83; represented in pvt. collections. Trustee Dallas Mus. Art, 1978-84. Mem. Tex. Designer/Craftsmen, Craft Guild Dallas, Fiber Artists Dallas, Dallas Art Edn. Assn., Tex. Art Edn. Assn., Nat. Art Edn. Assn., Dallas Counselors Assn. (pres. 1968), Delta Delta Delta.

HULL, PEGGY FIESS, librarian; b. Hudson, N.Y., Nov. 18, 1950; d. Edward and Natalie (Zilboorg) Fiess; 1 child, Samira Kate. Student, Edinburgh (Scotland) U., 1970-71; BA, U. Wis., 1972; MS, Fla. State U., 1975. Libr. Career Edn. Ctr., Tallahassee, Fla., 1975-77; vol. Peace Corps, Yemen Arab Republic, 1977-79; tech. svc. libr. Chapel Hill (N.C.) Pub. Libr., 1981-82; cataloger Burroughs Wellcome Co., Research Triangle Park, N.C., 1982-83; head libr. and info. svcs. Glaxo Inc., Research Triangle Park, 1983-93; mgr. libr. svcs., 1994—. Mem. Spl. Librs. Assn. (chair pharm. divsn. 1990-91, mem. internat. rels. com. 1991-93, strategic planning com. 1990-91), Beta Phi Mu. Democrat. Unitarian. Office: Glaxo Inc 5 Moore Dr Durham NC 27709-4613

HULL, RITA PRIZLER, accounting educator; b. Lone Tree, Iowa, Mar. 29, 1936; d. Ernest Ralph and Mildred Lennis (Huskins) Prizler; m. J.W. Hull, May 29, 1954 (div. 1963); children: Mark, Marshall; m. John O. Everett, Sept. 1, 1976. BA in Acctg., Augustana Coll., Rock Island, Ill., 1967; MA in Acctg., Western Ill. U., 1973; PhD in Bus. Adminstrn., Okla. State U., 1978. CPA, Ill.; cert. internal auditor, Ill. Auditor Price Waterhouse & Co., Chgo., 1967-70; asst. prof. acctg. Bowling Green (Ohio) State U., 1976-78; assoc. prof. No. Ill. U., DeKalb, 1978-82; prof. Va. Commonwealth U., Richmond, 1982—. Contbr. articles, papers to profl. publs. Mem. AICPA, NOW (treas. Richmond chpt. 1987-88), Am. Soc. Women Accts. (treas. Richmond chpt. 1986-87, sec. 1987-88, pres. 1988-90, nat. bd. dirs. 1990-93, nat. sec. 1991-92, nat. v.p. 1992-93), Am. Acctg. Assn. (Trueblood seminars com. 1987-88, acctg. educator awards com. 1988-90, awards evaluation com. 1990-91, chmn.-elect gender issues in acctg. sect. 1991-92, chmn. 1992-93, coun. 1992-93), Inst. Internat. Auditors, Acad. Acctg. Historians. Democrat. Home: 810 Keats Rd Richmond VA 23229-6520 Office: Va Commonwealth U 1015 Floyd Ave Richmond VA 23284-4000

HULL, SHARON ANN, lobbyist; b. San Antonio, Nov. 16, 1947; d. Norman Leslie and Joyce Juliet (Haby) Harwell; m. M. Cordell Hull, Dec. 21, 1967 (div. May 1973); children: Lyndell Anne, Ashley Reneé. Student, Tex. Luth. Coll.; paralegal cert., U. Tex., 1965-67. Legis. liason Tex. Adult Probation Commn., Austin, 1975-81; lobbyist Booth, Lloyd & Simmons, Austin, 1981-83, pvt. practice, Austin, 1983—; participant in political activities with former husband Tex. state rep. for 6 yrs. Chmn. Bi-annual function Legislative Ladies Club, Austin, 1987-93; mem. strategic planning com. Laguna Gloria Women's Art Guild, Austin, 1993-94. Mem. Met. Club (social planning com.). Office: Sharon Hull & Assocs 1300 Guadalupe St Austin TX 78701-1643

HULL, SUZANNE WHITE, retired cultural institution administrator, writer; b. Orange, N.J., Aug. 24, 1921; d. Gordon Stowe and Lillian (Siegling) White; m. George I. Hull, Feb. 20, 1943 (dec. Mar. 1990); children: George Gordon, James Rutledge, Anne Elizabeth. BA with honors, Swarthmore Coll., 1943; MSLS, U. So. Calif., 1967. Mem. staff Huntington Libr., Art Gallery and Bot. Gardens, San Marino, Calif., 1969-86, dir. adminstrn. and pub. svcs., 1972-86, also prin. officer. Author: Chaste, Silent and Obedient, English Books for Women, 1475-1640, 1982, 88; editor: State of the Art in Women's Studies, 1986. Charter pres. Portola Jr. High Sch. PTA, L.A., 1960-62; pres. Children's Service League, 1963-64, YWCA L.A., 1967-69; mem. alumni council Swarthmore Coll., 1959-62, 83-86, mem.-at-large, 1986-89; mem. adv. bd. Hagley Mus. and Libr., Wilmington, Del., 1983-86, Betty Friedan Think Tank, U. So. Calif., 1985—; hon. life mem. Calif. Congress Parents and Tchrs.; bd. dirs. Pasadena Planned Parenthood Assn., 1978-83, mem. adv. com., 1983—; founder-chmn. Swarthmore-L.A. Connection, 1984-85, bd. dirs., 1985-92; founder Huntington Women's Studies Seminar, 1984, mem. steering com. 1984-91, mem. adv. bd., 1991—; bd. dirs. Pasadena Girls Club, 1988-91, mem. Organizing Com. Soc. for the Study of Early Modern Women, 1993—. Mem. Monumental Brass Soc. (U.K.), Renaissance Soc., Brit. Studies Conf., Western Assn. Women Historians, Authors Guild, Beta Phi Mu (chpt. dir. 1981-84). Home: 1465 El Mirador Dr Pasadena CA 91103-2727 Office: 1151 Oxford Rd San Marino CA 91108-1299

HULLINGER, CHARLOTTE M., psychotherapist; b. Houston, Apr. 1, 1934; d. Anton A. and Ada A. (Baepler) Froehlich; m. Robert Neil Hullinger, Sept. 1, 1957; children: Lisa, Jennifer, Robert Jr. AA, St. John's Coll., Winfield, Kans., 1953; BS, Luther Coll., Decorah, Iowa, 1958; MA, U. Cin., 1988. Ordained Internat. Coun. Community Churches, 1988. Elem. sch. tchr., 1953-55; adminstrv. asst. various, Cin., 1970-75; pvt. practice therapist Cin., 1988—; therapist Employee Asst. Program City of Cin., 1989—; dir. Wholistic Counseling and Ednl. Svcs. Cin., 1993—; therapist counseling week Sancta Sophia Seminary, Tahlequah, Okla., 1990-92; victim counselor Victim Svc. Ctr., 1988-89; founder, exec. Parents of Murdered Children, Inc., 1978-86; legal asst. Richard H. Glazer, Cin., 1974—; instr. So. Ohio Coll., Cin., 1978-80; apptd. Pres. Reagan's task force on law enforcement, 1980-83, Ohio adv. bd. on victims, 1980-83, City/County task force on victims, 1980-83, Ad. Bd. Nat. Victims of Crime, 1980-83. tech. asst. tng. cons. Nat. Orgn. Victim Assistance, Washington, 1986-90, cons. U.S. Dept. Justice, 1986-90. Recipient Edith Surgan award for outstanding leadership, Nat. Orgn. Victim Assistance, 1987; named one of ten top women of 1984, Cin. Enquirer. Home: 1739 Bella Vista Cincinnati OH 45237 Office: Pub Employees Assistance 50 E Hollister Cincinnati OH 45219

HULME, DARLYS MAE, banker; b. Buckingham, Iowa, Apr. 2, 1937; d. Leland James and Dorothy Mae (Nation) Philp; m. Harlan Dale Hulme, Dec. 4, 1955 (div. Nov. 1971); children: Debra Jean Hulme Hanneman, Richard Dale. Student Iowa Sch. Banking, 1974, Sch. Bank Adminstrn. U. Wis.-Madison, 1982. Bookkeeper, Farmers Savs. Bank, Traer, Iowa, 1954-55, asst. cashier, 1962-72, v.p., 1973-83, sr. v.p., 1983-93, exec. v.p., 1993—, also sec. bd. dirs.; acct. North Tama Housing, Inc., Traer, 1974—; sec. to bd. Talen, Inc., Talen Aviation, Ltd., Traer; cashier, sec. bd. dirs. Farmers Savs. Bank Trust, Vinton, Iowa, 1988—; dir., sec. to bd. Traer Nursing Care Ctr., Inc.; mem. Iowa State Banking Bd., 1985—. Mem. Nat. Assn. Bank Women (group treas. 1980-81, group v.p. 1981-82, group pres. 1982-83, state membership chair 1983-84, regional membership chair 1984-85), Iowa Bankers Assn. (mem. edn. com. 1985-86, Iowa Disting. Woman in Banking 1994). Republican. Methodist. Club: PEO (Traer) (corr. sec. 1988, v.p. 1991). Avocations: gardening, traveling. Home: 701 S Main St Traer IA 50675-1337 Office: Farmers Savs Bank 611 2nd St Traer IA 50675-1230

HULME, MARY ANN K., women's health nurse, administrator; b. Galion, Ohio, July 25, 1952; d. Walter Herman and Mary Elizabeth (Prim) Kumm; m. Roy Allan Hulme, Jan. 8, 1977; children: Eric A., Ann E. BSN, Capital U., 1974; MSN, Case Western Res. U., 1993. RN, Ohio; cert. in ob-gyn., neonatal nursing ANCC. Staff and charge nurse, labor and delivery St. Ann's Hosp., Columbus, Ohio, 1974-76, head nurse, dir. ob-gyn. outpatient clinic, 1976-77; clin. nurse, sr. clin. nurse, head nurse mgr. labor/delivery Univ. Hosps., Cleve., 1977-94; head nurse mgr. labor/delivery antepartum U. Hosps. Cleve., Cleve., 1994—; clin. instr. maternity and gynecology nursing Case Western Res. U., Cleve., 1986—. Contbr. articles to profl. jours. Recipient Silver medals U.S. Figure Skating Assn. Mem. ANA, Assn. Womens Health, Obstet. and Neonatal Nursing, Assn. Oper. Room Nurses, Ohio Nurses Assn., Lake Erie Coun. Nurse Execs., Cleve. Skating Club, Sigma Theta Tau. Lutheran. Home: 16070 S Park Blvd Cleveland OH 44120-1673

HULME, NANCY KENYON, educator; b. Upper Montclair, N.J.; d. Hallas Edwin and Margaret Louise (Williams) Kenyon; m. Robert DuBois Hulme, Sept. 11, 1954 (div. July 1966); children: Randall K., Michael H., Kimberly Dana. BFA, Swarthmore Coll., 1956; postgrad., U. N.H., 1969-70. Writer The Swarthmorean, Swarthmore, Pa., 1955, theatre critic, 1956-57; tchr. Rutgers Ave Sch., Swarthmore, Pa., 1965-68, George C. Baker Sch., Moorestown, N.J., 1968—. Mem. leadership coun. So. Poverty Law Ctr.; mem. faculty adv. coun., dist. human rels. com., textbook com. Moorestown Sch. Dist.; v.p. Jr. Women's Club, Swarthmore, 1964; bd. chmn. U.S. Census, Swarthmore, 1960; majority inspector (rep.) Election Polls, Swarthmore, 1964-65; sr. server Christ Ch., Riverton; parish rep. AIDS Com. of Diocese of N.J. Recipient Nat. Tchr. Recognition award Gov. Thomas Kean, N.J., 1989. Mem. NEA, Internat. Human Rels. Assn., Moorestown Edn. Assn., Burlington County Edn. Assn. Episcopalian. Home: 401 Shrewsbury Rd Riverton NJ 08077-1037 Office: George C Baker Sch 139 W Maple Ave Moorestown NJ 08057-1859

HULSEY, ELIZABETH BENBROOK, librarian; b. Jonesboro, Ark., Sept. 27, 1936; d. Orien Thurl and Olive May (Kerr) Benbrook; m. Jess Dale Hulsey, July 3, 1959; children: Charlotte Margaret Hulsey Taylor Weber, Edward Benbrook Hulsey. BA, Tex. Woman's U., 1958; MLS, U. Ill., 1959. Reference libr. U. Ill., Champaign-Urbana, 1959-62; head tech. svcs. Corpus Christi (Tex.) Pub. Libr., 1963-65; sch. libr. Cullen Jr. High Sch., Corpus Christi, 1965-66; freelance writer Stavanger, Norway, 1975-79; children's libr. Cypress Creek br. Harris County Pub. Libr., Houston, 1979, asst. br. libr., 1980-81, br. libr., 1981—. Mem. AAUW (1st v.p. Harris County Br. 1990—), Tex. Libr. Assn. Republican. Home: 3814 Stillview Dr Houston TX 77068-2917 Office: Harris County Pub Libr Cypress Creek Br 6815 Cypresswood Dr Spring TX 77379-7705

HULSLANDER, MARJORIE DIANE, auditor; b. Towanda, Pa., Mar. 8, 1938; d. Robert Alfred and Catharine Agnes (Brennan) Neiley; m. John Edgar Hulslander, June 14. 1958; children: Thomas Alfred, Cindy Lou Hulslander Loss, Timothy John. Bookkeeper G.L.F. Petroleum, Inc., Towanda, Pa., 1956-59; sec., treas. West Burlington Milk Producers, Troy, Pa., 1961-67; clk. Valley Stockyards, Inc., Athens, Pa., 1967-80; tax collector West Burlington Twp., Troy, Pa., 1968-87; auditor, chmn. Bradford County, Towanda, Pa., 1988-95. Committeewoman Bradford County Rep. Party, West Burlington Twp., 1980-95; Pres., founder Troy Fire Dept. Ladies Auxiliary Sta. 11, West Burlington Twp., 1988-90, treas., 1990-92; exec. Pa. State Auditors Assn., 1992-95; treas. Bradford County Rep. Women, Towanda, Pa., 1994-95; auditor State Rep. Women Fin. Records, 1994. Mem. Union Grange (#155 treas.). Republican. Episcopalian. Home: RD #3 Box 318 Troy PA 16947

HUMBACH, MIRIAM JANE, marketing and financial professional; b. N.Y.C., May 18, 1964; d. William Walter and Mildred (Wender) H. BA in Bus.-Econs./Psychology, SUNY-Oneonta, 1986. Fin./acctg. staff The N.Y. Times Co., N.Y.C., 1987-92, media svcs. rsch. asst., 1992-94; circulation/staff asst. N.Y. Times Co., N.Y.C., 1994—. Mem. NAFE. Home: 235 E 95th St # 12G New York NY 10128 Office: The New York Times Co 229 W 43rd St New York NY 10036

HUME, ELLEN HUNSBERGER, media analyst, journalist; b. Chevy Chase, Md., Apr. 24, 1947; d. Warren Seabury and Ruth (Pedersen) H.; m. John Shattuck, Feb. 14, 1991; 1 child, Susannah; stepchildren: Jessica, Rebecca, Peter. BA, Harvard U., 1968; PhD (hon.), Daniel Webster Coll., 1990. Reporter Somerville (Mass.) Jour., 1968-69; feature writer Santa Barbara (Calif.) News Press, 1969-70; pub. service dir., copy writer KTMS Radio, Santa Barbara, 1970-72; edn. reporter Ypsilanti (Mich.) Press, 1972-73; bus. reporter Detroit Free Press, 1973-75; met. reporter L.A. Times, 1975-77; congl. reporter L.A. Times, Washington, 1977-83; White House corr., polit. writer Wall St. Jour., Washington, 1983-88; exec. dir. Shorenstein-Barone Ctr. on Press and Politics Harvard U., Cambridge, Mass., 1988-93; moderator The Editors TV program, Montreal, Que., 1990-93; adj. lectr. Kennedy Sch. Govt., 1991-93, Medill Sch. Journalism, 1993-94; commentator Washington Week in Rev. PBS-TV, 1973-88, CNN, 1993—. Kennedy Inst. Politics fellow Harvard U., 1981, Woodrow Wilson fellow. Mem. Coun. of Fgn. Rels., Fund for Free Expression, Nat. Press Club (judge, Fourth Estate awards 1985, 86). Methodist. Office: Annenberg Washington Prog Ste 200 1455 Pennsylvania Ave NW Washington DC 20004-1008

HUME, SUSAN RACHEL, finance and economics educator; b. Englewood, N.J., Aug. 25, 1952; d. Philip and Anna Ann (Petrowski) Nachtigal; m. John Elliott Hume, Dec. 27, 1975; children: Philip John, Scot Elliott. BA, Douglass Coll., 1974; MBA, Rutgers U. Grad. Sch. Mgmt., 1976; postgrad., CUNY, 1988—. Bank analyst N.Y. Fed. Res. Bank, 1976-77, sr. credit analyst, 1977-79; sr. comml. loan officer 1st Pa. Bank, Phila., 1979-81; asst. v.p. Mfrs. Hanover Trust Co., N.Y.C., 1982-83, v.p., 1983-84, dept. head, hedge funding and asset liability mgmt., 1984-88; adj. assoc. prof. fin. and econs. Rider Coll., 1988-90; asst. adj. prof. Fairleigh Dickinson, Madison, N.J., 1991-93; adj. prof. dept. fin. and econs. Baruch Coll., N.Y.C., 1993—; mem. Douglass Alumnae Endowment Fund Fin. Com., 1985—, counselling for coll. srs. bus. opportunities, New Brunswick, N.J., 1988; mem. internat. seminar interest rate risk mgmt. N.Y. Inst. Fin., N.Y.C., 1990—. Mem. choir, Sunday Sch. tchr. Presbyn. Ch., Westfield; active Boy Scouts Am.; chairperson McGinn Elem. Sch. PTA Reading Program. Recipient Heller alumni award Rutgers U., 1976.

HUMMEL, DANA D. MALLETT, librarian; BA in Art History, Smith Coll., 1957; MA in Libr. and Info. Sci., Denver U., 1968; postgrad. Def. Lang. Inst., 1961, Instituto Mexicano-Norteamericano de Relationes Culturales, 1962, John F. Kennedy Ctr. for Spl. Warfare, 1974, Nat. War Coll., 1976, No. Va. Bus. Sch., 1978, Cath. U. Am., 1981. Head libr., administrn., Howard AFB Libr., C.Z., 1969-70; asst. libr. Holmes Intermediate Sch., 1970-71; tchr. Spanish and substitute tchr. J.E.B. Stuart High Sch., 1972-77; sec. Office of exec. dir.-Africa The World Bank, 1978-79; personal sec. to rector Falls Ch. (Va.), 1979-81; mgr. Info. Svcs. Ctr., BDM Internat. subs. Ford Aerospace Co., McLean, Va., 1981-88. Mem. vestry Falls Ch. Episcopal Ch., 1982; del. Republican State Conv., 1981, 86; pres. Ravenwood Civic Assn., 1979-80, 80-81, 81-82; rep. Mason Dist., Fedn. Civic Assns.; mem. ann. plan rev. task force Mason Dist., 1981-82; gov. trustee Fairfax County Pub. Libr. Bd., 1982-88; chmn. bd. trustees Fairfax County. Named Outstanding Woman of Yr., Fairfax County Bd. Suprs. & Com. of Women, 1982. Mem. AAUP, ALA, Am. Soc. for Info. Sci., Spl. Libr. Assn., Va. Libr. Assn., D.C. Libr. Assn., Women in Def., Jr. League Sarasota, Fla. Home: 7355 Villa D Este Dr Sarasota FL 34238-5649

HUMMEL, KAY JEAN, physical therapist; b. Cleve., Apr. 24, 1943; d. Lloyd Elmer and Olive Agnes (Latou) Hetherington; m. Charles William Hummel (div. Feb. 1984); children: Patrick H., Robin E. BA, Miami U., Oxford, Ohio, 1965; cert. in phys. therapy, Columbia U., N.Y., 1966. Lic. phys. therapist, La.; cert. ofcl. Games Uniting Mind and Body. Staff phys. therapist St. Joseph's Hosp., Chgo., 1966-68, Wrightwood Extended Care Facility, Chgo., 1967-68, Suburban Hosp., Bethesda, Md., 1969, Holy Cross Hosp., Silver Spring, Md., 1969-70; asst. chief phys. therapist Community Gen. Hosp., Syracuse, N.Y., 1970-76; itinerant phys. therapist Caddo Parish Schs., Shreveport, La., 1976—; pvt. practice Shreveport, 1985—. Mem. Coun. for Exceptional Children, U.S. Cerebral Palsy Athletic Assn. (regional classifier), Presbyn. Women's Club of Shreveport, Kappa Delta Alumni Assn. Office: Caddo Exceptional Sch 3202 William St Shreveport LA 71103

HUMMEL, MARILYN MAE, elementary education educator; b. Cleve., June 20, 1931; d. John Winfield and Meta E. (Timm) H. BS, Ohio U., 1953. Cert. elem. educator. Elem. tchr. Lakewood (Ohio) Bd. of Edn., 1953-83. Mem. Centennial Planning Com., Lakewood, Ohio 1989; vol. United Way, Lakewood Hosp. Jennings scholar, 1969-70; named Tchr. of the Yr., Franklin Sch., 1983. Mem. Coll. Club West, Delta Kappa Gamma, Kiwanis Club. Republican. Presbyterian.

HUMPHREY, DORIS DAVENPORT, consulting company executive, educator; b. Woodbury, Tenn., June 3, 1943; d. Luther and Gladys (Alexander) Davenport; m. John Sparkman Humphrey, Sept. 15, 1941 (dec.); children: Heather, Holly. BS, Middle Tenn. State U., 1965; MBE, Ga. State U., 1972, EdS, 1977; PhD, Ga. State U., 1983; postgrad. Bryn Mawr Coll., 1989. Sec., coordinator creative services, asst. to pres. Noble-Dury & Assocs., Nashville, 1965-69; asst. account exec. McCann-Erickson & Assocs., Atlanta, 1969-70; adj. and full-time instr. DeKalb C.C., 1970-79; coord. internship program Raymond Walters Coll., U. Cin., 1980-83, chmn. dept. office adminstrn., 1981-86; asst. dean bus. and office mgmt. Del. County C.C., Media, Pa., 1987-90; pres. Career Solutions Tng. Group, Paoli, Pa., 1990; lectr. in field; curriculum cons. Author: Northside Medical Center, P.C.: The Medical Secretary, 1980, The Medical Office: A Reference Manual, 1986, Pediatric Associates, P.C., 1988, Contemporary Medical Office Procedures, 1989, The Medical Manager, 1991, School to Work Series, 1994. Mem. Nat. Bus. Edn. Assn., Am. Vocat. Assn., Delta Pi Epsilon. Presbyterian.

HUMPHREY, KIMBERLY MICHELLE, pediatrician, educator; b. Blakely, Ga., Mar. 11, 1962; d. Calvin Walter and Helen Virginia (Grier) H. AB in Chemistry, Duke U., 1984; MD, U. Cin., 1988. Diplomate Am. Bd. Pediatrics. Resident in pediatrics Cardinal Glennon Children's Hosp., St. Louis, 1988-91; pvt. practice, Atlanta, 1991—; mem. faculty Morehouse U. Sch. Medicine, Atlanta, 1991—; mem. staff S.W. Hosp., Atlanta, Egleston Childrens Hosp., Atlanta, South Fulton Hosp., Atlanta; mem. cons. staff Kennestone Hosp., Marietta, Ga. Fellow Am. Acad. Pediatrics; mem. Internat. Coalition Women Physicians, Ga. Med. Assn., Alpha Kappa Alpha. Methodist. Home: 3605 John Carrol Dr Decatur GA 30034 Office: Southside Healthcare Inc 1039 Ridge Ave SW Atlanta GA 30315

HUMPHREY, MITZI GREENE, artist; b. Johnson City, Tenn., Feb. 10, 1936; d. Sterling Augustus and Alta Marie (Ferguson) Greene; m. Thomas MacGillivray Humphrey, June 4, 1957; children: Sheryl Lynn, Thomas MacGillivray Jr. and Elizabeth Eleanor (twins). BS in Art Edn., Fine Arts, U. Tenn., 1957; MA in British and Am. Lit., Auburn U., 1970; BFA in Painting and Printmaking, Va. Commonwealth U., 1988. Tchr. art, English Knoxville City Schs., 1957-59; dir., co-founder Wofford Coll. Art Gallery, Spartanburg, S.C., 1960-61; sec. chemistry dept. Newcomb Coll., New Orleans, 1962-63; asst. to dir. Scott-McKennis Gallery, Richmond, Va., 1975-76; curator nat. xerographic exhibit 1708 East Main Gallery, Richmond, Va., 1988-89; curator nat. book art exhibit Artspace, Richmond, Va., 1993-94, pres., 1992-94; adj. faculty English dept. J. Sargeant Reynolds C.C., Richmond, 1975-76, U. Richmond, 1982-84; instr. workshops Va. Mus. Fine Arts, 1990-91; instr. travel jour. workshop Valentine Mus., Richmond, 1992; lectr. women's resource ctr. U. Richmond, 1992; reps. women's caucus for art Nat. Book Art Conf., N.Y.C., 1989. Producer (ednl. videos) Art Ex Libris at Artspace, 1994, Clifford Edwards and Books as Icons in the Paintings of Van Gogh, 1994, Isota Epes and How Virginia Woolf Brought Me Up, 1994. Sec. Richmond Interfaith Coun., 1982-83; mem. Conservation Coun. Va., Richmond, 1989-94. Va. Commn. Arts grantee, 1989, 94. Mem. Internat. Soc. Copier Artists (Va. rep. 1980-91), Richmond Artists Assn. (pres. 1984-86) Women's Caucus Art (mem. exec. bd. 1991-93, grantee 1989), Briarwood Book Club, Phi Kappa Phi, Pi Lambda Theta. Independent. Presbyterian. Home: 2201 Conte Dr Midlothian VA 23113 Office: 300 N Lombardy Ave Richmond VA 23220

HUMPHREYS, KAREN M., judge; b. Ashland, Kans., Feb. 18, 1948; d. Frederick Mitchell and Carrie (Arnold) H. BA in History and Am. Studies, Univ. of Kans., 1970, JD, 1973. Bar: Kans. 1973, U.S. Dist. Ct. Kans. 1978, U.S. Supreme Ct. 1980. Estate and gift tax atty. IRS, Dept. of Treasury, 1973-75; staff atty. Legal Aid, 1975-76; founder, mng. atty. Senior Citizen Law Project, 1976-78; asst. U.S. atty. Topeka, Kans., 1978-83, Wichita, Kans., 1983-86; assoc. Redmond, Redmond & Nazar, 1986-87; staff atty. FDIC, 1987; dist. judge State of Kans., 18th Judicial Dist., 1987-93; magistrate judge U.S. Dist. Ct. Kans., Wichita, 1993—; bd. dirs. Women's Studies at Wichita State Univ., Kans. Health Inst. and Prairie View Inc.; advisory bd. Jr. League. Recipient Matrix award Women in Comm., 1989. Mem. Am. Bar Assn., Kans. Bar Assn., Wichita Bar Assn. (President's award for outstanding svc. 1988), Nat. Assn. of Women Judges, Wichita Women Attys. Assn. (Louise Mattox award 1994). Protestant. Office: US Courthouse 401 N Market St Rm 322 Wichita KS 67202*

HUMPHRIES, JOAN ROPES, psychologist, educator; b. Bklyn., Oct. 17, 1928; d. Lawrence Gardner and Adele Lydia (Zimmermann) Ropes; m. Charles C. Humphries, Apr. 4, 1957; children: Peggy Ann, Charlene Adele. BA, U. Miami, 1950; MS, Fla. State U., 1955; PhD, La. State U., 1963. Part-time instr. psychology dept. U. Miami, Coral Gables, Fla., 1964-66; prof. behavioral studies dept. Miami-Dade Community Coll., 1966—. Registered lobbyist State of Fla. Recipient cert. Appreciation Miami-Dade Community Coll. Prodr., prin. host (videos) Strategies in Global Modern Academia: Issues and Answers in Higher Education, 1993-94. Mem. AAUP (pres. Miami-Dade Community Coll. chpt. 1986—, sec., mem. exec. bd. Am. Assn. Univ. Profs. Fla. conf. 1986-90, v.p. 1986, 87, 88), AAUW (former v.p. Tamiami branch 1983-88) Biofeedback Soc. of Am. (pres. 1989—), Biofeedback Assn. Fla. (pres. 1990—), Internat. Platform Assn. (gov. 1979—, Silver Bowl award 1993), Am. Psychol. Assn., AAUW (life, appreciation award 1977), Am. Psychol. Soc. (charter), Fla. Psychol. Assn., Mexico Beach C. of C. (bus. 1991—), North Campus Speaker's Bur. (award for community lecture series), Physicians for Social Responsibility, Internat. Soc. for Study Subtle Energies and Energy Medicine (charter), Inst. Evaluation, Diagnosis and Treatment (past v.p. 1975-87, pres. 1987—, former bd. dirs.), Dade-Monroe Psychol. Assn., Assn. Applied Psychophysiology and Biofeedback, Noetic Scis., Colonial Dames 17th Century, N.Y. Acad. Scis. (life), Regines in Miami, Soc. Mayflower Descs. (elder William Brewster colony), Phi Lambda (founder's plaque 1976, appreciation award 1987), Phi Lambda Pi. Democrat. Clubs: Country of Coral Gables (life), Jockey (life). Editorial staff, maj. author: The Application of Scientific Behaviorism to Humanistic Phenomena, 1975, rev. edit., 1979; researcher in biofeedback and human consciousness. Home: 1311 Alhambra Cir Coral Gables FL 33134-3521 Office: Miami Dade CC North Campus 11380 NW 27th Ave Miami FL 33167-3418

HUMPHRIES, JUDY LYNN, lawyer, nurse; b. Charleston, W.Va., Nov. 20, 1946; d. Robert Elmer and Arravelva Virginia (Davis) H.; m. Michael Allen Grant, Dec. 29, 1971; children: Susan Lindley, Christopher Allen, Elizabeth Davis. BSN, W.Va. U., 1968; MS, U. Md., 1970; JD, William & Mary Coll., 1977. Bar: Va. 1977, W.Va. 1978, D.C. 1980. Instr. in psychiatric nursing W.Va. U., Morgantown, 1970-72, asst. prof. upper div. nursing, 1977-78; psychiat. nurse Veterans Hosp., Cin., 1972-73; asst. prosecutor Monongalia County, Morgantown, 1978-81; sole practice Fairmont, W.Va., 1980-90; instr. health law and med. ethics Fairmont State Coll., 1984-86, adj. prof., 1984-87; cons. J.B. Lippincott Pubs., Phila., 1985; asst. prosecuter Marion County, W.Va., 1986-88; bd. dirs. Fairmont Gen. Hosp. Inc., 1988-90. Bd. dirs. Monongalia County Youth Svcs. Ctr., 1981-83, Hope, Inc., Task Force on Domestic Violence, 1986-89. Mem. ABA, LWV. Democrat. Episcopalian. Home: 1160 Avalon Rd Fairmont WV 26554-5028

HUMPHRIES, KAREN ANN, bank examiner; b. Boston, Nov. 29, 1953; d. Joseph E. and Evelyn D. (Lopez) Flahive; m. Donald E. Humphries, Mar. 4, 1972; children: Bryan, Daniel. BS, U. Mass., Boston, 1983; MBA, Bentley Coll., 1985. With State St. Bank & Trust, Boston, 1983-88, credit officer, 1985-88; credit mgr. Warren Five Cents Savs. Bank, Peabody, Mass., 1988-91; examiner Comptr. of the Currency, Boston, 1991—. Religion tchr. CCD program St. Clement Cath. Ch., Somerville, Mass., 1983—, mem. parish pastoral coun., 1990—. Office: Comptr of Currency 150 Federal St Boston MA 02110-1745

HUNING, DEBORAH GRAY, actress, dancer, audiologist; b. Evanston, Ill., Aug. 23, 1950; d. Hans Karl Otto and Angenette Dudley (Willard) H.; divorced; 1 child, Bree Alyeska. BS, No. Ill. U., 1981, MA, 1983. Actress, soloist, dancer, dir. various univ. and community theater depts., Bklyn., Chgo. and Cranbrook, B.C., Can., 1967—; ski instr. Winter Park (Colo.) Recreation Assn., 1975-79; house photographer C Lazy U Ranch, Granby, Colo., 1979; audiologist, ednl. programming cons. East Kootenay Ministry of Health, Cranbrook, 1985-89; ind. video prodn./asst., 1991—; owner Maxaroma Espresso and Incredible Edibles, 1993—; master of ceremonies East Kootenay Talent Showcase, EXPO '86, Vancouver B.C., Can., 1986; creator, workshop leader: A Hearing Impaired Child in the Classroom, 1986. Producer, writer, dir., editor (video) Down With Decibels, 1992; author: Living Well With Hearing Loss: A Guide for the Hearing-Impaired and Their Families, 1992. Sec., treas. Women for Wildlife, Cranbrook, 1985-86; assoc. mem. adv. bd. Grand County Community Coll., Winter Park, Colo., 1975-77; assoc. mem. bd. dirs. Boys and Girls Club of Can., Cranbrook, 1985. Mem. Internat. Marine Animal Trainers Assn.

HUNKELE, MARGARET MARY, radiologic technologist; b. Bklyn., Dec. 26, 1960; d. Lester Martin and Agnes Veronica (Tarpey) H. Radiologic licensure, Bartone Sch. of Radiography, Bklyn., 1987; AS, Empire State, Marymount, N.Y.C., 1990. Cert. radiologic technologist Am. Registry Radiologic Technologists. Staff technologist N.Y.U. Hosp., 1987-88; lead technologist Mitchell M. Bashiri, M.D., Bklyn., 1988-89; clin. instr. Bryman Sch., Phoenix, Ariz., 1990—. Recipient Regents scholarship Bd. Regents, N.Y., 1974, Nat. Edn. Dept. award of excellence, Washington, 1975. Mem. Am. Soc. Radiologic Technologists. Home: PO Box 54351 Phoenix AZ 85078

HUNNICUTT, BARBARA ISERT, biology educator; b. Louisville, June 29, 1943; d. Fred John and Joey (Crume) Isert; m. M. Kermit Hunnicutt, Mar. 23, 1969 (div. Feb. 1991); children: Jeffrey, Heather, Laura. BS in Math. and Biology, U. Tex., Arlington, 1965; EdD in Sci. Edn., U. Ga., 1969. Tchr. math. and biology Lake Brantley H.S., Forest City, Fla., 1976-78; instr. Gen. Edn. Diploma, and ESL, Seminole C.C., Sanford, Fla., 1978-81, prof. math., 1981-84, prof. biology, honors dir., 1984—, v.p. faculty senate, 1992-93, also past chmn. staff and program devel.; treas. Fla. Honors Coun., 1991—. Author: (lab. manuals) Special Problems in Biology, 1987, Biology, 1988. Mem. exec. bd. Seminole Work Opportunity Program, Casselberry, Fla., 1984-93; vol. painter wall murals for chs. and daycare, Mobile, Ala., 1972-75, Orlando, Fla., 1976—. Recipient Outstanding Leadership in Edn. award Ctrl. Fla. Consortium for Women, 1989. Mem. AAUW (treas. 1980-94, exec. bd., presiding ptnr. investment group 1991-92, treas. 1994-96), Nat. Collegiate Honors Coun., Fla. Assn. C.C.'s (exec. bd., v.p., pres. 1981-94). Roman Catholic. Home: 1007 Cathy Dr Altamonte Springs FL 32714-7216 Office: Seminole CC 100 Weldon Blvd Sanford FL 32773

HUNSLEY, LILLA MAY, school nutrition program director; b. Denver, Oct. 20, 1939; d. Gilbert and Elanor May (Anderson) H. BA in Elem. Edn., Mt. Marty Coll., Yankton, S.D., 1965; MS in Nutrition, Iowa State U., 1978. Cret. edn. dir. and adminstr., Ga.; lic. dietitian, Ga. Tchr. St. Jospeh Sch., Pueblo, Colo., 1959-62, Holy Trinity Sch., Hardington, Nebr., 1962-68; missionary work Cath. Ch., Guatemala, 1968-72; coord. nutrition edn. State of Iowa, Des Moines, 1978-84; dir. sch. nutrition program Gwinnett County Pub. Schs., Lawrenceville, Ga., 1984—; apptd. by Gov. Zell Miller to bd. trustees The Pub. Sch. Employees' Retirement Sys., 1994-98. Mem. Am. Sch. Food Svc. Assn. (mem. nutrition standards com. 1990-93), Ga. Sch. Food Svc. Assn. (legis. chmn. 1990-93, pres. 1994-95, Josephine Martin award 1992). Home: 270 Thornbush Trce Lawrenceville GA 30245-7472

HUNSPERGER, ELIZABETH JANE, art and design consultant, educator; b. Phila., Aug. 30, 1938; d. Francis Charles and Elizabeth Julia (Rudolph) Thorpe; m. Robert George Hunsperger, Sept. 13, 1958; 1 child, Lisa Marie. AA in Design, Santa Monica Coll., 1974; student, UCLA, 1975-76; BA in Art History, U. Del., 1978; postgrad., Rutgers U., 1978-81; MA in Edn., Del. State Coll., 1993. Designer Huntingdon Mills, Phila., 1960-63, Rothschild's, Ithaca, N.Y., 1963-65, Cornell U., Ithaca, 1965-67; freelance designer, Malibu, Calif., 1967-76; art and design cons., lectr. Art & Sci. Assocs., Newark, Del., 1980—; art tchr. Cath. Diocese of Wilmington, 1988—; with Leech Sch., 1994; bd. dirs. Gallery 20, Newark, Del., 1982-86. Exhibitions include: Malibu Art Assn. Show, 1973, 74, Newark Art Show, 1987, 88. Founding mem. bd. dirs., v.p. Newark Housing Ministry, Inc., 1983—, pres., 1989-91; mem. social concerns com. and drug and alcohol task force Del.; active Coun. Exceptional Children. Episcopal. Recipient Outstanding Svc. award YWCA, Santa Monica, Calif., 1972, Award of Recognition, Missionhurst, 1982, Gov.'s Vol. of the Yr. award State of Del., 1990. Mem. Nat. Art Edn. Assn., Am. Craft Coun., Art Educators of Del., Debutante Assembly Club (N.Y.C.). Home: 1014 New London Rd Newark DE 19711-2116

HUNSTEIN, CAROL, judge; b. Miami, Fla., Aug. 16, 1944. AA, Miami-Dade Jr. Coll., 1970; BS, Fla. Atlantic U., 1972; JD, Stetson U., 1976. Bar: Ga. 1976; U.S. Dist. Ct. 1978; U.S. Ct. Appeals 1978; U.S. Supreme Ct. 1989. Legal practice Atlanta, 1976-84; judge Superior Ct. of Ga. (Stone Mt. cir.), 1984-92; justice Supreme Ct. of Ga., Atlanta, 1992—; chair Ga. Commn. on Gender Bias in the Judicial System 1989—; pres.-elect Coun. of Superior Ct. Judges of Ga. 1990—. Recipient Clint Green Trial Advocacy award 1976, Women Who Made A Difference award Dekalb Women's Network 1986. Mem. ABA, Atlanta Lawyers Club, Dekalb Lawyers Assn., Ga. Assn. of Women Lawyers, Nat. Assn. of Women Judges (dir. 1988-90), State Bar Ga., Decatur-DeKalb Bar Assn., Ga. Assn. Criminal Defense Lawyers, Ga. Trial Lawyers Assn., Commercial Real Estate Women's Assn., Sigma Delta Kappa. Office: Supreme Ct Ga 523 State Judicial Bldg Atlanta GA 30334*

HUNT, ANDREA C., nurse; b. Kingston, Jamaica, Aug. 10, 1946; d. Rupert A. and Mavis C. Atkins; m. Robert T. Hunt, Feb. 24, 1979; children: Ian Jason, Simon Christopher. BSN, U. Cen. Fla., 1986; BSc, U. Guelph, Canada, 1969; MS, U. Cen. Fla., 1991. Cert. diabetic educator. Agrl. officer Min. Agrl., Kingston, Jamaica; lectr. Coll. Bahamas, Nassau; staff nurse, med. surg. Orlando Regional Med. Ctr., Fla.; sr. community health nurse Orange County Health Dept., Orlando, Fla.; insvc. edn. coord. Spl. Care Home Health, Inc., Sunrise, Fla.; supr. nursing Pulse Health Svc., Lauderhill, Fla. Recipient Jamaican Govt. scholar, 1967. Mem. Fla. Nurses Assn., South Fla. Assn. Nurse Educators, South Fla. Assn. Diabetes Educators.

HUNT, CATHY S., secondary education educator; b. Sycamore, Ill., Nov. 2, 1955; d. Robert C. Sr. and Marilyn J. (Jones) Smith; m. David G. Hunt, Sr. (div); children: David G. Jr., Tanya N. BS, Western Ill. U., 1977; MEd, Nat. Lewis U., 1989; postgrad., No. Ill. U., Gov. State U., St. Xavier, U. San Diego. Home econs. tchr. Valley View Schs., Romeoville, Ill., 1978-80, Oswego (Ill.) Sch. Dist. 308, 1980—; asst. girls softball coach Westview Mid. Sch., Romeoville, 1980; track coach Traughber Jr. High, Oswego, 1981, 83, 84, costume designer, 1980, 82, mem. sch. improvement team, 1988—, mem. core team and crisis team, 1991—, athletic dir., 1994—. Chair Multiple Sclerosis Bike in Hike, Sycamore, Ill., 1985-86; asst. regional dir., dist. dir. Jaycees, Sycamore, 1987-90; active Easter Seals Telethon, Aurora, Ill., 1994. Named Outstanding Young Woman of Am., Jaycees, 1987, Outstanding Dist. Dir., 1987-88, Outstanding State Chmn., 1988-89. Mem. Ill. Vocat. Assn., Ill. Vocat. Home Econs. Assn., Phi Delta Kappa (v.p. 1992-93, pres. 1993-94). Home: 15 Greenbriar Montgomery IL 60538 Office: Traughber Jr HS Franklin & Polk Oswego IL 60543

HUNT, EFFIE NEVA, former college dean, former English educator; b. Waverly, Ill., June 19, 1922; d. Abraham Luther and Fannie Ethel (Ritter) H. A.B., MacMurray Coll. for Women, 1944; M.A., U. Ill., 1945, Ph.D., 1950; postgrad., Columbia U., 1953, Univ. Coll., U. London, 1949-50. Keypunch operator U.S. Treasury, 1945; spl. librarian Harvard U., 1947, U. Pa., 1948; Instr. English U. Ill., 1950-51; librarian Library of Congress, Washington, 1951-52; asst. prof. English Mankato State Coll., 1952-59; prof. Radford Coll., 1959-63, chmn. dept. English, 1961-63; prof. Ind. State U., 1963-86; dean Ind. State U. (Coll. Arts and Scis.), 1974-86, dean and prof. emerita, 1987—. Author articles in field. Fulbright grantee, 1949-50. Mem. AAUP, MLA, Nat. Council Tchrs. English, Am. Assn. Higher Edn., Audubon Soc. Home: 3325 Wabash Ave Terre Haute IN 47803-1660 Office: Ind State U Root Hall Eng Dept Terre Haute IN 47809

HUNT, F. V. See VANCE-HUNT, FLORENCE

HUNT, HELEN, actress; b. L.A., June 15, 1963; d. Gordon H. TV appearances include Amy Prentiss, The Swiss Family Robinson, The Fitzpatricks, It Takes Two, Having Babies, Land of Little Rain, Weekend, Mary Tyler Moore Show, Family, St. Elsewhere; TV movies include Pioneer Woman, All Together Now, Death Scream, The Spell, Transplant, Angel Dusted, Child Bride of Short Creek, The Miracle of Cathy Miller, Desperate Lives, Quarterback Princess, Bill: On His Own, Choices of the Heart, Sweet Revenge, Why Are You Here?, Murder In New Hampshire: The Pamela Smart Story, 1991, In the Comfort of Darkness, 1992; TV series Mad About You, 1992— (Emmy nomination, Lead Actress - Comedy, 1993, 94, Golden Globe award for Best Actress, musical or comedy, 1994, 95); films include Rollercoaster, 1977, Girls Just Want To Have Fun, 1985, Trancers, 1985, Empire, 1985, Peggy Sue Got Married, 1986, Project X, 1987, Miles From Home, 1988, Next Of Kin, 1989, The Waterdance, 1992, Only You, 1992, Bob Roberts, 1992, Mr. Saturday Night, 1992, Kiss of Death, 1995. Office: care Connie Tavel 9171 Wilshire Blvd Ste 436 Beverly Hills CA 90210

HUNT, LINDA, actress; b. Morristown, N.J., Apr. 2, 1945. Student, Interlochen Arts Acad., Mich., Goodman Theatre and Sch. of Drama, Chgo. Stage appearances include Hamlet, 1972, 74, The Soldier's Tale, 1974, The Knight of the Burning Pestle, 1974, Down by the River Where Waterlilies are disfigured Every Day (off-Broadway debut) 1975, Ah, Wilderness (Broadway debut) 1975, The Rose Tattoo, 1977, Five Finger Excuse, 1975, The Recruiting Officer, 1978, Elizabeth Dead, 1980, A Metamorphis in Miniature (Obie award), 1983, Mother Courage and Her Children 1983, Top Girls (Obie award) 1983, Little Victories, 1983, End of the World, 1983, (Tony nomination 1984), Aunt Dan and Lemon, 1985, The Cherry Orchard, 1988; films include Popeye, 1980, The Year of Living Dangerously, 1982 (Acad. award Best supporting actress 1983), Dune, 1984, The Bostonians, 1984, Eleni, 1985, Silverado, 1985, Waiting for the Moon, 1987, She-Devil, 1989, Kindergarten Cop, 1990, If Looks Could Kill, 1991, Rain Without Thunder, 1993, Twenty Bucks, 1993, Younger and Younger, 1993, Ready to Wear (Prét-a-Portér), 1994; TV appearance in Ah, Wilderness, 1976, Fame (series) 1978, The Room, 1987, Chico Mendes: Voice of the Amazon, 1989, The Room Upstairs (T.V. movies) 1987, Distant Lives (host) 1989, Space Rangers (series), 1993. Office: care William Morris Agy 151 EL Camino Beverly Hills CA 90212*

HUNT, MARIE FERGUSON, financial executive; b. Pinehurst, N.C., Nov. 12, 1948; d. James Archie and Nell (Lewis) Ferguson; m. Robert Lee Hunt, Apr. 14, 1971 (div. Oct. 1991); children: Lisa Hunt Jones, Audrey Lee. Student, Raleigh Sch. Data Processing, 1968; cert. programmer, Rsch. Tech. Inst., 1969; student, Sandhills Community Coll., 1975, 77. Acctg. clerk Orkin Exterminating Co., High Point, N.C., 1970-71; full charge bookkeeper, front desk clerk Hyland Hills Lodge and Restaurant, Southern Pines, N.C., 1971-74; head cashier Pinehurst (N.C.) Hotel and Country Club, 1974-76, project analyst, 1976-80, supr. customer svc. dept., 1980-83; asst. mgr. Westlake Pla. Hotel, Westlake Village, Calif., 1983-84; accts. payable clerk Evergreen Mgmt. Corp., Southern Pines, 1985; full charge double-entry bookkeeper Southern Pines Elks and C.C., 1986; front office mgr. Embassy Suites, Oxnard, Calif., 1986; fin. officer Village of Pinehurst, 1987—. Recipient Acctg./Fin. Mgmt. award State of N.C. Dept. of State Treas., 1989. Mem. Internat. Pers. Mgmt. Assn., Govt. Fin. Officers Assn., N.C. Fin. Officers Assn., N.C. Local Govt. Investment Assn. Methodist. Office: Village of Pinehurst 10 Village Way Pinehurst NC 28374

HUNT, MARTHA, sales executive, researcher; b. N.Y.C., May 17, 1924; d. Paul Andrew and Monika (Dobberstein) Pankau; children: Philip Brian Hunt, Susan Monica Hunt. Student, Syracuse U., 1943-47. Asst. controller Commonwealth Fund, N.Y.C., 1947-50; sales tech. Caldwell & Bloor, Mansfield, Ohio, 1958-61; sales promotion mgr. Vita Craft Corp., Shawnee, Kans., 1964-90, cons., 1990—; mem. Meeting Planners Internat., Kans. City, 1982—. Author and editor: cookbooks, 1965—. Pres. League Women Voters, Akron, Ohio, 1951-53; gov. Soroptimist Internat. of Am., 1978-80 (bd. dirs., Phila. 1978-80); pres. Soroptimist Internat. Kans. City, 1973-74; bd. dirs. Kans. City, Mo. cpt. Shepherd's Ctr., 1972—; nat. bd. dirs. Shepher's Ctrs. Am., 1990—; bd. dirs. Rose Brooks Ctr., 1979-86, v.p., 1984-85; bd. dirs., founder Safehome, Inc., 1979—; pres. Metro Citizens Crusade Against Crime, Kans. City., 1983. Recipient Meritorious Svc. award, Kans. City Police Dept., 1975, Disting. Govs. award, Soroptimist Internat. Am., Phila., 1978-79, 79-80, Woman of Distinction award Santa Fe Trl. Girl Scouts, 1993. Mem. Kappa Kappa Gamma (pres. 1948-49), Alumnae Assn. (N.Y.C.). Republican. Presbyterian.

HUNT, MARY REILLY, organization executive; b. N.Y., Apr. 17, 1921; d. Philip R. and Mary C. (Harten) Reilly; m. Robert R. Hunt, Apr. 10, 1943,; children: Marianne Schram, Philip R., Robert R., Elise Paul. Student, CCNY, 1939. Tax investigator Ind. Dept. Revenue, 1970-80; pres. Ind. Right to Life, 1973-77; treas. Nat. Right to Life Com., Washington, 1974, 77, 78, mem. exec. com., 1974, 76-81, vice chmn., 1976, exec. dir., 1978, dir. devel., 1979-94, v.p. devel., 1994—, hon. bd. mem., 1983—; pres. Mary Reilly Hunt & Assoc., Inc., South Bend, Ind., 1985—. Bd. dirs., v.p. YWCA, 1968-73, bd. dirs. Mental Health Assn. St. Joseph Co., 1972-78; candidate for state legis., 1988; mem. St. Joseph County Rep. precinct com., South Bend, 1964-79, alt. del. to Nat. Rep. Conv., 1976, 84, 88, 92. Mem. NAFE, Women Bus. Owners, South Bend Symphony Women's Assn. Republican. Roman Catholic. Office: Nat Right to Life Com 1102 N Lafayette Blvd South Bend IN 46617-1136

HUNT, PAMELA RALSTON, public relations professional; b. Marine City, Mich., Aug. 30, 1962; d. James Wallis Ralston and Judith Anne Leonard Lester. AA, St. Clair C.C., Port Huron, Mich., 1982; BS, Grand Valley State Univ., 1987. News reporter, announcer Sta. WPHM Radio, Port Huron, Mich., 1982-84, Sta. WGVU-FM Radio, Allendale, Mich., 1985-87; with pub. rels. staff Haworth, Inc., Holland, Mich., 1987-90; pub. rels. acct. supv. Sefton Assocs, Inc., Grand Rapids, Mich., 1990-94; dir. pub. rels. Aves Inc., Grand Rapids, 1994—. Co-chair publicity Food and Wine Symposium, Sta. WGVU/WGVK, Grand Rapids, 1991-92; comm. cons. S.E. Econ. Devel., Grand Rapids, 1993-94. Mem. Pub. Rels. Soc. Am. (accredited, state conf. com. 1991-93, Honorable Mention award 1993). Office: Aves Inc 50 Monroe NW Ste 400 Grand Rapids MI 49503

HUNT, PATRICIA JACQUELINE, mathematician, system manager, graphics programmer; b. Pasadena, Calif., Feb. 20, 1961; d. Daniel Joseph and Jacqueline (Vautrain) Collins; m. Daniel Phillip Hunt, Oct. 10, 1987. BS in Applied Math., U. Calif., Santa Barbara, 1983; MS in Applied Math., Naval Postgrad. Sch., 1988. Mathematician Computer Ctr. Naval Postgrad. Sch., Monterey, Calif., 1983-87; computer analyst Metro Info. Svcs., Virginia Beach, Va., 1988-90; system mgr., computer analyst Lockheed Engring. and Sci. Corp., Hampton, Va., 1990—; instr. NASA Engr.'s Week, 1992. Mem. Math. Assn. Am., Assn. Computing Machinery (graphics spl. interest group). Home: 317 Willow Bend Ct Chesapeake VA 23323-1057 Office: Lockheed Engring/Sci Corp 144 Research Dr Hampton VA 23666

HUNT, VANESSA ANN, civilian employee; b. Dayton, Ohio, Sept. 12, 1956; d. Wade Thomas and Peggie Ann (Allen) H. BA in Polit. Sci., Wright State U., 1979; MA in Edn., Tuskegee Inst., 1983; postgrad., Def. Systems Mgmt. Coll., L.A., 1985-86. Res. tchr. Dayton Bd. Edn., 1980-81, 85; grad. asst., asst. dir. profl. edn. Tuskegee (Ala.) Inst., 1981-83; logistics mgmt. specialist L.A. AFB, 1985—. Mem. Internat. Leadership Conf., Bahamas Faith Ministry and 700 Club, Jerusalem, 1993. Recipient performance award Dept. Air Force, 1991, 92. Mem. NAFE, Air Force Assn., Soc. Logistics Engrs., Phi Delta Kappa, Kappa Delta Pi. Office: Hdqrs Space & Missile Systems Ctr Ste 2208 ALK 155 Discoverer Blvd Los Angeles AFB CA 90245-4692

HUNTE, BERYL ELEANOR, mathematics educator, consultant; b. N.Y.C.. BA, CUNY-Hunter Coll., 1947; MA, Columbia U., 1948; PhD, NYU, 1965. Tchr. maths. Friends Sem., N.Y.C., 1957-62; asst. prof. maths. Rockland C.C., Suffern, N.Y., 1962-63; instr. maths., supr. tchr. trainees NYU, N.Y.C., 1964; chmn. dept. math. Borough of Manhattan C.C., N.Y.C., 1964-67, 70-73, prof. maths, 1970—, acting dean students, 1985-87, acting dean acad. affairs, 1987-88; dean for spl. projects CUNY, 1988-89; assoc. U. Seminar on Higher Edn., Columbia U., N.Y.C., 1989—. Author: (with others) (textbook) Mathematics Through Statistics, 1973. Mem. YWCA Greater N.Y. NSF fellow, summer 1960, 1963-64, Chancellor's Faculty fellow CUNY, 1980. Mem. N.Y. Acad. Scis., Am. Math. Soc., CUNY Acad. for Humanities and Scis. (bd. dirs. 1991—, first v.p. 1994—), UN Assn. N.Y.C. (bd. dirs., sec. 1980-86). Office: Borough Manhattan CC 199 Chambers St New York NY 10007-1079

HUNTER, ANN ARNOLD, publishing executive; b. Washington, July 22, 1941; d. James Chapman and Grace Dinsmore (Watson) Arnold; m. Stephen R. Hunter, July 29, 1959; children: Cynthia Ann Hunter Wallen, Alice Theresa Hunter Smith, Robert Harry, Maud Arnold Hunter Fogle. Grad., George Mason High Sch., 1958. Pres. AAH Graphics, Seven Fountains, Va., 1973—. Author: A Century of Service: The Story of the DAR, 1991; contbr. essays to newspapers; prodn. editor jour. Ednl. Tech. Rsch. and Devel. Bd. dirs. Am. Lung Assn. of Va., Winchester, 1984—, Shenandoah County Hist. Assn., Woodstock, Va., 1993—, Fort Valley Mus., Inc., 1976—. Mem. Bookbuilders of Washington, DAR (state rec. sec. 1992-95, state treas. 1983-86, nat. fin. chmn. 1989-95, nat. chmn. revision of bylaws 1991-93, State Outstanding Jr. Mem. 1976), Nat. Press Club. Republican. Office: AAH Graphics PO Box 95 Seven Fountains VA 22652

HUNTER, ANNE GRAVES, counselor; b. Albemarle County, Va., Feb. 4, 1934; d. Andrew Leslie and Ladys Marshall Graves; m. E. Sidney Hunter Jr., 1956 (div. 1976); children: E. Sidney III, James Andrew, Robert S., Bruce A., Mary Frances. RN, Grace Hosp. Sch. Nursing, 1954; BS magna cum laude, Old Dominion U., 1978, MS in Edn., 1985. Cert. Nat. Bd. Cert. Counselors; family therapy cert. Ea. Va. Med. Sch. RN DePaul Hosp., Norfolk, Va., 1978-79; clin. mgr. for mental health, chem. dependency, pain mgmt. DePaul Hosp., Norfolk, 1979-90; clin. therapist Crossroads Clin. Svcs., Virginia Beach, Va., 1988-91, Pembroke Counselings Svcs., Virginia Beach, 1991-93, Anne G. Hunter, LPC, NCC, Virginia Beach, 1993—. Bd. mem. Mental Health Assn. Tidewater; bd. mem., facilitator Amputee Support Group; facilitator SHARE, 1982—. Mem. ACA, Va. Counselors Assn., Lic. Profl. Counselors Hampton Roads, Mid-Atlantic Group Psychotherapy Soc., Phi Kappa Phi, Alpha Chi. Methodist. Office: 448 Viking Dr Ste 230 Virginia Beach VA 23452

HUNTER, BARBARA WAY, public relations executive; b. Westport, N.Y., July 14, 1927; d. Walter Denslow and Hilda (Greenawalt) Way; m. Austin F. Hunter, Jan. 24, 1953; children: Kimberley, Victoria. BA, Cornell U., 1949. Assoc. editor Topics Pub. Co., N.Y.C., 1949-51; publicist Nat. Dairy Product Corp., N.Y.C., 1951-53; account exec. Sally Dickson Assn., 1953-56; assoc. D-A-Y Pub. Relations (div. Ogilvy & Mather Co.), N.Y.C., 1964-70, exec. v.p., 1970-84, pres., 1984-89; pres. Hunter MacKenzie, Inc., 1989—; bd. dirs. Mr. Steak Inc., Denver. Trustee Cornell U., Ithaca, N.Y., 1980-85; bd. dirs. Point O'Woods Assn., Fire Island, N.Y., 1980-87. Recipient Sparkplug award Internat. Foodservice Mfrs. Assn., 1970, Matrix award N.Y. Women in Communications Inc., 1980, Entreprenurial Woman award Women Bus. Owners, 1981, Nat. Headliner award Women in Communications Inc., 1984. Mem. Pub. Relations Soc. Am. (pres. 1984, pres.-elect 1983, treas. 1982, pres. N.Y. chpt. 1978, John Hill award N.Y. chpt. 1986, Nat. Gold Anvil award 1993), Internat. Pub. Rels. Assn., Found. Pub. Relations Research and Edn. (trustee 1982, 84), Women's Forum, Cornell Club of N.Y. Club: The Club at Point O'Woods. Home: 137 E 38th St New York NY 10016 Office: Hunter MacKenzie Inc 41 Madison Ave New York NY 10010

HUNTER, BILLIE MARIE, social worker, educator; b. Dallas, Aug. 10, 1936; d. Alvis W. and Margie B. (Hall) Lindsey; m. E. Royce Hunter, Aug. 30, 1955; children: Gina Marie, Lindsey Royce, Hollianne. BA, U. Sci. and Arts in Okla., Chickasha, 1980; MSW, U. Okla, 1983. Lic. clin. social worker, Okla. Realtor OK, 1969-80; social worker Dept. Human Svcs., Ct. Related and Community Svcs., Anadarko, Norman, OK, 1980-85; therapist Cen. Okla. Community Mental Health Ctr., Norman, 1985-86; program dir. Esteem Counseling Ctr. Tulsa Psychiatric Ctr., 1986-88; program mgr. eating disorders unit Hillcrest Hosp., Tulsa, 1988-89; social worker/therapist Sigonella Naval Air Sta., Italy, 1989-92; familty advocacy rep. Family Svc. Ctr. Naval Surface Warfare Ctr., Dahlgren, Va., 1992-93; dist. coord. Children's Initiative Network Century Healthcare, Inc., Tulsa, 1993—; tchr. Tulsa Jr. Coll., 1986-87; adj. asst. prof. in social work U. Okla., 1994-95. Vol. Tulsa chpt. ARC, 1987-88. Office: Children's Initiative Network 326 W 11th St Shawnee OK 74801

HUNTER, CECILIA AROS, librarian, archivist; b. Tucson, Nov. 18, 1941; d. Jose Aviña and Josephine (Marchello) Aros; m. Louis Gerald Nuttycombe, Aug. 19, 1961 (dec. July 1965); children: Louis Garfield; m. Leslie Gene Hunter, Aug. 15, 1969; children: Daniel Aros, Joseph Aros, Raquel Aviña. BA, U. Ariz., 1969, MLS, 1991; MA, Tex. A&I U., 1976. Cert. social studies tchr., Arizl; cert. social studies tchr., libr., computer literacy midmgmt., Tex. Tchr. Kingsville (Tex.) Ind. Sch. Dist., 1975-80; prin. Epiphany Episcopal Sch., Kingsville, 1980-84; libr. and tech. coord. Santa Gertrudis Ind. Sch. Dist., Kingsville, 1984-90; archivist South Tex. Archives, Tex. A&M U., Kingsville, 1992—; mem. adv. bd. Teacching and Computers Scholastic Publs., N.Y.C., 1987-90. Co-author: Historic Kingsville, 1994; columnist on tech., The Social Studies Texan, 1989—; co-author computer software Spanish Missions of Texas, 1986. Mem. exec. com. Kleberg county Dem. Com., Kingsville, 1978—; election judge Kleberg County, 1980—; mem. Kleberg County Libr. Bd., 1980-83; vestrywoman Epiphany Episcopal Ch., 1985-88; preservation officer Kingsville Hist. Commn., 1992—. Recipient Friend of Computer Edn. award Tex. Computer Edn. Assn., 1986, award for using microcomputers Follett County, 1987; fellow NEH, Rutgers U., 1983, Columbia U., 1986, Fulbright-Hays fellow, China, 1984. Mem. ALA (Reforma scholar 1990), Am. Assn. Sch. Librs. (award for using microcomputers 1987), Soc. Am. Archivist, Soc. Southwestern Archivist, Delta Kappa Gamma, Phi Delta Kappa, Phi Alpha Theta, Pi Sigma Alpha. Home: 811 W Alice Ave Kingsville TX 78363-4262 Office: Tex A&M U Archives Campus Box 134 Kingsville TX 78363

HUNTER, GEORGIA L., clergywoman; b. Wiergate, Tex., June 14, 1938; d. George Clavert and Leria (Thomas) Spikes; m. LeRoy Hunter, Feb. 2, 1967; children—Balenda M. Spikes, Maria A. Spikes. Student Bible Moody Bible Inst; MDiv Universal Life Ch. Sch., Modesto, Calif. Ordained to ministry Christian Meth. Episcopal Ch., 1983. Counselor Ill. Dept. children and Family Services, Freeport, 1970-74; food service dir. Retirement Inc., Freeport, 1978—; pastor Christian Meth. Episcopal Ch., Madison, Wis., 1983-91; asst. pastor Miles Meml. Christian Meml. Episcopal Ch., Rockford, Ill., 1993; pastor Christ Mission Christian Meth. Episcopal Ch., Milw., 1993; corr. Jour. Standard, Freeport, 1982-83; chairperson expansions and missions sect. Milw. dist. Christian Meth. Episcopal Ch.; mem. Com. Milw. Dist. Leadership Tng. Sch.; coord. Interdenominational Theol. Ctr. Ext. Program, Atlanta. V.p. Freeport Bd. Edn., 1977—; pres. Ch. Women United, Freeport, 1970-83; asst. dir. youth Rockford and Vicinity Dist. Assn., 1980-82; sec. Freeport Good Samaritan Refuge House. Recipient Human Relations award City Council Freeport, 1974, Spiritual Achievement award Martin Luther King Ctr., Freeport, 1983, Good Neighbor award Freeport Jour. Standard, 1983, Achievement award Ch. Women United, 1983. Mem. Fully Gospel Women Assn. (bd. dirs., coord.), Young Adult Christian Women (pres.). Democrat. Avocations: bowling; researcher; reading; sewing; writing poetry. Home: 846 E Pleasant St Freeport IL 61032-5861

HUNTER, HOLLY, actress; b. Atlanta, Mar. 20, 1958; d. Charles Edwin and Opal Marguerite (Catledge) H. BFA, Carnegie-Mellon U., 1980. Appeared in feature films Broadcast News, 1987 (Best Actress award N.Y. Film Critics Circle 1988, Best Actress award Berlin Film Festival 1988, Nat. Bd. Review award, Acad. award nominee best actress), Raising Arizona, 1987, Always, 1990, Miss Firecracker, 1989, Once Around, 1991, The Piano, 1993 (Best Actress award, Cannes Film Festival, 1993, Best Actress - Drama, Golden Globe, 1994, Academy Award, Best Actress, 1993), The Firm, 1993 (Acaemy award nominee, Best Supporting Actress, 1993); TV prodns. Roe vs. Wade (Best Actress Emmy award 1989); Broadway stage prodns. Crimes of the Heart, The Wake of Jamey Foster; regional stage prodns. Buried Child, A Doll's House, Artichoke; other stage prodns. include A Lie of the Mind, L.A., Battery, N.Y.C., Miss Firecracker Contest, The Person I Once Was, N.Y.C.; cable TV prodns. Crazy in Love, 1992 (Ace award nominee), The Positively True Adventures of the Alleged Texas Cheerleader Murdering Mom, 1993 (Best Actress award Am. TV Awards, Emmy award - Outstanding Lead Actress in a Miniseries or Special, Cable Ace award, Best Actress in a Movie or Miniseries). Bd. dirs. Calif. Abortion Rights Action League. *

HUNTER, JUDY BRYANT, air transportation executive; b. Amherst, Tex., May 24, 1944; d. Arthur Laverne and Edith Grace (Enloe) Bryant; m. William J. Hunter, Aug. 11, 1962 (div. Mar. 1981); remarried Aug. 24, 1984. Student, Levelland (Tex.) Jr. Coll., 1964, Tex. Tech U., 1967. Supr. scheduling Weber Aircraft, Gainesville, Tex., 1974-78, supr. purchasing, 1978-81, mgr. purchasing, 1981—. Mem. NAPM-Dallas, Am. Purchasing Assn., Kiwanis (bd. dirs. Gainesville chpt.). Republican. Baptist. Home: 1002 Aspen Rd Gainesville TX 76240-2945 Office: Weber Aircraft 2000 Weber Dr Gainesville TX 76240-9399

HUNTER, KIM (JANET COLE), actress; b. Detroit, Nov. 12, 1922; d. Donald and Grace Mabel (Lind) Cole; m. William A. Baldwin, Feb. 11, 1944 (div. 1946); 1 dau., Kathryn Emmett; m. Robert Emmett, Dec. 20, 1951; 1 son, Sean Emmett. Ed. pub. schs.; student acting with, Charmine Lantaff Camine, 1938-40, Actors Studio. First stage appearance, 1939; played in stock, 1940-42; Broadway debut in A Streetcar Named Desire, 1947; appeared in (tour) Two Blind Mice, 1950, Darkness at Noon, N.Y.C., 1951, The Chase, 1952, N.Y.C., They Knew What They Wanted, N.Y.C., 1952, The Children's Hour, N.Y.C., 1952, The Tender Trap, N.Y.C., 1954, Write Me a Murder, N.Y.C., 1961, Weekend, N.Y.C., 1968, The Penny Wars, N.Y.C., 1969, (tour) And Miss Reardon Drinks a Little, 1971-72, The Glass Menagerie, Atlanta, 1973, The Women, N.Y.C., 1973, (tour) In Praise of Love, 1975, The Lion in Winter, N.J., 1975, The Cherry Orchard, N.Y.C., 1976, The Chalk Garden, Pa., 1976, Elizabeth the Queen, Buffalo, 1977, Semmelweiss, Buffalo, 1977, The Belle of Amherst, N.J., 1978, N.H., 1986, The Little Foxes, Mass., 1980, To Grandmother's House We Go, N.Y.C, 1980, Another Part of the Forest, Seattle, 1981, Ghosts, 1982, Territorial Rites, 1983, Death of a Salesman, 1983, Cat on a Hot Tin Roof, 1984, Life with Father, 1984, Sabrina Fair, 1984, Faulkner's Bicycle, 1985, Antique Pink, 1985, A Delicate Balance, 1986, Painting Churches, 1986, Jokers, 1986, Remembrance, 1987, Man and Superman, 1987-88, N.Y.C., The Gin Game, Lancaster, Pa., 1988, A Murder of Crows, N.Y.C., 1988, Watch on the Rhine, 1989, Suddenly Last Summer, 1991, A Smaller Place, 1991, Open Window, Houston, 1992, The Cocktail Hour, Pitts., 1992, The Belle of Amherst, Vero Beach., Fla., Palm Beach, Fla., Chester, Mass., 1992, Conn., 1993, The Eye of the Beholder, N.Y.C., 1993, Love Letters, Springfield, Mass., 1993, Worcester, Mass., 1993, Northhampton, Mass., 1994, Do Not Go Gentle, Bristol, Pa., 1994, The Gin Game, Chester, Mass., 1994—, tour, 1994-95; frequent appearences summer stock and repertory theater, 1940—; appeared Am. Shakespeare Festival, Stratford, Conn., 1961; film debut The Seventh Victim, 1943, films include Tender Comrade, 1943, When Strangers Marry (re-released as Betrayed), 1944, You Came Along, 1945, A Canterbury Tale, 1949, Stairway to Heaven, 1946, A Streetcar Named Desire (Oscar award best supporting actress), Anything Can Happen, 1952, Deadline U.S.A., 1952, Storm Center, 1956, Bermuda Affair, 1957, The Young Stranger, 1957, Money, Women, and Guns, 1958, Lilith, 1964, Planet of the Apes, 1968, The Swimmer, 1968, Beneath the Planet of the Apes, 1970, Escape from the Planet of the Apes, 1971, Dark August, 1975, The Kindred, 1987, Two Evil Eyes, 1991; TV debut Actors' Studio program, 1948; TV appearences include Requiem for a Heavyweight, 1956, The Comedian, 1957, Give Us Barabbas, 1961, 63, 68, 69, Love, American Style, Colombo, Cannon, Night Gallery, Mission Impossible, The Magician, 1972-73, Marcus Welby, Hec Ramsey, Griff, Police Story, Ironside, Medical Center, Bad Ronald, Born Innocent, 1974, Ellery Queen, 1975, Lucas Tanner, This Side of Innocence, Once an Eagle, Baretta, Gibbsville, Hunter, 1976, The Oregon Trail, 1977, Project UFO, Stubby Pringle's Christmas, 1978, Backstairs at the White House, 1979, Specter on the Bridge, 1979, Edge of Night, 1979-80, FDR's Last Year, 1980, Skokie, 1981, Scene of the Crime, 1984, Three Sovereigns for Sarah, 1985, Hot Pursuit, 1985, Private Sessions, 1985, Martin Luther King, Jr., The Dream and the Drum, 1986, Drop Out Mother, 1987, (mini-series) Cross of Fire, 1989, Murder, She Wrote, 1990, Vivien Leigh: Scarlett and Beyond, 1990, Bloodlines: Murder in the Family, 1993, Class of '96, 1993, All My Children, 1993, Hurricane Andrew, 1993, L.A. Law, 1994, Mad About You, 1994; recordings include From Morning 'Til Night (and a Bag Full of Poems), 1961, Come, Woo Me, 1964, The Velveteen Rabbit, 1989; author Kim Hunter: Loose in the Kitchen, 1975. Recipient Donaldson award forest supporting actress in A Streetcar Named Desire 1948, also on Variety N.Y. Critics Poll 1948, for film version 1952, winner Look award, Hollywood Fgn. Corrs. Golden Globe award, Emmy nominations for Baretta 1977, Edge of Night 1980, Fla. Carbonell (for Big Mama in Cat on a Hot Tin Roof) award 1984. Mem. Acad. Motion Picture Arts and Scis., ANTA, Actors Equity Assn. (council 1953-59), Screen Actors Guild, AFTRA.

HUNTER, KIM ANTOINETTE, state official; b. Houston, June 23, 1965; d. Lawrence Nathaniel and Brenda (Herson) H. BA in Journalism, La. State U., 1987. Reporter Sta. WBRZ-TV, Baton Rouge, 1987-89; news anchor, reporter Sta. KPLC-TV, Lake Charles, La., 1989-91; press sec. Office of Gov., State of La., Baton Rouge, 1992—; disting. spkr. La. State U., Baton Rouge, 1992, 94; guest spkr. Nat. Gov. Assn., Austin, 1992; state del. Very Spl. Arts Exch., Sicily, Italy, 1993. Bd. dirs. La. Adult Literacy Com., Baton Rouge, 1992-93, N.G. Youth Challenge, Baton Rouge, 1993—; state rep. Pres. Nat. Svc. Program, Baton Rouge, 1993—. Recipient Top TV award Nat. Big Bros./Big Sisters, 1991, Outstanding Svc. award La. Emergency Preparedness Assn., 1994; named Outstanding Young Woman, 1988. Mem. Nat. Assn. Govt. Communicators (mem. gov. coun.), Assn. State Communicators (bd. dirs.). Democrat. Roman Catholic. Home: 1522 Fig St Baton Rouge LA 70802 Office: State of La Office of Gov PO Box 94004 Baton Rouge LA 70804-9004

HUNTER, MARGARET KING, architect; b. Balt., May 13, 1919; d. Talmage Damron and Margaret Julie (Greenough) King; m. Edgar Hayes Hunter, May 8, 1943; children—Christopher King, Margaret Greenough. A.B., Wheaton Coll., 1941; postgrad., Smith Coll. Sch. Architecture, 1941-42, Harvard Grad. Sch. Design, 1942-45. Draftsman H.V. Lawrence; landscape architect H.V. Lawrence, Mass., 1940, Antonin Raymond; architect Antonin Raymond, N.Y.C., 1942-43; designer Raymond Loewy, N.Y.C., 1943; partner E.H. & M.K. Hunter (architects-planners), Hanover, N.H., 1945-66, Raleigh, N.C., 1969—; owner Heritage Antiques, Raleigh, 1971—; writer Pencil Points, 1942-45; traveling exhibit of work, 1963-66; design instr. N.C. State U., 1968; lectr., writer architecture, conservation, 1945—. Author: Your Own Kitchen and Garden Survival Book, 1978, The Indoor Garden: Design, Construction, and Furnishing, 1978; Important works include Laconia (N.H.) State Sch. Dormitories, 1955, N.H. Toll Rd. Structures, 1955, Children's Study Home, N.H. State Hosp., 1954, apts. and classroom bldg., Dartmouth, 1960, House for Life mag., 1956, Colby Jr. Coll. Art Center and Sci. Bldg., New London, N.H., 1962; classroom bldg. Dormitories Bridgton Acad, Maine, 1964, Loon Mountain Ski Area, Lincoln, N.H., 1966; dormitory, Conn. Coll., New London, 1965, twenty year campus plan, N.C. Central U., Durham, 1971, Student Internat. Meditation Soc. Acad., Santa Barbara, Calif., Clearwater Office Park, 1972, N.C. Central U. Law Sch., 1974, Hunter's Creek Townhouses, 1983. Chmn. Dance Com., Hanover, 1964-66; v.p. Culture Arts for Students, Raleigh, 1970; N.H. del. 1st Internat. Conf. Women Engrs. and Scientists, 1964; mem. edn. com. N.C. Land Use Congress, 1971, chmn. soils com., 1974, dir., 1976-78. Recipient Progressive Architecture Mag. award, 1946, 47; award N.H. State Office Bldg. Competition, 1950. Mem. AIA (chmn. pub. relations N.H. chpt. 1953-54), Soc. Women Engrs., Soil Conservation Soc., Constrn. Specifications Inst. Presbyterian. Club: Women's (Raleigh). Home: 3808 Tall Tree Pl Raleigh NC 27612 Office: PO Box 30632 Raleigh NC 27622-0632

HUNTER, MARILYN SUE, controller; b. Indpls., Mar. 2, 1958; d. Forest Cameron and Rosemary Alice (Keller) Gill; m. Edward Lowell Hunter, Sept. 28, 1985; children: Cathy A., Christina M., Chelsea E. Cert. in bus. studies, Ind. U., Indpls., 1984. Office mgr. Nexxus of Ind., Inc., Indpls., 1979-81, CMT, Inc., San Antonio, 1981-82, TAB Precision Tools, Inc., Indpls., 1982-83; paraprofl. Peachin Schwartz & Peachin, P.C., Indpls., 1983-87; contr. Huck Heating and Air Conditioning, Inc., Indpls., 1987—. Sci. scholar Purdue Sch. Sci. Indpls., 1989, 90. Roman Catholic. Office: Huck Heating & A/C Inc 5412 Rock Hampton Ct Indianapolis IN 46268-1029

HUNTER, MARSHA L., lawyer; b. Tallahassee; d. Emmett Marshall and Marjorie Louise (Roth) H.; children: Sarah Maddin, Henry Wyche. AA, Greenbrier Coll., 1968; BA, Hollins Coll., 1970; JD, So. Meth. U., 1978. Bar: Tex. 1978. Atty. Lone Star Gas Co., Dallas, 1986—. Will Wilson fellow, 1976, Shell Found. fellow, 1977. Mem. Tex. Bar Assn. (instr. 1985), Dallas Bar Assn., Fed. Energy Bar Assn. Republican. Methodist. Home: 3511 Mockingbird Ln Dallas TX 75205 Office: Lone Star Gas Co 301 S Harwood St Dallas TX 75201

HUNTER, MEREDITH KAYE, surgical, orthopaedic nurse; b. Washington, June 9, 1958; d. Charles and Nettie Lou (Price) Wissler; m. Jack Arthur Hunter, July 7, 1989; children: Donald Michael, Robert Charles. AAS in Nursing summa cum laude, No. Va. Community Coll., Annandale, 1992. Dental mgr. Dr. Charles Wissler, McLean, Va., 1976-92; ortho, neuro surg. and pediatric nurse Mt. Vernon Hosp., Alexandria, Va., 1992-93, charge nurse acute joint replacement unit, 1993-94, unit dir. nursing, 1994—; counselor P.W. Women's Aid, Woodbridge, Va., 1978-81. Mem. People for the Am. Way, L.A., 1981-86. Mem. ANA, Va. Nurses Assn., Phi Theta Kappa. Office: 3000 McComas Way Kensington MD 20707

HUNTER, MIRIAM EILEEN, artist, educator; b. Cin., June 6, 1929; d. James R. and Bertha (Oberlin) H. BS, Ball State U., 1951, MA in Art, 1957; MA in Christian Edn., Wheaton Coll., 1958; EdD, Nova U., 1979. Tchr. art and English, Madison-Marion Consol. Schs., 1951-52; tchr. art Wheaton Coll., Ill., 1952-84, chair art dept., 1969-70, 75-79; asst. prof. art Fine Arts Gallery, Chgo., then assoc. prof., 1971-84; dir. Sch. Edn., Calvin Simmons Coll., Lawrenceville, Ga., 1984—; freelance art cons.; broker First Am. Nat. Securities Corp., 1982—; div. mgr. A.L. Williams Corp., Chgo. and Lilburn, Ga., 1982—; mgr. House of Frames, Frameland, Ltd. Edit. Galleries, 1985-88. Vol., Cook County Hosp., Chgo., 1955-58; mem. Wheaton Human Relations Orgn., 1965-67. Recipient Ingersol award for painting, 1946, 47; 2d place award DuPage Sesquicentennial, 1968; Outstanding Alumnus award Ball State U., 1975. Mem. Nat. Assn. Securities Dealers, Ill. Art Edn. Assn., Nat. Soc. Lit. and the Arts, Art Inst. Chgo., Delta Phi Delta, Sigma Tau Delta, Kappa Delta Pi. Home: 8725 Lake Dr Lithonia GA 30058-6529

HUNTER, NANCY DONEHOO, education educator; b. Atlanta, July 11, 1956; d. Joseph Andrew and Sophia (Sellers) Donehoo; m. Charles James Hunter IV, Dec. 1, 1979; children: Katherine Elizabeth, Charles James V. BA, Asbury Coll., 1981; MA, Morehead (Ky.) State U., 1984; postgrad., U. Ky., 1989. Dir. Christian edn. 1st United Meth. Ch., Clewiston, Fla., 1981-82; assoc. prof. Maysville (Ky.) C.C., 1983—; mem. partnership coordination coun. Destination Graduation, Frankfort, Ky., 1989-91; tutor trainer Ky. Literacy Coun., Frankfort, 1990—. Author: Peer Tutor Trainer Manual, 1989. Bd. dirs. Community Literacy Coun., Mason County, Ky., 1988—; choir dir. Trinity Meth. Ch., Maysville, 1990—. Recipient Vol. Svc. award Mason County Schs., 1987, 91; grantee U.S. Dept. Edn., 1989-91. Mem. ASCD, Internat. Reading Assn., Nat. Assn. Devel. Educators, Coll. Reading and Learning Assn., Ky. Assn. Devel. Educators (treas. 1989-90, conf. dir. 1989—). Home: PO Box 203 Washington KY 41096-0203 Office: Maysville Community Coll US 68 Maysville KY 41056

HUNTER, PAMELA ANN, veterinarian, educator; b. Washington, Feb. 12, 1955; d. Melvin L. and Audrey Jean (Perry) Ailer. BS in Zoology, Howard U., 1976; BS in Animal Sci., Tuskegee U., 1980, DVM, 1981. Staff fellow NIH, Bethesda, Md., 1981-83; rsch. assoc. Fla. A&M U., Tallahassee, Fla., 1985-86, asst. prof., 1986-93, assoc. prof., 1993—; vet. med. officer Bur. Land Mgmt., Reno, Nev., 1993; cons. FAMU, Tallahassee, 1986—. Vol. Sr. Citizen Coun., Tallahassee, St. Francis Wildlife Program, Thomasville, Ga., Nat. Zool. Soc., Washington. Mem. AVMA, Am. Assn. Women in Bus., Am. Soc. Animal Sci., Fla. Wildlife Assn., Delta Sigma Theta, Friends Nat. Zoo. Office: Fla A&M U 103 S Perry-Paige Tallahassee FL 32301

HUNTER, SALLY IRENE, interior designer; b. East Liverpool, Ohio, Oct. 8, 1936; Charles E. and Thelma E. (Rice) H. BA, Kalamazoo Coll., 1958. Certified Am. Soc. Interior Designers. Interior designer The Higbee Co., Cleve., 1958-70; interior designer, v.p., dir. of design Harrisons Fine Furniture and Interiors, Lakewood, Ohio, 1970—. Mem. Nat. Trust for Hist. Preservation, Cleve. Mus. Natural History. Mem. Am. Soc. Interior Designers (profl.), Cleve. Mus. Art, Cleve. Zool. Soc. Home: 22535 Detroit Rd Cleveland OH 44116-2056 Office: Harrisons Fine Furniture & Interiors 14518 Detroit Ave Cleveland OH 44107-4317

HUNTER, SUE PERSONS, former state official; b. Hico, Tex., Aug. 21, 1921; d. David Henry and Beulah (Boatwright) Persons m. Charles Force Hunter; children: Shelley Hunter Richardson, Kathy Hunter McCullough, Margaret Hunter Brown. BA, U. Tex., 1942. Air traffic controller CAA (now FAA), San Antonio and Houston, 1942-52; writer Bissonet Plaza News, 1969-72; coordinator Goals for La., 1971-74; adminstrv. dir. Jeff Publs. Inc., 1974; press sec. Jefferson Parish Dist. Atty., 1972-75, communications cons., 1975-78; adminstr. Child Support Enforcement Div., 1979-85; contbg. editor The Jeffersonian, 1975-76. Pres. United Ch. Women East Jefferson (La.), 1958-59, LWV Jefferson Parish, La., 1961-64; pres. LWV La., 1961-64, 67-71, also bd. dirs., 1962-67, pres. bd. dirs., 92—; mem. probation services com. Community Services Council, Jefferson, 1966-73, v.p., 1970-72; mem. Library Devel. Com. La., 1967-71, Nat. Com. for Support of Pub. Schs., 1967-72; mem. Goals Found. Council Met. New Orleans, 1969-75, sec. 1970, 72; mem. Goals La. Task Force State and Local Govt., 1969-70; pres. MMM Investment Club, 1969-72; bd. dirs. New Orleans Area Health Planning Council, 1969-75, Friends of Westminster Tower, 1986, Coun. for Internat. Visitors, 1990—, chmn., 1991-93, programmer, 1994—; bd. dirs. Jefferson Twenty Five, 1991—; mem. adv. council La. State Health Planning, 1971-76; title I adv. council La. State Dept. Edn., 1970-72; vice chmn. Jefferson Women's Polit. Caucus, 1977-78, chmn., 1979, treas., 1980; bd. dirs. New Orleans Area/Bayou-River Health Systems Agy., 1978-82, pres., 1980, 81; mem. Task force for La. Talent Bank of Women, 1980; exec. bd. La. Child Support Enforcement Assn., 1980-86, pres., 1982-84; bd. dirs., legis. chmn. Nat. Child Support Enforcement Assn., 1983-86; mem. Gov.'s Commn. on Child Support Enforcement, 1984-88; mem. La. Statewide Health Coordinating Council, 1980-83, mgmt. com. edn. fund League of Women Voters La., 1988-89. Recipient Outstanding Citizens award Rotary Club, Metairie, La., 1962, River Ridge award, 1976. Mem. Am. Assn. Individual Investors (pres. New Orleans chpt. 1986-88), New Orleans Panhellenic (pres. 1956-57), Fgn. Rels. Assn. (bd. dirs. New Orleans chpt. 1992—), Les Pelicaneers (pres. 1988-90), Earn and Learn Investment Club (pres. 1992-94), Alpha Xi Delta. Presbyterian (elder). Home: 210 Stewart Ave New Orleans LA 70123-1457

HUNTER-GAULT, CHARLAYNE, journalist; b. Due West, S.C., Feb. 27, 1942; d. Charles S.H. Jr. and Althea Hunter; m. Walter Storall (div.); 1 child, Susan; m. Ronald Gault, 1971; 1 child, Chuma. Attended, Wayne State U., Detroit; BA in Journalism, U. Ga., 1963. With The New Yorker, 1963-67; editor Trans-Action Mag., 1967; investigative reporter, anchorwoman local evening news WRC-TV; also with N.Y. Times; with MacNeil/Lehrer Report PBS, 1978—, became nat. correspondent, 1983, now chief nat. correspondent. Author: In My Place, 1992; contbr. various publs. Recipient NYT Publisher's award, 2 Emmys for national news and documentaries, the Nat. Urban Coalition for Dist. Urban Reporting, George Foster Peabody award for Excellence in broadcast Journalism. Office: MacNeil/Lehrer Newshour 356 W 58th St New York NY 10019-1896*

HUNTINGTON, MARY C., elementary school educator; b. West Hebron, N.Y., May 23, 1923; d. Fred and Agnes (Scott) Cary; m. David Huntington, July 17, 1949; children: Scott Lee, Debra Dee. BEd, Oneonta (N.Y.) State Coll., 1946; postgrad., Cornell U., 1952-53, U. Maine, 1963-64, Elmira (N.Y.) Coll., 1977-78. Cert. tchr., N.Y. Elem. tchr. Pine Bush, N.Y., 1946-51, Ithaca, N.Y., 1951-53, Maine, 1959-64; substitute tchr. Alfred and Almond, N.Y., 1976—. Mem. Alfred (N.Y.) Village Planning Bd., 1974-86; mem. grants com. Bethesda Found., 1985-91, sec. 1990-91, pub. rels. chair 1992; v.p. LWV, Maine, 1958-64; bd. dirs. Camp Fire Girls coun., Hornell, N.Y., 1976-84, Hornell Symphony; bd. dirs. Bethesda Hosp., 1975-85; mem. So. Tier Health Mgmt. Bd., 1980-85; trustee Alfred Meth. Ch., 1993. Mem. AAUW (v.p. 1988—), Woman's Golf Assn. (v.p. 1992—). Republican. Home: 5470 Jericho Hill Rd Alfred Station NY 14803-9743

HUNTINGTON, MARY LEE, educational counselor; b. Brainerd, Minn., May 13, 1959; d. Robert Nathan and Mildred Evelyn (Moen) MacLeod; m. Mark Louis Huntington, June 2, 1990; children: Bradley James, Jason Scott. BS, U. Wis., 1981; MS, San Diego State U., 1988. Cert. tchr., Calif. Tchr., coach Waukesha (Wis.) Pub. Schs., 1981-84; various positions Moorhead, Minn., 1984-88; social worker New Alternatives, Inc., San Diego, 1988-91; tchr. San Diego C.C., 1988-93; vocat. case mgr. ConServ Co., San Diego, 1991-93; dir. guidance Santa Fe Cath. High Sch., Lakeland, Fla., 1993—. Mem. Am. Sch. Counseling Assn., Am. Assn. for Counseling & Devel., Phi Kappa Phi. Office: Santa Fe Cath High Sch 3110 Highway 92 E Lakeland FL 33801

HUNTLEY, DIANE E., dental hygiene educator; b. Concord, N.H., Oct. 1, 1946; d. George Williams and Esther A. (Gadwah) H. AS, Fones Sch. Dental Hygiene, Bridgeport, Conn., 1966; BA, U. Bridgeport, Conn., 1968; MA, SUNY, Buffalo, 1971; PhD, Kans. State U., 1985. Registered dental hygienist. Dental hygienist various gen. practice dentists Conn., Colo., 1966-76; clin. instr. Fones Sch. Dental Hygiene, 1971-74; asst. prof. U. Colo. Dental Sch., Denver, 1974-76; asst. prof. dental hygiene Wichita (Kans.) State U., 1976-82, assoc. prof., 1982—; vol. hygienist Good Samaritan Clinic, Wichita, 1989-90, 92—. Contbr. articles to profl. jours. Mem. dental adv. bd. United Meth. Urban Ministries, Wichita, 1990-92. Mem. AAUP (Wichita State U. chpt. sec.-treas. 1988-91), Am. Assn. Dental Schs., Wichita Dental Hygienists' Assn. (pres. 1982-83, treas. 1988-90, trustee 1990-91), Kans. Dental Hygienists' Assn. (del. 1989-93), Am. Dental Hygienists' Assn. (editl. dir. 1983-85, historian 1993), Phi Kappa Phi, Alpha Eta. Office: Wichita State U 1845 Fairmount St Wichita KS 67260-0144

HUNTOON, CAROLYN LEACH, physiologist; b. Leesville, La., Aug. 25, 1940; m. Harrison H. Huntoon; 1 child, Sally Ann. BS in Biology, Northwestern State Coll., Natchitoches, La., 1962; degree in med. technol., Ochsner Found. Hosp., New Orleans, 1962; MS in Physiology, Baylor U., 1966, PhD, 1968. Head endocrinology lab. NASA Johnson Space Ctr., Houston, 1968-74, head endocrine and biochemistry labs., 1974-76, spl. asst. to dir., 1976-77, chief space metabolism and biochemistry br., 1976-77, chief biomed. labs. br., 1977-84, assoc. dir., 1984-87, dir. space and life scis., 1987-94, dir., 1994—; mem. astronaut selection bd. NASA-Johnson Space Ctr., 1978, 84, 85, 87, 89, 91, dep. chief for personnel devel. astronaut office, 1980, 84, 85, 87. Contbr. articles to profl. jours. With USAF, 1985—. Recipient Arthus S. Fleming award, Career Achievement award Nat. Civil Svc. League, Paul Bert award, Hubertus Strughold award, Yuri Gagarin medal USSR Fedn. Cosmonatuics, 1987, Presdl. Rank Meritorious Exec. award, 1991, Disting. Rank award, 1993; named Outstanding Alumna Northwestern State U., 1977, Outstanding Woman in Sci., Am. Women in Sci., Disting. profl. Woman of Yr., U. Tex. Health Sci. Ctr., 1985, Outstanding Scientist, State of Tex., 1991. Fellow Am. Astronautical Soc. (Lovelace award 1991), Aerospace Med. Assn. (Louis H. Bauer Founder's award); mem. AIAA, Assn. Bus. and Profl. Women, Am. Physiol. Soc., Endocrine Soc., Internat. Acad. Astronautics. Office: NASA Johnson Space Ctr 2101 Nasa Rd 1 # 1 Houston TX 77058-3607*

HUNTOON, DONNA R., commissioner; b. Redford, Mich., Dec. 1, 1929; d. Cortland Osmun and Ota (Fish) Richards; m. Stephen John Huntoon, Aug. 17, 1956 (dec. Nov. 1977); 1 child, Bonny. Diploma, Pontiac Bus. Inst., 1949, Chapin Coll. Bus., 1981. Acct. McManus, John & Adams Adv., Bloomfield Hills, Mich., 1949-52; asst. credit mgr. Aurora Gasoline Co., Detroit, 1952-56; co-mgr. Shasta Farms, Clarkston, Mich., 1956-74; dist. office mgr. Mich. State Rep., Clarkston, Mich., 1979-87; trustee, precinct del. White Lake (Mich.) Twp., 1986-90; jury commr. Oakland County, Lansing, Mich., 1987-90; Oakland County jury commr. Pontiac, Mich., 1990—; mobile home commr. apptd. by Gov. Engler, Lansing, 1992—; mem. finance com. Oakland County, Pontiac, Mich., 1993—, vice chair pub. svc. com., 1990—; vice chair judiciary com. Mich. Assoc. Counties, Lansing, 1993—. Editor: (book) Phenomenological Study of Female Sexual Response as Affected by Sexual Distress Therapy, 1981. leader, judge 4-H, Clarkston, Mich., 1968-74; mem. bd. dirs. YWCA, Pontiac, Mich., 1992-93; mem. Mich. Assn. Counties, Lansing, 1990—, Nat. Assn. Counties, Washington, 1990—. Republican. Home: 9785 Crosby Lake Rd Clarkston MI 48346 Office: Oakland County 1200 N Telegraph Rd Pontiac MI 48341-1043

HUNTRESS, BETTY ANN, former music store proprietor, educator; b. Poughkeepsie, N.Y., Apr. 29, 1932; d. Emmett Slater and Catherine V. (Kihlmire) Brundage; m. Arnold Ray Huntress, June 26, 1954; children: Catherine, Michael, Carol, Alan. BA, Cornell U., 1954. Tchr. high sch., Bordentown, N.J., 1954-55; part-time asst. to prof. Delta Coll., Northwood Inst., Midland, Mich., 1958-71; part-time tchr. Midland Pub. Schs., 1968-79, 83—; owner, mgr. The Music Stand, Midland, 1979-82. Bd. dirs. Midland Center for Arts, 1978-86 ; v.p. MCFTA (Arts Center), 1980-84 ; mem. charter bd. mgrs. Matrix Midland Ann. Arts and Sci. Festival, 1977-80; cons. Girl Scouts U.S., 1964-76; mem. Mich. Internat. Council, 1975-76; bd. dirs. Literary Council Midland County, 1986—, sec., 1987-91. Named Midland Musician of Yr., 1977. Mem. Music Soc. Midland Center for Arts (dir. 1971-86, chmn. 1976-79), AAUW (dir. 1962-73, pres. 1971-73, mem. Mich. state div. bd. 1973-75, 1st v.p. Mich. state div. 1983-85 , bd. dirs. 1993—, outstanding woman as agt. of change award 1977, fellowship grant named in her honor 1976), Midland Symphony League Soc. (2d v.p.), LWV (bd. dirs. 1986-90), Community Concert Soc., Women's Study Club of Midland, Friends of Libr.,Kappa Delta Epsilon, Pi Lambda Theta, Alpha Xi Delta. Republican. Presbyterian. Home: 5316 Sunset Dr Midland MI 48640-2536

HUNTTING, CYNTHIA COX, artist; b. San Francisco, Sept. 2, 1936; d. E. Morris and Margaret (Storke) Cox; m. Edward Tyler Huntting Jr., Mar. 8, 1969 (div. 1974). BA, Smith Coll., 1958; San Francisco Art Inst., 1959. Artist Emporium White House, San Francisco, 1958-61; artist, staff Pace Program Stanford U., 1962-64; artist World Affairs Council No. Calif., San Francisco, 1964-67; artist pvt. practice San Francisco, 1968—; mem. Modern Art Council Bd. San Francisco Mus. Modern Art, 1970-78. Active Jr. League San Francisco, Inc. Republican. Episcopalian. Clubs: Town and Country, Metropolitan, Calif. Tennis. Home and Office: 2720 Lyon St San Francisco CA 94123-3815

HUNYADI, CSILLA, economist, consultant; b. Hajduszoboszlo, Hungary, Apr. 25, 1958; came to U.S., 1987; d. Gyorgy Hunyadi and Julianna (Szomoru) Fazekas; m. R. Surendra Kumar; children: Brahma, Laavanya, Vinitha. MA, Budapest (Hungary) U. Econs., 1981, PhD, 1984. Rsch. asst. Ctrl. Statis. Office, Budapest, 1981-83; asst. prof. Budapest U. Econs., 1983-87, W.Va. State Coll., Institute, 1989—; editor Sure Pub. Co., Hurricane, W.Va., 1989-93; v.p. Zenith Consulting Group, Inc., Hurricane, 1993-94. Author: Big Bang and Acceleration, 1994; editor: (newsletter) Hungary Today, 1989-93. Rsch. fellow Yale U., 1987-88. Mem. AAAS, Internat. Trade and Fin. Assn., Assn. Comparative Econs. Studies, Internat. Soc. Inventory Rsch. Office: WVa State Coll Institute WV 25112

HUOT, RACHEL IRENE, cell biologist; b. Manchester, N.H., Oct. 16, 1950; d. Omer Joseph and Irene Alice (Girard) H. BA in Biology cum laude, Rivier Coll., 1972; MS in Biology, Cath. U. Am., 1976, PhD in Biology, 1980. Sr. technician Microbiol. Assocs., Bethesda, Md., 1974-77; chemist Uniformed Svcs. Univ. of Health Scis., Bethesda, 1977-79; biologist Nat. Cancer Inst., Bethesda, 1979-82; postdoctoral fellow S.W. Found. for Biomed. Rsch., San Antonio, 1982-85, asst. scientist, 1985-87, staff scientist, 1987-88; instr. U. Tex. Health Sci. Ctr., San Antonio, 1988-89; asst. prof., dir. basic urologic rsch. La. State U., New Orleans, 1990—; judge sr. div. Alamo Regional Sci. Fair, San Antonio, 1989-90. Contbr. articles to profl. jours. Vol. ARC; active Stephen Ministry. NSF grantee, 1972-74; recipient NIH Rsch. Svc. award, 1983-86, Searle Young Investigator award, 1994. Mem. AAAS, LWV, AAUW, Am. Soc. for Microbiology, Am. Assn. Cancer Rsch., Am. Soc. Cell Biology, Fedn. Am. Scientists, Sci. Club (pres. 1971-72), Soc. for In Vitro Sci., N.Y. Acad. Scis., St. Vincent De Paul Soc., Sierra Club, Fedn. Am. Soc. Experiment Biology, Sigma Xi, Iota Sigma Pi, Delta Epsilon Sigma. Democrat. Roman Catholic. Home: 3440 Edenborn Ave Apt 5 Metairie LA 70002-3334 Office: La State U Sch Medicine Dept Urology 1542 Tulane Ave New Orleans LA 70112-2865

HUPALO, MEREDITH TOPLIFF, artist, illustrator; b. Tarpon Springs, Fla., Apr. 28, 1917; d. Walter and Maurine (Martin) Topliff; cert. in design Pratt Inst., 1938; m. Nicholas Hupalo, July 13, 1940 (dec. Sept. 1977); children: Walter Topliff, John Nicholas. One-woman shows: Tarpon Springs Public Libr., 1945, Valley Stream (N.Y.) Mus., 1962, Contemporary Arts, Inc., N.Y.C., 1966, Jet Clubs Internat., N.Y.C., Henry Waldinger Libr., Valley Stream, N.Y., 1977, East River Savs. Bank, Valley Stream, 1978; two-person show: Art League of Daytona Beach, 1986; represented in permanent collection Valley Stream Pub. Libr., Tarpon Springs (Fla.) Pub. Libr., Eastern Airlines Exec. Offices, N.Y.C.; tchr. printmaking Nassau County (N.Y.) Home Extension Svc.; art adviser Valley Stream Mus., 1962-64; illustrator Eastern Airlines, 1964-68; artist Shell Oil Co., 1968-70; designer Continental Can Co., N.Y.C., 1970-73; art tchr. Astor (Fla.) Community Ctr., 1980-82. Active Mt. Dora Ctr. for the Arts of Lake County, 1991. Recipient spl. award oil painting 34th Nat. Spring Exhbn. Nat. Art League L.I., 1964, gold medal in oil painting 35th Membership Show, 1965; 1st pl. fine art Fla. Silver Springs Arts & Crafts Festival, 1980; 1st place award Umatilla Fall Festival (Fla.), 1983 merit award, 1985; merit award Tampa Realistic Artists, 1984; Best in Show award Nat. League Am. Pen Women, 1984; 1st pl. Fla. Extension Homemakers Cultural Arts; Award of Distinction, Pioneer Art Settlement, 1987, Honorable Mention Pioneer Art Settlement, 1991, 1st Pl. award Ann. Lake County Juried Art Show Mt. Dora Ctr. for Arts, 1992, Best in Show and 1st in Graphics awards Umatilla Fall Festival, 1993. Mem. Fla. Watercolor Soc. (assoc., participating artist II), Nat. Art League L.I. (treas. 1959-60), Art League of Daytona Beach (Lillian Gittner Meml. award 1988), Nat. League Am. Pen Women (Fla. br. 1987, v.p. 1991), Mus. Arts and Scis., DeLand Mus., Astor Area C. of C. (dir. 1981-82). Methodist. Works include Paintings With Markers, 1972. Home: 55809 Dale Cir Astor FL 32102-2628

HURD, GALE ANNE, film producer; b. L.A., Oct. 25, 1955; d. Frank E. and Lolita (Espiau) H. Degree in econs. and communications, Stanford U., 1977. Dir. mktg. and publicity, co-producer New World Pictures, L.A., 1977-82; pres., producer Pacific Western Prodns., L.A., 1982—. Producer: (films) The Terminator, 1984 (Grand Prix Avoriaz Film Festival award), Aliens, 1986 (nominated for 7 Acad. awards, recipient Best Sound Effects Editing award, Best Visual Effects award Acad. Picture Arts & Scis.), Alien Nation (Saturn award for best sci. fiction film), The Abyss, 1989 (nominated for 4 Acad. awards, Best Visual Effects award), The Waterdance, 1991 (2 1FP Spirit awards, 2 Sundance Film Festival awards), Cast A Deadly Spell, 1991 (Emmy Award), Raising Cain, 1992, No Escape, 1994, Safe Passage, 1994; exec. producer: (films) Tremors, 1990, Downtown, 1990, Terminator 2, 1991 (winner 3 acad. awards); creative cons. (TV program) Alien Nation, 1989-90. Juror Focus Student Film Awards, 1989, 90, Nicholl Fellowship Acad. Motion Picture Arts & Scis., 1989—; mem. Show Coalition, 1988—; mem. Hollywood (Calif.) Women's Polit. Com., 1987—; bd. dirs. Earth Communications Office, 1990—; mem. U.s. Film Festival Juror; bd. dirs. ARtists Rights Found. Recipient Spl. Merit award Nat. Assn. Theater Owners, 1986, Stanford-La Entrepreneur of Yr. award Bus. Sch. Alumni L.A., 1990, Fla. Film Festival award, 1994. Mem. AMPAS (producer's br. exec. com. 1990—), Am. Film Inst. (trustee 1989—), Americans for a Safe Future (mem. bd dirs. 1993—), Women in Film (bd. dirs. 1989-90), Feminist Majority, Phi Beta Kappa. Office: Pacific Western Prodns 270 N Canon Dr # 1195 Beverly Hills CA 90210-5323

HURD, SUZANNE SHELDON, federal agency health science director; b. Elmira, N.Y., Dec. 17, 1939; d. Victor Sheldon H. BS, Bates Coll., 1961; MS, U. Wash., 1963, PhD, 1967. Post-doctoral fellow U. Calif., Berkeley, 1967-69; grants assoc. NIH, Bethesda, Md., 1969-70; health sci. adminstr. Nat. Heart, Lung and Blood Inst., Bethesda, 1970-78, dep. dir. div. lung diseases, 1979-84; dir. div. lung diseases Nat. Heart, Lung and Blood Inst., Bethesda, 1984—; acting dir. Nat. Inst. Nursing Rsch., Bethesda, 1994-95. Mem. Am. Thoracic Soc. Office: Nat Heart Lung and Blood Inst Div Lung Diseases 5333 Westbard Ave # 6a16 Bethesda MD 20816-1423

HURD-GRAHAM, ROBIN J., sales and marketing executive, consultant; b. West Chester, Pa., Dec. 25, 1957; d. George A. and Winifred A. (Pines) Hurd; m. John G. Graham Sr., Mar. 18, 1978 (div. June 1985); 1 child, John G. Jr. BS in Biology, Ariz. State U., 1984. Corp. officer, asst. br. mgr. ops. Valley Nat. Bank, Phoenix, 1978-86; owner Dinner for Two Catering, Phoenix, 1985-87; field svc. zone mgr. Ford Motor Co., Detroit, 1987-89; owner, ptnr., mgr. MMI Co., Ellicott City, Md., 1989-91; exec. v.p. sales and mktg. Telemktg. Advantage, Malvern, Pa., 1992-94; owner, pres. R.J. Graham Consulting, West Chester, Pa., 1994—; instr. Pa. State U., 1994—, West Chester Adult Sch. Night, 1994—. Author: (poetry) The Mourning After Love, 1993. Pack leader Boy Scouts Am., Carrollton, Tex., 1988-89; instr. Jr. Achievement of Phoenix, 1984-85; mem. adv. bd. Comprehensive Employment Svc. Mem. NAFE, ASTD, Chester County Chamber of Bus. & Industry, Jack and Jills Am., Inc. (com. chair 1982), Alpha Kappa Alpha Sorority Inc. Home: 145 E Miner St West Chester PA 19382

HURET, MARILYNN JOYCE, library administrator; b. N.Y.C., Dec. 5; d. Hyman and Clara (Weinberg) Moskowitz; m. Barry Saul Huret, Feb. 11, 1961; children: Abbey Beth, Eric Alan. BA in Math., Adelphi U., 1961. Tchr. math. Dist. 281, Robbinsdale, Minn., 1974-77; puzzle constructor Marvel Comics, N.Y.C., 1982-88, Great Puzzle Catalog, N.Y.C., 1982-83; adminstr. David Libr. of Am. Revolution, Washington Crossing, Pa., 1988—. Coop. weather observer Sta. WOR, N.Y.C., 1965-71; severe storm weather spotter NOAA, 1972-77, Mpls., 1977-79, Racine, Wis., 1980—, Phila.; commr. pub. safety City of Golden Valley, Minn., 1972-77; judge Delaware Valley Sci. Fairs, Phila., 1984—; dep. coord. emergency mgmt. Lower Makefield Twp., Pa., 1989—; bd. dirs. Delaware Valley Philharmonic Orch. Recipient Svc. Appreciation award Golden Valley City Coun., 1977. Mem. LWV, AAUW (editor Makefield Area Connections 1993—, Named Gift award 1994), Spl. Libr. Assn. (assoc.), Am. Cryptogram Assn., Nat. Puzzlers League, Bucks County Librs. Assn., Adelphi U. Alumni Assn., Toastmasters. Home: 484 Kings Rd Yardley PA 19067-4652 Office: David Libr of Am Revolution PO Box 748 Washington Crossing PA 18977-0748

HURLEY, CHERYL JOYCE, book publishing executive; b. Pitts., Oct. 30, 1947; d. John and Violet Dernorsek; m. Kevin Hurley, July 27, 1974. Lang. and lit. cert., Université de Lyon, France, 1968; AB, Ohio U., 1969; MA, U. Mich., 1971. Research assoc. MLA, N.Y.C., 1972-74, dir. spl. programs, 1974-79; pub. The Library of America, N.Y.C., 1979—, pres., 1988—; cons. in field. Contbr. articles to profl. jours. Trustee French Inst./Alliance Francaise, 1992—, exec. com., 1994—; mem. libr. com. Hort. Alliance of Hamptons, 1989—; mem. benefit com. Hampton Libr., 1988—. Rackham fellow, 1969-70. Mem. Grolier Club, Century Assn., Bridgehampton Club, Phi Beta Kappa. Home: 4 E 88th St New York NY 10128-0556 Office: Libr of Am 14 E 60th St New York NY 10022-1006

HURLEY, GINA SAPIENZA, publishing and public relations executive; b. N.Y.C., May 21, 1966; d. Joseph N. and Geraldine F. (Adami) Sapienza; m. Richard W. Hurley, Sept. 10, 1989; 1 child, Parker Gerald. Student, Mercy Coll. Book critic The Sentinel, New Windsor, N.Y.; publicity mgr. Gleneida Pub. Mem. Pubs. Publicity Assn. Democrat. Roman Catholic. Home and Office: 1116 Continental Manor New Windsor NY 12553

HURLEY, MARY CAROLINE, educator; b. Evanston, Ill., Jan. 16, 1950; d. Jerome Edward and Dorothy Barbara (Evert) H. BA in English, Loyola U., Chgo., 1971, MEd in Reading and Learning Disabilities, 1977, postgrad., 1987—. Reading clinician Loyola U., Chgo., 1976-77; chmn. dept. reading, English Orr Community Acad., Chgo., 1977-79, chmn., mgr., instr. English, 1979-82, program coord., 1981-85, instr. English, 1981-84; program coord. Senn Met. Acad., Chgo., 1985-87; asst. prin. Lincoln Elem. and Jr. High Sch., Dolton, Ill., 1987-88; instr. English, dir. attendence Senn Met. Acad., 1988-89, instr. English, 1989-92, English chair, 1992—; del. profl. personnel adv. com. Senn Met. Acad., 1991-92. Mem. Rogers Park Hist. Soc., Chgo., Children's Home and Aid Soc. Ill., Chgo., House of Good Shepherd, Chgo. Mem. Nat. Staff Devel. Coun., Nat. Sch. Bds. Assn., Am. Fedn. Tchrs., Edit. Projects in Edn., Assn. Supervision and Curriculum Devel., Assn. Outcome Based Edn., Phi Delta Kappa (exec. bd. 1988—). Home: 7250 N Oakley Ave Chicago IL 60645

HURLEY, ROSE ANN, federal agency administrator; b. Detroit, Apr. 18, 1957; d. Roy Franklin and Genella (Rose) Staples; m. Jay Dwight Hurley, Jan. 2, 1982. A in Acctg., Trident Tech. Coll., 1992; postgrad. in bus. tech. and acctg., Charleston So. U., 1992—. Accounts maintainence clk., acctg. technician Govt. Long Beach (Calif.) Naval Sta., 1982-83, acctg. technician, agt. cashier, 1983-84; mil. pay clk. Govt. Norfolk (Va.) Naval Air Sta., 1984-85, lead mil. pay clk., 1985-87; sales clk. Summerville, S.C., 1987; civilian pay technician Govt. Naval Weapons Sta., Charleston, S.C., Govt. Defense Acctg. Office, Charleston, 1993—; sales clk. Ben Franklin Retail Store, Benton, Ky., 1977-78, P.N. Hirsh Retail Store, Benton, 1977-78; dept. mgr. Wal-Mart Retail Store, Benton, 1978-82; temporary worker Norrell Svcs., Long Beach, 1982. Recipient Cert. Recognition, VITA, 1992. Mem. Am. Soc. Mil. Comptrollers (Continuing Edn. grantee 1992), Inst. Mgmt. Accts., Federally Employed Women, Trident Tech. Coll. Alumni Assn. Republican. Baptist. Home: 5803 Robinhood Dr Charleston SC 29406-2733 Office: Defense Acctg Office 1545 2d St W Ste C Code BLN Charleston SC 29408-1968

HURST, AMANDA CADY, youth agency executive; b. Chgo., Nov. 26, 1951; d. John Foss and Helen (Freres) Pontanini; m. Richard C. Hurst, Jan. 3, 1970 (div. June 1976); 1 child, Richard Darian Hurst. Cert. Assault Counseling Techniques, Edgewater/Uptown Mental Health, 1987; cert. Community Svc. Mgmt., Roosevelt U., 1988-89. Staff Chgo. Women's Liberation Union, 1975-76; founder, chmn. Uptown Women's Coalition, Chgo., 1988-89; founding and steering commn. mem. Soc. Women in Philosophy, Chgo., 1984-88; founder, dir. Vega Youth Network, Chgo., 1981-85; exec. dir. The Centre, Inc., Chgo., 1985—; coun. mem. City Chgo./Youth Coord. Com., 1986-89; ofcl. state rep. Am. Double-Dutch League, Chgo., 1987-88; pres. Alternative Schs. Network, Chgo., 1992—; founding mem., pres. Just Us For Youth/Children's Legal Clinic, 1992—; founding mem. Magenta Soc., 1993. Mem. adv. bd. Chgo. Police Dept./24th Dist. Steering Com., Chgo., 1988-90; mem. Roosevelt U. Am. Policy Studies Ctr., Chgo., 1987-88; mem. child welfare com. Chgo. Bar Assn., 1991. Named WBBM Citizen of Week, Sta. WBBM-AM News Radio, Chgo., 1985. Mem. Nat. Soc. Fund Raising Execs., Internat. Platform Assn. Office: The Centre Inc 119 W Hubbard Ste 502 Chicago IL 60610

HURST, AMELIA, cardiovascular technician; b. Phila., June 7, 1953; d. Raymond and Betty Jean (Hamilton) Webb; m. James Hurst, June 20, 1975 (div. May 1991); children: Jason, Nicole. BS, Morehead (Ky.) State U., 1975. Cert. cardiovascular technician. Cardiovascular technician St. Joseph's Hosp., Lexington, Ky., 1976-81; sonographer Cardiac Ultrasound, Lexington, 1989—; cardiovascular technician/supr. Cardiology Assocs., Lexington, 1981—. Mem. Am. Cert. Technician Assn., Nat. Echocardiography Assn. Baptist. Home: 108 Lige Ct Nicholasville KY 40356-2209 Office: Cardiology Assocs 1401 Harrodsburg Rd Lexington KY 40504-3751

HURST, ANNA PACE, school system administrator; b. Prentiss, Miss., Dec. 31, 1950; d. Spurgeon Eugene and Lillian (Fontenberry) P.; m. Edward Carter Hurt, July 20, 1974; children: Jana Elise, Jessica Elizabeth. BS, U. So. Miss., 1972, M Adminstrn., 1985, postgrad., 1990; M Elem. Edn., William Carey Coll., 1976. Elem. tchr. Orleans Parish Sch. Bd., New Orleans, 1972-74; elem. tchr. Ocean Springs (Miss.) Sch. Dist., 1974-86, adminstrv. asst., 1986-91, dir. fed. programs and adminstrn., 1991—, dist. coord., 1991-94; accreditation evaluator Miss. Dept. Edn., Jackson, 1987-94, adminstrv. trainer, 1991-94; developer Ocean Springs Adopt-A-Sch. Program, 1987-94. Editor (newsletters) Springing Toward Excellence, 1992-93, What's Springing, 1993, (manual) Ocean Springs Teacher Resource Manual, 1986-94; co-editor handbook: What To Know, 1986-87. Bd. dirs. Ocean Springs Edn. Found., 1992—. Mem. Miss. Staff Devel. Coun. (pres.-elect), Miss. Assn. Sch. Adminstrs., Miss. Assn. Fed. Adminstrs. Program Dirs. (regional rep.), Nat. Assn. Reading, Nat. Staff Devel. Coun., Ft. Maurepas Reading Assn., Ocean Springs C. of C. (bd. dirs. 1986—), Lions. Baptist. Office: Ocean Springs Sch Dist 1600 Government St PO Box 7002 Ocean Springs MS 39564-7002

HURST, CHRISTINA MARIE, respiratory therapist; b. San Diego, Jan. 29, 1955; d. Harvey Joseph Breighner and Doris Romaine March-Breighner; children: Heather Erin, Ian Richard. AAS, Del. Tech. Coll., 1989. Cert. and registered respiratory therapist. Respiratory therapist Med. Ctr. Del., Christiana, 1989—; instr. basic. cardiopulmonary rescusitation, Wilmington, Del., 1989-90; speaker Senate Labor Rels. Com., 1987. Vol. preschool asthma program Am. Lung Assn. Del., Wilmington, 1989, Del. Epilepsy Found. Wilmington, 1988-90; exec. coun. State Adv. Coun. for Svcs. to Handicapped, Dover, Del., 1989-90; charter mem. parent support group Children with Epilepsy, Wilmington, 1988-90. Mem. Am. Assn. for Respiratory Care, Epilepsy Found. Am., Phi Theta Kappa. Home: 518 Pheasant Run Bear DE 19701-2720 Office: Med Ctr Del Stanton Ogletown Rd Newark DE 19713

HURST, JANE D., community health nurse, nursing educator; b. Philpsburg, Pa., Feb. 18, 1943; d. Don R. and Inez N. (Dobbins) m. Marion Fieldon Hurst, Jan. 3, 1965; children: Dana Lynn, Jacqueline Leigh. ASN, Pensacola (Fla.) Jr. Coll., 1963; BS, U. of So. Miss., 1983; MSN, U. Ala, Birmingham, 1984, DSc in Nursing, 1991. RN, Miss. Office nurse Office of Melvin Young, MD, Pensacola, Fla.; staff nurse nursery Riverside Meth. Hosp., Columbus, Ohio; nurse mgr. Laurel Wood Adolescent Unit, Meridian, Miss.; instr. East Ctrl. C.C., Decatur, Miss. Contbr. articles and rsch. to profl. jours. Mem. ANA (del. nat. conv. 1989, bd. dirs. DBA #16), Nat. League Nursing, Sigma Theta Tau.

HURST, LINDA GIBSON, office manager; b. Butler, Ala., June 13, 1953; d. Tobia Young and Devon (Giles) Gibson; 1 child, Lloyd Benjamin. BSBA, Livingston (Ala.) U., 1973; postgrad., Inst. Fin. Edn., Denver, 1984; BS in Fin., Ohio State U., 1989. Civilian pay liaison USAF, RAF Lakenheath, Suffolk, Eng., 1973-76; title clk. Big Country Dodge, Abilene, Tex., 1979; inventory mgmt. clk. non-appropriated funds mgmt. br. USAF, Dyess AFB, Tex., 1979-81; payroll clk., cashier Coca-Cola Bottling Co., Montgomery, Ala., 1981-83; human resources compensation rep. Silverado Banking, Denver, 1984-86; office mgr. Office Furniture Maintenance Corp., Upper Marlboro, Md., 1990-93, Blue Rents, Inc., Mobile, Ala., 1993—; accounts payable cons. Columbia Savs. & Loan, Denver, 1986. Vol. Pineview Manor Nursing Home, Clinton, Md., 1990-93; treas. adult ladies Sunday sch. class Clinton Bapt. Ch., 1991-93; pres. Music Boosters Club, Gwynn Park Mid. Sch., Brandywine, Md., 1990-91; mem. Prince Georges County Parents Music Students, Landover, Md., 1991-93; outreach leader adult ladies sunday sch. class Cottage Hill Baptist Ch., 1994. Mem. NAFE, AAUW, Am. Soc. Women Accts. (reporting chmn. 1994), Ohio State U. Alumni Assn. (life), Newark AFB Wives Club (sec. 1988-89). Home: 4370 Sawyer Ave Mobile AL 36619-9773 Office: Blue Rents Inc 1601 S Beltline Hwy Mobile AL 36606-2741

HURST, LINDA WHITTINGTON, educational curriculum writer; b. Norfolk, Va., July 19, 1949; d. Leroy and Minnie Estella (Burgess) Whittington; m. Donald Grayson Hurst, Aug. 28, 1971; children: William Christopher, Donald Geoffrey. BS in Secondary Edn., Old Dominion U., 1971, MS in Edn., 1978; postgrad., East Tex. State U., 1982-89. Cert. tchr., Tex. Tchr. Tidewater Christian High Sch., Virginia Beach, Va., 1971-73, Victory Christian Sch., Norfolk, Va., 1976-78; substitute tchr. Dallas Ind. Sch. Dist., 1981-84, tchr., 1984-88; grad. asst. East Tex. State U., Commerce, 1988-89, adj. instr., 1989-91; owner, writer-editor Helping Hand Ednl. Svc. and Supplies, Garland, Tex., 1989—; ednl. cons. H.O.P.E. for Tex., Austin, 1991—. Author, editor elem. curriculum The Classics, 1989-92, children's mag. Treasure Box, 1992. Sec. Parent Awareness League, Mesquite, Tex., 1990-91. Mem. Phi Delta Kappa. Home and Office: 5006 Barcelona Dr Garland TX 75043-5101

HURST, MARJORIE JACKSON, lawyer, association executive; b. Springfield, Mass., Oct. 14, 1946; d. Morris Joseph Jackson and Rosa Lee (Hill) Gooding; m. Frederick Ashley Hurst, Sr., July 16, 1966; children: Tiffani, Frederick Jr., Justin. BA, Howard U., 1968; MEd, U. Mass., 1973; JD, Western New Eng. Coll., 1985. Dir. fin. aid Daniel Hale Williams U., Chgo., 1977-78; legal sec. Schwartz & Freeman, Chgo., 1979-81, Altheimer & Gray, Chgo., 1981-82; legal rschr. law dept. City of Springfield, Mass., 1984-85, asst. city solicitor law dept., 1987-89; pvt. practice Springfield, 1985-92; ptnr. Sapirstein & Hurst, P.C., Springfield, 1992—; mem. faculty Mass. Continuing Legal Edn., Boston, 1993—; mem. merit selection panel magistrate judge U.S. Dist. Ct. Mass., 1994. Sec. Beautillion Greater Springfield, Inc., 1993—; pres., bd. dir.s YWCA Western Mass., Springfield, 1993—; bd. dirs. Greater Springfield Bus. Devel. Corp., 1993—. Recipient Meritorious Svc. to Community award Gov. of Commonwealth of Mass., 1989, Community Svc. citation Mass. State Senate, 1989, Mass. Ho. Reps., 1989, Proclamation, Mayor of Springfield, 1989. Mem. ABA, Mass. Bar Assn., Hampden County Bar Assn., Hampden County Bar Advs. (bd. dirs. 1993—), Springfield C. of C. (mem. women's partnership 1992—). Democrat. Office: Sapirstein & Hurst PC 1365 Main St Springfield MA 01103

HURST, MARY JANE, English language educator; b. Hamilton, Ohio, Sept. 21, 1952; d. Nimrod and Leckie (Brumback) Gaines; m. Daniel L. Hurst, June 5, 1974; 1 child, Katherine Jane. BA summa cum laude, Miami U., 1974; MA, U. Md., 1980, PhD, 1986. Tchr. Groveport (Ohio) High Sch., 1974-77; teaching asst. U. Md., College Park, 1978-79, master tchr., 1979-82; asst. prof. Tex. Tech U., Lubbock, 1986-92, assoc. prof., 1992—; vis. scholar Stanford U., summer 1987; steering com. Nat. Cowboy Symposium, Lubbock, 1988-89. Author: The Voice of the Child in American Literature, 1990; tech. editor: HTLV-I and the Nervous System, 1989; contbr. articles to profl. jours. Mem. Lubbock Cultural Affairs Coun., 1986-92, All Saints Episcopal Sch. Parent's Orgn., Lubbock, 1986—, Lubbock Symphony Guild, 1992—; vol. Meals on Wheel, Lubbock, 1986—, Habitat for Humanity, Lubbock, 1986—. Mem. AAUW (alt. fellowships panel in linguistics 1988-90), AAUP (regional v.p. 1990—), MLA, Linguistic Soc. Am., Am. Classical League, Linguistic Assn. S.W., Coll. Tchrs. English Tex., South Cen. Modern Lang. Assn., Lake Ridge Country Club, Phi Beta Kappa, Phi Kappa Phi, Sigma Tau Delta, Alpha Lambda Delta. Office: Tex Tech U Dept English Lubbock TX 79409

HURST, SHARLEENE PAGE, state legislator; b. Northampton, Mass., Apr. 30, 1959; d. Benjamin William and Shirley Ann (Weiner) Dempsey; m. Lee E. Hurst III, Apr. 27, 1986. File processor Liberty Mus. Inst. Co., 1985-89, rater I, 1989-90, reconciliation asst. grad. 5, 1990-91; mem. N.H. Ho. of Reps., 1990—, mem. standing com. corrections and criminal justice, 1993—, constn. and statutory rev. com., 1991-94, mem. state and fed. rels. com., 1994—, cllk., 1995—, gender equity in sports study com., chmn., 1991—, legis. task force on AIDS, 1993—; mem. standing com. on state and fed. rels., 1994—, mem. state septic adv. com., 1994—, mem. state and fed. rels. com., 1994—, apptd. clk., 1995; conf. attendee Maine Rep. State Com. Sch. of Campaign Mgmt., 1984, Young Rep. Nat. Leadership Conf., Washington, 1985, Norman Blackwell's Sch. Youth Campaign Mgmt., Nashua, N.H., 1986, N.H. Rep. State Com. Sch. of Campaign Mgmt., 1986, N.H. Sch. Bd. Assn., 1989, State Conv., 1989, New Eng. Rep. Day in Washington, 1989, N.H. State Conf. on Kids-at-Risk, 1990, Nat. Common Cause Conf. on State Leadership, Washington, 1991, Conf. on Substance Abuse in the Criminal System, Portsmouth, 1993. Bd. dirs. Hampton Sch. Bd., 1989-92, bd. rep. for transp. com., 1991-92, prin. search com., 1991, rep. to Hampton Mcpl. budget com., 1989, dist. clk., 1987-89; mem. Hampton Mcpl. Budget Com., 1986-90; mem. adv. bd. Rockland, Maine Libr., 1982-84; co-chmn. Mayor's Adv. Com. on Alternative Energy, Northampton, 1980-81; mem. Hampshire County Energy Policy Congress, 1980; pres. Hampshire County, Mass. Young Dems., 1980; assoc. mem. Northampton Energy Resource Commn., 1980-81; chmn. Maine Young Rep. State Conv., 1984; sec. Hampshire County Dem. Com., 1978-82, Rockland (Maine) Rep. City Com., 1984, New Eng. Coun. Young Reps., 1985-87, New Eng. Young Rep. Conv., 1985; del. to Mass. Dem. State Conv., 1979, 1981, Maine Rep. State Conv., 1984, Young Rep. Nat. Conv., N.H., 1985, N.H. Rep. State Conv., 1986, 90, 92; del.-at-large Rep. Nat. Conv., 1984; Rep. nominee for Rockingham County Commr., 1984; active Maine Young Rep. State Fedn., 1982-84, Young Rep. Nat. Platform Com., 1985, Maine Rep. State Conv. Planning Com., 1984, N.H. Rep. Trust, 1989, Hampton Rep. Town Com., 1986—, New Eng. Rep. Coun., 1991—. Mem. Citizens for Term Limits, N.H. Tourism Caucus, Order of Women Legislators. Republican. Methodist. Home: PO Box 1572 38 Mill Rd Hampton NH 03842-2237 Office: NH Ho of Reps State House Concord NH 03301

HURST, STACY JOHNSON, fundraiser; b. Pine Bluff, Ark., Feb. 11, 1962; d. James Leonard and Katherine (Karlovic) Johnson; m. Howard Cates Hurst, Aug. 4, 1993. BA in Comm., U. Ark., 1984. Found. assoc. Ark. Children's Hosp. Found., Little Rock, 1985-87, dir. corp. devel., 1987-89, dir. telethon, 1989-94, v.p., 1994—. Co-editor (mag.) Interaction, 1994. Active Jr. League Little Rock, Friends of the Rep.; pres. Episcopal Churchwomen, Little Rock, 1991. Mem. Nat. Soc. Fund Raising Execs. (v.p. philanthropy), Assn. Healthcare Philanthropy, Delta Delta Delta Alumnae (pres.). Home: 4608 Club Rd Little Rock AR 72207 Office: Ark Children's Hosp Found 800 Marshall Little Rock AR 72202

HURT, NANCY S., law librarian; b. Corpus Christi, Tex., Aug. 14, 1959; d. Roy Monroe and Mary Caroline (Redwine) Hurt. AA, Del Mar Coll., Corpus Christi, 1979; BA cum laude, Corpus Christi State U., 1981; MLIS, U. Tex., 1984, Cert. of Specialization, 1985. Libr. aide Parkdale Libr./City of Corpus Christi, 1974-81; prin. libr. aide La Retama Libr./City of Corpus Christi, 1982; asst. br. mgr. McCreless Libr./City of San Antonio, 1984-85; info. svcs. mgr. McCamish & Martin, P.C., San Antonio, 1985-93; law libr. corp. libr. USAA, San Antonio, 1993—; ptnr., gen. mgr. Grim Reader Mystery Catalog. Bd. dirs. Friends of San Antonio Pub. Libr., 1991—; bd. advisors Accusearch of Tex., 1992—. Recipient Vol. of the Yr. award United Way of San Antonio, 1991. Mem. ALA, Am. Assn. Law Librarians. Office: United Svcs Automoblie Assn C-3-W USAA Bldg San Antonio TX 78288

HURT, TERESA ANN, handwriting analyst; b. Spokane, Wash., Jan. 5, 1954; d. Alexander Lazarus and Pauline Joyce (Hodgson) Birch; m. Robert Earl Hurt, Aug. 11, 1973 (div. Jan. 1986); 1 child, Melinda Eslie Ann. Student, Spokane C.C., 1992—. Cert. in behavioral profiling and forensic document examinations, Am. Bd. Forensic Examiners. Owner Profl. Handwriting Analysis, Spokane, 1986—; instr. Spokane Falls C.C., 1989-92, 92-94. Mem. Am. Handwriting Analysis Found. (cert., com. mem.), Coun. Graphological Soc., Nat. Assn. Document Examiners, Nat. Questioned Document Assn., Human Graphics Ctr. Office: Profl Handwriting Analysis 10 N Post St Ste 550 Spokane WA 99201-0705

HURTADO, TRACY ELLEN, accountant; b. Roseville, Calif., Aug. 4, 1968; d. Corydon Dicks and Nancy (Trott) H. BS in Acctg. cum laude, Calif. State U., Sacramento, 1991. CPA, Nev. Sr. acct. audit Deloitte & Toche LLP, Reno, Nev., 1991—. Mem. Nev. Soc. CPAs, Inst. Mgmt. Accts. (sec. 1994—), Delta Sigma Pi (dist. dir. U. Nev.-Reno chpt. 1991-93). Office: Deloitte & Touche LLP 50 W Liberty St Ste 900 Reno NV 89501

HURTUBIS, CYNTHIA MARIE, artist, designer; b. Rochester, N.Y., Feb. 19, 1966; d. Edward William and Mary Leona (Carmosky) H. BFA in Design, Colo. State U., 1988; postgrad., Acad. of Art Coll., San Francisco, 1993—. Designer Interior Architects, L.A., 1989-90, PHH Walker, L.A., 1990, Hefferlin Architects, L.A., 1990-91; designer, artist, pres., owner Hurtubis Design, San Mateo, Calif., 1991—; western regional applications engr. Ashlar, Inc., Sunnyvale, Calif., 1992-93. Mem. PEO (social chair 1992-94), Berkeley Macintosh User Group, Calif. Vellum User Group, Kappa Delta. Roman Catholic. Office: Hurtubis 126 12th Ave San Mateo CA 94402

HURWITZ, ELLEN STISKIN, college president, historian; b. Stamford, Conn., May 4, 1942; d. D.O. Bernard and Marjorie (Kanter) Stiskin; children: Jason, Sarah. BA, Smith Coll., 1964; MA, Columbia U., 1965, PhD, 1972. Vis. asst. prof. Wesleyan U., Middletown, Conn., 1972-73; asst. prof. Lafayette Coll., Easton, Pa., 1974-80, assoc. prof., assoc. dean, 1980-88; dean acad. affairs Ill. Wesleyan U., Bloomington, 1988-89, provost, dean of faculty, 1989-92; pres. Albright Coll., Reading, Pa., 1992—; cons. Nat. Faculty Arts and Scis., Inst. for Ednl. Mgmt., Harvard U., 1990. Author: Andrej Bogoljubskij: Man and Myth, 1972. NEH fellow, 1973-74. Mem. AAAS, Am. Assn. Higher Edn., Phi Beta Kappa. Office: Albright Coll PO Box 15234 Reading PA 19612-5234*

HURWITZ, JOHANNA (FRANK), author, librarian; b. N.Y.C., Oct. 9, 1937; d. Nelson and Tillie (Miller) Frank; m. Uri Hurwitz, Feb. 19, 1962; children: Nomi, Beni. BA, Queens Coll., 1958; MLS, Columbia U., 1959. Libr. children's sect. N.Y. Pub. Libr., 1959-64; lectr. in children's lit. Queen's Coll., N.Y.C., 1965-69; libr. Calhoun Sch., N.Y.C., 1968-75, New Hyde Park (N.Y.) Sch. Dist., 1975-77; libr. children's sect. Great Neck (N.Y.) Pub. Libr., 1978-92. Author: Busybody Nora, 1976, Nora and Mrs. Mind-Your-Own-Business, 1977, The Law of Gravity, 1978, Much Ado About Aldo, 1978, Aldo Applesauce, 1979, New Neighbours for Nora, 1979, Once I Was a Plum Tree, 1980, Superduper Teddy, 1980, Aldo Ice Cream, 1981, Baseball Fever, 1981, The Rabbi's Girls, 1982, Tough-Luck Karen, 1982, Rip-Roaring Russell, 1983, DeDe Takes Charge!, 1984, The Hot and Cold Summer, 1984, The Adventures of Ali Baba Bernstein, 1985, Russell Rides Again, 1985, Hurricane Elaine, 1986, Yellow Blue Jay, 1986, Class Clown, 1987, Russell Sprouts, 1987, The Cold and Hot Winter, 1988, Teacher's Pet, 1988, Anne Frank: Life in Hiding, 1988, Hurray for Ali Baba Bernstein, 1989, Russell and Elisa, 1989, Astrid Lindgren: Storyteller to the World, 1989, Class President, 1990, Aldo Peanut Butter, 1990, School's Out, 1991, E Is for Elisa, 1991, Roz and Ozzie, 1992, Ali Baba Bernstein, Lost and Found, 1992, The Up and Down Spring, 1993, Make Room for Elisa, 1993, Leonard Bernstein: A Passion for Music, 1993, New Shoes for Silvia, 1993, A Word to the Wise, 1994, School Spirit, 1994, A Llama in the Family, 1994. Recipient Bluebonnet award Tex. Libr. Assn., 1987, Sunshine State award Fla. Libr. Assn., 1990, Miss. Children's Book award Miss. Libr. Assn., 1990, S.C. Children's Book award, 1990, Garden State award N.J. Sch. Libr. Assn., 1991, 94, Weekly Reader Book Club award, 1993. Mem. PEN, Author's Guild, Soc. Children's Book Writers, Amnesty Internat. Address: 10 Spruce Pl Great Neck NY 11021-1904

HUSBY, JEAN ANN, marketing educator, consultant; b. Superior, Wis., Jan. 16, 1960; d. Walter Joseph and Irene Kay (Kubalak) Urbaniak; m. Bradley David Husby, Dec. 28, 1985. AAS, We. Wis. Tech. Coll., LaCrosse, 1982; BS, U. Wis.-Stout, 1987, MS, 1993. Cert. mktg. educator. Customer svc. rep. Consumers Coop. Assn., Menomonie, Wis., 1983-84; advt. mgr. Dunn County News and Shopper, Menomonie, 1984-87; mktg. educator U. Wis.-Stout, Menomonie, 1987-90; mktg. instr. Chippewa Valley Tech. Coll., Eau Claire, Wis., 1990—; advisor Wis. Mktg. and Mgmt. Assn., Eau Claire, 1990—. Mem. NEA, Mktg. Edn. Assn., Am. Vocat. Assn., Wis. Vocat. Assn., Wis. Mktg. Edn. Assn., Wis. Edn. Assn. Coun., Distributive Edn. Clubs Am. (pres. 1977-78), Delta Epsilon Chi (pres. 1981-82). Roman Catholic. Home: E2508 470th Ave Menomonie WI 54751-6100 Office: Chippewa Valley Tech Coll 620 W Clairemont Eau Claire WI 54701

HUSLIG, MARY ANN, medical librarian; b. Kansas City, Kans., July 24, 1947; d. Walter Leroy and Mary Agnes (Kelly) Hubbel; m. Dennis Michael Huslig, July 11, 1970; children: Mark Andrew, Dawn Marie. BS in Bus. Mgmt., Emporia State U., 1969, MS in Libr. Sci., 1970. Assoc. librarian St. Mary's Coll., Leavenworth, Kans., 1970-71; librarian/instr. Cen. Mo. State U., Warrensburg, 1971-72; librarian Bergan High Sch., Peoria, Ill., 1976-77; instr. LTA program Ill. Cen. Coll., East Peoria, Ill., 1977-84; librarian Ill. Cen. Coll., East Peoria, 1978-84; head tech. svcs. Chgo. Coll. Osteo. Medicine, 1984-86; asst. dir. Chgo. Coll. Osteopathic Medicine, Downers Grove, Ill., 1986-93; coord. libr./ednl. resource ctr. Healthcare COMPARE Corp., Downers Grove, 1993—. Pastoral minister St. Louise de Marillac Ch., LaGrange Park, Ill., 1991—; bd. dirs. Chgo. Marriage Encounter, 1987-89, 92—; v.p. PTO, Forest Rd. Sch., LaGrange Park, 1985-86. Mem. Med. Libr. Assn., Ill. Libr. Assn., Health Sci. Librarians of Ill. (bylaws com. chair 1990-92). Roman Catholic. Home: 526 Beach Ave LaGrange Park IL 60525-5716 Office: Healthcare COMPARE Corp 3200 Highland Ave Downers Grove IL 60515-1282

HUSMAN, LOIS ARLENE, psychotherapist; b. Chgo., July 24, 1937; s. Nathan H. and Harriet (Bernstein) Schwartz; m. David L. Husman, Jan. 23, 1957 (div. Mar. 1969); children—Melinda, Lori. Student Northwestern U., 1954-57; B.G.S., Roosevelt U., 1972; M.S.W., U. Ill., 1974. Social worker A.E.R.O. spl. edn. sch., 1974-79; psychotherapist in pvt. practice, Chgo., 1979—. Mem. Chgo. Symphony Orch. Assn., Art Inst. Chgo., Chgo. Council Fgn. Relations, Nat. Assn. Social Workers, Am. Orthopsychiat. Assn. Home: 1430 N Astor St Apt 10C Chicago IL 60610-1646 Office: 111 N Wabash Ave Ste 1202 Chicago IL 60602-2001

HUSSELMAN, GRACE, innkeeper, educator; b. Paterson, N.J., July 24, 1923; d. Edward and Lydia (Kliphouse) Van Allen; B.A., William Paterson Coll.; m. Samuel Husselman, June 3, 1944; children—Samuel Glenn, Howard Lloyd. With personnel office Wright Aero. Corp., Fairlawn, Pub. 1942-45; library asst. Wyckoff (N.J.) Pub. Library, 1964-66; library dir. Allendale (N.J.) Pub. Library, 1967-81; elem. sch. tchr., assoc. ednl. media specialist, 1981-84; owner Ye Olde Buckmaster Inn, 1984—. Reading Merit Badge counselor Boy Scouts Am.; pioneer guide Pioneer Girls, nat. youth v.p., sec. friendship circle; sec. bookstore com. Christian Growth Ministries; sec. Ladies Aid Soc., Shrewsbury Community Ch.; bd. deacons Shrewsbury Community Ch.; bd. dirs. Shrewsbury Library, Vt. Mem. N.J., Bergen-Passaic library assns., Hist. Soc. of Shrewsbury (pres./sec.), Kappa Delta Pi. Club: Captains and Mates Yacht. Home: Lincoln Hill Rd Shrewsbury VT 05783

HUSSELS MAUMENEE, IRENE E., ophthalmology educator; b. Bad Pyrmont, Germany, Apr. 30, 1940. MD, U. Gottingen, 1964. Cert. Am. Bd. Ophthalmology, Am. Bd. Med. Genetics. Rsch. asst. U. Hawaii, 1968; vis. genetics Population Genetics Lab., 1968-69; fellow dept. medicine Johns Hopkins U., 1969-71; ophthalmology preceptorship Wilmer Inst. Johns Hopkins Hosp., 1969-71, from asst. prof. to assoc. prof. Wilmer Ophthalmology Inst., 1972-87, prof. ophthalmology and medicine, divsn. med. genetics Wilmer Ophthalmology Inst., 1987—; dir. Johns Hopkins Ctr. Hereditary Eye Disease, Wilmer Inst., 1979—; cons. John F. Kennedy Inst. Visually & Mentally Handicapped Children, 1974—; dir. Low Vision Clinic, Wilmer Inst., 1977-88; vis. prof. French Ophthalmology Soc., Paris & French Acad. Medicine, 1988; advisor Nat. Eye Inst. Task Forces, 1976, 81. Mem. AMA, Am. Soc. Human Genetics, Am. Acad. Ophthalmology, Assn. Rsch. Vision & Ophthalmology, Internat. Soc. Genetic Eye Disease, Am. Ophthalmology Soc., Pan Am. Assn. Ophthalmology. Office: Johns Hopkins Hosp Ctr Hereditary Eye Diseases 600 N Wolfe St # 517 Baltimore MD 21287-0002

HUSSEY, ELIZABETH SUE, veterinarian; b. St. Louis, Nov. 19, 1962; d. John Edwin and Janet Sue (Lane) H. BA in Polit. Sci., U. Mo., 1984, DVM, 1989. Assoc. vet. Horton Animal Hosp., Columbia, Mo., 1989—. V.p., bd. dirs. Ctrl. Mo. Humane Soc., 1989—; guest host The Pet Place-Sta. KFRU Radio, Columbia, 1990—; bd. dirs. Columbia Bd. Health, 1992-93. Mem. AVMA, Mo. Vet. Med. Assn. (mem. animal welfare com.), Columbia/Boone County Vet. Med. Soc. (sec.-treas.). Democrat. Home: 655 North Rte O Rocheport MO 65279 Office: Horton Animal Hosp 1700 1-70 Dr SW Columbia MO 65203

HUSTON, ANJELICA, actress; b. L.A., July 8, 1951; d. John and Enrica Huston; m. Robert Graham, 1992. Student, Loft Studio. Actress appearing in Hamlet, Roundhouse Theatre, London, Tamara, Il Vittorale Theatre, L.A.; appeared in films including A Walk with Love and Death, 1969, Hamlet, 1969, Sinful Davey, 1969, Swashbuckler, 1976, The Last Tycoon, 1976, The Postman Always Rings Twice, 1981, This is Spinal Tap, 1984, The Ice Pirates, 1984, Prizzi's Honor, 1985 (Academy award for best supporting actress 1985, N.Y.Film Critics award 1985, L.A. Film Critics award 1985), Captain Eo, 1986, Gardens of Stone, 1987, The Dead, 1987 (Best Actress award Ind. Filmakers 1987), Mr. North, 1988, A Handfull of Dust, 1988, Witches, 1989, Crimes and Misdemeanors, 1989, Enemies, A Love Story, 1989 (Acad. award nomination 1990), The Grifters, 1990 (Acad. award nomination 1991), The Addams Family, 1991, The Player, 1992, Addams Family Values, 1993, Manhattan Murder Mystery, 1993, The Crossing Guard, 1994, The Perez Family, 1994; TV films include the Cowboy and the Ballerina, 1984, Faerie Tale Theatre, A Rose for Miss Emily, Lonesome Dove, 1989, Family Pictures, 1993, And The Band Played On, 1993. Office: Internat Creative Mgmt 8942 Wilshire Blvd Beverly Hills CA 90211*

HUSTON, BEATRICE LOUISE, banker; b. Grantsburg, Wis., Dec. 26, 1932; d. Elvin and Fay Cynthia (Sybrant) H.; m. Gerald W. Huston, June 30, 1951 (dec.); 1 child, Linda Sandell. BA, Met. State U., Minn., 1992. With Northwest Bus. Service, Mpls., 1950-51, Progressive Machine Co., Huntington Park, Calif., 1951-52; v.p. and corp. sec. Apache Corp., Mpls., 1954-87; v.p. stock transfer Norwest Bank, Minn., 1987—. Mem. Am. Soc. Corp. Secs. Lutheran. Home: 8264 Xerxes Ave S Minneapolis MN 55431-1003 Office: Norwest Bank 6th and Marquette Minneapolis MN 55402

HUSTON, DEVERILLE ANNE, lawyer; b. Great Falls, Mont., Mar. 2, 1947; d. Orion Joseph and Beverly Rosemary (Mower) H. BA, U. Minn., 1969; JD, William Mitchell Coll. Law, 1975. Bar: Minn. 1975, Ill. 1976,

U.S. Dist. Ct. (no. dist.) Ill. 1976). Assoc. Sidley & Austin, Chgo., 1977-83, ptnr., 1983—. Fellow Am. Bar Found.; mem. ABA, Ill. State Bar Assn., Chgo. Bar Assn., Chgo. Fin. Exch., Law Club. Office: Sidley & Austin 1 First National Plz Chicago IL 60603*

HUSTON, HARRIETTE IRENE OTWELL (REE HUSTON), retired county official; d. Harry C. Otwell and Fannie (Mitchell) Otwell Geffert; m. Dan E. Huston, Jan. 21, 1951; children: Terry Dane, Dale Curtis, Ronald William, Randall Philip. BS, Kans. State Coll., 1951. Cert. life ins. agt., Wash.; cert. wastewater operator in tng., Wash. Tchr. Kans., Ill., 1955-68; assoc. home economist McCall's Patterns Co., N.Y.C., 1959-62; counselor, owner Dunhill of Seattle Personnel, 1968-75; enrollment officer, trainer, adminstrv. sec. Teller Tng. Insts., Seattle, 1975-76; life and health ins. agt. Lincoln Nat. Sales, Seattle, 1976-77; office mgr., adminstrv. sec. ARA Transp. Group, Seattle, 1977-78; asst. to the pres. Pryde Corp., Bellevue, Wash., 1978-80; sr. sec. Municipality of Met. Seattle, 1980-92, project asst., 1992-93; adminstrv. specialist II King County Dept. Met. Svcs. (formerly Municipality of Met., 1993-95; ret., 1995—. Co-author: Homemaking textbook, 1956; contbr. articles to profl. jours.. Sec. exec., mem. gen. bd. Bellevue Christian Ch., Disciples of Christ, 1976-77, 86-87, chmn. flowers com., 1978-83, elder, 1978, deacon, 1987; bd. dirs., sec. Surrey Downs Comty. Club, Bellevue, 1983-85; mem. choir Sequim Presbyn. Ch., 1994—; vol. leader, coord. Linking Home and Sch. Through the Workplace, 1992-93. Recipient Clothing award check McCall's Patterns Co., N.Y.C., 1962, Certs. of Merit Metro Hdqrs., Seattle, 1981, 82, 83, 86, 89. Mem. Bellevue Bridge Club. Home: 1783 E Sequim Bay Rd Sequim WA 98382

HUSTON, KATHLEEN MARIE, library administrator; b. Sparta, Wis., Jan. 7, 1944; d. Orlin Runde and Kathleen (Dwyer) A.; m. Gregory T. Raab, May 9, 1970; 1 child, Steven G. Raab; m. James L. Huston, July 9, 1988. BA, Edgewood Coll., 1966; MLS, U. Wis., Madison, 1969. Libr. Milw. Pub. Libr., 1969-90; city libr. Milw. Pub. Libr. System, 1991—; com. mem. Libr. Svcs. Constrn. Act, 1989-92, System & Resource Libr. Adminstrs. of Wis., Madison, 1991—. Mem. TEMPO, Milw., 1991—, Profl. Dimensions, Milw., 1986—. Mem. ALA, Wis. Libr. Assn., Rotary. Office: Milwaukee Pub Libr 814 W Wisconsin Ave Milwaukee WI 53233-2309

HUSTON, LEONA M., speech pathologist; b. Mt. Pleasant, Mich., May 9, 1951; d. Joseph Thomas and Helen Jane (Diehl) H. BS, Cen. Mich. U., 1973, MA, 1975. Speech therapist Victoria Infirmary, Glasgow, Scotland, 1975-76, Mich. Assn. for Better Hearing and Speech, Lansing, 1976-77, Tuscola Intermediate Sch. Dist., Caro, Mich., 1977—. Mem. coun. on ministries com. Caro United Meth. Ch., 1983, pastor-parish relationships com. 1990-93. Mem. ASHA, TTT, PEO. Home: 227 W Grant St Caro MI 48723-1517 Office: Tuscola Intermediate Sch 1385 Cleaver Rd Caro MI 48723-9378

HUSTON, MARGO, journalist; b. Waukesha, Wis., Feb. 12, 1943; d. James and Cecile (Timlin) Bremner; student U. Wis., 1961-63; A.B. in Journalism, Marquette U., 1965; m. James Huston, Dec. 9, 1967 (div.); 1 son, Sean Patrick. Editorial asst. Marquette U., Milw., 1965-66; feature editor, reporter Waukesha Freeman, 1966-67; feature reporter Milw. Jour., 1967-70; reporter Spectrum, women's and food sections, 1972-79, editorial writer, 1979-84, polit. reporter, 1984—, asst. picture editor, 1985-91, copy editor, 1992—; instr. mass communications U. Wis., Milw. Recipient Penney-Mo. award for consumer abortion series, 1975, Pulitzer Prize for investigation into plight of elderly, 1977, Clarion award, 1977, Knight of Golden Quill award, Milw. Press Club, 1977, Wis. AP writing award, 1977, special award Milw. Soc. Profl. Journalists, 1977, Penney-Mo. Paul Myhie award for excellence, 1978; By-Line award Marquette U. Coll. of Journalism, 1980; Wis. UPI best editorial award, 1982; Wis. Women's Network award for journalist achievement for women's issues, 1983, Dick Goldensohn Fund award, 1991; Wis. Arts Bd. Literary Arts grantee, 1992. Mem. Nat. News Council (dir.), Investigative Reporters and Editors, Nat. Conf. Editorial Writers, Sigma Delta Chi. Club: Milw. Press. Office: Milwaukee Journal 333 W State St Milwaukee WI 53203-1305

HUSZAR, ARLENE CELIA, lawyer; b. N.Y.C., May 1, 1952; d. Charles and Dora (Toffoli) H.; m. Victor M. Yellen, May 6, 1978; 1 child: Mariette Huszar Yellen. BA, Fla. Atlantic U., 1973; JD, U. Fla., 1976. Bar: Fla. 1977, U.S. Dist. Ct. (mid. and no. dists.) Fla. 1978, U.S. Ct. Appeals (5th and 11th cirs.) 1978, D.C. 1979, U.S. Supreme Ct. 1982. Pvt. practice Gainesville, Fla., 1977-80; mng. atty. Fla. Instl. Legal Svcs., Gainesville, 1980—. Author: (with others) Termination of Parental Rights, 1992, Adoption, 1990. Mem. City of Gainesville Citizens Adv. Com. for Community Devel., 1976-79, Fla. Bar Com. on the Legal Needs of Children, 1984-85, steering com. juvenile law sect. Nat. Legal Aid and Defender Assn., 1986-87; vice chmn. Alachua County Citizens Adv. Com., Dept. Criminal Justice Svcs., 1986—; precinct committeewoman Alachua County Dem. Exec. Com., 1986—. Named one of Outstanding Young Women of Am., 1975. Mem. LWV, Assn. Trial Lawyers Am., Nat. Assn. Counsel for Children, Eighth Jud. Cir. Bar Assn. (bd. dirs. 1994—). Roman Catholic. Office: Fla Instl Legal Svcs 1110-C NW 8th Ave Gainesville FL 32601

HUTCHEON, LINDA ANN, English language educator; b. Toronto, Aug. 24, 1947; d. Vincent Roy and Elisa (Rossi) Bulfon Bortolotti; m. Michael Alexander Hutcheon, May 30, 1970. B.A., U. Toronto, 1969, Ph.D., 1975; M.A., Cornell U., 1971. Vis. prof. U. Toronto, 1980-81, 81-82, 84-85; prof. McMaster U., Hamilton, Ont., Can., 1976-88, U. Toronto, 1988—; assoc. editor RS/SI, Toronto and U. Toronto Quarterly, 1993—; mem. editorial bd. Texte, Toronto, 1983—, English Studies in Can., 1984-94, Italian Canadiana, 1984—, Textual Practice, 1985—, Canadian Review of Comparative Literature, 1987—, Can. Poetry, 1987-93, PMLA, 1990-92, Essays on Can. Writing, Contemporary Literature, 1992—, Modern Fiction Studies, 1993—, Contemporary Literature, 1992—, CLIO, 1994—. Author: Narcissistic Narrative, 1980 (Choice award 1980-81), Formalism & the Freudian Aesthetic, 1984; A Theory of Parody, 1985, A Poetics of Postmodernism, 1988, The Canadian Postmodern, 1988, The Politics of Postmodernism, 1989, Splitting Images, 1991, Irony's Edge, 1994. Fellow Woodrow Wilson Found., 1969, Social Scis. and Humanities Research Council Can., 1983, 93—, Can. Council, 1972-75; Killam Found., 1978-80, 86-88, Connaught, 1991-92, Guggenheim, 1992-93. Mem. Assn. Can. Univ. Tchrs. English (exec. mem. 1979-81), Can. Comparative Lit. Assn. (sec.-treas. 1981-83), MLA (del. assembly 1985-88, exec. coun. 1992—).

HUTCHESON, ELIZABETH BRUNK, retired association executive; b. Pitts., Apr. 12, 1920; d. Henry Edward and Cornelia A. (Steeb) Brunk; m. Thomas Jewett Hutcheson, Nov. 13, 1944 (div. Dec. 1950); 1 child, Sara Elizabeth Hutcheson Akehi. BA in Edn., U. Pitts., 1941, MBA, 1950. Program dir. YWCA Greater Pitts., 1950-56, dir. downtown br., 1956-61, assoc. exec. dir. met. assn., 1961-68; field cons. ea. region Nat. Bd. YWCA of U.S.A., N.Y.C., 1968-71, interim exec., cons., 1984—; exec. dir. YWCA Buffalo and Erie County, 1971-83. Bd. dirs., past pres. Buffalo Area Coun. Chs., 1976-94; dir. exec. com. Concerned Ecumenical Ministries, Buffalo, 1980—; founder, bd. dirs. Coalition Common Ground, 1992—; steering com. Common Ground Network, Washington, 1993—. Capt. U.S. Army, 1942-45. Recipient Women's Achievement award NOW, 1974, Community Achievement award Urban League, 1975, Appreciation award Women in Community Svc., 1980, Community Svc. to Women award Every Woman Opportunity Ctr., 1985, Community Svc. award Coun. Chs., 1990. Lutheran. Home: 554 Tacoma Ave Buffalo NY 14216-2405

HUTCHESON, JUDY ANN, computer systems specialist; b. Chattanooga, Tenn., Mar. 18, 1952; d. Kenneth Arnold and Bessie Ray (McSpadden) H.; m. Rodney Alan Morgan, Aug. 1, 1971 (div. Aug. 14, 1974); m. James Harvey Cash, June 6, 1993. AS, Pellissippi State C.C., 1988. Programming technician Tenn. Valley Authority, Knoxville, 1975-90; systems analyst Baker, Worthington et al, Knoxville, 1990-93; EDI coord. Transp. Data Network Internat., Atlanta, 1993—. Author: (poetry) American Anthology of Poetry, 1985. Recipient Nat. Outstanding Achievement award Federally Employed Women, 1988, Tribute to Women award Knoxville YWCA, 1987, Outstanding Achievement award Knoxville Chpt. FEW, 1987, Tenn. Valley Authority Employee Silver Honor award, 1988, Outstanding Achievement award Chattanooga Chpt. FEW, 1988. Democrat. Home: 3527 Quiet Creek Rd Marietta GA 30060

HUTCHINGS, BRENDA SUE, geriatrics nurse, health facility administrator; b. Charleston, W.Va., May 7, 1949; d. Luther E. and Thelma Ethel (Walls) Wilkinson; m. Geoffrey K. Hutchings, Dec. 19, 1970; children: Gennifer, Gretchen, Ginger. BSN, East Tenn. State U., Johnson City, 1971, postgrad. RN, Tenn.; cert. quality assurance profl., Tenn. Staff nurse Unicoi County Meml. Hosp. and Long Term Care Facility, Erwin, Tenn., 1971-72, charge nurse, 1972-73, inservice dir., 1973-79, quality assurance dir., 1979-84; dir. nursing Life Care Ctr. of Erwin, 1989-91; pres. Quality Mgmt. Assocs., Inc., 1991—; corp. cons. Life Care Ctrs. Am., 1989—, mem. med. adv. bd.; mem. home health adv. bd. Unicoi County; mem. adv. bd. Apple Rehab. Svcs. Deconess Downtown Christian Ch., bd. dirs., mem. edn. com.; mem. Bluff City Mid. Sch. PTA, Bluff City, Tenn. Mem. Nat. Assn. Quality Assurance Profls., Alzheimer's Disease and Related Disorders Assn., Tenn. Health Care Assn. (Disting. Profl. Svc. award 1991), Life Care Ctrs. Am. (quality assurance com.), Tenn. Nurses Assn. (pub. co-chmn. dist. 5), Tenn. Health Care Assn./Dirs. of Nursing Assn. (state bd. 1989-90, v.p.-elect 1990—, DON of Yr. in Tenn. award 1989-90). Home: RR 4 Box 1645 Elizabethton TN 37643-9201

HUTCHINGS, LEANNE VON NEUMEYER, communications executive, research consultant, writer; b. L.A.; d. F. Louis and Greta Catherine (Clifford) von Neumeyer; children: Marc Lane, Kristin LeAnne, Michael Lane, Jamie Laird, Jeremy Leif, Breton Louis. Student Brigham Young U., 1962. Researcher, writer, owner Heritage Tree, Arcadia, Calif., 1970—; internat. bd. advisors, dir. protocol, mem. scholarship grant review com. Neeley Scholarship Found., 1988-89; dir. pub. communications Ch. of Jesus Christ of Latter-day Saints, Foothill and Glendale regions, Calif., 1975-92, dir. community relations, 1984-92, asst. dir. area coun., 1984; adminstrv. asst., mem. grant propsal review com. Calif. Pub. Affairs Dept., L.A., 1990—; seminar coord. R.E.D.I., Inc., L.A., 1982-91, corp. rels. dir., 1984-91; design cons. H.M.J. Jewelers, L.A., 1985—; supr. Rexall Internat., So. Calif. Leadership, 1995—; mem. nat. adv. coun. motion picture studio Brigham Young U., Provo, Utah, 1986-89; adminstrv. dir. Pasadena Geneal. Libr., Calif., 1977-82; writer, co-producer KBIG, Sideband Div. Radio, L.A., 1979-80; exec. assoc adminstr. Calif. Bicentennial Found. for the U.S. Constitution, 1987; regional cons. Latter-Day Sentinel Newspaper, L.A., 1985-89; mem. Scholarship Found., L.A., 1985-89, exec. dir., 1988-89; mem. Brigham Young U. Marriott Sch. Bus. Mgmt. Soc., L.A., 1990—; mem. com. on child pornography legis. L.A. County Commn. on Obscenity & Pornography, 1988-91, chmn. pub. info. portfolio com., 1988-91, artist. Author: Honored Heritage, 1975, Woman's Place of Honor, 1976, Prologue and Tapestry, 1976, Moments with the Prophets, 1977, Southern California: The Earthquake Threat, 1981, Quake!: Preparing Home, Family and Community, 1982, The Peregrine Papers, 1986; columnist HeritageTree Foothill Intercity News, 1977-79; contbg. writer Women's Exponent Southern Calif. edit.; Sentinel; journalism series, 1978-80; also articles, collected works, stage trilogy; art exhibits include Wilshire Alma Exhibit, 1985, The Grand Artists Hall, 1986-88. Pres. Daus. Utah Pioneers-Los Angeles County, 1983-85; dir. protocol L.A. County Law Enforcement Conf., 1990; dir. recept. protocol State of Calif. Law Enforcement Conf. of Child Porngraphy, 1990; chmn. So. Calif. Task Force on Pornography, 1989-92; instr. earthquake preparedness and survival Arcadia chpt. ARC, L.A., 1983-85; mem. Community Coordinating Coun., Arcadia, 1983-86; mem. exec. bd. Calif. Utah Women, L.A., 1977-79, 85-86, chmn. L.A. County Commn. Pub. Rels. Portfolio, 1988; exec. dir. Neeley Scholarship Found., 1989-91; coord. planning com. California '96: One Hundred Fifty Years LDS Sequicentennial, 1994—; display coord. L.A. Hills Visitors Ctr., 1994—; lineage rsch. dir. von Neumeyer-Burches & Assocs., 1992—. Recipient Best of Exhibit award Sculptor's West Workshop, 1982, cert. of recognition L.A. County, 1989, cert. appreciation L.A. County, 1990. Mem. Assn. Latter-Day Media Artists (assoc. editor Voice of ALMA 1978-83, exec. bd. 1977-81, chmn. spl. events, 1985-90, internat. bd. govs. fellow 1981-83), Am. Film Inst., LDS Bookseller's Assn., Deseret Bus. and Profl. Assn., Marriott Bus. Mgmt. Soc. (L.A. chpt.), Assn. L.D.S. Pub. Rels. Profls., Nat. Mus. Women in the Arts (charter), Arcadia Tournament of Roses Assn., Arcadia C. of C. (chmn. industry commn. of women's div. 1983-85, mem. exec. bd. 1985-86), Internat. Platform Assn. Republican. Mem. Ch. of Jesus Christ of Latter-Day Saints. Avocations: sculpting, oil painting. Office: 1591 E Temple Way Los Angeles CA 90024-5801

HUTCHINS, CARLEEN MALEY, acoustical engineer, violin maker, consultant, writer, educator; b. Springfield, Mass., May 24, 1911; d. Thomas W. and Grace (Fletcher) Maley; m. Morton A. Hutchins, June 6, 1943; children: William Aldrich, Caroline. AB, Cornell U., 1933; MA, NYU, 1942; DEng (hon.), Stevens Inst. Tech., 1977; DFA (hon.), Hamilton Coll., 1984; DSc (hon.), St. Andrews Presbyn. Coll., 1988; LLD (hon.), Concordia U., Montreal, Que., Can., 1992. Tchr. sci. Woodward Sch., Bklyn., 1934-38, Brearley Sch., N.Y.C., 1938-49; asst. dir., asst. prin. All Day Neighborhood Schs., N.Y.C., 1943-45; sci. cons. Coward McCann, Inc., 1956-65, Girl Scouts Am., 1957-65, Nat. Recreation Assn., 1957-65; permanent sec. Catgut Acoustical Soc., Montclair, N.J., 1962—. Author: Life's Key, DNA, 1961, Moon Moth, 1965, Who Will Drown the Sound, 1972; author (with others): Science Through Recreation, 1964; Editor: (2 vols.) Musical Acoustics, Part I, Violin Family Components, 1975, Musical Acoustics, Part II, Violin Family Functions, 1976, The Physics of Music, 1978, Research Papers in Violin Acoustics 1973-1994, 1995; contbr. articles to profl. jours. in Sci. Am., Jour. of the Acoustical Soc. Am., Physics Today, Am. Viola Soc., Catgut Acoustical Soc. Martha Baird Rockefeller Fund for Music grantee, 1966, 68, 74; Guggenheim fellow, 1959, 61; recipient several spl. citations in music; grantee Nat. Sci. Found., 1971, 74. Fellow AAAS (electorate nominating com. 1974-76, Outstanding Performance in the Scis. award 1994), Audio Engring. Soc. (life), Acoustical Soc. Am. (emeritus, membership com. 1980-86, exec. council 1984-87, medal and awards com. 1987-89, nominating com. 1987-88, Silver Acoustics Medal 1981, tech. com. music. acoustics 1964—, chmn. pres.'s ad hoc com. 1987-88, archives com. 1988—, mem. com. on women 1989—); mem. So. Calif. Violin Makers Assn. (hon.), Viola da Gambda Soc. Am. (hon.), Scandinavian Violin Makers Assn. (hon.), N.Y. Viola Soc., Guild Am. Luthiers, Am. Viola Soc., Violoncello Soc., Amateur Chamber Music Players Assn., Am. Philos. Soc. (award violin acoustics 1968, 81), Sigma Xi, Pi Lambda Theta, Alpha Xi Delta. Clubs: Three O'Clock, Dot & Circle, others. Home and Office: Catgut Acoustical Soc Inc 112 Essex Ave Montclair NJ 07042-4121

HUTCHINS, CYNTHIA BARNES, special education educator; b. Macon, Ga., Apr. 29, 1954; d. Robert O. and Emily Ann (Coody) Barnes; m. Joe Thrash Hutchins, June 15, 1975; children: Joey, Jason. BS in Edn., U. Ga., 1976, MEd, 1981. Cert. tchr., Ga. Tchr. Bethlehem (Ga.) Elem. Sch., 1976-78, Winder (Ga.) Elem. Sch., 1983-85, Auburn (Ga.) Elem. Sch., 1985-92; tchr., staffing coord. Bramlett Elem. Sch., Auburn, 1992—; mem. spl. edn. adv. com., mem. inclusion task force, mentor tchr., tchr. support specialist Barrow County, 1990—. Sunday sch. tchr. Midway Meth. Ch., Carl, Ga., 1975-80, 90-93; leader Boy Scouts Am., Barrow County, 1986-90; active PTO. Mem. Coun. for Exceptional Children, Alpha Delta Kappa. Home: 1165 Bankhead Hwy Winder GA 30680

HUTCHINS, JOAN MORTHLAND, manufacturing executive, farmer; b. Pasadena, Calif., Aug. 8, 1940; d. Andrew and Constance Amelia (Gordon-Grant) Morthland; m. Ian Elcock Bush, Sept. 16, 1967 (div. 1972); children: Andrew Elcock, Georgia Ramsay; m. Warren Clifton Hutchins, Feb. 23, 1973; children: Alan Stewart, Paul Morthland. AB, Radcliffe Coll., 1961; hon. degree, Royal Coll. Music, London, 1979; AAS, SUNY, Farmingdale, 1985. Jr. mathematician Shell Devel. Co. (Shell Oil), Emeryville, Calif., 1961-63; mathematician Corp. for Econ. and Indsl. Rsch., London, 1964-65; mgmt. cons. McKinsey & Co., N.Y.C., 1965-67, investment mgr. family accounts, 1974-86; v.p. devel. Compotite Corp., L.A., 1985-87, pres., 1987-89, pres., chief exec. officer, 1989—; pres., chief exec. officer MBH Farms, Inc., Elizaville, N.Y., 1986—. Editor McKinsey & Co. Mgmt. Scis. News Bull., 1965-67; contbr. articles to profl. jours. Mem. bd. overseers Harvard U., Cambridge, Mass. 1994—, mem. overseers vis. com. athletic dept., 1986-91; pres. Harvard-Radcliffe Club of L.I., 1988-90; dir., v.p. Royal Music Found., N.Y.C., 1978—; trustee Bowdoin Coll. Summer Music Festival, Brunswick, Maine, 1978-88, L.I. Biol. Assn., Cold Spring Harbor, N.Y., 1986-88. Mem. Am. Nat. Standards Inst. (nat. waterproofing standards com. 1988—), Harvard U. Alumni Assn. (bd. dirs. 1990-93). Home: 8 Seawanhaka Pl Oyster Bay NY 11771-1629 Office: Compotite Corp 355 Glendale Blvd Los Angeles CA 90026-5032

HUTCHINS, KAREN LESLIE, psychotherapist; b. Denver, Sept. 9, 1943; d. Kimball Frederick and Bonnie Illa (Small) H.; divorced; 1 child, Alec Klinghoffer. BA, U. Denver, 1965; MA, George Washington U., 1972. Lic. profl. counselor clin. hypnotherapist; cert. chem. dependency specialist. Tchr. Washington D.C. Sch., 1966-70; asst. housing adminstr. George Washington U., Washington, 1970-72; counselor/instr. No. Va. C.C., Annandale, Va., 1972-77, Austin (Tex.) C.C., 1977-80; co-owner Hearts Day Care, Austin, 1980-81; supr./therapist MaryLee Resdl. Treatment, Austin, 1981-82; child protective svc. worker Dept. Human Resources, Austin, 1982-84; probation officer Adult Probation Travis County, Austin, 1984-90; lead therapist Cottonwood Treatment Ctrs., Bastrop, Tex., 1990-91; psychotherapist Austin, 1991—. Author conf. presentation: Beyond Survival, 1990-92, Why Me? vs. Spirtuality, 1993, Integrating the Wounded Soul, 1994, Ritually Abused Children, 1994. Vol. trainer Hotline, Austin, 1993—. Mem. Am. Counseling Assn., Tex. Counseling Assn. Democrat. Jewish. Office: Cicada Recovery Svcs 3004 S 1st St Austin TX 78704-6373

HUTCHINS, KELLY, healthcare management vocational consultant; b. Wilmington, Del., Jan. 23, 1964; d. Roy Austin and Irby Ruth (Whitehurst) H. BA in Psychology, N.C. State U., 1986; MEd in Counselor Edn., Miss. State U., 1990, PhD candidate, 1992-93. Cert. rehab. counselor. Intern The Women's Ctr., Raleigh, N.C., 1984-85; elem. supr. It's Academic Preschool, Cary, N.C., 1986; instr. Roanoke Chowan Tech. Inst., Ahoskie, N.C., 1986-87; practicum student Miss. Vocat. Rehab., Starkville, Miss., 1989; vocat. evaluator I Miss. Vocat. Rehab., Columbus, Miss., 1990; vocat. evaluator II Miss. Vocat. Rehab., Starkville, Miss., 1990-92; grad. asst. Career Devel. Project, Miss. State, 1992-93; personal care attendant Gulfport, Miss., 1993-94; vocat. cons. Crawford & Co., Healthcare Mgmt., Gulfport, Miss., 1993—; rehab. cons. Sims and Assocs., Jackson, Miss., 1991-93; univ. supr. group and individual supervision for Master's level rehab. and cmty. counseling students Miss. State U., 1991-93, instr., 1992. Psychology dept. rep. to Edn. Coun., N.C. State U., 1985-86; fin. chmn. Carolinas Psychology Conf., Raleigh, N.C., 1986; sec. CESA, 1989-90, pres., Fall 1990; mem. Mayor's Com. on Disability Awareness, Starkville, 1991-93. Named Counselor Edn. Dept. Outstanding Master's Student, Miss. State U., 1990-91, Woman of Achievement by Gulfport Bus. and Profl. Women, 1994—. Mem. Am. Counseling Assn., Am. Rehab. Counseling Assn., Nat. Rehab. Assn., Rehab. Assn. of Miss. Home: 1916 2nd St # 1 Gulfport MS 39501-2122 Office: Crawford & Co 951 Vision Oaks Blvd Ste 1 Gulfport MS 39507-3818

HUTCHINSON, ANN, program coordinator; b. East Stroudsburg, Pa., May 15, 1950; d. David Ellis and Susie (Ingalls) H.; m. Paul Harrison McAllister, Jan. 2, 1986. BS in Vocat. Edn., Fla. Internat. U., 1985; MBA, Pepperdine U., 1990. Cert. advanced vocat. tchr., Fla. Motorcycle technician Ft. Lauderdale, Fla., 1973-78, machinist, 1978-79; instr., motorcycle tech. Sheridan Vocat. Tech. Sch., Hollywood, Fla., 1979-85; adminstr., tng. program Am. Honda Motorcycle Div., Torrance, Calif., 1985-86, curriculum developer motorcycles svc. tech., 1986-90, coll. program coord., 1990—; chmn. high tech. acad. steering coms. Pasadena (Calif.) United Sch. Dist., 1991—. Builder, supporter Fla. Sheriff's Youth Ranches, 1988—. Recipient State of Ky. Colonel award, 1990. Mem. Am. Motorcycle Assn., Am. Vocat. Assn., ASTD, Vocat. Indsl. Clubs Am. (cochmn. motorcycle tech. com. 1988-90, automotive nat. tech. com. 1990—, advisor Hollywood, Fla. 1979-85), ASCD, Toastmasters Internat. Office: Am Honda Motor Co Inc 1919 Torrance Blvd Torrance CA 90501-2722

HUTCHINSON, BARBARA WINTER, middle school educator; b. Pitts., Dec. 20, 1952; d. Raymond Francis and Dorothy (Kunkel) Winter; m. Matthew Hutchinson, June 8, 1973; children: Matthew Martin, Jennifer Elizabeth. BA, Westminster Coll., 1974. Cert. tchr., Pa. Tchr. Shaler Area Sch. Dist., Glenshaw, Pa., 1975-84; tchr. North Allegheny Sch. Dist., Pitts., 1984—, staff devel. leader, 1991—; mem. dist. adv. coun. North Allegheny Sch. Dist., Pitts., 1993—, mem. prof. issues com., 1993—; presenter coop. learning workshops. Author: Primary Assistance, 1979, History of the Avonworth School District, 1990; co-author curriculum materials. Mem. Cmty. Presbyn. Ch. Ben Avon, Pa., 1976—; pres., program dir. Ben Avon Area Hist. Assn., 1988—; bd. dirs., sec., program chair Avon Club Found., 1990-93; mem. Ben Avon Centennial Com., 1990-93; co-leader local troop Girl Scouts U.S., 1991-92; bd. dirs. Sacred Heart Sch., Pitts., 1991-92. Mem. Am. Fedn. Tchrs., North Allegheny Fedn. Tchrs. (mem. exec. coun. 1992—), Pa. Fedn. Tchrs., Kappa Delta Pi. Home: PO Box 93 105 Dogwood Ln Connoquenessing PA 16027 Office: Marshall Middle Sch 5145 Wexford Run Rd Wexford PA 15090-7458

HUTCHINSON, BRENDA LAVONNE, county official; b. L.A., Dec. 1, 1954; d. Theodore and Charleszette (Wingate) Collins; m. Roscoe Carl Hutchinson, Dec. 16, 1975 (div. Oct. 1982); children: LaToya N., Jason D., Bryce D. BA, Calif. State U., Long Beach, 1978, MPA, 1982; postgrad., U. La Verne, Calif., 1991—. Cert. network adminstr. Student affairs asst. U. So. Calif., L.A., 1978-81, student affairs counselor, 1981, adminstr. acad. standards, 1981-84, mgr. petitions dept., 1984-86; acad. and admissions counselor Nat. U., Westminster, Calif., 1987-88; prin. student affairs officer Drew U. Medicine and Sci., L.A., 1987-88, dir. student svcs., 1988-91; records mgr. County of Riverside, Calif., 1991—; founder, owner Promoters Acad. Success, Riverside, 1991—; lectr. II, Calif. State U., Dominguez Hills, 1982-83; instr. L.A. C.C. Dist., 1983-86; adj. instr. Drew U. Coll. Allied Health, 1987-88, clin. instr., 1988-91. Scholar L.A. Times, 1972. Mem. ASPA, Assn. Records Mgrs. and Adminstrs. (session monitor internat. conf. 1993), Western Govtl. Rsch. Assn., County Clk. Assn. Calif., AAUW.

HUTCHINSON, ELEANOR LOUISE, nurse; b. Mpls., Nov. 9, 1928; d. Paul Carl Theodore and Amanda Marie (Doell) Ewert; R.N., Swedish Hosp., Mpls., 1951; B.S. in Nursing Edn., U. Minn., 1956; m. Richard Westervelt Hutchinson, Mar. 6, 1965; children—David Henry, Susan Elizabeth. Instr., clin. supr. pediatrics Hennepin County Gen. Hosp., Mpls., 1956-60; supr. pediatric and young adult unit Fairview Hosps., Mpls., 1961-67; dir. nursing, staff devel. coordinator Indianola (Iowa) Long-Term Care Facility, 1973-80; DON Madison County Meml. Hosp., Winterset, Iowa, 1980-92; DON The Village, 1992—. Mem. Nat. Nurses Assn., Nat. League Nursing, AAUW, U. Minn. Alumni Ass., Koinonia Group. Presbyterian. Club: Order Eastern Star. Home: PO Box 397 Indianola IA 50125-0397 Office: 1203 N E St Indianola IA 50125-1117

HUTCHINSON, JANET LOIS, historical society administrator; b. Washington, May 2, 1917; d. Lewis Orrin and Gertrude Elizabeth Hutchinson; divorced; 1 child, Jefferson Troy Siebert. Grad., So. Sem. and Jr. Coll., Buena Vista, Va., 1936; student, N.Y. Sch. Expression, 1923-30, Christine Dobbins Sch. Dance; studied with, Maude Adams, Clare Tree Major, 1934-35. Owner Broadlawn Inn Art Gallery, Camden, Maine, 1955-64; dir. Old Merchants House Mus., N.Y.C., 1962-63, Hist. Soc. Martin County, Stuart, Fla., 1965-91, Elliott Mus., Stuart, 1965-91; dir. House of Refuge Mus., Stuart, 1965-91, dir. emeritus, 1991—; pres., editl. cons. Hutchinson/Paige, Stuart, 1991—. Author: Tiny Timid's Christmas Wish, 1953, The History of Martin County, 1975; host: (TV interview show) Chronicle. Active Nat. Hist. Preservation Soc., Nat. History Soc., Fla. History Soc.; bd. dirs. Pioneer Occupationa Ctr. for Handicapped, St. Michael's Pvt. Sch.; adv. bd. St. Joseph's Coll. and Fla. Inst. of Tech. Named Woman of Yr., AAUW, 1975. Mem. DAR (Halpatiokee chpt.), Antique Car Assn., Smithsonian Instn., Nat. Soc. Lit. and Arts, Nat. Pen Women (hon. mem.), Salmaqundi Club, Nat. Arts Club. Home: 1023 NW Spruce Ridge Dr Stuart FL 34994-9513

HUTCHINSON, LESLIE E, state legislator, fiscal programs manager, consultant; b. Balt., Oct. 14, 1961; d. P. David Hutchinson and J. Leslie (Wilson) Duer; 1 child, Brent David. Student, Essex Community Coll., 1979-82, Villa Julie Coll., 1981-82, Johns Hopkins U., 1984—. V.p. Family Days, Inc., Balt., 1982; asst. clinic coordinator Johns Hopkins U., Balt., 1983-84, adminstrv. asst., 1984-85, budget coordinator, 1985-86; fiscal programs mgr. Balt. County Govt. Criminal Justice Coordinator's Office, Balt., 1986—; mem. Md. Ho. of Reps., Annapolis; cons. Ctr. for Hosp. Fin. and Mgmt. Johns Hopkins U., Balt., 1986-87, Plake Properties, Inc., Balt., 1987—. Mem. Dean's Ad Hoc Com. on Status of Women, Johns Hopkins U., 1985; adv. com. United Way of Johns Hopkins U., 1985-86; exec. dir. Family Day '87, Balt. 1987; campaign coordinator for United Way, Criminal Justice Coordinator's Office, 1987; mem. Am. Council of Young Polit. Leaders, Washington, 1987; treas. Hutchinson Com. for Good Govt., Hutchinson for Senate Com., Balt.,1987—; sec. Balt. County Young Dems., 1987-88; v.p. programs Maryland Young Dems., 1987-88; elected mem. Md. Dem. State Cen. Com., 1986-1990. Named Outstanding Young Dem. of Yr., 1987. Methodist. Office: Md Ho of Reps State Capitol Annapolis MD 21401*

HUTCHINSON, MARTHA LUCLARE, pathologist; b. Alton, Ill., Oct. 26, 1941; d. Elmer Frank and LuClare (Hall) H.; m. Marshall Edward Kadin, June 15, 1980. BS, Iowa State U., 1963; PhD, Purdue U., 1970; MD, Case Western Res. U., 1974. Intern Cleve. Met. Gen. Hosp., 1974-75; resident U. Calif., San Francisco, 1975-77, U. Wash., Seattle, 1977-79; asst. prof. Purdue U., West Lafayette, Ind., 1970, U. Wash., Seattle, 1979-84; assoc. prof. pathology Tufts U., Boston, 1984—; dir. cytopathology New Eng. Med. Ctr. Hosps., Boston, 1984—. Co-investigator devel. and testing of automated devices to facilitate cytology (pathology) diagnosis, 1986—. NIH grantee, 1986, 89, 92. Mem. AMA, Am. Soc. Clin. Pathology, Coll. Am. Pathologists, Internat. Soc. Analytical Cytology, Internat. Acad. Pathology, Am. Soc. Cytology, Internat. Soc. Analytical Cytology. Home: 103 Clinton Rd Brookline MA 02146-5812 Office: New Eng Med Ctr 750 Washington St Boston MA 02111-1533

HUTCHINSON, SHARON MARKHAM, instructional technology consultant; b. Evansville, Ind., Mar. 17, 1948; d. Henry Evans and Margie (VanCleve) Markham; m. David Lee Hutchinson, May 31, 1969; children: Jennifer, Clare. BS, Ind. State U., 1971; MA, U. Louisville, 1974; postgrad., Murray State U., 1974-78, U. Ky., 1986-87, 89-90. Cert. elem. edn. tchr., spl. edn. tchr., instrnl. supr., elem. prin., computer applications tchr., Ky. Tchr. Jefferson County Bd. Edn., Louisville, 1971-74, Ctrl. City (Ky.) Bd. Edn., 1974-76; tchr. Christian County Bd. Edn., Hopkinsville, Ky., 1976-86, dir. spl. edn., 1987-89, tchr., 1990-94; instructional tech. cons., Dept. Edn. State of Ky., Frankfort, 1994—; mem. steering com. Prism Project, Frankfort, Ky., 1992—; computer lab. dir. Gov.'s Scholars Program, Frankfort, 1987-90; presenter at confs. Recipient Young Career Woman award Bus. and Profl. Women, 1974. Mem. AAUW, P.E.O., Delta Kappa Gamma, Phi Delta Kappa.

HUTCHINSON, VIRGINIA NETTLES, librarian; b. Richmond, Va., Feb. 7, 1936; d. Joseph and Virginia (Davies) Nettles; m. John Michael Robin H., Oct. 3, 1959; children: Catherine Pierce, Peter Anthony. BA in English Lit., Mary Washington Coll., 1958. Librarian D.C. Pub. Library, Washington, 1958-59, 66-67; asst. to communications cons. Govt. Employees Ins. Co., Washington, 1973-78, librarian, 1978—. Mem. ALA, ASTD, Am. Mgmt. Assn., Soc. for Human Resources Mgmt., Spl. Librs. Assn. Home: 113 Hesketh St Chevy Chase MD 20815-4222 Office: Govt Employees Ins Co Goodwin Learning Ctr GEICO Pla Washington DC 20076

HUTCHISON, DEBORAH L., critical care nurse; b. Manhattan, Kans., Jan. 8, 1953; d. Patrick J. Sr. and Charlene S. (Baughman) Donnellan; m. James C. Hutchison III, Aug. 7, 1981; children: Todd, Jason, Tommy, Cynthia, Susan, Melissa. Diploma, St. John's Sch. Nursing, 1989; BS in Psychology cum laude, S.W. Mo. State U., 1983, MS in Biology, 1986. RN; cert. critical care. Grad. teaching asst. S.W. Mo. State U., Springfield; burn technician St. John's Hosp., Springfield, nurse, surg. intensive care unit. Mem. Am. Assn. Critical Care Nurses.

HUTCHISON, DEBORAH VIRGINIA, public health nurse, medical/surgical nurse; b. Atlanta, Mar. 24. AS in Nursing, Ga. State U., 1979. RN, Ga.; cert. med./surg. nurse. Staff nurse newborn nursery Grady Hosp., Atlanta, 1971-84, med./surg. staff nurse, 1988—; staff nurse geriatrics VA Med. Ctr., Atlanta, 1984-85; personal care coord. Fulton County Dept. Health, Atlanta, 1985-86; staff nurse substance abuse Community Psychiat. Ctrs. Parkwood Hosp., Atlanta, 1989-90; sr. staff nurse Govt. of Ga., Atlanta, 1986—, Cobb County Health Dept., Austell, Ga.; med.-surg. nurse Henry W. Grady Meml. Hosp. Mem. NAACP, Nat. League Nurses, Nat. Assn. Practical Nurse Edn., Ga. Nurses Assn. (med.-surg. coun.). Mem. AME Ch.

HUTCHISON, ELIZABETH MAY, nurse; b. Broomfield, Colo., Apr. 14, 1924; d. Percy William and Frances May (Cram) Marion; m. James Donald Hutchison, Dec. 9, 1945; children: John William, Daniel James, Janet May Morrell, Ronald Raymond. RN, U. Denver, 1945. Polio staff nurse Children's Hosp., Denver, 1945-53; home care staff nurse Weld County Health Dept., Greeley, Colo., 1970-73; community health coord. for adult health Boulder (Colo.) County Health Dept., 1973-87. Author: Adult Health Conference Protocol, 1985; editorial staff: Lafayette History Book, 1989. Mem., historian, co-dir. Lafayette Miners Mus., Lafayette Hist. Soc., 1978-95. Recipient Recognition award Boulder County, 1981, Appreciation award Boulder City-County Health Dept., 1976. Mem. Non-Practicing and Part-time Nurses Assn., DAR. Democrat. Methodist. Home: 778 Applewood Dr Lafayette CO 80026-8908 Office: Lafayette Miners' Mus 108 E Simpson Lafayette CO 80026

HUTCHISON, GENA LYNN LASSMANN, human resources administrator; b. Kingsville, Tex., July 25, 1963; d. Richard Allan and Marjorie Jean (Miller) Lassmann; m. Michael C. Hutchison Jr., Feb. 1, 1986 (dec. June 1993). BBA in Bus. Stats., U. Tex., 1985; MBA in Mgmt., U. Houston, 1990. Sales compensation analyst Variable Annuity Life Ins. Co. (VALIC), Houston, 1986-87, sales compensation supr., 1987; sr. compensation analyst Am. Gen. Corp., Houston, 1987-88, compensation mgr., 1988-90, compensation/human resources info sys. mgr., 1990-92, human resources info. sys. project leader, 1992-93, human resources info. sys. mgr., 1994—. Mem. Am. Compensation Assn., Human Resources System Profls. Episcopalian. Office: Am Gen Corp 2929 Allen Pky # A39 03 Houston TX 77019-2119

HUTCHISON, JANE CAMPBELL, art history educator, researcher; b. Washington (D.C.), July 20, 1932; d. James Paul and Leone Bailey (Warrick) H. BA fine arts, Western Maryland Coll., 1954; MA art history, Oberlin Coll., 1958; PhD art history, U. Wis., 1964. Tech. illustrator/ Dept. Model Basin U.S. Navy, Washington (D.C.), 1954-56; rsch libr. Toledo Mus. of Art, 1957-59; teaching asst. U. Wis., Madison, 1959-60,61-63; vis. asst. prof. Temple U., Phila., summer 1968; from instr. to assoc. prof. U. Wis., Madison, 1964—, prof., 1975—, dept. chmn., 1977-80, 92-93; cons. NEH, Washington (D.C.), 1972-77, Inst. Internat. Edn., N.Y.C., 1977,82,89, Nat. Gallery of Art, Washington, 1982-83, Rijksmuseum, Amsterdam, 1984, Cin. Art Mus., 1990—. Author: Master of the Housebook, 1972, Early German Artists, vol. I, 1980, vol. II, 1981, vol. III, 1991, Albrecht Dürer: A Biography, 1990, German edit., 1994. Grad. fellow Oberlin Coll., 1955-57, fellow U. Wis., 1959-60, 61-63, Fulbright fellow Rijksuniversiteit Utrecht, Netherlands, 1960-61, rsch. grantee NEH, Germany, 1982, German Acad. Exch. Svc., Germany, summer 1989; Grant in aid Am. Coun. Learned Soc., Amsterdam, 1984; recipient Alumni award Western Md. Coll. Trustees, 1987. Mem. AAUP (pres. Madison chpt. 1979-81), Internat. Coun. Mus., Am. Assn. Mus., Medieval Acad. Am., Coll. Art Assn., Univ. Club U. Wis. (bd. dirs. 1976-80, pres. 1980), Wis. Assn. Scholars (v.p. Madison chpt. 1990—), Midwest Art History Soc. (pres. 1983-85), Historians of Netherlandish Art (sec.-treas. 1995—), Print Coun. Am. Home: 2261 Regent St Madison WI 53705-5321 Office: U Wis Dept Art History 800 University Ave Madison WI 53706-1479

HUTCHISON, KAY BAILEY, senator; b. Galveston, TX, July 22, 1943; d. Allan and Kathryn Bailey; m. Ray Hutchison. BA, U. Tex., 1992, LLB, 1967. Bar: Tex. 1967. TV news reporter Houston, 1969-71, pvt. practice law, 1969-74; press sec. to Anne Armstrong, 1971; vice chmn. Nat. Transp. Safety Bd., 1976-78; asst. prof. U. Tex., Dallas, 1978-79; sr. v.p., gen. counsel Republic of Tex. Corp., Dallas, 1979-81; of counsel Hutchison, Boyle, Brooks & Fisher, Dallas, 1981-91; mem. Tex. Ho. of Reps., 1972-76; elected treas. of Tex., 1990, U.S. senator from Tex., 1993—. Fellow Am. Bar Found., Tex. Bar Found.; mem. ABA, State Bar of Tex., Dallas Bar Assn., U. Tex. Law Alumni Assn. (pres. 1985-86). Republican.

HUTCHISON, MICHELE VERONICA, accountant; b. Phila., July 28, 1957; d. Patrick William and Jane Marie (des Garennes) Gagliano; m. Andrew F. Hutchison, Dec. 4, 1989; children: Steven M., Amanda J. AS magna cum laude, Montgomery County C.C., 1982; BBA magna cum laude, Temple U., 1988. Cert. mgmt. acct. Control clk. North Penn Hosp., Lansdale, Pa., 1975-78, gen. ledger clk., 1978-80, acctg. supr., 1980—, controller, 1994. Vol. Cmty. Accounts, Phila.; mem. devel. bd. Lansdale Cath. H.S., 1992—. Mem. Inst. Mgmt. (nat. bd. dirs., treas. Mid. Atlantic coun. 1993-94, pres. Nortn Pa. chpt. 1992-93, dir. meetings 1991-92, dir. acad. rels. 1990-91, dir. cert. mgmt. accts. programs 1989-90), Beta Gamma Sigma, Golden Key Nat. Honor Soc. Republican. Roman Catholic. Office: North Penn Hosp 100 Medical Campus Dr Lansdale PA 19446

HUTCHISON, PAT, nurse, administrator; b. Omaha, Mar. 4, 1943; d. Earl Edward and Sylvia Lorraine (Kronen) Moore; m. James M. Hutchison, June 23, 1963; children—Michael, Danny. Diploma in nursing, St. Joseph's Sch. Nursing, 1968; student Central Ariz. Coll., 1976-82; BS in Health Service Adminstrn., U. Phoenix, 1983; BS in Nursing, U. Phoenix, 1988. R.N.; cert. in advanced cardiac life support, Ariz. Nurse Armish Maag Hosp., Teheran, Iran, 1969-71; supr. Hoemako Hosp., Casa Grande, Ariz., 1973-84; asst. dir. nursing Casa Grande Regional Med. Ctr., 1984-86, nursing supr., 1986—. Nursing chmn. ARC, Casa Grande, 1986—, also bd. dirs., instr. disaster tng., 1982—; instr. cardiopulmonary resuscitation Am. Heart Assn., Casa Grande, 1978—. Recipient Care award Ariz. Hosp. Assn., 1984, Service and Appreciation award Bus. and Profl. Women's Assn., 1984. Mem. Ariz. Nurses in Mgmt., Emergency Nurses Assn. Democrat. Roman Catholic. Avocations: traveling; camping; boating; reading. Home: 1308 N Center Ave Casa Grande AZ 85222-3408 Office: Casa Grande Regional Med Ctr 1800 E Florence Blvd Casa Grande AZ 85222-5303

HUTTENSTINE, MARIAN LOUISE, journalism educator; b. Bloomsburg, Pa., Jan. 26, 1940; d. Ralph Benjamin and Marian Louise (Engler) H. BS, Bloomsburg State U., 1961, MEd, 1966; postgrad., Rutgers U., 1962-63; PhD, U. N.C., 1985. High sch. English & journalism tchr., dept. chmn., 1961-66; asst. prof. Lock Haven (Pa.) U., 1966-73, assoc. prof. English, 1973-74; teaching asst., lectr. Sch. Journalism, U. N.C., Chapel Hill, 1974-76; cons., dir. Diener & Assocs., Research Triangle Park, N.C., 1975-86; asst. prof. journalism, Coll. Comm. U. Ala., Tuscaloosa, 1977-93; assoc. prof. comm. Coll. Comm. and Fine Arts Jacksonville State Univ., 1993—. cons. various publs., Ala., 1977—. Contbr. papers to profl. lit. Adult leader, vol. worker Episc. Ch., 1994—. NDEA fellow, Newspaper Fund fellow Rutgers U., 1962-63. Mem. ACLU, NAFE, Assn. Edn. in Journalism and Mass Communication, Nat. Fedn. Press Women, Ala. Media Profls. (Communicator of Yr. 1994), Kappa Tau Alpha, Ala. SPJ Club. Home: 494 Fomby's Ferry Rd Ohatchee AL 36271-5146 Office: Jacksonville State Univ Coll Comm and Fine Arts Jacksonville AL 36265-9982

HUTTNER, MARIAN ALICE, library administrator; b. Mpls., Apr. 10, 1920; d. Frederick August and Hilda Christina (Anderson) Huttner; m. Russell R. Christensen, Apr. 15, 1950 (div. 1961). BA summa cum laude, Macalester Coll., 1941; BS in Library Science, U. Minn., 1942. Jr. libr. U. Minn., Mpls., 1941-42, libr., 1942-43, sr. libr., 1943-44, prin. libr. serials, 1944-46, prin. libr. archives, 1946-53; serials libr. Hamline U., St. Paul, 1954-56; adult libr. Mpls. Pub. Libr., 1956-60, rsch. asst., 1961-64, adult group cons., 1964-67, head sociology dept., 1967-69, head main libr. subject depts., 1969-75; dep. dir. Cleve. Pub. Libr., 1976-85, interim dir., 1986; automated systems cons., 1987—; adj. prof. Case Western Res. U., 1983-84; lectr. Kent State U., 1982-83. Author: Program for Branches of the Cleveland Public Library, 1976; contbr. articles to profl. jours. Mem. ALA (reference services com. 1973-76), Minn. Library Assn. (sec. 1961-67), Ohio Library Assn. (awards com. 1984-85). Democrat. Presbyterian. Home: 8102 Highwood Dr B218 Bloomington MN 55438-1047

HUTTON, DONNA MARIE, civilian military employee; b. Oak Ridge, Tenn., July 7, 1953; d. Gerald Lincoln and Virginia Hewitt H. BA in Psychology, Cath. U. Am., 1975, postgrad., 1978-80; MS in Contract and Acquisition Mgmt., Fla. Inst. Tech., 1993. Info. specialist U.S. Office Pers. Mgmt., Washington, 1981-85; contracting officer U.S. Army/Walter Reed Army Med. Ctr., Washington, 1985—, chief svcs. br., 1994—; trainer, tchr. in related bus. fields U.S. Army. Youth counselor, psychol. counselor Montgomery County Govt., 1970-85. Mem. Nat. Contract Mgmt. Assn., Psi Chi. Roman Catholic. Office: Directorate of Contracting Walter Reed Army Med Ctr Washington DC 20307

HUTTON, LAUREN (MARY LAURENCE HUTTON), actress, model; b. Charleston, S.C., 1944; d. Laurence Hutton. Student, U. Fla., Sophia Newcombe Coll. Fashion model, 1960—. Actress: (feature films) Paper Lion, 1968, Little Fauss and Big Halsey, 1970, Pieces of Dreams, 1970, The Gambler, 1974, Gator, 1976, Welcome to L.A., 1977, Viva Knievall, 1977, A Wedding, 1978, American Gigolo, 1980, Zorro, the Gay Blade, 1981, Paternity, 1981, Lassiter, 1984, Once Bitten, 1985, A Certain Desire, 1986, Malone, 1987, Guilty As Charged, 1991, My Father, The Hero, 1994; (TV movies) Someone's Watching Me, 1978, Institute for Revenge, 1979, The Cradle Will Rock, 1983, Starflight: The Plane that Couldn't Land, 1983, Scandal Sheet, 1985, Timestalkers, 1987, Perfect People, 1988, Fear, 1990; (TV series) The Rhinemann Exchange, 1977, (stage prodn.) Extremities. Office: Creative Artists Agy 1888 Century Park E Suite 1400 Los Angeles CA 90067 also: Ford Models Inc 344 E 59th St New York NY 10022-1570*

HUVAL, BARBARA JANE, English language professional educator; b. New Orleans, La., Nov. 20, 1936; d. Barnie Perry and Hazel Dorothy (Saleeby) Bobbitt; m. John C. Huval, Sept. 11, 1955 (dec.); children: Bonnie Dawn, Bambi Diana, John Phillip. BA, Lamar U., 1978, MA, 1980; PhD, Rice U., 1985. Tchr. typing, shorthand Port Arthur (Tex.) Coll., 1954-56; assoc. prof. English Lamar U., Port Arthur, 1983—, dept. head liberal arts, 1987—; coord. inmate instrn., 1994—. Bd. dirs. Port Arthur Coun. Camp Fire, 1980—, Port Arthur Comty. Retirement Home, 1988—. Office: Lamar U Port Arthur PO Box 310 Port Arthur TX 77641-0310

HUXLEY, LAURA ARCHERA, humanist, psychologist, writer; b. Turin, Italy, Nov. 2, 1914; came to U.S., 1937; d. Felice and Fede (Bellini) A.; m. Aldous Huxley, Mar. 19, 1956 (dec. Nov. 1963). Studies in violin and music, C. Flesh, Berlin, G. Enesco, Paris; diploma in Prof. of Music, Conservatory of St. Cecilia, Rome, 1929; student, Curtis Inst., Phila., 1938-40; D of Human Svcs. (hon.), Sierra U., 1981. Concert violinist Europe and U.S., 1927-39; violinist L.A. Philharm. Orch., 1944-47; free-lance assoc. producer documentary films U.S.; film editor RKO, L.A., 1948-51; pvt. practice psychotherapy L.A., 1952-70; lectr. Seminarist Human Potential Movement, 1964—; founder, dir. Our Ultimate Investment, L.A., 1978—, an orgn. for the nurturing of the possible human. Author: You Are Not the Target, 1963, This Timeless Moment, 1969, rev., 1991, Between Heaven and Earth, 1974, rev., 1991, One a Day Reason to be Happy, 1986, rev., 1991; (with Dr. Piero Ferrucci) The Child of Your Dreams, 1987, rev., 1992. Recipient Maharishi award World Govt. of the Age of Enlightenment, 1981; honoree UN, NYC, 1978, World Health Fedn. for Devel. and Peace, 1990, Maharishi Found. Mem. Authors Guild, Assn. for Humanistic Psychology, Assn. for Transpersonal Psychology, The Huxley Inst. Address: Our Ultimate Investment PO Box 1868 Los Angeles CA 90028

HUXTABLE, ADA LOUISE, architecture critic; b. N.Y.C.; d. Michael Louis and Leah (Rosenthal) Landman; m. L. Garth Huxtable. AB magna cum laude, Hunter Coll.; postgrad., Inst. Fine Arts, NYU; hon. degrees, Harvard U., Yale U., NYU, Washington U., U. Mass., Oberlin Coll., Miami U., R.I. Sch. Design, U. Pa., Radcliffe Coll., Oberlin Coll., Smith Coll., Skidmore Coll., Md. Inst., Mt. Holyoke Coll., Trinity Coll., LaSalle U., Pace Coll., Pratt Inst., Colgate U., Hamilton U., Williams Coll., Rutgers U., Finch Coll., Emerson Coll., C.W. Post Coll. at L.I. U., Cleve. State U., Bard Coll., Fordham U., Parsons Sch. Design, Mass. Coll. Art. Asst. curator architecture and design The Museum of Modern Art, N.Y.C., 1946-50; Fulbright fellow for advanced study in architecture and design Italy, 1950, 52; free-lance writer, contbg. editor to Progressive Architecture and Art in America, 1950-63; architecture critic N.Y. Times, N.Y.C., 1963-82; mem. editorial bd. N.Y. Times, 1973-82; Cook lectr. in Am. instns. U. Mich., 1977; Hitchcock lect. U. Calif.-Berkeley, 1982; corp. vis. com. Harvard U. Grad. Sch. Design, Sch. Visual and Environ. Arts; bd. dirs. N.Y. Landmarks Conservancy; mem. adv. bd. Am. Trust Brit. Libr.; bd. dirs. Ctr. Study Am. Architecture Columbia U.; archtl. cons. Nat. Gallery, London, J. Paul Getty Trust, L.A., San Francisco Pub. Libr., Mus. Contemporary Art, Chgo. Author: Pier Luigi Nervi, 1960, Classic New York, 1964, Will They Ever Finish Bruckner Boulevard?, 1970, Kicked a Building Lately?, 1976, The Tall Building Artistically Reconsidered: The Search for a Skyscraper Style, 1985, Goodbye History, Hello Hamburger 1986, Architecture Anyone? 1986. Recipient 1st Pulitzer prize for disting. criticism, 1970, Spl. award Nat. Trust for Historic Preservation, 1971, Archtl. Criticism medal AIA, 1969, medal for lit. Nat. Arts Club, 1971, Diamond Jubilee medallion City N.Y., 1973, Mayor's Cultural award, 1984, Woman of Yr. award AAUW, 1974, Sec.'s award for conservation U.S. Dept. Interior, 1976, Thomas Jefferson medal U. Va., 1977, Archtl. Criticism medal Acad. d' Architecture Française, 1988; Guggenheim fellow for studies in Am. architecture, 1958, MacArthur fellow, 1981-86, Henry Allen Moe prize Humanities Am. Philosophical Soc., 1992. Fellow Am. Acad. Arts and Scis., N.Y. Inst. Humanities, Royal Inst. Brit. Architects (hon.), AAAL; mem. AIA (hon.), Am. Acad. Arts and Letters, Am. Acad. Arts and Scis., Soc. Archtl. Home: 969 Park Ave New York NY 10028-0322

HUYER, ADRIANA, oceanographer, educator; b. Giessendam, The Netherlands, May 19, 1945; arrived in Can., 1950; came to U.S., 1975; d. Jacob Catharinus and Sophia (Van Loon) H.; m. Robert Lloyd Smith. BS, U. Toronto, 1967; MS, Oreg. State U., 1971, PhD, 1974. Scientific officer Marine Scis. Branch, Ottawa, Can., 1967-73; rsch. scientist Marine Environ. Data Svc., Ottawa, Can., 1974-75; rsch. assoc. Oreg. State U., Corvallis, 1975-76, rsch. asst. prof., 1976-79, asst. prof., 1979-80, assoc. prof., 1980-85, prof., 1985—; vis. scientist Csiro Marine Labs, Hobart, Australia, 1988. Contbr. articles to profl. jours. Mem. AAAS, Am. Meterol. Soc., Am. Geophys. Union, Can. Meterol. and Oceanographic Soc., Am. Soc. Limnology and Oceanography. Office: Coll Oceanography Oreg State Univ Corvallis OR 97331

HUYSMAN, ARLENE WEISS, psychologist, educator; b. Phila.; d. Max and Anna (Pearlene) Weiss; B.A., Shaw U., 1973; M.A., Goddard Coll., 1974; Ph.D., Union Inst. Grad., 1980; m. Pedro Camacho; children: Pamela Claire, James David. Actress, dir. Dramatic Workshop, N.Y.C., 1956-68; music and drama critic and columnist Orlando (Fla.) Sentinel Star, 1966-68; psychodramatist Volusia County Guidance Center, Daytona Beach, Fla., 1966-68; free-lance journalist, 1968-70; psychodramatist Psychiat. Inst., Jackson Meml. Hosp., Miami, 1972-77, dir. Adult Day Treatment Center, 1974-77, dir. Lithium Clinic, 1976-77; psychodramatist South Fla. State Hosp., Hollywood, 1971-72; psychotherapy supr., neurosci. program coord. Miami Heart Inst., 1984—, clin. dir. Family Workshop, 1985—, clin. dir. Adult Day Treatment Ctrs., 1987—; founder, dir. Geriatric Adult Day Treatment Ctrs.; adj. asst. prof. Med. Sch., U. Miami, 1976—; adj. prof., Union Inst., 1992—; specialist in B. Polar Disorders, U. Wis., 1980—; mem. adv. panel Fine Arts Council Fla., 1976-77; mem. Fla. Gov.'s Task Force on Marriage and the Family Unit, 1976, 89-90; vol. Rec. for Blind, 1974—. Recipient Best Dirs. award and Best Actress award Fla. Theatre Festival, 1967. Mem. Am. Psychol. Assn., Fla. Psychol. Assn., Dade County Psychol. Assn. (bd. dirs.), Mental Health Assn. Dade County, Internat. Assn. Group Psychotherapy, Union Inst. Grad. Alumni Assn. (bd. dirs., southeastern rep., pres.-elect), Am. Soc. Aging, Am. Assn. Group Psychotherapy and Psychodrama, Moreno Acad., Fedn. Partial Hospitalization Study Groups, World Fedn. Mental Health, Fla. Assn. Practicing Psychologists (bd. dirs., pres. 1987-88, treas. 1990—). Office: Ctr Psychol Growth 3050 Biscayne Blvd Miami FL 33137-4143

HWANG, CORDELIA JONG, chemist; b. N.Y.C., July 14, 1942; d. Goddard and Lily (Fung) Jong; m. Warren C. Hwang, Mar. 29, 1969; 1 child, Kevin. Student Alfred U., 1960-62; BA, Barnard Coll., 1964; M.S., SUNY-Stony Brook, 1969. Rsch. asst. Columbia U., N.Y.C., 1964-66; analytical chemist Veritron West Inc., Chatsworth, Calif., 1969-70; asst. lab. dir., chief chemist Pomeroy, Johnston & Bailey Environ. Engrs., Pasadena, Calif., 1970-76; chemist Met. Water Dist. So. Calif., Los Angeles, 1976-79, rsch. chemist 1980-91, sr. chemist 1992—; mem. Joint Task Group on Instrumental Identification of Taste and Odor Compounds, 1983-85, instr. Citrus Coll., 1974-76; chair Joint Task Group on Disinfection by-products: chlorine, 1990. Mem. Am. Chem. Soc., Am. Water Works Assn. (cert. water quality analyst level 3, Calif.-Nev.), Am. Soc. for Mass Spectometry. Office: Met Water Dist So Calif 700 Moreno Ave La Verne CA 91750-3303

HWANG, MIRIAM, information technology specialist; b. Highland Park, Ill., Dec. 25, 1951; d. Kao and Sheila (Chen) H.; m. Craig Tilbury Jones, Jan. 18, 1986; children: Austin Tilbury, Alexander Hwang. BA with honors, U. Wis., 1974. Programmer Liberty Mut. Ins., Boston, 1977-78; sales rep., sr. cons. Tymshare, N.Y.C., 1978-80; mgr. tech. and mktg. investment group and asset svcs. Citibank, N.Y.C., 1980-81; tech. cons. Info. Builders Inc., N.Y.C., 1981-82; sr. systems analyst, then project leader HBO, N.Y.C., 1982; database mgr. Time Video Info. Svc. Time Inc., N.Y.C., 1982-83, mgr. personal computer tng., 1984-87, mgr. end-user svcs., 1987-89, dir. end-user computing, 1989-92, dir. emerging techs., 1992—. Active Dwight Englewood PTA, Christian Children's Fund. Mem. Symbol Users Group, Microsoft Corp. Users, N.Y. Lotus Notes Users Group. Office: Time Inc 1271 Avenue Of The Americas New York NY 10020-1300

HYATT-SMITH, ANN ROSE, non-profit organization executive, consultant; b. Portchester, N.Y., Sept. 25, 1953; d. David M. and Lenore (Moerschelle) Hyatt; m. Geoffrey D. Smith, June 24, 1984; children: Rachel Elana, Joshua Richard Lev. BA in Lit., State U. Coll., Oneonta, N.Y., 1975; M in Profl. Studies, New Sch. for Social Research, 1986. Asst. to sec.-gen. Israel Interfaith Com., Jerusalem, 1977-79; field rep. United Jewish Appeal/Fedn. Jewish Philanthropies, N.Y.C., 1979-81; asst. v.p. United Way of N.Y.C., 1981-83; dir. devel. Hebrew Arts Sch., Merkin Concert Hall, N.Y.C., 1983-84; asst. dir. devel. St. Vincent's Hosp. and Med. Ctr. N.Y., N.Y.C., 1984-86; program mgr. Bernd Brecher and Assocs., Inc., N.Y.C., 1986-88; pres. Hyatt Smith Assocs., White Plains, N.Y., 1988-91; dir. devel. The Shield Inst., N.Y.C., 1991-95; dir. devel. and alumni rels. Sch. Law, Pace U., White Plains, N.Y., 1995—; adj. faculty New Sch. for Social Research and Learning Alliance. V.p., treas. Village Ind. Dems., N.Y.C., 1985-86. Mem. Nat. Soc. Fund Raising Execs. (advanced cert. fund raising exec.), Assn. Devel. Officers, Planned Giving Group of Greater N.Y., Assn. Healthcare Philanthropy, Women in Fin. Devel. Jewish. Office: Pace U Sch Law 78 N Broadway P306 White Plains NY 10603

HYDE, GERALDINE VEOLA, secondary education educator, retired; b. Berkeley, Calif., Nov. 26, 1926; d. William Benjamin and Veola (Walker) H.; m. Paul Hyde Graves, Jr., Nov. 12, 1949 (div. Dec. 1960); children: Christine M. Graves Klykken, Catherine A. Graves Hackney, Geraldine J. Graves Hansen. BA in English, U. Wash., 1948; BA in Edn., Ea. Wash. U., 1960, MA in Edn., 1962. Cert. tchr. K-16, Wash.; life cert. specialist in secondary edn., Calif. English educator Sprague (Wash.) Consol. Schs., 1960-62, Bremerton (Wash.) Sch. Dist., 1962-63, Federal Way (Wash.) Sch. Dist., 1963-66; English, journalism and Polynesian humanities educator Hayward (Calif.) Unified Sch. Dist., 1966-86. Charter mem. Hist. Hawai'i Found., Honolulu, 1977—; founding mem. The Cousteau Soc., Inc., Norfolk, Va., 1973—; life mem. Hawai'ian Hist. Soc., Honolulu, 1978—; mem. Moloka'i Mus. and Cultural Ctr., Kaunakaka'i, 1986—, Bishop Mus. Assn., Honolulu, 1973—, Mission House Mus., Honolulu, 1994, Bklyn. Hist. Assn., N.Y., 1994, Berkshire Family History Assn., Pittsfield, Mass., 1994, Richville (N.Y.) Hist. Assn., 1994. Mem. Nat. Parks and Conservation Assn., Nature Conservancy of Hawai'i, Smithsonian Inst. (contbg.), Nat. Geog. Soc., Nat. Trust Historic Preservation, USS Constitution Mus., Jr. League Spokane, U. Wash. Alumni Assn. (life), Ea. Wash. U. Alumni Assn. (life). Episcopalian. Home: 306 W Meadowbrook Dr Midland MI 48640-3453 also (winter): PO Box 1598 Kaunakaka'i Moloka'i HI 96748

HYDE, JEANETTE W., ambassador; b. Hamptonville, N.C., June 15, 1938; m. Wallace Nathaniel Hyde. Student, Wake Forest U., 1956-58; BA, Delta State U. English tchr. Greenville, Miss., 1962-63, Iraklion, Crete, 1964; social worker Fayetteville, N.C., 1965-67, court counselor, 1967-71, ptnr., operator women's retail bus., 1971-78; with N.C. Bd. Transportation, 1977-84; founder, bd. dir. Triangle Bank and Trust, Raleigh, N.C., 1987-93; amb. to Barbados, St. Vincent, St. Lucia and Dominica, 1993—; bd. dirs. N.C. Global Transpark. Bd. dirs. N.C. Child Advocacy Inst., Outward Bound of N.C., Capital City Club of Raleigh, Sch. of Social Work, U. N.C.; chair Women's Club of Raleigh. Recipient Outstanding Pub. Svc. award Cumberland County N.C. Mem. Kappa Delta Pi. Office: PO Box 302 FPO AA 34055*

HYDEN, DOROTHY LOUISE, consulting company owner; b. Fort Collins, Colo., July 19, 1948; d. Douglas Stewart and Elizabeth Lenore (Stewart)

Neilson; m. Michael J. Daley, Dec. 27, 1969 (div.); 1 child, Shannon; m. Howard E. Hyden, July 17, 1976; children: Kent Stewart, Tiffany Nicole. BA, U. Calif., Santa Barbara, 1970; MBA, Pepperdine U., 1980. Head tchr. Sawyer Bus. Coll., Anaheim, Calif., 1974-75, admissions rep., 1975-76; mktg. specialist Anthony Schs., Orinda, Calif., 1976-77; adminstrv. dir. Escrow Tng. Ctr., Orinda, Calif., 1977-78; pvt. practice consulting Mpls., 1979-88; exec. v.p., owner Hyden & Hyden, Mpls., 1988—. Mem. ASTD, NAFE, PEN, NEHGS, Soc. Preservation New Eng. Antiquities, Wayland (Mass.) Hist. Soc., Pepperdine U. Alumni Assn., Internat. Platform Assn., Edmond Rice (1638) Assn., Clan MacKay Soc., Littleton Family Assn., Watertown Geneal. Soc., Milwaukee County Geneal. Soc., Wis. State Geneal. Soc. Republican. Episcopalian. Home: 7415 Hyde Park Dr Edina MN 55439-1741

HYLAND, KATHLEEN JEANNE, technology transfer and training program director; b. Hayward, Calif., Nov. 20, 1951; d. Robert Francis and Eileen Frances (Smith) H. BS, U. Tenn., 1974. Elem. sch. tchr. Farragut Hills Sch., Knoxville, Tenn., 1974-85; tng. and devel. specialist Oak Ridge (Tenn.) Associated Univs., 1985-86, sr. tng. and devel. specialist, 1986-88, program mgr., 1988-91, asst. program dir., 1991-92, program dir., 1992—. Author: Training the Occasional Trainer, 1992, (tng. manual) Technology Transfer in the Department of Energy, 1993. Vol. tutor, 1980—. Home: 1924 Marty Cir Knoxville TN 37932

HYLAND, VIRGINIA LING, small business owner; b. North Plainfield, N.J., Sept. 20, 1947; d. James C. and Juliet (Tchou) Ling.; m. Dale J. Hyland, June 7, 1967; children: Devin K., Christopher. Cert. in Ct. Reporting, Tampa Coll., 1975. Dep. ofcl. Conley & Swain, St. Petersburg, Fla., 1975-76; reporter Jud. Reporters, St. Petersburg, 1976-77; reporter, owner Suncoast Reporting Svcs., St. Petersburg, 1977—. Mem. Fla. Court Reporters Assn. (bd. dirs. 1983-85, 87-89, chief examiner 1986-89, mem. coms., v.p. 1994-95), Nat. Court Reporters (chief examiner 1986-89). Democrat. Office: Suncoast Reporting Svcs 501 1st Ave N Ste 508 Saint Petersburg FL 33701-3723

HYMAN, BETTY HARPOLE, technical equipment consultant; b. Jasper, Tex., Nov. 20, 1938; d. Russell Charles and John Francis (Hilton) Harpole; m. Arthur Siegmar Hyman (dec.); children: Norma Sullivan, Eric, Jonathan, Lee Ann; m. Gerald J. Sprute. BA in Psychology, U. Tex., San Antonio, 1979. Spl. project coord. Tex. Stores, San Antonio, 1975-79; communications cons. Southwestern Bell Tel., Midland, Tex. and San Antonio, 1980-82; tech. cons. AT&T, San Antonio, 1983-85, 88—, Intelliserve Corp., Dallas, 1987-88; cons. IMS Group, San Antonio, 1985-87. Mem. devel. com. San Antonio Spl. Olympics, San Antonio Conservation Soc., 1975-94, San Antonio World Affairs Coun., 1985-92, 1994—; bd. dirs S.Tex. Chidren's Habilitation Ctr., San Antonio, 1985-87; mem. Riverfront task force in Asheville. Mem. Am. Bus. Women's Assn. (program com. 1987-88), Tex. Tennis Assn. (ranked player 1976-90), Prime Time Tennis Club (v.p. 1985-86), Blue Ridge Dance Club (pres. 1993-94). Republican. Episcopalian. Home: 14426 Brook Hollow Blvd San Antonio TX 78232-3830 Office: 107 W Nakoma San Antonio TX 78216

HYMAN, ELAINE, artist; b. N.Y.C., Aug. 24, 1925; d. Harry and Dora (Himelstein) Lubart; m. Julian Bennett Hyman, Oct. 18, 1950; children: Steven E., Mona Rubin, Harvey A. BA, NYU, 1945; attended, Syracuse U. Grad. instr. Syracuse (N.Y.) U., 1946-47; trustee Bergen Mus., Paramus, N.J., curator of art, 1985, 86, 87. Solo shows include Adelphi U., 1969, Bodley Gallery, N.Y.C., 1973, 78, 82, Bergen County Mus., 1974, Moore Gallery, Aspen, Colo., 1976; exhibited in group shows at Caravan House, N.Y.C., 1971, World Trade Ctr., N.Y.C., 1978, Lever House, N.Y.C., 1979, 81, Kornbluth Gallery, Fairlawn, N.J., 1984, 85, 88, others; represented in permanent collections Snite Mus., Notre Dame U., Fordham U. Law Ctr., Norfolk (Va.)-Chrysler Mus., also pvt. collections in U.S. and Europe. Mem. Print Club N.Y. (trustee 1993-94). Democrat. Jewish. Home and Office: 281 Barr Ave Teaneck NJ 07666

HYMAN, MARY BLOOM, science education programs coordinator; m. Sigmund M. Hyman, 1947; children: Carol Ann Hyman Williams, Nancy Louise. BS, Goucher Coll., 1971; MS, Johns Hopkins U., 1977. Asst. dir. Edn. Md. Sci. Ctr., Balt., 1976-81, dir. edn., 1981-90; coord. sci. edn. programs, inst. child care edn. programs Loyola Coll., Balt., 1990—; trustee Goucher Coll. Mem. Baltimore County Pub. Schs. Com. for Sch.-Based and Sch.-Linked Child Care. Recipient Disting. Women award Gov.'s Office, Annapolis, Md., 1981; Meritorious Svc. award Johns Hopkins U., 1983; Outstanding Svc. to Sci. Edn. award. Assn. Sci. Dept. Chairmen of Balt. County Pub. Schs., 1989. Mem. Md. Assn. Sci. Tchrs. (bd. dirs.), Md. Math. Coalition, Phi Beta Kappa, Phi Delta Kappa. Home: 10815 Longacre Ln Stevenson MD 21153

HYMAN, PAULA E(LLEN), history educator; b. Boston; d. Sydney Max and Ida Frances (Tatelman) H.; m. Stanley Harvey Rosenbaum, June 7, 1969; children: Judith Hyman Rosenbaum, Adina Hyman Rosenbaum. B.J.Ed., Hebrew Coll., Brookline, Mass., 1966; B.A., Radcliffe Coll., 1968; M.A., Columbia U., 1970, Ph.D., 1975. Asst. prof. Columbia U., N.Y.C., 1974-81; assoc. prof. history Jewish Theol. Sem., N.Y.C., 1981-86, dean Sem., Coll. Jewish Studies, 1981-86; Lady Davis. vis. assoc. prof. Hebrew U. of Jerusalem, 1986; Lucy Moses prof. history Yale U., New Haven, 1986—. Series editor Ind. U. Press. Bloomington, 1982-95; contbg. editor Sh'ma Mag., N.Y.C., 1977—; author: From Dreyfus to Vichy, 1979, The Emancipation of the Jews of Alsace, 1991, Gender and Assimilation in Modern Jewish History, 1995; co-author: The Jewish Woman in America, 1976; co-editor: The Jewish Family; Myths and Reality, 1986; contbr. articles to pubis. Vice chmn. Zionist Acad. Coun., N.Y.C., 1982-83. NEH summer grantee, 1977;Am. Coun. Learned Socs. fellow, 1978; grantee N.Y. Council for Humanities, 1980, NEH fellow, 1986-87. Mem. Am. Hist. Assn. (com. 1983), Assn. for Jewish Studies (bd. dirs. 1978-81, 83-85, 86—, v.p. for mem., 1994—), Leo Baeck Inst. (bd. dirs. 1979—), Yivo Inst. for Jewish Rsch., Phi Beta Kappa. Jewish. Office: Yale U Dept History New Haven CT 06520

HYMAN, TRINA SCHART, illustrator; b. Phila., Apr. 8, 1939; d. Albert Henry and Margaret Doris (Bruck) Schart; m. Harris Joel Hyman, May 29, 1959 (div. 1968); 1 child, Katrin. Student, Phila. Mus. Sch. Art, 1956-59, Boston Mus. Sch. Fine Arts, 1959-60, Konstfackskolan, Stockholm, 1960-61. Free-lance illustrator, 1961—; art dir. Cricket mag., LaSalle, Ill., 1971-79, staff artist, 1979-88; greeting card artist, designer Pawprints Inc., Jaffrey, N.H., 1980—; free-lance figurine designer The Franklin Mint, Franklin Ctr., Pa., 1982—. Author: How Six Found Christmas, 1969, Self-Portrait, 1979; reteller: Sleeping Beauty, 1975, Little Red Riding Hood, 1983; illustrator 132 books including St. George and the Dragon, 1984 (Caldecott medal 1985). Recipient Horn Book award for illustration Boston Globe, 1973, Caldecott Honor Book award ALA, 1989. Mem. Graphic Artists Guild, Soc. Children's Book Writers (Golden Kite award 1984).

HYMES, NORMA, internist; b. N.Y.C., July 20, 1949; d. Richard and Ellen (Posner) H.; m. Vincent M. Esposito, Nov. 1978 (div.); l child, Richard Hymes-Esposito. BS, Oberlin Coll., 1971; MD, Mt. Sinai, 1975. Diplomate Bd. of Internal Medicine. Intern, resident Maimonides Med. Ctr., Bklyn., 1975-78; internist Manhattan Health Plan, N.Y.C., 1978-81, Manhattan Med Group, P.C., N.Y.C., 1981-92, N.Y. Med. Group, P.C., 1992—. Mgr. The Colonnade Condominium, N.Y.C., 1982-85; trustee N.Y. Soc. For Ethical Culture, N.Y.C., 1989-93. Mem. Am. Coll. of Physicians, Am. Med. Women's Assn. Office: NY Med Group 172 Amsterdam Ave New York NY 10023-5034

HYNAN, LINDA SUSAN, psychology educator; b. Ft. Sill, Okla., Nov. 20, 1953; d. Christy J. and Barbara Jean (Camp) Genzel; m. Edward F. Hynan, Feb. 3, 1973; 1 child, Patrick Shane. MS, U. Ill., 1982, PhD, 1993. Tchg. asst., rsch. asst. dept. psychology U. Ill., Urbana, 1980-91; rsch. asst. dept. psychology Del. State Coll., Dover, 1983—; asst. prof. dept. psychology and inst. grad. stats. Baylor U., Waco, Tex., 1991—; cons. Infosphere Devel. Systems, Waco, Tex., 1986—; reviewer Allyn & Bacon/Simon & Schuster, Needham Heights, Mass., 1992, 95, Harcourt Brace Coll. Publs., 1994, Worth Pubs., Inc., 1995. Contbr. chpt. to book Cognitive Bias, 1990, articles to profl. jours. Fellow U. Ill., 1988-89. Mem. APA, Am. Edn. Rsch. Assn., Am. Psychol. Soc., Am. Statis. Assn., Ea. Psychol. Assn., McLennan County Psychol. Assn., Midwestern Psychol. Assn., Psychometric Soc., Soc. for Judgement and Decision-Making, Soc. for Applied Multivariate Rsch., Soc. for Math. Psychology, Southwestern Psychol. Assn., Ctrl. Tex. Women's Alliance, Thyroid Found. Am., Inst. Math. Statistics, Am. Radio Relay League, Am. Numismatic Assn., Phi Kappa Phi. Home: 1312 Western Ridge Dr Waco TX 76712-8709 Office: Baylor U Psychology Dept and Inst Grad Stats PO Box 97334 Waco TX 76798-7334

HYNES, MARY ANN, publishing executive, lawyer; b. Chgo., Oct. 26, 1947; d. Ernest Mario and Emma Louise (Noto) Iantorno; m. James Thomas Hynes, Jan. 25, 1969; children: Christina, Nicholas. BS, Loyola U.; JD, John Marshall Law Sch., 1971, LLM in Taxation, 1975; MBA, Lake Forest Grad. Sch. Bus., 1993. Bar: Ill. 1971, U.S. Dist. Ct. (no. dist.) Ill. 1971. Exec. editor, law editor Commerce Clearing House, Inc., 1971-79, asst. sec, counsel, 1979-80; gen. counsel Commerce Clearing House, Inc., Chgo., now atty. rights and permissions. V.p., bd. dirs., exec. com. Chgo. Crime Commn.; mem. nat. strategy forum Midwest Coun. Nat. Security; adv. coun. Chgo. Symphony Orch. Chorus; deanery del. Chgo. Archdiocesan Pastoral Coun.; pres. local sch. bd., 1984-87; corp. coun. inst. planning com. Northwestern U. Sch. Law; mem. pres.' coun. Mus. Sci. and Industry, Chgo. Mem. ABA (coun., corp. law depts. com., litigation sect.), Ill. Bar Assn. (corp. law dept. sect. chair), Chgo. Bar Assn., Internat. Bar Assn., Women's Bar Assn., Ill. (former bd. dirs., found. adv. bd.), Internat. Fedn. Women Lawyers, Am. Corp. Counsel Assn., Am. Soc. Corp. Secs., Computer Law Assn., Justinian Soc. Lawyers, Law Club Chgo., Legal Club Chgo. (exec. com. 1987), Chgo. Club. Roman Catholic. Office: Commerce Clearing House Inc 2700 Lake Cook Rd Riverwoods IL 60015*

HYUN, CHRISTINA YOUNG, librarian; b. China, Dec. 20, 1947; d. Chang Jin and Sok Il (Lee) H.; m. Joseph E. Allen, Jr., 1974; children: Carl E., Nina Michelle. BA, Ewha Women's U., Seoul, 1969; MLS, U. Mich., 1986; Cert. of Libr. Mgmt., U. Wis., 1989. Libr. tech. asst. U. No. Ala., Florence, 1980-85; cataloger intern Kresge Bus. Libr./U. Mich., Ann Arbor, 1985-86; rsch. asst. U. Mich., Ann Arbor, 1986; head of cataloging dept. Warren Wilson Coll. Libr., N.C., 1986-87; dir. support svcs. Beloit (Wis.) Pub. Libr., 1987-89; head tech.-automation svcs. dept. Glen Ellyn (Ill.) Pub. Libr., 1990—; book reviewer Librs. Unltd., Inc. Artist: (watercolor) Still Life, 1983 (1st prize). Vol. coord. DuPage Prevention Partnership in Ill., 1992-93; mem. Rep. com. mem., Wis., 1987; bd. dirs. LWV, Wis., 1988-89, Naperville (Ill.) Arts Coun., 1990-91; nominated to run for election for trustee of of Libr. Bd. in DuPage County, Warrenville, Ill., 1993. Recipient top prize for acting UN Rep./Mock UN Conf., 1969; Ill. local del. to White House Conf. on Libr. Info. and Sci., 1992. Mem. ALA (interviewer oral history project for Disting. Am. Women 1989-90, chmn. com.), Chinese Am. Libr. Assn. (exec. b. 1987-90), Asian-Pacific ALA (com. 1993-94), AAUW, Am. Soc. Info. Sci., Libr. Adminstrs. Conf. of No. Ill. Tech. (v.p. 1992-93), State Literacy Coun. Methodist. Office: Glen Ellyn Pub Libr 596 Crescent Blvd Glen Ellyn IL 60137

IADAROLA, ANTOINETTE, college president. BA cum laude, Saint Joseph Coll., West Hartford, Conn., 1962; MA, Georgetown U., 1968; student, Oxford U., England, 1970; Fulbright Scholar, London Sch. Econs., 1971-73; PhD, Georgetown U., 1975; postgrad., Yale U., 1976-77. Asst. to grad. dean Georgetown U., Washington, 1968-71; dir. grants, asst. prof. history Saint Joseph College, 1974-78, dir. grants, chair dept. history, 1978-80, spl. asst. to pres. planning and ednl. affairs, chair dept. history, 1981-83; administrv. intern to pres. and provost Hood College, Frederick, Md, 1980-81; provost, dean of faculty College of Mount Saint Joseph, Cin., 1983-86, Colby-Sawyer Coll., New London, N.H., 1986-92; pres. Cabrini Coll., Radnor, Pa., 1992—; Mem. exec. com. Mercy Higher Edn. Colloquium, 1977-81; cons. Am. Coun. Edn., Ctr. Leadership Devel. and Acad. Adminstrn., 1980—; bd. dirs. Am. Conf. Acad. Deans, 1987-90; chair Strategic Planning Com., Coll. Mt. St. Joseph, 1983-86, Com. Chief Acad. Officers, Greater Cin. Consortium colls. and Univs., 1985-86, Teaching/Learning Com. Coeducation Transition, Colby-Sawyer Coll., 1989-92. Contbr. articles to profl. jours. Cons. YWCA, 1974-76, Farmington C. of C. Teenage Scholarship Program, 1976-79; bd. dirs. Ursuline Acad., Cin., 1983-86, Private Industry Coun., Cin., 1983-86, N.H. Humanities Coun., 1987-92, vice chair 1989-90; mem. adv. com. civic literacy, Women's City Club, Cin., 1984-86, devel. com. Shakers Village, Enfield, N.H., 1989-92; chair Town/Gown Community Forum, New London, N.H., 1986-92; coord. ecumenical adult edn. program, Our Lady of Fatima ch., New London, 1987-92. Fellow Georgetown U., 1968-71, Yale U., 1976-77, Danforth Assoc., 1976-86, Am. Coun. Edn. Fellowship in Acad. Administrn., 1980-81; grantee Inst. Internat. Edn. to Oxford U., 1970, NEH, 1979; Fulbright Scholar, 1971-73; recipient Dist. Alumna award Saint Joseph college, 1982. Mem. AAUP, Am. Assn. Higher Edn., Am. Hist. Assn., League of Women Voters. Office: Cabrini Coll 610 King of Prussia Rd Radnor PA 19087

IADAVAIA, ELIZABETH ANN, marketing professional; b. N.Y.C., June 28, 1960; d. Vincent Anthony and Sally (D'Angelo) I. BA in Econs., Georgetown U., 1982. Rsch. asst. Montefiore Hosp. Neurophysiology Labs., N.Y.C., 1979-80; in mktg. rsch. Sch. Bus. Adminstrn. Georgetown U., Washington, 1981-82; adminstrv. asst. Kolter Devel. Corp., N.Y.C., 1983-85; dir. ops. Merrill Lynch Realty, Stamford, Conn., 1985-88, Crown Group Real Estate Devel. & Fin., White Plains, N.Y., 1988-92; dir. mktg. The Equitable, New Hyde Park, N.Y., 1992—. Mem. St. Catherines Parish Coun., Bronxville. Winner 13th Ann. Life Ins. Mktg. and Rsch. Assn. Agy Bull. contest. Mem. N.Y. State MBA Assn., Sch. of the Holy Child Alumni Assn. (bd. dirs., chmn. Rye, N.Y. chpt. 1983—), Georgetown U. Alumni Assn. (class chmn. 1986—), Women in Sales Assn. (v.p. 1993—), Nat. Second Mortgage Assn., VIP Young Adult Club (pres. 1985-87). Home: 17 Archer Dr Bronxville NY 10708

IASIELLO, DOROTHY BARBARA, brokerage company executive; b. Bklyn., Oct. 6, 1949; d. Albert William and Josephine (Accardo) Rehorn; m. John Joseph Iasiello Jr., May 5, 1974. AAS in Mktg., N.Y.C. Community Coll., 1969; BS in Econs., Coll. Staten Island, 1978. With Lady Manhattan, N.Y.C., 1969-70; sec. Biscayne Fed. Savs. and Loan Assn., Miami, Fla., 1971, Morgan Guaranty Trust Co., N.Y.C., 1971-78; with mcpl. bond dept. J.P. Morgan Securities, N.Y.C., 1978-81, asst. treas. sales, 1981-84, asst. v.p. sales, 1984-88, v.p. sales adminstrn. mgmt., 1988-91, v.p. sales, 1991—. Roman Catholic. Office: JP Morgan Securities 60 Wall St New York NY 10005-2807

IBANEZ, JANE BOURQUARD, stress management consultant; b. New Orleans, Oct. 11, 1947; d. Albert John and Josephine (Vachetta) Bourquard; m. Manuel Luis Ibanez, Oct. 16, 1970; children: Juana, Vincent, William. BS, U. New Orleans, 1970. Lab. researcher in organic chemistry U. New Orleans, 1967-68, genetics lab. instr., 1968-69, fitness instr., 1972-90, yoga and meditative instr., 1972-90, stress mgmt. instr., 1980-90; profl. lectr., stress mgmt. cons., 1972—; bd. examiners Tex. Supreme Ct., 1993—. Author producer: (audiotapes) Childhood Stress, 1985, Yoga Workout, 1985, Jane's Way Mini Workout, 1986. Chmn. Tex. A&M U.-Kingsville Fund for Instnl. Advancement, Kingsville, 1989—, also presdl. asst.; pres. Am. Cancer Soc., Kingsville, 1992-94; mem. devel. bd. Spohn Kleberg Hosp., Kingsville, 1990—, trustee, 1991-93; chmn. devel. bd. Am. Heart Assn., Kingsville, 1990—; bd. dirs. Corpus Christi Women's Shelter, Kingsville Action Network, 1992-95; trustee South Tex. Ranching and Heritage Festival, 1992—; mem. bd. dirs. Tex. Supreme Ct. Bd. Law Examiners, 1993—. Mem. AAUW, Kingsville Garden Club, U. New Orleans Fitness Club (pres. 1975-89). Roman Catholic. Home: 905 N Armstrong Ave Kingsville TX 78363-3687 also: 2319 Prentiss Ave New Orleans LA 70122-5309

IBARRA, ANGELINE, small business owner; b. Strasburg, N.D., Aug. 2, 1936; d. Ignatz and Johanna (Zacher) Reinbold; m. John Christian Ibarra, Dec. 12, 1970; children: John Christian, Peter. BA in Criminal Justice, Met. State U., 1988; BS, Met. State, St. Paul, 1992. Office mgr. Indsl. Innovators, St. Paul; clerical/adminstrv. support Higher Edn. Assistance Found., St. Paul; rsch. vol. Washington County Mus., Stillwater, Minn.; crisis line vol. Family Violence Network, Lake Elmo, Minn. Food columnist Stillwater Gazette. Bd. dirs. Valley Coop, 1989-91; den leader Cub Scouts. Mem. Archeology Club (Twin Cities), St. Paul Hiking club, Audubon Soc. Home: 2644 Edgewood Ct Stillwater MN 55082-5343

ICE, CAROL STANLEY, computer specialist, small business owner; b. Sistersville, W.Va., July 17, 1952; d. Bernard Louis and Hilda Maye (Stroehman) Stanley; m. James R. Ice, June 6, 1972; children: Charles, Trevor. AAS, Parkersville (W.Va.) C.C., 1987; BA, Glenville State Coll., 1990. Pers. clk. Manville, Vienna, W.Va., 1989-90; sec. Simonton Bldg. Prod, Pennsboro, W.Va., 1991; bus. office mgr. Edward D. Jones, Vienna, 1992; owner Desktop Pub. Custom Comm., Vienna, 1991—; computer specialist Resource Cons. Devel., Inc., Parkersburg, W.Va., 1993—. Active Ea. Stars, Sistersville, 1972—. Mem. AAUW, Profl. Women's Assn., Mid Ohio Valley C. of C. (mem. women's conf. com.), Vienna Women's Club, Bus. Profl. Women. Home: 1725 Woodland Dr Vienna WV 26105

ICE, JOAN ELIZABETH, real estate sales associate; b. Olympia, Wash., Aug. 9, 1938; d. Ira James McCullough and Myrtle Elizabeth (Nefstad) McCullough Shriner; m. Rodney Dean Ice, Mar. 21, 1958; children: Randal Dean, Rex Daryl, Ronald Dale. BS, U. Cen. Okla., Edmond, Okla., 1981. V.p. Triar Enterprises, Edmond, 1976—. Lectr. Christian women's groups, 1971—. Baptist. Home: 78 Beverly Rd NE Atlanta GA 30309-2646 Office: Triar Enterprises PO Box 3042 Edmond OK 73083-3042

ICHINO, YOKO, ballet dancer; b. L.A.. Studies with Mia Slavenska, L.A. Mem. Joffrey II, N.Y.C., Joffrey Ballet, N.Y.C., Stuttgart Ballet, Fed. Republic Germany; tchr. ballet, 1976; soloist Am. Ballet Theatre, 1977-81; guest appearances, 1981-82; prin. Nat. Ballet Can., Toronto, Ont., 1982-90; tchr. Cullberg Ballet, Sweden, 1994—, Nat. Ballet Sch., 1994—, Ballet de Monte-Carlo, 1994—; various guest appearances including World Ballet Festival, Tokyo, 1979, 85, Tokyo Ballet, 1980, with Alexander Godunov and Stars, summer, 1982, Sydney Ballet, Australia, N.Z. Ballet, summer 1984, Ballet de Marseille, 1985-87, Deutsche Opera Ballet Berlin, 1985-90, Munich Opera Ballet, 1987-90, Australian Ballet, 1987, 89, Staatsoper Berlin, 1989-90, Komische Opera, Berlin, 1991-93, David Nixon's Dance Theater, Berlin, 1990-91, Birmingham Royal Ballet, 1990-93, Deutsche Opera Ballet, Berlin, 1994-95; tchr. numerous ballet workshops. First Am. women recipient medal Third Internat. Ballet Competition, Moscow, 1977. Office: Ballet Met 322 Mt Vernon Ave Columbus OH 43215

IDOUX-LONSDALE, NANCY KAY, cost accountant; b. Belleville, Ill., July 19, 1958; d. Vincent John and Jean Ellen (Grosspitch) I.; m. Robert Harold Lonsdale, Apr. 10, 1994. BA in Acctg., Ill. Wesleyan U., 1980; MBA, So. Ill. U., 1987. Acctg. clk. Firestone Tire & Rubber Co., Bloomington, Ill., 1979-80; inventory/cost acct. Estech, Inc., Fairview Heights, Ill., 1980-81, mgr., nat. supply and dist. acct., 1981-83, fin. analyst, 1983-85; chief purser Carnival Cruise Lines, Miami, Fla., 1985-90; cost acct. Harcros Pigments Inc., Fairview Heights, 1990—. Mem. Alpha Omicron Pi (chpt. advisor 1991-92). Home: 22 S 21st St Belleville IL 62223 Office: Harcros Pigments Inc 11 Executive Dr Ste 1 Fairview Heights IL 62208

IDSO, DEBRA JEAN, bridal wear designer; b. San Diego, Mar. 3, 1965; d. John and Linda Ruth (George) Fabrello; m. Kevin Earl Idso, May 24, 1986. Student, Western Wash. U., 1983-84, Seattle Ctrl. C.C., 1986-87. Custom seamstress Victoria's Bridal, Seattle, 1987-90; dispatcher Hobart Corp., Redmond, Wash., 1990-93; owner Idso Custom Bridal, Marysville, Wash., 1988—. Mem. Beta Sigma Phi (treas. Delta Pi 1993—). Democrat. Roman Catholic. Office: Idso Custom Bridal 4107 79th Pl NW Marysville WA 98271

IGLEWSKI, BARBARA HOTHAM, microbiologist, educator; b. Freeport, Pa., Mar. 23, 1938; married, 1965; 2 children. BS, Allegheny Coll., 1960; MS, Pa. State U., 1962, PhD in Microbiology, 1964. Instr. Oregon Health Sci. U., 1968-69, asst. prof., 1969-73, assoc. prof., 1973-79, prof. microbiology, 1970-86; prof., chair dept. microbiology and immunology U. Rochester (N.Y.) Sch. Medicine and Dentistry, 1986—, vice provost for rsch. and grad. affairs, 1995—; mem. bacterial and mycotic disease study sect., NIH, 1979-83;mem. rsch. and tng. com. Nat. Cystic Fibrosis Found., 1981-84, vaccine related biol. product com., 1981-82. Fellow Pa. State U., 1964-65, U. Colo. Med. Ctr., 1965-66, Pub. Health Rsch. Inst. N.Y., 1966-68; sr. fellow Walter Reed Army Inst. Rsch., 1976-77. Fellow Am. Acad. Microbiology; mem. Am. Soc. Microbiology (pres. 1987-88, chair publ. bd. 1990). Office: Univ of Rochester Dept of Microbiology & Immunology; 601 Elmwood Ave Rochester NY 14642-0001

IGNATONIS, SANDRA CAROLE AUTRY, special education educator; b. Dixon Mills, Ala., June 6, 1942; d. Charles Franklin Autry; m. Algis Jerome Ignatonis, June 15, 1968; children: Audra Carole, David Jerome. BA, Samford U., 1964; cert. in Gifted Edn., Kennesaw State U., 1989. Cert. tchr., Ga. Tchr. Jefferson County Bd. Edn., Birmingham, Ala., 1964, Huntsville (Ala.) Bd. Edn., 1964-71, Epiphany Cath. Sch., Miami, Fla., 1981, Cobb County Bd. Edn., Marietta, Ga., 1982, Bartow County Bd. Edn., Cartersville, Ga., 1990-92; mem. Sch. Self-Governance Com., Emerson, Ga., 1990-91, Soccer Adv. Bd., Marietta, 1985-89; judge, mem. Social Sci. Fair Competitions, Huntsville, 1964-71. Team mom Metro N. Youth Soccer Assn., Marietta, 1991-92; block parent Somerset Subdivision, Marietta, 1982-86; polit. chmn. Student Nat. Edn. Assn., Samford U., Birmingham, Ala., 1963-64. Recipient grant Samford U. Faculty, 1963. Mem. Ga. Supporters of Gifted, Profl. Assn. Ga. Educators. Republican. Roman Catholic. Home: 300 Somerset Ln Marietta GA 30067

IGNATOWICZ, NANCY RAE, critical care nurse; b. Kankakee, Ill., July 14, 1957; d. Raymond Paul and Florence Beatrice (Reniche) I. Diploma, Mennonite Hosp. Sch. Nursing, 1978; postgrad., Ill. State U., U. Wis., Oshkosh, Kankakee Community Coll.; BS in Health Arts, Coll. St. Francis, 1992. RN, Ill., Wis.; cert BCLS, ACLS, PALS, mobile intensive care nurse, trauma nurse specialist. Staff nurse ICU/CCU Riverside Med. Ctr., Kankakee, charge nurse neuro-med. module, charge/staff nurse emergency room; staff nurse ICU, critical care unit Mercy Med. Ctr., Oshkosh; staff devel. coord. emergency dept., case mgr. Riverside Med. Ctr., Kankakee, Ill.; rsch. coord. Riverside Med. Ctr. Mem. AACN, Emergency Nurses Assn., Rsch. Spl. Group, Soc. Critical Care Medicine.

IGNATZ, AMY MARTIN, chemical engineer; b. Grove City, Pa., May 4, 1967; d. David Ferree and Patricia Jean (Swank) Martin; m. Thomas Stephen Ignatz, Jr., July 14, 1990; 1 child, Erica Jane. BS in Engring., U. Pitts., 1989. Chem. engr. U.S. Dept. Labor, Mine Safety & Health Adminstrn., Pitts., 1989—. Republican. Roman Catholic. Home: 202 3rd St Pittsburgh PA 15225-1337 Office: US Dept Labor Mine Safety & Health Adminstrn PO Box 18233 Pittsburgh PA 15236-0233

IKEDA, DONNA RIKA, state senator; b. Honolulu, Aug. 31, 1939; d. William G. and Lillian (Kim) Yoshida; div.; children: Rika, Aaron, Julie. BA in Speech, U. Hawaii. Substitute tchr., 1969-71; legis. rschr. Hawaii Rep. Rsch. Office, 1971-74; asst. v.p. Grand Pacific Life Ins. Ltd., Honolulu, 1989—; mem. Hawaii Ho. of Reps., 1974-86, Hawaii Senate, 1987—. Office: Hawaii Senate Hemmeter Bldg Rm 503 235 S Beretania St Honolulu HI 96813

IKINS, RACHAEL ZACOV, writer, illustrator, photographer; b. Auburn, N.Y., July 5, 1954; d. Samuel Theodore and Phyllis Sylvia (Zacovitch) Killian; m. Phillip M. Ikins, Jan. 23, 1987. BS in Child and Family Studies, Syracuse (N.Y.) U., 1982. Pvt. practice sign lang. interpreter for the deaf Syracuse, 1980-81, Bd. of Coop. Ednl. Svcs., Syracuse, 1980-83; photographer, author greeting cards, Syracuse and Skaneateles, N.Y., 1985—, advertisements, West Columbia, S.C., 1985—. Author poetry. Recipient Honorable Mention, World of Poetry, 1991, New Eng. Writer's Conf., 1991. Jewish. Home and Office: 2636 E Genesee St Syracuse NY 13224-1521

IKLE, DORIS MARGRET, energy conservation company executive; b. Frankfort, Germany, May 28, 1928; came to U.S., 1937, naturalized, 1945; d. Richard and Sonia (Pappenheimer) Eisemann; m. Fred Charles Ikle, Dec. 23, 1959; children—Judith, Miriam. B.A., NYU, 1949, M.A., 1953; postgrad. Columbia U., 1957. Economist, Nat. Bur. Econ. Research, N.Y.C., 1949-54, Am. Bankers Assn., 1954-56, Rand Corp., Santa Monica, Calif., 1957-60; Inst. Energy Analysis, Washington, 1976-77; cons. U.S. Dept. Commerce, Washington, 1975-76; founder, pres. Conservation Mgmt. Corp., Bethesda, Md., 1977—; adv. council Am. for Energy Independence, 1985—; cons. in field. Author: New Approach to the Index Number Problem, 1977, The Complete Energy Audit Book, 1980, (software) RCS and CACS Audit Systems, 1984. Contbr. articles to profl. jours. Home: 7010 Glenbrook Rd Bethesda MD 20814-1223 Office: Conservation Mgmt Corp 7300 Pearl St Bethesda MD 20814-3321

ILANIT, TAMAR, psychologist; b. Tel Aviv, May 5, 1929; d. Aharon and Ada (Berman) Pougatch; came to U.S., 1950, naturalized, 1970; grad. Levinski Tchr. Sem., 1949; Ph.D., U. So. Calif., 1959; m. Apr. 15, 1948; children—Rona, Gill. Research dir. United Cerebral Palsy Assn., Los Angeles, 1959-61; instr. Pepperdine U., Los Angeles, 1962-64; spl. cons. White Meml. Med. Center, Los Angeles; pvt. practice clin. psychology, Los Angeles, 1963—; mem. disability evaluation panel Social Security Adminstrn., 1961-85. Mem. Am. Psychol. Assn., Los Angeles County Psychol. Assn., Sigma Xi, Phi Beta Kappa, Phi Kappa Phi. Jewish. Contbr. articles to profl. jours. Office: 1964 Westwood Blvd # 430 Los Angeles CA 90025 Office: 8618 So Sepulveda # 330 Los Angeles CA 90045

ILCHMAN, ALICE STONE, college president, former government official; b. Cin., Apr. 18, 1935; d. Donald Crawford and Alice Kathryn (Biermann) Stone; m. Warren Frederick Ilchman, June 11, 1960; children: Frederick Andrew Crawford, Alice Sarah. BA, Mt. Holyoke Coll., 1957; MPA, Maxwell Sch. Citizenship, Syracuse U., 1958; PhD, London Sch. Econs., 1965; LHD, Mt. Holyoke Coll., 1982, Franklin and Marshall Coll., 1983. Asst. to pres., mem. faculty Berkshire C.C., 1961-64; lectr. Ctr. for South and S.E. Asia Studies U. Calif., Berkeley, 1965-73; prof. econs. and edn., dean Wellesley (Mass.) Coll., 1973-78; asst. sec. ednl. and cultural affairs Dept. State, 1978; asso. dir. ednl. and cultural affairs Internat. Communication Agy., 1978-81; advisor to sec. Smithsonian Instn., 1981; pres. Sarah Lawrence Coll., Bronxville, N.Y., 1981—; intern, asst. to Sen. John F. Kennedy, 1957; dir. Peace Corps Tng. Program for India, 1965-66; chmn. com. on women's employment NAS. Author: The New Men of Knowledge and the New States, 1968, (with W.F. Ilchman) Education and Employment in India, The Policy Nexus, 1976. Trustee Mt. Holyoke Coll., 1970-80, Mass. Found. for Humanities and Pub. Policy, 1974-77, East-West Center, Honolulu., 1978-81 Expt. in Internat. Living, The Markle Found., The Rockefeller Found., The U. of Cape Town, South Africa, Corp. Adv. Bd., Hotchkiss Sch.; mem. Smithsonian Council, Yonkers Emergency Fin. Control Bd., 1982-88, Am. Ditchley Found. Program Com., Internat. Research and Exchange Bd., Com. for Econ. Devel.; bd. dirs. N.Y. Telephone Co., Seligman Group of Investment Cos. Mem. Nat. Acad. Pub. Adminstrn., NOW Legal Def. Edn. Fund, Coun. Fgn. Rels., Cosmpolitan Club (N.Y.C.), Century Assn. (N.Y.C.), Bronxville Field Club. Home: 935 Kimball Ave Bronxville NY 10708-5507 Office: Sarah Lawrence Coll Office of the President Bronxville NY 10708

ILDERTON, JANE WALLACE, small business owner; b. Gainesville, Ga., Mar. 10, 1936; d. William Lewis and Fay E. (Montgomery) Wallace; m. James Wilson Ilderton, June 12, 1954; children: James Wilson Jr., Mark Joseph, Andrew William. Grad. high sch., Gainesville. Owner, operator Designs by Jane, Charleston, S.C.; mfr., designer SGM Baby Bags Co., 1988—. Mem. Market Mchts. Assn., Charleston Trident C. of C., Smocking Arts Guild of Am., Longstreet Soc. (charter), United Daus. Confederacy (charter). Episcopalian. Office: Designs by Jane 188 Meeting St Charleston SC 29401-3138

ILES, EILEEN MARIE, bank executive, controller; b. Highland Park, Ill., Sept. 29, 1965; d. Dennis Jay and Ida Sigrid (Calderelli) Connolly; m. Kenneth Robert Iles, Dec. 14, 1985; 1 child, Kevin Andrew. Student, U. Ill., Chgo., 1983-85; BBA in Acctg. and Mktg. Mgmt., U. N.Mex., 1988, M in Acctg., 1992. Acct. Charter Bank for Savs., Albuquerque, 1989-90, bank acctg. supr., 1990-91, asst. contr., 1991—, asst. v.p., 1992—; instr. acctg. U. N.Mex., Albuquerque, 1994—; cons. in field. Mem. Inst. Mgmt. Accts.

ILITCH, MARIAN, professional hockey team executive; m. Michael Ilitch; children: Denise Ilitch Lites, Ron, Mike Jr., Lisa Ilitch Murray, Atanas, Christopher, Carole. Owner, sec.-treas. Detroit Red Wings, Detroit Tigers Baseball Team, 1993—; sec.-treas. Little Caesar Internat., Olympia Arenas, Inc., Fox Theatre. Recipient Pacesetter award, 1988, Michiganian of Yr. award, 1988, Nat. Preservation award Nat. Trust Hist. Preservation, 1990. Office: Detroit Red Wings 600 Civic Center Dr Detroit MI 48226-4419 also: Detroit Tigers Tiger Stadium Detroit MI 48216*

ILLIG, SUE ANN, chemical engineer, research executive; b. Pitts., Aug. 20, 1961; d. Eugene Gregory and Bernice Louise (McGuire) I. BS in Chem. Engring., Carnegie Mellon U., 1983. Rsch. engr. paper latex rsch. Dow Chem. Co., Midland, Mich., 1983-87; sr. devel. engr. Plastics Tech. Svc. and Devel., Midland, 1987-90; project leader Plastics Applications Devel., Granville, Ohio, 1990-92; rsch. leader Fabricated Products Rsch., Granville, 1992-94; group leader Fabricated Products Rsch. & Devel., Granville, 1995—. Adult leader, founder Ch. Youth Ministry, Columbus, Ohio, 1991—; founder, steering team leader Young Adults Faith Devel. Series, Columbus, 1992—; fund raiser event co-chair Soc. to Prevent Blindness, Columbus, 1993. Mem. Soc. Plastic Engrs. Roman Catholic. Office: Dow Chem Co PO Box 515 Granville OH 43023

ILLNER-CANIZARO, HANA, physician, oral surgeon, researcher; b. Prague, Czechoslovakia, Nov. 2, 1939; came to U.S., 1968; d. Evzen Pospisil and Emilie (Chrastna) Pospisilova; m. Pavel Illner, June 14, 1963 (div. 1981); children: Martin Illner, Anna Illner; m. Peter Corte Canizaro, Nov. 1, 1982. MD, Charles U., Prague, 1961. Diplomate State Bd. Oral Surgery, 1963. Resident in oral surgery Inst. of Health, Pribram, Czechoslovakia, 1961-63; attending physician Oral Surgery Clinic, Prague, 1963-68; rsch. assoc. dept. surgery U. Tex. Southwestern Med. Sch., Dallas, 1969-72, instr. surgery, 1972-74; instr. surgery U. Wash. Sch. Medicine, Seattle, 1974-77; asst. prof. surgery Cornell U. Med. Coll., N.Y.C., 1977-81, assoc. prof. surgery, 1981-83; assoc. prof. surgery Tex. Tech U. Health Scis. Ctr., Lubbock, 1984-88, prof. surgery, 1988—; site visitor NIGMS Postdoctoral Tng. Grant, Bethesda, Md., 1987. Mem. editorial bd. Circulatory Shock, N.Y.C., 1981—; manuscript reviewer Surgery, Gynecology and Obstetrics, Chgo., 1985—; contbr. chpts. to books, numerous articles to profl. jours. NIH grantee, 1979-83, 87-92; Tex. Tech U Health Scis. Ctr. grantee, 1985, 86; U.S. Dept. of Army grantee, 1988-90; Fogarty Sr. Internat. fellow, 1991-92. Mem. Shock Soc. Home: 4622 8th St Lubbock TX 79416 Office: Tex Tech U Health Scis Ctr 3601 4th St Lubbock TX 79430

IMAN (IMAN ABUDULMAJID), model; b. Somalia, July 25, 1955; m. Spencer Haywood (div. 1987); 1 child, Zulekha; m. David Bowie, Apr. 24, 1992. Student, U. Nairobi, Kenya. Joined Wilhelmina Model Inc., 1975; introduced to U.S. Iman's Kikois. Appearences include (films) The Human Factor, 1979, Out of Africa, 1985, Star Trek VI, 1986, No Way Out, 1987, Surrender, 1987, House Party II, 1991, Exit to Eden, 1994; (TV series) Miami Vice, The Cosby Show, In the Heat of the Night. Office: Writers and Artists Agy 924 Westwood Blvd Ste 900 Los Angeles CA 90024*

IMBROGNO, CYNTHIA, judge. BA, Ind. Univ. of Pa., 1970; JD cum laude, Gonzaga Univ. Sch. of Law, 1979. Law clk. to Hon. Justin L. Quackenbush U.S. Dist. Ct. (Wash. ea. dist.), 9th circuit, 1980-83; law clk. Wash. State Ct. of Appeals, 1984; civil rights staff atty. Ea. Dist. of Wash., 1984-85, complex litigation staff atty., 1986-88; with Preston, Thorgrimson, Shidler, Gates & Ellis, 1988-90, Perkins Coie, 1990-91; magistrate judge U.S. Dist. Ct. (Wash. ea. dist.), 9th circuit, Spokane, 1991—. Office: US Courthouse PO Box 263 920 Riverside Ave W 8th Fl Spokane WA 99210*

IMPELLIZERI, MONICA, pension fund administrator, consultant; b. N.Y.C., June 7, 1920; d. Benjamin and Elizabeth (Priolo) LoPinto; m. Mario E. Impellizeri, June 8, 1941; children: MaryLou, LilaMonica. Student, NYU, 1952-55, 55-57. Asst. advt. mgr. Lily Tulip Cups, Inc., N.Y.C., 1940-45; asst. pub. sch. adminstr. N.Y.C. Bd. of Edn., 1950-68; cons. Imperllizeri Assocs., Inc., Ft. Lee, N.J., 1972—, v.p., 1985—. Author: Yesterday's Tomorrow, 1982; one woman shows include East End Arts Coun., Riverhead, N.Y., 1991; exhibited in Parrish Art Mus., Southampton, N.Y., 1974; artist in oils and water colors. Volunteer art instr. Westchester (N.Y.) Nursing Homes, 1965-71; bd. trustees Friends of Westhampton Free Libr., Westhampton Beach, N.Y., 1985—, Westhampton Free Libr., Westhampton Beach, 1990—. Recipient St. Gaudens medal, N.Y.C., 1936. Mem. Am. Contract Bridge League, Bus. and Profl. Lodge (bd. trustees Queens, N.Y. chpt. 1970—), Southampton Artists, Westhampton Artists.

IMPERATO, ANDREA ECK, sales and marketing executive; b. Bethlehem, Pa., Oct. 31, 1962; d. Charles Anthony Bottiglieri and Almeda Louise (Eck) Migliazza; m. Anthony Richard Imperato, June 11, 1989 (div. Dec. 1993); 1 child, Anthony Richard. Degree in Bus./Mktg., Northampton C.C., 1982. Acct. exec. Christmas Club a Corp., Boston, 1980-86; acct. exec/, theatre dir. Steppin' Out Mag., Cherry Hill, N.J., 1987-88; admissions dir. John Casablancas Select Model Mgmt., Phila., 1986-89; sales rep., property mgr. Hillside Glen Devel., Eastchester, N.Y., 1989-90; mktg. rep. Sammons Comm., Easton, Pa., 1992-94; regional sales mgr. Independence Comm./ Muzak, Norristown, Pa., 1994—. Mem. AFTRA, NAFE, Assn. Cable Trainers, Two Rivers C. of C. (women in bus., downtown revitalization com. 1993). Republican. Lutheran. Office: Independence Comm Inc-Muzak 960 Rittenhouse Rd Norristown PA 19403

IMPERIALI, BEATRICE, financial and corporate communications executive; b. Naples, Italy, Apr. 6, 1957; d. Gian Luca and Luisa (Asquer) I. BA magna cum laude, Boston Coll., 1980; MA, Johns Hopkins U., 1982. Assoc. Greenwich (Conn.) Assocs., 1982-83; v.p. Bankers Trust Co., N.Y.C., 1983-89; sr. v.p. Ruder-Finn, Inc., N.Y.C., 1990—. Del. Commn. of European Communities Press and Info. Service, Washington, 1981; del. Commn. European Communities to the UN, N.Y.C., 1979.

INCLÁN, HILDA MARIANNE, magazine editor, business owner; b. Havana, Cuba, June 4, 1946; came to U.S., 1960, naturalized, 1976; d. Clemente and Rosa Blanca (Guas) Inclán; m. Marcos Gagligarcia, Sept. 2, 1967 (div. 1975); 1 child, Marcos Clemente. BA cum laude in Mass Communications, U. Miami, 1969. Reporter Hollywood (Fla.) Sun-Tattler 48, 1966-67, Ft. Lauderdale (Fla.) News, 1968-70; Latin community writer, daily columnist Miami (Fla.) News, 1970-78; editor-in-chief Intimidades Mag., Virginia Gardens, Fla., 1978-83; editor, owner Ind. Editorial Services, Miami, Fla., 1983-86; pub., editor-in-chief, owner Cruise n' Travel-En Espanol Mag. and Ind. Pub. Co., Inc., Miami, 1984—; founding news bureau chief U.S. Info. Agy., Radio Marti Program, Miami, 1986-87. Mem. Republican Presdl. Task Force, 1981—, U.S. Senate's Rep. Inner Circle, 1987—. Recipient community service awards from civic orgns. and local schs., local awards for maj. stories on Latin lifestyle and investigative pieces on corruption, Emmy award for documentary on Castro and Drugs, WLTV, 1984. Mem. Women in Communication, Nat. Assn. Female Execs., Mental Health Assn. Dade County, Phi Beta Kappa. Roman Catholic. Club: Coconut Grove Sailing. Office: 10371 SW 44th St Miami FL 33165-5607

INDERMARK, ELLEN ANN, therapist; b. Blue Mound, Ill., Apr. 27, 1933; d. Russel Dole and Julia (Hayden) Meachum; m. Roger Indermark, Nov. 27, 1952; children: Christine Indermark Diamond, Sheila Indermark Boehner, John, George. BA, Sangamon State U., 1986, MA, 1988. Mgmt. positions Ill. Bell Telephone Co., Springfield, Ill., 1958-85; therapist, cons. Lutheran child and family /DCFS Gateway Found., Springfield, Ill., 1985-89; owner, therapist Stillmeadow Counseling Ctr., Springfield, Ill., 1989—. Mem. ACA, Am. Assn. Marraige and Family Therapy, Ill. Alcohol and Drug abuse Profl. Cert. Assn., Inc., Chi Sigma Iota. Home: RR 7 Stillmeadow Springfield IL 62707 Office: Stillmeadow Counseling Ctr 833 S 4th St Springfield IL 62705

INDERSTRODT, LINDA DARLENE, accountant; b. Richmond, Ind., Dec. 30, 1950; d. Charles and Catherine (Elstro) Shaffer; m. Charles Inderstrodt, July 5, 1972; children: Phyllamania, David. AAS in Acctg., I. V. Tech., 1992; BS in Bus. Adminstrn., Ind. Wesleyan, 1994. Mgr. Safeway Taxi, Richmond, Ind., 1980-92; acct. YWCA, Richmond, 1992—; part-time instr. acctg. I. V. Tech., 1994—. Mem. Inst. Mgmt. Accts., Alpha Upsilon Omega. Home: 203 N 4th St Richmond IN 47374 Office: YWCA PO Box 2430 Richmond IN 47375

INDICK, JANET, sculptor, educational administrator; b. Bklyn., Mar. 3, 1932; d. Charles and Sarah (Goldsmith) Suslak; m. Benjamin Philip Indick, Aug. 23, 1953; children: Michael Cory, Karen Leigh Indick Maizel. B.S. in Art, Hunter Coll., 1953, postgrad., 1953; postgrad. New Sch., 1961-62. Tchr. kindergarten pub. schs., Elizabeth, N.J., 1953-54; dir. nursery sch. Teaneck Jewish Ctr., N.J., 1964-92. Commns. include sculpture for Netzach Yisroel, Teaneck Jewish Ctr., 1974, Etz Chaim 1981, Sanctuary Wall Menorah 1983, Temple Beth Rishon, Wyckoff, N.J., 1981, 83, Menorah, Franklin Lakes Pub. Sch., 1983, North Shore Synagogue, Syosset, N.Y., 1993, Temple Sharey Telfilo Israel, South Orange, N.J., 1993; one-woman shows include Discovery Art Gallery, Clifton, N.J., 1976, Mari Art Gallery, Westchester, N.Y., 1983, Hebrew Tabernacle, N.Y.C., 1984, Chubb Corp., Basking Ridge, N.J., 1985, Edward Williams Gallery, Fairleigh Dickinson U., Hackensack, N.J., 1986, Vineyard Gallery, N.Y.C., 1986, Maurice M. Pine Gallery, Fairlawn (N.J.) Pub. Libr., 1990, Quietude Garden Gallery, East Brunswick, N.J., 1991-92, Bergen Mus. Art & Sci., Paramus, N.J., 1994; juried exhbns. include Morris (N.J.) Mus., 1979, 84, Newark Mus., 1982, Jersey City Mus., 1983, Hebrew Tabernacle, N.Y.C., 1984, Parsons Gallery, N.Y.C., 1984, Lillian Heidenberg Gallery, N.Y.C., 1984—, Shering-Plough Corp., Madison, N.J., 1987, Kerygma Gallery, Ridgewood, N.J., 1989—, Marabella Gallery, N.Y.C., 1989, So. Vt. Art Ctr., Manchester, 1990; Nat. Assn. Women Artists Traveling Exhbns., 1989-90, Fgn. Traveling Exhbns., India, 1989-90, Columbus (Ohio) Mus. Fine Art, 1989-90, Balt. Mus. Art, 1989-90; represented in collections Jane Voorhees Zimmerli Art Mus. Rutgers U., New Brunswick, N.J., Bergen Mus., Paramus, N.J., Weingroup Equities Corp., N.Y.C., Hubbards Cupboard Corp., Edison, N.J., Rosenthal Art Equities, N.Y.C., Franklin Lakes (N.J.) Pub. Schs., Temple Beth Rishon, Wykoff, N.J., North Shore Synagogue, Sysosset, N.Y., Temple Sharey Tefilo, South Orange, N.J. Advisor Teaneck Arts Adv. Bd., 1982—. Recipient Sculpture awards Nat. Assn. Painters and Sculptors, 1970-80, Sculpture award Art in the Park, Paterson, N.J., 1977, Merit award IFFRA/AIA Forum on Religion, Art and Architecture, 1984, H.W. Frismuth Bronze Sculpture award Catherine Lorillard Wolfe Art Club, 1992; N.J. State Council Arts fellow, 1981. Mem. Nat. Assn. Women Artists (treas. 1990-94, juror, Pauline Law sculpture prize 1974, Clara Shainess Meml. award 1994), N.Y. Soc. Women Artists (chmn. juror 1990-94), Sculptors Internat. N.Y. (exec. bd. 1990-91), Women's Caucus Art (chmn. juror). Democrat. Jewish. Home: 428 Sagamore Ave Teaneck NJ 07666-2626 also: care Lillian Heidenberg Gallery 50 W 57th St New York NY 10019-3914

INFANTE, DAISY INOCENTES, sales and real estate executive, marketing executive; b. Marbel, The Philippines, Aug. 3, 1946; came to U.S., 1968; d. Jesus and Josefina (Inocentes) I.; children: Desiree Josephine, Dante Fernancio, Darrell Enerico; m. Rosben Reyes Ogbac, Jan. 30, 1987. AA with highest honors, Notre Dame of Marbel, Philippines, 1963; AB in English magna cum laude, U. Santo Tomas, Manila, 1965, BS in Psychology, 1966; MA in Communications, Fairfield U., 1971. Columnist, writer Pinoy News mag., Chgo., 1975-76, Philippine News, Chgo., 1977-80; cons. EDP Cemco Systems, Inc., Oak Brook, Ill., 1980-81; pres. Daisener, Inc., Downers Grove, Ill., 1980-82; cons. EDP Robert J. Irmen Assocs., Hinsdale, Ill., 1981-82; pres. Data Info. Systems Corp., Downers Grove, Ill., 1982-84; broker, co. mgr. Gen. Devel. Corp., Chgo., 1984-86; columnist, writer Via Times, Chgo., 1984-86; owner, pres. Marbel Realty, Chgo., 1984-88; exec. v.p. Dior Enterprises, Inc., Chgo., 1986-88; real estate sales mgr. M.J. Cumber Co., Grand Cayman, Cayman Islands, 1988-89, Vet. Real Estate, Orlando, Fla., 1989-90; sales mgr. All Star Real Estate, Inc., Orlando, 1990-92; ruby network mktg. exec. Melaleuca, Inc., 1991—; pres. Dior Enterprises, Inc., Orlando, 1992—. Author: Poems of My Youth, 1982; (lyrics and music) My First Twenty Songs, 1981; featured contbr. poems; American Poetry Anthology, vol. VIII, no. 4, Best New Poets of 1987; inventor fryer-steamer. Sec. Movement for a Free Philippines, 1984. Mem. NAFE, Am. Soc. Profl. Exec. Women, Philippine C. of C. (sec. Chgo. chpt. 1985), Bayanihan Internat. Ladies Assn., Lions (twister Fil-Am. club 1978-79). Roman Catholic.

INFINGER, GLORIA ALTMAN, nursing administrator; b. Charleston, S.C., Feb. 16, 1941; d. Norman B. and Gladys V. Risher; m. Norman M. Infinger, May 21, 1961; children: Robert M., Michael S. Diploma, Med. U.S.C., 1962. RN, S.C.; cert. nurse adminstr., register cen. svc. technician. Nurse Med. U. S.C. Med. Ctr., Charleston, 1962-68, nursing supr., asst. dir. evening shift, 1974-86, mgr. sterile processing, 1986-94; office nurse John Aycock, M.D., Mt. Pleasant, S.C., 1968-69; asst. head nurse Charleston Meml. Hosp., 1969-73; sterile processing cons., 1994. Mem. AHA, Am. Soc. for Hosp. Ctrl. Svc. Pers., S.C. Assn. for Hosp. Ctrl. Svc. Pers. (founder 1992), N.C. Assn. for Hosp. Ctrl. Svc. Pers., Internat. Assn. Hosp. Ctrl. Svc. Material Mgmt., S.C. State Employees Assn. Office: Med U SC Med Ctr EH 123 Childrens 171 Ashley Ave Charleston SC 29425

INGA, KANDRA JOYCE (KANDRA BAKER), actress, sales and marketing professional; b. Northridge, Calif., Dec. 18, 1959; d. Mel Frank and Joyce (Harrison) Baker; m. Joseph Vincent Inga, Sept. 14, 1985. BS summa cum laude, Calif. Luth. U., 1978. Nat. sales mgr. Tech Distributing, Canoga Park, Calif., 1979-81; v.p. sales and mktg. Morris Inc., Torrance, Calif., 1985—; dir. children's music Hope Chapel, Hermosa Beach, Calif., 1988—; dir. children's plays, 1989—; dance performer Norris Theatre, Palos Verdes, Calif., 1991, 92, 93. Appeared in film Eternity, 1990, Double O Kio, 1992, A Million to Juan, 1993, Better Harvest, 1993, Ava's Magical Adventure, 1994; (video) L.A. Bodyworks, 1990, Rock-A-Long with Bo Peep, 1992, (TV) Knots Landing, 1987, (theatre) The Outcasts of Poker Flat, 1983 (Best Actress 1983); co-prodr. (video) Computer Tng. Series, 1990, Learning DOS, 1990 (Am. Film award 1990). Mem. AFTRA, SAG, Women in Entertainment, Hope in Action, Media Focus (merchandising com. 1994). Republican. Home: 1746 Spreckels Ln Redondo Beach CA 90278-4734 Office: Morris Inc 2707 Plaza Del Amo Ste 601 Torrance CA 90503-7230

INGAGLIATO, SUSAN PATRICIA, surgical nurse; b. Takoma Park, Md., Nov. 30, 1954; d. Alfred Carmine and Claudia Ann (Robbins) I.; m. Manuel Serna Pena, July 7, 1990. ADN, Montgomery Coll., Takoma Park, 1985. RN, D.C.; cert. clin. nurse for ENT, plastic surgery and oral surgery. Staff nurse Sibley Meml. Hosp., Washington, 1985-87, nurse in oper. rm., 1987—. Mem. Am. Assn. Oper. Rm. Nurses (mentor Project Alpha). Office: Sibley Meml Hosp 5255 Loughboro Rd NW Washington DC 20016-2698

INGALLS, EVE, artist; b. Cleve.; d. Albert and Eileen (Brodie) I. Student, Skowhegan Sch. Art, 1954, 59; BA, Smith Coll., 1958; BFA, Yale U., 1960, MFA, 1962. Mem. Paula Allen Gallery, N.Y.C., 1987-88, Soho 20 Gallery, N.Y.C., 1980—; vis. instr. Yale U., New Haven, 1979; instr. SUNY, Coll. at Purchase, 1985; vis. asst. prof. Trinity Coll., Hartford, Conn., 1991; instr. Silvermine Sch. Art, New Canaan, Conn., 1972—. One person shows include Conn. Commn. on Arts, 1985, Paula Allen Gallery, 1987, 88, Soho 20 Gallery, 1990, 92, 95, Virginia Miller Gallery, 1993; exhibited in group shows at Sordoni Art Gallery, Wilkes-Barre, Pa., 1985, Columbus (Ga.) Mus. Arts, 1985, Cleve. Mus. Art, 1986, Aldrich Mus. Contemporary Art, Ridgefield, Conn., 1987, New Britain (Conn.) Mus. Am. Art, 1989, Kulturforum Mönchengladbach, Mönchengladbach, Germany, 1989, The Bruce Mus., Greenwich, Conn., 1991, The Lyman Allyn Mus., New London, Conn., 1992.

INGALLS, JEREMY, poet, educator; b. Gloucester, Mass., Apr. 2, 1911; d. Charles A. and May E. (Dodge) Ingalls. AB, Tufts Coll., 1932, AM, 1933; student, U. Chgo., 1938-39; LHD, Rockford Coll., 1960; LittD, Tufts U., 1965. Asst. prof. English Lit. Western Coll., Oxford, Ohio, 1941-43; resident poet, asst. prof. English lit. Rockford (Ill.) Coll., 1948-50, successively assoc. prof. English and Asian studies, prof., chmn. div. arts, chmn. English dept., 1950-60; Fulbright prof. Am. lit., Japan, 1957; Rockefeller Found. lectr. Kyoto Am. Studies seminar, 1958. Author: A Book of Legends, 1941, The Metaphysical Sword, 1941, Tahl, 1945, The Galilean Way, 1953, The Woman from the Island, 1958, These Islands Also, 1959, This Stubborn Quantum, 1983, Summer Liturgy, 1985, The Epic Tradition and Related Essays, 1989; translator (from Chinese) A Political History of China, 1840-1928 (Li Chien-Nung), 1956, The Malice of Empire (Yao Hsin-Nung), 1970, (from Japanese) Tenno Yugao (Nakagawa), 1975. Recipient Yale Series of Younger Poets prize, 1941, Shelley Meml. award, 1950, and other awards for poetry; apptd. hon. epic poet laureate United Poets Laureate Internat., 1965; Guggenheim fellow, 1943, Chinese classics rsch. fellow Republic of China, 1945, 46, Am. Acad. Arts and Letters grantee, 1944, Ford Found. fellow Asian studies, 1952, 53. Fellow Internat. Inst. Arts and Letters; mem. MLA (chmn. Oriental-western lit. rels. conf.), Assn. Asian Studies (life), Authors Guild, Poetry Soc. Am., New Eng. Poetry Soc., Dante Soc. Am. (life), Phi Beta Kappa, Chi Omega. Episcopalian. Home: 6269 E Rosewood St Tucson AZ 85711-1638

INGALLS, MARIE CECELIE, former state legislator, retail executive; b. Faith, S.D., Mar. 31, 1936; d. Jens P. and Ida B. (Hegre) Jensen; m. Dale D. Ingalls, June 20, 1955; children: Duane, Delane. BS, Black Hills State Coll., 1973, MS, 1978. Elem. tchr. Meade County Schs., Sturgis, S.D., 1957-72, Faith Sch. Dist. 46-2, 1973-76; elem. prin. Meade Sch. Dist. 46-1, Sturgis, 1976-81; owner, operator Ingalls, Sturgis, 1978-91; mem., asst. majority whip S.D. House Reps., Pierre, 1986-92. Sec. S.D. Rep. Orgn. Recipient Woman of Achievement award City of Sturgis, 1986. Mem. S.D. Cattlewomen, S.D. Stockgrowers (edn. chair), S.D. Farm Bur. (bd. dirs. dist. V), S.D. Retailers Assn. (bd. dirs., sec.-treas.), S.D. Ins. Commn., Faith C. of C. (pres. 1989), Sturgis C. of C. (bd. dirs.) Optimists, Zonta. Republican. Lutheran. Home: PO Box Pox # 31 Mud Butte SD 57758 Office: Ingalls 1032 Main St Sturgis SD 57785-1523

INGELL, DEBORA RIDENOUR, business analyst; b. Coshocton, Ohio, Mar. 20, 1961; d. Robert Allen Ridenour and Mary Lou Ridenour Cline; m. John Fredrick Ingell, June 13, 1987. BBA in Fin. and Mgmt., U. Cin., 1984. Auditor Gen. Acctg. Office, Cin., 1981-83; systems analyst GE, Erie, Pa., 1984-87; fin. analyst Siemens Transmission Sys., Phoenix, 1987-89; fin. planning supr. Tandem Computers, Austin, Tex., 1989-94. Mem. Toastmasters. Home: 9579 S Bellmore Ln Highlands Ranch CO 80126

INGIS, GAIL, interior designer, educator, writer; b. U.S., Nov. 1, 1935; d. Bernard and Claire Gerber; m. Thomas H. Claus; children: Linda, Richard, Paul. Student in bus. Bklyn. Coll., 1953; grad. in interior architecture and design N.Y. Sch. Interior Design, 1973, BFA, 1980; postgrad. Pratt Inst., N.J. Inst. Tech., Parsons Sch. of Design. Prin. Ingis Design Assoc., Woodcliff Lake, N.J., 1970—; interior designer The Design Store, locations in Washington, Md., N.J., 1977-78; prof. Kean Coll., Union, N.J., 1977-80, The King's Coll., Briarcliff Manor, N.Y., 1980-82, N.Y. Sch. Interior Design, 1980-82; mem. design staff Bloomingdale's, N.Y.C., 1981-82; founder, prin. Interior Design Inst. (merged with Berkeley Coll. Bus.), Woodcliff Lake, N.J., 1982-91, chmn. interior design dept., 1988-91; head interior designer Africa Inland Mission, Pearl River, N.Y., 1991—; founder D'Image Inc., Saddle River, N.J., 1986. Troop leader Girl Scouts U.S., N.Y.C. and Woodcliff Lake, 1964-69. Mem. Am. Soc. Interior Designers (admissions com. N.J. chpt. 1978, edn. chmn. 1978-86, 94—, co-chmn. pro-licensing com. 1984-86, com. legis. for interior designers 1988-90, bd. dirs. 1985-87, 94—, service awards 1978, 83-87), AIA profl. affiliate, Inst. Bus. Designers, U.S. Profl. Tennis Assn. (cert. tennis instr.), Illuminating Engring. Soc. N.Am., Interior Design Educators Coun. Home: 68 Montvale Ave Montvale NJ 07645 Office: 135 Crooked Hill Rd Pearl River NY 10965-1147

INGLE, JANET EMILEE, social worker; b. Jasper, Ala., Jan. 23, 1953; d. John Dewey and Margaret (Morris) Black; m. Ronald E. Ingle, Oct. 7, 1971 (dec. Jan. 1987); 1 child, Lila Gail. Student, Walker Jr. Coll., Jasper, 1971-72; BA in Sociology, U. Ala., Birmingham, 1975, postgrad., 1981-82. Social worker Dept. Human Resources, Jasper, 1977-79, Beacon House Juvenile Home, Jasper, 1979-80, Cordova (Ala.) Nursing Home, 1983-84; dir. Daybreak-Spouse Abuse, Jasper, 1987—; exec. dir. Daybreak, Jasper, 1983. Co-chair Share-A-Toy, Jasper, 1993. Mem. AAUW, Ala. Coalition Against Domestic Violence (sec. 1989-90, pres. 1991-92, nominee woman of yr. 1992), Pilot Club Jasper. Mem. Church of Christ. Home: 336 Highland Ave Cordova AL 35502

INGLEHART, MARITA ROSCH, psychologist, educator and researcher; b. Ludwigshafen, Germany, Aug. 23, 1951; came to U.S., 1984; d. Karl Julius and Rita (Schreck) Rohr; m. Ekkehard Rosch, Aug. 13, 1973 (div. May 1978); m. Ronald Franklin Inglehart, Apr. 5, 1986; children: Ronald Charles, Marita Helen; stepchildren: Elizabeth, Rachel. Diploma in psychology, U. Mannheim, Germany, 1975, PhD, 1978, Habilitation, 1983. Asst. prof. U. Mannheim, 1975-78; rsch. scientist Ctr. for Decision Making, U. Mannheim, 1978-83; pvt. dozent U. Mannheim, 1983-90; vis. prof. U. Mich., Ann Arbor, 1984-86; rsch. assoc. Ctr. for Rsch. on Learning and

Teaching, U. Mich., Ann Arbor, 1986-93; assoc. prof. Dental Sch., adj. assoc. prof. dept. psychology U. Mich., Ann Arbor, 1993—; vis. prof. U. Mich., Ann Arbor, 1984-86, adj. asst. prof., 1986-93. Author: Critical Life Events, 1988, Reactions to Critical Life Events, 1991; editor: Integration of Immigrants, 1979. Mem. APA, Am. Psychol. Soc., German Soc. Psychology, European Assn. Exptl. Social Psychology. Roman Catholic. Home: 2626 Geddes Ave Ann Arbor MI 48104-2715 Office: U Mich Dept Psychology E Eng 580 Union Dr Ann Arbor MI 48109-1346

INGLÉS, PAMELA ANNE, paralegal; b. San Pedro Sula, Honduras, Aug. 7, 1971; came to U.S., 1972; d. Steven Thomas and Lilian Patricia (Soto) I. BA, Tulane U., 1994. Litigation paralegal Henican, James & Cleveland, Metairie, La., 1993—.

INGLETT, BETTY LEE, retired media services administrator; b. Augusta, Ga., Oct. 6, 1930; d. Wilfred Lee and Elizabeth Arelia (Crouch) I. BS in Edn., Ga. State Coll. for Women, 1953; MA in Library, Media and Edn. Adminstrn., Ga. So. U., 1980; EdD in Edn. Adminstrn., Nova U., 1988. Tchr. James L. Fleming Elem. Sch., Augusta, Ga., 1953-63, Murphey Jr. High Sch., Augusta, 1963-64, Sego Jr. High Sch., Augusta, 1964-68, Glenn Hills High Sch., Augusta, 1968-75; media specialist Nat. Hills Elem. Sch., Augusta, 1975-80; prin. Lake Forest Elem. Sch., Augusta, 1980-84, Joseph R. Lamar Elem. Sch., Augusta, 1984-86; dir. ednl. media services Richmond County Bd. Edn., Augusta, 1986—; owner, operator Betty Inglett Enterprises, Augusta. Contbr. articles to profl. jours. Bd. dirs. Am. Heart Fund, 1975-80, Am. Cancer Fund, 1986—; del. Dem. State Conv., 1982; council mem. PTA. (life), 1985. Named Adminstr. of Yr., 1988-89. Mem. Richmond County Edn. Assn. (sec. v.p. 1961-63, Adminstr. of Yr. 1989-90), AAUW (v.p. 1957-59), NEA, Ga. Assn. Edn., Ga. Assn. Ednl. Leaders, Ga. Library Media Dept., Ga. Library Assn., Ga. Assn. Instructional Tech., Ga. Assn. Curriculum Instructional Supr., Profl. Leadership Assn., Cen. Savannah River Area Library Assn., Alpha Delta Kappa, Phi Delta Pi, Phi Delta Kappa. Baptist. Office: Ednl Media Svcs 3148 Lake Forest Dr Augusta GA 30909-3029

INGMAN, ANNETTE VIOLA, accountant; b. Gardner, Mass., Oct. 2, 1954; d. Joseph Arthur and Marie Cecilia (Allain) Bastarache; m. John E. Ingman, Oct. 6, 1972 (div. 1988). AS in Bus. Tech., Mt. Wachusett C.C., Gardner, Mass., 1985; BSBA in Acctg., U. Ariz., 1993. Furniture packer Heywood Wakefield Co., Gardner, Mass., 1972-74; upholsterer George B. Bent Co., Gardner, 1974-79; bookkeeper asst. Wood's Ambulance Inc., Gardner, 1979-81; office mgr. Dr. Charles E. Martel, Gardner, 1981-86; sr. bookkeeper Mt. Wachusett C.C., Gardner, 1986-88, Behavioral Health Svcs., Yuma, Ariz., 1994—; home health aide Homecare of So. Ariz., Tucson, 1988-92; part-time bookkeeper Vivace Restaurant, Tucson, 1993-94. Coord., fund raiser Spring Hill, Ashby, Mass., 1980; vol. EMT, Royalston (Mass.) Fire Dept., 1986-88, Templeton (Mass.) Fire Dept., 1987-88; fin. mgr. for ind. blind person, Tucson, 1989-93. Mem. Inst. Mgmt. Accts. (assoc.).

INGOLD, CATHERINE WHITE, academic administrator; b. Columbia, S.C., Mar. 15, 1949; d. Hiram Hutchison and Annelle (Stover) White; m. Wesley Thomas Ingold, June 13, 1970; 1 child, Thomas Bradford Hutchison. Student, U. Paris-Sorbonne, 1969; BS in French with honors, Hollins Coll., 1970; MA in Romance Langs., U. Va., 1972, PhD in French, 1979; DHum honoris causa, Francis Marion U., Florence, S.C., 1992. Assoc. prof. romance langs. Gallaudet U., Washington, 1973-88, dir. hons. program, 1980-85, dean arts and scis., 1985-86, provost, v.p. acad. affairs, 1986-88; pres. Am. U. of Paris, 1988-92, Curry Coll., Milton, Mass., 1992—; pres. N.E. region Nat. Collegiate Honors Coun., 1983-84. Bd. dirs. Am. Sch. of Paris; vestry Christ Ch., Alexandria, Va. Recipient Prix Morot-Sir de Langue et Littérature françaises (Hollins). Mem. MLA, Nat. Collegiate Honors Coun., Lychnos Soc. (U.Va.), Phi Beta Kappa. Episcopalian. Home: 956 Brush Hill Rd Milton MA 02186-1227 Office: Curry Coll 1071 Blue Hill Ave Milton MA 02186-2395

INGRAM, HELEN HENLEY, quality assurance professional, nurse, consultant; b. Manakin, Va., Mar. 11, 1923; d. Harry Hamilton and Ida Lee (Staples) Henley; m. Blaine Grant Ingram, Nov. 24, 1949; children: Connie Rae, Shirley Blaine. Grad., Stuart Circle Nursing Sch., Richmond, Va., 1944; student in pub. health, U. N.C., 1944-45; student, U. Mich., 1947-49; BSN, Ariz. State U., 1968. RN, Va., Mich., Ariz. Pub. health nurse Richmond Health Dept., 1945-47, Washtenaw Health Dept., Ann Arbor, Mich., 1947-49; nursing supr. Maricopa County Health Dept., Phoenix, 1963-66, supr. nursing programs, 1970-80, coord. quality assurance, 1980-87; assoc. prof. nursing Ariz. State U., Tempe, 1967-69; quality assurance cons., Phoenix, 1987—; speaker APHA, Washington, 1986, Houston Health and Human Svcs. Dept., 1986, Ft. Worth Health Svcs., 1987. Touring docent Phoenix Art Mus., 1987—; mem. Phoenix Art Mus., Valley Artist League. Recipient quality assurance achievement award for Maricopa County, Nat. Assn. Counties, 1985; scholar Va. Nurses Assn., 1944, Ariz. State U., 1968. Mem. AAUW, ANA, Nat. Quality Assurance Assn., Planned Parenthood. Home and Office: 2020 E Solar Dr Phoenix AZ 85020-5645

INGRAM, JOHNNYE HUGHES, artist, educator; b. Silverton, Tex., Apr. 28, 1904; d. James Monroe and Maude Ethel (McCann) Hughes; m. Abner Clay Ingram, July 17, 1922 (dec.); 1 child, Clark Hughes Ingram. Grad. high sch., Winnfield, La., 1922. Tchr. ceramics, china painting Smackover, Ark., 1936-45; art lectr. various schs. and orgns., Ark., 1940-80; art tchr. Singer Sewing Machine Studio, El Dorado, Ark., 1976-83, South Ark. U., El Dorado, 1982-83, South Ark. Art Ctr., El Dorado, 1984; art lectr. Ark. Oil & Brine Mus., Smackover, 1991—; art tchr., Smackover, 1970-88; art lectr. Springhill (La.) Art League, 1986; judge Ouachita County Fair, Camden, Ark., 1985-87, Columbia County Fair, Magnolia, Ark., 1980, Union County Fair, El Dorado, 1960-69; mem. bd. visual arts South Ark. Art Ctr. Active gray lady svc. ARC, Smackover, 1960-69, Easter Seals, Smackover, 1955; bd. dirs. Tuberculosis Bd. Union County, El Dorado, 1935, Union County Human Svcs., 1985-90, Ret. Sr. Vol. Program, 1982; active Maple Ave. Bapt. Ch. Mem. South Ark. Art Ctr. (bd. dirs. 1985-91), United Daus. Confederacy. Home: 600 E 12th St Smackover AR 71762-2125

INGRAM, JUDITH MYRNA, university specialist; b. Atlanta, Aug. 29, 1942; d. Thaddius Slater and Georgia (Williams) Allen; m. Ronald Nathaniel Myrick, June 6, 1965 (div. May 1968); children: Monica Lynn Myrick, Jill Jeanine Myrick; m. Nathaniel Bruce Ingram, Dec. 23, 1993. BA, Spelman Coll., 1964; MFA, Fla. State U., 1979. Youth program dir. Young Women's Christian Assn., Atlanta, 1964-66, 68-69; drama specialist City of Atlanta Parks & Recreation, 1969-75; registration specialist Ga. State U., Atlanta, 1981-82, conf. coord., 1982-88, adminstrv. coord., 1988-91, program specialist, 1991, unit head pub. svc., 1991-92; program devel. specialist Ga. State U., 1992—. Author: (play) Weavers of Dreams of Spells of Blues n' Things, 1977. Bd. dirs. Neighborhood Arts Ctr., 1987-90; mem. campaign staff Ivan Allen for mayor, 1961. Named Woman of Achievement Young Women's Christian Assn., 1991; Ga. Humanities Coun. grantee, 1990; Diguid Found. fellow, 1977. Democrat. Methodist. Office: Ga State U Div Continuing Edn PO Box 4044 Atlanta GA 30302-4044

INGRAM, MARGI, real estate broker; b. Central, Ala.; d. Jack and Dru (Graham) I. BS, U. Ala., 1969, postgrad., 1971-72. Tchr. pub. schs. Birmingham, Ala., 1970-78; broker Gilliland & Co., Birmingham, 1978-79; broker, pres. Ingram & Assocs., Birmingham, 1979—; mktg. cons. Collateral Mktg., Birmingham, 1982-84, Royal Homes, Inc., 1982—, Gibson-Anderson-Evins, 1983—, City Fed. Savs. & Loan Assn., 1983-85. Bd. dirs. Humane Soc. Birmingham, 1980. Named Bus. Exec. of Yr. Birmingham Bus. Jour., 1985. Mem. Nat. Assn. Realtors, Ala. Assn. Realtors, Birmingham Bd. Realtors, Fed. Land Inst., Sales Mktg. Execs. Internat., Birmingham C. of C. Democrat. Episcopalian. Office: Ingram Hayes & Assocs 2336 20th Ave S Birmingham AL 35223-1006

INGRAM, SHIRLEY JEAN, social worker; b. Louisville, Oct. 22, 1946. BA in Social Sci., U. Hawaii, Pearl City, 1979; MSW, Fla. State U., 1982. Lic. clin. social worker, Fla.; bd. cert. diplomate social worker, qualified clin. social worker, Md.; cert. family mediator Fla. Supreme Ct., 1991. Case mgr. Geriatric Residential Treatment Ctr., Crestview, Fla., 1982-84; case mgmt. supr. Okaloosa Guidance Ctr., Fort Walton Beach, Fla., 1984-86; family counselor Harbor Oaks Hosp., Fort Walton Beach, 1986-87; pvt. practice Fort Walton Beach, 1987—. Mem. Mental Health Assn. Okaloosa County (sec. bd. dirs. 1988—, mem. adv. bd. dirs. Area Agy. on Aging, chmn. adv. bd. dirs., Okaloosa County Area Agy. on Aging, pres.), NASW, Long Term Care Ombudsman Coun., AAUW, Sertoma. Home: 502 Regatta Cir Niceville FL 32578-2448 Office: Ste 31 348 Miracle Strip Pkwy Fort Walton Beach FL 32548

INKELLIS, BARBARA G., lawyer; b. Rockville Ctr., N.Y., Apr. 8, 1949; d. Adolph J. and Edith (Zackowitz) Greenberg; m. Steven Alan Inkellis, May 19, 1979; children: Elizabeth, David. AB, Dickinson Coll., 1971; MEd., George Washington U., 1973, JD, 1978. Bar: D.C. 1978, U.S. Dist. Ct. D.C. 1979. Assoc. Bracewell & Patterson, Washington, 1978-79, Fried, Frank, Harris, Shriver & Jacobson, Washington, 1979-81; gen. counsel Cambridge Info. Group, Bethesda, Md., 1981—. Mem. ABA. Office: Cambridge Info Group 7200 Wisconsin Ave Bethesda MD 20814-4807

INKSTER, CHRISTINE DAVIS, librarian, educator; b. Scranton, Pa., Aug. 3, 1943; d. Gordon W. and Mary Elizabeth (Murphy) Davis; m. Robert Paul Inkster, June 7, 1965; children: Matthew, John, Benjamin. BA in English, U. Wyo., 1965, MA in English, 1975; MLS, U. Pitts., 1979. English tchr. Wash. Jr. High Sch., Chgo. Heights, Ill., 1965-66, Laramie (Wyo.) Jr. High Sch., 1966-68, 79-89, Laramie (Wyo.) High Sch., 1969-75, Ea. Wyo. Coll., Torrington, 1975-78; ref. libr., assoc. prof. St. Cloud (Minn.) State U., 1989—; teacher, trainer Wyo. Writing Project, Laramie, 1979-89. Contbr. articles to profl. jours. Vol. Sch. Dist. 742, St. Cloud, 1989—. Mem. NEA, AAUW (newsletter editor 1990—, Outstanding Newsletter award 1991, 92, ednl. equity chair 1994—), Minn. Ednl. Media Orgn. (region chair 1992-94, Emerging Leader award 1991), Phi Kappa Phi (chpt. sec. 1992—), Phi Delta Kappa. Democrat. Lutheran. Home: 716 10th Ave S Saint Cloud MN 56301 Office: St Cloud State U Learning Res Svcs CH311D Saint Cloud MN 56301

INMAN, CLAUDIA JEAN, banker; b. Portland, Oreg., Oct. 23, 1942; d. Claude John and Dorothy Caroline (Svarvari) Forrette; m. Charles Dibert, June 28, 1970 (div. Dec. 1977); m. Robert Willard Inman, Apr. 12, 1980; 1 child, Brian Dibert. Student, Portland State Coll., 1970-88, Lewis & Clark Coll., 1979; banking degree, U. Wash., 1983. Proof transit clk. Bank of Calif., Portland, 1960-62, 68-69; proof and transit clk. LaSalle Nat. Bank, Chgo., 1963-65; with computer payroll and ops. Bank of Calif., Portland, 1969, ops. officer, 1974-75, liaison officer, 1975-79, credit officer, 1979-80, corp. loan officer, asst. v.p., 1980-86, asst. v.p. real estate loans, 1986-89, v.p. real estate loans, 1990-93; v.p. comml. loans Bank of Vancouver, Wash., 1993—; bd. dirs. Machinists and Boilermakers Fed. Credit Union, 1983-88. Vol. Oreg. Art Mus. Rental Sales Gallery, Portland, 1987—; participant women in pvt. sector Am. bus.-culture class Internat. Devel. Ctr. Japan, Williamette U., Salem, 1988-91; mem. Women in Action, 1993—. Mem. Oreg. Mortgage Bankers Assn. (com. 1988-91), Oreg. Bankers Assn. (com. 1980—), Robert Morris Assocs. (bd. dirs. Oreg. 1991), Bank Adminstrn. Inst. (bd. dirs. 1984-87), Fin. Women Internat. (nat. bd. dirs. 1985-86), Women in Action, Robert Morris Assocs., Vancouver C. of C., Rotary. Democrat. Roman Catholic. Home: 4660 SW Ormandy Way Portland OR 97221-3116 Office: Bank of Vancouver 109 E 13th St Vancouver WA 98666-9988

INNISS-BREWER, YVONNE, nurse, insurance company administrator; b. Sanicholas, Aruba, Netherlands Antilles, Mar. 10, 1948; came to U.S., 1975.; d. William Conrad and Ruby Marion (Edwards) I. BS in Human Services, N.H. Coll., 1984; MS in Urban Studies, So. Conn. State U., 1986; Lic. Practical Nurse, John Radcliffe Sch. of Nursing, Oxford, Eng., 1969; MALS, Wesleyan U., 1990. Asst. charge nurse Churchill Hosp., Oxford, Eng., 1971-75; claims reviewer Aetna Life and Casualty, Hartford, Conn., 1975-77; lic. processor Hartford Steam Boiler, 1977-79, supr. claim services, 1979-82, mktg. asst., 1982-87, 88, exec. asst., 1988—. Mem Wadsworth Atheneum, Hartford, 1986—; mem. town com. A Conn. Party, 1992-93, sec., 1990-92. Mem. Internat. Platform Assn. Anglican. Home: 71 Imlay St # B Hartford CT 06105-3609 Office: Hartford Steam Boiler Inspection and Ins Co One State St Hartford CT 06012-3001

INSALACO, BARBARA ANN, artist, art gallery owner; b. Johnson City, N.Y., Aug. 13, 1946; d. Joseph Peter and Julianna Michaelina (Talkiewicz) Bryk; m. Dennis Richard Insalaco, July 15, 1967; 1 child, Gaetano. BFA, SUNY, Buffalo, 1969. Owner Gallery 1100 Niagara, Buffalo. Solo exhbns. include Albright-Knox Art Gallery, Buffalo, 1982, Finger Lakes C.C., Canandaigua, N.Y. 1983, Art Gallery Niagara County C.C., Sanborn, N.Y., 1984, Roberson Ctr. for Arts and Scis., Binghamton, N.Y., 1984, Visual Edits. Gallery, Rochester, N.Y., 1985, Toledo Trust Atrium Gallery, 1986, Glass Grower's Gallery, Erie, Pa., 1987, Barbara Schuller Gallery/A.R.T., Buffalo, 1990, Gallery 1100/Niagara, 1992, 93, Roberson Mus., 1993; group exhbns. include Pastel Soc. Am., N.Y.C., 1982, Daemen Coll. Gallery, Amherst, N.Y., 1983, Mus. Art, Sci. & Industry, Bridgeport, Conn., 1985, Albright-Knox Gallery, (graphics control corp. award 1982), 1981, 87, Three Rivers Exhbn., Pitts., 1986, N.Y. State Mus., 1989, Galerie Tamenaga, N.Y.C., 1991, 92, others; represented in permanent collections Albright-Knox Gallery, Charles Burchfield Ctr., Buffalo, Columbia-Greene C.C., Hudson, N.Y., U. Wis. Stout Inst., Menomonie, Buffalo Sem., Robert Ctr. for Arts and Scis., Park Ridge Ctr., Rochester, Strategic Investments, Buffalo, Security Mut. Life Ins. Co. of N.Y., Binghamton, Emporia (Kans.) State U., Chase Lincoln First, Orchard Park, N.Y. Recipient Best of Show and Purchase award Columbia-Greene C.C., 1983, Purchase award and travel stipend Judith Selkowitz Fine Arts, Inc., 1984; Creative Artitsts Program Svcs. graphics fellow N.Y. State Coun. Arts, 1978. Home: PO Box 474 Buffalo NY 14205-0474

INSARDI, NINA ELIZABETH, benefits administrator; b. Port Chester, N.Y., Dec. 8, 1960; d. Albert Charles and Dorothy Elizabeth (Adis) I. BA in English magna cum laude, U. Richmond, 1982. Exec. sec. CBS Inc., N.Y.C., 1984-85, adminstrv. asst., 1985-86, supr. insured plans, 1986-87, mgr. benefits adminstrn., 1987-89, mgr. benefits comm., 1989—. Editor newsletter CBS Benefits Bull. Tutor Literacy Vols. of Am., Westchester, N.Y., 1989-94; fundraising vol. U. Richmond, N.Y. Alumni Chpt., 1993—; election dist. leader Rye (N.Y.) Dem. Com., 1992—. Mem. Phi Beta Kappa. Democrat. Presbyterian. Office: CBS Inc 51 W 52nd St New York NY 10019

INSCHO, BARBARA PICKEL, mathematics educator; b. Bristol, Tenn., May 25, 1936; d. Robert Roger and Willa Etta (McCarter) Pickel; children: Sara Inscho Johnson, Paula Inscho Trentham. AA, BS, Tenn. Wesleyan Coll., 1957; MS, U. Tenn., Knoxville, 1977; postgrad., U. of the South, 1962-66. Cert. tchr., Tenn. Tchr. math. Sevier County H.S., Sevierville, Tenn., 1957-58, Cocoa (Fla.) H.S., 1958-62, Princeton (N.J.) H.S., 1963-65; assoc. prof. math. Hiwassee Coll., Madisonville, Tenn., 1966-69, 85-88; tchr. math. Madisonville H.S., 1972-83, Maryville (Tenn.) H.S., 1983-85, 88—; adj. prof. math. Tenn. Wesleyan Coll., Athens, 1983-85. Co-author: Basic Skills Practice Book, 1986. V.p. Monroe County Dem. Women, Madisonville, 1990-92; mem. Maryville Coll. Cmty. Choir, 1992-93; tchr. Sunday sch. 1st Bapt. Ch., Madisonville, 1990-92. Recipient Tandy Tech. Scholars award of excellence in math., sci. and computer sci. Tex. Christian U., 1994; NSF grantee, 1962-66; named Tchr. of Yr., Hiwassee Coll., 1986-87. Mem. NEA, Tenn. Edn. Assn., East Tenn. Edn. Assn. (pres. 1982-83, exec. com. 1976-84), Maryville Edn. Assn. (pres. 1991-92), Nat. Coun. Tchrs. Math., Tenn. Math Tchrs. Assn., Smoky Mountain Math. Edn. Assn. Methodist. Home: 1518 Raulston Rd Maryville TN 37803-2861 Office: Maryville H S Math Dept 825 Lawrence St Maryville TN 37803

INSCHO, JEAN ANDERSON, social worker; b. Camden, N.J., Oct. 31, 1936; d. George Myrick and Alfrida Elizabeth (Anderson) Hewitt; m. James Ronald Inscho, June 4, 1955 (div. Mar. 1982); children: James Ronald Jr., Cynthia Ann, Michael Merrick. BA, Fla. Atlantic U., 1971; MA in Coll. Teaching, Auburn U., 1974. Lic. bachelor social worker. Instr. So. Union State Jr. Coll., Wadley, Ala., 1973-75; social worker Jefferson County Dept. Human Resources, Birmingham, Ala., 1976-77, Shelby County Dept. Human Resources, Columbiana, Ala., 1977-78, Houston County Dept. Human Resources, Dothan, Ala., 1978—; adj. instr. Troy State U., Dothan, 1982—. Bd. dirs., v.p. Adolescent Resource Ctr., 1992-93, sec., 1993-95; mem. Alzheimer's Assn., Dothan Area Bot. Gardens. EPDA fellow Auburn U., 1973, 74. Mem. Ala. State Employees Assn. (v.p. Wiregrass chpt. 1987-91, Dist. VII SEA-PAC rep. 1994), Ala. Master Gardeners, Wiregrass Master Gardeners (pres. 1994—), Am. Daffodil Soc. Episcopalian. Office: Houston County Dept Human Resources 1605 Ross Clark Cir SE Dothan AL 36302

INSELBERG, RACHEL, education educator, researcher; b. Manila, Jan. 2, 1934; came to U.S., 1955; d. Melecio and Rosalia (Medrano) Marzan; m. Edgar Inselberg, Aug. 12, 1956; 1 child, Louise Jesse. BS, Philippine Women's U., Manila, 1954; MS, U. Ill., 1956; PhD, Ohio State U., 1960. Tchr. nursery sch. Philippine Women's U., Manila, 1954-55; tchr. 3d grade Pleasant (Ohio) Sch., 1956-57; teaching asst. Ohio State U., Columbus, 1957-59; asst. prof. Carnegie Inst. Tech. Carnegie Inst. Tech., Pitts., 1961-65; from asst. to assoc. prof. Western Mich. U., Kalamazoo, 1966-73, prof., 1973—. Contbr. articles to prof. jours. Active Dem. Campaign, Kalamazoo, 1984, 86, 88. Fulbright scholar, 1955; U. Ill. fellow, 1955; grantee U.S. Office Edn., 1963, Western Mich. U., 1972, 79, 87, Bronson Clin. Investigative Unit, 1987. Mem. Am. Ednl. Rsch. Assn., Nat. Assn. for the Edn. Young Children, Soc. for Rsch. Child Devel., Phi Kappa Phi. Jewish. Home: 3006 Winchell Ave Kalamazoo MI 49008-2176 Office: Western Mich U Kalamazoo MI 49008

INSELMAN, LAURA SUE, pediatrician; b. Bklyn., Nov. 2, 1944; d. Alexander M. and Rae (Bloom) Inselman. BA, Barnard Coll., 1966; MD, Med. Coll. Pa., 1970. Diplomate Am. Bd. Pediatrics, Am. Bd. Pediatric Pulmonology. Intern and resident St. Lukes Hosp. Ctr., N.Y.C., 1970-73; fellow in pediatric pulmonary disease Babies Hosp., N.Y.C., 1973-76; chief pediatric pulmonary div. Interfaith Med. Ctr., Bklyn., 1976-81; chief pediatric pulmonary div. North Shore Univ. Hosp., Manhasset, N.Y., 1981-86; clin. dir. pediatric pulmonary div. Newington Con. Children's Hosp., 1987-92; assoc. pulmonologist, med. dir. dept. respiratory care A.I. duPont Inst., Wilmington, Del., 1992—; asst. prof. pediatrics Cornell U. Med. Coll., N.Y.C., 1981-86; asst. clin. prof. pediatrics, Yale U. Sch. Medicine, New Haven, 1987-92; asst. prof. pediatrics, U. Conn. Health Ctr., Farmington, 1987-92; assoc. prof. pediatrics, Jefferson Med. Coll. Thomas Jefferson U. Hosp., Phila., 1992—; mem. staff Good Samaritan Hosp., West Islip, N.Y., 1982-87. Bd. dirs. Am. Lung Assn. Nassau-Suffolk, East Meadow, N.Y., 1983-86, Del., 1992—. Fellow Am. Acad. Pediatrics, Am. Coll. Chest Physicians; mem. Am. Thoracic Soc., Am. Fedn. Clin. Research, N.Y. Acad. Medicine, Harvey Soc., Soc. Pediatric Research. Office: AI DuPont Inst 1600 Rockland Rd Wilmington DE 19803-3616

INSPRUCKER, NANCY RHOADES, air force officer; b. Fort Campbell, Ky., June 16, 1959; d. Glen Lee and Mary Josephine (Lasell) Rhoades; m. John L. Inspruckeer III, July 20, 1991. BS in Astro Engring., U.S. Air Force Acad., 1981; MS in Aero. and Astronaut. Engring., Stanford U., 1985. Commd. 2d lt. U.S. Air Force, 1981, advanced through grades to maj., 1993; satellite test engr. space div. Los Angeles, 1981-84; instr. dept. astronautics USAF Acad., Colorado Springs, Colo., 1985-88; chief payload devel. and integration divsn. Office Sec. Air Force, L.A. AFB, 1988-90, chief mission processing divsn., 1990-92; chief sys. engr. Office Def. Landsat, Pentagon, Washington, 1992-94, chief sys. engr. divsn. Office of Space Sys. Office Asst. Sec. Air Force, 1994—. Recipient Medal of Merit, Nat. Air Force Assn., 1985; named Colorado Springs Mil. Woman of Yr., Gazette Telegraph newspaper, 1987. Mem. Air Force Assn., Am. Astronautical Soc., Soc. Women Engrs. Avocations: aerobics, long distance running, sewing. Home: 2202 Central Ave Vienna VA 22182 Office: The Pentagon Washington DC 20050

INTILLI, SHARON MARIE, television director, small business owner; b. Amsterdam, N.Y., Aug. 11, 1950; d. Francisco Joseph Intilli and Virginia Eleanor (Tallman) Monaco. Cert., Paralegal Inst., 1973; BA in Psychology, Fordham U., 1995. Group assoc. editor Matthew Bender & Co., N.Y.C., 1974-77; prodn. sec. 20/20 program, ABC, N.Y.C., 1977-78, prodn. assoc., 1979-80, program prodn. asst., 1980-82; legal contract adminstr. ABC Sports, N.Y.C., 1978-79; assoc. dir. Capital Cities/ABC, N.Y.C., 1982—; dir., assoc. dir. freelance projects; owner GrrenBeing, Inc. Contbg. editor Bender's Forms of Discovery, Vols. 15 & 16, 1975. Mem. Bd. Health, Hillsdale, N.J., 1989—. Recipient Outstanding Individual Achievement cert. Nat. Acad. TV Arts & Scis., 1980-81. Mem. Dirs. Guild of Am.

INTRATER, CHERYL WATSON WAYLOR, risk management consultant; b. Montreal, Que., Can., Sept. 8, 1943; naturalized, 1978; d. Alan Douglas and Jean Mary (Hughes) Watson; m. Donald L. Intrater, Nov. 11, 1990. BBA, Ga. State U., 1980, postgrad. Supr. div. Liberty Mut., Atlanta, 1969-76; instr. ins. DeKalb Community Coll., Clarkston, Ga., 1978-79; mgr. div. Kemper Group, 1979-85; owner, pres. h.m.s. Co. Ins. Svcs. (name changed to Ins. Support Svcs., Inc.), Overland Park, 1986-91; lectr. in field; v.p., ins. cons. Fortune and Co. Risk Mgrs. Inc., 1987—; adv. coun. Johnson County Community Coll. Ins. Inst., Overland Park, Kans.; interim dir. profl. continuing edn. Johnson County C.C., 1994; owner Career Trend, 1994—. Contbr. articles to profl. jours. Vol. Girl Scouts U.S.A. Leadership Devel., 1987—. Mem. Ins. Women of Greater Kansas City-Nat. Assn. Ins. Women (pres. 1989-90, Rookie of Yr. 1985, Best Speaker Kansas City State, Mo. 1987, named Region V Ins. Profl. of Yr. 1992, cert. profl. ins. woman, Outstanding Mem. of Yr. 1992), Mission Area C. of C. (chmn. budget and fin. com. 1994—), Toastmasters Internat. (past dist. officer, parliamentarian 1991—, named able toastmaster). Republican. Avocations: sky diving, fencing, running, reading, traveling. Office: 6800 College Blvd Ste 219 Overland Park KS 66211

INTRILIGATOR, DEVRIE SHAPIRO, physicist; b. N.Y.C.; d. Carl and Lillian Shapiro; m. Michael Intriligator; children: Kenneth, James, William, Robert. BS in Physics, MIT, 1962, MS, 1964; PhD in Planetary and Space Physics, UCLA, 1967. NRC-NASA rsch. assoc. NASA, Ames, Calif., 1967-69; rsch. fellow in physics Calif. Inst. Tech., Pasadena, 1969-72, vis. assoc., 1972-73; asst. prof. U. So. Calif., 1972-80; mem. Space Scis. Ctr., 1978-83; sr. rsch. physicist Carmel Rsch. Ctr., Santa Monica, Calif., 1979—; dir. Space Plasma Lab., 1980—; cons. NASA, NOAA, Jet Propulsion Lab.; chmn. NAS-NRC com. on solar-terrestrial rsch., 1983-86, exec. com. bd. atmospheric sci. and climate, 1983-86, geophysics rsch. bd., 1983-86, geophysics study com., 1983-86; U.S. nat. rep. Sci. Com. on Solar-Terrestrial Physics, 1983-86; mem. adv. com. NSF Divsn. Atmospheric Sci. Co-editor: Exploration of the Outer Solar System; contbr. articles to profl. jours. Recipient 3 Achievement awards NASA, Calif. Resolution of Commendation, 1982. Mem. AAAS, Am. Phys. Soc., Am. Geophys. Union, Cosmos Club. Home: 140 Foxtail Dr Santa Monica CA 90402-2048 Office: Carmel Rsch Ctr PO Box 1732 Santa Monica CA 90406-1732

INVERSO, MARLENE JOY, optometrist; b. Los Angeles, May 10, 1942; d. Elmer Encel Wood and Sally Marie (Sample) Hirons; m. John S. Inverso, Dec. 16, 1962; 1 child, Christopher Edward. BA, Calif. State U., Northridge, 1964; MS, SUNY, Potsdam, 1975; OD, Pacific U., 1981. Cert. doctor optometry, Wash., Oreg. English tchr. Chatsworth (Calif.) High Sch., 1964-68, Nelson A. Boylen Second Sch., Toronto, Ont., Can., 1968-70, Gouverneur (N.Y.) Jr.-Sr. High Sch., 1970-74, 76-77; reading resource room tchr. Parishville (N.Y.) Hopkinton Sch., 1974-75; coordinator learning disability clinic SUNY, Potsdam, 1975-77; optometrist and vision therapist Am. Family Vision Clinics, Olympia, Wash., 1982—; mem. adv. com. Sunshine House St. Peter Hosp., Olympia, 1984-86, Pacific U. Coll. Optometry, Forest Grove, Oreg. 1986. Contbr. articles to profl. jours. Mem. Altrusa Svc. Club, Olympia, 1982-86; tchr. Ch. Living Water, Olympia, 1983-88, Olympia-Lacey Ch. of God, 1989—, sec. women's bd., 1990; bd. advisors Crisis Pregnancy Ctr., Olympia, 1987-89; den mother Cub Scouts Am. Pack 202, Lacey, Wash., 1987-88; vol. World Vision Countertop ptnr., 1986—. Fellow Coll. Optometrists in Optometric Devel.; mem. Am. Optometric Assn. (sec. 1983-84), Assn. Children and Adults with Learning Disabilities, Optometric Extension Program, Sigma Xi, Beta Sigma Kappa. Home: 4204 Timberline Dr SE Olympia WA 98503-4443

INZANO, KAREN LEE, advertising agency executive; b. Cleve., July 27, 1946; d. William and Edith (Fisher) Phipps; children: Thomas, Laura, Sharon. Student, Litschert Sch. of Comml. Art, Cleve., 1970-72. Pres., founder AK Graphics Inc., Lakewood, Colo., 1973—; instr. advt. and small bus. Red Rocks Community Coll., 1983-90, mem. mktg. adv. bd., 1986-88. Chmn. Ch. Adminstrv. Bd.; active caucus Colo. Rep. Com., 1980, Green Mountain Homeowners, Lakewood, 1980-84; sr. v.p. Lakewood on Parade, 1985-86; bd. dirs. Lakewood Sister Cities Internat., 1980-89, Lakewood Civic Found., 1986-94; vol. Children's Advocacy Ctr., 1994—; mem. D.A.'s Adv.

Bd., 1992-94. Named State Champion of Free Enterprise Salesman With A Purpose, 1985; recipient Disting. Svc. award Sister Cities Internat., 1984. Mem. Jefferson County C. of C. (bd. dirs. 1980-90, chmn. bd. 1988-89, Small Bus. Person of Yr. 1982), Denver Advt. Fedn. Typographers Internat. Assn., Mac User's Group # 2, Edn. 2000 #3, Woman Bus. Owners. Home and Office: 778 S Alkire St Lakewood CO 80228-2508

INZINGA, JACQUELINE MARIE, counselor; b. Rochester, N.Y., Feb. 26, 1967; d. Bradley Richard and Connie Marie (Casciani) Gisel; m. Christopher R. Inzinga, Oct. 5, 1991. BS in Criminology & Criminal Justice, Niagara U., 1989, MS in Sch. Counseling, 1991. Cert. sch. counselor, N.Y. Residence counselor Women's Place, Rochester, 1990-93; employment cons. Rochester Rehab. Ctr., Webster, N.Y., 1992-93, placement specialist, 1993—. Mem. ACA, Am. Rehab. Counseling Assn. Democrat. Roman Catholic. Home: 580 Adams Rd Webster NY 14580-1144

IP, ANNA YEH, pharmaceutical engineer; b. Taipei, Taiwan, Nov. 27, 1963; came to U.S., 1972; d. Dixon T. S. and Isabella (Teng) Yeh; m. Michael Tze Ngai Ip, Aug. 12, 1990. BSChemE, U. Calif., Berkeley, 1987. Engr.-in-tng. Student rsch. asst. neonatology dept. Stanford (Calif.) Med. Ctr., summer 1983; student trainee immunology dept. DNAX Rsch. Inst., Palo Alto, Calif., summer 1985, 86; student rsch. asst. biochem. engring. group dept. chem. eng. U. Calif., Berkeley, 1986-87; chem. engr. materials and chem. engrin. lab. SRI Internat., Menlo Park, Calif., 1987-92; pharm. engr. dept. pharmacology and drug delivery Amgen Inc., Thousand Oaks, Calif., 1992—; cons. Oculex Pharms., Palo Alto, 1993—. Mem. AICE, Am. Assn. Aerosol Rsch., Fine Particle Soc., Tau Beta Pi. Office: Amgen Inc 1840 Deltavilland Dr Thousand Oaks CA 91320-1789

IRANI, KATIE D., medical educator, rehabilitation services professional; b. Bombay, Aug. 18, 1933; came to U.S., 1969; d. Rustomji N. and Gulcher R. (Kanga) Desai; m. Dinshaw K. Irani, Oct. 15, 1961; children: Adel, Maynaaz. MBBS, Grant Med. Coll., Bombay, 1957. Diplomate Am. Bd. Phys. Medicine and Rehab. Asst. med. officer pub. health dept., dir. outpatient family planning clinic Bombay Mcpl. Corp., 1958-62; pvt. practice Bombay, 1963-66, 67-69; instr. dept. phys. medicine and rehab. Baylor Coll. of Medicine, Houston, 1973-74, asst. prof., 1974—; chief physical medicine and rehab. dept. Harris County Hosp. Dist., Ben Taub Gen. Hosp., Houston, 1990—; chief phys. medicine and rehab. svc. Harris County Hosp. Dist., Houston, 1990—. Pres. Zoroastrian Assn. of Houston, 1983-85, mem. exec. coun., 1980-84, 86-88, 90-92; mem. exec. com., med. dir. 7th N. Am. Zoroastrian Congress, 1990; mem. at larger indian Med. Assn., Houston, 1983. Mem. AMA (physician recognition award 1982), Am. Assn. Electrodiagnostic Medicine, Tex. Med. Assn., Acad. Phys. Medicine and Rehab., Assn. Acad. Medicine, Houston Phys. Medicine and Rehab. Soc. (founder, sec., v.p., pres. 1982-83). Zoroastrian. Home: 5035 W Bellfort Houston TX 77035 Office: Ben Taub Gen Hosp 1504 Taub Loop Houston TX 77030-1608

IRANI, SHEILA ZARAH, marketing professional; b. L.A., July 17, 1962; d. Raymond R. and Nayer (Ghadessi) I. BA in Psychology, UCLA, 1984, BA in Econs., 1984, MBA, 1987. Adminstrv. asst. various law firms, 1982-84; sales asst. Paine Webber Jackson & Curtis, Inc., Calif., 1983; rsch. analyst Merril Lynch Comml. Real Estate, Calif., 1984; fin. anlayst Calmark Asset Mgmt., Calif., 1984-85; software cons. various cons. cos., Calif., 1986-87; corp. fin. assoc. Shearson Lehman Hutton, N.Y.C., 1987; mktg. rep. The Voucher Corp., Calif., 1988-90; sr. cons. The Voucher Corp., 1990-94, nat. dir. transit svcs., 1990-94; v.p. mktg. Commuter Transp. Svcs., L.A., 1994—. Big Sister Big Sister of L.A., 1992; bd. dirs. Univ. Cath. Ctr., UCLA, 1991; bd. dirs. Speech and Lang. Devel. Ctr., Buena Park, 1993. Mem. Assn. Child Care Consul, Orange County Employee Benefit Coun., Soc. of Human Resource Mgrs., Assn. Commuter Transp., Am. Passenger Transport Assn. Democrat. Office: Commuter Transp Svcs Ste 300 3550 Wilshire Blvd Los Angeles CA 90010

IRBY, D. GAIL, federal agency administrator; b. Frankfurt, Germany, Nov. 2, 1954; d. Al Charles and Mary (Price) I. BS in Edn. and Journalism, U. Okla., 1973; MA in Journalism, U. Tex., 1988; student, Command and Staff. Coll., 1988-89. Commd. 2d lt. U.S. Army, 1976, advanced through the grades to lt. col., 1993; assoc. editor Soldier Mag., U.S. Army, 1989-90, exec. editor, 1990-91; exec. adminstrn. officer, directorate for info. systems for C4 The Pentagon, Washington, 1991-92; pub. affairs officer Defense Nuclear Agency, Washington, 1992—. Office: Def Nuclear Agency 6801 Telegraph Rd Rm 113 Alexandria VA 22310*

IRELAND, BARBARA HENNIG, newspaper editor; b. Batavia, N.Y., May 13, 1946; d. John Chester and Mae Electa (Schlagenhauf) Hennig; m. Allyn Lloyd Lamb, May 1, 1963 (div. 1979); children: Jeffrey Allyn, Celia Catherine; m. Corydon Boyd Ireland, May 25, 1985 (div. 1994). BA, Cornell U., 1969. English tchr. Homer (N.Y.) High Sch., 1969-70, Port Byron (N.Y.) High Sch., 1973; reporter Auburn (N.Y.) Citizen, 1973-77; copy editor Albany (N.Y.) Knickerbocker News, 1977; copy editor Buffalo News, 1977-80, editor Sunday mag., 1980-85, editorial writer, 1985-89, editor editorial page, 1989—. John S. Knight fellow Stanford U., 1988-89. Mem. Nat. Conf. Editorial Writers, Phi Beta Kappa. Office: Buffalo News PO Box 100 1 News Plaza Buffalo NY 14240

IRELAND, KATHY, actress; b. Santa Barbara, Calif., 1963; d. John and Barbara I.; m. Greg Olsen, 1988. Appearances in Sports Illustrated's Ann. Swimsuit Issues, 25th Anniversary Show Swimsuit Edit.; films include: Alien from L.A., 1988, Necessary Roughness, 1991, Mom and Dad Save the World, 1992, National Lampoon's Loaded Weapon I, 1993, The Player, Mr. Destiny, Amore, Backfire; TV appearances include: Beauty and the Bandit, Danger Island, Down the Shore, The Edge, Tales from the Crypt, Without a Clue, Grand, Charles in Charge, Perry Mason, Boy Meets World, Melrose Place, The Watcher. Office: The Sterling/Winters Co Ste 1640 1900 Avenue Of The Stars Los Angeles CA 90067-4308

IRELAND, MARDY SANDERS, psychologist; b. El Paso, Tex., Jan. 31, 1948; d. Aaron Perry and Betty Mae (Gelein) Sanders; m. George Bradley Gascoigne, Apr. 7, 1988 (div. May 1993). BA, Duke U., 1970; EdD, U. Hawaii, 1972, PhD, 1976. Clin. psychologist Aiea (Hawaii) Mental Health Clinic, 1977, U. Hawaii, 1978-80, The George Washington U., Washington, 1980-84, Kaiser Permanente, Martinez, Calif., 1984-88; core faculty Profl. Sch. Psychology, San Francisco, 1993—; pvt. practice clin. psychology Berkeley, Calif., 1988—; adj. faculty Santa Clara (Calif.) U., 1988-93; clin. supr. faculty The Psychotherapy Inst., Berkeley, 1988—. Author: (book) Reconceiving Women, 1993; contbr. articles to profl. jours. Mem. APA, Am. Art Therapy Assn., Nat. Register of Health Svc. Providers. Office: 2820 Adeline St Berkeley CA 94703

IRELAND, NORMA OLIN, writer, scholarly, researcher; b. Wadsworth, Ohio, Mar. 27, 1907; d. Carl Leroy and Jessie (Latimer) Olin; m. David Eugene Ireland, Aug. 15, 1931 (dec. 1970). AB, U. Akron, 1928; BS Libr. Studies, Western Reserve U., 1929. Part-time circulation Akron (Ohio) Pub. Libr., 1923-28; reference libr. U. Akron, 1929-36, instr. night sch., 1935; acting asst. libr. Pomona Coll. Libr., Claremont, Calif., 1936-37; acting reference libr. Glendale (Calif.) Pub. Libr., 1937-38; instr. reference work U. So. Calif. Libr. Sch., L.A., 1938-39; acting head Edn. Libr. U. So. Calif., L.A., 1939; co-dir. Ireland Book & Libr. Svc., Altadena, Calif., 1942-50; cataloger Calif. Tech., Jet Propulsion Libr., Pasadena, Calif., 1960-63; freelance indexer McGraw Hill, Stanford U. Press, World Affairs Yearbook, 1966, 67, 68—; nat. chmn. jr. mems. roundtable Am. Libr. Assn., 1939-40, Nat. Contesters Assn., 1953-54. Author: Index to Women, 1989, Index to America, vols. 3, 4, 1989, numerous other books; co-author Index to Fairy Tales, 1989; columnist Fallbrook (Calif.) Enterprise, 1980-87; contbr. articles to profl. jours. Recipient Disting. Alumni award U. Akron, 1979; named to Hall of Fame U. Akron, 1979. Mem. Fallbrook Women's Club (hon.), Nat. Soc. Mayflower, Phi Mu. Republican. Congregationalist.

IRELAND, PATRICIA, association executive; b. Oak Park, Ill., Oct. 19, 1945; d. James Ireland and Joan Filipek; m. James Humble, 1968. Grad., Univ. Miami Law Sch., 1975. Flight attendant Pan Am. World Airlines, 1967-75; ptnr. Stearns, Weaver, Miller, Weissler, Alhadeff and Sitterson, Miami; legal counsel Dade County and Fla. NOW; dir. Project Stand Up for Women NOW, initiator Global Feminist Conf.; NOW rep. European Parliament, Nat. Congress Brazilian Women, German-Am. Women's Confs., Cuban Women's Fedn., European Women's Solidarity Conf., England's Nat. Abortion Campaign; exec. v.p. NOW, from 1987, pres., 1991—. Contbr. law rev. Univ. Miami Law Sch. Office: NOW 1000 16th St NW Ste 700 Washington DC 20036-5705*

IRICK, DAWN RENEE, mortgage loan officer; b. Huntington, Ind., Nov. 13, 1962; d. James Dale and Beverly Ann (Vought) Shivley; m. Troy Don Irick, Oct. 12, 1985; children: Patrick James Ryan, Molly Anna Marie. G-rad. high sch., Huntington. Bookkeeper First Nat. Bank, Huntington, 1982-85, mortgage loan officer, 1991—; loan processor Valley Am. Fank, South Bend, Ind., 1985-86; consumer loan officer Star Fin. Bank, Columbia City, Ind., 1986-91. Mem. Huntington County Leadership Coun., Huntington, 1994; vol. United Way Fund Dr., Columbia City, Ind., 1989, Boy Scouts Am. Fund Dr., Huntington, 1993, Huntington County Rep. party, Huntington, 1992; co-chmn., bd. mem. Columbia City Mr. Miss Program, 1986—; bd. dirs. Huntington County Children's Choir, Trinity United Meth. Ch. Children's Coun. Mem. Forks of the Wabash Pioneer Festival, Am. Cancer Soc., Psi Iota Xi. Republican. Methodist. Home: 3208 Brampton Dr Huntington IN 46750-2206

IRISH, JEAN DARLENE, psychologist; b. Kittery, Maine, Dec. 17, 1951; d. Eugene Leon and Betty Ann Frances (Alley) I. BA, U. So. Maine, 1978; MA, U. Miss., 1982, PhD, 1986. Lic. psychologist, Maine. Rsch. asst. psychology U. Miss., Oxford, 1981-83; live-in house mgr. North Miss. Retardation Ctr., Oxford, 1983-84; psychol. intern U. Maine, Orono, 1984-85; asst. core group leader Jackson Brook Inst., South Portland, Maine, 1989; pvt. practice Gorham, Maine, 1989—; Head Start cons. Region II Mental Health Ctr., Oxford, 1983-84; adj. faculty U. So. Maine, Sanford, 1989. Contbr. articles to profl. jours. Organizer Neighborhood Crime Watch, Standish, Maine, 1992. Mem. APA, Maine Psychol. Assn. (pres. 1993-94, legis. com. 1992-95), Soc. Maine Psychologists, Maine Profl. Study Group. Office: 510 Main St Gorham ME 04038

IRMIERE-MARCHITTO, AMY FRANCES, futures compliance securities trader; b. Paterson, N.J., Apr. 23, 1961; d. Frank Nicholas and Amedia Delores (Contini) Irmiere; m. Michael Otto Marchitto, Aug. 23, 1987; 1 child, Michael Frank. BS in Pub. Health Adminstrn. and Econs., Livingston Coll., 1984. Cert. paralegal, futures compliance. With Drexel Burnham Lambert, N.Y.C., 1983-90, N.Y. stock exchange options fl. broker, 1987-89, Am. stock exchange options fl. broker, 1989-91; asst. v.p. Smith Barney Future Compliance, N.Y.C., 1991—. Republican. Roman Catholic. Home: 4 Avery Dr Old Bridge NJ 08857-3602

IROM, ELANA HARRIET, psychotherapist, consultant; b. Bklyn.; d. Sidney and Bessie (Nussbaum) Walfish. BSW, Adelphi U., 1978, MSW, 1979. Bd. cert. diplomate; lic. social worker, N.Y. Pvt. practice N.Y.C., 1980—; clin. coord., supr. YMCA Outreach Svcs., Bay Shore, N.Y., 1980-83; adj. prof. Adelphi U., Garden City, N.Y., 1983-84; cons. therapist Pavlin-Lungen Assocs., Gt. Neck, N.Y., 1983-85; staff psychotherapist Washington Square Inst., N.Y.C., 1984-91; staf therapist, supr. Inst. for Psychotherapeutic Advancement, N.Y.C., 1987-90; lectr., instr. Marymount Manhattan Coll., N.Y.C., 1986-88. Mem. Profl. Soc. Washington Square Inst., Am. Assn. Psychotherapists (planning com. 1990—, chmn. N.E. region 1991-93).

IRVINE, PHYLLIS ELEANOR KUHNLE, academic administrator; b. Germantown, Ohio, July 14, 1940; d. Carl Franklin and Mildred Viola (Erisman) Kuhnle; m. Richard James Irvine, Feb. 15, 1964; children: Mark, Rick. BSN, Ohio State U., 1962, MSN, 1979, PhD, 1981; MS, Miami U., Oxford, Ohio, 1966. Staff nurse VA Ctr., Dayton, Ohio, 1962-66; mem. nursing faculty Miami Valley Hosp. Sch. Nursing, Dayton, 1968-78; teaching asst., lectr. Ohio State U., Columbus, 1979-82; assoc. prof. Ohio U., Athens, 1982-83; prof., dir. N.E. La. U., Monroe, 1984-88; prof., dir. sch. nursing Ball State U., Muncie, Ind., 1988—. Reviewer Health Edn. Jour., Phila., 1987, Main Indianapolis, 1992—; contbr. articles to profl. jours. Mem. Mayor's Commn. on Needs of Women, La., 1984-88; 1st v.p., bd. dirs. United Way of Ouachita, La., 1986-88. Mem. ANA, Ind. Nurses Assn., Ind. Coun. Deans & Dirs. of Nursing Edn. (pres. 1992-96), Internat. Coun. Women's Health Issues (bd. dirs. 1986-92), Assn. for the Advancement Health Edn., Sigma Theta Tau. Office: Ball State U Cn418 Nursing Muncie IN 47306

IRVINE, ROSE LORETTA ABERNETHY, retired communications educator, consultant; b. Kingston, N.Y., Nov. 14, 1924; d. William Francis and Julia (Flynn) A.; m. Robert Tate Irvine Jr., Dec. 18, 1965 (dec. June 1968). BA, Coll. St. Rose, 1945; MA, Columbia U., 1946; PhD, Northwestern U., 1964. Tchr. English Kingston High Sch., 1946-47; tchr. English and speech Croton-Harmon High Sch., Croton-on-Hudson, N.Y., 1947-49; instr. speech SUNY, New Paltz, 1949-53; asst. prof. SUNY, New Platz, 1953-57, assoc. prof., 1957-64, prof. speech communication, 1964-85, prof. emeritus, 1985—; guest prof. Yousoi U., Seoul, Republic Korea, 1970; U.S. del. U.S. Bi-Nat. Conf., Manila, 1976; adv. bd. Rondout Nat. Bank Norstar (now Fleet Bank), 1973-85; U. Chancellor's adv. bd. SUNY Senate, Albany, 1974-80; guest prof. Celtic lore Princess Grace Libr., Monaco, 1987; cons., rschr., writer, 1985—; presenter in field. Contbr. articles to Speech Teacher, Educational Forum, Readers Theatre, others. Mem. Nat. Jr. League, Kingston, 1958-90; dir. Puppet Theater for Srs., N.Y., 1982-83; mem. pres. adv. com. Ulster County C.C., 1986—. Honor Tuition scholar Coll. St. Rose, Albany, N.Y., 1941; named Outstanding Educator of Am., 1971. Mem. AAUW (liaison SUNY New Paltz 1966-85), Speech Comm. Assn. (mem. legis assembly 1967-68), N.Y. State Speech Assn. (emeritus), Zeta Phi Eta, Delta Kappa Gamma, Kappa Delta Pi, Pi Lambda Theta. Roman Catholic. Home: 105 Lounsbury Pl Kingston NY 12401-5231 Office: SUNY New Paltz NY 12561

IRVING, AMY, actress; b. Palo Alto, Calif., Sept. 10, 1953; m. Steven Spielberg, Nov. 27, 1985 (div.); 1 child, Max Samuel; m. Bruno Barreto, 1990; 1 child, Gabriel Davis Barreto. Student, Am. Conservatory Theatre, London Acad. Dramatic Art. Films include Carrie, 1976, The Fury, 1978, Voices, 1979, Honeysuckle Rose, 1980, The Competition, 1980, Yentl, 1983, Mickey and Maude, 1984, Crossing Delancey, 1988, (voice) Who Framed Roger Rabbit, 1988, A Show of Force, 1990, (voice) An American Tail: Fievel Goes West, 1991, Benefit of the Doubt, 1993, Kleptomania, 1994; TV appearances include: The Rookies, Policewoman, Happy Days; TV movies James Dean, 1975, James A. Michener's Dynasty, 1976, Panache, 1976, Anastasia: The Mystery of Anna, 1986, Heartbreak House, 1986, Rumpelstiltskin, 1986, The Turn of the Screw, 1989; miniseries Once an Eagle, 1976-77, The Far Pavilions, 1984, Twilight Zone, 1994; appeared as Juliet in Romeo and Juliet, Seattle Repertory Theatre, 1982-83; appeared on Broadway in Amadeus, 1981-82, Heartbreak House, 1983-84, Broken Glass, 1994, off Broadway The Road to Mecca, 1988, The Heidi Chronicles, 1990-91.

IRVING, BRENDA A., secondary education educator; b. St. Louis, May 11, 1947; d. Fred V. and Corzetta (Jones) I. BS, Lincoln U., 1969; EMR cert., Harris-Stowe U., 1972; MA, N.E. Mo. State U., 1978; student, Paris Am. Acad., 1978. Cert. home economics, Mo. Tchr. St. Louis (Mo.) Pub. Schs., 1969—; sec. adv. bd. DePaul's Hosp., St. Louis, 1971-73. Camp dir. Girl Scout Coun. Greater St. Louis, 1970-86, bd. mem., 1975-79; asst. dir. St. Louis (Mo.) Progressive Christian Edn., 1976-79, Mo. Progressive Christian Edn., St. Louis, Kansas City, 1987—; dir. Mo. Progressive Missionary Baptist Conv., Congress of Christian Edn., 1993; sec. 27th Ward Polit. Orgn., St. Louis, 1984; mem. Congress Christian Edn.; tchr. Midwest Region Congress Christian Edn. Progressive Nat. Bapt. Conv. Inc., Washington, 1991—. Recipient Thanks badge Girl Scout Coun. St. Louis, 1972, 20 Yr. Svc. award Greater Mt. Carmel Bapt. Ch., St. Louis, 1987; Mo. Home Econs. Assn. exec. bd. scholar, 1994. Mem. Am. Home Econs. Assn., Mo. Home Econs. Assn. (bd. dirs. 1986-89, scholarship com. 1992—, chmn. 1994—, sec. dist. B 1993—), Mo. Home Econs. Tchrs. Assn., St. Louis Tchrs. Home Econs. Assn. (pres. 1987-89), Mo. Vocat. Assn., Lincoln U. Alumni Assn., Delta Sigma Theta (parliament 1968-69), Phi Delta Kappa. Baptist. Home: 4919 Lotus Ave Saint Louis MO 63113-1704

IRVING, JOYCE ARLENE, social worker, consultant; b. LaGrange, Tex., Aug. 8, 1945; d. Major Lee and Cora (Williams) Brown; m. Daniel Lamar Irving, Dec. 4, 1966; children: Dana Lorraine, Jerren Alan. AA, Sacramento City Coll., 1971; BA, Calif. State U., Sacramento, 1975, MSW, 1978. Program and tng. asst. Social Scis. Tng. Div., Sacramento, 1965-73; investigator, interviewer Social Svcs. Fraud Unit, Sacramento, 1973-76; social worker Sacramento County Social Svcs., 1976-80; casework specialist Calif. State Dept. Youth Authority, 1980-86, background investigator, 1986-88, casework specialist, 1988—; historian, editor Jack & Jill of Am., Sacramento, 1986-89, program dir., 1990—; cons. Group Home Inc., Sacramento, 1989-90. Mem. Assn. Black Correctional Workers (treas., exec. bd. 1988-90, Pres.'s award 1985, 89), Black Child Inst., Calif. Correctional Peace Officers Assn. (exec. bd. Sacramento chpt. 1990—), Nat. Assn. Univ. Women, Delta Sigma Theta. Home: 9845 Florin Rd Sacramento CA 95829-9311 Office: Calif Dept Youth Authority 3001 Ramona Ave Sacramento CA 95826-3814

IRWIN, G. STORMY, retired paper manufacturing professional; b. Melrose Park, Ill., Sept. 4, 1929; d. Charles W. and Mary E. (Worthley) I. With Zellerbach Paper Co. (div. Mead Co.), Sacramento, 1952-85, ret., 1985. Mng. editor, pub., owner Women in Softball mag. (Women in Sports 1957-72), 1957-78. Coach, mgr., participant Sacramento City Leagues. Recipient 1st place awards for continuous coverage of softball for non-daily pubsl. under 50,000 circulation Nat. Softball Broadcasters and Writers Assn., 1965, 66, 67, 69, 71, 72, 73; won 31 titles for volleyball, basketball, flag football and softball participation. Home: 1945 Piner Rd Lot 85 Santa Rosa CA 95403-6909

IRWIN, JAYNE WILLIAMS, social service agency administrator, business executive; b. Warren, Ohio, Apr. 12, 1945; d. Harold Verne and Helen Virginia (Shaffer) Williams; m. William Archibald Irwin, June 30, 1973; children: David Kean, Martha Anne. BS in Math. and Physics, Bowling Green State U., 1968; MS in Human Devel., Family Studies, Pa. State U., 1984; postgrad., Ohio State U.; spl. studies, Family Life Inst., 1984-93, Lycoming Valley Assn. for Deaf, 1991-92. Math. tchr. Castalia (Ohio) H.S., 1968; sci., math., physics tchr. North H.S., Columbus, Ohio, 1968-74; teaching asst. individual and family studies Pa. State U., State Coll., Pa., 1982-84; family and individual therapist Tressler Luth. Svcs. Assocs. Family & Children's Svcs., Williamsport, Pa., 1984-93; founding dir., adminstr., cons., workshop leader Awareness Comm., Inc., Williamsport, 1993—; co-owner, pres. ATAC...Corp., Williamsport. Author: Windows: Reredos of St. Paul's, 1992. Vol. to Deaf Students Loyalsock Sch. Dist., Williamsport, 1991-92; pres. MicroComputer User's Group, State Coll., Pa., 1992; sr. warden, vestry mem. St. Paul's Episcopal Ch., Lock Haven, Pa., 1993—. Named Outstanding Tchr., Columbus Pub. Schs., 1971; recipient Presidential Sports award, 1993. Mem. NAFE. Home: 323 Irwin St Lock Haven PA 17745-2315 Office: ATAC Corp 1738 E 3rd St # 301 Williamsport PA 17701-3862

IRWIN, LINDA BELMORE, consultant; b. Portland, Oreg., Apr. 29, 1950; d. Calvin C. and Dorothy B. (Belmore) Harper; m. Michael Hugh Irwin, June 24, 1989. Student Portland State U., 1968-72. With Hyatt Regency-New Orleans, 1975-78, catering Hyatt-Regency-Capitol Hill, Washington, 1978-80, dir. catering Hyatt-Anaheim, Calif., 1978-80; mgr. Dockside Yacht Sales, Annapolis, Md., 1981-85; dir. sales and mktg. Loew's Hotel, 1985-86; dir. mktg. Annapolis Marriot, 1986-88; ind. mktg. cons., Washington and Dallas, 1988—; ambassador State of Md., Annapolis, 1986-88; mktg. chair Tourism Council Annapolis and Anne Arundel County; curricula advisor Anne Arundel Community Coll.; mem. fund raising com. Ch. Circle Beautification Trust. Mem. Nat. Banquet Mgrs. Guild (founder Los Angeles chpt.), Nat. Assn. Female Execs. (area dir. 1985—), Annapolis C. of C. (ambassador 1985-88), Greater Washington Soc. of Assn. Execs., Anne Arundel Trade Council, Md. Tourism Council (adv. bd.), Internat. Platform Assn. Republican. Episcopalian. Avocations: sailing, travel, literature, calligraphy, ballet.

IRWIN, MICHELLE KATHLEEN, artist, educator; b. Boston, July 23, 1950. BA in Edn., So. Conn. State U., 1972; MA in Tech. Edn., W.Va. U., 1987; postgrad., Internat. Sch., London, Eng., 1973. Cert. tchr., Calif. Tchr. trainer Nat. Tchr. Tng. Coll., Maseru, Lesotho, Africa, 1975-77, crafts technician mohair spinning project, 1977-79; office mgr. Bus. Internat., San Francisco, 1980-83; muralist Marine World/Africa U.S.A., Vallejo, Calif., 1984; bd. dirs., adv. bd. mem. Precita Eyes Mural Arts Ctr., San Francisco, 1984—; artist, cons. Learning Through Edn. in the Arts Project, San Francisco, 1989—, Dr. Charles R. Drew Sch., San Francisco, 1990—; instr. computers New Coll. of Calif., San Francisco, 1994—; cons. San Francisco Unified Schs., 1989—. Author, artist: Resources in Technology, Vols. I and II, 1983; muralist Food for the People, 1988. Vol. S.H.A.R.E. Self-Help Food Distbn., San Francisco, 1988-92. Mem. NEA, Am. Fedn. Tchrs., Calif. Fedn. Tchrs. Home and Office: 3030 Ingalls Ave San Francisco CA 94124

IRWIN, MIRIAM DIANNE OWEN, book publisher, writer; b. Columbus, Ohio, June 14, 1930; d. John Milton and Miriam Faith (Studebaker) Owen; m. Kenneth John Irwin, June 5, 1960; 1 child, Christopher Owen Irwin. BS in Home Econs., Ohio State U., 1952, postgrad. in bus. adminstrn., 1961-62. Editorial asst. Am. Home Mag., N.Y.C., 1953-56; salesman Owen Realty, Dayton, Ohio, 1957-58, Clevenger Realty, Phoenix, 1958-59; home economist Columbus and So. Ohio Electric Co., 1959-60; pub. Mosaic Press, Cin., 1977—; pub. distbr. D'Bridge Email Systems N.Am. (a Mosaic Press div.), 1991—; owner Bibelot Bindery, 1987—. Author: Lute and Lyre, 1977, Forty is Fine, 1977, Miriam Mouse's Survival Manual, 1977, Miriam Mouse's Costume Collection, 1977, Miriam Mouse's Marriage Contract, 1977, Miriam Mouse, Rock Hound, 1977, Silver Bindings, 1983; editor: Tribute to the Arts, 1984; contbg. author Publisher's Favorite, 1988; illustrator: Corals of Pennekamp, 1979. Daytime crew chief Wyoming Life Squad, Ohio, 1966-71. Mem. Miniature Book Soc. (past bd. dirs., chairperson 1987-89), Am. Philol. Assn., DAR. Presbyterian. Avocation: book collecting. Home and Office: 358 Oliver Rd Cincinnati OH 45215-2615

ISAAC, BINA SUSAN, data processing executive; b. Nainital, India, Jan. 9, 1958; came to U.S. 1980; d. Rajan Kurian and Susan (Thomas) George; m. Mathew Isaac, July 14, 1980; children: Sonya Susan, Shawn George. BA, Sarah Tucker Coll., Tirunelveli, India, 1978; MA, Madurai U., India, 1980; MEd, U. Toledo, 1981, MBA, 1984. Coord. computer svcs. and computer ctr. Lourdes Coll., Sylvania, Ohio, 1984-85; dir. computer svcs. and computer ctr. Lourdes Coll., Sylvania, 1985—, part-time instr., 1985—; instr. Lifelong Learning Ctr., Sylvania, 1985—. Mem. Assn. Systems Mgmt., Ohio Assn. Ind. Rsch., SIG 3X Inc. (spl. interest group). Home: 7328 Gibley Park Toledo OH 43617 Office: Lourdes Coll 6832 Convent Blvd Sylvania OH 43560-2891

ISAAC, YVONNE RENEE, construction company executive; b. Cleve., Apr. 13, 1948; d. Leon Warren and Vernice Leona (Hallom) I.; m. Harold E. Rhynie, Dec. 30, 1984. BA, Sarah Lawrence Coll., 1970; MS, Rensselaer Poly. Inst., 1973, BArch, Poly. Inst., 1976. Market researcher GE Co., Phila., 1971-72; cons., planner SPA/Redco (subs. Perkins & Will), Chgo., 1972-75; sr. assoc. Perkins & Will, N.Y.C., 1975-76, project mgr., 1978-81; supply assoc. Mobil Oil Corp., N.Y.C., 1976-78; project mgr. Ehrenkrantz Group, P.C., N.Y.C., 1981-84; asst. dir. Met. Transp. Authority, N.Y.C., 1984-86; group dir. N.Y.C. Health & Hosps. Corp., N.Y.C., 1986-92; v.p. McDevitt Street Bovis, Atlanta, 1992—; vis. assoc. prof. Pratt Inst., Bklyn., 1977; asst. prof. Columbia U. Grad. Sch. Architecture and Planning, N.Y.C., 1977-78. Mem. games adv. team Atlanta Paralympic Orgn. Com., 1995—. Democrat. Home: 1194 Rosedale Rd NE Atlanta GA 30306-2558 Office: McDevitt Street Bovis 700 Central Pky Ste 1400 Atlanta GA 30328

ISAAC NASH, EVA MAE, educator; b. Natchitoches Parish, La., July 24, 1936; d. Earfus Will Nash and Dollie Mae (Edward) Johnson; m. Will Isaac Jr., July 1, 1961 (dec. May 1970). BA, San Francisco State U., 1974, MS in Edn., 1979, MS in Counseling, 1979; PhD, Walden U., 1985; diploma (hon.), St. Labre Indian Sch., 1990. Nurse's aide Protestant Episcopal Home, San Francisco, 1957-61; desk clk. Fort Ord (Calif.) Post Exchange, 1961-63; practical nurse Monterey (Calif.) Hosp., 1963-64; tchr. San Francisco Unified Schs., 1974; counselor, instr. City Coll. San Francisco, 1978-79; tchr. Oakland (Calif.) Unified Sch. Dist., 1974—; pres. sch. adv. coun., Oakland, 1977-78, faculty adv. coun., 1992-93; advt. writer City Coll., San Francisco, 1978; instr. vocat. skill tng., Garfield Sch., Oakland, 1980-81; pub. speaker various edn. insts. and chs., Oakland, San Francisco, 1982—; lectr. San Jose State U., 1993. Author video tape Hunger: An Assassin in the Classroom, 1993-

94. Recipient Community Svc. award Black Caucus of Calif. Assn. Counseling and Devel., 1988, Cert. of Recognition, 1990; named Citizen of the Day, Sta. KABL, 1988. Mem. ASCD, Internat. Reading Assn., Nat. Assn. Female Execs., Am. Personnel and Guidance Assn., Calif. Personnel and Guidance Assn., Internat. Platform Assn. (Hall Fame 1989, Profl. Speaking cert. 1993), Phi Delta Kappa. Democrat. Office: Oakland Unified Sch Dist 1025 2nd Ave Oakland CA 94606-2212

ISAACS, AMY FAY, political organization executive; b. Phoenix, Nov. 11, 1946; d. Richard and Bessie (Wagner) Hamburger; m. John David Isaacs, Oct. 6, 1974; children: Rachel Elizabeth, Stanley Richard. Student, U. Cologne, Germany, 1967-68; BA, Am. U., 1969; MA, Sch. for Internat. Tng., Brattleboro, Vt., 1970. With AID, Washington, 1965-66; tchr. English, Turkish Am. Univs. Assn., Istanbul, 1969; direct mail and fundraising cons., Washington, 1986-87; sr. coord. communications Planned Parenthood Fedn. Am., Washington, 1987-89; various positions Ams. for Dem. Action, Washington, 1969-86, nat. dir., 1989—. Observer del. Liberal Internat., Stockholm, 1984; del. Am. Coun. on Germany, Berlin, Dallas, 1985-87; mem. fin. com. Dukasis for Pres., Washington, 1987-88; mem. quality of care com. Group Health Assn., Washington, 1987-93. Democrat. Jewish. Home: 2018 Pierce Mill Rd NW Washington DC 20010 Office: Ams for Dem Action 1625 K St NW # 210 Washington DC 20006-1401

ISAACS, ANDREA, dancer, choreographer; b. Chgo., July 16, 1952; d. William H. and Sally (Shapiro) I. BFA, U. Ill., 1975; MA, U. Iowa, 1985. Cert. secondary tchr. Founder, artistic dir., pres. Moving Images Dance Co., Chgo. and Troy, N.Y., 1976—; artist-in-residence Ill. Arts Council, Chgo., 1978-86; dance dir. Emma Willard Sch., Troy, 1986-94; editor The Enneagram Monthly, 1994—. Choreographer: Village, 1985, Travelers, 1986 Dancing with a Foot in Two Worlds, 1988, Sacred Dream, 1989, Raven, 1990, Borrowed Ledges, Cocoon and Trinity, 1992, Avalon, 1992, Awakening, 1992, No Slack for You, 1993, Walking to the Falls, 1993, Northern Lights, 1993, Red Sea, 1994, Don't Worry Be Happy, 1994. Ill. Arts Coun. fellow, 1980; Ill. Arts Coun. grantee, 1978-86; recipient N.Y. State Arts Decentralization awards, 1988, 89, 90, 92, 93. Mem. Dance Alliance (chmn. 1987—), Chgo. Dance Arts Coalition. Home and Office: RD 6 Box 21 Sweetmilk Creek Rd Troy NY 12180

ISAACS, HELEN COOLIDGE ADAMS (MRS. KENNETH L. ISAACS), artist; b. N.Y.C., Jan. 17, 1917; d. Thomas Safford and Martha (Montgomery) Adams; student Miss Hewett's classes, N.Y.C., Miss Porter's Sch., Farmington, Conn., Fontainbleau (France) Sch. Art and Music, 1935, Art Students League, 1936; m. Kenneth L. Isaacs, Mar. 10, 1949; children: Kenneth Coolidge, Anne Isaacs Merwin. Represented by Child's Gallery, Boston. One-woman shows at Child's Gallery; group shows: 3 times at Allied Artists, N.Y., Boston Arts Festival; portraits of various prominent persons; murals in various pub. bldgs., Boston, Rochester, N.Y., Pittsfield, Mass., Daytona, Fla.; represented in painting and drawing collections Fogg Mus., Cambridge, Mass., Nat. Mus. Women in the Arts, Washington, Whaling Mus., New Bedford, Mass. Mem. Colonial Dames Am., Colony Club (N.Y.C.), Chilton Club (Boston). Home: 68 Beacon St Boston MA 02108-3422

ISAACSON, ARLINE LEVINE, food and beverage executive, hotel executive; b. Bklyn., Jan. 28, 1946; d. Harry and Sally (Fogelman) Levine; m. Leslie Robert Isaacson, Oct. 31, 1964 (div. July 1970); 1 child, Eric Michael. AAS in Hotel and Restaurant Mgmt., N.Y.C. Tech. Coll., 1983. Restaurant and lounge mgr. Holiday Inn, N.Y.C., 1982-83; mgr. Astors, St. Regis Hotel, N.Y.C., 1983-84; banquet and conf. mgr. Mariner 15 Conf. Ctr., N.Y.C., 1984-85; dir. banquets, confs. and sales Sardi's Restaurant Corp., N.Y.C., 1985-87; dir. catering sales Days Inn Hotel, N.Y.C., 1987-91; catering sales mgr. St. Moritz on the Park Hotel, N.Y.C., 1991-92; dir. catering Roosevelt Hotel, N.Y.C., 1992-93; catering sales mgr. Sheraton Park Ave., N.Y.C., 1993—. Dem. vol. Koch Relection Campaign, N.Y.C., 1985. Mem. Food and Beverage Mgrs. Assn. (sec. 1984-88, 91, exec. dir. 1995—), Roundtable for Women in Food Svc. (treas. 1986-87), Meeting Planners Internat., Soc. Incentive Travel, Hotel Sales and Mktg. Assn., Internat. Food Svc. Execs., N.Y.C. Tech. Coll. Alumni Assn. (bd. dirs. 1986—, v.p. 1986-87). Jewish. Avocations: dancing, travel, theatre, gourmet cooking. Home: 1836 E 18th St Brooklyn NY 11229-2965 Office: Sheraton Park Ave Hotel 45 Park Ave New York NY 10016-3406

ISAACSON, EDITH LIPSIG, civic leader; b. N.Y.C., Jan. 18, 1920; d. I.A. and Bertha (Evans) Lipsig; m. Selian Hebald; children: Anne Mandelbaum, Selian Jr.; m. William J. Isaacson. Student, Radcliffe Coll., 1936-39, 41; LLB, St. Lawrence U., 1943. Pres. Forest Knolls Corp., N.Y.C., 1960—, Norman Homes Corp., N.Y.C., 1968—; bd. govs. Medford Leas Residents Assn., 1990-92, v.p., 1991-92. Author biographies Am. artists; writer club handbooks. Fellow Pierpont Morgan Library, N.Y.C.; mem. Carnegie Council Ethics Internat. Affairs, founders com. Am. Symphony Orch., N.Y., 1962; nat. sec. Women's Am. Orgn. Rehab. through Tng., 1950; trustee Allergy Found. Am.; bd. govs. Medford Leas Residents Assn., 1991. Mem. Radcliffe Coll. Alumnae Assn. (chmn. clubs 1966). Clubs: Harvard (N.Y.C.), Cosmopolitan (N.Y.C.) (bd. govs. 1987—); Radcliffe (pres. Washington chpt. 1969) (pres. N.Y. chpt. 1959, 63, bd. sponsors 1974).

ISABELLA, MARY MARGARET, lawyer; b. Pitts., Oct. 16, 1947; d. Sebastian C. and Joanna C. (Ferris) I. BS in Biology, Duquesne U., 1969; cert. med. technologist, Mercy Hosp., Pitts., 1970; JD, Duquesne U., 1975. Bar: Pa. 1976, U.S. Dist Ct. (we. dist.) Pa. 1976, U.S. Supreme Ct. 1982. Sole practice Pitts., 1977—; instr. Wheeling (W.Va.) Coll., 1978-80. mem. coun. Brentwood Whitehall Assn., Pitts., 1984-90; bd. dirs. Dukes Ct. Duquesne U.; bd. govs. Law Alumni Assn., treas., 1993, sec., 1994—. Mem. ABA, Pa. Bar Assn., Allegheny County Bar Assn., Delta Theta Phi (past asst. dist. chancellor). Republican. Roman Catholic. Lodge: Italian Sons and Daughters of Am. (trustee local chpt.). Office: 4101 Brownsville Rd Bldg 200 Pittsburgh PA 15227-3336

ISAY, JANE FRANZBLAU, publisher; b. Cin., Aug. 24, 1939; d. Abraham Norman and Rose (Nadler) Franzblau; children: David Avram, Joshua Daniel. AB, Bryn Mawr Coll., 1961. First reader Harcourt, Brace Co., 1963; asst. editor, then assoc. editor Yale U. Press, 1964-66, editor, then exec. editor, 1966-79; assoc. publisher Basic Books Inc., N.Y.C., 1979, co-pub., exec. v.p., 1979-83; v.p., dir. electronic and tech. pub. Harper & Row, 1983-84; v.p., pub. Touchstone Books, Simon & Schuster, N.Y.C., 1985-87; editorial dir. trade books Addison-Wesley Pub. Co., 1987-91, v.p., 1990-91; pub. Grosset Books G.P. Putnam's, N.Y.C., 1991—; bd. advisers pub. program NYU; mem. adv. bd. Wesleyan U. Press; bd. dirs. The New Press, 1994—. Bd. dirs. Ezra Acad., New Haven, 1964-79, Yale U. Friends of Hillel, 1965-68, Women's Media Group; mem. vis. com. Harvard Grad. Sch. Edn. Fellow Timothy Dwight Coll., Yale U., 1969—. Mem. Assn. Am. Pubs. (chair freedom to read com. 1990-94), Jewish Publ. Soc. (bd. dirs. 1990-94). Office: Grosset Books 200 Madison Ave New York NY 10016-3901

ISBELL, VIRGINIA, state legislator; b. Chinook, Mont., May 8, 1932; d. Domenico Renda and Bessie M. (Newton) Renda; cert. med. sec. No. Mont. Coll., 1953; m. Donald D. Isbell, Oct. 11, 1953; children—David, Daniel, Mahealani, Iwalani, Richard. Tchr., Kona (Hawaii) Schs., 1962-72; mgr. Wilmot Boone, M.D., Allan Hubacker, M.D., Kona Coast Med. Group, Inc., Kailua, Kona, Hawaii, 1972-78; mem. Hawaii Ho. of Reps., 1980—. Bd. dirs. Kona Family YMCA; founder West Hawaii Fund. Named Woman of Yr., Mayor's award, 1980. Democrat. Mem. Ch. of Jesus Christ of Latter-day Saints. Club: Soroptimist (past pres.). Office: State Office Tower 235 S Beretania St Rm 1101 Honolulu HI 96813*

ISELIN, SALLY CARY, writer; b. Nahant, Mass., June 16, 1915; d. Charles Pelham and Edith Goddard (Roelker) Curtis; m. Lewis Iselin, June 14, 1935 (dec.); children: Edith Byron, Sarah Cary. Student, Harvard U., 1933. Editorial asst. sports and fgn. news depts. Newsweek mag., N.Y.C., 1942-45; soc. and non-fiction editor Town & Country Mag., N.Y.C., 1945-48; reporter, researcher Life Mag., N.Y.C., 1948-50; writer-contact CBS, N.Y.C., 1951; fashion editor Women's Home Companion, N.Y.C., 1956; freelance writer. Fund raiser Planned Parenthood, 1935—, Robert Kennedy for Senate, 1964. Mem. Colony Club, Fashion Group, Century Assn. Democrat. Episcopalian. Home: 11 E 73rd St New York NY 10021

ISENOR, LINDA DARLENE, grocery retailer, marketing professional; b. Calgary, Alta., Can., Oct. 3, 1955; d. Frank Carl and Mavis Ella (Jarnett) Kachmarski; m. Larry Douglas Isenor, Oct. 13, 1973. Diploma in mktg., So. Alta. Inst. Tech., Calgary, 1988. Cert. travel cons. Calgary Bd. Edn. Cashier to asst. mgr. G&S Restaurants Balmoral Ltd., Calgary, 1972-74; cashier, supr. Calgary Coop. Assn. Ltd., 1974-75, supr., 1975-78, head cashier, 1978-80, asst. grocery merchandiser, 1980-81, grocery merchandising specialist, 1981-82, grocery procurement specialist, 1982-83, grocery mktg. supr. for pricing and costing, 1983-93; grocery mktg. mgr., 1993—. Office: Calgary Coop Assn Ltd, 200 S 8500 MacLeod Trail SE, Calgary, AB Canada T2H 2N1

ISHIKAWA-FULLMER, JANET SATOMI, psychologist, educator; b. Hilo, Hawaii, Oct. 17, 1925; d. Shinichi and Onao (Kurisu) Saito; m. Calvin Y. Ishikawa, Aug. 15, 1950; 1 child, James A.; m. Daniel W. Fullmer, June 11, 1980. BE, U. Hawaii, 1950, MEd, 1967; MEd, U. Hawaii, 1969, PhD, 1976. Diplomate Am. Acad. Pain Mgmt. Instr. Honolulu Bus. Coll., 1953-59; instr., counselor Kapiolani Community Coll., Honolulu, 1959-73; prof., dir. counseling Honolulu Community Coll., 1973-74, dean of students, 1974-77; psychologist, v.p., treas. Human Resources Devel. Ctr., Inc., Honolulu, 1977—; cons. United Specialties Co., Tokyo, 1979, Grambling (La.) State U., 1980, 81, Filipino Immigrants in Kalihi, Honolulu, 1979-84, Legis. Ref. Bur., Honolulu, 1984-85, Honolulu Police Dept., 1985; co-founder Waianae (Hawaii) Child and Family Ctr., 1979-92. Co-author: Family Therapy Dictionary, 1991, Manabu: The Diagnosis and Treatment of a Japanese Boy with a Visual Anomaly, 1991; contbr. articles to profl. jours. Commr. Bd. Psychology, Honolulu, 1979-85; co-founder Kilohana United Meth. Ch. and Family Ctr., 1993—. Mem. APA, ACA, Hawaii Psychol. Assn., Pi Lambda Theta (sec. 1967-68, v.p. 1968-69, pres. 1969-70), Delta Kappa Gamma (sec., v.p., scholarship 1975, Outstanding Educator award 1975, Thomas Jefferson award 1993, Francis E. Clark award 1993). Home: 154 Maono Pl Honolulu HI 96821-2529 Office: Human Resources Devel Ctr 1750 Kalakaua Ave Apt 809 Honolulu HI 96826-3725

ISIDORO, EDITH ANNETTE, horticulturist; b. Albuquerque, Oct. 14, 1957; d. Robert Joseph and Marion Elizabeth (Miller) I. BS in Horticulture, N.Mex. State U., 1981, MS in Horticulture, 1984; postgrad., U. Nev., Reno, 1992—. Range conservationist Soil Conservation Service, Estancia, Grants, N.Mex., 1980-82; lab. aide N.Mex. State U. Dept. Horticulture, Las Cruces, 1982, 83-84; technician N.Mex. State U. Coop. Extension Service, Las Cruces, 1983-84, county agrl. extension agt., 1985; area extension agr. U. Nev., Reno, Fallon, 1985—; hay tester Nev. Agrl. Services, Fallon, 1988-92. Mem. AAUW, Am. Soc. Hort. Sci., Am. Horticulture Soc., Am. Botany Soc., Am. Horticulture Therapy Assn., Alpha Zeta, Pi Alpha Psi. Home: 3900 Sheckler Rd Fallon NV 89406-8202 Office: Churchill County Coop Extension 1450 Mclean Rd Fallon NV 89406-8880

ISIK, TELA MAE, obstetrical/gynecological nurse practitioner; b. Springfield, Mo., Sept. 25, 1944; d. Vincent James and Ella Mae (Boyd) Rinaldi; m. Ahmet Ozer Isik, Apr. 5, 1973; children: Deniz James, Suzan Michelle. Diploma, Presbyn. U. Hosp. Sch. Nursing, 1966; BSN, Tex. Christian U., 1984; MPA, Troy State U., 1987. RN, Pa., Tex. Staff nurse John J. Kane Hosp., Pitts., 1966-70; commd. 2d lt. USAF, 1970, advanced through grades to maj., served in various locations, 1970-90; asst. charge nurse Obs. USAF, Fed. Republic Germany, 1976-77; ob.-gyn. nurse practitioner USAF, Ellsworth AFB, S.D., 1978-82, Carswell AFB, Tex., 1982, Incirlik Air Base, Turkey, 1984-87, RAF, Lakenheath, U.K., 1987-90; ret. USAF, 1990; ob.-gyn. nurse practitioner Ft. Worth Pub. Health Dept., 1990-92, Tarrant County Hosp. Dist., 1992—. Mem. ANA, NAACOG (cert.), Tex. Nurses' Assn., Uniformed Nurse Practitioner Assn., Tex. Nurse Practitioners, Sigma Theta Tau. Home: 564 Greenway Dr Saginaw TX 76179 Office: John Petersmith Hosp Health Ctr for Women 1400 S Main St Ste 211 Fort Worth TX 76104

ISLER, ERIKA LISBETH, journalist; b. N. Tarrytown, N.Y., Apr. 8, 1967; d. Robert Klaus and Sally Layne (von Holzhausen) Isler. BS in Mag. Journalism, Syracuse U., 1989. Asst. editor N.Y. Daily News, N.Y.C., 1988; staff writer Syracuse Herald Jour., 1989; assoc. editor Magazineweek, N.Y.C., 1989-90, sr. editor, 1990-91, west coast editor, 1991-92; west coast editor Cowles Business Media's Folio: First Day, Folio: Magazine, 1992—. Mem. Women in Communications, Western Publs. Assn. Home: 1978 Azure Way Encinitas CA 92024

ISLER, VICKI JAN, lawyer, educator; b. Elizabeth, N.J., July 29, 1955; d. Sidney and Dorothy (Millberger) I; m. J. Mitchell Grossman, June 12, 1977; children: Lisa, Drew and Jenna (twins). BA, Colgate U., 1977; JD, Yeshiva U. Cordozo Sch. of Law, 1980. Bar: N.J. 1980, U.S. Dist. Ct. N.J. 1980, U.S. Dist. Ct. (so. and ea. dists.) N.Y. 1985, U.S. Supreme Ct. 1986. Dep. atty. gen. environ. protection sect. div. law and pub. N.J. Atty. Gen.'s Office, Environ. Protection sect., Trenton, 1980-84; assoc. Brenner Wallack & Hill, Princeton, N.J., 1984, Budd, Larner, Kent, Gross, Rosenbaum, Picillo, Greenberg & Sade, Short Hills, N.J., 1985-87, Farer Siegal Fersko, P.A., Westfield, N.J., 1987-89; ptnr. Giordano, Halleran & Ciesla, Middletown, N.J., 1989—; adj. prof. environ. law Seton Hall U. Law Sch., Newark, 1987—; lectr., seminar panelist, 1986-93. Author: N.J. Environmental Law Treatise, 1991; mem. editorial bd. Jersey Lawyer. Mem. adv. bd. Environ. Expo, 1986—, ECRA; mem. Indsl. Site Adv. Bd.; violist Plainfield (N.J.) Symphony Orch., 1980-86; vice chair curriculum adv. bd. Inst. for Continuing Legal Edn., 1987—. George Cobb fellow, 1974; named Belkin scholar, 1979. Mem. ABA, N.J. Bar Assn. (chmn. Environ. Law Sect. 1988-89, del. bd. govs. 1987—, editorial bd.), LWV. Office: Giordano Halleran & Ciesla 125 Half Mile Rd Middletown NJ 07748

ISOM, HARRIET WINSAR, ambassador; b. Heppner, Oreg., Nov. 4, 1936; d. Blaine Eugene and Evelyn (Struve) I. BA, Mills Coll., 1958; MALD in Law and Diplomacy, Tufts U., 1960. Joined Fgn. Svc., U.S. Dept. State, Washington, 1961; various positions in Africa and Asia; dep. chief mission Am. Embassy, Bujumbura, Burundi, 1974-77; consul Am. Consulate, Medan, Sumatra, Indonesia, 1977-78; polit. counselor Am. Embassy, Jakarta, Indonesia, 1978-81; chargé d'affaires Am. Embassy, Vientiane, Laos, 1986-89; sr. assignments officer Bur. Pers. Dept. State, Washington, 1982-84, dir. Korean affairs Bur. East Asian and Pacific Affairs, 1984-86; amb. to Republic of Benin, Cotonou, 1989-92, Republic of Camaroon, Yaounde, 1993—. Address: Am Embassy Yaounde Dept State Washington DC 20521

ISRAEL, LESLEY LOWE, political consultant; b. Phila., July 21, 1938; d. Herman Albert and Florence (Segal) Lowe; m. Fred Israel, Dec. 18, 1960; children: Herman Allen, Sanford Lawrence. BA, Smith Coll., 1959. Dir. media advance Humphrey for Pres., Washington, 1967-68, dir. politic. intelligence, 1972; dir. scheduling Bayh for Pres., Washington, 1971; spl. asst. Jackson for Pres., Washington, 1975-76; coordinator nat. labor Kennedy for Pres., Washington, 1979-80; sr. v.p. The Kamber Group, Washington, 1981-87; pres., chief exec. officer Politics, Inc., Washington, 1987—; bd. dirs. The Kamber Group, Washington. Pres. Jewish Cmty. Ctr. of Greater Washington, Rockville, Md., 1981-83; bd. mgrs. Adas Israel Synagogue, 1981-83; mem. Dem. Charter Commn., 1982-83, Dem. Del. Selection Commn., 1983-84, Dem. Site Selection Com., 1989-90, 90—; Nat. Dem. Club, 1986—; chmn. Washington Regional Bd., ADL, 1991-94; mem. Nat. Commn. ADL, 1991-94, nat. exec. commn., 1994—; chmn. Washington Bd. Friends of Tel Aviv U. Recipient Spl. Service award Jewish Community Ctr., 1984; named one of 100 Most Powerful Women, Washingtonian mag., 1990. Jewish. Home: PO Box 69 Royal Oak MD 21662-0069 Office: Politics Inc 1920 L St Ste 700 NW Washington DC 20036-5004

ISRAEL, LYNNE CHARLENE, occupational therapist; b. L.A., Mar. 20, 1946; d. Wayne Edwin and Evelyn Elizabeth (Firnhaber) Thomsen; m. Barry John Israel, June 22, 1968; children: Alison, Ashley, Brenna. BS, San Jose State U., 1968. SIPT cert. by Sensory Integration Internat. Occupational therapist Rehab. Svcs. Columbus Ga., 1969, Good Samitarian Hosp., Balt., 1970-72, Nat. Naval Med. Ctr., Bethesda, Md., 1972-74, Fairfax County Pub. Schs., Va., 1975-77; pvt. practice Washington, 1977—; cons. occupational therapy D.C. Cmty. Svcs., 1985-92, United Cerebral Palsy, 1983-87, 92—. Mem. Washington Ind. Svcs. for Ednl. Resources, Am. Occupational Therapy Assn., D.C. Occupational Therapy Assn. Democrat. Office: 1700 Kalorama Rd NW Washington DC 20009

ISRAEL, MARGIE OLANOFF, psychotherapist; b. Atlantic City, Apr. 30, 1927; d. Herman and Mary (Salter) Olanoff; m. Allan Edward Israel, Sept. 20, 1953; 1 child, Janet. Student U. Miami, 1945-46, 50, Am. Acad. Dramatic Arts, 1946-47; BA in Psychology cum laude, Hunter Coll., 1970; MSW with honors in fieldwork, Hunter Sch. Social Work, 1972; psychoanalytic tng. N.Y. Soc. Freudian Psychologists, 1965-70, Manhattan Ctr. for Advanced Psychoanalytic Studies, 1972-74, 76. Bd. cert. diplomate in clin. social work Am. Bd. Examiners of Clin. Social Workers. Celebrity interviewer Lunchin' with Marge radio show Sta. WFPG, Atlantic City, 1947-48; co-host Steel Pier Midnight radio show, 1949; publicity writer Hy Gardner Astor Hotel, N.Y.C., 1948; writer theatrical interviews Miami (Fla.) Daily News, 1950-51; sec. to exec. dir. Hebrew Old Age Ctr., Atlantic City, 1951-55; sec. to dir. TV-films and radio Nat. Office, Am. Cancer Soc., N.Y.C., 1959-66, asst. to dir. TV-films and radio, 1966-70; social worker Bellevue Hosp., N.Y.C., 1972-76; field instr. socialwork N.Y. U., 1975-76; pvt. practice psychotherapy, N.Y.C., 1973—, Providence, 1991—. Fellow N.Y. State Soc. Clin. Social Work, Am. Orthopsychiat. Assn.; mem. NASW (diplomate), Nat. Fedn. Socs. Clin. Social Work (com. on psychoanalysis), Acad. Cert. Social Workers, N.Y. Acad. Scis., Psi Chi. Home and Office: 319 E 24th St Apt 8A New York NY 10010-4038 Office: 111 Everett Ave #3 Providence RI 02906

ISRAELOV, RHODA, financial planner, writer, entrepreneur; b. Pitts., May 20, 1940; d. Joseph and Fannie (Friedman) Kreinen; divorced; children: Jerome, Arthur, Russ. BS in Hebrew Edn. Herzlia Hebrew Tchr.'s Coll., N.Y.C., 1961; BA in English Language and Lit. U. Mo.-Kansas City, 1965. Cert. Fin. Planner, CLU; registered fin. and estate planning practioner. Tchr. Hebrew, various schs., 1961-79; ins. agt. Conn. Mut. Life, Indpls., 1979-81; fin. planner Smith Barney, Inc., Indpls., 1981—, v.p., 1986—; instr. for mut. fund licensing exams. Pathfinder Securities Sch., Indpls., 1983-87; cons. channel 6 News, 1984-85. Weekly fin. columnist Indpls. Bus. Jour., 1982—; bi-weekly fin. columnist Jewish Post & Opinion, 1982-86; regular guest WTUX Radio; monthly columnist, sr. Beacon. Recipient Gold Medal award Personal Selling Power, 1987; named Bus. Woman of Yr. Network of Women in Bus., 1986. Mem. Inst. Cert. Fin. Planners, Nat. Assn. Life Underwriters, Women's Life Underwriters' Conf. (treas. Ind. chpt. 1982, v.p. chpt. 1983), Internat. Assn. Fin. Planners (v.p. Ind. chpt. 1983-84, bd. dirs., sec.), Am. Soc. CLU, Women's Life Underwriters Conf., Nat. Coun. Jewish Women, Nat. Assn. Profl. Saleswomen , Nat. Speakers Assn. (pres. Ind. chpt. 1986-87, treas.), Registry Fin. Planning Practitioners. Lodge: Toastmasters (chpt. ednl. v.p. 1985-86), Soroptimists (bd. dirs.). Avocations: piano, folk, square and ballroom dancing, theatre. Office: Smith Barney Bank One Center Tower 111 Monument Circle Ste 3100 Indianapolis IN 46204

ISTOMIN, MARTA CASALS, performing arts administrator; b. P.R., Nov. 2, 1936; d. Aquiles and Angelica M. (Martinez) Montanez; m. Pablo Casals, Aug. 3, 1957 (dec. 1973); m. Eugene Istomin, Feb. 15, 1975. Student, Mannes Coll. Music, N.Y.C., 1950-54; Mus.D. (hon.), World U., P.R., 1972; L.H.D. (hon.), Marymount Coll., 1975; Doctorate (hon.), U. P.R., 1984, Dickinson Coll., Carlisle, Pa., 1986; D (hon.), Shenandoah Coll., 1986, Interam. U., P.R., 1989. Prof. cello Conservatory Music, San Juan, P.R., 1961-64; vis. prof. cello Curtis Inst., Phila., 1974-75; co-chmn. bd., music dir. Casals Festival, 1974-77; artistic dir. John F. Kennedy Center for Performing Arts, Washington, 1980-90; dir. gen. Evian Music Festival, France, 1990—; pres. Manhattan Sch. Music, N.Y.C., 1992—; mem. Nat. Coun. on Arts, 1990; cons. Latin Am. ednl. projects. Trustee Marlboro Sch. Music and Festival; trustee Marymount Sch., N.Y.C., World U. Recipient Puerto Rican Fedn. Women's Clubs award, 1967; award for cultural achievements City of San Juan, 1975; Nat. Conf. Puerto Rican Women award, 1975; Casita Maria medal for outstanding contbns. to culture N.Y.C., 1978; Outstanding Contbns. Performing Arts in Nation's Capitol award, 1983; Family Place Outstanding Community Service award, 1986; Mayor's Excellence in Service Arts award, Washington, 1986; Nat. Fedn. Music Clubs citation, 1987; named Outstanding Woman of Yr. P.R., 1975; Woman of Achievement Sta. WETA-TV, Washington, 1981; Order of Isabella the Cath. govt. Spain, 1986; Officer, Order Arts and Letters govt. France, 1986; Officer's Cross Order Merit govt. Fed. Republic Germany, 1987. Mem. Nat. Coun. on the Arts. Roman Catholic.

ITNYRE, JACQUELINE HARRIET, programmer; b. Camden, N.J., May 13, 1941; d. John Harold and Harriet Geraldine (Rankine) Bruynell; m. Thomas James Itnyre, Oct. 13, 1968 (dec. 1978); children: Beth Thierry, John. AS in Engring., Mercer County Coll., 1961; BA in Liberal Studies, San Jose State U., 1980, MLS, 1981. Media ctr. mgr. Milpitas (Calif.) Unified Sch. Dist., 1975-81; tech. libr. Lockheed Missiles and Space Co., Sunnyvale, Calif., 1981, programmer, 1982-83; with ground support dept. Challenger-Space Lab 2 Lockheed Missiles and Space Co., Palo Alto, Calif., 1984-85; systems mgr. gen. clin. rsch. ctr. Stanford (Calif.) U. Med. Sch., 1985-87, computing systems specialist divsn. epidemiology, 1988—. Edna B. Anthony scholar San Jose State U., 1981. Mem. Assn. for Computing Machinery, ALA, Nature Conservancy, Sierra Club. Home: 2463 Louis Rd Palo Alto CA 94303-3608

ITSON, SONJA PATRICE, information systems executive; b. Denver, Dec. 22, 1943; d. Raymond G. and Gladys F. (Mills) Green; m. Joe A. Itson, Sept. 17, 1966; 1 child, Erica Rae. BA in Geology, Occidental Coll., 1966; MS in Geology, San Diego State U., 1971. Technician Dept. Water Resources State of Wash., Olympia, 1966-68; researcher Scripps Instn. of Oceanography, La Jolla, Calif., 1971-74; instr. geology dept. San Diego State U., 1974; with County of San Diego, 1974—; planner, planning chief, zoning adminstr. mem. planning and environ. rev. bd. County of San Diego, 1986—; regional urban info. system chief County of San Diego, 1990-94, county bldg. offcl., 1994—. Bd. dirs., pres., fin. officer Homeowners Assn., San Diego, 1986—. Mem. NAFE, Assn. Environ. Profls. (charter), Urban and Regional Info. Systems Assn. (charter, chair com. and sect. pres. 1990—), Am. Planning Assn., Internat. Assn. Runners and Walkers (vol.), Calif. Elected Women's Assn., Toastmasters (pres., dist. historial San Diego chpt. 1979, 80), Sigma Delta Epsilon (treas. 1973-74). Home: 3633 Seahorn Cir San Diego CA 92130-1017 Office: County of San Diego 5201 Ruffin Rd Ste B San Diego CA 92123-4310

ITTELSON, MARY ELIZABETH, museum director; b. Dayton, Ohio; d. Richard W. and Lois (Koblitz) I.; m. Richard Carl Tuttle. BA, NYU, 1979; MBA, Stanford U., 1985. Dir., choreographer Premiers Dance Theatre, N.Y.C., 1976-78; exec. dir. Crossroads Inc., N.Y.C., 1978-79; asst. prof. dance Northwestern U., Evanston, 1979-83; assoc. McKinsey & Co., Inc., Chgo., 1985-88; acting dir. Mus. Contemporary Art, Chgo., 1988-89; assoc. dir. Mus. Contemporary Art, 1989—. Choreographer: (dance) In Three Places, 1977, Garland Epitaphium, 1981, Sir Gawain and the Green Knight, 1982, Little Children Lost, 1983. Am. Dance Festival fellow, 1980. Office: Mus Contemporary Art 237 E Ontario St Chicago IL 60611-3204

ITTNER, HELEN LOUISE, entrepreneur; b. Saginaw, Mich., June 12, 1935; d. David Harvey and Helen (Austin) Jones; m. Frederick E. Ittner; children: David (dec.), Philip. BA, St. Mary's Coll., 1981. Pres. H.L.I. Enterprises, Inc., Moraga, Calif., 1988—. Mem. Moraga Sch. Bd., 1981-85, pres., 1984-85; bd. dirs. Hospice of Contra Costa, 1990-94, Hearst Monument Found., 1992—; directress Altar Guild, St. Stephen's Episcopal Ch., 1993-95. Mem. AAUW (Disting. Woman award 1991). Republican. Episcopalian. Home: 1858 School St Moraga CA 94556-1729

IVANICK, CAROL W. TRENCHER, lawyer; b. Springfield, Mass., Mar. 6, 1939; d. Joseph George and Daisy Wolf; m. Michael Ira Trencher, July 30, 1960 (div. Feb. 1984); children: Christopher, Daniel, Deborah; m. Peter Alan Ivanick. BA, Wellesley Coll., 1959; JD, Yale U., 1962. Bar: N.Y. 1963. Assoc. Cleary, Gottlieb et al, N.Y.C., 1962-67; ptnr. Dewey, Ballantine, Bushby, Palmer & Wood, N.Y.C., 1976—; chmn. adv. com. Pension Benefit Guaranty Corp., Washington, 1978-80; visiting lectr. Yale Law Sch., New Haven, Conn., 1978-79, 82-83. Home: 110 Riverside Dr New York NY 10024 Office: Dewey Ballantine 1301 Avenue Of The Americas New York NY 10019-6092

IVENS, MARY SUE, microbiologist, mycologist; b. Maryville, Tenn., Aug. 23, 1929; d. McPherson Joseph and Sarah Lillie (Hensley) I.; B.S., E. Tenn. State U., 1949; M.S. (NIH research trainee), Tulane U. Sch. Medicine, 1963;

Ph.D., La. State U. Sch. Medicine, 1966; postgrad. Oak Ridge Inst. Nuclear Studies, Emory U. Sch. Medicine. Dir. microbiol. and mycol. labs. Lewis-Gale Hosp., Roanoke, Va., 1953-56; rsch. mycologist Ctrs. Disease Control, Atlanta, 1957-60; rsch. assoc. La. State U. Sch. Med., 1963-66, instr. medicine, 1966-72, instr. Microbiology, 1966-72, clin. prof., 1972—; dir. mycology lab, La. State U. Sch. Med., 1963-72; lectr. Sch. Dentistry, La. State U. Med. Ctr., 1968-70; assoc. prof. natural scis. Dillard U., New Orleans, 1972—; assoc. Marine Biol. Lab., Woods Hole, Mass., 1978— ; cons. in field. Commr. WHO conf. on ctr. for Mycotic sera 1969; chmn. Gold Medal Award Com. Sigma Xi, 1978; mem. La. assn. def. counsel expert witness bank, 1985—; bd. dirs. La. coun. Girl Scouts U.S., Community Relationships Greater New Orleans, Zoning Bd. River Ridge (La.); mem. exec. bd. River Ridge Civic Assn., 1982—, sec., 1982-84; chmn. pers. bd. Riverside Bapt. Ch., River Ridge; dir. Outreach First Baptist Ch., New Orleans, 1989—. Recipient Rosicrucian Humanitarian award, 1981; Macy fellow, MBL, Woods Hole, 1978-79; grantee NSF, NIH; diplomate Am. Bd. Microbiology. Mem. Internat. Soc. Human and Animal Mycology, Med. Mycological Soc. Am., Am. Soc. Microbiology (nat. com. on membership 1983-87), AAAS, Nat. Inst. Sci., Sigma Xi. Author articles in field. Home: 408 Berclair Ave New Orleans LA 70123-1504 Office: Dillard U Div Natural Sci New Orleans LA 70122

IVERSEN-GOULSON, CORINNE G., insurance company executive, adjuster; b. Denver, Sept. 9, 1953; d. James Lowell and Betty Erma Davenport. Cert. in gen. ins., Ins. Inst. Am., Malvern, Pa., 1986, A in Claims, 1987, A in Mgmt., 1993; cert. in liability claims law, Am. Ednl. Inst., Basking Ridge, N.J., 1990. Inside/outside agt. Northwestern Mut. Life, Billings, Mont., 1973-75; bookkeeper Sky Aviation, Worland, Wyo., 1975-76, office mgr., 1976-77; corp. pres. Sky Aviation Inc., Worland, Wyo., 1977-80; sales mgr. Serlkay, Inc., Worland, Wyo., 1980-82; adjuster trainee GAB Bus. Svcs., Inc., Thermopolis, Wyo., 1982-83; adjuster GAB Bus. Svcs., Inc., Rock Springs, Wyo., 1983-88; supervising adjuster GAB Bus. Svcs., Inc., Cheyenne, Wyo., 1988-90; br. mgr. GAB Bus. Svcs., Inc., Missoula, Mont., 1990—. Gov.'s appointee Wyo. Commn. for Women, Worland, 1981-83, Wyo. Coun. for the Humanities, Rock Springs, 1983-86; charterer Hot Springs Assist, Thermopolis, Wyo., 1983; mem. First Presbyn. Ch., Missoula, 1990—. Mem. Nat. Assn. Ins. Women (Claims Profl. of Yr. region IX 1993, Mont. state dir. elect 1994-95), Ins. Women of Missoula (pres. 1993-94, edn. chmn. 1991-92), S.E. Wyo. Ins. Assn. (treas. 1990-91, legis. chmn. 1989-90), Wyo. Claims Assn., Mont. State Adjusters Assn., Western Mont. Adjusters Assn. Presbyterian. Home: PO Box 5523 Missoula MT 59806-5523 Office: GAB Bus Svcs Inc PO Box 4107 Missoula MT 59806-4107

IVERSON, CAROL JEAN, library media specialist; b. Villisca, Iowa, July 2, 1937; d. Paul Gerald and Garnet Blanche (Dunn) Smith; m. Merlin Gerald Iverson, June 11, 1961; children: Robert Mark, Jean Marie Iverson Howe. BA, U. No. Iowa, 1960. Elem. tchr. Manning (Iowa) Community Schs., 1957-58, Mason City (Iowa) Sch. Dist., 1960-61, Manson (Iowa) Community Schs., 1961-63, Blooming Prairie (Minn.) Community Schs., 1963-64, 65-66; elem. tchr., K-12 librarian Rockwell (Iowa) Swaledale Community Schs., 1973-80; libr. media specialist Mason City Sch. Dist., 1980—. County co-chair Cerro Gordo County Reps., Howard Baker campaign, 1979; campaign worker DuKakis for Pres., 1987. Mem. AAUW (pres. 1993—, v.p. 1989-91), NEA (del. rep. assembly), Iowa State Edn. Assn. (del., resolutions com. 1975-78), Iowa Ednl. Media Assn. (legis. chair 1987-89), Delta Kappa Gamma (pres. 1986-88), Phi Delta Kappa (v.p. 1990-92). Democrat. Lutheran. Home: 429 20th Pl SW Mason City IA 50401-6428

IVES, ADRIENE DIANE, real estate executive; b. Washington, Oct. 6, 1951; d. Edwin Forrest and Carolyn Elizabeth (Wray) Warner; m. Perry Nelson Ives, May 12, 1972; children: Jesse Warner, James Robert. BS, U. Md., 1973. Tchr. Charles County (Md.) Bd. Edn., 1973-83, Broad Creek Day Sch., Ft. Washington, Md., 1983-85; sales counselor L.K. Farrall, Ltd., Camp Springs, Md., 1985-90; tchr. real estate Farrall Inst., Waldorf, Md., 1990—; assoc. broker Century 21, Donald & Assocs. Inc., Ft. Washington, 1990—; tchr. Christian Children's Ministry, Washington, 1982-83; v.p. The Warner Corp., Washington, 1982-83; bd. dirs. Nat. Plumbing Supply, Inc., Washington; devel. agt. Burgundy Farm Country Day Sch., Alexandria, Va., 1986-91; isntr. real estate edn. Farrall Inst., 1990. Author: Nat. City Christ Church, 1988, 89; contbr. articles to jours. Bd. dirs. Broad Creek Country Day Sch., 1982-83; bd. deaconesses Nat. City Christian Ch., Washington, 1989-91. Recipient Citizenship award Prince Georges County Police, Forestville, Md., 1986. Mem. Nat. Assn. Realtors (cert. residential specialist), Md. Assn. Realtors (Grad. Realtors Inst.), Prince Georges Assn. Realtors (edn. com. orientation subcom. 1990—, Outstanding Realtors Educator of Yr. award 1990), Women's Coun. Realtors (sec.-treas. 1992-93, pres. elect 93, pres. 1994, Leadership Tng. Grad. award, 1993), Realtors Nat. Mktg. Inst. (residential sales coun. 1985—, realtors polit. action com. 1989-90), Realtors Brokerage Coun., Md. Cert. Residential Specialists Coun. (chmn. realtor fair com.). Republican. Mem. Christian Ch. (Disciples of Christ). Office: Century 21 Donald and Assocs 10903 Indian Head Hwy Ste 307 Fort Washington MD 20744-4000

IVES, CYNTHIA JANE, music director, organist; b. Oklahoma City, Dec. 12, 1966; d. Myrl Wayne and Alice June (Davis) I. BS in Instrumental Music Edn., U. Ctrl. Okla., 1993; postgrad., St. John's U., Collegeville, Minn., 1994—. Cert. tchr. music, theory and instrumental music, K-12, Okla. Asst. dir., accompanist St. Charles Borromeo Cath. Ch., Oklahoma City, 1985-88; asst. Office of Worship, Oklahoma City, 1987-88; music dir., organist St. Patrick Cath. Ch., Oklahoma City, 1988-92; music tchr., music dir. Taize prayer and life teen program St. Eugene Cath. Ch., Oklahoma City, 1991-94; choir dir., organist St. Anthony (Minn.) Cath. Ch., 1994; dir. liturgy and music Holy Spirit Cath. Ch., St. Cloud, Minn., 1994—. Recipient Music, State, Regents and Found. scholarships U. Ctrl. Okla., 1989-93, Sch. Theology fellowship St. John's U., Collegeville, 1994. Mem. Nat. Assn. Pastoral Musicians (chpt. dir. 1988-90). Democrat. Roman Catholic. Home: 605 8th Ave N Apt # 1 Saint Cloud MN 56303

IVESTER, VICKY JO, sales professional; b. Atlanta, July 27, 1951; d. Thomas Bryan and Duane (Neureuther) I. BBA, U. Ga., 1973; MBA, Ga. State U., 1982. Lic. real estate broker. Mgmt. trainee Citizens and So. Nat. Bank, Atlanta, 1973-75; sales merchandiser Chesebrough-Ponds, Inc., Atlanta, 1975; sales rep., key accounts Clairol, Inc., Macon and Atlanta, Ga., 1975-81; account mgr. Pepperidge Farm, Atlanta, 1982-84; dist. sales mgr., account mgr., mktg. mgr. Coca-Cola USA, Atlanta, Albuquerque, Dallas and St. Louis, 1984-88; real estate broker CAMCO Realty, Albuquerque, 1989-91; registered sales asst. Prudential Securities, Inc., Albuquerque, 1991-92; area sales mgr. Nordic Track, Inc., Albuquerque, 1992-93; inside sales mgr. Kyser Co., Inc., Albuquerque, 1993-94; pres., owner Melon Rags, Inc., Albuquerque, 1994—. Pres. and founder Acad. Ridge East Neighborhood Assn., Albuquerque, 1989-91; founder U. Ga. Alumni Group, Albuquerque, 1989-92. Mem. Am. Mktg. Assn. (bd. dirs. 1983-84), NAFE. Presbyterian. Home: 10821 Malagueña Ln NE Albuquerque NM 87111 Office: Melon Rags Inc 5850 Eubank Blvd NE Ste B49 Albuquerque NM 87111

IVEY, ELIZABETH S., acoustician, physicist; b. Schenectady, N.Y., Apr. 21, 1935; married, 1957 (div.), remarried, 1982; 5 children. BS in Physics, Simmons Coll., 1957; MA in Teaching, Harvard U., 1959; PhD in Mech. Engring. Acoustics, U. Mass., 1976. Prof. physics Simmons Coll., 1958-59, Bucknell U., 1960-63; prof. physics Colo. State U., Ft. Collins, 1964-68, assoc. dean faculty, 1982-85, Louise Wolff Kahn prof., from 1985; prof. physics Smith Coll., 1969-90, chmn. dept. physics, 1983-90; provost Macalester Coll., St. Paul, 1990—, now provost, dir.; vis. prof. Yale U., 1982. Bd. dirs. Minn. Inst. Talented Youth, 1990—, World Press Inst., 1990-93, St. Paul Area United Way, 1990—. Recipient Woman Engr. award Soc. Women Engrs., 1988. Mem. AAAS, Acoustical Soc. Am., Am. Assn. Physics Tchrs. Office: Macalester Coll Office of the Provost 1600 Grand Ave Saint Paul MN 55105-1801

IVEY, JAN DENISE, health services administrator; b. Birmingham, Ala., Aug. 2, 1955; d. Eugene Bryant and Marjorie Jean (Young) I. BSN, U. Ala Sch. Nursing, 1977, MS in Nursing, 1982. Cardiovascular clin. specialist Med. Coll. Va., 1982-88; nurse Med. Coll. Va., Richmond, 1989; critical care nurse Chippenham Med. Ctr., Richmond, Va., 1989-93; adminstrv. coord. Heart Ctr., The U. of Va. Health Scis. Ctr., Charlottesville, 1993-94; patient care svc. mgr. Thoracic and Cardiovascular Svcs., U. Va. Health Scis. Ctr., 1994—. Missionary Mission World Presby. Ch. Am. Recipient Doris B. Yingling Rsch. award. Mem. AACN, Sigma Theta Tau, Omicron Delta Kappa.

IVEY, JEAN EICHELBERGER, composer; b. Washington, July 3, 1923; d. Joseph S. and Elizabeth (Pfeffer) Eichelberger. AB magna cum laude, Trinity Coll., 1944; MusM in Piano, Peabody Conservatory, 1946; MusM in Composition, Eastman Sch. Music, U. Rochester, 1956; D of Music, U. Toronto, 1972. Founder electronic music studio, mem. composition faculty Peabody Conservatory, Johns Hopkins U., Balt., 1969—, dept. coord., 1982-86, 91—; music panelist Nat. Endowment for the Arts, 1989-91. Performer piano recitals, concert tours including own compositions, U.S., Mex., Europe; composer: for solo voice and orch. Tribute: Martin Luther King, 1969, Testament of Eve, 1976; for orch. Sea-Change, 1979, Voyager for Cello and Orchestra, 1987, Short Symphony, 1988, Sonata da Chiesa, 1993, Forms in Motion, 1994, My Heart is Like a Singing Bird, 1994, Flying Colors, 1994; opera The Birthmark, 1982, also choral and vocal chamber music, instrumental solos, ensembles, music for films and TV; subject TV documentary A Woman Is-A Composer; recorded Folkways, 1967, 73, Composers Records, Inc., 1974, 88, Grenadilla, 1987; contbr. to Electronic Music: A Listeners Guide, 1972; contbr. articles to mus. publs. Recipient residencies at MacDowell Colony and Yaddo, Disting. Alumni award Peabody Conservatory, 1975, Peabody Dir.'s Recognition award, 1988, Disting. Achievement citation Nat. League Am. Pen Women, 1988, Artists' Fellowship award N.Y. Found. for Arts, 1992; grantee Nat. Endowment Arts, 1978, 83, Martha Baird Rockefeller Fund, Am. Music Ctr.; Guggenheim fellow, 1986. Mem. ASCAP (ann. awards since 1972), Am. Soc. Univ. Composers (editor newsletter 1968-70), Phi Beta Kappa, Sigma Alpha Iota (composer-judge). Home: 320 W 90th St Apt 3A New York NY 10024-1617 Office: Johns Hopkins U Peabody Conservatory Baltimore MD 21202

IVEY, JERRY WAVE, school program coordinator; b. Bristol, Va., Feb. 19, 1946; d. Orville Kenneth and Rowena Lucille (Cowden) Necessary; m. William Irvin Ivey III, Jan. 27, 1968; children: William Irvin IV, Andrew Mitchell. BS, Emory (Va.) and Henry Coll., 1968. Office mgr. phys. therapy Bass Meml. Bapt. Hosp., Enid, Okla., 1982-88; rels. vol. programs Helena (Ark.)-W. Helena Sch. Dist., 1988—; cons. and presenter of workshops. Mem. Task Force for Prevention of Sch. Violence, Helena, 1993—. Mem. Nat. Sch. Pub. Rels. Assn., Ark. Sch. Pub. Rels. Assn., Citizens for Better Schs. (founder), Delta Kappa Gamma (hon.). Methodist. Office: Helena-W Helena Sch Dist 898 N Sebastian St West Helena AR 72390-1805

IVEY, JUDITH, actress; b. El Paso, Tex., Sept. 4, 1951; d. Nathan Aldean and Dorothy Lee (Lewis) I.; m. Tim Braine, 1989; children: Maggie, Thomas Carter. BS, Ill. State U., 1973. Actress in stage plays: The Sea, 1974, The Philanthropist, Hay Fever, Romeo and Juliet, Two Gentlemen of Verona, Mourning Becomes Electra, 1975, Don Juan, Cactus Flower, As You Like It, Design for Living, 1976, The Goodbye People, The Moundbuilders, Oh, Coward, Much Ado About Nothing, 1977-78, Bedroom Farce, 1979, Dusa, Fish, Stas and VI, 1980, Piaf, 1980-81, The Dumping Ground, 1981, The Rimers of Eldritch, 1981, Pastorale, 1982, Two Small Bodies, 1982, Steaming, 1982-83 (Tony award 1983, Drama Desk award 1985), Second Lady, 1983, Hurlyburly, 1984 (Tony award 1985, Drama Desk award 1985), Precious Sons, 1986, Blithe Spirit, 1987, Mrs. Dally Has a Lover, 1988, Park Your Car in Harvard Yard, 1991; films include: Harry and Son, 1984, The Lonely Guy, 1984, The Woman in Red, 1984, Compromising Positions, 1985, Brighton Beach Memoirs, 1986, Hello Again, 1987, Sister Sister, 1988, Miles from Home, 1988, Love Hurts, 1989, In Country, 1989, Alice, 1990, Everybody Wins, 1990, Pay Dirt, 1992, There Goes the Neighborhood, 1992; TV films include: The Shady Hill Kidnapping, 1980, Dixie Changing Habits, 1982, We Are The Children, 1986, The Long, Hot Summer, 1985, Decoration Day, 1990, The Betty Broderick Story, 1992, On Promised Land, 1994; TV series: Down Home, 1990-91, Designing Women, 1992-93, The Five Mrs. Buchanans, 1994. Office: care Bresler Kelly Kipperman 15760 Ventura Blvd Ste 1730 Van Nuys CA 91436

IVINS, MOLLY, writer. BA, Smith Coll.; MA in Journalism, Columbia U.; postgrad., Inst. Polit. Sci., Paris. Former reporter The Houston Chronicle, The Mpls. Star Tribune, The New York Times; former columnist The Dallas Times Herald; co-editor The Texas Observer, 1970-76; columnist Fort Worth Star-Telegram. Author: Molly Ivins Can't Say That, Can She?, 1991, Nothin' But Good Times Ahead, 1993. Office: Fort Worth Star-Telegram 1005 Congress Ave Rm 920 Austin TX 78701

IVORY, GOLDIE LEE, social worker, educator; b. Chgo., Apr. 19, 1926; d. Percey Carr and Edna M. (Scott) Carr Williams; B.S., Ind. U., 1949; M.A., U. Notre Dame, 1956; M.S.W., Ind. U.-Purdue U., Indpls., 1977. Registered cert. clin. social worker Ind. m. Sam Ivory, Aug. 7, 1947; children: Kenneth L., Kevin D. Juvenile probation officer St. Joseph County Juvenile Probation Dept., South Bend, Ind., 1949-56, intake supr., 1956-59; chief probation officer South Bend City Ct., 1959; psychiat. social worker Beatty Meml. Hosp., Westville, Ind., 1960; instr. sociology Ind. U., South Bend, 1960-67; relocation rep. Urban Redevel. Commn., South Bend, 1960-62; social worker Elkhart (Ind.) Community Schs., 1962-66, supr. social services, 1966-69, dir. human relations, 1970-87; mem. faculty Goshen (Ind.) Coll., 1971—, asst. prof. social work, 1971-81, adj. prof. social work, 1981-91; assoc. prof. social work emeritus Goshen Coll., 1993—; pvt. practice social work, Ivory Caring Corner, 1981-87; family therapist Family Learning Ctr., South Bend, Ind., 1987-94, clinician emeritus, 1994—. workshop cons. human social services; instr. sociology and social work St. Mary's Coll., 1967-69, dir. Upward Bound program, 1970; guest lectr. dept. sociology U. Swaziland, 1983. Recipient Human Service award Acad. Human Services, 1974-75, Merit award Indpls. Public Schs. Dept. Social Work, 1977, Designation BCD award Am. Bd. Examiners in Clin. Soc., 1985; plaque for community services Mayor of Elkhart, 1981; Black Achiever award in edn. Ind. Black Expo, 1983; State chpt. Delta Kappa Gamma scholar, 1969-70. Registered clin. Social worker. Mem. Nat. Assn. Social Workers, Nat. Assn. Black Social Workers, Acad. Cert. Social Workers, The Links, Delta Kappa Gamma, Delta Sigma Theta, Alpha Delta Mu. Methodist. Club: Altrusa. Author articles in field. Home: 1309 Bissell St South Bend IN 46617-2108 Office: 2720 California Rd Elkhart IN 46514-1220

IWAMASA, GAYLE YURI, psychologist, educator; b. L.A., Oct. 4, 1964; d. Gilbert Hiroshi and Grace Yuki (Matsueda) I. BA, U. Calif., Santa Barbara, 1986; MS, Purdue U., 1988, PhD, 1992. Lic. psychologist, Ind., health svc. provider in psychology. Postdoctoral fellow U. Calif., San Francisco, 1992-93; asst. prof. Ball State U., Muncie, Ind., 1993—. Contbr. articles to profl. jours. Mem. APA (Minority fellow 1986-89, Sci. Directorate Dissertation grantee 1991, Dissertation award 1993), Am. Psychol. Soc., Asian-Am. Psychol. Assn., Assn. Advancement Behavior Therapy, Midwestern Psychol. Assn., Soc. Personality Assessment. Office: Ball State U Dept Psychol Sci Muncie IN 47306

IWANSKI, MARY, parochial school educator; b. Sacramento, Feb. 12, 1947; d. John Joseph Iwanski and Philomena Astorino Iwanski Glassy. BS, Ill. Benedictine Coll., Lisle, 1969; MS, U. Wis., Milw., 1973; postgrad., Corcordia U., River Forest, Ill., 1992-93, U. Calif., 1980-82, 91. Cert. high sch. tchr., Ill.; joined Inst. Blessed Virgin Mary, 1964. Tchr. high sch. physics and math. Loretto Cath. Ctrl. High Sch., Sault Sainte Marie, Mich., 1969-71; tchr. high sch. algebra and phys. sci. Sault Area Pub. High Sch., Sault Sainte Marie, 1971; tchr. high sch. geometry and physics St. Francis High Sch., Wheaton, Ill., 1971-72; tchr. math., physics, physical sci. Unity Cath. High Sch., Chgo., 1972-76; jr. high sch. tchr. math. and sci., cons. Our Lady of the Assumption, Carmichael, Calif., 1976-82; 8th grade tchr. math. and sci. St. John of the Cross Sch., Western Springs, Ill., 1982-88; high sch. math. tchr. Mother McAuley Liberal Arts High Sch., Chgo., 1989—; sci. cons. St. John of the Cross Sch., 1982-88, math. coach/cons., 1983-88; mem. faculty/staff coun. Mother McAuley Liberal Arts High Sch., Chgo., 1990-93, math. Macs team coach, 1994—. Recipient Photography award Joliet (Ill.) Park Dist., 1977; nominated for Heart of the Sch. award, 1994-95. Mem. Math. Assn. Am., Nat. Coun. Tchrs. Math., Nat. Cath. Ednl. Assn., Sigma Pi Sigma. Office: Mother McAuley Liberal Arts High Sch 3737 W 99th St Chicago IL 60642-3321

IWASIW, ORYSIA IRENE, insurance executive; b. N.Y.C., Dec. 13, 1961; d. John and Maria (Stzonyk) I. BBA in Honors, Hofstra U., 1983. Claims supr. Liberty Mutual Ins. Co., Mitch Field, N.Y., 1984-86; account mgr. Am. Internat. Group, N.Y.C., 1986-92; account exec. Zurich Am. Ins. Co., N.Y.C., 1992—. Mem. St. Barts Cmty. Club, Manhattan Soc., Beta Gamma Sigma. Roman Catholic.

IWEKA, VANESSA ANN, nurse-midwife, educator; b. Jackson, Ala., Feb. 27, 1957; d. Willie James and Addie Mae (Moore) Hightower; m. Kingsley Eloka Iweka, June 10, 1981; children: Evette, Emmanuel, Phillip. Cert., S.W. State Tech. Coll., Mobile, Ala., 1975; BSN, U. South Ala., 1983; nurse-midwife cert., U. So. Calif., 1988. LPN, RN; cert. nurse-midwife; cert. ARC instr. Staff nurse Springhill Meml. Hosp., Mobile, U. So. Calif. Med. Ctr., L.A.; staff nurse, childbirth instr. King/Drew Med. Ctr., L.A., staff nurse, midwife; nurse-midwifery instr. King/Drew Med. Ctr., 1991—; rev. instr. RONA Ednl. Inst., L.A. Mem. NAACOG, Am. Coll. Nurse-Midwives, Calif. Nurses Assn., Phi Theta Kappa.

IZAC, SUZETTE MARIE, air force officer; b. Coronado, Calif., Nov. 8, 1950; d. Edouard V. M. Jr. and Betty Ross (Allen) I.; m. Gregory F. Howell, Apr. 8, 1971 (div. 1974); 1 child, Roxanne Elizabeth Howell-Izac. BA in English, Calif. State U., Fullerton, 1977; MS in Pub. Adminstrn., Troy State U., 1982; student, Squadron Officer Sch., 1983, 84, Air Command & Staff Coll., 1987. Commd. 2d lt. USAF, 1979, advanced through grades to maj.; asst. chief ctrl. base adminstrn. USAF, Aviano Air Base, Italy, 1979-80, asst. exec. officer, group commdr., 1980, exec./adminstrv. support officer for dep. commdr. for ops., 1980-82; chief base adminstrn. divsn. Tempelhof Ctrl. Airport USAF, West Berlin, Germany, 1982-85; ops. officer Milw. mil. entrance processing sta. USAF, 1988-91; wing exec. officer 31g bombardment wing USAF, Grand Forks, N.D., 1991, chief wing exercises 319 air refueling wing, dep. wing insp., 1991-92; asst. prof. aerospace studies AFROTC detachment 845 Tex. Christian U., Ft. Worth, 1985-88. Treas., bd. dirs., dancer N.D. Ballet Co.; bd. dirs. North Valley Arts Assn., Grand Forks, 1992-94; dancer Bowman Sch. of Dance, 1994—. Mem. Air Force Assn. (life), Entomol. Soc. Am., Zeta Tau Alpha (life). Home: 1201 W Curie Ave Santa Ana CA 92707-3838

IZZO, LUCILLE ANNE, sales representative; b. Rochester, N.Y., Apr. 1, 1954; d. Peter George and Dorothy June (Cusimano) I. Grad. high sch., Rochester. Regional sales mgr. T.R. Miller Co., Inc., New Milford, Conn., 1986-87; program mgr. Jr. Achievement SW Conn., Stamford, 1987-88, adviser, cons., 1986-93; sec. Eastman Kodak Co., Rochester, 1972-84; consumer products sales rep. Eastman Kodak Co., Oklahoma City, 1984-86; copy products sales rep. Eastman Kodak Co., Stamford, 1988-91; office imaging sales rep. Eastman Kodak Co., Hartford, Conn., 1992—; grad. asst. Dale Carnegie Human Rels. Course, 1987, 1988. Bus. cons. Region One Jr. Achievement Conf., 1988, 90; guest speaker West Conn. Jr. Achievement Conf., 1990; adviser, recruiter Greater Rochester Jr. Achievement, 1980-83, Small Bus. Owner, Accessorize, 1994—. Mem. NAFE, Am. Mgmt. Assn. Home: Bldg 205 166 Old Brookfield Rd Danbury CT 06811-4030 Office: Eastman Kodak Co Riverbend Exec Park 77 Hartland St Hartford CT 06108

IZZO, MARY ALICE, real estate broker; b. Mesa, Ariz., Aug. 5, 1953; d. Edward Lee and Evangeline Lauda (Gorraiz) Meeker; m. Michael David Izzo, Dec. 26, 1971; children: Michael Wade, Clinton Jarred, Antoinette Marie. Student, Pioneer Coll., 1977, Yavapai Coll., 1984-93. Cert. realtor, Ariz. Sales agt. Babbit Bros., Flagstaff, Ariz., 1970-76; owner Cottonwood (Ariz.) Tees, 1978-84; realtor Weston Realty, Cottonwood, 1985-86, Coldwell Banker Mabery Real Estate, Cottonwood, 1986-89; sales agent, assoc. broker The Glenarm Land Co., Cottonwood, 1989-94; office mgr., sec. Izzo & Sons Contracting, 1985—, Wilhoit Water Co., 1991-93. Auhtor: Current Customer Cook Book, 1984. Bd. dirs. cub scouts Boy Scouts Am., 1984, 87; bd. dirs. AYSO Soccer, Verde Valley, Ariz., 1984-87, 92—, coach tournament all girls' traveling team, 1993—; leader youth group, Cottonwood. Democrat. Roman Catholic. Home: PO Box 2002 Cottonwood AZ 86326-2002 Office: The Glenarm Land Co 408 S Main St Cottonwood AZ 86326-3903

JABLON, SUSAN NESBITT, artist, educator; b. Buffalo, Dec. 1, 1950; d. Carl G. Jr. and Edith Ann (Ganzenmuller) Nesbitt; m. Alan Jablon, Apr. 24, 1980; children: Emily Agree, Samuel Philip. BA, Wells Coll., 1972. Dir. pers. Daus. of Charity, Binghamton, N.Y., 1972-82; dir. sales promotion and advt. Security Mut. Life, Binghamton, 1982-84; tchr. art, Binghamton, 1972—. Group shows include Broome County Arts Coun., 1992-93; one woman show Binghamton Plz. Gallery, City Hall, 1995; represented in pvt. collections. Mem. Fine Arts Soc. Home: 2204 Acorn Dr Vestal NY 13850-2602 Studio: 138 Baldwin St Johnson City NY 13760

JABLONS, JANE ELLEN, lawyer; b. Bklyn., May 10, 1953; d. Abraham Harry and Anita (Rosenberg) J. BS, Cornell U., 1975; postgrad. law sch., U. Mich., 1975-76; JD, NYU, 1978. Bar: N.Y. 1979, U.S. Dist. Ct. (so. dist.) N.Y. 1982. Assoc. Dewey Ballantine Bushby Palmer & Wood, N.Y.C., 1978-82, Guggenheimer & Untermyer, N.Y.C., 1982-85; assoc. Kelley Drye & Warren, N.Y.C., 1985-87, ptnr., 1988—. Mem. ABA, Phi Kappa Phi. Office: Kelley Drye & Warren 101 Park Ave New York NY 10178-0062

JACK, JANIS GRAHAM, judge; b. 1946. RN, Thomas Sch. Nursing, 1969; BA, U. Balt., 1974; JD cum laude, South Tex. Coll., 1981. Real estate saleswoman Tompkins Young Real Estate, 1975-77, Robert S. Morgan, 1978-80; shareholder White Horse Restaurant, Houston, 1980-81; pvt. practice Corpus Christi, Tex., 1981-93; judge U.S. Dist. Ct. (so. dist.) Tex., Corpus Christi, 1994—. Mem. adv. bd. Nueces County Juvenile Citizens; former mem. Coastal Bend Coun. for Deaf, Planned Parenthood of South Tex., South Texans for Choice; active YWCA, Spohn Hosp. Found., Sta. KEDT Radio, Corpus Christi Art Mus., Tex. Med. Assn. Aux., Nueces County Med. Assn. Aux., Tex. State Aquarium. Mem. ABA, Tex. Bar Found., State Bar Tex., Coll. State Bar Tex., Tex. Acad. Family Law Specialists, Corpus Christi Bar Assn., Corpus Christi Family Law Assn., Order of Lytae, Phi Alpha Delta. Office: US Dist Ct 521 Starr Corpus Christi TX 78206*

JACK, MINTA SUE, hospital department head; b. Huntsville, Tex., Aug. 24, 1935; d. Clinton Orrin and Dorris Eugenia (Pierce) Bunn; m. Samuel Garred Jack, Jr., June 8, 1957 (div. 1984); children: Samuel Garred III, Paul Alan. BA with distinction, U. N.Mex., 1957. Cert. secondary educator. High sch. tchr. Albuquerque Pub. Schs., 1957-58; bd. dirs. Delta Delta Delta, Reno, 1962-63; com. chmn. Tustin (Calif.) Sch. Dist. PTO, 1965-70, Red Hill Luth. Sch., Tustin, 1970-74; bd. dirs. Assistance League of Tustin, 1972-83, Performing Arts Ctr. Guilds, Orange County, Calif., 1983-88; bd.d irs. Delta Delta Delta, Orange County, Calif., 1987-91; dir., vol. Western Med. Ctr., Santa Ana, Calif., 1986—. Vol. leader Boy Scouts/Little League, Tustin, 1966-72; vol. Olympic Organizing Com., L.A., 1984; assoc. Mexican Am. Nat. Women, Santa Ana, 1988-90; mem. Freedom Found./Valley Forge, Santa Ana, 1988-90. Recipient Writing award, 1989, Newsletter award, 1991, Community Svc. award Disneyland, 1981, Amelia Earhart award U. Calif., 1989, Ernestine Grigsby award Delta Delta Delta, 1989; named Woman of Yr. nominee Panhellenic Assn., 1989. Mem. AAUW, So. Calif. Assn. Dirs. of Vol. Svcs. (bd. dirs. 1987-91), Am. Soc. Dirs. Vol. Svcs. (membership com. 1989), Assistance League of Tustin (pres. 1980-81), Westmed Gold Club (membership com. 1986-92), Chapman Univ. Music Assocs. (bd. dirs. 1987-92), Mortar Bd., Delta Delta Delta (pres. 1988-89, bd. dirs. 1988-91), Dirs. Vols. in Agencies, Phi Kappa Phi, Phi Alpha Theta, Pi Lambda Theta. Episcopalian. Home: 7634 Appaloosa Trail Orange CA 92669 Office: Western Med Ctr 1001 N Tustin Ave Santa Ana CA 92705

JACK, NANCY RAYFORD, supplemental resource company executive, consultant; b. Hughes Springs, Tex., June 23, 1939; d. Vernon Lacy and Virginia Ernestine (Turner) Rayford; m. Kermit E. Hundley, Dec. 19, 1979; 1 child by previous marriage, James Bradford Jack, III. Cert. in bus. adminstrn., Keller Grad. Sch. Mgmt., 1980; cert. in acctg., Harper Coll., 1972, cert. in corp. law and tax law, paralegal, 1973. Sr. sec. Gould, Inc., Rolling Meadows, Ill., 1971-73; staff asst. Gould, Inc., 1973-74, asst. sec., 1974-77, corp. sec., 1977-89, v.p., 1985-89; pres. The Corp. Ofcl. Sec., Wheaton, Ill., 1989-92, Corp. Minutes and more, Wheaton, 1992—. Recipient cert. of leadership YWCA Met. Chgo., 1975. Mem. Fair Oaks Ranch Golf and

Country Club, Beta Sigma Phi. Home: 1040 Creekside Dr Wheaton IL 60187-6173

JACK, PHYLLIS HARRIS, corporate family strategist, educational consultant; b. Charlotte, N.C., Aug. 23, 1934; d. William Thomas and Connie LaVerne (Childers) Harris; children: Michael Harris, Julie Dawn Jack Rodgers. BA, U. N.C., 1965, MEd, 1969; postgrad., North Tex. State U., 1982-83. Cert. tchr., N.C., Tex. Elem. tchr. Chapel Hill (N.C.) Pub. Schs., 1965-68; staff devel. coordinator Learning Inst. N.C., Durham, 1969-72; child devel. specialist Tex. Dept. Human Resources, Ft. Worth, 1975-77; child care tng. coordinator North Tex. State Univ., Denton, 1978-81; dir., owner Resources for Children, Inc., Ft. Worth, 1984-88; pvt. practice Ft. Worth, 1988—; instr. Tarrant County Jr. Coll., Ft. Worth, North Tex. State U., 1982—; frequent guest speaker; appearances on TV; coord. for tng. in establishment of pub. sch. kindergarten program in State of N.C., 1972-73; cons. for family support svcs. State Dept. Pub. Instrn., Raleigh. Contbg. author: Room to Grow; mem. editorial rev. bd. Child Care Quar., Austin, 1984—. Trustee Tarrant County Youth Collaboration, 1982-86; bd. dirs. Tarrant County Med. Aus., 1983-84; adv. bd. Ft. Worth's A Better Childhood Com., 1990—; coord. Tex. State Parent Action, 1989—; gov.'s task force mem. Head Start Collaboration, 1991—. Recipient Brous Outstanding Advocate award, 1984. Mem. Nat. Assn. for the Edn. of Young Children (gov. bd. nominee 1988—, nat. field rep. 1983—), Tex. Assn. for the Edn. of Young Children (state pres. 1982-83, Adminstr. of the Yr. award 1993), Ft. Worth Assn. for the Edn. of Young Children (pres. 1976-78), So. Assn. for Children Under Six (com. chair 1978-80, conf. co-chair 1987), Rotary, Phi Beta Kappa, Phi Delta Kappa. Methodist. Club: Ft. Worth Woman's (v.p. and auditor 1983-86). Lodge: Rotary.

JACKLE, KAREN DEE, real estate executive; b. Santa Ana, Calif., June 26, 1945; d. Franklin Suits and Dorothy (Miller) Todd; m. Paul Herman Jackle, Oct. 12, 1968; children: Lara Irene, Julie Maureen. BA in History, Calif. State U., Long Beach, 1967. Elem. tchr. L.A. City Schs., 1967-68; social worker Los Angeles Dept. Pub. Social Svcs., 1968-70; with Seablue Pools, Salisbury, Rhodesia, 1970; co-owner, property mgr., appraiser Paul Jackle & Assocs., Inc., Huntington Beach, Calif., 1971—; property mgr., appraiser Paul Jackle & Assocs., Huntington Beach, Calif., 1973-86; property developer, mgr. Paul Jackle & Assocs., Huntington Beach, 1986—; pres. June Coast Corp., 1993—. Mem. Sister City Club, Huntington Beach, 1986—. Mem. AAUW (chmn. edn. found. 1991-92, chmn. membership 1992-94, mem. mentoring program 1990-94, Mentor award 1991), Nat. Assn. Women in Constrn., H. Seacliff Homeowners Assn. (block rep.), Amigos de Bolsa Chica. Office: 18652 Florida St Ste 300 Huntington Beach CA 92648

JACKMAN, MICHELE, management consultant; b. L.A., Aug. 18, 1944; d. Michael and Grace (DeLeo) Pantaleo; m. Jarrell C. Jackman, Sept. 7, 1968; 1 child, Renee Grace. BA in Polit. Sci., U. Calif., Davis, 1966; MSW in Social Policy, Cath. U., 1980; MA in Human Rels. Mgmt., U. Okla., 1980. Social worker Los Angeles County, 1966-70; supr., trainer Santa Barbara (Calif.) County, 1970-74; mgr. Drug/Alcohol program U.S. Army, Western Europe, 1974-78; analyst, cons. Office Dep. Chief of Staff Pers. U.S. Army, Washington, 1978-80; trainer, cons. Profit Systems, Internat., Santa Barbara, 1980—; lectr. organizational psychology U. Calif., Santa Barbara; cons. numerous agys., orgns. Co-author: Choices/Challenges Teacher's Guide, 1985; author: (tape) Humor at the Workplace, 1988, Star Teams, Key Players, 1991; profiled in: Management: Function and Strategy, 1994; contbr. chpts. to books. Bd. dirs. Women's Cmty. Ctr.; cmty. advisor Jr. League, 1991-93. Recipient Commdr.'s medal for Disting. Civilian Svc. U.S. Army, 1977, Bus. Personality of Yr., 1992 Bus. Digest. Mem. NAFE, OAS, NASW (chmn. local chpt.), ASTD, UN Instl. Assn., Inst. Noetic Scis., Santa Barbara C. of C. (Bus. award Coun. of High Edn./Industry 1986), Univ. Club, Native Daus. of Golden West. Office: Profit Systems Internat Tng and Mgmt Systems 5266 Hollister Ave Ste 101 Santa Barbara CA 93111-2066

JACKMAN, VIRGINIA GLORIA, artist, educator; b. Miles City, Mont., Nov. 14, 1921; d. John Edison and Lula May (Wilson) Campbell; m. Robert Kenneth Jackman, Aug. 5, 1944; children: Thomas, Luana, Douglas. MFA, Mont. State U., 1943; postgrad., Otis Art Inst., UCLA. Cert. tchr. Artist Walt Disney Studio, Burbank, Calif., 1943-46; tchr. Burbank Unified Sch. Dist., 1960-85; artist, 1970-90; resident artist Burbank City Park & Recreations, Burbank, 1987, 88; tchr., workshop leader Mont., Calif., 1979-90; faculty mem. Burbank Adult Sch., The Jade Fon summer watercolor workshop, Monterey, Calif. One-person shows include Waterworks Gallery, Custer County Art Ctr., Guild Hall Galleries, London; exhibited in group shows including Brand Libr. Gallery, Descanso Gardens; represented in permanent collections Home Savs. and Loan, Utah State U. Gallery, Bertha Eccles Found., Swains Pvt. Coll., Joseph Hughes Pvt. Collection; featured artist in Am. Artist mag., Dec. 1993; contbr. articles to profl. jours. Recipient Watercolor West award, 1972, Purchase award Home Savs. and Loan All City Show, L.A., 1976, Purchase award Brand X, 1980, Women Painters West awards, 1978, 79, 80, San Bernardino Mus. Fine Arts Inst. Juried Shows awards, 1978, 79, 80. Mem. Women Painters West, Fine Arts Inst., Watercolor West (signature mem.), Mont. Watercolor Soc. (signature mem.), Valley Watercolor Soc.

JACKOWIAK, PATRICIA, lawyer; b. Chgo., Feb. 3, 1959; d. Leonard John and Margaret Mary (Iozzi) J. BA, Loyola U., Chgo., 1981; JD, John Marshall Law Sch., 1984. Bar: Ill. 1985. Asst. state's atty. Cook County, Chgo., 1987-89, supr. trial atty. bur. child support enforcement, legal advisor law student's spl. and perjury projects, chmn. employee rels. com., 1988-89, com. mem. domestic rels. div. Pro-se task force, 1989; dep. commr. Consumer Protection div. Dept. Consumer Svcs. City of Chgo., 1989—; summer atty. Ct. Claims and Antitrust divsn. Office of Ill. Atty. Gen., 1985, 86; com. mem. domestic rels. divsn. Cook County The Pro-Se Task Force Com.; mem. Chgo. divsn. Ford Consumer Appeals Bd., 1989-92, chair, 1991-92. Pres. Santa Lucia Sch. Bd., Chgo., 1987—; chairperson Santa Lucia Parish Carnival Com., 1987—; chairperson employee rels. com. Child Support div., 1988-89; dir. religious edn. Santa Lucia Parish, 1985—; mem. freshman recruiting and fundraising coms. Parents Assocs. Loyola U., Chgo., 1987-90; mem. elder care task force Dept. Health, Aging and Disability, Dept. Consumer Svcs. City of Chgo., 1989—; commencement speaker St. Barbara High Sch., Chgo., 1993, bd. dirs., 1994—. Recipient Local Parish award Cath. Youth Orgn./Archdiocese of Chgo., 1991; disting. elem. grad. award Nat. Cath. Ednl. Assn., Santa Lucia Sch., 1994. Mem. ABA, Nat. Indsl. Scale Assn., Nat. Conf. Weights and Measures, Blue Key, Pi Sigma Alpha. Democratic. Roman Catholic. Office: Dept Consumer Svcs 121 N La Salle St Chicago IL 60602-1202

JACKSON, ADRIENNE ANGELA, vice principal; b. L.A., July 18, 1960; d. Harold Coyage and Clora (Ellis) J. BA, Chapman U., Orange, Calif., 1982, MA, 1988. Teaching and Adminstrv. Svcs. Cert., Calif. Dance instr. Centinela Valley Union High Sch. Dist., Lawndale, Calif., 1987-90; dir. of activities Tustin (Calif.) Unified Sch. Dist., 1990-93; vice prin. Grossmont (Calif.) Union High Sch. Dist., 1993—. Mem. ASCD, NAACP, Nat. Coalition of 100 Black Women (founding mem. San Diego chpt.), Phi Delta Kappa, Delta Gamma. Office: Monte Vista High Sch 3230 Sweetwater Springs Blvd Spring Valley CA 91977

JACKSON, ALEXINE CLEMENT, community volunteer; b. Sumter, S.C, June 10, 1936; d. William Alexander and Frances Lawson Clement; m. Aaron Gordon Jackson, June 21, 1958; children: Gordon, Celia, Emily, Juliet, Scott. BA in English, Spelman Coll., 1956; MA in Speech Pathology and Audiology, U. Iowa, 1958. Pres. Washington Performing Arts Soc., 1990-92; v.p. YWCA of U.S.A., N.Y.C., 1991—; bd. dirs. Black Women's Agenda, Washington, 1988—, Wolf Trap Found. Performing Arts, Vienna, Va., 1990—. Home: 11815 Piney Glen Ln Potomac MD 20854

JACKSON, ALICE HUMBERT, retired psychologist and educator; b. Buffalo, Sept. 22, 1914; d. Herbert Earl and Eula (Brainard) Humbert; m. A. Leon Jackson, Nov. 1953 (div. 1964); 3 stepchildren. BA, U. Mich., 1936, MA, 1937; PhD, U. So. Calif., 1953. Cert. tchr., Mich.; standard designated svc. credential, life tchr., sch. psychologist, supr., cons., coord., prin., pupil pers., Calif. Tchr. pub. schs., Mich., Calif., 1937-43, 46, 49; psychometrist Calif. Test Bur., Hollywood, 1947-49; coord. sch. psychologists Los Angeles County Supt. Schs., L.A., 1950-55; prof. Ea. N.Mex. U., Portales, 1965-70, dir. Head Start regional tng., 1966-70; prof., dir. Kindergarten Insts. Tex. Woman's U., Denton, 1970-72; prof. head start supplementary tng. Redlands (Calif.) U., 1972-73; sch. psychologist Covina (Calif.) Valley Unified Sch. Dist., 1973-80. Author audio-visual curriculum activities in elem. reading and arithmetic, 1967-69; editor: Performance Based Activities for Kindergarten, 1971. Pres. Hosp. Auxs. Kans., 1964; mem. adv. bd. Head Start, Rogers, Ark., 1986-88; mem. Fed. Women's Club, Kans., N.Mex., 1954-66. With USN, 1944-46. Mem. AAUW, Pi Lambda Theta. Home: 5411 Rolling Green Rd Arlington TX 76017-6237

JACKSON, ANNE (ANNE JACKSON WALLACH), actress; b. Allegheny, Penn., Sept. 3, 1926; d. John Ivan and Stella Germaine (Murray) J.; m. Eli Wallach, Mar. 5, 1948; children: Peter, Roberta, Katherine. Studied with Sanford Meisner and Herbert Berghof at Neighborhood Playhouse, with Lee Strassberg at Actor's Studio. Profl. debut: Cherry Orchard; mem. Am. Repertory Co.; Broadway plays include: Summer and Smoke, Oh, Men! Oh, Women!, Middle of the Night, Major Barbara, Rhinoceros, Luv, Waltz of the Toreadors, Diary of Anne Frank, 1978, Twice Around the Park, 1982-83, Nest of the Woodgrouse, 1984, Café Crown, 1989, Love Letters, 1991-92, Lost in Yonkers, 1992, In Person, 1993, The Flowering Peach, 1994, off-Broadway plays: The Typists, The Tigers; film appearances include: So Young, So Bad, 1950, Secret Life of an American Wife, 1968, Dirty Dingus McGee, 1970, Lovers andOther Strangers, 1970, The Shining, 1980, Sam's Son, 1985, Funny About Love, 1992, Folks, 1992; TV appearances include: 84 Charing Cross Road, Private Battle, Everything's Relative, 1987; TV films: Family Man, Golda I and II, Out on a Limb, Baby M, 1988; author: (autobiography) Early Stages, 1979. Recipient Obie award. Office: care Paradigm Clifford Stevens 200 W 57th St New York NY 10019

JACKSON, ANNE MCEWEN, dean; b. Litchfield, Ill., Feb. 25, 1956; d. David Alonzo and Mina Jean (Miller) J. AB, Ill. Coll., 1978; MA, Sangamon State U., 1990. From asst. dean to dean students MacMurray Coll., Jacksonville, Ill., 1979—; therapist for Community Counseling; homebound tchr. Sch. Dist. 117. Bd. dirs. Women's Crisis Ctr. Mem. AAUW, AACD, Am. Coll. and U. Housing Assn., Am. Sch. Counseling Assn., Am. Coll. Pers. Assn., Ill. Assn. Women Deans, Adminstrs. and Counselors, Jacksonville Jr. Women's Club (chmn. com. 1990-91), Phi Delta Kappa. Home: 325 N Westgate Jacksonville IL 62650-2129 Office: MacMurray Coll 447 E College Ave Jacksonville IL 62650-2590

JACKSON, BARBARA W., school system administrator; b. Eudora, Ark., Feb. 13, 1929; d. John Leonard Sr. and Elise (Thompson) Wall; children: John David, Cheryl Lynn Jackson Woodberry, Charles Robert. BS, Ark. State Tchrs. Coll., 1949; MEd, U. Ga., 1968, EdS, 1973, EdD, 1983. Cert. counseling and sch. psychologist, Ga. Psychologist Clarke County Sch. Dist., Athens, Ga., counselor elem.; counselor elem.-title III Franklin County Sch. Dist., Royston, Ga.; coord. chpt. I and testing Clarke County Sch. Dist., Athens. Contbr. articles to profl. jours. Mem. APA, ASCD, Nat. Assn. Sch. Psychologists, Ga. Assn. Sch. Psychologists, Ga. ASCD, Ga. Ednl. Rsch. Assn., Profl. Assn. Ga. Educators, Alpha Chi, Kappa Delta Pi, Phi Kappa Phi, Delta Kappa Gamma.

JACKSON, BECKY GAIL, critical care nurse; b. Dallas, Nov. 8, 1960; d. Glen Ray Bennett and Shirley McCormick Owens; m. Gary Todd Jackson, May 8, 1986 (div. Feb. 1990); children: Jeremy, Jennifer. LPN, Moore Norman Votech, 1981; ADN, Okla. City C.C., 1990; BSN, U. Okla., Oklahoma City, 1994. LPN; cert. ACLS, BLS instr., intra aortic balloon pump specialist. Staff nurse Norman (Okla.) Regional Hosp., 1981-91, asst. nurse mgr., 1991—; coord. open heart recovery Norman Regional Hosp., 1992—, chair-elect care com., 1993—, cons. safety com., 1993—. Mem. AACN, Okla. Nurses Assn. Democrat. Baptist.

JACKSON, BEVERLEY JOY JACOBSON, columnist, lecturer; b. L.A., Nov. 20, 1928; d. Phillip and Dorothy Jacobson; student U. So. Calif., UCLA; m. Robert David Jackson (div. Aug. 1964); 1 child, Tracey Dee. Daily columnist Santa Barbara (Calif.) News Press, 1968-92, Santa Barbara Independent, 1992—; nat. lectr. Santa Barbara History, History of China Recreated, Chinese Footbinding, Shoes for Bound Feet, China Today; free lance writer, fgn. corr. Bd. dirs. Santa Barbara br. Am. Cancer Soc., 1963—; mem. art mus. coun. L.A. Mus. Art, 1959—, mem. costume coun., 1983—; docent L.A. Mus. Art, 1962-64; mem. exec. bd. Channel City Club (formerly Channel City Women's Forum), 1969—; mem. adv. bd. Santa Barbara Mus. Natural History, Coun. of Christmas Cheer, Women's Shelter Bldg., Direct Relief Internat., Nat. Coun. Drug and Alcohol Abuse, Am. Oceans Campaign; mem adv. bd. Hospice of Santa Barbara, 1981—, Stop AIDS Coun., Arthritis Found.; bd. dirs. So. Calif. Com. for Shakespear's Globe Theatre; chmn. Santa Barbara Com. for Visit Queen Elizabeth II, 1982—; founder costume guild Santa Barbara Hist. Soc.; curator Chinese collections Santa Barbara Hist. Mus.; adv. bd. Santa Barbara Choral Soc.; hon. bd. Santa Barbara Salvation Army, Ensemble Theatre Santa Barbara; adv. bd. Storyteller Sch. Homeless Children. Author: Dolls and Doll Houses of Spain, 1970, (with others) I'm Just Wild About Harry, 1979, Spendid Slippers: The History of Chinese Footbinding and Lotus Shoes, 1994. Home: PO Box 5118 Santa Barbara CA 93150-5118

JACKSON, CAROL E., federal judge. BA, Wellesley Coll., 1973; JD, U. Mich., 1976. With Thompson & Mitchell, St. Louis, 1976-83; counsel Mallinckrodt, Inc., St. Louis, 1983-85; magistrate U.S. Dist. Ct., Ea. Dist. Mo., 1986-92, dist. judge, 1992—; adj. prof. law Washington U., 1989-92; mem. Eigth Cir. Adv. Com., Ea. Dist. Mo. Adv. Com. Trustee St. Louis Art Mus., 1987-91; dir. Hyde Park Renovation Effort, 1984-85, bi-state chpt. ARC, 1989-91, Sherwood Forest Camp, Inc., Mo. Bot. Garden. Mem. Nat. Assn. Women Judges, Fed. Magistrate Judges Assn., Mo. Bar, St. Louis County Bar Assn., Bar Assn. Metro. St. Louis, Mound City Bar Assn., Lawyers Assn. St. Louis. Office: US Courthouse 1114 Market St Saint Louis MO 63101-2043*

JACKSON, CHARLOTTE DENISE CAVE, critical care nurse; b. Miami, Fla., Nov. 3, 1956; d. Charles Cave and Bernice (Harp) Foster; m. Wesley Wendell Jackson, July 5, 1975; children: Charnice Wendetta, LaTesha Marie, Aleesia Danielle. ADN, Miami Dade Community Coll., 1984. CCRN, BLS instr., ACLS instr. Staff nurse Cedars Med. Ctr., Miami, 1984-85; charge/staff nurse Augusta Regional Med. Ctr., Augusta, Ga., 1985—. Mem. AACN. Home: 3630 Munich Dr Augusta GA 30906-4082

JACKSON, CHRISTINE OSBURN, association executive; b. Marion, Ala., Aug. 1; d. Roland Lee and Cornelia (Scott) Osburn; m. E. L. Jackson (dec.); children: Kathy, Kim, Moshe. AS, Stillman Coll., 1950; BS in Home Econs., Tenn. A&I U., 1953. County home demonstration agt. Auburn (Ala.) U. Ext. Svc., 1953-63; tchr. sci. Elmore County Sch. System, Tallahassee, Ala., 1961-63; asst. home demonstration agt. Clemson U. Ext. Svc., Charleston, S.C., 1963-65; tchr. sci. and English Bapt. Hill High Sch., Yonges Island, S.C., 1966; br. exec. Charleston YWCA, 1966-69; exec. dir. YWCA Greater Charleston, 1969—. State chairperson Foster Care Review Bd., 1984-91, also bd. dirs.; former sec. Charleston County Dem. Women's Club; bd. dirs. Interfaith Crisis Ministry. Mem. LWV, Am. Bus. and Profl. Women, Tri-County Assn. Execs., Sigma Gamma Rho. Home: 892 Dills Bluff Rd Charleston SC 29412

JACKSON, DORIS KELLY, principal; b. Wilmington, N.C., Mar. 23, 1938; d. Le Roy and Janie (Grady) Kelly; m. Robert Travis Jackson, Nov. 3, 1962 (div. Aug. 1981); children: Robert Jr., Kelli, Shawn. BS, Cheyney U., 1960, MS, 1991; MS, Temple U., 1978. Cert. tchr. elem. edn., reading specialist, media specialist, elem. supr., secondary prin., Pa. Tchr. Coatesville (Pa.) City Sch. Dist., 1960-62; curriculum writer Capitol Cities Inc., Phila., 1976-77; tchr. Sch. Dist. Phila., 1963-73, reading specialist, 1973-87, in-svc. instr., 1980-82, instrl. supr., 1988-91, reading specialist, 1991—; cons. social studies textbook, Phila., 1986. Co-editor: (mag.) Alert, 1979; editor: (video scripts) Training Development Standards of AT&T, 1979-80. Mem. steering com. Careers in Comms. Tech., Office of Multi-Media, Sch. Dist. Phila., 1981-89; exec. com. PATHS, Sch. Dist. Phila., 1990, 91; mem. long range planning com. Colonial Sch. Dist., Plymouth Meeting, Pa., 1990; grad. coun. rep. Grad. Student Assn., Cheyney, 1990-91; bd. dirs. Am. Women's Heritage Soc., Phila., 1989-93. Recipient Cert. of Recognition Phila. Bd. Edn., 1983, Cert. of Recognition City Coun., 1983, Cert. of Appreciation Ada H. H. Lewis Mid. Sch., 1983, Cert. of Award Mid. Sch. Sci. Fall Retreat, 1990, Plaque of Recognition Bicentennial Commn. U.S., 1991; grantee Pa. Dept. Edn., 1981, Phila. Assn. Sch. Adminstrs., 1991. Mem. ASCD, Assn. Ednl. Comms. and Tech. (evaluator instrl. materials 1988-89), Nat. Coun. Tchrs. English (liaison rep. 1977-80), Women in Edn., Phila. Fedn. Tchrs., Black Women's Edn. Alliance, Delaware Valley Assn. Black Sch. Educators, Cheyney U. of Pa. Alumni Assn., Alumni Assn. Temple U., Kappa Delta Pi, English Club Phila. (v.p. 1976-79), Optimist (charter). Republican. Home: 32 Corson Rd Conshohocken PA 19428-2103 Office: Sch Dist Phila 21st And Pky Philadelphia PA 19103

JACKSON, DOROTHY FAYE GREENE, nursing educator; b. Marlin, Tex., Mar. 18, 1947; d. Shellie Tom and Ruby Lee (O'Neal) Greene; m. David Lee Jackson, Jr., Dec. 20, 1967; children: David Lee III, Danese. AAS, Odessa Coll., 1967; BSN, West Tex. State U., 1977; MSN, U. Tex., Galveston, 1980. RN, Tex. Staff nurse Med. Ctr. Hosp., Odessa, Tex., 1967-68, charge nurse CCU, 1968-72, mgr. quality assurance and infection control, 1979-80, dir. nursing, critical care and edn., 1980-81, bd. mgrs. Med. Ctr. Hosp., 1988-89; instr. nursing Odessa Coll., 1972-79, 81-94, dept. chair, 1993; asst. prof. Sch. Nursing Tex. Tech. U. Health Scis. Ctr., Odessa, 1993—, advanced practice nurse Sch. Medicine and Family Practice, 1993—; mem. adv. bd. Head Start, Odessa, 1981—; cons. to long term care facilities, Odessa, 1991—, clin. specialist in gerontological nursing, 1994—; v.p. Seabury Nursing Home, 1985—; presenter Nat. Conf. on Gerontol. Nursing Edn., Norfolk, Va., 1992. Bd. dirs. Odessa Cultural Coun., 1989—, Midland-Odessa Symphony and Chorale, 1991—. Mem. ANA, Deans and Dirs. for Schs. Nursing for State Tex., Altrusa Internat., Jr. League Odessa, Phi Delta Kappa, Sigma Theta Tau, Alpha Kappa Alpha. Episcopalian. Home: 410 E 42nd St Odessa TX 79762-6856 Office: Tex Tech U Univ Health Scis Ctr W 4th St Odessa TX 79763

JACKSON, GERALDINE, entrepreneur; b. Barnesville, Ga., Oct. 30, 1934; d. Charles Brown and Christine (Maddox) J.; 1 child, Prentiss Andrew. Nurses aide Grady Hosp., Atlanta; mail handler U.S. Post Office, Cicero, Ill.; sec., tour guide Walgreens Lab., Chgo.; credit clk. Sterling Jewelers, Atlanta; owner, broker Gerris Automobile Leasing Svc., Atlanta. Mem. Nat. Law Enforcement Officer Meml. Fund, Rep. Nat. Com.; active Sacred Heart League. Mem. AARP, DAV, NAACP, NAFE, Nat. Assn. Police Orgn. (assoc. mem. presdl. task force), Internat. Assn. Chief Police, Ga. Sheriff's Assn., Nat. Right to Life. Democrat. Home and Office: 1890 Myrtle Dr SW Apt 422 Atlanta GA 30311-4954

JACKSON, GLENDA, actress; b. Birkenhead, Cheshire, Eng., May 9, 1936; d. Harry and Joan J.; m. Roy Hodges (div.); 1 son, Daniel. Ed., West Kirby County Grammar Sch. for Girls; DLitt (hon.), U. Liverpool, 1978; LLM (hon.), U. Nottingham, 1992. M.P. for Labor Party representing Hampstead and Highgate, Parliament, London; Dir. United Brit. Artists, 1983—; MP for Hampstead and Highgate, 1992—. Made stage debut as student in Separate Tables, Worthing, Eng., 1957; first appeared London (Eng.) stage as Ruby in All Kinds of Men, Arts Theatre, 1957; appeared in Hammersmith, 1962, The Idiot, 1963, Alfie, 1963; joined Royal Shakespeare Co. and appeared in exptl. Theatre of Cruelty season, L.A.M.D.A., 1964, Stratford season, 1965; played Princess of France in Love's Labour's Lost, Ophelia in Hamlet; reader in The Investigation, 1965; appeared as Charlotte Corday in Marat-Sade, 1965, and repeating performance in N.Y. debut at Martin Beck Theatre, 1965 (Variety award as most promising actress); appeared as Eva in Puntila at Aldwych Theatre, 1965, as Masha in Three Sisters at Royal Ct., 1967, as Tamara Fanghorn in Fanghorn at Fortune, 1967, as Katherine Winter in Collaborators, 1973, as Solange in The Maids, 1974, as Hedda Gabler, 1975, as Vittoria Corombona in The White Devil, 1976, Scenes from an Execution, 1990, Mother Courage, 1990; appeared on stage in Rose, N.Y.C., London, 1980-81, Phaedra, N.Y.C., 1984-85, Strange Interlude, 1985, Macbeth, 1988; appeared in numerous films, 1968— including Women in Love (Acad. award for Best Actress 1970), Sunday, Bloody Sunday, The Music Lovers, Marat-Sade, Negatives, Mary Queen of Scots, Triple Echo (being reissued as Soldier in Skirts), The Nelson Affair, A Touch of Class (Acad. award for Best Actress 1974), 1973, The Maids, The Romantic Englishwoman, The Incredible Sarah, Nasty Habits, House Calls, Lost and Found, 1979, Health, 1980, Hopscotch, 1980, Stevie, 1981, The Return of the Soldier, 1982, Giro City, Turtle Diary, 1986, Beyond Therapy, 1987, Salome's Last Dance, 1988, Business as Usual, 1988, The Rainbow, 1989, The Visit; also numerous TV appearances, 1960— including (series) Elizabeth R., The Patricia Neal Story, 1981, Sakharov, 1984, Strange Interlude, 1988, The House of Bernarda Alba, 1991. Office: Lioner Larner Ltd 130 W 57th St New York NY 10019-3325

JACKSON, JANE W., interior designer; b. Asheville, N.C., Aug. 5, 1944; d. James and Willie Mae (Stoner) Harris; m. Bruce G. Jackson; children: Yvette, Scott. Student, Boston U., 1964; BA, Leslie Coll., 1967; postgrad., Artisan Sch. Interior Design, 1980-82. Tchr. Montessori, Brookline, Mass., 1969-72; interior designer, owner Nettle Creek Shop, Honolulu, 1980-88; owner Wellesley Interiors, Honolulu, 1988—. Active Mayor's Com. for Small Bus., Honolulu, 1984. Mem. Honolulu Club. Democrat. Office: Wellesley Interiors PO Box 1365 Kaneohe HI 96744-1365

JACKSON, JANET DAMITA, singer, dancer; b. Gary, Ind., June 16, 1966; d. Joseph and Katherine J.; m. James DeBarge, 1984 (div. 1985). Albums include Janet Jackson, Dream Street, 1984, Control, 1986, Rhythm Nation 1814, 1991, janet, 1993; actress (TV series) Good Times, 1977, A New Kind of Family, Diff'rent Strokes, Fame; (films) Poetic Justice, 1993 (Academy award nomination Best Original Song 1993). Recipient 6 Am. Music awards, 1987, 1988, 1991, 5 Grammy nominations, MTV Video Vanguard award, 1990, Grammy award, Best R&B song 1994 for "That's the Way Love Goes" with Terry Lewis and James Harris III; MTV Best Female Video for "If". Office: A & M Records Inc 1416 N La Brea Ave Los Angeles CA 90028-7563*

JACKSON, JANET ELIZABETH, municipal judge, association executive; b. Randolph, Va.; d. Robert and Joan (Morton) J.; 1 child, Harrison Michael Sewell. BA, Wittenberg U., 1975; JD, George Washington U., 1978. Bar: Ohio 1978, U.S. Dist. Ct. (so. dist.) Ohio 1979, U.S. Dist. Ct. (no. dist.) Ohio 1983. Asst. atty. gen. Office Ohio Atty. Gen., Columbus, 1978-80, chief crime victims compensation sect., 1980-82, chief workers compensation and civil rights sects., 1983-87; with Sindell, Sindell & Rubenstein, Cleve., 1982-83; judge Franklin County Mcpl. Ct., Columbus, 1987—, adminstrv. and presiding judge, 1992; atty. gen.'s ethics and profl. responsibility adv. coun.; joint task force gender bias Ohio Supreme Ct. and Ohio State Bar Assn.; mem. com. to study impact of substance abuse on cts., Supreme Ct., 1989-90. Chair bd. trustees YWCA; vice-chair bd. trustees, mem. exec. com. United Way Franklin County; chair Right from the Start Community Forum; bd. dirs. Met. Women's Ctr., 1980-86, S.E. Community Mental Health Ctr., 1987, Columbus Urban League, 1987-90, Maryhaven, 1987-89, Riverside Meth. Hosp.; trustee Wittenberg U.; chair task force child care City of Columbus; vol. Columbus Pub. Schs.; past mem., chairperson Minority Task force on AIDS; mem. AIDS community adv. coalition, 1987-90, task force domestic violence, 1988; mem. svc. team Explorer Divsn. Boy Scouts Am. Recipient Sharon Wilkin award Met. Women's Ctr., Dr. Martin Luther King Jr. Humanitarian award Love Acad., 1987, Polit. Leadership award 29th Dist. Citizens' Caucus, 1987, Citizenship award Omega Psi Phi, 1987, Outstanding Accomplishments award Franklin County Dem. Women, 1988, Community Svc. award Met. Dem. Women's Club, 1989, Warren Jennings award Franklin County Mental Health Bd., 1989, Martin Luther King Jr. Humanitarian award Columbus Edn. Assn., 1991, Women of Achievement award YWCA, 1992, Citizen's award Columbus Assn. Edn. Young Children, 1993, Citations award Pi Lamda Theta, 1993, Blue Chip award Social Svcs., 1994. Mem. Nat. Conf. Black Lawyers (Disting. Barrister award 1988, John Mercer Langston award 1994), Ohio State Bar Assn. (coun. dels. 1993—, commn. racial and ethnic fairness, bd. govs. women in the profession sect.), Columbus Bar Assn., Women Lawyers Franklin County, The Links, Inc. (pres. Twin Rivers chpt. 1992-94), Columbus Mortar Bd. Alumni Club, Golden Key Nat. Honor Soc. (hon.). Home: 2865 Castlewood Rd Columbus OH 43209 Office: Franklin County Mcpl Ct 375 High St 13D Columbus OH 43215

JACKSON, JANET SUE JEAN, nurse; b. Kingman, Kans., July 26, 1957; d. James Walker and Allegra Marie (Long) Reynolds; divorced; m. Dean Alvin Jackson, Nov. 5, 1989; stepchildren: Brian, Scott, Jeff. BS in Family and Child Devel., Kans. State U., 1979; BSN, Wichita State U., 1982; MEd,

Alberton's Coll. of Idaho, 1993. Program coord. Kans. State U., Manhattan, 1977-80; staff nurse emergency room St. Joseph's Med. Ctr., Wichita, 1982-83; staff nurse/maternal-child USAF, Austin, Tex., 1983-86; social actions officer Idaho Air Nat. Guard, Boise, 1986-93; staff nurse, labor and delivery St. Luke's Regional Med. Ctr., Boise, 1986-93; adj. faculty Boise State U., 1989-93; practicum on counseling Ctr. for New Directions, Boise, 1992, 93; workshops in coms. Skills and Stress mgmt. for the Idaho Air Nat. Guard, Boise, 1990-93. Pres. Teenage Reps., Manhattan, 1974. Capt. USAF, 1986-93. Mem. Step Family Assn. of Am., Assn. of Women's Health, Obstetric and Neonatal Nurses, Am. Assn. Counseling and Devel., Idaho Counseling Assn., Nat. Guard Assn.

JACKSON, JEAN THERESE, surgeon; b. Marquette, Mich., Apr. 12, 1931; d. Charles Arthur and Kathleen Louise (Olivier) J. BS, Coll. St. Teresa, 1955; MS, Boston Coll., 1961; MD, Loyola U., Maywood, Ill., 1973. Diplomate Am. Bd. Plastic Surgery. Intern and resident in gen. surgery and plastic surgery Loyola U. Affiliated Hosps., Maywood, 1973-79; commd. maj. U.S. Army, 1979, advanced through grades to col., 1990; staff plastic surgeon Letterman Army Med. Ctr., San Francisco, 1979-82, chief plastic surgery svc., 1982-88; chief plastic surgery svc. Madigan Army Med. Ctr., Tacoma, 1988-92; chief plastic surgery svc., dir. residency program William Beaumont Army Med. Ctr., El Paso, Tex., 1992-93, chief plastic surgery svc., dep. dir. med. edn., 1993—. Fellow ACS; mem. Am. Assn. Plastic and Reconstructive Surgery. Republican. Roman Catholic. Office: William Beaumont Army Med Ctr OGME El Paso TX 79920

JACKSON, JEWEL, retired state youth authority executive; b. Shreveport, La., June 3, 1942; d. Willie Burghardt and Bernice Jewel (Mayberry) Norton; children: Steven, June Kelly, Michael, Anthony. With Calif. Youth Authority, 1965—, group supr., San Andreas and Santa Rosa, 1965-67, youth counselor, Ventura, 1967-78, sr. youth counselor, Stockton, 1978-81, parole agt., 1986, treatment team supr., program mgr., Whittier and Ione, 1981-91; retired, 1991; pres. Valley Paralegal Svc., Stockton. Avocations: reading, horseback riding, writing poetry and short stories, stamp collecting. Home: 2416 Hall Ave Stockton CA 95205-8422

JACKSON, JOY JUANITA, educator; b. New Orleans, Oct. 8, 1928; d. Oliver Daniel and Oneida Christina (Drouant) Jackson; student La. State U., 1946-49; B.A., Tulane U., 1951, M.A., 1958, Ph.D., 1961. Feature writer New Orleans Times-Picayune, 1951-56; instr. Nicholls State Coll., Thibodaux, La., 1961-62, asst. prof., 1962-66; asst. prof. Southeastern La. U., Hammond, 1966-68, asso. prof., 1968-73, prof. history, 1973—, dir. Center for Regional Studies and univ. archives, 1982—. AAUW Irma E. Voight fellow, 1960-61. Mem. Am., La. (dir. 1966-68, pres. 1977-78), So. Hist. Assn., S.E. La. Hist. Assn. (pres. Hammond 1978), Oral History Assn. Author: New Orleans in the Gilded Age, 1969, Where the River Runs Deep, 1993. Home: 1411 University Dr Hammond LA 70401-1738

JACKSON, JUDITH ANN, elementary education educator; b. Picayune, Miss., June 22, 1944; d. Roy Austin and Oleta Maria (Atkinson) Calhoun; m. David Harris Jackson, Dec. 31, 1965 (dec. Oct. 1990); children: Stacy Ann, William Austin. AA, Pearl River Jr. Coll., 1964; BS, U. So. Miss., 1966. Cert. elem. tchr. Reading tchr. Purvis (Miss.) Elem., 1965-66; 1st grade tchr. Bertie Rouse Sch., Picayune, 1966-68; 4th grade tchr. Scott County Christian Sch., Harperville, Miss., 1971-72; presch. dir., tchr. Forest (Miss.) Bapt. Ch. Kindergarten, 1984-87; elem. tchr. Gulfview Elem., Hancock County, Miss., 1993—. Home: 836 Longo St Waveland MS 39576

JACKSON, KAREN RENEE, school system administrator; b. Cleve., Sept. 13, 1948; d. Edward David and Vivian LaMar (Eanes) Dickson; m. Aquine Jackson; children: Kimberly Michelle, Kathryn Camille. BA, U. Wis., 1970; MS, U. Wis., Milw., 1974; PhD, U. Wis., 1988. Lic. dir. pupil svcs.,spl. edn., instrn., secondary sch. adminstr., guidance counselor, dist. adminstr. Social planner Social Devel. Commn., Milw., 1970-71; adminstr. Job Corps-YWCA, Milw., 1971-74; guidance counselor Horlick H.S., Racine, Wis., 1974-78; guidance counselor Whitefish Bay (Wis.) H.S., 1978-84, assoc. prin., 1984-89; dir. student svcs. Shorewood (Wis.) Sch. Dist., 1989—. Bd. mem. St. Charles Youth & Family Svc., Wauwatosa, Wis., Children Family Svcs., West Allis, Wis. Mem. The Links, Inc., U. Wis.-Milw. Alumni Assn. (bd. mem.), GetAway Club, Phi Delta Kappa, Pi Lambda Theta, Alpha Kappa Alpha. Democrat. Presbyterian. Home: 9920 W Greenwood Ter Milwaukee WI 53224 Office: Sch Dist Shorewood 1701 E Capitol Dr Shorewood WI 53211

JACKSON, KARLA RENEE, social worker; b. Columbia, Mo., Jan. 19, 1961; d. Frederick Eugene and Maribeth (Buescher) J. B in Social Work, Columbia Coll., 1991. Victim advocate, counselor The Shelter, Columbia, 1986-92; cmty. support worker McCambridge Ctr. for Women, Columbia, 1991—; owner, mgr. Helping Hands, Columbia, 1988—. Commr. Columbia Human Rights Commn. 1992—, chair edn. and outreach subcom. Mem. Nat. Assn. Social Workers (cert. social worker), Mo. Assn. for Social Welfare. Democrat. Methodist. Home: 819 W Worley St Columbia MO 65203-2682

JACKSON, LAURA JEAN, sales representative, aerobics/fitness instructor; b. San Francisco, Sept. 2, 1955; d. Allen Boing and Ida (Miele) J. LPN, Brooke Army Med. Ctr., 1976; Cert. Dental Technician, R.I. Jr. Coll., 1979; BA in Biology (Physiology), San Francisco State U., 1985. Cert. pulmonary resuscitator. Nurse R.I. Hosp., Providence, 1976-78; dental asst. various dentists, Providence, San Francisco, 1978-85; exercise physiologist Marshall Hale Sports Medicine, San Francisco, 1985-89; owner, pres. TruBody Co., San Francisco, 1985-89; aerobics instr. Nob Hill Club, Fairmont Hotel, San Francisco, 1985-88; tech. sales rep. indsl. maintenance supplies Mantek, Dallas, 1989—; aerobics instr. Oakland Hill Tennis Club, Oakland, Calif., 1992-94, Telegraph Hills Club, San Francisco, 1994, Advantage Fitness, San Francisco, 1994. Creator fitness program TruBody Fitness, 1986. Served with U.S.Army, 1975-78. Mem. Calif. Pioneer Soc., IDEA. Roman Catholic. Office: Laura Jackson DBA Mantek 15 Heritage St Oakland CA 94605-4606

JACKSON, LOLA HIRDLER, art instructor; b. Faribault, Minn., Mar. 2, 1942; d. Earl Arthur and Marian Barbara (Pavek) Hirdler; children: Carilyn, Cherilyn, Marc. BS in Art Edn., Mankato State U., 1972, MA, 1975. Cert. tchr. Instr. art YWCA, Mankato, 1968-70; art instr. Mankato Area Vocat. Tech. Inst., 1971-72; pres., tchr., art dir. Jackson Studios, Mankato, 1969-78; art tchr. New Richland (Minn.) High Sch., Mankato (Minn.) State U., 1973-74; pres. Lola Ltd. Lt'ee Art Distbn., N.C., 1976—; tchr. art Lincoln Sch. Math. and Sci. Tech., Greensboro, N.C., 1988-90, chmn. dept., 1988, 89-90; tchr., chmn. art dept. Shallotte Mid. Sch., 1990—; instr. art Brunswick C.C., Supply, N.C., 1990—; staff artist The Reporter, 1970-73; pres., bd. dirs. Fine Arts Inc., Gallery 500, Mankato, 1972-75. Bd. mem. Mankato Area Found., 1976-83. Recipient award Busch Found. Minn. Arts Coun., Nat. Endowment Arts, 1974. Mem. Profl. Pictures Framers Assn., N.C. Assn. of Edn. Republican. Roman Catholic.

JACKSON, LYNN ROBERTSON, lawyer; b. Montgomery, Ala., Nov. 20, 1947; d. Arthur Borders Jr. and Mozelle (Martin) Robertson; m. George Thomas Jackson, Aug. 16, 1969; children: Katherine, William Borders. BS, U. Ala., 1970; JD, Faulkner U., 1979. Bar: Ala. 1981, U.S. Dist. Ct. Ala. 1984. Ptnr. Jackson and Faulk, Clayton, 1981-83, Andrews and Jackson, Clayton, 1983-84; pvt. practice Clayton, 1984-92; ptnr. Jinks, Smithart & Jackson, Clayton, 1992—; chair mandatory legal edn. Ala. State Bar, 1990—; mem. permanent code com., bench and bar rels. com. Ala. State Bar. City atty. City of Clayton, 1984—; bd. trustees Town and County Libr., Clayton, 1990—; trustee Ala. Law Found., 1989—. Mem. ABA, Ala. State Bar Assn. (bar commr. 1985—), Assn. Trial Lawyers Am. Episcopalian. Home: Licklog Farm Clayton AL 36016 Office: Jinks Smithart and Jackson Court Sq Clayton AL 36016

JACKSON, MAE BOGER, executive adminstrative assistant, secretary; b. Winston-Salem, N.C., May 19, 1963; d. Billy Charles and Leona (Heath) Key; m. John Talbert Jackson, June 13, 1987; 1 child, Thomas William. Student, U. N.C., Charlotte, 1981-83; BS, Johnson Bible Coll., 1986. Cert. profl. sec. Adminstrv. asst., exec. sec. The Shelton Cos., Winston-Salem, 1986-88; office automation specialist, personnel mgr. POPI Temp. Svcs., Winston-Salem, 1988-90; exec. asst. Inmar Enterprises, Inc., Winston-Salem, 1990-92, Chesapeake Display and Packaging co., Winston-Salem, 1992—. Mem. NAFE, Profl. Secs. Internat. (treas. 1990, v.p. 1991, pres.-elect 1992, pres. 1993-94, Winston-Salem Sec. of Yr. 1991, Winston-Salem Outstanding Mem. of Yr. 1993), Assn. Info. Systems Profls., Office Automation Soc. Internat. Mem. Christian Ch. Home: 310 Gatewood Dr Winston Salem NC 27104-2432 Office: Chesapeake Display & Packaging Co PO Box 12669 Winston Salem NC 27117

JACKSON, MARY CATHERINE, tax assessor; b. Boston, May 31, 1950; d. Arthur W. and Mary (Connolly) Barry; m. Richard T. Jackson, July 30, 1977; stepchildren Eileen D. Jackson Nicosia, Kristine L. Jackson Twarog. BS in Edn., Northeastern U., 1973. Buyer Gilchrist Dept. Store, Boston, 1973-77; program auditor Hyuman Resources dept. City of Buffalo, 1979-83, assessor trainee, 1983-88, real property tax assessor Assessment dept., 1988—. Committeewoman Erie County Dem. Party, Buffalo, 1984-86; mem. North Buffalo Community Devel. Corp., 1984-85, Buffalo-Dortmund Sister City Com., 1985—, Buffalo-Tver Sister City Com., 1992—; bd. dirs. North Buffalo Community Devel. Corp., sec., 1984-85. Recipient Home Beautification award City of Buffalo, 1989. Mem. Internat. Assn. Assessing Officers, N.Y. Assessors Assn., Erie County Assessors Assn. (bd. dirs., sec. 1991—), Buffalo and Erie County Zool. Soc. (photo award). Democrat. Roman Catholic. Office: City of Buffalo Dept Assessment Rm 101 3 Niagara Sq City Hall Buffalo NY 14202

JACKSON, MARY JANE MCHALE FLICKINGER, principal; b. Cleve., Feb. 23, 1938; d. Thomas William Flickinger and Margaret Julia (Lydon) Flickinger Nichols; m. Robert Lowell Jackson, June 27, 1959; children: Julia Anna Jackson Sommers, Patricia L. Jackson Haggenjos, Margaret Jacqueline Jackson Tyler. BS in Speech, St. Louis U., 1959; postgrad., U. Copenhagen, 1961-62; MS in Spl. Edn., Southern Ill. U., 1965; EdD, George Washington U., 1977. Cert. tcht. Md. 1972. Tchr. Ritenour Sch. Dist., Overland, Mo., 1959-60; tutor Spl. Sch. Dist. Handicapped, St. Louis, 1960-61; tchr. Rugaards Franske Skole, Copenhagen, Denmark, 1961-62; substitute tchr., primary tchr. St. Louis and Ladue, Mo., 1962-65; tchr. L.A. City Schs., 1966-67, Woodlin Elem. Sch., Silver Spring, Md., 1967-68; various teaching positions, 1968-71, 73-81; asst. prin. Ritchie Park Elem. Sch., Rockville, Md., 1971-73, various supr. positions, 1974-79; asst. prin. Stephen Knolls Sch., Kensington, Md., 1981-88, prin., 1988—; v.p. Concerned Citizens Exceptional Edn., Washington, 1968-70; surrogate parent Assn. Retarded Citizens, Washington. Bd. dirs. Archdiocesan of Washington, 1986-91; pres. Bd. Edn., Washington, 1990-91; bd. dirs. United Cerebral Palsy, Montgomery County, 1992—; presenter Young Adult Insts. Internat. Conf., 1994. Recipient Lisa Kane award, 1964. Mem. Wash. Hearing Soc. (bd. dirs. 1969-81), Coun. Exceptional Children (exec. bd., pres. Montgomery county chpt. 1992-93, polit. action coord. for Md. fedn. 1993, exec. com. divsn. of internat. spl. edn. and svcs. 1993), Alexander Graham Bell Assn. (pub. rels. com. 1979—), Rotary. Roman Catholic. Home: 9900 Georgia Ave T-11 Silver SPring MD 20902 Office: Stephen Knolls Sch 10731 St Margaret's Way Kensington MD 20895

JACKSON, MARY L., health services executive; b. Phila., June 25, 1938; d. John Francis and Helen Catherine (Peranteau) Martin; m. Howard Clark Jackson III, Dec. 17, 1954; children: Michael, Mark, Brian. Student Bucks County Community Coll., 1977-83. Asst. mgr. retail div. Sears Roebuck & Co., Bensalem, Pa., 1972-77; educator, adminstr., dir. Trevose Behavior Modification Program, Pa., 1975—, leadership tng. workshops, 1979—; participant rsch. studies in field; salesman Makefield Real Estate, Morrisville, Pa., 1977-78; mortgage fin. cons. Tom Dunphy Real Estate, Feasterville, Pa., 1978-81; weight loss cons., Hulmeville, Pa., 1984—, also TV and radio appearances on behavior modification for weight loss and maintenance. Coauthor: The Official Calorie Book; pub., columnist monthly newsletter The Modifier, 1977—. Recipient Chapel of Four Chaplain award, 1977. Mem. Assn. Advancement of Behavior Therapy, Bucks County Bd. Realtors, Hulmeville Hist. Soc. (a founder, charter mem.). Democrat. Presbyterian. Avocations: reading, classical music, speed walking, knitting, fishing. Home: 218 Main St Hulmeville PA 19047

JACKSON, MELISSA MARGARET, real estate appraiser, marketing executive; b. Trenton, N.J., Jan. 26, 1962; d. William Tuttle and Shirley Marie (Sagi) J. BS in Mktg. and Spanish, Susquehanna U., 1984. Lic. real estate salesperson, N.J., residential real estate appraiser, N.J. Regional mktg. mgr. Cardell and Assocs., Inc., Morristown, N.J., 1984-87; asst. dir. mktg. and customer svc. Capital Adv. Group Inc., Parsippany, N.J., 1987-88; dir. ops. Zoch and Zoch Fin. Group, Inc., Fairfield, N.J., 1988-90; mortgage loan officer First Nat. Mortgage Co. N.J., Inc., Hamilton Square, 1990-93; v.p. mktg. United Evaluators, Inc., Whippany, N.J., 1993-95; pub. rels. dir. Peak Chiropractic Care, Princeton, N.J., 1995—; real estate sales assoc. Fox & Lazo Realtors, Hamilton, N.J., 1994—; pres. Pebble Beach Traders, Laurence, N.J., 1994—; real estate sales assoc. AAA Conti Realty, Mercerville, N.J., 1992—. Mem. NAFE, Internat. Assn. Fin. Planners, Internat. Assn. Bank Women, Mercer County Bd. Realtors, Sierra Club, Sigma Kappa (pres. Epsilon Delta chpt. 1981-82, treas. corp. bd. 1988-92). Republican. Presbyterian. Home: 40 Merritt Dr Lawrenceville NJ 08648-3157

JACKSON, PAMELA ZIEMER, accounting educator; b. Mt. Clements, Mich., Feb. 5, 1955; d. Rudolph Frederick and Eiko (Iwata) Ziemer; m. Philip James Jackson, June 15, 1985; children: Nathan Philip, Megan Elise. BS in English Edn., U. Ga., 1978; MBA, Augusta Coll., 1982; PhD in Bus. Adminstrn. and Acctg., U. Ga., 1990. CPA, Ga. Secondary sch. English tchr. Columbia County Bd. Edn., Evans, Ga., 1978-80; staff acct., auditor Baird and Co., Augusta, Ga., 1982-85; prof. acctg. Augusta Coll., 1989—. Co-author: Encyclopedia of Journal Entries, 1993; contbr. articles to profl. jours. Mem. Ga. Soc. CPAs, Inst. Mgmt. Accts. (dir. manuscripts 1991-94, treas. 1992-94, v.p. adminstrn. 1994, Manuscript award 1992, 93), Phi Kappa Phi. Office: Augusta Coll Sch Bus Adminstrn 2500 Walton Way Augusta GA 30904-2200

JACKSON, PATRICIA ARVIN, technology director; b. Richmond, Va., Sept. 30, 1945; d. Edwin Hazen and Ruth Natalie (Dee) Arvin; m. Donne Matthew Storino, July 11, 1970 (div. Aug. 1984); children: Michael Francis Storino, Andrew Matthew Arvin Storino; m. Michael Wilson Jackson, Aug. 24, 1991. BS in Math., U. Richmond, 1967. Programmer, analyst Divsn. Automated Data Processing, Sovran Bank, Richmond, Va., 1967-71, Printronics Corp., J.C. Penney Corp., Data Concepts, N.Y.C., 1967-71; sr. systems analyst divsn. justice and crime prevention Commonwealth of Va., Richmond, 1971-75; analyst, cons. self-employed, Richmond, 1975-81; systems devel. supr. Dept. Info. Technology, Richmond, 1981-85, chief systems engr., 1985-88; info. tech. mgr. Coun. on Info. Mgmt., Richmond, 1988-91, acting dir., 1991-92, dir., 1992-94; rsch. assoc. Va. Polytechnic Inst. and State U., Blacksburg, 1994—; bd. dirs. Blacksburg (Va.) Electronic Village, 1993-95; adv. bd. State Technologies, Inc., Albany, N.Y., 1992-93; VA film adv. bd. Commonwealth of Va., Richmond, 1993. Episcopalian. Home: 731 Blakeston Dr Richmond VA 23236

JACKSON, PATRICIA JORDAN, school system administrator; b. Tulsa, Mar. 31, 1933; d. Amiel Ralph and Lois Lucile (Cheairs) Jordan; m. Frank Andrew Jackson, Nov. 3, 1957 (dec. Nov. 1993); children: Catherine, Drew. BA, Ark. Tech. U., Russellville, 1954; MEd, U. Ark., 1978, EdD, 1983. Cert. adminstr., elem. prin., elem. tchr., media specialist, Ark. Elem. tchr. Springdale (Ark.) Pub. Schs., 1956-78, dir. instrn., 1978-84; dir. pers. Ft. Smith (Ark.) Pub. Schs., 1984-88, asst. supt. for pers. and support svcs., 1988—. Adv. trustee Sparks Regional Med. Ctr., 1995—. Fulbright scholar to France, Bordeaux, 1955-56. Mem. Am. Assn. Sch. Adminstrs., Am. Assn. Sch. Pers. Adminstrs., Ark. Assn. Ednl. Adminstrs. (Ednl. Adminstr. of Yr. 1994), Phi Delta Kappa, Delta Kappa Gamma. Methodist. Office: Ft Smith Pub Schs PO Box 1948 Fort Smith AR 72902

JACKSON, PATRICIA LEE (MRS. CLIFFORD L. JACKSON), psychologist; b. N.Y.C.; d. Albert George and Lisbeth P. (Lee) Scharf; B.A., Barnard Coll.; M.A., Ph.D., Tchrs. Coll. Columbia U.; m. Clifford L. Jackson. Dir. psychol. testing R. H. Macy & Co., Inc., 1941-49; employment dir. Alexander's Dept. Stores, Inc., Bronx, N.Y., 1949-52; asst. prof. psychology Hunter Coll., N.Y.C., 1951-66, asso. prof., 1966-77, coordinator of counseling services, 1959-71; research dir. Klein Inst. for Aptitude Testing, Inc., N.Y.C., 1953-59, asst. v.p., 1957-59; pvt. practice in psychotherapy, 1964—. Trustee Alfred Adler Inst.; v.p. bd. trustees Ch. of Healing Christ (Emmet Fox Ch.), N.Y.C. Mem. AAAS, Am. Assn. Counseling & Devel., Am. Psychol. Assn., Am. Statis. Assn., Am. Group Psychotherapy Assn., N.Y. Soc. Clin. Psychologists. Author articles in field. Home: 518 Hawkins Ave Lake Ronkonkoma NY 11779-2327

JACKSON, PAULETTE WHITE, nursing administrator, agency executive; b. New Orleans, Jan. 19, 1949; d. Lawrence III and Velma (Jones) White; m. Robert Wardell Tate, June 30, 1964 (div. 1969); children—Robert Jr., Detra Jeanene; m. Tommy Lee Jackson, July 20, 1974; 1 child, Byron. B.S. in Nursing, Southeastern La. U., 1980. Staff nurse Capitol Home Health, Baton Rouge, 1980-81; dir. nursing svc. Hill Haven Nursing Home, Baton Rouge, 1981; nephrology nurse BMA Baton Rouge, 1981-82; staff nurse Ammon's Home Health, Baton Rouge, 1981-83; supr. Greenwell Springs Hosp., La., 1983; owner, adminstr. Faith Home Health Svcs., Baton Rouge, 1983—; pres., owner Abundant Life Nursing Svc., Inc., Baton Rouge, 1989—, Gloryland Med. Transp. Svcs., Baton Rouge, La., 1992. Recipient Outstanding Bus. Achievement award Wybirk & Assocs. Inc., 1984. Mem. Beta Beta Beta. Democrat. Avocations: reading; skating; swimming. Home: 5589 Monarch Ave Baton Rouge LA 70811-5633 Office: Faith Home Health Svcs 1718 Wooddale Blvd Baton Rouge LA 70806-1507 also: Faith Home Health Svc Inc 6144 Highway 74 Saint Gabriel LA 70776-4554

JACKSON, REBECCA DOROTHY, medical educator, researcher; b. Columbus, Ohio, Aug. 18, 1955; d. William Edward and Dorothy Patricia (Woytowicz) J.; m. W. Jerry Mysiw, July 23, 1988; children: Natalie Rebecca Mysiw, Alexander William Mysiw. BS, Ohio State U., 1975, MD, 1978. Intern, resident Johns Hopkins U., Balt., 1978-81; fellow Ohio State U., Columbus, 1981-83, asst. prof., 1983-89, assoc. prof., 1989—; endocrinologist, prin. investigator Ohio State U. Ctr. for NIH sponsored Womens Health Inst. Contbr. articles to profl. jours. Named YWCA Woman of Achievement, Ohio Women Hall of Fame by Ohio OBES, Profl. of Yr. by Pilot Club; NIH scholar. Mem. ACP (chair womens com.), Am. Soc. Bone & Mineral Metabolism, Endocrine Soc., Am. Fedn. Clin. Rsch. Office: Ohio State U N1111 Doan Hall 410 W 10th Columbus OH 43210

JACKSON, REBECCA R., lawyer; b. Ark., 1942. BA magna cum laude, St. Louis U., 1975, JD, 1978. Bar: Mo. 1978, Ill. 1979. Atty. Bryan Cave, St. Louis. Mem. ABA. Office: Bryan Cave One Met Sq 211 N Broadway Saint Louis MO 63102-2750*

JACKSON, RUTH MOORE, academic administrator; b. Potecasi, N.C., Sept. 27, 1938; d. Jesse Thomas and Ruth Estelle (Futrell) Moore; m. Roderick Earle Jackson, Aug. 14, 1965; 1 child, Eric Roderick. BS in Bus., Hampton Inst., 1960; MSLS, Atlanta U., 1965; PhD, Ind. U., 1976. Asst. edn. libr. Va. State U., Petersburg, Va., 1965-66, head reference dept., 1966-67, asst. prof., 1976-77, assoc. prof., program coord., 1977-84, interim dept. chair, 1978-79; teaching fellow Ind. U., Bloomington, Ind., 1968, vis. lectr., 1971-72; asst. dir. librs. U. N. Fla., Jacksonville, 1984-88; dean univ. librs. W.Va. U., Morgantown, W.Va., 1988—; pers. cons. Va. State U., 1980; archival cons. N.C. Ctrl. U., Durham, N.C., 1984-85; automation cons. W.Va. Acad. Libr. Consortium, 1991—. Editor: W.Va. U. Press, 1990—; contbr. to books. Active Big Brother/Big Sister of Am., Jacksonville, Fla., 1985-88; den leader Boy Scouts of Am., Petersburg, Va., 1976-78. U.S. Office Edn. fellow, 1968-71, Rsch. fellow So. Fellowships Found., 1973-74; recipient Outstanding Alumni award Hampton Inst., 1980, Non-Italian Woman of Yr. award, 1992, Disting. West Virginian award Gov. W.Va., 1992. Mem. NAFE, ALA, Southeastern Libr. Assn. (mem. standing com.), Assn. Coll. and Rsch. Librs. (mem. standing com., mem. Fla. chpt.), W.Va. Libr. Assn., Libr. Info. Tech. Assn., Coalition for Networking, Coun. of State Univ. Librs. (founding mem.), Alpha Kappa Alpha. Democrat. Roman Catholic. Home: 775 Springbranch Rd Morgantown WV 26505-3575 Office: W Va Univ Main Libr PO Box 6069 Morgantown WV 26506-6069

JACKSON, SALLY DEE, public relations executive; b. Columbus, Ohio, Oct. 7, 1946; . Jay Greene and Ann Elizabeth (Rodgers) J. Grad., The Masters Sch., Dobbs Ferry, N.Y., 1964; AA, Bradford Coll., 1966; BA, Columbia U., 1970. Asst. producer Boston Transcription Trust, 1970-71; registrar Berkshire Music Ctr., Boston Symphony Orch., 1970-71; editorial asst. Harvard U., Cambridge, Mass., 1972-73; script supr. Leonard Bernstein at Harvard U., Cambridge, 1973; dir. pub. relations ADS, Inc., Cambridge, 1974-75; account exec. Communique Inc., Boston, 1975-77, Arnold & Co., Boston, 1977-80; pres. Jackson & Co., Boston, 1980—. Contbr. articles to profl. jours. Mem. Gov.'s Com. on Small Bus., Boston, 1985-87; dir. Ford Hall Forum, Boston, 1986—; chmn. program com. State House Conf. on Small Bus., Boston, 1987. Clubs: Advt. of Greater Boston; Annisquam Yacht. Office: Jackson & Co 29 Commonwealth Ave Boston MA 02116

JACKSON, SHARON BROOME, elementary educator; b. Sarasota, Fla., Sept. 3, 1952; d. Stanley Frank and Aileen Rita (Murphy) Broome; m. Thomas Harold Jackson Jr., Nov. 22, 1975; children: Thomas Harold III, Stanley David. Student, Ga. So. Coll., 1970-71; BS in Edn., U. Ga., 1973, MS in Edn., 1976; postgrad., West Ga. Coll., 1976. Cert. tchr. Kindergarten-8th grades, Ga., supervising tchr. child abuse edn., drug/alcohol awareness tchr. Tchr. 7th and 8th grades Winder-Barrow Mid. Sch., Winder, Ga., 1973-75; tchr. 5th and 6th grades Dunson Elem. Sch., LaGrange, Ga., 1975-80; tchr. 4th grade Oconee County Schs., Watkinsville, Ga., 1980—; presenter, tchr. tng. Ga. Assn. Marine Sci. Educators, 1990; presenter tchr. stress mgmt. workshop, Watkinsville, 1990. Vol. local shelter for the homeless, local soup kitchen; mem. 1st United Meth. Ch., pres. United Meth. Women's Circle. Named Oconee County Tchr. of Yr., 1989-90; one of 20 tchrs. statewide chosen to participate in Marine Sci. Edn. program, 1989. Mem. Profl. Assn. Ga. Educators, Ga. Sci. Tchrs. Assn., Nat. Coun. Tchrs. Math. Home: 1021 Rossiter Ter Watkinsville GA 30677-5124 Office: Oconee County Intermediate Sch Colham Ferry Rd Watkinsville GA 30677

JACKSON, SHARON JUANITA, management consultant; b. Modesto, Calif., Sept. 21, 1938; d. H. Edward and Beatrice C. (Wright) Melin; m. John L. George, Apr. 27, 1956 (div. 1974); children: Terri A., Tami L., Timothy J., Tobin E. BS in Edn. magna cum laude, Calif. State U., Hayward, 1965; MEd Guidance and Counseling, Hardin-Simmons U., 1976; MBA in Mgmt., Golden Gate U., 1984. Cert. elem. edn., Calif., elem., secondary counseling, Tex. Tchr. elem. Hayward (Calif) Unified Sch. Dist., 1965-73; tchr. diagnostics, group therapist Tex. Youth Coun., Brownwood, 1974-75; assoc. dir. New Directions Psychiat. Half Way House, Abilene, Tex., 1975-77; exec. dir. Mental Health Assn., Abilene, 1977-78, San Francisco, 1979-84; pres. Health Mktg. & Mgmt., San Francisco, 1983—; exec. dir., cons. Vision of Am. At Peace, Berkeley, Calif., 1984, Oakes Children's Ctr., San Francisco, 1985-87; mktg. dir. Mental Health Providers of Calif., 1987-90; prin., v.p. health care devel. Sakhalin region, Russia Health Marketing and Mgmt., 1990-92; instr. managed care U. San Francisco, 1994; sr. assoc. Behavioral Health Systems, dir. nat. practice 1991-92; founding exec. dir., v.p. adminstrn. Planet Live Earthbeat TV, Inc.; bd. dirs. PL Enterprises, Inc.; vis. lectr. McMurry Coll., Abilene, 1976-78; cons. Dyess AFB, Abilene, 1976-78, Abilene Youth Ctr., 1976-78; speaker in field, 1979—. Chair Commn. on Status of Women of Marin County, Calif., 1985—; mem. adv. com. Displaced Homemaker Project, Sacramento, 1985-90; founder, Children's Mental Health Policy Bd., 1984-90; pres. Artisans Gallery, Mill Valley, Calif., 1984—. Grantee Fed. Dept. Justice, Brownwood, 1975, pvt. community founds., Calif., 1979-87. Mem. NAFE, Council of Calif. Mental Health Contractors, Am. Soc. Profl. Exec. Women. Avocations: travel, gourmet cooking, hiking, public speaking. Home and Office: PO Box 2392 Mill Valley CA 94942

JACKSON, SHIRLEY ANN CARROLL, school counselor; b. Mpls., May 29, 1945; d. Donald A. and Dorothy R. (Carley) Carroll; m. Ralph William Jackson, Dec. 17, 1966; children: Christopher, Mark, Natalie. BS, U. Minn., St. Paul, 1967; MED, U. Wis., River Falls, 1992. Cert. sch. counselor, Minn., vocat. home econs. tchr. Spl. edn. mentally handicapped tchr. Chester (Ohio) Elem. Sch., 1967-70; home visitor early childhood edn. Mounds View Dist. 621, Roseville, Minn., 1982; guidance resource ctr. specialist Mounds View High Sch., Arden Hills, Minn., 1985-92; sch. counselor White Bear Lake (Minn.) High Sch. North, 1992; student assistance program counselor Westmoreland (Tenn.) High Sch., 1993-94. Lay mem. ann. conf. and adminstrv. bd. Grace United Meth. Ch., Mpls., 1976—; exec. bd. N.W. YMCA, St. Paul, 1989-93; mem. exec. bldg. com. 1st United Meth. Ch., Hendersonville, Tenn., 1993-94. Mem. NEA, Am. Counseling Assn., Minn. Counseling Assn., Minn. Sch. Counselor Assn., Minn. Assn. Counseling and Devel., Minn. Edn. Assn., Tech Prep Network.

JACKSON, SILVIA PATRICIA, doctor of Oriental medicine, researcher; b. Lima, Peru, Dec. 19, 1958; d. Robert Conrad and Dory Ariansen Cespedes. D of Oriental Medicine, Shanghai, China, 1987, Acad. of Traditional Medicine, Hong Kong, 1988; postgrad. hon. cert., Commonwealth Inst. Acupuncture, Queensland, Australia, 1988; Med. Diploma, Tex. Coll., Dallas, 1989; postgrad., Internat. U. Sri Lanka, Colombo, 1988. Acupuncturist Acupuncture Assocs., Dallas, 1989-90; med. asst. Orange County Renal, Irvine, Calif., 1992-93; ppub. rels./recruit mgr. acupuncture clinic asst. dir. South Baylo U., U. Oriental Medicine, Garden Grove, Calif., 1993; in pvt. practice Oriental Medicine Naturopathic Inst., Sumner, Wash., 1993—; photographer, Lima, 1977-93; researcher in acupuncture and herbology in drug withdrawal and immunodeficiency; asst. membership mgr. World Trade Ctr., Irvine, 1991. Photographer documentaries to support Wycliff's Bible Orgn. in the mountain/jungles of Peru. Recipient Letter of Appt., Pres. of Internat. Acupuncture Sci. Isnt., Korea, 1988. Mem. Orange County C. of C. (amb.), Toastmassters Internat.

JACKSON, SUSANNE LEORA, graphics firm chief executive officer; b. Rochester, N.Y., June 9, 1934; d. Daniel T. and Gertrude (Grantham) Sheriff; m. David K. Jackson, Mar. 12, 1954; children: Jonnie Sheehan, Jaynette Kettler. Student, Santa Fe Sch. Art, 1952-53, Midwestern U., 1953-55. Supr. ANR Prodn. Co., Houston, 1976-83; v.p. Robinhawk Drafting & Design, Houston, 1983-85; pres. Houston Creative Connections, 1985—; advt. & mktg. dir. Geotech Assn., Houston, 1989-90; past pres. Am. Inst. Design & Drafting, 1984-86. Design cons.: (mag.) Urbane, 1989-94. Mem. Mus. Fine Arts, Houston, 1988-94, Greater Houston Partnership, 1989-94; bd. dirs. Literacy Advance, 1993-94. Recipient Scholarship Santa Fe Sch. Art., 1952-53, Colo. Sch. Art, 1953. Mem. NAFE, Houston Advt. Fedn. (Silver and Merit awards 1989, Merit award 1990, Bronze award 1991, 2 Bronze awards 1992, 2 Gold and 3 Merit awards 1992, Gold and Bronze awards 1994), Greater Heights C. of C. (bd. dirs. 1994), Rotary (treas. 1992, pres.-elect 1993, pres. 1994), U.S. C. of C. (Blue Chip Enterprise award 1993). Republican. Episcopalian. Office: Houston Creative Connection Ste 675 701 N Post Oak Rd Houston TX 77024

JACKSON, SUZANNE ELISE, health education coordinator; b. Webster, Mass., Mar. 1, 1942; d. John Edward and Marguerite Emmaline (Plante) Baczek; m. Dale Lynne Bagby, Sept. 28, 1968 (div. July 1975); m. Stephen Harvey Jackson, July 12, 1975; 1 child, Gabrielle Benette. Diploma, Henry Heywood Hosp., 1963; BA, U. Redlands, 1975. RN Calif. Clin. instr. surgery Henry Heywood Hosp., Gardner, Mass., 1963-64; asst. head nurse Los Gatos/SCC Valley Hosp., San Jose, Calif., 1964-68; head nurse oper. rm. Good Samaritan Hosp., San Jose, Calif., 1970-76; corp. officer SHJ Corp., San Jose, Calif., 1976—; health edn. coord. Ac. Medicine Symposium, Monte Sereno, Calif., 1980—; design cons. Suzanne Jackson Designs, Monte Sereno, Calif., 1986—; pres. Calif. Med. Assn. Alliance, 1994—, also bd. dirs., 1986—. Pres. SCC Med. Assn. Aux., San Jose, 1985-86; leader, sch. coord. Girl Scouts U.S., Los Gatos, 1983-89; fundraiser Hillbrook Sch., Los Gatos, 1983-90; bd. dirs. LWV, Los Gatos, 1986-90; mem. Monte Sereno City Coun., 1994—. Recipient Gilbert & Sullivan Soc. Gypsy Robe, 1984. Mem. Santa Clara County Med. Alliance (bd. dirs. 1980—), Brandies U. Women, Capitol Club Silicon Valley. Republican. Office: 15984 Grandview Ave Monte Sereno CA 95030-3118

JACKSON, SUZANNE RENEE, accountant; b. Abington, Pa., Oct. 16, 1963; d. John Robert and Nancy Miller Gottshall; m. Kris Michael Jackson, May 21, 1988; children: Kristopher Bennett, Griffin Kyle. BSBA in Acctg., Bloomsburg U., 1985. CPA, Pa. Staff supr. Stiteler, Douglas & Clarke, Ltd., West Chester, 1985-91; assoc. Douglas & Assocs., West Chester, Pa., 1991—. Mem. ambassador com. C. of C., West Chester, 1990-92. Mem. AICPA, Pa. Inst. of CPA, Inst. Bus. Appraisers, IMA (dir. student activities, Valley Forge, Pa., 1989-92, profl. devel. 1988-89), Women's Referral Network (treas. 1993—). Republican. Presbyterian.

JACKSON, VALERIE PASCUZZI, radiologist, educator; b. Oakland, Calif., Aug. 25, 1952; d. Chris A. and Janice (Mayne) Pascuzzi; m. Price A. Jackson, Jr., July 24, 1976; children: Price Arthur III. AB, Ind. U., 1974, MD, 1978. Diplomate Am. Bd. Radiology. Intern, resident in diagnostic radiology Ind. U. Med. Ctr., 1978-82; from asst. prof. radiology to prof. radiology Ind. U. Sch. Medicine, Indpls., 1982-94, John A. Campbell prof. radiology, 1994—; dir. residency program radiology Ind. U. Sch. Medicine, 1994—. Contbr. over 50 articles to profl. jours., chpts. to books. Fellow Am. Coll. Radiology (chair 3 coms.), Soc. Breast Imaging (pres. 1990-92); mem. AMA, Am. Inst. Ultrasound in Medicine, Am. Roentgen Ray Soc., Radiol. Soc. N.Am., Alpha Omega Alpha. Office: Indiana U Sch Med Dept Rad 1001 W 10th St Indianapolis IN 46202

JACKSON, VIVIAN MICHELE, school administrator; b. Yonkers, N.Y., Feb. 17, 1953; d. Evelyn Green Alexander-Booker; m. Harry R. Jackson, Jr., Dec. 25, 1976; children: Joni Michele, Elizabeth Rountree. BA in Edn., Wittenberg U., 1975; MA in Edn., Northeastern U., 1980; MA in Theology, Logos Bible Coll., Fla., 1986. Tchr. Cleve. Pub. Schs., 1975-77, Cin. Pub. Schs., 1977-78, Boston Pub. Schs., 1978-79; grad. asst. Northeastern U., Boston, 1979-80; pres. Word of Life Broadcast Christian Hope Ctr., Corning, N.Y., 1981-84, assoc. pastor, 1981-88; founder, dir. Hope Christian Acad., Corning, 1987-88; founder, dir. Hope Christian Acad., College Park, Md., 1989—, dir. children's ministry, 1989-94; dir. children's ministry HCC, College Park, 1989-92; prof. Hope Bible Coll., 1994—; assoc. pastor Hope Christian Ch., 1994—; cons. Hope Christian Ch., 1988—. Named one of Outstanding Young Women of Am., 1981, 84. Office: Hope Christian Ch 5301 Edgewood Rd College Park MD 20740-4699

JACKSON, WENDY S LEWIS, social worker; b. Grand Rapids, Mich., May 9, 1965; d. Thomas James and Karen Susan (Kinard) L. BS, U. Mich., 1987, MSW, 1989. Investigator def. D.C. Pub. Defender Officer, Washington, 1985; program asst. Detroit Urban League, 1989; coord. housing Ann Arbor (Mich.) Housing Commn., 1989-90; sr. assoc. United Way, Grand Rapids, 1990-93; program coord. The Grand Rapids Found., 1993—; mgr. database Kent County Emergency Needs Task Force, Grand Rapids, 1990—, editor, 1990—; sec. Kent County Emergency Food Subcom., Grand Rapids, 1990—; mem. Kent County Domestic Violence Coordinating Com., Grand Rapids, 1990—; mem. pub. affairs com. Mich. League for Human Svcs., Lansing, 1990—. Contbr. articles to profl. jours. Vol. Blodgett Meml. Med. Ctr., Grand Rapids, 1982—; mem. task force Citizens League, Grand Rapids, 1990—; mem. pub. affairs task force United Way, Lansing, 1990—. Recipient Leadership award Kiwanis Club, 1983; Old Kent Bank and Trust scholar, 1983-87. Mem. NASW, Nat. Assn. Black Social Workers, U. Mich. Social Work Govs. (bd. mem. 1991—), U. Mich. Alumni Assn., Women's Leadership Coun., Urban League. Democrat. Episcopalian. Home: 624 Pleasant St SE Grand Rapids MI 49503-5531 Office: The Grand Rapids Found 209-C Waters Bldg 161 Ottawa AVe NW Grand Rapids MI 49503

JACKSON-LEE, SHEILA, congresswoman; b. Queens, N.Y., Jan. 12, 1950; m. Elwyn C. Lee; 2 children. BS, Yale U.; JD, U. Va. Sr. counsel select com. on assassinations U.S. Ho. of Reps., 1977; trial atty. Fulbright and Jaworski, 1978-80; sr. atty. United Energy Resources, Inc., 1980; assoc. judge Houston Mcpl. Ct., 1987-89; mem. Houston City Coun., 1990-94, 104th Congress from 18th Tex. dist., 1995—. Democrat. Office: US House Reps 1520 Longworth House Office Bldg Washington DC 20515*

JACOBOWITZ, ELLEN SUE, former museum administrator; b. Detroit, Feb. 21, 1948; d. Theodore Mark and Lois Clairesse (Levy) J. BA, U. Mich., 1969, MA, 1970. Curator Phila. Mus. Art, 1972-90; administr. Cranbrook Inst. Sci., Bloomfield Hills, Mich., 1991-94. Author: The Prints of Lucas Van Leyden, 1983, American Graphics: 1860-1940, 1982. Past bd. dirs. Print Coun. Am., Balt., 1972-74, Netherlands Am. Amity Trust, Washington, 1982-84, Nat. Coun. Jewish Women, Detroit, 1990-91; mem. Am. Jewish Com., 1991—. Mem. Am. Assn. Mus., Leadership Oakland, Womens Luncheon Club.

JACOBS, CHRISTIE JEAN, lawyer; b. Damariscotta, Maine, Aug. 27, 1961; d. Winton O'Brien and JoAnn (Waltz) J. AB, Vassar Coll., 1983; JD, Cath. U. of Am., 1990. Bar: D.C. 1990. Paralegal specialist Nationwide Info. Svcs., Albany, N.Y., 1984-86; customer svc. rep. Blue Cross & Blue Shield, Albany, 1986-87; legal intern U.S. Dept. Labor, Washington, 1988-89; legal intern IRS, Washington, summer 1989, atty. adviser, 1990—; arbitrator Autoline Dispute Resolution Better Bus. Bur., Buffalo, 1986-87; student rep. faculty com. Appointments and Promotions, Washington, 1988-89. Tax preparer Vol. Income Tax Assistance, Washington, 1987—; police liaison Beat 27 Citizens Assn., 1994—. Recipient Spl. Merit award U.S. Dept. Labor, 1988. Mem. ABA (student liaison sect. on taxation 1989-90, appointee to com. on sales, exchs. and basis 1990—), D.C. Bar, Moot Ct. Assn., Nat. Panel Consumer Arbitrators. Democrat. Home: 1617 E St SE Washington DC 20003-2446 Office: IRS Office of Chief Counsel 1111 Constitution Ave NW Washington DC 20224-0001

JACOBS, DELORES HAMM, educator; b. Tuscaloosa, Ala., Mar. 1, 1947; d. Howard Murphy and Nellie Mae (Booth) Hamm; m. Paul Thomas Jacobs, June 1, 1966; 1 child, Michael Paul. BS in Secondary Edn., U. Ala., 1971; BS in Middle Sch. Edn., Samford U., 1991; MA in Secondary Edn., U. Ala., Birmingham, 1974. Title I reading tchr. Locust Fork (Ala.) High Sch., 1971-74; tchr. English Locust Fork High Sch., 1974-85; speech instr. Pizitz Middle Sch., Vestavia Hills, Ala., 1985-86, tchr. English, instr., 1986—. Contbr. poetry to various poetry publs. and editorials to Tuscaloosa News, Vestavia Hills edn. newsletters, Am. Poetic Soc. poetic vols. Bd. dirs. First Ch. of the Nazarene Pre-Sch. and Daycare Sch., Vestavia Hills, 1987-93, ch. organist, 1976—; sch. rep. United Way; rep. Heart Fund, Jefferson County, Ala. Mem. NEA, Ala. Edn. Assn., So. Assn. of Schs. (accreditation com.), Nat. Coun. Tchrs. English, Ala. Reading Assn., Vestavia Hills Garden Club, Chi Delta Phi. Republican. Office: Pizitz Middle School 2020 Pizitz Dr Vestavia Hills AL 35216

JACOBS, ELEANOR, art consultant, retired art administrator; b. N.Y.C., July 25, 1929; d. Samuel and Mary (Praw) Cohen; m. Raymond Jacobs, Dec. 29, 1955; children: Susan, Laura. BA, NYU, 1979. Co-founder, v.p. The Earth Shoe Co., N.Y.C., 1969-79; art adminstr. Print Dept., Sotheby's, N.Y.C., 1980-81; exec. asst. Care, N.Y.C., 1982-84; exec. adminstr. Hirschl & Adler Galleries, N.Y.C., 1984-93; art cons. Recipient Founders Day award NYU, N.Y.C., 1978. Mem. Nat. Arts Club (gov. 1989—, exhbns. com. 1984—, curatorial com. 1990—, founder, editor exhibiting artists newsletter 1987—).

JACOBS, ELEANOR ALICE, retired clinical psychologist, educator; b. Royal Oak, Mich., Dec. 25, 1923; d. Roy Dana and Alice Ann (Keaton) J. B.A., U. Buffalo, 1949, M.A., 1952, Ph.D., 1955. Clin. psychologist VA Hosp., Buffalo, 1954-83; EEO counelor VA Hosp., 1962-79, chief psychology service, 1979-83; clin. prof. SUNY, Buffalo, 1950-83; speaker on psychology to community orgns. and clubs, 1952—; Mem. adult devel. and aging com. NICHD, HEW, 1971-75. Researcher for publs. on hyperbaric medicine, hyperoxygenation effect on cognitive functions in aged. Recipient Outstanding Superior Performance award Buffalo VA Hosp., 1958, Spl. Recognition award SUNY, Buffalo, Spl. Recognition award SUNY, 1971; W.L. McKnight award Miami Heart Inst., 1972; Adminstrs. commendation VA, 1974; Dirs. commendation VA Med. Center, Buffalo, 1978; Disting. Alumni award SUNY, Buffalo, 1983; named Woman of Yr. Bus. and Profl. Women's Clubs, Buffalo, 1973. Mem. Am. Psychol. Assn., Eastern Psychol. Assn., N.Y. State Psychol. Assn., Am. Group Psychotherapy Assn., Am. Soc. Group Psychotherapy and Psychodrama, Psychol. Assn. Western N.Y. (Disting. Achievement award 1976), Group Psychotherapy Assn. Western N.Y., Undersea Med. Soc., Sigma Xi. Home: 221 Pleasant Ave N, Ridgeway, ON Canada L0S 1N0

JACOBS, ILENE B., electrical equipment company executive, treasurer; b. Boston, May 12, 1947; d. William and Sylvia (Mintz) Brenner; m. Richard B. Jacobs, June 15, 1969; children: Aaron, Wendy. BA, U. Mass., 1969; cert. in adv. mgmt. prog., Harvard U., 1982. Cash mgmt. officer Shawmut Bank of Boston, 1969-74; mgr. money and banking Digital Equipment Corp., Maynard, Mass., 1974-80, asst. treas., 1981-84, v.p., treas., 1984—; bd. dirs. Little Switzerland, Inc., Arkwright Mut. Ins. Co. Mem. Nat. Assn. Corp. Treas. (bd. dirs.), Soc. Internat. Treas. Republican. Jewish. *

JACOBS, JANE, author; b. Scranton, Pa., May 4, 1916; d. John Decker and Bess Mary (Robison) Butzner; m. Robert Hyde Jacobs, Jr., May 27, 1944; children—James Kedzie, Edward Decker, Mary Hyde. Author: Downtown Is For People in The Exploding Metropolis, 1959, The Death and Life of Great American Cities, 1961, The Economy of Cities, 1969, The Question of Separatism, 1980, Cities and the Wealth of Nations, 1984, (juvenile) The Girl on the Hat, 1989, Systems of Survival, 1992. Address: care Random House 201 E 50th St New York NY 10022-7703

JACOBS, KAREN LOUISE, medical technologist; b. Kingston, N.Y., May 7, 1943; d. William Charles and Vera Elizabeth (Kelly) Jacobs; BS in Applied Tech., Empire State Coll., 1976; MS in Pub. Service Adminstrn., Russell Sage Coll., 1982. Sr. lab. technician, hosp. lab. supr. City of Kingston (N.Y.) Labs., 1962-68; sr. rsch. asst. Dudley Obs., Albany, N.Y., 1972-75; lab. adminstr. Albany Med. Coll., 1976—, mem. faculty, 1982—; mem. infection control com. and subcoms. on AIDS mgmt. and human immunodeficiency virus universal precautions Albany Med. Ctr. Infection Control, 1987—. Bd. dirs. chpt. Leukemia Soc. Am., 1983-87; judge sci. and tech. summer issue on excellence in Am. U.S. News and World Report; vol. asst. naturalist Five Rivers Environ. Ctr. Mem. Clin. Lab. Mgmt. Assn. (del. citizen amb. program to China 1989), Am. Soc. Clin. Pathologists, Sierra Club, Earthwatch, Nat. Speleological Soc., Helderburg-Hudson Grotto. Home: 11 Eastmount Dr # 202 Slingerlands NY 12159-2168 Office: Albany Med Coll Div Hematology and Oncolgy 47 New Scotland Ave Albany NY 12208-3479

JACOBS, LINDA ROTROFF, elementary education educator; b. Peebles, Ohio, June 10, 1942; d. Joseph Harold Rotroff and Mary Lucille (Peterson) Nixon; m. Donald Eugene Jacobs, Nov. 29, 1968; 1 child, Donald Brett. BS in Edn., Ohio State U., 1963; MA in Edn., U. Cin., 1968; postgrad., U. Cin., Miami U., Xavier U., 1968—, Coll. Mt. St. Joseph, 1968—. Cert. tchr., Ohio. Tchr. kindergarten Forest Hills Bd. Edn., Cin., 1963-74, Chillicothe (Ohio) Bd. Edn., 1974-77, Forest Hills Bd. Edn., Cin., 1977—; tchr. reading adult edn. Cin., 1975; tchr. kindergarten Mercer Elem. Forest Hills, Cin., 1977—; cooperating tchr. student tchrs. Ohio U., U. Cin., No. Ky. U., 1965—; tchr. summer sch. 4th, 5th, and 6th grades math./lang. arts, Cin., 1964-68, kindergarten and 1st grade Forest Hills, Cin., 1978-82; tchr. rep. Head Start, Chillicothe, 1975-77; kindergarten coord. Forest Hills and Hamilton County, Cin., 1965-70, 83-85; mem. supt.'s coun. Forest Hills, Cin., 1979, 82, 88; tchr. rep. PTA, Cin., 1967, 73, 82, 89; facilitator Forest Hills Summer Sch., 1993, 94; master tchr./advisor entry tchrs. Forest Hills, 1993—; career mentor Ashford-McCarthy Resources, Inc., 1993-94; coord. early entrance screening Hamilton County, 1994, 95, faculty mem. Intervention Based Multifaceted Evaluation Com., 1994, 95, mem. Collaboration Team for Inclusion of Spl. Children, 1994, 95. Co-author: Getting Ready for Kindergarten, 1978, Intervention Assistance Team Handbook, 1992; author: Parenting Tips, 1982. Cons. Women Helping Women, Cin., 1989. Named Hamilton County Tchr. of Yr., 1965. Mem. NEA, Nat. PTA (rep.), Tchrs. Applying Whole Lang., Ohio Edn. Assn. (del. 1965), Southwestern Ohio Edn. Assn., Forest Hills Educators Assn. (sec. 1964-68, Martha Holden Jennings scholar 1976-77), DAR, Alpha Kappa Delta (sec. 1975—). Mem. Ch. of Christ.

JACOBS, MARIAN, advertising agency owner; b. Stockton, Calif., Sept. 11, 1927; d. Paul (dec.) and Rose (Sallah) J. AA, Stockton Coll. With Bottarini Advt., Stockton, 1948-50; pvt. practice Stockton, 1950-64; with Olympius Advt., Stockton, 1964-78; pvt. practice Stockton, 1978—; pres. Stockton Advt. Club, 1954, Venture Club, Stockton, 1955; founder Stockton Advt. and Mktg. Club, 1981. Founder Stockton Arts Comms., 1976, Sunflower Entertainment for Institutionalized, 1976, Women Execs., Stockton, 1978; founding dir. Pixie Woods, Stockton; bd. dir. Goodwill Industries, St. Mary's Dining Room, Alan Short Gallery. Paul Harris fellow Rotary Club, 1994; recipient Woman of Achievement award San Joaquin County Women's Coun., Stockton, 1976, Achievement award San Joaquin Delta Coll., Stockton, 1978, Friend of Edn. award Calif. Tchrs. Assn., Stockton, 1988, Stanley McCaffrey Disting. Svc. award, U. of the Pacific, Stockton, 1988, Athena award for Businesswoman of Yr. Greater Stockton C. of C., 1989, Role Model award Tierra del Oro Girl Scouts U.S., 1989; named Stocktonian of the Yr. Stockton Bd. of Realtors, 1978, Outstanding Citizen Calif. State Senate & Assembly, 1978; the Marian Jacobs Writers & Poets Symposium was established in her honor. Republican. Roman Catholic. Home and Office: 4350 Mallard Creek Cir Stockton CA 95207-5205

JACOBS, MARISA FRANCES, lawyer; b. Phila., Aug. 13, 1957; d. Irving and Sylvia Sonia (Silver) J. BA, Dickinson Coll., 1978; JD, Columbia U., 1981. Atty. Reavis & McGrath, N.Y.C., 1981-87; v.p. Prism Assocs., N.Y.C., 1987-89; sec., assoc. gen. counsel Cooper Cos., Inc., Ft. Lee, N.J., 1989—. Active Lenox Hill Hosp., N.Y.C., 1987-89; mem. bus. and profl. women's com. United Jewish Appeal, 1993—. Mem. ABA, Bar Assn. City of N.Y. Office: The Cooper Cos Inc 1 Bridge Plz Ste 600 Fort Lee NJ 07024

JACOBS, MARY LEE, lawyer; b. Pitts., June 29, 1950; d. George and Mary Jane (Swinderman) Jacobs. B.A. in History, Wellesley Coll., 1972; J.D., Boston U., 1975. Bar: Mass. 1975, U.S. Dist. Ct. Mass. 1976, U.S. Ct. Appeals (1st cir.) 1978, U.S. Supreme Ct. 1981. Assoc. Moulton & Looney, Boston, 1978-80; assoc. Nutter, McClennen & Fish, Boston, 1980-84; gen. counsel Tufts U., Medford, Mass., 1984—. Mem. ABA, Boston Bar Assn., Women's Bar Assn. Mass. Office: Tufts Univ Ballou Hall 3d Fl Braintree MA 02184*

JACOBS, ROSETTA See LAURIE, PIPER

JACOBS, RUTH ANN, program director; b. Toledo, Apr. 5, 1954; d. Ralph Clare and Toshi (Murakami) J.; m. Nathan Douglas Jacobs. Student, U. Toledo, 1980-81; A. in Electronic Engring. Tech., Stautzenberger Coll., 1986; student, Owens Tech. Coll., 1990, Heidelberg Coll., 1991. Cert. netware instr., netware engr. Ranch hand H.H. Green Ranch, Houston, 1973; tropical fish breeder Silent World, Gretna, La., 1974-75; machine operator Lindsay Design Assocs., Toledo, 1975; mem. sales Colony Generator, Toledo, 1976; control clk. Union 76 Oil Co., Millbury, Ohio, 1976-85; fabrication T.L. Industries, Toledo, 1986; biomed. engring. temp Med. Coll. Ohio, Toledo, 1986-87, computer technician, 1994—; program coord. Stautzenberger Coll., Toledo, 1987—. Vol. zookeeper Toledo Zoo, 1986-88. Mem. Mensa, Internat. Soc. Cert. Electronic Technicians (cert., journeyman in computers 1990). Home: 581 Colima Dr Toledo OH 43609 Office: Stautzenberger Coll 5355 Southwyck Blvd Toledo OH 43614

JACOBS, SHARON LEE, nurse; b. Windber, Pa., Dec. 29, 1948; d. Donald Andrew and Betty I. (Cummings) Galloway; m. Ernest R. Jacobs, May 23, 1970; children: Jennifer L., Jonathan R., M. Rachel. Diploma, We. Pa. Hosp. Sch. Nursing, Pitts., 1969; postgrad., Coll. St. Francis, Joliet, Ill. Cert. infection control practitioner. Staff nurse oper. rm. West Penn Hosp., Pitts., 1969-70; staff nurse labor/delivery Alexandria (Va.) Hosp., 1970-71; staff nurse, infection control nurse Canonsburg (Pa.) Gen. Hosp., 1971-78; staff nurse South Hills Convalescent Ctr., Canonsburg, 1978-79; infection control nurse, employee health nurse Canonsburg Gen. Hosp., 1979-86; infection control coord. Shadyside Hosp., Pitts., 1986-90; infection control practitioner St. Clair Hosp., Pitts., 1990—; cons. Mt. Lebanon Surg. Ctr., Pitts., 1994. Contbr. articles to profl. jours. Mem. Assn. for Profls. in Infection Control and Epidemiology Inc. (v.p. Three Rivers/Pitts. chapt. 1991-92). Home: 1208 Harvest Ct Bridgeville PA 15017 Office: St Clair Hosp 1000 Bower Hill Rd Pittsburgh PA 15243

JACOBS, SUE CARROL, psychologist, educator; b. Phoenix, June 25, 1945; d. Ernest Neal and Dorothy Carroll (Jones) Jacobs; m. Albert John Szymanski Jr., Aug. 15, 1970 (div. 1980). BA, Antioch Coll., 1968; ABD, Columbia U., 1971; MA, Norwich U., 1983; PhD, U. So. MIss., 1989. Lic. psychologist, Mass. Career counselor Clackamas C.C., Oregon City, Oreg., 1980-85; psychology intern Palo Alto (Calif.) VA Med. Ctr., 1987-88; rsch. fellow Behavioral Medicine Deaconess Hosp., Boston, 1988-90; staff psychologist Behavior Med. Hosp. and Deaconess Hosp., Boston, 1990-94; instr. in medicine Harvard U., Boston, 1990-94; scientist Mind/Body Med. Inst., Boston, 1990-94; assoc. prof. Dept. Counseling U. N.D., 1994—; outpatient psychologist New Eng. Meml. Hosp., Stoneham, Mass., 1989-93. Contbr. chpt. to book The Wellness Book, 1992; contbr. articles to profl. jours. Mem. APA, Assn. for Advancement of Behavior Therapy, Soc. for Behavioral Medicine, Gerontol. Assn. Am., Am. Heart Assn. Office: Dept Counseling U ND PO Box 8255 Grand Forks ND 58202-8255

JACOBS, SUZANNE, state legislator; b. Chgo., July 6, 1936; d. Saul Wolff and Ruth (Margolis) J.; m. Gerald William Saperstein, Dec. 20, 1959 (div. 1974); children: Natalle Saperstein Eisner, Hilary Saperstein Shenfeld; m. Earl Stewart Hamburger, Aug. 27, 1976; stepchildren: David Hamburger, Steven Hamburger, Joel Hamburger. BA, U. Calif., 1958; MS in Edn., Nat. Louis U., Evanston, Ill., 1972; postgrad., Vanderbilt U., 1981-84. Tchr. 4th, 6th, and 8th grade Pub. and Pvt. Sch. Systems, Chgo., 1960-70; dir. The Tchr. Ctr., Arlington Heights Sch. Dist., Ill., 1972-76; mgr. coop. edn. Oakton C.C., Des Plaines, Ill., 1977-83; legis. asst. Florida Legis., 1985-90; mem. Fla. Ho. Reps., Tallahassee, 1992, 94—; vice chair, higher edn. oversight com. Fla. Ho. Reps., mem., fin. and taxation com., chair, aging and human svcs. com., mem., corrections com. Featured in 60 Minutes TV Show, 1994. Bd. dirs. Anti Defamation League of Palm Beach County, 1993—, The Homeless Coalition of Palm Beach County, Inc., 1990-93, Caldwell Theatre Co., 1993—, Jewish Federation Task Force on Social Justice, 1990-93; pres. Cmty. Counseling Svcs of Boca, Inc., 1991—, NOW, 1991-92; founding bd. dir. Aid to Victims of Domestic Assault Shelter, Inc., 1986; legis. com. chair Palm Beach County Dem. Exec. Com., 1988-90, program chair, 1990-92; del. Dem. Nat. Convention, 1988; coord. South Palm Beach County Dem. Predsl. Campaign, 1988. Recipient Outstanding Legislator Consumers Rights award Acad. Fla. Trial Lawyers, 1994; named Freshman Friend of Edn. by Fla. Teaching Profession and United Faculty of Fla., 1994. Democrat. Jewish. Office: Fla Ho Reps 302 House Office Bldg Tallahassee FL 32399 also: Ste 5 990 S Congress Ave Delray Beach FL 33445

JACOBSEN, BETTY, artist, art educator; b. S.I., N.Y., Oct. 12, 1954; d. Kurt R. and Borghild (Tvede) J. BA, Montclair State Coll., 1980; MA, NYU, 1992. Artist, 1954—; tchr. art Bound Brook (N.J.) Sch. Dist., 1980-82, Warren (N.J.) Sch. Dist., 1980-82, Union Cath. Regional High Sch., Scotch Plains, N.J., 1982-85, Summit (N.J.) Sr. High Sch., 1985-86, Hunterdon Central Regional High Sch., Flemington, N.J., 1986—; resident artist Skidmore Coll., Saratoga Springs, 1989, Va. Ctr. Creative Arts, Sweet Briar, 1989, Millay Colony for Arts, Austerlitz, N.Y., 1991, Dorland Mountain Arts Colony, Temecula, Calif., 1993. Editorial artist the Home News Daily Newspaper, 1985-86; artist: Kalliope: A Journal of Women's Art: The Spiritual Quest, 1989. Mem. N.J. Edn. Assn. Home: 1720 Wrightstown Rd Newtown PA 18940 Office: Hunterdon Central Regional High Sch 84 Rt 31 Flemington NJ 08822

JACOBSEN, CHARLENE MARIE, music educator, band director; b. Chgo., Nov. 21, 1942; d. Edmund S. and Florence D. (Krause) Berchert; m. Lloyd H. Jacobsen, July 11, 1970 (dec. May, 1992); 1 child, Gretchen M. BS in Music Edn., Ea. Ill. U., 1964; MS in Music Edn., U. Ill., 1968; postgrad., Vander Cook Coll. of Music, Chgo., 1988-92. cert. tchr. music. elem., secondary, jr. coll., Ill. Tchr. Dixon (Ill.) Pub. Schs., 1964-66; tchr. River Trails Pub. Sch., Mt. Prospect, Ill., 1966-73, Mt. Prospect, 1980—; tchr. Immanuel Sch., Des Plaines, Ill., 1976-77; parish music dir. Immanuel Luth. Ch., Des Plaines, 1986-88; founding mem. Fine Arts Network, Arlington Heights, Ill., 1989-92. chair person, 1992-93. Mem. NEA, Ill. Edn. Assn., River Trails Edn. Assn. (pres. 1969-71, chair person 1969-73, negotiating team 1989-92), Music Educators Nat. Conf. (registered music educator), Ill. Music Educators Assn., Alumni Assn. Ea. Ill U., U. Ill. Home: 802 E Jennifer Ct Arlington Heights IL 60004-4000 Office: River Trails Middle Sch 1000 N Wolf Rd Mount Prospect IL 60056-1597

JACOBSEN, JOSEPHINE, author; b. Coburg, Ont., Can., Aug. 19, 1908; d. Joseph Edward and Octavis (Winder) Boylan; m. Eric Jacobsen, Mar. 17,

1932; 1 son, Erlend Ericsen. Grad., Roland Park Country Sch., 1926; LHD (hon.), Coll. Notre Dame Md., 1974, Goucher Coll., 1974; MDiv. (hon.), St. Mary's Seminary & Coll., 1988; hon. degree, Johns Hopkins U., 1993. Critic; short story writer; lectr.; poetry cons. Library of Congress, 1971-73, hon. cons. in Am. letters, 1973-79; v.p. PSA, 1979-80. Author: The Human Climate, 1953, For the Unlost, 1948, The Animal Inside, 1966, (with William Mueller) The Testament of Samuel Beckett, 1968, Genet and Ionesco Playwrights of Silence, 1968, The Shade-Seller: New and Collected Poems, 1974, A Walk With Raschid and Other Stories, 1978 (Notable Books of 1978), The Chinese Insomniacs, New Poems, 1981, Adios Mr. Moxley, 1986, The Sisters: New and Selected Poems, 1987, Distances, 1992; writing also included O. Henry Awards Prize Stories, 1967, 71, 73, 76, 85, 93, Fifty Years of the American Short Story, 1970, On the Island: Stories, 1989, Best Poems, 1991, Pushcart Prizes, 1991. Mem. lit. panel Nat. Endowment for Arts, 1980-84. Recipient MacDowell Colony fellow; Yaddo fellow; Am. Acad. Poets fellow, 1987; recipient Shelly Meml. award for life work PSA, 1993. Mem. Am. Acad. Arts and Letters (Svc. to Lit. award 1982, Lenore Marshall award for best book of poetry pub. in U.S. in 1987, 1988), PEN (nominee Faulkner award for fiction 1990). Democrat. Roman Catholic. Home: 13801 York Rd Cockeysville MD 21030-1804

JACOBSEN, MAGDALENA GRETCHEN, mediator, federal agency executive; b. N.Y.C., July 26, 1940; d. Carl J. and Helen (Faber) J.; m. Bruce Donald Henricus, Dec. 20, 1986. Cert. labor studies, AFL-CIO, 1971; cert. labor studies, bargaining and arbitration, Harvard U., 1973; cert. indsl. rels., U. Calif., San Francisco, 1975; BS, U. San Francisco, 1987; MS, Golden Gate U., 1989. Sec. CBS TV, Hollywood, Calif., 1962-65; flight attendant Continental Airlines, L.A., 1965-69, mgr. labor rels., 1972-76; local union official, sec.-treas. steward and stewardess divsn. ALPA, Washington, 1966-72; commr. Fed. Mediation and Conciliation Svcs., San Francisco, 1976-89, Portland, Oreg., 1992-93; dir. employee rels. City and County of San Francisco, 1989-92; bd. Nat. Mediation Bd., Washington, 1993—. Mem. Indsl. Rels. Rsch. Assn. (mem. exec. bd. 1980—, pres. San Francisco chpt. 1985-87). Office: Nat Mediation Bd 1301 K St Ste 250 East Washington DC 20572

JACOBSEN, SHARON ELAINE, nuclear materials management professional; b. Oliver Springs, Tenn., Jan. 25, 1957; d. Donnie Cordell and Daisy Louise (Bunch) Longmire; m. Daniel Craig Jacobsen, Dec. 23, 1975; 1 child, Eric Conrad. BSBA, U. Tenn., 1985. Data processing technician Union Carbide Corp., Oak Ridge, Tenn., 1979-81, computing analyst, 1982-84; sect. mgr. nuclear materials mgmt. and safeguards sys. Martin Marietta Energy Sys., Inc., Oak Ridge, 1985-89, dept. mgr. nuclear materials mgmt. and safeguards sys., 1990-93, mgr. Ctr. for Info. Security Tech., 1994, dept. mgr. comm. and security, 1994—; mem. nat. and internat. nuclear material task forces and coms. Dept. Energy, Nuclear Regulatory Commn., Oak Ridge and Washington, 1984—; tech. expert nuclear materials info. sys. U.S. Del. Nuclear Weapons Safety, Security and Dismantlement, Washington, 1991—. With USN, 1974-78. Mem. Nat. Mgmt. Assn. (chair awards com. 1991-93, chair pub. rels. com. 1993—), Inst. Nuclear Materials Mgmt. (com. chair 1984—). Home: 4600 Gillcrest Dr Knoxville TN 37938 Office: Martin Marietta Energy Sys 1099 Commerce Park Oak Ridge TN 37830-8027

JACOBSEN, SUSAN MARIE, art museum educator and program director; b. Tyler, Minn., June 25, 1949; d. Henry M. and Wilburta (Sanderson) J.; m. Jerome A. Downes, Apr. 26, 1980 (dec. Aug. 10, 1993). Student, U. Minn., 1967-68; BA, S.W. State U., Marshall, Minn., 1982. Intern edn. div. Mpls. Inst. Arts, 1972-73, coord. art program for tchrs. and students, 1973-74, coord. young people's program, 1974-88, supr. young people's program, 1988-89, supr. pub. programs, 1989—; instr. Compas, St. Paul, 1974-75; mem. adv. bd. edn. dept. Minn. Mus. Art, St. Paul, 1978-79; mem. adv. bd. Children's Mus., St. Paul, 1979-82. Author exhbn. and children's gallery guides Mpls. Inst. Mem. oper. support rev. panel community group II, Minn. Arts Bd., 1986-88, Whittier Youth Adv. Com. Mem. Nat. Art Edn. Assn., Minn. Art Edn. Assn., Am. Assn. Mus., Minn. Assn. Mus. Home: 515 5th Ave SE Apt 1 Minneapolis MN 55414-1641 Office: The Mpls Inst Arts 2400 3rd Ave S Minneapolis MN 55404-3506

JACOBSON, ANNA SUE, finance company executive; b. Ft. Smith, Ark., Aug. 13, 1940; d. Ray Bradley and Joy Anna (Person) McAlister, (stepfather) Cleve J. McDonald, Sr.; m. Lyle Norman Jacobson, Nov. 23, 1958; children: Lyle Michael, Daniel Ray, Julie Anne, Eric Joseph. Cert. in Fin. Planning, Coll. for Fin. Planning, 1984. Certified fin. paraplanner. Office mgr. Twin Cities Lithographic Inst., St. Paul, 1963-66; sec., St. Paul, Mpls., 1971-78; asst. to pres., office mgr. Planners Fin. Svcs., Mpls., 1978-85, asst. corp. treas., 1987-88; fin. paraplanner McAlmont Investment Co., Mpls., 1985—, office mgr., 1988—; registered rep. McAlmont Investment Co., 1989—; ind. fin. cons.; bd. dir. Planners Fin. Svcs.; mem. bd. advisors Coll. for Fin. Planning, Denver, 1982—; v.p., CFO J&J Specialty Co., 1993—; speaker various orgns. Co-creator Paraplanning Profession Advisor; mem. firm McAlmont Investment Co., 1987—, Mpls., 1987—. Del. Dem. Farmer Labor Com., St. Paul, 1980; campaign chmn. mayoral election, Roseville, Minn., 1983, county commr., city coun. election, Roseville, 1980, 84; local chmn. for passage of ERA, Minn.; mem. Am. Lung Assn., St. Paul, Ramsey Found. of Minn., Como conservatory Hist. Soc.; past. pres. PTA, Minn.; mem. exec. coun. Boy Scouts Am., 1977-81; mem. adv. bd. Sch. Dist. 623, Roseville, Minn., 1978-81; fund raising com. mem. Twin Cities Pub. TV Sta., 1975—. Recipient Volunteerism award State of Minn., 1981, Cert. of Appreciation Minn. Bicentennial Com., 1976; named 1st Fin. Paraplanner in history of industry. Mem. Internat. Assn. Fin. Planning, Twin Cities Assn. Fin. Planners, Internat. Assn. Bus. and Profl. Women (bd. dirs. 1977-86, pres. 1980-82, Woman of Yr. 1982), Minn. Women's Consortium, Como Conservatory Hist. Soc., Concordia Acad. Booster Club, Beta Sigma Phi Nu Phi Mu Chpt. Democrat. Lutheran. Avocations: tennis, riding, reading, piano, harp. Home: 2171 Dellwood Ave Saint Paul MN 55113-4329

JACOBSON, ANNETTE MOFF, chemical engineer; b. Latrobe, Pa., May 6, 1957; d. Charles James Jr. and Mary Agnes (Antinori) Moff; m. Donald Bruce Jacobson, Aug. 22, 1981; children: Jennifer Lynn, Amanda Rose. BSChE, Carnegie Mellon U., 1979, PhD in Chem. Engring., 1988. Chem. engr. PPG Inds., Inc., Pitts., 1979-81, Sr. rsch. engr., 1981-85; assoc. dir. colloids, polymers & surface program Carnegie Mellon U., Pitts., 1988-89, lectr. in chem. engring., 1988—, dir. colloids, polymers & surface program, 1989—; lectr. dept. chem. engring. Carnegie Mellon U., 1989—; workshop lectr. in field. Inventor in field. Amoco Found. fellow, 1986-88, Carnegie Mellon U. Women's Clan scholar, 1978-79, Babcock & Wilcox scholar Carnegie Mellon U., 1977-79; recipient G.D. Parfitt award Chem. Engring. Student Group, 1987. Mem. AICE, Am. Chem. Soc., Internat. Assn. Colloid and Interface Scientists, Sigma Xi (corr. sec. 1994—).

JACOBSON, CAROL PHYLLIS, management analyst; b. Detroit, Feb. 1, 1942; d. Walter Alozy and Stephanie (Romas) Kulson; m. Alexander Maclean Kennedy, June 24, 1967 (dec. June 1977); 1 child, Douglas Maclean Kennedy Jacobson; m. William Charles Jacobson, Feb. 24, 1979. BA, Wayne State U., 1964, M in Urban Planning, 1968. Regional planner S.E. Mich. Coun. of Govts., Detroit, 1965-69; city planner City of Detroit, Mich., 1970-73; outdoor recreation planner U.S. Dept. of the Interior, Nat. Pk. Svc., Washington, 1974-87; mgmt. analyst U.S. Environ. Protection Agy., Washington, 1987—. Roman Catholic. Office: US Environ Protection Agy 401 M St SW Washington DC 20460-0002

JACOBSON, ELAINE ZEPORAH, clinical psychologist; b. Bklyn., Feb. 10, 1942; d. Julius Y. and Eleanor (Lebowitz) Finkelstein; m. Howard Jacobson, June 10, 1965; children: Michael, Daniel, Joel, David. AB summa cum laude, Bklyn. Coll., 1963; PhD, Adelphi U., 1968. Lic. psychologist, Ill. Staff psychologist Staten Island (N.Y.) Mental Health Soc., 1967-68; staff psychologist Adler Zone Ctr., Champaign, Ill., 1968-71, chief psychologist mentally ill children's program, 1981-82; rsch. cons. Eric Clearinghouse, Urbana, Ill., 1976-77, Mediax, Urbana, 1977-78; assoc. psychotherapist Family Svc. Champaign County, Champaign, 1977-81, 84-85; staff psychologist Wizo Found., Jerusalem, 1979-80; clin. supr. dept. psychology and psychol. clinic U. Ill., Champaign, 1986-88; pvt. practice Champaign, 1977-81, 84—; founding chair Patient Adv. Bd. dept. ob-gyn., Carle Hosp., Urbana, 1972-74. Active Hillel Found., U. Ill., 1975—; Zionist affairs chair Hadassah, Champaign, 1980-83. USPHS fellow Adelphi U., 1963-67. Mem. APA, Ill. Psychol. Assn., Champaign Area Psychol. Soc. (officer 1993-94), Phi Beta Kappa. Democrat. Jewish. Office: 1 Greencroft Dr Champaign IL 61821-5118

JACOBSON, HELEN GUGENHEIM (MRS. DAVID JACOBSON), civic worker; b. San Antonio; d. Jac Elton and Rosetta (Dreyfus) Gugenheim; m. David Jacobson, Nov. 6, 1938; children: Elizabeth, Dorothy Miller. BA, Hollins Coll. With news and spl. events staff NBC, N.Y.C., 1933-38. 1st v.p. San Antonio, Bexar County coun. Girl Scouts U.S.A., 1957-63; Tex. State rep. UNICEF, 1964-69; bd. dirs. U.S. com. UNICEF, 1970-80, hon. bd. dirs., 1980—; bd. dirs. Nat. Fedn. Temple Sisterhoods, 1973-77, Temple Beth-El Sisterhood, Youth Alternatives, Inc.; bd. dirs. Community Guidance Ctr., chmn. bd., 1960-63; bd. dirs. Sunshine Cottage Sch. for Deaf Children, chmn. bd., 1952-54; pres. Child Welfare Coun., 1968-70; pres. bd. trustees San Antonio Pub. Libr., 1957-61; trustee Nat. Coun. Crime and Delinquency, 1964-70, San Antonio Mus. Assn., 1964-73; bd. dirs. Cancer Therapy and Rsch. Found. South Tex., 1977—, sec., 1977-83; pres. S.W. region Tex. Coalition for Juvenile Justice, 1977-79; chmn. Mayor's Commn. on Status of Women, 1972-74; del. White House Conf. on Children, 1970; mem. Commn. on Social Action of Reform Judaism, 1973-77; chmn. Foster Grandparent project Bexar County Hosp. Dist., 1968-69; sec. Nat. Assembly for Social Policy and Devel., 1969-74; pres. women's com. Ecumenical Ctr. for Religion and Health, 1975-77; chmn. criminal justice planning com. Alamo Area Coun. of Govts., chmn., 1975-77, 1987-88; mem. Tex. Internat. Women's Yr. Coordinating Com., 1977; co-chmn. San Antonio chpt. NCCJ, 1980-84; chmn. United Negro Coll. Fund Campaign, 1983, 84; sec. nat. bd. Avance, Inc., 1991-93; trustee Target 90/Goals for San Antonio, 1986-90; hon. mem. bd. dirs. Witte Mus., 1994—. Recipient Headliner award for civic work San Antonio chpt. Women in Communications, 1958, Nat. Humanitarian award B'nai B'rith, 1975, City of Peace award, 1991; named Vol. Woman of Yr. Express-News, 1959, Spl. Svc. award Tex. Soc. Psychiat. Physicians, 1994; honoree San Antonio chpt. NCCJ, 1970, Nat. Jewish Hosp., 1978; inductee San Antonio Women's Hall of Fame, 1986, others. Mem. Nat. Coun. Jewish Women (Hannah G. Solomon award 1979), Internat. Women's Forum, San Antonio 100, Argyle Club. Home: 207 Beechwood Ln San Antonio TX 78216-7345

JACOBSON, JUDITH HELEN, state senator; b. South Bend, Ind., Feb. 26, 1939; d. Robert Marcene and Leah (Alexander) Haxton; m. John Raymond Jacobson, 1963; children—JoDee, Eric, Wendy. Student U. Wis.-Milw. and Madison, 1957-60; BS Mont. Tech, Butte, Mont., 1995. Mem. Mont. Senate, 1980—, majority whip, 1987, minority whip, 1989, chair com. on coms., fin. and claims. Democrat. Lutheran. Office: Mt State Senate State Capitol Helena MT 59620*

JACOBSON, LESLIE SARI, biologist, educator; b. N.Y.C., May 22, 1933; d. William and Gussie (Mintz) Goldberg; m. Homer Jacobson, Aug. 18, 1957; children: Guy Joseph, Ethan Samuel. BS, Bklyn. Coll., 1954, MA, 1955; postgrad., Columbia U., 1956; postgrad. (NIH fellow), Calif. Inst. Tech., 1960; Ph.D., NYU, 1962. Instr. dept. biology Bklyn. Coll., 1954-57, fellow dept. chemistry, 1961-63, prof. health sci., 1974—, dean Sch. Gen. Studies and Continuing Higher Edn., 1974-80, dean Grad. Studies and Continuing Higher Edn., 1980-82, dean Grad. Studies, 1980-88, dean Grad. Studies and Rsch., 1988-89, prof. dept. health and nutritions scis., 1989—, exec. dir. Applied Scis. Inst., 1994—; instr. dept. nursing L.I. Coll. Sch. Nursing, 1958; asst. prof. biology L.I. U., Bklyn., 1963, prof. biology, 1963-74, dean Grad. Sch., 1973-74, nat. program chmn. Assn. Continuing Higher Edn., 1978, nat. bd. dirs., 1978-81, pres.-elect, 1980-81, pres., 1981-82; bd. dirs. Center for Labor and Mgmt., N.Y.; dir. N.Y. Regional Cabinet Adult Continuing Edn., 1982—; mem. adv. com. on minorities Coun. Grad. Schs., 1987-90, svcs. com. Grad. Record Exam. Bd., 1990-93, chmn. Acad. policy com. all-univ. senate CUNY, 1992—; bd. dirs. Hyperion Capital Mgt.; invited speaker at nat. meetings Issues in Higher Edn. Vice pres. Alpha Sigma Lambda Found., 1983-88; v.p. Mapleton Midwood Community Health Bd. Inc., 1990—; v.p. B'nai B'rith Hillel JACY Assn., 1986-93; bd. dirs. Meth. Hosp., 1989—; v.p. Am. Lung Assn. of Bklyn. Recipient Founders Day award NYU, 1961, N.Y. Outstanding Adult Educator award, N.Y.C., 1978, Nat. Merit award, Assn. Continuing Higher Edn., 1984, Leadership award, 1986, Citation for svc. to community N.Y.C. Coun., 1987, Citation for excellence in edn. Bklyn. Boro Pres., 1987, Citation for outstanding svc. to community N.Y. State Assy., 1987, N.Y. State Senate, 1987. Mem. Sigma Xi, Alpha Sigma Lambda (nat. pres. 1978-80). Office: Bklyn Coll Dept Health and Nutrition Scis Bedford Ave # H Brooklyn NY 11210

JACOBSON, MINDY LEINER, art psychotherapist, educator; b. N.Y.C., July 25, 1954; d. Murray and Joan Lois (Rubenstein) Leiner; m. Christopher Harold Jacobson, Mar. 9, 1980 (div. 1984); 1 child, Stephanie Beth. Student, Union Coll., Schenectady, 1972-74; BA, SUNY, Stony Brook, 1975; MCAT in Creative Arts Therapies, Hahnemann U., 1978; cert. in adminstrn. social svcs., Temple U., 1985. Cert. open water diver. Sr. art psychotherapist Friends Hosp., Phila., 1978—; pvt. practice Phila., 1982—; asst. clin. prof. Hahnemann U. Phila., 1979—, continuing edn. instr., 1990-91; clin. instr., supr. trenton (N.J.) State Coll., 1989; cons. U.S. Naval Regional Med. Ctr., Phila., 1978; faculty mem. Ea. Regional Conf. on Multiple Personality Disorders, 1988—; articles reviewer Dissociation, 1989, 93; presenter in field. Contbr. articles to profl. jours. Speaker on preventive child abuse Jewish Fedn. Phila., 1988, 89; asst. Brownie leader Girl Scouts U.S.A., Melrose Park, Pa., 1988-91; treas. Phila. Sea Horses, 1990-93. Mem. Am. Art Therapy Assn. (registered profl. 1980, editor film/video jour. 1994—), Internat. Soc. for Study Multiple Personality Disorders/Dissociative States (profl.), Delaware Valley Art Therapy Assn. (profl., treas. 1979-82, newsletter com.). Democrat. Jewish. Office: Friends Hosp 4641 Roosevelt Blvd Philadelphia PA 19124-2399

JACOBSON, SANDRA A., medical educator, physician; b. Vancouver, Wash., Mar. 21, 1953; d. Oliver Charles and Frieda Marie (Lemme) Jacobson; m. Ronald Page Hammer Jr., Dec. 5, 1986. BA in Psychology summa cum laude, U. Hawaii, 1976, MD, 1987. Psychiatry residency Sch. of Medicine UCLA, L.A., 1991; rsch. fellow UCLA Sch. of Medicine, L.A., 1992, asst. clin. prof., 1992-93; asst. prof. Tufts New England Med. Ctr., Boston, 1993—. Contbr. to profl. jours. Recipient Familian Rsch. award Familian Found., 1991; Laughlin fellow Am. Coll. Psychiatrists, 1991. Mem. Am. Psychiatric Assn., Mass. Psychiatric Soc., Am. Assn. Geriatric Psychiatry, Soc. Neuroscience, Assn. Woman Psychiatrists. Office: Tufts New England Med Ctr 750 Washington St #1007 Boston MA 02111

JACOBSON, SUSAN DENE, librarian; b. St. Paul, Sept. 13, 1949; d. Payson Bernard and Shirley Thelma (Goldman) J. Student, Conn. Coll., 1967-69; BA, Bowdoin Coll., Brunswick, Maine, 1971; MS, Simmons Coll., Boston, 1972. Acquisitions libr. Yale U., New Haven, Conn., 1972-74; head acquisitions libr. Youngstown (Ohio) State U., 1974—; bd. dirs., insight leader, game leader, coord. of monitors English Festival Youngstown State U. Bd. dirs. alumni coun. Bowdoin Coll., 1976-80. Mem. ALA (co-chmn. libr.-vendor rels. discussion group 1982-83, chmn. computer applications in librs. subcom. 1984-85), Phi Kappa Phi. Office: Youngstown State U WF Maag Libr 410 Wick Ave Youngstown OH 44555-0001

JACOBSON, WENDEE ELIZABETH, English language educator; b. Quincy, Mass., Oct. 30, 1957; d. Walter Edwin and Beverly Jean (Bishop) J. BA in English, Lake Erie Coll., 1981; MA in English, U. Iowa, 1986. English instr. Cen. Ariz. Coll., Coolidge, 1988-89, Pima Coll., Tucson, 1988-89, Alfred (N.Y.) State Coll., 1989—. Author poetry. Mem. AAUW, Nat. Coun. English, Nat. Women's Studies Assn. Office: Alfred State Coll Dept English Alfred NY 14802

JACOBY, ANNE CATHERINE, supervisory nurse; b. Lincoln, Nebr., July 5, 1950; d. Billy Burton and Arleen Mae (Heinz) Michael; m. Jonathon L. Jacoby; children: Melissa Anne, Matthew David. BSN, U. Nebr. Coll. Nursing, 1972; postgrad., The Meth. Hosp., 1980; MSN, U. Nebr. Coll. Nursing, 1982; PhD in Nursing, Tex. Woman's U., 1988. CCRN, ACLS. Staff nurse med. ICU U. Nebr. Hosp., Omaha, 1972-74; staff nurse coronary care, ICU Immanuel Med. Ctr., Omaha, 1974-77; staff nurse coronary care Tufts New England Med. Ctr., Boston, 1978-79; staff nurse respiratory ICU Mass. Gen. Hosp., Boston, 1977-79; asst. prof. Tex. Woman's U. Coll. Nursing, Dallas, 1988-89; coord. pulmonary rehab. program Presbyn. Hosp. Dallas, 1989-90, staff nurse coronary care, 1987-92; supr. nurse rsch. Presbyn. Hosp. Dallas Inst. Exercise and Environ. Medicine, 1992-93; supr. nurse Smith Nursing Svc., Dallas, 1993—. Contbr. articles to profl. jours. Named Notable Woman Tex., Young Community Leaders Am. mem. ANA, AACN, Am. Heart Assn., Sigma Theta Tau. Office: Smith Nursing Svc 8330 Meadow Rd # 114 Dallas TX 75231

JACOBY, TAMAR, journalist, author; b. N.Y.C., Nov. 28, 1954; d. Irving and Alberta (Smith) J. Grad., UN Internat. Sch., N.Y.C., 1972; BA, Yale U., 1976. Writer, editor Hudson Rsch. Europe, Paris, 1976-77; editorial staff N.Y. Rev. Books, 1977-81; dep. editor Op-Ed Page N.Y. Times, 1981-87; sr. writer Newsweek, N.Y.C., 1987-89, justice editor, 1988-89; self employed author, 1989—; lectr. Yale U., New Haven, Conn., 1986-90; instr. The New Sch. for Social Rsch., N.Y.C., 1991. Author articles for Fgn. Affairs, The New Republic, Times Lit. Commentary, Dissent, The Washington Monthly, others. Fellow Nat. Endowment for the Humanitites, 1992, Alicia Patterson journalism fellow, 1990. Mem. Coun. Fgn. Rels., Helsinki Watch. Home: 118 N Mountain Ave Montclair NJ 07042

JACOX, ADA KATHRYN, nurse, educator; b. Centreville, Mich.; d. Leo H. and Lillian (Gilbert) J. BS in Nursing Edn., Columbia U., 1959; MS in Child Psychiat. Nursing, Wayne State U., 1965; PhD in Sociology, Case Western Res. U., 1969. R.N. Dir. nursing Children's Hosp.-Northville State Hosp., Mich., 1961-63; assoc. prof., then prof. Coll. Nursing Univ. Iowa, Iowa City, 1969-76; prof., assoc. dean Sch. Nursing U. Colo., Denver, 1976-80; prof., dir. rsch. ctr. sch. nursing U. Md., Balt., 1980-90, dir. ctr. for health policy rsch., 1988-90; prof. sch. nursing, Independence Found. chair health policy Johns Hopkins U., Balt., 1990—; co-chmn. panels to develop clin. guidelines for pain mgmt. U.S. Agy. for Health Care Policy and Rsch., 1990-94. Co-author: Organizing for Independent Nursing Practice, 1977 (named Book of Yr., Am. Jour. Nursing); A Process Measure for Primary Care: The Nurse Practitioner Rating Form, 1981 (named Book of Yr., Am. Jour. Nursing). Editor: Pain: A Sourcebook for Nurses, 1977 (named Book of Yr., Am. Jour. Nursing). Chair AIDS study sect. NIH, 1990-92. Carver fellow U. Iowa, 1972; cert. Disting. Achievement in Nursing Rsch. and Scholarship Alumni Assn. Columbia U. Tchrs. Coll., 1975, Disting. Alumna award Wayne State U. Coll. Nursing, 1994. Fellow Am. Acad. Nursing; mem. ANA (dir. 1978-82, 1st v.p. 1982-84), AMA (mem. health policy agenda work group 1983-86), Am. Nurses Found. (pres. 1982-85), Am. Acad. Nursing, Nat. Acad. Scis. (com. on nat. needs for biomed. and rsch. pers. 1984-87), Inst. of Medicine, Wayne State U. Alumni Assn. (Disting. Alumni award 1994). Office: Johns Hopkins U Sch Nursing 1830 E Monument St Baltimore MD 21205-2114

JACOX, MARILYN ESTHER, chemist; b. Utica, N.Y., Apr. 26, 1929; d. Grant Burlingame and Mary Elizabeth (Dunn) J. BA, Syracuse U., 1951; PhD, Cornell U., 1956; ScD (hon.), Syracuse U., 1993. Postdoctoral research assoc. U. N.C., Chapel Hill, 1956-58; fellow in fundamental research Mellon Inst., Pitts., 1958-62; research chemist Nat. Bur. Standards, Washington, 1962—; fellow Nat. Bur. Stds. (Nat. Inst. Stds. & Tech.), Gaithersburg, Md., 1986—. Mem. editorial bd. Revs. Chem. Intermediates, 1984-89, Jour. Chem. Physics, 1989-91; contbr. numerous articles to profl. jours. Recipient Gold medal U.S. Dept. Commerce, 1970, Fed. Women's award, 1973, Samuel Wesley Stratton award, 1973, Lippincott award, 1989, Hillebrand prize Chem. Soc. Washington, 1990, WISE Lifetime Achievement award, 1991. Fellow AAAS, Am. Phys. Soc., Washington Acad. Scis. (Phys. Sci. award 1968); mem. Am. Chem. Soc., Exec. Women in Govt. (sec. 1981, vice-chmn. 1982), Inter-Am. Photochemical Soc. (exec. com. 1978-79), Sigma Xi (pres. elect NBS chpt. 1987-88, pres. 1988-89). Office: Nat Inst Standards & Tech Molecular Physics Division Gaithersburg MD 20899

JACQUARD, CHERYL ANNE, administrator; b. Queens, N.Y., Apr. 6, 1959; d. Genevieve Toratunio. Gen. mgr. Hyaid Group, Hicksville, N.Y.; supr. ADA Computer Svcs., Hauppauge, N.Y. Office: Hyaid Group 12 Comml St le NY 11801

JACQUENEY, STEPHANIE A(LICE), lawyer; b. Freeport, N.Y.; d. Theodore and Mona (Graubart) J. BS, Cornell U., 1979; MPA, JD, Syracuse U., 1982. Bar: N.Y. 1983, U.S. Dist. Ct. (so. and ea. dists.) N.Y. 1983. Law clk. to U.S. atty. U.S. Dist. Ct. (No. Dist.) N.Y., Syracuse, 1981-82; assoc. Olwine, Connelly, Chase, O'Donnell & Weyer, N.Y.C., 1982-84, Cadwalader, Wickersham & Taft, N.Y.C., 1984-87; asst. counsel Manhattan Cable TV, Inc., N.Y.C., 1987-89, gen. counsel, 1989-90, v.p., gen. counsel, 1990-92; v.p. legal dept. Time Warner Cable of N.Y.C., 1992-94; dir. bus. affairs Radio City Music Hall Prodns., N.Y.C., 1994—. Mem. ABA, N.Y. State Bar Assn., Assn. of Bar of City of N.Y. (com. on arbitration 1984-88), N.Y. County Lawyers Assn. Office: Radio City Music Hall Prodn Rockefeller Ctr 1260 Ave of the Americas New York NY 10020

JACQUES, DIANA LYNN, realtor; b. Winchester, Mass., Sept. 14, 1949; d. Richard Edwin and Rita M. (Pender) Hunt; children: Cari Lynn, Michelle Lynn. Broker Realty Execs., Scottsdale, Ariz. Author: Girlfriends, 1992. Co-chair Ballet Arizona, 1993. Office: Realty Execs 6263 N Scottsdale Rd # 140 Scottsdale AZ 85250-5402

JACQUES, SHARON ANNE, artist, consultant; b. New Orleans, June 14, 1956; d. Charles Gustave and Melrose Josephine (Payne) J.; m. Luis Cruz Azaceta, May 15, 1982; 1 child, Dylan Jacques Cruz Azaceta. BFA, La. State U., 1977, MFA, 1982. Artist educator, program dir. The Mus. Modern Art, N.Y.C., 1983-91; artist educator, lectr. The New Mus. Contemporary Art, N.Y.C., 1988-91; artist, cons. The Contemporary Arts Ctr., 1993—; lectr. in field. Mem. N.Y. Roundtable Art Edn. Democrat. Roman Catholic. Home: 4100 Prytania St New Orleans LA 70115 Studio: 3831 Tchoupitoulas St New Orleans LA 70115

JAEGER, BERNICE MARY, hotel facility administrator; b. Cin., July 27, 1934; d. Frank Charles and Bertha Marie (Grosser) Smith; m. Ivan Jaeger, June 20, 1955; children: Ginger, Jackie, Judi. AA, Clark County C.C., Las Vegas, Nev., 1973, AAS, 1974; BA, U. Nev., Las Vegas, 1985. Cert. reality therapist (mgmt. specialist). Conv. sales sec. Riviera Hotel, Las Vegas, 1973-77, adminstrv. asst., hotel dir., 1977-80; exec. sec. Aladdin Hotel, Las Vegas, 1980-84; dir. temporary svcs. Flextime, Las Vegas, 1984-85; asst. gen. mgr. Continental Hotel/Casino, Las Vegas, 1985—; speaker, faculty mem. Internat. Gaming and Bus. Exposition, Las Vegas, 1991. Featured annually Disting. Women in So. Nev., Las Vegas. Named Working Mother of Yr., Mother of the Yr. Award, Las Vegas, 1981. Mem. Phi Kappa Phi, Phi Lambda Alpha. Office: Continental Hotel/Casino 4100 Paradise Rd Las Vegas NV 89109-6561

JAEGER, ELIZABETH MARY, artist, art restorer; b. Geneva, Ill., Apr. 1, 1954; d. John Justin and Eleanore Frances (Wermuth) J.; m. Stephen Lawson, May 21, 1979. BFA in Painting, U. Notre Dame, 1976; MFA in Painting, W.Va. U., 1978. Art restorer Garo, Morgantown, W.Va., 1989—. Exhibited in one woman shows including Edinburgh, Scotland, 1984, 85, 86, 88, Morgantown, W.Va., 1993; group exhbns. incl. Charleston, W.Va., 1991, 93, 95, Chgo., Ill., 1994; author: Neolithic Stone Circles and Contemporary Art in the Landscape, 1984, An Atlas of Known Places, 1987. Grantee Scottish Arts Coun., 1986, 88, W.Va. Divsn. Culture and History, 1992.

JAESCHKE, SARAH ANN, systems programmer, consultant; b. Chgo., July 20, 1950; d. Carl H. and Lenora M. (Yates) J. BS, So. Ill. U., 1972; MS, U. Ill., Chgo., 1979; postgrad., Northwestern U., 1982-84. Tchr. math. Glenbrook North High Sch., Northbrook, Ill., 1973-81; systems mktg. rep. Control Data Bus. Info. Svcs., Chgo., 1981-82; programmer analyst Resources, Inc., Northbrook, 1984-85; sr. statis. programmer G.D. Searle & Co., Skokie, Ill., 1985; software engr. Allergan Humphrey, San Leandro, Calif., 1986-87; data processing mgr. Onsite Systems, Berkeley, Calif., 1987-88; systems analyst TRW, Berkeley, 1988-90; cons. Ingres Corp., Alameda, Calif., 1990-91; systems analyst Pacific Bell Info. Svcs., San Ramon, Calif., 1992; systems programmer Pillsbury Madison & Sutro, San Francisco, 1992—. Canvasser, Green Party of Calif., Berkeley, 1991. Mem. NOW, ACLU, Pub. Citizen, Greenpeace. Office: Pillsbury Madison & Sutro 114 Sansome St # 416A San Francisco CA 94104-3803

JAFFE, BARBARA, university administrator; b. Cleve., June 7, 1955; d. Bernard and Bertha (Marin) J.; m. Howard I. Langer, Oct. 16, 1983; children: Bernard Samuel, Martin Jaffe. AB cum laude, Harvard-Radcliffe

Coll., 1977; MBA, Harvard Bus. Sch., 1979. Spl. projects coord. Phila. Inquirer and Daily News, 1979-82; asst. to mng. editor Phila. Daily News, 1982-84; dir. ext. svcs. Temple U., Phila., 1985-90, assoc. vice provost for continuing edn., 1990—. Exec. com. mem. Jewish Fedn. Greater Phila., 1991—; bd. dirs. Community Hebrew Schs. Greater Phila. Mem. ASTD, Nat. Univ. Continuing Edn. Assn. (instnl. rep. 1985—), Harvard Bus. Sch. Alumni Club (sec. 1985-86). Office: Temple Univ Ctr City 1616 Walnut St Philadelphia PA 19103

JAFFE, LOUISE, English language educator, creative writer; b. Bronx, N.Y., May 17, 1936; d. Joseph and Anna (Movitz) Neuwirth; m. Steven Jaffe, Aug. 26, 1962 (div. 1975); 1 child, Aaron Lawrence; m. Leo Gerber, 1993. BA, Queens Coll., 1956; MA, Hunter Coll., 1959; PhD, U. Nebr., 1965; MFA, Brooklyn Coll., 1991. Instr. Kingsborough Community Coll., Bklyn, 1965-67, asst. prof., 1967-70, assoc. prof. English, 1970-88, prof., 1989—. Author: Hyacinths and Biscuits, 1985, Wisdom Revisited, 1987, Light Breaks, 1995, also numerous poetry and fiction stories. Mem. editorial bd. Community Review CUNY, 1984—; faculty adv. student lit. mag., 1983—. Recipient First prize N.Y. Poetry Forum, 1980, First prize, First honorable mention Shelley Soc. N.Y., 1983, 84, and others. Mem. Mensa, Poets and Writers Inc., Shelley Soc. of N.Y., Feminist Writers Guild, Writers Union. Democrat. Jewish. Avocations: creative writing, scrabble, crossword puzzles, people-watching, attending and giving poetry readings. Home: 2411 E 3rd St Brooklyn NY 11223-5357 Office: Kingsborough Community Coll Oriental Blvd Brooklyn NY 11235-4906

JAFFE, RONA, author; b. N.Y.C., June 12, 1932; d. Samuel and Diana (Ginsberg) J. BA, Radcliffe Coll., 1951. Sec. N.Y.C., 1952; assoc. editor Fawcett Publs., N.Y.C., 1952-56. Author: The Best of Everything, 1958, Away From Home, 1960, The Last of the Wizards, 1961, Mr. Right Is Dead, 1965, The Cherry in the Martini, 1966, The Fame Game, 1969, The Other Woman, 1972, Family Secrets, 1974, The Last Chance, 1976, Class Reunion, 1979, Mazes and Monsters, 1981, After the Reunion, 1985, An American Love Story, 1990. Office: Janklow & Nesbit Assocs 598 Madison Ave New York NY 10022-1614*

JAFFE, SUSAN, ballerina; b. Washington; m. Paul Connelly. Student, Md. Sch. Ballet; student, Sch. Am. Ballet, Am. Ballet Theatre Sch. With Am. Ballet Theatre II, 1978-80; with Am. Ballet Theatre, 1980—, soloist, 1981-83, prin., 1983—. Repertoire includes: Le Corsaire, Apollo, La Bayadere, Bouree Fantastique, Carmen, Cinderella, Concerto, Duets, Giselle, The Guards of Amager, Push Comes to Shove, Symphonie Concertante, Ballet Imperial, Coppelia, Etudes Giselle, Jardin auxLilas, Romeo and Juliet, The Sleeping, Other Dances, Theme and Variations, SwanLake, La Sylphide, Undertow, Voluntaries, Dim Lustre, Manon, Gala Performance, Don Quixote, Cruel World, Sextet, others; created role Lynne Taylor-Corbett's Great Galloping Gottschalk, Bruch Violin Concerto No. 1, Serious Pleasures; appeared Spoleto in An Evening of Jerome Robbins Ballets, 1982; appeared with Kirov Ballet, 1988; guest appearances with The Royal Swedish Ballet, The Royal Danish Ballet, The English Nat. Ballet. Recipient N.Y. Woman-Lancome Paris Woman of Yr. award, 1989. Office: Am Ballet Theatre 890 Broadway New York NY 10003-1211

JAFFE, SUSAN LYNN, retired manufacturing company executive; b. N.Y.C.; d. Irving and Beatrice (Albert) J.; m. Irwin R. Tane; children by previous marriage: Robert Wayne, Stephen Mark. BS, Boston U., 1964; postgrad., Hofstra U., C.W. Post U. Elem. sch. tchr. Long Beach, N.Y., 1964-67; pres. Fashions by Appointment, Glen Cove, N.Y., 1967-71; adminstrv. asst. Peerless Sales Corp., Elmont, N.Y., 1967-71; sales mgr., then mktg. dir. United Utensils Co., Inc., Port Washington, N.Y., 1973-78; v.p. ops. and control United Molded Products div. United Utensils Co., Inc., Port Washington, 1978-80; v.p. mktg. Utensco, Port Washington, 1980-88; bd. dirs. Peerless Aerospace Corp. Co-inventor plastic container and handling assembly. Bd. trustees Am. Jewish Congress; mem. Dirs. Circle, Folger Shakespeare Libr.; life mem. Hadassah, Ronald McDonald House; mem. Friends of the Arts-L.I. U., Inner Circle-Nassau County Mus. Art; friend N.Y. Pub. Libr. Mem. Boston U. Alumni Assn. Home: 249 12th Ave Sea Cliff NY 11579-1021 Office: PO Box 735 Glenwood Landing NY 11547-0735

JAFFE, SUZANNE DENBO, investment banker, entrepreneur; b. Washington, Apr. 17, 1943; d. Milton Carl and Beatrice (Altman) Denbo; m. Howard M. Jaffe, Sept. 10, 1967 (div. 1973). BA, U. Pa., 1965; postgrad., NYU, 1965-67. Picture researcher Time, Inc., N.Y.C., 1967-68; analyst L.M. Rosenthal & Co., N.Y.C., 1968-69, Standard & Poor's Intercapital, Inc., N.Y.C., 1969-70; portfolio mgr., ptnr. Century Capital Assocs., N.Y.C., 1971-81; v.p. Highland Capital Corp., N.Y.C., 1982; exec. v.p. Lehman Mgmt. Co., Inc., N.Y.C., 1982-83; dep. compt. N.Y. State, N.Y.C., 1983-85; pres. S.D.J. Assocs., N.Y.C., 1985-89; mng. dir. Angelo, Gordon & Co., N.Y.C., 1990-93, Hamilton & Co., N.Y.C., 1994—; bd. dirs. Crossroads Capital LP, Hartford, Conn., Olin Corp.; bd. dirs., treas. Rsch. Corp.; trustee U.S. Social Security-Medicare, Washington, 1984-90; mem. adv. coun. Employees Retirement Income Security Act, U.S. Dept. Labor, Washington, 1985-88. Bd. dirs. Fordham U., 1984—, mem. exec. com., 1992—, chmn. audit and fin. com., 1992—; assoc. trustee U. Pa., Phila., 1987—, treas. trustees coun. Penn women, 1991—; bd. dirs. Planned Parenthood, N.Y.C., 1976-83, Investor Responsibility Rsch. Ctr., 1984-85, Coun. Governing Bds. State Colls. and Univs.; mem. N.Y. women in bus. com. Overseas Edn. Fund Internat.; mem. adv. com. Children's Aid Soc. Mem. Internat. Women's Forum (bd. dirs., sec.), Women's Forum (pres. 1992—, bd. dirs., treas. 1987-89), Fin. Women's Assn. (treas. 1985-87), Columbia U. Grad. Sch. Bus. Adv. Bd., Harmonie Club (N.Y.C.), Econ. Club (N.Y.C.). Democrat. Jewish. Home: 784 Park Ave 5A New York NY 10021 Office: Hamilton & Co 45 Rockefeller Plz Ste 2602 New York NY 10111

JAFFE, SYLVIA SARAH, art collector, former medical technologist; b. Detroit, May 16, 1917; d. Sam and Rose (Rosmarin) Turner; BS in Med. Tech., U. Wis., 1940; m. David Jaffe, Nov. 8, 1942. Med. technologist Watts Hosp. Lab., Durham, N.C., 1940-45; rsch. hematology technologist in leukemia Sloan Kettering Meml. Hosp. Lab., N.Y.C., 1946-47; chief med. technologist in hematology Arlington (Va.) Hosp. Lab., 1948-55; chief technologist in diagnostic hematology Georgetown U. Hosp., Washington, 1959-70; collector 19th century and 20th century art, 1970—. Art collections include spl. collection of Winslow Homer Wood, block engravings and collection by 19th Century French graphic artist. Mem. Col. Williamsburg (Va.) Found., hon. citizen. Mem. Am. Soc. Med. Technologists, Am. Soc. Clin. Pathologists (assoc.), Am. Women in Sci., Corcoran Gallery Art, Pa. Acad. Fine Arts, Sierra Club, Nat. Wildlife Fed., World Wildlife Fund., Nat. Audubon Soc., Nat. Trust Hist. Preservation, The Washington Print Club, U. Wis. Alumni Assn., Boston Mus. Arts, Nat. Mus. Women in Arts (charter), Sierra Club, Greenpeace, Soc., Wilderness Soc. Democrat. Jewish. Club: Pioneer Women. Contbr. articles to profl. socs. Address: 1913 S Quincy St Arlington VA 22204

JAFFEE, SANDRA SCHUYLER, financial executive; b. N.Y.C., Dec. 18, 1943; d. I.M. and P.B. Schuyler; m. Carl Daniel Jaffee, Aug. 19, 1964; 1 child, Evan Schuyler. B.A., Tufts U., Medford, Mass. Vol. U.S. Peace Corps, 1966-68; mgmt. cons., 1968-71; budget analyst N.Y. City Bur. of Budget, 1971-74; asst. v.p. Citibank, N.Y.C., 1974-76, v.p. ops., 1976-78, pres. capital markets sources, 1978-81, sr. v.p. new ventures U.S. consumer group, 1981-86; exec. v.p., chief adminstrv. officer N.Y. Stock Exchange, 1986-90; consulting dir. APM, Inc., N.Y.C., 1990—. Chmn. Children's Heart Fund, N.Y. Hosp., 1985-90. Recipient Women Achievers in Bus. award YWCA, 1978. Office: APM Inc 1675 Broadway New York NY 10019-5818

JAGACINSKI, CAROLYN MARY, psychology educator; b. Orange, N.J., Apr. 12, 1949; d. Theodore Edward and Eleanor Constance (Thys) Jagacinski; m. Richard Justus Schweickert, Dec. 27, 1980; children: Patrick, Kenneth. AB with honors in psychology, Bucknell U., 1971; MA in Psychology, U. Mich., 1975, PhD in Psychology and Edn., 1978. Rsch. assoc. U. Mich., Ann Arbor, 1978-79; rsch. assoc. Purdue U., West Lafayette, Ind., 1979-80, vis. asst. prof., 1980-83, rsch. psychologist, 1983-86, vis. lectr., 1986-88, asst. dean, 1988-89, asst. prof. psychology, 1988-94, assoc. prof., 1994—. Contbr. articles to profl. jours. U. Mich. predoctoral fellow, 1977-78, dissertation grantee, 1977-78; Exxon Edn. Found. grantee, 1983-84. Mem. APA, Midwestern Psychol. Assn., Soc. for Judgment and Decision Making, Am. Ednl. Rsch. Assn., Psychonomic Soc., Sigma Xi, Psi Chi. Office: Purdue Univ Dept Psychol Scis West Lafayette IN 47907

JAGIELLA, DIANA MARY, lawyer; b. Chgo., Sept. 16, 1959; d. John James and Mildred Helen (Lapinskas) J.; m. Charles John Thorbjornsen, June 9, 1984; children: Kenneth James, Rachael Frances, Lauren Kellie. BA, Purdue U., 1983; JD, DePaul U., 1987; postgrad., U. Chgo., 1989—. Bar: Ill. 1987, U.S. Dist. Ct. (cen. dist.) Ill. 1987, U.S. Ct. Appeals (7th cir.) 1989. Assoc. Hinshaw & Culbertson, Chgo., 1987-88, Howard & Howard, Attys., P.C., Peoria, Ill., 1991—; atty. CilCorp, Inc., Peoria, 1988-91. Contbr. articles to legal jours. Chmn. Police and Fire Commn., Peoria, 1990—; mem. allocation panel United Way, Peoria, 1991—; mem. spl. com. Peoria C. of C., 1989-90; pres., bd. dirs. Abuse Shelter, Peoria, 1991-92; mem. Rotary North Peoria Sch. Bd., 1989—. Sheridan scholar, 1986; recipient Recognition award Women's Law Caucus, 1986. Mem. ABA (environ. sect.), Ill. Bar Assn. (environ. sect.), Peoria Bar Assn. (chmn. law day 1990-91, pres. women lawyers sect. 1988-90). Republican. Roman Catholic. Office: Howard & Howard Attys PC 321 Liberty St Peoria IL 61602-1403

JAGO, DEIDRE ELLEN BERGUSON, exercise and sport science educator, tennis coach; b. Blossburg, Pa., May 26, 1948; d. Walter Bernard and Iris Lorraine (Strong) Berguson; m. John William Jago, May 29, 1971; children: Jocelyn Anne, William Thomas. BS in Health and Phys. Edn. cum laude, East Stroudsburg (Pa.) U., 1970, MEd in Phys. Edn., 1972. Instr. rating U.S. Profl. Tennis Registry. Tchr. T.A. Edison High Sch., Elmira Heights, N.Y., 1970-71; grad. asst. East Stroudsburg U., 1971-72; instr. health and phys. edn. Pa. State U., Hazleton, 1972-76, asst. prof. exercise and sport sci., 1976—, women's tennis coach, 1974-92, men's tennis coach, 1987—, mem. senate, 1979-91; women's volleyball coach, 1992—; participant People to People Citizen Amb. Women in Sport Del. to Russia and Belarus, 1993. Instr. trainer water safety Hazleton chpt. ARC, 1976—; mem. Hazleton Area Sch. Bd., 1987—, v.p., 1989, pres., 1990; mem. consistory Christ Ch., United Ch. of Christ, 1986-88, sec., 1986-87; participant People to People Citizen Amb., Women in Sport Del. to Russian and Belarus, 1993; Pa. Intercollegiate Athletic Assn. Volleyball and Swimming Ofcl., 1993—; bd. mgrs. Hazelton area Pub. Libr., 1987-89, 94, bd. trustees, 1987-89, 95. Recipient vol. svc. award Hazleton chpt. ARC, 1990. Mem. AAHPERD, AAUW (Risk Challenge award Pa. divsn. 1989, named gift to Marilyn Kreidler Gardner Endowment Hazleton br. 1989), U.S. Profl. Tennis Registry. Home: 20 Lissa Ln Sugarloaf PA 18249-9701 Office: Pa State U Highacres Hazleton PA 18201

JAGODZINSKI, CECILE MARIE, librarian; b. Buffalo, N.Y., Oct. 15, 1951; d. Edwin and Dorothy Evelyn (Majchrowicz) J. BA in English, Canisius Coll., 1978; MLS, SUNY, Buffalo, 1979; CAS in Libr. Sci., U. Chgo., 1985; MA in English, Northwestern U., 1988. Cert. tchr. English 7th-12th grade, N.Y., cert. pub. libr., N.Y. Tchr. English various schs., Buffalo, 1972-78; libr. I Buffalo and Erie County Pub. Libr., Buffalo, 1979-80; asst. libr. Quincy (Ill.) Coll., 1980-83; cataloger Northwestern U. Law Libr., Chgo., 1983-84, head retrospective conversion project, 1984-86; mgr. tech. svcs. AMA Libr., Chgo., 1986-88; cataloger Ill. State U., Normal, 1988-89, head catalog dept., 1989-93, coord. collection mgmt., 1993—. Contbr. book revs. and articles to acad. jours. Scholar Canisius Coll., 1969, N.Y. State Bd. Regents, 1969, U. Chgo. Grad. Libr. Sch., 1983. Mem. ALA, MLA, Assn. Coll. and Rsch. Librs., Soc. for History of Authorship, Reading, and Publishing, Renaissance English Text Soc., Beta Phi Mu. Office: Ill State U Milner Libr Campus Box 8900 Normal IL 61790-8900

JAHN, BILLIE JANE, nursing educator, consultant; b. Byers, Tex., Dec. 12, 1921; d. Thomas Oscar and Molly Verona (Kennemer) Downing; student Scott and White Sch. Nursing, 1941-42, U. Mich., 1973-75; BSN, Wayne State U., 1971; MS, East Tex. State U., 1976, PhD, 1982; m. Edward L. Jahn, Dec. 6, 1942; children: Antoinette R., James T., Thomas L., Edward L., Janette E. Staff nurse Warren Meml. Hosp., Centerline, Mich., 1957-61; supr. nursing svc. Mich. Dept. Mental Health, Northville, 1962-71, Franklin County (Tex.) Hosp., 1972-74; instr. nursing Paris (Tex.) Jr. Coll., 1975-80; nurse educator VA, Waco, Tex., 1981-82; exec. v.p., dir., sr. nursing cons. Dos Cabezas, Inc., Mt. Vernon, Waco and Temple, Tex., 1981—; adj. faculty U. Tex.-Arlington, 1985—; mem. dept. phys. medicine and rehab. Scott and White Hosp., Temple, Tex., 1985—; head nurse dept. phys. med. and rehab., nurse researcher biosci., 1990; cons. East Tex. State U., Texarkana, 1978—; adj. faculty U. Tex.-Arlington. Vol., ARC, 1971—; den mother Boy Scouts Am., 1960-62; sec. PTA, Warren, Mich., 1960-62; v.p., Temple, Tex., 1957-58. Mem. AAAS, AAUP, NAFE, Nat. League Nursing, Nat. Assn. Rehab. Nurses (rev. bd. Rehab. Nursing Inst. 1986—, Rsch. Grant Panel, 1992—, Rehab. Nursing Found., 1989—), Tex. League Nursing, Am. Assn. Curriculum and Supervision, Phi Delta Kappa, Kappa Delta Pi.

JAHN, SHARON ELISABETH, animal health technologist, consultant; b. Mill Valley, Calif., July 22, 1947; d. John Kendrick and Doris Vivian (Voigts) Bloom; m. Larry Wyatt Jahn, June 21, 1969 (div.). BS, U. Calif., Davis, 1969, MS, 1993. Lic. animal health tech., Calif. Staff rsch. assoc. Animal Resources Svc. U. Calif., Davis, 1972-74, asst. environ. health and safety tech., 1976-77, assoc. environ. health and safety specialist, 1977—; cons. Lab. Animal Biotech Cos., others, 1989—; mem. subcom. for animal tech. tng. Sch. Vet. Medicine U. Calif., Davis, 1981, animal tech. tng. selection com., 1981, staff to com. Chancellor's Animal Use and Care Adminstrv. Adv. Com., 1982—, mem. Solano County Scholarship Com., U. Calif., Davis, 1991, 93; mem. subcom. for developing and evaluating tng. programs for mem. instns. Calif. Biomed. Rsch., 1986-88; judge Calif. Biomed. Rsch. Assn. Ann. Essay Contest, 1991—; active Calif. Consumer Affairs Animal Health Tech. Job Task Rev. Com., 1990. Mem. Am. Assn. Lab. Animal Sci. (cert. lab. tech. 1974, cert. lab. animal tech. 1981, Al Edward award no. Calif. br. 1984, tech. recognition award nat. 1984, com. lab. animal techs. 1985-89, br. pres.'s com. 1987-88, workshop chmn. 38th annual mtg. 1987, animal tech. cert. bd. 1989-95, trustee, dist. 8 rep. 1989-92, audiovisual rev. com. 1989-90, rev. 1992-93, chair animal tech. cert. bd. 1994-95, bd. dirs. No. Calif. br. 1984-90, tech. br. rep. 1984-86, regional examining bd. 1985-93, pres. 1987, 88, workshop chair dist. 8 conv., learning resources/poster session chair dist. 8 conv. 1988, chair edn. 1989-91, interim chair local arrangements com. 1995 ann. meeting 1991-93, No. Calif. br. mem. nominations and awards com. 1992). Office: Office of Campus Vet Environ Health & Safety U Calif Davis CA 95616-8545

JAHNKE, JESSICA JO, university administrator, dean; b. Appleton, Wis., Nov. 4, 1949; d. Howard Tod Jahnke and Evelyn Marie Appleton Blunck. BS in Secondary English Edn., Silver Lake Coll., Manitowoc, Wis., 1971; MA in Humanities/English, Roosevelt U., Chgo., 1975; PhD in Edn., Ohio State U., 1981. Tchr. Hauser Jr. High Sch., Riverside, Ill., 1971-73; instr. Coll. Edn. Ohio State U., Columbus, 1981-82, dir. accreditation and state evaluation Coll. Edn., 1981-84, coord. program devel./adminstrn. Office Acad. Affairs, 1984-85; asst. prof. edn., exec. asst. to pres. U. Maine, Farmington, 1985-88, assoc. prof. edn., 1988-90, chair dept. elem., secondary and early childhood edn., 1988-90; dean Ctr. for Tchr. Edn. Shawnee State U., Portsmouth, Ohio, 1990—; presenter in field. Contbr. articles to profl. jours. Mem. ASCD, Am. Ednl. Rsch. Assn., Am. Assn. Colls. Tchr. Edn. (instl. rep.). Office: Shawnee State U 940 2d St Portsmouth OH 45662

JAHNKE, PAMELLA EMRICK, emergency nurse; b. Indpls., May 2, 1956; d. Harold Benjamin and Betty Mae (Cunningham) Emrick; m. Lawrence Everett Jahnke, Aug. 16, 1975; children: Leslie Ann, Kimberly Diane. ADN, U. Indpls., 1976; BS in Health Arts, Coll. St. Francis, 1984; BSN, Ball State U., 1990. RN, Ind.; CEN; cert. instr. BLS and ACLS, Am. Heart Assn. and TNCCI, ENPC. Charge nurse cardiopulmonary unit Midwest Med. Ctr., Indpls., 1984; staff and charge nurse ICU Community Hosp. East, Indpls., 1976-84, staff and charge nurse level II emergency dept., 1984-91; coord. patient care emergency/admitting, level III RN Ind. U. Med. Ctr., U. Hosp., Indpls., 1991-92; emergency level III staff nurse Community Hosp., East Indpls., 1992—. Jr. troop leader Girl Scouts U.S., Indpls., 1991-92; mem. Children's Mus., Indpls., 1987—, Indpls. Zoo, 1987—, Hoosier Environ. Coun., Indpls., 1991—. Mem. ANA, Emergency Nurses Assn. (cert., trauma nurse provider/instr. nursing practice com., pres. Ind. state chpt. 1995), Ind. State Nurses Assn., Emergency Med. Svc. Coun., Sigma Theta Tau. Baptist. Home: 6250 Woburn Dr Indianapolis IN 46250-2740 Office: Community Hosp East 1500 N Ritter Ave Indianapolis IN 46219-3095

JAHR, JOANNE BARBARA, research librarian; b. Madison, Wis., July 25, 1943; d. Bert Norman and Jean Renee (Sardy) J. AB, Bklyn Coll., 1969; MLS, Pratt Inst., 1972. Staff asst. N.Am. Jewish Students Network, N.Y.C., 1970-75; staff assoc. Conf. Pres. Major Am. Jewish Orgns., N.Y.C., 1975-79; nat. program coordinator Assn. Reform Zionists Am., N.Y.C., 1979-82; asst. to exec. v.p. Jewish Braille Inst. Am., N.Y.C., 1982-87, library adminstr., 1987-90. Editor: Guide to Jewish Student Groups, 1973, Likutim mag., 1983—. Mem. exec. com. Jewish Frontier mag., 1983-1989; bd. dirs. Assn. Reform Zionists Am., 1984—. Mem. ALA, Am. Friends of Peace Now, N.Am. Serials Interest Group, Assn. Jewish Libraries. Democrat. Office: Readmore Inc 22 Cortlandt St New York NY 10007

JAILLITE, JOYCE ANN, computer analyst; b. Marion, Kans., Sept. 5, 1948; d. Edgar Worall and N. Virginia (Potts) J. AB, Ctrl. Meth. Coll., 1970; MA, U. Mo., 1975. Short term missionary United Meth. Ch., Albuquerque, N.Mex., 1970-72; libr. tech. Ctrl. Meth. Coll., Fayette, Mo., 1972-73; head libr. Columbia (Mo.) Coll., 1975-78; head reference libr. N.E. Mo. State U., Kirksville, 1978-81; dir. Mid-Mo. Libr. Network, Columbia, 1981-84; sr. bus. analyst Contract Svcs., Kansas City, Mo., 1982-93; with M.I.S. Lister-Petter Inc., Olathe, Kans., 1993—. Vol. Kansas City Pub. T.V., 1989—, Restart, Kansas City, 1991—; chair outreach com. Blue Ridge United Meth. Ch., Kans. City, 1994—. Mem. Order Amaranth (grand rep. Kans. 1995—), Order White Shrine (worthy shephardess 1994—), Order Ea. Star (assoc. conductress 1994-95). Home: 814 South Lake Dr Independence MO 64053-1838

JAIN, KARUNA M., software consultant; b. Bombay, Mar. 9, 1961; came to U.S., 1992; d. Mahendrakumar G. and Bimla M. (Panday) J. BS in Physics, Bombay U., Bombay, 1981; MS in Physics, Bombay U., 1983; postgrad. dipl. in computer sci., Datamatics, Bombay, 1984. Lectr. in physics Khalsa Coll., Bombay, 1983-84; computer programmer Suburban Computer Ctr., Bombay, 1984-85; sr. cons. A.F. Ferguson & Co., Bombay, 1985-92; cons. ITT, Hartford, Conn., 1992, Oracle Corp., Redwood Shores, Calif., 1993; sr. system analyst Transnational Computer Tech., El Segundo, Calif., 1993—; cons. Infocom Cons., Inc., N.J., 1991-92. Home: 3217 Overland Ave #9105 Los Angeles CA 90034

JAKAB, IRENE, psychiatrist; b. Oradea, Rumania; came to U.S., 1961, naturalized, 1966; d. Odon and Rosa A. (Riedl) J. MD, Ferencz József U., Kolozsvar, Hungary, 1944; lic. in psychology, pedagogy, philosophy cum laude, Hungarian U., Cluj, Rumania, 1947; PhD summa cum laude, Pazmany Peter U., Budapest, 1948; Dr honoris causa, U. Besançon, France, 1982. Diplomate Am. Bd. Psychiatry. Rotating intern Ferencz József U., 1943-44; resident in psychiatry Univ. Hosp., Kolozsvar, 1944-47, resident in neurology, 1947-50; resident internal medicine Univ. Hosp. for Internal Medicine, Pécs, Hungary, 1950-51; chief physician Univ. Hosp. for Neurology and Psychiatry, Pécs, 1951-59; staff neuropathol. rsch. lab. Neurol. Univ. Clinic, Zurich, 1959-61; sect. chief Kans. Neurol. Inst., Topeka, 1961-63; dir. rsch. and edn., 1966; resident psychiatry Topeka State Hosp., 1963-66; asst. psychiatrist McLean Hosp., Belmont, Mass., 1966-67; assoc. psychiatrist McLean Hosp., 1967-74; prof. psychiatry U. Pitts. Med. Sch., 1974-89, prof. emerita, 1989—, co-dir. med. student edn. in psychiatry, 1981-89; dir. John Merck Program, 1974-81; mem. faculty dept. psychiatry Med. Sch., Pecs, 1951-59; asst. Univ. Hosp. Neurology, Zurich, 1959-61; assoc. psychiatry Harvard U., Boston, 1966-69, asst. prof. psychiatry, 1969-74, program dir. grad course mental retardation, 1970-87; lectr. psychiatry, 1974—. Author: Dessins et Peintures des Aliénés, 1956, Zeichnungen und Gemälde der Geisteskranken, 1956; editor: Psychiatry and Art, 1968, Art Interpretation and Art Therapy, 1969, Conscious and Unconscious Expressive Art, 1971, Transcultural Aspects of Psychiatric Art, 1975; co-editor: Dynamische Psychiatrie, 1974; editorial bd.: Confinia Psychiatrica, 1975-81; contbr. articles to profl. jours. Recipient 1st prize Benjamin Rush Gold medal award for sci. exhibit, 1980, Bronze Chris plaque Columbus Film Festival, 1980, Leadership award Am. Assn. on Mental Deficiency, 1980; Menninger Sch. Psychiatry fellow, Topeka, 1963-66. Mem. AMA, Am. Psychol. Assn., Am. Psychiat. Assn., Société Medico Psychologique de Paris, Internat. Rorschach Soc., N.Y. Acad. Scis., Internat. Soc. Psychopathology of Expression (v.p. 1959—), Am. Soc. Psychopathology of Expression (chmn. 1965—, Ernst Kris Gold Medal award 1988), Royal Soc. of Medicine (overseas fellow), Internat. Soc. Child Psychiatry and Allied Professions, Internat. Assn. Knowledge Engrs. (v.p. for medicine), Deutschsprachige Gesellschaft für Psychopathologie des Ausdruckes (hon. Prinzhorn prize 1967), Hungarian Psychiat. Assn. (hon. 1992). Home and Office: 74 Lawton St Brookline MA 02146-2501

JAKOBE, VIRGINIA ELLIS, retired educator; b. Molino, Mo., Sept. 10, 1922; d. Clyde William and Lucy (Baker) Ellis; m. Henry George Jakobe Sr., Feb. 23, 1963; 1 child, Henry George. BS, NE Mo. State U., 1946; MA, Columbia U., 1960. Cert. elem. art tchr., Mo., N.Y. Tchr. Ellis Sch., Molino, 1941-43; tchr. art and English Marceline Sch., Mo., 1943-44; remedial tchr. Berkley Sch., Mo., 1944-46; tchr. elem. art Maplewood Sch., Mo., 1946-54, Univ. City Schs., Mo., 1954-63, Saranac Lake (N.Y.) Cent. Schs., 1970-90. Editor Show Me Art, 1962-64; originator The Children's Art Exhibit Saranac Lake Cen. Sch., 1970—. Pres. Saranac Lake./N.Y. PTA., 1968-69, St. Louis County Art Tchrs. Assn., 1954-55. Mem. N.Y. State Art Tchrs. Assn., Paint and Palette Artists Assn., Delta Kappa Gamma (sec.). Republican. Episcopalian. Home: 12 Rockledge Rd Saranac Lake NY 12983-1928

JAKUBOWSKI, AUDREY FEDYSZYN, pharmaceutical regulatory affairs administrator; b. Dunkirk, N.Y., Oct. 6, 1942; d. Stanley Joseph and Irene Mary (Piglowski) Fedyszyn; divorced; children: Lara and Alex Jakubowski; m. Gerald S. Lazarus, Apr. 7, 1990. BA, Seton Hill Coll., Greensburg, Pa., 1964; PhD, SUNY, Buffalo, 1975. Assoc. dir. U.S. regulatory affairs Westwood Pharms., Buffalo, 1980-83, dir. U.S. regulatory affairs, 1983-86; dir. internat. regulatory affairs Bristol Myers Co., Wallingford, Conn., 1986-89; exec. dir. regulatory affairs DuPont Merck Pharm. Co., Wilmington, Del., 1989-94, v.p. world wide regulatory affairs, 1994—; postdoctoral fellow Buffalo Children's Hosp., 1978-80, Roswell Park Meml. Inst., Buffalo, 1975-78. Contbr. articles to profl. jours. Mem. Drug Info. Assn., Regulatory Affairs Profl. Soc., PMA Regulatory Affairs Com. (steering com.), Sigma Xi. Home: 2027 Spruce St Philadelphia PA 19103-5623 Office: DuPont Merck Pharm Co Barley Mill Plz # 27 Wilmington DE 19880

JAKUS, STEPHANIE, writer, composer, musician, instructor; b. Melrose Park, Ill., Nov. 8, 1926; d. Victor and Anna (Yutelis) Novicky; div.; children: Aldie, Larry. MusB in Piano, Chgo. Musical Coll., 1950; MusM in Music Composition, Am. Conservatory Music, 1961; studied piano with Ruth Wilkins Tyer, Howard Wells, Margery Giles, Mollie Margolies, studied theory and composition with Rosseter G. Cole, Leo Sowerby, studied musicology with Hans Rosenwald. Journalist Garfield News and Austinite, Chgo., 1946; piano accompanist Stone Camryn Sch. of Dance, Chgo., 1947-50, Charlene Rose Sch. Dance, River Forest, Ill., 1951-54; co-prodr., dir. Backyard Frolics, River Forest, 1959-61; piano tchr. River Forest, 1947-75; journalist Oak Leaves, Oak Park, Ill., 1968-70; free lance writer Cherry Circle Mag., Chgo., 1970-75; freelance writer various mags., 1975—; mem. adv. coun. St. Paul Fed. Music Contests, Chgo., 1977-79. Author: Alone...Woman in Maturity, 1978, The Sick Society Part 1 - The Medical Profession, The Courtship of Mary Todd (play); composer musical: In the Park; composer various art songs, pop songs, vocal and theatrical songs, chamber music, orchestral music, piano theory, piano concerto, piano solos, arrangements for young piano students, four players at 1 piano, 2 pianos. Vol. Dem. Senators Adlai Stevenson, Ted Leverenz, River Forest, 1974, Dem. Senator Alan Cranston, Forest Park, 1983; v.p., dir. MacDowell Artists Assn., Oak Park, 1952-60; leader Com. to Join Triton Coll., River Forest, 1970; sec., treas. Soc. Am. Musicians, Chgo., 1975-80. Named 1st Place winner in piano Chgo. Tribune Music Festival, 1946, 1st Place winner for play on A. Lincoln, Ill. Sesquicentennial, 1968. Ecumenical Ch. Home and Office: 918 La Costa Cir # 1 Sarasota FL 34237

JALALI, BEHNAZ, psychiatrist, educator; b. Mashad, Iran, Jan. 26, 1944; came to U.S., 1968; d. Badiolah and Bahieh (Shahidi) Samimy; m. Mehrdad Jalali, Sept. 18, 1968. MD, Tehran (Iran) U., 1968. Rotating intern

Burlington County Meml. Hosp., Mt. Holly, N.J., 1968-69; resident in psychiatry U. Md. Hosp., Balt., 1970-73; asst. prof. psychiatry dept. psychiatry Sch. Medicine Rutgers U., Piscataway, N.J., 1973-76, Yale U., New Haven, Conn., 1976-81; assoc. clin. prof. psychiatry Yale U., New Haven, 1981-85; assoc. clin. prof. psychiatry dept. psychiatry UCLA, 1985-94, clin. prof. psychiatry dept. psychiatry Sch. Medicine, 1994—; dir. psychotherapy Sch. Medicine Rutgers U., Piscataway, 1973-76; dir. family therapy unit dept. psychiatry Yale U., New Haven, 1976-85; chief clin. svcs., mental health clin. coord., med. student educator West L.A. VA Hosp., 1987—. Author: (with others) Ethnicity and Family Therapy, 1982, Clinical Guidlines in Cross-Cultural Mental Health, 1988; contbr. articles to profl. jours. Fellow Am. Psychiatric Assn., Am. Orthopsychiatry Assn., Am. Assn. Social Psychiatry; mem. Am. Family Therapy Assn., So. Calif. Psychiatric Assn. (chair com. for women 1992), World Fedn. Mental Health. Home: 1203 Roberto Ln Los Angeles CA 90077 Office: UCLA Dept Psychiatry West LA VAMC MHC B116912 11301 Wilshire Blvd Los Angeles CA 90073

JAMES, AMABEL BOYCE, freelance writer; b. Balt., Oct. 13, 1952; d. John Cowman George and Barbara Allen (Cobb) Boyce; m. Hamilton Evans James, Aug. 25, 1973; children: Meredith Evans, Rebecca Lee, Hamilton Boyce. AB, Wellesley Coll., 1974. Chartered fin. analyst, 1981. Systems analyst John Hancock Mut. Life Ins. Co., Boston, 1974-75; asst. buyer Lord & Taylor, N.Y.C., 1975; economist Lionel D. Edie, N.Y.C., 1977, E.F. Hutton & Co., N.Y.C., 1978-79, Schroder Capital Mgmt., N.Y.C., 1979-82; freelance writer N.Y.C., 1984—; cons. Keck & Co., N.Y.C., 1984. Editor, contbr. author numerous articles to popular mags., newsletters. Vol. Jr. League City of N.Y., 1975—; bd. dirs. Friends Henry St. Settlement House, 1977-80, Voluntary Assn. for Sr. Citizen Activities, 1984—, pres., 1994-95; cum laude spkr. Garrison Forest Sch., 1993. Named Margaret Brand Smih lectr. So. Meth. U. Sch. Continuing Edn., 1980. Mem. N.Y. Soc. Security Analysts/Fin. Analyst Fedn., River Club of N.Y.C., Colony Club, Tokeneke Club, Wee Burn Country Club. Republican. Episcopalian. Home and Office: 1001 Park Ave New York NY 10028-0935 Home: 51 Contentment Island Darien CT 06820 Also: Wequetonsing MI 49740

JAMES, ANTOINETTE MARY, economics educator; b. Brockton, Mass., Nov. 10, 1960; d. Richard William and Claire Annette (Wallace) J. BS in Resource Econs. cum laude, U. Vt., 1982; MS in Agrl. and Natural Resource Econs., Colo. State U., 1984; PhD in Econs., U. N.H., 1993. Instr. U. N.H., 1991-92, 93; asst. prof. econs. Randolph-Macon Woman's Coll., 1993—; bd. dirs. Tacomis Fed. Credit Union, Washington, treas., 1986, pres. 1987-88. Contbr. articles to profl. jours. Democrat. Roman Catholic. Office: Dept Econs Randolph Macon Womans Coll 2500 Rivermont Ave Lynchburg VA 24503

JAMES, BARBARA WOODWARD, small business owner, interior designer, antique appraiser, consultant; b. Owensboro, Ky., Feb. 14, 1936; d. J.T. and Thelma (Newman) Woodward; m. William E. James, Feb. 19, 1951 (div. June 1953); 1 child, Keith Douglas. Vice pres., Fla. Containers Inc., Sebring, 1978-81; v.p. Libra Ltd., 1980-88, Barda Svcs. Inc., Tampa, Fla., 1981-87; v.p., gen. mgr., owner BJ's Lounge of Tampa, Inc., 1981-86; founder, owner Flamingo Bar and Grill, Clearwater, Fla., 1986-89, BJ's Lounge, Tampa, 1989-94, The Clique, 1994—. Democrat. Roman Catholic.

JAMES, CLARITY (CAROLYNE FAYE JAMES), mezzo-soprano; b. Wheatland, Wyo., Apr. 27, 1945; d. Ralph Everett and Gladys Charlotte (Johnson) J. Mus.B., U. Wyo., 1964; Mus.M., Ind. U., 1967. Cert. instr. Radiance Technique. Assoc. prof. voice Radford (Va.) U., 1990—; asst. prof. voice U. Iowa, Iowa City, 1968-72. Debut in opera as Madame Flora in: The Medium, St. Paul Opera, 1971; also sang role with Houston Grand Opera, 1972, Opera Theatre St. Louis, 1976, Augusta (Ga.) Opera Co., 1976; N.Y.C. Opera debut as Baroness in: The Young Lord, 1973; N.Y.C. Opera debut as Widow Begbick in Mahogonny, Opera Co. of Boston, 1973; created role Mother Rainey in: The Sweet Bye and Bye, 1973; Mrs. G. in: Captain Jinks, 1976; Mrs. Cratchit in A Christmas Carol (Musgrave), 1979; created Mrs. Doc in world premiere of A Quiet Place (Leonard Bernstein), Houston, 1983; debut Chgo. Lyric Opera, 1983, Vienna Staatsoper, 1986, National Symphony, 1986, Phila. Orch., 1986; numerous appearances with opera cos. throughout U.S. and fgn. countries including, Dallas Civic Opera, Cin. Opera Co., Netherlands Opera, Amsterdam, Florentine Opera. Rec. artist. Martha Baird Rockefeller grantee; Met.; Opera Assn. grantee; recipient Lillian Garabedian award Santa Fe Opera, 1967; Corbett Found. grantee, 1968; named Young Artist Nat. Fedn. Music Clubs, 1972. Office: Radford U Dept Music Radford VA 24142

JAMES, CLAUDIA ANN, business educator and trainer, motivational speaker; b. Kansas City, Mo., July 23, 1948; d. Claude Jr. and Edna Mae (Henderson) Hinton; m. Wavy L. James, Oct. 21, 1967 (dec. Apr. 1991); children: Edward Allan, Sheryl Evonne. AA, Maple Woods C.C., Kansas City, Mo., 1987; BSE cum laude, Mo. Western State Coll., St. Joseph, 1989. Fin. sec. EBC, Kansas City, Mo., 1977-87; instr. Capital City Bus. Coll., Kansas City, Mo., 1989-90, Career Point Bus. Sch., Kansas City, Mo., 1990-91; owner James Ednl. Meetings/Seminars, Kansas City, Mo., 1992—; instr. Am. Mgmt. Assn., 1993—, Mo. Western State Coll., St. Joseph, 1993—, Independence (Mo.) Sch. Dist., Park Hill Sch. Dist., Kansas City, Mo., North Kansas City Sch. Dist., 1993—, Maple Woods C.C., Kansas City, 1990—, Johnson County C.C., Overland Park, Kans., 1994—; guest spkr. on radio and TV. Mentor WNET-SBA, Kansas City, 1992—. Higgs Art scholar, 1987. Mem. Home Bus. Connection (v.p. 1994), Mo. Home Based Bus. Assn. (pres. 1994—), Clay County Women's Exch. (networking chair 1993—), Platte County Women's Exch., Kansas City C. of C., Mo. Western State Coll. Alumni Assn., Kappa Delta Phi. Democrat. Baptist. Office: James Ednl Meetings/Seminar 1001 NE 86th St Kansas City MO 64155

JAMES, DOT (DOROTHY ANN JAMES), researcher, writer, fund-raiser, editor; b. San Antonio, Sept. 14, 1938; d. Royal Percy and Eloise (Ohlen) J. BA in History, So. Meth. U., 1960; MA in Edn., Stanford U., 1962; postgrad., U. San Francisco, 1984-85, U. Santa Cruz, 1987-88. Cert. in secondary edn., Calif., human svcs. counseling. Mgmt. analyst Dept. of Navy, Treasure Island, Calif., 1963-65; tchr. pub. high sch. Gilroy, Calif., 1965-69, Caldwell, Idaho, 1969-71; editor in chief Venus mag., Palo Alto, Calif., 1973-75; ptnr., chief exec. officer F.S. Button Mfg. Co., San Jose, Calif., 1975-83; exec. dir. AIDS Found. of Santa Clara County, San Jose, Calif., 1983-84; free-lance mgmt. cons. and writer San Jose, 1984—; office mgr. Adult Independence Devel. Ctr., Santa Clara, Calif., 1987; dir. vols. Emergency Housing Consortium, San Jose, 1987-88; coord. community devel. Shelter Against Violent Environments (S.A.V.E.), Fremont, Calif., 1988; with devel. office Santa Clara U., 1988-90; prin. Paladin Editorial Svcs., San Jose, 1990—. Designer/mfr. feminist slogan buttons housed in Women's Collection, Smithsonian Inst., Washington; contbr. monographs and articles to profl. pubs. Active various women's rights, environ., animal welfare, orgns. for developmentally and physically disabled, gay rights, pub. health groups, 1962—; bd. dirs. Aris Project, Campbell, Calif., 1987-88; crisis intervention counselor Suicide Crisis Svc. of Santa Clara County, San Jose; commr. City of San Jose Human Rights Commn. Grantee Nat. Def. Edn. Act, 1967, Coe Found., 1969; Nonprofit Orgn. Mgmt. Inst. scholar, 1984. Mem. Stanford Bay Area Profl. Women, Nat. Soc. of Fundraising Execs., Santa Clara County Hist. and Geneal. Soc. Democrat.

JAMES, ELIZABETH JOAN PLOGSTED, pediatrician, educator; b. Jefferson City, Mo., Jan. 15, 1939; d. Joseph Matthew Plogsted and Maxie Pearl (Manford) Plogsted Acuff; m. Ronald Carney James, Aug. 25, 1962; children: Susan Elizabeth, Jason Michael. BS in Chemistry, Lincoln U., 1960; MD, U. Mo., 1965. Diplomate Am. Bd. Pediatrics, Am. Bd. Neonatal-Perinatal Medicine. Resident physician pediatrics U. Mo. Hosps. & Clinics, Columbia, 1965-68, fellow in neonatology, 1968-69; dir. neonatal-perinatal medicine Children's Hosp. U. Mo. Hosps. & Clinics, 1971—; fellow in neonatal-perinatal medicine U. Colo. Hosps., Denver, 1969-71; from asst. to assoc. prof. pediatrics and obstetrics sch. medicine U. Mo., 1971-83, prof. child health and obstetrics, 1983—; dir. med. student edn. program dept. child health sch. medicine U. Mo., Columbia, 1989—. Mem. editl. bd. Mo. Medicine, 1983—; contbr. chpts. to books and articles to profl. jours. Fellow Am. Acad. Pediatrics (sect. neonatal-perinatal medicine); mem. Mo. State Med. Assn., Boone County Med. Soc., Alpha Omega Alpha. Roman Catholic. Office: U Mo Hosps & Clinics Children's Hosp 1 Hospital Dr Columbia MO 65212

JAMES, GENEVA BEHRENS, secondary school educator; b. Marietta, Minn., Mar. 23, 1942; d. Siegfried and Dora (Schoenrock) Behrens; BS, Mankato State U., 1963; m. Howard James, Aug. 2, 1963; children: Scott, Dawn. Tchr. English high schs., Minn., 1964-65; instr. acctg., Adult Continuing Edn., Bellevue, Nebr., 1971-75, dir. Adult Basic Edn. Ctr., 1974-91, vol. coordinator, 1983-91, instr. secondary schs., 1980—, instr. computer literacy, 1984-91; Pilot Computer Program, 1987-88, seminar presenter Nebr. State Adult Edn. Assn., 1986, Commn. on Adult Basic Edn., 1987; mem. review bd. English curriculum, 1985-86, Bellevue (Nebr.) Pub. Schs. Computer Utilization Com., 1992—; mem. adv. bd. adult edn., 1993—. Mem. exec. com. Boy Scouts Am., 1974-80; mem. metro community PLUS task force, 1986-88. Mem. AAUW, Nat. Assn. Public and Continuing Adult Edn., Adult and Continuing Edn. Assn. Nebr., NEA, Nat. Council Tchrs. English, WHAR Investment Club (pres.), Alpha Delta Kappa (chmn. scholarship com. 1985-86, 91—). Republican. Lutheran. Home: 1314 Hansen Ave Bellevue NE 68005-3016 Office: Bellevue West High Sch 1501 Thurston Ave Bellevue NE 68005

JAMES, GRACIE MAE, public health administrator; b. Pine Bluff, Ark., Nov. 30, 1952; d. William Henry James and Parlee (Cook) Taylor. BA, U. Ark., Pine Bluff, 1973; MA, Ohio State U., 1974. Substitute tchr. Columbus (Ohio) Pub. Schs., 1974; instr. Clemson (S.C.) U., 1975-77, Tri-County Tech. Coll., Pendleton, S.C., 1976-77; teaching assoc. Ohio State U., Columbus/Mansfield, 1977-82; vis. instr. Denison U., Granville, Ohio, 1981; social program developer Ohio Dept. Health, Columbus, 1982-84, info. mgr., 1984-87, health planning adminstr., 1988—; freelance actor/announcer various orgns., Ohio and vicinity, 1982—; grad. rep. Ohio State Union Bd., Columbus, 1980-82. Author: (one act play) Missing You, 1986; contbg. author: (plays) This Is Not a Test, 1985, Our Target Is, 1987, Ornaments, 1987. Inagural mem. Columbus Symphony Cmty. Choir, 1990; bd. mem. Columbus Nat. Theatre, 1988-89. Named Outstanding Supporting Actress Little Theatre Off Broadway, Grove City, Ohio, 1985, Ctr. Stage Theatre, Columbus, 1986, Outstanding Young Woman in Am. Ohio Ho. of Reps., Columbus, 1983. Mem. AFTRA. Office: Ohio Dept Health 246 N High St Columbus OH 43266-0588

JAMES, JEANNETTE ADELINE, state legislator, accountant; b. Maquoketa, Iowa, Nov. 19, 1929; d. Forest Claude and Winona Adeline (Meyers) Nims; m. James Arthur James, Feb. 16, 1948; children: James Arthur Jr., Jeannette, Alice Marie. Student, Merritt Davis Sch. Commerce, Salem, Oreg., 1956-57. Payroll supr. Gen. Foods Corp., Woodburn, Oreg., 1956-66; cost acctg., inventory control clk. Pacific Fence & Wire Co., Portland, Oreg., 1966-67, office mgr., 1968-69; substitute rural carrier U.S. Post Office, Woodburn, 1967-68; owner, mgr., acct. and tax preparer James Bus. Svc., Goldendale, Wash., 1969-75, Anchorage, 1975-77, Fairbanks, Alaska, 1977-94; mem. Alaska Ho. of Reps., Juneau, 1993—; workshop and seminar leader, 1989-91; instr. workshop Comm. Dynamics, 1988. Vice chmn. Klickitat County Dems., Goldendale, 1970-74; bd. dirs. Mus. and Art Inst., Anchorage, 1976-80; pres. Anchorage Internat. Art Inst., 1976-78; chmn. platting bd. Fairbanks North Star Borough, 1980-84, mem. Planning Commn., 1984-87; treas., vice chmn. 18th Dist. Reps., North Pole, Alaska, 1984-92; mem. City of North Pole Econ. Devel. Com., 1992-93. Mem. Internat. Tgn. in Comm. (winner speech contest 1981, 86), North Pole C. of C., Emblem Club, Rotary (treas. North Pole 1990), Eagles, Women of Moose. Presbyterian. Home: 3068 Badger Rd North Pole AK 99705

JAMES, JULIE ANN, congressional staff member; b. Evergreen Park, Ill., July 9, 1949; d. Arthur George and Franca (Zecchi) Christenson; m. Alvin Clark James Jr., Oct. 11, 1969; children: Sara, Laura, Elizabeth. Student, Pitzer Coll., 1967-68; BA, Oreg. State U., 1970; postgrad., Portland State U., 1972-78, Lewis & Clark, 1990-91. Rsch. asst. Kaiser Found. Health Svcs. Rsch. Ctr., Portland, Oreg., 1968-73; assoc. dir. Northwest Oreg. Health Systems, Portland, Oreg., 1973-77, Oreg. Cancer Ctr., Portland, Oreg., 1977-78; ind. cons. Bend, Oreg., 1990-91; minority profl. staff mem., congressional staff Com. on Fin., U.S. Senate, Washington, 1991—; mem. appeals bd. Oreg. Cert. of Need, Salem, Oreg., 1985-88; coun. mem. Oreg. Health Coun., Salem, Oreg., 1981-89. Chmn. bd. Deschutes County Libr. Bd., Bend, Oreg., 1987-91; mem. sch. bd. Bend-Lapine Sch., Bend, Oreg., 1988-89. Office: Finance Com 203 Hart Senate Office Bldg Washington DC 20510

JAMES, KAY LOUISE, management consultant, healthcare executive; b. Little Rock, Feb. 13, 1948; d. Charles Robert and Mary Virginia (Morgan) J. BA, Vanderbilt U., 1970; MBA, U. Chgo., 1986. Diplomate Am. Coll. Healthcare Execs.; CPA, Ill., Mo. Mgr. Wallace Community Mental Health Ctr., Nashville, 1973-78; sr. cons. Ernst & Whinney, Washington, 1978-79; sr. cons. Ernst & Whinney, Chgo., 1979-81, mgr., 1981-84; dir. Am. Hosp. Supply Corp., Evanston, Ill., 1984-85; mgr. Am. Hosp. Supply Fin. Corp., Evanston, 1985-86; sr. mgr. KPMG Peat Marwick, Kansas City, Mo., 1986-89, ptnr., 1989-92; ptnr. Katz, James & Assocs., Inc., Plymouth Meeting, Pa., 1992-93; pres. James Mgmt. Assocs., Inc., Nashville, 1994—; speaker healthcare topics various grad. programs and profl. assns.; mem. Women's Leadership Forum of Dem. Nat. Com. Reviewer The Coming Home Program, San Francisco, 1993. Mem. AICPA, Am. Hosp. Assn., Med. Group Mgmt. Assn., Healthcare Fin. Mgmt. Assn. Democrat. Office: James Mgmt Assocs 3200 W End Ave Ste 500 Nashville TN 37203-1322

JAMES, LESLIE, communications executive; b. Salt Lake City, June 30, 1964; d. Marlynn Rees and Jane Marie (Brown) J. Student, Brigham Young U., 1983-87; BS, U. No. Colo., 1989. Sales rep. Sprint Comm., Denver, 1990-92; account mgr. Sprint Comm., Salt Lake City, 1992—. Mem. Ams. Freedom Festival, Provo, Utah, 1992, 94. Mem. AAUW, Am. Mgmt. Assn., Utah Industry Tech. Assn., Utah Telecomm. Mktg. Assn., Provo/Orem C. of C. Republican. Mem. LDS Ch. Office: Sprint Comm 560 E 200 S # 250 Salt Lake City UT 84102-2021

JAMES, MAGNA M., psychologist; b. Curacao, Netherlands Antilles, Mar. 23, 1961; came to U.S., 1962; d. Everard and Sarah Lilia (Adolph) J. BA in Psychology, Oakwood Coll, 1982; MA in Psychology, Ohio State U., 1984, PhD in Psychology, 1988. Lic. psychologist, Ala. Grad. teaching assoc. Ohio State U., Columbus, 1984-86; counseling fellow Ga. State U., Atlanta, 1986-87; prof. U. Tenn., Chattanooga, 1987-89, counselor, 1989-94; prof. psychology Oakwood Coll., Huntsville, Ala., 1989-94; pvt. practice Jonesboro, Ga., 1994—. Past mem. Big Bros. Big Sisters Orgn., 1991-92. Recipient Rsch. award Sears Roebuck Co., 1990. Mem. APA (minority fellow 1982-85), Assn. Social and Behavioral Scientists, Southeastern Psychol. Assn. Seventh-day Adventist. Office: Affiliated Counseling Svcs 7099 Tara Blvd Jonesboro GA 30236

JAMES, MARIE MOODY, clergywoman, musician, vocal music educator; b. Chgo., Jan. 23, 1928; d. Frank and Mary (Portis) Moody; m. Johnnie James, May 25, 1968. B Music Edn., Chgo. Music Coll., 1949; MusM, Roosevelt U., 1969, MA, 1976; DD, Internat. Bible Inst. and Sem., Plymouth, Fla., 1985. Ordained to ministry Pentecostal Ch., 1976; cert. vocal music tchr., Ill. Key punch operator Dept. Treasury, Chgo., 1950-52; tchr. Posen-Robbins Bd. Edn., Robbins, Ill., 1952-59; tchr. vocal music Englewood High Sch., Chgo., 1964-84; music counselor Head Start, Chgo., 1965-66; exec. dir. House of Love DayCare, 1983, 88, Mary P. Moody Christian Acad., 1989, supt., 1989; dir. Handbell Choir for Srs. Maple Park United Meth. Ch., 1988-92. Composer, arranger choral music: Hide Me, 1963, Christmas Time, 1980, Come With Us, Our God Will Do Thee Good, 1986, The Indiana House, 1987, Behold, I Will Do a New Thing, 1989, Glory and Honor, 1992. Organist Allen Temple A.M.E. Ch., 1941-45; asst. organist Choppin A.M.E. Ch., 1945-49; organist-dir. Progressive Ch. of God in Christ, Maywood, Ill., 1950-60; missionary Child Evangelism Fellowship, Chgo., 1955-63; unit leader YWCA, New Buffalo, Mich., 1956-58; min. of music God's House of All Nations, Chgo., 1960-80; pastor God's House of Love, Prayer and Deliverance, Robbins, 1982—; chmn. Frank and Mary Moody Scholarship Com., 1984—; dir. music Christian Women's Ourtreach Ministry, 1984-88; mem. Robbins Community Coun., 1987-88; camp counselor Abraham Lincoln Ctr., 1951-53. Coppin A.M.E. Ch. scholar, 1946. Mem. Music Educators Nat. Conf., Good News Club (tchr. 1987-90, Robbins, Ill.). Home: 8154 S Indiana Ave Chicago IL 60619-4712

JAMES, MARILYN SHAW, secondary education educator, social service worker; b. Chgo., Apr. 6, 1926; d. Harry and Louise A. (Milkey) Shaw; m. Eugene Nelson James, June 17, 1950; children: Jim, Mark, Katherine, Caroline. BS, Carthage Coll., 1947; MA, U. Iowa, 1954. Tchr. home econs. Highland Park (Ill.) High Sch., 1947-50, Hampshire (Ill.) High Sch., 1950-51; instr. home econs. No. Ill. U., DeKalb, 1963-65; tchr. Winkie Bear, Sycamore, Ill., 1970-71; sub. tchr. DeKalb and Sycamore Sch. Dists., 1969—, Hinckley-Big Rock, Ill., 1973-80; homemaker coord. Family Svc. Agy., DeKalb, 1980-88. Stage mgr. Stage Coach Players, DeKalb, 1954—; moderator First Congl. Ch., DeKalb, 1983-84; v.p. Kishwaukee Symphony Assocs., 1988-90, pres., 1990, mem. adv. com. on elder concerns, 1991—; bd. dirs. Family Svc. Agy., DeKalb, 1971-79. Named Stage Coacher of Yr., Stage Coach Players, 1990. Mem. AAUW (v.p., scholar 1980, 1990, 93, 94), LWV (legis. chairperson 1983), DeKalb County Home Economists, DeKalb Drama Club (pres. 1986-87), Univ. Women's Club (pres. 1991), Family Svc. Aux. (v.p.), DeKalb Women's Club. Democrat. Home: 212 Tilton Park Dr DeKalb IL 60115-1942 Office: Family Svc Agy 3131 Sycamore Rd De Kalb IL 60115

JAMES, MARY LYNN, financial analyst; b. Tulsa, July 16, 1949; d. Earl Wilder Drake Jr. and Sarah Mary Truscott; m. Wilburn Dwight James, June 14, 1975; 1 child, Peter Allen. Student, Okla. State U., 1967-68, Am. Christian Coll., 1972-73; AS, Tulsa Jr. Coll., 1989; BBA Fin., Northeastern Okla. State U., Tulsa, 1993. Various positions First Nat. Bank and Trust Co., Tulsa, 1968-69; sec. State Dept. of Vocat./Tech. Edn., Stillwater, Okla., 1969-71; legal sec. Jacobus, Green and Eldridge, Tulsa, 1973-75; asst. br. mgr. Republic Bank, Tulsa, 1975-76; sr. asst. treasury Parker Drilling Co., Tulsa, 1980-81; analyst Amoco Corp./Amoco Prodn. Co., Houston, Tulsa, 1981-94; tchr., facilitator/trainer Amoco Corp., Tulsa, 1989-94. Author poem. Pres. Lioness (Women's Assn. as Aux. to Lions Club Am.), Sugarland, Tex., 1983-84, v.p., 1982-83; sec. Young Reps., Stillwater, Okla., 1967-70; pres., leader Boy Scouts Am., Tulsa, Broken Arrow, Okla., 1975-81, sr. class advisor Dulles High Sch., Sugarland, 1984; mem. asset and liability com. to bd. dirs. Red Crown Fed. Credit Union. Named Outstanding Achievement Centennial Celebration, Amoco Corp., 1989. Mem. Univ. Cen. Tulsa Fin. Assn. (charter, advisor), Nat. Mktg. Assn., Am. Bus. Women's Assn. (bd. dirs.), Amoco Golf Assn. (bd. dirs.).

JAMES, MARY SPENCER, nursing administrator; b. London, Ont., Can., July 10, 1949; d. Richard Spencer and Helen Frances (Winterbottom) James; m. Robert Peter Owler, Oct. 4, 1969 (div. June 25, 1975). AA, Norwich U., 1969; Nursing Diploma, Toronto (Ont.) Gen. Hosp., 1973; BA in Psychology, U. Vt., 1975. RN, Calif. Staff nurse Toronto Gen. Hosp., 1973-77, Stanford (Calif.) U. Hosp., 1977-81, B.C. Children's Hosp., Vancouver, 1981-83; sr. staff nurse King Abdul Aziz Mil. Hosp., Tabuk, Saudi Arabia, 1983-84, Charter Med. Ltd./Tawam Hosp., Al Ain, Abu Dhabi, UAE, 1984-87; nurse Dubai Petroleum Co., UAE, 1987-88; nursing dir. Ygia Polyclinic, Limassol, Cyprus, 1988-89; nurse Stat Travelers, Inc., L.A., 1990-91; staff nurse Lucile Salter Packard Children's Hosp. at Stanford, Palo Alto, Calif., 1991-92; field nurse H.S.S.I. Home Care and Olsten Healthcare, Milbrae and San Francisco, 1992-93; nursing dir. CHS Home Health Agy., San Francisco, 1993-94; liaison nurse coord. United Nursing Internat., San Francisco, 1994—. Home: 500 Beale St Apt 407 San Francisco CA 94105-2030

JAMES, SANDRA MAY, journalist; b. Kingston, Jamaica, Apr. 16, 1954; d. Adolphos James and Winnifred Broderick Pantaleo. BS, Hunter Coll., 1979; MS, Columbia U., 1981. Staff writer Paterson (N.J.) News, 1982-83, Gannett Westchester, N.Y., 1983-87, Hartford (Conn.) Courant, 1987—; editor West Indian Am. Newspaper, Hartford, 1991—. Mem. West Indian Social Club (pub. rels. 1990-91).

JAMES, VIRGINIA LYNN, contracts executive; b. March AFB, Calif., Feb. 6, 1952; d. John Edward and Azella Virginia (Morrill) Anderson; children: Raymond Edward, Jerry Glenn Jr. Student, Sinclair Community Coll., 1981-83, U. Tex., San Antonio, 1980, Redlands U., 1986, San Diego State U., 1994. With specialized contracting USAF, Wright-Patterson AFB, Ohio, 1973-77; with logistics contracting USAF, Kelly AFB, Tex., 1977-81; contract specialist USAF, Wright-Patterson AFB, Ohio, 1981-84; spl. asst. Peace Log, Tehran, Iran, 1977; acting chief of contracts cruise missile program Gen. Dynamics/Convair, San Diego, 1984-86; contracts mgr. VERAC, Inc., San Diego, 1986-90, Gen. Dynamics, San Diego, 1990-92; mgr. contracts Scientific-Atlanta, San Diego, 1992-93; dir. contracts GreyStone, San Diego, 1993—; cons. Gen. Dynamics, San Diego, 1985, Efratrom, 1986. Mem. Nat. Assn. Female Execs., Nat. Mgmt. Assn., Nat. Contract Mgmt. Assn. Republican. Office: GreyStone Tech 15010 Ave of Science Ste 200 San Diego CA 92128

JAMES, VIRGINIA SCOTT, elementary school educator; b. Mobile, Ala., Feb. 5, 1955; d. Timothy Varian and Sarah (Watts) Scott; m. Jeffery Thomas Heathcock, June 7, 1980 (widowed, July 1988); m. Colvin Jerome James, Mar. 22, 1991. BS, Mobile Coll., 1978; grad. in pub. speaking, Dale Carnegie Sch., 1978. Cert. tchr. grades kindergarten through 8, Ala. Tchr. grades 1 and 2 Cypress Shores Christian Sch., Mobile, 1983-84; tchr. grade 2 Irvington Christian Sch., Mobile, 1984-85; early intervention tchr. reading and math. grades 1 through 8 Riggins Elem. Sch., Birmingham, Ala., 1985—. Sponsor various 3rd through 5th grade Just Say No Clubs, Riggins Elem. Sch., 1986—; choir Warrior United Meth. Ch. Mem. Ala. Edn. Assn., Birmingham Edn. Assn., Birmingham Area Reading Coun., Ala. Classroom Tchrs. (social dir. Birmingham chpt. 1991-92). Methodist. Home: 3680 Goblers Knob Rd Warrior AL 35180-3118

JAMES, VIRGINIA STOWELL, retired elementary education educator; b. New Britain, Conn., July 9, 1926; d. Austin Leavitt and Doris Carolyn Stowell; m. William Hall James, June 24, 1950; 1 child, Hillery. BA, Middlebury Coll., 1947; MA, Yale U., 1955; PhD, U. Conn., 1988. Cert. tchr. Elem. tchr. Bd. Edn., Westport, Conn., 1950-58; art tchr. grades 6-9 Wallingford (Conn.) Bd. Edn., tchr. gifted/talented grades 4-5, kindergarten, 1958-91; ret., 1991. Contbr. articles to profl. jours. Mem. NEA, AAUW, ASCD, Nat. Art Edn. Assn., Nat. Assn. for Gifted Children, Conn. Assn. for the Gifted, Conn. Edn. Assn., Phi Delta Kappa, Pi Lambda Theta, Delta Kappa Gamma. Address: PO Box 234 Northford CT 06472

JAMESON, DOROTHEA, sensory neuroscientist; b. Newton, Mass., Nov. 16, 1920; d. Robert and Josephine (Murray) Jameson; B.A., Wellesley Coll., 1942; M.A. (hon.), U. Pa., 1973, DSc (hon.) SUNY, 1989; m. Leo M. Hurvich, Oct. 23, 1948. Research asst. Harvard, 1941-47; research psychologist Eastman Kodak Co., Rochester, N.Y., 1947-57; research scientist N.Y.U., 1957-62; vis. scientist Venezuelan Inst. Sci. Research, 1965; research asso. to prof. Psychol. and Inst. Neurol. Scis., U. Pa., 1962-74, Univ. prof. U. Pa., 1975—; vis. prof. Center Visual Sci., U. Rochester, 1974, Columbia U., 1974-76, fall 1986; vis. com. of bd. overseers Harvard U., 1989—; cons. in field. Mem. Nat. Adv. Eye Council, NIH, 1985-89; corp. bd. Woods Hole Oceanographic Inst., 1978-84, 85-91, life mem., 1991—; U.S. Nat. Com. Internat. U. Psychol. Scis., 1985-91; Nat. Acad. Sci.-NCR Commn. on Human Resources, 1977-80, chmn. com. on vision, 1980-81; mem. rsch. & evaluation com. The Lighthouse, 1993—. Recipient I.H. Godlove award Inter-Soc. Color Council, 1973; Alumnae Achievement award Wellesley Coll., 1974; Deane B. Judd award Assn. Internationale 'de Couleur, 1985; Hermann von Helmholtz award Cognitive Neurosci. Inst., 1987; fellow Center for Advanced Study in the Behavioral Scis., 1981-82. Fellow AAAS, Soc. Exptl. Psychologists (Howard Crosby Warren medal 1971), Am. Psychol. Assn. (Disting. Sci. Contbn. award 1972), Am. Acad. Arts and Scis., Optical Soc. Am. (Tillyer medal 1982); mem. NAS (com. on human rights 1994—), Am. Psychol. Soc. (William James fellow 1989), Assn. Research in Vision and Ophthalmology, Internat. Brain Research Orgn., Internat. Research Group Color Vision Deficiencies, N.Y. Acad. Sci., Psychonomic Soc., Soc. Neurosci., Sigma Xi. Co-author: The Perception of Brightness and Darkness, 1966; co-author introduction and English translation: Outlines of a Theory of the Light Sense, 1964 (E. Hering); co-editor, author chpt.; Visual Psychophysics: Handbook of Sensory Physiology, Vol. VII/4, 1972; contbr. to History of Psychology in Autobiography, 1989; contbr. articles to profl. jours. Office: U Pa 3815 Walnut St Philadelphia PA 19104-3604

JAMESON, JULIANNE, clinical psychologist; b. L.A., Apr. 22, 1943; d. Walter McClure and Anne Virginia (Walther) J.; m. Russell Larson, Oct. 9, 1970 (div. Mar. 1973). BA, UCLA, 1965; MS, Calif. State U., L.A., 1973; PhD, Calif. Grad. Inst., 1982. Lic. psychologist, Calif. Tchr. L.A. Unified

Sch. Dist., 1965-70; sch. psychologist West Covina (Calif.) Unified Schs., 1973-85; ednl. psychologist, Covina, Calif., 1980—; pvt. practice clin. psychology Covina, 1984—; provider Blue Shield, L.A., 1989—, LifeLink, L.A., 1991—, U.S. Behavioral Health, L.A., 1991—; assessor HelpNet, 1992, PPO Alliance, 1994, CompPsych, 1994. Mem. APA, Calif. State Psychol. Assn. Mem. APA. Office: 750 Terrado Plz Ste 121B Covina CA 91723-3419

JAMESON, PATRICIA MARIAN, government agency administrator; b. Pitts., Mar. 17, 1945; d. Vernon L. and Dorothy Leam (Wilson) J.; B.A., Northwestern U., 1967; M.A., Ohio State U., 1969, with HUD, 1970—, project mgr., Detroit, 1976-77, acting dir. housing mgmt., 1978, dep. area mgr. Milw. Area Office, 1978-85, acting area mgr., 1979-80, 82, regional dir. adminstrn. Chgo. Regional Office, 1985—. Mem. Chgo. Council on Fgn. Relations. Recipient Quality Performance award HUD, 1973, 75, 80, Outstanding Performance award, 1980, 85, 87, 88, 90, 91, 92, 94, Disting. Svc. award 1992; NDEA fellow, 1967-69. Mem. Nat. Assn. Female Execs., NOW, ACLU, Women in Mgmt., Fed. Execs. Inst. Alumni Assn., Phi Beta Kappa, Pi Sigma Alpha. Office: 77 W Jackson Blvd Fl 25 Chicago IL 60604-3511

JAMESON, PAULA ANN, lawyer; b. New Orleans, Feb. 19, 1945; d. Paul Henry and Virginia Lee (Powell) Bailey; children: Paul Andrew, Peter Carver. B.A., La. State U., 1966; J.D., U. Tex., 1969. Bar: Tex. 1969, D.C. 1970, Va., 1973, N.Y. 1978, U.S. Dist. Ct. D.C. 1970, U.S. Dist. Ct. (ea. dist.) Va. 1976, U.S. Ct. Appeals (D.C. cir.) 1972, U.S. Ct. Appeals (4th cir.) 1976, U.S. Ct. Appeals (5th cir.) 1978, U.S. Supreme Ct. 1973, U.S. Ct. Appeals (2d cir.) 1985. Asst. corp. counsel D.C. Corp. Counsel's Office, 1970-73; sr. asst. county atty. Fairfax County Atty.'s Office, Fairfax, Va., 1973-77; atty. Dow Jones & Co., Inc., Princeton, N.J., 1977-79, house counsel, 1979-81, asst. to chmn. bd., 1981-83, house counsel, dir. legal dept., 1983-86; sr. v.p., gen. counsel, corp. sec., PBS, Alexandria, Va., 1986—; bd. dirs. Advanced TV Test Ctr. Inc. Mem. ABA, Fed. Communications Bar Assn., D.C. Bar Assn., N.Y. State Bar Assn., Assn. of Bar of City of N.Y., Am. Pub. TV Prodr. Assn. (chair), Copyright Soc. USA (former trustee). Democrat. Roman Catholic. Office: PBS 1320 Braddock Pl Alexandria VA 22314

JAMESON, PENNY BROOKE, clinical psychologist; b. La Jolla, Calif., Sept. 12, 1942; d. Hubert E. and Betty (Rodolf) Brooke; m. Kenneth Peter Jameson, Jan. 5, 1966; children: Rex, Matthew. BA, Stanford U., 1964; MA, U. Wis., 1969, PhD, 1974. Vol., tchr. Peace Corps, Frankfield, Jamaica, 1964-66; tchr. East Jr.-Sr. High Sch., Madison, Wis., 1966-67; prof. St. Mary's Coll., Notre Dame, Ind., 1971-90; NIMH postdoctoral trainee, rsch. fellow U. Utah, Salt Lake City, 1990-93; clin. psychology intern U. Colo. Sch. Health Scis., Denver, 1993—; cons. Inst. for Internat. Edn., Lima, Peru, 1975. Contbr. articles to profl. jours., chpts. to books. Bd. dirs. various daycare ctrs., South Bend, Ind., 1973-90. Recipient Reinhold Niebuhr award U. Notre Dame, 1982; Maria Pieta award St. Mary's Coll., 1985, Spes Unica award, 1988, Sears leadership award, 1990; Lilly teaching award Lilly Found., 1986;fellow NIMH, 1967-70. Mem. APA, Soc. for Rsch. in Child Devel. Roman Catholic. Office: Colo Psychiat Hosp Div Clin Psychology 4200 E 9th Ave Denver CO 80262

JAMES-ROLLOCKS, ETHLYN A., health facility administrator; b. James Hill, Clarendon, Jamaica, Oct. 12, 1942; d. Herbert Samuel and Birdella (Ferguson) James; m. Hugh W. Rollocks, Feb. 12, 1974; children: Adrian James, Nadia Alexis. S.R.N., Amersham Gen. & High Wycombe, Eng., 1964; Midwifery Pt.I., U. Leeds, Women's Hosp., Eng., 1965; postgrad., Nuffield Maternity Hosp., 1966; BSN magna cum laude, U. Detroit, 1984, MS in Adminstrn., 1986. RN, Mich. Dir. nursing Ford Convalescent Ctr., Highland Park, Mich.; quality assurance coord., audit coord., nursing supr. Kirwood Gen. Hosp., Detroit; supr. nursing Henry Ford Hosp., Detroit, assoc. adminstr. nursing. Mem. adv. bd. Sch. Nursing, U. Detroit, Detroit Pub. Schs.; pres. Ethlyn Rollocks Enterprises Inc.; bd. dirs. St. Christopher House, Detroit, 1992—; lectr. in field. U. Pa. fellow, 1989. Mem. Sigma Theta Tau. Home: 1955 Balmoral Dr Detroit MI 48203-1403

JAMISON, CHERYL LYNETTE, conference planner; b. Chgo., May 26, 1955; d. Louis Jamison and Bertha (McGee) Calvert. BA in psychology, Cedarville Coll., 1976; MEd, U. Mo., 1979. Cert. Conf. Mgr., 1991. Coord., counselor Univ. Mo., Columbia, Mo., 1978-80; rsch. analyst Mo. House of Rep., Jefferson City, 1981-82; communications dir. Wheat for Congress Camp., Kansas City, Mo., 1982; leg. dir. Congressman Alan Wheat, Washington, 1983-84; conf. mgr. Mo. Leg. Black Caucus, Jefferson City, 1985; mgmt. analyst Dept. Consumer & Regulatory Affairs, Washington, 1985-86, Office of Housing Reorganization, Washington, 1986-87; chief materials mgmt. div. Dept. Pub. Assisted Housing, Washington, 1987-91; dir. spl. events Congressional Black Caucus Found., Washington, 1991-93; CEO, ptnr. Better than Perfect Events, Washington, 1993—. Named Supr. of Yr. Dept. Pub. & Assisted Housing, Washington, 1988. Mem. Nat. Coalition of Black Meeting Planners, Black Pub. Rels. Soc. Washington, Women of Washington. Office: Better Than Perfect Events 4516 S Dakota Ave NE Washington DC 20017-2752

JAMISON, JUDITH, dancer; b. Phila., May 10, 1943; d. John J. Student, Fisk U., Phila., Phila. Dance Acad. (now U. of Arts); studied with, Anthony Tudor, John Hines, Delores Brown, John Jones, Joan Kerr, Madame Swaboda. Dancer Alvin Alley's Am. Dance Theatre, N.Y.C., 1965-80; artistic dir. Alvin Ailey's Am. Dance Theatre, N.Y.C., 1990—; dancer, choreographer touring U.S., Europe, Asia, S.Am., Africa, 1980—; formerly with Maurice Hines Dance Sch., N.Y.C.; founder Jamison Project, 1988; vis. disting. prof. Univ. of Arts; guest assoc. artistic dir. 30th ann. tour Alvin Ailey's Am. Dance Theatre, 1990—; guest appearences with Harkness Ballet, Am. Ballet Theatre, San Francisco Ballet, Dallas Ballet. N.Y. dance debut in Agnes DeMille's "The Four Marys", 1965; starring role created for her in Joseph's Legend (John Neumeier), Vienna Opera, Le Spectre de la Rose (Maurice Bejart), Brussels, Paris, N.Y.C.; performed in Maskela Language, 1969, Cry, 1971, Choral Dance, 1971, Mary Lou's Mass, 1971, The Lark Ascending, 1972, The Mooche, 1975, Passage, 1978; star Broadway show Sophisticated Ladies, 1980; choreographer Divining Hymn for Alvin Ailey Am. Dance Theatre, works for Maurice Bejart, Dancers Unltd. Dallas, Washington Ballet, Jennifer Muller/The Works, Alvin Ailey Repertory Ensemble, Ballet Nuevo Mundo de Caracas, also for opera Boito's Mefistofele for Opera Co. Phila.; subject of PBS spl. The Dancemaker; subject of book Aspects of a Dancer; author: Dancing Spirit, 1993. Recipient Dance Mag. award, 1972, Key to the City of N.Y., 1976, Disting. Service award Mayor of N.Y.C., 1982, Disting. Service award Harvard U., 1982, Spirit of Achievement award Nat. Women's Divsn. Yeshiva U. Albert Einstein Coll. Medicine, 1992, Golden Plate award Am. Acad. Achievement, 1993. Address: Alvin Ailey Am Dance Theater 211 W 61st St 3rd Fl New York NY 10023

JAMISON, SUSAN CLAPP, librarian; b. Pitts., Mar. 21, 1929; d. Harlan Luther and Irene Julia (Krause) Clapp; m. Robert Beatty Jamison, Dec. 19, 1947; children: Linda Jamison Larkin, Stephen Robert. BA in History and English, Coll. Staten Island, CUNY, 1971; M.A. in Am. Studies, U. Del., 1972, Am. History, 1974; MLS U. Md., 1979; postgrad. Ind. U. of Pa., 1991—. Bus. asst. Dr. Robert L. Jacobson, 1960-71; real estate sales Walter Reno Watson Agy., Staten Island, N.Y., 1960-63; tchr. Dover High Sch. (Del.), 1973-75; adj. prof. Wilmington Coll., New Castle, Del., 1975—; asst. dir. Dover Pub. Library, 1980-85; dir. Corbit-Calloway Meml. Library, Odessa, Del., 1975-91; grant writer Del. Humanities Forum Coun., Wilmington, 1979-81, mem., 1991—; mem. speakers bur., 1982-83, evaluator, 1978—; pres. Cen. Del. Libr. Consortium, 1982-85. Author: The Face of a Town: the Corbit-Calloway Meml. Library, 1979; author 8 books and programs Yesterday & Today, series 1979-81; contbr. articles to profl. jours; editor and project dir., Six Tricentennial Views of Kent County, 1983-85; author, advisor A Legacy from Del. Women, 1987. Active in Odessa Women's Club, Del., 1975—; host of open house Christmas In Odessa, 1976—; founder, chmn. Septemberfest, 1982; art chmn. Del. Fed. Women's Clubs, 1980-82; publicity chmn. Kent County Tricentennial Commn., Dover, 1983. Recipient Facts on File award for reference pub. ideas, 1985. Mem. ALA (Del. councilor 1989-91), Kent Library Network (v.p. 1982-84, pres. 1984-85), Del. Library Assn. (pres. pub. library div. 1979-81, pres. 1985-86, councilor to ALA 1989-91), Del. Folklife Assn. (treas. 1987-91), Del. Humanities Forum Coun. Home: Starr-Lore House Main St Odessa DE 19730-9999 Office: Corbit-Calloway Meml Libr 2D And High St Odessa DE 19730

JANDA, MARY BETH, accountant; b. Green Bay, Wis., Jan. 6, 1960; d. Alvin Allen and Evelyn Jane (Blotz) J. BBA, U. Wis., Oshkosh, 1982. CPA. Acct. Sentry Ins., Stevens Point, Wis., 1983-86; sr. acct. Am. Family Ins., Madison, Wis., 1986—. Mem. Inst. Mgmt. and Acctg., Jaycees.

JANECEK, LENORE ELAINE, insurance specialist, consultant; b. Chgo., May 2, 1944; d. Morris and Florence (Bear) Picker; M.A.J. in Speech Communications (talent scholar), Northeastern Ill. U., 1972; postgrad. (Ill. Assn. C. of C. Execs. scholar) Inst. for Organizational Mgmt., U. Notre Dame, 1979-80; M.B.A., Columbia Pacific U., 1982; cert. in C. of C. mgmt. U. Colo., 1982; m. John Janecek, Sept. 12, 1964; children: Frank, Michael. Adminstrv. asst., exec. dir. Ill. Mcpl. Retirement Fund, Chgo., 1963-65; personnel mgr. Profile Personnel, Chgo., 1965-68; personnel rep. Marsh Instrument Co., Skokie, Ill., 1971-73; restaurant mgt. Gold Mine Restaurant and What's Cooking Restaurant, Chgo., 1974-76; pres., owner Secretarial Office Services, Chgo., 1976-78; founder, pres. Lincolnwood (Ill.) C. of C. and Industry, 1978-85; pres. Lenore E. Janecek & Assocs., Lincolnwood, 1985—; rep. 10th dist. U.S. C. of C., 1978—; appointee Health Care Reform Task Force, 1992—; apptd. by Pres. Bill Clinton Selective Svc. Bd., 1993—; apptd. by Gov. Jim Edgar Ill. Health Care Cost Containment Coun., 1994—. Mem. mktg. bd. Niles Twp. Sheltered Workshop; pres. Lincolnwood Sch. Dist. 74 Sch. Bd. Caucus; bd. mem., officer, founder Ill. Fraternal Order Police Ladies Aux.; bd. dirs., officer Lincolnwood Girl's Softball League, PTA; bd. dirs. United Way, 1982-83; mem. sch. curriculum com. Lincolnwood Bd. Edn.; appointed by Pres. Reagan to the Selective Svc. Bd., 1983; pres. United Way, Skokie Valley, Ill., 1989; pres., founder Leadership Ill., 1992—, Twp. Coord. and Health Care advisor, Gov. Jim Edgar, Ill., 1990—. Named Disting. Grad. of Yr. Nat. Honor Soc., 1985; chosen one of Top 100 Women Leaders in Am., 1988; recipient Outstanding Woman in Healthcare Mgmt. award Women Health Exec. Network, 1994. Mem. NAFE, Am. Notary Soc., Hadassah. Jewish. Office: 4433 W Touhy Ave Ste 405 Lincolnwood IL 60646

JANEWAY, ELIZABETH HALL, author; b. Bklyn., Oct. 7, 1913; d. Charles H. and Jeannette F. (Searle) Hall; m. Eliot Janeway (dec. 1993); children: Michael, William. Student, Swarthmore Coll.; A.B., Barnard Coll., 1935; Ph.D. in Lit. (hon.), Simpson Coll., Cedarcrest Coll., Villa Maria Coll.; D.H.L. (hon.), Russell Sage Coll., 1981, Florida Internat. U., 1988, Simmons Coll., 1989. Assoc. fellow Yale. Author: The Walsh Girls, 1943, Daisy Kenyon, 1945, The Question of Gregory, 1949, The Vikings, 1951, Leaving Home, 1953, Early Days of the Automobile, 1956, The Third Choice, 1959, Angry Kate, 1963, Accident, 1964, Ivanov Seven, 1967, Man's World, Woman's Place, 1971, Between Myth and Morning: Women Awakening, 1974, Powers of the Weak, 1980, Cross Sections: From a Decade of Change, 1982, Improper Behavior, 1987; contbr. to: Comprehensive Textbook of Psychiatry, 2d edit, 1980, Harvard Guide to Contemporary American Writing, 1979, also short stories and critical writing in periodicals and newspapers. Past chmn. N.Y. State Coun. Humanities; past bd. dirs. NOW Legal Def. and Edn. Fund, Fedn. State Humanities Coun.; bd. dirs. Nat. Cultural Alliance. Recipient educator's award Delta Kappa Gamma, 1972; named Disting. Alumna Barnard Coll., 1979; recipient Medal of Distinction, 1981. Mem. Authors Guild (council), Authors League Am. (council), PEN, Phi Beta Kappa (hon.). Home: 350 E 79th St New York NY 10021-9202

JANIAK, CATHY LYNN, sales consultant; b. Summit, N.J., Oct. 25, 1950; d. Anthony Tyrone and Jane (LaMaster) Cuva; m. Richard Walter Janiak, Sept. 10, 1968; children: Jacqueline, Jeffrey. BBA, Georgian Ct. Coll., 1986; postgrad., Monmouth Coll. Teller Supreme Savs. and Loan, Irvington, N.J., 1972-73; with claims svcs. State Farm Ins., Summit, N.J., 1981-83; substitute tchr. Toms River (N.J.) Bd. Edn., 1986-87; sr. svc. analyst N.J. Bell, Toms River, 1982-84, sales cons., 1987—. Vol. Artist Guild, Island Heights, N.J., 1982; historian Welcome Wagon, Toms River, 1984-85. Recipient 1st pl. Latin category Star Dust Ball, Meadowlands, N.J., 1992. Home: 1119 Kells Ct Toms River NJ 08753-3162 Office: 79 Hwy 37 West Toms River NJ 08753

JANICE, BARBARA, illustrator; b. Brooklyn, N.Y., Jan. 25, 1949; d. Irving and Blanche (Lass) Rothman; 1 child, Stacey-Alissa Mirsky. BS in Biology, L.I. U., 1971; studied with Susan Moscowitz, John Broccoli. Staff illustrator Courier-Life Pubs., Bklyn., 1975-78, The Village Voice, N.Y.C., 1978-80; art dir., dept. anatomy SUNY Health Sci. Ctr., Bklyn., 1989-91; freelance illustrator Walt Disney Prodns., N.Y.C., 1990—, Orlando, Fla., 1990—; art dir. EuroDisney, Paris, 1990—; illustrator EuroDisney, Orlando, N.Y.C., 1991—; dir. Barbara Janice Graphics, N.Y.C. and Fla., 1980—; guest speaker Pratt Sch. Art & Design, Bklyn., 1991. Illustrator: Current Operative Urology, 6th edit., 1989, A Historical Profile of the Children's Medical Center, 1990, 2d rev. edit., 1992, The Day the Alphabet Was Born, 1991; represented in permanent collections SUNY Health Sci. Ctr., EuroDisney, Paris. Vol. artist Coalition for the Homeless, N.Y.C., 1985, 91, AIDS Coalition, Ft. Lauderdale, N.Y.C., 1992—. Recipient 1st place N.Y. Art Critics award, 1984, other awards for illustrations, 1990-91. Mem. Assn. Med. Illustrators, Soc. Illustrators (1st place 34th ann. exhbn. 1991, 2d place 33d ann. exhbn. 1990), Graphic Artists Guild (profl. rep.). Jewish. Home: 3881 NW 122d Ter Sunrise FL 33323 Office: Walt Disney Prodns 3881 NW 122nd Ter Sunrise FL 33323-3360

JANIGA, MARY ANN, educator and artist; b. Lackawanna, N.Y., June 14, 1950; d. Jacob and Julia (Zatlukal) Mazurchuk; m. William B. Janiga, Nov. 23, 1972; children: Nicholas, Matthew. BS, SUNY, Buffalo, 1972, MS, 1974, postgrad., 1991—. Tchr. art Buffalo Pub. Schs., 1972—; art facilitator Olmsted Sch., Buffalo, 1985—, liaison to Albright-Knox Art Gallery, 1994—. Exhibited in group shows Cheektowaga (N.Y.) Art Guild, 1979, Erie County Parks Art Festival, 1979, Lockport Art Festival, 1980, Allentown Art Exhibit, Kennan Ctr. Recipient various awards for art; grantee Buffalo Tchr. Ctr., 1986-90, Olmstead Home Sch. Assn., 1991, 93, Allentown Village Soc., 1994. Mem. NEA, Olmsted Home Sch. Assn., Lancaster High Sch. Home Sch. Assn., SUNY-Buffalo Alumni Assn., PTA (life), Buffalo Tchrs. Fedn., Buffalo Fine Arts Acad., Buffalo Soc. Natural Scis., Zool. Soc. of Buffalo. Office: Olmsted Sch Amherst & Lincoln Pky Buffalo NY 14216

JANKLOW, LINDA LEROY, civic worker, volunteer; b. L.A., Apr. 17, 1938; d. Mervyn LeRoy and Doris (Warner) Vidor; m. Morton Lloyd Janklow, Nov. 27, 1960; children: Angela Janklow Harrington, Lucas Warner. BA, Smith Coll., 1959. Vice chmn., mem. exec. com., bd. dirs. Lincoln Ctr. Theater, N.Y.C., 1979-91, chmn., 1991—. V.p., treas. Vidor Found., N.Y.C., 1978—; chmn. ArtsConnection, N.Y.C., 1979—; founding trustee, mem. exec. com., chmn. collection com. Am. Mus. of Moving Image, N.Y.C., 1979—; mem. adv. coun. Tisch Sch. Arts, NYU, 1980-91; mem. adv. bd. Guggenheim Mus., N.Y.C., 1986-91; pres., chief exec. officer Janklow Found., N.Y.C., 1988—; trustee Nat. Coun. for Families and TV, L.A., 1989-92; bd. dirs. The New 42d St., N.Y.C., 1990—. Office: Lincoln Ctr Theater 150 W 65th St New York NY 10023-6903

JANNEY, KATHARINE THAMSIN, information scientist; b. Silver Spring, Md., Jan. 16, 1953; d. Werner L. and Anne H. Janney; m. Will Roberts; 1 child, Sofia Rhiannon Janney-Roberts. BA, Grinnell Coll., 1974; MLIS, U. Calif., Berkeley, 1987. Database mgr. U. Art Mus./Pacific Film Archives, Berkeley, 1986-91; database info. specialist Continuum Prodns., Bellevue, Wash., 1991—; cons., 1990-91. Mem. ASIS, ALA, Mus. Computer Network (co-chair SIG cataloging and vocabulary). Office: Continuum Prodns 15395 SE 30th Pl Ste 300 Bellevue WA 98103

JANOVEC, MADELINE MEZA, artist, educator; b. L.A., Feb. 14, 1935; d. Joachim Joseph and Martha (Meza) J.; m. Morton Kaplan, 1964 (div. 1973); 1 child, Pietra Anna Kaplan Tate. BS, Portland (Oreg.) State U., 1971. Instr. art Clark Community Coll., Vancouver, Wash., 1978—, Mt. Hood Community Coll., Gresham, Oreg., 1989-91; vis. art faculty Exploration of Visual Lang., The Evergreen State Coll., Olympia, Wash., 1987-88; co-leader Contemporary Art Tours to Western Europe, 1986—. Exhibited in 25 one-woman shows and 30 group shows. Mem. Women's Caucus for Art (founding pres. Portland, 1987-91, Oreg. chpt.). Home: [illegible] Janovec Ln Washougal WA 98671 also: 902 SE Franklin Portland OR 97202 Studio: 544 SE Oak St Portland OR 97214-1122

JANOW, LYDIA FRANCES, meeting planner; b. N.Y.C., Dec. 2, 1957; d. John and Angie (Bizzios) J. BA cum laude, CCNY, 1978; grad., CBS Div. Publ., 1984. Registered meeting planner. Exec. sec. Family Weekly Mag., N.Y.C., 1978-81; asst. mdse. mgr. Family Weekly Mag., 1981-83; spl. events mgr. Family Weekly/USA Weekend, N.Y.C., 1983-86; mgr. meetings & events Mag. Pubs. Assn., N.Y.C., 1986-88; conv. svcs. mgr., sales & catering mgr. Sheraton Heights Hotel, Hasbrouck Heights, N.J., 1989-91; conf. mgr. Aviation Week Group McGraw Hill Inc., N.Y.C., 1991-93, dir. tradeshows and confs., 1993—. Editor: Newsletter Heights Hotel, 1991; contbr. articles to profl. jours. Camp counselor, Hellenic-Am. Neighborhood Action Com., N.Y.C., 1974-78; tchr., Sunday sch., St. Spyridon Ch., N.Y.C., 1974-80. Mem. IAEM, Internat. Soc. Meeting Planners, Meeting Planners Internat. Greek Orthodox. Home: 29 Levitt Ave Bergenfield NJ 07621

JANSEN, BONNIE, federal agency administrator. BA in Comm, Wash. State U., 1984; student, George Mason U., 1990-91. Asst. press sec. to Senator Slade Gorton, Wash., 1984-87; dir. pub. affairs Office of Special Adviser to the Pres. for Consumer Affairs, The White Ho., Washington, 1987-91, FCC, Washington, 1991—. Mem. Phi Kappa Phi. Office: Fed Trade Commn Public Affairs 6th & Pennsylvania Ave NW Washington DC 20580-0002*

JANSON, BARBARA JEAN, publisher; b. Mason City, Iowa, Mar. 7, 1942; d. Harley Arnold and Helen Victoria (Henrickson) J.; m. W. John Shallenberger, Feb. 24, 1963 (div. Sept. 1980); children: Mona, Ann; m. John Batty Henderson, Sept. 8, 1984 (div. 1990). BS in Math., Iowa State U., 1965; MS in Math., Trinity Coll., 1970; MBA, U. R.I., 1982. Cert. math. tchr., Iowa, N.Y., Conn. Math. tchr. Pub. High Schs., Avon, Farmington, Bloomfield, Conn., 1966-68, Ulster Acad., Kingston, N.Y., 1971-73; math. instr. Ulster County Community Coll., Kingston, 1973; math. editor Houghton Mifflin Co., Boston, 1974-77; math. instr. Bristol County Community Coll., Fall River, Mass., 1977-78; asst. dir. editorial Am. Math. Soc., Providence, 1978-81, dir. of publ., 1982-85; pres. Janson Publs., Inc., Providence, 1985—; rep. sci. publ. com. Am. Heart Assn., 1986-90; mem. R.I. State Adv. Commn. on Librs.; mem. R.I. Legis. Commn. for Math. and Sci. Edn., 1991; mem. adv. com. R.I. State Systemic Initiative in Math. and Sci. Editor: Scholarly Publishing: Managing Today, Planning for Tomorrow, 1986. Bd. dirs. Planned Parenthood of R.I., Providence, 1986-87, First Parish Unitarian Ch., Beverly, Mass., 1975-76; mem. steering com. Am. Math. Project, Berkeley, Calif., 1986-92; mem. oversight com. Resources Math. Reform Ednl. Devel. Ctr., Newton, Mass.; adv. mem. R.I. State Coun. on Librs. Recipient Mortar Bd. award Iowa State U., 1965. Mem. Soc. for Scholarly Publishing (bd. dirs. 1986-90, chair annual meeting 1985), N.Y. Acad. Sci., AAAS, Am. Math. Soc., Math. Assn. Am., Nat. Council Tchrs. Math., Assn. Am. Publishers (jours. com. 1983-85), Nat. Assn. Women Bus. Owners, LWV. Unitarian. Home: 8 Jackson Pond Dedham MA 02026-5524 Office: Janson Publs Inc 450 Washington St Ste 107 Dedham MA 02026-4449

JANSON, DIANE MARIE, school psychologist; b. Glen Ridge, N.J., Dec. 5, 1952; d. Owen Francis and Margaret Elizabeth (Faust) Rabbitt; m. John M. Janson, Oct. 26, 1975; children: Michael, Melissa. BA, Jersey City State Coll., 1974, MA, 1979; MA, Kean Coll. of N.J., 1985; D in Psychology, Rutgers U., 1992. Art tchr. Keansburg (N.J.) BOE, 1974-81, sch. psychologist, 1987-88, 91-93; guidance counselor St. Vincent Acad., Newark, 1982-86; instr. Rutgers U., New Brunswick, N.J., 1988-89, dir. child study team, 1992—; cons. Morris Union Jointure Commn., New Providence, N.J., 1989-91; clinician Rutgers Psychol. Clinic, New Brunswick, 1987—; sch. psychologist Berkeley Heights (N.J.) Bd. Edn., 1993—. Den mother cub scout troop Boy Scouts Am., Piscataway, N.J., 1990. Mem. APA, Nat. Assn. Sch. Psychologists, N.J. Assn. Sch. Psychologists, N.J. Coll. Admissions Counselors Assn. Home and Office: 408 Shirley Pkwy Piscataway NJ 08854

JANSSEN, EUNICE CHARLENE, healthcare facility administrator; b. Urania, La., Mar. 23, 1948; d. Luther Clarence and Eunice Bobby (Pendarvis) Smith. BS in Nursing, Humboldt State U., 1970; MS in Nursing, Calif. State U., Fresno, 1980. Dir. nurses, asst. adminstr., coord. patient care svcs. Mad River Community Hosp., Arcata, Calif.; nursing supr. Fresno (Calif.) Community Hosp. Mem. Am. Soc. Healthcare Risk Mgmt., CANA (region 9 nurses interest group). Home: 1220 Winchester Ave Mc Kinleyville CA 95521

JANSSEN, MARYBETH, engineering educator; b. Tulsa, May 1, 1956; d. Henry Floyd and Bessie Viola (Barr) Kinyon; m. Lawrence Eric Janssen, Dec. 23, 1977 (div. Oct. 1987). Grad. H.S., Los Gatos, Calif. Cert. airframe and powerplant mechanic, FAA. Jet engine mechanic USAF, 1976-84; flight engr. USAFR McChord AFB, Tacoma, 1984-86; flight attendant Trans World Airlines, St. Louis, 1986-89, airframe and powerplant mechanic, 1989-90; airframe and powerplant mechanic Am. Airlines, Inc., Tulsa, 1990-92; tech. crew chief instr. Am. Airlines, Inc., Ft. Worth, 1992—. Jet engine technician Mo. Air N.G., St. Louis, 1987-90, Okla. Air N.G., Tulsa, 1990-92, non-commd. officer-in-charge maintenance tng., 1993—. Tech. Sgt. USAF, 1976-84. Decorated Air Force Achievement medal and Meritorious Svc. medal USAF, Robins AFB, Ga., 1983, Meritorious Svc. medals Mo. Air Nat. Guard, St. Louis, 1990, Okla. Air Nat. Guard, Tulsa, 1993. Mem. NAFE, Aircraft Mechanics Fraternal Assn., Am. Legion. Home: 7709 Briarcliff Ct Ft Worth TX 76180

JANTI, LISA, educator, administrator, arts consultant; b. Warsaw, Poland, July 5, 1933; d. Vladimir and Elizabeth (Gordon) Montwill; divorced; 1 child, Shireen. Student in Liberal Arts, U. Miami, 1951-52; student in Pub. Adminstrn., U. Ariz., 1967-71; MS in Edn., Nat. U., San Diego, 1981. Actress L.A., 1954-67; exec. dir. Child Devel. Ctrs., Tucson, 1967-72; spl. asst. Mayor Tom Bradley, L.A., 1975-80; instr. Nat. Univ., San Diego, 1981-85; cons. dept. cultural affairs and Mayor's office City of L.A., 1985—; exec. dir. Art on Wheels, L.A., 1992—; lectr. in field. Author, cons. (document) Youth Arts Advocacy Program City of L.A., 1993; author, editor El Ruisenor/Nightingale mag., 1993; editor, reader (cassette) Meditations from Writings of Baha "U" llah, 1983. Bd. dirs. L.A. Cities in Schs., 1992—; co-chair adv. com. Urban Pride, L.A., 1992—; chmn. L.A. Baha'i Assembly, 1975-80; coord World in Transition Pub. Forum series. Recipient Commendation, L.A. Mayor Tom Bradley, 1993, Commendation, Puebla (Mex.) City Coun., 1991, Commendation, Nat. Indian Arts and Edn. Alliance, 1977.

JANZEN, NORINE MADELYN QUINLAN, medical technologist; b. Fond du Lac, Wis., Feb. 9, 1943; d. Joseph Wesley and Norma Edith (Gustin) Quinlan. BS, Marian Coll., 1965; med. technologist St. Agnes Sch. Med. Tech., Fond du Lac, 1966; MA, Cen. Mich. U., 1980; m. Douglas Mac Arthur Janzen, July 18, 1970; 1 son, Justin James. Med. technologist Mayfair Med. Lab., Wauwatosa, Wis., 1966-69; supr. med. technologist Dr.'s Mason, Chamberlain, Franke, Klink & Kamper, Milw., 1969-76, Hartford-Parkview Clinic, Ltd., 1976-94, Med. Sci. Labs., Wauwatosa, Wis., 1994—; coord. health in bus. Hartford Parkview Clinic, 1990-91, drug program coord., 1991-94; co-chair joint mtg. Clin. Lab. Mgrs. Assn. and Wis. Assn. Med. Tech., 1993-94. Substitute poll worker Fond du Lac Dem. Com., 1964-65; mem. Dem. Nat. Com., 1973—. Mem. Am. Soc. Med. Tech. (people to people clin. lab. scientist del. to People's Republic of China 1989), Nat. Soc. Med. Technologists (awards com. 1984-87, 88-91, chmn. 1986-88, nominations com. 1989-92), Wis. Assn. Med. Tech. (exec. sec. 1991—), Wis. Assn. Med. Technologists (chmn. awards com. 1976-77, 84-85, 86-87, treas. 1977-81, pres.-elect 1981-82, pres. 1982-83, dir. 1977-84, 85-87, Mem. of Yr. 1982, numerous svc. awards, chair ann. meeting 1987-88), Am. Soc. Med. Technologists, Clin. Lab. Mgmt. Assn. (co-chair joint meeting 1993-94), Wis. Assn. Med. Tech. (co-chair joint meeting 1993-94), Milw. Soc. Med. Technologists (pres. 1971-72, bd. dir. 1972-73), Communications of Wis. (originator, chmn. 1977-79), Southeastern Suprs. Group (co-chmn. 1976-77), LWV, Alpha Delta Theta (nat. dist. chmn. 1967-69, nat. alumnae dir. 1969-71), Alpha Mu Tau. Methodist. Home: N98 W 17298 Dotty Way Germantown WI 53022 Office: Med Scis Lab 11021 W Alank Ct Ste 110 Wauwatosa WI 53226

JARABA, MARTHA E. (BETTY JARABA), secondary school educator; b. San Pedro Sula, Honduras, Feb. 27, 1949; d. G.E. and Francisca L. (Reynaud) Donaldson; m. Jaime I. Jaraba; children: Janine, Jimmy. BA in French, Spanish, La. State U., 1972. Cert. tchr. French, Spanish, ESL. El Paso (Tex.) Ind. Sch. Dist.; examiner for Ednl. Testing Svc.; mentor New Tchrs. Assistance Program; presenter in field. Published author. Panelist Tex. Commn. on the Arts; bd. mem. City of El Paso Arts Resource Dept. Named Tchr. of Yr., Tex. Tchr. Task Force. Mem. NEA, TESOL, Tex. TESOL, Tex. State Tchrs. Assn., El Paso Tchrs. Assn. Home: 6629 Camino Fuente Dr El Paso TX 79912-2407

JARMAN, KATHLEEN DOWTY, vocational consultant; b. Lafayette, La., Nov. 27, 1948; d. Forrest K. and Eleanor (Hutto) D.; m. G. William Jarman, Jan. 25, 1969 (div. 1988); children: Jennifer, Kent. BS, La. State U., 19709, MA, 1989. Lic. profl. counselor, La.; lic. rehab. counselor, La.; cert. case mgr. Tchr. elem. Ea. Baton Rouge Parish Sch. Bd., 1970-73; career counselor La. State U., Baton Rouge, 1987-89; career cons. Bellsouth Svcs., Baton Rouge, 1990-92; vocat. cons. Crawford Helathcare Mgmt., New Orleans, 1992—. Mem. Jr. League New Orleans. Home: 1316 Washington Ave New Orleans LA 70130-5750 Office: Metairie 3850 N Causeway Blvd Ste 950 Metairie LA 70002-1752

JARRELL, IRIS BONDS, elementary educator, business executive; b. Winston-Salem, N.C., May 25, 1942; d. Ira and Annie Gertrude (Vandiver) Bonds; m. Tommy Dorsey Martin, Feb. 13, 1965; 1 child, Carlos Miguel; m. 2d, Clyde Rickey Jarrell, June 25, 1983; stepchildren—Tamara, Cris, Kimberly. Student U. N.C.-Greensboro, 1960-61, 68-69, 74-75, Salem Coll., 1976; B.S. in Edn., Winston-Salem State U., 1981; postgrad. Appalachian State U., 1983; M in Elem. Edn., Gardner-Webb Coll., 1992. Cert. tchr., N.C.Tchr. Rutledge Coll., Winston-Salem, 1982-84; owner, mgr. Rainbow's End Consignment Shop, Winston-Salem, 1983-85; tchr. elem. edn. Winston-Salem/Forsyth County Sch. System, 1985—. Contbr. poetry to mags. Mem. Assn. of Couples for Marriage Enrichment, Winston-Salem, 1984-86, Forsyth-Stokes Mental Health Assn., 1985-86; mem. Planned Parenthood. Mem. Internat. Reading Assn., N.C. Assn. Adult Edn., Forsyth Assn. Classroom Tchrs., Nat. Assn. Female Execs., NOW, Greenpeace, World Wildlife Fund, KlanWatch. Democrat. Baptist. Avocations: singing, writing, sewing, gardening, reading. Home: 101 Cheswyck Ln Winston Salem NC 27104-2905

JARRELL, PATRICIA LYNN, photojournalist; b. South Charleston, W.Va., Jan. 21, 1952; d. Ronald Eugene and Barbara Anne (Hill) J.; m. Timothy James Shortt, Mar. 10, 1990. Photographer PCA Internat., Tampa, Fla., 1974-77, Linwood/Gittings, Houston, 1977-78; sr. photographer Gittings/Neiman Marcus, Dallas, 1978-80; studio photographer PCA Internat., Dallas and Orlando, 1980-85; photographer, mgr. Charlton Studios, Altamonte Springs, Fla., 1985; photographer Fla. Today/Gannett, Melbourne, Fla., 1985—; mem. discussion panel covering tragedy Fla. Press Women, 1989. Works exhibited at So. Newspaper Pubs. Assn., 1989, Armory Art Ctr., West Palm Beach, Fla., 1994. Recipient Photojournalism/Spot News award Internat. Soc. Newspaper Design, 1986-87, award of excellence in photojournalism Soc. Newspaper Design, 1986-87, Best News Photography award Fla. Press Club, 1987, Clarion/News Photography award Women in Comms., 1988, 1st Pl./Spot News Fla. Soc. Newspaper Editors, 1988, 1st Pl. News Photography award Fla. Press Women, 1988, 1st Pl. Color Feature award Fla. Soc. Newspaper Editors, 1990. Mem. NOW, Nat. Press Photographers Assn. Democrat. Home: 1802 Crane Creek Blvd Melbourne FL 32940 Office: Fla Today Newspaper Gannett Plaza PO Box 419000 Melbourne FL 32941-9000

JARRETT, ALEXIS, insurance professional; b. Independence, Kans., July 2, 1948; d. Robert Patterson and Betty June (Johnson) J.; m. Victor K. O'Yek, Apr. 12, 1987. BS, U. Minn., Duluth, 1970; postgrad., U. Mo. Lic. in Property and Casualty Ins., Ind., Life and Health Ins., Ind., Life Underwriting Tng. Coun. fellow; cert. coach, Minn. Tchr. Esko (Minn.) Pub. Schs.; pvt. practice Schererville, Ind.; asst. dir. athletics, head coach U. Mo., Columbia; women's basketball and softball color analyst Regional Radio Sports, N.W. Ind. Contbr. articles on sports to newspapers. Sponsor Lake County (Ind.) H.S. Girls Basketball Banquet; mem. adv. bd. indsl. rsch. liason program Ind. U., Bloomington; bd. dirs. Samaritan Counseling Ctr. N.W. Ind., pres. 1994; bd. dirs. VNA Found., sec.-treas., 1994; mem. mktg. and promotional subcom. Ind. U. N.W. Scholarship Fundraiser Com.; celebrity Am. Heart Assn. Celebrity Dinner; v.p. S.W. Lake divsn. Am. Heart Assn., 1992, 93, 94. Mem. Nat Life Underwriters, Lake County Med. Soc. Alliance (pres.), Am. Bus. Womens Assn. (pres. New Image chpt. 1983, Woman of Yr. 1993) Ind. State Med. Assn. Alliance (chair media rels. 1990-91, 93-94, treas. 1992-93). Address: 2330 Wicker Blvd Schererville IN 46375-2810

JARRETT, CHERYLANNE CAMPBELL, counselor; b. Richmond, Va., Oct. 16, 1952; d. Kenenth Raymond and Anne (Hathaway) Campbell; m. W. Patrick Jarrett, June 7, 1986; 1 child, Benjamin Campbell Jarrett. BS in Psychology, James Madison U., 1975; MS in Rehab. Counseling, Va. Commonwealth U., 1978. Lic. profl. counselor; nat. cert. counselor. Probation and parole officer, drug specialist Va. Div. Community and Prevention Svcs., Richmond, 1977-79; counselor Woodrow Wilson Rehab. Ctr., Fishersville, Va., 1980-81, Human Resources, Inc., Richmond, 1981; vocat. cons. Crawford Rehab. Svcs., Richmond, 1981-82; rehab. coord. Underwriters Adjusting Co., Richmond, 1982-84; counselor The Next Step, Inc., Richmond, 1984-85; dir. family care program for chem. dependency treatment Poplar Springs Hosp., Petersburg, Va., 1985-91; pvt. practice counseling Richmond, 1985—; pvt. contractor C & P Telephone Co., Richmond, 1987, 90. Vol. Chesterfield County Libr., Richmond, 1993—. Mem. Am. Counseling Assn., Assn. Mental Health Counselors Am., Va. Assn. Clin. Counselors. Office: 10109 Krause Rd Chesterfield VA 23832-6573

JARRETT, GRACIE MAE, junior high school guidance counselor; b. Kansas City, Kans., Feb. 8, 1944; d. Hosea George Washington and Sylvia Ann (McCluney) Canady; m. Gennie Jarrett, Jr., July 11, 1987; children: Tony Jarrett, André D. Oden, Dale Marie Jarrett. AA, Coffeyville (Kans.) JUCO, 1964; BS, Kans. State Coll., 1968; MS, Troy (Ala.) State U., 1975. Cert. tchr.; cert. guidance counselor. Nurse aide, cashier Kansas City U. Med. Ctr., 1962-67; phys. edn. tchr. Kansas City Mo. Dist., 1968-73; sch. social worker Okaloosa County Schs., Ft. Walton Beach, Fla., 1973-76; spl. agt. tng. FBI, Quantico, Va., 1976; substitute tchr. Berryessa Sch. Dist., San Jose, Calif., 1976; personal lines underwriter Reliance Ins. Co., Shawnee Mission, Kans., 1977-81; vocat. edn. counselor Operation P.U.S.H., Kansas City, Mo., 1981; casemanager Kansas Youth Trust, Kansas City, Kans., 1982-83; guidance counselor Sch. Dist. #204, Bonner Springs, Kans., 1983—; trainer, spkr. U. Mo., Kansas City, 1989—; trainer Adult Illiteracy Program, Kansas City, 1993-94; del. Minority Leadership Tng., Bonner Spring, 1995. Co-sponsor, chaperone Spl. Olympics of Fla., Fort Walton Beach, 1973-75; vol. Community Action Program, Kansas City, 1978-82, Hotline, Kansas City, 1978-80; mem. Kansas Polit. Action, Bonner Springs, 1994—; nominating com. Senator Al Ramirez, Bonner Springs, 1991-93. Scholarship Delta Sigma Theta, 1964; named Kappa Sweetheart Kappa Alpha Psi. Mem. NEA, ACA, NAACP (bd. dirs. 1977—), Kans. Nat. Edn. Assn. (commr. 1990, pres. 1990), Bonner Springs KNEA (pres., rep., del. 1982—), Delta Kappa Gamma. Baptist. Home: 1746 S 98th St Kansas City KS 66111-3528 Office: Robert E Clark Jr High 420 N Bluegrass St Bonner Springs KS 66012-1608

JARRETT, JOY ALLYSON, management consultant; b. Athens, Ga., Aug. 20, 1959; d. James Augustus and Margaret Alice (Houston) J. BA, U. Ga., 1981. Sales rep. Lee Jofa, Atlanta, 1981-82; sr. account mgr. Geiger Internat., N.Y.C., 1982-87, Knoll Internat., L.A., 1987-89; west coast market dir. Sign Techs. Ltd., L.A., 1989-90; project mgr. Zornizer & Assocs., L.A., 1990-92; project dir. World Bus. Network, Atlanta, 1992-93; internat. trade mgr. Bachman Internat., Atlanta, 1993-94; dir. spl. projects Project Mgmt. Svcs., Inc., Atlanta, 1994—; project cons. Nestle/Carnation Corp., Glendale, Calif., 1990-92, SAG, Hollywood, Calif., 1992-93, Atlantic Records, L.A., 1991-92, Berger & Norton, L.A., 1991-92. Coord. Cerebral Palsy Found., L.A., 1988; com. coord. Sojourn Soc., L.A., 1989; com. dir. Homeless Task Force, L.A., 1990-92. Presbyterian.

JARRETT, RUTH, financial executive; b. Bklyn., Feb. 11, 1942; d. Ernest David and Joyce (Litzky) Kurnow; m. Jeffrey Edward Jarrett, June 16, 1963; children: Michael Philip, Debra Lynn, Daniel Mark. BS in Edn., N.Y.U., 1963; MS in Acctg., U. R.I., 1980. Survey analyst Soc. of the Plastics Industry, N.Y.C., 1963-81; cons. Technic, INc., Cranston, R.I., 1981; fiscal mgr. Univ. R.I. Found., Kingston, R.I., 1981-88; chief fin. officer Univ. R.I. Found., Kingston, 1988—. Bd. dirs. Lit. Vols. of Am., South County R.I. Br., 1993; pres. Jewish Community Coun., Kingston, 1991-93, treas., 1993—. Recipient Founder's Day award N.Y.U., 1963. Mem. Assn. Profl. and Acad. Univ. Women, Triangle Club, South County Hadassah (treas. 1989—, Woman of Yr. 1994), Beta Alpha Psi. Office: U RI Found 21 Davis Hall Kingston RI 02881

JASHINSKY, JUDY FAYE, artist, educator; b. Oconto Falls, Wis., Dec. 27, 1947; d. Walter Alfred and Ruby Faye (Tousey) J.; m. Lawrence A. Finfer, Oct. 15, 1971. BS, U. Wis., Stevens Point, 1970; MFA, Mich. State U., 1973. Instr. Oakland U., Rochester, Mich., 1974, Lansing (Mich.) C.C., 1973-78, Prince George's C.C., Largo, Md., 1980-86, Trinity Coll., Washington, 1984-87, West Shore C.C., Scottville, Mich., 1990—; panelist Censorship in Arts Trinity Coll., 1991, Arts Club, 1992; visual arts panelist Arlington Commn for Arts, 1993, 94; panelist Takoma Metro Arts Ctr., 1994; bd. dirs. Washington Project for the Arts, 1990—, coordinator Open Studio, 1991, 93, mem. outreach com., 1992; lectr. in field. Solo exhbns. include Gallery K, Washington, 1985, Clare Spitler-Works of Art, Ann Arbor, Mich., 1986, 89, Gallery 10, Washington, 1987, Washington Project for the Arts, 1989, Rosenberg Gallery Goucher Coll., Balt., 1994; traveling exhbn. Va. Ctr. Creative Arts, Sweet Briar, 1993, Susquehanna Art Mus., Harrisburg, Pa., 1992, 93, Franz Bader Gallery, Washington, 1992; group shows include Mus. Temporary Art, Washington, 1979, Washington Project for the Arts, 1983, 84, Emily Harvey Gallery, N.Y.C., 1982, Smithsonian Mus. Natural History, Washington, 1984, Kathleen Ewing Gallery, Washington, 1986, Städtische Galerie, Regensburg, West Germany, 1988-89, Strathmore Hall, Washington, 1986, Fondo del Sol Visual Arts Ctr., Washington, 1990, 92, Arlington (Va.) Art Ctr., Arts 901, Washington, 1991, Rockville (Md.) Arts Place, 1991, 92, Mahler Gallery, Washington, 1992, D.C. Arts Ctr., 1993, Artist Space, N.Y.C., 1993-94, Emerson Gallery McLean (Va.) Project for the Arts, 1993, Drawing Ctr., N.Y.C., 1993, Corcoran Gallery of Art, 1994; represented in permanent collections Art Inst. Chgo., Detroit Inst. Art, Springfield (Mo.) Art Mus., Va. Ctr. Creative Arts, Cranbrook Mus. Art, Manufacturers Hanover Trust, Smith-Barney, Great Lakes Bancorp, U. Mich. Sch. Medicine; subject newspaper, mag. articles. Va. Ctr. for Creative Arts resident fellow, 1983, 85, 89, 90, 93, painting residency, Rome, 1986, New Forms Regional grantee Painted Bride, 1993; Individual Artist grantee D.C. Commn. on Arts and Humanities, 1981, 86-88. Home: 1219 C St SE Washington DC 20003

JASICA, ANDREA LYNN, mortgage banking executive; b. Orlando, Fla., Aug. 21, 1945; d. Walter S. and Florence E. (Pasek) J. AA in Pre Bus. Adminstrn. cum laude, Orlando Jr. Coll., 1965; BS with honors, Rollins Coll., 1976. Sec. Am. Mortgage Co. Fla. Inc., Orlando, 1965-68; closing specialist Charter Mortgage Co., Orlando, 1968-70, Gen. Guaranty Mortgage Co. Inc., Winter Park, Fla., 1971; sr. loan processor C.E. Brooks Mortgage Co. Inc., Orlando, 1971-79; v.p. mktg. Twin Homes Ltd., Orlando, 1980-83; asst. v.p., mgr. region Atlantic Mortgage and Investment Corp. subs. Atlantic Nat. Bank, Orlando, 1984-86; v.p. Commerce Nat. Mortgage Co., Winter Park, 1987-88; supr. Bur. of Census, U.S. Dept. Commerce, Orlando, 1990; investor, 1990—; real estate assoc. Atlantic-to-Gulf Realty Inc., 1972-73, Medel Inc., Maitland, Fla., 1973-74; instr. Mortgage Personnel Svcs. Inc. Contbr. articles to profl. jours. Home: 1011 E Harwood St Orlando FL 32803-5706

JASINSKI-CALDWELL, MARY L., company executive; b. Chester, Pa., May 8, 1959; d. A. Robert and Helen M. Jasinki; m. William A. Caldwell, Aug. 4, 1990; 1 child, Helaina M. Student, Loyola Coll., Balt., 1980; BS, Goldey Beacom Coll., Wilmington, Del., 1983. Registered orthotic fitter; cert. sr. pharmacy technician. Gen. mgr., treas., trustee corp. pension plan City Pharmacy Inc., Elkton, Md.; jr. ptnr. City Pharmacy, Elkton, Md., 1994; disc jockey, promoter Garfield's Restaurant, Elkton; editl. writer local newspapers; pro-life columnist KC newsletter. Creator ednl. program PARTICIP.A.A.T.E. For Life. Bd. dirs. Md. Right to Life, 1993-94, co-chmn. Cecil County chpt.; founder PARTICIP.A.A.T.E. for Life, Cecil County; advisor Cecil County Pro-Life Coalition; pro-life educator; bd. dirs. Mission Am., Inc. Recipient J.W. Miller award, Outstanding Achievement in Excellence award K.C., 1994; Alpha Chi scholar, Lindback scholar. Mem. NAFE, Am. Mgmt. Assn., Nat. Fedn. Ind. Bus., Cecil County C. of C., Bd. Orthotic Cert., Goldey Beacom Coll. Alumni Assn., Alpha Phi. Republican. Roman Catholic. Avocations: home improvement, gardening, social concerns, pro-life education, reading. Office: City Pharmacy Inc 723 N Bridge St Elkton MD 21921-5309

JASON, J. JULIE, lawyer; b. Owensboro, Ky., May 14, 1949; d. Richard and Grazina Pauliukonis; m. Marius J. Jason, Dec. 19, 1970; children: Ilona, Leila. BA, Baldwin-Wallace Coll., 1971; JD, Cleve. State U., 1974; LLM, Columbia U., 1975. Bar: Ohio 1974, N.Y. 1976, U.S. Dist Ct. (so. dist.) N.Y. 1976, U.S. Ct. Appeals (2d cir.) 1976, U.S. Supreme Ct. 1978. Pvt. practice N.Y.C., 1974-78; asst. gen. counsel Paine Webber, N.Y.C., 1978-83; pres. P.W. Trust and Paine Webber Futures Mgmt. Co., N.Y.C., 1983-88; sr. fin. svcs. atty. Donovan, Leisure, Newton & Irvine, N.Y.C., 1988-89; co-founder, mng. dir. Jackson, Grant & Co., Stamford, Conn., 1989—; arbitrator NYSE, AAA. Author: You & Your 401-K, 1995. Mem. ABA, AAUW (chair scholarship com. 1992-93), Nat. Assn. Securities Dealers (cert., arbitrator), Investment Co. Inst., The Corp. Bar, Am. PenWomen, Columbia U. Alumni Club of Fairfield County (pres. 1993-94), Women in Mgmt. (former officer), Jr. League of Greenwich. Office: Jackson Grant & Co 1177 High Ridge Rd Stamford CT 06905-1211

JASON, JUDY BOYER, writer; b. Reading, Pa., Sept. 9, 1942; d. James Howard and Madeline Agnes (Kerchner) Boyer; m. Gary Cooper Lohman, Jan. 22, 1978; children: Sharon Cristine, Valerie Madelyn, Monica Leigh, Christiane Noelle. BA, U. Md., 1979; MFA, Am. U., 1984. Writer, editor HUD, Washington, 1973-77; editor Exec. Office of the Pres., Washington, 1977; writer, editor Comsat, Clarksburg, Md., 1980-81; vis. artist Artists in the Schs. Program, Balt., 1982-86; poet in the schs. Md. State Arts Coun., Balt., 1982-86; writing tchr. Montgomery County Secondary Schs., Rockville, Md., 1984-88; writer, acting dir. U.S. Dept. Agr., Washington, 1989-92; fiction and poetry writer Sideling Press, Asheville, N.C., 1994—; lit. cons. Montgomery County Pub. Sch. System. Rockville, 1986. Author: (poetry book) Collage, 1984; contbr. poems and short stories to literary jours. Organizer and facilitator midlife support group, Family Life Ctr., Frederick, Md., 1993-94; activist Women in Edn., Rockville, 1985-87; vol. NOW, Washington, 1980-83; rep. Fed. Women's Program, Washington, 1975, 91. Grantee Charlotte W. Newcombe Found., Princeton, N.J., 1982-83; recipient Presdl. Excellence in Edn. award White House, 1987, Adminstr.'s Golden Pen award U.S. Dept. Agr., Washington, 1988, cert. of Merit, 1991. Mem. AAUW, Asheville Art Mus. Edn. Org., Poets and Writers. Home: 12105 Merricks Ct Asheville NC Office: Sideling Press Asheville NC

JASPER, ANNETTE FRANCES, computer software company executive, consultant; b. Miami, Fla., Oct. 27, 1965; d. Matathias E. and Zora E. Frances; m. Warren Joseph Jasper, June 21, 1992. BS in Mgmt. Info. Sys., Fla. State U., 1987; MBA, U. N.C., 1992. Project leader, sys. analyst, programming specialist Andersen Cons., Miami, 1987-90; product mgr. Q & E Software, Raleigh, N.C., 1992-93; pres., CEO Custom Data Sys., Inc., Cary, N.C., 1993—. Mem. Nat. Assn. Women Bus. Owners, Ind. Computer Cons. Assn., Carolina Harmony-Sweet Adelines Internat. (bd. dirs. 1994—). Home: 127 Donna Pl Cary NC 27513

JAUDZEMIS, KATHLEEN A., judge; b. Omaha, Nebr., Jan. 18, 1949. BA, Univ. of Nebr., 1971, MA, 1976; JD, Univ. of Nebr. Law Coll., 1982. Bar: Nebr., U.S. Dist. Ct. Nebr., U.S. Ct. Appeals (8th cir.). Tchr. St. Paul pub. schs., Nebr., 1971-74, Lincoln pub. schs., Nebr., 1974-79; atty. Cline, Williams, Wright, Johnson & Oldfather, 1982-91; magistrate judge U.S. Dist. Ct. Nebr., 8th circuit, Omaha, 1992—. Mem. Am. Bar Assn., Nebr. Bar Assn., Fed. Magistrate Judges Assn., Nat. Assn of Women Judges. Office: Edward Zorinsky Fed Bldg PO Box 336 215 N 17th St Omaha NE 68101-4910*

JAUNDALDERIS, JULIA LEE, software engineer; b. Neubrüke, Germany, Nov. 28, 1961; came to U.S., 1963; d. Imants and Virginia Lee (Wine) J. BS in Computer Sci., We. Wash. U., Bellingham, 1984; MS, U. Wash., 1991. Cert. nat. note investor. Analyst Pacific N.W. Bell, Bellevue, Wash., 1984-87; software engr. U.S. West Comms., Bellevue, 1987-94; sr. software engr. GTE, Bothell, Wash., 1994—; stained glass designer; real estate investor. Athletes' Village liaison 1990 Goodwill Games, Seattle, 1990; v.p. Wash. State Coun. for Self-Esteem, Bothell, 1993-94. Home: PO Box 1605 Bothell WA 98041-1605

JAUQUET-KALINOSKI, BARBARA, library director; b. Crystal Falls, Mich., Mar. 12, 1948; d. Herbert Francis and Lenore Mary (Roell) Jauquet; m. Gregory Clem Kalinoski, Nov. 12, 1983; children: Stacia Amee, Sara Amee, Michael Thomas and Thomas Michael (twins.). BS, No. Mich. U., 1970; MLS, Western Mich. U., 1974. Adminstrv. asst. Mid-Peninsula Libr. System, Iron Mountain, Mich., 1970-74, asst. dir., 1975-79; periodical libr. U. Wis., Superior, 1980; dir. N.W. Regional Libr., Thief River Falls, Minn., 1981—; mem. libr. devel. & svcs. adv. com. Dept. Edn., Minn.; mem. planning, evaluation, reporting curriculum com. for sch. dist. Treas. St. Bernard's Home/Sch. Assn., treas.; mem. Thief River Falls Acad. Booster's Club. Named Woman of Honor, AAUW, 1990. Mem. ALA, Minn. Libr. Assn. (continuing edn. com.), Thief River Falls C. of C., Toastmasters, Rotary (past pres.). Roman Catholic. Office: NW Regional Libr 101 1st St E Thief River Falls MN 56701-2041

JAVAN, MARJORIE J(ANE), artist, consultant; b. Peckville, Pa., Dec. 6, 1936; d. Joseph and Vivien Scott (Reedy) Browning; m. Ali Javan, Apr. 12, 1962 (div. May 1988); children: Maia, Lila. BS, Trenton State Coll., 1957. Artist, tchr. Exptl. Etching Studio, Inc., Boston, 1970-80; advt. mgr. Laser Sci., Inc., Cambridge, Mass., 1981-86; cons. Haber-Schaim, Belmont, Mass., 1986-88; graphic artist Marjorie Javan Graphics, Boston, 1988-93; corp. art cons. Mourlot Art Cons., Boston, 1993—. Dir. First Night Boston, Inc., 1992—. Mem. Iternat. Assn. Hand Paper Makers, Am. Print Alliance, Inc. (bd. dirs. 1992—), Boston Printmakers, Inc. (pres. exec. bd. 1985—), Coll. Art Assn. Home: 47 Harvard St Charlestown MA 02129

JAVITCH, ANKI (ANN LOUISE) WOLF, psychologist; b. Newton, Mass., Oct. 30, 1949; d. Leo E. and Natalie (Wasserman) Wolf; m. David Gerald Javitch, Apr. 15, 1978; children: Matthew Ethan, Jacob Micah. BA, Russell Sage Coll., 1971; MEd, Boston Coll., 1972; PhD, Ohio State U., 1980. Learning disabilities specialist Concord (Mass.) Pub. Schs., 1972-74; learning disabilities specialist supr. Hudson (N.H.) Pub. Schs., 1975-77; sr. clin. supr. Valley Adult Counseling Ctr., Milford, Mass., 1980-81; pvt. practice Newton, Mass., 1981-90; clin. therapist Coping with Pregnancy/Parenting Experiences (C.O.P.E.), Boston, 1984-90; cons. Javitch Assoc., Newton, 1990—. Bd. dirs. Cambridge Sch. of Weston, Mass., 1986-93, Newton Symphony Orch., 1991—. Mem. APA. Office: Javitch Assocs 133 Waban Ave Waban MA 02168-2101

JAY, NORMA JOYCE, artist; b. Wichita, Kans., Nov. 11, 1925; d. Albert Hugh and Thelma Ree (Boyd) Braly; m. Laurence Eugene Jay, Sept. 2, 1949; children: Dana Denise, Allison Eden. Student Wichita State U., 1946-49, Art Inst. Chgo., 1955-56, Calif. State Coll., 1963. Illustrator Boeing Aircraft, Wichita, Kans., 1949-51; co-owner Back Door Gallery, Laguna Beach, Calif., 1973-88. One-woman shows include Milcir Gallery, Tiburon, Calif., 1978, Newport Beach City Gallery, 1981; group shows include Am. Soc. Marine Artists ann. exhbns., N.Y.C., 1978-86, Peabody Mus., Salem, Mass., 1981, Mystic Seaport Mus. Gallery, Conn., 1982-85, 1982-95, Grand Cen. Galleries, N.Y., 1979-84, The Back Door Gallery, Laguna Beach, Calif., 1973-88, Mariners' Mus., Newport News, Va., 1985-86, Nat. Heritage Gallery of Fine Art, Beverly Hills, Calif., 1988—, Md. Hist. Mus., 1989, Kirsten Gallery, Seattle, 1991-93, R.J. Schaefer Gallery Mystic (Conn.) Seaport Mus., 1992, Vallejo Gallery, Newport Beach, Calif., 1992, Caswell Gallery, Troutdale, Oreg., 1994, Columbia River Maritime Mus., Astoria, Oreg., 1994, Coos Art Mus., Coos Bay, Oreg., 1994, Arnold Art Gallery, Newport, Conn., 1994; represented in permanent collections including James Irvine Found., Newport Beach, Niguel Art Assn., Laguna Niguel, Calif., Deloitte, Haskins & Sells, Costa Mesa, Calif., M.J. Brock & Sons Inc., North Hollywood, Calif., others. Recipient Best of Show award Ford Nat. Competition, 1961, First Pl. award Traditional Artists Exhbn., San Bernadino County Mus., 1976, Artist award Chriswood Gallery Invitational Exhbn., Rancho California, Calif., 1973. Fellow Am. Soc. Marine Artists (charter); mem. Niguel Art Assn. (first pres. 1968, hon. life mem. 1978), Artists Equity, Am. Artists Profl. League. Republican.

JAYNE, CYNTHIA ELIZABETH, psychologist; b. Pensacola, Fla., June 5, 1953; d. Gordon Howland and Joan (Rockwood) J. AB, Vassar Coll., 1974; MA, SUNY, Buffalo, 1978, PhD, 1983. Lic. psychologist, Pa. Instr. dept. psychiatry Temple U. Sch. Medicine, Phila., 1982-84, asst. prof., 1984-85, asst. dir. outpatient services, asst. dir. residency tng., 1982-85, clin. asst. prof., 1985—; pvt. practice psychology Phila., 1985—. Contbr. articles to profl. jours. Soc. for Sci. Study Sex scholar, 1981; Sigma Xi grantee, 1981, Kinsey Inst. Dissertation award, 1983. Mem. APA, Ea. Psychol. Assn., Soc. for Sci. Study Sex (bd. dirs. 1984-86).

JAYSON, MELINDA GAYLE, lawyer; b. Dallas, Sept. 29, 1956; d. Robert and Louise Adelle (Jacobs) J. BA, U. Tex., 1977, JD, 1980. Bar: Tex. 1980, U.S. Dist. Ct. (no. dist.) Tex. 1980, U.S. Ct. Appeals (5th and 11th cirs.) 1981, U.S. Dist. Ct. (so. dist.) Tex. 1989, U.S. Ct. Appeals (8th cir.) 1990, U.S. Supreme Ct. 1991. Assoc. Akin, Gump, Strauss, Hauer & Feld, Dallas, 1980-86, ptnr., 1987—; mem. panel securities arbitrators, Dallas adv. coun. Am. Arbitration Assn. Mem. Am. Jewish Com., Dallas, 1982—. Named one of Outstanding Young Women Am., 1983. Mem. Nat. Assn. Securities Dealers (arbitrator), Tex. Bar Assn., Dallas Bar Assn. Office: Akin Gump Strauss Hauer & Feld LLP 1700 Pacific Ave Ste 4100 Dallas TX 75201-4618

JAZAIE, TAMARA MICHELLE, protective services official; b. Orange, Calif., Mar. 16, 1962; d. Robert Edward and Paula Joline (Ritchey) Watkins; m. Ric Hirbod, Aug. 17, 1989 (div. Mar. 1991). AA, Orange Coast Coll., 1983. Teaching asst. Fairview State Hosp., Costa Mesa, Calif., 1984-88; office mgr. Med. Bd. Calif., Santa Ana, 1988-89, Dental Bd. Calif., Santa Ana, 1989-91; correctional officer Calif. Youth Authority, Whittier, 1991—. Mem. Alpha Gamma Sigma. Democrat. Office: California Youth Authority 13200 S Bloomfield Norwalk CA 90650

JEANSONNE, ANGELA LYNNE, senior analyst; b. Honolulu, Oct. 3, 1961; d. Charles Preston and Beverly Jean (Ulstad) McKinney; m. William C. Jeansonne, June 11, 1988. BA, Am. U., 1984; MA, George Washington U., 1992. Legis. analyst Sch. Bd. Assn., Washington, 1983-84; edn. analyst Ind. Fed., Washington, 1984-86; analyst Xerox Corp., Arlington, Va., 1986-88; sr. analyst Student Loan Mktg. Assn., Washington, 1988—. Recipient acad. scholars Am. Univ., Washington, 1982-84, Bryce Harlow scholarship, 1991. Mem. AAUW, Bus. and Profl. Women. Republican. Methodist.

JECKLIN, LOIS UNDERWOOD, art corporation executive, consultant; b. Manning, Iowa, Oct. 5, 1934; d. J.R. and Ruth O. (Austin) Underwood; m. Dirk C. Jecklin, June 24, 1955; children: Jennifer Anne, Ivan Peter. BA, State U. Iowa, 1992. Residency coord. Quad City Arts Coun., Rock Island, Ill., 1973-78; field rep. Affiliate Artists, Inc., N.Y.C., 1975-77; mgr., artist in residence Deere & Co., Moline, Ill., 1977-80; dir. Vis. Artist Series, Davenport, Iowa, 1978-81; pres. Vis. Artists, Inc., Davenport, 1981-88; pres., owner Jecklin Assocs., 1988—. asst. to exec. dir. Walter W. Naumburg Found., N.Y.C., 1990—; cons. writer's program St. Ambrose Coll., Davenport, 1981, 83, 85; mem. com. Iowa Arts Coun., Des Moines, 1983-84; panelist Chamber Music Am., N.Y.C., 1984, Pub. Art Coun., Cedar Rapids, Iowa, 1984; panelist, mem. com. Lt. Gov.'s Conf. on Iowa's Future, Des Moines, 1984; trustee Davenport Mus. Art, 1975-95, Nature Conservancy Iowa, 1987-88; mem. steering com. Iowa Citizens for Arts, Des Moines, 1970-71; bd. dirs. Tri-City Symphony Orchestra Assn., Davenport, 1968-83; founding mem. Urban Design Council, HOME, City of Davenport Beautification Com., all Davenport, 1970-72; bd. gov. Am. Craft Mus., N.Y.C., 1995—. Recipient numerous awards Izaak Walton League, Davenport Art Gallery, Assn. for Retarded Citizens, Am. Heart Assn., Ill. Bur. Corrections, many others; LaVernes Noyes scholar, 1953-55. Mem. Am. Coun. for Arts, Nat. Assn. Performing Art's Mgrs. and Agents, Am. Symphony Orch.

League, Crow Valley Golf Club, Outing Club, Rotary. Republican. Episcopalian. Home and Office: 2717 Nichols Ln Davenport IA 52803-3620

JEDYNAK, BEVERLY L., public relations executive; b. Chgo., Dec. 10, 1952; d. Leonard Joseph and Adele Astrid (Martens) J. Student, Dana Coll., 1970-71. Sec. Martin E. Janis & Co., Inc., Chgo., 1971-77, acct. exec., 1977-79, sr. acct. exec., 1979-81, v.p., 1981-86, sr. v.p., 1986-90, exec. v.p., 1990—. Treas., bd. dirs. Chgo. Bible Soc., 1991—; pres. bd. dirs. Park View Luth. Sch., Chgo., 1987-90, 94—, founder, 1987; mem., chmn. various coms. Park View Luth Ch., Chgo., 1971—, ch. organist.

JEFF, GLORIA JEAN, federal government administrator; b. Detroit, Apr. 8, 1952; d. Doris Lee and Harriette Virginia (Davis) J. BSE in Civil Engring., U. Mich., 1974, MSE, 1976, M in Urban Planning, 1978; cert. profl. program in Urban Transp., Carnegie Mellon U., 1979. Prin. planner, program analyst, equipment engr. Southeastern Mich. Transp. Authority, 1976-81; divsn. adminstr., multi-regional planning divsn. Mich. Dept. Transp., 1981-83, divsn. adminstr., urban transp. planning divsn., 1983-85, asst. dep. dir. Bur. of Transp. Planning, 1985-90, dep. dir. Bur. Transp. Planning; assoc. adminstr. for policy Fed. Hwy. Adminstrn., U.S. Dept. Transp., Washington, 1993—; adj. prof. Coll. Architecture and Urban Planning, U. Mich., Ann Arbor, 1988—; chair standing com. on planning Mississippi Valley Conf. State Hwys. and Transp. Ofcls., 1987-89, vice chair strategic issues com., 1990-94; mem. Transp. Rsch. Bd., 1989—. Bd. dirs. Capitol chpt. Child and Family Svcs. of Mich. Inc., 1990-93, chair long-range planning com., 1991-93, sec. bd. dirs., 1993. Recipient Young Engr. of Yr. award Detroit chpt. Soc. Women Engrs., 1979, Young Engr. of Yr. award Detroit chpt. NSPE, 1979, Disting. Alumni award U. Mich., 1991, 92, Regional Amb. award S.E. Mich. Assn. Govts., 1993, others. Mem. Am. Assn. Hwy. and Transp. Ofcls. (mem. model adv. tech. com. 1988-91, mem. econ. expansion and devel. com. 1990-91, vice chair intermodal issues com. 1990-93), Am. Planning Assn. (v.p. for programs Planning and the Black Cmty. div. 1990-92, mem. nat. membership com. 1990-92, chair transp. planning div. 1994—, pres. Mich. chpt. 1990-91), Am. Inst. Cert. Planners, U. Mich. Alumni Assn. (bd. dirs. 1985-90), U. Mich. Coll. Architecture Alumni Soc., Delta Sigma Theta, others. Office: Dept Transp Policy Office 400 7th St SW Washington DC 20590

JEFFERDS, MARY LEE, environmental education executive; b. Seattle, July 16, 1921; d. Amos Osgood and Vera Margaret (Percival) J.; AB, U. Calif. at Berkeley, 1943, gen. secondary teaching cert., 1951; MA, Columbia U., 1947; cert. Washington and Lee U., 1945. Sec. Fair Play Com. Am. Citizens Japanese Ancestry, 1943-44; adminstrv. asst. U.C. Alumni Assn. book Students at Berkeley, 1949; dir. Student Union Monterey Jr. Coll., 1949-50; mgr. Nat. Audubon Soc. Conservation Resource Ctr., Berkeley, 1951-66; dir. Nat. Audubon Soc. Bay Area Ednl. Svcs., 1966-71; curriculum cons. Project WEY, U. Calif. Demonstration Lab. Sch., Berkeley, 1972-83. Cons. Berkeley Sch. Dist., Alameda County Schs. Mem. land- use com. Environ. Edn. com. East Bay Mcpl. Utility Dist., 1968-87; mem. steering com. Nat. Sci. Guild, Oakland Mus., 1970-76; community adviser Jr. League of Oakland, 1972-76. Mem. Berkeley Women's Town Coun., 1970-91; mem. NAACP.; bd. dirs. East Bay Regional Park Dist., 1972-91, pres., 1978-80, 88-90; bd. dirs. Save San Francisco Bay Assn., 1969-91, People for Open Space, 1977-86, Calif. Natural Areas Coordinating Coun., 1968-90, Living History Ctr., 1982-85; mem. steering com. Bay Area Environ. Edn. Alliance, 1982-85, regional planning com. Assn. of Bay Area Govts., 1988-91, exec. com. Citizens for Eastshore State Park, 1985—; v.p. Friends of Bot. Garden, U. Calif., Berkeley, 1976-80, trustee, 1986—. With USAAF, 1944-46. Recipient Merit award Calif. Conservation Coun., 1953; Woman of Achievement award Camp Fire Girls, 1976; Merit award Am. Soc. Landscape Architects, 1979, Conservation award Golden Gate Audubon Soc., 1985, Benjamin I. Wheeler medal, 1991; mem. Am. Farmland Trust. Mem. AAUW (Calif. com. 1970-73), Prytanean Alumnae, Inc. (pres. 1969-71, chmn. adv. coun. 1971-73, adv. com. Urban Creeks Coun. 1986-91), Nature Conservancy (chmn. no. Calif. chpt. 1970-71), LWV, Regional Parks Assn. (citizens com. to complete the refuge), Nat. Women's Polit. Caucus, Golden Gate Audubon Soc., Sierra Club (environ. edn. com. No. Calif. chpt. 1973-77), U. Calif. Alumni Assn., Inst. Calif. Man in Nature, Calif. Assn. Recreation and Park Dists. (v.p. 1978-81, 1988-90, Oustanding Bd. Mem. award 1989), Preserve Area Ridgelands, Calif. Native Plant Soc., Planning and Conservation League, Urban Ecology, Cousteau Soc., Soroptomists, Pi Lambda Theta, Mortar Board, Gavel (pres.). Democrat. Mem. adv. com. Natural History Guide Series U. Calif. Press, 1972-91. Home: 2932 Pine Ave Berkeley CA 94705-2349

JEFFERS, IDA PEARLE, management consultant, volunteer; b. Houston, Tex., Sept. 5, 1935; d. Stanford Wilbur and Ida Pearle (Kinkead) Oberg; m. Samuel Lee Jeffers, Aug. 29, 1956; children: John Laurence (dec.), Julie Elizabeth Flynn, Melinda Leigh. Student, U. Colo., 1953-56; BA in History, U. N.Mex., 1957. Asst. to mayor City of Albuquerque, 1978, dir. capital improvements, 1979-81; pres. Orgn. Plus, 1988—; guest lectr. U. N.Mex. Albuquerque Pub. Sch., 1968-71. Chmn. Comprehensive Plan Rev., Bond Issue, various coms., Albuquerque, 1968—; mem. Middle Rio Grand Coun. Govts., Albuquerque, 1972-74; mem. Environ. Planning Commn., Albuquerque, 1972-77, chmn. 1975-76; chmn. Citizen Adv. Group, Community Devel., Albuquerque, 1974-75; mem. Jr. League, Albuquerque, 1966—, bd. dirs. 1970-76; mem. N. Mex. Architect, Engrs. Joint Practice Bd. 1978-85, chmn. 1983-85; treas. St. Mark's Episcopal Ch., 1983-86; pres. Eldorado High Sch. Parents, Albuquerque, 1985-86; pres. Regional Conservation Land Trust, Albuquerque, 1987-91; trustee Found., Study and Care of Organic Brain Damage, Houston, 1972-82, pres. 1982-94; mem. Urban Transp. Planning Policy Bd., 1972-74; chmn. community advisors Albuquerque Youth Symphony, 1985-91; founder, chair Friends of Sandia (N.Mex.) Sch., 1965-68, chmn. devel. pre-sch. bd., 1974; mentor Leadership Albuquerque, 1987-91; bd. dirs. Good Govt. Group, Albuquerque, 1988-92, treas. 1988-92; mem., treas. Albuquerque Arts Alliance, 1988-91; mem. Albuquerque All Faiths, All Faith's Receiving Home Aux., 1964-68, sec. 1966, Jr. Women Club, 1963-66, Chaparral Coun. Girl Scouts leaders, 1971-73, selections chmn., 1973-74, Albuquerque Tutorial Coun., 1967-69; foundation bd. Albuquerque Youth Symphony, 1995—. Recipient Disting. Pub. Svc. award, State of N. Mex., 1975, Disting. Woman of N. Mex. award, N.Mex. Women's Polit. Caucus, 1976, Golden Talon award Eldorado High Sch., Albuquerque, 1985, Panhellenic Coun. Disting. Alumnae award 1979. Mem. Rotary, Delta Gamma (pres. 1963-67, chmn. collegiate adv. bd. 1968-71, Cable and Shield awards 1970, 77). Republican. Episcopalian.

JEFFERSON, CLAIRE EATON, meetings executive; b. Balt., Dec. 8, 1940; d. Clarence Leroy and Jennie (Bierner) Eaton; m. Milton Earl Jefferson, Sept. 21, 1974. Cert., Balt. C.C., 1961. Exec. sec. Balt. Life Ins. Co., Balt., 1961-71; sec. Balt. Sunpapers, Balt., 1971-74; asst. to pres. A/V Edn. Products, Balt., 1974-76; retail mgr. Spectrum 39, Balt., 1976-85, security mgr., 1985-90; meetings mgr. Am. Med. Dirs. Assn., Columbia, Md., 1990—. Active Gov.'s Adv. Com. State of Md.-Ocean City. Mem. Balt. Alumnae Assn. (pres. 1989-93), Chi Sigma (nat. pres. 1979-80, chair membership com.). Home: 5514 Edna Ave Baltimore MD 21214-2311 Office: Am Med Dirs Assn 10480 Little Pat Pky #760 Columbia MD 21044

JEFFERSON, DENISE, dance school director; b. Chgo.. Studied ballet with, Edna L. McRae; BA, Wheaton Coll.; MA, NYU. Co-founder, co-dir. Chgo. Dance Ctr.; tchr. dance U. Ill., Chgo.; with Pearl Lang Dance Co.; mem. dance faculty Sch. Arts NYU, Alvin Ailey Dance Ctr., 1975—; dir. Alvin Ailey Am. Dance Ctr. Scholarship program, 1980-84, Alvin Ailey Dance Ctr., 1984—; remedial writing tchr. Seek program Hunter Coll.; developed modern dance program Benedict Coll.; guest tchr. U.S., internat.; mem. internat. team dance profls. Dutch govt. to evaluate Dance acads. in Holland, 1990; adjudicator Arts Recognition, Talent Search Confederation Nat. de Danse, Fedn. Interprofl. de la danse, 1992. Grantee Nat. Endowment Arts and Humanities; scholar Marthe Graham Sch. Contenporary Dance. Mem. Internat. Assn. Blacks in Dance (co-chair), Nat. Assns. Schs. Dance (bd. dirs. 1989-91, program evaluator, mem. commn. accredation), N.Y. State Coun. Arts (dance panel, appeal panel). Office: Alvin Ailey Am Dance Ctr 211 W 61st St 3d Fl New York NY 10023*

JEFFERSON, SANDRA TRAYLOR, choreographer, ballet coach; b. Tarboro, N.C., Feb. 28, 1942; d. Charles Labon and Doris Vivian (Parker) Traylor; m. Milton Franklin Jefferson, July 2, 1960; children: Mark Franklin, Todd Christopher. Student, Parks Sch. Dance, Petersburg, Va., 1947-58, Sch. of the Richmond (Va.) Ballet, 1958-60; diploma, Julia Mildred Harper Sch. Dance, Richmond, 1960; studied with Robert David Brown, Sterling, Va., 1978-80. Soloist Ballet Impromptu, Richmond, 1958-60; freelance dance instr. Chantilly, Va., 1968-70; ballet coach Artistic Skating Club of Sterling, 1980; founder, dir. Ballet for Skaters, Manassas, Va., 1980-89; artistic dir., cons. in choreography No. Va. Artistic Skating Club, Manassas, 1986-89; artistic dir. Skating Club of Manassas, 1989; founder, dir. Ballet for Skaters, Seabrook, Md., 1989-94; choreographer, ballet coach Nat. Capitol Dance and Figure Club, Seabrook and Washington, 1989-94; founder, dir. Ballet for Figure Skaters, Sterling, Va., 1993-94; students include nat. medalists in the U.S. and Can. and mems. Can. World Team, U.S. Olympic Sports Festival Team; freelance choreographer, ballet coach, Sterling, 1993—. Developer: Brosano Technique Vocabulary of Movement, 1986, Free Form Ballet, 1993; co-developer (artistic skating technique) Brosano Technique, 1981. Social dir. Jaycee-ettes, Winchester, Va., 1963-67. Recipient Achievement award Jaycee-ettes, 1963, 64, 65, 66, 67, U.S. S.E. Soc. Roller Skating Tchrs. Am. award, 1988, World Decoration of Excellence award Am. Biog. Inst., 1989. Mem. Profl. Dance Tchrs. Assn. Methodist. Home and Office: 507 S Maple Ct Sterling VA 20164

JEFFERY, DIANE LYNNE ROLLINS, human resources manager; b. Oklahoma City, Sept. 24, 1962; d. Roger William and Joan Josephine (Heller) Rollins; m. Mark Adrian Jeffery, July 3, 1988. BA, Wheaton Coll., 1984; MPA, U. Mass., 1987. Pers. officer Dept. Pub. Works, Boston, 1987-88; mgr. human resources Dept. Revenue, Boston, 1988—. Bd. dirs. LWV, Norwood, Mass., 1993, membership chair, co-chair domestic violence com., Boston, 1993. Recipient Citation for Outstanding Performance, Commonwealth of Mass., 1988, Cert. Recognition, Commonwealth of Mass., 1988. Mem. Internat. Pers. Mgmt. Assn. (pres.-elect 1992, pres. Mass. chpt. 1993), Am. Soc. Pub. Adminstrs. (coun. mem. Mass. chpt. 1993). Home: 41 Fisher St Norwood MA 02062 Office: Dept Revenue 100 Cambridge St Boston MA 02204

JEFFERY, GINA MARIE, insurance company official; b. Jamaica, N.Y., Feb. 17, 1965; d. Angelo Joseph and Anna Marie (Laine) Avignone; m. Scott Anthony Jeffery, Apr. 17, 1993. BA in Sociology, SUNY, Albany, 1987; postgrad., Northeastern U. Coord. pers. South Nassau Communities Hosp., Oceanside, N.Y., 1987-88; human resources asst. Mass. Casualty Ins. Co., Boston, 1988-90, human resources rep., 1990—. Mem. New Eng. Human Resources Assn. Office: Mass Casualty Ins Co 711 Atlantic Ave Boston MA 02111

JEFFREY, NOELA MARY, publishing executive; b. Reading, Pa., Dec. 11, 1941; d. John Theodore and Mary M. (Linkowski) Slapikas; m. Alexander MacLean Jeffrey, June 22, 1968; children: Alexander Maclean Jr., Douglas Duart. BA, Seton Hill Coll., 1963. Corr. Harcourt, Barce, Javanovich, N.Y.C., 1963-65; editor Publs. of Most. Reverend Fulton J. Sheen, N.Y.C., 1965-68; editor, assoc. pub. Wells Pubs., Pasedena, Calif., 1985-91; principal Noel Jeffrey Editorial Svcs., 1991—. Editor Printing Jour., 1988, PINC Newsletter and Blueline, American Printer Mag., 1993—; contbr. articles to profl. jours. Bd. dirs. Graphic Arts Literacy Alliance, Pitts., 1990—; mem. adv. com. graphics comms. dept. Pasadena City Coll., 1988—; various bd. positions Pasadena Jr. Philharmonic Com., 1982-86, assoc. 1986—; cmty. svc. positions, Little League, PTA, 1972—. Named Pioneer of Yr. Printing Industries So. Calif., 1990. Mem. In Plant Mgmt. Assn., L.A. Phil. Affiliates. Democrat. Roman Catholic. Home: 330 Rosita Ln Pasadena CA 91105-1437

JEFFREY, SHIRLEY RUTHANN, publisher; b. Durant, Okla., Aug. 5, 1936; d. Hubert D. and Pauline (Blain) Carr; m. Dwight W. Jeffrey, Oct. 6, 1966; children: Robin Kimberly Reese, Paula Cherie Lyon, Michelle Jolie Jeffrey. AA, El Camino Coll., Gardena, Calif., 1962; BA, U. So. Calif., L.A., 1966. Cert. Ikebana tchr., Tokyo. Publisher Pelican Publs., Denton, Tex. Co-author: Gesneriad Judges Manual, 1989; author/editor: Internat. Cookbook, 1990, Episcias, 1990; contbr. articles to various jours. Hdqs. worker Rep. Ctrl. Com., Denton, 1988, coord. vols., 1993-94, mem. exec. com., precinct chmn., 1994—; bd. dirs. Am. Cancer Soc., Denton, 1975-77; referee U.S. Soccer Fedn., Denton, 1980-81. Mem. NAFE, Nat. Assn. Securities Dealers (registered rep.), U.S. SEC (registered investment advisor) Gesneriad Soc. Internat. (pres. 1987-90), North Tex. African Violet Judges Coun. (pres. 1975-76), First African Violet Soc. of New Orleans (pres. 1973-74), Nat. Assn. Parliamentarians, Tex. State Assn. Parliamentarians, Am. Gloxinia and Gesneriad Soc. (sr. judge), Am. Assn. Ret. Persons (chpt. bd. dirs. 1992—), others. Episcopalian. Home: 1918 Williamsburg Row Denton TX 76201-2227 Office: Pelican Publs PO Box 720 Denton TX 76202-0720

JEFFREY-SMITH, LILLI ANN, biofeedback specialist, educator, administrator; b. Bedford, Ind., 1944; d. Charles Constantine and Adelai (Malon) Jeffrey-Smith. Grad. Ind. Bus. Coll., 1963; B.S., Ind. U., 1973; grad. Psychosomatic Medicine Clinic, Berkeley, Calif. (accredited by Albert Einstein Coll. Medicine); PhD in Behavioral Sci., Kennedy-Western U., 1988. Cert. biofeedback specialist. Project assoc., stress mgmt. clinician City of Indpls., 1973-79; cons. Airport Med. Clinic, Indpls., 1981; outreach coord. Abbott-Northwestern Hosp., Mpls., 1981; dir. biofeedback dept. Sister Kenney Inst., Mpls., 1979-81, Noran Neurol. Clinic, Mpls., 1981-83; instr., dir. Biofeedback Tng. and Treatment Ctr., Edina, Minn., 1979—; pres. Biofeedback Rsch. and Devel. Co. Ltd., Edina, 1983—; cons. to biofeedback depts. St. Joseph Hosp., Mankato, Minn., 1984—, Lakeview Clinic, Waconia, Minn., 1983, Psychiat. Clinic of Mankato, 1983—, Fairview Ridges Hosp., Burnsville, Minn., 1987—. Author, narrator health and wellness tape series. Mem. Republican Presdl. Task Force, 1984—, NSC, 1985; co-chmn. Mayor's Handicapped Task Force, Indpls., 1975; founder, pres. Miss Wheel Chair of Ind., Inc. Named Hon. Lt. Gov., State of Ind., 1978; given Key to the City of Indpls., 1973, Flag of the City of Indpls., 1975. Mem. Am. Inst. Stress, N.Y. Acad. Sci., AAAS, Edina C. of C., Minn. Women's Network, Biofeedback Soc. Am., Biofeedback Soc. Minn., Am. Assn. Control Tension, Am. Assn. Behaviorial Therapists, Am. Assn. Biofeedback Clinicians, Nat. Assn. Women Bus. Owners, Soc. Open Focus and Tng. Rsch., Assn. Trainers in Clin. Hypnosis, Internat. Stress and Tension Control Assn., Minn. Assn. Rehab. Providers, Nat. Assn. Exec. Women, Internat. Platform Assn. Avocations: music, stamp collecting, shooting, poetry. Office: Biofeedback Tng & Treatment Ctr 7300 France Ave S Ste 200 Minneapolis MN 55435-4542

JEFFRIES-ASHFORD, ALECIA, accounting analyst; b. Chapel Hill, N.C., June 28, 1964; d. James William and Esther Jerlene (Hayes) J.; m. Jerry L. Ashford, Oct. 8, 1994. BS in Acctg., Elon Coll., 1987; postgrad., Lindenwood Coll., 1991—. With accounts receivable dept. Roche Biomed. Labs., Burlington, N.C., 1984-86; asst. mgr. Ashby's Ltd., Durham, N.C., 1987-88; placement dir. Rutledge Coll., Durham, 1988-89; cash mgmt. analyst DNS/MEMC Electronic Materials (formerly Monsanto Electronic, St. Peters, Mo., 1989, cost analyst, 1989-90; corp. property acct. DNS/MEMC Electronic Materials (formerly Monsanto Electronic Materials), St. Peters, Mo., 1990—; cost analyst Smiths Industries, Grand Rapids, Mich., 1992-94; fin. analyst United Techs. Automotive, Dearborn, Mich., 1994—. Bd. dirs. Grand Rapids Urban League, 1993; active Big Brother/Big Sister, Grand Rapids, 1993—; bd. dirs. fin. Grand Rapids Urban League, 1993—; cons. Grand Rapids Jr. Achievement, 1992—. Mem. NOW, NAFE, Nat. Assn. Accts., Inst. Mgmt. Accts., Profl. Women's Alliance. Home: 12970 E Outer Dr Detroit MI 48224 Office: United Techs Automotive 5200 Auto Club Dr Dearborn MI 48126-9982

JEGEN, SISTER CAROL FRANCES, religion educator; b. Chgo., Oct. 11, 1925; d. Julian Aloysius and Evelyn W. (Bostelmann) J. BS in History, St. Louis U., 1951; MA in Theology, Marquette U., 1958, PhD in Religious Studies, 1968; hon. degree, St. Mary of the Woods, Terra Haute, Ind., 1977. Elem. tchr. St. Francis Xavier Sch., St. Louis, 1947-51; secondary tchr. Holy Angels Sch., Milw., 1951-57; coll. tchr. Mundelein Coll., Chgo., 1957-91; prof. pastoral studies Loyola U., Chgo., 1991—; adv. coun. U.S. Cath. Bishops, Washington, 1969-74; trustees Cath. Theol. Union, Chgo., 1974-84. Author: Jesus the Peace Maker, 1986, Restoring Our Friendship with God, 1989; co-author: (with Byron Sherwin) Thank God, 1989; editor: Mary According to Women, 1985. Participant Nat. Farm Worker Ministry, Fresno, Calif., 1977—; mem. Pax Christi, U.S.A., 1979—, Jane Addams Conf., Chgo., 1989. Recipient Loyola Civic award Loyola U., Chgo., 1981; named one of 100 Women to Watch Today's Chgo. Woman, 1989. Mem. Cath. Theol. Soc. Am., Coll. Theology Soc., Cath.-Jewish Scholars Dialog, Liturgical Conf. Democrat. Roman Catholic. Home: Wright Hall 6364 N Sheridan Rd Chicago IL 60660-1726 Office: Loyola U Inst Pastoral Studies 6525 N Sheridan Rd Chicago IL 60626-5311

JEHLEN, CHRISTY CAROL COKER, association executive; b. Conway, Ark., Feb. 29, 1960; d. Otis Ray Coker and Peggy Ann (Hager) Coker-Gandy; m. John Ervin Jehlen Jr., June 27, 1981; 1 child, Jordan Blakely. B of Sci. Edn., U. Ark., 1982, MA, 1983. Comm. instr. Univ. Ark., Fayetteville, 1982-86; dir. placement and edn. Cooper Communities, Inc., Bella Vista, Ark., 1986-88; gen. mgr. Dental Implant Ctr., Fayetteville, 1988-89; mktg. specialist, workshop lectr. State of Ark. Dept. Human Svcs., Russellville, 1989-94; comm. instr. Petit Jean Tech. Coll., Morrilton, Ark., 1993-94; exec. dir. River Valley United Way, Russellville, Ark., 1994—. Coord. Welfare Reform Task Force, Pope County, Ark., 1990-94; chair Ark. River Valley Resource Fair Com., 1993-94; mem. Drug and Gang Task Force, Pope County, 1993. Recipient Outstanding Citizenship, Ark. Gov., 1993, Pub. Svc. Recognition award Welfare Reform Task Force, Pope County, 1993. Mem. NAFE. Democrat. Methodist. Office: River Valley United Way Inc PO Box 636 500 W Main St Ste 216 Russellville AR 72811

JEHLEN, PATRICIA D., state legislator; b. Austin, Tex., Oct. 14, 1943; d. Paul Kindred Jr. and Ruth Miller (Zumbrunnen) Deats; m. Alain Peter Jehlen, Aug. 29, 1969; children: Nicholas, Wendy, Peter. BA, Swarthmore Coll., 1965; MA in Teaching, Harvard U., 1969. Rschr. Harvard Sch. Edn., Cambridge, Mass., 1966-67; tchr. history Brookline (Mass.) High Sch., 1968-71; mem. Somerville (Mass.) Sch. Com., 1976-91; legislator Mass. Ho. of Reps., Somerville, 1991—. VISTA vol. Cook County Migrant Coun., Chicago Heights, Ill., 1965-66. Democrat. Unitarian-Universalist. Home: 67 Dane St Somerville MA 02143-3730 Office: Mass House of Reps Boston MA 02133

JELESKO, CHRISTINA HUTCHINS, minister; b. San Jose, Calif., May 16, 1961; d. Bruce Allen and Bessie May Hutchins; m. John Gene Jelesko, July 7, 1984. BS in Biochemistry with honors, U. Calif., Davis, 1983; MDiv, Harvard U. Div. Sch., 1991. Ordained to ministry United Ch. of Christ, 1992. Lab. technician II City of San Jose (Calif.) Water Pollution Control, 1981-85; biochem. rsch. technologist II Neo Rx, Corp., Seattle, 1986-88; student assoc. minister South Action (Mass.) Congl. Ch., 1989-91; sr. minister Mira Vista United Ch. of Christ, El Cerrito, Calif., 1992—; spokesperson Plymouth Congl. Ch., Seattle at Iglesia Morava, Managua, Nicaragua, 1988; guest preacher, speaker No. Calif. conf. United Ch. of Christ, 1992—. Author: (poetry) Ruah: The Power of Poetry, 1993. Vol. Habitat for Humanity, Inc., Americus, Ga., 1978; commencement speaker Harvard U. Div. Sch., Cambridge, Mass., 1991; keynote speaker Martin Luther King Jr. Celebration, NAACP, El Cerrito, Calif., 1993, Religious Coalition for Reproductive Rights, 1993; homeless advocate, speaker Greater Richmond Interfaith Program, El Cerrito, 1993-94. Recipient Billings Preaching prize Harvard U., 1990, 91; Thayer Scholar of Divinity Harvard U., 1991. Mem. NOW, Greater Richmond Interfaith Program, No. Calif. Conf. United Ch. of Christ (com. mem. 1993—), NAACP, United Ch. of Christ Friends of Open and Affirming (resident theologian 1994—), Parents and Friends of Lesbians and Gays. Democrat. United Ch. of Christ. Office: Mira Vista United Ch Christ 7075 Cutting Blvd El Cerrito CA 94530

JENKINS, BARBARA ALEXANDER, pastor; b. Ft. Bragg, N.C., Oct. 13, 1942; d. Archie Herman Alexander and Hattie Elizabeth (Thigpen) Truitt; m. Warren Keith Jenkins, Aug. 22, 1964 (div. Sept. 1980); children: Pamela, Eric, Jason. BS, Ea. Mich. U., 1964, postgrad., 1964-66; postgrad., Duke U., 1978; DD (hon.), Ch. of Christ Bible Coll., Madras, India, 1988. Ordained to ministry, World Faith Clinic Inc., 1983, A.M.E. Zion Ch., 1982. Min. World Faith Clinic Inc., Fayetteville, N.C., 1981-83, A.M.E. Zion Ch., Fayetteville, 1982-84; pastor Noah's Ark Ministry, Fayetteville, 1985-86; founder, pastor Rainbow Tabernacle of Faith Ministries, Inc., Winston-Salem, N.C., 1984—; founder Rainbow Raleigh (N.C.) Outreach Ministries, 1986—, Rainbow Tabernacle of Faith, Charlotte, N.C., 1987—; dir. Spotlight on Truth Internat. Radio Ministries, Winston-Salem, 1985—, overseer hdqs. Ogun State, Nigeria, 1992; founder Rainbow Internat. Crusade Ministry, Winston-Salem, 1986—; dean Rainbow Inst. Commensurate Studies, Winston-Salem, 1985—; mem. Internat. Conv. Faith Ministries, Tulsa, 1989—. Author: Guidelines for Ministers, 1994; contbr. articles to religious jours. Concert vocalist N.C. Black Repertory Co., Winston-Salem, 1987, 88; youth coord. Jerry Lewis Muscular Dystrophy Telethon, Raleigh, 1987, 88; guest speaker Wake Forest U., Winston-Salem, 1991. Recipient Outstanding Svc. award Rainbow Tabernacle Faith, Inc., 1987; scholar March of Dimes-Easter Seals, 1960-64. Mem. N.C. Women in Ministry (bd. dirs.), NAFE, Delta Sigma Theta (project coord. 1979-80). Democrat. Office: Rainbow Tabernacle Faith Ministries Inc 4091 New Walkertown Rd Winston-Salem NC 27105 also: 1119 Cypress Cir Winston-Salem NC 27106

JENKINS, BILLIE BEASLEY, film company executive; b. Topeka, June 27, 1943; d. Arthur and Etta Mae (Price) Capelton; m. Rudolph Alan Jenkins, Nov. 1, 1935; 1 child, Tina Caprice. Student, Santa Monica City Coll., 1965-69. Exec. sec. to v.p. prodn. Screen Gems, L.A., 1969-72; exec. asst. Spelling/Goldberg Prodns., 1972-82; dir. adminstrn. The Leonard Co./Mandy Films, 1982-85, v.p., 1985-87; exec. asst. to pres. and chief oper. officer 20th Century Fox Film Corp., L.A., 1986-87, dir. adminstrn., 1987-90, dir. prodn. svcs. & resources Fox Motion Pictures div., 1990-92; program coord. Am. Film Inst. Gary Hendler Minority Filmmakers Program, 1990-93; pres., CEO Masala Prodns., Inc., 1991—. Asst. to exec. producer: (films) War Games, 1984, Spacecamp, 1986; (movies for TV) Something about Amelia, 1984, Alex, The Life of a Child, 1985; (series) Paper Dolls, 1985, Cavanaughs, 1987, Charlie's Angels, Rookies, others. Commr. L.A. City Cultural Heritage Commn., 1992-93. Named Woman of Excellence by Western L.A. County Coun. Boy Scouts Am., 1991. Mem. NAFE, Women in Film Assn. (pres. 1991, 92, advisor to exec. bd.), Black Women's Network, Am. Film Inst., Ind. Feature Prodns./West, Motivating Our Students Through Experience (exec. bd. mem.).

JENKINS, BRENDA GWENETTA, early childhood education specialist; b. Durham, N.C., Aug. 11, 1949; d. Brinton Alfred and Ophelia Arden (Eaton) Jenkins. BS, Howard U., 1971, MEd, 1972, Cert. Advanced Spl. Edn., 1975; postgrad. Trinity Coll., Am. U., U. D.C., 1976—. Cert. aerobics instr. Nat. Dance-Exercise Instr.'s Tng. Assn. Cheerleader coach Howard U., Washington, 1971-86; aerobics instr. D.C. Pub. Schs., 1982—, tchr., 1972—; v.p. Nerdlihc Corp., Washington, 1985—; co-owner Fantasia Early Learning Acad., 1985—; ptnr. Jenkins, Trapp-Dukes and Yates Partnership; aerobic instr. for handicapped Council for Exceptional Children, Washington, 1982, recreation svcs. City of Rockville, Md., 1986—; instr. Washington Tchrs.; instr. aerobics Langdon Park Recreation Ctr. Washington Dept. Recreation, 1988-93, You Fit, Inc. Nat. Children's Ctr., Washington, 1991—, Anthony Bowen YMCA, Washington, 1992-93; instr. health and nutrition support, Rockville, Md., 1992; instr., coach Maryvale Pom Pom/cheerleaders, Montgomery County, Md., winter 1992; step aerobic instr. Nat. Children's Ctr., 1991—; master tchr. Cooperating Tchr. Corps, 1993—; bldg. rep. Washington Tchrs. Union AFT, AFL-CIO, 1987-89, 91-94, asst. bldg. rep., 1990-91; elected. v.p. spl. edn. Washington Tchrs. Union Local # 6, 1994; developer, coord. My Spl. Friend program, 1984—; trainer AIDS in the Workplace, 1990; developer BJ's Thinking Cap, 1991, Learning Creations, 1994; presenter numerous workshops, seminars; supr. foster grandparent program Sharpe Health Sch., 1988—; trainer Early Childhood Substance Abuse Project Tng., spring and summer, 1992-93; mental health trainer Metro. Foster Grandparent Program, Washington, 1992-93; mem. presch. adv. bd. D.C. Pub. Schs., 1992-93, mem. coordinating curriculum coun., 1994—; curriculum writer, trainer, summer 1993; master tchr. Coop. Tchr. Corps, 1993—; del. numerous confs. Recipient Conscientious Service award D.C. Pub. Schs., 1985; Outstanding Recognition award Howard U. Alumni Cheerleaders Assn., 1984 (award renamed The Brenda G. Jenkins Outstanding Cheerleader Award, 1987); Outstanding Service awards Kappa Delta Pi, 1978, 79, 81, 82, 84; citation Washington Tchrs. Union, 1985; Appreciation cert. D.C. Dept. Recreation, 1985, others; nominee Agnes Meyer Outstanding Tchr. award, 1988, Theodore R. Hogans Jr. Pub. Service award, 1988, Outstanding Svc. and Leadership award Howard U. Alumni Cheerleaders Assn., 1994; Spl. Edn. grantee D.C. Pub. Sch. State Office, 1993, Citibank, 1994. Mem. Am. Fedn. Tchrs., D.C. Parents and Friends of

Children with Spl. Needs (bd. dirs.), Theta Alpha chpt. Kappa Delta Pi (exec. com.), Howard U. Alumni Cheerleaders Assn. (co-founder 1977, pres. elect 1990-94). Democrat. Avocations: alumni cheerleading, fashion design, cooking, dancing, poetry writing.

JENKINS, CAROL ANNE, educator; b. Kearny, N.J., Mar. 1, 1945; d. Lawrence Augustine and Sara (Ball) J. BA, Malone Coll., 1968; MA in Religious Edn., Chgo. Grad.Sch. Theology, 1969; MA in Sociology, Western Mich. U., 1972; PhD in Sociology, Kans. State U., 1986. Asst. prof., program dir. various orgns., Grand Rapids and Livonia, Mich., 1970-73; asst. prof. Judson Coll., Elgin, Ill., 1973-74, No. State Coll., Aberdeen, S.D., 1974-75, Henry Ford Community Coll., Dearborn, Mich., 1975-76, Wheeling (W.Va.) Coll., 1976-78, Tabor Coll., Hillsboro, Kans., 1978-82; instr. Kans. State U., Manhattan, 1982-85; assoc. prof. Biola U., La Mirada, Calif., 1985-92; prof. Glendale (Ariz.) C.C., 1992—; bd. dirs., chairwoman bd. Faculty Student Union, La Mirada, Christian Conciliation Svcs. of Orange County, Calif.; chair Maricopa C. C. Dist. Sociology Instructional Coun., 1992-93; cons. in field. Author: Thanatology: Discussions On Death & Dying, 1986, Social Problems: Issues and Their Opposing Viewpoints, 1987, Toward An Understanding of Social Thought, 1987, Toward an Understanding of Sociological Theory, 1989; contbr. chpts. to books and articles to profl. jours. Vol. umpire Hillsboro Recreation Dept., 1980-82; speaker Kiwanis, Hillsboro, 1981, Marquette High Sch., 1982; vol. Cedar Hill Mobile Country Club, Fullerton, Calif., 1986-92. Instnl. Rsch. grantee, 1990-91, 91-92. Mem. Am. Sociol. Assn. (exec. coun., awards chair, sect. undergrad. edn. 1993-96), Pacific Sociol. Assn. (program chair 1988), Midwest Sociol. Assn. (undergrad. edn. com. 1982-85), Rural Sociol. Soc. (com. 1988-90), Assn. Christians Tchg. Sociology (nat. program chair 1981, 92, 90), Religious Edn. Assn., AAUW, Nat. Assn. Ethnic Studies, William Lock Singers Players, Alpha Kappa Delta. Mennonite. Home: 19502 N 98th Ave Peoria AZ 85382-4113

JENKINS, CLARA BARNES, psychology educator; b. Franklinton, N.C.; d. Walter and Stella (Griffin) Barnes; BS, Winston-Salem State U., 1939; MA, N.C. Ctl. U., 1947; EdD, U. Pitts., 1964; postgrad., N.Y.U., 1947-48, U. N.C.-Chapel Hill, 1963, N.C. Agrl. and Tech. State U., 1971; m. Hugh Jenkins, Dec. 24, 1949 (div. Feb. 1955). Tchr. pub. schs., Wendell, N.C., 1939-43, Wise, N.C., 1943-45; mem. faculty Fayetteville State U., 1945-53, Rust Coll., Holly Spring, Miss., 1953-58; asst. prof. Shaw U., 1958-64; prof. edn. and psychology St. Paul's Coll., Lawrenceville, Va., 1964—; vis. prof. edn. Friendship Jr. Coll., Rock Hill, S.C., summer 1947, N.C. Agrl. and Tech. State U., 1966-83. Former mem. bd. dirs. Winston-Salem State U. Notary pub., N.C.; bd. dirs. annual giving fund U. Pitts.; United Negro Coll. Fund Faculty fellow, 1963-64; Am. Bapt. Conv. grantee, 1963-64. Mem. AAUP, Nat. Soc. for Study Edn., NEA, AAUW, Am. Hist. Assn., Va. Edn. Assn., Am. Acad. Polit. and Social Sci., AAAS, Internat. Platform Assn., Assn. Tchr. Educators, History Edn. Soc., Doctoral Assn. Educators, Am. Assn. Higher Edn., Am. Soc. Notaries, Acad. Polit. Sci., Am. Psychol. Assn., Soc. Research in Child Devel., Am. Soc. Notaries, Jean Piaget Soc., Philosophy of Edn. Soc., Soc. Profs. Edn., Am. Soc. Notaries, Leadership Coun., So. Poverty Law Ctr., Phi Eta Kappa, Zeta Phi Beta, Phi Delta Kappa, Kappa Delta Pi. Episcopalian. Home and Office: St Paul's Coll 920 Bridges St Henderson NC 27536-3736

JENKINS, FRANCES OWENS, retail owner; b. Leonard, Tex., Nov. 12, 1924; d. R. Melrose and Maureen (Durrett) Owens; m. William O. Jenkins (div. 1961); children: Steven O., Tamara. Student theatre arts East Tex. State U., 1939-42, Ind. U., 1945-48, U. Tenn., 1954-56. Fashion model Rogers Modeling Agy., Boston, 1950-52, Rich's, Knoxville, Tenn., 1955-60; owner, instr. Arts Sch. of Self-Improvement and Modeling, Knoxville, 1959-69; owner, pres. Fran Jenkins Boutique, Knoxville, 1964—; cons. Miss Am. Pageant, Knoxville, 1958-66. Actress Carousel Theatre, Knoxville, 1955-58. Home: 8833 Cove Point Ln Knoxville TN 37922-6402

JENKINS, GENI LOUISE EVANS, home health nurse; b. Chula Vista, Calif., Sept. 26, 1954; d. Howard Eugene and Gladys Louise (Phinney) Evans; m. Larry Joseph Jenkins, May 24, 1985; children: Gretchen Dawn, Thomas Glenn. ADN, Walla Walla (Wash.) C.C., 1984; BSN, Lewis Clark State Coll., 1992. RN, Wash., Idaho, Oreg.; cert. home health nurse. Staff oncol. nurse St. Joseph's Regional Med. Ctr., Lewiston, Idaho, 1984-86; office nurse Southway Internists, Lewiston, 1986-90; office urol. nurse D.A. Shrader, MD, Lewiston, 1990-91; home health nurse St. Joseph's Regional Med. Ctr., Lewiston, 1991-93; DON Able Home Health Svcs., Inc., Lewiston, 1993—; speaker in field. Mem. Idaho Nurses Assn., Nat. League of Nursing. Home: 1315 Boston St Clarkston WA 99403-2425

JENKINS, JANET E., state legislator, lawyer; b. Omaha, Jan. 22, 1941; d. Albert Eldon and Callie Elizabeth (Cowan) Clark; children: Jay Allen, John Richard, Janell Elizabeth, Lucille Jenkins. BS, So. Oreg. State Coll., 1962; JD magna cum laude, Gonzaga U., 1982. Bar: Idaho; cert. libr. Sch. libr. Corbett (Oreg.) Sch. Dist., 1972-76; tchr. Gresham (Oreg.) Sch. Dist., 1975-77, Wood River Jr. High Sch., Hailen, Idaho, 1978; law clerk U.S. Dist. Ct. (ea. dist.) Wash., Spokanne, 1982-83; atty. Hannon, Jenkins & Assocs., Coeur d'Alene, Idaho, 1983-88, Jenkins & Leggett, Coeur d'Alene, 1989-92; mem. Idaho Ho. Reps., 1990—; pvt. practice atty. Coeur d'Alene, 1993—. Mem. AAUW, NOW, Idaho State Bar. Democrat. Methodist. Home: 1627 Boyd Coeur D Alene ID 83814 Office: Idaho House of Reps State Capitol Boise ID 83720*

JENKINS, JUDITH ALEXANDER, bank consultant; b. Fort Sill, Okla., Oct. 14, 1940; d. James Buchanan and Gerry Lee (Gibbs) Permenter; m. Robert Miles Turner, Oct. 28, 1962 (div. 1972); m. Clarence Withers Alexander, Dec. 19, 1975 (div. Jan. 1987); m. David Claude Jenkins, Apr. 23, 1994. Student, U. Okla., 1958-59; B.A. in English, U. Tulsa, 1962; M.B.A., U. Okla., 1969; postgrad., U. St. Thomas, 1975-78. Asst. cashier So. Nat. Bank of Houston, 1971-73, asst. contr., 1973-74, asst. v.p. and asst. contr., 1974, v.p., contr., 1974-77, sr. v.p., contr., 1977-79; cons., 1979—. Mem. NOW, Nat. Audubon Soc., Beta Gamma Sigma, Gamma Phi Beta. Office: 2211 Norfolk Ste 612 Houston TX 77098

JENKINS, KATHERINE ERSKINE, advertising executive; b. N.Y.C., Dec. 3, 1948; d. William Coventry and Frances (Thomson) Erskine; m. George Patrick Ziller, Jan. 10, 1980 (div. June 1981); m. Dale Aubrey Jenkins, Dec. 3, 1987; 1 child, Grace Aubrey. BA, Barnard Coll., 1986. Asst. beauty editor Vogue Mag., 1973-76; creative group head Grey Advt., 1976-78; agy. group head Sacks & Rosen, 1978-79; v.p., group supr. Young & Rubicam, 1979-83; v.p., assoc. creative dir. Saatchi & Saatchi, 1983-85; dir. worldwide promotion Time Mag., 1985-87; pres. Erskine Jenkins, Creative Cons., 1988-91; v.p., copy group supr. Thomas G. Ferguson Assocs., Inc., Parsippany, N.J., 1991-92, v.p., creative group supr., 1992, sr. v.p., creative group dir., 1992—. Co-author: Scavullo on Beauty, 1976. Chair alumnae annual fund Spence Sch., N.Y.C., 1993—; mem. Tuxedo Park Garden Club, N.Y., 1991—, Friends of Valley Hosp., Tuxedo Park, 1993—. Recipient Clio Gold, 1985, 93, Art Dirs. Club (3), 1979, One Show, 1979. Mem. Advt. Women of N.Y. (Addy award 1986), Tuxedo Club (Tuxedo Park, N.Y.). Republican. Presbyterian. Home: West Lake Rd Tuxedo Park NY 10987 Office: Thomas G Ferguson Assocs Inc 30 Lanidex Plz W Parsippany NJ 07054

JENKINS, LINDA DIANE, accountant; b. Detroit, Jan. 8, 1960; d. Robert A. Martinez and Marillyn June (Owens) Scheere; m. George Edwin Jenkins, Oct. 21, 1978 (div. May 1992); children: Stephanie Marie, Mark Richard. Student, RETS Electronics Sch., Detroit, 1978; AA in Bus. Adminstrn. with honors, St. Petersburg Jr. Coll., Tarpon Springs, Fla., 1987; BS in Acctg., U. South Fla., 1991. CPA, Fla. Acct. Carl Lawson & Assocs., Inc., New Port Richey, Fla., 1986-88, Garcia & Ortis PA CPA's-GOC Inc., St. Petersburg, Fla., 1992; treas. New Life Foursquare Gospel Ch., Bayonet Point, Fla., 1988-90; fin. adminstr. M.P. Spychala & Assocs., Inc., Safety Harbor, Fla., 1988-91; project acct., network adminstr. Harbour Assocs. Constrn. Co., Tampa, Fla., 1992-94; acct. sole practicioner Linda D. Jenkins CPA, Clearwater, Fla., 1994—. Mem. FICPA. Home: 1701 Marion St Tampa FL 34616 Office: Linda D Jenkins CPA 1701 Marion St Clearwater FL 34616

JENKINS, LOUISE SHERMAN, nursing researcher; b. Normal, Ill., Jan. 19, 1943; d. Fred and Zylpha Louise (Garrett) Sherman; m. Gary L. Jenkins, Oct. 30, 1965 (div. July 1976). Diploma, Evanston Hosp. Sch. Nursing, 1963; BS, No. Ill. U., 1979; MS, U. Md., Balt., 1982, PhD, 1985. Asst. head nurse intensive care Community Meml. Hosp., LaGrange, Ill., 1963-65; head nurse coronary care Luth. Gen. Hosp., Park Ridge, Ill., 1965-69; nurse clinician hemodialysis unit Evanston Hosp., Evanston, Ill., 1969-74; head nurse Skokie Valley Community Hosp., Skokie, Ill., 1974-75; faculty dept. continuing edn. Northwest Community Hosp., Arlington Heights, Ill., 1975-80; Walter Schoeder chair nursing rsch. U. Wis. Milw. Sch. Nursing and St. Luke's Med. Ctr., Milw., 1987—. Mem. editl. rev. bd. Jour. Cardiopulmonary Rehab., Nursing Rsch.; mem. editl. bd. Cardiovasc. Nursing. Vice chmn., chmn.-elect Coun. Cardiovasc. Nursing, Dallas, 1989—; bd. dirs. Am. Heart Assn., Milw., 1988—, fellow coun. on cardiovasc. nursing. Fellow, clin. nurse scholar Robert Wood Johnson Found., U. Calif., San Francisco, 1985-87. Mem. Am. Assn. Cardiovasc. and Pulmonary Rehab. (bd. dirs.-at-large 1993—), Wis. Nurses Assn. (bd. dirs. 1988-90), Midwest Nursing Rsch. Soc. (gov. bd. 1993-95), Coun. Nurse Rschrs., Soc. Behavioral Medicine, Sigma Xi, Sigma Theta Tau. Office: U Wis Sch. Nursing PO Box 413 Milwaukee WI 53201-0413

JENKINS, LUCINDA SUE, healthcare financial consultant; b. Springfield, Mo., Jan. 28, 1953; d. Roger Wesley and Dorothy June (Williams) J. BBA, U. Mo., 1986, MBA, 1987. Mgr., contract officer We. Mo. Area Health Edn. Ctr., Kansas City, 1972-82; adminstrv. asst. St. Joseph Hosp., Kansas City, 1982-83; mgr. client services United Healthcare Systems, Overland Park, Kans., 1983-85; graduate coordinator Small Bus. Inst., Kansas City, 1986—; fin. cons. Econ. Devel. Agy., Kansas City, 1986-88; strategic planner Midwest Community Health Corp., 1988-89; v.p. Para Fin. Healthcare Cons., 1989—; bd. dirs. NW Mo. Area Health Edn. Ctr., St. Joseph, 1980-82; adv. council Metro Area Health Edn. Found., Kansas City, 1980-82. Adminstrv. staff, U. Mo. Sch. Med. Study Tour, Republic of China, 1981. Recipient Dean Banking Fin. Scholarship Boatman's Bank, 1986; named Young Entrepreneur of the Yr., U. Mo. Entrepreneurial Com., 1986. Mem. Healthcare Fin. Mgmt. Assn., MBA Execs., Am. Mgmt. Assn., Am. Mktg. Assn., Bus. and Profl. Women's Found. (recipient scholarship 1986). Home: 1300 E Gartner Rd Naperville IL 60540-8222 Office: PARA Ltd 261 E Colorado Blvd Pasadena CA 91101-1903

JENKINS, MARGARET BUNTING, human resources executive; b. Warsaw, Va., Aug. 3, 1935; d. John and Irma (Cookman) Bunting; children: Sydney, Jr., Terry L. Student Coll. William and Mary, 1952; AA in Bus. Adminstrn., Christopher Newport U., 1973; BA in Human Resource Devel., St. Leo Coll., 1979; M in Human Resources, George Washington U., 1982; PhD in Human Rsch. Mgmt., Columbia Pacific U., 1986. Rehab. counselor York County Schs., Yorktown, Va.; mgr. Waterfront Constrn. Co., Seafood Corp., Seaford, Va., 1960-72; labor rels. specialist NWS, Yorktown, 1974-77, staffing specialist, 1977-78; position classification specialist NWS/SUPSHIP, Newport News, Va., 1978-81; supr. personnel mgmt. specialist SupSHIP, Newport News, 1981-90; pers. mgmt. specialist NWS/Y, Yorktown, Cheatham and Williamsburg, Va., 1990-94; bd. dirs. various health orgns.; owner Jenkins Consulting. Recipient Navy Meritorious Civilian Svc. award SUPSHIP, Newport News, 1990, 2 Navy commendations, others. Mem. AAUW, Fedn. Women's Clubs, Sierra Club, Audubon Soc., Nature Conservancy, Classification & Compensation Soc. (pres. 1984), 4-Alumni Assn., Human Resources Mgmt., Toastmasters Internat. (pres. 1985-87, various offices, awards). Methodist. Home and Office: PO Box 203 Seaford VA 23696-0203

JENKINS, MARIE HOOPER, manufacturing company executive, engineer; b. Alexandria, La., Apr. 22, 1929; d. Jesse Joseph and Katie B. Hooper; m. Charles Edward Jenkins, Jan. 28, 1950 (div. May 1990); children: Nancy Marie von Minden, Charles Edward Jr.. B.S. in Chem. Engring., U. Wash., 1956. Founder, prin. Decision Systems, Austin, Tex., 1975-76; chmn. bd., pres. NAPP Inc. and subsidiary LACE Engring., 1977—. Active Leadership Tex. program, Leadership Am., 1988, Tex. Found. for Women's Resources; bd. dirs. Com. Wild Basin Wilderness, 1993—. Mem. Am. Inst. Chem. Engrs. (chmn. Mojave Desert sect.), Calif. Soc. Profl. Engrs. (founding sec., treas. Desert Empire chpt.), Tex. Soc. Profl. Engrs., Nat. Soc. Profl. Engrs., Leadership Tex. Alumni Assn., Leadership Am. Alumnae Assn., Nat. Property Mgmt. Assn., Nat. Contract Mgmt. Assn., Greater Austin C. of C. (exec. com. North Cen. area coun.). Episcopalian. Home: 3710B Meredith St Austin TX 78703-2021 Office: NAPP Inc & LACE Engring 2104 Kramer Ln Austin TX 78758-4045

JENKINS-ANDERSON, BARBARA JEANNE, pathologist, educator; b. Chgo.; d. Carlyle Fielding and Alyce Louise (Walker) Stewart; m. Sidney Bernard Jenkins, Sept. 22, 1951 (div. June 1970); children: Kevin Jenkins, Judy Kelly, Sharolyn Sanders, Marc Jenkins, Kayla French; m. Arthur Eugene Anderson, Sept. 30, 1972. BS, U. Mich., 1950; MD, Wayne State U., 1957. Diplomate Am. Bd. Pathology. Assoc. prof. pathology Wayne State U. Med. Sch., Detroit, 1973—; adminstrv. med. dir. DMC Univ. Labs., Detroit, 1988—; chief pathology DRH/UHC Hosp., Detroit, 1990—. Recipient Leonard Sain award U. Mich., 1980. Mem. Alpha Omega Alpha. Office: DMC Univ Labs 4201 St Antoine Detroit MI 48201-1998

JENKINSON, JUDITH APSEY, librarian; b. Monroe, Mich., Apr. 9, 1943; d. Robert Henry Williams and Caroline (Pardee) Stephenson; m. Arnold Apsey, July 1, 1962 (div. 1977); 1 child, Amy Lou; m. Leif Jenkinson, May 21, 1977, 1 stepchild, Karl J. A.A., Alpena Community Coll., 1964; B.A., Mich. State U., 1966; Arts M.L.S., U. Mich., 1969. Elem. tchr., Lincoln, Mich., 1966-68, high sch. librarian, 1969-72; elem. librarian, Ketchikan, Alaska, 1972-75, 90—, high sch. librarian, 1975-90; mem. City Coun., Ketchikan City, Alaska, 1993—. Mem. Ketchikan Community Coll. Council, 1980-84, pres., 1984-85; del. Alaska Democratic Conv., 1982, 88, 92; dir., producer, actress, mem. stage crew First City Players, 1972—; mem. Ketchikan Greater Dem. Precinct's Com., 1988—, vice chair, 1992—; commr. Ketchikan Gateway Borough Planning Commn., 1989-93, vice-chair, 1992-93. Mem. ALA, NEA, AAUW, NOW, LWV, Ketchikan Edn. Assn., NEA-Alaska, Women's Internat. League for Peace and Freedom, Alaska Library Assn. VFW Aux., Swinging Kings Square Dancers (pres. 1985-86), Eagles, Women of the Moose, Delta Kappa Gama. Home: PO Box 5342 Ketchikan AK 99901-0342 Office: 1900 1st Ave Ketchikan AK 99901

JENKS, ZOYA ELAINE, librarian; b. Chgo., Mar. 13, 1933; d. Abraham and Anna (Frumkin) Hochstein; m. George Merritt Jenks, Mar. 7, 1957; children: Darrell, Mark, Andrew. BA, UCLA, 1956; MLS, Clarion U., 1983. Prin. lit. asst. UCLA, 1956-57; tutor history U. Tasmania, Hobart, Australia, 1963-66; lectr. music Bucknell U., Lewisburg, Pa., 1967-83, catalog libr., 1983-89; head catalog dept. Bucknell U., Lewisburg, 1990—; reviewer Australian Broadcasting Commn., Hobart, 1963-66. Mem. ALA, Pa. Libr. Assn. (chair acad. and rsch. 1988, bd. dir. 1995—). Democrat. Home: 202 N 2d St Lewisburg PA 17837 Office: Bucknell U Bertrand Libr Lewisburg PA 17837

JENKS-DAVIES, KATHRYN RYBURN, retired daycare provider, civic worker; b. Lynchburg, Va., Oct. 9, 1916; d. Charles Arthur and Jessie Katherine (Moorman) Ryburn; m. Thomas Edgar Jenks Jr., Sept. 9, 1941 (dec. June 1975); children: Thomas Edgar III, Jessika, Timothy; m. Robert E. Davies, Dec. 27, 1986. BS, State Tchr. Coll., 1938; postgrad., Mary Washington Coll., 1947-48, U. Va., 1957-58, William and Mary Coll., 1967-68, Va. Commonwealth U., 1969-70. Elem. tchr. various schs., Grundy, Va., 1939-41; phys. therapist U.S. Army, Ft. Bragg, N.C., 1942; operator motor pool U.S. Army, Ft. Still, Okla., 1943-44; occupational therapist U.S. Army, Augusta, Ga., 1944-45; instr. phys. edn. King George (Va.) High Sch., 1947-48; instr. phys. edn. Stafford (Va.) High Sch., 1949-50, substitute tchr., 1950-53; owner, dir. Kay's Kindergarten, Fredericksburg, Va., 1959-82. Featured in Fredericksburg Times mag., The Free Lance-Star and Richmond Newspapers. Counselor Girl Scouts U.S.A., Grundy, Va., 1939-41; life mem. Kenmore Assn., 1949—; mem. Hist. Fredericksburg Found., Inc., 1953—, Mental Health Bd., 1978-84; founder Fort Franklin Found., 1968-78; mem. Fredericksburg Clean Community Commn., 1976—; rep. United Way, Fredericksburg; instr. art ceramics Community Ctr. Fredericksburg, 1950-80; bd. dirs. Miss Fredericksburg Fair Pageant, 1965-88; participant community parades; coord. Fredericksburg Agrl. Fair 18th Century Craft People and Artisans, 1988-93, also others; bd. dirs. Antique Farm Implements, Gas and Steam Engines, 1989-93; active State Fair of Va., Am. Heritage Showcase endl. reenactment Pioneer Farmstead, 1981—. Recipient Virginia Ellison Vol. Svc. award Fredericksburg Clean Community Commn., 1976-87, Recognition of Svc. award, 1983-84, 1st, 2nd. and 3rd pl. trophies community parades, awards radio Stas. WFLS and WFVA, 1949-89; honored by Kiwanians for travelogue for fund raiser, 1994. Mem. AAUW (advt. chmn. travelogue 1971-89, Donor Honoree award 1983, bd. dirs. 1971-79), Lioness Club (bd. dir. 1968-87, Lioness Tamer 1984, Tongue Wagger 1985), Soroptimist Internat. Fredericksburg (life mem., sec. 1971-73, pres. 1973-75, bd. dirs. 1971-78, co-chmn. Soroptimist Travelogue 1991-93, First Class Pub. Recognition Trophy 1986, Women Helping Women award 1982, named 1 of 5 who have made a difference in cmty. 1994), Order of Eastern Star, Nat. League of Fredericksburg (bd. dir., Svc. Recognition Trophies 1963, 69, 80), Izaac Walton League (bd. dir. Dog Mart parade 1965-72). Republican. Episcopalian. Home: 8 Blair Rd Fredericksburg VA 22405-3025

JENNEMANN, KAREN SUE, judge; b. Louisville, Dec. 6, 1955; d. Noel and Meta Sue (Scales) Lemons; m. Thomas Joseph Jennemann, Aug. 3, 1974 (div. Sept. 1988); 1 child, Thomas William Noel. BS in Edn. with honors., No. Ariz. U., 1977; postgrad., U. Louisville, 1978-79; JD, Coll. William and Mary, 1983; postgrad., Coll. of William and Mary, 1980-83, Coll. of William and Mary. Bar: Va. 1983, U.S. Dist. Ct. (ea. dist.) Va. 1983, U.S. Dist. Ct. (mid. dist.) Fla. 1984, U.S. Ct. Appeals (4th cir.) 1983, U.S. Dist. Ct. (no. dist.) Fla. 1987, U.S. Ct. Appeals (11th cir.) 1988. Law clk. to Presiding Justice Hon. Robert G. Doumar, U.S. Dist. Ct., Norfolk, Va., 1983-84; assoc. atty. Smith & Hulsey, 1984-88; ptnr. Mahoney, Adams & Criser, Jacksonville, Fla., 1988-93; bankruptcy judge U.S. Bankruptcy Ct. (Fla. mid. dist.), 11th circuit, Orlando, 1993—; atty., guardian Guardian Ad Litem Program, Jacksonville, 1985—. Asst. editor: Dickens Studies Newsletter. Bd. dirs. Jacksonville Legal Aid Soc., 1984-86. Named Outstanding Senior, Highest Ranking Scholar; recipient Frier Found. scholarship. Mem. ABA, Jacksonville Bar Assn. (chmn. Bankruptcy Law Sec. 1988-90), Fla. Bar Assn. Legal Needs Children, Fla. Bar Assn. (publ. chairperson, exec. coun. of bus. law sect.), Kappa Delta Pi, Phi Kappa Phi. Methodist. Office: US Courthouse 135 W Central Ave 9th Fl Orlando FL 32801*

JENNESS, M. EMILY, systems training consultant; b. Memphis, Tenn., Aug. 16, 1968; d. Paul Emerson and Marion Evelyn (Duggan) Andrews; m. Timohty M. Jenness, July 5, 1990. BS Indsl. Tech., So. Ill. U., 1990; BA Bus. Mgmt., U. Md., 1992. Office mgr. Arid Land Survey, Inc., Tucson, Ariz., 1986-87; asst. v.p. Scott-European Corp., Reston, Va., 1994—; cons. Booz-Allen & Hamilton, Vienna, Va., 1994—. Campaign asst. Orgn. to Elect a Dem. Gov., Tucson, 1986; student leader mil./3481 & 3483 Student Squadrons, Monterey, Calif., San Angelo, Tex., 1987-89; vol. English tutor for Russians, Jewish Vol. Svcs., Balt., 1993-94; U. Md. alumna vol. U. Md. Internat. Dept., College Park, 1993-94. Sgt. USAF, 1987-93, England. Recipient Aerial Achievement medals USAF, John Levitow Leadership award, others. Mem. Soc. Mil. Comptrollers, U. Md. U. Coll. Alumni Assn. Home: 1298 Holmespun Dr Pasadena MD 21122

JENNESS, REBECCA ESTELLA, artist, educator; b. L.A., Aug. 16, 1946; d. Russell Albert and Estella Virginia (Guzman) J. Student, Cape Sch. Art, Provincetown, Mass., 1971; diploma, Vesper George Sch. of Art, 1972; BFA, Southeastern Mass. U., 1981. mem. panel R.I. State Coun. on the Arts, 1989-93; mem. adv. bd. Warwick Art Mus., R.I., 1990-94, New Eng. Found. on the Arts, Boston, 1990-94, Sarah Doyle Gallery, Brown U., 1991-94; mem. multicultural art literacy coun. State Coun. on the Arts, R.I., 1991-94. Exhibited in group shows at Soviet Hall of Art, Moscow, 1988, U. N.H., 1989, Fitchburg Art Mus., 1990, R.I. Sch. Design Mus. of Art, 1992-93. Art advocate Perishable Theater, Providence, 1993, New Eng. conf., Providence, 1993; artists for food Amos House, Providence, 1993. Democrat. Home: 12 Elgin St Providence RI 02906-2622 Studio: 220 Weybosset St Fl 4 Providence RI 02903-3712

JENNETT, SHIRLEY SHIMMICK, hospice executive, nurse; b. Jennings, Kans., May 1, 1937; d. William and Mabel C. (Mowry) Shimmick; m. Nelson K. Jennett, Aug. 20, 1960 (div. 1972); children: Jon W., Cheryl L.; m. Albert J. Kukral, Apr. 16, 1977 (div. 1990). Diploma, Rsch. Hosp. Sch. Nursing, Kansas City, Mo., 1958. RN, Mo., Colo., Tex., Ill. Staff nurse, head nurse Rsch. Hosp., 1958-60; head nurse Penrose Hosp., Colorado Springs, Colo., 1960-62, Hotel Dieu Hosp., El Paso, Tex., 1962-63; staff nurse Oak Park (Ill.) Hosp., 1963-64, NcNeal Hosp., Berwyn, Ill., 1964-65, St. Anthony Hosp., Denver, 1968-69; staff nurse, head nurse, nurse recruiter Luth. Hosp., Wheat Ridge, Colo., 1969-79; owner, mgr. Med. Placement Svcs., Lakewood, Colo., 1980-84; vol., primary care nurse, admissions coord., team mgr. Hospice of Metro Denver, 1984-88, dir. patient and family svcs., 1988, exec. dir., 1988—; mem. adv. com. Linkages Assn. for Older Adults, Denver, 1989-90. Community liaison person U. Phoenix, 1988-90. Mem. Nat. Hospice Orgn. (bd. dirs. 1992—), Colo. Hospice Orgn. (bd. dirs., pres. 1991-93), NAFE. Republican. Mem. Ch. of Religious Sci. Office: Hospice of Metro Denver 3955 E Exposition Ave Ste 500 Denver CO 80209-5033

JENNEY-WEST, ROXANNE ELIZABETH, special agent, accountant; b. Balt., Jan. 12, 1960; d. C.L. and Dorothy (Berger) Jenney; m. Daniel Eugene West, Oct. 27, 1984; children: Colleen Jenney, Daniel Eugene Jr., Mary Elizabeth. BS in Acctg., U. Md., 1983. CPA, Md. Staff acct., asst. contr. B.F. Saul Co., Chevy Chase, Md., 1981-84; contr., chief fin. officer FWB Bancorp., Rockville, Md., 1984-86, Mercy Med. Svcs. Inc., Las Vegas, Nev., 1986-89; owner, pres. Jenneywest Fin. Svcs., Inc., Las Vegas, Nev., 1989-91; spl. agt. FBI, Phila., 1992—. Mem. AICPA, NAFE, U.S. C. of C.

JENNI, CATHERINE BRINCKERHOFF, counseling education director; b. San Francisco, Calif., Aug. 8, 1945; d. Elmer Ellsworth and Anne Hobron (Dyer) Brinckerhoff; m. Thomas Stanton Cory, Juen 23, 1968 (div. Dec. 1984); children: Jeffrey Michael, Elizabeth Anne, Benjamin Thomas; m. Donald Allison Jenni, Jan. 3, 1986; stepchildren: Robert, William Karen, Thomas. BA in Psychology, Stanford U., 1967, MA in Child Devel., 1970; PhD in Psychology, Saybrook Inst., 1990. Lic. clin. counselor, Mont. Vol. U.S. Peace Corps, Liberia, West Africa, 1968-69; head tchr. Bing Nursery Sch. Stanford (Calif.) U., 1970-71; instr. early childhood edn. Solano C.C., Suisun City, Calif., 1971-82; intern in psychology U. Calif., San Francisco, 1983-84, Interlogue, Santa Rosa, Calif., 1984-85; vis. instr. family rels. U. Mont., Missoula, 1986-87, counseling psychologist, 1988-90, assoc. prof. counselor edn., 1990—; cons. in field. Contbr. articles to profl. jours. Trustee Sch. Dist. # 1, Missoula, 1989-93. Recipient 1st prize Mont. Outdoor Photography, 1993. Mem. ACA, Am. Assn. Profl. Psychology, Assn. Humanistic Psychology. Home: 17 Greenbrier Dr Missoula MT 59802-3353 Office: U Mont Sch Edn Missoula MT 59812

JENNINGS, ANN SANDERS, human resources manager; b. Augusta, Ga., June 14, 1966; d. Conrad Wienges and Alice (Haskell) Sanders; m. Horace Smith Jennings, June 12, 1993. BA in English, Randolph-Macon Woman's Coll., 1988; MA in Human Resource Devel., Marymount U., 1994. Mgr. Ctr. for Pers. Rsch. Internat. Pers. Mgmt. Assn., Alexandria, Va., 1989-94; human resource mgr. EB Svcs., Inc., Charlotte, N.C., 1994—. Coord. job bank Randolph-Macon Woman's Coll. Alumnae, Washington, 1993. Washington Pers. Assn. scholar, 1994. Mem. ASTD, Soc. for Human Resource Mgmt., Jr. League. Episcopalian. Office: EB Svcs Inc 4801 Chastain Ave # 10 Charlotte NC 28217

JENNINGS, CAROL, marketing executive; b. Marion, Ohio, Oct. 2, 1945; d. Richard P. and Mary (LeMaster) J.; m. John Putnam Merrill Jr., Jan. 3, 1981. BA, Miami U., Oxford, Ohio, 1967. News editor Penton Pub. Inc., Cleve., 1967-69; pub. rels. exec. Cen. Nat. Bank, Cleve., 1969-71; dir. pub. rels. New Eng. Conservatory of Music, Boston, 1971-74, Bklyn. Acad. Music, N.Y.C., 1974-75; account exec., supr. Hill and Knowlton, N.Y.C., 1975-81, from v.p. to mng. dir., 1981-87; sr. v.p., gen. mgr. Hill, Hilliday, Connors, Cosmopolus, Boston, 1987, Hill and Knowlton, Boston, 1987-90; dir. corp. communications Bain and Co., Boston, 1991—. Office: Jennings & Co 20 University Rd Cambridge MA 02138

JENNINGS, DEBORAH KAY SHIELDS, elementary education educator; b. McMinnville, Tenn., Dec. 27, 1954; d. Arthur Waterman and Nancy Clare (Dollins) Shields; m. William Kenneth Jennings, Dec. 22, 1972; children: Andrea Gail, William Kenneth, Samantha Kaye, Laura Nancy Ellen, Christina Sue. BS, Tenn. Tech. U., Cookeville, 1975, MA, 1978, EdS, 1991. Waitress So. Belle Foods, McMinnville, Tenn., 1971-73; substitute tchr. Warren County Schs., McMinnville, 1973-75, elem. tchr., 1975—. Troop leader Girl Scouts U.S., Warren County, 1986-88. Mem. AAUW (sec. 1984-86, pres. 1991-94). Home: 314 Stagecoach Trail McMinnville TN 37110 Office: Warren County Mid Sch 200 Caldwell St Mc Minnville TN 37110-8400

JENNINGS, DEBRA VERA, lawyer; b. Meridian, Miss., Oct. 20, 1960; d. Rudolph and Fannie Mae (Cole) J. BA in Polit. Sci., U. Houston, 1981; JD, South Tex. Coll., 1986. Officer U.S. EEOC, Houston, 1986-89; loan adminstr. First City Nat. Bank, Houston, 1989-91; atty. Debra Jennings & Assocs., Houston, 1991—. Bd. dirs. Lawndale Art and Performance Ctr., Houston, 1993—, Milan House AIDS hospice, Houston, 1993. Kellogg scholar, 1981, scholar South Tex. Coll. Law Alumni Assn., 1985. Baptist. Home: 4915 Austin # 3 Houston TX 77004 Office: Debra Jennings & Assocs 3401 Louisiana Ste 110 Houston TX 77002

JENNINGS, MADELYN PULVER, communications company human resources executive; b. Saratoga Springs, N.Y., Nov. 23, 1934; d. George Joseph and Martha (Walsh) Pulver. BA in Bus. and Econs., Tex. Woman's U., 1956. Asst. dir. pub. rels. Slick Airways, Dallas, 1956-58, VIP Svcs., Inc., N.Y.C., 1958; asst. to pres. Smith, Dorian & Burman, Hartford, Conn., 1959; bus. mktg. planning GE, Bridgeport, Conn., 1960-68, mgr. manpower planning, 1968-71, mgr. environ. support operation, 1971-73, mgr. employee rels., 1973-76; v.p. human resources Standard Brands, Inc., N.Y.C., 1976-80; sr. v.p. pers. Gannett Co., Arlington, Va., 1980—; corp. adv. bd. NOW legal def. and edn. fund; adv. com. U. Ill. Inst. Labor and Indsl. Rels.; former mem. sec's. commn. on achieving necessary skills U.S. Dept. of Labor, former mem. adv. com. Fed. Workforce Quality Assesment. Mem. assocs. coun. Sch. Bus. and Pub. Mgmt., George Washington U.; former trustee Russell Sage Coll.; former bd. dirs. Am. Press Inst.; bd. dirs. U.S. Com. for UNICEF, Tex. Woman's U. Found., Corp. Yaddo, Ctr. Leadership and Career Studies, Emory U.; former chair, mem. exec. com. and adv. coun. human resources mgmt. conf. bd. Internat. Alliance; mem. bd. visitors John S. Knight Fellowship; mem. SCANS 2000 program Johns Hopkins Inst. for Policy Study; bd. advisors Catalyst; mem. UCLA Human Resources Outlook Panel. Mem. Human Resources Roundtable, Soc. for Human Resource Mgmt. (bd. dirs.), Sr. Pers. Execs. Roundtable, Am. Newspaper Pubs. Assn. (past chair human resources com., exec. com.), Labor Policy Assn. (bd. dirs.), Bus. Roundtable (employee rels. com.). Home: 3520 Duff Dr Falls Church VA 22041-1415 Office: Gannett Co Inc 1100 Wilson Blvd Arlington VA 22234-0001

JENNINGS, MARCELLA GRADY, rancher, investor; b. Springfield, Ill., Mar. 4, 1920; d. William Francis and Magdalene Mary (Spies) Grady; student pub. schs.; m. Leo J. Jennings, Dec. 16, 1950 (dec.). Pub. relations Econolite Corp., Los Angeles, 1958-61; v.p., asst. mgr. LJ Quarter Circle Ranch, Inc., Polson, Mont., 1961-73, pres., gen. mgr., owner, 1973—; dir. Giselle's Travel Inc., Sacramento; fin. advisor to Allentown, Inc., Charlo, Mont.; sales cons. to Amie's Jumpin' Jacks and Jills, Garland, Tex. Investor. Mem. Internat. Charolais Assn., Los Angeles County Apt. Assn. Republican. Roman Catholic. Home and Office: 509 Mt Holyoke Ave Pacific Palisades CA 90272-4328

JENNINGS, NANCY ANN, retired elementary education educator; b. Bristow, Okla., July 11, 1932; d. John Linard and Charlie Estelle (Hooper) Stucker; m. Jerald Leon Jennings, June 4, 1951; children: Jan, Catherine Jennings Hackman, Elizabeth Jennings Pineda. BS, U. Okla., 1956; MS, Washburn U., Topeka, Kans., 1974. Cert. elem. tchr., Kans. Tchr. Whitson Grade Sch. Dist. 501, Topeka, 1970-75, Delia Grade Sch Dist. 321, St. Marys, Kans., 1978-79, Silver Lake (Kans.) Grade Sch. Dist. 372, 1979-85, ret., 1985. Mem. Kans. Hist. Soc. Mem. NEA (life), AAUW (bd. dirs.), Topeka Area Ret. Tchrs. Assn. (v.p. 1992-93), DAR (regent Topeka chpt. 1989-91, sec.-treas. N.E. dist. Kans. 1992-95, chmn. pres.-gen.'s project state com. 1992-95), Internat. Reading Assn. (sec. 1983-84), Topeka Aux. Kans. Engring. Soc. (pres. 1987-88), Woman's Club (2d v.p. 1989-91), P.E.O. Kans. (corr. sec. 1993—, guard 1994—, pres. 1995—), Alpha Delta Kappa (pres. 1989-91), Kappa Delta Pi, Alpha Phi (2d v.p. 1989-90). Presbyterian. Home: 11340 NW 13th St Topeka KS 66615-9620

JENNINGS, SHARON ANN, secondary school educator; b. Detroit, July 15, 1944; d. Donald Ogden and Gladys Elizabeth (Pierce) Moss; m. Steven Richard Jennings, Aug. 16, 1964 (div. 1983); children: Matthew Thomas, Timothy Mark, Peter Tyson. AA, Highland Community Coll., 1964; BS, No. Ill. U., 1974; MEd, U. Ill., 1984. Med. sec. McDonough Hosp., Macomb, Ill., 1964-66; order sec. Wurlitzer, DeKalb, Ill., 1966-68; bus. tchr. Pearl City (Ill.) Schs., 1983—; adult edn. tchr. Highland Community Coll., Freeport, Ill., 1985—, writer career curriculum for tech. prep; network coord. Pearl City Schs., 1989—; mem. bus. tchr. program devel. team Stephenson Area Vocat. Edn. System, Freeport, 1983—. Grantee U. Ill., 1991, Black Dot, 1986, Vitner's, 1993. Mem. Ill. Bus. Edn. Assn., No. Ill. Bus. Edn. Assn., Delta Pi Epsilon. Home: 630 Alamo Dr Freeport IL 61032 Office: Pearl City Schs 100 S Summit Pearl City IL 61062

JENNINGS, SUSAN JANE, lawyer; b. Providence, June 23, 1952; d. John Edward and Betty Jean (Frost) Stedman; m. James Albert Jennings, Jan. 2, 1982; children: Olivia Arden, Caroline Alexis, Susan Alexandra. BA, Ind. U., 1973; JD, Tex. Tech U., 1978; LLM in Taxation, So. Meth. U., 1985. Bar: Tex. 1978, U.S. Dist. Ct. (no. dist.) Tex. 1979, U.S. Tax Ct. 1986. Advanced mktg. cons. Southwestern Life Ins., Dallas, 1978-81; asst. gen. counsel Res. Life Ins., Dallas, 1981-85; gen. counsel, corp. sec., v.p. Life Ins. Co. SW, Dallas, 1986—; of counsel Erhard, Ruebel and Jennings, Dallas, 1981—; mem. bd. dirs. Tex. Legal Reserve Officials Assn., 1994—. Contbr. articles to profl. jours. Mem. ABA (mem. editor's pub. bd., TIPS sect., 1993—), Dallas Bar Assn. (sec. corp. counsel sect. 1994—), Kappa Delta (pres. Dallas alumnae 1983-84), Phi Delta Phi. Republican. Presbyterian. Clubs: Lone Star Masters Swim Team (Dallas). Lodge: Daus. of Penelope. Home: 4001 Miramar Ave Dallas TX 75205-3129 Office: Life Ins Co SW 1300 W Mockingbird PO Box 47421 Dallas TX 75247

JENNINGS, TONI, state senator, construction company executive; b. Orlando, Fla., May 17, 1949; d. Jack C. and Margaret (Murphy) J. BA, Wesleyan Coll., Macon, Ga., 1971; postgrad., Rollins Coll., 1972-73. Pres. Jack Jennings and Sons, Inc., Gen. Contractors, Orlando, 1973—; mem. Fla. Ho. of Reps., 1976-80; mem. Fla. Senate, 1980—, Republican leader pro tempore, 1982-83, 85, 86, Rep. leader, 1984, 86-88. legis. del. Orange County, 1980-82, 86-88; chmn. econ. profl. and utility regulation; mem. appropriations, Sub A, Ins., Regulated Industries, Rules and Calendar, Transp. coms. Active Sr. Citizens Adv. Council, Rep. Women's Federated Club of Winter Park, Orlando Women's Rep. Club Federated. Recipient Spl. Commendation award Fla. Restaurant Assn., 1979, Meritorious Service award Fla. Fedn. Humane Socs., 1979, Disting. Alumni award Wesleyan Coll., 1981, Freedom award Women for Responsible Legislation, 1982, Support of Law Enforcement award Fla. Sheriffs Assn., Outstanding Efforts award Tampa Missing Children Help Ctr., 1983, Outstanding Svc. award Grocers' Assn. Fla., 1983, Legis. award Fla. , 1983, Legis. award Fla. Chiropractic Assn., 1983, 86, Appreciation award Fla. Med. Assn. and Physicians of Fla., 1983, Second Ann. Frank J. Fahrenkopf, Jr. Outstanding State Minority Leader award, 1988, Annual Legis. award for Leadership in Econ. Devel. Legislation award Fla. C. of C., 1987; Legislator of Yr. Orange County Young Rep. Club, 1980-81. Mem. Orlando Area Bd. Realtors (Friend of Realtors award 1989), Builders and Contractors, Cen. Fla. Builders Exch., Delta Kappa Gamma, Phi Kappa Phi, Kappa Delta Epsilon. Office: State Capitol Senate House Tallahassee FL 32301*

JENNINGS, SISTER VIVIEN ANN, academic administrator; b. Jersey City, May 18, 1934; d. Eugene O. and Alice (Smith) J. BA, Caldwell Coll., 1960; MA in English, Cath. U. Am., 1966; MS in Telecommunications, Syracuse U., 1980; PhD in English, Fordham U., 1972; EdD (hon.), Providence Coll.; LittD (hon.), Caldwell Coll. Assoc. prof. English Caldwell Coll., 1960-69; instr. broadcasting writing Syracuse U., 1979-80; with community affairs dept. Sta. WIXT TV, Syracuse, N.Y., 1980; dir. telecommunications Barry U., 1982-83; dir. pub. affairs Cath. Telecommunications Network Am., 1983-84; pres. Caldwell Coll., 1984-94; originator, designer campus TV studios Caldwell Coll., Barry U.; curriculum planner, coord. new grad.-level curriculum in telecommunications Barry U.; lectr. on ednl. and media issues. Producer: Centenary Journey, 1981, Advent Vesper Chorale, 1981, American Immigrant Church, 1982, Las Casas: Ministry of Presence, 1987; co-producer: The Boat People, 1980. Founder, dir. Children's TV Experience; founder Project Link Ednl. Ctr., Newark. Recipient Gov.'s Pride N.J. Albert Einstein award for edn., 1989. Mem. Assn. Cath. Colls. (coord. nat. teleconf.), Assn. Ind. Colls. (pres.'s group). Office: Caldwell Coll 9 Ryerson Ave Caldwell NJ 07006-6195

JENNINGS, VIVIEN LEE, bookstore management and licensing executive; b. Little Rock, Mar. 7, 1945; d. Loron and Mildred Louise (Wright) Bolen. B.A., Rhodes Coll., Memphis, 1967. Women's fiction cons. Ballantine Books, Inc., N.Y., 1981-82, Berkeley Pub. Group, N.Y., 1982-83; pres. Rainy Day Books, Inc., Fairway, Kans., 1975—. Editor nat. weekly bus. letter Boy Meets Girl, 1981-86; exec. editor serialized women's fiction project Day Dreams Universal Press Syndicate, 1984. Bd. dirs. Coterie Children's Theatre, 1994. Author: The Romance Wars; contbr. articles to profl. publs. Featured on nat. pub. radio and nat. tv programs. Mem. Romance Writers Am. Inc. (bd. dirs. 1982-83), Am. Booksellers Assn., Greater Kansas City C. of C., Soc. of Fellows Nelson-Atkins Mus. of Art, Hist. Kansas City Found., U. Mo. Kansas City Womens Coun., Friends Planned Parenthood. Episcopalian. Clubs: Cen. Exchange (Kansas City). Home: 5413 Norwood Rd Shawnee Mission KS 66205-2649 Office: Rainy Day Books Inc 2812 W 53d St Fairway KS 66205

JENS, ELIZABETH LEE SHAFER (MRS. ARTHUR M. JENS, JR.), civic worker; b. Monroe, Mich., Jan. 25, 1915; d. Frank Lee and Mary (Bogard) Shafer; m. Arthur M. Jens, Jr., Aug. 14, 1937; children: Timothy V., Christopher E., Jeffrey A. Student, Kalamazoo Coll., 1932-34, U. Wis., 1935, Northwestern U., 1934-36, BS, 1936; postgrad. Wheaton Coll., 1965; Lic. Practical Nurse, Triton Coll., 1968-69; Gray lady, Hines, (Ill.) Hosp., 1948-49, 51-53; vol. Elgin (Ill.) State Hosp., 1958-72; writer Newsletter Vol. Planning Coun., 1960-62; mem. Family Svc. Assn. Du Page County; vol. coord., chmn. bd. dirs., treas. Thursday Evening Club, social club for recovering mental patients Du Page County, 1966—; vol. FISH orgn., 1973-84. Bd. dirs. Du Page County Mental Health Soc., 1962-68, sec., 1963-64, 65-68, chmn. forgotten patient com., 1963-68, chmn. new projects, 1965-68; co-chmn. Glen Ellyn unit Cen. Du Page Hosp. Assn. Women's Aux., 1959-60; bd. dirs. chmn. com. on pesticides, Ill. Audubon Soc., 1963-73; mem. Ill. Pesticide Control Com., 1963-73, Citizens Com. Dutch Elm Disease, Glen Ellyn, 1960; bd. dirs. Natural Resources Coun. Ill., 1961-67, sec., 1961-64; bd. dirs. Du Page Art League, 1958-68, chmn. bd., 1961-63, Paint-out chairperson, 1968-84, 91—, chmn. new bldg. com., 1968-75, Best in Show award 1991; bd. dirs. mem. planning com., publicity chmn. Du Page Fine Arts Assn., 1965-67; bd. dirs. Friends Libr. Glen Ellyn, 1967-68; mem. adv. bd. Rachel Carson Trust for Living Environment 1971-74; bd. dirs. Mental Health Assn. of Du Page, 1973—, sec., 1973-75, pres., 1980-81, chmn. community liaison, 1981—, chmn. action group, 1976—; mem. Du Page Subarea adv. coun. Suburban Cook County-Du Page County Health Systems Agy., 1977-83; bd. dirs. Du Page County Comprehensive Health Planning Agy., 1976, DuPage County Bd. of Health, 1987—; mem. DuPage County Mental Health Adv. Bd., 1977—; mem. com. on midlife and older women Ill. Commn. on Status of Women, 1978-85; bd. dirs., publicity chmn., DuPage County Coun. Vol. Coords., 1977-78; bd. dirs., membership chmn. Homemakers Equal Rights Assn. in DuPage County, 1979-84; publicity chmn., v.p. Homemakers Coalition for Equal Rights, 1984—, pres. 1986—; mem. ERA Ill. Bd., 1987—, v.p. 1994—; mem. DuPage County Health Planning Coun., 1984-94, chairperson task force on residences for mentally ill, 1990-93; mem. Community Care Coalition of DuPage County, 1988-93, NAACP; mem. pub. rels. com. Bethlehem Ctr. Food Bank of DuPage County, 1987-89; tour guide Stacy's Tavern-Glen Ellyn Hist. Mus., 1986—; chmn. Grass Roots Com. to Pass Ill. Marital Property Act, 1982—; mem. adv. bd. Older Adult Inst. Coll. DuPage, 1989-94; del. for Mental Health Assn. Du Page to DuPage County Consortium, 1989—, Prevention and Intergenerational Task Force, 1991—; vol. Hospice of DuPage, 1990—; bd. dirs. Friends of Furred and Feathered, 1992—, v.p., 1992-94; bd. dirs. Dupage area Older Women's League, chairperson publicity, 1992— (recipient Wonderful Older Woman ann. award. 1990); with clown ministry Fox Valley unity Ch., 1991—. Hon. mention in Nat. Sonnet contest, 1967; Vol. of Yr. Ill. Mental Health Assn., 1975; Svc. award Ill. Rehab. Assn., 1980; named DuPage County Outstanding Woman Leader in Arts and Culture W. Suburban YWCA, 1984, Friend of the Mentally Ill, Alliance for the Mentally Ill of Dupage County Ann. award, 1988, Adade Wheeler award Coll. of DuPage, 1994. Mem. Mental Health Assn. DuPage, Wilderness Soc., Humane Soc. U.S., Nat. Trust for Hist. Preservation, Du Page County Hist. Soc. (life), Glen Ellyn Hist. Soc. (life), Nat. Audubon Soc., Nat. Writers Club (monthly meeting chmn. Midwest chpt. 1973-74, 4th award Ann. Mag. Con. test 1978), DuPage Art League (hon. life, Best of Show award 1991), Defenders of Wildlife, Theosophical Soc. Am. (Quest Study Group 1992—), Nature Conservancy Ill. (hon.), Chgo. Art Inst. (life), Ill. Assn. Mental Health (dir. 1966-68), Amnesty Internat., Pi Beta Phi. Writer column Mental Health and You for Press Publs., 1969-90, Life Newspape Newspapers, 1984, Herald Newspapers, 1986-94; author: The Jewelled Flower: The True Account of a Courageous Young Man's Life and Death By His Own Hand, 1987. Home: 22 W 210 Stanton Rd Glen Ellyn IL 60137

JENSEN, ANNE TURNER, automobile service company executive; b. Upper Providence Twp., Pa., Sept. 15, 1926; d. Ellwood Jackson and Elizabeth Addis (Downing) Turner; student Hood Coll., 1944-45, Phila. Coll. Pharmacy and Sci., 1945-46, 47-48; m. Harry Frederick Jensen, Jr., Apr. 13, 1946; children—Frederick Howard, Richard Jordan, Peter Hielm. Legal sec. Robertson & Turner, Media, Pa., 1950-51; sec. Luncheon-is-Served, Media, 1951-53; asst. sec., treas. Delvale Realty Corp., Media, 1955-59; bookkeeper Turner Realty Co., 1960-64, William H. Turner, Atty., 1960-64, Media Auto Service, 1957-64; sec. Media Auto Service, Inc., 1957—. Capt. Heart Fund Dr., 1958-60. Republican. Presbyterian. Clubs: DAR (chpt. regent 1971-74, state corr. sec. 1977-80, nat. chmn. 1974-77), Daughters of Am. Colonists, Daughters of Colonial Wars (state treas. 1974-77, 80-83), Magna Carta Soc., Daus. of 1812, Navy League U.S. (N.Y. Coun.), Am. Legion.

JENSEN, ANNETTE M., mental health nurse, administrator; b. Albert Lea, Minn., Jan. 16, 1952; d. Oliver H. and Ardis R. (Nelson) J. BSN, Winona (Minn.) State U., 1974; postgrad., Calif. Coll. Health Scis. Staff nurse in adolescent psychiatry C.B. Wilson Ctr., Faribault, Minn., 1974-76, 79-80, Abbott Northwestern Hosp., Mpls., 1981-82; charge nurse in child psychiatry Med. Coll. Ga., Augusta, 1983-87; adminstr. child psychiat. program Charter Hosp. of Augusta, 1987-91; staff educator/quality mgmt. in psychiatry Ga. Regional Hosp. at Augusta, 1990-92; team leader child psychiatry Charter Peachford Hosp., Atlanta, 1992—. Active Girl Scouts Am. Mem. NAFE, AAUW, ANA, Ga. Nurses Assn., Assn. Child/Adolescent Psychiat. Nurses, Am. Camping Assn. Presbyterian. Home: 725 Josh Ln Lawrenceville GA 30245-3157

JENSEN, CAROLYN JEAN, energy company executive; b. Visalia, Calif., Nov. 7, 1947; d. Charles Thomas and Bette Jean (Williamson) Madden; m. Robert Laurits Jensen, Apr. 6, 1968 (div. Dec. 1980); children: Francene Ann, Christene Ann, Jeanne Marie. AA, Coastline Coll., 1978, AA in Energy Mgmt., 1982; BSBA in Mktg. & Fin., U. Phoenix, 1992, MA in Orgnl. Mgmt., 1995. Conservation rep. So. Calif. Edison, Santa Ana, Calif., 1978-80; conservation, load mgmt. planning cons. So. Calif. Edison, Rosemead, Calif., 1980-81; energy svcs. rep. So. Calif. Edison, Santa Ana, Calif., 1981-89, energy svcs. supr., 1989-91; project mgr. So. Calif. Edison, Rosemead, 1991-92, program mgr., 1992-93, rsch. adminstr., 1993-94, 1994—; corp. speaker So. Calif. Edison, Rosemead, 1994-97; ad hoc com. Women in ASHRAE, Atlanta, 1991-94. Tech. cons., author: (energy innovation) Calif. Energy Commn. Papers, Dept. of Energy Award Projects, 1988, 89, 90, 91, (innovative design) Orange County Urban Rail, 1992. Advisor Rails for Trails, EOS, Laguna Beach, Calif., 1992-94. Named Exemplary vol. Carnation Co., 1985, 86; recipient Mktg. award Edison Elec. Inst., 1988, 89, Govt. Affairs award ASHRAE, 1990, 91. Mem. NAFE, ASHRAE (chair tech. energy com. 1993-94, mem. govt. affairs com. 1990-92), Women in Engring. Advocates, Wycliffe Assocs., PTO (vol. 1985). Republican. Presbyterian. Office: So Calif Edison 2244 Walnut Grove Ave Rosemead CA 91770

JENSEN, CYNTHIA ANN, marketing professional; b. Phoenix, Sept. 24, 1953; d. Harold Emery and Jacqueline A. (Funk) Canterbury; m. Paul Eldredge Jensen, Jan. 25, 1975; children: Elizabeth Ann, Natalie Marie. Student, Ariz. State U., 1971-72; BS, U. Ariz., 1974. From exec. trainee to asst. buyer May Co. Dept. Stores, Los Angeles, 1975-77; dept. mgr. Bullocks Dept. Stores, Phoenix, 1977-78; real estate sales assoc. Jim Daniel & Assocs. Realtors, Phoenix, 1978-79; asst. buyer Broadway Southwest, Mesa, Ariz., 1979-82; mgr. Peat, Marwick, Mitchell & Co. (name now KPMG Peat Marwick), Phoenix, 1982-87, Lewis & Roca Lawyers, 1987-92; dir. media and cmty. rels. State Bar Ariz., 1992-93; pvt. practice as mktg. cons., 1992-93; dir. client svcs. Jennings Strouss & Salmon, Phoenix, 1993—; cons. Lannan & Cleverly Property Mgmt. Inc., Tempe, Ariz., 1985-86. Mem. long range planning com. Cactus Pine council Girl Scouts U.S., 1984, new dimensions foundations com. Phoenix Symphony Orch., 1983-84, religious edn. bd. Encanto Community Ch., 1980-82, 87-89, 94—, hospitality com., 1984-87. Mem. Internat. Assn. Bus. Communicators (profl. devel. com. 1984-85, v.p. profl. devel., bd. dirs. 1985-86, treas. 1986-87, Service award 1985), Pub. Relations Soc. Am. (awards com. 1989, Copper Quill award 1990), Meeting Planners Internat. (program com. 1984-85, mem. membership com. 1985-86, chmn. 1986-87, bd. mem. 1987-88, sec. 1988-89, awards com. 1987-88, fundraising com. chair 1987-88, by law revision com. 1988-89, Meeting Planner of Yr. Ariz. Sunbelt chpt. 1989), Nat. Assn. Law Firm Mktg. Aminstrs. (NALFMA) (nat. awards com. 1987-88, nat. awards com. chair 1988-89, sec. bd. dirs. 1989-90, mem. membership com. 1991-92, 1st place award for firm newsletter, 1988), Phoenix Met. C. of C. (communications coun. 87-88). Republican. Home: 7107 N 6th Ave Phoenix AZ 85021 Office: Jennings Strouss & Salmon 2 N Central Ave Phoenix AZ 85004

JENSEN, CYNTHIA KAY, social worker; b. Hampton, Iowa, Nov. 30, 1954; d. Elmer George and Kathleen Jeanette (White) Kraft; m. Donald George Jensen, June 27, 1975; children: Daniel George, Michelle Kay. BA in English, Milton Coll., 1978. Bldg. and rental property asst. mgr. Helgesen Realty, 1980-84; with acctg. and computer cons. sales dept. Equity Mgmt. Svcs., 1984-87; with furniture sales dept. Janesville Comfort Shoppe, 1986-89; with sales and framing dept. Joan Blackbourn, Concepts in Art, 1989-90; adoption counselor Cmty. Adoption Ctr., Inc., 1990—. Active Marshall Middle Sch. PTA, Janesville, 1990—, Craig H.S. PTO, Janesville, 1993—. Mem. AAUW (book discussion chair 1979—).

JENSEN, DEBORAH ANN, photographer; b. Santa Rosa, Calif., Dec. 21, 1952; d. David Laurens and Barbara (Hackler) Jordan; m. William Jensen; children: Natalie, Trudie, Erik. Student, Mesa Jr. Coll., San Diego, 1976. Metal sculptress Hallmark Stores, 1973-76; piano instr. Calif., 1976-77; pvt. wedding photographer, keyboardist, florist San Diego, 1977-82, pvt. wedding photographer, 1977—; group leader, photographer, videographer Weight Watchers, San Diego, 1987-89. Pianist Christian Congregation, Sacramento, 1975—. Mem. Bridal Mart Am. (assoc.). Office: Bill & Debbie Jensens Economy Photo Sacramento CA 95823

JENSEN, DELORES (DEE JENSEN), physical education educator; b. Harvey, N.D., Apr. 20, 1944; m. Owen Jensen, Dec. 28, 1968. BS, Valley City State U., 1966; MA, No. Ariz. U., 1973. Master cert. official track and field, level 1 coaching cert. Bus., phys. edn. instr. Hatton (N.D.) Pub. Schs., 1966-72; phys. edn. instr. Midway Sch. Dist., Inkster, N.D., 1972-74; student svcs. asst., women's track coach N.D. State Coll. Sci., Wahpeton, 1974-77, bus. instr., women's track coach, 1974—; mem. exec. com. Nat. Athletic Ofcls. Com., 1984-94; co-mgr. Nat. Sports Festival, Baton Rouge, 1985; mem. Xth Pan Am. Games Ofcls. Selection Com., 1985-86, Olympic Trials Ofcls. Selection Com., 1988, Centennial Olympic Games Ofcls. Selection Com., 1993—; mem. exec. com. U.S. Olympic Sports Festival, 1987—; bd. dirs. U.S.A. Track & Field. Mem. U.S.A. Track and Field Site Selection Com., 1992—; head mgr. Goodwill Games, 1990, U.S. Olympic Sports Festival, Norman, Okla., 1989, U.S.A. vs. Great Britain, 1993; ofcl. U.S. Olympic Trials, 1992. Named Olympic ofcl. Track and Field, 1984, Coach of Yr., Nat. Jr. Coll. Track Coaches Assn., 1986, Xth Pan Am. Games ofcl., 1987, Internat. Spl. Olympics ofcl., 1991; recipient Svc. award U.S. Women's Track Coaches Assn., 1989, Andy Bakjian award Nat. Track & Field Ofcls. Com., 1993. Mem. AAUW (treas. 1982-85), U.S. Women's Track and Field Coaches Assn. (exec. com. 1986-88), NJCAA Men's and Women's Track Coaches Assn. (v.p. 1991—), Kiwanis (bd. dirs. 1989-91), Alpha Delta Kappa (chpt. pres. 1976-78, treas., exec. com. N.D. chpt. 1982-84). Home: 1621 5th St N Wahpeton ND 58075-3301 Office: ND State Coll Sci Old Main Wahpeton ND 58076

JENSEN, ETHEL ROXANNE, hotelier; b. Minot, N.D., Oct. 5, 1938; d. Lyle James Thompson and Hazella Marion (Jones) Blake; m. J. Walter Richard Peters, Nov. 14, 1959 (div. 1975); 1 son, J. Chandler; m. Ivan Raymond Jensen, June 1, 1978. Cert. secondary tchr., N.D. Adminstrv. officer U. N.D. Grad. Sch., Grand Forks, 1974-78; owner, mgr. Ambassador Motel, Grand Forks, 1978-91; exec. dir., Prairie Harvest Human Svcs. Fdn., 1991—, exec. com., bd. dir., chmn. bd. com. 1993—; mem. N.D. Ho. of Reps., 1989, 91. Author weekly newspaper column Valley View, 1980-82. Bd. dirs. Greater Grand Forks Symphony, 1979-80; founding mem., treas. Greater Grand Forks Arts and Humanities Coun., 1980-81; charter v.p. Greater Grand Forks Conv. Bur., 1981-82, pres., 1982-83, 83-84; chmn. Affordable Housing Coun. Home Loan Bank of Des Moines, 1990-92. Mem. Am. Hotel/Motel Assn., Greater Grand Forks Hotel/Motel Assn. (pres. 1979-81), Phi Beta Kappa. Unitarian. Club: Quota (treas. 1982-83). Lodge: Rotary, Lioness (charter pres. 1982-83). Avocations: art, music, lit. Home: 3707 Belmont Rd Grand Forks ND 58201-7813 Office: Prairie Harvest Found 930 N 3d St Forks ND 58201

JENSEN, HANNE MARGRETE, pathology educator; b. Copenhagen, Dec. 9, 1935; came to U.S., 1957; d. Niels Peter Evald and Else Signe Agnete (Rasmussen) Damgaard; m. July 21, 1957 (div. Apr. 1987); children: Peter Albert, Dorte Marie, Gordon Kristian, Sabrina Elisabeth. Student, U. Copenhagen, 1954-57; MD, U. Wash., 1961. Resident and fellow in pathology U. Wash., Seattle, 1963-68; asst. prof. dept. pathology U. Calif. Sch. Medicine, Davis, 1969-79, assoc. prof., 1979—, dir. transfusion svc., 1973—; McFarlane prof. exptl. medicine U. Glasgow, Scotland, 1983. Mem. No. Calif. Soc. for Electron Microscopy, U.S. and Can. Acad. of Pathology, Am. Cancer Soc., Am. SOc. Clin. Pathologists, Am. Assn. for Advancement of Sci., Am. Assn. of Blood Banks, Calif. Blood Bank System, People to People Internat., Internat. Platform Assn; fellow Pacific Coast Obstetrician and Gynecol. Soc., Coll. of Am. Pathologists. Office: U Calif Sch Medicine Dept Pathology Davis CA 95616

JENSEN, HELEN, musical artists management company executive; b. Seattle, June 30, 1919; d. Frank and Sophia (Kantosky) Leponis; student pub. schs., Seattle; m. Ernest Jensen, Dec. 2, 1939; children: Ernest, Ronald Lee. Co-chmn., Seattle Community Concert Assn., 1957-62; sec. family concerts Seattle Symphony Orch., 1959-61; hostess radio program Timely Topics, 1959-60; gen. mgr. Western Opera Co., Seattle, 1962-64, pres. 1963-64; v.p., dir., mgr. pub. rels. Seattle Opera Assn., 1964-83, preview artists coord., 1981-84; bus. mgr. Portland (Oreg.) Opera Co., 1968, cons., 1967-69; owner, mgr. Helen Jensen Artists Mgmt., Seattle, 1970-92. First v.p. Music and Art Found., 1981-84, pres. 1984-85. Recipient Cert., Women in Bus in the Field of Art, 1973, award Seattle Opera Assn., 1974, Outstanding Svc. award Music and Art Found., 1984, Women of Achievement award Women in Communications, 1992. Mem. Am. Guild Mus. Artists, Music and Art Found. (life), Seattle Opera Guild (life, bd. dirs. 1988-92, pres., award of distinction 1983, parliamentarian 1987-89), Ballard Symphony League (sec.), Portland Opera Assn., Portland Opera Guild, Seattle Civic Opera Assn. (pres. 1981—), 200 Plus One, Aria Preview, Lyric Preview Group (chmn. 1988-92), Past Pres. Assembly (pres. 1977-79, parliamentarian 1987-89), Pres.'s Forum (1st v.p. 1990-91, program vice chmn. 1987-88, pres. 1991-92), North Shore Performing Arts Assn. (pres. 1981), Women of Achievement (past pres's. assembly, chmn.), Pres.'s Forum (pres. 1991-92), Woman's Century Club (chmn. art, drama, music dept. 1992-93), Helen Jensen Hiking Club. Home: 19029 56th Ln NE Seattle WA 98155-3156 Office: 716 Joseph Vance Bldg Seattle WA 98101

JENSEN, HELENE WICKSTROM, nutritionist, educator; b. Carthage, Mo., Mar. 3, 1929; d. Frank Emil and Lois (Stroup) Wickstrom; m. Robert Gordon Jensen, Dec. 20, 1947; children: Gordon Lee, Jeffrey Alan. BS, U. Mo., 1951; MS, U. Conn., 1983. Registered dietitian. Dietitian-in-charge U. Mo., Columbia, 1952-56; therapeutic dietitian Windham Community Meml. Hosp., Willimantic, Conn., 1967, dir. food service, 1967-72; dir. sch. lunch program Windham Pub. Schs., Willimantic, 1963-66; lectr. U. Conn., Storrs, 1972-78, leader ednl. outreach program, 1979-92; cons. Recipient award Met. Life Ins. Co., 1985, Czajowski Nutrition award U. Conn., 1989, Disting. Alumna award U. Conn. Agr. and Natural Resources Alumni Assn., 1989. Mem. Am. Dietetic Assn. (presenter), Am. Sch. Food Svc. Assn. (exec. bd. 1989-91, presenter), Soc. Nutrition Edn., Conn. Sch. Food Svc. Assn. (com. mem.), Conn. Nutrition Coun. (presenter), Conn. Dietetic Assn. (presenter, Dietitian of Yr. 1987), Phi Kappa Phi, Gamma Sigma Delta. Home: 186 Chaffeeville Rd Storrs Mansfield CT 06268-2637

JENSEN, JAKKI RENEE, retail company executive; b. Eugene, Oreg., Mar. 1, 1959; d. Philip William Jensen and Mary Katherine (Sommers) Henderson; m. Johnny Claiborne Hawthorne, May 7, 1983. Student, Oreg. State U., 1977-78; student (hon.), Portland State U., 1978-81. With Nordstrom Inc., Beaverton, Oreg., 1981—; mgr. cosmetics Nordstrom Inc., Beaverton, 1984; mgr. cosmetics Nordstrom Inc., Walnut Creek, Calif., 1984-86, buyer cosmetics, 1986-88; buyer cosmetics Nordstrom Inc., San Francisco, 1988-93; area mdse. mgr. Nordstrom Own Product, San Francisco, 1993—. Affiliate, vol. San Francisco Soc. for Prevention of Cruelty to Animals, 1990—. Republican. Home: 118 Costanza Dr Martinez CA 94553-6600 Office: 865 Market St San Francisco CA 94103-1900

JENSEN, JANE MARY, periodontist; b. St. Paul, Aug. 25, 1951; d. Vernon John and Margaret Joan (Garvey) Hermes; m. Robert Lyle Jensen Jr., July 7, 1973; children: Aric, Cristin, Andrew. AA, Ottumwa Heights Coll., 1971; grad. in dental hygiene, U. Minn., 1973, BS, 1975, DDS, 1977, MS in Dentistry, 1980. Cert. periodontist. Periodontist Drs. Robert and Jane Jensen, Maplewood, Minn., 1979—; clin. instr. Sch. Dentistry, U. Minn., 1978—. Contbr. articles to profl. jours. Mem. Home and Sch. Assn. St. Jude's Sch. Mahtomedi, Minn. Mem. ADA, Minn. Dental Assn. (del. 1988—, co-chairperson legis. com.), Am. Acad. Periodontology (Balint Orban award), Midwest Soc. Periodontists, Minn. Assn. Periodontists (pres. 1988-89), St. Paul Dist. Dental Soc. (pres. 1994-95, treas. 1986-89, mem. exec. coun. 1990-93), Phi Theta Kappa, Omicron Kappa Upsilon. Roman Catholic. Office: 2480 White Bear Ave N Saint Paul MN 55109-5121

JENSEN, JUDY DIANNE, psychotherapist; b. Portland, Oreg., Apr. 8, 1948; d. Clarence Melvin and Charlene Augusta (Young) J.; m. Frank George Cooper, Sept 4, 1983; stepchildren: Pamela Cooper, Brian Cooper. BA in Sociology and Anthropology with honors, Oberlin Coll., 1970; MSW, U. Pitts., 1972; postgrad., U. Wis., 1977. Lic. clin. social worker, marriage and family therapist, Oreg. Social worker Day Hosp. Western Psychiat. Inst. and Clinic, Pitts., 1972-73, South Hills Child Guidance Ctr., Pitts., 1973-74; mem. drug treatment program Umatilla County Mental Health Clinic, Pendleton, Oreg., 1975-77; social worker Children's Svcs. Div. State of Oreg., Pendleton, 1978-80, therapist intensive family services project, 1980—, dir. intensive family services project, 1986—; pvt. practice Pendleton, 1980—. NIMH grantee, 1970-72; NDEA fellow 1977; Gen. Motors scholar Oberlin Coll., 1966-70. Mem. Am. Assn. Marriage and Family Therapists (clin.), Nat. Assn. Social Workers. Home: 325 NW Bailey Ave Pendleton OR 97801-1604 Office: PO Box 752 Pendleton OR 97801-0752

JENSEN, KATHERINE KEMP, insurance company executive; b. Canandaigua, N.Y., July 22, 1955; d. Harry Frederick and Charlotte Ruth (Doebereiner) Kemp; m. Fred E. Jensen, Mar. 7, 1987; stepchildren: Brett, Stacey, Marceil. BA, Siena Coll., 1976. Cert. property and casualty ins. instr. Dir. local programs N.Y. State Assembly, Albany, 1976-77; assoc. realtor Grad. Realtor Inst. LaLonde Realty, Inc., Fairport, N.Y., 1978-81; ops. unit mgr. Allstate Ins. Co., Rochester, N.Y., 1981-84; adminstrv. svcs. mgr. Allstate Ins. Co., Rochester, 1984-88; market sales mgr. Allstate Ins. Co., Jamestown, 1988-92; agy. mgr. Allstate Ins. Co., Jamestown, N.Y., 1992—. Chmn. N.Y. State Teen Age Reps., 1973-74; mem. N.Y. State Rep. Platform Com., 1974; mem. Perinton Rep. Com., 1978-88, chmn., 1985-88; mem. Zoning Bd. Appeals, Perinton, N.Y., 1981-88, chmn., 1985-88; mem. Warren County Rep. Exec. Com., Pa. Recipient Mary Ann award N.Y. State Reps., 1974. Mem. Am. Mgmt. Assn., Ind. Ins. Agts. Assn. N.Y., Inc., Western Pa. Paint Horse Club, Chautauqua Region Life Underwriters, Jamestown Area C. of C., Empire State Paint Horse Club (pres. 1986-87). Home: RR 1 Columbus PA 16405-9801 Office: Allstate Ins Co 560 W 3rd St Jamestown NY 14701-4733

JENSEN, SUSAN ANN, advertising executive; b. Ashton, Idaho, Oct. 30, 1946; d. Orville Arnold and Irma Hazel (Kortesoja) Jensen; m. Paul Singer, Oct. 1, 1983. BA, U. Oreg., 1971; MBA, U. Wash., 1974. Dir. research Cole Weber, Seattle, 1972-75, v.p., 1975-79; v.p. Ogilvy Mather, N.Y.C., 1979-84; sr. v.p. Rapp Collins, N.Y.C., 1984-87, Wells, Rich, Greene, N.Y.C., 1987-89; ptnr. Jensen & Singer, N.Y.C., 1989-94, Jackson, Wyo., 1994—. Mem. Direct Mktg. Assn. Republican. Mem. Unitarian Ch. Home: PO Box 20183 Jackson WY 83001

JENSEN-MORAN, JOAN MARY, elementary education educator, consultant, coach; b. Chgo., Sept. 25, 1952; d. Axel Fred and Mary J. (Maes) Jensen; m. Gregory Keith Moran, Sept. 6, 1980. BS in Edn., Western Ill. U., 1974; MS in Edn., No. Ill. U., 1978. Cert. tchr., Ill. Part-time office clk. Dallas Distbrs., Chgo., 1968-69; part-time lifeguard Chgo. Park Dist., 1970-73, part-time recreation leader, 1974; tchr., coach East Coloma Sch., Rock Falls, Ill., 1974—; part-time recreation specialist Woodhaven Lakes, Sublette, Ill., 1975-79; cons. Ill. State Bd. of Edn., Springfield, 1984—; instr. NDEITA, Ill., 1988—; facilitator Project Wild, Ill., 1990—. Contbr. numerous articles to profl. jours. Mem. grad. adv. outdoor edn. com. Lorado Taft Campus, 1979-80; instr. ARC, Rock Falls, 1978—, Am. Heart Assn., Rock Falls, 1978—; mem. Phys. Devel. and Health Adv. Com., Springfield, 1991—; fitness del. to Russia and Hungary, 1992. Named one of Outstanding Young Women Am., 1986; recipient Alumni award Western Ill. U., 1993, Disney Am. Tchr. award, 1993. Mem. AAPHERD, Ill. Assn. Health, Phys. Edn., Recreation and Dance (presenter, presider convs., v.p. elect teenage youth 1989, v.p. 1990, pres.-elect 1993, pres. 1994, county rep. No. dist. 1985, treas. 1987-88, awards chair 1986, pres.-elect, pres. 1988-90, advisor, newsletter editor 1991—, Ill. Mid. Sch. Phys. Edn. Tchr. of Yr. 1992, Midwest Mid. Sch. Phys. Edn. Tchr. of Yr. 1993, Western Ill. Master Tchr. 1993), NEA, Ill. Edn. Assn. (region 20 newsletter editor 1984-85, treas., exec. bd. 1985-90), East Coloma Edn. Assn. (chief negotiator 1989-91, regional coun. rep. 1989-92, v.p. 1982, pres. 1983-84), Environ. Edn. Assn. Ill. (exec bd., rep.). Democrat. Lutheran. Home: 1903 E 41st St Sterling IL 61081-9419 Office: East Coloma Sch 1602 Dixon Rd Rock Falls IL 61071-1999

JENSON, KATHY LAVON, marketing director; b. Bismarck, N.D., Oct. 24, 1943; d. Edward Michael and Clara Catherine (Ficker) Degen; m. Roy Kenneth Jenson, Oct. 22, 1977; children: Patricia, Elizabeth. BS in Math., N.D. State U., 1965; MBA in Mktg., U. St. Thomas, 1980. System mgr. Control Data Corp., Bloomington, Minn., 1965-74; major acct. mgr. Digital Equip Corp., Mpls., 1974-80; mgr. strategic planning Control Data Corp., Bloomington, 1980-87; area applications sales mgr. Wang Labs., Mpls., 1987-89; nat. sales mgr. Faxbank Inc., St. Paul, 1990-91; dir. mktg. & sales Solutronix Corp., Eden Prairie, Minn., 1991-92; mktg. dir. NCS, Edina, Minn., 1992—; Minn. quality examiner; guest speaker in field. Vol. Guthrie Theater, Mpls., 1991—, Children's Theater, Mpls., 1991—, Bel Canto Voices, Mpls., 1990—, Regional Dance Competitions, Mpls., 1987—; com. mem. Bloomington C. of C., 1987-88. Mem. Assn. Field Svc. Mgrs., Am. Electronic Assn. (internat. com. 1991—), Soc. Consumer Affairs Profls., Am. Mktg. Assn., Sales and Mktg. Execs., Am. Soc. Quality Control, Minn. Quality Award Com. (Minn. Quality Award examiner 1994).

JERACE, CHARLOTTE LOUISE, writer, consultant; b. Rockland, Maine, Nov. 17, 1942; d. Max and Ida (Shapiro) Gopan; m. Harvey Cohen, Aug. 22, 1964 (div. Oct. 1971): children: Scott, Melissa; m. Michael Crawley Jerace, July 12, 1986. MEd, Antioch U., 1981. pres. Coast-to-Coast Prodns., Truro, Mass., 1990—. Agt. Aetna Life Ins. Co., Boston, 1975-80; mng. editor Employee Comm. Svcs., Natick, Mass., 1980-85; sr. mgr. KPMG Peat Marwick, Boston, 1985-94; prin. Buck Consultants, Boston, 1994—. Author: A Survivor's Manual, 1978, Facing the Future, 1980, Secret Hiding Places, 1994; author short story. Chmn. Truro Beach Commn., 1993—; pres. Boston chpt. Eleanor Roosevelt group Hadassah, 1968-70, mem., 1966—. Recipient Telly award, 1990, 91, 92, Award of Excellence Bus. Ins. Mag., 1993. Mem. Internat. Assn. Bus. Communicators (Award of Excellence 1992), New. Eng. Employee Benefits Coun. Democrat. Jewish.

JERGE, MARIE CHARLOTTE, minister; b. Mineola, N.Y., Dec. 26, 1952; d. Charles Louis and Helen Marie (Scheld) Scharfe; m. James Nelson Jerge, Aug. 27, 1977. AB, Smith Coll., 1974; MDiv, Luth. Theol. Sem. of Phila., 1978. Pastor St. Mark Evang. Luth. Ch., Mayville, N.Y., 1978-88; co-pastor Zion Evang. Luth. Ch., Silver Creek, N.Y., 1983-88; asst. to the bishop Upstate N.Y. Synod, Buffalo, 1988—; bd. dirs. Acad. Preachers, Phila., 1982—. Chairperson Chautauqua County Commn. of Family Violence and Neglect, Mayville, 1981-82, bd. dirs., 1978-88. Named one of outstanding Young Women in Am., 1980. Home: 370 Borden Rd Buffalo NY 14224-1713 Office: Upstate NY Synod 49 Linwood Ave Buffalo NY 14209-2203

JERNIGAN, MARIAN SUE, fashion merchandising educator; b. Chattanooga, Dec. 18, 1940; d. John Marion and Coye M. (Cunningham) Hayes; m. G. William Jernigan, Dec. 22, 1969. BS, Purdue U., 1962, MS, 1964, PhD, 1968. Exec. trainee Hutzler Bros. Co., Balt., 1963-64; dept. mgr. L.S. Ayres & Co., Lafayette, Ind., 1964-65; instr. Purdue U., W. Lafayette, Ind., 1965-66; asst. prof. La. State U., Baton Rouge, 1968-73; assoc. prof. Fla. State U., Tallahassee, 1973-76, N. Tex. State U., Denton, 1976-83; acting dir. N. Tex. State U., 1980-83; prof. fashion merchandising Tex. Woman's U., Denton, 1983—; mem. exec. com. Tex. Coun. Faculty Governance Orgns., 1992-96. Co-author: Merchandising Mathematics for Retailing, 1984, 2d edit., 1992, Fashion Merchandising and Marketing, 1990. pres. Internat. Toastmistress, Lewisville, Tex., 1983. Mem. Fashion Group Internat., Internat. Textile and Apparel Assn., Am. Collegiate Retailing Assn., Am. Assn. Family and Consumer Scis., Costume Soc. Am., Tex. Home Econs. Assn. (div. sec.), Delta Kappa Gamma, Alpha Lambda Delta, Omicron Nu, Phi Kappa Phi, Phi Upsilon Omicron, Zeta Tau Alpha (advisor student chpts.). Methodist. Office: Tex Woman's U PO Box 22509 Denton TX 76204-0509

JERNIGAN, TAMARA E., astronaut; b. Chattanooga, Tenn., May 7, 1959; d. Terry L. and Mary P. J. BS in Physics with honors, Stanford U., 1981, MS in Engineering Science, 1983; MS in Astronomy, U. Calif., Berkeley, 1985; PhD in Space Physics and Astronomy, Rice, 1988. Rsch. scientist Theoretical Studies Branch NASA, 1981-85, astronaut candidate, 1985, astronaut, 1986—, mission specialist Space Shuttle Columbia, 1992; administrator sci. experiments Space Shuttle Endeavor, 1995. Mem. Am. Astron. Assn., Am. Physical Soc., U.S. Volleyball Assn. Office: NASA Johnson Space Ctr Astronaut Ofc Houston TX 77058*

JERNIGAN, TRACEY A., quality assurance executive; b. Crestview, Fla., Jan. 23, 1960; d. W.A. (Jake) and Claire (Covell) J. Attended, Gulf Coast C.C., Panama City, Fla., 1979-80, U. So. Fla., 1980-82; degree in Info. Mgmt. and Programming with honors, Data Processing Inst., 1983. Mgr. tng. and edn. Didas Corp., Destin, Fla., 1987-89; co-founder, dir. tng. and edn. Group 400, Destin, 1989-91; dir. quality tng. and edn. Precision Industries, Ft. Walton Beach, Fla., 1991—. Bd. dirs. Focus Ctr. Sci. Mus.; mem. Jr. League of Ft. Walton Beach. Mem. Am. Soc. Quality Control, Am. Soc. Training and Devel., Internat. Customer Svc. Assn., IBM Edn. Ctr., Am. Productivity and Quality Ctr. Republican. Presbyterian. Home: 2705 Hwy 98 E Unit 1 Destin FL 32541-3400 Office: 151 Mary Esther Blvd Ste 503 Mary Esther FL 32569

JESSEE, S. LEE, environmental protection specialist; b. Roanoke, Va., Jan. 5, 1954. Student, Va. Poly. Inst. & State U., 1972-74; AAS in Engring., New River C.C., Dublin, Va., 1976; BA, Trinity Coll., Washington, 1990. Cert. engring. technologist; cert. hazardous substance incident response mgr. Site planner Long, Brown & Assocs., Fairfax, Va., 1976-77, Patton, Harris, Rust & Assocs., Fairfax, 1977-79; environ. engr. SCS Engrs., Reston, Va., 1979-84; head environ. program dept. Nat. Naval Med. Command, Bethesda, Md., 1984-89; environ. protection specialist U.S. Dept. Energy, Washington, 1990—; agy. rep. geog. info. systems subcom. Natural Resources & Environ. subcom.; mem. site-specific conceptual design com. Superconducting Super Collider, Dept. Energy; subteam head Tiger Team Environ., Stanford Linear Accelerator Ctr., 1991; mgr. Doe Nepa Info. Sys.; develer Pres. Coun. Environ. Quality, Nat. Corporate Nepa Info. Resource for Internet, 1995. Naval on-scene comdr. Montgomery (Md.) County Local Emergency Planning & Response Com. Mem. Internat. Assn. for Impact Assessment, Met. Washington Fed. Safety Coun., Hazardous Materials Control Rsch. Inst. Home: 105 Hopeland Ln Sterling VA 20164 Office: US Dept Energy 1000 Independence Ave SW Washington DC 20585

JESSEP, JANE NORDLI, elementary education educator; b. Bridgeport, Conn., Oct. 30, 1947; d. William and Elizabeth (Glenn) Nordli; m. John Jessep, Dec. 16, 1978 (div. 1985); 1 child by previous marriage, Tara Walsh. BS, Skidmore Coll., 1969; M Voice, Manhattan Sch. Music, 1977; postgrad., Lincoln Ctr. Inst., 1992-94. Cert. tchr., Conn. Tchr. music Title I Schs., Omaha, 1970-71, Hillspoint Sch., Westport, Conn., 1971-72, Coleytown Jr. High Sch., Westport, 1977-82, Hart Sch., Stamford, Conn., 1984-85, Hurlbutt Elem. Sch., Weston, Conn., 1985—; soloist New Haven Opera, 1974-77, Delphi Opera, Conn., 1980-84; chorister Am. Guild Musical Artists, 1976-83; chorus mem. Met. Opera, N.Y.C., 1980-83, N.Y.C. Ballet, 1980-86; tchr. music history Adult Edn. Program, Westport, 1984-87. Vol. AIDS hospice Bread and Roses. Mem. NEA, LWV, Conn. Edn. Assn., Weston Tchr. Assn., Music Educators Nat. Conf. (cert. music educator), New Eng. Assn. Schs. and Colls. (steering com. 1990-92). Democrat. Home: 26 Glen Rdg Wilton CT 06897-4037

JESSUP, JAN AMIS, arts volunteer, writer; b. Chgo., Aug. 10, 1927; d. Herman Harvey and Anita (Lincoln) Sinako; m. Everett Orme Amis, Dec. 20, 1970 (dec. Nov. 1981); m. Joe Lee Jessup, Apr. 16, 1989. BA, U. Minn., 1948; postgrad., Rutgers U., 1969-70. bd. dirs., exec. com. Broward Ctr. for Performing Arts Pacers, Fort Lauderdale, Fla., 1985-88, pres., 1987-88; speaker U. Internat. Bus., Beijing, 1985. Active various not-for-profit orgns. including Girl Scouts U.S., Boy Scouts Am., Presbyn. Ch. among others; mem. Beautification Com., Lighthouse Point, Fla., 1978-89, sec., 1988-81; rep. to Fla. Art Orgns., 1987-88; bd. dirs. Archways, Ft. Lauderdale, 1987-91; trustee Miami City Ballet, 1991-93; adv. bd. Guild of the Palm Beaches, 1992—. Mem. Nat. Soc. Arts and Letters, Am. Symphony Orch. League (vice chmn. 1989-90, sec. vol. coun. 1986-87, v.p. 1987-88, pres. elect 1988-90, pres. 1989-90, advisor 1990-91), Fla. Philharm. Orch. (bd. govs. 1981—, v.p. representing all affiliates 1985-87, 92, 94, exec. com. 1989-93, v.p. individual giving 1991-92, bd. dirs. 1994—, chmn. affiliate com. 1994—), The Opus Soc. (bd. dirs/exec. com. 1981—, chmn. 1981-85), Fort Lauderdale Philharm. Soc. (bd. dirs. 1986—), Opera Soc. (sec. 1986-87, v.p. pub. rels. 1987-88), Opera Guild, Inc. (bd. dirs. 1993—), Gold Coast Jazz Soc. (bd. dirs. 1992—, v.p. 1994—), Boca Raton Resort and Club, Royal Palm Yacht Club, Royal Palm Country Club, Women's Club, Sea Grape Garden Club (past pres.). Republican. Home: 133 Coconut Palm Rd Boca Raton FL 33432-7975

JETER, ANNE PEARL, guidance, marriage, family and child counselor; b. East St. Louis, Ill.; d. Jeff Mills and Annie Louise (Swanson) Ware; m. Roy Jeter, Oct. 31, 1952; children: Brian, Kevin, Roy Jr., Wanda, Kimberly, Phyllis. AA, Allan Hancock Coll., Santa Maria, Calif., 1966; BA, Chapman U., 1970, MA, 1971; PhD, U.S. Internat. U., 1978. Employee rels. officer USAF, Vandenberg AFB, Calif., 1971-72; guidance counselor 30 MSSO/MSE USAF, Vandenberg AFB, 1973—; edn. svcs. officer USAF, Germany, 1980, Sicily, 1985; adj. instr. Lompac (Calif.) Adult Sch., 1971-74, U.S. Internat. U., San Diego, 1978-79; Chapman U., Orange, Calif., 1978-92, Allan Hancock Coll., Santa Monica, Calif. 1978-80; marriage, family and children counselor Mt. Zion Missionary Ch., Grover City, Calif., Family Support Ctr. Vandenberg AFB. Pres. Robinson Sch. PTA, 1954; bd. dirs. Lompac Mental Health, 1978-79. Mem. ACA, Air Force Assn. (v.p. edn. Goddard chpt., chair edn. Calif. chpt.), Beta Phi Sigma (recording grammeteus 1974-80).

JETER, KATHERINE LESLIE BRASH, lawyer; b. Gulfport, Miss., July 24, 1921; d. Ralph Edward and Rosa Meta (Jacobs) Brash; m. Robert McLean Jeter, Jr., May 11, 1946. BA, Newcomb Coll. of Tulane U., 1943; JD, Tulane U., 1945. Bar: La. 1945, U.S. Dist. Ct. (we. dist.) La. 1948, U.S. Tax Ct. 1965, U.S. Supreme Ct. 1971, U.S. Dist. Ct. (ea. dist.) La. 1975, U.S. Ct. Appeals (5th cir.) 1981, U.S. Dist. Ct. (mid. dist.) La. 1982. Assoc. Montgomery, Fenner & Brown, New Orleans, 1945-46, Tucker, Martin, Holder, Jeter & Jackson, Shreveport, 1947-49; ptnr. Tucker, Jeter, Jackson and Hickman and predecessors, Shreveport, 1980—; judge pro tem 1st Jud. Dist. Ct., Caddo Parish, La., 1982-83; mem. adv. com. to joint legis. subcom. on mgmt. of the community; pres. YWCA of Shreveport, 1963; hon. consul of France; Shreveport, 1982-91; pres. Little Theatre of Shreveport, 1966-67; pres. Shreveport Art Guild, 1974-75; mem. task force crim justice La. Priorities for the Future, 1978; pres. LWV of Shreveport, 1950-51. Recipient Disting. Grad. award Tulane U., 1983. Mem. Am. Law Inst., La. State Law Inst. (mem. coun. 1980—, adv. com. La. Civil Code 1973-77, temp. ad hoc. com. 1976-77, sr. officer 1993—), Am. Law Inst., Pub. Affairs Rsch. Coun. (bd. trustees 1976-81, exec. com. 1981—, area exec. committeeman Shreveport area 1982), ABA, La. Bar Assn., Shreveport Bar Assn. (pres. 1986), Nat. Assn. Women Lawyers, Shreveport Assn. for Women Attys., C. of C. Shreveport (bd. dirs. 1975-77), Order of Coif, Phi Beta Kappa. Contbr. articles on law to profl. jours. Home: 3959 Maryland Ave Shreveport LA 71106-1021 Office: 401 Edwards St Ste 905 Shreveport LA 71101-3146

JETER, MARY JANE, insurance executive; b. New Kensington, Pa., Aug. 13, 1948; d. Pete and Ann (Brook) Tromza. Cert., Ins. Inst., Malvern, Pa., 1979; BSBA, U. Hartford, 1994. Claim supr. Aetna Life & Casualty, Hartford, Conn., 1978-79, asst. adminstr., 1979-81, claim supt., 1981-82, sr. analyst, 1982-84, project coord., 1984-85, sr. rsch. assoc., 1985-88, mgr. pub. policy, 1988-90, dir. law dept., 1990-92, claim cons., 1992—. Author: (manuals) Emerging Conceptions of Injury, 1988, The Availability and Affordability of Property/Casualty Insurance, 1986. Mem. CPCU (dir. Conn. chpt. 1990-94), Alpha Chi. Republican. Roman Catholic. Home: 105 Craigemore Cir Avon CT 06001-3418 Office: Aetna Life & Casualty 151 Farmington Ave Hartford CT 06156-0002

JEVNE, JOAN JANET, artist; b. Taipei, Taiwan, Feb. 10, 1946; came to U.S., 1967; d. Chi an dAu-thou (Lin) Chen; m. Terry Bryon Jevne, Feb. 9, 1966; children: Jonathan, Priscilla, Patricia. Artist, tchr. Minot AFB (N.D.) Arts & Crafts, 1984; tchr. art elem. sch. Lansford, N.D., 1994. Exhibitor st. fairs, art shows, Fargo, N.D., Bismarck, N.D., Mandan, N.D., Minot, 1987—. Recipient Best of Show N.D. State Fair Art Dept., Minot, 1983, People's Choice award Down Town St. Fair, Minot, 1984, Quick Draw Artist award Rough Rider Internat. Art Show, Williston, N.D., 1991. Mem. Sheyenne Valley Arts and Crafts, East Grand Forks Art Coun., Bismarck Art and Galleries Assn. Mem. Nazarene Ch. Home: Rt 1 Box 17A Lansford ND 58750

JEWELL, BARBARA CHRISTENSEN, accountant; b. Racine, Wis., Mar. 16, 1954; d. Richard William and Rita Natalie (Thomas) Christensen; m. David Gene Jewell, Aug. 15, 1987. BS in Acctg., U. Wis., Parkside; MBA in Fin., U. Wis., Whitewater. CPA. Staff acct. Cutler-Hammer, Inc., Milw., 1977-78, supr. cost reporting, 1978-79; supr. gen. acctg. J.I. Case Co., Racine, 1979-80, budget analyst, 1980-83, sr. fin. analyst, 1983-88; mgr. fin. planning & analysis automation product divsn. Square D Co., Milw., 1988-89; dir. fin. Square D Co., Milw., and Raleigh, N.C., 1989-92; divsn. contr. nameplate divsn. W.H. Brady Co., Hillsborough, N.C., 1992-93; corp. contr. TSR, Inc., Lake Geneva, Wis., 1993—; mem. adj. faculty acctg. & fin. U. Wis.-Parkside, Kenosha, 1985-89. Instr. Jr. Achievement Project Bus., Milw., 1978. Mem. Inst. Mgmt. Accts. (pres. Racine/Kenosha 1985-86, v.p. adminstrn. Racine/Kenosha 1984-85). Office: TSR Inc 201 Sheridan Springs Rd Lake Geneva WI 53147

JEWELL, LINDA CAROL, principal; b. Colorado Springs, Aug. 1, 1949; d. Robert Claire and Joan Joyce (Short) De Mark; m. Charles Russell Jewell, Aug. 21, 1971. BA, Phillips U., 1971; MEd, No. Ariz. U., 1994. Cert. secondary music educator, elem. prin. Music tchr. Lincoln and Eisenhower Elem. Schs., Enid, Okla., 1972-73, Mohave Mid. and Pima Elem. Schs., Scottsdale, Ariz., 1974-75, Navajo Elem. Sch., Scottsdale, 1975-78, Cherokee and Paiute Elem. Schs., Scottsdale, 1979-80; music tchr. Hopi Elem. Sch., Scottsdale, 1980-92, asst. prin., 1992—; dist. music coord. Hopi Elem. Sch., 1991—. Mem. ASCD, Music Educators Nat. Conf., Scottsdale Edn. Assn., Scottsdale Music Tchrs. Home: 11238 S Mandan St Phoenix AZ 85044-1811 Office: Hopi Elem Sch 5110 E Lafayette Blvd Phoenix AZ 85018-4433

JEWELL, MARTHA PEARL, marketing professional; b. Brimfield, Ohio, Oct. 10, 1940; d. Roy Delbert and Johnnie Belle (Smith) McPherson; m. Richard Lee Jewell, Oct. 13, 1956; children: Melany Elaine, Brian Lee, Kenneth Richard. Student, U. Kansas, 1974, Dale Carnegie, Kansas City, Mo., 1974, U. Mo., Kansas City, 1975-76. Successively treas., gen. sales mgr., exec. v.p. Arrow Forklift Parts Co., Inc., Kansas City, 1971-81; pres. Jewell Mktg. Service, Inc., Kansas City, 1981—, Matrix Dimensions, Inc., Kansas City, 1986-87. Film producer The Master Key, 1986. Treas. Wesleyan Service Guild, Kansas City, 1975. Mem. Nat. Assn. Women Bus. Owners (spl. projects chmn. 1982), Smithsonian Inst., Creative Film Soc., Visual Music Alliance, Nat. Arbor Day Found., Christian Bus. and Profl. Women (chmn. 1973-74), Sales and Mktg. Execs., Material Handling Equipment Dealers Assn., Kansas City Direct Mktg. Assn. Presbyterian. Home and Office: PO Box 514 Naples NC 28760-0514

JEWETT, KATHRYN JENSEN, nurse, researcher; b. Ellsworth, Maine, Mar. 5, 1942; d. Carl Aggerholm and Edith Mae (Nelson) Jensen; m. David Stuart Jewett, Oct. 13, 1963; children: Carl David, Mark William, Eric Stuart. AA in Nursing, Va. Intermont Coll., 1962; BSN, U. Md., 1989. RN, Md. Charge nurse NYU Hosp., N.Y.C., 1962-63; obstet. practice office nurse Mason Williams, M.D., Norfolk, Va., 1964-65; office nurse, operating rm. nurse Thomas Holmes, M.D., Pensacola, Fla., 1964; lamaze instr. Childbirth Edn. Assn., Springfield, Va., 1970-81; CPR instr. Montgomery Coll., Germantown, Md., 1984-88; clinic nurse Children's Hosp. Nat. Med. Ctr., Rockville, Md., 1984; chief nurse Noyes Children's Ctr., Rockville, Md., 1983-87; surg. practice office mgr. J.S. McCarrick, M.D., Rockville, Md., 1988-89; clin. nurse specialist in surg. and plastic surgery Nat. Naval Med. Ctr., Bethesda, Md., 1989-90; HIV rschr. Henry M. Jackson Found. Navy Hosp., Bethesda, Md., 1990—. Author: (handbook) Birth of a Family, 1972. Mem. ANA, Sigma Theta Tau, Phi Kappa Phi. Home: 25742 Ridge Rd Damascus MD 20872-1852 Office: Henry M Jackson Found 8901 Wisconsin Ave PO Box 207 Bethesda MD 20889

JEYNES, MARY KAY, college dean; b. Miami, Fla., Oct. 31, 1941; d. Nasrallah and Martha (Jabaly) Demetry; m. Paul Jeynes, Sept. 30, 1978. BS, Fla. State U., 1963. Program dir. Orange County YMCA, Orlando, Fla., 1964-69, Ea. Queens YMCA, Belrose, N.Y., 1970-73; regional coord. N.Y. State Park and Recreation Commn., N.Y.C., 1974-77; dir. health, fitness and recreation YWCA of N.Y.C., 1978-79; dean continuing edn. and adult programs Marymount Manhattan Coll., N.Y.C., 1980—. Office: Marymount Manhattan Coll 221 E 71st St New York NY 10021-4501

JEZL, BARBARA ANN, chemist, automation consultant; b. Pitts., June 7, 1947; d. James L. and Elizabeth (Bannister) J. BS in Chemistry, U. Del., 1969, PhD in Organic Chemistry, 1974. Jr. chemist Am. Cyanamid, Pearl River, N.Y., 1969-70; NSF postdoctoral assoc. U. Cin., 1974-76; inst. application specialist E.I. DuPont de Nemours & Co., Wilmington, Del., 1976-79, mem. computing staff, 1979-84, staff specialist, 1985-93, sr. rsch. chemist scientific computing divsn., 1993—. Author: Science, 1990; contbr. articles to profl. jours. Bd. dirs. Unitarian-Universalist Fellowship of Newark, 1981-85, pres., chmn. bd., 1986-87, rep. Delaware Valley Area Coun., Phila., 1983-85, v.p. Fellowship of Newark, 1984-85. Mem. AAAS, IEEE, Am. Chem. Soc., Assn. for Computing Machinery, Macintosh Sci. and Tech. Assn. (bd. dirs., co-chmn. tech. adv. com. 1990—). Home: 5448 W Pinehurst Dr Wilmington DE 19808-2619 Office: EI duPont de Nemours & Co Exptl Sta PO Box 80320 Wilmington DE 19880-0320

JHABVALA, RUTH PRAWER, author; b. Cologne, Germany, May 7, 1927; lived in India, 1951-75; came to U.S., 1975; d. Marcus and Eleonora (Cohn) Prawer; m. Cyrus S. H. Jhabvala, 1951; 3 children. MA, London U., DLitt (hon.). Author: (novels) To Whom She Will, 1955, The Nature of Passion, 1956, Esmond in India, 1957, The Householder, 1960, Get Ready for Battle, 1962, A Backward Place, 1965, A New Dominion, 1972, Heat and Dust, 1975 (Booker award for fiction Nat. Book League 1975), In Search of Love and Beauty, 1983, Three Continents, 1987, Poet and Dancer, 1993; (short story collections) Like Birds, Like Fishes and Other Stories, 1964, A

Stronger Climate: Nine Stories, 1968, An Experience of India, 1971, How I Became a Holy Mother and Other Stories, 1976, Out of India: Selected Stories, 1986; (film scripts) The Householder, 1963, (with James Ivory) Shakespeare Wallah, 1965, (with Ivory) The Guru, 1968, Bombay Talkie, 1970, Autobiography of a Princess, 1975, Roseland, 1977, Hullabaloo over Georgie and Bonnie's Pictures, 1978, (with Ivory) The Europeans, 1979, Jane Austen in Manhattan, 1980, (with Ivory) Quartet, 1981, Heat and Dust, 1983, The Bostonians, 1984, The Courtesans of Bombay, 1985, A Room With A View, 1986 (Writers Guild of Am. award for best adapted screenplay 1986, Academy award for best adapted screenplay 1986), (with John Schlesinger) Madame Sousatzka, 1988, Mr. and Mrs. Bridge, 1990, Howards End, 1992 (Academy award for best adapted screenplay 1992), The Remains of the Day, 1993 (Academy Award nomination for best adapted screenplay 1993), Jefferson in Paris, 1995. Guggenheim fellow, 1976; Neil Gunn. Internat. fellow, 1979; MacArthur Found. fellow, 1984-89. Home: 400 E 52nd St New York NY 10022-6404*

JILER, LINDA CERISE, fire emergency dispatcher, consultant, writer; b. Santa Monica, Calif., Dec. 30, 1956; d. Milton John "Jack" Jiler and Peggy Jean Williams. AA, Lassen Coll., 1979, Cert. Forestry Technician, 1980. Cert. Calif. Dept. Forestry and Fire Protection Fire Acad., 1990. Fire clk./firefighter-wildland Lassen Coll. Contract Crew, Susanville, Calif., 1976-77; forestry technician (fire) U.S. Forest Svc. Lassen Nat. Forest/Eagle Lake Ranger Dist., Eagle Lake Ranger Dist., Calif., 1977-80; dist. personnel technician U.S. Dept. Interior-Bur. Land Mgmt., Susanville Dist., Calif., 1981-86; wildland firefighter/dispatcher Lassen Coll. Contract Fire Crew, Susanville, Calif., 1986-87; fire and aviation program asst. U.S. Dept. Interior Bur. Land Mgmt., Calif. State Office, Sacramento, 1987-89; 9-1-1 interagy. fire dispatcher Calif. Dept. Forestry and Fire Protection, Camino, 1989-93; 9-1-1 interagency emergency commd. ctr. operator Calif. Dept. Forestry and Fire Protection, Camino Interagency Emergency Command Ctr., 1990-93; cons. info. svcs. Sacramento, 1993—; speaker in field; pub. info. officer USDA-FS, U.S. Dept. Interior-Bur. Land Mgmt., CDF, 1983-93. Author: How to Get A Job with the Federal Government, 1983, rev. edit., 1985, 86, Injury and Claim Processing Manual, 1985, Demobilization Training Guide, 1985, Train-the Trainer Wildland Fire Timekeeping Procedures, 1985, (manual) California State Office SOP for Intelligence Gathering, 1987-88; co-author: (manual) California Interagency Mobilization Guide, 1988, Bur. of Land Management's State Policy for Handling of Burn Victims, 1988. Recipient Cert. of Appreciation, Lassen County Bd. Supvs., 1986, 87, Cert. of Appreciation and Cert. of Recognition for Outstanding Performance, U.S. Forest Svc. Pacific S.W. Region, 1987, Nat. Wildland Coord. Group award for Outstanding Performance, U.S. Forest Svc. Pacific N.W. Region and Wallow Whitman Nat. Forest, 1986, Superior Achievement and Profl. Contbns. award U.S. Dept. Agriculture Forest Svc. and U.S. Dept. Interior Bur. Land Mgmt., 1990; cert. Appreciation Eldorado Bd. Suprs. U.S. Forest Svc., 1992, Recognition award Oakland Athletics Baseball Club, 1987, Recognition award San Diego Padres Baseball Club, 1988. Mem. Calif. State Employees Assn. (classification rep. 1989-93), Calif. Profl. Firefighters, Chronic Fatigue Immune Dysfunction Syndrome Support Groups, Nat. Wildlife Fedn., Nat. Trust for Hist. Preservation, Nat. Audubon Soc., Nat. Conf. Incident Command System Fin. Officers, Nat. Australian Shepherd Club Am., Sigma Kappa (alumni past pres.). Democrat.

JIMENEZ, BETTIE EILEEN, retired small business owner; b. LaCygne, Kans., June 8, 1932; d. William Albert and Ruby Faye (Cline) Montee; m. William R. Bradley, Aug. 21, 1947 (div. Sept. 1950); 1 child, Shirley; m. J.P. Jimenez, Feb. 20, 1951 (div. Nov. 1978); children: Pamela, Joe Jr., Robin Michelle. Student, Ft. Scott Jr. Coll., Paola, Kans., 1979-81. Reporter LaCygne Jour., 1943-45; union recorder I.L.G.W.U., Paola, 1956-57; mgr. Estes Metalcraft, Osawatomie, Kans., 1977-82; owner El Rey Tavern, Osawatomie, 1980-95; ret., 1995. Home: 516 Walnut Ave Osawatomie KS 66064-1254

JIMENEZ, JOSEPHINE SANTOS, portfolio manager; b. Lucena, Quezon, Philippines, June 6, 1954; came to U.S., 1972; d. Jose Hirang and Virginia Villapando (Santos) J. BS, NYU, 1979; MS, MIT, 1981. Securities analyst Mass. Mut. Life Ins. Co., Springfield, 1982-83; investment officer One Fed. Asset Mgmt., Boston, 1984-87; sr. analyst, portfolio mgr. Emerging Markets Investors Corp., Washington, 1988-91; mng. dir., portfolio mgr. Montgomery Asset Mgmt., San Francisco, 1991—. Mem. Inst. Chartered Fin. Analysts. Office: Montgomery Asset Mgmt 600 Montgomery St San Francisco CA 94111-2702

JIMENEZ, TESSIE CASIANO, realtor; b. Manila, May 13, 1936; came to U.S., 1960, naturalized, 1970; d. Andrew Manglicmot and Irene (Paranada) Casiano; m. Rodolfo Jimenez, May 29, 1960; 1 child, Jonathan Casiano. AA, U. of East, Manila, 1956, student, 1956-60; grad. med. technologist, de Paul Hosp., Va., 1962; cert. profl. achievement, U. Calif., Irvine, 1993. Real estate salesman Better Homes Realty, Union City, Calif., 1975-80, Property Profls., Fremont, Calif., 1981-90, Trout Real Estate, Newark, Calif., 1991-92, Security West Realty, Fremont, 1993—. Mem. Nat. Assn. Realtors, Calif. Assn. Realtors, South Alameda Assn. Realtors (Multi-Million Dollar Club 1977-92, Master Achievement award 1989), No. Calif. Filipino Assn. Roman Catholic. Home: 2117 Arapaho Pl Fremont CA 94539-6562 Office: Security West Realty 39500 Stevenson Pl Ste 106 Fremont CA 94539-3102

JIMMINK, GLENDA LEE, elementary school educator; b. Lamar, Colo., Feb. 13, 1935; d. Harold Dale and Ruth Grace (Ellenberger) Fasnacht; m. Gary Jimmink, Oct. 24, 1964 (div. 1984); 1 child, Erik Gerard. BA, U. LaVerne, Calif., 1955. Tchr. elem. grades Pomona (Calif.) Unified Sch. Dist., 1955-61, Palo Alto (Calif.) Unified Sch. Dist., 1961-65, San Rafael (Calif.) Sch. Dist., 1966—; mem. curriculum coun. San Rafael Sch. Dist., 1983-90, 94—, mentor tchr., 1989-90, mem. social studies steering com., 1990—; charger mem. Marin County Curriculum Connection, 1991—. Artist, pub. (calendar) Dry Creek Valley, 1987; author: World Geography Resource Handbook for Tchrs., 1990, others. Mem. Marin Arts Coun., San Rafael, 1988—, Big Bros.-Big Siters, San Rafael, 1986-93, PTA, San Rafael, 1988—, Earthwatch, 1990—. Mem. NEA, Calif. Tchrs. Assn., San Rafael Tchrs. Assn., Nat. Wildlife Soc., Sierra Club, Gualala Arts Assn. Office: Davidson Mid Sch 225 Woodland Ave San Rafael CA 94901-5098

JIRKANS, MARIBETH JOIE, educator, school counselor; b. Cleve., May 3, 1945; d. Raymond Wenceslaus and Elsie Koryta J.; children: Annemarie Gurchik, Keith Robert Gurchik. Student, U. Vienna, Austria, 1965; BS in Edn., Coll. Mt. St. Joseph, 1967; MEd, Cleve. State U., 1984; postgrad., U. Akron, 1986-88, Kent State U., 1989—. Cert. elem., spl. edn. and adult edn. tchr., counselor. Tchr. North Olmstead (Ohio) City Schs., 1967-76; tchr. adult edn. Polaris Vocat. Sch., Middleburg Heights, Ohio, 1978; tchr. adult edn., ESL Lakewood (Ohio) City Schs., 1978-79; tchr. 2d grade Saint Rose Sch., Cleve., 1979-80; tchr. learning disabilities Cleve. Pub. Schs., 1980-85; tutor handicapped Cleve. Christian Home, 1982-84; elem. sch. counselor Cleve. Pub. Schs., 1985—; counselor West Side Community Mental Health Ctr., Cleve., 1983-84; sales mgr. Field Enterprises Inc., Cleve., 1977-82. Contbr. articles to newspapers. Vol. Fairview Gen. Hosp., Cleve., 1959-63, Cerebral Palsy Camp, 1959-63, Allen Halfway House for Children, Cin., 1963-67; co-founder Westshore Separated, Divorced and Remarried Caths., Cleve., 1975-85; chairwoman North Olmsted Jr. Women's Club; mem. parish coun. St. Brendan Ch., North Olmsted, 1975-87; mem. com. Cleve. Symphony, Cleve. Art Mus. Recipient Speaker's United Torch award United Way, Cleve., 1st Pl. prize in clothing design Stretch & Sew, 1975, 1st Pl. prize in needlepoint Framemakers Art, 1983. Mem. AACD, N.E. Ohio Counselor Assn., Coun. for Exceptional Children, Am. Sch. Counselor Assn., Internat. Assn. Marriage and Family Counselors, NOW, ASCD, Gestalt Inst., Audubon Soc., Eagle Valley Athletic Club, Greenpeace, Sierra Club, Cleve. Natural History Mus., North Coast Sailing Club, Holden Arboretum, Pi Lambda Theta. Democrat. Home: 727 Tollis Pky Cleveland OH 44147-1813

JIVIDEN, LORETTA ANN HARPER, secondary school educator; b. Charleston, W.Va., Jan. 30, 1939; d. Murry Deane and Marie Frances (Allison) Harper; m. Gay Melton Jividen, Jan. 30, 1959; children: Jon David, Ann Marie. BA in Sociology, N.C. State U., 1970, MEd in Curriculum and Instrn., 1979. Tchr. Our Lady of Lourdes, Raleigh, N.C., 1970-72; tchr. Wake County Pub. Sch. System, Raleigh, 1972-87, supr. Academically Gifted Program, 1987-90, tchr., 1990-92, math., computer specialist, 1992—; bd. dirs. Durant Rd. Elem. Sch. Found., Inc. Co-author: The EXCEL Program grant for Wake County Pub. Sch. System; past editor Special Edit., Parent Edit., Wake County Pub. Schs. Special Programs newsletters. Mem. NEA, Coun. for Exceptional Children, Assn. Classroom Tchrs., N.C. Edn. Assn., N.C. Assn. for the Gifted (pres. elect 1988-90, pres. 1991-93), N.C. Assn. Sch. Adminstrs., Parents for Advancement of Gifted Edn. (past v.p., past bd. dirs.), Nat. Assn. Gifted Children, Nat. Coun. Tchrs. Math., N.C. Assn. for the Gifted and Talented (Tchr. of Yr. award 1984), N.C. Edn. Assn., Delta Kappa Gamma Soc. Internat. (past pres., past coordinating coun. pres.). Home: 12501 Shallowford Dr Raleigh NC 27614-9664 Office: Durant Rd Elem Sch 9901 Durant Rd Raleigh NC 27614-9369

JOBE, MURIEL IDA, medical technologist; b. St. Louis, Apr. 17, 1931; d. Ernest William and Mable Mary (Hefflinger) Meissner; m. James Joseph Jobe, Sr., May 17, 1952 (dec. 1984); children: James J. Jr., Timothy D. (dec. 1976), Jonathan J., Daniel D. BS, Wash. U., St. Louis, 1971; med. technologist tng., Mo. Bapt. Hosp., St. Louis, 1973-74; postgrad., Webster U., St. Louis, 1981-83. Cytogenetic tech. St. Luke's Hosp., St. Louis, 1963-65; med. technologist Mo. Bapt. Hosp., St. Louis, 1974-76, 82-84, sr. instr., 1976-82, lead technologist, 1985; mgr., clin. instr. St. Louis U. Hosp., 1985—; mem. student selection com. Mo. Bapt. Hosp. Med. Technologists, St. Louis, 1975-78; observer Nat. Com. Clin. Lab. Standards, Villanova, Pa., 1989-90, advisor, 1991-92, 93—. Author: (with others) Clinical Hematology: Principles, Procedures, Correlations, 1991, (with others) 8th Revision PER Handbook, a Review Manual for Clinical Laboratory Exams., 1992. Counselor La Leche League; participant Ecology Day; community rels. chmn. The Life Seekers, St. Louis. Mem. Am. Soc. Clin. Pathologists (staff asst. 1984, 86, 88, 89, 94, dir. workshops 1990, 91, bd. dirs. 1990-92, state advisor 1992—, chmn. regional adv. com., adminstrv. bd. assoc. mem. sect., regional assoc. mem. award 1994), Am. Assn. Clin. Chemists, Am. Soc. Med. Tech. (dir. workshop 1984), Mo. Soc. Med. Tech. (pres. 1985-86), Clin. Lab. Mgrs. Assn. (chmn. devel. St. Louis chpt.). Mem. United Ch. of Christ. Office: St Louis U Hosp Hematology Lab 4 FDT 3635 Vista Ave Saint Louis MO 63110-2539

JOCHENS, SANDRA JEAN, emergency room nurse; b. Wayne, Nebr., Dec. 25, 1948; d. Harvey G. and Bonnie (Phillips) Aevermann; m. Lon R. Jochens, June 5, 1971; children: Lori, Pamela. Grad. in nursing, Lincoln (Nebr.) Gen. Hosp., 1971; BSN, U. Nebr., Omaha, 1990; MA in Mgmt., Bellevue Coll., Columbus, Nebr., 1995. RN, Nebr.; CEN; cert. ACLS, trauma nurse core course, oncology nurse. Charge nurse med.-surg. unit Columbus Community Hosp., 1971-73, house supr., 1973-82, charge nurse, asst. coord. emergency rm. outpatient report clin., 1982—; mem. adv. bd. Transitional Living Ctr. for Boys, Columbus, 1990—. Mem. Columbus Women's Club, 1978-80; mem. adv. bd. jr. high sch., Columbus, 1984-90; campaigner United Way, Columbus, 1989-90; bd. dirs. Am. Heart Assn., Columbus, 1987-89. Recipient svc. award Columbus Community Hosp., 1991. Mem. ANA, Emergency Nurses Assn., Sigma Theta Tau Inc. Internat. Republican. Lutheran. Home: 3160 31st Ave Columbus NE 68601 Office: Columbus Community Hosp 3111 19th St Columbus NE 68601

JOCHMANN, SISTER ROSE, treasurer of religious order; b. Appleton, Wis., Mar. 31, 1943; d. Edward Joseph and Rosella Mary (Hoelzel) J. BS, St. Norbert Coll., 1969; MSA, Notre Dame U., 1986. Tchr. various grade schs., Green Bay, Casco, De Pere, Wis., 1963-81; prin. Holy Cross Grade Sch., Green Bay, 1981-83; treas. Sisters of St. Francis of the Holy Cross, Green Bay, 1983—; coordinator Oneida (Wis.) Indian Summer Session, 1977-80; pres. Green Bay Diocese Sisters Council, 1979-81; mem. Just Labor Relations Task Force, 1983-87; coordinator Social Justice Coordinator, Sisters of St. Francis of the Holy Cross, 1985-88. Chairperson Fiscal Concerns Com., 1986-90. Mem. Nat. Assn. Treasurers of Religious Insts., Corp. Responsibility Coalition for State of Wis. Roman Catholic.

JOCKISCH, RHONDA DIANE, pharmacist; b. Manito, Ill., Apr. 3, 1969; d. Lawrence Roy and Diane Mae (Rauch) J. BS, St. Louis Coll. Pharmacy, 1992. Registered pharmacist. Organist St. Luke's Luth., San Jose, Ill., 1982-84, St. Johns Luth., Topeka, Ill., 1984-90, Christ Luth., Delevan, Ill., 1992—; pharmacy tech. Super X, Pekin, Ill., 1988, 89, Walgreens, Peoria, Ill., 1990, Pekin (Ill.) Hosp., 1991; pharmacist Kewanee (Ill.) Hosp., 1992-93, St. Mary Med. Ctr., Galesburg, Ill., 1993-94, Pekin Meml. Hosp., 1994—. Mem. Am. Pharm. Assn., Ill. Pharmacists Assn., Nat. Assn. Retail Execs. Democrat. Lutheran. Home: 1018 S 13th St Pekin IL 61554-4956 Office: Pekin Meml Hosp 600 S 13th St Pekin IL 61554-4969

JOFEN, JEAN, foreign language educator. BA, Bklyn. Coll., 1943; MA, Brown U., 1945; PhD, Columbia U., 1960; MS, Yeshiva U., 1961. Cert. sch. psychologist, N.Y. Teaching fellow Brown U., 1943-44; lectr. adult edn. Bklyn. Coll., 1951-61; assoc. prof. Yeshiva U., N.Y.C., 1955-62; assoc. prof., chmn. dept. Germanic and Slavic langs. Bernard M. Baruch Coll., N.Y.C., 1962-77, prof., 1977—, chmn. dept. modern langs., 1977-83, chmn. dept. Germanic, Hebraic and Oriental langs., 1983—, bd. govs., 1973—; mem. adv. bd. Jewish Studies CUNY, 1986; lectr., speaker various sci., civic and religious orgns. and socs. in U.S. and Europe; scholar abroad, Vienna, Austria, 1991. Author: A Linguistic Atlas of Eastern European Yiddish, 1964, rev. edit., 1967, Das letzte Geheimnis (in German), 1972, The Jewish Mystic in Kafka, 1987, (textbooks) Yiddish for Beginners, 1963, Yiddish Literature for Beginners, 1972, (with Y. Kerstein) Hebrew for Beginners, 1975, (with E. Mok) Chinese for Beginners, 1980; editor Elizabethan Concordance series: The Concordance of The Works of Christopher Marlowe, 1979, A Concordance to The Shakespeare Apocrypha, 3 Vols., 1987; Nat. Endowment for Humanities; assoc. editor Jour. Evolutionary Psychology; contbr. numerous articles to profl. jours. Recipient Nat. Jewish Culture Found. award, 1963, Kohut Found. award, 1966, Bernard M. Baruch Coll. medal for 35 yrs. svc., AAUW award, 1968, 69, others; fellow Inst. for Yiddish Lexicological Rsch. CUNY, 1963—; grantee Ford Found., 1970, Population Coun. Rockefeller Inst., 1970-71, Rsch. Found. CUNY, 1985, Lucius N. Littauer Found., 1986, Austrian Fed. Ministry for Sci. and Rsch., 1991. Fellow Jewish Acad. Arts and Scis.; mem. Am. Assn. Tchrs. German, MLA, AAUP, Am. Assn. Profs. Yiddish (pres.), Am. Psychol. Assn., Marlowe Soc. Am. (founder 1975, pres. 1975-84, organizer 1st. Internat. Congress in Eng. 1983), Mich. Acad. Arts and Scis., Acad. Scis. and Humanities CUNY, Sigma Alpha. Address: 1684 52nd St Brooklyn NY 11204-1418

JOFFRE, AUDREY GLASS, accountant; b. Jersey City, Feb. 14, 1934; d. Emanuel and Regina (Lynn) Glass; m. Peter Libman, 1954 (div.); m. Jack Joffre, Apr. 13, 1973. BA, Baylor Coll. Women, 1955; MEd, Memphis Stte U., 1964; cert. acctg., State Tech. Inst., Memphis, 1990. Speech therapist Memphis City Schs., 1959-66, tchr. English-speech, 1966-90, guidance counselor, 1976-90; acct. Joffre & Womack, P.C., Memphis, 1990—. Mem. bd., pres. Anshei Sphard Beth El Emety Synagogue Sisterhood, 1989-91, various chairs, v.p., 1978—, mem. bd., 1983—; bd. mem., treas., sec. Plough Towers Jewish Housing Devel. Corp., 1983—, v.p., pres. Democrat. Home: 5761 Barfield Cir Memphis TN 38120-2054 Office: Joffre & Womack PC 4821 American Way Ste 208 Memphis TN 38118-2453

JOHANN, SUSAN WALTHER, photographer; b. Bklyn., Dec. 21; d. Herbert and Betty (Mayer) Walther; m. Dallas Don Johann, June 15, 1944; children: Cameron, Trevor. BA, Immaculate Heart Coll., 1964. Actress, singer Broadway play Mame, N.Y.C., 1969, Papermill Playhouse, N.J., 1972; singer, concert artist, nationally and internationally, 1972-84; photographer various mags. including Smart, N.Y. Times, Mirabella, Chgo. Mag., Lears, Am. Theater, Opera News; photographer fine arts, exhbns. at the Platinum Gallery, Santa Fe, 1993, 94, Condeso, Lawler Gallery, N.Y., 1994; contbg. photographer: Shooting Stars, 1992. Exec. com. Parents Against Lead in Schs., N.Y., 1992-93; co-chair Child's Environment Alliance, N.Y., 1993-94. Office: 594 Broadway # 808 New York NY 10012

JOHANSEN, KAREN LEE, sales executive; b. Sheldon, Iowa, Dec. 5, 1945; d. Alvin Anthony and Marjory Gertrude (Kuiper) Eich; m. Pete Brunsting, May 15, 1964 (div. Dec. 1983); children: Jeffrey, Keri Christensen; m. Alan Brockberg, Oct. 30, 1988 (div. Apr. 1991); m. Alan Johansen, Aug. 21, 1993. Student, Sioux Valley Hosp. Sch. Nsg., 1963-65; grad., S.D. Police Acad., 1978; postgrad., Phoenix Paralegal Inst., 1981-82. Owner Redwood Steak House and Lounge, White, S.D., 1975-76; dep. sheriff Brookings (S.D.) County Sheriff's Office, 1978-79; clk. of ct. City of Gillette, Wyo., 1980-82; child support enforcement officer Campbell County, Gillette, 1982-84; jud. asst. Wyo. Dist. Ct., Sheridan, 1984-85; office mgr. Felt & Martin Law Firm, Billings, Mont., 1985-87; owner paralegal svcs. office, Pipestone, Minn., 1987-89; dist. agt. Prudential Ins. Co. Am., Pipestone, 1989-91; sales mgr. Prudential Ins. Co. Am., Austin, Minn., 1991-93; mgr. S.W. Minn. Prudential Ins. Co., Worthington, Minn., 1993-94; cons. Aanenson Agy., Inc., Fulda, Slayton, Minn., 1994—; estate planner, Austin and Pipestone, 1989—. Asst. Campaign to Re-Elect Andy Steensma, Pipestone, 1990; mem. Ihlen (Minn.) City Coun., 1990; chair Brookings Summer Art Festival, 1976-79, chair, 1977-79, chair entertainment, 1976. Mem. Nat. Assn. Life Underwriters, Elks. Democrat. Mem. Assembly of God. Office: Prudential Ins Co PO Box 367 339 Oxford Worthington MN 56187

JOHANSEN, MARJORIE HARKINS, librarian; b. Salem, Oreg., Sept. 9, 1938; d. Lewis Charles Harkins and Marjorie (Fossum) Boring; 1 child, Christopher. BA, Oreg. State U., 1960; MLS, San Jose State U., 1981. Reference libr. Burlingame (Calif.) Pub. Libr., 1982-86, San Francisco (Calif.) State U., 1987-90; bus. reference libr. San Mateo (Calif.) Pub. Libr., 1990—. Mem. ALA, Calif. Libr. Assn. Democrat. Episcopalian. Office: San Mateo Pub Libr 55 W 3rd Ave San Mateo CA 94402-1513

JOHANSSON, TERI-LYNNE HEAD, software engineer; b. Fayetteville, N.C., Dec. 30, 1960; d. John Leslie and Nancy Jean (Grothe) Head; m. Kjell Arne Johansson, Oct. 9, 1993. AS in CIS and AA in Math., Brevard C.C., 1987; AS in Mktg. Mgmt., Valencia Community Coll., 1988; BS in Mktg. and BS in Computer Sci., Fla. So. Coll., 1989; MS in MIS, U. Tex., Dallas, 1992, MBA, 1993. Data processing supr. Wilson, Wheeler & Schmidt, Orlando, Fla., 1987-89; systems engr. Electronic Data Systems, Plano, Tex., 1989-91; software engr. Ericsson Network Systems, Richardson, Tex., 1991—; math. tutor local high schs., 1985—. Mem. Assn. for Software Engring. Excellence, NAFE, Phi Theta Kappa. Republican. Office: Ericsson Network Systems MS L-05 730 International Pky Richardson TX 75081-2843

JOHMANN, NANCY, librarian; b. N.Y.C., Apr. 18, 1948; d. Robert Richard and Mary Stewart (Heath) J. BA, SUNY, Cortland, 1970; MLS, SUNY, Geneseo, 1971. Reference libr. Yonkers (N.Y.) Pub. Libr., 1971-76; cons., coord. Mass. Bd. Libr. Commrs., Boston, 1976-78; head info. and reference dept. Bridgeport (Conn.) Pub. Libr., 1979-84, asst. city libr., 1984-91, city libr., 1992—. Pres. bd. trustees Greater Bridgeport Symphony Orchestra, 1987-94. Treas. bd. trustees Greater Bridgeport Symphony Orchestra, 1987. Mem. ALA, Conn. Libr. Assn. Office: Bridgeport Pub Libr 925 Broad St Bridgeport CT 06604-4812

JOHN, YVONNE MAREE, artist, interior designer; b. Leeton, New South Wales, Australia, Sept. 8, 1944; came to U.S., 1966; d. Percy Edward and Gladys May (Markham) Thomas; m. Michael Peter John, Aug. 20, 1966; children: Michael Christian, Stephen Edwin Dennis. Student, Buenaventura Coll., 1969, U. Calif., Santa Barbara, 1975; cert., United Design Guild, 1975; AA, Interior Design Guild, 1976; Diploma, Internat. Correspondence Sch., 1976. Designer Percy Thomas Real Estate, Leeton, 1960-66; cosmetologist, artist Bernard's Hair Stylists, Ventura, Calif., 1966-67, 74-73; cosmetologist Banks Beauty Salon, Chgo., 1968-69; owner, mgr. Yvonne Maree Designs, Ventura and Olympia, Wash., 1978—; owner, cosmetologist Mayfair Salon, Leeton, 1962-66; owner, mgr. Y.M. Boutique, Griffith, Australia, 1965-66. Contbr. numerous short stories and poems to newspapers; artist numerous pen and ink drawings; exhibited one-person show Royal Mus. Sydney, Australia, 1954; exhibited group shows Ventura County Courthouse, 1970, Wash. Women in Art, Olympia, 1990, Timberland Libr., Olympia, 1990, Maska Internat. Gallery, Seattle, 1991, Nat. Hqrs. of Am. Soc. Interior Designers, Washington, 1992, Michael Stone Collection, Washington, 1992, Mus. Modern Art, Bordeau, France, 1993; 1st release of ltd. edit. prints, 1992; exhibited oil painting and drawing Hargis Unique Gallery, Pomona, Calif., 1994. Artist Ventura County Gen. Hosp., 1970's. Recipient Cash and Cert. awards Sydney Newspapers, 1950's, Ribbon awards Sydney County Fairs, 1950's. Mem. Am. Platform Assn. Office: Yvonne Maree Designs PO Box 2143 Olympia WA 98507-2143

JOHNNIE, CANDACE CARLSON, engineer; b. Hancock, Mich., Oct. 29, 1951; d. Thomas Roy Carlson and Dolores Anita (Kittell) J.; m. Daniel Harry Johnnie Jr., July 3, 1976. BSChE, U. Utah, 1975, BS in Econs., 1978. Process chem. engr. Process Design-Fluor Corp., Irvine, Calif., 1975-82; internat. mktg. Fluor Corp., Irvine, Calif., 1981-83; project engr. Rockwell, Anaheim, Calif., 1983-84, 84-88, project mgr., 1988-93, engring. mgr., 1993—, tech. svcs. mgr., 1993—; cons. in field. Contbr. articles to profl. jours. Vol. O.C. Corp. Investment Ctr., Anaheim, 1989; Young Women's Comm Act-YWCA, Anaheim, 1989; with Youth Motivation Task Force, Anaheim, 1991; advisor engring. Explorer Post. Recipient Women of Achievement awards Santiago Coll., 1989, 90, 92. Fellow Inst. Advancement Engring.; mem. AIChE, Nat. Mgmt. Assn., Soc. Women Engrs. (past pres.). Home: 242 La Cuesta San Clemente CA 92672

JOHNS, BEVERLEY ANNE HOLDEN, special education administrator; b. New Albany, Ind., Nov. 6, 1946; d. James Edward and Martha Edna (Scharf) Holden; m. Lonnie J. Johns, July 28, 1973. BS, Catherine Spalding Coll., Ky., 1968; MS, So. Ill. U., 1970; postgrad., Western Ill. U., 1973-74, 79-80, 82, U. Ill., 1984-85. Cert. adminstr., tchr. Ill. Demonstration tchr. So. Ill. U., Carbondale, 1970-72; instr. MacMurray Coll., Jacksonville, Ill., 1977-79, 90-93; intern Ill. State Bd. Edn., Springfield, 1981; program supr. Four Rivers Spl. Edn. Dist., Jacksonville, Ill., 1972—; chmn. Ill. Edn. of the Handicapped Coalition, 1982—; conf. coord. Ill. Alliance, Champaign, 1982—; bd. dirs. Jacksonville Area Assn. Retarded Citizens, v.p., 1993-94; lectr. to profl. confs.; cons. in field. Author: Report on Behavior Analysis in Edn., 1972, (with U. Carr) Techniques for Managing Verbally and Physically Aggressive Students, 1995; editor: Position Papers of Ill. Council for Exceptional Children, 1981; contbr. articles to profl. jours. Govt. rels. chmn. Internat. Council Exceptional Children, 1984-87; fed. liason Ill. Adminstrs. Spl. Edn., 1985-86. So. Ill. U. fellow, 1968; resolution honoring Beverly H. Johns 60th Ann. Internat. Coun. for Exceptional Children Conv., 1982; cert. of recognition Ill. Atty. Gen., 1985. Recipient Lifetime Achievement award Ill. Coun. for Exceptional Children, 1989; named Jacksonville Woman of the Yr. Bus. and Profl. Women, 1988, First Lady Ill. Coun. Exceptional Children, 1993, Unsung Hero Jacksonville Jour.-Carrier, 1993. Mem. ASCD, Assn. Retarded Citizens (com. 1982—), Ill. Coun. for Children With Behavioral Disorders (founder, past pres., presdl. award 1985), pres. Ill. div. for learning disabilities 1991-92, Ill. Alliance for Exceptional Children (v.p 1982—), Ill. Coun. Exceptional Children (past pres., chmn. govt. rels. com. 1982—, governing bd. 1984—, Presdl. award 1983), West Cen. Assn. for Citizens with Learning Disabilities (founder, com. chair 197—), Delta Kappa Gamma (chpt. pres. 1988-90, state exec. bd. 1991—), Phi Delta Kappa. Roman Catholic. Avocation: world travel. Home: PO Box 340 Jacksonville IL 62651-0340 Office: Four Rivers Spl Edn Dist 936 W Michigan Ave Jacksonville IL 62650-3113

JOHNS, CAROL JOHNSON, physician, educator; b. Balt., June 18, 1923; d. Ashmore Clark and Elsie Greacen (Carstens) Johnson; BA, Wellesley Coll., 1944; MD, Johns Hopkins U., 1950; DHL (hon.), Coll. Notre Dame of Md., 1981; m. Richard James Johns, June 27, 1953; children: James Ashmore, Richard Clark, Robert Shanard. Intern, Johns Hopkins Hosp., 1950-51, asst. resident in medicine, 1951-53, fellow, 1953-54, physician outpatient dept., 1953-64, dir. Sarcoid Clinic, 1962-93, active staff, 1964—, dir. med. clinic, 1967-76, dir. hosp. quality assurance, 1974-79, mem. hosp. med. bd., 1971-79; asst. in medicine Johns Hopkins U., 1951-58, instr., 1958-67, asst. prof., 1967-71, assoc. prof., 1971—, adv. bd. Applied Physics Lab., 1974-78; acting pres. Wellesley Coll., 1979-81, asst. dean, dir. continuing edn., 1981-93; chmn. bd. Balt. City PSRO, 1975-79; pres. Internat. Sarcoid Conf., 1984; mem. pulmonary allergy adv. com. FDA, 1973-75; faculty adv. editorial bd. Johns Hopkins U. Press, 1981-84. Contbr. articles to med. jours., chpts. in textbooks. Mem. vestry Ch. of Redeemer, 1967-70, sr. warden, 1976-79, layreader; bd. trustees Calvert Sch., 1968-72; trustee Wellesley Coll., 1971-90, exec. com., 1971-80, 84-90, chmn. nat. devel. fund, 1975-80, trustee fin. com., 1979-90, chmn. trustee faculty relations com., 1984-90, trustee emeritus, 1990—; trustee St. Paul's Sch. for Girls, 1973-75; bd. dirs. Stetler Rsch. Fund for Women, 1971-79, 84-93; mem. Armed Forces Epidemiol. Bd., 1985-90; bd. regents Uniformed Svcs. Univ. Health Scis., 1985, vice-chair, 1988—. Named Med. Woman of Yr. Med. Coll. Pa.,

1984. Mem. Am. Clin. Climatol. Assn. (v.p. 1987, coun. 1994—), Am. Thoracic Soc., Balt. City Med. Soc., Johns Hopkins Med. Surg. Assn. (sec.-treas. 1981-87, pres. 1987-89), Johns Hopkins Women's Med. Alumni Assn. (pres. 1957-59, dir.), Md. Med. Chirurg. Faculty (coun. 1978-79), Soc. Med. Coll. Dirs. Continuing Edn., Alliance for Continuing Med. Edn. (coun. 1987-93), Phi Beta Kappa, Sigma Xi, Alpha Omega Alpha (bd. dirs. 1978-87, v.p. 1985-86, pres. 1986-87), Johns Hopkins Club, Wellesley Coll. Club, Mt. Vernon Club, Cosmos Club. Episcopalian. Home: 203 E Highfield Rd Baltimore MD 21218-1105 Office: Johns Hopkins Sch Medicine 858 Ross Bldg 720 Rutland Ave Baltimore MD 21205

JOHNS, CATHERINE, radio personality; b. Ft. Wayne, Ind., Nov. 3, 1952; d. Richard and Barbara Johns; married, Aug. 24, 1991. Student, Western Ill. U., Valparaiso U. Reporter WHBF-TV, Rock Island, Ill.; reporter, editor WRBC, Jackson, Miss.; morning drive anchor WQSA, Sarasota, Fla.; anchor, editor, reporter KEYH, Houston; midday co-anchor WERE, Cleve.; reporter WLS-AM, Chgo., 1979—, talk show host, 1990—. 'Fangette', NFG, 1969—. Office: WLS-AM 190 N State St Chicago IL 60601-3302

JOHNS, DELORAS KIM, escrow officer; b. Hement, Calif., Feb. 10, 1957; d. Charles Richard Curtis and Sylvia Patricia (McCoy) Curtis-Young; m. Joseph Franklin Johns, June 7, 1982 (div. Dec. 1987); 1 child, Brian Patick Curtis. Courier Empire Title Co., Nevada City, Calif., 1980, rec. clk., 1980-82, customer svc. officer, 1983-84, title officer, 1984-86, escrow sec., 1986-89; escrow officer Empire Title Co., Grass Valley, Calif., 1989-91, 91-93, adminstrv. asst., 1991; escrow officer Fidelity Title Ins., Grass Valley, Calif., 1993-94, Penn Valley, Calif., 1994—. Youth liaison Youth Self Help, Nevada City, 1976; mem. Welcome Wagon Club, Nevada County, Calif., 1975-76; notary pub., Calif., 1994—. Republican. Office: Fidelity Title Ins 11248 Pleasant Valley Rd Penn Valley CA 95946-9413

JOHNS, LEE RHEA, nurse; b. Birmingham, Ala., Aug. 7, 1956; d. Llewellyn William Jr. and Jane Elizabeth (Green) Johns. BS in Sociology, Jacksonville (Ala.) State U., 1978; BS in Nursing, U. Ala., Birmingham, 1983; grad., Sch. Aerospace Medicine, Brooks AFB, Tex., 1989. RN, Ala., S.C.; oncology cert. nurse. Staff oncology nurse U. Ala. Med. Ctr., 1983-84; staff hospice nurse AMI Brookwood Med. Ctr., Birmingham, 1984-86; patient care coord. oncology unit Bapt. Med. Ctr. Montclair, Birmingham, 1986-87, staff nurse one day surgery dept., 1987-88; hospice nurse clinician Greenville (S.C.) Hosp. System, 1988-92, oncology nurse clinician, 1992—; flight nurse aeromed. evacuation USAFR, Charleston AFB, S.C., 1989—; instr. flight nurse USAFR, 1994—. With USNG, 1986-88; capt. USAFR, 1988—, Persian Gulf War, 1990-91. Decorated S.W. Asia medal with 2 devices, Nat. Def. medal, Acheivement medal. Mem. Oncology Nursing Soc. (v.p. Birmingham chpt. 1986-88), Nat. Hospice Orgn., Aerospace Med. Assn., Res. Officers Assn., Jacksonville State U. Alumni Assn. (pres. Jefferson/Shelby County chpt. 1988), Palmetto Ski and Outing Club, Greenville Singles Club (v.p. 1989-90). Republican. Roman Catholic. Office: Greenville Hosp System 701 Grove Rd Greenville SC 29605-4295

JOHNS, MARY E., law librarian; b. Davenport, Iowa, Apr. 27, 1953; d. Donald S. and Elizabeth C. Blackman; m. Christopher K. Johns, Aug. 25, 1973; 1 child, Eric Robert. AB, U. Calif., Berkeley, 1977; MLS, La. State U., 1982. Cataloger La. State U. Law Libr., Baton Rouge, 1982-84, head cataloging, 1984-87, 89—, acting head tech. svcs., 1987-89. Mem. Am. Assn. Law Librs. Home: 864 Albert Hart Dr Baton Rouge LA 70808-5807 Office: La State U Law Libr Baton Rouge LA 70803

JOHNS, ROBIN FOELL, medical-surgical nurse; b. Abington, Pa., Oct. 21, 1961; d. Nelson Albert and Janet Alice (Lindsay) F. ADN, Wake Tech. Coll., 1984; BSN, Barton Coll., 1990; MSN, U. N.C., Chapel Hill. RN, N.C.; cert. CPR instr., ACLS instr., med.-surg. nursing. Staff nurse Wake Med. Ctr., Raleigh, N.C., 1984-86, preceptor, 1986-90; asst. prof. Barton Coll., Wilson, N.C., 1990—; cons. in field, Raleigh, 1987—. Vol. ARC, Raleigh, 1987—. Mem. AACCN, Sigma Theta Tau (scholar 1990), Alpha Chi. Home: 8412 Evans Mill Pl Raleigh NC 27613 Office: Barton Coll Wilson NC 27893

JOHNS, SUSAN D., state senator; b. Oct. 7, 1954. BA, Georgetown Coll., MA. Mem. Ky. State Senate from 36th Dist., 1991—; chmn. senate econ. devel., tourism, and energy com. Ky. State Senate, chmn. legis. program rev., investigations com., former vice chmn. senate health and welfare com.; v.p. Republic Bank & Trust Co. Former tchr., ofcl. Ky. Dept. Edn., corp. mgr. Presbyn. Ch. USA. Recipient Outstanding Legislator award Ky. Assn. for the Edn. of Young Children, Ky. Victims Coalition, Voice of Children award Community Coordinated Child Care; named One of 10 Best Legislators in Ky., Lexington Herald-Leader. Mem. NEA, Ky. Edn. Assn., Louisville Women's Polit. Caucus, St. Matthews Bus. & Profl. Women's Assn. Democrat. Baptist. Home: 3120 Runnymede Rd Louisville KY 40222 Office: Ky State Senate State Capitol Frankfort KY 40601*

JOHNSON, ADDIE COLLINS, secondary education educator, former dietitian; b. Evansville, Ind., Feb. 28; d. Stewart and Willa (Shamell) Collins; m. John Q. Johnson, Sept. 6, 1958 (dec. Aug. 1991); 1 child, Parker. BS, Howard U., 1956; MEd, Framingham State Coll., Mass., 1967. Registered dietitian, Mass. Dietitian Boston Lying-In Hosp., 1957-61; dietitian Diet Heart Study, Harvard U. Sch. Pub. Health, Boston, 1962-63; tchr. Foxboro (Mass.) Pub. Sch., 1967—; dietitian Sch. Medicine Boston U., 1975-77, Westinghouse Health Systems, Boston; faculty Dept. Nursing Boston State Coll., 1979-82; nutrition cons. Head Start program Westinghouse Sch., Boston, 1979-82; instr. dept. nursing U. Mass., 1981—, Bridgewater (Mass.) State Coll., 1982—; mem. state adv. coun. Dept. Edn Bur. Nutrition Edn., 1981-83; participant NSF Project Seed, 1992. Bd. dirs. Norfolk-Bristol County Home Health Assn., Walpole, Mass., 1975-78; presenter Nat. Social Studies Assn., Boston, 1984-85; instr./trainer health svcs. edn. ARC, 1987-90. Mem. AAUW, NAACP (life), Am. Dietetic Assn., Am. Home Econs. Assn., Ea. Mass. Home Econs. Assn. (bd. dirs. 1978), Mass. Tchrs. Assn. (higher edn. com. 1984-87), Soc. Nutrition Edn., Delta Kappa Gamma (journalist Iota chpt. 1986-88, membership com. 1988-92, v.p. 1994), Delta Sigma Theta. Home: 92 Morse St Sharon MA 02067-2719 Office: Foxboro Pub Schs Mechanic St Foxboro MA 02035-2028

JOHNSON, ALICE ELAINE, retired academic administrator; b. Janesville, Wis., Oct. 9, 1929; d. Floyd C. and Alma M. (Walthers) Chester; m. Richard C. Johnson, Sept. 25, 1948 (div. 1974); children: Randall S., Nile C., Linnea E. BA, U. Colo., 1968. Pres., administrator Pikes Peak Inst. Med. Tech., Colorado Springs, Colo., 1968-88; mem. adv. com. to Colo. Commn. on Higher Edn., 1979-80, State Adv. Coun. on Pvt. Occupational Schs., Denver, 1978-86; mem. tech. adv. com. State Health Occupations, 1986-88; bd. dirs. All Souls Unitarian Ch., Colorado Springs, 1990—, mem. celebration team, 1990-91, pres. bd. trustees, 1991-93. Mem. Colo. Pvt. Sch. Assn. (pres. 1981-82, bd. dirs. 1976-88, Outstanding Mem. 1978, 80), Phi Beta Kappa. Democrat. Unitarian.

JOHNSON, ANGELA, children's book author; b. Tuskegee, Ala., June 18, 1961; d. Arthur and Truzetta (Hall) J. Author: Tell Me a Story, Mama, 1989 (Sch. Libr. Jour. Best Books list 1989), Do Like Kyla, 1990, When I Am Old with You, 1990 (Ezra Jack Keats award U.S. Bd. on Books for Young People 1990, Coretta Scott King Book award 1990), One of Three, 1991, The Leaving Morning, 1992, The Girl Who Wore Snakes, 1993, Julius, 1993, Toning the Sweep, 1993 (Young Adult Libr. Svcs. Assn. Best Book for young adults list 1994), Shoes Like Miss Alice's, 1994, Joshua By the Sea, 1994, Joshua's Night Whispers, 1994, Mama Bird, Baby Bird, 1994, Rain Feet, 1994. Child development worker, vol. Svc. to Am., Ravenna, Ohio, 1981-82. Office: care Orchard Books 95 Madison Ave Fl 11 New York NY 10016-7801*

JOHNSON, ANNE ELIZABETH, executive assistant; b. Springfield, Mass., Nov. 3, 1955; d. Michael Francis Xavier and Miriam Rose (Coombs) Gigliotti. NSCC, Beverly, Mass., 1976. Cert. med. transcriptionist. Home health aide Sr. Home Care Svcs., Gloucester, Mass., 1974-76; lab asst., EKG technician, phlebotomist Addison Gilbert Hosp., Gloucester, Mass., 1976-80; exec. asst. MGA Inc., Gloucester, Mass., 1980-83, 85—; med. asst. Cape Ann Med. Ctr., Gloucester, 1983-84; dance instr., 1973-80. Sec. Am. Cancer Soc., Gloucester, 1978-79; polit. asst. Dem. Party, Gloucester, 1974-85; active People for the Ethical Treatment of Animals. Mem. NAFE, Mass. Soc. for Prevention of Cruelty to Animals, Doris Day Animal League, Surfrider Found. Roman Catholic. Home: 27 Exchange St Gloucester MA 01930-3449 Office: MGA Inc 42 Rogers St Gloucester MA 01930-5009

JOHNSON, AUDREY ANN, options trader, stockbroker; b. Chgo., June 7, 1954; d. Elmer and Diane Ann (Vassiv) J. Student, North Ctrl. Coll., 1972-75, U. Ill. Registered stockbroker, real estate salesperson, Ill. Real estate salesperson Century 21 Cahill Bros., Chgo., 1975-80; stockbroker Charles Schwab, Chgo., 1980-87; Chgo. Bd. Options Exch. floor trader Drexel Burnham, Chgo., 1987-90; pvt. practice Chgo., 1990—; options broker, stockbroker Profl. Trader's Inst. Securities, Chgo., 1990—; arbitrator Chgo. Bd. Options Exch., 1989-92; guest spkr. Chgo. TV Channel 26, 1993-94; participant in NAFTA. Mem. Nat. Assn. Securities Dealers, Ind. Floor Members Assn., Chgo. Bd. Options Exch., Palos Hills Horseman's Assn. Democrat. Roman Catholic. Home: 9174 South Rd Palos Hills IL 60465

JOHNSON, BADRI NAHVI, sociology educator, real estate business owner; b. Tehran, Iran, Dec. 1, 1934; came to U.S., 1957; d. Ali Akbar and Monir (Khazraii) Nahvi; m. Floyd Milton Johnson, July 2, 1960; children: Robert, Rebecca, Nancy, Shahla. BS, U. Minn., 1967, MA, 1969; postgrad. Stenographer Curtis 1000, Inc., St. Paul, 1958-62; lab. instr. U. Minn., Mpls., 1966-69, teaching asst., 1969-72; chief exec. officer Real Estate Investment and Mgmt. Enterprise, St. Paul, 1969—; instr. sociology Anoka-Ramsey Community Coll., Coon Rapids, Minn., 1973—; pub. speaker, bd. dirs., sponsor pub. radio KFAI, Mpls., 1989-93; established an endowed scholarship for women Anoka Ramsey C.C., 1991. Radio talk show host KCW, Brookline Parks, Minn., 1993. Organizer Iranian earthquake disaster relief, 1990. Recipient Earthquake Relief Orgn. citation Iranian Royal Household, 1968. Mem. NEA, Minn. Edn. Assn., Sociologists of Minn., U. Minn. Alumni Assn., Minn. Club. Home: 1726 Iowa Ave E Saint Paul MN 55106-1334 Office: Anoka-Ramsey Community Coll 11200 Mississippi Blvd NW Minneapolis MN 55433-3499

JOHNSON, BARBARA ANNE UMBERGER, business owner, editor, publisher; b. Staunton, Va., Feb. 16, 1939; d. Gordon William and Billie Lois (Patton) Umberger; m. Gilbert Dixon Johnson, Jan. 23, 1960; children: Gilbert Scott, William Bryant. AAS, Indian Valley Colls., 1976; BA in Anthropology, George Washington U., 1978; MS in Counseling and Guidance, Nova U., 1981. Tech. editor Electronic Data Systems Corp., Alexandria, Va., 1978—, pub. affairs mgr.; product implementation mgr., account mgr. Policy Mgmt. Systems Corp., Columbia, S.C., 1984; entrepreneur Editorial Resources, Unltd., Columbia, 1988; columnist Mil. Families, 1979-80. Editor, pub. South Carolina Association of Naturalists: The First Ten Years, 1993; author news column Military Families, 1979-80; contbr. book revs. to profl. jours.; founder, pub. monthly newsletters Mechanics Lien Bull., Pub. Record Report, Capital Corner; pub. S.C. Naturalists Notes. Campaigner Rep. Party, Columbia; mem. environ. adv. bd. Cen. Midlands Regional Planning Coun.; mem. Solid Waste Mgmt. Task Force; mem. Leadership Columbia, 1993-94; mem. Main Street Devel. Assocs., 1993—. Cpl. USMC, 1957-60. Mem. NAFE, LWV, Soc. for Tech. Comms., Nat. Contract Mgrs. Assn., Media Women S.C., S.C. C. of C., Columbia C. of C. (chair enterprisers network, riverfront planning com., small bus. devel. bd.), Ret. Officers Wives Club (v.p. 1987—), Sertoma (v.p. Richland club 1992, pres. Richland club 1993, chmn. bd. dirs. 1994). Methodist.

JOHNSON, BETH EXUM, lawyer; b. Beaumont, Tex., July 4, 1952; d. James Powers Jr. and Betty Jean (Clement) Exum; m. Walter William Johnson, Apr. 25, 1981; 1 child, Stratton William. BA in Psychology, Tulane U., 1974; JD, Loyola U., New Orleans, 1985; LLM in Energy and Environ., Tulane U., 1989. Bar: La. 1985, Tex. 1993, U.S. Dist. Ct. (ea. dist.) La. 1985, U.S. Dist. Ct. (we. and mid. dists.) 1989. Paralegal McCloskey, Dennery, Page & Hennesy, New Orleans, 1975-80; oil and gas abstractor of title Frawley, Wogan, Miller & Co., New Orleans, 1980-82; assoc. trust counsel, asst. v.p. and trust officer Hibernia Nat. Bank, New Orleans, 1985—; mem. faculty La. succession practice Tulane U., New Orleans, 1990—, environ. law practice, 1991—; mem. fundraising com. New Orleans Pro Bono Project. Mem. New Orleans Estate Planning Coun.; mem. fundraising com. New Orleans Pro Bono Project. Mem. ABA, La. Bar Assn., New Orleans Bar Assn., Assn. Employee Benefit Planners New Orleans, Friends City Park, Premier Athletic club, Rivercenter Tennis Club, Cavalier King Charles Spaniel Club, Phi Alpha Delta, Kappa Alpha Theta. Home: 959 Harrison Ave New Orleans LA 70124-3837 Office: Hibernia Nat Bank 313 Carondelet St Rm 321 New Orleans LA 70130-3178

JOHNSON, BETSEY LEE, fashion designer; b. Hartford, Conn., Aug. 10, 1942; d. John Herman and Lena Virginia J.; m. John Cale, Apr. 4, 1966; 1 child, Lulu; m. Jeffrey Olivier, Feb. 7, 1981. Student, Pratt Inst., N.Y.C., 1960-61; B.A., U. Syracuse, 1964. Editorial asst. Mademoiselle mag., 1964-65; ptnr., co-owner Betsey, Bunky & Nini, N.Y.C., from 1969; owner retail stores N.Y.C, L.A., San Francisco, Coconut Grove, Fla., Venice, Calif., Boston, Chgo., Seattle. Prin. designer: Paraphernalia (owned by Puritan Fashions, Inc.), 1965-69; designer, Alvin Duskin Co., San Francisco, 1970; head designer: Alley Cat by Betsey Johnson, div. LeDamor, Inc., 1970-74; freelance designer for, Jr. Womens div. Butterick Pattern Co., 1971, Betsey Johnson's Kids Children Wear for new div, Shutterbug, Inc., 1974-77, Betsey Johnson for, Jeanette Maternities, Inc., 1974-75; designer first line womens clothing for, Gant Shirtmakers, Inc., 1974-75; Tric-Trac by Betsey Johnson, Womens Knitwear, 1974-76; children's wear for Butterick's Home Sewing catalog, from 1975; head designer jr. sportswear co.: childrens wear for Star Ferry by Betsey Johnson and Michael Milea, 1975-77; owner, head designer, B.J., Inc., designer wholesale co., N.Y.C., 1978, pres., treas., B.J. Vines, N.Y.C., owner, Betsey Johnson store, N.Y.C., from 1979 (Recipient Mademoiselle mag. Merit award 1970, Coty award 1971, 2 Tommy Print awards 1971); owner 3 retail stores in N.Y.C., 3 in L.A., 1 San Francisco, 1 in Miami, 1 in Chgo., 1 in Seattle. Mem. Coun. Fashion Designers Am., Women's Forum. Office: Betsey Johnson Co 209 W 38th St New York NY 10018-4405 also: 110 E 9th St Ste A889 Los Angeles CA 90079*

JOHNSON, BETTY ANNE, nurse; b. Centerville, Iowa, Sept. 14, 1924; d. Delazon Marion and Lucy Glen (Guernsey) Wilson; m. Vern William Johnson (dec. Oct. 1966); children: Richard Hugh, Russell William, John Allen. Grad., St. Joseph Sch. Nursing, Ottumwa, Iowa, 1946; BS in Health Arts, Coll. of St. Francis, Joliet, Ill., 1982. RN, Iowa. Tchr. Albany Sch., Bloomfield, Iowa, 1942-43; nurse Ottumwa Hosp., 1946-49, 78-83, Balboa Hosp., San Diego, 1949-50, Davis County Hosp., Bloomfield, Iowa, 1951-52, 74-78; nurse, pediatrics dept. St. Joseph Hosp., Ottumwa, 1967-73; nurse Glenwood (Iowa) State Hosp. for Retarded, 1973-74; substitute house parent Rainbow Acres, Ranch for Handicapped Adults, Camp Verde, Ariz., 1984-87; supr. Foothills Care Ctr., Cottonwoord, Ariz, 1985-87; with Kachine Point Health Ctr., Sedona, Ariz, 1987-89; nurse Easter Seals East Camp, Va., 1990, Good Samaritan Care Ctr., Ottumwa, Iowa, 1991; day substitute Child Care Ctr., Dallas; RN Vista Woods, Dallas. Home: 425 S Willard St Ottumwa IA 52501-5032

JOHNSON, BETTY LOU, secondary education educator; b. Stockwell, Ind., Apr. 4, 1927; d. Paul Stanley Jones and Ethel Leona (Royer) J.; m. Kenneth Odell Johnson, Aug. 5, 1950; children: Cynthia Jo (Mrs. James P. Greaton), Gregory Alan. BS in Home Econs., Purdue U., 1948; postgrad., Northwood Inst. Culinary Arts, 1981, 83. Cert. home economist. Tchr. LaCrosse (Ind.) Jr.-Sr. High Sch., 1948-49, Wendell L. Willkie High Sch., Elwood, Ind., 1949-51, Thomas Carr Howe High Sch., Indpls., 1951-57; substitute tchr. Gt. Oaks Joint Vocat. Sch. Dist., Cin. Mem. AAUW, Am. Home Econs. Assn. (life), Ohio Home Econs. Assn. (life), John Purdue Club (dir.), Purdue U. Alumni Assn. (life), Gamma Sigma Delta. Home: Indian Hill Village 8360 Arapaho Ln Cincinnati OH 45243-2718

JOHNSON, BETTY MARIE, administrator; b. Rockford, Ill., Mar. 5, 1931; d. Martin Carl and Hildur Marie (Tinberg) J. Diploma, Swedish Am. Hosp., 1951; BSN, U. Minn., 1955; MSN, U. Colo., 1962; PhD, U. Wis., 1970. Staff nurse Swedish - Am. Hosp., Rockford, Ill., 1951-52, Swedish Hosp., Mpls., 1952-55; ednl. dir. Swedish - Am. Hosp., 1955-61; asst. prof. Case Western Reserve U., Cleve., 1962-66; acad. advisor U. Wis., Madison, 1969-70, asst. prof., 1970-74; dean, prof. U. S.C., Columbia, 1975-80; dir. continuing edn. project for deans Am. Assn. Colls. of Nursing, Washington, 1981-83; vis. prof. Med. Coll. Ga., Augusta, 1983-84, U. Utah, Salt Lake City, 1984; dir. essentials project Am. Assn. Colls. of Nursing, Washington, 1985-87; vis. prof. U. Va., Charlottesville, 1980-81, prof., acting assoc. dean, 1987-91; prof., dept. chmn. U. Va. Clinch Valley Coll., Wise, 1991—; mem. site visitor nat. arthritis bd. NIH, Bethesda, Md., 1977-82; peer reviewer Jour. Profl. Nursing, Washington, 1985—, Nursing and Health Care, N.Y., 1993—; cons. in field. Contbr. articles to profl. jours. Bd. dirs. Hope House for Abused Women, Norton, Va., 1992—. Recipient cert. of merit U. S.C., 1980. Mem. AAUW, Am. Assn. Univ. Adminstr., Am. Assn. Higher Edn., Nat. League Nursing (accreditation site visitor 1977-80), Va. Assn. Colls. of Nursing, Sigma Theta Tau, Pi Lambda Theta. Home: 715 Tiffany Dr Gaithersburg MD 20878 Office: Clinch Valley Coll U Va College Ave Wise VA 24293

JOHNSON, BEVERLY, model, actress; b. Buffalo, Oct. 13, 1952; m. Billy Potter, 1971 (div.), Danny Sims, 1977 (div.); 1 child, Anansa. Attended, Northeastern U., Bklyn. Coll. Model Ford Modeling Agy., 1972-77, Elite Modeling Agy., 1977; now with Wilhemina Agy.; model Virginia Slims, 1985, Revlon Cosmetics. Actress (documentary) Land of Negritude, 1975, Ashanti, 1978, The Meteor Man, 1993, National Lampoon's Loaded Weapon 1, 1993; singer (albums) Beverly Johnson, 1978, Don't Lose the Feeling, 1980; author: Beverly Johnson's Guide to a Life of Beauty, 1981, True Beauty, 1994; guest host (TV) Video Soul. Recipient Ikoyi award, 1975, Capri award for most outstanding model, 1975, Image award for achievement in fashion NAACP, 1990; named one of 10 Best-Coiffured Women by Helene Curtis, 1975. 1st African-Am. model to appear on the cover of Vogue, 1974, Elle, 1975; appeared on the cover of Glamour mag. 6 times, 1971-73; represented in Matchbox Toys' Real Model doll collection, 1990. Office: Beverly Glen Enterprise 250 W 40th St 4th Fl New York NY 10018*

JOHNSON, BEVERLY PHILLIPS, bank officer; b. Richmond, Va., May 14, 1963; d. Harold Thomas and Betty Lucille (Trammell) Phillips; m. Robert Mark Johnson, Nov. 29, 1985; children: Margaret Elizabeth, Laura Ellen. BS, Lee Coll., Cleveland, Tenn., 1985. Comptroller Frank White Co., Cleveland, Tenn., 1983-86; credit analyst 1st Am. Nat. Bank, Chattanooga, 1986-88; mortgage banker 1st Am. Nat. Bank, Cleveland, Tenn., 1988-89; comml. real estate banker 1st Am. Nat. Bank, Chattanooga, 1989-92; comml. lender Am. Nat. Bank & Trust Co., Cleveland, Tenn., 1992—. Div. campaign chairperson United Way, Bradley County, Cleveland, 1987-90, 93; treas. Cleveland Cmty. Concert Assn., 1989—; mem. leadership Cleveland, 1991-93; blockwalkers capt. Am. Heart Assn., 1993; bd. dirs. Cleve. Family YMCA, 1993—, First United Meth. Child Devel. Ctr., 1992—. Mem. Cleveland/Bradley Home Builders Assn. (assoc.), Cleveland Bd. Realtors (assoc.), Cleveland Country Club (assoc.), Jaycees, Civitan (bd. dirs. Cleveland chpt. 1984-91, 93—, Chattanooga chpt. 1991-92), United Way Pillars Club, Lee Coll. Pres. Circle, Cleveland/Bradley C. of C. (econ. devel. coun. 1992—). Republican. United Methodist. Home: 1220 Bramblewood Trl NW Cleveland TN 37311-4107 Office: Am Nat Bank & Trust Co PO Box 1149 Cleveland TN 37364-1149

JOHNSON, BRENDA LEE, elementary school principal, reading educator; b. Jamestown, N.Y., Oct. 5, 1950; d. Herbert Edwin and Betty Lou (Steck) J. Student, U. Buffalo, 1971; BA in Edn., SUNY, Fredonia, 1971, MEd in Reading, 1975, CAS, 1991. Cert. elem. and reading tchr., sch. dist. adminstr., sch. adminstr. and supr. Tchr. remedial reading Jamestown Pub. Schs., 1980-81; tchr. Panama (N.Y.) Cen. Sch., 1972-80, reading educator, 1981-91; elem. prin. Pine Valley Cen. Sch., 1991-95, R.R. Rogers Sch., Jamestown City Schs., 1995—; reading educator and developer Program for at Risk Students, Jamestown Boys and Girls Club and Pvt. Industry Coun., 1987-90. Mem. NAESP, ASCD, AAUW, N.Y. State ASCD, Western N.Y. ASCD, Internat. Reading Assn. (pres., bd. dirs. Chautauqua coun. 1984-91), Nat. Coun. Tchrs. English, Sch. Adminstrs. Assn. N.Y. State, N.Y. State ACE, Women of Moose, Order Ea. Star, Delta Kappa Gamma, Phi Delta Kappa (corr. sec. 1993—). Home: 240 Valley View Ave Jamestown NY 14701-8417 Office: RR Rogers Sch Jamestown NY 14701

JOHNSON, BROOKE BAILEY, television executive; b. L.A., May 12, 1951; d. Edwin Beauvais and Jeanne (Foote) Bailey; m. Peter Michael Johnson, Sept. 18, 1982; children: Bailey Peter, Lee Keating. BA, Northwestern U., 1973, MS in Journalism, 1974. Promotion dir. Sta. KGUN-TV, Tucson, 1975-77; asst. programming dir. Sta. WLS-TV, Chgo., 1977-82; dir. programming Sta. WABC-TV, N.Y.C., 1982-89; became v.p. programming Arts & Entertainment Network, N.Y.C., 1989, now sr. v.p. programming and production. Mem. NOW. Mem. Nat. Cable Acad., Cable TV Assn., NATAS, Nat. Assn. TV Program Execs. (Iris award), Kappa Alpha Theta. Office: A & E Television Network 235 E 45th St New York NY 10017-3305*

JOHNSON, CANDICE ELAINE BROWN, pediatrics educator; b. Cin., Mar. 21, 1946; d. Paul Preston and Naomi Elizabeth (Lind) Brown; m. Thomas Raymond Johnson, June 30, 1973; children: Andrea Eleanor, Erik Albert. BS, U. Mich., 1968; PhD, Case Western Reserve U., 1973, MD, 1976. Diplomate Am. Bd. Pediat. Intern, resident Rainbow Babies & Children's Hosp./Metro. Gen. Pediatrics, 1976-78; fellow in ambulatory pediatrics Metro. Gen. Hosp., Cleve., 1978-79; asst. prof. pediat. Case Western Reserve U., Cleve., 1980-90, assoc. prof. pediat., 1990—; mem. Lederle Spkr.'s Bur. Am. Cyanamid, Pearl River, N.Y., 1992-94; mem. rev. panel NIH, Washington, 1993. Contbr. articles profl. jours. Active 1st Unitarian Ch., Shaker Hgts., Ohio, 1982-94. Mem. Women Faculty Sch. Medicine (v.p. 1991-93), Southern Utah Wilderness Alliance, Harvard Club of Cleve., Sierra Club. Democrat. Home: 3062 Huntington Cleveland OH 44120 Office: Dept Pediat Met Health Med Ctr 2500 MetroHealth Dr Cleveland OH 44108

JOHNSON, CAROL ANN, accountant; b. Ruston, La., Dec. 15, 1963; d. Wayne Dale and Martha Rachel (Wiggins) J. BS in Acctg., La. Tech. U., 1985; postgrad., Georgetown U., 1991—. Tax acct. EDS, Dallas, 1985-89, Mobil Corp., Fairfax, Va., 1989—. Docent Boyhood Home of Robert E. Lee, Alexandria, Va., 1992—. Mem. Inst. Cert. Mgmt. Accts. Office: Mobil Corp 3225 Gallows Rd Rm 3A806 Fairfax VA 22037

JOHNSON, CAROLYN JEAN, law librarian; b. Beaver Dam, Wis., Nov. 7, 1938; d. Henry William and Bernice Mae (Haas) Krueger; m. Robert Edward Johnson, June 19, 1960; children: Eric Steven, Kristin Elizabeth. BS in Edn., Wartburg Coll., 1960. Tchr. various locations, 1960-64, Hennepin County Library, 1972-81; libr. 3M Tech. Libr., St. Paul, 1981-86; law libr. 3M Ctr. Law Libr., St. Paul, 1986—. Mem. Am. Assn. Law Libraries, Minn. Assn. Law Libraries. Lutheran. Office: 3M Co Ctr Law Library PO Box 33355 Bldg 220-12E-02 Saint Paul MN 55133-3355

JOHNSON, CARYN See GOLDBERG, WHOOPI

JOHNSON, CATHY, accountant; b. L.A., Apr. 18, 1953; d. Grover Cleveland and Naomi Esther (Johnson) Williams; 1 child, Milton Clyde JOrdan, Jr. AA, Sacramento City Coll., 1984; BS, Calif. State U., Sacramento, 1987. Acctg. clerk Texaco Oil Co., L.A., 1973-75; bookkeeper Nichols Inst., San Juan Capistrano, Calif., 1980, Matsukas Bros. Paper Co., L.A., 1981; acct. 1st Nationwide Bank, Sacramento, 1988; bookkeeper Calif. Optometric Credit Union, Sacramento, 1989-90; acct. Planning and Conservation League, Sacramento, 1990-91; prin. Budget Bookkeeping, Rancho Cordova, Calif., 1991—. Contbr. United Negro Coll. Fund, N.Y.C., 1988; Christmas vol. Salvation Army Outreach Svc., Sacramento, 1990, Iraq relief vol. St. Ignatius Parish, Sacramento, 1991; big sister The Birthing Project, Sacramento, 1990-91. Marion Muddox scholar Calif. State U., 1986. Mem. Nat. Assn. Accts., Calif. State U. Alumna, Sacramento Bus. Chpt. Office: Budget Bookkeeping PO Box 2904 Rancho Cordova CA 95741-2904

JOHNSON, CHARLENE ELIZABETH, language arts consultant, educator; b. Aurora, Ill., June 7, 1933; d. Floyd Clark and Marion Priscilla Smith; m. Bennett F. Johnson, July 25, 1955 (div. 1961): children—Roderick Julian, Marshall Floyd. BSE, Butler U., 1960, MSE, 1968, EdS, 1982; EdD in Leadership in Early and Mid. Childhood Nova U., 1992. Classroom tchr. Indpls. Pub. Schs., 1960-68, reading tchr., 1968-71, lang. arts cons., 1972-82, reading tchr., 1982-90; condr. parent workshops in reading Flanner House, 1980, 4 parent workshops, N.E. orgns., 1988. Author: Parent Primer, 1979.

Instrumentalist, Butler U. Orch., 1971-92, C 2d Christian Ch. String Ensemble, Indpls. Philharm. Orch.; trainer reading tutors Pub. Housing Authority; vol. Ptnrs. Edn., Harshman Jr. High Sch.; conducted workshops for Even Start Parents, 1990-92; adult edn. tchr. Even Start Family Literacy Program, 1990—. Pres. Christian Women's Fellowship. Mem. Nat. Assn. Edn. Young Children, Internat. Reading Assn., Indpls. Reading Assn., Ind. Reading Assn., Nat. Council Negro Women, NEA, Indpls. Edn. Assn., Ind. State Tchrs. Assn., NAACP, Indian Assn. for Edn. of Young Children, Midwest Assn. for Edn. of Young Children, Nat. Assn. for Edn. of Young Children, Delta Sigma Theta, Sigma Alpha Iota, Phi Delta Kappa.

JOHNSON, CHERYL DENISE, special education educator; b. Meridian, Miss., May 20; d. David Arnold and Toreatha (Means) J. BS in Edn., U. Ala., 1982, MA, 1984, EdS, 1992. Tchr. spl. edn. Perry County Bd. Edn., Marion, Ala., 1982-83; instr. spl. needs Partlow State Sch., Tuscaloosa, Ala., 1983-84; tchr. spl. edn. Tuscaloosa County Bd. Edn., 1984-94, Tuscaloosa City Bd. Edn., 1994—. Mem. com. Adopt-a-Sch., Brookwood, 1987-90; sch. organizer United Cerebral Palsy Telethon, Tuscaloosa, 1988. Mem. NEA, Coun. for Exceptional Children, Kappa Delta Pi, Alpha Kappa Alpha. Democrat. Methodist. Home: 2501 15th St E Apt A Tuscaloosa AL 35404-4143 Office: Tuscaloosa Mid Sch 315 Mcfarland Blvd E Tuscaloosa AL 35405

JOHNSON, CHERYL L., legislative staff member; b. New Orleans, May 8, 1960; d. Austin Jr. and Cynthia Terry (Davis) J. BS in Journalism, U. Iowa, 1977-80; JD cum laude, Howard U., 1981-84. Bar: D.C., 1988. Assoc. Stoel, Rives & Boley, 1984-85; rsch. asst., 1985-88; staff dir., sub-com. on librs. and memls. Com. on House Adminstrn., Washington, 1989-91; staff dir. sub-com. on oversight and investigations Ho. Com. on Post Office and Civil Svc., Washington, 1991—. Office: Ho Com Post Office & Civil Svc 219 Cannon House Office Bldg Washington DC 20515*

JOHNSON, CHRISTINE ANN, nurse; b. Omaha, Nebr., Aug. 23, 1951; d. Ralph James and Marlene (Marlenee) Matney; m. Timothy Carl Johnson, Aug. 1, 1970; children: Erik Carl, Christine Nicole. Cert. practical nurse, Met. Tech. Community Coll., 1973; BA cum laude, Creighton U., 1989. LPN, Nebr.; cert. pregnancy exercise instr.; cert. lactation cons. EKG technician Bishop Clarkson Meml. Hosp., Omaha, 1971-74, lic. practical nurse, 1978—, instr. pregnancy exercise, 1984-86, instr. sibling preparation, 1985-86, instr. breastfeeding, 1985-95; LPN Cons. in Cardiology, P.C., Omaha, 1974-78; tchr. asst. Creighton U. Dept. Psychology, Omaha, 1987-88; lactation cons. Bergan Mercy Med. Ctr., Omaha, 1994—; teaching asst. dept. psychology, child psychology, adolescent psychology, devel. psychology Creighton U., 1987-88. Assoc. editor: (cons.'s corner) Jour. Human Lactation, 1994. Sec. United Meth. Women First United Meth. Ch., 1984-85, chmn. 1985-86; vol. Radio Talking Book, 1985; mem. Omaha Pub. Schs. Superintendent's Task Force on Human Growth and Devel., 1986. Mem. Internat. Lactation Cons. Assn., Psi Chi. Methodist. Home: 4618 N 129th Ave Omaha NE 68164-1708 Office: Bergan Mercy Med Ctr 7500 Mercy Rd Omaha NE 68124

JOHNSON, CHRISTINE MARIE, promotions professional; b. Willmar, Minn., July 1, 1967; d. Charles Leroy Johnson and Sandra Marie Sandin. BS in Mktg. and Comm., Babson Coll., 1989; cert. legal studies, Lake Washington Coll., 1994. Retail sales mgr. Lechmere Sales Inc., Cambridge, Mass., 1990-92; sales rep. corporate divsn. Minolta Corp., Seattle, 1992-93; legal sec. Law Offices of Steven G. Toole, Seattle, 1994; legal asst. John Blackburn Law Offices, Seattle, 1994; promotions dir. Sta. KCMU, Seattle, 1994—; owner One Love Music Co., Seattle, 1994—. Music reviewer Sta. KCMU, 1994—. Animal care vol. Humane Soc., Bellevue, Wash., 1994. Recipient Women's award for vocat. excellence State of Wash., 1994. Mem. NAFE. Republican. Home: 2305 First Ave # 111 Seattle WA 98121

JOHNSON, CHRISTY LYNN RODEHEAVER, nurse; b. Macon, Ga., Nov. 11, 1956; d. Charles Stewart and Dorothy (Roper) Rodeheaver; m. Herbert Clay Johnson Jr., June 5, 1974. ADN, Gordon Coll., 1977; cert. RN 1st asst., Delaware Community Coll., 1989; BA in Health Care Bus., Stephens Coll., 1991; BSN, N.Y. State Regents Coll., 1994. RN first asst., Ga.; cert. nurse oper. rm. Staff nurse med./surg. unit HCA Coliseum Med. Ctrs., Macon, Ga., 1977-79, head nurse med./surg. unit, 1979-82, staff nurse oper. rm., 1982-89, RN 1st asst., 1989—. Mem. Assn. Oper. Rm. Nurses, Southeastern Surg. Nurses Assn., Ga. Nurses Assn., Nat. League for Nursing, Registered Nurse First Assts. Home: RR# 5 Box 117 Forsyth GA 31029

JOHNSON, CINDA HAWKS, publishing company executive, financial consultant; b. Rochester, N.Y., Sept. 15, 1948; d. Thomas Harris and Marion (Jones) Hawks; m. Winthrop D. Johnson, Aug. 28, 1968; children: Cory, Lindsay. AA, Stephens Coll., Columbia, Mo., 1968; BA, U. Colo., 1970; MBA, U. Rochester, 1979, postgrad. Project dir. Walker & Dunlap, Washington, 1970-73; dir. program devel. Gananda Devel. Corp., Rochester, 1973-74; fin. coord. Dept. Community Devel., Rochester, 1975-77; mgr. treasury ops. Sybron Co., Rochester, 1979-83; v.p. fin. Cyberlynx, Inc., Boulder, Colo., 1983-88; chief fin. officer, treas. New Hope Communications, Inc., Boulder, 1988-92, pres., chief oper. officer, 1992-94; CEO 4 Health, Inc., Boulder, Colo., 1994—. Bd. dirs. Rochester YMCA, 1979-83, vice chair 1981-83, chair fin. com., 1979-80; bd. dirs. Compeer Program of Rochester Health Assn., 1980-83. Mem. Chief Fin. Officer's Exec. Group-Nat. Products Industry (bd. dirs. 1989—), Chief Fin. Officer's Roundtable Group, Profl. Women's Group. Congregationalist. Home: 3756 Wonderland Hill Ave Boulder CO 80304 Office: New Hope Communications 1301 Spruce St Boulder CO 80302

JOHNSON, CINDY COBLE, councilwoman, personnel consultant; b. El Paso, Tex., Aug. 20, 1956; d. Walter Mylen and Dewyria Shirley (Hendrix) Coble; m. David Johnson, Feb. 8, 1974; children: David, Luke, Phillip. Grad. high sch., Plattsmouth, Nebr. OB technician Clarkson Hosp., Omaha, 1975-76; pers. asst. Target, Lincoln, Nebr., 1985-86; loan adminstr. 1st Nat. Bank, Lincoln, 1987-91; mem. Lincoln City Coun., 1991-94; pers. cons. Talent +, Lincoln, 1994—; mem. Community Devel. Task Force, Lincoln, 1993-94, Joint Budget Com., Lincoln, 1993-94, Highlands Tech. Park Com., Lincoln, 1993-94. Pres. MADD, Lancaster County, 1985-91; chair Traffic Safety Com., Lincoln, 1989-94; trustee Lighthouse-At Risk Youth, Lincoln, 1993-94; bd. dirs. People's City Mission, Lincoln, 1993-94; active MAD DADS. Recipient Bradley Cuda Meml. award Lincoln Bd. Realtors, 1990, Svc. to Mankind award Sertoma, 1991, Pub. Svc. award U.S. Dept. Transp., 1991, Ptnrs. in Prevention award Lincoln Coun. on Alcoholism and Drugs, 1994. Mem. Lincoln Ind. Bus. Assn., C. of C. Home: 6109 NW 7th Lincoln NE 68521 Office: Talent + 3883 Normal # 204 Lincoln NE 68508

JOHNSON, CIRI DIANE, graphic design firm owner; b. Ann Arbor, Mich., Aug. 19, 1956; d. Paul Christian and Genevieve Ruth J. Student, U. Ariz., 1974-76, U. Oreg., 1976-78; BFA, San Francisco Art Inst., 1980; MA, NYU, 1982. Artist asst. Lucio Pozzi, N.Y.C., 1983-85; editor, art dir. New Observations Mag., N.Y.C., 1985-91; owner Ciri Johnson Design, Bklyn, 1988-91, Tucson, 1991—; asst. tchr. Parson's Sch. Design, N.Y.C., 1985-86; instr. NYU, 1982. Prin. works published in The National Poetry Magazine of Lower East Side, 1988-90; designed promotional piece for Elisa Monte Dance Co. chosen for reproduction in 1991 Artist's Market. Mem. Resources for Women, Tucson Ad Club (Bronze Addy award for mag. advt. campaign, Merit cert. 1992, Gold Addy award for art exhbn. catalog, Bronze Addy for self-promotion 1993). Democrat. Office: 6651 N Campbell Ave Tucson AZ 85718-1363

JOHNSON, CLARICE P., manager procurement and materials planning; b. Madison, N.C., Dec. 15, 1941; d. George Taylor and Betty Mae (Preston) Penn; m. William Howard Johnson, June 22, 1962; children: William Jr., Renata. BS in Biology, Upsala Coll., 1974, BSBA, 1983; MS, N.J. Inst. Tech., 1990. Mfg. biologist Organon, Inc., West Orange, N.J., 1975-80, prodn. supr., 1980-84, mfg. supr., 1982-84, sr. regulatory assoc., 1984-85, mgr. prodn. and inventory control, 1985-89, mgr. procurement and materials planning, 1989—; edn. counselor, Organon, Inc., 1988—; lectr., guest cons. Jersey City (N.J.) State Coll., 1990, Cenogenics, Old Bridge, N.J., 1989; mem. Organon Gender Focus Group, West Orange, 1993—. Author: Vendor Certification, 1990. Pres. College Park Neighborhood Assn., South Orange, N.J., 1983-87; mem. South Orange Community Rels. Bd., 1981-88; tutorer Essex County C.C., Newark, 1989. Mem. Am. Prodn. and Inventory Control Soc. (v.p. mem. 1993-94, Mem. of Yr. 1993, CPIM, company coord. 1992-93, Company of Month award 1992), Nat. Assn. Purchasing Mgmt., Am. Soc. Quality Control, AAAS, Internat. Soc. Pharm. Engrs. Democrat. Home: 429 Wilden Pl South Orange NJ 07079-2518 Office: Organon Inc 375 Mount Pleasant Ave West Orange NJ 07052-2798

JOHNSON, CLAUDIA CHRISTINA, geological researcher; b. St. Louis, Apr. 7, 1955; d. Magdalene Maria (Wengritzky) McNeely; m. Erle G. Kauffman, Sept. 16, 1989. BA, U. Colo., 1981, MS, 1984, PhD, 1993. Rsch. asst. U. Colo., Boulder, 1980-84, teaching asst., 1982-83, 87-89, instr., 1990, coord. phys. geology labs., 1991; rsch. assoc. Earth Systems Sci. Ctr. Pa. State U., University Park, 1993; instr. U. No. Colo., 1990, U. Colo., 1990; cons. and presenter in field. Contbr. articles and abstracts for profl. jours. Univ. West Indies acad. scholar, 1982; faculty fellow U. Colo., 1987, Zena Hutner Andrews fellow, 1991-92; grantee Paleont. Soc., Geol. Soc. Am., Gulf, Arco, Amoco, Marathon, Shell. Mem. AAUW, Geol. Soc. Am., Paleont. Soc. Office: Pa State U Earth Systems Sci Ctr 248 Deike Bldg Univ Park PA 16802-2711

JOHNSON, CONSTANCE ANN TRILLICH, minister, small business owner, librarian, lawyer, writer, researcher, lecturer; b. Chgo., Apr. 16, 1949; d. Lee and Ruth (Goodhue) Trillich; m. Robert Dale Neal, Dec. 25, 1972 (div. 1988); 1 child, Adam Danforth; m. Lewis W. Johnson Jr., Feb. 14, 1990. BA in French, U. Tenn., 1971, cert. Sorbonne, 1970; MLn, Emory U., 1979; JD, Mercer Law Sch., 1982; postgrad. Internat. Sem., 1991—. Bar: Ga. 1982; cert. Reiki therapist level III. Reservationist AAA, Tampa, Fla., 1971-72; libr. tech. asst. I, Mercer U., Macon, Ga., 1973-74, libr. tech. asst. II, 1974-78; teaching asst. Mercer Law Sch., Macon, 1981; asst. prof. Mercer Med. Sch., Macon, 1980-82; pvt. practice, Macon, 1982-86; min. Ch. Tzaddi, 1986-89; writer/researcher ADC Project, 1988-89; min. Alliance of Divine Love, 1988—; of counsel Read Found., Evansville, Ind., 1989; mgr. Lifestream Assocs., 1989; freelance editor Page Design Co., 1989; assoc. AA Computer Care, Winter Park, Fla., 1989; founder House of the Lord, 1989—; rsch. asst. Ctr. Constl. Studies, Macon, 1983; instr. bus. Wesleyan Coll., Macon, 1982; owner Christian Computer Care, Winter Park, Fla., 1990—. Mem. Ch. of Religious Rsch. Inc., 1992—. Editor (periodical) Ray of Sunshine, 1989; assoc. prof. libr. sci., Internat. Sem., Plymouth Fla., 1991. Bd. dirs. Unity Ch., Middle, Ga., 1987, Sec., 1987. Bd. dirs. Macon Council World Affairs, 1981-82, Light of Creative Awareness, Northville, Mich., 1989; mem. Friends Emory Libraries, Atlanta, 1980-87; mem. Friends Eckerd Coll. Library, St. Petersburg, Fla., 1980-87. Mem. ABA, Am. Soc. Law and Medicine, Am. Judicature Soc., DAR (Kaskaskia chpt.), Mercer U. Women's Club (treas. 1974, pres. 1986, bd. dirs. 1987), Am. Assn. U. Women, Friends of the Libr., Mid. Ga. Gem and Mineral Soc., Macon Mus. Arts and Scis., Nat. Fedn. Spiritual Healers Am., La Leche League (sec. 1985), Phi Alpha Delta. Republican. Office: Christian Computer Care 1416 Pelican Bay Trl Winter Park FL 32792-6131

JOHNSON, CRYSTAL DUANE, psychologist; b. Houston, Mar. 2, 1954; d. Alton Floyd and Duane (Mullican) J.; m. Donald Beecher Hart, Mar. 21, 1989. BA, U. Tex., 1983, MS, 1985. Lic. profl. counselor, psychol. assoc., marriage and family therapist; cert. chem. dependency specialist. Student devel. specialist U. Tex., Tyler, 1985-86, intake counselor, 1986-88; staff psychologist Sabine Valley Ctr., Longview, Tex., 1987-88, Mental Health/Mental Retardation Ctr. of East Tex., Tyler, 1988-89; pvt. practice psychologist Tyler, 1989—; counselor Juvenile and Adult Probation Depts., 1988—, ICF/MR Residential Homes, 1991—; spl. edn. counselor, 1990—; counselor Child Protective Svcs., 1991—. Mem. Smith County Humane Soc., Tyler, 1985—, Humane Soc. of the U.S., Washington, 1987—, Am. Soc. Prevention Cruelty to Animals, 1987—, Nat. Wildlife Fedn., 1986—, World Wildlife Fedn., 1986—. Mem. Am. Psychol. Assn., Tex. Psychol. Assn., East Tex. Psychol. Assn.

JOHNSON, D'ELAINE ANN HERARD, artist; b. Puyallup, Wash., Mar. 19, 1932; d. Thomas Napoleon and Rosella Edna (Berry) Herard; m. John Laffette Johnson, Dec. 22, 1956. B.F.A., Central Wash. U., 1954; M.F.A., U. Wash., 1958, postgrad. U. London, 1975—; postgrad U. Wash., 1975—. Instr. art Seattle Pub. Schs., 1954-78, Mus. History and Industry, Seattle, 1954-56; dir. Mt. Olympus Estate, Edmonds, Wash., 1971; cons. art groups, Wash. State, 1954—. lectr. Cen. Wash. State U., Seattle PTA, Creative Arts Assn., Everett, Everett Community Coll., Women's Caucus for Art, Seattle, numerous others; served as art juror for numerous shows. Founder Mt. Olympus Preserve for Arts, Edmonds, Wash., 1971, sponsor art events, 1971—; active Wash. Coalition Citizens with Disabilities. Exhibited in group shows: Fry Art Mus., Seattle, 1964, Seattle Art Mus., 1959, Henry Art Gallery, Seattle, Vancouver Maritime Mus., B.C., Can., 1981, N.S. Art Mus., Can., 1971, Whatcom Mus., Bellingham, Wash., 1975, State Capitol Mus., Olympia, Wash., 1975, Corvallis State U., Oreg., 1982, Newport Mus., Oreg., Nat. Artist Equity, 1972, Belluvue Art Mus., Seattle, 1989, Rosicrusian Egyption Mus., San Jose, Calif., 1990, St. Mark's Cathedral, Seattkem 1991, Sidney Mus. and Arts Assn., Port Orchard, Wash., 1991, Bellvue Art Mus., 1992, Pacific Arts Ctr. Hauberg Gallery, Seattle, 1992, Bon Marche Gallery, Seattle, 1992, Northeast Trade and Exbn. Hall, 1993, Edmonds (Wash.) Art Mus., 1993, Ilwaco (Wash.) Heritage Mus., 1993, Robert Frey Gallery, Seattle, 1994; over 300 exhibits 1950—, over 1200 paintings through 1970; Illustrator: The Bing Crosby Family Music Books for Children, 1961; TV art instr. TV-9 U. Wash., 1968. Elected to Wash. State Art Commn. Registry, Olympia, 1982; recipient numerous awards. Mem. Nat. Artist Equity, Internat. Soc. Artists, The Cousteau Soc., Am. Council for Arts, Nat. Women's Studies Assn., Assn. Am. Culture, Internat. Platform Assn., Nat. Pen Women Assn., Kappa Delta Pi, Kappa Pi. Avocations: scuba diving, camping, travel, violin, writing. Home and Office: 16122 72d St Ave W Edmonds WA 98206-4517

JOHNSON, DIANA LEE, insurance specialist; b. Cin., Oct. 7, 1952; d. Earl Richard and Rosemary (Fey) Peterson; m. William W. Johnson, Apr. 7, 1978; children: Anthony Joseph, Scott Alan, Brandi Marie, Gregory James. BA in Math., Miami U., Oxford, Ohio, 1975. Rate analyst Ohio Casualty Group, Hamilton, 1976-89, tech. analyst, 1989—. Recipient Intro to Ins. cert. Ins. Inst. Am., 1991, Intro to Claims cert. Ins. Inst. Am., 1992, Supervisory Mgmt. cert. Ins. Inst. Am., 1994. Mem. Ins. Data Mgmt. Assn. (test grader 1993—, designation 1993). Home: 335 Belle Ave Hamilton OH 45015-1104 Office: Ohio Casualty Group Ins Cos 136 N 3rd St Hamilton OH 45025-0002

JOHNSON, DIANE LYNN, publishing executive, consultant; b. N.Y.C., Apr. 26, 1945; d. Lawrence Schlesinger and Rita (Gorman) Kingsley; m. Arnold Krull, Mar. 6, 1969 (div. Mar. 1973); m. Martin A. Johnson, Aug. 19, 1981. Student, New Sch. of Social Rsch., N.Y.C., 1967-69. Ops. mgr. Cambist Films, Inc., N.Y.C., 1963-69; pres. Fantasy Jewelry, Inc., N.Y.C., 1973-75; v.p., media Dynamic House/Tele House, Inc., N.Y.C., 1973-75; v.p., gen. mgr. Columbia Communications, Inc., N.Y.C., 1975-80; pres. Pub. Dynamics, Inc., Stamford, Conn., 1982—; cons. Key Pub., Inc., Katonah, N.Y., 1978-80, Milan Schuster, Inc., N.Y.C., 1980-81. Mem. Literacy Vols. Am., N.Y.C., 1973-75; big sister Big Sister Program, N.Y.C., 1973-75; tchrs. aide Jewish Community Ctr. Nursery Sch., Stamford, 1981-82; group leader Smokers Anonymous, Stamford, 1988—. Mem. Landmark Club (Stamford, Conn.). Jewish. Home: 1 Strawberry Hill Ct Apt 3H Stamford CT 06902-2529 Office: Publishing Dynamics Inc 15 Bank St Stamford CT 06901-3008

JOHNSON, DIANE MARIE, art educator; b. Sioux Falls, S.D., Apr. 24, 1958; d. Calvin Theodore and Darlene Evelyn (Wettestad) J. Fashion merchandising grad., Spencer (Iowa) Sch. Bus., 1977; BA in Art Edn., U. No. Iowa, 1981. Art tchr. grades K-12 Cedar Valley Community Sch., Farnhamville, Iowa, 1981-89; art tchr. grades 6-12 Denver (Iowa) Community Sch., 1989—. Various commd. work including Cedar Valley Community Sch., 1982-89; group shows include Stumme Art Show, 1989 (2d pl.), Art Educators Invitational at Blanden Meml. Art Mus., Ft. Dodge Iowa, 1988; works include town logo and motto, Farnhamville, 1988, watercolor paintings. Mem. Mus. Women in the Arts, NEA, Iowa State Edn. Assn., Art Educators Iowa, Nat. Art Edn. Assn., Denver Edn. Assn. Home: 125 E Franklin St Denver IA 50622-0338 Office: Denver Secondary Sch 541 E Eagle St Denver IA 50622-0384

JOHNSON, DONNA LYNN, critical care nurse; b. Bitburg, Fed. Republic Germany, Jan. 31, 1958; d. Bill and Bernice R. (Staudt) J. BSN, Northwestern State U., 1980. RN, La.; CCRN. Nurse SICU Schumpert Med. Ctr., Shreveport, La., 1981-87, adminstrv. supr., 1987-89; relief nurse ICU Riverside Community Hosp., Bossier, La., 1982-83, Minden (La.) Med. Ctr., 1983-86; recovery coord. La. Organ Procurement Agy., Shreveport, 1989-94; dir. critical care La. State U. Med. Ctr., Shreveport, 1994—; preceptor Northwestern State U., Shreveport, 1983-89. Mem. AACN (pres. 1992—), N.Am. Transplant Coord. Orgn., Krewe of Aesclepius. Home: 448 Huron St Shreveport LA 71106-1648 Office: La State U Med Ctr 1501 Kings Hwy Shreveport LA 71130

JOHNSON, DORA MYRTLE KNUDTSON, principal; b. Bryant, S.D., Sept. 4, 1900; d. Knudt Guttorm and Margit Knudtson; m. Arthur Johnson, Jan. 31, 1949 (dec. Aug. 1949); 1 stepdaughter, Doris Miller. BA, St. Olaf Coll., 1923; MA, U. Wash., Seattle, 1941. Sr. high sch. tchr. math. Gaylord (Minn.) Sch. Dist., 1923-26, Madison (S.D.) Sch. Dist., 1926-43; dean of girls Madison (S.D.) Sch. Dist., S.D., 1932-41; prin. Madison (S.D.) Sch. Dist., 1941-43; high sch.tchr. math. Kansas City (Mo.) Sch. Dist., 1943-49; dean of women Mo. Christian Coll., Columbia, 1950-57; ret. Mo. Christian Coll., 1958; cons. AAUW, Kansas City, 1969-71. Editor: A History of the Mo. Div. of AAUW, 1946-76. Mem. AAUW (state pres. Madison, S.D., state chmn., fellowship found. Kansas City 1963-67, state pres. Kansas City 1967-69, nat. com. for edni. found. D.C. chpt. 1971-75, honorary life mem. 1989, Significant Svc. award 1989), Internat. Assn. of Univ. Women (Ednl. Found. award), Internat. Rels. Coun., Friends of Art. Democrat. Lutheran. Home: 10000 Wornall Rd Apt 1402 Kansas City MO 64114-4363

JOHNSON, DORIS ANN, educational administrator; b. Marinette, Wis., Dec. 4, 1950; d. Jerome Louis and Jean Fern (Henry) La Plant; m. Daniel Lee Leonard, June 10, 1972 (div. June 1987); children: Jeremiah Daniel, Erica Leigh, Wesley Cyril; m. Paul Robert Johnson, Oct. 21, 1989; stepchildren: Kindra Michelle, Tanya Mari. Student, U. Wis., Oshkosh, 1969-70; BA in Edn., U. Wis., Eau Claire, 1973; MS in Edn., U. Wis., Whitewater, 1975; postgrad., Oreg. State U., 1988—. Reading specialist Brookfield (Wis.) Cen. High Sch., 1975-79; lead instr. N.E. Wis. Tech. Coll., Marinette, 1979-87; dir. adult basic edn. Umpqua C.C., Roseburg, Oreg., 1987—; founding bd. dirs. Project Literacy, Umpqua Region, Roseburg, 1989—; mem. adv. bd. Umpqua Cmty. Action Network, Roseburg, 1987-94; mem. State Dirs. of Adult Edn., Oreg., 1987—, vice chair, 1992-93, chair, 1993-94; mem. Adminstrn. Assn., Roseburg, 1989—, chair, 1993-94, 94-95; bd. dirs. Greater Douglas United Way, 1994—; adv. bd. Oreg. Literacy Line, 1994—. Coauthor literacy module Communication Skills, 1988; author ednl. curriculum. Bd. dirs. St. Joseph Maternity Home, Roseburg, 1987-90, founding mem.; mem. Literacy Theater, Roseburg, 1988—, Greater Douglas United Way Bd., 1994—; mem. Project Leadership, Roseburg, 1988-89; mem. adv. bd. Oregon Literacy Line, 1994—; mem. Roseburg Valley Rep. Women, 1994—. State legalizatoin assistance grantee Fed. Govt., 1988-94, homeless literacy grantee Fed. Govt., 1990-91, family literacy grantee Fed. Govt., 1990-91, family literacy grantee Fed. Govt., 1991-93, intergenerational literacy grantee State of Oreg., 1991, literacy expansion grantee Fed. Govt., 1992-93, literacy outreach grantee Fed. Govt., 1992-95, staff devel. spl. projects grantee Fed. Govt., 1992-93. Fellow Nat. Inst. Leadership Devel., Am. Assn. Adult and Continuing Edn., Oreg. Assn. Disabled Students, Oreg. Developmental Edn. Studies, Oreg. Assn. for Children with Learning Disabilities, Tchrs. of English to Spkrs. of Other Langs., Western Coll. Reading and Learning Assn., Am. Assn. Women in Coll. and Jr. Coll., Roseburg Valley Rep. Women, Altrusa Internat. Club of Roseburg (chair literacy com. 1993-94, 94-95), Rep. Women. Republican. Lutheran. Home: 761 Garden Grove Roseburg OR 97470 Office: Umpqua CC PO Box 967 Roseburg OR 97470

JOHNSON, DOROTHY PHYLLIS, counselor, art therapist; b. Kansas City, Mo., Sept. 13, 1925; d. Chris C. and Mabel T. (Gillum) Green; B.A. in Art, Ft. Hays. State U., 1975, M.S. in Guidance and Counseling, 1976, M.A. in Art, 1979; m. Herbert E. Johnson, May 11, 1945; children—Michael E., Gregory K. Art therapist High Plains Comprehensive Mental Health Assn., Hays, Kans., 1975-76; art therapist, mental health counselor Sunflower Mental Health Assn., Concordia, Kans., 1976—, co-dir. Project Togetherness, 1976-77, coordinator partial hospitalization, 1978—, out-patient therapist, 1982—; dir. Swedish Am. State Bank, Courtland, Kans., 1960—, sec., 1973-77. Mem. Kans., Am. art therapy assns., Am. Mental Health Counselors Assn., Am. Counseling Assn., Kans. Counseling Assn., Assn. for Humanistic Psychologists, Assn. Transpersonal Psychologists, Assn. Specialists in Group Work, Phi Delta Kappa, Phi Kappa Phi. Contbr. articles to profl. jours. Home: PO Box 200 Courtland KS 66939-0200 Office: 520 Washington St # B Concordia KS 66901-2117

JOHNSON, EDDIE BERNICE, congresswoman; b. Waco, Tex., Dec. 3, 1935; d. Lee Edward and Lillie Mae (White) J.; m. Lacy Kirk Johnson, July 5, 1956 (div. Oct. 1970); 1 child, Dawrence Kirk. Diploma in Nursing, St. Mary's Coll. of South Bend, 1955; BS in Nursing, Tex. Christian U., 1967; MPA, So. Meth. U., 1976; LLD (hon.), Bishop Coll., 1979, Jarvis Coll., 1979, Tex. Coll., 1989, Houston-Tillotson Coll., 1993, Paul Quinn Coll., 1993. Chief psychiat. nurse psychotherapist Vets. Hosp., Dallas, 1956-72; state rep. Tex. Ho. Reps. Dist. 33-0, Dallas, 1972-77; regional dir. HEW, Dallas, 1977-79; exec. asst. to adminstr. for primary health care policy HEW, Washington, 1979-81; v.p. Vis. Nurse Assn. of Tex., Dallas, 1981-87; mem. Tex. State Senate, dist. 23, 1986-1992, 103rd Congress from 30th Tex. dist., Washington, D.C., 1993—; cons. div. urban affairs Zales Corp., Dallas, 1976-77; exec. asst. personnel div. Neiman-Marcus, Dallas, 1972-75; pres. Eddie Bernice Johnson & Assocs., Inc., Metroplex News, Dallas-Ft. Worth Airport. Bd. dirs. ARC. Recipient Citizenship award Nat. Conf. Christians and Jews, 1985; named an Outstanding Alumnus St. Mary's Coll. of Nursing, 1986. Mem. Alpha Kappa Alpha. Office: US Ho of Reps 1123 Longworth HOB Washington DC 20515

JOHNSON, EDNA SCOTT, English language educator, volunteer; b. Sioux Falls, S.D., Aug. 15, 1913; d. George Emil and Emma Erika (Pearson) Nelson; m. Preston William Scott, May 29, 1939 (dec. Apr. 1969); children: William Scott (dec. 1969), Gregory N. Scott; m. Merritt W. Johnson, Jan. 1, 1973 (dec. May 1978). BA, U. S.D., 1936. Cert. secondary tchr. English instr. Beresford (S.D.) High Sch., 1936-39; pres. Hecla (S.D.) Sch. Bd., 1950-63, Assn. Sch. Bds., S.D., 1954-60; del. to White House Conf. on Edn., 1955; cons. Am. Social Hygiene Soc., 1956; exec. com. Gov.'s Lay Conf. Edn., S.D., 1962; mem. Landmarks Commn., 1975-84. Author: School Board Members Handbook, 1957, Brown County History, 1981, Bethlehem Lutheran Church History, 1984, (booklet) Railroads of Brown County, 1984; editor Brown County LWV Bull., 1991-92. Den mother Cub Scouts, 1951-61; leader Brown County Sch. Dist. Reorganization Bd., S.D., 1953-57; mem. devel. com. U. S.D., 1958-66; pres. Brown County Libr. Bd., 1958-77, S.D. PTA, 1960-62, Brown County Hist. Soc., 1984-88, Community Concerts Bd., Aberdeen, 1981-85; gen. chmn. Diamond Jubilee, Hecla, 1960-61, Declaration of Independence Celebration, Brown County, 1976, Brown County State Centennial Celebration, S.D., 1988-90; bd. dirs. Aberdeen United Way, 1983-84; sheriff Dakota Midlands Western Corral, pres. 1989-91; bd. pres. Dakotah Prairie Mus., 1968-72; mem. Bethlehem Luth. Ch. Choir. Recipient Outstanding Svc. award U. S.D., 1956, Outstanding Sch. Bd. Mem. award S.D. Sch. Bd. Assn., Sch. Bell award S.D. Sch. Bd. Assn., 1984; named First Lady of Aberdeen, 1984. Mem. AAUW (pres.), NEA, S.D. Edn. Assn., P.E.O., O.E.S., Aberdeen Area Arts Coun., Fedn. Women's Clubs, N.S.U. Faculty Wives, Aberdeen Area Geneal. Soc., Chi Omega, Delta Kappa Gamma. Home: 4136 Greenwood Ln Aberdeen SD 57401-9501

JOHNSON, ELAINE BOWE, college dean, educational consultant; b. Seattle, May 22, 1940; d. Lyman Campbell Bowe and Elaine Ingeborg Larson; m. H. Thomas Johnson, July 17, 1971; 1 child, Thomas Christian. BA, Mills Coll., 1962; MA, Ind. U., 1964; PhD, U. Oreg., 1968. Instr. U. Oreg., Eugene, 1963-68; chair, asst. dean, assoc. prof. English Huron Coll., London, Ont., Can., 1968-78; instr. liberal studies dept. Western Washington U., Bellingham, 1979-82; chmn. English dept. Charles Wright Acad., Tacoma, 1982-88; lectr. Pacific Luth. U., Tacoma, 1982-88; assoc. dean lang. and lit. Mt. Hood Community Coll., Gresham, Oreg., 1988—; cons. in field. Contbr. articles to profl. jours. Recipient Outstanding Tchr. award U. Chgo., 1987, Disting. Tchrs. award Charles Wright Acad., 1988; Woodrow Wilson fellow, 1962-63, Hon. fellow Huron Coll., 1982, Ind. Studies in the Humanities fellow Coun. for Basic Edn. and NEH, 1987; Peris H. Coleman scholar Mills Coll., 1962. Mem. MLA (pres. Oreg. writing and English adv. com. 1992-94), Assn. Oreg. C.C. Humanities Adminstrs., Am. Assn. Women in Jr. and C.C., NAt. Coun. Tchrs. English. Office: Mt Hood Community Coll 26000 SE Stark St Gresham OR 97030

JOHNSON, ELAINE GLENN, accountant; b. Louisville, Miss., Mar. 15, 1943; d. Joe Johnson and Carrie Geneva (Crosby) Glenn; m. Herman Johnson, Dec. 10, 1960; children: Pamela, Herman II, Joseph, Tessa, Verna, Ivan. AS, Triton Coll., 1985; BA in Acctg., Rosary Coll., 1987, MBA in Fin., 1988. Cost. acctg. Entenmann's Inc., Northlake, Ill., 1980-83; bus. mgr. Westside Holistic Family Ctr., Chgo., 1983-88; v.p. fin. Bethel New Life Inc., Chgo., 1988-90; pres., CEO Advance Mgmt. Solutions Inc., Chgo., 1990—. Chair audit com. Nat. Assn. Negro Bus. and profl. Women; founding mem., treas. West Suburban Ednl. and Cultural Found.; pres. WSE and C Found., Oak Park Women's Exchange. Home: 325 Rowan Ct Naperville IL 60540 Office: Advance Mgmt Solutions Inc 4909 W Division St Chicago IL 60651

JOHNSON, ELAINE MCDOWELL, federal government administrator; b. Balt., June 28, 1942; d. McKinley and Lena (Blue) McDowell; m. Walter Johnson; children: Nathan H. Murphy, Michael W. Murphy. BA, Morgan State U., Balt., 1965; MSW, U. Md., 1971, PhD, 1988. Drug abuse adminstr., acting regional dir. State Md. Drug Abuse Adminstrn., Balt., 1971-72; social sci. analyst, pub. health advisor Nat. Inst. Drug Abuse, Rockville, MD, 1972-76, dep. dir., dir. div. community assistance, 1976-82, dep. assoc. dir. for policy devel., 1981-82, dir. div. prevention and communications, 1982-85; dep. dir. Nat. Inst. on Drug Abuse, 1985-88; exec. asst. to adminstr. Alcohol, Drug Abuse & Mental Health Adminstrn., Rockville, MD, 1985; dir. Office for Substance Abuse Prevention, 1988-94; acting adminstr. Alcohol, Drug Abuse and Mental Health Adminstrn., Rockville, Md., 1992; acting adminstr. Substance Abuse and Mental Health Svcs. Adminstrn., Rockville, Md., 1992-94, dir. Ctr. Substance Abuse Prevention, 1995—; chmn. interdepartmental work group White House Domestic Policy Staff, 1980-81; expert cons. in field. Active Presbyterian Ch., Balt., 1979—. Recipient Secretary's commendation HHS, 1989, Disting. Svc. award, 1990, Pride Bldg. Bridges award, 1991, Nat. Fedn. Parents Nat. Leadership award, 1991, Nat. Coun. on Alcoholism and Drug Dependence Ind., Pres. award for outstanding fed. leadership, 1991, Presdl. Meritorious Exec. Rank award, 1991, Presdl. Meritorious Disting. Rank award, 1993. Mem. NASW, ASPA, Sr. Execs. Assn., Fed. Exec. Inst. Alumni Assn. Office: Substance Abuse & Mental Health Svcs Adminstrn 5600 Fishers Ln Rom 12-105 Rockville MD 20857*

JOHNSON, ELIZABETH DIANE LONG, lawyer; b. Pasadena, Calif., Nov. 16, 1945; d. Volney Earl and Sylvia Irene (Drury) Long; m. Lynn Douglas Johnson, Oct. 22, 1966; 1 child, Barbara Annette. BA, U. of Houston, 1967; JD, Rutgers U., 1980. Bar: N.J. 1980, U.S. Dist. Ct. N.J. 1980, Pa. 1984, U.S. Supreme Ct. 1986. Pvt. practice Riverside, N.J., 1980—; pub. defender Riverside Twp., 1988-91; speaker Bur. Comprehensive Justice Ctr. Burlington County, 1987-89. Del. Women in Law to Peoples Republic of China Citizen Amb. Program of People to People Internat., 1989; mem. Orchid Found., 1989—, rec. sec., 1991—; mem. Tenby Chase Civic Assn., Delran, N.J., 1972-87, treas., 1976, v.p., 1974; trustee Drenk Mental Health Ctr., 1988—, pres., 1991—. Mem. N.J. Women Lawyers Assn., Burlington County Bar Assn. (chmn. bench and bar com. 1989-91), Burlington County Bar Found. (trustee 1988-91, treas. 1988-90, v.p. 1990-91, pres. 1991-92), Soc. for Right To Die, Nat. Trust for Hist. Preservation, Mensa, Rotary (sec. Riverside 1991-92, v.p. 1992-93, pres.-elect 1993-94, pres. 1994-95), Delta Gamma. Methodist. Office: 23 Scott St Ste C PO Box 274 Riverside NJ 08075

JOHNSON, ELIZABETH HILL, foundation administrator; b. Ft. Wayne, Ind., Aug. 21, 1913; d. Harry W. and Lydia (Buechner) Hill; m. Samuel Spencer Johnson, Oct. 7, 1944 (dec. 1984); children: Elizabeth Katharine, Patricia Caroline. BS summa cum laude, Miami U., Oxford, Ohio, 1935; MA in English Lit., Wellesley Coll., 1937; postgrad., U. Chgo., 1936. Cert. tchr., Ohio. Pres., co-founder S.S. Johnson Found., Calif. Corp., San Francisco, 1947—. Mem. Oreg. State Bd. Higher Edn., Eugene, 1962-75, Oreg. State Edn. Coord. Com., Salem, 1975-82, Assn. Governing Bds., Washington, 1970-80, chairperson, 1975-76; mem. Oreg. State Tchr. Standards and Practices Commn., Salem, 1982-89; bd. dirs. Lewis and Clark Coll., Portland, Oreg., 1985—, Pacific U., Forest Grove, Oreg., 1982—, Sunriver Prep. Sch., 1983-92, Oreg. Hist. Soc., Portland, 1985—, Cen. Oreg. Dist. Hosp., Redmond, 1982—, Oreg. High Desert Mus., 1984—, Bend, Oreg., Health Decisions, 1986-92, Ctrl. Oreg. Coun. Aging, 1991—. Lt. USNR, 1943-46. Named Honoree March of Dimes White Rose Luncheon, 1984; recipient Aubrey Watzek award Lewis and Clark Coll., 1984, Cen. Oreg. 1st Citizen award, Abrams award Emanuel Hosp., 1982, Pres. award Marylhurst Coll., 1991, Thomas Jefferson award Oregon Historical Soc., 1993. Mem. Am. Assn. Higher Edn., Am. Assn. Jr. Colls., ASCD, Soroptimists (hon.), Francisca Club, Town Club, Univ. Club, Waverley Club, Beta Sigma Phi, Phi Beta Kappa, Phi Delta Kappa, Delta Gamma. Republican. Lutheran. Home: 415 SW Canyon Dr Redmond OR 97756-2028 Office: S S Johnson Found 441 SW Canyon Dr Redmond OR 97756-2028

JOHNSON, ELIZABETH JANE, controller, accountant; b. Muskegon, Mich., May 5, 1958; d. William Harvey and Erika Berta (Mueller) Paulson; m. Thomas Allen Brozek, June 24, 1978 (div. Sept. 1988); children: Stephen, Jessica; m. James Alan Johnson, Sept. 21, 1991; 1 child, Lucas. AA with honors, Muskegon C.C., 1978; B in Bus. Adminstrn. cum laude, Grand Valley State U., 1981; postgrad., Western Mich. U., 1991. CPA, Mich., cert. mgmt. acct., Mich. Revenue agt. IRS, Muskegon, 1980-85; sr. staff acct. DeBoer, Baumann & Co., CPAs, Grand Haven, Mich., 1985-87; internal auditor JSJ Corp., Grand Haven, 1987-91; contr. RAM Electronics, Inc., Fruitport, Mich., 1991—. Mem. fin. com. Ctrl. United Meth. Ch., Muskegon, 1990-91, Sunday sch. tchr., 1989—; mem., musician West Mich. Concert Winds, Muskegon, 1978—; mem. U.S. 31/Sternberg Rd. Interchange Com., Norton Shores, Mich., 1986-93. Mem. AICPA, Inst. Mgmt. Accts., Mich. Assn. CPAs. Home: 4916 Dorchester Dr Norton Shores MI 49441 Office: RAM Electronics Inc 259 N 3d Ave Fruitport MI 49415

JOHNSON, ELIZABETH MOSIER, retired college administrator, counselor; b. Pilares de Nacozari, Mex., Feb. 2, 1914; d. McHenry and Louise (Laurance) Mosier; m. Ronald Lee Johnson, Aug. 14, 1936 (dec. May 11, 1967); children: William Laurance, Ann Johnson Hertel. BA in English Lit. with honors, Scripps Coll., 1935; MA in History, Claremont Coll., 1939, postgrad., 1967-72. Alumnae rep. Scripps Coll. Bd. Trustees, Claremont, 1945-50; pres. Coachella Valley chpt. Am. Field Svc., Indio, Calif., 1966-67; resident adviser Scripps Coll., 1967-68, dir. fin. aid, 1968-80; analyst Calif. Student Aid Commn., Sacramento, 1968-86; acting dean of students Scripps Coll., 1974-75; vol. hospice and sr. peer counselor Pomona (Calif.) Valley Svcs., 1980-93; retired, 1993; evaluator advanced tech. on use of fed. money, Washington, 1984. Vol. Pilgrim Pl., Claremont, 1993—, Joselyn Ctr. for Srs., Claremont, 1993—. Recipient Disting. Svc. award Calif. Assn. Student Fin. Aid Adminstrs., 1980. Mem. P.E.O. (chpt. O rec. sec. 1993-94, del. state conv. 1992, 93), Mt. San Antonio Gardens Club (area rep. coun. 1993-94). Home: 880 W Harrison Ave Claremont CA 91711-4128

JOHNSON, ELLEN SCHULTZ, retired music librarian, researcher; b. Beatrice, Nebr., Apr. 11, 1918; d. P. Daniel and Justina (Wiebe) Schultz; m. Dale M. Johnson, May 12, 1944; children: Richard, Dorothy, Brenda. BA, Friends U., 1939; BLS, U. Ill., 1941. Head libr. Friends U., Wichita, Kans., 1946-47; head circulation and reference libr., music lectr. Wichita State U., 1959-68; head circulation dept., catalog libr., music lectr. Western Ky. U., Bowling Green, 1968-73; head cataloging dept. U. Kans., Lawrence, 1973-77, libr. archives of recorded sound, 1977-88, emeritus, 1988—; prin. investigator Associated Audio Archives, Washington, 1986-87. Author: Leslie Bassett, A Bio-Bibliography; contbr. articles to Flute Talk, Am. Music Tchr., Coll. Band Dirs. Nat. Assn. jour. Recipient cert. recognition Audio Engring. Soc., 1986; NEH grantee, 1986-87. Mem. AAUP (officer 1959—), Internat. Assn. Sound Archives (chmn. copyright com. 1984—, contbr. phonographic bull. 1986—), Sonneck Soc., Music Libr. Assn., Assn. for Recorded Sound Collections (assoc. audio archives com. 1984-88), Nat. Fedn. Music Clubs, Lawrence Bus. and profl. Women's Club (past pres.), Sigma Alpha Iota. Republican. Unitarian. Home: 3112 Longhorn Dr Lawrence KS 66049-1958

JOHNSON, ELSIE LORRAINE, realtor; b. Cavalier, N.D., Mar. 1, 1929; d. Norman Ervin and Josephine (Staldt) Restemayer; m. Harold Norman Johnson, Sept. 24, 1948 (dec. Apr. 1989); 1 child, Merilynn. Student, Aakers Bus. Coll., Grand Forks, N.D., 1946-47, U. N.D., 1965-76. Sec. Tweet Food Store, East Grand Forks, Minn., 1947; office mgr. Atlantic Commn. Co., Grand Forks, 1947-48; asst. v.p. 1st Bank Grand Forks, Grand Forks, 1951-84; realtor Belmont Realtors, Grand Forks, 1985—; pres. Grand Forks Bd. Realtors, 1993-94. Asst. treas. N.D. State Easter Seal Bd., Bismarck, 1987-93; dir. Grand Forks County Coun. Aging, Grand Forks, 1987-94; mem. United Health Svcs., Grand Forks, 1993-95; treas. PEO, 1991-93; organizer network for women Community Input, 1980; dist. governor Quota Internat., 1977-78. Mem. Grand Forks C. of C., 1985. Republican. Lutheran. Office: Belmont Realtors 2211 S Washington St Grand Forks ND 58201-6345

JOHNSON, EVELYN BRYAN, flying service executive; b. Corbin, Ky., Nov. 4, 1909; d. Edward William and Mayme Estelle (Fox) Stone; grad. Tenn. Wesleyan Jr. Coll., 1929; student U. Tenn., 1930-32; m. Wyatt J. Bryan, Mar. 21, 1931 (dec. 1963); m. 2d, Morgan N. Johnson, Feb. 25, 1965 (dec. 1977). With Morristown (Tenn.) Flying Service, Inc., 1947—, chief flight instr., 1949—, sec.-treas., 1949-62, pres., 1962-82; mgr. Moore Murrell Airport, 1962—. Gov.'s appointee Tenn. Aero. Commn., 1983-86, v. chmn., 1987-89, chmn., 1989—. Recipient Carnegie Hero medal, 1958, Service to Mankind award Morristown Sertoma Club, 1981, Kitty Hawk award FAA, 1991, Friends of Aviation award Tenn. Aviation Assn., 1992, Stewart G. Potter Aviation Edn. award Aviation Distbrs. and Mfrs. Assn., 1992, Elder Statesman of Aviation award Nat. Aeronautics Assn., 1993; named Flight Instr. of Yr., Nashville dist., 1973, 79, So. region, 1979, Nat., 1979 (all FAA); Outstanding Alumnus, Tenn. Wesleyan Coll., 1981, Women in Aviation Pioneers Hall of Fame, 1994. Mem. Morristown Area C. of C., Nat. Assn. Flight Instrs. (dir., treas. 1987-89, award 1992), Ninety-Nines, Whirly Girls (plaque 1992), Aircraft Owners and Pilots Assn., CAP, Silver Wings (Woman of Yr. 1981, bd. dirs. 1987—, Carl Fromhagen award 1992, Ninety-Nines Award of Merit 1994). Republican. Baptist. Home: RR 1 Jefferson Cy TN 37760-9801 Office: PO Box 1013 Morristown TN 37816-1013

JOHNSON, FANNIE MIRIAM HARRIS, performing company executive; b. Birmingham, Ala., Sept. 11, 1938; d. Moses and Fannie (Williams) Harris; m. Edward L. Johnson, Feb. 13, 1960; children: Angela Fanita, Danielle Nicole. BA, Johnson C. Smith U., Charlotte, N.C., 1958; MA, UCLA, 1967. Cert. tchr., N.C., Ala., Calif. Tchr. Spanish Dunbar High Sch., Bessemer, Ala., 1959-61; tchr. English/drama Simi Valley (Calif.) Unified Sch. Dist., 1979-82; chief exec. officer Miriam & Co. Performing Arts, Moreno Valley, Calif., 1981—; cons. Boy's Club, San Fernando, Calif., 1975-76; cons., leader YWCA, Girl's Club, Moreno Valley, Calif., 1990—; tutor lit. program Riverside County Libr., Moreno Valley, 1990—. Writer, dir. plays: Family Reunion, 1981, Easterlude, 1982; writer, producer play: Worship Experience in the Arts, 1986; author: You Are Mine, 1970. Asst. sec. Fair Housing Coun., Simi Valley, Calif., 1972; pres. Community Devel., Pacoima, Calif., 1976-77; 2nd v.p. NAACP, Moreno Valley, Calif., 1994—. Recipient Outstanding Svc. award NAACP, San Fernando, 1975, Achievement award City Coun., L.A., 1976, Leadership award Ebony Women, Thousand Oaks, Calif., 1980. Mem. Nat. Pen Women, Writer's Guild Am., Optimist Interant., Delta Sigma Theta (sec. 1970-73, svc. award 1972). Democrat. Methodist. Office: Miriam & Co Performing Arts PO Box 7751 Moreno Valley CA 92552-7751

JOHNSON, FRANCES R., educational assessment administrator, photographer; b. Detroit, June 24, 1926; d. Fritz Loba and Grace Kathleen (Hutchings) Radford; m. Edward Stone Johnson, July 7, 1951; children: Kathleen Kobosh, Gregory Stone, Carl Radford. B in Design, U. Mich., 1948, MA in Edn. Psychology, 1969; BS in Edn., Wayne State U., 1949. Lic. profl. counselor. Art tchr. Detroit Bd. Edn., 1949-52; art tchr. Huron Valley Bd. Edn., Milford, Mich., 1961-71, alternative tchr. in art, 1971-80, guidance counselor, 1980-84; tchr. photography and hypnosis Pima C.C., Green Valley, Ariz., 1985-90; substitute tchr. Livingston County, Mich., 1991—. One-woman shows for photography include Unity Ch., Tuscon, S.W. Savs., Continental, Western Savs., Great Am. Bank, Arizona Bank; exhbns. include Ariz. State Art Show, 1987, Nat. League Am. PEN Women Biennial Competition, Washington, 1988, 92, No. Nat. Art Exhbn., Rhinelander, Wis., 1988, Hill Top Gallery, Nogales, Ariz., 1989, others; also various pvt. collections. Vol. crisis hotline Casa de Esperanza, Green Valley, Ariz., 1987-91; co-tchr. Parents Anonymous Program, Green Valley, 1989-91. Recipient numerous 1st, 2nd, 3d Place and Honorable Mention awards for photography. Mem. NEA (life), ACA, Am. Assn. Med. Hypnoanalysts (assoc.), Mich. Edn. Assn. (life), Mich. Counseling Assn. (legis. mem.), Nat. Bd. Cert. Counselors, Nat. League Am. PEN Women (corr. sec. Sonora br. 1988-91). Home: 7018 Colonial Oaks Waterford MI 48327

JOHNSON, FREDDIE LEE, nurse; b. Oklahoma City, Feb. 17, 1928; d. Fred Crader and Julia Martha Melrose Williams; m. Marion Ernest Johnson, Aug. 23, 1944; children: Freddie Doyle and Eddie Ernest (twins), Judy LaWants Johnson Thompson. ADN, Okla. State U., Oklahoma City, 1973. Nurse registrar Nurse Registry divsn. Okla. State Employment Svc., Oklahoma City, 1969-73; interviewer Okla. State Employment Svc., Oklahoma City, 1973-79, sr. interviewer, 1979-80; profl. pvt. duty nurse. Democrat. Roman Catholic. Home: 2536 Cedar Park Dr Oklahoma City OK 73120

JOHNSON, GERALDINE ESCH, language specialist; b. Steger, Ill., Jan. 5, 1921; d. William John Rutkowski and Estella Anna (Mannel) Pietz; m. Richard William Esch, Oct. 12, 1940 (dec. 1971); children: Janet L. Sohngen, Daryl R., Gary Michael; m. Henry Bernard Johnson, Aug. 23, 1978 (dec. 1988). BSBA, U. Denver, 1955, MA in Edn., 1958, MA in Speech Pathology, 1963; vocat. credential, U. No. Colo., 1978, postgrad.; postgrad., Metropolitan State Coll., U. Colo., Colo. State U., Colo. Sch. of Mines. Cert. speech therapist, Colo.; cert. tchr., Colo. Tchr. music Judith St. John Sch. Music, Denver, 1946-52; tchr. West High Sch., Denver, 1955-61, chmn. bus. edn. dept., 1958-61, reading specialist, 1977-78; speech therapist, founder South Denver Speech Clinic, 1965-71; tchr. Educationally Handicapped Resource Rm., Denver, 1971-74, Diagnostic Ctr., The Belmont Sch., Denver, 1974-77; speech-lang. specialist elem. and jr. high schs., Denver, 1978-86; itinerant speech-lang. specialist various elem. and jr. high schs., Denver, 1978—; ret. Denver Pub. Sch. System, 1986; home lang tchr. Early Childhood Edn., Denver, 1975; mem. Ednl. TV Adv. com., Colo.; sec. Cen. Bus. Edn. Com., Colo; tchr. letter writing clinics, local bus., Denver, 1960—. Former judge Colo. State Speech Festivals; demonstrator, lectr. Speech-Lang. and Learning Disabilities area Colo. Edn. Assn., 1971-73; vol. communications and prereading skills tchr. YMCA. Recipient Spl. Edn. award Denver Pub. Schs., 1986. Mem. Speech-Lang.-Hearing Assn. (cert.), U. Denver Sch. Bus. Alumni Bd., Beta Gamma Sigma, Kappa Delta Pi, Delta Pi Epsilon. Home: 14050 E Linvale Pl # 502 Aurora CO 80014

JOHNSON, GLENDA GREENE, program analyst; b. Crosby, Tex., Aug. 30, 1950; d. Isaiah and Flora Lee (Holmes) Greene; 1 child, Glynn Garnett. BS in Bus. Edn., Prairie View A&M U., 1972; MPA, Tex. So. U., 1980; MA in Polit. Sci, U. Houston, 1994, postgrad., 1990—. Cert. tchr. learning disabled, Tex. Presdl. mgmt. intern NASA Space Shuttle Crew Systems, Houston, 1980-82, jr. program analyst, 1982-86; program analyst NASA Mission Planning/Space Station, Houston, 1986-94; sr. program analyst info. systems NASA-Johnson Space Ctr., Houston, 1994—. V.p. Egret Bay Condominium Assn, Webster, Tex., 1991-94; com. mem. City of Webster, 1993-94; coun. mem. Fed. Women's Program Coun., Houston, 1994—. Mem. Am. Polit. Sci. Assn., Am. Soc. Pub. Adminstrn., NAt. Mgmt. Assn., Clear Lake Bay Area Jack & Jill (sgt.-at-arms 1986-94). Office: NASA Johnson Space Ctr NASA Rd I/PR2 Houston TX 77058

JOHNSON, GLORIA LEE, publisher, writer; b. Fruitland, Idaho, Feb. 16, 1931; d. Clayton Everett and Norma May (Doty) Anderson; m. Robert Lee Johnson, June 28, 1948; children: Randall, Dann, Kim, Brigette, Jauna. Office staff Voght Transfer, Ontario, Oreg., 1946-47; dental asst. Daniels DMD, Ontario, 1948-49; receptionist, asst. Peffley MD, Arco, Idaho, 1960-61; asst., x-ray technician Hodge MD, Blackfoot, Idaho, 1963-64; floral designer Vonnie's Flowers, Newberg, Oreg., 1968-69; mgr. breeding farm, trainer Stature Arabians, Dayton, Oreg., 1969-89; exec., owner Color Photo Ads Inc., Dayton, 1984-89; editor, pub. Kingsong Pubs., Salem, Oreg., 1990—. Charter mem., sec. Snake River Valley Art Assn., Ontario, 1956; chmn. mother's march Crippled Children's Fund., Butte County, Idaho, 1960; sec. Humane Soc., Yamhill County, Oreg., 1974; charter mem., publicity Beauty Pageant, Butte County, 1960. Recipient Cert. Recognition award Blue Book Arabian Industry, 1983. Mem. Oreg. Assn. Christian Writers, Internat. Platform Assn. Office: Kingsong Pubs 3160 Windsor Ave NE Salem OR 97301-1766

JOHNSON, GRACE FLORENCE, accounting educator; b. Jamaica, N.Y., May 4, 1960; d. Stephen S. and Marie J. Pardi. BS in Bus. Adminstr., U. South Fla., 1986, M in Acctg., 1988. CPA, Fla.; CMA. Chief acct. Poynter Inst. for Media Studies, St. Petersburg, Fla., 1983-89; asst. prof. Marietta (Ohio) Coll., 1989—. Author: Information Technology in Accounting Using Pacioli, 1995; contbr. chpts. encyc. Trustee First City Recovery Ctr., Marietta, 1993—. Mem. Inst. Mgmt. Accts. (sec. 1989—, dir. acad. rels.), W.Va. Soc. CPAs, Small Bus. Inst. Dir.'s Assn. (editor newsletter 1994—). Office: Marietta Coll Dept Econ Mgmt & Acctg Marietta OH 45750

JOHNSON, GWENAVERE ANELISA, artist; b. Newark, S.D., Oct. 16, 1909; d. Arthur E. and Susie Ellen (King) Nelson; m. John Wendell Johnson, Dec. 17, 1937; 1 child, John Forrest. Student, Mpsl. Sch. Art, 1930; BA, U. Minn., 1937; MA, San Jose State U., 1957. Cert. gen. elem., secondary, art tchr., Calif. Art tchr., supr. Austin (Minn.) Schs., 1937-38; art tchr. Hillbrook Sch., Los Gatos, Calif., 1947-52; art tchr., supr. Santa Clara (Calif.) Pub. Schs., 1952-55; art tchr., dept. chmn. San Jose (Calif.) Unified Schs., 1955-75; owner Tree Tops studio, San Jose, 1975—. Juried shows: Los Gatos Art Assn., 1976-79, 85-88, Artist of Yr., 1988 (1st and 2d awards), 83, 84 (Best of Show awards), Treeside gallery, 1991, Los Gatos, 1980, 81 (1st awards); Livermore Art Assn., 1977 (2d award), Los Gatos Art Mus., 1981 (1st award), 82 (2d award), 91 (best of show award), Rosicrucean Mus., 1983, Centre d'Art Contemporian, Paris, 1983; creator Overfelt portrait Alexian Bros. Hosp., San Jose, Calif., 1977; exhibited in group shows ann. Garden Art Show, 1981-95, Triton Art Mus., 1983-95. Recipient Golden Centaur award Acad. Italia, 1982, Golden Album of prize winning Artists, 1984, Golden Flame award Academia Italia, 1986, others. Mem. San Jose Art League, Los Gatos Art Assn. (Artist of Yr. 1988, 2d, 3d awards), Santa Clara Art Assn. (Artist of Yr. 1983, 3 First awards 1989, 2d award in spl. merit achiever's exhbn. 1992, 3 First awards in merit achiever's exhbn. 1993), Soc. Western Artists, Nat. League Am. Penwomen (corr. sec., Merit Achiever award), Los gatos Art Assn., Santa Clara Art Assn., San Jose Art League. Home and Office: 2054 Booksin Ave San Jose CA 95125-4909

JOHNSON, GWENDOLYN ALBERTA, artist, educator; b. Knoxville, Tenn., July 15, 1950; d. Clifford Rubin and Frajan (McGowan) Campbell; m. James W. Johnson, May 28, 1983 (div.). BS in Art and Edn., Tenn. State U., 1973; postgrad., U. Tenn., 1976. Artist-in-residence Dept. Def. Schs., Ludwigsburg, Germany, 1976-77; freelance artist Houghton Mifflin Co., Boston, 1979-83; co-owner, mgr. Johnson & Campbell, photography and mktg. co., Knoxville, 1982—; tchr. art mid. sch. Knox County Schs., Knoxville, 1990—; coord. outreach program Dulin Gallery Art, Knoxville, 1980-81, cons., 1990-91; cons. Knoxville Mus. Art, 1992-94, Pellissippi State U., Knoxville, 1992-93, Children's Mus., Knoxville, 1993—. One-woman shows include Oak Ridge Art Ctr., Beck Culter Ctr.; exhibited in group shows at Ebony Imagery II, 1989, Nat. Urban League, 1990, Knoxville Mus. Art, 1991, Pellissippi State U., 1992, Martin Luther King Exhibits, 1992, Malcolm X Exhibits, 1992, Oil Pastel Assn. United Pastels Am., 1992, Huntington Mus. Art, 1992, SAF/NEH, 1992, N.Y. 96th Annual Art Club, 1992, 27th Annual Wyo. Art Show, 1992, Children's Mus., 1993, Road Ctr., 1993, Annual Tenn. Valley Women's Conf., 1993, Assn. for Visual Artists, 1993, Ctrl. South Art Exhibit, 1993, Ebony Imagery IV, 1994; represented in permanent collections at Oak Ridge Art Ctr. Bd. dirs. Kuumba Festival, Knoxville, 1993—, YWCA, Knoxville, 1994—; artist-in-residence Shades of Hope, Knoxville, 1994. Recipient Women in the Art award, 1980, Art for the Blind award, 1980, Recognition award Knoxville Art Festival, 1981, Kuumba award Appalachian Art Soc., 1991, Best of Show award Ebony and Imagery III, 1992, Collector's Choice award Savannah Nat., 1993, Faces of My People award YWCA, 1994. Mem. Oil Pastel Assn., United Pastel Soc. Am., Pastel Soc., Assn. for Visual Arts, Nat. Women Assn. Women in Arts, N.Y. Art Club. Home and Studio: 2344 Washington Ave Knoxville TN 37917-6958

JOHNSON, HEIDI SMITH, science educator; b. Mpls., June 1, 1946; d. Russell Ward and Eva Ninette (Holmquist) Smith; m. Alan C. Sweeney, Dec. 21, 1968 (div. 1977); m. Robert Allen Johnson, July 17, 1981. BA, U. Calif., Riverside, 1969; MA, No. Ariz. U., 1992. Park ranger U.S. Nat. Parks Svc., Pinnacles Nat. Monument, 1972-73; aide Petrified Forest Mus. Assn., Ariz., 1973-75; dispatcher police dept. U. Ariz., Tucson, 1975-76; communications operator II dept. ops. City of Tucson, 1976-78; dispatcher Tucson Police Dept., 1978-82, communications supr., 1982-85, communications coord., 1985; substitute tchr. Bisbee (Ariz.) Pub. Schs., 1985-91; instr. English Cochise Community Coll., Douglas, Ariz., 1990-92; tchr. English/creative writing Bisbee H.S., 1992-93; tchr. phys. sci. and geology Lowell Mid. Sch., Bisbee, 1993—; GEd tchr. Cochise County Jail, 1988-89; owner Johnson's Antiques and Books, Bisbee, 1990—. Assoc. editor Ariz. Fossil Record. Trustee Bisbee Coun. on Arts and Humanities, 1986-88; pres. Cooper Queen Libr. Bd., Bisbee, 1988-91; book sales chmn. Shattuck Libr., Bisbee Mining Mus., 1987-92. Mem. Mid-Am. Paleontol. Soc., N.Mex. Geol. Soc., Ariz. Geol. Soc., Paleontol. Soc. So. Ariz., So. Calif. Paleontol. Soc. Roman Catholic. Home: PO Box 1221 Bisbee AZ 85603-2221

JOHNSON, ISCEOLA ACQUILLA WINBUSH, educational program specialist; b. Baton Rouge, Feb. 10; d. William Ward and Clementine (Johnson) W.; m. Samuel M. Johnson, Dec. 24, 1943; 1 child, Colette Acquilla Johnson Norman. BS, Southern U., 1946, BA, 1948, MEd, 1961. Cert. tchr., Calif.; cert. tchr., adminstr., La. Tchr. Feliciana Parish Sch., St. Francisville, La., 1944-46; tchr. East Baton Rouge Parish, 1946-56, supervising tchr., 1956-85; supr., program specialist Ravenswood Sch. Dist., Palo Alto, Calif., 1985—; pvt. cons., Foster City, Calif., 1987—; cons. Dept. Edn., Baton Rouge, 1983-85. Author: Where the Mississippi Flows by Unnoticed, 1977, Combatting Teen-age Pregnancy, 1986, (handbook) Reaching for Distant Hills. V.p. Y.W.C.A., Baton Rouge, 1980-84; supr. 4-H Club, Baton Rouge, 1960-80; collector March of Dimes, ARC, Baton Rouge, 1960-84; leader Community Svcs./Homeless and Children, East Palo Alto, 1987—. Named Christian Woman of Yr., Allen Chapel, 1983, Outstanding Community worker Alpha Kappa Alpha Sorority, 1991, Outstanding educator East Baton Rouge Sch. System, 1982; recipient Recognition Svc. award Hammond, La. chpt. Delta Sigma Theta, 1980. Mem. NAFE, Les Professionals (founder, pres. 1980-85), Top Ladies of Distinction, Interfaith Ministers' Wives (v.p. 1993), Ministers' Wives (pres. 1990-93), Alpha Kappa Alpha, Delta Kappa Gamma Internat. (v.p. 1990). Home: 902 Beach Park Blvd # 136 Foster City CA 94404

JOHNSON, JACQUELINE DOLORES, community health nurse; b. N.Y.C., Apr. 28, 1948; d. Thomas Frank and Geraldine Louise (Riddick) J. BSN, L.I. U., 1974; MPH, Johns Hopkins U., 1985. RN, N.Y.; cert. community health nurse, ANCC. Pub. health nursing supr. Vis. Nurse Assn. N.Y., N.Y.C., 1974-76; commd. U.S. Army, 1976, advanced through grades to lt. col., 1988; med./surg. nurse Brooke Army Med. Ctr., Ft. Sam Houston, Tex., 1976, community health nurse, 1976-78; chief preventive medicine U.S. Army Med. Dept. Activity, Aberdeen Proving Ground, Md., 1979-80; community health nurse U.S. Army Med. Dept. Activity, Ft. Irwin, Calif., 1980-81, Ft. Irwin, 1981-82, Ft. Belvoir, Va., 1982-84; dir. preventive medicine U.S. Army Med. Dept. Activity, Ft. Drum, N.Y., 1988-92; chief community health nurse Med. Dept. Activity, Ft. Carson, Colo., 1992-93; chief pub. health and safety dept. U.S. Med. Dept. Activity, Ft. Carson, Colo., 1993—; mem. minority human immunodeficiency virus adv. group Office of Surgeon Gen., Washington, 1990—. Mem. ANA, APHA. Office: Pub Health & Safety Dept US Army MEDDAC Fort Carson CO 80913

JOHNSON, JACQUELINE JAY, nurse; b. Granite Falls, Minn., Jan. 29, 1964; d. Paul Marvin and Jane Ellen (Arnold) J. BA in Nursing, Luther Coll., 1986; MA in Mgmt., St. Mary's Grad. Sch., 1993. RN, Minn. Staff nurse Mayo Med. Ctr., Rochester, Minn., 1986-93, nurse mgr., 1993—; exch.

nurse Mayo Jacksonville, Mayo Med. Ctr., Rochester, 1988-89, Mayo Scottsdale, 1992. Howard Winholz mgmt. scholar Mayo Med. Ctr., 1991. Mem. Am. Assn. Critical Care Nurses (Rochester chpt.), Minn. Nurses Assn., Dist. F Coun. Nurse Mgrs. Home: 822 9th St SE Rochester MN 55904-7304 Office: Mayo Med Ctr-RMH 201 W Center St Rochester MN 55902-3003

JOHNSON, JAMIESON DREGALLO, women's athletics director; b. June 24, 1951; d. Frank and Phyllis Arlene (Griffiths) Dregallo; m. Stephen B. Johnson; children: Lindsay Benedict, Christopher Sheldon. BA with honors, Lindenwood Coll., St. Charles, Mo., 1973; M Sport Sci., U.S. Sports Acad., Mobile, Ala., 1987. Cert. life K-12 health and phys. edn. tchr., Mo. Tchr. phys. edn. Berkeley Sch. Dist., St. Louis, 1973-77; asst. to headmaster for girls activities Casady Sch., Oklahoma City, 1977-81; dir. women's sports Tex. Mil. Acad., San Antonio, 1981-82; varsity coach, dormitory head Berkshire Sch., Sheffield, Mass., 1982-86; dir. fitness Danbury Health Racquetball Club, Bethel, Conn., 1987-88; dir. women's athletics Greens Farms (Conn.) Acad., 1988—; personal trainer, Greens Farms, 1987—. Mem. Am. Coll. Sports Medicine (cert. fitness instr.), Am. Coun. Exercise, Fairchester Athletic Assn. (sec., treas. 1992—). Episcopalian. Home: 26 Penfield Pl Bridgeport CT 06605 Office: Greens Farms Acad 35 Beachside Ave Greens Farms CT 06436

JOHNSON, JAN KINSLEY, artist; b. South Paris, Maine, Apr. 14, 1929; d. Chester C. and Ruth Sawin (Holt) Kinsley; m. Richard E. Johnson, Feb. 3, 1951. Grad., Sch. of Mus. of Fine Arts, Boston, 1981, 5th yr. cert., 1982; BFA, Tufts U., 1986. Artist Harwich, Mass., 1977—. One woman shows include Harvard Law Sch., Cambridge, Mass., 1984, Higgins Gallery, Cape Cod C.C., Barnstable, Mass., 1990; exhibited in group shows at Berkshire Mus., Pittsfield, Mass., 1982, Copley Soc., Boston, 1988. Recipient Drawing award Cape Cod Conservatory, 1973. Mem. Women's Caucus for Art. Home: 151 Belmont Rd West Harwich MA 02671

JOHNSON, JANE DRENNAN, sculptor, interior designer; b. L.A., May 21, 1940; d. Harold Perry and Evelyn Isabel (Chivers) Drennan; m. Kenneth Frank Johnson, June 11, 1961; children: Erik Allan, Mark Drennan. BA with honors, U. Calif., Berkeley, 1962; postgrad., Coll. Marin, 1990—, Calif. Coll. Arts & Crafts, 1991. Cert. interior designer, Calif. Tchr. singing and guitar Orinda (Calif.) Community Ctr., 1973-83; solo musician pvt. parties, fundraisers, convalescent homes, 1973-85; mgr. bus. office Interior Design Showroom/Galleria Design Ctr., San Francisco, 1979-87; owner Jane D. Johnson, Interiors, Orinda, 1987—, Jane D. Johnson, Sculpture, Orinda, 1989—. Exhbns. include SOMAR Gallery, San Francisco, 1992, Coll. of Marin Art Gallery, Kentfield, Calif., 1992, San Francisco Women Artists Gallery, San Francisco, 1992, 93, Berkeley (Calif.) Art Ctr. Assn. Gallery, 1993, Bedford Gallery, Walnut Creek, Calif., 1994, Internat. Sculpture Ctr. Biennial Sculpture Conv., San Francisco, 1994, many others. Vol. Alta Bates Hosp., Berkeley, 1979; active Orinda Art Assn., 1975-79. Nat. Home Fashions League, San Francisco, 1987, San Francisco Women Artists, 1991-93, San Francisco Mus. Modern Art, 1990—, Oakland Mus., 1991—, De Young & Asian Mus., San Francisco, 1990—. Mem. Internat. Sculpture Ctr., Calif. Coun. for Interior Design Cert., U. Calif. Berkeley Alumni Assn. (life), U. Calif. Berkeley Coll. Environ. Design Alumni Assn. (charter), Marin Arts Coun., Nat. Mus. Women in Arts. Democrat. Presbyterian. Home: 134 Orchard Rd Orinda CA 94563-3831

JOHNSON, JANE OLIVER, artist; b. Fresno, Calif., Jan. 3, 1929; d. Evan Donaca Oliver and Adaline Dorinda (Nelson) Edwards; m. Vernon Reddinger Allen, Aug. 11, 1946 (div. 1963); children: Lue Elizabeth, Mark Laroy, Stuart Vernon; m. Loren Theodore Johnson, Mar. 8, 1981. Student, Fresno City Coll., 1952-55, Fresno State, 1955-60, Hayward State Coll., 1965-70. Tech. artist Hughes, Northrup, Lockheed, Magnavox, L.A., 1972-84; artist Neighborhood Gallery, L.A., 1976-80. Works exhibited at Beyond Baroque, San Jose Mission, Tribal Treas., Calico Gallery. Mem. state ctrl. com. Calif. Dem. Party, 1993—; active 34th Assembly Dist. Exec. Bd., 1993—; elected San Bernardino County Dem. Ctrl. Com., 1994—. Mem. High Desert Cultural Arts, Bus. and Profl. Women (sec. 1980), Hesperia Dem. Club (mem. environ. women's caucus 1993—, pres. 1994), Mus. Contemporary Art (L.A.), Sierra Club. Home: PO Box 1323 Lucerne Valley CA 92356-1323

JOHNSON, JANE PENELOPE, freelance writer; b. Danville, Ky., July 1, 1940; d. Buford Lee Carr and Emma Irene (Coldiron) Sebastian; m. William Evan Johnson, July 15, 1958; children: William Evan Jr., Robert Anthony. Grad., Famous Writer's Sch. Fiction, Westport, Conn., 1967; grad. writer's div., Newspaper Inst. Am., N.Y.C., 1969; LittD (hon.), The London Inst. Applied Rsch., 1993. Freelance writer Lexington, Ky., 1969—. Contbr. poetry to Worldwide Poetry Anthologies; contbr. articles to mags. Patron Menninger. Ennobled by Prince John, The Duke of Avram, Tasmania, Australia; semifinalist N.Am. Poetry Open; recipient 2 Editor's Choice awards for poetry Nat. Libr. of Poetry, 1994. Mem. NAFE, Smithsonian Assocs., Peale Ctr. for Christian Living, Sweet Adelines, Internat. Soc. Poets (life, advisor), Internat. Platform Assn., Nat. Writer's Club. Democrat. Office: PO Box 8013 Lexington KY 40504

JOHNSON, JANE TRUESDALL, artist; b. Lakewood, Ohio, June 4, 1943; d. James and Alice (Kilner) Truesdall; m. James Moore Johnson, Aug. 28, 1965 (div. 1974); children: Peter Turley, Jesse Denny. AA, Briarcliff Coll., 1963; BA, Rollins Coll., 1965; postgrad., Corcoran Sch. Art, 1980-86. One person shows include Galleria Beretich, Claremont, Calif., 1993, McNair Gallery, Telluride, Colo., 1993-94, Mahler Gallery, Washington, 1994; pub. catalog of paintings; contbr. photographs and articles to mags. and newspapers. Founder, organizer Tough Love Parent Group, Washington, 1989; head fundraising auction Sheridan Sch., Washington, 1983; auction asst. Sidwell Friend's Sch., Washington, 1976-78; vol. Source Theater, Washington, 1988-89. Recipient Drawing award Art League of Alexandria, 1987. Mem. Artists Equity, Arlington Arts Ctr., A Salon Artist Coop., Washington Project for the Arts. Office: Jackson Sch Arts Ctr R St and Avon Pl NW Washington DC 20007

JOHNSON, JANET A., law educator, academic dean; b. Bridgewater, Iowa, Mar. 10, 1940; d. Leland Russell and Viola Lydia (Pfundheller) Taylor; m. Kenneth L. Johnson, Jan. 8, 1960 (div. 1981); children: Rodger (dec.), Sheri; m. Burton M. Leiser, Aug. 12, 1984; stepchildren: Shoshana, Illana, Phillip. AB U. Ill.-Chgo., 1968; JD Drake U., 1972; LLM U. Va., 1984. Bar: Iowa 1972. Cts. specialist Iowa Crime Commn., 1972-73; asst. prof. Law Sch., Drake U., Des Moines, 1973-75, assoc. prof., 1975-77, prof., 1977-78; assoc. judge Iowa Ct. Appeals, Des Moines, 1978-83; dean Sch. Law, Pace U., White Plains, N.Y., 1983-89, prof., 1989—; mem. Grievance Com. N. Jud. Dist., State N.Y., 1989-93, chairperson 1994—; mem. Local Conditional Release Commr., Westchester County, 1989—; mem. Iowa Bd. of Parole, 1975-78. Contbr. articles to legal publs. Vice chmn. adv. com. State Corrections Master Plan, 1977-78; bd. mem. Iowa Civil Liberties Union, 1974-76. Mem. ABA, Iowa Bar Assn., Assn. Bar City N.Y., Westchester Women's Bar Assn., Westchester County Bar Assn. Office: Pace U Sch Law 78 N Broadway White Plains NY 10603-3710

JOHNSON, JANET B., state legislator; b. Mar. 5, 1940; m. Dennis Johnson; 3 children. Student, U. Minn. Owner small bus.; mem. Minn. Senate. Mem. Democratic Farm Labor Party. Lutheran. Office: Minn State Senate State Capital Saint Paul MN 55155*

JOHNSON, JANET DROKE, legal secretary; b. Bristol, Tenn., Feb. 26, 1961; d. Jimmie D. and Nancy Belle (Sluder) Droke; m. Danny Ray Wilson, June 17, 1978 (div. May 26, 1986); children: Leslie Ann, Laurie Elizabeth; m. Edwin Keith Johnson, June 26, 1987. AA, East Tenn. State U., 1980; student, Milligan Coll., Johnson City, Tenn., 1988-89. With Sullivan County Election Commn., Blountville, Tenn., 1978; sec. Kelly svcs., Blountville, 1978-80; legal sec. Boarman & Vaughn, Johnson City, 1980-84; legal asst. Bob McD. Green and Assocs., Johnson City, 1985-89; fed. judicial sec. to U.S. cir. judge U.S. ct. Appeals, 4th Cir., Abingdon, Va., 1989—; mem. adv. bd. Legal Assistant Program, Milligan Coll., Johnson City, 1988-89. Asst. ch. clk. Bluff City Bapt. Ch., 1994—. Mem. ABA (assoc.) Tenn. Paralegal Assn. (treas. 1989, pub. rels. dir. 1990), Fed. Judicial Secs. Assn., Res. Officers Assn. Ladies Club. Republican. Home: PO Box 727 Bluff City TN 37618-0727 Office: US Court of Appeals 4th Cir PO Box 868 Abingdon VA 24212-0868

JOHNSON, JANET GRAY ANDREWS, clinical social worker; b. Raleigh, N.C., Jan. 14, 1956; d. Junius Jackson and Alma Gray (Goff) Andrews; m. Charles Lavon Johnson, Jr., June 23, 1990. BSW, N.C. State U., 1978; MSW, U. N.C., 1980; MBA, Meredith Coll., Raleigh, 1987. Diplomate clin. social work; cert. clin. social worker, N.C.; cert. Acad. Cert. Social Workers. Social worker Johnston County Dept. Social Svc., Smithfield, N.C., 1980-81; clin. social worker Johnston County Mental Health, Smithfield, 1981-84; clin. social worker Holly Hill Hosp., Raleigh, 1984-87, geriatric program coord., 1987-90, adult clin. svcs. coord., 1990-91; dir. adult program Coastal Plain Hosp., Rocky Mount, N.C., 1991-93; clin. case mgr. Value Behavioral Health, Research Triangle Park, N.C., 1993-94; social work clin. specialist Dorothea Dix Hosp., Raleigh, N.C., 1994—; chair geriatric adv. bd. Holly Hill Hosp., 1989-91; bd. dirs. Johnston County Coun. on Aging, Smithfield, 1982-84; founder/facilitator Johnston County Alzheimers's Family Support Group, Smithfield, 1982-84. Recipient humanitarian awards. Mem. NASW (bd. dirs. N.C. chpt. 1990-94, chair eastern dist. 1991-94, co-chair Wake County chpt. 1990-91, Social Worker of Yr. award N.C. chpt. 1992). Office: Dorothea Dix Hosp 820 S Boylan Ave Raleigh NC 27603

JOHNSON, JANET HELEN, Egyptology educator; b. Everett, Wash., Dec. 24, 1944; d. Robert A. and Jane N. (Osborn) J.; m. Donald S. Whitcomb, Sept. 2, 1978; children: J.J., Felicia. BA, U. Chgo., 1967, PhD, 1972. Instr. Egyptology U. Chgo., 1971-72, asst. prof., 1972-79, assoc. prof., 1979-81, prof., 1981—; dir. Oriental Inst., 1983-89; research assoc. dept. anthropology Field Mus. of Natural History, 1980-84, 94—. Author: Demotic Verbal System, 1977, Thus Wrote Onchsheshonqy, 1986, 2d revised edit., 1991, (with Donald Whitcomb) Quseir al-Qadim, 1978, 80; editor: (with E.F. Wente) Studies in Honor of G.R. Hughes, 1977, Life in a Multi-Cultural Society, 1992. Smithsonian Instn. grantee, 1977-83; NEH grantee, 1978-81, 81-85; Nat. Geog. Soc. grantee, 1978, 80, 82. Mem. Am. Rsch. Ctr. in Egypt (bd. govs. 1979—, exec. com. 1984-87, 90—, v.p. 1990-93, pres. 1993—). Office: U Chgo Oriental Inst 1155 E 58th St Chicago IL 60637-1540

JOHNSON, JANET LOU, real estate executive; b. Boston, Aug. 22, 1939; d. Donald Murdoch and Helen Margaret (Slauenwhite) Campbell; m. Walter R. Johnson, Mar. 31, 1962; children—Meryl Ann, Leah Kathryn, Christa Helen. Student Boston U., 1959, Gordon Coll., Hamilton, Mass., 1962-64. Administr., account exec. Fuller/Smith & Ross, Boston, 1958-63; adminstr. Walter R. Johnson, P.E., Gloucester, 1970-76; broker Realty World, Gloucester, 1976-77, Hunneman & Co., Gloucester, 1977-79; pres., owner Janet L. Johnson Real Estate, Gloucester, 1979—. Mem. Mass. Assn. Realtors (bd. dirs. 1985-87), Nat. Assn. Realtors, Cape Ann C. of C., Cape Ann Bd. Realtors (pres. 1984-85, state dir. 1985-86), Greater Salem Bd. Realtors. Home: 35 Norseman Ave Gloucester MA 01930-1026 Office: Janet L Johnson Real Estate 79 Rocky Neck Ave Gloucester MA 01930-4180

JOHNSON, JEAN ELAINE, nursing educator; b. Wilsey, Kans., Mar. 11, 1925; d. William H. and Rosa L. (Welty) Irwin. B.S., Kans. State U., 1948; M.S. in Nursing, Yale U., 1965; M.S., U. Wis., 1969, Ph.D., 1971. Instr. nursing Iowa, Kans. and Colo., 1948-58; staff nurse Swedish Hosp., Englewood, Colo., 1958-60; in-svc. edn. coord. Gen. Rose Hosp., Denver, 1960-63; rsch. asst. Yale U., New Haven, 1965-67; assoc. prof. nursing Wayne State U., Detroit, 1971-74, prof., 1974-79; dir. Ctr. for Health Rsch., 1974-79; assoc. dir. oncology nursing Cancer Ctr. U. Rochester, N.Y., 1979-93; prof. nursing U. Rochester, 1979—; Rosenstadt prof. health rsch. Faculty Nursing U. Toronto, 1985. Contbg. author: Handbook of Psychology and Health, vol. 5, 1984; contbr. articles to profl. jours. Recipient Bd. Govs. Faculty Recognition award Wayne State U., 1975, award for disting. contbn. to nursing sci. Am. Nurses Found. and ANA Coun. for Nurse Rschrs., 1983, Grad. Teaching award U. Rochester, 1991, Disting. Rschr. award Oncology Nursing Soc., 1992, Outstanding Contbns. to Nursing and Psychology award divsn. of health psychology APA, 1993; NIH grantee, 1972-95. Fellow AAAS, APA (Outstanding Contbns. to Nursing and Psychology award 1993), Acad. for Behavioral Medicine Rsch., Am. Psychol. Soc.; mem. ANA (chmn. coun. for nurse rschrs. 1976-78, commn. for rsch. 1978-82), Inst. Medicine NAS (com. on patient injury compensation 1976-77, membership com. 1981-86, gov. coun. 1987-89), Sigma Xi, Omicron Nu, Phi Kappa Phi. Home: 1412 East Ave Rochester NY 14610-1619 Office: U Rochester Sch of Nursing 601 Elmwood Ave Rochester NY 14642-0001

JOHNSON, JEAN URBATI, school librarian; b. Somerville, Mass., June 25, 1931; d. James Theodore and Mary Imelda (Manning) Urbati; children: Kathryn Mary, Jill Ann. BE, U. Conn., 1953; postgrad., So. Conn. State Coll., 1965-69. Cert. media specialist, libr. Sch. libr. Calvin Leete Sch., Guilford, Conn., 1968—; tchr. Higher Order Thinking Skills Calvin Leete Sch., Guilford, 1992—. Named Outstanding Elem. Tchr. Am., 1975. Mem. NEA, Conn. Edn. Assn., Conn. Ednl. Media Assn., So. Conn. Reading Coun., Guilford Edn. Assn., Phi Mu (life, treas. 1952-53). Republican. Roman Catholic. Office: Calvin Leete Sch S Union St Guilford CT 06437

JOHNSON, JEANNE MARIE, nurse psychotherapist, clinical nurse specialist; b. N.Y.C.; d. Hector J. and Jean (Bershacht) Streyckmans; 1 child, Robert M. AAS, Queens Coll., 1963; BSN, Adelphi U., 1967, MSN, 1973; postgrad., Karen Horney Inst., N.Y.C., 1981-82. Cert. clin. nurse specialist. Pub. health nurse Nassau County Dept. Health, Mineola, N.Y., 1963-69; instr. nursing Molloy Coll., Rockville Centre, N.Y., 1977-78; cmty. mental health nurse, psychotherapist Cmty. Mental Health Ctr. Nassau County, Westchester County, N.Y., 1969-89; nurse psychotherapist Cen. Nassau Guidance and Counseling Svc., Inc., Hicksville, N.Y., 1990-91; geriatric psychotherapist New Hope Guild, 1989; pvt. practice as nurse/psychotherapist, 1988—; substitute sch. nurse Wantagh Sch. Dist., 1991—, Bethpage Sch. Dist., 1995—; disaster team nurse ARC, 1979—. Mem. ANA, N.Y. State Nurses Assn., Network of Clin. Nurse Specialists, Sigma Theta Tau. Home: 112 Hawthorn St Massapequa Park NY 11762-2001

JOHNSON, JENNIE, chaplain, social worker; b. Houston, Sept. 18, 1952; d. James L.C. and Marilyn Mildred (Frazier) J. BS in Social Work, Tex. Woman's U., 1976; postgrad., Bishop's Sch. of Theology, Denver, 1979-80, Samaritan Theol. Sem., L.A., 1982-84, Episcopal Theol. Sem., Austin, Tex., 1986-87. Cert. social worker, Tex. Comdr. 94th Ord. Det. USAR, Ft. Carson, Colo., 1978-80; evaluator 1st maneuver tng. command USAR, Denver, 1980-81; prodn. control planner Elmo Semiconducter, L.A., 1981-83; quality control planner TRW Def. and Space Guidance, L.A., 1983-84; dir. chpt. svcs. Greater Amarillo (Tex.) Red Cross, 1985-86; chaplain Austin State Hosp., 1987-88, Brackenridge Hosp., Austin, 1988-91, Hospice Austin, 1992—; conveener Integrity Austin, 1989-90, 92-94; presenter conf. Nat. Episcopal AIDS Coalition, Cin., 1990, mem., 1990—. Founding bd. dirs. Out Youth Austin/YWCA, 1990-92; mem. Tex. AIDS Network, Austin, 1992—; foster parent Casey Family Program, Austin, 1992—; diocesan del. St. Michael's Episcopal Ch., Austin, 1988—, vestry/jr. warden, 1993-95; mem.-at-large Women for Social Witness Network, Nat. Episcopal Ch., 1992—; mem. Episcopal Womens Caucus, 1992—, Tex. Hospice Orgn., 1992—, presenter state conf., 1995, Order of St. Luke the Physician, 1984—. 1st lt. U.S. Army, 1975-80. Democrat. Office: Hospice Austin 3710 Cedar St Austin TX 78705

JOHNSON, JERMICKO SHOSHANAH, fashion designer; b. Chgo., Aug. 20, 1954; d. Albert Johnson and Teary Watson-Johnson. Student, Art Inst. Chgo., 1972, U. Chgo., 1972; cert., Cosmopolitan Sch. Bus., 1973. Designer apprentice Stanley Korshak, Chgo., 1971; with Eucos, Inc., Evanston, Ill., 1972-73, Fureal, Ltd., Skokie, Ill., 1973-74; tchr. Chgo State U., 1974-75; fashion designer, coordinator Pier 1 Imports, Ft. Worth, 1975-77; designer Revere Sportswear, Chgo., 1977-79; pres. Jermicko Shoshanah Johnson Originals, Chgo., 1979—, JJ Hobeau Inc., Chgo., 1987—; founder adult edn. fashion design program Olive-Harvey Coll., Chgo. State U.; faculty adviser Acad. Fashion and Merchandising, 1981, Ray Vogue Sch. Fashion Design, 1982, instr., 1979-87; fashion designer HJ, Inc., 1979-82; mem., com. chmn. for art, entertainment, and media mgmt. Columbia Coll., Chgo. Active Girl Scouts U.S. Chgo. Pub. Sch. Art Soc.-Sch. Art Inst. grantee, 1971; Stanley Korshak grantee, 1971, Oscar Arronson grantee, 1970. Mem. Chgo. Fashion Group Guild, Chgo. Fashion Exchange, League of Black Women, Fashion Group. Jewish. Office: 1229 N Northbranch 3208 N Clifton Chicago IL 60657

JOHNSON, JETSIE WHITE, nurse, consultant; b. Newport News, Va., Apr. 7, 1944; d. Breavoid Milton and Jetsie (Johnson) White; m. Henry Johnson Jr., Feb. 24, 1963; children: Cheryl Johnson Holmes, Henry Breavoid, Daryl Jay, Shamala Michelle. AAS magna cum laude, Thomas Nelson Community Coll., Hampton, Va., 1974; BS, Hampton U., 1985, MSN, 1987. RN, Va.; cert. family nurse practitioner, psychiat. clin. nurse specialist. Staff nurse Hampton Gen. Hosp., 1974-77; nurse practitioner Alvin Bryant, M.D., Hampton, 1978-80, VA Med. Ctr., Hampton, 1980-81; staff nurse VA Med. Ctr., Richmond, Va., 1983-84; nurse practitioner Naval Regional Med. Ctr., Norfolk, Va., 1981-82; nurse supr. Commonwealth Health Care, Hampton, 1982—; staff nurse Med. Coll. of Va., Richmond, 1988; nurse practitioner Ea. State Hosp., Williamsburg, Va., 1984-91; preceptor Old Dominion U., Norfolk, 1981-82, Hampton U., 1988-89; hon. instr. nurse practitioner program Med. Coll. of Va., 1979-80; cons. Alvin Bryant, M.D., 1981-91; mem. adv. coun. Hampton U. Nursing Ctr., 1989-90; pres. Minority Cancer Task Force, Hampton, 1989-92; corr. sec. Dept. Mental Health/Mental Retardation and Substance Abuse Svcs. Nurse Practitioner Practice Group, 1989-91. Co-leader Girl Scouts U.S., Hampton, 1985-86; v.p. La Progressive Ten, Hampton, 1982; pres. Young Profls. of Tidewater, Hampton, 1980-81. Recipient Cert. of Appreciation, Minority Cancer Task Force, 1985; NIMH Tng. grantee Dept. HHS, 1985, 86. Mem. Va. Coun. Nurse Practitioners, Phi Theta Kappa, Sigma Theta Tau. Democrat. Home: 66 Santa Barbara Dr Hampton VA 23666-1638

JOHNSON, JO ANN, nursing educator; b. Orlando, Fla., May 31, 1938; d. Joe Wynne and Posy (Edwards) Prichard; m. David L. Johnson, Aug. 3, 1963; children: Leslie Ann, David Wynne. BSN, Vanderbilt U., 1960; MA, Columbia U., 1962; MPA, U. So. Calif., 1972, D of Pub. Adminstrn., 1973. Pub. health nurse County of Orange, Fla., 1960-61; instr. nursing U. Va., 1962-64; asst. prof. nursing Calif. State U., L.A., 1965-75, assoc. prof. nursing, from 1975, now full prof. nursing, now chmn. dept. nursing, 1987—. HEW spl. fellow U. So. Calif., 1972. Office: Calif State U-LA Dept Nursing 5151 State University Dr Los Angeles CA 90032-4221

JOHNSON, JOAN, state senator; b. Denver, Oct. 4, 1943. BA, U. Colo., 1965. Mem. state senate dist. 24; pub. rels. cons., writer Creative Assocs. Unltd., Englewood, Colo.; Mem. Colo. Adv. Com. on Intergovtl. Rels., Gov.'s AIDS Coun. Mem. Nat. Fedn. Press Women (Nat. Comm. award), Colo. Press Women (State Comm. award), Westminster Newcomers Club, Colo. Press Assn. (assoc.), Colo. Broadcasters (assoc.); bd. trustees Adams County Libr. Roman Catholic. Democrat. Office: Senate House State Capitol Denver CO 80203*

JOHNSON, JOAN BRAY, insurance company consultant; b. Kennett, Mo., Nov. 19, 1926; d. Ples Green and Mary Scott (Williams) Bray; m. Frank Johnson Jr., Nov. 6, 1955; 1 child, Victor Kent. Student, Drury Coll., 1949-51, Cen. Bible Inst. and Coll., 1946-49. Staff writer Gospel Pub. Co., Springfield, Mo., 1949-51; sec. Kennett Sch. Dist. Bd. Edn., 1951-58; spl. features corr. Memphis Press-Scimitar, 1959-60; sec. to v.p. Cotton Exchange Bank, Kennett, Mo., 1959-60; proposal analyst Aetna Life Ins. Co., El Paso, Tex., 1960-64, pension adminstr., 1964-71; office mgr. Brokerage div. Aetna Life Ins. Co., Denver, 1971-78; office adminstr. Life Consol. div. Aetna Life Ins. Co., Oakland, Calif., 1979-82; office adminstr. PFSD div. Aetna Life Ins. Co., Walnut Creek, Calif., 1983-86; office adminstr. PFSD-Health Mktg. div. Aetna Life Ins. Co., Sacramento, Calif., 1986-89; regional adminstr. Aetna Life Ins. Co., Hartford, Conn., 1989-91; cons. Aetna Life Ins. Co., Riverside, Calif., 1991—. Officer local PTA, 1964-71; pres. Wesley Service Guild, 1968-71; den mother Boy Scouts Am. Recipient Life Service award PTA, 1970. Fellow Life Office Mgmt. Assn. (instr. classes); mem. DAR (regent Silver State Nev. chpt. 1994-96), Assn. Bus. and Profl. Women, Life Underwriters Assn., Last Monday Club, Opti-Mrs., Allied Arts Club. Democrat. Methodist. Home: 2415 La Estrella St Henderson NV 89014-3608 Office: 1677 N Main Ste 250 Santa Ana CA 92701

JOHNSON, JOANNE MARY, marketing and real estate executive, real estate broker; b. Bklyn., Mar. 28, 1947; d. John Peter and Anne Marie (Alesi) Da Prato; m. John Daryl Johnson, Feb. 15, 1969; children: Jodi Lynn Johnson Pieczynski, Shaun Bryan. AA, Ariz. State U., 1994; postgrad., U. No. Tex., 1987-94; student, Univ. No. Tex., 1987—. CFP. Profl. asst. Price Waterhouse, N.Y.C., 1983-86, supr., 1986-90; mgr. Price Waterhouse, Dallas, 1990-94; mktg. profl. Park Cities Ford, Dallas, Ariz., 1994—. Editor: (newsletters) Real Estate Update, 20/20 Vision; freelance editor: Modern Screen's Country Music Special; contbr. poetry to National Poetry's Far Off Places. Bd. dirs., v.p. Tex. Soc. To Prevent Blindness, also chmn. pub. rels. com. Mem. NAFE, Nat. Assn. Real Estate Editors, The Susan Komen Found., North Tex. Assn. Real Estate Profls., Assn. Acctg. Mktg. Execs., Inc., Brookhaven Country Club (Dallas). Repubican. Roman Catholic. Home: Unit 1336 1312 Royal Palm Ln Carrollton TX 75007 Office: Park Cities Ford 3333 Inwood Rd Dallas TX 75235

JOHNSON, JOSEPHINE LYNN, lawyer; b. Washington, Pa., Nov. 25, 1958; d. Robert H. and Natalie F. (Collins) Johnson; m. Ralph J. Cessar, May 28, 1983 (div. Feb. 1992); children: Jacob and Brian Cessar (twins). BA in Polit. Sci., Chatam Coll., Pitts., 1980; JD, Duquesne U., Pitts., 1983. Bar: Pa. 1983, U.S. Dist. Ct. (we. dist.) Pa. 1983. Atty. Eckard & Clausner, Mt. Pleasant, Pa., 1983-84; mng. atty. Hyatt Legal Svcs., Pitts., 1984-87; atty. Ceisler, Richman, Smith, Washington, Pa., 1987-89, Binotto, Sweat & Johnson, Washington, Pa., 1989-93; mng. atty. Raphael, Ramsden, Behers & Frantz, P.C., Washington and Pitts., 1993—; mem. com. Washington County Rules Com., Washington, Pa., 1991—, chmn., 1995; sect. mem. family law div. Pa. Bar, 1987—. Active Dem. Party, Washington, Pa., 1976—; bd. dirs. Easter Seals Soc., Washington, 1988-89; mem. Daus. of Current Events, Washington, 1989-92; mem. Washington County Coun. Econ. Devel., 1991—; bd. dirs. Mental Health Assn., 1994—. Named to Outstanding Young Women of Am., 1984. Mem. Pa. Bar Assn. (lectr.), Washington County Bar Assn., Washington Bus. and Profl. Assn. (2d v.p. 1992-93, 1st v.p. 1993-94, pres. 1994-95, Young Careerist 1991). Episcopal. Office: Raphael Ramsden et al 15 W Beau St Ste 2 Washington PA 15301-6805

JOHNSON, JOY ANN, diagnostic radiologist; b. New Richmond, Wis., Aug. 16, 1952; d. Howard James and Shirley Maxine (Eidem) J.; m. Donald G. Nieto, June 24, 1989. BA in Chemistry summa cum laude, U. No. Colo., 1974; D of Medicine, U. Colo., 1978. Diplomate Am. Bd. Radiology, Nat. Bd. Med. Examiners. Resident in radiology U. Colo., 1978-81, fellow in radiology, 1981-82; asst. prof. diagnostic radiology and pediatrics, chief sect. pediatric radiology Clin. Radiology Found. U. Kans. Med. Ctr., Kansas City, 1982-87; radiologist Radiology Assocs. Ltd., Kansas City, Mo., 1987-92; mem. staff Bapt. Med. Ctr., Kansas City, Mo., 1987-92; radiologist Children's Mercy Hosp., Kansas City, 1992—; assoc. prof. U. Mo., Kansas City, 1992—; speaker Radiol. Soc. Republic of China, 1985. Contbr. articles to med. jours. Nat. Cancer Inst. fellow, 1982. Mem. AMA, Am. Coll. Radiology, Radiol. Soc. N.Am., Am. Inst. Ultrasound in Medicine (mem. program com. Kansas City 1984), Soc. Pediatric Radiology, Am. Assn. Women in Radiology, Lambda Sigma Tau. Office: Childrens Mercy Hosp-Dept Rad 2401 Gillham Rd Kansas City MO 64108-4619

JOHNSON, JUDITH ALENE, community counselor; b. Casper, Wyo., Jan. 24, 1962; d. Richard Cabell and Betty Louise (Darnell) J. BA in Elem. Edn., U. No. Colo., 1985, MA in Rehab. Counseling, 1990, postgrad., 1994—. Cert. elem. tchr., Colo. Child care worker Gayle's Child Care Svc., Greeley, Colo., 1982-85; elem. tchr. Cherry Creek Sch. Dist., Englewood, Colo., 1985-87; social work asst. New Life Ctr., Greeley, 1988-90; vocat. counselor South Platte Valley Bd. Coop. Edn. Svcs., Ft. Morgan, Colo., 1990-91; community counselor 19th Jud. Dist. Atty.'s Office, Greeley, 1991—; reviewer career devel. video rev. Colo. State U., Ft. Collins, 1990; adv. mem. Ea. Plains Profl. Devel. Ctr., Ft. Morgan, 1990-91; guest speaker Inside Greeley, TV show, 1991; presenter Career Inst. East, Ft. Morgan, 1991. Mem. human rights com. Centennial Devel. Svcs., Greeley, 1991-92; bd. dirs. Weld County chpt. Nat. Multiple Sclerosis Soc., Greeley, 1991-92; mem. Greeley Juvenile Firesetter Task Force, 1991—. Grantee Ea. Plains Profl. Devel. Ctr., 1990, Gov.'s Job Tng. Office, 1991, Bloedorn Found., 1991. Mem. ACA, Am. Probation and Parole Assn., Colo. Counseling Assn., Colo. Juvenile Coun., NAFE. Democrat.

JOHNSON, JUDITH ANNE, accountant; b. Peoria, Ill., Aug. 29, 1961; d. Richard John and Karin Anne (Jacobson) Hanson; m. Steven Ryan Johnson, Sept. 28, 1991. BA, Carthage Coll., 1983. Cert. managerial acct. and mgr. Staff acct. Elco Industries, Inc., Rockford, Ill., 1984-87, cost acctg. mgr., 1987-93, sr. acct., 1993—. Treas. coun. Faith Luth. Ch., 1991—; chairperson Women of Faith, 1993—. Mem. Inst. Managerial Accts. Home: 5036 Larchmont Pl Rockford IL 61114 Office: Elco Industries Inc PO Box 7009 1111 Samuelson Rd Rockford IL 61125

JOHNSON, KATE, dancer. Studied with Manuel Alum. Dancer Feld Ballet, N.Y.C., Rosalind Newman and Dancers, N.Y.C., Hannah Kahn Dance Co., N.Y.C., until 1982, Paul Taylor Dance Co., N.Y.C., 1982-90, White Oak Dance Project, N.Y.C., 1990—; guest artist N.Y.C. Ballet, 1988. Orignated roles in Mark Morris's Motorcade, A Lake, Mosaic and United; danced in shows including Going Away Party, Pas de Poisson. Recipient Dance Mag. award, 1994. Office: White Oak Dance Project care Edgar Vincent Assocs 157 W 57th St # 502 New York NY 10019-2210*

JOHNSON, KATHARYN PRICE (MRS. EDWARD F. JOHNSON), civic worker; b. Smyrna, Del., Mar. 24, 1897; d. Lewis M. and Jennie Cairl (Smithers) Price; grad. Centenary Coll., 1915; student Goucher Coll., 1915-18; m. Edward F. Johnson, Nov. 16, 1920; children—Edward A., Jane Cairl Johnson Kent. With Liberty Loan Com. for Md. and Liberty Loan Assn. of Balt., 1918-20; pres. Women's Guild Hitchcock Meml. Ch., 1930-32; dir. Scarsdale Woman's Club, 1933-36; dir. White Plains Thrift Shop, 1930-43, pres, 1936-43; mem. exec. com. Scarsdale Community Fund, 1934-38; active Scarsdale council Girl Scouts, 1937-53, commr., 1939-41, now hon. mem. Scarsdale-Hartsdale council, 1953-69; mem. region 2 com. Girl Scouts U.S.A., 1942-56, mem. nat. bd., exec. com., 1947-55, chmn. orgn. and mgmt. dept., 1952-55, mem. nat. field com., 1943-55, mem. equipment service com. 1956-69, mem. internat. com., 1956-60, mem. meml. gifts com., 1974-81; mem. Bd. Edn., Scarsdale, N.Y., 1943-46; disaster chmn. Scarsdale chpt. ARC, 1942-45; mem. Commn. Human Rights, 1958-69, Commn. Status of Women, 1957-69; rep. World Assn. Girl Guides and Girl Scouts to UN, 1957-71, mem. NGO com. on UNICEF, 1965-72, sec., 1968-70; participant World Confs., World Assn. Girl Guides and Girl Scouts, Greece, 1960, Denmark, 1963, Japan, 1966, Finland, 1969, Can., 1972, Eng., 1975, Iran, 1978, World Conf., U.S., 1984. Recipient Juliette Low World Friendship medal Girl Scouts USA, 1984. Mem. Nat. Council Women U.S., Scarsdale Hist. Soc., Olave-Baden-Powell Soc. (founder), Pi Beta Phi. Republican. Presbyterian. Clubs: Scarsdale Woman's (life), Scarsdale Golf, Nat. Women's Republican; Shenorock Shore. Home: 165 Brewster Rd Scarsdale NY 10583-2021

JOHNSON, KATHERINE ANNE, health research administrator, lawyer; b. Medford, Mass., Apr. 20, 1947; d. Lester and Eileen Anne (Henaghan) J. BS, La. State U., 1969; MSA, George Washington U., 1972; JD, Cath. U., 1985. Bar: Md. 1985. Pub. health adviser HHS, Washington, 1970-76; dir. plan implementation SE Colo. Health Systems Agy, Colorado Springs, 1976-78; sr. mng. assoc. CDP Assocs., Inc., Atlanta, 1978-87, dir. legal affairs, 1986-87; v.p. Cancer CarePoint Inc., Atlanta, 1987; sr. mgr. Salick Health Care, Inc., Bethesda, Md., 1987-89; pvt. practice atty. cons., Potomac, Md., 1989-90; assoc. dir. for adminstrn. San Antonio Cancer Inst., 1990—; speaker in field. Contbr. articles to profl. jours. Vol. Ct.-Apptd. Spl. Adv. for Abused Children. Mem. Md. Bar Assn., Nat. Health Lawyers Assn., Am. Acad. Hosp. Attys., Assn. for Health Svcs. Rsch. Office: San Antonio Cancer Inst. 8122 Datapoint Dr Ste 600 San Antonio TX 78229-3264

JOHNSON, KATHERINE HOLTHAUS, health care marketing professional; b. Denver, Mar. 19, 1961; d. William Philip and Barbara Kristine (Nielsen) Holthaus; m. Robert Scott Johnson; children: Katie Maree, Brian David. B in Applied Math. Engring., U. Colo., 1983; MBA, U. Denver, 1992. Acctg. intern Cooper, Haugen & Co., CPAs, Englewood, Colo., 1982-84; market analyst mktg. dept. Porter Meml. Hosp., Denver, 1985-88; account exec. Tallant LaPointe & Ptnrs., Inc., Englewood, 1988-92; advt. mgr. Micromedex, Inc., Denver, 1992-93; mktg. cons. Highlands Ranch, Colo., 1993—. Judge, vol. 4-H Clubs, Met. Denver, 1979—; supt. Sunday sch. Ascension Luth. Ch., Littleton, Colo., 1985-87. Recipient 2 Advantage awards Adventist Health System, 1987. Mem. Soc. for Healthcare Planning and Mktg., Am. Hosp. Assn., Acad. for Health Svcs. Mktg., Am. Mktg. Assn., Alpha Chi Omega. Republican.

JOHNSON, KAY DURBAHN, real estate manager, consultant; b. Crookston, Minn., Apr. 4, 1937; d. Wilbert John and Frieda (Johnson) Durbahn; m. Ray Arvin Johnson, May 14, 1960; children: Sherry Kay Johnson Johnston, Diane Rosalind Johnson Peterson, Laura Faye Johnson. BA, U. Minn., 1959. Reference analyst Indsl. Rels. Ctr. U. Minn., Mpls., 1959-61; real estate mgr. Minnetonka, Minn., 1976—; ptnr. Broadmoor Plantation Investors, Fargo, N.D., 1976—; v.p. D&T Property, Inc., Minnetonka, 1990—, also bd. dirs.; tax reduction cons. R.A. Johnson & Assocs., Minnetonka, 1985—. City of Minnetonka Planning Commn., 1972-74, vice chair, 1973-74; mem. Land Use Task Force, 1972-74; liaison Ridgedale Devel., 1972-74; chair Evangelism Bd. Minnetonka Luth. Ch., 1974-76, 85-87, chair Stewardship Bd., 1992-94, mem. choir; mem. GMC Motorcoach Assn. Mem. Mpls. Inst. Arts, Minnetonka Ctr. for Arts. Republican. Home: 2227 Platwood Rd Minnetonka MN 55305

JOHNSON, KELLY ANNE, art director; b. Balt., June 8, 1962; d. Alfred Clarke Johnson and Marguerite Eileen Walsh. AAS in Comml. Art, Austin C.C., 1993. Media specialist Austin (Tex.) C.C., 1984; designer City of Austin Electric Utility, 1984-85, Best Printing Co., Austin, 1987-88; art dir. Green Pea Design, Austin, 1988-90, Optical Soc. Am., Washington, 1990-91, The Nature Conservancy, Arlington, Va., 1991—; art and design cons. Search for Common Ground, Washington, 1992—. Vol. Greater D.C. Cares, Washington, 1993—; vol. usher The Shakespeare Theatre, Washington, 1993—. Mem. Am. Inst. Graphic Arts, Soc. Nat. Assn. Publs. (co-founder, co-chair assn. electronic pub.'s user group 1990-93), Austin Graphic Arts Soc. (pres. 1984-90, Presdl. award 1988), Art Dirs. Club Met. Washington. Democrat. Unitarian. Home: 7524 Broadcloth Way Columbia MD 21046 Office: The Nature Conservancy 1815 N Lynn St Arlington VA 22209

JOHNSON, LADY BIRD (MRS. LYNDON BAINES JOHNSON), widow of former President of U.S.; b. Karnack, Tex., Dec. 22, 1912; d. Thomas Jefferson Taylor; B.A., U. Tex., 1933, B.Journalism, 1934, D.Letters, 1964; LL.D., Tex. Woman's U., 1964; D.Letters, Middlebury Coll., 1967; L.H.D., Williams Coll., 1967, U. Ala., 1975; H.H.D., Southwestern U., 1967; m. Lyndon Baines Johnson (36th Pres. U.S.), Nov. 17, 1934 (died Jan. 22, 1973); children: Lynda Bird Johnson Robb, Luci Baines. Mgr. husband's congl. office, Washington, 1941-42; owner, operator radio-TV sta. KTBC, Austin, Tex., 1942-63, cattle ranches, Tex., 1943—. Hon. chmn. Nat. Headstart Program, 1963-68, Town Lake Beautification Project; also cotton and timberlands, Ala. Mem. Advisory council Nat. Parks, Historic Sites, Bldgs. and Monuments; bd. regents U. Tex., 1971-77, mem. internat. conf. steering com., 1969; trustee Jackson Hole Preserve, Am. Conservation Assn., Nat. Geog. Soc.; founder Nat. Wildflower Research Ctr., Austin, 1982. Recipient Togetherness award Marge Champion, 1958; Humanitarian award B'nai B'rith, 1961; Businesswoman's award Bus. and Profl. Women's Club, 1961; Theta Sigma Phi citation, 1962; Disting. Achievement award Washington Heart Assn., 1962; Industry citation Am. Women in Radio and Television, 1963; Humanitarian citation Vols. of Am., 1963; Peabody award for White House TV visit, 1966; Eleanor Roosevelt Golden Candlestick award Women's Nat. Press Club; Damon Woods Meml. award Indsl. Designers Soc. Am., 1972; Conservation Service award Dept. Interior, 1974; Disting. award Am. Legion, 1975; Woman of Year award Ladies Home Jour., 1975; Medal of Freedom, 1977; Nat. Achievement award Am. Hort. Soc., 1984. Life mem. U. Tex. Ex-Students Assn. Episcopalian. Author: A White House Diary, 1970. Address: LBJ Libr 2313 Red River Austin TX 78705*

JOHNSON, LEAYN HUTCHINSON, nursing educator, mental health nurse; b. Elizabeth, Pa., June 3, 1936; d. Ernest Eba and Edna (Caley) Hutchinson; m. Donald E. Johnson, Mar. 10, 1959; children: Donna Lynn, Donald E. Diploma, McKeesport Hosp. Sch. Nursing, 1957; BSN cum laude, Wright State U., 1975; MS, Ohio State U., 1977; PhD in Psychology, U.S. Internat. U., 1987. RN, Calif. From lectr. to asst. prof. U. Hawaii, Honolulu; clin. nurse specialist Our Self Counseling Ctr., Santa Ana, Calif.; asst. prof. Calif. State U., Long Beach; assoc. prof. Mem. ANA, Calif. Nurses Assn., Sigma Theta Tau. Home: 16932 Edgewater Huntington Beach CA 92649

JOHNSON, LILLIAN BEATRICE, sociologist, educator, counselor; b. Wilmington, N.C., Nov. 8, 1922; d. James Archie and Mary Gaston (Atkins) J. A.A., Peace Coll., 1940; B.R.E., Presbyterian Sch. Christian Edn., 1942; M.S., N.C. State U., 1965, Ph.D., 1972. Dir. Christian edn. First Presbyn. Ch., Pensacola, Fla., 1945-47, Greenwood, S.C., 1947-48, Durham, N.C., 1948-51; club dir. Army Spl. Services, No. Command, Japan, 1951-53; teenage dir. YWCA, Washington, 1953-56, assoc. exec. Honolulu, 1956-59, exec. dir. Tulsa, 1959-62; instr. N.C. State U., 1962-72; asst. prof. Greensboro Coll., 1972-75; mem. faculty sociology dept. Livingston U., 1975-89, emerita prof., 1989—; pvt. practice family counselor, Fayetteville, N.C., 1989—. Ct. counselor, mediator Cumberland County Dispute Resolution Ctr. Mem. Nat. Coun. Family Rels. Home: 405A Tradewinds Dr Fayetteville NC 28314-2449 Office: 155 Gillespie St Fayetteville NC 28301-5670

JOHNSON, LINDA ARLENE, petroleum transporter; b. Sparta, Wis., Mar. 6, 1946; d. Clarence Julius and Arlene Mae (Yahnke) Jessie; children: Darrick, Larissa. With Union Nat. Bank & Trust Co., Sparta, 1964-69, Hill, Christensen & Co., CPA's, Tomah, Wis., 1969-75; owner Johnson of Wis. Oil Co., Inc., Tomah, 1969-95; with Larry's Express, Inc., Tomah, 1975-78; owner Johnson Rentals, 1979—, Johnson of Wis. Transport Co., Inc., Tomah, 1982—. Mem. St. Paul's Luth. Ch., Tomah. Mem. Petroleum Marketers Assn. Am., Nat. Assn. Convenience Stores, Nat. Fedn. Ind. Bus., Am. Trucking Assn., Wis. Assn. Convenience Stores, Petroleum Marketers Assn. Wis., Wis. Ind. Businessmen, Inc., Tomah Area C. of C., Tomah Area Credit Union (bd. dirs., 1993-94). Home and Office: Rt 1 Box 428 Tomah WI 54660-2011

JOHNSON, LINDA KAYE, art educator; b. Port Lyautey, Morocco, Africa, Feb. 6, 1956; d. Arthur Joseph and Iona Belle (Marshall) J. BFA, Radford U., 1980; MS in Art Edn., Fla. State U., 1994. Art instr. dept. psychology Fla. State U., Tallahassee, summers 1985,86; art instr. Western Psychiat. Inst. and Clinic, Pitts., summers 1987-89, Blacksburg (Va.) Mid. Sch., 1981; jeweler Treasure Hut, Tallahassee, 1981-83, Gem Collection, Tallahassee, 1983-85; art instr. Havana (Fla.) Elem., 1985-87, Cobb Mid. Sch., Tallahassee, 1987-89, Raa Mid. Sch., Tallahassee, 1989-90, Deerlake Mid. Sch., Tallahassee, 1990—; participant Nat. Assessment of Edn. Progress, Fla. Team, 1994; chmn. Winter Festival Youth Art Show, Tallahassee, 1992, 93; participating artist Very Spl. Arts Festival, Tallahassee, 1986-90; field test coord. Fla. Int. for Ar Edn.-CHAT, Tallahassee, 1992, 93; co-chair Arts for a Complete Edn. Coalition, 1993—. Grantee Leon County Tchr.'s Assn., Tallahassee, 1992, Gadsden (Fla.) Edn. Found., 1987, 86; named Mid. Sch. Art Educator of Yr., State of Fla., 1993. Mem. Profl. Art Instrs. Near Talla (pres. 1991-93), Fla. Art Educators Assn., Nat. Art Educators Assn., Fla. Tchng. Profession, NEA.

JOHNSON, LINDA THELMA, information specialist; b. New Britain, Conn., May 18, 1954; d. Oren and Lois Elizabeth (Armstrong) J.; 1 child, Portia Lauren. BS in Econs., Va. State U., 1978; cert. in computer programming, Morse Sch. Bus., 1978; cert. in legal assisting, Morse Sch. Bus., Hartford, Conn., 1994. Programmer analyst Vitro Automation Industries, Silver Spring, Md., 1980-83; sr. analyst Sci. Mgmt. Corp., Lanham, Md., 1984-86; sr. programmer analyst Applied Mgmt. Scis. Inc., Silver Spring, 1986; programmer analyst Computer Data Systems Inc., Rockville, Md., 1986-88; project leader systems cert. dept. Arbitron Co., Laurel, Md., 1988-90; systems analyst Engring. and Econ. Rsch., Inc., Vienna, Va., 1990; computer cons. Comsys Tech. Svcs. Inc., Rockville, 1990, CPU Inc., Fairfax, Va., 1991; quality assurance cons. Cigna Corp., Bloomfield, Conn., 1992; info. systems specialist The Travelers Ins. Group, Hartford, Conn., 1992—; mem. rsch. bd. advisors The Am. Biographical Inst., Inc. Mem. NAFE, NAACP, Am. Bus. Women's Assn. Democrat. Baptist. Home: 386 Park Ave Bloomfield CT 06002-3106

JOHNSON, LINNEA R., judge; b. 1946. BA, Univ. of Ga.; JD, Stetson Univ., 1971. Asst. state atty. Dade County, Fla.; asst. U.S. atty. Fla. so. dist.; magistrate judge U.S. Dist. Ct. (Fla. so. dist.), 11th circuit, Miami, 1987—. Office: US Courthouse 300 NE First Ave Rm 131 Miami FL 33132*

JOHNSON, LISA MARY, violinist, educator; b. Vancouver, B.C., Can., Oct. 25, 1956; came to U.S., 1974; d. Goodwin Walin and Mary Edna (Driscoll) J.; m. Oliver Sylvan Pinchot, May 20, 1990. B Profl. Studies, Empire State Coll., 1980; MM, Yale U., 1980. Violinist New Haven (Conn.) Symphony, 1979-81, Houston Symphony Orch., 1982-83; asst. concertmaster Ea. Music Festival, Greensboro, N.C., 1984-94; violin tchr. Calif. Inst. of the Arts, Valencia, 1993-94; violinist L.A. Chamber Orch., 1984-94. Democrat. Home: 511 S Hudson Ave Pasadena CA 91101

JOHNSON, LIZABETH LETTIE, insurance agent; b. Dallas, Aug. 24, 1957; d. Winfred Herschel Johnson and Mary Francis (Flowers) Goff; children: Brandi, Elissa. Student, Georgetown (Ky.) Coll., 1975-76, U. Ky., 1976-78. Staff analyst Met. Ins. Co., Lexington, 1979-81, ins. agt., 1981-82; sr. account agt. Allstate Ins. Co., Lexington, 1982—. Vol. Big Bros./Big Sisters, 1979-84, Life Adventure Camp, 1989-92; hotline counselor Lexington Rape Crisis Ctr., 1984-92, bd. dirs., 1988-91; vol. Christians in Comty. Svc., 1986-93; mem. Bluegrass Adoptive Parent Support Group, 1985-92. Fellow Life Underwriting Tng. Council; mem. NAACP, Nat. Assn. Life Underwriters, Progressive Execs. Democrat. Baptist. Office: Allstate Ins Co 694 New Circle Rd NE Rm 3 Lexington KY 40505-4513

JOHNSON, LOIS ANN, patient educator; b. Jersey City, Nov. 2, 1937; d. John Milton and Sadie Marie (Arbogast) Herrold; m. Lewis Clifford Johnson, Aug. 26, 1961; children: Lisa, Ann, Dosa. Diploma, Del. Hosp. Sch. Nursing, 1958; BSN, U. Del., 1960. RN, Del. Instr. Del. Hosp. Sch. Nursing, Wilmington, 1960-65, Nursing Sch. Wilmington, 1965-85; patient educator Med. Ctr. Del., Wilmington, 1986—; pres. Clin. Testing Assocs., Inc., Claymont, Del., 1982—. Contbr. to profl. publs. Mem. Am. Assn. Diabetes Educators (cert.), Am. Diabetes Assn., Tri-State Assn. Diabetes Educators, Am. Heart Assn. (instr.), Christian Bus. and Profl. Women's Assn. Home: 121 Hilldale Ct Claymont DE 19703-1306 Office: Med Ctr Del 501 W 14th St Wilmington DE 19899

JOHNSON, LOLA N., advertising and public relations executive, educator; b. Austin, Dec. 28, 1942; d. Alton E. and Evelyn M. (Quast) Milbruth; m. Dennis D. Johnson, June 15, 1963 (div. July 1973); children: Brenda J., Erik B. Attended, Coll. of St. Thomas. Pub. rels. account rep. Karkerr Assocs. Advt. and Pub. Rels., Bloomington, Minn., 1973-78; comm. mgr., mgr. Norwest Bank Mpls., 1978-83; dir. media rels., account supr. Edwin Neuger & Assocs. Pub. Rels., Mpls., 1983-85; v.p., mng. dir. The Richards Group, Mpls., 1985-86; owner, pres. PR Plus, Edina, Minn., 1986—; mem. cmty. faculty, instr., counselor Met. State U., Mpls., St. Paul, 1980—. Cons. comm. United Way, Mpls., 1982. Recipient Gold award United Way Mpls., 1982. Home and Office: PR Plus 6400 Barrie Rd # 1103 Minneapolis MN 55435

JOHNSON, LUAN, disaster preparedness consultant, researcher; b. Provo, Utah, Apr. 27, 1956; d. Jack R. and Colleen (Kesler) J. BA, Brigham Young U., 1981, MA, 1984; PhD, U. Wash., 1994. Dir. Teaching Resource Ctr., Provo, 1980-84; teaching asst. communications dept. Brigham Young U., Provo, 1982-83; counselor Master Acad., Salt Lake City, 1985; ednl. designer, program mgr. City of Sunnyvale, 1986-90; teaching asst., rsch. asst., speech communications dept. U. Wash., Seattle, 1991-93; program mgr. City of Seattle, 1993—. Pres. Youth Assn. Retarded Children, Brigham City, 1976-77. Mem. Phi Kappa Phi. Mormon. Avocation: collecting and flying kites. Home: 21329 76th Ave W # 11 Edmonds WA 98026 Office: SPAN 9792 Edmonds Way # 112 Edmonds WA 98020

JOHNSON, LYNDA JOAN HEMPELMANN, county administrator; b. Phila., Dec. 30, 1956; d. H. Kurt and Joan Edna (Leyrer) Hempelmann; m. Walter Monroe Johnson III, Nov. 13, 1976; children: Kyle Christopher, Kendal Lyn. Grad. high sch., Perkasie, Pa. Mem. Richland Twp. (Pa.) Planning Commn., 1982-89, chmn., 1984-88; mem. Quakertown Area Planning Com., Richland Twp., 1990-92; mem. Richland Twp. Bd. of Suprs., 1990-94, chmn., 1991-92; mem. staff Bucks County Treas. Office, Doylestown, Pa., 1994—. Mem. Pennridge Rep. Club, Perkasie, 1992—, North Pa. Coun. Rep. Women, 1992—, Bucks County Coun. Rep. Women, Doylestown, 1992—, Pa. State Coun. Rep. Women, 1992—, Nat. Coun. Rep. Women, 1992—; campaign coord. Richland Twp. and Richlandtown Borough Greenwood for Congress, 1992; bd. dirs. Emergency Outreach Quakertown, Pennridge, Palisades, 1992—, pres., 1994—. Mem. Pa. Assn. Twp. Suprs., Bucks County Assn. Mcpl. Ofcls., Pa. State Assn. Mcpl. Planners, Nat. Fedn. Bus. and Profl. Women's Clubs (legis. chmn. Quakertown chpt. 1993), Upper Bucks Sertoma Club. Lutheran. Home: 1151 Farm House Ln Quakertown PA 18951-2440 Office: Bucks County Treas Office 55 E Court St Doylestown PA 18901

JOHNSON, LYNN BARBARA, artist, civic worker; b. N.Y.C., Jan. 23, 1933; d. Carl Lincoln (stepfather) and Mary Catherine (Albert) Nelson; m. Frederick Hannan Johnson, Dec. 14, 1957; children: Christopher H., Laura B., Thor A. AA with honors, Stockton Jr. Coll., 1952; BFA, BA, U. Wash., 1954. With Standard Oil Co., San Francisco, 1956-57; tchr. Menlo Park (Calif.) Pvt. Sch., 1957-58, Niantic (Conn.) Pub. Sch., 1961-63; pvt. tchr. art San Diego, 1968-69; art dealer Kenneth Behm Galleries, Seattle and Bellevue, Wash., 1981-84; juror N.W. Internat. Women's Conf. Art Exhbn. One-woman shows include Menlo Park Show, 1958-59, Hartford Conn. Amory Show, 1965, Converse Gallery Annual Show, 1965, San Diego Watercolor Annual, 1967, Northwest Watercolor Annual, 1972. Active numerous civic orgns.; founder Niantic (Conn.) Outdoor Art Show, 1962; co-founder Bellevue Jazz Festival, 1977; mem. Bellevue Sch. Dist. Citizens' Task Force, 1979-80, Wash. State Ad Hoc Com. on Arts, 1977-79; mem. Bellevue Centennial Steering Com., 1988, Bellevue Sch. Dist. Affirmative Action Com., 1989—; mem. citizens' coodinating com. King County Centennial, 1988; chmn. Bellevue City Arts Commn., 1980-81, 83; co-founder, pres. Seattle-King County Community Arts Network, 1986-87; co-founder Bellevue Allied Arts Coun., 1981, Wash. State Art Alliance, 1979; v.p. Found. for Internat. Understanding through Students, U. Wash., 1987-88; del. Wash. Rep. Com., 1987-88; bd. dirs. Seattle Opera Guild, 1990-94, Seattle Group Theatre, 1990-93; pres. Bel Canto Opera Group, 1990—; founding mem. Women Together U.S./U.S.S.R., 1990—; vol. Sta. KCTS-TV, 1991—; founding chmn. Bellevue Cmty. Diversity Awards, 1993—; active Burke Mus., Pacific Sci. Ctr., City of Bellevue Transit Adv. Group, 1993-94; mem. art exhbn. and media coms. N.W. Internat. Women's Conf., 1993-95. Recipient numerous awards for watercolors, Calif., N.Y., Conn.; World of Difference award Sta. KIRO-TV, 1990; finalist Priz de Paris, Vogue mag., 1954; Nat. Assn. Fgn. Student Affairs travel grantee, 1987. Mem. AAUW (Wash. chpt. bd. dirs., chmn. Wash. divsn. nominating com., cultural rep., v.p. Conn. bd., nat. assn. diversity adv. group 1991-93, mem. coll./univ. rels. 1993—, named Gift Honoree 1990), San Diego Watercolor Soc. (profl.), Wash. Arts Alliance, Native Am. Studies Assn., Seattle Art Mus. (native arts coun.), Bellevue Art Mus. (founding, docent coun. 1978), Seattle Opera Guild (bd. dirs. 1990-94), Nat. Mus. Women Arts (charter mem.), U. Wash. Alumni Assn. (life, reunion class of 1954 com.), Women's Univ. Club, Overlake Rep. Women's Club, Lambda Rho. Home: 2202 102d Pl SE Bellevue WA 98004

JOHNSON, MADELINE MITCHELL, retired administrative assistant; b. Cleve., Oct. 24, 1930; d. Maidlon and Katherine (Reynolds) Mitchell; m. Elvyn Frank Johnson, Dec. 4, 1954. BS, Case Western Res. U., 1976. Adminstrv. asst. Fed. Res. Bank Cleve., 1950-92, tng. coord. data svcs., 1988-92, ombudsman rep., 1989-92; ret., 1992; mem. tng. task force bd. govs. FRS, Washington, 1987-92. Chair bd. trustees Affinity Bapt. Ch. Mem. Am. Bus. Women's Assn. (pres. 1986-88, Woman of Yr. Cleve. chpt. 1987), Nat. Coun. Negro Women, Top Ladies Distinction (Top Lady of Yr. 1993-94). Home: 1410 Cleveland Heights Blvd Cleveland OH 44121-1603

JOHNSON, MARGARET ANN, library administrator; b. Atlanta, Aug. 11, 1948; d. Odell H. and Virginia (Mathiasen) J.; m. Lee J. English, Mar. 4, 1978; children: Carson J., Amelia J. BA, St. Olaf Coll., 1970; MA, U. Chgo., 1972; MBA, Met. State U., 1990. Music cataloger U. Iowa Librs., Iowa City, 1972-73; analyst Control Data Corp., Bloomington, Minn., 1973-75; br. libr. St. Paul (Minn.) Pub. Librs., 1975-77; head tech. svcs. St. Paul (Minn.) Campus Librs., U. Minn., 1977-86; collection devel. office U. Librs., U. Minn., Mpls., 1987-90; asst. dir. St. Paul (Minn.) Campus Librs., U. Minn., 1987—; libr. cons. Mekerere U., Kampala, Uganda, 1990, U. Nat. Rwanda, 1990, Inst. Agriculture and Vet. Hassan II, Rabat, Morocco, 1992—. Author: Automation and Organizational Change in Libraries, 1991; (bimonthly column) Technicalities Jour.; editor Guide to Tech. Svcs. Resources, 1994, Recruiting, Educating and Tng. Librarians for Collection Devel., 1994, Collection Mgmt. and Devel., 1994; contbr. articles to profl. jours. Recipient Samuel Lazerow Rsch. fellowship Assn. Coll. and Rsch. Librs., Inst. for Sci. Info., 1987. Mem. ALA, Minn. Libr. Assn., Internat. Assn. Agrl. Librs. and Documentatists, Assn. for Internat. Agrl. and Extension Edn., U.S. Agrl. Info. Network, Women in Devel. Office: U of Minn Librs St Paul Campus Librs 1984 Buford Ave Saint Paul MN 55108

JOHNSON, MARGARET H, welding company executive, author; b. Chgo., June 3, 1933; d. Harold W. and Clara J. (Pape) Glavin; m. Odean Jack Johnson, Nov. 18, 1950; children: Karen Ann, Dean Harold. Student Moody Bible Inst., 1976-78. V.p., sec. Seamline Welding, Inc., Grayslake, 1956—, dir.; trustee SWCEPS, Grayslake, 1963—. Author: Living Faith, 1973, 80, Lord's Ladder of Love, 1976, God's Rainbow, 1982; contbr. articles to religion mags. Life mem. Rep. Presdl. Task Force, 1982—, trustee, 1986-88; charter founder Ronald Reagan Rep. Ctr., 1987; mem. Lake View Neighborhood Group, Chgo., Small Group Ch. Community; active Mary, Seat of Wisdom Cath. Women's Club, 1970-90, renew facilitator 1986-88, cochairperson 1986-88; Sunday sch. tchr., 1985; mem. St. Gilbert's Parish, 1990—. Mem. ASCAP, Fedn. Ind. Small Bus., Internat. Platform Assn., Women's Aglow Fellowship Internat., Grayslake C. of C.. Exch. Club Grayslake, Grayslake Devel. Corp. Home: 20 Hawley Ct Grayslake IL 60030-1517

JOHNSON, MARGARET HILL, educational administrator; b. Dundee, Scotland, June 26, 1923; came to U.S., 1946, naturalized, 1957; d. John Barnet and Isabella Rae (Watson) Hill; children: Ann Hill Doughty, James Appleton Doughty (dec.), Joanna Elizabeth Doughty Going. Student Inverness (Scotland) Royal Acad., 1940, Edinburgh (Scotland) Royal Coll. Art, 1940-43; Doctor in Edn., U. Mass., Amherst, 1985. Latin and remedial English tutor Harvey Sch., N.Y.C., 1947-52; tchr. athletics Pingree Sch. for Girls, Hamilton, Mass., 1959-61, Shore Country Day Sch., Beverly, Mass., 1952-59; asso. dir. Theodore S. Jones & Co., design mgmt. cons., Milton, Mass., 1961-72; dir. career planning and placement Mass. Coll. Art, 1972—, coordinator human services; design cons. Theodore S. Jones & Co.; Fulbright advisor Mass. Coll. Art, 1974—; speaker Lesley Coll., 1977, Cambridge (Mass.) Community Schs., 1977—, MIT, Harvard U., R.I. Sch. Design, Hofstra U. Served with Brit. Women's Royal Naval Service, 1943-46. Mem. Am. Craft Coun., Am. Assn. Mus., Boston Soc. Architects, Coll. Placement Coun., Am. Assn. Higher Edn., Coll. Art Assn. Am., Eastern Coll. Employer Network, Internat. Educators Network. Author: (with others) Your Future in Art and Design, 1977. Home: PO Box 75 Marshfield Hills MA 02051-0075 Office: 621 Huntington Ave Boston MA 02115

JOHNSON, MARGARET KATHLEEN, business educator; b. Baylor County, Tex., Oct. 30, 1920; d. George W. and Julia Rivers (Turner) Higgins; m. Herman Clyde Johnson, Jr., July 27, 1949 (dec.); 1 child, Carolyn Kay. B.S., Hardin-Simmons U., 1940; M.Bus. Edn., North Tex. State U., 1957, Ed.D., 1962. Clk. Farmers Nat. Bank, Seymour, Tex., 1940-41; adminstrv. sec. U.S. Navy, Corpus Christi, Tex., 1941-46; adminstrv. asst. Hdqrs. 8th Army, Yokohama, Japan, 1946-49; instr. Coll. Bus. Adminstrn., U. Ark., 1957-60; teaching fellow Sch. Bus. Adminstrn., North Tex. State U., 1960-62, instr., 1962-63; asst. prof. bus., tchr. edn. and secondary edn. Tchrs. Coll., U. Nebr., Lincoln, 1963-65; asso. prof. Tchrs. Coll., U. Nebr., 1966-70, prof., 1970—; guest lectr. U. N.Mex., 1967, Curriculum Devel. in Bus. Edn., N.S. Dept. Edn., 1969, North Tex. State U., 1970, East Tex. State U., 1972; in Policies Commn. for Bus. and Econ. Edn., 1979-83. Author: Standardized Production Typewriting Tests series, 1964-65, National Structure for Research in Vocational Education, 1966; co-author: Introduction to Word Processing, 1980, 2d edit., 1985, Introduction to Business Communication, 1981, 2d edit., 1988; editor: Nat. Bus. Edn. Assn. Yearbook, 1980. Recipient

United Bus. Edn. Assn. award as outstanding grad. student in bus. edn. North Tex. State U., 1957; award for outstanding service Nebr. Future Bus. Leaders Am., 1968; Mountain-Plains Bus. Edn. Leadership award, 1977; merit award Nebr. Bus. Assn., 1979. Mem. Nat. Bus. Edn. Assn. (exec. bd. 1975, 76-78), Mountain-Plains Bus. Edn. Assn. (exec. sec. 1970-73, pres. 1975), Nebr. Bus. Edn. Assn. (pres. 1966-67), Nebr. Council on Occupational Tchr. Edn., Delta Pi Epsilon. Office: U Nebr 529 Nebraska Hall Lincoln NE 68588

JOHNSON, MARGARET LITTLEFIELD, account manager, sales; b. Camden, Maine, Mar. 30, 1961; d. Donald Hanson and Ruth Frances (Littlefield) Carr; m. Jon Frederick Johnson, Mar. 14, 1981 (dec. Feb. 23, 1994); 1 child, Jennifer Littlefield Johnson. Student, Braniff Edn. Systems, Dallas, 1980. Novell cert. sales profl. Sales assoc. LaVerdiere's Super Drug, Camden, Maine, 1977-80; travel counselor Coronet Travel Ltd., St. Louis, 1980-81, Huffman Travel, St. Louis, 1981-82; sales & mgr. Columbia MicroSystems, St. Louis, 1982-84; sales, acct. mgr. Sextant Computer Systems, St. Louis, 1984-92; acct. mgr., sales J & G Computer Solutions, St. Louis, 1992—; grad asst. Dale Carnegie Ctr. for Excellence, St. Louis, 1993—. Contbr. articles to profl. publs. Chmn. Parks & Recreation Bd., Maplewood, Mo., 1987—; founder, pres. Maplewood Arts Coun., St. Louis, 1988—; campaign writer in field, St. Louis, 1989—; co-chmn. Mayoral Race-Bob Scheidt, Maplewood, 1993, Citizens Against Mandatory Fees, Maplewood, 1994. Mem. St. Louis Wang Users Soc. (v.p. 1988-91), St. Louis Chpt. NOMDA/LANDA (pres. 1992—, Landa chpt. adv. coun. 1992—). Republican. Methodist. Office: J&G Computer Solutions 8664 Olive Blvd Saint Louis MO 63132-2509

JOHNSON, MARIAN ILENE, education educator; b. Hawarden, Iowa, Oct. 3, 1929; d. Henry Richard and Wilhelmina Anna (Schmidt) Stoltenberg; m. Paul Irving Jones, June 14, 1958 (dec. Feb. 1985); m. William Andrew Johnson, Oct. 3, 1991. BA, U. La Verne, 1959; MA, Claremont Grad. Sch., 1962; PhD, Ariz. State U., 1971. Cert. tchr., Iowa, Calif. Elem. tchr. Cherokee (Iowa) Sch. Dist., 1949-52, Sioux City (Iowa) Sch. Dist., 1952-56, Ontario (Calif.) Pub. Schs., 1956-61, Reed Union Sch. Dist., Belvedere-Tiburon, Calif., 1962-65, Columbia (Calif.) Union Sch. Dist., 1965-68; prof. edn. Calif. State U., Chico, 1972-91. Home: 26437 S Lakewood Dr Sun Lakes AZ 85248-7246

JOHNSON, MARLENE M., government executive; b. Braham, Minn., Jan. 11, 1946; d. Beauford and Helen (Nelson) J.; m. Peter Frankel. BA, Macalester Coll., 1968. Founder, pres. Split Infinitive, Inc., St. Paul, 1970-82; pres., bd. dirs. Face to Face Health and Counseling Clinic, 1977-78; with Working Opportunities for Women, 1977-82; lt. gov. State of Minn., St. Paul, 1983-91; sr. fellow Family Support Project, Ctr. for Policy Alternative, 1991-93; assoc. adminstr. for adminstrn. GSA, Washington, 1994—; founder, past chmn. Nat. Leadership Conf. Women Execs. in State Govt.; mem. exec. com., midwestern chair Nat. Conf. Lt. Govs.; mem. adv. bd. Ctr. for Children in Poverty, Columbia U. Chmn. Minn. Women's Polit. Caucus, 1973-76, Dem.-Farmer-Labor Small Bus. Task Force, 1978, Child Care Task Force, 1987, Nat. Conf. Lt. Govs., 1987; dir. membership sect. Nat. Women's Polit. Caucus, 1975-77; vice chmn. Minn. Del. to White House Conf. on Small Bus., 1980; co-founder Minn. Women's Campaign Fund, 1982; founder, past chmn. Nat. Leadership Conf. Women Execs. in State Govt., 1983; bd. dirs. Nat. Child Care Action Campaign; chair Children's 2000 Commn., 1990; candidate for Mayor St. Paul, Minn. Recipient Outstanding Achievement award St. Paul YWCA, 1980, Disting. Svc. award St. Paul Jaycees, 1980, Disting. Citizen citation Macalester Coll., 1982, Disting. Contbns. to Families award Minn. Coun. on Family Rels., 1986, Minn. Sportfishing Congress award, 1986, Royal Order of Polar Star Govt. Sweden, 1988, Children's Champion award Def. Fund, 1989, Jane Preston award Minn. State Coun. on Vocat. Tech. Edn., 1989, Legis. Leadership award Am. Fedn. Tchrs., 1991; named One of Ten Outstanding Young Minnesotans, Minn. Jaycees, 1980; Swedish Bicentennial Commn. grantee, 1987. Mem. Nat. Assn. Women Bus. Owners (past pres.).

JOHNSON, MARLYS DIANNE, utility company executive; b. Akron, Iowa, Mar. 31, 1948; d. Harry J. and Alvina (Jurgensen) Nannen; m. Randall Lee Johnson, June 27, 1970; children: Amy Lyn, Ann Marie. BS, Augustana Coll., 1970; MBA, U. S.D., 1985. Clk. City of Sioux City, Iowa, 1970-74; ops. mgr. Dain Bosworth, Sioux City, 1974-77; mgmt. trainee Iowa Pub. Svc. Co., Sioux City, 1977-79; adminstrv. asst. to treas. Iowa Pub. Service Co., Sioux City, 1979-81; asst. treas. Midwest Energy Co., Sioux City, 1981-85, v.p., treas., 1985-90; v.p. customer rels. Iowa Public Svc. Co., Sioux City, 1991-92; mgr. consumer affairs Midwest Power Systems Inc., Sioux City, 1992—; bd. dirs. Wallace Tech. Transfer Found. of Iowa, Siouxland Ventures, Inc., Iowa Inst. for Low-Income Housing, Energy and Telecomm., Mid-Sioux Opportunity Inc. Sec.-treas. Akron Pub. Libr., 1970-80, also bd. dirs.; v.p. fin. Prairie Gold coun. Boy Scouts Am.; active Girls Inc., 1989—, treas., 1992-93, chmn. fundraising com., 1994; chairperson fin. YWCA, Sioux City, 1983; mem. investments subcom. Marian Health Ctr., Sioux City, 1985-88; bd. dirs. Sioux City Stationery Co., 1986-94. Mem. Am. Gas Assn. (consumer affairs com. 1991-92), Sioux City C. of C. (community involvement com., Main St. Downtown Tree com.), Edison Electric Inst. (customer svcs. com. 1991-92), Quota Internat. (treas. 1982-83), Toastmasters (historian 1979-80), Rotary Internat. Republican. Lutheran. Home: 521 Reed St Akron IA 51001 Office: Midwest Res Inc 401 Douglas St Sioux City IA 51101-1480

JOHNSON, MARY ALICE, magazine editor; b. Rochester, Ind., Apr. 16, 1942; d. Nolan Lee and Alice Lavida (Ruede) Lewis; m. Manford Warren Johnson, May 28, 1960; children: Nola (dec.), John Jay, June Jeannette Johnson Sorber. Grad. high sch., Hillsboro, Oreg., 1960. Owner, baker, decorator Mary's Custom Cakes and Cake Parts, St. Helens, Oreg., 1980-87; creator Sweet Tooth Confections Candy, 1981—; founder, mng. editor Sugar Art Sharing Confectionary Ideas mag., 1986-88; chmn. Sugar Art Ltd. Partnership, McMinnville, Oreg., 1986-93, Temptations Party Plan, McMinnville, 1987-88; owner Double Rainbow Enterprises, McMinnville, 1993—; creator products for hobbyist and handicapped decorators, 1989—; tchr. cake decorating, candy and gingerbread houses, 1981—; cons., presenter cake decorating and sugar art demonstrations, various youth clubs and area high schs. Author: ABC Bible, 1967, I Can See God In Everything, 1975, The Wedding Book, 1983, Friends Feasts & Fellowship, 1992, God and Money, 1992, Looseleaf Pattern Library, 1992, Mary's Cook Book, 1993, It's Time to Oil the Lamps, 1994. Leader, Country Kids and Friends 4-H, St. Helens, 1979-85; organizer rural fire dept., Rainier, Oreg.; Sunday sch. tchr. Luth. Ch., 1956-74, officer women's groups, 1960-77; sec. Tualitan Vallye Rabbit Breeders Assn., 1964-67, fair dinner booth chmn., 1965-66; ballot clk. Columbia County Election Bd., 1972-80; decorated cake supt. Columbia County Fair, 1983-85; decorations chmn. Christian Women's Club, McMinnville, 1989-90; founder youth hobby club Pettis Fours Club, 1989. Winner awards for entries in numerous county and state fairs, cake shows. Mem. Women Entrepreneurs Oreg., Internat. Cake Exploration Soc. Republican. Lutheran. Office: Double Rainbow Enterprises 1301 N Hwy 99W #298 McMinnville OR 97128

JOHNSON, MARY BETTINA BLACK, physical education educator, athletic trainer; b. Salt Lake City, Mar. 2, 1952; d. Wayne Lythgoe and Bettina Loewen (Rothrock) Black; m. Carl Lowell Johnson, July 26, 1974; 1 child, Robert Wayne Rā. BS, U. Utah, 1974, MS, 1984, PhD, 1990. Cert. tchr., Utah. Phys. edn. tchr. Mt. Jordan Jr. High Sch., Sandy, Utah, 1974-78, Alta High Sch., Sandy, Utah, 1978-84; adj. faculty U. Utah, Salt Lake City, 1986-89; assoc. athletic trainer U.S. Olympic Com., Colorado Springs, Colo., 1986; athletic trainer Salt Lake Sports Medicine, 1987-89; grad. asst. athletic trainer U. Utah Athletics, Salt Lake City, 1985-89; asst. prof. athletic tng./pre-phys. therapy San Diego State U., 1989-93; asst. prof., dir. athletic tng. dept. human performance Met. State Coll. Denver, 1993—. contbr. articles to profl. jours. Named one of Outstanding Young Women of Am., 1979; Affirmative Action grantee, Rsch. scholar and Creative Arts grantee San Diego State Univ. Mem. AAHPERD, Nat. Athletic Trainers Assn. (cert., grad. student scholarship 1984, membership rsch. grant 1990), Far West Athletic Trainers Assn., Rocky Mountain Athletic Trainers Assn., Colo. Athletic Trainers Assn., Calif. Athletic Trainers Assn., Utah Athletic Trainers Assn. Democrat. Office: Met State Coll Denver Dept HPSL Campus Box 25 Po Box 173362 Denver CO 80217-3362

JOHNSON, MARY ELIZABETH, retired speech educator; b. Powhatan Pt., Ohio, Mar. 10, 1905; d. John McFadden and Nancy Ramsay (Shannon) J. BA, Muskingum Coll., New Concord, Ohio, 1926; MA, U. Mich., 1933; postgrad., Northwestern U., 1956, 60, Ohio State U., 1946, 68. Cert. in edn., speech correction, Ohio, 1960. Tchr. Moundsville (W.Va.) High Sch., 1926-37, dean of girls, 1935-37; chmn. English dept. Martins Ferry (Ohio) High Sch., 1937-44, instr. speech, 1944-48; asst. prof. Muskingum Coll., 1948-52, assoc. prof. speech, 1952-72, emeritus assoc. prof., 1972—; chmn. drama and poetry reading conf. Muskingum Coll., 1946-68, communications area, 1950-53, acting chmn. dept. speech, 1965-66, adviser Nat. Collegiate Players, 1957-65; author Ohio dist. state scholarship tests in English for secondary schs., 1941, 43, 46. V.p. Women's Forum, New Concord, 1966-67; mem. First Community Village Coun., Columbus, Ohio, 1984, 85; chmn. Children's Hosp. Twig #15, Columbus, 1987, 88. Mem. AAUW, Am. Assn. Retired Persons, Am. Speech and Hearing Assn., Ohio Speech and Hearing Assn., Comparative Edn. Soc. (seminar and field study in Europe 1967), Ohio Ret. Tchrs. Assn., Heritage Club, Parchment Club (pres. New Concord 1968, 78), Delta Kappa Gamma Internat. (pres. Psi chpt.), Alpha Delta State 1941-43, pres. Alpha Psi chpt. 1951, state recording sec. 1965-67). Presbyterian.

JOHNSON, MARY ELIZABETH, elementary education educator; b. St. Louis, Sept. 17, 1943; d. Richard William Blayney and Alice Bonjean (Taylor) Blayney Needham; m. Clyde Robert Johnson, Aug. 31, 1963; children: Brian (dec. 1991), Elizabeth Johnson Meyer, David. BS cum laude, U. Ill., 1966; MA, Maryville U., 1990; postgrad., So. Ill. U., 1990. Cert. elem. tchr., Ill., Mo. Tchr. Hazelwood Sch. Dist., Florissant, Mo., 1971-93, positive intervention tchr., 1989-91; Author play: Say No to Drugs, 1991. Author: Secret Study Skills for Third Graders, 1990. Mem. Hazelwood Schs. Music Boosters, 1980-88; mem. coms. Townsend PTA, Florissant, 1976—; contbr. Schlarship Run-Walk, 1982—; mem. Children's United Rsch. Effort in Cancer, 1986—; vol. Spl. Love, Inc., camp for children with cancer, 1986—; active The Children's Inn, Bethesda, Md., 1990—, Bailey Scholarship Fund, U. Ill. Fred S. Bailey scholar, 1962-66, Edmund J. James scholar, 1964-65; named Townsend Tchr. of Yr., 1989-90. Mem. NEA, Kappa Delta Pi, Alpha Lambda Delta, Phi Kappa Phi. Baptist. Home: 12 Shamblin Rd Florissant MO 63034-1354 also: 5230 E Brown Rd Apt 114 Mesa AZ 85205-4364

JOHNSON, MARY LOU, lay worker; b. Moline, Ill., July 15, 1923; d. Percy and Hope (Aulgur) Sipes; m. Blaine Eugene Johnson, May 30, 1941; children: Vivian A. Johnson Sweedy, Michael D., Amelia Johnson Harms Thomas, James Michael (dec.). Grad. high sch., Moline. Chmn. Christian edn. 1st Christian Ch., Moline, 1971-73, 77-79, 84-86, elder, 1973-76, 77-80, chmn. official bd., 1979-81, dir. Christian edn., 1988-93, ret., 1993; Sunday sch. tchr. 1st Christian Ch, Moline, 1958-84; cluster del. Christian Chs. Ill. and Wisc., Moline, 1988-89. Author: (poem) What Is A Mother?, 1965. Officer (various) PTA, Moline, 1952-75 (hon. life mem. State of Ill. 1972); leader, dist. dir. Girl Scouts U.S. Moline, 1955-65; skywatcher USAF Ground Observer Corps, Moline, 1955-57; vol. telethon coord. Muscular Dystrophy Assn., Moline, 1971—; del. lt. gov's. Commn. on Aging, Springfield, Ill., 1990. Recipient numerous appreciation awards Muscular Dystrophy Assn., 1964-93. Republican. Home: 2014 9th St Moline IL 61265-4779

JOHNSON, MARY MURPHY, social services director; b. N.Y.C., Mar. 5, 1940; d. Richard and Nora (Greene) Murphy; m. Noel James Johnson, Oct. 8, 1961; children: Valerie Johnson Cross, Donna Homan, Noreen Marie Pettitt, Richard. BA in English/History magna cum laude, Jacksonville State U., 1983, MA in History, 1984; B in Social Work magna cum laude, 1988. Cert. gerontology specialist. Asst. activities dir. Jacksonville (Ala.) Nursing Home, 1985-86; social services dir. Beckwood Manor, Anniston, Ala., 1987—; Cons. in field. Editor: Vladivostak Diary, 1987. Mem. Ala. Archaeol. Soc., Coosa Valley Archaeol. Soc. (sec. 1982-87), Soc. Ala. Archivists, Human Svcs. Coun., Vietnam Vets. of Am., Phi Eta Sigma, Phi Alpha Theta, Sigma Tau Delta, Omicron Delta Kappa. Russian Orthodox. Clubs: Non Commd. Officers Ladies Aux. (pres. 1970-71), Non Commd. Officers Wives (Germany) (pres. 1965-66).

JOHNSON, MARY SUSAN, transportation company professional; b. Bloomingdale, Ind., Nov. 19, 1937; d. William Blaine Shade and Goldina VandaVeer (Newlin) Brown; children: Roger, Tisa, Julia, Angela, Robert, William. Grad. high sch., Rockville, Ind. Sec., treas. Tri-State Transport, Inc., 1968-73; road driver Roadway Express, Chicago Heights, Ill., 1977—, safety team capt., 1991-92, 94; completed Passport Tour (Abate), 1990, 94; mem. Roadway Express Dist. Road Team Dist. 12, 1995. Mem newsletter com. focus group Roadway Express; mem. focus group Kenworth Driver's Bd., 1992-94. Recipient rodeo awards. Mem. Am. Motorcycle Assn., Am. Bikers Aim Toward Edn., Am. Radio Relay League, Am. Radio Emergency Svc. (Lake County), Internat. Platform Assn., Stars Radio Club, Harley Owners Group (newsletter editor Calumet region, Hammond, Ind.), Ladies of Harley, Kankakee Valley Harley Owners Group, Porter County Harley Owners Group. Home and Office: PO Box 316 Griffith IN 46319-0316

JOHNSON, M(ARY) SUSAN, school counselor; b. Parson, Kans., Aug. 17, 1953; d. Kirby R. and Dorothy A. (Purkey) Killough; m. Fred Wilber Johnson Jr., Nov. 17, 1973; 1 child, Brian Kirby Johnson. BS in Bus. Edn., Pitts. State U., 1973, MS in Counseling, 1985. Sec. Am. Nat. Ins., Pitts., 1974-77; pers. asst. Kans. Power and Light Co., Topeka, 1977-80; bus. edn. instr. Oswego (Kans.) High Sch., 1980-85, counselor, 1985—; bd. dirs. Oswego Found. for Edn., Found. for CLASS, Columbus, Labette County Correctional Camp, Oswego, CLASS, Ltd., Columbus; cons. S.E. Kans. Edn. Svc. Ctr., Girard, Kans., 1990—. Cubmaster Cub Scouts of Am., Oswego, 1988-90; bd. dirs. Oswego Econ. Devel. Com., 1984-87; soccer coach Oswego Recreation Commn., 1989-90. Mem. ACA, S.E. Kans. Counseling Assn. (pres. 1991-92), Kans. Counseling Assn. (human rights chair), Kans. Sch. Counselors Assn. (membership chair 1992-93, awards chair 1993-94, pub. rels. chair 1994—), Kans. Career Devel. Assn. Office: Oswego High Sch PO Box 129 Oswego KS 67356-0129

JOHNSON, MARYANNA MORSE, business owner; b. Oxford, Miss., Dec. 21, 1936; d. Hugh McDonald and Anna Sullivan (Virden) Morse; children: Julianna, Hunter, Cynthia, Capp. Student, Miss. U. for Women, 1957; BSN cum laude, Tex. Woman's U., 1986. RN, Tex. Owner MJM & Assocs., Boulder, Colo., 1968—; health promotion cons., 1986—. Mem. Sigma Theta Tau. Home: 3102 Bell Dr Boulder CO 80301-2277

JOHNSON, MARYBETH CASS, public relations executive; b. Evanston, Ill., Oct. 5, 1955; d. Richard Lewis and Mary Stuart Cass; m. Scott B. Johnson. BA in Journalism, Ohio State U., 1977; M in Pub. Affairs, Columbia Coll., Chgo., 1986. Field rep. St. Jude Children's Rsch. Hosp., Columbus, Ohio, 1977-80; pub. affairs specialist City of Chgo., 1981-85; press sec. Ill. State Senate, Chgo., 1986-89; acct. supr. Burson-Marsteller, Chgo., 1990-93; dir. pub. rels. Ameritech Cellular Svcs., Hoffman Estates, Ill., 1993—. Bd. regents Mercy Home for Boys and Girls, Chgo., 1991—; spokesperson Ill. Dem. Party, Chgo., 1986-92. Mem. Chgo. Women in Govt. Rels. (chair pub. rels. com. 1982-92), Women in Mgmt., Women in Wireless. Office: Ameritech Cellular Svcs 2000 W Ameritech Center Dr Hoffman Estates IL 60195-5000

JOHNSON, MARYL RAE, cardiologist; b. Fort Dodge, Iowa, Apr. 15, 1951; d. Marvin George and Beryl Evelyn (White) J. BS, Iowa State U., 1973; MD, U. Iowa, 1977. Diplomate Am. Bd. Internal Medicine; diplomate of Subspeciality of Cardiovascular Diseases. Intern, U. Iowa Hosps., Iowa City, 1977-78, resident 1978-81, fellow, 1979-82; assoc. in cardiology U. Iowa Hosps. and Clinics, Iowa City, 1982-86, asst. prof. medicine cardiovascular div., 1986-88; asst. prof. medicine Med. Ctr. Loyola U., 1988-92, assoc. prof. 1992-94; assoc. prof. Rush U., 1994—; med. dir. cardiac transplantation U. Iowa Hosp., 1986-88, assoc. med. dir. cardiac transplantation Loyola U., 1988-94; assoc. med. dir. Rush Heart Failure and Cardiac Transplant Program, 1994—. Mem. Nat. Heart Lung and Blood Adv. Council, Bethesda, Md., 1979-83, biomed. rsch. tech. rev. com. NIH, 1990-93 (chairperson 1992-93). Barry Freeman scholar, 1974; recipient Jane Leinfelder Meml. award U. Iowa Coll. Medicine, 1977, Clin. Investigator award NIH, 1981, New Investigator Research award, NIH, 1986. Mem. AMA, Internat. Soc. Heart and Lung Transplantation, Am. Heart Assn., Am. Fedn. Clin. Research, AAAS, Am. Coll. Cardiology, ACP, Ill. State Med. Soc., Chgo. Med. Soc., Order of the Rose, Alpha Lambda Delta, Phi Kappa Phi, Iota Sigma Pi, Alpha Omega Alpha.

JOHNSON, MAXINE FRAHM, bank executive; b. Mason City, Iowa, Dec. 18, 1939; d. Peter Jr. and Emily Marian (Bistline) Frahm; m. Robert W. Johnson, June 3, 1962; children: Brenda Lynn, Janine Suzanne. BA, Grinnell Coll., 1961; MBA, U. Pitts., 1976. Cert. fin. planner; cert. trust and fin. advisor. Contract writer Bankers Life Co., Des Moines, 1961-62; music tchr. Haworth (N.J.) Pub. Sch., 1962-63; pvt. practice Setauket, N.Y., 1963-65, Joliet, Ill., 1965-70, Glenshaw, Pa., 1970-76; trust officer Pitts. Nat. Bank, 1976-82; sr. trust officer Bank of New England, N.A., Boston, 1982-84, v.p., 1984-90, head personal trust administrn., 1990-91; v.p. R.I. Hosp. Trust Nat. Bank, 1991—; faculty mem. New Eng. Banking Inst., 1984—; adj. faculty Northeastern U., Dedham, Mass., 1989—. Author: Implications of the Generation Skipping Transfer Tax for Trust Administrators, 1980. Sec. bd. dirs. Children's Mus. R.I. Mem. AAUW, Inst. Cert. Fin. Planners, Boston Estate Planning Coun., R.I. Estate Planning Coun., Chaminade Club, Pi Kappa Lambda, Delta Gamma Sigma. Office: RI Hosp Trust Nat Bank One Hosp Trust Pla T 03 01 Providence RI 02903-2449

JOHNSON, MELINDA See CUMMINGS, SPANGLER

JOHNSON, MILDRED GRACE MASH, investment company executive; b. Castle Rock, Wash., Mar. 3, 1922; d. Percival and Hilda C. (Nyberg) M.; widowed, 1988; children: John, Joy, Judy, Chris, Steven. Student, U. Wash. V.p. Johnson Constrn. Co., Seattle, 1950-58, pres., 1988-91; v.p. Johnson Investment Co., Seattle, 1950-58, pres., 1988—. Deacon U. Presbyn. Ch., Seattle, 1981—. Mem. Am. Bus. Women's Assn. (v.p. 1979-89, Woman of Yr. 1981), Apt. Assn., Master Builders, Daus. Nile, Order of Ea. Star. Republican. Home: 3812 E McGilvra St Seattle WA 98112

JOHNSON, MILDRED SNOWDEN, nursing educator, retired; b. Elgin, Tex., Nov. 15, 1915; d. Milton Foy and Pearl Mae (DeLoach) Snowden; children: Roy B. Johnson, Betty Carol Johnson. BSN, U. Tex., Galveston, 1965; MSN, U. Tex., Austin, 1972. Cert. clin. nurse spl. adult psychol./mental health. Psychiatric nurse tech. State Hosp., Austin, 1959-63; head nurse Holy Cross Hosp., Austin, 1967, St. David's Hosp., Austin, 1968-69; acting dir. Ctrl. Tex. Coll., Kileen, Tex., 1969-70; asst. prof. nursing U. Tex., Galveston, 1970-93; ret., 1993. Mem. ANA, Nat. League Nursing, Tex. Nurses Assn., Tex. League Nursing, Sigma Theta Tau Internat. Home: 2116 Fordham Ln Austin TX 78723-1332

JOHNSON, MONICA LYNN, elementary education educator; b. Dubuque, Iowa, Mar. 8, 1962; d. Hugo and Arlene Isabel (Netzer) Fritz; children: Justus, Kyle. BS, No. Ill. U., 1985. Elem. art educator Saratoga Elem. Sch., Morris, Ill., 1987-92, 94—, Immaculate Conception Sch., Morris, Ill., 1991-92, Troy Shorewood-Dist. 30C, Joliet, Ill., 1992-94; muralist Saratoga Sch., Morris, 1990, Immaculate Conception Sch., Morris, 1991, Mary Crest Sch., Joliet, 1991, Troy Shorewood Sch., Joliet, 1993; owner Monicom, Personalized Children's Books, Morris. Mem. Nat. Art Edn. Assn., Ill. Art Edn. Assn.

JOHNSON, NANCY K., judge; b. Cin.. BA, Univ. of Cin., 1975, JD, 1978. Bar: Ohio 1978, Tex. 1980. Asst. atty. gen. Ohio, 1978-80, Tex., 1980-81; asst. U.S. atty. Tex. So. Dist., 1982-90; magistrate judge U.S. Dist. Ct. (Tex. so. dist.), 5th circuit, 1990—. Mem. Fed. Bar Assn., Houston Bar Assn. Office: Federal Bldg 515 Rusk St Rm 7019 Houston TX 77002-2600*

JOHNSON, NANCY LEE, congresswoman; b. Chicago, Ill., Jan. 5, 1935; d. Noble Wishard and Gertrude Reid (Smith) Lee; m. Theodore H. Johnson, July 16, 1958; children—Lindsey Lee, Althea Anne, Caroline Reid. B.A., Radcliffe Coll., 1957; postgrad., U. London, 1957-58. Vice chmn. Charter Commn. New Britain, Conn., 1976-77; mem. Conn. Senate from 6th dist., 1977-82, 98th-104th Congresses from 6th Conn. dist., Washington, 1983—; mem. ways and means com., subcom. health, chair oversight com.; Pres. Friends of Libr., New Britain Pub. Libr., 1973-76, Radcliffe Club No. Conn., 1973-75; bd. dirs., pres. Sheldon Cmty. Guidance Clinic, 1974-75; dir. religious edn. Unitarian Universalist Soc. New Britain, 1967-72, pres., 1973-75; bd. dirs. New Britain Symphony Soc., 1975-77, Plainville Group Home, 1975-76, United Way New Britain, 1976-79. Lectr. Am. art New Britain Mus. Am. Art, 1968-71. Recipient Outstanding Vol. award United Way, 1976; English Speaking Union grantee, 1958-59. Republican. Home: 141 S Mountain St New Britain CT 06052-1511 Office: Ho of Reps 343 Cannon Washington DC 20515-0706

JOHNSON, NANCY TEAGUE, critical care nurse; b. Hickory, N.C., Nov. 27, 1950; d. Troy V. and Mae (Bolick) Teague; m. Gary Lee Johnson, Dec. 22, 1968; children: Andrew L., Cantresa L. ADN, Catawba Valley Tech. Coll., 1985; BSN summa cum laude, Winston-Salem State U., 1992. RN, N.C.; cert. BLS, ACLS, PALS Am. Heart Assn. Sec. Plastic Packaging, Inc., Hickory, 1970-78, 81-83; staff nurse, charge nurse Catawba Meml. Hosp., Hickory, 1985—. Del. People to People Internat., People's Republic China, 1990. Mem. ANA, AACN. Methodist. Home: RR 1 Box 47 Taylorsville NC 28681-9706

JOHNSON, NORMA HOLLOWAY, federal judge; b. Lake Charles, La.; d. H. Lee and Beatrice (Williams) Holloway; m. Julius A. Johnson, June 18, 1964. B.S., D.C. Tchrs. Coll., 1955; J.D., Georgetown U., 1962. Bar: D.C. 1962, U.S. Supreme Ct. 1967. Pvt. practice law Washington, 1963; atty. civil divsn. Dept. Justice, Washington, 1963-67; asst. corp. counsel Office of Corp. Counsel, Washington, 1967-70; judge D.C. Superior Ct., 1970-80, U.S. Dist. Ct. (D.C. dist.), Washington, 1980—. Bd. dirs. Judiciary Leadership Devel. Coun. Fellow Am. Bar Found.; mem. Nat. Bar Assn., Fed. Judges Assn., Am. Judicature Soc., Supreme Ct. Hist. Soc., Am. Inns of Ct. (William Bryant inn). Office: US Dist Ct US Courthouse 3rd & Constitution Ave NW Washington DC 20001*

JOHNSON, NORMA J., specialty wool grower; b. Dover, Ohio, Aug. 30, 1925; d. Jasper Crile and Mildred Catherine (Russell) J.; m. Robert Blake Covey, Oct. 7, 1951 (div. 1960); 1 child, Susan Kay. Student Heidelberg Coll., 1943; cert. drafting techniques Case Sch. Applied Sci., 1944; student Western Res. U., 1945-47, Ohio State U., 1951, Muskingum Coll., 1965; AA, Kent State U., 1979, Buckeye Joint Vocat. Sch., 1979-84. Instr. arts and crafts Univ. Settlement House, Cleve., 1944; mech. drafstwoman Nat. Assn. Civil Aeros., Cleve., 1944-46; mfrs. rep. Nat. Spice House, 1947-49; tchr. econs., home econs., English, math, history, high sch., Tuscarawas County Sch. System, New Philadelphia, Ohio, 1962-69; owner, mgr., operator Sunny Slopes Farm, producer of specialty wools and grains, Dover, Ohio, 1969—. Tchr., Meth. Sunday Sch., 1956-61; chaplain Winfield PTA, 1960; program dir. Brandywine Grange, 1960-62; troop leader Girl Scouts U.S.A., 1961-70; mem. assoc. bd. Norma Johnson Conservation Ctr. Recipient cert. of merit Tuscarawas County Schs., 1965, Ohio Wildlife Conservation award Tuscarawas County, 1972, 1st and 3d premiums for handspinning fleece, Ohio State Fair, 1984, 8th and 10th premiums, Mich. Stat Fair, 1985, proclamation of appreciation Bd. Commrs. Tuscarawas County, 1990, Zeisberger-Heckewelder medal Ohio State Ho. Reps. presented by Tuscarawas County Hist. Soc., 1992., State of Ohio Senate honor for commitment to conservaiton edn., 1992, Community Svc. award VFW, 1992. Mem. Mid States Wool Growers, Am. Angus Assn., Am. Tree Farm System, Nat. Arbor Day Found., Nat. Wildlife Fedn., Nat. Trust for Hist. Preservation, Ohio Nut Growers Assn., Midwest Weavers Assn., Canton Weavers and Spinners, Ohio Hist. Soc., Ohio Arts and Crafts Guild, Tuscarawas County Geneal. Soc., Inc., Tuscarawas County Hist. Soc. Bldg. designed and constructed interior facilities for the Scheuer-Haus. Home and Office: 4033 State Route 39 NW Dover OH 44622-7237

JOHNSON, PATRICIA DUREN, health insurance company executive; b. Columbus, Ohio, Oct. 22, 1943; d. James and Rosetta J. Duren; m. Harold H. Johnson, Jr., Dec. 25, 1965; 1 child, Jill. BS in Edn., Ohio State U., 1965. Tchr. various locations, 1966-72; sales rep. ITT Hartford, Portland, Oreg., 1972-73; sr. v.p. Blue Cross of Calif., 1975-92; gen. mgr. preventive care Blue Cross of Calif., Westlake, 1992—. Mem. editorial adv. bd. RN Times. Mem. community adv. bd. KCET, L.A.; mem. Coalition of 100 Black Women; bd. dirs. Am. Cancer Soc., 1988-92. Mem. Am. Hosp. Assn.,

Women in Health Adminstrn., Delta Sigma Theta. Office: Blue Cross of Calif PO Box 9078 Oxnard CA 93031-9078

JOHNSON, PATRICIA GAYLE, corporate communication executive, writer; b. Conway, Ark., Oct. 23, 1947; d. Rudolph and Frances Modene (Hayes) J. Student U. Calif., Irvine, 1965-68. Advance rep. Disney on Parade, Los Angeles, 1971-75; mktg. dir., dir. field ops. Am. Freedom Train, 1975-77; publ. rels. mgr. Six Flags, Inc., Los Angeles, 1977-81; mgr. corp. communications Playboy Enterprises, Inc., Los Angeles, 1981-82; external rels. mgr. Kal Kan Foods, Inc., Los Angeles, 1982-86; v.p. Daniel J. Edelman, Inc., 1986-88; sr. v.p. Amies Advt. and Pub. Rels., Irvine, 1988-89; dir. pub. rels. World Vision, Monrovia, Calif., 1989-92; v.p. The Bohle Co., L.A., 1992—; lectr. U. So. Calif., UCLA, Calif. State U., Northridge, Calif. State U., Dominguez Hills. Bd. dirs. Jeopardy Youth Gang Intervention Program. Mem. Pub. Rels. Soc. Am. (past officer), Pub. Affairs Council, Delta Soc. (advisor). Mem. Foursquare Gospel Ch. Collaborator TV scripts; contbr. articles to various consumer and profl. mags. Office: The Bohle Co 1999 Ave of Stars Los Angeles CA 90067

JOHNSON, PATRICIA MARY, publisher; b. Evanston, Ill., Mar. 14, 1937; d. Harold W. and Florence M. (Miller) J.; children: William, Nancy, Richard. Degree in Interior Design LaSalle U., Chgo., 1972; student Art Inst., Chgo., 1970-73. Interior design communicator, producer/host weekly syndicated cable TV program on interior design, 1980-86; owner Design Communications, Rosenhayn, N.J., 1976; exec. dir., founder Corp. for Disabled/Handicapped, 1985—, A Positive Approach, Inc. Author; Eliminating Barriers From Your LIfestyle, 1988, Guide to Securing Housing for People with Developmental Disabilities, 1993; pub. (mags.) A Positive Approach, 1985—, An Approach to Barrier Free Design, 1992; prodr. A Guide to Securing Independent Housing for Individuals with Disabilities, 1994. Recipient award N.J. Gov., 1985, Practitioner of Yr. award N.J. Rehab. Assn., 1987, Humanitarian Service award United Cerebral Palsy, 1987, Jefferson award NBC, 1988, Healing Community United Nations Pub. award, 1989, Community Svc. award Pres. George Bush, 1991. Office: PO Box 910 Millville NJ 08332-0910

JOHNSON, PAULINE BENGE, nurse, anesthetist; b. London, Ky., May 10, 1932; d. Chester G. and Bertha M. (Hale) Benge; m. Scottie W. Johnson, Apr. 29, 1950 (dec. 1976); children: Rita Johnson, Nita Johnson Yaw, Gina Johnson Carlson. AA, U. Ky., 1968; diploma, U. Cin. Sch. Nurse Anesthesia, 1971; BS summa cum laude, U. Cin., 1974, M., 1977, D., 1981. RN, Ohio, Ky., Tenn., Ind., W.Va., Fla., Tex.; cert., lic. RN anesthetist. Staff anesthetist Jewish Hosp., Cin., 1971-72, Mercy North Hosp., Hamilton, Ohio, 1972-86, Ft. Hamilton Hosp., Hamilton, 1972-86, McCullough-Hyde Hosp., Oxford, Ohio, 1986-88; freelance anesthetist multiple hosps. Ohio, Ky., 1982-88; staff anesthetist, ind. contractor Shriner Burn Inst., Cin., 1989; pres., staff anesthetist, ind. contractor multiple hosps. Pauline B. Johnson Co., Inc., Ohio, Ky., Tenn., Ind., W. Va., Fla., Tex., 1989—. Ch. clk. Lindenwald Bapt. Ch., Hamilton, 1955-72, mem. 1955-85, instr., 1955-76; mem. 1st Bapt. Ch., Hamilton, 1985—, NOW, 1978—, nominating com. major polit. party, Hamilton, 1986-89; mem., med. com. Planned Parenthood, Hamilton, 1987—. Scholar U. Cin., 1969-71, 77-81; recipient Spl. Recognition Higher Edn., Laurel County Homecoming, London, Ky., 1988. Mem. Am. Assn. Nurse Anesthetists (speaker nat. conv. 1982, speaker rsch. forum nat. meeting 1989, mem. nominating com. 1978), Ohio State Assn. Nurse Anesthetists (state bd. dirs. 1989-92, 88-90, 79-80, chair bylaws com. 1991-92, 92-93, nominating com. 1993-94, chair edn. com. 1990-91, pres. 1982-84, state editor Highlights 1974-82, co-chair state meeting 1982, pres. dist. 5 Cin. 1978, govt. rels. chpt. Greater Cin. chpt. 1976-87, speaker meetings), Kappa Delta Pi. Home: 128 S F St Hamilton OH 45013-4710

JOHNSON, PENELOPE B., librarian; b. Lewiston, Maine, Nov. 26, 1946; d. Wesley I and Bertha (Leavitt) J.; m. Milton F. Bornstein, July 12, 1969. BA, U. Maine, 1969; MS, Simmons Coll., 1970; CAGS, Boston U., 1978. Cert. profl. librarian. Children's libr. Wilmington Mem'l Libr., Wilmington, Mass., 1970-71, Worcester Pub. Libr., Worcester, Mass., 1971-79; children's cons. Ctrl. Mass. Regional Libr. System, Worcester, Mass., 1979-80; divsn. head Worcester Pub. Libr., Worcester, Mass., 1980-87, assoc. libr., 1987-91, head libr., 1991—. Pres. YMCA of Ctrl. Mass., 1989-91, bd. dirs., 1979-95; mem. exec. com. City Adminstrv. Affairs Assn., 1993-95. Mem. ALA, New England Libr. Assn., Mass. Libr. Assn., Simmons Coll. Alumni Assn. (pres. grad. sch. libr. and info. 1990-91). Office: Worcester Pub Libr 3 Salem Sq Worcester MA 01608

JOHNSON, RAMONA ELIZABETH, physician; b. LaCrosse, Wis., Dec. 12, 1951; d. Marion Butcher and Bernice Naomi (Rittenhouse) J.; children: Amanda, Elizabeth. BS in Zoology, U. Wis., 1972, MD, 1977; MS in Preventive Medicine and Environ. Health, U. Iowa, 1982. Diplomate Am. Bd. Family Practice, Am. Bd. Quality Assurance and Utilization Rev. Physician. Fellow assoc. U. Iowa Family Practice, Iowa City, 1980-82; clin. physician Irvine (Calif.) Walk-In Med. Group, 1985-94; med. officer Orange County Pub. Health Dept., Santa Ana, Calif., 1987-94; med. dir. Met. Life, Orange, Calif., 1991—; clin. asst. prof. family practice U. So. Calif., L.A., 1984—; med. cons. Cost Care, Inc., Huntington Beach, Calif., 1986-89, Employee Benefits Am. Adminstrn. Corp., Newport Beach, Calif., 1990-91. Contbr. articles to profl. jours. Fellow Am. Acad. Family Physicians; mem. Am. Coll. Med. Quality, Wesleyan Med. Fellowship. Office: Met Life 200 S Manchester Ste 720 Orange CA 92668

JOHNSON, RAYMONDA THEODORA GREENE, humanities educator; b. Chgo., Jan. 12, 1939; d. Theodore T. and Eileen (Atherley) Greene; m. Hulon Johnson, June 27, 1964; children: David Atherley, Theodore Cassell, Alexander Ward. BA in English, DePaul U., 1960; MA in English, Loyola U., Chgo., 1965. Cert. high sch. English tchr., Ill. Tchr. high sch. English, Chgo. Pub. Schs., 1960-65; instr. English, Harold Washington Coll. (formerly Loop Coll.), City Coll., Chgo., 1965-66, asst. prof., 1966-91, assoc. prof., 1991—, faculty advisor coll. newspaper, 1989-92, pres. faculty coun., 1990-92, chairperson English and Speech Dept., 1992—, chair coll. assessment planning com., 1995—. Middle sch. v.p. parents coun. Latin Sch., Chgo., 1974-76, trustee, 1987-93; cubmaster, leader cub scouts Boys Scouts Am., Chgo., 1974-81; active black creativity adv. com. Mus. Sci. and Industry, Chgo., 1984—. Recipient svc. award religious edn. program St. Thomas the Apostle Ch., Chgo., 1984. Mem. Twigs Mothers Club (pres. 1982-84), Alpha Kappa Alpha. Democrat. Roman Catholic. Home: 6747 S Bennett Ave Chicago IL 60649-1031 Office: Harold Washington Coll Rm 602A 30 E Lake St Chicago IL 60601-2420

JOHNSON, REBECCA BELL, enterostomal therapy nurse; b. Lewes, Del., Dec. 30, 1948; d. Walter James and Ruth Eleanor (Hastings) Bell. Student, Mitchell Coll., 1966-68; ADN, Del. Tech. Community Coll., 1978; diploma in enterostomal therapy, Harrrisburg Hosp., 1980. Cert. in enterostomal therapy. Staff nurse Nanticoke Meml. Hosp., Seaford, Del., 1978-80; instr. ostomy and skin care Nanticoke Meml. Hosp., Methodist Manor House, Del. Hospice, Seaford, Del., 1980—; staff nurse oper. rm. Nanticoke Meml. Hosp., Seaford, 1980-85, enterostomal therapy nurse, 1980—, nurse mgr., 1988—; lectr. Convatec, Inc., 1989, instr., 1987, 86. lectr. Convatec, Inc., 1989, instr., 1987, 88; initiator preventive skincare program Lifecare, Lofland Park, 1992. Mem. exec. bd. dirs. Sussex County chpt. Am. Cancer Soc., 1987. Mem. Wound, Ostomy and Continence Nursing, Am. Assn. Enterostomal Therapy Nurses, United Ostomy Assn. Democrat. Methodist. Home: Rt 4 Box 53 Seaford DE 19973 Office: Nanticoke Meml Hosp 801 Middleford Rd Seaford DE 19973-3698

JOHNSON, ROBYN M(ARIA) A(NNETTE), arts and visual design educator; b. Boston, July 25, 1955; d. Louis Charles and Veronica (Henry) J.; children: Roginald T., Rheeyan M.A., Rynique M.A. Student, Boston U., 1976-78; cert. of completion, Paris Fashion Inst., 1982; BFA, Mass. Coll. Art, 1983, postgrad., 1985. Cert. tchr., Mass. Arts educator Wellesley (Mass.) Pub. Schs., 1984-85; tchr. Boston Pub. Schs., 1985—; area coord. Action Boston Community Devel., 1975-81; instr. illustrating Newbury St. Sch. Fashion Design, Boston, 1987-88; arts instr. Boston Parks and Recreation, 1992; co-dir. Action Boston Community Devel., 1976-81, councilor, 1976-79; freelance designer, D.B.A. Obynee's Artfordable Fashions. Campaign worker Imee Jackson for City Coun., Boston, 1989-90. Named Most-Outstanding Designer, Beantown Prodns., Boston, 1979; recipient Charlotte Demsey award United South End Settlements, Boston, 1983, Frances Thompson award Mass. Coll. Art, 1982. Mem. Boston Afro Am. Artists (rec. sec. 1989, 1st pl. award 1989, 91), Eastern Star Juridiction Mass., Inc. Pentecostal-Apostolic. Home: 6 Kerr Pl Boston MA 02120 Office: Gavin Middle Sch South Boston MA 02120

JOHNSON, ROMANZA LAMOYNE, home economist; b. Scottsville, Ky., Dec. 1, 1939; d. John Coyner and Virginia Hall (Sledge) Oliphant; m. Ralph Eugene Johnson, June 22, 1961. BS in Home Econs., Western Ky. U., 1960, MA, 1968; postgrad., U. Tenn. Tchr. home econs. Scottsville High Sch., Ky., 1960-65, Western Ky. U., 1965-70; home economist Bowling Green (Ky.) Mcpl. Utilities, 1970-93. Contbr. articles to profl. jours. Hostess Eastwood Bapt. Ch., 1975—, chmn. pulpit flowers; bd. dirs. Ky. Heart Assn., 1978-88, chmn. pub. rels., 1980-81, 81-82, Ky. vice chmn., 1983-84, Ky. chmn. bd., 1984-86; mem. health com. Barren River Area Devel. Dist., 1979; mem. adv. coun. Home-Health Agy. City-County Hosp., 1974-94, v.p. and sec.; mem. Vols. in Action, 1981—, Bowling Green Interagy.; mem. adv. coun. head Start of Bowling Green. Recipient Farm-City Activities award Warren County, 1972, 73, 74, Nat. Alma award, 1973, Honor award Warren County Soil Conservation Dist., 1974, Girls Club award, 1978-82, Vol. award Ky. Heart Assn., 1983; named Outstanding Citizen Bowling Green, 1976, Citizen of Yr. Optimist Club, 1984, recipient Hertiage award Landmark Assn., 1988. Mem. Am. Home Econs. Assn. (mem. nat. program com., pub. relations com.), Ky. Home Econs. Assn., Ky. Home Econs. in Bus. (nominating chmn. 1977-78, mem. com. 1978-79, nat. edn. and personal devel. com. 1977-78, 78-79, others), Bluegrass Elec. Womens Roundtable Assn. (pres. 1975-76, co-chmn. nat. meeting 1976, other positions), Ky. Nutrition Council (bd. dirs. 1977-80, treas. 1978-79, vice chmn. 1979-80, 80-81, pres. 1981-82, counselor 1981-82, Bowling Green area Nutrition Council chmn. 1984-85), Bowling Green-Warren County Home County Home Econmist (pres. 1968), Bowling Green Dist. Home Econs. Tchrs. (pres. 1963). Home: 3341 Cemetery Rd Bowling Green KY 42103-9063

JOHNSON, RONDA JANICE, fundraising consultant; b. Muleshoe, Tex., Sept. 28, 1943; d. Randolph Revere and Betty Jo (Pool) J. BS in Edn., U. Tex., Austin, 1966; MBA, Houston Bapt. U., 1980. Cert. fund raising exec. Tchr. Galena Park Ind. Sch. Dist./Houston Ind. Sch. Dist., 1966-68; adminstrv. asst. Houston-Galveston Area Coun., 1968-69, Johns Hopkins U. Applied Physics Lab., Columbia, Md., 1969-73; dir. adminstrn. Edmondson Coll. Bus., Chattanooga, 1973-76; dir. Branell Women's Coll., Atlanta, 1976-78; dir. devel. U. Tex. Health Sci. Ctr., Houston, 1978-84, Houston Symphony Orch., 1984-85, Houston Child Guidance Ctr., 1985-87; pres. ctrl. divsn. Douglas M. Lawson Assocs., Inc., Houston, 1987—; instr. Vol. Support Ctr., Houston, 1992, continuing edn. div. Rice U., Houston, 1992. Adv. bd. Houston Achievement Pl., 1992; bd. dirs. Escape Ctr., Houston, 1992—. Named Woman of the Yr., 1994. Mem. Nat. Soc. Fundraising Execs. (bd. dirs. 1989—, pres. 1994—), Planned Giving Coun., Houstonian Network. Republican. Home: 5612 Saint Moritz St Bellaire TX 77401-2617 Office: Douglas M Lawson Assocs 4801 Woodway Dr # 382W Houston TX 77056

JOHNSON, ROSE CARMEN, management executive; b. Bronx, N.Y., Nov. 3, 1942; d. Samie Najeeb and Carmen Marie (Torres) Kiamie; m. J. Walter Johnson, Aug. 27, 1966 (div. Mar. 1993); children: Gregory, Glenn. AAS, Latin Am. Inst., 1962; BFA, Marymount Coll., 1964. Bilingual sec., translator Gen. Foods Corp., White Plains, N.Y., 1964-68; mgr. human resources Primerica, Greenwich, Conn., 1976-88; v.p. Sonique Employment, White Plains, 1988-89, Windsor Mgmt. Corp., N.Y.C., 1989—. Mem. NOW, Am. Contract Bridge Orgn. (pres. 1991-93), N.Y. Real Estate Bd. Home: 2-1 Steven Dr Ossining NY 10562 Office: Windsor Mgmt Corp 286 Fifth Ave New York NY 10001-4512

JOHNSON, ROSEMARY WRUCKE, personnel management specialist; b. Leith, N.D., Sept. 21, 1924; d. Rudolph Aaron and Metta Tomina (Andersen) Wrucke; m. Robert Johnson Jr., Sept. 28, 1945 (div. 1964). Student, George Washington U., 1944-45, 47, Nat. Art Sch., Washington, 1943-45. Supr. Displaced Persons Commn., Frankfurt, Germany, 1950-52, FBI, Washington, 1952-81; cons. position mgmt. orgn. design Arlington, Va., 1981—. Mem. NAFE, Classification and Compensation Soc., Soc. FBI Alumni (membership chmn. 1985-91), Internat. Platform Assn. Lutheran. Home and Office: 2525 10th St N Apt 820 Arlington VA 22201-1968

JOHNSON, RUBY LAVERNE, retail executive; b. Ada, Okla., Oct. 31, 1917; d. James Lee and Minta Estelle (Speights) Eppler; m. Albert Howard Johnson, Dec. 22, 1938; children: Phyllis, Richard, Jim, Bruce. With So. Bell Telephone, Ada, 1936-38; founder, owner, buyer Johnson's Furniture, Bossier City, La., 1963—. Mem. La. Home Furniture Assn., Bossier City C. of C., Univ. Club Shreveport. Home: 3376 Jon Rd Shreveport LA 71119-2236 Office: Johnson's Furniture 921 Westgate Ln Bossier City LA 71112-3595

JOHNSON, RUTH ALLEN, elementary school educator; b. Saltillo, Miss., Dec. 11, 1941; d. William Henry and Ruby R. (Harwood) Nichols; m. Charles Lee Johnson, Nov. 10, 1962; children: Stephen Lee, William Allen. BS, Miss. State U., 1963; MEd, U. Miss., 1975, EdS, 1978. Cert. elem. tchr., Miss. Elem. tchr. Lee County Schs., Tupelo, Miss., 1962-69, Columbus (Miss.) Pub. Schs., 1969-71, Tupelo City Schs., 1971-94; instr. adult basic edn. Itawomba C.C., 1994—; chairperson 5th Grade Reading Curriculum, Tupelo, 1980-94; cons. Cooperative Learning in Elem. Classroom, Portfolio Assessment, Miss. Writing/Thinking Inst. Named Profl. Educator of Yr. Columbus City Schs., 1969-71, one of 2000 Notable Am. Women. Mem. AAUW, Miss. Profl. Educators, ASCD, Delta Kappa Gamma (pres. 1987-89), Phi Delta Kappa (sec. 1978-79). Baptist. Home: 1222 Oakview Dr Tupelo MS 38801-1604

JOHNSON, SALLY JOANN, marketing professional; b. Flint, Mich., July 10, 1949; d. Bernard L. and Emma Jeanne (Maxson) J.; m. Douglas Sweet, Apr. 1, 1973 (div.); children: Dan Sweet, Jesse Sweet, Caitlin Sweet. BA in Sociology, Ohio U., 1990. Case mgr. Clark Ctr. for Children, Marietta, Ohio, 1983-87; dir. Child Assault Prevention Project, Marietta, 1985-87; childcare dir. Marietta YMCA, 1987-89; dir. women's ctr. Marietta Meml. Hosp., 1989-93, mktg. specialist, 1993—; trainer Wash. State C.C., Marietta, 1992—; co-founder Sexual Assault Intervention Network, Marietta, 1990-93. Telesis mem. C. of C. Leadership Program, Marietta, 1990. Named Citizen of Yr., Civitan, Washington County, 1993. Home: 800 E Montgomery St Marietta OH 45750-1714

JOHNSON, SHARON DENISE, office administrator, assistant treasurer; b. Kans. City, Mo., Nov. 18, 1947; d. Leland Earl and Leona (Gover) Dailey; m. Herbert Johnson, Oct. 27, 1973. AA in Studio Art, Met. C.C., Kans. City, Mo., 1967; BA in Studio Art, U. Mo., Kans. City, 1969, MPA, 1976. Draftsman, stat. analysis JBM & Assoc., Kans. City, 1969-73; office mgr., adminstr. Felix Camera & Video, Overland Park, Kans., 1976-93; office mgr., asst. treas. Hedlund & Assoc., Mission, Kans., 1993—. Chair fin. com. Lutheran Ch. of Resurrection, Prairie Village, Kans., 1992—, chair computer com., 1993—, mem. coun., 1991—. Mem. Inst. Mgmt. Accts., William Jewell Fine Arts Guild, Phi Kappa Phi. Republican. Home: 8404 Meadow Ln Leawood KS 66208 Office: Hedlund & Assoc 5909 Martway Mission KS 66202

JOHNSON, SHELLI WRIGHT, lawyer; b. LaPorte, Ind., Apr. 1, 1953; d. Burdette Baxter and Doris Dunfee (Childs) Wright; m. James Alan Johnson, May 22, 1980; children: Andrew James, Scott Robert, Jenna Marie. BS, Ball State U., 1975; JD, Valparaiso U., 1979. Bar: Ind. 1979, U.S. Dist. Ct. (no. and so. dists.) Ind. 1979. Tchr. lang. arts Coffee County Schs., Douglas, Ga., 1975-76; assoc. Law Offices of Larry W. Rogers, Portage, Ind., 1979-83, Harper & Rogers, Valparaiso, Ind., 1983-85, Law Offices of James A. Johnson, Portage, 1985-89, Law Offices Shelli Wright Johnson, Valparaiso, 1989—; tchr. family law, bankruptcy Sawyer Bus. Coll., Merrillville, Ind., 1990. Fundraiser Valparaiso U. Community-Univ. Fund Raising Campaign; buyer Porter County 4-H Celebration Sale; founder, adminstr. Doris Wright Meml. Scholarship Fund. Mem. ABA, Ind. Bar Assn. (family and juvenile law sect., bankruptcy and creditors rights sect.), Porter County Bar Assn., Porter County Am. Inns of Ct., Women Lawyers Assn. Lake and Porter Counties, The Attys. Group, Northwest Ind. Archeol. Assn., Porter County Celebration Sale Auction Com., Ball State U. Found. (philanthropy adv. com.), Delta Theta Phi. Methodist. Home: 555 N County Rd 300 E Valparaiso IN 46383 Office: 304 W Us Highway 6 Valparaiso IN 46383-7911

JOHNSON, SHIRLEY ELAINE, management consultant; b. Terre Haute, Ind., Sept. 15, 1946; d. Mervil Ray and Sarah Kathryn (Tucker) W.; children from a previous marriage: Richard Alan, Gary Michael; m. James E. DeHainaut, May 1, 1993; stepchildren: Jenifer L., Aimee L. DeHainaut. BA, DePaul U., 1991. Sec. to v.p. fin. Cenco Inc., Oak Brook, Ill., 1972-74, exec. asst. to group pres., 1974-75, asst. to chmn., 1975-77, corp. personnel/office mgr., 1977-80; corp. sec. Acadia Petroleum Corp., Denver, 1980-82; mgr. office Chapman, Klein & Weinberg, PC, Denver, 1982-84; asst. to chmn. The Heidrick Ptnrs., Inc., Chgo., 1984-92, v.p., 1992—. Mem. NAFE, Am. Mgmt. Assn., Exec. Women Internat., The River Club, Rsch. Roundtable. Home: 3312 Summerhill Dr Woodridge IL 60517 Office: The Heidrick Ptnrs Inc 20 N Wacker Dr Ste 2850 Chicago IL 60606-3101

JOHNSON, STACI SHARP, lawyer; b. Dallas, July 3, 1960; d. William Wheeler and Rublyin (Slaughter) S.; m. Byron Wade Johnson, Jan. 8, 1984; 1 child, Mollie Beatrice. BA in Dance, U. Tex., 1983, BA in Govt., 1983; JD, Tex. Tech. U., 1987. Bar: Tex. 1987, U.S. Dist. Ct. (ea. dist.) Tex. 1989, U.S. Dist. Ct. (no. dist.) Tex. 1990, U.S. Supreme Ct. 1991. Law clk. Dist. Atty.'s Office, Lubbock, Tex., 1987; rsch. asst. law libr. Tex. Tech. U., Lubbock, 1985-87; assoc. Henderson Bryant & Wolfe, Sherman, Tex., 1987-93, Law Offices of Richard E. Harrison, 1993—. Vol. Lubbock Crisis Ctr., 1985-87; mem. outreach com. Grace United Meth. Ch., Sherman, 1992; judge law and psychology Jan. term session Austin Coll., Sherman, Tex., 1992. Recipient Pro Bono Svc. award Legal Svcs. North Tex., 1991; named one of Outstanding Young Women of Am., 1987. Mem. Tex. Bar Assn., Tex. Young Lawyers Assn., Tex. Assn. Def. Counsel (co-author workers' compensation newsletter 1988), Grayson County Bar Assn. (mem. county law libr. com. 1989—, chair 1989-90, pres. 1990-91, sec. 1988-89, pres.-elect 1989-90, chair successful nomination of Judge R.C. Vaughan for Tex. Bar Found.'s Outstanding Jurist award 1990, chair minimum continuing legal edn. video presentations 1990-93, chair Law Day program 1992), Coll. of State Bar Tex., Phi Delta Phi. Methodist. Home: 1704 Glenway Dr Sherman TX 75092-3228 Office: Law Offices Richard E Harrison 123 N Crockett St Sherman TX 75090-5994

JOHNSON, SUSAN ELEANOR, writer, sociologist; b. Rockford, Ill., Apr. 3, 1940; d. Harold Adams and Margaret Dale (Madden) J.; life ptnr. Constance Wolfe. AB, Bryn Mawr Coll., 1962; MA, U. Wis., 1965, PhD, 1974. Instr. U. Wis., Madison, 1967-69; lectr., instr. U. Minn., Duluth, 1971-73, 76, 77; asst. prof. Cook Coll., Rutgers U., New Brunswick, N.J., 1974-75; adj. faculty Antioch U. West, Seattle, 1982, 84, 86; pvt. practice writer, rsch. cons. Anchorage, 1991—. Author: Staying Power: Long Term Lesbian Couples, 1990, When Women Played Hardball, 1994, For Love and For Life, 1995. Mem. NOW, Am. Sociol. Assn., Soc. for Am. Baseball Rsch., All-Am. Girls Profl. Baseball League Players Assn. Unitarian. Office: 308 G St Ste 312 Anchorage AK 99501-2135

JOHNSON, SUZANNE CURTIS, advertising and public relations executive; b. Anna, Ill.; d. Edward Earl Jr. and Juanita Curtis; m. Don Edwin Johnson, Aug. 23, 1959; children: Jennifer, Marc Wade. BS in English, Millikin U., 1960; MS in Journalism and Pub. Relations, So. Ill. U., 1985. Admissions counselor Millikin U., Decatur, Ill., 1980-88; devel. cons. John A. Logan Coll., Carterville, Ill., 1987; owner Suz-and Co., Pinckneyville, IL, 1990—, "Duffies" by Suz-, Pinckneyville, IL, 1990—. Co-author U.S.A. Parents' College Survival Handbook, 1986-87; staff writer (mag.) Accent on Southern Illinois, 1982-84; contbr. articles to mags. and newspapers. Trustee U. of the Ozarks, Clarksville, Ark., 1979-85; pres. Millikin U. Parents Assn., Decatur, Ill., 1980-84; county organizer Girl Scouts U.S.A.; founder Jr. Women's Club, Pinckneyville, Ill.; publicity chmn. ARC, Rep. Women, Perry County, Ill.; Ill. del. White House Conf. on Children and Youth. Named to Outstanding Young Women of Am., AAUW. Mem. Pub. Relations Soc. Am., Nat. Council for Resource Devel., AAUW (past pres. county and state coms.), Kappa Tau Alpha, Phi Kappa Phi, Pi Kappa Delta, Pi Beta Phi. Presbyterian. Home and Office: PO Box 467 605 W South St Pinckneyville IL 62274-1236

JOHNSON, SYLVIA SUE, university administrator, educator; b. Abiline, Tex., Aug. 10, 1940; d. SE Boyd and Margaret MacGillivray (Withington) Smith; m. William Ruel Johnson; children: Margaret Ruth, Laura Jane, Catherine Withington. BA, U. Calif., Riverside, 1962; postgrad., U. Hawaii, 1963. Elem. edn. credential, 1962. Mem. bd. regents U. Calif.; mem. steering com. Citizens Univ. Com., chmn., 1978-79; bd. dirs., charter mem. U. Calif.-Riverside Found., chmn. nominating com., 1983—; pres., bd. dirs. Friends of the Mission Inn, 1969-72, 73-76, Mission Inn Found., 1977—, Calif. Bapt. Coll. Citizns Com., 1980—; bd. dirs. Riverside Comty. Hosp., 1980—, Riverside Jr. League, 1976-77, Nat. Charity League, 1984-85; mem. chancellors blue ribbon com., devel. com. Calif. Mus. Photography. Named Woman of Yr., State of Calif. Legislature, 1989, 91, Citizen of Yr., C. of C., 1989. Mem. U. Calif.-Riverside Alumni Assn. (bd. dirs. 1966-68, v.p. 1968-70).

JOHNSON, THEA JEAN, systems engineer; b. Conshohocken, Pa.; d. Andrew Edward and Mary Rachel (Hillyard) Lewis; m. Lewis Edward Johnson, Apr. 30, 1966; 1 child, Vanessa Rachel. BS in Indsl. Mgmt., Temple U., 1968; Diploma in Computer Systems Engring., IBM Edn. Ctr., N.Y.C., 1968; AMA Cert., Villanova U., 1976. Acctg. clk. Bell Telephone, Conshohocken, Pa., 1960-63; adminstrv. mgmt. trainee IBM, Phila., 1963-65; systems engr. IBM, various, 1965-70; cons. in field various, 1971-80; asst. dir. PIA, Washington, 1980-82; sr. cons. RGI, Falls Church, Va., 1981-84; pres. NESS, Reston, Va., 1984—. Facilitator/co-author: (book) Lifelong Learning, 1992 (plaque 1992), others. Bd. dirs. Reston Community Assn., 1988-89; mem. Fairfax County Commn., 1989-92; nat. del. Dem. Nat. Conv., San Francisco, 1984; chair Fairfax County Coun. Arts, 1993; fgn. rels. commr. Internat. Children's Festival, Wolf Trap; deacon Martin Luther King Ch.; co-chairperson Va. del. White House Conf. on Small Bus., 1995. Recipient Svc. award U.S. Dept. Health and Human Svcs., Washington, 1992, citation Outstanding Vol. Reagan/Bush, Washington, 1985, others. Mem. Network Entrepreneurial Women (charter mem.), LWV (exec. bd. Reston chpt. 1989-91), Va. Assn. Female Execs. (adv. bd. 1989-93), Jack and Jill of Am. (treas./parliamentarian Reston chpt. 1980-90), Alpha Kappa Alpha. Democrat. Baptist. Home: 2022 Swans Neck Way Reston VA 22091 Office: Ness Inc Ste 2B 2022 Swans Neck Way Reston VA 22091-4035

JOHNSON, TRICIA HALL, archery range and retail shop owner; b. Putnam, Conn., Jan. 20, 1965; d. Arthur Marvin Hall and Marcia Monroe Bartman; m. Richard Andrew Johnson Jr., Dec. 8, 1985; 1 stepchild, Richard Andrew Johnson III. Grad. high sch., Willimantic, Conn. From co-owner to owner Hall's Arrow Indoor Archery Range, Manchester, Conn., 1982—; dir. Conn. State Archery Instr.'s Certification Sch.; coord. archery tournaments; instr., mgr. Olympic-bound archers. Fundraiser Jr. Olympic Archery Devel. Program. Mem. Nat. Field Archers Assn. (1st place world pro champion 1988, 1st place outdoor pro champion 1988, 89, 91, 1st place indoor pro champion 1989, 91), Profl. Archers Assn. (1st place indoor pro champion 1987, 88, 1st place outdoor pro champion 1991, 93, 94), Nat. Archery Assn., Mass. Field Archers Assn. (life), Coaches Alliance. Democrat. Home: Route 197 # 234 Woodstock CT 06281-1637 Office: Hall's Arrow Indoor Archery 291 Middle Tpke W Manchester CT 06040-3834

JOHNSON, VICKI R., insurance company executive; b. Glens Falls, N.Y., June 19, 1952; d. Leonard H. and Rose (Petrosky) J. AB, Franklin and Marshall Coll., 1974; postgrad. U. Portland, 1979-80; MBA, UCLA, 1986. ChFC, CLU. Group mgr. The Prudential, San Diego, 1974—; mem. Oreg. Accident and Health Claim Assn., 1976-81. Pres., Ridgeview Condominium Assn., 1978-81; mem. Los Angeles Olympic Organizing Com., 1984; active San Diego Employee Benefit Coun. Fellow Life Mgmt. Inst.; mem. AAUW (Del Mar-Levcadia br.), Nat. Health Underwriters, UCLA Alumni Bd. (dir. at large, exec. MBA). Presbyterian. Home: 1691 Neptune Ave Encinitas CA 92024-1051 Office: 9171 Towne Centre Dr Ste 380 San Diego CA 92122-1237

JOHNSON, VICTORIA KAPRIELIAN, medical educator; b. The Bronx, N.Y., June 30, 1959; d. Walter V. and Julia (Hachigian) K.; m. Lemmuel Owen Johnson Jr., 1990. BA, Brown U., 1981; MD, UCLA, 1985. Diplomate Am. Bd. Family Practice. Resident Duke-Watts Family Practice, Durham, N.C., 1985-88; fellow UCLA Family Medicine, L.A., 1988-89; asst. clin. prof. Duke U. Med. Ctr., Durham, N.C., 1989—; chief, divsn. predoctoral edn. and faculty devel., dept cmty and family medicine Duke U., Durham, N.C., 1994—, fellowship dir., dept. cmty. and family medicine, 1994—; dir. inpatient svc. Div. Community Medicine Duke U., 1989-90, dir. sports medicine, 1989-94, dir. arts medicine, 1989—, dir. predoctoral edn, 1990—. Mem. Am. Acad. Family Physicians (pub. com. 1985, mental health com. 1986-88), N.C. Acad. Family Physicians (edn. com. 1989-90, med. sch. affairs 1990—, chair of com. 1991—), Soc. Tchrs. Family Medicine (steering com., predoc dir. working groups, 1995—). Office: Duke U Div Family Medicine PO Box 3886 Durham NC 27710-0001

JOHNSON, VIRGINIA ALMA FAIRFAX, ballerina; b. Washington, Jan. 25, 1950; d. James Lee and Madeline (Murray) J. Student, pub. schs.; grad., Academy Wash. Sch. Ballet. Prin. ballerina Dance Theatre Harlem, N.Y.C., 1969—; prin. dancer Star World Ballet, Australia, 1979; guest artist Washington Ballet, Capitol Ballet, Detroit Symphony, Eugene Ballet, 9th Internat. Festival of Dance in Cuba, 1984, 10th Festival, 1986. Debut as Giselle, London Coliseum, 1984; performed solo Concert Socials at Marymount Coll., N.Y.C., 1978, The White House, 1980, 81; (PBS spl.) as Blanche in A Streetcar Named Desire, (BBC documentary) Ballerina; other prodns. include Magic of Dance, 1979, Dance in America, 1977, Creole Giselle on NBC, 1987, Ginastera, 1993; appeared in film A Piece of the Action, 1977. Recipient Monarch award Nat. Coun. Culture and Art, N.Y.C., 1983, Young Achiever award Nat. Council Women, 1985, Dance Mag. award, 1991. Mem. Alpha Kappa Alpha (hon.). Office: Dance Theatre Harlem 466 W 152nd St New York NY 10031-1896 also: 133 W 71st St New York NY 10023*

JOHNSON, YVONNE AMALIA, elementary education educator, science consultant; b. DeKalb, Ill., July 1, 1930; d. Albert O. and Virginia O. (Nelson) J. BS in Edn., No. Ill. State Tchrs. Coll., 1951; MS in Edn., No. Ill. U., 1960. Tchr. Love Rural Sch., DeKalb, 1951-53, West Elem. Sch., Sycamore, Ill., 1953—; Ill. honors sci. tchr. Ill. State U., 1985-87; sci. cons. Ednl. Svc. Ctr. 1, Rockford, Ill., 1986—; faculty NASA's Ednl. Workshop for Elem. Sch. Tchrs.; participant Lewis Rsch. Ctr., 1988—; faculty coord., 1990-91; LEEP - Lewis Rsch. Ctr., 1993—; summer adventures tchr. Ferm: Lab. Batavia, 1993-94. Contbr. articles to profl. publs. Bd. dirs. Sycamore Pub. Libr., 1974-84, pres. bd. dirs., 1984—. Named DeKalb County Conservation Tchr., 1971, Gov.'s Master Tchr., State of Ill., 1984, Outstanding Agrl. Tchr. in the Classroom Dekalb County Farm Bur., 1993; grantee NSF, 1961, 62, 85, 86, 87; Sci. Lit. grantee State of Ill., 1992-94. Mem. NEA, ASCD, NSTA (cert. in elem. sci.), Ill. Sci. Tchrs. Assn., Ill. Edn. Assn., Sycamore Edn. Assn., Coun. for Elem. Sci. Internat. Office: West Elem Sch 240 Fair St Sycamore IL 60178-1641

JOHNSON, ZOE ANN, accounting executive; b. Madison, Wis., Oct. 26, 1960; d. Gordon Heldt and Betty Ann (Rynders) J. BBA with distinction, U. Wis., 1982; MBA, U. Tex., Dallas, 1991. CPA, Wis., Tex. Sr. auditor Arthur Andersen & Co., Dallas, 1982-85; contr. Lyn Zanville, Inc., Dallas, 1985-86; mgr. gen. acctg. Meth. Hosps. Dallas, 1986-89, mgr. planning, 1989-91; chief fin. officer Presbyn. Hosp. Kaufman, Tex., 1991-93; controller HealthCor, Inc., Dallas, 1993—; chmn. bd. dirs. Meth. Hosp. Employees Credit Union, 1990-92. Mem. Healthcare Fin. Mgmt. Assn. Republican. Presbyterian. Office: HealthCor Inc 5720 LBJ Fwy Dallas TX 75240

JOHNSON-CHAMP, DEBRA SUE, lawyer, educator, writer; b. Emporia, Kans., Nov. 8, 1955; d. Bert John and S. Christine (Brigman) Johnson; m. Michael W. Champ, Nov. 23, 1979; children: Natalie, John. BA, U. Denver, 1977; JD, Pepperdine U., 1980; postgrad. in library sci. U. So. Calif., 1983—. Bar: Calif. 1981. Sole practice, Long Beach, Calif., 1981-82, Los Angeles, 1981-87, Woodland Hills, Calif., 1993—; legal reference librarian, instr. Southwestern U. Sch. Law, Los Angeles, 1982-88; adj. prof. law, 1987-88; atty. Contos & Bunch, Woodland Hills, 1988-93. Editor-in-chief: Southern Calif. Assn. Law Libraries Newsletter, 1984-85. Contbr. articles to profl. journs. Mem. law rev. Pepperdine U., 1978-80. West Pub. Co. scholar, 1983; trustee United Meth. Ch., Tujunga, Calif., 1986-88. Recipient H. Wayne Gillis Moot Ct. award, 1980, Vincent S. Dalsimer Best Brief award, 1979. Mem. ABA, So. Calif. Assn. Law Libraries, Am. Assn. Law Libraries, Calif. Bar Assn., Southwestern Affiliates, Friends of the Library Los Angeles. Democrat. Home and Office: 5740 Valerie Ave Woodland Hills CA 91367-3967

JOHNSON GRAHAM, JENNIFER, social services administrator; b. Fayetteville, N.C., Nov. 28, 1960; d. Edward Jenner and Gloria (Einspahr) Johnson; children: Christopher, Sean. BS in Orgnl. Comm. Mgmt., U. Wyo., 1982; MS in Edn., Northwestern State U., Natchitoches, La., 1991. Tech. supr. Law Sch. U. Wyo., Laramie, 1982-86; tchr. Trinity Presch., Natchitoches, 1989-91; exec. dir. Cane River Children's Svcs., Natchitoches, 1992—; mem. rate setting rev. bd. Office Cmty. Svcs., La. Dept. Health and Hosps., Baton Rouge, 1993-94. Mem. exec. bd., treas.-sec. Crisis Pregnancy Ctr., 1988-92; treas.-sec. exec. coun. Christ the King Luth. Ch., 1986-94, tchr. supt., 1992-94; com. chmn. Natchitoches Arts Coun., 1990-94. Recipient Life Saving/CPR award Am. Heart Assn., 1990. Mem. Nat. Assn. Bus. and Profl. Women, La. Assn. Child Care Agys. (v.p. residential divsn. 1992—, mem. govt. rels. La. Legislature com. 1992—, sec. 1994—), Natchitoches C. of C., Natchitoches Art Gallery (founding mem. 1990), Assn. Preservation of Hist. Natchitoches, Dixie Youth Baseball (coach 1990-94), Delta Delta Delta Alumnae (pres. 1984-86). Republican. Lutheran. Office: Cane River Children's Svcs 524 4th St PO Box 2453 Natchitoches LA 71457

JOHNSON-KIMBALL, KAREN ANGELA, retail executive; b. Little Falls, N.Y., Oct. 7, 1957; d. John William and Catherine Elisabeth (Ciuffa) Johnson; m. Wayne Michael Kimball, May 23, 1981. AAS in Travel and Tourism, Herkimer (N.Y.) County C.C., 1977; BSBA, BS in Mktg., Franklin Pierce Coll., 1986. Northeast regional comm. mgr. Roy F. Weston Inc., Concord, N.H., 1978-91; prin. Garbos, Concord, 1988—; pres. Egyptian Treasures, Concord, 1992—. Driving coord. Am. Cancer Soc., Concord, 1993; caretaker SPCA/Hospice, Concord, 1993-94; event planner Kimball-Jenkins Estate, 1994; mem. publicity com. Capitol Ctr. for the Arts, 1994. Democrat. Mem. Congl. Ch. Home and Office: 139 Oak Hill Rd Concord NH 03301

JOHNSON-LEESON, CHARLEEN ANN, insurance agent, elementary education educator; b. Battle Creek, Mich., June 10, 1949; d. Kenneth Andrews Leeson and Ila Mae (Weed/Lesson) McCutcheon; m. Lynn Boyd Johnson, Aug. 8, 1970; children: Eric Andrew, Andrea Marie. BA, Spring Arbor Coll., 1971; MS, Reading Specialist, Western Ill. U., 1990. Cert. elem. and secondary tchr., Mich., elem. tchr., Ill., reading K-9, Ill. Tchr. Hanover (Mich.) Horton Schs., 1972-73, Virden (Ill.) Elem. Sch., 1984-90; ins. agt. State Farm Ins., Virden, Ill., 1990—; collegiate and jr. high sch. cheerleading advisor in field; course leader Agt. Schs. 1, 2, and 3. Music dir., pianist Zion Luth. Ch., Farmersville, Ill., 1979-88, organist, pianist Olvie St. Friends, Battle Creek, 1961-67. Recipient Honor the Educator award World Book, 1988, 89, Soaring Eagle award, 1991; Wilson Stone scholar, 1990, Mich. State scholar, 1967. Mem. AUA, Internat. Reading Assn., Alpha Upsilon Alpha. Home: RR 1 Box C77 Virden IL 62690-9801 Office: State Farm Ins 1024 N Springfield St Virden IL 62690-1030

JOHNSON-LIBKIND, JEAN SUE See LIBKIND, JEAN SUE JOHNSON

JOHNSON-TURCHICK, SHARON MARIE, controller, accountant; b. Pitts., Aug. 21, 1967; d. James Joseph and Dolores Jean (Blosl) Johnson; m. Stephen Andrew Turchick, Apr. 17, 1993. BS in Acctg., Duquesne U., 1989. Staff sr. acct. Arthur Andrews & Co., Pitts., 1988-92; corp. contr. Sauer Industries Inc., Pitts., 1992—. Mem. AICPA, Pa. Inst. CPAs. Roman Catholic. Office: Sauer Industries Inc 4960 USX Tower 600 Grant St Pittsburgh PA 15219-2702

JOHNSTON, CAROL ELIZABETH, English language educator; b. Norwood, Mass., Nov. 16, 1948; d. Charles James and Dorothy (Veator) Ingalls; m. Richard Johnston, Mar. 9, 1973 (div. 1993); 1 child, Catherine Faith. BA, Rollins Coll., 1970; MA, U. Fla., 1972; PhD, U. S.C., 1980. Tchr. English Colleton County Schs., Walterboro, S.C., 1972-73, Collier County Schs., Naples, Fla., 1973-75; asst. prof. Clemson (S.C.) U., 1980-88, assoc. prof., 1988—. Author: Thomas Wolfe: A Descriptive Bibliography, 1987; editor S.C. Rev., 1983—; cons. editor Thomas Wolfe Rev., 1992—; contbr. over 20 articles to profl. jours. Grantee NEH, 1983-87. Recipient numerous NEA awards Nat. Endowment for Arts, 1983-87. Mem. MLA, So. Atlantic MLA, Philol. Assn. Carolinas, Thomas Wolfe Soc. (bd. dirs. 1988—, Zelda Gitlin award 1989, Honors Prof. of Yr. 1989, Harriet Holman award for faculty excellence 1993). Roman Catholic. Home: 102 Carriage Ln Pendleton SC 29670-9685 Office: Clemson U English Dept Clemson SC 29634

JOHNSTON, DONNA R., management information specialist; b. Milw., Mar. 21, 1957; d. Frank V. and Ruth R. (Siettmann) Haybeck; m. Thomas H. Johnston, Apr. 13, 1974; children: Jason W., Heather Rose. AD, U. Wis., Waukesha, 1989; BBA, U. Wis., Whitewater, 1993. Ops. network analyst Johnson Controls, Milw., 1981-89; adminstr. U. Wis., Whitewater, 1982-93; staff auditor Deloitte & Touche, Milw., 1993-94; computer specialist U. Wis., Whitewater, 1994—. Mem. Inst. Mgmt. Accts. Home: S79 W36986 Timber Ct Eagle WI 53119

JOHNSTON, GESSICA T., emergency physician; b. New Haven, May 11, 1940; d. George Leonard and Sadie (Grabel) Trager; m. Melvin M. Johnston, Mar. 8, 1989. BA, Cornell U., 1961; PhD, U. Calif., Berkeley, 1965; MD, U. Calif., L.A., 1971. Diplomate Am. Bd. Emergency Medicine. Asst. dir. emergency medicine Yuma Regional Med. Ctr., Yuma, Ariz., 1994—. Patent Yin Yang Clasp, 1993. Recipient Jewerly Gold Medal award INPEX, 1994. Office: 6800 S Strand Ave # 25 Yuma AZ 85364

JOHNSTON, GWINAVERE ADAMS, public relations consultant; b. Casper, Wyo., Jan. 6, 1943; d. Donald Milton Adams and Gwinavere Marie (Newell) Quillen; m. H.R. Johnston, Sept. 26, 1963 (div. 1973); children: Gwinavere G., Gabrielle Suzanne; m. Donald Charles Cannalte, Apr. 4, 1981. BS in Journalism, U. Wyo., 1966; postgrad., Denver U., 1968-69. Editor, reporter Laramie (Wyo.) Daily Boomerang, 1965-66; account exec. William Kostka Assocs., Denver, 1966-71, v.p., 1969-71; exec. v.p. Slottow, McKinlay & Johnston, Denver, 1971-74; pres. The Johnston Group, Denver, 1974-92; chair, CEO The Johnston-Wells Group, Denver, 1992—; adj. faculty U. Colo. Sch. Journalism, 1988-90. Bd. dirs. Leadership Denver Assn., 1975-77, 83-86, Mile High United Way, 1989—, Colo. Jud. Inst., 1991—. Fellow Am. Pub. Rels. Soc. (pres. Colo. chpt. 1978-79, bd. dirs. 1975-80, 83-86, nat. exec. com. Counselor's Acad. 1988-93, sec.-treas. 1994, pres.-elect 1995, profl. award Disting. Svc. award 1992); mem. Colo. Women's Forum, Rocky Mountain Pub. Rels. Group (founder), Denver Athletic Club, Denver Press Club. Republican. Home: 717 Monaco Pky Denver CO 80220-6040 Office: The Johnston Wells Group 1512 Larimer St Ste 720 Denver CO 80202-1622

JOHNSTON, JOCELYN STANWELL, legal assistant; b. Evanston, Ill., Feb. 16, 1954; d. Gerald and Dorothy Jeanne (Schoenfeld) Stanwell; m. Thomas Patrick Johnston, Nov. 28, 1986. BA, U. Minn., 1981; cert., Inst. Paralegal Tng., Phila., 1986. Paralegal Fredrikson & Byron P.A., Mpls., 1981, 84, Reed, Smith, Shaw and McClay, Phila., 1984-85, McCausland, Keen & Buckman, P.C., Radnor, Pa., 1985-86, Harris, Guenzel, Meier & Nichols, P.C., Ann Arbor, Mich., 1986-87, Conner & Bentley, P.C., Ann Arbor, 1987-88, Cichocki & Armstrong, Ltd., Oak Park, Ill., 1988-90, Bishop and Bishop, Oak Brook, Ill., 1994—, Marten, Breen & Merrick, Oak Park, 1994—. Mem. ACLU, Nat. Abortion Rights Action League, Ill. Paralegal Assn. Democrat. Home: 258 Iowa St Oak Park IL 60302-2346 Office: Bishop and Bishop 1111 W 22d St Ste C-40 Oak Brook IL 60521 also: Marten Breen & Merrick 1010 Lake St Ste 604 Oak Park IL 60301

JOHNSTON, JOSEPHINE ROSE, chemist; b. Cranston, R.I., Aug. 9, 1926; d. Robert and Rose (Varca) Forte; m. Howard Robert Johnston, Mar. 7, 1949; 1 child, Kevin Howard. Student, Carnegie Inst., 1945-47; BS, Mich. State U., 1972, MA, 1973; postgrad., MIT, 1973—. Med. technologist South Nassau Community Hosp., Rockville Centre, N.Y., 1947-50; med. technologist Mich. State U., East Lansing, 1950-53, faculty specialist, 1966-76; dept. pathology Albany (N.Y.) Med. Ctr., 1953-54; med. lab. supr. Bulova Watch Co., Jackson Heights, N.Y., 1954-57; sr. chemistry technologist Mid Island Hosp., Bethpage, N.Y., 1958-66; sr. rsch. assoc. Uniformed Svcs. Univ., Bethesda, Md., 1976-78; asst. to chmn. dept. physiology Uniformed Svcs. Univ., Bethesda, 1978-82, assoc. to chmn., 1982—. Author: Patriarch: The Life of T.J. Haddy, 1994; contbr. articles to profl. jours. Danzinger Found., Lauderdale, Fla. Mem. Analytical Chem. Soc., Data and Electronic Soc., Internat. Platform Assn. Lutheran. Office: 6813 Woodville Rd Mount Airy MD 21771-7611

JOHNSTON, JUDY ANN, dietitian; b. Spirit Lake, Iowa, May 23, 1951; d. Leonard Lessie and Mary Katheryn (Beseau) Heldt; m. Bill Burt Johnston, Sept. 19, 1975; 1 child, Lorien Kay. BS in Dietetics and Instnl. Mgmt., Kans. State U., 1973, MS in Adult Edn., 1975. Registered, lic. dietitian. Clin. dietitian St. Francis Regional Med. Ctr., Wichita, Kans., 1973-75, teaching dietitian, 1975-76; chief clin. svcs. Osteo. Hosp., Wichita, 1976-77; dir. nutritional svcs. Riverside Hosp., Wichita, 1977-90; dir. Kans. LEAN, Wichita, 1990—; speaker in field; advisor credentialing office Kans. Dept. Health and Environ., Topeka, 1989—. Author: (cookbook) Holiday Cuisine, 1981, (booklet) Get to the Point, 1980; developer board game Jack Sprat's Table, 1991. Pres. pastoral coun. St. Joseph Ch., 1989-92; chair Younger Girl Oper. Unit Wichita Area coun. Girl Scouts U.S.A., 1985—. Recipient Thank You award Wichita Area coun. Girl Scouts U.S.A., 1989. Mem. Wichita Dist. Dietetic Assn. (pres. 1978-80), Kans. Dietetic Assn. (chmn. coun. on practice 1984-87, del. to Am. Dietetic Assn. 1990-93, lobbyist 1983-89, Young Dietitian award 1976, Anita Owen award for Innovation in Nutrition Edn. 1994). Roman Catholic. Home: 444 N Sheridan St Wichita KS 67203-5264 Office: Kans LEAN 130 S Market St 6th fl Wichita KS 67202

JOHNSTON, MARGUERITE, journalist, author; b. Birmingham, Ala., Aug. 7, 1917; d. Robert C. and Marguerite (Spradling) J.; m. Charles Wynn Barnes, Aug. 31, 1946; children: Susan, Patricia, Steven, Polly. A.B., Birmingham-So. Coll., 1938. Reporter Birmingham News, 1939-44; Washington corr. Birmingham News, Birmingham Age-Herald, London Daily Mirror, 1945-46; columnist Houston Post, 1947-69, fgn. news editor, mem. editorial bd., 1969-85, assoc. editor editorial page, 1972-77, asst. editor editorial page, 1977-85; lectr. in field, 1947—; instr. creative writing U. Houston, 1946-47, lectr. feature writing, 1965-66; lectr. Baker Coll., Rice U., 1977-78; del. Asian Am. Women Journalists Conf., Honolulu, 1965, 1st World Conf. Women Journalists, Mexico City, 1969. Author: Public Manners, 1957, A Happy Wordly Abode, 1964, Houston: The Unknown City, 1836-1946, (Winedale Historical Ctr. Ima Hogg award, Otis Lock award East Tex. Historical Assn.), 1991. Bd. dirs. Tex. Bill of Rights Found., 1962-64; bd. dirs. Planned Parenthood, 1953-55, Population Inst., 1985—; mem. Mcpl. Art Commn., 1971-76, Houston Com. Fgn. Relations. Recipient Theta Sigma Phi Headliner award, 1954, 1st ann. award of merit Houston Com. Alcoholism, 1956, cert. of merit Gulf Coast chpt. Am. Soc. Safety Engrs., 1960, Agnese Carter Nelms award Planned Parenthood, 1968, Sch. Bell award Tex. State Tchrs. Assn., 1974, 75, Gold Key award Nat. Council Alcoholism, 1975, Global award Population Inst., 1981. Mem. Tex. Soc. Architects (hon.), Philos. Soc. Tex., Phi Beta Kappa, Pi Beta Phi. Home: 5319 Cherokee St Houston TX 77005-1701

JOHNSTON, MARILYN FRANCES-MEYERS, physician, medical educator; b. Buffalo, Mar. 30, 1937; B.S., Dameon Coll., 1966; Ph.D., St. Louis U., 1970, M.D., 1975. Diplomate Am. Bd. Pathology, Diplomate Nat. Bd. Med. Examiners. Fellow in immunology Washington U., St. Louis, 1970-72; resident in pathology Washington U. Hosp., St. Louis, 1975-77, St. John's Mercy Med. Ctr., St. Louis, 1977-79; research fellow hematology St. Louis U. Sch. Medicine, 1979-80; instr. biochemistry St. Louis U., 1972-75, asst. prof. pathology, 1980-87, assoc. prof. 1987—, dir. transfusion service, 1980—; med. dir. Mo./Ill. Regional Red Cross, 1983—; area chmn. for inspection and accreditation Am. Assn. Blood Banks, Arlington, Va., 1984. Author: Transfusion Therapy, 1985. Recipient Transfusion Medicine Acad. award Nat. Heart, Blood and Lung Inst., 1984; Goldberger fellow AMA, 1979. Mem. Am. Assn. Blood Banks, Am. Assn. Immunologists, Sigma Xi. Office: St Louis U Hosps 1325 S Grand Blvd Saint Louis MO 63104-1029

JOHNSTON, MARJORIE DIANE, computer programming executive, analyst; b. Fullerton, Calif., Sept. 19, 1943; d. Earl Lawrence Whipple and Ruth Juanita (Long) Purcell; children: Stephen, Deborah. Grad computer programming LaSalle U., Chgo., 1973; BSBA U. Phoenix, 1994. Computer programmer Los Alamos (N.Mex.) Nat. Lab., 1972-81, cons. control data, 1984-89, sr. analyst, programmer, 1989—; contract programmer Computer Assistance, Inc., Tulsa, 1981-82; profl. svcs. analyst Control Data Corp., Denver, 1982-84, Los Alamos, 1984-89. Mem. Order Eastern Star (past matron), Toastmasters Internat. Home: 950 Santa Clara Pl Los Alamos NM 87544-3209

JOHNSTON, NANCY DAHL, data processing specialist, paralegal; b. Waco, Tex., Sept. 18, 1954; d. Howard Edward and Gladys Marie (Haynes) Dahl; children: Russell Edward, Dennis Aaron. Student, Tex. Woman's U., Denton, Victor Valley Coll., Victorville, Calif.; cert., Nat. Acad. Paralegal Studies, 1991. Accounts mgr. Pacific Physicians' Svcs., Loma Linda, Calif., 1978-81; data processing coord. Denton County, 1986-89; customer svc. mgr. Jet-Line Svc., Inc., Portland, Maine, 1989-92; exec. sec. to state court adminstr. State of Maine, Standish, Maine, 1993—. Vol. Maine Audubon Soc., Global Response, Com. for Responsible Transp. Mem. NAFE, Maine Assn. Paralegals, Mcpl. Software Users Group (sec. 1988-89), Greenpeace. Home and Office: PO Box 185 Standish ME 04084-0185

JOHNSTON, NANCY JEAN, computer software products executive; b. Englewood, N.J., July 27, 1952; d. Fredrick Lorenz and Elizabeth Penn (Hammond) McGowan; m. Larry Leonard Johnston, Nov. 27, 1982. Degree in Bus. Adminstrn., W.Va. Wesleyan, 1972; cert. Japanese Lang., Tokyo Lang. Inst., 1986. Sales mgr. IBM Internal Systems Devel., Franklin Lakes/Montvale, N.J., 1972-81; corp. program mgr. Office Systems Software Strategy, Purchase, N.Y., 1981-84; info. systems dir. IBM Asia Pacific Hdqrs., Tokyo, 1984-85, office systems edn. dir., 1985-86; lab. tech. asst. IBM Software Devel. Lab., Dallas, 1986-88; world trade process cons. IBM Software Svc. and Support, Dallas, 1988-90; Asia Pacific product mgr. IBM Office Applications, Dallas, 1990—. Polit. adminstr. Reps. for Bush, Southlake, Tex., 1990. Mem. Southlake C. of C., Tokyo Am. Club, Southlake Women's Club. Republican. Methodist. Home: 910 Emerald Blvd Southlake TX 76092-8895

JOHNSTON, PAMELA LOUISE, assistant United States attorney; b. Sacramento, Calif., 1962; d. Ted Yates and Margaret Johnston. BS in Botany, U. Calif., Davis, 1984; JD, U. Calif., Berkeley, 1987. Bar: Calif., 1987. Law clk. U.S. Dist. Ct., Montgomery, Ala., 1987-88, U.S. Ct. Appeals (5th cir.), Dallas, 1988-89; litigation assoc. Irell & Manella, L.A., 1989-91; asst. U.S. atty. U.S. Attys. Office Crtl. Dist. Calif., L.A., 1991—; spl. counsel L.A. Community Projects for Restoration, 1992—. Mem. Order of Coif. Democrat. Office: US Attys Office 312 N Spring St Los Angeles CA 90012

JOHNSTON, PAMELA MCEVOY, clinical psychologist; b. Forest Hills, N.Y., Mar. 8, 1937; d. Renny T. and Pamela (Sweeny) McE.; m. Percy H. Johnston, Jr. (dec.); children: Michael B. Anderson, Jeffery A. Thomas, Candy L. Watts, Kenneth L. Anderson. BA, U. La Verne, 1978, MS, 1980; PhD, U.S. Internat. U., 1982. Instr. psychology-sociology Allan Hancock Coll., Santa Maria, 1977-78; mental health asst. Santa Barbara City Alcoholism Dept., 1977-78; gen. mgr. Profl. Suites, San Diego, 1978-81; therapist Chula Vista (Calif.) Community Counseling Ctr., San Diego, 1978-85; research asst. U.S. Internat. U., 1979-82; rsch. coordinator Mil. Family research Ctr., San Diego, 1981-82; assoc. dir. Acad. Assoc. Psychotherapists, 1982-86; pvt. practice, San Diego, 1982—; pres. Borrego Springs Med. Clinic, 1987-90, 91—; bd. dirs. Women's Internat. Ctr., 1984-86. Bd. dirs. San Diego County Mental Health Assn., 1978-84, Chula Vista Counseling Ctr., 1978; mem. Delinquency Prevention Commn., 1978; bd. dirs. North City Interfaith Coun., Escondido, Calif., 1990-92, Civic Fedn., 1993—. State fellow, 1979, 80, 81, 82, Calif. State scholar, 1976-77. Mem. Am. Psychol. Assn., Calif. State Psychol. Assn., Am. Assn. Marriage and Family Therapists, Calif. Assn. Marriage and Family Therapists, Borrego Springs C. of C. (pres.-elect 1994—), Rotary Internat. Republican. Roman Catholic. Home: PO Box 1198 Borrego Springs CA 92004-1198

JOHNSTON, REBECCA LEIGHAN, computer graphics specialist; b. Latrobe, Pa., Oct. 2, 1953; d. W. Merle and Martha Jane (Bash) Clawson; m. William Merrill Johnston, May 12, 1984. Visual Comm., Art Inst. Pitts., 1973. Graphic designer Allegheny Intermediate Unit, Pitts., 1974-82; computer graphics designer Slidemasters Inc., Pitts., 1982-87; computer graphics specialist Westinghouse Electric Corp., Pitts., 1987-90, prodn. coord., 1990—. Home: 65 N Fremont Ave Pittsburgh PA 15202-3219 Office: Westinghouse Electric Corp 11 Stanwix St Pittsburgh PA 15222-1312

JOHNSTON, SHERYL L., communications executive; b. Portland, Oreg., Feb. 18, 1944; d. Frank F. and Edith A. (Vallereux) Neels; m. Robert K. Johnston, Feb. 14, 1973; 1 child, James Patrick. Student, Portland State U., 1962-65, 67-68, Sch. of the Art Inst., Chgo., 1972-74, Northwestern U., 1975; BA, Columbia Coll., Chgo., 1993. Adminstrv. asst. Art Inst. Chgo., 1971-75; asst. editorial dir. Sta. WLS-TV, Chgo., 1975-76; dir. pub. rels. Prime Time Sch. TV, Chgo., 1976-77; v.p. J. Walter Thompson Co., Chgo., 1977-82; pres. Sheryl Johnston Communications, Chgo., 1982—; tchr. Columbia Coll., 1991. Mem. Country Music Assn. (pub. rels. com. 1981, 82, 85). Democrat. Episcopalian. Office: 623 W Oakdale Chicago IL 60657-5309

JOHNSTON, SUSAN LEFFERT, psychologist; b. Syracuse, N.Y., Jan. 15, 1955; d. David Jerome and Lillian (Weiner) Leffert; m. Frank C. Johnston, July 26, 1981. BA, Univ. at Albany, 1977, PhD, 1984; MA, EdM, Columbia U., 1979. Lic. psychologist, N.Y. Sch. psychologist Madison/Oneida County BOCES, Verona, N.Y., 1979-80; psychology intern Univ. at Buffalo Counseling Svc., Amherst, N.Y., 1983-84; counselor Counseling Ctr., SUNY, Brockport, 1984-90; asst. psychologist Oak Orchard Community Health Ctr., Brockport, 1985-86; psychologist in ind. practice Rochester, N.Y., 1989—. Mem. APA, N.Y. State Psychol. Assn., Genesee Valley Psychol. Assn. (treas. 1991-94), Rochester Area Assn. Clin. Psychologists, Nat. Register Health Svc. Providers in Psychology. Democrat. Jewish. Home: 2200 Westfall Rd Rochester NY 14618 Office: 480 White Spruce Blvd Rochester NY 14623

JOHNSTON, VIRGINIA EVELYN, editor; b. Spokane, Wash., Apr. 26, 1933; d. Edwin and Emma Lucile (Munroe) Rowe; student Portland Community Coll., 1964, Portland State U., 1966, 78-79; m. Alan Paul Beckley, Dec. 26, 1974; children—Chris, Denise, Rex. Proofreader, The Oregonian, Portland, 1960-62, teletypesetter operator, 1962-66, operator Photon 200, 1966-68, copy editor, asst. women's editor, 1968-80; spl. sects. editor (UPDATE), 1981-83, 88—; editor FOODday, 1982—; pres. Matrix Assos., Inc., Portland, 1975—, chmn. bd., 1979—; cons. Dem. Party Oreg., 1969, Portland Sch. Dist. No. 1, 1978. Mem. Eating and Drinking Soc. Oreg. (past pres.), We. Culinary Inst. (mem. adv. bd.), Portland Culinary Alliance (mem. adv. bd.), Internat. Food Media Conf. (mem. adv. bd.). Democrat. Editor Principles of Computer Systems for Newspaper Mgmt., 1975-76. Home: 4140 NE 137th Ave Portland OR 97230-2624 Office: Oregonian Pub Co 1320 SW Broadway Portland OR 97201

JOHNSTONE, PAULA SUE, medical technologist; b. Springfield, Mo., July 5, 1947; d. Nathan Paul and Ima Louise (Glenn) Johnstone. BS, S.W. Mo. State U., 1969. Cert. med. technologist Am. Soc. Clin. Pathologists. Vol., Cox Med. Ctr., Springfield, 1964-68; lab., office aide Springfield Med. Lab., 1964-68; chief technologist Springfield Gen. Osteo. Hosp., 1969-73; staff technologist St. John's Regional Health Ctr., Springfield, 1973-75, evening supr., 1975-76, asst. adminstrv. dir., 1976-86; clin. lab. coordinator, 1986-89; lab. computer coord., 1989—. Dir., Glidewell Bapt. Ch. Tng., Springfield, 1984-85, chmn. budget and fin. com. 1986-87; pres. MER class Broadway Bapt. Ch., 1993-94. Mem. NAFE, Am. Soc. Med. Technologists, Nat. Cert. Agy. Med. Lab. Personnel, Mo. Soc. Med. Technologists (pres. 1976-77, columnist newsletter 1976-77), S.W. Mo. State U. Alumni Assn. Baptist. Clubs: Nat. Travel, Frommer's Dollarwise Travel Club.

Avocations: European travel; reading; knitting; house plants. Home: 1107 W Farm Rd 64 Springfield MO 65803-9622 Office: St John's Regional Health Ctr 1235 E Cherokee St Springfield MO 65804-2203

JOHNSTONE, ROSE MAMELAK (MRS. DOUGLAS JOHNSTONE), biochemistry educator; b. Lodz, Poland, May 14, 1928; d. Jacob Shea and Esther (Rotholz) Mamelak; m. Douglas Johnstone, Aug. 9, 1953; children: Michael, Eric. BSc, McGill U., 1950, PhD, 1953. Nat. Cancer Inst. of Can. fellow Nat. Inst. for Med. Rsch., London, and Strangeway Rsch. Lab., Cambridge, Eng., 1954-56; research asso. McGill-Montreal Gen. Hosp. Research Inst., 1956-60; faculty McGill U., Montreal, Que., Can., 1961—; asso. prof. biochemistry McGill U., 1967-76, prof., 1977—, chmn. dept., 1980-90; Gilman Cheney chair of biochemistry, 1985—. Contbr. articles to profl. jours. Grantee Nat. Cancer Inst. Can., 1965-67, Med. Rsch. Coun. of Can., 1965—, NIH, 1987-90, 92—. Fellow Royal Soc. Can. (treas. 1991-94); mem. McGill Assn. U. Tchrs. (treas., membership sec. 1967-70), Biol. Chemists Am., Can. Biochem. Soc. (pres. 1985-86), Internat. Assn. Women Bioscientists (sec. 1985-88). Home: 4064 Oxford, Montreal, PQ Canada H4A 2Y4 Office: McGill Univ McIntyre Med Sci Ctr, Dept Biochemistry 3655 Drummond, Montreal, PQ Canada H3G 1Y6

JOHNSTONE, SALLY MAC, educational association administrator, psychology educator; b. Macon, Ga., Dec. 8, 1949; d. Ralph E. and Maxine A. J.; m. Stephen R. Tilson, 1977; 1 child, Emma. BS, Va. Poly. Inst., 1974, MS, 1976; PhD, U. N.C., 1982. Lectr. European div. U. Md., Heidelberg, Fed. Republic of Germany, 1982-84; instr. psychology U. Md., College Park, 1984-89, asst. dean, 1984-86, dir. Ctr. for Instructional Telecom., 1986-89; dir. Western Coop. for Ednl. Telecom., Boulder, Colo., 1989—; cons. Grand Valley State U., Grand Rapids, Mich., 1989, Can. Distance Learning Devel. Centre, Edmonton, Alta., Can., 1989, Program for Educating Nurses via Satellite Links, Charleston, W.Va., 1986-89, Fairleigh Dickinson U., Teaneck, N.J., 1990, Northwest Legis. Leadership Forum, Seattle, 1990, Pacific Northwest Econ. Region, Whistler, B.C., 1991, Calif. State U. System, 1993; invited panelist U.S. Dept. Edn., Washington, 1990—, Aspen Inst., Washington, 1990, Pacific Northwest Econ. Region, 1991-92; presenter Pacific Rim Pub. U. Pres. Conf. Asia Found., Bangkok, Thailand, 1990, workshops Pacific Telecom Coun., Honolulu, 1991, Nat. U. Continuing Edn. Assn., Miami, Fla.; keynote speaker Mountain States Community Coll. Assn., Farmington, N.Mex., 1991; speaker EDUCOM, San Diego, 1991, edn. commn. States' Legislator's Workshop, Cin., 1992, State Higher Edn. Exec. Officer's Meeting, Jackson, Wyo., 1992, Calif. State U. Project DELTA Workshop, Sacramento, 1993, higher edn. conf. NEA, New Orleans, 1993, meeting Nat. Assn. State Univs. & Land Grant Colls. Distance Edn. & Telecomm. Working Group; witness U.S. Senate Subcom. Edn., Humanities and Arts, Washington, 1991; leader faculty devel. workshop Athabasca U., Alta., Can., 1992; study advisor Corp. Pub. Broadcasting, 1993; panelist ann. meeting Am. Assn. Colls., 1994, Pacific Mountain Network, 1994, keynote regional meeting Am. Assn. Continuing Edn., 1994; bd. mem. Okla. State U. Inst. Telecomm. Co-author: (with Witherspoon and Wasem) Rural TeleHealth: Telemedicine, Distance Education and Informatics, 1993; co-editor: (with Markwood) New Pathways to a Degree: Technology Opens the College, 1994. Mem. Ednl. Access Com., Prince George's County, Md., 1986-89; sci. fair judge U. Hills. Elem. Sch., Md., 1986-89. Grantee Annenberg/CPB Project, 1988, 91-93, Fund for Improvement of Postsecondary Edn., 1993, Dept. Commerce Nat. Telecomms. and Info. Adminstrn., 1994, U.S. Dept. Edn., 1991; recipient Disting. Rsch. award Nat. U. Continuing Edn. Assn., 1989. Mem. Am. Psychology Assn., Internat. Teleconferencing Assn.

JOHS, SHARON CATHERINE, psychological and educational consultant; b. Linton, N.D., May 15, 1951; d. Michael M. and Irene (Dosch) J.; children: Stacy Marie, Shannon Lee, Destry Timothy. BS, No. State U., 1983, MSEd, 1984; postgrad., Moorhead State U., 1986—. Lic. sch. psychologist, Minn.; cert. sch. psycologist, S.D.; lic. profl. counselor, S.D.; nationally cert. sch. psychologist. Rehab. counselor S.D. Dept. Vocat. Rehab., Aberdeen, 1984-85; program dir. Resource Ctr. for Women, Aberdeen, 1985-86; sch. psychologist Aberdeen Area Spl. Edn. Coop., Pierre, S.D., 1986-92; owner, dir. Psyc/Ed Consulting, Aberdeen, 1992—; adj. faculty instr. Sisseton-Wahpeton C.C., Sisseton, S.D., 1985-86; spl. edn. coord. office Indian edn. Bur. Indian Affairs, Sisseton; cons. Standing Rock Agy., Cheyenne-Eagle Butte Agy., Ft. Totten Agy., Sisseton Agy., Crow Creek Agy., and Theodore Jamerson Sch., 1992—. Mem. Nat. Assn. Sch. Psychologists, S.D. Assn. Sch. Psychologists, S.D. Counseling Assn., Coun. for Exceptional Children, Phi Delta Kappa, Pi Gamma Mu. Office: Psyc/Ed Consulting 819 S 11th St Aberdeen SD 57401

JOICE, NORA LEE, clinical dietitian; b. Kearney, Nebr., Mar. 5, 1948; d. Frank Rogers and Clarrisa Blanche (Drinnan) Jackson; m. David Wayne Joice, Dec. 21, 1973. BS, U. Ariz., 1971. Registered dietician; lic. dietician. Clin. dietitian St. Francis Hosp., Tulsa, 1972-76; pub. health nutritionist Tulsa City County Health Dept., 1976-81; clin. dietitian City of Faith Hosp., Marriott Corp., Tulsa, 1982-84, asst. chief dietitian, 1984-86, chief clin. dietitian, 1986-87, clin. nutrition specialist, 1987-89; cons. dietitian in long-term health facilities Marriott Corp., Tulsa, 1990-92; pvt. practice cons. dietitian Tulsa, 1992—; clin. dietitian Broken Arrow (Okla.) Med. Ctr., 1993-94. Mem. Okla. Dietetic Assn., Am. Dietetic Assn., Okla. Cons. Dietitians in Health Care Facilities, Dietitians in Gen. Clin. Practice. Democrat. Pentecostal. Home and Office: 2320 S Urbana Ave Tulsa OK 74114-3627

JOLIVET, ANNA MARY, retired school system administrator, association executive; b. Tucson, Nov. 24, 1928; d. Joe Turner and Sadie Osborne; m. Clarence Warner Jolivet, June 7, 1952; children: Clarence Michael, Leslie Cecilia. BA in Elem. Edn., U. Ariz., 1950, MEd in Elem. Edn., 1965, EdS in Ednl. Adminstrn., 1972, EdD, 1976. Cer. tchr., prin., supt., Ariz. Tchr. Spring/Dunbar Elem.-Jr. High Sch. Tucson Pub. Schs. Dist. # 1, 1950-59, helping tchr. music dept., tchr. Booth Elem. Sch., 1961-67, prin. Richey Elem. Sch., 1967-70, prin. Cragin Elem. Sch., 1970-75; lectr. Coll. Edn. U. Ariz., Tucson, 1976; adminstrv. asst. learning and staff devel. Tucson Unified Sch. Dist. # 1, 1976-80, dir. planning svcs., 1980-89, asst. supt. high sch. region, 1989; cons. ednl. adminstrn., curriculum devel., 1989—; organizing dir. Tucson Assn. for Child Care, 1970; mem. adv. bd. U. Ariz. Cultural Affairs; speaker AAUW, Nat. Assn. Sch. Pers., Rocky Mountain Ednl. Rsch. Assn. Conf., Nat. Coun. Adminstrv. Women Edn., Ariz. Black Town Hall, Baha'i Faith/ UN Assn. So. Ariz. Pres. Camp Fire Tucson, Inc., 1969-71, adv. bd.; pres. Downtown Devel. Corp., Tucson, 1988-90, Tucson Partnership, Inc., 1990-92; allocations divsn. chmn. United Way Tucson, 1982-84, exec. bd., bd. dirs.; v.p. Am.-Israel Friendship League, Tucson, 1989—, coord. high sch. youth exch., 1990—; exec. com. Tucson Community Found., 1990—, chair discretionary grants, 1993; vice chmn. Tucson Pima County Community Profile, 1991—; chair Sahuaro Coun. Girl Scouts, nominating com.; chair Older Adults Svc. and Info. Sys., 1992-94, Tucson Fund Raising Rev. Bd., Tucson Urban League, 1988-89, guild pres., 1983-84; exec. bd. Tucson Tomorrow; active Ariz. Adv. Health Coun., Tucson Bicentennial Com., Health Systems Agy. Screening com., Goals for Tucson; block grant com. Ariz. Dept. Health, chair proposal revs. 1981, 82; chmn. subcom. Crippled Children's Svc.; trustee Mt. Calvary Bapt. Ch., Tucson Mus. Art, 1988-92; bd. dirs. Ariz. Acad. Phoenix, 1983-86; active Tucson/ Pima Libr.; nat. bd. dirs. YWCA of U.S.A., N.Y.C., 1982—, past mem. nat. nominating com.; past bd. dirs. YWCA Tucson, past chmn. pers. Recipient Women on Move award, YWCA Tucson, 1982, Alumni Achievement award U. Ariz., 1983, Phenomenal Woman award U. Ariz. Black Alumni, 1990. Mem. NEA, ASTD, ASCD (state sec. 1981-82, state pres. 1982-83, nat. bd. dirs. 1982-83, exec. coun. 1984-87), Coun. Ednl. Facility Planners Internat. (interface project), Nat. Assn. Elem. Sch. Prins., Nat. Coun. Adminstrv. Women in Edn., Am. Ednl. Rsch. Assn., Am. Assn. Sch. Adminstrs., Ariz. Edn. Assn., Ariz. Sch. Adminstrs., Inc. (region 5 legis. rep.), NAACP (life), Exec. Women's Coun. (v.p. 1992-93), Pi Lambda Theta (past v.p. Alpha Alpha chpt.), Delta Kappa Gamma, Phi Delta Kappa, Alpha Delta Kappa, Alpha Kappa Alpha (past mem. nat. constn. com., past far western region parliamentarian, chair far west regional conf. com. 1986, past pres. Tucson chpt., past treas., undergrad. acad. scholarship). Democrat. Home: 8818 E Harborage Dr Tucson AZ 85710-6225

JOLLY, ALLENE R., anesthesiology nurse; b. Memphis, Mar. 28, 1952; d. Allen Candler and Norma Rose (Goldman) Craven; m. David W. Jolly, July 10, 1970; children: Hope, David W., Brandi Nicole. AS, Itawamba Jr. Coll., Fulton, Miss., 1976; BS in Anesthesia, U. Miss., 1985. Cert. in anesthesiology. Staff nurse, neonatal ICU Gilmore Meml. Hosp., Amory, Miss.; ICU supr. Houston (Miss.) Community Hosp.; staff nurse anesthetist Aberdeen-Monroe County Hosp., Monroe, Miss., Clay County Med. Ctr., West Point, Miss.; chief nurse anesthetist Bapt. Meml. Hosp. Union County, New Albany, Miss. Mem. Am. Assn. Nurse Anesthetists. Home: 1169 CR 101 New Albany MS 38652-9804

JOLLY, BARBARA LEE, hospital pharmacy management company executive; b. Central City, Nebr., Dec. 23, 1952; d. Louis Carl and Elizabeth (Mesner) Lindahl; m. William C. Zimmerman, June 2, 1973 (div. Aug. 1986); m. Daniel Ehs Jolly, May 7, 1988; 1 stepchild, Farrell Elisabeth Ehs Jolly. BS in Pharmacy, U. Mo., Kansas City, 1976, MPA, 1984. Registered pharmacist. Pharmacy supr. Truman Med. Ctr., Kansas City, Mo., 1976-87; dispensing dept. mgr. Nursing Ctr. Svcs., Hilliard, Ohio, 1988-90; v.p. Pharmacy Systems, Inc., Dublin, Ohio, 1990—; trustee Ohio Cancer Pain Initiative, Columbus, 1987—. Bd. dirs. Open Church, Inc., Columbus, 1991—; mem. social svcs. bd. Salvation Army, Kansas City, 1986-88; co-dir. Siouxland Hotline, Inc., Sioux City, Iowa, 1972-73; med. missionary, Honduras, 1992-94; del. to state conv. Easter Seals of Ohio, Columbus, 1989-91. Recipient Outstanding Vol. award Salvation Army, Kansas City, 1987. Mem. Am. Soc. Hosp. Pharmacists, Ohio Soc. Hosp. Pharmacists, Ohio Pharmacists Assn., Ky. Soc. Hosp. Pharmacists, Midwest Pain Soc., Pi Alpha Alpha (pres. 1983-84). Mem. United Ch. of Christ. Home: 5322 Bay Meadows Ct Columbus OH 43221-5703

JONAS, RUTH HABER, psychologist; b. Tel Aviv, Aug. 24, 1935; d. Fred S. and Dorothy Judith (Bernstein) Haber; m. Saran Jonas, Sept. 16, 1956; children: Elizabeth, Frederick. AB, Barnard Coll., 1957; MA, New Sch. for Social Rsch., 1977, PhD, 1987. Lic. psychologist, N.Y. 1st and 2d yr. intern clin. psychology NYU Med. Ctr.-Bellevue Hosp., N.Y.C., 1985-87; postdoctoral rsch. fellow NYU Med. Ctr., N.Y.C., 1987-88; clin. instr. psychiatry NYU Sch. Medicine, N.Y.C., 1987, clin. asst. prof. psychiatry, 1991; sr. psychologist forensic svc. Bellevue Hosp., N.Y.C., 1988—; pvt. practice psychology N.Y.C., 1988—. Fellow Am. Orthopsychiat. Assn.; mem. APA, N.Y. State Psychol. Soc., Manhattan Psychol. Assn., Am. Heart Assn. (fellow stroke coun.). Office: 200 E 33d St # 10B New York NY 10016

JONASSON, OLGA, surgeon, educator; b. Peoria, Ill., Aug. 12, 1934; d. Olav and Swea C. (Johnson) J. MD, U Ill., Chgo., 1958; DSc, Newberry (S.C.) Coll., 1982. Diplomate Am. Bd. Surgery (bd. dirs. 1988-94). Intern and resident U. Ill. Rsch. & Ednl. Hosps., 1959-64; prof. surgery U. Ill., 1975-87; chief of surgery Cook County Hosp., Chgo., 1977-86; chmn., prof. dept. surgery Ohio State U., Columbus, 1987-93; mem. staff U. Ill. Hosps., Chgo., 1993—. Markle scholar John & Mary Markle Found., 1969. Fellow ACS; mem. Am. Surg. Assn. Office: Am Coll Surgeons Surg Svcs Dept 55 E Erie St Chicago IL 60611-2731

JONDAHL, TERRI ELISE, sales and marketing professional; b. Ukiah, Calif., May 6, 1959; d. Thomas William and Rebecca (Stewart) J. AA in Bus. Adminstrn., Mendocino Coll., 1981; BA in Adminstrn. and Mgmt., Columbia Pacific U., 1993. Sec. to planning commn. County of Mendocino, Ukiah, Calif., 1977-80; office systems analyst County of Mendocino, Ukiah, 1980-83; micro systems analyst Computerland of Annapolis, Md., 1983-84; controller Continental Mfg. Inc., Nacogdoches, Tex., 1984-87; mktg. mgr. Continental Mfg. Inc., Nacogdoches, 1987-89, dir. sales and mktg., 1989—, sec., treas., 1985—; pres. Jondahl & Assocs.; owner, Jondahl & Assocs., Nacogdoches; cons. acct. Drosia Trading Inc., Nacogdoches, 1988-89; mem. JSEC com. Tex. Employment Commn., 1990—. Co-author: National Federation of Business & Professional Women Local Organization Revitalization Plan, 1989. Mem. mktg. edn. adv. coun. Nacogdoches Ind. Sch. dist., 1989. Mem. NAFE, Tex. Fedn. Bus. and Profl. Women (dist. dir. 1989-90, 3d v.p. 1991-92, 1st v.p. 1992-93, pres.-elect 1993-94, state pres. 1994—), Nacogdoches Bus. and Profl. Women (pres. 1987-88), Ukiah Bus. and Profl. Women (pres. 1981-82), Nacagdoches County C. of C. (small bus. adv. com. 1990). Home: 1069 Woodhaven St Nacogdoches TX 75961-9613 Office: Continental Mfg Inc 2306 S Rayburn Dr Nacogdoches TX 75961-7438

JONES, ALICE JANE, soil scientist, educator, federal agency administrator; b. Michigan City, Ind., Apr. 9, 1953; d. Harry William and Helen Zell (Moore) J.; m. Lloyd Norman Mielke, Oct. 22, 1988; children: Janet, Steve. BS Biology, Ecology, Mich. Tech. U., 1975; MS Soil Fertility, Mont. State U., 1978; PhD Soil, Physics Engring., Utah State U., 1982; Bus. Mgmt. cert., U. Nebr. Lincoln, 1992. Grad. rsch. asst. plant and soil sci. dept. Mont. State U., 1976-78; rsch. asst. agronomy dept. Wash. State U., 1978-79; grad. rsch. asst. soil sci. and biometeorology dept. Utah State U., 1979-80; instr. plant and soil sci. dept. Mont. State U., 1980-81, asst. prof. western triangle agrl. rsch. ctr., 1983-85; asst. prof. biology dept. Mont. Coll. Mineral Sci. and Tech., 1981-83; asst. prof., extension specialist agronomy dept. U. Nebr. Lincoln, 1985-88, assoc. prof., extension specialist agronomy dept., 1988—, vice chair agronomy dept., 1991-92, asst. dean, adminstrv. intern agrl. rsch. divsn., 1991-92; program mgr. natural resources food and social scis. divsn. USDA Cooperative State Rsch. Svc., Washington, 1992-93; dir. sustainable agriculture USDA, Washington, 1993-94; cons. and presenter in field. Contbr. numerous articles to profl. and popular jours., abstracts, author video prodns., computer software. Recipient Soil and Water Conservation Steward award State of Nebr., 1987, Outstanding Ednl. Aids Blue Ribbon award Am. Soc. Agrl. Engrs., 1987-91; numerous grants in field. Mem. Soil Sci. Soc. Am. (chair divsn. S6 1993-94), Soil and Water Conservation Soc. (fellow, mem. numerous coms., state commendation award 1987, pres'. citation award 1987, 88, internat. commendation award 1988, pres. Lincoln NE chpt., bd. dirs. 1989-92, vice pres. 1991-92), Internat. Soil Tillage Rsch. Orgn., Am. Soc. Agronomy (pub. rels. com. 1991—, fellow award com. 1992—), Nebr. Coop. Extension Assn. (outstanding new specialist award 1988), Sigma Xi, Gamma Sigma Delta (award com., Phi Sigma, Epsilon Sigma Phi. Office: Univ of Nebraska Lincoln 279 Plant Sci Lincoln NE 68588

JONES, ANITA KATHERINE, computer scientist, educator; b. Ft. Worth, Mar. 19, 1942; d. Park Joel and Helene Louise (Voigt) J.; m. William A. Wulf, July 1, 1977; children: Karin, Ellen. AB in Math., Rice U., 1964; MA in English, U. Tex., 1966; PhD in Computer Sci., Carnegie Mellon U., 1973. Programmer IBM, Boston, Washington, 1966-69; assoc. prof. computer sci. Carnegie-Mellon U., Pitts., 1973-81; founder, v.p. Tartan Labs. Inc., Pitts., 1981-87; free-lance cons. Pitts., 1987-88; prof., head computer sci. dept. U. Va., Charlottesville, 1988-93; dir. def. rsch. and engring. Dept. Def., Washington, 1993—; mem. Def. Sci. Bd., Dept. Defense 1985-93, USAF Sci. Adv. Bd. 1980-85; bd. dirs. Sci Applications Internat. Corp.; trustee Mitre Corp., 1989. Editor: Perspectives on Computer Science, 1977, Foundations of Secure Computation, 1971. Recipient Air Force Meritorious Civilian Svc. award, 1985. Mem. IEEE, Assn. Computing Machinery (editor-in-chief Transactions on Computer Sys. 1983—), Sigma Xi.

JONES, BARBARA CHRISTINE, educator, linguist, creative arts designer; b. Augsburg, Swabia, Bavaria, Fed. Republic Germany, Nov. 14, 1942; came to U.S., 1964, naturalized, 1971; d. Martin Walter and Margarete Katharina (Roth-Rommel) Schulz von Hammer-Parstein; m. Robert Edward Dickey, 1967 (div. 1980); m. Raymond Lee Jones, 1981. Student U. Munich, 1961, Philomatique de Bordeaux, France, 1962; BA in German, French, Speech, Calif. State U., Chico, 1969, MA in Comparative Internat. Edn., 1974. Cert. secondary tchr., community coll. instr., Calif. Fgn. lang. tchr. Gridley Union High Sch., Calif., 1970-80, home econs., decorative arts instr., cons., 1970-80, English study skills instr., 1974-80, ESL coordinator, instr. Punjabi, Mex. Ams., 1970-72, curriculum com. chmn., 1970-80; program devel. adviser Program Devel. Ctr. Supt. Schs. Butte County, Oroville, Calif., 1975-77; opportunity tchr. Esperanza High Sch., Gridley, 1980-81, Liberty High Sch., Lodi, Calif., 1981-82, resource specialist coordinator, 1981-82; Title I coordinator Bear Creek Ranch Sch., Lodi, 1981-82, instr., counselor, 1981-82; substitute tchr. Elk Grove (Calif.) Unified, 1982-84; freelance decorative arts and textiles designer, 1982-85; internat. heritage and foods advisor AAUW, Chico, Calif., 1973-75; lectr. German, Schreiner Coll., Kerrville, Tex., 1993. Workshop dir. Creative Arts Ctr., Chico, 1972-73; workshop dir., advisor Bus. Profl. Women's Club of Gridley, 1972-74; v.p. Golden State Mobile Home League, Sacramento, 1980-82; mem. publicity Habitat for Humanity, Kerrville br., 1992-94. Designer weavings-wallhangings (1st place 10 categories, Silver Dollar Fair, Chico, 1970). Mem. AAUW (publicity dir. cultural activities Kerrville br. 1991-92), Am. Cancer Soc. (publicity 1992-95), United European Am. Club, Am. Assn. German Tchrs., U.S. Army Res. Non-Commd. Officer's Assn. (ednl. adv. 1984-86), German Texan Heritage Soc., Kappa Delta Pi. Avocations: weaving, fiber designs, swimming, skiing, internat. travel and culture. Home: 2894 Lower Turtle Creek Rd Kerrville TX 78028-9743

JONES, BEVERLY ANN MILLER, nursing administrator, patient services executive; b. Bklyn., July 14, 1927; d. Hayman Edward and Eleanor Virginia (Doyle) Miller. BSN, Adelphi U., 1949; m. Kenneth Lonzo Jones, Sept. 5, 1953; children: Steven Kenneth, Lonnie Cord. Chief nurse regional blood program ARC, N.Y.C., 1951-54; asst. dir., acting dir. nursing M.D. Anderson Hosp. and Tumor Inst., Houston, 1954-55; asst. dir. nursing Sibley Meml. Hosp., Washington, 1959-61; assoc. dir. nursing svc. Anne Arundel Gen. Hosp., Annapolis, Md., 1966-70; asst. adminstr. nursing Alexandria (Va.) Hosp., 1972-73; v.p. patient care svcs., Longmont (Colo.) United Hosp., 1977-93; pvt. cons., 1993—; instr. ARC, 1953-57; mem. adv. bd. Boulder Valley Vo.-Tech Health Occupations Program, 1977-80; chmn. nurse enrollment com. D.C. chpt. ARC, 1959-61; del. nursing adminstrs. good will trip to Poland, Hungary, Sweden and Eng., 1980. Contbr. articles to profl. jours. Bd. dirs. Meals on Wheels, Longmont, Colo., 1978-80, Longmont Coalition for Women in Crisis, Applewood Living Ctr., Longmont; mem. Colo. Hosp. Assn. Task Force on Nat. Commn. on Nursing, 1982; mem. utilization com. Boulder (Colo.) Hospice, 1979-83; vol. Longmont Police Bur., Colo.; mem. coun. labor rels. Colo. Hosp. Assn., 1982-87; mem.-at-large exec. com. nursing svc. adminstrs. Sect. Md. Nurses' Assn., 1966-69; mem. U. Colorado Task Force on Nursing, 1990; vol. Champs program St. Vrain Valley Sch. Dist.; vol. Longmont Police Dept. Mem. Am. Orgn. Nurse Execs. (chmn. com. membership svcs. and promotions, nominee recognition of excellence in nursing adminstrn.), Colo. Soc. Nurse Execs. (dir. 1978-80, 84-86, pres. 1980-81, mem. com. on nominations 1985-86). Home: 853 Wade Rd Longmont CO 80503-7017

JONES, BLANCHE, nursing administrator, orthopaedic and gerontology consultant; b. Edgecombe, N.C., Nov. 11, 1935; d. Cosevelt Ewuell and Evelyn (Jones) Harrison. Diploma, CUNY Hunter Coll., 1971; AAS, CUNY Medgar Evers Coll., 1986; BS in Cmty. Health, Gerontology and Med. Surg. Sci., St. Joseph's Coll., 1990. RN, N.Y.; RN in med.-surg., ANCC. Nurse aide Bellevue Hosp., N.Y.C., 1958-61, lic. practical nurse, 1961-71, staff nurse, 1971-72, head nurse, 1972-77; head nurse Coney Island Hosp., Bklyn., 1978-90, clin. supr., 1990—. Contbr. articles to profl. jours. Bd. dirs. Baisley Park Neighbors Inc., Jamaica, N.Y., 1968—. Mem. Orthopaedic Nurses Assn., N.Y. Nurses Assn. (del. 1972), Bowling League, Fishing Club, Target Pistol Club. Democrat. Baptist. Home: 15026 119th Ave Jamaica NY 11434-2009 Office: Coney Island Hosp 2600 Ocean Pky Brooklyn NY 11235-7701

JONES, BRENDA GAIL, school district administrator; b. Winnipeg, Man., Can., Nov. 5, 1949; d. Glen Allen and Joyce Catherine (Peckham) McGregor. BA, San Francisco State U., 1972; MA, U. San Francisco, 1983. Cert. tchr., sch. adminstr., Calif. Tchr. Lakeport (Calif.) Unified Sch. Dist., 1973-82, asst. prin., 1982-88, dir. ednl. svcs., 1988—; instr. English Mendocino Coll., Ukiah, Calif., 1977-82. Mem. Assn. Calif. Sch. Adminstrs. (past pres. 1987, Lake County charter), Order Ea. Star (worthy matron Clear Lake chpt. 1995). Democrat. Episcopalian. Home: 1315 20th St Lakeport CA 95453-3051 Office: Lakeport Unified Sch Dist 100 Lange St Lakeport CA 95453-3297

JONES, CAROLINE ROBINSON, advertising executive; b. Benton Harbor, Mich.; d. Ernest and Mattie Robinson; 1 child, Anthony R. BA, U. Mich., 1963. Copywriter J. Walter Thompson, N.Y., 1963-68, v.p., co-creative dir. Zebra Assocs., Inc., N.Y., 1968-71; copywriter Kenyon & Eckhardt, N.Y., 1971-74; ptnr., creative dir. Black Creative Group, N.Y., 1974-77; v.p., creative group head Batten, Barton, Durstine & Osborn, Inc., N.Y., 1977; exec. v.p., creative dir. Mingo-Jones Advt., N.Y., 1978-86; pres. Caroline Jones Advt. Inc., N.Y.C., 1986—. Bd. dirs. N.Y. Advt. Council, L.I.U., Smithsonian Ctr. Advt. History, Women's Forum. Recipient creative advt. awards Clio, One Show, ANNY, NYMRAD, Art Dirs., CEBA, Ad Woman of Yr., 1990, and others, Matrix award Women in Comm.; mem. Com. of 200. Mem. N.Y.C. Partnership, N.Y. Home: 200 E 65th St New York NY 10021-6603 Office: Caroline Jones Inc 415 Madison Ave New York NY 10017-1111

JONES, CAROLYN ELLIS, publisher, retired employment agency and business service company executive; b. Marigold, Miss., Feb. 21, 1928; d. Joseph Lawrence and Willie Decelle (Forrest) Peeples; m. David Wright Ellis, May 30, 1945 (div. 1966); children—David, Lyn, Debbie, Dawn; m. Frank Willis Jones, Jan. 1, 1980. Student La. State U., 1949. Owner, mgr. Personnel and Bus. Service, Inc., Greenwood, Miss., 1962-88, now v.p.; owner Honor Pub. Co., Greenwood, 1988—. Author: The Lottie Moon Storybook, 1985; Editor: An Old Soldier's Career, 1974. Contbr. articles to religious and gen. interest publs. Mem. adv. bd. career edn. Greenwood Pub. Schs., 1975-76, mem. adv. bd. vocat.-tech. dept., 1975-88; conf. leader Miss. Bapt. Convention Singles Retreat, 1980; Mission Service Corps del. Home Mission Bd., So. Bapt. Conv., Hawaii, 1979. Mem. Greenwood C. of C. (edn. com. 1980—, guest speaker career day program local high sch.), Mothers Against Drunk Drivers, Altrusa Internat., Nat. Fedn. Ind. Bus., Miss Delta Rose Soc., Miss. Native Plant Soc., Gideon Aux. (pres. 1986-88). Avocations: writing, rose exhibitions. Office: Honor Pub 802 W President Ave Greenwood MS 38930-3326

JONES, CAROLYN EVANS, small business owner; b. Middleboro, Mass., Sept. 5, 1931; d. King Israel and Kleo Estelle (Hodges) Evans; m. John Homer Jones, Sept. 9, 1966 (dec. July 1986); 1 child, David Everett. BA in English, Tift Coll., 1952; M of Religious Edn., Carver Sch. Missions and Social Work (now So. Bapt. Theol. Sem.), 1958; BA in Art, Mercer U., 1982. Cert. secondary tchr., Ga. Tchr. McDuffie County Bd. Edn., Thomson, Ga., 1952-53, Colquitt County Bd. Edn., Norman Park, Ga., 1953-55; missionary Home Mission Bd. SBC, New Orleans and Macon, 1958-66; spl. edn. tchr. Bibb County Bd. Edn., Macon, 1968-70, 75-79; owner, operator Laney Co. Imprinted Specialties, Macon, 1986—. Contbr. numerous articles and poems to profl. jours. Bible tchr. YWCA, Macon, 1980-85; deacon 1st Bapt. Ch., Macon. Mem. Promotional Products Assn. Internat., Macon-Bibb County C. of C., Internat. Tng. in Comm., Alumnae Assn. Tift Coll. (exec. com.), Greater Macon Women Bus. Owners Club, Ad Club of Cen. Ga. Democrat. Office: Laney Co Imprinted Specialties 2451 Kingsley Dr Macon GA 31204-1718

JONES, CATHERINE ANN, library administrator; b. Conneaut, Ohio, Apr. 30, 1936; d. Leo Joseph and Mary Louise (McGinty) Delanty; m. Thomas Michael Jones, May 18, 1957; 1 child, Michael S. BA in English, U. Ala., 1965; MLS, Cath. U. Am., 1969; MA in Govt., George Washington U., 1980. Chief reference libr. Exec. Office of Pres. Office of Mgmt. and Budget, Washington, 1968-72; assoc. dir. Washington office ALA, 1972-73; asst. univ. libr. George Washington U., Washington, 1973-78; chief congl. reference div. Congl. Rsch. Svc., Libr. of Congress, Washington, 1978—; adj. prof. Cath. U. Am., Washington, 1983—. Fellow Spl. Librs. Assn. (pres. Washington chpt. 1980-81, 81-82, nat. treas. 1988-91, Pres.'s award 1987, editor jour. issues summer 1988; mem. D.C. Libr. Assn. (pres. 1977-78,, profl. devel. com. 1992—), Cath. U. Alumni Assn. (pres. 1977-78, Alumni Achievement award 1994). Roman Catholic. Office: Libr Congress Congl Reference Div CRS Independence Ave & 1st St SE Washington DC 20540-7420

JONES, CHRISTINE MASSEY, furniture company executive; b. Columbus, Ga., Nov. 7, 1929; d. Lewis Everett and Donia (Spivey) Massey; divorced; children—James Raymond, Jr., James David. Student, Ga. Southwestern Coll., 1947-48. With Muscogee Mfg. Co., Columbus, Ga., 1948-56; sec. to pres. Muscogee Mfg. Co., 1956; sec. to pres. and treas., corp. sec. Haverty Furniture Cos., Inc., Atlanta, 1956-59, sec. to pres. and treas., 1959-63, sec. to pres., 1963-72, sec. to pres., adminstrv. asst., 1972-74, sec. to pres., admintrv. asst., asst. corp. sec., 1974-78, corp. sec., 1978-86, corp. sec., asst. v.p., 1986-93; v.p. stockholder rels., sec. Haverty Furniture Cos., Atlanta, 1993—. Mem. Am. Soc. Corp. Secs. (securities industry com.).

Home: 5245 Chemin De Vie NE Atlanta GA 30342-2547 Office: 866 W Peachtree St NW Atlanta GA 30308-1123

JONES, CLAIRE BURTCHAELL, artist, teacher, writer; b. Oakland, Calif.; d. Clarence Samuel and Florence Mallett (Hinchman) Burtchaell; m. E.C. Jones; children: Holland Mallett, Lela Claire, S. Evan. AB, Stanford U.; postgrad. Laguna Beach Sch. Art, 1972-73, San Diego Art Acad., 1980-82. Free lance art tchr., Park Ridge, Ill., 1967; tchr. Jade Fon Group, Pacific Grove, Calif., 1972-73, Merced Coll., Sierra Mountains, Calif., 1973; free lance pvt. workshop, painting for commns. and galleries, Calif., 1973—. Author: First The Blade (annual collection), 1939; Arrows in the Air, 1947-51; Utah Sings, 1953. Editor: Watercolor West Newsletter, 1978-83. Contbr. articles to profl. jours. Recipient numerous awards for artwork. Mem. San Diego Mus. Art Artists Guild, Nat. Mus. Women in the Arts (founding mem.), Assn. Western Artists (bd. dirs. 1970-71), Watercolor West (bd. dirs. 1978-81, 86—), San Diego Art Inst. (bd. dirs. 1976-78), Stanford Alumni Assn., Literati West (founder, sec.-treas. 1994—).

JONES, CYNTHIA TERESA CLARKE, artist; b. Bklyn., Aug. 12, 1938; d. Arthur Ottio and Emma (Gibbs) Clarke; m. Robert H. Jones. Apr. 21, 1968 (div. Sept. 1977); 1 child, Kim Marie. Student, Bklyn. Mus., 1954-57, Art Career Sch., 1958, Hunter Coll., N.Y.C., 1963-65. One woman shows include Queens Borough Pub. Libr., Jamaica, N.Y., 1986, Baruch Coll., 1972; exhibited in group shows Queens Coun. on Arts Exhibit at Gertz Dept. Store, 1972, Queens Coll. Arts Festival, 1972, Dist. Coun. 37, First Art Exhbn., 1972, Artist Equity Group Shows Union Carbide, 1975, 77, Queensborough Community Coll. Invitational Show at Holocaust Resource Ctr., 1985, Pen and Brush, 1990, AQA Gallery, 1990, AQA at Chung Cheng Gallery at St. Johns U., 1987-90, Lowenstein Libr. Gallery Fordham U., 1989, Arlington Arts Ctr., 1991, Pursuit of Peace Ceres Gallery, 1991; designer cover Rsch. Papers Stats. Dept. Bernard M. Baruch Coll., 1973; works reprinted in Locally Speaking Local 384 newsletter. Donator work to MUSE Gallery, 1990, to Hale House Ctr., Inc.; active Women's Caucus for Art. Recipient Joseph Grumbacher Co. award, 1958, Scholastic Art award and key, 1957, Fine Arts award Queensboro Soc., 1973, Outstanding Painting award, 1973, France Lieber Meml. award Nat. Assn. Women Artists, Inc., 1992, two certs. of merit Latham Found., 1956-58; scholar Latham Found., 1958. Mem. Artists Equity Assn., Inc. N.Y., Alliance of Queens Artists, Coll. Art Assn., Queens Coun. on Arts, Ind. Arts Assn., Arlington Arts Ctr. Va., Queensboro Coll. Art Gallery (assoc.), Nat. Assn. Women Artists, Print Club, Guild Am. Papercutters. Office: 11332 Mayville St Jamaica NY 11412-2410

JONES, DALE CHERNER, marketing executive; b. Chgo., Apr. 22, 1948; d. Morris and Rose (Fidelman) Cherner; m. Jerome J. Jones, Dec. 16, 1973 (div. Feb. 1985); m. Edward Louis Kathrein, Oct. 24, 1987; stepchildren: Janet Kirkwood, Brian Kathrein. BA, Northwestern U., 1968, M in Mgmt., 1986. Manuscripts librarian Chgo. Hist. Soc., 1968-69; mktg. coord. Perkins & Will Architects & Engrs., Chgo., 1969-73; owner Mktg. & Mgmt. Cons., Evanston, Ill., 1974-77; mktg. adminstr. Grumman-Butkus (formerly Enercon Ltd.), Evanston, 1977-79; assoc., mktg. dir. H.W. Lochner, Inc., Chgo., 1979-82; prin., owner JCS, Inc., Evanston, 1982-83; prin., dir. mktg. Schirmer Engrng. Corp., Deerfield, Ill., 1983-88; pres., COO, ptnr. R.E. Timm & Assocs., Hinsdale, Ill., 1990—; mktg. advisor Chgo. chpt. Ill. Soc. Profl. Engrs., 1980—. Contbr. articles to profl. jours. Fellow Soc. for Mktg. Profl. Svcs. (founder Chgo. chpt., nat. bd. dirs. 1984-86, pres. 1979-82, Cert. of Achievement 1982); mem. AIA (affiliate; mem. adv. coun. 1984-86, Cert. 1985); ABWA (founder Chgo. chpt., treas. 1973-74, pres. 1974-75, Bus. Woman of Yr. 1974), Profl. Svcs. Mgmt. Assn., Am. Mgmt. Assn., Kellogg Alumnae Club, Northwestern Club of Chgo. Office: RE Timm & Assocs Inc 8330 S Madison St Hinsdale IL 60521-6215

JONES, DIANA MITCHEN, school psychologist; b. Crossett, Ark., Sept. 16, 1946; d. Joseph Henry and Eliza Jane (Zazzi) Mitchen; m. Daniel Elven Jones, Apr. 17, 1965; children: Dana Leigh, David Michael. BA in Psychology, So. Conn. State U., 1972; MS in Psychology, U. New Orleans, 1984, PhD in Counselor/Edn., 1993. Lic. profl. counselor; cert. sch. psychologist, supr. of sch. psychol. svcs. Dean of admissions and devel. St. Martin's Episcopal Sch., Metairie, La., 1982-86; dir. admissions Louise S. McGehee Sch., New Orleans, 1986-87; sch. psychologist Orleans Parish Schs., New Orleans, 1987—; adj. asst. prof. U. New Orleans, 1993—. Mem. Women in Action, Tulane Women's Assn., New Orleans, 1993-94. Mem. Am. Counseling Assn., Assn. for Adult Devel. Aging, Chi Sigma Iota. Office: Support and Appraisal New Orleans Pub Schs 3510 General DeGaulle Dr New Orleans LA 70114

JONES, DONNA JO, educator; b. Council Bluffs, Iowa, Nov. 29, 1943; d. Donald Dwane and Ida Josephine (Beeks) J.; m. Ronald E. Jones, Feb. 17, 1967 (div. June 1968); m. V. Dennis Rutledge, Apr. 6, 1984; stepchildren: Loretta Adams, Pamela Rutledge, Deborah Lee. BA in Sociology, Tarkio Coll., 1965; MA in Sociology, U. Mo., 1970, PhD in Sociology, 1991. Instr. St. Louis U. Sch. Medicine, 1971-74; counselor, reproductive decisions Reproductive Health Svcs., St. Louis, 1974-84; rsch. asst. Ctr. Rsch. Social Behavior, Columbia, Mo., 1974-79; parenting advocate Parent Infant Interaction Program, St. Louis, 1979-81; coord. community activities Desegregation St. Louis Pub. Schs., 1981-84; coord. mothers march March of Dimes, Springfield, Mo., 1984-85; coord. Parents as Tchrs. The Parenting Place, Springfield Pub. Schs., 1985-86; dir. The Parenting Place, Forest Inst. Profl. Psychology, Springfield, 1986-88; asst. prof. Drury Coll., Springfield, 1991—; cons. Springfield/Greene County Librs., 1992—; adj. prof. and instr. S.W. Mo. State U., Springfield, 1986-90, Drury Coll., 1989-91; cons. Springfield Cmty. Needs Assessment. Co-author: Readings in Health Care, 1970, Involving Significant Others, 1979; co-editor: Midwest Feminist Papers, 1992, 93, 94; editor newsletter Tapestries, 1992—. Pres., v.p. Ozark Lakes Area Disciples of Christ Women's Work, 1985-89; founder local chpt. Nat. Soc. Fundraising Execs., Springfield, 1985-90; bd. dirs. Mo. Victim Ctr., Springfield, 1991—; founder, bd. dirs. Parent Teen Adv. Com., Springfield, 1986-89; founder, mem. Discovery Ctr., Springfield, 1986-88; mem. Interfaith AIDS Network, Springfield, 1991—; mem. Ozark Greenways. Recipient Laing Bible award Tarkio Coll., 1962, Disting. Gregory award U. Mo., 1965, 66, PTA Vol. award St. Louis, 1984. Mem. Am. Sociol. Assn., Mo. Sociol. Soc. (pres.-elect 1994—), Am. Soc. Sex Educators, Counselors and Therapists, Midwest Sociol. Soc. (com. mem., chair acad. freedom and responsibility com. 1993—), Midwest Sociologists for Women in Soc., Sociologists for Women in Soc. Office: Drury Coll Behavioral Sci Dept 900 N Benton Springfield MO 65802

JONES, DONNA MARIE, public administrator, lawyer; b. Chgo., Mar. 2, 1950; d. Nathaniel Beck Jr. and Merle Rowe; children: André Jamal, Aerle Taree. BA, U. Wis., 1972, JD, 1978; MPA, CUNY, 1984. Bar: Wis. 1979, U.S. Dist. Ct. (we. dist.) Wis. 1979. Recruitment-selection specialist U. Wis. System, Madison, 1973-75; pers. analyst City of Madison, 1975, asst. to city atty., 1976, contract compliance officer, 1979-82, 83-85, asst. to mayor, 1988-89; exec. asst. to dir. Maricopa County Human Resources Dept., Phoenix, 1982-83; dir. Office of Disadvantaged Bus. Devel. Milwaukee County, Milw., 1985-88; interim pers. mgr. Supreme Ct. of Wis., Madison, 1989; dir. Office of Affirmative Action and Compliance U. Wis., Madison, 1989-94, sr. adminstrv. program specialist, 1994—; bd. govs. State Bar Wis., Madison, 1990-92, program. co-chair com. for participation of women in the bar, 1990, 92; mem. nat. steering com. Nat. Conf. on Women and the Law, San Antonio, 1978-79. Author articles, book revs. and poetry. Bd. dirs. Child Devel., Inc., Madison, 1976; Wis. del. Nat. Observance of Internat. Women's Yr., Houston, 1977-78; bd. dirs. South Madison Neighborhood Ctr., 1981-82, Ko-Thi Dance Co., Inc., 1985-88, Dane County Cultural Affairs Commn., Madison, 1991-94. Named Woman of Distinction, Madison YWCA, 1982, one of Am.'s top bus. and profl. women Dollas and Sense Mag., 1992; Nat. Urban fellow, 1982. Mem. Madison NAACP, Legal Assn. for Women, Am. Assn. for Affirmative Action, Urban League of Greater Madison, Wis. Minority Women's Network, Wis. Women's Network. Office: Univ of Wisconsin 179-A Bascom Hall 500 Lincoln Dr Madison WI 53706-1380

JONES, DONNA MARILYN, real estate broker, legislator; b. Brush, Colo., Jan. 14, 1939; d. Virgil Dale and Margaret Elizabeth (McDaniel) Wolfe; m. Donald Eugene Jones, June 9, 1956; children: Dawn Richter, Lisa Shira, Stuart. Student, Treasure Valley Community Coll., 1981-82; grad., Realtors Inst. Cert. residential specialist. Co-owner Parts, Inc., Payette, Idaho, 1967-79; dept. mgr., buyer Lloyd's Dept. Store, Payette, Idaho, 1979-80; sales assoc. Idaho-Oreg. Realty, Payette, Idaho, 1981-82; mem. dist. 13 Idaho Ho. of Reps., Boise, 1987-90, mem. dist. 10, 1990—; assoc. broker Classic Properties Inc., Payette, 1983-91; owner, broker ERA Preferred Properties Inc., 1991—. Co-chmn. Apple Blossom Parade, 1982; mem. Payette Civic League, 1968-84, pres. 1972; mem. Payette County Planning and Zoning Commn., 1985-88, vice-chmn. 1987; field coordinator Idaho Rep. Party Second Congl. Dist., 1986; mem. Payette County Rep. Cen. Com. 1978—; precinct II com. person, 1978-79, state committeewoman, 1980-84, chmn. 1984-87; outstanding county chmn. region III Idaho Rep. Party Regional Hall of Fame, 1985-86; mem. Payette County Rep. Women's Fedn., 1988—, bd. dirs., 1990-92; mem. Idaho Hispanic Commn., 1989-92, Idaho State Permanent Bldg. Adv. Coun., 1990—; bd. dirs. Payette Edn. Found., 1993—, Western Treasure Valley Cultural Ctr., 1993—; nat. bd. dirs. Am. Legis. Exchange Coun., 1993—; mem. legis. adv. coun. Idaho Housing Agy., 1992—; committeeperson Payette County Cen.; chmn. Ways and Means Idaho House of Reps., 1993—; Idaho chmn. Am. Legis. Exchange Coun., 1991—. Recipient White Rose award Idaho March of Dimes, 1988; named Payette/Washington County Realtor of Yr., 1987. Mem. Idaho Assn. Realtors (legis. com. 1984-87, chmn. 1986, realtors active in politics com. 1982—, polit. action com. 1986, polit. affairs com. 1986-88, chmn. 1987, bd. dirs. 1984-88), Payette/Washington County Bd. Realtors (v.p. 1981, state dir. 1984-88, bd. dirs 1983-88, sec. 1983), Bus. and Profl. Women (Woman of Progress award 1988, 90, treas. 1988), Payette C. of C., Fruitland C. of C., Wiesr C. of C.. Republican. Home: 1911 1st Ave S Payette ID 83661-3003 Office: ERA Preferred Properties 1610 6th Ave S Payette ID 83661-3348

JONES, DOROTHY JOANNE, social services professional; b. L.A.; d. Joseph Anthony and Florence (Chaffin) Ghiotto; divorced; children: Teri McKane, Carole Thompson, Christopher Jones. BA, La Verne U., 1980; MS, Calif. State U., Fullerton, 1983. Lic. marriage, family/child counselor. Dep. sheriff L.A. County Sheriff Office, 1972-76; dir. A.I.C., L.A., 1976-80; mgr. McDonnell Douglas, Long Beach, Calif., 1980-93; pvt. practice Los Alamitos, Calif., 1985—; cons. L.A. County, 1993-94. Author: When to Say No, 1983. Mem. Ctr. for Performing Arts, L.A., 1976&, Transpacific Mgmt., Long Beach, 1982-83. Recipient Spl. Svc. award Assn. Labor and Mgmt., Orange County, Calif., 1983. mem. Employee Assistance Profls. Assn. (pres. 1980-82), Alcoholism Info. Ctr. (v.p. 1980-91), Counseling Assocs. (v.p. 1976-83), Calif. Assn. Marriage and Family Therapists (cons. Los Angeles County 1993—). Democrat. Episcopalian. Office: Ste 201 10741 Los Alamitos Los Alamitos CA 90720

JONES, EDITH HOLLAN, federal judge; b. Phila., Apr. 7, 1949; BA, Cornell U., 1971; JD with honors, U. Tex., 1974. Bar: Tex. 1974, U.S. Supreme Ct. 1979, U.S. Ct. Appeals (5th and 11th cirs.), U.S. Dist. Ct. (so. and no. dists.) Tex. Assoc. Andrews & Kurth, Houston, 1974-82, ptnr., 1982-85; judge U.S. Ct. Appeals (5th cir.), Houston, 1985—. Gen. counsel Rep. Party of Tex., 1981-83. Mem. ABA, State Bar Tex. Presbyterian. Office: US Ct Appeals 8631 US Courthouse 515 Rusk Ave Houston TX 77002-2603*

JONES, EDITH IRBY, physician; b. Conway, Ark., Dec. 23, 1927; d. Robert and Mattie (Buice) Irby; m. James Beauregard Jones, Apr. 16, 1960 (dec. Oct. 1989); children: Gary, Myra, Keith. BS, Knoxville Coll., 1948; MD, U. Ark., 1952. Intern Univ. Hosp., Little Rock, Ark., 1952-53; gen. practice medicine Hot Springs, Ark., 1953-59; resident in internal medicine Baylor Coll. Medicine, Houston, 1959-62; practice medicine specializing in internal medicine Houston, 1962—; mem. staff Meth. Hosp., Houston, Hermann Hosp., Houston, Riverside Gen. Hosp., Houston, St. Elizabeth Hosp., Houston, St. Anthony Ctr., Houston, St. Joseph Hosp., Houston, Thomas Care Ctr., Houston; mem. staff Town Park, Houston, chief of staff; clin. asst. prof. medicine Baylor Coll. Medicine, U. Tex. Sch. Medicine, Houston; dir. Prospect Med. Lab.; bd. dirs., sec. Mercy Hosp. Comprehensive Health Care Group; ptnr. Jones, Coleman and Whitfield; grand med. examiner Ct. Calanthe Jurisdiction, Tex.; cons. Social Security Agy., Tex. Pub. Welfare Dept., Vocat. Rehab. Assn., Tex. Rehab. Commn.; bd. dirs. Standard Savs. Assn., Houston; numerous others. Contbr. articles to profl. jours. Bd. dirs. Houston Internat. U., Drug Addiction Rehab. Enterprise, March of Dimes, Houston, Odessey House, Houston; mem. adv. bd. Houston Council on Alcoholism; mem. com. for revising justice code, Harris County, Tex.; chmn. bd. trustees Knoxville Coll.; impartial hearing officer Houston Ind. Sch. Dist.; trustee Mut. Assn. for Profl. Service; mem. Community Welfare Planning Assn., Friends of Youth, Human Services Adv. Council, Houston; mem. bd. visitors U. Houston; numerous others. First black to receive BS and MD degrees from U. Ark; Dr. Edith Irby Jones Day proclaimed by State of Ark., 1985, City of Little Rock, 1985, City of N.Y.C., 1986; named One of 30 Most Influential Black Women Houston, 1984; inducted into Tex. Black Women's Hall of Fame, 1986; commended by Calif. Senate, 1969; proclaimation by city council, Houston, 1985, Mayor of Houston, 1986; recipient cert. of citation Ho. of Reps. State of Tex., 1986; portrait placed in entrance hall U. Ark. for Med. Scis., 1985; numerous others. Mem. AMA, Am. Med. Women's Assn. (v.p. Houston chpt.), Nat. Med. Assn. (past pres.), Lone Star Med. Assn., Harris County Med. Assn., Houston Med. Forum, Tex. Assn. Disability Examiners, Bus. and Profl. Women, Nat. Council of Negro Women, Inc. (v.p. Dorothy Height chpt.), NAACP, PTA, YMCA, Alpha Kappa Mu, Delta Sigma Theta, Eta Phi Beta. Democrat. Clubs: Links, Inc., Top Ladies of Distinction, Girl Friends, Inc., Women of Achievement, Inc. (Hall of Fame 1985). Lodge: Order Eastern Star. Home: PO Box 14207 Houston TX 77221-4207 Office: 2601 Prospect St Houston TX 77004-7737

JONES, ELAINE HANCOCK, humanities educator; b. Niagara Falls, N.Y., Feb. 17, 1946; d. Roy Elmer and June Edna (Clark) Hancock; m. Ralph Jones III, Oct. 9, 1971 (div. June 1981). AAS in Comml. Design, U. Buffalo, 1962; BFA, SUNY, Buffalo, 1971, MFA in Painting, 1975; postgrad., Fla. State U., 1993—. Med. illustrator Roswell Park Meml. Inst., Buffalo, 1967-70; designer, animator Acad. McLarty Film Prodns., Buffalo, 1970-73; publs. designer Buffalo/Erie County Hist. Soc., 1974-78; dir. publs. Daemen Coll., Amherst, N.Y., 1978-80; owner, art dir. Plop Art Prodns., Melbourne, Fla., 1981-86; instr. humanities Brevard C.C., Melbourne, 1986—. One-woman shows include SUNY, Buffalo, 1974, Upton Gallery, N.Y., 1975, Gallery Wilde, Buffalo, 1978; exhibited in group shows at Fredonia Coll., N.Y., 1975, Upton Gallery, 1975, Brevard Art Mus., Melbourne, Fla., 1987. Mem. docent program Brevard Art Mus./Sci. Ctr., Melbourne, 1983-84; officer Platinum Coast chpt. Sweet Adelines Internat., 1984-90. Nat. Merit scholar, 1971-75; recipient cert. of merit Curtis Paper Co., 1977; N.Y. State Coun. on Arts grantee, 1975. Republican. Home: 2240 Sea Ave Indialantic FL 32903-2524 Office: Brevard CC Liberal Arts Dept 3865 N Wickham Rd Melbourne FL 32935-2310

JONES, ELIZABETH WINIFRED, biology educator; b. Seattle, Mar. 8, 1939; d. Kenneth Clifford Harris and Dorothea (Dowty) J. BS, U. Wash., 1960, PhD, 1964. Postdoctoral fellow MIT, Cambridge, 1964-67, instr. in biology, 1967-69; asst. prof. Case Western Res. U., Cleve., 1969-74; assoc. prof. Carnegie Mellon U., Pitts., 1974-82, prof., 1982--; vis. scientist Sch. Medicine Wash. U., 1981-82; adj. prof. in psychiatry U. Pitts., 1985—; mem. genetics tng. com. NIH, Bethesda, Md., 1972-73, mem. genetics study sect., 1976-80, 84-86, chair, 1990-93. Editor: Molecular Biology of the Yeast Saccharomyces, 2 vols., 1981, 92, Molecular and Cellular Biology of the Yeast Saccaromyces, 2 vols., 1991, 92; editor Genetics, 1980—, Yeast, 1984—, Molecular Biology of the Cell., 1992—; assoc. editor Ann. Rev. of Genetics, 1990—. Recipient Rsch. Career Devel. award NIH, 1971-74, 75-77. Fellow AAAS; mem. Am. Soc. Microbiology, Am. Soc. Cell Biology (coun. 1992—), Genetics Soc. Am. (pres. 1987), Am. Soc. Human Genetics. Office: Carnegie Mellon U 4400 5th Ave Pittsburgh PA 15213-2617

JONES, ERIKA ZIEBARTH, lawyer; b. Washington, June 10, 1955; d. Thomas Arthur and Ruth (Helm) Ziebarth; m. Gregory Monroe Jones, June 2, 1978; 1 child, Katherine Anne. AB, Georgetown U., 1976, JD, 1980. Bar: D.C. 1980, U.S. Ct. Appeals (D.C. cir.) 1987, U.S. Supreme Ct. 1987. Atty., regulatory analyst U.S. Office Mgmt. and Budget, Washington, 1980-81; spl. counsel Nat. Hwy. Traffic Safety Adminstrn., Washington, 1981-85, chief counsel, 1985-89; of counsel Mayer, Brown and Platt, Washington, 1989-90, ptnr., 1991—. Bd. dirs. Immaculata Coll. High Sch., 1985-88. Mem. ABA, Fed. Bar Assn., Women's Bar Assn. D.C., D.C. Bar Assn., Phi Beta Kappa. Republican. Roman Catholic. Home: 6612 31st Pl NW Washington DC 20015-2302 Office: 2000 Pennsylvania Ave NW Washington DC 20006-1812

JONES, ETTA, singer. Albums include Lonely and Blue, 1962, Don't Go To Strangers, Christmas with Etta Jones, Ms. Jones To You, 1976, My Mother's Eyes, 1977, If You Could See Me Now, 1978, Save Your Love For Me, 1980 (Emmy award nominee 1981), Love Me With All Your Heart, 1983, Fine and Mellow, 1987, I'll Be Seeing You, 1987, Nice Sugar, 1990, Reverse the Charges, 1993. Office: Houston Person 160 Goldsmith Ave Newark NJ 07112-2001*

JONES, HELENE RASBERRY, nursing educator; b. Weleetka, Okla., Apr. 16, 1940; d. John Milburn and Florence Loretta (King) Rasberry; m. Thomas Graves Jones, June 29, 1974; children: Kimberly Anne, Kendall Lee. BSN, Okla. Bapt. U., 1962; MN, Emory U., 1970. RN, Okla., Miss. Instr. Bapt. Sch. Nursing, Oklahoma City, 1963-66; staff nurse Presbyn. Hosp., Oklahoma City, 1966-67; instr. William Rufus King State Tech. Inst., Selma, Ala., 1967-69; prof. Sch. Nursing U. Miss., Jackson, 1970-80, coord., asst. prof., 1986-90; asst. DON div. staff devel. Univ. Hosp., Jackson, 1990—; assoc. prof. U. Tulsa, 1981; asst. dir., coord. divsn. staff devel. Hillcrest Med. Ctr., 1983-86; cons. Miss. Regional Med. Program, Jackson, 1972; chair accreditation rev. com. Schs. Nursing and bd. trustees instns. higher learning, Jackson, 1979-80. Mem. coms. health check and awards, Jackson, 1986-90, Am. Heart Assn., 1986-90, PTA, Jenks, Okla. and Jackson, 1970-84; Citizens Better Edn., Jackson, 1978-80. Lt. U.S. Army, 1961-63. Mem. ANA, Miss. Nurses Assn. (dist. #13 nurse educator II award 1993), Sigma Theta Tau. Republican. Baptist. Home: 65 Glenway Pl Brandon MS 39042-2530 Office: UMC/Univ Hosp 2500 N State St Jackson MS 39216-4505

JONES, JAMIE DENISE See WATFORD, JAMIE DENISE

JONES, JAN LAVERTY, mayor; m. Ted Jones. Grad. Stanford Univ. Mayor, City of Las Vegas. Office: Office of Mayor City Hall 10th Fl 400 Stewart Ave Las Vegas NV 89101-2942*

JONES, JANE ELIZABETH, artist, art educator; b. Phillipsburg, N.J., Jan. 20, 1934; d. Lester Albert and Anna (Matviak) Brower; m. Elwyn Jones; children: Jeffrey Lee, Teresa Lynn. Grad. h.s., Easton, Pa. Designer, mfr. Jones Palettes, Dallas, Tex., 1973-76; designer palettes Plastiform, Dallas, 1976-94; art educator Jane E. Jones Studio, Dallas, 1974—; tchr. Art Critique Programs Sherman (Tex.) Art League, 1993, Waterloo Water Color Assn., Austin, Tex., 1992-93, design seminars, color seminars, Ft. Worth Woman's Club Art Dept., 1992-93. Artist: water colors have been chosen for Southwestern Watercolor Soc. Ann. Membership Show, 1972-94 (Edgar Whitney award 1990), Nat. Water Color Show Okla., 1988 (Best of Show), Salmagundi Club Competition, N.Y. (House of Hewyward award 1988); patentee: Watcr Color Palettes. Recipient Floral award, named Honored Artist, Dallas Civic Garden Club, 1993. Mem. Southwestern Watercolor Soc. (signature mem.), Artists and Craftsmen Assn. (hon. mention 1989, Merit award 1991, signature mem.), Allied Artists of Am., Dallas Women's Caucus for Arts, Tex. Watercolor Soc., Nat. Watercolor Soc., Ky. Watercolor Soc. Home and Office: 5914 Bent Trl Dallas TX 75248-2720

JONES, JANET DULIN, writer, film producer; b. Hollywood, Calif., Sept. 6, 1957; d. John Dulin and Helen Mae (Weaver) J. BA, Calif. State U., Long Beach, 1980. Developer mini-series and TV series Embassy Communications, Los Angeles, 1981-84; assoc. to producer Hotel Aaron Spelling Prodns., Los Angeles, 1984-85; writing intern Sundance Film Inst., Los Angeles, 1985; feature film story analyst Carson Prodns., Los Angeles, 1985-86; freelance screenplay and play writer Los Angeles and N.Y.C., 1986—. Author (screenplays) Fade Away, 1986, Alone in the Crowd, 1987, Story of the Century, 1988, The Long Way Home, 1989, (play) Cousin Judy, 1989, The Set-Up, 1990, Roommates, 1991, Local Girl, 1991, Dickens and Crime, 1992, (books) Little Bear Books, Vols. 1-5, A Weighty, Waity Matter—My Adventures with India, 1992, Coming and Going,. 1993, Watching the Detectives, 1994, The Ambassadors, 1994. Bd. dirs. Sterling Cir. of Aviva Ctr. for Girls, 1990; bd. dirs., recording sec., steering com. The Creative Coalition, 1991-92. Mem. ACLU, Earth Communication Office (TV and film coms.), Writers Guild Am., Ind. Feature Project, Am. Film Inst., Sundance Film Inst. (pre-selection com. 1985-87), People for Am. Way, Habitat for Humanity, Amnesty Internat., Delta Gamma.

JONES, JANET IRENE, human resources specialist; b. Portsmouth, N.H., Dec. 30, 1943; d. Ronald Edward Simpson and Elizabeth (Staples) Singer; m. Harry Walter Jones, Feb. 1974 (div. 1982); children: Michael Paul, Curtis Kevin. BS in Music Edn., U. N.H., 1965, MEd in Counseling Psychology, 1974. Cert. tchr., N.H., mental health counselor, Mass.; nat. cert. profl. counselor. Educator mucis, dir. music Supervisory Union # 6, Exeter and Stratham, N.H., 1965-72; co-dir. drug treatment naval disciplinary command Portsmouth Naval Prison, 1973-74; substitute tchr. Portsmouth and Rye (N.H.) Schs., 1974-75; guidance counselor Air Force Adult Edn., Pease AFB, N.H., 1975-82; dir. family support ctr. Air Force Family Support Agy., Plattsburgh AFB, N.Y., 1982-83; dir. guidance Air Force Adult Edn. Ctr., Plattsburgh AFB, N.Y., 1983-87; assst. dir. edn. Air Force Adult Edn. Ctr., Griffiss AFB, N.Y., 1987-89; dir. Air Force Adult Edn. Ctr., Hanscom AFB, Mass., 1989-92; mgr. occupational tng. Air Force Human Resource Devel. Ctr., Eglin AFB, Fla., 1992—; sr. faculty Cambridge Coll., 1991-92; adj. prof. Boston U. prison program, 1991-92; workshop presenter and designer; symposium organizer. Advisor, trainer Caminemos program Bay State Prison, 1991-92, cons. Vietnam veterans PTSD group, 1991-92. Mem. ACA (chair com.), Mil. Educators and Counselors Assn. (sect. v.p. 1987-90, pres. 1990-91, bd. dirs. 1991-93, Disting. Svc. award 1990), Assn. Multicultural Counseling and Devel. (com. 1990—, Profl. Svc. award 1992), Gulf States Pers. Coun., Gulf Coast Tng. Coun. Home: PO Box 1852 Eglin AFB FL 32542-0852 Office: Air Force Human Resouce Devel Ctr 108 N Mccarthy Ave Ste 1 Eglin AFB FL 32542-5626

JONES, JANET VALERIA, psychiatric nurse; b. Detroit, June 14, 1942; d. Frederick Leopold and Anne Elizabeth (Doege) J.; m. Calvin L. Jones, Dec. 12, 1960; children: Cherie L., Mark A. ASN, U. Guam, 1974; BSN with honors, Stephen F. Austin State U., 1982; MS in Allied Health, U. Tex., Tyler, 1985; MSN in Nurse Administration, Tex. Women's U., Dallas, 1991. RN, Calif., Tex. Staff nurse Barstow (Calif.) Community Hosp.; instr. Stephen F. Austin State U., Nacogdoches, Tex., Tyler Jr. Coll., Rusk, Tex.; RN III Tex. Dept. Corrections, Tenn. Colony, Tex.; nurse supr. geriatric/med. unit Rusk (Tex.) State Hosp.; asst. dir. nursing Terrell (Tex.) State Hosp.; lectr., speaker and presenter in field. Contbr. poem to poetry jour.; columnist: State Hosp. Newsletter; Lectr. to ch. and sch. orgns. Mem. ANA, Tex. Nurses Assn., Am. Psychiat. Nurses Assn. Home: RR 2 Box 527 Rusk TX 75785-9802

JONES, JANICE ANN, counselor; b. Balt., Oct. 14, 1952; d. Elmer John and Ernestine Marie (Davis) Mangold; m. John Alan Jones, June 2, 1973; children: Aaron, Nicholas. AA, Harford Community Coll., 1985; BS, U. Md., 1991; MA, U. Cin., 1993, postgrad. Lic. social worker, Ohio. Lic. day care provider Aberdeen, Md., 1982-85; presch. tchr. Calling All Kids, Las Vegas, 1986-89; owner, operator Kids Country Haven, Mt. Airy, Md., 1989-92; counselor U. Cin., 1992-94; counselor-trainee South Community, Centerville, Ohio, 1993; area coord. Adventures in Real Communication, Cleve., 1993-94; area coord. High Sch. Fgn. Exch. program Adventures in Real Communication; adj. prof. U. Cin., 1994. ESL tutor Adventures in Real Communications; chair PTO, also sch. vol.; den leader Cub Scouts Am. Mem. ACA, Ohio Assn. Counseling and Devel., Chi Sigma Iota, Alpha Lambda. Democrat. Home: 200 Fairfield Ct Springboro OH 45066-9267

JONES, JANON J., county recreation manager; b. Lawrenceville, Ga., Dec. 5, 1960; d. William Sanford and Eleanor Jean (Suddeth) Jones. BS in Human Svcs. Adminstrn., Mercer U., 1982, BS in Phys. Edn., 1982; MA in Phys. Edn., U. Ga., 1986. cert. health and phys. edn. tchr. Asst. coach Mercer U., Atlanta, 1982-83; tchr. DeKalb Coll., Mercer U., Atlanta, 1986-87; head reciever, stocker Drug Emporium, Norcross, Ga., 1982-85; teaching asst. U. Ga., Athens, 1985-86; sales rep. D & J Sales and Svc., Duluth, Ga., 1987-89; recreation leader Gwinnett County Parks & Recreation,

Lawrenceville, Ga., 1990, recreation supr., 1990-92, recreation coord., 1992-94, recreation mgr., 1994—; fundraising chair Gwinnett Safe Kids Coalition, Lawrenceville, 1994—. Chair blood drive Mercer U., 1980-82; coach, mgr. Lawrenceville Athletic Assn., 1994; vol. Gwinnett Coun. Child Abuse, Lawrenceville, 1994—. Mem. Nat. Recreation & Parks Assn., Nat. Youth Sport Coaches Assn., Ga. Recreation & Parks Assn., Atlanta Lawn Tennis Assn. Home: 1459 Bridgestone Dr Lawrenceville GA 30245

JONES, JEANNINE ANN, executive; b. Albion, Mich., Jan. 11, 1936; d. Milton Roderick and Florence Kathleen (Hillis) Sova; m. James Milton Jones, Oct. 22, 1966. Student, Mills Coll., 1953-56. Data mgr., reviewer Valley Med. Review, Altadena, Calif., 1984; medicare/DRG coder Huntington Meml. Hosp., Pasadena, Calif., 1984-88; owner, chief cons. Medi-Rx Health Record Cons., Sunland, Calif., 1973—; founder, past pres. Profl. Health Record Cons., L.A. Author: Coding Manual for SNF's, 1982, Coding Manual for Physicians, 1989, Coding Advisor, 1991. Past pres. Fatimas of the Fez, Glendale, Calif., 1981; mem. C. of C., Sunland-Tujunga, Calif., 1979—. Mem. Am. Health Info. Mgmt. Assn., Am. Acad. Procedural Coders, Calif. Health Info. Assn. (mem. coding and reimbursement com. 1990-92), Greater L.A. Coding Network (hon. life mem., founder, past pres. 1986-87). Home and Office: Medi-Rx Health Record Cons 7942 Le Berthon St Sunland CA 91040-2220

JONES, JOAN MEGAN, anthropologist; b. Laramie, Wyo., Sept. 7, 1933; d. Thomas Owen and Lucille Lenoir (Magill) J; m. James Caldwell Merritt, June 20, 1980. BA, U. Wash., 1956, MA, 1968, PhD, 1976. Mus. educator Burke Mus. U. Wash., Seattle, 1969-72; anthropologist Quinault Indian Nation, Taholah, Wash., 1976-77; researcher, corp. officer Profl. Anthropology Consulting Team/Social Analysts, Seattle, 1977-79; research assoc. dept. anthropology U. Wash., Seattle, 1982-91; research investigator Dept. Social and Health Services State of Wash., Seattle, 1977; vis. lectr. Dept. Anthropology U. B.C., Vancouver, 1978; research specialist Artsplan Arts Alliance Wash. State, Seattle, 1978; vis. instr. Dept. Anthropology Western Wash. U., Bellingham, 1981; cons. in field. Author: Northwest Coast Basketry and Culture Change, 1968, Basketry of Quinault, 1977, Native Basketry of Western North America, 1978, Art and Style of Western Indian Basketry, 1982, Northwest Coast Indian Basketry Styles. Wenner-Gren Found. Anthrop. Research fellow, 1967-68; Ford Found. fellow, 1972-73; Nat. Mus.'s. Can. grantee, 1973-74. Fellow Am. Anthrop. Assn., Soc. Applied Anthropology; mem. Nat. Assn. Practicing Anthropologists, Assn. Women in Sci., Skagit Valley Weavers Guild (v.p. Skagit County chpt. 1985-86, 89-90, corr. sec. 1988-89), Whidbey Weavers.

JONES, JULIA HUGHES, state official; b. Camden, Ark., Sept. 9, 1939; d. James Harvey and Alice (Chandler) Rumph; m. James H. Jones (dec.); children: David Hughes, Betsy Hughes Landman, Lori Hughes. Student, Tex. Women's U., U. Ark., Fayetteville, U. Ark., Little Rock. Chief investigator Office Prosecuting Atty., Little Rock, 1973-76; cir. clk. Pulaski County, Little Rock, 1976-78; state auditor State of Ark., Little Rock, 1981—; bd. dirs. State Bd. Fin., 1981—; trustee Bd. Pub. Employees Retirement Sys., 1981—. Author: (reference book) Encyclopedia of the Future, 1993; contbr. articles to profl. jours. Chair Ark. Dem. Conv., 1982; del. Dem. Nat. Conv., 1988. Named one of Outstanding Women in Ark. Politics, George C. Douthit Scholarship Trust, 1989. Mem. Nat. Assn. State Auditors, Comptrollers and Treas., Nat. Assn. Unclaimed Property Adminstrs., Internat. Assn. Clks., Recorders, Election Officials and Treas., Govt. Fin. Officers Assn., Assn. Govt. Accts. (Outstanding Fin. Mgr. Yr. ctrl. Ark. chpts. 1993), Women Execs. in State Govt. (founding mem.). Office: Office of Auditor 230 State Capitol Little Rock AR 72201-1059

JONES, JULIA PEARL, elementary school educator; b. Kesler, W.Va., Nov. 22, 1942; d. Wallace Leon and Wilda Thelma (Doss) Frazier; m. James Victor Jones, Jr., Nov. 26, 1961; children: Julie Lorraine Lynch, Jamie Lynn Dunston. BS in Elem. Edn. cum laude, Memphis State U., 1979; MEd cum laude, U. Va., 1986. Cert. elem./mid. sch. prin., supr., K-7th grade tchr., art tchr. Tchr. 4th grade Spotsylvania County (Va.) Schs., 1979-91, reading resource specialist, 1991—. Mem. ASCD, Nat. Tchrs. Assn., Va. Edn. Assn., Spotsylvania Edn. Assn., Nat. Congress of Parents and Tchrs., Internat. Reading Assn., Va. Reading Assn., Rappahannock Reading Coun. (past pres., Reading Tchr. of Yr. 1993-94), Kappa Delta Pi, Phi Delta Kappa, Order Ea. Star. Methodist. Home: 5414 Jamie Ct Fredericksburg VA 22407

JONES, JULLIA ANN, nurse; b. Indpls., May 2, 1949; d. Quincy Lon and Shirley Ann (DeMoss) Brock; m. Arthur Eugene Jones, Apr. 6, 1967; children: Jeannette Marie Jones Burge, Tonya Lorrain. ADN, Skagit Valley Coll., 1982; student, SUNY, Albany, 1989—. LPN, Wash., Miss., Ind., Fla. Nurses aide, emergency med. technician Med. Pers. Pool, San Diego, 1976-79; LPN United Gen. Hosp., Sedro-Woolly, Wash., 1983, Meridian (Miss.) Regional Hosp., 1983-84, Norrell Healthcare and Am. Nursing Care, Indpls., 1984-93, Marion County Jail, Ocala, Fla., 1993—; med. instr., extern coord., med. coord. Pontiac Bus. Inst., Indpls., 1986—. Home: 16667 SW 35th St Ocala FL 34481 Office: Prison Health Svcs 101 Lukens Dr New Castle DE 19720

JONES, KATHLEEN ANN, nuclear medicine technologist; b. Allentown, Pa., July 15, 1964; d. Edward Thomas and Catherine Marie (Steve) Jones. BS in Nuclear Med. Tech. magna cum laude, Cedar Crest Coll., Allentown, Pa., 1986. Cert. in nuclear med. tech. Staff nuclear med. technologist Lehigh Valley Hosp., Allentown, 1986—, clin. coordinator, 1988—. Editor ednl. programs Greater N.Y. chpt. Jour. Nuclear Med. Tech., 1990-93. Mem. Soc. Nuclear Medicine (technologist sect. bylaws chmn. 1990-91, area councilor 1991-92, technologist sect. treas. Greater N.Y. chpt. 1988-90, pres.-elect 1992-93, pres. 1993-94, awards chmn. 1995), Lehigh Valley Soc. Nuclear Med. Technologists (sec. 1987-88, pres. 1989-90, nominating chmn. 1990-91, bylaws com. 1991—), Del. Valley Soc. Nuclear Medicine Technologists. Democrat. Roman Catholic. Home: 1234 California Ave Whitehall PA 18052-4634 Office: Lehigh Valley Hosp 1200 S Cedar Crest Blvd Allentown PA 18103-6248

JONES, KATHLEEN LOUISE, educator; b. Escondido, Calif., Oct. 29, 1949; d. Kenneth Gilbert and Lois Ruth (Bowman) Finney; m. George Lawrence Jones, Oct. 20, 1973; children: Joshua, Erin. BA, San Diego State U., 1971; MA, Calif. State U., Sacramento, 1992. Tchr. Santee (Calif.) Sch. Dist., 1971-74, Yuba City (Calif.) Unified Sch. Dist., 1974-80, Pleasant Valley Sch. Dist., Penn Valley, Calif., 1980—; cons. Sacramento Regional Tech. Consortium, 1990-93; dir. Project CREATE, Penn Valley, 1987-89. Recipient Golden Apple award Pleasant Valley Sch. Dist. Parent Club, 1988. Mem. ASCD, Computer Using Educators. Office: Pleasant Valley Sch Dist 14804 Pleasant Valley Rd Penn Valley CA 95946

JONES, KATHRYN ANN, writer, artist; b. L.A., Oct. 12, 1956; d. Samuel Andrew and Wanda Faye (Smith) J.; m. Dan F. Malone, June 27, 1981. BA in English and Journalism, Trinity U., San Antonio, 1979. Staff writer Corpus Christi (Tex.) Caller-Times, 1979-81, Harte-Hanke Comm., Austin, Tex., 1981, Dallas Times Herald, 1984-86, Dallas Morning News, 1986-91; bur. chief MIS Week, Fairchild Pubs., Dallas, 1982-84; freelance writer Time, Life, D Mag., N.Y.C. and Dallas, 1991-93; contract writer N.Y. Times, 1993—. co-author: How to Be Happily Employed in Dallas-Fort Worth, 1990, Fort Worth, 1990; contract writer N.Y. Times, 1992—; exhibited in group show Dallas Women's Caucus for Art, 1991, 94. Recipient award of excellence Dallas Press Club, 1988. Mem. Assn. Women Journalists (bd. dirs. 1993), Dallas Women's Caucus for Art, Southwestern Watercolor Soc., Trinity Arts Guild. Home: 5140 Malinda Ln N Fort Worth TX 76112

JONES, KATHRYN CHERIE, pastor; b. Breckenridge, Tex., Nov. 26, 1955; d. Austin Thomas and Margaret May (Mohr) J. BA, U. Calif., San Diego, 1977; MDiv, Fuller Theol. Sem., 1982. Assoc. pastor La Jolla (Calif.) United Meth. Ch., 1982-84; pastor in charge Dominguez United Meth. Ch., Long Beach, Calif., 1984-88, San Marcos (Calif.) United Meth. Ch., 1988-90; dir. The Walk to Emmaus Program, The Upper Room, Nashville, 1990—; coord. chaplains Pacific Hosp., Long Beach, 1986-88. Bd. dirs. So. Calif. Walk to Emmaus Cmty., L.A., 1987-88, San Diego chpt., 1988-90. Mem. Christian Assn. Psychol. Studies, Evangs. for Social Action. Democrat. Office: The Upper Room 1908 Grand Ave PO Box 189 Nashville TN 37202-0189

JONES, LAURA ANN, radio announcer, production assistant; b. Mishawaka, Ind., Oct. 22, 1968; d. Michael David Jones and Susan Lynn (Gebel) Moore. BS in Telecommunications, Ball State U., 1990. Announcer, news anchor Sta. WCRD Radio, Muncie, Ind., 1989; producer, dir. Ball State U. Journalism Workshop, Muncie, 1989; announcer, recording engr., producer, news anchor Sta. WBST Radio, Ball State U., Muncie, 1988-90; voice over announcer Rutter Communications, Muncie, 1990-91; announcer Sta. WOKZ-Radio, Muncie, 1991; copywriter, producer, announcer WIFF Radio-TV 7, Auburn, Ind., 1991-93; announcer WFWI-FM, Fort Wayne, Ind., 1993—; engr. Sta WKJG (NBC), Ft. Wayne, Ind., 1992—. Contbg. writer, photographer: Deadline Music Mag., 1990-91. Recipient David Letterman Intern award, 1990. Mem. Women in Communications (sec. 1988-90), Alpha Epsilon Rho (rec. sec. 1989-90). Democrat. Home: 608 Vance Ave Fort Wayne IN 46805-2144

JONES, LAURIE LYNN, magazine editor; b. Kerrville, Tex., Sept. 2, 1947; d. Charles Clinton and Jean Laurie (Davidson) J.; m. C. Frederick Childs, June 26, 1976; children: Charles Newell (Clancy), Cyrus Trevor; 1 stepchild, Ariel Childs. B.A., U. Tex., 1969. Asst. to dir. coll. admissions Columbia U., N.Y.C., 1969-70; asst. to dir. Office Alumni-Columbia U., N.Y.C., 1970-71; asst. advt. mgr. Book World, 1971-72, Washington Post-Chgo. Tribune, 1971-72; editorial asst. N.Y. Mag., N.Y.C., 1972-74, asst. editor, 1974, sr. editor, 1974-76, mng. editor, 1976-92; mng. editor Vogue Mag., N.Y.C., 1992—. Mem. Am. Soc. Mag. Editors, Women in Coummunication, Advt. Women N.Y. Republican. Methodist. Home: 40 Great Jones St New York NY 10012-1115 also: 62 Giles Hill Rd Redding Ridge CT 06876 Office: Vogue Magazine 350 Madison Ave New York NY 10017-3704

JONES, LEAH LOU, medical technologist; b. Woods County, Okla., Aug. 10, 1933; d. Charles A. and Leah Vashti Hogan; m. Loren Eugene Jones, Jan. 12, 1954; children: Michael Eugene, Lauren Frances. BA, Friends U., 1954. Med. technologist Hutchinson (Kans.) Clinic, 1965-67, Cen. Kans. Med. Ctr., Great Bend, 1967-79, Pratt (Kans.) Med. Arts, 1979-89, Hutchinson Clinic, 1989—. Mem. choir Pratt United Meth. Ch., 1986—; supporting mem. Met. Opera Guild. Mem. Am. Soc. Med. Tech., Kans. Soc. Med. Tech. (dist. rep. 1985-86, bd. dirs. 1986-92, 94—, sci. assembly microbiology chair 1992-94), Am. Soc. Microbiology, S.W. Assn. Clin. Microbiology (bd. dirs. 1994—), Kans. Soc. Med. Tech., Pratt Music Club (pres. 1988-92). Republican. Home: 22807 S Lerado Rd Langdon KS 67583-9049

JONES, LEONADE DIANE, newspaper publishing company executive; b. Bethesda, Md., Nov. 27, 1947; d. Leon Adger and Landonia Randolph (Madden) J. BA with distinction, Simmons Coll., 1969; JD, Stanford U., 1973, MBA, 1973. Bar: Calif. 1973, D.C. 1979. Summer assoc. Davis Polk & Wardwell, N.Y.C., summer 1972; securities analyst Capital Rsch. Co., L.A., 1973-75; asst. treas. Washington Post Co., 1975-79, 86-87, treas., 1987—; dir. fin. services Post-Newsweek Stas., Inc., Washington, 1979-84, v.p. bus. affairs, 1984-86; bd. dirs. Am. Balanced Fund, Inc., Income Fund Am., Inc., Growth Fund Am., Inc.; mem. investment mgmt. subcom. of benefit plans com. Am. Stores Co., 1992—. Treas., bd. dirs. Big Sisters Washington Met. Area, 1984-85; bd. dirs. D.C. Contemporary Dance Theatre, 1987-88, Washington Performing Arts Soc., 1990—; mem. adv. coun. Charlin Jazz Soc., 1988-92; mem. adv. bd. Sta. WHMM-TV, 1989-93; asst. chmn. budget and audit D.C. chpt. Met. Washington, Edges Group, Inc., 1989-93; mem. adv. coun. Bus. Sch., Stanford U., 1991—, bd. visitors Law Sch., 1982-84, 93—; trustee Am. Inst. Mng. Diversity, Inc., 1991—; mem. corp. Simmons Coll., 1992—. Recipient Candace award for bus., 1992, Serwa award, 1993; named to D.C. Woman's Hall of Fame, 1992. Mem. ABA, Calif. Bar Assn., D.C. Bar Assn., Stanford U. Bus. Sch. Alumni Assn. (bd. dirs. 1986-88, pres. Washington-Balt. chpts. 1984-85), Nat. Assn. Corp. Treas. Office: Washington Post Co 1150 15th St NW Washington DC 20071-0002

JONES, LILLIE AGNES, retired educator; b. Leroy, Iowa, Nov. 25, 1910; d. Orace Wesley and Lorena Floy (Buffum) Davis; m. John Hammond Jones, May 27, 1938 (dec. Aug. 1994); children: John Harry, Mary Agnes Jones Edwards. BA, Colo. State Coll. Edn., 1937. Cert. elem. tchr., Colo. Elem. tchr. Weld County Sch. Dist. 8l, Kersey, Colo., 1930-34, Weld County Sch. Dist. 12l, Erie, Colo., 1934-38, Longmont (Colo.) Pub. Schs., 1955-59, Adams County Sch. Dist. 12, Thornton, Colo., 1959-67, Littleton (Colo.) Pub. Schs., 1967-69; Farmington (N.Mex.) Pub. Schs., 1969-76, ret., 1976; cataloger Longmont Pub. Libr., 1953-55. Kersey High Sch. scholar, 1928. Mem. AAUW (life, past treas. Longmont), Nat. Ret. Tchrs. Assn., N.Mex. Ret. Tchrs. Assn. (life), Pub. Employees Retirement Assn., Colo. Ret. Sch. Employees Assn., Alpha Delta Kappa (rec. sec. Farmington 1975-76, sec. Sun City, Ariz. 1980, historian 1982). Democrat. Home: Sun Grove Resort Village 10134 W Mohawk Ln # 1017 Peoria AZ 85382-2251

JONES, LINDA ISLES, English language educator, association executive; b. Belmont, N.C., Sept. 19, 1943; d. Hiawatha and Blondine (Henderson) Isles; m. Nathaniel Jones, Dec. 19, 1966; 1 child, Natalie Lauren Jones Cloud. BS in English, N.C. A&T State U., 1965; MEd, Converse Coll. English tchr. J.A. Chandler High Sch., Weldon, N.C., 1965-66, Beck High Sch., Greenville, S.C., 1966-70, Hughes Mid. Sch., Greenville, 1970-74; English instr. Greenville (S.C.) Tech. Coll., 1974—; tchr. tng. workshops Greenville (S.C.) City Pers., Bi lo Groceries, Greenville, Greenville Hosp. Sys.; tchr. improve project sys. S.C. Tech. Colls.; bd. dirs. Southeastern Conf. for Tchr. in Two-Yr. Colls., 1987-90, 94—. Pres. bd. dirs. YWCA, Greenville, 1994—; bd. dirs. Greenville County Literacy; active Greenville Coalition for Women on Bds. and Commns., 1990-93, Woman's Way Coun., Greenville. Leadership in Higher Edn. cert. Bapt. Conv. S.C., 1992. Mem. Alpha Kappa Alpha (pres. 1990-94, Homie Regulus Basileus 1994), Delta Kappa Gamma. Baptist. Home: 400 Griffin Rd Greenville SC 29607-5126

JONES, LINDA R. WOLF, organization executive; b. Jersey City, Sept. 4, 1943; d. Eugene Leon and Lottie (Pinkowitz) Rubin; m. Frank Paul Jones, Oct. 21, 1973 (div. Nov. 1987); 1 child, Elisabeth Noel. AB, Bryn Mawr Coll., 1964; MA, Yale U., 1968; DSW, Yeshiva U., N.Y.C., 1985. Dir. planning and tng. N.Y.C. Dept. Employment, 1971-77; dir. legislation N.Y.C. Community Devel. Agy., 1977-78; supervisory legis. analyst N.Y.C. Human Resources Adminstrn., 1978; sr. policy analyst Community Svc. Soc. N.Y., 1978-85; dir. pub. policy YMCA Greater N.Y., 1985-89; dir. spl. projects Phoenix House, N.Y.C., 1990-92; dir. income security policy Community Svc. Soc., N.Y.C., 1992-94; exec. dir. Therapeutic Communities Am., Washington, 1994—; mem. adj. extension faculty Cornell U./N.Y. State Sch. Indsl. and Labor Rels., N.Y.C., 1975-80; dir. Nonprofit Coordinating Com. N.Y., N.Y.C., 1986-94, Govt. Affairs Profls., N.Y.C., 1989-94. Author (book) Eveline M. Burns and the American Social Security System 1935-60, 1991; mem. editorial bd. New Eng. Jour. Human Svcs., 1981—; contbr. articles to profl. jours. Mem. Civic Affairs Forum, N.Y.C., 1985-94; mem. legis. task force N.Y. State Gov.'s Office Vol. Svc., N.Y.C., 1987-90. Mem. Women in Govt. Rels., Am. Pub. Welfare Assn. (dir. 1982), Bryn Mawr Club Westchester (bd. dirs., past pres. 1974-94), Bryn Mawr Club Washington, Princeton Club. Home: 825 Underwood St NW Washington DC 20012 Office: Therapeutic Communities Am 1818 N St NW Ste 300 Washington DC 20036

JONES, LORELLA MARGARET, physics educator; b. Toronto, Ont., Can., Feb. 22, 1943; came to U.S., 1948; d. Donald Cecil and F. Shirley (Patterson) J. BA, Harvard U., 1964; MSc, Calif. Inst. Tech., 1966, PhD, 1968. From postdoctoral fellow to instr. Calif. Inst. Tech., Pasadena, 1967-68; asst. prof. physics U. Ill., Urbana, 1968-70, assoc. prof. physics, 1970-78, prof. physics, 1978—. Author ednl. physics software. Fellow Am. Phys. Soc. (div. particles and fields); mem. AAUP (chpt. pres. 1989-91). Office: Univ of Ill Dept Physics 1110 W Green St Urbana IL 61801-3003

JONES, LYNLEY EIKEN, management specialist; b. Ft. Walton Beach, Fla., Dec. 15, 1965; d. Edwin Lee Eiken and Faith Freeman; m. Rex Randall Jones, Oct. 21, 1989. BA in Community and Regional Planning, U. So. Miss., 1987. Planner, intern Emergency Mgmt., Jackson County, Miss., 1986, So. Miss. Planning and Devel. Dist., Gulfport, Miss., 1986-87; spring intern Hattiesburg (Miss.) C. of C., 1987; asst. planner Calcasieu Parish Planning Dept., Lake Charles, La., 1987-90; dir. outreach/mktg. First United Meth. Ch., Lake Charles, 1990-93; mgmt. specialist Mayor's Office, Lake Charles, 1993—. Bd. dirs. Samaritan Counseling Ctr., Lake Charles, 1989-92, S.W. La. Vol. Ctr., Lake Charles, 1991-93, Jr. League of Lake Charles, Inc., 1994-95; sec. Mayor's Commn. for Women, Lake Charles, 1990-93; mem. Calcasieu Parish Drug Free Schs. Taskforce, Lake Charles, 1992—. Named to Outstanding Young women, 1986; named Am. Bus. Woman of Yr., Novelle Chpt., ABWA, Lake Charles, 1990, Young Careerist, Bus. & Profl. Women Lake Charles, 1994-95. Democrat. Methodist. Home: 2526 21st St Lake Charles LA 70601 Office: City of Lake Charles Mayors Office 326 Pujo St Lake Charles LA 70601

JONES, MALLORY See DANAHER, MALLORY MILLETT

JONES, MARCIA A., legislative staff member, lawyer; b. Austin, Tex., Jan. 11, 1961; d. Paul Byron and Sheila (Gallagher) J. BA in Econs., Georgetown U., 1984; JD, George Washington U., 1990. Staff mem. to Rep. Don Young, Washington, 1981-85, Senator Frank H. Murkowski, Washington, 1985-87; with Jellinek, Schwartz, Connolly & Freshman, Washington, 1987-88; legis. dir. and tax counsel to Senator John B. Breaux, Washington, 1988—. Mem. ABA, Tax Coalition. Roman Catholic. Office: Sen John Breaux D-La 516 Hart Senate Office Bldg Washington DC 20510*

JONES, MARGARET DORIS, small business owner; b. Mechanicsville, Md., June 15, 1942; d. George Henry and Cora Madeline (Goldsmith) Murphy; m. Joseph Paul Jones, Jr., Sept. 3, 1960; children: Joseph Paul Jones III, Margaret Dedie. Student, U. Md., 1972-74, George Washington U., 1969, Mgmt. Devel. Ctr. Md., 1978, grad. Realtors Inst. Telephone operator C&P Telephone Co., Md., Leonardtown, 1960-62; tchr., tchr's aid Leonardtown Bd. Edn., 1967-70; with trial magistrate's system, 1970-71; dist. ct. clk. St. Mary County Dist. Ct., Leonardtown, 1971-86, mem. grievance com., 1976-77; assoc. L. K. Farrell Realtors, Ltd.; owner Jones Countryside Antiques, Crafts and Collectibles. Sec., v.p. Hollywood Ladies Aux. Fire Dept., Md., 1965-70; sec. Oakville Elem. Sch. PTA, Mechanicsville, 1968; mem., chmn. Father Andrew White PTA, Leonardtown, 1972-80; worker St. Mary Ryken PTA, Leonardtown, 1976-84; coordinator Dist. Ct. United Way campaign, 1984; past mem. Fraternal Order of Police Sec. for Domestic Abuse/Sexually Assaulted Task Force, St. Mary's County. Named to Sales Club Hall of Fame, 1992. Mem. So. Md. Bd. Realtors (Disting. Sales Assoc. of Yr. 1989). Democrat. Roman Catholic. Avocations: sewing; art; family history. also: L K Farrall Realtors Ltd PO Box 716 Lexington Park MD 20653-0716

JONES, MARGARET HYLTON, public relations executive; b. Welch, W.Va., Feb. 12, 1947; d. Robert Logan and Margaret Marie (Hylton) J.; m. Virgil Agan Hartley, Sept. 1, 1973 (div. Sept. 1993). BA, Emory U., 1969. Assoc. editor alumni publs. Emory U., Atlanta, 1969-79; dir. external affairs Atlanta Coll. Art, 1980-83; pub. info. officer DeKalb County Govt., Decatur, Ga., 1983-90; pres. Margaret Jones and Assocs., Stone Mountain, Ga., 1991—. State com. mem. Democrats of Ga., 1988—; pres. Am. Cancer Soc., DeKalb County, 1994; bd. dirs., chair legis. com. Ga. Head Injury Assn., 1991—. Mem. Am. Assn. Polit Cons., Pub. Rels. Soc. Am. (bd. dirs.), Ga. C. of C. (pub. rels. com. chair 1991—). Episcopalian. Home and Office: 1081 New Gibraltar Sq Stone Mountain GA 30083

JONES, MARGUERITE JACKSON, English language educator; b. Greenwood, Miss., Aug. 12, 1949; d. James and Mary G. (Reedy) Jackson; m. Algee Jones, Apr. 4, 1971; 1 child, Stephanie Nerissa. BS, Miss. Valley State U., 1969; MEd, Miss. State U., 1974; EdS, Ark. State U., 1983; postgrad. U. Ark., 1982. Tchr. English Henderson High Sch., Starkville, Miss., 1969-70, creative writing Miami (Fla.) Coral Park, 1970-71, English, head dept. Marion (Ark.) Sr. High Sch., 1971-78, East Ark. Community Coll., Forrest City, 1978-79; migrant edn. supr. Marion (Ark.) Sch. Dist., 1979-83; mem. faculty Draughons Coll., Memphis, 1978-83; assoc. prof. State Tech., 1984—; cons. writing projects; condr. workshops for ednl., bus., civic groups. Bd. dirs. Bountiful Blessings Christian Acad., Memphis; dir. Leadership Tng. Inst. for 4th Eccles. Jurisdiction, Tenn.; Christian edn. dir. Temple Deliverance-The Cathedral Bountiful Blessings, Memphis. Mem. ASCD, Nat. Coun. Tchrs. English, Ark. Assn. Profl. Educators, Memphis Assn. Young Children, Tenn. Assn. Young Children, Nat. Assn. Young Children, Phi Delta Kappa. Home: 1239 Meadowlark Ln Memphis TN 38116-7801 Office: State Tech Inst 5983 Macon Cove Memphis TN 38134-7693

JONES, MARIE MILIE, lawyer; b. Greensburg, Pa., Jan. 27, 1963; d. Robert John and Josephine Mary (Cirucci) Milie; m. Cameron W. Jones. BA, Duquesne U., 1985, JD, 1987. Bar: Pa. 1987, U.S. Supreme Ct. 1991, W. Va. 1994. Assoc. Meyer, Darragh, Buckler, Bebenak & Eck, Pitts., 1987-92, jr. ptnr., 1992—; chair edn. com. Pa. Defense Inst., Harrisburg, 1992—, treas., 1994—. Vol. Make-A-Wish Found., Pitts., 1990—. Mem. ABA, Pa. Bar Assn., Allegheny County Bar Assn., Def. Rsch. Inst. Republican. Roman Catholic. Home: 1120 Graham Blvd Pittsburgh PA 15235-2722 Office: Meyer Darragh Buckler Bebenek & Eck 2000 Frick Bldg Pittsburgh PA 15219-6101

JONES, MARLENE WISEMAN, elementary education educator, reading specialist; b. Zanesville, Ohio, Oct. 8, 1939; d. Mark Andrew Wiseman and Elizabeth Wiseman (Wilkins) Doughty; m. Herbert Pearce Jones, Sept. 2, 1961. BS in Edn., Muskingum Coll., New Concord, Ohio, 1962; MEd, Ohio U., Zanesville, 1984. Elem. tchr. Zanesville City Schs., 1962-65, reading specialist, 1967—; reading instr. Ohio Univ., Zanesville, 1984, Muskingum Area Tech. Coll., Zanesville, 1991-94. Co-author book Diagnosis for Reading, 1975; creator Games for Reading, 1973. Recipient Outstanding Elem. Tchr. award, 1973. Mem. NEA, Ohio Edn. Assn., Zanesville Edn. Assn., Heisey Collectors of Am., Zanesville Art Ctr., Order Ea. Star. Democrat. Lutheran. Home: 2219 Hazel Ave Zanesville OH 43701-2022 Office: Zanesville City Schs 160 N 4th St Zanesville OH 43701-3518

JONES, MARLYNN RUTH, university official; b. Petersburg, Va., Feb. 11, 1963; d. Dossie Nickles and Grover Seline (Johnson) J. AB in Journalism, U. N.C., 1984; MS in Mass Communications, Va. Commonwealth U., 1987. Grad. intern athletics dept. Va. Commonwealth U., Richmond, 1985-86; sec.-receptionist Duke U. Publs./Graphic Arts Svcs., Durham, N.C., 1986; mgmt. trainee Thalhimer Bros., Inc., 1987; advt. mgr. The NCAA News, NCAA, Overland Park, Kans., 1987-91; asst. athletic dir. N.C. A&T State U., Greensboro, 1991-93; asst. mgr. Jones N.Y. Factory Store, 1993-94; interi, dir. of scholarships N.C. Ctrl. U., Durham, N.C., 1994—; proctor Ednl. Testing Svcs., Durham, 1986-87, asst. supr., Kans., 1989-91. Contbr. poems to profl. publs. (Golden Poet award 1988, 89, Silver Poet award 1990). Herman Lehman Ednl. Fund. scholar, 1980-84; Va. Commonwealth U. fellow, 1985-86. Mem. NAFE, Nat. Assn. Collegiate Women Athletic Adminstrs., Nat. Assn. Collegiate Dirs. of Athletics, U.S. Basketball Writers Assn., Coll. Sports Info. Dirs. Am., Delta Sigma Theta. Democrat. Episcopalian. Home: 2916 Kanewood Dr Durham NC 27707

JONES, MARY ELLEN, biochemist; b. La Grange, Ill., Dec. 25, 1922; d. Elmer E. and Laura A. (Klein) J.; children: Ethan Vincent Munson, Catherine Laura Munson. BS, U. Chgo., 1944; PhD, Yale U., 1951. AEC fellow, Am. Cancer Soc. fellow, assoc. biochemist Mass. Gen. Hosp., Boston, 1951-57; asst. prof. grad. dept. biochemistry Brandeis U., Waltham, Mass., 1957-60, assoc. prof., 1960-66; assoc. prof. dept. biochemistry Sch. Medicine, U. N.C., Chapel Hill, 1966-68, prof. depts. biochemistry and zoology, 1968-71; prof. dept. biochemistry Sch. Medicine, U. So. Calif., 1971-78; prof., chmn. dept. biochemistry Sch. Medicine, U. N.C., Chapel Hill, 1978-89, Kenan prof. biochemistry, 1980-95, prof. emeritus biochemistry, 1995—; mem. study sect. Am. Cancer Soc., 1971-73, mem. com. biochemistry and endocrinology, 1991-94, NIH, 1971-75; mem. sci. adv. bd. Nat. Heart, Lung and Blood Inst., 1980-84; mem. metabolic biology study sect. NSF, 1978-81; mem. VA Merit rev. bd., 1975-78; mem. life sci. com. NASA, 1976-78; pres. Chairs of Assn. Med. Sch. Depts. Biochemistry, 1985; mem. Nat. Adv. Gen. Med. Scis. Council, 1988-91. Am. Cancer Soc. scholar, 1957-62; NIH grantee, 1957-94; NSF grantee, 1957-90. Mem. NAS, AAAS, Am. Acad. Arts and Scis., Am. Chem. Soc. (councilor 1975-79, nominating com. 1971-72, chair biochem. divsn. 1973-74), Am. Soc. Biol. Chemists (councilor 1975-78, 81-84, pres. 1986), Am. Philos. Soc., Inst. Medicine of Nat. Acad. Scis. (councilor 1984-87), Assn. Women in Sci., N.Y. Acad. Sci., Sigma Xi. Democrat. Unitarian. Clubs: Appalachian Mountain, Sierra. Contbr. numerous articles on biochem. research to sci. publs.; editorial bd. Jour. Biol. Chemistry, 1975-80, 82-87, Cancer Research, 1982-86; assoc. editor Can.

Jour. Biochemistry, 1969-74. Office: U NC Dept Biochemistry and Biophysics Chapel Hill NC 27599-7260

JONES, MARY EMMA B., counselor; b. Izmir, Turkey, Nov. 10, 1944; came to U.S., 1946; d. Lawrence Hartwell Brown and Erma Marie (Carl) Macfie; m. Robin Dee Jones, Sept. 11, 1966; children: Darcy Marie, Samuel Evan. BA in English, Campbell U., 1967; MEd in Mid. Grades, North Ga. Coll., 1984; cert. edn. specialist in sch. counseling, U. Ga., 1991, postgrad. Cert. sch. counselor, Ga. Tchr. high sch. Harnett County Schs., Lillington and Buies Creek, N.C., 1967-69; craftsperson (weaver) Jugtown Pottery, Seagrove, N.C., 1969-70; designer, weaver Wolf Pen Crafts, Young Harris, Ga., 1970-78; instr. weaving Campbell Folk Sch., Brasstown, N.C., 1977-78; tchr. Union County Mid. Sch., Blairsville, Ga., 1978-90; sch. counselor St. Joseph Sch., Athens, Ga., 1990-94; intern in counseling psychology Park Ctr., Ft. Wayne, Ind., 1994—; leader workshop Postponing Sexual Involvement, Blairsville, Ga., 1984; ; counselor Ctr. for Counseling, U. Ga., Athens, 1992-93, supr., 1993. Active PTA, Harnett County, N.C., 1967-69, Union County, 1978-90; leader workshop Lions-Quest Skills Adolescence, Blairsville, 1988-90, Students Organized to Assist to Resist, Blairsville, 1990-91; active St. Joseph Sch. PTA, Athens, 1990-94. Named STAR Tchr., Union County Schs., C. of C. and Bus. Coun. Ga., 1984. Mem. APA (student affiliate), Am. Counseling Assn., Am. Sch. Counselor Assn., Assn. Specialists Group Work, Assn. Women Psychology.

JONES, MARY LOUISE HELFRICH, hospital and nursing administrator; b. Dover, Del., Sept. 7, 1944; d. Anthony G. and Mary Jane (Brown) Helfrich; m. William Frank Jones, June 6, 1965; children: Michelle Lynn, Matthew Sean. Diploma, Washington Hosp. Ctr., 1965; BSN cum laude, Southern Coll., Collegedale, Tenn., 1980; MSN, U. Fla., 1985, PhD, 1994. RN, D.C., Fla., Pa.; cert. nurse adminstr.; cert. childbirth educator. Adminstrv. dir. maternal child div. Pa. Hosp., Phila., 1994—, also dir. edn. and rsch. pediatric svcs., co-dir./dir. perinatal; v.p. patient care svcs./women's svcs. Fla. Hosp., Orlando, 1974-94; cons. for program/space planning, family centered perinatal svcs. Contbr. articles to profl. pubs. Area leader, walking mother March of Dimes, 1981-88; mem. exec. bd. Parent Resource Ctr., 1989-93; bd. dirs. Healthy Start Coalition, 1993-94. Mem. AWHONN (Fla. congress on nursing orgns.), Nat. Perinatal Assn., So. Regional Nursing Soc., Fla. Healthy Mothers/Healthy Babies Coalition, Coun. Nurse Rschrs., Commn. on Future of Nursing in Fla., Fla. Orgn. Nurse Execs., Sigma Theta Tau, Alpha Theta, Theta Epsilon (pres. 1994). Roman Catholic.

JONES, MAXINE HOLMES, librarian; b. St. Louis, May 18, 1929; d. Clay and Clara Viola (Peterson) Holmes; m. Rolland W.T. Jones, Sept. 5, 1948 (div. June 1976); children: Jan Kathryn, Erick. BS in Edn. and English, SW Mo. State U., 1968; MA in Edn. and Media, Ohio State U., 1973; PhD in Instrn. Media and Tech., U. Wis., 1981. Cert. tchr., Mo., Tex. Tchr. English, De Soto (Mo.) Pub. Schs. Dist. 73, 1968-69, dir. media, 1973-76; libr. Jefferson R-7 Sch. Dist., nr. Festus, Mo., 1969-72, Parkway Sch. Dist., St. Louis County, Mo., 1976-77; rsch. assoc. Ohio State U., Columbus, 1972-73; project asst. Bureau of Audio Visual Instruction U. Wis. Extension, Madison, 1977-82, supervisory teaching asst. Sch. Libr. Sci., 1980; writer, researcher, Springfield, Ill., 1983-88; libr. Grand Prairie (Tex.) Ind. Sch. Dist., 1988—. Contbg. author: Video Involvement for Libraries: A Current Awareness Package for Librarians, 1981; author: See, Hear, Interact: Beginning Developments in Two-way Television, 1985; also articles. Pres. LWV Jefferson County Mo., 1973-75. Mem. ALA, Tex. Libr. Assn., Soc. Children's Book Writers (pres. North Ctrl. Tex. chpt. 1990-91). Lutheran. Home: 1819 Marble Dr Apt 1061 Arlington TX 76013-6144

JONES, MEREDITH J., federal government official; b. Hartford, Conn., Mar. 24, 1948; d. Cyril Johnstone and Rose Victoria (Randolph) Jones. BA, Swarthmore Coll., 1968; JD, Yale U., 1974. Bar: N.Y. 1975, Calif. 1983, D.C. 1994. Assoc. Cleary, Gottlieb, Steen & Hamilton, N.Y.C., 1974-83; ptnr. Chickering & Gregory, San Francisco, 1983-86; sr. counsel Bechtel Financing Svcs., Inc., San Francisco, 1986-93; gen. counsel Nat. Oceanic & Atmospheric Adminstrn., Washington, 1993-94; chief cable svcs. bur. FCC, Washington, 1994—. Mem. Calif. Assn. Black Lawyers, Bar Assn. City of N.Y. Democrat. Office: Cable Svcs Bur FCC 1919 M St NW Washington DC 20554

JONES, NANCY GALE, retired biology educator; b. Gaffney, S.C., Nov. 12, 1940; d. Louransey Dowell and Sarah Louise (Pettit) J. BA, Winthrop Coll., 1962; MA, Oberlin Coll., 1964; postgrad., Duke U. Marine Biology Lab., 1963, Marine Biol. Lab., Woods Hole, Mass., 1964, N.C. State U., 1965, Ohio State U., 1966, Ariz. State U., 1970. Lectr. biology Oberlin (Ohio) Coll., 1964-66; from instr. to asst. prof. zoology Ohio U., Zanesville, 1966-73; media specialist Muskingum Area Vocat. Sch., Zanesville, 1973-74; salesperson Village Bookstore, Worthington, Ohio, 1975; mem. planned giving adv. com. Winthrop U. Vol. hortitherapist for retarded adults Habilitation Svcs., Inc. Gaffney, S.C., 1977-80; vol. dir. emergency assistance to needy PEACHcenter Ministries, Gaffney, 1991-94. Mem. Sigma Xi (assoc.). Baptist. Home: 1643 W Rutledge Ave Gaffney SC 29341-1023

JONES, NANCY LANGDON, financial planner, investment advisor; b. Chgo., Mar. 24, 1939; d. Lewis Valentine and Margaret (Seese) Russell; m. Lawrence Elmer Langdon, June 30, 1962 (div. 1970); children: Laura Kimberley, Elizabeth Ann; m. Claude Earl Jones, Jan. 1, 1973. BA, U. Redlands, Calif., 1962; MS, Coll. for Fin. Planning, 1991. CFP; registered investment advisor; accredited tax advisor. Bookkeeper Russell Sales Co., Santa Fe Springs, Calif., 1962-70; office mgr. Reardon, McCallum & Co., Upland, Calif., 1970-77; broker, assoc. ERA Property Ctr., Upland, 1977-84; registered rep. Fin. Network Investment Corp., Pasadena, Calif., 1984-92; pvt. practice fin. planning Upland, 1984—; ptnr. Jones, Graham & Assocs., Registered Investment Advisors, Upland, Calif., 1994; adj. faculty Coll. Fin. Planning, Denver, 1986-94; mem. nat. comprehensive exam. question writing com. CFPs Bd. Stds., 1994-95; del. U.S. fin. and investment leaders study mission to the People's Republic of China and Hong Kong, 1993. Leader Spanish Trails coun. Girl Scouts U.S., 1974-81; mem. exec. com. Corp. 2000 Coun., San Antonio Cmty. Hosp. Recipient Hon. Svc. award Valencia Elem. Sch., 1978. Mem. SAG, Inland Soc. of Tax Cons., Estate Planning Coun., Internat. Assn. Fin. Planners (pres. San Gabriel Valley chpt. 1987-88, mem. exec. bd. So. Calif. conf. 1992—), Am. Bus. Women's Assn. (sec. Upland chpt. 1989-90, gen. chmn. 1995 Pacific Spring conf., Woman of Yr. award 1988), Inst. CFPs San Gabriel Valley Soc. (pres. 1992-93, chmn. 1993-94, bd. dirs. 1990—), Nat. Coun. Exchangers (sec. 1986-87), Inland Soc. Tax Cons., Estate Planning Coun. Pomona Valley, Women's Bus. Network (pres. 1987-88), Registry of Fin. Planning Practitioners, Inland Valley Profl. Aux. (charter, bd. dirs. 1991-92), Assistance League of Upland, Upland C. of C. Home and Office: 2485 Mesa Ter Upland CA 91784-1078

JONES, NANCY THOMPSON, voice educator; b. Humansville, Mo., Oct. 31, 1938; d. Guy Hill and Noveta Luelle (Brown) Thompson; m. Russell Ransom Jones, June 23, 1962; children: Beverly, Steven. MusB, Coll. Conservatory of Music, Cin., 1960; MS, Pittsburg (Kans.) State U., 1962. Pvt. voice tchr. Kans. and Mo., 1959—; adj. prof. voice Baker U., Baldwin, Kans., 1967-70, Park Coll., Parkville, Mo., 1971-73, St. Mary Coll., Leavenworth, Kans., 1973-76, William Jewell Coll., Liberty, Mo., 1976-86; prof. voice Ctrl. Meth. Coll., Fayette, Mo., 1987—, dir. opera workshop, 1987—, interdisciplinary specialist in value-centered curriculum, 1991—; part time educator Pittsburg State U., 1973-90. Performer numerous recitals, 1958—, also recordings; vocalist with Kansas City Lyric Opera, 1967-92. Mem. choir United Meth. Ch., Marshfield, 1987-94; spokesperson Ellis-Fischel Cancer Ctr., Columbia, Mo., 1993—. Curators' faculty scholar Curators of Ctrl. Meth. Coll., 1992-94; faculty grantee William Jewell Coll., 1980; recipient Barrows award for European Study, Geraldine Barrows, 1977. Mem. Am. Guild Musical Artists, Actors' Equity Assn., Music Educators' Nat. Conf., Mo. Music Educators Assn., Coll. Music Soc., Phi Beta Arts Fraternity (v.p. 1989—), Mu Phi Epsilon. Home: 208 N Church St Fayette MO 65248 Office: Ctrl Meth Coll 411 Central Methodist Sq Fayette MO 65248

JONES, NORMA LOUISE, librarian, educator; b. Poplar, Wis.; d. George Elmer and Hilma June (Wiberg) J. BE, U. Wis.; MA, U. Minn., 1952; postgrad. U. Ill., 1957; PhD, U. Mich., 1965; postgrad., NARS, 1978, 79, 80, Nova U., 1983—. Librarian Grand Rapids (Mich.) Public Schs., 1947-62; with Grand Rapids Public Library, 1948-49; instr. Central Mich. U., Mt. Pleasant, 1954, 55; lectr. U. Mich., Ann Arbor, 1954, 55, 61, 63-65, asst. prof., 1966-68; librarian Benton Harbor (Mich.) Public Schs., 1962-63; asst. prof. library sci. U. Wis., Oshkosh, 1968-70; assoc. prof. U. Wis., 1970-75, prof., 1975—, chmn. dept. library sci., 1980-84, exec. dir. librs. and learning resources, 1987-93; dir. Adult Ctr., 1993—. Recipient Disting. Teaching award U. Wis.-Oshkosh, 1977. Mem. ALA (chmn. reference cons. 1975), Wis. Libr. Assn., Assn. Libr. and Info. Sci. Educators, Spl. Libr. Assn., Wis. Spl. Libr. Assn., Soc. Am. Archivists, Wis. Assn. Acad. Librs., Phi Beta Kappa, Phi Kappa Phi, Pi Lambda Theta, Beta Phi Mu, Sigma Pi Epsilon. Home: 1220 Maricopa Dr Oshkosh WI 54904-8121

JONES, ORA MCCONNER, foundation administrator; b. Augusta, Ga., Jan. 2, 1929; d. Landirs and Mamie (Elderidge) Williams; m. Walter R. McConner, June 27, 1953 (div.); 1 child, Susan L.; m. Courtney P. Jones, Feb. 14, 1991. BA, Paine Coll., Augusta, 1949; MA, Boston U., 1951; EdD, Nova U., Ft. Lauderdale, Fla., 1982. Instr. Paine Coll., Augusta, 1951-55; tchr. Chgo. Pub. Schs., 1956-66, adminstr., 1966-79, asst. supt., 1979-89, supt. dist. 6, 1989-91; exec. dir. Branch County Cmty. Found., Coldwater, Mich., 1991—. Danforth study grantee, 1955; recipient Image award League of Black Women, 1974, Silver Beaver award Boy Scouts Am., 1985; named Educator of Yr. Chgo. Black Sch. Educators, 1984; recipient Outstanding Educator's award Beatrice Coffee's, 1989. Mem. Am. Assn. Sch. Adminstrs., Nat. Alliance of Black Sch. Educators, Coun. for Exceptional Children, Profl. Women's Aux. of Provident Hosp., Alpha Gamma Psi, Phi Delta Kappa. Episcopalian. Club: Altrusa (v.p., sec.). Home: 10591 Simco Dr Coldwater MI 49036 Office: Branch County Cmty Found 116 N Clay St Coldwater MI 49036

JONES, PATRICIA ANN, assistant administrator; b. Balt., Feb. 13, 1948; d. Robert Stewart and Lois Carmel (Harris) Funk; divorced; 1 child, Stephanie Marie. AA in Bus. Mgmt. and Adminstrn., Essex C.C., 1988; BS in Bus. Mgmt. cum laude, Towson State U., 1994. Dept. clk. Western Electric, Hunt Valley, Md., 1966-73; adminstrv. asst. theater dept. Essex C.C., Balt., 1985-88; exec. sec. Calvert Wholesale Florist, Balt., 1988-89; asst. adminstr. Magnetic Resonance Imaging Ctr.-St. Joseph Hosp., Towson, Md., 1989—; part-time receptionist Dr. Norris L. Horwitz, Balt., 1986-88. Stage mgr. Cockpit-in-Ct. Theatre, Essex C.C., Balt.; sec., leader women's group New Life Prayer Group, 1975-87; active Nat. Mus. Women in Arts. Mem. NAFE, AAUW, Am. Mgrs. Assn., Md. Radiol. Mgrs. Assn., Md. Med. Group Mgmt. Assn. (3d party com., managed care com.), Balt. Coun. on Fgn. Affairs, Business Women of Balt. (charter, treas. 1993—), Christian Bus. and Profl. Women's Club (chair adv. bd. 1971-78). Home: Box 9724 Baldwin MD 21013 Office: BCIC Assoc PC 124 Sister Pierre Dr Towson MD 21204

JONES, PATRICIA LOUISE, elementary counselor; b. Moorhead, Minn., Aug. 20, 1942; d. Harry Wilfred and Myrtle Louise Rosenfeldt; m. Edward L. Marks (div.); m. Curtis C. Jones, July 16, 1973; children: Michon, Andrea, Nathan, Kirsten, Leah. BS, Moorhead State U., 1965; MS, Mankato State U., 1990. Cert. K-12 sch. counselor, Minn. Tchr. Anoka (Minn.) Hennepin Schs., 1966-68; pvt. practice Youth Ctr., Truman, Minn., 1969-72; bookkeeper Fairmont (Minn.) Glass & Sign, 1973, Truman Farmers Elevator, 1973-87; libr. Martin County Libr., Truman, 1988-89; sch. counselor St. James (Minn.) Schs., 1989—; coord. Internat. Fun Fest, St. James, 1992; originator, advisor Armstrong After Sch. Hispanic Club, St. James, 1991—. Coord. Truman Days Parade, 1991, 92, 94, 95; mem. adv. bd. Watonwan County Big Buddy Program, 1993—. Mem. Am. Counseling Assn., Am. Sch. Counselors Assn., Minn. Sch. Counselors Assn., S.W. Minn. Counselors Assn. (Elem. Counselor of Yr. 1993). Office: Saint James Sch Dist 1273 10th Ave N Saint James MN 56081-2029

JONES, PRISCILLA LEE, mental health nurse, therapist; b. Ft. Ord, Calif., Jan. 7, 1950; d. Mary Elizabeth (Clark) Jones; m. Douglas E. Sipple, Feb. 22, 1986 (div.); 1 child, Jacob D. AA in Psychology, U. Del., 1985; ADN, Del. Tech. and Community Coll., 1985; BS in Psychology, Wilmington Coll., 1987. RN, Del. Nurse rehab. dept. Alfred I. duPont Inst., Wilmington, Del., 1985-86; nurse emergency dept. St. Francis Hosp., Wilmington, 1986; psychiat. charge nurse Meadowwood Adolescent Hosp., New Castle, Del., 1990-91; nurse emergency dept. Beebe Med. Ctr., Lewes, Del., 1991-92; family practice nurse Dr. John Giuliano, Lewes, Del., 1992—; pvt. practice Millsboro, Del., 1992—. Author: A Christmas Poem, 1990. Mem. Mayflower Soc., DAR. Republican. Methodist. Office: Beebe Med Ctr Dr John Giuliano RR 26 Millville DE 19970

JONES, REBECCA ALVINA PATRONIS, nurse; b. Quincy, Fla., Sept. 14, 1952; d. Eugene T. Patronis and Ada Lee (Allen) Poole; m. Robert Gerald Jones, Dec. 29, 1979; 1 child, Aislan Hlynn. BS in Nursing, U. Fla., 1974; MS in Nursing, U. S.C., 1988; D in Nursing Sci., Ind. U., Indpls., 1991. RN, Tex., Ind., Pa.; cert. in nursing adminstrn. advanced. Team leader, teaching staff nurse Shands Teaching Hosp., Gainesville, Fla., 1974-76; commd. 1st Lt. U.S. Army, 1976, advanced through grades to lt. col., held various nursing positions, 1976-83, resigned, 1983; discharge planning coord. Gorgas Army Hosp., Panama City, Panama, 1984-86; nursing rsch. asst. U. S.C., Columbia, 1986-87; asst. dir. nursing Kershaw County Meml. Hosp., Camden, S.C., 1988-89; assoc. instr. Ind. U., Indpls., 1989-91; asst. prof., assoc. dir. nursing La Salle U., Albert Einstein Med. Ctr., Phila., 1991-94; dir., assoc. prof. dept. nursing and health scis. Tex. A&M U., Corpus Christi, 1994—. Contbr. articles to profl. jours. Mem. Am. Coll. Healthcare Execs., Midwest Nursing Rsch. Soc., Nat. League Nursing, Am. Orgn. Nurse Execs., Ea. Nursing Rsch. Soc., Coun. on Grad. Edn. for Adminstrn. in Nursing (sec.), Tex. League for Nursing, Tex. Nurses Assn., So. Nursing Rsch. Soc., Am. Nurses Assn., N.E. Orgn. Nurses, Sigma Theta Tau. Republican. Presbyterian. Home: 5422 Pressler Dr Corpus Christi TX 78412 Office: Tex A&M U Dept Nursing & Health Scis Sch of Nursing Corpus Christi TX 78412

JONES, RENEE KAUERAUF, health care administrator; b. Duncan, Okla., Nov. 3, 1949; d. Delbert Owen and Betty Jean (Marsh) Kauerauf; m. Dan Elkins Jones, Aug. 3, 1972. BS, Okla. State U., 1972, MS, 1975; PhD, Okla. U., 1989. Statis. analyst Okla. State Dept. Mental Health, Okla. City, 1978-80, divisional chief, 1980-83, adminstr., 1983-84; assoc. dir. HCA Presbyn. Hosp., Okla. City, 1984—; adj. instr. Okla. U. Health Sci. Ctr., 1979—; assoc. staff scientist Okla. Ctr. for Alcohol and Drug-Related Studies, Okla. City, 1979—; cons. in field. Assoc. editor Alcohol Tech. Reports jour., 1979-84; contbr. articles to profl. jours. Mem. assoc. bd. Hist. Preservation, Inc., treas. 1994. Mem. APHA, Assn. Health Svcs. Rsch., Alcohol and Drug Problems Assn. N.Am., Am. Sleep Disorders Assn., N.Y. Acad. Scis., So. Sleep Soc. (sec.-treas. 1989-91), Phi Kappa Phi. Democrat. Methodist. Home: 401 NW 19th St Oklahoma City OK 73103-1911 Office: HCA Presbyn Hosp NE 13th at Lincoln Blvd Oklahoma City OK 73104

JONES, RICKIE LEE, singer, songwriter; b. Chgo, Ill., Nov. 8, 1954. Albums include: Rickie Lee Jones, 1979, Pirates, 1981, The Magazine, Girl at Her Volcano, Flying Cowboys, 1989, Pop Pop, 1991, Traffic from Paradise, 1993; songwriter: Easy Money, Chuck E.'s in Love, 1977, numerous others. Recipient Grammy awards 1979, 89, Rolling Stone mag. Music awards 1979, 81. Office: Geffen Records 1755 Broadway New York NY 10019-3743*

JONES, ROSEMARIE FRIEDA, service executive; b. Heidelberg, Federal Republic of Germany, May 15, 1950; came to U.S., 1952; d. Duane W. Blodgett and Imargard P. (Reinmuth) Boczanski; m. Curtis B. Jones, June 3, 1989; children: Spencer E. Jones, Steven T. Kratzer. BS in Bus. Edn., U. Nebr., 1972, MEd, 1980. Instr. Columbus (Ga.) Vo-Tech., 1975-76; adminstrv. asst. to commdr. 1st Infantry Div., Goeppingen, Federal Republic of Germany, 1976-79; grad. asst. U. Nebr., Lincoln, 1979-80; instr. bus. occupations S.E. Community Coll., Lincoln, 1980-84; br. mgr. Imprimis, Dallas, 1985—; adv. bd. Dallas County Community Coll., Brookhaven Coll., curriculum writer Eastfield Community Coll., Dallas; speaker in field. Recipient Victor Trophy Sales and Mktg. Execs. Dallas, 1991. Mem. Am. Mgmt. Soc., Assn. Information Systems Profls. (pres. 1984). Home: 1615 Auburn Dr Richardson TX 75081-3046 Office: Imprimis 1717 Main St Ste 3390 Dallas TX 75201-7348

JONES, ROSEMARY, education director; b. Washington, Pa., Aug. 15, 1951; d. Roy F. and Grace Vivian (Beton) J. BA in Sociology, Ohio State U., 1974, MA in Pub. Adminstrn., 1977. Mgmt. analyst office planning studies Ohio State U., Columbus, 1974-76; staff assoc., edn. rev. com. Ohio Gen. Assembly, Columbus, 1977-78; from adminstr. to asst. dir. info. systems and rsch. Ohio Bd. Regents, Columbus, 1978-90; from project dir. instl. rsch. to dir. rsch. planning Lakeland C.C., Mentor, Ohio, 1990-93; dist. dir. instl. planning evaluation Cuyahoga C.C., Cleve., 1994—; cons. Ohio Bd. Regents, Columbus, 1990-91; mem. NPECSS planning com. U.S. Dept. Edn., 1994—. Consumr adv. bd. United Health Plan, Columbus, 1978-82, chair, 1980-82; vol. Ronald McDonald House, Columbus, 1989, operating bd. mem., 1989; bd. dirs. Netcare Found., Columbus, 1988; state and regional conf. chair ASPA, Columbus, 1981, 83-84; steering com. Ctrl. Ohio Salute to Pub. Employees, Columbus, 1983. Mem. Assn. Instl. Rsch., Ohio Conf. for Coll. and Univ. Planning, Ohio Assn. Instl. Rsch. (two-yr. campus coun. rep.), Cleve. Planning Forum, Soc. for Coll. and Univ. Planning, Cleve. Commn. on Higher Edn. Strategic Planning com. (temp. chair 1991). Office: Cuyahoga CC 700 Carnegie Ave Cleveland OH 44115-2833

JONES, ROXANNE HARPER, state legislator; b. N.C., May 3, 1928; d. Gilford and Mary (Bruton) Harper; m. James H. Jones, 1957 (dec.); children: Patricia Hill, Wanda. Student pub. schs. Bd. dirs. Pa. Minority Bus. Devel. Authority, Pa. Legis. Black Caucus, 1985—, Pa. Intra-Govtl. Long Term Care Coun.; mem. urban affairs and housing com., minority chmn. pub. health and welfare com., mem. aging and youth com., mem. consumer protection and professional licensure com. Pa. State Senate, 1985—. Recipient Nat. Welfare Rights Orgn. Leadership award Nat. Welfare Rights Orgn., 1972, Woman of Yr. award Zeta Phi Beta, 1985, Achievement cert. Nat. Coun. Negro Women, 1985. Bd. dirs. Ams. for Democratic Action; mem. children's health adv. coun. Pa. Trauma Systems Found., 1985—; co-chmn. Coalition Concerned Citizens; exec. dir. Phila. Citizens in Action; mem. Allegheny West Found. Mem. Apostolic Ch. Home: 2330 W Allegheny Ave Philadelphia PA 19132-1422 Office: Pa State Senate State Capital Harrisburg PA 17101

JONES, SALLY DAVIESS PICKRELL, writer; b. St. Louis, June 4, 1923; d. Claude Dildine and Marie Daviess (Pittman) Pickrell; m. Charles William Jones, Sept. 2, 1943; 1 son, Matthew Charles. Student, Mills Coll., Oakland, Calif., 1941-43, U. Calif.-Berkeley, 1944, Columbia, 1955-58. Author: (novel) The Lights Burn Blue, 1947. Mem. AAUW, UN Women's Guild, Fgn. Policy Assn., Nat. Coun. Women, Asia Soc., English-Speaking Union, Met. Mus. Art, Internat. Platform Assn., Women's Internat. Forum. Episcopalian. Address: 311 E 58th St New York NY 10022-2003

JONES, SANDRA, electronics executive; b. Frankfurt, Fed. Republic Germany, Oct. 5, 1946; came to U.S., 1949; d. Irving and Lena (Kooningstein) Zak; m. Charles E. Jones, Dec. 18, 1973; stepchildren: Katherine Jones Mearns, Terry Jones, Cynthia E. Jones. Grad. sch. grad. Mgr. ops. J&L Builders, Cleve., 1968-71; v.p. Sabin Machine Co., Cleve., 1971-75; pres. Security Products Col, Cleve., 1975—, also bd. dirs., 1975-90; pres. Sandra Jones & Co., Chardon, Ohio, 1990—; spokesperson Electronic Security Industry; participant Consumer Products Safety Commn.; industry rep. Ad Hoc Window Falls Com. Bd. dirs. Nat. Burglar and Fire Alarm Assn., Security Industry Assn. (bd. dirs. 1985—, v.p. 1986-88, pres. elect 1988—, exec. dir.), Nat. Assn. Wholesalers (trustee 1986—, bd. dels.). Jewish. Office: 10100 Sherman Rd Chardon OH 44024-9443

JONES, SARA CAROLYN NOLEN, school counselor; b. Birmingham, Ala., Jan. 24, 1943; d. Daniel Edward and Louise (Johnson) Nolen; m. Ernest Gordon Jones, Oct. 4, 1969; children: Kimberly Brooke, Austin Edward. BFA, U. Ga., 1965; MEd, Ga. State U., 1992. Tchr. art Charlotte (N.C.) Mecklenburg Schs., 1966, Fulton County Sch. Dist., Atlanta, 1966-71; receptionist Nolen & Assocs. Inc., Atlanta, 1989; counselor Walnut Grove Elem. Sch. Gwinnett County Sch. System, Suwanee, Ga., 1991—. Tchr. Sunday sch. Wienca Rd. Bapt. Ch., Atlanta, 1984-92. Mem. Am. Sch. Counseling Assn., Am. Counseling Assn., Ga. Sch. Counselors Assn. Republican. Home: 1425 Vernon North Dr Atlanta GA 30338

JONES, SHARON FRANK, appraiser; b. Tulsa, Okla., July 5, 1960; d. Percy Dan and Eloise (Curry) Frank; divorced; children: Renisha F. Thomas, Andre F. BAA in Acctg., Baker Coll., 1992. Appraiser City of Flint, Mich., 1989—; sec. bd. Chrysalis, Inc., Flint, 1993-94. Recipient Award of Achievement, Nat. Assn. Black Accts., 1991-92, women of Achievment award YWCA, 1992. Mem. Nat. Soc. Pub. Accts., Inst. Mgmt. Accts. (treas. 1990-91, pres. 1991-92). Office: City of Flint 1101 S Saginaw St Flint MI 48502-1416

JONES, SHEILA MCLENDON, construction company executive; b. Bennettsville, S.C., July 11, 1965; d. Charlie Garrett and Ruby (Hatcher) McLendon; m. James Robert Jones, July 24, 1987; children: Robert Shane, Ashley Sunny. Student, Chesterfield/Marlboro Tech., 1981. Nurse asst. Marlboro Park Hosp., Bennettsville, S.C., 1983-84; inspectopr INA Bearing Co., Inc., Cheraw, S.C., 1985; with Big Apple Fashions, Cheraw, S.C., 1985; inspector ADS Co., Inc., Star, N.C., 1985-86; machine operator Legg's Hosery, Rockingham, N.C., 1986-87; masonry cons. Robert Jones Masonry, Morven, N.C., 1987—. Democrat. Baptist. Home and Office: 128 N Church St Morven NC 28119

JONES, SHERYL LEANNE, paralegal; b. Burlington, Iowa, Jan. 5, 1959; d. Leo F. and Mary E. (Hudson) Wallace; m. Paul W. Jones, July 14, 1984. BA in Spanish Lit. and Lang., U. Kans., 1981, BSBA, 1982; cert. legal asst., S.W. Mo. State U., 1989; AS in Legal Asst. Studies, Drury Coll., 1991. Legal sec. Pratt & Fossard, Springfield, Mo., 1984-87; paralegal Pratt, Fossard & Rahmeyer, Springfield, Mo., 1987—; adj. faculty, mem. com. dept. office systems & tech. Ozark Tech. Coll., Springfield, 1992-93; mem. adv. bd. dept. paralegal studies Drury Coll., Springfield, 1988-90; lectr. seminar Mo. Bar Assn., 1990. Contbr. articles to legal jours. Mem. Nat. Assn. Legal Secs. (cert. profl. legal sec. 1989, Continuing Legal Edn. award 1989, 92), Nat. Assn. Legal Assts. (cert. legal asst. 1990, cert. specialist in litigation 1992), Nat. Fedn. Paralegal Assns., Mo. Assn. Legal Secs. (parliamentarian, chair various coms. 1986—, Outstanding Membership Idea 1986, Legal Sec. of Yr. 1991), S.W. Mo. Paralegal Assn. (chair various coms. 1987—, bd. dirs. 1993—), Greene County Legal Secs. Assn. (pres., v.p., sec., gov., alt. gov., rep. Nat. Assn. Legal Secs., Outstanding New Mem. 1987, 88, Legal Sec. Yr. 1991), Springfield Mo. Alumnae Panhellenic (v.p., sec., treas., pres. 1994—), Sigma Kappa (pres., v.p., panhellenic rep., various coms., alumnae Springfield chpt., coord. dist. housing 1992-93, corp. fin. coord. 1993—, v.p. nat. housing corp. 1993—). Home: 1149 E Greenwood St Springfield MO 65807-3714 Office: Pratt Fossard & Rahmeyer 1200 E Woodhurst Dr A-200 Springfield MO 65804-4259

JONES, SHIRLEY, actress, singer; b. Smithton, Pa., July 31, 1934; d. Paul and Marjorie (Williams) J.; m. Jack Cassidy, Aug. 5, 1956 (div. 1975); children: Shaun, Patrick, Ryan; m. Marty Ingels, 1977. Grad. high sch., 1952; student, Pitts. Playhouse. Appeared with chorus South Pacific, 1953, in Broadway prodn. Me and Juliet, 1954; other state appearences include The Beggar's Opera, 1957, The Red Mill, 1958, Maggie Flynn, 1968, On a Clear Day, 1975, Show Boat, 1976, Bitter Suite, 1983; films include role of Laurey in Oklahoma, 1954, later stage tour Paris and Rome, sponsorship U.S. Dept. State, Carousel, 1956, April Love, 1957, Never Steal Anything Small, 1959, Bobbikins, 1959, Elmer Gantry, 1960 (Acad. Best Supporting Actress award 1961), Pepe, 1960, The Two Rode Together, 1961, The Music Man, 1962, The Courtship of Eddie's Father, 1963, A Ticklish Affair, 1963, Bedtime Story, 1964, The Secret of My Success, 1965, Fluffy, 1965, The Happy Ending, 1969, The Cheyenne Social Club, 1970, Beyond the Poseidon Adventure, 1979, Tank, 1984, There Were Times, Dear, 1985; night club tour with husband, 1958, later TV and summer stock; star TV series The Partridge Family, 1970-74, Shirley, 1979; guest star: TV series McMillan, 1976; TV films include: Silent Night, Lonely Night, 1969, But I Don't Want To Get Married!, 1970, The Girls of Huntington House, 1973, The Family Nobody Wanted, 1975, The Lives of Jenny Dolan, 1975, Winner Take All, 1975, Yesterday's Child, 1977, Evening in Byzantium, 1978, Who'll Save Our Children, 1978, A Last Cry for Help, 1979, The Children Of An Lac, 1980, Inmates: A Love Story, 1981, There Were Times Dear, 1987; one-woman concert: TV series Shirley Jones' America 1981; author: Shirley and Marty: An Unlikely Love Story, 1990. Nat. chairwoman Leukemia Found. Named Mother of Yr. by Women's Found., 1978.

JONES, SONIA JOSEPHINE, advertising agency executive; b. Belize, Brit. Honduras, Nov. 9, 1945; came to U.S., 1962, naturalized, 1986; d. Frederick Francis and Elsie Adelia (Gomez) Alcoser; m. John Marvin Jones, Mar. 21, 1970; children: Christopher William Edward, Joshua Joseph Paul. Student, Lamar U., 1964-66. With Foley's Federated Dept. Store, Houston, 1965-67; media buyer Vance Advt., Houston, 1967-68; media buyer, planner O'Neill & Assocs., Houston, 1968-75; media supr. Ketchum Houston, 1975-76; v.p., media dir. Rives Smith Bladwin Carlberg/Y & R, Houston, 1976-86; sr. v.p. media dir. Black Gillock & Langberg, Houston, 1986-89; pres. JMM Group, Inc., Houston, 1989—; lectr. U. Houston, 1983—. Vol. Women in Yellow, Houston, 1966; mem. St. Thomas High Sch. Mothers Club, 1992—; translator vol. St. Cecilia Clinic, 1993—; mem. sch. bd. St. Cecilia Cath. Sch., St. Thomas High Sch. Women's Club, fundraising vol., 1992—. Mem. Houston Advt. Fedn. Republican. Office: JMM Group Inc 2500 City West Blvd Ste 300 Houston TX 77042

JONES, SUSAN DORFMAN, real estate broker, writer; b. N.Y.C., Oct. 4, 1939; d. Joseph and Sarah (Sorrin) Dorfman; m. William Harry Jones, Sept. 18, 1960; children: Jeffrey Scott, Eric David, Timothy Mark. BA, Syracuse U., 1961. Pres., owner Antiques Corp. Am., 1972-77; pres., owner Susan & Sons Antiques, 1977—; communications officer Riggs Bank, Washington, 1978-81; mgr. publs. Potomac Electric Power Co., Washington, 1981-82; sr. mgr. corp. communications MCI Corp., Washington, 1982-83; dir. corp. communications Sears World Trade, Washington, 1983-85; dir. corp. communications and govt. rels. Oxford Devel. Corp., Bethesda, Md., 1985-87; communications expert pub. health svc./health and human svcs. U.S. Alcohol, Drug Abuse, Mental Health Adminstrn., Rockville, Md., 1989-91; real estate broker Weichert/Shannon & Luchs, Washington, 1991—; freelance writer, cons., Washington, 1975-92; radio personality Sta. 4KQ, Brisbane, Australia, 1962; adj. prof. comms. Am. U., Washington, 1978-82. Author, editor, project mgr. corp. ann. reports. Recipient 1st pl. award for columns N.Y. Press Assn., 1961, Gold Quill award Internat. Assn. Bus. Communicators, 1980. Mem. Internat. Assn. Bus. Communicators (treas. 1981), Nat. Assn. Bank Women, Women in Telecommunications, Nat. Press Club, Pub. Rels. Soc. Am. Democrat. Jewish. Home and Office: 3777 Oliver St NW Washington DC 20015 Office: 5035 Wisconsin Ave NW Washington DC 20016

JONES, SUSAN EMILY, fashion educator, administrator, educator; b. N.Y.C., Sept. 9, 1948; d. David and Emily Helen (Welke) J.; m. Henry J. Titone, Jr., Oct. 21, 1974 (div. 1980); m. Douglas S. Robbins, Aug. 21, 1985. B.F.A., Pratt Inst., Bklyn., 1970. Designer Sue Brett, N.Y.C., 1970-74; prof. fashion Pratt Inst., Bklyn., 1972-80, prof., 1980—, chairperson fashion dept., 1981-83, chairperson merchandising and design programs fashion dept., 1983—; computer software cons., 1988-89; internat. observer Jeunes Createurs de Mode, Paris, 1987, judge, 1988; U.S. rep. SAGA Internat. Design Ctr., Copenhagen, 1992. Recipient Young Am. Designer award Internat. Ladies Garment Workers Union, 1970. Mem. Fashion Group (regional com. 1983-87, membership com. 1990-93), National Retail Fedn., Under Fashion Assn. Home: 220 Willoughby Ave Brooklyn NY 11205-3805 Office: Pratt Inst Dept of Fashion Design 200 Willoughby Ave Brooklyn NY 11205-3817

JONES, SUSAN MATTHEWS, elementary educator; b. Pueblo, Colo., Nov. 2, 1945; d. Zolton and Cecilia (Barnhoft) Orosz. BS in Edn., Ark. State U., 1968. Cert. elem. tchr., Ark., Okla., art tchr., Ark., Okla., Mo. 1st grade tchr. Cherokee Elem. Sch., Hardy, Ark., 1969-70, Madill (Okla.) Elem. Sch., 1979-86, T. G. Smith Elem. Sch., Springdale, Ark., 1986—; high sch. art tchr. Warren County R-III Sch., Warrenton, Mo., 1970-74; jr. high art tchr. Moore (Okla.) West Ju. High Sch., 1974-75; presenter workshops in math and reading. Creator, pub. memory aid books and posters, 1984—. State recognition exemplary grantee Ark. Dept. Edn., 1988-89, Christa McAuliffe fellowship program grantee, 1990-91. Mem. NEA, ASCD, Ark. Edn. Assn., Ark. Reading Coun. Home: 1623 Terry Fayetteville AR 72703

JONES, SUSAN REBECCA, social services administrator; b. Portland, Maine, Feb. 27, 1962; d. Allan Author and Joanne Marie (Partridge) J. BA, U. Maine, 1984, MS, 1989. Exec. dir. Rape Crisis Ctr., Inc., Portland, Maine, 1991—. Adv. bd. mem. Portland Sch. Human Sexuality, 1991—; com. mem. United Way, Portland, 1992—. Mem. NOW (Greater Portland chpt.), Planned Parenthood of New Eng., Maine Coalition Against Rape (sec. exec. com. 1993—), C. of C. Office: Rape Crisis Ctr Inc 1000 Shore Rd Ft Williams Cape Elizabeth ME

JONES, SUSAN RUSSELL, actress; b. Bryn Mawr, Pa., Aug. 23, 1967; d. Thomas Owen Jones and Mary Louise (Mahon) Russell. BFA, Cath. U. Am., 1988; postgrad., Cir. in the Sq., 1990-91. Actress Royal Ct. Theatre, N.Y.C., 1980-81, NRF Callan Players, Washington, 1984, Arena Theatre Workshop, Washington, 1985, Hartke Theatre Workshop, Washington, 1986, Studio Theatre, Washington, 1987, Circle in the Sq. Workshop, N.Y.C., 1989, North Theatre Group, L.A., 1991—. Appeared in film Julia, 1978. Vol. AIDS Project L.A., 1991-93. Mem. SAG. Democrat. Roman Catholic.

JONES, SUZANNE P., public relations executive; b. Niagara Falls, N.Y., Sept. 4, 1946; d. Morris G. and Betty (Connolly) J. BA in English, Niagara U., 1969; MA in Theater, U. Conn., 1971. Editor Niagara Observer, Niagara Falls, 1971-74, Niagara Free Press, Niagara Falls, 1974-75; pub. info. dir. City of Niagara Falls, 1975-76; advt. dir. Orion Enterprises, Lewiston, N.Y., 1976-79; v.p. Bozell and Jacobs Pub. Rels., N.Y.C., 1980-86, Porter/Novelli, N.Y.C., 1987-93; dir. inhouse pub. rels. Black & Decker Household Products, Shelmar, Conn., 1991-93; dir. in-house pub. rels. Black & Decker Household Products, Sheldon, Conn., 1993—. Mem. Theatre Hist. Soc., Larchmont Manor Soc., Larchmont Hist. Soc., Friends Niagara U. Theatre, Niagara U. Coun. Democrat. Roman Catholic. Home: 3 Washington Sq # 4A Larchmont NY 10538-2032

JONES, VALÉRIA, artist; b. Atlantic City, Jan. 17, 1954; d. Frank Lewis and Mary Halth (Hunter) J. BFA, Moore Coll. Art, 1981. Photographer Westsider Weekly, N.Y.C., 1982, Valéria Jean Photography, Inc., Atlantic City, 1982—, Casino Assn. of N.J., Atlantic City, 1989; art tchr. Hebrew Acad. of Atlantic County, Margate, N.J., 1987-88; photojournalist Mainland Jour., Pleasantville, N.J., 1988-89. Exhibited in group shows at Goldie Palley Gallery, Phila., 1981—, Ocean City (N.J.) Art Ctr., 1985, Lawrence Gallery, N.Y.C., 1989, Heritage Art Ctr., Phila., 1990; contbr. poems to profl. publs. Vol. Convenant House of N.J., Atlantic City, 1991. Named One of Best New Poets of 1988, Am. Soc. Poetry, 1988, cert. for lyric writing excellence Platinum Records, 1993. Mem. Am. Soc. Media Photographers. Democrat. Baptist. Home: 116 MLK Blvd Atlantic City NJ 08401

JONES, VALERIE KAYE, insurance company executive; b. Cleve., Oct. 26, 1956; d. Daniel Edward and Katherine (Donaldson) J. BS with high honors, Ohio U., 1978; postgrad., Cleve. State U. Lic. ins. agt. Asst. personnel dir. The Higbee Co., Cleve., 1977-78; tchr. learning disabilities and behavior disorders Cleve. Heights-Univ. Heights (Ohio) Sch., 1978-83; mem. ins. specialist CUNA Mut. Ins. Group, Madison, Wis., 1983-84, rep. group coverages, 1984-87, field communications adminstr. cen. dist., 1987-88, sr. field comms. adminstr., 1988-93; sr. dist. account cons., 1993-94; mktg. support mgr. east ctrl. mktg. divsn. CUNA Mut. Ins. Group, Madison, Wis., 1994—; bd. sec. Liberty Hill Credit Union, Cleve., 1978-83. Asst. to dir. directory project Cuyahoga Spl. Edn. Service Ctr., 1974; mem. 21st Dist. Congl. Caucus, Cleve., 1984. Mem. Nat. Assn. Female Execs., Delta Sigma Theta. Democrat. Home: 14840 Greenview Rd Detroit MI 48223-2329 Office: CUNA Mut Ins Group 20800 Civic Center Dr Southfield MI 48076-4117

JONES, VIRGINIA MCCLURKIN, social worker; b. Anniston, Ala., Mar. 13, 1935; d. Louie Walter and Virginia Keith (Beaver) McClurkin; m. Charles Miller Jones Jr., Mar. 16, 1957; children: Charles Miller III, V. Grace. BA, Agnes Scott Coll., 1957; M.A., U. Tenn., 1965, MS in Social Work, 1979. Instr. English, U. Tenn., Knoxville, 1967-71; religious edn. dir. Oak Ridge Unitarian Ch., 1972-73, 76-78; co-owner, mgr. The Bookstore, 1973-76; instr. English, Roane State Community Coll., 1975-80; pvt. practice clin. social work, Oak Ridge, 1980—; cons. Mountain Community Health Ctr., Coalfield, Tenn., 1980-83, Valley Ridge Hospice, 1987-89. Bd. dirs. Anderson County Ctr. Community Justice. Mem. Nat. Assn. Social Workers, Oak Ridge Ministerial Assn., Knoxville Area Agnes Scott Alumnae (pres.), Concord Yacht Club, Rotary. Democrat. Episcopalian. Contbr. articles to newspapers. Office: 1345 Oak Ridge Tpke # 358 Oak Ridge TN 37830-6416

JONES, WINONA NIGELS, library media specialist; b. St. Petersburg, Fla., Feb. 24, 1928; d. Eugene Arthur and Bertha Lillian (Dixon) Nigels; m. Charles Albert Jones, Nov. 26, 1944; children: Charles Eugene, Sharon Ann Jones Allworth, Caroline Winona Jones Pandorf. AA, St. Petersburg Jr. Coll., 1965; BS, U. South Fla., 1967, MS, 1968; Advanced MS, Fla. State U., 1980. Libr. media specialist Dunedin (Fla.) Comprehensive High Sch., 1967-76; libr. media specialist, chmn. dept. Fitzgerald Middle Sch., Largo, Fla., 1976-87; dir. Media Svcs. East Lake High Sch., Tarpon Springs, Fla., 1987-93, ret., 1993. Active Palm Harbor and Pinellas County Hist. Soc.; del. White House Conf. for Libr. and Info. Svcs. Named Educator of Yr. Pinellas County Sch. Bd. and Suncoast C. of C., 1983, 88, Palm Harbor Woman of Yr. Palm Harbor Jr. Women's Club, 1989. Mem. ALA (coun. 1988-92), NEA, AAUW, Fla. Assn. Media in Edn. (pres.), U. So. Fla. Alumni Assn., Assn. Ednl. Communication and Tech. (div. sch. media specialist, coms.), Am. Assn. Sch. Librs. (com., pres.-elect 1989, pres. 1990-91, past pres., exec. bd. 1991-92), Southeastern Libr. Assn., Fla. Libr. Assn., Assn. Supervision and Curriculum Devel., Fla. State Libr. Sci. Alumni, U. South Fla. Libr. Sci. Alumni Assn. (pres. 1991-92, 92-93), Phi Theta Kappa, Phi Rho Pi, Beta Phi Mu, Kappa Delta Pi, Delta Kappa Gamma (parliamentarian 1989-90, legis. chmn. 1990), Inner Wheel Club, Pilot Club, Civic Club, Order of Eastern Star (Palm Harbor, past worthy matron). Democrat. Home: 911 Manning Rd Palm Harbor FL 34683-6344 Office: 1300 Silver Eagle Dr Tarpon Springs FL 34689-9101

JONES-ATKINS, DEBORAH KAYE, state official; b. Bradenton, Fla., July 2, 1958; d. Ralph and Jewelle Vanessa (Gayle) Jones; m. Larry Bobby Atkins, July 30, 1983; 1 child, Omari Gayle Jones-Atkins. AS with distinction, Monroe Community Coll., Rochester, N.Y., 1986, cert. in human svcs, 1986; BIS candidate, Va. State U., 1976-79, 94—, student, 1990—. Credit investigator Sears Roebuck & Co., Rochester, N.Y., 1980; customer svc. rep. B. Forman Co., Rochester, 1980-81; youth counselor Brighton Youth Agy., Rochester, 1976-81; staff asst. Makro Inc., Capitol Hts., Md., 1981-82; customer svc. rep. MetroVision Inc., Capitol Hts., 1983-84; teen parent counselor Urban League of Rochester, 1985; job developer YWCA of Rochester, 1985-87; program coord. Urban League of Rochester, 1988; prog. support technician, sr. Dept. Med. Assistance Svcs., Commonwealth of Va., Richmond, 1989—. Mem. Women's Resource Ctr., Richmond, 1989—; heir link The Links Inc., Rochester, 1982—; vol. United Negro Coll. Fund Telethon, Rochester, 1988, N.Y. State Dept. Labor Career Edn. Expo, 1989, WXXI Auction 21, Rochester, 1989, YMCA Greater Rochester, 1989, Arts Coun., Richmond, Richmond Children's Festival, 1989, Sci. Mus. Va., Richmond, 1989, Arts Coun. Richmond 15th Ann. June Jubilee, 1990, Children's Book Festival, 1990, Maymont Found. Flower Garden Show, 1990, 91, Va. Spl. Olympics, 1990—, Jr. League Richmond 45th Book and Author Dinner, 1990, dinner asst. ticket chairperson 46th Book and Author Dinner, 1991, hostee 45th Dinner, Children's Book Festival Arts Coun. Richmond; mem. agy. svc. com. Friends Assn. for Children, 1990—, student adv. com. Va. Commonwealth U. Health Svcs., 1991, Friends of Art Richmond Mus. Fine Arts, 1991, membership com., audience devel. com., Richmond Profl. Women's Network; placement counselor Placement Com. Jr. League Richmond, 1991, mem. tng. com., 1991, adv. com. Children's Mus. Richmond; mem. exec. bd. YWCA of Richmond, 1992-95; mem. policy bd. Jr. League Richmond, 1992-93. Mem. NAFE, Nat. Coun. Negro Women, Jr. League of Rochester, Nat. Trust Hist. Preservation, Richmond Profl. Women's Network (rec. sec., exec. bd. 1992—), Richmond Jaycees. Democrat. Home: 5207 Cutshaw Ave Richmond VA 23226

JONESCO, JANE RIGGS, lawyer, development officer; b. Delaware, Ohio, Feb. 7, 1949; d. Edgar Gray and Bettie Pauline (Lowther) Riggs; m. John Michael Jonesco, Aug. 8, 1970; children: Amy Jane, John Michael III, Michael Andrew, Katherine Elizabeth. BA, Ohio Wesleyan U., 1971; JD, DePaul U., 1980. Bar: Ohio 1980. Atty. in pvt. practice Oberlin, Ohio, 1981-91; dir. planned giving Oberlin Coll., 1991—; mem. adminstrn. and profl. coun. Oberlin Coll., 1992-93. Mem. Oberlin Bd. Edn., 1987-93, v.p., 1988-89, pres., 1990-93; founder, mem. Oberlin Interagy. Coun., 1990-93; mem. Oberlin Community Svcs. Coun., 1986-90; mem. Oberlin Bicentennial Commn., 1985-86; pres., mem. Oberlin Baseball Softball Fedn., 1981-86; mem. Nat. Planned Giving Coun., No. Ohio Planned Giving Coun.; mem. Jr. League of Columbus, 1979-80. Episcopalian. Home: 440 E College St Oberlin OH 44704 Office: Oberlin Coll 208 Bosworth Hall Oberlin OH 44074

JONES-LUKÁCS, ELIZABETH LUCILLE, physician, air force officer; b. Norfolk, Va.; d. Oliver C. and Gertrude (Layden) Jones; B.S., Oglethorpe U., 1955; m. Michel J. Lukacs (dec.); children—Amanda, Laurel, Angelique, Klara. Intern Beth Israel Hosp., N.Y.C., 1964-65; family practice medicine, Goshen, N.Y., 1965-73, Buckingham, Va., 1973-78; commd. maj. U.S. Air Force, 1978; flight surgeon, Andrews AFB, Md., 1978-85, chief exec. med. program, 1991—; unit charge physician Student Health Ctr., U. Md., College Park, 1985-91. Col. USAFR, commd. 459th USAF Clinic. Diplomate, fellow Am. Bd. Family Practice. Mem. Am. Med. Womens Assn. (pres. Br. I), Assn. Aerospace Physicians, Aerospace Med. Assn., Md. Thoroughbred Breeders. Episcopalian. Author: The Curies Radium & Radioactivity, 1962; The Golden Stamp Book of Flying Animals, 1963. Home: 4310 Woodberry St Hyattsville MD 20782-1173 Office: MGMC Dept FP Andrews AFB Washington DC 20331

JONES-LYONS, MONIKA, data processing executive; b. Burlington, Vt., May 7, 1949; d. Paul and Frieda (Windisch) Desforges; m. Dennis E. Jones (div. 1974); children: Dennis E. Jr., Anthony B. V.p., data processing mgr., mktg. services officer, customer support rep. Exchange Bank & Trust, Tampa, Fla., 1974-82; asst. v.p., v.p. data processing First Fla. Bank. N.A., Tampa, 1982-90; dir. profl. svcs. Systems Mgmt. Engring., Inc., Tampa, 1990-91, EMP Leasing Inc., Tampa, 1991-92; database mgr. OKRA Mktg. Corp., Tampa, 1992-94, 2nd v.p., mktg. mgr., 1994—. Mem. Am. Inst. Banking (edn. adminstr. Tampa chpt. 1979-83, Banker of Yr. Tampa chpt. 1981-82), Nat. Assn. Female Execs. Home: 17923 Holly Brook Dr Tampa FL 33647-2245 Office: EFCI 5100 W Lemon St Ste 200 Tampa FL 33609

JONES-SMITH, JACQUELINE, federal commission administrator, lawyer; b. Bronx, N.Y., Nov. 5, 1952. BA, Swarthmore Coll., 1974; MLS, Syracuse U., 1978; JD, Am. U., 1984. Bar: Md. 1985, U.S. Dist. Ct. Md. 1986, U.S. Ct. Appeals (9th cir.) 1987, U.S. Supreme Ct. 1988, U.S. Ct. of Appeals (D.C. Cir.) 1988. Systems libr., div. mgr. MAXIMA Corp., Rockville, Md., 1979-85; asst. city atty. Montgomery County, Rockville, Md., 1985-87; staff atty. Office of Gen. Counsel, Fed. Election Commn., Washington, 1987-89; chmn. Consumer Product Safety Commn., Bethesda, Md., 1989-94, commr., 1994—. Mem. ABA, Nat. Bar Assn., Md. State Bar Assn. Democrat. Office: US Consumer Product Safety 4430 East West Hwy Ste 725 Bethesda MD 20814-4408

JONG, ERICA MANN, writer, poet; b. N.Y.C., Mar. 26, 1942; d. Seymour and Eda (Mirsky) Mann; m. Michael Werthman, 1963 (div. 1965); m. Allan Jong (div. Sept. 1975); m. Jonathan Fast, Dec. 1977 (div. Jan. 1983); 1 child, Molly; m. Kenneth David Burrows, Aug. 5, 1989. B.A., Barnard Coll., 1963; M.A., Columbia U., 1965. Faculty, English dept. CUNY, 1964-65, 69-70, overseas div. U. Md., 1967-69; mem. lit. panel N.Y. State Council on Arts, 1972-74; faculty Breadloaf Writers Conf. Middlebury, Vt., 1982; mem. faculty Saltzburg Seminar, Saltzburg, Austria, 1993. Author: (poems) Fruits & Vegetables, 1971, Half Lives, 1973, Loveroot, 1975, At the Edge of the Body, 1979, Ordinary Miracles, 1983, Becoming Light: Poems New and Selected, 1992; (novels) Fear of Flying, 1973, How to Save Your Own Life, 1977, Fanny: Being the True History of the Adventures of Fanny Hackabout-Jones, 1980, Parachutes & Kisses, 1984, Serenissima, 1987, Any Woman's Blues, 1990, (poetry and non-fiction) Witches, 1981, (juvenile) Megan's Book of Divorce, 1984, (memoir) The Devil At Large, 1993, (autobiography) Fear of Fifty, 1994. Woodrow Wilson fellow; recipient Bess Hokin prize Poetry mag., 1971; named Mother of Yr., 1982; Nat. Endowment Arts grantee, 1973. Mem. PEN, Authors Guild U.S.A. (coun. 1975—, pres. 1991-93), Poets and Writers Bd., Writers Guild Am.-West, Poetry Soc. Am. (Alice Faye di Castagnola award 1972), Phi Beta Kappa. Office: K D Burrows 425 Park Ave New York NY 10022-3506

JONG, MAY LANE, administrative aide; b. L.A., Sept. 7, 1951; d. Don Suey and Frances Jong. BS in Bus. Edn., Calif. State U., Long Beach, 1974, MPA, 1992. Clk. typist III police dept. City of Long Beach, 1974-76, sec. police dept., 1977-84, legis. asst. legis. dept., 1984-85, clk. typist IV pers. dept., 1985-86, adminstrv. aide II dept. human resources, 1987—, asst. to dep. city mgr., 1992. Robert M. Odell Endowed scholar Calif. Soc. Mcpl. Fin. Officers, 1991; Patricia Harris Roberts fellow, 1990; cert. Leadership Long Beach, 1994. Am. Soc. for Pub. Adminstrn. (mem. L.A. met. chpt., chpt. liaison Nat. Young Profls. Forum), Western Govt. Rsch. Assn., Mcpl. Mgmt. Assts. So. Calif., Phi Alpha Alpha. Republican. Methodist. Office: City of Long Beach 13th Fl 333 W Ocean Blvd Long Beach CA 90802

JONG, THERESA ANN, human resource executive; b. Chgo., Aug. 27, 1965; d. Ronald Walter and Marilyn Ruth (Krase) W. BS, San Diego State U., 1989. Dir. personnel and facilities Guild Mortgage Co., San Diego, 1988. Vol. Easter Seals Soc. San Diego, 1988—, Am. Heart Assn., 1989—, Zool. Soc. San Diego, 1986—; coord. (ETC) mgmt. employee transp. San Diego Traffic Demand, 1989—. Mem. Pers. Mgmt. Assn. Roman Catholic. Office: Guild Mortgage Co 9160 Gramercy Dr San Diego CA 92123-4020

JONKER, PAMELA LYNN, artist; b. Denver, Apr. 25, 1947; d. William Espy and Geraldine Marie (Plumb) Ingram; m. L. Anton Jonker, Mar. 17, 1968 (div. Feb. 1994); children: Stephanie Lynn, Stacey Marie. BA in Polit. Sci., The Colo. Coll., 1969; postgrad., Calif. State U., Fresno, 1989-92. Artist-sculptor, painter, ceramist, fiber arts Fresno, Calif. and, Espanola, N.Mex., 1979—; devel. coord. Fresno Arts Coun., 1992-93. Fiber artist/quilt hangings, 1980—; wheel-thrown manipulated ceramic bowls, 1992—; author: (exhibit catalog) Calif. State U. Fresno/Phebe Conley Gallery, 1992. Mem. Am. Quilter's Soc., Am. Craft Coun., Fresno Arts Coun., Kappa Alpha Theta. Office: Rt 3 Box 1333-9 Espanola NM 87532

JONKOUSKI, JILL ELLEN, materials scientist, ceramic engineer, educator; b. Chgo.; d. Joseph and Ruth Jonkouski. BS in Ceramic Engring., U. Ill., MS in Ceramic Engring. Former researcher Battelle Meml. Inst., Columbus, Ohio; former ceramic engr. Austenal Dental, Inc., Chgo.; former rsch. scientist BIRL Indsl. Rsch. Lab. Northwestern U., Evanston, Ill.; ceramics mfg. engr., program mgr. conservation fossil rsch. Programs and Facilities Mgmt. divsn. U.S. Dept. Energy, Argonne, Ill., 1991—; past adj. faculty Triton Coll., River Grove, Ill.; presenter Nat. Thermal Spray Conf., 1991, 92, Pacific Coast regional meeting Am. Ceramic Soc., 1994, Coal-Fired Sys. 94, 1994. Mem. Am. Ceramic Soc. (spkr., tech. presenter 1983, 84, chair Chgo.-Milw. sect. 1993-94), U.S. Figure Skating Assn., U. Ill. Alumni Assn. Office: US Dept Energy Program/Facilities Mgmt Div 9800 S Cass Ave Argonne IL 60439-4899

JOOS, OLGA MARTÍN-BALLESTERO DE, Spanish language educator; b. Zaragoza, Spain, May 2, 1944; came to U.S., 1973; d. Luis and Olga Helena (Hernandez) Martin-Ballestero; m. William Joseph Joos, Oct. 9, 1973; children: Catalina, Louis, Olga, William. Grad., U. Zaragoza, Spain, 1969; postgrad., UNF. Substitute lang. tchr. Assumption Sch., 1989-91, Bolles Sch., 1991-93; h.s. Spanish tchr. Douglas Anderson Sch. of Arts, Jacksonville, Fla., 1994—. Home: 2641 River Rd Jacksonville FL 32207

JORDAN, BARBARA C., lawyer, educator, former congresswoman; b. Houston, Feb. 21, 1936; d. and Arlyne J. BA in Polit. Sci. and History magna cum laude, Tex. So. U.; LLB, Boston U., 1959. Bar: Mass. 1959, Tex. 1959. Pvt. practice, adminstrv. asst. to county judge County of Harris, Tex.; mem. Tex. Senate, 1966-72; pres. pro tem, chmn. Labor and Mgmt. Relations Com. and Urban Affairs Study Com.; mem. 93d-95th congresses from 18th Dist. Tex., 1972-78; mem. com. judiciary, com. govt. ops.; mem. spl. task force 94th Congress; mem. steering and policy com. House Democratic Caucus; Lyndon B. Johnson pub. svc. prof. U. Tex., Austin, 1979-82, Lyndon B. Johnson Centennial chair in nat. policy, 1982—; mem. UN panel on multinat. corps. in South Africa and Namibia; keynote speaker Nat. Dem. Conv., 1976; dir. numerous cos. Author: Barbara Jordan: A Self Portrait, 1979; editor (with Elspeth Rostow) The Great Society: A Twenty-Year Critique; host PBS TV series Crisis to Crisis with Barbara Jordan, 1982; contbr. articles to profl. jours. Trustee Henry J. Kaiser Family Found.; mem. presdl. adv. bd. Ambassadorial Appts., 1979-81; hearings officer Nat. Inst. Edn. Hearings minimum competency testing; founder, bd. dirs. People for the Am. Way. Recipient Eleanor Roosevelt Humanities award State of Israel Bonds, 1984, 21st Charles Evans Hughes Gold medal NCCJ, 1987, Harry S. Truman Pub. Svc. award Harry S. Truman Scholarship Found., 1990, Elmer B. Staats Pub. Svc. Careers award, 1990, Tom C. Clark Equal Justice Under Law award, 1991, Bess Wallace Truman award, 1992, Nat. Civil Rights Mus. Freedom award, 1992, Eleanor Roosevelt Val-Kill award, 1992, 77th Spingarn award NAACP, 1992, Nelson Mandela Health and Human Rights award, 1993; named one of Ten Women of Yr., Time mag., 1976, first choice for Women Who Could Be Appointed to Supreme Ct., Redbook mag., 1979, one among 100 Most Influential Women in Am., Ladies Home Jour., 1980, One of 25 Most Influential Woman in Am., World Amanac, 1986, Best Living Orator, Internat. Platform Assn., 1984, One of Most Influential Women of 20th Century, Nat. Women's Hall of Fame, 1993; inducted into Nat. Women's Hall of Fame, 1990, The African-Am. Hall of Fame, 1993; elected to Tex. Women's Hall of Fame, 1984; 1990 edit. Ann. Survey of Am. Law dedicated in her name, 1990. Fellow Am. Bar Found.; mem. ABA, Tex. Bar Assn., Mass. Bar Assn., Houston Bar Assn., D.C. Bar, NAACP, Delta Sigma Theta. Baptist. Office: U Tex Lyndon B Johnson Sch Pub Affairs Austin TX 78713

JORDAN, BARBARA MAY, speech pathologist; b. Camden, N.J., Oct. 11, 1954; d. James T. and Lillian M. (Steventon) J. BS summa cum laude, West Chester State Coll., 1976; postgrad., Temple U., 1978; MA, Trenton State Coll., 1982. Cert. in speech pathology. Speech pathologist Elwyn Inst., Phila., 1977; developer presch. spl. needs program Medford (N.J.) Twp. Bd. Edn., 1977-86; developer speech and lang. dept. for sch.-aged children Tabernacle (N.J.) Bd. Edn., 1978; pvt. practice speech/lang. pathology Shamong, N.J., 1984—. Mem. Am. Speech-Lang.-Hearing Assn. (Continuing Edn. award 1993), N.J. Speech and Lang. Assn., Phi Beta Kappa, Kappa Delta Pi. Office: 384 Indian Mills Rd Shamong NJ 08088

JORDAN, BERNICE BELL, elementary education educator; b. Calvert, Tex.; d. Ocie Wade and Nannie B. (Westbrook) Bell; m. William B. Jordan, Sept. 28, 1956; children: Beverly, Terrence, Keith Jordan. BA, San Jose State Coll., 1959, MA, 1985; student, Prairie View A and M, Tex. Western Coll. Cert. elem. edn., fine arts, multi-cultural. Writer curriculum guide, fine arts Alum Rock Union Elem. Sch. Dist., San Jose, Calif.; writer sch. plan Goss Elem.; tchr. 3rd grade Alum Rock Union Elem. Sch. Dist., San Jose; adv. com., tchr.-cons. San Jose Area Writing Project, San Jose U., 1992—. Mem. Assn. for Supervision and Curriculum Devel., Alum Rock Edn. Assn., Calif. Tchrs. Assn., Calif. Reading Assn., Calif. Elem. Edn. Assn., Santa Clara County Reading Coun., NEA, Alpha Delta Kappa. Home: 3282 Fronda Dr San Jose CA 95148-2015

JORDAN, BETTY SUE, retired special education educator; b. Lafayette, Tenn., Sept. 4, 1920; d. Aubrey Lee and Geneva (Freeman) West; m. Bill Jordan, Oct. 22, 1950; 1 child, L. Nicha. Student, David Lipscomb Coll., 1939-41; BS, U. Tenn., 1943; registered dietitian Duke U. Hosp., 1945; MEd, Clemson U., 1973. Dietitian U. Ala., Tuscaloosa, 1945-46, Duke U., Durham, N.C., 1946-48, Stetson U., DeLand, Fla., 1948-50, Furman U., Greenville, S.C., 1950-52; elem. tchr. Greenville County Schs., S.C., 1952-66, tchr. orthopedically handicapped, 1966-85; with Shriners Hosp. for Crippled Children Sch.; pres. Robert Morris S.S. class U. Meth. Ch., 1992. Mem. NEA, Assn. Childhood Edn. (treas. 1980-85), United Daus. Confederacy (pres. Greenville chpt. 1978—), Greenville Woman's Club (exec. bd. 1991—), Lake Forest Garden Club (pres. 1970-71, 77-79, 80-81, historian 1981-87, 1st v.p., 1991-92, Woman of Yr. awards 1991, 92, Rachel McKaughan Horticulture award 1992, Lois Russel Arrangement award 1993), Greater Greenville Rose Soc. (pres. 1983-84), Am. Rose Soc. (accredited rose judge 1986, rose arrangement judge, cons., Rosarian), Clarice Wilson Garden Club (pres. 1987-89, Woman of Yr. 1991, Award for Arrangements), Delta Kappa Gamma (pres. Tau chpt. 1976-78, state chmn. communications 1979-81, state chmn. rsch. 1983-85, leadership/mgmt. seminar Austin, Tex. 1989), Kappa

Kappa Iota (state pres. 1972-73, conclave pres. 1983-85), Democrat. Methodist. Avocations: collecting antiques, growing roses, flower arranging. Home: 21 Lisa Dr Greenville SC 29615-1350

JORDAN, BRENDA LOUVA, gerontology clinical nurse specialist; b. Milford, Conn., Oct. 23, 1948; d. Elton Wesley and Grace Louva (Simonson) Latham; m. Paul James Danz, Sept. 6, 1969 (div. July 1979); 1 child, Heather Diane Danz; m. James Robert Jordan, Apr. 15, 1981; 1 child, Nathaniel James Jordan. BS, U. Bridgeport, 1970; MS, U. N.H., 1991. From charge nurse medicine to charge nurse psychiatry West Haven (Conn.) VA Hosp., 1970-72; staff nurse psychiatry Yale New Haven Hosp., 1972-74, head nurse neuropsychiatry, 1974-77; nursing instr. Mary Hitchcock Meml. Hosp. Sch. Nursing, Hanover, N.H., 1977-78; asst. prof. nursing N.H. Tech. Coll., Claremont, 1978-81; cons. nursing edn. Cornish, N.H., 1981-82; nursing supr. Mary Hitchcock Meml. Hosp., Hanover, 1982-83, dir. nursing, 1983-85, nursing supr., 1985-91, nursing edn. coord., 1992—; dir. nursing Kendal at Hanover, 1991-92; nursing instr. nursing update Office of Continuing Edn. in Health Scis., Dartmouth-Hitchcock Med. Ctr., Hanover, 1981, 82, 83, nurse educator varied workshops, 1984—; planner/coord. New Eng. Grad. Nursing Edn. Consortium, 1993—. Asst. editor (newsletter) Rsch. Rev.: Studies in Nursing Practice, 1989-91. Bd. dirs. Cornish (N.H.) Sch. Bd., 1988-92, chair, 1992—; troop leader Girl Scouts U.S., Cornish, 1981-87, community chair, 1981-87. Mem. N.H. Nurses Assn. (Grafton county dir. 1980-82, chairperson ad hoc com. econ. and gen. welfare 1982-83, chairperson commn. on econ. and gen. welfare 1983-84), Gerontologic Soc. Am., Sigma Theta Tau. Democrat. Methodist.

JORDAN, JEANETTE ELISABETH, human resources administrator; b. Munich, Germany, Apr. 9, 1953; came to U.S., 1972; m. James Morton Jordan, Apr. 10, 1974; 1 child, Corinne Elisabeth. AA in Liberal Arts, Atlantic C.C., 1976; BS in Comms., U. Minn., 1980. Cert. indsl. rels. adminstr. Human rels. generalist Unisys Corp., Eagan, Minn., 1978—. Mem. Soc. Logistics Engrs. (vice chair ops. 1986-87, 89-90, exec. bd. 1986-89, membership com. 1988-89, Chpt. Chmn. award 1986), Twin Cities Pers. Orgn. Home: 4397 N Woodgate Ln Eagan MN 55122-2281

JORDAN, JENNIFER CAMERY, Olympic committee official, lawyer; b. Dayton, Ohio, May 9, 1963; d. J. Richard Jordan and Anne Scott Camery. BA in Sports Promotion, Ind. U., 1986, JD cum laude, 1992. Bar: N.Y. 1993. Mem. press ops. staff Liberty Weekend, N.Y.C., 1986; mktg. mgr. The Maple Ctr., Beverly Hills, Calif., 1986-89; mgr. main press ctr. The Goodwill Games, Seattle, 1990; mem. press advance staff The White House, Washington, 1990-92; dir. media svcs. World Univ. Games, Buffalo, 1992-93; mgr. venue press Atlanta Com. for Olympic Games, 1993—; assoc. instr. Ind. U. Sch. Law, Bloomington, 1991-92; spl. events cons. Perelman, Pioneer & Co., L.A., 1989—, The Harbor Festival Found., N.Y.C., 1992—, Martin Luther King, Jr. Fed. Holiday Commn., Atlanta, 1993—. Mem. N.Y. State Bar Assn., Ind. U. Alumni Assn., Phi Delta Phi. Home: 303 River Glen Dr Roswell GA 30075 Office: Atlanta Com for Olympic Games 250 Williams St Ste 6000 Atlanta GA 30303

JORDAN, JUDITH VICTORIA, clinical psychologist, educator; b. Milw., July 28, 1943; d. Claus and Charlotte (Backus) J.; m. William M. Redpath, Aug. 11, 1973. AB, Brown U., 1965; MA, Harvard U., 1968, PhD, 1973. Diplomate Am. Bd. Profl. Psychology. Psychologist Human Relations Service, Wellesley, Mass., 1971-73; assoc. psychologist McLean Hosp., Belmont, Mass., 1978-93, psychologist, 1993—, dir. women's studies program, 1988—, dir. tng. in psychology, 1991, dir. Women's Treatment Network, 1992—; vis. scholar Stone Ctr. Wellesley Coll., 1985—; asst. prof. psychiatry Harvard Med. Sch., 1988—; cons. in field. Author: Empathy and Self Boundries, 1984, Women's Growth in Connection, 1991, (with others) The Self in Relation, 1986; editor, author: Relational Self in Women. Mem. Am. Psychol. Assn., Mass. Psychol. Assn. (bd. dirs. 1983-85), Phi Beta Kappa. Office: McLean Hosp 115 Mill St Belmont MA 02178-1048

JORDAN, KAREN LEIGH, travel editor; b. Freeport, Tex., Nov. 20, 1954; d. Matt Culum and Laura Louise (English) Arrington; m. William David Jordan, May 8, 1982; 1 child, Lauren Kathryn. BA in Journalism magna cum laude, Tex. A&M U., 1976. Intern Wall St. Jour., Dallas, summer 1976; asst. news editor Abilene (Tex.) Reporter-News, 1976-77; sports copy editor Dallas Morning News, 1977-79, asst. travel editor, 1979-81, travel editor, 1981—; judge journalism competition Univ. Interscholastic League, Tex., 1976. Contbg. writer (guidebook) Fodor's Tex., 1983—; writer (guidebook) Fodor's Dallas-Fort Worth, 1983—; copy editor Dallas-Ft. Worth Metroplex Football mag., 1978-80. Teaching asst. Garden Ridge Ch. of Christ, Lewisville, Tex., 1988—. Recipient State Headline Writing award AP Mng. Editors, 1977; named one of Outstanding Young Women of Am., 1982. Mem. Soc. Am. Travel Writers (writing, editing and photography awards 1981—), Phi Kappa Phi, Sigma Delta Chi, Alpha Lambda Delta. Office: Dallas Morning News Comm Ctr PO Box 655237 Dallas TX 75265-5237

JORDAN, LINDA SUSAN DARNELL, elementary school educator; b. Greenville, Tex., Sept. 5, 1955; d. Charles Albert and Dorothy Nell (Everheart) Darnell; m. Mark Alan Jordan, Sept. 1, 1979; children: Sarah Tison, Michael Albert. BE, East Tex. State U., 1977. Cert. elem. edn. tchr. 1-8, secondary edn. tchr. 9-12. County ext. agt. Tex. A & M U., Wise County, Tex., 1977-81; tchr. Decatur (Tex.) Ind. Sch. Dist., 1981-87, 91—; tech. planning com. Decatur Ind. Sch. Dist., 1991—, campus improvement com., 1992—. Sun. sch. educator First United Meth. Ch., Decatur, 1992—, acolyte coord., 1990-91, Sun. sch. coord., 1989-90; mem. Decatur Jr. Woman's Club, 1977-79. Recipient Apple of the Month award Twin Lakes Hosp., 1992. Mem. Tex. Classroom Tchrs. Orgn. Home: Rte 2 Box 478 Decatur TX 76234 Office: Decatur Elem Sch 1300 Deer Park Rd Decatur TX 76234

JORDAN, LOIS HEYWOOD, real estate developer; b. Salem, Oreg., Apr. 22, 1913; d. Frank Hall and Winnifred E.(Heywood) Reeves; m. Edmund A. Jordan, Nov. 19, 1936 (dec. Dec. 1982); children: Jolie Mae, E. Andrew Jr., Jennifer Loie. Student, Oreg. State U., 1931-33, N.W. Sch. of Art, Portland, Oreg. Dress designer Portland, 1933-36, real estate developer, 1955—; pres. Jordan Developers, Portland, 1987—. Pres. Alameda Sch. PTA, Portland, 1960; v.p. Ainsworth Sch. PTA, Portland, 1964; pres. Alameda Garden Club, Portland, 1956, Women's Convalescent Home, Portland, 1957; v.p. sec. SW Hills Residential League, Portland, 1968; v.p. Friends Marquam Ravine, Portland, 1976; bd. dirs. Friendly House, Portland, 1986. Mem. Sons and Daus. of Oregon Pioneers (bd. dirs.), Multnomah Athletic Club, Pi Beta Phi (mgr. Oreg. State chpt. 1932-33). Republican. Prebyterian.

JORDAN, LORI ANN, oncological nurse; b. Frackville, Pa., May 3, 1960; d. Louis and Florence (Kryscio) J. Diploma, Pottsville Hosp. Sch. Nursing, 1981. Inpatient oncology nurse Jefferson Univ. Hosp., Phila., 1981-84; outpatient chemo-therapy nurse I. Brodsky and Assocs./Hahnemann U., Phila., 1984-86; staff clinician Caremark Homecare, Malvern, Pa., 1986-88, nursing supr., 1988-90, nurse mgr., 1990-93; regional infusion clin. program mgr. Olsten Kimberly Quality Care, Broomall, Pa., 1993-94, divsnl. infusion program mgr., 1994—. Producer: (ednl. video) A World of Difference, 1989; author teaching manual: A World of Difference, 1989. Mem. AIDS waiver com. State of Pa., Harrisburg, 1988-89. Mem. Intravenous Nursing Soc., Oncology Nurses Soc. Democrat. Home: 271 Windermere Ave Lansdowne PA 19050 Office: Olsten Kimberly Quality Care 660 Clark Ave King of Prussia PA 19406

JORDAN, LORNA, news director; b. Washington, D.C., Nov. 3, 1958; d. Edwin C. and Mary (Kahle) J.; m. John A. Romano, Aug. 30, 1986. PhB, Miami U., 1981. News reporter Sta. WING-AM, Dayton, Ohio, 1981-84, Sta. WHIO-AM, Dayton, Ohio, 1984-85, Sta. WKRC-AM, Cin., 1985-87; from news reporter to news dir. Sta. WVXU-FM, Cin., news dir., 1988—; stringer Nat. Pub. Radio, Washington, 1987—, CBS News, N.Y., 1987-88; instr. Xavier U., 1991—. Bd. dirs. YWCA, Kettering, Ohio, 1985-87; bd. dirs. statehouse com. Ohio Ednl. Broadcasting. Mem. Soc. for Profl. Journalists, Kappa Delta. Office: WVXU FM Radio Station 3800 Victory Pky Cincinnati OH 45207-1035

JORDAN, MARY LEE, bookkeeper; b. Cin., Oct. 22, 1931; m. T. Paul Jordan, July 29, 1975 (dec. 1988); children: Aaron, Marc, Carrie. BS in Edn., U. Cin., 1965, AA, 1984. First grade tchr. St. Louis County, Mo., 1963-65; first grade, kindergarten tchr. Cin., 1965-80; sec. personnel dept. Longview State Hosp., 1983; word processor Nat. Inst. Occupational Safety & Health, 1984; bookkeeper L. Levine & Co., Inc., 1985-88; Bd. dirs., membership chmn., newsletter co-producer Cin. Alliance for the Mentally Ill, 1983-86; park ranger U.S. Nat. Park Svc., Cin., 1993—. Author: History of Camp Dennison, Ohio, 1956. Pres. Cin. chpt. Zero Population Growth, 1976. Mem. AAUW (v.p. Cin. br. 1994—, bd. dirs. 1970-71), LWV (pres. N.C. br. 1994—, program coord. 1970-71), Am. Horse Show Assn., Ohioana Libr. Assn., DAR (vice-regent, mus. trustee Mariemont, Ohio chpt. 1988-89, regent 1990-91). Home: 27 Sherry Rd Cincinnati OH 45215

JORDAN, MICHELLE DENISE, lawyer; b. Chgo., Oct. 29, 1954; d. John A. and Margaret (O'Dood) J. BA in Polit. Sci., Loyola U, Chgo., 1974; JD, U. Mich., 1977. Bar. Ill. 1977, U.S. Dist. Ct. (no. dist.) Ill. 1978. Asst. state's atty. State's Attys. Office, Chgo., 1977-82; pvt. practice Chgo., 1983-84; with Ill. Atty. Gen.'s Office, Chgo., 1984-90, chief environ. control div., 1988-90; ptnr. Hopkins & Sutter, Chgo., 1991-93; apptd. dep. regional adminstr. region 5 U.S. EPA, Chgo., 1994—. Active Operation Push, Chgo., 1971—. Recipient Kizzy Image Achievement and Svc. award, 1990; named in Am.'s Top 100 Bus. and Profl. Women, Dollars and SenseMag., Chgo., 1988. Mem. Ill. Bar Assn., Chgo. Bar Assn. (bd. mgrs., chmn. criminal law com. 1987-88, mem. hearing divsn., jud. evaluation com. 1987-88, exec. coun. 1987-88), Cook County Bar Assn., Nat. Bar Assn., Alpha Sigma Nu. Democrat. Baptist. Office: US EPA 19th Flr 77 W Jackson Chicago IL 60604

JORDAN, MICHELLE HENRIETTA, public relations company executive; b. Sussex, Eng., Sept. 19, 1948; came to U.S., 1975; d. Raymond Cameron and Liliane (Ambar) J.; m. Billy Owens, 1994. Student, Sorbonne, 1966-67. With Coordinated Mktg. Services Ltd., London, 1967-71; dir. Spectrum Public Relations, London, 1971-74; with Rowland Co., N.Y.C., 1975-87, exec. v.p., 1987-91; sr. v.p., mng. dir. mktg. svcs. div. Hill and Knowlton, N.Y.C., 1991-94; prin. The Dilenschneider Group, N.Y.C., 1994; v.p. Digital Pictures, San Mateo, Calif., 1994—. Mem. Mayor N.Y.C. Commn. Status Women, 1980-86; bd. dirs. New Dramatists, Relition in Am. Life, 1992-94. Recipient Matrix award N.Y. Women in Communications, 1990. Mem. Players Club. Office: Digital Pictures 1825 S Grant San Mateo CA 94402

JORDAN, SANDRA, public relations professional; b. Pasadena, Tex., Oct. 10, 1952; d. Royal Wilson and Kathryn Ann (Speck) J.; m. William Anderson Mintz, Aug. 10, 1974 (div. 1980). B of Journalism, U. Tex., 1974. Reporter Austin (Tex.) American Statesman, 1974-76; news dir. KTAE Radio, Taylor, Tex., 1974-76; dir. of news and info. Inst. of Texan Cultures, San Antonio, 1976-82; pub. rels. dir. San Antonio Mus. Assn., 1982-83; dir. news/info. Univ. Tex., San Antonio, 1983-86; sr. publicist Rogers & Cowan, Inc., Washington, 1986-87; communications dir. NARAL, Washington, 1987-88; assoc. Parker, Vogelsingers & Assocs., Washington, 1988-90; pub. rels. and mktg. dir. Girl Scout Coun., Washington, 1990—; pub. rels. cons. YWCA, Washington; judge, ad contest, Women in Communications, Iowa, 1992; workshop organizer Washington Ind. Writers, 1990; mem. publicity com. CASE Conf., San Antonio, 1986, Smithsonian Nat. Assoc. Prog., San Antonio, 1980. Contbg. author: Folk Art in Texas, 1985. Prog. cons. KLRN-TV (pub. TV) San Antonio, 1981, 82; del. Dem. Nat. Conv., Taylor, 1976; docent Kennedy Ctr., Washington, 1989. Recipient Apex '91, '92 and '93 awards, Communications Concepts, 191, Design honors, Tex. Assn. of Mus., 1993. Mem. Women in Communications (D.C. chpt., mem. literacy project 1992, mentoring program), Women in Advt. and Mktg., Am. Soc. Assn. Execs., The Writers Ctr. Home: 6305 E Halbert Rd Bethesda MD 20817 Office: Girl Scout Council of Nation's Capitol 2233 Wisconsin Ave NW Washington DC 20007-4104

JORDAN, SANDRA DICKERSON, law educator; b. Phila., Dec. 3, 1951; m. Byron Neal Jordan, July 21, 1973; children: Nedra Catherine, Byron Neal II. BS in Edn., Wilberforce U., 1973; JD, U. Pitts., 1979. Bar: Pa. 1979, U.S. Dist. Ct. (we. dist.) Pa. 1979, U.S. Ct. Appeals (3d cir.) 1979. Asst. U.S. atty. U.S. Dept. Justice, Pitts., 1979-88; assoc. ind. counsel Ind. Counsel-Iran/Contra, Washington, 1988-91; prof. U. Pitts. Sch. Law, 1988—, assoc. dean, 1993—; mem. hearing com. disciplinary bd. Pa. Supreme Ct., Pitts., 1989—; lectr. U.S. Dept. Justice, Pa. Trial Judges Assn., Acad. Trial Lawyers, Pa. Bar Inst. Author tng. video in field, 1982; contbr. articles to profl. jours. Vice pres. Health and Welfare Planning Commn., Pitts., 1986-89; mem. Program to Aid Citizen Enterprise, Pitts., 1983—. Mem. ABA (mem. white collar crimes com. 1988—), Homer S. Brown Law Assn., Allegheny County Bar Assn., Nat. Bar Assn., Urban League (v.p. Pitts. chpt. 1988-90), Alpha Kappa Mu, Alpha Kappa Alpha. Office: U Pitts Law Sch 3900 Forbes Ave Pittsburgh PA 15213

JORDAN, SHARIE CECILIA, industrial artist; b. Grand Rapids, Mich., Sept. 12, 1961; d. Erwin Francis and Ardis Jean (Gilbert) Schmuker; m. Thomas William Jordan, Dec. 4, 1982. Fashion cons. Mullberry Bush, Houghton Lake, Mich., 1982-84; freelance artist Houghton Lake, Mich., 1984-90; owner Jordan Illustration and Design, Houghton Lake, Mich., 1991—; cons. Buyers Guide Weekly, Houghton, 1988-90. Founding chmn. Annual Meml. Day Parade, Houghton Lake, 1992—. Recipient Emily Hilton-Janice Reeney Art award, 1979. Mem. Eagle Aux. (chaplain 1991-92, activity chmn. 1991-93, trustee 1992-94, v.p. 1994—, Outstanding Vol. Work and Svc. award 1991-92, MRS-Eagle award 1991-92).

JORDAN, SHARON LEE, librarian, educator; b. Long Beach, Calif., Jan. 19, 1946; d. Harold Wilson and Nina Pearl (Campbell) Chapman; m. Frank Cody Jordan, Jan. 1, 1984. BA, Calif. State U., Chico, 1968, MA, 1975; MLS, San Jose State U., 1980. Life K-14 teaching credentials, Calif. Tchr. Coacti-Anderson (Calif.) Union High Sch., 1969-79; data processor, sr. computer programmer Lockheed Missiles & Space Co., Sunnyvale, Calif., 1980-83; dist. libr. Highland Sch. Dist., Cowiche, Wash., 1983-88; libr., tchr. Port Townsend (Wash.) Sch. Dist., 1988—. Mem. NEA, Wash. Edn. Assn. (former v.p., sec., treas., grievance chmn., assembly rep., head negotiator Cowiche), Wash. Libr. Media Assn. (conf. presenter), Escapees (winter grievance chmn.), Ladies Aux. VFW, Order Ea. Star, Phi Kappa Phi, Phi Delta Kappa. Republican. Home: PO Box 429 Chimacum WA 98325 Office: Port Townsend High Sch 1500 Van Ness Port Townsend WA 98368

JORDAN, SHIRLEY DRAKE, writer; b. Overton, Tex., Feb. 7, 1935; d. Clarence Troy and Ina L. (Brewer) Drake; m. Joseph Robert Jordan, Mar. 21, 1952; children: Sherrill Patrice Jordan Colarusso, Martin Drake. Student, Camden Clark Sch. Nursing, Parkersburg (W.Va.) Bus. Coll. Asst. State Farm Ins. Agy.; county editor Times Leader Newspaper, Martins Ferry, Ohio, 1964-65; office nurse Curtiss Clinic, Chagrin Falls, Ohio, 1973-78, Fleming, Blaylock and Higgins Med. Office, Winter Park, Fla., 1980-81; with State Farm Ins., J. Jordan Agy., Saint Augustine, Fla. Author column Here's To You Kids for Salem, Ill. newspaper, 1947-49; contbr. articles, poems to profl. publs. Pres. Jr. Women's Club, Grayville, Ill., 1961-62; co-dir. ann. event St. Augustine Writers Conf. Recipient award Am. Legion, 1949, Woman of Yr. award Beta Sigma Phi, 1975. Mem. Am. Poetry Assn., Marsh Creek Women's Assn. (pres. 1991—), Am. Bus. Women's Assn. (v.p., State Bull. award 1983), St. Augustine Scriveners Soc. (founding mem.), Marsh Creek Country Club (bd. dirs. 1992-94). Home: 309 Amelia Ct Saint Augustine FL 32084-7658 Office: State Farm Ins J Jordan Agy 1011 Ala Beach Blvd Saint Augustine FL 32084

JORDAN, SHIRLEY JEAN, psychologist; b. Oblong, Ill., May 4, 1947; d. Melvin Franklin and Bernice (Shepard) J. BA in Psychology summa cum laude, John Wesley Coll., 1969; MA in Ednl. Psychology, Mich. State U., 1971; PhD in Counseling Psychology, Tex. Woman's U., 1985. Lic. psychologist, Tex. Instr. social scis. John Wesley Coll., Owosso, Mich., 1969-72; dean of women John Wesley Coll., Owasso, Mich., 1970-72; coord. vol. svcs., juvenile caseworker Genesee County Probate Ct., Flint, Mich., 1972-74; grad. teaching fellow psychology dept. Tex. Woman's U., Dallas, 1974-79, assoc. counselor Counseling Ctr., 1976; adminstr. neuropsychol. testing North Tex. State U., Denton, 1978-79; clin. intern. Terrell (Tex.) State Hosp., 1979-80; psychometrician, therapist Office of Dr. Stricklin pvt. practice, 1979-84; psychotherapist Office of Dr. Mccreary pvt. practice, 1984-85; pvt. practice counseling psychologist, 1985-87; founder counseling ctr. Prince of Peace Luth. Ch., Carrollton, 1986-87; sr. lectr. psychology dept. U. Bophuthatswana, Mmabatho, 1988-91; pvt. practice, 1991—; radio talk show host Bophuthatswana Radio, Mmabatho, 1990-91. Mem. APA, South African Psychol. Assn. Home: 18050 Kelly Blvd # 812 Dallas TX 75287 Office: 3610 N Josey Ln Ste 221 Carrollton TX 75007

JORDAN, SUSIE LINTON, electronics company buyer and planner; b. Hattiesburg, Miss., Mar. 3, 1955; d. Jack and Gwendolyn Yvonne Linton; m. Thomas G. Jordan, Jan. 19, 1973; children: Tasha Dawn, Chrystal Skye. Grad. H.S., Hattiesburg. Inventory control coord. Hercules Inc., Hattiesburg, 1977-90; material control specialist Avex Electronics, Huntsville, Ala., 1990; material planner Avex Electronics, Huntsville, 1990-91, sys. applications admistr., 1991, prodn. and bus. planner, 1991-92, sr. bus. planner, 1992-93, sr. bus. unit planner, 1993-94, account specialist II, 1994, sr. buyer, planner, 1994—. Mem. NAFE, Nat. Mgmt. Assn. (Avex chpt.). Baptist. Home: 24959 Bubba Trail Athens AL 35611 Office: Avex Electronics 4807 Bradford Dr Huntsville AL 35807

JORDEN, ELEANOR HARZ, linguist, educator; b. N.Y.C.; d. William George and Eleanor (Funk) Harz; m. William J. Jorden, Mar. 3, 1944 (div.); children: William Temple, Eleanor Harz, Marion Telva. A.B., Bryn Mawr Coll., 1942; M.A., Yale U., 1943, Ph.D., 1950; D.Litt. (hon.), Williams Coll., 1982; D.H.L. (hon.), Knox Coll., 1985; D. Langs. (hon.), Middlebury Coll., 1991; D. Univ. (hon.), U. Stirling, Scotland, 1993. Instr. Japanese Yale U., 1943-46, 47-48; dir. Japanese lang. program and Fgn. Service Inst. Lang. Sch., Am. Embassy, Tokyo, 1950-55; sci. linguist Fgn. Service Inst., Dept. State, Washington, 1959-69; acting head Far East langs., 1961-64, chmn., 1964-67, 69, chmn. Vietnamese lang. div., 1967-69; vis. prof. linguistics Cornell U., 1969-70, prof., 1970-87, Mary Donlon Alger prof. linguistics, 1974-87, prof. emeritus, 1987—; Bernhard disting. vis. prof. Williams Coll., 1985-86; vis. prof. Williams Coll., 1986-87, adj. prof., 1987-92; dir. Japanese FALCON program, 1972-87; Univ. prof., Disting. fellow Nat. Fgn. Lang. Ctr. Sch. Advanced Internat. Studies Johns Hopkins U., 1987-91; acad. dir. Exchange: Japan's Tchr. Tng. Inst., 1988—, for high sch. tchrs., 1993—; sr. cons. prep. framework Japanese lang. curriculum and Japanese coll. bd. exam, 1991-93; dir. SPENG Program, 1980—; co-dir. Survey on Japanese Lang. Study, 1988-92; guest scholar Wilson Ctr. Smithsonian Instn., 1982; cons., permanent mem. exec. com. Nat. Assn. Self-Instructional Lang. Programs, pres., 1977-78, 84-85; mem. Fulbright-Hays Com. on Internat. Exchange Scholars, 1972-75; mem. area adv. com. for East Asia, 1972-76; chmn. Social Sci. Research Council Task Force on Japanese Lang. Tng., 1976-78; mem. adv. com. Japan Found., 1979-81; mem. Lang. Attrition Project, 1981-87; advisor Centre for Japanese Studies, Stirling U., Scotland, 1988-92; mem. Yale U. Coun. com. Langs. and Lit., 1990—. Author: (with Bernard Bloch) Spoken Japanese, 1945, Syntax of Modern Colloquial Japanese, 1955, Gateway to Russian, 1961, Beginning Japanese, Part 1, 1962, Part 2, 1963, (with Sheehan, Quang and others) Basic Vietnamese, vols. I, II, 1965, (with Quang) Vietnamese Familiarization Course, 1969, (with Hamako Chaplin) Reading Japanese, 1976, (with Mari Noda) Japanese: The Spoken Language, part 1, 1987, part 2, 1988, part 3, 1990, (with Richard Lambert) Japanese Language Instruction in the U.S.: Resources, Practice and Investment Strategic, 1992. Decorated Order of Precious Crown Emperor of Japan, 1985; recipient Superior Svc. award Dept. State, 1965, Japan Found. and Social Sci. Rsch. Coun. sr. fellow, 1976, Toyota award Twentieth Anniversary Fund grantee, 1978; Japan Found prize, 1985, Papalia award for Excellence Tchr. Tng., 1993, N.E. Conf. award Disting. Svc. and Leadership in Profession, 1994. Mem. Assn. Asian Studies (v.p. 1979-80, pres. 1980-81), Linguistic Soc. Am., Am. Council Tchrs. Fgn. Langs., Nat. Assn. Self-Instrnl. Language Programs (pres. 1978, 85, disting. dir. 1991—), Assn. Tchrs. Japanese (exec. com., pres. 1978-84), Japan Soc. N.Y. (bd. dirs. 1982-88). Office: 3300 Darby Rd Ste 1302 Haverford PA 19041-1067

JORGENSEN, ANN, farmer; b. Cedar Rapids, Iowa, Sept. 16, 1940; d. Kenneth Edward and Velma Ann (Baumhoefener) Fry; m. Marlyn L. Jorgensen, Feb. 27, 1961; children: Christopher, Peter, Timothy, Jennifer. BA, U. Iowa, 1962. Lic. commodity broker. Tax acct. Bill Burrell Tax Svc., Urbana, Iowa, 1968-70, Hansen Acctg., Vinton, Iowa, 1970-75; commodity broker First Mid. Am., Cedar Rapids, 1975-85; owner Lakeview Enterprises, Osage Beach, Mo., 1975-85; v.p., treas. Timberlane Hogs, Ltd., Garrison, Iowa, 1971—; mng. ptnr., owner Jorg-Anna Farms, Garrison, 1963—; pres., founder Farm Home Offices, Vinton, 1981—; bd. dirs. Farm Bureau Mutual Funds, Des Moines; commr. Interstate Agrl. Grain Commn. Midwest Compact, 1986-88; mem. Agriculture Products Adv. Bd., Des Moines, 1990—; speaker in field. Author: Put PaperWork in its Place, 1982; contbr. articles to profl. jours. Mem., chair Iowa Arts Coun., 1973-79; regent Iowa Bd. Regents, 1979-85; dir., pres. Iowa Alcoholic Beverages Commr., Des Moines, 1985-88; nat. chair Tauke for U.S. Senate, Iowa, 1987-88; bd. dirs. Iowa Dept. Econ. Devel., 1988—; chair bd. Iowa Rural Devel. Coun., 1991—. Named to Iowa Vol. Hall of Fame, 1989. Mem. Vinton Am. Assn. U. Women (various offices 1980—), Iowa Pub. TV Found. (sec. 1987—). Home: 1965 64th St Garrison IA 52229-9647 Office: Farm Home Offices PO Box 840 Vinton IA 52349-0840

JÖRGENSEN, BETH ELLEN, Spanish language educator; b. S.I., N.Y., Oct. 11, 1953; d. Charles William and Dorothy (Gralow) J.; m. Thomas Scott Covell; children: Megan J., Benjamin J. BA in Spanish with high honors, Oberlin Coll., 1975; MA in Spanish, U. Wis., 1978, PhD in Spanish-Am. Lit., 1986. Teaching asst. U. Wis., Madison, 1976-82, lectr. dept. Spanish and Portuguese, 1982-83; asst. prof. Spanish U. Rochester, N.Y., 1986-93, assoc. prof. Spanish, 1993—, chair dept. modern langs. and cultures, 1994—; assoc. chair undergrad. programs modern langs. and cultures U. Rochester, 1993-94, undergrad. advisor Spanish, mem. steering com. Multimedia Ctr., mem. study abroad com. Coll. Arts and Scis., 1993-94, dean's fellow, 1987-88; assoc. Susan B. Anthony Ctr. for Women's Studies, mem. seminar and speakers com., 1992-94; manuscript appraiser U. Tex. Press, U. Ariz. Press; book reviewer Hispanic Review, Letras Femeninas; presenter in field. Author: The Writing of Elena Poniatowska: Engaging Dialogues, 1994; contbr. articles to profl. jours. Vilas fellow U. Wis., 1978-79, Dipman Grad. fellow Oberlin Coll., 1984-85. Mem. MLA, Am. Assn. Tchrs. Spanish and Portuguese, L.Am. Studies Assn., Midwest MLA, N.E. MLA, New England Coun. L.Am. Studies, Assn. de Literatura Femenina Hispánica, Feministas Unidas, Phi Beta Kappa (Iota of N.Y., chpt. pres. 1992-94). Office: U Rochester Modern Langs and Cultures Rochester NY 14627

JORGENSEN, ELAINE MARION, psychologist, educator; b. Bklyn., Nov. 17, 1958; d. James Walter and Marion Doris (Faulstich) J.; 1 child, Evan Jay Stern. BS, Pace U., 1980, MS, 1982, D of Psychology, 1986. Lic. psychologist, N.Y., N.J.. Sch. psychologist Oceanside (N.Y.) Sch. Dist., 1982-84; adj. psychology instr., asst., then assoc. prof. Pace U., N.Y.C., 1982—; mgmt. trainer, cons. Mitchell & Assocs. Cons. Firm, Caldwell, N.J., 1982—; staff psychologist JFK Med. Ctr., Edison, N.J., 1986-92, sr. psychologist, 1992-94. Mem. Nat. Assn. Sch. Psychologists (speaker), Am. Psychol. Assn. (speaker).

JORGENSEN, JUDITH ANN, psychiatrist; b. Parris Island, S.C.; d. George Emil and Margaret Georgia Jorgensen; BA, Stanford U., 1963; MD, U. Calif., 1968; m. Ronald Francis Crown, July 11, 1970. Intern, Meml. Hosp., Long Beach, 1969-70; resident County Mental Health Services, San Diego, 1970-73; staff psychiatrist Children and Adolescent Services, San Diego, 1973-78; practice medicine specializing in psychiatry, La Jolla, Calif., 1973—; staff psychiatrist County Mental Health Services of San Diego, 1973-78, San Diego State U. Health Services, 1985-87; psychiat. cons. San Diego City Coll., 1973-78, 85-86; asst. prof. dept. psychiatry U. Calif., 1978—, assoc. prof. dept. psychiatry, 1991—; chmn. med. quality rev. com. Dist. XIV, State of Calif., 1982-83. Mem. Am. Psychiat. Assn., San Diego Soc. Psychiat. Physicians (chmn. membership com. 1976-78, v.p. 1978-80, fed. legis. rep. 1985-87, fellowship com. 1989), Am. Soc. Adolescent Psychiatry, San Diego Soc. Adolescent Psychiatry (pres. 1981-82), Calif. Med. Assn. (former alternate del.), Soc. Sci. Study of Sex, San Diego Soc. Sex Therapy and Edn. (cert. sex therapist), San Diego County Med. Soc. (credentials com. 1982-84). Club: Rowing. Office: 470 Nautilus St Ste 211 La Jolla CA 92037-5970

JORGENSEN, JUDITH STRONG, public relations executive; b. Los Angeles, May 9, 1959; d. James Knox and Mary Elizabeth (Leonard) Strong; m. Gregory Arnold Jorgensen, Apr. 25, 1987. AB in Comparative Lit., Occidental Coll., 1981; MS in Journalism, Northwestern U., 1982. With Harcourt Brace Jovanovich, N.Y.C., 1983-84, Esquire Mag. Group Inc.,

N.Y.C., 1984-87; mgr. pub. rels. Esquire Mag., N.Y.C., 1987; group mgr. pub. relations Hearst Mags., N.Y.C., 1987-88; mgr. publicity Condé Nast Publs. Inc., N.Y.C., 1988-89; dir. communications Mag. Pubs. of Am., N.Y.C., 1989—. Mem. Pub. Rels. Soc. Am., N.Y. Women in Communications, N.Y. Jr. League. Office: Mag Pubs of Am 575 Lexington Ave New York NY 10022-6102

JORGENSEN, LOU ANN BIRKBECK, social worker; b. Park City, Utah, May 14, 1931; d. Robert John and Lillian Pearl (Langford) Birkbeck; student Westminster Coll., 1949-51; B.S., U. Utah, 1953, M.S.W., 1972, D.S.W., 1979; grad. Harvard Inst. Ednl. Mgmt., 1983; m. Howard Arnold Jorgensen, June 9, 1954; children: Gregory Arnold, Blake John, Paul Clayton. Social work adminstr. nursing home demonstration project, dept. family and community medicine U. Utah Med. Ctr., Salt Lake City, 1972-74; mental health ednl. specialist Grad. Sch. Social Work, U. Utah, 1974-77, 77-80, asst. prof., 1974-80, assoc. prof., 1980-94, prof., 1994—, dir. doctoral program, 1984-89, assoc. dean, 1986-94; regional mental health cons. Bd. dirs. Info. and Referral Ctr., 1975-82, United Way of Utah, 1976-82, Pioneer Trail Parks, 1977-83, Rowland Hall-St. Marks Sch., 1980-86; Salt Lake County housing commr., 1980-86, Utah State Health Facilities Bd., 1991—, chair, 1994; pres. Human Svcs. Conf. for Utah, 1979-80; bd. dirs. Alzheimer Assn., Utah chpt., 1990—, Salt Lake County Coalition Bus. and Human Svcs., 1990-94, Town Club 1990-93, Valley Mental Health Bd., 1990—. Mem. Coun. on Social Work Edn., Commn. Women in High Edn., Nat. Assn. Social Workers (pres. Utah chpt. 1978-79), Adminstrs. of Public Agys. Assn., Human Svcs. Assn. Utah, Jr. League of Salt Lake City, Phi Kappa Phi. Republican. Episcopalian. Clubs: Town. Author: Explorations in Living, 1978, Social Work in Business and Industry, 1979; Handbook of the Social Services, 1981; contbr. articles to profl. jours. Home: 1458 Kristianna Cir Salt Lake City UT 84103-4221 Office: U Utah Grad Sch Social Work Social Work Bldg #324 Salt Lake City UT 84112

JORGENSON, MARY ANN, lawyer; b. Gallipolis, Ohio, 1941. BA, Agnes Scott Coll., 1963; MA, Harvard U., 1964; JD, Case Western Res. U., 1975. Bar: Ohio 1975, N.Y. 1982. Ptnr., chair firm's corp. practice Squire, Sanders & Dempsey. Office: Squire Sanders & Dempsey 4900 Society Ct 127 Public Sq Cleveland OH 44114

JORNEAUX, YVE, librarian; b. Ft. Wayne, Ind., June 30, 1953; d. Howard O. and Dardanella (Pinson) Jornod; m. Joseph R. Guastafeste, June 30, 1992. BS with honors, Ball State U., 1975; MLS, Rosary Coll., 1989; post-grad., U. Chgo., 1991—. Freelance musician Chgo., Ft. Wayne, 1975-88; info. mgr. mktg. intensive group Booz Allen & Hamilton, Chgo., 1988-90; rsch. and mktg. cons. Chgo., 1991; mgr. libr. and info. svcs. Winston & Strawn, Chgo., 1991-94; editor, pub. Qualitative Bull's-Eye, Chgo., 1994—; adj. prof. Rosary Coll. Grad. Sch. of Libr. and Info. Sci., River Forest, Ill., 1991—. Author: (with others) Manual of Online Searching Strategies, 1991.

JOSE, PHYLLIS ANN, librarian; b. Detroit, Mar. 15, 1949; d. William Henry and Isobel Eleanor (Mundle) J. BA, Mich. State U., 1971, MA, 1972; MA in Libr. Sci., U. Mich., 1975. Libr. aide audio-visual div. Dearborn (Mich.) Dept. Librs., 1973-76, libr. gen. info. div., 1976-77; reference libr. dir. Oakland County (Mich.) Libr., 1977-93, dir. libr. svcs., 1994—. Mem. Southfield Economic Devel. Corp., 1980-91, Southfield Tax Increment Fin. Authority, 1981-91, Southfield Local Devel. Fin. Authority, 1989-91; chairperson WOLF Adv. Coun. Librs., 1989-90; coord. Southfield Arts Festival, 1984, 85. Mem. ALA, Mich. Libr. Assn. (ALA chpt. councilor 1986-90), MLA treas. 1991-93). Presbyterian. Office: Dept 453 1200 N Telegraph Rd Pontiac MI 48341-1032

JOSEFOWITZ, NATASHA, syndicated columnist; b. Paris, Oct. 31, 1926; d. Myron T. and Tamara (Fradkin) Chapro; m. Sam Josefowitz, May 15, 1949; children: Nina, Paul. MSW, Columbia Sch. Social Work, 1965; Doctorans, Lausanne U., Switzerland, 1974; PhD, Sussex Coll., Eng., 1977. Prof. social work Lausanne U. Child Guidance Clinic, Switzerland, 1965-74; lectr., psychologist Lausanne U., Switzerland, 1972-74; prof. mgmt. U. N.H., 1974-80, Coll. Bus., San Diego State U., 1980-84; syndicated columnist, 1985—. Author: Paths to Power, 1980, Is This Where I Was Going?, 1983, You're the Boss, 1985, Natasha's Words for Friends, Families, and Lovers, 1986, Fitting In: How To Get a Good Start in Your New Job, 1988, 100 Scoops of Ice Cream: Tiny Tales for Children, 1988; co-author: Love Secrets, 1992. Named Woman of Yr. Women in Mgmt. Assn., 1988, Woman of Yr. Charter 100, 1992, One of San Diego's Top Gun Bus Jour., 1993. Mem. Nat. Tng. Lab. (emeritus 1985), Rotary. Home and Office: 2235 Calle Guaymas La Jolla CA 92037-6915

JOSELL, JESSICA (JESSICA WECHSLER), public relations executive; b. Balt., June 17, 1943; d. Maury J. and Rose E. (Lodin) Snyder; m. Neil B. Josell, Apr. 30, 1965 (dec. Nov. 1967); m. Steven James Wechsler, Jan. 12, 1980. BA, U. Fla., 1965. V.p., gen. mgr. Morton Dennis Wax & Assocs., N.Y.C., 1976-81; v.p. The Raleigh Group, Ltd., N.Y.C., 1981-87; pres. Josell Communications, Inc., N.Y.C., 1981—; exec. officer, bd. dirs. The Bridge, Inc., N.Y.C. Mem. N.Y. Women in Film and TV, Internat. Teleproduction Soc. Office: Josell Communications Inc 185 W End Ave Apt 22C New York NY 10023-5569

JOSEPH, CATHERINE BOYLAN, poetry therapist and educator; b. Manhattan, N.Y.; d. George and Gertrude (Brogan) Boylan; m. William Marshall Joseph; 1 child, Karen Lynne. BA, Hofstra U., 1941; MA, Adelphi U., 1950; postgrad., Cornell U., 1966, Syracuse U., 1967, Fordham U., 1969. Cert. tchr., N.Y.; cert. poetry therapist. Past instr. Adelphi U., Garden City, N.Y.; tchr. Roslyn (N.Y.) High Sch. and L.I. Schs., 1950-78; poetry therapist Mineola, N.Y.; workshop leader, lectr. New Sch., N.Y. Author: newspaper by-line The Mending Wall, 1994-95, also poems. Recipient NDEA Grad. scholarship Syracuse U., 2 social studies scholarships Cornell U. Mem. Internat. Arts as Medicine Assn., Internat. Assn. U. Women, AAUW, Nat. Coalition of Arts Therapy Assn., Nat. Assn. Poetry Therapy, Am. Legion Aux. Roman Catholic.

JOSEPH, EDITH HOFFMAN, retired editor; b. Syracuse, N.Y., Jan. 4, 1928; d. Max and Ida (Hodis) Finkelstein; m. Irving Hoffman, Sept. 4, 1949 (dec. Dec. 1965); children: Kenneth R., Maxine E. Neuhauser; m. William Jacob Joseph, May 19, 1968; stepchildren: David E., Harlan L., Saul J., Gail C. BS in Journalism/Bus. Adminstrn., Rider Coll., 1949. Copywriter advt. Swern's-Lit Bros., Trenton, N.J., 1949-51; pub. info. asst. N.J. Div. Pensions, Trenton, 1967-69; pub. rels. asst. N.J. Dept. Labor & Industry, Trenton, 1969-70; mng. editor newsletter N.J. Dept. Environ. Protection, Trenton, 1971-74; environ. news editor N.J. Dept. Environ. Protection-N.J. Outdoors Mag., 1974-84; editor newsletter N.J. Dept. Environ. Protection-Environ. News, 1985-90; editor environ. news sect. N.J. Dept. Environ. Protection-N.J. Outdoors Mag., 1991. Contbr. articles to profl. jours. Home: 8 Llanfair Ln Trenton NJ 08618-1012

JOSEPH, EDNA WHITEHEAD (MRS. LAWRENCE J. JOSEPH), tax financial consultant, former banker; b. Everett, Mass., Feb. 4, 1924; d. Alfred Edward and Mary Kathleen (Butler) Whitehead; attended Winthrop Schs., Boston U., Am. Inst. Banking, Lee Real Estate Inst.; m. Lawrence James Joseph, May 30, 1958. With Nat. Shawmut Bank (name now Shawmut Bank of Boston, N.A.), 1941-55, 57-84, asst. tax officer, 1965-69, tax officer, 1969-79, sr. trust officer, 1979-84; owner The Old Looking Glass, antiques; income tax mgr. Sam C. Charlson, Manhattan, Kans., 1955-57. Bd. dirs. Found. of Hope, Boston; mem. Republican Nat. Com., Women's Rep. Club Essex County, Nat. Fedn. Rep. Women. Mem. Fiduciary Tax Assos., Mass. Bankers Assn. (vice chmn. taxation com. 1971-72, chmn. 1972-73, tax cons. com. 1975-84), Nat. Assn. Bank Women, Am. Inst. Banking, Nat. Early Am. Glass Club (founders chpt.), North Shore Antique Assn., Soc. Preservation New Eng. Antiquities, Friends of Sandwich Mus., Woman 76 (Boston organizing com.), Soc. Jesus in New Eng. (liaison com. 1974-75, exec. com. 1975-76), Mus. Fine Arts, Bostonian Soc., Victorian Soc., Essex Inst., Peabody Mus., Jones Gallery Glass and Ceramics. Home: 8 Laurel Rd Lynnfield MA 01940-1512

JOSEPH, ELEANOR ANN, hospital association administrator; b. Cleve., Mar. 6, 1944; d. Emil and Eleanor (Leelais) Dienes; m. Abraham Albert Joseph, Oct. 28, 1984. BS in Math. cum laude, Cleve. State U., 1978, MPA in Health Care Adminstrn., 1991. Cert. profl. for healthcare quality, coding specialist, procedural coder, accredited records technician, 1967. Asst. dir. med. records Suburban Hosp., Warrensville Heights, Ohio, 1963-77; coder Shaker Med. Ctr., Shaker Heights, Ohio, 1965, Huron Rd. Hosp., Cleve., 1965; instr. Cuyahoga C.C., Cleve., 1970-72; dir. med. records Hillcrest Hosp., Mayfield Heights, Ohio, 1977-84; med. records technician Vis. Nurse Assn., Cleve., 1985; coord. med. record svcs. Ctr. for Health Affairs Greater Cleve. Hosp. Assn., 1985-88, dir. coding svcs. Ctr. Health Affairs, 1988-89; dir. health record svcs. Ctr. for Health Affairs/Greater Cleve. Hosp. Assn., 1989—; cons. in field, Cleve., 1976—; mem. speakers' bur. Hillcrest Hosp., Mayfield Heights, 1978-84; mem. adv. com. Cuyahoga C.C., 1973-80; cons. Suburban Pavilion Manor Care Nursing Homes, Luth. Home, Cleve., 1976-88; condr. seminars in field. Co-author: (manual) Quality Assurance Program for Medical Records Department, 1981, Dollars and Sense: A Reference Guide to Coding and Prospective Payment System Reimbursement Issues, 1988; co-editor: Care and Management of Health Care Records, 1988, 92. Active Holden Arboretum, Kirtland, Ohio, 1975—, Ohio Hist. Soc., Columbus, 1975—, mem. adv. task force Cert. program in Med. Office mgmt., Lakeland C.C., 1992—. Mem. Am. Acad. Procedural Coders (treas. local chpt. 1994—), Am. Med. Record Assn. (mem. long term care sect., cons. roster 1976, charter mem. assembly on edn. 1989), Am. Health Info. Mgmt. Assn. (quality assurance sect., long term care sect., ambulatory records sec. 1992—), Am. Guild Patient Accounts Mgrs., Nat. Assn. for Healthcare Quality, East Ohio Med. Record Assn., N.E. Ohio Med. Record Assn. (mem. audit com., membership com., bylaws com., pub. rels. com., counselor 1983, ednl. com. 1984, 87, chmn. nominating com. 1986, treas. 1979, v.p. 1980, pres. elect 1981-82, pres. 1982-83, mem. cons. com. 1987-91), Ohio Med. Record Assn. (mem. legis. com. 1989-90, bylaws com. 1983-84, nominating com. 1982-83, med. record coun. 1985-92, alt. del. 1982, del. for state assn. mems. at nat. ann. mtg. Am. Med. Record Assn. 1989, 90), Am. Coll. Healthcare Execs., Ohio Assn. Healthcare Quality, Ohio Health Info. Mgmt. Assn. (project leader-alliances 1992-94, data quality and reimbursement coun. 1992—, liaison to ambulatory sect. of Am. Health Info. Mgmt. Assn. 1994—), Northeast Ohio Health Info. Mgmt. Assn. (chair coding roundtable 1993—), Soc. Clin. Coders. Democrat. Lutheran. Office: Greater Cleve Hosp Assn Ctr for Health Affairs 1226 Huron Rd Cleveland OH 44115-1702

JOSEPH, GERI MACK (GERALDINE JOSEPH), former ambassador, educator; b. St. Paul, June 19, 1923. B.S., U. Minn., 1946; LL.D. (hon.), Bates Coll., 1982. Staff writer Mpls. Tribune, 1946-53, contbg. editor, 1972-78; amb. to The Netherlands The Hague, 1978-81; sr. fellow internat. programs Hubert H. Humphrey Inst. Pub. Affairs, U. Minn., 1984-94; dir. Mondale Policy Forum, 1990-94; bd. dirs. Nat. Dem. Inst. for Internat. Affairs, George A. Hormel Co., Honeywell; mem. U.S. Pres.'s Commn. on Mental Health, Minn. Supreme Ct. Commn. on Mentally Disabled and the Cts., com. on Mid. East, The Brookings Inst., 1987; mem., bd. dirs. The German Marshall Fund, 1987—. Vice chmn. Gov.'s Commn. on Taxation, 1983-84; trustee Carleton Coll., 1975-94; mem. Democratic Nat. Com., 1960-72, vice chmn., 1968-72; co-chairperson Minn. Women's Campaign Fund, 1982-84; co-chmn. Atty. Gen.'s Com. on Child Abuse within the Family, 1986. Office: U Minn Humphrey Ctr 301 19th Ave S Minneapolis MN 55455-0429

JOSEPH, HARRIET, English literature educator; b. Montreal, Mar. 14, 1919; came to U.S., 1944; d. Samuel and Hanna Mai (Brown) Bloomfield; m. Edward D. Joseph, Aug. 16, 1942; children: Leila Muriel, Alan Pinto, Brian Daniel. BA, McGill U., Montreal, Que., 1941; MA, Bryn Mawr Coll., 1942. Instr. to assoc. prof. English lit. Pace U., Pleasantville, N.Y., 1966-81; prof. Pace U., Pleasantville, 1981—. Author: Shakespeare's Son-in-Law: Man & Physician, 1964; contbr. articles on Eng. litr. to jours. Active LWV, Scarsdale, N.Y. Mem. MLA, Internat. Shakespeare Assn., Shakespeare Assn. Am., Am. Jewish Congress, Women's Am. Orgn. for Rehab. Through Tng., Author's League, AAUW. Home: 9 Putnam Rd Scarsdale NY 10583-2009 Office: Pace U Bedford Rd Pleasantville NY 10570-1002

JOSEPH, JEAN, artist; b. New Rochelle, N.Y., Jan. 28, 1914; d. Barnet and Alimeta Edna (Calder) J.; m. Paul Heinz Mertens, Oct. 19, 1941 (dec. Oct. 1979); children: Bruce, Mark, Gail. Student, Art Students League, 1930-34, U. Miami, 1935. Freelance artist. One woman shows at Manhasset Libr., 1974, Unitarian Soc., 1984; exhibited in group shows at Wildenstein Galleries, N.Y., 1952, 53-55 tour (Internat. Hallmark awards, 1952, 53-55), Nat. Acad. Design, 1953 (Allied Artists of Am. award 1953), Fire House Gallery, 1973, Port Washington Libr., 1977, Unitarian Universalists Soc., Plandome, N.Y., 1977, Lincoln House, 1980 (sculpture prize), Port Washington Libr., 1981 (hon. mention), Nassau County Mus. Fine Art, 1983, Heckscher Mus., 1986 (Top of the Eighties award 1986), Nassau County Mus. Art, 1986 (Silver award 1986), 88 (hon. mention), Discovery Gallery, N.Y., (Jurors Merit award, 1993), 1992. Vol. 1000 hours St. Francis Hosp., Roslyn, N.Y., 1970-75. Recipient Hon. Mention award Cannon Photo Contest, 1986. Home and Studio: 11 Chanticlare Dr Manhasset NY 11030

JOSEPH, LURA ELLEN, librarian, geologist; b. Tulsa, Jan. 24, 1947; d. Don Roscoe and Ruth Elizabeth (Taplin) J. Student, St. Paul Bible Coll., 1965-67, Pan Am. Coll., 1967-68; BA in Anthropology, U. Okla., 1971, MS in Geology, 1981; MA in Psychology with honors, U. Cen. Okla., 1992; M of Libr. and Info. Studies, U. Okla., 1994. Cert. petroleum geologist. Exploration geologist Getty Oil Co., Oklahoma City, 1977-84; geologist Harper Oil Co., Oklahoma City, 1984-86, consulting geologist, 1986-88; sr. geologist Grace Petroleum, Oklahoma City, 1988-93, cons. geologist, 1993-95; phys. scis. libr. N.D. State Univ. Libr., Fargo, 1995—. Author: (with others) Hugo Reservoir I, 1971; contbr. articles to profl. jours. Active adv. coun. New Life Ranch, Inc., Colcord, Okla. Mem. Am. Assn. Petroleum Geologists, Oklahoma City Geol. soc., Sigma Gamma Epsilon, Psi Chi. Republican. Mem. Independent Evangelical Ch. Office: ND State U Libr PO Box 5599 Fargo ND 58105

JOSEPH, MARILYN SUSAN, gynecologist; b. Bklyn., Aug. 18, 1946; d. S. Seymour and Maxine Laura (Stern) J.; m. Warren Erwin Regelmann, Dec. 20, 1969; children: Adam Gustave, David Joseph. BA, Smith Coll., 1968; MD cum laude, SUNY Downstate Med. Ctr., Bklyn., 1972. Diplomate Am. Bd. Ob-Gyn, Nat. Bd. Med. Examiners. Intern U. Minn. Hosps., 1972-73, resident in ob-gyn, 1972-76; med. fellow specialist U. Minn., 1972-76, asst. prof. ob-gyn, 1976—, dir. women's clinic, 1984—. Author: Differential Diagnosis Obstetrics, 1978. Fellow Am. Coll. Ob-Gyn (best paper dist. VI meeting 1981); mem. Am. Assn. Gynecol. Laparoscopy, Hennepin County Med. Soc., Minn. State Med. Assn., Mpls. Council Ob-Gyn, Minn. State Ob-Gyn Soc. Jewish. Office: Boynton Health Svc 410 Church St SE Minneapolis MN 55455-0346

JOSEPH, ROSALINE RESNICK, hematologist/oncologist; b. N.Y.C., Aug. 21, 1929; d. Joseph and Malca (Rosenberg) Resnick; m. Robert J. Joseph, Jan. 2, 1954; children: Joy S., Nina B. AB, Cornell U., 1949; MD, Women's Med. Coll. Pa., Phila., 1953; MS, Temple U., 1958. Intern Kings County Hosp., Bklyn., 1953-54; resident Phila. Gen. Hosp., 1954-55, Temple U. Hosp., 1955-57; instr. dept. medicine Temple U. Med. Ctr., Phila., 1957-60; assoc. in medicine Temple U. Med. Ctr., 1960-63, asst. prof. medicine, 1963-69, assoc. prof. medicine, 1969-77; course co-coordinator Sys. Oncology Interdisciplinary Course, 1968-73; prof. medicine, dir. Med. Coll. Pa., Phila., 1977; course coordinator Med. Coll. Pa., 1978, dir. hematology/oncology, to date; pres. med. staff Med. Coll. Pa., 1990—. Contbr. articles to profl. jours. Del. dir. Am. Cancer Soc., 1989—. Recipient Lindback award for disting. teaching, Christian & Mary Lindback Found., 1982, Am. Cancer Soc. Div. Disting. Svc. award, 1987. Fellow ACP; mem. Am. Soc. Hematology, Am. Soc. Clin. Oncology, Alumni Assn. Med. Coll. Pa. (pres. 1988-90). Office: Med Coll of Pa 3300 Henry Ave Philadelphia PA 19129-1121

JOSEPH, SANDRA CAROL, psychologist; b. Mt. Airy, N.C., June 7, 1941; d. Otis William and Ruth Mildred (Gates) Holder; widowed, June, 1976; 1 child, David Marcus. BA in Edn., Wake Forest U., 1963, MA in Psychology, 1983; postgrad., Wayne State U., 1994—. Intern St. Joseph Mercy Hosp., Pontiac, 1984-85, Hawthorn Ctr., Northville, 1985-86; consulting sch. psychologist Ednl. Resources, St. Clair Shores, Mich., 1986-87; dir. Joseph Consulting Svcs., P.C., Oak Park, Mich., 1986—; child and family therapist Mich. Family Inst., Oak Park, Mich., 1993—; cons. Out Wayne County Head Start, Wayne, Mich., 1987-89, Hillsdale (Mich.) Sch. Dist., 1988-89; presenter numerous seminars. Creator Raising Emotionally Healthy Children program. Adv. bd. Com. Children's T.V., 1988-90. Grad. Profl. scholar, 1981-82, 84; Thomas Rumble fellow, 1983. Mem. APA, Mich. Psychol. Assn., Mich. Assn. Profl. Psychologists, Mich. Com. Prevention Child Abuse. Office: Joseph Cons Svcs PC 25900 Greenfield Rd # 208 Detroit MI 48237

JOSEPH, SUSAN B., lawyer; b. N.Y.C., June 1, 1958; d. Alfred A. and Bella (Muniches) J. BS in Econ. and Bus. Mgmt., Ramapo Coll. of N.J., 1981; JD cum laude, Seton Hall U., 1985. Bar: N.J. 1985, U.S. Dist. Ct. N.J. 1985, N.Y. 1988, U.S. Dist. Ct. (so. and ea. dist.) N.Y. 1991. Legal asst. Prudential Ins. Co. Am., Newark, 1982-85; assoc. Fox & Fox, Newark, 1985-86, Elkes, Maybruch & Weiss, P.A., Freehold, N.J., 1986-87; asst. counsel N.Am. Reins. Corp., N.Y.C., 1987-90; assoc. Mark D. Lefkowitz, Esq., 1991; mgr. GRE Ins. Group, Princeton, N.J., 1991; atty. GRE Ins. Group, N.Y.C., 1992—. Vol. campaign Bill Bradley for Senate, 1984, 90; vol. Starlight Found., N.Y.C., 1988—. Mem. ABA, N.J. State Bar Asn. (sect. on entertainment and arts law, newsletter editor 199-93, bd. dirs., ins. law com. 1993—), N.Y. State Bar Assn. (sect. on entertainment, arts and sports law). Democrat. Jewish. Home: 747 Valley St Apt 3K Maplewood NJ 07040-2663

JOSEPHS, BABETTE, legislator; b. N.Y.C., Aug. 4, 1940; d. Eugene and Myra A. Josephs; children: Lee Aaron Newberg, Elizabeth Newberg. BA, Queens Coll., 1962; JD, Rutgers U., 1976. Sole practice Phila., 1976-78; exec. dir. Nat. Abortion Rights Action League of Pa., Phila., 1978-80, Citizens Coalition for Energy Efficiency, Phila., 1980-81; pvt. practice cons., fundraiser Phila., 1981-84; mem. Pa. Ho. of Reps., Phila., 1984—. Bd. dirs. ACLU. Mem. Phila. Bar Assn. Democrat. Jewish. Office: Pa Ho of Reps State Capitol Harrisburg PA 17120*

JOSEPHS, EILEEN SHERLE, mediator, financial consultant; b. Johnstown, Pa.; d. David and Freda (Beerman) Venetsky; m. Gerald Lisowitz, June 27, 1953 (div. 1968); children: Mara Lisowitz, Carlyn Lisowitz Walker; m. Marvin Josephs, May 25, 1969 (div. 1988); m. Michael N. Berger, Aug. 28, 1993. BS cum laude, U. Pitts., 1956, MA, 1969. Cert. mediator. Tchr. Pitts. Pub. Schs., 1958-59; tchr. mil. Ft. Lee, Va., 1960; docent edn. staff Carnegie Inst., Pitts., 1971-77; real estate developer, sales rep. Equity Real Estate, Pitts., 1977-79; women's div. buyer and retail cons. Coach House Stores, Pitts., 1980; ptnr., mediator Divorce and Separation Ctr., 1980—; ptnr. Mediation Masters, Pitts., 1992—; guest lectr. U. Pitts., 1982-88, Duquesne U., Pitts., 1994, Community Coll., Pitts., 1988-91, co founded Michael Berger Gallery, 1995, others. Author: Landmark Mediations-Long Term Marriage, 1992, Divorce Agreements and Landmark Adoption Mediation Resulting in Shared Parenting, 1993, Expanding Non-Adversarial Dispute Resolution in Business Practice, 1993; contbr. articles to profl. jours. Pub. co-chair Three Rivers Arts Festival, Pitts., 1965; found. bd. dirs. Group Against Smog & Pollution, Pitts., 1967-70; bd. dirs. nat. Coun. Jewish Women, Pitts., 1979; vol. Pitts. Mediation Ctr., 1988—. Senatorial scholar U. Pitts., Marshal scholar, 1954. Mem. Pitts. Plan Art, Acad. Family Mediators (cons. 1985—, presentor workshops 1988, 89, 90, 92), Family Mediation Coun. Western Pa. (charter, bd. dirs. 1992—), Greater Pitts. Bd. Realtors. Office: Mediation Masters 7514 Kensington St Pittsburgh PA 15221

JOSEPHSON, DIANA HAYWARD, aerospace executive; b. London, Oct. 17, 1936; came to U.S., 1959; d. Robert Hayward and Barbara (Clark) Bailey. BA with honors, Oxford U., Eng., 1958, MA, 1962; M in Comparative Law, George Washington U., 1962. Bar: Eng. and Wales 1959, D.C. 1963. Assoc. Covington & Burling, Washington, 1959-68; asst. dir. Office of the Mayor, Washington, 1968-74; exec. dir. Nat. Capital Area ACLU, Washington, 1975-78; dep. asst. adminstr. policy and planning, satellites NOAA, U.S. Dept. Commerce, Washington, 1978-82; pres. Am. Sci. and Tech. Corp., Bethesda, Md., 1982-83, Space Am., Bethesda, 1983-85; v.p. mktg. Arianespace, Inc., Washington, 1985-87; v.p. Martin Marietta Comml. Titan Inc., Washington, 1987-89; dir. bus. devel. Martin Marietta Advanced Launch Systems, Denver, 1989-90, Martin Marietta Civil Space and Communications Co., Denver, 1990-93; dep. under sec. of commerce for oceans and atmosphere NOAA, U.S. Dept. Commerce, Washington, 1993—; mem. Space Applications Bd., Nat. Rsch. Coun., 1988-89, comml. space transp. adv. commn., U.S. Dept. Transp., Washington, 1984-85; adv. bd. Washington Space Bus. Roundtable, 1985-87. Mem. D.C. Law Revision Commn., Washington, 1975-78, D.C. Internat. Women's Yr. State Coordinating Com., 1977. Recipient Gold medal for Disting. Svc., U.S. Dept. Commerce, 1981. Mem. Am. Astronautical Soc. (bd. dirs. 1985-88), Nat. Space Club (bd. govs.), Women in Aerospace, Washington Space Bus. Roundtable (adv. bd. 1985-87). Office: Dept of Commerce Nat Oceanic & Atmospheric Admin 14th & Constitution Ave NW Washington DC 20230

JOSHI-PETERS, KARUNA LAXMIPRASAD, psychologist; b. Patan, Gujerat, India, July 18, 1944; came to U.S., 1971; d. Laxmiprasad Chunilal and Leelvati Laxmiprasad (Shukla) Joshi; m. Ramashanker Misra, May 10, 1965 (div. July 1977); m. Michael Wood Peters, Sept. 8, 1977; children: Adrian Manoj Rohit, Julian Vikram Suhas. BA in English Lit. with honors, Banaras Hindu U., Varanasi, India, 1960, MA in Philosophy, 1962; MA in Psychology, U. Hawaii, 1990, PhD in Psychology, 1992. Lic. clin. psychologist, Hawaii. Jr. rsch. fellow Banaras Hindu U., 1962-64, lectr., 1963; lectr. Patna (India) U., 1964-65; sr. rsch. asst. Indian Inst. Tech., Kanpur, India, 1965-71; teaching asst. dept. philosophy U. Hawaii, Honolulu, 1975-76; psychol. intern Oreg. Health Scis. U., Portland, 1991-92; psychol. examiner spl. svcs. State of Hawaii Dept. Edn., Honolulu, 1992; psychologist State of Hawaii Dept. Health, Kaneohe, 1993; pvt. practice psychology Kaneohe, 1993—; organizer Hawaii Neuropsychology Group, Kaneohe, 1990—. Author rsch. papers in field. East West Ctr. grantee, 1971-75; jr. rsch. fellow Univ. Grants Commn., New Delhi, India, 1962-64. Mem. APA, Hawaii Psychol. Assn., Nat. Acad. Neuropsychology, Internat. Neuropsychol. Soc. Democrat. Office: 46-001 Kamehameha Hwy Ste 419B Kaneohe HI 96744-3711

JOSKOW, RENEE W., dentist, educator; b. N.Y.C., Mar. 15, 1960; d. Melvin Lawrence and Eunice Lila (Levine) J. BA, SUNY, Binghamton, 1981; MPH, Columbia U., 1985, DDS, 1985. Gen. practice resident Hackensack (N.J.) Med. Ctr., 1985-86; pvt. faculty practice, gen. practitioner Columbia Sch. of Dental and Oral Surgery, N.Y.C., 1986-90; asst. prof., dentistry Columbia Univ., N.Y.C., 1986—; pvt. practice gen. dentistry N.Y.C., 1990—; cons. alternative delivery systems Columbia Sch. Dental and Oral Surgery, N.Y.C., 1985-86, admission com., 1988-92; cons. Prudential Ins. Co., 1994—; chairperson Frederick Birnberg Award Com., 1986-90; clin. program coord. Health of the Pub. Grant Columbia Sch. Pub. Health, 1987-88; dir. freshman dental courses Columbia U., N.Y.C., 1987—; workshop leader Columbia U. Sch. Dental and Oral Surgery, 1993, Columbia Presbyn. Med. Ctr., 1993. Guest lectr. Inst. for Child Devel.-Community Outreach Lectr. on Oral Health, Hackensack Med. Ctr., 1986. Recipient L.I. Acad. of Odontology award, N.Y., 1985, Ella Marie Ewell award for Meritorious Svc., Columbia Univ., 1985, Alumni award for Excellence in Preventive Dentistry, Columbia Univ., N.Y., 1985. Fellow N.Y. Acad. Dentistry, Acad. Gen. Dentistry; mem. ADA, Am. Assn. Women Dentists (faculty advisor 1986—), 1st dist. Dental Soc., Columbia U. Alumni Assn. (com. chair 1989—), Julliard Evening Divsn. Chorale (Shiatsu therapist), Columbia Student Honor and Rsch. Soc. (faculty advisor 1986—), Nat. Assn. Women Bus. Owners, Dental Honor Fraternity, Omicron Kappa Upsilon. Office: 29 W 57th St New York NY 10019-3406

JOURDAIN, ALICE MARIE, philosopher, retired educator; b. Brussels, Mar. 11, 1923; came to U.S., 1940, naturalized, 1948; d. Henri and Marthe (van de Vorst) J.; m. Dietrich von Hildebrand, July 16, 1959. Student, Manhattanville Coll., 1942-44; PhD, Fordham U., 1949; D honoris causa, U. Steubenville, Ohio, 1987. Mem. faculty dept. philosophy Hunter Coll., CUNY, 1947—, prof., 1971-84; vis. prof. U. de los Andes, Bogotá, Colombia, summer 1955, Thomas More Inst., Rome, Spring 1985, Catechetical Inst., Yonkers, N.Y., 1985, Notre Dame Catechetical Inst., Arlington, Va., summer 1986, 87, 88; lectr. Internat. Congress on Family, Caracas, Venezuela, 1985; lectr. various instns., The Netherlands, Germany, Austria, Mex., Can., Colombia, Liechtenstein, Eng., U.S. Author: Greek Culture: The Adventure of the Human Spirit, 1966, Introduction to a Philosophy of Religion, 1971, By Love Refined, 1988, By Grief Refined, 1994; (with D. von

Hildebrand) Graven Images, 1957, Art of Living, 1965, Situation Ethics, 1966. Recipient William O'Brien award Newman Club, 1963. Roman Catholic.

JOVANOVITCH, MILENA, editor, journalist; b. London, July 26, 1951; came to U.S., 1958; d. Stevan and Mirjiana (Tupanjanin) J. BA, Smith Coll., 1973. Adminstr. asst. Coun. Fgn. Rels., N.Y.C., 1974-76; reporter N.J. Herald, Newton, 1976-79, Westchester-Rockland Newspapers, White Plains, N.Y., 1979-84; contbg. reporter N.Y. Times, 1984—; program mgr. Prodigy Svcs. Co., White Plains, 1987—. Mem. Soc. Profl. Journalists, Women in Comms.

JOY, ATHALIE DORIS, clinical psychologist, consultant; b. Bridgeport, Conn., June 22, 1940; d. James Vincent and Athalie (Goodman) J.; m. Peter S. Gold, Dec. 30, 1988. BA, Manhattanville Coll., 1962; PhD, SUNY, Buffalo, 1977. Lic. psychologist, N.Y. Clin. supr. West N.Y. Inst. Psychotherapies, Niagara Falls, 1979-81; program dir. Buffalo Gen. Hosp., 1981-84; pvt. practice Williamsville, N.Y., 1984—; v.p. Erie Niagara Counselling Assocs., Williamsville, N.Y., 1986—; assoc. med. dir. mental health svcs. Ind. Health Assn., Williamsville, N.Y., 1992—; clin. asst. prof. SUNY, Buffalo, 1977—; founding mem. Behavioral Healthcare Network, Buffalo, 1993. Cons. Planned Parenthood Buffalo and Erie County, 1993. Mem. APA, N.Y. State Psychol. Assn., Western N.Y. Psychol. Assn. Office: 5500 Main St Williamsville NY 14221

JOYCE, ANN IANNUZZO, art educator; b. Scranton, Pa., May 23, 1953; d. Albert Joseph and Lucy (Guimento) Iannuzzo; m. Patrick Francis Joyce, July 23, 1977; children: Ryan Patrick, Shawn Patrick. BFA, Maryland Inst., Balt., 1975; MS, U. Scranton, 1988; postgrad., Pa. State U., 1990—. Mech. artist Internat. Corr. Schs., Scranton, Pa., 1975-77; layout artist Lynn Orgn., Wilkes-Barre, Pa., 1977-78; prodn. coord. Jewelcor Merchandising, Wilkes-Barre, 1978-82; adj. lectr. Kings Coll., Wilkes-Barre, 1981-89; art dir. WVIA-TV Pub. Broadcasting, Pittston, Pa., 1985-86; publs. dir. U. Scranton, 1986-89; asst. prof. King's Coll., Wilkes-Barre, 1989—; exec. bd. v.p. Northeastern Pa. Writing Coun., Wilkes-Barre, 1993—; edn. co-chair Northeast Pa. Ad Club, 1994—. Cub Scout leader Boy Scouts Am., Moosic, Pa., 1992—. Mem. ASCD, Nat. Art Edn. Assn., Am. Inst. Graphic Arts (Phila. chpt.), Calligraphers Guild, Artists for Art, Pa. Art Edn. Assn., Pa. Alliance Arts Edn. Democrat. Roman Catholic. Home: 812 Grace Ln Moosic PA 18507-1610 Office: King's Coll 133 N River St Wilkes Barre PA 18711

JOYCE, BERNITA ANNE, federal government agency administrator; d. Albert A. and Margaret C. Joyce. BA, Duchesne Coll.; MBA, U. Santa Clara, 1968, PhD, 1974; m. Kenneth B. Lucas, Aug. 2, 1975. With Wolfe & Co., CPA's, Washington, 1971-72; fin. dir. Nat. Forest Products Assn., Washington, 1972-74; budget and fiscal officer ICC, Washington, 1974-77, Office Mgmt. and Budget, 1977-80; asst. dir. mgmt. svcs. Bur. Mines, Dept. Interior, 1980-85, asst. dir. Office Policy Analysis Dept. Interior, 1985—. Author: Financial Viability of Private Elementary Schools. Mem. AICPA, Sr. Execs. Assn., Exec. Women in Govt., Assn. Govt. Accts., Assn. for Pub. Policy Analysis and Mgmt., Beta Gamma Sigma. Home: 6001 Bradley Blvd Bethesda MD 20817-3807

JOYCE, CAROL BERTANI, social studies educator; b. N.Y.C., Apr. 9, 1943; d. Joseph and Ethel Marie (Bracchi) Bertani; m. William Leonard Joyce, Aug. 13, 1967; children: Susan A., Michael J. BA, Coll. New Rochelle, 1964; MA, St. John's U., 1966; postgrad., U. Mich., 1970-71. Cert. tchr., N.J., N.Y., Mass., Mich. Tchr. Christ the King High Sch., Middle Village, N.Y., 1966-67, Willow Run High Sch., Ypsilanti, Mich., 1967-68, Notre Dame Acad., Worcester, Mass., 1974-81, Salesian High Sch., New Rochelle, N.Y., 1981-82, Ursuline Sch., New Rochelle, 1982-88, Burlington Twp. (N.J.) Schs., 1988-89; edn. planner N.J. Dept. Edn., Trenton, 1989-91; tchr. Princeton (N.J.) Regional Schs., 1991—; participant Tri-States Global Workshop, Boylston, Mass., 1980, NEH summer seminar fellowship U. Mass. Dartmouth, North Dartmouth, 1993, Tchrs. Inst. in History, Princeton U., summer 1994; tchr., counselor European tour Am. Leadership Study Group, 1987; master tchr. DeWitt-Wallace World History Tchrs. Summer Inst., Woodrow Wilson Nat. Scholarship Found., Princeton, 1992. Tchr. religious edn. various parishes in Mass., N.Y., 1974-83; chair edn. com. LWV, Pelham, N.Y., 1983-84; vol. Profl. Roster, Princeton, 1989, Profl. Svc. Group, New Brunswick, N.J., 1991; panelist N.J. Bar Found. High Sch. Curriculum Panel on Law-Related Edn., 1993—. Grantee Women's Ctr. U. Mich., 1970-71. Mem. Nat. Coun. for Social Studies (participant social studies coun. meeting N.E. regional conf. 1981), Nat. Coun. for History Edn. Home: 99 Mccosh Cir Princeton NJ 08540-5626 Office: Princeton High Sch 151 Moore St Princeton NJ 08540-3399

JOYCE, DEBBIE GOODMAN, real estate company executive; b. West Jefferson, N.C., Dec. 13, 1955; d. Grover Arnold and Sue Ann (Bledsoe) G.; m. Philip Hardin Joyce, June 12, 1982; 1 child, Benjamin Houston. BS in Mgmt., Guilford Coll., 1978. Owner, pres. Legend Properties, Inc., Greensboro, N.C., 1986—. Mem. Nat. Home Builders Assn., Greensboro Home Builders Assn., Cmty. Assns. Inst. Office: Legend Properties Inc 503 State St Greensboro NC 27405

JOYCE, JUANITA SANDGREN, educational administrator; b. Mineola, N.Y., Sept. 10, 1950; d. Walter Harold and Gertrude Anna (Brunner) S.; m. Robert Lee Joyce, Oct. 22, 1983. BS, SUNY, Cortland, 1972; MS, U. Okla., 1973; cert. of advanced study, Old Dominion U., 1990. Cert. supr. of instrn., tchr. of hearing impaired. Tchr. asst. Mill Neck (N.Y.) Manor, summer 1972; tchr. Hampton (Va.) City Schs., 1973-79, program coord., 1979-93, dir. spl. edn., 1993—. Mem. Speech and Hearing Assn. Va., Va. Coun. Adminstrs. of Spl. Edn. Lutheran.

JOYCE, MARY ANN, principal; b. Bklyn., May 29, 1935; d. Alfred and Antoinette (Polito) Lo Sasso; m. Michael J. Joyce, Jr., Mar. 2, 1957 (dec. 1982); children: Michael, Debra Grammer, Patricia Sommers. BA in Elem. Edn., Social Scis., Mount St. Mary Coll., 1972; MS in Elem. Edn., Reading, SUNY, New Paltz, 1975, CAS in Ednl. Adminstrn., 1983. Cert. tchr. N-6, N.Y., reading tchr., K-12, N.Y., sch. dist. administr., N.Y., sch. administr./supr., N.Y. Tchr. grades 3 and 4 Temple Hill Sch., Newburgh, N.Y., 1972-74, tchr. reading, 1974-83, tchr. gifted and talented, 1976-83, asst. prin., 1983-85; prin. Horizons-on-the-Hudson Magnet Sch., Newburgh, 1985—; tchr. summer sch. Newburgh (N.Y.) Free Acad., 1976-81; adj. prof. SUNY, New Paltz, 1989-91; nat. review panelist Blue Ribbon Sch. Competition, 1991, 92, FIRST family-sch. partnership program, 1992; speaker numerous confs., seminars. Recipient Elem. Sch. Recognition award U.S. Dept. Edn., 1989-90, 93-94, Excellence in Adminstrn. award Mid-Hudson Sch. Study Coun., 1993, award for Outstanding Leadership, Achievements and Contributions Toward Making the Edn. of our Nation's Youth a Safe and Productive Experience, 1991. Mem. ASCD, Am. Assn. Female Execs., Nat. Assn. Elem. Sch. Prins. (Excellence in Edn. award 1990, 94), State Adminstrs. Assn. N.Y. State (Elem. Schs. Excellence award 1990, 94), Newburgh Suprs. and Adminstrs. Assn., United Univ. Profs., Delta Kappa Gamma. Office: Horizons-on-the-Hudson Magnet Sch 137 Montgomery St Newburgh NY 12550-3636

JOYCE, MICHELLE MARIE, communications and marketing professional; b. Hartford, Conn., July 25, 1966; d. John Roger Sr. and Katherine Aileen (Pound) Berube; m. Robert Steven Joyce, Sept. 27, 1991; children: Robert, John. Student, U. Conn., 1984-87. Receptionist St. Thomas Aquinas, Storrs, Conn., 1985-87; policy typist Nat. Wide Ins., Syracuse, N.Y., 1987; coop. rels. asst. Ea. Milk Producers, Syracuse, 1987-88; comms. and tng. trainee August Max Woman, Enfield, 1988-94; mktg. asst. Women's Specialty Retailing, Enfield, 1994—. Asst. dir. Holy Family Folk Choir, Enfield, Conn., 1991—. Democrat. Roman Catholic. Home: 5B The Hamlet Enfield CT 06082 Office: Women's Specialty Retailing 100 Phoenix Ave Enfield CT 06082-4499

JOYE, AFRIE SONGCO, minister; b. Guagua, Pampanga, Philippines, Aug. 8, 1942; d. Emilio Lelay and Elmerita (Atienza) Laus Songco; m. Charles James Joye, Aug. 28, 1971. BA in Christian Edn., Harris Meml. Coll., Manila, 1963; MA in Christian Edn., Scarritt Grad. Sch., Nashville, 1970; PhD in Theology and Religious Edn., Sch. Theology at Claremont, Calif., 1990. Dir. Christian edn. First United Meth. Ch., Naga, Philippines, 1963-66; dist. Christian Edn. coord. Bicol-Palawan Region of United Meth. Ch., 1963-66; dir. Christian Edn. Cen. United Meth. Ch., Manila, 1966-68; dir. youth ministry and student ctr. Cen. United Meth. Ch., 1970-71; instr. psychology and Christian edn. Philippin Christian Coll./Harris Meml. Coll., Manila, 1970-71; dir Christian Edn. Aldersgate United Meth. Ch./John Wesley United Meth. Ch., Charleston, S.C., 1971-74; instr. Palmer Coll., Charleston, S.C., 1972-74; nat. dir. Christian edn. in Asian and Native Am. chs. Gen. Bd. Discipleship, Nashville, 1976-79, nat. dir. Christian edn. in small membership chs., 1979-83; cons.-trainer in Christian edn., 1983-87; minister Christian edn. Community United Meth. Ch., Huntington Beach, Calif., 1987-90; assoc. minister Laguna Hills (Calif.) United Meth. Ch., 1990-92; co-pastor Hollywood (Calif.) First United Meth. Ch., 1992-94; sr. pastor St. Paul's United Meth. Ch., 1994—. Editor: Program Ideas and Training Designs for Pacific and Asian American Church Schools, 1981; contbr. articles to profl. jours. Nat. mem. Bread for the World, Fellowship of Reconciliation, Amnesty Internat. Coolidge Colloquium fellow, Assn. for Religion and Intellectual Life, 1989. Mem. AAUW (life), Nat. Christian Educators Fellowship, Am. Acad. Religion, Assn. of Profs. and Researchers of Religious Education, Nat. Fedn. Asian Am. United Meth., Religious Edn. Assn.

JOYNER, DARLA JEAN, trade association executive; b. Sioux Falls, S.D., Dec. 4, 1947; d. John Jay and Darlene Dorothy (Loe) Anderberg; m. John A. Joyner, Dec. 7, 1968; children: Jay Arthur, Amy Renee, Evan James. AA, Arapahoe Community Coll., 1974; postgrad., Met. State Coll., Denver, 1974-78; cert., Inst. Organizational Mgmt., Boulder, Colo., 1986. Layout artist JC Penney, Denver, 1973-74; gen. mgr. Bozeman (Mont.) Area C. of C., 1978-83, exec. v.p., chief exec. officer, 1983—; state adv. coun. Mont. Small Bus. Adminstrn.; S.W. Mont. adv. bd. Horizon Airlines. Editor Ignacio Chieftain mag., 1971-72, Beverage Analyst Mag., 1972-73. Trustee Belgrade (Mont.) City-County Planning Bd., 1986—, Belgrade Sch. Dist., 1990—, vice chair, 1990-93; bd. dirs. Big Bros. and Sisters, Bozeman; bd. dirs., steering com. Mike Mansfield Found. Sgt. USMC, 1966-69. Mem. Am. C. of C. Execs (del. 1989-90), Mountain States Assn. C. of C. (pres. bd. dirs. 1990-91), Mont. Assn. Chamber Execs. (pres. 1987-88), Bus. Profl. Women (v.p. Bozeman chpt. 1982-83, Outstanding Young Woman award 1983, Woman of Achievement award 1985), Gallatin Performing Art Ctr. (sec., bd. dirs. 1989—), Mont. SBA (adv. coun. 1992—), Mont. State Rural Devel. Coun. (exec. com.), Mus. Rockies, Rotary.

JOYNER, DEE ANN, bank official; b. Alton, Ill., Feb. 26, 1947; d. T. Claxton and Dorothy M. (Troeckler) Burroughs; m. Orville Joyner, Mar. 15, 1973; 1 child, Dawn L. Kotva. BA in Govt., So. Ill. U., 1971, MS in Govt., 1973; MBA, St. Louis U., 1985. Adminstrv. asst. So. Ill. U., Edwardsville, 1970-72; staff assoc. Marshall Kaplan, Gans and Kahn, Washington, 1972-73; dir. community affairs East-West Gateway Coordinating Council, St. Louis, 1973-78; exec. dir. Coro Found., St. Louis, 1978-80, St. Louis County Econ. Council, Clayton, Mo., 1985-89; planning dir. St. Louis County, 1980-84; chief of staff to county exec. St. Louis County, Clayton, Mo., 1989-90; sr. v.p. Commerce Bank St. Louis, 1990—. Bd. dirs. Confluence, St. Louis, 1983-89, Civil Svc. Bd., University City, Mo., 1984-93, Better Bus. Bur., 1991-93, Tax Increment Financing Commn./Indsl. Devel. Authority, University City, 1993—, Alzheimers Assn., 1992—, Girl Scout Coun. of Greater St. Louis, 1993—, Boys and Girls Town, 1994—; active St. Louis Counts, 1987—; chmn. Sold On St. Louis campaign, 1988-90. Recipient Joseph E. Boland Meml. Outstanding Alumnus award St. Louis U., 1992, Spl. Leadership award YWCA, St. Louis, 1987. Mem. Leadership St. Louis, So. Ill. U. (bd. dirs. 1989-90, Alumnus of Yr. 1984), Rotary, Univ. Club (bd. dirs. 1994). Office: 8000 Forsyth Blvd Saint Louis MO 63105-1707

JOYNER, JO ANN, geriatrics nurse; b. Glenwood, Ga., Mar. 9, 1947; d. Roy and Lucille (Mercer) Powell; m. Henry Gene Lamb, Dec. 3, 1965 (div. 1984); children: Henry G. Lamb, Jr., Roy, Melinda, Jody; m. Robert Eugene Joyner, June 14, 1991. Diploma, Swainsboro Vocat./Tech., 1979; student, Ga. So. Coll., 1980. LPN, Ga. Staff nurse Meadows Meml. Hosp., Vidalia, Ga., 1980-82; staff nurse in ICU and critical care unit Toombs Alcohol and Drug Abuse Ctr., Vidalia, 1982-84; charge nurse Conners Nursing Home, Glenwood, Ga., 1984-85; supr. Bethany Nursing Ctr., Vidalia, 1990-92, charge nurse, 1985-92; nurse Claxton (Ga.) Nursing Home, Toombs Nursing and Intermediate Care Home, Lyons, Ga., 1992-93; with Laurens Convalescent Ctr., Dublin, Ga., 1993-94, staff nurse, 1994; staff nurse Meadow Brook Manor, 1994—; mem. ind. nursing registry, Claxton; nurse Meml. Med. Ctr., Savannah, Ga.; office nurse Montgomery County Correctional Inst., Mt. Vernon,m Ga. Democrat. Apostolic. Home: 315 Clover St East Dublin GA 31021

JOYNER KERSEE, JACQUELINE, track and field athlete; b. East St. Louis, Ill., Mar. 3, 1962; d. Alfred Sr. and Mary Joyner; m. Bob Kersee, Jan. 11, 1986. BA in History, UCLA, 1985. Winner 4 consecutive Nat. Jr. Pentathlon Championships; silver medalist, heptathlon Olympics, 1984; winner heptathlon Goodwill Games, Moscow, 1986; winner heptathlon, world record of 7161 points U.S. Olympic Festival, 1986; winner USA/Mobil Outdoor Track and Field Championship, 1987; winner, long jump and heptathlon World Track and Field Championships, 1987; gold medalist, long jump 24'3'12 and decathlon, world record 7291 Olympics, 1988; Grand Prix Indoor Champion, winner indoor world record 55m hurdlers 7:37, 1989; gold medalist, heptathlon, bronze medalist, long jump Olympics, Barcelona, Spain, 1992; winner heptathlon Goodwill Games, St. Petersburg, Russia, 1994. Recipient Sullivan award, 1987, Jesse Owens award Am. Black Achievement award Ebony Mag., 1987, Gold medal heptathlon World Track and Field Championships, 1993, Jim Thorpe award, 1993, Jackie Robinson "Robie" award, 1994, Grand Prix Outdoor Champion, 1994; named Athlete of Yr. Track & Field News, 1986, Female Athlete of Yr. AP, 1987, 1st Female Athlete of Yr. award Sporting News, 1988; holder Am. record in long jump, 1994. Office: JJK & Assocs Ste 105 3466 Bridgeland Dr Bridgeton MO 63044

JUAREZ, MARETTA LIYA CALIMPONG, social worker; b. Gilroy, Calif., Feb. 14, 1958; d. Sulpicio Magsalay and Pelagia Lagotom (Viacrusis) Calimpong; m. Henry Juarez, Mar. 24, 1984. BA, U. Calif., Berkeley, 1979; MSW, San Jose State U., 1983. Lic. clin. social worker; cert. in eye movement desensitization and reprocessing. Mgr. Pacific Bell, San Jose, Calif., 1983-84; revenue officer IRS, Salinas, Calif., 1984-85; social worker Santa Cruz (Calif.) County, 1985, Santa Clara County, San Jose, 1985—; co-chair Inter-Agy. Coun. of South Santa Clara County. Recipient award Am. Legion, 1972. Mem. NASW, Nat. Coun. on Alcoholism, Assn. Play Therapists. Democrat. Roman Catholic.

JUBINSKA-CHRISTIANSEN, PATRICIA ANN, ballet instructor, choreographer; b. Norfolk, Va., Nov. 10, 1949; d. Joseph John and Lucy (Babey) Topping; m. Paul Christiansen, June 5, 1971; children: Vanessa Meredith, Courtney Hilary. Student, Md. State Ballet Sch., 1959-60, Sch. Am. Ballet, N.Y.C., 1960-67; BA, R.I. Coll., 1976; postgrad., Wesleyan U. Mem. N.Y.C. Ballet, 1968-72; freelance artist Chamber Ballet of L.A., San Antonio Ballet, Md. State Ballet, 1972-81, 92-95; artistic dir. Blackstone Valley Ballet, Harrisville, R.I., 1983-84; freelance artist Am. Ballet, Pascoag, R.I., 1984-92. Home: 1264 Round Top Rd Harrisville RI 02830-1013

JUCEAM, ELEANOR PAM, behavioral sciences educator; b. Bklyn., June 24, 1936; d. Simon and Berta (Field) Pam; m. Robert Emanuel Juceam, May 24, 1970; children: Daniel James, Jacquelyn Brooke, Gregory Andrew. B.A., Brandeis U., 1958; M.A., NYU, 1960, NYU, 1963; Ph.D., NYU, 1969. Exec. asst. to pres. Queensboro Community Coll., CUNY, 1969-72, assoc. dean coll., 1969-72, dir. spl. programs CUNY, 1972-73, univ. dir. spl. programs, 1978-79; dept. chmn., prof. behavioral scis. Hostos Community Coll., CUNY, 1981—; mem. pres. coun. Brandeis U., Waltham, Mass., 1972—. Recipient Founders Day award NYU, 1969. Mem. City U. Women's Coalition, NOW. Jewish. Home: 106 Hemlock Rd Manhasset NY 11030-1214 Office: Hostos Community Coll Dept Behavioral Social Scis 500 Grand Concourse Bronx NY 10451-5323

JUDD, JACQUELINE DEE (JACKIE JUDD), journalist, reporter; b. Johnstown, Pa., Nov. 29, 1952; d. Myer and Lillian J.; m. Michael James Shulman, Oct. 6, 1985; 2 children. BA in Journalism and Polit. Sci., Am. U., 1973. Reporter WKXL Radio, Concord, N.H., 1974-75, WBAL Radio, Balt., 1975-76; reporter, anchor All Things Considered, Morning Edit., Nat. Pub. Radio, Washington, 1976-82; news anchor, reporter, anchor CBS Radio, N.Y.C., 1982-87; reporter ABC TV, Washington, 1987—. Recipient Overseas Press Club citation Overseas Press Club, N.Y.C., 1989, Emmy award Am. Acad. Arts and Scis., N.Y.C., 1990, Lodestar award Am. U., 1993, Dupont award, 1994. Mem. Radio TV Corr. Assocs. of Capital Hill (exec. com. 1993—), Am. Fedn. Radio and TV Artists. Office: ABC News Washington Bur 1717 Desales St NW Washington DC 20036-4407

JUDD, WYNONNA, vocalist, musician; b. 1964; d. Naomi Judd; 1 child, Elijah. Mem. country & western mus. duo The Judds; now pursuing solo career; songs include Had A Dream, 1983, Mama He's Crazy, 1984, Why Not Me, 1984, Love Is Alive, 1985, Have Mercy, 1985, Rockin' with The Rhythm, 1985, Grandpa, 1986; albums include The Judds, Why Not Me?, Rockin' with The Rhythm, Christmas Time With the Judds, Heartland, 1987, River of Time, 1989, Love Can Build A Bridge, 1990, Wynonna, 1992, Tell Me Wy, 1993, Greatest Hits Vols. I and II; co-author: (with Naomi Judd) Love Can Build a Bridge, 1993. Recipient: Grammy award, 1985, 86, 87, 89, duet award (with Naomi Judd), Acad. Country Music award, 1985-91, Vocal Duo award (with Naomi Judd), Country Music Assn. award, 1984-91, 2 Grammy nominations, 1994. *

JUDELL, CYNTHIA KOLBURNE, craft company executive; b. N.Y.C., Mar. 23, 1924; d. Luma L. and Stella E. (Robins) Kolburne; m. Samuel Judell, Oct. 30, 1949; children: Joy C., Neil H.K. BSEE, Antioch Coll., Yellow Springs, Ohio, 1945; MA, Columbia U., 1948. Cert. secondary tchr. Engr., Jet Propulsion Lab., Pasadena, Calif., 1946-47; tchr. math., sci. Leonard Sch. for Girls, N.Y.C., 1948-49; substitute tchr. Bd. Edn., Ridgefield, Conn., 1964-67; part-time tchr. Bd. Edn., Brookfield, Conn., 1967-73; owner T W M Enterprises, Wilton, Conn., 1976—. Dep. registrar of voters Town of Wilton, 1977-93; elected mem. Bd. of Tax Rev., Wilton, 1980-87; treas. Town Assn., Inc., Wilton, 1980-84. Recipient Intergroup scholar Columbia U., 1948. Mem. LWV (budget chair, treas. Conn. chpt. 1978-86, treas. Wilton chpt. 1986-88), Conn. Soc. Women Engrs. (treas. 1971-72). Office: T W M Enterprises PO Box 266 Wilton CT 06897-0266

JUDGE, DOLORES BARBARA, real estate broker; b. Plymouth, Pa.; d. Benjamin F. and Lottie (Kwiatkoski) Demsky; m. Richard James Judge, July 11, 1964; children: Susan, Nancy, Richard Jr. Student, North Harris County Coll., 1984-85, U. Tex., 1985, Houston Community Coll., 1988-89. Real estate agt. comml. real estate cos. in area, 1981-84; owner D-J Investment Properties, Conroe, Tex., 1984—; mem. first adv. bd. First Nat. Title Co., Conroe, 1989-90. Chmn. North Houston Econ. Devel. Showcase, 1990; bd. dirs. Montgomery County Crime Stoppers, Inc., 1993—. Mem. Comml. Real Estate Assn. Montgomery County (pres. 1986, 87, bd. dirs. 1988), Conroe C. of C. Office: D-J Investment Properties 130 Jeb Stuart Ln Conroe TX 77302-1149

JUDGE, ROSEMARY ANN, oil company executive; b. Jersey City; d. Frank T. and Frances M. (O'Brien) J. A.B., Seton Hall U. Exec. sec. Socony Vacuum, N.Y.C., 1944-56; sec., confidential asst. to v.p. and dir. Socony Mobil, N.Y.C., 1956-59; sec., confidential asst. to pres. Mobil Oil Co. Div., N.Y.C., 1959-61; sec., adminstrv. asst. to pres. Mobil Oil Corp., N.Y.C., 1961-69; adminstrv. asst. to chmn. Mobil Oil Corp., 1969-71, asst. to chmn., sec. exec com., 1971-84, corp. sec., 1975-76; asst. to chmn., sec. bd. and exec. com. Mobil Corp., 1976-84; pres. Mobil Found., N.Y.C., 1973-85. Mem. bd. regents Seton Hall U., 1982-88. Club: Women's Econ. Round Table.

JUDSON, BARBARA MICHAEL, business proposal manager; b. Goshen, Ind., Apr. 19, 1938; d. Ernest William and Dorothy Anne (Bartlett) Scully; children: Jennifer Beth, Rebecca Anne. BA, Calif. State U., 1962. Proposal mgr. Parker Hannifin Corp., Irvine, Calif., 1987-93, Rogerson Corp., Irvine, Calif., 1986. Home: 34142 Selva Rd Apt 216 Dana Point CA 92629-3780

JUDY, NANCY ELIZABETH, county commissioner; b. East Orange, N.J., Dec. 19, 1931; d. Ellsworth Rodman and Mary Ethel (Luppert) Bailey; m. Robert Walter Judy, Nov. 13, 1954; children—Robin Ann, Matthew Rodman. B.A., Pa. State U. Mem. sch. bd. Dallas Ind. Sch. Dist., 1972-76; exec. dir. Dallas County Rep. Party, 1977; county commr. Dallas County Commrs. Ct., 1979-94. Chmn. Regional Transp. Council, 1983—, Dallas County Civil Service Commn., 1983—, chmn. 1983—; mem. Regional Transp. Coun. 1981-91, chmn. 1985-86; bd. dirs. Dispute Mediation Service of Dallas County, 1980-85, Dallas Alliance; bd. dirs. Rep. Men's Club of Dallas County, Youth and Family Impact Bd., 1993—; precinct chmn. Dallas County Rep. Party, 1964-76; com. mem. Air Carrier Policy Com., 1992—, others. Mem. Dallas Assembly, Dallas Arboretum and Bot. Garden, Dallas Mus. Fine Arts. Roman Catholic. Address: 3346 Mayhew Dr Dallas TX 75228 Office: County Judge & Commissioners County Administration Bldg 411 Elm St Dallas TX 75202

JUE, SUSAN LYNNE, interior designer; b. Berkeley, Calif., July 7, 1956; d. Howard Lynn and Rosie (Fong) J. AA with honors, Cabrillo Coll., 1977; BA, Calif. Coll. Arts and Crafts, 1979. Interior designer Lucasfilm Ltd., San Anselmo, Calif., 1980-81, Whisler-Patri Architects and Planners, San Francisco, 1982, Barry Reischmann Design Studio, San Francisco, 1983, Kaplan, McLaughlin, Diaz Architects and Planners, San Francisco, 1984-85; Gensler & Assocs., Architects San Francisco, 1985, Hirano Assocs., San Francisco, 1987-88, Clocktower Design, San Ramon, Calif., 1988-89, Reel/Grobman & Assocs., San Francisco, 1989-90; interior designer Primo Angeli Inc., San Francisco, 1990-92, Guillermo Rossello, Architect, Berkeley, Calif., 1992—. Recipient No. Calif. Home & Garden Design Achievement award 1992. Mem. Inst. Bus. Designers (newsletter editor No. Calif. chpt. 1987-88, resource index com. 1987-88, chmn. graphic com. 1987-88, Ronald McDonald House com. 1988-89, chmn. Salvation Army project com. 1990-91, chmn. Bread and Roses project com. 1991, chmn. Ctr. for AIDS, 1991-92, bd. dirs. 1991—, Cert. of Appreciation 1989, 91, 92, Cmty. Svc. Program award 1993), Designers Lighting Forum. Home: 241 Stanford Ave Kensington CA 94708

JUETTE, GISELLE C., volunteer; b. Nordhausen, Harz, Germany, Nov. 8, 1931; d. Albert Fritz and Elsa Clara (Beegen) Juette; m. Roland J. Braun, May 12, 1956 (dec. Feb. 1990); children: Beate Elsa Braun, Bertram D. Braun, Burkhard R. Braun. Student, Victoria U., Manchester, Eng., 1952; Staatsexamen, Georgia Augusta U., Goettingen, Germany, 1953; diploma, Fremdsprachen/Dolmetshes Inst., Goettingen, Germany, 1953. Translator Brown Doveri & Co., Baden, Switzerland, 1953-58; substitute tchr. German, English Vestal (N.Y.) Cen. High Sch., 1970-89; docent Lower Cape Fear Hist. Soc., Wilmington, N.C., 1990—. Mem. Internat. Assn. Univ. Women, AAUW (bd. dirs. Wilmington br. 1990). Republican. Lutheran. Home: 3112 Lantern Way Wilmington NC 28409

JUHLIN, DORIS ARLENE, French language educator; b. Atlanta, Dec. 1, 1942; d. Lawrence Alfred and Doris (South) J. BA, Greenville (Ill.) Coll., 1964; MA, Baldwin-Wallace Coll., 1979. Cert. elem. and secondary French and reading tchr., Ohio. Tchr. French Cleve. Bd. Edn., 1965—; chmn. bldg. activities Cleve. Pub. Schs., 1983—, writer French curriculum, 1980; workshop presenter Ohio Modern Lang. Tchrs.' Assn., Columbus, Ohio, 1978. Dir. jump for heart sch. program Am. Heart Assn., 1986-90; v.p. Women's Ministries Internat.; speaker, editor ann. program resource books Free Meth. Ch., Indpls., 1985—; sec. Free Meth. Ohio Conf. Bd. Camping Dirs., Mansfield, Ohio, 1990-94; organist, Sunday Sch. tchr. Free Meth. Ch., Westlake, Ohio, 1964—; vol. Nat. Welsh Home for Aged, Rocky River, Ohio, 1970—; mem. task force Edn. 2000, 1992-93. Jennings scholar Martha Holden Jennings Found., 1980. Mem. Ohio Fgn. LAng. Assn., Cleve. Tchrs. Union, Nat. Audubon Soc., Mensa (gifted child coord. 1985-94, columnist Graffiti 1986-94). Democrat. Home: 3745 W 213th St Fairview Park OH 44126-1216 Office: Wilbur Wright Mid Sch 11005 Parkhurst Cleveland OH 44111

JUISTER, BARBARA JOYCE, mathematics educator; b. Ottawa, Ill., Sept. 4, 1939; d. Ralph Edward and Imogene (Wilson) Weber; m. Robert Milton Gibson, Sept. 9, 1959 (dec. May 1961); 1 child, Robert Milton Jr.; m. Charles Harry Juister, Apr. 2, 1966 (div. Dec. 30, 1991); children: Charles Edward, Leslie Elizabeth. BS in Math. Edn., Ill. State U., 1961; MA in Math. Teaching, Purdue U., 1965. Tchr. math. Lew Wallace High Sch.,

Gary, Ind., 1961-63, Paxton (Ill.) High Sch., 1963-64; prof. math. Elgin (Ill.) C.C., 1964—; reviewer textbooks for numerous pubs., 1977—; article reviewer Math. Tchr. mag., 1983—; reviewer modules Univ. Math. Applications Project, 1978—. Treas. Sybaquay coun. Girl Scouts U.S.A., 1985-92; elder 1st Presbyn. Ch., Elgin, 1986-92; del. Nat. Coun. Girl Scouts U.S.A., 1993—. Recipient Faculty Mem. of Yr. award Ill. C.C. Trustees Assn., 1992, Ctrl. region Outstanding Faculty Mem. award Assn. C.C. Trustees, 1993, Excellence in Tng. award Nat. Inst. Staff and Organizational Devel., 1993, Leader award for Edn. Elgin YWCA, 1994. Mem. Math. Assn. Am. (vis. lectr. 1981-92, bd. dirs. Ill. sect. 1985-94, chmn. 1992-93), Am. Math. Assn. 2-Yr. Colls. (libr. subcom. edn. com. 1990-91, Ill. del. to Del. Assembly 1992—), Ill. Math. Assn. C.C. (sec. 1978-83, pres. 1984-85, Disting. Svc. award 1992), Nat. Coun. Tchrs. Math. (speaker nat. meeting 1988), Ill. Coun. Tchrs. Math. (program com. 1988-89, speaker), No. Ill. Assn. Tchrs. Math. (bd. dirs. 1994—), Consortium for Math. and Its Applications, Altrusa Internat. Svc. Club. Presbyterian. Office: Elgin CC Math Dept 1700 Spartan Dr Elgin IL 60123

JUKES, BETTY C., performing arts consultant, fundraiser; b. Feb. 29, 1932; d. C.E. and Dorothy (Barber) Saunders; m. Harry T. Jukes, July 4, 1963; 1 child, Harry Samuel II. Bd. dirs. Houston Youth Symphony and Ballet, Houston, 1974—; founding dir. Tex. Music Festival, 1990; founder Houston's Internat. Mayor's Ball, founder Spl. Event March of Dimes; past exec. com., bd. mem. Internat. Inst. Edn. Home Hosp. for VIPs; coord. dinner and sci. seminar World Wildlife for His Royal Highness the Prince Philip; founding mem. Theatre Under the Stars Aux.; coord. 25th Ann. Original Astronauts Mercury Seven. Founding mem. Charles A. Lindbergh Meml. Found, Mpls., 1979—; founder Proud Ptnr. Mayor's Luncheon, Mayor's Ball; co-founder Houstonian of Yr. Dinner, 1973-90; founding com. mem. Houston Festival; founder ann. concert Music, The Internat. Lang.; mem. Houston Symphony Soc., Houston Grand Opera, Houston Ballet.; life mem. Meth. Hosp. Aux.; founding mem., life Mercury Seven Found., Orlando, Fla., 1987—. Mem. Nat. Soc. Fund Raising Execs., Houston Jr. Woman's Club (hon., founder), The Woman's Club (life, past pres.), Cancer League (life), Mental Health Assn. (life), others.

JULANDER, PAULA FOIL, association administrator; b. Charlotte, N.C., Jan. 21, 1939; d. Paul Baxter and Esther Irene (Earnhardt) Foil; m. Roydon Odell Julander, Dec. 21, 1985; 1 child, Julie McMahan Shipman. Diploma, Presbyn. Hosp. Sch. Nursing, Charlotte, N.C., 1960; BS magna cum laude, U. Utah, 1984; MS in Nursing Adminstrn., Brigham Young U., 1990. RN, Utah. Nurse various positions Fla. and S.C., 1960-66; co-founder, office mgr. Am. Laser Corp., 1970-79; gen. staff nurseoper. rm. Salt Lake Surg. Ctr., Salt Lake City, 1976-79; self employed Salt Lake City; teaching asst. U. Utah, Salt Lake City; rep. Utah State Legislature Coms., 1989-92; demo. nominee lt. gov., 1992; adj. faculty Brigham Young U. Coll. Nursing, 1987—; bd. dirs. Companion Fin. Corp.; mem. Utah state exec. bd. U.S. West Comm., 1993—; bd. regents Calif. Lutheran U. Pres. Utah Nurses Found., 1986-88; mem. Statewide Task Force on Child Sexual Abuse, 1989-90, Utah Nursing Resource Study, 1985—, State Feasibility Task Force for Nurses, 1985—, LWV, Women's Polit. Caucus, Statewide Abortion Task Force, 1990; bd. dirs. Community Nursing Svc. Home Health Plus, 1992—. Mem. ANA (del. conv. 1986-90), Utah Nurses Assn. (legis. rep. 1987-88, pres.), Nat. Orgn. Women Legislators, Sigma Theta Tau, Phi Kappa Phi (Susan Young Gates award 1991). Home: 1467 Penrose Dr Salt Lake City UT 84103-4466 Office: Utah Nurses Assn 455 E 400 S Ste 402 Salt Lake City UT 84111-3008

JULIAN, CYNTHIA ANN, accountant; b. Dallas, Oct. 17, 1958; d. Billy Wayne Presley and Willie Mae (Sanders) Presley Wilcox; m. Paul David Julian, Mar. 3, 1984. AA in Acctg., Mountain View Coll., 1981; BBA in Acctg., U. Tex., 1989. CPA, Tex., CMA. Cash disbursements clk. Drawing Bd. Greeting Cards, Dallas, 1979-81; rev. acctg. clk. Sunbelt Airlines, Camden, Ark., 1981-84; bookkeeper Crown Office Supply, Tyler, Tex., 1984-85; bookkeeper, adminstrv. asst. Motion Industries, Inc., Tyler, Tex., 1985-90; staff acct. Rex-Hide, Inc., Tyler, 1990—. Company leader Am. Heart Assn. Heart Walk, Tyler, 1993, 94; tabulator Childrens Miracle Network Telethon, Tyler, 1990—. Mem. AICPA, Tex. Soc. CPAs, E. Tex. Chpt. Tex. Soc. CPAs, Inst. Mgmt. Accts. (pres.-elect Tyler chpt., pres. Tyler chpts. 1994—, v.p. 1993-94). Home: 7915 CR 118 Bullard TX 75757 Office: Rex-Hide Inc 705 S Lyons PO Box 4726 Tyler TX 75712

JULIEN, GAIL LESLIE, model, public relations professional; b. L.I., N.Y., Apr. 13, 1940; d. David William Syme and Virginia Martha (Burth) Miller; m. Michael Louis Woodman, Sept. 12, 1958 (div.); children: Jho'meyr Renei, Sabrina Michelle; m. Francis Dana Julien, Dec. 24, 1977. Diploma in modeling, Coronet of Calif., 1960; grad., Am. Beauty Finishing Sch., 1961. Playboy bunny Playboy Club, Kansas City, Mo., 1970-72; Gremlin girl AMC, Kansas City, 1972; Dodge girl Dodge, Kansas City, 1972-73; owner, pres. Gail Woodman Enterprises Inc., Overland Park, Kans., 1972-76; sales rep. Kansas City Brit. Motors, Lenexa, Kans., 1976-78; dir. pub. rels., mktg. Downtown Air Ctr., Kansas City, 1978-80; dir. pub. rels., media rels. Bretney Corp., Kansas City, 1980-82; v.p. Nuwalters Co., Overland Park, 1983-84; regional mgr. aviation Multi Svc. Corp., Overland Park, 1984—; rep. Nat. Bus. Aircraft Assn., 1984—, Can. Bus. Aircraft Assn., 1984—, Nat. Aircraft Transp. Assn., 1984—, Abbotsford Internat. Airshow, 1991. Author: Physician's Nutritional Guide, 1984; author numerous poems, self improvement and modeling course. Vol. Live On Stage '88 (AIDS), Santa Ana, Calif., 1988, St. Joseph Hosp., Kansas City, 1986-88; v.p. Young Dems., Midland, Mich., 1960; active Northshore Animal League, Christian Children's Fund, City of Hope, L.A., 1991; bd. dirs., fundraiser Make A Wish of Tri Counties. Recipient Outstanding Sales Achievement award Brit. Leyland, 1976-77. Mem. Am. Bus. Women's Assn. Home: 28129 Peacock Ridge Dr Apt 312 Palos Verdes Peninsula CA 90274-7121 Office: Multi Svc Corp 8650 College Blvd Shawnee Mission KS 66210-1820

JULIFS, SANDRA JEAN, community action agency executive; b. Jersey City, July 12, 1939; d. Roy Howard and Irma Margrete (Barkhausen) Walters; m. Harold William Julifs, July 22, 1961; children: David Howard, Steven William. BA, U. Va., 1961; postgrad., U. Minn., 1962-63, Mankato State Coll., 1963. Cert. comty. action profl. Tchr. St. James (Minn.) Pub. Schs., 1961-62; substitute tchr. Sleepy Eye (Minn.) Pub. Schs., 1963-67, home bound tutor, 1967; lay reader, rater U. Wis., Stevens Point, 1968; co-founder Family Planning Service Portage County, Stevens Point, 1970-72; family planning dir. Tri-County Opportunities Coun., Rock Falls, Ill., 1971-77; energy programs coord. Tri-County Opportunities Coun., Rock Falls, 1977-78, planner, EEO officer, 1978-83, pres., chief exec. officer, 1983—; sec. Ill. Ventures for Comty. Action Springfield, 1983-91. Mem. Nat. Cmty. Action Found., Washington, 1987—; bd. dirs. Twin Cities Homeless Coalition, 1989—; adv. coun. Sauk Valley Coll. Human Svcs., 1990—; mem. Whiteside County Overall Econ. Devel. Coun., 1990—, adv. coun. Inst. for Social and Econ. Devel., 1992—; cons. com. No. Ill. Synod Evang. Luth. Ch. Am., 1993—, churchwide assembly del., 1995. Recipient Appreciation award Western Ill. Agy. on Aging, 1980, 81, Spl. Recognition award Ill. Head Start and Day Care Assn., Recognition award Ill. Community Action Fund, 1984. Mem. AAUW, NAFE, Am. Soc. Pub. Adminstrn., Whiteside County Welfare Assn., Lee County Welfare Assn. (sec.-treas. 1983-84), Nat. Comty. Action Assn., Ill. Comty. Action Assn. (com. chair 1985-88, dir. exec. com. 1986—, treas. 1988, 89, sec. 1989, 90, v.p. 1991-93, pres. 1993—, Recognition award 1985-94). Lutheran. Office: Tri-County Opportunities Coun 405 Emmons Ave PO Box 610 Rock Falls IL 61071

JUMBELIC, MARY IRENE, forensic pathologist, educator; b. Balt., July 30, 1956; d. Stephen and Esther Irene (Ruth) J.; m. Marc Jay Safran, Nov. 30, 1986; children: Joshua Jumbelic, David Jumbelic. BA in Biology cum laude, U. Md., 1979, MD, 1983. Diplomate Am. Bd. Pathology. Mem. rsch. staff Martin Marietta Labs., Balt., 1977-81; intern in gen. surgery Union Meml. Hosp., Balt., 1983-84, resident in pathology, 1984-85; resident in pathology North Western U. Hosp., Chgo., 1985-87; fellow in forensic pathology Cook County Office of Med. Examiner, Chgo., 1987-88, dep. med. examiner, 1988-90; forensic pathologist, coroner's physician Peoria (Ill.) County Coroner's Office, 1990-94; anatomic pathologist St. Francis Hosp. Pathology Assn., Peoria, 1990-94; pvt. practice Peoria Heights, Ill., 1990—; clin. instr. pathology U. Ill. Coll. of Medicine, Peoria, 1991-93, clin. asst. prof. pathology, 1993—; mem. forensic sci. adv. bd. Ill. State Police, Springfield, 1992—, forensic adv. bd. to atty. gen. on child death and serious injury, Chgo., 1993—; mem. Sexual Assault Med. Work Group, Chgo., 1993—; staff physician Pediatric Resource Ctr., Peoria, 1994—; lectr. in field. Contbr. articles to profl. jours. Balt. Med. Soc. scholar, 1980-82. Mem. AMA (alt. del. 1994—), Am. Acad. Forensic Scis., Am. Profl. Soc. on the Abuse of Children, Internat. Soc. Prevention of Child Abuse and Neglect, Nat. Assn. Med. Examiners, Ill. State Med. Soc., Ill. Soc. Pathologists, Peoria County Med. Soc., Phi Kappa Phi. Office: 4617 N Prospect Rd Ste 9 Peoria Heights IL 61614-6450

JUNCK, MARY, newspaper publishing executive. Pub., pres. St. Paul Pioneer Press, St. Paul, until 1993; pub. The Baltimore Sun, 1993—. Office: Baltimore Sun 501 N Calvert St Baltimore MD 21278*

JUNG, DORIS, dramatic soprano; b. Centralia, Ill., Jan. 5, 1924; d. John Jay and May (Middleton) Crittenden; m. Felix Popper, Nov. 3, 1951; 1 son, Richard Dorian. Ed., U. Ill., Mannes Coll. Music, Vienna Acad. Performing Arts; student of, Julius Cohen, Emma Zador, Luise Helletsgruber, Winifred Cecil. Debut as Vitellia in: Clemenza di Tito, Zurich (Switzerland) Opera, 1955, other appearances with, Hamburg State Opera, Munich State Opera, Vienna State Opera, Royal Opera Copenhagen, Royal Opera Stockholm, Marseille and Strasbourg, France, Naples (Italy) Opera Co., Catania (Italy) Opera Co., N.Y.C. Opera, Met. Opera, also in Mpls., Portland, Oreg., Washington and Aspen, Colo.; soloist: Wagner concert conducted by Leopold Stokowski, 1971; with, Syracuse (N.Y.) Symphony, 1981, voice tchr., N.Y.C., 1970—. Home: 40 W 84th St New York NY 10024

JUNG, HILDA ZIIFLE, physicist; b. Gretna, La.; d. William Christian and Leonora Margaret (Giboney) Ziifle; m. Julius Robert Jung Jr., Nov. 2, 1968. BS, Tulane U., 1943. Engring. release clk. Higgins Aircraft Co., Michoud, La., 1943-44; rsch. physicist So. Regional Rsch. Ctr., USDA, New Orleans, 1944-79; retired, 1979. Contbr. articles to profl. jours.; patentee chem. process. Named Woman of Yr. New Orleans Fed. Exec. Bd., 1978. Mem. AAAS, AARP (program dir. Terrytown chpt. 1991-95, chmn. social com. 1989), Am. Chem. Soc. (sec. La. sect. 1977), Orgn. Profl. Employees Dept. Agrl. (life, pres. 1978, Profl. of Yr. 1979), Am. Legion Aux., Nat. Assn. Ret. Fed. Employees (life, 1st v.p., legis. chmn. 1980, pres. 1981, 92, pub. rels. officer 1984, 89-91, newsletter editor 1993, program chair 1995), Sigma Xi. Lutheran.

JUNGBLUTH, CONNIE CARLSON, senior tax compliance specialist; b. Cheyenne, Wyo., June 20, 1955; d. Charles Marion and Janice Yvonne (Keldsen) Carlson; m. Kirk E. Jungbluth, Feb. 5, 1977; children: Tyler, Ryan. BS, Colo. State U., 1976. CPA, Colo. Sr. acct. Rhode Scripter & Assoc., Boulder, Colo., 1977-81; mng. acct. Arthur Young, Denver, 1981-85; asst. v.p. Dain Bosworth, Denver, 1985-87; v.p. George K. Baum & Co., Denver, 1987-91; acct. Ariz. Luth. Acad., 1994-95; sr. tax acct. Ernst & Young, L.L.P., Phoenix, 1995—. Active Denver Estate Planning Coun., 1981-85; organizer Little People Am., Rocky Mountain Med. Clinic and Symposium, Denver, 1986; adv. bd. Children's Home Health, Denver, 1986-89; fin. adv. bd. Gail Shoettler for State Treas., Denver, 1986; campaign chmn. Kathi Williams for Colo. State Legislature, 1986; mem. Sch. dist. 12 Colo. Edn. Found. Bd., 1991, Napa Sch. Dist. Elem. Site Com., 1992-94. Named one of 50 to watch, Denver mag., 1988. Mem. AICPA, Colo. Soc. CPAs (strategic planning com. 1987-89, instr. bank 1983, trustee 1984-87, pres. bd. trustees 1986-87, bd. dirs. 1987-89, chmn. career edn. com. 1982-83, pub. svc. award 1985-87), Colo. Mcpl. Bond Dealers, Metro North C. of C. (bd. dirs. 1987-90), Denver City Club (bd. dirs. 1987-88), Phi Beta Phi.

JUNKER, CHRISTINE ROSETTA, swine production executive; b. Burlington, Iowa, June 10, 1953; d. Roland Lee and Janet Elaine (Kapotas) Wiemann; 1 child, Nolan Robert. Assocs. of Animal Sci., Hawkeye Inst. Tech., 1977; student, U. No. Iowa, 1984-85, 94—. Drafstman Confinement Specialists, Mediapolis, Iowa, 1973-75; herdsman X-L Pork, Cedar Falls, Iowa, 1976-77; livestock specialist Tasco, Inc., Shell Rock, Iowa, 1977-81; problem accounts specialist I.F.G. Leasing, Parkersburg, Iowa, 1981-86; pres. Pork Purveyors, Ltd., Parkersburg, 1986-88, 89—; gen. mgr. div. Pork Purveyors Doane Farm Mgmt. Co., Parkersburg, 1988-89; founder div. Pork Purveyors, Ltd. Craft Store, Parkersburg, 1990-92; mem. adv. com. animal sci. dept. Hawkeye Inst. Tech., Waterloo, Iowa, 1988-94; coord. Parkersburg Econ. Devel., 1990-92; mem. Iowa Small Bus. Adv. Bd., 1992—; mng. dir. Surg. Device Internat., Inc., 1992—. Producer children's album with 5 original songs, 1989; contbr. articles to profl. jours. Mediator Iowa Farmer/Creditor Mediation Svc., 1987—; dir. choir Calvary Bapt. Ch., 1991-92; mem. jud. nominating commn. Iowa Dist. Two-A, 1992—. Named Outstanding Alumni All Agrl. Club, Hawkeye Inst. Tech., 1979, Citizen of Yr., Parkersburg, Iowa, 1991; recipient Iowa Community Betterment Leadership award, 1991, Gov.'s Volunteerism award, 1992. Home: PO Box 596 Parkersburg IA 50665 Office: Pork Purveyors Ltd PO Box 596 215 3d St Parkersburg IA 50665

JUNKER, PATRICIA A., sales executive; b. Peoria, Ill., Dec. 29, 1945; d. Raymond Starts and Flora Dora (Wyss) J.;m. Daniel E. Smith, Feb. 14, 1970 (div. Aug. 1971). Student, Marin C.C., 1980-86; BS in Orgnl. Behaviour, U. San Francisco, 1989. From travel cons. to asst. mgr. World Wide Travel, Peoria, Ill., 1967-71, mgr., 1971-73; sales rep. KLM Royal Dutch Airlines, Des Moines, Iowa, 1977-80, San Francisco, 1980-86, L.A., 1986-92; dist. mgr. sales KLM Royal Dutch Airlines, Orlando, 1993—; cons. Midtown Travel and TravelDesk, San Francisco, 1973-76; mem. mktg. project Europe By Design, 1989-90. Recipient Kaspar Press Advt. award. Mem. Nat. Assn. Profl. Saleswomen (past bd. dirs. No. Calif.), Travel Industry Adv. Bd., Acad. Pacific Bus. and TVL Coll.-Hollywood, Assn. for Promotion of Tourism to Africa, Inst. Cert. Travel Agts. (cert. travel cons. 1980, co-coord. Iowa study group program 1978-80). Office: KLM Royal Dutch Airlines 201 E Pine St # 1400 Orlando FL 32801

JURCZYK, JOANNE MONICA, technical analyst; b. Orange, Calif., Dec. 27, 1958; d. Edward Joseph and Helen Imogene (Shelly) J. BSBA in Econs., Chapman U., 1981. Guest rsch. specialist Disneyland-Walt Disney Co., Anaheim, Calif., 1985-88, guest rsch. coord., 1988-89, guest rsch. survey ops. supr., 1989-91, indsl. engring. tech. analyst, 1991-92; pricing coord. Kirk Paper Corp., Downey, Calif., 1995—; active Work Exposure Day, Disneyland/U. Disneyland, Anaheim, 1990. Assoc. Met. Mus. Art, 1991—; active youth motivation task force Orange County Unified Sch. Dist., 1992; mem. Orange County chpt. Habitat for Humanity. Mem. Am. Film Inst. Democrat. Roman Catholic. Office: Kirk Paper Corp 7500 Amigos Ave Downey CA 90242

JURGENSEN, KAREN, newspaper editor. BA in Eng., U. N.C., 1971. Editorial and feature writer, columnist, editorial page layout editor Charlotte (N.C.) News, 1972-75; writer, editor Sea Grant Coll. Program U. N.C., Raleigh, 1976-79; from asst. lifestyle editor to lifestyle editor Miami News, 1979-82, asst. city editor, 1982; topics editor, life dept. USA Today, Arlington, Va., 1982; spl. projects editor, life dept. USA Today, 1983-85, dep. mng. editor, life dept., 1985-86, mng. editor, cover stories dept., 1986-87, sr. editor, days/spl. projects, 1987-91, editor of editorial page, 1991—; participant Penney-Mo. Workshop, Columbia, Mo., 1981, Am. Press Inst. Workshops, 1981, 84, newspaper execs. mktg. sem. Am. Newspaper Pubs. Assn., 1986. Bd. vis. Chapel Hill Sch. Journalism and Mass Comm., U. N.C. Exchange scholar U. P.R., 1969-70. Mem. Am. Soc. Newspaper Editors (chair/vice chair press bar com. 1993-95, convention com. 1991-94, vice chair convention com. 1995—, vice chair, chair literacy com. 1989-91, future of newspapers com. 1988-90, 91, writing awards bd. 1989-91), Internat. Women's Media Found., Nat. Conf. Editorial Writers, New Directions News (bd. dirs.). Office: USA Today 1000 Wilson Blvd Arlington VA 22229-3991

JURIGA, ROSEMARIE, social service administrator; b. Akron, Ohio, Sept. 4, 1949; d. Emil Paul and Wanda Theresa (Pelka) J. AAS in Community Svcs., U. Akron, 1977, BA in Social Work, 1981; MS in Social Adminstrn., Case Western Res. U., 1992. Lic. social worker, Ohio. Office supr. Vocat. Devel. Ctr., Akron, 1978-80; assoc. exec. dir. Goodwill Industries of Akron, 1980-82; coord. Akron Community Svc. Ctr. and Urban League, 1982-84; dir. Akron 70001, 1984-90; exec. dir. Tri-County Ind. Living Ctr., Akron, 1990—; commn. grant rev. U.S. Dept. Edn., Washington, 1993-95; dean appointment Summit County Adv. for Mandel Sch. of Applied Social Sci., Cleve., 1992—. Bd. dirs. Cath. Commn., Akron, 1986—; bd. dirs., treas. Women's Entrepreneurial Growth Orgn., Akron, 1991-93; bd. dirs. United Way Women, Akron, 1993; cand. sch. bd. Akron Sch. Bd., 1993; mem. Mayor's Commn. on Children, Akron, 1994, allocations panel United Way of Summit County, 1986-92. Named Employer of Yr., Summit County Com. on Employment and Advocacy of Persons with Disability, 1994, Woman of Yr., Women's History Project of Summit County, Akron, 1994. Mem. NASW, Women's Network of Akron. Office: Tri-County Ind Living Ctr 680 E Market St Ste 205 Akron OH 44304-1640

JURKA, EDITH MILA, psychiatrist, researcher; b. N.Y.C., Dec. 4, 1915; d. Charles Anton and Edith Dorothy (Schevcik) J. BA, Smith Coll., 1936; postgrad., Charles U., Prague, Czechoslovakia, 1936-38; MD, Yale U., 1944. Diplomate Am. Bd. Psychiatry and Neurology. Intern in children's med. svc. Bellevue Hosp., N.Y.C., 1944-45, asst. alienist, 1947-49; rotating intern Gallinger Hosp., Washington, 1945-46; intern N.Y. State Psychiat. Inst., N.Y.C., 1946-47; asst. psychiatrist Mt. Sinai Hosp., N.Y.C., 1949-51; pvt. practice N.Y.C., 1949—; asst. psychiatrist Roosevelt Hosp., N.Y.C., 1954-57; chief psychiatrist Pleasantville (N.Y.) Cottage Sch., 1961-74; bd. dirs. intuition network Inst. Noetic Scis. Fellow Am. Orthopsychiat. Assn.; mem. Am. Psychiat. Assn., N.Y. Coun. Child and Adolescent Psychiatry, N.Y. County Med. Soc., N.Y. State Med. Soc. Home: 16 Apple Bee Farm Ln Croton-on-Hudson NY 10520 Office: 116 E 66th St New York NY 10021-6547

JURKUS, JANICE MARGARET, optometric educator; b. Milw., Feb. 20, 1950; d. Zanner Casper Jurkus and Alice Regina (Kuzminski) Jurkus-Reed. BS, Ill. Coll. Optometry, 1972, OD, 1974; MBA, Loyola U., 1978. Registered optometrist. Tchr., staff dr. Ill. Coll. Optometry, Chgo., 1974, chmn. optometric sci., 1982-85, assoc. prof., 1983—; rsch. cons. Wesley-Jesson, Inc., Chgo., 1975-83; optometric practice cons. Jessen-Wesley & Assocs., Chgo., 1986—; continuing edn. lectr. state, local and nat. optometric groups, 1975—. Cons. editor: Contact Lens Forum, 1986-91; contbr. articles to profl. jours. Mem. adv. bd. St. Joseph's Carondelet Child Care Ctr., Chgo., 1985—; vol. 43d Ward Dem. Com., Chgo., 1990—. Fellow Am. Acad. Optometry; mem. Am. Optometric Assn., Internat. Assn. Contact Lens Educators (exec. bd. 1990-94), Assn. Optometric Contact Lens Educators (vice chair 1991-93, chmn. 1994—, outstanding svc. award 1992). Office: Ill Coll Optometry 3241 S Michigan Ave Chicago IL 60616

JURRUS, KATHLEEN SUE, post anesthesia care nurse; b. Toledo, July 30, 1949; d. Earl Martin and Rae Grace (Koch) J. Diploma in nursing, Flower Hosp. Sch. Nursing, Toledo, 1970; Assoc. in Respiratory Therapy Health Tech., U. Toledo, 1976; BSN, Toledo/Med. Coll. of Ohio, 1994. RN, Ohio; cert. post anesthesia nurse, ACLS, respiratory therapy technician. Staff nurse ICU/CCU St. Luke's Hosp., Maumee, Ohio, 1970-74, staff therapist respiratory therapy, 1974-76, asst. dir. respiratory therapy, 1976-78, staff nurse PACU, 1991—; staff nurse Post Anesthesia Care Unit Flower Hosp., Sylvania, Ohio, 1978-84, 86-94, staff nurse Post Anesthesia Care Unit, Outpatient Surgery, 1986-94; head nurse Post Anesthesia Care Unit Toledo Clinic Outpatient Surgery Ctr., 1984-86; mem. Am. Bd. Post Anesthesia Nursing Certification, 1988-94, treas., 1989-93. Mem. AACN, Am. Soc. Post Anesthesia Nurses (charter mem.), Ohio Post Anesthesia Nurses Assn. (pres. 1983-84, bd. dirs. 1978—), N.W. Ohio Post Anesthesia Nurses Assn. (pres. 1983-84, bd. dirs. 1986—), Mich. Assn. Post Anesthesia Nurses, Sigma Theta Tau. Lutheran. Office: St Lukes Hosp Post Anesthesia Care Unit 5901 Monclova Rd Maumee OH 43537-1899

JURSKIS, SNIEGA MARIA (SNIEGUOLE JURSKYTE), architectural designer; b. Kaunas, Lithuania, Aug. 5, 1932; came to U.S., 1949; d. Alfonsas and Ona (Tallat-Kelpsa) J.; m. John Robert Gamble, Aug. 5, 1961 (div. Sept. 1964). Assoc. degree in Tech., Temple U., 1954. Lead designer United Engrs. & Constructors, Inc., Phila., 1960-86. Sec. Lithuanian-Am. Cmty. Nat. Exec. Com., 1970-72; tchr. Lithuanian Heritage Sch. Phila., 1959-62; announcer, editor Lithuanian Radio Hour Phila., 1951-67. Mem. Fedn. Lithuanian Women's Clubs (chmn. human rights com. 1978-82), Phila. Club (chmn. 1982—). Republican. Roman Catholic.

JURY, DEBRA E. (DEBBIE JURY), emergency nurse, consultant, author, educator; b. Las Cruces, N.Mex., Mar. 22, 1957; d. Robert Charles and Elois (Awalt) Aylett; m. Jeffrey Paul Jury, Mar. 29, 1986; children: Dana Renee, Travis Adair, Zane William. ADN, N.Mex. State U., 1977; postgrad., Calif. State U., Carson, 1990—. CEN; trauma nurse course cert. Staff nurse Meml. Gen. Hosp., Las Cruces, 1977-78, team leader, 1978, asst. charge nurse, 1978-79, asst. IV therapist/chemotherapist, 1979-80, asst. charge nurse, 1983; office RN Richard H. Higgs M.D., Las Cruces, 1980-83; staff nurse Clovis (Calif.) Community Hosp., 1983-84, staff triage nurse, 1984-94; emergency med. svcs. specialist, tng. officer Fresno County Dept. Health, Fresno, Calif., 1994—; cons. RN preceptor, lectr., nurse educator Genentech, San Francisco, 1985—. Contbr. articles to profl. jours. Voting mem. Community Hosps. of Ctrl. Calif., Fresno, 1987—. Named Emergency Nurse of the Yr., Mid-Valley Emergency Nurses, 1990, scholarship, 1993. Mem. Emergency Nurses Assn. (fundraising chair 1989, pres.-elect 1990, pres. 1991, past pres. 1992, chair emergency nurse of yr. com. 1993, 94), Am. Trauma Soc., Calif. Emergency Nurses Assn. (co-chair membership 1994), Calif. Nurses Assn. (co-chair program com. region 5 RN of Yr. Com. 1993-94), Safety Belt Safe, Scottish Soc. Ctrl. Calif. Democrat. Office: Emergency Med Svcs PO Box 11867 Fresno CA 93775

JUST, GEMMA RIVOLI, advertising executive; b. N.Y.C., Nov. 29, 1921; d. Philip and Brigida (Consolo) Rivoli; B.A., Hunter Coll., N.Y.C., 1943; m. Victor Just, Jan. 29, 1955. Copy group head McCann Erickson, N.Y.C., 1958-62; copy. supr. Morse Internat., N.Y.C., 1962-67; v.p., dir. creative svcs. Deltakos div. J. Walter Thompson, N.Y.C., 1967-75; v.p., copy dir. Sudler & Hennessey, div. Young & Rubicam, N.Y.C., 1980-87; sr. v.p., assoc. creative dir. copy, 1987-88, ret., 1989. Mem. Episcopal Ch. Women of Incarnation, N.Y.C., also ch. altar guild and acolyte. Named Best Writer, Art Dirs. Club N.Y., 1979, Best Writer Young & Rubicam, 1981; recipient Aesulapius awards Modern Medicine mag., 1980-88. Mem. Coun. Communications Socs., Pharm. Advt. Coun., Am. Med. Writers Assn. (exec. com. 1973). Home: 155 E 38th St Apt 5D New York NY 10016-2663

JUSZCZAK, LINDA JOY, nursing educator; b. July 15, 1951. BSN, Skidmore Coll., 1973; MSN, U. Colo., 1974; MPH, U. Minn., 1982, certs., 1981, 82. Cert. nurse practitioner in pedatrics. Staff nurse Children's Hosp. Nat. Med. Ctr., Washington, 1974-75; staff nurse Yale New Haven (Conn.) Hosp., 1975-77, pediatric clin. nurse specialist, 1977-80; instr. pediatric nursing Yale U. Sch. Nursing, 1977-80; pediatric nurse practitioner Dept. Pediatrics Montefiore Med. Ctr., Bronx, N.Y., 1982-87; program dir. The Bronx Consortium for Adolescent Health Montefiore Med. Ctr., 1984-86, program dir. Bronx Adolescent Consultation, Health Program, 1986-87; clinic dir. Far Rockaway High Sch. Clinic North Shore U. Hosp., Manhasset, N.Y., 1987-92; project dir. Far Rockaway, Intermediate Sch. 53 Clinic North Shore U. Hosp., Manhasset, 1992—; frequent participant confs., workshops; contbr. articles to profl. jours. Reviewer Am. Jour. Nursing, 1986, Jour. of Developmental and Behavioral Pediatrics, 1989-93; mem. Jour. Adv. Com. of Soc. for Adolescent Medicine. Mem. insvc. com. Greater N.Y. March of Dimes, 1982-83, planning com. for reference guide on nutrition mgmt. of pregnant adolescents Divsn. of Maternal Child Health, Dept. Health and Human Svcs., City of N.Y. Mayor's Child Health Adv. Coun.'s work group on sch. health; acting chairperson steering com. Coalition for Sch.-Base Primary Care, N.Y.C., 1992-93, co-chairperson, rsch. and evaluation com., 1992—, co-chairperson steering com., 1993—. Fellow Nat. Assn. of Pediatric Nurse Practitioners and Nurses; mem. APHA, Soc. for Adolescent Medicine. Office: North Shore U Hosp 300 Community Dr Manhasset NY 11030

KABACK, ELAINE, career counselor, consultant; b. Phila., Feb. 22, 1939; d. Sol and Evelyn Zitman; children: Douglas, Stepen, Michelle. Student Pa. State U., 1956-58; B.A., Temple U., 1960; M.S., Calif. State U., 1977. Cert. career counselor. Tchr. English Sayre Jr. High Sch., Phila. Public Schs., 1960-62; tchr. English and history Beth Tfiloh Pvt. Day Sch., Balt., 1968-72; mgmt. cons., trainer SWA, Palos Verdes, Calif., 1975-85; counselor Career Planning Ctr. and Mid-Life Ctr., Long Beach City Coll., 1977-78; dir. program devel. Univance Career Ctrs., Inc., Los Angeles, 1978-80; pvt. practice career counseling, 1980—, outplacement cons. Exec. Horizons, Inc., Newport Beach, Calif., 1985—; coord. career transition program, trainer, instr. UCLA Extension, 1980—; cons. in career systems, outplacement and orgnl. devel. Pres. Palos Verdes chpt. NOW, 1974-76; treas. S.W. chpt. Nat. Women's Polit. Caucus, 1973, 78; bd. dirs. STEP Adult Edn. Programs, Palos Verdes, 1974—, cert. community coll. life counselor, Calif.; cert. tchr., Pa. Mem. Calif. Counseling and Devel., Am. Counseling Assn., Orgn. Devel. Network, Phi Kappa Phi. Office: 11340 W Olympic Blvd Ste 255 Los Angeles CA 90064-1612

KABAT, LINDA GEORGETTE, civic leader; b. Cleve., Nov. 26, 1951; d. Michael G. and Georgette (deVos) Paul; m. John Edward Kabat Jr., Apr. 23, 1977; 1 child, Susan Marie. Student, Cleve. Inst. Music, 1969-72. With sales dept. Higbee Co., Fairview Park, Ohio, 1972; customer svc. rep. Ashland Chem. Co., Cleve., 1972-74, Celanese Corp., Lakewood, Ohio, 1974-76; with sales dept. May Co., North Olmsted, Ohio, 1979; customer service rep. Diamond Shamrock Corp., Cleve., 1979-82; in sales May Co., North Olmsted, 1989—. Chpt. pres. Cath. War Vets. Aux., Cleve., 1973-75, pres. Ohio, 1975-77, nat. sec., 1977-79, state sec., 1991-92. Mem. Mu Phi Epsilon (pres. 1971-72, historian 1970-71). Republican.

KABAT, SYRTILLER DÉLORES MCCOLLUM, marriage, family, child counselor; b. Tampa, June 18, 1937; d. Theodore and Katie (McCoy) McCollum; m. Lucien Kabat, July 16, 1965; children: Luke, Michael (adopted), Soon Yun Kwon (adopted), Debi Estell (adopted). BA, Montclair State Coll., 1960; MA in Psychol., Wright Inst., 1972, PhD, 1975. Cert. tchr. N.J., Calif.; lic. profl. counselor Calif., Mo.; cert. Nat. Bd. Cert. Counselors, Am. Bd. Med. Psychotherapists, MFCC. Asst. prof. counseling San Jose (Calif.) St. U., 1972-79; prof. John F. Kennedy U., Orinda, Calif., 1974-83; instr. U. Mo., Kansas City, 1984-86; pvt. practice marriage, family, child counselor Kansas City and Lee's Summit, Mo., 1984—. Contbr. articles to profl. jours. Bd. dirs. Ravenswood Sch. Dist., Palo Alto, Calif., 1967-75; pres. Lee's Summit Housing Commn., 1987—, Adolescent Resource Com., Kansas City, 1987, Shekinah Found., 1987—. Mem. Am. Assn. Marriage and Family Therapists, Mo. Assn. Marriage and Family Therapists, Calif. Assn. Marriage and Family Therapists (v.p.), Am. Assn. Counseling and Devel. Home: 410 SE Independence Ave Lees Summit MO 64063-2854 Office: 120 SE Second St Suite 106 Lee's Summit MO 64063

KABRIEL, MARCIA GAIL, psychotherapist; b. El Reno, Okla., Jan. 8, 1938; d. Gail Frederick and Katherine (Marsh) Slaughter; m. J. Ronald Kabriel, May 25, 1957 (div. Sept. 1985); children: Joseph Charles, Jeffrey Gail, Jae B. BA, U. Okla., 1965, MSW, 1968; postgrad. Am. U. Psychiat. social worker Dept. Mental Hygiene, N.Y.C., 1968-69; psychiat. social worker Washington Hosp. Ctr., 1970-72, assoc. mem. dept. psychiatry, 1972-75, sr. psychotherapist Counseling Ctr., 1972-75; psychotherapist Md. Inst. Pastoral Counseling, Annapolis, Md., 1972—; chief dept. social svcs. Washington Hosp. Ctr., 1979-82, cons. spl. projects, 1974-82; supr. continuing protective svcs. State Md., 1983-91; supr. rsch. project on child sexual abuse for AACO, 1991-93; forensic social worker Anne Arundel Cir. Ct., 1991—; exec. v.p. Kent Island Transport, Inc., 1985—; field instr. Cath. U., Washington, 1973-75, U. Md., 1976-91; adjunct prof. U. Md. 1992-94. Mem. Nat. Assn. Social Workers, Acad. Cert. Social Workers (bd. cert. diplomate). Democrat. Presbyterian. Home: 1416 Regent St Annapolis MD 21403-1247 Office: 104 Forbes St Suite F Annapolis MD 21404

KACHUR, BETTY RAE, elementary education educator; b. Lorain, Ohio, June 12, 1930; d. John and Elizabeth (Stanko) K. BS in Edn., Kent State U., 1963; MEd, U. Ariz., 1971. Cert. tchr.; cert. in reading. Tchr. Lorain City Schs., 1961-94. Mem. AAUW (social com.), Internat. Reading Assn. (by-laws com. Ohio Coun.), Daniel T. Gardner Reading Assn. (pres. 1978-79, treas. 1988-94). Mem. United Ch. of Christ.

KACIR, BARBARA BRATTIN, lawyer; b. Buffalo, Ohio, July 19, 1941; d. William James and Jean (Harrington) Brattin; m. Charles Stephen Kacir, June 3, 1973 (div. Aug. 1977). BA, Wellesley Coll., 1963; JD, U. Mich., 1967. Bar: Ohio 1967, D.C. 1980. Assoc. Arter & Hadden, Cleve., 1967-74, ptnr., 1974-79; ptnr. Jones, Day, Reavis & Pogue, Washington, 1980-83, Cleve., 1983—; instr. trial tactics Case-Western Res. U., Cleve., 1976-79; legal rep. for Warner Bros., Twentieth-Century Fox, MGM/UA, Universal, Orion, Columbia, Buena Vista, Paramount, Tri-Star in Ohio litigation. Mem. nat. com. visitors, nat. fund raising com. U. Mich. Mem. ABA, Ohio Bar Assn., D.C. Bar Assn., Cleve. Bar Assn. (trustee 1973-76, treas. 1978-79), Assn. Trial Lawyers Am., Am. Law Inst., Def. Rsch. Inst. Republican. Office: Jones Day Reavis & Pogue 901 Lakeside Ave E Cleveland OH 44114-1190

KACUBA, ALICE MARIE, nurse; b. Montrose, Pa., July 7, 1960; d. Leonard and Dolores (Monahan) K. Diploma, Robert Packer Hosp., 1981; BSN, U. Md., 1993. RN, Pa., Md.; cert. CCRN. Staff nurse, ICU Robert Packer Hosp., Sayre, Pa., 1981-83, The Traveling Nurse Corps., Malden, Mass., 1983-86; clin. nurse IV The Nat. Insts. Health, Bethesda, Md., 1986—. Mem. AACN, ANA, Oncology Nursing Soc. Office: NIH Bldg 10/7050 900 Rockville Pke Bethesda MD 20892

KADEN, ELLEN ORAN, lawyer, broadcasting corporation executive. AB, Cornell U., 1972; MA, U. Chgo., 1973; JD, Columbia U., 1977. Bar: N.Y., 1978. Law clerk U.S. Dist. Ct. (so. dist.) N.Y., 1977-78; asst. prof. Columbia U. Sch. Law, 1978-82, assoc. prof., 1982-84; now exec. v.p., gen. counsel, sec. CBS Inc., N.Y.C., 1991—; reporter jud. coun. 2nd Cir. Adv. Comm. on Planning for Dist. Cts., 1979-81. Office: CBS Inc 36th Fl 51 W 52nd St Fl 36 New York NY 10019-6119

KADISH, ANNA STEIN, pathologist, educator, researcher; b. Mexico City, Feb. 27, 1942; came to U.S., 1942; d. Emanuel and Rosa (Herzig) Stein; m. Lawrence J. Kadish, July 1, 1965; children: Debbrah, Rachel, Sam. BA, Barnard Coll., 1963; MD, Harvard U., 1967. Diplomate Am. Bd. Pathology. Resident in pathology Alber Einstein Coll. Medicine, Bronx, N.Y., 1967-69, 71-72, Roosevelt Hosp., N.Y.C., 1970-71; from asst. to assoc. prof. pathology Albert Einstein Coll. Medicine, 1972-84, prof., 1984—, vice chmn., 1993—, dir. residency tng., 1993—; attending pathologist Bronx Mcpl. Hosp., 1972—. Contbr. articles to profl. jours. Chmn. bd. edn. Solomon Schechter Sch., White Plains, N.Y., 1986-92. Grantee NIH, Am. Cancer Soc. Office: Albert Einstein Coll Medicine 1300 Morris Park Ave U421 Bronx NY 10461

KADISH, KATHERINE, artist, art educator. BFA, Carnegie Mellon U., 1961; MA, U. Chgo., 1966. co-dir. art gallery Harpur Coll. SUNY, Binghamton, 1963-66; curator, slide and print collection dept. art and art history, SUNY Binghamton, 1963-66, vis., adj. asst. prof. dept. art and art history, 1974-82; master tchr. N.Y. State Summer Sch. Visual Arts, 1979-82; asst. prof. art Broome C.C., Binghamton, 1982-84; vis. lectr. art dept. Ohio State U., Columbus, 1985-86; artist-in-residence Montpelier Cultural Arts Ctr., Laurel, Md., 1986; adj. assoc. prof. dept. art and art history Wright State U., Dayton, Ohio, 1987-88; vis. asst. prof. dept. art Wittenberg U., Springfield, Ohio, 1989-90, vis. assoc. prof., 1992; vis. artist Arrowmont Sch. Arts and Crafts, Gatlinburg, tenn., 1992—, Cleve. Inst. Art, 1994. Solo exhbns. include Denison U., Granville, Ohio, 1975, Eisenhower Coll., Seneca Falls, N.Y. 1976, Hobart Coll., Geneva, N.Y., 1977, Arnot Art Mus., Elmira, N.Y., 1978, SUNY Buffalo, 1980, Va. Ctr. Creative Arts, Sweet Briar, 1981, Univ. Art Gallery SUNY Binghamton, 1981, SUNY Plattsburgh, 1981, Atlantic Gallery, N.Y.C., 1983, Wheaton Coll. Watson Gallery, Norton, Mass., 1984, NW La. U., Natchitoches, 1985, Leigh Gallery, London, 1985, 87, Springfield (Ohio) Art Mus., 1986, Malton Gallery, Cin., 1986, 88, Montpelier Cultural Arts Ctr., Laurel, Md., 1986, Nanjing (People's Republic of China) Arts Coll., 1987, Clemson (S.C.) U. Gallery, 1992, Roberta Kuhn Gallery, Columbus, Ohio, 1992, Yvonne Rapp Gallery, Louisville, 1992, Marta Hewett Gallery, Cin., 1994, Dayton (Ohio) Art Inst., 1994, Gallery East and West, Chgo., 1995, Interchurch Ctr. Gallery, N.Y.C., 1995; group and exhbns. include Libr. Congress, Washington, 1973, Galerie de l'Esprit, Montreal, Que., Can., 1975, Evans Gallery, Toronto, Ont., Can., 1975, Pleiades Gallery, N.Y.C., 1976, Okla. Art Ctr., Okla. City, 1976, Empire State Plz., Albany, 1977, SUNY, Albany, 1981, N.Y. State Mus., Albany, 1981, U. N.D., Grand Forks, 1983, Whitney Mus. Am. Art/Downtown, N.Y.C., 1983, Quinton Green Fine Arts, London, 1984, Hopkins Gallery Ohio State U., Columbus, 1986, Davis Gallery U. Akron, Ohio, 19990, Cadogan Contemporary Gallery, London, 1990, Ohio Arts Invitational, Tokyo, 1991, Oxford (Eng.) Gallery, 1993, Anita Shapolsky Gallery, N.Y.C., 1995, others; represented in public and corp. collections Baldwin & Whitney Corp., Dayton, Broome C.C., Binghamton, N.Y., Charter Oaks Bank, Columbus, 1st Federal of Boston, Cin., Fries and Fries Corp., Cin., GTE Corp., Indpls., Herbert F. Johnson Mus. Cornell U., Ithaca, N.Y., Marine Midland Bank, Binghamton, Metel Corp., Cin., N.Y. State Coun. Arts, N.Y.C., SUNY Coll. at Cortland, Success Group, Inc., Columbus, Va. Ctr. Creative Arts, others. Recipient Profl. Devel. award Ohio Arts Coun., 1988, 90, 1st Annual Artist-in- Residency award Montpelie Cultural Arts Ctr., 1986, Profl. Devel. Assistance award Ohio Arts Coun., 1993; Creative Artists Pub. Svc. Program grantee N.Y. State Coun. on Arts, 1973, Travel grantee Unied Bd. Christian Higher Edn. in Asia, 1986; Residency fellow Yaddo, 1977, 78, 80, Tyrone Guthrie Ctr. for Arts, Ireland, 1988, Va. Ctr. Creative Arts, 1978-82, 87, 89, Vt. Studio Colony, 1990. Home: 1062 State Rte 343 Yellow Springs OH 45387 also: 222 W 14th St New York NY 10011

KAEL, PAULINE, film critic, author; b. Petaluma, Calif., June 19, 1919; d. Isaac Paul and Judith (Friedman) K.; 1 child, Gina James. Student, U. Calif., Berkeley, 1936-40; LLD (hon.), Georgetown U., 1972; D. Arts and Letters (hon.), Columbia Coll., Chgo., 1972; LittD (hon.), Smith Coll., 1973, Allegheny Coll., 1979; LHD (hon.), Kalamazoo Coll., 1973, Reed Coll., 1975, Haverford Coll., 1975; DFA (hon.), Sch. Visual Arts, N.Y.C., 1980. Movie critic New Yorker mag., 1968-91. Author: I Lost it at the Movies, 1965, Kiss Kiss Bang Bang, 1968, Going Steady, 1970, Deeper into Movies, 1973 (Nat. Book award 1974), Reeling, 1976, When the Lights Go Down, 1980, 5001 Nights at the Movies, 1982, enlarged edit., 1991, Taking It All In, 1984, State of the Art, 1985, Hooked, 1989, Movie Love, 1991, For Keeps, 1994; contbg. author: The Citizen Kane Book, 1971; contbr. to numerous other mags. Recipient George Polk Meml. award, 1970, Front Page award Newswomen's Club N.Y., 1974, 83; Guggenheim fellow, 1964. Mem. Phi Beta Kappa (hon.). Office: New Yorker Mag 20 W 43rd St New York NY 10036-7400

KAESS, GAIL, county employee; b. Detroit, Nov. 24, 1939; d. Charles Francis and Thelma Inez (Cooke) White; m. Frederick Charles Kaess, III, Oct. 29, 1959; children: Kathrine Elizabeth, Frederick Charles IV. Student, Hillsdale (Mich.) Coll., 1959, 60, 61; BA, Mich. State U., 1962. Pres. Detroit Awareness Tour Svc., Detroit, 1978-84; dist. adminstr. Senator John Kelly, Detroit, 1984-88; exec. asst. Wayne County Exec. Office, Detroit, 1988—; pres. Mich. Mcpl. League, 1988-89; chair-elect. S.E. Mich. Coun. Govts.; chmn. Wayne County Solid Waste Commn., Mich. Mcpl. Liability Pool; trustee Mich. Mcpl. League Found. Mem. coun. City of Grosse Pointe Farms, Mich., 1979—; pres. Jr. League of Detroit, 1976-78; trustee Brighton (Mich.) Hosp., 1990—. Named Parent of Yr., Grosse Pointe Sch. System, 1973, Vol. of Yr., United Way of S.E. Mich., 1980, Regional Amb., S.E. Mich. Coun. Govts., 1988; Taubman County fellow Harvard U. John F. Kennedy Sch. Govt., 1993. Mem. Mich. Mcpl. League (life). Republican. Presbyterian. Home: 155 Irvine Ln Grosse Pointe MI 48236-2951 Office: Wayne County Exec Office 600 Randolph Detroit MI 48226

KAGAN, JULIA LEE, magazine editor; b. Nurnberg, Fed. Republic Germany, Nov. 25, 1948; d. Saul and Elizabeth J. (Koblenzer) K. A.B., Bryn Mawr Coll., 1970. Researcher Look Mag., N.Y.C., 1970-71; editorial asst., asst. editor McCall's Mag., N.Y.C., 1971-74, assoc. editor, 1974-78, sr. editor, 1978-79; articles editor Working Woman mag., N.Y.C., 1979-85, exec. editor, 1985-88; editor Psychology Today, 1988-90; sr. editor McCalls, 1990-91; contbg. editor Working Woman, 1991-93; editor-in-chief Lamaze Parents' Mag., 1992-93, Lamaze Baby Mag., 1993; spl. projects dir. Child Mag., 1993-94; sr. v.p. EDK Assocs., N.Y.C., 1994; psychology and health dir. Fitness Mag., N.Y.C., 1995—; vis. J. Stewart Riley prof. journalism Ind. U., 1991-93. Co-author: Manworks: A Guide to Style, 1980; contbg. author: The Working Woman Success Book, 1981, The Working Woman Report, 1984. Pres. Appleby Found., N.Y.C., 1982-84. Recipient 2d Ann. Advt. Journalism award Compton Advt., 1983. Mem. Am. Soc. Mag. Editors, Am. Soc. Pub. Opinion Researchers, Womens Media Group (bd. dirs.), Journalism and Women Symposium (treas. 1993-94). Club: Princeton (N.Y.C.). Home: 523 W 121st St Apt 42 New York NY 10027-5901

KAGAN, SUSAN LYNN, secondary school educator; b. Roslyn, Ill., Oct. 16, 1948; d. Eric and Marge Miller; m. H. George Kagan (div. Nov. 1989); children: Erica, Aaron. BA, U. South Fla., 1971; MA, Nova U., 1978. Tchr. Killian and Sunset High Schs. Dade County, Miami, Fla., 1971-77; tchr., chairperson Boca Mid. Sch. Palm Beach County, Boca Raton, Fla., 1987—, ESOL coord., 1991-92; mem. Dade County Textbook Commn., Miami; del. Mid. Sch. Conf., Toronto, Can., 1989; sponsor L'Amitie, Miami, 1971-75; sponsor Spanish Nat. Honor Soc., Boca Raton (Fla.) H.S., mem. steering com., tchr. adv. placement program in Spanish lang., mem. principal's Cabinet; attendant It's A "Block" Thing, Ashboro, N.C. Vol. Devon Aire Elem. Sch., Miami, 1982, Whispering Pines Elem. Sch., Boca Raton, 1987, Coral Sunset Elem. Sch., Boca Raton, 1988; vol., tchr. Temple B'nai Israel, Boca Raton, 1986-87. Mem. NEA, Fgn. Lang. Assn., Nat. Coun. English Tchrs., Classroom Tchrs. Assn., Nat. Mid. Sch. Tchrs. Home: 7705 Kenway Pl Boca Raton FL 33433

KAGEY, F. EILEEN, retired educator; b. Lima, Ohio, July 29, 1925; d. Joseph Leonard and Florence Elizabeth (Niles) K.; B.S. in Edn., Ball State U., 1952; M.S. in Edn., Ind. U., 1955. Sec., Gen. Electric Co., Ft. Wayne, Ind., 1943-45, 48-49, Farnsworth Telephone and Radio Corp., Ft. Wayne, 1945-48; H.A. Jeep prof. Ball State U., 1949-52; elem. tchr. Harmar Sch., Ft. Wayne, 1952-54, Emerson Sch., Gary, Ind., 1954-58, Sch. 52, Indpls., 1959-61, George Kuny Sch., Gary, 1961-90, ret.; sec. to v.p. Rsch. and Rev. Svc. of Am., Indpls., 1958-59. Active Calumet Corner chpt. Sweet Adelines, Inc., Munster, Ind., 1977-83, pub. rels. chmn. 1980-82, bd. dirs., 1981-82. Mem. NEA (life), Am. Fedn. Tchrs. (bldg. rep. Local 4 1979-89), Ind. State Tchrs. Assn., Assn. Supervision and Curriculum Devel., Ind. Assn. Supervision and Curriculum Devel., AAUW (v.p. in-charge program), Kappa Delta Pi. Democrat. Roman Catholic. Author: (juvenile) Jeremy: the People-Dog, 1974. Home: 3040 W 39th Pl Gary IN 46408-1908

KAGGEN, LOIS SHEILA, non-profit organization executive; b. N.Y.C., Jan. 2, 1944; d. Elias and Sylvia (Muntner) K.; m. Harold Jay Burns, June 29, 1969 (dec. June 1975); 1 child, David Henry (dec.); m. Michael Francis McCann, Sept. 26, 1984. BS in Fine Arts, Skidmore Coll., 1964; postgrad., Cooper Union, 1967-70; MA in Art Edn., CCNY, 1973; postgrad., NYU, 1987—. Founder, pres. Resources for Artists With Disabilities, N.Y.C., 1987—; mem. adv. com. Art in Edn. Project Ctr. for Safety in Arts, N.Y.C., 1987; cons. Ea. Paralyzed Vets. Assn., Guggenheim Mus. Art, N.Y.C., 1990, Queens Ind. Living Ctr.; bd. advisors The Ind. Arts Gallery, Jamaica, N.Y, 1987—; mem. steering com. Ann. Disablity Ind. Day March, 1992—; mem. media outreach, 1992; art presenter in field. Photography exhbns. include 80 Washington Sq. East Galleries, N.Y.C., 1977, Soho Photo Gallery, N.Y.C., 1978, 4th St. Photo Gallery, N.Y.C., 1979, Leslie-Lohman Gallery, N.Y.C., 1980, 81, Window Gallery, N.Y.C., 1980, Mus. Gallery, N.Y.C., 1980, Donnell Gallery, 1981; exhbn. organizer: various African-American Artists with Disabilities', Artists with Physical Disabilities' exhbns.; contbr. articles, photographs to profl. jours. Mem. disability rights steering com. 501 Dem. Club for Persons with Disabilities, 1987-88, mem. exec. com., 1990—; active Disabled in Action of Greater N.Y., 1989—, Manhattan Borough Pres. Adv. Com. on Disabled, 1988—, Mayor's Adv. Com. on People with Disabilities, N.Y.C., 1991-93, Citywide Coalition on Disability, N.Y.C., 1994. Grantee Whitney Mus. Am. Art, 1967, Stanford U., 1968; Cooper Union scholar, 1967-70; recipient Chancellor's Svc. award NYU, 1987, Appreciation cert. Manhattan Borough Pres., 1991. Office: Resources Artists with Disabilities 77 7th Ave PH H New York NY 10011-6645

KAGIWADA, HARRIET HATSUNE NATSUYAMA, engineering educator; b. Honolulu, Sept. 2, 1937; d. Kenjiro and Yakue Natsuyama; children: Julia, Conan. BA, U. Hawaii, 1959, MS, 1960; PhD, Kyoto U., 1965. Math. Rand Corp., Santa Monica, Calif., 1961-68, cons., 1968-77; adj. assoc. prof. U. So. Calif., L.A., 1974-79; sr. scientist Hughes Aircraft Co., El Segundo, 1979-87; chief engr. Infotec Devel. Inc., Camarillo, 1987-89; prof. systems engring. Calif. State U., Fullerton, 1990—. Author: Invariant Imbedding and Time-Dependent Transport Processes, 1963, System Identification: Methods and Applications, 1974, Integral Equations via Imbedding Methods, 1974, Multiple Scattering Processes: Inverse and Direct, 1975, Numerical Derivatives and Nonlinear Analysis, 1986. Mem. IEEE, AAAS, Inst. Advanced Engring., Grad. Women in Sci. (pres. 1990-91), Phi Beta Kappa. Office: Calif State U Fullerton CA 92634

KAHANA, EVA FROST, sociology educator; b. Budapest, Hungary, Mar. 21, 1941; came to U.S., 1957; d. Jacob and Sari (Mayer) Frost; m. Boaz Kahana, Apr. 15, 1962; children: Jeffrey, Michael. BA, Stern Coll., Yeshiva U., 1962; MA, CCNY, CUNY, 1965; PhD, U. Chgo., 1968; HLD (hon.), Yeshiva U., 1991. Nat. Inst. on Aging predoctoral fellow U. Chgo. Com. on Human Devel., 1963-66; postdoctoral fellow Midwest Council Social Research, 1968; with dept. sociology Washington U., St. Louis, 1967-71, successively research asst., research assoc., asst. prof.; with dept. sociology Wayne State U., Detroit, 1971-84, from assoc. prof. to prof., dir. Elderly Care Research Ctr., 1971-84; prof. Case Western Res. U., Cleve., 1984—, Armington Prof., 1989-90, chmn. dept. sociology, 1985—, dir. Elderly Care Research Ctr., 1984—, Pierce and Elizabeth Robson prof. humanities, 1990—; cons. Nat. Inst. on Aging, Washington, 1976-80, NIMH, Washington, 1971-75. Mem. editorial bd. Gerontologist, 1975-79, Psychology of Aging, 1984-90, Jour. Gerontology, 1990-94, Applied Behavioral Sci. Rev., 1992—; contbr. articles to profl. jours., chpts. to books (recipient Pub.'s prize 1969). Bd. dirs. com. on aging Jewish Community Fedn., Cleve.; vol. cons. Alzheimer's Disease and Related Disorders Assn., Cleve. NIMH Career Devel. grantee, 1974-79, Nat. Inst. Aging Merit award grantee, 1989—; Mary E. Switzer Disting. fellow Nat. Inst. Rehab., 1992-93; recipient Arnold Heller award excellence in geriatrics and gerontology Menorah Park Ctr. for Aged, 1992; named Disting. Geontological Rschr. in Ohio, 1993. Fellow Gerontol. Soc. Am. (chair behavioral social sci. com. 1984-85, Disting. Mentorship award 1987); mem. Am. Sociol. Assn. (coun. sect. on aging 1985-87), Am. Psychol. Assn., Soc. for Traumatic Stress, Wayne State U. Acad. Scholars (life). Office: Case Western Res U Dept of Sociology Mather Meml 226 Cleveland OH 44106-1749

KAHL, MARY KATHERINE, lawyer; b. N.Y.C., Dec. 3, 1951; d. Harry Russell Kahl and Mary Virginia (Callcott) Hall; m. Neil Greenblatt, Aug. 17, 1986 (div. Feb. 1989). BA in Am. Studies, Barnard Coll., 1972; JD, N.Y. Law Sch., 1976. Bar: Tex. 1977, Maine 1987. City solicitor City of Saco (Maine), 1987-89; corp. counsel City of South Portland (Maine), 1991—. Author: Ballot Box 13, 1981. Mem. ABA (Maine liaison/contact person for govt. and publ. sector lawyers div.), Nat. Inst. Mcpl. Law Officers (recorder mcpl. ops. sect.), Maine State Bar Assn., State Bar Tex. Democrat. Office: City of South Portland 25 Cottage Rd S Portland ME 04106-3699

KAHLER, ELIZABETH SARTOR (MRS. ERVIN NEWTON CHAPMAN), physician; b. Washington, Oct. 20, 1911; d. Armin Adolphus and Lenore Elome (Sartor) K.; m. Dr. Ervin Newton Chapman, Feb. 24, 1942 (dec. Apr. 1987). B.S., George Washington U., 1933, M.A., 1935, M.D. with distinction, 1940. Intern Gallinger Municipal Hosp. (now D.C. Gen. Hosp.), Washington, 1940-41; resident Children's Hosp., Washington, 1941-42; practice medicine Washington, 1942-78; assoc. univ. physician George Washington U., 1942-50; examining physician YWCA, 1942-45; courtesy staff Washington Hosp. Center, until 1978, George Washington U. Hosp., until 1978; physician for health services br. resources div. Bur. Social Services and Resources Social Services Adminstrn. D.C. Dept. Human Services, 1953-75; sch. physician D.C. pub. schs., 1959-89; mem. cons. com. for practical nursing program D.C. Pub. Schs., 1962-70. Everitt-Pomery trustee Wilson Coll., 1993—; vol. Widowed Persons Svc., 1993—; mem. exec. com. Nat. Voluntary Orgns. for Ind. Living for Aging, 1978-82, liaison from Am. Med. Women's Assn., 1975-82; mem. nat. program com. Camp Fire Girls Inc.; treas. Women's Assn. of Nat. Presbyn. Ch., 1981-83, fin. chmn., 1983-85, 87-89, asst. treas., 1989-91, chmn. memls. 1985-87, 91-93, cir. leader, 1994—, nat. pres. ch. memls. com., 1986—, mem. libr. com. 1991—, Stephen min., 1993—. Mem. AMA, Women's Med. Soc. D.C. (pres. 1950-51), Am. Med. Women's Assn. (pres. 1957-58, treas. Past Presidents Club 1976-78), Med. Soc. D.C. (life, chmn. com. on medicine and religion 1967-72, aging com. 1985-86, 88, mem. pub. info. and edn. com. 1986), D.C. Assn. Mental Health, Am. Heart Assn., Columbian Women of George Washington U. (life). Republican. Presbyterian. Home: 2600 36th St NW Washington DC 20007-1419 Office: 3601 Davis St NW Washington DC 20007-1428

KAHLER, KATHRYN SCHILLER, communications executive; b. Denton, Tex., Aug. 18, 1953; d. James Harlan and Martha Pearla (Speer) K. BA in Sociology, Tulane U., 1975; MA in Mass Comm., U. Minn., 1977. Writer, editor U. Minn. News Svc., Mpls., 1976-77; freelance health writer Twin Cities Reader, Mpls., 1977; health/scis. reporter The Jour.-News, Nyack, N.Y., 1977-83; nat. corr. Newhouse Newspapers, Washington, 1983-93; comm. dir. U.S. Dept. Edn., Washington, 1993—; chmn. bd. dirs. Nat. Bldg. Corp., 1991-93; adviser WHO, Commn. on Health and Environ., 1990; freelance writer The Boston Globe, Regardie's, Southern Mag., Dallas Morning News Mag., Am. Way, Spl. Report: Personalities. Editorial advisor to editorial bd. Tulane U. pubs. Panelist Washington Week in Rev., Washington Waypoints; hon. chmn. fundraiser for Youth Comm.; bd. dirs. USA Vote; judge Robert F. Kennedy awards, John Hancock awards, Nat. Press Club consumer awards, numerous other journalism contests; spkr. various press, edn., cmty. events. Vis. fellow Woodrow Wilson nat. fellow, 1992—; recipient Pub. Svc. award AP Mng. Editors Assn., 1982, Cert. of Merit, ABA, 1992. Mem. Nat. Press Club (chmn. bd. govs. 1988-90, 92-93, pres. 1991), USA Vote (bd. dirs.), Nat. Press Bldg. Corp. (bd. dirs.). Democrat. Methodist. Home: 3020 Tilden St NW Apt 304 Washington DC 20008 Office: US Dept Edn 400 Maryland Ave SW Washington DC 20202

KAHLEY, KAREN ELIZABETH, accountant; b. York, Pa., Apr. 29, 1957; d. Edward Paul Bortner and Sarah Virginia (Clark) Elicker; m. Jerry Lee Kahley, Apr. 25, 1980; children: Jamie, Justine, Janna. BS in Acctg., York Coll., 1989. Cost acct. Maple Press Co., York, Pa., 1989-92; instr. acctg. Yorktowne Bus. Inst., York, 1990—; fixed asset acct. Graham Packaging Co., York, 1992—. Mem. Inst. Mgmt. Accts.

KAHLOW, BARBARA FENVESSY, statistician; b. Chgo., June 26, 1946; d. Stanley John and Doris (Goodman) Fenvessy; m. Lloyd Fitch Reese, Dec. 6, 1969 (div. 1977); m. Allan Howard Young, Mar. 31, 1979 (div. 1982); m. Ronald Arthur Kahlow, Sept. 28, 1985 (div. 1990). BA, Vassar Coll., 1968. Statistician U.S. Govt./Dept. HEW, Nat. Ctr. Health Statistics, 1968-70, Nat. Ctr. for Ednl. Statistics, 1970-72, Exec. Office of Pres. Office Mgmt. and Budget, Washington, 1972—. Author: Motor Vehicle Accident Deaths in the U.S.: 1950-69, 1970; contbr. articles to profl. jours. Recipient Quality Svc. award HEW, 1971, Spl. Performance award Office Mgmt. and Budget, 1982, 89, 94; N.Y. State Regents scholar, 1964-68. Mem. Am. Statis. Assn., Foggy Bottom Assn., League of Rep. Women of D.C., Friends of the Kennedy Ctr., Friends of the Corcoran, Smithsonian Assocs., Washington Vassar Club, Univ. Club Washington. Republican. Episcopalian. Home: Apt 404 2555 Pennsylvania Ave NW Washington DC 20037-1640 Office: Office Mgmt and budget 6025 NEOB Washington DC 20503

KAHN, CAROLE, journalist; b. N.Y.C., Feb. 17, 1937; d. Saul and Mae (Sheweloff) K. BA, Bklyn. Coll., 1957; MS in Journalism, Columbia U., 1960. Feature writer Conn. Sun. Herald, Bridgeport, 1962-68; investigative reporter Hartford Times, 1968-70, Boston Herald Traveler, 1970; co-anchor, assoc. producer Conn. Pub. TV, Hartford, 1970-71; dir. info. City of N.Y., BPSSA Sr. Programs, 1973-74; dir. broadcast film Consumers Union, Mt. Vernon, N.Y., 1974-77; co-producer, writer Buyline: Betty Furness, WNBC-TV, N.Y.C., 1977-80; econ./fin. producer NBC News, N.Y.C., 1980—. Producer/writer ednl. film: The Six Billion $ Sell, 1976 (Learning AV award 1976), Kicking Tires is Not Enough, 1976; script editor, reporter documentary: War Called Peace, 1980. Pres. 522 Apts. Corp., N.Y.C., 1983-85, bd. dirs., 1982. Recipient Peabody award for Buyline: Betty Furness, Regents U., Ga., 1977, Emmy award NATAS, 1977, 78, 79, Wilbur award Religious Pub. Rels. Coun., 1990, CPA award for Chinese Econs., N.Y. State Soc. CPAs, 1990, Equality, Dignity and Independence award Nat. Easter Seal Soc., 1991; Corp. for Pub. Broadcasting career fellow, 1970. Office: NBC News 30 Rockefeller Plz New York NY 10112-0001

KAHN, FAITH-HOPE, nurse, administrator, writer; b. N.Y.C., Apr. 25, 1921; d. Leon and Hazel (Cook) Green; RN, Beth Israel Med. Center, N.Y.C., 1942; student N.Y. U., 1943; m. Edward Kahn, May 29, 1942; children: Ellen Leora, Faith Hope II, Paula Amy. First scrub nurse operating room Beth Israel Hosp., N.Y.C., 1942; supr., operating room Hunts Point Gen. Hosp., 1942; gynecol. reconstrn. procedures researcher Phoenixville

(Pa.) Gen. Hosp., 1943, Sydenham Hosp., N.Y.C., 1945; supr. ARC Disaster Field Hosp., Queens, N.Y., 1950-51; adminstr., mgr. team coordinator Dr. Edward Kahn, FACOG, Queens Village, N.Y., 1945—. Inventor, publicity chmn. Girl Scouts U.S.A., 1953; exec. dir. publicity Woodhull Schs., 1956-60, pres., 1961-62; exec. dir. publicity N.Y. Dept. Parks Figure Skating, 1956-70; exec. dir. publicity and applied arts St. John's Hosp., Smithtown, N.Y., 1965-66; state advisor N.Y., U.S. Congressional Adv. Bd., Washington, 1981—; nat. adv. bd. Am. Security Council, 1978—; founder Am. Security Found.; bd. trustees, Am. Police Hall of Fame and Mus., 1983—; mem. Republican Presdl. Task Force, 1986, Statue of Liberty and Ellis Island Centennial Commn., N.Y., 1986—. Recipient citation ARC, 1951, Am. Law Enforcement Officers Assn., Bronze medal Am. Security Council Ednl. Found., 1978, spl. recognition award Center Internat. Security Studies, 1979, Meml. Plate, Patriots of Am. Bicentennial, 1976, Great Seal of U.S.A. Plate, cert. Am. Sons Liberty, 1987, Good Smaritan award, 1987, Justice award Cross of Knights, 1987 Knights of Justice award, 1987; named Knight Chevalier Venerable Order of Michael the Archangel, 1987. Fellow, World Lit. Acad. (life), Acad. Nat. Law Enforcement (hon.); mem. Am. Acad. Ambulatory Nursing Adminstrn., Nurses Assn., Nat. League Nursing, Am. Coll. Obstetricians and Gynecologists, Nat. Assn. Physicians' Nurses, Nat. Critical Care Inst., Assn. Operating Room Nurses, AAAS, Nat. Assn. Female Execs., N.Y. Acad. Scis., Am. Police Acad. (cert. appreciation 1979, 83), Am. Fedn. Police, The Retired Officers Assn., Internat. Platform Assn., Security and Intelligence Found. (cert. appreciation 1986), Internat. Intelligence and Orgnd. Crime Investigators Assn., Smithtown Hist. Soc., Nat. Audubon Soc., NRA. Clubs: Tiyospaye, Paul Revere, Sterlingshire Woman's. Author, editor: The Easy Driving Way for Automatic and the Standard Shift, 1954; (with Edward Kahn) The Pelvic Examination, Outline and Guide for Residents, Internes and Students, 1954; (with Edward Kahn) Traction Hysterosalpingography for Uterine Lesions, 1949; contbr. articles profl. and lay jours. Home and Office: 21316 85th Ave Hollis Hills NY 11427-1324

KAHN, JENETTE SARAH, publishing company executive; b. Altoona, Pa., May 16, 1947; d. Benjamin and Rosalind (Aronson) K. BA cum laude, Radcliffe Coll, 1968. Co-founder, editor Kids mag., Cambridge, Mass., 1970-73; creator, editor Dynamite mag., 1973-74; pub., editor Smash mag., 1974-76; pub. DC Comics, N.Y.C., 1976-81, now pres., pub., editor-in-chief. Jr. council Mus. Modern Art, 1975-81; active Big Sisters and Big Brothers, from 1978; mem. nat. adv. coun. Nat. Network of Runaways and Youth Svcs.; pres. Wonder Woman Found. Grantee Kress Found., 1969. Office: DC Comics 666 Fifth Ave New York NY 10019*

KAHN, LINDA MCCLURE, maritime industry executive; b. Jacksonville, Fla.; d. George Calvin and Myrtice Louise (Boggs) McClure; m. Paul Markham Kahn, May 20, 1968. BS with high honors, U. Fla.; MS, U. Mich., 1964. Actuarial trainee N.Y. Life Ins. Co., N.Y.C., 1964-66, actuarial asst., 1966-69, asst. actuary, 1969-71; v.p., actuary US Life Ins., Pasadena, Calif., 1972-74; mgr. Coopers & Lybrand, Los Angeles, 1974-76, sr. cons., San Francisco, 1976-82; dir. program mgmt. Pacific Maritime Assn., San Francisco, 1982—. Bd. dirs. Pacific Heights Residents Assn., sec.-treas., 1981; trustee ILWU-PMA Welfare Plan, SIU-PD-PMA Pension and Supplemental Benefits Plans, 1982-90, Seafarers Med. Ctr., 1982-90, others. Fellow Soc. Actuaries (chmn. com. on minority recruiting 1988-91, chmn. actuary of future sect. 1993—), Conf. Actuaries in Pub. Practice; mem. Internat. Actuarial Assn., Internat. Assn. Cons. Actuaries, Actuarial Studies Non-Life Ins., Am. Acad. Actuaries, Western Pension Conf. (newsletter editor 1983-85, sec. 1985-88, treas. 1989-90), Actuarial Club Pacific States, San Francisco Actuarial Club (pres. 1981), Met. Club, Commonwealth Club, Soroptimists Club (v.p. 1973-74). Home: 2430 Pacific Ave San Francisco CA 94115-1238 Office: Pacific Maritime Assn 550 California St San Francisco CA 94104-1006

KAHN, MADELINE GAIL, actress; b. Boston; d. Bernard B. Wolfson and Paula Kahn. BA, Hofstra U.; trained as opera singer; ArtsD (hon.), Boston Conservatory. Appeared in: satirical revue Upstairs at the Downstairs, N.Y.C., 1966-67, New Faces of 1968, Booth Theatre, N.Y.C., Candide, Philharmonic Hall, 1968, Two by Two, Imperial Theatre, N.Y.C., 1970-71, Broadway mus. Two by Two; motion picture appearances include What's Up Doc?, 1972, Paper Moon, 1973 (Academy award nomination 1973, Golden Globe award nomination), From the Mixed-up Files of Mrs. Basil E. Frankweiler, 1973, Blazing Saddles, 1974 (Academy award nomination 1974, First Ann. Acad. of Humor award 1975), Young Frankenstein, 1974 (Golden Globe award nomination), At Long Last Love, 1975, The Adventure of Sherlock Holmes' Smarter Brother, 1975, Won-Ton-Ton, the Dog Who Saved Hollywood, 1976, High Anxiety, 1977, The Cheap Detective, 1978, The Muppet Movie, 1979, Simon, 1980, Happy Birthday Gemini, 1980, Wholly Moses!, 1980, First Family, 1980, History of the World, Part I, 1981, Yellowbeard, 1983, Slapstick of Another Kind, 1984, City Heat, 1984, Clue, 1985, (voice) My Little Pony, 1986, (voice) An American Tail, 1986, Betsy's Wedding, 1990, Shadows and Fog, 1992, Mixed Nuts, 1994; stage appearances in Boom Boom Room, Vivian Beaumont Theater, 1973 (Tony nominee, Drama Desk award), Broadway prodn. On the 20th Century, 1978 (Tony nominee), Born Yesterday, 1989 (Tony nominee), Broadway prodn. The Sisters Rosensweig (Tony Award Best Actress in a Play), 1992-93; in ABC-TV afterschool special, 1986-87 (Emmy award); star TV series Oh, Madeline, ABC, from 1983 (People's Choice award), Mr. President, FOX-TV, 1987; appeared as Madame Arcati in Blithe Spirit, Santa Fe Festival Theater, 1983. Recipient Disting. Service award Hofstra Alumni Assn., 1975. *

KAHN, MARILYN ZELDIN, artist, art educator; b. N.Y.C., Nov. 21, 1928; d. Jacob and Sarah Zeldin; m. Ernest Joseph Kahn, June 4, 1950; children: David Lawton, Richard Barry. Cert., Traphagen Sch., N.Y.C., 1948, Bklyn. Mus. Sch., 1949, Art Students League, N.Y.C., 1950. Art tchr. studio classes Sharon, Mass., 1960—; juror Mansfield Art Festival, 1985, Easton Art Festival, 1987, Stoughton Art Assn. Show, 1988, 94. One-woman show Moosehill Sanctuary Gallery, Sharon, Mass., 1992, Stonehill Coll., Easton, Mass., 1987, Caccivio & Sons Gallery, 1990-92, Cambridge Art Assn. Gallery, 1968—; group shows include Wenninger's Gallery, Rockport, Mass., 1970-89, Attleboro (Mass.) Mus., 1972, Easton Art Festival, 1989. Pres. Sharon (Mass.) League of Women Voters, 1975-76; chairperson Sharon (Mass.) Planning Bd., 1980, 85, active, 1976-86. Recipient numerous 1st Prizes, and other honorable mentions. Mem. Nat. Mus. Women in Arts, New Eng. Watercolor Soc. (assoc.), Cambridge Art Assn., Sharon Creative Arts Assn. (program co-chair 1993-95, past pres. 1972, 73). Home: 114 Ames St Sharon MA 02067

KAHN, NANCY VALERIE, publishing company executive, consultant; b. N.Y.C., Dec. 15, 1952; d. Alfred Joseph and Miriam (Kadin) K. BA magna cum laude, Princeton U., 1974. Dir. prodn. and devel. Bus. Rsch. Publs., Inc.-MacRAE's Directories, N.Y.C., 1984-86; assoc. pub., exec. editor Monitor Pub. Co., N.Y.C., 1987-88; dir. new product devel. Gale Rsch. Inc., N.Y.C., 1988-89; pub., editorial dir. directories and info. devel. Adweek/BPI Comms., N.Y.C., 1989-93; v.p. Everlink Corp., N.Y.C., 1993-94; prin. Info. Enterprises, N.Y.C., 1994—. Univ. scholar Princeton U., 1974. Mem. Info. Industry Assn., Directory Pubs. Forum NorthAm., Washington Directory Assn., Princeton Club. Office: Info Enterprises PO box 826 New York NY 10021

KAHN, SANDRA S., psychotherapist; b. Chgo., June 24, 1942; d. Chester and Ruth Sutker; m. Jack Murry Kahn, June 1, 1965; children: Erick, Jennifer. BA, U. Miami, 1964; MA, Roosevelt U., 1976. Tchr. Chgo. Pub. Schs., 1965-67; pvt. practice psychotherapy, Northbrook, Ill., 1976—. Host Shared Feelings, Sta. WEEF-AM, Highland Park, Ill., 1983—; author: The Kahn Report on Sexual Preferences, 1981, The Ex Wife Syndrome Cutting The Cord and Breaking Free After The Marriage Is Over, 1990; columnist Single Again mag. Mem. Ill. Psychol. Assn., Chgo. Psychol. Assn. (past pres. 1990). Jewish. Office: 2970 Maria Dr Northbrook IL 60062-2017

KAHN, SUSAN BETH, artist; b. N.Y.C., Aug. 26, 1924; d. Jesse B. and Jenny Carol (Peshkin) Cohen; m. Joseph Kahn, Sept. 15, 1946 (dec.); m. Richard Rosenkranz, Feb. 1, 1981. Grad., Parsons Sch. Design, 1945; pupil, Moses Soyer, 1950-57. Subject of: book Susan Kahn, with an essay by Lincoln Rothschild, 1960; One-man shows Sagittarius Gallery, 1960, A.C.A., Galleries, 1964, 68, 71, 76, 80, Charles B. Goddard Art Center, Ardmore, Okla., 1973, Albrecht Gallery Mus. Art, St. Joseph, Mo., 1974, N.Y. Cultural Center, N.Y.C., 1974, St. Peter's Coll., Jersey City, 1978, Heidi Neuhoff Gallery, N.Y.C., 1989; exhibited in group shows Audubon Artists, N.Y.C., Nat. Acad., N.Y.C., Springfield (Mass.) Mus., City Center, N.Y.C., A.C.A., Galleries, N.Y.C., Nat. Arts Club, N.Y.C., Butler Inst., Youngstown, Ohio, Islip Art Mus., East Islip. N.Y., 1989, Fine Arts Mus. of S., Mobile, Ala., 1989, Chatanooga Regional History Mus, 1989, Longview (Tex.) Mus. Art, 1989, ; represented in permanent collections, Tyler (Tex.) Mus., St. Lawrence U. Mus., Canton, N.Y., Fairleigh Dickinson U. Mus., Rutherford, N.J., Syracuse U. Mus., Sheldon Swope Gallery, Terre Haute, Ind., Montclair (N.J.) Mus. Fine Arts, Butler Inst. Am. Art, Youngstown, Ohio, Reading (Pa.) Mus., Albrecht Gallery Mus. Art, St. Joseph(Mo.), Cedar Rapids (Iowa) Art Center, N.Y. Cultural Center, N.Y.C., Edwin A. Ulrich Mus., Wichita, Kans., Wichita State U., Johns Hopkins Sch. Advanced Internat. Studies, Washington, Joslyn Mus., Omaha, U. Wyo., Laramie. Recipient Knickerbocker prize for best religious painting, 1956; Edith Lehman award Nat. Assn. Women Artists, 1958; Simmons award, 1961; Knickerbocker Artists award, 1961; Nat. Arts Club award, 1967; Knickerbocker Medal of Honor, 1964; Famous Artists Sch. award, 1967. Mem. Nat. Assn. Women Artists (Anne Barnett Meml. prize 1981, Solveig Stromsoe Palmer Meml. award 1987, Dorothy Schweitzer award 1990), Artists Equity, Met. Mus., Mus. Modern Art, Nat. Assn. Women Artists (meml. award 1987).

KAHN-FEUER, LOIS HENNING, clinical social worker, educator; b. Chgo., Aug. 16, 1943; d. Alexander M. and Marian I. (Mesigal) Henning; children: Samantha, Jason, Aaron. BS, Boston U., 1965; MS, So. Ill. U., 1982; MA, Fielding Inst., Santa Barbara, Calif., 1992, postgrad., 1992—. Lic. clin. social worker, Minn. Owner Kahn-Feuer & Assocs., St. Paul, 1983-92; ptnr. Kahn-Feuer & Johnston, St. Paul, 1992—; pres. Workplace Am., Inc., St. Paul, 1988—. Author: (booklet) An Understanding of Why We do What We Do, 1988, An Understanding of Eating Disorders, 1988, An Understanding of Chemical Dependency, 1988. Mem. APA, Minn. Psychol. Assn., Am. Counseling Assn., Inst. Chem. Dependency Profls. Minn. Office: Kahn-Feuer & Johnston 26 E Exchange # 102 Saint Paul MN 55101

KAIDO, BONNELL DOLORES, medical education administrator; b. Cooperstown, N.Y., Dec. 5, 1951; d. Samuel Wellington and Bernadette Elizabeth (Rafferty) K. AAS in Bus., SUNY, 1972; BS in Bus., Coll. of St. Rose, 1974; MS in Edn., U. Albany, 1978. Bus. educator Sharon Springs Cen. Sch., 1975-80; supr. The Mary Imogene Bassett Hosp., Cooperstown, 1980-82, coord. med. edn., 1982-86, asst. dir. med. edn., 1986—; mem. svcs. com. Assn. for Hosp. Med. Edn., 1989—, vice chair mem. com., 1991—; office tech. adv. com. SUNY, Cobleskill, 1988—; dir. Med. Alumni Assn. MIBH, Cooperstown, 1988—; speaker Alliance for Continuing Med. Edn., 1991, Assn. Hosp. Med. Edn. Spring Inst., 1988-91, 94, N.J. Assn. Med. Edn. New Directions in Med. Edn., 1988, N.J. Med. Soc., Coun. Adminstrn. Direct in Med. Edn. Workshop, 1986, 89, chmn.-elect, 1988-91, chair, 1992-94; instr. emergency med. svcs. Otsego County Emergency Svcs.; mem. regional EMS faculty N.Y. State Dept. Health, 1995—. Mem. Otsego EMS Coun., CPR instr. ARC, Am. Heart Assn.; capt. Cooperstown Fire Dept. Emergency Squad, 1992—; mem. Adirondack-Appalachian Regional Emergency Med. Svcs. Coun., 1990—, League of Women Voters. Mem. LWC, Delta Kappa Gamma, Delta Pi Epsilon. Democrat. Roman Catholic. Office: The Mary Imogene Bassett Hosp One Atwell Rd Cooperstown NY 13326

KAIGE, ALICE TUBB, retired librarian; b. Obion, Tenn., Jan. 27, 1922; d. George Easley and Lucile (Merryman) Tubb; m. Richard H. Kaige, Aug., 1952; children: Robert H., Richard C., John S. (dec.). BA, Vanderbilt U., 1944; BS in Libr. Sci., Geo. Peabody Coll., 1947. Libr. Martin (Tenn.) High Sch., 1946-47, Demonstration Sch. Geo. Peabody Coll. Joint U. Librs., Nashville, Tenn., 1947-52; acquisitions libr. Lincoln Libr., Springfield, Ill., 1967-70; office coord. Springfield (Ill.) Chpt. ACLU, 1974; staff rep. Am. Fed. State, County & Mcpl. Employees, Springfield, 1975; libr. Ill. Dept. of Commerce and Community Affairs, Springfield, 1976-89. Vice chmn. Women's Internat. League for Peace and Freedom, 1969-70, various coms., 1970—; treas. Cen. Ill. Women's Lobby, 1971-72; com. on local govt. League of Women Voters, 1973-76; career day com. Urban League Guild, 1970-71; mem. NAACP,steering com. Springfield chpt. ACLU, 1974-75; co-founder West Side Neighborhood Assn., Springfield, 1977. Recipient Elizabeth Cady Stanton award, Springfield Women's Political Caucus, 1982. Mem. Sangamon County Hist. Soc., NOW, Women's Internat. League for Peace and Freedom, War Resisters League, LWV, Springfield Women's Polit. Caucus. Home: 701 S State St Springfield IL 62704

KAIKOW, RITA ELLEN, library media specialist; b. Bklyn., Mar. 18, 1947; d. Solomon and Sylvia (Bitkoff) K. BA, Queens Coll., 1968, MLS, 1971. Tchr. Bklyn., 1968-70; libr. media specialist Oceanside (N.Y.) High Sch., 1971—; liaison Nassau Sch. Libr. System, Carle Place, N.Y., 1980— (Outstanding Leadership, Dedication and Svc. as Facilitator award 1988), facilitator S.W. cluster, S.W. Nassau County, N.Y., 1985-94; mem. taskforce White House Conf. on Libr. and Info. Svcs. Author: (mag.) The Book Report, 1991. Mem. ALA, Am. Assn. Sch. Librs., N.Y. State United Tchrs., N.Y. Libr. Assn. (sch. libr. media sect.), Nassau County Libr. Assn., Oceanside Fedn. Tchrs., L.I. Sch. Media Assn. (v.p. 1987-92, co-pres. 1992—), Libr. and Info. Tech. Assn., Soc. Sch. Librs. Internat., Freedom to Read Found., Beta Phi Mu. Office: Oceanside High Sch 3160 Skillman Ave Oceanside NY 11572-4495

KAIL, MARIA-FRANZISKA, international development association executive; b. Bitburg, Germany, Dec. 21, 1959; came to U.S., 1980; d. Herbert and Anna Helene (Reiter) K.; m. Richard Lawrence Moss, Feb. 18, 1989. Student, Corcoran Sch. Art, 1987-93, Skidmore Coll., 1993. Lang. sec. World Bank, Washington, 1980-83, sr. staff asst. dept. West Africa, 1983-87, adminstr., mgr., 1987-93, ops. analyst Nigeria, 1993—. Fundraiser United Way, Washington, 1992. With U.S. Army, 1977-79. Home: 5909 Ramsgate Rd Bethesda MD 20816-1127

KAISER, ANTOINETTE PERRONE, communications executive; b. Pittston, Pa., Feb. 22, 1935; d. Rosario Peter and Annunziata Clementina (Franco) Perrone; m. Robert G. Kaiser, June 22, 1969 (dec. Feb. 1979); 1 child, Kyle Kaiser Swiat. BS in Bus., Empire State Coll., Buffalo, 1984. Asst. mgr. Marine Midland Bank, N.A., Tonawanda, N.Y., 1969-72; dist. ops. officer Marine Midland Bank, N.A., Buffalo, 1972-73, br. ops. officer, 1973-76; gen. mgr. STI-CO Industries, Inc., Buffalo, 1976-79, pres., chief exec. officer, 1979—. Apptd. to def. adv. panel Gov. Mario Cuomo, 1990. Fellow Radio Club of Am.; mem. Am. Prodn. and Inventory Control Soc., Assn. PUb. Safety Communications Officers (comml. adv. com.). Office: STI-CO Industries Inc 11 Cobham Dr # 656 Orchard Park NY 14127-4101

KAISER, CHARLENE BETH, physician; b. Ill., Nov. 14, 1945. BA, U. Colo., 1967; MD, Albert Einstein Coll. Medicine, 1972; MPH, Yale U., 1982. Cert. indsl. hygienist. Med. dir. FNP, Inc., Palm Springs, Calif. Mem. Am. Coll. Preventive Medicine, Am. Acad. Dermatology. Home: 11429 Artesia Morongo Valley CA 92256 Office: FHP Inc 501 S Palm Canyon Dr Palm Springs CA 92262

KAISER, JEAN MORGAN, real estate broker; b. Johnson City, Tenn., June 28, 1932; d. Samuel Harold and Mabel Loretta (Burleson) Morgan; m. Edward Latham Kaiser, June 21, 1957; children: Gary Charles, Janet Lynne. Grad., Realtors Inst., 1978. Cert. real estate broker. Copywriter, announcer Sta. WGRV, Greeneville, 1952-58; exec. dir. Washington County United Fund, Abingdon, Va., 1961; personnel sec. Hubbard Aluminum Products Co., Abingdon, 1962-63; exec. sec. Roy Heyse and Assocs., Prairie Village, Kans., 1969-72; realtor assoc. Claiborne Co., Bartlesville, Okla., 1973-77; sec., treas. Blasting Svcs. Inc., Bartlesville, 1985—, Elko Inc., Bartlesville, 1987—; pres. Kaiser Realty/Better Homes and Gardens, Bartlesville, 1977—; Okla. Real Estate Commr., Oklahoma City, 1984-88; mem. rsch. bd. advisors Am. Biog. Inst., Inc. Mem. Women's Council Realtors, Real Estate Educators Assn., Bartlesville Bd. Realtors (bd. dirs. 1981-83), Okla. Assn. Realtors (bd. dirs. 1987—), N.E. Okla. Bd. Realtors (bd. dirs.), Nat. Assn. Real Estate Lic. Law Ofcls. (legis. and interstate coop. coms. 1986-87), Okla. Cert. Residential Specialists (forum com. 1986-87). Democrat. Office: Kaiser Realty/Better Homes Gardens 2450 S Washington Blvd Bartlesville OK 74006 also: 412 S Main St Grove OK 74344-3327

KAISER, LINDA SUSAN, state commissioner, lawyer; b. Alexandria, Va., Apr. 7, 1956; d. Thomas Raymond Kaiser and Joanne May (Wilber) Raynolds. BA, Pa. State U., 1978; JD, U. Pitts., 1981. Asst. counsel Pa. Ins. Dept., Harrisburg, 1981-85; sr. counsel Cigna Corp., Phila., 1985-92; asst. gen. counsel Reliance Ins. Co., Phila., 1992-95; ins. commr. Commonwealth of Pa., Harrisburg, 1995—; mem. property casualty steering com. Ins. Fedn. Pa., Phila., 1992—; alternate Pa. Workers Compensation Gov. Bd., 1993—. Pres. Huntington's Disease Soc. of Am., Del. Valley, Phila., 1993. Mem. Soc. Chartered Property Casulaty Underwriters, ABA, Nat. Assn. Ind. Insurers, Order of Coif, Barristers. Office: 1326 Strawberry Sq Harrisburg PA 17120

KAISER, LISA ROSE, nurse anesthetist; b. St. Louis, Mar. 30, 1965; d. Earl Leroy and Mary Lou (Kramer) Zimmer; m. Robert John Kaiser, Nov. 22, 1986; 1 child, Natalie Rose. Grad., St. Lukes Sch. Nursing, St. Louis, 1986; student, U. North Fla., 1985, 86-87; BSN, U. Mo., St. Louis, 1989; MSN in Anesthesia, Bradley U., 1994. RN; cert. BLS, ACLS. RN ICU, CCU, SICU St. Luke's Hosp., Jacksonville, Fla., 1986-87; RN RICU St. Luke's Hosp., Chesterfield, Mo., 1987-89, RN recovery rm., 1989-93; nurse anesthetist St. Anthony's Med. Ctr., St. Louis, 1994—. Vol. tchr. prenatal an infant care low income pregnant teenagers, 1989; mem. Nursing Christian Fellowship, 1983-86, Fla. Nursing Assn., 1986-87. Meml. Aux. scholar U. North Fla., 1987. Mem. Mo. Nursing Asnm., Am. Assn. Nurse Anesthetists. Roman Catholic. Home: 169 Rockaway O'Fallon MO 63366

KAISER-BOTSAI, SHARON KAY, early childhood educator; b. Waterloo, Iowa, Aug. 9, 1941; d. Peter A. Ley and Lorraine (Worthington) Burton; m. Hugh W. Kaiser, Aug. 28, 1968 (div. 1981); 1 child, Kiana; m. Elmer E. Botsai, Dec. 5, 1981; children: Kiana, Don, Kurt. BSBA, U. Ariz., 1963; MEd, U. Hawaii, Honolulu, 1970; postgrad., Hawaii Loa Coll., 1971, U. Hawaii, 1972-88. Cert. elem. edn. tchr., Hawaii. Sec. Donald M. Drake, San Francisco, 1964-66; tchr. St. Mark's Kindergarten, Honolulu, 1966-73; head tchr. Cen. Union Preschool, Honolulu, 1967-77; tchr. Waiokeola Preschool, Honolulu, 1974-76, 77-88; tchr. staff instruction Honolulu Dist. Dept. of Edn., 1989-90; tchr. students of ltd. English proficiency Kaahumanu Sch., Honolulu, 1990-94; tchr. kindergarten Palolo Sch., Honolulu, 1991-93; pvt. instr. in Hawaiian dance, 1977-79; workshop leader marine sea crafts Sea Grant Inst. for Marine Educators, 1977, HAEYC Conf., 1979, 82, 84, 85, 86, chair workshops in music and creative drama, 1977, drama workshop, 1994; speaker Celebration of Life Sta. KHON-TV, 1979; workshop leader MECAP Conf., 1985; mem. com. Improvement Symphony Performance for Preschoolers, 1977; art advisor, coord. Sunday sch. program Waiokeola Ch., 1973, speaker creative communication, 1984; validator accreditation program Nat. Acad. for Edn. of Young Children, 1986—; asst. to co-chair conf. Hawaii Assn. for Edn. Young Children, 1987-88; Hawaii State Tchrs. Assn. rep. Palolo Sch., 1993. Author: Creative Dramatics, 1990; co-author: Preschool Activities, 1990. Actress Presido Playhouse, San Francisco, 1962, Little Theatre, Honolulu Zoo, 1976; instr. spl. edn. students Kaneohe YWCA, 1967; troop co-leader Girl Scouts U.S.A., 1981-84; bd. dirs. Zoo Hui, 1984-86; trustee, stewardship chmn. Waiokeola Ch., 1986-88. Mem. Hawaii Assn. for Edn. of Young Children (First recipient Phyllis Loveless Excellence in Teaching award 1979), Delta Delta Delta. Lutheran. Home: 321 Wailupe Cir Honolulu HI 96821-1524

KAISERLIAN, PENELOPE JANE, publishing company executive; b. Paisley, Scotland, Oct. 19, 1943; came to U.S., 1956; d. W. Norman and Magdalene Jeanette (Houlder) Hewson; m. Arthur Kaiserlian, June 29, 1968; 1 child, Christian. B.A., U. Exeter, Eng., 1965. Copywriter, sales rep. Pergamon Press, Elmsford, N.Y., 1965-68; exhibits mgr. Plenum Pub., N.Y.C., 1968-69; asst. mktg. mgr. U. Chgo. Press, 1969-76, mktg. mgr., 1976-83, assoc. dir., 1983—. Mem. Soc. for Scholarly Pub., Am. Geog. Assn., Quadrangle Club. Office: U Chgo Press 5801 S Ellis Ave Chicago IL 60637-1404

KAJI, HIDEKO KATAYAMA, pharmacologist; b. Tokyo, Jan. 1, 1932; came to U.S., 1954; d. Sakae and Tsuneko (Matsuda) Katayama; m. Akira Kaji, Aug. 23, 1958; children: Kenneth, Eugene, Naomi, Amy. BS, Tokyo Coll. Pharmacy, 1954; MS, U. Nebr., 1956; PhD, Purdue U., 1958. Vis. scientist Oak Ridge (Tenn.) Nat. Lab., 1962-63; assoc. U. Pa., Phila., 1963-64; rsch. assoc. The Inst. Cancer Rsch., Phila., 1965-66, asst. mem., 1966-76; vis. mem. Max Planck Inst. Molek. Gen., Berlin, 1972-73, Nat. Inst. Med. Rsch., London, 1973; assoc. prof. Jefferson Med. Coll., Phila., 1976-82; vis. prof. Wistar Inst., Phila., 1984-85; prof. pharmacology and structural biology Jefferson Med. Coll., Phila., 1983—; cons. Nippon Paint Co., Ltd., Tokyo, 1990—, Coatesville (Pa.) VA Hosp., 1982-84. Contbr. articles to profl. jours. Fellow NIH (bd. dirs. 1986-89); mem. Am. Soc. Biochemistry and Molecular Biology, Am. Soc. Pharmacol. and Exptl. Therapeutics, Am. Soc. Microbiology, Sigma Xi. Home: 334 Fillmore St Jenkintown PA 19046-4328 Office: Jefferson Med Coll 1020 Locust St Philadelphia PA 19107-6731

KALAF, ABBIGAIL STEPHENS, therapist; b. Paris, Dec. 14, 1964; came to U.S., 1966; d. William Curtis and Joan Carol (Fischer) Stephens; m. Bill Anthony, Aug. 29, 1987. BS in Psychology, Gardner-Webb U., Boiling Springs, N.C., 1987; MS in Community Counseling, Ga. State U., 1990; diploma in Christian counseling, Psychol. Studies Inst., Atlanta, 1990; cert. risk reduction instr., Prevention Rsch. Inst., Lexington, Ky., 1990. Lic. profl. counselor Ga., N.C. Therapist Family Recovery, Inc., Cumming, Ga., 1990-94; resdl. counselor, area dir., adj. faculty Gardner-Webb U., Boiling Springs, N.C., 1994—; contract therapist Ga. Highlands Med. Svcs., Inc., Cumming, 1990-92; instr. risk reduction program North Ga. DUI Educators, Inc., Cumming, 1990-92. Econs. cons. Ctrl. Forsyth H.S., Jr. Achievement, Cumming, 1990-91; mem. Citizens Adv. Coun. for Mental Health, Mental Retardation and Substance Abuse, 1991-94, chmn., 1992-93; mem. pub. edn. com. Forsyth County Youth Coalition, 1993-94; Sunday sch. tchr. North Lanier Bapt. Ch., Cumming, 1993-94. Mem. ACA, Assn. for Religious and Value Issues in Counseling. Republican. Baptist. Home: Gardner-Webb U Box 6016 Boiling Springs NC 28017

KALAYJIAN, ANIE SANENTZ, educator, consultant, psychotherapist, nurse; b. Aleppo, Syria; came to U.S., 1971; d. Kevork and Zabelle (Mardikian) K.; m. Shahé Navasart Sanentz, Dec. 16, 1984. BS L.I. U., 1979; MEd, Columbia U., 1981, EdD, 1985, profl. nurses tng. course, 1984; cert. photography, Pratt Inst., 1979. R.N., N.Y.; cert. psychiat. mental health specialist; Dutch diplomate in logotherapy. Psychiat. nurse Met. Hosp., N.Y.C., 1979-84; staff psychiat. mental health nurse Manhattan Bowery Project, N.Y.C., 1978-86; instr. Hunter Coll., N.Y.C., 1980-82; prof. Bloomfield Coll., N.J., 1984-85; lectr. Jersey City Coll., 1985; prof. Seton Hall U., South Orange, N.J., 1985-87; assoc. prof. grad. program St. Joseph Coll., 1987-91; prof. John Jay Coll. Criminal Justice Fairleigh Dickinson U., 1991-92, vis. prof., 1991-92, Pace U., N.Y.C. Active com. for presdl. task force on nursing curriculum Soc. for Traumatic Stress Studies; co-founder, East coast coord. Mental Health Outreach to Earthquake Survivors in Armenia; dir. Julia Richman-Pace Univ.-N.Y. State Bd. Edn.-Visiting Nurse Svc.-Partnership program, 1991-92. Recipient Clark Found. scholarship award, 1985; rsch. grantee Pace U., 1992; Endowed Nursing Edn., Columbia U., scholar, 1984; Armenian Relief Soc. scholar, 1976-77, Armenian Students Assn. Am. scholar, 1976-78. Fellow Am. Orthopsychiat. Assn., N.Y. State Nursing Assn. (planning com. nursing edn.); mem. Coun. on Continuing Edn., Psychiat. and Mental Health Nursing (coun.), Am. Psychiat. Nurses Assn. (internat. coun. psychologists, internat. trauma councilors), Inst. for Psychodynamics and Origins of Mind, Armenian Students Assn. (treas. 1980-81, pres. 1981-83, scholarship chairperson 1983-85, v.p. Cen. Exec. Com. 1987-88, pres. 1988-89, elected nat. pres. 1988-90), Armenian Info. Profls. (corr. sec.), Armenian-Am. Soc. for Studies on Stress and Genocide (founder, pres. 1988—), N.Y. Registered Nurses' Assn. (chairperson edn. com., 1989—), World Fed. for Mental Health (UN rep., treas., sec., UN com. on human rights, 1994—), Univ. for Peace (coresponding sec. UN com.), Internat. Soc. Tramatic Stress Studies (v.p. N.Y. chpt. 1993—), Am. Info. Profls. (corr. sec. 1993—), Kappa Delta Pi (advisor 1989-90), Sigma Theta Tau. Avocations: aerobics, photography, acting, logotherapy. Office: 130 W 79th St New York NY 10024-6477

KALB, VIRGINIA GROVER, school library administrator, educator; b. Trenton, N.J., Apr. 19, 1936; d. Charles Rue and Mary Beatrice (App) Grover; m. John Garrison Kalb, Dec. 21, 1957; children: John Charles, Thomas Rue. BA, William Smith Coll., Geneva, N.Y., 1958; MA, Calif.

State U., Long Beach, 1976. Cert. in elem. edn., libr. svcs., adminstrv. svcs., Calif. Libr. media specialist Montebello (Calif.) Unified Sch. Dist., 1976-84, coord. media svcs., 1984—; asst. prof. Calif. State U., L.A., 1987-93; lectr. Calif. State U., Long Beach, 1990—. Author column in Sch. Libr. Media Quar., 1988-91. Mem. ALA, Am. Assn. Sch. Librs., Calif. Media and Libr. Educators Assn. (pres. 1987-88), So. Calif. Coun. on Lit. for Children and Young People, Phi Kappa Phi. Office: Montebello Unified Sch Dist 123 S Montebello Blvd Montebello CA 90640

KALIN, KARIN BEA, educator, consultant; b. N.Y.C., June 22, 1943; d. Lawrence Leon and Celia (Siskind) Elkind; children: Laura, Howard. BS, SUNY, Oswego, 1965; MS, CUNY, 1967. Cert. social studies tchr., N.Y. Tchr. Benjamin Franklin High Sch., N.Y.C., 1965-66, Grover Cleveland High Sch., Ridgewood, N.Y., 1967-73; tchr. Aviation High Sch., Long Island City, N.Y., 1979—, sex equity coord., 1982-90, local equal opportunity coord., 1983-91, sch. recruiter, 1985-91; curriculum developer OEO, N.Y.C. Bd. Edn., fall 1985; panelist Aerospace Edn. Workshop for Elem. Tchrs., Career Exploration Seminar, Aerospace Edn. Conf., 1990, East Meadow (N.Y.) Sch. Dist., 1989—; cons. Coll. Aeros., N.Y., 1986; cons. Profl. and Clerical Employees of Internat. Ladies Garment Workers Union, N.Y.C., 1989; with L.I. Coun. for Equal Edn. and Employment, 1990. Mem. Women on Job, Port Washington, N.Y., 1986-91; mem. com. Nassau Dem. Com., Westbury, N.Y., 1988—; mem. L.I. Coun. Equal Edn. and Employment, 1990—, Coalition To Advocate for Women of Color in Edn. William Robertson Coe fellow, 1992; grantee Columbia U., 1967, 69, N.Y.C. Bd. Edn., 1983, Nat. Coun. for Humanities, 1985, Project Voice/Move, 1984-85. Mem. AAUW (roundtable on gender equity in classroom 1992), NAFE, NOW (chair women and employment com. 1987-90, chair consciousness raising com. 1982), LWV, N.Y. State Alliance for Women and Girls in Tech., N.Y. State Tchrs. Union, Acad. Polit. Sci., Nat. Women's Polit. Caucus (bd. dirs., chair polit. action com.). Jewish. Home: 700 Barkley Ave East Meadow NY 11554-4501 Office: Aviation High Sch 36th St Queens Blvd Long Island City NY 11101

KALINA, MICHELLE LOUISE, reading skills educator; b. N.Y.C., Sept. 16, 1947; d. Henry Jean Nibur and Pearl (Arnheim) Chandler; m. Michael A. Kalina, Feb. 9, 1969. BA in History, CCNY, 1969; MS in Edn. and Reading, Calif. State U., Hayward, 1974; EdD in Curriculum, Theory and Instrnl. Design, U. San Francisco, 1991. Instr. history, reading San Francisco adult edn. divsn. Presidio San Francisco, 1970-77; instr. reading adult divsn. Oakland (Calif.) Pub. Schs., 1973-74; instr. reading Foothill C.C. dist. DeAnza Coll., 1975; instr. reading, writing, ESL San Mateo C.C. coll. dist. Can. Coll., Redwood City, Calif., 1976-79; instr. reading, basic skills Sierra C.C., Rocklin, Calif., 1979—; ind. reviewer Houghton Mifflin, Scott Foresman & Co., Townsend Press, Wadsworth Pub., West Pub., 1982—; adj. prof. curriculum and instrn. U. San Francisco, 1992; coord. LARC rsch. grant Sierra and Napa Colls., 1992-93; test evaluator Clinch Valley Coll., U. Va., 1993; cons. L.A. Harbor Coll., 1993, Elk Grove (Calif.) Unified, 1993-94; pres. faculty senate Sierra Coll., co-chair classroom feedback project, mem. ednl. requirements com., curriculum coun., title 5 implementation task force; condr. workshops and presentations in field. Commr. ednl. policy commn. Calif. C.C. League. Sr. fellow Ctr. for Outcome-Based Edn., San Francisco, 1991-94. Mem. ASCD, NEA, Internat. Reading Assn., Am. Ednl. Rsch. Assn., No. Calif. Coll. Reading Assn. (pres.-elect, sec.), Orton Dyslexia Soc., Sierra Coll. Faculty Assn. (chair contract, negotiator), Pi Lambda Theta. Office: Sierra Coll 5000 Rocklin Rd Rocklin CA 95677-3397

KALIPOLITES, JUNE E. TURNER, rehabilitation professional; b. Grasmere, N.H., Aug. 10, 1932; d. Louis O. and Edith Mae (Allen) Turner; m. Nicholas G. Kalipolites, Feb. 12, 1955; children: George, Stephanie, Athena. AA, Hesser Coll., Manchester, N.H., 1977; B of Gen. Studies, U. N.H., 1980; MS in Rehab. Adminstrn. and Svcs., So. Ill. U., Carbondale, 1982; EdD in Ednl. Adminstrn., Vanderbilt U., 1992. Cert. rehab. counselor. Office mgr. Harris Upham and Co., Inc., Manchester; mgr. Amoskeag Bank & Trust Co.; rehab. counselor Div. Vocat. Rehab., Nashua, N.H.; rehab. cons. N.H. Divsn. Vocat. Rehab., Concord, 1986—, tng. coord., 1993-94; tng. coord. N.H. Div. Vocat. Rehab., Concord, 1993—. Author: Profile of Women in Rehabilitation Administration: A Common Theme, 1992, Projects with Industry: A Unique Concept for Providing Rehabilitation Services to Persons with Severe Disabilities, 1982. LaVerne Noyes scholar. Mem. NAFE, ACA, Am. Rehab. Counseling Assn., Nat. Rehab. Assn. (nat. bd. dirs. 1994—), Nat. Rehab. Counseling Assn. (bd. dirs. 1986-87), Nat. Rehab. Adminstrn. Assn. (nat. bd. dirs. 1983-87, 92-94), N.E. Rehab. Counseling Assn. (pres. 1987, bd. dirs. 1986-88), N.H. Rehab. Assn. (bd. dirs. 1977—, treas: 1978, 89-92, sec. 1977-78), Nat. Assn. Ind. Living, Rho Sigma Chi, Chi Sigma Iota. Democrat. Greek Orthodox. Home: 668 Lake Ave Manchester NH 03103-3538 Office: NH Div Vocat Rehab 78 Regional Dr Concord NH 03301-8508

KALISCH, BEATRICE JEAN, nursing educator, consultant; b. Tellahoma, Tenn., Oct. 15, 1943; d. Peter and Margaret Ruth Petersen; m. Philip A. Kalisch, Apr. 17, 1965; children—Philip P., Melanie J. BS, U. Nebr., 1965; MS, U. Md., 1967, PhD, 1970. Pediatric staff nurse Centre County Hosp., Bellefonte, Pa., 1965-66; instr. nursing Philipsburg (Pa.) Gen. Hosp. Sch. Nursing, 1966; pediatric staff nurse Greater Balt. Med. Center, Towson, Md., 1967; asst. prof. maternal-child nursing Am. U., 1967-68; clin. nurse specialist N.W. Tex. Hosp., Amarillo, 1970; assoc. prof. maternal-child nursing, curriculum coordinator nursing Amarillo Coll., 1970-71; chmn. baccalaureate nursing program, asso. prof. nursing U. So. Miss., 1971-74; prof. nursing, chmn. dept. parent-child nursing U. Mich. Sch. Nursing, Ann Arbor, 1974-86; Shirley C. Titus Disting. prof. U. Mich. Sch. Nursing, 1977—, Titus Disting. prof. nursing mgmt., 1989—; prin., dir. nursing consultation svcs. Ernst & Young, Detroit, 1986-89; prin. investigator USPH grant to study image of nurses in mass media and the informational quality nursing news, U. Mich., 1977-86, prin. investigator to study intrahosp. transport of critically ill patients, 1991—; prin. investigator to study use of HIA nurse in N.Y.C. labor market, U. Mich.; prin. investigator to study the impact of managed care on critical care, U. Mich.; vis. Disting. prof. U. Ala., 1979, U. Tex., 1981, Tex. Christian U., 1983. Author: Child Abuse and Neglect: An Annotated Bibliography, 1978; co-author: Nursing Involvement in Health Planning, 1978, Politics of Nursing, 1982, Images of Nurses on Television, 1983, The Advance of American Nursing, 1986, revised, 1994, The Changing Image of the Nurse, 1987; co-editor: Studies in Nursing Mgmt.; contbr. articles to profl. jours. Recipient Joseph L. Andrews Bibliog. award Am. Assn. Law Libraries, 1979; Book of Yr. award Am. Jour. Nursing, 1978, 83, 86, 87, Outstanding Achievement award U. Md., 1987, Distinguished Alumni award U. Nebr., 1985, Shaw medal Boston Coll., 1986; USPHS fellow. Fellow Am. Acad. Nursing; mem. Am. Nurses Assn., Am. Pub. Health Assn., Am. Hosp. Assn., Am. Orgn. Nurse Execs., Sigma Theta Tau, Phi Kappa Phi. Presbyterian. Home: 27675 Chatsworth St Farmington MI 48334-1821 Office: U Mich Sch Nursing 400 N Ingalls St Ann Arbor MI 48109-2003

KALISH, KATHERINE MCAULAY, lawyer; b. Pinehurst, N.C., Aug. 6, 1945; d. Hugh Page and Exie Katherine (Beasley) McAulay; m. David Marcus Kalish, Jr., June 18, 1967; children: David Marcus, Page McAulay. B.A., Agnes Scott Coll., 1966; J.D., Mercer U., 1979. Bar: Ga. 1979, U.S. Dist. Ct. (mid. dist.) Ga. 1979, U.S. Ct. Appeals (5th cir.) 1981, U.S. Ct. Appeals (11th cir.) 1982. Elem. sch. tchr. Clayton County, Jonesboro, Ga., 1966-67; in office claims adjuster C.N.A., Atlanta, 1967-68; customer account auditor So. Ry., Atlanta, 1968-69; office mgr. David M. Kalish, DDS, Macon, Ga., 1971-73; asst. city atty. Macon, 1979-81; sole practice, Macon, 1981—. judge pro hac Mcpl. Ct. City of Macon, Ga., 1981-82. Mem. Career Women's Network of Macon, Temple Beth Israel Sisterhood, Macon; bd. dirs. Ctr. for Continuing Edn. Women, Macon, 1981-90, Macon Fire and Police Pension Bd., 1983-91, Porter Found., 1985—, chair, 1990, 91. Mem. Macon Bar Assn., Ga. Bar Assn., ABA, YLS Coll. Placement and Forums Com., LWV. Democrat. Home: 4800 N Mumford Rd Macon GA 31210-4039 Office: 3110 Ridge Ave Macon GA 31204-2329

KALISKI, MARY, psychologist; b. Bratislava, Czechoslovakia, Dec. 9, 1938; came to U.S., 1950; d. Frank and Margaret (Fleischman) Reichenthal; m. Thomas Kaliski, Sept. 21, 1957; children: Karen, Kenneth. BS summa cum laude, C.W. Post Coll., 1978; MS, profl. diploma, St. John's U., 1980, PhD, 1987. Psychologist North Shore Schs., L.I., 1977-79, Herricks Schs., L.I., 1979—; speaker in field. Chief psychologist Stepfamily Found. L.I., 1987-92; bd. dirs. Nassau Psychol. Svcs. Inst., 1989—. Mem. Am. Psychol. Assn., Nassau County Psychol. Assn., Sch. Coun. N.Y. State Psychol. Educators.

KALLAS, JACQUELINE HEATHER, television producer; b. Paris, July 7, 1958; came to U.S., 1961; d. James Gus and Darlean Phyllis Kallas. BA in Comm., U. Calif., San Diego, 1979. Writer, reporter KGTV-TV 10, San Diego, 1978-80; newscaster IMN Regional Radio, KOSI & KTLK Radio Stas., Denver, 1980-82; producer, reporter KRMA TV 6, Denver, 1982-83; news producer KMGH TV 7, Denver, 1983-85; spl. projects producer KRON TV, San Francisco, 1986-90; producer ABC's PrimeTIME Live, N.Y.C., 1990—; career sponsor Foxcroft Continuing Career Series, Middleburg, Va., 1993. Author: (poetry book) A Women's Anthology of Poetry, 1981. Recipient Hon. Mention, RFK awards. Mem. NAFE, Am. Biog. Inst. Office: Primetime Live 147 Columbus Ave New York NY 10023-5900

KALLGREN, JOYCE KISLITZIN, political science educator; b. San Francisco, Apr. 17, 1930; d. Alexander and Dorothea (Willett) K.; m. Edward E. Kallgren, Feb. 8, 1953; children: Virginia, Charles. BA, U. Calif., Berkeley, 1953, MA, 1955; PhD, Harvard U., 1968. Jr. researcher to asst. researcher Ctr. Chinese Studies U. Calif., Berkeley, 1961-65, research assoc., 1965—, chair, 1983-88; assoc. dir. Inst. of East Asian Studies, Berkeley, 1987—; from lectr. to prof. polit. sci. emeritus U. Calif., Davis, 1965—; cons. in field. Contbg. editor: Asean and China: An Evolving Relationship, 1988, Academic Exchanges: Essays on the Sino-American Experience, 1987, Developing a Nation State: China After Forty Years, 1990; editor: Jour. Asian Studies, 1980-83, Asian Survey, 1991—; contbr. articles to profl. jours. and chpts. to books. Ford Found. awardee, 1978-79. Mem. Am. Polit. Sci. Assn., Assn. Asian Studies (bd. dirs.), Nat. Com. U.S./China Rels., U.S. Com. on Security and Coop. in Asia Pacific. Home: 28 Hillcrest Rd Berkeley CA 94705-2807 Office: U Calif Inst East Asian Studie E Berkeley CA 94720

KALLMAN, KATHLEEN BARBARA, marketing and business development professional; b. Aurora, Ill., Mar. 23, 1952; d. Kenneth Wesley and Germaine Barbara (May) Eby. Legal sec. Sidley & Austin, Chgo., 1973-76, Winston & Strawn, Chgo., 1976-78; exec. sec. Beatrice Cos., Inc., Chgo., 1978-81, adminstrv. asst., 1981-83, asst. to chmn. bd. dirs., 1983-84, asst. v.p., 1984-85; pres., mng. dir. Stratxx Ltd., Charlotte, N.C., 1985—. Mem. Chgo. Coun. on Fgn. Rels., 1986—. Mem. Am. Soc. Profl. and Exec. Women, Nat. Assn. Women Bus. Owners, Charlotte Women Bus. Owners Assn., Charlotte Assn. Profl. Saleswomen. Office: Stratxx Ltd PO Box 470008 Charlotte NC 28247-0008

KALLNER, NINA CORY, educator; b. Colfax, Ind., Sept. 19, 1921; d. Herschel Floyd and Lena Jeanette (Hutchison) Cory; m. Robert Clayton Kallner; children: Beverly Kay Kallner Schwinn, Linda Carol Kallner Gale. BS, Ball State U., 1961, MA, 1966. Cert. elem. edn. tchr., libr. sci. Tchr. Anderson Community Schs., Anderson, Ind., 1961-64, 65—. Mem. AAUW (pres. local chpt. 1982, 85-86, 92-93), Kappa Delta Phi. Democrat. Mem. Disciples of Christ Ch. Home: 2527 Albert St Anderson IN 46012-3208

KALMANIR, KAREN ANN, lawyer; b. Los Angeles, June 15, 1958; d. Thomas John and Frances (Brown) K. AB in History, Stanford U., 1980; JD, Lewis and Clark Coll., 1984. Bar: Md. 1986, D.C. 1986. Law clk. to legal counsel U.S. Senate, Washington, 1985-86; trial atty. criminal div. U.S. Dept. Justice, Washington, 1986-87; asst. state's atty. State's Atty.'s Office, Montgomery County, Md., 1987-89; assoc. Miles & Stockbridge, Balt., Md., 1989-90; asst. U.S. atty. criminal divsn. U.S. Atty.'s Office Eastern Dist. Calif., Fresno, 1990—; moot ct. judge Georgetown U. Law Sch., Washington, 1987. Office: US Atty's Office 1130 O St Fresno CA 93721

KALMAN-SNYDER, ABBE LYNN, artist, elementary school teacher; b. N.Y.C., Sept. 27, 1950; d. Theodore Kalman and Beatrice (Rosen) Levey; divorced; 1 child, Todd Snyder. BA Elem. Edn., Fairleigh Dickinson U., Madison, N.J., 1970; MA in Reading, William Paterson Coll., 1978. Cert. reading tchr. K-12, elem. sch. tchr., N.J. 5th grade tchr. Harrington Park (N.J.) Bd. Edn., 1970-75; reading coord. Vernon (N.J.) Twp. Bd. Edn., 1975-76; adminstrv. asst. Eas. Bldg. & Utility Co., Inc., Pompton Lakes, N.J., 1983-94; owner, artist Kalman Originals, Hewitt, N.J., 1991—; cons. Stepping Stone Day Nursery, River Edge, N.J. Artist: (dimensional acrylics) works have appeared in solo exhibitions at Tappan (N.Y.) Libr., John Harms Art Ctr., N.J., Chestnut Ridge Village, N.Y., Ringwood Commons, N.J., Custom Touch Gallery, N.J.; galleries showing her work include Custom Touch, West Milford, N.J., Sidney Rothman, Barnegat Light, N.J., The Nathans Gallery, West Paterson, N.J., Galerie 32, Milburn, N.J.; juried shows Atrium Art Gallery, Morristown, N.J., Art-Mine Registry, Soho, N.Y. and others. Mem. Morris County Art Assn., Allied Artists of Am. (assoc.), Ringwood Manaor Art Assn., Salute to Women in Arts. Jewish. Home: 26 Yancey Terr Hewitt NY 07421

KALMBACH, TERESA ELLEN, human resources professional; b. Portland, Oreg., Apr. 22, 1963; d. Brian Frederick Kalmbach and Mildred Ann (Nichols) Reppeto. BS, Oreg. State U., 1985; cert. in Human Resources, U. Wash., 1994. Mgr. Jay Jacobs, Inc., Seattle, 1985-88; mgr. sr. sta. Hertz Corp., Seattle, 1988-94; mgr. human resources Furon Co., Seattle, 1994—. Vol. big sister United Way, King County, Wash., 1993—. Home: 11122 SE 316th Pl Auburn WA 98092

KALMUS, ELLIN, art historian, educator; b. N.Y.C.; d. Victor and Mata (Heineman) Roudin; m. Murray L. Silberstein, Oct. 6, 1949 (dec. 1968); children: James, Barbara Silberstein Keezell, John; m. Allan H. Kalmus, May 16, 1969. BA cum laude, Vassar Coll., 1946. Asst. dept. publs. and exhbns. Mus. Modern Art, N.Y.C., 1946-49; asst. tchr. Mus. Modern Art, 1950; lectr. Riverdale Country Sch., N.Y.C., 1970—, Dalton,Trinity, Columbia Grammar, Birch Wathen Schs., N.Y.C., 1971-83, Fifth Ave. Presbyn. Ch., St. James Episcopal Ch., N.Y.C., 1982-83; lectr. pvt. groups N.Y.C., 1975—; mem. vis. com. photograph and slide libr. Met. Mus. Art, N.Y.C., 1978—, lectr., 1986, 87; mem. teaching staff Ethical Culture Sch. for Adult Edn., New Sch. for Social Rsch., 1980-81; Paris lectr. Friends of Vieilles Maisons Francaises, 1988; series lectr. Darien Cmty. Assn., 1988—, London Lectr. Arts Club of London, 1990; lectr. Albert Einstein Coll. of Medicine, 1993, Christie's, 1994. Trustee, head edn. com. Riverdale Country Sch., N.Y.C., 1978-84. Pierpont Morgan Libr. fellow, 1986, Frick Collection fellow, 1992. Mem. Phi Beta Kappa, Cosmopolitan Club, Sunningdale Club (Scarsdale, N.Y.). Home: 125 E 72d St New York NY 10021-4299

KALMUS, HOPE RENEE, lawyer; b. L.A., May 28, 1963; d. Michael and Lillian (Richman) K. BA in Psychology, Calif. State U., Northridge, 1985; JD, U. Calif., San Francisco, 1988. Bar: Calif. 1989. Law clk. U. Calif. Regents Gen. Counsel, Berkeley, summer 1986; tutor, discussion group leader Hastings Coll. Law Hastings Coll. of the Law, San Francisco, 1986-88; jud. extern Calif. Ct. Appeals, San Francisco, 1988; assoc. Knapp, Petersen & Clarke, Universal City, Calif., summer 1987, 88-89; atty. So. Calif. Edison Co., 1989-90; rsch. atty. L.A. Superior Ct., 1990—. Outreach coord., coach L.A. City Spl. Olympics, 1990—. Mem. LA. County Bar Assn., Hastings Coll. of the Law (bd. govs. 1993—, sec. L.A. chpt. 1991-92, v.p. L.A. chpt. 1992-93, pres. L.A. chpt. 1993-94, bd. mem. L.A. chpt. 1994—). Office: LA Superior Ct Dept 14 111 N Hill St Los Angeles CA 90012-3117

KALNAY, EUGENIA, government official, meteorologist; b. Buenos Aires, Oct. 1, 1942; came to U.S., 1971; d. Jorge and Susana (Zwicky) K.; m. Alberto Mario Rivas, July 24, 1965 (div. 1981); 1 child, Jorge Rodrigo; m. Malise Cooper Dick, July 13, 1981. Lic. in meteorology, U. Buenos Aires, 1965; PhD in Meteorology, MIT, 1971. Asst. prof. U. Uruguay, Montevideo, 1971-73; rsch. assoc. MIT, Cambridge, 1973-75, asst. prof. meteorology, 1975-76, assoc. prof., 1977-78; sect. head NASA Goddard Space Flight Ctr., Greenbelt, Md., 1979-82, br. head, 1983-86; chief devel. div. Nat. Weather Svc., NOAA Nat. Meteorology Ctr., Washington, 1987—; mem. several coms. NRC, NAS, Washington; prin. investigator NASA, 1973—; adj. prof. meteorology U. Md., 1980-83. Editor several jours.; contbr. over 100 articles to sci. jours. Recipient medal for exceptional svc. NASA, 1981; silver medal Dept. Commerce, 1990, gold medal, 1993, Jule Charney Am. Meterol. Soc. award, 1995. Mem. Am. Meteorol. Soc. Home: 8103 Sligo Creek Pky Takoma Park MD 20912-6205 Office: Nat Meteorol Ctr NOAA Washington DC 20006

KALSOW, KATHRYN ELLEN, library clerk; b. Stevens Point, Wis., Dec. 31, 1938; d. Wilbert Otto and Vivian Frances (Peterson) K. BA, Luther Coll., 1961. Libr. clk. Luther Coll. Libr., Decorah, Iowa, 1961—. Del. county conv. Rep. com., Decorah, Iowa, 1970-84, state conv., Des Moines, 1970-84; del. Nat. Fedn. Rep. Women, Washington, 1971. Mem. AAUW (treas. 1966-68, 79-81, internat. rels. area rep. 1975-77, 85-87, 90-92, named Gift Honoree, 1982), UN Assn. of USA, Iowa Libr. Assn. Lutheran. Home: Luther Coll Instrnl Media 700 College Dr Decorah IA 52101

KALTENBORN, MARILYN MAYES, lawyer; b. Margaretville, N.Y., July 20, 1949; m. H. Stanley Kaltenborn Jr., Aug. 7, 1971. BA, William Smith Coll., 1971; JD, Union U., 1974. Bar: N.Y. 1975. From atty. trainee to dir. taxpayer svcs. divsn. N.Y. State Dept. Tax and Fin., Albany, 1974—. Contbr. tax articles to profl. jours. Active Capital Dist. chpt. Embroiders Guild, Albany, 1987, Hudson-Mohawk Weaver's Guild, Albany, 1990. Mem. Normanside Country Club (gov. 1993—). Office: NY State Dept Tax and Fin Bldg # 9 W A Harriman Campus Albany NY 12227

KALUPA, ALICE FAYE, air transportation executive; b. Minden, La., Jan. 5, 1944; d. Van Andrew and Gladys Drummond; m. James Edward Kalupa, Oct. 12, 1973; children: Tony V. Bettis, Kimberly M. Wilson. Student, U. P.R., 1972-74; BA, Miami Dade U., 1976. Adminstr. P.R. Mil. Academy, Guayanabo, 1971-73; pub. rels. exec. The Jet Ctr., Van Nuys, Calif., 1977-87, liaison for customers and refurbishing ctr., 1979-87, founded charter dept., 1980-87; gen mgr. Spectrum Air, Van Nuys, 1987-88, v.p., 1988—. Mem. Nat. Bus. Aircraft Assn., Nat. Airline Transp. Assn. Office: Spectrum Air 7435 Valjean Ave Ste 200 Van Nuys CA 91406-2902

KAMA, KATHRYN PAMELA, nurse anesthesist, small business owner; b. Jacksonville, Fla., Aug. 7, 1943; d. Kenneth Leroy And Katherine Tsilta (Beat) Ward; m. Peter Kama (div.); 1 child, Shaun Pele. Diploma in nursing, Berkshire Med. Ctr., Pittsfield, Mass., 1965; AA, Orange Coast Coll., Costa Mesa, Calif., 1978; cert. nurse anesthetist, Va. Med. Ctr., Albany, N.Y., 1977. RN, cert. nurse anesthetist, Calif., N.Y., Mass., Wash., Oreg. Staff nurse Lakeview Hosp., Madigan Army Hosp., Tacoma, Wash., 1970-71, Calif. U. Med. Ctr., Irvine, 1971-75; registered nurse anesthetist VA Med. Ctr., Long Beach, Calif., 1977-91; nurse anesthetist pvt. practice, 1991-93; pres. Mamma Kama Podns., Huntington Beach, Calif., 1993—. Capt. Army Nurse Crops, 1963-69, Vietnam. Mem. Vietnam War Vets. Home and Office: Mama Kama Prodns 7715 Newman Ave Ste 303 Huntington Beach CA 92647

KAMALI, NORMA, fashion designer; b. N.Y.C., June 27, 1945; d. Sam and Estelle (Mariategui) Arraez. Grad., Fashion Inst. of Tech., 1965. Established Kamali Ltd., N.Y.C., 1967-78; owner, designer On My Own Norma Kamali, N.Y.C., 1978—. Designer costumes for Emerald City in The Wiz, 1977, for Twyla Tharp dance In the Upper Room, 1986, parachute designs Met. Mus. of Art, N.Y.C., 1977; prodr., dir. (video) Fall Fantasy; dir. (video) Fashion Aid, 1985. Recipient Coty award for women's fashion design, 1981, Coty Return award, 1982, Coty Hall of Fame award, 1983, Ernie awards Earnshaw Rev., 1983, award Fashion Inst. Design and Merchandising, 1984, award Coun. Fashion Designers Am., 1983, 85, Salute to Women award N.Y. Fashion Group, 1986, Disting. Architecture award N.Y. chpt. AIA, 1986, Outstanding Grad. award Pub. Edn. Assn. N.Y., 1988, award of merit Internat. Video Competition, 1988, Am. Success award Fashion Inst. Tech., 1989. Office: 11 W 56th St New York NY 10019-3902*

KAMATOY, LOURDES AGUAS, artist; b. San Fernando, Pampanga, Philippines, June 29, 1945; came to U.S., 1966; d. Juan Gutierrez and Segunda Mercado (De La Cruz) Aguas; m. Ernesto Gabriel Kamatoy, Apr. 28, 1973; 1 child, Lisette Marie. BA in English, U. Santo Tomas, Manila, Philippines, 1964; MA in Ednl. Theatre, NYU, 1972; overseas cert. theatre, Rose Bruford Coll. Speech, Kent, Eng., 1966. Supr. Arthur Andersen & Co., N.Y.C., 1966-73; instr. theatre U. So. Ind., Evansville, 1973-75; pres. Bodega, Evansville, 1975-79; artist rep. Lulu Represents, Chgo., 1986-92; ptnr. MK Videostar, Chgo., 1989-92; account exec. Kamatoy Creative, Encino, Calif., 1992—. Pres. Evansville Arts and Edn. Coun., 1983; v.p. U. Evansville Theatre Soc., 1984; panelist Ind. Arts Commn., Indpls., 1985; bd. dirs. Arts Insight, Indpls., 1985, USI Soc. Arts & Humanities, Evansville, 1988. Roman Catholic. Office: 4630 Woodley Ave # 105 Encino CA 91436

KAMBIC, HELEN ELIZABETH, biochemist; b. Elizabeth, N.J., Apr. 24, 1946; d. Wallace Chester and Klara Pauline (Wnek) Jablonski; m. George Xavier Kambic, Aug. 16, 1969; children: Kathleen, Danielle, Peter. BS, St. Francis Coll., Loretto, Pa., 1967; MS, Fordham U., 1969. Instr. Coll. of St. Elizabeth, Convent Station, N.J., 1968-69; rsch. scientist Kidney Disease Inst., N.Y. State Dept. Health, Albany, 1969-72; staff project scientist Cleve. Clinic Found. Biomed. Engring., 1972—. Author: Plasmapheresis Historical Perspective, 1983; editor: Vascular Graft Update: Safety and Performance, 1986, Biomaterials' Mechanical Properties, 1994; mem. editl. bd. Jour. Biomed. Mech. Behavior, Materials and Engring., 1990; contbr. articles to profl. publs., chpts. to books. Recipient Rsch. prize in urology Am. Acad. Pediatrics, 1991. Fellow Am. Inst. Chemists; mem. ASTM (vice chmn. 1983—), Am. Soc. Artificial Internal Organs (trustee 1991—, editorial bd. 1986-89, membership com. 1981-84, chmn. 1985, Rsch. award 1993), Internat. Soc. Artificial Organs (program com. 1985, 89), Soc. for Biomaterials, Am. Chem. Soc., Acad. Surg. Rsch. Roman Catholic. Office: Cleve Clinic Found Biomed Engring 9500 Euclid Ave Cleveland OH 44195-0002

KAMERMAN, SHEILA BRODY, educator, social worker; b. Jan. 7, 1928; d. S. Lawrence and Helen (Golding) Brody; m. Morton Kamerman, Sept. 11, 1947; children: Nathan Brody, Elliot Herbert, Laura Kamerman-Katz. B.A., NYU, 1946; M.S.W., Hunter Coll., 1966; D. Social Welfare, Columbia U., 1973. Social worker N.Y.C. Dept. Social Svcs., 1966-68; social work supr. Bellevue Psychiat. Hosp., 1968-69; from rsch. assoc. to sr. rsch. assoc. Columbia U. Sch. Social Work, 1971-79, assoc. prof. social policy and planning, 1979-81; prof. Sch. Social Work Columbia U., 1981—; assoc. prof. Hunter Coll. Social Work, 1977-79; chmn. NAS-NRC panel on work, family and community, 1980-82; mem. Com. Child Devel. Rsch. and Pub. Policy, 1983-88; mem. com. on prenatal care Inst. Medicine, 1986-88; cons. in field; mem. numerous social welfare coms. and adv. bds.; mem. Gov. Cuomo's Task Force on Poverty and Welfare Reform, 1986-87, adv. com. on Work and Family, 1987-88, UN Expert groups on social welfare and family policies. Author: (with Alfred J. Kahn) Not for the Poor Alone, 1975, Social Services in the United States, 1976, Social Services in International Perspective, 1977, Family Policy: Government and Families in Fourteen Countries, 1978, Child Care, Family Benefits and Working Parents, 1981, Parenting in an Unresponsive Society, 1980, Maternity and Parental Benefits and Leaves, 1980, Helping America's Families, 1982, Maternity Policies and Working Women, 1983, Income Transfers for Families with Children, 1983, Child Care: Facing the Hard Choices, 1987, The Responsive Work Place, 1987, Child Support: From Debt Collection to Social Polciy, 1988, Mothers Alone: Strategies For a Time of Change, 1988, Privatization and the Welfare State, 1989, Social Services for Children, Youth and Families in the United States, 1990, Child Care, Parental Leave, and the Under 3's, 1991, A Welcome For Every Child, 1994; contbr. numerous articles to profl. jours. Recipient Hexter award Hunter Coll. Sch. Social Work, 1977, Nat. Leadership award in Social Policy, Heller Sch. Brandeis U., 1989; named to Hunt Coll. Hall of Fame, 1981; fellow Ctr. Advanced Study in Behavioral Scis., 1983-84. Mem. NASW, Am. Pub. Welfare Assn., Assn. Policy Analysis and Mgmt., Phi Beta Kappa. Home: 1125 Park Ave New York NY 10128-1243

KAMIL, ELAINE SCHEINER, physician, educator; b. Cleve., Jan. 26, 1947; d. James Frank and Maud Lily (Severn) Scheiner; m. Ivan Jeffery Kamil, Aug. 29, 1970; children: Jeremy, Adam, Megan. BS magna cum laude, U. Pitts., 1969, MD, 1973. Diplomate Am. Bd. Pediats., Am. Be. Pediat. Nephrology. Intern in pediats. Children's Hosp. Pitts., 1973-74, resident in pediats., 1974-76; clin. fellow in pediat. nephrology Sch. Medicine, UCLA, 1976-79, acting asst. prof. pediats., 1979-80; rsch. fellow in nephrology Harbor-UCLA Med. Ctr., Torrance, Calif., 1980-82; med. dir. The Children's Clinic of Long Beach, Calif., 1984-87; med. dir. pediat. nurse practitioner program Calif. State U., Long Beach, 1984-87; asst. clin. prof.

pediats. Sch. Medicine, UCLA, 1988-90, assoc. clin. prof. pediats., 1991—; assoc. dir. pediat. nephrology and transplant immunology Cedars-Sinai Med. Ctr., L.A., 1990—; adj. asst. prof. pediats. Harbor-UCLA, Torrance, Calif., 1983-87, UCLA, 1987-88; cons. in pediat. nephrology Hawthorne (Calif.) Cmty. Med. Group, 1981—. Author chpts. to books; contbr. articles to profl. jours. Mem. AAUW, Am. Soc. Nephrology, Am. Soc. Pediat. Nephrology, Am. Fedn. Clin. Rsch., Internat. Soc. Nephrology, Internat. Soc. Pediat. Nephrology, Internat. Soc. Peritoneal Dialysis, Renal Pathology Soc., Nat. Kidney Found. So. Calif. (mem. med. adv. bd. 1987—, rsch. com. 1987-90, chmn. pub. info. med. adv. bd. 1988-92, mem. handbook com. 1988, co-chair med. adv. bd. cmty. svcs. com. 1992-93, chair-elect patient svcs. and cmty. edn. com. 1993-94, chair patient svcs. and cmty. edn. com. 1994—, kidney camp summer vol. physician 1988-91, 93, 94, Arthur Gordon Meml. Rsch. scholar 1981, Continuing Svc. award 1991, Exceptional Svc. award 1992), Alpha Omega Alpha, Phi Beta Kappa. Office: Cedars-Sinai Med Ctr 8700 Beverly Blvd Los Angeles CA 90048

KAMIN, KAY HODES, financial planner, lawyer, historian, educator; b. Chgo., July 3, 1940; d. Barnet and Eleanor (Cramer) Hodes; m. Malcolm S. Kamin, June 12, 1963; children—Kim Alison, Kyle Barret. BA, Vassar Coll., 1961, MA, U. Chgo., 1962, PhD, 1970, CFP, 1992; JD cum laude, Northwestern U., 1981. Bars: Ill. 1981, U.S. Dist. Ct. (no. dist.) Ill. 1981. Registered investment adviser, Ill. History tchr. Lincoln Park High Sch., Chgo., 1963-67; social studies coord. U. Chgo., 1968-69; assoc. prof. edn. Rosary Coll., River Forest, Ill., 1970-76; jud. law clk. Ill. Appellate Ct., Chgo., 1981-83; assoc. Mayer, Brown & Platt, Chgo., 1983-85; v.p., gen. counsel Glencorp Inc., 1985-93, also bd. dirs.; pres. Sutton Place Fin., Inc., Chgo., 1993—. Co-author: Contract Law, 1983; contbr. articles to profl. jours. Pres. Chgo. Coun. for Social Studies, 1967-69; bd. govs., life mem. Chgo. Art Inst., 1974—; pres. Soc. for Contemporary Art, 1974-76; pres. Sedoh Found., 1986—; bd. dirs. Women's Bd. Northwestern U.; fellow U. Chgo. Grad. Sch., 1967-70 . Mem. ABA, Chgo. Bar Assn. Club: Arts, John Evans (Northwestern U.). Avocations: golf, jogging, skiing, art collecting. Office: Sutton Place Financial Inc 1305 N Sutton Pl Chicago IL 60610-2007

KAMINKER, VALERIE JACQUELINE, management consultant; b. Lake Forest, Ill., May 21, 1967; d. Jean Marcel Henri and Helene K. BS in Fin. and Entrepreneurial Studies, Babson Coll., 1988. Fin. analyst Bull Groupe, Paris, 1988; acctg. analyst IBM, Southbury, Conn., 1989-90, auditor, 1990-91; internat. acct. IBM, Mt. Pleasant, N.Y., 1991-92; mgmt. cons. A.T. Hudson, London, 1992—. Home: 1055 Peppertree Dr #303 Sarasota FL 34242

KAMINSKI, MARGARET, librarian; b. Detroit, Mar. 16, 1944; d. John Joseph and Gertrude (Malak) K. BFA, Wayne State U., 1966, MSLS, 1969. Artist Henry Ford Hosp., Detroit; reference librarian Detroit Pub. Libr., 1969-74, 76-85, pub. rels. librarian, 1974-76, 1st asst. branches, 1985—; producer, presenter travel slide programs Detroit Pub. Libr., 1976—, Ont. Archaeol. Soc., Sinte Gleska Coll., 1981, also various pub. librs. Author: Martinis, 1972, La Vida de la Mujer, 1979, Guatemalan Diary, 1982; editor: Moving to Antarctica, 1975; editor (jour.) Moving Out: A Feminist Lit. & Arts Jour., 1970—. Sec. Friends of Polish Art, Detroit, 1984-91. Mini-grantee Mich. Coun. for Arts, 1975, 80—. Mem. NOW (sec. Macomb County chpt. 1993—), UAW, Detroit Pub. Libr. Staff Assn. (newsletter editor 1970-73). Democrat. Home: 22333 Hanson Ct Saint Clair Shores MI 48080 Office: Franklin Branch Library 13651 E McNichols Detroit MI 48205

KAMINSKY, ALICE RICHKIN, English language educator; b. N.Y.C.; d. Morris and Ida (Spivak) Richkin; m. Jack Kaminsky; 1 son, Eric (dec.). B.A., NYU, 1946, M.A., 1947, Ph.D., 1952. Mem. faculty dept. English NYU, 1947-49, Hunter Coll., 1952-53, Cornell U., 1954-57, Broome Community Coll., 1958-59, Cornell U., 1959-63; mem. faculty dept. English SUNY, Cortland, 1963—, prof., 1968-91, prof. emeritus, 1991—, faculty exchange scholar. Author: George Henry Lewes as Critic, 1968, Logic: A Philosophical Introduction, 1974; editor: Literary Criticism of George Henry Lewes, 1964, Chaucer's Troilus and Criseyde and the Critics, 1980, The Victim's Song, 1985; contbr. articles and revs. to numerous jours. Mem. MLA, Chaucer Soc. Office: SUNY Coll Dept English Cortland NY 13045

KAMISAR, SANDRA LEE, federal agency administrator, publishing consultant; b. Washington, Apr. 15, 1937; d. Harry and Betty (Bass) K. AA, George Washington U., 1956; cert. med. sec., Strayer Bus. Coll., Washington, 1957. With Office of Prevention, Edn. and Control Nat. Heart, Lung and Blood Inst., Bethesda, Md., 1957—, chief pubs. mgmt. sect., supr. writing and editing Office of Prevention, Edn. and Control, 1977—; cons. printing and pub. NIH, Bethesda, 1979—. Editor: Dietary Management of Hyperlipoproteinemia. Trustee Temple Shalom, Chevy Chase, Md., 1982—; v.p. Mid-Atlantic coun. Union Am. Hebrew Congregations, Washington, 1994, chmn. comm. com., 1992, mem. comm. com., N.Y., 1994. Democrat. Home: 6140 Utah Ave NW Washington DC 20015-2462

KAMM, CAROL ANN, realtor; b. St. Louis, Nov. 30, 1951; d. Hubert Ronald and Mary Martha (Brandt) Smith; m. William Albert Kamm, Aug. 12, 1973; children: Jeremy, Peter, Zachary. AA, Pierce Coll., Woodland Hills, Calif., 1971; BS, Concordia Tchrs. Coll., Seward, Nebr., 1973. Realtor Prudential Carolinas Realty, Charlotte, N.C., 1990—. Hotline counselor Crisis Pregnancy Ctr., Charlotte, 1990-94. Home: 7744 Krefeld Glen Dr # 1612 Charlotte NC 28227 Office: Prudential Carolinas Realty 4529 Sharon Rd Charlotte NC 28211-3521

KAMMERER, EMILY M., insurance examiner; b. Ridgway, Ill., Sept. 21, 1942; d. James Willard and Mary Aliene (Jones) Goforth; m. Thomas Anthony Pearce, Sept. 2, 1962 (div. May 1986); children: Rebecca Lynn Noe, Thomas Anthony II; m. William Jerald Kammerer, Nov. 1, 1993. AS, Belleville Area Coll., 1972; BS in Transp., Travel and Tourism, St. Louis U., Cahokia, Ill., 1979. Van. dept. mgr. Sun Oil Co., Tulsa, 1979-87; transp. mgr. Twin Tour's Co., Lodi, Calif., 1987-89; transp. broker Am. Trucking Co., Richmond, Va., 1989-91; ins. examiner Blue Cross Blue Shield Okla., Tulsa, 1991—. Speaker Christian Coalition, Berryhill, Okla., 1993. Capt. U.S. Army, 1976-79. Mem. Nat. Mgmt. Assn., Alpha Chi. Republican. Baptist. Home: 14527 S Maple Pl Glenpool OK 74033-4016 Office: 1215 S Boulder Tulsa OK 74119

KAMMEYER, SONIA MARGARETHA, real estate agent; b. Stockholm, June 21, 1942; came to U.S., 1964; d. Bengt Henrik and Margot Elsa M. (Hodin) Sjoberg; m. Whitman Ridgway, June 13, 1964 (div. 1978); children: Sean, Siobhan; m. Kenneth C.W. Kammeyer, Dec. 28, 1982. Student, Fleisher's Art Meml. Sch., Phila., 1966-69. With Ben Bell Real Estate, Lanham, Md., 1972-73, Robert L. Gruen Real Estate, Silver Spring, Md., 1973-81, Panarama Real Estate, Silver Spring, 1981-82, Long & Foster Real Estate, Inc., Silver Spring, 1982—. Named to Montgomery County Bd. Realtors Hall of Fame, 1994. Mem. Montgomery County Bd. Realtors, Montgomery County Realtors Hall of Fame, Howard County Bd. Realtors, Washington D.C. Bd. Realtors, Swedish Profl. Women. Home: 14600 Tri-adelphia Mill Rd Dayton MD 21036-1217 Office: Long & Foster Real Estate 5520 A Norbeck Rd Rockville MD 20853

KAMP, KAREN SUE, computer project administrator; b. Chgo., Nov. 10, 1950; d. Everett and Verbena Ann (Bolhuis) K.; m. Donald E. Winter, Dec. 31, 1982 (div. 1986). BS in Bus. Adminstrn., U. Ariz., 1985. Tng. analyst/developer ManTech Advanced Systems, Sierra Vista, Ariz., 1983-88, 90-92; human factors analyst Jet Propulsion Labs., Pasadena, Calif., 1988-90; ops. analyst SAIC, Inc., Sierra Vista, 1992; computer based tng. mgr. TRW Unmanned Aerial Vehicle Ctr., Sierra Vista, 1992—. Sec. City of Sierra Vista Environ. Affairs Commn., 1993-94; vol. Nature Conservancy, Ramsey Canyon, Ariz., 1991-93. Staff sgt. U.S. Army, 1974-82. Recipient Bear Down award Ariz. Alumni Assn., 1994. Mem. Sierra Vista Area U. Ariz. Alumni Club (v.p. 1992-94, pres. 1994—). Office: TRW UAV Ctr 1838 S Paseo San Luis Sierra Vista AZ 85635-4612

KAMPF-SINGMAN, CINDY ALISE, public relations executive; b. Honolulu, Aug. 14, 1961; d. Joel and Isobel Linda (Cohen) Kampf; m. Robert Jay Singman, June 19, 1994. BA, Muhlenberg Coll., 1983; MS, Syracuse U., 1985. Project mgr. Hemming and Gilman, Inc., N.Y.C., 1985-86; asst. account exec. Dorf & Stanton Communications, Inc., N.Y.C., 1986-87; spl. events coord. Dorf & Stanton Communications, Inc., 1987-88; account exec. Keyes Martin Pub. Rels., Springfield, N.J., 1988-90; pres. Cin-Sational Publicity and Events, Inc., West Orange, N.J. and Bethesda, Md., 1990—; pub. rels. cons. various orgns., 1985—. Active Young Benefactors Smithsonian, Washington; area chmn. Hands Across Am., N.J., 1986; mem. young profls. com., bd. dirs. Cancer Care of N.J., Millburn; fundraiser spl. events Am. Indian Coll. Fund. Mem. Pub. Rels. Soc. Am., Pro Bono, Muhlenberg Metro Alumni Assn., Newhouse Alumni Assn. Home and Office: Cin-Sational Publicity & Events Inc 5225 Pooks Hill Rd # 609 S Bethesda MD 20814

KAMPITS, EVA, educator, consultant; b. Budapest, Hungary, Feb. 22, 1946; came to U.S., 1951; d. Ernest Michael and Ilona (Gondi) K.; m. Dan Catalin Stefanescu, Aug. 4, 1979; children: Andreea N., Cristina F. Cert., U. Innsbruck, Austria, 1963; BA, Harvard U., 1968; MA, Boston Coll., 1971, PhD, 1977. Instr. freshman seminars MIT, Cambridge, 1973-80, freshman advisor, 1975-80, sophomore advisor, 1976-80, adminstrv. officer Artificial Intelligence Lab., 1967-78, asst. to dir. Lab. for Computer Sci., 1987-88, rsch. affiliate Media Lab., 1987-88; acad. dean Pine Manor Coll., Chestnut Hill, Mass., 1980-94, dir. sponsored programs, grad. sch. dean, 1994; dir. sch./coll. rels. New Eng. Assn. Schs. & Colls., Inc., Bedford, Mass., 1994—; chmn., trustee NERComp, 1985-91; mem. NEARnet; co-chair Gov.'s Ednl. Tech. Adv. Coun.; mem. steering com. Mass Telecomputing Coalition. Mem. bd. editors NERComp Jour. Founding mem. bd. visitors Brimmer and May Sch., Chestnut Hill, Mass., 1992-94. Mem. MLA, Soc. for Advancement of Scandinavian Study, Assn. for Computing Machinery. Republican. Roman Catholic.

KAN, DIANA ARTEMIS MANN SHU, artist; b. Hong Kong, Mar. 3, 1926; came to U.S., 1949, naturalized, 1964; d. Kam Shek and Sing-Ying (Hong) K.; m. Paul Schwartz, May 24, 1952; 1 son, Kan Martin Meyer Sing-Si. Student, Art Students League, 1949-51, Beaux Arts, Paris, 1951-52, Grande Chaumiere, Paris, 1951-52. Fgn. corr., city editor Cosmorama Pictorial Mag., Hong Kong, 1968; art reviewer Villager, N.Y.C., 1960-69; lectr. Birmingham So. U., N.Y. U., Mills Coll., St. Joseph's Coll., Phila. Mus., Smithsonian Instn. Author: White Cloud, 1938, The How and Why of Chinese Painting, 1974; One-man shows, London, 1949, 63, 64, Paris, 1949, Hong Kong, 1937, 39, 41, 47, 48, 52, Shanghai, 1935, 37, 39, Nanking, 1936, 38, Macao, 1947, 48, Bankok, 1947, Casablanca, 1951, 52, San Francisco, 1950, 67, N.Y.C., 1950, 54, 59, 67, 71, 72, 74, 78, Naples, 1971, Elliot Mus., Stuart, Fla., 1967, 73, Bruce Mus., Greenwich, Conn., 1969, Nat. Hist. Mus., Taipei, Taiwan, 1971, N.Y. Cultural Center Mus., 1972, Galerie Barbarella, Palm Beach, Fla., 1972, Hobe Sound (Fla.) Galleries, 1976, 81, Nat. Arts Club, 1979, Dyansen Galleries, 1987-90 others; exhibited in group shows Allied Artists of Am., 1957-90, Royal Acad. Fine Arts, London, 1963-64, Royal Soc. Painters, London, 1964, Nat. Arts Club, N.Y.C., 1964-90, Am. Water Color Soc., N.Y.C., 1966-90, Nat. Acad., N.Y.C., 1967-90, Charles and Emma Frye Mus., Seattle, 1968, Willamette U., Salem, Oreg., 1968, Columbia (S.C.) Mus. Art, 1969, Audubon Artist, 1974-90, Evansville (Ind.) Mus., 1991, Dyansen Gallery, Boston, 1991; represented permanent collections, Met. Mus. Art, Phila. Mus. Art, Nelson Gallery, Elliot Mus., Fla., Bruce Mus., Dalhousie U., Atkin Mus., Kansas City, Nat. Hist. Mus., Taipei; subject of film Eastern Spirit, Western World—A Profile of Diana Kan. Recipient Summer Festival award N.Y.C., 1959, 1st Prize Nat. Art Club, 1982; named most Outstanding Profl. Woman of the Yr., Washington Sq. chpt. N.Y. League Bus. and Profl. Women's Club, 1971, 79, Gold medal of honor Knickerbocker Artists, 1990, Gold medal of honor Audubon Artists, 1991; Diana Kan Appreciation Day proclaimed by Mayor of Boston, 1991; offl. citation proclaimed by Pres. Senate of Mass., 1991. Fellow Royal Soc. Arts; mem. Pen and Brush Club (dir. 1968, Brush Fund award 1968, Alice S. Buell Meml. award 1969, Margaret Sussman award 1991), Nat. Acad. Design (assoc., John Pike Meml. award 1987, cert. of merit 1991), Am. Watercolor Soc. (traveling award 1968, Marthe T. McKinnon award 1978, dir. 1975-77), Art Students League, Nat. League Pen Women, Audubon Artists (v.p. 1983), Allied Artists Am. (Barbara Vassilieff Meml. award 1969, Ralph Fabri Meml. award 1975, corr. sec. 1975-78), Catharine Lorillard Wolf Art Club (Anna Hyatt Huntington bronze medal 1970, 74, Gold medal of honor 1982). Clubs: Overseas Press Am., Lotos, The Nat. Arts (N.Y.C.). Home: 15 Gramercy Park S New York NY 10003-1705

KANCHE, PEGGY GOODWYN, criminal justice consultant; b. Birmingham, Ala., Nov. 10, 1942; d. Leon Branton and Julia (Lawley) Goodwyn-Stewart; m. Michael Gregory Kanche, Jr., May 4, 1985. BA, Huntingdon Coll., 1965; student, Fla. State U., 1969-70; MS, Auburn U., 1970. Chief probation officer Cir. Ct. Family Ct., Montgomery, Ala., 1970-74; dep. dir. Ala. Dept. Youth Svcs., Montgomery, 1974-84; dir. Johnson County Dept. Corrections, Olathe, Kans., 1985-92; program dir. Concept, Inc./Eloy (Ariz.) Fed. Detention Ctr., 1994—; instr. Troy (Ala.) State U., 1970-74; mem. adv. bd. Lewis U. Spl. Svcs. Ctr., 1978-84; mem. Task Force on Justice in Sentencing, Laurel, Md., 1993—; steering com. Women in Corrections Com., Laurel, 1993—. Mem. Jr. League Adv. Com., Montgomery, 1970-84, Quota Internat., Montgomery, 1980-84, State Adv. Group on Juvenile Justice, Montgomery, 1982-84. Named Outstanding Jaceette, Montgomery (Ala.) Jaycees, 1970. Mem. Am. Correctional Assn. (various coms. 1970—, cons. 1992—), Kans. Community Corrections Assn. (pres. 1988-90), Kans. Correctional Assn. (pres. 1992), Kans. Sentencing Commn. (field svcs. task force 1991-92). Methodist. Office: Concept Inc Eloy Fed Detention Ctr Eloy AZ 85231

KANCHIER, CAROLE, psychologist; b. Winnipeg, Manitoba, Can.; came to U.S., 1993; d. Michael and Mary (Dyma) K. BA in Social Scis., U. Manitoba, Winnipeg, Can., BEd in Guidance and Counseling, MEd in Guidance and Counseling; PhD in Counseling Psychology, U. Calgary, Alberta, Can., 1981. Registered psychologist; cert. tchr. Dir. arts and crafts Winnipeg Parks Bd.; dir. women's phys. edn. Daniel McIntyre Collegiate, Winnipeg; dir. publicity Royal Winnipeg Ballet; dir. guidance and counseling Kelvin H.S., Winnipeg; dir. rsch. Thomson and Lightstone, Calgary, 1981-82; instr. edn. psychology U. Calgary, 1981-82; edn. and psychology cons. Vogue Bus. Svcs., Calgary, 1981-82; faculty edn. psychology and adult edn. U. Alta., Edmonton, 1983-92; pres. Questers Consulting, Mountain View, Calif., 1983—; vis. fellow Inst. Transpersonal Psychology, Palo Alto, Calif., 1990; chair career change Nat. Career Devel. Assn., Alexandria, Va., 1989-93; exec. bd. Life Plan Ctr., San Francisco, 1993—; instr., advisor adult edn. credentialing program U. Calif, Santa Cruz, 1994—. Author: Dare to Change Your Job--And Your Life, 1991 (Best Can. popular book 1992); contbr. articles to profl. jours. including Encyclopedia of Career Decisions and Work Issues, The Career Devel. Quarterly, Internat. Jour. for Advancement of Counseling, Jour. Employment Counseling, Am. Counselor, etc. Mem. ASTD, Am. Psychol. Assn., Am. Counseling Assn., Inst. Noetic Scis., Can. Assn. Adult Edn., Canadian Psychol. Assn. Home and Office: 555 W Middlefield Rd S 206 Mountain View CA 94043

KANDEL-ENGLANDER, ELIZABETH, psychology educator; b. L.A., June 4, 1963; d. Stephen David and Anne Oakes (Finkelstein) Kandel; m. Michael Kandel Englander, Oct. 11, 1992. BA, U. Calif., Berkeley, 1985; MA, U. So. Calif., 1987, PhD, 1989. Staff psychologist Tri-City Mental Health Ctr., Boston, 1989-91; NIMH postdoctoral rsch. fellow U. N.H., Durham, 1990-92; asst. prof. Westfield (Mass.) State Coll., 1992-93, Bridgewater (Mass.) State Coll., 1993—; mem. adj. faculty Lasell Coll., Newton, Mass., 1991, Fisher Coll., Boston, 1992.; presenter in field. Contbr. articles to Chgo. Tribune, USA Today, and other newspapers and profl. jours. Recipient Recognition Excellence in Rsch. award Psi Chi, 1987, Grad. Sch. Merit Tuition award U. So. Calif., 1988-89, Grad. and Profl. award U. So. Calif., 1989, NIMH Rsch. Sci. award U. N.H., 1990-92, Tech. Assistance award NIMH, 1991; Presdl. Undergrad. fellow U. Calif., 1984, All-Univ. Predoctoral Merit fellow Grad. Sch. U. So. Calif., 1985-88; Student Travel grantee NSF, 1986. Mem. Am. Psychol. Assn., Am. Criminological Soc., Am. Profl. Soc. Abuse of Children, Phi Beta Kappa. Office: Bridgewater State Coll Dept Psychology Bridgewater MA 02325

KANDELMAN, HARRIET A., management and business educator. PhD, U. Oreg., 1980. Prof. bus. adminstrn. U. Portland, Oreg., 1981-88; prof. mgmt. and labor rels. Sangamon State U., Springfield, Ill., 1988-92; prof. of mgmt. and bus. Barat Coll., Lake Forest, Ill., 1992—.

KANE, ALICE THERESA, lawyer; b. N.Y.C., Jan. 16, 1948. AB, Manhattanville Coll., 1969; JD, NYU, 1972; grad., Harvard U. Sch. Bus. Program Mgmt. Devel., 1985. Bar: N.Y. 1973, U.S. Dist. Ct. (so. dist.) N.Y. 1974. Atty. N.Y. Life Ins. Co., N.Y.C., 1972-83, v.p., assoc. gen. counsel, 1983-85, v.p. dept. personnel, 1985, sr. v.p., gen. counsel, 1986-89, corp. sec., 1989-92, exec. v.p., gen. counsel, sec., 1992—. Mem. ABA (chmn. employee benefits com., tort and ins. practice sect. 1984-85, mem. corp., banking and bus. law sects., tort and ins. practice sects.), Assn. of Life Ins. Counsel (deps. solvency com.). Office: NY Life Ins Co 51 Madison Ave New York NY 10010-1603*

KANE, ANNETTE P., religious organization executive; b. Trenton, N.J., May 2, 1933; d. Theodore P. and Stella (Mackiewicz) Pieslak; m. Joseph P. Kane, Sept. 6, 1958; children: Paula M., Stephen J., Brian P., Christine A. BA, Trinity Coll., Washington, 1954; MA, U. Pa., 1956. Asst. prof. Rosemont (Pa.) Coll., 1955-58; asst. prof. Trinity Coll., Washington, 1958-61, editor alumni jour., 1973-79; program dir. Nat. Coun. Cath. Women, Washington, 1979-86, exec. dir., 1986—. Bd. dirs. Nat. Coun. Aging, Washington, 1985-87, CARA-Ctr. for Applied Rsch. in Apostolate, Washington, 1989—. Office: Nat Coun Cath Women 1275 K St NW Ste 975 Washington DC 20005-4006*

KANE, CAROL, actress; b. Cleve., June 18, 1952. Stage debut in The Prime of Miss Jean Brodie, 1966; other N.Y.C. theatre appearances include Ring 'Round the Bath Tub, 1972, The Tempest, 1974, 80, The Effect of Gamma Ray on Man-in-the-Moon Marigolds, 1978, Are You Now or Have You Ever Been?, 1978, Benefit of a Doubt, 1978, Tales from Vienna Woods, 1979, Sunday Runners in the Rain, 1980, Macbeth, 1980, The Fairy Garden, 1984, The Debutante Ball, 1988, Frankie and Johnny in the Clair de Lune, 1988; film appearances include Carnal Knowledge, 1971, Desperate Characters, 1971, Wedding in White, 1972, The Last Detail, 1974, Dog Day Afternoon, 1975, Hester Street, 1975 (Acad. award nomination for Best Actress), Harry and Walter Go to New York, 1976, Annie Hall, 1977, Valentino, 1977, The World's Greatest Lover, 1977, The Mafu Cage, 1978, When a Stranger Calls, 1979, The Muppet Movie, 1979, The Sabiana, 1979, Les Jeux, 1980, Pandemonium, 1982, Norman Loves Rose, 1982, Can She Bake A Cherry Pie?, 1983, Over the Brooklyn Bridge, 1984, Racing With the Moon, 1984, The Secret Diary of Sigmund Freud, 1984, Transylvania 6-5000, 1985, Jumpin' Jack Flash, 1986, The Princess Bride, 1987, Ishtar, 1987, License to Drive, 1988, Scrooged, 1988, Sticky Fingers, 1988, Flashback, 1990, Joe Versus the Volcano, 1990, The Lemon Sisters, 1990, My Blue Heaven, 1990, Ted and Venus, 1991, In the Soup, 1992, Adams Family Values, 1993, When a Stranger Calls Back, 1993, Even Cowgirls Get the Blues, 1993, Baby on Board, 1993; TV series Taxi, 1981-83, All is Forgiven, 1986, American Dreamer, 1990, (voice) Alladin, 1994; TV films An Invasion of Privacy, 1983, Burning Rage, 1984, All is Forgiven, 1986, Drop Out Mother, 1988; TV spls. Shelly Duvall's Tall Tales and Legends: Case at the Bat, 1985, Bob Goldthwait—Don't Watch This Show, 1986, Paul Reiser: Out on a Whim, 1987, Rap Master Ronnie-A Report Card, 1988, Tales from the Crypt, 1992. Recipient Emmy award for outstanding supporting actress in a comedy series, 1981. Office: Krost/Chapin Artists Talent Agy 9911 W Pico Blvd Penthouse I Los Angeles CA 90035*

KANE, CAROLE LEE, principal; b. Akron; d. Hubert E. and Marian Blair (Dunbar) Sickinger; m. Robert Martin Kane; children: Kathleen, Kelly, Kerry, Kevin. BA, Occidental U., 1958; MEd, LaVerne Coll., 1978. Tchr. Pleasant Valley Sch., Groton, Conn., 1958-61, Pierson Sch., Clinton, Conn., 1961-64, Sierra Gardens Sch., Roseville, Calif., 1971-78; prin. Sierra Gardens Sch., Roseville, 1986-92; tchr. in charge, vice prin. Cirby Woodbridge, Roseville, 1978-85; coord. of alternate edn. Eich Jr. High Sch., Roseville, 1985-86; prin. Kaseberg Sch., Roseville, 1992—; bd. dirs. Calif. Sch. Leadership Acad., Chapman Coll., Sacramento, Calif. Pres. Women in Leadership, Placer County, 1982-83. Recipient Community Svc. award PTA, 1983. Mem. AAUW (pres. 1978079, v.p. sect. state rep. 1970—, Outstanding Woman award 1987), Bus. and Profl. Women, Assn. Calif. Sch. Adminstrs. (past pres. 1993, state rep. 1987—), Soroptimist Internat. (v.p. 1986-93, bylaws chair), Phi Delta Kappa. Home: PO Box 461 Rocklin CA 95677 Office: Kaseberg Sch 1040 Main St Roseville CA 95678

KANE, CECELIA DRAPEAU, state legislator, registered nurse; b. Concord, N.H., Oct. 12, 1915; d. Esdras and Marguerite Elizabeth (Carter) Drapeau; m. Thomas J. Kane, Jan. 23, 1986 (dec.); children: Maureen, Cheryl, Charlene, Thomas D. Diploma, Sch. Nursing, 1938; postgrad., 1939. Legislature N.H. House of Reps., Portsmouth, N.H., 1988—. Mem. Cath. Daughters Am., Portsmouth, 1987, Dem. State Com., 1942—, N.H. OWLS, 1990—; bd. registrars Supr. of Checklist, Portsmouth, 1987—; bd. dirs. Betty's Dream, Portsmouth, 1990—. Democrat. Roman Catholic. Home: 391 Colonial Dr Portsmouth NH 03801-4706 Office: NH State Senate State Capitol Concord NH 03301*

KANE, ELLEN LOUISE, writer; b. White Plains, N.J., Oct. 17, 1938; d. Waldemar and Alida (Decker) Laine; m. William F. Kane, May 22, 1966; children: Andrew William, Joel Decker. Student, SUNY, Albany, 1956-59; AA in Liberal Arts, Tompkins-Cortland C.C., 1987. Feature writer, reporter, editor The Knickerbocker News, Albany, N.Y., 1959-68; wire svc. editor The Citizen, Auburn, N.Y., 1968-70; rsch. assoc., editor Chronicle Guidance Publs., Moravia, N.Y., 1978-83; writer, editor, graphic designer, owner Paragraphics, Moravia, 1983—. Mem. NAFE. Democrat. Office: Paragraphics RD3 Box 132 Moravia NY 13118-9522

KANE, GRACE MCNELLY, maternal/women's health and pediatrics nurse; b. Auburn, Ill., Mar. 31, 1939; d. Irving Benjamin and Ruby Louise (Stinnett) McNelly; m. Robert John Kane, July 23, 1960; children: Scott Robert, Timothy Phillip, Pamela Colette, Glenn Randall, Andrew Keith, Bruce Ryan. Diploma, Mem. Hosp. Sch. Nursing, Springfield, Ill., 1960; BS in Profl. Arts, St. Joseph's Coll., North Windham, Maine, 1985. RN, Ill.; cert. in occupational hearing conservation, fetal monitoring I and II. Staff nurse nursery-newborn units Walther Meml. Hosp., Chgo., 1962-67; staff nurse rooming-in nursery Luth. Gen. Hosp., Park Ridge, Ill., 1977=85; staff nurse med.-surg. unit Swedish Covenant Hosp., Chgo., 1989; staff nurse occupational clinic Rush-Presbyn-St. Luke's, Elk Grove Village, Ill., 1988; staff replacement nurse Nursefinders, Arlington Heights, Ill., 1989-90; staff nurse newborn nursery Alexian Bros. Med. Ctr., Elk Grove Village, 1990-91; nurse Kingsley Med. Ctr., Arlington Heights, Ill., 1991-92. Home: 675D Versailles Cir Elk Grove Village IL 60007

KANE, KAREN MARIE, public affairs consultant; b. Colorado Springs, Colo., Mar. 7, 1947; d. Bernard Francis and Adeline Marie (Logan) K. Student, Mills Coll., Oakland, Calif., 1965-66; BA, U. Wash., 1970, MA, 1973, PhC, 1977, postgrad. Pub. affairs cons., housing subcom. Seattle Ret. Tchrs. Assn., 1981-84; pub. affairs cons. 1st U.S. Women's Olympic Marathon Trials, 1982-83, Seattle, 1985—. Contbr. articles to newsletters and mags. Vol. city coun. campaigns, Seattle; bd. dirs. Showboat Theatre Found./Bravo (formerly Showboat Theatre Found.), 1984—; hist. preservation chmn. LWV, Seattle, 1989—; hist. preservation chmn., sec. bd. trustees, mem. exec. com. Allied Arts of Seattle, 1987—; mem. Mayor's Landmark Theatre Adv. Group, 1991-93; mayoral appointee as commr. on Pike Pl. Market Hist. Commn., Seattle, 1992—. Recipient Award of Honor Wash. Trust for Hist. Preservation, 1990, Recognition award Found. for Hist. Preservation and Adaptive Reuse, Seattle, 1991; Am. Found. grantee, 1989, 91. Mem. Am. Assn. Univ. Women, Mills Coll. Alumnae Assn., U. Wash. Alumni Assn., Nat. Trust for Hist. Preservation, Hist. Hawai'i Found., Found. for San Francisco's Archtl. Heritage, Internat. Platform Assn. Office: Allied Arts of Seattle 105 S Main St Seattle WA 98104-2515

KANE, LUCILE MARIE, archivist, historian; b. Maiden Rock, Wis., Mar. 17, 1920; d. Emery John and Ruth (Coty) Kane. BS, River Falls State Tchrs. Coll., 1942; MA, U. Minn., 1946. Tchr. Osceola (Wis.) High Sch., 1942-44; asst. publicity dept. U. Minn. Press, Mpls., 1945-46; rsch. fellow, editor Forest Products History Found., St. Paul, 1946-48; curator manuscripts Minn. Hist. Soc., St. Paul, 1948-75; sr. rsch. fellow Minn. Hist. Soc., 1979-85, sr. rsch. assoc. emeritus, 1985—, mem. hon. counc., 1988—; state archivist, 1975-79. Author: A Guide to the Care and Administration of Manuscripts, 2d edit, 1966, (with Kathryn A. Johnson) Manuscripts Collections of the Minnesota Historical Society, Guide No. 2, 1955, The Waterfall That Built a City, 1966 (updated edit. pub. as The Falls of St. Anthony,

1987), Guide to the Public Affairs Collection Minn. Historical Society, (with Alan Ominsky) Twin Cities: A Pictoral History of Saint Paul and Minneapolis, 1983; Editor, transl., editor: Military Life in Dakota, the Jour. Philippe Regis de Trobriand, 1951; editor: (with others) The Northern Expeditions of Major Stephen H. Long, 1978; contbr. articles to profl. jours. Recipient Disting. Service award Western History Assn., 1982, Disting. Service award Minn. Humanities Commn., 1983, Award of Distinction Am. Assn. State and Local History, 1987. Fellow Soc. Am. Archivists, 1958. Home: 1298 Fairmount Ave Saint Paul MN 55105-2703 Office: 345 Kellogg Blvd W Saint Paul MN 55102-1903

KANE, MARGARET BRASSLER, sculptor; b. East Orange, N.J., May 25, 1909; d. Hans and Mathilde (Trumpler) Brassler; m. Arthur Ferris Kane, June 11, 1930; children: Jay Brassler, Gregory Ferris. Student, Packer Collegiate Inst., 1920-26, Syracuse U., 1927, Art Students League, 1927-29, N.Y. Coll. Music, 1928-29, John Hovannes Studio, 1932-34; PhD (hon.), Colo. State Christian Coll., 1973. head craftsman sculpture, arts and skills unit ARC, Halloran Gen. Hosp., N.Y., 1942-43; jury mem. Bklyn. Mus., 1948, Am. Machine & Foundry Co., 1957; com. mem. An Am. Group, Inc. Work exhibited at Jacques Seligmann Gallery, N.Y., Whitney Ann. Exhbns., all Sculptors Guild Mus. and Outdoor Shows, Nat. Sculpture Soc. Ann. Bas-Relief Exhbn., 1938, Whitney Mus. Sculpture Festival, 1940, Bklyn. Mus. Sculptors Guild, 1938, Bklyn. Soc. Artists, 1942, Lawrence (Mass.) Art Mus., 1938, N.Y. World's Fair, 1939, Sculptors Guild World's Fair Exhbn., 1940, Robinson Gallery, N.Y., 1939, Traveling Mus. and Instns., 1938, Lyman Allyn Mus., 1939, Met. Mus., Internat. Exhbns., 1940, 1949, Roosevelt Field Art Ctr., N.Y.C., 1957, Phila. Mus., N.Y. Archtl. League, Nat. Acad., Penn. Acad., Chgo. Art Inst., Am. Fedn. Arts, Riverside Mus., Montclair Mus., Grand Cen. Art Galleries, Lever House, N.Y.C., 1959-81, Rye (N.Y.) Library, 1962, Lever House Sculptors Guild Ann. Exhbn., 1973-81, N.Y. Bot. Garden, 1981, Sculptors Guild 50th Anniversary Exhbn., Lever House, 1987-90, 1st Bi-Coastal exhibits San Francisco, Collection Donald Trump, 1988, Collection Rene Anselmo, 1991, Shidoni Galleries, Santa Fe, N.Mex., 1989, Am. Sculpture, Hofstra Mus., 1990; permanent collections Zimmerli Art Mus., Rutgers U., N.J., 1992, Nat. Mus. Am. Art, Smithsonian Instn., Washington, 1993; nat. tour. Am. sculpture by EducArt Projects Inc., 1992; also exhbns. of nat. scope, 1938—; solo sculpture exhbn., Friends Greenwich (Conn.) Library, 1962; executed plaque for Burro Monument, Fairplay, Colo.; exhibited N.Y. Bank for Savs., 1968, Mattatuck Mus., Con., 1967, Lamont Gallery, N.H., 1967, Phila. Art Alliance Exhibition Sculpture of the American Scene, 1987, Am. References (Artists) Chicago, 1989—; executed: 18 foot carving in limewood depicting History of Man; reprodns. in Contemporary Stone Sculpture, 1970, Contemporary American Sculptures, Am. References, Chgo., 1989—; contbr. articles to mags.; feature article in Greenwich (Conn.) Time, 1990, 93. Recipient Anna Hyatt Huntington award, 1942; Am. Artists Profl. League and Montclair Art Assn. Awards, 1943; 1st Henry O. Avery Prize, 1944; Sculpture Prize Bklyn. Soc. Artists, Bklyn. Mus., 1946; John Rogers Award, 1951; Lawrence Hyder Prize, 1952, 54; David H. Zell Meml. Award, 1954, 63; hon. mention U.S. Maritime Commn., 1941 and; A.C.A. Gallery Competition, 1944; Med. of honor for sculpture Nat. Assn. Women Artists, 1951; Med. of honor for sculpture Nat. Acad. Galleries, N.Y.; prize for carved sculpture, 1955; animal sculpture, 1956; 1st award for sculpture Greenwich Art Soc., 1958, 60; 1st award for sculpture Annual New Eng. Exhbns., Silvermine, Conn. Fellow Internat. Inst. Arts and Letters (life); mem. Nat. Assn. Women Artists (2nd v.p. 1943-44), Nat. League Am. Pen Women, Inc. (OWL award for the Arts 1991), The Pen and Brush (emeritus 1992), Artists Coun. U.S.A., Bklyn. Soc. Artists, Greenwich Soc. Artists (mem. coun.), Internat. Sculpture Ctr., Internat. Soc. Artists (charter), Sculptors Guild, Inc. (lifetime mem., 1993—, sec. to exec. bd. 1942-45, chmn. exhbn. com. 1942, 44), Silvermine Guild Artists, Nat. Trust for Hist. Preservation. Home and Studio: 30 Strickland Rd Cos Cob CT 06807-2729

KANE, MARILYN ELIZABETH, small business owner; b. Butler, Pa., May 7, 1941; d. James and Anna (Supko) Holot; m. Paul D. Kane Sr., May 6, 1961; children: Kristina Marie, Paul D. Jr., Marilyn E. Grad. high sch., Butler, Earl Wheeler Modeling, Pitts., 1960; student, Palmer Talent Agy., N.Y.C., 1983—, UCLA, 1988. Cert. to teach modeling through World Modeling Assn. Exec. dir. Kane Finishing and Modeling Sch., Butler, 1970—; former instr. personal devel. Butler County Community Coll.; exec. dir. Kane Model and Talent Mgmt., Butler, 1970—. Fashion photographer Kane Sch. and Mgmt., 1980—; pageant dir. Miss Butler County USA, Cameo Model USA, Butler, 1977—; pageant judge various local, state, nat. levels competitions, 1970—. Mem. NAFE, World Modeling Assn. (life, Dir. of Yr. award 1978, 79, 85, Jr. Internat. Fashion Model award 1979, 80, 81, 83). Democrat. Byzantine Catholic. Home: 203 Reiber Ave Butler PA 16001-3126 Office: Kane Finishing & Modeling Sch 1022 N Main St Butler PA 16001-1956

KANE, NANCY JUNE, psychotherapist; b. Milw., Aug. 6, 1953; d. Elbert Edwin and Gloria (Bixby) Allison; m. Raymond Allen Kane, Aug. 6, 1977; children: Eric, Krista. BS, U. Wis., 1975; MS in Counselor Edn., No. Ill. U., 1980; postgrad., Gestalt Inst., Chgo., 1981. Assoc. dean of students Trinity Coll., Deerfield, Ill., 1980-82; psychotherapist, pvt. pracitce Grace Family Counseling, Northbrook, Ill., 1982—; adj. prof. Moody Bible Inst., Chgo., 1992—; conf. and workshop speaker, various women's groups and churches in Chicago suburbs, 1984—. Cmty. outreach chair PTA, Arlington Heights, Ill., 1993. Named to Outstanding Young Women of Am., 1987. Mem. Am. Counseling Assn., Ill. Mental Health Counselors Assn., Ill. Counseling Assn. Office: Grace Family Counseling 1501 Shermer Rd Northbrook IL 60062

KANE, PATRICIA LANEGRAN, language professional, educator; b. St. Paul, June 23, 1926; d. Walter B. and Lita E. (Wilson) Lanegran; m. Donald Patrick Kane, Apr. 1, 1947; children: Laura Kane Gustafson, Maura L. B.A. cum laude, Macalester Coll., St. Paul, 1947; M.A., U. Minn., 1950, Ph.D., 1961. Mem. faculty Macalester Coll., 1950-91, prof. English, 1971-91, DeWitt Wallace prof., 1978-91, prof. emeritus, 1992—, chmn. dept., 1977-86, faculty assoc., office of v.p. acad. affairs, 1979-83; mem. Minn. planning com. nat. identification project advancement women in acad. adminstrn. Nat. Council Edn., 1979-81. Co-author: A St. Paul Omnibus, 1979; Contbr. articles to profl. jours. Recipient Jefferson prize for teaching excellence, 1980, Disting. Alumni citation Macalester Coll., 1992; Danforth grantee, 1957-58. Mem. MLA, Soc. Study So. Lit. Office: Macalester Coll Saint Paul MN 55105

KANE HITTNER, MARCIA SUSAN, bank executive; b. N.Y.C., June 4, 1959; d. Howard Eugene and Sydell (Friedman) Kane; m. Ellis Hittner, May 23, 1993. Cert. fin. planning, NYU, 1980, BA in Communications, 1986. Pension specialist Union Dime Savs. Bank, N.Y.C., 1978-81; money market specialist Goldome (formerly Union Dime Savs. Bank), N.Y.C., 1981-82; customer svc. unit mgr. Citibank, N.A., N.Y.C., 1982-85, keogh product mgr., 1986-87, shareholder communications mgr., 1988-89, asst. v.p., tax shelter conversion mgr., 1990-93, asst. v.p. tech. request interface and control dept., 1993—. Author: (with others) Critical Reading-Level G, 1980. Bd. dirs. Forest Hills Owners Corp., N.Y.C., 1991-92. Mem. N.Y. Bus. and Profl. Women's Club. Office: Citibank NA 1 Court Sq 35th Fl Long Island City NY 11120

KANENAKA, REBECCA YAE, microbiologist; b. Wailuku, Hawaii, Jan. 9, 1958; d. Masakazu Robert and Takako (Oka) Fujimoto; m. Brian Ken Kanenaka, Nov. 10, 1989; 1 child, Kent Masakazu. Student, U. Hawaii, Manoa, 1976-77; BS, Colo. State U., 1980. Lab. asst. Colo. State U., Ft. Collins, 1979-80; microbiologist Foster Farms, Livingston, Calif., 1980-81; microbiologist Hawaii Dept. Health, Lihue, 1981-86, Honolulu, 1986—. Mem. Am. Soc. Microbiology (Hawaii chpt.), Nat. Registry of Microbiologists, Am. Soc. Microbiology. Clubs: Brown Bag (Lihue) (pres. 1985-86); Golden Ripples (4-H leader). Home: 1520 Liholiho St Apt 502 Honolulu HI 96822-4093 Office: Hawaii Dept Health Lab 1250 Punchbowl St Honolulu HI 96813-2428

KANESTA, NELLIE ROSE, chemical dependency counselor; b. Zuni, N.Mex., Aug. 8, 1939; d. Paxton E. and Bessie (Thompson) Boone; m. Patrick Tsethlikia, Apr. 10, 1959 (div. Mar. 1973); children: Nina, Frederick William, Pamela, Judson, Marie Christine, Paxton, Clifford. Student, U. N.Mex., Gallup, 1994-95, U. N.Mex., Gallup, 1994-95, U. Minn., Duluth, 1987-88. Alcoholism counselor Zuni (N.Mex.) Indian Hosp., 1985-86; counselor Friendship Svcs., Inc., Gallup, N.Mex., 1986-87; trainer Hazelden Found., Center City, Minn., 1987-88; intense residential guidance counselor Ramah (N.Mex.) Navajo Dormitory, 1988-89; Title V counselor, dir. Pine Hills (N.Mex.) Schs., 1989-91, phys. ednl. aide, 1992-93, group home life skills counselor, 1993—; counselor Zuni Pub. Health Svc. Indian Hosp., 1985, Regional Conf. on Children of Alcoholics, Albuquerque, 1985; insvc. tng. confs. Western N.Mex. U., 1986, Native Am. Cultural Issues in Substance Abuse, Coll. of Santa Fe, 1986, Chem. Dependency and Intervention, The N.Mex. Alcoholism and Drug Abuse Counselors, 1986, In-Svc. Tng. on Battered Families and Its Relation to Alcohol/Drug Abuse, 1987, N.Mex. Alcoholism and Drug Abuse Counselors Assn., 1986-88, Hazelden Chem. Dependency Counselor Tng. Program, 1988; family advocate for mentally ill Zuni Pub. Health Svc., 1993-94. Home: PO Box 9 Zuni NM 87327 Office: Ramah Navajo Sch Bd Inc PO Drawer H Pine Hill NM 87357

KANE-VANNI, PATRICIA RUTH, lawyer, consultant; b. Phila., Jan. 12, 1954; d. Joseph James and Ruth Marina (Rameriz) Kane; m. Francis William Vanni, Feb. 14, 1980; 1 child, Christian Michael. AB, Chestnut Hill Coll., 1975; JD, Temple U., 1985. Bar: Pa. 1985, U.S. Ct. Appeals (3d cir.) 1988. Freelance art illustrator Phila., 1972-80; secondary edn. instr. Archdiocese of Phila., 1980-83; contract analyst CIGNA Corp., Phila., 1983-84; jud. aide Phila. Ct. of Common Pleas, 1984; assoc. atty. Anderson and Dougherty, Wayne, Pa., 1985-86; atty. cons. Bell Telephone Co. of Pa., 1986-87; sr. assoc. corp. counsel Independence Blue Cross, Phila., 1987—; cons. Coll. Consortium on Drug and Alcohol Abuse, Chester, Pa., 1986-89; speaker in field. Contbr. articles and illustrations to profl. mags. Judge Del. Valley Sci. Fairs, Phila., 1986, 87; Dem. committeewomen, Lower Merion, Pa., 1983-87; ch. cantor, soloist, mem. choir Roman Cath. Ch.; mem. Phila. Assn. Ch. Musicians, also bd. dirs. Recipient Legion of Honor award Chapel of the Four Chaplins, 1983. Mem. ABA, Pa. Bar Assn., Phila. Bar Assn. (Theatre Wing), Phila. Assn. Def. Counsel, Phila. Vol. Lawyers for Arts (bd. dirs.), Nat. Health Lawyers Assn. (spkr. 1994 annual conv.), Hispanic Bar Assn. Democrat. Home: 119 Bryn Mawr Ave Bala Cynwyd PA 19004-3012 Office: Ind Blue Cross Legal Dept 36th Fl 1901 Market St Philadelphia PA 19103-1400

KANFER, RUTH, psychologist; b. St. Louis, Feb. 1, 1955; d. Frederick H. and Ruby Kanfer. BA, Miami U., Oxford, Ohio, 1976; MA, PhD, Ariz. State U., 1981. Med. psychology intern health scis. ctr. U. Oreg., Portland, 1980-81; NIMH postdoctoral fellow U. Ill., Champaign, 1981-83, vis. asst. prof. psychology, 1983-84; asst. prof. psychology U. Minn., Mpls., 1984-89; office naval rsch. summer faculty rsch. fellow USN Personnel Rsch. and Devel., San Diego, 1987; vis. scholar Stanford U., Palo Alto, Calif., 1988; assoc. prof. psychology U. Minn., Mpls., 1989-93; prof., 1993—. Editl. bd. Jour. Applied Psychology, 1990-94, Orgnl. Behavior and Human Decision Processes, 1989—, Applied Psychology: An Internat. Rev., 1991—, Basic and Applied Social Psychology, 1994—, Contemporary Psychology, 1992—; co-editor: Abilities Motivation and Methodology: The Minnesota Symposium on Learning and Individual Differences, 1989; contbr. articles to profl. jours. Fellow NIMH, 1976; recipient Disting. Scientific award for early career contribution to psychology APA, 1989. Fellow APA, Am. Psychol. Soc.; mem. Acad. Mgmt. Assn. (Outstanding Publ. in Orgnl. Behavior award 1989), Internat. Assn. Applied Psychology, Psychonomic Soc., Midwestern Psychol. Assn., Sigma Xi. Office: U Minn Dept Psychology Elliott Hall 75 E River Rd Minneapolis MN 55455-0280

KANG, BANN C., immunologist; b. Kyungnam, Korea, Mar. 4, 1939; d. Daeryong and Buni (Chung) K.; came to U.S., 1964, naturalized, 1976; A.B., Kyungpook Nat. U., 1959, M.D., 1963; m. U. Yun Ryo, Mar. 30, 1963. Intern, L.I. Jewish Hosp.-Queens Hosp. Center, Jamaica, N.Y., 1964-65, resident in medicine, 1965-67; teaching assoc. Kyungpook U. Hosp., Taegu, Korea, 1967-70; fellow in allergy and chest Creighton U., Omaha, 1970-71; fellow in allergy Henry Ford Hosp., Detroit, 1971-72; clin. instr. medicine U. Mich. Hosp., Ann Arbor, 1972-73; asst. prof. Chgo. Med. Sch., 1973-74; chief allergy-immunology Mt. Sinai Hosp., Chgo., 1975—; asst. prof. Rush Med. Sch., Chgo. 1975-84, assoc. prof., 1984-86; assoc. prof. U. Ky. Coll. Medicine, 1987-92, prof., 1992—; cons. allergy-immunology Edgewater Hosp., Chgo., St. Anthony's Hosp., Chgo., 1976—, Nat. Heart, Lung, Blood Inst., 1979—; mem. Exptl. Transplantation Adv. Bd., Ill., 1985-86, Diagnostic and Therapeutic Tech. Assessment (AMA), 1987—, Gen. Clin. Rsch. Com. (NIH), 1989-93; adv. com. Ctr. for Biologics and Rsch., FDA, 1993—; counselor Chgo. Med. Soc., 1984-86, mem. policy com., adv. com. to health dept. Chgo. and Cook County, 1984-86. Recipient NIH award U. Mich., 1972-73. Diplomate Am. Bd. Internal Medicine, Am. Bd. Allergy-Immunology. Fellow ACP, Am. Acad. Allergy; mem. Am. Fedn. Clin. Research, AMA, Inter-Asthma Assn. Contbr. over 40 articles to profl. jours. Home: 2716 Martinique Ln Lexington KY 40509-9509 Office: U Ky Coll Medicine K528 Albert B Chandler Med Ctr 800 Rose St Lexington KY 40536

KANG, JULIANA HAENG-CHA, anesthesiologist; b. Mokpo, Cheonnam, People's Republic of Korea, July 1, 1941; came to U.S., 1965; d. Jonan and E-E-Suk (Lee) Kang; m. Chang-Song Choi; children: Mee-Kyung, Mee-Ae, Han-Bae. MD, Yonsei U., Seoul, People's Republic of Korea, 1965. Diplomate Am. Bd. Anesthesiology. Intern Pittsfield (Mass.) Gen. Hosp., 1965-66; asst. prof. biology Yonsei U., 1965; resident in anesthesiology D.C. Gen. Hosp., 1966-67, Yale-New Haven (Conn.) Hosp., 1967-69; asst. prof. anesthesiology U. Conn., Farmington, 1970-75, 82-85; vice chairperson anesthesia dept. Conn. Surgery Ctr., Hartford, Conn., 1985-86; med. dir., chairperson anesthesia dept. Conn. Surgery Ctr., Hartford, 1986—. Fellow Am. Coll. Anesthesiologists; mem. Am. Med. Women's Assn., Am. Soc. Ambulatory Surgery Anesthesia, Am. Soc. Anesthesiologists, Conn. Soc. Anesthesiology, Nat. Abortion Rights Action League, Naral Polit. Arm of Pro-Choice. Office: Conn Surgery Ctr 81 Gillett St Hartford CT 06105-2630

KANICK, VIRGINIA, radiologist; b. Coaldale, Pa., Nov. 10, 1925; d. Martin and Anna (Pisklak) K. BA, Barnard Coll., 1947; MD, Columbia U., 1951. Diplomate Am. Bd. Radiology. Intern Western Reserve U. Hosps., Cleve., 1951-52; resident in radiology St. Luke's Hosp., N.Y.C., 1952-55, attending radiologist, 1955-74; acting dir. radiology St. Luke's Roosevelt Hosp., N.Y.C., 1981-84, dep. dir. of radiology, 1984-89; ptnr. West Side Radiology, N.Y.C., 1989—; clin. prof. radiology Coll. Physicians and Surgeons Columbia U., N.Y.C., 1975—; pres. Med. Bd. St. Luke's Roosevelt Hosp., 1980-82. Contbr. articles to profl. jours. Bd. dirs. Health System Agy. of N.Y.C., 1978-81. Fellow Am. Cancer Soc., 1955. Fellow Am. Coll. Radiology; mem. Am. Roentgen Ray Soc., Radiol. Soc. N.Am., N.Y. County Med. Soc. (sec., dir. 1978—), N.Y. State Radiol. Soc. (bd. dirs. 1975—). Republican. Roman Catholic. Home: 560 Riverside Dr Apt 17B New York NY 10027-3202 Office: West Side Radiology 1090 Amsterdam Ave New York NY 10025-8104

KANIN, FAY, screenwriter; b. N.Y.C.; d. David and Bessie Mitchell; m. Michael Kanin (dec.); children: Joel (dec.), Josh. Student, Elmira Coll., L.H.D. (hon.), 1981; B.A., U. So. Calif. mem. western regional exec. bd., judge Am. Coll. Theatre Festival, 1975-76; appointed v.p. Marstar Prodns., L.A. Writer: (with Michael Kanin) screenplays including The Opposite Sex, Teacher's Pet; Broadway plays including His and Hers, Rashomon, Grind (Tony nomination 1985); writer, co-producer TV spls. including Friendly Fire, ABC-TV (Emmy award for best TV film, San Francisco Film Festival award, Peabody award), Hustling (Writers Guild award for best original drama), Tell Me Where It Hurts (Emmy award, Christopher award); Heartsounds (Peabody award). Mem. Writers Guild Am. West (pres. screen br. 1971-73, Val Davies award 1975), Am. Film Inst. (trustee), Acad. Motion Picture Arts and Sci. Found. (past pres., v.p.), Nat. Ctr. Film and Video Preservation (co-chmn.).

KANNE, ELIZABETH ANN ARNOLD, secondary school educator; b. Atlanta, Sept. 16, 1945; d. Robert Earl and Elizabeth Ann (Jetton) A.; m. Robert Edward Lee, Jr., Aug. 20, 1967 (div. Oct. 1977); children: Robert Edward III, Edward Andrew; m. William Rudolph Kanne, Jr., June 4, 1979; 1 child, William Edward. BA, Furman U., 1967; MA, U. S.C., 1978. Cert. elem., early childhood, mid. sch. tchr., S.C. 1st grade tchr. Aiken (S.C.) County Schs., 1967-70, 4th and 5th grade tchr., 1978-90, guidance counselor, 1990-92, 6th grade math. tchr., 1992—; mem. S.C. Curriculum Congess, Columbia, 1991—, Dist. Screening Team, Aiken, 1991—, Sch. Improvement Coun., Aiken, 1992—. S.C. Ednl. Improvement Act grantee State Dept. Edn., 1991-92, 93-94. Mem. NEA, S.C. Edn. Assn., S.C. Mid. Sch. Assn., Aiken County Edn. Assn. Office: Schofield Mid Sch 220 Sumter St NE Aiken SC 29801-4499

KANORA, LINDA JANE, controller; b. Waterville, Maine, Sept. 20, 1956; d. George H. and Ruth P. (Gibbs) Goforth; m. Douglas J. Kanora, Dec. 5, 1975; 1 child, James M. Kanora. BS cum laude, Mansfield State U., 1984. Controller Binsky & Snyder, Plainfield, N.J., 1985—. Mem. Constrn. Fin. Mgmt. Assn. Office: Binsky & Snyder Inc 965 Highway 22 W N Plainfield NJ 07060

KANT, GLORIA JEAN, neuroscientist, researcher; b. Chgo., June 6, 1944; d. Hans Georg and Jo Sefa (Pick) K.; m. Philip Herbert Balcom, July 1, 1967 (div. 1976). BS in Chemistry, Mich. State U., 1965; PhD in Physiol. Chemistry, U. Wis., 1969. Chemist dept. psychiatry Walter Reed Army Inst. Rsch., Washington, 1970-71, neurochemist dept. microwave rsch., 1971-77, neurochemist dept. med. neuroscis., 1977-87, chief dept. med. neuroscis., 1987—. Mem. editorial bd. Pharmacology, Biochemistry and Behavior, 1991—; contbr. over 70 articles to sci. jours. Mem. AAAS, Soc. for Neurosci., Am. Soc. for Pharmacology and Exptl. Therapeutics, Internat. Behavioral Neurosci. Soc., Women in Neurosci. Home: 1124 Dennis Ave Silver Spring MD 20901-2171 Office: Walter Reed Army Inst Rsch Dept Med Neurosci Washington DC 20307

KANTER, ROSABETH MOSS, management educator, consultant, writer; b. Cleve., Mar. 15, 1943; d. Nelson Nathan and Helen (Smolen) Moss; m. Stuart Alan Kanter, June 20, 1963 (dec. Mar. 1969); m. Barry Alan Stein, July 2, 1972; 1 child, Matthew Moss Kanter Stein. BA in Sociology magna cum laude, Bryn Mawr Coll., 1964; MA, U. Mich., 1965, PhD, 1967; postgrad., Harvard U. Law Sh., 1975-76; MA (hon.), Yale U., 1978, Harvard U., 1986; DSc (hon.), Bucknell U., 1980, Babson Coll., 1984, Bryant Coll., 1986, Bentley Coll., 1990; LHD (hon.), Antioch U., Westminster Coll., 1984, Suffolk U., N. Adams State Coll., 1987, Colby-Sawyer Coll., 1988, U. New Haven, 1989; DCL (hon.), Union Coll., 1987; LLD (hon.), Regis Coll., 1987; DSS (hon.), Fla. Internat. U., 1990; DHL (hon.), SUNY Inst. Tech., 1991, Dowling Coll., 1991, Claremont Coll., 1992, Monmouth Coll., 1994. Vis. prof. mgmt. Harvard U., 1973-74, MIT, 1979-80; from assoc. to asst. prof. Brandeis U., 1967-77; prof. Yale U., 1977-86; Class of 1960 prof. mgmt. Harvard U. Bus. Sch., 1986—; trustee Coll. Retirement Equities Fund, N.Y., 1985-89, Am. Leadership Forum, Houston, 1982-86; dir. Ctr. for New Democracy, Washington, 1985-87; mem. work group on entrepreneurship Pres.'s Commn. Indsl. Competitiveness, 1984; Govs.'s innovation adv. com. Commonwealth of Mass, chair subcom., 1986; mem. Spl. Commn. on Employee Involvement and Ownership, Mass., 1986-87; mem. Gov.'s Commn. Rev. Anti-Takeover Laws, Mass. 1988; mem. Gov.'s Counc. Econ. Growth, Mass., 1994—; Katz-Newcomb lectr. in social psychology U. Mich., 1986; Disting. speaker Orgn., Theory, Careers and Women in Mgmt. divs. Nat. Acad. Mgmt., 1987, Eastern Acad. Mgmt., 1993; Centenniel lectr. APA, 1992; Lilly Found. Disting. lectr. Nat. Assn. Community Leadership Orgns., 1985; Leavey Disting. lectr. U. Santa Clara, 1984; vis. scholar Newberry Libr. Program in Humanities, Chgo., 1973, Norwegian Rsch. Coun. on Sci., and Humanities, Oslo, 1980; Kellogg Found. 50th Anniv. lectr. Am. Assn. Higher Edn., 1979, Blazer lectr. U. Ky., 1974, Davidson lectr. U. N.H., 1975; Sigma Chi scholar-in-residence Miami U., Oxford, Ohio, 1978; bd. dirs. Am. Productivity and Quality Ctr., Houston. Author: Work and Family in the U.S., 1977, Men and Women of the Corporation, 1977 (C. Wright Mills award 1977), 93, The Change Masters, 1983, (with M.S. Dukakis) Creating The Future: The Massachussetts Comeback and Its Promise for America, 1988, When Giants Learn to Dance, 1989 (Johnson Smith Knisely Exec. Leadership award 1990), (with B.A. Stein and T.F. Jick) The Challenge of Organizational Change: How Companies Experience It and Leaders Guide It, 1992; 5 other books, also monographs; mem. editorial bd. Human Resource Mgmt. jour., 1982-89, Orgn. Dynamics jour., 1983-85, 89, Jour. Bus. Venturing, 1985-89, Jour. Contemporary Bus., 2987-89, others; adv. bd. Society jour., 1987-89; editor Harvard Bus. Rev., 1989-92; contbr. over 150 articles to profl. jours., books, mags. (articles Harvard Bus. Rev. McKinsey award). chmn. bd. Goodmeasure Inc., 1977—; bd. dirs. NOW Legal Def. and Edn. Fund, N.Y.C., 1979-86, 93—, Ctr. New Democracy, Washington, 1985-88, Am. Prodn. and Quality Ctr., Houston, 1989—, Econ. Policy Inst., 1994—; incorporator Babson Coll., 1984-87, Boston Children's Mus., 1984—, Mt. Auburn Hosp., 1991—; bd. overseers Malcolm Baldrige Nat. Quality Award U.S. Dept. Commerce, 1994—. Guggenheim fellow; numerous rsch. grants; named Woman of the Yr. New Eng. Women's Bus. Owners, 1981, Internat. Assn. Personnel Women, 1981, MS mag., 1985; named to Cleve. Heights High Sch. Hall of Fame, 1986, Working Woman Hall of Fame AT&T/Working Women mag., 1986, Ohio Women's Hall of Fame, 1990; recipient Athena award Intercollegiate Assn. Women Students, 1980, Gold medal award Big Sister Assn. Greater Boston, 1985, Women Who Make a Difference award Internat. Women's Forum, 1988, Richard M. Cyert award Profl. Excellence Carnegie-Mellon U. Grad. Sch. Indsl. Adminstrn., 1989, Project Equality award, 1n's and Colitis Found. award, 1993, Disting. Scholar award Acad. Mgmt., 1994. Fellow Acad. Mgmt. (Disting. speaker mgmt. cons. divsn. 1985, women in mgmt. divsn. 1987, orgn. mgmt. theory divsn. 1994, Disting. Scholar award OMT divsn. 1994), Am. Soc. Quality & Participation, World Productivity Cong. (Ams. divsn.); mem. Am. Sociol. Assn. (exec. coun. 1982-85), Eastern Sociol. Soc. (exec. com. 1975-78, Gellman award 1978), Soc. for Advancement of Socio-Econs., Com. of 200 (founder), Internat. Women's Forum, Coun. on Fgn. Rels. Office: Harvard U Grad Sch Bus Adminstrn Soldiers Field Boston MA 02163

KANTNER, HELEN JOHNSON, church education administrator; b. Chgo., Oct. 22, 1936; d. Wilbert E. and Edna M. (Benson) Johnson; m. Robert O. Kantner, Aug. 22, 1959; children: Robert O. Jr., Sheryl Jackson. BA, Wheaton Coll., 1958; MS in Education, Youngstown State U., 1987. Asst. to prin. 1st Bapt. Day Sch., West Palm Beach, Fla., 1970-72; elem. tchr. Am. Heritage Schs., Ft. Lauderdale, Fla., 1973-76; social studies tchr. Champion High Sch., Warren, Ohio, 1977-88; edn. dir. Ocean Dr. Presbyn. Ch., North Myrtle Beach, S.C., 1988—. Vice pres. bd. dirs. Horry County (S.C.) Arts Coun. Youngstown State U. scholar. Mem. NEA, Ohio Edn. Assn., Champion Classroom Tchrs. Home: 3610 Golf Ave Little River SC 29566 Office: 410 6th Ave S North Myrtle Beach SC 29582-3306

KANTROWITZ, JOANNE SPENCER, writer; b. Marquette, Mich., Dec. 6, 1931; d. Robert S. and Doris Margaret (Jorgensen) Spencer; m. Nathan Kantrowitz, June 2, 1958; children: Alexander Fraser, Edward Fraser. BA, Mich. U., 1953; MA, U. Chgo., 1957, PhD, 1967. Editor, writer Irving-Cloud Publishing, Chgo., 1954-56; writer, social activist Tarrytown, N.Y., 1980—; dir. communications Profl. Women in Constrn., 1985-89, cons., 1989—; lectr. Kent State U., Marymount Coll., Vassar Coll., Pratt Inst., 1957-76. Spl. editor women and poverty issue Westchester Women's News, 1984; author: Dramatic Allegory, 1975; contbr. articles to profl. jours. Bd. dirs. Asbury Terrace, Tarrytown, 1983-93; women's adv. bd. Westchester County, 1984-86; sec. for Christian edn. Westchester-Rockland Reformed Ch. Women, 1982-85; campaign mgr. N.Y. State Assembly candidate, Yonkers, 1984; active Voter Registration Project, 1984; publicity mgr. ERA campaign, Westchester NOW, 1981, program planning, 1980-83, steering com. 1980-88, chair 20th birthday gala, 1986, chair task force on religion & morality, 1983-86, v.p. publicity, 1983-86; asst. to pres. NAACP, Tarrytown, 1992-94, coun., 1994—. Grantee Am. Coun. Learned Soc., 1971, Medieval Soc. Am., 1973; recipient Leadership awards Profl. Women in Constrn., 1987, NAACP, Tarrytown, 1994. Home and Office: 122 Mckeel Ave Tarrytown NY 10591-3426

KANTROWITZ, SUSAN LEE, lawyer; b. Queens, N.Y., Jan. 15, 1955; d. Theodore and Dinah (Kotick) Kantrowitz; m. Mark R. Halperin; 1 child, Jacob Josef Kantrowitz-Sirotkin. BS summa cum laude, Boston U., 1977; JD, Boston Coll., 1980. Bar: Mass. 1982. Assoc. producer Sta. KOCE-TV, Huntington Beach, Calif., 1980-81; account exec. Bozell & Jacobs, Newport Beach, Calif., 1981; atty. WGBH Ednl. Found., Boston, 1981-84, dir. legal affairs, 1984-86, gen. counsel, dir. legal affairs, 1986—; v.p., gen. counsel, 1993. Co-Author: Legal and Business Aspects of the Entertainment, Publishing and Sports Industries, 1984. Mem. ABA, Mass. Bar Assn., Boston Bar Assn.

KANY, JUDY C(ASPERSON), health policy analyst, former state senator; b. June 29, 1937; d. Helmer C. and Florence P. Casperson; m. Robert Kany,

Aug. 16, 1958; children: Kristin, Geoffrey, Daniel. BBA, U. Mich., 1959; MPA, U. Maine-Orono, 1976. Mem. Maine Ho. Reps., 1975-82, Maine Senate, 1982-92; project dir. for health professions regulations Med. Care Devel., Augusta, Maine, 1993—. chmn. Maine's Adv. Commn. on Radioactive Waste, 1981-87, Joint Standing Com. Legal Affairs, Joint Standing Com. on State Govt., 1982-86, Joint Standing Com. Energy and Natural Resources, 1983-84, 89-90, Joint Standing Com. Banking and Ins., 1991-92, com. Maine Lakes, 1990-92; mem. Commn. on Maine's Future, 1976, 87-89; mayor Waterville, Maine, 1988-89. Democrat. Home: PO Box 508 Belgrade Lakes ME 04918-0508 Office: Med Care Devel 11 Parkwood Dr Augusta ME 04330

KAO, YASUKO WATANABE, library administrator; b. Tokyo, Mar. 30, 1930; came to U.S., 1957; d. Kichiji and Sato (Tanaka) Watanabe; m. Shih-Kung Kao, Apr. 1, 1959; children: John Sterling, Stephanie Margaret. B.A., Tsuda Coll., 1950; B.A. in Lit., Waseda U., 1955; M.S.L.S., U. So. Calif., 1960. Instr., Takinogawa High Sch., Tokyo, 1950-57; catalog librarian U. Utah Library, 1960-67, Marriott Library, 1975-77, head catalog div., 1978-90; dir. libr. Teikyo Loretto Heights U., 1991—. Contbr. articles to profl. jours. Vol., Utah Chinese Am. Community Sch., 1974-80, Asian Assn. Utah, 1981-90. Waseda U. fellow, 1958-59. Mem. ALA, Asian Pacific Librs. Assn., Assn. Coll. and Research Libraries, ALA Library and Info. Tech. Assn., Colo. Library Assn., Utah Coll. Library Council, Beta Phi Mu. Address: 3801 W Wagontrail Dr Littleton CO 80123

KAPELMANN, BARBARA ANN, physician, educator; b. N.Y.C., Apr. 30, 1949; d. Leonard A. and Helen (Hass) K.; m. Lawrence William Koblenz, Mar. 24, 1979; 1 child, Adam. BA, Barnard Coll., 1970; MS in Microbiology, Yale U., 1972; MD, Yeshiva U., 1975. Diplomate Am. Bd. Internal Medicine, Am. Bd. Gastroenterology. Intern St. Lukes-Roosevelt Hosp.-Columbia U., N.Y.C., 1975-76, resident, 1976-78; asst. attending physician in gastroenterology Beth Israel Hosp., N.Y.C., 1982-88, assoc. attending physician in medicine and gastroenterology, 1988—; clin. instr. in medicine Mt. Sinai Sch. of Medicine, N.Y.C., 1981-87, asst. clin. prof. medicine, 1987—; bd. dirs. Beth Israel Med. Ctr., N.Y.C., 1984—; vis. clin. fellow Columbia U. Coll. of Physicians and Surgeons, N.Y.C., 1975-80; attending physician courtesy staff Doctors Hosp., N.Y.C., 1983—. Co-author: Gastroenterology for the House Officer, 1989; contbr. articles to profl. jours. Fellow ACP, Am. Coll. Gastroenterology; mem. Am. Women's Med. Assn., Women's Med. Assn. N.Y.C. (officer), Am. Gastroent. Assn., Am. Assn. for Study of Liver Diseases, Am. Soc. for Gastrointestinal Endoscopy, Am. Med. Informatics Assn., N.Y. Acad. Gastroenterology, N.Y. Soc. for Gastrointestinal Endoscopy. Office: 944 Park Ave New York NY 10028

KAPITAN, MARY L., retired nursing administrator, educator; b. Lawrence, Mass., July 9, 1920; d. Vincent and Concetta (Tomaselli) Zazzo; m. John A. Kapitan, Sept. 6, 1947. Diploma, Somerville (Mass.) Hosp., 1944; BS in Nursing Edn., DePaul U., Chgo., 1960, MS in Nursing Adminstrn., 1962. RN; lic. health facility adminstr., Ind. Occupational health nurse E. I. duPont de Nemours & Co., Lincolnwood, Ill., Senco Corp., Newtown, Ohio; asst. prof. psychiat. and med. nursing No. Ky. U., Highland Heights; nursing coord. VA Hosp., Butler, Pa.; instr. psychiat. nursing Ohio Valley Community Hosp., McKees Rocks, Pa.; dir. nursing svc. Presbyn. Home, Evanston, Ill., Edgewater Hosp., Chgo., Franklin Blvd Hosp., Chgo. 1st lt. U.S. Army Nurse Corps, 1944-47. Mem. ANA, Am. Asn. Occupational Health Nurses, Am. Coll. Health Facility Adminstrs., Ohio Nurses Assn., Ill. Nurses Assn., Ind. Nurses Assn., Mass. Nurses Assn., Southwestern Ohio Assn. Occupational Health Nurses (chmn. legislation and edn. com.), Women in Mil. Svc. for Am. (charter), Women's Meml. Found.

KAPITAN-WHITE, ELSA KAREN, regulatory affairs specialist, technical writer; b. Dhahran, Saudi Arabia, Aug. 12, 1959; came to U.S., 1967; d. John Rudolph and Christine C. (Saari) Kapitan; m. James M. Mazzullo, May 1, 1982 (div. Jan. 1987); m. Eric R. White, July 16, 1994. BS in Geology, Centenary Coll., Shreveport, La., 1981; MS in Geology, Tex. A&M U., 1983. Cert. in tech. writing. Sci. editor Ocean Drilling Program, College Station, Tex., 1984-90; regulatory analyst K.W. Brown Environ. Svcs., Houston, 1990-93; regulatory affairs specialist Mitchell Energy & Devel. Corp., The Woodlands, Tex., 1993—; cons. Ocean Drilling Program, 1990—. Editor procs. and reports. Pres. LWV of the Brazos Valley, Bryan-College Station, 1986-88. Named Woman of Excellence, Fedn. of Houston Profl. Women, 1993. Mem. Assn. Earth Sci. Editors (chair awards com. 1993—), Assn. for Women Geoscientists (Lone Star chpt. newsletter editor 1988—), Houston Geol. Soc., Soc. for Tech. Comm., Air and Waste Mgmt. Assn. Unitarian Universalist. Home: 23906 Hunter Spring Cir Spring TX 77373-6331 Office: Mitchell Energy & Devel Co PO Box 4000 The Woodlands TX 77387-4000

KAPLAN, CAROLYN SUE, educator; b. Childress, Tex., June 23, 1944; d. Irving and Juliette (Weiner) Kohn. Student, C.W. Post Coll. Cert. tchr., N.Y. Tchr. N.Y.C. Bd. Edn., 1966-79, 91—; sec. Borough of Manhattan Community Coll., N.Y.C., 1975-76, N.Y.C. Housing Authority, 1984-90; with Headstart program United People's Meth. Ch., 1993. Mem. legis. adv. com. N.Y. State Senate, Albany, 1991—; vol. Queens Woman's Ctr., 1994—; tutor adult literacy program Queens Librs., 1994—. Mem. Assn. for Childhood Edn. Internat. Home: 19806 Pompeii Ave Jamaica NY 11423-1422

KAPLAN, ERICA LYNN, typing and word processing service company executive, pianist; b. Jamaica, N.Y., Aug. 6, 1955; d. George William and Raylia (Eagle) Kaplan; m. James Laurence Kellermann, Feb. 26, 1982. B in Mus., Manhattan Sch. Music, N.Y.C., 1976, M in Mus., 1979. Clk. dept. edn. 92d St. Y, N.Y.C., 1972-76, assoc. dept. pub. rels., 1977-78, catalogue coord., sec. to exec. dir., 1978, assoc. dept. performing arts, 1978-79, assoc. dir. dept. publs., 1979-80; pres. Erica Kaplan Typing/Word Processing/Music Svcs., N.Y.C., 1980—; piano soloist Huntington (N.Y.) Philharmonia, 1975; rehearsal pianist, performance accompanist The Mikado, Playwrights Horizons, N.Y.C., 1975, Fiona in Swan Song, N.Y.C., 1986; mus. dir., accompanist A Salute to Vaudeville/A Tribute to Fred Astaire, N.Y.C., 1980—; mus. dir., pianist Portrait of a Man, Hyde Pk. (N.Y.) Festival Theatre, 1981, Am. Renaissance Theater, N.Y.C., 1982, 86, The Fantasticks, Dalton Sch., N.Y.C., 1983; performance accompanist Okla., Theatreworks, Bklyn., 1984; resident pianist Am. Renaissance Theater, N.Y.C., 1981—; audition accompanist Interboro Repertory Theater, N.Y.C., 1986—; accompanist, vocal lessons class Stuyvesant Adult Ctr., N.Y.C., 1988—, The Singing Experience, 1990-91; mus. dir. Gift of the Magi, 1991. Translator and annotator with additional mus. examples: L'Anacrouse dans la Musique Moderne, 1978; composer (songs) Four by Feiffer, 1978, Hey Boys, 1984, Unborn Child, 1988, Neighbor, 1991; arranger Postcards from the Apple, 1993. Mem. New Eng. Anti-Vivisection Soc., Boston, 1982—, Nat. Anti-Vivisection Soc., 1988—, Common Cause, Washington, 1983—, SANE/FREEZE, 1988—. Mem. Am. Fedn. Musicians, NAFE, Union Concerned Scientists, Mensa. Democrat. Jewish. Avocations: theater, travel.

KAPLAN, FRAN BETH, social worker, consultant; b. Lafayette, Ind., Feb. 9, 1947; d. George and Lillian (Blecher) K.; m. Reuben Levisohn; 1 child, Aaron. BA with honors, U. Wis., 1968; MSW, U. Mich., 1972. Nat. cert. nurturing program trainer/cons. Community worker, tchr. United Migrant Opportunity Svcs., Milw. and so. Fla., 1968-72; instr. dept. sociology Northeastern Ill. U., Chgo., 1972-73; dir. Downtown Ctr. YWCA, Milw., 1973-74; clinic adminstr. Summit Med. Ctr., Milw., 1975-78; exec. dir., pres. bd. Bread and Roses Women's Health Ctr., Milw., 1978-86; dir. Israel Child Protection Assn., Tel Aviv, 1984-86; coord. nurturing program Walker's Point Youth and Family Ctr., Milw., 1986-91; program devel. mgr. Family Svc. of Milw., 1991-92; cons. social worker in pvt. practice Milw., 1987—; spl. projects dir. Nurturing Network, Milw., 1988—; internat. liaison Family Devel. Resources, Inc., Park City, Utah, 1988—; psychotherapist in pvt. practice, Milw. and Tel Aviv, 1984-91. Author: Implementation Manual and Resource Guide for Group and Home-based Nurturing Programs, 1994; co-author family life edn. program. Organizer Mitzvah Dalkon, Israel, 1984-86; founder, pres. bd. Children's Discovery Ctr., Milw., 1975-79; founder/convenor Milw. Feminist Therapy Network, Milw., 1979-83. Recipient Leadership in Prevention award Wis. Com. for Prevention of Child Abuse, 1991, Community Svc. award Milw. Common Coun., 1991. Mem. NASW (Wis. Social Worker of Yr. 1992), Child Abuse Prevention Network (program com. chair 1987-93). Jewish. Office: Nurturing Program Tng and Cons 3125 N 50th St Milwaukee WI 53216

KAPLAN, HELENE LOIS, lawyer; b. N.Y.C., June 19, 1933; d. Jack and Shirley (Jacobs) Finkelstein; m. Mark N. Kaplan, Sept. 7, 1952; children: Marjorie Ellen, Sue Anne. AB cum laude, Barnard Coll., 1953; JD, NYU, 1967; LLD (hon.), Columbia U., 1990. Bar: N.Y. 1967. Pvt. practice law N.Y.C., 1967-78; ptnr. Webster & Sheffield, N.Y.C., 1978-86, counsel, 1986-90; of counsel Skadden, Arps, Slate, Meagher & Flom, N.Y.C., 1990—; bd. dirs. The May Dept. Stores Co., Met. Life Ins. Co., Chem. Banking Corp., Chem. Bank, Mobil Corp., Nynex, Coun. Fgn. Rels. Trustee N.Y. Coun. for the Humanities, 1976-82, chmn., 1978-82; trustee Barnard Coll., 1973—, chmn. 1984-94, Columbia U. Press, 1977-80, MITRE Corp., 1978—, N.Y. Found., 1976-86, Mt. Sinai Hosp. Med. Ctr. and Med. Sch., 1977—, vice chmn., John Simon Guggenheim Meml. Found., 1981—, NYU Law Ctr. Found., 1985-87, Carnegie Corp. N.Y., 1979—, vice chmn., 1981-84, chmn., 1984-91; trustee Inst. for Advanced Study, 1986—, Neuroscis. Rsch. Found., 1986-92, Am. Mus. of Natural History, 1989—, Am. Trust for Brit. Libr., 1991-93, Com. for Econ. Devel., 1993—, Commonwealth Fund, 1990—, J. Paul Getty Trust, 1992—; mem. adv. com. of U.S. Sec. of State on South Africa, 1986-88; mem. N.Y. State Gov.'s Task Force on Life and the Law, 1985-90; trustee N.Y.C. Pub. Devel. Corp., 1978-83, vice chmn., 1979-82; trustee Olive Free Library; bd. dirs. Am. Arbitration Assn., 1978-82, Catskill Ctr. for Conservation and Devel., 1981—; mem. Women's Forum, Inc., 1982—; mem. Rockefeller U. Coun., 1984-94; mem. Bretton Woods Com., 1985—; mem. Carnegie Coun. on Adolescent Devel., 1986—, Carnegie Commn. on Sci., Tech. and Govt., chair task force on sci. and tech. and jud. decision making, 1988-93; ptnr. N.Y.C. Partnership, 1987-92. Mem. ABA, AAAS, N.Y.C. Bar Assn. (treas. 1991-93, chair task force on sci. and tech. and judicial decision making, com. on philanthropic orgns., 1975-81, recruitment of lawyers 1978-82, com. on profl. responsibility 1980-83), N.Y. State Bar Assn., Am. Philos. Soc., Cosmopolitan Club, Coffee House Club, Century Assn. Home: 146 Central Park W New York NY 10023-2005 Office: 919 3rd Ave Fl 29 New York NY 10022-3903

KAPLAN, HUETTE MYRA, business educator, training consultant; b. Chgo., July 11, 1933; d. Max and Jeannette (Smith) Lazan; m. Jerrold M. Kaplan, Feb. 14, 1954; children: Lawrence, Jeffrey. BS in Bus. Edn., DePaul U., 1971. Instr. Pub. Svc. Careers Program State of Ill., Chgo., 1971-72; instr., dir. Patricia Stevens Bus. Sch., Chgo., 1972; relocation mgr., tng. specialist, dir. tng. and devel. Zurich-Am. Ins. Cos., Chgo. and Schaumburg, Ill., 1972-80; pres., tng. cons. H.K. & Assocs., Lansing, Ill., 1980—; tng. dir. Calumet Area Lit. Coun., Hammond, Inc., 1985—; trainer Chgo. Literacy Coordinating Ctr., 1988-93; instr. Purdue U.-Calumet, Hammond, 1976—. Bd. dirs. Temple Beth El, Hammond, 1986-88, Calumet Area Literacy Coun., 1990-92, 94—, mem. task force Chgo. Coalition for Edn. and Tng. for Employment, 1984-86; literacy vol. tutor. Mem. ASTD, Nat. Bus. Edn. Assn., Kappa Gamma Pi. Jewish. Home and Office: HK & Assocs 2843 192D St Lansing IL 60438

KAPLAN, (NORMA) JEAN GAITHER, retired tutor, reading specialist; b. Cumberland, Md., Dec. 14, 1927; d. Frank Preston and Elizabeth (Mcneil) Gaither; m. Robert Lewis Kaplan, Dec. 4, 1959; 1 child, Benjamin Leigh. AB in Edn., Madison Coll., Harrisonburg, Va., 1950; MA in Edn., U. Va., 1956; postgrad., U. Va., William & Mary, 1958-61; reading specialist degree, U. Va., 1976. Tchr. Frederick County Sch. System, Winchester, Va., 1950-51, Washington County Sch. System, Hagerstown, Md., 1951-55, Charlottesville (Va.) Sch. System, 1955-60, York County (Va.) Sch. System, 1962, Newport News Sch. System, Denbigh, Va., 1963, Internat. Sch. Bangkok, 1965-67; tutor Reston Reading Ctr., Fairfax County, Va., 1972-74; tutor homebound, substitute tchr. Fairfax County Sch. Systems, 1974-78; pvt. practice pvt. tutor McLean/Middleburg, Va., 1978-89; pres. Tutorial Svcs., Inc., McLean, 1985-87; sec. The Rumson Corp., Middleburg, 1981-95. Mem. No. Va. Conservation Coun., Fairfax County, 1976-81; bd. dirs. Nat. Environ. Leadership Coun. Mem. AAUW, LWV, Bangkok Am. Wives Assn., Tuesday Afternoon Club (pres. 1974-75), Ayr Hill Garden Club, Soc. John Gaither Descs. Inc., Kappa Delta Pi, Alpha Sigma Tau. Home and Office: PO Box 1943 Middleburg VA 22117-1943

KAPLAN, JOCELYN RAE, financial planning firm executive; b. Lynbrook, N.Y., Apr. 23, 1952; d. Eugene S. and Adeline (Dembo) K. B.S., Northwestern U., 1975. Cert. fin. planner. Ins. agt. Fidelity Union Life Ins. Co., College Park, Md., 1976-77, Bankers Life Ins. Co., Rockville, Md., 1977-80; fin. planner Reutemann & Wagner, McLean, Va., 1980-82; fin. planning casewriter McLean Fin. Group, 1982-83; dir. fin. planning DeSanto Naftal Co., Vienna, Va., 1983-85; pres. Advisors Fin., Inc., Falls Church, Va., 1985—. Founding mem., treas. Congregation Bet Mishpachah, Washington, 1981, v.p., 1982, pres., 1983. Recipient Nat. Quality award Nat. Assn. Life Underwriters, 1978; Agt. of Yr. award Gen. Agt. and Mgrs. Assn., 1978. Mem. Internat. Assn. Fin. Planners, Inst. Cert. Fin. Planners, Registry of Fin. Planning Practitioners. Home: 1045 N Utah St #611 Arlington VA 22201 Office: Advisors Fin Inc 131 Great Falls St # 300 Falls Church VA 22046-3402

KAPLAN, JUDITH HELENE, corporate professional; b. N.Y.C., July 20, 1938; d. Abraham and Ruth (Kiffel) Letich; m. Warren Kaplan, Dec. 31, 1958; children: Ronald Scott, Elissa Aynn. BA, Hunter Coll., 1955; post-grad., New Sch. for Social Rsch., 1955-56. Registered rep. Herzfeld & Stern, N.Y.C., 1963; agt. New York Life Ins. Co., N.Y.C., 1964-69; registered rep. Scheinman, Hochstin & Trotta, 1969-70; v.p. Alpha Capital Corp., N.Y.C., 1970-74; pres. Tipex, Inc., N.Y.C., 1966-84; v.p. Alpha Pub. Relations, N.Y.C., 1970-73; pres. Utopia Recreations Corp., 1971-73, Howard Beach Recreation Corp., 1972-73; chmn. bd. Alpha Exec. Planning Corp., 1970-72; field underwriter N.Y. Life Ins. Co., 1974-75; pres. Action Products Internat. Inc., 1978-87, chairperson, 1980—, Ronel Industries, Inc., 1982-84; participant White House Conf. on Small Bus., 1979; founder Women's History Mus., Judith Kaplan & Warren Kaplan's Women's History Collection Cen. Fla. Community Coll., Ocala, 1991. Author: Woman Suffrage, 1977; co-author: Space Patches-from Mercury to the Space Shuttle, 1986; contbg. editor: Stamp Show News, M & H Philatelic Report; creator, producer Women's History series of First Day Covers, 1976-81; contbr. articles to profl. jours. Active Wyo. adv. on woman suffrage; trustee Found. for Innovative Lifelong Edn. Inc., 1986-88. Named Outstanding Young Citizen Manhattan Jaycees, Small Bus. Person of Yr. State of Fla, 1986. Mem. NOW (ins. coord. nat. task force on taxes, v.p. N.Y. chpt., co-founder Ocala/Marion County chpt. 1982, bd. women's adv. coun. Ocala and Marion Counties 1986-88), Nat. Women's Polit. Caucus, Women Leaders Round Table, Nat. Assn. Life Underwriters, Assn. Stamp Dealers Am., Am. First Day Cover Soc. (life), Am. Philatelic Soc. (life), Bus. and Profl. Women, AAUW. Home: 577 Silver Course Cir Ocala FL 34472-2200 Office: 344 Cypress Rd Ocala FL 34472-3102

KAPLAN, LAURA GARCIA, disaster preparedness consultant; b. Hollywood, Fla., Mar. 11, 1957; d. Thomas Tubens and Felicia (Acebal) Garcia; m. Steven Kaplan; 1 child, Kristin. BSEE, U. Miami, 1979. Utilities exec. Fla. Power and Light Co., Miami, 1980-93, ops. mgr. Dade County, 1991-93; pres. L.G.K. Assocs., Ft. Lauderdale, Fla., 1993—. Author: Disaster Can Happen Anywhere in the World. . .Are You Prepared?, 1994. Counselor Soc. Abused Children, Kendall, Fla., 1985-86; instr. Jr. Achievement, Miami, 1986-87, Adult Illiteracy Program, 1987; bd. dirs. YWCA, 1988-92. Early admission scholar U. Miami, 1975; recipient Hurricane Andrew Hero award Dade County Rebuilding Program. Mem. Leadership Miami Assn., Greater Miami C. of C. Republican. Roman Catholic. Club: Hurricane. Home: 12302 NW 19th St Plantation FL 33323-2100 Office: LGK Assocs 110 SE 6th St Fort Lauderdale FL 33301

KAPLAN, MADELINE, legal administrator; b. N.Y.C., June 20, 1944; d. Leo and Ethel (Finkelstein) Kahn; m. Theodore Norman Kaplan, Nov. 14, 1982. AS, Fashion Inst. Tech., N.Y.C., 1964; BA in English Lit. summa cum laude, CUNY, 1982; MBA, Baruch Coll., 1990. Free-lance fashion illustrator N.Y.C., 1965-73; legal asst. Krause Hirsch & Gross, Esquires, N.Y.C., 1973-80; mgr. communications Stroock & Stroock & Lavan Esquires, N.Y.C., 1980-86; dir. adminstrn. Cooper Cohen Singer & Ecker Esquires, N.Y.C., 1986-87, Donovan Leisure Newton & Irvine Esquires, N.Y.C., 1987-93, Proskauer Rose Goetz & Mendelsohn, 1993—. Contbr. articles to profl. jours. Founder, pres. Knolls chpt. of Women's Am. Orgn. Rehab. Through Tng., Riverdale, N.Y., 1979-82, v.p. edn., Manhattan region, 1982-83. Mem. ASTD, Assn. Legal Adminstrs. (program com.), Soc. Human Resources Mgmt., Exec. MBA Alumni Assn. (bd. dirs.), Sigma Iota Epsilon (life). Office: 1583 Broadway New York NY 10036

KAPLAN, MURIEL SHEERR, sculptor; b. Phila., Aug. 15, 1924; d. Maurice J. and Lillian J. (Jamison) Sheerr; BA, Cornell U., 1946; postgrad. Sarah Lawrence Coll., 1958-60, U. Calif. at Oxford (Eng.), summer 1971, U. Florence (Italy), summer 1973, Art Students League, N.Y.C., summers 1975-89, New Sch., N.Y.C., 1974-78, m. Murray S. Kaplan, June 3, 1946 (dec.); children: Janet Belsky, James S., S. Jerrold, Amy Sheerr Eckman. Exhbns. at Women's Clubs in Westchester, 1954-60, Allied Artists Am., 1958-73, Nat. Assn. Women Artists, 1966-89, Bklyn. Mus., 1968, Sculptors Guild, 1972, Bergen County (N.J.) Mus., 1974; 2-person shows: Camino Real Gallery, Boca Raton, Fla., 1980; represented in group shows at Norton Art Gallery, Palm Beach, Fla., 1980, Govt. Ctr., West Palm Beach, Fla., 1984, Northwood U. Gallery, 1993; represented in permanent collections Israel, Columbia U., Brandeis U., U. Tex., Harvard Law Sch., 1990; executed twin 30 foot cor-ten steel sculptures, Tarrytown, N.Y., 1972, 2 large rotating steel sculptures Art Park, Trans-Lux Corp., 1978; art cons., interior designer, 1971-89; sec. commn. to establish art mus. in Westchester, 1956; chmn. Westchester Creative Arts Festival, 1956. Bd. dirs. Fedn. Jewish Philanthropies, 1956; chmn. 1st Sta. WNET, Channel 13 Art Auction; mem. com. art in pub. places, Palm Beach County, Fla., 1984; mem. art adv. com. Boca Raton Mus. Art, 1987-93; bd. dirs. Palm Beach County Cultural Coun. of Arts, 1992-94; tchr. sculpture Armory Arts Ctr., Palm Beach, 1987-92, bd. dirs., 1992—. Recipient prizes Nat. Assn. Women Artists, 1966, Westchester Women's Club, 1955, 56, Allied Artists Am., 1969, Artists Guild, Palm Beach, 1987, 88, 90, 91, 92, 93, 94. Mem. NAD, Art Students League N.Y. Nat. Assn. Women Artists, Allied Artists Am., Nat. Sculpture Soc., Internat. Sculpture Ctr., Portraits Inc. N.Y. Address: 339 Garden Rd Palm Beach FL 33480-3221

KAPLAN, ROXANNE SALCH, writer; b. Bronx, N.Y., Oct. 7, 1953; d. Edward Thomas John and Eleanor Marion Anne (Ziehl) Salch; m. Stephen Kaplan, Feb. 27, 1982; children: Jennifer, Victoria. AS in Bus. Adminstrn., Queensborough Community Coll., CUNY, 1979; student, Queens Coll., CUNY. Corr. sec., rschr. Parapsychology Inst. Am., Vampire Rsch. Center, South Setauket, N.Y., 1974-77; assoc. dir., travel coord. Parapsychology Inst. Am., Vampire Rsch. Center, Elmhurst, N.Y., 1977—; writer, 1985—. Contbg. author: In Pursuit of Premature Gods and Contemporary Vampires, 1976, Vampires Are, 1984, True Tales of the Unknown, Vols. I, II, III, 1985-91; co-author: The Amityville Horror Hoax, 1995. Singer Queensborough Chorus. Office: Parapsychology Inst Am PO Box 252 Elmhurst NY 11373

KAPLAN, SUSAN, lawyer. BA summa cum laude, Hofstra U., 1971; JD, Columbia U., 1974. Bar: N.Y. 1975, U.S. Dist. Ct. (so. and ea. dists.) N.Y. 1975. Assoc. Patterson Belknap & Webb, N.Y.C., 1974-76; asst. dist. atty. Nassau County, N.Y., 1976-81; asst. chief prosecution Office Profl. Discipline, State of N.Y., 1981-83; dep. dir. prosecution Office Profl. Discipline State of N.Y., 1983-85; pvt. practice N.Y.C., 1985—; mem. adv. bd. Employee Assistance Program Health Care Network, 1988—; lectr. in field. Contbr. articles to profl. jours. Mem. adminstrv. bd. Soc. Meml. Sloan-Kettering Cancer Ctr., 1975-78; mem. adv. coun. Nassau County Boy Scouts Am., 1977-87, v.p., 1981-84; sec., bd. dirs. Harkness Ballet Found., 1980-86. Assoc. fellow N.Y. Acad. Medicine 1990-91, fellow 1992—. Fellow N.Y. Bar Found.; mem. N.Y. State Bar Assn. (com. on pub. health 1975-78, com. on profl. discipline 1983-90, com. on health law 1985-88, 92—, com. to confer with state med. soc. 1985—, vice chair 1986-87, chair 1987-92). Office: 165 W End Ave Apt 27P New York NY 10023-5536

KAPLAN, SUSAN, lawyer; b. Worcester, Mass., July 27, 1958; d. Alvin H. and Elaine (Levy) K.; m. Matthew T. Gerson, Nov. 1, 1987; 1 child. BA, Bowdoin Coll., 1980; JD, Georgetown U., 1983. Chief counsel/counsel Constitution subcom. U.S. Senate Judiciary Com., Washington, 1987—. Office: US Senate Judiciary Com 524 Dirksen Washington DC 20510

KAPLAN ROWE, PHYLLIS DEEN, environmental scientist, research administrator; b. Everett, Wash., Feb. 9, 1931; d. Phillips Deen and Hazel Marion (Morseth) R.; m. Fred Kaplan, Aug. 1957 (div. 1974); children: Harold Deen, Madeleine Marie Kaplan Fusi. BA, U. Wash., 1953; MA, Brandeis U., 1956; PhD in Chemistry, U. Cin., 1967. Rsch. assoc. med. ctr. U. Cin., 1968-71, asst. prof. environ. health, 1971-77; sr. rsch. toxicologist Am. Cyanamid Co., Pearl River, N.Y., 1977-82; engring. cons. Am. Standards Testing Bur., N.Y.C., 1982-83; adminstr. preclin. internat. R&D Allergan, Inc., Irvine, Calif., 1983-87, dir. internat. R&D Europe & Middle East, 1987-90; dir. tech. affairs In Vitro Internat. Inc., Irvine, Calif., 1990-92, La Haye Labs., Inc., Redmond, Wash., 1992—; chem. spectroscopist Syntex Corp., 1967-68; lectr. Coll. Arts & Scis., U. Cin., 1972-73, Coll. Nursing, 1973-74; adj. prof. NYU, 1982-83; chem. cons. J.T. Baker Chem. Co., Phillipsburg, N.J., 1982-83; mgmt. cons. HM Assn., Irvine, Seattle, 1990—. Author: Review of Transition Metal Chemistry, 1975; editor children's books, 1990—. Grantee NIH, 1957-59, 59-60; Rsch. grantee Nat. Inst. Occupational Safety & Health, 1971-76. Mem. Am. Chem. Soc. (Petroleum Rsch. Fund grantee 1965-66), Internat. Soc. Ocular Toxicology (bd. dirs. 1988-90), N.Y. Acad. Sci., Assn. Rsch. in Vision and Ophthalmology, Sigma Xi. Home: 526 1st Ave S Apt 525 Seattle WA 98104-2863

KAPP, ELEANOR JEANNE, impressionistic artist, writer, researcher; b. Hagerstown, Md., Oct. 16, 1933; d. James Norman and Nellie Belle (Welty) Weagley; m. Alan Howard Kapp, Sept. 25, 1972. Cert., L.A. Interior Design, 1969; student, U. Utah, 1976-82. Artist Farmers Ins. Group, L.A., 1960-63; interior designer W&J Sloane, Beverly Hills, Calif., 1965-70; ski resort exec. Snowpine Lodge, Alta, Utah, 1970-84; dir. mktg. and pub. rels. Alta Resort Assn., 1979-84; free-lance photographer Alta, 1979—; bus. owner Creative Art Enterprises, Sandy, Utah, 1984-85; artist-resident Collector's Corner Art Gallery, San Ramon, Calif., 1991—; owner Art of Jeanne Kapp, Lafayette, Calif., 1985—; artist-resident St. Germain Gallery, Tiburon, Calif., 1993—, Regional Art Ctr. Gift Store, Walnut Creek, Calif., 1994—, Valley Art Ctr., Walnut Creek, 1995—. Author, pub.: The American Connection, 1985, 91; author, prodr. (documentary) A Look at China Today, 1981; photographer: Best of the West, 1983. Promotion liaison Alta Town Coun., 1980-84; floral decorator Coun. State Govts., Snowbird, Utah, 1976; photographer Utah Dems., Salt Lake City, 1981; exhibit curator Salt Lake County Libr. System, 1982, founder Alta Br. Libr., 1982; fundraiser Friends of Libr., Alta, 1982; mem. Alta Town-Libr. Adv. Bd., 1983. Recipient Cert. of Appreciation, Salt Lake County Libr. System, 1981, Cert. of Recognition, Gov. Cal Rampton, Salt Lake City, 1972-74, Calendar Cover award Utah Travel Coun., 1981, Internat. Invitational Art Exhibit, Centre Internat. D'Art Contemporain, Paris, 1983. Mem. Internat. Platform Assn., Diablo Art Assn. (pub. rels. chmn. 1987, Hon. Mention award 1989), Concord Art Assn. (1st pl. award 1991), Alamo and Danville Artist's Soc. (cir. leader 1990—, Hon. Mention award 1991, chmn. art exhbn. 1993, chmn. art program 1994), Las Junas Artist Assn. (juror's asst. 1992, 2d pl. award 1992, curator art exhbn. 1995). Home: 411 Donegal Way Lafayette CA 94549

KAPPA, MARGARET MCCAFFREY, resort hotel consultant; b. Wabasha, Minn., May 14, 1921; d. Joseph Hugh and Verna Mae (Anderson) McCaffrey; B.S. in Hotel Mgmt., Cornell U., 1944; grad. Dale Carnegie course, 1978; cert. hospitality housekeeping exec.; m. Nicholas Francis Kappa, Sept. 15, 1956; children—Nicholas Joseph, Christopher Francis. Asst. exec. housekeeper Kahler Hotel, Rochester, Minn., 1944; exec. housekeeper St. Paul Hotel, 1944-47, Plaza Hotel, N.Y.C., 1947-51; exec. housekeeper, personnel dir. Athearn Hotel, Oshkosh, Wis., 1952-58; dir. housekeeping The Greenbrier, White Sulphur Springs, W.Va., 1958-84; cons., 1984—; tchr. housekeeping U.S. and fgn. countries; cons.; vis. lectr. Cornell U. Author: (with others) Managing Housekeeping Operations, 1989. Pres. St. Charles Borromeo Parish Assn., White Sulphur Springs, 1962, v.p., 1980, 82; tech. adv., host 2 ednl. videos Am. Hotel and Motel Assn., 1986; host Kappa on Kleanings for video Spectra Vision AHMA Ednl. Inst, 1994. Recipient diploma of honor Société Culinaire Philanthropique, 1961. Mem. AARP, Cornell Soc. Hotelmen (pres. 1980-81, exec. com. 1981-82), Nat. Exec. Housekeepers Assn. (pres. N.Y. chpt. 1950), N.Y.U. Hotel and Restaurant Soc. (hon. life), Nat. Woman's Quota (charter mem. Greenbrier County), St. Charles Parish Assn., White Sulphur Springs Busy Bees, AARP, Senior

Friends. Republican. Roman Catholic. Home and Office: 207 Azalea Trl White Sulphur Springs WV 24986-2001

KAPPEL, MARLENE PHYLLIS, accountant; b. Detroit, Oct. 14, 1962; d. Fred and Frieda (Gendler) Sherman; m. Jerold M. Kappel, Jan. 8, 1984. Student, Baker Coll., 1991-93, Henry Ford Coll., 1993—. Acct. Wrubel, Wesley & Co. CPAS, Farmington Hills, Mich., 1980-88; acct. sec. Oak Park, Mich., 1988-90; acct. Max. M. Fisher, Detroit, 1990-94; pres. MPK Profl. Svcs., 1994—. Tutor Oakland County Literacy Program, Oakland County, Mich., 1985—. Jewish. Home: 1209 Woodfield Oaks Dr Apopka FL 32703-3618

KAPPELMAN, PEGGY A., college administrator; b. Lexington, Mo., Nov. 11, 1955; d. Charles M. and Bettie J. (Inbody) Blair; m. John J. Kappelman, Aug. 26, 1979; children: Kyla Lyn, Karly Ann, John Konner. BS in Home Econs. in Bus., Cen. Mo. State U., 1978, postgrad., 1993—; postgrad., Park Coll., 1990-92. Store mgr. Rader's Inc., Higginsville, Mo., 1977-82; data entry clk. Timothy H. Thurmon, CPA, Higginsville, 1983-85; instr. Internat. Acad. Merchandise Design, Kansas City, Mo., 1987-88; instr. Park Coll., Kansas City, Mo., 1988—, program adminstr. interior design dept., 1989—; asst. sales rep. Lucia Dave Parker, Overland Park, Kans., 1987—; cons. Mary Kay Cosmetics, Dallas, 1988—. Chmn. King and Queen Contest Higginsville Country Fair, 1978-80, The Country Fair Quilt Show, 1982-89. Mem. Fashion Group of Kansas City (chmn. career seminar 1992), Fashion Group Internat., Smocking Arts Guild Am. (chmn. regional seminar 1982). Lutheran. Home: 104 E 13th St Higginsville MO 64037 Office: Park College 934 Wyandotte Kansas City MO 64105

KAPTUR, MARCIA CAROLYN, congresswoman; b. Toledo, Ohio, June 17, 1946. B.A., U. Wis., 1968; M. Urban Planning, U. Mich., 1974; postgrad., U. Manchester, (Eng.), 1974. Urban planner; asst. dir. urban affairs domestic policy staff White House, 1977-79; mem. 98th-103rd Congresses from 9th Ohio dist., Washington, D.C., 1983—; mem. Appropriations com., subcom. Agrl., D.C., Veterans, HUD, indep. agys. Bd. dirs. Nat. Ctr. Urban Ethnic Affairs; adv. com. Gund Found.; exec. com. Lucas County Democratic Com.; mem. Dem. Women's Campaign Assn. Mem. Am. Planning Assn., Am. Inst. Cert. Planners, NAACP, Urban League, Polish Mus., U. Mich. Urban Planning Alumni Assn. (bd. dirs.), Polish Am. Hist. Assn. Roman Catholic. Clubs: Lucas County Dem. Bus. and Profl. Women's, Fulton County Dem. Women's. Office: US House of Reps 2104 Rayburn Washington DC 20515

KARABATSOS, ELIZABETH ANN, aerospace industry executive; b. Geneva, Nebr., Oct. 25, 1932; d. Karl Christian and Margaret Maurine (Emrich) Brinkman; m. Kimon Tom Karabatsos, Apr. 21, 1957 (div. Feb. 1981); children: Tom Kimon, Maurine Elizabeth, Karl Kimon. BS, U. Nebr., 1954; postgrad., Ariz. State U., 1980; Cert. contemporary exec. devel., George Washington U., 1985; M Orgnl. Mgmt., U. Phoenix, 1994. Instr. bus. Fairbury (Nebr.) High Sch., 1954-55; staff asst. U.S. Congress, Washington, 1955-60; with Karabatsos & Co. Pub. Relations, Washington, 1960-73; conf. asst. to asst. adminstr. and dep. adminstr. Gen. Services Adminstrn., Washington, 1973-76; dir. corr. Office Pres.-Elect, Washington, 1980; assoc. dir. adminstrv. services Pres. Personnel-White House, Washington, 1981; dept. asst.to Sec. and Dep. Sec. Def., Washington, 1981-86, asst. to, 1987-89; dir. govt. and civic affairs McDonnell Douglas Helicopter Co., Mesa, Ariz., 1989-90, gen. mgr. gen. svcs., 1990-92, co. ombudsman, community rels. exec., 1992-95; cons., counselor dispute resolution Ariz., 1995—. Mem. Nat. Mus. Women in Art, Washington; bd. dirs. U.S. C. of C. Com. on Labor & Tng.; mem. Gov.'s Sci. and Tech. Com.; mem. Ariz. Com. Employer Support the Guard and Res., 1991; active Gov. Com. for Ariz. Clean and Beautiful, World Affairs Coun. Ariz. Mem. AAUW, Women in Def., Am. Arbitration Assn., Ariz. Dispute Resolution Assn., Order Eastern Star, Pi Omega Pi, Pi Beta Phi. Episcopalian. Home: 7818 E Montebello Ave Scottsdale AZ 85250-6173

KARAIM, BETTY JUNE, librarian; b. Devils Lake, N.D., May 27, 1936; d. Erick Henry and Anna Caroline (Steen) Keck; m. William James Karaim, Dec. 7, 1955 (dec. 1983); children: Reed, Lisa, Ryan, Lynn, Rachel, Lee, Lara. BS in Edn., Mayville (N.D.) State U., 1958; postgrad., U. N.D., summer 1961; MLS, U. Okla., 1972; postgrad., No. Mont. Coll., 1979, 81. Libr. Cando (N.D.) High Sch., 1960-62; asst. libr., tchr. Mayville State Coll., 1962-79; libr. Havre (Mont.) Pub. Schs., 1979-82; libr. dir. Mayville State U., 1982—. Mem. ALA, NEA, Assn. of Coll. and Rsch. Librs. (nat. adv. coun. 1990—), Mountain Plains Libr. Assn., N.D. Libr. Assn. (chair acad. sect. 1987-88), N.D. Edn. Assn. (chpt. pres. 1985-89), N.D. Pub. Employees Assn. Democrat. Home: 320 1st St NW Mayville ND 58257-1107 Office: Mayville State U 330 3rd St NE Mayville ND 58257-1217

KARAKEY, SHERRY JOANNE, financial and real estate investment company executive, interior designer; b. Wendall, Idaho, Apr. 16, 1942; d. John Donald and Vera Ella (Frost) Kingery; children: Artist Roxanne, Buddy (George II), Kami JoAnne, Launi JoElla. Student, Ariz. State U., 1960. Corp. sec., treas. Karbel Metals Co., Phoenix, 1963-67; sec. to pub. Scottsdale (Ariz.) Daily Progress, 1969-72; with D-Velco Mfg. of Ariz., Phoenix, 1959-62, dir., exec. v.p., sec., treas., 1972-87; mng. ptnr. Karitage, Ltd., Scottsdale, 1987—.

KARALEKAS, ANNE, publishing executive; b. Boston, Nov. 6, 1946; d. Christus and Helen (Vogiantzis) K. AB, Wheaton Coll., Norton, Mass., 1968; AM, Harvard U., 1969, PhD, 1974. Chief project mgr. def. and arms control project Commn. on Orgn. of Govt. for Conduct of Fgn. Policy, Washington, 1974-75; sr. staff mem. Senate Select Com. on Intelligence, Washington, 1975-78; sr. assoc. McKinsey & Co., Washington, 1978-85; mktg. mgr. The Washington Post, 1985-87, dir. mktg., 1987-89; pub. Washington Post Mag., 1989—, dir. specialty products group, 1993—. Author: History of the CIA, 1976; contbr. articles and book revs. to profl. publs. Advisor fgn. policy Mondale-Ferraro Presdl. Campaign, Washington, 1984; trustee Wheaton Coll., Norton, 1985-88. Mem. Council on Fgn. Relations, Phi Beta Kappa. Greek Orthodox. Office: The Washington Post 1150 15th St NW Washington DC 20071-0002

KARAN, DONNA (DONNA FASKE), fashion designer; b. Forest Hills, N.Y., Oct. 2, 1948; m. Mark Karan; 1 child, Gabrielle. BFA, Parsons Sch. Design, 1987. With Addenda Co., to 1968; with Anne Klein & Co., N.Y.C., 1968-84; co-designer Anne Klein & Co., 1971-74, designer, 1974-84; owner, designer, ptnr., CEO Donna Karan Co., N.Y.C., 1984—. Showed first complete collection for Anne Klein & Co. in 1974; collaberator on Anne Klein collections with Louis dell'Olion. Recipient Coty award, 1977, Awards Coun. of Fashion Designers of Am., 1985, 86, 92, Frontrunner award Sara Lee Corp., 1992; co-recipient (with Louis dell'Olio) Coty Return award, 1981, Coty Hall of Fame citation, 1982, Coty award, 1984. Office: Donna Karan Co 550 7th Ave New York NY 10018-3203*

KARAVITE, CARLENE MARIE, psychologist, real estate property manager; b. Detroit, Jan. 17, 1939; d. Carl John Daniels and Leota Mae Hobbs Dunham; m. Charles George Schwartz Jr., Nov. 22, 1958 (div. 1980); children: Craig William, Charles Michael, Christine Marie Schwartz Milano; m. James Karavite, Jan., 1985. Student, U. Detroit, 1956-57, Oakland C.C., 1972-73, Oakland U., Rochester, Mich., 1973-74; BA cum laude, Wayne State U., 1990; MS in Clin. Psychology, Ea. Mich. U., 1992. Ltd. lic. psychologist, Mich. Sec. Reichhold Chem., Inc., Ferndale, Mich., 1957-59; bookkeeper Bee Kalt Travel, Royal Oak, Mich., 1978-79; optometric asst. Belmont Vision Ctr., Detroit, 1979-80; sec., data staff Dale L. Prentice Co., Oak Park, Mich., 1980-85; real estate agt. Berridge & Morrison, Royal Oak, Mich., 1985-86, Coldwell Banker Real Estate, Birmingham, Mich., 1987-89; salesperson AT&T, Troy, Mich., 1989; property mgr. Leota Dunham, Royal Oak, 1976—; ltd. lic. psychologist Midwestern Edn. Resource Ctr., Bloomfield Hills, Mich., 1994—, Advanced Counseling Svcs., P.C., Southfield, Mich., 1994—. Vol. and child advocate Family Focus, Birmingham, 1976-78, ct. apptd. supr., 1990-92. Named Outstanding Young Woman of the Yr. Jr. Women's Club of Am., 1966. Mem. Christian Assn. for Psychol. Studies, Mich. Psychol. Assn. (assoc.), Mich. Women Psychologists. Home: 226 E Windemere Royal Oak MI 48073-2678

KARBON, KELLY ANNE, auditor; b. Lapeer, Mich., Oct. 10, 1957; d. Gerald Donald and Monai Ann (Martin) White; m. Paul Alan Karbon, Apr. 23, 1983. BA, Alma Coll., 1979; M in Internat. Mgmt., Am. Grad. Sch. Internat. Mgmt., 1981. CPA, Ariz.; cert. mgmt. acct.; lic. real estate salesperson. Staff auditor Prudential Ins. Co., Scottsdale, Ariz., 1981-83, acctg. supr., 1983; sales assoc. Coldwell Banker Real Estate, Phoenix, 1984-87; owner, mgr. Kelly's Yogurt & Ice Cream, Inc., Scottsdale, 1987-88; acct. Mitchell Sweet & Assoc., Tempe, Ariz., 1989, asst. mgr. audit dept., 1989-90, acctg. mgr., 1990-93; sr. auditor Am. West Airlines, Inc., Tempe, 1994—. Advisor Jr. Achievement, Scottsdale, 1981-82. Mem. Inst. Mgmt. Accts., Inst. Internal Auditors, Scottsdale Bd. Realtors. Office: Am West Airlines Inc 4000 E Sky Harbor Blvd Phoenix AZ 85034

KARDON, JANET, museum director, curator; b. Phila.; d. Robert and Shirley (Drasin) Stolker; m. Robert Kardon, Nov. 19, 1955; children: Ross, Nina, Roy. BS in Edn., Temple U.; MA in Art History, U. Pa. Lectr. Phila. Coll. Art, 1968-75, dir. exhbns., 1975-78; dir. Inst. Contemporary Art, Phila., 1978-89, Am. Craft Mus., N.Y.C., 1989—; cons., panel mem. Nat. Endowment for Arts, 1975—; mus. panel mem. Pa. Coun. on Arts, Phila., 1988—; U.S. commr. Venice Biennale, Venice, 1980. Curated and created essays for 30 exhbns., including Labyrinths, Time, Artists Sets and Costumes, Laurie Anderson, Robert Mapplethorpe, David Salle, Gertrude and Otto Natzler; editor: Twentieth Century American Craft: A Centenary Project, 1900-1920. Grantee Nat. Endowment for Arts, 1978. Mem. Assn. Art Mus. Dirs. Club: Cosmopolitan. Home: Rittenhouse Pla 1901 Walnut St Apt 21A Philadelphia PA 19103-4664 Office: Am Craft Mus 40 W 53d St New York NY 10019

KAREN, LINDA TRICARICO, fashion designer; b. Bklyn., June 8, 1961; d. John William and Phyllis Jean (D'Addario) T. Student, Bucks County Community Coll., 1978-79; AAS, Fashion Inst. Tech., 1992. Retail mgr. Canadians, Brooks, Casual Corner, 1980-83; coord. sales and design Sure Snap Corp., N.Y.C., 1983-84; asst. designer E.S. Sutton Inc., N.Y.C., 1984-86; designer Good 'N Plenty Inc., N.Y.C., 1986-90; designer, merchandiser Leonard A. Feinberg, Inc., N.Y.C., 1991—; free-lance illustrator, designer. Contbr. fashion trend reports, Milan, Italy, 1984, Rome, 1985, Milan and Florence, Italy, 1986, London and Paris, 1987, Montreal, Can., 1988, 94, L.A., 1993. Mem. Fashion Soc., NAFE. Democrat. Roman Catholic. Home: 316 Berry Rd Monroe NY 10950

KARKUT, BONNIE LEE, dental office manager; b. Muskegon, Mich., Feb. 7, 1934; d. Fay Henry Hohenstein and Doris Catherine (Nelson) Collins; m. Joseph Paul Karkut, Dec. 29, 1956; children: Deborah, Joseph, Bradley, Elizabeth. BA in Speech Pathology, Mich. State U., 1955; postgrad. studies, U. Hawaii, 1956, U. Mich., Saginaw, 1959. Cert. speech pathologist. Speech pathologist Pub. Schs., Muskegon, Mich., 1955-56, Saginaw, Mich., 1956-59; office mgr. Dental Office, Naples, Fla., 1984—. Pres. Saginaw (Mich.) County Dental Aux., 1978-79. Mem. AAUW, Fla. Dental Assn. (dental asst. and aux. sect.), Delta Zeta (program chmn. 1988-89), Panhellenic Soc. Republican. Roman Catholic. Home: 2570 Crayton Rd Naples FL 33940-4020 Office: Dental Office 850 Central Ave Ste 103 Naples FL 33940-6099

KARL, HELEN WEIST, pediatric anesthesia educator, researcher; b. N.Y.C., Oct. 28, 1948; d. Edward C. and Louise (Stursberg) Weist; m. Stephen R. Karl, June 1, 1974 (div. 1990); children: Katherine L., Thomas R., John W. BA in Philosophy, Smith Coll., 1970; MD, U. Va., 1976. Diplomate Am. Bd. Anesthesiology, Nat. Bd. Med. Examiners. Intern in surgery Hartford (Conn.) Hosp., 1976-77, resident in anesthesia, 1977-79; fellow in pediatric anesthesiology Children's Hosp. of Phila., 1979-81; staff anesthesiologist St. Christopher's Hosp. for Children, Phila., 1981; asst. prof. anesthesiology and pediatrics Pa. State U., Hershey, 1981-90; asst. prof. anesthesiology U. Washington, 1990—; Parker B. Francis fellow in pulmonary rsch. Pa. State U., Hershey, 1986-88. Contbr. articles to profl. jours. Grantee Am. Lung Assn. of Pa., 1986-88. Fellow Am. Acad. Pediatrics (sec. on anesthesiology com. on drugs 1989—); mem. Am. Soc. Anesthesiologists (task force for preparation self-evaluation exam. 1982-83), Am. Med. Women's Assn., Internat. Anesthesia Rsch. Soc., Wash. Soc. Anesthesiologists, Anesthesia Patient Safety Found. Office: Children's Hosp & Med Ctr 4800 Sand Point Way NE Seattle WA 98105-3916

KARLE, ISABELLA, chemist; b. Detroit, Dec. 2, 1921; d. Zygmunt Apolonaris and Elizabeth (Graczyk) Lugoski; m. Jerome Karle, June 4, 1942; children: Louise Hanson, Jean Marianne, Madeleine Tawney. BS in Chemistry, U. Mich., 1941, MS in Chemistry, 1942, PhD, 1944; DSc (hon.), U. Mich., 1976, Wayne State U., 1979, U. Md., 1986; LHD (hon.), Georgetown U., 1984. Assoc. chemist U. Chgo., 1944; instr. chemistry U. Mich., Ann Arbor, 1944-46; physicist Naval Rsch. Lab., Washington, 1946—; Paul Ehrlich lectr. NIH, 1991; mem. exec. com. Am. Peptide Symposium, 1975-81, adv. bd. Chem. and Engring. News, 1986-89. Mem. editorial bd. Biopolymers Jour., 1975—, Internat. Jour. Peptide Protein Rsch., 1981—; contbr. articles to profl. jours. Recipient Superior Civilian Service award USN, 1965, Fed. Women's award U.S. Govt., 1973, Annual Achievement award Soc. Women Engrs., 1968, Annual Achievement award U. Mich., 1987, Dexter Conrad award Office Naval Rsch., 1980, WISE Lifetime Achievement award Women in Sci. and Engring., 1986, award for disting. achievement in sci. Sec. of Navy, 1987, Gregori Aminoff prize Swedish Royal Acad. Scis., 1988, Adm. Parsons award Navy League U.S., 1988, Ann. Achievement award CCNY, 1989; Bijvoet medal U. Utrecht, The Netherlands, 1990, Vincent du Vigneaud award Gordon Conf. (Peptides), 1992, Bower Sci. award Franklin Inst., 1993; named to Michigan Women's Hall of Fame, 1989, Chem. Scis. award Nat. Acad. Scis., 1995. Fellow Am. Acad. Arts Scis., Am. Inst. Chemists. (Chem. Pioneer award 1984); mem. NAS (Chem. Scis. award, 1995), Am. Crystallographic Assn. (pres. 1976), Am. Chem. Soc. (Garvan award 1976, Hillebrand award 1970), Am. Phys. Soc., Am. Philos. Soc., Biophys. Soc. Home: 6304 Lakeview Dr Falls Church VA 22041 Office: Naval Rsch Lab Code 6030 Washington DC 20375-5341

KARLIN, MARCIA SUSAN, artist; b. Lakewood, Ohio, July 14, 1949; d. Donald Francis and Barbara Elizabeth (Sollenberger) Brown; m. Larry Michael Karlin, Aug. 29, 1971; children: Matthew, Lindsay. Student, U. Mich., 1967-69; BA with highest honors, U. Iowa, 1972. Artist Ill. Artisans Program, Chgo., 1986—, Artisan Shop & Gallery, Wilmette, Ill., 1986—, Gallery 500, Elkins Park, Pa., 1990—, Vale Craft Gallery, Chgo., 1993—. Editor newsletter FACET, Chgo., 1991-95; featured artist Great Am. Quilts, 1987, Visions: Quilts of a New Decade, 1990, Sunday Chgo. Tribune, 1991, Contemporary Quilts Wall Calendar, 1992, Sunday Chgo. Sun-Times, 1993, Artists and Graphic Designers Market, 1995. Recipient Judges Merit award So. Arts Fedn., 1988, Best of Show award Virginia Churchill Bath, 1990, 2d Place award Fla. State U., 1993, Juror's Outstanding Commendation award Chautauqua Crafts Alliance, 1993. Mem. Chgo. Artists' Coalition, Am. Craft Coun., Studio Art Quilt Assocs., Surface Design Assn., Coun. of Am. Embroiders, Am. Quilter's Soc., Phi Beta Kappa.

KARLL, JO ANN, state agency administrator, lawyer; b. St. Louis, Nov. 16, 1948; d. Joseph H. and Dorothy Olga (Pyle) K.; m. William Austin Hernlund, Sept. 9, 1990. Bar: Mo. 1993. Ins. claims adjuster, 1967-88; state rep. Mo. Gen. Assembly dist. 104, 1991-92; mem. from dist. 105 Mo. Gen. Assembly, 1992-93; dir. Mo. State Divsn. Worker's Compensation, Jefferson City, 1993—. Mem. exec. bd. Jefferson County Dem. Club, 1988-92; committeewoman Jefferson County Ctrl. Dem. Com., Rock Twp., 1988-91; bd. dirs. Mid-East Area Agy. on Aging, 1991-93. Mem. NOW, LWV, Women Legislators of Mo. (treas. 1991-93), Mo. Women's Network, Nat. Women's Polit. Caucus, Bus. and Profl. Women's Clubs (treas. 1987-89), Rock Twp. Dem. Club, Meramec-High Ridge Twp. Dem. Club. Democrat. Office: Mo St Divsn Worker's Compensation 3515 W Truman Blvd Jefferson City MO 65102

KARLOVEC, SHELLEY TAYLOR, sales service manager; b. Council Grove, Kans., July 24, 1958; d. Byron Eugene and Barbara Frances (Elliott) Taylor; m. Bradley Don Karlovec, Mar. 9, 1991. BS in Edn., Memphis State U., 1980. Substitute tchr. Shelby County Schs., Memphis, 1980-81; receptionist Exec. of Memphis, 1981-82, customer svc. rep., 1982-83; sales svc. rep. Champion Internat., Oxford, Miss., 1983-84; ter. sales rep. Champin - U.S. Plywood, Charlotte, N.C., 1984-87; sales svc. mgr. U.S. Plywood - Georgia Pacific, Gaylord, Mich., 1987—. Bd. dirs. Big Bros./Big Sisters, 1991; chair fun drive United Way, Gaylord, 1993-94, v.p., 1994—; counselor Evang. Free Ch.; active Alpinfest Bd., Cmty. Found. Mem. Rotary. Republican. Home: 509 S Court St Gaylord MI 49735 Office: Georgia Pacific Corp 2212 Dickerson Rd Gaylord MI 49735

KARMAN, ROBIN-ADAIR, real estate company executive; b. Covington, Va., Jan. 31, 1955; d. Louis A. and Barbara L. (DeSanto) K. Student, Wilmington (Del.) Coll., 1975-76, Cleve. State U., 1976-77. V.p. Mid-Atlantic Communities, Plymouth Meeting, Pa., 1979-87; pres., ptnr. Mid-Atlantic Sales & Mktg., Plymouth Meeting, Pa., 1987-90; CEO Karman Communities Corp., New Hope, Pa., 1990—. Coun. mem. governing body Borough of New Hope, 1992; bd. mem. Bucks County Family Svcs., 1993—. Home: 39 S Sugan Rd # 446 New Hope PA 18938-1428

KARMEL, ROBERTA SEGAL, lawyer, educator; b. Chgo., May 4, 1937; d. J. Herzl and Eva E. (Elin) Segal; m. Paul R. Karmel, June 9, 1957 (dec. Aug. 1994); children: Philip, Solomon, Jonathan, Miriam. B.A., Radcliffe Coll.; LL.B., NYU, 1962. Bar: N.Y. 1962, U.S. Dist. Ct. (so. and ea. dists.) N.Y. 1964, U.S. Ct. Appeals (2d cir.) 1968, U.S. Supreme Ct. 1968, U.S. Ct. Appeals (3d cir.) 1987. With SEC, 1962-69, 77-80, asst. regional adminstr., until 1969; commr. SEC, Washington, 1977-80; assoc. firm Willkie Farr & Gallagher, N.Y.C., 1969-72; partner firm Rogers & Wells, N.Y.C., 1972-77, 80-85, of counsel, 1987-94; of counsel Kelley Drye & Warren, N.Y.C., 1995—, ptnr., 1987-94, of counsel, 1995—; adj. prof. law Bklyn. Law Sch., 1973-77, 82-85, prof., 1985—, co-dir. Ctr. for Study of Internat. Bus. Law; bd. dirs. Mallinckrodt Group, Inc., Kemper Nat. Ins. Cos.; trustee Practicing Law Inst. Author: Regulation by Prosecution, 1982; contbr. articles to legal publs. Fellow Am. Bar Found.; mem. ABA, Assn. Bar City N.Y., Am. Law Inst., Fin. Women's Assn. Home: 26 Hopke Ave Hastings On Hudson NY 10706-2310 Office: Kelley Drye & Warren 101 Park Ave New York NY 10178-0002

KARNATH, JOAN EDNA, editor; b. St. Paul, July 14, 1947; d. Charles Omar and Marie Edna (Gorg) League; m. Richard John, July 24, 1971 (div. Mar. 1981). BS in Elem. Edn., Winona State U., 1970, MS in Elem. Edn., 1978. Tchr. Ind. Sch. Dist. 234, Rushford, Minn., 1971-82; beauty cons. Mary Kay Cosmetics, Dallas, 1982-84; hostess Ramada Hotel, Inc., St. Paul, 1983-84; coord., computer ctr. 3M Co., St. Paul; lead editor Unisys Corp., St. Paul, 1984—; mem, sec. Rushford Edn. Assn., 1971-82. Editorial advisor Info. DesigNews, 1990—. Precinct Chairwoman Ind. Reps., Winona, 1980-81; Sec. Eden Home Assn., Eagan, 1987-92. Recipient award of merit Soc. Tech. Comm., 1989, 94, award of distinction, 1993, 94, Unisys Achievement award, 1990. Mem. AAUW, NEA, Minn. Edn. Assn., U. Minn. Global Edn. Com., Profl. Editors Network, Unisys Profl. Women's Forum, Toastmasters Internat. Republican. Roman Catholic. Home: 4423B Clover Ln Saint Paul MN 55122-2437 Office: Unisys Corp 2276 Highcrest Rd Saint Paul MN 55113-2529

KARNATH, LORIE MARY LORRAINE, bank officer, consultant; b. Chgo.; d. Albert Welch and Carole Margaret (Bohrer) K. m. Robert Emil Roethenmund, Jan. 8, 1994. BA, Fordham U., 1981; MBA, Inst. Superior des Etudes Adminstrv., Fontainebleau, France, 1990. Loan officer Chem. Bank, N.Y.C., 1981-84; team leader Credit Suisse, N.Y.C., 1984-86; assoc. Kidder, Peabody, N.Y.C. and Madrid, 1986-91; cons. E.M.C. Group, Hamburg, Fed. Republic of Germany, 1991—. Contbg. author: Adventure Challenge, 1988; contbg. editor Next Mag., 1984-85. Mem. N.Y. Acad. Scis., Explorers Club (internat. mem.). Home: 6 Passage Chesnard, La Couture Boussey 27750, France

KARNES, LUCIA ROONEY, psychologist; b. Moncton, N.B., Can., Mar. 9, 1921; d. Charles William and Jean Waring (Robson) Rooney; m. Thomas Campbell Karnes, June 7, 1946; children; Eleanore, Campbell, Timothy, Charles. BS, Ga. State Coll., 1942; MA, Emory U., 1946; PhD, U. N.C., 1967. Tchr. Decatur Girls High, Decatur, Ga., 1942-46; tchr. Summit Sch., Winston-Salem, N.C., 1947; prof. Salem Coll., Winston-Salem, 1949-54, 60-77; lang. therapist Bowman Grey Sch. Medicine, Winston-Salem, 1950-57, Orton Reading Ctr., Winston-Salem, 1957-72; dir. Ctr. for Spl. Edn., Salem Coll., Winston-Salem, 1972-77; pvt. practice psychology Winston-Salem, 1977—; dyslexic cons. Jefferson Acad., Winston-Salem, 1980—, Greenfield Sch., Wilson, 1986—, Wingate (N.C.) Coll., 1988—. Creator Using Computers in Psychology courses, 1972; author (video) Teaching Dyslexics, 1975. Founder, pres. state bd. LWV, Winston-Salem, 1953; pres. state bd. AAUW, Winston-Salem, 1950-54; bd. dirs. YWCA, Winston-Salem, 1950-54; v.p. bd. dirs. Arts Coun., Winston-Salem, 1954-60. Named Outstanding Reading Tchr., Reading Assn., Winston-Salem, 1982. Mem. Orton Dyslexia Soc. (v.p. bd. dirs. 1960-77), Am. Psychol. Assn., N.C. Psychol. Assn., Assn. for Children with Learning Disabilities (v.p. bd. dirs. 1972—), Sorosis Club, Delta Kappa Gamma. Democrat. Presbyterian. Home: 200 Lamplighter Cir Winston Salem NC 27104-3419

KARNOWSKY, DEBORAH A., advertising agency executive. V.p., sr. v.p. W.B. Doner & Co., Southfield, Mich., until 1989; exec. v.p., creative dir. Lintas Campbell-Ewald, Warren, Mich., 1989—. Recipient numerous creative awards; named Midwest Creative All-Star, AdWeek MAg., 1991. Office: Lintas Campbell-Ewald 30400 Van Dyke Ave Warren MI 48093*

KAROL, MERYL HELENE, immunotoxicology educator; b. N.Y.C., Aug. 10, 1940; m. Paul Jason; children: Darcie, Deverin, Meredith. BS, Cornell U., 1961; PhD, Columbia U., 1967. NIH fellow SUNY-Stony Brook, 1967-68; research assoc. U. Pitts., 1974-76, research asst. prof., 1976-79, assoc. prof., 1979-85, prof. environ. and indsl. health, 1985—; advisor numerous govt. health adv. bds., agys.; lectr. in field. Assoc. editor Jour. Chem. Rsch. in Toxicological Environ. Health, Toxicology and Ecotoxicology News; mem. editl. bd. Methods in Toxicology; contbr. articles to profl. jours. Recipient Women in Sci. award U. Mich., 1986, Rachel Carson award, 1993. Mem. AAAS, Am. Chem. Soc., Am. Thoracic Soc., Am. Conf. Govt. Indsl. Hygienists, Soc. Toxicology (v.p. 1993, pres. 1994, Frank R. Blood award), N.Y. Acad. Scis., Am. Assn. Immunologists. Avocations: sports, decorating, design, travel. Office: U Pitts Dept Environ Occupational Health 260 Kappa Dr Pittsburgh PA 15238-2818

KARP, JUDITH ESTHER, oncologist, science administrator; b. San Diego, July 15, 1946; d. Louis Moses and Bella Sarah (Perlman) K.; m. Stanley Howard Freedman, Sept. 21, 1975. BA in Chemistry, Mills Coll., Oakland, Calif., 1966; MD, Stanford U., 1971. Diplomate Am. Bd. Internal Medicine. Intern in medicine, jr. resident in medicine Stanford Hosps., 1971-72; asst. resident in medicine Johns Hopkins Hosp., 1972-73; clin. and rsch. fellow oncology Johns Hopkins Med. Sch., 1973-75, instr. oncology and medicine, 1975-78, asst. prof., 1978-85, assoc. prof., 1985-92; spl. asst. to dir. Nat. Cancer Inst., NIH, 1990-94, asst. dir. applied sci., 1995—; mem. consensus com. Immuno-compromised Host Soc., 1987-88. Recipient Aurelia Henry Reinhardt prize Mills Coll., 1966, Cancer Rsch. award Washington chpt. Awards for Rsch. Coll. Scientists, 1975; San Diego Heart Assn. grantee, 1965-67; Am. Cancer Soc. Jr. clin. faculty fellow, 1976-79; recipient Resolution of Commendation, State of Md., 1982, Recognition award City of Balt., 1984. Mem. Am. Soc. Hematology, Am. Soc. Clin. Oncology, Cell Kinetics Soc. (clin. counsellor governing council 1985-87), Am. Soc. Microbiology, Immunocompromised Host Soc., Internat. Soc. Exptl. Hematology, Nat. Bd. Med. Examiners, Phi Beta Kappa. Democrat. Jewish. Home: 3422 Manor Hill Rd Baltimore MD 21208-1824 Office: Nat Cancer Inst Rm 11a27 Bethesda MD 20892

KARPAN, KATHLEEN MARIE, former state official, lawyer, journalist; b. Rock Springs, Wyo., Sept. 1, 1942; d. Thomas Michael and Pauline Ann (Taucher) K. B.S. in Journalism, U. Wyo., 1964, M.A. in Am. Studies, 1975; J.D., U. Oreg., 1978. Bar: D.C. 1979, Wyo. 1983, U.S. Dist. Ct. Wyo., U.S. Ct. Appeals (D.C. and 10th cirs.). Asst. news editor Cody Enterprise, Wyo., 1964; press asst. to U.S. Congressman Teno Roncalio U.S. Ho. of Reps., Washington, 1965-67, 71-72, adminstrv. asst., 1973-74; asst. news editor Wyo. Eagle, Cheyenne, 1967; free-lance writer, 1968; teaching asst. dept. history U. Wyo., 1969-70; desk editor Canberra Times, Australia, 1970; dep. dir. Office Congl. Relations, Econ. Devel. Adminstrn. U.S. Dept. Commerce, Washington, 1979-80, atty. advisor Office of Chief Counsel, Econ. Devel. Adminstrn., 1980-81; campaign mgr. Rodger McDaniel for U.S. Senator, Wyo., 1981-82; asst. atty. gen. State of Wyo., Cheyenne, 1983-84, dir. Dept. Health and Social Services, 1984-86, sec. of state, 1987-94. Del. Dem. Nat. Conv., San Francisco, 1984, Atlanta, 1988, N.Y.C., 1992;

mem. bd. govs. Nat. Dem. Leadership Coun., drafting com. Dem. Nat. Platform, Santa Fe, 1992. W.R. Coe fellow, 1969. Mem. Wyo. Bar Assn., Bus. and Profl. Women, Rotary, Zonta. Roman Catholic. Home: 410 W 2nd Ave Cheyenne WY 82001-1211 Office: Wyo Sec of State State Capitol Cheyenne WY 82002

KARPATKIN, RHODA HENDRICK, consumer information organization executive, lawyer; b. N.Y.C., June 7, 1930; d. Charles and Augusta (Arkin) Hendrick; m. Marvin Karpatkin, June 16, 1951 (dec.); children: Deborah Hendrick, Herbert Isaac, Jeremy Charles. BA, Bklyn. Coll., 1951; LLB, Yale U., 1953. Bar: N.Y. 1954. Pvt. practice law, 1954-74; ptnr. Karpatkin & Karpatkin, 1958-61, Karpatkin, Ohrenstein & Karpatkin, N.Y.C., 1961-74; pres. Consumers Union of U.S. Inc., Yonkers, N.Y., 1974—; pres. Internat. Orgn. Consumers Unions, 1984-91, v.p., 1991—; Spl. counsel for decentralization N.Y.C. Bd. Edn., 1969-70; adj. prof. dept. urban studies Queens Coll., 1972-74; commr. Nat. Commn. on New Tech. Uses of Copyrighted Works, 1975-78; mem. Pres.'s Com. Trade Policy and Negotiation, 1993—. Contbg. author: Current School Problems, 1971, Consumer Education in the Human Services; contbr. articles to profl. publs. Mem. Local Sch. Bd. 5, N.Y.C., 1966-70, chmn., 1967-69; mem. Community Sch. Bd. 3, N.Y.C., 1970-71; mem. com. acad. freedom ACLU, 1973-84; mem. Pres.'s Commn. for Nat. Agenda for the Eighties., 1979-80; trustee Pub. Edn. Assn., 1972-85. Mem. ABA (commn. on law and the economy 1976-79, commn. to reduce costs and delay 1978-84, commn. access to justice 2000 1993—), Assn. of Bar of City of N.Y. (com. consumer affairs 1969-80, chmn. 1974-79, com. on internat. human rights 1980-83, audit com. 1982-83, com. Ea. European affairs), Nat. Inst. for Dispute Resolution (bd. dirs. 1982-89), Assn. Yale Alumni (rep.-at-large 1982-85). Office: Consumers Union US Inc 101 Truman Ave Yonkers NY 10703-1057

KARPELLS, SHARON THERESA, molecular biologist, laboratory administrator; b. N.Y.C., Nov. 1, 1961; d. Charles Thaddeus and Mary Edwina (Baisley) K. BA, Coll. of Our Lady of the Elms, Chicopee, Mass., 1983; MS, U. Mass., 1987, PhD, 1989. Postdoctoral rsch. assoc. U. Wash., Seattle, 1989-91, VA Med. Ctr., Seattle, 1991-92; dir. Molecular Biology Lab. Baystate Med. Ctr., Springfield, Mass., 1992—. Contbr. sci. rsch. articles to profl. jours. Mem. AAAS, Am. Soc. for Human Genetics. Office: Baystate Med Ctr 759 Chestnut St Springfield MA 01199-1001

KARPEN, MARIAN JOAN, financial executive; b. Detroit, June 16, 1944; d. Cass John and Mary (Jagiello) K. AB, Vassar Coll., 1966; postgrad. U. Paris at Sorbonne, N.Y. U. Grad. Sch. Bus., 1974-77. New Eng. corr. Women's Wear Daily, Fairchild Publs.-Capital Cities Communications, 1966-68, Paris fashion editor, TV and radio commentator Capital Cities Network, 1968-69; fashion editor Boston Herald Traveler, 1969-71; nat. syndicated newspaper columnist and photojournalist Queen Features Syndicate, N.Y.C., 1971-73; account exec. Blyth Eastman Dillon, N.Y.C., 1973-75, Oppenheimer, N.Y.C., 1975-76; v.p., mcpl. bond coordinator Faulkner Dawkins & Sullivan (merged Shearson Hayden Stone), N.Y.C., 1976-77; mgr. retail mcpl. bond dept. Warburg Paribas Becker-A.G. Becker (merger Becker Paribas into Merrill Lynch), N.Y.C., 1977-79, sr. v.p. and prin., 1977-84; sr. v.p., ltd. ptnr. Bear Stearns & Co., 1984-87, assoc. dir., 1987-90; pres., prin. The EuroEast Group, Inc., N.Y.C., 1990—; founder, pres. CEO The Forum WorkTalk..., Inc., N.Y.C., 1992—; writer, lectr. fin. seminars, 1978—; former mem. bus. adv. council U.S. Rep. Senate. Founder, pres. WorkTalk, St. John the Martyr Ch., N.Y.C., 1992, creator newsletter "The WorkTalk Times"; mem. benefit com. March of Dimes, 1983; mem. Torchlight Ball com. Internat. Games for Disabled, 1984, other benefit coms.; friend vol. Whitney Mus. Am. Art. Recipient Superior Prodn. award Becker Paribas, 1983. Mem. Nat. Assn. Securities Dealers (registered rep.), N.Y. Stock Exchange (registered rep.), N.Y.C. Women's Econ. Roundtable, Am. Soc. Profl. and Exec. Women, AAUW, U.S. Figure Skating Assn., Fishing Club of Am. (angler's honor roll), English Speaking Union, Vassar Club N.Y. (bd. dirs., mem. exec. com., ex-officio), Skating Club (N.Y.C. and Boston). Past editorial bd. Retirement Planning Strategist; contbr. articles and photographs to newspapers and mags. Office: WorkTalk 184 E 76th St and Washington Ave New York NY 10021

KARPIEL, DORIS CATHERINE, state legislator; b. Chgo., Sept. 21, 1935; d. Nicholas and Mary (McStravick) Feinen; m. Harvey Karpiel, 1955 (div.); children—Sharon, Lynn, Laura, Barry. A.A., Morton Jr. Coll., 1955; B.A., No. Ill. U., 1976. Real estate sales assoc. Bundy-Morgan BHG; coordinator Bloomingdale Twp. Republican Presdl. Hdqrs., Ill., 1960, 64, 68; former pres. Bloomingdale Twp. Rep. Orgn.; mem. Twp. Ofcls. of Ill.; trustee Bloomingdale Twp., 1974-75, supr., 1975-80; precinct committeewoman Bloomingdale Twp. Rep. Central Com., 1972, chmn., 1978-80; mem. Ill. Ho. of Reps., 1979-82, Ill. State Senate from 25th Dist., 1984—. Mem. Am. Legislators Exchange Council, Rep. Orgn. Schaumberg Twp.; former sec. DuPage County Suprs. Assn.; former sec. DuPage County Twp. Ofcls.; mem. DuPage County Women's Rep. Orgn., Meml. Hosp. Guild, Am. Cancer Soc. Mem. LWV, DuPage Bd. Realtors, Pi Sigma Alpha. Clubs: Bloomingdale Roselle and Streamwood Country, University Women's, St. Walters Women's. Office: Ill State Senate State Capitol Springfield IL 62706 Address: 1076 Ridgefield Cir Carol Stream IL 60188*

KARR, CAROLYN P.G., lawyer; b. San Francisco, Dec. 14, 1953; d. Lawrence and Doris E. (Holt) Goldberg. AA, Louise Salinger Acad. Fashion, 1977; student, Gemological Inst. Am., 1978-80; BA summa cum laude, UCLA, 1988; JD, Stanford U., 1991. Bar: Calif. 1991, D.C. 1994. Assoc. Milbank, Tweed, Hadley & McCloy, L.A., 1991-93, Curtis, Mallet-Prevost, et al, Washington, 1993-94; atty. advisor Office of Gen. Counsel, U.S. Agy. for Internat. Devel., Washington, 1994—; intern Internat. Inst. for Unification of Pvt. Law, Rome, Italy, 1990; vis. faculty U. Autonoma de Baja Calif., Mexico, 1992. Sec., treas. Citizens Com. to Preserve Beverly Hills (Calif.) Landmarks, 1986-88. Mem. U.S. Com./Internat. Coun. Monuments and Sites, World Affairs Coun., Smithsonian Instn., Nat. Trust for Hist. Preservation, Phi Beta Kappa. Democrat. Office: Office of Gen Counsel USAID Dept State Bldg 320 21st St NW Washington DC 20523

KARR, ELIZABETH HARDEN, educator; b. Springfield, Mass., Aug. 29, 1923; d. Raymond Leo and Hannah Harden (Hersey) Flanagan; m. Christy Karr, Dec. 22, 1945 (div. Sept. 1978); children: Christy Jr., Richard Harden, Elizabeth Hersey Rodbell. BA summa cum laude, Brown U., 1945; MA in Tchg., Am. Internat. Coll., 1974, postgrad., 1986. Tchr. MacDuffie Sch., Springfield, 1965-69, Ursuline Acad., Springfield, 1969-72; tchr., chmn. English dept. Springfield Pub. Schs., 1972-93; adj. prof. Am. Internat. Coll., 1993—. Contbr. articles to profl. jours. Mem. Friends of the Libr., Springfield; patron Springfield Libr. & Museums Assn., 16 Acres Civic Assn. Mem. Nat. Coun. Tchrs. English, Am. Fedn. Tchrs., Springfield Fedn. Tchrs., Coll. Club (Springfield), DAR, NOW, Mayflower Soc. Mass., English Speaking Union, Phi Beta Kappa. Home: 1091 S Branch Pkwy Springfield MA 01118-1930

KARRER, CAROL CONVERSE, nurse educator; b. Columbus, Ohio, Dec. 10, 1940; d. Edward Beck and Elma Louise (McClain) Converse; m. George Henry Karrer, Aug. 26, 1961; children: Andrew (dec.), Matthew, James. Dipl. Nursing, Grant Hosp. sch. Nursing, Columbus, 1961; BSN, Ohio State U., 1963, MSN, 1964, PhD in Family Rels. and Human Devel., 1984. RN, Ohio. Staff nurse, asst. head nurse Grant Hosp., Columbus, 1961-63; instr., rsch. assoc. Ohio State U. Sch. Nursing, Columbus, 1964-67; organist and presch. music tchr. St. Andrew Presbyn. Ch., Columbus, 1967-71; instr. nursing Grant Hosp. Sch. Nursing, Columbus, 1971-72; nursing coord. Ohio State U. Sch. Nursing, Columbus, 1973-75; asst. prof. nursing Ohio Wesleyan U., Delaware, 1976-80; prof. nursing Franklin U., Columbus, 1981—; cons. evaluator North Cen. Assn. Colls. and Schs., Commn. on Instns. of Higher Edn., Chgo., 1991—. Contbr. articles to profl. jours., chpt. to book. Ohio State U. Home Econs. Alumni Assn. rsch. grantee, 1978. Mem. Mid-Ohio Nurses Assn. (pres. 1986-90), Ohio Bd. Nursing (chmn. ednl. adv. com. 1989-90). Home: 536 Haymore Ave N Worthington OH 43085-2445

KARRER, JENNIFER HILL, neurophysiologist; b. Nashville, July 7, 1956; d. Robert Milton Hill and Peggy Jane (Hudgens) Sewall; m. Rathe Stevens Karrer, Mar. 8, 1930; children: Kimberly, Jacqueline, Cynthia. BS, U. Tenn., 1985, PhD, 1988; MS, U. Mont., 1986. Rsch. asst. U. Mont., Missoula, 1985-86; teaching assoc. U. Tenn., Knoxville, 1986-88; asst. prof. U. Wis., Oshkosh, 1988-93; researcher U. Kans. Med. Ctr., Kansas City, 1993—. Contbr. articles to profl. jours. Mem. Soc. Neurosci. Democrat. Home: 302 Homestead Dr Lawrence KS 66049 Office: U Kans Med Ctr Physiology Dept Kansas City KS 66160

KARRER, TRACY ANNE, sensory analyst; b. Akron, Nov. 8, 1954; d. Max Crawford and Joanne Barbara (Sherts) K. BA in Theatre, Eckerd Coll., 1976; postgrad., City Coll., Santa Barbara, 1980-83; BA in Psychobiology, U. Calif., 1985; PhD in Physiol. Psychology, Yale U., 1991. Florist, clk. Nelsons Greenhouse Gallery, Santa Cruz, Calif., 1984; bookstore clk. Upstart Crow & Co., Santa Cruz, 1984-85; assoc. rsch. scientist Yale U., New Haven, 1989-91; sr. sensory analyst Internat. Flavors and Fragrance, Union Beach, N.J., 1992—. Contbr. articles to profl. jours. Grass Found. fellowship Woods Hole Labs., 1987, Friday Harbor Lab., 1986. Mem. Assn. for Chemoreception Scis. Office: Internat Flavors and Fragrances R&D 1515 Hwy 36 Union Beach NJ 07735

KARSEN, SONJA PETRA, retired Spanish educator; b. Berlin, Apr. 11, 1919; came to U.S., 1938, naturalized, 1945; d. Fritz and Erna (Heidermann) K. Titulo de Bachiller, 1937; BA, Carleton Coll., 1939; MA (scholar in French), Bryn Mawr Coll., 1941; PhD, Columbia U., 1950. Instr. Spanish Lake Erie Coll., Painesville, Ohio, 1943-45; instr. modern langs. U. P.R., 1945-46; instr. Spanish Syracuse U., 1947-50, Bklyn. Coll., 1950-51; asst. to dep. dir. gen. UNESCO, 1951-52, Latin Am. Desk, tech. assistance dept., 1952-53, mem. tech. assistance mission Costa Rica, 1954; asst. prof. Spanish Sweet Briar Coll., Va., 1955-57; assoc. prof., chmn. dept. Romance langs. Skidmore Coll., Saratoga Springs, N.Y., 1957-61, chmn. dept. modern langs. and lits., 1961-79, prof. Spanish, 1961-87, prof. emerita, 1987; cons. Hudson-Mohawk Assn. Colls. and Univs., 1990; Faculty rsch. lectr. Skidmore Coll., 1963; Fulbright lectr. Free U., Berlin, 1968; mem. adv. and nominating com. Books Abroad, 1965-67. Author: Guillermo Valencia, Colombian Poet, 1951, Educational Development in Costa Rica with UNESCO's Technical Assistance, 1951-54, 1954, Jaime Torres Bodet: A Poet in a Changing World, 1963, Selected Poems of Jaime Torres Bodet, 1964, Versos y prosas de Jaime Torres Bodet, 1966, Jaime Torres Bodet, 1971, Ensayos de Literatura E Historia Iberoamericana/Essays on Iberoamerican Literature and History, 1988, Papers on Foreign Languages, Literature and Culture, 1982-87, 88, Bericht Über Den Vater: Fritz Karsen 1885-1951, 1993; translator: The Role of the Americas in History (Leopoldo Zea), 1992; editor Lang. Assn. Bull., 1980-83; mem. editorial adv. bd. Modern Lang. Studies; contbr. articles to profl. jours. Decorated chevalier dans l'Ordre des Palmes Académiques, 1964; recipient Leadership award N.Y. State Assn. Fgn. Lang. Tchrs., 1973, 76, 78, Nat. Disting. Leadership award, 1979, Disting. Service award, 1983, 86, Capital Dist. Fgn. Language Disting. Service award, 1987; recipient Spanish Heritage award, 1981, Alumni Achievement award Carleton Coll., 1982; exchange student auspices Inst. Internat. Ednl. at Carleton Coll., 1938-39; Buenos Aires Conv. grantee for research in Colombia, 1946-47; faculty research grantee Skidmore Coll., summer 1959, 61, 63, 64, 67, 69, 70, 73, ad hoc faculty grantee, 71, 78, 85. Mem. Am. Assn. Tchrs. Spanish and Portuguese, Nat. Assn. Self-Instructional Lang. Programs (v.p. 1981-82, pres. 1982-83), AAUW, AAUP, MLA (del. assembly 1976-78, Mildenberger medal selection com 1984-86), El Ateneo Doctor Jaime Torres Bodet (founding mem.), Nat. Geog. Soc., Asociación Internacional de Hispanistas, UN Assn. U.S.A., Am. Soc. French Acad. Palms, Fulbright Alumni, Phi Sigma Iota, Sigma Delta Pi. Home: 1755 York Ave Apt 37A New York NY 10128-6875

KARSON, CATHERINE JUNE, computer programmer, consultant; b. Salt Lake City, Jan. 26, 1956; d. Gary George and Sylvia June (Naylor) Anderson; m. Mitchell Reed Karson, June 14, 1987; 1 child, Rhonda. A in Gen. Studies, Pima C.C., Tucson, 1989, AAS in Computer Sci., 1990. Night supr. F.G. Ferre & Son, Inc., Salt Lake City, 1973-76, exec. sec., 1977-79; operating room technician Cottonwood Hosp., Salt Lake City, 1976-77; customer svc. rep., System One rep. Ea. Airlines, Inc., Salt Lake City and Tucson, 1979-88; edn. specialist Radio Shack Computer Ctr., Tucson, 1988-89; programmer/analyst Pinal County DPIS, Florence, Ariz., 1989-90; systems analyst Carondelet Health Svcs., Tucson, 1990; programmer/analyst Sunquest Info. Sys., Tucson, 1990-94, sr. tech. proposal specialist, 1994—; cons. Pinal County Pub. Fiduciary, Florence, 1990, UBET, Barbados, W.I., 1990—, numerous clients, Tucson, 1990-93. Mem. bus. adv. coun. Portable Practical Ednl. Preparation, Inc., Tucson, 1990-91. Mem. Nat. Sys. Programmer Assn. Republican. Jewish. Home: 6066 N Serendipity Ln Tucson AZ 85704

KARU, GILDA M(ALL), lawyer, government official; b. Oceanport, N.J., Dec. 1, 1951; d. Harold and Ilvy (Meriloo) K.; m. Frederick F. Foy, May 23, 1981. AB, Vassar Coll., 1974; JD, Ill. Inst. Tech., 1987. Bar: Ill. 1987, U.S. Dist. Ct. (no. dist.) Ill. 1987. Quality control reviewer Food and Nutrition Svc. USDA, Robbinsville, N.J., 1974-77, team leader, 1977-78, supr., 1978-81; sect. chief Food and Nutrition Svc. USDA, Chgo., 1981—; employer adviser Ctr. for Rehab. and Tng. Disabled Persons, Chgo., 1986-93; chief mgmt. negotiator for collective abargaining agreement Nat. Treasury Employees Union, 1990. Bd. dirs., legal counsel, regional dir. North Ctrl. Estonian Am. Nat. Coun., N.Y.C.; v.p. 1st Estonian Evang. Luth. Ch., Chgo., treas., 1994—; mem. Chgo. Vol. Legal Svcs., Friends of Arlington Heights Meml. Libr.; vol. dep. voter registration officer Cook County, Ill.; pres. Arlington Heights, Mt. Prospect, Buffalo Gfove area LWV. Recipient cert. of recognition William A. Jump Meml. Found., 1987, Arthur S. Flemming award Washington Downtown Jaycees, 1987, Ill. Dem. Ethnic Heritage award, 1989, cert. of appreciation Assn. for Persons with Disabilities in Agr., 1992, Group Honor award for work on 1993 Miss. River Flood Disaster Relief, Sec. of USDA, 1994. Mem. ABA, NAFE, LWV (bd. dirs. 1992—), Ill. Bar Assn., Chgo. Bar Assn., Baltic Bar Assn., Am. Pub. Welfare Assn., Internat. Platform Assn., Mensa, Vassar Club (chpt. treas. 1988-90, v.p. 1990-91, coord. pub. rels. 1991—). Office: USDA Food and Nutrition Svc 20th Fl 77 W Jackson Blvd Chicago IL 60604-3507

KASA, PAMELA DOROTHY, lawyer; b. 1943. BSChemE, Rensselaer Poly. Inst., 1965; JD, Georgetown U., 1968; LLM, NYU, 1980. Sr. patent atty. Bristol-Myers Squibb Co., N.Y.C., 1976-78, counsel, 1982-89, asst. gen. counsel, 1989-90, assoc. gen. counsel, 1990—, corp. sec., 1982—, v.p., 1985—; assoc. counsel Clairol, Inc., 1978-80, v.p., counsel, 1980-82. Office: Bristol-Myers Squibb Co 345 Park Ave New York NY 10154-0004

KASAJU, ELENA VLADIMIROVNA, accountant, consultant; b. Moscow, Nov. 15, 1961; d. Vladimir and Galina Dergacheva; m. Purushottam B. Kasaju, March 29, 1984; 1 child, Pujan. MS in Econs., Moscow Inst. Nat. Econ., 1983; B Bus. Adminstrn. in Acctg. summa cum laude, Northeast La. U., 1994, MBA, 1994. CPA, CMA, CIA. Economist Spl. Constrn. Bur. Acad. Sci., Moscow, Russia, 1983—; staff acct. KPMG Peat Marwick LLP, Houston, 1994. Named All American Scholar U.S. Achievement Acad. Mem. Inst. Internal Auditors, Inst. Cert. Mgmt. Accountants, Beta Alpha Psi, Beta Gamma Sigma. Home: 1955 Fountainview # 84 Houston TX 77057

KASAKOVE, SUSAN, interior designer; b. Newark, N.J., Nov. 11, 1938. BFA, U. Buffalo, 1958, Hunter Coll., 1960; postgrad., N.Y. Sch. of Interior Design, 1960-64, New Sch. for Social Rsch., 1967-68, Pratt Inst., 1968-69. Asst. interior designer Rodgers Assocs., N.Y.C., 1964-66; interior designer Walter Dorwin Teague Assocs., N.Y.C., 1966-70; sr. interior designer N.Y. State Facilities Devel. Corp., N.Y.C., 1970—. Reading tutor Vols. for Children's Svcs., N.Y.C., 1976-82; chair Friends of White Plains (N.Y.) Symphony, 1981-83; vol. dept. Asian Studies Met. Mus. Art, N.Y.C., 1988—, vol. guide edn. dept., 1978—; Rep. treas. 11th Ward, Yonkers, N.Y., 1979-81. Recipient Outstanding Svc. to Sch. award Rockland County (N.Y.) Lions Club, 1955. Mem. Environ. Design Rsch. Assn. Home: 793 Palmer Rd Apt 3F Bronxville NY 10708-3337 Office: NY State Facilities Devel Corp 909 3d Ave New York NY 10022

KASAKS, SALLY FRAME, apparel executive; b. 1944. With Lord & Taylor, Garfinckels, Saks Fifth Avenue, N.Y.C., 1966-83; pres., CEO AnnTaylor, Inc., N.Y.C., 1983-85; chmn., CEO Talbots, Inc., Hingham, Mass., 1985-88; pres. Abercrombie & Fitch (divsn. The Limited, Inc.), Columbus, Ohio, 1989-92; chmn., CEO AnnTaylor Stores Corp. and AnnTaylor, Inc., N.Y.C., 1992—. Office: AnnTaylor Stores Corp 142 W 57th St New York NY 10019*

KASCHAK, LILLIAN ANNE, financial fund executive; b. Plymouth, Pa.; d. Stanley and Mary Christine (Sinkiewicz) Javer; student Wyo. Sem., Dean Sch. Bus., 1946-47, Wilkes Coll., 1952-53; m. Joseph V. Kaschak; 1 son, Thomas J. Sr. clk. Prudential Ins. Co., Kingston, Pa., 1953-58; with advt. dept. Wyoming Valley Distbg. Co., Wilkes-Barre, Pa., 1968-69; adminstrv. mgr. Keystone Welfare & Pension Funds, Wilkes-Barre, 1969-82; with Sheetmetal Workers Welfare Fund, Wilkes-Barre, 1982—; partner Kaschak & Slesinski, 1977—. Mem. Eastern Pa. Adminstrs. Assn. (sec.-treas. 1975-79), Tri-County Personnel Assn. (publicity chmn. 1976-78), Madam Curie Soc. Roman Catholic. Clubs: Quota (membership chmn. 1972-79), Wyoming Valley Ski. Home and Office: 306 Stephanie Dr Plymouth PA 18651-2011

KASCUS, MARIE ANNETTE, librarian; b. Boston, June 2, 1943; d. Anthony Joseph and Mildred (Lochiatto) Martucci; m. Joseph Edward Kascus, July 3, 1966. BA, Northeastern U., Boston, 1966; MSLS, U. Ill., 1969. Libr. asst. Boston Pub. Libr. Br., East Boston, Mass., 1961-66; rsch. asst. Hanscom AFB/Decision Scis. Lab., Bedford, Mass., 1964-66; asst. binding libr. Univ. Ill., Champaign-Urbana, 1970-72; head serials dept. Cen. Conn. State Univ., New Britain, 1972—, collection mgmt. coord., 1984-86; abstracter ABC-CLIO, Santa Barbara, Calif., 1979—; indexer Productivity, Inc., Stamford, Conn., Cambridge, Mass., 1981-86; mem. editorial bd. Cataloging and Classification Quart., 1984—; cons. Post Coll., Waterbury, Conn., 1986, State of Conn. Pers. Div., Hartford, Conn., 1987-88, Choice Mag., Middletown, Conn., 1990—; mem. program adv. bd. Sixth Off-Campus Libr. Svcs. Conf., 1992-93; mem. ASIS Thesaurus of Info. Sci. and Librarianship Adv. Bd., 1993; presenter at profl. confs. Referee and contbr. articles to profl. jours; presenter at profl. confs. Cons. New Eng. Assn. Schs. and Colls., Newton, Mass., 1990, 92, CCSU Found./George R. Muirhead Scholarship Fund, New Britain, Conn., 1991, Harriet Kiser Opera Fund, Hartford, 1991—. Recipient Sears B. Condit award for excellent scholarship Sears Roebuck, Inc., Boston, 1966, Alumni award for profl. promise Northeastern U., Boston, 1966; AAUP Faculty Rsch. grantee Cen. Conn. State U., New Britain, 1991; Higher Edn. Act fellow U.S. Govt. U. Ill., Champaign, 1969-70. Mem. AAUP, ALA, Assn. Coll. and Rsch. Librs. (del. at large), Am. Soc. Indexers (Conn. chpt. pres. 1988—, organizer, voting rep. Nat. Info. Standards Orgn. 1995—), Phi Delta Kappa, Phi Kappa Phi, Pi Sigma Alpha, Beta Phi Mu. Office: Cen Conn State Univ 1615 Stanley St New Britain CT 06053-2439

KASEMAN, DIANNE FISHER, nurse educator; b. Rochester, Pa., Aug. 19, 1940; d. Henry Ashley and Eleanor Marie Fisher; m. Mansfield M. Kaseman, June 17, 1979; children: Roger, Laura. BSN, U. Fla., 1962; MS, Fla. State U., 1974, PhD, 1978. Dir. Leon County Mental Health Assn., Tallahassee; researcher, author, asst. prof., asst. to dean Fla. State U., Tallahassee, 1971-79; assoc. prof., grad. dean Howard U. Coll. Nursing, Washington, 1980-87; rsch. assoc. Georgetown U., Washington, 1987-89; assoc. prof., dir. program devel. George Mason U. Sch. Nursing, Fairfax, Va., 1990—; nat. cons., peer reviewer, div. nursing and Bur. Health Professions, USPHS; pvt. cons. in gerontol. nursing, edn. and adminstrn. Grantee in field. Mem. NLN (site visitor 1981-89), Nat. Coun. on Aging, D.C. League Nursing (v.p. 1988-90), Md. Nurses Assn., Gerontol. Soc. Am., U.S. Pub. Health Assn., Sigma Theta Tau.

KASE-POLISINI, JUDITH BAKER, educator; b. Wilmington, Del., Dec. 13, 1932; d. Charles Robert and Elizabeth Edna (Baker) Kase; BA, U. Del., 1955; MA, Case Western Res. U., 1956; m. James F. Polisini; stepchildren: James, Elizabeth, John, Katherine, Ann. Tchr., dir. children's theatre Agnes Scott Coll., 1956, U. Tenn., 1957, U. Md., Germany, 1958-60, Denver Civic Theatre, Denver U., Kent Sch., 1960-61; dir. children's theatre U. N.H., Durham, 1962-69; dir. theatre resources for youth, Somersworth, N.H., 1966-69; assoc. prof. theatre U. South Fla., Tampa, 1969-74, assoc. prof. edn., 1975-83, prof., 1984—, artistic dir. ednl. theatre, 1976—; project dir. Hillsborough County Artists-in-Schs. Evaluation and Inservice Project, 1980-82; dir. Internat. Ctr. for Studies in Theatre Edn. Bd. dirs. Fla. Alliance for Arts Edn., sec., 1976-77, vice-chmn., 1979-82, chmn. 1982-84; chmn. Wingspread Conf. on Theatre Edn., 1977; drama adjudicator Nat. Arts Festival, Ministry of Edn., Bahamas, 1975, 76, 79, 80; regional chmn. Alliance for Arts Edn., chmn. nat. adv. council, mem. edn. adv. com., 1986—; trustee Children's Theatre Found.; bd. dirs. Am. Theatre of J.F. Kennedy Ctr. for Performing Arts, 1991-93, Coll. Bus., 1993—; cons. theatre edn. and prodn.; steering com. Arts for a Complete Edn., 1991—. Recipient Disting. Book of Yr. award, 1989. Fellow Am. Theatre (bd. dirs. 1990); mem. Children's Theatre Assn. Am. (pres.-elect 1975-77, pres. 1977-79, chmn. symposia 1981-85, spl. recognition citation 1984), Am. Theatre Assn. (chief div. pres.'s coordinating council 1977-78 commn. on theatre edn. 1982—, elected), Am. Alliance for Theatre and Edn. (dir. & project dir. theatre literacy collaborative study Internat. Ctr. for Studies in Theatre Edn., Presdl. award 1992), Speech Communication Assn. (membership dir. 1961), Southeastern Theatre Confs. (Sara Spencer award 1980), Fla. Theatre Confs. (Disting. Career award), Nat. Theatre Conf., Internat. Assn. Theatres for Children and Youth, Internat. Amateur Theatre Assn. (N.Am. bd. dirs.), Fla. Assn. for Theater Edn. (theatre edn. of yr. award 1986), Fla. Dept. Edn. Arts Complete Edn. Steering com., Tampa Mus. Democrat. Episcopalian. Club: Carrollwood Village. Author: The Creative Drama Book: Three Approaches, other books; editor: Creative Drama in a Developmental Context; Children's Theatre, Creative Drama and Learning, Drama as a Meaning Maker, Introduction to Drama Teacher Resource Guide, The Arts: Interconnecting Pathways to Human Experience; contbr. articles to profl. jours.; pub. playwright 3 plays. Home: 5321 Taylor Rd Lutz FL 33549-4823 Office: U South Fla Dept Secondary Edn Tampa FL 33620

KASHDIN, GLADYS SHAFRAN, painter, educator; b. Pitts., Dec. 15, 1921; d. Edward M. and Miriam P. Shafran; m. Manville E. Kashdin, Oct. 11, 1942 (dec.). BA magna cum laude, U. Miami, 1960; MA, Fla. State U., 1962, PhD, 1965. Photographer, N.Y.C. and Fla., 1938-60; tchr. art, Fla. and Ga., 1956-63; asst. prof. humanities U. South Fla., Tampa, 1965-70, assoc. prof., 1970-74, prof., 1974-87, prof. emerita, 1987—; works exhibited in 58 one-woman shows, 38 group exhbns.; maj. touring exhibits include: The Everglades, 1972-75; Aspects of the River, 1975-80; Processes of Time, 1981-91; represented in permanent collections: Taiwan, Peoples Republic of China, Columbus Mus. Arts, LeMoyne Art Found., Tampa Internat. Airport, Tampa Mus. Art, Kresge Art Mus., U. So. Fla.; lectr.; adv. bd. Hillsborough County Mus., 1975-83. Mem. U. S. Fla. Status of Women Com., 1971-76, chmn., 1975-76. Recipient Women Helping Women in Art award Soroptimist Internat., 1979, Citizens Hon. award Hillsborough Bd. County Commrs., 1984, Mortar Bd. award for teaching excellence, 1986. Mem. AAUW (1st v.p. Tampa br. 1971-72), Phi Kappa Phi (chpt.-pres. 1981-83, artist/scholar award 1987). Home: 441 Biltmore Ave Temple Ter FL 33617-7207 Office: U South Fla CPR # 107 Humanities Dept Tampa FL 33620

KASHLAK, NANCY LYNN, pediatrics nurse; b. Coaldale, Pa., July 29, 1952; d. Joseph and Florence Louise (Hagadish) K. Diploma, Montgomery Hosp. Sch. of Nursing, 1973; BS in Profl. Arts, St. Joseph's Coll., 1975; cert. PNP in Hematology and Oncology, Children's Hosp. of Phila. and Widener U., 1980; MS in Health Edn., St. Joseph's U., 1985, Post-Master's cert. in Health Adminstrn., 1986; MSN, Gwynedd-Mercy Coll., 1993. RN, Pa., Va.; cert. PNP, pediatric oncology nurse. Staff nurse Children's Hosp. of Phila., 1973-76, 1982-86; charge nurse pediatrics Rockingham Meml. Hosp., Bellows Falls, Vt., 1976-77; primary nurse pediatrics Mary Hitchcock Meml. Hosp. Dartmouth-Hitchcock Med. Ctr., Hanover, N.H., 1977-80; asst. head nurse St. Christopher's Hosp. for Children, Phila., 1980-81; pediatric nurse practitioner oncology/hematology U. Va. Sch. Medicine, Charlottesville, 1986-91; pediatric nurse practitioner South Phila. Pediatrics, 1991—; instr. clin. faculty U. Va. Sch. of Nursing, Charlottesville, 1988-91; clin. instr. Del. County Community Coll., Media, Pa., 1991, 93, 94; contbg. mem. Pediatric Oncology Group, 1988-91; facility rep. nursing com. Children's Cancer Study Group, 1991; mem. childhood cancer com. Am. Cancer Soc., VA div., Richmond, Va., 1988-91; mem., career mentor St. Joseph's Coll., Windham, Maine, 1990—; health cons. Early Childhood Edn. Linkage Sys., Pa. chpt., Am. Acad. Pediatrics, 1993—; clin. preceptor Sch. Nursing U. Pa., Phila., 1994—. U. Va. facility rep. Jason's House, Surfside Beach, S.C., 1987-91. Fellow Nat. Assn. Pediatric Nurse Assocs. and Practitioners; mem. Assn. Pediatric Oncology Nurses, St. Joseph's Coll. Alumni Assn., Montgomery Hosp. Sch. Nursing Alumni Assn., Sigma Theta Tau. Office: South Phila Pediatrics 1400 S 5th St Philadelphia PA 19147-5919

KASI, LEELA PESHKAR, pharmaceutical chemist; b. Bombay, July 15, 1939; came to U.S., 1971; d. Subbaraman and Lakshmi (Shastri) Peshkar; m. Kalli R. Kasi, June 10, 1971. BS, U. Bombay, India, 1958; PhD, U. Marburg, W. Germany, 1968. Jr. chemist Khandelwal Labs., Bombay, India, 1958-59; trainee Farbwerke Hoechst, Frankfurt, W. Germany, 1960; teaching asst. U. of Marburg, W. Germany, 1967-68; sr. chemist Boehringer-Knoll Ltd., Bombay, India, 1969-71; mgr. quality control U. Tex.-M.D. Anderson Cancer Ctr., Houston, Ind., 1972-77; asst. chemist U. Tex.-M.D. Anderson Cancer Ctr., Houston, 1979-90; assoc. chemist U. Tex. M.D. Anderson Cancer Ctr., Houston, 1990—; assoc. prof. chemistry U. Tex.-M.D. Anderson Cancer Ctr., Houston, 1993—, assoc. prof., 1993—, dir. Exptl. Nuclear Medicine Lab., 1987—; mem. grad. faculty U. Tex., 1984-90. Asst. editor Jour. Nuclear Medicine, 1984-89; contbr. articles to profl. jours. Co-investigator, investigator several rsch. grants and contracts from fed. and state agys. and pvt. industries, 1986—. Mem. AAAS, Am. Assn. Cancer Rsch., Soc. of Nuclear Medicine, Sigma Xi. Home: 4710 Mcdermed Dr Houston TX 77035-3706 Office: U Tex MD Anderson Cancer Ct 1515 Holcombe Blvd Houston TX 77030-4095

KASINDORF, BLANCHE ROBINS, educational administrator; b. N.Y.C., May 18, 1925; d. Samuel David and Anna (Block) Robins; B.A., Hunter Coll., 1944; M.A., N.Y.U., 1948; postgrad. Cornell U., 1946-50; m. David Kasindorf, July 1, 1960. Tchr. pub. schs., Bklyn., 1945-56; instr. Bklyn. Coll., 1956-57; asst. in research for Puerto Rican Study Ford Found. and N.Y.C. Bd. Edn., 1956-57; asst. prin. N.Y.C. Pub. Schs., 1957-59; research assoc. ednl. program rsch. and stats. N.Y.C. Bd. Edn., 1959-63, coordinator spl. edn. liaison div. child welfare for Bur. Curriculum Research, 1963-64; jr. prin., integration coordinator Bklyn. Sch. Dist. 44, 1964-65; prin. Pub. Sch. 7-8, Bklyn., 1965-87; cons. to numerous social agys. Mem. NEA, Council Exceptional Children, N.Y.C. Elementary Sch. Prins., Council Supervisory Assns. Contbr. to profl. publs.; also editor instructional materials. Home: 1655 Flatbush Ave Brooklyn NY 11210-3276

KASKINEN RIESBERG, BARBARA KAY, author, composer, songwriter, musician, music educator; b. Manistee, Mich., June 26, 1952; d. Norman Ferdinand and Martha Agnes (Harju) Kaskinen; m. David H. Riesberg, Feb. 14, 1985 (div.). AA, Broward Community Coll., Coconut Creek, Fla., 1978; BA with honors, Fla. Atlantic U., 1981; postgrad., Nova U., 1989, Fla. Atlantic U., 1992—. Instr. adult piano Atlantic High Sch., Delray Beach, Fla., 1981-82; organist, combo dir. Affirmation Luth. Ch., Boca Raton, Fla., 1981-86; studio musician, composer/arranger Electric Rize Prodns., Margate, Fla., 1982—; ind. instr. piano, electronic keyboard and guitar. Margate, 1979—; bass and keyboard player Electric Rize Band, Margate, 1982—; in-house composer and arranger Hansen House, Miami Beach, Fla., 1987-88; co-founder Oasis Coffee House, Boca Raton, Fla., 1990—; co-owner Electric Rize Pub., 1991—; grad. tchg. asst. Fla. Atlantic U., 1994—, asst. dir. T.O.P.S. Piano Camp, 1994—. Author: Barbara Riesberg's Adult Electronic Keyboard Course Book I, 1988, Books II and III, 1989. Reporter Coalition to Stop Food Irradiation, Broward, Fla., 1989. Mem. NOW, ASCAP, Fla. Atlantic U. Alumni Assn., Nat. Guild Piano Tchrs., Broward County Music Tchr.'s Assn., Fla. State Music Tchr.'s Assn., Music Guild of Boca Raton. Home: 6601 NW 22nd St Pompano Beach FL 33063-2117

KASLEY, HELEN MARY, corporate secretary, legal counsel; b. Chgo., May 9, 1951; d. John F. and Michaeline J. (Wesolowski) Czachorski; m. William L. Kasley, Aug. 18, 1973; children: Joseph Anthony, Gabrielle Alexandra. BA, Bradley U., 1973, MA, 1978; MEd, U. Ill., Champaign, 1974; JD, U. Chgo., 1986. Bar: Calif. 1986, U.S. Dist. Ct. (no. dist.) Calif. 1986, U.S. Ct. Appeals (9th cir.) 1986; cert. sch. psychologist, Ill., cert. tchr. social and emotional disorders, Ill., cert. tchr. early childhood spl. edn., Ill. Disseminator Precise Early Edn. of Children with Handicaps outreach inst. child behavior & devel. U. Ill., 1975-76; head tchr. ctr. study early childhood devel. Bradley U., Peoria, Ill., 1976-77, rsch. and teaching asst. psychology dept., 1976-78; sch. psychologist Tazewell-Mason Counties Spl. Edn. Assn., Pekin, Ill., 1978-82, Cath. Social Svc., Peoria, 1983; assoc. atty. McCutchen, Doyle, Brown & Enersen, San Francisco, 1986-90; sec., legal counsel Calif. Water Svc. Co., San Jose, 1990—. Mem. mng. bd. U. Chgo. Legal Forum, 1984-85. Mem. Am. Corp. Counsel Assn., Am. Soc. Corp. Secs., Inc., Bar Assn. Calif. Office: Calif Water Svc Co 1720 N 1st St San Jose CA 95112

KASMAN, MARLENE N., psychologist; b. Bklyn., July 12, 1939; d. Philip J. and Frieda (Backinoff) Noumoff; m. Richard B. Kasman, June 30, 1963; children: Lawrence Paul, Laine Beth Kreindler. BA, Adelphi U., 1960, PhD, 1966, postgrad., 1972, 85. Cert. addiction specialist, Am. Acad. Health Care Providers in the Addictive Disorders, psychologist, N.Y. Psychotherapist Cumberland County Guidance Ctr., Fayetteville, N.C., 1963-65; staff psychotherapist Mid Nassau Community Guidance Ctr., Hicksville, N.Y., 1966-67; pvt. practice East Northport, N.Y., 1967—; staff therapist Pederson-Krag Clin., Huntington, N.Y., 1967-72; Listed Nat. Register Health Care Providers in Psychology, L.I. Referral Svc.; dir. Eating Disorders Program, Pederson-Krag Ctr., coord. externship, supr., 1972—; affiliate clin. prof. psychology St. John's U.; adj. prof. psychology L.I. U.; adj. clin. assoc., Pace U. Mem. Am. Psychol. Assn., N.Y. State Psychol. Assn., Suffolk County Psychological Assn. (pres.-elect, member-at-large, co-chair independent practice com., recording sec.), Am. Group Psychotherapy Assn., Eastern Group Psychol. Assn., Adelphi Soc. Psychoanalysis and Psychotherapy, Am. Anorexia/Bulimia Assn., Nat. Anoretic Aid Soc. Home and Office: 163 Town Line Rd East Northport NY 11731-3916

KASMER, IRENE, fashion and textile executive; b. Bilky, Czechoslovakia, Sept. 24, 1926; came to the U.S., 1948; d. Izidor and Malvina Amalia (Klein) Markovic; m. Gerald Stuart Kasmer, Aug. 29, 1954; children: Jeff Anthony, Bruce Neal, Lauren Michele. AA in Art, LATTJ Coll., L.A., 1953. Designer Bell Sportswear, L.A., 1948-50; prof. costume design, lectr. L.A. Trade Tech. Coll., 1951-54; chief designer, dir. Ardee Sportswear, L.A., 1951-66; pres. Irene Kasmer Inc., L.A., 1966—; founder, pres. Modac Mus. Fashion Designers and Creators, L.A., 1994—, also bd. dirs.; cons., designer, 1951—; pres. Mus. Fashion Designers and Creators, L.A., 1991—. Fashion adv. com. to mayor, L.A., 1970—. Recipient Young Designer award Calif. Stylist, 1957, Mayda award May Co., 1960, Trend Setting Toby award, 1962, Designer award Monsanto and DuPont, 1960-65. Mem. Fashion Group Internat. (bd. dirs. 1960—), Textile Group Internat. (bd. dirs. 1987—). Home: 315 S Bedford Dr Beverly Hills CA 90212-3724 Office: 910 S Los Angeles St Ste 302 Los Angeles CA 90015-1726

KASMIR, GAIL ALICE, insurance company official, accountant; b. N.Y.C., Aug. 19, 1958; d. Fred and Evelyn Silvie (Mailman) K. BSBA summa cum laude, U. Cen. Fla., 1979. CPA, Fla. Acct. Ernst and Young, Orlando, Fla., 1979-83; fin. mgr. Harcourt Brace Jovanovich (Harvest Life Ins. Co.), Orlando, Fla., 1983-85; sr. v.p., treas., sec., cons. to bd. dirs., mem. investment com. LifeCo Investment Group, Inc. and subs. Nat. Heritage Life Ins. Co., Maitland, Fla., 1985-89, exec. v.p., 1991-94; bd. dirs., exec. v.p., sec.-treas., CFO Nat. Heritage Life Ins. Co., LifeCo Investment Group, Inc., LifeCo Mktg. Svcs. Vol. Am. Cancer Soc., 1987—, Am. Soc. for Cancer Research, 1987—. Fellow Life Office Mgmt. Assn.; mem. AICPAs, Fla. Inst. CPAs, Ins. Acctg. and Systems Assn., Beta Alpha Psi, Beta Gamma Sigma. Republican. Jewish. Home: 1351 Richmond Rd Winter Park FL 32789 Office: Life Co Investment Group Inc 390 N Orange Ave 23d Fl Orlando FL 32801-1640

KASPERSON, JEANNE XANTHAKOS, librarian, editor, educator; b. Southbridge, Mass., Feb. 3, 1938; d. James and Mary (Mitsakos) Xanthakos; m. Roger Eugene Kasperson, Sept. 6, 1959; children: Demetri Alexander, Kyra Eleni. BA with honors in English, Clark U., 1959; postgrad. in L.S., U. Chgo., 1959-60, MA in English, 1962; MS in L.S., Simmons Coll., 1967. Asst. librarian circulation and reference Edn. Library, U. Chgo., 1959-60; asst. acquisitions librarian Wilbur Cross Library, U. Conn., Storrs, 1964-66; asst. to chief bibliographer Mich. State U. Library, East Lansing, 1966-67; research librarian Hazard Assessment Group, Clark U., Worcester, Mass., 1977-78, Center Tech., Environ., and Devel., 1979-90, George Perkins Marsh Inst., Marsh Libr., 1991—; sr. rsch. assoc. World Hunger Program, Brown U., 1986—; editor Aquarius Project, 1972-73; dir. publs. CENTED, 1983—. Co-editor: Water Re-use and the Cities (best sci. book award 1977), 1977; Risk in the Technological Society, 1982; co-author, co-editor: Natural Hazards Observer, 1984; Perilous Progress: Managing the Hazards of Technology, 1985 (Choice Outstanding Acad. Books 1987); Nuclear Risk Analysis in Comparative Perspective, 1986, Corporate Management of Health and Safety Hazards, 1988, Global Environmental Change: The Contributions of Risk Analysis and Management, 1990, Managing Nuclear Accidents: A Model Emergency Plan for Power Plants and Communities, 1992, Preparing for Nuclear Power Plant Accidents, 1995; contbg. editor Environment 1987-92; bd. editors Risk Abstracts, 1988—, book rev. editor, 1990—; contbr. articles to profl. jours. Exec. bd. Woodstock Library Assn., 1974-75, v.p., 1975-77, pres., 1978-80, book selection com., 1980-85; pres. N. Woodstock Library Assn., 1977-82. Mem. ALA, AAUW, N.Y. Acad. Sci., Soc. Risk Analysis, Union of Concerned Scientists, Research Com. Disasters, Internat. Disaster Inst., Internat. Assn. Impact Analysis, Spl. Librs. Assn., Am. Soc. Environ. History, Soc. Internat. Devel., U.S. Agrl. Info. Network, Assn. Population Family Planning Librs. Info. Ctrs. Internat., Nat. Hazards Soc. Democrat. Greek Orthodox. Office: Brown Univ World Hunger Program PO Box 1831 Providence RI 02912-1831

KASS, ANDREA MICHELLE, educator; b. Bklyn., Feb. 1, 1968; d. Arnold Joseph and Harriet Leah (Segal) K. BA, Hofstra U., 1990; MS, Adelphi U., 1992. Cert. speech-hearing tchr., N.Y. Tchr. speech-hearing handicapped South Huntington Union Free Sch. Dist., Huntington Station, N.Y., 1990-91, East Williston Union Free Sch. Dist., Old Westbury, N.Y., 1992—; pvt. practice Woodbury; dir. fundraisers of speech clinic Hofstra U.; grad. rsch. asst. to chairperson speech dept. Adelphi U., 1991. Mem. Am. Speech, Lang. and Hearing Assn. (cert.), Sigma Pi (sec. Hempstead, N.Y. chpt. 1989, pres. 1989-90). Home: 20 Gloria Dr Woodbury NY 11797-2106

KASS, SUSAN, artist; b. Fall River, Mass.; d. Bernard Charles and Jeanette (Silver) K.; m. Alex Johnson; children: Nicholas, Gabriel. BS in Design, Cornell U.; cert. in art edn., CUNY, 1990, MFA in Painting, 1992. Instr. modern dance U. Va., Charlottesville, 1975-76; guest tchr. performance art SUNY, Buffalo, 1977; guest tchr. performance video RISD, Providence, 1979; guest tchr. Düsseldorf (Germany) Kunstakademie, 1980; tchr. painting and dance children's program Queens Coll., CUNY, 1990, 91, grad. asst., 1992; pvt. tchr. drawing, Merrick, 1993—; art instr. N.Y. Inst. Tech., 1994; art educator Islip Art Mus., 1994; writer, dir., producer videotapes and films, 1975-84; founding mem. Colab Artists Group, N.Y.C., 1977; founder Point Reyes Dance Palace, Point Reyes Station, Calif., 1975. One-woman shows Anthology Film Archives, N.Y.C., 1977, Internat. Cultural Ctr., Antwerp, Belgium, 1978, RISD, 1979, Di Appel Galerie, Amsterdam, The Netherlands, 1979, U. Calif.-Berkeley Art Mus., 1979; 2-woman shows Whitney Mus., N.Y.C., 1978, Holly Solomon Gallery, N.Y.C., 1978; group shows include Art Inst. Chgo., 1979, Long Beach (Calif.) Mus. Art, 1979, Folkwang Mus., Essen, Germany, 1979, Mus. Modern Art, Paris, 1980, Venice Biennale, 1980, Mus. Contemporary Art, La Jolla, Calif., Mus. Contemporary Art, Chgo., 1981, Everson Mus., Syracuse, N.Y., 1981, Staftisches Kunstmuseum, Bonn, Germany, 1981, Neue Gesellshaft fur Bildende Kunst, Berlin, 1982, Van Abbemuseum, Amsterdam, 1983, Kroller Muller Museum, Amsterdam, 1984, Parrish Art Mus., Southhampton, N.Y., 1994. Queens Coll. fellow Chautauqua Sch. Art Colony, summer 1993. Mem. Coll. Art Assn., Nat. Mus. Women. Home: 30 Lincoln Blvd Merrick NY 11566-4013 Studio: 10-20 45th Rd Long Island City NY 11101

KASSEBAUM, NANCY LANDON, senator; b. Topeka, July 29, 1932; d. Alfred M. and Theo Landon; children: John Philip, Linda Josephine, Richard Landon, William Alfred. BA in Polit. Sci, U. Kans., 1954; MA in Diplomatic History, U. Mich., 1956. Mem. Maize (Kans.) Sch. Bd., 1972-75; mem. Washington staff Sen. James B. Pearson of Kans., 1975-76; mem. U.S. Senate from Kans., 1979—, mem. fgn. relations com., labor and human resources com., Select com. indian Affairs. Republican. Episcopalian. Office: US Senate 302 Russell Senate Bldg Washington DC 20510

KASSEWITZ, RUTH EILEEN BLOWER, retired hospital executive; b. Columbus, Ohio, May 15, 1928; d. E. Wallett and Helen (Daub) Blower; BS in Journalism-Mgmt., Ohio State U., Columbus, 1951; m. Jack Kassewitz, July 28, 1962 (dec.); 1 stepchild, Jack. Copywriter, Ohio Fuel Gas Co., Columbus, 1951-55, Merritt Owens Advt. Agy., Kansas City, Kans., 1955-56; account exec. Grant Advt., Inc., Miami, Fla., 1956-59; account supr. Venn/Cole & Assocs., Miami, 1959-67; dir. communications Ferendino/Grafton/Candela/Spillis Architects & Engrs., Miami, 1967-69; dir. communications Dade County Dept. Housing and Urban Devel., Miami, 1969-72; dir. communications Met. Dade County Govt., 1972-78; adminstr. pub. rels. U. Miami/Jackson Meml. Med. Ctr., 1978-90, ret., 1990. Pres., U. Miami Women's Guild, 1973-74; bd. dirs. Girls Scouts Tropical Fla., 1974-76, 81-83, Lung Assn. Dade-Monroe Counties, 1976-87; mem. exec. com. Miami-Dade Community Coll. Found., 1984—; pres. Mental Health Assn. Dade County, 1982; mem. Miami Ecol. and Beautification Com., 1978—, also vice-chmn.; bd. govs. Barry U., Miami, 1981-83; trustee Nat. Humanities Faculty, 1981-83; trustee, sec. United Protestant Appeal, 1984—; treas., past chmn. Health, Edn., Promotion Council, Inc.; adv. bd. Miami's for Me, 1987-88; mem. Coral Gables Cable TV Bd., 1983-86; ch. moderator Plymouth Congl. Ch., 1986-88; community adv. bd. Jr. League Greater Miami, Inc., 1989-92; founding mem. Nat. Honor Roll Women in Pub. Rels., No. Ill. U., 1993. Recipient Disting. Service award Plymouth Congl. Ch., Miami, 1979; Ann Stover award, 1983, Golden Image award Fla. Pub. Rels.Assn. 1987; named Woman of Yr., Plymouth Congl. Ch., U. Miami Med. Sch., 1991. Fellow Public Relations Soc. Am. (pres. South Fla. chpt. 1969-70, nat. chmn. govt. sect. 1973-74, nat. dir. 1974-78; continuing edn. council 1981-83; Silver Anvil award 1973, Assembly del. 1970-73, 86-89, Paul M. Lund Pub. Svc. award 1993); mem. Women in Comm. (pres. Greater Miami chpt. 1962-63; Clarion award 1973, 75, Community Headliner 1985), Miami Internat. Press Club (bd. dirs. 1986-87, treas. 1992), Greater Miami C. of C. (gov. 1983-86), Rotary Club of Miami (bd. dirs., 1988—, pres. 1993-94). Home: 1136 Aduana Ave Miami FL 33146-3206

KASSEY, JACQUELYN MARIE BONAFONTE, pediatrics nurse; b. Middletown, Conn., May 11, 1960; d. Benjamin John Bonafonte and Carol Ann (Amato) Woodmancy; m. Mark George Kassey, Sept. 11, 1986. Diploma, Ona M. Wilcox Sch. Nursing, 1981; AA, Middlesex Community Coll., 1984; student, St. Joseph's Coll., West Hartford, Conn. RN, Conn.; cert. med.-surg. nurse, pediatric nurse, pediatric advanced life support. Staff nurse med./surg. unit Middlesex Meml. Hosp., Middletown, 1981-82, 83-84; staff nurse SICU Hartford (Conn.) Hosp., 1982-83, Newington (Conn.) VA Med. Ctr., 1984-86; staff nurse respiratory care New Britain (Conn.) Meml. Hosp. (now Hosp. for Special Care), 1987-90; staff nurse pediatrics, medically complex children Hosp. for Special Care, 1990—. Mem ANA, Soc. Pediatric Nurses. Home: 168 Royal Oak Dr Southington CT 06489

KASSOY, HORTENSE (HONEY KASSOY), artist; b. N.Y.C., Feb. 14, 1917; d. Adolph and Mary (Apfel) Blumenkranz; m. Bernard Kassoy, June 30, 1946; children: Meredith, Sheila. Diploma, Pratt Inst., 1936; BS, Columbia U., 1938, MA, 1939; student, Parsons Sch. Design, Paris, U. Colo., 1966, NYU, 1966-67; studied with Sahl Swarz, Chaim Gross and Oronzio Maldarelli. Solo exhbns. include Caravan House Gallery, 1974, Women in the Arts Gallery, 1978, Ward-Nasse Gallery, 1986, Pioneer Gallery, Cooperstown, N.Y., 1987, 91; group exhbns. include Bronx (N.Y.) Mus., 1971, 75, 85-86, Toledo Mus. Art, Toronto Mus. Art, Hudson River Mus., Bklyn. Mus., New Age Gallery, Lever House, Bklyn. Coll., Fordham U., Lehman Coll., Cork Gallery, Nat. Acad. Design; permanent collections include Slater Meml. Mus. Co-chair visual arts Bronx (N.Y.) Coun. on Arts, 1973-76. Fellow Va. Ctr. for Creative Arts, 1986, 88, 89, 92; recipeint 1st prize in watercolor Painters Day at N.Y. World's Fair, 1940. Mem. Am. Soc. Contemporary Artists (v.p. 1989-94, awards 1979, 80, 83, 90, 92), N.Y. Artists Equity Assn. (v.p., bd. dirs. 1971-83), Internation Assn. Art (corr. sec. 1979—, del. to 10th Congress 1983), Contemporary Arts Guild (rec. sec.). Home: 130 Gale Pl Apt 6B Bronx NY 10463-2853 also: Butternut Hill RR 1 Box 74 Burlington Flats NY 13315-9728

KASTEN, BETTY LOU, state legislator; b. Sharon, Pa., Apr. 6, 1938; d. Louis and Betty Todut; m. David Kasten; children: Tod Louis, Elaine Katherine. BA, U. Denver, MS. Rancher, farmer; mem. Mont. Ho. of Reps., 1989—; past bd. trustees Mid River Telephone; past mem. Mont. Health Sys. Agy., Ea. Sub-Area Coun. Kellogg fellow Mont. State U. Mem. Mont. Farm Bur., Mont. Stockgrowers, Mont. Woolgrowers, Mont. Grain Growers, McCone County Cowbelles, Brockway Homemakers. Republican. Home: HC 77 Box A-14 Brockway MT 59214-9701 Office: Mont Ho of Reps State Capitol Helena MT 59620-0001*

KASTEN, CHRISTI LEE, financial services manager; b. Lebanon, Oreg., June 11, 1964; d. B. Donn Bass and Barbara G. (Davis) Powell; m. James M. Kasten, Sept. 10, 1988. BS in Polit. Sci., Oreg. State U., 1986; MPA, Portland State U., 1993. With office of mgmt. & budget City of Corvallis (Oreg.), 1988-92; fin. svcs. mgr. The Pvt. Industry Coun., Inc. & The Oreg. Consortium, Albany, 1992—. PArticipant LEadership Corvallis, 1993. Mem. Am. Soc. Pub. Adminstrs. Office: The Oreg Consortium 260 SW Ferry Ste 102 Albany OR 97333

KASTENS, BEVERLY ANN, special and elementary education educator; b. Wichita, Kans., June 22, 1941; d. Ray Francis and Ava Marie (Lambert) Poole; children: Kelly, Cyndi; m. Gary Michael Kastens, Apr. 22, 1978. BA in Elem. Edn. magna cum laude, Wichita State U., 1973; MS in Edn., Kans. State U., 1980. Cert. tchr., Kans. Math. lab. instr. Goddard (Kans.) Sch. Dist., Unified Sch. Dist. #265, 1973-74, reading lab. instr., 1975-76, 8th grade remedial reading tchr., 1976, 6th grade tchr., 1977-78, 5th grade tchr., 1979-91, tchr. gifted grades K-9, 1992—; faculty advisor Intermediate Learning Ctr., Goddard, 1979, 81, 83, gifted screening com., 1980-83, dept. head, 1984-91; curriculum com. Unified Sch. Dist. #265, Goddard, 1987-88. Author: (teaching curriculum) Christmas Traditions, 1979, (poetry) Memoirs of Grandma, 1979, Memoirs of Student, 1982. Facilitator Wichita (Kans.) Park Bd., 1988-89; cast Voices of Ctrl. Community, Wichita, 1990—, Majesty of Christmas-Easter, Wichita, 1990—. Named Master Tchr., Intermediate Learning Ctr., Goddard, 1985, 87, 89; recipient grant in literature Kans. State Dept. Edn., Topeka, 1987. Mem. Nat. Assn. for Gifted Children, Nat. Rsch. Ctr. on the Gifted and Talented, Kans. Nat. Edn. Assn. (negotiator 1973-91, faculty rep.-negotiation team NEA, Goddard 1985-88). Republican. Mem. Church of God. Home: 547 Pamela Wichita KS 67212 Office: Clark Davidson Sch 333 S Walnut Goddard KS 67052

KASTER, LAURA A., lawyer; b. N.Y.C., May 24, 1948. BA, Tufts U., 1970; JD magna cum laude, Boston U., 1973. Bar: Mass. 1973, Ill. 1975. Law clk. to Hon. Frank M. Coffin U.S. Ct. Appeals (1st cir.), 1973-75; ptnr. Jenner & Block, Chgo. Co-author: Sanctions in Federal Litigation, 1991; co-editor: The Attorneys' Guide to the Seventh Circuit Court of Appeals, 1987; note editor Law Rev. Boston U., 1973-72; contbr. articles to profl. jours. Fellow Am. Bar Found.; mem. ABA, Ill. State Bar Assn., 7th Cir. Bar Assn.

KASTNER, CYNTHIA, lawyer; b. Woonsocket, R.I., July 22, 1948; d. Everett Lathrop and Edith Stark; m. Robert W. Kastner, June 26, 1971. BA, Rutgers U., Newark, 1970; postgrad., Cornell U., 1970-71; JD, Seton Hall U., 1973. Bar: N.J. 1973, U.S. Dist. Ct. N.J. 1973, U.S. Supreme Ct. 1984. Assoc. Wharton, Stewart & Davis, Somerville, N.J., 1973-76; v.p., gen. counsel AT&T Consumer Products, Parsippany, N.J., 1976—. Mem. adminstrv. coun., pres. Women's Circle, Sunday sch. tchr. New Providence (N.J.) Meth. Ch. Mem. ABA, N.J. Bar Assn., N.J. Assn. Corp. Counsel. Home: 70 Lacey Ave Gillette NJ 07933-1407 Office: AT&T Consumer Products 5 Wood Hollow Parsippany NJ 07054-6440

KASWELL, MARYANN MCCARTHY, lawyer; b. Butte, Mont., June 28, 1947; d. George D. McCarthy and Mary A. Kiely; divorced; 1 child, Mack G. AB, Chestnut Hill Coll., 1969; JD, Cath. U., 1981. Govt. rels. counsel Consumer Bankers Assn., Arlington, Va., 1981-83; fed. regulatory counsel Credit Union Nat. Assn., Washington, 1984; dep. dir. legislation Office of Thrift Supervision, Washington, 1985-87, spl. asst., 1987-89, sr. counsel, 1989-91; assoc. gen. counsel Thrift Depositor Protection Oversight Bd., Washington, 1991—. Roman Catholic. Home: 7610 Glendale Rd Chevy Chase MD 20815 Office: Thrift Depositor Pro Oversight Bd 808 17th St NW Washington DC 20232

KATCHUR, MARLENE MARTHA, nursing administrator; b. Belleville, Ill., Dec. 20, 1946; d. Elmer E. and Hilda B. (Gutherz) Wilde; m. Raymond J. Katchur, Feb. 22, 1969; 1 child, Nickolas Phillip. BSN, So. Ill. U., 1968; MS in Health Care Adminstrn., Calif. State U., L.A., 1982. RN; cert. critical care nurse. Staff nurse, head nurse, nursing supr. U. So. Calif Med. Ctr. LA County, 1968-81, assoc. dir. nursing, internal medicine nursing, 1981-83, internal medicine nursing info. systems coord., 1983-89, patient-centered info. systems cons., 1989-90, nursing info. systems cons. for pediatrics, psychiatry and ICU, 1990-92, psychiat. nursing svcs. human resources and info. systems, 1992-94; nursing supr. adminstrv. nursing office, 1994—. Mem. Sheriff's Relief Assn. Mem. AACCN, NAFE, AAUW, Nat. Critical Care Inst. Edn., Am. Heart Assn., So. Ill. U. Alumni Assn. (life), Health Svcs. Mgmt. Forum, Orgn. Nurse Execs. Calif. (membership com.), Am. Soc. Profl. and Exec. Women, Soc. Clin. Data Mgmt. Systems (bd. dirs. 1990-91), Soc. Med. Computer Observers (charter), Am. Legion Aux., Nat. Hist. Soc., Job's Daus. (past honor queen). Office: LA County U So Calif Med Ctr 1200 N State St Los Angeles CA 90033-4525

KATES, DEE TAMAR, banker; b. Lexington, Ky., Aug. 29, 1963; d. Robert Aaron Rothman and Sherran Sue (Simson) Blair; m. Jeffrey Kates, Oct. 24, 1987; children: Andrea Erin, Kevin Matthew. BS, Babson Coll., 1985. Mktg. rep., salesperson Computer Info. Sys., Braintree, Mass., 1985-86; v.p., sec. First Cmty. Bank, Whitehall, Ohio, 1986—; also bd. dirs. First Cmty. Bank, Whitehall; bd. dirs. First City Bank, Columbus, Ohio. Advisor Temple Israel Youth Group, Columbus, 1987-89; asst. coach Bexley (Ohio) H.S. Field Hockey, 1988-90. Mem. Whitehall C. of C. (sec. 1992-93, pres. 1994—), Pride of Whitehall (trustee 1994—). Office: First Cmty Bank 4300 E Broad St Whitehall OH 43213

KATHAN, JOYCE C., social worker, administrator; b. Middletown, Conn., Oct. 28, 1931; d. Herbert G. and Mabel Elizabeth (Lee) Clark; m. Boardman W. Kathan, Aug. 17, 1952; children: Nancy Lee, David Wardell, Robert Boardman. B of Social Work magna cum laude, Southern Conn. State U., 1976. Dir. sr. citizen programs Town Woodbury (Conn.); dist. dir. Coun. Greater Boston Camp Fire Girls; participant Global Assembly of Women and Environ., 1991; mem. adv. bd. VNA Health Care, 1985—. Co-author: Youth Where the Action Is, 1970, (with others) Management of Hazardous Agents, Vol. 2: Social and Political Aspects, 1992. Bd. dirs. Waterbury YWCA, 1977-83, rec. sec. Recipient Outstanding Conn. Women award, 1987. Mem. NASW, AAUW (com. mem. pub. policy com. 1985-89, mem. local and state coms. 1978-94, Award for Outstanding Cmty. Svc. Conn. chpt. 1994), LWV (pres. Cheshire chpt. 1989-93), Conn. LWV (mem. pub. policy com. 1988—), Conn. Assn. Sr. Ctr. Pers. (charter mem., sec., Svc. award 1986), Western Conn. Area Agy. Aging (mem. prospect commn. on aging 1979-89, chair 1979-87), Western Conn. Agy. Aging (bd. dirs. 1986-92, pres. 1990-92), Conn. Soc. Gerontology.

KATO, PAMELA KIYOMI, lawyer; b. Mountain View, Calif., Oct. 24, 1964; d. George Mas and Satsuki May (Sugimoto) K. BA, U. Calif., Santa Barbara, 1987; JD, Santa Clara U., 1990. Bar: U.S. Dist. Ct. (no. dist.) Calif., 1991, U.S. Ct. Appeals 1991. Asst. dist. atty. Santa Cruz County, Santa Cruz, Calif., 1991—. Office: 701 Ocean St Santa Cruz CA 95060

KATSON, ROBERTA MARINA, economist; b. Albuquerque, Oct. 5, 1947; d. Robert V. and Penelope (Papafrangos) Katson; student Emory U., 1966-67, Ga. State U., 1967-69; m. Cyrus Butner, 1980; children: Justin Cyrus, Renee Alexis. BA, U. N.Mex., 1974, MA, 1977. Gen. mgr. Window Rock (Ariz.) Motor Inn, Navajo Reservation, 1972-73; research asst. dept. econs. U. N.Mex., Albuquerque, 1974-75, research asso. Resource Econ. Group, 1975-77; economist program analysis Econ. Devel. Adminstrn., Dept. Commerce, Washington, 1977-79; economist Dept. Energy, Washington, 1979-84; cons. Calligraphic Design, Fairfax, Va., 1986-88, owner, 1989-91; economist Office of Fin. Mgmt., Adminstrn. for Children and Families, Dept. of HHS, Washington, 1991—. Mem. Phi Kappa Phi, Omicron Delta Epsilon. Democrat. Contbr. articles to profl. jours. Home: 10722 Midsummer Dr Reston VA 22091-5115 Office: HHS/ACF/OFM 370 L'Enfant Promenade SW Washington DC 20447

KATZ, ANDREA G., pediatrician; b. Newark, Feb. 21, 1963; d. Allan and Marion Ruth (Davidson) Maitlin; m. Eric D. Katz, May 27, 1990. BA, U. Pa., 1984; MD, N.Y. Med. Coll., 1988. Resident The N.Y. Hosp.-Cornell Med. Ctr., 1988-91; with Summit/Warren Pediatrics, 1991-94, Watchung

(N.J.) Pediatrics, 1994—. Fellow Am. Acad. Pediatrics. Office: Watchung Pediatrics 20 Shawnee Dr Ste C Watchung NJ 07059

KATZ, BARBARA ANN, sales executive; b. St. Louis, Jan. 15, 1962; d. Edward and Joyce Lorraine (Gilbert) K. BSBA in Mktg., U. Mo. Sales rep., regional mgr. Vance Pub. Credit and Rating Svc., Overland Park, Kans., 1984-88; pharm. rep. Lederle Labs. Divsn. Am. Cyanamid, Wayne, N.J., 1988-90; oncology rep. Lederle Oncology Divsn., Wayne, N.J., 1991-92; oncology specialty rep. Immunex Biotech Corp., Seattle, 1993—. Bd. dirs. Children's Mercy Cancer Ctr., Kansas City, 1994. Home and Office: 1036 NE Kenwood Ct Lees Summit MO 64064-1767

KATZ, HILDA, artist; b. June 2, 1909; d. Max and Lina (Schwartz) K. Student, Nat. Acad. Design; student (3 awards; New Sch. Social Research scholarship), 1940-41. Author: (under pen name Hulda Weber) poems including numerous anthologies, spl. ltd. edit., 1987-88, Author's Limited Edition Original Manuscript-36 Poems, 1994; anthologies include The Bloom, 1984-85, 87, Perfume and Fragrance, 1988, 89, Lightning & Rainbows, 1989, 90; contbr.: numerous poems, short stories to books and mags. including Humpty Dumpty's Mag. (publ. for children); contbr. commemorative poetry to mus. and govt. including Pres. Ronald W. Reagan, 1985, Pres. Chaim Herzog of Israel, 1987, series of poems in N.Y. State Mus. of Albany, 1987, 89, Yad Vashem Meml. Archives, Jerusalem, 1987, Mus. of Jewish Heritage, 1988, 89, Jewish Theol. Sem. of Am., 1989, Ft. Lewis Coll. Found., 1990, Jewish Nat. and Univ. Libr., Jerusalem, 1990, The Simon Wiesenthal Ctr., U.S.A., 1990, U.S. Holocaust Meml., Washington, 1991, Libr. Congress, Washington, 1991, 92; one-woman exhbns. include Bowdoin Coll. Art Mus., 1951, Calif. State Library, 1953, Print Club Albany, N.Y., 1955, U. Maine, 1955, 58, Jewish Mus., 1956, Pa. State Tchrs. Coll., 1956, Massillon Mus., 1957, Ball State Tchrs. Coll., 1957, Springfield (Mass.) Art Mus., 1957, Miami Beach (Fla.) Art Ctr., Richmond (Ind.) Art Assn., 1959, Old State Capitol Mus. La., other exhbns. include: Corcoran Bienniale Library of Congress, Am. in the War Exhbn, N.Y. State Mus. of Albany, 1989, Jewish Theol. Sem. of Am., 1989, 26 mus., Am. Drawing anns. at: Albany Inst., Nat. Acad. Design, Conn. Acad. Fine Arts, Bklyn. Mus., Delgado Mus., Art-U.S.A., 1959, Congress for Jewish Culture, Met. Mus. Art., Springfield (Mo.) Art Mus., Children's Mus. Hartford, Conn., Miniature Printers, Peoria (Ill.) Art Ctr., Pa. Acad. Fine Arts, Originale Contemporate Graphic Internat., France, Bezalel Nat. Mus., Israel, Venice (Italy) Bienniale, Royal Etchers and Painters Exchange Exhibit, Eng., Bat Yam Mus., Israel, Paris, France, 1958, 59, Am.-Italian Print Exchange, numerous libraries, artists socs., invitational exhbns. include, Rome, Turin, Venice, Florence, Naples (all Italy), Nat. Academe Muse, France, Israel, USIA exhbns. in, Europe, S. Am., Asia, Africa; represented spl. collections, U.S. Nat. Mus., 1965, U. Maine, 1965, Library of Congress, 1965-71, Met. Mus. Art, 1965-66, 80, Nat. Gallery Art, 1966, Nat. Collection Fine Arts, 1966-71, 78, Nat. Air and Space Mus., 1970, N.Y. Pub. Library, 1971, 78, U.S. Mus. History and Tech., 1972, Naval Mus., 1972, Ft. Lewis Coll., Durango, Colo., 1980-81, Boston Pub. Library, 1980-81, Israel Nat. Mus., Jerusalem, 1980-81, State Mus. Albany, N.Y., 1980, N.Y. State Mus. Archives, Albany, 1979-89; also represented in permanent collections U.S. Nat. Mus., U. Maine, Libr. of Congress, Met. Mus. Art, Nat. Coll. Fine Arts, D.C., Nat. Gallery Art, D.C., Nat. Air and Space Mus., D.C., N.Y. Pub. Libr., Nat. Mus. History and Tech., Bklyn. Mus., New Britain Mus. Am. Art, Mus. of City of N.Y., Jewish Mus. of N.Y., N.Y. State Mus. of Albany, Israel Mus., Jerusalem, Boston Pub. Libr., Ft. Lewis Coll. Art Mus., Colo., Balt. Mus. Art, Franklin D. Roosevelt, Fogg Mus., Harvard, Santa Barbara (Calif.) Art Mus., Syracuse U., Colorado Springs Fine Arts Ctr., Pennell Collection, Am. Artists Group Prize at Samuel Golden Coll., U. Minn., Calif. State Library, Pa. State Library, Bezalel Nat. Mus., Smithsonian Archives Am. Art (art and poetry), 1979-93, Washington, Archives and State Mus. Albany, N.Y. (120 works), Newark Pub. Library, Libr. of Congress, Washington, Addison Gallery Am. Art, Bat Yam Municipal Mus., Safed Mus., Israel, Pa. State Tchrs. Coll., Richmond Art Assn., Peoria (Ill.) Art Ctr., Boston Pub. Library, St. Margaret Mary Sch. Art, Musee Nat. d'Art Modern, Yad Vashem Meml. Archives, Jerusalem (poetry), 1987, N.Y. State Mus. and Archives, Columbia U. Librs., U. at Albany, SUNY; spl. collections paintings, drawings and prints acquired by 19 nat. and internat. mus./archives including U.S. Nat. Mus., Washington, 1965, Univ. Maine Art, 1965, Libr. Congress, Washington, 1965, 71, Met. Mus. N.Y., 1965, 80, Nat. Coll. Fine Arts, 1966, 71, 78, Nat. Gallery Art, 1966, Nat. Air & Space Mus., 1966, N.Y. Pub. Libr., 1971, 78, Nat. Mus. History/Tech., 1971, Bklyn. Mus. Art, 1978, Mus. City N.Y., 1978, Jewish Mus. N.Y., 1979, N.Y. State Mus. Albany, N.Y., 1979-90, Israel Mus., 1980, Ft. Lewis Coll. Mus., 1980, Smithsonian, 1979, Yad Vashem Meml. Mus./Archives, 1987, Mus. Jewish Heritage, N.Y., 1989, Jewish Theological Seminary Am., 1989, Jewish Nat. & Univ. Libr., Israel, 1990. Represented as artist and poet: Miss. Art Assn. Internat. Water Color Club award 1947, 51, New Haven Paint and Clay Club, purchase award Peoria Art Ctr. 1950, Print Club Albany 1962, also Library of Congress, U. Minn., Calif. State Library, Met. Mus. Art, Pa. State Tchrs. Coll., Art Assn. Richmond, Ind., N.Y. Pub. Library, Newark Pub. Library, St. Margaret Mary Sch. Art Coll., landscape award Soc. Miniature Painters, Gravers and Sculpture, James Joyce award Poetry Soc. Am. 1975; presented spl. commemoration to Yad Vashem Meml. Hist. Site, Jerusalem, 1987; named to Exec. and Profl. Hall of Fame (plaque of honor 1966); all art works, paintings, drawings, prints, print blocks acquired by 19 nat. or internat. mus., librs., archives, spl. permanent collections; original manuscripts, including spl. author's limited editions acquired by 14 nat. or internat. mus., librs., archives, spl. permanent collections under pen name Hulda Weber. Recipient World Order of Narrative Poets, Founder and Ednl. and Cultural Support honor for Mus. and Librs., U. Art Mus., U. Librs. of SUNY, Albany, 1994; named Membro Honoris Causa dell'Accademia di Scienze, Letteri, Arti Classe Accademica "Nobel", Milan, 1974, 75, Classe Storia Letter-Atura Americana, Milan, 1978, Exec. and Profl. Hall of Fame-Life, 1966, A Dau. of Mark Twain, 1970. Fellow Internat. Acad. Poets (founder 1977), Met. Mus. Art; mem. Soc. Am. Graphic Artists (group prize 1950), Print Club Albany (N.Y.), Boston Printmakers (award 1955), Washington Printmakers (exhbns.), Conn. Acad. Fine Arts, Am. Color Print Soc., Audubon Artists (group exhbns., award 1944), Phila. Watercolor Club (life, group exhbns.), Nat. Assn. Women Artists (hon. life, award 1945, 47), Print Council Am., Hunterdon Art Center, Internat. Platform Assn., Poetry Soc. Am., Artists Equity N.Y., Authors Guild, Inc., Accademia Di Scienze, Lettere, Arti-Milano, Italy (Consigliere, named hon. mem. as artist 1974, author/poet 1975, Nobel designate 1978); Academia Di Scienze. Lettere, Arti, Classe, Daughter of Mark Twain (hon. life). Office: 915 West End Ave Apt 5D New York NY 10025-3503

KATZ, HOPE N., journalist; b. Phila., July 8, 1964; d. Joel S. and Bobbi A. (Brownstien) K. Studied abroad, Tel Aviv U., 1983-84; BA in Communications, U. Pa., 1986; postgrad., George Washington U., 1988-89, 91—. Cert. massage therapist with touching the goddess pregnancy and therapeutic specialty. Staff writer Today's Post, King of Prussia, Pa., 1984-86, Dominion Post, Morgantown, W.Va., 1986-87; asst. editor Miami (Fla.) Herald, 1987-88; editor Adler Pub. Co., Washington, 1988-89; assoc. editor New Miami mag., 1989—;, 1989-91; publs. specialist George Washington U., Washington, 1991—; freelance writer Washington, 1993—. Founder The Writing's on the Wall. Mem. NOW, Save the Whales. Democrat. Jewish. Home: 7 W Braddock Rd Alexandria VA 22301

KATZ, JANE, educator; b. Sharon, Pa., Apr. 16, 1943; d. Leon and Dorothea (Oberkewitz) Katz; B.S. in Edn., CCNY, 1963; M.A., NYU, 1966; M.Ed., Columbia Tchrs. Coll., 1972, Ed.D., 1978. Mem. faculty Bronx C.C., CUNY, 1964—, prof. phys. edn., 1972—; mem. U.S. Round-the-World Synchronized Swim Team, 1964; synchronized swimming solo tour of Eng., 1969; founding co-organizer, coach 1st Internat. Israeli Youth Festival Games, 1970; mem. winning U.S. Maccabiah Swim Team, 1957; vice chmn. Metro Master AAU Swim Team, 1974—; mem. AAU Nat. Masters All-Am. Swimming Team, 1974—, synchronized swimming solo champion, 1975; speaker, judge in field. Trainee Fed. Adminstrn. Aging, 1971-72; mem. Internat. Hall. of Fame, Ft. Lauderdale, Fla. Named Healthy Am. Fitness Leader U.S. Jaycees and the Pres's. Coun. on Phys. Fitness, 1987, Outstanding Masters Synchroured Swimming, 1987; winner CCNY Towsend Harris Acad. medal, 1989. Mem. AAHPER, U.S. Com. Sports for Israel (dir., co-chmn. women's swimming com. 1970—), Nat. Jewish Welfare Bd., Internat. Aquatics. Author: Swimming for Total Fitness, A Progressive Aerobic Program, 1981, rev. ed. 1993, Swimming Through Your Pregnancy, 1983, W.E.T. Workouts: Water Exercises and Techniques to Help You and Tone Up Aerobically, 1985, Fitness Works: Blueprint for Lifelong Fitness, 1988, Swim 30 Laps in 30 Days, 1991, The Workstation Workout, 1994; author: (video) The W.E.T. Workout, 1994; papers in field. Address: 400 2nd Ave Apt 23B New York NY 10010-4052

KATZ, JERI BETH, lawyer; b. Washington, Nov. 6, 1964; d. Stanley J. and Paula (Goldberg) K.; m. Daniel Alan Ezra, June 19, 1988 (div. Dec. 1990). BA, U. Md., 1987; JD, Cath. U., Washington, 1990. Bar: Md. 1990, D.C. 1991, U.S. Ct. Appeals (6th cir.) 1991, U.S. Ct. Internat. Trade 1992. Assoc. Winston & Strawn, Washington, 1990; ptnr. Law Offices Royal Daniel, Washington, 1990-94, Daniel & Katz, Breckenridge, Colo., 1994—. Home: P O Box 6602 Breckenridge CO 80424 Office: Daniel & Katz 130 Ski Hill Rd P O Box 567 Breckenridge CO 80424

KATZ, JOETTE, judge; b. Bklyn., Feb. 3, 1953. BA, Brandeis U., 1974; JD, U. Conn., 1977. Bar: Conn. 1977. Pvt. practice, 1977-78; asst. pub. defender Office Chief Pub. Defender, 1978-83; chief legal svcs. Pub. Defender Svcs., 1983-89; judge Superior Ct., 1989-92; assoc. judge Conn. Supreme Ct., Hartford, 1992—; instr. U. Conn. Sch. law, 1981-84. Office: Conn Supreme Ct Drawer Z Sta A 231 Capitol Ave Hartford CT 06106-1537*

KATZ, LOIS ANNE, internist, nephrologist; b. Rockville Centre, N.Y., Dec. 1, 1941; d. Irvin Martin and Frances (Berenstein) Fradkin; m. Arthur A. Katz, Aug. 18, 1962; children: David, Brian. BA, Wellesley Coll., 1962; MD, NYU, 1966. Diplomate Am. Bd. Internal Medicine, Am. Bd. Nephrology. Intern medicine Bellevue Hosp., NYU, N.Y.C., 1966-67, resident medicine, 1967-68; sr. resident medicine N.Y. Hosp., N.Y.C., 1968-69; chief resident medicine N.Y. VA Med. Ctr., N.Y.C., 1969-70, fellow nephrology, 1970-71, staff physician, 1970-74, assoc. chief nephrology, 1974—, assoc. chief of staff ambulatory care, 1980—; asst. prof. clin. medicine NYU Sch. Medicine, N.Y.C., 1974-79, assoc. prof., 1979—. Blood drive chmn. Beth Emeth Synagogue, Larchmont, N.Y.; alumna admission rep. Wellesley-in-Westchester, N.Y.; bd. mem. Women's Med. Assn., N.Y.C., 1986—. Fellow ACP; mem. Am. Soc. Nephrology, Am. Med. Women's Assn., Soc. Gen. Internal Medicine, Women in Nephrology (treas. 1985-89), Am. Soc. Hypertension, Sigma Xi, Alpha Omega Alpha. Jewish. Office: Dept Vets Affairs Med Ctr 423 E 23d St New York NY 10010

KATZ, MARTHA LESSMAN, lawyer; b. Chgo., Oct. 28, 1952; d. Julius Abraham and Ida (Oiring) Lessman; m. Richard M. Katz, June 27, 1976; children: Julia Erin, Meredith Evin. AB, Washington U., St. Louis, 1974; JD, Loyola U., Chgo., 1977. Bar: Ill. 1977, U.S. Dist. Ct. (no. dist.) Ill. 1977, Calif. 1981, U.S. Dist. Ct. (so. dist.) Calif. 1981, U.S. Dist. Ct. (no. dist.) Calif. 1982, Md. 1993, U.S. Supreme Ct. 1993, D.C. 1994. Assoc. Fein & Hanfling, Chgo., 1977-80, Rudick, Platt & Victor, San Diego, 1981-82, 84-91; asst. sec., counsel Itel Corp., San Francisco, 1982-84; ptnr. Katz & Mann, Attys. at Law, 1991-94. Active Friends of Mayor's Commn. on Women. Mem. ABA (corp. banking and bus. law, real property and law mgmt. sects), Calif. State Bar Assn., Md. Bar Assn., Ill. State Bar Assn., San Diego County Bar Assn., Lawyers Club San Diego, Bar Assn. Balt. City, Career Women's Network, Anti-Defamation League (regional bd., civil rights com., chair govt. affairs com.), Phi Beta Kappa. Jewish.

KATZ, MICHELE WYNNE, marketing professional; b. Buena Park, Calif., Dec. 21, 1962; d. Milton and Piri (Gross) K. BA, UCLA, 1984, MBA, 1989. Account coord. Needham Harper Worldwide/Rubin Postaer & Assocs., L.A., 1985-87; dir. mktg. Taco Bell Corp., Irvine, Calif., 1989—. Vol. Pediatric Cancer Rsch. of Children's Hosp. of Orange County. Mem. Anderson Mgmt. Alumni Assn., Kappa Kappa Gamma. Democrat. Jewish. Office: Taco Bell Corp 17901 Von Karman Ave Irvine CA 92714-6212

KATZ, MIRIAM LESSER, psychotherapist, educator; b. Petah-Tikva, Israel, Aug. 29, 1942; came to U.S., 1965; d. Kurt and Ilse (Fliess) Lesser; m. Adrian Izhack Katz, Mar. 31, 1965; 1 child, Iris Ellen. Diploma in nursing, Beilinson U. Tel-Aviv, 1962; B Gen. Studies, Roosevelt U., Chgo., 1976; MA, U. Chgo., 1977. RN Ill.; lic. psychotherapist Am. bd. Med. Psychotherapist. Head nurse Beilinson Med. Ctr. Tel-Aviv U., Petah-Tikva, 1962-65; operating room nurse Yale U. Med. Ctr., New Haven, 1965-67; surg. nurse U. Chgo. Med. Ctr., 1968-75; rsch. asst. dept. child psychiatry U. Chgo., 1976-80, child and adolescent psychotherapist, 1980—, lectr. in psychiatry, 1988—; psychiat. cons. Head Start, Chgo., 1979-80. Contbr. articles to profl. jours. Mem. Am. Psychol. Assn., Am. Assn. Counseling Psychologists, Am. Counseling Assn., World Fedn. Mental Health. Home: 1125 E 53rd St Chicago IL 60615-4410 Office: U Chgo Dept Psychiatry 5841 S Maryland Ave Chicago IL 60637-1463

KATZ, PHYLLIS POLLAK, magazine publisher and editor; b. N.Y.C., Dec. 29, 1939; d. Henry Abraham and Rose (Chaiken) P.; m. Edward Katz, Sept. 12, 1971; children: Charles Daniel, Jacob Evan. B.A., Cornell U., 1961; postgrad., U. Pa., 1961-68, Am. Sch. Classical Studies, Athens, 1964-66. Dept. asst. Univ. Mus., U. Pa.; lectr. NYU, 1970-71; asst. editor Archaeology mag., N.Y.C., 1968-72; editor Archaeology mag., 1972-87, pub., 1978—. Mem. archaeol. excavations, Gordion, Turkey, 1965, Porto Cheli, Greece, 1965, Samothrace, Greece, 1966, Torre del Mordillo, Italy, 1967. Heinemann fellow, 1964-66. Mem. Archaeol. Inst. Am. Jewish. Office: Archaeology 135 William St New York NY 10038-3805

KATZ, RENÉE SUE, psychologist. BA summa cum laude, U. Wash., 1980; MSW, U. Calif., Berkeley, 1982; PhD, Calif. Sch. Prof Psychology, Berkeley, 1988. Lic. psychologist and clin. social worker, Calif. Patient and family counselor Merrit-Peralta Med. Ctr., Oakland, Calif., 1981-85; pvt. practice San Francisco, 1986—; mem. faculty San Francisco State U., 1986-91; therapist Palo Alto (Calif.) Ctr. for Stress Related Disorders, 1988-90; outpatient therapist Stanford (Calif.) U. Med. Ctr., 1989-90; staff psychologist Addictions Inst., Menlo Park, Calif., 1989—; cons., trainer in field. Author, editor: Countertransference and Older Clients, 1990; contbr. numerous articles to profl. jours. Mem. APA, NASW, Am. Soc. on Aging, Phi Beta Kappa. Office: 1220 Universtiy Dr Ste 101 Menlo Park CA 94025

KATZ, SUSAN AUDREY, communications executive, producer, director, writer; b. Bklyn., May 14, 1956; d. Nathan and Pearl (Kron) K.; m. Stephen Anthony Sheehan, Aug. 31, 1986. BA in TV-Radio with honors, Bklyn. Coll., 1978; cert. in film, NYU, 1987. Assoc. producer BC Presents Sta. WNYC-TV, N.Y.C., 1977-78; traffic producer Sta. WNEW-TV, N.Y.C., 1978-79, syndicated tape mgr., 1979-80; promotion mgr. Sta. WWYZ-FM, Waterbury, Conn., 1980-82; dir. promotions Sta. WATR-TV, Waterbury, 1980-82; dir. creative services Sta. WTXX-TV, Waterbury, 1980-85; editor in chief Bandshell Publs., Bklyn., 1985—; co-owner, pres. Katz Sheehan Media, Inc., Bklyn. and Bridgeport, Conn., 1985—. Dir. Campbell's Soup film commls., 1990—. Newsletter editor N.Y. State Senator Marty Markowitz, 1978—; dir. advt. Bucci for Bridgeport mayor, 1989; exec. producer Taste of Bridgeport, 1988, Ganim for Bridgeport mayor, 1991; active numerous corp., comml. and polit. prodns. Recipient Telly awrd, 1985, 94, Echo award Direct Mktg. Assn., 1986, Cindy award, 1994. Mem. Conn. Assn. Prodn. Profls. (exec. coun.), Assn. Ind. Viedo and Filmmakers Inc., Internat. TV Assn. Democrat. Jewish. Office: Katz Sheehan Media Inc 120 Pinewood Trl Bridgeport CT 06611-3313

KATZ, TONNIE, newspaper editor. BA, Barnard Coll., 1966; MSc, Columbia U., 1967. Editor, reporter newspapers including The Quincy Patriot Ledger, Boston Herald Am., Boston Globe; Sunday/projects editor Newsday; mng. editor Balt. News Am., 1983-86, The Sun, San Bernardino, Calif., 1986-88; asst. mng. editor for news The Orange County Register, Santa Ana, Calif., 1988-89, mng. editor, 1989-92, editor, v.p., 1992—. Office: Freedom Newspapers Inc Orange County Register 625 N Grand Ave Santa Ana CA 92701-4347

KATZ, VERA, mayor, former college administrator, state legislator; b. Dusseldorf, Germany, Aug. 3, 1933; came to U.S., 1940; d. Lazar Pistrak and Raissa Goodman; m. Mel Katz (div. 1985); 1 child, Jesse. BA, Bklyn. Coll., 1955, postgrad., 1955-57. Market research analyst TIMEX, B.T. Babbitt, N.Y.C., 1957-62; mem. Oreg. Ho. of Reps., Salem; former dir. devel. Portland Community Coll., from 1982; mayor City of Portland, Oreg., 1993—; mem. Gov.'s Council on Alcohol and Drug Abuse Programs, Oreg. Legis., Salem, 1985—; mem. adv. com. Gov.'s Council on Health, Fitness and Sports, Oreg. Legis., 1985—; mem. Gov.'s Commn. on Sch. Funding Reform; mem. Carnegie task Force on Teaching as Profession, Washington, 1985-87; vice-chair assembly Nat. Conf. State Legis., Denver, 1986—. Recipient Abigail Scott Duniway award Women in Communications, Inc., Portland, 1985, Jeanette Rankin First Woman award Oreg. Women's Polit. Caucus, Portland, 1985, Leadership award The Neighborhood newspaper Portland, 1985, Woman of Achievement award Commn. for Women, 1985, Outstanding Legis. Advocacy award Oreg. Primary Care Assn., 1985, Service to Portland Pub. Sch. Children award Portland Pub. Schs., 1985. Fellow Am. Leadership Forum (founder Oreg. chpt.); mem. Dem. Legis. Leaders Assn., Nat. Bd. for Profl. Teaching Standards. Democrat. Jewish. Office: Office of the Mayor City Hall Rm 303 1220 SW Fifth Ave Portland OR 97204*

KATZ, VICTORIA MANUELA, public relations executive, educator, consultant; b. N.Y.C., Mar. 12, 1941; d. Isaac William and Sylvia (Katz) Penner; m. Ronald Mark Katz, Sept. 8, 1974. BA in Journalism, Hofstra Coll., 1962. Sr. editor real estate, fin. Long Island (N.Y.) Comml. Review, 1962-72; freelance writer, publicist N.Y., 1972-74; managing editor North Shore News Group, Smithtown, N.Y., 1974-88; dir. u. news svcs. SUNY, Stony Brook, 1988—; dir. Long Island Bus. Inc., Ronkonkoma, N.Y., 1965—; adj. journalism prof. C.W. Post, Greenvale, N.Y., 1986-88, Hofstra Coll., Hempstead, N.Y., 1987. Author: (study) Smithtown Minorities, 1983. Trustee Harbor County Day Sch., St. James, N.Y., 1977-93, mktg. and pub. rels. com. mem. United Way, L.I., 1988—; program com. mem. Mus. at Stony Brook, 1990-93. Recipient Media award for govtl. reporting Press Club L.I., 1987, 88. Mem. AAUW (past v.p.), Pub. Rels. Soc. Am., Soc. Profl. Journalists (nat. com. mem., co-chair chpt. health and welfare com., regional dir. 1994—), Press Club L.I. Chpt. Soc. Profl. Journalists (pres. 1974, treas. 1985-93, Deadline Club bd. 1994, program co-chair 1993, v.p. 1995). Home: 19 Millbrook Dr Stony Brook NY 11790-2930 Office: SUNY at Stony Brook Adminstrn Bldg 144 Stony Brook NY 11794

KATZBERG, JANE MICHAELS, health care administrator, consultant; b. Bklyn., Apr. 17, 1940; d. David Donn and Shirley (Ingram) Michaels; m. Mitchell Ronald Katzberg, Jan. 19, 1959; children: Michael Loren, Todd Alexander. BS, Adelphi U., 1961; M of Profl. Studies in Health Care Adminstrn., L.I. U., 1975. Cert. home economist, tchr., N.Y. Mgr. quality assurance Suffolk Physicians, Central Islip, N.Y., 1979-81; dir. quality assurance Community Hosp. of Glen Cove, N.Y., 1982-84; dir. intermediate care facilities program United Cerebral Palsy, Commack, N.Y., 1985-86; dir. svcs. for handicapped Town of Huntington, L.I., N.Y., 1986-95; pres., cons. Images, Dix Hills, N.Y., 1985-88; lectr. in field. Mem. Citizen's Adv. Com. for Handicapped, Town of Huntington 1985-86, Round Table Selection Com., C. of C. Found., Huntington Health and Human Svcs., Huntington Hosp. Cmty. Health Ctr. Bd. steering com.; mem. adv. bd. Dept. Social Svcs., Huntington, L.I. Devel. Ctr., Melville Estates; facilitator Nat. Orgn. Disability award, N.Y. State Eleanor Roosvelt award for Town Huntington; pres. Howell Rd. Sch. PTA, North Valey Stream, N.Y., 1973; meeting rep. N.Y. State Advocate for Disabled, 1986-95; mem. divsn. dirs. Cmty. Resource Dept., 1986-89, divsn. dirs. human svcs., 1989-95. Acad. scholar C.W. Post Coll., Greenvale, N.Y., 1974. Mem. Assn. Local Govt. Advocates for Disabled, Huntington C. of C. Republican. Jewish. Home: 81 Buttonwood Dr Dix Hills NY 11746-4804

KATZEN, SALLY, lawyer; b. Pitts., Nov. 22, 1942; d. Nathan and Hilda (Schwartz) K.; m. Timothy B. Dyk, Oct. 31, 1981; 1 child, Abraham Benjamin. BA magna cum laude, Smith Coll., 1964; JD magna cum laude, U. Mich., 1967. Bar: D.C. 1968, U.S. Supreme Ct. 1971. Congl. intern Sente Subcom. on Constl. Rights, Washington, 1963; legal rsch. asst. civil rights div. Dept. Justice, Washington, 1965; law clk. to Judge J. Skelly Wright U.S. Ct. Appeals (D.C. cir.), 1967-68; assoc. Wilmer, Cutler & Pickering, Washington, 1968-75, ptnr., 1975-79, 81-93; gen. counsel Coun. on Wage and Price Stability, 1979-80; dep. dir. for policy, 1980-81; adminstr. Office of Info. and Regulatory Affairs, Office of Mgmt. and Budget, Washington, 1993—; pub. mem. Adminstrv. Conf. U.S., 1988-93, govt. mem. and vice chair, 1993—; mem. exec. com. Prettyman-Leventhal Inn of Ct., 1988-90, counselor, 1990-91; mem. Jud. Conf. for D.C. Cir., 1972-91, 83-92; adj. prof. Georgetown U. Law Ctr., 1988, 90, 92. Editor-in-chief U. Mich. Law Rev., 1966-67. Mem. com. visitors U. Mich. Law Sch., 1972—. Fellow ABA (ho. of dels. 1978-80, 89-91, coun. adminstrv. law sect. 1979-82, chmn. adminstrv. law and regulatory practice sect. 1988-89, governing com. forum com. communications law 1979-82, chmn. standing com. Nat. Conf. Groups 1989-92); mem. D.C. Bar Assn., Women's Bar Assn., FCC Bar Assn. (exec. com. 1984-87, pres. 1990-91), Women's Legal Def. Fund (pres. 1977, v.p. 1978), Order of Coif. Home: 4638 30th St NW Washington DC 20008-2127 Office: Info & Regulatory Affairs Office Mgmt & Budget Old Exec Office Bldg Rm 350 Washington DC 20503

KATZENSTEIN, THEA, retail executive, jewelry designer; b. N.Y.C., Mar. 30, 1927; d. Carl E. and Lillian (Rosenblatt) Schustak; m. William Katzenstein, Sept. 10, 1950; children: Leo, Ranee. Student, Sarah Lawrence Coll., 1948-50; BS, Columbia U., 1962, MA, 1967. Pres. Gallery A., N.Y.C., 1967-71, Melita, N.Y.C., 1972-77, TK Studio, Coral Gables, Fla., 1977—; adj. prof. of jewelry Fla. Internat. U., 1989-90; enamelling instr. U. Miami, 1991. Author: Early Chinese Art and The Pacific Basin, 1967; painting, graphics and jewelry represented in numerous pvt. collections. Trustee Miami Metro Zoo, 1994—. Mem. Soc. N.Am. Goldsmiths, Enamel Guild South, Nat. Enamelist Guild, Fla. Soc. Goldsmiths (pres. S.E. chpt.), Fla. Craftsmen, Zonta (sec. Coral Gables chpt. 1989-90). Democrat. Jewish. Home: 9 Island Ave # 1501 Miami Beach FL 33139

KATZOWITZ, LAUREN, philanthropic and non-profit consultant; m. Marc Shenfield. BS in Comparative Lit. with honors, Brandeis U., 1970; MS with honors, Columbia U., 1971. With, Newsweek mag., then Phila. Bull.; freelance writer, editor, cons., until 1975; cons. Ford Found., 1972-75; mgr. PBS programs Exxon Corp., 1978-81, Great Performances, Live From Lincoln Ctr., Dance in America, NOVA, The MacNeil/Lehrer Report; communications mgr. Exxon Rsch. and Engring. Co., 1981-84; regional liaison Europe and Africa, Exxon Corp., 1984-86; exec. dir. Found. Svc., 1986—; pres. LK Consulting, Croton on Hudson, N.Y., 1986—. Pres. Bronx Ednl. Svcs. Named one of 12 Women to Watch in the Eighties, Ladies' Home Jour., 1979. Regional Finalist Pres.'s Commn. on White House fellow, 1984. Office: LK Consulting 4 Hamilton Ave Croton On Hudson NY 10520-2521

KAUFFMAN, KAETHE COVENTON, art educator, artist, author; b. Washington, Aug. 12, 1948; d. Richard G. and Kathleen B. (Coventon) K.; m. James William Hite, Oct. 23, 1983; children: James Haydn, Kauffman Hite. BA, U. Wash., 1970, U. Nev., 1975; MFA, U. Calif., Irvine, 1978; PhD, Union Inst. Cin., 1989. Art dept. faculty U. Nev., Las Vegas, Mount St. Mary's Coll., L.A.; chmn. art dept. Sierra Nevada Coll., Incline Village, 1989-91, assoc. prof., 1991—; mem. faculty dept. art U. Calif., Irvine; mem. editorial adv. bd. Collegiate Press. Author: Sex and the Avant-Garde: A Gender Revolution in the Visual Arts 1830-1993, Female Forms of Originality and the New, Women Artists in the Avant-Garde, How Art Professors Teach Avant-Garde Values, Women Artists Deconstruct the Male Avant-Garde, A Modern Renaissance of the Arts; columnist: Lake Tahoe World newspapers; art exhibited at Utrecht, Holland, 1977, Inst. Modern Art, Brisbane, Australia, 1978, George Patton Gallery U. Melbourne, Australia, 1979, Newport Harbor Art Mus., Calif., 1980, Fiberworks Gallery, Berkeley, Calif., 1981, Galerie Triangle, Washington, 1982, Nev. Mus., Reno, 1983, Schoharie Nat., Cobleskill, N.Y., 1984, Pinnacle Gallery, N.Y., 1986, Space Gallery, Las Vegas, Nev., 1988, Manville Gallery, U. Nev., Reno, 1989, Galerie Art-Jeunesse, Montreal, Que., 1990, Kleinert Gallery, N.Y., 1991, West Gallery, Claremont Grad. Sch., 1992, Sierra Nev. Coll. Art Gallery, Lake Tahoe, Nev., 1995, Exhbn. Hall U. Prague, Czech Republic, CERES Gallery, N.Y.; represented in permanent collections Women's Studio Workshop, N.Y.C., Calif. Mus. Photography, L.A., Fluor Corp., L.A., Harris Found., Las Vegas, Nev., Computer Scis. Corp., L.A., Sheraton Plaza Inn, L.A., Glendale Fed. Bank, L.A. Juror 3d biennial Nev. Craft Show. Recipient Max H. Block award for Humanism; Laguna Beach Festival of the Arts fellow; TOSCO Corp. grantee; Artists grantee Sierra Arts Found. Mem. Orgn. for Ind. Artists, Nat. Mus. Women in Arts, Women's Caucus for Art, Nat. Assn. Women Artists, Ceres Gallery.

KAUFFMAN, SANDRA DALEY, state legislator; b. Osceola, Nebr., Jan. 26, 1933; d. James Richard and Erma Grace (Heald) Daley; m. Larry Allen Kauffman, Sept. 4, 1955; children: Claudia Kauffman Boosman, Matthew Allen. BA, U. Nebr., 1954; postgrad., U. Kansas City, summer 1957. Tchr. Falls City (Nebr.) High Sch., 1954-55, Westport High Sch., Kansas City, Mo., 1955-59; sales rep. Manson Industries, Topeka, Kans., 1974-75; dir. pub. affairs Bishop Hogan High Sch., Kansas City, 1985-86; mem. Mo. Ho. of Reps., Jefferson City, 1987—. Mem. Kansas City Citizens Assn., 1981—, Kansas City Consensus, 1985—; mem. women's coun. U. Mo., Kansas City, 1986—; mem. Carondelet Aging Svcs. Adv. Bd., 1992—, mem. rsch. mental health bd., bd. govs., 1992—. Recipient Friend of Edn. award Ctr. Edn. Assn., 1986; named Mem. of Yr., Mo. Congress Parents and Tchrs., 1979. Mem. Am. Legis. Exch. Coun., Nat. Coun. State Legislatures, Nat. PTA (hon. life), Mo. PTA (hon. life), South Kansas City C. of C., Grandview C. of C., Women C. of C., Mo. Women's Coun. on Econ. Devel. and Tng. Republican. Methodist. Home: 620 E 90th Ter Kansas City MO 64131-2918 Office: Mo Ho of Reps State Capitol Jefferson City MO 65101*

KAUFMAN, DEBRA RENEE, sociology and women's studies educator; b. Cleve., Apr. 2, 1941; d. Max and Ida (Hoffman) Horwitz; m. Michael William Kaufman, Aug. 25, 1963; children: Alana, Marc. BA, U. Mich., 1963, MA, 1966; PhD, Cornell U., 1976. Asst. prof. SUNY, Albany, 1974-76; asst. prof. Northeastern U., Boston, 1976-81, assoc. prof., 1981-86, prof., coord. women's studies, 1986—, Matthews Disting. prof., 1994—; vis. scholar Union Coll., Schenectady, 1974; Klein lectr., 1987; vis. scholar, prof. Brigham Young U., Provo, Utah, 1993; reader NSF, Washington, 1993; referee jours. Author: Rachel's Daughters, 1991; co-author: Achievement and Women, 1982; editor: Public/Private Spheres, 1989; contbr. articles to profl. jours. Active Nat. Coun. on Edn., Boston, 1987—; mem. adv. bd. Program on Women's Studies, Princeton, N.J., 1983-88, Sister Spirit, Boston, 1985-87. Mellon fellow Wellesley (Mass.) Coll. Ctr. for Rsch. on Women, 1983-84; vis. scholar Radcliffe Coll. Murray Rsch. Ctr., Cambridge, Mass., 1989-90. Mem. Am. Sociol. Assn., Am. Soc. Religion, Sociologists for Women in Soc. (life; mem. adv. bd.), Ea. Sociol. Soc., Phi Kappa Phi. Democrat. Jewish. Office: Northeastern U 515 Holmes 360 Huntington Ave Boston MA 02115-5096

KAUFMAN, DENISE NORMA, psychologist, addictions counselor, educator; b. Trenton, N.J., Feb. 7, 1954; d. Charles Edwin and Luella (Barcroft) Farr; m. Peter Alan Kaufman, May 15, 1986 (div. Nov. 1989). BS, Trenton State Coll., 1976, MEd, 1977; EdD, Temple U., 1983. Cert. tchr. health, driver edn., spl. edn., N.J., cert. sch. psychologist, cert. addictions counselor, cert. in student pers. svcs., N.J. Health edn. tchr., dept. dir. Haddon Heights (N.J.) Pub. Schs., 1976-81; tchr. educationally handicapped adolescents Haddon Twp. (N.J.) High Sch., 1984-85; tchr. educationally handicapped adolescents, psychologist Archway Programs, Atco, N.J., 1984-90; tchr., psychologist Ferris Sch. for Boys, Dept. Children, Youth and Families, Wilmington, Del., 1991-92; tchr., cons. psychologist Willingboro (N.J.) Twp. Pub. Schs., 1991-92; pvt. practice psychology, addictions counselor Haddon Heights, 1979—; psychologist Atlantic County Spl. Svcs. Sch. Dist., Mays Landing, N.J., 1992-93; prof., supr. student interns Rowan Coll. of N.J., Glassboro, 1993—; adj. prof. psychology Camden County Coll., Blackwood, N.J., 1993—; mem. Gov. Brendan Byrne's Smoking and Health Com., 1978-80; assoc. prof. health edn. Mercer County Community Coll., Trenton, 1981; program dir. Phila. (Pa.) Health Mgmt. Corp., 1982; cons. Clearview Regional High Sch., Jr. High Sch. Pub. Sch. Dist., 1986—, Lower Camden County Regional Sch. Dist., 1986—; lectr. Assn. Schs. and Agys. for the Handicapped, 1986—; cons., lectr. Charter Fairmont Inst., Phila., 1991—. Instr. Camden chpt. ARC, S.E. Pa. chpt. Am. Heart Assn.; lectr., cons. Haddon Heights (N.J.) Rotary, 1988—. Mem. APA, Eta Sigma Gamma, Kappa Delta Pi. Republican. Jewish. Home: 1604 Chestnut Ave Haddon Heights NJ 08035-1506 Office: Rowan Coll of NJ Dept Spl Edn Svcs and Instrn Robinson Hall Glassboro NJ 08028

KAUFMAN, ELAINE SUE SOMMERS, special education educator; b. Bklyn., Dec. 25, 1933; d. Samuel and Lily Vivian (Schiller) Sommers; m. Harold Alexander Kaufman, June 24, 1956; children: Michele Beth, Roy Sommers. BA, Bklyn. Coll., 1955; MEd, U. Pitts., 1959. Cert. elem., spl. edn., reading tchr., reading specialist, N.Y., Pa., N.J. Elem. tchr. East Meadow (N.Y.) Pub. Schs., 1955-56, Pitts. Pub. Schs., 1956-61; elem. tchr. Piscataway (N.J.) Bd. Edn., 1961-63, supplemental tchr., 1972-80, learning strategist, 1980-82, tchr. handicapped, 1982—; cons. Piscataway Adult Edn. Adv. Coun., 1975—. Editor: (booklet) Multi-Ethnic Traditional Cooking for the Microwave, 1991; contbg. food editor (newsletter) In Common, 1992; contbr. articles to local newspaper. Counselor Piscataway Helpline, 1971-73; pres. Women's Am. ORT, Piscataway, 1970-73, North Cen. N.J. regional v.p., 1973-75; v.p. Pitt Dames, U. Pitts., 1957-58; trustee Anshe Emeth, 1977-78, v.p., pres. Couples Club, 1977-79; active Planned Parenthood. Frick Commn. scholar, 1958; Piscataway Bd. Edn. grantee, 1990-91, grantee Innovative Ideas in Teaching. Mem. NEA, NOW, AAUW, N.J. Edn. Assn., Piscataway Tchrs. Assn., Middlesex Reading Coun. (membership chmn. 1987-88, parliamentarian 1988-90, news reporter 1992, Outstanding Contbr. award 1987), Brandeis Women's Assn. (life Middlesex chpt.), Phi Kappa Delta. Home: 142 Fountain Ave Piscataway NJ 08854-4607 Office: Schor Mid Sch N Randolphville Rd Piscataway NJ 08854

KAUFMAN, JAN CARYL, educational administrator, clergywoman, lawyer; b. Balt., June 24, 1955; d. Stanley and Joyce (Jacobson) K. BA, Goucher Coll., 1974; B Hebrew Lit., Balt. Hebrew Coll., 1974; MA in Hebrew Lit., Hebrew Union Coll., N.Y.C., 1979; JD, George Washington U., 1988. Bar: Pa. 1988, D.C. 1989; Rabbi, 1979. Assoc. dir. B'nai B'rith Found., U. Md., College Park, 1979-81; mem. faculty upper sch. Charles E. Smith Jewish Day Sch., Rockville, Md., 1981-91; rabbi Congregation Kol Ami, Annapolis, Md., 1986-88; dir. Jewish Study Ctr., Washington, 1988-92; prin. Solomon Schechter H.S., N.Y.C., 1991-94; dir. spl. projects Rabbinical Assembly Jewish Theol. Sem., N.Y.C., 1994—; founder, sec. Aleph-Bet Jewish Day Sch., Annapolis, 1987-92. Mem. Rabbinical Assembly (com. Jewish law and standards 1991—), N.Y. Bd. Rabbis. Democrat. Home: 215 W 101st St New York NY 10025 Office: Jewish Theol Sem 3080 Broadway New York NY 10027

KAUFMAN, JANICE HORNER, foreign language educator; b. Mattoon, Ill., Apr. 30, 1949; d. Daniel Ogden and Julia Betty (McDermid) Horner; m. Richard Boucher Kaufman, June 24, 1972; children: Julia Ogden, Richard Pearse. AB, Duke U., 1971; MA in Liberal Studies, Hollins Coll., 1979; postgrad., NYU, 1986, U. Va., Charlottesville, 1991—. Tchr. Roanoke (Va.) City Pub. Schs., 1971-72, North Cross Sch., Roanoke, Va., 1974-82; instr. in French Va. Poly. Inst. and State U., Blacksburg, 1984-86, 88, 90, 94, asst. dir fgn. lang. camps, 1984-85, administrv. dir., 1986; French, English interpreter, translator Coll. Architecture and Urban Studies, Blacksburg, 1988; instr. ESL U. Community Internat. Coun., Cranwell Internat. Ctr., Blacksburg, 1987-89; instr. French Hollins Coll., Roanoke, Va., 1989-90, Radford (Va.) U., 1989, 90; grad. teaching asst. U. Va., Charlottesville, 1992; student counselor Am. Inst. Fgn. Study, Greenwich, Conn., 1977; session leader Russell County Pub. Schs., Lebanon, Va., 1985, Va. Assn. Ind. Schs., Richmond, 1986; reader Mountain Interstate Fgn. Lang. Conf., Radford U., 1990, East Carolina U., Greenville, N.C., 1991, Va. Poly. Inst. and State U., Blacksburg, 1992, Clemson (S.C.) U., 1993, Va. Fgn. Lang. Conf., Richmond, 1993, African Lit. Assn. Conf., Guadeloupe, 1993; faculty cons. advanced placement exam in French, Ednl. Testing Svc., Trenton State Coll., 1991, 92, 93, 94. Mem. Jr. League of Roanoke Valley, Inc., 1975—; treas. Women of Christ Ch., 1984-86; Sunday sch. tchr. Christ Episc. Ch., Blackburg, 1987-89; co-coord. jr. high youth group St. Timothy's Episc. Ch., Herndon, Va., 1994—. Mem. MLA, Am. Assn. Tchrs. French, African Lit. Assn., South Atlantic MLA (presenter 1994), Pi Delta Phi. Home: 900 Barker Hill Rd Herndon VA 22070

KAUFMAN, JUDY, librarian; b. N.Y.C., July 24, 1947; d. George and Roslyn (Weinstein) Leiderman; m. Peter S. Kaufman, June 18, 1972 (div. Aug. 1988); children: Rachel, Daria. BA magna cum laude, Brown U., 1969; MusM, SUNY, Stony Brook, 1970; MLS, SUNY, Buffalo, 1974. Reference libr., cataloger music libr. SUNY, Buffalo, 1974-76; acting head music libr. Cornell U., Ithaca, N.Y., 1976; head music libr. SUNY, Stony Brook, 1977-87, asst. dir. librs. for pers., 1987-93; asst. univ. libr. for pers. and adminstrn. U. Calif., Irvine, 1994—. Co-chmn. campus com. Mid-Suffolk NOW, Stony Brook, 1990-92. Recipient Chancellor's award for excellence in librarianship SUNY, 1979. Mem. ALA, Phi Beta Kappa, Beta Phi Mu. Home: 35 Whitman Ct Irvine CA 92715 Office: U Calif Main Libr PO Box 19557 Irvine CA 92713

KAUFMAN, LINDA ANN, educator, composer, writer; b. Trenton, N.J., Dec. 13, 1937; d. Charles H. Walcoff and Lillian Alperin Robins; m. Irwin Sidney Friedman, May 18, 1968 (dec. Apr. 1984); children: Deborah Ruth, Miriam Judith; m. Albert Norman Kaufman, Nov. 2, 1990. BA, Rutgers U., Newark, 1959. Diploma in music ministry. High sch. English tchr. Clark (N.J.) Regional High Sch., 1959-61, McArthur High Sch., Hollywood, Fla., 1967-70; music tchr. Temple Beth El, Hollywood, 1970-75; English and music tchr. Hollywood Fellowship, 1975-78; vice prin. Bowen's Mill Christian Ctr., Fitzgerald, Ga., 1978-83; music and Bible tchr. Grace Fellowship, Tulsa, 1987-89; ESL tchr. L.A. Unified Sch. Dist., 1989-90; music and Bible tchr., ch. music cons. Eagles' Nest Fellowship, San Antonio, 1992—; head drama dept. New Covenant Fellowship, San Antonio, 1985-87. Composer, lyricist, concept for musical comedy Estherella, 1993; writer, composer, lyricist musical for children Nothing Ever Happens in a Small Town, 1993. Recipient Globe award for best mus. score San Antonio Arts Coun., 1993. Mem. Temple Beth El Sisterhood, Hadassah. Jewish. Home: 3910 Creek Spg San Antonio TX 78230-2061

KAUFMAN, NANCY J., health foundation executive; b. Milw., Mar. 1, 1949; d. Wesley Paul and Wilma Barbara (Kluger) Foreman; m. Ira Ray Kaufman, Jan. 7, 1973; 1 child. BS in Nursing, U. Wis., 1971, MS in Adminstrv. and Preventive Medicine, 1983. RN, Wis., N.J. Dir. Wis. Controlled Substances Bd. and Gov.'s Coun. on Alcohol and Drug Abuse, Madison, 1972-74; prevention coord. Wis. Bur. Alcohol and Other Drug Abuse, Madison, 1974-79, supr. prevention and tng. unit, 1979-82; dir., nat. prevention evaluation rsch network Alcohol, Drug Abuse and Mental Health Adminstrn., Madison, 1978-82; coord. health block grant Wis. Div. Health, Madison, 1982, dir. maternal and child health, 1982-84, chief family and community health, 1982-83; dep. dir. Bur. of Pub. Health, Madison, 1983-91; v.p. Robert Wood Johnson Found., Princeton, N.J., 1991—; mem. prevention, treatment and tng. grant rev. com. Nat. Inst. on Drug Abuse, Rockville, Md., 1979-81; cons. Nat. Cancer Inst., Bethesda, Md., 1982; cons., mem. adv. bd. Nat. Eldercare Inst. for Health Promotion, Am. Assn. Ret. Persons, Washington, 1988-93; mem., chmn. perinatal grant rev. com. Office Substance Abuse Prevention, Rockville, 1989-91. Author: Preventing the Transmission of HIV through Serologic Screening, 1986; co-editor: Handbook for Prevention Evaluation, 1980; co-dir. media campaign Osteoporosis: Stop the Lady Killer, 1987 (Clarion award Nat. Women in Comm. 1987). Bd. dirs. Alliance for Children and Youth Found., Madison, 1979-91, AIDS Resource Ctr. Wis., Milw., 1986-87; mem. Madison Pub. Health Commn., 1989-91; sec. Friends of WHA-TV, Madison, 1989-90, pres., 1991. Recipient Clarion award Nat. Women in Comm., 1985, Sec.'s award for excellence in govt. svc. Wis. Dept. Health and Human Svcs., 1990. Mem. APHA (co-founder alcohol, tobacco and drug sect., chmn. 1981-84, 94—, mem. governing coun. 1982-84, 90-92, publs. bd. 1984-90, editor search com. Am. Jour. Pub. Health 1991), Soc. for Prevention Rsch. Office: Robert Wood Johnson Foundation Box 2316 1 College Rd E Princeton NJ 08543-2316

KAUFMAN, PAULA T., librarian; b. Perth Amboy, N.J., July 26, 1946; d. Harry and Clara (Katz) K.; m. L. Ratner, 1989. AB, Smith Coll., 1968; MS, Columbia U., 1969; MBA, U. New Haven, 1979. Reference librarian Columbia U., N.Y.C., 1969-70, bus. librarian, 1979-82, dir. library services, 1982-86, dir. acad. info. services, 1986-87, acting v.p., univ. librarian, 1987-88; dean of librs. U. Tenn., Knoxville, 1988—; ref. coord. McKinsey & Co., N.Y.C., 1970-73; founder, ptnr. Info. for Bus., N.Y.C., 1973-76; prin. ref. libr. Yale U., New Haven, 1976-79; bd. dirs. Rsch. Librs. Group, Ctr. Rsch. Librs. Contbr. articles to mags., 1983—. Mem. ALA, Soc. for Scholarly Pub. Ctr. Rsch. Librs. Group (bd. dirs.), Solinet (bd. dirs., chmn. 1992-93).

KAUFMANN, SYLVIA NADEAU, office equipment sales company executive; b. Eagle Lake, Maine, Dec. 1, 1940; d. Edwin Joseph Nadeau and Emily (Beaulieu) Gadbois; m. Max Daniel Kaufmann, Sept. 21, 1958 (div. 1985); children: Mark A., Laura A., Max D. Jr. Grad. high sch., East Hartford, Conn., 1958. Registered arbitrator Am. Registry Arbitrators. Bookkeeper United Bank and Trust, Hartford, Conn., 1959-66; real estate agt. Barcombe Agy., South Windsor, Conn., 1967-74; sales rep. Duplicating Methods Co., East Windsor, Conn., 1974-80; gen. mgr., officer Duplicating Methods Co., East Windsor, 1980—; bd. dirs. Enfield (Conn.) Community Fed. Credit Union. Commr. ethics commn. Town of Enfield, Conn. Mem. Nat. Office Machine Dealers Assn., North Cen. Conn. C. of C., Bus. Profl. Women Greater Hartford, Exec. Females Inc. Democrat. Roman Catholic. Home: 6 Hoover Ln Enfield CT 06082-5314 Office: Duplicating Methods Co 170 North Rd East Windsor CT 06088-9678

KAUGER, YVONNE, state supreme court justice; b. Cordell, Okla., Aug. 3, 1937; d. John and Alice (Bottom) K.; m. Ned Bastow, May 8, 1982; 1 child, Jonna Kauger Kirschner. BS magna cum laude, Southwestern State U., Weatherford, Okla., 1958; cert. med. technologist, St. Anthony's Hosp., 1959; J.D., Oklahoma City U., 1969, LLD (hon.), 1992. Med. technologist Med. Arts Lab., 1959-68; assoc. Rogers, Travis & Jordan, 1970-72; jud. asst. Okla. Supreme Ct., Oklahoma City, 1972-84, justice, 1984-94; vice chief justice Okla. Supreme Ct., 1994—; mem. appellate div. Ct. on Judiciary; mem. State Capitol Preservation Commn., 1983-84; mem. dean's adv. com. Oklahoma City U. Sch. Law; lectr. William O. Douglas Lecture Series Gonzaga U., 1990. Founder Gallery of Plains Indian, Colony, Okla., Red Earth (Down Towner award 1990), 1987; active Jud. Day, Girl's State, 1976-80; keynote speaker Girl's State Hall of Fame Banquet, 1984; bd. dirs. Lyric Theatre, Inc., 1966—, pres. bd. dirs., 1981; past mem. bd. dirs. Civic Music Soc., Okla. Theatre Ctr., Canterbury Choral Soc.; mem. First Lady of Okla.'s Artisans' Alliance Com. Named Panhellenic Woman of Yr., 1990, Woman of Yr. Red Lands Coun. Girl Scouts, 1990, Washita County Hall of Fame, 1992. Mem. ABA (law sch. accreditation com.), Okla. Bar Assn. (law schs. com. 1977—), Washita County Bar Assn., Washita County Hist. Soc. (life), St. Paul's Music Soc., Iota Tau Tau, Delta Zeta (Disting. Alumna award 1988, State Delta Zeta of Yr. 1987, Nat. Woman of Yr. 1988). Episcopalian.

KAUL, INGE ANNELIES, human development specialist; b. Wiesbaden, Germany, Aug. 18, 1944; came to U.S., 1976; d. Heinrich and Annelies K.; m. Edward Hurwitz, 1987. MA, U. Frankfurt, Germany, 1969; PhD, Konstanz (Germany) U., 1972. Asst. prof. U. Konstanz, 1972-75; social affairs officer UN, N.Y.C., 1976-80; asst. rep. UN Devel. Programme, Laos, 1981-83; dep. rep. UN Devel. Programme, Afghanistan, 1983-86; from sr. evaluation officer to sr. policy analyst UN Devel. Programme, N.Y.C., 1986-89, dir. human devel. report office, 1989—. Contbr. articles to profl. jours. Mem. Peace and Devel. Inst. (bd. advisors 1993—), Soc. for Internat. Devel. (bd. dirs. 1993). Office: UNDP 1 UN Plz New York NY 10017

KAULKIN, DONNA BROOKMAN, editor, writer; b. Phila., May 2, 1943; d. Philip and Minnie (Markovitz) Brookman; m. Marvin Kaulkin, Jan. 20, 1963 (div. 1981); children: Andrew Jon, Michael. BA, Georgetown U., 1977. Mng. editor U.S. Pharmacopeia, Rockville, Md., 1978-83; editorial dir. World Aviation Directory, Washington, 1984—, China Buyer's Guide, 1987—, Internat. Air Show Directories, 1987-92, Milestones in Aviation, 1990, Asia/Pacific Aviation, 1991, Airport Business Opportunities, 1991, 92, 93, Overhaul & Maintenance, 1993—, Aviation in Ireland, 1991, Regional Report: Russia and the Newly Independent States, 1993, Regional Report: China, 1994; playwright: Woman at the Washington Zoo, 1980; contbr. many poems, stories, articles to profl. jours. and newsletters. Founder Women's Ctr. Montgomery County, Md., 1975; crisis counselor Crisis Ctr. Montgomery County, 1983-84; speaker, 1983-84. Mem. Internat. Aviation Women's Assn., Aviation Space Writers Assn., Aero Club Washington (bd. dirs.), Internat. Aviation Club, UNIFEM, Am. News Women's Club. Democrat. Jewish. Avocations: acting, directing, playwriting, travel, theater, music. Home: 4200 Cathedral Ave NW Apt 711 Washington DC 20016-4934 Office: McGraw-Hill World Aviation Directory 1200 G St NW Washington DC 20005

KAVADAS-PAPPAS, IPHIGENIA KATHERINE, preschool administrator, teacher, consultant; b. Manchester, N.H., Oct. 24, 1958; d. Demetrios Stefanos and Rodothea (Palaiologou) K.; m. Constantine George Pappas, July 29, 1979; children: George Demetrios, Rodothea Constance. BA, U. Detroit, 1980; MAT summa cum laude, Oakland U., 1985. Cert. tchr., Mich. Pre-sch. tchr. Assumption Nursery Sch., St. Clair Shores, Mich., 1977-80, interim dir., 1984, bd. dirs., 1980—; Sunday sch. tchr. Assumption Greek Orthodox Ch., St. Clair Shores, 1985—; chairperson pre-sch. curriculum com. Greek Orthodox Archdiocese Dept. Religious Edn., Brookline, Mass., 1987—; cons. Assumption Nursery Sch., 1985—. Co-author: Preschool Curriculum Manual for Greek Orthodox Archdiocese, 1990, Preschool Curriculum for National Use, 1991. Mem. Assumption Greek Orthodox Ch. Philoptochos Soc., 1978-87; trustee Assumption Nursery Sch., 1979—, Sunday sch. presch. tchr., 1985—; vol. svcs. Bemis Elem. Sch., Boulan Park Mid. Sch., 1991-92. Recipient Vol. Svc. award Angus Elem. Sch., 1989. Mem. Nat. Assn. for the Edn. Young Children. Office: Assumption Greek Orthodox 21800 Marter Rd Saint Clair Shores MI 48080-2464

KAVALER, LUCY ESTRIN, author and editor; b. N.Y.C., Aug. 29, 1930; d. Lazar I. and Helen (Vishniac) Estrin; m. Arthur R. Kavaler; children: Roger, Andrea. BA magna cum laude, Oberlin (Ohio) Coll., 1950; postgrad., Columbia U., 1970. Assoc. editorial dir. PW Comms., N.J., 1975-89; editorial dir. AIN Co., N.Y.C., 1989-91. Author: The Private World of High Society, 1960, Mushrooms, Molds and Miracles, 1965, The Astors, 1966, Freezing Point, 1970, Noise the New Menace, 1975, A Matter of Degree, 1981, The Secret Lives of the Edmonts, 1989, Heroes and Lovers, 1995, others. Recipient Best Books of the Yr. award ALA, AAAS, others. Mem. Am. Med. Writers Assn., Nat. Assn. Sci. Writers, Authors Guild, Am. Soc. Journalists and Authors, PEN Am. Ctr., Internat. Sci. Writers Assn.

KAVALER-ALDER, SUSAN, clinical psychologist; b. N.Y.C., Jan. 31, 1950; d. Solomon and Alice (Zelikow) Weiss; m. Thomas Kavaler, July 12, 1970 (div. 1975); m. Saul Michael Adler, Aug. 14, 1983. PhD in Clin. Psychology, Adelphi U., 1974. Psychologist Beth Israel Hosp., N.Y.C., 1974-76, Manhattan Psychiat. Children's Ctr., N.Y.C., 1977-80; pvt. practice psychotherapy-psychoanalysis, N.Y.C., 1976—; condr. writing groups; founding dir. Object Rels. Inst., mem. faculty, supr. Inst. Devel. Psychology; mem. faculty Postgrad. Ctr. Mental Health, N.Y.C., 1984-86, 90—; mem. faculty, supr. Nat. Inst. Pychotherapies, N.Y.C., 1985—; bd. dirs., supr. Bklyn. Inst. Psychotherapy and Psychoanalysis, 1985—, mem. psychoanalytic inst. faculty; bd. dirs. Women and Psychoanalysis; adj. prof. Fordham U.; founding exec. dir. Object Rels. Inst. Psychotherpy and Psychoanalysis; spkr. pvt. seminars, writing groups. Author: The Compulsion to Create, A Psychology for Study of Women Artists, Thw Creative Mystique; contbr. chpts. to books, 32 articles to profl. jours. Recipient Postgrad. Ctr. Hon. award, 1984, 85. Mem. NAFE, Am. Psychol. Assn. (bd. dirs., chairperson pub. info. com. for psychoanalysis div.), Nat. Inst. for Psychotherapies Profl. Assn. (chair writing group 1984-90, cert. psychoanalyst, psychotherapist), Postgraduate Psychoanalytic Soc. (speaker). Office: 115 E 9th St New York NY 10003

KAVNER, JULIE, actress; b. Sept. 7, 1951. Grad., San Diego U. Actress: (TV series) Rhoda, 1974-78 (Emmy award 1978), The Tracey Ullman Show, 1987-90, The Simpsons, (voice only) 1990— (TV movies) Katherine, 1975, No Other Love, 1979, Revenge of the Stepford Wives, 1980, Dont' Drink the Water, 1994, (TV spl.) The Girl Who Couldn't Lose, 1975, (feature films) National Lampoon Goes to the Movies, 1981, Bad Medicine, 1985, Hannah and her Sisters, 1985, Radio Days, 1987, Surrender, 1987, New York Stories, 1989, Awakenings, 1990, This Is My Life, 1992, Shadows and Fog, 1992, I'll Do Anything, 1994, Forget Paris, 1995, (stage prodn.) Particular Friendships, 1981. *

KAWAZOE, ROBIN INADA, federal official; b. Wilkinsburg, Pa., Jan. 13, 1959; d. George and Hanako (Nishio) Inada; m. Howard Eugene Kawazoe, Oct. 23, 1982; children: Amy, Steven. BA, U. Md., 1982. Program analyst Alcohol, Drug Abuse & Mental Health Adminstrn., Rockville, Md., 1981-85, 85-87, com. mgmt. officer, 1985, extramural programs officer, 1987-88; spl. asst. Nat. Inst. on Drug Abuse, Rockville, 1988-91, dep. dir. Office Sci. Policy and Comm., 1991-94, acting dir. Office Sci. Policy and Comm., 1995—. Recipient Recognition award Pub. Health Svc., 1992. Office: NIH/Nat Inst on Drug Abuse 5600 Fishers Ln Rm 10A-55 Rockville MD 20857

KAWCZYNSKI, DIANE MARIE, elementary and middle school educator, composer; b. Milw., Jan. 22, 1959; d. Adalbert Lawrence and Joan (Zernia) K. BMus, Lawrence U., 1981; MMus, U. Wis., 1985. Cert. music tchr., Va. Suzuki violin instr., string methods instr. Brandon (Manitoba, Can.) Univ. Sch. Music, 1982-83; violin/viola instr., univ. prep program U. Wis. Sch. of Music, Madison, 1983-85; elem. and middle sch. string instr. Albuquerque Pub. Schs., 1985-86; middle sch. string and chorus instr. Ft. Morgan (Colo.) Pub. Schs., 1986-87; elem. string instr., middle sch. orchestra instr. Norfolk Pub. Schs., 1987—. Mem. NEA, Am. String Tchr. Assn., Music Educators Nat. Conf. Home: 860 Gas Light Ln Virginia Beach VA 23462-1232

KAWMY, SUSAN YOST, educational consultant; b. Bklyn., Feb. 14, 1950; d. John Gantt and June Ardith (Goodman) Yost; m. Karim Fred Kawmy, Aug. 17, 1974; children: Jumana Maria, Rashad Fouad, Marya Melissa, Elie Wadiah. BS, Colo. State U., 1972; MEd, U. Ariz., 1973. Resource tchr. Edn. Svc. Unit, Hastings, Nebr., 1973-74, 85-87, Scottsdale (Ariz.) Pub. Schs., 1974-76; resource tchr., cons. Universal Am. Sch., Kuwait, 1977-78, Am. Sch. Kuwait, 1979, Al Bayan Sch., Kuwait, 1979-82; pvt. practice Susan Kawmy Lang. and Learning Specialist, Kuwait, 1976-84; resource tchr., diagnostician Hastings Pub. Schs., 1986-87, 90-91; spl. edn. cons. Kawmy and Assocs., Kuwait, 1987-89; outreach project dir. Kuwait Spl. Edn. Soc., 1989—; pvt. practice Cairo, 1991—, Dubai, Kuwait, 1992, Jeddah, Saudi Arabia, 1992-93, Riyadh, Saudi Arabia, 1993—; cons. Al Bayan Sch., Ctr. for Evaluation and Teaching; founder, mem. sch. bd. Khalifeh Sch.; designer mainstream support team Kuwait Pvt. Schs.; spl. cons. New Spl. Needs Sch., Kuwait, Spl. Edn. Libr. for Women, Jeddah. Mem. Mental Health Specialists Support Group. Mem. Kuwait Spl. Edn. Soc., YWCA Internat. Club. Republican. Episcopalian. Home: Joumaiah Bottling Co, PO Box 210, Riyadh Saudi Arabia also: c/o Dr J G Yost Rte 4 Box 4 Hastings NE 68901

KAY, ELIZABETH ALISON, zoology educator; b. Kauai, Hawaii, Sept. 27, 1928; d. Robert Buttercase and Jessie Dowie (McConnachie) K. BA, Mills Coll., 1950, Cambridge U., Eng., 1952; MA, Cambridge U., Eng., 1956; PhD, U. Hawaii, 1957. From asst. prof. to prof. zoology U. Hawaii, Honolulu, 1957-62, assoc. prof., 1962-67, prof., 1967—; research assoc. Bishop Mus., Honolulu, 1968—. Author: Hawaiian Marine Mollusks, 1979, Shells of Hawaii, 1991; editor: A Natural History of the Hawaiian Islands, 1972, 94. Chmn. Animal Species Adv. Commn., Honolulu, 1983-87; v.p. Save Diamond Head Assn., Honolulu, 1968-87, pres., 1987—; trustee B.P. Bishop Mus., Honolulu, 1983-88. Fellow Linnean Soc., AAAS; mem. Marine Biol. Assn. (Eng.), Australian Malacol. Soc. Episcopalian. Office: U Hawaii Manoa Dept Zoology 2538 The Mall Honolulu HI 96822-2233

KAY, HERMA HILL, law educator; b. Orangeburg, S.C., Aug. 18, 1934; d. Charles Esdorn and Herma Lee (Crawford) Hill. BA, So. Meth. U., 1956; JD, U. Chgo., 1959. Bar: Calif. 1960, U.S. Supreme Ct. Law clk. to Justice Roger Traynor, Calif. Supreme Ct., 1959-60; asst. prof. law U. Calif., Berkeley, 1960-62; assoc. prof. U. Calif., 1962, prof., 1963, dir. family law project, 1964-67, Jennings prof., 1987—, dean, 1992—; co-reporter uniform marriage and div. act Nat. Conf. Commrs. on Uniform State Laws, 1968-70; vis. prof. U. Manchester, Eng., 1972, Harvard U., 1976; mem. Gov.'s Commn. on Family, 1966. Author: Text Cases and Materials on Sex-based Discrimination, 3rd edit., 1988, Supplement, 1994; (with R. Cramton, D. Currie and L. Kramer) Conflict of Laws: Cases, Comments, Questions, 5th edit., 1993; contbr. articles to profl. jours. Trustee Russell Sage Found., N.Y., 1972-87, chmn. bd., 1980-84; trustee , bd. dirs. Equal Rights Advs. Calif., 1976—, chmn., 1976-83; pres. bd. dirs. Rosenberg Found., Calif., 1987-88, bd. dirs. 1978—. Recipient rsch. award Am. Bar Found., 1990, award ABA Commn. Women in Profession, 1992, Marshall-Wythe medal, 1995; fellow Ctr. Advanced Study in Behavioral Sci., Palo Alto, Calif., 1963. Mem. Calif. Bar Assn., Bar U.S. Supreme Ct., Calif. Women Lawyers (bd. govs. 1975-77), Am. Law Inst. (mem. coun. 1985-), Assn. Am. Law Schs. (exec. com. 1986-87, pres.-elect 1988, pres. 1989, past pres. 1990), Am. Acad. Arts and Scis., Order of Coif (nat. pres. 1983-85). Democrat. Office: U Calif Law Sch Boalt Hall Berkeley CA 94720

KAY, KELLY W., lawyer; b. Houston, June 14, 1954; d. Rayford G. and Patsy A. (Crow) K. BA, Southwestern U., 1975; MFA, U. Tex., 1978; JD, Columbia U., 1982. Bar: Calif. 1983, U.S. Dist. Ct. (cen. dist.) Calif. 1983, U.S. Ct. Appeals (9th cir.) 1987. Assoc. Stutman, Treister & Glatt, L.A., 1982-85, Rosenfeld, Meyer & Susman, Beverly Hills, Calif., 1985-90; sr. counsel Sony Pictures Entertainment, Burbank, Calif., 1990—; mem. bd. dirs. L.A. Internat. Gay & Lesbian Film & Video Festival, v.p. 1994—. Bd. trustees Life AIDS Lobby, Sacramento, 1987—. Mem. L.A. County Bar Assn. (vice chair individual rights sect. 1985—, trustee 1988-90, chmn. 1991—), L.A. Lawyers for Human Rights (bd. govs., pres. 1988). Office: Sony Pictures 10202 West Washington Blvd Culver City CA 90232

KAYAR, SUSAN RENNIE, physiologist; b. Highland, Ill., May 17, 1953; d. Sedat Arif and Ruth Annalea (Houseman) K. BS, U. Miami, Fla., 1974, PhD, 1978. Rsch. asst. Everglades Nat. Park, Flamingo, Fla., 1978-79; rsch. assoc. U. Colo., Boulder, 1979-81; rsch. fellow U. Colo., Denver, 1981-84, U. Bern, Switzerland, 1984-89; instr. U. Medicine & Dentistry of N.J., Piscataway, 1989-90; physiologist Naval Med. Rsch. Inst., Bethesda, Md., 1990—. Contbr. numerous articles to profl. jours. Maytag fellow U. Miami, 1974-77, Fogarty Found. fellow Swiss NSF, 1984-85; Nat. Merit scholar U. Miami, 1971-74; NRC/NIH grantee, 1981-84, Am. Heart Assn. grantee, 1989-90. Mem. Am. Physiol. Soc., Microcirculatory Soc., Internat. Soc. Oxygen Transport to Tissue, Capital Hiking Club. Office: Nat Naval Med Ctr Naval Med Rsch Institu Bethesda MD 20889-5607

KAYE, CELIA ILENE, pediatrics educator; b. July 12, 1943; m. Tod B. Sloan. BS, Wayne State U., 1965, MS, 1968, MD, 1969, PhD, 1975. Diplomate Am. Bd. Pediatrics, Am. Bd. Med. Genetics; lic. physician, Mich., Ill., Tex. Resident in pediatrics Bronx (N.Y.) Mcpl. Hosp. Ctr., 1969-71, U. Ill. Hosp., Chgo., 1971-72; fellow in biochem. genetics Children's Meml. Hosp., Chgo., 1972-75; instr. pediatrics Northwestern U. Coll. Medicine, Chgo., 1974-75; from asst. prof. to assoc. prof. pediatrics U. Ill. Coll. Medicine, Chgo., 1975-89; chmn. divsn. genetics dept. pediatrics Cook County Hosp., Chgo., 1975-80, attending physician divsn. genetics, dept. pediatrics, 1980-89; dir. sect. genetics and genetics lab., divsn. pediatrics Luth. Gen. Hosp., Park Ridge, Ill., 1980-89, co-med. dir. Perinatal Ctr., 1986-89; dep. chmn. Santa Rosa Children's Hosp. Activities, co-dir. clin. cytogenics lab. U. Tex. Health Sci. Ctr., San Antonio, 1990—, prof. depts. pediatrics and cellular and structural biology, 1990—, chief sect. of metabolism, 1990—, vice chmn. dept. pediatrics, 1993—, co-dir. cytogenetics lab., 1990—; mem. quality assurance com. cytogenetics lab. dept. cellular and structural biology U. Tex. Health Sci. Ctr., 1991—, chair clin. faculty promotions com. dept. pediatrics, 1991—, chair com. for devel. plan for selection, evaluation and promotion of clin. faculty dept. pediatrics, 1990-91, med. perinatal mktg. com. dept. pediatrics, 1990-91, mem. residency adv. com. dept. pediatrics, 1990—; mem. clin. coord. com., 1990—, ad hoc clin. care com., 1990—, MSRDP adv. bd., 1991-93, search com. chmn. dept. medicine, 1992-93; dir. sect. genetics, Ctr. Craniofacial Anomalies, U. Ill. Coll. Medicine, Chgo., 1975-85; mem. med. adv. bd. Santa Rosa Children's Hosp., 1990-91, dir. med. edn., 1991—, exec. com., 1992—, medicine policy com., 1992—, chair med. edn. com., 199—; assoc. med. dir. cytogenetics lab. Santa Rosa Med. Ctr., San Antonio, 1991—; vis. assoc. prof. pediatrics Rush-Presbyn.-St. Luke's Med. Ctr., Chgo., 1979-89; mem. Genetics Task Force Ill., 1981-89, sec., 1981-83, pres., 1983-85; mem. genetics svc. com. Tex. Genetics Network, 1989—, chmn., 1992—; del. Nat. Coun. Regional Genetics Networks, 1992—, mem. exec. com., 1993—; mem. Ill. Genetic and Metabolic Diseases Adv. Bd., 1984-89, chmn. lab. subcom., 1985-89; mem. sci. adv. com. Tex. Dept. Health, 1992—; mem. steering com. Children's Regional Health Care Network, San Antonio, 1992-93; moderator genetics sect. So. Soc. for Pediatric Rsch. Annual Meeting, 1993—; mem. mgmt. com. Children's Regional Health Care System, San Antonio, 1993—; mem. instl. rev. bd. Cook County Hosp., Chgo., 1975-80, Luth. Gen. Health Care System, Park Ridge, Ill., 1988-89; mchmn. pediatric edn. com. Luth. Gen. Hosp., Park Ridge, 1981-86, chmn. pediatric bioethics com., mem. faculty adv. com., 1986-89; cons. Med. Ctr. Hosp. Ward and Nursery, Bapt. Hosp. System, Santa Rosa Children's Hosp., Meth. Hosp., Humana Women's Hosp. Mem. adv. bd. Am. Jour. Med. Genetics; reviewer Am. Jour. Human Genetics, Pediatric Dermatology; contbr. articles to profl. jours., chpts. to books. Mem. program planning com. March of Dimes Defects Found., Chgo., 1985-89, mem. health profl. adv. com., 1983-89, chmn. health profl. adv. com., 1981-83, mem. health profl. adv. com. South Ctrl. Tex. chpt., 1989-90; bd. dirs., exec. com. Harkness House for Children, Winnetka, Ill., 1988-89; mem. Ill. Spina Bifida Assn., 1983-89; exec. bd. El Valor Corp. for Handicapped Children, Chgo., 1980-81; mem. med. adv. com. Tex. State Sickle Cell Assn., 1990—. Fellow Am. Coll. Med. Genetics (founding, edn. com. 1993—); mem. AMA, Am. Soc. Human Genetics (info. and edn. com. 1990—), Am. Acad. Pediatrics (genetics sect., judge sci. awards uniformed svcs. sect. 1992-93), Soc. for Pediatric Rsch., Teratology Soc., Soc. for Inherited Metabolic Diseases, So. Soc. for Pediatric Rsch., Tex. Med. Soc., Tex. Genetics Soc., Tex. Pediatric Soc., Bexar County Med. Sc Soc. Office: U Tex Health Sci Ctr Genetics Dept 7703 Floyd Curl Dr San Antonio TX 78284-6200

KAYE, ELLEN JANE, journalist, consultant; b. Boston, Sept. 19, 1932; d. Leo and Dorothy (Lebowich) Eskin; m. Sanford Redmond, Dec. 31, 1957 (div. Nov. 1960); 1 child, Sanford; m. Robert Kaye, Nov. 17, 1960; 1 child, Anthony Edward. BA, Goucher Coll., 1952. Asst. to advt. mgr. Alfred A. Knopf Inc., N.Y.C., 1954-56; cover copywriter Dell Pub., N.Y.C., 1956-58; writer Fairchild Publs., N.Y.C., 1965-68; freelance author, 1965-91; columnist Sunday Mag., Phila. (Pa.) Inquirer, 1976-91; collage jewelry maker, 1990—; info. cons. various fundraising charitable orgns. Vol. worker with sch. age children People's Emergency Ctr., Phila. Recipient Press award Phila. Chpt. Am. Soc. Interior Designers, 1988. People's Emergency Ctr. Svc. award, 1994. Democrat. Jewish.

KAYE, GAIL LESLIE, healthcare consultant; b. Upland, Pa., Aug. 6, 1955; d. Ronald E. and Doris T. (Welfley) K. BS, Welseyan Coll., 1977; MS, Ohio State U., 1982, PhD, 1989. Lic. profl. clin. counselor; registered dietitian. Asst. dir. food svc., chief clin. dietitian Albert Einstein Med. Ctr., Phila., 1983; asst. prof. Ind. State U., Terre Haute, 1983-85; nutrition cons. Ohio State U. Hosp. Clinics, Columbus, 1986-88, grad. rsch. asst., 1986-89; legis. rep. Ohio Assocs. Counseling and Devel., Columbus, 1988-89; rsch. cons. State Dept. Edn., Columbus, 1988-89; lectr. counselor edn. Ohio State U., Columbus, 1989—; program devel. and clin. rschr. Ross Labs., Columbus, 1990-94; pres. Kaye Consultation Svcs., Inc., 1994—. Inventor in field; contbr. articles to profl. jours. Recipient Pres. award Ohio Mental Health Counselors Assn., 1990. Mem. ACA, Am. Mental Health Counselors Assn., Am. Assn. Specialists Group Work, Am. Dietetics Assn., Ohio Counseling Assn. (chair public policy and legis.), Ohio Assn. Specialists in Group Work, Ctrl. Ohio Counseling Assn., Soc. for Behavioral Medicine. Home: 365 Helmbright Dr Gahanna OH 43230 Office: Ross Labs 625 Cleveland Ave Columbus OH 43215

KAYE, JANET MIRIAM, psychologist; b. New Haven, Mar. 2, 1937; d. Al and Rose (Marcus) Sovitsky; m. Donald Kaye, June 26, 1955; children: Kenneth, Karen, Kendra, Keith. BS, NYU, 1958, MA, 1960; PhD, Med. Coll. of Pa., 1980. Clin. instr. Med Coll. of Pa., Phila., 1980-82, asst. prof., 1982-86, assoc. prof., 1986—. Contbr. articles to profl. jours. Mem. Am. Assn. Cancer Edn., APA, Am. Soc. Clin. Hypnosis, Soc. Health & Human Values, Gerontol. Soc. of Am., Am. Soc. Psychiat. Oncology, Coll. of Physicians of Pa., Internat. Soc. Exptl. Hypnosis. Office: Med Coll Pa 3300 Henry Ave Philadelphia PA 19129-1121

KAYE, JENNIFER LYNN, healthcare executive; b. Vallejo, Calif., Oct. 15, 1964; d. Edward Humphrey and Susan Kathy (Album) Bogart. BA in Psychology, U. Va., 1987. Programmer analyst U. Va. Med. Ctr., Charlottesville, 1987-88; personal computer cons. Northwestern U., Chgo., 1988-90; rsch. analyst Blue Cross Blue Shield Minn., St. Paul, 1990-93; mgr. nat. sales Pharmacy Gold, Inc., St. Paul, 1993-94; sr. dir. mktg. and ops. Group Health Cooperative of Eau Claire, Altoona, Wis., 1994—; instr. Grad. Mgmt. Admissions Test preparatory course, Bar Bri, Mpls., 1990-92. Vol. adult self-sufficiency program Project for Pride in Living, Mpls., 1991; vol. mission control officer, 1st flight launch action group (1st flag) Minn. Air Nat. Guard Mus., Mpls., 1994. Mem. Am. Coll. Healthcare Execs.

KAYE, LORI, travel academy executive, consultant; b. N.Y.C.; d. Eldin Bert and Katherine Angeline Onsgard; student Detroit Inst. Art, 1951, 56, U. N.Mex., 1960. Actress, radio and TV commls., 1951-82; actress Warner Brothers, 1960-64; dir., v.p. John Robert Powers Schs., Los Angeles, 1961-71; v.p. Electron Industries, Torrance, Calif., 1963-65; owner, v.p., Lawrence Leon Photography Studio, Los Angeles, 1964-68; pres. Lori Kaye Cosmetics, Hollywood, Calif., 1964-70; co-owner, v.p. K and S Employment, Calif. Fashion Mart, 1965-67; dir., internat. cons. Airline Schs. Pacific, Van Nuys, Calif., 1972-74; dir. Caroline Leonetti Ltd. Sch., Hollywood, 1976-79; pres., Lori Kaye's Internat. Travel Acad., North Hollywood, Calif., 1980—; internat. cons. Internat. Career Acad., Van Nuys, 1978—, Glendale Coll. Bus. and Paramed. (Calif.), 1980—, Acad. Pacific, Hollywood, 1981—; pres. Molori Publs., Studio City, Calif., 1981—; cons. A&T Inst. Travel and Tourism, 1982; lectr., 1969—. Dir. project Camarillo State Hosp., 1963-69; cons. Job Corps. Recipient Mental Health Achievement award, 1967. Mem. Nat. Assn. Female Execs., Assn. for Promotion of Tourism Africa, AAU, Screen Actors Guild, AFTRA, Smithsonian Assocs., Am. Soc. Travel Agents, Internat. Airlines Travel Agents Network, Internat. Air Transport Assn., Soc. Travel Agents in Govt., Calif. Assn. Pvt. Postsecondary Schs., U.S. Masters-Internat. Swim Club, Nat. Geog. Soc., Internat. Platform Assn., Better Bus. Bur. (also arbitrator), L.A. World Affairs Coun., Universal City- No. Hollywood C. of C. Paintings included in UNICEF collection, 1967; hostess TV talk show The New You, KTTV, Hollywood, 1964-65. Office: Internat Travel Ctr 12123 Magnolia Blvd North Hollywood CA 91607-2609 also: Lori Kayes Internat Travel Acad 12123 Magnolia Blvd North Hollywood CA 91607-2609

KAYE JOHNSON, SUSAN, educational consultant; b. N.Y.C., Jan. 23, 1932; d. Albert and Goldie (Feldman) Sroge; m. Carroll F. Johnson, Jan. 16, 1990; children from previous marriage: Richard M. Kaye, Gillian Kaye Karran. BA in History, Bklyn. Coll., 1953, MS in Counseling, 1958; MEd in Adminstrn., Columbia U., 1976, EdD in Adminstrn., 1978. Cert. adminstr., supr. N.Y., N.J., guidance counselor, history tchr., N.Y. Tchr. 3d grade Ollie Perry Storm Sch., San Antonio, 1954-55; tchr. social studies Jr. High Sch. 214, Bklyn., 1955-57; guidance counselor Jr. High Schs. 214 and 510, Bklyn., 1957-59; evaluation asst., coord. career devel. Great Neck (N.Y.) Pub. Sch., 1966-71, dir. chpt. I, 1971-79; dir. pupil svcs. Bellmore-Merrick High Sch. Dist., Long Island, N.Y., 1979-83; asst. supt. schs. Longwood Sch. Dist., Middle Island, N.Y., 1983-89; supt. schs. Florham Park (N.J.) Pub. Schs., 1989-92; ednl. cons. Longboat Key, Fla., 1992—; chair women's caucus Am. Assn. Sch. Adminstrs., 1980-82. Co-author: An Analysis of Problems in a School District, 1980, Managing Schools in Hard Times, 1981. Assoc. trustee Dowling Coll., Long Island, 1983-87; trustee Women Svcs. Divsn., Brookhaven, N.Y., 1986, Brookhaven Twp. Youth Bd., 1987, Adult Sch., Florham Park, 1989-92. Mem. AAUW, NOW, Archael. Inst. Am., Phi Delta Kappa. Home and Office: 2077 Gulf of Mexico Dr Longboat Key FL 34228

KAZENAS, SUSAN JEAN, accounting manager; b. Oregon, Ill., Dec. 29, 1956; d. Charles Leroy and Vera Jean (Groenhagen) K. BS, Northwestern U., 1982. CPA, Ill., 1985. Acctg. analyst Allstate Ins. Co., Northbrook, Ill., 1977-80; asst. dir. Steel Tank Inst., Deerfield, Ill., 1980-85; owner, acct. Decker Drug, Oregon, Ill., 1981-84; acct., auditor Crone, Kipp & Blomgren, Rockford, Ill., 1984-87; acct., internal auditor Woodward Gov. Co., Rockford, 1987-88; acct., sr. cons. McGladrey & Pullen, Rockford, 1988-90; cons. mgr. BDO Seidman, Rockford, 1990-92, Chgo., 1992-93; acctg. mgr. Danfoss Electronic Drives, Rockford, Ill., 1993—. Bd. dirs. pub. info. Am. Cancer Soc., Winnebago County, Ill., 1988-92. Mem. AICPA, Ill. CPA Soc. (No. chpt. sec. 1988-89, pres. 1989-90, state bd. dirs. 1993-95), Inst. Mgmt. Accts. Home: 8463 Center Ct Belvidere IL 61008-8591 Office: Danfoss Electronic Drives 2995 Eastrock Dr Rockford IL 61109-1737

KAZMAREK, LINDA ADAMS, secondary education educator; b. Crisfield, Md., Jan. 18, 1945; d. Gordon I. Sr. and Annie Ruby (Sommers) Adams; m. Stephen Kazmarek, Jr., Aug. 2, 1981. B of Music Edn., Peabody Conservatory of Music, 1967; postgrad., Morgan U., Towson U. Cert. advanced profl. tchr., K-12, Md.; nat. cert. tchr. Mayron Cole piano method. Organist, choir dir. Halethorpe United Meth. Ch., Balt., min. music, 1978-92, 93—; organist, choir dir. Olive Branch United Meth. Ch., 1973-77; 1978-92, 93—; piano tchr. Modal Cities Program, Balt., Balt. Community Schs; tchr. vocal music Balt. City Schs., 1967—; min. music Halethorpe Meth. Ch., 1993—; pvt. tchr. piano and organ. Composer: A Family of Care (award), 1991, Praise Song, 1992, Thy Way, Lord, 1993, I Asked the Lord, 1993, Peace and Rest, 1994, Sing Praise to Jesus, 1994, Trilogy for piano solo, 1994, Shine Your Light, 1994. Concert performer for Meth. Bd. Child Care, 1989, Balt. S.W. Emergency Svcs., 1991, Halethorpe Meth. Ch., 1994; guest performer Balt. City Tchrs. Appreciation Banquet, 1991. Recipient vol. award for music enrichment summer program, 1973, award for voluntarism Fund. for Ednl. Excellence, 1985; Fund for Ednl. Excellence grantee, 1988. Mem. NEA, Md. State Tchrs. Assn., Balt. City Tchrs. Assn., Md. Music Educators Assn., Music Educators Nat. Conf., Md. State Music Tchrs. Assn., Nat. Music Tchrs. Assn., Washington Songwriters Assn., Christian Song Writers Assn., Gospel Music Assn., Peabody Alumni Assn.

KEAL, MARY ELIZABETH, accountant; b. Mpls., Dec. 25, 1940; d. John Francis and Eleanor Marie (Hofmaster) Braden; m. Charles Robert Keal, Feb. 2, 1963; children: Daniel Robert, Maria Denise, James Patrick, Laura Elaine. BA, U. Minn., 1962; BS, Winona State U., 1982, MBA, 1987. CPA, cert. mgmt. acct. Fin. analyst IBM, Rochester, Minn., 1982-93; cost acctg. mgr. Advt. Unltd., Sleepy Eye, Minn., 1994—. Office: Advt Unltd 1000 Hwy 4 S Sleepy Eye MN 56085

KEARFOTT, KIMBERLEE JANE, nuclear engineer, educator; b. Oakland, Calif., Jan. 30, 1956; d. William Edward and Edith (Chamberlin) K. BSc, St. Mary's U., Halifax, N.S., Can., 1975; ME in Nuclear Engring., U. Va., 1977; ScD, MIT, 1980. Coop. engr. Babcock & Wilcox Co., Lynchburg, Va., 1975-77; rsch. asst. Mass. Gen. Hosp., Boston, 1980; asst. prof. Cornell U. Med. Sch., N.Y.C., 1980-84; rsch. assoc. Sloan-Kettering Cancer Ctr., N.Y.C., 1980-84; from asst. to assoc. prof. Ariz. State U., Tempe, 1984-89; assoc. prof. Ga. Inst. Tech., Atlanta, 1989-93; assoc. prof. Med. Sch. Emory U., Atlanta, 1990-93; prof. U. Mich., Ann Arbor, 1993—; adj. asst. prof. Mass. Coll. Pharmacy, Boston, 1980. Contbr. articles to Jour. Health Physics, Jour. of Nuclear Medicine, Jour. Computer Assisted Tomography, Jour. Med. Physics. Bd. dirs. Health Physics Soc., 1992-95. Recipient Tetalman award Soc. Nuclear Medicine, 1991, Anderson award Health Physics Soc., 1992. Mem. Am. Nuclear Soc., Soc. Nuclear Medicine, Assn. Women in Sci., AAUW, IEEE, Soc. Women Engrs., Order of the Engr., Health Physics Soc. Office: U Mich Dept Nuclear Engring Ann Arbor MI 48109-2104

KEARNEY, PATRICIA ANN, university administrator; b. Wilkes-Barre, Pa., May 15, 1943; d. William F. and Helen L. (Hartz) K. BA, Mich. State U., 1965; MSEd, Ind. U., 1966. Head resident advisor Western Ill. U., Macomb, 1966-68; asst. v.p. SUNY, Buffalo, 1968-70; asst. dean student life Lock Haven (Pa.) State Coll., 1970-72; dir. residential life U. Calif., Davis, 1974-83, bus. mgr., 1983-85, dir. housing and food services, 1985-90, asst. vice chancellor student affairs, 1990—; speaker nat. and state convs. Contbr. articles to profl. jours. Mem. Am. Coll. Personnel Assn. (pres.), Assn. Coll. and U. Housing Officers Internat., Sierra Club. Home: 714 Borchard Ct Woodland CA 95695-5002 Office: U Calif 127 Student Housing Davis CA 95616

KEARNEY, SHEILA JANE, lawyer; b. Paterson, N.J., Dec. 16, 1961; d. John James and Rita Barbara (Burke) K. BA cum laude, Fairfield U., 1983; JD, George Washington U., 1986. Bar: N.Y. 1987, U.S. Dist. Ct. (so. dist.) N.Y. 1987, D.C. 1989. Assoc. Shearson Lehman Bros., Inc., N.Y.C., 1986-87; regional atty. Nat. Assn. Securities Dealers, N.Y.C., 1987-89, sr. regional atty., 1989-90, regional counsel, 1990-91; assoc. counsel N.Y. Life Ins. Co., N.Y.C., 1991-93, asst. gen. counsel, 1993-94, assoc. gen. counsel, 1994—. Mem. ABA, Securities Industry Assn., Am. Coun. Life Insurers (com. securities regulation adn ins. broker-dealer subcom.), Rep. Nat. Lawyers Assn., D.C. Bar Assn., Fairfield U. Alumni Club N.Y. (pres. 1988-90, bd. dirs. 1990—), Phi Delta Phi. Republican. Roman Catholic. Home: 101 W 87th St Apt 7B New York NY 10024 Office: NY Life Ins Co 51 Madison Ave New York NY 10010-1603

KEARNEY NUNNERY, ROSE, nursing administrator, educator, consultant; b. Glen Falls, N.Y., July 8, 1951; d. James J. and Helen F. (Oprandy) K.; m. Jimmie E. Nunnery. BS with honors, Keuka Coll., 1973; M of Nursing, U. Fla., 1976, PhD, 1987. Asst. prof. La. State U. Med. Ctr., New Orleans, 1976-87, U. of South Fla., Tampa, 1987-88; project coord. indigent health care U. Fla., Gainesville, 1984-85; dir. nursing programs SUNY, New Paltz, N.Y., 1988-94; project dir. MS in gerontol. nursing advanced nursing edn. grant U.S. Health Resources and Svcs. Adminstrn. Div. Nursing, 1992-94. Bd. dirs. Ulster County unit Am. Cancer Soc., 1991-94, nursing edn. com, 1990-92; bd. dirs. Mid-Hudson Consortium Advancement Edn. for Health Profls., 1988-94, nursing edn. com., 1988-92, scholarship com., 1989-93, com. chair, 1990-93, treas., 1992-94; profl. devel. program SUNY, Albany, 1989-92; adv. coun. Ulster C.C., 1989-94; adv. regional planning group for early intervention svcs. United Cerebral Palsy Ulster County Inc., Children's Rehab. Ctr., 1989-91; mem. Ulster County adv. com. Office for Aging, 1991-94; state del. S.C. State Conf. on Aging, 1995. Mem. ANA, Nat. League for Nursing, Sigma Theta Tau. Roman Catholic. Home and Office: 41 S Shore Ct Hilton Head Island SC 29928

KEARNS, JANET CATHERINE, corporate secretary; b. Chgo., Oct. 29, 1940; d. Casimir J. and Eleanor (Galus) Kubik; m. Edward P. Kearns, May 4, 1975. Grad., Madonna High Sch., 1958. Legal sec. Seyfarth, Shaw, Fairweather & Geraldson, Chgo., 1960-66; sec. to pres. Bowey's, Inc., Chgo., 1966-69, Sealy, Inc., Chgo., 1969—; corp. sec. Sealy, Inc., 1977-89; adminstrv. sec. RHR Internat. Co., Wood Dale, Ill., 1989—. Asst. dir. religious edn. St. Matthew Parish, Glendale Heights, Ill., 1988-89. Office: RHR Internat Co 220 Gerry Dr Wood Dale IL 60191-1139

KEARNS, MERLE GRACE, state senator; b. Bellefonte, Pa., May 19, 1938; d. Robert John and Mary Catharine (Fitzgerald) Grace; m. Thomas Raymond Kearns, June 27, 1959; children: Thomas, Michael, Timothy, Matthew. B.S., Ohio State U., 1960. Tchr. St. Raphael Elem. Sch., Springfield, Ohio, 1960-62; substitute tchr. Mad River Green dist., Springfield, 1972-78; instr. Clark Tech. Coll., Springfield, 1978-80; commr. Clark County, Ohio, 1981-91; state senator from 10th Ohio dist. 1991—; chair, Senate Human Svcs. and Aging Comm.; vice chair, Senate Agrl. Com.; co-chair, Supreme Ct. Domestic Violence Com.; mem. Joint Com. Agy. Rule Review; pres. bd. county commrs., 1982, 83, 86, 87, 90, v.p., 1985, 88, 89. dirs. Springfield Symphony, 1980-86, Arts Council, 1980-85, County Commrs. Assn. of Ohio, sec., 1988, 2d v.p., 1989-90, 1st v.p., 1990; mem. exec. com. Springfield Republicans, 1984—. Ohio State U., scholar, 1957-59; named Woman of Yr. Springfield Pilot Club, 1981, Wittenberg Woman of Accomplishment, 1991, Watchdog of Treasury, 1991. Mem. LWV (bd. dirs. 1964-78, pres. 1975-78), Rotary, Omicron Nu. Roman Catholic. Avocations: reading, golf. Home: 2664 Brookdale Dr Springfield OH 45502-9109 Office: Senate Annex Ground Fl Columbus OH 43266

KEARSE, AMALYA LYLE, federal judge; b. Vauxhall, N.J., June 11, 1937; d. Robert Freeman and Myra Lyle (Smith) K. B.A., Wellesley Coll., 1959; J.D. cum laude, U. Mich., 1962. Bar: N.Y. 1963, U.S. Supreme Ct. 1967. Assoc. Hughes, Hubbard & Reed, N.Y.C., 1962-69; ptnr. Hughes, Hubbard & Reed, 1969-79; judge U.S. Ct. Appeals (2d cir.), 1979—; lectr. evidence N.Y. U. Law Sch., 1968-69. Author: Bridge Conventions Complete, 1975, 3d edit., 1990, Bridge at Your Fingertips, 1980; translator, editor: Bridge Analysis, 1979; editor: Ofcl. Ency. of Bridge, 3d edit, 1976; mem. editorial bd. Charles Goren, 1974—. Bd. dirs. NAACP Legal Def. and Endl. Fund, 1977-79; bd. dirs. Nat. Urban League, 1978-79; trustee N.Y.C. YWCA, 1976-79, Am. Contract Bridge League Nat. Laws Commn., 1975—; mem. Pres.'s Com. on Selection of Fed. Jud. Officers, 1977-78. Named Women's Pairs Bridge Champion Nat. div., 1971, 72, World div., 1986, Nat. Women's Teams Bridge Champion, 1987, 9o, 91. Mem. ABA, Assn. of Bar of City of N.Y., Am. Law Inst., Lawyers Com. for Civil Rights Under Law (mem. exec. com. 1970-79). Office: US Ct Appeals US Courthouse Foley Sq New York NY 10007-1501*

KEASBEY, VICTORIA IRENE, computer scientist; b. Yonkers, N.Y., Sept. 23, 1955; d. Alan and JoAnne (Calton) Peterson; m. Timothy Woodwell KEasbey, June 21, 1986; children: Michael, Athena, Karina. Cert. in keypunching, Hudson Valley Community Coll., 1976, cert. in computer ops., 1980; AAS in Data Processing, Dutchess Community Coll., Poughkeepsie, N.Y., 1983; student, Mt. St. Mary Coll., 1991—. Keypunch operator N.Y. State Dept. Taxation & Fin., Albany, 1976; computer operator Pawling (N.Y.) Rubber Corp., 1980-81; computer scientist Texaco, Inc., Glenham, N.Y., 1984—. Member Dutchess County Girl Scouts New Hackensack, Wappingers Falls, N.Y., 1991—; editor, linesetter Wappinger Jr. High Sch. Drama Club, Wappingers Falls, 1990—; brochure creator Prevention Players-Wappingers Falls Jr. High Sch., 1991—; asst. cubmaster Boy Scouts Am., Pawling, 1987. Baptist. Office: Texaco Inc Old Glenham Rd Glenham NY 12727-0254

KEATH, KATHLEEN CLAIRE, auditor; b. Wilmington, Del., Aug. 1, 1966; d. John Joseph and margaret Ann (Mitchell) K. BS in Acctg., U. Del., 1990. CPA; cert. mgmt. acct., cert. internal auditor. Bookkeeper Godwin Enterprises, Inc., Newark, Del., 1984-86; acct./bookkeeper White Oak, Inc., Newark, 1986-88; staff acct. Whisman & Assocs., CPA, Wilmington, 1988-89; paraprofl. McBride, Shopa & Co., CPA, Greenville, Del., 1989-90; income tax preparer H&R Block, Inc., Wilmington, 1990; staff acct. Daney, Cannon, Truitt & Sarnecki, Wilmington, 1991-92; sr. staff auditor Artisans' Savs. Bank, Wilmington, 1992-93, dir. internal audit, 1993—; pvt. tax and audit practice Newark, 1992—; external auditor Kiwans of Wilmington, 1992—; speaker Mil. Order of World Wars, 1993. Mem. Del. Soc. CPAs (industry com. mem. 1993—), AICPAs, Inst. Internal Auditors, Inst. Mgmt. Accts. Roman Catholic. Office: Artisans Savs Bank PO Box 908 9th and Tatnal Wilmington DE 19899

KEATING, MARGARET JOAN, bank executive; b. San Francisco, Aug. 21, 1944; d. William F. and Margaret (Walitsch) de Ryk; m. John Joseph Keating Jr., Jan. 8, 1966; children: Patrick, Jinny. Loan underwriter Lafayette (Calif.) Fed. Savings, 1981-83; sr. underwriter 1st Security Savings & Loan, Danville, Calif., 1983; v.p. Home Owners Fed., Danville, Calif., 1983-86, Arden Mortgage Corp., Lafayette, 1986, Plaza Savings & Loan, Santa Ana, Calif., 1987; br. mgr. no. region BancPlus Mortgage, San Diego, 1987-89; regional v.p. for Pacific Coast, NVR Mortgage, Pleasanton, Calif., 1989—. Mem. Calif. Assn. Residential Lenders (bd. dirs. 1991, pres.-elect 1992), Calif. Assn. Mortgage Brokers. Republican. Office: NVR Mortgage 5000 Hopyard Rd Ste 440 Pleasanton CA 94588-3352

KEATING, MARGARET MARY, entrepreneur, management consultant; b. Chgo., Feb. 18, 1950; d. Jeremiah Joseph and Margaret Mary (Donnelly) K. Student, Harvard U., 1986-87; cert. in law, U. Mass., 1993; postgrad., Emmanuel Coll., 1994, Simmons Coll., 1994—. Sr. merchandiser J.C. Penney Co., Chgo., 1971-73, dist. mgr. fashions, 1973-75, regional mgr., 1976-78; gen. mgr. merchandise J.C. Penney Co., Aurora, Ill., 1978-82; co-founder, exec. v.p., dir. mktg. The Pres. Mgmt. Group, Inc., Hingham, Mass., 1984-88; pres., dir. Keating Konsult, Inc., Accord, Mass., 1988—; v.p., co-founder Video Tours, Inc., Hartford, Conn., 1986-87. Mem. Advocates for Moral and Ethical Treatment by Divorce Attys., Accord, Mass., 1991—. Mem. NAFE, LWV, Nat. Assn. for Women in Careers, Nat. Womens Polit. Caucus, Am. Mgmt. Assn., Ctr. for Entrepreneurial Mgmt. Democrat. Office: Keating Konsult Inc PO Box 171 Accord MA 02018-0171

KEATING, PAMELA JOAN, nurse anesthetist; b. Chgo., Mar. 30, 1950; d. Harry Atkinson and Margaret Pruit (Keith) Ruyter; m. Kevin Thomas Keating, June 27, 1976. BS in Psychology, Loyola U., Chgo., 1972; diploma in nursing with honors, Luth. Gen. and Deaconess Hosp., Park Ridge, Ill., 1976; diploma in nurse anesthesia, Ravenswood Hosp., Chgo., 1981; MS in Nursing with distinction, DePaul U., 1992; postgrad., Loyola U., Chgo., 1994—. RN, Ill. Lab. technician Bio-Labs, Inc., Northbrook, Ill., 1973; staff nurse surg. unit, then alcoholism treatment unit Luth. Gen. Hosp., Park Ridge, 1973-76; nurse anesthetist, instr. Ravenswood Hosp. Med. Ctr., Chgo., 1981—, asst. program dir. Sch. of Anesthesia, 1992—. Mem. Am. Assn. Nurse Anesthetists (cert.), Ill. Assn. Nurse Anesthetists. Home: 1115 S Seminary Ave Park Ridge IL 60068-4369 Office: Ravenswood Hosp Med Ctr 4550 N Winchester Ave Chicago IL 60640-5205

KEATINGE, CORNELIA WYMA, architectural preservationist consultant, lawyer; b. Poughkeepsie, N.Y., July 22, 1952; d. Edwin R. and Josephine B. (Brazis) Wyma; m. Robert Reed Keatinge, Aug. 21, 1982; 1 child, Courtney Elizabeth. BArch, U. Ky., 1974; MA in History and Theory of Architecture, U. Essex, Colchester, Eng., 1976; JD, U. Denver, 1982. Bar: Colo. 1982. Archtl. historian Kans. State Hist. Soc., Topeka, 1975-77; hist. architect Nat. Park Service, Denver, 1977-79; assoc. Richard E. Young, Denver, 1982-84; hist. architect Colo. Hist.Soc., Denver, 1984-86; sole practice, cons. architecture Denver, 1986; hist. preservation specialist Adv. Council Hist. Preservation, Golden, Colo., 1986—. Vol. Denver Art Mus., 1980—, Jr. League Denver, 1983—. Rotary fellow, 1974-75; recipient Spl. Achievement award, Nat. Park Service, 1980. Mem. ABA. Home: 460 S Marion Pky # 1904 Denver CO 80209-2544 Office: 730 Simms St Ste 401 Golden CO 80401-4798

KEATON, DIANE, actress; b. Santa Ana, Calif., Jan. 5, 1946. Student, Neighborhood Playhouse, N.Y.C., 1968. Appeared on N.Y. stage in Hair, 1968, Play It Again Sam, 1969, The Primary English Class, 1976; appeared in numerous films including Lovers and Other Strangers, 1970, Play It Again Sam, 1972, The Godfather, 1972, Sleeper, 1973, The Godfather Part II, 1974, Love and Death, 1975, I Will, I Will...For Now, 1975, Harry and Walter Go To New York, 1976, Annie Hall, 1977 (Best Actress Acad. award 1978, Brit. Acad. Best Actress award 1978, N.Y. Film Critics Circle award 1978, Nat. Soc. Film Critics award 1978), Looking for Mr. Goodbar, 1977, Interiors, 1978, Manhattan, 1979, Reds, 1981 (Acad. award nominee), Shoot the Moon, 1982, Little Drummer Girl, 1984, Mrs. Soffel, 1984, Crimes of the Heart, 1986, Radio Days, 1987, Baby Boom, 1987, The Good Mother, 1988, The Lemon Sisters, 1990, The Godfather Part III, 1990, Father of the Bride, 1991, Manhattan Murder Mystery, 1993, Look Who's Talking Now, 1993 (voice), Father of the Bride 2, 1995; (TV movie) Running Mates, 1992, Amelia Earhart, 1994; dir. film: Heaven, 1987, Wildflower, 1991; accomplished artist and singer; author book of photographs: Reservations, 1980; editor: (with Marvin Heiferman) Still Life, 1983, Mr. Salesman, 1994. Recipient Golden Globe award, 1978. Office: John Burnham William Morris Agy 151 S El Camino Dr Beverly Hills CA 90212-2704*

KEATON, FRANCES MARLENE, sales representative; b. Redfield, Ark., July 1, 1944; d. John Thomas and Pauline (Hilliard) Wells; m. Larry Ronald Keaton, Sept. 17, 1946. Cert. in acctg., Draughon's Sch. Bus., 1972. Lic. ins. agt. Acctg. supr. Home Ins. Co., Little Rock, 1962-70; auditor St. Paul Ins. Co., Little Rock, 1970-74; spl. agt. Continental Ins. Co., Little Rock, 1974—. Vol. Ark. Sch. for the Blind, Little Rock, 1968. Mem. Little Rock Field Club, Casualty Roundtable, Auditor's Assn., Ins. Women, Underwriters Roundtable, The Executive Female, Ind. Ins. Agts. Assn., Profl. Ins. Assn. Democrat. Methodist. Home and Office: 111 Red River Dr Sherwood AR 72116-5851

KEATOR, CONSTANCE L., accountant; b. Susquehanna, Pa., Aug. 2, 1956; d. A. Robert and Lucille V. (Cheatham) K. BBA, William & Mary Coll., 1978. Acct. Spivey Rentals, Inc., Hampton, Va., 1978—. Vice chmn. Dist. 2 Planning Commn. Framework Task Force, Newport News, Va., 1990-93; chmn. Hilton Village Archtl. Rev. Bd., Newport News, 1991-92. Mem. Va. Jaycees (regional dir. 1994-95), Hampton Roads Jaycees (pres. 1992-93, Outstanding Pres. of Qtr. 2qtrs 1993, Va. Jaycees).

KEATS, PATRICIA HART, counselor, educator; b. Boise, Idaho, July 18, 1946; d. Robert James Hart and Joyce Elizabeth (Shroyer) Smith; m. Theodore Eliot Keats, Mar. 30, 1974; 1 child, Ian. AS, Piedmont Coll., 1982; BS, Mary Baldwin Coll., 1983; MEd, U. Va., 1986, EdD, 1992. Cert. Am. Bd. Radiologic Tech.; cert. Nat. Bd. Cert. Counselors; lic. profl. counselor, Va. Rsch. asst. U. Va., Charlottesville, 1982-83, 86-87; counselor Charlottesville, 1986—; mem. faculty, counselor Piedmont Community Coll., Charlottesville, 1987—; Honor lectr. Mary Baldwin Coll., 1988. Pres. Charlottesville Cmty. Children's Theatre, 1974-84, 78; mem. Charlottesville Light Opera Co., 1978—; supr. Albemarle County Fair, 1988—; exec. com. Jefferson Cmty. Theatre, 1991; bd. dirs. Epilepsy Assn. Va., 1993—. Mem. AACD, Am. Soc. Radiologic Tech., Psi Chi, Chi Sigma Iota. Home: 421 Key West Dr Charlottesville VA 22901-8423

KEDDERIS, PAMELA JEAN, insurance company executive; b. Waterbury, Conn., May 15, 1956; d. Leo George and Evelyn Helen (Fenske) K. Student, U. Nice, 1976-77; BA, Assumption Coll., 1978; MBA, U. New Haven, 1981. Credit analyst, Citytrust Bank, Bridgeport, Conn., 1980-81, sr. credit analyst, 1981-82, fin. analyst, 1982-83, seminar instr., 1981-83; planning analyst Continental Ins. Co., N.Y.C., 1983-84, sr. planning analyst, 1984-85, dir. planning, 1985-87, asst. v.p. 1987-92, v.p., 1992—; mem. Planning Forum. Mem. NAFE, Nat. Assn. Ins. Women, North Shore Animal League. Democrat. Lutheran. Avocations: music, traveling. Home: 1166 Schmidt Ln New Brunswick NJ 08902

KEDJIDJIAN, CATHERINE BRIGGS, writer, consultant; b. Bryn Mawr, Pa., Mar. 27, 1967; d. Berton and Mary Jayne (Briggs) Winograd; m. Ohan Anton Kedjidjian, Sept. 29, 1990. BS, Ind. U., 1989. Writer, cons. Hewitt Assocs., Lincolnshire, Ill., 1989-91; freelance writer Highland Park, Ill., 1991—. Mem. NOW, Chgo. Women in Pub.

KEE, BERTHINIA, minister; b. Suffolk, Va., June 9, 1940; d. Clarence and Berneathia (Thompson) H.; m. Frank Kee, Nov. 2, 1958; children: Frank Jr., Anita Marie, George Eric, Randy Antonio, Sybrella Nanette, James Randolph, Collette Verita. Student, Mattatuck Coll., 1979, Hartford Sem., 1985. Ordained to ministry Penecostal Ch., 1981. Deaconess True Holiness Ch., Waterbury, Conn., 1979-80, asst. pastor, 1980-82; founder, pastor Macadonia Ch., Waterbury, 1982—; jr. choir dir., Sunday sch. and Bible tchr. Mt. Olive Ch., Waterbury, 1965-79. Bd. dirs. Prison Fellowship, Peace Dale, R.I., 1990. Mem. Charismatic Bible Ministries. Office: Macadonia Ch 769 N Main St Waterbury CT 06704-3512

KEE, SHIRLEY ANN, elementary education educator; b. Ewing, Mo., Dec. 21, 1935; d. Marion L. and Ida (Pauline) Becktell; m. Byron Eugene Kee, Aug. 18, 1956; children: Daniel G., Kristin S. Student, Western Ill. U., 1954-59, Ball State U., 1969-70; BA, Trinity Christian Coll., 1975; MEd, U. Ill., 1982. Tchr. 1st grade La Harpe (Ill.) Grade Sch., 1958-60, South Holland (Ill.) Sch Dist. 151, 1960-66, 68, 1971; tchr., adminstr. St. Andrews Nursery Sch., Homewood, Ill., 1972-73; tchr. 1st, 2d grades North Palos Dist. 117, Hickory Hills, Ill., 1975-84, Mansfield (Ohio) City Schs., 1984—. Pres. Parent Edn. Groups, Palos Park, Ill., 1974-81. Mem. AAUW, Alpha Kappa (historian, sec., pres.-elect, pres.). Presbyterian. Home: 770 Courtwright Blvd Mansfield OH 44907-2128

KEEBLE, KATHARINE BROWNLEE, media specialist; b. Claysville, Pa., May 2, 1950; d. Frank Lyle and Katharine Louise (Buchanan) Brownlee; m. Donald Wayne Keeble, Dec. 31, 1972; 1 child, Adrienne Keegan. BA in Edn., U. N.C., 1972; postgrad., Fla. So. Coll., 1982, Ga. State U., 1983-84, Wayne State U., 1994—. Tchr. Westarea Sch., Fayetteville, N.C., 1972-74; media specialist King (N.C.) Sch., 1974-75, Christ the King Sch., Atlanta, 1975-76; tchr. 1st United Meth. Sch., Kissimmee, Fla., 1981-83; media specialist ReedyCreek Elem. Sch., Kissimmee, Fla., 1983-84; media specialist, tchr. Holly (Mich.) Sch. Dist., 1992-93; media specialist Walled Lake (Mich.) Schs., 1993—. Area coord. Youth Understanding Fgn. Exch. Students program, Detroit, 1991-92. Mem. ALA, Am. Assn. Sch. Librs., Mich. Assn. Media Edn., Assn. Educators in Comms. and Tech., Mensa, Phi Beta Kappa, Phi Delta Kappa. Home: 32350 Chestnut Run Dr Bloomfield Hills MI 48302-1113 Office: Walled Lake Schs 8500 Ladd Rd Walled Lake MI 48390

KEEBLER, LOIS MARIE, elementary school educator; b. Jasper, Ala., Nov. 24, 1955; d. Roosevelt T. and Marie (Smiley) K. Student, Cen. State U., Wilberforce, Ohio; cert., North Ala. Regional Hosps., 1981. Cert. tchr., Ala. Tchr. Mamani Vallied Children Devel. Ctr., Dayton, Ohio. Vol. pub. schs. Democrat. Baptist.

KEE BORGES, SAUNDRA ALICE, city manager, lawyer; b. Montclair, N.J., June 21, 1959; d. William Henry Jr. and Edith Hope (Wells) Kee; m. Peter L. Borges, Nov. 15, 1986; children: Garrett, Julian, Adriana. BS, Trinity Coll., 1981; JD, U. Conn., 1984. Bar: Conn. 1984, U.S. Dist. Ct. Conn. 1985, U.S. Ct. Appeals (2d dist.) 1985. Spl. counsel City of Hartford, Conn., 1984-87, asst. corp. counsel, 1987-93, sr. asst. corp. counsel, 1993, city mgr., 1993—. Bd. dirs. Legal Aid Soc., 1993—, Conn. Valley Girl Scouts, 1993—, Christmas in July, 1994—; mentor Trinity Coll., 1994—, U. Conn. Law Sch., 1994—. Mem. ABA, George Crawford Law Assn. Office: City Hall 550 Main St Hartford CT 06103

KEECH, ELOWYN ANN, interior designer; b. Berrien County, Mich., Oct. 5, 1937; d. Earl Docker and Elizabeth Hall (Paullin) Stephenson; 1 child, Robert Earl. Cert. contract interior designer. Print designer, copywriter newspaper accounts, dept. stores, resorts, svc. orgns., industry, 1957-75; freelance interior designer, photoset and video set designer, St. Joseph, Mich., 1975—; owner Fog Horn Records & Tapes. Bd. dirs. Blossomland United Way, 1981-86; bd. dirs., mem. steering and long-range planning coms. United Way Mich., 1980-87. Designer interiors 1st Fed. Savs. & Loan Assn., Three Oaks, Mich., 1975, Holland (Mich.) Cen. Trade Credit Union, 1978, 1st. Fed. Savs. & Loan Assn., Holland, 1978, Yonker Realty, Co., Holland, 1979, People's Bank of Holland, 1979, exec. offices Whirlpool Corp., 1980—, human resources St. Joe div., 1985, Claeys Residence, 1984, Calley Dental Office, 1985, Sarett Nature Ctr., 1985, Imperial Printing, 1986, Miller Residence, 1986, Schraders Super Market, 1986, Dave's Garage, 1987, Merritt Residence, 1987-88, Smith Residence, 1988, Emergency Shelter Svcs. 1991, Butzbach Residence, 1992, Merritt Residence, Del Mar, Calif., 1993-94, Fister Better Homes & Gardens Conf. Room, 1994, Vanderbogh Residence, 1994-95, S.W. Mich. Regional Airport, 1994—, other contract and residential projects. Trustee Mich. Martime Mus., 1994—. Mem. AIA (profl. affiliate S.W. Mich. chpt.), Nature Conservancy, Sarett Nature Ctr., Nat. Trust Hist. Preservation, Assn. Great Lakes Maritime History, Econ. Club of S.W. Mich., Am. Rottweiler Club, Rotary. Home and Office: 375 Ridgeway St Saint Joseph MI 49085-1062

KEEFE, CAROLYN JOAN, tax accountant; b. Huntington Park, Oct. 11, 1926; d. Paul Dewey and Mary Jane (Parmater) K. AA, Pasadena (Calif.) City Coll., 1947; BA, U. So. Calif., 1950. Tax acct. Shell Oil Co., L.A., 1950-71; tax acct. Shell Oil Co., Houston, 1971-91, ret., 1991. Advisor Midwest Mus. of Am. Art, 1993—; vol. Houston Mus. of Fine Arts, 1991—; vol. docent Houston Mus. of Natural Sci., 1991—, Theatre Under the Stars, 1991—, Houston Pub. TV Channel 8, Houston, 1989—. Mem. LWV, Inst. Mgmt. Accts. (life), Desk and Derrick Club (bd. dirs. 1994—), Houston Alumni Club of Alpha Gamma Delta, USC Houston Alumni Club. Christian Scientist. Home: #203D 4615 N Braeswood Blvd Houston TX 77096-2823

KEEGAN, JANE ANN, insurance executive, consultant; b. Watertown, N.Y., Sept. 1, 1950; d. Richard Isidor and Kathleen (McKinley) K. BA cum laude, SUNY-Potsdam, 1972; MBA in Risk Mgmt., Golden Gate U., 1986. CPCU. Comml. lines mgr. Lithgow & Rayhill, San Francisco, 1977-80; risk mgmt. account coordinator Dinner Levison Co., San Francisco, 1980-83; ins. cons., San Francisco, 1983-84; account mgr. Rollins Burdick Hunter, San Francisco, 1984-85; account exec. Jardine Ins. Brokers, San Francisco, 1985-86; ins. cons., San Francisco, 1986-87, ins. adminstr. Port of Oakland, 1987—, risk mgr., 1989—. Vol. San Francisco Ballet vol. orgn., 1981—, Bay Area Bus., Govt. ARC disaster conf. steering com., 1987-88, 89, 90, 91-92; mem. Nob Hill Neighbors Assn., 1982—. Mem. Nat. Safety Mgmt. Soc., CPCU Soc. (spl. events chairperson 1982-84, continuing profl. devel. program award 1985, 88, chair loss prevention), Risk and Ins. Mgr. Soc. (dep., sec. 1990—, dir. legis. 1993, dir. conf.). Democrat. Roman Catholic. Home: 1065 Las Gallinas San Rafael CA 94903

KEEGAN, MARY BARDEN, volunteer; b. Yonkers, N.Y., Nov. 18, 1921; d. James J. and Mary Agnes (Linehan) Barden; m. James Magner Keegan, June 12, 1948; children: James, Patrick, Colleen, Kathleen, Michael. BS in Edn., Columbia U., 1943, MA in Pers. Adminstrn., 1944. Mem. World Svc. Coun. YWCA of U.S.A, N.Y.C., 1962—; first pres., founder Women's Pub. Rels. Coun., St. Joseph's Hosp., Houston, 1963-66; bd. dirs., v.p. YWCA, Houston, 1965-71, Houston Area Urban League, 1981-86; Houston chair 1st Nat. Women's Conf., Houston, 1977; pres. U.S. del. Friendship Among Women, St. Paul, 1979—; co-chair Women in Devel. Adv. Com. Voluntary Fgn. Aid, Dept. of State, Washington, 1983-93; founder, CEO, chmn. bd. End Hunger Network, Houston, 1985-95; bd. dirs. Citizens Network for Fgn. Affairs, Washington, 1987—; U.S. dep. observer to Ireland Internat. Fund for Ireland, Washington, 1990-92; bd. dirs. St. Joseph Hosp. Found., Houston, 1984—, 1st v.p. exec. com., 1994, pres., 1995; bd. dirs., mem. exec. com., chmn. pub. affairs com. U. St. Thomas, Houston, 1994—; mem. adv. com. Houston Food Bank, St. Jude Children's Rsch. Hosp., St. Joseph Hosp. Benefit "For Our Children's Future", Fox TV; mem. internat. adv. com. Counterpart; trustee, advisor Care. Recipient Brotherhood award NCCJ, 1981, Spl. Fundraiser award YWCA, Houston, 1981, Outstanding Woman award YWCA, 1986, Whitney M. Young Vol. Yr., Houston Area Urban League, 1987, U.S. Presdl. Hunger award Pres. U.S., 1987, Martin Luther King Jr. Life and Legacy award, 1989; named Houston's Pioneer Houston Woman's Club, 1975. Mem. Fedn. Profl. Women, Houston Forum. Home: 121 N Post Oak Ln # 2304 Houston TX 77024

KEEGAN, PATRICIA MARY, operations research analyst; b. Amsterdam, N.Y., Oct. 10, 1942; d. John Patrick and Mary Phillips K.; m. Robert C. McClenon, Jan. 15, 1977; children: Daniel R. Keegan-McClenon, Mary Cecelia Keegan-McClenon. BA in Math., Am. U., 1966; MS in Ops. Rsch., George Washington U., 1981. Mathematician U.S. Naval Weapons Lab., Dahlgren, Va., 1966-67; mem. tech. staff Computer Sci. Corp., Falls Church, Va., 1967-74; sr. analyst GE, Arlington, Va., 1974-76; tech. staff SAI Comsystems, McLean, Va., 1976-78; ops. rsch. analyst Essex, Alexandria, Va., 1978-83; consulting analyst Synectics Corp., Fairfax, Va., 1983—. V.p. Walter H. McClenon Fund, Washington, 1979—. Mem. Ops. Rsch. Soc. Am., Washington Ops. Rsch. Coun. Home: 1119 S Carolina Ave SE Washington DC 20003-2205 Office: Synectics 10400 Eaton Pl Fairfax VA 22030-2208

KEEGAN, SHANNON MARIE, artist; b. Long Beach, Calif., July 22, 1953; d. Robert Charles and Diana Leilani (Colburn) K.; children: Dylan Greenwalt, Lauren Greenwalt. Cert. professionalism, Rocky Mountain Sch. Art, Denver, 1973. Designer, illustrator Denver, 1973-75, Addison Wesley Pub., Menlo Park, Calif., 1975-76; instr., dept. head Rocky Mountain Coll. Art, Denver, 1974-75, 76-82; creative dir. Grant Comm., Boulder, Colo., 1982-89, Environ. Comm., Boulder, 1989-91; prin., dir. Keegan Illustration Advt. Design, Boulder, 1991-93; writer, illustrator Beaverton, Oreg., 1993—. Author, illustrator: Haunted Tacos, 1991; illustrator: Biz Kids Guide to Success, 1991; illustrator, designer Winter's Orphans, 1993, Heetunka's Harvest, 1994. Recipient awards Am. Corp. Identity, N.Y., 1988, 89, Addy awards Advt. Assn.,Rocky Mountain area, 1989, Silver medal Art Dirs. Club, Denver, 1989.

KEEGAN-CORSELLO, ROBYN, financial planner; b. Worcester, Mass.. AAS, Fashion Inst. Tech., N.Y.C., 1973; Cert. in Fin. Planning, Adelphi U., 1987. Registered investment advisor. V.p. Keegan Fin. Cons., Seaford, N.Y., 1983-87; pres. Keegan Fin. Planning, Inc., Seaford, 1988—; investment officer European Am. Bank/ABN AMRO Investment Svcs., Merrick, N.Y., 1993—. Mem. Internat. Assn. Fin. Planning, Inst. Cert. Fin. Planners. Office: ABN-AMRO Investment Svcs Inc 2085 Merrick Rd Merrick NY 11566

KEELER, LYNNE LIVINGSTON MILLS, psychologist, educator, consultant; b. Detroit, Sept. 18, 1934; d. Robert Livingston Mills Staples and Lyda Charlotte (Diehr) Staples; m. Lee Edward Burmeister, July 16, 1955 (div. 1982); children: Benjamin Lee, Lynne Ann; m. Robert Gordon Keeler, Oct. 26, 1986. BS magna cum laude, Ctrl. Mich. U., 1957; MA, U. Mich., 1965; student, Marygrove Coll., Cen. Mich. U., 1971-74. Ltd. lic. psychologist, sch. psychologist; cert. social worker, elem. permanent cons. and tchr. for mentally handicapped. First grade tchr. Shepherd (Mich) Schs., 1957-59; tchr. Kingston (Mich.) Schs., 1959-65; tchr. educationally handicapped Rialto (Calif.) Unified Sch. Dist., 1965-66; tchr., cons. Tuscola Int. Sch. Dist., Caro, Mich., 1966-71; sch. psychologist Huron Int. Sch. Dist., Bad Axe, Mich., 1971-74, Tuscola Int. Sch. Dist., Caro, 1974-89; instr. Delta Coll., University Center, Mich., 1976-88; tchr. spl. day classes Victorville (Calif.) High Sch., 1989; sch. psychologist Bedford (Ind.) Schs., 1990-91; clin. psychologist ACT team and outpatient therapy Sanilac County Mental Health Svcs., Sandusky, Mich., 1991—; cons. sch. psychologist Marlette (Mich.) Schs., 1982-86, Bartholomew Pub. Schs., Columbus, Ind., 1989, Johnson County Schs., Franklin, Ind., 1990; clin. psychologist Thumb Family Counseling, Caro, 1985-88; personnel com. Team One Credit Union, 1993. Conf. presenter in field. Del. NEA-Mich. Edn. Assn. Rep. Assemblies, 1970-89; pres., auction chmn. Altrusa Club, Marlett, 1982-88; style show chmn. Marlette Band Boosters, 1983; mem. exec. bd. Lawrence County Tchrs. Assn., Bedford, 1991; mem. Sanilac Symphonic Band, 1993-94; bd. dirs. Team One Credit Union, 1994—. Fed. govt. grantee Wayne State U., 1968. Mem. Am. Federated State and Mcpl. Employees (chairperson #219 1993 , chairperson #15 chpt. 1994), Ind. State Tchrs. Assn. (rep. assembly del. 1991), Ind. Assn. Sch. Psychologists (pub. rels. bd. 1990-91), Lions Club Internat. Democrat. Methodist. Home: 6726 Clothier Rd Clifford MI 48727-9501 Office: Sanilac County Cmty Mental Health 190 N Delaware St Sandusky MI 48471-1009

KEELEY, G(RAZINA) CHRIS, human resources professional; b. Sakai, Lithuania, Aug. 30, 1939; d. Stanley and Marija (Mozuraitis) Abramovicius; m. Robert E. Keeley, July 31, 1965; children: Robert A., Lara J. BA, U. Chgo., 1963, MAT, 1975, MBA, 1979. Cert. compensation profl. Tchr. Chgo. Bd. Edn./Cath. Sch. Bd., 1964-68; instr. Little Co. of Mary Hosp., Evergreen Park, Ill., 1975-76; asst. dir. ednl. tng. Personnel and Labor Rels./U. Chgo., 1976-81; dir. personnel svcs. Chgo. State U., 1981-83; dir. human resources Indian U./Purdue U., Indpls., 1983—. Author: Progressive Discipline: Supervisor's Guide to Managing Performance, 1987. Bd. dirs. Christamore House, Indpls., 1985—. Recipient Outstanding Leadership award Midwest Coll. and Univ. Personnel Assocs., 1988, others. Mem. U. Chgo. Bus. Sch. Alumni (co-founder, v.p. programs 1987—), U. Chgo. Women's Bus. Group (co-founder, pres. 1980—), Am. Compensation Assn., Am. Soc. Healthcare Human Resources (Lit. award 1988), Soc. for Coll. and Univ. Planning, Coll. and Univ. Personnel Assn. (chair midwest sect. 1983—). Office: Ind Univ Purdue U Indpls 620 Union Dr Indianapolis IN 46254

KEELEY, IRENE PATRICIA MURPHY, federal judge; b. 1944. BA, Coll. Notre Dame, 1965; MA, W.Va. U., 1977, JD, 1980. Bar: Va. Atty. Steptoe & Johnson, Clarksburg, W.Va., 1980-92; dist. judge U.S. Dist. Ct. (no. dist.), W. Va., 1992—; adj. prof. law coll. law W.Va. U., 1990-91. Bd. dirs. United Way Harrison County; mem. vis. com. Coll. Law W.Va. U., 1987-91. Mem. ABA (antitrust sect., tort and ins. practice sect., litigation sect., forum com. health care), W.Va. State Bar (law and medicine com., spl. com. professionalism), W.Va. Law Inst., Harrison County Bar Assn., Def. Trial Counsel W.Va., Def. Rsch. Coun., Am. Assn. Hosp. Attys., Nat. Health Lawyers Assn., W.VA. Soc. Hosp. Attys., Am. Soc. Law and Medicine, Harrison County C. of C., Clarksburg Country Club, Oral Lake Fishing Club, Immaculate Conception Roman Cath. Ch. Office: US Courthouse PO Box 2808 500 W Pike St Rm 202 Clarksburg WV 26302-2808*

KEELING, ELIZABETH BURFOOT, health facility administrator; b. Wills Point, Tex., Jan. 23, 1959; d. Charles Andrews and Elizabeth Ligon (Wilson) Burfoot; m. Robert Walton Keeling, Aug. 31, 1985. ADN, La. Tech. U., 1983; BSN, N.E. La. U., 1985; MSN, U. Tex. Sch. Nursing, Arlington, 1991. RN, Tex., La. Staff nurse St. Francis Med. Ctr., Monroe, La., 1983-85; staff nurse Valley Bapt. Med. Ctr., Harlingen, Tex., 1985-86, nurse mgr., 1986-88, MIS coord., 1988-89; staff nurse Meth. Med. Ctr., Dallas, 1989-91, asst. dir. nursing, 1991-92, edn. dir., 1992-93, dir. women and children's svcs. and edn., 1993-94; asst. adminstr. patient care svcs. Med. Ctr. Mesquite, Tex., 1994—. Mem. ANA, Tex. Nurses Assn., Tex. Orgn. Nurse Execs., Tex. Soc. Healthcare Educators (bd. dirs. 1992-94), Dallas Area Soc. Healthcare Educators (pres.-elect 1991-92, pres. 1992-94), Sigma Theta Tau. Home: 8410 Van Pelt Dr Dallas TX 75228-5952 Office: Med Ctr Mesquite 1011 N Galloway Ave Mesquite TX 75149

KEEN, KATHLEEN THOMAS, neonatal nurse practitioner; b. Havre de Grace, Md., Nov. 15, 1948; d. Carroll Cole and Doris Jean (Schaffer) Thomas; m. John Pratt Wright, Feb. 1967 (div. 1975); children: Cary John, Renee Nicole; m. Raymond Wallace Keen, June 1976 (div. 1983); 1 child, Catherine Mary. AA in Nursing, Harford C.C., Bel Air, Md., 1973; BSN with honors, U. Md., 1976, MS with honors, 1994. RN, Md.; cert. in neonatal intensive care nursing; cert. neonatal nurse practitioner. Staff nurse Harford Meml. Hosp., Havre de Grace, 1973-86, head nurse, 1978-80; staff nurse Johns Hopkins Bayview Med. Ctr., Balt., 1986-92; neonatal nurse practitioner Johns Hopkins Bayview Med Ctr., Balt., 1993-94, Sinai Hosp., Balt., 1994—. Recipient Nursing scholarship State of Md., 1993. Mem. Nat. Assn. Neonatal Nurses, West-East Chesapeake Assn. Neonatal Nurses, Sigma Theta Tau. Democrat. Home: 10 Shannon Dr Bel Air MD 21014 Office: Sinai Hosp of Baltimore 2401 W Belvedere Ave Baltimore MD 21215

KEEN, MARIA ELIZABETH, retired educator; b. Chgo., Aug. 19, 1918; d. Harold Fremont and Mary Eileen Honore (Dillon) K. AB, U. Chgo., 1941; postgrad., U. Wyo., summer 1943; MA, U. Ill., 1949; postgrad., U. Mich., 1957. Tchr. high sch. Wyo., 1942-43, Mich., 1943-44; tchr. Am. Coll. for Women, Istanbul, Turkey, 1944-47; mem. faculty U. Ill., Urbana, 1947-88, prof. emerita, 1988—. Mem. Champaign Community Devel. Com. Mem. AAUW, AAUP (past treas.), AAAS, LWV, Animal Protection Inst., Defenders of Wildlife, Am. Inst. Biol. Scis., Nat. Coun. Tchr. Educators, U. Ill. Athletic Assn. (sec., bd. dirs.), Ont. Geneal. Soc., Orton Dyslexia Soc., Art Inst. Chgo., Women's Philharm. (charter), Women in Arts (charter), Women's Humane Soc., Illini Union (faculty staff social com.), Nat. Humane Soc., Phi Kappa Epsilon (hon.). Baptist. Home: 608 S Edwin St Champaign IL 61821-3834

KEENAN, BARBARA MILANO, judge. Former judge U.S. Cir. Ct. (19th cir.) Va., U.S. Ct. Appeals of Va.; judge Supreme Ct. Va., McLean; now assoc. justice Supreme Ct. Va., Richmond. Office: Supreme Ct 100 N 9th St Richmond VA 23219

KEENAN, CELESTINE, accountant; b. Walnut Creek, Calif., Nov. 16, 1959; d. Roger Derrill and Beverly (Andrew) K.; children: Timothy Andrew Keenan, William Stelios Keenan-Glover. BS Bus. Adminstrn., Calif. State U., 1994. Bookkeeper, accounts payable mgr. Mountain Sports, Chico, Calif., 1990-94; software cons. Mike Darrow, Gen. Contractor, Chico, Calif., 1994; accountant Tri Counties Bank, Chico, Calif., 1994—. Recipient Alfred B. Konuwa Achievement in Microeconomics award Butte Coll., 1991. Mem. Inst. Mgmt. Accts., Beta Gamma Sigma. Roman Catholic. Office: Tri Counties Bank 15 Independence Circle Chico CA 95926

KEENAN, DEIRDRE ANN BRADBURY, manufacturing executive, business educator, consultant; b. Providence, Mar. 7, 1952; d. John Joseph and Marion Damon (Shute) Bradbury; m. Thomas Keenan, Nov. 15, 1975 (div. Dec. 1980); 1 child, Victoria Irene. BA in Govt. and Law, Lafayette Coll., 1973. Supr. Procter & Gamble Mfg. Co., S.I., N.Y., 1973-76; mgr. warehouse dept. Procter & Gamble Mfg. Co., 1976-79, mgr. shortening and oils dept., 1979-81, fin. mgr. food plant, 1981-82, mgr. personnel, 1982-86, mgr. total quality and pub. affairs, 1986-91; ptnr. Avraham Y. Goldratt Inst., New Haven, Conn., 1991—; cons. Procter & Gamble, S.I., 1982—, Cin., 1989-91. Trustee Lafayette Coll., 1985-90. Mem. Lafayette Coll. Alumni Assn. (pres. 1992-94, Clifton P. Mayfield award), Maroon Club (Easton, Pa., pres. 1987-89). Roman Catholic. Office: Avraham Y Goldratt Inst 442 Orange St New Haven CT 06511

KEENAN, RETHA ELLEN VORNHOLT, nurse, educator; b. Solon, Iowa, Aug. 15, 1934; d. Charles Elias and Helen Maurine (Konicek) Vornholt; BSN, State U. Iowa, 1955; MSN, Calif. State U., Long Beach, 1978; m. David James Iverson, June 17, 1956; children: Scott, Craig ; m. Roy Vincent Keenan, Jan. 5, 1980. Publ. health nurse City of Long Beach, 1970-73, 94—, Hosp. Home Care, Torrance, Calif., 1973-75; patient care coord. Hillhaven, L.A., 1975-76; mental health cons. InterCity Home Health, L.A., 1978-79; instr. Community Coll. Dist., L.A., 1979-87; instr. nursing El Camino Coll., Torrance, 1981-86; instr. nursing Chapman Coll., Orange, Calif., 1982, Mt. Saint Mary's Coll., 1986-87; cons., pvt. practice, Rancho Palos Verdes, Calif., 1987-89. Contbg. author: American Journal of Nursing Question and Answer Book for Nursing Boards Review, 1984, Nursing Care Planning Guides for Psychiatric and Mental Health Care, 1987-88, Nursing Care Planning Guides for Children, 1987, Nursing Care Planning Guides for Adults, 1988, Nursing Care Planning Guides for Critically Ill Adults, 1988.

Cert. nurse practitioner adult and mental health, 1979; mem. Assistance League of San Pedro, Palos Verdes, Calif. NIMH grantee, 1977-78. Mem., Nurses Assn., Calif. Nurses Assn., Am. Nurses Assn., Sigma Theta Tau, Phi Kappa Phi, Delta Zeta. Republican. Lutheran. Avocations: travel, writing, reading. Home: 27849 Longhill Dr Rncho Pls Vrd CA 90274-3908

KEENAN-ABILAY, GEORGIA ANN, service representative; b. Denver, Oct. 3, 1936; d. Lawrence Edward and Helen Kathleen (Gray) K.; m. Charles Henry Dupree, May 31, 1958 (div. Nov. 1977); children: Phoenix, Therese, Mark, John; m. Joseph D. Abilay, Nov. 26, 1988. BA, Regis Coll., 1968; MA, St. Thomas U., 1978. With reservations United Airlines, Denver, 1956-57; stewardess Trans World Airlines, Chgo., 1957-58; in elem. edn. Notre Dame Sch., Denver, 1969-72; dir. religious edn. Notre Dame Parish, Denver, 1972-77, Archdiocese Denver, 1977-80; v.p., treas. Kilfinane and Cook, Denver, 1980-82; dir. human resources Cosmopolitan Hotel, Denver, 1982-83, Kaanapali Beach Hotel, Lahaina, Hawaii, 1983-85, Royal Lahaina Resort, Hawaii, 1985-90; corp. dir. human resources Hawaiian Hotels and Resorts, Lahaina, 1988; dir. human resources Rock Resorts Lanai Resorts Ptnrs., Island of Lanai, 1990—; trainer Amfac Hotels and Resorts, Hawaii, 1984-86; vice chmn. Maui Hotel Assn., 1987; bd. dirs. Project 714, Lahaina, 1987. Bd. dirs. Archdiocesan Women's Bd., Denver, 1981-83, Passages, Denver, 1980-83, Maui Econ. Devel. Bd., Kahalui, 1984; chairperson Charity Walk, 1984-86. Named Handicapped Employer of Yr., State of Hawaii, 1987. Mem. Council Hawaii Hotels, Am. Soc. Personnel Assn. Club: Distributive Edn. of Am. (Hawaii) (bd. dirs. 1984—). Home: PO Box 721 Lanai City HI 96763-1090 Office: Lanai Resort Ptnrs PO Box 774 Lanai City HI 96763-0774

KEENE, PAMELA DIANE, engineering draftsman; b. Campton, Ky., May 8, 1966; d. Roscoe and Monella (Spencer) K. Student, Sinclair C.C., Dayton, Ohio, 1987—. Stenography clk. U.S. Air Force ASD/B1, Wright-Patterson AFB, Ohio, 1985-87; sec., stenographer U.S. Air Force Civil Engring., Wright-Patterson AFB, 1987-89, engring. draftsman, 1989-94; founding ptnr. United CAD Svcs. and Tng. Inc., Huber Heights, Ohio, 1994—. Vol. instr. ARC, Dayton; rescue diver, emergency med. technician Box 21 Rescue Squad, Dayton. Mem. Federally Employed Women. Baptist. Home: 6107 Leyden Ln Huber Heights OH 45424-3459

KEENE, SUSIE MILLER (SUSIE HORNE), retired library media specialist; b. Robinson Creek, Ky., Nov. 8, 1929; d. Lee Joseph and Jessie (Ison) Horne; m. Bruce E. Keene, Apr. 6, 1950; 1 child, Rebecca Lynn. BS, Pikeville Coll., 1961; MA, Eastern Ky. U., 1969, postgrad., 1974. Tchr. Pike County Bd. Edn., Robinson Creek, 1949-51; tchr., instr. art Virgie (Ky.) Grade Sch., 1958-61; instr. art Robinson Creek Elem. Sch., 1961-67; libr. media specialist George F. Johnson Elem. Sch., Virgie, 1967-92; ret., 1992. Bd. dirs. Pike County ARC, 1976-78. Mem. NEA, AAUW (2d v.p. 1978-80), Ea. Ky. Media Assn. (pres. 1988-89), Pike County Media Assn. (past pres.), Ky. Libr. Assn. (bd. dirs.), Ky. Dept. Edn. Media Cadre, Delta Kappa Gamma, Alpha Gamma (1st v.p. 1993-95). Democrat. Baptist.

KEENE-BURGESS, RUTH FRANCES, army official; b. South Bend, Ind., Oct. 7, 1948; d. Seymour and Sally (Morris) K.; m. Leslie U. Burgess, Jr., Oct. 1, 1983; children: Michael Leslie, David William, Elizabeth Sue, Rachael Lee. BS, Ariz. State U., 1970; MS, Fairleigh Dickinson U., 1978; grad., U.S. Army Command and Gen. Staff Coll., 1986. Inventory mgmt. specialist U.S. Army Electronics Command, Phila., 1970-74, U.S. Army Communications-Electronics Material Readiness Command, Fort Monmouth, N.J., 1974-79; chief inventory mgmt. div. Crane (Ind.) Army Ammunition Activity, 1979-80; supply systems analyst Hdqrs. 60th Ordnance Group, Zweibruecken, Fed. Republic Germany, 1980-83; chief inventory mgmt. div. Crane (Ind.) Army Ammunition Activity, 1983-85, chief control div., 1985; inventory mgmt. specialist 200th Theater Army Material Mgmt. Ctr., Zweibruecken, 1985-88; analyst supply systems U.S. Armament, Munitions and Chem. Command, Rock Island, Ill., 1988-89; specialist logistics mgt. U.S. Army Info. Systems Command, Ft. Huachuca, Ariz., 1989—. Mem. Federally Employed Women (chpt. pres. 1979-80), NAFE, Soc. Logistics Engrs., Assn. Computing Machinery, Am. Soc. Public Adminstrn., Soc. Profl. and Exec. Women, Assn. Info. Systems Profls., AAAS, NOW. Democrat.

KEENER, ELAINE FATELY, art therapist; b. Alexandria, Va., Sept. 13, 1936; d. Thomas and Mildred (Monroe) Fately; m. Howard Nelson Keener Jr., Mar. 30, 1963 (div. May 1986); children: Christine Keener Cintron, Thad Thomas. BA, Ohio Wesleyan U., 1959; MA, Vt. Coll., 1979; BFA, U. N.C., Greensboro, 1994. Social worker Boston City Missionary Soc., Charlestown Armed Svcs, YMCA, Kanawha County Schs., Charleston, W.Va., 1974-76; art therapist Charleston Area Med. Ctr., 1976-78, Highland Hosp., Charleston, 1978-80, Lakin (W.Va.) State Hosp., 1980-86; activities dir. Triad United Meth. Home, Winston-Salem, N.C., 1986-92; art therapist Charter Hosp., Winston-Salem, 1994—. One-woman shows include Arbor Acres, Winston Salem, 1995; exhibited in group shows at UNCG, 1994, Greensboro Coll., 1994. Home: 2865 Farmbrook Rd Winston-Salem NC 27103-6217 Office: 3637 Old Vineyard Rd Winston Salem NC 27103

KEENER, MARY LOU, lawyer; b. Flint, Mich., Aug. 9, 1944; d. Robert Sherman Keener and Rosemary (Kowalski) Brady. BSN, Cath. U. Am., 1966; MN, Emory U., 1972; JD, Cath. U. Am., 1982. Bar: Ga. 1983, Md. 1983, Supreme Ct. Ga. 1992. Congl. caseworker Congressman D. W. Riegle, Jr., Washington, 1969-71; asst. prof. dept. nursing Ga. State U., Atlanta, 1972-76; exec. dir. Ga. Nurses Assn., Atlanta, 1976-79; atty. Arfken, Caldwell, Steckel & Mack, Atlanta, 1982-84, Lavigno & Dawkins, Conyers, Ga., 1985, Butler & McDonald, Atlanta, 1986-88, Law Offices Mary Lou Keener, Atlanta, 1989-93; gen. counsel Dept. Vet. Affairs, Washington, 1993—. Bd. dirs. Ga. Vietnam Vets. Leadership Program, 1983-93, chmn., 1984-86, Atlanta Vietnam Vets. Bus. Assn., 1989-93; mem. adv. bd. Agent Orange Class Assistance Program, 1989-93. Lt. USN, 1966-69, Vietnam. Recipient Nat. Svc. Def. medal, Vietnam Svc. medal, Republic of Vietnam Campaign medal, Air Force Commendation medal; named Winner Nat. Moot Ct. Competition, 1980. Mem. ABA, ANA (bylaws com. 1978-82), Am. Trial Lawyers Assn., Ga. Trial Lawyers Assn. (LAWPAC 1992-93, legis. com. 1992-93), Ga. Underwriting Assn. (bd. dirs. 1991-93), Atlanta Bar Assn., Atlanta Vietnam Vets. Bus. Assn. (bd. dirs. 1989-93). Office: Dept Vets Affairs 810 Vermont Ave NW Washington DC 20420

KEENER, POLLY LEONARD, illustrator; b. Akron, Ohio, July 14, 1946; d. George Holman and Alice June (Bolinger) Leonard; m. Robert Lee Keener, Dec. 29, 1967; children: Robert Edward Alan, June Whitney. Student, Kent State U., 1967, Princeton U., 1968, 73; BA, Conn. Coll., 1968. Cert. tchr., Ohio. Illustrator Akron, 1969—; instr. cartooning Northeastern Ohio Univs. Coll. Medicine, 1992—; instr. cartooning U. Akron, 1979—, instr. soft sculpture, 1979-84; cartoon text writer Prentice Hall Pubs., Englewood Cliffs, N.J., 1985—; pres. Keener Corp., Akron, 1977—; judge arts and crafts competition, Akron, 1982—. Author: Cartooning, 1992; illustrator: Eat Dessert First, 1987, It's Our Serve, 1989, 80+ Great Ideas For Making Money At Home, 1992; contbr. articles to profl. jours. Trustee Stan Hywet Hall Found., Akron, 1972—; trustee and v.p. Women's History Project, Akron, 1993—; v.p. Jr. League, Akron, 1988-89, Western Res. Acad. Women's Bd., Hudson, Ohio, 1987-88; active Women's Bd. Blossom Music Ctr., Penninsula, Ohio, 1969—. Named Woman of Yr. Women's History Project Ohio, 1989; recipient Unsung Hero award Jr. League Akron, 1988. Mem. AAUP, DAR (trustee, recording sec. Cuyahoga-Portage chpt. 1992—), Nat. Cartoonists Soc. (sec.-treas. Ohio/Mich. chpt. 1994—), Soc. Illustrators, Coll. Art Assn., Portage Country Club. Episcopalian. Home: 37 Elmdale Ave Akron OH 44313-7645

KEENEY, REGINA MARKEY, lawyer; b. Sumter, S.C., Aug. 20, 1955; d. John Patrick and Margaret Mary (Rogers) Markey; m. Terence J. Keeney, Aug. 16, 1980; children: Teresa Marie, Anne Mairead. BS, Georgetown U., 1977; JD, Harvard U., 1980. Bar: D.C. Assoc. Hamel, Park, McCabe & Saunders, Washington, 1980-83; atty., advisor FCC, Washington, 1983-85, bur. chief Wireless Telecom. Bur., 1994—; sr. counsel comm. Senate Commerce Com., Washington, 1985-94. Roman Catholic. Office: FCC Pvt Radio Bur 1919 M St NW Washington DC 20554

KEEP, JUDITH N., federal judge; b. Omaha, Mar. 24, 1944. B.A., Scripps Coll., 1966; J.D., U. San Diego, 1970. Bar: Calif. 1971. Atty. Defenders Inc., San Diego, 1971-73; pvt. practice law, 1973-76; asst. U.S. atty. U.S. Dept. Justice, 1976; judge Mcpl. Ct., San Diego, 1976-80; judge U.S. Dist. Ct. (so. dist.) Calif., San Diego, 1980—, chief judge, 1991—. Office: US Dist Ct 940 Front St Rm 6 San Diego CA 92101-0010*

KEES, BEVERLY, newspaper editor; b. Mpls., June 4, 1941; d. Burton Joseph and Dorothy Ann (White) K. BA, U. Minn., 1963. Reporter Mpls. Star, 1963-69, sect. editor, 1969-72; rsch. planning analyst Mpls. Star and Tribune Co., 1972-73; asst. mng. editor Mpls. Tribune, 1973-81; exec. editor Grand Forks (N.D.) Herald, 1981-84; editor Post-Tribune, Gary, Ind., 1984-88; exec. editor Fresno (Calif.) Bee, 1988-93; vis. profl. scholar Freedom Forum First Amendment Ctr. Vanderbilt U., 1993-94; editor-in-resident The Freedom Forum Pacific Coast Ctr., Oakland, Calif., 1994—; part-time journalism instr. Coll. St. Thomas, St. Paul, 1974. Author: Wonderful Ways With Chicken, 1970, Cook with Honey, 1973, Basic Breads Around the World, 1977; co-author Fondue on the Menu, 1970. Bd. dirs. greater Grand Forks Symphony Assn., 1982-84, Grand Forks chpt. Am. Red Cross, 1981-84, FKJN Pub. Radio Sta., 1981-84; mentor Career Beginnings Gary Ind. high schs., 1986-88; pres. Minn. Arts Forum, 1980-81; sec. The Acad., 1990-91, v.p., 1991-92, pres., 1992-93. Mem. Am. Soc. Newspaper Editors (chair bulletin com. 1989-90), Internat. Press Inst. (Am. com. bd. 1988—), Associated Press Mng. Editors Assn. (bd. dirs. 1985-91, sec. 1994), Minn. Alumnae Club (pres. 1977), U. Minn. Alumni Assn. (bd. dirs. 1975-79, exec. com. 1976-79). Episcopalian. Home: 201 Harrison St Apt 1127 San Francisco CA 94105 Office: Freedom Forum Pacific Coast Ctr 70 Washington St Ste 210 Oakland CA 94607

KEESEE, PATRICIA HARTFORD, volunteer; b. Nashville, Apr. 29, 1928; d. William Donald and Mary Carolyn (Gwyn) Hartford; m. Thomas Woodfin Keesee Jr., June 26, 1953; children: Thomas Woodfin III, Anne Hartford Keesee Niemann; 1 stepson: Allen P.K. Keesee. BA in English, Radcliff Coll., 1950; BA in Environ. Scis., SUNY, Purchase, 1977. Lab. asst. Rockefeller U. (formerly Rockefeller Inst. Med. Rsch.), N.Y.C., 1951-54. Chmn. Byram com. Nature Conservancy, Bedford, 1978-81; mem. Conservation Bd. Town of Bedford, 1978-88, Westchester County Environ. Mgmt. Commn., 1979-88, Coun. of N.Y. Botan. Garden, Bronx, 1982—, Wetlands Commn., Bedford, N.Y., 1988—; trustee Lower Hudson chpt. Nature Conservancy, Katonah, N.Y., 1980-90, 91—, chmn., 1983-86; pres. Fed. Conservationists of Westchester County, Purchase, 1985-87; trustee N.Y. State Bd. Nature Conservancy, Albany, 1983-91, vice-chmn., 1986-88. Mem. N.Y. Acad. Scis., Garden Club Am. (conservation com. 1983-85, vice chmn. conservation com. 1985-87, bd. dirs. 1989-91, vice chmn. scholarship com. 1991-93). Episcopalian. Home: 140 Sarles St Rd # 3 Mount Kisco NY 10549-2812

KEESHEN, KATHLEEN KEARNEY, public relations consultant; b. N.Y.C., Dec. 4, 1937; d. James William and Hannah Pauline (Mansfield) Kearney; 1 child (by previous marriage), John Christopher Day; m. Walt Keeshen Jr.; stepchildren: Michael Patrick, Walt John III, Kathleen Marie, William Thomas, Ralph Timothy. BA in English, U. Md., 1959, MA in Journalism, 1973, PhD in Am. Studies, 1983; postgrad., Stanford U., 1988—. Cert. profl. sec. Congl., legal, med., acad., corp. sec. various orgns., East and Midwest, 1954-63; staff and mgmt. positions IBM, Washington, Md., 1963-73; lab. communications mgr. Systems Communications Div. IBM, Manassas, Va., 1974-76; communications staff corp. hdqrs. IBM, Armonk, N.Y., 1977-83; communications and community rels. mgr. Almaden Rsch. Ctr. IBM, San Jose, Calif., 1983-92; prin. Keeshen Comm., Coyote (Calif.) Press., 1992—. Contbr. articles to profl. jours.; lectr. in field. Adv. bd. Freinds of San Jose Pub. Libr., 1987—, Silicon Valley Info. Ctr., 1986-92, Media Report to Women; mem. corp. task force Stanford U. Inst. for Rsch. on Women and Gender, 1990—, affiliated scholar, 1992-94, assocs. bd., 1994—; affiliated scholar Beatrice M. Bain Rsch. Group U. Calif., Berkeley, 1994—. Mem. Am. Journalism Historians Assn., Assn. for Edn. in Journalism and Mass Comm., Women in Comm., Am. Studies Assn., Dean's First Edition Club, Coll. of Journalism U. Md., San Jose Rotary Club, San. Jose Profl. Womens Literary Assn., Calif. Writers Club, Sigma Delta Chi, Alpha Xi Delta. Office: Keeshen Comm Coyote Press PO Box 13154 Coyote CA 95013-3154

KEESLING, KAREN RUTH, lawyer; b. Wichita, Kans., July 9, 1946; d. Paul W. and Ruth (Sharp) K. BA, Ariz. State U., 1968, MA, 1970; JD, Georgetown U., 1981. Bar: Va. 1981, Fla. 1981. Asst. dean of women U. Kans., Lawrence, 1970-72; exec. sec. , sec.'s adv. com. on rights and responsibilities of women HEW, Washington, 1972-74; dir. White House Office of Women's Programs, Washington, 1974-77; head civil rights and equal opportunity sect., Gov. Div., Congl. Rsch. Svc. Libr. Congress, Washington, 1977-80; legis. aide Sen. Nancy Kassebaum, Washington, 1979-81; mem. pers. office staff Office of Pres.-elect, Washington, Jan. 1981; pvt. practice Falls Church, Va., 1981-88, 90-92, 1993—; dept. for equal opportunity dept. Dept. Air Force, Washington, 1981-82, dep. asst. sec. manpower res. affairs and installations, 1982-83; prin. dep. asst. sec. manpower res. affairs Dept. Air Force, 1983-87; prin. dep. asst. sec. readiness support dept. Dept. Air Force, Washington, 1987-88, prin. dep. asst. sec. manpower and res. affairs, 1988, asst. sec. manpower and res. affairs, 1988-89; acting wage and hour adminstr. U.S. Dept. Labor, Washington, 1992-93; bd. advisers Outstanding Young Women Am., 1983-90; acting wage and hour adminstr. U.S. Dept. Labor, 1992-93. Mem. Nat. Fedn. Republican Women's Club, Washington, 1975, Nat. Women's Polit. Caucus, Washington, 1980. Named one of Ten Outstanding Young Women of Am., 1975; recipient Ariz. State U. Alumni Achievement award, 1976, Elizabeth Boyer award Women's Equity Action League, 1986, Meritorious Civilian award USAF, 1987, Woman of Distinction award Nat. Conf. Coll. Women, Student Leaders and Women of Distinction, 1988, Exeptional Civilian Svc. award USAF, 1988. Mem. Va. Bar Assn., Fla. Bar Assn., Va. Fedn. Bus. and Profl. Women's Clubs (2d v.p. 1987-88, 1st v.p. 1988-89, pres.-elect 1989-90, pres. 1990-91), No. Va. Women Atty.'s Assn. (steering com. 1990—), Va. Bus. and Profl. Women's Found. (trustee 1985-93), The Women's Inst. Inc. (adv. coun. 1985—), U.S. Com. for the UNIFEM (gen. counsel 1983—), P.E.O. (Wichita), Pi Beta Phi. Home: 7124 Sanford Ct Annandale VA 22003-1726 Office: 252 N Washington St Falls Church VA 22046-4500

KEESLING, KRISTINE LOUISE, hotel sales and marketing executive; b. Riverside, Calif., Oct. 27, 1950; d. Arthur Lawrence and Constance Eugenia (Betts) K. AA, Riverside City Coll., 1970; BA, San Diego State U., 1972. Office asst. Kelly Svcs., Inc., Riverside and San Diego, 1968-73; mountain hostess Vail (Colo.) Assocs., 1973-77; sales sec. AIRCOA, Vail, 1977-78; dir. sales and mktg. AIRCOA, Vail, Summit County, Albuquerque, Santa Fe, 1978-85; asst. mgr. AIRCOA, Orlando, Fla.; mgr. AIRCOA, Beaver Creek, Colo., 1985-87; mgr. sales and front office Pickett Suite Hotels, Tampa, Durham, 1988-89; dir. sales and mktg. Embassy Suites, Napa, Calif., 1989-91; nat. sales mgr. Embassy Suites, South Lake Tahoe, Calif., 1991—. Mem. South Lake Tahoe Airport Commn., 1994—. Scholar Riverside Panhellenic, 1970. Mem. Am. Soc. Assn. Execs. (bd. dirs., coms. 1979—), Meeting Profls. Internat. (bd. dirs., coms. 1979—), Soc. Govt. Meeting Planners (bd. dirs., coms. 1983—), Hotel Sales and Marketers Assn. Internat. (cert. hospitality sales exec., bd. dirs., coms. 1979-89), Nat. Tour Assn. (cert. tour profl., conv. vol. 1979—). Republican. Methodist. Office: Embassy Suites Resort Lake Tahoe 4130 Lake Tahoe Blvd South Lake Tahoe CA 96150

KEGLEY, JACQUELYN ANN, philosophy educator; b. Conneaut, Ohio, July 18, 1938; d. Steven Paul and Gertrude Evelyn (Frank) Kovacevic; m. Charles William Kegley, June 12, 1964; children: Jacquelyn Ann, Stephen Lincoln Luther. BA cum laude, Allegheny Coll., 1960; MA summa cum laude, Rice U., 1964; PhD, Columbia U., 1971. Asst. prof. philosophy Calif. State U., Bakersfield, 1973-77, assoc. prof., 1977-81, prof., 1981—; vis. prof. U. Philippines, Quezon City, 1966-68; grant project dir. Calif. Council Humanities, 1977, project dir. 1980, 82; mem. work group on ethics Am. Colls. of Nursing, Washington, 1984-86. Author: Introduction to Logic, 1978; editor: Humanistic Delivery of Services to Families, 1982, Education for the Handicapped, 1982; mem. editorial bd. Jour. Philosophy in Lit., 1979-84; contbr. articles to profl. jours. Bd. dirs. Bakersfield Mental Health Assn., 1982-84, Citizens for Betterment of Community. Recipinet Outstanding Prof. award Calif. State U., 1989-90, Golden Roadrunner award Bakersfield Community, 1991. Mem. N.Y. Acad. Scis., Philosophy of Sci. Assn., Soc. Advancement Am. Phil. soc. (chmn. Pacific div. 1979-83, nat. exec. com. 1974-79), Philosophy Soc., Soc. Interdisciplinary Study of Mind, Am. Philosophical Assn., Dorian Soc., Phi Beta Kappa. Democrat. Lutheran. Home: 7312 Kroll Way Bakersfield CA 93309-2320 Office: Calif State U Dept Philosophy & Religious Studies Bakersfield CA 93311

KEHLER, ABBEJEAN, economist, educator; b. Balt., June 12, 1952; d. Richard Jay and Mary Elizabeth (Lenhardt) K. BS in Edn., U. N.D., 1975, MEd, 1977. Instr. dept. econs. Wichita State U., 1977-8; instr., asst. dir. Ctr. Econ. Edn. Ball State U., Muncie, Ind., 1978-80; instr. dept. econs. Ind. U., Bloomington, 1980-81; field dir. Fla. Coun. Econ. Edn., Tampa, 1981-86; assoc. dir. Cen. Ohio Ctr. Econ. Edn. Ohio State U., Columbus, 1986-93, dir. Cen. Ohio Ctr. Econ. Edn., 1993—; pres. Ohio Coun. Econ. Edn., Columbus, 1991—; mem. social studies adv. com. Ohio Dept. Edn., Columbus, 1992-94. Editor profl. newsletters. Recipient Univ. Teaching award Joint Coun. Econ. Edn., 1989. Mem. Nat. Assn. Econ. Educators (long-range planning com. 1990-93, 94—), Columbus Assn. Bus. Economists, Nat. Coun. Social Studies, Phi Delta Kappa, Omicron Delta Epsilon. Office: Ohio State Univ 160 Ramseyer Hall 29 W Woodruff Ave Columbus OH 43210-1177

KEHOE, SUSAN, quality project manager; b. Cleve., Dec. 5, 1947; d. John William and Mary Margaret Kehoe; m. Gerald Nicholas, May 15, 1970 (div.); children: Patricia, Mark; m. George Vivier, Sept. 19, 1992. BA, U. Detroit, 1970; MA, Oakland U., 1980, PhD, 1983. Cert. secondary tchr., Mich. Trainer ESL Utica Community Schs., Mich., 1974-78; coord. program Oakland Univ., Rochester, Mich., 1980-83; adj. prof. mktg. Wayne State Univ., Detroit, 1983-85, U. Mich., Ann Arbor, 1984-85; pres., owner The Kehoe Group, Birmingham, Mich., 1983-89; trainer, program designer Gen. Motors, Detroit, 1984-89; trainer, cons. Nat. Steel, Ecorse, Mich., 1984-89; tng. specialist electronics div. Ford Motor Co., Dearborn, Mich., 1990-92, program dir. quality oper. systems, 1991-92; project mgr. Ford Motor Co. Powertrain, 1992—. Presenter Nat. Reading Conf., 1981, 83, Internat. Reading Assn., 1982, Am. Edn. Rsch. Assn., 1982, Conf. on Coll. Composition, 1984. Mem. Am. Soc. For Tng. and Devel., Nat. Soc. Performance in Instrn. Avocations: art, travel, music. Home: 2477 Hickory Glen Dr Bloomfield Hills MI 48304-2207 Office: Ford Motor Co Powertrain Ops 3001 Miller Rd Dearborn MI 48121

KEHR, BARBARA SHOEMAKER, educational supervisor; b. Chester, Pa., Mar. 7, 1956; d. Elmer Ellsworth and Frances Alma (Alexander) Shoemaker; m. David Allan Kehr, Nov. 22, 1980; 1 child, Matthew David. AB in Humanities, Muhlenberg Coll., 1978; MA in Reading, Hood Coll., 1982; MS in Sch. Adminstrn., Western Md. Coll., 1995. Cert. elem. profl., reading specialist. Tchr. Waynesboro (Pa.) Area Sch. Dist., 1978-90, comm. arts. coord., 1990—; instr. Pa. State U., Mont Alto, 1992—; chair reading dept. Waynesboro Area Sch. Dist., 1990—, lead tchr., 1990-92; trainer reading workshop, writing workshop, portfolio assessment numerous local sch. dists., Adams County, Pa., 1992—. Lead tchr. profl. devel. grantee South Ctrl. Lead Tchr. Ctr., New Oxford, Pa., 1991, 92, 93, 95, grantee Bus. and Edn. Standing Together, Franklin County, Pa., 1992. Mem. ASCD, Internat. Reading Assn., Nat. Coun. Tchrs. English, Phi Delta Kappa. Republican. Lutheran. Home: 47 Fish And Game Rd Littlestown PA 17340 Office: Summitview Elem 840 E 2nd St Waynesboro PA 17268-2392

KEHRET, PEG, writer; b. LaCrosse, Wis., Nov. 11, 1936; d. Arthur Robert and Elizabeth (Showers) Schulze; m. Carl Edward Kehret, July 2, 1955; children: Bob. C., Anne M. Kehret Konen. Student, U. Minn., 1954-55. trustee Pacific Northwest Writers Conf., Seattle, 1983-86. Author: Vows of Love and Marriage, 1979, Refinishing and Restoring Your Piano, 1985, Winning Monologs for Young Actors, 1986, Deadly Stranger, 1987 (Children's Choice award 1988), The Winner, 1988, ENCORE!—More Winning Monologs for Young Actors, 1988, Nightmare Mountain, 1989 (Young Hoosier Book award 1992, Golden Sower award Nebr. Libr. Assn. 1993, Iowa Children's Choice award 1994), Wedding Vows, 1989, Sisters, Long Ago, 1990, Cages, 1991, Acting Natural, 1992, Terror At The Zoo, 1992, Horror At The Haunted House, 1992, Night of Fear, 1994, Richest Kids in Town, 1994, Cat Burglar on the Prowl, 1995, Danger at the Fair, 1995, Bone Breath and the Vandals, 1995, (plays) Cemeteries Are a Grave Matter, 1977, Let Him Sleep 'Till It's Time for His Funeral, 1978, Spirit!, 1979 (Forest Roberts Playwriting award No. Mich. U. 1979, Best New Play award Pioneer Drama Svc. 1980), Dracula, Darling, 1980, Charming Billy, 1981, (musical) Bicycles Built for Two, 1985; contbr. 300 articles and short stories to mags. Vol. Humane Soc., SPCA, Bellevue, Wash., 1975—; bd. dirs. Bellevue Playbarn, 1975-78, Alzheimer's Assn., Bellevue, 1982. Recipient Achievement award Pacific N.W. Writers, Celebrate Lit. award N.W. Reading Coun. of Internat. Reading Assn., 1993. Mem. Author's Guild, Soc. Children's Book Writers, Seattle Freelancers. Office: Curtis Brown Ltd Ten Astor Pl New York NY 10003

KEIFFER, MARGUERITE MAY, music teacher; b. Portland, Oreg., Oct. 6, 1931; d. Harold Charles and Alice May (Davis) Elkinton; m. Gerald Allen Keiffer, Mar. 19, 1955; children: Gerald, Jr., Brian, Karen. BS, Linfield Coll., 1953; postgrad., Portland State U., 1953-54, U. Portland, 1954-55. Social worker I Columbia County Welfare, St. Helens, Oreg., 1953-54; social worker II Multnomah County Welfare, Portland, 1954-57; piano tchr. Keiffer's Piano Studio, Ukiah, Calif., 1963—. Author short stories, 1993-94. Republican. Baptist.

KEIL, MARILYN MARTIN, artist; b. Balt., Nov. 6, 1932; d. Francis and Mary Blanche (Murphy) Martin; m. Herbert Bruce Keil, Dec. 18, 1954; children: Braden, Mary-Beth, Sue-Ann, Nancy, Bryant. Student, Corcoran Sch. Art, Washington, 1991-94, U. Md., 1994—. active art in embassies program U.S. Dept. State. One-woman show Ralls Collection, Washington, 1993; exhibited in group shows at Rockville Art League (watercolor winner), 1991, Corcoran Sch. of Art, 1994, Nat. Cathedral, Washington, 1994. Bd. dirs. Potomac Glen Civic Assn., Potomac, Md., 1988-94. Mem. Rockville Art League, Nat. Mus. Women in the Arts (charter). Home: 11540 South Glen Rd Potomac MD 20854

KEILLOR, SHARON ANN, computer company executive; b. St. Thomas, Ont., Can., July 10, 1945; d. Mary Keillor; m. Russel C. Jones; children: Kimberly Nicole, Tamara Melissa. BSChemE, U. Western Ont., 1968; diploma mech. engring., Imperial Coll. Sci. and Tech., London, 1972; PhDME, U. London, 1972; MBA in Bus. Mktg./Fin., Ohio State U., 1976. Asst. prof., faculty engring. and applied sci. Meml. U. Nfld., St. John's, Can., 1972-76; assoc. dir. div. continuing edn., budget planning and fin. U. Mass., Amherst, 1977-78, spl. asst. to provost, 1978-80; corp. mgr. software svcs. tng. Digital Equipment Corp., Stow, Mass., 1980-83, corp. mgr. digital mgmt. edn. and office automation, 1982-83, corp. mgr. software svcs., software engring., 1983-91, v.p. computer spl. systems, 1989-91; v.p. bus. and mktg. mgmt. The Software Group, Stow, Mass., 1991-93, v.p. shared engring. svcs., 1993—; vis. asst. prof. faculty engring. sci. U. Western Ont., London, Can., 1973, 75. Athlone fellow; Nat. Rsch. Coun. Can. scholar. Mem. IEEE, Soc. Women Engrs., Am. Soc. Engring. Edn. Home: 12 Boysenberry Dr Hockessin DE 19707-2128 Office: 2 Penns Way New Castle DE 19720-2409

KEIM, BETTY ADELE T., mayor; b. California, Pa., Nov. 14, 1935; d. Glenn L. and F. Edith (Carson) Tinley; m. Richard P. Keim, Mar. 2, 1957 (dec. Sept. 1987); children: Susan Keim Rohrer, Sheila Marie (dec.), Karen Keim Smoot, R. Paul Jr., David C., Katherine A. Grad. nursing, Allegheny Gen. Hosp., Pitts., 1956; student, U. Pitts., 1957-58; BS in Nursing Edn., U. Kans., 1965. RN, Kans., Pa. Nurse biochemistry and nutrition rsch. dept. U. Pitts., St. Margaret's Hosp., 1956-57; pres. Jr. League, Wyandotte, Johnson County, Kans., 1975-76; founding pres. Kans. Action for Children, Topeka, 1978-80; founding mem. Kans. Children's Endowment Fund, Topeka, 1981; pres. Aux. to Kans. Dental Assn., Topeka, 1983-84, United Community Svcs., Johnson County, 1985-87; adv. mem. bd. trustees Bethany Med. Ctr., Kansas City, Kans., 1986-89; dir. Bethany Med. Ctr. Found., Kansas City, Kans., 1989—; pres. Johnson County C.C. Found., 1990-92. Author resource documents. Bd. mem. Community Blood Ctr., Kansas City, Mo., 1988—; mem. Leadership Kans., Topeka, 1991; mem. bd. govs. Am. Royal, Kansas City, Mo., 1990—; precinct committeewoman, Mission Hills, Kans., 1988—; active City Coun., Mission Hills, 1989—, pres., 1991-93, mayor, 1993—; mem. bd. zoning appeals, Mission Hills, 1987-89. Recipient Ann. Child Advocacy award Kans. Action for Children, 1981, Child Abuse Prevention award Kans. Com. for Prevention Child Abuse,

1979, Community Svc. award Jr. League, 1978; named Milton E. Erickson Citizen of Yr. United Community Svcs., Johnson County, 1988, Woman of Yr. Aux. Kans. Dental Assn., 1986. Mem. Allegheny Gen. Hosp. Nurse Alumni Assn., ANA, Kans. State Nurses Assn., Kans. U. Med. Ctr. Nurse Alumni Assn., Jr. League Wyandotte and Johnson Counties Kans., Rep. Elephant Club, Sigma Theta Tau. Presbyterian.

KEIPER, MARILYN MORRISON, educator; b. South Gate, Calif., June 12, 1930; d. David Cline and Matilda Ruth (Pearce) M.; m. Edward E. Keiper, June 18, 1962; children: Becky S. Swickard, Edward M. BA, Calif. State U., L.A., 1954; postgrad., UCLA, 1968. Elem. tchr. Rosemead (Calif.) Sch. Dist., 1954—; recreation leader L.A. County, 1951-62. 2d leader 1st Ch. Christ Scientist, Arcadia, Calif., 1991-94; mem. cons. Janson Adv. Group, Rosemead, 1985—; bd. dirs. Janson PTA, Rosemead, 1985—; participant Sta. KNBC Spirit of Edn., 1990-92. Named Tchr. of the Yr., L.A. County, 1983-84. Fellow Rosemead Tchrs. Assn., Delta Kappa Gamma.

KEISEL, MAURINE LILLEY, rehabilitation nurse; b. Corry, Pa., Oct. 31, 1939; d. Maurice D. and Violet S. (Vettenburg) Lilley; m. Glenn L. Keisel, Apr. 7, 1962; children: G. Adam, Glenda (Sunny), Mark. Diploma in nursing, Hamot Hosp. Sch. Nursing, 1961. RN; CRRN, Rehab. Nursing Certification Bd. RN Bethesda Childrens Home, Meadville, Pa., 1961-62; staff RN Ashtabula (Ohio) Gen. Hosp., 1969-71; coord., supr. restorative nursing program Ashtabula Medicare Ctr., 1975-87; co-owner, cons. Keisel Phys. Therapy, Ashtabula, 1989—; parish nurse, health ministries coord. Bethany Luth. Ch., Ashtabula, 1992—; cons. in field. Active Ashtabula Nursing Homes. Mem. ANA, Ohio Nurses Assn., Assn. Rehab. Nurses, Health Ministries Assn., Nurses Christian Fellowship. Lutheran. Home: 3016 S Ridge W Ashtabula OH 44004 Office: Keisel Phys Therapy 416 W 27th St Ashtabula OH 44004

KEISER, CAROL JANE, artist; b. Springfield, Mass., Jan. 15, 1945; d. Donald Joseph and Muriel L. (Moulton) K.; m. David Mischke, June 21, 1968 (div. 1980); 1 child, Jude; m. James William Hunt, Oct. 2, 1987. Student, U. N.H., 1963-67, Ohio State U., 1968-69; MEd, Antioch Grad. Sch., Putney, Vt., 1971-72; postgrad., Art Student's League of N.Y., 1982. Self-employed artist working in clay, painting, and tiles, 1970—; owner Studio Tile, Putney, 1985-93, Stoneware Pottery, Putney, 1970-80; work influence includes several years of travel and work in San Miguel de Allende, Mex.; handpainted tiles represented in about 50 galleries throughout the U.S.; painting exhbns. mostly in New Eng. One-woman shows include Interiors, Artisan Gallery, Northampton, Mass., 1993, Remembered Moments, 1991, Paintings from Mexico, River Valley Playhouse, Putney, 1988; group shows include Tile Paintings, Newbury Soc. of Arts and Crafts, Boston, 1993, Woodstock (Vt.) Gallery, 1993, Works from Mexico, Bellows Falls Trust, Putney, 1992, Hands of the Goddess, Michelson Gallery, Amherst, Mass., 1992, Beyond the Borders, Gerard Gallery, Windsor, Vt., 1990, Stratton (Vt.) Arts Festival, 1988, 90-93, more. Mem. Planning Commn., Putney, 1976-78. Recipient Jurors award of Distinction, Stratton Arts Show, 1993; invited to design ornament for White House Christmas tree, 1993; painting selected to appear in Hands of the Goddess calendar, 1992; drawing selected for greeting card design, Frog Hollow Craft Ctr., Middlebury, Vt., 1989; recipient grant to attend bus. seminars at Am. Woman's Devel. Corp., N.Y.C., New Woman mag., 1985. Mem. Newbury Soc. of Arts and Crafts, N.H. League of Arts and Crafts, Vt. State Craft Ctrs. at Middlebury, Burlington, Manchester and Windsor. Democrat. Unity.

KEISER, MEGAN MARIE, neuroscience nurse specialist; b. Ann Arbor, Mich., Aug. 22, 1964; d. Franklin Delano McDonald and Mary Patricia (Ranere) Currier; m. Edward Vincent Keiser, Aug. 3, 1991; 1 child, Kristi Marie; 1 child by previous marriage, Johnathon Welch. BSN, U. Mich., 1986, MS in Med.-Surg. Nursing, 1990. RN, Mich., Calif.; cert. BCLS, ACLS, clin. specialist in med.-surg. nursing; cert. neurosci. RN. Nursing asst. in neuroscis. U. Mich. Hosp., Ann Arbor, 1984-86, staff nurse neuroscis., 1986-90; clin. nurse specialist in neurosurgery Detroit Receiving Hosp., 1990-92; clin. nurse specialist Comprehensive Epilepsy Program, L.A., 1993-94; BLS instr. Am. Heart Assn., 1990. Mem. AACN, ANA, Am. Assn. Neurosci. Nurses, Epi Found. of Am., Case Mgmt. Soc. Am. Roman Catholic.

KEISKER, KRISTIE LYNN, neonatal intensive care nurse; b. Louisville, Oct. 27, 1954; d. William Nolan and Mary Jane K.; m. Stephen Joseph Mattingly, Sept. 8, 1979 (div. Jan., 1986); children: Wesley Nolan, Aaron Stuart. BS, U. Ky., 1976; AS in Nursing with highest honors, Jefferson C.C., Louisville, 1990. RN, Ky.; cert. EMT, Ky. Law Enforcement Coun.; lic. ins. adjuster, Ky. Lab. technician, rsch. asst. Whipp Mix Corp., Louisville, 1976-78; police officer, police detective Jefferson County Police Dept., Louisville, 1978-84; claims rep. (auto) State Farm Ins., Louisville, 1985-88; staff nurse Alliant Health Systems, Louisville, 1990—; neonatal advanced life support nurse Alliant Med. Systems, Louisville, 1993, extracorporeal life support specialist, 1993, neonatal cardiovascular team, 1994. Recipient Exceptional Merit medal Jefferson County Police Commanding Officers Assn., 1985. Home: 9308 Wimbley Ct Louisville KY 40241

KEISTER, JEAN CLARE, lawyer; b. Warren, Ohio, Aug. 28, 1931; d. John R. Keister and Anna Helen Brennan. JD, Southwestern, 1966. Bar: Calif. 1967, U.S. Supreme Ct. 1972, U.S. Dist. Ct. (so. dist.) Calif. 1988. Legal writer Gilbert Law Summaries, L.A., 1967; instr. Glendale (Calif.) Coll. Law, 1968; pvt. practice Glendale, 1967-70. Mem. Themis Soc., 1989-93. Recipient Golden Poet award World of Poetry. Mem. Burbank Bar Assn. (sec. 1993), Lancaster C. of C., Palmdale C. of C. Office: 1321 W Burbank Blvd Burbank CA 91506

KEISTLER, BETTY LOU, accountant, tax consultant; b. St. Louis, Jan. 2, 1935; d. John William and Gertrude Marie (Lewis) Chancellor; m. George E. Keistler, Aug. 3, 1957 (div. Mar. 1981); children: Kathryn M. Morrissey, Deborah J. Birsinger. AS, St. Louis U., 1956; BBA, U. Mo., 1986. Asst. treas. A. G. Edwards & Sons, St. Louis, 1956-57; owner, mgr. B. L. Keistler & Assoc., St. Louis, 1969-82; contr. Family Resource Ctr., Inc., St. Louis, 1982-87; registered rep. Equitable Fin. Svcs., Mo., 1987-88; bus. mgr. Mo. Bapt. Coll., St. Louis, 1987-88, Barnes Hosp. Sch. of Nursing, St. Louis, 1989-91, U. South Fla., St. Petersburg, 1991—; cons. in field, 1982-91; registered rep. Equitable Fin. Svcs., 1987-88; adminstrv. and profl. coun. mem. U. South Fla., 1994. Treas. Pkwy. Townhouses at Village Green, Chesterfield, Mo., 1985-87; exec. core United Way Greater St. Louis, 1984-91; mem. U. Mo. Alumni Assn., 1987-91; rep. to the bd. alumni assn. U. Mo., St. Louis, 1988-91; mem. bldg. and grounds com., Sunday sch. gen. sec., trustee Pasadena Bapt. Ch. Scholar Phillip Morris Corp., St. Louis, 1982-84. Mem. Am. Bus. Womens Assn. (v.p. 1978-79, pres. Lewis & Clark chpt. 1979-80, treas. nat. conv. 1981, pres. ADITI chpt. 1988-90, Sand & Sea chpt. 1992—, Woman of Yr. 1979-80, 94-95), U. South Fla. Women's Club, Am. Soc. Women Accts., Ind. Accts. Mo. (sec. 1978-79, v.p. 1980-81, state sec. 1978-79), St. Louis Women's Commerce Assn., 1904 World's Fair Soc., Internat. Platform Assn., Am. Biog. Inst. (hon. advisor, rsch. bd. advisors nat. divsn. 1991), NAFE, Alpha Sigma Lambda (life, treas. 1985-87). Republican. Home: 6973 Place De La Paix South Pasadena FL 33707

KEITH, CAMILLE TIGERT, airline marketing executive; b. Ft. Worth, Feb. 27, 1945; d. Marvin and Catherine Frances (Tuscany) K. Student, Tex. Tech U.; BA in Broadcasting and Journalism, Tex. Christian U., 1967. Pub. relations, publicity mgr. Sta. WFAA-TV, Dallas; media relations dir. Read-Poland Pub. Relations Co., Dallas; pub. relations dir. Southwest Airlines Co., Dallas, 1972-76, asst. v.p. pub. relations, 1976-78, v.p. pub. relations, 1978-84, v.p. spl. mktg., 1984—; chair Tex. Travel Summit, 1992, 93; mem. adv. bd. bus. leaders coun. City of Dallas Mktg. adn Promotions. Com. Bd. dirs. Dallas Repertory Theatre, Communities in Schs., Vis. Nurses of Dallas, Vis. Nurses Tex,. United Cerebral Palsy Dallas, Press Club. Dallas Found., Shared Housing, , Project Independence for Older Ams., Jr. Achievement Dallas, exec. com. 1991—; mem. adv. bd. sch. journalism com. Tex. Christian U.; mem. advt. com. Tex. Tech U., Women's Ctr. of Dallas, adv. bd.; deacon, dept. chmn. ch. growth Cen. Christian Ch., mem. adv. bd. nat. task force on comm.; sr. nat. v.p. Children Am. Revolution Women's Resource Ctr. YWCA, Dallas; bd. dirs. Dallas/ Ft. Worth Area Tourism Coun., Dallas Heart Assn.; bd. advs. Nat. Coun. on Aging; Gov.'s adv. bd. tourism, com. of 60 Tex. Dept. Commerce; v.p. pub. rels. Freedom Found., Dallas, 1989-94; pres. bus. womens group. Ctrl. Christian Ch., Christian Women's Fellowship; mem. adv. bd. Girl Scouts Am., Dallas, Sr. Citizens Greater Dallas, Ret. Sr. Vol. Program, Okla. Bus. and Leadership Coun., Okla. Dept. Aging, Tex. Dept. Aging; lay rep. Nat. Eldercare Inst. on Elder Abuse and State Long Term Care Ombudsman Svc., SR. Tex. Newspaper, Dallas Travel and Tourism Acad., Dallas Ind. Sch. Dist., Tex. Dept. Health; active adminstrn. on aging project eldercare strategy task force Region VI Dept. Health and Human Svcs. Named Rising Star, Tex. Bus. Mag., 1984; names to Hall of Fame, Tex. Tech. Sch. Mass Comm.; recipient Women Helping Women Maura award Women's Ctr., Dallas, Nat. Heatlines award Women in Comms., 1994. Mem. Discover Tex. Assn. (bd. dirs.), Tex. Pub. Relations Assn., Tex. Travel Industry Assn. (exec. com. 1990—, chair elect), Women in Comm., Inc. (Excellence in Comm. award), 500, Inc., Women Entrepreneurs of Tex. (adv. bd.), Tex. Children of the Am. Revolution (nat. chmn.), Tex. Women's Alliance, Exec. Women Dallas (bd. dirs. 1991-92, v.p. programs 1992-93, pres.-elect 1994-95, pres.), Dallas C. of C. (pub. service com.), Children of the Am. Revolution (sr. nat. v.p. 1988-90, sr. nat. chaplain 1990-92, hon. v.p.), Press Club Dallas (pres. 1988-89), Dallas Advt. League (pres. 1980-81), Bill Kerrs Community Svc. award), Leadership Tex. Alumni Assn. Office: Southwest Airlines Co PO Box 36611 Dallas TX 75235-1611

KEITH, CAROLYN AUSTIN, secondary school counselor; b. Mobile, Ala., July 15, 1949; d. Lloyd James Jr. and Aletia Delores (Taylor) Austin; m. Carlos Lamar Keith Sr., Aug. 14, 1971; children: Carlos Lamar Jr., Carolyn Bernadette Austin Keith. BA in English and History, Mercer U., 1971; cert. in gifted edn., Valdosta State Coll., 1979, MEd in Counseling, 1982, postgrad., 1987. Tchr. English Crisp County High Sch., Cordele, Ga., 1971-77; tchr. gifted Tift County Jr. High Sch., Tifton, Ga., 1977-81, Dooly County Sch. System, Vienna, Ga., 1981-82; counselor Worth County High Sch., Sylvester, Ga., 1982-86, Monroe Comprehensive High Sch., Albany, Ga., 1986-91, Dougherty Alternative Sch., Albany, 1991—; cons. Ga. State U., Atlanta, 1986-89, Dept. Family and Children Svcs., Albany, 1993, 94. Mem. West Point Parent's Club, U.S. Mil. Acad., 1992—, Dougherty County Commn. on Children/Youth, Albany, 1991-95; mem. adv. bd. Southwest Ga. Prevention Resource Ctr. Named Vol. of Yr., Dougherty County Coun. on Child Abuse, 1993, Student Assistance Program Counselor of Yr. for State of Ga., 1994. Mem. Am. Counseling Assn., Ga. Sch. Counselors Assn. (sec. 2d dist. 1985-91, Counselor of Yr. 1993), Am. Sch. Counselors Assn., Nat. Bd. Cert. Counselors, Ga. Lic. Profl. Counselors, South Ga. Regional Assn. Lic. Profl. Counselors. Democrat. Roman Catholic. Office: Dougherty County Altern Sch 600 S Madison St Albany GA 31701

KEITH, EFFIE MELTON, school system administrator; b. Mobile, Ala., June 1, 1946; d. Joseph R. and Effie (Reynolds) Melton; m. Gert Keith, May 8, 1974. BS in English Edn., Fla. State U., 1973; M in English, Valdosta State Coll., 1988, M in Adminstrn. and Supervision, 1989, edn. specialist adminstrn., supervision, 1991. Cert. tchr., Ga. Tchr. Godby H.S., Tallahassee, 1972-74, Brooks County Jr. H.S., Quitman, Ga., 1974-78, Brooks County H.S., Quitman, Ga., 1978-88; curriculum dir. Brooks County Bd. Edn., Quitman, Ga., 1988—. Effie Keith Day, City of Quitman, 1988. Mem. NEA, ASCD, Nat. Coun. for Tchrs. English, Ga. ASCD, Ga. Assn. of Curriculum and Instrnl. Supervision, Ga. Assn. Ednl. Leaders, Phi Delta Kappa (v.p. 1993-94). Home: Rt 3 Box 170 Quitman GA 31643

KEITH, JENNIE, anthropology educator/administrator, writer; b. Carmel, Calif., Nov. 15, 1942; d. Paul K. and Romayne Louise (Fuller) Hill; m. Marc Howard Ross, Aug. 25, 1968 (div. 1978); 1 child, Aaron Elliot Keith Ross; m. Roy Gerald Fitzgerald, June 21, 1980; 1 child, Kate Romayne Keith-Fitzgerald. BA, Pomona Coll., 1964; MA, Northwestern U., 1966, PhD, 1968. NIMH fellow Paris, 1968-70; asst. prof. anthropology Swarthmore Coll., 1970-76, assoc. prof., 1976-82, prof., 1982—, Centennial prof. anthropology, 1990—, chmn. sociology and anthropology, 1987-92, provost, 1992—; mem. rsch. edn. rev. com. NIMH, Washington, 1979-82; co-dir. workshop on age and anthropology Nat. Inst. Aging, Washington, 1980-81, task group leader nat. rsch. plan on aging, 1981; mem. human devel. rev. bd. NIH, 1985-89; mem. adv. coun. Brookdale Found., 1990-93; bd. dirs. Kendal Corp. Author: Old People, New Lives, 1977, 2nd paperback edit., 1982 (Am. Jour. Nursing Book of Yr. 1978), Old People as People, 1982, (with others) The Aging Experience, 1994; co-editor: New Methods for Old-Age Research, 1980, 2nd edit., 1986, Age in Anthropological Theory, 1984; mem. editl. bd. Geronotologist, 1981-89, Jour. Gerontology, 1987-91, Jour. of Aging Studies, 1989—; assoc. editor Rsch. on Aging, 1981-88. Bd. dirs. Cmty. Svcs., Folsom, Pa., 1980-82, Inst. Outdoor Awareness, Swarthmore, 1980—; bd. dirs. Kendal-Crosslands, 1987-92, chmn., 1989-92. Conf. grantee Nat. Inst. Aging, 1980, rsch. grantee, 1982-90. Fellow Am. Anthrop. Assn., Gerontol. Soc. Am. (exec. bd. behavioral and social scis. sect. 1985-87, program chmn. 1989, chair 1989-90, publs. com. 1993—); mem. Assn. Anthropology and Gerontology (founder, sec. 1980-81). Office: Swarthmore Coll Office of the Provost Swarthmore PA 19081

KEITH, LINDA GAIL, school administrator; b. Ardmore, Okla., Aug. 13, 1946; m. Velter D. Keith, Jan. 15, 1966; children: Rebecca, Christy, Michelle. BS in BA, Southeastern Okla. State U., 1989. Receptionist Hallett Constrn. Co., Boone, Iowa, 1964-66, payroll clk., 1966-69; libr. asst. Lone Grove (Okla.) Pub. Schs., 1979-85, fin. sec., 1985-88, bus. mgr., 1988—. Vice mayor Lone Grove City Coun., 1992-94, mem. coun., 1991—; freeholder Lone Grove City Charter Coun., 1985. Mem. Lone Grove Ednl. Support Pers., Lone Grove C. of C.

KEITH, MARY AGNES, food scientist, educator; b. Bellefonte, Pa., Apr. 12, 1947; d. Robert Bruce and Rose Alma (Gillespie) K. BS in Secondary Edn. and Chemistry, Pa. State U., 1969, MS in Food Sci., 1979, PhD, 1983; cert., Swahili Lang. Inst., 1989. Home econs. vol. U.S. Peace Corps-Paraguay, Washington, 1970-75; internat. job counselor Internat. Agriculture Programs Pa. State U., University Park, 1976-82; asst. prof., extension specialist Ill. Cooperative Extension U. Ill., Urbana, 1983-88; nutritionst, missionary Maryknoll (N.Y.) Lay Mission Program, 1989-91; pvt. practice Urbana, 1991-92; dir. house ops., adminstr., trainer summer mission program St. Augustine's Cath. Ctr., U. Fla., Gainesville, 1992—; food safety cons. EFNEP Ill. Cooperative Extension, 1991; faculty liaison Internat. Colloquium, Urbana, 1983-87; speakers bur. Office Internat. Affairs, Champaign, Ill., 1985-88. Co-author: Food Safety for Dietitians, 1991. Translator Champaign-Urbana Com. on Sanctuary, 1984-88. Mem. Inst. Food Technols. (del. 1987-88, chair lecture com. 1987-88, Pitts. sect. fellow 1979, Foremost-McKesson fellow 1980), Assn. Women in Internat. Devel., Am. Home Econs. Assn., Internat. Assn. Milk, Food and Environ. Sanitarians. Democrat. Roman Catholic. Home: 2106 E Annie St Tampa FL 33612

KEITH, PAULINE MARY, artist, illustrator, writer; b. Fairfield, Nebr., July 21, 1924; d. Siebelt Ralph and Pauline Alethia (Garrison) Goldenstein; m. Everett B. Keith, Feb. 14, 1957; 1 child, Nathan Ralph. Student, George Fox Coll., 1947-48, Oreg. State U., 1955. Illustrator Merlin Press, San Jose, Calif., 1980-81; artist, illustrator, watercolorist Corvallis, Oreg., 1980—. Author 5 chapbooks, 1980-85; editor: Four Generations of Verse, 1979; contbr. poems to anthologies and mags. and articles to mags.; one-woman shows include Roger's Meml. Libr., Forest Grove, Oreg., 1959, Corvallis Art Ctr., 1960, Human Resources Bldg., Corvallis, 1959-61, Chintimini Sr. Ctr., 1994—, Corvallis Pastoral Counciling Ctr., 1992-94, Parteral Counseling Ctr., 1993, 94, Hall Gallery, Sr. Ctr., 1993, 94, Consumer Power, Philomath, Oreg., 1994; exhibited in group shows at Hewlett-Packard Co., 1984-85, Corvallis Art Ctr., 1992, Chintimini Sr. Ctr., 1992, Hall Gallery, Corvallis, 1994. Co-elder First Christian Ch. (Disciples of Christ), Corvallis, 1988-89, co-deacon 1980-83, elder, 1991-93; sec. Hostess Club of Chintimini Sr. Ctr., Corvallis, 1987, pres. 1988-89, v.p., 1992—. Recipient Watercolor 1st price Benton County Fair, 1982, 83, 88, 89, 91, 2d prize, 1987, 91, 3d prize, 1984, 90, 92. Mem. Oreg. Assn. Christian Writers, Internat. Assn. Women Mins., Am. Legion Aux. (elected poet post II Covallis chpt. 1989-90, elected sec. 1991-92, chaplain 1992-93, 94-95, v.p. 1994-95). Republican. Office: 304 S College Newberg OR 98132

KEITH, PENNY SUE, mayor, educator; b. Louisville, Sept. 15, 1949; d. John G. Jr. and Edna Lee (Butler) K. AS, U. Ky., 1974; BS, U. Louisville, 1978, MEd in Spl. Edn., 1982, MEd in Curriculum Studies, 1984. Cert. tchr., Ky. Adv. tchr. St. Stephan Martyr Sch., Louisville, 1978-80; tchr. learning disabled students South Oldham Mid. Sch., Crestwood, Ky., 1980-87; dir., prodr. WSOM News, 1988—; pub. rels. liason South Oldham Mid. Sch., 1987-90; mayor City of Parkway Village, Ky., 1990—; prodr./dir. WSOM News, South Oldham Middle Sch., 1988—, WSOH News, South Oldham High Sch., 1994—. Editor: Through the Eyes of 6th Graders, 1978, Interview with Famous People in the Louisville Times, 1987, An Interview with Diane Sawyer, Louisville Mag.. Nov. 1992. Commr. City of Parkway Village, Louisville, 1982-85, 88-89; treas., 1986; mem. Regional Airport Authority, Louisville, 1992-93; mem. Community Adv. Com., Louisville, 1992. Mem. NEA, Ky. Mcpl. League, Ky. Cols., Oldham County Edn. Assn., Atwood Sr. Citizens (pres. 1985-90). Democrat. Methodist. Home: 850 Melford Ave Louisville KY 40217-2006 Office: South Oldham Mid Sch 6403 W Highway 146 Crestwood KY 40014-9570

KEKATOS, DEPPIE-TINNY Z., microbiologist, researcher, lab technologist; b. Buffalo, Oct. 16, 1960; d. Soter Spyros and Mary Soter (Kassimis) Zarifopoulos; m. Dion Kekatos; 1 child, Mary. BS, CUNY, 1983; MS, St. John's U., Jamaica, N.Y., 1986. Lic. lab. technologist, N.Y. Clin. lab. technologist trainee Booth Meml. Hosp., Flushing, N.Y., 1986-87; clin. lab. technologist L.I. Jewish Hosp., New Hyde Park, N.Y., 1988-89, Elmhurst (N.Y.) Hosp., 1990—. Mem. Am. Pharm. Assn., St. John's U. Alumni Fedn. Home: 25-34 Crescent St Apt 5K Long Island City NY 11102 Office: Elmhurst Hosp 79-01 Broadway Elmhurst NY 11373

KEKELIS, LINDA SUE, educational researcher, consultant; b. Cleve., Dec. 9, 1952; d. George Baker and Sue (Bender) K.; m. Norman Kwockchung Wong, Dec. 9, 1981; 1 child, Kyle Segan. BA, San Francisco State U., 1977; MA, U. So. Calif., 1982; PhD, U. Calif., Berkeley, 1993. Counselor Clearwater Rsch., Cloverdale, Calif., 1972-73; teaching asst. linguistics dept. U. So. Calif., L.A., 1978-79, rsch. asst., 1981-84; rsch. specialist U. Calif. Sch. Optometry, 1983-86; instr. San Francisco State U., 1984; teaching asst. Blind Children's Ctr., L.A., 1980-81, cons., 1984-85; coord. parent edn., Montclair Community Play Ctr., Oakland, Calif., 1990-91, pres., 1991-92; exec. dir. Academy Street Assocs., Oakland, 1993—; counsellor Commodore Stockton Sch., San Francisco, 1973-74; classroom aide Sierra Sch., El Cerrito, Calif., 1992-94. Author, editor: The Development of Social Skills by Blind and Visually Impaired Students, 1993; contbr. articles to profl. jours. Bd. dirs. Blind Babies Found., San Francisco, 1994-96. Fellow Soroptimists, 1986; grantee March of Dimes, 1986-88. Mem. AAUW (grantee 1993-94). Democrat. Office: Academy Street Assocs 5931 Broadway Oakland CA 94618

KELEHEAR, CAROLE MARCHBANKS SPANN, administrative assistant; b. Morehead City, N.C., Oct. 2, 1945; d. William Blythe and Gladys Ophelia (Wilson) Marchbanks; m. Henry M. Spann, June 5, 1966 (div. 1978); children: Lisa Carole, Elaine Mabry; m. Zachariah Lockwood Kelehear, Sept. 15, 1985. Student Winthrop Coll., 1963-64; grad. Draughon's Bus. Coll., 1965; cert. in med. terminology Greenville Tech. Edn. Coll., 1972; grad. Millie Lewis Modeling Sch. Office mgr. S.C. Appalachian Adv. Commn., Greenville, 1965-68, Wood-Bergheer & Co., Newport Beach and Palm Springs, Calif., 1970-72; asst. to Dr. J. Ernest Lathem, Lathem & McCoy, P.A., Greenville, 1972-75, Gov. Robert E. McNair, McNair, Konduros, Corley, Singletary and Dibble Law Firm, Columbia, S.C., 1975-77; office mgr. Dr. James B. Knowles, Greenville, 1977-78; office mgr. Constangy, Brooks & Smith, Columbia, 1978-83; legal asst. to sr. ptnr. William L. Bethea Jr., Bethea, Jordan & Griffin, P.A., Hilton Head Island, S.C., 1983-88; adminstrv. asst./paralegal to Dr. Rajko D. Medenica, Hilton Head Island, 1988—; notary pub.; vol. Ladies aux. Greenville Gen. Hosp., 1966-72, South Coast Hosp., Laguna Beach, Calif., 1973, St. Francis Hosp, Greenville, 1974-76, Hilton Head Hosp., 1983-92. Mem. Hilton Head Hosp. Aux., Profl. Women's Assn. Hilton Head Island, Am. Bus. Women's Assn., Nat. Assn. Female Execs., Am. Soc. Notaries, Beta Sigma Phi. Home: PO Box 21174 Hilton Head Island SC 29925-1174

KELEN, JOYCE ARLENE, social worker; b. N.Y.C., Dec. 5, 1949; d. Samuel and Rebecca (Rochman) Green; m. Leslie George Kelen, Jan. 31, 1971; children: David, Jonathan. BA, Lehman Coll., 1970; MSW, Univ. Utah, 1974, DSW, 1980. Recreation dir. N.Y.C. Housing Authority, Bronx, 1970-72; cottage supr. Kennedy Home, Bronx, 1974; sch. social worker Davis County Sch. Dist., Farmington, Utah, 1976-86; clin. asst. prof. U. Utah., Salt Lake City, 1976—; sch. social worker Salt Lake City Sch. Dist., 1986—; cons. in field, Salt Lake City, 1981—. Editor: To Whom Are We Beautiful As We Go?, 1979; contbr. articles to profl. jours. Utah Coll. of Nursing grantee, 1985. Mem. Nat. Assn. Social Workers (chairperson Gerontology Council, 1983-84, Utah Sch. Social Worker of Yr., 1977), NEA, Utah Edn. Assn., Davis Edn. Assn. Democrat. Jewish. Home: 128 M St Salt Lake City UT 84103-3854 Office: Franklin Elem Sch 1100 W 400 S Salt Lake City UT 84104-2334

KELLAIGH, KATHLEEN, conservatory artistic director; b. N.Y.C., June 28, 1955; d. Joseph Anderson and Alice Rendell (French) Kelly; m. Joel Wayne Robertson, Oct. 1, 1988; children: Christopher, Sarah. BFA summa cum laude, U. Ill., 1976. Performer United Stage, Mich., 1977-78, Hartman Stage, Conn., 1978-79, Guiding Light-CBS TV, N.Y.C., 1979-81; dir. Center Stage Bravo, 1981-82; performer Nassau Rep., N.Y., 1983-84, Sail-Away Prodns., World Cruises, 1983-86; producer (transferred from City of London Festival) Narnia, Adonai Arts Found., N.Y.C., 1986; performer All My Children, N.Y.C., 1987, America's Most Wanted, Fox TV, N.Y.C., 1988; producer, assoc. producer Adonai Arts Found., N.Y.C., 1988-90; founder, artistic dir. Action Theatre Conservatory, Clifton, N.J., 1990—; dir. Waldwick, N.Y.C., 1992, An Evening of Ed Dixon One-Acts, N.Y.C., 1994; make-up artist Sarah Caldwell's Bicentennial Prodn., Pa., 1976; make-up artist, instr. Nat. Acad. Dance, 1974-77; playwright-in-residence Little Theatre/Genesis Guild, Ill., N.Y., 1971-72, 81-90; artistic dir. Art for God's Sake, Montclair, N.J., 1992, 94. Author: (plays) The Separate World, 1971, Chapter 33, 1981, Alternatives, 1993, Bridges, 1993, The Music's Not So Beautiful Anymore, 1994; lyricist for musical Beauty and the Beast, 1989. Chmn. Episcopal Peace Fellowship, N.Y.C., 1982-86; mem. Diocesan Task Force on World Peace, N.Y., 1982-88. Phi Kappa Phi Acad. scholar, 1975-76. Mem. Am. Fedn. TV and Radio Artists, Screen Actors Guild, Actors Equity Assn., Actors Fund, Episcopal Actors Guild, Genesius Guild (sec. 1987-88), Phi Kappa Phi.

KELLAM, DIANE CELINE FIDI, insurance executive; b. New Britain, Conn., July 6, 1950; d. Victor C. Sr. and Filomena (Lombardo) Fidi; m. David Corbin Kellam III, Feb. 11, 1977. Student, Cath. U. Am., 1967. Personal ins. mgr. Charles H. McDonough Sons, Inc., Bloomfield, Conn., 1978-82; ins. account exec. H.D. Segur, Inc., Waterbury, Conn., 1982-85; v.p. ISU Internat., San Francisco, 1985-89; pres., chief exec. officer ISU East, Inc., Farmington, Conn., 1989-94; exec. Am. Phoenix Corp., Avon, Conn., 1994—; adv. bd. Conn. Inst., also nat. spkr. Mem. Jr. League of Greater New Britain, New Britain Gen. Hosp. Aux. (corporator), St. Francis Hosp. & Med. Ctr., Catholic Family Svcs. (adv. bd., bd. trustees), Hospice of Greater New Britain. Mem. Hartford Assn. of Ins. Women, Nat. Assn. Ins. Women, Mary Immaculate Acad. Alumni Assn. (treas.), New London County Mut. Ins. Adv. Coun., VFW Post 511 Women's Aux. Roman Catholic. Home: 108 Adams St New Britain CT 06052-1222 Office: 270 Farmington Ave Ste 305 Farmington CT 06032-1909

KELLAM, NORMA DAWN, medical, surgical nurse; b. Benton Harbor, Mich., June 13, 1938; d. Edgar Arnold and Bernice (Cronk) K. AA, San Bernardino Valley Coll., 1958; student, Calif. State Coll., Long Beach, 1961-1964, 1965, 1966, 1967; BS, San Diego State Coll., 1961; MS, Calif. State U., Fresno, 1972. Nursing instr. Porterville (Calif.) State Hosp., 1968-69; staff nurse Northside Psychiat. Hosp., Fresno, 1969-72; nursing instr. Pasadena (Calif.) City Coll., 1972-73; night shift lead Fairview Devel. Ctr., Costa Mesa, Calif., 1973—. Contbr. articles to newspapers. Vol. Spanish translator for Interstitial Cystitis Assn. Recipient Cert. of Appreciation for vol. work Interstitial Cystitis Assn. Mem. Calif. Nurses Assn., Am. Urol. Assn. Allied, Phi Kappa Phi.

KELLER, ANNE HURD, artist; b. Evanston, Ill., June 30, 1933; d. Howard Joseph and Anna Catherine (Hurd) K. BA, Manhattanville, 1955; MA, Ill. Inst. Tech., 1967. Stylist, photographer A. George Miller, Chgo., 1955-60, Shigeta-Wright, Chgo., 1961; artist self-employed Chgo., 1961—. Roman Catholic.

KELLER, BARBARA LYNN, special education educator; b. Great Falls, Mont., July 18, 1941; d. Edward Jerome and Alvina Elizabeth (Kampsnider) Daly; m. Ray B. Keller, Dec. 28, 1961; 1 child, Forest Ry. Student, Ea. Mont. Coll., 1967-69; BA, U. Mont., 1976; postgra., Mont. State U., 1976-79, No. Mont. Coll., 1989-91. Tchr. grades 1-4 Pub. Schs. Birch Creek Hutterite Colony, Dupuyer, Mont., 1962-63; tchr. grade 2 Pub. Sch. Blackfeet Indian Reservation, Heart Butte, Mont., 1963-64; tchr. reading remediation Pub. Sch., Fort Benton, Mont., 1967-68; tchr. emotionally disturbed Manzanita Ranch Residential Sch., Hyompom, Calif., 1968-69; tchr. reading remediation Pub. Schs., Bigfork, Mont., 1975-78; tchr. ESL Flathead C.C., Kalispell, Mont., 1978-82; pvt. practice tchr. reading, ESL, emotionally disturbed Bigfork, 1982-85; tchr. spl. edn. Pub. Schs. Blackfeet Indian Reservation, Browning, Mont., 1985-94; tchr. study skills and reading Browning (Mont.) H.S., 1994—; pres. Eagle's View Publs., Bigfork, 1989—; author-in-residence Am. Edn. Inst., 1994—. Author: Reading Pals--A Handbook for Volunteers, 1990, Reading Pals--A Teacher's Manual, 1990, The Parents' Guide--Studyng Made Easy, 1991, Gifts of Love and Literacy--A Parent's Guide to Raising Children Who Love to Read, 1993, Read with Your Child--Make a Difference, 1994; (ednl. program) Studying Made Easy--The Complete Program, 1992. Reading cons. Personal Vol. Svc., Bigfork, 1970—, Browning, Mont., 1985—. Recipient Author of Yr. award Am. Edn. Inst., 1993. Mem. ASCD, Internat. Reading Assn., Am. Fedn. Tchrs., Literacy Vols. Am., Glacier Reading Coun., Learning Disabilities Assn., COSMEP Internat. Assn. Ind. Publishers. Home: PO Box 1814 Browning MT 59417 Office: Eagles View Publs 750 Cascade Ave Bigfork MT 59911-3625

KELLER, CHRISTINE, lawyer; b. Montclair, N.J., May 8, 1943; d. Edward Demarest and Ruth Ada (Dosch) K. BA, Rice U., 1965; JD, Duke U., 1969. Bar: Tex. 1969. Atty. Great So. Life, Houston, Tex., 1969-81; v.p., gen. counsel, sec. Great So. Life, Houston, 1982-84; pvt. practice lawyer Houston, 1984-85; assoc. Greer, Herz & Adams, Galveston, Tex., 1986-87; ptnr. Greer, Herz & Adams, Galveston, 1988-94, of counsel, 1995—. Commr. Galveston Housing Authority, 1994—. Dir. Ronald McDonald House, Galveston, 1990—, 1894 Grand Opera House, Galveston, 1992—; dir., pres., sec.-treas. The Children's Ctr., Galveston, 1990—. Mem. ABA, State Bar Tex., Kiwanis. Democrat. Methodist. Home: 1702 Church Galveston TX 77550 Office: Greer Herz & Adams One Moody Plaza Galveston TX 77550

KELLER, DARLA LYNN, financial manager, organization consultant; b. Lemon, S.D., Jan. 7, 1956; d. Donald Dwight and Bonna Claire (Gilbert) K.; m. Jerry Jerome Eskridge, Aug. 27, 1984 (div. Dec. 1988); children: Lisha Saree, Aram Josias. Diploma, Minn. Sch. Bus., 1975. Sec. Hirschfield's Inc., Mpls., 1974-75, Lionel D. Eide & Co., Mpls., 1975-76; client adminstr. Resource Trust Co., Mpls., 1976-81; family office mgr. Archer & Daniels Families, Mpls., 1981-93; cons. Larry Wilson Enterprises, Mpls., 1987-89, founder, pres. Dellwood Fin. Svcs. Co., Mpls., 1992—. Treas. Como Park Elem. Sch. PTA, St. Paul, 1989-91; treas. St. Croix Valley coun. Girl Scouts U.S.A., 1986-91, mgr. east cen. svc. unit, 1990-91. Home: 1315 Dale St N Saint Paul MN 55117-4123 Office: Dellwood Fin Svcs Co 105 S 5th St Ste 712 Minneapolis MN 55402-1208

KELLER, DOROTHY MARGARET MILLER, elementary education educator; b. Crafton, Pa., June 2, 1910; d. George Walter and Edna Lida (Daum) Miller; m. Frank Rugh Keller, Sept. 7, 1935; children: Marjorie Ann Hottel, Nancy Louise Wilson, David Frank. BS in Edn., U. Pitts., 1934. Cert. tchr. kindergarten through high sch. With H. C. Frick Sch. for Pitts. Tchrs., 1928-31; tchr. Shady Side Jr. Acad., Pitts., 1931-34; arts and crafts tchr. Pitts. (Pa.) Pub. Sch. Humboldt Sch., 1934-35; tchr. in ch. sch. classes and depts. Coraopolis United Meth. Ch., 1935-48, Ravenna, Ohio, 1948-53, dept. supt., 1955-70. Co-editor: Historic Calendar, 1988, Original Pen and Ink Drawings Historic Landmarks 200th Ann. book of Moon Twp., Pa. Bd. dirs., sec. Moon Twp. Pks. and Recreation Bd., Coraopolis, 1963-70; organizer property given to Moon Twp., Robin Hill Pk. nature preserve and cultural ctr., 1971-79, West Area Conservation Coun., Pa., 1970; active PTA, Coraopolis and Ravenna, pres. 1949-51, 55-57, 61-63; mem. adminstrv. bd. United Meth. Ch., Coraopolis. Named Woman of Yr., Moon Twp. Jaycees, 1968, Western Br. Pitts. YWCA, 1965, Garden Club Dist. of Western Pa., Pitts., 1966-71, Woman of Yr. for Community Activities, 1971, Woman of Yr., Coraopolis-Sewickley AAUW, 1994; recipient conservation award DAR, 1991. Mem. AAUW, We. Area Art League (Moon Twp., Coraopolis), Old Moon Twp. Hist. Soc. (co-editor Bicentennial History Book 1988), Am. Assn. Ret. Persons, United Meth. Women. Republican. Methodist. Home: 213 Oakhaven Dr Coraopolis PA 15108-2935

KELLER, JULIE ELIZABETH, elementary and learning disabilities educator; b. Portsmouth, Ohio, Jan. 29, 1960; d. Charles Curtis and Mary Margaret (Greer) Caulley; m. Paul Jeffrey Keller, Nov. 4, 1978; children: Jennifer, Joshua. Student, Shawnee State U., 1987-88, Ohio U., 1987-88; BS in Edn., U. Rio Grande (Ohio), 1989-90; postgrad., Ohio U., 1994—. Cert. elem. tchr., learning disabilites tchr., Ohio. Priv. music tchr. Minford, Ohio, 1979-86; sch. bus driver Minford Local Sch. Dist., 1985-89; vol. tchr. aide Minford Primary Shc., 1988-89; in-sch. suspension monitor Green Local Sch. Dist., Franklin Furnace, Ohio, 1990-91; learning disabilites tchr., asst. basketball coach Wheelersburg (Ohio) Elem. Sch., 1991—; adult basic edn. instr. Northwest Local Sch. Dist., Minford Ctr., 1991-92; priv. home tutor Wheelersburg Schs., 1991-92; com. person U. Rio Grande Grad. Program, 1990-91, bd. of review mem., 1992—; cons. appendix to bd. policy Emergency Procedure Plan, 1990. Author: (booklet) Athletic, Activity Handbook, 1991 (bd. recognition award 1991); designer In-Sch. Suspension Program, 1990 (bd. recognition award 1991). Program dir. Music Recital and Review, Minford, 1983-86, Daily Vacation Bible Sch. Fairview Bapt. Ch., Minford, 1984-86; activity asst. Silver Spurs 4-H Club, Minford, 1989-91; pianist Fairview Missionary Bapt. Ch., 1973-94; asst. musician, choir mem. Wheelersburg Baptist Ch., 1994—. Recipient Ohio Student Choice award, Rio Grande, 1989. Mem. Wheelersburg Edn. Assn. (spl. areas rep. liaison com. 1992—, exec. com. 1992—, negotiating com. 1994—), Wheelersburg 200 Club, Wheelersburg PTO. Republican. Baptist. Home: 687 Gleim Rd Wheelersburg OH 45694 Office: Wheelersburg Elem Sch 1731 Dogwood Ridge Rd Wheelersburg OH 45694-9474

KELLER, KAREN JEAN, therapist; b. Grand Forks, N.D., July 5, 1960; d. Robert Ernest and Dorothy Louise (McGrath) Pribula; children: Elizabeth Jean, Megan Louise. BS in Natural Sci., U. N.D., 1982, BS in Psychology, 1986, MA in Counseling, Guidance, 1991; postgrad., Union Inst. Lic. profl. counselor. Instr. piano Grand Forks, 1985-91; dir., adminstr. Psychosocial Rehab. Ctr., Grand Forks, 1992—; pvt. practice therapist, owner Personal Devel. Ctr., Grand Forks, 1992—. Mem. ACA, N.D. Counseling Assn., Am. Mental Health Counselors Assn., North Valley Mental Health Assn. (pres. 1994). Roman Catholic. Office: Personal Devel Ctr PO Box 14072 Grand Forks ND 58208

KELLER, LAURA CHANCE, elementary school educator; b. Gary, Ind., June 24, 1948; d. Earl Eugene and Norma June (Clements) Chance; m. Larry Eugene Keller, Aug. 25, 1968 (div. 1979); children: Julene Elizabeth, Hillary Alexis; m. Robert Eugene Hurst, Aug. 8, 1981. BS, U. Ill., 1972, MEd, 1976. Cert. tchr., K-9. Tchr. 4th grade Champaign (Ill.) Pub. Schs., 1972—. Mem. Champaign Edn. Assn. (grievance chairperson 1978-81, v.p. 1983-87), Champaign Fedn. Tchrs. (v.p. 1989—), Champaign County NOW (convenor/pres. 1978-79, Celebration of Feminism award 1983), Alpha Lambda Delta, Phi Kappa Phi, Kappa Delta Pi. Home: 1007 W John St Champaign IL 61821-3905 Office: Westview Elem Sch 703 S Russell St Champaign IL 61821-4420

KELLER, SHARON PILLSBURY, speech pathologist; b. L.A., Sept. 28, 1935; d. Edward Gardner and Iris Noriene (Hager) Pillsbury; m. Clarence Stanley Keller (dec. 1982); children: Jann Kathleen, Jennifer Beth, Lauren Elaine. AA, Chaffey Community Coll., Alta Loma, Calif., 1971; BA, U. La Verne, 1978, MS in Communicative Disorders, 1983. Lic. speech pathologist, sch. audiometrist, calif.; life svc. credential clin. and rehabilitative, Calif. Lang. speech and hearing specialist Chino (Calif.) Unified Schs., 1978-86, Rim of the World Sch. Dist., Lake Arrowhead, Calif., 1986—; speech and lang. pathologist Lake Arrowhead Elem. Sch., 1986-89, Valley of Enchantment Elem. Sch., Lake Arrowhead, Calif., 1989—; cons. Assn. Speech and Hearing Svcs., Chino, 1984; former cons. infant lang. devel., teenage parent program Buena Vista Continuation H.S., Boys' Republic H.S., Chino; trainer pre-sch. and parent/child interaction Headstart, Chino; active Home program Mountain Cmtys., San Bernardino County Pre-Sch., 1988-89. Anchor Mountain Cmtys. News, Falcon Cable TV. Mem. bd. deacons, moderator Presbyn. Ch., 1991-94, 94—, mem. English handbell choir, 1988-92, children's storyteller, pastor nominating com., 1994—. Mem. AAUW (rec. sec.), Am. Speech-Lang. Hearing Assn. (cert. clin. competence speech-lang. pathologist), Calif. Speech and Hearing Assn., Calif. Tchrs. Assn., Delta Kappa Gamma. Republican. Home: PO Box 1745 Crestline CA 92325-1745 Office: Valley of Enchantment Elem Sch PO Box 430 Lake Arrowhead CA 92352-0430

KELLER, SHIRLEY INEZ, accountant; b. Ferguson, Iowa, Sept. 15, 1930; d. Adelbert Leslie and Inez Marie (Abbey) Hilsabeck; m. Earl Wilson Keller, Feb. 2, 1957 (dec. 1987); children: Earl William, Cynthia Marie, Eric Walter, Kenneth Paul. Student, U. Iowa, 1949-51; AS, Cameron U., 1971, BS, 1973; postgrad., Arapahoe Community Coll., 1986. High speed radio operator U.S. Army Signal Corps, N.Y.C., Japan, 1951-57; auditor U.S. Dept. Justice, Washington, 1973-76, U.S. Dept. Energy, Oklahoma City, 1976-83, U.S. Dept. Interior, Albuquerque, 1983-86; acct. U.S. Dept. Interior, Denver, 1986—; seminar instr. U.S. Dept. Interior, Denver, other cities, 1989-94. Author: Oil and Gas Payor Handbook, 1993. Scorekeeper Boy's Baseball, Lawton, Okla., 1964-72; den mother Boy Scouts Am., Lawton, 1965-66. Sgt. U.S. Army, 1951-57. Decorated Merit Unit Commendation. Mem. Toastmasters (sec. Buffalo chpt. 1990-93, Competent Toastmaster 1993). Democrat. Roman Catholic. Home: PO Box 280535 Lakewood CO 80228-0535

KELLER, SUSAN AGNES, insurance officer; b. Moline, Ill., July 12, 1952; d. Kenneth Francis and Ethel Louise (Odendahl) Hulsbrink. Grad. in Pub. Relations, Patricia Stevens Career Coll., 1971; grad. in Gen. Ins., Ins. Inst. Am., 1986. CPCU; lic. ins. and real estate agt.; notary public. Comml. lines rater Bitiminous Casualty Corp., Rock Island, Ill., 1973-78; with Roadway Express, Inc., Rock Island, 1978-81; front line supr. Yellow Freight System, Inc., Denver, 1982-83; supr. plumbing and sheet metal prodn. Bell Plumbing and Heating, Denver, 1983-84; v.p. underwriting farm/ranch dept. Golden Eagle Ins. Co., San Diego, 1985—; cons. real estate foreclosure County Records Svc., San Diego, 1986-89; tchr. Ins. Inst. of Am., 1991. Vol. DAV, San Diego, 1985—; tchr. IEA and CPCU courses. Mem. Soc. CPCU (pres., bd. dirs.), Profl. Women in Ins., NAFE. Roman Catholic. Home: 790 Camino De La Reina Apt 163 San Diego CA 92108-3227 Office: Golden Eagle Ins Co 3420 Camino Del Rio Ste 200 San Diego CA 92108

KELLERMAN, FAYE MARDER, novelist, dentist; b. St. Louis, July 31, 1952; d. Oscar and Anne (Steinberg) Marder; m. Jonathan Seth Kellerman, July 23, 1972; children: Jesse Oren, Rachel Diana, Ilana Judith, Aliza Celeste. AB in Math, UCLA, 1974, DDS, 1978. Author: The Ritual Bath, 1986 (Macavity award best 1st novel 1986), Sacred and Profane, 1987, The Quality of Mercy, 1989, Milk and Honey, 1990, Day of Atonement, 1991, False Prophet, 1992, Grievous Sin, 1993, Sanctuary, 1994, Justice, 1995; contbr. short stories to Sisters in Crime vols. 1 & 3, Ellery Queen Mag., A Woman's Eye, Women of Mystery, the year's 2d finest crime: mystery stories, The Year's 25 Finest Mystery and Crime Stories, A Modern Treasury of Great Detective and Murder Mysteries. UCLA rsch. fellow, 1978. Mem. Mystery Writers of Am. (So. Calif. bd. dirs.), Womens' Israeli Polit. Action Com., Sisters in Crime. Jewish.

KELLERMAN, SALLY CLAIRE, actress; b. Long Beach, Calif., June 2, 1937; d. John Helm and Edith Baine (Vaughn) K.; m. Richard Edelstein, Dec. 19, 1970; 4 step-daughters; m. Jonathan Krane, 1980. Student, Los Angeles City Coll., Actor's Studio, N.Y.C. Stage appearances include Singular Man, N.Y.C., Breakfast at Tiffany's; films include Reform School Girl, 1959, The Third Day, 1965, The Boston Strangler, 1968, The April Fools, 1969, M*A*S*H, 1970 (Acad. award nominee 1970, Golden Globe award 1970), Brewster McCloud, 1970, Last of the Red-Hot Lovers, 1972, Slither, 1973, Reflection of Fear, 1973, Lost Horizon, 1973, Rafferty and the Gold Dust Twins, 1975, The Big Bus, 1976, Welcome to L.A., 1977, The Mouse and His Child, 1977 (voice), Magee and the Lady, 1978, It Rained All Night The Day I Left, 1978, A Little Romance, 1979, Foxes, 1980, Loving Couples, 1980, Serial, 1980, Head On, 1980, September Gun, 1983, Moving Violations, 1985, Lethal, 1985, Back to School, 1986, That's Life, 1986, Meatballs III, 1987, Three for the Road, 1987, Someone to Love, 1987, Paramedics (voice), 1988, You Can't Hurry Love, 1988, All's Fair, 1989, Limit Up, 1989, The Secret of the Ice Cave, 1990, Happily Ever After, 1990 (voice), The Player, 1992, Younger and Younger, 1993, Mirror, Mirror 2: Raven Dance, 1994, Ready to Wear (Prêt-à-Porter), 1994; also TV roles Chrysler Theatre, Mannix, It Takes a Thief; TV films Verna: USO Girl, 1978, For Lovers Only, 1982, Dempsey, 1983, Secret Weapons, 1985, Elena, 1985, Boris and Natasha, 1992; miniseries Centennial, 1978-79. Recipient nominations Acad. and Golden Globe awards for MASH. Mem. Actor's Equity, AFTRA. Office: The Gersh Agency 232 N Canon Dr Beverly Hills CA 90210*

KELLETT, SUSAN SHULER, elementary school educator; b. Indpls., Mar. 15, 1940; d. Lacey Lee and Marie Lillian (Cook) Shuler; m. Roger Bulkeley Kellett, Dec. 30, 1962; children: Cordelia Edwards, Mary Newton. BA, Smith Coll., 1962. Tchr. Brooklin (Maine) Schs., 1978—. Author: (poetry) Dream Fishing, 1993, Penelope's Fifth Letter, 1994.

KELLEY, BETTY MARIE, restaurant owner, cook; b. Oil City, Pa., Feb. 23, 1955; d. Robert Charles Miles and Ethel Eleanor (Kelley) Miles. Grad. high sch., high sch., Titusville, Pa. lectr. Cambridge Grange, 1990—. Owner Betty's Restaurant, Cambridge Springs, Pa., 1980—. Mem. Cambridge Pride: Coming Alive, 1992-93; chairperson Cambridge Springs Community Picnic, 1992, 93, 94; mem. Cambridge Springs Discover Days Com., 1994; mem. Prison Runathon com. State Correctional Inst., Cambridge Springs, 1993, 94. Mem. U.S. C. of C., Cambridge Grange (chaplain 1987-90, lectr. 1990—). Republican. Baptist. Office: 164 Venango Ave Cambridge Springs PA 16403-1038

KELLEY, CYNTHIA, nursing administrator; b. Birmingham, Ala., May 15, 1955; d. Richard Bennett and Audrey Faye (Malone) Parkes; divorced; children: Katie Lynne, Brandi Elise, Amy Catherine, Jesse Tyler. Diploma, Jackson Meml. Hosp., Miami, 1978; AS/AA, Miami-Dade C.C., 1978; postgrad., Barry U., 1990—. Cert. neonatal intensive care nurse. Asst. head nurse pediatrics, clin. supr. Jackson Meml. Hosp., Miami, 1975-83; staff nurse Bapt. Hosp., Miami, 1983-87; nurse mgr. materials mgt. and ctrl. svc. supply South Miami Hosp., Miami, 1987—; lectr. in field. Vol. South Fla. Hist. Mus. Mem. ANA, Neonatal Nurses Assn., South Fla. perinatal Network, Dade County C. of C., Kendall/Hammocks Optimist Clubs.

KELLEY, CYNTHIA JO, laboratory administrator; b. Tulsa, Apr. 20; d. Joseph Mayo and Edna Pauline (Phillips) Redditt; m. William Robert Kelley, Oct. 31, 1970; children: William Michael, Shannon Paige. BS in Chemistry, Okla. Coll. Liberal Arts, 1970; Med. Technologist, Mercy Hosp., Oklahoma City, 1971. Cert. Am. Soc. Clin. Path. Bd. Registry. Med. technologist Oklahoma City Clinic, 1972-76; med. technologist, researcher U. Nebr. Med. Ctr., Omaha, 1976-81; med. technologist Creighton Path. Assocs.-Creighton U., Omaha, 1981-86; lead med. technologist St. Francis Hosp., Tulsa, 1986—, lectr. Sch. Med. Tech., 1986-94; lab. mgr. rsch. Belton (Mo.) Hosp., 1994—. Vol. Union Pub. Schs., Tulsa, 1988-94; deacon First Christian Ch., Tulsa. Mem. Clin. Lab. Mgrs. Assn., Pi Beta Phi Parents Orgn. Democrat. Mem. Disciples of Christ Ch. Home: 11920 Windsor Leawood KS 66209 Office: Rsch Belton Hosp 17065 S H Hwy Belton MO 64012

KELLEY, DELORES GOODWIN, state legislator; b. Norfolk, Va., May 1, 1936; d. Stephen Cornelius and Helen Elizabeth (Jefferson) Goodwin; m. Russell Victor Kelley, Jr., Dec. 26, 1956; children: Norma Kelley Johnson, Russell III, Brian. BA, Va. State Coll., 1956; MA, NYU, 1958, Purdue U., 1972; PhD, U. Md., 1977. Dir. religious edn. N.Y.C. Protestant Coun., Bronx, 1959-60; tchr. N.Y.C. Pub. Schs., Bklyn., 1962-64, Ctrl. Sch. Dist., Plainview, N.Y., 1965-66; asst. prof. Morgan State U., Balt., 1966-70; prof. speech comms. and English Coppin State Coll., Balt., 1973—; legislator Md. Ho. of Dels., Annapolis, 1991-94, state senator, 1995—; panelist, reviewer NEH, Washington, 1978-82; mem. editorial bd. Md. English Jour., Salisbury, 1980-88; dean Coppin State Coll., Balt., 1979-82; fellow Am. Coun. on Edn., Washington, 1982-83; vice chair bd. dirs. Harbor Bank Md., 1982—; mem. jud. proceedings com. Md. State Senate, chair joint com. fed. rels., legis. com., women legislators of Md. Editor (monograph) Concepts of Race, 1981; moderator (TV series) Teaching Writing: Process Approach, 1982. Sec. Md. Dem. Party, Annapolis, 1986-90; bd. dirs. Balt. Urban League, 1986-89; pres. Black Jewish Forum, Balt., 1990-92; commr. Md. Commn. on Values, Annapolis, 1980-85; bd. dirs. Balt. Mental Health Systems, 1991—; host Internat. Visitors Ctr., 1976—; commn. mem. Md. Commn. Hereditary and Congenital Disorders, Balt., 1993—. Fellow Purdue U., 1970-72; grantee Md. Com. for Humanities, Balt., 1977-78, NEH, Washington, 1988-89. Mem. Inst. for Govtl. Svcs. (bd. dirs. 1993-94), Nat. Polit. Congress Black Women (bd. dirs., Balt. chair 1993-94). Baptist. Office: 209 Senate Office Bldg Annapolis MD 21401 also: 6660 Security Blvd Ste 10 Baltimore MD 21207

KELLEY, FLORENCE MARIA, real estate administrator; b. Chgo., Nov. 3; d. Clarence and Margarite Hope (Ioas) Ullrich; m. Lawrence Welsford Kelley, July 19, 1957; 1 child, Kevin Andrew. BA, DePauw U., 1953. Sec., head ins. dept. Olympic Maritime S.A., Monte Carlo, Monaco, 1954-57; sec. MMM, Key West, Fla., 1961; realtor assoc. Grubb & Ellis Residential, Honolulu, 1976-80, Urner & Assocs., Inc., Honolulu, 1980-93. Mem. Spiritual Assembly of Baha'is of Ko'olaupoko, 1977—, chmn., 1985-88, sec., 1989—; dir. office external affairs Baha'is of Hawaiian Islands, 1980-94; exec. dir. Hawaii Baha'i Cmty., 1994—. Office: Hawaii Baha'i Cmty 3264 Allan Pl Honolulu HI 96817

KELLEY, HEATHER RYAN, artist, educator; b. New Haven, Jan. 19, 1954; d. Charles Peter and Jeanne Therese (Burr) Ryan; m. Frank Whitney Kelley Jr., Dec. 29, 1973 (div. Jan. 1988); 1 child, Matthew Ryan. BFA, So. Meth. U., 1975; MA, Northwestern U., 1984. Vis. lectr. McNeese State U., Lake Charles, La., 1981-83, asst. prof., 1984-89, assoc. prof. art, 1990—, coord. works in paper exch., 1988—. Exhibited in numerous one-person shows including Irving (Tex.) Arts Ctr., 1992, 94, Evelyn Siegel Gallery, Fort Worth, Tex., 1994, Still Zinsel Contemporary Fine Art, New Orleans, 1993; group shows include La. State U., Baton Rouge, 1992 (1st Place award), Mainstreet Fine Arts Exhbn., Fort Worth, 1993 (cash award 1993), Cheekwood Nat. Contemporary Painting Exhbn., Nashville, 1993 (Jurors Mention 1993), Masur Mus., Monroe, La., 1994 (Best of Show). Contbr. work to ann. auction S.W. La. AIDS Coun., Lake Charles, 1992, 93. Project Assistance grantee Calcasieu Arts and Humanities Coun., 1991. Mem. Coll. Art Assn. Office: McNeese State U Art Dept Ryan and Sale Sts Lake Charles LA 70609

KELLEY, SISTER HELEN, hospital executive; b. Niagara Falls, N.Y., July 25, 1922; d. Robert Vincent Jr. and Helen Gertrude (O'Neil) K. BSN, Cath. U., 1953; MHA, St. Louis U., 1957; postgrad., Cath. U., Seton Hall, Wayne U., St. Louis U. RN, D.C., N.Y., Mass., Mo. Tchr. elem. and jr. high sch. Endicott, N.Y., 1942-50; faculty divsn. nursing St. Joseph Coll., Emmitsburg, Md., 1953-55; adminstr., pres. bd. dirs. St. Agnes Hosp., Balt., 1958-62; asst. adminstr. Sisters of Charity Hosp., Buffalo, N.Y., 1962-64; adminstr., pres. bd. dirs. Carney Hosp., Boston, 1964-69; provincial councilor Daughters of Charity, Northeast Province, 1969-71; internat. work with Vincentian priests Mex., Rep. Panama, 1971-73; adminstr., pres. Our Lady of Lourdes Hosp., Binghamton, N.Y., 1973-76; pres. Nat. Cath. Health Assn., St. Louis, 1976-78; exec. dir. Laboure Ctr., 1979-82; adminstr. St. Louise House, Albany, N.Y., 1982-83; dir. mktg., plannig Carney Hosp., 1983-85; assoc. dir. Intercounty Home Health Care Agy. Diocese of Albany, 1985-86; dir., coord. health and social svcs. Cath. Worker of Niagara Falls, 1986-88; dir./coord. clin. svcs. Cath. Charities' Programs Adult Mentally Retarded Developmental Disabilities, Bklyn. and Queens, N.Y., 1988-91; v.p. mission svcs. Sisters of Charity Hosp., Buffalo, 1991—; mem. bd. Filmore Leroy Residents Assn., FLARE, Inc., Buffalo; bd. dirs. St. Mary's Hosp., Rochester; trustee Good Samaritan Hosp., Pottsville, Pa.; participant internat. Commns. Daus. of Charity, 1968; pres. bd. trustees Carney Hosp., Our Lady of Lourdes Hosp., St. Agnes Hosp.; chair, participant profl. religious cmty. studies; cons., spkr. Mercy Hosp., Pitts., St. Mary's Hosp., Amsterdam, N.Y.; mem. couns., coms. nursing, pers., profl. practice, other groups. Recipient Community Svc. award Cedar Grove Civic Assn., Boston, Ladies of Charity, Binghamton, CHA Pres., St. Louis. Fellow Am. Coll. Healthcare Execs.; mem. Am. Acad. Cath. Leadership. Office: Sisters of Charity Hospital 2157 Main St Buffalo NY 14214-2648

KELLEY, JACQUELYN LARSON, gerontologist; b. Palo Alto, Calif., Oct. 28, 1945; d. John Monroe and Glendora Drusilla (Sampson) Larson; m. Stephen Earl Kelley, Dec. 24, 1963 (div. 1994); children: Kristina Leona Jane, Stephenie Victoria. AA, Coll. San Mateo, 1974; BS summa cum laude, Coll. Notre Dame, Belmont, Calif., 1980; postgrad., San Francisco State U., 1980-82, Coll. Notre Dame, 1992-94. ESL aide Cabrillo Unified Sch. Dist., Half Moon Bay, Calif., 1975-76; community services specialist Ret. Sr. Vol. Program, Menlo Park, Calif., 1980-82, dir., 1982-83; dir. vol. services Vis. Nurse Assn. San Francisco, 1983-85; gerontology specialist San Jose (Calif.) Office on Aging, 1986-90, gerontology supr., 1990-92; analyst San Jose Dept. Human Resources, Retirement Benefits, 1992-94; v.p. clin. and edn. svcs. York County (Pa.) Family Svc. Assn., 1994—; lectr. San Jose State U., 1991-93. Founder Ocean Shore Resident's Assn., Half Moon Bay, 1976; founder Friends of RSVP Inc., Redwood City, Calif., 1983. Mem. Internat. Soc. for Retirement Planning (chpt. pres., bd. dirs. 1985—, v.p. 1991—), Nat. Coun. Aging, Am. Soc. on Aging (com. chmn. 1984-87, chmn. retirement program planning com. 1988-90, chair recreation and leisure planning com. 1990—), Assn. Profl. Vol. Mgrs. (founder, chmn. 1984-87, trainer), Nat. Recreation and Park Assn. (aging task force 1989-91, founding pres. aging and leisure sect. 1991-94), Calif. Park and Recreation Soc. (bd. dirs., founder, pres. aging sect. 1988-90), Alpha Gamma Sigma, Delta Epsilon Sigma, Kappa Gamma Pi. Democrat. Lutheran. Home: 6060 Gensemer Ln Harrisburg PA 17111 Office: York County Family Svc Assn 1 Market Place West York County PA 17401

KELLEY, KARA JANE, public affairs executive; b. Las Vegas, Aug. 6, 1968; d. Donald Ray and Penelope Josephine (Bellavia) K.; m. Joseph J. Panebianco. BA in Polit. Sci., U. Nev., Las Vegas, 1992, BA in Communications, 1992. Asst. media buyer R&R Advt., Las Vegas, 1987-89; pres., owner KJK Enterprises, Las Vegas, 1991—; dir. pub. affairs Altamira Communications Group, Las Vegas, 1991-92; issues analyst The McMullen Strategic Group, 1993—. Vol. We Can, Inc., Las Vegas, 1987-89, KNPR, Pub. Radio, Las Vegas, 1988-89. Recipient Ned Dey Meml. scholarship U. Nev., 1989, Women in Communications scholarship, 1989, Leadership scholarship, 1990, Milken scholarship, 1990, Lynn Shoen scholarship, 1990. Mem. Golden Key, Phi Kappa Phi, Pi Sigma Alpha, Phi Alpha Delta. Office: KJK Enterprises 1350 E Flamingo Rd Ste 463 Las Vegas NV 89119

KELLEY, KATHLEEN ULAND, accountant; b. Jeffersonville, Ind., Feb. 16, 1956; d. Franklin Joseph and Ruth (Morgan) U.; m. Mark Charles Kelley, Sept. 21, 1986; children: Eoghan, Eamon, Aoibhinn, Eibhlyn. BS in Acctg., Ohio State U., 1978. CPA, N.H., Del.; cert. fraud examiner. EDP auditor E.I. DuPont de Nemourse Co., Wilmington, Del., 1978-81; staff adminstr. U. Mass., Amherst, 1981-85; auditor Brown U., Providence, R.I., 1985-88; pvt. practice Randolph, N.H., 1988—; rsch. and publs. chairperson Assn. Coll. and Univ. Auditors, 1986-88; guest lectr. HERS program Wellesley (Mass.) Coll., 1986-92, North Country Ednl. Found., Gorham, N.H., 1990—, FHA-HERO, N.H., 1993. Editor: (booklet) Internal Auditing in Universities, 1987; contbr. articles to profl. jours. Treas. St. Kieran's Ch., Berlin, N.H., 1990-93; mem. Randolph Dem. Com., 1993—; bd. dirs. C. of C., Berlin, 1994. Mem. AICPA, AAUW (treas. 1990-94, found. chair and membership chair 1992-94, pres. 1994—, Pathfinders grantee 1992-94), N.H. Soc. CPAs. Roman Catholic. Office: RR 1 Box 1045 Berlin NH 03570-9714

KELLEY, LINDA EILEEN, marketing specialist, sales consultant; b. Osceola, Iowa, June 10, 1950; d. Marion Gale and Frances (Steele) McKinnie; m. Dennis Dean Kelley, Aug. 3, 1969 (div. 1980); 1 child, Jennifer Lynne. Student, U. No. Iowa, 1969. Classified advt. mgr. Creston (Iowa) News-Advertiser, 1971-79, advt./promotion mgr., 1981-82; classified advt. promotion specialist Des Moines Register & Tribune, 1979-81; assoc. cons. K. Bordner Cons., Inc., Bloomington, Minn., 1982-84; sales devel. rep. Mpls. Star & Tribune, 1983-90; pres. Cities Best Mktg. Advt. Agy., Bloomington, 1990—; pres. Cities Best Mktg., Inc., 1989—; instr. Hennepin Jr. Coll.,

Mpls.; small bus. advt. Author: Retail Advertising for the Small Business, 1986—. Methodist. Office: Cities Best Mktg Inc 10740 Lyndale Aves Bloomington MN 55420

KELLEY, LINDA SUSAN, healthcare consulting executive; b. Bangor, Maine, July 12, 1955; d. Franklin R. and Janet M. (Knauf) Heyner; m. Michael S. Kelley, May 4, 1985; children: Stacie Leigh, Jason Thomas. Med. asst. cert., Bryman Sch., 1973; RN, No. Essex C.C., Haverhill, Mass., 1982; BSBA, N.H. Coll., 1989; postgrad., Simmons Coll., 1991—. Cert. med. asst. Dental/law sec. Joseph Haggerty, Concord, Mass., 1973-74; med. sec. Lexington Eye Assocs., Concord, 1974-75; office mgr./med. asst. Martin C. Gross, MD, Concord, 1975-78; office mgr. Stephen A. Smith, MD, Concord, 1978-80; adminstr. Billerica (Mass.) Walk-In Med., 1980-82; v.p., founder M. M. Consulting, Inc., Scottsdale, Ariz., 1982—; dir. mgmt. info. sys./adminstrn. Visiting Nurse, Arlington, Mass., 1989-93; cons. Health Northeast, Manchester, N.H., 1989-90. Co-author: (manual) Paper Chase-How to Win, 1992. Recipient N.H. Coll. Alumni scholarship N.H. Coll., Manchester, 1988-89, Shoehorn award Bd. Dirs. Vis. Nurse and Cmty. Health, 1992. Mem. NAFE, Am. Coll. Healthcare Execs. (affiliate), Delta Profl. Adv. Com. (founder), U.S. Olympic Com. Office: M M Consulting 14718 N 100th Way Scottsdale AZ 85260

KELLEY, LISA STONE, public guardian, conservator; b. Sacramento, Calif., Mar. 10, 1947; d. John William and Coral Frances (Roberts) Stone; m. Charles B. Kelley, Oct. 7, 1967 (div. Feb. 1987); children: Brian Christopher, Darren Matthew. Student, Sacramento City Coll., 1965-67, AA in Social Sci., 1978; BA in Social Work with honors, Calif. State U., Sacramento, 1982, MSW with honors, 1985; postgrad. in Psychology, Calif. Coast U., 1994—. Lic. clin. social worker, Calif. Pharmacy clerk S. Sacramento Pharmacy, 1966-68; temp. med. asst. Sacramento, 1978-80; adv., counselor El Dorado Women's Info. Ctr., Placerville, Calif., 1982; dep. patients rights adv. Sacramento County Office Patients Rights, 1983-84; sch. social worker Elk Grove (Calif.) Unified Sch. Dist., 1984-85; mental health counselor Sacramento Mental Health Ctr., 1986; dep. pub. guardian/conservator Sacramento County, 1986—. Mem. NASW, Sacramento County Employees Orgn., Am. Orthopsychiat. Assn., Menninger Found., Calif. State U. Alumni Assn., Calif. Coast U. Alumni Assn., Phi Kappa Phi. Democrat. Office: Sacramento County Pub Guardian/Conservator 4875 Broadway Ste I Sacramento CA 95820-1500

KELLEY, LOIS ELIZABETH, arts administrator, consultant; b. Peoria, Ill., Jan. 20, 1922; d. Doran A. Dieter and Sylvia Irene Huntington; m. George Thomas Edwards (div. 1949); children: George Thomas Jr., William Clarke; m. Russell Eugene Kelley (dec. June 1981); 1 child, Kathleen Lee. Student, Miss Brown's Bus. Sch., Milw., 1941, U. Ala., Tuscaloosa, 1941; cert. in arts adminstrn., Golden Gate U., 1976. Flight attendant Pan Am. World Airways, 1943-45; legal sec. Helliwell & Clarke, Miami, Fla., 1948; arts adminstr. San Mateo County Fair Arts, San Mateo, Calif., 1972-90; gallery chmn. Foster City (Calif.) Arts and Culture Commn., 1974-93; arts adminstr., pres. Peninsula Art Assn., 1994—. Chmn. Foster City Bicentennial Commn., 1974-78; vice chmn. San Mateo County Arts Coun., 1972-76; pres. Women's Caucus for Art, San Mateo, 1992-93; pres. bd. dirs. San Mateo County Fair and Expn., 1985-86; mem. No. Calif. arts adv. bd. to CAL-EXPO, 1972-94; founder Foster City Art League; jr. leader Girl Scouts U.S.A., Foster City, 1968; initiator, establisher Redwood Grove at San Mateo County Fairgrounds, 1985. Recipient award of appreciation San Mateo County Fair Assn., 1977, 91, Gavel award, 1986; outstanding svc. award dist. IV, Calif. Parks and Recreation Soc., 1992, Outstanding Dedicated Svc. award City of Foster City Arts, 1992. Home: 171 Flying Cloud Isle Foster City CA 94404

KELLEY, LYN SCHRAFF, insurance broker; b. Cleve., Mar. 30, 1956; d. Albert Gerald Schraff and Mary Patricia (McCarty) Urban; m. Kevin E. Kelley, Feb. 28, 1949. BBA, Cleve. State U., 1982, MBA, 1990. V.p., mgr. comml. property dept. Johnson & Higgins, Cleve., 1977—; bd. dirs. Ct. Community Svc. Agy. Mem. leadership devel. program United Way, 1991, also mem. allocations panel. Mem. Exec. Women's Roundtable, Women's City Club. Roman Catholic. Home: 27631 Whitehill Cir Cleveland OH 44145-1217 Office: Johnson & Higgins 1301 E 9th St Ste 1900 Cleveland OH 44114-1890

KELLEY, MARY ELIZABETH (LAGRONE), computer specialist; b. Temple, Tex., Feb. 12, 1947; d. Harry John and Mary Erma (Windham) LaGrone; m. Roy Earl Kelley, May 10, 1968; children: Roy John, James Lewis, Joanna Marylu. BS, U. Mary Hardin-Baylor, 1968. Cert. tchr., Tex. Math tchr. Killeen (Tex.) High Sch., 1977-78; clk. typist Readiness Region VIII, Aurora, Colo., 1979; statis. clk. Fitzsimons Army Med. Ctr., Aurora, 1980-81, mgmt. asst., 1981-83; clk. typist Corpus Christi (Tex.) Army Depot, 1984; mgmt. asst. Health Care Studies and Clin. Investigation Act, Fort Sam Houston, Tex., 1984-85; computer programmer/analyst Health Care Systems Support Act, Fort Sam Houston, 1985-88, computer systems analyst, 1988-92, computer specialist, 1992—; tchr. Fitzsimons Army Med. Ctr., 1978-79, cons., 1978-79. Author: (databases) Health Care Management System, 1988-94. Vol. Heidi Search Ctr., San Antonio, 1990, Friends of Safe House, Denver, 1980-83, Parents Encouraging Parents, Denver, 1979-83. Recipient achievement medal for civilian svc. Dept. Army, 1991. Mem. DAR, Daus. of Republic of Tex., United Daus. of Confederacy, Tex. Soc. of Mayflower Descs., Alpha Chi, Delta Psi Theta, Sigma Tau Delta. Roman Catholic.

KELLEY, PATRICIA HAGELIN, geology educator; b. Cleve., Dec. 8, 1953; d. Daniel Warn and Virginia Louise (Morgan) Hagelin; m. Jonathan Robert Kelley, June 18, 1977; children: Timothy Daniel, Katherine Louise. BA, Coll. of Wooster, 1975; AM, Harvard U., 1977, PhD, 1979. Instr. New Eng. Coll., Henniker, N.H., 1979; asst. prof. U. Miss., University, 1979-85, assoc. prof., 1985-89, acting assoc. vice chancellor acad. affairs, 1988, prof., 1989-92, assoc. dean, 1989-92; program dir. NSF, Washington, 1990-92; prof., chmn. dept. geology U. N.D., Grand Forks, 1992—. Contbr. articles to profl. jours. Deacon Bethel Presbyn. Ch., Olive Branch, Miss., 1985-90. Rsch. grantee NSF, 1986-89, 90—; NSF fellow, 1976-79. Mem. AAAS, Paleontol. Soc. (coun. 1984-85, chair SE sect. 1984-85), Geol. Soc. Am., Paleontol. Rsch. Inst., Soc. Econ. Paleontologists and Mineralogists, Sigma Xi, Phi Beta Kappa. Presbyterian. Office: U ND Dept Geology & Geol Engring PO Box 8358 Grand Forks ND 58202-8358

KELLEY, ROSEMARY REGINA, bank executive; b. Rockville Centre, N.Y., Jan. 3, 1966; d. Leo Martin and Rosemary Regina (Burns) Walsh; m. Timothy Edward Kelley, Oct. 16, 1993. BA, Manhattanville Coll., 1987; MBA, Columbia U., 1991. Analyst Morgan Stanley & Co., N.Y.C., 1987-89; assoc. The Sanwa Bank Ltd., N.Y.C., 1991-93; asst. v.p. Deutsche Bank AG, N.Y.C., 1993—.

KELLEY, SHEILA SEYMOUR, public relations executive, crisis consultant; b. Bronxville, N.Y.; d. William Joseph and Jane (Seymour) K.; m. Robert Max Kaufman, 1959. BA magna cum laude, Syracuse U., 1949. Reporter Yonkers Herald Statesman, N.Y.C., 1950; reporter, editor Close Up column Herald Tribune, N.Y.C., 1950-53; writer, producer Sta. WNBC-TV, N.Y.C., 1953-54; media cons. to Senator Jacobs K. Javits, N.Y.C., 1956-74; press sec. Senator Jacobs K. Javits, Washington, 1958-61; account supr., v.p. Harsne Rotman Druck, N.Y.C., 1961-76; founder, pres. VOTES, Inc., N.Y.C., 1973-75; v.p. Doremus Pub. Rels., N.Y.C., 1976-86, sr. v.p., 1987-90, mng. dir., exec. v.p., 1990; exec. v.p. Gavin Anderson & Co., N.Y.C., 1990—. Mem. Pub. Rels. Soc. Am. (accredited), Women Execs. Pub. Rels. (pres. 1987-88), Phi Beta Kappa. Republican. Office: Gavin Anderson & Co 1633 Broadway New York NY 10019

KELLEY, WENDY THUE, fine art advisor, consultant; b. Santa Monica, Calif., July 4, 1941; d. Horace Wendel and Marjory (Simmons) Thue; children: David Byron Jr., Christopher S., Jennifer M. AA, Stephens Coll., 1960; BA, Phillips U., 1963; postgrad., NYU, 1987-90, Instituto Allende, San Miguel de Allende, 1993—. Cert. tchr., Conn. Asst. dir. Hotline of Greenwich, Conn., 1978-80; corp. sales dir. Saugatuck Gallery, Westport, Conn., 1983-85; founder, dir. Artworks Fine Art Advisors, Old Greenwich, 1985; curator exhbns. Home Box Office/Time Warner, N.Y.C., Keren Devel., Tarrytown, N.Y., 1993-94; cons. Aetna, Cornell Med. Ctr., Time-Warner, Apple Computer, Marriott Corp. Exhibited in group show including Nacional de Bellas Artes, 1993. Bd. dirs. YMCA, 1987-93; tchr. Literacy Vol. of Am. TESOL, Stamford, Conn., 1993; mem. NOW, 1976—; docent art history Greenwich Sch. System, Conn., 1991. Mem. The Guild (corp. cons.), Art in Am. Guide (art advisor), Silvermine Arts Ctr., Kappa Alpha Theta. Office: Artworks Fine Art Advisors 15 Potter Dr Old Greenwich CT 06870-1507

KELLEY-BROCKEL, KATHLEEN FRANCES, principal; b. Phila., Apr. 4, 1948; d. James J. and Frances M. (Stiegler) Kelley; m. Thomas E. Hoats, Aug. 8, 1970 (div. Jan. 1989); children: Christina, Melissa, Michael; m. Robert L. Brockel Sr., Sept. 28, 1991; children: Robert, Scott, Arlene, Curt. BS, Coll. Misericordia, 1970; MS, Marywood Coll., 1983; student, Lehigh U., 1993. Cert. prin., Pa. Tchr. grade 4 Allentown (Pa.) Sch. Dist., 1970; tchr. grades 3, 4 and 5 St. Paul's Sch., Allentown, 1979-87; prin. Christ the King Sch., Whitehall, Pa., 1987-93; asst. prin. So. Lehigh Mid. Sch., Center Valley, Pa., 1993—. Mem. ASCD, Pa. ASCD, Nat. Assn. Secondary Sch. Prins. Roman Catholic. Office: So Lehigh Mid Sch 3715 Preston Ln Center Valley PA 18034

KELLISON, DONNA LOUISE GEORGE, accountant, educator; b. Hugoton, Kans., Oct. 16, 1950; d. Donald Richard and Zepha Louise (Lowry) George. BA in Elem. Edn. with honors, Anderson (Ind.) U., 1972; MS in Elem. Edn., Ind. U., 1981. CPA, Ind.; lic. tchr., Ind. Tchr. elem. Maconaquah Sch. Corp., Bunker Hill, Ind., 1972-73; office mgr. Eskew & Gresham, CPA's, Louisville, Ky., 1973-78; para-profl. Blue & Co., Indpls., 1979-83, tax compliance specialist, 1983-84, tax sr., 1984-86, tax supr., 1986-87, tax mgr., 1987-90, tax prin., 1990-92, tax sr. mgr., 1992-94, dir., 1995—. Vol. Children's Clinic, Indpls., 1985—. Mem. AICPA, Ind. CPA Soc. (tax inst. com. 1989-93, chairperson 1993-94, govt. rels. com. 1994—), Toastmasters (sec. Indpls. 1986). Presbyterian. Home: 9318 Embers Way Indianapolis IN 46250-3419 Office: Blue & Co PO Box 80069 Indianapolis IN 46280-0069

KELLOGG, ANN MARIE, publishing executive, consultant; b. Pitts., Oct. 2, 1939; m. Eugene Krasnoff (div.); children: Peter Lawrence, Stephanie Ann; m. Jack L. Kellogg, Nov. 10, 1979. BS, U. Wis., 1961. Prodn. and bus. mgr. Collective Advt., Inc., Princeton, N.J., 1973-83; dir. publs. Community Pride, Inc., Princeton, 1983-87, Exclusive Publs., Ltd./Relocation Guides, Boca Raton, Fla., 1987-94. Chair Abortion Law Reform Com. of N.J., Princeton, 1967-71. Mem. Fla. Mag. Assn., Soroptimist Internat. (pres. Pompano Beach, Fla. chpt. 1991-92). Home and Office: Red Cloud Indian Sch Pine Ridge SD 57770

KELLS, ELIZABETH COREY, publisher, author; b. Ogdensburg, N.Y., Nov. 15, 1929; d. Albert B. and Inez M. (MacCallum) Corey; m. James M. Guthe, Jan. 2, 1951 (div. 1985); children: David, Steven, Susan Guthe Mazzon, Carl; m. Robert T. Kells, Jan. 17, 1987. BA, Boston U., 1969; EdM, Harvard U., 1975. Lic. capt. USCG. Assoc. dir. Ctr. for Continuing Edn. Bentley Coll., Waltham, Mass.; exec. dir. Wash. Literacy, Seattle, until 1979; resident carver Wendell Gilley Mus., Southwest Harbor, Maine, 1982-83; pres. Pubs. N.E., Seattle, 1983—. Author: Want To Carve a Duck?, 1983, Taking Notes in the Classroom, 1993. Mem. Harvard Club Palm Beaches. Home: 103 Aqua Ra Drive Jensen Beach FL 34957-2674

KELL-SMITH, CARLA SUE, federal agency administrator; b. Highland Park, Mich., Sept. 15, 1952; d. Carl William and Margie May (Cannon) Bodner; m. Joseph Mark Kell, Oct. 10, 1971 (div. Dec. 1980); m. Richard Charles Smith, Jan. 28, 1989; Student, Anderson Coll., 1970-71, Glendale Coll., 1976-77, Ariz. State U., 1978-79, Mesa Coll., 1979-80. Private tutor English, Fed. Republic of Germany, 1971-74; office mgr. Bell & Schore, Rochester, Mich., 1974-75, COL Press, Phoenix, 1978-80; publicity mgr. O'Sullivan Woodside & Col, Phoenix, 1980-81, gen. mgr., 1982-84; pub. relations/promotion cons. GPI Publs., Cupertino, Calif., 1985; pub. cons., 1985-88; project adminstr. FAA, 1986—; account coord. Bernard Hodes Advt., Tempe, Ariz., 1981; cons. freelance mktg., Phoenix, 1983. Vol., Fiesta Bowl Parade Com., Phoenix, 1983, FAA Airport Improvement Project. Office: 789 Pepper Dr San Bruno CA 94066-2935

KELLUM, CARMEN KAYE, apparel company executive; b. Greensburg, Pa., Oct. 15, 1952; d. Bruce Lowell and Mildred Louise (Montgomery) Taylor; m. John Douglas Kellum, Aug. 2, 1975 (div. May 1987). Student, MacMurray Coll., 1971-72, Elgin Community Coll.; AA, Coll. DuPage, 1975; BA with honors, Nat. Coll. Edn., 1978. Cert. tchr. Aide occupational therapy Mercy Ctr., Aurora, Ill., 1972-76; tchr. behavior disorders Lake Park High Sch., Roselle, Ill., 1978-80, Salk Pioneer Sch., Roselle, 1980-81; mgr. So-Fro Fabrics Stores, Lombard, Joliet & Chgo., Ill., 1981-84; offshore coord. Florsheim Shoe Co., Chgo., 1984-90; mgr. Linens N Things, Rolling Meadows, Ill., 1990-91; mgr. House of Fabrics, Aurora, Ill., 1992-94, Glen Ellyn, Ill., 1994; merchandise mgr. T.J. Maxx, West Dundee, Ill., 1994—. Mem. Orton Dyslexia Soc., Nat. Assn. Female Exec., Kappa Delta Pi. Lutheran. Home: 30 W 156 Wood Ct and Hwy 59 PO Box 8137 Bartlett IL 60103 Office: TJ Mazz 870 N Main St West Dundee IL 60118

KELLY, ANN TERESE, elementary education educator; b. St. Louis, Jan. 29, 1954; d. Robert Victor and Mary Magdalen (Debrecht) K. BS in Elem. Edn., U. Mo., St. Louis, 1977, postgrad., 1978-79, 86-88; postgrad., Webster U., St. Louis, 1990, U. Mo., Columbia, 1990-92. Tchr. 4th grade St. Paul (Mo.) Sch., 1974-75, Assumption Sch., O'Fallon, Mo., 1977-79; tchr. grades 6 to 8 St. Raphael, St. Louis, 1979-86; tchr. grade 7 Our Lady of Sorrows, St. Louis, 1986-88, tchr. grade 5, 1988—; tchr. trainer Sci. Olympiad, St. Louis, 1987—; presenter weather workshops, 1991—; trainer Gr. 5 Developmental Approaches in Sci. and Health, 1993, Archdiocese of St. Louis, 1994; Am. Meteorol. Soc./Nat. Oceanic and Atmospheric Adminstrn. workshop presenter Maury Project oceanographic studies, 1994. Mem. Nat. Sci. Tchrs. Assn., Sci. Tchrs. Mo. Roman Catholic. Home: 10126C Puttington Dr Saint Louis MO 63123-5258 Office: Our Lady of Sorrows 5831 S Kingshighway Blvd Saint Louis MO 63109-3571

KELLY, ANNE CATHERINE, retired city official; b. Buffalo, Mar. 6, 1916; d. John Patrick and Elizabeth Marie (Edwards) Donohue; m. Thomas Edward Kelly, Apr. 19, 1941 (dec. 1993); children: Maureen Anne Kelly, Michael Thomas, Edward John, Kevin Joseph, Theresa Elizabeth Callahan. Student SUNY-Buffalo. Tchr., St. Teresa Sch., Buffalo, 1956-64; clk. City of Buffalo, 1964, sec. to comptroller, 1967-70, coun. clk., 1970-76, sr. coun. clk., 1976-81. Com. woman N.Y. Democratic Com., 1970-87, mem. exec. bd., 1970—; vice chmn. Erie County Dem. Com., 1985—; past pres. Mercy League of Buffalo Mercy Hosp., Nash Ladies Guild, South Side Dem. Club; mem. Women for Downtown Buffalo. Roman Catholic. Clubs: Daus. of Erin, Nash Ladies. Lodge: KC (past pres. Nash guild). Home: 9 Haig Pl # 404 Dunedin FL 34698-8547

KELLY, BEVERLY BEEBE GRIMES, retired learning consultant; b. Waterford, Conn., July 11, 1930; d. Arthur Russell and Cornelia Louise (Avery) Grimes; m. Thomas Joseph Kelly, Oct. 28, 1950; 1 child, Susan Elizabeth. AS, Mitchell Coll., 1950; BS, Coll. of William and Mary, 1958; MA, Seton Hall U., 1966, post master's cert learning disabilities, 1973. Cert. kindergarten through grade 8 tchr., learning disabilities tchr./cons., reading, spl. edn., adminstrn. and supervision. Tchr. Montville (Conn.) Sch. Bd., 1952-55, Rochester (N.Y.) Sch. Bd., 1955-56, Richmond (Va.) Sch. Bd., 1956-58, Montclair (N.J.) Sch. Bd., 1960-62, Charlotte (N.C.) Sch. Bd., 1962-64, Wilmington (Del.) Sch. Bd., 1964-66, San Juan (P.R.) Sch. Bd., Antilles Svc. Command, 1966-69; Tchr. Middletown (N.J.) Sch. Bd., 1969-71, learning cons., child study team chair, 1971-83; pvt. practice, learning cons. Flagler County, 1985—. Organizer fund-raising events Am. Cancer Soc., Flagler County, Fla.; active Girl Scouts U.S., 1986-89; mem. sch. bd. adv. com. Palm Coast Civic Assn., 1988—. Mem. NEA (life), AARP, DAR, AAUW (life., br. v.p. 1984-86, pres. 1986-88, Fla. state membership v.p. 1990-94, v.p. dir. programs 1994—, Woman As Agt. of Change-Fla. award 1988, Assn. Membership Recruitment 4th pl. award 1985, State Membership V.P. Plan award 1991, LEAP award for state diversity 1994), Learning Cons. Assn. N.J., N.J. Edn. Assn. (life), Assn. Learning Cons., Irish Social Club, Pine Lakes Women's Golf Club (sec. 1989-90, membership chair 1993—), Phi Delta Kappa (newsletter editor 1992, Tchr. of the Year Selection com., 1990—). Episcopalian. Home: 3 Fernham Ln Palm Coast FL 32137-8105

KELLY, CAROL WHITE, company executive; b. Shreveport, La., Dec. 23, 1946; d. Verlin Ralph and Mary Louise (Humphries) White; m. James Patrick Kelly, June 6, 1968; children: Mary Louise, Christopher John. BA, Centenary Coll. La., Shreveport, 1968. Corp. sec., treas. Kelly & Assocs., Atlanta, 1986—. Mem. Ga. Baptist Med. Guild (life), Atlanta Hist. Soc., Atlanta Ballet Guild (life), Internat. Platform Assn., High Mus. Art, Episcopal Ch. Women (sec.-treas. 1976-80), Chi Omega Alumnae Assn. (pres. 1979-80). Office: Kelly & Assocs PC 200 Galleria Pky NW Ste 1510 Atlanta GA 30339-5946

KELLY, CHRISTINE ANN, small business owner, educator; b. Bklyn., May 11, 1952; d. William John and Joan Ellen (Sullivan) K. AAS in Acctg., Kingsborough Community Coll., 1973; BS in Phys. Edn., Bklyn. Coll., 1976. Cert. physical edn. tchr., N.Y. Head softball coach C.W. Post Coll., Greenvale, N.Y., 1979-84; sales mgr. Karnival Sports Ctr., Bklyn., 1984-88; owner, founder Shortstop Silkscreening, S.I., N.Y., 1988—; tchr. St. Edmund High Sch., Bklyn., 1979-81; adj. lectr. Kingsborough Community Coll., Bklyn., 1984—; head coach softball Empire State Games, N.Y., 1987-89. Bd. dir. holiday basketball tournament Tournament of Champions, N.Y., 1986—. Mem. Screen Printing Assn. Internat., N.Y. Bd. Ofcls. for Women Sports. Democrat. Roman Catholic. Office: Shortstop Silkscreening 1235 Bay St Staten Island NY 10305-3111

KELLY, DAWN, business educator; b. Peoria, Ill., Oct. 4, 1957; d. Donald G. and Lynda R. (Jackson) K.; m. Thomas Francis Reed, June 22, 1991. BA, U. Ill., 1979, MBA, 1981; PhD, Northwestern U., 1988. Asst. prof. U. Wis., Milw., 1986-91; assoc. prof. U. Calgary, Alta., Can., 1991-92; vis. assoc. prof. Northwestern U., Evanston, Ill., 1992-93; adj. assoc. prof. bus. U. Mich., Ann Arbor, 1993-94; vis. assoc. prof. dept. mgmt. and mktg. Coll. of Bus., U. Limerick, Ireland, 1994—. Contbr. articles to profl. jours., chpts. to books. Mem. Acad. Mgmt. Office: Dept Mgmt and Mktg, Coll of Bus, Univ Limerick, Limerick Ireland

KELLY, DEBRA LEAH, financial executive; b. Bethesda, Md., Aug. 2, 1953; d. Alan Graham Settles and Marcia Marie (Russell) Stroble; m. Thomas Joseph Kelly, July 9, 1994; children: John Thomas, Rhiannon Leah, Mikael Logan. BS in Bus. with distinction, Ind. U., Gary, 1982. CPA, Md. Sr. auditor Laventhol & Horwath, Washington, 1982-85; asst. contr. Jurgovan & Blair, Potomac, Md., 1985-86; controller Tactical Systems Corp., El Cajon, Calif., 1986-91; contr. Ctr. for Strategic and Internat. Studies, Washington, 1991-94; controller Northwind Enterpirse, Inc., 1994—; acctg./fin. cons. Mem. NAFE, Assn. Govt. Accts., Md. Assn. CPA's, Beta Alpha Psi, Beta Gamma Sigma, Omicron Delta Epsilon.

KELLY, DOROTHY PAMLYN, psychologist, consultant; b. Salt Lake City, Nov. 5, 1943; d. James Edsil and Vergie Dorothy (McDaniel) Henderson (div. 1983); children: Kristin Michelle, Alexis Pamlyn. BA in Psychology, Calif. State U., Hayward, 1973, MS in Edn., 1975; MS in Clin. Psychology, Pacific Grad. Sch. Psychology, 1982, PhD in Clin. Psychology, 1990. Lic. psychologist, Ariz., Calif. Co-facilitator Inst. for Effectiveness, San Jose, Calif., 1975-77; dir. advanced officer tng. program Sunnyvale (Calif.) Police Dept., 1978-79; intern psychiat. svcs. Children's Hosp., San Francisco, 1981-82; pvt. practice clin. psychology Novato, Calif., 1976—; psychol. asst. Rivka Kaplowitz, PhD, Fairfield, 1990—; owner, CEO Human Resource Concepts, Novato, 1991—; dir. Regency Affiliates, 1993—; adv. bd. mem. Solano Park Hosp., Fairfield. Mem. APA, Calif. Psychol. Assn., Calif. Assn. Marriage and Family Counselors, Pi Gamma Mu. Home: 10 Winged Foot Dr Novato CA 94949-5909 Office: 634 Webster St Fairfield CA 94533-6214

KELLY, EILEEN PATRICIA, management educator; b. Steubenville, Ohio, Oct. 24, 1955; d. Edward Joseph and Mary Bernice (Cassidy) K. BS, Coll. Steubenville, 1978; MA, U. Cin., 1979, PhD, 1982. LPA, Ohio; sr. profl. in human resources. Lectr. U. Cin., 1981-82; asst. prof. bus. Creighton U., Omaha, 1982-87, chmn. mgmt., mktg. and systems dept., 1986-88, assoc. prof., 1987-88, coordinator project Minerva, 1987-88; assoc. prof. La. State U., Shreveport, 1988-93, chmn. dept. mgmt. and mktg., 1988-93; assoc. prof., chmn. mgmt. dept. Ithaca (N.Y.) Coll., 1993—; comml. arbitrator, 1988—. Contbr. articles to profl. jours. and acad. presentations. Mem. Acad. Mgmt., Acad. Legal Studies in Bus., Soc. Human Resource Mgmt., Soc. for Bus. Ethics, Soc. for History in the Fed. Govt., Beta Gamma Sigma (faculty adviser 1985-88, 92-93). Roman Catholic. Office: Ithaca Coll Sch Bus Ithaca NY 14850

KELLY, GLENDA MARIE, former mayor; b. San Diego, June 3, 1944; d. Glenn Adrian and Donna Louise (Embrey) Molsberry; m. Ronald Worth Campbell, June 3, 1962 (div. 1969); children: Gina Marie, Chad Loren; m. Dennis Patrick Kelly, Sept. 18, 1970. BS in Sociology cum laude, Mo. Western State Coll., 1989. Legal sec. Stanley S. Kalender, St. Joseph, Mo., 1960-88; dep. mayor City of St. Joseph, 1986-89, mayor, 1989-94; Dem. nominee for State Rep. Mo., 1994—. Mem. Buchanan County Social Welfare Bd., 1979-85; mem. steering com. YWCA Women's Abuse Shelter, 1980; vice chair, chair budget com. Citizen's Adv. Commn., 1980-81; mem. task force Mo-Kan Regional Food Bank, 1981-83, City St. Joseph Fair Housing, 1984, Pony Express Region Tourist Info. Ctr., 1982, bd. dirs., 1983; bd. dirs. Pony Express Hist. Assn., 1983-84, Econ. Opportunity Corp., 1984-85, YWCA, 1985-86, Mo. Mcpl. League, 1990—, St. Joseph Hist. Soc., 1979-80, sec., 1979-80; mem. St. Joseph City Coun., 1986, Governance Coun. Cmty. Based Health Care for Children, 1994—. Recipient Outstanding Community Vol. award United Way, Civic Recognition award City St. Joseph, Vol. award VFW Aux., 1980, Recognition award St. Joseph's br. NAACP, 1990, James C. Kirkpatrick Good Govt. award Northwest Mo. Press Assn., Historic Preservation award for Leadership in Historic Preservation Issues St. Joseph Landmark Commn., 1993; named Woman of Month by YWCA, 7/93, Outstanding Woman of Yr. YWCA, 1993. Mem. LWV (bd. dirs. St. Joseph area, co-chair local govt. com. 1978-79, chair budget com. 1979-80, 1st v.p. 1981, chair drug awareness com. 1981, pres. 1985-86), St. Joseph Area C. of C. (urban action com. 1985, econ. devel. coun. 1988—, bd. dirs. 1994—). Democrat. Roman Catholic. Home: 3415 N 3rd St Saint Joseph MO 64505-3046

KELLY, JANET LANGFORD, lawyer; b. Kansas City, Mo., Nov. 27, 1957. BA, Grinnell Coll., 1979; JD, Yale U., 1983. Bar: N.Y. 1985, Ill. 1989. Law clerk to Hon. James J. Hunter III U.S. Ct. Appeals (3rd cir.), 1983-84; ptnr. Sidley & Austin, Chgo., 1984—. Sr. editor Yale Law Jour., 1983. Office: Sidley & Austin 1 First Nat Plz Chicago IL 60603*

KELLY, JOAN LARSON, association executive; b. Platteville, Wis., July 31, 1927; d. Irving P. and Willah (Johnson) P.; m. Thomas Wylie Kelly, Sept. 7, 1973. BS, U. Toledo, 1949; MBA, The George Wash. U., 1983. Buyer R.H. Macy & Co., Toledo, 1949-51; tchr. The Internat. Sch., Medellin, Columbia, 1952-53, The Am. Sch. in Japan, 1953-64; dir. communications VISTA, Washington; dir. photography The Peace Corps, Washington, 1968-70; dir. pub. rels. PBS, 1970-71, The Am. Assn. State Colls. & Univs., Washington, 1971-73, The Sci. Mus., St. Paul, 1973-76, U.S. Commn. Civil Rights, Washington, 1977-78, HCRS Dept. Interior, Washington, 1978-81; v.p. Drake Beam Morin, Washington, 1980-83; account exec. Hill & Knowlton, Washington, 1983-85; mgr. bus. ptnrships. AARP, Washington, 1985—. Author: Visit With Me In Japan, 1964, The Geisha Cookbook, 1973, Irish Wit & Humor, 1974. Mem. Nat. Press Club, Fed. City Club. Office: AARP 601 E St NW Washington DC 20049-0001

KELLY, KATHLEEN S(UE), educator; b. Duluth, Minn., Aug. 6, 1943; d. Russell J. and Idun N. Mehrman; m. George F. Kelly, Apr. 29, 1961; children: Jodie A., Jennifer L. AA, Moorpark (Calif.) Coll., 1971; BS in Journalism, U. Md., College Park, 1973, MA in Pub. Rels., 1979, PhD in Pub. Communication, 1989. Accredited pub. rels.; cert. fundraising exec. Dir. pub. info. Bowie (Md.) State Coll., 1974-77; asst. to dean, instr. Coll. Journalism U. Md., College Park, 1977-79, assoc. dir. devel., 1979-82; v.p. Mt. Vernon Coll., Washington, 1982-83; dir. devel. U. Md., College Park, 1983-85, assoc. dean, lectr. Coll. Journalism, 1985-88, asst. dean Coll. Bus. and Mgmt., 1988-90; assoc. prof. U. S.W. La., 1991—; cons. NASA, NIH, Mt. St. Marys Coll., 1986—; lectr. CASE, Pub. Rels. Soc. Am., 1987—. Author: Fund Raising and Public Relations: A Critical Analysis, 1991. Named Outstanding Faculty Mem., Panhellenic Assn., Univ. Md., 1986; 1991 Pride Book award winner Speech Communication Assn., 1991, John

Grenzebach award winner for rsch. on philanthropy CASE and Am. Assn. Fund-Raising Coun., 1991, PRIG award winner for outstanding dissertation Internat. Communication Assn., 1990. Mem. Pub. Rels. Soc. Am. (chmn. ednl. and cultural orgn. sect. 1989, pres. Md. chpt. 1986-87, Pres.' Cup 1981, nat. bd. dirs. 1994-96), Nat. Soc. Fund Raising Execs. (mem. rsch. coun., N.H. coun. support and advancement of Edn., women's forum 1983), Women in Higher Edn., Phi Kappa Phi. Democrat. Home: 1033 Rue Bois De Chene Breaux Bridge LA 70517-6735 Office: U SW La Dept Comm PO Box 43650 # U Lafayette LA 70504-3650

KELLY, KATHRYN ELIZABETH, toxicologist; b. Montreal, Mar. 10, 1958; d. Paul Brendan Jr. and Barbara Alden (Carter) K. AB, Stanford U., 1979; MPH, Columbia U., 1982, Dr.P.H., 1985. Environ. scientist Dames & Moore, White Plains, N.Y., 1979-80; environ. toxicologist Dames & Moore, Cranford, N.J., 1980-82; CEO Environ. Toxicology Internat., Inc., Seattle, 1985—; pres. Alden Analytical Labs., Inc., Seattle, 1988-94; program dir. risk assessment and toxicology ERM Group of Cos., 1994—. Speaker on toxicology, risk assessment and risk communication; contbr. articles to profl. jours. Mem. Soc. Environ. Toxicology and Chemistry, Soc. Risk Analysis, Am. Coll. Toxicology. Office: Environ Toxicology Internat Inc 600 Stewart St Ste 700 Seattle WA 98101-1217

KELLY, KRISTINE JOAN, telecommunications industry executive; b. Easton, Pa., Mar. 24, 1951; d. Edward and Edith M. (Vosper) Falco; m. Eric V. Ottervik, Dec. 3, 1976 (div. Jan. 1987); m. Gerard J. Kelly, Aug. 22, 1992. AA, Northampton Coll., 1981, AAS, 1980; BA summa cum laude, Lehigh U., 1984. Mgr. telecommunications dept. Lehigh U., Bethlehem, Pa., 1972-80, dir. telecommunications dept., 1984-86; sr. cons. Flack & Kurtz Cons. Engrs., N.Y.C., 1986-88; asst. v.p. worldwide telecommunications Chem. Bank, N.Y.C., 1988-89, v.p. telecom. svcs., 1989-94; v.p. global tech. J.P. Morgan, N.Y.C., 1994—. Recipient Achievement award Women's Inner Circle; Williams scholar Lehigh U., 1982-84. Mem. IEEE (assoc.), NAFE, Phi Beta Kappa. Home: 6 Glenmere Dr Chatham NJ 07928-1308 Office: JP Morgan 60 Wall St New York NY 10260-0060

KELLY, LUCIE STIRM YOUNG, nursing educator; b. Stuttgart, Germany, May 2, 1925; came to U.S., 1929; d. Hugo Karl and Emilie Rosa (Engel) Stirm; m. J. Austin Young, Aug. 30, 1946 (div. Feb. 1971); m. Thomas Martin Kelly, 1972; 1 child by previous marriage, Gay Aleta (Mrs. Donald Meyer). BS, U. Pitts., 1947, MLitt, 1957, PhD (HEW fellow), 1965; D in Nursing Edn. (hon.), U. R.I., 1977; LHD (hon.), Georgetown U., 1983; DSc (hon.), Widener U., 1984, U. Mass., 1989; D of Pub. Svc. (hon.), Am. U., 1985. Instr. nursing McKeesport (Pa.) Hosp., 1953-57, asst. adminstr. nursing, 1966-69; asst. prof. nursing U. Pitts., 1957-64, asst. dean, 1965; prof., chmn. nursing dept. Calif. State U., Los Angeles, 1969-72; co-project dir. curriculum research Nat. League for Nursing, 1973-74; project dir. patient edn., office consumer health edn., also adj. assoc. prof. community medicine Coll. Medicine and Dentistry N.J.-Rutgers Med. Sch., 1974-75; prof. pub. health and nursing Sch. Pub. Health and Sch. Nursing Columbia U., N.Y.C., 1975-90; prof. emeritus Sch. Pub. HEalth and Sch. Nursing Columbia U., N.Y.C., 1990—; assoc. dean acad. affairs Sch. Pub. Health Columbia U., N.Y.C., 1988-90, hon. prof. nursing edn. Tchrs. Coll., 1977-93, acting head div. health adminstrn. Sch. Pub. Health, 1980-81, 86-88; on leave as exec. dir. Mid-Atlantic Regional Nursing Assn., 1981-82; cons. U. Nev., Las Vegas, 1970-72, Ball (Ind.) State U., 1971, Long Beach (Calif.) Naval Hosp., 1971-72, Travis AFB, Calif., 1972, Comprehensive Health Planning, Los Angeles, 1970-72, Brentwood VA Hosp., Los Angeles, 1971-72, Central Nursing Office VA, Washington, 1971—, N.J. Dept. Higher Edn., 1974-78, John Wiley Pub., 1974-76, Sch. Nursing Am. U. Beirut; mem. spl. med. adv. group VA Dept. Medicine and Surgery, Washington, 1980-84; cons. nursing com. AMA, 1971-74, Citizen's Com. for Children, N.Y.C.; v.p. Pa. Health Council, 1968-69; sec. Allegheny County (Pa.) Comprehensive Health Planning, 1969; mem. adv. com. physicians assts. Calif. Bd. Med. Examiners, 1970-72; mem. adv. com. Cancer Soc., Los Angeles, 1970-72; com. nursing VA, Washington, 1971-74, regional med. programs, Pa., 1967-69, Calif., 1970-72; mem. spl. adv. council on med. licensure and profl. conduct N.Y. State Assembly, 1977-79; mem. nat. adv. com. Encore (nat. YWCA postmastectomy group rehab. project), 1977-83; mem. ethics com. Palisades Gen. Med. Ctr., 1993—; lectr., cons., guest (Beijing Med. Coll. (China), 1982, Aga Khan U., Pakistan, 1990; bd. visitors U. Pitts. Sch. Nursing, 1986-93; nat. and internat. lectr. Author: Dimensions of Professional Nursing, 6th edit., 1991, The Nursing Experience: Trends Challenges, Transitions, 2d edit., 1992; contbg. editor Jour. Nursing Adminstrn., 1975-82; mem. editorial bd. Nurse Practitioner, 1976-82; columnist Nursing Outlook, editor-in-chief, 1982-91; bd. advs. Nurses Almanac, 1978, Nurse Manager's Handbook, 1979, Nursing Administration Handbook, 1992; mem. editorial adv. bd. Am. Health, 1981-91; edit. adv. bd. Jour. Public Health, 1992—, chair. 1993—; edit. adv. bd. Nursing and Health Care, 1991—; contbr. articles to profl. jours. Bd. dirs. ARC, Los Angeles, 1971-72, Vis. Nurse Service N.Y., 1980—, mem. exec. com., chmn. human resources, 1989—; bd. dirs. Concern for Dying, 1983-89; trustee Calif. State Coll. Los Angeles Found., 1971-72, U. Pitts, 1984-90, mem. exec. com. 1988-90; chair bd. visitors U. Pitts. Sch. Pub. Health, 1988; bd. visitors U. Miami Sch. Nursing, 1986—; mem. health services com. Children's Aid Soc., N.Y., 1978-84; v.p. Am. Nurses Found., 1980-82; mem. nat. adv. council on nurse tng. HRA, 1981-85. Named Outstanding Alumna U. Pitts. Sch. Nursing, 1966; recipient Hon. Recognition award, Am. Nurses Assn., 1992, Disting. Alumna award, U. Pitts. Sch. Nursing, 1981, Shaw medal Boston Coll., 1985, Bicentennial Medallion of Distinction U. Pitts., 1987, R. Louise McManus Medallion for Disting. Service to Nursing, Tchrs. Coll. Columbia U., 1987; named Pa. Nurse of Year, 1967; no Roll of Honor N.J. State Nurses Assn., 1990. Fellow Am. Acad. Nursing, N.Y. Acad. Medicine (assoc.); mem. ANA (dir. 1978-82, Hon. Recognition 1992), Am. Pub. Health Assn. (Ruth Freeman Pub. Health Nursing award 1993), Pa. Nurses Assn. (pres. 1966-69), Nat. League Nursing (bd. govs. 1991-93, bd. nurses' ednl. funds 1993—), U. Pitts. Sch. Nursing Alumni (pres. 1959), Am. Hosp. Assn. (com. chmn. 1967-68), Assn. Grad. Faculty Community Health/Public Health Nursing (v.p. 1980-81), Sigma Theta Tau Internat. (sr. editor jour. Image 1978-81, pres.-elect 1981-83, pres. 1983-85, nat. campaign chair Ctr. for Nursing Scholarship 1987-89, chair devel. com. 1989—, Memtor award 1993), Pi Lambda Theta, Alpha Tau Delta (certificate of merit); mem. bd. Nurses' Ednl. Funds, 1993—. Home: 6040 Boulevard E Apt 11G West New York NJ 07093-3809

KELLY, MARGARET BLAKE, auditor, state official; b. Crystal City, Mo., Sept. 17, 1935; d. Emory and Florine (Stovesand) Blake; m. William Clark Kelly; children: Kevin, Tom, John. BSBA, U. Mo., 1957; MBA, S.W. Mo. State U., 1975; D in Bus. Adminstrn. (hon.), S.W. Bapt. U., 1986. CPA, Mo. Acct. Williams-Keepers, Columbia and Jefferson City, Mo., McNabb, Westermann, Mitchell & Branstetter, Springfield, Mo., Fox & Co., Springfield; county auditor Cole County, Mo., 1982-84; state auditor State of Mo., Jefferson City, 1984—. Recipient Faculty-Alumni Gold Medal award U. Mo., 1985. Mem. Am. Inst. CPA's, Assn. Govt. Accts., Nat. State Auditors Assn. (past pres.), Nat. Assn. State Auditors, Comptrollers, and Treas., Am. Soc. Women Accts., Am. Womens Soc. CPAs, Mo. Soc. Cert. Pub. Accts., Women Execs. in State Govt., Govt. Fin. Officers Assn., Delta Gamma. Republican. Baptist. Lodge: Zonta. Office: Mo State Auditor's Office 224 State Capitol PO Box 869 Jefferson City MO 65102-0869

KELLY, MARGIE EILENE, corporation executive; b. Somerset, Pa., Oct. 15, 1951; d. Theodore Roosevelt and Aretta Mae (Hetrick) Stoner; m. Harris G. Custer, July 4, 1969 (div. 1977); m. Richard Earl Burkett, Mar. 20, 1982 (div. 1991); 1 child, Tracy Sue; m. Charles Thomas Kelly, May 1, 1993. AA, Cambria Rowe Bus. Coll., 1971. Sec. Stoner Enterprises, Inc., Friedens, Pa., 1969-77, computer operator, 1977-82; pres. Stoner Quality Water, Inc. (formerly Stoner Enterprises), Friedens, 1992—. Republican. Home and Office: Stoner Enterprises Inc Stoner Quality Water Inc Rte 1 Friedens PA 15541-9801

KELLY, MARGUERITE STEHLI, fashion executive, consultant; b. N.Y.C., June 9, 1931; d. Henry E. and Grace (Hays) Stehli; m. Charles J. Kelly, Jr., Dec. 23, 1962; children: Marguerite Grace, Lisa Stehli. BA, Bryn Mawr Coll., 1953. Exec. trainee Macy's, N.Y.C., 1953-54, asst. buyer, 1954-57; buyer Bloomingdale's, N.Y.C., 1957-63; pres. Maggie, Inc., Wayzata, Minn., 1964-86; also brs. Maggie, Inc., Georgetown, D.C., 1964-70, Locust Valley, N.Y., 1970-75; ret., 1986; founder Workshop for Learning, 1987—. Mem. com. for spl. fund Foxcroft Sch., Middleburg, Va., 1974-76, trustee, 1978-87; mem. alumnae coun. Brearley Sch., N.Y.C., 1973-75; trustee Abbott Northwestern Hosp., Mpls., 1984-86; co-founder Citizens for Colin Powell 1996 Presdl. Draft Movement, 1996—. Episcopalian. Home: 3018 N St NW Washington DC 20007-3404

KELLY, MARIE THERESA, secondary education educator, accountant; b. Houston, June 29, 1960; d. Lowell Paul and Marolyn (Jamail) Thies; m. Michael Anthony Kelly, May 28, 1983; children: Amanda, Jacob. BBA, Stephen F. Austin U., 1982, MBA, 1987. CPA; cert. bus. and math tchr., Tex. Acct. White, Petrov & McHone, CPAs, Houston, 1982-83; acct.-CPA Alexander & Rogers, CPAs, Lufkin, Tex., 1983-84; contr. Nacoma Consol., Nacogdoches, Tex., 1984-85; CPA-ptnr. Crowell & Rhodes, CPAs, Nacogdoches, 1985-87; instr. acctg. Stephen F. Austin U., Nacogdoches, 1987-91; tchr. bus. and math. Douglass (Tex.) Ind. Sch. Dist., 1991—. Treas. Peace Officers' Spl. Support Enterprise, Nacogdoches, 1991-93. Mem. Tex. State Bd. Pub. Accountancy, Tex. Soc. CPAs. Office: Douglass Ind Sch Dist PO Box 38 Douglass TX 75943-0038

KELLY, MARY JOLSON, town agency administrator; b. Fairfield, Conn., Dec. 17, 1930; d. Alfred James and Justine Elizabeth (Houlihan) Jolson; divorced; children: Martin, Katie, Alfred, Patrick, John. BS, Russell Sage Coll., 1953; MS, U. Bridgeport, 1981. Cert. tchr. phys. edn., Conn. Playground supr. Town of Fairfield Recreation, 1952-57; tchr. phys. edn. City of Norwalk, Conn., 1953-54; tchr. phys. edn. Town of Fairfield, 1954-57, social worker, 1981-85, 86-87, acting dir. social svcs., 1985-86, dir. social svcs., 1987—. Elected to representative town meeting Town of Fairfield, 1980; chmn. patchworking Laura1ton Hall, Milford, Conn., 1987-89; chmn. Salvation Army, Fairfield, 1990-94; cons. United Home, Fairfield, 1990-94. Recipient Claven award Lauralton Hall, 1988. Democrat. Roman Catholic. Home: 76 Wakeman Rd Fairfield CT 06430 Office: Social Svcs Independence Hall Annex 725 Old Post Rd Fairfield CT 06430

KELLY, MARY LEE, university administrator; b. Bklyn., Aug. 16, 1963; d. Thomas J. and Anne D. (Tauckus) K. BA, Swarthmore Coll., 1981-85; MBA, Columbia U., 1991. Paralegal Hogan and Hartson, Washington, 1985-87; editorial asst. Defenders of Wildlife, Washington, 1987-89; univ. planning officer L.I. U., Brookville, N.Y., 1991—. Vol. Children's Hope Found., N.Y.C., 1991—, North Shore U. Hosp., Manhasset, N.Y., 1993—. Eugene Lang Grad. Incentive fellow, Swarthmore Coll., 1989; recipient Allied-Signal Corp. scholarship, Columbia U., 1990. Mem. Young Profls. Group of Fgn. Policy Assn. Democrat. Roman Catholic. Home: 47-27 Little Neck Pkwy #3J Little Neck NY 11362 Office: LI Univ University Ctr Brookville NY 11548

KELLY, MAXINE ANN, property developer; b. Ft. Wayne, Ind., Aug. 14, 1931; d. Victor J. and Marguerite E. (Biebesheimer) Cramer; m. James Herbert Kelly, Oct. 4, 1968 (dec. Apr. 74). BA, Northwestern U., 1956. Sec., Parry & Barns Law Offices, Ft. Wayne, 1951-52; trust sec. Lincoln Nat. Bank & Trust Co., 1956-58; sr. clk. stenographer div. Mental Health, Alaska Dept. Health, Anchorage, 1958-60; office mgr. Langdon Psychiat. Clinic, 1960-70; propr. A-1 Bookkeeping Svc., 1974-75; ptnr. Gonder-Kelly Enterprises & A-is-A Constrn., Wasilla, Alaska, 1965-92; sales assoc. Yukon Realty/Gallery of Homes, Wasilla, 1989; sec. Rogers Realty, Inc., Wasilla, 1989, MMC Constrn., Inc., 1992—. Dir. Alaska Mental Health Assn., Anchorage, 1960-61; pres., treas. Libertarian Party Anchorage, 1968-69, Alaska Libertarian Party, 1969-70. Mem. AAUW (life), Anchorage C. of C., Whittier Boat Owners Assn. (treas. 1980-84). Home: 8651 Augusta Cir Anchorage AK 99504-4202

KELLY, MERCEDES DALE, financial services company executive; b. New Orleans, Feb. 13, 1953; d. Morris Clement and Mercedes (Lewis) K.; children: Kimkya Laini, Kamal Yosef. BA, Vassar Coll., 1975; MSW, La. State U., 1981; postgrad., Internat. Factoring Inst., Orlando, Fla., 1993. Cert. factoring specialist. Counseling dir. Total Community Action, New Orleans, 1976-77; dir. East Baton Rouge Consumer Protection Ctr., 1977-79; profl. advocate Advocacy Ctr., Baton Rouge, 1981-83; exec. dir. Family Quest, Inc., Zachary, La., 1984-85; social work cons. La. State Dept. Edn., Baton Rouge, 1986-87; vol. svcs. dir. Hospice Found., Baton Rouge, 1986-87; program dir. United Way, New Orleans, 1988-93; social svc. practitioner San Bernadino (Calif.) County, 1989-93; owner Kelly's Brokerage and Fin. Svcs., Redlands, Calif., 1993—; cons. Boys and Girls Club, Redlands, 1993, Community Action Group, Redlands, 1993; factoring broker Kelly's Brokerage and Fin. Svcs., Redlands, 1993—. Contbr. articles to profl. jours. Bd. dirs. YWCA, Redlands, 1993; mem. Leadership Redlands, 1993. Named to Registry of Achievement, Am. Biog. Inst., 1994, Registry of Honors, Internat. Biog. Ctr., Cambridge, Eng., 1994. Mem. NAFE, Nat. Alliance Black Entrepreneurs, Womens Referral Svc., Nat. Assn. Factoring Profls., Redlands C. of C. Democrat. Roman Catholic. Office: Kelly's Brokerage/Fin Svcs PO Box 7003 Redlands CA 92375-0003

KELLY, MICHELE, family counselor; b. Kingston, Pa., Dec. 14, 1958; d. Joseph Francis and Margaret (James) Pugliese; m. Mark Francis Kelly, Mar. 6, 1982; children: Mark Shemus, Luke Joseph. BA in Psychology, Wilkes U., 1980; MA in Counseling, Marywood Coll., 1982. Sec., 1976-82, sales ptnr., 1982—; counselor Kingston, Pa., 1992—; pres. Depression After Delivery, Inc., 1994—; coord., co-facilitator Depression and Anxiety after Delivery N.E. Pa., 1989-91; coord. postpartum depression adv. bd. Nesbitt Meml. Hosp., Kingston, 1990, initiator med. conf. postpartum disorders, 1990, vol. conf. com. Vol. telephone counselor Depression After Delivery, 1989-92, bd. trustees, 1990-94; active Youth Ministry Program, 1979, Marriage Sponsor Program, 1993—. Mem. APA, Postpartum Support Internat. Office: 601 Wyoming Ave Kingston PA 18704

KELLY, NANCY FOLDEN, arts administrator; b. Fredericksburg, Va., Oct. 28, 1951; d. Virgil Alvis Jr. and Frances Virginia (DeShazo) Folden; m. Frank R. Kelly, Aug. 11, 1973. BA in Theaatre Arts, Va. Poly. Inst. and State U., 1973; MFA in Theatre Directing, So. Meth. U., 1975. Coord. student programs Lincoln Ctr. Inst., N.Y.C., 1976-79; dir. N.Y.C. Opera Nat. Co. and edn. dept. Lincoln Ctr., 1979-93, mem. coun. on ednl. programs, 1979-93; mng. dir. Broadway Arts Theatre for Young Audiences, 1994—.

KELLY, NANCY FRIEDA WOLICKI, lawyer; b. Chgo., Sept. 8, 1953; d. Samuel and Ingrid (Rappel) W.; B.A. in Journalism and Sociology, U. Ariz., 1974, J.D., 1977. Bar: Ariz., 1977; law clk. Ariz. Ct. Appeals, 1977-78; legis. asst. fgn. policy and armed svcs. health, staff atty. Billy Carter investigation to U.S. Sen. Dennis DeConcini, 1979-81; staff dir. Senate Subcom. on Alcoholism and Drug Abuse, Washington, 1981-84; mem. staff Senator Gordon J. Humphrey, Washington, 1984-87; coord. adv. com. Voluntary Fgn. U.S. Aid, 1987; sr. analyst legal and drug related issues President's Commn. on the HIV Epidemic, 1987-88; sr. policy analyst Commn. Exec. Legis. Jud. Salaries, 1988-89; counselor Sec. Energy, 1989-93; sr. cons. Kelly, Anderson, Pethick & Assocs., Washington, 1993—. Recipient William Spaid Meml. award U. Ariz. Coll. Law, 1977, Senate commendation for Billy Carter investigation, 1980. Mem. Ariz. Bar Assn., Phi Kappa Phi. Jewish. Office: 1020 19th St NW Ste 800 Washington DC 20036

KELLY, PAMELA J., accountant; b. Breckenridge, Minn., Oct. 25, 1948; d. John T. and Anita Ruth (Knudsen) Sanker; m. James Wayne Kelly, May 10, 1969 (div. May 1993); children: Jamison Marc, Brian Lee. BA in Music Edn., Concordia Coll., Moorhead, Minn., 1969; BS in Indsl. Adminstrn., Iowa State U., 1980. CPA, Iowa. Band and choir tchr. Danube (Minn.) Ind. Schs., 1969-70; orch. tchr. Raleigh (N.C.) City Schs., 1972-73; French and English tchr. Bethel Acad., Kinston, N.C., 1974; jr. high sch. music tchr. Lenoir County Schs., Kinston, 1974-76; in-charge staff auditor McGladrey Pullen, Des Moines, 1980-82; with internal auditing dept. Am. Fed. Savs. & Loan, Des Moines, 1982-84; v.p. fin. Gentry, Ltd., Des Moines, 1984-89; dir. property mgmt. adminstrn. R&R Investors, Ltd., West Des Moines, Iowa, 1989—; mem. acct. adv. bd. Am. Inst. Bus., Des Moines, 1988-94. Chairperson Holy Trinity Luth. Ch., Ankeny, Iowa, 1991. Recipient Elijah Watts Sells award AICPA, 1980. Mem. Iowa Soc. CPAs, Mensa, Des Moines Choral Soc., Phi Beta Kappa. Home: 909 SE Kensington Rd Ankeny IA 50021 Office: 4401 Westown Pkwy Ste 212 West Des Moines IA 50266

KELLY, PATTY, elementary education educator, business owner; b. Cohoes, N.Y., May 31, 1936; d. Daniel J. and Lucie Anne (Montmarquet) K.; m. W. Umenhofer; children: Kelly, Judith Lucie, Danny, John; m. Jose Botello, May 7, 1968 (div. Jan. 1974); 1 child, Jennifer; m. Leon Conner, Apr. 3, 1974; children: Patrick, Michael. AA, Ariz. Western Coll., 1986; BA in Edn., No. Ariz. U., 1990. Bank teller N.Y.C., 1954-56; postal person Fremont, Calif., 1966-67; dealer Las Vegas, 1967-68, camera girl, 1970-72, cocktail waitress, 1968-74, bartender, 1971-74; grape picker Dateland, Ariz., 1975-76; bus. owner, mgr. Dateland, 1974—, post person, 1982-90; 6th grade tchr. Dateland, Ariz., 1990—. pres. sch. bd., Dateland, 1985-90. Mem. Phi Theta Kappa. Democrat. Home: H C Box 6 Dateland AZ 85333

KELLY, PEGGY DOBBS, health supervisor; b. Palatka, Fla., July 27, 1949; d. Thomas and Mary (Kummer) Dobbs; divorced; children: Claire Francine, Mary Katherine. Student, U. Montevallo; AA, Sacred Heart Coll., 1967; BS in Health, Phys. Edn., Recreation and Dance, St. Bernard Coll., 1970. Tchr. K-12 Fla. Schs., 1970—; health supr. N.E. Fla. Ednl. Consortium, Palatka, 1988—. Coord. child abuse prevention project U. Fla., Gainesville, 1985-87; field rep. Gateway coun. Girl Scouts Am., Jacksonville, Fla., 1974-76; coord. ch. youth choir and liturgy, 1981-85; coun. chair, coord. Drug Prevention, 1983-85; youth trainer in AIDS/Peer Edn., 1991—. Named Outstanding Woman in Putnam County, Palatka Daily News, 1986. Mem. Fla. Assn. Profl. Health Educators (cert. health educator, sec./bd. govs. 1990-94), Fla. Alcohol and Drug Abuse Assn., Fla. Sch. Health Assn. Democrat. Roman Catholic. Office: NE Fla Ednl Consortium 3841 Reid St Palatka FL 32177

KELLY, SHARON PRATT, former mayor; b. Washington, Jan. 30, 1944; d. Carlisle and Mildred (Petticord) Pratt; children: Aimee Arrington, Drew Arrington; m. James Kelly III, Dec. 7, 1991; 1 child, Khrys Kelly. BA, Howard U., 1965, JD, 1968. Bar: D.C. 1970, U.S. Dist. Ct. D.C. 1970, U.S. Ct. Appeals (D.C. cir.) 1970, U.S. Tax Ct. 1970. Assoc. Pratt & Queen, P.C., Washington, 1971-76; lawyer, prof. Antioch Sch. Law, Washington, 1972-76; assoc. gen. counsel Potomac Electric and Power Co., Washington, 1976-79, dir. consumer affairs, 1979-83, v.p. consumer affairs, 1983-86, v.p. pub. policy, 1986-89; mayor Washington, D.C., 1990-94. Chmn. Ea. regional caucus Dem. Nat. Com., Washington, 1976-85, treas., 1985-89; nat. committeeperson D.C. State Com., Washington, 1977—. Recipient Disting. Svc. award Fedn. Women's Clubs, 1986, Nat. Assn. Black Women Attys., 1987, 88, Presdl. award NAACP, 1983, Disting. Leadership award United Negro Coll. Fund, 1985. Mem. Women's Rsch. and Ednl. Inst. (bd. dirs. 1986-88), D.C. Unified Bar, D.C. Bar Assn., Links Club, Jack & Jill Club. Home: 1525 Iris St NW Washington DC 20012 Office: Office of Mayor 1 Judiciary Sq 441 4th St NW Washington DC 20001

KELLY, SUE W., congresswoman; b. Lima, Ohio, Sept. 26, 1936; m. Edward; 4 children. BA, Denison U., 1958; MA in Health Advocacy, Sarah Lawrence Coll., 1985. Researcher New England Inst. Med. Rsch., 1958; tchr. John Jay Jr. H.S., 1962-63, Harvey Sch.; real estate rehabilitator, 1963—; campaign coord. Rep. Hamilton Fish, N.Y., 1971-72; intern Ruth Taylor Home, 1973-74; florist, owner Somerstown Flower Shop, 1978-79; patient advocate St. Luke's Hosp., 1984-87; adj. prof. of health advocacy Sarah Lawrence Coll., 1987-92. Office: US House Reps 2354 Rayburn House Office Bldg Washington DC 20515-3219*

KELLY, TISH, state legislator; m. John Kelly; 3 children. BA, U. Md. Mem. N.D. Ho. of Reps., 1975-89; mem. legis. coun.; mem. constn. celebration com.; mem. appropriations, legis procedure coms.; mem. N.D. Senate, 1990—; mem. appropriations com.; active Close Up Found. Democrat. Home: 404 S University Dr Fargo ND 58103-1765 Office: ND Senate State Capitol Bismarck ND 58505*

KELLY, VIRGINIA ANN, education educator, research consultant; b. N.Y.C., Feb. 25, 1956; d. Joseph Neil and Marilyn Theresa (Murphy) Ruocco; m. William Michael Kelly, Oct. 6, 1984; children: Drew Thomas, Charles Joseph. BS, SUNY Geneseo, 1978; MEd, Pa. State U., 1980; PhD, U. N.C. Greensboro, 1993. Nat. cert. counselor; cert. sch. guidance counselor, N.C. Rsch. asst. Pa. State U., University Park, 1979-80; supr. Young Adult Inst., N.Y.C., 1980-82; dir. Cath. Charities, Bklyn., 1982-84; tng. specialist Chase Manhattan Bank, N.Y.C., 1984-86; guidance counselor Guilford County (N.C.) Schs., Greensboro, 1986-88; grad. asst. U. N.C. Greensboro, 1988-91, statis. cons., 1991-93; asst. prof. U. Cin., 1993—; rsch. cons. Aring Inst., Cin., 1993—, Transitions, Inc., Covington, Ky., 1993—; coord. Summer Inst. Counseling and Sch. Psychology. Co-author (manual) Say Yes to Yourself, 1990; ad hoc editor Jour. Counseling and Devel.; contbr. articles to profl. jours. Mem. League Women Voters, Cin., 1993-94; mem. and speaker Aring Family Network. Grantee U.S. Dept. Edn., 1990-91, Provostal Support Instrnl. Devel., 1994. Mem. Am. Counseling Assn., Ohio Counseling Assn. Democrat. Home: 4002 Ballard Ave Cincinnati OH 45209-1718 Office: U Cin Coll Edn Divsn Human Svcs 522 Teachers Coll Cincinnati OH 45221

KELLY-CHARLES, PATRICIA CHARLENE, counselor; b. Omak, Wash., Oct. 27, 1946; d. Lawrence V. and Ethel G. (Voyles) Forsythe; m. Richard W. Dunkin, Aug. 13, 1966 (div. 1971); children: Nikki J. Dunkin Brown, Jason L. Dunkin; m. Patrick J. Charles, Oct. 31, 1993. Lic., Mr. Lee's Sch. Cosmetology, 1966; BA, East Wash. U., 1988. Registered counselor. Hairdresser Garards, Spokane, Wash., 1966-68, Martins, Twisp, Wash., 1968-71; youth specialist Youth Resource Ctr., Everett, Wash., 1978-83; dir. residential substance abuse program Okanogan (Wash.) County Juvenile, 1983-86; project coord. Omak (Wash.) S.D., 1986-87; JTPA counselor Employment Security, Omak, 1987-88; student assistance program dir. Methow Valley S.D., Twisp, 1988-91; prevention/intervention specialist North Ctrl. ESD, Wenatchee, Wash., 1991—; cons. Okanogan County Drug Prevention Program, 1988—; presenter workshops in field, 1988—. Coord. spl. events Health Week, Symposium at Risk Youth Conf., 1992—; bd. dirs. Okanogan County Health Dept. Teen Health Line, 1991—, Cmty. Action, Okanogan, 1990-91. Named Educator of Yr., 1988. Office: North Ctrl ESD PO Box 1846 Wenatchee WA 98801

KELLY-MACKENZIE, JILL WHITTIER, clinical psychologist; b. Boston, Aug. 12, 1947; d. Sumner Gage and Jessie (Johnston) W.; married; children: Jennifer, Heather, Elizabeth. BA, Mt. Holyoke Coll., 1969; MA, Wayne State U., 1976, PhD, 1978. Pvt. practice clin. psychology Birmingham, Mich., 1976—. Author: The Golden Fairy, 1990, Jennifer, 1991. Pres., sec. Woodbrook Nursery Sch. Bd., Bloomfield Hills, Mich., 1981-84; mem. Kirk in the Hills Nursery Sch. Bd., Bloomfield Hills, 1989—; pres. Kirk Nursery Sch., 1993—; active Kaleidoscope Steering Com., Bloomfield Hills, 1983-86, Cranbrook/Kingswood Schs. Mothers Coun., Bloomfield Hills, 1983—; sch. rep. Birmingham Bloomfield Families in Action, 1988-91; freedom writer Amnesty Internat., N.Y.C., 1988-92. Mem. Am. Psychol. Assn., Mich. Psychol. Assn., Mich. Women Psychologists, Kirk in the Hills Garden Guild (sec. 1993—). Republican. Presbyterian. Office: 1050 Webster Birmingham MI 48009-6963

KELM, BONNIE G., art museum director, educator; b. Bklyn., Mar. 29, 1947; d. Julius and Anita (Baron) Steiman; m. William G. Malis; 1 child, Michael Darren. BS in Art Education, Buffalo State U., 1968; MA in Art History, Bowling Green (Ohio) State U., 1975; PhD in Arts Adminstrn., Ohio State U., 1987. Art tchr. Toledo Pub. Schs., 1968-71; ednl. cons. Columbus (Ohio) Mus. Art, 1976-81; prof. art Franklin U., Columbus, 1976-88; legis. coord. Ohio House of Reps., Columbus, 1977; pres. bd. trustees Columbus Inst. for Contemporary Art, 1977-81; tech. asst. cons. Ohio Arts Coun., Columbus, 1984-88; dir. Bunte Gallery Franklin U., Columbus, 1978-88; dir. art mus. Miami U., Oxford, Ohio, 1988—; assoc. prof. Miami U., 1988—; grant panelist Ohio Arts Coun., Columbus, 1985-87, 91—; art book reviewer William C. Brown Pub., Madison, Wis., 1985-92; mem. acquistions adv. bd. Martin Luther King Ctr., Columbus, 1987-88; field reviewer Inst. Mus. Svcs., Washington, 1990—; chairperson grant panel Art in Pub. Places, 1992—; trustee Ohio Mus. Assn., 1993—. Contbr. articles to profl. publs.; author, editor (mus. catalogues) Connections, 1985, Into the Mainstream: Contemporary Folk Art, 1991, Testimony of Images: PreColumbian Art, 1992. Founding mem., mem. adv. coun. Columbus Cultural Arts Ctr., 1977-81; coord., curator Cultural Exch. Program, Honolulu-Columbus, 1980; mem. acad. women achievers YWCA, 1991; guest speaker 1991 Scholastic Arts Award, Cin., 1991; keynote speaker Ohio Mus. Assn., ann. meeting, 1992; speaker Internat. Coun. Mus. Triennial Conf., Quebec City, 1992;

session chair Midwest Mus. Assn. ann. meeting, St. Louis, 1993. Recipient Gelpe award YWCA, 1987, Cultural Advancement of City of Columbus award, The Columbus Dispatch, 1984, Disting. Svc. award, Columbus Art League, 1984, Critic's Choice award Found. for Community of Artists, N.Y., 1981; Fulbright scholar USIA, 1988 (The Netherlands); NEH fellow East-West Ctr., Honolulu, 1991. Mem. Am. Assn. Mus. (advocacy task force), Assn. of Coll. and Univ. Mus. and Galleries, Midwest Mus. Assn., Fulbright Assn., Coll. Arts Assn., Internat. Coun. Mus., Ohio Mus. Assn. (bd. dirs. 1993—). Office: Miami U Art Mus Patterson Ave Oxford OH 45056-1605

KELM, LINDA, opera singer; b. Salt Lake City, Dec. 11, 1944; d. Robert Gordon and Hettie Frances Kelm. Studies with Elizabeth Hayes Simpson, Salt Lake City, 1963-75; studies with Jennie Tourel, Aspen, Colo., 1968; studies with Judith Oas, N.Y.C., 1975-84, L.A., 1994—. Profl. debut in Der Ring des Nibelungen, 1977; performed in Die Walküre and Götterdämmerung, 1977-83; sang title role in Turandot, 1979, Salome, 1984, Fidelio, 1987, Elektra, 1990, Tristan und Isolde, 1991; performed with: Rai Radio Orch. (Rome), Residentie Orkest of Holland, Minn. Orch., Utah Symphony, Opera Orch. N.Y., Chgo. Symphony, San Francisco Symphony, St. Louis Symphony, Pitts. Symphony, Balt. Symphony, Denver Symphony, Detroit Symphony, Seattle Symphony, N.J. Symphony, L.I. Philharm., San Antonio Symphony, Houston Grand Opera, N.Y.C. Opera, San Francisco Opera, Deutsche Oper/Berlin, Associaciones Bilbania de Amigos de Opera-Bilbao, Spain, Hamburgische Staatsoper, Mexico City Opera, Ky. Opera, Utah Opera, Portland Opera, Greater Miami Opera, L.A. Philharm., City of Birmingham Symphony Orch., Tokyo Symphony Orch., Orchestre de Bordeaux-Aquitaine, Cin. Orch., Phoenix Symphony Orch., Bklyn. Philharm. Orch., Symphony of the New World, Philippine Youth Symphony Orch., Spokane Opera; sang role of Brünnhilde, Seattle Wagner Festival, 1986, 87; appeared in maj. opera houses throughout the world; Met. Opera debut Brünnhilde in Siegfried, 1988; Avery Fisher Hall debut, 1987; Carnegie Hall debut, 1988, Concertgebouw debut, 1983, Royal Festival Hall debut, 1989, May Festival debut, 1986; rec. debut Helmwige in Deutsche Gramophon, Die Walküre Met. Opera, 1988 (Grammy award). Nat. Fedn. of Women's Club scholar, 1968; grantee PEO Sisterhood, 1979, Nat. Inst. of Music Theatre grantee, 1979, 80. Mem. Am. Guild of Musical Artists, Internat. Order of Job's Daughters (past Bethel guardian, majority mem.). Methodist. Home: c/o 2744 Grandview Cir Salt Lake City UT 84106 Address: 1263 Robinson Ave # 31 San Diego CA 92103-4468

KELSCH, RAEANN, state legislator; m. Thomas D. Kelsch; 3 children. BBA, U. N.D. Mem. N.D. Ho. of Reps.; vice chmn. judiciary com., mem. govt. and vets. affairs com. Bd. dirs. United Way; active AID, Inc. Republican. Home: 1411 Second St NW # 6 Mandan ND 58554 Office: ND Ho of Reps State Capitol Bismarck ND 58505*

KELSEY, EDITH JEANINE, psychotherapist, consultant; b. Freeport, Ill., Oct. 15, 1937; d. John Melvin and Florence Lucille (Ewald) Anderson; divorced; children: Steven Craig, Kevin John. Student, Pasadena Coll., 1955-58; BA in Psychology, Calif. State U., San Jose, 1980; MA in Counseling Psychology, Santa Clara U., 1984. Lic. marriage, family and child counselor. Counselor, cons., cert. trainer Values Tech., Santa Cruz, Calif., 1981—, dir. research, 1982-84; intern in counseling Sr. Residential Services, San Jose, 1983-84; psychotherapist Process Therapy Inst., Los Gatos, Calif., 1983-86, Sexual Abuse Treatment Ctr., San Jose, 1984-87; cons. in field, Santa Clara Valley, 1982—; trainer, cons. Omega Assoc., 1987-88; teaching asst. Santa Clara U., 1987-88; pvt. practice psychotherapy, cons., tng., 1987—. Contbr. articles to profl. jours. Vol. Parental Stress Hotline, Palo Alto, Calif., 1980-85. Mem. Am. Assn. Marriage and Family Therapists, Am. Soc. Aging, Calif. Assn. Marriage and Family Therapists (clin.), Sierra Club. Democrat. Presbyterian. Home: 431 Casita Ct Los Altos CA 94022 Office: 153 Forest Ave Palo Alto CA 94301-1615

KELSEY, FRANCES OLDHAM (MRS. FREMONT ELLIS KELSEY), government official; b. Cobble Hill, Vancouver Island, Can., July 24, 1914; came to U.S., 1936, naturalized, 1956; d. Frank Trevor and Katherine (Stuart) Oldham; m. Fremont Ellis Kelsey, Dec. 6, 1943; children—Susan Elizabeth, Christine Ann. B.Sc., McGill U., 1934; M.Sc., 1935; Ph.D., U. Chgo., 1938, M.D., 1950. Instr., asst. prof. pharmacology U. Chgo., 1938-50; editorial assoc. AMA, Chgo., 1950-52; assoc. prof. pharmacology U. S.D., 1954-57; med. officer FDA, Washington, 1960—; dir. div. sci. investigations FDA, 1967—. Author: (with F.E. Kelsey, E.M.K. Geiling) Essentials of Pharmacology, 1960. Recipient Pres.'s award for Distinguished Fed. Civilian Service (refusal to approve coml. distbn. thalidomide in U.S.), 1962. Mem. Am. Soc. Pharmacology and Exptl. Therapeutics, Soc. Exptl. Biology and Medicine, Am. Med. Writers Assn., Teratology Soc., Sigma Xi, Sigma Delta Epsilon. Home: 5811 Brookside Dr Bethesda MD 20815-6669 Office: FDA Office of Compliance 7520 Standish Pl Rockville MD 20855-2737

KELSO, ANN BREEDING, fine arts education curator; b. Hollywood, Fla., Sept. 21, 1945; d. Harvey James and Ruth (Lige) Breeding; m. John Russell Kelso, July 22, 1972 (div. Feb. 1984); 1 child, Anna Liege. BA in Fgn. Lang., U. Ky., 1967; MA in History of Art, Ohio State U., 1971. Curatorial intern Lowe Art Mus., Coral Gables, Fla., 1972; adj. faculty Fla. Atlantic U., Boca Raton, Fla., 1972-73, 78; lectr. Miami (Fla.) Dade Community Coll., 1974, with art-music workshop, 1980-81; lectr.-cons., 1972—; adj. faculty music dept. Miami Dade (Fla.) Community Coll., 1991; curator of edn. Ctr. for the Fine Arts, Miami, 1987-92, High Mus. of Art, Atlanta, Ga., 1992—; mem. Artists in Edn. Panel, Ga. Coun. for Arts, 1994; field reviewer Inst. Mus. Svcs., 1994. Contbg. editor African Art: An Essay for Teachers, 1993. Recipient Nat. award for graphics Mead Paper Co., 1989, Gold Medal of Honor, S.E. Mus. Educators Publ. Design, 1994. Mem. Am. Assn. of Mus., Inst. Mus. Svcs., Nat. Art Edn. Assn., Fla. Art Edn. Assn. (dir. mus. divsn.), Ga. Art Edn. Assn. (dir. mus. divsn., Mus. Educator of Yr. 1993). Home: 2420 Mitchell Rd Marietta GA 30062-5321 Office: High Mus of Art 1280 Peachtree St NE Atlanta GA 30309

KELSO, BECKY, state legislator; b. 1948; m. Michael Kelso; 2 children. BA in Comm., U. Minn. Mem. Minn. Ho. of Reps., 1986—; mem. capital investment com., mem. edn. com., mem. regulated industries and energy com., mem. transp. and transit com. Home: 60 S Shannon Dr Shakopee MN 55379-8025 Office: Minn State Senate State Capital Saint Paul MN 55155 also: 415 State Office Bldg Saint Paul MN 55155*

KELSO, GWENDOLYN LEE, silver appraiser, consultant; b. Washington, Jan. 5, 1935; d. Leon Hugh and Katherine Estelle (Henderson) K. Mgr. Shaw & Brown Co., Washington, 1967-71, Chas. Schwartz & Son, Washington, 1972-76; silver appraiser, Washington, 1976—; ptnr. The Silver Lion, Washington, 1983-85; owner, mgr. The Rampant Lion, Washington, 1985—; cons. FBI and law enforcement agys. and ctrs., 1982—; cataloguer and conservator hist. silver belonging to USN and U.S. Naval Acad., 1987—; appraiser presentation silver aboard U.S. Naval vessels and at installations, 1986-88; cataloguer, conservator silver Forbes Mag. Collection, N.Y.C., 1989; mem. USS Alexandria Commissioning Com., 1990; conservator State of Md. for preservation Battleship USS Md. presentation silver, 1990; instr. USN pers. for care and maintenance preservation silver. Author: United States Navy Presentation Silver- a History and a Manual for its Care and Preservation, 1989, Silver Reflections an American Naval History, 1991. Mem. Internat. Soc. Appraisers (scholar 1989), Am. Soc. Appraisers, Appraisers Assn. Am., Silver Soc. (London), NAFE, U.S. Naval Inst., Newcomen Soc. U.S. Republican. Episcopalian. Home: 3731 39th St NW Washington DC 20016-5522 Office: The Rampant Lion PO Box 5887 Washington DC 20016-1487

KELSO, MARY CATHERINE, controller; b. Neptune, N.J., Oct. 24, 1964; d. David and Esther Veronica (Cassidy) K. AA, Brookdale C.C., Lincroft, N.J., 1984; BS, Monmouth Coll., 1986, MBA, 1993; postgrad., Fairleigh Dickinson U. Mgr. operational review MCOSS, Inc., Red Bank, N.J., 1992-93; mgr. acctg. MCoss, Inc., Red Bank, N.J., 1988-92, fin. analyst, 1987-88, staff acct., 1986-87; controller The Presbyn. Home at Monroe, Inc., Jamesburg, N.J., 1993—. Mem. Inst. of Mgmt. Accounts, Coll. Healthcare Execs. (student chpt. of Am.). Office: Presbyn Home at Monroe One David Brainerd Dr Jamesburg NJ 08831

KEMMERER, SHARON JEAN, computer systems analyst; b. Sellersville, Pa., Apr. 11, 1956; d. John Musselman and Esther Jone (Landis) K. BS, Shippensburg U., 1978; MBA, Marymount Coll., 1982. Mgmt. analyst Navy Internat. Logistics, Phila., 1978-81; computer systems analyst Navy Supply Systems Commn., Crystal City, Va., 1981-86, Nat. Inst. Standards and Tech., Gaithersburg, Md., 1986—; bd. dirs. ComSci, Derwood Sta.; adult tutoring, 1991—. Contbr. articles, poetry to newspapers; author publs. Deacon Alexandria (Va.) Ch., 1985-86, v.p. coun., 1985; moderator Lung Assn., Fairfax, Va., 1986; vol. Project Heart, Washington, 1986-87, Montgomery County Health Buddy, 1988—, Stepping Stones Shelter for Homeless, 1989-91, Pets on Wheels, 1994—, Stewardship Com., 1995—. Lutheran. Office: NIST/CSL Gaithersburg MD 20899

KEMNA, MARGARITA ELISABETH, medical technologist; b. Weisbaden, West Germany, Dec. 21, 1947; d. Robert. I. and Elli E. (Mahler) K. BS in Med. Technology, Hartwick Coll., 1969; cert., United Hosp. Sch. Med. Tech., Pt. Chester, N.Y., 1969. Technologist lab. VA Med. Ctr., Iowa City, 1969-71, Bklyn. Jewish Hosp., 1971-77; sr. instr. microbiology Sch. Med. Tech. Albany (N.Y.) Med. Ctr. Hosp., 1977-82; supr. mycology lab. Wadsworth Ctr. for Labs. and Rsch. N.Y. State Dept. Health, Albany, 1982-93; mgr. mycology reference lab. dept. dermatology Case Western Res. U., Cleve., 1993—; Com. mem., chmn. public employees fedn. health and safety com. Dept. Health, Albany, 1990-93; mem. adv. com. med. tech. program Hudson Valley C.C., Troy, N.Y., 1991-93. Contbr. rsch. articles to sci. jours. and procs. Named one of Outstanding Young Women of Am., 1979. Mem. Internat. Soc. Human and Animal Mycology, Mycology Soc. of the Ams., Am. Soc. Clin. Pathologists (registered med. technologist), Am. Soc. Microbiology, Med. Mycology Soc. of the Ams., Med. Mycol. Soc. N.Y., Omicron Sigma. Office: Case Western Res U Dept Dermatology Mycology Reference Lab Cleveland OH 44106

KEMP, ANN, retired librarian; b. Providence, Ky., Aug. 2, 1941; d. Charlie and Rubye (Sigler) Kemp Page. BA, Belmont U., 1964; MLS, Vanderbilt U., 1965, postgrad., 1968-79. Cert. tchr., Ky. Libr. Nashville Pub. Libr., 1965, U. Louisville Libr., 1965-67, Dawson Springs (Ky.) Ind. Schs., 1967-93; ret., 1993; instr. Murray (Ky.) State U., 1973-78. Baptist. Home: 113 Woodlawn Dr Madisonville KY 42431

KEMP, BETTY RUTH, librarian; b. Tishomingo, Okla., May 5, 1930; d. Raymond Herrell and Mamie Melvina (Hughes) K.; BA in Libr. Sci., U. Okla., 1952; MS, Fla. State U., 1965. Extramural loan libr. U. Tex., Austin, 1952-55; libr. lit. and history dept. Dallas Pub. Libr., 1955-56, head Oaklawn Br., 1956-60, head Walnut Hill Br., 1960-64; dir. Cherokee Regional Libr., LaFayette, Ga., 1965-74; dir. Lee County Libr., hdqrs. Lee-Itawamba Libr. System, Tupelo, Miss., 1975-92; bd. libr. commrs. State of Miss., 1979-83, chmn., 1979-80. Chmn. Chickasaw Hist. Soc., 1994—; active LWV, Native Am. Chickasaw Nation, United Meth. Women. Mem. AAUW, ALA, Nat. Soc. Daus.Am. Colonists, Nat. Soc. U.S. Daus. of 1812, United Daus. of the Confedercy, Nat. Soc. Dames of Ct. of Honor, Am. Indian Cultural Soc. (Norman Okla.), First Families Twin Ters., Beta Phi Mu. Democrat. Home: 3313 Winchester Cir Norman OK 73072-2937 Office: Kemp Rsch & Cons Svc PO Box 7720531 Norman OK 73070

KEMP, GINA CHRISTINE, rehabilitation services professional; b. New Orleans, June 5, 1968; d. Donald Rue and July Carol (Sallee) K.; m. Patrick E. Hutto, May 15, 1994; 1 stepchild, Patrick B. BA in Psychology, So. Coll., Collegedale, Tenn., 1989; MA in Edn., U. Ga., 1991. Sociology tchr. So. Coll., 1989; counselor offender rehab., GED examiner IW Davis Detention Ctr., Jefferson, Ga., 1991; counselor offender rehab. drug specialist Alcovy Diversion Ctr., Monroe, Ga., 1991—; boot camp officer Ga. Dept. Corrections. Mem. ACA, Nat. Bd. Cert. Counselors, Internat. Assn. Addictions and Offender Counseling, Chi Sigma Iota, Psi Chi. Republican. Adventist. Home: 4077 Wedgefield Cir Decatur GA 30035-2392 Office: Alcovy Diversion Ctr PO Box 1600 Monroe GA 30655-6600

KEMP, H. JANE, librarian; b. Davenport, Iowa, Apr. 10, 1944; d. Milton and Henrietta Jane (Bonnell) Zagel; m. Donald R. Kemp, Apr. 25, 1969; 1 child, Anna Mary Amanda. BA, U. Iowa, 1966; MLS, U. Pitts., 1971. Libr. Luther Coll., Decorah, Iowa, 1981—. Bibliographer: (book) Letters of Gerhard Marcks, 1991; contbr. articles to profl. jours. Grantee Am. Luth. Ch., 1988, 92. Mem. ALA, Art Librs. Assn. N.Am., Am. Assn. Mus., Assn. Coll. and Rsch. Libr. (pres. Iowa chpt. 1989), Iowa Libr. Assn. (exec. bd. 1991-93). Democrat. Lutheran. Office: Luther Coll Preus Libr 700 College Dr Decorah IA 52101-1045

KEMP, JEANNE FRANCES, office manager; b. L.A., Dec. 8, 1942; d. Damian Thomas and Helen Catherine (Bohin) Hanifee; m. Don H. Kemp, Dec. 16, 1966 (div. 1972). AB, San Francisco State U., 1965. Food svc. technician United Air Lines, San Francisco, 1961-65; clk. N.Y. Life Ins., San Francisco, 1965-66; inventory clk. Ingersoll-Rand, San Francisco, 1966; advt./order clk. Patrick's Stationers, San Francisco, 1966-67; sec. Dartmouth Travel, Hanover, N.H., 1967-68, Olsten Temp. Svcs., N.Y.C., 1968-70; office mgr. Brown U. Devel., N.Y.C., 1970-73; asst. dir. Cen. Opera Svc., N.Y.C., 1974-85; office mgr., sec. Payne, Thompson, Walker & Taaffe, San Francisco, 1986—. Editor: Career Guide...Singers, 1985, Operas...for Children, 1985; asst. editor COS Bull., 1976-85; editorial asst.: Who's Who in Opera, 1975. Democrat. Roman Catholic. Office: Payne Thompson Walker & Taaffe 235 Montgomery St Ste 760 San Francisco CA 94104-2910

KEMP, MAE WUNDER, real estate broker, consultant; b. Balt.; d. Edward J. and Helen (Robel) Wunder; m. George C. Segerman, May 17, 1941 (div. 1959); children: Barbara, George C.; m. Robert B. Kemp, July 23, 1960 (dec. 1989). BA, Notre Dame Coll., 1941. Pres. Realty Sales corp., Balt., 1958-60; records mgmt. cons. Boeing Co., Seattle, 1960-65; v.p., real estate broker Satellite Realty, Mercer Island, Wash., 1973-76; real estate broker Washington Properties Real Estate, Seattle, 1970-76; assoc. broker John L. Scott Real Estate, Seattle, 1976-92; tech. adviser of real estate North Seattle Community Coll., 1973-80. Mem. Seattle Women's Commn., 1973; precinct committeewoman Seattle Rep. Com., 1973; v.p. Freedoms Found., Valley Forge, Pa., 1974; past pres., pres. emeritus Hawthorne Hills Community Club, Inc., Seattle, 1974-90; chmn. Seattle's First Citizen Award. Recipient 5 State Regional Chmn. award, Woman of Yr., Omega Tau Rho medal Nat. Assn. Realtors, Seattle, Sales Assoc. of Yr. award Seattle Real Estate Bd., Outstanding Woman in Real Estate award Past Pres. Club, Woman of Day award Sta. KIXI, CBS. Mem. Wash. Assn. Realtors, Seattle-King County Bd. Realtors (bd. dirs.), Nat. Assn. Real Estate Brokers, Women's Assn. Hilton Head Island, Wash. Athletic Club, Country Club Hilton Head (mem. com., house com.), Navy League of U.S., Hilton Head Island Coun. Republican. Roman Catholic. Home: 37 Club Course Dr Hilton Head Island SC 29928-3137

KEMP, SUZANNE LEPPART, educator, clubwoman; b. N.Y.C., Dec. 28, 1929; d. John Culver and Eleanor (Buxton) Leppart; m. Ralph Clinton Kemp, Apr. 4, 1953; children—Valerie Gale, Sandra Lynn, John Maynard, Renee Alison. Grad. Ogontz Jr. Coll., 1949; B.S., U. Md., 1952. Elem. sch. tchr. Mem. Nat. Soc. Women Descs. of Ancient and Hon. Arty. Co., Nat. Soc. Daus. of Founders and Patriots of Am. (corr. sec.), Nat. Soc. Sons and Daus. of Pilgrims, Nat. Soc. U.S. Daus. of 1812 (chpt. organizing Md. state pres. 1977-79, chpt. v.p. 1979—), Nat. Soc. New Eng. Women (colony pres. 1978-80, Nat. Soc. Colonial Dames XVII Century (state chmn. heraldry and coats of arms 1977-79), Nat. Soc. D.A.R. (chpt. regent 1970-73, chpt. v.p., Md. soc. chmn. transp. 1976-79), Md. State Officers Club, Md. Hist. Soc., Friends of Animals, Defenders of Animal Rights Inc., U. Md. Alumni, English Speaking Union, Star Spangled Banner Flag House Assn., Potter-Balt. Clayworks, Balt. Mus. Art, Walters Art Gallery, Dames of the Court of Honor, Kappa Delta Alumni. Clubs: Baltimore Country; Lago Mar (Ft. Lauderdale, Fla.); Roland Park Women's; Woodbrook-Murray Hill Garden Club, Federation Garden Clubs. Editor; The Spinning Wheel, 1973-76. Home: 7 Ruxton Green Ct Ruxton MD 21204

KEMPE, SUSANNA VICTORIA, marketing professional; b. Burlington, Vt., Aug. 22, 1966; d. Herbert Ernst and Victoria (Lane) K. MA, Cambridge U., 1987. From mktg. asst. to conf. producer Inst. for Internat. Rsch., London, 1988-90; conf. dir. Centaur Publs., London, 1990-91; European mktg. mgr. Seminar Centre Inst. for Internat. Rsch., Frankfurt, Germany, 1991; group mktg. dir. Inst. for Internat. Rsch., London, 1991-92; v.p. mktg. Am. Inst. Inst. for Internat. Rsch., N.Y.C., 1992—; faculty Mktg. Fedn., Washington, 1993. Office: American Inst 708 3d Ave 4th Fl New York NY 10021

KEMPER, DORLA DEAN (DORLA DEAN EATON), real estate broker; b. Calhoun, Mo., Sept. 10, 1929; d. Paul McVey and Jesse Lee (McCombs) Eaton; student, William Woods Coll., 1947-48; B.S. in Edn., Cen. Mo. State U., 1952; m. Charles K. Kemper, Mar. 1, 1951; children: Kevin Keil, Kara Lee. Tchr. pub. schs., Twin Falls, Idaho, 1950-51, Mission, Kans., 1952-53, Burbank, Calif., 1953-57; real estate saleswoman, Minn., 1967-68, Calif., 1971-73; Deanie Kemper, Realtor (name changed to Deanie Kemper, Inc. Real Estate Brokerage 1976), Loomis, Calif., 1974-76, pres., 1976-91; sr. couns. Capital Holding Corp., Louisville, 1991-93, dir. Pres., Battle Creek Park Elem. Sch. PTA, St. Paul, 1966-67; mem. Placer County (Calif.) Bicentennial Comm., 1976; mem. Sierra Coll. Adv. Com., 1981—; active Placer County Hist. Soc. Named to Million Dollar Club (lifetime) Sacramento and Placer County bds. realtors, 1978-94; designated Grad. Realtors Inst., Cert. Residential Specialist. Mem. Nat. Assn. Realtor, Calif. Assn. Realtors, Nat. Assn. Real Estate Appraisers, Placer County (mem. profl. standards com.) bds. realtors, DAR (chpt. regent 1971-73, organizing chpt. regent 1977—, dist. dir. 1978-80, state registrar Calif. 1980-82, state vice regent 1982-84, state regent 1984-86, nat. resolutions com., nat. recording sec. gen., 1986-89), DAR (nat. chmn. units overseas 1983-86), Daus. Am. Colonists, Colonial Dames Am., Dames Ct. of Honor, Internat. Platform Assn. Republican. Mem. Christian Ch. Clubs: Hidden Valley Women's (pres. Loomis club 1970-71), Auburn Travel Study (pres. 1979). Home: 8165 Morningside Dr Loomis CA 95650-9185

KEMPER LITTMAN, MARLYN, information scientist; b. Balt., Mar. 26, 1943; d. Louis and Augusta Louise (Jacobs) Janofsky; m. Bennett I. Kemper, Aug. 1, 1965 (dec. June 1987); children: Alex Randall, Gari Hament, Jason Myles; m. Lewis Littman, Apr. 22, 1990. BA, Finch Coll., 1964; MA in Anthropology, Temple U., Phila., 1970; MA in Library Sci., U. S. Fla., 1983; PhD in Info. Sci., Nova Southeastern U., 1986. Dir., Hist. Broward County Preservation Bd., Hollywood, Fla., 1979-87; automated systems librarian Broward County Main Library, Ft. Lauderdale, Fla., 1983-86; assoc. prof., dir. info. sci. doctoral program Nova U., Ft. Lauderdale, 1987-90. Pub. info. officer Broward County Hist. Commn., 1975-79. Vice chmn. Broward County Library Adv. Bd., 1987-92. Bd. dirs. Ctrl. Agy. Jewish Edn., 1992-94. Recipient Judge L. Clayton Nance award, 1977; Broward County Hist. Commn. award, 1979. Mem. ALA, IEEE, Am. Soc. for Info. Sci., Assn. Computing Machinery, Beta Phi Mu, Phi Kappa Phi. Author: A Comprehensive Documented History of the City of Pompano Beach, 1982 A Comprehensive History of Dania 1983, Hallandale, 1984, Deerfield Beach, 1985, Plantation, 1986, Davie, 1987, Networking: Choosing A Lan Path to Interconnection, 1987, (with others) Mosaics of Meaning, New Ways of Learning; author weekly columns Ft. Lauderdale News, 1975-79; author chpts. to books; contbr. articles to Microcomputer Environment: Management Issues, and articles to profl. jours. and procs. Home: 2845 NE 35th St Fort Lauderdale FL 33306-2007 Office: Nova U Sch Computer & Info Sci 3100 SW 9th Ave Fort Lauderdale FL 33315

KEMPF, JANE ELMIRA, marketing executive; b. Phila., Sept. 28, 1927; d. Albert Thomas and Alice (Gaston) Mullen; m. Peter Kempf, Sept. 4, 1948 (dec. Mar. 1985); children: Peter Albert, Jan Michael, Richard Allen, Jeffery Val. Grad. high sch., Yeadon, Pa. News dir. Sta. WIFF, Auburn, Ind., 1968-69; city editor The Evening Star, Auburn, 1969-76, columnist, 1969—; paralegal Warren Sunday Atty., Auburn, 1977-85; mktg. mgr. City Nat. Bank, Auburn, 1986-89; with communications mktg. Lincoln Fin. Corp., Ft. Wayne, Ind., 1989-90; prin. JK Communications Bus. Svcs., Auburn, Ind., 1990—; bd. dirs. Tri-County Power Wash, Inc. Contbr. articles to profl. jours. Mem. Auburn Network Enterprising Women, Ladies Literary Club, PEO Sisterhood (past pres.), Auburn C. of C. (past sec., bd. dirs.). Republican. Presbyterian. Home: 1117 Packard Pl Auburn IN 46706 Office: JK Communicatons Bus Svcs PO Box 430 Auburn IN 46706-0430

KEMPF, MARTINE, voice control device manufacturing company executive; b. Strasbourg, France, Dec. 9, 1958; came to U.S., 1985; d. Jean-Pierre and Brigitte Marguerite (Klockenbring) K. Student in Astronomy, Friedrich Wilhelm U., Bonn, Fed. Republic of Germany, 1981-83. Owner, mgr. Kempf, Sunnyvale, Calif., 1985—. Inventor Comeldir Multiplex Handicapped Driving Systems (Goldenes Lenkrad Axel Springer Verlag 1981), Katalavox speech recognition control system (Oscar, World Almanac Inventions 1984, Prix Grand Siecle, Comite Couronne Francaise 1985). Recipient Medal for Service to Humanity Spinal Cord Soc., 1986; street named in honor in Dossenheim-Kochersberg, Alsace, France, 1987; named Citizen of Honor City of Dossenheim-Kochersberg, 1985, Outstanding Businessperson of Yr. City of Sunnyvale, 1990. Office: 1080 E Duane Ave Ste E Sunnyvale CA 94086-2628

KEMPLEY, RITA A., film critic, editor; b. Frankfort, Ky., Sept. 12, 1945; d. Noah and Musaetta (Lathrem) Abrams; m. William Holcomb Kempley, June 31, 1968 (div. 1978); m. Edward Ronald Schneider, Aug. 11, 1986. BJ, U. Mo., 1967. Reporter Copley News Svc., La Jolla, Calif., 1967-68; assoc. editor John F. Holman & Co., Washington, 1968-71; reporter Graphic Arts Mag., Washington, 1972-75; freelance editor-writer Washington, 1975-76; mng. editor Washington Dossier, 1977-79; editor/critic Washington Post, 1979—; commentator Sta. WETA, 1989—. Mem. Newspaper Guild, Kappa Tau Alpha. Office: The Washington Post 1150 15th St NW Washington DC 20071-0001

KENAS, JANE HAMILTON, musician; b. Fond du Lac, Wis., June 17, 1951; d. Vern Aaron and Marilyn Jane (Bluemke) K. MusB, U. Wis., Stevens Point, 1975; MA, Northeastern Ill. U., 1987. Staff accompanist dept. music Northeastern Ill. U., Chgo., 1982—; music dir. USO Tour to Europe, Germany, 1973; cantorial soloist Temple Beth El, Northbrook, Ill.; music dir., composer Papai Players Theatre Co., Palatine, Ill.; accompanist Maine Twp. Choir, Park Ridge, Ill. Composer: (mus. play) The Adventures of Goldilocks, 1990; (one-act opera) Romance Novel, 1993. Office: Northeastern Ill U 5500 N Saint Louis Ave Chicago IL 60625-4625

KENDALL, DEBORAH A., legislative staff director; b. Taiwan, Jan. 29, 1955. BS, George Mason U., 1977. Caseworker Rep. Richard Bolling, 1979-82; sr. caseworker Rep. Alan Wheat, 1982-85; legis. dir. Rep. Frank McCloskey, 1985-87; staff dir. Subcom. Postal Pers. & Modernization, 1987-89, Subcom. Postal Ops. & Svcs., 1990-92, Subcom. Civil Svc., House Com. Post Office & Civil Svc., Washington, 1993—. Office: Subcommittee on Civil Svcs 122 Cannon House Office Bldg Washington DC 20515*

KENDALL, DOLORES DIANE PISAPIA, artist, author, marketing executive; b. Newark, N.J., June 1, 1946; d. Dominick Pisapia and Ann Fanfone Pisapia Kendall. Grad. Berkeley Bus. Coll., East Orange, N.J., 1965; postgrad. Middlesex County Coll., Edison, N.J., 1966-67, Rutgers U., 1967-69, Todd Butler Art Workshop, Edison, 1964-74, Art Inst. Boston, 1976, Graham Art Studio, Boston, 1975-77, Sch. Visual Arts, N.Y.C., 1978, NYU, 1977, Advt. Club N.Y., 1978. Proofreader, supr. N.J. State Diagnostic Ctr., Menlo Park, N.J., 1965-75; apprentice, instr. Graham Art Studio, Boston, 1975-77; dir. direct mktg. Boardroom Reports Inc., N.Y.C., 1977-82; pres., chief operating officer Roman Managed Lists, N.Y.C., 1982; dir. direct mktg. Mal Dunn Assocs., N.Y.C., 1983; dir. lists and card deck mgmt. Warren, Gorham & Lamont Inc., N.Y.C., 1984-86, direct mktg. cons., 1986-87; v.p., Marketry, Inc., N.Y.C. and Bellevue, Wash., 1987-93; cons. direct mktg., N.Y.C., 1993—. Exhibited in group art shows: N.Y.C., Boston, Middlesex County, N.J., Somerset County, N.J., Morris County, N.J., 1965-74, Greenwich Village Art Show, N.Y.C., 1972, Graham Art Studio, Boston, 1975-77; represented in numerous pvt. art collections throughout the U.S. Author: My Eyes Are Windows, 1972, Feelings and Thoughts (poetry), 1979, The Direct Marketing Handbook, 2d edit., 1992; contbr. articles to profl. jours. Recipient Desi award Direct Mail Mktg. Promotion Package, 1980, Poetry award One Mag., 1972, Internat. Cert. of Recognition for List Day, 1982. Mem. Direct Mktg. Assn. (Echo awards bd. judges 1982-85, List Day lectr., N.Y.C.), Can. Direct Mktg. Assn., Internat. Poetry Assn. (Clover Collection of Verse VI 1973, Danae in Clover 1973—), Direct Mktg. Creative Guild, Nat. Mail Order Assn. (adv. bd. 1979-80), Nat. Assn. Female Execs., NOW, Direct Mktg. Club N.Y.C., Internat. Platform Assn., Nat. Bus. Circulation Assn. Home: 530 2nd Ave New York NY 10016-8207

KENDALL, JANE LOUISE, management consultant; b. Cadillac, Mich., July 30, 1948; d. Robert Llewellyn and Betty Louise (Powers) K.; m. Jeffrey T. Guillemette, Aug. 27, 1971 (div. 1979); children: Gina, Mara, Kendall; m. Dan Michael Swank, Nov. 14, 1980 (div. 1990). BS, U. Mich., 1970; MBA, DePaul U., 1994. Pvt. practice dental hygienist Grand Rapids, Mich., 1970-71, Jackson, Mich., 1971-78; co-owner Kendall Enterprises, Jackson, 1978-80, Swank & Swank, Jackson, 1980-84; dir. govt. affairs Am. Dental Hygienists Assn., Chgo., 1984-94; sr. cons. Orion Internat., Ltd., Ann Arbor, Mich., 1995—; rep. Mich. Dental Hygienists Statewide Health Coordinating Com., Lansing, Mich., 1976-79; mem. profl. rels. adv. coun. Delta Dental Plan of Mich., Lansing, 1977-79; mem. steering com. U.S. Dept. Health and Human Svcs., Denton, Tex., 1985-86; charter bd. dirs. Coalition for Oral Health, Washington. Mem. adv. com. Ferris State Coll., Big Rapids, Mich., 1976-79; panelist Hew Rsch. Project, Washington, 1978; deacon First Presbyn. Ch., Jackson, 1980-83, Glen Ellyn, Ill., 1989-92, fund raising campaign bd., Glen Ellyn, 1991. Recipient Outstanding Alumnae award U. Mich., 1990. Mem. APHA, Am. Mgmt. Assn., Am. Soc. Assn. Execs. (cert.), Chgo. Soc. Assn. Execs. (mem. govt. affairs com. 1989-90, mem. adv. com. 1988-90, DePaul scholar 1986). Home: 371 N Park Blvd Glen Ellyn IL 60137 Office: Orion Internat Ltd 555 Briarwood Cir Ste 140 Ann Arbor MI 48108

KENDALL, KAY LYNN, interior designer; b. Cadillac, Mich., Aug. 20, 1950; d. Robert Llewellyn and Betty Louise (Powers) K.; 1 child, Anna Renee Easter. BFA, U. Mich., 1973. Draftsman, interior designer store planning dept. Jacobson Stores, Inc., Jackson, Mich., 1974-79; sr. interior designer store planning dept. Jacobson Stores, Inc., Jackson, 1981—; prin. Kay Kendall Designs, Jackson, 1979—; cons. in field. Bd. dirs. Big Bros./Big Sisters of Jackson County. Mem. Am. Soc. Interior Designers (profl. mem., assoc. Cen. Mich. chpt.). Home: 6890 Ann Arbor Rd Jackson MI 49201-9623 Office: Jacobson Stores Inc 3333 Sargent Rd Jackson MI 49201-8847

KENDALL, LAUREL ANN, geotechnical engineer; b. Detroit, Dec. 4, 1956; d. James McNair and Dorothy Mildred (Frost) K. BSE in Environ. Sci., U. Mich., 1979, MSCE, 1983. Registered profl. engr., Mich., Ill., Ohio. Student engr. Bechtel Assocs. P.C., Ann Arbor, Mich., 1979, geotech. engr., 1980-81; geotech. engr. Bechtel Civic & Mineral Corp., Gaithersburg, Md., 1981-82, Bechtel Power Corp., Midland, Mich., 1983-84; project mgr. NTH Cons., Ltd., Farmington Hills, Mich., 1984-90; sr. project engr., site mgr., gen. mgr. solid waste ops. Environ. Quality Co., Ypsilanti, Mich., 1990—; instr. Lawrence Inst. Tech., Southfield, Mich., 1985-91, Wayne State U., 1991—. Mem. ASCE (chmn. geotech. com. 1985-87, bd. dirs. 1987-89, officer 1989—), Mich. Soc. Profl. Engrs. (officer 1990-95), Engring. Soc. Detroit. Congregationalist. Office: Wayne Disposal Inc 1349 Huron St Ypsilanti MI 48197-9701

KENDALL, SCIPIARUTH, programmer, analyst; b. Boston, May 29, 1955; d. Scipio Hoover and Connie Lee (Lester) K. BS in Computer Info Systems, Calif. Polytech. U., Pomona, 1986. Noncommd. lab. tech. USAF-George AFB, Victorville, Calif., 1977-81; lab. asst. Covina (Calif.) Reference Lab., 1981-85; credit processor Informative Rsch., Inc., Anaheim, Calif., 1985; inventory specialist Washington Inventory Inc., Riverside, Calif., 1985; tax asst. Borsch Tax Svc., Fullerton, Calif., 1986; phlebotomist Meth. Hosp., Arcadia, Calif., 1986; eligibility worker County of L.A., El Monte, Calif., 1986-87; programmer analyst L.A. County, Downey, Calif., 1987-92, Riverside Dist. Atty., 1992—; enlisted lab. technician USAFR, March AFB, Calif., 1981-89, commd. Med. Svc. Corps, 1990—. Canvasser U.S. Savs. Bond of L.A. County, Downey, 1988; fundraiser Brotherhood Crusade and United Way, Downey, 1988; walker March of Dimes L.A. County, Downey, 1989, 90. With USAF, 1977-81, USAFR, 1981—. Recipient Community Support award L.A. County Data Processing Dept., 1990. Mem. NAFE, Orange County Women Networkers, Data Processing Mgmt. Assn., Assn. Med. Surgeons U.S., Res. Officers Assn., Computer Security Inst., IEEE, Toastmasters Internat., Soc. Air Force Res. Med. Svc. Corp., Air Force Assn. Office: Riverside Dist Atty Law Enforcement Systems 4075 N Main St Riverside CA 92501-3707

KENDALL-TACKETT, KATHLEEN ANN, developmental psychologist, researcher, writer; b. Ogden, Utah, Nov. 21, 1959; d. Leland Dale and Josephine Patricia (Jones) Kendall; m. Douglas William Tackett, Aug. 1, 1981; children: Kenneth Jmes, Christopher William. BA, Calif. State U., Chico, 1982, MA, 1984; PhD, Brandeis U., 1990. Prin. investigator childhood victimization study Giarretto Inst., San Jose, Calif., 1985-87; field ops. coord. infant health and devel. program Stanford (Calif.) U., 1985-87; rsch. fellow Family Rsch. Lab. U. N.H., Durham, 1990-92; asst. rsch. scientist Stone Ctr. Wellesley (Mass.) Coll., 1992-94; lectr. psychology Brandeis U., 1994; dir. The Perinatal Edn. Group, Framingham, Mass., 1993-94, Henniker, N.H., 1994—. Author: Postpartum Depression, 1993; assoc. editor: The Advisor, 1992—; editorial cons. and contbg. author to profl. jours. Leader La Leche League, Framingham, 1992-94, Concord, N.H., 1994—. Recipient Rsch. Svc. award NIMH, 1990-92, Outstanding Rsch. Study award Am. Profl. Soc. on Abuse of Children, 1994, Presdl. Honor Roll award Am. Profl. Soc. on Abuse of Children, 1994; Schulman Caplan and Univ. fellow Brandeis U., Waltham, Mass., 1987-90, grad. rsch. fellow Nat. Inst. Justice, 1989. Mem. Assn. for Women in Sci. (Rsch. award 1989), Mass. Profl. Soc. on Abuse of Children (bd. dirs. 1991-93, v.p. for edn. 1992-93, chair nominating com. 1993—). Evangelical. Office: The Perinatal Edn Group 34 Western Ave Henniker NH 03242

KENDRICK, CHERYL DONOFRIO, public relations and marketing professional; b. Troy, N.Y., Feb. 10, 1948; d. Frank Charles and Norma (Martorelli) Donofrio; m. Carleton R. Ayers (div.); children: Joshua Royse, Benjamin Lawrence; m. Ronald Howard Kendrick, June 10, 1989. Student, St. Lawrence U., 1966-69; première degrée, U. Rouen, France, 1968-69; BA in French and English, U. Conn., 1970; postgrad., San Diego State U., 1975-77. Mgr. pub. rels. J.W. Robinson's, San Diego, 1977-81; dir. pub. rels., asst. store mgr. Neiman Marcus, San Diego, 1981-88; dir. Office Procotol Office of Mayor, San Diego, 1988-89; dir. community rels. and devel. Grossmont Hosp., La Mesa, Calif., 1989-93; prin. C.D. Comms., San Diego, 1993—. Bd. dirs. L.E.A.D. San Diego, Inc., 1987—, Sr. Cmty. Ctrs., San Diego, 1989; pres. bd. dirs. NCCJ, 1993—. Mem. Pub. Rels. Soc. Am. Republican.

KENLEY, ELIZABETH SUE, commerce and transportation executive; b. Kansas City, Mo., Oct. 4, 1945; d. Ralph Raymond and Josephine Allen (Wells) Cummins. BS, Kans. U., 1968, MPA, 1972. Asst. city mgr. Winfield (Kans.), 1968-70; adminstrv. asst. Kansas City (Mo.) Police Dept., 1970; cons., 1973; with E.I. DuPont Co., Kingwood, Tex., 1974—, regional tech. buyer, 1977-79, cons., plant start up, 1979, regional tech. buyer, 1980-82; internat. project buyer Aramco, Houston, 1982-86, quality assurance liaison, supr. refinery no. area projects unit, 1986-89, owner, pres. Internat., Inc., Houston, 1988—. Mem. Houston C. of C., Am. Mgmt. Assn. Home: 9632 Briar Forest Dr Houston TX 77063-1007 Office: 2230 Harbor St Houston TX 77020-7506

KENLEY-LETTS, RUTH, film producer. films include: The Cormorant, 1983, Morphine and Dolly Mixtures, 1990, Rebecca's Daughters, 1992, Franz Kafka's It's a Wonderful Life, 1994 (Acad. award for Best Live Action Short Film 1994). *

KENNAN, ELIZABETH TOPHAM, college president; b. Phila., Feb. 25, 1938; d. Frank and Henrietta (Jackson) Topham; m. Michael Burns, 1986; 1 child, Frank Alexander Kennan. BA summa cum laude, Mt. Holyoke Coll., 1960; MA, St. Hilda's Coll. Oxford U., Eng., 1962; PhD, U. Wash., 1966; LHD (hon.), Trinity Coll., Washington, 1978, Amherst Coll., 1980, St. Mary's Coll., 1982, Oberlin Coll., 1983; LLD (hon.), Smith Coll., 1984; LittD (hon.), Cath. U. Am., 1985, U. Mass., 1988. Asst. prof. history Cath. U. Am., Washington, 1966-70, assoc. prof., 1970-78, dir. mediaeval and Byzantine studies program, 1970-78, dir. program in early Christian humanism, 1974-78; pres. Mt. Holyoke Coll., South Hadley, Mass., 1978—; lectr. in field; dir. NYNEX Corp., White Plains, N. Y., N.E. Utilities, Hartford, Conn., The Putnam Funds Inc., Ky. Home Mut. Life Ins. Co., Louisville, Talbots; cons. to various colls.; pres. Five Colls., Inc., 1985-94; dir. Coun. on Libr. Resources, 1982—, Consortium on Financing Higher Edn., 1994—; past mem. Indo-U.S. Subcom. of Am. Secretariat. Translator, author: (with John D. Anderson) On Consideration (St. Bernard of Clairvaux), 1976; contbr. articles to profl. publs. Mem. Dana Found., Higher Edn. Program Commn., 1986—; trustee U. Notre Dame, South Bend, Ind. Named Tchr. of Yr., Cath. U. Am., 1977; Marshall scholar, 1960; Woodrow Wilson fellow, 1962. Mem. Mediaeval Acad. Am. (coun. 1984-86), Coun. on Fgn. Rels., Folger Shakespeare Library, Phi Beta Kappa. Home and Office: Mt Holyoke Coll Pres' House Pres' Office South Hadley MA 01075

KENNARD, CINNY CLARE, news correspondent; b. New Haven, Conn., Dec. 28; d. John Edward and Mary (Powers) K. BS, Northeastern U., 1977. Corr. Sta. WNLK, Norwalk, Conn., 1977-79, Sta. WANE-TV, Ft. Wayne, Ind., 1980-82, KHOU-TV, Houston, 1982-88, Sta. WFAA-TV, Dallas, 1988-92; corr. CBS News, L.A., 1992-93, Moscow, 1993-94, London, 1994—. Recipient Columbia U./Du Pont award, 1992. Roman Catholic. Office: CBS News Fgn Desk London 524 W 57th St New York NY 10019-2902

KENNARD, JOYCE L., judge. Former judge L.A. Mcpl. Ct., Superior Ct., Ct. Appeal, Calif.; assoc. justice Calif. Supreme Ct., San Francisco, 1989—. Office: Calif Supreme Ct South Tower 303 2nd St San Francisco CA 94107

KENNEDY, ADRIENNE LITA, playwright; b. Pitts., Sept. 13, 1931; d. Cornell Wallace and Etta (Haugabook) Hawkins; m. Joseph C. Kennedy, May 15, 1953 (div. 1966); children: Joseph C., Adam. BS, Ohio State U., 1953; student creative writing, Columbia U., 1954-56; student playwrighting, New Sch. Social Research, Am. Theatre Wing, Circle in the Sq. Theatre Sch., 1957-58, 62. Mem. playwriting unit Actors Studio, N.Y.C., 1962-65; lectr. Yale U., New Haven, 1972-74; CBS fellow Sch. Drama, N.Y.C., 1973; lectr. Princeton (N.J.) U., 1977; vis. assoc. prof. Brown U., 1979-80; rep. to conf. Internat. Theatre Inst., Budapest, 1978; vis. lectr. Harvard U., 1990, 91. Author: (plays) Funnyhouse of a Negro, 1964, Cities in Bezique, 1965, A Rat's Mass, 1966, A Lesson in Dead Language, 1966, The Lennon Plays, 1968, Sun, Cities of Bezique, 1969; A Movie Star Has To Star in Black and White, 1976, Ohio State Murders, She Talks to Beethoven, 1990; (memoirs) People Who Led to My Plays, 1987 (Manhattan Borough Pres.'s award 1988), Letter to My Students, 1992; commd. Royal Ct., London, 1968, Lancashire Lad; commd. by Empire State Youth Inst., 1979, Onestes, Electra, Juilliard Sch. Music, 1980, Black Children's Day, Rites and Reason, Brown U., 1980; represented in numerous anthologies Norton Anthology of Am. Lit. Recipient Obie award, 1964, Pierre Lecomte du Novy award Lincoln Ctr., 1994, award Am. Acad. Arts and Letters, 1994; fellow Guggenheim Found., 1968, Rockefeller Found., 1967-68, NEA, 1993, Lila Wallace Readers Digest, 1994, Yale U., 1974-75; grantee Nat. Endowment Arts, 1973, Rockefeller Found., 1974, Creative Artists Pub. Svc., 1974; Disting. lectr. U. Calif., Berkeley, 1980, 86. Mem. PEN (bd. dirs. 1976-77).

KENNEDY, BARBARA ELLEN PERRY, art therapist; b. Columbus, Ohio, Apr. 22, 1937; d. Donald Earl Perry and Elsie Irene (Strait) Modglin; m. Marvin Roosevelt Kennedy, July 1, 1955 (div. Sept. 1969); children: Sherry Lynn Kennedy Anderson, Michelle Reneé Kennedy Byrd. AS in Mental Health Technology cum laude, Purdue U., 1975, BA in Psychology, 1976; MA in Art Therapy, Wright State U., 1990. Registered art therapist; cert. social worker; cert. marriage and family therapist. Probation officer intern Allen County Juvenile Probation Dept., Ind., 1975; prodn. supr. asst. Allen County Assn. for Retarded, Ft. Wayne, Ind., 1975, relief supr. semi-ind. living, 1975-76; occupational therapist asst. Logansport (Ind.) State Hosp., 1977; rehab. therapist Richmond (Ind.) State Hosp., 1977—, recreation therapy dir. acute intensive treatment unit, 1983-85, dir. art therapy dept., 1986—; pvt. counselor Mental Health Assn., Richmond, 1986; art therapy counselor Battered Women's Shelter, Richmond, 1986; counselor Dayton (Ohio) Pub. Schs., Family Svc. Assn., 1989-90, expressive therapy counselor; lectr. in field of mental health and art therapy. Author, editor: Mental Stimulation Activities, 1992. Mem. com. LWV, Richmond, 1977-80; publicity officer USCG Aux., Richmond, 1985; chairperson legis. group AAUW, Richmond, 1982-84; bd. dirs. Community Coun. on Disabilities Awareness, Richmond, 1985-86; vol. ARC, Muncie, Ind. and Ft. Wayne, 1969-73; vol. tutor Adult Literacy Resource Ctr., 1991—. Recipient Merit scholarship Purdue U., 1971-76, Gov.'s Showcase award State of Ind., 1990. Mem. Am. Art Therapy Assn., Buckey Art Therapy Assn., Ind. Art Therapy Assn. (v.p. 1992-95), Mensa. Reorganized Ch. of Jesus Christ of Latter-day Saints. Office: Richmond State Hosp 498 NW 18th St Richmond IN 47374

KENNEDY, BEVERLY (KLEBAN) BURRIS, financial consultant, agent, registered representative; b. Pitts., Sept. 23, 1943; d. Jack and Ida (Davis) Kleban; m. Thomas E. Burris, Dec. 31, 1967 (div.); 1 child, Laura Danielle Burris; m. Ed A. Kennedy, Jan. 14, 1984; stepchildren: Kathleen, Patricia, Thomas. BS, Pa. State U., 1964; postgrad., Va. Commonwealth U., 1967. Founder, exec. dir. Broward Art Colony, Inc., Broward County, Fla., 1978-80; dir. sales Holiday Inn, Plantation, Fla., 1980-81; agent, registered rep. Equitable Life Assurance Soc., Ft. Lauderdale, Fla., 1982—; pres. Fin. Planning Svcs. Assn., Inc., Ft. Lauderdale, Fla., 1984-86; owner, fin. cons. Beverly B. Kennedy & Assocs., Ft. Lauderdale, Fla., 1982—; adv. bd. Transflorida Bank, 1983-88; bd. arbitration Nat. Assn. Securities Dealers, Inc., 1992. Talk show host Sta. WWNN, 1992-93. Bd. dirs. Community Appearance Bd., 1988-89, Riverwalk, Ft. Lauderdale, 1988-89; trustee Police and Fireman Fund of Fort Lauderdale, 1990-91; appointed by gov. to Fla. State Bd. Profl. Engrs., 1988-91; cons. Com. on Fin. for Nat. Coun. examiners for Engring and Surveying, 1990-91; Rep. nominee for U.S. Congress 20th dist. Fla., 1992, 94. Named Woman of the Year (Bus. for Profit), Women in Communications, Broward County, 1986, Bus. & Profl. Women, 1988-89, oustanding alumni, Pa. State Univ. Coll . Edn., 1988-89. Mem. Internat. Assn. Fin. Planning, Nat. Assn. Life Underwriters, East Broward Fed. Women's Rep. Club (pres. 1992-93).

KENNEDY, CHERYL LYNN, museum director; b. Pekin, Ill., Nov. 25, 1946; d. Paul Louis and Ann Marie (Bingham) Wieburg; m. Roger Nicholas Kennedy, Feb. 7, 1966; children: Kurt Alan, Kimberly Ann. Grad. high sch., Pekin, Ill. Prin., and profl. quilter Mahomet, Ill., 1976-81; program coord. Early Am. Mus., Mahomet, 1981-85; dir. Early Am. Mus. Champaign County Forest Preserve, Mahomet, 1986—; chmn. Ill. quilt documentation project Early Am. Mus. and Land of Lincoln Quilt Assn., 1986—. Historian Meth. Local History Com., Mahomet, 1984-86; chair The Attractions Coun., Champaign-Urbana Conv. and Visitors Bur. Mem. Midwest Mus. Coun., Am. Assn. Mus., Am. Assn. State and Local History Mus., Assn. Ill. Mus. and Hist. Socs. (past pres., Heritage Awareness chair), Ill. Heritage Assn., Ill. State Hist. Soc. (bd. dirs.), Champaign County Hist. Soc., Nat. Quilt Assn., Am. Quilt Soc., Antique Quilt Study Group, Quilt Conservancy, Nat. Soc. Fundraising Execs., Rural Ptnrs. (bd. dirs.). Home: 219A S Lake of the Woods Rd Mahomet IL 61853 Office: Early Am Mus PO Box 1040 Mahomet IL 61853-0669

KENNEDY, CHERYL NOBLE, occupational health nurse; b. Kinston, N.C., May 21, 1948; d. Lynwood and Hilda Grace (Lee) Noble; m. Tony Earl Kennedy, Mar. 6, 1982; 1 child, Joseph John. Diploma, Petersburg (Va.) Gen. Hosp., 1969. RN, Va., N.C.; cert. occupational health nurse. Staff nurse Vis. Nurse Assn., Richmond, Va.; charge nurse vascular surgery unit McGuire Vets. Hosp., Richmond, Va.; occupational health nurse Guilford East Textiles, Kenansville, N.C.; employee health nurse City of Kinston. Mem. Am. Assn. Occupational Health Nurses, N.C. Assn. Occupational Health Nurses, N.C. Coastal Plains Assn. Occupational Health Nurses (cert.). Office: City of Kinston PO Drawer 339 Kinston NC 28502

KENNEDY, CORNELIA GROEFSEMA, federal judge; b. Detroit, Mich., Aug. 4, 1923; d. Elmer H. and Mary Blanche (Gibbons) Groefsema; m. Charles S. Kennedy, Jr. (dec.); 1 son, Charles S. III. B.A., U. Mich., 1945, J.D. with distinction, 1947; LL.D. (hon.), No. Mich. U., 1971, Eastern Mich. U., 1971, Western Mich. U., 1973, Detroit Coll. Law, 1980, U. Detroit, 1987. Bar: Mich. bar 1947. Law clk. to Chief Judge Harold M. Stephens, U.S. Ct. of Appeals, Washington, 1947-48; assoc. Elmer H. Groefsema, Detroit, 1948-52; partner Markle & Markle, Detroit, 1952-66; judge 3d Judicial Circuit Mich., 1967-70; dist. judge U.S. Dist. Ct., Eastern Dist. Mich., Detroit, 1970-79; chief judge U.S. Dist. Ct., Eastern Dist. Mich., 1977-79; circuit judge U.S. Ct. Appeals, (6th cir.), 1979—. Mem. Commn. on the Bicentennial of the U.S. Constitution (presdl. appointment). Recipient Sesquicentennial award U. Mich. Fellow Am. Bar Found.; mem. ABA, Mich. Bar Assn. (past chmn. negligence law sect.), Detroit Bar Assn. (past dir.), Fed. Bar Assn., Am. Judicature Soc., Nat. Assn. Women Lawyers, Am. Trial Lawyers Assn., Nat. Conf. Fed. Trial Judges (past chmn.), Fed. Jud. Fellows Commn. (bd. dirs.), Fed. Jud. Ctr. (bd. dirs.), Phi Beta Kappa. Office: US Ct of Appeals 744 US Courthouse 231 W Lafayette Blvd Detroit MI 48226-2799

KENNEDY, DEBRA JOYCE, marketing professional; b. Covina, Calif., July 9, 1955; d. John Nathan and Drea Hannah (Lancaster) Ward; m. John William Kennedy, Sept. 3, 1977 (div.); children: Drea, Noelle. BS in Communications, Calif. State Poly. U., 1977. Pub. rels. coord. Whittier (Calif.) Hosp., 1978-79, pub. relations mgr., 1980; pub. rels. dir. San Clemente (Calif.) Hosp., 1979-80; dir. pub. rels. Garfield Med. Ctr., Monterey Park, Calif., 1980-82; dir. mktg. and community rels. Charter Oak Hosp., Covina, 1983-85; mktg. dir. CPC Horizon Hosp., Pomona, 1985-89; dir. mktg. Sierra Royale Hosp., Azusa, 1989-90; mktg. rep. PacifiCare, Cypress, 1990-92; regional medicare mgr. Health Net, Woodland Hills, Calif., 1992—. Mem. Am. Soc. Hosp. Pub. Rels., Healthcare Mktg. Assn., Healthcare Pub. Rels. and Mktg. Assn., Covina and Covina West C. of C., West Covina Jaycees. Republican. Methodist. Club: Soroptimists. Contbr. articles to profl. jours.

KENNEDY, ELIZABETH, health facility administrator; b. Binghamton, N.Y., Mar. 19, 1944; d. Robert D. and Doris Beverly (Bryde) Courtright; m. Leon C. Kennedy, Aug. 29, 1964; children: Andrew, Tracey, Brian, Kristie. AAS, Ind.-Purdue U., 1986. RN, Ind.; lifetime ARC nurse. Asst. DON Ligonier Health Facility Arbors at Ft. Wayne, Ind.; staff nurse Mark Souder, M.D., Auburn, Ind.; DON Summit House, Ft. Wayne, Ind., Kendallville (Ind.) Nursing Home, Lifecare Ctr., Lagrange, Ind.; nursing supr. Allen Home Care, Allen Home, Health and Hospice Care, Ft. Wayne; instr. ARC. Recipient Scottish Rite Nursing scholarship. Home: 5135-6 Stone Hedge Rd Fort Wayne IN 46835

KENNEDY, ELIZABETH ANN, elementary school educator; b. Sacramento, Calif., Dec. 11, 1914; d. George Francis and Margaret Virtue (Robinson) McDonell; m. James Francis Kennedy, June 20, 1942 (dec. Oct. 1991); children: Judith Drew, James P., Susan Wingard. AB in Math., U. Calif., Berkeley, 1936. Cert. tchr. Tchr. math. Calif. Jr. High Sch., Sacramento, 1937; tchr. Sacramento City Schs., 1937-72. Pres., auditor, budget chmn. Sacramento Suburban Rep. Women, 1953—, treas., 1993—; tournament chmn. Am. River Women's Golf Tournament, 1987, 88. Recipient PTA award, 1967. Mem. AAUW. Home: 5611 Seward Ct Sacramento CA 95819-1820

KENNEDY, EVELYN SIEFERT, foundation executive, textile restoration specialist; b. Pitts., Nov. 11, 1927; d. Carmine and Assunta (Iacobucci) Rocci; BS magna cum laude, U. R.I., 1969, MS in Textiles and Clothing, 1970; cert. appraiser of personal property; m. George J. Siefert, May 30, 1953 (div. 1974); children: Paul Kenneth, Carl Joseph, Ann Marie; m. Lyle H. Kennedy, II, Oct. 12, 1974 (div. Feb. 1986). With Pitts. Pub. Schs., 1945-50; with Goodyear Aircraft Corp., Akron, Ohio, 1950-54; clothing instr. Groton (Conn.) Dept. Adult Edn., 1958-68; pres. Sewtique, Groton, 1970, Sewtique II, New London, Conn., 1986; v.p. Kennedy Capital Advisors, Groton, 1973-85, Kennedy Mgmt. Corp., Groton, 1974-85, Kennedy InterVest, Inc., Groton, 1975-85; pres., exec. dir. P.R.I.D.E. Found., Inc., Groton, 1978—; clothing cons. Coop. Extension Service, Dept. Agr.; internat. lectr. on clothing for disabled and elderly; adj. faculty U. Conn., Eastern Conn. State Coll., St. Joseph Coll.; hon. prof. U. R.I., assoc. prof., 1987—; fed. expert witness Care Label Law, FTC, 1976; mem. Major Appliance Consumer Action Panel, 1983-89. Regional adv. coun. SBA active corps Execs., Hartford, 1985—; bd. dirs. Small Bus. Devel. Ctr., 1989—, Easter Seal Rehab. Ctr. Southeastern Conn.; bus. adv. council U. R.I., 1979—, trustee, 1985—; active LWV; mem. Groton Vocat. Edn. Adv. Council. Recipient award of distinction U. R.I., 1969, Adv. of Yr. SBA. 1984, Outstanding Svc. in Community, 1991; named Woman of Yr. Bus. and Profl. Women's Club, 1977, Conn. Home Economist of Yr., 1987. Mem. Internat. Sleep Council (consumer affairs rep., Small Bus. Adminstrn. award 1991), Internat. Soc. Appraisers (cert. appraiser personal property, panelist FMHA roster, farmer's credit mediator 1989—), Nat. Assn. Bedding Mfrs., Conn. Home Economists in Bus. (founder 1977, Women of Yr. 1987), Nat. Home Economists in Bus. (chmn. internat. relations, nat. fin. chmn. 1986), Am. Home Econs. Assn., Coll. and Univ. Bus. Instrs. of Conn., Am. Occupational Therapy Assn. (resource cons. 1986—), Southeastern Women's Network, Fashion Group, Omicron Nu, Phi Kappa Phi. Democrat. Roman Catholic. Clubs: New London Zonta, Bus. and Profl. Women's (Outstanding Women of Year 1977). Author: Dressing With Pride, 1980, Clothing Accessibility: A Lesson Plan to Aid the Disabled and Elderly, 1983. Office: 391 Long Hill Rd Groton CT 06340-1293

KENNEDY, FAYE, retired social worker, author; b. Kansas City, Mo., Apr. 3, 1931; d. Wiley Choice and Zella Rae (Jackman) K.; m. Patrick Joseph Daly, Jan. 7, 1961. AA, Pasadena City Coll., 1951; BA, Hunter Coll., 1955; cert., Alliance Francaise, Paris, 1956. Vocat. counselor N.Y. State Divsn. Employment, N.Y.C., 1957-65; social worker N.Y. State Div. Parole, N.Y.C., 1965-77. Author: Good-bye, Diane, 1976, Aloha Can Mean Danger, 1995; assoc. editor Afro-Hawaii News, 1990-92. Mem. Hawaii Adv. Com. U.S. Civil Rights Commn., Honolulu, 1990—; mem. Hawaii State Commn. on Status of Women, Honolulu, 1993—; mem. Martin Luther King Jr. Commn., Honolulu, 1989-93; del. state conv. Hawaii Dem. Party, Honolulu, 1982, 84, 86, 88, 90, 92, Hawaii Dem. Party State Cen. Com., 1994—; mem. bd. dirs. Hawaii Literacy, Inc., 1987—, Hawaii Youth at Risk, 1991-94. Recipient Gov.'s Cert. of Appreciation, State of Hawaii, 1989-93, Making of the King Holiday award Martin Luther King Jr. Commn., 1991, Outstanding Achievement award Hawaii Literacy, Inc., 1988, 92, Outstanding African Ams. citation Afro-Hawaii News, 1992, Hawaii Personalities Recognition citation RSVP mag., 1989. Mem. Hawaii Women's Polit. Caucus (v.p. programs 1990—, bd. dirs.), Hawaii Yacht Club. Democrat. Home: 3071 Felix St Honolulu HI 96816

KENNEDY, JANICE MARIE, accountant; b. Wichita, Kans., Jan. 4, 1943; d. Oren L. and Jean H. (Harrison) Shelley; m. David W. Kennedy, Aug. 29, 1964; children: Christopher L., Drue D. BS in Bus. Adminstrn., U. Kans., 1964; MS in Acctg., Wichita State U., 1981. CPA, Kans. Staff acct. Kennedy and Coe, CPAs, Wichita, 1981-84; pvt. practice acctg. Wichita, 1984-89; ptnr. A. Leon Prior & Assocs, CPA's, Wichita, 1989-94; pvt. practice acctg. Wichita, 1994—. Adv. bd. Kans. Children's Svc. League, Wichita, 1984-92; treas., bd. dirs. adv. bd. Literacy Vols. of Am., Wichita, 1986—; pres. Wichita Downtown Lions Club, 1994-95; treas. Kans. Lions Band Found., Inc., 1992—, mem. planning commn. USA/Can. Lions Leadership Forum, 1994. Mem. Nat. Assn. Accts. (treas., pres. 1981-82, nat. dir. 1993-95),, AICPAs, Kans. Soc. CPAs (com. mem.), Am. Soc. Women Accts. (bd. dirs., v.p. 1982-83). Republican. Episcopalian. Home: 6211 Beachy St Wichita KS 67208-2622 Office: 343 N Market Wichita KS 67202-2009

KENNEDY, JOAN CANFIELD, volunteer; b. Washington, Mar. 24, 1931; d. Austin Francis and Gertrude Rita (MacBride) Canfield; m. Keith Furnival Kennedy, Feb. 11, 1956; children: Joseph Keith, Austin Robert, Thomas Canfield, Richard Furnival. BA, Coll. New Rochelle, 1953. trustee Ctr. Preventive Psychiatry, White Plains, N.Y., 1973-85, Catawba Lands Conservancy, 1992-95; dir. Scarsdale chpt. LWV, 1974-85, Charlotte-Mecklenburg (N.C.) chpt., 1985-89, pres., 1989-93, dir., 1993-95; dir. Coll. of New Rochelle Alumnae Assn., 1977-81, 89-92; chmn. Coun. Human Rels., Scarsdale, N.Y., 1983-85; bd. dirs. New Neighbors League, 1986-87, Shalon Homes, 1987-88. Recipient Ursulas Laurus Citation, 1968, Angela Merici award, 1988; named New Neighbor of Yr. New Neighbors League, 1987. Mem. Niantic Bay Yacht Club, Larchmont (N.Y.) Yacht Club. Roman Catholic. Home: 1441 Carmel Rd Charlotte NC 28226-5011

KENNEDY, JOANN, artist, educator; b. Chgo., June 17, 1950; d. Frank Joseph and Therese Katherine (Engelhardt) Mueller; m. John Fluent, Sept. 4, 1971 (div. May 1976); children: Benjamin, Molly; m. Samuel Joseph Kennedy, Oct. 9, 1982. BFA, No. Ill. U., 1988, MA, 1991, MFA, 1994. Typesetter, draftsperson, keyline illustrator Motorola, Schaumburg, Ill., 1976-84; instr. Harper Coll., Palatine, Ill., 1993—. Home: 1414 Eton Dr Arlington Heights IL 60004

KENNEDY, KAREN LEIGH, benefits compensation analyst; b. Raleigh, N.C., May 3, 1961; d. Larry Donald and Julia Brown (Pittman) Reece. AAS in Acctg., Wake Tech. Coll., Raleigh, N.C., 1982. Cert. compensation profl. Payroll acct. State Budget and Mgmt., Raleigh, N.C., 1983-84; payroll and taxes acct. Fed. Pacific Electric, Raleigh, 1985-86; payroll and fixed assets acct. Sumitomo Electric, Raleigh, 1986-87; sr. compensation and benefits analyst Post Software Internat., Wake Forest, N.C., 1987—. Mem. Internat. Found. Employee Benefit Plans, Am. Compensation Assn. Democrat. Baptist. Office: Post Software Internat PO Box 631 Wake Forest NC 27588

KENNEDY, KATHLEEN, film producer. Student, San Diego State U. With KCST, San Diego; pres. Amblin Entertainment, Universal City, Calif. Prodr.: (film) E.T. The Extra Terrestrial, 1982, Poltergeist, 1982, Indiana Jones and the Temple of Doom, 1984; co-producer: (films) Gremlins, 1984, Fandango, 1985, The Goonies, 1985, Back to the Future, 1985, Young Sherlock Holmes, 1985, The Color Purple, 1985, The Money Pit, 1986, An American Tail, 1986, Innerspace, 1987, Batteries Not Included, 1987, Empire of the Sun, 1987, Who Framed Roger Rabbit, 1988, The Land Before Time, 1988, Indiana Jones and the Last Crusade, 1989, Dad, 1989, Back to the Future Part II, 1989, Always, 1989, Gremlins 2: The New Batch, 1990, Joe Versus the Volcano, 1990, Arachnophobia, 1990, Cape Fear, 1991, Hook, 1991, Noises Off, 1991, A Far Off Place, 1992, Alive, 1993, Jurassic Park, 1993; exec. prodr.: Schindler's List, 1993, A Dangerous Woman, 1993, The Flintstones, 1994. Office: 650 Bronson Clinton 100 Los Angeles CA 90004*

KENNEDY, KATHY IRENE, public health researcher; b. Yonkers, N.Y., May 25, 1956; d. John James Kennedy and Jean Marie (Baldassare) Jarusinsky; m. Walter Benson Vernon, Sept. 6, 1980; children: Margaret Amelia, Gordon Fitzgerald. AB in Psychology, Boston Coll., Chestnut Hill, Mass., 1978; MA in Psychology, Assumption Coll., Worcester, Mass., 1981; postgrad., U. N.C., 1981-82, 91—. Rsch. asst. Med. Found., Boston, 1976; teaching asst. dept. psychology Boston Coll., Chestnut Hill, 1978; rsch. asst. Mass. Mental Health Ctr., Boston, 1978-79; teaching asst. dept. psychology Assumption Coll., Worcester, 1979-80; project asst. Family Health Internat., Rsch. Triangle Park, N.C., 1980-82, rsch. analyst, 1983, sr. rsch. analyst, 1984-87, rsch. assoc., 1988-90, sr. rsch. assoc., 1991-93; prin. rsch. scientist, 1994—; bd. dirs. Nat. Coalition Nat. Family Planning, 1987—; profl. adv. Internat. Lactation Cons. Assn., 1992—; tech. adv. Inst. Reproduction Health, Georgetown U., 1985—; adj. faculty Wellstart Lactation Program, San Diego, 1991—; presenter, trainer in field. Contbr. numerous articles to profl. jours. Recipient numerous scholarships and grants in field. Mem. AAUW, APHA. Home: 2201 S Fillmore St Denver CO 80210 Office: Family Health Internat 2224 Chapel Hill - Nelson Hwy Durham NC 27713

KENNEDY, KIMBERLY KAYE, history educator, bookkeeper; b. Naples, Fla., Nov. 2, 1961; d. George Eugene and Viola (Passmore) K. BA, Valdosta Coll., 1989, MA, 1990. Mgr. asst. Avon Products, Valdosta, 1983-88; bookkeeper Kennedy Rentals, Valdosta, 1983—; history educator Ga. Mil. Coll., Valdosta, 1993—; owner Kennedy Rentals, Valdosta, 1994—. Author: What Rainbow Means, 1976 (Internat. Order of Rainbow 1st pl. award 1986), (with others) Reflections, 1978. Recipient Grand Cross of Color Internat. Order of Rainbow, 1977. Mem. Order Ea. Star (worthy matron 1982-83). Democrat. Methodist. Home: 3647 Guest Rd Valdosta GA 31602 Office: Ga Mil Coll 3010 Robinson Rd Moody AFB GA 31699-1518

KENNEDY, LINDA MANN, neuroscience educator, researcher; b. Malden, Mass., July 29, 1939; d. Alfred William Mann and Etta May (Maglue) Stenquist; m. Richard Dearman Kennedy, Apr. 15, 1961; children: Pamela Lee, Ruth Alexander. Diploma in nursing, New England Deaconess Hosp., 1959; AB, Simmons Coll., 1975; PhD, Harvard U., 1980. RN, Mass. Staff nurse Lahey Clinic, Boston, 1959-61, various hosps., Mass., Ga., 1962-72; tchg. asst. Simmons Coll., Boston, 1972-75; vis. rsch. fellow Cornell U., Ithaca, N.Y., 1978-81; rsch. assoc. Worcester (Mass.) Found. Exptl. Biology, 1980-83; rsch. asst. prof. Clark U., Worcester, 1983-84, asst. prof., 1984-91, assoc. prof., 1991—; vis. scientist Weizmann Inst. Sci., Rehovot, Israel, 1991-92; co-founder, co-dir., dir. interdisciplinary neurosci. program Clark U., Worcester, 1984-91, 94—; mem. adv. panel sensory sys. program NSF, Washington, 1993—; mem. area grant study sects. NIH, Nat. Inst. for Neurol. and Comm. Disorders and Stroke, Nat. Inst. for Deafness and Other Comm. Disorders, Washington, 1988-89. Mem. editl. com. Univ. Press New England, 1989-91; contbr. articles to profl. jours. Mem. conservation com. Town of Framingham, Mass., 1973-74. Recipient Grad. fellowship for women Danforth Found., 1975-79, Rsch. Svc. award NIH, 1980-83, multiple Rsch. grants NSF, NIH, 1978—. Mem. New Eng. Psychol. Assn. (hon.), Assn. Chemoreception Scis. (exec. bd. councilor 1986-88), Soc. for Neurosci., Soc. for Values in Higher Edn., European Chemoreception Orgn., Internat. Brain Rsch. Orgn., Assn. for Women in Sci., Assn. Univ. Profs. Unitarian. Home: 98 Waterford Dr Worcester MA 01602 Office: Clark Univ Dept Biology Worcester MA 01610

KENNEDY, MARY VIRGINIA, diplomat; b. Pocatello, Idaho, Sept. 5, 1946; d. Charles Millard and Martha Lorissa (Evans) K. BA, U. Denver, 1968, MA, 1969; MAT, U. Idaho, 1971. Tchr. cert. Idaho. Recreation aide ARC, South Vietnam, 1969-70; ops. officer State Dept. Ops. Ctr., Washington, 1977-78; spl. asst. amb. Philip Habib, Washington, 1979-80, Sec. State, Washington, 1980-81; econ. officer U.S. Embassy, Cairo, Egypt, 1981-84; consul Am. Consulate, Adana, Turkey, 1985-88; Pearson fellow Office Cong. Bereuter Ho. Reps., 1988-89; exec. asst. Dept. Sec. State, Washington, 1989-91; dep. chief mission Dept. State U.S. Embassy, Kuwait, 1991-93; consul gen. Am. Consulate, Karachi, Pakistan, 1994—. Mem. Am. Fgn. Svc. Protective Assn. (bd. dirs. 1988-91), Phi Beta Kappa, Mortar Bd. Home: Amcongen-Exec, Unit 62400 Box 126, APO AE 09814-2400

KENNEDY, MAUREEN AGNES, advertising agency market researcher; b. Washington, Feb. 15, 1946; d. Daniel Bernard and Ann Aurelia (Caldwell) Kennedy; m. James H. Mangan, Sept. 10, 1977 (div. Oct. 1987); 1 child, James Daniel. BA, U. Md., 1970. Dir. rsch. Daniel J. Edelman, Washington, 1976-80; v.p., rsch. dir. N.Am. Mktg., Richmond, Va., 1980-83; pres. Mangan & Smith Rsch., Richmond, 1983-84; dir. mktg. Comms. Resource Group, Richmond, 1984-85, The Bomstein Agy., Washington, 1985—; adj. faculty Va. Commonwealth U., Richmond, 1980-83. Recipient Golden Candlestick award Am. Mktg. Assn., 1985. Roman Catholic. Home: 4446 1st Pl South Arlington VA 22204 Office: The Bomstein Agy 2201 Wisconsin Ave NW Washington DC 20007

KENNEDY, MERI BETH, women's health nurse; b. Decatur, Ill., Mar. 29, 1956; d. Joe D. and Goldie L. (Owens) K.; m. Donald Fluker, Oct. 28, 1978; children: Ryan, Meryn. Student, U. Ill., 1974-75; BSN, U. Iowa, 1978; MS, U. Mich., 1989. RN, Mich. Rsch. asst., project mgr. U. Mich. Sch. Nursing, Ann Arbor, 1987, lectr., 1988; nurse practitioner Planned Parenthood Mid-Mich., Ann Arbor; lectr., student counselor U. Mich. Sch. Nursing, Ann Arbor, 1989; nurse practitioner U. Mich. Health Ctrs., Brighton and Ann Arbor, 1990—; adj. faculty U. Mich. Sch. Nursing, 1993—, bd. dirs. North Campus Nursing Ctr., 1994—. Hartwell C. Howard scholar, LuAnn Gerlach scholar; Rackham Minority fellow. Mem. ANA, Mich. Nurses Assn., Mich. Assn. Nurse Practitioners Reproductive Health, Sigma Theta Tau. Office: 2200 Green Rd Ann Arbor MI 48105

KENNEDY, PATRICIA JOYCE, artist, educator; b. Newark, Jan. 23, 1943; d. Joseph James and Adele Romalda (Chumicki) Wegrocki; m. Gregory Patrick Kernahan, June 20, 1964 (dec. Mar. 1968); children: Kevin Gregory, Sean Patrick; m. Edward Felix Kennedy, Nov. 14, 1970; 1 child, Brendan Edward. AA, Fashion Inst. Tech., N.Y.C., 1963; BA, Georgian Ct. Coll., 1978; MS, Bank St. Coll., N.Y.C., 1990. Cert. art edn., supr., N.J. Publicity coord. Fredrica Furs, N.Y.C., 1963-64; art dept. chair Mater Dei H.S., New Monmouth, N.J., 1978-93; instr. art history Ocean C.C., Toms River, N.J., 1991—; lectr. Soc. Scribes, N.Y.C.; cons. internat. calligraphy confs., Trenton and Hoboken, N.J., 1981-83. Exhbns. include Scripps Coll., Calif., 1988, Monmouth Reform Temple, 1988, 89, 90, 91, 92, 93, Monmouth Mus., Lincroft, N.J., 1989, Bank St. Coll., N.Y.C., 1990, U. Portland, Oreg., 1991, Ocean County Coll., Toms River, N.J., 1992, 93, 94, Orgn. Ind. Artists, N.Y.C., 1994; represented in pvt. collections in N.Y., N.J., Fla., Ill., Calif.; collage artist; creator hand lettered and bound books. Mem. Guild Creative Artists, Jersey Shore Calligrapher's Guild (pres., founder 1982-85), Womens Caucus for Art, Soc. Scribes, Coll. Art Assn., Archaeol. Inst. Am., Gold Star Wives Am. Home and Office: 24 Irving Pl Red Bank NJ 07701

KENNEDY, SANDRA DENISE, state representative; b. Oklahoma City, Dec. 25, 1957; d. Leland and Doll B. (Alford) K.; 1 child, Mahogany Renee Cherry. Student, Phoenix Coll., 1975-76, So. Mountain Community Coll. and Ariz. State U., 1976-86. Acct. Kennedy and Assocs., Phoenix, 1983—; state rep. Ariz. Ho. of Reps., Phoenix, 1986—; del. Fgn. Relations Conf. Am. Council Young Polit. Leaders, Washington, 1987, alternate del. Commn. Internat. Trade State Fed. Assembly, Washington, 1987. Bd. dirs. Ariz. Cactus Pine Girl Scouts, Phoenix, 1987—. Mem. Nat. Conf. State Legislators, Nat. Black Caucus State Legislators, Order Women Legislators, Nat. Assn. Exec. Women Inc. Baptist. Home: 2333 E Wier Ave Phoenix AZ 85040-2657 Office: Ariz State Sen State Capitol Phoenix AZ 85007*

KENNEDY, SUSAN JEAN, system analyst; b. New Haven, July 3, 1963; d. Charles and Marie (Dwyer) K. BS, Quinnipiac Coll., 1985, postgrad. Programmer analyst Blue Cross/Blue Shield, North Haven, Conn., 1985-86; system specialist So. New Eng. Telecomm., New Haven, 1986-89, 93—; programmer analyst Gen. Reins., Stamford, Conn., 1989-90; sr. analyst Sikorsky Aircraft, Stratford, Conn., 1990-92, BC/BS, North Haven, 1992. Home: 83 Manorwood Dr Branford CT 06405 Office: So New Eng Telecomm 4th fl 545 Long Wharf Dr 10-30-10 New Haven CT 06511

KENNEDY-SHIELDS, KATHLEEN ANN, health care administrator; b. Bklyn., Sept. 9, 1951; d. Vincent B. and Ann M. (Dunlap) Kennedy; m. Paul J. Shields, May 6, 1977; 1 child, Christopher Ryan. BA, U. South Fla., 1973; MS magna cum laude, St. Johns U., 1977. Child care worker Mission of Immaculate Virgin, S.I., 1973-74, caseworker, 1974-76; caseworker N.Y. State Office Mental Retardation and Devel. Disabilities, S.I., 1976-77; team leader S.I. Devel. Ctr., 1977-78, placement specialist, 1978-80, program planning specialist, 1980-83, community service adminstr., 1983-86; dir. S.I. Planning and Devel., 1986-93; dir. devel. Ind. Living Assn., Bklyn., 1993—; project cons. to numerous orgns. including On Your Mark, Inc., S.I., Assn. for Children with Retarded Mental Devel., N.Y.C., St. Lucy's Old Roman Cath. Cathedral, Bklyn., Eden II for Autistic Children, S.I., and many others; dir. planning Willowbrook Closure Exec. Task Force, 1986-87; presenter N.Y.C. Rent Stabilization Bd., 1994. Active Commr.'s Task Force for Redesign of N.Y.C. Service Delivery System, 1989, N.Y. State Task Force of Needs and Assessment and Evaluation, 1988-92, Commr.'s Task Force on Strategic Planning in N.Y.C., 1988-92, S.I. Cmty. Bd. II, S.I. Interagy. Coun. on Aging, co-chair social activities com.; panelist Commr.'s Forum Planning for the Future, 1988; den mother Boy Scouts Am., S.I., 1988-89; mem. info. exch. com. S.I. Regional Retardation and Devel. Disabilities. Named Woman of Yr. on Your Mark, Inc., 1989; recipient Commendation Mission of Immaculate Virgin, 1989, Commendation Ind. Living Assocs., 1990. Mem. Am. Mgmt. Assn., Am. Women in Econ. Devel., Mid Island Kiwanis (chair priority one children birth to 5). Roman Catholic. Home: 650 Victory Blvd Apt 4B Staten Island NY 10301-3545 Office: Ind Living Assn 110 York St Brooklyn NY 11201

KENNELLY, BARBARA B., congresswoman; b. Hartford, Conn., July 10, 1936; d. John Moran and Barbara (Leary) Bailey; m. James J. Kennelly, Sept. 26, 1959; children: Eleanor Bride, Barbara Leary, Louise Moran, John Bailey. BA in Econs, Trinity Coll., Washington, 1958; grad., Harvard-Radcliffe Sch. Bus. Adminstrn., 1959; M.A. in Govt, Trinity Coll., Hartford, 1971. Mem. Hartford Ct. of Common Council, 1975-79; sec. of state State of Conn., Hartford, 1979-83; mem. 98th-103rd Congresses from 1st Dist. Conn., Hartford, 1982—; mem. chief majority dep. whip, budget com., House adminstrn. com., subcoms. librs. and memls., office systems, accts., ways and means, subcom. trade. Trustee Trinity Coll., Hartford, Conn.; previously active in numerous civic, polit., and govt. orgns. in Greater Hartford, Conn. Democrat. Roman Catholic. Office: 201 Cannon HOB Washington DC 20515

KENNELLY, SISTER KAREN MARGARET, college administrator; b. Graceville, Minn., Aug. 4, 1933; d. Walter John Kennelly and Clara Stella Eastman. BA, Coll. St. Catherine, St. Paul, 1956; MA, Cath. U. Am., 1958; PhD, U. Calif., Berkeley, 1962. Joined Sisters of St. Joseph of Carondelet, Roman Cath. Ch., 1954. Prof. history Coll. St. Catherine, 1962-71, acad. dean, 1971-79; exec. dir. Nat. Fedn. Carondelet Colls., U.S., 1979-82; province dir. Sisters of St. Joseph of Carondelet, St. Paul, 1982-88; pres. Mt. St. Mary's Coll., L.A., 1989—; cons. N. Cen. Accreditation Assn., Chgo., 1974-84, Ohio Bd. Regents, Columbus, 1983-89; trustee colls., hosps., Minn., Wis., Calif., 1972—; chmn. Sisters St. Joseph Coll. Consortium, 1989-93. Editor, co author: American Catholic Women, 1989; author: (with others) Women of Minnesota, 1977. Fulbright fellow, 1964, Am. Coun. Learned Socs. fellow, 1964-65. Mem. Am. Hist. Soc., Am. Cath. Hist. Soc., Medieval Acad., Am. Assn. Rsch. Historians on Medieval Spain. Roman Catholic. Home and Office: Mt St Marys Coll 12001 Chalon Rd Los Angeles CA 90049

KENNER, CAROL J., federal judge; b. 1950. BA, Syracuse U.; JD, New Eng. Sch. Law. Bar: Mass. 1978. Judge U.S. Bankruptcy Ct. Mass., Boston. Office: Fed Office Bldg 10 Causeway St Boston MA 02222-1047*

KENNER, MARILYN SFERRA, civil engineer; b. Youngstown, Ohio, Oct. 16, 1959; d. Joseph James and Mary (Conti) Sferra; m. Walter Sherden Kenner, July 7, 1984. B in Engring., Youngstown State U., 1982. Registered profl. engr., Ohio. Design and constrn. engr. Mahoning County Engr.'s Office, Youngstown, 1982-89, chief dep. engr., 1989—; mem. engring. dean search com. Youngstown State U. Mem. Mahoning Valley Soc. Profl. Engrs. (pres., v.p. 1990-93, treas. 1987-90). Democrat. Roman Catholic. Home: 6941 Lockwood Blvd Youngstown OH 44512 Office: Mahoning County Engr Office 940 Bears Den Rd Youngstown OH 44511

KENNER, MARY ELLEN, marketing and communications executive; b. Darlington, Wis., Jan. 7, 1941; d. Horace James and Adean Elizabeth (McDonald) Smith; BS, Marquette U., 1963, MBA, U. West Fla., 1988, cert. assn. exec., 1994; m. John Miller Kenner, Sept. 27, 1975. Fashion dir. spl. events Federated Store, Milw., 1962-63; mktg. ofcl. Ohio Bell and Wis. Telephone Cos., 1963-66; coll. mktg. instr. Milw. Inst. Tech., 1966-67; advt. positions AT&T and Wis. Telephone Co., 1967-78; advt. dir. No. States Power Co., Mpls., 1978-83; pres. Kenner Enterprises, 1983—; adj. prof. U. West Fla., 1988-89; dir. mktg. and communications Printing Industries Am., Alexandria, Va., 1989-91; dir. mktg. and pub. rels. Am. Production & Inventory Control Soc., 1992—; mem. steering com. 1st Conf. Consumerism. Recipient Clio award, 1974, Effie award, 1978, 79, 81. Mem. Am. Mktg. Assn., Am. Soc. Assn. Execs. (cert. assn. exec.), Direct Mktg. Assn Wash., Minn. Ctr. Arts, Milw. Advt. Club (dir. 1969-72, sec. 1973-76), U. West Fla. and Marquette U. alumni assns., Belleek Collectors Club. Roman Catholic. Home: 2211 Marthas Rd Alexandria VA 22307-1827

KENNERK, VICKIE-LYNN, high school counselor; b. Muncie, Ind., May 8, 1948; d. Raymond Keith and Katherine (Rooker) Foust; m. Mark Steven Carey, July 17, 1971 (dec. Nov. 1980); m. James Paul Kennerk, July 2, 1982. BS in Edn., Ball State U., 1969, MA in Elem. Edn., 1970; counseling cert., Tex. Woman's U., 1992, mid-mgmt. cert., 1993. Cert. elem. tchr., K-12 counselor. 3rd grade tchr. Anderson (Ind.) Schs., 1970-71, Maple Valley Schs., Vermontville, Mich., 1971-72; 6th grade tchr. N.W. Allen County Schs., Huntertown, Ind., 1972-83; 6th grade tchr. McKinney (Tex.) Ind. Sch. Dist., 1983-89, elem. counselor, 1989-92; vocat. counselor, lead counselor McKinney H.S., 1992—. Group leader McKinney Ind. Sch. Dist. New Focus, 1989—; mem. McKinney Edn. Found., 1992—, Tex. Sch. Improvement Initiative Office of Accountability. Mem. ASCD, Tex. Assn. for Supervision and Curriculum Devel., Tex. Edn. Agy., Tex. Counseling Assn., Am. Legion Aux. Office: McKinney Ind Sch Dist 1400 W Wilson Cir McKinney TX 75069

KENNETT, MARY JOSEPHINE, molecular biologist; b. Spokane, Wash., Mar. 11, 1959; d. George F. and Bessie L. Kennett. BS in Vet. Sci., Wash. State U., 1981, DVM, 1984; MS in Biology, Walla Walla Coll., 1987. Gen. practice clinician Plaza Vet. Clinic, Walla Walla, Wash., 1984-86; mem. biology faculty Columbia Basin Coll., Pasco, Wash., 1987-89, Walla Walla C.C., 1989-93; molecular biology fellow U. Mo., Columbia, 1993—; with DNS sci. I, NSF, Cold Spring Harbor, 1991, DNA sci. II, 1993. Mem. PEO, AMVA, Grange, Phi Kappa Phi. Methodist. Home: 509 Laurel Dr Columbia MO 65203-1379

KENNETTE, JENNIE LAURA FAKES, medical/surgical nurse; b. Hanston, Kans., Jan. 16, 1935; d. Jack Delmont and Bertha Mabel (Law) Fakes; m. Leslie Cleland Koontz, Dec. 4 1958 (dec.); children: Kim, Lynn, Gay, Jan, Jay, Lee; m. Robert Ray Hamill, Oct. 21, 1979 (div.); m. Russell T. Kennette Jr., Nov. 17, 1990. ADN, Barton County Community Coll., 1971; BSN, U. Wyo., 1988. RN; cert. med.-surg. nurse, pediatrics nurse, gerontol. nurse. Staff nurse clin. level III Laramie County Hosp., Cheyenne, Wyo.; asst. head nurse DePaul Hosp., Cheyenne; charge nurse St. Catherine's Hosp., Garden City, Kans.; DON Spearville (Kans.) Dist. Hosp.; charge nurse Meml. Hosp. Laramie County, Laramie County Hosp., Cheyenne, Wyo.; supr. Wyo. Retirement Ctr. Mem. ANA. Home: PO Box 841 Basin WY 82410-0841

KENNON, PAMELA CANERDAY, secondary school educator; b. Opelika, Ala., Nov. 9, 1961; d. Thomas Donald and Norma (Fowler) Canerday; m. John Carlton Kennon, Jr., Jan. 12, 1985; children: Kate, Carly, Jake, Sam. Student, Chipola Jr. Coll., Marianna, Fla., 1980-81; BS in Edn. cum laude, U. Ga., 1984; MEd, Brenau U., 1994. Phys. edn. tchr. Greensboro (Ga.) Primary Sch., 1984-85; tchr. 2d grade Jefferson (Ga.) Elem. Sch., 1985-93; tchr. 4th grade Oconee County Intermediate Sch., Watkinsville, Ga., 1993—; softball coach Jefferson (Ga.) High Sch., 1988-92, Oconee County High Sch., 1993—. Named Tchr. of Yr., Tchr. of Month Jefferson Elem. Sch., 1988, 90. Mem. Golden Key Hon. Soc. Baptist. Home: 1640 Barnett Shoals Rd Watkinsville GA 30677 Office: Oconee County Intermediate Sch Watkinsville GA 30677

KENNY, JANICE MARIE, psychologist; b. Zanesville, Ohio, Jan. 31, 1925; d. Joseph and Clara Catherine (Cervenka) Schmidt; m. Carl Maclaren Hobkirk, June 12, 1946 (div. 1954); children: Linda Kay, Steven Lawrence; m. Ben R. Kenny, Feb. 21, 1959; children: Charlotte Louise, Susan Michelle. BA, U. N.C., 1946; BS, St. Lawrence U., 1949; MA, Temple U., 1953, U. Pa., 1956; PhD, U. Pa., 1957. Lic. psychologist, Pa., N.J. Asst. in psychology U. Pa., Phila., 1953-54, assoc. in psychology, 1954-56; intern VA Hosp., Perry Point, Md., 1956-57; psychologist Phila. State Hosp., 1957-61; exec. dir. Delaware Valley Psychol. Ctrs., Phila., 1961—; dir. Continuing Edn. Abroad, Inc., Phila., 1983—. Fellow Pa. Psychol. Assn. (treas. 1977-81, pres. 1982-83), Phila. Soc. Clin. Psychologists (pres. 1976-77, Disting. Svc. award 1978), Quick Buck Prosperity Club (pres.). Home: 701 Jade Rd Yardley PA 19067-3011 Office: Delaware Valley Psychol Ctrs 1536 Pratt St Philadelphia PA 19124

KENNY, SHIRLEY STRUM, college administrator; b. Tyler, Tex., Aug. 28, 1934; d. Marcus Leon and Florence (Golenternek) S.; m. Robert Wayne Kenny July 22, 1956; children: David Jack, Joel Strum, Daniel Clark, Jonathan Matthew, Sarah Elizabeth. BA, BJ, U. Tex., 1955; MA, U. Minn., 1957; PhD, U. Chgo., 1964; LHD (hon.), U. Rochester, 1988. Chair English dept. U. Md., College Park, 1973-79, provost Arts and Humanities, 1979-85; pres. CUNY Queens Coll., Flushing, 1985-94, SUNY, Stony Brook, 1994—; bd. dirs. Toys 'R' Us, Computer Assocs., Chem. Bank Regional Adv. Bd. Author: The Conscious Lovers, 1968, The Plays of Richard Steele, 1971, The Performers and Their Plays, 1982, The Works of George Farquhar, 2 vols., 1988; editor: British Theatre and the Other Arts, 1984; contbr. numerous articles to profl. jours. Bd. dirs. Carnegie Found. for the Advancement of Teaching, Assn. Am. Colls. and Univs., Citizens Com. for N.Y.C., Goodwill of Greater N.Y., Long Island Assn. Recipient Disting. Alumnus award U. Chgo. Club Washington, 1980, Svc. and Leadership award N.Y. Urban League, 1988; named Outstanding Woman, U. Md., 1983, Outstanding Alumnus, U. Tex. Coll. Communication, 1989. Mem. Am. Handel Soc., Am. Soc. for 18th Century Studies, Bibliog. Soc. Va., Sigma Alpha Iota. Office: SUNY PO Box 0701 Stony Brook NY 11794-0701

KENT, JILL ELSPETH, academic healthcare administrator, lawyer, former government official; b. Detroit, June 1, 1948; d. Seymour and Grace (Edelman) K.; m. Mark Elliott Solomons, Aug. 20, 1978. BA, U. Mich., 1970; JD, George Washington U., 1975, LLM, 1979. Bar: D.C. 1975. Mgmt. intern U.S. Dept. Transp., Washington, 1971-73; staff analyst Office Mgmt. and Budget, Exec. Office of Pres., Washington, 1974-76; legis. counsel U.S. Treasury Dept., Washington, 1976-78; dir. legis. reference div. Health Care Financing Adminstrn., Washington, 1978-80; sr. budget examiner Office Mgmt. and Budget, Exec. Office Pres., Washington, 1980-84; chief Treasury, Gen. Services, OMB, 1984-85; dep. asst. sec. for departmental fin. and planning U.S. Dept. Treasury, 1985-86; dep. asst. sec. for dept. fin. and mgmt., 1986-88; asst. sec. of treasury, 1988-89, CFO, U.S. Dept. State, 1989-93, acting under sec. of state for mgmt., 1991; exec. devel. program Office Mgmt. and Budget, 1984; CFO George Washington U. Med. Ctr., Washington, 1993—; prin. Coun. Excellence in Govt., 1993—; adj. prof. pub. policy U. Md., 1993—; bd. dirs. Mobile Med. Care Inc., 1987-91. Trustee Newport Sch., 1988-91; bd. trustees Washington Civic Symphony, 1994—. Recipient Adminstrs. award Health Care Financing Adminstrn., 1980; named one of Top 40 Performers, Management mag., 1987, Disting. Svc. award Dept. Treasury, 1989, Am. Assn. Govt. Accts. award, 1992, Disting. Svc. award Dept. State, 1993. Mem. ABA, D.C. Bar Assn., Pres's. Council on Mgmt. Improvement, Exec. Women in Govt. (treas. 1991-92, pres. 1992-93), Va. Assn. of Female Exec. (adv. coun. 1990). Republican. Home: 2419 California St NW Washington DC 20008-1615 Office: George Washington Med Ctr Washington DC 20037

KENT, JULIE ANN, ballet dancer, actress, model; b. Bethesda, Md., July 11, 1969; d. Charles Lindbergh and Jennifer Elsie (Machirus) Cox. Grad. high sch., Potomac, Md. Apprentice Am. Ballet Theatre, N.Y.C., 1985-86, mem. corps de ballet, 1986-1990, soloist, 1990-93, prin. dancer, 1993—. Starring role (film) Dancers, 1986; performed as a guest artist nationally and internationally. Recipient Prix de Lausanne Internat. Ballet competition, 1986, 1st prize at Erik Bruhn Competition in Toronto, 1993; named one of 50 Most Beautiful People, People Mag., 1993. Office: Am Ballet Theatre 890 Broadway Fl 3 New York NY 10003-1211*

KENT, LINDA GAIL, dancer; b. Buffalo, Sept. 21, 1946; d. Jerol Edward and Dorismae (Kohler) K. BS, Juilliard Sch., 1968. Dancer Alvin Ailey Am. Dance Theater, 1968-74, then prin. dancer, 1970-74; prin. dancer Paul Taylor Dance Co., N.Y.C., 1975-89; faculty Juilliard Sch., 1984—; artist-in-residence Union Theological Seminary, N.Y. Mem. Am. Guild Mus. Artists, Actors Equity. Democrat. Unitarian. Home: 175 W 92nd St New York NY 10025 Office: 552 Broadway New York NY 10012-3922

KENT, M. ELIZABETH, lawyer; b. N.Y.C., Nov. 17, 1943; d. Francis J. and Hannah (Bergman) K. AB, Vassar Coll. magna cum laude, 1964; AM, Harvard U., 1965, PhD, 1974; JD, Georgetown U., 1978. Bar: D.C. 1978, U.S. Dist. Ct. D.C. 1978, U.S. Ct. Appeals (D.C. cir.) 1978, U.S. Supreme Ct. 1983, U.S. Dist. Ct. Md. 1985. From lectr. to asst. prof. history U. Ala., Birmingham, 1972-74; assoc. Santarelli and Gimer, Washington, 1978; sole practice Washington, 1978—. Mem. Ripon Soc., Cambridge and Washington, 1968-93; rsch. dir. Howard M. Miller for Congress, Boston, 1972; vol. campaigns John V. Lindsay for Mayor, 1969, John V. Lindsay for Pres., 1972, John B. Anderson for Pres., 1980. Woodrow Wilson fellow 1964-65; Harvard U. fellow 1968-69. Mem. ABA, ACLU, D.C. Bar Assn., Women's Bar Assn., Women's Legal Def. Fund, D.C. Assn. Criminal Def. Lawyers, Superior Ct. Trial Lawyers Assn., Nat. Women's Polit. Caucus, Phi Beta Kappa. Republican. Home: 35 E St NW Apt 810 Washington DC 20001-1520 Office: 601 Indiana Ave NW Ste 605 Washington DC 20004-2907

KENT, MAEREA JACKSON, elementary education educator; b. DeFuniak Springs, Fla., Mar. 5, 1965; d. K. P. and Edna Mae (Watts) Jackson; m. Steven John Kent, Dec. 21, 1985; children: Phillip Steven, Hannah Lynn. AA, Okaloosa-Walton Jr. Coll., 1985; BS in Edn., U. West Fla., 1987. Cert. tchr. elem. edn. and early childhood edn. Tchr. 1st grade Maude Saunders Elem. Sch., DeFuniak Springs, 1987—, mem. sch. improvement team, writing com., 1993—, ann. staff editor, 1993—, chair math com., grade level chair, mem. planning com., group leader Wax Mus.; tchr. rep. PTO. Co-coord. Hometown Christmas Pageant, DeFuniak Springs, 1993; coord. Miss DeFuniak Springs Pageant, 1994. Mem. AAUW, Bus.

and Profl. Assn., Beta Sigma Phi (Gamma Sigma chpt., Cancer Walk-a-Thon 1992, membership com., yearbook organizer 1993—, rec. sec. 1993, v.p. 1994, named Pledge of Yr. 1993). Democrat. Baptist.

KENT, ROBERTA B., literary consultant; b. N.Y.C., Sept. 7, 1945; d. Robert B. and Rose (Linker) K. BA magna cum laude, NYU, 1967, MA, 1969; postgrad., Princeton U., 1967-68. Asst. to head literary dept. Creative Mgmt. Assocs., N.Y.C., 1969-70; asst. to pres. Curtis Brown Ltd., N.Y.C., 1970-72, literary agt., v.p. dept. motion pictures, 1978-79; ptnr., literary agt. W.B. Agy., N.Y.C., 1972-78; literary agt., v.p. dept. motion pictures Kohner-Levy Agy., Los Angeles, 1979-81; literary agt. The Ufland Agy., Beverly Hills, Calif., 1981-83; literary agt., v.p. literary dept. S.T.E. Representation, Ltd., Beverly Hills, 1983-91; ind. cons. Cowling, Heysell, Plouse, Ingalls & Moore, Medford, Oreg., 1991—. Mem. Phi Beta Kappa. Democrat. Office: Cowling Heysell Plouse Ingalls & Moore 717 Murphy Rd Medford OR 97504

KENT, SHEILA KELLY, community volunteer; b. Chehalis, Wash., Oct. 20, 1932; d. John Caesar Jr. and Gladys Marie (Meenach) Kelly; m. Harry Christison Kent, Aug. 18, 1956 (dec. Apr. 1991); children: Colleen Kent de Ruiz, Bruce Kelly. BA with great distinction, Stanford U., 1953; postgrad., Golden Gate Coll., 1953-54, Whittier Coll., 1955. Cert. tchr., Calif. Jr. acct. Perkins & Trousdale, CPAs, San Francisco, 1953-55; tchr. kindergarten Glendora (Calif.) Sch. Dist., 1955-56. Spl. mem. United Meth. Women, 1979, dist. pres., 1989-93; vol. Santa Shop (Jeffco Action Ctr.), 1984—; mem. fin. com. Ch. Women United in Colo., 1994—. Mem. AAUW (named gift edn. found. 1982), Phi Beta Kappa. Democrat. Home: 5131 Jellison Ct Arvada CO 80002-3257

KENYON, JANE JENNIFER, poet, writer; b. Ann Arbor, Mich., May 23, 1947; d. Reuel Baldwin and Pauline Celeste (Miller) K.; m. Donald Hall, Apr. 17, 1972. BA, U. Mich., 1970, MA, 1972. Author: (poetry) From Room to Room, 1978, The Boat of Quiet Hours, 1986, Let Evening Come, 1990, Constance, 1993; translator: Twenty Poems of Anna Akhmatova, 1985. Recipient Sara Teasdale award Wellesley Coll., 1991, gift St. Botolph Club, 1991, PEN/Voelcker award for poetry, 1994; creative writing fellow Nat. Endowment for the Arts, 1981, N.H. Coun. on Arts fellow, 1984, Guggenheim grantee, 1992. Democrat. Congregationalist. Home: Eagle Pond Farm Danbury NH 03230 Office: care Graywolf Press 2402 University Ave Ste 203 Author Mail Saint Paul MN 55114

KEOGH, HEIDI HELEN DAKE, publishing executive; b. Saratoga, N.Y., July 12, 1950; d. Charles Starks and Phyllis Sylvia (Edmunds) Dake; m. Randall Frank Keogh, Nov. 3, 1973; children: Tyler Cameron, Kelly Dake. Student, U. Colo., 1972. Reception, promotions Sta. KLAK, KJAE, Lakewood, Colo., 1972-73; account exec. Mixed Media Advt. Agy., Denver, 1973-75; writer, mktg. Jr. League Cookbook Devel., Denver, 1986-88; chmn., coordinator Colorado Cache & Creme de Colorado Cookbooks, 1988-90; speakers bur. Mile High Transplant Bank, Denver, 1983-84, Writer's Inst., U. Denver, 1988; bd. dirs. Stewart's Ice Cream Co., Inc., Jr. League, Denver. Contbr. 6 articles to profl. jours. Fiscal officer, bd. dirs. Mile High Transplant Bank; blockworker Heart Fund and Am. Cancer Soc., Littleton, 1978—, Littleton (Colo.) Rep. Com., 1980-84; fundraising vol. Littleton (Colo.) Pub. Schs., 1980—; vol. Hearts for Life, 1991—, Gathering Place, 1991—, Oneday, 1992, Denver Ballet Guild, 1992—, Denver Ctr. Alliance, 1993—. Mem. Jr. League Denver (pub. rels. bd., v.p. ways and means 1989-90, planning coun./ad hoc 1990-92, sustainer spl. events 1993-94), Community Emergency Fund (chair 1991-92), Jon D. Williams Cotillion at Columbine (chmn. 1991-93), Columbine Country Club, Gamma Alpha Chi, Pi Beta Phi Alumnae Club (pres. Denver chpt. 1984-85, 93-94). Episcopalian. Home: 63 Fairway Ln Littleton CO 80123-6648

KEOHANE, NANNERL OVERHOLSER, college president, political scientist; b. Blytheville, Ark., Sept. 18, 1940; d. James Arthur and Grace (McSpadden) Overholser; m. Patrick Henry III, Sept. 16, 1962 (div. May 1969); 1 child, Stephan; m. Robert Owen Keohane, Dec. 18, 1970; children: Sarah, Jonathan, Nathaniel. BA, Wellesley Coll., 1961, Oxford U., Eng., 1963; PhD, Yale U., 1967. Faculty Swarthmore Coll., Pa., 1967-73, Stanford U., Calif., 1973-81; fellow Ctr. for Advanced Study in the Behavioral Scis. Stanford U., 1978-79, 87-88; pres., prof. polit. sci. Wellesley (Mass.) Coll., 1981-93, Duke U., Durham, N.C., 1993—; bd. dirs. IBM. Author: Philosophy and the State in France: The Renaissance to the Enlightenment, 1980; co-editor: Feminist Theory: A Critique of Ideology, 1982. Trustee Colonial Williamsburg Found., 1988—, Ctr. for Advanced Study Behavioral Scis., Stanford U., 1991—; mem. adv. com. to dir. NIH, 1993—; mem. MIT Corp., 1992—; mem. Trilateral Commn., 1992—; mem. Commn. for a Competitive N.C. Marshall scholar, 1961-63; AAUW dissertation fellow. Fellow Am. Acad. Arts and Scis., Am. Philos. Soc.; mem. Coun. on Fgn. Rels., Saturday Club (Boston), Watauga Club (N.C.), Phi Beta Kappa. Democrat. Episcopalian. Office: Duke Univ 207 Allen Bldg Durham NC 27708-0001

KEPNER, RITA MARIE, sculptor, writer, editor, educator, public affairs officer, marketing and communications professional; b. Binghamton, N.Y., Nov. 15, 1944; d. Peter Walter and Helena Theresa (Piotrowski) Kramnicz; m. John C. Matthiesen; 1 child, Stewart. Student, Elmira Coll., 1962-63; BA, SUNY, 1966; postgrad., Okla. U., 1988, Seattle Pacific U., 1991, Western Wash. U., 1991, 92, diplome of merit (hon.), Acad. Bedriacense, Calvatore, Italy, 1984. Instr. exptl. coll. U. Wash., 1972-74; instr. sculpture internship program Evergreen Coll., Olympia, Wash., 1974-78; informal visual arts amb. between U.S. and Poland, 1976-81; pres. fed. women's program coun. Seattle dist., 1985-86; fed. women's program mgr., Schweinfurt, Fed. Republic Germany, 1986-87, Wiesbaden, Fed. Republic Germany, 1988; artist-in-residence City of Seattle, 1975, 77-78; del. Internat. Sculptors Conf., Toronto, Ont., Can., 1978; writer, editor, pub. affairs specialist Seattle dist. U.S. Army C.E.; pub. affairs officer Wiesbaden Milcom Hdqrs., 1987-88, editor, Schweinfurt, 1986-87; instr. writing & editing for mgrs. Dept. of Navy, Bremerton, Wash., 1991-93; apptd. disaster assistance spokesperson and pub. affairs officer Region X, pub. info. officer, Fed. Emergency Mgmt. Agy., mid-western U.S., 1993, So. Calif., 1993, Northridge, Calif., 1994—, States of Ga., Oreg., Wash. and Alaska, 1994, No. Calif. floods, 1995. One-woman shows include Willoughby Wallace Meml. Gallery, Branford, Conn., 1967, Penryn Gallery, Seattle, 1970, 73, 76, Haines Gallery, Seattle, 1975, Zoliborz Gallery, Warsaw, Poland, 1981, Yorkshire 510, Norman, Okla., 1988; group shows include SUNY, Binghamton, 1966, Manawata Art Gallery, Palmerston North, N.Z., 1976, Modern Art Mus., Seattle, 1976, Portland (Oreg.) Art Mus., 1976, Hajnowka (Poland) Gallery, 1977, Die Roemer Gallery, Wiesbaden, Fed. Republic Germany, 1988, Blue Heron Gallery, Port Hadlock, Wash., 1991-92, Quimper Arts, Bruskin Gallery, Port Townsend, Wash., 1993, 94; major works include Peace Pipe, Zalaegerszeg, Hungary, Human Forms in Balance, City of Seattle, 1975, Unity, City of Znin, Poland, 1976, Rough to Smooth, Seattle Pub. Libr., 1978; commd. U.S. Army Corps of Engrs., 1995; contbr. articles to N.W. Arts, Seattle Post-Intelligencer, Leonardo mag., Polska Panorama, Poland mag. Founder Bainbridge Island Arts Coun., 1984; VISTA vol., 1982-84; bd. dirs. Aradia Med. Clinic, Seattle, 1972-74; founder Chimacum (Wash.) Sch. Dist. Learning Boosters, 1989; loaned exec. to govt. campaigns United Way, 1989; trainer for campaign cords. and key workers, 1989; 1st aid trainer Medic I, Seattle, 1989-91; elected chair Marrowstone Island Groundwater Com.; mem. adv. com. Seawater Intrusion Team Dept. of Ecology, Wash. State; pres. Marrowstone Island Community Assn., 1993-94. Recipient merit award for superior journalistic achievement U.S. Army CE, 1984, 85, 2d place news category competition award, 1985, 86; suggestion award Dept. Army, 1984, ofcl. commendation Dept. of Army, 1985, 86, 87, 90, Dept. of Navy, Puget Sound Naval Shipyard, 1990, 91, Achievement cert. Washington Assn. Educators of the Talented and Gifted, 1990, Specialist Achievement award, 1991, Recognition cert. FEMA, 1993 (3), 1994; named Citizen of Yr., City of Marrowstone Island, Wash., 1994; Kosciuszko Found. grantee, 1975, 76, 79, 81. Mem. Internat. Artists Cooperation (Edewecht, Fed. Republic Germany), N.W. Multihull Assn. (commodore 1974), Marrowstone Island Community Assn. (pres. 1993). Holder USCG capt. lic. for passenger carrying aux. sailing vessels up to 50 tons, 1980—. Home: 8643 Flagler Rd Nordland WA 98358-9600

KERBER, BONNIE M., human resources executive; b. Lincoln, Nebr., Sept. 1, 1952; d. Sherman Wayne and Betty Louise (Gorsline) Mills; m. Garry Leonard Ruppert, July 31, 1971 (div. Dec. 1981); m. William Edward Kerber, May 9, 1987; 1 child, Robert Sherman. BBA, U. Iowa, 1980. Pers. mgmt. specialist VA Med. Ctr., Iowa City, 1976-80; asst. pers. officer VA Med. Ctr., Martinsburg, W.Va., 1980-81, Augusta, Ga., 1982-84; labor rels. specialist VA Ctrl. Office, Washington, 1984-86, 88-93, Dept. Navy, Washington, 1986-88; chief human resources mgmt. VA Med. Ctr., Omaha, 1993—. Mem. Healthcare Human Resource Mgmt. Assn. of Midlands, Soc. Fed. Labor Rels. Profls. Office: Dept Vets Affairs 4101 Woolworth Ave Omaha NE 68105

KERBER, LINDA KAUFMAN, historian, educator; b. N.Y.C., Jan. 23, 1940; d. Harry Hagman and Dorothy (Haber) Kaufman; m. Richard Kerber, June 5, 1960; children: Ross Jeremy, Justin Seth. AB cum laude, Barnard Coll., 1960; MA, NYU, 1961; PhD, Columbia U., 1968; DHL, Grinnell Coll., 1992. Instr., asst. prof. history Stern Coll., Yeshiva U., N.Y.C., 1963-68; asst. prof. history San Jose State Coll., (Calif.), 1969-70; vis. asst. prof. history Stanford U., (Calif.), 1970-71; asst. prof. history U. Iowa, Iowa City, 1971-75, prof., 1975-85; May Brodbeck prof. U. Iowa, 1985—; vis. prof. U. Chgo., 1991-92. Author: Federalists in Dissent: Imagery and Ideology in Jeffersonian America, 1970, paperback edit., 1980, Women of the Republic: Intellect and Ideology in Revolutionary America, 1980, paperback edit., 1986; co-editor: Women's America: Refocusing the Past, 1982, 4th edit., 1995; co-editor: U.S. History As Women's History, 1995; mem. editl. bd. Signs: Jour. Women in Culture and Society, Law and History Rev.; contbr. articles and book revs. to profl. jours. Fellow Danforth Found., Barnard Coll., NEH, 1976, 83-84, 94, Am. Coun. Learned Socs., 1975, Nat. Humanities Ctr., 1990-91, Guggenheim Found., 1990-91. Mem. Orgn. Am. Historians (pres.-elect 1995), Am. Hist. Assn., Am. Studies Assn. (pres. 1988), Am. Soc. for Legal History, Berkshire Conf. Women Historians. Jewish. Office: U Iowa Dept History Iowa City IA 52242

KERBIN, DIANE LEITHISER, history educator; b. Havre de Grace, Md., Oct. 20, 1941; d. William Austin and Mildred (Tweed) Leithiser; m. William Howard Kerbin, June 8, 1963; children: Laura, William. BA, Western Md. Coll., Westminster, 1963; MEd, Salisbury (Md.) State U., 1984. Cert. Secondary History, Social Studies, Md. Tchr. Worcester County Bd. Edn., Newark, Md., 1963-65; exec. sec. Pocomoke City (Md.) C. of C. and Bus. Assn., Md., 1979-81; adult lit. program coord. Worcester County Libr., Snow Hill, Md., 1982-83; counselor Worcester County Health Dept., Snow Hill, Md., 1983-84; tchr. Worcester County Bd. Edn., Newark, Md., 1984—; mem. sch. Improvement Team, Pocomoke, Md., 1991-92, Sch. Improvement Adv. Com., 1990-91, 92—. Past mem. Jr. Woman's Club, Pocomoke City, Md., 1970-75, Worcester County (Md.) Garden Club, 1970-80; vol. tutor Citizens Involved with Today's Youth, Pocomoke City, Md., 1992—. Named Pocomoke Mid. Tchr. of Yr., 1993-94. Mem. Nat. Coun. for Social Studies, Orgn. of Am. Hist., Alpha Delta Kappa. Democrat. Episcopalian. Office: Pocomoke Mid Sch 800 8th St Pocomoke City MD 21851-1599

KERBIS, GERTRUDE LEMPP, architect; m. Walter Peterhans (dec.); m. Donald Kerbis (div. 1972); children: Julian, Lisa, Kim. BS, U. Ill.; MA, Ill. Inst. Tech.; postgrad., Grad. Sch. Design, Harvard U., 1949-50. Archtl. designer Skidmore, Owings & Merrill, Chgo., 1954-59, C.F. Murphy Assocs., Chgo., 1959-62, 65-67; pvt. practice architecture Lempp Kerbis Assocs., Chgo., 1967—; lectr. U. Ill., 1969; prof. William Rainey Harper Coll., 1970—, Washington U., St. Louis, 1977, 82, Ill. Inst. Tech., 1989-91; archtl. cons. Dept. Urban Renewal, City of Chgo.; mem. Northeastern Ill. Planning Commn., Open Land Project, Mid-North Community Orgn., Chgo. Met. Housing and Planning Council, Chgo. Mayor's Commn. for Preservation Chgo.'s Hist. Architecture; bd. dirs. Chgo. Sch. Architecture Found., 1972-76; trustee Chgo. Archtl. Assistance Ctr., Glessner House Found., Inland Architect Mag.; lectr. Art Inst. Chgo., U. N.Mex., Ill. Inst. Tech., Washington U., St. Louis, Ball State U., Muncie, Ind., U. Utah, Salt Lake City. Prin. archtl. works include U.S. Air Force Acad. dining hall, Colo., 1957, Skokie (Ill.) Pub. Library, 1959, Meadows Club, Lake Meadows, Chgo., 1959, O'Hare Internat. Airport 7 Continents Bldg, 1963; prin. developer and architect: Tennis Club, Highland Park, Ill., 1968, Watervliet, Mich. Tennis Ranch, 1970, Greenhouse Condominium, Chgo., 1976, Webster-Clark Townhouses, Chgo., 1986, Chappell Sch., 1993; exhibited at Chgo. Hist. Soc., 1984, Chgo. Mus. Sci. and Industry, 1985, Paris Exhbn. Chgo. Architects, 1985, Spertus Mus.; represented in permanent archtl. drawings collection Art Inst. Chgo. Active Art Inst. Chgo.. Recipient award for outstanding achievement in professions YWCA Met. Chgo., 1984. Fellow AIA (bd. dirs. Chgo. chpt. 1971-75, chpt. pres. 1980, nat. com. architecture, arts and recreation 1972-75, com. on design 1975-80, head subcom. inst. honors nomination); mem. Chgo. Women in Architecture (founder), Chgo. Network, Internat. Women's Forum, Arts Club Chgo., Cliff Dwellers (bd. dirs. 1987-88, pres. 1988, 89), Lambda Alpha. Office: Lempp Kerbis Assocs 172 W Burton Pl Chicago IL 60610-1310

KERCE, ELYSE WOFFORD, psychologist; b. Yoakum, Tex.; d. Vernon Rutledge Wofford and Maybelle Elizabeth (Pipkin) Holland; m. Paul S. Kerce (div.); children: Stephen P., Kevin L., Jeffrey W. BA in Social Ecology, U. Calif., Irvine, 1976; MS in Indsl. and Orgnl. Psychology, Calif. State U., Long Beach, 1979; PhD in Social and Orgnl. Psychology, Claremont Grad. Sch., 1987. Teaching asst. psychology dept. Pitzer Coll., 1979; rsch. asst. Claremont (Calif.) Grad. Sch., 1980, mem. rsch. team and orgnl. rsch. and problem solving team, 1983-85; pers. rsch. psychology Navy Pers. R & D Ctr., San Diego, 1981, 82, 86—; orgnl. cons., 1979-85; instr. Saddleback Coll., 1983-85. Contbr. articles to profl. publs. Calif. State grad. fellow, 1977-81, fellow Claremont Grad. Sch., 1982, Haynes dissertation fellow, 1985-86. Mem. APA. Democrat. Episcopalian. Office: Navy Pers R & D Ctr 53335 Ryne Rd San Diego CA 92152-7207

KERESTY-HERITAGE, LYNNE JUDITH, administrative assistant; b. Phila., Aug. 14, 1943; d. Joseph Stephen and Charlotte Anna (Ogden) Keresty; divorced; children: Robert C., David M., Patricia L. Student, Atlantic County C.C., 1992—. Regional sr. control clk. Ea. Seaboard Prudential Life Ins. Co., 1961-68; sales clk, mgr. summer store Kranich Dress Shoppe, 1964-68; account receivable bookkeeper Holy Redeemer V.N.A., 1983-88; office bus. mgr. Phys. Therapy Svcs., 1989; sec. to nutritional svcs. dept. Burdette Tomlin Meml. Hosp., Cape May Court House, N.J., 1990, dir.'s asst., 1991—. Organizer Lower Twp. Crime Watch Program, Cape May County, N.J., 1990. Recipient N.J. Safety Patrol award North Wildwood (N.J.) Police, 1956, 58. Mem. NAFE, Future Bus. Leaders Am. (del. 1958-61). Republican. Methodist. Home: 10 Harmony Ln N Cape May NJ 08204-3514 Office: Burdette Tomlin Meml Hosp 2 Stone Harbor Blvd Cape May Court House NJ 08210-2171

KERKEL, LYNN, middle school educator; b. Baton Rouge, Nov. 14, 1942; d. Peter Phillip and Rosa Emaline (Dunnam) K.; m. James O. Skidmore, Dec. 23, 1972 (div. Jan. 6, 1978). AA, Mt. San Antonio Jr. Coll., 1962; BE, Kent State U., 1965, MEd in Reading, 1973. Cert. elem. educator, reading specialist, Ariz., Mich. Elem. educator Willoughby (Ohio) Eastlake Bd. Edn., 1965-84, mid. sch. educator, 1984—; inservice instr. Willoughby-Eastlake Bd. Edn. Recipient Jennings grant Martha Holden Jennings Found., 1992; Named to South High Sch. Hall of Fame Willoughby-Eastlake Bd. Edn., 1989; Jennings grantee Martha Holden Jennings Found., 1992, scholar, 1978-79. Mem. NEA (rep. 1979—), AAUW, Willoughby Eastlake Tchr. Assn. (past pres. 1981-86, grievance co-chair 1965—), Galilee Shrine #41 Order of the White Shrine of Jerusalem, Am. Profl. Partnership for Lithuanian Edn., Ohio Edn. Assn. (rep. 1970—), Northeastern Ohio Edn. Assn., Internat. Reading Assn., Delta Kappa Gamma Soc. Internat. Democrat. Methodist. Home: 5457D Millwood Ln Willoughby OH 44094-3263

KERKLO, NORMA JEAN, information systems specialist; b. McKeesport, Pa., Dec. 6, 1947; d. John and Edythe (Steiner) Moore; m. John M. Kerklo, Sept. 8, 1964 (div. 1989); children: Mark, Michelle. AA in Journalism, Riverside City Coll.; BA in Tech. Writing, U. Colo. Comm. coord. U. Tex., El Paso; journalist Norco (Calif.) Pony Express; pub. info. asst. State Bd. for C.C. and Occupational Edn., Denver, 1984-85; from assoc. tech. writer to sr. tech. writer McData Corp., Broomfield, Colo., 1986-92; trainer, tech. writer Micro Decisionware, Inc., Boulder, Colo., 1992—. Mem. Soc. for Tech. Comm. (sr. mem., competition mgr. 1990, awards mgr. 1992-93, Achievement award 1991), Soc. for Computing and Informational Processing. Home: 1364 Elmer Dr Denver CO 80233-3571 Office: Micro Decisionware 2995 Wilderness Pl Boulder CO 80301

KERKOVIUS, RUTH, artist; b. Berlin, June 9, 1921; raised in Riga, Latvia; came to U.S., 1949; m. Jay L. Johnson. Student, U. Munich, 1946-48, Pratt Graphic Art, 1958-62, Art Students League, 1951-53, 86-88; hon. degree in textile engring., Ga. Tech., 1955. Head mill designer Wamsutta Mills, New Bedford, Mass., 1949-52; car upholstery designer Chicopee Mills, Johnson & Johnson, N.Y. & Ga., 1953-58; printmaker etcher Assoc. Am. Artist, Weyhe, Main Galleries, N.Y., Ariz. and Chgo., 1962-85; painter, sculptor, 1988—. Represented in collections at IBM Gallery, Bell Telephone, Mobil, Exxon, Mayo Clinic, Mus. Fine Arts, Boston, Pa. Acad. Fine Arts, Phila., Mus. Western Art, Ft. Worth, U. Chgo., Cin. Art Mus., Pepsi-Cola, De Pauw U., Greencastle, Ind., also numerous pvt. collections. Home: 145 E 16th St New York NY 10003 Studio: 426 E 91st St New York NY 10128

KERLEY, JANICE JOHNSON, personnel executive; b. Coral Gables, Fla., Nov. 28, 1938; d. Howard Love and Lois Dean (Austin) Johnson; m. Bobby Joe Kerley, May 16, 1959; children: Janice Elisabeth Kerley Smothers, Meredith Ann Kerley Tucker. AA, Stephens Coll., 1958; B in Music Edn., U. Miami, Fla., 1960. Tchr. Dade County Pub. Schs., Miami, 1960-69; asst. to v.p. engr. Racal-Milgo, Inc., Miami, 1972-80; dir. sales and mktg. B. Joe Kerley, Realtor, Miami, 1980-83; dir. customer service, ops. mgr. Modern-Age Furniture Co., Miami, 1983-85; chief exec. officer Adia Pers. Svcs., Greensboro, Winston-Salem, N.C., 1985—. Named Small Bus. Person of Greensboro, Greensboro C. of C., 1988, Remarkable Woman of Greensboro, Greensboro Coll. Honor Soc., 1991. Mem. Am. Bus. Women's Assn. (nat. bd. dirs. 1978-79, trustee nat. scholarship fund 1978-79, named one of top ten businesswomen, 1988). Office: Adia Pers Svcs 315B Pomona Dr Greensboro NC 27407-1621 also: 4300 Indiana Ave Ste 35 Winston Salem NC 27105-2512

KERLINGER, KATHLEEN FAITH, bank executive; b. Apr. 16, 1960. BS in Acctg. and Fin. cum laude, CUNY, 1990. Sec. to v.p. of sales Interstate Cigar Co., Westbury, N.Y., 1978-80; sec. to fin. contr. for Visa credit card sector Chase Manhattan Bank, N.A., Lake Success, N.Y., 1980-82; sec. to exec. v.p. and CFO midmarket aerospace hardware mfr. Hi-Shear Industries, Inc., North Hills, N.Y., 1982-84; sr. adminstrv. sec. N.Y. br. comml. lending dept. Standard Chartered Bank, N.Y.C., 1984-85, office mgr. N.E. regional office, 1985-89, field auditor, 1989-91; asst. v.p., ops. mgr. ABN-Amro/LaSalle Bus. Credit, Inc. (formerly Standard Chartered Bank/Stan Chart Bus. Credit, Inc.), N.Y.C., 1991-94; sr. field examiner Sanwa Bus. Credit, Teaneck, N.J., 1994—. Office: Sanwa Bus Credit Corp 500 Glenpointe Ctr W Teaneck NJ 07666

KERN, ANGELINE FRAZIER, educational administrator; b. Jackson, Tenn., Apr. 27, 1939; d. William Raymond and Sarah Louise (Harris) Frazier; divorced; children: Tiffany Louise, Kevin James. BA, Lambuth Coll., Jackson, 1961; MA, Memphis State U., 1962; postgrad., U. Tenn., 1963. Cert. assessor trainer, Nat. Assn. Secondary Sch. Prins. Tchr. phys. edn. Jackson City Schs., 1960-62; tchr. English, guidance counselor Georgian Hills Jr. High Sch., Memphis, 1962-65; guidance counselor Colonial Jr. High Sch., Memphis, 1965-70; adminstrv. asst. Kingsbury High Sch., Memphis, 1970-72; prin. Avon Elem. Sch., Memphis, 1972-77, Balmoral Elem. Sch., Memphis, 1977-93, Cordova Sch., 1993—. Mem. adv. bd. East Memphis YMCA, 1984-87; mem. Memphis City Beautiful Commn., 1985-89; pres. St. John's Creek Home and Garden Club, Memphis, 1968-70. Recipient Youth Svc. award YMCA, Memphis, 1983, Vol. Recognition award, 1986; finalist Rotary Club Prin. of Yr. award, 1989. Mem. NEA, Nat. Assn. Elem. Sch. Prins., Assn. for Sch. Curriculum Devel., Tenn. Assn. Elem. Sch. Prins. (fall conf. planning com. 1985), Memphis Pub. Sch. Prins. Assn. (auditing com. 1983-85), Memphis State U. Rebounders, Educators Bridge Club, Phi Delta Kappa, Delta Kappa Gamma (fin. chmn. Epsilon chpt. 1976-84, corr. sect. 1990-92). Republican. Roman Catholic. Office: Cordova Sch 900 Sanga Rd Cordova TN 38018

KERN, CONSTANCE ELIZABETH, real estate broker; b. Cleve., Dec. 18, 1937; d. Walter Anthony and Irene (Davies) Matthews; divorced; children: James, David, Douglas, Kathleen. Student, John Carroll U., 1957, Case Western Res. U., 1958; BA in Speech and English, Marietta (Ohio) Coll., 1959; postgrad., Sul Ross State U., Midland, Tex., 1967-68, Comml. Coll. Real Estate, Ft. Worth, 1984, 86. Cert. tchr., Ohio, Tex.; lic. real estate broker, Tex. Tchr. South Euclid and Lyndhurst (Ohio) Schs., 1959-60; sec. Pan Am. Petroleum, Midland, 1960-61; tchr. St. Ann's Sch., Midland, 1967-69; real estate agt. McAfee & Assocs., Arlington, Tex., 1985-86; real estate broker Constance Kern Real Estate, Arlington, 1986—; property mgr., 1986—; oil operator, investor, Midland and Arlington, 1975-92. Vol. Pink Ladies Midland Meml. Hosp., 1970-73; troop leader Brownies Girl Scouts Am., Midland, 1971; vol. speech therapist Children's Service League Cerebral Palsy Ctr., Midland, 1975-76. Mem. Pi Kappa Delta. Republican. Roman Catholic.

KERN, EDNA RUTH, insurance executive; b. Rochester, N.Y., Dec. 31, 1945; d. Carl H. and Mildred B. (Fronk) McRorie; m. Charles E. Kern, Nov. 1, 1968 (div. July 1975); 1 child, Barbara Renee. BBA summa cum laude, Tex. Wesleyan Coll., 1978. CLU; ChFC; registered health underwriter. Pvt. detective Statewide Detective Agy., Orlando, Fla., 1968-78; agt. Pacific Mut. Ins., Ft. Worth, 1978-79, Conn. Mut. Ins., Ft. Worth, 1979-83; gen. agt. Gen. Am. Life Ins., Ft. Worth, 1983-85; ins. owner Kern & Assocs., Ft. Worth, 1985—; life underwriters tng. fellow. Pres. All Svs. Hosp. Execs. Forum, Ft. Worth, 1986-87, Women's Health Forum, 1994—; bd. dirs. YWCA, 1984-85. Mem. Ft. Worth Assn. Life Underwriters (bd. dirs. 1986-91, moderator 1984-86, chmn. health com., chmn. edn. com. 1986-88), Tarrant County Assn. Health Underwriters (pres. 1986-87), Sales and Mktg. Exec. Club (sec. Ft. Worth chpt. 1994-95, v.p. 1986-87, bd. dirs. 1985-87), Nat. Assn. Health Underwriters (nat. sec.-treas. 1990-91, Disting. Svc. award), Tex. Assn. Health Underwriters (state sec., bd. dirs. 1987-88, pres. 1988-90, Outstanding Texan of Yr. award, Hollis Roberson award), Sales and Mktg. Execs. Ft. Worth (sec. 1994—), Mensa. Republican. Office: Kern & Assocs PO Box 331296 Fort Worth TX 76163-1296

KERNAN, BARBARA DESIND, senior government executive; b. N.Y.C., Jan. 11, 1939; d. Philip and Anne (Feuer) Desind; m. Joseph E. Kernan, Feb. 14, 1973. BA cum laude, Smith Coll., 1960; postgrad. Oxford U., 1963; MA, Harvard U., 1963; postgrad. in edn. policy George Washington U., 1980. Editor Harvard Law Sch., 1960-62; tchr. English, Newton High Sch. (Mass.), 1962-63; editor Allyn & Bacon Pubs., Boston, 1963-64; edn. assoc. Upward Bound, Edn. Assocs., Inc., Washington, 1965-68; edn. program specialist Title I, Elem. and Secondary Edn. Act, U.S. Office Edn., 1969-73; fellow Am. Polit. Sci. Assn., Senator William Proxmire and Congressman Alphonzo Bell, 1973-74; spl. asst. to dep. commr. for elem. and secondary edn. and dir. dissemination, sch. finance and analysis, U.S. Office Edn., 1975-77, chief program analysis br. div. edn. for disadvantaged, 1977-79; chief grant program coordination staff Office Dep. Commr. for Ednl. Resources, 1979-80; chief priority concerns staff Office Asst. Sec. Mgmt., U.S. Dept. Edn., Washington, 1980-81; dir. div. orgnl. devel. and analysis Office of Dep. Undersec. for Mgmt., 1981-86; Sr. Exec. Svc. candidate on spl. project to improve status of women Sec. Transp., Washington, 1983-84; inducted Sr. Exec. Svc., 1986; assoc. adminstr. for adminstrn. Nat. Hwy. Traffic Safety Adminstrn., U.S. Dept. Transp., 1986—, career devel. leader to presdl. mgmt. interns, 1989-91. Recipient awards U.S. Office Edn., 1969, 71, 77, U.S. Dept. Edn., 1981-86, U.S. Dept. Transp., 1991, Small Agy. Coun., 1990; scholarships U. Mich., 1956-58, Smith Coll., 1958-60, Harvard U., 1962-63; Am. Polit. Sci. Assn. fellow, 1973-74; Sr. Exec. fellow John F. Kennedy Sch. Govt. Harvard U., 1983.

KERN-FOXWORTH, MARILYN LOUISE, journalism educator; b. Kosciusko, Miss., Mar. 4, 1954; d. Jimmie and Manella (Dickens) Kern; m. Gregory Lamar Foxworth, July 3, 1984; 1 child, Gregory Lamar II. BS, Jackson State U., 1974; MS, Fla. State U., 1976; PhD, U. Wis., 1982. Pub. rels. asst. Sta. WJTV, Jackson, Miss., 1974; communications specialist Fla. State U., Tallahassee, 1974; advt. coordinator City of Tallahassee, 1975-76; coll. rels. rep. GTE Automatic Electric, Northlake, Ill., 1977; AM traffic mgr. Sta. WWQM Radio, Madison, Wis., 1978-79; prodn. mgr. Sta. WHA-AM, Madison, 1979-80; columnist, reporter Mid-West Observer, Madison, 1979-80; asst. prof. U. Tenn., Knoxville, 1980-87; prof. Tex. A&M U., College Station, 1987—. Assoc. editor Nashville Banner, 1983; contbr. chpt. to Dictionary Lit. Biography, 1985; contbr. articles to mags. including Black Collegian (Unity award 1985). Co-chair advisory Phyllis Wheatley YWCA, Knoxville, 1983-85. Amon Carter Evans scholar U. Tenn., 1983; Agnes Harris fellow AAUW, 1991-92; fellow Am. Press Inst., 1988, Poynter Inst., 1988; recipient Kizzy award Black Women's Hall of Fame, Chgo., 1980, Pathfinder award Pub. Rels. Inst., 1988, PRSSA Adviser of Yr., Kreightaun Under-40 award Assn. for Men Educators in Journalism and Men in Comm., 1993; named Women of Achievement, U. Tenn., 1983; 1st black person in U.S. to receive PhD in Advt. and Pub. Rels.; Tex. State Senate Proclamation, 1993. Me. Pub. Rels. Soc. Am. (accredited; Recognition of Excellence 1985), Assn. for Ednl. Journalism (nat. com., Rsch. award 1980), Nat. Communication Assn. (planning com.), Black Media Assn., Alpha Kappa Alpha. Home: 3710 Stillmeadow Dr Bryan TX 77802-3913 Office: Tex A&M U Dept Journalism 230 Reed McDonald College Station TX 77843-4111

KERNS, PEGGY SHOUP, state legislator; b. Columbus, Ohio, Mar. 17, 1941; d. Ronald Traxler and Marie (Strausbaugh) Shoup; m. Pat L.J. Kerns, Nov. 9, 1963; children: Jerry, Deborah. BA, Duquesne U., 1963. Editor co. newspaper Samsonite Corp., Denver, 1978-83; mgr. customer svc. dept. Mt. Med. Equipment, Littleton, Colo., 1983-88; mem. State Ho. of Reps., Colo., 1989—; mem. bd. trustees Aurora (Colo.) Regional Med. Ctr., 1984—. Mem. coun. City of Aurora, 1983-89, mayor pro tem., asst. minority leader, 1993-94, minority leader, 1994—. Named Bus. and Profl. Women's Woman of Yr., 1991, Legislator of Yr. Colo. Assn. Commerce and Industry, 1993, Colo. Sch. Nurses Assn., Colo. Children's Campaign, 5th Most Effective Legislator by Colo. Bus. Mag., 1994, Legislator of Yr. by AP, 1994. Mem. AAUW, LWV, Aurora C. of C. (Woman of Yr. 1989), BPW. Democrat. Roman Catholic. Home: 1124 S Oakland St Aurora CO 80012-4260 Office: State Ho Reps State Capitol Denver CO 80201

KERPER, MEIKE, family violence, sex abuse and addictions educator, consultant; b. Powell, Wyo., Aug. 13, 1929; d. Wesley George and Hazel (Bowman) K.; m. R.R. Milodragovich, Dec. 25, 1963 (div. 1973); children: Dan, John, Teren, Tina, Stana. BS, U. Mont., 1973; MS, U. Ariz., 1975; postgrad. Ariz. State U., 1976-78, Columbia Pacific U., 1990—. Lic. marriage & family therapist, Oreg.; cert. domestic violence counselor, alcoholism and drug abuse counselor, mental health profl. and investigator. Family therapist Cottonwood Hill, Arvada, Colo., 1981; family program developer Turquoise Lodge, Albuquerque, 1982; co-developer abusers program Albuquerque Shelter Domestic Violence, 1984; family therapist Citizens Coun. Alcoholism and Drug Abuse, Albuquerque, 1984-86; pvt. practice cons. and trainer family violence and treatment, Albuquerque, 1987—; developer sex offender program Union County, Oreg. Co-author: Court Diversion Program, 1985; author Family Treatment, 1982. Lobbyist CCOPE, Santa Fe, 1983-86; bd. dirs. Union County Task Force on Domestic Violence, 1989-91; developer Choices program treatment of sex offenders and victims Union, Wallowa and Baker Counties, Oreg.; mem. Child Abuse Prevention Team, Union County, Baker County and Wallowa County, Oreg. Recipient commendation Albuquerque Shelter Domestic Violence, 1984. Mem. Assn. for the Treatment Sexual Abusers, Nat. Assn. Marriage and Family Therapists, Nat. Assn. Alcoholism Counselors, Delta Delta Delta. Republican. Episcopalian. Club: PEO. Avocations: Art history; reading; Indian culture; swimming; public speaking. Home: 61002 Love Rd Cove OR 97824-8211

KERR, ALVA RAE, writer, editor, association executive; b. Borger, Tex., July 29, 1926; d. Rene Lawerence and Georgia Margaret (Jones) McDonald; m. Gary Karp, Jan. 23, 1946 (dec. 1969); children: Pamela Karp Roper, Victoria, Richard; m. Glenn Enevold Kerr, Nov. 18, 1977. Student U. of Ams., Mex., 1970; BA, U. Houston, 1972; MA, George Washington U., 1975. Real estate broker Coldwell Banker Realtors, McLean, Va., 1975-83, writer, editor, D.C. area, 1984; writer, editor Nat. Capital chpt. Multiple Sclerosis Soc., Washington, 1984-86; corr. sec. UN World Com. Decade of Disabled Persons, Washington, 1985-86; writer, editor Retired Officers Assn. of Houston, 1990—; lectr. Nat. Security Agy., Fort Meade, Md., 1983, Somerset Civic Assn., Fairfax, Va., 1983, B'nai Brith, McLean, 1984, also others. Vol. spl. asst. on community program Nat. Orgn. on Disability, Washington, 1985-86; active Soc. for Performing Arts of Harris County, 1986-88. Recipient Commendátiere for Outstanding Newsletter, Ret. Officers Assn., 1994. Mem. AAUW, Scriptwriters of Houston, Campanille Writer's Group, Assn. Adms.-Texas Navy, Phi Delta Gamma (pres. 1984-86). Avocations: writing, music. Home: 17006 Hillswind Cir Spring TX 77379-4505

KERR, JEAN, writer; b. Scranton, Pa., July 10, 1923; d. Thomas J. and Kitty (O'Neill) Collins; m. Walter Kerr, Aug. 16, 1943; children: Christopher, John and Colin (twins), Gilbert, Gregory, Katharine. B.A., Marywood Coll., 1943; M.F.A., Cath. U. Am., 1945; L.H.D., Northwestern U., 1962, Fordham U., 1965. Author: (plays) Jenny Kissed Me, 1948, (with Walter Kerr) Thank You, Just Looking, 1949 (produced on Broadway as Touch and Go, 1949), (with Eleanor Brooke) King of Hearts, 1954, (with Kerr) Goldilocks, 1958, Mary, Mary, 1961, Poor Richard, 1965, Finishing Touches, 1973, Lunch Hour, 1980; (essays) Please Don't Eat the Daisies, 1957, The Snake Has All the Lines, 1960, Penny Candy, 1970, How I Got to Be Perfect, 1978; adapter: (plays) (with Kerr) The Song of Bernadette, 1944, Our Hearts Were Young and Gay, 1946, The Big Help, 1947, The Good Fairy, 1955. Recipient Campion award, 1971, Laetare medal Univ. Notre Dame, 1971. Mem. Nat. Inst. Social Scis. Democrat. Roman Catholic. Home: 1 Beach Ave Larchmont NY 10538-4004*

KERR, LISA ANN, clinical scientist; b. New Castle, Pa., July 12, 1963; d. Walter Allen and Donna Miriam (Eshbaugh) K.; m. Robert Ilowite. BA, U. Pa., 1987; MBA, Fairleigh Dickinson U., 1995. Rsch. asst. U. Pa., Phila., 1984-87, rsch. coord., 1988-89; clin. rsch. asst. Immunobiology Rsch. Inst., Annandale, N.J., 1989-90; assoc. clin. scientist Bristol-Myers Squibb Co., Princeton, N.J., 1990-91; clin. scientist, 1991-92; ops. analyst Bristol-Myers Squibb Co., Princeton, N.J., 1992-93, mgr. clin. ops., 1993—. Contbr. articles to profl. jours. Recipient Yale U. scholarship, summer 1982. Mem. Soc. for Neuroscience, British Brain Rsch. Assn., British Brain and Behavior Soc., Assocs. Clin. Pharmacology. Republican. Methodist. Home: 12 Greenwood Ct Branchburg NJ 08876 Office: Bristol-Myers Squibb Co Rte 206 and Province Line Rd Princeton NJ 08543

KERR, MABEL DOROTHEA, psychiatrist, educator; b. Toronto, Ont., Can. (parents Am. citizens); d. George Houston and Mabel (Wark) Kerr; B.S., Ohio State U., 1944; M.D., Columbia, 1950. Intern dept. medicine St. Luke's Hosp., N.Y.C., 1950-51, resident, 1951-52; psychiat. resident Payne Whitney Clinic, N.Y. Hosp., 1952-57; practice medicine, specializing in psychiatry, N.Y.C., 1954—; assoc. attending psychiatrist N.Y. Hosp., 1979—; clin. asst. prof. psychiatry Cornell U. Med. Coll., 1968-79, clin. assoc. prof., 1979—; asst. med. examiner, officer chief med. examiner City of N.Y., 1957-66. Pres., Elmora Found. Fellow N.Y. Acad. Medicine; mem. AMA, Am. Psychiat. Assn., Women's Med. Soc. N.Y. State, Am. Med. Women's Assn. Address: 449 E 68th St New York NY 10021

KERR, NANCY HELEN, psychology educator; b. L.A., June 27, 1947; d. Edmund James and Sally (Byrd) K.; m. David Foulkes, Apr. 19, 1978. BA, Stanford U., 1969; PhD, Cornell U., 1974. Asst. prof. psychology U. Wyo., Laramie, 1974-78; vis. asst. prof. psychology Emory U., Atlanta, 1978-79, vis. asst. prof. psychiatry, 1979-82; vis. asst. prof. psychology Mercer U., Macon, Ga., 1982-83; asst. prof. to prof. psychology Oglethorpe U., Atlanta, 1983—, chair div. behavioral scis., 1989—. Contbr. articles to profl. jours. Recipient James McKeen Cattell award, 1990. Mem. Am. Psychol. Soc., Psychonomic Soc., Southeastern Psychol. Assn. Office: Oglethorpe U 4484 Peachtree Rd NE Atlanta GA 30319-2737

KERR, NANCY KAROLYN, pastor, mental health consultant; b. Ottumwa, Iowa, July 10, 1934; d. Owen W. and Iris Irene (Israel) K. Student Boston U., 1953; AA, U. Bridgeport, 1966; BA, Hofstra U., 1967; postgrad. in clin. psychology Adelphi U. Inst. Advanced Psychol. Studies, 1968-73; MDiv Associated Mennonite Bibl. Sems., 1986; m. Richard Clayton Williams, June 28, 1953 (div.); children: Richard Charles, Donna Louise. Ordained pastor Mennonite Ch., 1987; inducted pastor Presbyn. Ch., Can., 1992. Pastoral counselor Nat. Council Chs., Jackson, Miss., 1964; dir. teen program Waterbury (Conn.) YWCA, 1966-67; intern in psychology N.Y. Med. Coll., 1971-72; rsch. cons., 1972-73; coord. home svcs., psychologist City and County of Denver, 1972-75; cons. Mennonite Mental Health Svcs., Denver, 1975-78; asst. prof. psychology Messiah Coll., 1978-79; mental health cons., 1979-81; called to ministry Mennonite Ch., 1981, pastor Cin. Mennonite Fellowship, 1981-83, coord. campus peace evangelism, 1981-83, mem. Gen. Conf. Peace and Justice Reference Council, 1983-85; instr. Associated Mennonite Bibl. Sems., 1985; teaching elder Assembly Mennonite Ch., 1985-86; pastor Pulaski Mennonite Ch., 1986-89; v.p. Davis County Mins.' Assn., 1988-89; exec. dir., pastoral counselor Bethesda Counseling Svcs., Prince George B.C., 1989—; bd. dirs. Tri-County Counselling Clinic, Memphis, Mo., 1980-81; spl. ch. curriculum Nat. Council Chs., 1981; mem. Cen. Dist. Conf. Peace and Justice Com., 1981-89; mem. exec. bd. People for Peace, 1981-83. Mem. Waterbury Planned Parenthood Bd., 1964-67; mem. MW Children's Home Bd., 1974-75; bd. dirs. Boulder (Colo.) ARC, 1977-78; mem. Mennonite Disabilities Respite Care Bd., 1981-86; active Kanloops Presbytery Presbyn. Ch. Can., 1992—. Mem. APA (assoc.), Soc. Psychologists for Study of Social Issues, Christian Assn. Psychol. Studies, Davis County Mins. Assn. (v.p. 1988-89), Prince George Ministerial Assn. (chmn. edn. and Airport chapel coms. 1990-92).

KERR, REBECCA ANN, accounting educator; b. Columbia, S.C., Dec. 17, 1952; d. Hamilton Westlake and Barbara (Brown) K.; m. David Thomas Spell, Jr., May 10, 1975 (div. 1987). BS, U. S.C., 1975, MBA, 1984, M in Acctg., 1991. CPA, Fla. Staff acct. Gen. Constrn. Co., Columbia, 1975-77, comptr., 1977-80; acctg. instr. Midlands Tech. Coll., Columbia, 1984—. Treas. Jr. Woman's Club of Columbia, 1979. Mem. S.C. Assn. of Acctg. Instrs. (pres. 1990-91, liasion com. chair 1991-92), Inst. of Mgmt. Accts. (Columbia chpt. pres. 1994-95, v.p. edn. 1992-93, v.p. community svc. 1993-94), S.C. Assn. of CPAs (assoc.). Office: Midlands Tech Coll Beltline Blvd Columbia SC 29202

KERR, SYLVIA JOANN, educator; b. Detroit, June 19, 1941; d. Frederic Dilmus and Maud (Dirst) Pfeffer; m. Norman Story Kerr, Aug. 6, 1933; children: David, Kathleen. BA, Carleton Coll., 1963; MS, U. Minn., 1966, PhD, 1968. Asst. prof. Augsburg Coll., Mpls., 1968-71; instr. Anoka Ramsey Community Coll., Coon Rapids, Minn., 1973-74; from asst. prof. to full prof. Hamline U., St. Paul, 1974—. Contbr. numerous articles to profl. jours. NIH fellow U. Minn., 1972, 74-75. Office: Hamline U Dept Biology 1536 Hewitt Ave Saint Paul MN 55104-1284

KERR, WILMA ERNESTINE, construction company executive officer; b. Gunnison, Colo., Mar. 5, 1933; d. Ernest Franklin Reppy and Edith Irene (Evans) Stein; m. M. Keith Kerr, Aug. 4, 1957; children: David William, Patricia Jo Anne Christ, Karen Kay Gordon, Robert Keith. AS in Solar Constrn., Lane C.C., Eugene, Oreg., 1983, AS in Energy Mgmt. Tech., 1984. Cert. Oreg. Dept. Energy auditor. Corp. sec. Kerr Bros. Inc., Cottage Grove, Oreg., 1971-84; energy analyst Brown & Caldwell Engrs., Eugene, Oreg., 1984-87; cons. City of Springfield, Oreg., 1987-90; owner, mgr. Kerr Builders Inc., Creswell, Oreg., 1991—; mid. mgmt. vol. Oreg. State U. Ext., Eugene, 1990-94. Vol. Oreg. State U.-Lane Ext., Eugene, 1991—. Mem. Phi Theta Kappa. Republican. Presbyterian. Office: Kerr Builders Inc PO Box 844 Creswell OR 97426

KERSCHNER, BARBARA BUCKLEY, real estate developer; b. Gainesville, Fla., Aug. 28, 1926; d. Rolf Kennard and Margaret Mabel (Crawford) Buckley; m. Nolan Kellerman Kerschner, Mar. 2, 1945; children: Steven Nolan, Amy Margaret, Andrew Buckley, Sarah Ivy. BS, Sacred Heart U., Conn., 1978. Treas. Nolan K. Kerschner Co. Inc., Norwalk, Conn., 1964-94; owner Andrews Constrn. Co., Inc., Norwalk, 1994—. Bd. dirs., treas. Arts Coun., Norwalk, 1978-82, Human Svcs. Coun., 1990—; chmn. Dist. E. Dem. Com., 1983-87; mem. Norwalk Bd. Estimate and Taxation, 1984-88; vice chmn. Norwalk Dem. Town Com., 1988-94, treas. 1984-88; mem. Conn. Dem. State Cen. Com., 1990-94; mem. Congl. Ch. Coun., 1989—; formerly bd. dirs. Norwalk Econ. Opportunity Now, Inc. Home: 23 Splitrock Rd Norwalk CT 06854-4713 Office: Kerschner Cos 5 Eversley Ave Norwalk CT 06851-5821

KERSHAW, CAROL JEAN, psychologist; b. New Orleans, Apr. 11, 1947; d. Neal Howard and Gloria Jackson (Moss) Perkins; m. John William Wade, Aug. 20, 1983; stepchildren: Chris Wade, Stephen Wade, Tiffany Wade. BS in Secondary Edn., U. Tex., 1969; MS in Speech Communication, North Tex. State U., 1971, MEd in Counseling, 1976; EdD in Counseling, East Tex. State U., 1979. Lic. psychologist, Tex. Assoc. prof. DeVry Inst., Dallas, 1971-73; instr., counseling psychologist East Tex. State U., Commerce, 1976-78; counselor, instr. Tarrant County Jr. Coll., Hurst, Tex., 1971-74; dir. spl. svcs. Goodwill Industries, Dallas, 1974-76; marriage and family therapist, cons. mental health clinic Tex. Dept. Mental Health and Retardation, Greenville, 1977-79; asst. prof., dir. grad. program in marriage & family therapy Tex. Woman's U., Denton, 1980-83; coord. child devel. dept. Tex. Woman's U., Houston, 1983-88; pvt. practice Inst. for Family Psychology, Houston, 1986—; co-dir. Milton H. Erickson Inst. Houston, 1986—; bd. dirs. Milton H. Erickson Inst. Tex., Houston, 1986—; internat. presenter in field. Author: Therapeutic Metaphor in the Treatment of Childhood Asthma: A Systemic Approach, Ericksonian Monographs, Vol. 2, 1986, The Couple's Hypnotic Dance, 1992, The Healing Power of the Story, Ericksonian Monographs, Vol. 9, 1994; co-author: Psychotherapeutic Techniques in School Psychology, 1984, Learning to Think for an Organ, Bridges of the Bodymind, 1980, Restoring the Mind: Using Therapeutic Narrative in Psychotherapy in Ericksonian Methods, 1994, Healing the Body/Mind: A New Model For Using Group Hypnotism With Chronic Illness, Erickson Monographs, Vol. 11, 1995. Sec. Tex. Assn. for Marriage and Family Therapy, 1978-80. Recipient Visionary award, Meritorious Svc. award Tex. Assn. for Marriage & Family Therapy, 1980. Mem. Am. Psychol. Assn, Am. Assn. for Marriage and Family Therapy (clin., approved supr.), Soc. for Exptl. & Clin. Hypnosis, Am. Soc. for Clin. Hypnosis (cons.), Internat. Soc. for Clin. & Exptl. Hypnosis, Psi Chi. Democrat. Methodist. Office: Inst for Family Psychology 2012 Bissonnet St Houston TX 77005-1647

KERSTING, LISA GAYLE, librarian; b. Wichita; d. Evelyn A. (Schwartz) K. BS in Family Scis., Emporia State U., 1987. Resource libr. Andra Design Assocs., Wichita, 1987-94; libr. Motional Images Multimedia, Kansas City, Kans., 1994—. Named one of Outstanding Young Women of Am., 1986; Nat. Collegiate Home Econs. grantee, 1986, Acad. All-Am. grantee U.S. Achievement Acad., 1986. Mem. Order Ea. Star, Internat. Order of Rainbow for Girls (mem. jr. exec. com. 1986-89, mother advisor 1988-94). Republican. Presbyterian. Home: 12116 Norwood Leawood KS 66209 Office: Motional Images Multimedia 1140 Adams Ste 100 Kansas City KS 66103

KERSTNER, PATRICIA LOUISE, psychologist; b. Phila., Mar. 14, 1948; d. William Louis and Anna Marie (Litschauer) K.; m. Patrick B. Romine, May 18, 1985 (div. Aug. 1992). BA, Pa. State U., 1970; MA, U. Wyo., 1980; PhD, Ariz. State U., 1986. Instnl. aide Hunterdon (N.J.) State Sch., 1972-74; counselor Wyo. Youth Outreach Pl., Laramie, 1974-80; program supr. Vol. Sheltercare, Kennewick, Wash., 1980-81; staff psychotherapist Ctr. for Behavioral Health, Mesa, Ariz., 1982-86; staff psychologist Ctr. for Women's Health, Mesa, 1986-89; grad. asst. Ariz. State U., Tempe, 1981-82, faculty assoc. women's studies, 1984-94, cons. psychologist, 1989—; pvt. practice Ahwatukee Psychol. Svc., Tempe, 1989—; clin. specialist U. Phoenix, 1991—. Mem. AACD (chairperson com. on women 1989-90), Am. Mental Health Counselors Assn. (s.w. dist. cons. 1988-90, Grad. Student Rsch. award 1983), Am. Psychol. Assn., Ariz. Counselors Assn. (pres. 1988-89, Profl. Counselor of Yr. 1987). Office: U Phoenix Phoenix AZ 85040

KERT, BERNICE GALANSKY, writer; b. St. Louis, Oct. 4, 1923; d. Gus D. and Mary (Katanik) Galansky; m. Morley J. Kert, Jan. 14, 1945 (dec. May 1990); children: Elizabeth, Kathryn Green, Charles. BA, U. Mich., 1944. Teaching fellow dept. English U. Mich., Ann Arbor, 1946-47; editl. bd. The Hemingway Rev., Moscow, Idaho, 1992—. Author: (biographies) The Hemingway Women, 1983, Abby Aldrich Rockefeller, 1993. John Simon Guggenheim Meml. Found. fellow, N.Y.C., 1988; scholar-in-residence Bellagio (Italy) Study Ctr., 1991. Mem. J.B. Berland Found., The Hemingway Soc., Hillcrest Country Club, Authors Guild. Democrat. Jewish.

KERTZ, MARSHA HELENE, accountant, educator; b. Palo Alto, Calif., May 29, 1946; d. Joe and Ruth (Lazear) K. BSBA in Acctg., San Jose State U., 1976, MBA, 1977. CPA, Calif., cert. tax profl. Staff acct. Steven Kroff & Co., CPA's, Palo Alto, 1968-71, 73-74; contr. Rand Teleprocessing Corp., San Francisco, 1972; auditor, sr. acct. Ben F. Priest Accountancy Corp., Mountain View, Calif., 1974-83; tchr. San Jose Unified Regional Occupation Program, San Jose, 1977; pvt. practice accounting San Jose, 1977—; lectr. San Jose State U., 1977—. Mem. AICPA, Nat. Soc. of Tax Profls., Am. Inst. Tax Studies, Am. Acctg. Assn., Calif. Soc. CPAs, Beta Alpha Psi, Beta Gamma Sigma. Democrat. Jewish. Home: 4544 Strawberry Park Dr San Jose CA 95129-2213 Office: San Jose State U Acctg & Fin Dept San Jose CA 95192

KERWIN, MARY ANN COLLINS, lawyer; b. Oconomowoc, Wis., Oct. 16, 1931; d. Thomas Patrick and Florence Mary (Morris) Collins; m. Thomas Joseph Kerwin, Dec. 27, 1954; children: Thomas, Edward, Gregory, Mary, Anne, Katherine, John, Michael. BA, Barat Coll., 1953; JD, U. Denver, 1986. Bar: Colo. 1987. Tchr. Country Grade Sch., Wheaton, Ill., 1953-54; travel agt. Chgo. Athletic Club, 1954-55; legal intern City Atty.'s Office, Denver, 1985, Dist. Atty.'s Office, Denver, 1985; atty. Kerwin and Assocs., Denver, 1987-92, Decker, DeVoss & O'Malley, P.C., Denver, 1992-93, King Peterson Brown, LLC, Englewood, Colo., 1993-95, Daniel F. Lynch, P.C., Denver, 1995—; legal compliance dept. editor United Banks Colo., Inc., Denver, 1988-93. Author: (with others) The Womanly Art of Breastfeeding, 1958, revised edit. 1991; contbr. articles to profl. jours. Mem. Colo. Breatfeeding Task Force mem., 1990-93; adv. bd. St. Luke's Woman's Hosp., Denver, 1986—, Colo. Sudden Infant Death Syndrome Program, 1992-94; sch. bd. Christ the King Sch., Denver, 1970-73; great books leader Jr. and Collegiate Great Books, Denver, 1963-82; marriage spkr. Cath. Archdiocese, Denver, 1965-75; co-founder, bd. dirs. La Leche League Internat., Franklin Park, Ill., 1956—, founder state orgn., 1960—, chmn. bd. 1980-83, sec. 1988-91. Named One of Ten Outstanding Alumnus Barat Coll., 1988. Mem. Colo. Bar Assn., Colo. Women's Bar Assn., Denver Bar Assn., Colo. Alumnae Assn. (pres. 1968-70), Theresians (pres. 1974-76). Home: 200 Cherry St Denver CO 80220-5638 Office: Daniel F. Lynch PC 4704 Harlan St Ste 610 Denver CO 80212

KERY, PATRICIA ANN, legislative director; b. Danbury, Conn., Sept. 5, 1960; d. James R. and Mariellen A. (Keenan) K. BA, U. Conn., 1982; MPA in Tax Policy, George Washington U., 1989. Intern Conn. State Gen. Assembly, Hartford, 1979; adminstrv. asst. Ratchford for Congress Com., Danbury, 1980, rsch. dir., 1982, campaign mgr., 1984; legis. intern Conn. Dept. on Aging, Hartford, 1982; legis. aide to Rep. William Ratchford U.S. Ho. Reps., Washington, 1982-84, legis. dir. to Rep. Marcy Kaptur, 1985-88, sr. legis. asst. dir. to Rep. Barbara Kennelly, 1988—. Democrat. Roman Catholic. Office: US Ho Reps 201 Cannon House Office Bldg Washington DC 20515

KERZ, LOUISE, historian; b. N.Y.C., Sept. 16, 1936; d. Louis and Catharine (Sohn) Tittmann; m. Leo Kerz, Apr., 1965 (dec. 1976); children: Jonathan, Antony. Student, Queens Coll., 1954-56, Marymount Coll., 1972-74. Theatre producer Leo Kerz Prodns., N.Y.C., 1960-74; theatrical curator N.Y. Cultural Ctr., N.Y.C., 1974, Theatre of Max Reinhardt, 1974, N.Y. Pub. Libr., N.Y.C., 1984, Calif. Mus. Sci. and Industry, L.A., 1985, The Demille Dynasty, 1984; rsch. cons. CBS: On the Air, 1978, Smith-Hemion TV Prodns., L.A., 1987—, The Phantom of the Opera, 1995; dir. rsch. Greengage Prodns., L.A., 1988; rsch. cons. TV Acad. Hall of Fame and Tony Awards telecasts. Prodr. (Broadway prodn.) Rhinoceros, 1961; contbg. editor N.Y.C. Access, 1983; picture editor: The DeMilles: An American Family, 1988; curator/dir. Exhibit Broadway, 1995. Vol. Persian Gulf war Am. Jewish Congress, Israel, 1991. Mem. Theatre Libr. Assn. Democrat. Home: 333 E 69th St New York NY 10021

KESCHL, CONSTANCE FRANCES, home economics educator; b. Elizabeth, N.J., Mar. 31, 1949; d. Michael Peter and Helen Ann (Pazahanich) Lokuta; m. Dennis Lee Keschl, Sept. 5, 1970; children: Dennis Kurt, Thomas Michael. BS in Home Econs., Mansfield State Coll., 1971. Cert. home econs. tchr., N.J., Maine. Instr., curriculum developer child care Perth Amboy (N.J.) Adult Sch., 1975-76, educator family life/consumer edn., coord. home econs. dept., 1976, supr. sch. cafeteria, 1976, project dir., 1976-78; home econs. educator Livermore Falls (Maine) High Sch., 1979-87; home econs. educator, dept. chairperson Gardiner (Maine) Area High Sch., 1987-93; health/nutrition coord. Head Start No. Kennebec and Somerset Counties, Waterville, Maine, 1993—; substitute tchr. Manville (N.J.) Pub. Schs., Middlesex (N.J.) Pub. Schs., Union County Tech. Inst. and Vocat. Ctr., Scotch Plains, N.J., 1978-79; cooperating tchr. U. Maine, Farmington, 1980—. Grantee Carl D. Perkins, 1987. Mem. NEA, Maine Tchrs. Assn., Maine Home Econs. Assn., Pine Tree Quilters Guild Inc., Backroad Quilters, Cabin Fever Quilters. Roman Catholic. Home: 316 Wings Mls Rd Belgrade ME 04917 Office: KVCAP-Head Start PO Box 1529 Waterville ME 04903-1529

KESSEL, BRINA, ornithologist, educator; b. Ithaca, N.Y., Nov. 20, 1925; d. Marcel and Quinta (Cattell) K.; m. Raymond B. Roof, June 19, 1957 (dec. 1968). BS (Albert R. Brand Bird Song Found. scholar), Cornell U., 1947, PhD, 1951; MS (Wis. Alumni Research Found. fellow), U. Wis.-Madison, 1949. Student asst. Patuxent Research Refuge, 1946; student teaching asst. Cornell U., 1945-47, grad. asst., 1947-48, 49-51; instr. biol. sci. U. Alaska, summer 1951, asst. prof. biol. sci., 1951-54, assoc. prof. zoology, 1954-59, prof. zoology, 1959—, head dept. biol. scis., 1957-66; dean U. Alaska (Coll. Biol. Scis. and Renewable Resources), 1961-72, curator terrestrial vertebrate mus. collections, 1972-90, curator ornithology collection, 1990—, adminstrv. assoc. for acad. programs, grad. and undergrad., dir. acad. advising, office of chancellor, 1973-80; project dir. U. Alaska ecol. investigation for AEC Project Chariot, 1959-63; ornithol. investigations NW Alaska pipeline, 1976-81, Susitna Hydroelectric Project, 1980-83. Author book, monographs; contbr. articles to profl. jours. Fellow AAAS, Am. Ornithologists' Union (v.p. 1977, pres.-elect 1990-92, pres. 1992-94), Arctic Inst. N.Am.; mem. Wilson, Cooper ornith. socs., Soc. for Northwestern Vertebrate Biology, Pacific Seabird Group, Assn. Field Ornithologists, Sigma Xi (pres. U. Alaska 1957), Phi Kappa Phi, Sigma Delta Epsilon. Office: U Alaska Museum PO Box 80211 Fairbanks AK 99708-0211

KESSELHAUT, AMY BETH, art historian; b. Livingston, N.J., July 1, 1966; d. Arthur M. and Nancy S. (Slater) K. BS, U. So. Calif., 1988; postgrad., U. Calif., Santa Barbara. Fin. analyst Continental Bank, N.Y.C., 1988-90; asst. v.p. Security Pacific Bank, N.Y.C., 1990-91, Daiwa Bank, L.A., 1991-92; asst. to dir. edn. Santa Barbara Mus. Art, 1992—; tour guide Contemporary Arts Forum, U. Art Mus., Santa Barbara. Contbr. art revs. profl. jours. Coord. events L.A. Works, 1991-92; vol. N.Y. Cares, 1990-91. Mem. Am. Assn. Mus. Home: 235 Pacific Oaks # 204 Goleta CA 93117

KESSINGER, MARGARET ANNE, education educator; b. Beckley, W.Va., June 4, 1941; d. Clisby Theodore and Margaret Anne (Ellison) K.; m. Loyd Ernst Wegner, Nov. 27, 1971. MA, W.Va. U., 1963, MD, 1967. Diplomate Am. Bd. Internal Medicine and Med. Oncology. Internal medicine house officer U. Nebr. Med. Ctr., Omaha, 1967-70, fellow med. oncology, 1970-72, asst. prof. internal medicine, 1972-77, assoc. prof., 1977-90, prof., 1990—, assoc. chief oncology/hematology sect., 1988-91, chief oncology/hematology sect., 1991—. Contbr. articles to profl. publs. Fellow ACP; mem. Am. Assn. Cancer Edn., Am. Soc. Clin. Oncology, Am. Assn. Cancer Rsch., Internat. Soc. Exptl. Hematology, Am. Soc. Hematology, Sigma Xi, Alpha Omega Alpha. Republican. Methodist. Office: U Nebr Med Ctr 600 S 42d St Omaha NE 68198

KESSLER, DEBBIE THERESA, sales professional; b. Mattoon, Ill., Sept. 9, 1960; d. Kurt and Gertrude (Rehberger) K. Automobile sales cons. K.C. Summers Buick, Mattoon, Ill., 1977—. Recipient Buick Profl. Salesmaster award, Toyota Pride award. Mem. Eagles, Am. Legion, Women of the Moose. Republican. Lutheran. Office: KC Summers Buick PO Box 769 Mattoon IL 61938-0769

KESSLER, GLADYS, federal judge. BA, Cornell U., 1959; LLB, Harvard U., 1962. Staff atty. enforcement divsn. Nat. Labor Rels. Bd., 1962-64; legis. asst. Sen. Harrison A. Willians, N.J., 1964-66, Rep. Jonathan B. Bingham, 1966-68; staff atty. office labor rels N.Y.C. Bd. Edn., 1968-69; ptnr. Berlin, Roisman and Kessler (and successor firms), 1969-77; assoc. judge D.C. Superior Ct., 1977-94; judge U.S. Dist. Ct. D.C., Washington, 1994—; asst. lectr. law sch. George Washington U., 1971-73; del. to judicial adminstrn.

divsn. D.C. Superior Ct., 1985-90; mem. adv. bd. Ctr. for Dispute Settlement Inst. for Judicial Adminstrn., State Justice Inst., mem. adv. com. nat. judicial edn. project on domestic violence; mem BNA adv. bd. Alternative Dispute Resolution Report, 1987-90; mem. family law cirriculum planning com. Georgetown U.; lead judge permanency planning project Nat. Coun. Juvenile and Family Ct. Judges; chair Nat. Conf. on Bioethics, Family and the Law, D.C., 1991; mem. faculty Nat. Inst. Trial Advocacy. Contbr. articles to legal jours. Recipient Women Lawyer of Yr. award Women's Bar Assn., 1983, Svc. award D.C. Coalition Against Domestic Violence, 1987, Judicial Excellence award Trial Lawyers Assn. Washington, 1987. Fellow Am. Bar Found.; mem. ABA (judicial adminstrn. divsn., com. on bioethics and AIDS, adv. com. on youth, alcohol and drug problems, nat. adv. bd. on child support and criminal justice, individual rights and responsibilities sect.), Am. Judicature Soc. (bd. dirs. 1985-89), NOW Legal Def. and Edn. Fund, Inc., Nat. Assn. Women Judges (v.p. 1979-81, pres. 1981-82), Nat. Ctr. for State Cts. (bd. dirs. 1984-87), Women's Legal Def. Fund (founding pres. 1971), Women Judges' Fund. for Justice (bd. dirs. 1980—), Found. for Women Judges (pres. 1980-82), Pres.'s Coun. Cornell Women, Thurgood Marshall Am. Inn. Ct. Office: US Courthouse 333 Constitution Ave NW Rm 6333 Washington DC 20001*

KESSLER, JEAN S., business analyst; b. New Brunswick, N.J., Oct. 20, 1954; d. John S. and Henrietta Marguerite (Pasquier de Lumeau) Kessler; m. Michael P. Gutzan, Sept. 16, 1984; AAS with highest honors, Middlesex County Coll., 1981; AS in Mgmt. Edison State Coll., 1990, postgrad., 1990—. Cert. profl. ins. woman. Pres. Continental Ins. Co., Cranbury, N.J., 1981-89; exec. sec. Am. Reliance Ins. Co., 1989-92; assoc. underwriter, bus. analyst, Sprint, 1992-95. Recipient Sec. of Yr. award Profl. Secs. Internat. Cert. profl. sec. Mem. NAFE, Profl. Secs. Internat., Nat. Assn. Ins. Women (nominating com. 1990), Mensa, Nu Tau Sigma. Office: Three Bala Plz W Bala Cynwyd PA 19004

KESSLER, JOAN F., lawyer; b. June 25, 1943; m. Frederick P. Kessler, Sept. 1967; 2 children. BA, U. Kans., 1961-65; postgrad., U. Wis., 1965-66; JD cum laude, Marquette U., 1968. Law clk. Hon. John W. Reynolds U.S. Dist. Ct. (ea. dist.) Wis., Milw., 1968-69; assoc. Warschafsky, Rotter & Tarnoff, Milw., 1969-71; pvt. practice Milw., 1971-74; assoc. Cook & Franke, S.C., Milw., 1974-78; U.S. atty. Eastern Dist. Wis., Milw., 1978-81; ptnr. Foley & Lardner, Milw., 1981—; lectr. profl. responsibility U. Wis. Law Sch., Marquette U. Law Sch., Milw.; mem. bd. govs. State Bar of Wis., 1985-89, 90-92, 93—, chair, 1993; mem. Jud. Coun. Wis., Madison, 1989-92; mem. Milw. Bd. Attys. Profl. Responsibility, 1979-85, bd. dirs. family law sect. State Bar of Wis., 1991-94. Bd. dirs. Legal Aid Soc., 1974-78, v.p., 1978, Urban League, 1980-82, Womens Bus. Initiative Corp., 1989-91, Girl Scouts Am., Milw., 1994—; chair adv. com. Wis. Dept. Industry, Labor & Human Rels., 1976-78; bd. dirs., pres. Voters for Choice in Wis., 1989-93; active Tempo. Profl. Dimension. Fellow Am. Acad. Matrimonial Lawyers (bd. govs. 1990—); mem. ACLU. Office: Foley & Lardner 777 E Wisconsin Ave Milwaukee WI 53202-5302

KESSLER, KENDALL SEAY FERIOZI, artist; b. Washington, Nov. 4, 1954; d. Dan John and Anne Fletcher (Trotter) Feriozi; m. Clyde Thomas Kessler, June 25, 1977; 1 child, Alan. BA in Art Edn., Va. Polytech. Inst. & State U., 1976; MFA in Painting & Printmaking, Redford U., 1983. Tchr. art, Spanish Cherrydale Christian Sch., Arlington, Va., 1976-77; tchr. community arts sch. Radford (Va.) U., 1980-82, adminstr., 1982-83; tchr. art Fine Arts Ctr., Pulaski, Va., 1984; instr. art Radford U., 1985-87, 88-93, interim gallery dir., 1987-88; freelance profl. artist, tchr. Radford, 1993—. Illustrator (poetry books) Shooting Creek, 1982, Dancing at Big Vein, 1987, Preservations, 1989. Officer PEO Sisterhood, Radford, 1992-94, mem., 1989—; mem. Lamplighters, Radford Pub. Libr., 1991—, Valley-Wide Newcomers, Radford, 1993—. Mem. Nat. Mus. Women in Arts, Blacksburg Regional Art Assn., Lynwood Artists, Piedmont Arts Assn. Home: PO Box 3612 Radford VA 24143-3612

KESSLER, LEONA HANOVER, interior designer; b. Phila., Sept. 15, 1925; d. Herman and Ida (Gleaner) Hanover; B.S. in Textile Engrng. (Sara Tyler Wister scholar), Phila. Coll. Textiles and Sci., 1948; m. Sydney Kessler, Aug. 28, 1948; children—Andrew Louis, Todd Hanover. Pvt. practice interior design and cons. Lee Kessler Interiors, Phila., 1957—; textile designer, stylist, color cons.; mem. faculty Moore Coll. Art, 1970-72, Art Inst. Phila., 1973-78, Phila. Coll. Textiles and Sci., 1972-81; juror textile design and interior design; works exhibited designer showcases, local house tours, faculty shows. Named Alumnus of Month, Textile Engr., 1971. Mem. Am. Soc. Interior Designers (dir. Pa. East chpt. 1967-78, chpt. recognition awards 1974, 80). Author: That Which Was Once a Warp, 1971; contbr. articles and photographs to mags. and newspapers. Address: 101 Hawthorne Ct Wyomissing PA 19610

KESSLER, LYNN FRIEDMAN, clinical psychologist; b. N.Y.C., Sept. 7, 1938; d. Sylvan and Bertha (Brown) Henline; m. Gerald L. Friedman, June 15, 1960 (div.); children: Lisa, Douglas, Kenneth, Cynthia; m. Irving Kessler. BA in Child Devel., Vassar Coll., 1960; MA in Speech Pathology, Calif. State U., Northridge, 1968; MA in Counseling Psychology, Loyola Marymount U., 1977; PhD in Clin. Psychology, Fielding Inst., 1986. Lic. clin. psychologist, Calif.; lic. speech pathologist; lic. marriage and family child therapist; cert. gen. edn. tchr., Calif. Classroom tchr. Ithaca (N.Y.) Pub. Schs., 1960-62; staff speech pathologist, intern supr. Community Speech and Hearing Ctr., Encino, Calif., 1967-75; staff speech pathologist West Valley Ctr. Ednl. Therapy, Canoga Park, 1980-82; psychologist Forensic Psychology Assocs., Sherman Oaks, Calif., 1984-87; pvt. practice speech pathology, pvt. practice marriage, family and child counseling, pvt. practice in clin. psychology; founder, exec. dir. Adoption Rsch. Ctr., Sherman Oaks, 1993—. Activist Death Penalty Focus, L.A., Social Justice, L.A. Mem. APA, Am. Speech and Hearing Assn. (cert. clin. competence), Calif. Speech and Hearing Assn., Calif. Psychol. Assn., L.A. Psychol. Assn.

KESSLER, SHERI ARDEN, secondary school educator; b. Bklyn., Mar. 25, 1957. BA in English, SUNY, Binghamton, 1978; MS in English Edn., SUNY, New Paltz, 1988. Tchr. English, N.Y. Massage therapist N.Y., 1982-85; English tchr. Rondout Valley Sch. Dist., Accord, N.Y., 1985—. Mem. N.Y. State United Tchrs. Office: Rondout Valley Sch Dist PO Box 9 Accord NY 12404

KESSLER-HODGSON, LEE GWENDOLYN, actress, corporate executive; b. Wellsville, N.Y., Jan. 16, 1947; d. James Hewitt and Reba Gwendolyn (Adsit) Kessler; m. Bruce Gridley, June 22, 1969 (div. Dec. 1979); m. Jeffrey Craig Hodgson, Oct. 31, 1987. BA, Grove City Coll., 1968; MA, U. Wis., 1969. Prof. Sangamon State U., Springfield, Ill., 1969-70; pers. exec. Bullock's, L.A., 1971-74; owner Brunnen Enterprises, L.A., 1982—. Author: A Child of Arthur, 1981; producer, writer play including Anais Nin: The Paris Years, 1986; actress appearing in TV movies, mini-series including Roots, 1978, Backstairs at The White House, 1979, Blind Ambition, 1980, Hill Street Blues, 1984-87, Murder By Reason of Insanity, 1985, Hoover, 1986, Creator, 1987, Our House, 1988, Favorite Son, 1988, Lou Grant 1983, 84, Barney Miller, 1979, L.A. Law, 1990, Hunter, 1991, (screenplay) Settlers Way, 1988; recurring role TV series Matlock, L.A. Law, numerous others. Knapp Prize fellow U. Wis., 1969. Mem. AFTRA, SAG, Actors Equity Assn. Republican. Mem. Ch. Scientology. Home: 5629 Terrace Dr La Crescenta CA 91214-1548

KESTER, DIANE KATHERINE DAVIES, library educator; b. Oak Park, Ill., Nov. 21, 1937; d. Will Sullivan and Gladys Charlotte (Krafft) Davies; m. Daniel Douglas Kester, Feb. 15, 1960; children: Donald Warren, Daniel Douglas Jr., David Carl, Dawn Katherine, Deneen Wilson Marshall. BA/BS, Tex. Woman's U., 1959; MEd, East Carolina U., 1970, MLS, 1974, EdS, 1984; PhD, U. N.C., Chapel Hill, 1990. Libr. Runnels Jr. High Sch., Big Spring, Tex., 1959-60; coord. librs. Howard Co. Schs., Big Spring, Tex., 1966-67; media specialist Ea. Wayne Jr. High Sch., Goldsboro, N.C., 1967-87; instr. East Carolina U., Greenville, N.C., 1987-90, asst. prof., 1990—; cons. Wayne Co. Librs., Goldsboro, 1987—. Editor: N.C. Ednl. Media Assn. Newsletter, 1984-93. Cons. Girl Scouts U.S.A., Goldsboro, 1970—; instr. Am. Nat. Red Cross, Wayne Co., 1967—. Grantee N.C. Assn. Sch. Librs., 1987-88; fellow Margaret Kalp, U. N.C., 1985. Mem. Am. Libr. Assn., Am. Assn. Sch. Librs., Assn. Specialized & Coop. Libr. Agencies, Libr. & Info. Tech. Assn., Assn. for Ednl. Communications and Tech.,Assn. Libr. & Info. Sci. Educators, N.C. Libr. Assn., N.C. Assn. Sch. Librs., N.C. Assn. Ednl. Comm. and Tech. Methodist. Home: 105 Longview Dr Goldsboro NC 27534-8871 Office: East Carolina U Sch Edn Dept Libr Studies and Ednl Tech Greenville NC 27858

KESTNER, HEIDI TERESA, physician assistant; b. Bethesda, Md., Nov. 12, 1960; d. Alvin Knight and Jane (Sturgis) K. AA in Math. and Sci., Montgomery Coll., 1982; BS in Med. Sci., Alderson Broaddus Coll., 1985. Cert. physician asst. Surg. physician asst. Harbour Hosp. Ctr., Balt., 1986-88, Sibley Meml. Hosp., Washington, 1989—. Mem. Am. Acad. Physician Asst., Md. Acad. Physician Asst., Goshen Scout Alumni Assn. (sec. 1991—). Home: 10213 Conover Dr Silver Spring MD 20902-4847

KESTON, JOAN BALBOUL, government agency administrator; b. N.Y.C., Feb. 6, 1937; d. Sol and Adele (Gredinger) Balboul; (div. Mar. 1986); children: Lisa, Vicky, Sol. BA, N.Y.U., 1958; postgrad., Rutgers U., 1959; MPA, U. So. Calif., 1981, D in Pub. Adminstrn., 1991. Br. mgr. Social Security Adminstrn., Rockville, Md., 1978-86; exec. dir., pres. Pub. Employees Roundtable, Washington, 1984-94, pres., 1994—; exec. asst. to dir. adminstrn. and mgmt. Office of Sec. of Def., Arlington, Va., 1994—. Editor: (book) Hagadah, 1972, (newsletter) Unsung Heroes, 1986; co-author: (booklet) How to Celebrate Public Service Recognition Week, annually, 1986-94. Recipient Office of Sec. of Defense Outstanding Performance award, 1991, PRes. Coun. Mgmt. Improvement Cert. Mgmt. Excellence, 1988. Mem. ASPA (Pres. award 1990), Federally Employed Women, Am. Fgn. Svc. Assn., Drs. Pub. Adminstrn. Assn. of U. So. Calif., Am. Consortium Pub. Arminstrn., Sr. Exec. Assn., Consortium of Pub. Arminstrn., World Affairs Coun., Inter Policy Inst. Jewish. Home: 330 Lynn Manor Dr Rockville MD 20850-4429

KESWANI, SATTY GILL, reproductive endocrinologist; b. Punjab, India, Jan. 4, 1932; came to U.S., 1958; d. Ujagar Singh and Mohindar (Kaur) Gill; m. Moti Sugnomal Keswani, Aug. 4, 1962; children: Raj Moti, Sonia. AA, U. Santo Tomas, Manila, 1950; Med. Diploma, Lady Hardinge Med. Coll., New Delhi, 1955. Intern in ob.-gyn and surgery Lady Hardinge Med. Coll. Women, New Delhi, 1956-57, with ob-gyn. and surgery, 1957-63; resident in ob.-gyn. St. Luke's Hosp., N.Y.C., 1959-60, Meth. Episcopal/Jefferson Med. Coll., Phila., 1960-61, Margaret Hague Maternity Hosp., Jersey City, N.J., 1961-63; with obstet. anesthesia Margaret Hague Maternity Hosp., Jersey City, 1963-65; rsch. fellow infertility & gynecology-endocrinology N.Y. Med. Ctr., 1965-72; pvt. practice Livingston (N.J.) Fertility, 1972—. Author: (with others) The Women's Complete Health Book, 1994. Named Woman of Yr., John Greco Found., 1986. Fellow Am. Coll. Obstetrics and Gynecology, Internat. Coll. Surgeons, Royal Soc. Health; mem. Am. Fertility Soc., Am. Med. Women Assn. (v.p. fin. 1994), N.Y. Acad. Scis., N.J. Am. Med. Women Assn. (pres. 1972-74), Med. Women Internat. Assn. (non-govtl. orgn. rep. to UN 1993-94). Home and Office: Livingston Fertility 176 W Mt Pleasant Ave Livingston NJ 07039

KETRON, CARRIE SUE, secondary school educator; b. Clifton, Tex.; d. Randolph Allen and Mary (Waggoner) Ogden; m. N.M. Ketron, Aug. 4, 1984; children: John, Robert. B of Applied Arts and Scis., U. North Tex., 1990, MEd, 1993. Tchr. Duncanville (Tex.) High Sch., 1982—. Named Tchr. of Yr. Tex. Vocat. Tech. Assn., 1990. Mem. Golden Key Honor Soc., Am. Vocat. Assn., Cosmetology Instructors' of Pub. Schs. (parlimentarian 1989-90), Vocat. Indsl. Clubs Am. (advisor 1986-93), Iota Lambda Sigma Sigma, Phi Theta Kappa, Alpha Chi. Baptist. Home: PO Box 381356 Duncanville TX 75138

KETT, KATHLEEN MARIE, maternal nurse, consultant; b. Wisconsin Rapids, Wis., Mar. 29, 1951; d. Alex Frank and Dorothy Lucille (Gaulke) Macha; m. Jeffrey Allen Kett, Oct. 2, 1971; children: Andrew, JoAnne. BSN, U. Wis., Milw., 1972, MSN, 1988; postgrad., Marquette U., 1994—. Staff nurse Sheboygan (Wis.) Meml. Hosp., 1972-74, Columbia Hosp., Milw., 1974-76, St. Mary's Hosp., Milw., 1976-78; staff nurse Columbia Hosp., Milw., 1978-81, head nurse mgr., 1981-84; prenatal support nurse Wis. Ind. Physician Assn., Milw., 1988-89; physiologic diagnostic svcs. nurse adminstr. TOKOS Med. Corp., Milw., 1989-92, account rep., insvc. educator, 1991-92; sales specialist, insvc. educator Healthdyne Perinatal Svcs., Milw., 1992-93, rsch. cons., educator, 1993—; prenatal care coordination home vis. nurse Sinai Samaritan Med. Ctr., 1993—; cons. Milw. Based Home Care Agy., 1984-88. Recipient State Nurse traineeship State of Wis., Milw., 1986, Sigma Theta Tau Eta Nu Scholarship, 1994. Mem. NAACOG, Wis. Assn. for Perinatal Care (treas. 1988-92), U. Wis.-Milw. Alumni Assn. (pres., bd. dirs. 1990-92). Lutheran. Home: 1951 W Rochelle Ave Milwaukee WI 53209

KETTLE, SALLY ANNE, consulting company executive, educator; b. Omaha, Feb. 2, 1938; d. Harry Eugene and Elaine Josephine (Winston) Smiley; m. William Frederick Kettle, July 20, 1968 (div. 1973); children: Christopher, Winston. BEd, U. Nebr., 1960, postgrad. Cert. tchr., S.C., Nebr. Tchr. Omaha Pub. Schs., Omaha, 1966-72; owner, mgr. The Rick Rack, Ltd., Lakewood, Colo., 1974-75; coord. merchandising communications 3M, St. Paul, 1978-80, sr. coord. internat. corp. comm., 1981-83; corp. dir. communications Intran Corp., St. Paul, 1984; pres. Sally Kettle & Co., Bloomington, Minn., 1985—; tchr. TV U. Omaha, 1968-69; mem. cmty. faculty Met. State U., Mpls., 1983-90, St. Olaf Coll., Northfield, Minn., 1992—; mem. adj. faculty U. Minn. Sch. Journalism and Mass Comm., Mpls., St. Thomas U., 1994—. TV hostess City of Bloomington Cable TV, 1984-86. Co-founder Women's Resource Ctr., bd. dirs., mem. adv. bd., 1978-88; chair 13th Precinct, Bloomington, 1978-83; bd. dirs. 41st Sen. Dist., Bloomington, 1982-83; cable TV commr. Bloomington City Coun., 1984-85; pub. rels. com. U.S. Olympic Festival, 1989-90; bd. dirs. Minn. Prayer Breakfast Bd., 1984—; mem. Better Bus. Bur.; founder Ad Rev. Coun.; v.p. Christian Mgmt. Assn., Minn.; internat. com. bd. Carlson Grad. Sch. Mgmt., U. Minn.; mem. state cen. com. and platform commn. DFL, 1988-90; bd. dirs. Fellowship Christian Athletes, 1988-89. Named one of Outstanding Young Women of Am., 1965. Mem. Am. Advt. Fedn. (conf. com. 1985-87, pub. svc. com. 1986-88), Pub. Rels. Soc. Am., Advt. Fedn. Minn. (bd. dirs. 1982-86), Women's Econ. Roundtable, Internat. Platform Assn., Nat. Grad. Women's Honor Soc., Minn. Press Club (co-chair newsmaker com., bd. dirs. 1989-92), Phi Delta Gamma, Kappa Alpha Theta. Home: 13390 Gunflint Path Apple Valley MN 55124-7376

KETTULA, RUBY JEAN, fish farmer, county supervisor; b. Galesville, Ill., Mar. 14, 1932; d. Silas and Frona (Whitt) Perry; m. Hugo W. Kettula; children: Linda, Richard, David, Kay, Kathy. Grad. high sch., Eagle River, Wis., 1950. Telephone operator Commonwealth Telephone, Eagle River, 1947-52; fish farmer Seven Pines Fishery, Inc., Lewis, Wis., 1957—; supr. Polk County, Balsam Lake, Wis., 1992—; apptd. to govs. coun. on mandates, 1994—; newsletter editor Wis. Aquaculture, Lewis, 1967—. Town clk. Town of Clam Falls, Lewis, 1979-91. Mem. Wis. Aquaculture Assn. (sec.). Home: 1029 Clam Falls Dr Box 15 Lewis WI 54851

KEULEGAN, EMMA PAULINE, special education educator; b. Washington, Jan. 21, 1930; d. Garbis H. and Nellie Virginia (Moore) K. BA, Dumbarton Coll. of Holy Cross, 1954. Cert. tchr. elem. and spl. edn. Tchr. St. Dominic's Elem. Sch., Washington, 1954-56, Sacred Heart Acad., Washington, 1956-59, Our Lady of Victory, Washington, 1959-63, St. Francis Acad., Vicksburg, Miss., 1963-78; tchr. Culkin Acad., Vicksburg, 1978-91, substitute tchr. spl. edn., 1991—. Treas. PTA, Vicksburg, 1980. Mem. Internat. Reading Assn. (pres. Warren County chpt.), Colonial Dames 17th Century (state v.p. 1987-89, state pres. 1989, hon. state pres. 1991—), Daus Am. Colonists (state pres. 1992-94, hon. state pres. 1994—, 1st v.p. 1991, 2d v.p. 1989, chaplain 1985-89), DAR (chpt. regent 1967-69, sec. 1994). Republican. Roman Catholic. Home: 215 Buena Vista Dr Vicksburg MS 39180 Office: Jett Elem Sch 4232 Warrenton Rd Vicksburg MS 39180

KEWLEY, SHARON LYNN, systems analyst, consultant; b. Geneseo, Ill., Sept. 23, 1958; d. James Leslie and Geraldine (Myers) K. BBA with honors, U. Miami (Fla.), 1988. Gen. agent Varvaris & Assocs., Cedar Rapids, Iowa, 1981-84; programmer, analyst U. Miami, Coral Gables, Fla., 1984-88; systems analyst Metro Dade County, Miami, 1988-91, Nat. Coun. on Compensation Ins., Boca Raton, Fla., 1991-93; owner Boca Byte, Boca Raton, Fla., 1993—; owner Boca Byte, Boca Baton, Fla. Mem. NAFE, Kendall Jaycees, Nat. Gold Key Honor Soc., PADI Divemaster. Republican. Lutheran. Office: Boca Byte PO Box 7072 Boca Raton FL 33432

KEY, KAREN LETISHA, pharmaceutical executive; b. Sanford, N.C., Jan. 17, 1957; d. Kermit Lee and Ruth (Whitaker) K. BS in Phys. Edn., Appalachian State U., 1978; MBA, U. N.C., 1993. Profl. sales rep. Burroughs Wellcome Co., Florence, S.C., 1982-84; field trainer Burroughs Wellcome Co., Kernersville, N.C., 1984-87; field mgmt. trainee then asst. product mgr. Cardiovasculars/Antivirals/Psychotropics, Research Triangle Park, N.C., 1987-90, dist. sales mgr. psychiatry, 1990-91, asst. to sr. v.p. prodn. and engring., 1991-92, mgr. mktg. tng. and devel., 1991-92, product mgr. neuromuscular blockers, 1993—. Choir mem. Lakewood Bapt. Ch., tchr. Sun. sch. Republican. Baptist. Office: 3030 Cornwallis Rd Durham NC 27709

KEY, MARCELLA ANN, computer information specialist; b. St. Louis, Nov. 26, 1947; d. Wallace Albert and Dorothy (Croskery) F.; m. Philip Odell, Nov. 18, 1967; children: Heather Colleen, Philip Sean. BA in English magna cum laude, U. Mo., St. Louis, 1969. Info. operator Southwestern Bell Tel., St. Louis, 1965-69; army procurement intern U.S. Army Mobility Equipment Command, St. Louis, 1969-70; army contract price analyst U.S. Army Weapons Command, Rock Island, Ill., 1970-72; army data processing intern U.S. Army Mgmt. Engring. Tng. Activity, Rock Island; computer programmer U.S. Army Logistics Mgmt. System Activity, St. Louis, 1973-77; computer specialist USRCPAC, 1977, U.S. Army Logistics Mgmt. System Activity, St. Louis, 1977-80; computer specialist, cons., instr. U.S. Army Mobility Equipment Command, Rock Island, 1980-88; data bas adminstr. U.S. Army Aviation Systems Command, St. Louis, 1988-91, project mgr., 1991—; pres., v.p., sc., Army Data Base Users' Group, Rock Island, 1982-85; dir. Epochs Bethel #2, Hazelwood, Mo., 1989-93, guardian sec., 1993—. Co-Author: Orgn. Study of the Automation, 1983, An Info. Mgmt. Evaluation, 1987. Guardian Treas. Jobs Daughters Bethel #5, 1986-88; Troop com. mem. Boy Scouts Am., St.Charles, 1992—. Mem. Army Materiel Command Data Base Users Group. Ind. Dutch Reformed. Home: 4251 Greensboro Dr Saint Charles MO 63304-1612 Office: US Aviation Troop Command 4300 Goodfellow Blvd Saint Louis MO 63120-1798

KEY, MARY POMROY, marriage, family and child counselor, educator; b. Pasadena, Calif., July 16, 1960; d. David Henry and Nancy Joy (Hunecke) Pomroy; m. Scott Benson Key, July 27, 1991; 1 child, Jonathan Benson. BS in Psychology magna cum laude, Calif. Bapt. Coll., 1981, MS in Counseling Psychology, 1984; PhD, U. So. Calif., 1994. Program counselor Beverly Manor, Riverside, Calif., 1981-83; marriage, family and child counselor in pvt. practice, 1983-88; counseling psychologist I U. Calif., Riverside, 1990-91; counselor, supr. Christian Counseling Svc., Redlands, Calif., 1993—; adj. instr. dept. psychology Calif. Bapt. Coll., 1984-92. Leo Buscaglia scholar, 1990-91; Dean's Merit scholar U. So. Calif., 1987-90. Mem. APA, Am. Assn. for Counseling and Devel., Calif. Assn. Marriage and Family Counselors, Assn. for Student Devel. in So. Bapt. Colls. and Univs. (exec. coun., pub. rels. chair 1988-90). Democrat. Christian. Office: Christian Counseling Svc 51 W Olive Ave Redlands CA 92373

KEY, MARY RITCHIE (MRS. AUDLEY E. PATTON), linguist, author, educator; b. San Diego, Mar. 19, 1924; d. George Lawrence and Iris (Lyons) Ritchie; children: Mary Helen Key Ellis, Harold Hayden Key (dec.), Thomas George Key. Student, U. Chgo., summer 1954, U. Mich., 1959; M.A., U. Tex., 1960, Ph.D., 1963; postgrad., UCLA, 1966. Asst. prof. linguistics Chapman Coll., Orange, Calif., 1963-66; asst. prof. linguistics U. Calif., Irvine, 1966-71; assoc. prof. U. Calif., 1971-78, prof., 1978—, chmn. program linguistics, 1969-71, 75-77, 87—; cons. Am. Indian langs., Spanish, in Mexico, 1946-55, S.Am., 1955-62, English dialects, 1968-74, Easter Island, 1975, Calif. Dept. Edn., 1966, 70-75, Center Applied Linguistics, Washington, 1967, 69; lectr. in field. Author: Comparative Tacanan Phonology, 1968, Male/Female Language, 1975, Paralanguage and Kinesics, 1975, Nonverbal Communication, 1977, The Grouping of South American Indian Languages, 1979, The Relationship of Verbal and Nonverbal Communication, 1980, Catherine the Great's Linguistic Contribution, 1980, Polynesian and American Linguistic Connections, 1984, Comparative Linguistics of South American Indian Languages, 1987, General and Amerindian Ethnolinguistics, 1989, Language Change in South American Indian Languages, 1991; founder, editor: newsletter Nonverbal Components of Communication, 1972-76; mem. editoral bd. Forum Linguisticum, 1976—, Lang. Scis., 1978—, La Linguistique, 1979—, Multilingua, 1987—; contbr. articles to profl. jours. Recipient Friends of Libr. Book award, 1976, hon. mention, Rolex awards for Enterprise, project Computerizing the Languages of the World, 1990; U. Calif. Regent's grantee, 1974, Fulbright-Hays grantee, 1975; faculty rsch. fellow, 1984-85. Mem. Linguistic Soc. Am., Am. Dialect Soc. (exec. council; regional sec. 1974-83), Internat. Reading Assn. (dir. 1968-72), Delta Kappa Gamma (local pres. 1974-76). Office: U Calif-Irvine Dept Of Linguistics Irvine CA 92717

KEYAK, JOYCE HELENE, bioengineer; b. San Francisco, Aug. 18, 1960. BSME, U. Calif., Berkeley, 1989; postgrad., U. Calif., Berkeley/San Francisco. Engring. technician Rehab. R&D Svc., VA Med. Ctr., San Francisco, 1986-87, mech. engr., 1987—; co-investigator Rehab. R&D Svc. VA Med. Ctr., San Francisco, 1990—; cons. biomechanics rsch. U. Calif., Davis, 1990—, San Francisco, 1990-94. Contbr. articles to profl. jours. Grantee (3) Rehab. R&D Svc. Dept. of Vet. Affairs, 1989, 92. Mem. Am. Soc. of Biomechanics, Tau Beta Pi, Pi Tau Sigma. Office: Rehab R&D Svc VA Med Ctr 4150 Clement St San Francisco CA 94121-1598

KEYES, JOAN ROSS RAFTER, educator, author; b. Bklyn., Aug. 12, 1924; d. Joseph W. and Hermia (Ross) Rafter; m. William Ambrose, Apr. 26, 1947 (dec.); children: William, Peter, Dion, Alexandrea. BA, Adelphi U., Garden City, N.Y., 1945; MS, Long Island U., Greenvale, N.Y., 1973. Prodn. asst. CBS Radio, N.Y., 1943-44; cub news reporter Bklyn. Daily Eagle, 1945-46; advt. copywriter Gimbel's Dept. Store, N.Y., 1946-47; adj. prof. L.I. U., Greenvale, N.Y., 1984—; tchr. Port Wash. Pub. Schs., N.Y., 1970-94; lectr., cons. pub. sch. dists. nationwide, 1978—; workshop leader Tchrs. English to Speakers Other Langs. convs., 1981—. Author: Beats, Conversations in Rhythm, 1983, (video program) Now You're Talking, 1987, (computer program) Quick Talk, 1990; contbr. articles to ednl. mags. Lectr., catechist Our Lady of Fatima Ch., Port Washington, 1987—; vol. Earthwatch, Mallorca, 1988. Australia/New Zealand ednl. grantee Port Washington Pub. Schs., 1992. Mem. Tchrs. of English to Speakers of Other Languages, Am. Fedn. of Tchrs., N.Y. State United Tchrs., Port Wash. Tchrs. Assn. Republican. Roman Catholic. Office: Port Washington Pub Schs Campus Dr Port Washington NY 11050-3719

KEYES, KRISTIN LEIGH, public relations professional; b. Coronado, Calif., Jan. 27, 1958; d. Roy Vance and Sandra Leone (Odale) K.; m. John Denton Boyd, Dec. 9, 1984 (div. Dec. 1992). BA, U. Wash., 1981. Prodr. KING TV, Seattle, 1981-82; news dir., exec. prodr. KMTR TV, Eugene, Oreg., 1982-83; asst. news dir. KRIS TV, Corpus Christi, Tex., 1984; investigative reporter CJOB Radio, Winnipeg, Man., 1986-87; pub. rels. mgr. Computer Assocs., Vancouver and San Jose, 1987-91, Wordstar Internat., Novato, Calif., 1991-92; sr. pub. rels. mgr. McLean Pub. Rels., San Mateo, Calif., 1992-93; dir. corp. comm. HSC Software, Santa Monica, Calif., 1993—.

KEYES, SAUNDRA ELISE, newspaper editor; b. Salt Lake City, June 28, 1945; d. Vernon Harrison and Mildred (Wilkins) K.; m. William J. Ivey, June 13, 1969 (div. 1976). BA, U. Utah, 1966; MA, Ind. U., 1969, PhD, 1976. Tchr. Salt Lake City Pub. Schs., 1966-67; asst. prof. Fisk U., Nashville, 1971-76; reporter, city editor The Tennessean, Nashville, 1976-83; staff writer The Courier-Jour., Louisville, 1983-84; dep. mng. editor Orlando (Fla.) Sentinel, 1985-88; mng. editor Phila. Daily News, 1988-90; exec. editor, sr. v.p. Press-Telegram, Long Beach, Calif., 1991-93; mng. editor The Miami Herald, 1993—. Ford Found. fellow, 1978. Mem. Am. Soc. Newspaper Editors. *

KEYSER-FANICK, CHRISTINE LYNN, banker, marketing professional; b. Ft. Dodge, Iowa, Nov. 16, 1956; d. Archie Harlan and LaVonne Janette (Larsen) K. AA, Iowa Cen. Community Coll., Ft. Dodge, 1976; BA, U. No. Iowa, 1979; MA, Drake U., 1985; grad. with honors, Sch. Bank Mktg., Boulder, Colo., 1990. Educator Marshalltown (Iowa) Community Schs.,

1979-84; v.p. LaGrave Klipfel Clarkson, Inc., Des Moines, 1985-87; pub. rels. and mktg. cons. Des Moines, 1987-88; asst. prof. Drake U., Des Moines, 1988; dir. mktg. 1st Insterstate Bank, Des Moines, 1988-89; v.p. Am. Trust & Savings Bank, Dubuque, Iowa, 1989-94; sr. v.p. San Antonio Fed. Credit Union, 1994—; speaker leadership confs. various univs., 1985—; v.p. Women in Mgmt., 1991, pres.-elect, 1992-93, pres., 1993. Contbr. articles to Iowa Commerce Mag., 1988-93. Bd. dirs. Iowa Soc. to Prevent Blindness, Des Moines, 1987-91, Dubuque Main St. Ltd., 1990-93, v.p., 1993; bd. dirs. Dubuque Symphony Orch., 1990-93, Dubuque Coun. for Diversity, 1992-94; bd. dirs., bus. devel. chair Dubuque Main St., 1991-94; mem. pub. rels. com. San Antonio area coun. Girl Scouts, Inc., 1994—. Named New Bd. Mem. of Yr., Iowa Soc. to Prevent Blindness, 1988, Vol. of Yr., Iowa Main St., 1993; recipient Nat. Charlotte Danstrom Women of Achievement award, 1992. Mem. Pub. Rels. Soc. Am. (pres. Greater Dubuque chpt. 1993, v.p. 1991-92, San Antonio chpt. bd. dirs. 1995—, accredited), Bank Mktg. Assn. (adv. coun. 1989-93), ITS Inc. Mktg. Com., Advertisers of Dubuque (legis. chair 1990-93, bd. dirs. 1991-93), Dubuque Area C. of C. (membership adv. coun. 1993-94, media coord. Iowa Trade Symposium 1990). Home: 7114 Valley Trails San Antonio TX 78250-3477 Office: San Antonio Fed Credit Union PO Box 1356 San Antonio TX 78295-1356

KEYSTON, STEPHANI ANN, small business owner; b. Baytown, Tex., Aug. 6, 1955; d. Herbert Howard and Janice Faye (Stowe) Cruickshank; m. George Keyston III, Oct. 8, 1983; children: Jeremy George, Kristopher Samuel. AA with honors, Merced Coll., Merced, Calif., 1975; BA in Journalism with distinction, San Jose State U., 1976. Reporter, Fresno (Calif.) Bee, 1974-75; reporter, photographer Merced (Calif.) Sun-Star, 1974-77; pub. info. officer Fresno City Coll. (Calif.), 1977-80; dir. communications Aerojet Tactical Systems Co., Sacramento, 1980-83; co-owner, v.p. Keyco Landscape Contractor Inc., Auburn, Calif., 1984—. Co.-coordinator Aerojet United Way Campaign, 1981; Aerojet Tactical Systems Co. coordinator West Coast Nat. Derby Rallies, 1981-83. Mem. Internat. Assn. Bus. Communicators (dir. Sacramento chpt. 1983), Citrus Heights C. of C. (v.p. 1983). Republican. Home: 13399 Lakeview Pl Auburn CA 95602 Office: Keyco Landscape Contractor Inc 6216 Main Ave Ste C Orangevale CA 95662

KEZLARIAN, NANCY KAY, social services administrator; b. Royal Oak, Mich., Aug. 26, 1948; d. Barkev A. and Nancy (Israelian) K. Student, U. Vienna, Austria, 1969; BA, Albion Coll., 1970; MA in Theatre and TV, U. Mich., 1971; MA in Clin. Psychology, Pepperdine U., 1992. Cert. secondary tchr., Mich., Calif. Tchr. West Bloomfield Hills (Mich.) High Sch., 1971-76; tchr. ESL, L.A. Pub. Schs., 1976-80; personnel dir. Samuel Goldwyn Co., L.A., 1985-86; dir. adminstrn. and human resources (Norman Lear) Act III Communications, L.A., 1986-90; dir. programs Salvation Army Booth Meml. Ctr., L.A., 1993-94; asst. exec. dir. group home ops. Florence Crittenton Ctr., L.A., 1994—; owner, mgr. KAZ, hand painted clothing co., L.A., 1980-85. Writer, actress My Seventeenth Summer, The Big Blue Marble, 1979 (Emmy award for childen's TV programming). Named Tchr. of Yr., West Bloomfield Hills High Sch., 1976. Mem. SAG, Pers. and Indsl. Rels. Assn. (legis. rep. dist. 5 1989, 90), Calif. Assn. of Marriage and Family Therapists, L.A. Group psychtherapy Soc., Psi Chi.

KHALILI, MARYLOUISE DALLAL, management and marketing educator; b. Harlingen, Tex., Sept. 13, 1937; d. Tewfik Gabrial and Minerva (Laham) Dallal. BS in Bus., Central State U., 1961; MS in Bus., Calif. State U., Long Beach, 1971; PhD in Bus., U. Okla., 1990; cert. in communications, U. Hawaii, 1972. High sch. tchr. Okla., Calif. and Kans., 1961-71; dir. family planning Govt. of Iran, Tehran, 1972-76; prof. Oklahoma City U., 1976—; cons. Shifting Gears Unltd., Oklahoma City, 1985—; realtor ERA Bob Linn & Assocs., Oklahoma City, 1985—. Author: Sign of the Times, 1975. Vol. Planned Parenthood Am., Oklahoma City, 1976—, United Cerebral Palsy, Oklahoma City, 1989—, Mar. of Dimes, Oklahoma City, 1976-81; organizer Ptnrs. for Excellence in Edn., Okla., 1985—; campaigner Okla. Dems., 1987-88; vol. Salvation Army, Jesus Ho., Meals on Wheels. Mem. various mgmt. orgns., Delta Pi Epsilon (v.p. 1979-81, pres. 1981-82). Home: 2304 NW 28th St Oklahoma City OK 73107-2524 Office: Shifting Gears Unltd PO Box 12426 Oklahoma City OK 73157-2426

KHAN, ARFA, radiologist, educator; b. Srinagar, Kashmir, India, Dec. 4, 1943; came to U.S., 1966; d. Ghulam Rasool and Ruqia Hayat; m. Faroque A. Khan, Apr. 16, 1966; children: Arif O., Shireen. MBBS, Govt. Med. Coll., Kashmir, 1964. Diplomate Am. Bd. Radiology. Intern Barberton (Ohio) Citizen Hosp., 1966-67; resident in radiology L.I. Jewish Med. Ctr., New Hyde Park, N.Y., 1967-70, from instr. to assoc. prof. radiology, 1970-93, prof., 1993—, assoc. chmn. radiology, 1994—. Contbr. 47 articles to radiology jours. Mem. Am. Coll. Radiology, Am. Soc. Neuroradiology, Am. Soc. Head & Neck Radiology, Am. Soc. Thoracic Radiology, Radiol. Soc. N.Am. Democrat. Muslim. Office: 95 Karol Pl Jericho NY 11753

KHARASCH, VIRGINIA SISON, pediatric pulmonologist; b. Manila, Aug. 14, 1956; came to U.S., 1983; d. Gregorio Beljano and Luz (Mendoza) Sison; m. Sigmund Joseph Kharasch, Dec. 29, 1956. BS in Zoology, U. of Philippines, 1977, MD, 1981. Diplomate Am. Bd. Pediatrics. Resident in pediatrics Phoenix Hosp., 1983-84, Michael Reese Hosp./U. Chgo., 1984-86; mem. pediatric staff Michael Reese Health Plan and Hosp., Chgo., 1986-87; pediatric pulmonology specialist Harvard U./Children's Hosp., Boston, 1987-89; pediatrician Children's Hosp., Boston, 1990—, clin. dir. pulmonary div., 1992—; mem. faculty med. sch. Harvard U., Boston, 1990—; asst. prof. Boston U., 1992—; basic sci. researcher Harvard U. Sch. Pub. Health, 1987-90; cons. Cystic Fibrosis Ctr., Boston, 1987-90. Contbr. articles to med. jours. Rsch. fellow Nat. Rsch. Coun. of The Philippines, 1982. Fellow Am. Acad. Pediatrics; mem. AMA, Am. Coll. Chest Physicians, Pi Gamma Mu, Phi Kappa Phi, Phi Sigma. Office: Childrens Hosp 300 Longwood Ave Boston MA 02115-5737

KHASAT, NAMITA, financial executive; b. Hyderabad, India, May 11, 1960; came to U.S., 1981; d. Satish and Vijay Jaiswal; m. Nitya Prakash Khasat, Jan. 14, 1981; children: Vikram, Vivek. BA, St. Francis Coll., Hyderabad, 1978; MA, Osmania U., Hyderabad, 1980; MPA in Fin. and Computers, U. Del., 1983. Mgmt. analyst Del. Dept. Labor, Wilmington, 1983-84; budget analyst, bus. svcs. mgr. div. revenue Del. Dept. Fin., 1984-85; chief fin. officer, dir. fin. Del. YMCA, 1985-88; chief fin. officer Vis. Nurse Assn. of Del., Newark, 1990—. Recipient Acad. Gold Medal Osmania U., 1980, Athletic Individual Championship award, 1980. Home: 67 Willow Creek Ln Newark DE 19711-3430

KHASDAY, ALYCE FIELD, literary and film agent, psychic consultant; b. Bklyn., May 2, 1943; children: Jamie, Cortnie. Student, NYU, 1961-63; grad., La Varenne Culinary Inst. Sales mgr. Malom Lingerie, N.Y.C., 1962-66; sales coord. Sherman Underwear, N.Y.C., 1966-71; pub. rels. cons. Espon, Fla., 1977; organizer press confs. preventive medicine, 1977—; pres., fin. planner Greenbelt Equities, Inc., N.Y.C., 1982-84; archtl. planner, developer, pres. Kasday Design, N.Y.C., 1977-87; pres., syndicator, developer real estate, mgr. M & M Mgmt. Corp., Fla., 1984—; asst. chef to Isabelle Marique, N.Y.C., Albert Jorant, Paris; founder Psychic Life Counselling, Fla., 1990—; psychic cons. various orgns. including Am. Women in Radio and T.V. Office: 500 E 77th St Ste 519 New York NY 10021

KHEEL, CLAUDIA KATE, curator; b. Fulton, N.Y., Nov. 24, 1956. BA, Cornell U., 1978; MA, Tulane U., 1994. Instr. Tulane U., New Orleans, 1986, Herron Sch. Art, Ind. U.- Purdue U. at Indpls., 1989-92; curator fine arts Ind. State Mus., Indpls., 1987-93; curator visual arts La. State Mus., New Orleans, 1993—; panelist Am. Assn. State and Local History, Detroit, 1991; mem. design com. Arts Ind. mag., 1990-93; mem. planning com. Crossing Borders symposium, Indpls., 1989-90. Advisor Ind. Gov.'s Portrait Selection Com., Indpls., 1990. Recipient Award of Distinction Vol. and Info. Agy. New Orleans, United Way, 1986. Mem. Am. Assn. Mus., La. Assn. Mus., La. Art Conservation Alliance (newsletter editor 1993—), Hoosier Group, Inc. (hon.). Jewish. Office: La State Mus 614 St Ann St Arabi LA 70032

KHOURY, NANCY LITAKER, library director; b. Concord, N.C., Mar. 7, 1943; d. Richard Vernon and Lillian Brown (Efird) Litaker; m. Edward John Khoury, July 20, 1968; children: Whitney M., Jenny K. BA, U. N.C., 1965; MS, La. State U., 1968. Reference trainee Pub. Libr. of Charlotte and Mecklenburg County, Charlotte, N.C., 1965-67; head reference dept. Lake Charles (La.) Pub. Libr., 1969-73; head serials dept. McNeese State U. Libr., Lake Charles, 1973-82, head pub. svc., 1982-90, libr. dir., 1990—; Pres. Librs. S.W., Lake Charles, , 1991—; mem. adv. bd. Libr. Sci. Constrn. Act Baton Rouge, 1991—; mem. bd. regents Resource Sharing Task Force, Baton Rouge, 1991-93; mem. Lalinc Consortium, 1993—, exec. com., 1994—; assoc. mng. ptnr. L'Argent Investments, 1992-94, mng. ptnr., 1994—. Mem. Calcasieu Arts and Humanities Coun., McNeese Dean's Coun., McNeese State U. Diversity Awareness Com.; asst. dir. McNeese State U. self study for So. Assn. Colls. and Schs., 1993-96. N.C. State scholar, 1966. Mem. ALA, Southeastern Libr. Assn., La. Libr. Assn., Assn. Coll. and Rsch. Librs., Soc. S.W. Architects, La. Archives and Manuscripts Assn., Children's Mus., Calcasieu Preservation Soc., Calcasieu Hist. Soc. Republican. Episcopalian. Home: 519 Helen St Lake Charles LA 70601-5774 Office: McNeese State U PO Box 91445 Lake Charles LA 70609-1520

KIANG, ASSUMPTA (AMY KIANG), brokerage house executive; b. Beijing, Aug. 15, 1939; came to U.S., 1962; d. Pei-yu and Yu-Jean (Liu) Chao; m. Wan-lin Kiang, Aug. 14, 1965; 1 child, Eliot Y. BA, Nat. Taiwan U., 1960; MS, Marywood Coll., Scranton, Pa., 1964; MBA, Calif. State U., Long Beach, 1977. Data programmer IBM World Trade, N.Y.C., 1963; libr. East Cleve. Pub. Libr., 1964-68; lectr. Nat. Taiwan U., Taipei, 1971-73; with reference dept. U.S. Info. Svc., Taipei, 1971-74; v.p. Merrill Lynch, Santa Ana, Calif., 1977—. Author numerous rsch. reports in field. Founder Pan Pacific Performing Arts Inc., Orange County, Calif., 1987; treas. women league Calif. State. U., Long Beach, 1980-82. Mem. Chineses Bus. Assn. Soc. Calif. (chmn. 1987—, v.p. 1986-87), U.C.I. Chancellor's Club, Old Ranch Country Club. Democrat. Roman Catholic. Office: Merrill Lynch 2670 N Main St Santa Ana CA 92701-1224

KIBLER, RHODA SMITH, lawyer; b. Gainesville, Fla., Mar. 10, 1947; d. Chesterfield and Vivian Lee (Parker) Smith; children: John Vincent Cannon, Parker Smith Cannon. BA, Skidmore Coll., 1972; JD cum laude, Fla. State Univ., 1982. Bar: Fla. 1982. Research asst. to U.S. Senator, Washington, 1967-68; lobbyist Colo. Civil Rights Commn., Denver, 1974-75; intern Fla. Commn. on Human Relations, Tallahassee, 1981-82; atty. Office of Gen. Counsel Dept. Ins., Tallahassee, 1982-84, hosp. cost containment spl. counsel, 1984-86; ptnr. Kibler & Renard, Tallahassee, 1984-86, Ervin, Varn, Jacobs, Odom & Kitchen, Tallahassee, 1986-88; chmn. Global Enterprises, 1988—; del. S.E. U.S. Japan Assn., S.E. U.S. Korea Assn.; del. leader CIS, Republic of Argentina; adv. Internat. Telecom. Tenders Econ. Summit; legis. counsel Fla. Assn. HMO's, 1986-87, Fla. Council Internat. Bus. Devel.; vice chmn. HMO Rules Adv. Task Force, Health Policy Council; mem. Ins. Commr's. Task Force on Discrimination in Ins., Tallahassee, 1983-85, Task Force on Elimination of Discrimination in Statutes, Tallahassee, 1984-85; adv. Internat. Govt. Housing. Vice chmn. U.S. Constitutional Bicentennial Commn. Fla., 1992; mem. exec. com. Statute of Liberty-Ellis Island Centennial Commn., Fla., 1983-86; mem. trade and investment missions to Far East; bd. dirs. Anti-Recidivism Ctr., Denver, 1973-75, United Way Tallahassee, 1985-87, Capital Women's Network, Tallahassee, 1982-86, Big Bend Bus. Exchange; mem. LeMoyne Art Found., Tallahassee, 1984—; state chmn. Overseas Edn. Fund Women, Law, and Devel., 1984-85; mem. S.E. Regional Conf. on Constl. System. Fellow Am. Bar Found.; mem. Am. Judicature Soc., Nat. Inst. Trial Advocacy (diplomate), ABA (mem. sect. adminstrv. law, individual rights and responsibilities, taxation, ins. coms., forum com. internat. health law), Fla. Bar Assn. (chair com. individual rights and responsibilities 1986-87, chair ins. com. 1986, legis. com. Young Lawyers 1984, health law com., internat. law sect., jud. evaluation com. 1984, long-range planning com. 1987—, mem. spl. com. on gen. assembly 1988-89, spl. com. on ho. of dels. 1989—), Tallahassee Bar Assn., Fla. Assn. Hosp. Attys., Fla. Hosp. Assn., LWV, Tallahassee Assn. Women Lawyers, Tallahassee C. of C. (trustee's com. of 100, bd. regents Leadership Tallahassee, legis. affairs), Fla. C. of C. (steering com. internat. bus.), Leadership Fla. (del. leader People's Republic China), Fla. Women's Network (chair jud. appts. com. 1984-87). Clubs: Capital Tiger Bay, Gov.'s (Tallahassee), International, Fla. Econs. Office: Global Enterprises 4500 Shannon Lakes Plz Ste 1 Tallahassee FL 32308

KIBLER, VIRGINIA MARY, economist; b. Meadville, Pa., July 30, 1960; d. Richard Dale and Jean Katherine (Brunner) K. BS in Biology, Clarion (Pa.) U., 1982, BA in Econs., 1983; MS in Natural Resource Econs., Pa. State U., 1986. Rsch. asst. Pa. Dept. Agrl. Econs., University Park, 1984-85; office mgr. League of Conservation Voters, Washington, 1986; pvt. practice econ. cons. Washington, 1986-88; economist Office of Pesticide Program EPA, Washington, 1988-91, team leader, program analyst Office of Comptroller, 1991-94, economist Office of Water, 1994—; spl. asst. U.S. Senate, Washington, 1990. Contbr. articles to profl. jours. Vol. cook So Others May Eat/Homeless Shelter, Washington, 1988—; tutor Cmty. Club, Washington, 1989-92; sec., treas. Timberwood on the Park Homeowners Assn., Wheaton, Md., 1991-93. Named one of Outstanding Young Women of Am., 1986. Mem. EPA Breakfast Club (charter chpt. 8428), Toastmasters. Office: EPA Office of Water 401 M St # 4102 Washington DC 20460

KIBRICK, ANNE, nursing educator, university dean; b. Palmer, Mass., June 1, 1919; d. Martin and Christine (Grigas) Karlon; m. Sidney Kibrick, June 16, 1949; children: Joan, John. RN, Worcester (Mass.) Hahnemann Hosp., 1941; BS, Boston U., 1945; MA, Columbia Tchrs. Coll., 1948; EdD, Harvard U., 1958; LHD (hon.), St. Joseph's Coll., Windham, Maine, 1973. Asst. edn. dir. Cushing VA Hosp., Framingham, Mass., 1948-49; asst. prof. nursing Simmons Coll., Boston, 1949-55; dir. grad. div. Boston U. Sch. Nursing, 1958-63, dean, 1963-68, prof., 1968-70; chmn. dept. nursing Boston Coll. Grad. Sch. Arts and Sci., 1970-74; chmn. sch. nursing Boston State Coll., 1974-82; dean Sch. Nursing U. Mass., Boston, 1974-88, prof., 1988-93, prof. emeritus, 1993—; cons. div. nursing USPHS, 1964-68; cons. Nat. Student Nurses Assn., 1985-88; mem. nat. adv. council nurse tng. USPHS, NIH, 1968-73; cons. Hebrew U.-Hadassah Med. Orgn., Jerusalem, 1971—; mem. Inst. Medicine of Nat. Acad. Scis., 1972—, mem. steering com. costs of edn. of health professions, 1972-74; mem. Nat. Med. Audiovisual Tng. Center, 1972-76, Gov.'s Com. and Area Bd. Mental Health and Mental Retardation, Nat. Commn. for Study Nursing and Nursing Edn., 1970-73; mem. faculty com., regent's external degree program in nursing SUNY, 1974-82; mem. hosp. mgmt. bd. U. Hosp., U. Mass., 1976-81; dir. Medic Alert, Am. Jour. Nursing Co.; cons. Cumberland Coll. Health Scis., New South Wales, Australia, 1986, Menoufia U., Shibin El Kom, Egypt, 1987. Mem. editorial bd. Mass. Jour. Community Health. Bd. dirs. Brookline Mental Health Assn., Met. chpt. ARC, Children's Ctr. Brookline and Greater Boston, Inc., 1984-89, Boston Health Care for the Homeless, 1988-90; bd. dirs. Landy-Kaplan Nurses' Coun., 1992—, treas., 1994—. Fellow Am. Acad. Nursing; mem. Nat. Mass. Leagues Nursing (pres. 1971-73), Am. Nurses Assn., Mass. Nurses Assn. (dir. 1982-86), AIDS Internat. Info. Found. (founding mem. 1985), Mass. Nurses Found. (v.p. 1983-86), Nat. Acads. of Practice, Mass. Med. Soc. (bd. dirs. postgrad. med. inst. 1983—, exec. com. 1989—), Mass. Blueprint 2000, Sigma Theta Tau, Pi Lambda Theta. Home: 381 Clinton Rd Brookline MA 02146-4146

KICHTY, KRISTINE CLOSE, real estate property manager; b. Springdale, Pa., June 24, 1964; d. William Amos and Anne (Karan) Close; m. Michael Joseph Kichty, Oct. 6, 1991; children: Megan Nicole, William Andrew. A. in Bus. and Real Estate, Allegheny County C.C., Pitts., 1994; student, Thomas Edison Coll., Trenton, N.J., 1994—. Lic. real estate salesperson; cert. property mgr. candidate; accredited resdl. mgr. Resident mgr. Wilson Mgmt., Pasadena, Tex., 1987-90; property mgr. Arbors Mgmt. Inc., Pitts., 1991-92, McCormack Baron Mgmt. Svcs., St. Louis, 1992—; cons. Mary Kay Cosmetics Inc., Dallas, 1994—; instr. property mgmt. Allegheny County C.C., Pitts., 1993-94. Mem. Working Group on Cmty. Devel., Pitts., 1993-94; chmn. Positive Interaction Program, Houston, 1989-90; com. mem. strategic planning com. Plum Borough Sch. Dist. Recipient ARM Cert. of Achievement Inst. Real Estate Mgmt., 1993. Mem. Inst. Real Estate Mgmt. (sec. 1992, chmn. Accredited Redl. Mgr. com. 1994, programs chair 1994), Phi Theta Kappa. Democrat. Home: 845 Mount Hood Dr Pittsburgh PA 15239-2515

KICKERT, JULIANA ARLENE, private investor; b. Blue Island, Ill., Sept. 1, 1943; d. Robert J. and Delia (Vander Giessen) K.; m. Durwood Perry Long, July 14, 1973 (div. Oct. 1974). AA, U. Fla., 1963, BS, 1965; MS, Ind. U., 1971. Registered real estate sales, Ill., Chgo. Instr. Chgo. Bd. Edn., 1965-71; dir. legal office program Sauk Area Career Ctr., Crestwood, Ill., 1973-76; real estate sales Kahn Kaplan Realty, Inc., Chgo., 1977-86; pvt. investor Sedona, Ariz. Apptd. Yavapai County Mounted Posse Search and Rescue Team, 1994—. Recipient Life Time Coop. Sales award North Side Real Estate Bd., Chgo., 1984, Top 20 Residential Salesperson award Condex Info. Svcs., 1984, 86; named Ariz. Horseman of Yr. Bridle & Bit Newspaper, 1990. Mem. Verde Valley Horsemen's Coun., Yavapai, Sedona Saddle Club (founding mem., pres. 1990-92, bd. dirs. 1993-94). Republican. Home and office: PO Box 1047 Sedona AZ 86339

KICKISH, MARGARET ELIZABETH, elementary education educator; b. Atlantic City, N.J., Nov. 30, 1949; d. James Bernard and Margaret Elizabeth (Egan) Parlett; m. Robert Anthony Kickish, June 30, 1973; children: Eileen, Kathleen, Robert Jr. BS, Franciscan U., 1971; MEd, Trenton State Coll., 1977. Cert. elem. educator. Tchr. Our Lady Star of the Sea Sch., Atlantic City, N.J., 1971-75, Weymouth Twp. Elem. Sch., Dorothy, N.J., 1975-89; curriculum coord. Port Republic (N.J.) Sch., 1990-91; tchr. Brigantine (N.J.) Bd. Edn., 1991-94, supr. curriculum and instrn., 1995—; cognetics coach St. Joseph Sch., Somers Point, N.J., 1989—. Treas. PTA, Somers Point, 1987-89, pres., 1989-90; asst. coach Somers Point Softball Assn., 1991—; mem. St. Joseph Ch. Choir, Somers Point, 1985—. Mem. AAUW, NEA, ASCD, N.J. Edn. Assn. (treas. 1977-86), Prins. and Suprs. Assn., Coun. Exceptional Children, Assn. Learning Conss., Seashore Mother of Twins Club (pres. 1994—), South Jersey Irish Cultural Soc., Kappa Delta Phi. Democrat. Roman Catholic. Home: 526 9th St Somers Point NJ 08244-1458 Office: Brigantine Bd of Edn 301 E Evans Blvd Brigantine NJ 08203

KIDD, DEBRA JEAN, communications executive; b. Chgo., May 13, 1956; d. Fred A. and Jean (Pezzopane) Winchar; m. Kim Joseph Kidd, July 22, 1978; children: Jennifer Marie, Michele Jean. AA in Bus. with high honors, Wright Jr. Coll., 1977. Legal sec. Sidley & Austin, Chgo., 1977-80; investment adminstr. Golder, Thoma & Co., Chgo., 1980-81, exec. asst., 1981-84; sales rep. Dataspeed, Inc., Chgo., 1984, midwestern regional mgr. Dataspeed, Inc., Chgo., 1985; comm. cons. Chgo. Comm., Inc., Chgo., 1986-88; owner, founder Captain Kidd's Video, Niles, 1981-84. Vol. Am. Lung Assn., Chgo., 1979; vol. tchr. religious edn. Our Lady Mother of Ch., Norridge, Ill., 1981-83, St. Raymonds, Mt. Prospect, 1993-94; vol. Parents Who Care, 1988-94, pres., 1991-93; vol. PTA Lion's Park Sch., 1993—, bd. dirs., 1993-94, editor Lion's Roar, founder Young Journalist Club, 1994—; leader Girl Scouts, 1992—. Mem. NAFE, Nat. Assn. Bus. Women, Nat. Assn. Profl. Saleswomen, Phi Theta Kappa. Roman Catholic. Avocations: camping, skiing, snorkeling, sailing, reading, needlepoint.

KIDD, RITA CAROLYN, government process redesign consultant; b. Merced, Calif., Feb. 27, 1943; d. Vivian Grace (Reyburn) Broddrick-Hagan; m. James Tony Kidd, Feb. 24, 1962; 1 child, Alexandra Grace. Sec. Merced Planning Dept., 1960-61, Svc. Bur. Corp., San Jose, Calif., 1961-62, Mountain View (Calif.) Planning Dept., 1962-64; adminstrv. asst.. Syntex Labs., Palo Alto, Calif., 1965-69; stockbroker Harrison Fin. and Emmett Larkin, Sacramento, 1971-77; cons. on EEO law, affirmative action, pers. mgmt., Sacramento, Merced, 1974-80; asst. dir. project planning and devel. group Merced County Human Svcs. Agy., Merced, 1980-93; instr. Merced Coll., 1970-71, 77-79; cons. to govt. and industry in process redesign, 1993—. Mem., chmn. Merced Downtown Improvement Dist., 1977-79. Recipient recognition award Nat. Assn. Counties, 1987, 88, project award Urban and Regional Info. Systems Assn., 1991. Mem. Internat. Platform Assn. Democrat.

KIDDER, MARGOT, actress; b. Yellowknife, Can., Oct. 17, 1948; m. Tom McGuane, 1975 (div.); 1 dau., Maggie; m. John Heard. Student, U. B.C. Began career in Can. theater and TV; film debut in Gaily, Gaily, 1969; other films include Quackser Fortune Has a Cousin in the Bronx, 1970, Sisters, 1973, Black Christmas, 1974, A Quiet Day in Belfast, 1974, Gravy Train, 1974, Black Christmas, 1974, The Great Waldo Pepper, 1975, The Reincarnation of Peter Proud, 1975, 92 in the Shade, 1975, Superman, 1978, The Amityville Horror, 1979, Mr. Mike's Mondo Video, 1979, Miss Right, 1980, Superman II, 1980, Willie and Phil, 1980, Shoot the Sun Down, 1981, Heartaches, 1981, Some Kind of Hero, 1981, Trenchcoat, 1983, Superman III, 1983, Little Treasure, 1985, Speaking Our Peace, 1985, Little Treasure, 1985, The Canadian Conspiracy, 1986, Gobots: Battle of the Rock Lords (voice), 1986, Keeping Track, 1987, Superman IV: The Quest for Peace, 1987, Mob Story, 1990, The White Room, 1990, Crime and Punishment, 1992; dir., screenwriter And Again, 1975; starred in TV series Nichols, 1971-72, Shell Game, 1987, The Pornographer, 1993, Phantom 2040, 1994 (voice); TV movies Suddenly Single, 1971, The Bounty Man, 1972, Honky Tonk, 1974, Louisiana, 1984, The Glitter Dome, 1984, Such Dust as Dreams are Made Of, 1984, Picking Up the Pieces, 1985, Vanishing Act, 1986, Body of Evidence, 1987, Curiosity Killed, 1992, To Catch a Killer, 1992, One Woman's Courage, 1992, Windrunner, 1994; other TV appearances include Mod Squad. Office: Gold/Marshak and Assocs 3500 W Olive Ave Burbank CA 91505*

KIDMAN, NICOLE, actress; b. Hawaii, 1967; m. Tom Cruise, 1990; children: Isabella Jane Kidman, Connor Antony Kidman. Film appearences include BMX Bandits, 1983, Bush Christmas, 1983, Wills and Burke-The Untold Story, 1985, Windrider, 1986, The Bit Part, 1987, Emerald City, 1989, Dead Calm, 1989, Days of Thunder, 1990, Flirting, 1991, Billy Bathgate, 1991 (Golden Globe Award nomination 1992), Far and Away, 1992, Malice, 1993, My Life, 1993, Batman Forever, 1995, Portrait of a Lady, 1995; TV appearences include Bangkok Hilton, 1990 (Australian Film Inst. Best Actress in Miniseries), Vietnam (Australian Film Inst. Best Actress in Miniseries). Office: care Catherine Olin PMK Pub Rels 955 S Carrillo Dr #200 Los Angeles CA 90048*

KIDOKORO, YASUKO, physician; b. Japan, Feb. 21, 1940; d. Kenzo Ano. BS, Tokyo U., 1960, MD, 1964. Intern, 1964-65, resident in internal medicine, 1965-68, fellow in pulmonary medicine, 1968-70, 74-77, intern in pathology, 1977-78, resident in pathology, 1978-80, fellow in microbiology and infectious disease, 1983-84; dir. lab. Mission Bay Meml. Hosp., San Diego, 1991—. Office: Mission Bay Meml Hosp 3030 Bunker Hill St San Diego CA 92109

KIEFER, ANNE FLAVELLE, psychologist; b. West Hartford, Conn., Oct. 15, 1953; d. C. Raymond and Elizabeth Margaret (Herron) K.; m. C. Michael Wieghard, Dec. 21, 1977; children: Nicole, Ryan. BA, Ind. U., 1975, MSW, 1978; MA, U. Mo., 1982, PhD, 1988. Lic. psychologist, Kans. Clinician Family Svc. Assn., Indpls., 1978-79; supr. Johnson County Mental Health Ctr., Olathe, Kans., 1979—; pvt. practice Leawood, Kans., 1984—; cons., trainer Assocs. in Cons. and Tng., Leawood, 1990—. Contbr. articles to profl. jours. Mem. leadership com. Oak Hill Sch., 1994. Mem. APA. Office: Comprehensive Counseling 11111 Nall Ave Ste 218 Leawood KS 66211-1625

KIEFER, JACQUELINE LORRAINE, education educator, consultant; b. Dayton, Ohio, Nov. 6, 1947; d. Elmer Louis Kiefer and Lorraine (Siefert) K. BS in Educ., U. of Dayton, 1969; MED in Curr and Super., Wright STate U., 1978; MED, Wright State U., 1987. Sp. edn. tchr. Milton Union Village Sch., West Milton, Ohio, 1969-88; spl. edn. cons. Medina (Ohio) County Bd. Edn., 1988—; supr. part-time Amateur Trap Shooting Assn., Vandalia, Ohio, 1969-93. Author: Packets of Activities - Kids N Summer, math Box of Activities, Math Box. chairperson Disaster Services, Am. Nat. Red Cross, Dayton, Ohio, Fund raiser, Cancer Soc., Heart Assn., Dayton; mem. Women in Ednl. Leadership; vol. Miami Valley Hosp., Ohio Pub. Images, Miami Valley Spl. Edn. Regional Resource Ct. Recipient Disting. Service award, Spl. Olympics, Ohio, Cert. of Merit, Milton Union Sch., Council of Exceptional Children. Mem. Ohio Assn. Supr., N.E. Ohio Suprs. Assn., Coun. Exceptional Children, Assn. Curriculum Supervision, Lizotte Reading Coun., Assn. Curriculum Devel., Dayton Ski Club, Kappa Delta Pi, Phi Delta Kappa. Home: 10 W Sherry Dr Trotwood OH 45426 Office: Medina Bd Edn 144 N Broadway St Medina OH 44256-1902

KIEFER, RENATA GERTRUD, physician, economist, health consultant; b. Lorrach, Baden, Germany, July 4, 1946; came to U.S., 1970; d. Friedrich W. and Gertrud Anna (Keller) K.; m. James C. Bridgman. BA, Stanford U., 1963; MA, U. Calif., Berkeley, 1967; MD, U. Geneva, Switzerland, 1982; MPH, U. Calif., Berkeley, 1990. Asst. instr. dissection lab. dept.

morphology U. Geneva Sch. of Medicine, Switzerland, 1979-80; interim resident dept. diagnostic radiology Univ. Hosp., Geneva, 1980, intern physician, 1982-83; clin. fellow in pediatrics Harvard Med. Sch., Boston, 1983-85; resident physician Mass. Gen. Hosp., Boston, 1983-85; sr. resident dept. pediatrics U. Calif., San Francisco, 1985-86; attending physician emergency dept. Children's Hosp. Med. Ctr., Oakland, Calif., 1986—; fellow dept. epidemiology and internat. health U. Calif., San Francisco, 1988-90; German tech. cooperation expert tropical medicine & internat. pub. health Inst. for Health Sci. Rsch., Asuncion, Paraguay, 1990-94, vis. prof. epidemiol. and preventive medicine, 1992—; sci. methods advisor Nat. U. Asuncion, 1994—; cons. and presenter in field. Contbr. numerous articles to profl. jours. Named Internat. Health scholar U. Calif., 1990, AAUW fellow, 1968, Internat. scholar Swedish Inst., 1968, Fulbright scholar, 1962-64, ASSU scholar Stanford U., 1962-63; recipient MacJannet Found. award for Internat. Understanding, 1981. Address: 6 Locksley Ave 10A San Francisco CA 94122-3839

KIEFFER, SUSAN WERNER, geology educator; b. Warren, Pa., Nov. 17, 1942. BS in Physics and Math., Allegheny Coll., 1964; MS in Geol. Scis., Calif. Inst. Tech., 1967, PhD in Planetary Scis., 1971; DSc (hon.), Allegheny Coll., 1987. Postdoctoral research geochemist UCLA, 1971-73, asst. prof. geology, 1973-79; geologist U.S. Geol. Survey, Flagstaff, Ariz., 1979-90; prof. geology Ariz. State U., Tempe, 1988—, Regents prof., 1991-93; prof., head dept. geol. sci. U. B.C., Vancouver, Can., 1993—. Co-editor: (with A. Navrotsky) Microscopic to Macroscopic: Atomic Environments to Mineral Thermodynamics, 1985. Alfred P. Sloan Found. fellow, 1977-79; W.H. Mendenhall lectr., U.S. Geol. Survey, 1980; recipient Disting. Alumnus award Calif. Inst. Tech., 1982, Meritorious Svc. award Dept. Interior, 1986, Spendiarov award Soviet Acad. of Scis., 1990. Fellow Am. Geophys. Union, Am. Acad. Arts and Scis., Mineral. Soc. Am. (award 1980), Geol. Soc. Am. (Arthur L. Day medal 1992), Meteoritical Soc.; mem. NAS. Office: U BC Dept Geol Sci, 6339 Stores Rd, Vancouver, BC Canada V6T 1Z4

KIEKHAEFER, RUTH ANNE, healthcare executive; b. Lincoln, Nebr., Feb. 3, 1938; d. John Henry and Helen Anna (Kastner) Heins; m. Theodore Charles Kiekhaefer, Sept. 13, 1959; children: Kristin Dunn, Phillip, Anne, Michael. Student, Concordia Coll., Seward, Nebr., 1955-56; BS in Nursing, Nebr. U., 1959; postgrad., U. Ariz., 1963-64; M in Nursing, Kans. U., 1987; certificate, U. Kans., 1992. Cert. devel. specialist. Staff nurse Univ. Hosp., Omaha, 1959-60; pediatric instr. Children's Hosp., Omaha, 1960-62; staff nurse Tuscon Med. Ctr., 1963-64; tchr. Happy Time Nursery Sch., Superior, Nebr., 1970; dir. nursing svc. and edn. Good Samaritan Ctr., Superior, Nebr., 1971-73; dir. health Industry Resources, Inc., St. Joseph, Mo., 1981-83; cons. Progressive Evaluation and Rehab. Cons., Shawnee Mission, Kans., 1985; pres. Healthwise, Inc., St. Joseph, 1986—; cons. Med. Clinic St. Joseph, 1986—; instr. Mo. Western State Coll., 1992—. Mem. exec. bd. Family Guidance Ctr., 1992—. Mem. ANA, Am. Assn. Occupational Health Nurses, Clin. Nurse Specialist Coun., Nat. Wellness Assn., Mo. Nurses Assn. (bd. dirs. dist. 1 1988-90), Buchanan County Med. Aux. (pres. 1990), Mo. State Med. Assn. Aux. (v.p., state health chair 1992-93), Mo. Assn. Cardiovascular and Pulmonary Rehab. Specialists, N.W. Mo. Wellness Coun. (chair 1992), Sigma Theta Tau, Delta Delta Delta (Alumni pres. 1989-91). Republican. Lutheran. Home: 2 Evergreen Dr # 2rr Saint Joseph MO 64505-9660 Office: Healthwise Inc 1301 S Belt Hwy Saint Joseph MO 64507-2228

KIEL, CATHERINE ANN, public relations executive; b. Phila., Aug. 8, 1961; d. Seymour and Alice (Wolf) K. BA, BS, Miami U., Oxford, Ohio, 1983. Asst. to dir. spl. events Penn's Landing Corp. Phila. Tri-Centennial, 1982; account exec. Jessica Dee Communications, N.Y.C., 1983-85; v.p. Grossich & Ptnrs., Inc., N.Y.C., 1985-89; sr. v.p. G.S. Schwartz & Co. Inc., N.Y.C., 1989—; with Laws Hall & Assocs., Miami U., Oxford, 1983; pub. rels. cons. N.Y.C. Opera Guild, 1989-90. Mem. exec. com. John Ravitz Campaign, N.Y.C., 1988; exec. v.p. Eastside Young Reps. Club, N.Y.C., 1987-90. Recipient Ptnrship. in Edn. award N.Y.C. Bd. Edn., 1983, 88, Silver Anvil, Pub. Rels. Soc. Am., 1992, Big Apple, N.Y. chpt. Pub. Rels. Soc. Am., 1992, Creativity in Pub. Rels. award, 1994. Mem. Miami U. Alumni Club (pres. N.Y.C. chpt. 1988-94), Miami U. Alumni Assn. (bd. dirs. 1992—), N.Y. Jr. League. Home: 245 E 83rd St New York NY 10028 Office: GS Schwartz & Co Inc 470 Park Ave S New York NY 10016

KIENTZ, RENEE, newspaper editor. Lifestyle editor Features Desk Houston Chronicle. Office: Houston Chronicle Pub Co 801 Texas Ave Houston TX 77002-2907

KIER, DUANN, human resources consultant; b. Jackson, Miss., Jan. 3, 1955; m. Steven O. Brown. AA, Hinds C.C., Raymond, Miss., 1975; BA, Miss. Coll., 1977; M of Religious Edn., New Orleans Theol. Sem., 1980. Dir. programs YWCA, Nashville, 1987-92; dir. career edn. continuing studies Mid. Tenn. State U., Murfreesboro, 1991-92; pres. Ctr. for Pers. and Profl. Devel., Morganton, N.C., 1992—. Mem. AAUW (chair pub. rels. 1993, pres. 1992), Am. Bus. Women's Assn. (chair edn. com. 1993), Assn. for Psychol. Type, Assn. for Transpersonal Psychology, Global Intuition Network, Soc. Bus. and Profl. Women, Kiwanis (bd. dirs. 1993). Office: Ctr Pers and Profl Devel PO Box 1092 Morganton NC 28680-1092

KIES, COSETTE NELL, library science educator, consultant; b. Platteville, Wis., Sept. 2, 1936; d. Guerdon Francis and Gertrude Caroline (Pitts) K. B.S., U. Wis.-Platteville, 1957; M.A. in Art History, U. Wis.-Madison, 1961, M.A. in Library Sci., 1962; D.L.S., Columbia U., 1977. Art tchr. Grafton Pub. Schs., Wis., 1957-59; children's librarian Fond du Lac Pub. Library, Wis., 1962-63; sr. asst. librarian, asst. prof. U. Nebr., Lincoln, 1963-67; prof. asst. ALA, Chgo., 1968-69; library career cons. Ill. State Library, Springfield, 1969-71; asst. dir., personnel and pub. relations Ferguson Library, Stamford, Conn., 1971-74; asst. prof. Sch. Library Sci., Goerge Peabody Coll. for Tchrs., Nashville, 1975-78; assoc. prof. Sch. Library Sci., George Peabody Coll. for Tchrs., 1978-83; vis. assoc. prof. Sch. Library Sci., Simmons Coll., Boston, 1978; sr. lectr. Fulbright-Hays Program, Escola de Biblioteconomia, U. Fed. de Minas Gerais, Brazil, 1979-80; vis. prof. Escola de Biblioteconomia, U. Fed. de Paraiba, Joao Pessoa, Brazil, 1980; chmn., prof. dept. library and info. studies No. Ill. U., De Kalb, 1983-94, prof. dept. leadership and ednl. policy studies, 1994—; mem. planning com. Children's Lit. Inst., 1983—; speaker various orgns., radio and TV. Author: Problems in Library Public Relations, 1974, Projecting a Positive Image Through Public Relations, 1979, Occult Books in the Western World, 1986, Marketing and Public Relations for Libraries, 1987, Supernatural Fiction for Teens, 1987, 92, Horror Fiction for Young Adults, 1991, Presenting Lois Duncan, 1994; editor: The Literary Allusions Cookbook, 1982. Recipient George Virgil Fuller award Columbia U., 1976. Mem. ALA (life mem., pub. library assn. 1973—, adv. com. Office for Library Personnel 1979-83, chair nat. library week com. 1985-87, editor Recruitment Newsletter 1968-69, editor Fin. Assistance for Library Edn. 1970-73, recipient H.W. Wilson Recruitment award 1970), Assn. Library Services for Children (Newbery-Caldecott com. 1976, ad hoc com. to provide procs. for evaluation of exec. sec. 1976-78), Library Edn. Div. (chmn. fin. assistance for library edn. com. 1969-73, Beta Phi Mu award com. 1976), Assn. Library and Info. Sci. Edn. (communications com. 1978-80, coordinator joint library sch. reunion 1984-85), Women's Nat. Book Assn. (dir. pub. affairs, spl. asst. to pres. 1980-82, pres. Nashville chpt. 1981-83, adv. panel for status of women in pub. research project 1981—, newsletter editor 1980-82), Ill. Library Assn., Ill. Coalition Library Advocates (bd. dirs. 1984-86), Children's Internat. Edn. Ctr. (chmn. pub. relations com. 1981-83), Friends of No. Ill. U. Library. Home: 607 Normal Rd De Kalb IL 60115-2204 Office: No Ill U Dept Leadership/Ednl Policy De Kalb IL 60115*

KIESLICH, ANITA FRANCES, school system administrator; b. St. Albans, Vt., July 8, 1941; d. George E. and Doris E. (Rogers) Hilliker; m. Karl V. Kieslich, May 16, 1964; children: Karin, Karl John, Kathleen, Kevin. BEd, Johnson State Coll., 1964; MA, Wayne State U., 1974; specialist degree in reading, U. S.C., 1985. Cert. tchr., adminstr., counselor S.C. Tchr. Vt. Pub. Schs., Burlington, 1964, Georgia, 1967-68; sub. tchr. DOD Schs., Germany, 1965-67, Colo. Pub. Schs., Denver, 1968-72; tchr. reading DOD Schs., Turkey, 1972-75; guidance counselor, tchr. reading Millwood Elem. Sch., Sumter, S.C., 1975-89; asst. prin. Lemira Elem. Sch., Sumter, 1989-94; coord. parenting & extended day programs Sch. Dist. # 17, Sumter, 1994—; adj. instr. U. S.C., Sumter, 1990-91, Carolina Cent. Coll., Sumter, 1992—; presenter S.C. Palmetto's Tchrs. Assn., Charleston, 1992; grant reader DOE Washington, 1992; cons. on grants Sumter Dist. 17 Sch., 1992—; Parent As Tchr. educator, 1994; Motheread facilator, 1995. Author: Teaching Reading Through Bulletin Boards, 1989; host for daily T.V. show. Adv. bd. Boys and Girls Club, Sumter, 1989—; chmn. edn. Bicentennial Women's Club, Sumter, 1987-90; tchr. St. Jude's Cath. Ch., Sumter, 1988—; adv. bd. RSVP, Sumter, 1991—. Mem. S.C. Assn. Sch. Adminstrs., S.C. Assn. Elem. and Mid. Sch. Prins. (Asst. Principal of Yr. 1993), S.C. Assn. for Elem. Prins., Pee Dee Reading Assn., S.C. Assn. for Counseling and Devel., S.C. Network for Women Admistrs. in Edn., Phi Delta Kappa, Kappa Delta Epsilon (charter pres. 1962). Home: 22 Conyers St Sumter SC 29150

KIESLING, JUANITA HASELOFF, real estate broker; b. Vernon, TX, Jan. 23, 1935; d. Herbert Karl and Ottilie Rose (Obenhaus) H.; m. Ernst Willie Kiesling, Aug. 25, 1956; children: Carol, Chris, Max. BBA, Tex. Tech U., 1957, MBA, 1974. Instr. Tex. Tech U., Lubbock, 1971-76; real estate agt. Land and Assocs., Lubbock, 1977-80; owner, broker Chapman South, Realtors, Lubbock, 1980-82, Nita Kiesling, Realtors, Lubbock, 1982-88; v.p. WestMark, Realtors, Lubbock, 1988—; Bd. dirs. Lubbock Housing Fin. Corp. Bd. dirs. Am. Heart Assn., Lubbock, 1985-86; chmn. adv. council Lutheran Social Service, Lubbock, 1986-87; dir. Caprock Girl Scouts Council, Lubbock, 1984-88; com. chair Citizens Adv. Com. for Capital Improvements, Lubbock, 1985-86; budget div. United Way, Lubbock, 1986-88. Mem. Lubbock Bd. Realtors (Realtor of Yr. award 1986, chmn. bd. 1990), Tex. Assn. Realtors (chmn. fin. procedures com., mgtm. adv. com. 1986, bd. dirs. 1989-91), Sales Execs. Assn. (bd. dirs. 1983-84), Real Estate Brokerage Coun. (Tex. pres. 1989), Lubbock C. of C. (com. mem. 1982—), Toastmasters, Soroptimists (pres. 1987-88). Home: 4912 94th St Lubbock TX 79424-4812 Office: West Mark Realtors 7008 Indiana Ave Lubbock TX 79413-6114

KIESLING, L(AURA) LYNNE, economics educator; b. Pitts., June 14, 1965; d. David Lawrence and Kathryn (Jacobson) K. BS, Miami U., 1987; PhD, Northwestern U., 1993. Asst. prof. Coll. of William and Mary, Williamsburg, Va., 1992—. Mem. Am. Econ. Assn., Econ. History Assn., Cliometric Soc., Com. on the Status of Women in the Econs. Profession. Office: Coll of William and Mary 118 Morton Hall Williamsburg VA 23187

KIICK, KAREN MARIE, art educator; b. Easton, Pa., June 6, 1968; d. Kirby Miller and Judith Lynn (Haas) K. BS in Art Edn., Kutztown (Pa.) U., 1990. Children's counselor Mountain Lake Resort, Marshalls Creek, Pa.; social dir. Foxwood Farms Campground, Marshalls Creek; day camp dir. YMCA Camp Eljabar, Dingmans Ferry, Pa., 1990; resident asst. Kutztown U., 1988-90; cashier Weis Markets, East Stroudsburg, Pa., 1990—; art tchr. grade 6-7 East Stroudsburg (Pa.) Area Sch. Dist., 1990—; set designer East Stroudsburg Area Sch. Dist., 1992-93; pvt. art instr., Stroudsburg, 1990—. Mem. United Presbyn. Ch., East Stroudsburg, 1993-94. Mem. Monroe County Arts Coun. (3rd pl. mixed media 1993, 2d pl. sculpture, 1994), Nat. Art Edn. Assn., Pa. State Edn. Assn., Kappa Delta Pi. Democrat. Home: 201 Analomink St East Stroudsburg PA 18301 Office: East Stroudsburg Area Sch Dist 2000 Milford Rd East Stroudsburg PA 18301

KIJANKA, DOROTHY M., library administrator; b. Mt. Olive, Ill.; d. Michael and Catherine (Zupsich) Kaganich; m. Stanley J. Kijanka, Jr., Nov. 20, 1970 (dec. 1981). AB in History with honors, U. Ill.; MLS, Rutgers U. Reference librarian Greenwich Pub. Library, Conn., 1966-68; reference librarian Fairfield U., Conn., 1968-74, assoc. librarian, 1974-84; dir. Sacred Heart U. Library, Fairfield, 1984—; bd. dirs. Bibliomation, 1990—; chair Conn. Acad. Libr. Dirs., 1993—; panelist Off-Campus Libr. Svcs. Conf., 1993. Contbr. articles to profl. jours. Mem. ALA, Library Group of Southwestern Conn. (pres. 1977-78), Southwestern Conn. Library Council (trustee 1977-78), Fairfield County Library Adminstrs. Group (pres. 1986—), New Eng. Library Assn., Conn. Library Assn. (chmn. reference sect. 1975), Assn. Coll. and Rsch. Librs. (planning com. 1987—, mem. internat. rels. com. 1991), Libr. Adminstrn. and Mgmt. Assn. (orgn. com. 1987, risk mgmt. and ins. com. 1987—, mem. fund raising com. 1990, mentor 1990-92). Office: Sacred Heart Univ Library 5151 Park Ave Fairfield CT 06432-1000

KILBOURNE, BARBARA JEAN, health and human services executive; b. Milw., Mar. 21, 1941; d. Burton Conwell and Marjorie Janet (Tufts) K.; m. Kenneth Keith Kauffman, Feb. 10, 1962 (div. 1983). BA, U. Minn., 1972; MBA, Coll. St. Thomas, St. Paul, 1980. Adminstr. Ebenezer Soc., Mpls., 1974-85; v.p., dir. housing Walker Residence and Health Svcs., Inc., Mpls., 1985-88; exec. v.p. Oblate Ministries Health and Aging, West St. Paul, Minn., 1988-94; bd. dirs. Westminster Resident Svcs. Corp., St. Paul, River Region Health Svcs., Red Wing, Minn., 1990—, Sr. Housing, Inc., Mpls., 1986—, Ancilla Health Sys., Chgo., 1990-93; mem. commn. on aging Cath. Charities USA, Washington, 1989—; presenter workshops, symposia; cons., spkr. in field. Author: Family Councils in Nursing Homes, 1981. Chmn. bd. dirs. Dakota Inc., Eagan, Minn., 1985—; project chair Dialog 2000, Dakota County, Minn., 1988-91; chmn. bd. dirs. Minn. Assn. Homes for Aging, 1991-92. Mem. Gerontol. Soc. Am. Republican. Episcopalian. Home: 1021 Sibley Memorial Hwy Lilydale MN 55118-6100

KILBOURNE, DIANE CUSTEAU, special education educator; b. Glen Ridge, N.J., Feb. 25, 1946; d. Emile Michel and Helen Mildred (Lombard) Custeau; m. Lincoln F. Kilbourne, June 29, 1968 (div. Feb. 1984); children: Charles Evans III, Elizabeth Brooke. BA, Wells Coll., 1968; MA, Duquesne U., 1972. Cert. tchr., Fla. Sec. GE, Schenectady, N.Y., 1968-69; instr. Duquesne U., Pitts., 1970-72; client svcs. rep. Merrill Lynch, Pierce, Fenner & Smith, Inc., Schenectady, 1984-86; investment broker A.G. Edwards & Sons, Inc., Schenectady, 1986-89; instr. SUNY, Cobleskill, 1990; tchr. Taylor County Mid. Sch., Perry, Fla., 1990—. Bd. dirs. Alcoholism Coun. and Clinic, Schenectady, 1979-82. Named Outstanding Young Women of Am., 1978. Mem. NEA, FTP. Republican.

KILBURN, PENELOPE WHITE, data processing executive; b. Freeport, N.Y., June 25, 1940; d. William Prescott and Marian (Churchill) White; m. Edwin Allen Kilburn, Feb. 7, 1964; children: Penelope Allen, Nancy Kitchen. BA, Barnard Coll., 1962. Elem. sch. tchr. Holmdel (N.J.) Bd. Edn., 1975-78; tech. writer Continental Data Ctr., Neptune, N.J., 1983-86; with Johnson & Higgins, N.Y.C., 1986-89; asst. v.p., 1989-91; v.p. Johnson & Higgins, N.Y.C., 1991—. Active mem. Jr. League, Monmouth County, 1973-80, sustaining mem., 1980—; chmn. St. Georges refugee com., Rumson, N.J., 1981-83; mem. St. Georges By the River Altar Guild, Rumson. Mem. Soc. for Tech. Communication. Episcopalian. Office: Johnson & Higgins 125 Broad St New York NY 10004-2424

KILCHER, KATHERINE STARR, counselor; b. Hagerstown, Md., Apr. 29, 1954; d. James Conrad and JoAnn (Beachley) K.; m. William Henry Watkins IV, Nov. 1981 (wid. Oct. 1988); m. Charles Eugene Flournoy, Jr., Oct. 15, 1989; 1 child, Charles Eugene Flournoy, III. BS in Psychology, Lynchburg Coll., 1976; MA in Counseling Psychology, Towson State U., 1978. Lic. profl. counselor, Va.; lic. mental health counselor, Fla. Psychologist Cen. Va. Tng. Ctr., Lynchburg, 1978-79; therapist Cen. Va. Community Svcs., Lynchburg, 1979-87; counselor Magri, Kilcher & Jenkins Therapy Assns., Inc., Lynchburg, 1987—; employee assistance cons., Employee Assistance of Cen. Va., Inc., Lynchburg, 1983-84;. Bd. dirs. Woman's Resource Ctr., Lynchburg, 1980s. Named to Outstanding Young Women of Am., 1981. Mem. Am. Assn. Mental Health Counselors, Va. Counselors Assn., Fla. Counseling Assn., Am. Counseling Assn., Va. Assn. Clin. Counselors, Planned Parenthood of Blue Ridge, Mental Health Assn., NOW (pres. Lynchburg chpt. 1980-82), Chi Sigma Iota, Psi Chi. Episcopalian. Office: Magri Kilcher & Jenkins Therapy Assocs 1120 Mcconville Rd Ste A Lynchburg VA 24502-4534

KILDAY, EILEEN MARY, accountant, educator; b. New Britain, Conn., Apr. 8, 1952; d. Walter Warren and Claire Rose (Ryniec) K.; m. G. Stephen Christopher, Sept. 10, 1988. BS in Acctg., Russell Sage Coll., 1974; MS in Acctg., SUNY, Albany, 1976; postgrad., Drexel U., 1984-87. CPA, N.Y. Sr. auditor Ernst & Whinney, Hartford, Conn., 1976-79; sr. internal auditor, supv. external reporting Itek Corp., Lexington, Mass., 1979-81; mgr. corp. acctg., sys. specialist fin. planning dept. Centronics Data Computer Corp., Hudson, N.H., 1981-83; acctg. cons., pvt. practice Troy, N.Y., 1983—; asst. prof. acctg. Russell Sage Coll., Troy, 1984-85, 86-87; vis. asst. prof. acctg. Skidmore Coll., Saratoga, N.Y., 1992-94; vis. lectr. SUNY Albany, 1991-92. Past mem. fin. com. TRIP, Inc., Pahl House; treas. Troy area United Ministries. Mem. AICPAs, N.Y. State Soc. CPAs, Am. Soc. Women Accts., Inst. Mgmt. Accts. (past pres. Albany chpt., past mem. chpt. ops. com., nat. dir. 1991-93). Home: 203 10th St Troy NY 12180 Office: PO Box 1449 Troy NY 12181

KILDE, SANDRA JEAN, nurse anesthetist, educator, consultant; b. Eau Claire, Wis., June 25, 1938; d. Harry Meylan and Beverly June (Johnson) K. Diploma Luther Hosp. Sch. Nursing, Eau Claire, 1959; grad. anesthesia course Mpls. Sch. Anesthesia, 1967; BA, Met. State U., St. Paul, 1976; MA, U. St. Thomas, 1981; EdD, Nova U., 1987. RN, Wis., Minn. Operating room nurse Luther Hosp., Eau Claire, 1959-61, head nurse operating room, 1961-63; supr. operating room Midway Hosp., St. Paul, 1963-66; staff anesthetist North Meml. Med. Ctr., Robbinsdale, Minn., 1967-68; program dir. Mpls. Sch. Anesthia, St. Louis Park, Minn., 1968—; adj. assoc. prof. St. Mary's Coll., Winona, Minn., 1982—, program dir. Masters Degree Program, 1984—; ednl. cons. accreditation visitor Coun. on Accreditation of Nurse Anesthesia Ednl. Programs, Park Ridge, Ill., 1983-92, elected to coun., 1992—, vice chmn., 1994—; presentations in field. Recipient Good Neighbor award Sta. WCCO, Mpls., 1980, Disting. Alumni Achievement award Nova U., 1993. Mem. Am. Assn. Nurse Anesthetists (pres. 1981-82, pres. and bd. dirs. Edn. and Research Found. 1981-83, cert. profl. excellence 1976, Program Dir. of Yr. award 1992), Minn. Assn. Nurse Anesthetists (pres. 1975-76). Lutheran. Avocations: gardening, fishing, photography, choir directing, playing guitar and piano. Home: 11784 Madison St NE Minneapolis MN 55434-3008 Office: Mpls Sch Anesthesia 6715 Minnetonka Blvd Minneapolis MN 55426-3468

KILDOW, GLORIA JEAN, psychotherapist; b. Bessemer, Mich., Dec. 8, 1951; d. Bernard Thomas and Martha Jane (Lewandowski) Olejnicak; m. Ronald Lee Kildow, Oct. 1, 1977; stepchildren: Tina, Adria. BS, No. Mich. U., 1973; MA in Counseling, Oakland U., 1994. Lic. profl. counselor, Mich.; limited lic. psychologist, Mich. Substitute tchr. Oakland (Mich.) Schs., 1974-77, Sarasota (Fla.) Schs., 1974-77; tchr. Northwestern High Sch., Flint, Mich., 1977-78; prodn. specialist Truck & Bus divsn. GM, Pontiac, Mich., 1978-88, alt. EAP rep. UAW Local 594, 1988—; instr. Dale Carnegie courses Ralph Nichols Corp., Southfield, Mich., 1986-91. Mem. ACA, APA, UAW (civil rights standing com.), Am. Mental Health Counselors Assn., Mich. Assn. Counseling and Devel., Mich. Mental Health Counselors Assn., Oakland Assn. Counseling and Devel., Assn. for Religious and Value Issues in Counseling, Grad. Counseling Student Assn. Oakland U., Chi Sigma Iota. Home: 212 W Fairmont Ave Pontiac MI 48340-2740

KILDUFF, BONNIE ELIZABETH, director of expositions; b. Washington, Sept. 25, 1959; d. Macolm McGreggor and Betty (Alvino) K. Adminstr. Aircraft Owners & Pilot Assn., Bethesda, Md., 1977-79; mktg. pub. rels., meeting planning, exec. asst. Dairy and Food Inds. Supply Assn., Rockville, Md., 1979-89; dir. expns. Packaging Machinery Mfrs. Inst., Washington, 1989—; secmem. Trade Show Adv. Coun., Denver, 1992-94. Mem. Internat. Assn. Expn. Mgrs. (sec. found. com. 1994, mem. major trade show organizer 1991-94, mem. edn. com. 1992-94, cert. expn. mgr. 1993), Trade Show Bur., Women on Packaging, Confedn. of Organizers of Packaging Expns. Office: Packaging Machinery Mfrs Inst 4350 N Fairfax Dr Ste 600 Arlington VA 22205

KILE, CAROL ANN, lawyer; b. Cleve., Dec. 26, 1946; d. Walter John and Leona Eleanor (Koeppen) Ripich; m. William Simons Kile, Aug. 12, 1972; children: Evan William, Warren Ripich. BA cum laude, Wittenberg U., 1968; MA, U. Ariz., 1970; JD cum laude, Cleve. State U., 1991. Bar: Ohio, 1991. Tchr. Cleve. Pub. Schs., 1969-74; children's libr. Cuyahoga County Pub. Libr., Cleve., 1976-92; clerk externship Ohio 8th Dist. Ct. Appeals, Cleve., 1991; staff atty. Legal Aid Soc. Lorain County Inc., Elyria, Ohio, 1992—; lectr. on Islamic law and constitutional history, Cleve., 1987—. Contbr. articles to profl. jours. Com. woman Rocky River (Ohio) United Meth. Ch., 1980—. Recipient award for excellence in constl. law Fed. Bar Assn., 1989, Am. Jurisprudence award in constl. law, 1989. Mem. ABA, AAUW, LWV, Ohio Bar Assn., Phi Alpha Theta.

KILE, HEATHER LOUISE, pharmacist; b. Omaha, Sept. 10, 1964; d. Harlow Wayne and Linda Kay (Thomas) Inman; m. Todd Alan Kile, May 15, 1987. Student, U. Nebr., 1982-84, PharmD, 1988. Pharmacist Johnson Pharmacy, Council Bluffs, Iowa, 1988-93, Mayo Clinic, Scottsdale, Ariz., 1993—; pharmacist cons. Johnson Home Health Care Pharmacy, Council Bluffs, 1988-93. Mem. Am. Soc. Cons. Pharmacists, Ariz. Pharmacy Assn. Republican. Methodist. Home: 12705 N 78th St Scottsdale AZ 85260 Office: Mayo Clinic Pharmacy 13400 E Shea Blvd Scottsdale AZ 85260

KILGORE, JANICE KAY, musician, educator; b. Dallas, July 6, 1955; d. Jean Kendall and Dorothy Helen (King) K.; m. Albert Franklin Slatter, Jr., Mar. 24, 1979 (div. Jan. 1993). Student, Oral Roberts U., 1973-76; AA, Mountain View Coll., 1979; MusB, U. North Tex., 1983, M in Mus. Edn., 1990; postgrad. in recording technology, Cedar Valley Coll. Cert. music tchr., Tex. Tchr. aide ESL Dallas Pub. Schs., 1979, substitute tchr., 1979-83, class piano tchr., 1983-84, choir dir./class piano instr., 1988-90, orch. tchr., 1992—; asst. dir. Jazz Singers, Oral Roberts U., Tulsa, 1975-76; music dir., vocalist, keyboardist, booking agent, violist Janal, High Soc., Dallas Woodwind Ensemble Imperial String Quartet, Imperial Brass Ensemble, 1978—; music instr. Project Upward Bound, Denton, Tex., 1981; tchr. Waxahachie (Tex.) Ind. Sch. Dist., 1990-92, choir dir., coord. dept. voice; class keyboard instr. Baldwin Family Music, Dallas, 1987-89; music instr. North Lake Coll., Irving, Tex., 1990—; creator, dir. numerous outdoor concerts; owner Southwest Music Enterprises. Author: British English to American English Dictionary, 1994; composer (symphonic poem) Scottish Suite, 1977, (choral work) The Wisemen, 1990; contbr. articles to mags. dir. Urbandale Christian Ch., Dallas, 1977-79, Centenary United Meth. Ch., Dallas, 1984-85, First United Meth. Ch., Midlothian, Tex., 1985-87, St. Luke United Meth. Ch., Dallas, 1989-90, First United Meth. Ch., Waxahachie, 1990-93, Trinity United Meth. Ch., Duncanville, Tex., 1993-94. Recipient Missionary Svc. award United Meth. Women, 1986. Mem. Tex. Music Educators Assn. (presenter 1994), Tex. Choral Dir. Assn., Tex. Orch. Dirs. Assn., Dallas Music Educators Assn., Kappa Delta Pi, Pi Kappa Lambda. Republican. Home: 317 Oak Meadow Ln Cedar Hill TX 75104 Office: Dallas Pub Schs 3700 Ross Ave Dallas TX 75204

KILKELLY, MARJORIE LEE, state legislator; b. Hartford, Conn., Dec. 1, 1954; d. Bruce Hamilton and Corlys Lucille (Lux) Brewer; children: Jeffrey Jr. (dec.), Robert, Sarah A.E. BS in Human Services, N.H. Coll., 1986, MS in Community Econ. Devel., 1986. Asst. to dir. Lincoln County Summer Youth Employment Program, Wiscasset, Maine, 1978; coordinator Community Food & Nutrition Program Coastal Enterprises, Inc., Wiscasset, 1978-79, Coastal Econ. Devel. Corp., Wiscasset, 1979-80; dir. Head Start Program Coastal Econ. Devel. Corp., Bath, Maine, 1980-84; asst. instr. N.H. Coll., Manchester, 1985-86; dir. Jr. Tots Wiscasset Recreation Program, 1985-88; dir. food services Boothbay Sch. Dept., Boothbay Harbor, Maine, 1985-88; owner Hurricane Hill Catering Co., Wiscasset, 1989—; mem. Maine Ho. of Reps., Augusta, 1988—; house chair com. on agr., forestry and conservation, 1995-96; co-chmn. coastal caucus Maine Ho. of Reps., Augusta, candidate for speaker of house, 1992, candidate for house majority whip, 1994, chair agriculture, forestry and conservation com., 1995—; treas. Coastal Enterprises, Inc., Rundlet Block, Wis., 1981—; rep. to Internat. Conf. on Econ. Devel., New Delhi, 1983—; 3d Selectman Town of Wiscasset, 1993—. Mem. planning com. Blaine House Conf. on Families, 1979-80; active Maine Human Svcs. Coun. Sta. 23, Augusta, 1980-88; Sunday sch. tchr., lectr. St. Philips Episcopal Ch., Wiscasset, 1984-85, chmn. coord. com. food bank, 1986-88, candidate for sr. warden; chmn. Wis. Dem. Com., 1986; nat. chmn. Schs. S.O.S. Nat. Hunger Awareness Program, Denver, 1986. New England Rural fellow, Coun. State Govts. Toll fellow; grantee Maine Welfare Edn. Employment Tng. Program, 1983. Mem. Bus. and Profl. Women (Maine Young Career Woman award 1989), Huntoon Hill Grange Club, Lincoln County Pomona Grange Club, Sportsmans Alliance Club of Maine, Am. Coun. Young Polit. Leaders. Democrat. Episcopalian. Clubs: B.P.W. (Damariscotta, Maine); CONA (Newcastle, Maine). Home: PO Box 180 W Alna Rd Wiscasset ME 04578-0180 Office: Maine Ho Reps State Capitol Augusta ME 04333

KILLAM, EVA KING, pharmacologist; b. N.Y.C., Nov. 16, 1921; d. Charles H. and Louise C. (Richter) King; m. Keith F. Killam, Jr., May 12, 1955; children: Anne Louise, Paul Fenton, Melissa Helen. AB, Sarah Lawrence Coll., 1942; AM, Mt. Holyoke Coll., 1944; PhD in Pharmacology, U. Ill., 1953. Pharmacologist Army Chem. Center, Md., 1948-51; jr. rsch. pharmacologist, then assoc. rsch. pharmacologist UCLA Med. Sch., 1953-59; research asso. Stanford U. Med. Sch., 1959-68; prof. physiology U. Calif., Davis, 1968-72; prof. pharmacology U. Calif., 1972-91, prof. emeritus, 1991—; epilepsy adv. com. NIH, 1976-80; study sect. preclin. pharmacology NIMH, 1972-76. Co-editor: Handbook of Electroencephalography, Vol. 7, 1977; editor-in-chief: Jour. Pharmacology and Exptl. Therapeutics, 1978-91; edit. bd.: Soc. Exptl. Biology and Medicine, 1957-58, Internat. Jour. Neuropharmacology, 1962-68, Exptl. Neurology, 1980-83; contbr. articles to sci. jours. Fellow Am. Coll. Neuropsychopharmacology (counselor 1980-84, pres. 1988); mem. AAAS, Am. Soc. Pharmacology and Exptl. Therapeutics (counselor 1972-75, pres.-elect 1988, pres. 1989-90, Abel award 1954), Western Pharmacology Soc. (Council 1980-83, pres. 1984), Epilepsy Soc., Bd. Sci. Counselors, Nat. Inst. for Neurological and Communicature Disorders and Stroke, Sigma Xi. Office: U Calif Dept Med Pharmacology and Toxicology Sch Medicine Davis CA 95616

KILLAM, JILL MINERVINI, oil and gas company executive; b. Pitts., Sept. 6, 1954; d. Virginio Lucien and Helen Elizabeth (Safgren) Minervini; m. Clayton Henry Killam, June 4, 1973. AAS with high honors, Eastfield Jr. Coll., Mesquite, Tex., 1974; BBA with high honors, U. Tex., Arlington, 1985. CPA, Tex. Asst. to treas. CKB & Assocs., Dallas, 1985-89, v.p., chief acctg. officer, 1989-92; v.p., CFO Box Energy Corp. (formerly OKC Ltd. Partnership), Dallas, 1992—. Mem. AICPA (Elijah Watt Sells award 1985), Tex. State Bd. Pub. Accts. (lic., Spl. award for Outstanding Achievement 1986), Tex. Soc. CPAs (state and Dallas chpt.), Petroleum Accts. Soc. Dallas, Inst. Mgmt. Accts. Republican. Roman Catholic. Office: Box Energy Corp 8201 Preston Rd Ste 600 Dallas TX 75225-6211

KILLEA, LUCY LYTLE, state legislator; b. San Antonio, July 31, 1922; d. Nelson and Zelime (Pettus) Lytle; B.A., Incarnate Word Coll., San Antonio, 1943; M.A. in History, U. San Diego, 1966; Ph.D. in History, U. Calif., San Diego, 1975; m. John F. Killea, May 11, 1946; children: Paul, Jay. Research analyst for Western Europe, Army Intelligence, Spl. Br., Washington, 1944-48; adminstrv. asst. Dept. State, London, 1946; econ. officer Econ. Coop. Adminstrn., The Hague, Netherlands, 1949; research analyst CIA, Washington, 1948-56; part time book reviewer USIS, 1956-60; teaching and research asst. U. Calif., San Diego, 1967-72; exec. dir., exec. v.p. Fronteras de las Californias, San Diego, 1974-78; mem. City Council, San Diego, 1978-82, dep. mayor, 1982, mem. planning commn., 1978; mem. Calif. State Assembly, 1982-89; mem. Calif. State Senate, 1989—; lectr. socioeconomics of Baja, Calif. and Mex., Southwestern Coll., Chula-Vista, 1976; lectr. dept. history San Diego State U., 1976-77; participant, organizer, panelist, moderator confs. in field, U.S., Mex.; mem. Palm City Sanitation Dist., 1978-82, Met. Transit Devel. Bd., 1978-82. Regional Employment and Tng. Consortium Bd., 1978-80, City-County Reinvestment Task Force, 1978-80. Bd. trustees San Diego Zool. Soc., 1976-78; mem. San Diego County Cultural Heritage Com., 1971-78, vice chmn., 1973-75; mem. Hist. Site Bd., City San Diego, 1968-75, vice chmn., 1971-75; bd. dirs. San Diego Hist. Soc., 1971-77; chmn. Internat. Com. Conv. and Visitors Bur., 1978, host com., 1976-77; adv. bd. Sharp Hosp.; bd. dirs., com. mem. Friends of Library, U. Calif., San Diego; founding mem. Caridad Internacional; mem. James S. Copley Library Adv. Council, U. San Diego, 1981—; active community orgns. including LWV, Fine Arts Soc. San Diego, YWCA, San Diego Mus. Art, San Diego Chpt. ARC, Dimensions, Aardvarks Ltd., Pacific Beach Hist. Soc., San Diego Symphonic Assn. Research grantee, Justice Found., 1965, U. Calif., San Diego, 1971; recipient awards, Conf. Calif. Hist. Socs., 1966, Inst. for Protection of Children, City of Tijuana and Tijuana Com., 1966, Alice Paul Award, Nat. Women's Polit. Caucus, 1982; named one of 12 Women of Valor, Beth Israel Sisterhood of Temple Beth Israel, San Diego, 1966, Woman of Accomplishment, Bus. and Profl. Clubs. San Diego, 1979, Woman of Yr., San Diego Irish Congress, 1981; honored Leukemia Soc., 1980; named alumna of distinction Incarnate Word Coll., San Antonio, 1981. Mem. Nat. Women's Polit. Caucus, Calif., Women in Bus., Mus. Photog. Arts, San Diego Arts Center, Nat. Trust Historic Preservation, San Diego Hist. Soc. (life), San Diego County Congress of History, Travelers Aid Soc., Navy League, Vietnam Vets. Assn. Mid City C. of C., San Diego C. of C., Nat. Assn. State Legislatures, NCCJ, World Affairs Council, Am. Fgn. Service Assn., Incarnate Word Alumnae Assn., U. San Diego Alumni Assn., U. Calif. San Diego Alumni and Friends, Calif. Elected Women's Assn. for Edn. and Research (bd. 1980-85, sec., treas., 1980-81, v.p. 1982-85). Roman Catholic. Clubs: Catfish, Army-Navy (Arlington, Va.). Contbr. writings to publs. in field. Office: State Capitol Rm 4062 Sacramento CA 95814*

KILLEBREW, ELLEN JANE (MRS. EDWARD S. GRAVES), cardiologist; b. Tiffin, Ohio, Oct. 8, 1937; d. Joseph Arthur and Stephanie (Beriont) K.; B.S. in Biology, Bucknell U., 1959; M.D., N.J. Coll. Medicine, 1965; m. Edward S. Graves, Sept. 12, 1970. Intern, U. Colo., 1965-66, resident 1966-68; cardiology fellow Pacific Med. Center, San Francisco, 1968-70; dir. coronary care, Permanent Med. Group, Richmond, Calif., 1970-83; asst. prof. U. Calif. Med. Center, San Francisco, 1970-83, assoc. prof., 1983-93, clin. prof. medicine, Univ. Calif., San Francisco, 1992—. Contbr. chpt. to book. Robert C. Kirkwood Meml. scholar in cardiology, 1970; recipient Physician's Recognition award continuing med. edn., Lowell Beal award excellence in teaching, Permante Med. Group/House Staff Assn., 1992. Diplomate in cardiovascular disease Am. Bd. Internal Medicine. Fellow ACP, Am. Coll. Cardiology: mem. Fedn. Clin. Research, Am. Heart Assn. (research chmn. Contra Costa chpt. 1975—, v.p. 1980, pres. chpt. 1981-82, chm. CPR com. Alameda chpt. 1984). Home: 30 Redding Ct Belvedere Tiburon CA 94920-1318 Office: 280 W Macarthur Blvd Oakland CA 94611-5642

KILLGALLON, CHRISTINE BEHRENS, healthcare administrator; b. Portsmouth, Ohio, June 29, 1958; d. Carl William Behrens and Karin Rita (Roeder) Behrens-Ellis; m. William Casley Killgallon, June 21, 1989. AS in Sci., Brunswick Coll., 1979, AS in Nursing, 1981; BA in Econs., George Mason U., 1987; M in Healthcare Adminstrn., Xavier U., 1989. CCRN. Staff nurse Bath County Community Hosp., Hot Springs, Va., 1981-82; critical care nurse U. Va. Med. Ctr., Charlottesville, Va., 1982-85; med. paralegal Donahue, Ehrmantraut, Montedonico, Washington, 1986; adminstrv. intern U. Va. Med. Ctr., Charlottesville, 1987; adminstrv. resident Alleghany Regional Hosp., Lowmoor, Va., 1989—; bd. dirs. Odin Co. Mem. aux. Safe Harbor, St. Simons, Ga., 1991; active Med. Assistance Program, Brunswick, 1990, Rep. Women's Orgn., St. Simons, 1990; mem. found. bd. S.E. Ga. Regional Med. Ctr. mem. AACCN, Am. Hosp. Assn., Am. Coll. Healthcare Execs., Golden Isles Investment Club St. Simons (pres. 1994), Omicron Delta Epsilon Theta. Presbyterian. Home: 1335 Hilltop Rd Charlottesville VA 22903

KILLGORE, LE, journalist, political columnist; b. Poughkeepsie, N.Y., Mar. 16, 1926; m. James A. Killgore, July 24, 1948; children: Lynne, Robert, Andrew. BA in Romance Langs., Skidmore Coll., 1948; postgrad., Auburn U., 1961-62. Classroom tchr. music Stare Baldwin Sch., Dallas, 1949-50, The Little Sch., Dallas, 1950-51; substitute tchr. DOD Sch., Clark AB, Philippines, 1964-65, Dayton Ohio Schs., 1966-67, Jeb Stuart High Sch., Fairfax County, Va., 1967-68; staff writer Standard-Times, San Angelo, Tex., 1972-79, sr. staff writer, 1979-83, political affairs editor, 1983-92; polit. cons. San Angelo, Tex., 1992—; co-host radio/TV pub. affairs show. Staff writer, editor Officers Wives Club mags., Clark AB, Philippines, 1964, McClellan AFB, Calif., 1966, Panama Canal Zone, 1969-71. Recipient Overall Excellence in News Gathering award Headliners Club, 1973, Outstanding Continuous Coverage of Edn. award Tex. State Tchrs. Assn., 1977, Excellence in Health-related Reporting Tex. Med. Assn., 1977. Mem. Soc. Profl. Journalists (pres. San Angelo chpt. 1984, bd. dirs. 1986, 87, 89).

KILLINGSWORTH, KATHLEEN NOLA, artist, photographer, company executive; b. Eglin AFB, Fla., Sept. 5, 1952; d. Marlin Donald Evans and Winnifred Irene (Pelton) Yow; m. Thomas Marion, Dec. 31, 1973 (div. Feb. 1976). Grad. high sch., Myrtle Point, Oreg. Food svc. Internat. Trade Club, Mobile, Ala., 1970-73; food and beverage Gussies Restaurant and Night Club, Coos Bay, Oreg., 1973-77, Libr. Buttery and Pub, Las Vegas, Nev., 1977-79; beverage dir. Laughlin's (Nev.) Riverside Resort, 1979-80; food and beverage Hyatt Regency Maui, Lahaina, Hawaii, 1980-92; realtor assoc. Wailea (Hawaii) Properties, 1990; sole propr. K N Killingsworth Enterprises, Lahaina, 1990—; assoc. Kona Coast Resort II, 1992—; vol. Lahaina Arts Soc., 1992—; mem. Hui No'eau Visual Arts Ctr., Makawao, Maui, Hawaii, 1992—. Artist numerous watercolor and acrylic paintings; photographer nature greeting cards. Vol. The Word For Today, Lahaina, 1983-87, Kumalani Chapel, Kapalua, Hawaii, 1983-87, Maui Special Olympics, 1993—; founding mem. & vol. Maui Community Arts & Cultural Ctr.; supporter Teen Challenge, Lahaina, 1987—. Mem. Lahina Arts Soc., 1992—. Republican. Office: K N Killingsworth Enterprises PO Box 5369 Lahaina HI 96761-5369

KILLIPS, SALLY EILLEEN, artist; b. Westfield, Mass., Aug. 13, 1947; d. Charles Reid and Sadie (Premny) Moore; m. Joseph Paul Killips, Aug. 12, 1967; children: Sharon Leigh, Jennifer Leigh. Student, Westfield State Coll., 1965-67. One woman shows include Wolfwalker Gallery, Whale and the Bird, Earthworks Gallery, Remarque-Able Artistry Gallery, Wildlife of the World Gallery; exhibited in group shows St. Hubert's Giralda Wildlife Show, Madison, N.J., Flat Rock Brook Nature Ctr., Englewood, N.J., The Nature Ctr., Westport, Conn., Nat. Audubon Exhbn., L.A., Soc. Animal Artists Show, Park City, Utah, N.E. Audubon Exhbn., Sharon, Conn., Big Cats Exhbn., Douglas Gallery, Stamford, Conn., N.E. Hawk Symposium, Cape May, N.J.; invited artist The Animal Guernsey's Auctions, N.Y.C.; represented in numerous pub. and pvt. collections. Mem. Soc. Animal Artists. Home and Studio: 37 Birchwood Rd Southwick MA 01077

KILPATRICK, CAROLYN CHEEKS, state legislator, educator; b. Detroit, June 25, 1945; d. Marvell and Willa Mae (Henry) Cheeks; divorced; children: Kwame, Ayanna. AS, Ferris State Coll., Big Rapids, Mich., 1965; BS, Western Mich. U., 1972; MS in Edn., U. Mich., 1977. Tchr. Murray Wright High Sch., Detroit, 1972-78; mem. Mich. Ho. of Reps., Lansing, 1978—; Dem. whip, mem. appropriations com.; del. Dem. Convs., 1980, 84, 88. Rep. Detroit Substance Abuse Adv. Coun.; participant Mich. African Trade Mission, 1985, UN Internat. Women's Conf., 1986; del., participant Mich. Dept. Agr. to Nairobi (Kenya) Internat. Agrl. Show, 1986. Recipient Anthony Wayne award Wayne State U., Disting. Legislator award Gentlemen of Wall Street, Disting. Alumnus award Ferris State U., Burton-Abercrombie award 15th Dem. Congl. Dist. Mem. Nat. Orgn. 100 Black Women, Nat. Black Caucus of State Legislators (chairperson Mich. legis. session 1983-84), Nat. Order Women Legislators, Nat. Orgn. Black Elected Legis. Women (treas.). Mem. Pan African Orthodox Christian Ch. Office: House Reps State Capitol Lansing MI 48909*

KILSBY, MARY ELLEN, minister; b. L.A., June 20, 1934; d. Lester Eugene and Mary Anna (Erickson) Green; m. Graham Perry Kilsby, Feb. 11, 1956; children: Mary Kathleen, Richard Perry, Christi Ann, Robin Lynn. BA, Pomona Coll., 1956; MRel, Sch. of Theology, Claremont, Calif., 1971, MDiv, DMin, 1978. Various Christian edn. positions Claremont, to 1978; assoc. min. Claremont United Ch. of Christ, 1978-83; min., pastor Altadena (Calif.) United Ch. of Christ, 1983-88; sr. min., pastor 1st Congl. United Ch. of Christ, Long Beach, Calif., 1988—; speaker in field. Trustee Claremont Unified Sch. Bd., 1971-78. Home: 4647 E 4th St Long Beach CA 90814-3075 Office: 1st Congl Ch 241 Cedar Ave Long Beach CA 90802-3099

KIM, CHRISTINE S., physician; b. Seoul, Korea. MD, Ewha Womens U., 1967. Pvt. practice Atlanta, 1973-80, Danbury, Conn., 1988—; asst. prof. U. Conn. Med. Sch., Farmington, 1980-88. Home: 3 Apple Hill Ct South Salem NY 10590

KIM, JANET, bank officer; b. Seoul, Korea, May 29, 1964; d. Kee Joe and Hae Shim (Byun) K. BA, Washington U., 1986; M of Mgmt., J.L. Kellogg Sch. Mgmt., 1990. Clk. DGHK, Chgo., 1987-88; trust officer No. Trust, Chgo., 1988-90; assoc. mortgage derivative Bankers Trust, N.Y.C., 1990-92, assoc. equity derivatives, 1992-93; sr. v.p. structured equity derivatives marketer SG Warburg, N.Y.C., 1993—. Author: Handbook of Structured Equity Derivatives, 1994. Office: SG Warburg & Co 787 7th Ave # 26th St New York NY 10019-6018

KIM, MARLENE, economics educator; b. Gardena, Calif., Dec. 30, 1958; d. Leroy and Grace Miyeko (Tanouye) K. BA in Econs. and English, U. Calif., Berkeley, 1981, MA in Econs., 1984, PhD in Econs., 1990. Rsch. asst. Inst. Indsl. Rels., Berkeley, 1983-84; rsch. asst. pay equity litigation Calif. State Employees Assn., Oakland, 1985-89; asst. prof. econs. U. Wis., Milw., 1989-91, Rutgers U., New Brunswick, N.J., 1991—; trainer Ctr. for Ethics and Econ. Policy, Berkeley; advisor Equal Means mag., Berkeley; cons., Hoboken, N.J. Contbr. articles to profl. publs. Mem. Am. Econ. Assn., Internat. Assn. for Feminist Economists (bd. dirs. 1992—). Office: Rutgers U Labor Edn Dept Ryders Ln Clifton Ave New Brunswick NJ 08903

KIM, MYUNGHEE, adult and child psychiatrist, psychoanalyst; b. Pusan, Korea, Nov. 8, 1932; came to U.S. 1959; d. Too Soo and Boo Sil (Kim) K.; m. Peter Reimann, June 29, 1962; children: Kim, Hannah. MD, Seoul Nat. U., 1957; Psychoanalyst, NYU, 1981. Intern Hackensack (N.J.) Hosp., 1959-60; resident in psychiatry Grassland Hosp., Valhalla, N.Y., 1960-62, Bronx Mcpl. Med. Ctr., 1962-63; staff psychiatrist Roosevelt Hosp., N.Y.C., 1964-65; fellow in child psychiatry Union County Psychiat. Clinic, Plainfield, N.J., 1968-70; child psychiatrist Child Guidance and Family Svc., Orange, N.J., 1970-72; pvt. practice child and adult psychiatry, psychoanalysis Springfield, N.J., 1972—; cons. Headstart Nursery Sch., Orange, 1971-72; faculty in psychiatry Bergen Pane Hosp., Paramus, N.J., 1977-83; instr. psychiatry N.J. Med. Sch., Newark, 1988—; clin. asst. prof. U. Medicine and Dentistry N.J. Robert W. Johnson Med. Sch., 1991—; cons. to daycare ctr., 1993—. Editor N.J. Psychoanalytic Soc. Bull., 1992-94; contbr. articles to profl. jours. Mem. Am. Psychoanalytic Assn., Internat. Psychoanalytic Assn., Psychoanalytic Assn. N.Y., Am. Psychiatric Assn., N.J. Psychoanalytic Soc., Korean Psychoanalytic Study Group. Home and Office: 272 Short Hills Ave Springfield NJ 07081-1029

KIM, SANGDUK, biochemistry educator, researcher; b. Seoul, Korea, June 15, 1930; came to U.S., 1954; d. Tak Won and chungHee (Kil) K.; m. Woon Ki Paik, June 15, 1959; children: Margaret, Dean, David. MD, Korea U., Seoul, 1953; PhD, U. Wis., 1960. Intern Evang. Deaconess Hosp., Milw., 1954-55; rsch. assoc. U. Wis., Madison, 1959-61, U. Ottawa, Ont., Can., 1961-66; rsch. assoc. Fels Inst. Temple U., Phila., 1966-73, sr. investigator Fels Inst., 1973-78, assoc. prof. biochemistry Fels Inst., 1978-90, prof. biochemistry, 1990—. Author: (monograph) Protein Methylation, 1980; editor: Protein Methylation, 1990. NIH Rsch. grantee, 1973-81, NSF Rsch. grantee, 1979-85, Nat. Multiple Sclerosis Rsch. grantee, 1985—. Mem. Am. Soc. Biol. Chemists, Am. Assn. for Cancer Rsch., N.Y. Acad. Sci., Am. Chem. Soc., Am. Soc. for Neurochemistry. Home: 7818 Oak Lane Rd Cheltenham PA 19012-1015 Office: Temple U Fels Inst 3420 N Broad St Philadelphia PA 19140-5104

KIM, SYNJA P., corporate business planner; b. Seoul, Republic of Korea; came to U.S., 1967; d. Byung Jae and Jung-D (Kim) Park; m. Sang Joo Kim, Dec. 4, 1976. BS in Acctg., Va. Commonwealth U., 1971; MBA in Fin. and Multinat. Mgmt., U. Pa., 1986. Jr. analyst Am. Fgn. Ins. Assn., N.Y.C., 1971; internal auditor Ethan Allen, Inc., Danbury, Conn., 1972-74, sr. acct., 1975-77; sr. acct. Carolina Power & Light Co., Raleigh, N.C., 1978-79, fin. analyst, 1980-82, sr. fin. analyst, 1983-87; mgr. budget planning and fin. analysis Internat. Life and Group, CIGNA Worldwide, Phila., 1987-89; mgr. bus. planning CIGNA Internat. Fin. Svcs., Phila., 1989, dir. bus. planning, 1989—; pres. Inst. Korean-Am. Studies, 1979—; instr. Korean-Am. Lang. Sch., Research Triangle Park, N.C., 1979-81; guest speaker Raleigh C. of C., 1982; program coord. Nat. Coun. Internat. Visitors Ctr., Research Triangle Park, 1984-87; bd. dirs. Signex, Inc., 1990—; advisor to com. for internat. programs dynamics of orgn. U. Pa., Phila., 1993—; secured ofcl. visit His Excellency Seung-Soo Han, Amb. Republic of Korea to U.S., U. Pa. and City of Phila, 1993, also dinner speaker honoring him. Vol. YMCA, 1993—, ARC, 1993—, United Way, 1993—, mem. goal com., allocation com. southeastern Pa. chpt., 1993—. Fellow Life and Mgmt. Inst. (FLMI), 1993. Mem. Nat. Assn. Accts. Republican. Office: CIGNA Internat Fin Svcs Two Liberty Pl 55th Fl 1601 Chestnut St PO Box 7716 Philadelphia PA 19192

KIM, WILLA, costume designer; b. L.A.; d. Shoon Kwan and Nora Kim; m. William Pene Du Bois. Costume designer New Theatre for Now, Mark Taper Forum, L.A., 1969-70, Goodman Theatre, Chgo., 1978-79; set and costume designer Feld Ballet, Joffrey Ballet, Am. Ballet Theatre, San Francisco Ballet. Designer: (theatre) Red Eye of Love, 1961, Fortuna, 1962, The Saving Grace, 1963, Have I Got a Girl for You!, 1963, Funnyhouse of a Negro, 1964, Dynamite Tonight, 1964, A Midsummer Night's Dream, 1964, The Old Glory, 1964 (Obie award 1964-65), Helen, 1964, The Day the Whores Came out To Play Tennis, 1965, Sing to Me Through Open Windows, 1965, The Star King, 1965, Malcolm, 1966, The Office, 1966, Chu Chem, 1966, Hail Scrawdyke!, 1966, Scuba Duba, 1967, The Ceremony of Innocence, 1967, Promenade, 1969 (Drama Desk award 1969-70), Papp, 1969, Operation Sidewinder, 1970 (Drama Desk award 1969-70), Sunday Dinner, 1970, The Screens, 1971 (Maharam award 1971-72, Drama Desk award 1971-72, Variety N.Y. Drama Critics Poll award 1971-72), Sleep, 1972, Lysistrata, 1972, The Chickencoop Chinaman, 1972, Jumpers, 1974, Goodtime Charley, 1975 (Tony award nominee for best costume design 1975), The Old Glory: a trilogy, 1976, Dancin', 1978 (Tony award nominee for best costume design 1978), The Grinding Machine, 1978, Bosoms and Neglect, 1979, Sophisticated Ladies, 1981 (Tony award for best costume design 1981), Family Devotions, 1981, Lydie Breeze, 1982, Chaplin, 1983, Elizabeth and Essex, 1984, Song and Dance, 1985 (Tony award nominee for best costume design 1986), Long Day's Journey Into Night, 1986, The Front Page, 1986, Legs Diamond, 1989 (Tony award nominee 1989), The Will Rodgers Follies, 1991 (Tony award for best costume design 1991), Four Baboons Adoring the Sun, 1992, Tommy Tune Tonight!, 1993, Grease, 1994, Victor/Victoria, 1995; (ballets) Birds of Sorrow, 1962, Gamelan, 1963, Game of Noah, 1965, Daphins et Chloe, Papillon, Scenes for the Theatre, A Song for Dead Warriors, Shinju, Rodin, Dream Dances; (TV) The Tempest, 1981 (Emmy award 1981), Le Rossignol; (film) Gardens of Stone, 1987; (operas) The Magic Flute, Le Rossignol, Help, Help, the Gobolinks. Recipient Asian Woman of Achievement award Asian Am. Profl. Women, 1983. Democrat. Home: 250 W 82nd St New York NY 10024-5421*

KIMBALL, CATHERINE D., justice. Former judge La. Dist. Ct. (18th dist.); now assoc. justice Supreme Ct. of La. Office: 301 Loyola Ave New Orleans LA 70112-1800

KIMBALL, MICHEL TURNER, human services manager; b. Glen Ridge, N.J., Dec. 6, 1938; d. George B. and Dorothy Louise (Michel) Turner; children: Walker III, Steven, Joslin. BA, Wellesley Coll., 1961; MSW, Adelphi U., 1979. Cert. social worker, N.Y., Vt.; lic. ind. clin. social worker, Mass. Divsn. dir. outpatient svcs. United Counseling Svc. of Bennington (Vt.) County, Inc., 1973-86; exec. dir. PAHL, Inc., Troy, N.Y., 1986-90, Mental Health Assn. in Albany (N.Y.) County, Inc., 1991—; psychotherapist Bennington, Vt., 1985—. Contbr. articles to profl. jours. V.p. Project Against Violent Encounters, 1992—, Phoenix, Inc., 1986—. Mem. NOW (Vt. chpt.), Vt. NASW, Acad. Cert. Social Workers, N.Y. State Task Force for Residential Chem. Programs for Youth (treas. 1988-90), Coalition of Substance Abuse Svcs. of Northeastern N.Y. (v.p. 1988-90, chair treatment com. 1988-90), Alcohol and Substance Abuse Program Ctr. of Rensselaer County Unified Svcs. Democrat. Home: 8 Walloomsac Rd Bennington VT 05201-2138 Office: Mental Health Assn 95 Central Ave Albany NY 12206-3026

KIMBER, SARA ANN LOUISE, systems analyst; b. Cambridge, England, Sept. 1, 1961; came to U.S., 1967; d. Gordon and Yvonne Mary Elizabeth (Griffiths) K. BA, U. Mo., 1984, MS in Computer Sci., 1988. Systems analyst Chevron, San Ramon, Calif., 1988-93; product mgr. Velocity Software, Inc., Mountainview, Calif., 1993—. Planning commr. City of San Ramon, 1992—; City of San Ramon rep. Tasahara Valley Property Owners Assn., Contra Costa County, Calif., 1994; commn. liaison Gen. Plan Ubdate, San Ramon, 1992-94; vol. Mounted Patrol East Bay Regional Park Dist., 1994—. Mem. Contra Costa NOW (pres. 1992-94). Democrat. Home: 2653 Fountainhead Dr San Ramon CA 94583-1735 Office: Velocity Software Inc 1242 Wasatch Dr Mountain View CA 94040-3942

KIMBERLY, ANN GEYER, nursing administrator, medical/surgical nurse; b. Buffalo, Dec. 4, 1931; d. Robert C. and Rose Marie (Rogers) Geyer; children: John L. Kimberly III, Susan Kimberly Holker. Diploma in nursing, Buffalo Gen. Hosp., 1952; student, U. Va., 1971, 72, Roanoke Coll., Salem, Va., 1973, U. Miami, 1990. RN, N.Y., Tex., Fla., Va. Advt. and TV cons., Roanoke, Va., San Antonio, Ft. Lauderdale, Fla.; asst. to prof. SUNY, Buffalo; asst. dir. Alamo Area Tb Assn., San Antonio; nursing adminstr., pvt. duty nurse, Coral Springs, Fla.; bd. dirs. Nurses Profl. Registry, 1974—. Past mem. bd. dirs. Roanoke Symphony Soc., San Antonio Symphony Soc.; mem. Coral Springs Symphony Soc., Ft. Lauderdale Symphony Soc., Boca Raton (Fla.) Fine Arts Ctr., Light Brigade, Ft. Lauderdale, Hospice By Sea, Flagler Mus., Palm Beach, Fla., Haven-Boca Raton Friends Vietnam Meml. Recipient award San Antonio Conservation Soc., 1962. Mem. ANA, Fla. Nurses Assn. (del.), Nat. Assn. Orthopedic Nurses, Internat. Oceanography Assn., Nat. Hist. Preservation Soc., Fla. Hist. Preservation Soc., Nature Conservancy, Audubon Soc., Nat. Wildlife Assn., Williamsburg Found., Winterthur Guild, English Heritage Soc., Fla. Hist. Soc., Sierra Club. Republican. Episcopalian. Home: The Aristocrat 1200 Hibiscus Ave Apt 1103 Pompano Beach FL 33062

KIMBRELL, FRANCES ELIZABETH, health care administrator; b. Louisville, Ga., Apr. 29, 1948; d. James Ellis and Ethel Mae (Newman) Snider; m. Robert Lamar Kimbrell, June 5, 1966; children: Stephanie Ann, Robert Lamar Jr. LPN, Swainsboro (Ga.) Tech. Coll., Ga.; RN, Columbia (Tenn.) State Coll., 1983. RN, Tenn. Charge nurse Old Capitol Inn, Louisville, 1966—; office nurse pvt. dr. Louisville, 1966-80; charge nurse Merihil Nursing Home, Lewisburg, Tenn., 1980-81; nurse surg. dept. St. Thomas Hosp., Nashville, 1981-83; CCU care charge nurse Bedford County Hosp., Shelbyville, Tenn., 1986-92; adminstr., dir. profl. svcs. Res Care Home Health, Inc., Shelbyville, 1986—; adminstr., dir. profl. svcs. for multi locations ResCare Home Health, Shelbyville, Murfreesboro, Columbia, 1994—. Vol. Mothers March of Dimes, 1991, 92. Home: 422 Bethlehem Church Rd Shelbyv'lle TN 37160-6421 Office: Res Care Home Health Inc 738 N Main St Shelbyville TN 37160-2828

KIMBRIEL-EGUIA, SUSAN, engineering planner; b. San Francisco, July 22, 1949; d. Scott Slaughter and Kathleen (Edens) Smith; m. Floyd Thomas Kimbriel; 1 child, John Thomas; m. Candelario Eguia, Feb. 14, 1991; 1 child, Daniel. AA in Computer Sci., El Camino C.C., 1984. Engrng. planner, sys. adminstr. various mainframe and PC based sys. Northrop Aircraft, Hawthorne, Calif., 1982-91; PC cons. Moselle Ins. Corp., North Hollywood, Calif., 1989-94, Northrop Aircraft, 1991-94.

KIMBROUGH, FRANCES HARRIETT, psychologist; b. Bryan, Tex., Sept. 10, 1947; d. Wallace M. and Frances H. (James) K. BA, Tex. A&M U., 1969, MEd, 1971, PhD, 1981. Lic. psychologist; lic. profl. counselor, health svc. provider, family mediator, real estate broker; cert. secondary edn. counselor, spl. edn. counselor, Spanish/English. tchr. Head sportswear dept. Lester's Clothing Store, Bryan, 1970-71; tchr. Spanish S.F. Austin High Sch., Bryan, 1971-75; psychologist S.F. Austin High Sch., 1982-84; counselor Bryan High Sch., 1975-76; psychology intern Tex. A&M U., College Station, Tex., 1981-82; pvt. practice psychologist Bryan, 1985—; with Desert Hills Psychiat. Ctr., College Station, 1992—. Mem. adminstrv. bd. First United Meth. Ch., Bryan, 1993-94, tchr. Sunday Sch.; mem. Brazos County A&M Club, College Station. Named to Outstanding Young Women of Am. Mem. Am. Psychol. Assn., Tex. Psychol. Assn., Brazos Valley Psychol. Assn., Am. Counseling Assn., Am. Assn. Christian Counselors, Christian Counselors of Tex. Home: 501 E 29th St Bryan TX 77803 Office: 704-B E 29th St Bryan TX 77803

KIMBROUGH, SUZANNE LEE, counselor; b. Atlanta, Feb. 28, 1958; d. Robert Edgar and Frances Eugenia (Ezell) Lee; m. Robert Stanton Kimbrough, Sept. 26, 1992. BA, West Ga. Coll., 1979, MA, 1981. Lic. profl. counselor. Clin. assoc., asst. pub. rels. dir. Carroll County Crisis Intervention Ctr., Carrollton, Ga., 1980-81; counselor Student Devel. Ctr. West Ga. Coll., Carrollton, 1981; sales rep. Saber Freight Systems, Atlanta, 1981-86; nat. sales mgr. KES Irrigation, Atlanta, 1986-87; corp. recruiter Lucas Assocs., Atlanta, 1987-88; counselor Transitions, Atlanta, 1988-90; sr. counselor The Resource Ctr., Atlanta, 1990-91; dir. patient svc. Scott & Assocs.,

Atlanta, 1991-92; pvt. practice Atlanta, 1991—. Mem. Am. Counseling Assn. (profl.), Ga. Mental Health Counselors Assn., Phi Kappa Phi (life). Office: Ste 484 5575-B Chamldee Dunwoody Rd Atlanta GA 30338 also: 6810 Roswell Rd Ste 2-H Atlanta GA 30328

KIMES, BEVERLY RAE, editor, writer; b. Aurora, Ill., Aug. 17, 1939; d. Raymond Lionel and Grace Florence (Perrin) K.; m. James H. Cox, July 6, 1984. BS, U. Ill., 1961; MA in Journalism, Pa. State U., 1963. Dir. publicity Mateer Playhouse, Neff's Mills, Pa., 1962, Pavillion Theatre, University Park, Pa., 1963; asst. editor Automobile Quar. Publs., N.Y.C., Princeton, N.J., 1963-64, assoc. editor, 1965-66, mng. editor, 1967-74, editor, 1975-81; editor The Classic Car, 1981—. bd. corporators Mus. Transp., Brookline, Mass.; bd. trustees Nat. Automotive History Collection, Detroit Pub. Libr. Recipient Cugnot award Soc. Automotive Historians, 1978, 79, 83, 85, 86, Thomas McKean trophy, 1983, 85, 86, Moto award Nat. Assn. Automotive Journalists, 1984, 85, 86, Benz award, 1994. Mem. Internat. Motor Press Assn., Milestone Car Soc. (bd. dirs.), Soc. Automotive Historians (pres. 1987-89). Author: The Classic Tradition of the Lincoln Motor Car, 1968; (with R.M. Langworth) Oldsmobile: The First Seventy-Five Years, 1972; The Cars That Henry Ford Built, 1978; (with Rene Dreyfus) My Two Lives, 1983; (with Robert C. Ackerson) Chevrolet: A History from 1911, 1984; The Standard Catalog of American Cars 1805-1942, 1985; The Star and the Laurel: The Centennial History of Daimler, Mercedes and Benz, 1986; editor: Great Cars and Grand Marques, 1976; Packard: History of the Motor Car and the Company, 1979; Automobile Quarterly's Handbook of Automotive Hobbies, 1981, The Classic Car: The Ultimate Book About the World's Grandest Automobiles, 1990.

KIMMEL, A. JUNE MILLER, council executive; b. Detroit, May 27, 1931; d. Charles Kenneth and Alonda Sara (Donovan) Miller; m. Donald Loraine Kimmel Jr., June 16, 1960 (div. May 1983); children: Stephen Garrett, Charity Allen, Christopher Donald, Benjamin Haines. Grad., George Sch., 1949; student, Goucher Coll., 1949-51; BA, U. Pa., 1953. Prodn. editor Holiday Mag., Phila., 1953; rsch. assoc. Towers, Perrin, Forster & Crosby, Phila., 1954; admissions officer, dean's office Temple U. Med. Sch., Phila., 1958-60; reading cons. Mooresville (N.C.) City Schs., 1976-78; region dir. N.C. Coun. for Women, Charlotte, 1984—; mem. Domestic Violence Adv. Bd., Charlotte, 1986—. Author: (newsletter) Women's Issues, 1986—. Precinct chair Dem. Party, Davidson, N.C., 1973, 74, 75; chair Charlotte (N.C.) Solid Waste Adv. Com., 1978-80; mem. Mecklenburg Solid Waste and Hazardous Bd., Charlotte, 1980-84. Named Woman of the Yr., Coll. of Arts and Scis., U. N.C., Charlotte, 1990; recipient Women of Courage award Charlotte (N.C.)/Mecklenburg Women's Commn., 1992. Mem. AAUW, R.I. LWV (state bd. 1966), Barrington LWV (pres. 1967-69, Tribute 1969), Charlotte/Mecklenburg LWV (bd. mem. 1974-79, 94—)), N.C. LWV (bd. mem. 1980-93), Women's Agenda, N.C. Women's Polit. Caucus (pres. 1994, 95), SE Women's Studies Assn. Mem. Soc. of Friends. Home: PO Box 595 750 Dogwood Ln Davidson NC 28036 Office: NC Coun for Women 500 W Trade St # 360 Charlotte NC 28202

KIMMEL, CHARITY ALLEN, small business owner, writer; b. Balt., Jan. 5, 1961; d. Donald Lorraine and Alonda June (Miller) K. BA, Queens Coll. Bus. Adminstrn., 1984. With Charlotte (N.C.) Meml. Hosp., 1980-81, Old World Deli, Lake Wylie, S.C., 1984-85, Fortune Media/Charlotte Mag., 1985, ABM, Pineville, N.C., 1985-86, HESCO, Pineville, N.C., 1986, Internat. Bearings Co., Charlotte, 1986-87, The Herald, Rock Hill, S.C., 1987-88, Lake Wylie Mag., 1987-88; sales exec. HFH USA Corp., Charlotte, 1988-94; owner FWBC, Charlotte, 1994—. Author: The Man With The Golden Mask, 1994; newspaper writer. Democrat. Mem. Soc. of Friends.

KIMMEL, ELLEN BISHOP, psychologist, educator; b. Knoxville, Tenn., Sept. 16, 1939; d. Archer W. and Mary Ellen (Baker) Bishop; BA, U. Tenn., 1961; MA, U. Fla., 1962, PhD, 1965; div.; children: Elinor, Ann, Jean, Tracy. Asst. prof., rsch. assoc. Ohio U., 1965-68; asst. prof. U. South Fla., Tampa, 1968-72, assoc. prof., dir. Univ. Studies Coll., 1972-73, prof. psychology and ednl. psychology, 1975—, chair, 1992—; disting. vis. prof. psychology Simon Fraser U., Vancouver, B.C., Can., 1980-81; cons. numerous sch. systems, bus. and govt. Mem. Fla. Blue Ribbon Task Force on Juvenile Delinquency, 1976-77; mem. Fla. Gov.'s Commn. on Women, 1979-83; mem. adv. bd. Stop Rape, Good Govt., Inc.; bd. dirs. NCCJ. Recipient Outstanding Teaching award U. South Fla., 1978; Career Achievement award U. Tenn., 1983; 16 research grants. Fellow APA (governing council 1982-85, pres. div. 1986-88, Disting. Leadership award 1993), Am. Psychol. Soc. (charter fellow, conf. chair 1990), Am. Assn. Applied and Preventive Psychol. (charter fellow, program chair 1991, Disting. Edn. award 1994); mem. Women in Psychology, Southeastern Psychol. Assn. (pres. 1978-79), Athena Soc., Sigma Xi, Delta Kappa Gamma, Omicron Delta Kappa. Democrat. Contbr. articles to jours., chpts. to books. Office: U South Fla FAO 268 Tampa FL 33620

KIMMEL, JERRY LYNN TOUGHSTONE, artist; b. Jackson, Miss., Feb. 25, 1945; d. Roy Henry and Ruth Elizabeth (Smith) T.; m. James Ross Kimmel, Mar 25, 1967; children: Jamie Lynn, Julie Rene. BA, Baylor U., 1967; BFA, Southwest Tex. State U., 1985. Faculty Laguna Gloria Art Mus., Austin, Tex., 1987—, Hill County Arts Found., Ingram, Tex., 1992; workshop leader Laguna Gloria Art Mus. Sch., 1988-89; docent Tyler (Tex.) Art Mus., 1972. Represented in permanent collections and by AIR Gallery, Austin, Bowman Gallery, Portland, Tex., Robinson Galleries, Houston, Lightside Gallery, Santa Fe, N.Mex., Creative Art Gallery, San Antonio. Leader Girl Scouts Am., Austin, 1977-84, day camp art dir., 1983-84. NEA grantee, 1990. Mem. Tex. Photographic Soc., Tex. Fine Arts Assn., Austin Visual Arts Assn. (bd. dirs. 1984-86), Mus. Women in Arts D.C., Women and Their Work. Home: 3712 Capistrano Trail Austin TX 78739

KIMMEL, MARGARET ELIZABETH, music educator; b. Ottawa, Ill., Mar. 17; d. Frederick Ernest and Eleanor Letticia (Crowle) Ledrich; m. Allan Lee Kimmel, Mar. 21, 1953; children: Karl, Frederick. BA, Goddard Coll., 1975; MA, Columbia U., 1988. Singer, pianist Statler Hilton, N.Y.C., 1975-76; band leader Anele's of Queens, N.Y., 1983-84; keyboardist, accordian player QE2 Cruise Ship, 1985; tchr. N.Y.C. Bd. Edn., 1985-89, Bronx (N.Y.) House Music Sch., 1989—; pres. WUJ Prodns., N.Y.C., 1988—. Author: Bronx House Music School Series: Keyboard Books 1, 2 and 3. Home: 1631 Tenbroeck Ave Bronx NY 10461-2007

KIMMONS, MERRYL BANNISTER, media specialist; b. Abbeville, S.C., Dec. 1, 1955; d. James Daniel Jr. and Doris Jeanette (Pruitt) Bannister; m. Dick Scott Kimmons, Dec. 18, 1977; children: Merrick Bannister, Kayla McCain, Haley Jeanette. AB, Erskine Coll., 1978; MLS, U. S.C., 1989. Cert. sch. libr., S.C. Tchr. English Belton-Honea Path (S.C.) H.S., 1978-82; resident dir. Erskine Coll., Due West, S.C., 1979-86; media specialist Dixie High Sch., Due West, 1987—; libr. Due West Assoc. Reform Presbyn. Ch., 1990—. Mem. Assn. for Ednl. Comms. and Tech. of S.C., S.C. Assn. Sch. Librs., Abbeville Woman's Club (sustaining), Delta Kappa Gamma (sec. 1994—). Office: Dixie High Sch PO Box 158 1 Abbeville St Due West SC 29639

KIMURA, DOREEN, psychology educator, researcher; b. Winnipeg, Man., Can.; 1 child, Charlotte Vanderwolf. BA, McGill U., Montreal, Que., can., 1956, MA, 1957, PhD, 1961; LLD (hon.), Simon Fraser U., 1993. Lic. psychologist, Ont., Can. Lectr. Sir George Williams U. (now Concordia U.), Montreal, 1960-61; rsch. assoc. otol. rsch. lab. UCLA Med. Ctr., 1962-63; rsch. assoc. Coll. Medicine, McMaster U., Hamilton, Ont., 1964-67; assoc. prof. psychology U. Western Ont., London, 1967-74, prof., 1974—, coord. clin. neuropsychology program, 1983—; supr. clin. neuropsychology Univ. Hosp., London, 1975-83. Author: Neuromotor Mechanisms in Human Communication, 1993; contbr. numerous articles to profl. jours. Recipient Outstanding Sci. Achievement award Can. Assn. Women in Sci., 1986, John Dewan award Ontario Mental Health Found., 1992; fellow Montreal Neurol. Inst., 1960-61, Geigy fellow Kantonsspital, Zurich, Switzerland, 1963-64. Fellow Royal Soc. Can., Can. Psychol. Assn. (Disting. Contbns. to Sci. award 1985), Am. Psychol. Soc.; mem. Internat. Neuropsychol. Symposium, Acad. of Aphasia, Soc. for Neurosci. Office: U Western Ont, Dept Psychology, London, ON Canada N6A 5C2

KIMURA, KIMI TAKEUCHI, social worker, educator; b. Kyoto, Japan, Apr. 13, 1926; came to U.S., 1954; d. Kinzo Fujiwara and Miyo Takeuchi; divorced; 1 child, Fumi Kimura Inouye. BA, Doshisha Women's Coll., Kyoto, 1938; postgrad., Columbia U., 1955-56; MFA, Boston U., 1957. Cert. secondary English tchr., interpreter, Japan. Rsch. assco. South Manchurian RR Rsch., Toyko, 1936-41; travel cons. SITA Internat. Travel, N.Y.C., 1957-58; vis. prof. Howard U., Washington, 1958-59; overseas adv. Japan Pubs. Assn., Tokyo, 1959-68; asst. cultural attache Embassy of Japan, Washington, 1962-66; sr. rsch. assoc. Columbia U., N.Y.C., 1973-76; case worker Lenox Hill Neighborhood Assn., N.Y.C., 1977-78; ret., 1978; trade negotiator, various bus. firms, Tokyo, N.Y.C., 1945—; dir. social work Japan/Am. Assn., N.Y.C., 1983-84; cons. Nat. Theatre of Japan, Tokyo, 1966-73; fundraiser The Vol. Coun. of Philharmonic- Symphony Soc. N.Y. Inc., 1986—. Contbr. numerous features articles to jours.; producer various plays, 1957. Campaign worker Dem. Party, n.Y.C., 1976-78; vol. Lincoln Ctr. Performing Arts, Inc.; fundraiser Consol. Corp. Fund, 1992—. Recipient Translation award, Nat. Sci. Found., Washington, 1973-76, Older Am. Act, Title III, Washington, 1977—. Mem. Am. Ednl. Theatre (officer 1972-73, Citation 1973), N.Y. Philharmonic (assoc. mem., Citation 1989). Home: 350 65th St Bldg 1 Apt 12A Brooklyn NY 11220-4942

KIMURA, LILLIAN CHIYEKO, retired human service agency executive; b. Glendale, Calif., Apr. 7, 1929; d. Homer and Hisa (Muraki) Kimura; B.A., U. Ill., 1951, M.S.W., 1954; postgrad. Inst. for Nonprofit Mgmt., Columbia U., 1985. Program dir. Olivet Community Center, Chgo., 1954-68; dir. Olivet Service Area, Chgo. Commons Assn., 1968-71; program cons. Nat. Bd. YWCA of U.S.A., 1971-78; dir. mid-states region, 1978-80, exec. field services, 1980-83, asst. exec. dir., 1984-86, assoc. exec. dir., 1987-92, exec. cons. 1992—. Pres., Japanese Am. Service Com., 1973-79; bd. dirs. Nat. Japanese Am. Citizens League, 1972-79, 88-94, nat. pres., 1992-94; chairwoman bd. Pacific Citizens, 1988-92, gov., 1974-79, pres. N.Y. chpt., 1986-92, treas. 1990—. Recipient Racial Justice award YWCA of the U.S.A., 1988, Ambassador award YWCA of the U.S.A., 1993; decorated Order of the Precious Crown, Wisteria, Japanese Govt., 1993. Mem. Acad. Cert. Social Workers, Assn. Social Workers, Assn. Advancement of Social Work (bd. dirs.), Nonprofit Mgmt. Assn. (bd. dirs.)

KINARD, AGNES DODDS, historian, author, retired lawyer; b. Pitts.; d. Robert James and Agnes Julia Raw; m. Morton Frank, June 4, 1944 (div. 1958); children: Allan Dodds, Michael Robert, Marilyn Morton; m. James Pinckney Kinard, Dec. 27, 1961 (dec. Mar. 1994). BA in History cum laude, U. Pitts., 1936, LLB, 1939, JD, 1961; postgrad., Chatham Coll., 1980. Bar: Pa. 1940. Law researcher Reed, Smith, Shaw & McClay, Pitts., 1940-41; Lynne A. Warren, N.Y.C., 1940-41; exec. sec. Allegheny County War Price and Ration Bd., Pitts., 1941-44; British Colonies section chief, asst. to the deputy adminstr. Lend-Lease Adminstrn., Washington, 1944-46; women's editor, columnist Canton (Ohio) Economist, 1946-58; assoc. broker, sales Kelly Wood Real Estate, Pitts., 1959-72; broker, pres., co-owner Mountain Real Estate Co., Inc., Confluence, Pa., 1973-83. Author: Historical Survey of the Landscape Design Society of Western Pennysylvania, 1962-83, 1983, Celebration of Carnegie in Pittsburgh, 1981, The Jane Holmes Residence—A Century of Caring, 1982, Seasons of the Heart, 1988-89, Fanfare for Fifty Years, 1989, History of the Pittsburgh Symphony Association, 1939-1989, 1989, The First 100 Years of The Carnegie in Pittsburgh, 1995; commd. symphony by Nikolai Lopatnikoff for Pitts. Symphony Orch., 1972, works of John Lennon for Youth Symphony Orch., 1989. Bd. dirs. Pitts. Plan for Art, Sch. Vol. Assn., Pitts. Youth Symphony Orch. Assn., Pitts. Symphony Assn.; founder, mem. Rachel Carson Homestead Assn.; founder, pres. Pioneer Crafts Coun. (now Touchstone Crafts Ctr.); mem. women's com. Carnegie Mus. Art. Recipient Award of Merit Pitts. History and Landmark Found., Three Rivers Environ. award, 1993; named No. 60 of the First 100 Women Lawyers in Allegany County, Pa., 1992. Mem. Pitts. Civic Garden Ctr. (life), Nat. Coun. State Garden Clubs (life), Nat. Soc. Arts and Letters (life, landscape design critic), Landscape Design Soc. Western Pa. (founding bd. dirs., past pres., Helen S. Hull plaque for lit. hort. interest 1986), Kappa Kappa Gamma.

KINCAID, ELSIE ELIZABETH, educational therapist; b. Vernon, Tex., Nov. 29, 1929; d. Richard Oscar Paul and Bertha Rosanna (Quast) Schuetze; m. Richard Warren Kincaid, June 1, 1949; children: Carol Jean, Richard Warren, Sandra Elizabeth, Robert Rendall. AA, Del Mar Coll., 1949; BS magna cum laude, Tex. Agrl. and Industry U., 1976; MS, Corpus Christi (Tex.) State U., 1978; PhD, Columbia Pacific U., 1985. Dir., diagnostician, edn. therapist Corpus Christi Acad. Devel. Services, 1979-80; dir., diagnostician, ednl. therapist Corpus Christi Acad. Devel. Svcs., Corpus Christi, 1980-86; diagnostician, edn. therapist Corpus Christi Acad. Devel. Svcs., 1987-89; ednl. therapist Clinic for Learning Disabilities, Dallas, 1989; pvt. practice McKinney and Dallas, Tex., 1990-92, Plano, Tex., 1992—; spl. edn. substitute tchr. Corpus Christi Ind. Sch. Dist., 1986-88. Author: Reasoning Process As Early Intervention for Reading Disability, 1985, The Preschool Diagnostic Development Screening Test, 1987. V.p. Symphony Guild Corpus Christi, 1973; bd. dirs. Ada Wilson Hosp. for Children, Corpus Christi, 1986-89, Samaritan Counseling Ctr. of Coastal Bend, 1987-89 (v.p. 1988), Holy Family Sch., McKinney, 1990-92; mem. adv. bd. "Any Baby Can" Project, Corpus Christi, 1988-89; mem. High Risk Infant Task Force, Art Mus. So. Tex. and Corpus Christi, 1988-89; vol. Collin County Community Food Pantry, 1990-91. Mem. Jennete Hammer Guild (pres. 1984-85), CPA Wives (pres. 1970), Mental Health Assn. Collin County, Estate Garden Club (pres. 1981), Daus. of King (v.p. 1986-88), Plano Rep. Womens Club, Plano Chamber Orch. Encore, Kappa Delta Pi (xi Omicron chpt.), The Heard Natural Sci. Mus. and Wildlife Sanctuary of McKinney Guild. Republican. Episcopalian. Home and Office: 1820 Azurite Trl Plano TX 75075-2106

KINCAID, JAMAICA, writer; b. St. John's, Antigua and Barbuda, May 25, 1949; came to U.S., 1966; d. Annie Richardson; m. Allen Shawn; 1 child. Student pub. schs., St. John's; hon. degree, Williams Coll., 1991, L.I. Coll., 1991. Author: At the Bottom of the River, 1983 (Morton Dauwen Zabel award Am. Acad. and Inst. of Arts and Letters 1984), Annie John, 1985, A Small Place, 1988, Annie Gwen Lilly Pam and Tulip, 1989, Lucy, 1990, Autobiography of My Mother, 1994. *

KINCAID, JUDITH WELLS, electronics company executive; b. Tampa, Fla., July 1, 1944; d. George Redfield and Louise Wells (Brodt) K.; B.A., Stanford U., 1966, M.S. in Indsl. Engring., 1978; 1 dau., Jennifer Wells Maben. Scientific programmer med. research Stanford (Calif.) U., 1972-77; info. systems mgr. Hewlett Packard Corp., Palo Alto, Calif., 1978-84, mgr. strategic systems, 1985-81; direct mktg. database mgr. , 1991—. Mem. Am. Inst. Indsl. Engrs., Am. Prodn. Dir. Mktg. Assn., Inventory Control Soc. Office: Hewlett Packard Corp 5301 Stevens Creek Blvd Santa Clara CA 95052-8059

KINCAID, MARILYN COBURN, medical educator; b. Bennington, Vt., July 14, 1947; d. E. Robert and Jean A. (Flagg) Coburn; m. William Louis Kincaid, Dec. 21, 1970. AB, Mt. Holyoke Coll., 1969; MD, St. Louis U., 1975. Cert. Am. Bd. Ophthalmology, Am. Bd. Pathology. Asst. prof. ophthalmology & pathology U. Tex., San Antonio, 1982-86; assoc. prof. ophthalmology & pathology U. Mich. Med. Sch., Ann Arbor, 1986-87, St. Louis U. Sch. Medicine, St. Louis, 1989—; bd. dirs. Singular Vision Outreach, St. Louis. Author (book) Intraocular Lenses, 1989; contbr. articles to profl. jours. Fellow Am. Acad. Ophthalmology (Honor award 1990), Coll. Am. Pathologists; mem. Am. Assn. Ophthalmic Pathologists (sec.-treas. 1983-86). Office: St Louis U The Eye Inst 1755 S Grand Blvd Saint Louis MO 63104

KINCAID, TINA, entertainer, producer; b. Lenoir, N.C., Dec. 24, 1959; d. Joseph George and Betty Gail (Prestwood) K.; m. Stephen Kim Cretella, June 11, 1988 (div. May 1994). Student, Am. Theater Arts, 1979-81. Entertainer, 1979—; TV producer, actor Video Record Albums of Am., Pasadena, Calif., 1980-83; v.p. sales, mktg. prodns. Amity Sales Inc., Hudson, N.C., 1980—; co-founder, producer, singer T'NT Entertainments, Inc., Pasadena, 1981-83; founder, pres. ProductVision, Inc., L.A., 1984-86; co-founder, v.p. prodns. Kincaid Enterprises, Morganton, N.C., 1988-89; founder, owner VAT Pub., Hudson, 1989—; cons., owner Mary Kay Cosmetics, Hudson, 1989—; co-founder, v.p., performer Rappin' Grandmas, Inc!, Hickory, N.C., 1991—; entertainer, singer The Troy Cory China Goodwill Concert Tour, 1991. Actor, author TV spl. Catching Christmas, 1981; singer, author album Isn't A Shame, 1990, The Real Country, 1990; author, editor, pub: The Wedding Book, 1990, Recipes Of Love, 1991. Mem. SAG. Republican. Mem. Christian Ch. Home: 4491 Magnolia Ln Hudson NC 28638

KIND, ANNE WILSON, engineer; b. Carmel, Calif., Dec. 1, 1958; d. Patrick Wayne and Mary Elaine (Bryan) Wilson; m. David Lee Kind, June 5, 1992. AAS in Music, Everett C.C., 1981; BSME, Calif. State U., Long Beach, 1987. Lic. pilot, FAA. Engr. Rockwell-Aircraft Divsn., El Segundo, Calif., 1983-86, Rockwell-Satellite Divsn., Seal Beach, Calif., 1986-89; Engr. Rockwell-Space Divsn., Downey, Calif., 1989, Northrop B-2 Divsn., Pico Rivera, Calif., 1989-91, McDonnell Douglas-Space Sta., Huntington Beach, Calif., 1991-94; distbr. Amway Corp., Anaheim, Calif., 1993—. Pianist Ridgecrest Christian Ch., Albuquerque, 1982-83. Mem. Soaring Soc. Am. (Symons Wave meml. award 1993), Orange County Soaring Assn. (editor 1991-95, v.p. 1993, pres. 1994-95), Pres. award 1993), United Radio Amateur Club. Republican. Home and Office: 3050 W Ball Rd Trlr 77 Anaheim CA 92804-3803

KIND, PHYLLIS DAWN, immunologist; b. Sidney, Mont., July 31, 1933; d. Dan E. and Margaret (Erickson) K. B.A., U. Mont., 1955; M.S., U. Mich., 1956, Ph.D., 1960, postgrad. 1960-63. Instr., U. Colo.-Denver, 1963-65, asst. prof., 1965-71; research microbiologist NCI-NIH, Bethesda, Md., 1971-74; assoc. prof. dept. microbiology George Washington U., Washington, 1974-79, prof. and acting chair, 1979—; mem., chmn. NSF Grad. Fellowship Eval. Panel, Washington, 1979-81; ad hoc mem. of NIH Study sect., 1976—. Contbr. articles to profl. jours. NSF fellow, 1955-59; NIH fellow, 1963-64. Mem. Am. Soc. Microbiology (div. chmn. 1975-76), Am. Assn. Immunologists, Am. Soc. Histocompatibility and Genetics, AAAS, Soc. Exptl. Biology and Medicine, Assn. Women in Sci., NIDA (study sect. 1986-90), Sigma Xi, Phi Kappa Phi. Avocations: sailing, skiing, tennis, swimming, bird-watching. Office: George Washington U Med Ctr 2300 I St NW Washington DC 20037-2337

KINDBERG, SHIRLEY JANE, pediatrician; b. Newark, Feb. 4, 1936; d. John Bertil and Mabel Jacoba (deJonge) K.; m. Charles Dale Coln, May 12, 1962; children: Sara, Eric, Lois, Ruth, Mary. BS, Wheaton Coll., 1957; MD, Baylor U., 1961. Intern Tex. Children's Hosp., Houston, 1961-62; resident Children's Med. Ctr., Dallas, 1962-63; fellow in pediat. pulmonary disease U. Tex. S.W. Med. Sch., Dallas, 1963-64, fellow in pediat. infectious disease, 1965-67; pvt. practice gen. pediat. Dallas, 1969-81, pvt. practice newborns, 1981—. Active Northwest Bible Ch., 1972—. Fellow Am. Acad. Pediatrics; mem. Tex. Pediatric Assn., Dallas Symphony Assn., The Dallas Opera. Republican. Office: 3600 Gaston Ave Ste 406 Dallas TX 75246-2017

KINDER, KAREN DEANN, art educator; b. Webster, S.D., Dec. 8, 1950; d. Sidney Orville and Elsie Jean (Patton) Jacobson; m. Keith Lee Kinder, Aug. 2, 1980; children: Kevin Jacob, Kimberly Ann. BS in Edn. summa cum laude, No. State U., Aberdeen, S.D., 1973. Teaching cert. art K-12. Elem. art tchr. Sioux Falls (S.D.) Ind. Sch. Dist., 1973-83; art tchr. Madison (S.D.) Jr. High Sch., 1991, Brookings (S.D.) Mid. and Ctrl. Elem. Sch., 1991—; desktop pub. and computer graphic artist Dakota State U., Madison, 1991. One-person shows at Old Firehouse Gallery, Madison, 1990, S.D. State U., Brookings, 1991, No. State U., Aberdeen, S.D., 1991, Oscar Howe Art Ctr., Mitchell, S.D., 1991, Dakota State U., Madison, 1991; exhibited in group shows at LaGrange (Ga.) Nat. XU, 1990 (Jurors merit award 1990), Old Courthouse Mus., Sioux Falls, 1991, Six-State Competitive, McCook, Nebr., 1992 (Patron award 1992), Mitchell Juried Art Show, 1992 (2d pl. award 1992), Holiday Biennial, Spirit Lake, Iowa (merit award 1992), Nobles County Art in the Courtyard, Worthington, Minn., 1994 (Best of Show). Vol. Spl. Olympics, Sioux Falls, 1977-82. Mem. NEA. Baptist. Home: 521 12th St S Lot 3 Brookings SD 57006-3801 Office: Brookings Mid Sch 601 4th St Brookings SD 57006-2047

KINDZRED, DIANA, communications company executive; b. Chgo., Apr. 13, 1946; d. Bernell and Katherine L. (Gee) K. Student, Northwestern U., 1970-73. Owner, pres. Kindzred & Co. Comm., Chgo., 1978—. Contbr. articles to profl. jours. Co-founder mid-west div. Am. Sephardi Fedn., Evanston, Ill., 1990; coord. Amnesty Internat., Evanston, 1991. With U.S. Army, 1964-67. Democrat. Jewish. Home: 7333 N Ridge Blvd Apt 101 Chicago IL 60645-2070 Office: Kindzred & Co Comm 1440 S Indiana Ave Ste # 1004 Chicago IL 60605

KING, ALMA JEAN, former health and physical education educator; b. Hamilton, Ohio, Feb. 28, 1939; d. William Lawrence and Esther Mary (Smith) K. BS in Edn., Miami U., Oxford, Ohio, 1961; MEd, Bowling Green State U., 1963; postgrad., Fla. Atlantic U., 1969, '92, Nova U., Ft. Lauderdale, Fla., 1979. Cert. elem. and secondry tchr., Ohio, all levels incl. coll., Fla. Tchr. health, physical edn. Rogers Middle Sch., Broward County Bd. Pub. Instrn., 1963-64; assoc. prof. health, phys edn., recreation, dance Broward C.C., Fort Lauderdale, Fla., 1964-94; ret., 1994; dir. Intramurals and Extramurals Boward C.C., Fort Lauderdale, Fla., 1964-67, chair person Women's Affairs, 1978, health and safety com., 1975, faculty evaluation com. 1980-85, mem. faculty ins. benefits com. 1993-94. Sponsor Broward County Fire Fighters, Police; active mem. Police Benevolent Assn.; Historical Soc. Grantee Broward C.C. Staff Devel. Fund, 1988. Mem. AAHPERD, NEA, Fla. Edn. Assn., Fla. Assn for Health, Physical Edn., Recreation and Dance, Am. Assn. for Advancement of Health Edn., United Faculty of Fla., Fla. Assn. of C.C., Order of the Eastern Star (past Worthy Matron), Order of Shrine. Home: 4310 Buchanan St Hollywood FL 33021-5917

KING, AMANDA ARNETTE, elementary school educator; b. Conway, S.C., Feb. 6, 1951; d. James Hilton and Maisie (Dunn) Arnette; m. Roachel Dent King III, Dec. 31, 1972; children: Roachel Dent IV, Amanda Catherine. AB, Coker Coll., 1973. Tchr. Darlington (S.C.) County Sch. Dist., 1972-75, 78-81, James F. Byrnes Acad., Florence, S.C., 1981-88, Darlington County Sch. Dist., 1988—. Mem. Society Hill (S.C.) Rescue Squad. Woodmen of World. Recipient Golden Apple award, 1993-94, EIA grant, 1994-95. Mem. S.C. Coun. Tchrs. Math., Internat. Reading Assn., Palmetto State Tchrs. Assn. (mem. com.), Coker Coll. Alumni Assn. (2d v.p. 1988—, Outstanding Alumni com. 1989-90, 93—). Baptist. Home: PO Box 58 Society Hill SC 29593-0058

KING, BARBARA JEAN, nurse; b. Cape Girardeau, Mo., June 28, 1941; d. Otto Samuel and Goldie Elizabeth (Clover) Fowler; student Weatherford Jr. Coll., 1965; RN, John Peter Smith Hosp. Sch. Profl. Nursing, 1969. Cert. advanced cardiac life support; m. Charles Basil King, Jr., Sept. 4, 1972; children—Otto Samuel, Christopher Lee. Head nurse pediatrics and isolation County Hosp., also intensive care and coronary care units Small Gen. Hosp., Ft. Worth, 1969-72; dir. nursing service Jarvis Heights Nursing Center, Ft. Worth, 1976-77; dir. nursing services Ft. Worth Rehab. Farm, 1978-80; staff nurse, asst. supr. shift Decatur Community Hosp. (Tex.), 1983-85; staff nurse and supr. Burdgeport Hosp., Tex., 1986—; clin. supr., patient care coord. Hospice of Tijas; instr. vocat. nursing Cooke County Coll., Gainesville, Tex., 1981; clin. care supr. home health dept. Faith Community Hosp., 1992; patient care coord. Family Svcs. Home Health and Hospice, 1994; cons. convalescent centers and hosps. Chmn. child care com. Women of Moose, 1977—; ch. organist Zion Valley Cumberland Presbyterian Ch.; asso. organist St. Matthew Cumberland Presbyn. Ch. Served with M.C., USN, 1962-65. Mem. Dirs. Nursing Homes Assn. Tarrant County (v.p.). Democrat. Home: Route 1 RR 1 Box 198 Alvord TX 76225-9735

KING, BETTY, politician; b. Cleve., June 9, 1932; d. W. Griffin and Elizabeth (White) K. AS, Finch Coll., 1953; Cert., U. Poitier, France, 1971. Active profl. theatre N.Y., 1953-61; program officer African-Am. Inst., N.Y.C., 1962-63; exec. dir. Mozambique Inst., Dar-Es-Salaam, Tanzania, 1963-67; mng. dir. Continental Ore Ltd., Dar-Es-Salaam, 1967-71; adminstrv. asst. McGovern for Pres., Washington, 1972; cons. Nat. Women Polit. Caucus, Washington, 1973-74; program dir. D.C. Bicentennial Commn., Washington, 1974-75; cons. various polit. and women's orgns., 1975-78; spl. asst. to mayor D.C., 1979-90; cons. various polit. campaigns, Washington, 1972—. Co-author: Descendants of Thomas White, 1638, 1992; editor: (newsletter) Equal Writes, 1976-80. Vol. broadcaster Metro Washington EAR, Silver Spring, Md., 1990—; vol. Washington Readers for Blind, 1993; reader Braille Inst., Rancho Mirage, Calif., 1992-93; fundraiser various charitable and civic orgns., Washington, 1973—; mem.-at-large Ward 3 Dem. Com., 1991—; dep. dir. to mayor-elect Marion Barry Transition Team, 1994-

95. Recipient Leadership award Coalition for Women's Appointments, 1978, Community Svc. award Stein Dem. Club, 1989. Mem. Ams. for Dem. Action (exec. com. 1990—). Home: 2820 34th Pl NW Washington DC 20007

KING, BETTY F., health and social services administrator; b. Raleigh, N.C., Dec. 9, 1954; d. Odell and Frances (Chatham) K.; m. Joseph Donovan, Feb. 14, 1981. BS in Pub. Health, U. N.C., 1977, MS in Pub. Health, 1980. Asst. dir. U. Ariz., Tucson, 1981-84, Nat. Rural Health Assn., Kansas City, Mo., 1984-85; project dir. The Circle, McLean, Va., 1985-88; exec. dir. Internal Medicine Ctr. to Advance Rsch. & Edn., Washington, 1988-93; dir. Cochise County Health & Social Svcs., Bisbee, Ariz., 1993—. Office: Cochise County Health & Social Svcs 1415 W Melody Ln Bisbee AZ 85603

KING, BEVERLY SUE, information systems specialist; b. Covington, Ky., June 10, 1949; d. Lawrence Leo and Dorothy Eunice (Field) Black; m. Lloyd Thomas King, Feb. 11, 1967 (div. July 6, 1982); children: Kimberly Sue, Angela Carol. Student, U. Ky., 1971-82, No. Ky. U., 1980-82, Thomas More Coll., 1985. Mgmt. asst. IRS, Covington, Ky., 1982-83; computer programmer analyst Computer Svc., Covington, Ky., 1984-87; chief electronic filing Resources Mgmt., Covington, Ky., 1987; chief programming sect. Computer Svc., Covington, Ky., 1987-88; computer systems analyst Statistics of Income, Washington, 1989-90; chief SOI sect. Info. Systems, Covington, 1990-91, chief expert site sect., 1991-92; chief programming and support br. Internat., Washington, 1992; chief Automated Criminal Investigation Support, Florence, Ky., 1993—; co-op mentoring IRS-Resources Mgmt., Covington, 1991-92; deaf & hearing impaired mgr. IRS-Info. Systems, Covington, 1987-93, health improvement coord., 1991-92. Pres. Boone County Home Ext. Svc., 1977-79; mem. ladies group 1st Ch. of Christ, 1975. Named Fed. Employee of Yr., Greater Cin. Fed. Exec. Bd., 1987, Fed. Employee of Yr., Info. Systems Divsn., 1992; recipient Disting. Rating for Performance Mgmt. & Recognition System, Info. System Divsn., 1990, 91, 93. Mem. Fed. Employed Women (v.p. 1987, com. chair fed. women's program 1985-87), Assn. for the Improvement of Minorities, Hispanic Internal Revenue Employees, German Lang Soc. Home: 909 Arran Ct Union KY 41091 Office: Autom Crim Investigation 7940 Kentucky Dr Florence KY 41042

KING, BILLIE JEAN MOFFITT, professional tennis player; b. Long Beach, Calif., Nov. 22, 1943; d. Willard J. Moffitt; m. Larry King, Sept. 17, 1965. Student, Calif. State U. at Los Angeles, 1961-64. Amateur tennis player, 1958-67, profl., 1968—; mem. Tennis Challenge Series, 1977, 78; dir., ofcl. spokesperson World TeamTennis, Chgo., 1985—; Singles champion tournaments Wimbledon, 1966-68, 72, 73, 75, U.S. Open, 1967, 71, 72, 74, U.S. Hardcourt, 1966, Italian Open, 1970, West German Open, 1971, Australian Open, 1968, South African Open, 1966, 67, 69, U.S. Indoor, 1966-68, 71, U.S. Clay Court, 1971, French Open, 1972, Avon, 1980; doubles champion Wimbledon, 1961, 62, 65, 67, 68, 70-73, U.S. Open, 1965, 67, 74, 80, French, 1972, Italian, 1970, South African, 1967-70, Bridgestone, 1976, Virginia Slims, 1974, 76; mixed doubles champion Wimbledon, 1967, 71, 73, U.S. Open, 1967, 71, 73, French, 1967, 70, South African, 1967, Australian, 1968; winner 29 Virginia Slims singles titles, 1970-77, 4 Colgate titles, 1977, Fedn. Cup, 1963-67, 76-79, Wightman Cup, 1961-67, 70, 77, 78; World Tennis Team All-Star, 3 times; host Colgate women's sports TV spl. The Lady is a Champ, 1975; co-founder, dir. Kingdom, Inc., San Mateo, Calif.; sports commentator ABC-TV, 1975-78; co-founder, pub. WomenSports mag., 1974—; founder Women's Tennis Assn., 1973; first woman commr. (Team Tennis League) profl. sports history, 1984; TV commentator HBO-Sports Wimbeldon coverage; cons. Virginia Slims World Championship Series; bd. dirs. Challenger Ctr.; amb. Adventures in Movement Charity; nat. spokesperson Literary Vols. Am.; tennis tchr. to profls. Author: Tennis to Win, 1970, (with Kim Chapin) Billie Jean, 1974, (with Cynthia Starr) We Have Come a Long Way, The Story of Women's Tennis, 1988. Named Sportsperson of Yr., Sports Illustrated, 1972; Woman Athlete of Yr., A.P., 1967, 73, Top Woman Athlete of Yr., 1972; Woman of Yr., Time mag., 1976, One of 10 Most Powerful Women in Am., Harper's Bazaar, 1977, One of 25 Most Influential Women in Am., World Almanac, 1977, One of 100 Most Important Ams. of 20th Century, Life mag., 1990; named to Internat. Tennis Hall of Fame, 1987, Nat. Women's Hall of Fame, 1990; Lifetime Achievement award, March of Dimes, 1994. Office: World TeamTennis 445 N Wells St Ste 404 Chicago IL 60610-4512

KING, CAROLE, composer, singer; b. Bklyn., Feb. 9, 1942; m. Gerry Goffin; m. Charles Larkey; m. Rick Evers; m. Rick Sorensen, 1982; children: Louise, Sherry, Molly, Levi. Student, Queens Coll. Co-writer (with Gerry Goffin) numerous songs, 1960-68, including Will You Still Love Me Tomorrow?, He's a Rebel, Go Away, Little Girl, Up on the Roof, Natural Woman, The Locomotion, Take Good Care of My Baby, It's Too Late; albums include Tapestry, 1971 (4 Grammy awards), Simple Things, Pearls: Songs of Goffin and King, Wrap Around Joy, 1974, One To One, 1982, Speeding Time, 1983, Legacy, 1989; off-Broadway theater appearance in A Minor Incident, 1989; Broadway appearance inBlood Brothers, 1994. Inducted in Rock & Roll Hall of Fame, 1990. Office: Free Flow Prodns Inc 1209 Baylor St Austin TX 78703-4123 also: care Atlantic Records 75 Rockefeller Plaza New York NY 10019*

KING, CAROLYN DINEEN, federal judge; b. Syracuse, N.Y., Jan. 30, 1938; d. Robert E. and Carolyn E. (Bareham) Dineen; children: James Randall, Philip Randall, Stephen Randall; m. John L. King, Jan. 1, 1988. A.B. summa cum laude, Smith Coll., 1959; LL.B., Yale U., 1962. Bar: D.C. 1962, Tex. 1963. Assoc. Fulbright & Jaworski, Houston, 1962-72; ptnr. Childs, Fortenbach, Beck & Guyton, Houston, 1972-78, Sullivan, Bailey, King, Randall & Sabon, Houston, 1978-79; circuit judge U.S. Ct. Appeals (5th cir.), Houston, 1979—; mem. coun. Am. Law Inst., 1991—. Trustee, mem. exec. com., treas. Houston Ballet Found., 1967-70; trustee, mem. exec. com. U. St. Thomas, 1988—; mem. Houston dist. adv. council SBA, 1972-76; mem. Dallas regional panel President's Commn. White House Fellowships, 1972-76, mem. commn., 1977; bd. dirs. Houston chpt. Am. Heart Assn., 1978-79; nat. trustee Palmer Drug Abuse Program, 1978-79; trustee, sec., treas., chmn. audit com., fin. com., mem. mgmt. com. United Way Tex. Gulf Coast, 1979-85. Mem. ABA, Fed. Bar Assn., State Bar Tex., Houston Bar Assn., Am. Law Inst. (coun. mem. 1991—). Roman Catholic. Office: US Ct Appeals 11020 US Courthouse 515 Rusk St Houston TX 77002-2600*

KING, CHAROLETTE ELAINE, administrative officer; b. Baker, Oreg., Apr. 10, 1945; d. Melvin Howard and Rella Maxine (Gwilliam) Wright; m. Craig Seldon King, April 14, 1965; children: Andrea Karen, Diana Susan. Clerical positions various firms, Idaho, Va., Conn., 1964-71; nursing sec. VA, San Diego, 1974-77; sec. USN, Agana, Guam, 1972-73; procurement clk. USN, Bremerton, Wash., 1977-80; procurement clk. USN, San Diego, 1980, support svcs. supr., 1980-83, div. dir., 1983-87, program analyst, 1987-93, adminstrv. officer, 1993—. Recipient Model Agy. cup USN, San Diego, 1986. Republican. Office: USN Pub Works Ctr Code 139 2730 McKean St Ste 1 San Diego CA 92136-5294

KING, CHERYL ANN, critical care nurse; b. Charleston, S.C., Dec. 30, 1960; d. Howard R. and Eleanor (Griffith) Halpenny; m. Kenneth A. King, Dec. 17, 1986. Diploma, Barnes Hosp. Sch. Nursing, St. Louis, 1982; BSN, Webster U., 1992. RN, Mo.; cert. TNCC, ACLS, ABLS. Staff nurse emergency and cardiovascular recovery units DePaul Health Ctr., St. Louis, 1982-87; staff nurse Barnes Hosp., St. Louis, 1982, staff nurse psychiatry and emergency depts., 1987—. Mem. Nat. League Nursing, Emergency Nurses Assn. Home: 2944 Katie Ct Arnold MO 63010-3766

KING, CLAUDIA LOUAN, film producer, lecturer; b. Merced, Calif., May 1, 1940; d. Alvin Cecil and Thelma May (Matthew) K.; m. Douglas McLean, July 10, 1965 (div. 1975); children: Kia Gabrielle, Kendra Sue. BA, U. Calif., 1963; MA, Ind. U., 1969. Lectr. U. Fla., Gainesville, 1969-70; asst. prof. U. Nev., Las Vegas, 1973-79; producer Source 17 Prodns., Santa Monica, Calif., 1979-85; freelance producer Chico, Calif., 1985—. Author: Life Mastery: A Self-Esteem Handbook for Adults and Children, 1994, (screenplays) The Garden of Eden, 1983, My Sister's Keeper, 1986, (documentary) The Evolution of Women, 1988, 92 (short stories) In the Realm of the Invisible, 1991; prodr.: Rape is Everybody's Concern, 1978, Los Angeles Personally Yours, 1986; pub. Light Paths Communications, 1994—. Carnegie grantee, 1969; Nev. Endowment for Humanities grantee, 1978. Mem. Women in Film, Coll. Art Assn. Democrat. Home: PO Box 3576 Chico CA 95927-3576

KING, CORETTA SCOTT (MRS. MARTIN LUTHER KING, JR.), educational association administrator, lecturer, writer, concert singer; b. Marion, Ala., Apr. 27, 1927; d. Obidiah and Bernice (McMurray) Scott; m. Martin Luther King, Jr., June 18, 1953 (dec. Apr. 1968); children: Yolanda Denise, Martin Luther III, Dexter Scott, Bernice Albertine. A.B., Antioch Coll., 1951; Mus.B., New Eng. Conservatory Music, 1954, Mus.D., 1971; L.H.D., Boston U., 1969, Marymount-Manhattan Coll., 1969, Morehouse Coll., 1970; H.H.D., Brandeis U., 1969, Wilberforce U., 1970, Bethune-Cookman Coll., 1970, Princeton U., 1970; LL.D., Bates Coll., 1971. Voice instr. Morris Brown Coll., Atlanta, 1962; commentator CNN, Atlanta, 1980—; lectr., writer; founding pres., chief exec. officer Martin Luther King Jr. Ctr. for Nonviolent Social Change Inc. Author: My Life With Martin Luther King, Jr., 1969; contbr. articles to mags.; syndicated newspaper columnist N.Y. Times Syndication Sales Corp., 1986-90, United Features Syndicate, 1990-94; concert debut, Springfield, Ohio, 1948; numerous concerts throughout U.S., concerts, India, 1959, performances, Freedom Concert. Del. to White House Conf. Children and Youth, 1960; sponsor Com. for Sane Nuclear Policy, Com. on Responsibility, Moblzn. to End War in Viet Nam, 1966, 67, Margaret Sanger Meml. Found.; mem. So. Rural Action Project, Inc.; pres. Martin Luther King, Jr. Found.; chmn. Commn. on Econ. Justice for Women; mem. exec. com. Nat. Com. Inquiry; co-chmn. Clergy and Laymen Concerned about Vietnam, Nat. Com. for Full Employment, 1974; pres. Martin Luther King Jr. Center for Nonviolent Social Change; co-chairperson Nat. Com. Full Employment; mem. exec. bd. Nat. Health Ins. Com.; active YWCA; bd. dirs. So. Christian Leadership Conf., Martin Luther King, Jr. Found. Gt. Britain; trustee Robert F. Kennedy Meml. Found., Ebenezer Bapt. Ch. Recipient Outstanding Citizenship award Montgomery (Ala.) Improvement Assn., 1959, Merit award St. Louis Argus, 1960, Distinguished Achievement award Nat. Orgn. Colored Women's Clubs, 1962, Louise Waterman Wise award Am. Jewish Congress Women's Aux., 1963, Myrtle Wreath award Cleve. Hadassah, 1965, award for excellence in field human relations Soc. Family of May, 1968, Universal Love award Premio San Valentine Com., 1968, Wateler Peace prize, 1968, Dag Hammarskjold award, 1969, Pacem in Terris award Internat. Overseas Service Found., 1969, Leadership for Freedom award Roosevelt U., 1971, Martin Luther King Meml. medal Coll. City N.Y., 1971, Internat. Viareggio award, 1971, numerous others; named Woman of Year Utility Club N.Y.C., 1962, Woman of Year Nat. Assn. Radio and TV Announcers, 1968, UAW Social Justice award, 1980. Mem. Nat. Council Negro Women (Ann. Brotherhood award 1957), Women Strike for Peace (del. disarmament conf. Geneva, Switzerland 1962, citation for work in peace and freedom 1963), Women's Internat. League for Peace and Freedom, NAACP, United Ch. Women (bd. mgrs.), Alpha Kappa Alpha (hon.). Baptist (mem. choir, guild adviser). Club: Links (Human Dignity and Human Rights award Norfolk chpt. 1964). Address: Martin Luther King Jr Ctr 449 Auburn Ave NE Atlanta GA 30312

KING, DIANE MARIE, production administrator; b. Winchester, Mass., Jan. 7, 1960; d. Frank Anthony Cushenette and Etta Priscilla (Gentile) Nadeau; m. Brian Thomas King, May 12, 1990. BS, Fitchburg (Mass.) State Coll., 1983. Mktg. dir. Lustre Diamonds, Boston, 1983-85; mgr. Living Well Fitness Ctr., Cambridge, Mass., 1985-87; Desktop Pub. trainer Gemini Cons., Cambridge, 1987-89; assoc. systems engr. EDS, Bloomfield Hills, Mich., 1989-90; prodn. mgr. Gemini Cons., Cambridge, 1990-92; prodn. mgr. Coopers & Lybrand, Boston, 1992-95, nat. creative svcs. mgr., 1995—; v.p. Mktg. Mgmt. Assistance Program, Fitchburg, 1981-83. Roman Catholic. Home: 3-B Carnation Cir Reading MA 01867 Office: Coopers & Lybrand 1 Post Office Square Boston MA 02109

KING, EILEEN ELIZABETH, secondary education educator; b. Two Rivers, Wis., June 10, 1950; d. Milton James and Loyola Ann (Ellerman) Barry; m. Ervin R. King Jr., Sept. 22, 1973; children: Barry, Andy, Betsy. BA in Biology and Life Scis., Cardinal Stritch Coll., 1975. Cert. biology and life scis. tchr. Tchr. biology Ozaukee High Sch., Fredonia, Wis., 1974-75; tchr. sci. St. Peter Alcantara Sch., Port Washington, Wis., 1975-78; substitute tchr. Port Washington High Sch., 1978-92, tchr. biol., 1992—. Home: 3234 Highway W Port Washington WI 53074 Office: Port Washington High Sch 427 W Jackson St Port Washington WI 53074-1899

KING, ELAINE A., curator, art historian, critic; b. Oak Park, Ill., Apr. 12, 1947; d. Casimir Stanley and Catherine Mary (Chemle) Czerwien. BS, No. Ill. U., 1968, MA, 1974; PhD, Northwestern U., 1986. Intern George Eastman House, Rochester, N.Y., 1977; lctr. history of photography Northwestern U., Evanston, Ill., 1977-81; curator Dittmar Meml. Gallery, Evanston, 1978-81; dir. Artemesia Gallery, Chgo., 1976-77; dir. Carnegie-Mellon Art Gallery, Pitts., 1985-91; assoc. prof. history of art, Carnegie Mellon U., Pitts., 1981—; bd. dirs. Mountain Lake Criticism Conf., Blacksburg, Va., 1982-91; ind. curator, 1991—; exec. dir., chief curator Contemporary Art Ctr., Cin., Ohio, 1993-95; guest curator Pitts. Cultural Trust, 1992; art critic-in-residence U. Ariz., Tucson; guest curator in critical theory U. Cin.; organizing com. 1993 Hungarian Bienale Exhibition II, Győr, Hungary; panelist NEA Visual Arts, 1993; grant reviewer Inst. Mus. Sci., Washington, 1994, Ohio Arts Council fellowship and grant evaluator; mem. organizing com. Midwest Mus. Con., 1994-95. Active Dem. Party, Evanston, Ill., award judge, 1977-78, precinct capt. 1977. Curator and author: The Figure As Fiction, 1993, Alfred DeCredico: Drawings, 1985-93, Emily Cheng: Monoprints, 1993, (exhibition catalogues) Barry LeVa: 1966-88, Mel Bochner: 1973-85, Elizabeth Murray: Drawings: 1980-86, Michael Gitlin: Sculpture & Drawings, 1990, New Generations: Chgo., 1990, New Generations: N.Y., 1991, Magdalena Jetalova, 1991, Martin Puryear: Sculpture & Drawings, 1987, Abstraction/Abstraction, Tishan Hsu, Paintings, Drawings & Sculpture, 1987, N.Y. Painting Today, Michel Gerand: Drawings and Site Works, 1989, Drawings and Sculpture, 1990, Art in the Age of Information, 1993, Five Artists at the Airport: Insights into Public Art, 1992, Martha Rosler: In Place of the Public, 1994, Lyzabeth Sallan: 2 Installations Light Into Art: From Video to Virtual Reality (also booklet), David Humphrey: Paintings and Drawings 1987-95 (also catalogue), others; free lance art critic, Arts, Tema Celeste, & Sculpture; art critic in residence Delaware Contemporary Center for the arts, 1992, Mid-Atlantic Arts Fellow, 1991; editor Dialogue, Columbus, Ohio, 1984-89; contbr. articles to profl. jours. Recipient Hunt Art award, 1977; Art Critics fellow Pa. Coun. on Arts, 1985, Art Criticism fellow, 1989, 95; faculty research grantee, 1985, 87, 89-90. ArMem. Coll. Art Assn., Am. Assn. Mus., Assn. Historians of Am. Art, Internat. Assn. Art Critics (Am. sect.). Avocations: jogging, gardening, tennis, swimming, sailing. Office: Contemporary Arts Ctr 115 E 5th St Cincinnati OH 45202

KING, GLADYS DORMAN, corporate secretary, administrative executive; b. Wilmington, Del., Aug. 16, 1960; d. James Thomas and Geraldine Iva (deShong) Dorman; m. Paul Allen King, Oct. 20, 1984; 2 children. BA in English and Journalism, U. Del., 1983. Correspondence rep. Beneficial Nat. Bank, Wilmington, 1983-84; adminstrv. asst. Downtown Wilmington Improvement, 1984-85; exec. asst. to pres. TriMark, Inc., New Castle, Del., 1985—, corp. sec., 1989—; corp. sec. Mark Prodns., Ltd., New Castle, 1989—. Editor brochure Welcome to Wilmington, 1984. Republican. Presbyterian. Office: TriMark Inc 184 Quigley Blvd New Castle DE 19720-4104

KING, GLYNDA B., state legislator; b. Chattanooga, July 5, 1946; d. William Cass and Johnnie Olivan (Griffen) Bowman; m. Thomas Wayland King, Jan. 12, 1963; children: Denise Schön, Kelly Todd. Grad. high sch., Tyner, Tenn. Mem. Clayton County (Ga.) Drug Adv. Com., 1976—, Ga. Arts Caucus, Atlanta, 1991—, Clayton County Disabilities Early Intervention for Families and Children; bd. dirs. Clayton County Bd. Edn., 1983-89, Gov.'s Commn. on Mental Health, Mental Retardation and Substance Abuse, Atlanta, 1992—, Leadership Clayton; state rep. Ga. Gen. Assembly, Atlanta, 1991—; mem. success by six coun. United Way, Atlanta, 1992—; hon. life mem. E.J. Swint Elem. Sch. PTA, 1979—. Recipient Founders award 16th Dist. Ga. PTA, 1985. Mem. Mental Health Assn. Met. Atlanta (pres. 1992-93), Clayton County C. of C., Southlake Kiwanis. Democrat. Baptist. Home: PO Box 961032 Riverdale GA 30296-7032

KING, GWENDOLYN BAIR, former White House staff member, public speaker; b. Hartsville, S.C., Oct. 27, 1915; d. William Parlor and Mary Margaret (Scurry) Bair; m. LaBruce Ward King, Dec. 26, 1937; children: John LaBruce King, Margaret Gwendolyn King Farrow. AB, Coker Coll., 1936. With asst. pers. office Libr. Congress, Washington, 1937-39; sec., dir. Libr. Congress, Union Catalog, Washington, 1939-43; asst. to appointments sec. for the President The White House, Washington, 1953-69, dir. correspondence for Pat Nixon, 1969-74; pub. speaker on White House career Calif., 1977—. Contbr. to Presidential Records, The Nat. Archives, Washington, 1988. Dir. Speakers' Bur., Home Hospice, Santa Rosa, Calif., 1985, cert. caregiver, 1982-84; mem. Oakmont Archtl. Com., Santa Rosa Symphony League. Named Paul Harris Fellow, Rotary Internat., 1983, Citizen of the Day, KABL, San Francisco, 1983. Mem. AAUW, Newcomers Club (pres. Santa Rosa chpt. 1977-78), Oakmont Book Club (chmn. 1981-82), Oakmont Golf Club (sec. 1986), Saturday Afternoon Club. Republican. Home: 451 Pythian Rd Santa Rosa CA 95409-6346

KING, GWENDOLYN S., utility company executive, former federal official; b. East Orange, N.J.; d. Frank M. and Henryne (Walker) Stewart; m. Colbert I. King, July 3, 1961; children: Robert Franklin, Stephen Cranston, Allison Jennifer. BA cum laude, Howard U., 1962; postgrad., George Washington U.; hon. doctorate, U. Md., 1990, U. New Haven, 1992. With HEW, 1971-76; dir. div. consumer complaints HUD, Washington, 1976-78; legis. asst. to Sen. John Heinz Washington, 1978-79; dir. Commonwealth of Pa. Office, Washington, 1979-86; dep. asst. to the pres. and dir. Office Intergovtl. Affairs The White House, Washington, 1986-88; commr. Adv. Commn. on Intergovtl. Rels.; mem. Interagency Com. Women's Bus. Enterprise; dir. The White House Task Force on P.R.; exec. v.p. Gogol & Assocs., 1988-89; commr. Social Security Adminstrn., Balt., 1989-92; bd. dirs. Martin Marietta, Monsanto Co. Bd. dirs. Phila. Conv. and Vis. Bur. Recipient Drum Major for Justice award So. Christian Leadership Conf., 1990, Alumni award Howard U., 1991, Black Achievement Bus. and Fin. award Ebony Mag., 1992. Mem. Forum Exec. Women, Internat. Women's Forum. Office: PECO Engery Co 2301 Market St Philadelphia PA 19103-1338

KING, IMOGENE M., nurse, educator; b. West Point, Iowa, Jan. 30, 1923. Diploma, St. John's Hosp., 1945; B.S. in Nursing, St. Louis U., 1948; M.S. in Nursing, 1957; Ed.D., Columbia U., 1961; Ph.D. (hon.), So. Ill. U., 1980. Instr. med.-surg. nursing, asst. DON St. John's Hosp., St. Louis, 1947-58; asst. prof. nursing, then assoc. prof. Loyola U, Chgo., 1961-66; prof. grad. program in nursing Loyola U, 1972-80; prof. U. South Fla., Tampa, 1980-90, prof. emeritus, 1990—; asst. chief rsch. grants br. div. nursing HEW, Washington, 1966-68; prof., dean sch. nursing Ohio State U., Columbus, 1968-72; mem. def. adv. com. on women in svcs. Dept. Def., 1972-75; cons. VA Hosp., health care agencies. Author: Toward a Theory for Nursing, 1971, transl. to Japanese, 1975, A Theory for Nursing: Systems, Concepts, Process, 1981, transl. to Japanese, 1983, transl. to Spanish, 1985, Curriculum and Instruction in Nursing, 1986; contbr. articles in nursing to profl. jours., chpts. to books. Alderman, chmn. fin. com. Ward 2, Wood Dale, Ill., 1975-79; bd. dirs. operation PAR Inc., Pinellas County, Fla., 1990-92. Recipient Founders award St. Louis U., 1969, Recognition of Contbns. to Nursing Edn. award Columbia U. Tchrs. Coll., 1983, Disting. Scholar award U. So. Fla., 1988-89. Fellow Am. Acad. Nursing (hon. 1994); mem. ANA, Ill. Nurses Assn. (highest recognition award 1975, award 19th dist. 1975), Fla. Nurses Assn. (del. to ANA conv. 1982—, dir. region 2 1981-83, 2d v.p. 1983-85, Nurse of Yr. award 1984, Nursing Rsch. award 1985), Dist. IV Fla. Nurses Assn. (pres.-elect 1982-83, pres. 1983-84, del. Fla. Nurses Assn. 1981-93), Fla. Nurses Found. (sec. 1986-88, pres. 1988-91), Sigma Theta Tau Internat. Inc. (Delta Beta chpt., counselor 1981-83, pres.-elect 1986-87, pres. 1987-89, Disting. lectr. 1990-91, co-chair biennial conv. 1991, elected to nominating com. 1993—, Virginia Henderson fellow 1993-95, Founders award 1989), Phi Kappa Phi (scholar award 1988).

KING, JACQUELYN S., computer programmer; b. Lexington, Minn., Oct. 10, 1965; d. Rodney Lee and Rae Jean (Johnstone) K. BA in Math. with acad. honors, Alverno Coll., Milw., 1992. New accounts rep. Security Bank, Milw., 1988-92; actuarial technician Milliman & Robertson, Brookfield, Wis., 1992-94; computer programmer Applied Quoting Sys., Comml. Ins. Sys., Hartland, Wis., 1994—; programmer Blue Cross and Blue Shield, Milw., 1991; math. tutor Alverno Co., 1989-92. Mem. Soc. Actuaries. Roman Catholic.

KING, JANE CUDLIP COBLENTZ, volunteer educator; b. Iron Mountain, Mich., May 4, 1922; d. William Stacey and Mary Elva (Martin) Cudlip; m. George Samuel Coblentz, June 8, 1942 (dec. June 1989); children: Bruce Harper, Keith George, Nancy Allison Coblentz Patch; m. James E. King, August 23, 1991 (dec. Jan. 1994). BA, Mills Coll., 1942. Mem. Sch. Resource and Career Guidance Vols., Inc., Atherton, Calif., 1965-69, pres., CEO, 1969—; exec. asst. to dean of admissions Mills Coll., 1994—; part-time exec. asst. to dean of admissions Mills Coll., 1994—. Proofreader, contbr. Mills Coll. Quarterly mag. Life gov. Royal Children's Hosp., Melbourne, Australia, 1963—; pres. United Menlo Park (Calif.) Homeowner's Assn., 1994—; nat. pres. Mills Coll. Alumnae Assn., 1969-73, bd. trustees, 1975-83. Named Vol. of Yr., Sequoia Union High Sch. Dist., 1988, Golden Acorn award for outstanding svc. Menlo Park C. of C., 1991. Mem. AAUW (Menlo-Atherton branch pres. 1994—), Atherlons, Palo Alto (Calif.) Area Mills Coll. Club (pres. 1986), Phi Beta Kappa. Republican. Episcopalian. Home: 1109 Valparaiso Ave Menlo Park CA 94025-4412 Office: Menlo-Atherton H S Sch Resource Ctr Guid Vols 555 Middlefield Rd Atherton CA 94027

KING, JANE LOUISE, artist; b. South Bend, Ind., Aug. 9, 1951; d. Bill and Anne Luciel (Hopkins) Berta; m. Gerald William King Jr., July 7, 1973; children: Kelly Anne, Dinah Jolene. Student, Ind. U., South Bend, 1969-70, Ind. U., 1970-71; BFA, Ohio State U., 1973. Ind. artist Colo., 1974—; instr. Sangre de Cristo Art Ctr., Pueblo, Colo., 1982, Art Studio, Longmont, Colo., 1989. Exhibited oil and pastel paintings in numerous group shows including 5th Ann. Internat. Exhibit Kans. Pastel Soc., 10th and 22nd Ann. Pastel Soc. Am., N.Y., Colo. State Fairs, Poudre Valley Art League; prin. works represented in numerous pvt. collections; contbr. poems to At Days End, 1994. Leader 4-H Club, Longmont, 1986—; sec. Longmont Artists Guild Gallery, 1988-89, bd. dirs., 1989; supt. 1st Bapt. Ch., Longmont, 1990-91. Mem. Colo. Artists Assn. (area 1 rep. 1994), Longmont Artists Guild (Grumbacher award 1992), Longmont Arts Coun., Knickerbocker Artists N.Y, Audubon Artists N.Y. Republican. Home: 1508 Kempton Ct Longmont CO 80501-6716

KING, JENNIE LOUISE, research director; b. Ft. Hood, Tex., Nov. 27, 1962; d. Homer Lee and Jennie Louise (Smith) Walker; m. Philip Jerome King, Apr. 23, 1994. BA in Speech Comms., Columbus Coll., 1984; postgrad., Mercer U., 1987-90. Intern Senator Mack Mattingly, Washington, 1984, Congressman Richard Ray, Washington, 1984; rsch. asst. The Robinson Humphrey Co., Inc., Atlanta, 1985-89; mktg. asst. Norrell Corp., Atlanta, 1989-90; rsch. assoc. The Carter Ctr., Inc., Atlanta, 1990-93, dir. rsch., 1993-94; dir. rsch. Boys & Girls Clubs Am., Atlanta, 1994—. Vol. Richard Ray for Congress Campaign Com., 1984, The Atlanta Project, 1992; mem. adv. bd. Ga. Addiction Pregnancy and Parenting Family Enrichment Ctr., 1994—. Mem. NARAS (assoc.), Nat. Soc. Fundraising Execs., Atlanta Songwriters Assn. (v.p. 1992-93, bd. dirs. 1991-93, publicity chmn. 1991-93), Broadcast Music Inc., Nat. Acad. Songwriters, Am. Prospect Rsch. Assn. (pres. Ga. chpt. 1993-94), Nashville Songwriters Assn. Internat., Columbus Coll. Alumni Assn. Methodist. Office: Boys & Girls Clubs Am 1230 W Peachtree St NW Atlanta GA 30309

KING, JOANNE, psychologist; b. Salt Lake City, Nov. 21, 1955; d. Reed Kent and Wanda (Birch) K.; m. Jeffrey Bruce Leeson, Aug. 18, 1984 (div. July 1986). BS Elem. Edn., U. Utah, 1978; MS Ednl. Adminstrn., SUNY, Albany, 1984, CAS Ednl. Adminstrn., 1987; PhD Counseling Psychology, Ind. State U., 1993. Elem. sch. tchr. Jordan Sch. Dist., Salt Lake City, 1978-79, 80-81; resource specialist Missionary Tng. Ctr., Provo, Utah, 1981-83; asst. dir. Indonesia SUNY Edn. Program, Albany, 1984-85; rsch. assoc. SUNY, Albany, 1987; counselor Ind. State U., Terre Haute, 1988-91; family therapist Vigo County Welfare Dept., Terre Haute, 1990-91; psychology intern VA Med. Ctr., Lexington, Ky., 1991-92; psychologist Madison Ctr., South Bend, Ind., 1992—; cons. Washington Alternative Sch., Terre Haute, 1991, Crestwood Micro Systems, Inc., Latham, N.Y., 1987-88. Grad. fellow

Ind. State U., 1988-91, SUNY, Albany, 1983-84. Mem. APA, Am. Assn. Marriage and Family Therapy (affil.). Office: Madison Ctr 403 E Madison St South Bend IN 46617-2322

KING, JOYCE CALISTRI, columnist; b. Charleroi, Pa., May 26, 1927; d. Jeremiah James and Vera Colette (Hurley) Calistri; m. William Louis King, II, Dec. 22, 1951; children: Mari Joyce, William Louis, III, Donald II. BA, U. Pa. Coll. for Women, 1949. Tchr. Romper Room TV, WTPA-TV, Harrisburg, Pa., 1954-55, WGAL-TV, Lancaster, Pa., 1956-57; hostess, producer Joyce King Show, WHP-TV, Harrisburg, Pa., 1959-60; sta. mgr. WSUB-TV Cable, Shillington, Pa., 1969-70; publicity dir. Bavarian Festival, Barnesville, Pa., 1974-76; wine columnist Reading Eagle, Reading, Pa., 1978-91; feature writer Reading Eagle, 1978-91; freelance columnist newspapers, mags., 1972—; student activities dir. Reading Hosp. Sch. Nursing, Reading, Pa., 1965-69; newsletter editor Young Republicans, Harrisburg, Pa., 1949-50, AAUW, 1955-56; dir. publicity Green Hills Theatre, Reading, Pa., 1963-67; mem. Pres.'s Art Council. Alvernia Coll. Scholar Am. Legion, U. Pa., 1945. Mem. Am. Women Radio and TV (pres. 1960), AAUW (v.p. 1955). Republican. Roman Catholic. Home: 2624 Whittier Ave Reading PA 19608-1744

KING, KATHLEEN BERNADETTE, nurse educator; b. N.Y.C., Dec. 12, 1950; d. Thomas Francis and Sarah Ann (McKeon) K.; m. John Robert Laing, Nov. 19, 1983; children: James, Genevieve King. AS in Math. and Sci., Auburn C.C., 1970; BSN, SUNY, Brockport, 1973; MS, U. Rochester, 1976, PhD, 1984. Clin. specialist in surg. nursing U. Rochester (N.Y.) Med. Ctr., 1976; instr. dept. nursing Hartwick Coll., Oneonta, N.Y., 1976-79, asst. prof., 1979-80; rsch. asst., predoctoral fellow U. Rochester Sch. Nursing, 1980-84, Robert Wood Johnson clin. nurse scholar, 1984-86, asst. prof., clinician II in surg. nursing, 1986-92, assoc. prof., 1992—. Editor: Cardiovascular Nursing, 1992—; mem. editorial and rev. bds. numerous profl. jours.; contbr. articles to profl. jours. Bd. dirs. Dandelion Day Care Ctr., 1986-88, pres., 1988-91; cert. CPR instr. ARC, 1978-81. March of Dimes scholar, 1968. Mem. ANA (coun. nurse rschrs.), N.Y. State Nurses Assn. (sec. dist. 15 1977-79, bd. dirs. 1979-81), Genesee Valley Nurses Assn., Am. Assn. Critical Care Nurses , Am. Heart Assn. (coun. on cardiovascular nursing, bd. dirs. 1994—, co-chair planning com. ann. heart ball 1994), Am. Psychol. Assn. (health psychology divsn.), Sigma Theta Tau (editor newsletter 1987-90, pres. Epsilon Xi chpt. 1986-87, pres.-elect 1985-86), Sigma Xi. Home: 124 Trafalgar St Rochester NY 14619 Office: U Rochester Sch Nursing 601 Elmwood Ave Rochester NY 14642

KING, KATIE JOHNSON, school counselor; b. Paris, Ark., Jan. 31, 1952; d. Ruben Henry and Charlotte Mae (Newsom) Johnson; m. Stevie Preston King, Aug. 24, 1974; children: Stephanie Kay, Kimberly Faye. BS, Ark. Tech. U., 1974; MS, U. Ark., 1980, cert. edn. specialist, 1989. Cert. in phys. edn. and health, spl. edn./learning disabilities, elem. and secondary counseling, Ark. Health and sci. tchr. Mag. (Ark.) Pub. Schs., 1974-75; spl. edn. tchr. Mulberry (Ark.) Pub. Schs., 1975-79, sch. counselor, 1983—; mem. adv. bd. Ark. Valley Vo-Tech., Ozark. Co-author: The Power of Words, 1992. Mem. Crawford County Park Bd., Van Buren, Ark. Nominated Counselor of Yr., N.W. Ark. Counseling Assn. Mem. NEA, Ark. Edn. Assn., U.S. Tennis Assn., Lions, Beta Sigma Phi, Delta Kappa Gamma (Gladys J. McDonald scholarship 1991). Methodist.

KING, KAY SUE, investment company executive; b. Indpls., Sept. 14, 1948; d. George W. and Nadine M. K.; 1 child, Christopher G. Student, U. Ariz., 1966-70; BS in Edn., Ind. U., 1971; MA in Speech Communication, U. Hawaii, 1974. Tchr. Indpls. High Schs., 1971-1973; sec., treas. G. W. King Co., Indpls., 1974—; domestic sales mgr. Regal Travel, Indpls., 1975-90; pres., bd. dirs. K.S. King, Inc., Indpls., 1977—; mng. ptnr. K.S. King Co., Indpls., 1982—. Mem. pub. rels. com. Indpls. Zoolog. Xoc., 1976-85; vol. Indpls Humane Soc., 1966—, Indpls. Aid to Zoo Horse Show, 1974-78, Save the Ducks campaign, Indpls., 1978, Pan Am. Games Olympic Sports Com., Indpls., 1981-82; tchr. Sunday sch. Meridian St. Methodist Ch., Indpls., 1988-90. Elected Festival Princess 500 Festival Assn., Indpls., 1968. Mem. Internat. Assn. Bus. Communicators, Internat. Wildlife Fedn., Indpls. Zoolog. Soc. (charter), Indpls. Pub. Libr., Indpls. Children's Mus., Indpls. Ski Club, U. Ariz. Alumni Assn., Ind. Univ. Alumni Assn., Channel 20, Riviera Club, Meridian Hills Country Club, Delta Delta Delta. Home: 702 Holliday Ln Indianapolis IN 46260 Office: King Co 5665 N Meridian St Indianapolis IN 46208

KING, KAY WANDER, design educator, fashion designer, consultant; b. Houston, Oct. 16, 1937; d. Aretas Robert and Verna Elizabeth (Klann) Wander; m. George Ronald King, Feb. 21, 1960; 1 child, Collin Wander. BA, U. North Tex., 1959; M of Liberal Arts, Houston Bapt. U., 1991. Fashion designer Kabro Houston, Inc., 1959-66, Joe Frank, Inc., Houston, 1966-68; fashion dir. Foley's, Houston, 1968-70; prin. Kay King Designer/Cons., Houston, 1970—; chair fashion dept. Houston C.C., 1981—; mem. adv. bd. Spring (Tex.) Ind. Sch. Dist. Tech. Edn., 1990—; bd. dirs. Make It Yourself With Wool, Tex.; site evaluator Tex. Coordinating Bd. for Higher Edn., 1994. Designer Mrs. Am., 1966, Houston Oilers Cheerleaders, 1968-92, Astroworld and the Astrodome, 1968-69, Brian Boru Opera, 1991. Chair Guld Coast area United Cerebral Palsy Telethon, 1981, Whiteley Endowment Scholarship Awards, Houston, 1990-93; admr. Bedichek Faculty Devel. Grants, 1995; pres. Spring Br. Ind.Sch. dist. Coutn. PTAs, Houston, 1987-88; bd. dirs. Houston C.C. Found., 1988-93, Mus. Fine Arts Costume Inst., Huston, 1991—, acquisitions com. 1993—. Recipient Yellow Rose of Tex., Gov. Tex., 1982, Nat. Inst. for Staff and Orgnl. Devel. Teaching Excellence award U. Tex., 1993; named Woman to Watch, Hosuton Woman Mag., 1991, Woman of Excellence, Fedn. Houston Profl. Women, 1992; Bedichek Faculty Development grantee, 1986, 89, 90, 93, 94. Mem. Nat. PTA (life, hon., coun. pres. 1987-88), Costume Soc. Am. (awards chair 1992-93, exec. bd. dirs. and mem. sec. 1993—), Tex. Jr. Coll. Tchrs. Assn. (sect. chair 1990-92), Fashion Group Internat. (bd. dirs. 1969—, cultural exch. chair 1965-71, regional dir. 1969-70, program dir., chair career conf. 1994), Houston C.C. Women Adminstrs. Assn. (bd. dirs. 1993—, v.p. 1994-95, Star award 1989), Houston Fashion Designers Assn. (charter, publicity chair 1989-93, v.p. bd. dirs. 1993—), Fedn. Houston Profl. Women (bd. dirs., program dir. 1993, adminstrv. sec. 1994, pres.-elect 1995), Classy Clown Corps (charter 1994—), Zeta Tau Alpha (charity showhouse chair 1985, Nat. Cert. of Merit 1986). Office: Houston CC System 1300 Holman 319A Houston TX 77004-3898

KING, LAURA JANE, librarian, genealogist; b. Pemberville, Ohio, Jan. 19, 1947; d. Richard D. and Jessie Florence (Brown) Zepernick; m. Bruce William King, June 17, 1972; 1 child, Christian Andrew. BA, Bowling Green (Ohio) State U., 1969, MEd, 1976; postgrad. Kent State U. Cert. geneal. lectr.; cert. geneal. record searcher. County extension agt. home econs. Ohio Coop. Extension Svc., Paulding County, 1970-77; asst. dir., historian Pemberville Pub. Libr.; mem. PRIDE com., vocat. home econs. dept. Paulding Exempted Village, 1975—; instr. genealogy Continuing Edn. Bowling Green State U., Eastwood Sch. Dist. Community Edn. Mem. Paulding County Bicentennial Commn., 1975-77; organist 1st Presbyn. Ch., Pemberville, ruling elder, ch. historian; state chmn. Friends of Libr., 1992—; advisor 4-H. Recipient Tenure award Coop. Extension Svc., 1975; mem. Wood Counti Citizen's Com. for Bicentennial of U.S. Constn. and NW Ordinance; mem. Pemberville Sch. Adv. Com. Mem. Mary Sherman Hayes Soc. (sr. pres.), Flag of the U.S. of Am. (sr. state chmn., sr. state registrar 1994—) Children of the Am. Revolution, Ohio Geneal. Soc. (pres. Wood County chpt. 1978-80, chmn. pub. rels. chmn. 1982-83, chmn. First Families of Wood County com., state program chmn. ann. conf. 1991, 95, state chmn. History Writing Contest 1993), Berks County Geneal. Soc., Palatines to Am., DAR (vice regent chpt. 1975-77, regent chpt. 1979-83, registrar chpt. 1985—, state vice chmn. pages 1978-80, state chmn. lineage rsch. 1980-87, state and div. outstanding jr. mem. 1980, state chmn. membership commn. 1983-87, state recording sec. 1987-89, state corr. sec. 1989-92, area speaker's staff, state chmn. Friends of the Libr. 1992—), U.S. Daus. of 1812 (chmn. state insignia), First Families Ohio, Daus. Union Vets., Nat. Soc. Magna Charta Dames, Colonial Dames 17th Century, Daus. Am. Colonists (chpt. regent 1986—, state chmn. pub. rels., 1987, chmn. mideast region pub. rels.), Bus. and Profl. Women's Club (pres. Paulding 1975-76, v.p. 1974-75), Ohio Libr. Assn., Coun. Ohio Genealogists (v.p. 1992—), Colonial Order Crown of Charlemagne, SAR (medal of Appreciation). Club: Order Eastern Star. Corr. docent DAR Mus., Washington. Home: 14553 N River Rd Pemberville OH 43450-9797

KING, LINDA DARLENE WARDRUP, artist; b. Lynch, Ky., Feb. 1, 1946; d. Oscar England and Thelma (Onkst) Wardrup; m. David W. King, July 31, 1970; children: Jason Patrick, Jonathan David. Student, Ea. Ky. U., 1964-68. Quality control inspector Am. Greeting Inc., Corbin, Ky., 1970-72; aux. worker Laurel County Health Dept., London, Ky., 1972, health svc. aide, 1973, community health worker, 1974-81, clk. typist, 1982-84, adminstrv. sec., 1984-90; free-lance artist London, 1990—. Democrat. Baptist.

KING, LINDA MARIE, booking agent, tour manager; b. Whitestone, N.Y., Oct. 20, 1960; d. Robert Bittle and Dolores Grace (Atchinson) K. BS, U. Tenn., 1983; MA, Westminster Sem., 1987. Prodn. coord. GFI Prodns., Beverly Hills, Calif., 1989; mktg. rep. Harlem Globetrotters Internat., Hollywood, Calif., 1989-91; rd. mgr. Harlem Globetrotters, Hollywood, Calif., 1991-93, dir. booking, 1993—. Grad. scholar Westminster Sem., 1987. Mem. Kappa Alpha Theta. Office: Harlem Globetrotters Internat Inc 1000 S Fremont Ave Bldg 4A Alhambra CA 91803-1349

KING, LINDA ORR, museum director; b. Washington, June 21, 1948; d. William Baxter and Jayne (Reiser) Orr; m. James McClain King, June 3, 1947; children: David, Adam, Lindsay. BA, La. State U., 1970, MA in Fine Arts, 1971. Fine arts history asst. La. State U., Baton Rouge, 1967-70, grad. asst., 1970-71; assoc. curator La. State Mus., New Orleans, 1971-74; curator Coastal Ga. Hist. Soc./Mus. Coastal History, St. Simons Island, 1984-87; dir. Coastal Ga. Hist. Soc., St. Simons Island, 1987—. Co-editor: (photograph essay) George Francois Mugnier, 1975. Pres. Glynn County Soc. of St. Vincent de Paul, 1990-94; mem. adv. coun. on hist. preservation Coastal Regional Devel. Commn., 1987—, chmn., 1994-95; mem. Glynn County Courthouse Renovation Com., 1989—; Ga. state dir. S.E. Mus. Conf., 1990-94, also membership chair; mem. adv. coun. Brunswick Downtown Devel. Authority; mem. Leadership Glynn, 1992; mem. Commn. on Preservation of Ga. State Capitol. Recipient Kellogg Career Enhancement award Kellogg Found., 1989; Internat. Partnership Among Museums fellow to Sierra Leone, 1992. Mem. Ga. Assn. Mus. and Galleries (treas. 1987-89), Coastal Mus. Assn. (treas. 1987-89), Am. Assn. Mus., Low Country Mus. Network (treas. 1993, 94). Roman Catholic. Office: Mus of Coastal History PO Box 21136 Saint Simons Island GA 31522-0636

KING, LIS SONDER, public relations executive, writer; b. Roskilde, Denmark; came to U.S., 1956, naturalized, 1961; d. Carl Otto and Gerda Vohnsen (Sonder) Petersen; m. Robert King (div. 1972); 1 dau., Dorte; m. Theodore Allin Pace, 1972; grad. Roskilde Katedralskole, arts degree Sch. Fine Arts, Copenhagen, 1952. Feature writer Berlingske Tidende, Copenhagen, 1956-58; reporter, editor Moreau Pub. Co., Bloomfield, N.J., 1957-59; reporter, editor St. Thomas (V.I.) Daily News, Island Times, San Juan, P.R., 1962-63; editor The Advance, Dover, N.J., 1961-63; pub. relations dir. Fluid Chem. Co., Newark, 1963-64, Keyes, Martin & Co., Springfield, N.J., 1964-69; pres. Lis King Pub. Relations, Mahwah, N.J., 1969—; columnist Harris Pubs., N.Y.C., 1981—, Suburban News, Paramus, N.J., 1986—. Author, editor: St. Thomas Directory, 1962; author: Furniture: Make-Do, Make-Over, Make Your Own, 1977; contbr. articles to various pubs. Mem. Nat. Home Fashions League, Taxpayers Assn. Mahwah. Avocations: travel, gardening, reading, breeding Great Danes. Home and Office: 30 Dundee Ct PO Box 725 Mahwah NJ 07430-0725

KING, LISA, orthodontist; b. Shreveport, La., Nov. 19, 1962; d. Harry Garry and Joyce Lureline (Willis) K. BS, Centenary Coll. of La., 1984; DDS, U. Tenn., Memphis, 1988, MS in Orthodontics, 1990. Pvt. practice orthodontics Albuquerque, 1991—. Active Big Bros./Big Sisters, Albuquerque, 1994—. Southwestern Med. Sch. fellow in dentofacial deformities, 1991. Mem. ADA, Am. Assn. Orthodontists, Am. Assn. Women Dentists, Am. Cleft Palate Cranofacial Assn. Methodist.

KING, LUCY JANE, psychiatrist, health facility administrator; b. Vandalia, Ill., Dec. 23, 1932; d. Ira and Lucy Jane (Harris) K. AB, Washington U., St. Louis, 1954, MD, 1958. Diplomate Am. Bd. Psychiatry and Neurology, subspecialty Addiction Psychiatry. From instr. to assoc. prof. psychiatry dept. Washington U., 1963-74; prof. dept. psychiatry Med. Coll. of Va., Richmond, 1974-79; clin. prof. dept. psychiatry George Washington U., Washington, 1981-84, Ind. U. Med. Sch., 1994—; med. dir. chem. dependence treatment sect. Richard L. Roudebush VA Med. Ctr., Indpls., 1994—; mem. editorial bd. Annals of Clin. Psychiatry, 1989—. Author: (with others) Psychiatry in Primary Care, 1983; contbr. articles to profl. jours. Fellow Am. Psychiat. Assn.; mem. Am. Acad. Clin. Psychiatrists, Am. Med. Women's Assn., Am. Soc. Addiction Medicine (cert., dual diagnosis com. 1990—), Internat. House of Japan. Office: VA Med Ctr 116J Indianapolis IN 46222

KING, MARCIA, management consultant; b. Lewiston, Maine, Aug. 4, 1940; d. Daniel Alden and Clarice Evelyn (Curtis) Barrell; m. Howard P. Lowell, Feb. 15, 1969 (div. 1980); m. Richard G. King Jr., Aug., 1980. BS, U. Maine, 1965; MSLS, Simmons Coll., 1967. Reference, field advisory and bookmobile libr. Maine State Libr., Augusta, 1965-69; dir. Lithgow Pub. Libr., Augusta, 1969-72; exec. sec. Maine Libr. Adv. Com., Maine State Libr., 1972-73; dir. Wayland (Mass.) Free Pub. Libr., 1973-76; state libr. State of Oreg., Salem, 1976-82; dir. Tucson Pub. Libr., 1982-91; mgmt. cons. King Assocs., Tucson, 1991—. Past chmn. bd. dirs. Tucson United Way; past chmn. adv. bd. com. Sta. KUAT (PBS-TV and Radio); mem. adv. bd. Resources for Women, Inc.; chmn. Salvation Army. Mem. ALA, Pub. Library Assn., Ariz. State Library Assn., AAUW, Assn. Specialized and Coop. Library Agys. Unitarian. Office: King Assocs 7130 N Camino Caballos Tucson AZ 85743

KING, MARCIA JONES, potter, physicist; b. Oak Park, Ill., May 17, 1934; d. Walter Leland Jones and Florence W. (Dull) Anderson; m. James Craig King, Nov., 1953 (div. 1966); 1 child, James Craig King, Jr. BS, Johns Hopkins U., 1960, PhD, 1969. Elec. engr. Electronic Communications, Inc., Timonium, Md., 1959-63; research assoc. theoretical particle physics Syracuse (N.Y.) U., 1969-72; asst. editor The Physical Rev. Brookhaven Nat. Lab., Upton, N.Y., 1972-74; physicist Argonne (Ill.) Nat. Lab., 1974-78; pvt. practice potter and physicist Syracuse, N.Y., 1978—. Contbr. articles to profl. jours.; exhibitor pots throughout cen. N.Y. Mem. AAAS, Am. Physical Soc., Syracuse Ceramic Guild (pres. 1982-84), Phi Beta Kappa, Sigma Xi. Democrat. Home and Office: 228 Buckingham Ave Syracuse NY 13210-3024

KING, MARGARET ANN, communications educator; b. Marion, Ind., Feb. 27, 1936; d. Paul Milton and Janet Mary (Broderick) Burke; m. Charles Claude King, Aug. 25, 1956; children: C. Kevin, Elizabeth Ann, Paul S., Margaret C. Student, Ohio Dominican, 1953-56, U. Kans., 1980-81; BA in Communication, Purdue U., 1986, MA in Pub. Communication, 1990. Regional rep. Indpls. Juv. Justice Task Force, 1984-85; vis. instr. dept. communication Purdue U., West Lafayette, Ind., 1992; lectr. dept. communication, 1992—; bd. mem. Vis. Nurse Home Health Svcs. Charter bd. mem. Tippecanoe Coun. Drug & Alcohol, Lafayette, Ind., 1985; grad. mem. Leadership Lafayette, 1983. Purdue U. fellow, 1986-87. Mem. AAUW, Speech Comm. Assn. Am., Ctrl. States Comm. Assn. (conv. paper 1989), Internat. Platform Assn., Golden Key Nat. Hon. Soc., Phi Kappa Phi. Republican. Roman Catholic. Home: 1613 Redwood Ln Lafayette IN 47905-3939 Office: Purdue U Dept Communication West Lafayette IN 47907

KING, MARY CATHERINE (KAY KING), association executive; b. Portchester, N.Y., Feb. 22, 1954; d. Norman Edward and L. Elizabeth (Turnley) K.; stepdau. Mary Lorraine (Barden) K. BA, Vassar Coll., 1976; M International Affairs, Columbia U., 1979. Staff asst. to fellows in Europe and Africa, Coun. on Fgn. Rels., N.Y.C., 1980-81, edit. asst. Fgn. Affairs Mag., 1981-82, assoc. dir. project on European-Am. rels., 1983-87; sr. legis. asst. fgn. policy-def. Office Joseph R. Biden Jr. U.S. Senate, Washington, 1987-90; exec. dir. Assn. Profl. Schs. Internat. Affairs, Washington, 1990—; mem. group advisors Nat. Security Edn. Program, Washington; mem. nominating com. Alliance for Internat. Cultural and Edn. Exch., Washington, 1993—; mem. finalist selection com. Truman Scholars Program, Washington, 1992, 94, 95. Mem. Women's Fgn. Policy Group (bd. dirs. 1994—, chmn. mentoring com. 1994—), Coun. on Fgn. Rels., Am. Coun. on Germany (participant Young Leaders Conf. summer 1992). Democrat. Home: 2141 P St NW Washington DC 20037 Office: Assn Profl Schs Internat Affairs 2400 N St NW Washington DC 20037

KING, MICHELLE DAVIS, lawyer; b. N.Y.C., June 27, 1952; d. Joseph A. and Annette (Graber) Davis; m. Alfred A. King, Jr., June 16, 1991. BA, Boston U., 1974; JD, SUNY, Buffalo, 1977. Bar: N.Y., D.C. Atty. Dept. of Treasury, Washington, 1978-84; atty. Bur. Alcohol, Tobacco and Firearms, Washington, 1984-85, assoc. chief counsel adminstrn., 1985—; adj. instr. U. Md., College Park, 1984—. Author: Administrative Law Course Guide, 1990. Mem. N.Y. Bar Assn., D.C. Bar Assn. Office: Bur Alcohol Tobacco & Firearms Rm 6100 Washington DC 20226

KING, MONIQUE VIOLETTE, psychoanalyst; b. Paris, Apr. 30, 1932; came to U.S., 1950; d. Charles Kapel and Bertha (Simon) Wolf; m. Richard C. King, Dec. 19, 1950. BA, Case Western Reserve U., 1954, PhD in Chemistry, 1959, MD, 1965. Diplomate Am. Bd. Psychiatry and Neurology; cert. Am. Psychoanalytic Assn. Rsch. chemist phys.-organic chemistry Union Carbide, Cleve.; med. intern Univ. Hosps., Cleve.; resident adult and child psychiatry Hanna Pavilion, Cleve.; assoc. clin. prof. psychiatry Med. Sch. Case Western Reserve U., Cleve., 1994—; pvt. practice Cleve., 1970-94; tng. and supervising analyst Cleve. Psychoanalytic Inst., 1983-94; geographic regional tng. and supervising analyst for Ariz. So. Calif. Psychoanalytic Inst., L.A., 1994—; attending physician Univ. Hosps., Cleve.; mem. ednl. com. Cleve. Psychoanalytic Inst., 1983—, chairperson extension divsn., 1975-80; mem. Ctr. for Advanced Psychoanalytic Studies in Princeton, 1978—; tchr. pediatric dept. St. Luke's Hosp., 1972-75; presenter in field. Contbr. articles to profl. jours. Mem. Phi Beta Kappa, Sigma Xi, Alpha Omega Alpha. Home and Office: 7841 E Sabino Crest Pl Tucson AZ 85715

KING, NANCY, communications educator; b. Blytheville, Ark., May 10, 1945; d. Willie Lee and Janie (Jones) Garrett; m. Perry King, June 17, 1967; children: Perry Jr., Tiffany, Christopher. BA in Speech Communication, Calif. State U., L.A., 1974, MA in Speech Communication, 1981. Asst. supr. Pacific Telegraph & Telephone, 1968-70; computer operator West Coast Community Exch. Fenton & Lavine, L.A., 1970-71; computer operator So. Gas Co., L.A., 1972-81, communication cons., 1982—; devel. lang. specialist Charles Drew Headstart Program, L.A.; asst. prof. speech dept. Marymount Coll., Rancho Palos Verdes, Calif., 1986—; speechwriter various regional ofcls.; instr. Calif. State U., L.A., 1979-86; mem. Calif. Libr. Svcs. Bd., 1984—, pres., 1988-89, 90-91; mem. Calif. Libr. Networking Task Force, 1985—, Calif. Librs. Adv. Bd., 1984—, Orange County Friends of Libr. Found., 1988—, Calif. Alliance for Literacy Task Force, 1988, 89. Contbr. articles to profl. jours. Co-chmn. black coun. Orange County Hist. and Cultural Found., pres. bd., 1992; campaign mgr. Fran Williams for Santa Ana City Coun. Mem. NEA, Nat. Speech Communication Assn., Western Speech Communication Assn., Am. Fedn. Tchrs., AAUW, L.A. Southcentral Planning Coun. (bd. dirs.). Republican. Roman Catholic. Office: Marymount Coll 30800 Palos Verdes Dr E Palos Verdes Peninsula CA 90274-6299

KING, NANCY BARRETT, lawyer; b. Norwood, Mass., Aug. 7, 1952; d. Norman R. and Jean N. (Jordan) Barrett; m. Eugene R. King, Aug. 17, 1979; children: Caroline Barrett, Jordan Roberts. BA, U. Mass., 1975; JD, Cleve. State U., 1980. Staff atty. specializing in juvenile law Franklin County Pub. Defender Office, Columbus, Ohio, 1981—. Office: Franklin County Pub Defender Office 373 S High St Fl 12 Columbus OH 43215

KING, NINA DAVIS, journalist; b. Coco Solo, Panama, May 7, 1941; d. James White and Ruth (Steele) Davis. B.A. in French, U. N.C., 1963, M.A. in Comparative Lit. (Chancellors fellow), 1967; Ph.D. in English, Wayne State U., 1973. Lectr. Queens Coll., 1970-73; copy editor Newsday, L.I., N.Y., 1973-76; asst. news editor Newsday, 1976-77, asst. book rev. editor, 1977-79, book rev. editor, 1979-88; book editor The Washington Post, 1988—. Mem. Nat. Book Critics Circle, Phi Beta Kappa. Office: The Washington Post 1150 15th St NW Washington DC 20071-0001

KING, NORAH MCCANN, federal judge; b. Steubenville, Ohio, Aug. 13, 1949; d. Charles Bernard and Frances Marcella (Krumm) McCann; m. Tunney Lee King, March 22, 1975; children: Catherine, Colin, Hillary, Adrienne. BA cum laude, Rosary Coll., 1971; JD summa cum laude, Ohio State U., 1975. Bar: Ohio 1975, So. Dist. of Ohio 1980. Law clerk U.S. Dist. Ct., Columbus, Ohio, 1975-79; counsel Frost, King, Freytag & Carpenter, Columbus, Ohio, 1979-82; asst. prof. Ohio State U., Columbus, Ohio, 1980-82; U.S. magistrate judge U.S. Dist. Ct., Columbus, Ohio, 1982—. Recipient award of merit Columbus Bar Assn., 1990. Mem. Coun. U.S. Magistrate Judges, Fed. Bar Assn. Office: US Dist Ct 85 Marconi Blvd Rm 351 Columbus OH 43215-2823*

KING, PATRICIA ANN, law educator; b. Norfolk, Va., June 12, 1942; d. Addison A. and Grayce (Wood) K.; m. Roger W. Wilkins, Feb. 21, 1981; 1 child, Elizabeth. BA, Wheaton Coll., 1963; JD, Harvard U., 1969. Bar: D.C. 1969, U.S. Supreme Ct. 1980. Spl. asst. to chair EEOC, Washington, 1969-71; dep. dir. civil rights office HEW, Washington, 1971-73; prof. law Georgetown Law Ctr., Washington, 1973—; adj. prof. Sch. Hygiene and Pub. Health Johns Hopkins U., 1990—; bd. dirs. Wheaton Coll., Womens Legal Defense Fund. Co-author: Law, Science and Medicine, 1984; contbr. articles to profl. jours. Chmn. Redevelopment Land Agy., Washington, 1976-80. Fellow Hastings Ctr.; mem. Am. Soc. Law and Medicine, Am. Law Inst., Inst. Medicine.

KING, PATRICIA MILLER, library administrator, historian; b. Bklyn., July 26, 1937; d. Donald Knox and Amy Beatrice (Heyliger) Miller; m. Samuel W. Stein, Jan. 2, 1978 (dec. May 1988); 1 child by previous marriage, Victoria Elizabeth King. A.B., Radcliffe Coll., 1959, A.M., 1961; Ph.D., Harvard U., 1970. Teaching asst. Harvard U., 1965-70; asst. prof. Wellesley Coll., Mass., 1970-71; dir. research Haney Assocs., Concord, Mass., 1971-73; dir. Schlesinger Library, Radcliffe Coll., 1973—, dir. projects. Contbr. articles to profl. jours. Bd. dirs. Nat. Coun. for Rsch. on Women, N.Y.C., 1983-92, Database Task Force, 1986-90, treas., 1988-89, chmn. bd., 1989-92, fin. com., 1992—; trustee Boston Heart Found., 1988—. Grantee in field. Mem. Mass. Hist. Soc., Am. Antiquarian Soc., Orgn. Am. Historians, Am. Hist. Assn., Berkshire Conf. of Women Historians. Home: 2 Bradbury St # 26C Cambridge MA 02138-4806 Office: Radcliffe Coll Schlesinger Libr 3 James St Cambridge MA 02138-3766*

KING, PAULA ELAINE, lawyer, judge, novelist; b. Portland, Oreg., Dec. 8, 1951; d. Duane Marcellus and Elaine Marie (Johnson) Downing; m. Thomas J. King Jr., Nov. 27, 1987. BA in History, Whitman Coll., 1973; JD, U. Oreg., 1980. Bar: Oreg. 1981, U.S. Dist. Ct. Oreg. 1985. Exec. sec. Kneisel Travel, Portland, 1973; taxpayer rep. IRS, Springfield and Medford, Ill./Oreg., 1973-77; law clk. Hon. Michael R. Hogan, Eugene, Oreg., 1979-83; asst. atty. gen. Oreg. Dept. Justice, Salem, 1984-85; assoc. Dwyer, Simpson & Wold, Eugene, Bend & Medford, Oreg., 1985-91, Black, Chapman & Webber, Medford, 1992—; part-time instr. Roque C.C., Grants Pass, Oreg., 1976-77; mcpl. judge Mcpl. Ct., Talent, Oreg., 1989—; fiction panelist So. Oreg. State Coll. Writer's Conf., Ashland, 1993; lectr. Oreg. State Bar Speakers Bur., 1993. Author: (sci. fiction novels) Mad Roy's Light, 1990, Rinn's Star, 1990, Flare Star, 1992, Fallway, 1993, A Whisper of Time, 1994, Siduri's Net, 1994; columnist: Sci. Fiction and Fantasy Workshop, 1987-91; assoc. editor: Pandora, 1988-90; contbr. articles to profl. jours. Instr. Jackson/Josephine Legal Secs. Assn., Medford, Newport, Oreg., 1992, 93. Named John G. and Martha M. Kelly Nat. Merit scholar, 1969-73. Mem. Oreg. State Bar Assn., Sci. Fiction Writers Am. Democrat. Roman Catholic. Home: 4780 Andrews Rd Medford OR 97501-9688

KING, PAULA LEE, psychologist, consultant; b. Ashland, Ky., July 17, 1947; d. Max Emerson and Pauline (Hays) Turpin; m. Dick H. King, Feb. 21, 1974 (div. 1986); children: Tamara, Jacqueline. BA, Ariz. State U., 1969, PhD, 1985; MA, No. Ariz. U., 1972. Counselor Paradise Valley High Sch., Phoenix, 1972-75, Glendale (Ariz.) C.C., 1978-80; mem. high sch.-coll. rels. and continuing edn. staff No. Ariz. U., Flagstaff, 1975-78; pvt. practice Psychol. Ctr. for Human Concerns, Phoenix, 1980-92, Well Being Systems, Phoenix, 1992—; cons., workshop and seminar presenter to hosps., chs., community orgns., Phoenix, 1982—, Nat. Inst. for Clin. Application Behavioral Medicine, Hilton Head, S.C., 1993. Mem. ednl. team Shadow

Rock Ch., Phoenix, 1989—; mem. Phoenix Mayor's Youth Commn., 1992—. Mem. APA, Ariz. Psychol. Assn., Addiction Counselors. Office: Well Being Systems 2701 E Camelback Rd Ste 391 Phoenix AZ 85016-4307

KING, SALLY FIONA, executive; b. Carshalton, Surrey, Eng., June 7, 1958; came to U.S., 1981; d. Neil Mair and Dora (Morris) K.; m. Roger Michael Levin, July 11, 1986. Diploma, Croydon Coll., 1976; MBA, Columbia U., 1990. Exec. officer Dept. Health and Social Security, London, 1976-78; acct. exec. H & H Factors Ltd. (divsn Walter E. Heller), London, 1979-80, Walter E. Heller & Co., Inc., N.Y.C., 1981; exec. dir. Levin & Weissman, N.Y.C., 1982-91; sr. mgr., legal adminstrn. GE Co., Fairfield, Conn., 1991-93; exec. v.p., chief oper. officer CLexis Counsel Connect divsn. Am. Lawyer Media/Time Warner, N.Y.C., 1994—. Mem. ABA, Corp. Bar Assn., Large Law Dept. Coun. (exec. com. 1991—), Assn. Legal Adminstrs. Office: Counsel Connect Inc 600 3d Ave New York NY 10016

KING, SHARON L., lawyer; b. Ft. Wayne, Ind., Jan. 12, 1932. AB, Mt. Holyoke Coll., 1954; JD with distinction, Valparaiso U., 1957; LLM in Taxation, Georgetown U., 1961. Bar: Ind. 1957, D.C. 1958, Ill. 1962. Trial atty. tax divsn. U.S. Dept. Justice, 1958-62; ptnr. Sidley & Austin, Chgo. Fellow Am. Coll. Tax Counsel; mem. ABA (chmn. com. closely-held corps. taxation sect. 1979-81, regulated pub. utilities com. taxation sect. 1982-83, coun. dir. taxation sect. 1983-86), Chgo. Bar Assn. (bd. mgrs. 1973-75, chmn. fed. tax com. 1983-84), Ill. State Bar Assn. (counsel dir. sect. fed. taxation 1989-91), Women's Bar Assn. Ill. (bd. dirs. Found., v.p. Found., dir. scholarship). Office: Sidley & Austin 1 First National Plz Chicago IL 60603

KING, SHERYL JAYNE, secondary education educator, counselor; b. East Grand Rapids, Mich., Oct. 29, 1945; d. Thomas Benton III and Bettyann Louise (Mains) K. BS in Family Living, Sociology, Secondary Edn., Cen. Mich. U., 1968, M in Counseling, 1971. Educator Newaygo (Mich.) Pub. Schs., 1968-72; interior decorator Sue King Interiors, Grand Rapids, Mich., 1972-73; dir. girl's unit Dillon Family and Youth Svcs., Tulsa, 1973-74; mgr. Fellowship Press, Grand Rapids, Minn., 1974-76; educator, counselor Itasca Community Coll., Grand Rapids, 1977-81; dept. head Dist. 318, Grand Rapids, 1977-81, 85-87; bd. dirs., chairperson program com. Marriage and Family Devel. Ctr., Grand Rapids, 1985-89. Treas. Cove Whole Foods Coop., 1978-80; chmn. bd. Christian Community Sch., 1977-78; jr. high softball coach, 1983-86; mem. issues com. No. Minn. Citizens League, Grand Rapids, 1984—, Blandin Found. Study, 1985-86; chairperson Itasca County Women's Consortium, Grand Rapids, 1983-87; Women's Day Conf., Grand Rapids, 1983-87; bd. dir. audio tech. Fellowship of Believers, Grand Rapids, 1974-87, 90—, deaconess, 1974—; bd. dir. audio tech Camp Dominion, Cass Lake, Minn., 1976-80; mem. fitness com., chmn. aquatic com., YMCA, Grand Rapids, 1974-87. Recipient 6 Outstanding Svc. awards Fellowship of Believers, 1974-79. Mem. Alpha Delta Kappa. Republican. Home: 1914 Mckinney Lake Rd Grand Rapids MN 55744

KING, SIDSEL ELIZABETH TAYLOR (BETH KING), hotel catering-hospitality professional; b. Edmonton, Alta., Can., July 27, 1932; d. Claude L. and Sadie (Hommy) Taylor; m. Otis A. King, Mar. 21, 1953; children: Ronald R., Lori Beth. AAS in Hotel Mgmt. and Food Svc Industry, U. Alaska, 1989. Sec. Sheriff's Office Courthouse, Edmonton, 1950-51; new accounts clk. First Nat. Bank Anchorage, 1952-53; sec., receptionist rate clk. Alaska Freight Lines, Anchorage, 1954-59; co-owner King's Rentals, Anchorage, 1953—; sec. State of Alaska Dept. Fish and Game, Anchorage, 1959-64, Anchorage Sch. Dist., West High, Wendler and East High, Anchorage, 1964—; exec. sec. Anchorage Daily News, 1969-70; with freight svc. Anchorage Slnd., 1970-71; caterer Clarion Hotel, Anchorage, 1989—; ambassador Clarion Hotel, Anchorage, 1991, Red Cross person, 1990-91. Preservation charter mem. Nat. Soc. Hist. Preservation, 1980's, Nat. Women in the Arts, Washington, 1980's, Nat. Secs. Assn. Anchorage, 1959—. Mem. Alaska Watercolor Soc., U. Alaska-Anchorage Alumni. Home: PO Box 244304 Anchorage AK 99524-4304 Office: Regal Alaskan Hotel 4800 Spenard Rd Anchorage AK 99517-3200

KING, SUSAN BENNETT, retired glass company executive, dean; b. Sioux City, Iowa, Apr. 29, 1940; d. Francis Moffatt Bennett and Marjorie (Rittenhouse) Sillin; divorced. AB, Duke U., 1962. Legis. asst. U.S. Senate, Washington, 1963-66; dir. Nat. Com. for Effective Congress, Washington, 1967-71, Ctr. Pub. Financing of Election, Washington, 1972-75; exec. asst. to chmn. Fed. Election Commn., Washington, 1975-77; chmn. U.S. Consumer Product Safety Commn., Washington, 1978-81; dir. consumer affairs Corning (N.Y.) Glass Works, 1982, v.p. corp. communications, 1983-86; pres. Steuben Glass, N.Y.C., 1987-92; sr. v.p. corp. affairs Corning Inc., 1992—; del. Consumer Affairs Orgn. Econ. Cooperation and Devel., Paris, 1980-81; fellow Inst. Politics, Harvard U., Cambridge, Mass., 1981; fellow Sanford Inst. Pub. Policy, Duke U., Durham, N.C., 1995; bd. dirs. Coca-Cola Co. Trustee Duke U., Durham, N.C., 1987—, Eurasia Gound., Washington. Fellow Inst. Politics Harvard U., 1981, Stanford Inst. Pub. Policy, Duke U., 1995. Mem. Nat. Consumers League (pres. 1984-85), Am. Alliance Rights and Responsibilities, Nat. Pub. Radio Found., Health Effects Inst. Democrat.

KING, TERESITA LIM, gynecologist; b. Quezon City, Luzon, Philippines, Jan. 19, 1952; came to U.S., 1979; d. Fernando Go and Marina (Lim) K.; m. Andrew Steven Nakrin, July 5, 1979; 1 chld, Joy Cecille Grace Nakrin; adopted children: Chin Sui King-Nakrin, Annie Nakrin. BS, U. of Philippines, 1973, MD, 1977. Diplomate Am. Bd. Ob-Gyn. Intern Manila (Philippines) Med. Ctr., 1977-78; rural physician Republic of Philippines, Quezon City, 1978-79; staff physician Northwest Hosp., Chgo., 1979-80; resident ob-gyn. U. Ill., Chgo., 1980-84; staff physician, chief ob-gyn. Heritage Hosp., Tarboro, N.C., 1984-88; staff physician, chief gynecologist Community Hosp. of Rocky Mount, N.C., 1986—; tchr. birth control at pub. and pvt. high schs., Berwyn, Ill., Chgo., 1981-84; pub. health physician Cook County, Chgo., 1981-84. University scholar U. of Philippines, 1969-77. Fellow ACOG, Am. Bd. Obstetricians-Gynecologists; mem. Pre-Medicine Honor Soc., Phi Kappa Phi, Pi Gamma Mu. Roman Catholic. Office: 2807 Main St N Tarboro NC 27886-1903

KING CALKINS, CAROL COLEMAN, hospital administrator; b. L.A., May 31, 1949; d. Harold S. and Gladys (Blumenthal) Coleman; 1 child, Katrina Elizabeth King; m. Michael Steven Calkins, Oct. 10, 1987. BA in Psychology, U. Colo., 1972; MBA, U. No. Colo., 1982. Dir. group living Nat. Jewish Ctr. Immunology and Respiratory Medicine, Denver, 1980-82; dir. clin. support svcs. Nat. Jewish Ctr. Immunology and Respiratory Medicine, 1982-83, dir. spl. projects, 1983-84, asst. dir. adminstrv. svcs., 1984, dir. adminstrv. svcs., 1984—; speaker in field. Recorder improvement process coun. Jefferson County (Colo.) Schs., 1989. Mem. Colo. Hosp. Assn. Risk Mgrs., Am. Coll. Healthcare Execs., Assn. Commuter Transp. (v.p. Rocky Mountain chpt. 1992). Office: 1400 Jackson St Denver CO 80206-2761

KINGDON, MARY ONEIDA GRACE, elementary education educator; b. Canton, Ohio, Aug. 11, 1934; d. Virgil Ezra and Donnie Mabel (Rowe) Sell; m. Harold Ivor Edwin Kingdon, Feb. 22, 1957; children: Sheryl Lynn, Harold Ivor Edwin Jr., Jill Renée, James Todd Ezra. BA in History and Social Sci., Houghton Coll., 1956; postgrad., U. Ky., 1963-67, SUNY, Geneseo, 1969-71; MS in Edn., Alfred U., 1983. Cert. permanent N-6 elem. tchr., reading tchr., N.Y. Tchr. English, Cherry Street City Sch., Canton, 1956-57; tchr. English Mercer County Pub. Sch., Harrodsburg, Ky., 1963-64, Cardinal Valley Fayette County Sch., Lexington, Ky., 1965-67; intermediate tchr. Friendship (N.Y.) Cen. Sch., 1967—; primary tchr. Bearss Acad., Jackson, Miss., 1983-84. Mem. N.Y. State Tchrs. Retirement Assn. (Allegany and Cattaraugus counties del. 1985—), N.Y. State Union Tchrs., Friendship Cen. Sch. Tchrs. Assn. (sec. 1970-72, pres. 1982-83, 92-93). Republican. Mem. Wesleyan Ch. Home: RR 1 Box 14K Houghton NY 14744-9711 Office: Friendship Cen Sch Friendship NY 14735

KING-ETTEMA, ELIZABETH DOROTHY, video and film editor, writer, photographer; b. Morristown, N.J., Sept. 29, 1953; d. James Claude and Martha Helene (Dawson) King; m. Dale Frederic Ettema, Feb. 13, 1982; children: Taylor Braam, Claire Elizabeth. BA in Art History, UCLA, 1975; postgrad. U. N.Mex., 1977-78. Writer, Bettis & Parks Advt., Albuquerque, 1975-76; bus. mgr. N.Mex. Ballet Co., Albuquerque, 1976-78; asst. editor Dury Assocs., Los Angeles, 1978, Another Editing Pl., Los Angeles, 1978-79, Bullywood Prodn., Los Angeles, 1979, Alan Landsburg Prodn., Los Angeles, 1980-81, Columbia TV, Los Angeles, 1982-83; video editor Am. Film Inst., Los Angeles, 1983-85. Video editor Scenario, 1984, U.S. 49/Calif. 1, 1985; writer, photographer The Pumpkin Patch, 1990, Backyard Sunflower, 1993 (one of Outstanding Sci. Trade Books of Yr. for Children Nat. Sci. Tchrs. Assn. and Children's Book Coun.), Chile Fever, A Celebration of Peppers, 1995. Mem. Motion Picture and Videotape Editors Guild, Soc. Children's Book Writers. Democrat. Episcopalian. Club: Embroiderer's Guild of Am. (historian chpt. 1984-85, v.p., program chmn. 1987-88). Home and Office: 7235 Forbes Ave Van Nuys CA 91406-2736

KING GRISWOLD, KATHY ANN, cash manager, accountant; b. Danville, Pa., Apr. 25, 1957; d. Kenneth Albert and Mattie Jane (Boone) King; m. Keith Edwin Griswold, July 1, 1978; children: Kelsey Ann, Kyle Kenneth Edwin. AA, Ea. Nazarene Coll., 1978; BS, SUNY, Empire State Coll., Saratoga Springs, 1982; postgrad., SUNY, Saratoga Springs, 1991—. Bookkeeper, acct. Brophy, Dailey & Bonn, CPAs, Rochester, N.Y., 1978-81; asst. contr. Bathtique Internat., Ltd., Rochester, 1981-84; contr. Sugar Creek Stores, Inc., Rochester, 1984-91, treas., contr., 1991-93; cash mgr. Wegmans Food Markets, Inc., Rochester, 1993—; notary public State of N.Y., County of Monroe, Rochester, 1986—. Treas. Com. to Elect Keith Griswold, Rochester, 1985, 93. Mem. Treasury Mgmt. Assn., Inst. Mgmt. Accts. (dir. 1985—, Publicity award 1992), Treasury Mgmt. Assn. Western N.Y. (membership chair 1990-91, v.p., treas. 1991-92, pres. 1992-93, nominating chair 1993-94, Pres. award 1993). Republican. Methodist. Home: 1442 Crittenden Rd Rochester NY 14623 Office: Wegmans Food Markets Inc 1500 Brooks Ave Box 844 Rochester NY 14692-0844

KINGMAN, ELIZABETH YELM, anthropologist; b. Lafayette, Ind., Oct. 15, 1911; d. Charles Walter and Mary Irene (Weakley) Yelm; m. Eugene Kingman, June 10, 1939; children—Mixie Kingman Eddy, Elizabeth Anne Kingman. BA U. Denver, 1933, MA, 1935. Asst. in anthropology U. Denver, 1932-34; mus. asst. Ranger Naturalist Force, Mesa Verde Nat. Park, Colo., 1934-38; asst. to husband in curatorial work, Indian art exhibits Philbrook Art Ctr., Tulsa, 1939-42, Joslyn Art Mus., Omaha, 1947-69; tutor humanities dept. U. Omaha, 1947-50; chmn. bd. govs. Pi Beta Phi Settlement Sch., Gatlinburg, Tenn., 1969-72; asst. to husband in exhibit design mus. of Tex. Tech. U., 1970-75, bibliographer Internat. Ctr. Arid and Semi-Arid Land Studies, 1974-75; librarian Sch. Am. Research, Santa Fe, 1978-86; research assoc., 1986—; v.p. Santa Fe Corral of the Westerners, 1985-86. Mem. AAUW, LWV, Archeol. Inst. Am. (v.p. Santa Fe chpt. 1981-83), Santa Fe Hist. Soc. (sec. 1981-83). Home: 604 Sunset St Santa Fe NM 87501-1118 Office: Sch Am Rsch 660 Garcia St Santa Fe NM 87501

KINGSBURY, CAROLYN ANN, software systems engineer; b. Newark, Ohio, Aug. 4, 1938; d. Cecil C. Layman and Orpha Edith (Hisey) Layman Dick; m. L.C. James Kingsbury, Apr. 25, 1959; children: Donald Lynn, Kenneth James. BS in Math., BS in Info. and Computer Scis., U. Calif., Irvine, 1979; postgrad. West Coast U., 1982-84. Systems engr., analyst Rockwell Internat., Downey, Calif., 1979-84, system and software engr. Northrop Corp., Pico Rivera, Calif., 1984-89; systems engr. Hughes Aircraft Co., Long Beach, Calif., 1989-90, Fullerton, Calif., 1990-91. Pres. PTA, Manhattan Beach, Calif., 1971-73; Cub Scout den mother Boy Scouts Am., Manhattan Beach, 1972-73; mem. Fountain Valley Regional Hosp. Guild, 1993—. Recipient Service award Calif. Congress Parents and Tchrs., 1973, Leadership Achievement award YWCA, Los Angeles, 1980, 84, NASA Achievement awards, 1983. Mem. NAFE, AAUW, Nat. Mgmt. Assn., Newtowners Club (pres. 1962). Republican. Home: 11392 Stonecress Ave Fountain Valley CA 92708

KINGSLEY, EMILY PERL, writer; b. N.Y.C., Feb. 28, 1940; d. Alan F. and Florence (Schneider) Perl; m. Edwin H. Kaplin, July 15, 1963 (div. Feb. 1970); m. Charles R. Kingsley, June 25, 1972; 1 child, Jason. BA, Queens Coll., 1960. Book prodn. staff Harper, Harcourt Brace and Random House, N.Y.C., 1960-63; prodn. asst. Talent Assocs., N.Y.C., 1963-66; assoc. producer Everybody's Talking ABC-TV, L.A., 1966-67; researcher Dick Cavett Show ABC-TV, N.Y.C., 1967; talent coord. Emmy Awards Show CBS-TV, N.Y.C., 1970; writer Sesame Street Children's TV Workshop, N.Y.C., 1970—. Author teleplay Kids Like These, 1987 (Christopher award 1988, 1st prize Rehab. Insternat. Film Festival, Arc of Excellence award Nat. Assn. for Retarded Citizens of U.S., Nat. Easter Seals award). Co-chair Parent Assistance Com. on Downs Syndrome, White Plains, N.Y., 1976—; bd. dirs. Nat. Downs Syndrome Congress, chair adoption com., 1979-88. Recipient 10 Emmy awards, 6 Emmy award nominations Nat. Acad. TV Arts and Scis., Exceptional Svc. award Nat. Down Syndrome Congress, 1985, Media award MCCJ/ARC; named Humanitarian of the Yr., Girl Scouts U.S., 1988, Joseph P. Kennedy award, 1991. Home and Office: 226 S Greeley Ave Chappaqua NY 10514-3333

KINGSLEY, PATRICIA, public relations executive; b. Gastonia, N.C., May 7, 1932; d. Robert Henry and Marjorie (Norment) Ratchford; m. Walter Kingsley, Apr. 1, 1966 (div. 1978); 1 child, Janis Susan. Student, Winthrop Coll., 1950-51. Publicist Fountainebleau Hotel, Miami Beach, Fla., 1952; exec. asst. ZIV TV, N.Y.C., 1953-58; publicist Rogers & Cowan, L.A. and N.Y.C., 1960-71; ptnr. Pickwick Pub. Rels., L.A., 1971-80, PMK Pub. Rels., L.A., 1980—; adv. com. Women's Action for Nuclear Disarmament, Arlington, Mass., 1983—. Democrat. Office: PMK Pub Rels Inc 955 Carrillo Dr Ste 200 West Hollywood CA 90048-5400

KINGSLEY-ROACH, DIANE LYNN, accountant; b. Utica, N.Y., Apr. 8, 1967; d. Karl Kenneth and Theresa Rose (Cavaretta) Kingsley; m. John Patrick Roach, Mar. 9, 1991. AAS in Acctg., Mohawk Valley C.C., 1990; postgrad., SUNY, Utica/Rome, 1990-92. Teller Albany Savs. Bank, New Hartford, N.Y., 1987-90; asst. Christine's Office Svcs., Utica, 1990-91; office mgr. Midstate Steel, Utica, 1990-93; asst. bursar inst. tech. SUNY, Utica/Rome, 1993—; pvt. practice DKR Fin. Svcs., Utica, 1992—. Mem. Inst. Mgmt. Accts.

KINGSOLVER, BARBARA ELLEN, writer; b. Annapolis, Md., Apr. 8, 1955; d. Wendell and Virginia (Henry) K.; m. Joseph John Hoffmann, Apr. 15, 1985 (div.); 1 child, Camille. BA, DePauw U., 1977; MS, U. Ariz., 1981; LittD (hon.), DePauw U., 1994. Sci. writer U. Ariz., Tucson, 1981-85; freelance journalist Tucson, 1985-87, novelist, 1987—; book reviewer N.Y. Times, 1988—, L.A. Times, 1989—. Author: The Bean Trees, 1988 (Enoch Pratt Libr. Youth-to-Youth award 1988, Am. Libr. Assn. award 1988), Homeland and Other Stories, 1989 (Am. Libr. Assn. award 1990), Holding the Line: Women in the Great Arizona Mine Strike of 1983, 1989, Animal Dreams, 1990 (PEN West Fiction award 1991, Edward Abbey Ecofiction award 1991), Another America, 1992, Pigs in Heaven, 1993 (L.A. Times Fiction prize 1993, Mountains and Plains Fiction award 1993, Western Heritage award 1993, ABBY Honor Book 1994). Recipient Feature-writing award Ariz. Press Club, 1986; citation of accomplishment UN Nat. Coun. of Women, 1989; Woodrow Wilson Found./Lila Wallace fellow, 1992-93. Mem. PEN Ctr. USA West, Nat. Authors Guild, Nat. Writers Union, Phi Beta Kappa. Home and Office: PO Box 5275 Tucson AZ 85703-0275*

KINGSTON, MAXINE HONG, author; b. Stockton, Calif., Oct. 27, 1940; d. Tom and Ying Lan (Chew) Hong; m. Earll Kingston, Nov. 23, 1962; 1 child, Joseph Lawrence. B.A., U. Calif., Berkeley, 1962; hon. doctoral degrees, Ea. Mich. U., 1988, Colby Coll., 1990, Brandeis U., 1991, U. Mass., 1991, Starr King Sch. for the Ministry, 1992. Tchr. English, Sunset High Sch., Hayward, Calif., 1965-66, Kahuku (Hawaii) High Sch., 1967, Kahaluu (Hawaii) Drop-In Sch., 1968, Kailua (Hawaii) High Sch., 1969, Honolulu Bus. Coll., 1969, Mid-Pacific Inst., Honolulu, 1970-77; prof. English, vis. writer U. Hawaii, Honolulu, 1977; Thelma McCandless Disting. Prof. Eastern Mich. U., Ypsilanti, 1986, Chancellor's Disting. Prof. U. Calif., Berkeley, 1990—. Author: The Woman Warrior: Memoirs of a Girlhood Among Ghosts, 1976 (Nat. Book Critics Circle award for non-fiction; cited by Time mag., N.Y. Times Book Rev. and Asian Mail as one of best books of Yr. and Decade), China Men, 1981 (Nat. Book award; runner-up for Pulitzer prize; Nat. Book Critics Circle award nominee 1988), Hawai'i One Summer, 1987 (Western Books Exhbn. Book award, Book Builders West Book award), Tripmaster Monkey-His Fake Book, 1989 (PEN West Award in Fiction), Through the Black Curtain, 1988; contbr. short stories, articles and poems to mags. and jours., including Iowa Rev., The New Yorker, Am. Heritage, Redbook, Mother Jones, Caliban, Mich. Quarterly, Ms., The Hungry Mind Rev., N.Y. Times., L.A. Times; prodr., writer play The Woman Warrior, Berkeley Repertory Co., 1994, The Huntington Theater, Boston, 1994, The Mark Taper Forum, L.A., 1995. Recipient award Mademoiselle mag., 1977, Anisfield Wolf Book award, 1978, award Calif. Arts Commn., 1981, Hawaii award lit., 1982, Calif. Gov.'s award. art. 1989, Major Book Collection award Brandeis U. Nat. Women's Com., 1990, award lit. Am. Acad & Inst. Arts & Letters, 1990, Lila Wallace Reader's Digest Writing award, 1992, Spl. Achievement Oakland Bus. Arts award, 1994; named Living Treasure Hawaii, 1980, Woman of Yr. Asian Pacific Women's Network 1981, to Am. Acad. Arts & Scis., 1992. Office: Univ Calif Dept English 322 Wheeler Hall Berkeley CA 94720

KINKEAD, VERDA CHRISTINE, non-profit organization executive, consultant; b. Plant City, Fla., Feb. 12, 1931; d. Ernest Glenn and Mina Lee (Alexander) K. Diploma, Bronson Meth. Hosp. Sch. Nursing, Kalamazoo, 1952; BA in Humanities, Adrian Coll., 1963; MA Guidance-Counseling, Mich. State U., 1964. RN, Mich. Nurse Bronson Meth. Hosp., 1952-54; 2d sr. surg. nurse West Side Med. Group, Kalamazoo, 1954-60; mentor, resident asst. Adrian (Mich.) Coll., 1962-63; head resident Alma Coll., 1964-65, asst. dean student affairs, dean women, 1965-69; co-founder, co-dir. Handicappers Info. Coun. and Patient Equipment Locker, Inc., Alma, 1981-87, pres., chief exec. officer, co-chmn. bd. dirs., 1987—; ednl. asst. East Main Meth. Ch., Kalamazoo, 1959-60. Former editor Saginaw Valley Dynamo; editor Challenger newsletter, 1986—; contbr. poetry to various publs. Bd. dirs. Saginaw Valley br. Nat. Multiple Sclerosis Soc.; past treas.; sec. bd. dirs., fair sec. Gratiot Agrl. Soc., Ithaca, Mich., 1977-83; vol. counselor Gratiot County Mental Health Ctr., Alma, 1983—; chmn. Gratiot County Early Intervention Coun., 1989-90; organizer group facilitator Ptnrs. in Renewal, Alma, 1989—; lay speaker United Meth. Ch.; mem. Go Grow Gratiot, 1989—, co-chair awards com. 1989-90, chairperson, 1990-91. Recipient Outstanding Svc. award Mich. Coll. Pers. Assn., 1972, Saginaw Valley br. Multiple Sclerosis Soc., 1986, First Lady award Mich. Women's Commn., 1987, vol. leadership award Greater Mich. Found., 1988, Outstanding Alumni award Adrian Coll., 1988, Order of the Tartan Alma C. of C. Outstanding Citizen award, 1993; Paul Harris fellow Rotary Internat., 1994. Mem. AAUW (sec. Alma br. 1965), Order Eastern Star (chaplain 1988-89, assoc. conductress 1989-91, conductress 1991-93, assoc. matron 1993-94, starpoint Ruth 1994—), Alma Woman's Club (v.p. 1990, pres. 1991-92, 92-93), Rotary (handicapper com. 1991—, world community svc. com. 1992—, project SEVA com. co-chair 1991—, sgt. at arms 1993-94), Phi Delta Kappa. Republican. Home: 3060 N Union Rd Alma MI 48801-9740 Office: Handicappers Info Coun 1022 Michigan Ave Alma MI 48801-1330

KINNEY, LISA FRANCES, lawyer; b. Laramie, Wyo., Mar. 13, 1951; d. Irvin Wayne and Phyllis (Poe) K.; m. Rodney Philip Lang, Feb. 5, 1971; children: Cambria Helen, Shelby Robert, Eli Wayne. BA, U. Wyo., 1973, JD, 1986; MLS, U. Oreg., 1975. Reference libr. U. Wyo. Sci. Libr., Laramie, 1975-76; outreach dir. Albany County Libr., Laramie, 1975-76, dir., 1977-83; mem. Wyo. State Senate, Laramie, 1984-94, minority leader, 1992-94, with documentation office Am. Heritage Ctr. U. Wyo., 1991-94; assoc. Corthell & King, Laramie, 1994—; owner Summit Bar Rev., 1994—. Author: (with Rodney Lang) Civil Rights of the Developmentally Disabled, 1986; (with Rodney Lang and Phyllis Kinney) Manual For Families with Emotionally Disturbed and Mentally Ill Relatives, 1988, rev. 1991; Lobby For Your Library; Know What Works, 1992; contbr. articles to profl. jours; editor, compiler pub. relations directory for ALA, 1982. Bd. dirs. Big Bros./Big Sisters, Laramie, 1980-83, Am. Heritage Ctr., Friends of Cmty. Health, Children's Mus. Recipient Beginning Young Profl. award Mt. Plains Libr. Assn., 1980; named Outstanding Wyo. Libr. Wyo. Libr. Assn., 1977, Outstanding Young Woman State of Wyo., 1980. Mem. ABA, Nat. Confs. of State Legislatures (various coms. 1985-90). Democrat. Avocations: photography, dance, reading, traveling, languages. Home: 2358 Jefferson St Laramie WY 82070-6420 Office: Corthell & King 221 S 2nd Laramie WY 82070

KINNEY, MARJORIE SHARON, marketing executive, artist; b. Gary, Ind., Jan. 11, 1940; d. David H. and Florence C. Dunning; student El Camino Coll., 1957, 58; LHD (hon.), West Coast U., 1982, Coll. San Mateo, 1987-88; MBA, Pepperdine U., 1989; m. Daniel D. Kinney, Dec. 31, 1958 (div. 1973); children: Steven Daniel, Michael Alan, Gregory Lincoln, Bradford David; m. Bradley Thomas Jr., Nov. 9, 1985 (div. Apr. 1987). Ptnr., Kinney Advt. Inc., Inglewood, Calif., 1958-68; pres. Greeters of Am., 1967-69; chmn. Person to Person Inc., Cleve., 1969-72; pres. Kinney Mktg. Corp., Encino, Calif., 1972-80; sr. v.p. Beverly Hills (Calif.) Savs. & Loan Assn., 1980-84; chmn., pres. Kinney & Assocs., Dana Point, Calif., 1985—; dir. Safeway Stores, Inc., Chubb/Pacific Indemnity Co.; freelance artist; lectr. Bd. dirs. ARC, 1976-81, United Way, 1979-81; trustee West Coast U.; v.p., trustee Capestrano Valley Symphony, 1989—; adv. bd. U.S. Human Resources, Womens Legal Edn. Fund; briefing del. to Pentagon Fed. Res. Dept. and White House, 1986; pres. Santa Fe Rep. Women, 1987; co-chair Childcare Action Day, 1986; participant Women of Faith and Courage, program for homeless girls, 1987—; chair Caps for Calypso, clothing project for homeless, 1988; v.p. Laguna Beach Art-A-Fair, 1992—. Presbyterian. Office: 81 Palm Beach Ct Dana Point CA 92629-4526

KINOSIAN, JANET MARIE, journalist; b. Los Angeles, June 20, 1957; d. Kasper John and Carol Grace (Boghosian) K. BA in Psychology, UCLA, 1980; MA in Psychology, Loyola Marymount, 1987. Intern L.A. Mag., 1980-81; staff writer Orange County Media Group, Costa Mesa, Calif., 1982-84; contbg. editor Orange Coast Mag., Costa Mesa, Calif., 1984-91, Palm Springs Life mag., 1984—; pres. JMK & Co., Brentwood, Calif., 1991—. Contbr. numerous articles to regional and nat. mags. and newspapers; extensive reporting, writing L.A. Times; internationally syndicated by N.Am. Syndicate, Times of London, N.Y. Times Syndicate, L.A. Times Syndicate. Co-founder Campus Coalition for Peace, 1978, Internat. Women's Coalition, 1979; mem. Amnesty Internat., 1980-94, Child Help USA, 1985-94, Free Arts for Abused Children, 1991-94. Mem. APA, L.A. Press Club, Hollywood Women's Press Club, Calif. Assn. Ind. Writers, Am. Soc. Journalists, Pi Beta Phi.. Democrat. Presbyterian. Home and Office: 11692 Chenault St Apt 103 Los Angeles CA 90049-4529

KINSER, CYNTHIA D., judge; b. Pennington Gap, Dec. 20, 1951; d. Morris and Velda (Myers) Fannon; m. H. Allen Kinser, Jr., March 17, 1974; children: Charles Adam, Terah Diane. Student, Univ. of Ga., 1970-71; BA, Univ. of Tenn., 1974; JD, Univ. of Va., 1977. Bar: Va. 1977, U.S. Dist. Ct. (we. dist.) Va. 1977, U.S. Ct. Appeals (4th cir.) 1977, U.S. Supreme Ct. 1988. Law clk. to Judge Glen M. Williams U.S. Dist. Ct., 1977-78; pvt. law practice, 1978-90; commonwealth's atty. Lee County, Va., 1980-83; magistrate judge U.S. Dist. Ct. (we. dist.) Va., Abingdon, 1990—; trustee Chapter 7 Panel, U.S. Bankruptcy Ct., 1979-90. Mem. Va. Bar Assn., Va. Trial Lawyers Assn., Am. Bar Assn. Methodist. Office: US District Court PO Box 846 180 W Main St Abingdon VA 24210-0846*

KINSEY, SANDRA ANN, mathematics educator; b. Toledo, July 28, 1949; d. Howard E. and Marian R. (Lemond) K. BA, Mich. State U., 1971, MA, 1977. Cert. elem. edn. tchr., Mich. Tchr. elem. edn. Grand Rapids (Mich.) Pub. Schs., 1971-91, math specialist, 1991—; trainer Mich. Math. Insvc. Project, State Dept. Edn./We. Mich. U., 1992. Recipient Excellence in Edn. award Grand Rapids Found., 1992. Mem. Nat. Coun. Tchrs. Math., Mich. Coun. Tchrs. Math., Mich. State U. Alumni Assn. Democrat. Office: Math/Sci Acad 1440 Davis NW Grand Rapids MI 49504

KINSEY-CALORI, JOANNE, broadcasting firm executive; b. McKeesport, Pa., Sept. 3; d. George Morris and Pauline Vivian (Anderson) Kinsey; B.A., M.A. Ohio State U., 1976; Ph.D., Harvard U., 1982; children—Paula Christine, Kevin Kinsey. Reporter, Sta. WOSU, Ohio State U., Columbus, 1969-70; communications asst. dept. continuing edn. Ohio State U., 1970-72, pub. relations dir. Coll. Adminstrv. Sci., 1974-75, acting asst. prof. communications, psychology, 1971-76; editor Columbus region Internat. Harvester Corp., 1973-77; pres. Profl. Broadcasting Services, Redondo Beach, Calif., 1976—, also Paris, London, Lisbon, Washington; international cross-cultural photographer, writer, comm. cons. Photography showings London, Paris, Washington. Pres. PTA, Marburn, Ridgeview, Whetstone schs., Columbus, 1965-70; campaign mgr. Republican party, Franklin County, 1965-68. Recipient spl. award for outstanding community service Columbus Pub.

Schs. Mem. Nat. Acad. TV Arts and Scis., Women in Communications (Los Angeles chpt.), Pacific Pioneer Broadcasters, So. Calif. Wine Writers (charter mem.), Archaeology Soc. Columbus, Jr. League, Mirrors and Chimes, Phi Beta Kappa, Phi Kappa Phi. Presbyterian. Clubs: Worthington Music, Clintonville Women's, Columbus Players. Office: 225 N El Cielo Rd # 202 Palm Springs CA 92262-6914

KINSMAN, SARAH MARKHAM, investment company executive; b. L.A., Oct. 1, 1951; d. Robert Starr and Barbara Ann (Yates) K.; m. Kevin H. Olsen, Oct. 15, 1984 (div.); 1 child, Robert Kinsman. AB, UCLA, 1973; MBA, Harvard U., Boston, 1976. Account officer Citibank's World Corp. Group, N.Y.C., 1976-79; fin. mgr. Union Pacific Corp., N.Y.C., 1980-86; v.p./sr. transactor Citibank, N.A., N.Y.C., 1986-88; v.p. Bank N.Y., N.Y.C., 1988-92; sr. v.p. GE Capital, N.Y.C., 1992—. Com. chmn. Jr. League, N.Y.C., 1988—; mem. women's com. Am. Cancer Soc., N.Y.C., 1988-90. Mem. Assn. for Corp. Growth, Women's Harvard Bus. Sch. Club N.Y.C., Harvard Bus. Sch. Club N.Y.C., Harvard Bus. Sch. Club N.J., Phi Beta Kappa. Home: 2 Rowlands Rd Flemington NJ 08822 Office: GE Capital 335 Madison Ave New York NY 10017

KINSOLVING, SYLVIA CROCKETT, musician, educator; b. Berkeley, Calif., Sept. 30, 1931; d. Harold Waldo and Louise (Effinger) Crockett; m. Charles Lester Kinsolving, Dec. 18, 1953; children: Laura Louise, Thomas Philip, Kathleen Susan. AA in Voice, Piano magna cum laude, No. Va. Community Coll., 1983; BA, U. Calif., Berkeley, 1953. Solo vocalist various chs. Va., 1982—; pvt. tchr. piano Vienna, Va., 1983—; singer, soloist Unity Ch., Oakton, Va., 1980—, St. Andrew's Anglican Ch., Alexandria, Va., 1985—; active numerous local musical prodns., 1959—. Tour leader Vienna Newcomers, 1980. Mem. PEO, U. Calif. Alumni Club, Fairfax West Music Fellowship (sec. 1990—), Phi Theta Kappa, Pi Beta Phi. Democrat. Episcopalian. Home: 1517 Beulah Rd Vienna VA 22182-1417

KINZIE, JEANNIE JONES, radiation oncologist; b. Great Falls, Mont., Mar. 14, 1940; d. James Wayne and Lillian Alice (Young) Jones; m. Joseph Lee Kinzie, Mar. 26, 1965 (div. Sept. 1982); 1 child, Daniel Joseph; m. Johnson Wachira, Oct. 7, 1991. Student, Oreg. State U., 1960; BS, Mont. State U., 1961; MD, Washington U., 1965; postgrad., U. Phoenix, 1995—. Diplomate Am. Bd. Radiology. Intern. in surgery U. N.C., Chapel Hill, 1965-66; resident in therapeutic radiology Washington U., St. Louis, 1968-71, instr. in radiology, 1971-73; asst. prof. in radiology Med. Coll. of Wis., Milw., 1973-75; asst. prof. in radiology U. Chgo., 1975-78, assoc. prof. in radiology, 1978-80; assoc. prof. of radiation oncology Wayne State U., Detroit, 1980-85; prof. radiology U. Colo., Denver, 1985—; dir. radiation oncology U. Hosp., Denver, 1985-91; cons. Denver Vets. Hosp., Denver Gen. Hosp., Rose Med. Ctr., FDA Ctr. for Devices and Radiologic Health, Denver; sci. adv. bd. Cancer League Colo., 1985-88; examiner Am. Bd. Radiology, 1985-88; adv. physician Colo. Med. Found., 1988—; chmn. faculty promotion com. U. Colo. Health Scis. Ctr., 1988-89. Assoc. editor Internat. Jour. Radiation Oncology Biology and Physics; contbr. articles to profl. jours.; chpts. to books. NIH grantee, 1973-75; Am. Coll. Radiology fellow, 1984. Mem. AMA, Colo. Med. Soc., Denver Med. Soc. (del. to Colo. Med. Soc. Ho. of Dels. 1989—), Am. Coll. Radiology, Colo. Radiol. Soc., Rocky Mountain Oncology Soc. (bd. dirs. 1989-93, pres. 1991-93), Soc. Head and Neck Surgeons, Am. Radium Soc., Am. Soc. Therapeutic Radiologists, Am. Cancer Soc. (bd. dirs. Denver unit 1986-87), Am. Soc. Clin. Oncology, Wilderness Med. Soc., Xeriscape Colo. Republican. Lutheran. Home: PO Box 2767 Evergreen CO 80439-2767 Office: Radiation Oncology Box A031 4200 E 9th Ave Denver CO 80262-0001

KIOUSIS, LINDA WEBER, artist; b. Cleve., June 25, 1939; d. Kenneth Philip and Helen Marie (Glawe) Weber; m. Thomas Joseph Kiousis, Jr., Aug. 27, 1971. BS, Case Western Res. U., 1961, MA, 1962; Diploma, Cleve. Inst. Art, 1962. Dir. United Cerebral Palsy Assn. Workshop, Cleve., 1963-68; art tchr. Parma (Ohio) Pub. Schs., 1969-71; profl. designer Am. Greetings, Cleve., 1968-69, 71-75; freelance artist Brushstroke, Cleve., 1980-83, Paramount, Pawtucket, R.I., 1985-87. Exhibited in solo show at Apple Gallery, Boardman, Ohio, 1990; group shows include Butler Inst. Am. Art, Youngstown, Ohio, 1987, Chelsea Galleries, Cleve., 1990, Glass Growers Gallery, Erie, Pa. 1991, Sandusky (Ohio) Cultural Ctr., 1992, Great No. Corp. Ctr., Cleve., 1992, Mansfield Art Ctr., Ohio, 1992; represented in permanent collections at Soc. Corp., Binney and Smith, Inc., U. Mo.-Columbia and Arches Paper, Children's Oncology Svcs. Northeastern Ohio, Inc., Ronald McDonald House. Mem. Ohio Watercolor Soc., Pa. Watercolor Soc., Watercolor U.S.A. Honor Soc., Watercolor West.

KIPPER, BARBARA LEVY, corporate executive; b. Chgo., July 16, 1942; d. Charles and Ruth (Doctoroff) Levy; m. David A. Kipper, Sept. 9, 1974; children: Talia Rose, Tamar Judith. BA, U. Mich., 1964. Reporter Chgo. Sun-Times, 1964-67; photo editor Cosmopolitan Mag., N.Y.C., 1969-71; vice chmn. Charles Levy Co., Chgo., 1984-86, chmn., 1986—; pres. Charles and Ruth Levy Found., Chgo.; bd. dirs. Naral Found. Trustee Spertus Inst. Jewish Studies; exec. com. Golden Apple Found.; mng. dir. Joffrey Ballet, N.Y.C. and L.A.; trustee Roosevelt U., Chgo., Chgo. Hist. Soc. Recipient Deborah award Com. Women's Equality, Am. Jewish Congress, 1992; Shap Shapiro Human Rels. award The Anti-Defamation League of B'nai B'rith, 1993. Mem. Com. of 200, Coun. on Founds., Chgo. Women in Philanthropy, Social Venture Network, Chgo. Found. for Women, Chgo. Network, Women's Issues Network, The Standard Club. Jewish. Office: Chas Levy Co 1200 N North Branch St Chicago IL 60622-2410

KIPPUR, MERRIE MARGOLIN, lawyer; b. Denver, July 24, 1962; d. Morton Leonard and Bonnie (Seldin) Margolin; m. Bruce R. Kippur, Sept. 7, 1986. BA, Colo. Coll., 1983; JD, U. Colo., 1986. Bar: Colo. 1986, U.S. Dist. Ct. Colo. 1986, U.S. Ct. Appeals (10th cir.) 1987. Assoc. Sterling & Miller, Denver, 1985-88, McKenna & Cuneo, Denver, 1989-94; v.p., gen. counsel First United Bank, Denver, 1994—; lectr. trial practice, bankruptcy U. Colo., chpt. 9 bankruptcy and Real Estate Settlement Procedures Act. Author: Student Improvement in the 1980's, 1984, (with others) Ethical Considerations in Bankruptcy, 1985, Partnership Bankruptcy, 1986, Colorado Methods of Practise, 1988. Contract liaison Jr. League Denver, 1992-94; bd. dirs. Bylaws Parliamentarian, 1994-95. Mem. ABA, Colo. Bar Assn., Colo. Women's Bar Assn., Denver Bar Assn., Am. Judicature Soc., Am. Bankruptcy Inst., Gamma Phi Beta, Phi Delta Phi, Pi Gamma Mu. Democrat. Office: First United Bank 8095 E Belleview Ave Englewood CO 80111

KIRBY, DOROTHY MANVILLE, social worker; b. Burke, S.D., Oct. 23, 1917; d. Charles Vietz and Gail Lorena (Coonen) Manville; m. Sigmund Kirby, July 11, 1941 (div. 1969); children; Paul Howard, Robert Charles. BA, Wayne State U., 1970, MSW, 1972. Cert. social worker, Mich. Pvt. practice social work Allen Park, Mich., 1973—; conduct seminars on stress, personal effectiveness and communication for various orgns., hosps. and bus. Pres. Allen Park Symphony Orch., 1990-92. Mem. AAUW, Am. Group Psychotherapy Assn., Nat. Assn. Social Workers (clin.), Nat. Assn. Marriage and Family Counseling, Mich. Assn. Marriage and Family Counseling (sec. 1982), LWV (pres. Allen Park 1965-66). Presbyterian. Lodge: Soroptimists. Home and Office: 15720 Wick Rd Allen Park MI 48101-1535

KIRBY, JANE CROCKER, editor; b. Cambridge, Mass., Aug. 4, 1953; d. Gerard Leo and Gertrude Marie (Duffy) K.; m. George Webb Gager, Apr. 21, 1990. BS, Marymount Coll., Tarrytown, 1975. Registered dietitian, Mass. Staff dietitian Mass. Gen. Hosp., Boston, 1976-77; asst. food editor Good Housekeeping Mag., N.Y.C., 1977-79, Ladies' Home Journal, N.Y.C., 1979; food editor Glamour mag., N.Y.C., 1980—. Author: Glamour's Gourmet on the Run, 1989. Recipient Tastemaker award French's/Seagrams, 1989, Louis Pasteur award Mass. Dietetic Assn., 1989. Mem. Am. Dietetic Assn., Women in Comm., Inc., Les Dames d'Escoffier (v.p. 1989-90), N.Y. Women's Culinary Alliance. Democrat. Roman Catholic. Office: Glamour Mag. 350 Madison Ave New York NY 10017-3704

KIRBY, MARY MARGARET, foundation administrator; b. Chgo., Aug. 25, 1947; d. William Thomas and Evelyn Catherine (McAdams) K. BA in Lit., Cabrini Coll., Radnor, Pa., 1969; student, U. Vienna, 1968; postgrad., U. Wis., 1970-72. Art dir. Buhrmester Advt., Chgo., 1973-75; art dir., advt. dir. Brotman Theatres, Chgo., 1975-80; art dir., assoc. film buyer Plitt Theatres, Chgo., 1980-86; dir. MacArthur Found. Libr. Video Project, Chgo., 1988—; mem. adv. bd. Ctr. for New TV, Chgo., 1990—; rschr. Zoetrope Studios, San Francisco, 1986. Mem. Assn. Ind. Video and Film Makers, Chgo. Internat. Film Festival (documentary film jury), New TV Awards (jury). Office: MacArthur Found Library Video Project 1807 W Sunnyside Ave Chicago IL 60640-5804

KIRBY, MARY WEEKS, elementary education educator, reading specialist; b. Cheverly, Md., Nov. 23, 1947; d. Isaac Ralph and Dorothea (Huppert) Weeks; m. William Charlie Kirby, Feb. 14, 1976; children: Joie, Fatimah, Tariq. B in Music Edn., James Madison U., 1969; MEd, Va. Commonwealth U., 1976; cert. Writers' Digest Sch., 1988. Cert. tchr. of music, reading and elem., Va. Music instr. Charles City County Schs., Providence Forge, Va., 1969-70, Hanover Learning Ctr., Va., 1970-72; sales cons. Boykins's Music Shop, Richmond, Va., 1972-74; elem. tchr. New Kent Pub. Schs., Va., 1974—, writing cons., 1980—; owner/operator Wacky Timepieces; presenter ednl. and reading workshops, 1980-82. Sponsor Young Authors' Workshop, New Kent, 1985—; co-chmn., presentor Parents Anonymous of Va., 1984-88; trustee Islamic Ctr. of Va., 1985-88, sec., 1981-85; active Boy Scouts Am., Girl Scouts U.S., U.S. Naval Sea Cadet Corps. Mem. NEA, New Kent Edn. Assn. (officer 1977-81, 90-92, 94—), Va. Edn. Assn., Internat. Reading Assn., Va. State Reading Assn., Richmond Area Reading Council (sec. 1982-83, bd. dirs. 1992—), Sigma Alpha Iota (life). Avocations: needlework, reading, swimming. Home: 1309 Bull Run Dr Richmond VA 23231-5103 Office: New Kent Pub Schs Quinton VA 23141

KIRBY, SANDRA LEE, software support consultant; b. Duluth, Minn., Feb. 28, 1965; d. Marvin Dennis and Charlene Luverne (Nylander) Gunnarson; m. Emmett Michael Kirby, Aug. 7, 1993. AA, Willmar (Minn.) C.C., 1985; BS, Mankato State U., 1987. Staff acct. K-Tel, Plymouth, Minn., 1987-88; acctg. supr. Indsl. Lumber, Mpls., 1988-93; project mgr. Data Systems & Mgmt., St. Paul, 1993-95; software support cons. Lawson Software, Mpls., 1995—. Mem. Inst. Mgmt. Accts.

KIRCHER, ANNE CATHERINE, communications consultant; b. Portland, Oreg., Dec. 27, 1962; d. John Lawrence and Helen (Morris) K. Student, U. N.Mex., 1981-83. Planning and rsch. clk. Albuquerque Pub. Schs., 1985-89, desktop publisher, designer, 1989-90; pub. info. and comm. cons. Presbyn. Healthcare Svcs., Albuquerque, 1990—. Mem. N.Mex. Soc. Healthcare Mktg. and Pub. Rels. (sec. 1994—). Home: 2600 Virginia NE Albuquerque NM 87110 Office: Presbyn Healthcare Svcs 5901 Harper Dr NE Albuquerque NM 87109

KIRCHMAN, BUDAGAIL SIMMS, realtor; b. Sandusky, Ohio, Dec. 1, 1935; d. William Alexander and Dorathy (Valentine) Simms; children: Kimberly, Kevin, Karen. Student, Stetson U., U. Ariz.; cert. completion, U. Ctrl. Fla., 1983. Cons. Fla. Software, Inc., Altamonte Springs, Fla., 1967-77; adminstrv. asst. Theatre on Park, Winter Park, Fla., 1976-77; coord. for Seminole County Jack Eckerd for Gov. Campaign, 1977-78; pres. Bud-Rock Enterprises, Inc., 1979-80; with The Wall St. Col., Orlando, Fla., 1980-85; realtor, assoc., property mgr. of rentals A & A Real Estate, 1985-87; v.p., project mgr.-office mgr. Jackson Corp., 1987-89; realtor, assoc., property mgr. rentals RE/MAX Space Coast, Inc. and RE/MAX Svc. Team, Titusville, Fla., 1989-94. Vol. Com. Woman for Rep. Party, Jr. League of Orlando and Winter Park; Sunday sch. tchr., vestry lay reader Episcopal Ch.; legis. chmn. Bus. and Profl. Women's Club Complete Park; dir. Ctrl. Fla. Zoo; mem. aviation com. Orlando C. of C.; pres. Kennedy Condo Assn.; past vol. Thrift Shop, Orlando, Children's Theatre; past Girl Scout and Brownie leader; others. Home: 524 S Hopkins Ave Titusville FL 32796

KIRCHNER, ELIZABETH PARSONS, clinical psychologist; b. Balt., July 20, 1928; d. Wilber Fay and Marguerite Victoria (Lindsay) Parsons; m. Henry Paul Kirchner, Nov. 11, 1950; children: Peter, James, Robert. BS, Cornell U., 1950; MS, Pa. State U., 1952, PhD, 1955. Lic. psychologist, Pa. Pvt. practice State College, Pa., 1958—; mem. faculty dept. psychology Pa. State U., University Park, 1965-80; psychologist Buffalo State Hosp., 1959-61, U. Buffalo Med. Sch., 1961-64; cons. Pa. Correctional System, 1972-80, VA Hosp., Altoona, Pa., 1973-76, State Hosp. System Pa., 1975-78, Office of Juvenile Probation and Parole, Bellefonte, Pa., 1983-85, Centre Community Hosp., State College, 1984—, Multiple Sclerosis Soc., Pa., 1989—. Author: Assertive Training in Prison, 1973, Be Your Own Therapist, 1981, Coping with Chronic Illness, 1988; contbr. articles to profl. jours., newspapers. Bd. dirs. state and local ACLU, 1968-75; co-founder Environ. Forum, State College, 1985. Grantee NIH, 1971-73. Mem. LWV, Am. Psychol. Assn., Coun. Human Svcs., Art Alliance Cen. Pa., Pa. Guild Craftsmen, Sierra Club (officer), Sigma Xi. Office: 111 S Allen St Ste 2D State College PA 16801-4735

KIRK, BETH ANGELIA, clinical nurse; b. Vincennes, Ind., June 27, 1956; d. Harry Lee and Helen Annabell (Ellis) K. LPN, Ivy Tech., 1977; AN, Ind. U., 1986. RN, Ind. Assoc. dir. nursing Village Nursing Home, Sullivan, Ind., 1977; staff nurse Vincennes Nursing Home, 1977-78, Terre Haute (Ind.) Regional, 1978-79, St. Vincent Hosp., Indpls., 1979-81, Meth. Hosp. of Ind., Indpls., 1981-88; coord. gallstone lithotripsy, nurse Meth. Hosp.-Meridian Med. Group, Indpls., 1988-90; rsch. nurse Nasser, Smith & Pinkerton Cardiology, Indpls., 1990-92; clin. specialist Cook, Inc., Bloomington, Ind., 1992—. Office: Cook Cardiology PO Box 489 Bloomington IN 47401

KIRK, CAROL, lawyer, state ethics director; b. Henry, Ill., Dec. 23, 1937; d. Howard P. and Mildred Root McQuilkin; m. Robert James Kirk, Aug. 20, 1961; children: Kathleen, Nancy, Sally. BS in Music Edn., U. Ill., 1966; JD, Ind. U., Indpls., 1989. Bar: Ind. Pvt. piano tchr., 1957-85, pub. sch. music tchr., 1960-62; dir. Ind. Stae Ethics Commn., Indpls., 1989—; pres. Coun. on Govtl. Ethics Laws, (Internat.), 1993-94. Exec. editor Articles & Prodn. Ind. Law Rev., 1988-89. Mem. Met. Devel. Commn., Indpls, 1982-87; chair person Pub. Radio Adv. Bd., Indpls., 1983-84, treas. Cmty. Svc. Coun., Indpls., 1988. Invitee to Nat. 4H Congress, Chogo., 1956; named 4 H Family of Yr., Washington Twp., 4-H, Indpls., 1980, Vol. of Week, Voluntary Action Ctr., Indpls., 1980. Mem. LWV (pres. Indpls. 1979-83), Ind. Bar Assn., Indpls. Bar Assn., Phi Alpha Delta, Mu Phi Epsilon. Home: 1135 W 32nd St Indianapolis IN 46260 Office: State Ethics Commn 402 W Wasahinton Rm W189 Indianapolis IN 46204

KIRK, CLARA JEAN, social services administrator; b. Miss., Mar. 11, 1941; d. Hallase Isby; children: Sabrina, David, Benjamin, McKinnely, Charmaine. Coptic religion degree (hon.), Universal Tng. Sch., Chgo., 1963. Sec. Englewood Devel. Co., Chgo., 1985-89, 7th Dist. Sterring Co., Chgo., 1986-90; v.p. Universal Tng. Sch., 1990—; pres., founder West Englewood United Orgn./Clara's House Shelter, Chgo., 1983—. Treas. YCOME, 1990—; mem. Gov.'s Advistory Coun., 1993-94, Nat. Coalition for Homeless, 1988—. Mem. NOW, Chgo. Women Philanthrophy. Mem. Coptic Ch. Home: 7009 S Paulina St Chicago IL 60636 Office: West Englewood United Orgn 1650 W 62d St Chicago IL 60636

KIRK, FLORA KAY STUDE, artist, accountant, insurance company official; b. San Diego, Feb. 16, 1944; d. Lawrence Wilbur Stude and Lois Eileen (Johnson) Plunkett; m. Bobby Gene Kirkpatrick, Feb. 16, 1960 (div. 1974); children: Jeffery Lane, Ladina B.J. Kirkpatrick Wingfield; m. Charles Robert Kirk, June 11, 1977 (div.); 1 child, Robert Marcel. Student, Western Tex. Coll., 1973-74, Ft. Hays (Kans.) State Coll., 1974-75, U. Nebr., Kearney, 1988; AA, Mid-Plains C.C., North Platate, Nebr., 1987. Decorator, Snyder, Tex., 1960-73; bookkeeper, office mgr. Tri-State Constrn., Snyder, 1973-75; acct. Aid Feed Yard, Syracuse, Kans., 1975-77; agt., broker Woodmen Accident & Life Ins. Co., Lincoln, Nebr., 1977—; owner, mgr., artist Kirk's Pottery and Painting Studio, North Platte, 1984—; acct., corp. sec.-treas. Profl. Ag Products, Inc., North Platte, 1988-93; chmn. bd. Artists Coop. Art & Gift Gallery, North Platte, 1987—; mem. artist Artists in Embassies Program, Washington, 1991, 92; artist Carolyn Nelson Galleries, Pasadena, Calif., 1992. One-woman show Art & Gift Gallery, 1987-93, Morin-Miller Galleries, N.Y.C., 1989, Gt. Plains Regional Med. Ctr., 1989-93, Bismark State Coll., Arroyo Theatre Gallery, L.A., 1993, 94; exhibited in group shows Fiske Planetarium, Boulder (recipient 1st place award 1993), Nat. Arts Club, N.Y.C., 1987, Ariel Gallery, N.Y.C., 1988, Univ. Place Gallery, Lincoln, 1990-93, Gallery 525, Loveland, Colo., 1990, 91, C.W. Post Coll., L.I. U., 1990, U. Colo., 1990, Jacob Javits Fed. Bldg. Gallery, N.Y.C., 1991, 92, U.S. Ho. Reps., Washington, 1992, 94, Antiquarium Gallery, Omaha, Artel Gallery, White Crane Gallery, Omaha, 1993, Cork Gallery, Lincoln Ctr. Performing Arts, N.Y.C., Arroyo Theatre Gallery, L.A., 1993, 94; represented in permanent collections Mus. Cultural Exch., Cairo, Prarie Peace Park, Lincoln, Bismark State Coll. Chmn. North Platte Arts and Humanities Coun., 1991-92; vol. Kerry for Pres. Campaign, North Platte, 1992. Mem. Soc. Exptl. Artists, Nat. Soc. Painters in Casein and Acrylic (assoc.), Nat. Watercolor Soc. (assoc.), Visual Individual United (1st place award 1992), The Artel (merit award 1991), North Platte Art Guild, Platter Painters Art Club (pres. 1987-88, 1st place award 1987-91), Assn. Nebr. Art Clubs, Phi Theta Kappa. Democrat. Home: 1021 W 4th St North Platte NE 69101-3715

KIRK, LINDA SUE, information systems professional; b. Omaha, Jan. 19, 1953; d. Clebert Franklin and Bonnie Jean (Rosenkrans) Steidley; m. Wayne A. Kirk, June 28, 1980; children: Megan M., Jonathan J. BBA, Doane Coll., 1993. Computer operator Nat. Crane, Waverly, Nebr., 1971-72, ops. supr., 1973-74, programmer, 1974, systems analyst, 1975-76, mgr., 1977-84; mgr. systems and programming Sandoz, Lincoln, Nebr., 1984-93, assoc. dir. systems and programming, 1992—, dir. info. systems, 1994—. Leader Brownie Troop, Girl Scouts of Am., Lincoln, 1992-93. Mem. Am. Prodn. and Inventory Control Soc. (treas. 1982-83). Home: 4733 Happy Hollow Ln Lincoln NE 68516 Office: Sandoz PO Box 83288 Lincoln NE 68501

KIRK, LYNDA POUNDS, biofeedback therapist, neurotherapist; b. Corpus Christi, Tex., Dec. 17, 1946; d. James Arthur and Elizabeth Pauline (Sanders) Pounds; m. Edward C. Randolph Kirk, June 10, 1967; children: Leslie Jennifer, Edward Christopher. BA, U. Tex., Austin, 1977. Therapist Austin (Tex.) State Hosp., 1977-80; dir. stress mgmt. The Hills Med./Sports Complex, Austin, 1980-82; founder, owner Austin Biofeedback Ctr., 1982—, Health Mastery Concepts, Austin, 1982—; cons. State of Tex., Austin, 1983—, City of Austin, 1985—, Lower Colo. River Authority, Austin, 1984—. Author: (book/cassette series) Regenerative Relaxation, 1981; Urological Applications of Biofeedback, Stress Mastery and Peak Performance, 1986. Bd. dirs. South Austin Polit. Action Coalition, 1986-87, South Austin Civic Club, 1983—, pres., 1987; bd. dirs., treas. Texans for the Preservation of Hist. Structures, 1990—; bd. dirs. Austin Ctr. for Attitudinal Healing, 1992—. Mem. Assn. Applied Psychophysiology and Biofeedback, Internat. Soc. for Study of Subtle Energies and Energy Medicine, Biofeedback Soc. Tex. (pres. 1995-96, mem. exec. bd., citation award 1989), Behavioral Medicine Soc. Am., Am. Holistic Med. Assn., Nat. Registry of Neurofeedback Providers, Soc. for Study of Neuronal Regulation, Acad. Cert. Neurotherapists, Phi Beta Kappa. Episcopalian. Home: 420 Brady Ln Austin TX 78746-5502 Office: Austin Biofeedback Ctr 4207 James Casey St Ste 301 Austin TX 78745-1193

KIRK, REA HELENE (REA HELENE GLAZER), school administrator, educator; b. N.Y.C., Nov. 17, 1944; d. Benjamin and Lillian (Kellis) Glazer; 3 stepdaughters. B.A., UCLA, 1966; M.A., Eastern Mont. Coll., 1981; postgrad. U. So. Calif. Life cert. spl. edn. tchr., Calif., Mont. Spl. edn. tchr., Los Angeles, 1966-73; clin. sec. speech and lang. clinic, Missoula, Mont., 1973-75; spl. edn. tchr., Missoula and Gt. Falls, Mont., 1975-82; br. mgr. YWCA of L.A., Beverly Hills, Calif., 1989-91; sch. adminstrn., ednl. coord. Adv. Schs. of Calif., 1991—; dir. Woman's Resource Ctr., Gt. Falls, Mont., 1981-82; dir. Battered Woman's Shelter, Rock Springs, Wyo., 1982-84; dir. Battered Victims Program Sweetwater County, Wyo., 1984-88, Battered Woman's Program, San Gabriel Valley, Calif., 1988; mem. Wyo. Commn. on Aging, Rock Springs; mem. Community Action Bd. City of L.A. Pres., bd. dirs. battered woman's shelter, Gt. Falls, Woman's Resource Ctr., Gt. Falls; founder, advisor Rape Action Line, Gt. Falls; founder Jewish religious svcs., Missoula; 4-H leader; hostess Friendship Force; Friendship Force ambassador, Wyo., Fed. Republic Germany, Italy; mem. YWCA Mont. and Wyo. Recipient Gladys Byron scholar U. So. Calif., 1992, Dept. Edn. scholar U. So. Calif., 1994, honors Missoula 4-H; recognized as significant Wyo. woman as social justice reformer and peace activist Sweetwater County, Wyo.; nominated Wyo. Woman of the Yr., 1981, 82. Mem. Council for Exceptional Children (v.p. Gt. Falls 1981-82), Assn. for Children with Learning Disabilities (Named Oustanding Mem. 1982), Phi Delta Kappa, Delta Kappa Gamma, Psi Chi. Democrat. Jewish.

KIRK, SUSAN KAY, voters registration official; b. Evansville, Ind., Oct. 23, 1948; d. Frank H. and Giovannina (Franklin) Tilford; m. Lennis M. Kirk Jr., Nov. 4, 1967 (div. Sept. 23, 1987); 1 child, Wayne F. Dental asst. Dr. Eugene Brinker, Evansville, 1967-69; sec. Vanderburgh County Auditorium, Evansville, 1969-70; dep. Vanderburgh County Treas. Office, Evansville, 1970-72; supr. Vanderburgh County Election Office, Evansville, 1972-84, co-mgr., 1990—; bd. dirs. Vanderburgh County Voters Registration, Evansville, 1984—. Mem. acctg. staff, mem. fin. com. Rep. Hdqrs., Evansville, 1993—. Recipient Sagamores of the Wabash award, Gov. Robert Orr, Ind., 1986. Mem. Eagles (Aux. 427), Motor Belles (pres. 1986-87). Republican. Office: Voters Registration 1 NW Ml King Jr Blvd Evansville IN 47708

KIRKHAM, M. B., plant physiologist, educator; b. Cedar Rapids, Iowa; d. Don and Mary Elizabeth (Erwin) K. BA with honors, Wellesley Coll.; MS, U. Wis., PhD. Cert. profl. agronomist. Plant physiologist U.S. EPA, Cin., 1973-74; asst. prof. U. Mass., Amherst, 1974-76, Okla. State U., Stillwater, 1976-80; from assoc. prof. to prof. Kans. State U., Manhattan, 1980—; guest lectr. Inst. Water Conservancy and Hydroelectric Power Rsch., Inst. Farm Irrigation Rsch., China, 1985, Inst. Exptl. Agronomy, Italy, 1989, Agrl. U., Wageningen, Inst. for Soil Fertility, Haren, The Netherlands, 1991, Massey U., New Zealand, 1991; vis. scholar Biol. Labs., Harvard U., 1990; vis. scientist environ. physics sect. dept. sci. and indsl. rsch., Palmerston North, New Zealand, 1991; participant Internat. Grassland Congress, New Zealand, 15th Internat. Congress Soil Sci., Acapulco, Mex., 15th Internat. Soil Tillage Rsch. Orgn. Conf., Denmark; spkr. Internat. Symposium on Plant Growth and Environ., Seoul, 1993; mem. peer rev. panel USDA, Nat. Rsch. Initiative, Washington, 1994. Cons. editor Plant and Soil Jour., 1979—; mem. editl. bd. Field Crops Rsch. Jour., 1983-91; contbr. over 160 articles and papers to sci. jours. NSF postdoctoral fellow U. Wis., 1971-73, E.I. du Pont de Nemours and Co. summer faculty fellow, 1976; grantee NSF, USDA, Office Water Rsch. and Tech., U.S. Dept. Energy, Dept. Sci. and Indsl. Rsch., New Zealand; invited paper Internat. Grassland Congress, New Zealand. Fellow AAAS, Am. Soc. Agronomy (editorial bd. 1985-90), Soil Sci. Soc. Am. (travel grantee to internat. congress Japan 1990), Royal Meteorol. Soc., Crop Sci. Soc. Am. (editorial bd. 1980-84); mem. Am. Soc. Plant Physiology (editorial bd. 1982-87), Am. Soc. Horticultural Sci., Internat. Soil Tillage Rsch. Organ., Internat. Soil Sci. Soc. (elected 1st vice chmn. commn. soil physics 1994—), Bot. Soc. Am., Am. Meteorol. Soc., Société Française de Physiologie Végétale, Japanese Soc. Plant Physiology, Scandinavian Soc. Plant Physiology, N.Y. Acad. Sci., Soc. for Exptl. Biology (London), Growth Regulator Soc. Am., Water Environment Fedn., Phi Kappa Phi, Gamma Sigma Delta, Sigma Xi. Home: 1420 Mccain Ln Apt 244 Manhattan KS 66502-4680 Office: Kans State U Evapotranspiration Lab Manhattan KS 66505-5501

KIRKIEN-RZESZOTARSKI, ALICIA MARIA, academic administrator, researcher, educator; b. Lodz, Poland; came to U.S., 1965; d. Leszek Tadeusz and Francesca Irene (Mortkowicz) Kirkien. MS in Chem. Engring., Polish U. Coll., London, 1951; PhD, U. London, 1955. Asst. prof. chemistry U. W.I., Jamaica, 1956-59, assoc. prof., 1959-61; assoc. prof. U. W.I., Trinidad, 1961-65; assoc. prof. Trinity Coll., Washington, 1966-68, prof. chemistry, 1968-92, chair chemistry dept., 1969-91, prof. emeritus, 1992—; sr. rsch. assoc. George Washington U. Med. Ctr., Washington, 1984. One person show at Trinity Coll., Washington, 1994; watercolors exhibited in show at Sorrento, Italy, 1994; contbr. numerous articles to profl. publs. Sec., treas. Polish Vets. ASSC, Washington, 1981-83. Named one of Outstanding Educators of Am., 1973, 75; Univ. Coll. Sr. Rsch. fellow, 1965-66, 71, UCSB, 1967. Fellow Royal Inst. Chem. (Gt. Britain); mem. Md. Fedn. Art (Critics Choice award for pottery 1992), Am. Chem. Soc. (adv. bd. Chem. and Engring. News 1978-81), Chem. Soc. Gt. Britain, Polish Inst. Arts and Scis. of N.Y., Phi Beta Kappa. Republican. Roman Catholic. Home: 407 Buckspur Ct Millersville MD 21108-1764 Office: Trinity Coll 125 Michigan Ave NW Washington DC 20010-2916

KIRKLAND, BERTHA THERESA, project engineer; b. San Francisco; d. Lawrence and Theresa (Kanzler) Schmelzer; m. Thornton C. Kirkland, Jr.,

Dec. 27, 1937 (dec. July 1971); children: Kathryn Elizabeth, Francis Charles. Ed. pub. schs., Calif. Supr. hosp. ops. Am. Potash & Chem. Corp., Trona, Calif., 1953-54; office mgr., estimator T.C. Kirkland, elect. contractor, San Bernardino, Calif., 1954-58, estimator, sec./treas., bd. dir., 1958-74; estimator design-installation engr. Add-M Electric, Inc., San Bernardino, 1972-82, v.p., 1974-82; estimator, engr. Corona (Calif.) Indsl. Electric, Inc., 1982-83; project engr. Fischbach & Moore, Inc., L.A., 1984-91; project engr. cons. Fischbach & Moor, Inc., L.A., 1993-94. Mem. Arrowhead Country Club. Episcopalian. Home: 526 Sonora Dr San Bernardino CA 92404-1762

KIRKLAND, GELSEY, dancer; b. Bethlehem, Pa., 1953; m. Greg Lawrence. Student, Sch. Am. Ballet. With N.Y.C. Ballet, 1968-74, soloist, 1969-72, prin. dancer, 1972-74; ballerina Am. Ballet Theatre, 1974-81, 82-84; free-lance ballet teacher; guest artist Royal Ballet, London, 1980, 86, Stuttgart Ballet, 1980; teacher, coach Am. Ballet Theatre, 1992—. Created roles in ballets including: Firebird, 1970, The Goldberg Variations, Scherzo fantastique, An Evening's Waltzes, The Leaves are Fading, Hamlet, The Tiller in the Field, Four Bagatelles, Stravinsky Symphony in C, Song of the Nightingale Connotations, others; guest dancer Royal Ballet, London, 1980, 81, 86, Stuttgart Ballet, 1980; appeared in TV show The Nutcracker, 1977; author: (with Greg Lawrence) Dancing on My Grave, 1986, The Shape of Love: Footnotes on My Life, 1990, (with Greg Lawrence) The Little Ballerina and Her Dancing Horse, 1993. Office: care Dubé Zakin Mgmt Inc 67 Riverside Dr Apt 3B New York NY 10024-6165*

KIRKLAND, SALLY, actress; b. New York, NY, Oct. 31, 1944; d. Sally Kirkland; m. Michael Jarrett, 1975 (div.), Mark Hebert, 1985 (div.). founder, Sally Kirkland Acting Workshop, 1983; partner (with Daniel and Mark Buntzman), Artists Alliance Prodns., 1988—. Films include: (actress) The Thirteen Most Beautiful Women, 1964, Blue, 1968, Futz!, 1969, Coming Apart, 1969, Brand X, 1970, Going Home, 1971, The Way We Were, 1973, Cinderella Liberty, 1973, The Sting, 1973, The Young Nurses, 1973, Big Bad Mama, 1974, Bite the Bullet, 1975, Crazy Mama, 1975, Pipe Dreams, 1976, A Star Is Born, 1976, Hometown U.S.A., 1979, Private Benjamin, 1980, The Incredible Shrinking Woman, 1981, Human Highway, 1982, Love Letters, 1983, Fatal Games, 1983, The Killing Touch, 1983, Anna, 1987 (Golden Globe Award, 1988, Academy Award nom., 1988), Talking Walls, 1987, Melanie Rose, 1989, Crack in the Mirror, 1989, Paint It Black, 1989, Cold Feet, 1989, Best of the Best, 1989, Revenge, 1990, Bullseye, 1991, Two Evil Eyes, 1991, JFK, 1991, In the Heat of Passion, 1991, The Player, 1992, Blast 'Em, 1992, Primary Motive, 1992, Double Threat, 1992, Hit the Dutchman, 1993, Hollywoodland Forever, 1993 (also assoc. prodr.); (actress, exec. prodr.), Mom, 1993, Cheatin' Hearts, 1993, Eye of the Stranger, 1993, Gunmen, 1994; TV appearances include: Death Scream, 1975, The Kansas City Massacre, 1975, Griffin and Phoenix: A Love Story, 1976, Captains and the Kings, 1976, Shaughnessey, 1976, Stonestreet: Who Killed the Centerfold Model?, 1977, The Georgia Peaches, 1980, Willow B: Women in Prison, 1980, Summer, 1984, Death and Taxes, 1989, Largo Desolato, 1990, Heatwave, 1990, The Haunted, 1991, Double Jeopardy, 1992, The Woman Who Loved Elvis, 1993, Double Deception, 1993; guest on Falcon Crest, Steel Magnolias, Roseanne. supporter of StarServe and Heartstrings. Office: c/o Dale C. Olson & Associaties Carthay Cirle Suite 340 6310 San Vicente Blvd Los Angeles CA 90048*

KIRKPATRICK, ANNE SAUNDERS, systems analyst; b. Birmingham, Mich., July 4, 1938; d. Stanley Rathbun and Esther (Casteel) Saunders; m. Robert Armstrong Kirkpatrick, Oct. 5, 1963; children: Elizabeth, Martha, Robert, Sarah. Student, Wellesley Coll., 1956-57, Laval U., Quebec City, Can., 1958, U. Ariz., 1958-59; BA in Philosophy, U. Mich., 1961. Systems engr. IBM, Chgo., 1962-64; sr. analyst Commonwealth Edison Co., Chgo., 1981—. Treas. Taproot Reps., DuPage County, Ill., 1977-80; pres. Hinsdale (Ill.) Women's Rep. Club, 1978-81. Club: Wellesley of Chgo. (bd. dirs. 1972-73). Home: 524 N Lincoln St Hinsdale IL 60521-3447 Office: Commonwealth Edison Co 72 W Adams St Ste 1122 Chicago IL 60603-5105

KIRKPATRICK, ELEANOR BLAKE, civic worker; b. Mangum, Okla., Mar. 10, 1909; d. Mack Barkley and Kathryn (Talbott) Blake; m. John Elson Kirkpatrick, June 20, 1932; 1 child, Joan Elson. B.A. in French, Smith Coll., 1931; D.Humanities (hon.), Oklahoma City U., 1968. Ptnr. Kirkpatrick Oil Co., Oklahoma City, Kirkpatrick Oil & Gas, Oklahoma City. Bd. cons. Kirkpatrick Ctr., Oklahoma City; treas. Kirkpatrick Found., Oklahoma City. Named to Okla. Hall of Fame, Okla. Heritage Assn., Oklahoma City, 1975, Woman of Yr., Redlands Coun. Girl Scouts, 1991; recipient Outstanding Woman Okla. Soroptimist Club, 1966, Evergreen Disting. Service award Nat. Assn. Mature People, Okla., 1982, Bd. Trustees award Omniplex Sci. Mus., Oklahoma City, 1984, Wall of Fame award Oklahoma City Pub. Sch. Found., 1990, Humanitarian award Nat. Conf. Christians and Jews, 1990, Humanitarian award Nat. Arthritis Found., Okla. chpt., 1993, Ptnrs. award World Neighbors, 1991, Pathmaker award Oklahoma County Hist. Soc., 1992. Co-founder, hon. pres. Alliance Française, Oklahoma City; bd. dirs. Okla. City Art Mus.; mem. Oklahoma City Univ. Socs. Avocation: backgammon. Office: Kirkpatrick Oil Co PO Box 268822 Oklahoma City OK 73126-8822

KIRKPATRICK, JEANE DUANE JORDAN, political scientist, government official; b. Duncan, Okla., Nov. 19, 1926; d. Welcher F. and Leona (Kile) Jordan; m. Evron M. Kirkpatrick, Feb. 20, 1955; children: Douglas Jordan, John Evron, Stuart Alan. AA, Stephens Coll., 1946; AB, Barnard Coll., 1948; MA, Columbia U., 1950, PhD, 1968; postgrad. (French govt. fellow), U. Paris Inst. de Sci. Politique, 1952-53; LHD (hon.), Georgetown U., 1981, U. Pitts., 1981, U. Charleston, 1982, Hebrew U., 1982, Colo. Sch. Mines, 1983, St. John's U., 1983, Universidad Francisco Marroquin, Guatemala, 1985, Coll. of William and Mary, 1986, U. Mich., 1988, and others, Syracuse U., 1994. Asst. prof. polit. sci. Trinity Coll., 1962-67; assoc. prof. polit. sci. Georgetown U., Washington, 1967-73, prof., 1973—, Leavey prof., 1978—; sr. fellow Am. Enterprise Inst. for Pub. Policy Rsch., 1977—; mem. cabinet U.S. permanent rep. to UN, 1981-85. Author: Elections USA, 1956, Perspectives, 1962, The Strategy of Deception: A Study in World-Wide Communist Tactics, 1963, Mass Behavior in Battle and Captivity, 1968, Leader and Vanguard in Mass Society; The Peronist Movement in Argentina, 1971, Political Woman, 1974, The New Presidential Elite, 1976, Dismantling the Parties: Reflections on Party Reform and Party Decomposition, 1978, The Reagan Phenomenon, 1983, Dictatorships and Double Standards, 1982, Legitimacy and Force (2 vols.), 1988, The Withering Away of the Totalitarian State, 1990; syndicated columnist, 1985—; contbr. articles to profl. jours.; editor, contbr. various pubs. Trustee Helen Dwight Reid Ednl. Found., 1972—, pres., 1990—. Recipient Disting. Alumna award Stephens Coll., 1978, B'nai B'rith Humanitarian award, 1982, Award of the Commonwealth Fund, 1983, Gold medal VFW, 1984, French Prix Politique, 1984, Dept. Def. Disting. Pub. Svc. medal, 1985, Bronze Palm, 1992, Disting. Svc. medal Mayor of N.Y.C., 1985, Presdl. Medal of Freedom, 1985, Jamestown Freedom award, 1990, Centennial medal Nat. Soc. DAR, 1991, Disting. Svc. award USO, 1994. Mem. Internat. Polit. Sci. Assn. (exec. coun.), Am. Polit. Sci. Assn. (Hubert Humphrey award 1988), So. Polit. Sci. Assn. Office: Am Enterprise Inst 1150 17th St NW Washington DC 20036-4603

KIRKPATRICK, SUSAN ELIZABETH D., political scientist; b. Niagara Falls, N.Y., Oct. 6, 1950; d. George Leo Jr. and Bette (Wadsworth) Dischinger; m. Allan Thomson Kirkpatrick, July 1, 1972; children: Anne Thomson, Robert Wadsworth. BA, U. Mich., 1971; MEd, Harvard U., 1975; PhD, Colo. State U., 1995. Social studies tchr. Walsingham Acad., Williamsburg, Va., 1972-74; adminstr. Wentworth Inst. Tech., Boston, 1977-80; polit. scientist Colo. State U., Fort Collins, 1987-91; asst. prof. polit. sci. U. No. Colo., Greeley, 1992—. City coun. mem. City of Fort Collins, 1986-93, mayor, 1990-93; exec. bd. Colo. Mcpl. League, 1990-93; chair state bd. Outdoors Colo. Trust, 1993—. Mem. Jr. League Fort Collins (newsletter editor 1984), Am. Polit. Sci. Assn., Women in Mcpl. Govt. (sec. 1989), Great Outdoors Colo. Trust (bd. dirs. 1993—, chair 1994—). Home: 2312 Tanglewood Dr Fort Collins CO 80525

KIRKWOOD, CAROL ELAINE, lawyer; b. Edmonton, Alta., Can., Oct. 6, 1952; came to U.S., 1954; d. Dale and Bonnyle (Watts) Bowen; m. Mark Edgar Hammons, July 23, 1981 (div. July 6, 1989); children: Mark Edgar II, Kenneth Dale; m. Victor Lee Kirkwood, Mar. 29, 1991. BA, U. Okla., 1974; JD, Oklahoma City U., 1979. Bar: Okla. 1979, Tex. 1994, U.S. Dist. Ct. (no., ea. and we. dists.) Okla. 1980, U.S. Dist. Ct. (no. dist.) Tex. 1991, U.St. Ct. Appeals (1oth cir.) 1979, U.S. Ct. Appeals (5th cir.) 1994. Dep. chief fed. divsn. and asst. atty. gen. Atty. Gen.'s Office, State of Okla., Oklahoma City, 1978-81; ptnr. Hammons, Wolking and Hammons, Oklahoma City, 1981-89; sr. civil rights atty. Office for Civil Rights, Dept. of Edn., Dallas, 1989—. Pres. Canadian County Dem. Women, Oklahoma City, 1984-86. Named Outstanding Bus. Woman, Canadian County Bus. Assn., 1988. Mem. AAUW, Okla. Women's Lawyers Assn. (pres. 1983-84), Bus. and Profl. Women's Assn. (pres. 1985-88). Democrat. Baptist. Office: Office for Civil Rights Dept of Edn 1200 Main St Bldg 2600 Dallas TX 75202-4305

KIRKWOOD, EILEEN JANET, real estate developer; b. Dec. 14, 1942; children: Terry, Todd S. Student, Pa. State U., Kans. State U., Drexel U. Pres. TNT Sales Corp., Inc., Warminster, Pa., 1965-79, Nat. Redemption Corp., Inc., Chestnut Hill, Pa., 1980-81; builder, developer Seacrest Towers, North Wildwood, N.J., 1981-85; pres. Kirkwood Devel., Inc.; joint owner, gen. ptnr. Roosevelt Plaza Shopping Ctr. Kirkwood Devel. Inc./TSM Properties, Phila., 1986; developer residential subdivs. Shore Plaza Shopping Ctr., Northampton County, Va., 1989—. Office: PO Box 750 Exmore VA 23350-0750

KIRKWOOD, NANCY LYNNE, elementary education educator; b. Phila., June 6, 1961; d. Donald Francis and Joan Isabelle (Miller) Sleesman; m. James Mace, Oct. 4, 1986. BS of Edn., Millersville State Coll., 1983. Tchr., pre-kindergarten, asst. dir. Kinder-Care Learning Ctr., Camp Hill, Pa., 1983-85; remedial tchr. Upper Dauphin Area Schs., Elizabethville, Pa., 1985-86; tchr. York (Pa.) City Schs., 1986-87, Kindergarten-Kinder Care, Newark, Del., 1987-88, Millersburg (Pa.) Area Sch. Dist., 1988—; pharmacy technician Rite Aid Corp. Camp Hill, Pa., 1988—; pvt. tutor, Millersburg, 1989—; color guard advisor Millersburg Area High Sch. Band, 1988-92, Upper Dauphin Area High Sch. Band, Elizabethville, 1992—. Active N.Y. Skyliners Drum and Bugle Corp, 1991—. Mem. Nat. Coun. Curriculum and Devel., Nat. Coun. for Social Studies, Pa. State Edn. Assn. (bldg. rep. 1992-93), Pa. State Edn. Assn., Millersburg Area Edn. Assn. Republican. Lutheran. Home: 394 Rising Sun Rd Millersburg PA 17061

KIRMSE, SISTER ANNE-MARIE ROSE, nun, educator, researcher; b. Bklyn., Sept. 23, 1941; d. Frank Joseph Sr. and Anna (Keck) K. BA in English cum laude, St. Francis Coll., 1972; MA in Theology with honors, Providence Coll., 1975; PhD in Theology, Fordham U., 1989. Joined Sisters of St. Dominic, Roman Cath. Ch., 1960; cert. elem. tchr., N.Y. Tchr. elem. sch. Diocese Bklyn., 1962-73; instr. adult edn. Diocese Rockville Centre, N.Y., 1974—; dir. religious edn. St. Anthony Padua Parish, East Northport, N.Y., 1975-83; dir. spiritual programs Diocese of Rockville Centre, 1979—; demonstration tchr. Paulist Press, N.Y.C., 1968-70; cons. Elem. Sch. Catechetical Assocs., Bklyn., 1971-73; mem. adj. faculty grad. program Sem. Immaculate Conception, Huntington, N.Y., 1979-80; adj. instr. Molloy Coll., Rockville Centre, 1985, St. Joseph's Coll., Patchogue, N.Y., 1990-91; asst. to Rev. Avery Dulles, Fordham U., Bronx, 1988—, rsch. assoc. Laurence J. McGinley chair in religion and soc., 1989—. Recipient Dominican scholarship Providence (R.I.) Coll., 1973, Kerygma award Diocese Rockville Centre, 1980, Presdl. scholarship Fordham U., 1988; McGinley fellow Fordham U., 1988. Mem. Cath. Theol. Soc. Am., L.I. Women's Ordination Conf., Amnesty Internat. Democrat. Roman Catholic. Office: Fordham U Keating Hall 322 Bronx NY 10458

KIRON, DHEENA, accountant; b. Staten Island, N.Y., June 30, 1967; d. Krisnamurthy and Meera Sankaran; m. Ravi Kiron, Aug. 21, 1989; 1 child, Nikhil Raj. BA, Fairfield U., 1984. Acct. Price Waterhouse, Stamford, Conn., 1989-91; mgmt. acct. Guinness Import Co., Stamford, 1991-93. Republican. Hindu. Home: 15 Obed Hts Rd Old Saybrook CT 06475-1214 Office: Guiness Import Co 6 Landmark Sq Stamford CT 06901-2704

KIRSCHNER, BARBARA STARRELS, pediatric gastroenterologist; b. Phila., Mar. 23, 1941; m. Robert H. Kirschner. M.D., Woman's Med. Coll. of Pa., 1967. Diplomate Am. Bd. Pediatrics; cert. in pediatric gastroenterology and nutrition. Intern, U. Chgo., 1967-68, resident, 1968-70; Wyler Children's Hosp., U. Chgo., 1984—, assoc. prof. pediatrics, 1984-88; prof. pediatrics and medicine, 1988—, mem. com. on nutrition and nutritional biology. Contbr. articles to profl. jours. Recipient Davidson award in pediatric gastroenterology Acad. Pediatrics, 1993. Mem. Am. Gastroenterologic Assn., N.Am. Soc. Pediatric Gastroenterology, Soc. Pediatric Rsch., Alpha Omega Alpha. Office: U Chgo Med Ctr 5825 S Maryland Ave MC-4065 Chicago IL 60637-1470

KIRSCHNER, RUTH BRIN, elementary education educator; b. Mpls., Mar. 12, 1924; d. Sigman and Leah (Chazankin) Brin; m. Norman Bernard Kirschner, June 19, 1949; children: Sally Jo Kirschner Minsberg, William Arthur. BS cum laude, U. Minn., 1946. Primary tchr. Robert Fulton Sch., Mpls., 1946-52; elem. tchr. St. Louis Park (Minn.) Schs., 1962—; tchr. religious sch. Adath Jeshurun Synagogue, Mpls., 1946-83, Bnai Emet Synagogue, St. Louis Park, 1989—; primary tchr. Latch Key, Mpls., 1986-88; nursery sch. tchr. Westwood Luth. Ch., St. Louis Park, 1989—; customer svc. rep. Am. Automobile Assn., St. Louis Park, 1985—. Sec. 4th Dist. Dem. Com., St. Louis Park, 1986-90; state del. St. Louis Park Dem. Com., 1986, 88, 90; mem. Cmty. Rels. coun. St. Louis Park, 1986-88; mem. St. Louis Park Charter Commn., 1993—; pres. Friends of St. Louis Park Libr., 1987-88, sec., 1990—; pres. St. Louis Park Friends, 1991-92, 93-94; del. to 44th Dist. Dem. Farmer Labor Exec. Bd.; alt. to 5th Dist. Dem. Farmer Labor ctrl. com.; apptd. mem. charter commn. St. Louis Park, 1993—; mem. Visions, 1994; bd. dirs. Suburban Alliance, 1994. Mem. AAUW (sec.-treas. 1970-72, parliamentarian 1974-76), Lioness (pres. Lyn-Lake 1985-86, v.p. 1993-95), Alpha Delta Kappa (state scholarship chmn. 1988-90, sec. Gamma chpt. 1990—). Jewish. Home: 3135 Colorado Ave S Minneapolis MN 55416-2050

KIRSCHSTEIN, RUTH LILLIAN, physician; b. Bklyn., Oct. 12, 1926; d. Julius and Elizabeth (Berm) K.; m. Alan S. Rabson, June 11, 1950; 1 child, Arnold. B.A. magna cum laude, L.I. U., 1947; M.D., Tulane U., 1951; D.Sc. (hon.), Mt. Sinai Sch. Medicine, 1984; LL.D. (hon.), Atlanta U., 1985; DSc (hon.), Med. Coll. Ohio, 1986; LHD (hon.), L.I. Univ., 1991. Intern Kings County Hosp., Bklyn., 1951-52; resident pathology VA Hosp., Atlanta, Providence Hosp., Detroit, Clin. Ctr., NIH, Bethesda, Md., 1952-57; dep. dir. NIH, Bethesda, Md., 1993—; fellow Nat. Heart Inst. Tulane U., 1953-54; asst. dir. div. biologics standards NIH, 1971-72; dep. dir. Bur. Biologics, FDA, 1972-73, dep. assoc. commr. sci., 1973-74; dir. Nat. Inst. Gen. Med. Scis., 1974-93; dep. dir. NIH, Bethesda, 1993—; acting assoc. dir. women's health Nat. Inst. Gen. Med. Scis., 1974-93; acting dir. NIH, 1993, dep. dir., 1993—; mem. Found. Advanced Edn. Scis.; chmn. grants peer rev. study team NIH; mem. Inst. Medicine, NAS, 1982—; co-chair, sec. Spl. Emphasis Oversight Com. on Sci. and Tech., 1989—; co-chair PHS Coordinating Com. on Women's Health Issues, 1990—; mem. Office of Tech. Assessment Adv. Com. on Basic Rsch., 1989—. Recipient Superior Svc. award, 1980, Presdl. Disting. Exec. Rank award, 1985, Pub. Svc. award Fedn. Am. Socs. for Exptl. Biology, 1993, Pub. Svc. award, 1993, Nat. Pub. Svc. award Am. Soc. for Pub. Adminstrn./Nat. Acad. Pub. Adminstrn., 1994, Roger W. Jones award for exec. leadership American U., 1994. Mem. AMA (Dr. Nathan Davis award 1990), Am. Assn. Immunologists, Am. Assn. Pathologists, Am. Soc. Microbiology, Am. Acad. Arts and Scis. Home: 6 West Dr Bethesda MD 20814-1510 Office: NIH Shannon Bldg 1 Rm 126 9000 Rockville Pike Bethesda MD 20892

KIRSHBAUM, JANE KAPLAN, lawyer; b. Mpls., Oct. 27, 1964; m. David B. Kirshbaum, July 1, 1990; 1 child, Abby Elizabeth. BA, U. Wis., 1987; JD, U. Minn., 1991. Bar: Minn. 1991. Pvt. practice Plymouth, Minn., 1991-92; corp. employment counsel Best Buy Co., Inc., Eden Prairie, Minn., 1993—. Mem. ABA, Minn. State Bar Assn., Hennepin County Bar Assn. Jewish. Office: Best Buy Co Inc 7075 Flying Cloud Dr Minneapolis MN 55344

KIRSTEIN, NAOMI WAGMAN, travel agency executive; b. Israel, Mar. 23, 1937; came to U.S., 1939; BS in Pub. Relations and Communications, Boston U., 1958. With H.E. Harris and Co., 1958-61; coop. advt. mgr. Polaroid Corp., 1961-63; office mgr., pub. relations exec. N.Y. State Council on Arts, 1963-65; pub. relations dir. Mass. chpt. Heart Fund Assn., 1965-66; freelance pub. relations dir. Edward A. Finch Co., 1967-69; freelance pub. relations dir., pres. Rima Newmar Inc., 1970-71; owner, mgr. Wagman Travel, 1972-77, Custom Travel, Brookline, Mass., 1977—; owner Custom Spa Vacations, 1986—; spa cons. Author: Sun and Daughter Signs, 1974; contbr. articles to profl. publs. Mem. Am. Friends of Israel Soldiers (dir. N.E. region), Women in Travel, Food and Travel Writers Assn. (press mem.), Internat. Spa Profl. Assn. (founder, bd. dirs., primary officer, sec., chmn. internat., membership coms.), Tau Mu Epsilon. Jewish. Office: Custom Spa Vacations 1318 Beacon St Brookline MA 02146-3793

KIRTLEY, HATTIE MAE, realtor; b. Ludlow, Okla., July 9, 1934; d. Adam Marion and Hattie Ethel (Buttler) Williams; m. Albert David Kirtley, Aug. 21, 1954; children: Sharon Ann, Gary Dean. BS in Secondary Edn., Northwest Mo. State U., 1970; postgrad., Mo. Western, 1972. Cert. Mo. realestate salesperson. Waitress Greyhound Bus Depot, Wichita, Kans., 1951; telephone operator S.W. Bell Telephone Co., Wichita, 1952; key punch operator Cudahy Packing Co., Wichita, 1954, Kans. Gas & Electric Co., Wichita, 1955, Kans. State Income Tax Bur., Topeka, 1956, M.F.A. Dairy Breeders, Springfield, Mo., 1957; tchr. vocat. home econs. South Holt High Sch., Oregon, Mo., 1969-70; tchr. various schs., Cosby, Denton, Mo., Kans., 1971-72, 72-74; real estate salesperson Hatfield Realty, Staley Realty, Gen. Realty, St. Joseph, Mo., 1980-82, 82-84; realtor San Antonio Realty and Landmark Realty, Savannah, Mo., 1984—. Charter mem. Riverview Bapt. Ch., Wichita, Kans., 1951, Sharon Bapt. Ch., 1952, Kings Hwy. Bapt. Ch., 1953. Recipient Citation United Cerebral Palsey of Mo., 1970. Mem. Mo. Bd. Realtors. Baptist.

KIRTLEY, JANE ELIZABETH, professional society administrator, lawyer; b. Indpls., Nov. 7, 1953; d. William Raymond and Faye Marie (Price) K.; m. Stephen Jon Cribari, May 8, 1985. BJ, Northwestern U., 1975, MS in Journalism, 1976; JD, Vanderbilt U., 1979. Bar: N.Y. 1980, U.S. Dist. Ct. (we. dist.) N.Y. 1980, D.C. 1982, U.S. Dist. Ct. D.C. 1982, U.S. Ct. Appeals (4th cir.) 1982, U.S. Ct. Claims 1982, U.S. Ct. Appeals (D.C. cir.) 1985, U.S. Supreme Ct. 1985. Assoc. Nixon, Hargrave, Devans & Doyle, Rochester, N.Y., 1979-81, Washington, 1981-84; exec. dir. Reporters Com. for Freedom of Press, Washington, 1985—; adj. faculty Am. U. Sch. Communication, 1988—. Exec. articles editor Vanderbilt U. Jour. Transnat. Law, 1978-79; editor: The News Media and the Law, 1985—, The First Amendment Handbook, 1987, 2d edit., 1989, 3d edit., 1992, Agents of Discovery, 1991, 93; columnist: NEPA Bull., 1988—, Virginia's Press, 1991—; mem. editorial bd. Govt. Info. Quarterly. Bd. dirs. 1st Amendment Congress, Denver, Inst. for Comm. Studies, Cath. U. Am., Washington, Student Press Law Ctr., Washington; mem. steering com. Libel Def. Resource Ctr., N.Y.C., adv. bd. Pa. Ctr. for the 1st Amendment, University Park, Freedom Forum 1st Amendment Ctr., Nashville. Mem. ABA, N.Y. State Bar Assn., D.C. Bar Assn., Sigma Delta Chi. Home: 724 Franklin St Alexandria VA 22314-4104 Office: Reporters Com Freedom of Press 1101 Wilson Blvd Ste 1910 Arlington VA 22209

KIRWAN, KATHARYN GRACE (MRS. GERALD BOURKE KIRWAN, JR.), retail executive; b. Monroe, Wash., Dec. 1, 1913; d. Walter Samuel and Bertha Ella (Shrum) Camp; m. Gerald Bourke Kirwan Jr., Jan. 13, 1945. Student, U. Puget Sound, 1933-34; BA, BS, Tex. Woman's U., 1937; postgrad., U. Wash., 1941. Libr. Brady (Tex.) Sr. High Sch., 1937-38, McCamey (Tex.) Sr. High Sch., 1938-43; mgr. Milady's Frock Shop, Monroe, 1946-62, owner, mgr., 1962-93. Meml. chmn. Monroe chpt. Am. Cancer Soc., 1961—; mem. Snohomish County Police Svcs. Action Coun., 1971; mem. Monroe Pub. Libr. Bd., 1950-65, pres. bd., 1964-65; mem. Monroe City Coun., 1969-73; mayor City of Monroe, 1974-81; commr. Snohomish County Hosp. dist. 1, 1970-90, chmn. bd. commrs., 1980-90; mem. East Snohomish County Health Planning Com., 1979—; mem. Snohomish County Law and Justice Planning Com., 1974-78, Snohomish County Econ. Devel. Coun., 1975-81, Snohomish County Pub. Utility Dist. Citizens Adv. Task Force, 1983; sr. warden Ch. of Our Saviour, Monroe, 1976-77, 89, sr. warden, 1976-77, 89-90; mem. Monroe Breast Cancer Screening Project community planning group Fred Hutchinson Cancer Rsch. Ctrs., 1991-93. With USNR, 1943-46. Mem. AAUW, U.S. Naval Inst., Ret. Officers Assn., Naval Res. Assn., Bus. and Profl. Women's Club (2d v.p. 1980-82, pres. 1983-84), Washington Gens., Snohomish County Pharm. Aux., C. of C. (pres. 1972), Valley Gen. Hosp. Guild (pres. 1994), VAlley Gen. Hosp. Found. (sec. 1993—). Episcopalian. Home: 538 S Blakely St Monroe WA 98272-2402 Office: 108 W Main St Monroe WA 98272-1810

KISBY, LINDA JOY, nurse; b. Somers Point, N.J., May 10, 1961; d. Charles Ernest III and Margaret Ann (Storm) K. Student, Covenant Coll., 1979-80, Washington Bible Coll., 1980-83, Atlantic C.C., Mays Landing, N.J., 1990-92; ADN, Gloucester C.C., Sewell, N.J., 1993. RN, N.J. Pvt. duty nurse Kimberly Quality Care, 1989-94; nurse West Jersey Health Sys., Berlin, N.J., 1989-92, Atlantic City Med. Ctr., 1992—. With Names Project, Washington, 1992. Mem. Nat. League for Nurses (advocacy mem.), Assn. Nurses in AIDS Care (assoc.). Republican. Home: 39 Gulph Mill Rd Somers Point NJ 08244

KISCADEN, SHEILA M., state legislator; b. St. Paul, Apr. 21, 1946; d. Harvey Richard and Bea Mae (Conway) Martineau; m. Richard Craig Kiscaden, Sept. 12, 1970; children: Michael, Karen. BS in Edn., U. Minn., 1969; MS in Pub. Adminstrn., U. So. Calif., L.A., 1986. Tchr. So. St. Paul Secondary Schs., Minn., 1969-70, Jobs 70, Rochester, Minn., 1970-71; regional coord. Planned Parenthood, Rochester, Minn., 1971-76; vol. svc. coord. Olmsted County, Rochester, Minn., 1977-80, human svc. planner, 1980-82, legis. liaison, 1982-85; prin. Cons. Collaborator, Rochester, Minn., 1987—; senator Minn. State Senate, St. Paul, 1992—. Bd. dirs. Ability Bldg. Ctr. Found. Bd., Rochester, Minn., 1989-94, Dyslexia Inst. Minn., Rochester, Minn., 1989-94; team leader Global Vols., 1989—. Fulbright scholar, 1970. Mem. Phi Beta Kappa. Republican. Home: 724 11th St SW Rochester MN 55902 Office: Minn State Senate State Office Bldg # 143 Saint Paul MN 55155

KISER, ELIZABETH ROBERTSON, marketing professional, entrepreneur, inventor; b. Norfolk, Va., Dec. 30, 1962; d. William Dell and Marion Brown (Bowen) Robertson; m. Marshall Kent Kiser, June 4, 1983. BA magna cum laude, W.Va. U., 1987. Sales rep. The Office Place, Denver, 1988-90; mktg. coord. Olver Svcs. Inc., Blacksburg, Va., 1990-91; market rschr. Marshall Miller & Assoc., Bluefield, Va., 1992; mktg. coord. Einhorn Yaffee Prescott, PC, White Plains, N.Y., 1993, Cooper, Robertson & Ptnrs., N.Y.C., 1993-94; pres., mfr. Elizabeth's Originals, Ltd., Riverdale, N.Y., 1993—. Contbr. articles to profl. mags.; fashion accessory patentee of Aroolu Scarf Shapers. Leader, recycling feasibility author Bluefield 2000, 1992. Mem. Soc. Mktg. Profl. Svcs., Exec. Female, Phi Beta Kappa, Phi Alpha Theta. Democrat. Episcopalian. Address: 1714 Downey St Radford VA 24141

KISER, KAREN MAUREEN, medical technologist, educator; b. St. Louis, Sept. 28, 1951; d. Arthur John and Elizabeth M. (Boyer) Meier; m. Winston Kiser, July 21, 1973; children: Cynthia Kay, Jessica Lea. BS in Med. Tech., S.E. Mo. State U., 1973; MA in Health Care Edn., Cen. Mich. U., 1984. Part-time lab. asst. Luth. Med. Ctr., St. Louis, 1970-71; part-time lab. technician Jewish Hosp., St. Louis, 1972-73, med. technologist, 1973-77; assoc. prof., edn. coord. St. Louis C.C. at Forest Park, 1977—; on-site surveyor Nat. Accrediting Agy. for Clin. Lab. Sci., Chgo., 1986, 94; self-study reviewer, 1994; reviewer W.B. Saunders Co., Phila., 1986-91; speaker in field. Leader Girl Scouts U.S., 1986-90, 91-92, co-leader, 1990—; assoc. advisor Explorer Scouts, 1978-81; capt. United Way, St. Louis, 1989, 90, 93. Recipient Emerson Electric award for Teaching Excellence, 1993, Gov.'s award for Excellence in Teaching, 1993. Mem. NEA, Am. Soc. for Clin. Lab. Sci., Am. Soc. for Microbiology, Mo. Soc. for Med. Tech., Mo. Edn. Assn., Mo. Assn. Cmty. and Jr. Colls., Am. Soc. Clin. Pathologists. Office: Saint Louis CC 5600 Oakland Ave Saint Louis MO 63110-1316

KISER, NAGIKO SATO, retired librarian; b. Taipei, Republic of China, Aug. 7, 1923; came to U.S., 1950; d. Takeichi and Kinue (Sōma) Sato; m. Virgil Kiser, Dec. 4, 1979 (dec. Mar. 1981). Secondary teaching credential, Tsuda Coll., Tokyo, 1945; BA in Journalism, Trinity U., 1953; BFA, Ohio State U., 1956, MA in Art History, 1959; MLS, cert. in library media, SUNY, Albany, 1974. Cert. community coll. librarian, Calif., cert. jr. coll. tchr., Calif., cert. secondary edn. tchr., Calif., cert. tchr. library media specialist and art, N.Y. Pub. rels. reporter The Mainichi Newspapers, Osaka, Japan, 1945-50; contract interpreter U.S. Dept. State, Washington, 1956-58, 66-67; resource specialist Richmond (Calif.) Unified Sch. Dist., 1968-69; editing supr. CTB/McGraw-Hill, Monterey, Calif., 1969-71; multimedia specialist Monterey Peninsula Unified Sch. Dist., 1975-77; librarian Nishimachi Internat. Sch., Tokyo, 1979-80, Sacramento City Unified Sch. Dist., 1977-79, 81-85; sr. librarian Camarillo (Calif.) State Hosp. and Devel. Ctr., 1985-93. Editor: Short Form Test of Academic Aptitude, 1970, Prescriptive Mathematics Inventory, 1970, Tests of Basic Experience, 1970. Mem. Calif. State Supt.'s Regional Coun. on Asian Pacific Affairs, Sacramento, 1984-91. Library Media Specialist Tng. Program scholar U.S. Office Edn., 1974. Fellow Internat. Biog. Assn. (life); mem. ALA, Am. Biog. Inst. (life, dep. gov. 1988—), Claif. Libr. Assn., Med. Libr. Assn., Asunaro Shogai Kyoiku Kondankai (Lifetime Edn. Promoting Assn., Japan), The Mus. Soc., Internat. House of Japan, Matsuyama Sacramento Sister City Corp., Japanese Am. Citizens League, UN Assn. U.S., Ikenobo Ikebana Soc. Am., L.A. Hototogisu Haiku Assn., Ventura County Archeol. Soc., Internat. Platform Assn., Internat. Soc. Poets. Mem. Christian Science Ch. Office: Camarillo State Hosp & Devel Ctr Profl Libr PO Box 6022 Camarillo CA 93011-6022

KISH, KATHERINE MARIA, management consultant company executive; b. Hattiesburg, Miss., May 26, 1943; d. Louis S. and Maria (Rusynyk) K.; m. William D. Kraft, May 11, 1985; 1 stepchild, William D. Kraft III. BA, Allegheny Coll., 1965; MAT in Teaching, Antioch U., 1969. Coordinator, tchr. Lakewood (Ohio) Bd. Edn., 1965-68; cons. Fgn. Policy Assn., Pathe Newsfilm, Internat. Film Found., 1968-69; mktg. coordinator NBC Ednl. Enterprise, N.Y.C., 1969-74; dir. mktg. and spl. projects Harcourt Brace Jovanovich, Inc., N.Y.C., 1974-78; v.p. planning The Singer Co., Stamford, Conn., 1978-81; v.p. mktg. and sales Faxon Co., Westwood, Mass., 1981-82; pres. Market Entry, Inc., Cranbury, N.J., 1982—. Contbr. chpt. to book. Williams Coll. fellow, 1967, U. Hawaii fellow, 1968. Mem. ASTD, Assn. Media Producers (bd. dirs., officer 1976-81), Planning and Devel. Forum, Nat. Assn. Women Bus. Owners (N.J. program chmn., bd. dirs., v.p., pres.-elect), Nat. Found. Women Bus. Owners (bd. dirs.), N.J. Assn. Women Bus. Owners, Princeton Area C. of C. (chair edn. com., bd. dirs.). Democrat. Mem. Eastern Orthodox Ch. Home and Office: Market Entry Inc 18 George Davison Rd Cranbury NJ 08512

KISMARIC, CAROLE LEE, editor, writer, book packaging company executive; b. Orange, N.J., Apr. 28, 1942; d. John Joseph and Alice Felicia (Gruskos) K.; m. Charles Vincent Mikolaycak, Oct. 1, 1970. B.A. in Psychology, Pa. State U., 1964. Reporter, writer Parkersburg News, W. Va., summers 1960, 61; reporter, writer UPI, Columbus, Ohio, summer 1962; writer Conde Nast Publs., N.Y.C., 1964; picture editor, assoc. editor Time Life Book Div., N.Y.C., 1965-75; editorial dir. Aperture, Inc., N.Y.C., 1976-85; freelance pub. cons., editor, writer N.Y.C., 1985—; co-founder, co-owner book packaging co. Lookout Books, N.Y.C., 1990—; founder Lookout with Marvin Heiferman, comms. co.; mem. visual arts and policy panels NEA, Washington, 1977-81, 93; tchr. grad. sch. photography program Sch. Visual Arts, N.Y.C., 1990—. Author: Duel of the Ironclads, 1969, The Boy Who Tried to Cheat Death, 1971, The Rumor of Pavel and Paali, 1988, A Gift from Saint Nicholas, 1988, Forced Out: The Agony of the Refugee in Our Time, 1989, I'm So Happy, 1990, My Day, 1993, Talking Pictures, 1994; author, editor: The Photography Catalogue, 1976; contbr. numerous articles to profl. jours.; assoc. curator, From the Picture Press, Mus. Modern Art, 1973; co-curator travelling exhbns. L.A. Mcpl. Art Gallery: Forced Out: The Agony of the Refugee in Out Time, 1989-93, Internat. Ctr. of Photography, Talking Pictures, 1994—. Recipient award Communications Graphics Assn., 1971, 72; Book of Yr. award Am. Inst. Graphic Arts, 1974, 75, 91. Home: 64 E 91st St New York NY 10128-1359 Office: Lookout Books 1024 6th Ave New York NY 10018

KISNER, AUDREY HILDEGARD, advertising manager; b. San Diego, Dec. 10, 1964; d. Robert Kisner and Inga (Schroeder) Grove. Student, U. Santa Cruz, 1987; BA, U. Calif., Berkeley. Advt. mgr. Guess? Inc., L.A. and N.Y.C., 1987—. Office: Guess? Inc 150 S Rodeo Dr # 270 Beverly Hills CA 90212

KISSANE, MARY ELIZABETH, communications executive, consultant; b. Westchester, N.Y.; d. Thomas Patrick and Marion (O'Shea) K. BA cum laude, Iona Coll., 1982, MS in Corp. Communications with honors, 1990. Asst. to CFO Aspen Systems Corp., 1984; account supr. Charles Barker, Inc., 1984-86; communications mgr. BET Fin., Inc., 1987; assoc. Bliss, Barefoot & Assocs., 1988; asst. v.p. Georgeson & Co., 1989-92, v.p., 1992—. Home: 91 Summit Ave Bronxville NY 10708-1814 Office: Georgeson & Co Wall St Plz New York NY 10005

KISSIN, EVA H., educator; b. N.Y.C., Feb. 12, 1923; d. Samuel A. Hertz and Rose Harlam Rubenstein; m. Benjamin Kissin, July 1, 1950; 1 child, Ruth Helman. BA magna cum laude, Syracuse U., 1943; MA in English Edn., NYU, 1949, MA in Lit., 1973. Formerly tchr. Hunter Coll. High Sch., Ramaz Sch., Marymont Coll., N.Y.C., to 1983; adj. asst. prof. lit. NYU, N.Y.C., 1983—. Program chair for docents Bklyn. Mus., 1960-70. Mem. Cosmopolitan Club, Phi Beta Kappa. Home: 525 E 86th St New York NY 10028

KISTIAKOWSKY, VERA, physics researcher and educator; b. Princeton, N.J., Sept. 9, 1928; d. George Bogdan and Hildegard (Moebius) K.; m. Gerhard Emil Fischer, June 16, 1951 (div. 1970); children: Marc Laurenz Fischer, Karen Marie Fischer. A.B., Mt. Holyoke Coll., 1948, Sc.D. (hon.), 1978; Ph.D., U. Calif.-Berkeley, 1952. Staff scientist U.S. Naval Rsch. Def. Lab., San Francisco, 1952-53; fellow U. Calif.-Berkeley, 1953-54; rsch. assoc. Columbia U., N.Y.C., 1954-57, instr., 1957-59; asst. prof. Brandeis U., Waltham, Mass., 1959-62, adj. assoc. prof., 1962-63; staff mem. MIT, Cambridge, 1963-69, sr. rsch. scientist, 1969-72; prof. physics, 1972—. Author: Atomic Energy, 1959; One Way Is Down, 1967; contbr. articles on nuclear and elem. particle physics and astrophysics to profl. jours. Dir. Coun. for a Liveable World, Boston, 1983—. Recipient Centennial award Mt. Holyoke Coll., 1972. Fellow AAAS, Am. Phys. Soc. (councilor 1974-77); mem. Assn. for Women in Sci. (pres. 1982-83), Phi Beta Kappa (vis. scholar 1983-84, senator 1988—), Sigma Xi (lectr. 1990-92). Office: MIT 6-216 77 Massachusetts Ave Cambridge MA 02139-3594

KISTLER, DARCI ANNA, ballet dancer; b. Riverside, Calif., June 4, 1964; d. Jack B. and Alicia (Kinner) K.; m. Peter Martins, 1992. Student, Profl. Children's Sch., N.Y.C., Sch. Am. Ballet, N.Y.C. With N.Y.C. Ballet, 1980—, soloist, 1981-82, prin. dancer, 1982—; tchr. Sch. of Am. Ballet, 1994—. Performed roles in Andantino, Gershwin Concerto, Valse-Scherzo, Piano-Rag Music, Pastorale, Suite for Histoire du Soldat, N.Y.C. Ballet's Balanchine Celebration, 1993, Symphonic Dances, 1994, Apollo, 1994; performed in Film George Balanchine's The Nutcracker, 1993; danced with the Kirov, St. Petersberg, Russia; made appearence in PBS-TV Dance in America; author: Ballerina: My Story, 1993. Recipient Capezio Dance award, 1991, Dance Mag. award, 1992. Office: NYC Ballet NY State Theater 20 Lincoln Ctr Pla New York NY 10023

KISTNER, THELMA A., accountant, tax preparer; b. Everett, Pa., Aug. 20, 1942; d. Matthew Jr. and Catherine Elizabeth (Gamble) Swindell; m. Bernard Robert Kistner, Sept. 1, 1963. B in Mgmt. Acctg., LaSalle U., 1991. Enrolled agent. Acct. R.G. Blasiole, Pub. Acct., Greensburg, Pa., 1960-64; prin. T.A. Kistner, Acctg., Greensburg, 1960—; sr. acct., tax preparer Pitts. divsn. Supervalu, Inc. (formerly Charles Bros. Co.), Belle Vernon, Pa., 1964—; mem. adj. faculty LaSalle U., Mandeville, Pa., 1992—. Author: (manuals) Retail Accounting Manual, 1983, Retail Supermarket Front-End Procedures, 1984. Tchr. project bus. Jr. Achievement, Greensburg, 1991-92. Mem. Nat. Soc. Tax Profls. (cert.), Pa. Soc. Pub. Accts., Inst. Mgmt. Acctg. Sec. Home and Office: RD 11 Box 762 Greensburg PA 15601

KISVARSANYI, EVA BOGNAR, retired geologist; b. Budapest, Hungary, Dec. 18, 1935; came to U.S., 1957; d. Kalman and Ilona (Simon) Bognar; m. Geza Kisvarsanyi, July 3, 1956; 1 child, Erika G. Student, Eotvos Lorand U., Budapest, 1954-56; BS in Geology, U. Mo., Rolla, 1958, MS, 1960. Geologist Mo. Geol. Survey, Rolla, 1959-68; from rsch. geologist to sect. chief Mo. Dept. Natural Resources/Geol. Survey Program, Rolla, 1968-90; asst. dir. MODNR/Geol. Survey Program, Rolla, 1990-93; cons. Sarasota, Fla., 1993—. Editor geological guidebooks, 1976—; contbr. articles to profl. jours. Fellow Geol. Soc. Am. (mem. rep. 1985-93), Soc. Econ. Geologists (rsch. com. 1989-92); mem Sigma Xi (pres. Rolla chpt. 1990-91).

KISZKA, SONIA ANN, nurse practictioner, educator; b. N.Y.C., Apr. 4, 1938; d. Hermann William and Gertrude (Hohensteiner) Schumann; m. David F. Madden, Feb. 16, 1957 (div. Oct. 1975); children: David F., Michael P., Daniel J., Lisa M.; m. Lawrence F. Kiszka, Nov. 27, 1975; stepchildren: Lawrence V., Patricia, Valerie. AAS in Nursing cum laude, Maria Coll., Albany, N.Y., 1973; BS, Skidmore Coll., 1991; postgrad., St. Michael's Coll., Colchester, Vt., 1991—. Nat. cert. nurse practitioner in adult medicine, physician asst. Intensive/critical care nurse, dept. medicine Ellis Hosp., Schenectady, 1979-80, nurse practitioner dept. medicine, 1980-82, dir employee/student health svcs., 1982-85; asst. dir. health svc., health educator Skidmore Coll., Saratoga Springs, N.Y., 1985-89; dir. health svc. St. Michael's Coll., Colchester, Vt., 1989—; speaker colls. and profl. orgns. Contbr. articles to profl. jours. Bd. dirs. N.Y. State Coalition Nurse Practitioners, 1985-90. Mem. Vt. State Nurses Assn. (bd. dirs. 1990-93), Am. Coll. Health Assn. (Vt. rep., mem. task force on campus violence and human dignity, rep./speaker internat. conf. on sexual assault on campus), Vt. Nurse Practitioners Assn. (v.p. 1991-92). Roman Catholic. Office: St Michaels Coll Health Svc Winooski Park Colchester VT 05439

KITAGAWA, AUDREY EMIKO, lawyer; b. Honolulu, Mar. 31, 1951; s. Yonoichi and Yoshiko (Nagaishi) K. B.A. cum laude, U. So. Calif., 1973; J.D., Boston Coll., 1976. Bar: Hawaii, 1977, U.S. Dist. Ct. Hawaii, 1977. Assoc., Rice, Lee & Wong, Honolulu, 1977-80; sole practice, Honolulu, 1980—. Exec. editor Internat. Law Jour., 1976. Mem. Historic Hawaii Found., 1984. Mem. Hawaii Bar Assn., ABA, Assn. Trial Lawyers Am., Japan-Hawaii Lawyers Assn. (v.p. 1982—), Law Office Mgmt. Discussion Group, Hawaii Lawyers Care, Phi Alpha Delta. Republican. Club: Honolulu. Office: 820 Mililani St Ste 615 Honolulu HI 96813-2936

KITCHELL, B. KATHRYN, business owner; b. Tulsa, Oct. 8, 1949; d. James Joseph and Betty Helen (McClelland) Lawson; m. Robert G. Kitchell, Aug. 18, 1973. A in Bus., Okla. State U., 1969; grad., Stenotype Inst., Phila., 1977; student, U. Pa., 1982-83. Registered profl. reporter. Owner Jud. Data Svcs., Narberth, Pa., 1978—. Mem. Penn Valley Civic Assn., Union League of Phila. Mem. NAFE, U.S. Ct. Reporters Assn., Nat. Ct. Reporters Assn., Am. Mgmt. Assn., Pa. Ct. Reporters Assn., Penn Valley Womens Club, Kiwanis (City Line). Home: 622 Righters Mill Rd Penn Valley PA 19072

KITCHENS, PAMELA JANE, critical care nurse, educator; b. Birmingham, Ala., May 26, 1956; d. James E. and Katherine A. (Carlton) Waldrop; m. James Lewis, June 28, 1974; children: Heather, Tracy. ADN, Jefferson State Jr. Coll., Birmingham, 1978; BSN, U. Ala., Birmingham, 1988, postgrad., 1993—. Cert. BLS instr., ACLS instr., Ala. affiliate faculty mem. Am. Heart Assn. Home care nurse Home Health, Inc., Birmingham, 1984-85; clin. staff nurse, critical care Bapt. Med. Ctr.-Montclair, Birmingham, 1989-91, discharge planner, 1988-89; edn. coord. in critical care Ea. Health System Inc., Birmingham, 1989—. Mem. AACN (Excellence in Critical Care Edn. award Greater Birmingham chpt. 1992), Am. Heart Assn. (nurse edn. com.), Ala. Soc. for Healthcare Edn. and Tng. (chairperson ECC subcom.-Ala. affiliate 1990—, pres. region 2 1993-94), Emergency Nurses Assn. Office: Ea Health System Inc 50 Medical Park Dr E Birmingham AL 35235-3401

KITHCART, BEVERLY FRICK, educator, school counselor; b. Karnes City, Tex., Jan. 20, 1951; d. Jarrell Reese and Wilma Louise (Whigham) Frick; m. David E. Kithcart, July 14, 1973; children: Jacob Bryce, Lucas John. BS, Tex. Tech. U., 1972, MS, 1976; EdD, U. Houston, 1991. Lic. profl. counselor, Tex. Home econs. tchr. Crosbyton (Tex.) Ind. Sch. Dist., 1973-75; head resident Tex. Tech. U., Lubbock, 1975-76; asst. dir. San Juan Daycare, Austin, Tex., 1977; home econs. tchr San Benito (Tex.) Ind. Sch. Dist., 1977-78; home econs. tchr. Harlingen (Tex.) Consolidated Ind. Sch. Dist., 1986-88, teen parenting coord., 1988—; instr. U. Tex., Brownsville, 1991; presenter teen parenting programs and teen pregnancy issues to concerned groups in Tex., 1991—. Bd. dirs. Family Crisis Ctr., Harlingen, 1984-86, sec., bd. dirs. Horizon, Harlingen, 1988-89; state rep. Tex. Summit on Adolescent Pregnancy Prevention, Austin, 1992; chairperson Youth Leadership Harlingen, 1992-93. Named Family Educator of Month, Planned Parenthood, Cameron and Willacy Counties, 1982; grantee: Tex. Edn. Agy., 1990-93, 91-94. Mem. ACA, ASCD, PTA (pres. 1983—), Am. Sch. Counselor Assn., Jr. League of Harlingen, Tex. Assn. Sch.-Age Parents (bd. dirs.). Home: 1809 Mockingbird Ln Harlingen TX 78550-4363 Office: Harlingen Cons Ind Sch Dist 1201 Marshall St Harlingen TX 78550-4362

KITT, EARTHA MAE, actress, singer; b. North, S.C., Jan. 26, 1928; d. John and Anna K.; m. William McDonald, June 1960 (div.); 1 child, Kitt Shapiro. Grad. high sch. Soloist with Katherine Dunham Dance Group, 1948; night club singer, 1949—, appearing in France, Turkey, Greece, Egypt, N.Y.C., Hollywood, Las Vegas, London, Stockholm; actress: (plays) Dr. Faustus, Paris, 1951, New Faces of 1952, N.Y.C., Mrs. Patterson, N.Y.C., 1954, Shinbone Alley, N.Y.C., 1957, Timbuktu, 1978, Blues in the Night, 1985, (films) including New Faces, 1953, Accused, 1957, Anna Lucasta, 1958, Mark of the Hawk, 1958, St. Louis Blues, 1957, Saint of Devil's Island, 1961, Synanon, 1965, Up The Chastity Belt, 1971, Dragonard, Ernest Scared Stupid, 1991, Boomerang, 1992, also 2 French films, also numerous TV appearances including Cat Woman role in Batman series; star: (documentary film) All By Myself, 1982; albums include In Person at the Plaza, 1987, My Way: A Musical Tribute to Rev. Dr. Martin Luther King Jr., 1987; author: Thursday's Child, 1956, A Tart Is Not a Sweet, Alone With Me, 1976, I'm Still Here, 1990, Confessions of a Sex Kitten, 1991. Named Woman of Year Nat. Assn. Negro Musicians, 1968. Office: care Eartha Kitt 888 7th Ave 37th Fl New York NY 10106*

KITTLITZ, LINDA GALE, small business owner; b. Waco, Tex., Jan. 22, 1949; d. Rudolf Gottlieb and Lena Hulda (Landgraf) K. BA in Art, Tex. Tech. U., 1971. Sales rep. Taylor Pub. Co., San Francisco and Dallas, 1972-73, Internat. Playtex Corp., San Francisco, 1974-76, Faberge Inc., San Francisco, 1976-78, Soflens div. Bausch and Lomb Co., San Francisco, 1978-81, Ben Rickert Inc., San Francisco, 1981-86; mfr.'s sales rep. Dearing Sales, San Francisco, 1986-87; sales rep. Golden West Envelope Co., San Francisco, 1987-89; sales assoc. R.G. Creations, Inc., San Francisco, 1989-90; owner, mgr. Kittlitz & Assocs. (Custom Packaging and Printing Solutions), San Francisco, 1990—. Mem. NAFE, Profl. Women's Network San Francisco (bay area chpt.). Democrat. Baptist.

KITZMILLER, THELMA JEAN, systems analyst, sheep farmer; b. Hanover, Pa., Jan. 20, 1949; d. George Truman and Dorothy Virginia (Gist) Warehime; widowed; 1 child, Paul Dennis. Grad., high sch., 1967. Clk.-stenographer, sec. AEC, Germantown, Md., 1967-72, contract reports analyst, 1972-74, computer systems analyst, 1974-75; computer specialist Energy Rsch. and Devel. Adminstrn., Germantown, 1975-77; procurement info. systems analyst Dept. of Energy, Germantown, 1977-78; computer systems analyst Dept. of Navy, Mechanicsburg, Pa., 1978, computer specialist, 1978-80, lead systems analyst, 1980—. Leader Pa. 4-H Clubs, York, 1989—. Recipient various bus. awards. Office: Naval Sea Logistics Ctr PO Box 2060 5450 Carlisle Pike Mechanicsburg PA 17055-2411

KIVEL, MAXINE KESSLER (MICKIE KIVEL), public health advisor; b. Sebewaing, Mich., Aug. 8, 1934; d. Morris Bernard Kessler and Irene Nass; m. Joseph Kivel, June 16, 1956 (div. 1982); children: Karen Sue, Patricia Lynn. BA, U. Mich., 1956. Tech. writer, editor Atlanta Rsch. Corp., Alexandria, Va., 1965-68, Bell Tel. Labs., Whippany, N.J., 1968-69, U.S. FDA, Rockville, Md., 1970—. Editor: (tech. newsletter) Radiol. Health Bull., 1975-93, Med. Devices Bull., 1992-93, Mammography Matters, 1993—. Represented U.S. in World Bridge Olympiad, 1978, 86, 90. Recipient N.Am. Bridge Championship (Women's Pairs), 1986. Mem. Am. Contract Bridge League (life).

KIVELSON, MARGARET GALLAND, physicist; b. N.Y.C., Oct. 21, 1928; d. Walter Isaac and Madeleine (Wiener) Galland; m. Daniel Kivelson, Aug. 15, 1949; children: Steven Allan, Valerie Ann. AB, Radcliffe Coll., 1950, AM, 1951, PhD, 1957. Cons. Rand Corp., Santa Monica, Calif., 1956-69; asst. to geophysicist UCLA, 1967-83, prof., 1983—, also chmn. dept. earth and space scis., 1984-87; prin. investigator of magnetometer, Galileo Mission, Jet Propulsion Lab., Pasadena, Calif., 1977—; overseer Harvard Coll., 1977-83; mem. adv. coun. NASA, 1987-93; chair atmospheric adv. com. NSF, 1986-89, Com. Solar and Space Physics, 1977-86, com. planetary exploration, 1986-87, com. solar terrestial phys., 1989-92; mem. adv. com. geoscis. NSF. Editor: The Solar System: Observations and Interpretations, 1986; co-editor: Introduction to Space Physics, 1995; contbr. articlels to profl. jours. Named Woman of Yr., L.A. Mus. Sci. and Industry, 1979, Woman of Sci., UCLA, 1984; recipient Grad. Soc. medal Radcliffe Coll., 1983, 350th Anniversary Alumni medal Harvard U. Fellow AAAS, Am. Geophysics Union; mem. Am. Phys. Soc., Am. Astron. Soc., Internat. Inst. Astronautics (corr. mem.). Office: UCLA Dept Earth & Space Scis 6843 Slichter Los Angeles CA 90095-1567

KIVOWITZ, SHEILA, clinical social worker; b. N.Y.C., May 22, 1932; d. Jack and Roslyn (Berlin) Tobin; m. Bernard Kivowitz, Feb. 21, 1954; children: Meryl, Sharon, Susan. BA, Queens Coll., 1979; MSW, SUNY, Stony Brook, 1984. Cert. social worker. Paralegal For Our Children & Us, Hicksville, N.Y., 1980-81; clin. social worker Cath. Charities Mental Health Ctr., Commack, N.Y., 1986-91, Bay Shore, N.Y., 1991—. Mem. NASW, N.Y. State Soc. Clin. Social Work Psychotherapists (affiliate), South Shore Assn. for Ind. Living (past mem. exec. bd.). Democrat. Jewish. Home: 160 Allen Rd Rockville Centre NY 11570-1218

KIZER, CAROLYN ASHLEY, poet, educator; b. Spokane, Wash., Dec. 10, 1925; d. Benjamin Hamilton and M. (Ashley) K.; m. Stimson Bullitt, Jan., 1948 (div.); children: Ashley Ann, Scott, Jill Hamilton; m. John Marshall Woodbridge, Apr. 11, 1975. BA, Sarah Lawrence Coll., 1945; postgrad. (Chinese govt. fellow in comparative lit.), Columbia U., 1946-47; studied poetry with Theodore Roethke, U. Wash., 1953-54; LittD (hon.), Whitman Coll., 1986, St. Andrew's Coll., 1989, Mills Coll., 1990, Wash. State U., 1991. Specialist in lit. U.S. Dept. State, Pakistan, 1964-65; first dir. lit. programs Nat. Endowment for Arts, 1966-70; poet-in-residence U. N.C. at Chapel Hill, 1970-74; Hurst Prof. Lit. Washington U., St. Louis, 1971; lectr. Spring Lecture Series Barnard Coll., 1972; acting dir. grad. writing program Columbia, 1972; poet-in-residence Ohio U., 1974; vis. poet Iowa Writer's Workshop, 1975; prof. U. Md., 1976-77; poet-in-residence, disting. vis. lectr. Centre Coll., Ky., 1979; disting. vis. poet East Wash. U., 1980; Elliston prof. poetry U. Cin., 1981; Bingham disting. prof. U. Louisville, Ky., 1982; disting. vis. poet Bucknell U., Pa., 1982; vis. poet SUNY, Albany, 1982; prof. Columbia U. Sch. Arts, 1982; prof. poetry Stanford U., 1986; sr. fellow in humanities Princeton U., 1986; vis. prof. writing U. Ariz., 1989, 90, U. Calif., Davis, 1991; Cole Royalty chair U. Ala., 1995; participant Internat. Poetry Festivals, London, 1960, 70, Yugoslavia, 1969, 70, Pakistan, 1969, Rotterdam, Netherlands, 1970, Knokke-le-Zut, Belgium, 1970, Bordeaux, 1992, Dublin, 1993, Glasgow, 1994; sr. fellow humanities council Princeton U., 1986. Author: Poems, 1959, The Ungrateful Garden, 1961, Knock Upon Silence, 1965, Midnight Was My Cry, 1971, Mermaids in the Basement: Poems for Women, 1984 (Gov.'s award State of Wash. 1985, San Francisco Arts Commn. award 1986), Yin: New Poems, 1984 (Pulitzer prize in poetry 1985), The Nearness of You, 1987 (Theodore Roethke prize, 1988); Proses: On Poems & Poets, 1994, Picking & Choosing: Prose on Prose, 1995; editor: Woman Poet: The West, 1980, Leaving Taos, 1981, The Essential Clare, 1993, 100 Great Poems by Women, 1995; translator Carrying Over, 1988; founder, editor: Poetry N.W., 1959-65; contbr. poems, articles to Am. and Brit. jours. Recipient award Am. Acad. and Inst. Arts and Letters, 1985, Pres.'s medal Ea. Washington U., 1988. Mem. Amnesty Internat., PEN, Poetry Soc. Am. (Frost medal 1988, Masefield prize 1983), Acad. Am. Poets. Episcopalian. Address: 19772 8th St East Sonoma CA 95476

KIZER, JOANNE CALAMAN, real estate broker, small business owner; b. Sayre, Pa., Feb. 26, 1951; d. John T. Calaman and Mary E. (Gallagher) Farley; m. John F. Kizer III, June 3, 1972; children: John F. IV, James D. BS in Foods and Nutrition cum laude, Marywood Coll., 1973. Lic. real estate broker, Pa., GRI designation. Dietitian Polk (Pa.) State Sch. & Hosp., 1973-74; caseworker Bradford County Bur. Children's Svcs., Towanda, Pa., 1974-78; home and sch. visitor Towanda Area Schs., 1978-79; co-owner Designs for Living, Towanda, 1979-81; assoc. real estate agent Helen Dennis Real Estate, Towanda, 1981-83; assoc real estate broker Henry Dunn, Inc., Towanda, 1983-93; real estate broker, prin. JoAnne Kizer Real Estate, Towanda, 1994—. Trustee Guthrie Health Care System, Sayre, Pa., 1988—; bd. dirs. Robert Packer Hosp., 1989—; den leader Cub Scouts Pack 16 Boy Scouts Am., Towanda, 1991—; treas. Towanda Women's Civic League, 1976—. Mem. AAUW, Nat. Assn. Realtors, Pa. Assn. Realtors, Bradford County Bd. Realtors. Roman Catholic. Home: 6 Foster Rd Towanda PA 18848-1317

KJELGAARD, JULIA DEE, artist, educator; b. Bellefonte, Pa., Aug. 23, 1952; d. William Lewis and Barbara (Reichert) K.; m. F. Stephen Dobson, Feb. 14, 1982. BA, U. Calif., Santa Barbara, 1975; MFA, U. Mich., 1987. Resident printmaker Pyramid Atlantic, Washington, 1988-90; vis. asst. prof. U. Mich., Ann Arbor, 1990-91; asst. prof. U. Wyo., Laramie, 1991-94. Exhibited in numerous nat. and internat. exhbns. including the 5th Internat. Biennial Print Exhbn., Taipei, Taiwan (Hon. Mention), Internat. Triennial, Krakow, Poland, 1991, 4th Internat., Wakayama, Japan, 1991, 18th Inter Biennial, Ljubljana, Yugoslavia, 1989. Fellow Kala Inst., Berkeley, Calif., 1993-94; travel and rsch. grantee U. Wyo., 1992; recipient Best of Show award Ann Arbor Art Assn., 1987, Jurors award Hilo (Hawaii) Nat. Drawing Exhibit, 1991. Mem. Coll. Art Assn., Calif. Soc. Printmakers, So. Graphics Coun., Women's Caucus for the Arts. Home: 550 Dumas Dr Auburn AL 36830

KJOS, VICTORIA ANN, lawyer; b. Fargo, N.D., Sept. 17, 1953; d. Orville I. and Annie J. (Tanberg) K. BA, Minot State U., 1974; JD, U. N.D., 1977. Bar: Ariz. 1978. Assoc. Jack E. Evans, Ltd., Phoenix, 1977-78, pension and ins. cons., 1978-79; dep. state treas. State of N.D., Bismarck, 1979-80; freelance cons. Phoenix, 1980-81, Anchorage, 1981-82; asst. v.p., v.p., mgr. trust dept. Great Western Bank, Phoenix, 1982-84; assoc. Robert A. Jensen P.C., Phoenix, 1984-86; ptnr. Jensen & Kjos, P.C., Phoenix, 1986-89; assoc. Allen, Kimerer & LaVelle, Phoenix, 1989-90, ptnr., 1990-91; dir. The Yoga and Fitness Inst., Phoenix, 1994—; lectr. in domestic relations. Contbr. articles to profl. jours. Bd. dirs. Arthritis Found., Phoenix, 1986-89, v.p. for chpt. devel., 1988-89; bd. dirs. Ariz. Yoga Assn., 1993—, v.p., 1993—. Mem. ABA, ATLA, Ariz. Bar Assn. (exec. coun. family law sect. 1988-91), Maricopa Bar Assn. (sec. family law com. 1988-89, pres. family law com. 1989-90, judge pro tem 1989-91), Ariz. Trial Lawyers Assn.

KLAJBOR, DOROTHEA M., lawyer, consultant; b. Dunkirk, N.Y., Dec. 2, 1915; d. Joseph M., Sr., and Susan R. (Schrantz) K.; student George Washington U., 1949-52; JD, Am. U., Washington, 1956. Bar: D.C., 1957. From legal asst., legis. atty., atty., 2d asst. to Chief U.S. Marshal, civil rights compliance officer Dept. of Justice, Washington, 1938-70; supr. Town of Dunkirk, N.Y., 1973-76; mem. N.Y. State Liquor Authority, Buffalo, 1976-80. Bd. dirs. Center for Women Govt., Albany, N.Y., 1978-82, Dunkirk Sr. Citizens Ctr., 1983; mem. Chautauqua County Task Force on Aging, 1972-73, Town of Dunkirk Indsl. Devel. Agy., 1972-76, Chautauqua County Planning Bd., 1973-76, No. Chautauqua County Intermcpl. Planning Bd., 1974-76, Chautauqua County Overall Econ. Devel. Planning Bd., 1974-76, Literacy Vols., 1972-76, West Dunkirk Vol. Fire Dept., 1973—; adv. bd. Dunkirk Sr. Citizens, 1974-76; mem. women's div. N.Y. State Democratic Com. Mem. Am. Bar Assn. (life), Fed. Bar Assn., D.C. Bar, Women's Bar Assn. D.C. (life), AAUW, Nat. Lawyers Club, Cath. Daus. Am., No. Chautauqua Club Assocs. (life), Dunkirk Hist. Soc. (life), Kappa Beta Pi. Roman Catholic. Clubs: Chautauqua County Dem. Women's (treas. 1974-76), Zonta Internat. (chmn. com. on status of women; Industry Person of Yr. award 1980, Calista Jones award for advancement rights of women 1984), Fredonia Dem. Home: 91 Forest Pl Fredonia NY 14063-1701

KLAMERUS, KAREN JEAN, pharmacist, researcher; b. Chgo., Aug. 10, 1957; d. Robert Edward and Jane Mary (Nawoj) K.; m. Frederick P. Zeller. BS in Pharmacy, U. Ill., 1980; PharmD, U. Ky., 1981. Registered pharmacist Ky., Ill., Pa. Staff pharmacist Haggin Meml. Hosp., Harrodsburg, Ky., 1980-81, Regional Med. Ctr., Madisonville, Ky., 1982; critical care liasion Regional Med. Ctr., Madisonville, 1982; clin. pharmacist resident U. Nebr., Omaha, 1983; clin. pharmacist cardiothoracic surgery U. Ill., Chgo., 1983-88, clin asst. prof. dept. pharmacy practice, 1983-86, asst. prof., 1986-88, departmental affiliate dept. pharmaceutics, 1986-88; sr. pharmacokineticist Wyeth-Ayerst Rsch., Phila., 1988-91, asst. dir. clin. pharmacology, 1991—; cons. Dimensional Mktg. Inst., Chgo., 1983-88, Channing Weinbergs' Co., Inc., N.Y.C., 1983-88. Fellow Am. Coll. Clin. Pharmacy (mem. indsl. rels. com. 1995); mem. Am. Soc. Clin. Pharmacol. and Therapeutics, Mid-Atlantic Coll. Clin. Pharmacy (sec. 1991, pres. 1992-94). Office: Wyeth-Ayerst Rsch PO Box 8299 Philadelphia PA 19101-0082

KLAPPER, HARRIET THELMA, accountant; b. N.Y.C., May 20, 1929; d. Norbert and Steffie (Weinberger) Salzinger; m. Martin Klapper, Apr. 4, 1948; children: Iris, Norman. AAS, Sullivan County Community Coll., Loch Sheldrake, N.Y., 1967; BS magna cum laude, Fairleigh Dickinson U., 1973, MBA with honors, 1976. CPA, N.Y. Controller Sullivan County Community Coll., 1970-78; assoc prof. acctg. SUNY, New Paltz, N.Y., 1978-82; ptnr. Wilen, Klapper & Glassman CPAs, New Windsor, N.Y., 1982—. Mem. AICPA, N.Y. State Soc. CPA's, Assn. Women CPA's. Office: Wilen Klapper & Glassman 296 Temple Rd New Windsor NY 12553

KLAPPER, MOLLY, lawyer, educator; b. Berlin, Germany; came to U.S., 1950; d. Elias and Ciporah (Weber) Teicher; m. Jacob Klapper; children: Rachelle Hannah, Robert David. BA, CUNY, MA, 1964; PhD, NYU, 1974; JD, Rutgers U., 1987. Bar: N.J. 1987, U.S. Dist. Ct. N.J. 1987, N.Y. 1989, U.S. Dist. Ct. (so. and ea. dists.) N.Y. 1989, D.C. 1989, U.S. Supreme Ct. 1991, U.S. Ct. Appeals (2d cir.) 1992. Prof. English Bronx C.C., CUNY, 1974-84; law intern U.S. Dist. Ct. N.J., Newark, 1987; law sec. to presiding judge appellate div. N.J. Supreme Ct., Springfield, 1987-88; assoc. Wilson, Elser, Moskowitz, Edelman and Dicker, N.Y.C., 1988—. Author: The German Literary Influence on Byron, 1974, 2d edit., 1975, The German Literary Influence on Shelley, 1975; contbr. to profl. publs. NEH fellow, 1978; grantee Am. Philos. Soc., 1976. Mem. ABA (bankruptcy com.), N.Y. Bar Assn. (bankruptcy com.), D.C. Bar Assn. Office: Wilson Elser Moskowitz Edelman and Dicker 150 E 42d St New York NY 10017

KLARIC, BETTY, lawyer; b. Yorkville, Ohio, Nov. 25, 1931; d. Rade and Mary (Yurkovic) K. BA in Journalism, Ohio State U., 1953; JD magna cum laude, Cleve.-Marshall Coll. Law, 1984. Bar: Ohio 1984. Staff writer Brotherhood Locomotive Engrs., Cleve., 1953-55; reporter, environ. writer, 1st woman asst. city editor Cleve. Press, 1955-82; jud. law clk. 8th Dist. Ct. Appeals, Cleve., 1984-86; labor rels. specialist State Employment Rels. Bd., Cleve., 1986-88; staff atty. Office of Solicitor of Labor, U.S. Dept. Labor, Cleve., 1988—. 1st woman pres. in 33 yr. history Local 1, Am. Newspaper Guild, Cleve., 1967. Recipient Schlenz medal Water Pollution Control Fedn., 1979, Ohio Gov.'s award Gov. James Rhodes, 1976, Presdl. citation Pres. Richard Nixon, 1971, Nat. Headliner award Women in Comm., 1972, Edward J. Meeman Conservation award Scripps-Howard Found., 1969. Mem. ABA, Cleve. Bar Assn., ACLU. Office: US Dept Labor Office of Solicitor 881 Fed Office Bldg 1240 E 9th St Cleveland OH 44199

KLASING, SUSAN ALLEN, environmental toxicologist, consultant; b. San Antonio, Sept. 10, 1957; d. Jesse Milton and Thelma Ida (Tucker) Allen; m. Kirk Charles Klasing, Mar. 3, 1984; children: Samantha Nicole, Jillian Paige. BS, U. Ill., 1979, MS, 1981, PhD, 1984. Staff scientist Life Scis. Rsch. Office, Fedn. Am. Socs. Exptl. Biology, Bethesda, Md., 1984-85; assoc. dir. Alliance for Food and Fiber, Sacramento, 1986; postgrad. rschr. U. Calif., Davis, 1986-87; project dir. Health Officers Assn. Calif., Sacramento, 1987-89; cons. Klasing and Assocs., Davis, Calif., 1989—; mem. expert com. for substances-of-concern San Joaquin Valley Drainage Program, Sacramento, 1987, follow-up task force, 1990-91, drainage oversight com., 1992-94. Author: (chpt.) Consideration of the Public Health Impacts of Agricultural Drainage Water Contamination, 1991. Mem. AAAS. Office: Klasing and Assocs 515 Flicker Ave Davis CA 95616-0178

KLASSEK, CHRISTINE PAULETTE, behavioral scientist; b. Chgo., Dec. 28, 1947; d. Walter and Pauline (Bogolin) Strom; m. Alexander George Klassek, June 14, 1969; 1 child, Margaret Mary. BA in Applied Behavioral Sci., Nat. Louis U., Lombard and Evanston, Ill., 1989; cert. in leadership, Nat. Louis U., 1993. Asst. juvenile libr. Bolingbrook (Ill.) Fountaindale Libr., 1974-79; behavior modification counselor J.P. Kennedy Sch. for Exceptional Children, Palos Park, Ill., 1982-86; tchr. spl. edn. Little Friends Orgn., Downers Grove, Ill., 1986-89; program dir. Carmelite Carefree Village, Darien, Ill., 1989—. Treas. Young Democrats Will County, 1972; chmn., pres. bd. dirs. Dem. Women's Com. DuPage Twp., Ill., 1973-76; leader Campfire Girls Assn.; mem. adv. coun. case mgmt. Little Friends Assn., 1988; cert. pastoral min. care St. Charles Borromeo Pastoral Ctr.; vol. Pub. Action to Deliver Svc., Helping Hands Rehab. Ctr., Ray Graham; active Cath. Coun. Women; bd. dirs., mem. human rels. com. J.P. Kennedy Sch. Exceptional Children, 1985-86. Recipient cert. of appreciation Am. Cancer Soc., Hinsdale, Ill., 1991. Mem. LWV, Assn. Sr. Svc. Providers, Ill. Activity Profl. Assn., Ill. Activity Profl. Assn., Surburban Activity Therapists Assn., Jaycees. Roman Catholic. Home: 240 Davis Ln Bolingbrook IL 60440-2369 Office: Carmelite Carefree Village 8419 Bailey Rd Darien IL 60561-5361

KLATZKY, ROBERTA LOU, psychology educator; b. Duluth, Minn., Jan. 6, 1947; d. Arnold and Rena (Breslin) K.; m. Peter James Gesiwitz, Dec. 1, 1972. BS, U. Mich., 1968; PhD, Stanford U., 1972. Asst. prof. U. Calif., Santa Barbara, 1972-77, assoc. prof., 1977-82, prof. psychology, 1982-93; prof., dept. head Carnegie Mellon U., Pitts., 1993—. Author: Human Memory, 1980, Memory and Awareness, 1983. Ctr. for Advanced Study fellow, Stanford, Calif., 1982. Fellow APA, Am. Psychol. Soc.; mem. Psychonomic Soc. (mem. governing bd. 1993—), Phi Beta Kappa. Office: Carnegie Mellon Univ Dept Psychology Pittsburgh PA 15213

KLAUS, MARGARET ELIZABETH, pharmaceutical executive; b. Greencastle, Ind., Jan. 24, 1951; d. Earl Adam and Ruth Janet (Haley) K. BA, So. Ill. U., 1973, MS, 1975. Cert. in regulatory affairs. Research exploratory organic chemist Monsanto Co., St. Louis, 1974-78; spl. projects mgr. Monsanto Co., Brussels, 1978; coordinator product acceptability and environ. affairs Monsanto Co., St. Louis, 1979-81; product acceptance specialist Monsanto Co., 1982-83, acting mgr. product acceptability and environ. affairs, 1984, mgr. regulatory affairs, 1984-85; asst. dir. regulatory affairs Adria Labs., Columbus, Ohio, 1985-87; dir. regulatory compliance Erbamont, Stamford, Conn., 1987-89, Milan, 1987-89; exec. dir. Martec Pharm. Inc., Kansas City, Mo., 1988-89; dir. regulatory affairs The Nutra Sweet Co., Deerfield, Ill., 1989-94; pres., CEO The Klaus Group, Inc., Highland Park, Ill., 1994—; chmn. Biphenyl Industry Com., 1983-84, Phosphate Ester Ind. Com., 1983-84. Patentee in field. Mem. Regulatory Affairs Profls., Am. Chem. Soc., Drug Info. Assn., Internat. Assn. Polit. Cons., Bios. Home and Office: 1387 Linden Ave Highland Park IL 60035-3452

KLAUS, SUZANNE LYNNE, horticulturist, production specialist; b. Kansas City, Mo., May 2, 1956; d. John Wallace and Shirley Jane (Hoffman) K.; m. William D. Luebbert, Nov. 4, 1989. BS in Agriculture, U. Mo., 1978, MS in Horticulture, 1980. Prodn. mgr. John Klaus & Sons Greenhouses, Greenwood, Mo., 1972—; tchr. horticulture Longview C. of C., Lee's Summit, Mo., 1979-81; guest speaker, panel mem. Mo. State Florists Convs., 1981, 82, 86, 89; guest speaker St. Louis Growers Assn., 1985, Ohio Florists' Conf., 1986, Ball's Grow Show, 1987, Ark. State Growers Conf., 1988. Floriculture judge for nat. conv. Future Farmers Am., 1984—. Mem. Mo. State Florists' Assn. (bd. dirs. 1980-89, res. 1987-88), Floral Acad. Mo. (bd. dirs. 1986-87, pres.-elect 1988-89), Nat. Assn. Women in Horticulture (pres. 1989-90), Ohio Florists' Assn., Pointsettia Growers Assn., Nemokan Floral Assn. (bd. dirs. 1987-89). Republican. Roman Catholic. Home: PO Box 376 Greenwood MO 64034-0376

KLAVITER, HELEN LOTHROP, magazine editor; b. Lima, Ohio, Mar. 5, 1944; d. Eugene H. and Jean (Walters) Lothrop; m. Douglas B. Klaviter, June 7, 1969 (div. 1982); 1 child, Elizabeth. B.A., Cornell Coll., Mt. Vernon, Iowa, 1966. Communication specialist Coop. Extension Service, Urbana, Ill., 1969-71; mng. editor Poetry Mag., Chgo., 1973—; editorial cons. Harper & Row, N.Y.C., 1983-87. Bd. dirs. Ill. Theatre Ctr., 1989—, St. Clement's Open Pantry, 1990—, Episc. Diocese of Chgo. Hunger Commn., 1992—, Communications Commn., 1993—. Episcopalian. Home: 395 Dogwood St Park Forest IL 60466-1863 Office: Poetry Mag/Modern Poetry Assn 60 W Walton St Chicago IL 60610-3305

KLAW, BARBARA VAN DOREN, author, editor; b. N.Y.C., Sept. 17, 1920; d. Carl and Irita (Bradford) Van Doren; m. Spencer Klaw, July 5, 1941; children: Joanna Klaw Schultz, Susan Klaw (Del Tredici), Rebecca Klaw (Feldman), Margaret Klaw (Metcalfe). B.A., Vassar Coll., 1941. Writer-researcher OWI, Washington, 1942-43; reporter N.Y. Post, 1943-45; free-lance editor, writer, 1945-63; editor Am. Heritage mag., N.Y.C., 1963-88. Author: One Summer, 1936, One Winter, 1938, A Pony Named Nubbin, 1939, Joan and Michael, 1941, all under pseudonym Martin Gale; under pseudonym Eleanor Benton: The Complete Book of Etiquette, 1956; Camp Follower, 1944; editor folklore anthology, 1960. Home: 280 Cream Hill Rd West Cornwall CT 06796-1207

KLEBACK, LISA LYNN, computer graphics specialist; b. Parma, Ohio, July 20, 1963; d. Alexander Tibor and Ruth Alice (Krick) Nagy; m. James Michael Kleback, Sept. 12, 1987. Art found./fashion illustration student, Va. Commonwealth U., 1982-83; AA in Illustration, No. Va. Community Coll., 1985. Nurses aid Leewood Nursing Home, Springfield, Va., 1980; retail salesperson Adcom Inc., Springfield, 1984-85; graphic artist G.W. Press, Springfield, 1985-86; freelance prodn. artist McGraw Hill, Washington, 1987-88; prodn. artist Pub. Utilities Reports, Inc., Arlington, Va., 1986-88; computer graphics specialist CACI, Inc., Arlington, 1988—. Producer briefing charts for Sec. of Def. for Desert Shield/Desert Storm, 1991; exhibited in group shows Old Courthouse, Fairfax, Va., 1979 (3d place ribbon), "Spotlight on the Arts", 1992, Fairfax Art League. Recipient Commendation award (one), HQDA, 1988, Commendation awards (two), HQDA, 1989, Commendation awards (four), HQDA, 1990, Commendation awards (four), HQDA, 1991, Commendation awards (nine), HQDA, 1992, Cert. of Achievement, 1992. Mem. Springfield Art Guild. Presbyterian. Address: 8504 Paul Revere Ct Annandale VA 22003-4259

KLEBESADEL, HELEN RUTH, art educator, artist; b. Milw.; d. James Allen Klebesadel and Barbara Louise Richardson; life ptnr. Akeem L. Torres; stepchildren: Micahl, Daniel. BS, U. Wis., 1986, MFA, 1989. artist-in-residence State of Wis., Madison, 1978-81; vis. instr. art Beloit (Wis.) Coll., 1989-90. Owner Painted Ladies House Painting, Spring Green, Wis., 1972-78; tchg. asst. U. Wis., Madison, 1987-89; asst. prof. art Lawrence U., Appleton, Wis., 1990—. Exhbns. include Chosey Gallery, 1993, Wis. Acad. Arts, 1993, Bergstrom Mus., 1994. Vol. Wis. Family Farm Fund, 1986-89, Project Self Help and Awareness, 1984-89; mural coord. of vols. W.O.R.T. Cmty. Radio, Madison, 1991; leader, trainer No Limits for Women Artists, Wis., 1989—; bd. dirs. Breast Cancer Art Action Group, 1994—. CETA Arts grantee State of Wis., 1977; recipient Curators award Mus. Nat. Arts Found., 1989. Mem. Nat. Women's Studies Assn., Internat. Alliance of Women in Arts (bd. dirs.), Women's Caucus for Art (bd. dirs. 1990-92, 1st v.p. 1992-94, pres. 1994—), Wis. Women in Arts, Coll. Art Assn. Home: 2017 Jenifer St Madison WI 53704-5526 Office: Lawrence Univ Wriston Art Ctr Appleton WI 54912

KLEEMAN, NANCY GRAY ERVIN, special education educator; b. Boston, Feb. 19, 1946; d. John Wesley and Harriet Elizabeth (Teuchert) Ervin; m. Brian Carlton Kleeman, June 27, 1969. BA, Calif. State U., Northridge, 1969; MS, Calif. State U., Long Beach, 1976, Calif. State U., Long Beach, 1976; cert. resource specialist, Calif. State U., Long Beach, 1982. Cert. spl. edn., learning disabilities and resource specialist tchr., Calif. Tchr. spl. edn., resource specialist Downey (Calif.) Unified Sch. Dist., 1972-86; tchr. spl. day class Irvine (Calif.) Sch. Dist., 1986—; tutor in field; speaker Commn. for Handicapped, L.A., 1975; advisor Com. to Downey Unified Sch. Dist., 1976-82; co-owner ISIS Design Publs. Author: Rhyme Your Times, 1990; author numerous greeting cards. Vol. sec. UN, L.A., 1980-83; vol. coord., art dir., educator Sierra Vista Mid. Sch., Irvine, 1986-88; liaison Tustin (Calif.) Manor Convalescent Home and Regents Point Retirement Home, Irvine, 1988—; fundraiser Ronald McDonald House, Orange, Calif.; mem. Nat. Youth Svc., Washington; vol. Sr. Cheer Project. Recipient award Concerned Students Orgn., Downey, 1984; named Tchr. Yr. Sierra Vista Middle Sch., 1988. Mem. NEA, Irvine Tchrs. Assn., Calif. Tchrs. Assn., Am. Carousel Assn., Dogs for the Blind. Office: Irvine Unified Sch Dist 2 Liberty Irvine CA 92720-2536

KLEER, NORMA VESTA, critical care nurse; b. London, Apr. 23, 1933; d. Harold N. and Julia Bonanova (Ball-Dale) Wragg; divorced; children: Valerie Hamilton, David. Diploma, Torbay (South Devon, Eng.) Hosp., 1954, St. Francis Hosp., Trenton, N.J., 1964. Critical care nursing mgr. Bayfront Med. Ctr., St. Petersburg, Fla.; dir. nursing PRN Inc., St. Petersburg, Am. Healthcare Mgmt., St. Petersburg; nursing coord. Care Plus Inc. Hi-Tech. Home Infusion Co., Fla.; case mgr., DON Bayada Nurses Home Care Specialists, St. Petersburg, Fla.; DON Nurses PRN, Tampa Bay, Fla.; pioneer in devel. of EMS System, Pinellas Co. Mem. Fla. Emergency Nurses Assn. (founder, 1st pres.).

KLEIMAN, SYBIL ROSS, artist; b. Mineola, N.Y., Jan. 22, 1930; d. Harry and Martha C. (Markowitz) Ross; m. Henry Kleiman, May 3, 1953; children: Jerrold L., Barry A. BS in Biology, Adelphi U., 1950; MS in Art Edn., Hofstra U., 1974. Cert. tchr., N.Y. Master art counselor for gifted G.I.F.T. Inc., Brookville, N.Y., 1968-75; elem. art tchr. Baldwin (N.Y.) Pub. Schs., 1970-71; art instr., coord. B.O.C.E.S. Cultural Art Ctr., Syosset, N.Y., 1972-82; art cons. B.O.C.E.S. Art Program, Syosset, 1980-81; adj. lectr. Adelphi U., Garden City, N.Y., 1981-82; art historian, lectr. Wynmoor Village, Coconut Creek, Fla., 1985-88; judicator, lectr., 1994. Exhibited in group shows Broward Art Guild, 1987-94, Profl. Art Guild, 1987-95, Hollywood Art and Culture Ctr., 1987-90, Coconut Creek Art Guild, 1990-94, South Fla. Art Inst., 1990, Soc. 4 Arts, 1991, 94, Dover Gallery, Boca Raton, 1994, Nathan D. Rosen Art Gallery, 1994, Ft. Lauderdale Mus. Art; pvt. collections; featured artist XS Mag., 1994. Mem. 2 & 3: The Artist Orgn. (pres. 1991-92), Gallery Directory (coord.), Coconut Creek Art Guild (v.p. program chmn. 1990-94), Profl. Artists Guild of Boca Raton Mus. (corr. sec. 1994), Nat. Coun. for Jewish Women (historian), Scrabble Club of Wynmoor (dir. 1986-95). Home: 1801 Eleuthera Pt K-1 Cocunut Creek FL 33066

KLEIN, ANNE SCEIA, public relations executive; b. Phila., Apr. 25, 1942; d. Charles B. and Kathryn L. (Lucas) Sceia; m. Gerhart L. Klein, June 19, 1976. BS in Econs., U. Pa., 1964, MA in Communications, 1965. Promotion asst. S.E. Pa. Transit Authority, Phila., 1965; pub. rels. dir. Pa. Lung Assn., Phila., 1965-68; info. dir. H2L2 Architects, Phila., 1968; pub. rels. officer Girard Bank, Phila., 1969-76; acct. exec. Aitkin-Kynett Co., Inc., Phila., 1977; mgr. media rels. Sun Co., Radnor, Pa., 1978-80; mgr. exec. communications Sun Co., Radnor, 1980-82; pres. Anne Klein & Assocs., Inc., Mt. Laurel, N.J., 1982—. Mem. Ethics Com., Mt. Laurel, 1988-92; Citizens Adv. Com., Mt. Laurel, 1988-92. Recipient Super Communicator of 80's award Women in Communications, 1987, Tribute to Women in Industry award YMCA, 1990; named Small Bus. Person of Yr. So. N.J. C. of C., 1991. Fellow Pub. Rels. Soc. Am. (accredited, pres. Phila. chpt. 1979, mid-Atlantic chmn. 1984, assembly del. 1980-82, 88—, exec. com. Counselors Acad. 1990-91, Pepperpot awards, Coll. of Fellows 1991), Pub. Rels. Profls. So. N.J. (chmn. 1987—, pres. 1985-87), Forum Exec. Women (sec. bd. dis. 1981-83), Phila. Pub. Rels. Assn., Harbor League Club, U. Pa. Faculty Club, Kappa Delta. Office: 533 Fellowship Rd Ste 250 Mount Laurel NJ 08054-3412

KLEIN, CHARLOTTE CONRAD, public relations executive; b. Detroit, June 20, 1923; d. Joseph and Bessie (Brown) K. BA, UCLA, 1945. Corr. UPI, Los Angeles, 1945-46; staff writer CBS, Los Angeles, 1946-47; publicist David O. Selznick Studios, Culver City, Calif., 1947-49, Foladare and Assocs., Los Angeles, 1949-51; publicist to v.p. Edward Gottlieb & Assocs., N.Y.C., 1951-62; v.p. to sr. v.p. Harshe Rotman & Druck, N.Y.C., 1962-78; dir. press/govt. affairs Sta. WNET-TV, N.Y.C., 1978-79; pres. Charlotte C. Klein Assocs., N.Y.C., 1979-84; sr. v.p., group supr. Porter Novelli, N.Y.C., 1984-89; prin. Charlotte Klein Assocs., N.Y.C., 1989—; adj. prof. pub. rels. NYU. Contbr. articles to profl. jours. Bd. dirs. Manhattan chpt. Am. Cancer Soc., 1988-92. Recipient Cine Golden Eagle, 1977, Matrix award Women in Communications, 1975. Mem. Pub. Rels. Soc. Am. (accredited, pres. N.Y. chpt. 1985-86, Silver Anvil award 1978, John Hill award 1988), Women's Forum (bd. dirs. N.Y. chpt. 1986-87), Internat. Women's Forum (leadership com. chair dialogue for democracy 1993—), Women Execs. in Pub. Rels. (pres. 1965).

KLEIN, DYANN LESLIE, theater properties company executive; b. Clifton, N.J., June 1, 1951; d. Alfred L. and Florence (Slaff) K.; divorced. BA, Ohio State U., 1973; postgrad., Rutgers U., 1976, Sch. Visual Arts, 1983-86. Art therapist Jackson Meml. Hosp., Miami, Fla., 1973-74; prodn. asst. Dom Albi Assocs., N.Y.C., 1974-75; freelance prodn. asst. N.Y.C., 1975-76, freelance designer and stylist, 1976-80; pres. Props For Today, Inc., N.Y.C, 1980—; guest speaker Fashion Inst. of Tech., N.Y.C., 1987, mem. faculty; bd. dirs. Tipps Directory, N.Y.C. Mem. NAFE, Internat. Home Furnishings Assn., N.Y. Women in Film and TV, Pro New York. Jewish. Office: Props For Today Inc 121 W 19th St Fl 3D New York NY 10011-4114

KLEIN, EDITH MILLER, lawyer, former state senator; b. Wallace, Idaho, Aug. 4, 1915; d. Fred L.B. and Edith (Gallup) Miller; m. Sandor S. Klein (dec. 1970). BS in Bus., U. Idaho, 1935; teaching fellowship, Wash. State U., 1936; JD, George Washington U., 1946, LLM, 1954. Bar: D.C. 1946, Idaho 1947, N.Y. 1955, U.S. Supreme Ct. 1954. Pers. spec. Labor and War Depts., Wash., 1942-46; practice law Boise, Idaho, 1947—; judge Mcpl. Ct., Boise, 1947-49; mem. Idaho Ho. Reps., 1948-50, 64-68, Idaho Senate, 1968-82; atty. FCC Wash., 1953-54; FHA N.Y.C., 1955-56. Chmn. Idaho Gov.'s Commn. Status Women, 1964-72, mem. 1965-79, 82-92; mem. Idaho Gov.'s Coun. Comprehensive Health Planning, 1969-76, Idaho Law Enforcement Planning Commn., 1972-82, Nat. Adv. Commn. Regional Med. Programs, 1974-76, Idaho Endowment Investment Bd., 1979-82; trustee Boise State U. Found. Inc., 1973—; pres. Boise Music Week, 1991-94; bd. dirs. Harry W. Morison Found. Inc., 1978—, St. Alphonsus Regional Med. Ctr. Found., 1982—; past pres. bd. dirs. Boise Philharm. Assn., Boise Opera. Named Woman of Yr. Boise Altrusa Club, 1966, Boise C. of C., 1970, Disting. Citizen, Idaho Statesman 1970, Woman of Progress, Idaho Bus. Prof. Women, 1978; recipient Women Helping Women award Soroptomist Club, 1980, Stein Meml. award Y.M.C.A., 1983, Silver and Gold award for Outstanding Svc., U. Idaho, 1985, March of Dimes award to Honor Outstanding Women, 1987, Cert. of Appreciation by Boise Br., AAUW, 1990, Morrison Ctr. Hall of Fame award, 1990, Disting. Cmty. Svc. award Boise Area C. of C., 1995. Mem. DAR (regent Pioneer chpt. 1991-93). Republican. Congregationalist. Home: 1588 Lenz Lane PO Box 475 Boise ID 83701 Office: 1400 West One Plaza PO Box 2527 Boise ID 83701

KLEIN, ELAINE, magazine publishing executive; b. Bklyn., Mar. 12, 1929; d. Sidney and Bertha (Smith) Laks; m. Melvin Klein, Dec. 23, 1951; children: Cyd Robin Klein Tomack, Amy Susan Klein Len. Exec. sec. to pres. Muzak Corp., N.Y.C., 1949-55; expeditor The Van Ard Co., Forest Mills, N.Y., 1968-70; advt. sales mgr. Playbill mag., N.Y.C., 1970—. Mem. Nat. Assn.. Exec. Women, The New Dramatists, Friars Club, Mus. of Natural History. Democrat. Jewish. Office: Playbill Mag 52 Vanderbilt Ave New York NY 10017-3808

KLEIN, ELAYNE MARGERY, elementary education educator; b. L.I., N.Y., Apr. 25, 1947; d. Jack and Anne (Fialkow) K. BS, L.I. U., 1969, MS, 1972. Cert. elem. tchr., cert. in guidance edn., N.Y. Student tchr. 2nd, then 4th grades Robbins Lane Elem. Sch., Syosset, N.Y., 1968-69; tchr. 5th grade West Islip (N.Y.) Pub. Schs., 1969—; co-organizer/supr. 5th and 6th grade drama club West Islip Pub. Schs., 1972. Mem. AAUW, West Islip Tchrs. Assn., N.Y. State Congress Parents and Tchrs. (hon. life), Iota Alpha Pi. Office: Beach St Mid Sch Sherman Ave West Islip NY 11795

KLEIN, (MARY) ELEANOR, retired clinical social worker; b. Luzon, Philippines, Dec. 13, 1919; came to U.S., 1921; (parents Am. citizens); d. Roy Edgar and Edith Lillian Hay; m. Edward George Klein, June 24, 1955. BA, Pacific Union Coll., 1946; MSW, U. So. Calif., 1953. Lic. clin. social worker. Social worker White Meml. Hosp., Los Angeles, 1948-56; clin. social worker UCLA Hosp. Clinics, 1956-65, supr. social worker, 1965-67, assoc. dir., 1967-73, dir., 1973-82. Bd. dirs., treas. Los Amigos de la Humanidad, U. So. Calif. Sch. Social Work; hon. life mem. bd. dirs. Calif. div. Am. Cancer Soc., mem. vol. bd. Calif. div., 1964—, del. nat. dir., 1980-84, chmn. residential crusade for Orange County (Calif.) unit, 1985-86; bd. dirs. Vol. Ctr. Orange County West, 1988—, sec., 1991—. Recipient Disting. Alumni award Los Amigos de la Humanidad, 1984, Outstanding Performance award UCLA Hosp., 1968, various service awards Am. Cancer Soc., 1972-88. Fellow Soc. Clin. Social Work; mem. Nat. Assn. Social Workers (charter), Am. Hosp. Assn., Soc. Hosp. Social Work Dirs. (nat. pres. 1981, bd. dirs. 1978-82, life mem. local chpt.), Am. Pub. Health Assn. Democrat. Adventist. Home: 1661 Texas Cir Costa Mesa CA 92626-2238

KLEIN, ESTHER MOYERMAN (MRS. PHILIP KLEIN), author, retired publisher; b. Phila., Nov. 3, 1907; d. Louis and Rebecca (Feldman) Moyerman; BS, Temple U., 1929; student U. London, 1954; m. Philip Klein, Apr. 26, 1930; children: Arthur, Karen Louise Klein Mannes. Reporter, Phila. Jewish Times, 1925, Atlantic City Times, 1927; feature writer Pub. Ledger Syndicate, 1928-29, Pub. Ledger, Evening Bull., Phila. Record, 1929-32; pub. rels. counselor, editor Art Alliance Bull., 1945-49; commentator Sta. WPEN, 1949-53; pub. Phila. Jewish Times, 1953-74; author, hist. researcher, 1974—; lectr. women's clubs, 1951—; del. Internat. Conf. Residential Adult Edn., Holland, 1957, Germany, 1959; participant in first workshop Residential Adult Edn. for Adult Edn. Assn. U.S., 1954. Mem. Gov.'s Commn. on Charitable Orgns., 1969—; chmn. Rittenhouse Sq. Women's com. for Phila. Orch., 1957; organizer bicentennial women's com. Walnut St. Theatre; adv. com. Friends Nat. Independence Hist. Park; chmn. bicentennial program Beth Zion - Beth Israel Congregation; bd. dirs. Rittenhouse Found., Phila. Jewish Times Inst., also dir. ann. cooking festivals; exec. com. Long Beach Island Found. Arts and Scis., N.J.; bd. dirs. University City Sci. Ctr. Named Distinguished Dau. Pa.; recipient Gimbel Phila. award, 1975; awards Alumnae Girls High Sch., Phila. Art Alliance, Temple U., City Coun. Phila., Colonial Hist. Soc.; Klein Recital Hall at Temple U. named in her honor, Esther M. Klein Art Gallery named in her honor University City Sci. Ctr. Mem. Pa. Newspaper Pubs. Assn., Temple U. Alumni (honored at 80th anniversary, 1964), Phila. High Sch. for Girls Alumnae, Hannah Penn House, Emergency Aid of Pa., Chgo. Art Mus., Mus. Modern Art N.Y., Pan Am. Assn., Print Club. Author: A Guidebook to Jewish Philadelphia, 1965; International House Celebrity Cookbook, 1965; History and Guidebook of Fairmount Park, 1974. Address: 135 S 18th St Philadelphia PA 19103-5228

KLEIN, FAY MAGID, health administrator; b. Chgo., Jan. 12, 1929; d. Victor and Rose (Begun) Magid; m. Jerome G. Klein, June 27, 1948 (div. 1970); children: Leslie Susan Janik, Debra Lynne Maslov; m. Manuel Chait, Aug. 28, 1994. BA in English, UCLA, 1961; MA in Pub. Adminstrn., U. So. Calif., 1971. Cert. health adminstrn. Supr. social workers L.A. County, 1961-65; program specialist Econ. and Youth Opportunity Agy., L.A., 1965-69; sr. health planner Model Cities, L.A., 1971-72; dir. prepaid health plan Westland Health Svcs., L.A., 1972-74; exec. dir. Coastal Region Health Consortium, L.A., 1974-76; grants and legis. cons. Jewish Fed. Council of L.A., 1976-79; planning council Jewish Fed. Councils of So. Fla., Palm Beach to Miami, 1979-82; adminstrv. dir. program in kidney diseases Dept. Medicine UCLA, 1982-84; exec. dir. west coast Israel Cancer Rsch. Fund, L.A., 1984-94; cons. to non-profit orgns. Santa Monica, 1994—; cons. Arthritis Found., Los Angeles, 1984, Bus. Action Ctr., Los Angeles, 1982, Vis. Nurses Assn., Los Angeles, 1982. Charter mem. Los Angeles County Mus. of Art, Mus. of Contemporary Art, Los Angeles; cons. Los Angeles Mcpl. Art Gallery, 1979; mem. Art Council Wight Gallery, UCLA. Fellow U.S. Pub. Health, U. So. Calif., 1970-71. Mem. Am. Pub. Health, UCLA Alumni Assn. (life), U. So. Calif. Alumni Assn. (life).

KLEIN, FREDA, state agency administrator; b. Seattle, May 17, 1920; d. Joseph and Julia (Caplan) Vinikow; m. Jerry Jerome Klein, Oct. 20, 1946; children: Jan Susan Klein Waples, Kerry Joseph, Robin Jo Klein MacLeod. BA, U. Wash., 1942; MS, U. Nev., Las Vega, 1969, EdD, 1978. Owner, mgr. Smart Shop, Provo, Utah, 1958-60, Small Fry Shop, Las Vegas, 1961-66; vocat. counselor, test adminstr. Nev. Employment Security Dept., Las Vegas, 1966-77, local office mgr., 1978—. Contbr. articles to profl. jours. Exec. bd. Pvt. Industry Coun., Las Vegas, 1988—, Interstate Conf. on Employment Security Agys., Nev., 1988-90, Area Coordinating Com. for Econ. Devel., Las Vegas, 1988—. Recipient Achievement award Nev. Bus. Svc., 1990, Cert. of Spl. Cognition, 1992; named Outstanding Woman, Goodwill Industries sci. and rsch. divsn., 1977. Mem. AAUW, Internat.

Assn. Pers. in Employment Security, U. Nev. Las Vegas Alumni Assn., Henderson C. of C. (exec. bd. 1986—), Soroptimist Internat. (pres. 1987-88), Phi Kappa Phi (scholastic hon.). Home: 2830 Phoenix St Las Vegas NV 89121-1312 Office: Nev Employment Security 119 S Water St Henderson NV 89015-7221

KLEIN, GABRIELLA SONJA, communications executive; b. Chgo., Apr. 11, 1938; d. Frank E. Vosicky and Sonja (Kosner) Becvar; m. Donald J. Klein. BA in Comm. and Bus. Mgmt., Alverno Coll., 1983. Editor, owner Fox Lake (Wis.) Rep., 1962-65, McFarland (Wis.) Community Life and Monona Community Herald, 1966-69; bur. reporter Waukesha (Wis.) Daily Freeman, 1969-71; community rels. staff Waukesha County Tech. Coll., Pewaukee, Wis., 1971-73; pub. rels. specialist JI Case Co., Racine, Wis., 1973-75, corp. publs. editor, 1975-80; v.p., bd. dirs. publs. Image Mgmt., Valley View Ctr., Milw., 1980-82; pres. Communication Concepts, Unltd., Racine, 1983—; guest lectr. Alverno Coll., U. Wis.; adj. faculty U. Wis.-Parkside. Contbr. articles to profl. jours. Pres. Big Bros./Big Sisters Racine County. Recipient awards Wis. Press Assn., Nat. Fedn. Press Women; named Wis. Woman Entrepreneur of Yr., 1985. Mem. Internat. Assn. Bus. Communicators (accredited mem.; bd. dirs. 1982-85, various awards), Ad Club of Racine. Home: 3045 Chatham St Racine WI 53402-4001 Office: 927 S Main St Racine WI 53403-1524

KLEIN, GAIL BETH MARANTZ, freelance writer, dog breeder; b. Bklyn., Dec. 1, 1946; d. Herbert and Florence (Dresner) Marantz; m. Harvey Leon Klein, Mar. 17, 1979. AB cum laude, U. Miami, Coral Gables, Fla., 1968, MEd, 1969, MBA, 1977. Cert. residential contractor, Fla. Asst. dir. student activities Miami-Dade Community Coll., 1969-79, instr. photography for mentally retarded adults, 1974, acting dir. student activities, 1976, acting advisor student publs., 1978-79, asst. prof. bus. adminstrn., 1979; dog breeder Vizcaya Shepherds, Palm Beach Gardens, Fla., 1979—; trainer Dog Obedience and Conformation Show Handling, West Palm Beach, 1980—; owner, CEO Word Master Profl. Comm.; freelance writer WordMaster Profl. Comms.; mgr. proposal devel. specialist Profl. Food-Svc. Mgmt., Inc.; cons., speaker in field; appeared on various radio talk shows. Editor (booklet) 1978 Consumers Guide to Banking, 1978, (newsletter) Newsletter of German Shepherd Dog Club Ft. Lauderdale, Inc., 1980-83, Sunshine State Shepherd, 1988-89; contbr. articles to newspapers and mags. Chair spl. events com. Third Century U.S.A., Dade County, Fla., 1976; mem. adv. com., mktg. cons. YWCA of Greater Miami, 1976-79; mem. community rels. com. Greater Miami Jewish Fedn., 1976-79; mem. Met. Miami Art Ctr., 1977-79; vice chair appeals bd. Palm Beach County Animal Care and Control, 1989—, mem. pet overpopulation com., 1991—; co-developer, co-adminstr. OFA Verifications for German Shepherd Dogs, 1985—; pub. info. coord. Am. Kennel Club, Palm Beach County, 1991—. Recipient Job Training Partnership Act Employee of Yr. award State of Fla., 1994. Mem. Nat. Assn. Dog Obedience Instrs., Conformation Judges Assn. Fla., Inc., Palm Beach Users Group, Am. Sewing Guild, German Shepherd Dog Club Am., Inc. (hip dysplasia/orthopedic com. 1987-89), German Shepherd Dog Club of Can., Inc., German Shepherd Dog Club of Greater Miami (bd. dirs. 1981-82, 89—, rec. sec. 1977-78, corr. sec. 1978-80, life), Jupiter-Tequesta Dog Club, Inc. (pres. 1984-85, bd. dirs., various other offices, Gaines Sportsmanship award 1993), Obedience Tng. Club Palm Beach County, Inc. (AKC Cmty. Achievement Merit award 1994), Wolf Song of Alaska (grant/proposal writer), Hadassah (life), Alpha Lambda Delta, Epsilon Tau Lambda, Phi Kappa Phi, Mortar Board. Republican. Jewish. Home: 12956 Mallard Creek Dr Palm Beach Gardens FL 33418-8662

KLEIN, HARRIET FARBER, lawyer; b. Elizabeth, N.J., Apr. 30, 1948; d. Melvin Julius and Frances Mildred (Novit) Farber; m. Paul Martin Klein, Sept. 9, 1973; children: Andrew, Zachary. B.A. with honors, Douglass Coll., New Brunswick, N.J., 1970; J.D., Rutgers U., 1973. Bar: N.J. 1973, U.S. Dist. Ct. N.J. 1973. Jud. clk. chancery div. Superior Ct. N.J., 1973-74; assoc. Budd, Larner, Kent, Gross, Picillo & Rosenbaum, Newark, 1974-78; ptnr. Greenbaum, Rowe, Smith, Ravin & Davis (and predecessor), Woodbridge, N.J., 1979—; mem. N.J. State Bd. Bar Examiners, 1987-90, reader, 1977-87; mem. adv. com. on bar admissions N.J. Supreme Ct., 1987-90; mem. Essex-Newark Legal Svcs. Vol. Project, 1983-84. Pres. Sisterhood of Congregation B'nai Israel, Millburn, N.J., 1985-87, 1st v.p., 1993—. Mem. ABA, Essex County Bar Assn. (vice-chmn. com. on status of women in law firms 1988-90, vice-chmn. equity jurisprudence com. 1989-90, co-chmn. com. on women in the profession 1990—), N.J. Bar Assn. (labor and employment law sect.), Order of Barristers, Phi Alpha Theta. Home: 45 Ridgewood Ter Maplewood NJ 07040-2132 Office: Greenbaum Rowe Smith Ravin & Davis PO Box 5600 Woodbridge NJ 07095-0988

KLEIN, IRMA FRANCES, career development educator, consultant; b. New Orleans, Jan. 5, 1936; d. Harry Joseph and Gesina Frances (Bauer) Molligan; m. John Vincent Chelena (dec. 1963); 1 child, Joseph William; m. Chris George Klein, Aug. 14, 1965; 1 stepchild, Arnold Conrad. BS in Bus. Augustine Coll., postgrad. Mktg. Inst., Chgo., Loyola U., Chgo., Realtors Inst., Baton Rouge. Mgr. Stan Weber & Assocs., Metairie, La., 1971-75; tng. dir., 1975-81; cons. Coldwell Banker Comml. Co., New Orleans, 1981; dir. career devel. Coldwell Banker Residential Co., New Orleans, 1982-85; pres. Irma Klein Career Devel., Inc.; v.p. Klein Enterprises, Inc., 1994—; instr. U. New Orleans, Bonnabel High Sch., Realtors Inst., La. Real Estate Commn. Author: Career Development, 1982; Training Manual, 1978, Obtaining Listings, 1986, Participative Marketing, 1986, Marketing & Servicing Listings, 1987, Designing Training Curriculum, 1987. Active Friends of Longue Vue Gardens, La. Hist. Assn. Meml. Hall Found. Mem. La. Realtors Assn. (bd. dirs. 1973-74, grad. Realtors Inst. 1976), Jefferson Bd. Realtors (v.p. 1984), Edn. and Resources (cert., pres. La. chpt.), Rsch. Club of New Orleans (pres. 1984-85), Realtors Nat. Mktg. Inst. (amb. Tex. and La. 1985—, Outstanding Achievement award 1985, cert. broker 1980, residential specialist 1977), Nat. Assn. Realtors (nat. conv. speaker 1986), CRB (pres. La. chpt. 1982-83, chmn. edn.), CRS (pres. La. chpt. 1988-90), Forty Scholars Soc., Am. Dental Assts. Assn., Les Quarante Ecolieres. Republican. Roman Catholic. Clubs: Antique Study Group, Confederate Lit. (New Orleans) (pres.), Rsch. (New Orleans). Avocation: antiques.

KLEIN, JOAN DEMPSEY, judge; b. San Jose, Calif., Aug. 18, 1924; d. Edward Joseph and Estelle (Kottinger) Dempsey; m. Donrad Lee Klein, Mar. 16, 1963; children: Marc Dempsey Gross, Brad Hunter Gross; stepchildren: Karen Beth , Susan Linda. BA, San Diego State Coll., 1948; LLB, UCLA, 1955. Bar: Calif. 1955, U.S. Supreme Ct. 1964. Dep. atty gen., trial lawyer State of Calif., 1955-63; judge L.A. Mcpl. Ct., 1963-75, presiding judge, 1974; mem. L.A. Superior Ct., 1974-78; presiding justice Calif. Ct. Appeals, L.A., 1978—; prof. jud. adminstrn. U. So. Calif. 1974-75; mem. Calif. Coun. on Criminal Justice, 1970-74, Jud. Criminal Justice Planning Com., 1974-76; del. Nat. Adv. Commn. Criminal Justice Standards and Goals, Washington, 1973; chmn. adv. com. Calif. Hwy. Patrol, 1976; participant S. Am. Lecture Tour Internat. Communication Agy. Mem. adv. bd. Girls Week L.A. City Schs., Gifted Children's Assn., San Fernando Valley, Vol. League San Fernando Valley. Named Alumna of Yr. Law Sch. UCLA, 1963, Angel of Distinction L.A. Cen. City Assn., 1969, Woman of Achievement Calif. Fedn. Bus. and Profl. Women's Club, 1973, Mcpl. Ct. Judge of Yr. Calif. Trial Lawyers, 1973, Woman of Yr. L.A. Times, 1975; recipient Profl. Achievement award UCLA Alumni Assn., 1975, Myrtle Wreath award Hadassah, 1977, Community Woman of Achievement award Big Sisters L.A., 1979, cert. merit from Gov. Brown, 1979, Portrait in Excellence award B'nai Brith Women, Woman of the Yr. award Met. News, 1992, Woman of Vision award Valley Presbyn. Hosp., 1991. Mem. Internat. Fedn. Women Lawyers, Nat. Assn. Women Judges (founding and current pres.), Calif. Women Lawyers (pres. 1975), Calif. Judges Assn., L.A. County Bar Assn., Women Lawyers Assn., Bus. and Profl. Women's Club. (L.A. chpt.), Legion Lex. U. Soc. Calif., UCLA Law Sch. Alumni Assn. (past pres.). Democrat. Office: Ct Appeals 300 S Spring St Los Angeles CA 90013-1230*

KLEIN, JULIA MEREDITH, newspaper reporter; b. Phila., Dec. 11, 1955; d. Abraham and Murielle (Pollack) K. BA magna cum laude, Harvard U., 1977. Copy editor J.B. Lippincott, Phila., 1977; features reporter The Oakland Press, Pontiac, Mich., 1978; freelance writer, researcher, editorial cons., 1978—; reporter The Phila. Inquirer, 1983—. Mem. Soc. Profl. Journalists, Phi Beta Kappa. Home: 307 Monroe St Philadelphia PA 19147-3211 Office: Phila Inquirer 400 N Broad St PO Box 8263 Philadelphia PA 19101

KLEIN, KATHLEEN, critical care and clinical nurse specialist; b. Newark, N.J., Nov. 7, 1962; d. Henry George Sr. and Patricia (Scott) K. BSN, Fairleigh Dickinson U., 1984; MS, Rutgers State U. N.J., 1992. CCRN. Staff nurse N.Y. U. Med. Ctr., 1984-85, sr. staff nurse, 1985-87, nurse clin. sr. open heart recovery room, 1987-91, asst. clin. coord. orthopedics/neurology/neurosurgery, 1991-92; critical care nurse specialist Cathedral Healthcare System, Newark, N.J., 1992-93, Med. Ctr. of Cen. Ga., Macon, 1994—. Mem. AACN (mem. bd. dirs. N.J. chpt. 1993-94), Am. Nurses Assn., Sigma Theta Tau Internat. Alpha Tau. Office: Med Ctr Cen Ga 777 Hemlock St HB 125 Macon GA 31208

KLEIN, KATHRYN ANN, social worker; b. Milw., Aug. 25, 1961; d. Lawrence and Marilyn Frieda (Denney) K.; m. Frederick Pickering, Feb. 14, 1988 (div. Apr. 1992). BS in Psychology, Sociology, Carroll Coll., 1983; MSW, SUNY, Stony Brook, 1986. Lic. clin. social worker. Case mgr. YMCA Family Svcs., Bayshore, N.Y., 1986; project dir. YMCA Family Svcs., Mastic, N.Y., 1986-88; area mgr. Cmty. Health and Counseling Svcs., Millinocket, Maine, 1988-93, therapist, 1993-94, program svcs. coord., 1994—; pvt. practice clin. social worker Millinocket, 1993—; mem. adv. bd. Children's Emergency Response, Millinocket, 1992—. co-chair svc. provision, mem. com. Katahdin Area Resistance to Violence, Millinocket, 1990—; mem. MADE-IT Team-youth substance abuse prevention, Millinocket, 1993—; social work rep. Commn. to Evaluate Adequacy of Aid to Families with Dependent Children Need and Payment Standards, Augusta, 1990-91; bd. dirs., treas. Katahdin Friends, Inc., East Millinocket, 1990—. Mem. NASW. Democrat. Office: PO Box 401 Millinocket ME 04462

KLEIN, LAURA ROTER, physician, dermatologist; b. St. Charles, Mo., July 17, 1959; d. Alex Max and Shirley Mae (Slosberg) Roter; m. Jon B. Klein, June 12, 1983; children: Rachel, Sarah. BSN, Kans. U., Lawrence, 1981; MD, U. Louisville, 1988. Diplomate Am. Bd. Dermatology. Resident in internal medicine U. Louisville, 1988-89, resident in dermatology, 1989-92; dermatologist East Louisville Dermatology, Louisville, 1992—; clin. instr. div. dermatology U. Louisville, 1992—. Fellow Am. Acad. Dermatology; mem. AMA, Women's Dermatology Assn., Ky. Dermatology Assn. Jewish. Office: East Louisville Dermatology 4812 Us Highway 42 Ste 208 Louisville KY 40222-6358

KLEIN, LINDA ANN, lawyer; b. N.Y.C., Nov. 7, 1959; d. Gerald Ira Klein and Sandra Florence (Kimmel) Fishman; m. Michael S. Neuren, Sept. 23, 1985. BA cum laude, Union Coll., 1980; JD, Washington & Lee U., 1983. Bar: Ga. 1983, D.C. 1984, U.S. Dist. Ct. (no. and mid. dist.) Ga. 1985, U.S. Ct. Appeals (11th cir.) 1986. Assoc. Nall & Miller, Atlanta, 1983-86, Martin, Cavan & Andersen, Atlanta, 1986-90; ptnr. Martin, Cavan & Andersen, 1990-93, Gambrell & Stolz, 1993—; instr. Nat. Ctr. Paralegal Tng., Atlanta, 1986. Mem. ABA (editor Trial Techniques newsletter 1989, vice chmn. trial techniques com. 1989-90, chair elect 1990-91, chair 1991-92, vice chair Fidelity and Surety com. 1994—, mem. tort and ins. practice sect.), Ga. Bar Assn. (mem. adv. com. legis., vice chair profl. liability com., chair study com. on rules of practice 1987—, evidence study com. 1989-90, atty.'s role in post conviction com. 1989—, bd. govs. 1989—, mem. exec. com. 1992—, sec. 1994—), Atlanta Bar Assn. (bd. dirs. Atlanta Coun. on Young Lawyers 1986-89, chair commn. on uniform rules of ct. 1986), Coun. of Superior Cts. Judges (ex-officio uniform rules com.), Internat. Bar Assn., Phi Alpha Delta, Pi Sigma Alpha.

KLEIN, LINDA SIMET, healthcare educator, nurse practitioner; b. N.Y.C., Mar. 21, 1947; d. Franklyn Marshall Simet and Florence (Burton) Peate; m. Bruce R. Klein, June 23, 1968; 1 child, Vanessa Franklyn. BS, U. Vt., 1968; MSN, Pace U., 1982; MPH, Columbia U., 1991. Cert. nurse practitioner. Nurse practitioner Goldwater Meml. Hosp., N.Y.C., 1982-83, Beth Abraham Adult Day Care Ctr., Bronx, 1983-84; nursing instr. Columbia U., N.Y.C., 1984-88, dir. Divsn. Undergrad. Studies, 1985-88; dir. Continuing Edn. and Meeting Svcs. Nat. League for Nursing, N.Y.C., 1988-90; dir. mtkg. and devel. Healthcom Entreprises, Pound Ridge, N.Y., 1990-92; program supr. Triclinica Comms., N.Y.C., 1992-94; sr. ptnr. creative edn. Healthcom Enterprises, Pound Ridge, 1994—. Author, illustrator: IV Coloring Book; creative dir. The Analogy Book, 1993 (Rx Club award 1993); contbr. articles to profl. jours. Recipient Disting. Alumna awrd Pace U., 1992, Excellence Rx Club, 1993, Silver award for sales promotion Med. Mktg. Assn., 1994. Mem. APHA, Oncology Nursing Soc., Nephrology Nursing Soc., Gilda's Club (med. adv. bd. 1994—), Sigma Theta Tau. Home: 3 Linden Ave Park Ridge NJ 07656-1254 Office: Healthcom Enterprises PO Box 530 Pound Ridge NY 10576-0530

KLEIN, LUELLA VOOGD, obstetrics-gynecology educator; b. Walker, Iowa, Oct. 24, 1924; d. Elmer DeWitt and Leah (Stunkard) Bare; m. Alfred O. Colquitt. BA, U. Iowa, 1947, MD, 1949. Diplomate Am. Bd. Ob-Gyn (gen. bd. dirs., bd. dirs. div. maternal-fetal medicine). Intern Western Res. U., Cleve., 1949-50; resident in medicine, surgery and ob-gyn Cleve. City Hosp., 1950-55; U.S. Sr. Fulbright Rsch. scholar U. London Postgrad. Med. Sch., 1955-57; obstetric cons. Ga. Dept. Pub. Health, Atlanta, 1958-60; pvt. practice Atlanta, 1960-65; asst. dir. clin. rsch. Bristol Labs., Syracuse, N.Y., 1965-67; assoc. prof., dir. maternal and infant care project Emory U. Grady Meml. Hosp., Atlanta, 1967—; co-dir. Regional Perinatal Ctr., Charles Howard Candler prof., chmn. dept. ob-gyn Emory U. Sch. Medicine, Atlanta, 1986-93; bd. dirs. Alan Guttmacher Inst., N.Y.C., chmn., vice-chmn.; Maternal and Child Health Care governing coun. Am. Hosp. Assn., Chgo.; chmn. FDA Ob-Gyn Device Com., Washington, 1986-88. Recipient Elizabeth Blackwell award Am. Women's Med. Assn., 1986, Atlanta Woman History Maker award Am. Women's Assn., 1987, Daggett Harvey award Chgo. Maternity Ctr., Northwestern U., 1991, 40th Anniversary award FIGO, 1994. Fellow Am. Coll. Obstetricians and Gynecologists (pres., v.p., asst. sec. 1982-85, Disting. Svc. award 1994); mem. AMA, Ga. Obstet. and Gynecol. Soc. (pres.), Atlanta Obstet. and Gynecol. Soc. (pres.), Med. Assn. Ga. (chair maternal and child health care com.), Inst. Medicine, Marietta Country Club (Marietta, Ga.). Office: Emory U Grady Meml Hosp 69 Butler St SE Atlanta GA 30303-3033

KLEIN, MARY NOUVERTNE, otorhinolaryngology nurse; b. Newark, Aug. 30, 1954; d. Elwood and Marian (Barber) Nouvertne. Diploma in nursing, Keene State Coll., 1976; cert. in otorhinolaryngology, Meth. Hosp., 1979; BSN, U. Tex., Houston, 1988, MSN in Gerontology, 1992. Lic. long term care adminstr., Tex. Staff nurse Cheshire Hosp., Keene, N.H., 1976-77; asst. head nurse dept. otorhinolaryngology/head-neck surgery Baylor Coll. Medicine, 1979-89; staff nurse otorhinolaryngology/neurology ICU Meth. Hosp., Houston, 1977-79, nurse specialist otorhinolaryngology/neurology ICU & intermediate care, 1989-92; assoc. dir. skilled nursing facility St. Joseph Hosp., Houston, 1992-94; regional mgr. clin. svcs. Imperial Health Resources, Houston, 1994—; part-time faculty instr. San Jacinto Coll. for Long Term Care Adminstrn., 1994—. Vol. ombudsman Houston Area Agy. Aging, 1990-91; CPR instr., vol. Am. Heart Assn., Houston. Mem. ANA, AACN, Tex. Nurses Assn., Nat. Gerontol. Nursing Assn., Houston Gerontol. Soc., Soc. Otorhinolaryngology and Head-Neck Nurses, Inc. Home: 6602 Spring Cypress Klein TX 77379 Office: Imperial Health Resources 3555 Timmons Ln Ste 1550 Houston TX 77027

KLEIN, RUTH B., civic worker, packaging company executive, poet, author; b. Cin., Jan. 31, 1908; d. Samuel and Minnie (Schunke) Becker; student U. Calif. at Los Angeles, 1926-28, San Jose State Coll., 1928-29; m. Charles Henle Klein, Sept. 23, 1938; children—Betsy Klein Schwartz, Charles Henle, Carla Klein Fee III. Sec., Novelart Mfg. Co., Cin., 1960—, dir., 1960—. Vol. Aid to Visually Handicapped program Cin. sect. Nat. Council of Jewish Women, 1951-82, sec., 1954-56, 63-64, bd. dirs., 1952-70; bd. dirs. Civic Garden Center of Greater Cin., 1956-63, chmn. spl. services for aid to visually handicapped, 1952-82. Mem. Nat. Braille Assn., Greater Cin. Writers League, Verse Writers' Guild Ohio. Club: Contemporary Literary. Author: Latitude of Love; Longitude of Lust, 1979; contbr. poems to various anthologies. Home: 6754 Fair Oaks Dr Cincinnati OH 45237-3606

KLEIN, SAMI WEINER, librarian; b. Worcester, Mass., July 6, 1939; d. Phillip and Barbara Rose (Ginsberg) Weiner; m. Eugene Robert Klein, Oct. 22, 1961; children: Pamela, Jeffrey, Elizabeth. B.S., Simmons Coll., 1961; M.L.S., U. Md., 1973; postgrad., Johns Hopkins U., 1976-78. Chemist Hercules, Wilmington, Del., 1961-62, FDA, Washington, 1965-66; libr. NSWC, White Oak, Md., 1973-78; chief Hdqs. Libr. EPA, Washington, 1978-82; chief rsch. info. svcs. Rsch. Info. Ctr. Nat. Inst. Stds. and Tech., Gaithersburg, Md., 1982—; cons. in field; mem. librs. exec. coun. Met. Washington Coun. of Govts., 1981-82; elected mem. com. Fed. Libr. Info. Ctr., 1993-95, chair fin. working group, 1994—. Editor OIS Sci.-Tech Info; mem. editorial bd. Assn. Ofcly. Analyt. Chemists, 1985-92. Fed. govt. rep. Inst. for Sci. Info. Internat. Users Group, 1985-86; mem. edn. com. Fed. Libr. and Info. Ctr. Com., 1987-91. Recipient Gold medal Am. Soc. Chemists, 1961. Mem. ALA (sec.-treas. fEd. Librs. Round Table 1983-84, rep. to NITS 1984-90, bd. dirs. 1986-89, v.p. 1991, pres. 1991-92, nominations chair 1992-93, scholar 1994), Spl. Librs. Assn. (treas. info.-tech. group 1986-87, student loan com. 1984-85, mem. com. 1987-88), D.C. Law Librs. Soc. (NIST v.p. standards com. for women 1988, pres. 1989, elected to Comstar credit union bd. dirs. 1994—), Fed. Libr. and Info. Network (mem. exec. adv. com. 1989-91, sec. 1989, vice chair 1990, 91), Beta Phi Mu. Democrat. Jewish. Home: 11041 Woodelves Way Columbia MD 21044-1002 Office: Nat Inst Standards and Tech Route 270 Gaithersburg MD 20899

KLEIN, SNIRA L(UBOVSKY), Hebrew language and literature educator; came to U.S., 1959, naturalized, 1974; d. Avraham and Devora (Unger) Lubovsky; m. Earl H. Klein, Dec. 25, 1975. Tchr. cert., Tchrs. Seminar, Netanya, Israel, 1956; B. Rel. Edn., U. Judaism, 1961, M in Hebrew Lit., 1963; BA, Calif. State U., Northridge, 1966; MA, UCLA, 1971, PhD, 1983. Tchg. asst. UCLA, 1969-71; instr., continuing edn. U. Judaism, L.A., 1971-76, 94—, instr., 1975-84; instr. continuing edn. U. Judaism, Los Angeles, 1994—; vis. lectr. UCLA, 1985-91; adj. asst. prof. U. Judaism, 1984-94. Mem. Assn. for Jewish Studies, Nat. Assn. of Profs. of Hebrew, World Union of Jewish Studies. Jewish. Office: U Judaism 15600 Mulholland Dr Los Angeles CA 90077-1599

KLEINBERG, JUDITH G., lawyer; b. Hartford, Conn., Jan. 28, 1946; d. Burleigh B. and Ruth (Leven) Greenberg; m. James Paul Kleinberg, Aug. 30, 1970; children: Alexander, Lauren. BA cum laude, U. Mich., 1968; JD, U. Calif., Berkeley, 1971. Atty. pvt. practice, San Francisco, 1971-74; legal affairs reporter comml. and pub. TV, San Francisco, 1974-76; prof. law Mills Coll., Oakland, Calif., 1977-84; chief of staff The Global Fund for Women, Los Altos, Calif., 1987-88; pub. interest atty., non-profit corp. law/orgn. specialist alternative dispute resolution Palo Alto, Calif., 1988—; exec. dir. Kids in Common Collaborative, San Jose, Calif.; arbitrator/mediator, legal adv. for abortion rights, women and children's rights and environ. groups, Santa Clara County and Calif., 1980—; speaker in field. Mem. Calif. Law Rev. Bd. Editors, 1969-71. Mem. steering com. lawyers coun. No. Calif. sect. ACLU, bd. dirs., 1990-92; founder, chairperson No. Calif. Friends of Pediat. AIDS Found.; past pres. Com. for Green Foothills; bd. dirs. Palo Alto SAFE, MidPeninsula Support Network for Battered Women, 1990-92, Palo Alto Coun. PTAs, Leadership Palo Alto; pres. Palo Alto Stanford divsn. Am. Heart Assn.; v.p. Assn. for Sr. Day Health; founder Safer Summer Project; pres., legal counsel Calif. Abortion Rights Action League, 1980-86. Mem. Am. Arbitration Assn. (mem. atty. panel), Calif. Women Lawyers (v.p. 1986-88). Home: 722 Ashby Dr Palo Alto CA 94301

KLEINE, KAREN DIANNE, funeral director; b. Beatrice, Nebr., Mar. 9, 1944; d. Lloyd I. and Eloise M.E. (Stephenson) Metcalf; m. Larry G. Kleine, June 7, 1964; children: Kristine S., Jerry L., Janet Jo. Student, Nebr. Wesleyan U., 1962-63, U. Nebr., Lincoln, 1962-63, 82-83, U. Nebr., Kearney, 1982-83; grad., Dallas Inst. Funeral Svc., 1983. Lic. funeral dir. and embalmer, Nebr. Funeral dir. Livingston-Somdermann Funeral Home, Grand Island, Nebr., 1983-92; owner, operator Kleine Funeral Home, Grand Island, 1992—; eneculator Lions Eye Bank, 1985—. Vice chmn., chmn. Nebr. SIDS Found., 1985—; dir. Carpenter's Kids Choir, St. Paul's Luth. Ch., 1980-90. Mem. Nat. Funeral Dirs. Assn., Nebr. Funeral Dirs. Assn. (conv. and continuing edn. com. 1985-86, 93-94), Grand Island Heartland Singers (bd. dirs. 1972—), Altrusa, Kiwanis. Republican. Lutheran. Home: 2414 Vandergrift Grand Island NE 68803 Office: 3213 W North Front St Grand Island NE 68803

KLEINER, KATHLEEN ALLEN, psychology educator; b. Phila., Nov. 12, 1958; d. William Anton and Marjorie Anne (Fine) K.; m. Roy Owen Gathercoal, Aug. 9, 1988; 1 child, Glen William Gathercoal. AB, Franklin & Marshall Coll., Lancaster, Pa., 1981; MA, PhD, Case Western Res. U., 1985. Teaching asst. Franklin & Marshall Coll., 1980-81; rsch. asst. Case Western Res. U., Cleve., 1981-85; researcher U. Calif., Berkeley, 1985-87; asst. prof. psychology Ind. U.-Purdue U., Indpls., 1987-93; asst. prof. psychology, chair dept. psychology George Fox Coll., Newberg, Oreg., 1993—; summer faculty fellow Ind. U., Bloomington, 1988. Contbr. articles to profl. jours. Evaluation mem. Campaign for Healthy Babies, Indpls., 1990-92; active Yamhill County Commn. on Children and Families. Nat. Inst. Child Health and Human Devel. predoctoral fellow, 1981-85; Case Western Res. U. grad. alumni grantee, 1984, Project Devel. Program Interdisciplinary grantee Ind. U.-Purdue U., 1990, Intercampus Rsch. Funds, Ind. U., 1991. Mem. Am. Psychol. Soc., Midwest Psychol. Assn., Soc. Rsch. in Child Devel., Internat. Soc. Infant Studies, Psi Chi. Mem. Soc. of Friends. Home: 2504 Haworth Ave Newberg OR 97132 Office: George Fox Coll 414 N Meridian St Newberg OR 97132

KLEINER, SHIRLY ANN, accounting educator; b. Wamego, Kans., June 1, 1950; d. Edward Leroy and Twilla Lou (Fair) Leslie; m. David Allen Kleiner, Nov. 28, 1969; children: Brandi Kristi, Megan Amber, Travis David Edward. AA, Johnson County C.C., 1976; BA, Avila Coll., 1979; MBA, U. Kans., 1989. Cert. mgmt. acct.; cert. profl. sec. Loan closing sec. Capitol Fed. Savs. and Loan, Overland Park, Kans., 1970-71; adminstrv. asst. Thompson-Hayward Chem. Co., Kansas City, Kans., 1972-75; adj. instr. bus. Avila Coll., Kansas City, Mo., 1980-83; adj. instr. bus. Johnson County C.C., Overland Park, 1980-90, instr. acctg., 1990—; gen. cons. Small Bus. Devel. Ctr., Overland Park, 1989; gen. cons. SBDC, Overland Park, 1989—; book reviewer U. Kans., Lawrence, 1988-89. Facilities coord. Luth. Women's Missionary League, Kansas City, 1994—; active Redeemer Luth Ch., Olathe, Kans., 1979—. Mem. Inst. of Mgmt. Accts., Profl. Secs. Inst., Phi Delta Kappa, Phi Kappa Phi, Beta Gamma Sigma. Home: 15117 S Seminole Dr Olathe KS 66062-3004 Office: Johnson County CC 12345 College Blvd Overland Park KS 66210-1283

KLEINLEIN, KATHY LYNN, training and development executive; b. S.I., N.Y., May 2, 1950; d. Thomas and Helen Mary (O'Reilly) Perricone; m. Kenneth Robert Kleinlein, Oct. 30, 1983. BA, Wagner Coll., 1971, MA, 1974; MBA, Rutgers U., 1984. Cert. secondary tchr., N.Y., N.J., Fla. Tchr. English, N.Y.C. Bd. Edn., S.I., 1971-74, Matawan (N.J.) Bd. Edn., 1974-79; instr. English, Middlesex County Coll., Edison, N.J., 1978-81; med. sales rep. Pfizer/Roerig, Bklyn., 1979-81, mgr. tng. ops., N.Y.C., 1981-87; dir. sales tng. Winthrop Pharms. div. Sterling Drug, N.Y.C., 1987-88; dir. tng. Reuters Info. Systems, N.Y.C., 1988—; pres., dir. tng., Women in Transition, career counseling firm; pres. Kleinlein Cons.; pers. mgmt. officer U.S. Army Res., N.J., 1981-86; cons. Concepts & Producers, N.Y.C., 1981-85. Trainer United Way, 1982-83, mem. polit. action com., 1982—; mem. Rep. Presdl. Task Force, Washington, 1983—. Capt. U.S. Army, 1974-78. First woman in N.Y. N.G., 1974; first woman instr. Empire State Mil. Acad., Peekskill, N.Y., 1976. Mem. Nat. Soc. Pharm. Sales Trainers, Sales and Mktg. Execs., Am. Soc. Tng. and Devel., N.J. Assn. Women Bus. Owners, LWV, Matawan C. of C., Alpha Omicron Pi. Republican. Roman Catholic. Club: Atlantis Divers (N.Y.C.). Home: 1840 Hudson St Englewood FL 34223-6433 Office: Kleinlein Cons 1840 Hudson St Englewood FL 34223-6433

KLEINMAN, SUSAN PHYLLIS, travel writer and photographer; b. N.Y.C., Aug. 30, 1947; d. Sol and Hermina (Marder) K. BS, SUNY, Cortland, 1968; MS, U. Ill., Champaign-Urbana, 1973; PhD, U. Ill., 1978. CLU, chartered fin. cons., registered health underwriter. Tchr. phys. edn. John H. Glenn High Sch., Elwood, N.Y., 1968-71; substitute tchr. Chgo. Pub. Schs., 1973-74; instr. Oakton Community Coll., Morton Grove, Ill., 1974-77, U. Ill. Circle Campus, Chgo., 1974-76; vis. instr. U. Ill., Champaign-Urbana, 1977-78; asst. prof. health edn. U. Ill. Med. Ctr., Sch. Pub. Health, Chgo., 1978-81; sales rep. Paul Revere Cos., Arlington Heights, Ill., 1981-86; underwriter Sun Fin. Group, Rosemont, Ill., 1986-91; prin. Banks & Kleinman Enterprises, Around and About, Evanston, 1991—; head start cons. Kirschner Assocs., Chgo., 1975-77, Roy Littlejohn Assocs., Chgo., 1976-77; cons. health edn. Native Am. Edn. Service, Chgo., 1976-77. Contbr. articles to profl. jours. Pres. Chgo.-City com. U.S. Com. for UNICEF, 1992—. Mem. Nat. Assn. Life Underwriters (cert.), Nat. Assn.

Health Underwriters (registered), Chgo. Assn. Life Underwriters, Eta Sigma Gamma. Jewish. Home: 736 Ridge Ave Evanston IL 60202-2683 Office: Banks & Kleinman Enterprise PO Box 6077 Evanston IL 60204

KLEINROCK, VIRGINIA BARRY, public relations executive; b. Boston, Nov. 5, 1947; d. Robert Edmund and Anne Marie (Crowley) Barry; m. Lewis James Kleinrock, Dec. 15, 1984. AS, Garland Jr. Coll., Boston, 1967; BS, East Carolina U., 1969; MS, Simmons Coll., 1973; postgrad. Sch. Bus. Communications, Boston U., 1973, 86, 88. Tchr. Somerville (Mass.) Pub. Schs., 1969-70; tchr. Newton (Mass.) Pub. Schs., 1970-84, career edn. program coord., 1978-83; pres. Infinite Energy, Belmont, Mass., 1982—; cons. McKnight Pub. Co., Bloomington, Ill., 1976-82; publicity coord./intern Impact Communications, Boston, 1982. Contbr. articles to profl. jours. Recipient Commendation for Excellence for Pilot Occupational Training Program, New Eng. Assn. of Schs. and Colls., 1969. Mem. Pub. Rels. Soc. Am., Counselors Acad., The Fashion Group, The Publicity Club of New Eng. (Disting. Svc. award 1984), Internat. Platform Assn., Internat. Women's Writing Guild. Office: Infinite Energy 11 Hough Rd Belmont MA 02178-1104

KLEINSCHNITZ, BARBARA JOY, oil company executive, consultant; b. Granite Falls, Minn., Aug. 25, 1944; d. Arthur William and Joy Ardys (Roe) Green; m. Charles Lewis Kleinschnitz, Dec. 28, 1963; 1 child, Katheryn JoAnn Kleinschnitz Hartstock. BBA, U. Denver, 1983; student, Colo. Women's Coll. Leadman Schlumberger Well Services, Denver, 1968-76; supr., log processing Scientific Software-Intercomp, Denver, 1976-82; tech. cons. Tech. Log Analysis, Inc., Lakewood, Colo., 1982-83; customer support mgr. Energy Systems Tech., Inc., Englewood, Colo., 1983-86; cons. technical Littleton, Colo., 1986—; documentation specialist Q.C. Data, Inc., 1987-91; tng. specialist Advanced Data Concepts, Ft. Collins, Colo., 1991-93; tech. writer Computer Data Sys., Inc., Ft. Collins, 1993—; cons. Tech. Log Analysis, Inc., Denver, 1982-83, Energy Systems Tech., 1986—. Vol. Denver Police Reserve, 1973-75. Mem. NOW, NAFE, Assn. Women Geoscientists, Soc. Profl. Well Log Analysts (bd. dirs. 1989-90, v.p. 1990-91), Denver Well Log Soc. (bd. dirs. 1986-87, v.p. 1987-88, pres. 1988-89). Democrat. Roman Catholic. Home: 3024 Appaloosa Ct Fort Collins CO 80526-2646 Office: 2625 Redwing Rd Ste 120 Fort Collins CO 80526-2878

KLEIST, GLORIA ANN, quality engineer; b. Warren, Mich., May 2, 1943; d. Donald Paul Vandervest and Pauline Olga (Mackie) Rothgarn; m. Donald Edward Kleist, May 20, 1988 (div. 1993); children: Virginia Ann Barz, Steven Thomas Garwood, Christopher Michael Madrazo. AAS, Macomb County Coll., 1982; BS in Mgmt., Ctrl. Mich. U., 1989, MS in Adminstrn., 1993. Cert. quality engr. Metrology tech. LTV Corp., Sterling Heights, Mich., 1973-77; layout inspector Computer Peripherals, Rochester, Mich., 1978-79; quality engr. Chrysler Corp., Detroit, 1979; lab. inspector Massey Ferguson, Detroit, 1979-81; calibration specialist Volkswagen Am., Troy, Mich., 1982-88; quality engr. Aeroquip, Mt. Clemens, Mich., 1988-89, Geometric Results Ford, Dearborn, Mich., 1989-90, TRW-SSD, Sterling Heights, 1990-92; advance quality engr. Morton Internat., Ogden, Utah, 1992—; mem. adj. faculty Macomb County Coll., Warren, 1986-87. Workshop presenter Expanding Your Horizons Weber State U., 1993. Mem. Am. Soc. for Quality Control. Home: 5826 Club View Ln Ogden UT 84405-4900

KLEKODA-BAKER, ANTONIA MARIE, forensic handwriting specialist, consultant; b. Grand Rapids, Mich., June 30, 1939; d. Anthony Joseph and Adele Elizabeth (Fifelski) Zoppa; m. Raymond Syl Klekoda, Aug. 31, 1957 (div. 1977); children: Cecilia (dec.), Vanessa, Rhonda, Darla, Norman, Yvette, Patrice; m. Frederick John Baker, Dec. 31, 1986. Student, Davenport Coll., Grand Rapids, Mich., 1956, Aquinas Coll., Grand Rapids, Mich., 1957-58, 77. Cert. document examiner. Organist, choir dir. Basilica of St. Adalbert, Grand Rapids, Mich., 1957-62; music instr. Mich. Acad. of Music, Northern Mich., 1962-63; owner Handwriting Analysis Service, Grand Rapids, 1963-87; editor Garfield Park Assn., Grand Rapids, Mich., 1974-76; feature columnist Grand Rapids Press., 1966-76; staff Diocesan Pubs., Grand Rapids, 1977-85; musician, Convs., community theater, Western Mich. Author: A Guide for Document Examiners in Preparing Your Curriculum Vitae, 1991; contbr. over 4000 articles to profl. jours. and mags.; delivered over 3500 lectrs. Resource authority Grand Rapids Pub. Library, 1976—; organizer City Neighborhood Assn., Garfield Park, Grand Rapids, 1973, mem. Greater Grand Rapids Convention Bur., 1984-85. Recipient Safety Engrs. award W. Mich. Chpt. Soc. Safety Engrs., 1985, Holland Rotarian award, Holland, Mich. Rotary Club, 1985, Sparta Rotary award, Sparta, Mich. Rotary Club, 1986. Mem. Nat. Assn. Pastoral Musicians, Nat. Assn. of Document Examiners (edn. chmn. 1991, v.p. nominee 1992, pres. nominee 1992), Alliance Women Entrepreneurs, Grand Rapids Fedn. Musicians, Mich. Graphol. Resources (chairperson, Woman of Yr. 1986-87), Data Personnel Mgmt. Assn. Roman Catholic. Home and Office: 325 Aurora St SE Grand Rapids MI 49507-3123

KLEM, MARY THERESA, communications executive; b. Portland, Oreg., Feb. 12, 1961; d. Clayton Kelly and Gwendolyn Avonne (Yeo) Gross; m. John Martin Klem, Nov. 21, 1992. BA, U. Oreg., 1983. Staff writer North Columbia Reporter, Clatskanie, Oreg., 1983-84; news reporter Times Publs., Tigard, Oreg., 1984-86; pub. info. officer Oreg. Dept. Environ. Quality, Portland, 1986-87; pub. rels. officer Oreg. State Bar, Lake Oswego, 1987-89; corp. comm. mgr. Levi Strauss & Co., San Francisco, 1990—. Bd. dir. Goodwill Industries of San Francisco, San Mateo and Marin Counties, San Francisco, 1992-93. Mem. Internat. Assn. Bus. Communicators. Office: Levi Strauss & Co 1155 Battery St San Francisco CA 94111-1230

KLEMENS, SUSAN MARGARET, photo editor, photographer; b. Sydney, Australia, Oct. 27, 1954; d. Paul Gustav and Ruth Hannah (Weiner) K.; m. Daniel Alexander Root, Oct. 29, 1979; 1 child, Melinda Ida. BA in Photjournalism, Polit. Philosophy, Syracuse U., 1976. Photographer UPI, Washington, 1981; comml. photographer pvt. practice, Alexandria, Va., 1981-86; photo editor Nat. Geographic World, Washington, 1987, Gannett Rochester (N.Y.) Newspapers, 1988-89, Detroit News, 1989-90; assoc. editor, rschr. Time Life Books, Alexandria, Va., 1990-92; mgr. Content Prodn. Ctr. Picture Network Internat., Arlington, Va., 1993—. Recipient 3d pl. award feature photography White hOuse News Photographers Assn., Washington, 1981. Mem. Am. Soc. Picture Profls. Office: Picture Network Internat 2000 14th St N Arlington VA 22201

KLEPPER, ANNE, journalist, speechwriter; b. Denver, Sept. 19, 1920; d. Max and Ethel (Perlstein) Lopatin; m. Sidney Lester Klepper, Feb. 3, 1951; 1 child, Leslie Klepper Arkin. BA magna cum laude, U. Colo., 1942. Intern Nat. Inst. Pub. Affairs, Washington, 1942; panel asst. disputes Nat. War Labor Bd., Washington, 1942-45; dep., chief of agy. Nat. Railway Labor Panel, Washington, 1946-47; researcher, reporter Time, N.Y.C., 1948-54; speechwriter, spl. asst. to pres., dir. corp. contbns. Time Inc., 1955-73; sr. rsch. assoc., dir. contributions mgmt. inst. Conf. Bd., N.Y.C., 1974-93; bd. dirs. WNYC Found., N.Y.C., 1984—. Bd. dir. Nat. Charities Info. Bur., N.Y.C., 1969-81,. Mem. Phi Beta Kappa. Home: 520 E 90th St New York NY 10128-7850

KLEPPER, CAROL JEAN, mental health therapist; b. Wagner, S.D., July 17, 1933; d. Forrest Glenwood and Augusta Wilhamina (Mills) Herdman; m. Albert Raymond Klepper, May 14, 1955; children: James David, Leesa Lynn, Krista Patrice. BS in Psychology cum laude, S. Oreg. State Coll., 1987; MS in Counseling, Oreg. State U., 1989. Nat. cert. counselor, lic. profl. counselor. Dir. counseling Klamath Hospice, Klamath Falls, Oreg., 1990-91; staff therapist Klamath Mental Health Ctr., 1991-94; in-house counselor Wednesday's Child, 1995—; data rschr. Rich Pickett and Co., Klamath Falls, 1986-90; pre-commitment investigator Klamath Mental Health Ctr., 1991-94; EPSDT coord. County of Klamath, 1991-94. Mem. youth svcs. team local mid-schs., Klamath Falls, 1992-94; juvenile fire-setters network Klamath Falls Fire Dist. #1, 1992—; head start health bd., Klamath Falls, 1991—. Mem. Psi Chi. Democrat. Home: 8926 Hwy 66 Klamath Falls OR 97601

KLEPPER, ELIZABETH LEE, physiologist; b. Memphis, Mar. 8, 1936; d. George Madden and Margaret Elizabeth (Lee) K. BA, Vanderbilt U., 1958; MA, Duke U., 1963, PhD, 1966. Research scientist Commonwealth Sci. and Indsl. Research Orgn., Griffith, Australia, 1966-68, Battelle Northwest Lab., Richland, Wash., 1972-76; asst. prof. Auburn (Ala.) U., 1968-72; Plant physiologist USDA Agrl. Research Service, Pendleton, Oreg., 1976-85, research leader, 1985—. Assoc. editor Crop Sci., 1977-80, 88-90, tech. editor, 1990-92, editor, 1992—; mem. editorial bd. Plant Physiology, 1977-92; mem. editorial adv. bd. Field Crops Rsch., 1983-91; mem. editorial bd. Irrigation Sci., 1987-92; contbr. articles to profl. jours., chpts. to books. Marshall scholar British Govt., 1958-59; NSF fellow, 1964-66. Fellow AAAS, Crop Sci. Soc. Am. (fellows com. 1989-91), Soil Sci. Soc. Am. (fellows com. 1986-88), Am. Soc. Agronomy (monograph com. 1983-90); mem. Sigma Xi. Home: 1454 SW 45th Pendleton OR 98701 Office: USDA Argl Rsch Svc PO Box 370 Pendleton OR 98701

KLEPPINGER, MOSELLE LEE, public relations professional; b. Worland, Wyo., Mar. 2, 1956; d. Kenneth Myron and Moselle Loretta (Shelton) K.; m. Tim Lee Romanek, May 28, 1983 (div. 1987); m. Mark David Cheesbrough, Dec. 30, 1994. BS, U. Wyo., 1978, MA, 1980, postgrad., 1980—. Pub. rels. officer Natrona County Sch. Dist., Casper, Wyo., 1976; corr., intern Casper Star-Tribune, 1976-78; corr., intern KTWO-TV, Casper, 1978-79, reporter, 1979-87; asst. dir. pub. rels. Casper Coll., 1987-95; bd. dirs. Conv. and Visitors Bur., Casper C. of C., mem. mktg. com., 1992-94. Participant Leaderhsip Casper, 1990-91, co-chair, 1991-92; bd. dirs. Cultural Affairs Com. Chamber, Casper, 1988-94, Troopers Drum and Bugle Corps, Casper, 1989-93, Big Bros.-Big Sisters, Casper, 1991-94; mem. Stage III Cmty. Theatre, Casper, 1980-94, bd. dirs., 1980-87, pres. 1984-87. Recipient Hist. award Wyo. State Hist. Soc., 1987; named Outstanding Young Women of Am., 1987. Mem. Casper Area Mktg. Profls., Soroptimist Internat. (exec. bd. ctrl. Wyo. chpt. 1990-94). Methodist. Home: 717 Independence Dr Longmont CO 80501

KLIEBHAN, SISTER M(ARY) CAMILLE, academic administrator; b. Milw., Apr. 4, 1923; d. Alfred Sebastian and Mae Eileen (McNamara) K. Student, Cardinal Stritch Coll., Milw., 1945-48; B.A., Cath. Sisters Coll., Washington, 1949; M.A., Cath. U. Am., 1951, Ph.D., 1955. Joined Sisters of St. Francis of Assisi, Roman Catholic Ch., 1945; legal sec. Spence and Hanley (attys.), Milw., 1941-45; instr. edn. Cardinal Stritch Coll., 1955-62, assoc. prof., 1962-68, prof., 1968—, head dept. edn., 1962-67, dean students, 1962-64, chmn. grad. div., 1964-69, v.p. for acad. and student affairs, 1969-74, pres., also bd. dirs., 1974-91, chancellor, 1991—. Bd. dirs. Goals for Milw. 2000, 1980-83; treas. Wis. Found. Ind. Colls., 1974-79, 87-90, v.p., 1979-81, pres., 1981-83; bd. dirs. DePaul Hosp., 1982-91, Sacred Heart Sch. Theology, 1983—, Viterbo Coll., 1990—, Milw. Cath. Home, 1991—, St. Ann Adult Day Care, 1994—, Wis. Psychoanalytic Found., 1991—; mem. adv. bd. St. Camillus Campus, 1989—; bd. dirs. Internat. Inst. of Wis., 1984—, Mental Health Assn. Milwaukee County, 1983-87, Pub. Policy Forum, 1987-90, Better Bus. Bur. of Wis. Inc., 1989—; mem. TEMPO, 1982—, bd. dirs., 1986-89; bd. govs. Wis. Policy Rsch. Inst., 1987—. Mem. Am. Psychol. Assn., Rotary Club of Milw. (v.p., pres. elect 1992-93, pres. 1993-94), Phi Delta Kappa, Delta Epsilon Sigma, Psi Chi, Delta Kappa Gamma, Kappa Delta Pi.

KLIETHERMES, MARY ALICE, trade association administrator; b. Detroit, Oct. 27, 1960; d. George M. and Victoria (Ohanesian) Kurajian; m. Allen R. Kliethermes, Sept. 3, 1988. BA, U. Mich., 1982. Cert. bus. communicator. Sr. editor Entertainment Publs., Birmingham, Mich., 1984-85; copy editor Creative Universal, Warren, Mich., 1985-86; promotions adminstr. Soc. Mfg. Engrs., Dearborn., Mich., 1986—. Author: (with George M. Kurajian) Expanding Design Creativity, 1985. Recipient Galaxy award N.Y.C., 1990. Mem. Bus. and Profl. Advt. Assn., Direct Mktg. Assn. Detroit. Office: Soc Mfg Engrs 1 SME Dr PO Box 930 Dearborn MI 48121

KLIMA, MARTHA SCANLAN, state legislator; b. Balt., Dec. 3, 1938; d. Thomas Moore and Catherine A. (Stafford) Scanlan; m. James Patrick Klima Jr., Apr. 8, 1961; children: Jennifer, J. Patrick III, Andrew. AA, Villa Julie Coll., 1958. Med. stenographer U. Md. Med. Sch., Balt., 1958-63; mem. appropriations com. Md. Ho. of Dels., Annapolis, 1982—; sec. Cen. Md. Health Systems Agy., 1981-83; commr. State Planning Commn., State of Md., 1983—. Del. Rep. Nat. Conv. Dallas, 1984; bd. dirs. Greater Balt. Med. Ctr., Towson, 1986-91, Md. Spl. Olympics, 1987—. Named Freshman of Yr., Ho. of Dels., 1984, Woman of Yr. Towsontowne Bus. and Profl. Women's Club; recipient Gov.'s Citation for Outstanding Svc. to Citizens of Md., 1988, Pub. Svc. award for Outstanding Support to Balt. Assn. Retarded Citizens, Inc., 1994. Mem. Am. Legis. Exchange Coun. (state chmn. 1987—, Outstanding State Legislator award 1994), Women Legis. Md., Congress of PTA's (hon. life), Balt. County C. of C. (award of merit 1981), Exchange Club (Balt.). Republican. Roman Catholic. Home: 1403 Newport Pl Lutherville Timonium MD 21093-5920 Office: Ho Reps State Capital Annapolis MD 21401

KLIMCHAK, COLLEEN PAVICK, critical care nurse, nursing administrator; b. Latrobe, Pa., Aug. 30, 1960; d. Andrew Charles and Mary Margaret (Hohn) Pavick; m. Ronald C. Klimchak, Oct. 3, 1987; 1 child, Justin Robert. ADN, Westmoreland County Community Coll., Youngwood, Pa., 1981; BS in Nursing, Pa. State U., 1990; student, U. Pitts., 1978-79. RN med.-surg. pediatrics Jeannette (Pa.) Dist. Meml. Hosp., 1981-85; RN ICCU Latrobe (Pa.) Area Hosp., 1985-92, head nurse recovery rm., 1992—. Mem. ASPAN, Sigma Theta Tau. Home: 106 Rocky Mountain Ct Latrobe PA 15650-2409

KLINCK, CYNTHIA ANNE, library director; b. Salamanaca, N.Y., Nov. 1, 1948; d. William James and Marjorie Irene (Woodruff) K.; m. Andrew Clavert Humphries, Nov. 26, 1983. BS, Ball State U., 1970; MLS, U. Ky., 1976. Reference/ young adult libr. Bartholomew County Libr., Columbus, Ind., 1970-74; dir. Paul Sawyier Pub. Libr., Frankfort, Ky., 1974-78, Washington Twp. Pub. Libr., Dayton, Ohio, 1978—. Contbr. articles to profl. mags. Bd. dirs. Bluegrass Community Action Agy., Franfort, Ky., 1971-73; founder, bd. dirs. FACTS, Inc. (info. & referral), Frankfort, 1972-74; cofounder, bd. dirs. Seniors, Inc., Dayton, Ohio, 1980-81, 91—; trustee, officer South Community, Inc. Mental Health Ctr., Dayton, 1980-89. Mem. ALA, Am. Soc. for Info. Sci., Am. Soc. for Pers. Adminstrn., Ohio Libr. Assn. (chmn. legis. com.), Rotary Internat. Office: Washington-Centerville Pub Libr 111 W Spring Valley Rd Dayton OH 45458-1998

KLINCK, PATRICIA EWASCO, state official; b. Albany, N.Y., May 13, 1940; d. Albert C. and Mary Ann (Sopko) Ewasco; m. C. Hoagland Klinck, Jr., Sept. 12, 1970; 1 dau., Natalie Childs. B.A. in History, Smith Coll., 1961; M.S. in L.S, Simmons Coll., Boston, 1963; postgrad. in edn., SUNY, Albany, 1964-67; student sr. exec. program, Harvard U., 1989. Young adult worker Boston Pub. Libr., 1961-63; libr. dir. Colonie Central High Sch., Albany, 1963-67; libr. Libr./U.S.A., U.S. Pavilion, N.Y. World's Fair, summer 1965; libr. dir. Simon's Rock Coll., Gt. Barrington, Mass., 1967-70; regional dir. N.W. Regional Libr. Vt. Dept. Librs., Montpelier, 1970-72; dir. extension svcs. div. Vt. Dept. Librs., 1972-73, 73-74, acting asst. state libr., 1973, asst. state libr., 1974-77, state libr., 1977—; chmn. New Eng. Libr. Bd., 1979-81; vice chmn. Chief Officer State Libr. Agys., 1978-80, chmn., 1981-82; mem. White House Conf. Preliminary Design Commn., 1985-86, Gov.'s Telecomms. Tech. Coun. Vt., 1994—, Info. Resources Mgmt. Adv. Coun., 1993—. Bd. dirs. Vt. Hist. Soc., 1977—; mem. Vt. Bicentennial Commn., 1986-72; mem. Vt. Coun. on Humanities, 1987-91; incorporator Vt. Ctr. of the Book, 1993. Mem. ALA (legis. com. 1966-68), Assn. State Libr. Agys. (bd. dirs. with ALA 1986-88), Assn. Specialized and Coop. Libr. Agys. of ALA (bd. dirs.), New England Libr. Assn., Vt. Libr. Assn. Home: 47 Brewer Pky South Burlington VT 05403 Office: Vt State Dept of Librs 109 State St Montpelier VT 05609-0001

KLINE, BONITA ANN, middle school guidance counselor, educator; b. Charleroi, Pa., Sept. 25, 1952; d. Milton Paul Kobaly and Ann Marie (Gohosky) George; m. Dennis Charles Kline, Aug. 8, 1981. BS in Elem. Edn., U. Pitts., 1973; MEd, Calif. (Pa.) U., 1973; postgrad., U. Pitts., 1986—. Cert. elem. tchr., Pa., elem. guidance counselor, Pa., elem. prin., Pa. Juvenile probation officer Westmoreland County Court System, Greensburg, Pa., 1974; elem. tchr. Belle Vernon (Pa.) Area Sch. Dist., 1975—. Del. Mon Valley Ctrl. Labor Coun., Charleroi, Pa., 1988—. Mem. Ea. Pa. Profl. Womens Group, Tri-State Area Sch. Study Coun., PTO. Democrat. Roman Catholic. Home: RR 2 Box 268 C Belle Vernon PA 15012-9616 Office: Belle Vernon Area Sch Dist Circle Dr Belle Vernon PA 15012

KLINE, CAROLE JUNE, special education educator; b. Youngstown, Ohio, June 16, 1947; d. Stephen and Mary (Kuzniak) Yourst; m. Ronald Edward Kline, Aug. 3, 1968; children: Christopher John, Melinda Marie. BS in Elem. Edn., Kent State U., 1968, MEd in Spl. Edn., 1970; postgrad., L.I. U., 1987. Cert. tchr. spl. edn., elem. and nursery sch., N.Y. Libr. I reference rm. Kent (Ohio) State U., 1968; intermediate EMR tchr. Niles (Ohio) City Schs., 1969-75; tchr. elem. spl. edn. Fulton (N.Y.) City Schs., 1984-88; subs. tchr. Baldwinsville (N.Y.) Ctrl. Schs., 1982-84, resource tchr. jr. high sch., 1984, resource and spl. edn. tchr. jr. high sch., 1988—; homebound instr. Baldwinsville Ctrl. Schs., 1988-91. Active Seneca Gardens Homeowners Assn., Baldwinsville, 1978—, mem. Baldwinsville Community Band, 1988—. Mem. NEA, Nat. Edn. Assn. N.Y. (del. 1993, 94, 95), Baldwinsville Tchr.'s Assn. (exec. com. 1990—, bldg. rep. 1988—), Coun. for Exceptional Children (rsch. divsn. 1990—), Coun. for Children with Behavioral Disorders (divsn. for learning disabilities 1990—), Kent State Alumni Assn. Democrat. Roman Catholic. Home: 1607 S Ivy Trl Baldwinsville NY 13027-9047 Office: Durgee Jr High Sch E Oneida St Baldwinsville NY 13027

KLINE, EVELYN J., social worker; b. Littletown, Pa., June 25, 1937; d. Ammon Henry and Alice Amelia (Anthony) Rodgers; m. Eugene Raymond Kline, July 11, 1954 (div. 1991, dec. 1994); children: Stephen Eugene (dec.), Bradley Lee, Debra Helen. AA in Human Svcs., Harrisburg Area Community Coll., Pa., 1994; diploma Dental Asst., U. N.C., Chapel Hill, 1976. Sec. St. Marks Luthern Ch., Hanover, Pa., 1954-59; exec. sec. Alwine Brick Co., New Oxford, Pa., 1962-69; dental asst., office mgr. Mark S. Tome, DDS, Hanover, Pa., 1969-77; pub. affairs dir. Radio Hanover, Hanover, Pa., 1977-82; adult activities dir. YWCA, York and Hanover, Pa., 1982-88; case mgr., social worker Luthern Social Svcs., York, Pa., 1988—. Freelance writer: (newspapers) Evening Sun, Sunday News, 1977-82. Pres. Human Svcs. Orgn., Hanover, Pa., 1985; bd. dirs Displaced Homemakers, York, Pa., 1987; mem. Community Needs Coalition, St. Matthew's Lutheran Ch. Recipient Jefferson award WGAL-TV, Lancaster, Pa. Mem. AARP, Am. Bus. Women Assn. (v.p. 1982, Woman of the Yr. 1982), Hanover Dental Asst. (pres. 1974). Republican. Home: PO Box 1142 Brodbecks PA 17329 Office: Luthern Social Svcs 127 York St Hanover PA 17331

KLINE, LINDA, employment consultant; b. Boston, Aug. 8, 1940; d. George and Eva (Weiner) Kline; B.A. in Biology, Boston U., 1962. Pers. dir. Block Engring. Inc., Cambridge, Mass., 1964-66; brokerage mgr. Eastern Life Ins. Co. N.Y., Boston, 1966-68; mgr. direct placement Lendman Assos., N.Y.C., 1968-72; dir. women-in-mgmt. div. Roberts-Lund, Ltd., N.Y.C., 1972-77; prin. Kline-McKay, Inc., (name changed to Kline Cons., Inc. 1991), 1978-93; pres., mng. dir. The Arbor Group, Inc., N.Y.C., 1994—; exec. dir. Majority Money, women's network, 1976-79; tchr. fin. planning for women Marymount-Manhattan Coll., 1977; lectr. and/or cons. women's programs at several colls. and univs. and corps. Co-author: Career Changing: The Worry-Free Guide, 1982. Bd. dirs. Women Bus. Owners Edn. Fund, 1982-86, Mom's Amazing, 1985-88; community bd. dirs. Mt. Sinai Med. Ctr., 1984—; adv. counselor U.S. Small Bus. Adminstrn. WNET Program. Mem. Internat. Assn. Outplacement Profls., Women Bus. Owners N.Y. (bd. dirs. 1978-84), Nat. Coalition Women's Enterprise (adv. bd. 1988-89). Office: The Arbor Group Inc 9 E 37th St New York NY 10016

KLINE, MABLE CORNELIA PAGE, secondary education educator; b. Memphis, Aug. 20, 1928; d. George M. and Lillie (Davidson) Brown; 1 dau., Gail Angela Page. Student LeMoyne Coll.; BSEd, Wayne State U., 1948, postgrad. Tchr., Flint, Mich., 1950-51, Pontiac, Mich., 1953-62; tchr. 12th grade English, Cass Tech High Sch., Detroit, 1962—, coord. Study Skills Program; mem. English Book Selection com., 1986—. Life mem. YWCA, NAACP. Detroit Pub. Edn. Fund grantee, 1989. Mem. NEA (life), Assn. Supervision and Curriculum Devel., Am. Fedn. Tchrs., Nat. Council Tchrs. English, Wayne State U. Alumni Assn., Delta Sigma Theta. Episcopalian. Home: 555 Brush St Apt # 1512 Detroit MI 48226 Office: Cass Tech High Sch English Dept 2421 2d Ave Detroit MI 48201

KLINE, MARY FRANCES, graphic artist; b. Balt., Mar. 13, 1961; d. Robert Joseph and Catherie Marie (O'Brien) Hagen; m. Michael Richard Kline, Oct. 19, 1985; 1 child, John Patrick. BFA, Kutztown State U., 1983. Graphic designer Mark Trece, Inc., Balt., 1983-84, Eichhorn Printing Co., Balt., 1984-85, Bruning Paint Co., Balt., 1985-86; mgr. arts and graphics Crown Cen. Petroleum Corp., Balt., 1986-91; acct. exec. Moneypenny Graphics, Inc., 1991-92, The Collateral Group, Balt., 1992-93; account exec. Harvey & Daus., Inc., Hunt Valley, Md., 1993—. Mem. Am. Mktg. Assn. (bd. dirs. Balt. chpt.). Republican. Roman Catholic. Office: Harvey & Daughters Inc 116 Old Padonia Rd # C Cockeysville MD 21030-4918

KLINE, PAMELA IRIS, consulting company executive; b. Pitts., Aug. 23, 1958; d. Robert Edward and Rae R. Kline. Cert., U. Paris, Sorbonne, 1979; AB magna cum laude, Harvard U., 1980, MBA, 1984. Asst. staff mgr. Bell of Pa., Phila., 1980-82; product mgr. Visa Internat., San Francisco, 1983; v.p. Prognostics, Palo Alto, Calif., 1984-91; dir. Diefenbach/Elkins, San Francisco, 1991-92; ptnr. Regis McKenna, Inc., 1992—. Vol. San Jose Civic Lights, 1987; dir. Harvard/Radcliffe Fundraising, Boston, 1980—; chmn. Harvard/Radcliffe Schs. com., San Mateo County, 1985—. Mem. Young Profl. Woman Assn., Radcliffe Club (dir. 1987—), Harvard Club. Republican. Home: 570 Beale St Apt 416 San Francisco CA 94105-2025 Office: Regis McKenna Inc 1755 Embarcadero Rd Palo Alto CA 94303-3304

KLINE, VICKI ANN, stockbroker; b. Monterey, Tenn., Oct. 26, 1948; d. William John and Betty (Coleman) Harden; children: David, John, Lori, Lisa, Daniel. BS in Acctg., Nova U., 1983; MBA, Kent State U., 1994. CPA, Ohio. Internal auditor Roadway Svc., Akron, Ohio, 1984-85; acctg. mgr. A. Schulman Inc., Fairlawn, Ohio, 1985-93; stockbroker Butler Wick & Co., Inc., Kent, Ohio, 1993—. Mem. AICPA, Ohio Soc. CPAs, Inst. Mgmt. Accts. Home: 1282 Congress Lake Rd Mogadore OH 44260 Office: Butler Wick & Co Inc 149 N Water St Kent OH 44240-2418

KLINEFELTER, HYLDA CATHARINE, obstetrician-gynecologist; b. Gettysburg, Pa., Sept. 28, 1929; d. Roscoe Emanuel and Sara Catherine (Wagner) K.; m. Edward Ralph Kohnstam, June 18, 1955; children: Charles, Kathryn. Student, Gettysburg Coll., 1947-48; AB, U. Pa., 1951; MD, Med. Coll. Pa., 1955. Diplomate Am. Bd. Ob-Gyn. Rotating intern Phila. Gen. Hosp., 1955-56; resident in ob.-gyn. Presbyn. U. Pa. Med. Ctr., Phila., 1956-59; mem. teaching staff Med. Coll. Pa., Phila., 1959-62; rsch. asst. maternal and child health Pa. Hosp., Phila., 1964-66; co-supr. family planning clinic Presbyn. Hosp./U. Pa. Med. Ctr., 1967-68; ptnr. Media (Pa.) Clinic, 1969-81; pvt. practice, 1981-86; ptnr. Granite Run Ob.-Gyn. Assocs., Media, 1986—; mem. staff Riddle Meml. Hosp., vice chmn. ob-gyn., 1989-93, chmn. ob-gyn., 1993—. Contbr. articles to med. jours. Fellow ACOG; mem. AMA, Am. Med. Womens Assn. (past treas. dist. 25), Reproductive Medicine Assn., Am. Assn. Gyn. Laparoscopists, Internat. Soc. Gynecology Endoscopy, Delaware County Med. Soc., Pa. Med. Soc., Fox Valley Civic Assn., Soroptomist, Alpha Xi Delta. Republican. Lutheran. Home: 264 Ivy Ln Glen Mills PA 19342-1322 Office: Granite Run Ob Gyn Assn 10881W Baltimore Pike Ste 2303 Media PA 19063-5104

KLINEFELTER, KAY ANNE, business education educator; b. Bloomsburg, Pa., Sept. 8, 1948; d. Albert Wayne and Ruth Dugan Smeal; m. D. Kerry Klinefelter, Aug. 15, 1970; children: Kelly, Christopher. BS, Bloomsburg U., 1970, MS, 1974; postgrad., Millersville U., Carlow Coll., 1988—. Cert. bus. edn. tchr., Pa. Tchr., curriculum planner Millersburg (Pa.) High Sch., 1970—; tutor, Millersburg, 1970—; advisor to sch. paper Millersburg High Sch., 1983-92, yearbook advisor, 1980-82, class advisor, 1970—. Mem. Upper Dauphin Arts Alliance, Millersburg, 1993. Mem. Pa. State Edn. Assn. (sec. 1970—), Pa. Bus. Edn. Assn. (Tchr. of Yr. 1994), Millersburg Area Edn. Assn., Delta Kappa Gamma. Home: RR 1 Box 170 Millersburg PA 17061-9709

KLINEFELTER, SARAH STEPHENS, division dean, radio station manager; b. Des Moines, Jan. 30, 1938; d. Edward John and Mary Ethel (Adams) Stephens; m. Neil Klinefelter. BA, Drake U., 1958; MA, U. Iowa, Iowa City, 1968; postgrad., Harvard U., July, 1984, U. Wis., Sept., 1987, Vanderbilt U., 1991-92. Chmn. humanities dept. High Sch. Dist. 230, Orland Pk., Ill., 1958-68; chmn. communications and humanities div. Kirkwood Community Coll., Cedar Rapids, Iowa, 1968-78; prof. English Sch. of the

Ozarks, Point Lookout, Mo., 1978-86; gen. mgr. Sta. KSOZ-FM, Point Lookout, 1986-90; dean div. of performing and profl. arts Coll. of the Ozarks, Point Lookout, 1989—. Commr. Skaggs Community Hosp., Branson, Mo., 1986—; chmn. Branson Planning and Zoning Commn., 1983; project dir. Mo. Humanities Bd.; commr., examiner North Cen. Assn. Higher Edn., 1978-85; commr. Iowa Humanities Bd., 1971-78; mem. Taney County Planning and Zoning Commn., 1989—. Democrat. Presbyterian. Home: PO Box 828 Point Lookout MO 65726-0828 Office: Coll of the Ozarks Point Lookout MO 65726

KLING, PHRADIE (PHRADIE KLING GOLD), small business owner; b. N.Y.C., July 2, 1933; d. Samuel A. and Mary Leah (Cohen) K.; m. Lee M. Gold, Sept. 5, 1955 (div. 1976); children: Judith Eileen, Laura Susan, Stephen Samuel, James David. BA, Cornell U., 1955; MA in Human Genetics, Sarah Lawrence Coll., 1971. Genetic counselor assoc. Coll. Medicine and Dentistry N.J., Newark, 1970-73; assoc. genetic counselor Sarah Lawrence Coll., Bronxville, N.Y., 1970-73; genetic counselor N.Y. Fertility Rsch. Found., N.Y.C., 1971-73; staff assoc., genetic counselor depts. pediatrics, ob-gyn and neurology Columbia U. Coll. Physicians and Surgeons, N.Y.C., 1973-78; asst. in genetics St. Luke's Hosp. Ctr., N.Y.C., 1977-79; health program assoc. Conn. Dept. Health Svcs., Hartford, 1978-84; edn. cons. Conn. Traumatic Brain Injury Assn., Rocky Hill, 1984-85; office mgr. Anderson Turf Irrigation Inc., Plainville, Conn., 1986-92; owner, mgr. KlingWorks, contract adminstrn., Avon, Conn., 1992—; speaker, instr. on health and health ethics issues, Conn., N.Y., N.J., 1971-85; dir. confs. on genetics and traumatic brain injury, 1980-85; project dir. ednl. field testing Biol. Scis. Curriculum Study, 1981-83; scientist AAAS Sci.-by-Mail, 1991—. Mem. Farmington River Watershed Assn., Simsbury, Conn., 1988—; docent Sci. Mus. Conn., West Hartford, 1989-90. Recipient citation for dedicated svc. Conn. Safety Belt Coalition, 1985. Mem. AAAS, Am. Human Genetics Soc., Bus. and Profl. Microcomputer Users Group (bd. dirs.), Conn. Assn. for Jungian Psychology (bd. dirs.), Conn. Computer Soc., Hastings Ctr., Am. Mensa (chpt. coord. gifted children 1985—). Home and Office: 33 Hunter Rd Avon CT 06001-3618

KLINGBEIL-ROSE, DEBORAH, Christian Science nurse; b. Rhinelander, Wis., Sept. 20, 1951; d. Bruce Owen and Gloria Clara (Braun) Klingbeil; m. Alan M. Rose, 1982 (div. 1987). Student, Christian Sci. Benevolent Assn, Chestnut Hill, Mass., 1969-70, Tenacre Sch. Christian Sic., Princeton, N.J., 1970-72, Ardenwood Christian Sic. Bene., San Francisco, 1989-90. C.S. nurse, 1969—; adminstr. Grayhaven Sch. C.S. Nursing, Lansdale, Pa., 1991—; v.p. Spindrift Inc., Lansdale, 1993—. Contbr. articles to C.S. Jour., C.S. Sentinel, C.S. Monitor, various newspapers and other religious mags. C.S. Office: Grayhaven Sch 100 W Main St Ste 408 Lansdale PA 19446

KLINGENBURG, ANNE LOUISE, graphic design artist; b. Williamsport, Pa., June 30, 1935; d. George Milard and Frances Mary (Roberts) Williams; m. Neil A. Klingenburg, June 21, 1976 (div. July 1989); 1 child, Laura. Cert. advt. design, Ringling Sch. Art, 1956; student, Newark Sch. Fine-Indsl. Art, 1953-55, N.Y. Sch. Visual Art, 1991—. With Julian Burg Advt. Agy., Miami, Fla., 1957-59; separation artist Am. Greeting Card Co., Miami, 1959-62; promotion artist Miami News, Miami, 1962-64; with Lafond Advt. Agy., N.Y.C., 1965-66, Rodgers Studio, N.Y.C., 1966-68, Lasky Printing Co., Millburn, N.J., 1968-77; pvt. practice graphic design artist New Providence, N.J.; computer graphic artist Logical Design Solutions, Inc., New Providence, N.J. Commd. painting Footprints on the Moon, Print N.J., 1988 (in Air and Space Mus., OH).

KLINGENSMITH, THELMA HYDE (MRS. DON. J. KLINGENSMITH), retired educational administrator; b. Rauville, S.D., May 23, 1904; d. Eber Watson and Ida (Lebert) Hyde; B.A. magna cum laude, John Fletcher Coll., 1928; M.S. in Ed., U. N.D., 1962; m. Don Joseph Klingensmith, Sept. 11, 1930; children: Merle Joseph, Eunice Victoria Klingensmith Evans. Tchr. rural schs., Almont, N.D., 1922-24; exec. sec. Young People's Gospel League, Chgo., 1928-30; asst. supt. Ponca Meth. Indian Mission, Ponca City, Okla., 1936-43; tchr. English, Almont High Sch., 1951-54; supt. schs. Morton County, Mandan, N.D., 1959-73; mem. Am. Assn. Sch. Adminstrs. seminar to Russia, 1969, N.D. coun. of Sch. Adminstr. 1959—. Bd. dirs. N.D. div. Am. Cancer Soc., 1958-72, chmn. pub. edn. com., 1958-60, sec., 1960-66; sr. v.p. N.D. Young Citizens League, 1959-63, sr. pres., 1963-65; legis. rep. N.D. County Supts. Assn., 1963-66; vol. legis. lobbyist in family and edn. issues, 1959-89; mem. Vennard Coll. Tour of Holy Lands, 1973; vol. U.S. Ctr. for World Missions, Pasadena, Calif., 1989-90; adviser Morton County Libr. Bd., 1960—, trustee, 1977-83, 84-89; sec.-treas. Heart River Gospel Assn., 1950-66, sec.-treas., 1992, dir., 1950—; dir., treas. N.D. Action Com. for Environ. Edn., 1968-75; bd. dirs. Dickinson Coll. Found. 1969-88; v.p. West Wis. Conf., Women's Soc. Christian Svc., Methodist Ch., 1945-46; legis. rep. N.D. Woman's Christian Temperance Union, 1978-89; Western dist. coord. Christian Social involvement N.D. Conf., United Meth. Women, 1979-83; Western dist. coord. Christian Personhood, 1983-85; Dakota area del. Internat. Conf. Christian Heritage in Govt., United Meth. Ch., London, 1981; co-chmn. nat. Conv. Prohibition Party, 1983; treas. N.D. Coun. on Gambling Problems, 1985-88. Named N.D. Mother of the Yr., 1965; recipient citation for conservation edn. Nat. and N.D. wildlife fedns., 1974, Pres.' citation Vennard Coll., 1984, tribute and statuette N.D. Eagle Forum, 1985; honored as "The Pink Lady" N.D. Legis. Assembly, 1987. Mem. Mandan Hosp. Aux., Mandan Friends of the Libr., Am. Bible Soc., N.D. Libr. Assn. (trustee citation award 1980, cert. of appreciation 1982), N.D. Libr. Trustees Assn. (v.p. 1967-68, 74-76, sec. 1971-73, dir. 1976-82, pres. 1979-81), N.D. Wildlife Fedn. (chmn. essay contest 1973-78), Marquis Libr. Soc. (adv. mem.), Woman's Christian Temperance Union (treas. 1977-93). Clubs: Golden Grad of Vennard Coll. (pres. 1981-84) (University Park, Iowa); Zonta (dist. VII chmn. pub. affairs com. 1968-70; del. internat. convs. 1968, 70, 72). Editor: Almont Jubilee History Book, 1956; Morton County Elementary Tchrs. Bull., 1959-73. Home: 206 Collins Ave PO Box 663 Mandan ND 58554

KLINGER, JUDITH ANN, elementary education educator; b. Phila., Apr. 3, 1943; d. Ralph Paul and Margaret Elizabeth (Griffiths) Tarbutton; divorced; 1 child, Gayle Michele Grove. BS in Edn., Shippensburg State Coll., 1964, MEd, 1966; postgrad., Pa. State U., Millersville U., Shippensburg U., 1967-92. Cert. elem. tchr., Pa. Elem. educator Red Lion (Pa.) Area Sch. Dist., 1964-66, 70—, elem. libr. sci. educator, 1966-69; mem. lang. arts com. Red Lion Area Sch. Dist., 1988—, mem. whole lang. com., 1990—, assessment com., 1992—. Mem. Friends of Kaltreider Meml. Libr., Red Lion, 1989—; chmn. edn. com. St. Paul's United Meth. Ch., 1982-87, Sunday sch. supt., 1984-87, chmn. coun. on ministries, 1988-90. Mem. Order of Eastern Star (worthy matron 1974-75). Republican. Home: 706 S Main St Red Lion PA 17356-2605 Office: Mazie C Gable Elem Sch Cedar St Red Lion PA 17356-1199

KLINGER, PATRICIA, Congressional relations specialist; b. Pa., Sept. 14, 1958; d. Dean and Helen (Hornberger) K.; m. Francis Patrick Wathen II, Apr. 30, 1983 (separated); 1 child, Alexandra Lorraine Wathen. AA, Charles County C.C., La Plata, Md., 1988; student, U. Md. Congl. rels. specialist U.S. Dept. Transp., Washington, 1979-90, exec. asst., 1990-91, govt./pub. affairs specialist, 1991—. Fellow Coun. Excellence Govt. Office: US Dept Transp/RSPA 400 7th St SW Washington DC 20015

KLINGHOFFER, JUNE FLORENCE, physician, educator; b. Phila., Feb. 12, 1921; d. Harry and Esther (Uram) K.; m. Sidney U. Wenger, June 24, 1947; 1 child, Robert Klinghoffer Wenger. BA, U. Pa., 1941; MD, Woman's Med. Coll. Pa., Phila., 1945. Diplomate Am. Bd. Internal Medicine, Am. Bd. Rheumatology. Intern , then resident Albert Einstein Med. Ctr., Phila., 1945-47; fellow in pathology Woman's Med. Coll. Pa., 1947-48; prof. medicine Med. Coll. Pa., Phila., 1969—, Ethel Russell Morris prof. medicine, 1987—. Contbr. articles to med. jours. Recipient Lindback award for disting. teaching, 1965, Alumnae Achievement award Med. Coll. Pa., 1978. Fellow ACP, Phila. Coll. Physicians; mem. AMA, AAUP, Am. Med. Women's Assn., Assn. Am. Med. Colls., Am. Coll. Rheumatology, Alpha Omega Alpha. Home: 356 Meadow Ln Merion Station PA 19066-1331 Office: Med Coll Pa 3300 Henry Ave Philadelphia PA 19129-1191

KLINKENBERG, HILKA ELISABETH, management consultant; b. Bremen, Fed. Republic Germany, July 20, 1946; came to U.S., 1976; d. Lorenz and Agatha Margarete (Bohlen) K. BA, U. Toronto, Ont., Can., 1968. Mng. dir. Etiquette Internat., N.Y.C., 1989—. Contbr. monthly columns to Worldwide Practices Report, Agenda New York Mag. Vol. Vol. Svcs. for Children, N.Y.C., 1979-83, Helpline Telephone Crisis Counseling, N.Y.C., 1984-86; fund raising com. mem. Westchester Assn. for Retarded Citizens, White Plains, N.Y., 1991; fashion show coord. Guild for the Blind, N.Y.C., 1990. Mem. ASTD, NAFE, Am. Mgmt. Assn., Americas Soc., The Global Bus. Assn., Nat. Spkrs. Assn., Women in Comm. Office: Etiquette Internat 254 E 68th St New York NY 10021-6012

KLINKER, SHEILA ANN J., middle school educator, state legislator; m. Victor Klinker; children: Kerri, Kevin, Kelly. BS in Edn., Purdue U., MS in Elem. Edn., MS in Adminstrn. and Supervision. Tchr. Tecumseh Mid. Sch., 1982—; state rep. Ind. Ho. of Reps., Indpls., 1982—. Mem. St. Mary's Cathedral Parish; 1st woman appointee Tippecanoe Area Plan Commn.; bd. dirs. Lafayette Symphony, Opera de Lafayette, Tippecanoe County Chid Care, Purdue Musical Orgn.; past chairwoman pub. svc. divsn. United Way. Recipient Outstanding Svc. award Ind. Advocates for Children, Legis. award Assn. of RAAUW's Outstanding Woman in Politics, Woman of Distinction award Sycamore Girl Scout Coun., Salute to Women in Politics award, Outstanding Svc. for Pub. Interest award Ind. Optometric Assn., Pres.'s Spl. Svc. award Ind. Soc. Profl. Land Surveyors, Spl. Recognition award Ind. Chpt. NASW, Legis. Efforts Recognition award Ind. Residential Facilities Assn., Ind. Assn. for Counseling and Devel. Mem. Bus. and Profl. Women's Assn., Lafayette C. of C. (edn. com.), Delta Kappa Gamma, Phi Delta Kappa, Kappa Alpha Theta (mem. adv. bd.). Democrat. Home: 633 Kossuth St Lafayette IN 48905 Office: Ind Ho of Reps State House Third fl Indianapolis IN 46204*

KLINMAN, JUDITH POLLOCK, biochemist, educator; b. Phila., Apr. 17, 1941; d. Edward and Sylvia (Fitterman) Pollock; m. Norman R. Klinman, July 3, 1963 (div. 1978); children: Andrew, Douglas. AB, U. Pa., 1962, PhD, 1966. Postdoctoral fellow Weizmann Inst. Sci., Rehovoth, Israel, 1966-67; postdoctoral assoc. Inst. for Cancer Research, Phila., 1968-70, research assoc., 1970-72, asst. mem., 1972-77, assoc. mem., 1977-78; asst. prof. biophysics U. Pa., Phila., 1974-78; assoc. prof. chemistry U. Calif., Berkeley, 1978-82, prof., 1982—; mem. ad hoc biochemistry and phys. biochemistry study sects. NIH, 1977-84, phys. biochemistry study sect., 1984-88. Mem. editorial bd. Jour. Biol. Chemistry, 1979-84, Biofactors, 1991—, European Jour. Biochemistry, 1991—, Biochemistry, 1993—; contbr. numerous articles to profl. jours. Fellow NSF, 1964, NIH, 1964-66; Guggenheim fellow 1988-89. Mem. NAS, Am. Chem. Soc. (exec. coun. biol. div. 1982-85, chmn. nominating com. 1987-88, program chair 1991-92, Repligen award 1994), Am. Acad. Arts and Scis., Am. Soc. Biochemistry and Molecular Biology (membership com. 1984-86, pub. affairs com. 1987-94, program com. 1995), Sigma Xi. Office: U Calif Dept Chemistry Berkeley CA 94720

KLOC, EMILY ALVINA, elementary principal; b. Chgo., Apr. 8, 1933; d. Francis Joseph and Emily Mary (Gucwa) K. BMus, Mundelein Coll., Chgo., 1954; MEd, Loyola U., Chgo., 1960. Grade 2 tchr. Our Lady Help of Christians, Chgo., 1954-58; grades 5, 6, 7, 8 tchr. St. Mary of the Angels, Chgo., 1958-87, prin., 1987—. Mem. Near N.W. Orgn., Chgo., 1988—. Summer grantee U. Ill. NDEA Inst., Chgo., 1968; recipient Excellence in Mgmt. award Office Cath. Edn., Chgo., 1991, Tchr. Achievement award St. Mary of Angels Sch., Big Shoulders Fund, Chgo., 1992. Mem. ASCD, Nat. Cath. Educators Assn., Archdiocesan Prins. Assn. (chmn. coun. III-5A 1991—). Roman Catholic. Home: 1721 N Wood St Chicago IL 60622 Office: St Mary of the Angels 1810 N Hermitage Chicago IL 60622

KLOEPFER, MARGUERITE FONNESBECK, writer; b. Logan, Utah, Nov. 13, 1916; d. Leon and Jean (Brown) Fonnesbeck; m. Lynn William Kloepfer, Aug. 6, 1937; children: William Leon, Kenneth Lynn, Kathryn Kloepfer Ellis, Robert Alan. BS, Utah State U., 1937. Legal sec. Lynn W. Kloepfer, Atty., Ontario, Calif., 1958-74; freelance writer, novelist Ontario, Calif., 1974—. Author: Bentley, 1979, Singles Survival, 1979, But Where is Love, 1980, The Heart and the Scarab, 1981, Schatten in der Wuste, 1983; contbr. short stories to Seventeen, Women's Day, numerous others; contbr. articles on travel to profl. jours. Pres. Foothill chpt. Nat. Charity League Inc., Ontario, 1965-67, nat. pres., 1968-70; pres. Interfraternity Mother's Clubs council U. So. Calif., Los Angeles, 1971-72, mem. coordinating council, town and gown; pres. Law Aux. San Bernardino County, Calif., 1957-58, Law Aux. Calif., 1974-75. Mem. Moneytalkers Investment Club (pres. 1989). Club: Friday Afternoon (West San Bernardino County) (pres. 1986-87). Home: 306 E Hawthorne St Ontario CA 91764-1749

KLOESMEYER, ILIANA MARISA, public relations professional; b. Harrisburg, Pa., Sept. 28, 1958; d. Jan and Sonia (Plynaer) K. BA in Journalism, W.Va. U., Morgantown, 1978; cert., Katharine Gibbs, Boston, 1978-79; postgrad., Temple U., Phila., 1981-93. Sr. media buyer Sonder Sevitt Advt., Phila., 1983-85; mktg. dir. Cable AdNet, Malvern, Pa., 1985-86; media dir. Phila. Coca-Cola, 1986-91; dir. corp. comm., dir. investor rels. O'Brien Environ. Energy, Phila., 1991-92; pres. Iliana Koesmeyer, Inc., 1991—; contracts include Phila. Zoo, Phila. Mag. Counselor Women Organized Against Rape, Phila., 1981; com. mem. Am. Cancer Soc. Phila.; comm. chairperson, corp. fundraiser United Negro Coll. Fund, U.S. Ski Fedn.; co-chair Zoobilee, 1995, Acad. Ball, 1995. Mem. UNCF Sports (chmn. 1990-91), Alpha Xi Delta Alumni. Democrat. Presbyterian.

KLOPFLEISCH, STEPHANIE SQUANCE, social services agency administrator; b. Rupert, Idaho, Dec. 21, 1940; d. William Jaynes and Elizabeth (Cunningham) Squance; B.A., Pomona Coll., 1962; M.S.W., UCLA, 1966; m. Randall Klopfleisch, June 27, 1970; children—Elizabeth, Jennifer, Matthew. Social worker, Los Angeles County, 1963-67; program dir. day care, vol. services Los Angeles County, 1968-71; div. chief children's services Dept. Public Social Services, Los Angeles County, 1971-73, dir. bur. of social services, 1973-79; chief dep. dir. Dept. Community Services, Los Angeles County, 1979—;with Area 10 Devel. Disabilities, 1981-82; bd. dirs. Los Angeles Fed. Emergency Mgmt. Act, 1985-91, pres., 1987; bd. dirs. Los Angeles Shelter Partnership, Pomona Coll. Assocs., 1988—. Mem. Calif. Commn. on Family Planning, 1976-79; mem. Los Angeles Commn. Children's Instns., 1977-78; bd. dirs. United Way Info., 1978-79; chmn. Los Angeles County Internat. Yr. of Child Commn., 1978-79; bd. govs. Sch. Social Welfare, UCLA, 1981-84. Mem. Nat. Assn. Social Workers, Am. Soc. Pub. Adminstrn., Soroptimist Internat. (bd. dirs. 1989—, pres. L.A. chpt. 1993).

KLOSINSKI, DEANNA DUPREE, medical laboratory sciences educator; b. Goshen, Ind., Dec. 28, 1941; d. George C. and Gertrude (Todd) Dupree; m. Michael A. Klosinski, Jan. 30, 1965; children: Elizabeth, John, Robert, Lara. BS, Ind. State U., 1964; MS, Purdue U., 1972; PhD, Wayne State U., 1990. Diplomate in lab. mgmt. Am. Soc. Clin. Pathologists; cert. med. technologist. Med. technologist South Bend (Ind.) Med. Found., 1959-68; lab. specialist Home Hosp., Lafayette, Ind., 1968-74; program dir. Ind. Vocat. Tech. Coll., Lafayette, 1968-75; clin. asst. prof. Oakland U., Rochester, Mich., 1985—; adj. asst. prof. Wayne State U. and Mich. State U., Detroit, 1991—; program dir. William Beaumont Hosp., Royal Oak, Mich., 1979—. Author: (videotape, monograph) Blood Collection: The Difficult Draw, 1992; co-author: (videotape, monograph) Blood Collection: The Routine Venipuncture, 1989 (chpt.) Molecular Biology and Pathology, 1993. Mem. pastoral coun. St. Hugo Cath. Ch., Bloomfield, Mich., 1991-94. Named Outstanding Bus. Person Mich. Coun. on Vocat., 1992, Mich. Clin. Lab. Scientist, 1993, Am. Soc. Clin. Pathologists Tech. of Yr., 1994; rsch. grantee William Beaumont Hosp., 1989-90. Mem. Am. Soc. Clin. Pathologists (chmn. Tech. Sample 1984-93, Lab. Medicine editorial bd., editor Profl. Perspectives 1993, Technologist of Yr. 1994), Am. Soc. for Clin. Lab. Sci. (edn. sci. assembly, co-chair clin. lab. edn. conf. 1991), Mich. Soc. for Clin. Lab. Sci. (treas. 1984-86, 88-92, pres.-elect 1994-95), Assn. Women in Sci., Sigma Xi (Oakland U. chpt. sec. 1994-95), Alpha Mu Tau (scholarship award 1985, 87, 90), Delta Gamma Alumnae (treas. 1978-81, v.p. 91-93, pres. 93-95). Home: 90 Devon Rd Bloomfield Hills MI 48302 Office: William Beaumont Hosp 3601 W 13 Mile Rd Royal Oak MI 48073-6769

KLOSTER, AMY LAWSON, researcher; b. Oneonta, N.Y., Dec. 8, 1966; d. James Brooks and Dorothy Ann (Rydelek) L.; m. Brent M. Kloster, Nov. 14, 1992. BS in Biology and Chemistry, William Smith Coll., 1989. Rsch. asst. N.Y. State Agrl. Experiment Sta., USDA, Geneva, 1988-89, Cornell U. Med. Sch., N.Y.C., 1989-90; rsch. assoc. II Harvard Med. Sch., Boston, 1990-91; researcher James A. Baker Inst. for Animal Health, Cornell U., Ithaca, N.Y., 1992—. Mem. AAUW, LWV, SPCA. Home: 117 Roat St Ithaca NY 14850-2735 Office: JA Baker Inst Animal Health NY State Coll Vet Medicine Cornell U Ithaca NY 14853

KLOTZ, FLORENCE, costume designer; b. N.Y.C.; d. Philip K. and Hannah Kraus. Student, Parsons Sch. Design, 1941. Designer: Broadway shows Take Her She's Mine, 1960, Never Too Late, 1962, Nobody Loves An Albatross, 1963, On An Open Roof, 1963, Owl and the Pussycat, 1964, One by One, 1964, Mating Dance, 1965, The Best Laid Plans, 1966, Superman, 1966, Paris Is Out, 1970, Norman Is That You, 1970, Legends, Follies, 1971 (Drama Desk award, Tony award), A Little Night Music, 1973 (Drama Desk award, Tony award), Side By Side Sondheim, 1975, Pacific Overtures, 1976 (Drama Desk award, Tony award, Los Angeles Critic Circle award), On the 20th Century, 1978 (Drama Desk award), Broadway Broadway, Dancin' In The Streets, 1982, Grind, 1984 (Tony award), Jerry's Girls, 1985; (ballet-jazz opus) Antique Epagraph, N.Y.C.; Broadway musicals Rags, 1986, Roza, 1987; Ctr. prodns. Carousel, 1956, Oklahoma, 1956, Annie Get Your Gun, 1956, 4 Baggatelle; movies Something for Everyone, 1969, A Little Night Music, 1976 (Oscar nomination, Los Angeles Critic Circle award); ice shows John Curry's Ice Dancing, 1979; Broadway musical A Doll's Life; ballet 8 Lines, 1986, I'm Old Fashioned (Jerome Robbins), Ives Songs (Jerome Robbins), City of Angels, 1989 (Tony nominee, Outer Critics Circle award), Kiss of the Spider Woman (Tony winner, Drama Desk award winner), 1989, Showboat (Toronto, Can.), 1993. Democrat. Home: 1050 Park Ave New York NY 10028-1031*

KLUCZYNSKI, JANET, computer company marketing executive; b. Chgo., Aug. 5, 1955; d. Thomas Edward and Melanie Irene (Lakoma) K. BA in English cum laude, Dartmouth Coll., 1977; M in Mgmt., Kellogg Grad. Sch. Mgmt., 1980. Asst. product dir. McNeil Consumer Products Co. div. Johnson & Johnson, Ft. Washington, Pa., 1980-83; mktg. rep. IBM, Boston, 1984-87; assoc. cons. corp. competitive analysis Digital Equipment Corp., Concord, Mass., 1987-88; mktg. programs mgr. Stratus Computer, Inc., Marlboro, Mass., 1988—. Alumnae admissions interviewer Dartmouth Coll., class officer, 1992-97; mem. Jr. League Boston, 1984-89; English tutor, fundraiser, mem. bus. leaders bd. One with One, Brighton, Mass., 1986—. Mem. Kellogg Alumni Club of Boston (bd. dirs. 1991—). Democrat. Roman Catholic. Home: 282 Mount Auburn Watertown MA 02172 Office: Stratus Computer 55 Fairbanks Blvd Marlborough MA 01752

KLUGE, CHERYLE DARLENE JOBE, secondary education educator; b. Atlanta; d. Lonnie Dewitt and Gracie Beatrice (Shelton) Jobe. BS, Calif. State Poly. Coll., 1968; MEd, U. Houston, 1994. Cert. secondary English and Spanish tchr. Tchr. Ascension Parish Sch. Dist., Donaldsonville, La., 1968-69, Spring Br. Ind. Sch. Dist., Houston, Tex., 1979-91, Cypress-Fairbanks Ind. Sch. Dist., Houston, 1991—; tchr. Chinese Culture Ctr., Houston, 1990-92. Mem. ASCD, Nat. Assn. for Gifted Children, Nat. Coun. Tchrs. of English, Tex. Coun. Tchrs. of English, Tex. Assn. Gifted and Talented, Golden Key Nat. Honor Soc.

KLUGER, RUTH, German language educator, editor; b. Vienna, Austria, Oct. 30, 1931; came to U.S., 1947, naturalized, 1952; d. Viktor and Alma (Gredinger) Kluger Hirschel; m. Werner T. Angress, Mar. 1952 (div. 1962); children: Percy, Dan. B.A., Hunter Coll., N.Y.C., 1950; M.A., U. Calif.-Berkeley, 1952, Ph.D., 1967. Asst. prof. German lang. and lit. Case Western Res. U., 1966-70; assoc. prof. U. Kans., Lawrence, 1970-73; assoc. prof. U. Va., Charlottesville, 1973-75, prof., 1975-76; prof. U. Calif.-Irvine, 1976-80, 86-88, dir. Göttingen Study Ctr., Edn. Abroad Program, 1988-90; prof. Princeton U., 1980-86; editor German Quar., 1977-84. Author: The Early German Epigram: A Study in Baroque Poetry, 1971, Weiter leben Eine Jugend, 1992, Katastrophen. Uber deutsche Literatur, 1994; coor. editor Simon Wiesenthal Ctr. Annual, 1987; contbr. articles to profl. jours.; Rauriser Literaturpreis, 1993, Grimmelshausen-Preis, 1993, Niedersachsen Preis, 1993, Marie-Luise-Kaschnitz Pries, 1994. Am. Council Learned Socs. fellow, 1978. Mem. MLA (exec. coun. 1978-82), Am. Assn. Tchrs. German (exec. coun. 1976-81), Deutsche Akademie f394r Sprache und Dichtung, Lessing Soc. (pres. 1977-79). Democrat. Jewish. Home: 62 Whitman Ct Irvine CA 92715-4066 Office: U Calif Dept German Irvine CA 92717

KLUKA, DARLENE ANN, human performance educator, researcher; b. Berwyn, Ill., Oct. 6, 1950; d. Aloysius Louis and Lillian (Malkovsky) K. BA, Ill. State U., 1972, MA, 1976; PhD, Tex. Woman's U., 1985. Educator, coach Fenton High Sch., Bensenville, Ill., 1972-73, New Trier East High Sch., Winnetka, Ill., 1973-80; coach Bradley Univ., Peoria, Ill., 1980-82; grad. teaching asst. Tex. Woman's Univ., Denton, 1982-85; prof. Newberry (S.C.) Coll., 1985-86; prof., rschr., dir. Human Performance Ctr., Grambling (La.) State U., 1986-90; asst. prof. human studies and sport adminstrn. U. Ala., Birmingham, 1990-94, rschr., dir. Motor Behavior and Sports Vision Lab., 1990-94; dir. human performance lab B, grad. program dir. U. Ctrl. Okla., Edmond, 1994—; head of del. Internat. Olympic Acad., U.S. Olympic Com., Olympia, Greece, 1990; adv. bd. Women's Sports Found., 1992—; active U.S.A. Volley Sports Medicine and Performance Commn., 1994—; bd. dirs U.S.A. Volleyball. Author: Visual Skill Enhancement for Sport Exercises, 1989, Volleyball, 1989, 2d edit., 1992, Volleyball Drills, 1990; founding co-editor Internat. Jour. Sports Vision, 1991—; mem. edit. bd. Am. Volleyball Coaches Assn., 1988—; contbr. articles to profl. jours. Recipient Rsch. award So. Assn. Phys. Edn. Coll. Women. Mem. Nat. Assn. for Girls and Women in Sport (bd. dirs., exec. com. 1989-92, 93—, pres. 1990-91), Internat. Acad. Sports Vision (adv. bd. 1989—, v.p. 1993—), Am. Optometric Assn. (assoc., sports vision sect.), Am. Alliance for Health, Phys. Edn., Recreation and Dance (rsch. fellow, Taylor Dodson Young Profl. award So. Dist. 1991, bd. govs. 1993—), Internat. Coun. for Health Phys. Edn. and Recreation Sport and Dance (rsch. commn. 1993—), Women's Sports Found (internat. com. 1993—), Internat. Acad. Sports Vision, (v.p. 1993—), Internat. Assn. Physical Edn. and Sports for Girls and Women. Roman Catholic.

KLUTE, MARY CAROLYN, construction products distributor; b. Richmond, Ind., June 29, 1935; d. Paul Gerhardt and Nellie Kornelia (Stevens) Gahre; m. James Stanley Klute, June 13, 1954; children: Traci Lynn Klute Weaver, Scott Paul. BS in Edn., Wittenberg U., 1958. Lic. real estate salesman and broker. Tchr. Kettering (Ohio) Schs., 1958-60; real estate sales rep. Otto Realty, Richmond, 1971-88; pres., founder Am. Constrn. Products Inc., Richmond, 1988—; v.p., sec. Am. Metal Door Co., Inc., Richmond, 1964—; sec., founder Heritage Restoration, Inc., Richmond, 1976—; mem. bd. dirs. Trans National Gulf Assoc., 1994—. Author, pub.: (book series) Mother Always Said, Father Always Said, Dieters Always Say, Golfers Always Say, 1985. Active YWCA, Richmond, 1968-69; pres. Richmond (Ind.) Women's Golf Assn., 1981, 94. Winner Women's City Golf championship Richmond (Ind.) Women's Golf Assn., 1989, 94. Mem. Women's Trans Nat. Golf Assn. (bd. dirs. 1994—), Forest Hills Country Club (ladies golf chair 1983, 94), C. of C. (small bus. adv. com. 1993), North Palm Beach Country Club, Kappa Kappa Kappa. Republican. Lutheran.

KMET, REBECCA EUGENIA PATTERSON, pharmacist; b. Ellisville, Miss., June 17, 1948; d. Eugene Roberts and Ruth Winn (Pettis) Patterson; m. Joseph Paul Kmet, Mar. 29, 1969. BS in Pharmacy, U. Ariz., 1971; MBA, Nat. U., 1981. Pharmacist Santa Monica (Calif.) Bldg. Profl. Pharmacy, 1972-73, Vets. Hosp., West Los Angeles, Calif., 1973-74, Kaiser Med. Ctr., San Diego, Calif., 1979-82, Farmersville Drug Store, Farmersville, Calif., 1991—. Community svc. vol. Lt. USN, 1975-78. Recipient Presdl. Achievement award Rep. Party Nat. Congl. com. Mem. Wilson Assoc., Navy League, Naval Hist. Found., Marine Corps Hist. Found., U.S. English, Am. Immigration Control Fedn., Rho Chi, Kappa Epsilon, NSDAR. Independent. Episcopalian. Home: 985 Murphy Dr Lemoore CA 93245-2181

KNACK, PENNY ILONA, clinical psychologist; b. Queens, N.Y., Sept. 24, 1958. MA, Columbia U., 1981, MEd, 1982, MPhil, 1986, PhD, 1991. Lic. psychologist. Psychology intern Blythedale Children's Hosp., Valhalla, N.Y., 1985-86; psychologist Westchester Jewish Cmty. Svcs., Bedford Hills, Yorktown, N.Y., 1987—; pvt. practice Chappaqua, N.Y., 1991—; adj. faculty SUNY, Purchase, 1994—. Mem. Am. Psychol. Assn., Kappa Delta Pi. Office: One S Greeley Ave 203-C Chappaqua NY 10514

KNAFO, DANIELLE SYLVIA, clinical psychologist; b. Morocco, Mar. 18, 1953; came to U.S., 1953; d. Maurice and Rosine (Cohen) Knafo. BA magna cum laude, Tel Aviv U., Israel, 1977, MA magna cum laude, 1979; PhD, CUNY, 1987; cert. in psychoanalysis, NYU, 1992. Clin. psychology intern Bronx (N.Y.) Psychiatric Ctr., 1984-85; dir. psychol. svcs. St. Barnabas Hosp., Bronx, 1986-88; pvt. practice N.Y.C., 1987—; psychodiagnostician Holliswood (N.Y.) Hosp., 1988-89; supervising psychologist Bronx-Lebanon Hosp. Ctr., 1988-90; adj. lectr. CCNY, Bklyn. Coll., 1982-83; New Sch. Social Rsch., 1983-84; mem. faculty Eugene Lang Coll., 1989—, Tel-Aviv U., 1995—; clin. supr. grad. psychology program Pace U., 1988—; program content cons. telecourse on abnormal psychology, PBS. Author: Egon Schiele: A Self in Creation, 1993; reviewer jours. Hosp. and Cmty. Psychiatry, 1988—, Psychoanalytic Books, Contemporary Psychology. Counselor St. Vincent's Hosp. Rape Crisis Program, 1981-84; dir. Suicide Prevention Program, Bronx, 1986-88. Fellow NIMH, 1981, BRA Found. fellow, 1987, Faculty Devel. Fund fellow, 1991. Mem. Am. Psychol. Assn., N.Y. Acad. Scis., World Fed. for Mental Health, Internat. Psychohistory Assn. (rsch. assoc.), Israel Psychol. Assn., Women Psychoanalysts (study group). Office: 2166 Broadway # 14F New York NY 10024-9999

KNAPP, CANDACE LOUISE, sculptor; b. Benton Harbor, Mich., Feb. 28, 1948; d. Claire Warren and Frances Mary (Collins) K.; m. Björn Andrén, Mar. 3, 1988. BFA, Cleve. Inst. Art, 1971; MFA, U. Ill., 1974. Sculptures exhibited in numerous galleries and colls. including Northwood Inst. Collection, West Palm Beach, Fla.; represented in permanent collections at Malone & Hyde, Memphis, Mobil Oil Co., Stockholm, HageGården Music Ctr., Edane, Sweden, others; included in book Contemporary American Women Sculptors; numerous commns. including St. Vincent de Paul Cath. Ch., Arlington, Tex., Padre Pio Found., Cromwell, Conn., Temple Emanuel, Dallas, West Haven, Conn., Tampa (Fla.) Gen. Hosp. Helen Greene Perry traveling scholar, 1971. Mem. Assn. Fla. Liturgical Artists (co-founder).

KNAPP, JANIS ANN, elementary school educator; b. Coffeyville, Kans., Nov. 15, 1949; d. Harry Clarence and Dorothy (Lehr) Herman; m. Stephen Foxall Knapp, Feb. 12, 1972; children: Marysa Monica, Stephen Weslee, Alexandria Annastasia, Janna Jacqualan. BE, U. Kans., 1971; MEd, Pittsburg State U., 1983, EdS, 1986. Cert. elem. tchr., Fla. Tchr. Overland Park (Kans.) Elem. Sch., 1971-72, Alamo Heights (Tex.) Jr. High Sch., 1972-73, Hoover Elem. Sch., Bartlesville, Okla., 1974, 79-80, Limestone Elem. Sch., Bartlesville, 1975-76, Whittier Elem. Sch., Coffeyville, 1980-83, Edgewood Elem. Sch., Coffeyville, 1983-85, J.C. Mitchell Community Sch., Boca Raton, Fla., 1985-88; math. specialist Palm Beach County Schs., Riviera Beach, Fla., 1988-90; tchr. Meadow Park Elem. Sch., Palm Beach, Fla., 1990-91, Conniston Mid. Sch., Palm Beach, 1991-93, Pine Grove Elem. Sch., Delray Beach, Fla., 1993—. Vol. high sch. debate judge, Delray Beach, Fla., 1990; Heart Fund vol., Ft. Lauderdale, 1985-91; assoc. mem. Rep. Club, Boca Raton, 1990-91. Mem. ASCD, AAUW, Nat. Coun. Tchrs. of Math., Nat. Coun. Suprs. Math., South Fla. Ctr. for Exec. Educators, Fla. Coun. Tchrs. Math., Fla. Assn. Math. Suprs., Fla. ASCD, Palm Beach County Classroom Tchrs. Assn., Math. Assn. Am., Phi Delta Kappa, Alpha Phi (pres. alumni assn.). Roman Catholic. Home: 18755 Cape Sable Dr Boca Raton FL 33498-6377 Office: Pine Grove Elem Sch 400 SW 10th St Delray Beach FL 33444

KNAPP, MADONNA FAYE, property manager, administrator; b. Greenup, Ill., Nov. 13, 1933; d. Rella James Packer and Ruth Evelyn (Mills) Lam; m. Carl E. Helmick, Feb. 8, 1953 (div.); children: Carl E. Jr., Cheryl A. Helmick Pease, Madonna J. Helmick Zelazny, Timothy J.; m. Glenn E. Knapp, Sept. 24, 1982. Grad. high sch., Champaign, Ill. Notary pub., Ind. Justice of peace, Ill., 1957-61; owner, mgr. Feathercrafts, Champaign, Ill., 1961-64; hostess Town and Country Steak House, Champaign/Urbana, Ill., 1966-68; leasing agt. Pinehurse Village Apts., Indpls., 1976-78, Shortridge Mobile Home Park, Indpls., 1978-79; adminstr. Kingston Square Homes, Inc., Indpls., 1981—. Precinct committeewoman Champaign Dem. Com., 1966-67; mem. Indpls. Dem. Com., 1970, 91-92. Recipient letter of accomodation State's Atty. Piatt County, 1961. Mem. Internat. Platform Assn., Midwest Assn. HUD Mng. Agts., Fraternal Order Police. Democrat. Methodist. Home: 7168 Twin Oaks Dr Indianapolis IN 46226-5720 Office: Kingston Square Homes Inc 7171 Twin Oaks Dr Indianapolis IN 46226-5719

KNAPP, MILDRED FLORENCE, social worker; b. Detroit, Apr. 15, 1932; d. Edwin Frederick and Florence Josephine (Antaya) K.; BBA, U. Mich., 1954, MA in Community and Adult Edn. (Mott Found. fellow 1964), 1964, MSW (HEW grantee 1966), 1967. Dist. dir. Girl Scouts Met. Detroit, 1954-63; planning asst. Council Social Agencies Flint and Genessee County, 1965; sch. social worker Detroit public schs., 1967—; field instr. grad. social workers. Mem. alumnae bd. govs. U. Mich., 1972-75, scholarship chmn., 1969-70, 76-80, chmn. spl. com. women's athletics, 1972-75, class agt. fund raising Sch. Bus. Adminstrn., 1978-79; mem. Founders Soc. Detroit Inst. Art, 1969—, Friends Children's Mus. Detroit, 1978—, Women's Assn., Detroit Symphony Orch., 1982-89, Mich. Humane Soc., 1991—; vol. Coun. Detroit Symphony Orch., 1990—; trustee, fin. chmn. Children's Mus. Recipient various certs. appreciation. Mem. Nat. Assn. Social Workers, Acad. Cert. Social Workers, Nat. Community Edn. Assn. (charter), Outdoor Edn. and Camping Council (charter), Mich. Sch. Social Workers Assn. (pres. 1980-81), Detroit Sch. Social Workers Assn. (past pres.), Detroit Assn. U. Mich. Women (pres. 1980-82), Detroit Fedn. Tchrs. Methodist. Home: 702 Lakepointe St Grosse Pointe MI 48230-1706 Office: 8401 Woodward Ave Rm 211 Detroit MI 48202-2265

KNAPP, NANCY HAY, mental health administrator; b. Cleve., June 2, 1922; d. Henry Homer and Aurore Louise (LaCroix) Hay; m. Richard Dominick Knapp, Sept. 11, 1955; 1 child, Pamela Hay. BA, Hunter Coll., 1957; MSEd in Counseling Psychology, U. Pa., 1971, EdD in Counseling Psychology, 1987. Nat. cert. counselor; clin. assoc. Am. Bd. Med. Psychotherapists. Career and edn. counselor Johnson O'Connor Rsch. Found., N.Y.C., 1950-53; counselor, report writer The Pers. Lab., N.Y.C., 1953-63; cons. Chapel Hill, N.C., 1963-65; cons., Phila., 1965-69; counseling dir. Resources for Women U. Pa., Phila., 1972-78; dir. profl. svcs. Crossroads Career Planning Corp., Phila., 1978-80; dir. consultation and edn. Crozer-Chester Med. Ctr., Upland, Pa., 1980-90, chmn. staff tng. com., 1985-90; pvt. practice counseling, couples and family therapy, 1971—; mem. faculty Main Line Sch. Night, Ardmore, Pa., 1978-80; trainer Pa. Dept. Health, Harrisburg, 1982-85. Author: (tng. manuals) Prevention: Drug Misuse, 1983, Growing, Together, 1985. Bd. dirs. Resources for Women, U. Pa., Phila., 1976-80; mem. steering com. Coalition for Edn./Placement of Women, Phila., 1976-78, coord., 1978-80; mem. Chester (Pa.) Vocat./Ednl. Outreach, 1980-82, dir., 1982-84. Recipient Community Devel. award Pa. Cons. Edn. Coun., 1981; grantee Pa. Dept. Health, 1981, 83. Mem. Am. Counseling Assn., APA (assoc.), Cons. Assn. Greater Phila., Phi Delta Kappa. Home: 326 Sprague Rd Narberth PA 19072-1124

KNAPP, ROSALIND ANN, lawyer; b. Washington, Aug. 15, 1945; d. Joseph Burke and Hilary (Eaves) K.; B.A., Stanford U., 1967, J.D., 1973. Admitted to Calif. bar, 1973, D.C. bar, 1980; with Dept. Transp., Washington, 1973—, asst. gen. counsel legislation, 1979-81, dep. gen. counsel, 1981—. Mem. D.C. Bar Assn., Calif. Bar Assn. Office: 400 7th St SW Washington DC 20590-0001

KNAPP, SUSAN CANNONS, accountant; b. Nottingham, Eng., Jan. 9, 1945; came to U.S., 1947; d. William Charles and Constance Winifred (Barnard) Cannons; m. Bobby Lee Knapp, July 3, 1973; 1 child, Laurel Marie. Bachelor's degree, Ctrl. Fla. U., 1972; Master's degree, Drake U., 1990. CPA, CFP, Fla., Iowa. Acct. Seidman & Seidman, Orlando, Fla., 1972-73, Coopers & Lybrand, Kansas City, Mo., 1973-76; pvt. practice Susan C. Knapp CPA/Cons., Mission, Tex., 1976-77; supr. McGladrey, Marshalltown, Iowa, 1978-79; tax mgr. regional firm Tama, Iowa, 1979-85; pvt. practice Susan C. Knapp, CPAs, Marshalltown, 1985—; adj. instr. Buena Vista Coll., Marshalltown; bd. dirs. Farmers Savs. Inc., Garwin, Iowa. Bd. dirs. Iowa River Hospice, Marshalltown, 1988—, YMCA, Marshalltown, 1991—, Marshalltown Hosp. Found., 1992—. Mem. AAUW, AICPA, Am. Inst. Cert. Fin. Planners, Am. Women's Soc. CPAs, Iowa Soc. CPAs. Episcopalian. Office: 203 W Main St Marshalltown IA 50158-5845

KNASKO, SUSAN CAROLYN, psychologist; b. Natrona Heights, Pa., Feb. 12, 1955; d. John Joseph and Susanna Marie (Stonevice) K. BA, Indiana U. of Pa., 1976; MS summa cum laude, Pa. State U., 1982, PhD summa cum laude, 1985. Intern psychology New Castle (Pa.) Youth Devel. Ctr., 1976; forestry tech. U.S. Forest Svc., Marionville, Pa., 1978, Tonopah, Nev., 1979; supr. forestry tech. U.S. Forest Svc., Boise, 1980; rsch., teaching asst. Pa. State U., State College, 1980-86; staff scientist Monell Chem. Senses Ctr., Phila., 1990-93, sr. rsch. assoc., 1993—; cons. in field. Contbr. articles to profl. jours. Postdoctoral fellow Monell Chem. Senses Ctr., 1987-90; SEED Continuing Edn. grantee, Pa. State U., 1981, Olfactory Rsch. Fund grantee, N.Y.C., 1991. Mem. NAFE, Eastern Psychol. Assn., Assn. Chemoreception Scis., Environ. Design and Rsch. Assn., Assn. Consumer Rsch., Sierra Club, Amnesty Internat. Office: Monell Chem Senses Ctr 3500 Market St Philadelphia PA 19104-3308

KNAUER, VELMA STANFORD, retired savings and loan executive; b. Pottstown, Pa., July 4, 1918; d. Chester Miller and Pearl Fretz (Miller) Stanford. Student pub. schs.; m. Joseph Daniel Knauer, Feb. 17, 1940; children: Joseph Daniel, Susan Velma Knauer Metz. With U.S. Axle Co., Inc., Pottstown, 1936-45; with First Fed. Savs. & Loan Assn., Pottstown, 1953-88, contr., 1953-88, asst. treas., 1953-62, asst. sec., 1962-75, treas., 1976-89, ret., 1989. Mem. Am. Soc. Profl. and Exec. Women. Home: 970 Feist Ave Pottstown PA 19464-3955

KNAUER-ANDERSON, KAREN LEE, realtor; b. San Diego, Jan. 30, 1960; d. William Edward and Alta Jean (Hendricks) K.; m. Brent Allan Anderson, Mar. 22, 1986; 1 child, Carly Marie Anderson. Grad. high sch., El Cajon, Calif. Lic. contractor; lic. realtor, Mo. Sec. Accent Gen., Inc., Santee, Calif., 1981-82, Jean-Beck & Assocs., San Diego, 1982-84, Kertzman Contracting, Spring Valley, Calif., 1984-86; owner Karen Knauer Gen. Contractor, El Cajon, 1986-93; realtor Coleman Realtors, Inc., 1994—; mem. Tri-Lakes Bd. Realtors. Leader Dogwood Trails Daisy coun. Girl Scouts U.S. Mem. Assn. Builders & Contractors, Women Constrn. Owners & Execs., Am. Gen. Contractors, NAFE. Republican. Office: 681 Lone Hickory Rd Ozark MO 65721

KNAUST, CLARA DOSS, retired elementary school educator; b. Freistatt, Mo., Feb. 18, 1922; d. John Fredrick and Hedwig Louise (Brockschmidt) Doss; m. Donald Knaust, July 7, 1946 (dec.); children: Karen Louise, Ramona Elizabeth, Heidi Marie. BS in Edn., S.W. Mo. State U., 1969. Elem. tchr. Trinity Luth. Sch., Freistatt, 1942-46; tchr. kindergarten Trinity Luth Ch., Springfield, Mo., 1961-65, Redeemer Luth Ch., Springfield, 1962-63, 66-69; tchr. kindergarten Springfield R-12 Sch. System, 1969-70, 73-84, elem. tchr., 1970-73; elem. and kindergarten tchr. Springfield Luth. Sch., 1984-88; mem. planning bd. Early Childhood Conf., U. Mo., Columbia, 1977-80. Pres. Springfield Gen. Hosp. Guild, 1969-71; local and zone pres. Luth. Women's Missionary League, Springfield, 1986-94; historian Trinity Luth. Ch., 1985-94; chair bd. edn. Grace Luth. Ch., Tulsa. Mem. Assn. for Childhood Edn. Internat. (br. state pres. 1980-84, president's coun. 1983-85, Hall of Fame plaque 1988, state pres. 1989-93), Springfield Edn. Assn. (life), Springfield Luth. Sch. Assn. (pres. 1992-94), S.W. Dist. Kindergarten Assn. (pres. 1978-79), Alpha Delta Kappa. Home: Woodland Terr Apt 329 9524 E 71st St Tulsa OK 74133-5219

KNECHTEL, NANCY ELLEN, art history educator; b. Buffalo, Oct. 17, 1957; d. Robert P. and Ellen (John) K. BA, SUNY, Buffalo, 1979, MA, 1985. Asst. prof. art history Niagara County C.C., Sanborn, N.Y., 1985—, chmn. internat. edn., 1993, fine arts dept. coord., 1994—; sr. lectr. Niagara (N.Y.) U., 1986—; photog. archivist Pres.'s Office, SUNY, 1988—. Pictorial rschr.: Echoes in the Mist, 1991; contbr. Ency. 20th Century N.Am. Women Artists, 1993. Recipient Excellence in Teaching award SUNY, 1993, Nat. NISOD Excellence in Teaching award, 1994. Mem. Coll. Art Assn., Am. Assn. Tchrs. Italian. Home: 289 Pryor Ave Tonawanda NY 14150-7432 Office: Niagara County CC 3111 Saunders Settlement Rd Sanborn NY 14132-9460

KNEE, RUTH IRELAN (MRS. JUNIOR K. KNEE), social worker, health care consultant; b. Sapulpa, Okla., Mar. 21, 1920; d. Oren M. and Daisy (Daubin) Irelan; m. Junior K. Knee, May 29, 1943 (dec. Oct. 21, 1981). BA, U. Okla., 1941, cert. social work, 1942; MA, U. Chgo., 1945. Psychiat. social worker, asst. supr. Ill. Psychiat. Inst., U. Ill. at Chgo., 1943-44; psychiat. social worker USPHS Employee Health Unit, Washington, 1944-46, chief psychiat. social worker, 1946-49; psychiat. social work assoc. Army Med. Ctr., Walter Reed Army Hosp., Washington, 1949-54; psychiat. social work cons. HEW, Region III, Washington, 1955-56; with NIMH, Chevy Chase, Md., 1956-72; chief mental health care adminstrn. br. USPHS, 1967-72, assoc. dep. adminstr. Health Svcs. and Mental Health Adminstrn., 1972-73, dep. dir. Office of Nursing Home Affairs, 1973-74; long-term mental health care cons.; mem. com. on mental health and illness of elderly HEW, 1976-77; mem. panel on legal and ethical issues Pres.'s Commn. on Mental Health, 1977-78; liaison mem. Nat. Adv. Mental Health Coun., 1977-81. Mem. editorial bd. Health and Social Work, 1979-81. Bd. dirs. Hillhaven Found., 1975-86, governing bd. Cathedral Coll. of the Laity, Washington Nat. Cathedral, 1988-94. Fellow Am. Pub. Health Assn. (sec. mental health sect. 1968-70, chmn. 1971-72), Am. Orthopsychiat. Assn. (life), Gerontol. Soc. Am., Am. Assn. Psychiat. Social Workers (pres. 1951-53); mem. Nat. Conf. Social Welfare (nat. bd. 1968-71, 2d v.p. 1973-74), Inst. Medicine/Nat. Acad. Sci. (com. study future of pub. health 1986-87), Coun. on Social Work Edn., Nat. Assn. Social Workers (sec. 1955-56, nat. dir. 1956-57, 84-86, chmn. competence study com., practice and knowledge com. 1963-71), Acad. Cert. Social Workers (social work pioneer 1993), Am. Pub. Welfare Assn., DAR, U. Okla. Assocs., Woman's Nat. Dem. Club (mem. gov. bd. 1992—), Cosmos Club (Washington), Phi Beta Kappa (assoc. 1985—), Psi Chi. Address: 8809 Arlington Blvd Fairfax VA 22031-2705

KNEEBONE, ALICE JEANNETTE, child care coordinator; b. Boulder, Colo., July 28, 1956; d. John William and Miriam Alice (Alcorn) K. AS in Med. Assistance, Parks Coll., 1981. Proof operator, asst. supr. Nat. State Bank, Boulder, 1975-80; child care coord. Mothers of Presch. Children, Boulder, 1982—, Moments with Mothers, Boulder, 1992—; child care coord. Doorways Internat., Inc., Boulder, 1982—, bd. dirs. officer; sec., shipping and receiving mgr. Video Accessory Corp., Boulder, 1984-91; office mgr. Arapahoe Chiropractic Clinic, Boulder, Colo., 1991-92; Home Day Care, 1992—; child care lead tchr. Joy of Living, 1st Presbyn. Ch., 1993—. Author ednl. materials for working mothers; dancer, co-leader Polynesian Dance Troop, 1974—, Hawaiian-Tahitian Dance Troop, 1989—. Tchr. Sunday sch. 1st Presbyn. Ch., Boulder, 1980—; med. asst. blood bank Health Fair, Boulder, 1983; election judge Boulder County Clk. and Recorder Office, 1992—; vol. asst. Home Health Care, 1992—; vol. preparation com. Vacation Bible Sch. Mem. Nat. Assn. Med. Assts., Boulder Assn. Med. Assts., 1st Priority Christian Singles, 20/30 Something Christian Singles Social Club, 20/30 Something Christian Singles (Bible Study), Neighborhood Eco-Cycle Block (asst. to coord.), Ivy Rebekah Lodge (jr. past noble grand of ivy 1993, elevator fund raising 1991—, rep. to dist. 8 odd fellows orgn., chmn. hosp./shut-in visitation, program com. 1991-92, bereavement com. 1992-93, mem. program com., 1994, del. to Colo. assembly, 1994, mem. auditing com. 1995), Odd Fellows (UN pilgrimage for youth fund raising 1992—, elevator fund raising 1991—, delgate to internat. order, 1993—). Republican. Office: Internat 1st Presbyn Ch Boulder Moments with Mothers/Doorways 1820 15th St Boulder CO 80302-5494 also: Calvary Bible Evang Free Ch Mothers of Presch Children 3245 Kalmia Ave Boulder CO 80304 also: Arapahoe Chiropractic Clinic 2500 Broadway Boulder CO 80304

KNEPP, VIRGINIA LEE HAHN, legal assistant; b. South Bend, Ind., Nov. 1, 1946; d. Charles William and Mary Louise (Hunter) Hahn; m. James Patrick Knepp, Apr. 20, 1968; children: Meredith Leigh, Melanie Leigh. BS in Bus., Ind. U., 1971. Legal asst. Hahn, Walz, Knepp, Dvorak & Higgins, South Bend, Ind., 1983—; mem. Ind. allocation com. for Social Svc. Block Grants. Founder YWCA Women's Shelter, South Bend, 1978; founder, facilitator Women's Support Group, South Bend, 1979-90; vol. coord. Olympic Town Internat./Spl. Olympics, 1984-87, Kids Kingdom, South Bend, 1991, Children's Dispensary, South Bend, 1981-93, adv. coun., 1994, St. Joseph County Scholarship Found., 1990, Am. Cancer Soc., St. Joseph County, 1988-89; bd. dirs. Corvilla Inc., South Bend, 1989—; treas. Dvorak for State Rep., 1986—, Very Spl. Arts Ind., 1980—, South Bend Heritage Found., 1990—; active Gov. Bayh Commn., 1991—; chmn. Domestic Violence Prevention and Treatment Coun., Michiana Arts and Sci. Coun.'s Carnival for the Arts; bd. dirs. South Bend Heritage Found., 1991—. Mem. AAUW, Hoosier Art Patrons, Thalia Sorority (pres. 1988), Ind. Lawyers Aux. Home: 17725 Juday Lake Dr South Bend IN 46635-1758 Office: Hahn Walz Knepp Dvorak & Higgins 509 W Washington St South Bend IN 46601-1527

KNEPPER, ELIZABETH KORBER, office manager; b. Hyattsville, Md., Dec. 2, 1934; d. Otto Paul and Barbara (Schreiber) Korber; m. William Edward Knepper, Apr. 14, 1956; children: Julie Ann Knepper Markle, Holly Lynn. Grad., Washington Sch. Secs., 1953. Exec. sec. Nat. Canners Assn., Washington, 1953-56; adminstrv. sec. Fairchild Corp., Hagerstown, Md., 1956-65, 72-76; sec. Herald-Mail Co., Hagerstown, Md., 1969-72, Washington County, Hagerstown, Md., 1972-76; exec. sec. Fairchild Rep., Hagerstown, Md., 1978-83; office mgr. Washington County, States Attys. Office, Hagerstown, Md., 1984—. Republican. Home: 10818 Coffman Ave Hagerstown MD 21740-7628

KNEVALS, HARRIET JO, elementary education educator; b. Millburn, N.J., Dec. 20, 1942; d. Joseph Patrick and Celia (Winklestein) Dolcemaschio; m. Robert Paul Knevals, Apr. 4, 1982; 1 child, Jessica Mari. BS in Elem. Edn., Fairleigh Dickinson U., 1964; MA in Elem. Edn., Rutgers U., 1967. Secretarial aide Ashley Famous Artists, Beverly Hills, Calif., 1964; tchr. Quitman St. Sch., Newark, 1964—; tchr. SAT Review, Parsippany, N.J., 1993. Mem. LWV, Newark Tchrs. Union, Morris Sch. Dist. Home-Sch. Assns. (fund raiser 1987—). Republican. Home: 37 Sunderland Dr Morristown NJ 07960-3626

KNEZO, GENEVIEVE JOHANNA, science and technology policy researcher; b. Elizabeth, N.J., Aug. 8, 1942; d. John and Genevieve (Sadowski) K.; 1 child, Alexandra M. AB in Polit. Sci., Douglass Coll., Rutgers U., 1964; MA in Sci., Tech. and Pub. Policy, George Washington U., 1981; grad., Nat. Def. U., 1989. With Congl. Rsch. Svc., Libr. of Congress, Washington, 1967—, specialist in sci. and tech., 1979—, head sci., rsch. and tech. sect., 1986-88, sr. level specialist in sci. and tech. policy, 1991—. Author profl. publs. Mem. Phi Beta Kappa, Pi Sigma Alpha. Avocations: whitewater canoeing, hiking, gymnastics, classical music, community volunteer activities. Home: 606 Oakley Pl Alexandria VA 22302-3611 Office: Libr of Congress Congl Rsch Svc Sci Policy Rsch Divsn Washington DC 20540

KNIGHT, ALICE DOROTHY TIRRELL, state legislator; b. Manchester, N.H., July 14, 1903; d. Nathan Arthur and Clara (Stiles) Tirrell; m. Norman Knight, Nov. 15, 1952. B.A., U. N.H., 1925, postgrad., 1933; postgrad. Boston U., 1941-42. Tchr. Newton Falls (N.Y.) High Sch., 1925-26; prin. Oswegatchie (N.Y.) Union Sch., 1926-27, Bartlett Sch., Goffstown, N.H., 1932-35; home lighting specialist Pub. Svc. Co. N.H., Manchester, 1935-39; tchr. merchandising Mt. Ida Jr. Coll., Newton Centre, Mass., 1939-45; home svc. dir. Boyd Corp., Portland, Maine, 1945-47; dist. home economist Frigidaire Sales Corp., Boston, 1948-64; mem. N.H. Ho. of Reps., 1967-74, 76-78, 80-90; rep to N.H. Gen. Ct., 1967-91; mem. joint legis. com. on elderly affairs, 1983-87; pres. Greater Manchester Community Concert Assn., 1985-87; co-chmn. Goffstown Bicentennial Com. of the Constn., 1986—. Mem. budget com. Town of Goffstown, 1966-72; mem. Gov.'s Adv. Com. Alcoholism, 1972-73, 74-78, Statewide Health Coordinating Coun., 1977-78, N.H. Hist. Soc.; past pres. bd. dirs. Hillsborough County North Cancer Soc.; bd. dirs. N.H. Cancer Soc. Recipient award N.H. Program on Alcohol and Drug Abuse, 1971, 75, Gov.'s Recognition award Hillsborough County, 1986, Pub. Svc.award Union Pomona Grange, 1987. Mem. Nat. Home Fashions League (pres. 1957-58), Nat. Order State Legislators, Vis. Nurses Assn. (bd. dirs. Greater Manchester chpt. 1981-87), N.H. Coun. World Affairs, Nat. Grange (life), DAR (regent 1974-76), Nat. Order Women Legislators (treas. 1968-71), Manchester Bus. and Profl. Women (pres. 1972-74), Nat. Soc. New Eng. Women, Order Eastern Star (life), Soroptomist (life, Boston), Goffstown Unity Club, Goffstown Garden Club (pres. 1976-78), Goffstown Shirley Club (pres. 1977-78), Goffstown Hist. Soc. (life). Republican.

KNIGHT, ANGELIA DENYSE, counselor; b. Pontotoc, Miss., Dec. 10, 1965; d. H.G. and Virginia (Henry) K.; m. Frank Adams, Sept. 23, 1989. BA, Miss. State U., 1986, MS, 1989. Cert. counselor. Counseling intern Miss. State Univ. Counseling Ctr., 1988-89; university counselor N.W. Mo. State U. Counseling Ctr., 1989-94; dir. counseling and retention Miss. U. Women, Columbus, 1994—; presenter in field, 1989—. Pres. Venture Club of Maryville, Mo., 1993-94. Mem. Am. Counseling Assn., Am. Coll. Pers. Assn., Am. Coll. Counselors Assn., Assn. for Spiritual, Ethical and Religious Values in Counseling, Mo. Coll. Pers. Assn. Home: 519 West Edwards Maryville MO 64468 Office: Counseling & Retention MUW W-1624 Columbus MS 39701

KNIGHT, ATHELIA WILHELMENIA, journalist; b. Portsmouth, Va., Oct. 15, 1950; d. Daniel Dennis and Adell Virginia (Savage) K. B.A. with honors in English, Norfolk State Coll., 1973; M.A. with honors in Journalism, Ohio State U., 1974. Cert. tchr., Va. Aide D.C. Coop. Extension Service, 1969-72; sub. tchr. Portsmouth Pub. Schs., 1973; reporter Virginian Pilot, Norfolk, 1973, Chgo. Tribune, 1974; met. desk reporter Washington Post, 1975-81, investigative reporter, 1981—; lectr. high schs., colls. Recipient Mark Twain award, 1982, 87, Front Page award Washington-Balt. Newspaper Guild, 1982, Nat. award for edn. Edn. Writers Assn., 1987, Pub. Svc. award Md.-Del.-D.C. Press Assn., 1990, 93; Ohio State U. fellow, 1974, Nieman fellow Harvard U., 1985-86. Mem. Women in Comm., Nat. Assn. Black Journalists, Washington-Balt. Newspaper Guild, Investigative Reporters and Editors. Baptist. Home: 1435 4th St SW B507 Washington DC 20024-2213 Office: Washington Post 1150 15th St NW Washington DC 20071-0002

KNIGHT, BRENDA LEE, quality industrial engineer; b. Oil City, Pa., Aug. 22, 1958; d. Clarence Benjamin and Donna Jean (Grosteffon) K. BS in Indsl. and Ops. Engring., U. Mich., 1980; MBA, So. Ill. U., 1992. Cert. quality engr.; cert. quality auditor. Quality engr. Gen. Tire, Inc., Mt. Vernon, Ill., 1981—. Mem. Am. Soc. for Quality Control, Am. Inst. Indsl. Engrs., Am. Mgmt. Assn., Beta Gamma Sigma. Home: 4411 Woodglen Ln Mount Vernon IL 62864-2171 Office: Gen Tire Inc PO Box 1029 Mount Vernon IL 62864-1029

KNIGHT, FRANCES YOST, librarian; b. Louisville, Jan. 2, 1948; d. Frank Albert and Ruth Ritchey (Kasey) Yost; m. Thomas Frederic Knight, Jr., July 23, 1971; children: James Yost, Elizabeth June. BA in History of Art, Wellesley Coll., 1969; MS in Libr. and Info. Sci., Simmons Coll., 1991. Adminstrv. asst. MIT, Cambridge, Mass., 1969-72; asst. to the keeper of musical instruments Mus. of Fine Arts, Boston, 1973-79; libr. aide Burbank Elem. Sch., Belmont, Mass., 1987—. Mem. ALA, New Eng. Libr. Assn., Am. Assn. Sch. Librs., Mass. Libr. Assn. Methodist.

KNIGHT, IDA BROWN, retired elementary educator; b. Macon, Ga., Aug. 8, 1918; d. Morgan Cornelius and Ida (Moore) Brown; m. Dempsey Lewis Knight, Apr. 11, 1942; children: Lavera Knight Hughes, Eugene Charles. BS, Spelman Coll., 1940; MS, SUNY, Fredonia, 1958; postgrad., SUNY, 1974, U. Manchester, Eng., 1974. Cert. tchr. home econs. Clothing tchr. Bibb County Vocat. Sch., Macon, 1940-42; tchr. home econs. Ballard Normal Sch., Macon, 1943-45; elem. tchr. Jamestown (N.Y.) Pub. Schs., 1955-77. Bd. dirs. Jamestown Girls Club, 1960-78, Jamestown Cmty. Schs., 1989—; ch. organist, 1974-82; jr. bd. mem. Elizabeth Marvin Cmty. House, 1994—. Mem. AAUW, Chautauqua County Ret. Tchrs. Assn., N.Y. State Congress Parents and Tchrs. (hon. life), Links, Inc. (pres. Jamestown chpt.), Delta Kappa Gamma (corr. sec. 1963-64). Home: 140 Federal Pl Jamestown NY 14701-2010

KNIGHT, JACQUELYN BROWN, income tax consultant; d. Julius Lynn and Martha (Burns) Brown; children: Walter, Curtis, Martha, Julia. Student, Young Harris Coll., Ga., 1943, Cornett Bus. Coll., Va., 1946. Office mgr. Irrigation Systems, Inc., Ripon, Calif., 1968-73; prin. Knight Tax and Audit Svc., Modesto, Calif., 1976—. Mem. Calif. Soc. Enrolled Agts. (bd. dirs., sec. 1985-87), Inland Soc. Tax Cons. (treas. 1985-87). Episcopalian. Office: Knight Tax and Audit Svc 2921 Rimrock Ct Modesto CA 95355-4142

KNIGHT, JANE MILLER, nurse-midwife, air force officer; b. Hampton, Va., Oct. 8, 1950; d. Donald Alexander and Elizabeth Harriet (Wilgus) Miller; m. David Ray Knight, Nov. 12, 1988. BSN, Med. Coll. Va., 1972; MA in Guidance and Counseling, Hampton (Va.) Inst., 1984. RN, Va.; cert. nurse-midwife. Staff nurse Mary Immaculate Hosp., Newport News, Va., 1972, Potomac Hosp., Woodbridge, Va., 1973, N.E. Bapt. Hosp., San Antonio, 1973-74, Hampton Gen. Hosp., 1974-76; commd. 1st lt. USAF, 1976, advanced through grades to lt. col., 1993; staff nurse USAF Hosp., Barksdale AFB, La., 1976-78; staff nurse, midwife USAF Hosp., Langley AFB, Va., 1979-84; instr. USAF Nurse-Midwifery program Malcolm Grow USAF Med. Ctr., 1984-91; staff nurse-midwife 416th Med. Group, Griffiss AFB, N.Y., 1991-94; speaker on women's health issues; workshop leader. Decorated Air Force Commendation medal, Meritorious Svc. medal. Mem. Assn. Women's Health, Obstetric and Neonatal Nurses, Am. Coll. Nurse-Midwives, Air Force Assn., Am. Soc. Psychoprophylaxis in Obstetrics. Episcopalian. Home: 10210 Raygor Rd Colorado Springs CO 80908

KNIGHT, JANET ANN, elementary education educator; b. Covina, Calif., July 22, 1937; d. Arnold M. and Thelma (Lyle) Ostrum; m. Ronald L. Knight, Sept. 14, 1957; children: Barbara Lynne, Susan Kaye. BA in Edn., Cen. Wash. U., 1979; MA in Edn., Heritage Coll., 1992. Cert. elem, secondary tchr., Wash. 2nd grade tchr. Kennewick (Wash.) Pub. Schs., 1980-81, 1st grade tchr., 1981-85, 3rd grade tchr., 1985-93, 4th grade tchr., 1993—; mem. lang. arts dist. com. Kennewick Sch. Dist., 1985-89, curriculum, instr. com., 1989-92, dist. curriculum and instrn. renewal cycle for learning excellence, 1992-93, dist. assessment com., 1992—. Mem. Richland (Wash.) Light Opera Co., 1963-75. Mem. NEA, ASCD, Wash. Edn. Assn., Kennewick Edn. Assn., Wash. Orgn. Reading Devel., Benton County Coun. of Internat. Reading Assn., Order of Rainbow for Girls, Sigma Tau Alpha. Episcopalian. Home: 120 Heather Ln Richland WA 99352-9155 Office: Westgate Elem Sch 2514 W 4th Ave Kennewick WA 99336-3115

KNIGHT, JANICE ROCHESTER, counselor; b. Memphis, Jan. 24, 1943; d. Wilmer Cullen and Brooksie Ouida (Wilder) Rochester; m. Joe Darryl Knight, June 3, 1967; 1 child, Darryl Lee. BS, Memphis State U., 1965, MA in Edn., 1970. Cert. secondary tchr. and counselor, Miss. Tchr. English Desoto County Schs., Horn Lake, Miss., 1965-70, counselor, 1972-73, 88—; tchr. Am. lit., counselor So. Bapt. Ednl. Ctr., Memphis, 1974-88; leader seminars. Author poems; writer, broadcaster radio show Parenting Teens, 1990-94; contbr. articles to profl. jours. Co-house parent Desoto Sunrise Homes, Inc., 1993—. Mem. ACA, Miss. Profl. Educators, Miss. Sch. Counselors Assn. (bd. dirs. 1988—), Miss. Counselors Assn., Delta Kappa Gamma (sec. 1978—). Baptist. Home: 7477 S Ridge Dr Walls MS 38680 Office: Horn Lake High Sch 6125 Hurt Rd Horn Lake MS 38637

KNIGHT, JOAN ALDRICH, educator; b. Providence, Apr. 28, 1948; d. William Remington and Edna (Higginbottom) Aldrich; m. Philip Marshall, Nov. 18, 1967; children: Jennifer Aldrich, Jason Remington. BS, U. Vermont, 1970; MEd, Stetson U., 1981. Elementary tchr. Burlington, Vt., 1970-71; early childhood tchr Brooksville, Fla., 1971-77, early childhood tchr., dir., owner, 1977-82; early childhood tchr., dir. Casper, Wyo.; kindergarten tchr. Chpt. 1 Callaghan Meml. Sch., St. Albans, Vt., 1985—; ednl. cons. Early Prevention of Sch. Failure, Peotone, Ill., 1986—, nat. cons. Whole Lang., 1989—; instr. C.C. of Vt., St. Albans, 1987—, Coll. of St. Joseph's, Rutland, Vt., 1987—, Champlain Coll., 1995—. Author: It Happened by Chants, 1989, Knight Lights, 1991, Reading Recovery Training, 1993; co-author ednl. video Reading-Writing Connection, 1988. Reader nursing homes, St. Albans, 1989—. Named Outstanding Young Educator, Vt. Jaycees, 1987, Tchr. of Yr., U. Vt., 1991. Mem. Nat. Assn. Edn. of Young Children, Vt. Assn. Edn. of Young Children, Phi Delta Kappa. Republican. Congregationalist. Home and Office: 159 High St PO Box 1271 Saint Albans VT 05478

KNIGHT, MARGARET ELIZABETH, music educator; b. Biddulph, Staffordshire, Eng., July 3, 1938; came to U.S., 1972; d. William Bateman and Amy Elizabeth (Willshaw) Whitehurst; m. Richard Alan Scudder, Apr. 5, 1972 (div. Mar. 1979); m. Arthur James Knight, May 26, 1979. Grad., No. Sch. of Music, Manchester, Eng., 1959; student, Royal Acad. Music, 1958, diploma in sch. music and psychology, diploma in aural tng.; Assoc. in Piano Teaching, Royal Coll. Music. Lic. in voice culture, aural tng., sch. music and psychology. Asst. to head dept. music Thistley Hough Sch., Stoke, Eng., 1959-65; head dept. music Macclesfield (Eng.) High Sch., 1966-72; pvt. piano tchr. Shamong, N.J., 1972—; adj. mem. faculty dept. music Crewe (Eng.) Tchrs. Coll., 1963-72; dir. student activities South Jersey Music Tchrs. Assn., 1986-88; N.J. state rep. for Assoc. Bd. Royal Schs. Music, London, 1993—. sec. Conservative Party, Congleton, Eng., 1968-71; active Town Coun., Congleton, 1971-72. County Music scholar Cheshire County Coun., Chester, Eng., 1955. Mem. Music Tchrs. Nat. Assn., Nat. Guild Piano Tchrs. (judge 1987—), N.J. Music Tchrs. Assn. (dir. student activities 1988-92, pres. 1992-94). Episcopalian. Home: 3 Blueberry Rd Shamong NJ 08088-8627

KNIGHT, PATRICIA MARIE, eye care company executive; b. Schnectady, N.Y., Jan. 25, 1952; d. Donald Orlin and Mary Ann (Rooney) K. BS in Engring. Sci., Ariz. State U., 1974, MS in Chem. Engring., 1976; PhD in Biomed. Engring., U. Utah, 1983. Teaching and rsch. asst. Ariz. State U., Tempe, 1974-76; product devel. engr. Am. Med. Optics, Irvine, Calif., 1976-79, mgr. materials rsch., 1983-87; rsch. asst. U. Utah, Salt Lake City, 1979-83; dir. materials rsch. Allergan Med. Optics, Irvine, 1987-88, dir. rsch., 1988-91, v.p. rsch., devel. and engring., 1991—; Contbr. articles to profl. jours. Mem. Soc. Biomaterials, Am. Chem. Soc., Soc. Women Engrs., Assn. Rsch. in Vision and Opthalmology, Biomed. Engring. Soc. Office: Allergan Med Optics 9701 Jeronimo Rd Irvine CA 92718-2076

KNIGHT, SANDRA BLOOMSTER, emergency, critical care nurse; b. Ft. Pierce, Fla., Oct. 6, 1951; d. Otto Robert and Lorene Naomi (Herron) Bloomster; m. Keith Mathias Knight Sr., Mar. 19, 1977; 1 child, Keith Mathias. ASN, Miami Dade Coll., 1971; student, Fla. Internat. U., 1975-76, U. South Fla., 1976—. RN, Fla.; CEN, cert. PALS, ACLS, TNCC. Charge nurse emergency dept. Palmetto Gen., Hialeah, Fla., 1971-73, 74-76; staff nurse NICU Jackson Meml. Hosp., Miami, 1973; staff nurse emergency dept. South Miami Hosp., 1973-74; charge nurse emergency dept. Shands Teaching Hosp., Gainesville, Fla., 1976-78, Ft. Myers (Fla.) Community Hosp., 1978-80; mgr. The Family MedCenter, Ft. Myers, 1983-91; trauma cons. Lee Meml. Hosp., Ft. Myers, 1991-93, trauma nurse coord., 1993-94; emergency dept. clin. educator Naples (Fla.) Cmty. Hosp., 1995—; instr. pediat. advanced life support, Fla., 1989—; instr. Trauma Nurse Core Course, 1987—, instr. trainer, 1988—, nat. faculty, 1993—; co-chmn. Fla. State Trauma Com., 1988—. Reviewer EWA TNCC Manual, 4th edit.; mem. editl. bd., tech. advisor (nursing video series) Emergency Case Review. Mem. Am. Trauma Soc., Emergency Nurses Assn. (past sec. S.W. Fla. chpt. 1988, nat. TNCC faculty 1993—, pediat. com. 1993—).

KNIGHT, VIRGINIA CORK, investment banker, builder, developer; b. Washington, Nov. 18, 1952; d. Malcolm F. and Virginia (Cork) K. BA in Intenat. Studies, Va. Poly. Inst. and State U., 1975; Degree in Common Market Econs., Coll. Europe, Bruges, Belgium, 1977. Dir. program devel. Nat. Demonstration Water Project, Washington, 1978-80; pres. Med Data Services, Alexandria, Va., 1981-83; v.p., co-mgr. corp. fin. Ferris and Co., Washington, 1984-88; v.p., co-mgr.corp. fin. The Savoy Group, Washington, 1989; pres. Cork Builders and Developers, 1989—. Bd. dirs. The Source Theater, 1990—. Mem. MIT Enterprise Forum Washington-Balt. (bd. dirs. 1984—, chmn. 1986-87), Balt.-Washington Venture Group (bd. dirs. 1988—), LWV (bd. dirs. Alexandria chpt. 1983-86). Home: 1415 Mt Vernon Ave Alexandria VA 22301-1715 Office: CCI Internat Inc 403 E Nelson Ave Alexandria VA 22301-1612

KNISELY BONK, HELEN, corporate customs broker; b. Cleve., Apr. 12, 1950; d. Angelo and Laura (Kelepouris) Pappis; m. Robert B. Knisely Sr., July 5, 1969 (div. Dec. 1986); children: Robert Jr., Laura; divorced; 1 child, Alexandra. Degree in computer, AG Computer Tng., Cleve., 1984-93; student, Columbia Pacific U., 1989; B in Internat. Bus./Law, World Trade Inst., 1991; student. Lic. customs broker; cert. internat. law. Corp. customs broker Am. Greetings, others cos., worldwide locations, 1983—; pres., instr., seminar leader, cons. Internat. Trade Cons., Cleve., 1989—; co-pres. H & J Distributors, Cleve., 1993—; fgn. buyer Am. Greetings Corp., Cleve., 1990—. Author: (trade book) Foreign Trade Zones and Subzones, 1993; contbr. articles to profl. jours. Named Woman of Yr., Orgn. Women in Internat. Trade, 1992-93. Mem. NAFE, Internat. Freight Assn. (hon.), Women in Internat. Trade, C. of C. (student sponsor 1993—). Republican. Greek Orthodox. Home: 3209 Bay Landing Dr Westlake OH 44145 Office: Am Greetings Corp One American Rd Cleveland OH 44144

KNITTEL, DIANE LYNNE, insurance marketing executive; b. Warsaw, N.Y., Feb. 24, 1961; d. George Willard and Betty Jean (Wheeler) Sonricker; m. Philip James Knittel, June 3, 1989. BS in Microbiology, Pa. State U., 1983; Assoc. in Risk Mgmt., Ins. Inst. Am., 1993. Cert. profl. ins. woman. Agt. State Farm, Olean, N.Y., 1985; comml. marketer The Bowersox Ins. Agy., St. Louis, 1986-92, 94—; comml. mktg. mgr. The Warren Group, Chesterfield, Mo., 1992-94; tchr. Met. St. Louis (Mo.) Ins. Assn., 1992—. Mem. Met. St. Louis Ins. Assn. (bd. dirs. 1993—, v.p. 1994—), Nat. Assn. Ins. Women.

KNIZESKI, JUSTINE ESTELLE, insurance company executive; b. Glen Cove, N.Y., June 4, 1954; d. John Martin and Elsie Beatrice (Gozelski) Knizeski. B.A., Conn. Coll., 1976; M. Mgmt., Northwestern U., 1981. Customer service supr. Brunswick Savs., Freeport, Maine, 1977-79; investment analyst Bankers Life and Casualty Co., Chgo., 1980-83, dir. corp. planning and analysis, 1983-87; dir. budgets, cost acctg. Blue Cross/Blue Shield of Ill., 1987—. Chmn. bd. dirs. Alternatives, Inc., Chgo., 1984-87, vice chmn., 1987-91, sec., 1991-92, bd. dirs., 1983-84; mem. Chgo. Council Fgn. Relations, 1984-85. Mem. Planning Forum. Avocations: sailing; bicycling; traveling; painting.

KNOBLAUCH, CAROL JEAN, librarian; b. Washington, Apr. 21, 1949; d. Harold Carl and Willeta (Johnson) K. BS in Social Work, Ohio State U., 1972; MLS, Kent State U., 1975. Libr. asst. Pub. Libr. Columbus (Ohio) and Franklin County, 1972-74, media specialist Northside br., 1975-76, br. mgr. South High, 1976-78, br. mgr. Hilliard, 1978-80; sys. libr. Columbus Met. Libr., 1980-84; tech. libr. applications analyst Info. Dimensions, Inc., Dublin, Ohio, 1984-93; sr. product analyst Online Computer Libr. Ctr. Inc., Dublin, 1993-94, product mgr., 1994—; internat. exch. libr. Gloucestershire (Eng.) County Libr., 1979; adj. prof. Sch. Libr. and Info. Sci. Kent State U., Columbus, 1986-88. Mem. ALA, Ohio Libr. Assn. (divsn. coord. 1974—), Franklin County Libr. Assn. (pres. 1978). Office: Online Computer Libr Ctr 6565 Frantz Rd Dublin OH 43017

KNOEBEL, SUZANNE BUCKNER, cardiologist, medical educator; b. Ft. Wayne, Ind., Dec. 13, 1926; d. Doster and Marie (Lewis) Buckner. A.B., Goucher Coll., 1948; M.D., Ind. U.-Indpls., 1960. Diplomate: Am. Bd. Internal Medicine. Asst. prof. medicine Ind. U., Indpls., 1966-69, assoc. prof., 1969-72, prof., 1972-77, Krannert prof., 1977—; asst. dean rsch. Ind. U., Indpls., 1975-85; assoc. dir. Krannert Inst. Cardiology, Indpls., 1974-90; asst. chief cardiology sect. Richard L. Roudebush VA Med. Ctr., Indpls., 1982-90; editor-in-chief ACC Current Jour. Rev., 1992—. Fellow Am. Coll. Cardiology (v.p. 1980-81, pres. 1982-83); mem. Am. Fedn. Clin. Research, Assn. Univ. Cardiologists. Office: Ind U Sch Medicine 1111 W 10th St Indianapolis IN 46202-4800

KNOLL, FLORENCE SCHUST, architect, designer; b. Saginaw, Mich., May 24, 1917; d. Frederick E. and M. Haisting Schust; m. Hans G. Knoll, July 1, 1946 (dec. 1955); m. Harry Hood Bassett, June 22, 1958 (dec. 1991). Student, Cranbrook Art Acad., Bloomfield Hills, Mich., 1935-37, Archtl. Assn., London, 1938-39; B.Arch., Ill. Inst. Tech., Chgo., 1941; D.F.A. (hon.), Parsons Sch. Design, 1979. Archtl. draftsman, designer Gropius & Breuer, Boston, 1941; design dir. Knoll Planning Unit, 1942-55; pres. Knoll Internat., N.Y.C., 1955-65; pvt. practice architecture and designer Coconut Grove, Fla., 1965—. Recipient Ill. Inst. Tech. Hall of Fame award, 1982; recipient Athena award R.I. Sch. Design, 1982, others. Mem. AIA (recipient Gold medal for indsl. arts 1961), Indsl. Designers Am. (hon.).

KNOLL, JACQUELINE SUE, retired nurse; b. Harmon, Ill., Dec. 14, 1932; d. Francis Michael and Geraldine Oleta (Perkins) K. Diploma, Copley Meml. Hosp. Sch Nursing, Aurora, Ill., 1960; diploma flight nursing, Sch. Aerospace Medicine, Brooks Air Force Base, Tex., 1968; AA, Solano Community Coll., Fairfield, Calif., 1972; BA, Chapman U., 1975. RN. Commd. 2d lt. USAF, 1962, advanced through grades to maj., 1974; staff surg. nurse WD-Copley, Aurora, Ill., 1960-62; staff nurse gen. med. ward Toul-Rosierres Air Base, France, 1963-65, staff nurse obstetrics ward, 1965-66; charge nurse pediatric ward Vandenberg Air Force Base, Calif., 1966-67, charge male med. ward, 1967-68, asst. charge nurse combined med. ward, 1968-69; charge nurse Air Evacuation Staging Facility, Travis Air Force Base, Calif., 1971-74; flight nurse, flight nurse instr. 57th Aeromedical Evacuation Squadron, Clark Air Base, The Philippines, 1969-71. Judge H.S. speech contest VFW and Am. Legion, Yucaipa, Calif., 1985-89; mem. prisioner of war/missing in action Task Force Omega, Chgo., Task Force Omega of Ill., 1989-91. Decorated Air medal with oak leaf cluster, USAF Commendation medal, Vietnam Svc. medal, Republic of Vietnam Combat medal, Gallantry Cross medal. Mem. AAUW (life), AARP, VFW (life, sr. vice comdr. 1985-86), DAV (life), Nat. Alliance of Families (life), Vietnam Vets. Am. (life), VietNOW (life, dir. 1992), Vietnam Vets. Brevard, Fla., Air Force Assn. (life.), Res. Officer Assn. (life), Ret. Officers Assn. (life), Soc. Ret. Air Force Nurses, Am. Legion (life), Aero. Med. Evacuation Assn., Bravo (life), Rock Island Arsenal Officers Club, Good Sam RV Club (life), RVing Women. Democrat. Home: 2435A Madrid Dr Melbourne FL 32940

KNOPMAN, DEBRA S., hydrologist, federal agency administrator; b. Phila., Aug. 13, 1953; d. Harold L. and Minnette (Smulyan) Knopman; m. Donald Weightman, Sept. 29, 1985; children: Leah Alana, David Atwood. BA, Wellesley Coll., 1975; MSCE, MIT, 1978; PhD, Johns Hopkins U., 1986. Various positions as sci. writer and editor Washington, 1975-78; legis. asst. Daniel P. Moynihan, Washington, 1979-80; prof. staff mem. U.S. Senate Com. on Environ. and Pub. Works, Washington, 1980-83; student asst., office of groundwater U.S. Geol. Survey, Reston, Va., 1984-85, rsch. hydrologist, nat. rsch. program, 1985-86, hydrologist, br. of systems analysis, 1987-91, chief, br. or systems analysis, 1991-93; dep. asst. sec. water and sci. Dept. Interior, 1993—. Editor: Scientific Research in Israel, 1976; editor Geophysics News, 1990-92; contbr. articles to profl. jours. Henry R. Luce Found. scholar, Taiwan, 1978-79. Mem. Am. Geophys. Union (chair pub. info. com. 1990-92). Democrat. Jewish. Office: Dept Interior 1849 C St NW MS 6640 Washington DC 20240-0001

KNOTT, LOU, small business owner; b. Duncan, Okla., Feb. 12, 1943; d. Lonnie Austin Knott and Lorine (Gibson) Porter; m. John Carlysle Eichler, Apr. 18, 1966; children: Don, David, Ken, Kathy, Debbie, Robbie, Judy, Jerry, Barbara, Reenie, Molly. Student, Famous Artists Sch., 1967-69; BS in Anthropology, Mid. Tenn. State U., 1982; postgrad., Okla. U., 1982-83, Oklahoma City U., 1987. Nurse's aide Lindley Hosp., Duncan, 1965; bus. mgr. Hilda Patterson's Sch. of Dance, Duncan, 1973; owner Jelke Signs, Duncan, 1983—; designer and manufacturer clothing Horseman Enterprises, Lawton, Okla., 1992—; freelance comml. artist. Costume designer Lawton Civic Theatre, 1973; choreographer's aide Miss Charm Pageant, 1973. Republican. Episcopal. Office: Jelke Signs 506 W Elder Ave Duncan OK 73533-5844

KNOWLES, CAROLYN SUE EDWARDS, secondary education educator; b. May 14, 1947; d. Lewis and Willie Inez (Ford) Edwards; m. William Limbret Knowles, Aug. 1, 1970; children: Cory Limbret, Heather Shantay. BS, Alcorn State U., 1968; MA, Fisk U., 1974. Tchr. Hunter High Sch., Drew, Miss., 1968-70, North Scott Sch., Forest, Miss., 1970-71, Morton (Miss.) Attendance Ctr., 1971-87, Forest Mcpl. Sch., 1987—; chmn. sci. dept. Forest Mcpl. Sch. Dist., 1992-94. Sec. East Ctrl. Health System Agy., Newton, Miss., 1978-80, Scott County Dem. Exec. Com., Forest, 1972—; chmn. East Ctrl. Cmty. Action Agy., Forest, 1988-92; active VFW Women Aux., Forest, Scott County Colored Women Federated Club, Forest, 1992; leader Girl Scouts U.S., svc. unit co-chmn. Scott County; youth dir. Concord Bapt. Ch.; asst. youth dir. 3d New Hope Dist.; vol. leader 4-H Club, coord. Capitol regional vol., 1993-94. NSF grantee, 1971-74; named Star Tchr. MS Econ. Coun. by Star Student Darryl Harvey Morton Attendance Ctr. Mem. NEA (pres. Scott/Forest Assn. Educators 1968), Miss. Assn. Educators (bd. dirs. 1993—), Miss. Sci. Tchr. Assn., Nat. Sci. Tchrs. Assn., Zeta Phi Beta. Home: 430 George St Forest MS 39074-3412 Office: Hawkins Mid Sch 803 E Oak St Forest MS 39074-4601

KNOWLES, ELIZABETH PRINGLE, art museum director; b. Decatur, Ill., Jan. 9, 1943; d. William Bull and Elizabeth E. (Pillsbury) P.; m. Joseph E. Knowles; 1 child, Elizabeth Bakewell. BA in Humanities with honors, Stanford, 1964; MA in Art History, U. Calif., Santa Barbara, 1968; grad., Mus. Mgmt. Inst., 1984. Cert. jr. coll. tchr., Calif. Instr. art history Murray State U., Murray, Ky., 1967-68; instr. art history Santa Barbara Art Inst., 1969, Santa Barbar City Coll., 1969-70, 76-78; staff coord. docents Santa Barbara Mus. Art, 1974-78; instr. continuing edn. Santa Barbara City Coll., 1973-86; curator edn. Santa Barbara Mus. Art, 1978-86; assoc. dir. Meml. Art Gallery, Rochester, N.Y., 1986-88; instr. mus. studies Calif. State U., Long Beach, 1989; exec. dir. Lyman Allyn Art Mus., New London, Conn., 1989—. Contbr. essays to art catalogues. Board dirs., chmn. Met. Transit Dist., Santa Barbara, 1978-80; founding pres. Santa Barbara Contemporary Arts Forum, Santa Barbara, 1976-78; commr. Santa Barbara City Planning Commn., 1975-77. Kellogg Found. fellow Smithsonian Inst., 1985. Mem. Am. Assn. Mus. (treas. edn. com. 1986-88), Coll. Art Assn., New Eng. Mus. Assn. (v.p. 1993—). Office: Lyman Allyn Art Mus 625 Williams St New London CT 06320-4199

KNOWLES, JENNI SNODGRASS, youth ministry training director; b. Glendale, Calif., June 12, 1954; d. Cecil R. and Berneita A. (Greenlee) Snodgrass; m. John William Knowles, May 15, 1993. BS in Psychology, Grace Coll., 1976; MA in Youth Ministries, Denver Seminary, 1985. Youth guidance staff Detroit Youth for Christ, 1976-92; tng. dir. Young River Ministries, Farmington, Mich., 1992—; instr. Ashland Seminary, Detroit, 1990, William Tyndale Coll., Farmington, 1991—; tng. task force nat. youth event/Youth for Christ, Denver, 1991; tng. partnership, Youth Encounter, Detroit, 1993—. Presbyterian. Office: Young River Ministries PO Box 379 Farmington MI 48332

KNOWLES, JOCELYN WAGNER, health writer, women's health specialist; b. N.Y.C., Feb. 22, 1918; d. Frederick and Violet Alice (Swain) W.; m. Clive Dorman Knowles, 1950 (div. 1959); 1 child, Katherine Miranda. Student, London Sch. Econs., 1938; BS, Columbia U., 1939, MA, 1940; MPH, UCLA, 1970. Exec. dir. Nat. Physicians Forum, Inc., N.Y.C., 1945-49; West Coast editor Nat. Foremen's Inst. Prentice-Hall Co., L.A., 1959-68; writer, editor The Female Patient mag., N.Y.C., 1980-81; dir. Planned Parenthood of S.W., Silver City, N.Mex., 1981-83; freelance writer N.Y.C., 1977—; asst. to pres., lit. agt. Writers House, Inc., N.Y.C., 1989-92; book critic Kirkus Revs., 1989-90, Book of the Month Club, 1991—, Pubs. Weekly, 1991—. Contbr. articles to med. mags.; staff bookreviewer L.A. Times. First woman organizer Brotherhood of Railway Trainmen, 1945-47; publicist Farmers Union of Iowa, Des Moines, 1951, Golden Gate Arboretum, San Francisco, 1976; bd. dirs. Nat. Womens Health Network, 1981-85; apptd. to Sarasota (Fla.) Commn. on Status of Women, 1994—. NIH grantee U. Calif., L.A., 1968-70; Va. Ctr. for the Arts fellow, Charlottesville, 1976, Woolrich fellow Columbia U., N.Y.C., 1977, Wurlitzer Found. fellow, Taos, N.Mex., 1981. Jewish.

KNOWLES, LESLIE ANNE THORNTON, marketing professional; b. Memphis, Oct. 12, 1965; d. Robert Allen and Shirley Anne (Rogers) T. BBA in Econs., Memphis State U., 1987. With commodities rsch. dept. Allenberg Cotton Co., Memphis, 1987-92; mktg. rsch. analsyt Message Factors, Inc., Memphis, 1992—. Mem. AGD Alumnae (chpt. editor newsletter 1988-89, jr. circle chmn. 1989-90, Panhellenic rep. 1990-91, treas. 1991-92, 92-94). Republican. Baptist. Home: 1570 Hayne Rd Memphis TN 38119-6940 Office: Message Factors Inc Ste 208 2620 Thousand Oaks Blvd Memphis TN 38118-2458

KNOWLES, MARJORIE FINE, lawyer, educator, dean; b. Bklyn., July 4, 1939; d. Jesse J. and Roslyn (Leff) Fine; m. Ralph I. Knowles, Jr., June 3, 1972. BA, Smith Coll., 1960; LLB, Harvard U., 1965. Bar: Ala., N.Y., D.C. Teaching fellow Harvard U., 1963-64; law clk. to judge U.S. Dist. Ct. (so. dist.), N.Y., 1965-66; asst. U.S. atty. U.S. Atty.'s Office, N.Y.C., 1966-67; asst. dist. atty. N.Y. County Dist. Atty., N.Y.C., 1967-70; exec. dir. Joint Found. Support, Inc., N.Y.C., 1970-72; asst. gen. counsel HEW, Washington, 1978-79; insp. gen. U.S. Dept. Labor, Washington, 1979-80; assoc. prof. U. Ala. Sch. Law, Tuscaloosa, 1972-75, prof., 1975-86, assoc. dean, 1982-84; law prof., dean Ga. State U. Coll. Law, Atlanta, 1986-91, law prof., 1986—; cons. Ford Found., N.Y.C., 1973—, trustee Coll. Retirement Equities Fund, N.Y.C., 1983—; mem. exec. com. Conf. on Women and the Constn., 1986-88; mem. com. on continuing profl. edn. Am. Law Inst.-ABA, 1987-93. Contbr. articles to profl. jours. Am. Council Edn. fellow, 1976-77, Aspen Inst. fellow, Rockefeller Found., 1976. Mem. ABA (chmn. new deans workshop 1988), Ala. State Bar Assn., N.Y. State Bar Assn., D.C. Bar Assn., Am. Arbitration Assn. (panel arbitrators 1985—), Am. Law Inst. Office: Ga State U Coll Law University Plz Atlanta GA 30303

KNOWLES, PHYLLIS BRADFUTE, retired title insurance executive; b. Cin., Oct. 16, 1927; d. Fred Lott and Mary (White) Bradfute; m. Harry V. Knowles, Aug. 24, 1950 (div. 1973); children: Pamela A. Fleizach, Debra A. Zakarin. BA, Barnard Coll., 1950. Exec. sec. Carrie Chapman Catt Meml., N.Y.C., 1950-53; pres. Quinbee & Bradfute Internat. Promotions, Eastchester, N.Y., 1957-75; exec. mgr. Urban Developers, Phila., 1975-79, Gibraltar Title & Escrow Co. of Boca Raton, Fla., 1979-92; ret. Author: Records of the Town of Eastchester, 1994. Pres. LWV, Eastchester, 1954-56, Eastchester Hist. Soc., 1965-76, 92—; treas. West County Hist. Soc., 1970-76; treas. Univ. Arts League, Phila., 1977-79. Mem. DAR, 1st Families of Ohio. Republican. Methodist. Avocations: doll house building, historian, lectr., genealogist. Home: 71 Park Dr Yonkers NY 10707

KNOWLES, SUSAN WILLIAMS, art curator, critic; b. Washington, Sept. 1, 1952; d. Lawrence Harvey and Margaret Anderson Williams; m. E. Clifton Knowles, Apr. 8, 1978 (div. 1982). BA in Art History/French, Vanderbilt U., 1974, MA in Art History, 1986; MLS, George Peabody Coll., 1975. Curatorial asst. County Music Found., Nashville, 1974-75; libr. dir. Sevier Co. Pub. Libr., Sevierville, Tenn., 1975-78; children's libr. Cin. Pub. Libr., 1978-79; registrar Cheekwood Mus. Art, Nashville, 1981-85, curator collections, 1985-87; visual arts dir. Metro Arts Commn., Nashville, 1987-91; ind. curator, critic Nashville, 1991—; Map II reviewer Am. Assn. Museums, 1985—; panelist grants Tenn. Arts Commn., 1987—; project curator Tenn. exhibit Nat. Mus. Women in Arts, Washington, 1992-94; acting gallery dir. Middle Tenn. State U., 1992—. Critic New Art Examiner, 1985-92, Art Papers, 1984—, Nashville Scene, 1992—. Mem. bd. Visual Artists Alliance, Nashville, 1991—, Sinking Creek Film Festival, Nashville, 1990—, Tenn. Writers Alliance, Nashville, 1992-94; mem. bd. alumni rep. Vanderbilt Women's Ctr., Nashville, 1991-94. Home and Office: SW Knowles & Assocs 758 Roycroft Pl Nashville TN 37203

KNOWLTON, E(DITH) KATHERINE, clinical psychologist; b. New Haven, Sept. 17, 1949; d. Martin Perry Knowlton and Barbara Jane (Bramble) Lawrence; m. Stephen Robert Feldman, Feb. 22, 1986. BA, U. Chgo., 1971; PhD, U. Nebr., 1985. Lic. clin. psychologist, Wash. Tchr. English Dana Hall Sch., Wellesley, Mass., 1972-74; reporter, news anchor WCSH-TV, Portland, Maine, 1974-78; grad. instr. Antioch U., Seattle, 1986-87; clin. psychologist in pvt. practice Seattle, 1985—; clin. faculty dept. family medicine U. Wash., 1994—. Mem. AAUW, APA, Wash. State Psychol. Assn., N.W. Alliance for Psychoanalytic Study. Office: Seattle Psychol Svcs 216 1st Ave S Ste 333 Seattle WA 98104-2534

KNOWLTON, GRACE FARRAR, sculptor, photographer; b. Buffalo, Mar. 15, 1932; d. Frank Neff and Esther Sargeant (Norton) Farrar; m. Winthrop Knowlton, July 8, 1960 (div. 80); children: Eliza, Samantha. B.A., Smith Coll., 1954; M.A., Columbia U., 1981. Asst. to curator of graphic arts Nat. Gallery of Art, Washington, 1955-57; tchr. art Arlington Pub. Schs., Va., 1957-60; sculptor and photographer, 1960—. Avocations: tennis; bird-watching. Home and Studio: 67 Ludlow Ln Palisades NY 10964-1606

KNOWLTON, NANCY, biologist; b. Evanston, Ill., May 30, 1949; d. Archa Osborn and Aline (Mahnken) K.; m. Jeremy Bradford Cook Jackson; 1 child, Rebecca Knowlton. AB, Harvard U., 1971; PhD, U. Calif., Berkeley, 1978. Asst. prof. biology Yale U., New Haven, 1979-84, assoc. prof., 1984; biologist Smithsonian Tropical Rsch. Inst., Panama, Republic of Panama, 1985—; panelist animal learning and behavior NSF, Washington, 1989-92; vis. scholar Wolfson Coll., Oxford (Eng.) U., 1990-91. Editor Am. Scientist, 1981-90, Evolution, 1995—. NATO postdoctoral fellow NSF, Liverpool, Cambridge, Eng., 1978-79. Mem. AAAS, Ecol. Soc. Am., Soc. Study Evolution. Office: Smithsonian Tropical Rsch Institute Unit 0948 APO AA 34002-0948

KNOWLTON, SYLVIA KELLEY, physician; b. Huntington, Ind., June 8, 1949; d. Darwin Newton and Mary Lucille (Wilson) Kelley; m. Richard Levinson, June 19, 1977 (div. 1988); 1 child, Diana Nicole Levinson; m. Donald William Knowlton, Apr. 20, 1989; children: Fred, Bill. BS, Ind. U., 1977, MD, 1975. Diplomate Am. Bd. Internal Medicine, Am. Bd. Allergy and Immunology. Intern in internal medicine Mt. Sinai Med. Ctr., Miami Beach, Fla., 1976; resident in internal medicine U. Mich., Ann Arbor, 1976, U. Calif., Davis, 1976-77; fellow Nat. Jewish Hosp., Denver, 1977-79; pvt. practice Boca Raton, Fla., 1980—. Republican. Office: Delmar Office Park 7301 W Palmetto Park Rd Ste 10 Boca Raton FL 33433

KNOX, BETTY EMMETT, educational association executive; b. Gastonia, N.C., Feb. 9, 1934; d. James Wilson and Laura Marie (Fowler) Emmett; m. John Jackson Knox, Jr., Aug. 12, 1956 (dec. Apr. 1988); 1 child, Joy Lynne. AA, Gardner-Webb Coll., 1954; BS cum laude, Appalachian State U., 1956, MA, 1958; EdS in Counseling, N.C. State U., 1977, EdD, 1979. Nat. cert. counselor. Tchr. N.C. and Fla. schs., 1956-59; counselor N.C. schs., 1960-66, 67-74, 75-76; asst. dir. admissions U. N.C., Charlotte, 1966-67; pres. Counseling and Ednl. Cons. Svcs., Raleigh, N.C., 1977—; dir. devel., rsch. and planning, pers., publ. rels. Randolph Community Coll., Asheboro, N.C., 1983-85; exec. dir. N.C. Community Colls. Found., Inc., Raleigh, 1985-89; exec. dir. coll. advancement Cape Fear Community Coll., Wilmington, N.C., 1992-94; trustee Gardner-Webb U., Boiling Springs, N.C., 1985-88, 91-94. Contbr. articles to profl. jours. Bd. dirs. Counseling and Human Devel. Found., Alexandria, 1978-79, dir. emeritus, 1979—; bd. dirs., treas. Found. for Ednl. and Econ. Devel., Raleigh, 1990-91; bd. dirs. Forty For the Future, Raleigh, 1992-94. Mem. AAUW, ACA (pres. 1978-79), Am. Sch. Counselor Assn. (pres. 1974-75, Excellence in Rsch. award 1985), Nat. Coun. Resource Devel, N.C. Sch. Counselor Assn. (pres. 1970-71), N.C. Counseling Assn. (pres. 1974-75, Barrett Leadership award 1982, R. Anderson scholar 1970), N.C. Coun. Officers for Resource Devel (Crump Meml. scholar 1985), N.C. Assn. Instnl. Rsch., Execs. Club Raleigh, Phi Theta Kappa (hon., Mary B. Dowless award 1994). Baptist. Home: 5100 Sandelwood Dr Raleigh NC 27609-4425

KNOX, ELIZABETH LOUISE, community volunteer, travel consultant; b. Forest Hills, N.Y.; d. Frederick Conrad and Emma M. Wissel; m. Rudolph T. Haas Jr., Feb. 1944 (div. June 1955); 1 child, Rudolph T. III; m. James Henry Knox, Aug. 22, 1956 (dec. Feb. 1987),; children: Julie Frances, Alice Carrie. Student, Hunter Coll. Ret. co-owner Del Mar (Calif.) Travel Bur. Mem. nat. coun. Salk Inst., La Jolla, 1994—, v.p. women's assn., 1969-70, pres., 1970-72, trustee, 1981-82, chmn. Andy Williams golf tournament benefit, 1969-70, chmn. 30th anniversary com., 1990-92; co-chmn. fashion show benefit Bishop's Sch., La Jolla, 1967, chmn., 1968, trustee, devel. chmn., 1971—, v.p., 1980-82, pres., 1982-86, headmaster's adv. coun., 1986—; bd. dirs. women's aux. Scripps Meml. Hosp., La Jolla, 1963-64, co-chmn. candlelight ball, 1963; charter mem. La Jolla unit Children's Hosp., San Diego, 1956, chmn. ways and means La Jolla unit, 1956-59, chmn. 10th annual fair benefit, 1963, pres. La Jolla unit, 1965, bd. dirs. women's auxiliary, 1962-64, chmn. San Diego stadium premiere benefit, 1967; bd. regents Calif. Luth. Univ., 1994—. Recipient Nat. Lane Bryant award, 1966, Woman of Valor award Temple Beth Israel, 1967, Jonas Salk award of Congress Salk Inst., 1972, Pres.'s award Women's Assn./Salk Inst., 1978, Woman of Dedication award San Diego Door of Hope Aux./Salvation Army, 1986. Mem. La Jolla Beach and Tennis Club, Del Mar Turf Club. Home: 2688 Hidden Valley Rd La Jolla CA 92037

KNOX, GLENDA JANE, health and safety specialist, educator; b. Abernathy, Tex., Mar. 8, 1939; d. Raymond Arnold and Viola Jane (Melton) Boykin; m. William Gene Bright, Mar. 2, 1954 (dec. July 1974); children: Rocky Dwain, Jeannie Ann, Mary Jane, Tommy Lynn; m. Arthur Richard Knox, May 1, 1978; step-sons: Ricky Lynn Stinson, Tony Ray Knox; foster son, Roy David Haney. Grad., Comml. Coll., Baton Rouge, 1985; student, Odessa Coll., 1986-89. Cert. water safety instrn. trainer, health and safety specialist, infant, presch. and parent swimming instr. specialist. Sales clk. Flying B Western Wear, Odessa, Tex., 1975-76; mgr. Redondo Western Wear, Odessa, Tex., 1976-78, Andy's Western Wear, Odessa, Tex., 1978-79; owner Classy Original's Western Wear, Odessa, Tex., 1979-81; water safety instr. Odessa Family YMCA, 1979-82; water safety instr. Odessa Coll., 1981-83, water safety coord., 1983—, health and safety instr., 1987—, aquatics coord. continuing edn., 1983-92; instr. Arthritis Found. YMCA Aquatics Program, Odessa, 1990—, Aquatic Exercise Assn., Odessa, 1987—; instr. specialist ARC Adapted Aquatics, Midland, Tex., 1986—; lifeguard instr. trainer ARC, Odessa, 1979—, CPR instr. trainer, 1981—, 1st aid instr. trainer, 1981—, canoeing instr., 1988-91; water safety specialist Boy Scouts and Girl Scouts Am., Odessa, 1980—; 1st aid instr. Medic First Aid, Odessa, 1990—. Author, editor, artist: Water Aerobics, 1986; author, editor: Food Safety Svc., 1992; designer logo and pin West Tex. Ter. Am. Red Cross, 1988. Vol. Salvation Army, Odessa, 1979-83; mem. exec. bd. ARC, Odessa, 1992, nat. awards chmn., 1992—, health and safety chmn. region III, terr 3, 1987—. Recipient Outstanding Vol. Svc. award Commodore Longfellow Soc., 1994, Outstanding Vol. Svc. award ARC, 1994, others. Mem. NAFE, Commodore Longfellow Soc. (Outstanding Svc. award 1990), Smithsonian Inst., Nat. Trust for Hist. Preservation, Northshore Animal League (Benefactor award 1988, 89). Baptist. Home: 10177 W 26th St Odessa TX 79763 Office: Odessa Coll 201 West University Odessa TX 79764

KNOX, HAVOLYN CROCKER, financial consultant; b. Charlotte, N.C., Oct. 20, 1937; d. Earl Reid and Etta Lorain (Wylie) Crocker; m. Charles Eugene Knox, July 20, 1963 (div. 1981); children: Charles Eugene Jr., Sandra Leigh. Cert. Stenography, U. N.C., Greensboro, 1956. ChFC, CLU. Exec. sec. Stellings-Gossett Theatres, Inc., Charlotte, 1956-57; legal sec. McDougle, Ervin, Horack & Snepp, Charlotte, 1957, Pierce, Wardlow, Knox & Caudle, Charlotte, 1957-63; adminstrv. asst. Charlotte-Mecklenburg Planning Commn., 1980; exec. asst. Conn. Mut. Life Ins. Co., Charlotte, 1981-86; assoc. The Hinrichs Fin. Group, Charlotte, 1986-91, Lyn Knox & Assocs., Charlotte, 1991—. Ops. dir. Eddie Knox for Mayor campaign, Charlotte; campaign mgr. Herb Spaugh for City Coun., Charlotte, 1981, 83, 85; registration chmn. Kemper Open Golf Tournament, Charlotte, 1976-79; pres. The Legal Aux., Charlotte, 1972-73; bd. dirs. Oratorio Singers of Charlotte, 1986-93. Recipient William Danforth Found. award, 1955. Mem. Am. Soc. CLU and ChFC (bd. dirs. Charlotte chpt. 1994—), Nat. Assn. Life Underwriters, Charlotte Assn. Life Underwriters, Charlotte Estate Planning Coun. Republican. Presbyterian. Home: 2331 Carmel Rd Charlotte NC 28226-6322 Office: Lyn Knox & Assocs PO Box 4115 Charlotte NC 28226

KNOX, LINDA SUSAN, nursing administrator; b. Phila., Aug. 6, 1953; d. Andrew Donald and Irene Margaret (Hild) K. Diploma in Nursing, Hosp. of the U. Pa. Sch. Nursing, 1974; BSN, U. Pa., 1981, MSN, 1986. Staff nurse operating room Hosp. U. Pa., Phila., 1974-78, head nurse operating room, 1979, rsch. coord., 1980-83; rsch. coord. VA Med. Ctr., Phila., 1983-86; lectr. U. Pa. Sch. Nursing, Phila., 1986-92; nursing coord., night adminstr. Hosp. U. Pa., Phila., 1989-91, nurse mgr., clin. rsch. ctr., 1991—. Contbr. articles to jours. in field. chair annual giving Soc. of Alumni U. Pa. Sch. Nursing, 1991-93. Recipient Thomas B. McCabe Merit Achievement award, 1971-74, Profl. Nurse Traineeship award NIH, 1985-86. Mem. AACN, Am. Soc. Parenteral & Enteral Nutrition (chair nurses com., 1992-94, mem. bd. dirs.), Am. Soc. Law, Medicine & Ethics, Oncology Nursing Soc., The Hastings Ctr. Home: 6 E Windermere Terr Lansdowne PA 19050 Office: Hosp U Pa 3400 Spruce St Philadelphia PA 19104

KNOX, SARAH STUART, psychophysiologist, researcher; b. Cin., Nov. 21, 1946; d. Frank Samual and Mary Stuart (Duckworth) K.; m. Eje Thelin, Apr. 16, 1980 (div. 1986); 1 child, Vanessa Thelin-Knox. BA, U. N.H., 1968; MA and PhD, U. Stockholm, Sweden, 1981. Lic. psychologist, Sweden. Rsch. physiologist Nat. Inst. for Psychosocial Factors and Health, Stockholm, 1981-83; rsch. assoc. U. Stockholm, 1983-86, assoc. prof., 1986—; dir. rsch. group Karolinska Inst., Stockholm, 1983-87; assoc. prof. psychiatry Med. Sch. Wayne State U., Detroit, 1987-91; with Behavioral Medicine Br. Nat. Heart, Lung & Blood Inst., Bethesda, Md., 1991—; rsch. cons. WHO, Ljubliana, Yugoslavia, 1985, Nordic Working Group on Noise, Bergen, Norway, 1986; co-chair nat. workshop on biobehavioral mechanisms of lipid metabolism and atherosclerosis, Nat. Inst. Heart, Lung and Blood; lectr. in field. Contbr. articles to profl. jours. Grantee Swedish Work Environment Fund, 1981-82, 84, 85, 86, Swedish Dept. Environ. Conservation, 1983. Mem. AAAS, N.Y. Acad. Scis., Soc. Behavioral Medicine, Soc. Psychophysiol. Rsch. Home: 205 Fairgrove Cir Gaithersburg MD 20877-3474 Office: Nat Heart Lung & Blood Inst 7550 Wisconsin Ave Bethesda MD 20814-3559

KNUDSON, RUTH E., education educator; b. Phila., June 29, 1945; d. Robert J. and Ruth M. (Weisner) Rodisch; m. Karl J. Knudson, June 15, 1968; children: Robert K., Richard K. BA, Bryn Mawr Coll., 1967; MS, U. Wis., 1968; PhD, U. Calif., Riverside, 1988. English and reading tchr. Calif., La., Mass., 1969-77; supr. teaching edn. U. Calif. Sch. of Edn., Riverside, 1985-88, asst. head, edn. tchr., 1988-89, mem. faculty, 1989—; cons. pub. sch. dists., Calif., 1984-92; chair local arrangements Nat. Reading Conf., 1991; chair tchr. edn. com. U. Calif., Riverside, 1992-94. Contbr. articles to profl. jours. Advancement co-chair Boy Scouts Am., 1993—; tchr. Sunday Sch., First Bapt. Ch., Riverside, 1994—; vol. various other activities including Cub Scouts, Friends of the Libr., 1987—. Woodrow Wilson fellow, 1967-68; Presdl. grantee U. Calif., 1989; recipient Spencer award Spencer Found., 1989-90. Mem. Am. Ednl. Rsch. Assn., Nat. Conf. Rsch. on English, Nat. Coun. Tchrs. of English (rsch. co-chair com. on tracking and grouping practices 1991-93), Internat. Reading Assn., Phi Delta Kappa. Office: U Calif Sch of Edn Riverside CA 92521

KNULL, YOLANDA CHAVEZ, lawyer; b. Pasadena, Calif., June 20, 1949; d. Raul A. and Doris J. (Fields) Chavez; m. William H. Knull III, June 2, 1970; children: Anna, Warren. BA, Vassar Coll., 1970; postgrad., U. Va., 1976-77; JD, NYU, 1979. Bar: N.Y. 1980, Tex. 1986. Trust and estate adminstrn. atty. Morgan Guaranty, N.Y.C., 1979-81; atty. Shearman & Sterling, N.Y.C., 1981-86; assoc. Vinson & Elkins, Houston, 1986-91, ptnr., 1991—. Fellow Houston Bar Found.; mem. ABA (tax sect., real estate, probate & trust law sect.). Office: Vinson & Elkins LLP 3300 1st City Tower 1001 Fannin Houston TX 77002

KNUTH, CYNTHIA STROUT, educational consultant; b. Walpole, Mass.; d. Harold A. and Doris A. (Kendall) Strout; m. Count Adam Knuth. MA in Internat. Law and Govt., NYU. FAO Mission to Iraq, Baghdad, 1950-53; conf. precis-writer UN, Copenhagen, 1954-56; exec. sec. to UN legal counsel, N.Y.C., 1956-62, to pres. Gen. Assembly, 1962-63, UN Devel. Program, 1964-69; with Ctr. for Internat. Affairs, Harvard U., Cambridge, Mass., 1976-82; cons. to Bd. Regents of Higher Edn. in Mass., 1983-86. Founder Friends of the Wampanoag, Boston, 1986, Friends of Native Ams., 1989, Menotomy Indian Day, Arlington, Mass., 1991, Aberjona Indian Day, Winchester, Mass., 1992. Mem. Common Cause (exec. bd. Mass. 1986—), UN Assn. (exec. bd. 1970—), Boston Jazz Soc. (exec. bd. 1975—), Mystic River Watershed Assn. (exec. bd. 1991—), Phi Delta Kappa (2s v.p. Harvard U. chpt. 1990-92), Sierra Club/Thoreau Group (chair 1993), Walden Forever Wild (exec. bd. 1993-95). Home: 206 Massachusetts Ave Arlington MA 02174-8435

KOART, NELLIE HART, real estate investor and executive; b. San Luis Obispo, Calif., Jan. 3, 1930; d. Will Carleton and Nellie Malchen (Cash) Hart; m. William Harold Koart, Jr., June 16, 1951 (dec. 1976); children: Kristen Marie Kittle, Matthew William. Student Whittier Coll., 1947-49; BA, U. Calif.-Santa Barbara, 1952; MA, Los Angeles State Coll., 1957. Life diploma elem. edn., Calif. Farm worker Hart Farms, Montebello, Calif., 1940-48; play leader Los Angeles County Parks and Recreation, East Los Angeles, Rosemead, Calif., 1948-51; elem. tchr. Potrero Heights Sch. Dist., South San Gabriel, Calif., 1951-55, vice prin., 1955-57; real estate salesman William Koart Real Estate, Goleta, Calif., 1963-76, real estate investor KO-ART Enterprises, Goleta, 1976—, pres. Wm. Koart Constrn. Co., Inc., Goleta, 1975-91; real estate sales person Joseph McGeever Realty Co., Goleta, 1976-91; adv. bd. Bank of Montecito, Santa Barbara, Calif., 1983—. Editor: Reflections, 1972. Charter mem. Calif. Regents program Calif. Fedn. Republican Women, 1989; treas. Santa Barbara County Fedn. Republican Women, Alamar-Hope Ranch, 1981-82, treas. County Bd., 1983-84; treas. Com. to Recall Hone, Maschke and Shewczyk, Goleta, 1984; treas. Santa Barbara County Lincoln Club, 1983-87, bd. dirs., 1983-93; assoc. mem. state central com. Calif. Republican Party, 1985-87. Mem. Santa Barbara Apartment Assn., Antique Automobile Club of Am. (sec. treas. Santa Barbara 1980-84), Serena Cove Owners Assn. (sec.-treas, bd. dirs 1990—). Club: Santa Barbara County Lincoln Club. Avocations: swimming, numismatics, geneology, college and professional football. Office: KO-ART Enterprises PO Box 310 Goleta CA 93116-0310

KOBAYASHI, ANN H., state legislator; b. Honolulu, Apr. 10, 1937; m.; 3 children. Student Pembroke Coll., Northwestern U. Officer family corp.; former legis. aide, adminstrv. asst. Hawaii Senate, now mem. Senate from 14th Dist. Republican. Home: 3657 Waaloa Way Honolulu HI 96822-1150 Office: Senate House State Capitol Honolulu HI 96813*

KOBE, LAN, medical physicist; b. Semarang, Indonesia; naturalized; d. O.G. and L.N. (The) Kobe. BS in Physics, IKIP U., Bandung, Indonesia, 1964, MS in Physics, 1967; MS in Med. Physics and Biophysics, U. Calif.-Berkeley, 1975. Physics instr. Sch. Engring., Tarumanegara U., Jakarta, Indonesia, 1968-72; research fellow dept. radiation oncology U. Calif.-San Francisco, 1975-77; clin. physicist in residence dept. radiation oncology UCLA, 1977-78, asst. hosp. radiation physicist, 1978-80, hosp. radiation physicist, 1980—; instr. radiation oncology physics to resident physicians and med. physics graduate students. Contbr. sci. papers to profl. publs. Newhouse grantee U. Calif.-Berkeley, 1974-75, grantee dean grad. div. U. Calif.-Berkeley, 1975; recipient Pres. Work Study award U. Calif., Berkeley, 1974-75, Employee of Month award UCLA, 1983, Outstanding Service award UCLA, 1986; devel. Achievement award, UCLA, 1988. Mem. Am. Soc. for Therapeutic Radiology and Oncology, Am. Assn. Physicists in Medicine (nat. and So. Calif. chpts.), Am. Bd. Radiology (cert.), Am. Assn. Individual Investors (life). Office: UCLA Dept Radiation Oncology 200 UCLA Medical Plz Ste B265 Los Angeles CA 90024-6977

KOBER, ARLETTA REFSHAUGE (MRS. KAY L. KOBER), educational administrator; b. Cedar Falls, Iowa, Oct. 31, 1919; d. Edward and Mary (Jensen) Refshauge; BA, State Coll. Iowa, 1940; MA, U. No. Iowa; m. Kay Leonard Kober, Feb. 14, 1944; children: Kay Mary, Karilyn Eve. Tchr. high schs., Soldier, Iowa, 1940-41, Montezuma, Iowa, 1941-43, Waterloo, Iowa, 1943-50, 65-67, co-ordinator Office Edn. Waterloo Community Schs., Waterloo, Iowa, 1967-84; head dept. co-op. career edn. West High Sch., Waterloo, 1974-84. Mem. Waterloo Sch. Health Council; nominating com. YWCA, Waterloo; Black Hawk County chmn. Tb Christmas Seals; ward chmn. ARC, Waterloo; co-chmn. Citizen's Com. for Sch. Bond Issue; pres. Waterloo PTA Council, Waterloo Vis. Nursing Assn., 1956-62, 82—; pres. Kingsley Sch. PTA, 1959-60; v.p. Waterloo Women's Club, 1962-63, pres., 1963-64, trustee bd. clubhouse dirs., 1957-58; mem. Gen. Fedn. Women's Clubs, Nat. Congress Parents and Tchrs.; Presbyterial world service chmn. Presbyn. Women's Assn.; bd. dirs. Black Hawk County Republican Women, 1952-53, United Services of Black Hawk County, Broadway Theatre League, St. Francis Hosp. Found.; deacon Pres. Ch., 1995—. Mem. AAUW (v.p. Cedar Falls 1946-47), NEA, Internat. Platform Assn., LWV (dir. Waterloo 1951-52), Black Hawk County Hist. Soc. (charter), Delta Pi Epsilon (v.p. 1966-67), Delta Kappa Gamma. Club: Town (dir.) (Waterloo), P.E.O. Home: 3436 Augusta Cir Waterloo IA 50701-4608 Office: 503 W 4th St Waterloo IA 50701-1554

KOBER, DARLENE MARIE, marketing professional; b. Pitts., Feb. 3, 1963; d. Richard Donald and Anna Marie (Desiderio) Slavinsky; m. Brian Jon Kober, June 2, 1990. BSChemE, Bucknell U., 1985; MBA, Northwestern U., 1993. Cost engr. Air Products & Chems., Allentown, Pa., 1985-86, market devel. engr., 1986-87, project engr., 1987-90; sales engr. Air Products & Chems., Chgo., 1990-91; market mgr. Morton Internat., Chgo., 1991—. Divsn. coord. United Way Crusade of Mercy, Chgo., 1993. Office: Morton Internat 100 N Riverside Plz Chicago IL 60606-1518

KOBER, JANE, lawyer; b. Shamokin, Pa., May 17, 1943; d. Jeno Daniel and Angela Agnes (Kogut) DiRienzo; m. Arthur Kober, June 20, 1970 (div. 1975). AB, Pa. State U., 1965; MA, U. Chgo., 1966; JD, Case Western Res. U., 1974. Bar: Ohio, N.Y. Lectr. U. Baghdad, Iraq, 1966-67; editor, cons. Ernst & Young, Washington, 1968-70; law clk. to Hon. William K. Thomas U.S. Dist. Ct. (no. dist.) Ohio, Cleve., 1974-75; atty., ptnr. Squire, Sanders & Dempsey, Cleve. and N.Y.C., 1975-87; ptnr. Shea & Gould, N.Y.C., 1987-89, LeBoeuf, Lamb, Greene & MacRae, N.Y.C., 1989—. Mem. Union Club Cleve. Office: LeBoeuf Lamb Greene & MacRae 125 W 55th St New York NY 10019

KOBS, ANN ELIZABETH JANE, nursing administrator, consultant; b. Clinton, Iowa, Feb. 13, 1944; d. Francis Hubert and Leora Elizabeth (Sodeman) Boeker; m. Dennis Raymond Kobs, Oct. 15, 1966 (div. 1989); children: Michael, Peter, Amy. Diploma, Mercy Hosp. Sch. Nursing, 1965; BS in Nursing, Marycrest Coll., 1978; MS in Nursing Adminstrn., No. Ill. U., 1981. Staff charge nurse Mercy Hosp., Davenport, Iowa, 1965-66; clin. instr. Marycrest Coll., Davenport, 1967; health care cons., Chgo., 1973—; pre-reviewer for continuing edn. and career counselor in residence Ill. Nurses Assn., Chgo., 1978-80; career devel. cons. Ill. Hosp. Assn., Oak Brook, 1980-81, staff specialist nursing, 1981-83, dir. nursing, Naperville, 1983-84; dir. nursing surg./maternal-child health Alexian Bros. Med. Ctr., Elk Grove Village, Ill., 1984-87; dir. nursing svcs. Rochelle (Ill.) Community Hosp., 1987-89; cons. Medicus Systems Corp., 1989-91; assoc. dir. dept. performance measure interpretation Joint Commn. on Accreditation of Healthcare Orgns., 1991—; lectr. No. Ill. U., 1981-87, St. Xavier Coll., 1987; mem. faculty Aurora U., 1988-91; clin. teaching asst. U. Iowa, 1988—; expert witness for med. malpractice cases, 1987—. Contbr. numerous articles on materials mgmt., infection control, nursing and quality improvement, 1991—. Mem. City Beautification Commn. Rock Island, 1972-76, also sec., vice-chmn.; mem. com. perinatal health March of Dimes, 1991-93. Mem. Am. Orgn. Nurse Execs. (cons., legis. and regulation com. 1987-89), Ill. Orgn. Nurse Execs. (mem. exec. com., chmn. Task Force on Sunset Ill. Nursing Act 1984-87, pres. 1988-89, bd. dirs. 1984-92, archivist 1992—), Sigma Theta Tau. Roman Catholic. Editor: Ill. Nurses Assn. Directory of Baccalaureate Degree Completion Programs for RNs in Ill., 1979; writer, producer, dir.: Nursing: Opportunities Unlimited, 1980.

KOCEN, LORRAINE AYRAL, accountant; b. Levittown, N.Y., July 20, 1956; d. Edward Joseph and Joan Dorothy (Destefanis) Ayral; m. Ross Kocen, Oct. 4, 1981; 1 child, Daniel. BS, Hofstra U., 1978; MBA, U. Minn., 1985. Engr. Sperry Systems Mgmt., Great Neck, N.Y., 1978-81; fin. analyst ITT Consumer Fin. Corp., Mpls., 1981-84; cost acct. Mercy Med. Ctr., Mpls., 1984-85, contr., 1985-86; bus. segments acct. GTE, Thousand Oaks, Calif., 1986-88, Cerritos project acct., 1988-90, Cerritos project adminstr., 1990-92, fin. adminstr., 1992-93, sr. sales adminstr., 1993-94, adminstr. mobile comms., 1994—. Asst. editor newsletter Healthcare Fin. Mgmt. Assn., Mpls., 1985-86. Mem. archtl. com. Foxmoor Hills Homeowners Assn., Westlake, Calif., 1989. Office: GTE 3500 Willow Ln Thousand Oaks CA 91361

KOCH, CAROLE JACKSON, human resources executive; b. Evergreen Park, Ill., Feb. 25, 1951; d. Robert Lawrence Capman and Norma Gene (Benson) C.; m. Donald Charles Jackson, Sept. 24, 1976 (dec. Mar. 1984); m. Curtis Gerard Koch, Aug. 28, 1987. BA with honors, U. Ill., Chgo., 1972. Job analyst U. Ill., Chgo., 1973-76, personnel coordinator, 1976-80, assoc. personnel dir., 1980-83; dir. human resources U. Ill. Hosp. and Clinics, Chgo., 1983—. Mem. human resources coun. Met. Chgo. Healthcare Coun., 1987—. Mem. Coll. and Univ. Pers. Assn., Am. Soc. Healthcare Human Resources Adminstrn., Soc. Human Resource Mgmt. Office: U Ill Hosp 1740 W Taylor St Rm 1400 Chicago IL 60612-7236

KOCH, EDNA MAE, lawyer, nurse; b. Terre Haute, Ind., Oct. 12, 1951; d. Leo K. and Lucille E. (Smith) K.; m. Mark D. Orton. BS in Nursing, Ind. State U., 1977; JD, Ind. U., 1980. Bar: Ind. 1980, U.S. Dist. Ct. (so. dist.) Ind. 1980. Assoc. Dillon & Cohen, Indpls., 1980-85; ptnr. Tipton, Cohen & Koch, Indpls., 1985-93, LaCava, Zeigler & Carter, Indpls., 1993-94; assoc. Zeigler Carter Cohen & Koch, Indpls., 1994—; leader seminars for nurses, Ind. U. Med. Ctr., Ball State U., Muncie, Ind., St. Vincent Hosp., Indpls., Deaconess Hosp., Evansville, Ind., others; lectr. on med. malpractice Cen. Ind. chpt. AACCN, Indpls. "500" Postgrad. Course in Emergency Medicine, Ind. Assn. Osteo. Physicians and Surgeons State Conv., numerous others. Mem. ABA, ANA, Ind. State Bar Assn., Indpls. Bar Assn., Am. Soc. Law and Medicine, Ind. State Nurses Assn. Republican. Office: Zeigler Carter Cohen & Koch 8500 Keystone Xing Ste 510 Indianapolis IN 46240-2461

KOCH, KATHERINE R., communications executive; b. Pitts., Apr. 21, 1949; d. Irving Samuel Stapsy and Betty Ruth (Sachs) Blake; m. Stanley Christopher Brown, July 26, 1986; 1 child, Matthew. BFA, Rochester Inst. Tech., 1973. Instr. Ivy Sch. Profl. Art, Pitts., 1973-74; advt. dir. Buhl Optical Co., Pitts., 1974-77; pres., creative dir. Ambit Mktg. Comm., Ft. Lauderdale, Fla., 1977—; instr. Point Park Coll., Pitts., 1977-78. Mktg. dir. United Way Broward, Ft. Lauderdale, 1994, mem. exec. com., 1994—; mem. women's adv. bd. Plantation Gen. Hosp., 1993—; mem., comm. chair Broward Econ. Devel. Coun., 1994—. Mem. Greater Ft. Lauderdale Mktg. Alliance (chair 1993-94), Womens Exec. Club (pres.-elect 1994—). Office: Ambit Mktg Comm 888 E Las Olas Blvd # 520 Fort Lauderdale FL 33301

KOCH, KATHLEEN DAY, lawyer; b. St. Louis, Nov. 27, 1948; d. Edward J. and Margaret (Beckmeier) D.; children: Stefan, Martha, Rebecca. Student, Concordia Coll., River Forest, Ill., 1966-69; BS in Edn., U. Mo., 1971; JD, U. Chgo., 1977. Bar: Ill. 1977, D.C. 1978. Atty. HUD, Washington, 1977-79, U.S. Merit Sys. Protection Bd., Washington, 1979-84; sr. atty. U.S. Dept. Commerce, Washington, 1984-87; assoc. counsel to pres. White House, Washington, 1987-88; gen. counsel Fed. Labor Rels. Authority, Washington, 1988-91; spl. counsel Office Spl. Counsel, Washington, 1991—. Recipient Disting. Alumni award U. Mo.-St. Louis, 1990. Office: U S Office Spl Counsel 1730 M St NW 3d Flr Washington DC 20036-4505

KOCH, KIMBERLY ANN, broadcast executive; b. Chgo., May 5, 1964; d. Kenneth Alfred and Patricia Ann (Kelsey) K. BA magna cum laude, U. Utah, 1986. Camera operator Sta. KUTV (affiliate NBC), Salt Lake City, 1985-87; prodn. asst. Sta. KUED-TV (affiliate PBS), Salt Lake City, 1987-89, assoc. producer, 1989—. Mem. Women in Communications, Soc. Profl. Journalists, Phi Kappa Phi, Kaappa Tau Alpha, Phi Eta Sigma. Home: 7445 Tall Oaks Cir Park City UT 84060-5363 Office: Sta KUED-TV 101 Gardner Hall Salt Lake City UT 84112

KOCH, KIMBERLY ANN, marketing professional; b. Fort Knox, Ky., Oct. 29, 1965; d. George P. and Maureen R. (Burke) K. BBA in Fin., Loyola Marymount U., Calif., 1987; MBA in Mktg., Pepperdine U., 1995. Sales, fin. mgr. Campbell Automotive Group, Santa Ana, Calif., 1987-92; owner, cons. Alternative Concepts, Inc., Newport Beach, Calif., 1992-93; mktg. mgr. Cartel Mktg., L.A., 1993—. Ministres Our Lady Queen of Angels, Newport Beach, Calif., 1994. Mem. Nat. Assn. Female Execs., Loyola Marymount U. Pride of Lions (exec. bd. mem.). Republican. Roman Catholic. Office: Cartel Mktg Inc 9841 Airport Blvd Ste 1424 Los Angeles CA 90045

KOCH, LISA CHRISTIANSEN, healthcare consultant; b. Valparaiso, Ind., May 5, 1961; d. John and Julia (Svensli) C.; m. Christopher Jonathan Koch, Oct. 10, 1987 (div. Mar. 1991). AS in Nursing, Anderson Coll., 1983; BBA in Fin., Ohio State U., 1991. RN, Ind., Ohio. Nurse ICU St. Anthony Hosp., Michigan City, Ind., 1983-84, Mt. Sinai Hosp., Cleve., 1984-85; nurse ICU, dialysis Ohio State U. Hosps., Columbus, 1985-91, unit mgr., 1987, 88, 89; adminstr. Community Dialysis Ctr., Tampa, Fla., 1991-92; mgr. Ernst & Young LLP, Tampa, Fla., 1992—. Vol. Easter Seals, Columbus, 1985-91, Am. Heart Assn., Columbus, 1986; vol. Columbus Zoo, 1985-91, photographer, 1987; fundraiser Ohio State U. Recipient Summa award Ohio State U., 1987. Mem. Am. Nephrology Nurse Assn. (sec.-treas. 1987, 88, 89, pres. 1991), Ohio Nurses Assn., Fla. Orgn. Nurse Execs., Healthcare Fin.

Mgmt. Assn., Sons of Norway. Republican. Lutheran. Home: 10265 Gandy Blvd Saint Petersburg FL 33702 Office: Ernst & Young LLP 100 N Tampa St Ste 2200 Tampa FL 33602

KOCH, MARY COLLEEN, lawyer; b. Ft. Riley, Kans., Apr. 15, 1956; d. Ronald James and Mary Ann (Stanton) K. AB, U. Notre Dame, 1977; JD, John Marshall Law Sch., 1982. Atty. felony trial divsn. Cook County Pub. Defender, Chgo., 1981-94. Home: 3450 Lake Shore Dr Chicago IL 60657 Office: Cook County Pub Defender 2650 S Calif 7th Cl Chicago IL 60608

KOCH, VIRGINIA GREENLEAF, painter; b. Chgo., Aug. 28, 1925; d. William Henry and Henrietta Irene (Moser) Greenleaf; pupil of Ivan Olinsky, 1941-42; student Yale U., 1943-45; pupil of Robert Brackman, 1946; student Am. U., Washington, postgrad. 1956-57; pupil of Gene Davis, 1968-70; m. Henry Koch, Aug. 20, 1962 (dec.); children—Deidra G., William G. One-man shows at Studio Gallery, Washington, 1970, 72, 74 Haslem Gallery, Madison, Wis., 1971, In Town Gallery, Cleve., 1973, World Bank, Washington, 1972, Art League No. Va., 1973, Studio Gallery, 1976, Main St. Gallery, Boston, 1976, 77, 78, 79, 80, 81, 83, 87, 88, 89, Main St. Gallery, Nantucket, 1977, 82, 83, 84, 85, 86, 87, 88, 89, 91, 92, 93, 94, Gallery 124, N.Y.C., 1983; group shows include Maritime Mus., 1990, 91, Newport News, Va., 1971, 72, U. No. Va., 1973, U. Richmond (Va.), 1972, U. Md., 1975, Parsons Dreyfuss Gallery, N.Y.C., 1976, 77, Phillips Collection, Washington, 1989, Corcoran Gallery, 1975, 92, 93, Cooley Gallery, Old Lyme, Conn., 1991-94; represented in permanent collections Dept. of State, Washington, Cooley Gallery, Lyme Acad. of Fine Arts, Old Lyme, 1991-94, also various ambassadors' residences. Active Olde Town Citizens' Com., Alexandria, Va., 1964-73, Georgetown Citizens' Assn., Washington, 1971-75, Hosp. Thrift Shop, Nantucket, Mass., 1968-71, Nat. Symphony of Washington, D.C. Com., 1970—; bd. dirs. Arts Council of Nantucket. Mem. Studio Gallery, Foundery Group Women Painters, Artists' Equity, Art League Va., Art Found. Nantucket Conservation Assn., Nantucket Hist. Found.

KOCHANEK, NANCY CAROL, accountant; b. London, July 21, 1963; parents Am. citizens; d. Anthony Stanley and Hilde Elise (Hediger) K. BSBA in Acctg., Bucknell U., 1984. CPA, Md. Auditor Marriott Corp., Washington, 1984-86; fin. analyst Marriott Mgmt. Svcs., Washington, 1986-87, sr. fin. analyst, 1987-89; mgr. fin. adminstrn. and analysis Marriott Edn. and Health Care Svcs., Washington, 1989-90; dir. field support Marriott Mgmt. Svcs., Washington, 1990-92, v.p. fin. reporting and analysis, 1992—. Recipient Cert. of Merit, Pa. Inst. CPAs, 1984. Office: Marriott Internat One Marriott Dr 927.44 Washington DC 20058

KOCHANSKI, LOIS WHIDDEN, foundation administrator; b. San Angelo, Tex., Aug. 21, 1923; d. James Edgar and Bessie Mae (Mullican) Whidden; m. Joseph Thaddeus Kochanski, Jan. 21, 1949; children: Mary Ann Daly, James T., Constance Wetterer. BA, U. Tex., 1945. Intelligence analyst U.S. Office of Naval Intelligence, Arlington, Va., 1960-64; asst. to v.p. for acad. affairs George Washington U., Washington, 1964-67; exec. dir. Found. for Advanced Edn. in Scis., Bethesda, Md., 1970—. Author: The Mullican Family of Warren County, Tennessee, 1991. Mem. AAUW, NIH Camera Club, North Bethesda Camera Club, Soc. of Mayflower Descendants. Home: 6004 Manor Oak Way Bethesda MD 20814

KOCHANSKI, SUSAN DIANE, quality engineer; b. Richmond, Ind., Mar. 12, 1962; d. Kiffin Emil and Marieta Elvena (Vardaman) Gilbert; m. Mark Alan Kochanski, Aug. 14, 1982; children: Anna Marie, Sara Elizabeth. BS in Indsl. Engring., Purdue U., 1984. Process engr. Tex. Instruments, Midland, Tex., 1984-90; procurement quality engr. ATL, Bothell, Wash., 1991—; corp. sec. TransExploration, Bothell, 1994—. Mem. Am. Soc. Quality Control (cert. quality engr., cert. quality auditor). Methodist. Office: ATL PO Box 3003 Bothell WA 98041

KOCHAR, ARVIND KAUR, radiologist; b. Indore, India, Jan. 10, 1946; d. Darshan and Satwant Kaur Singh; m. Mahendr Singh Kochar, Dec. 20, 1968; children: Baltej (Baj), Ajay (Jay). MD, Med. Coll. Indore, 1968. Diplomate Am. Bd. Radiology. Intern Allegheny Gen. Hosp., Pitts., 1969-70; resident in radiology Deaconess Hosp., Milw., 1971-74; radiologist Lakeland Hosp., Elkhorn, Wis., 1980—. Mem. Am. Coll. Radiology, Am. Assn. Women Radiologists. Office: Lakeland Hosp PO Box 1002 Elkhorn WI 53121

KOCH-EILERS, EVAMARIA WYSK, oceanographer, educator; b. Porto Alegre, Brazil, May 11, 1961; came to U.S., 1985; d. Walter and Eva Margarethe Elsa Anna (Wysk) K. BS in Oceanography, U. Rio Grande, Brazil, 1984; MS in Botany, U. South Fla., 1988, PhD in Marine Sci., 1993. Rsch. asst. U. Rio Grande, 1980-85, U. South Fla., Tampa, 1985-89; biol. scientist Fla. Marine Rsch. Inst., St. Petersburg, 1988-89; rsch. scientist U. Conn./NOAA, Milford, 1993—. Contbr. to profl. publs. Mem. Brazilian Assn. Oceanography, Brazilian Phycological Soc., Estuarine Rsch. Fedn., Am. Soc. Limnology and Oceanography, Sigma Xi. Office: Univ of Conn/NOAA 212 Rogers Ave Milford CT 06460-6435

KOCHER, JUANITA FAY, auditor; b. Falmouth, Ky., Aug. 9, 1933; d. William Birgest and Lula (Gillespie) Vickroy; m. Donald Edward Kocher, Nov. 18, 1953. Grad. high sch., Bright, Ind. Bookkeeper Mchts. Bank and Trust Co., West Harrison, Ind., 1952-56, teller, asst. cashier, 1962-87, br. mgr., 1979-87, internal auditor, 1987—; bookkeeper Progressive Bank, New Orleans, 1956-58; with proof dept. 1st Nat. Bank, Cin., 1958-59; teller 1st Nat. Bank, Harrison, Ohio, 1959-62; bookkeeper Donald E. Kocher Constrn., Harrison, 1981—. Mem. Am. Bankers Assn., Ind. Bankers Assn. Home: 11277 Biddinger Rd Harrison OH 45030

KOCHTA, RUTH MARTHA, art gallery owner; b. N.Y.C., Jan. 5, 1924; d. Harry Joseph and Anna (Braun) Evers; m. Albert Emil Kochta, Nov. 7, 1948; children: Alan, Carol. Student, CUNY, Queens, 1965-68, Art Students League, 1970-75. Artist Queens, N.Y. and Lenox, Mass., 1965—; dir. Imperial Gallery, N.Y.C., 1981; owner, dir. Clark Whitney Gallery, Lenox, 1983—. Work exhibited at Nat. Acad., N.Y.C. 1969, Audubon Artists, N.Y.C. 1971, Heckscher Mus., Huntington, N.Y., 1972, Elizabet Ney Mus., Austin, Tex., 1972, Wadsworth Atheneum, Hartford, Conn., 1975, Philathea Mus., Ont., Can., 1976, New Britain (Conn.) Mus., 1978, Guild Gallery, N.Y.C. 1979, other exhibits. Recipient over 50 awards in various competitions.

KOCO, LINDA GALE, writer; b. Chgo., Ohio, Sept. 3, 1945; d. Peter Robert and Laura Sylvia (Albert) Young; m. Gary Paul Kocolowski, Dec. 20, 1968 (div. 1987); 1 child, Charles Adam. BA with honors, Lake Forest (Ill.) Coll., 1967. Cert. secondary sch. educator, Ill. English and writing tchr. Lake Forest High Sch., 1967-68; writer, copywriter Allstate Ins. Co., Northbrook, Ill., 1969-70; staff writer Nat. Underwriter Co., Cin., 1970-73, asst. editor, 1974-78; assoc. editor Nat. Underwriter Co., Lakewood, Ohio, 1988-92, sr. editor, 1992—; pvt. practice Lakewood, 1970—; founder, co-leader Cin. Poets' Workshop, 1973-78; founder, moderator Lakewood Poets Workshop, 1979-83; speaker numerous writing and bus. orgns., 1980—. Contbr. articles to numerous publs. Active Lakewood Congrl. Ch., 1984-92, chair diaconate, 1988-91; active Pilgrim Congrl. Ch., 1992—; learning ctr. vol. Madison Sch., Lakewood, 1984-88; parent mem. young author's com. Lakewood Bd. Edn., 1987-93. Mem. Poets League Greater Cleve., NAFE. Office: PO Box 771037 Lakewood OH 44107

KOCOUREK, SARAH SPRINGER, lawyer; b. Leesburg, Va., Aug. 25, 1956; d. Paul Le Baron and Mary Jean (O'Donnell) Springer; children: Kyle Thomas Doherty, Colin Brent Doherty; m. Karol Otto Kocourek, June 15, 1991. BA, U. S.C., 1977, JD, 1980. Bar: Tex., 1980, Miss., 1982. Staff atty. Tex. Dept. Community Affairs, Austin, 1980-81; assoc. atty. Bourdeaux & Jones, Meridian, Miss., 1981, Roy Pitts, Meridian, 1982-83; pvt. practice Meridian, 1983-85, 90-94; assoc. atty. Goldman, Dreyfus & Primeaux, Meridian, 1985-90; solo practice, 1990-94; chancery ct. judge dist. 12 Lauderdale and Clarke Counties, 1995—. Bd. dirs. Silver Cross Circle, Meridian, 1985—; bd. dirs., chpt. chmn. ARC, Meridian, 1986—. Recipient Pres.'s Pro Bono award Miss. Bar Assn., 1994; named Woman of Yr., The Meridian Star, 1993. Mem. ABA, Am. Trial Lawyers Assn., Miss. Trial Lawyers Assn., Lauderdale County Bar Assn. Republican. Episcopalian. Home: 7512 Confederate Dr Meridian MS 39305 Office: 500 Constitution Ave Meridian MS 39302

KODIS, MARY CAROLINE, marketing consultant; b. Chgo., Dec. 17, 1927; d. Anthony John and Callis Ferebee (Old) K.; student San Diego State Coll., 1945-47, Latin Am. Inst., 1948. Controller, div. adminstrv. mgr. Fed. Mart Stores, 1957-65; controller, adminstrv. mgr. Gulf Mart Stores, 1965-67; budget dir., adminstrv. mgr. Diana Stores, 1967-68; founder, treas., controller Handy Dan Stores, 1968-72; founder, v.p., treas. Handy City Stores, 1972-76; sr. v.p., treas. Handy City div. W.R. Grace & Co., Atlanta, 1976-79; founder, pres. Hal's Hardware and Lumber Stores, 1982-84; retail and restaurant cons., 1979—. Treas., bd. dirs. YWCA Watsonville,1981-84, 85-87; mem. Santa Cruz County Grand Jury, 1984-85. Recipient 1st Tribute to Women in Internat. Industry, 1978; named Woman of the Yr., 1986. Mem. Ducks Unltd. (treas. Watsonville chpt. 1981-89). Republican. Home and Office: 302 Wheelock Rd Watsonville CA 95076-9714

KODISH, ARLINE BETTY, principal; b. Alliance, Ohio, Sept. 20, 1934; d. Edward J. and Frances Harris; m. Phillip Kodish, June 13, 1954; children: Douglas, Lori D. M in Ednl. Adminstrn., U. Akron, 1979. Cert. prin., tchr., Ohio. Owner Shatto Acad., Akron, 1973—. Mem. NAESP. Office: Shatto Acad 707 Schocalog Rd Akron OH 44320-1035

KOEBEL, SISTER CELESTIA, health care system executive; b. Chillicothe, Ohio, Jan. 12, 1928. BS, Coll. of Mount St. Joseph, 1958; MHA, St. Louis U., 1964; D, U. Albuquerque, 1976. Asst. dir. nursing svcs. Good Samaritan Hosp. & Health Ctr., Dayton, Ohio, 1961-62; adminstrv. resident Providence Med. Ctr., Seattle, 1963-64; pres. St. Joseph Healthcare Corp., Albuquerque, 1964-85, Sisters of Charity Health Care Systems, Cin., 1985—. Mem. Am. Hosp. Assn. (adv. coun., 1987-88), N.Mex. Hosp. Assn. (treas. 1968-69, v.p. 1970, pres. 1972). Office: Sisters Charity Health Care System Inc 345 Neeb Rd Cincinnati OH 45233-5102

KOEHL, CAMILLE JOAN, accountant; b. Chgo., Nov. 9, 1943; d. Alfonse James and Genevieve V. (Riche) Daurio; children: David A., Laura L., Robert M., Karen M. BS in Acctg., De Paul U., 1976; postgrad., Roosevelt U., 1987—. CPA, Ill.; cert. fin. planner. Treas. Meritex Corp., Carpentersville, Ill., 1966-68; controller Di Com Corp., Glenview, Ill., 1968-73; v.p., treas. Ridge Road Co., Northbrook, Ill., 1982-87, Decker Gardens, Inc., Northbrook, 1979-87, S&L Engring. Co., Northbrook, 1973-87; ptnr. HJS Constrn. Co., Barrington Hills, Ill., 1979—; pres. Lé Tan Ltd., Palatine, Ill., 1984—, IMC Ltd., Barrington Hills, 1985—; owner Camille J. Koehl & Assoc., Barrington Hills, 1978—; pres. Koehl Constrn. and Devel. Corp., Barrington Hills, 1990—, Pressing Matters Ltd., East Dundee, Ill., 1990—. Mem. Internat. Bd. Cert. Fin. Planners, Ill. CPAs. Home and Office: 7 Bow Ln Barrington IL 60010

KOEHLER, IRMGARD KILB, dermatologist, educator; b. Freiburg, Germany, July 2, 1940; came to U.S., 1967; d. Johannes Ernst and Anna Magdalena (Grob) Kilb; divorced; children: Stephan Arpad, Dinah Anna. Attended, U. Munich, 1959-65; MD, Ind. U., 1969; postgrad., U. Chgo., 1975-78. Diplomate Am. Bd. Dermatology. Intern U. Munich, 1965-67, U. Chgo., 1971-73; pvt. practice Chgo., 1978; instr. Rush Med. Coll., Chgo., 1979-81; clin. assoc. prof. Chgo. Coll. Osteopathic Medicine, 1983-85; clin. asst. prof. U. Ill., Chgo., 1990—. Mem. AMA, Am. Acad. Dermatology, Chgo. Dermatol. Soc., Ill. Dermatol. Soc. Office: 150 N Wacker St Ste 2300 Chicago IL 60606

KOEHLER, SHARON KAY, hospice nurse; b. Marion, Ohio, Apr. 3, 1947; d. Richard Allen and Harriet Helen (Osmun) Sherman; m. Frederick J. Koehler, Sr., May 5, 1973; children: Kenneth Richard, Frederick John Jr. Grad., Lima Meml. Hosp. Sch. Nursing, 1968. RN, Fla., S.C. Charge nurse pediatrics Munroe Meml. Hosp., Ocala, Fla., 1969-71; office nurse Dr. James Casey, pediatrician, Ocala, 1971-73; phlebotomist Cen. Fla. Blood Bank, Orlando, 1973-74; pub. health nurse Richland/Lexington County Health Dept., Columbia, S.C., 1974-79; office nurse Dr. Bruce Marshall, surgeon, Clinton, S.C., 1981-83; sch. nurse Sebring (Fla.) Christian Sch., 1984-87; staff nurse Avon Park (Fla.) Cluster, 1987-88, Highlands County Home Health Agy., Sebring, Fla., 1988-90, Good Shepherd Hospice of Mid Fla., Sebring, 1990—; vol. speaker's bur. Good Shepherd Hospice, Sebring, 1987-90; organizer Hospice Svcs. Highlands County, Sebring, 1987-90. Bd. trustees Good Shepherd Hospice, Winter Haven, Fla., 1988-90; mem. Highlands County Sch. Health Adv. Com., 1984-87; sch. vol. Sun n Lake Elem. Sch., 1986-91, sch. adv. com., 1987—, Sebring Mid. Sch., Sebring H.S.; mem. Sebring H.S. Band Parents, 1993—, Soccer Boosters, 1994—, Improvement Team, 1994—; Sunday sch. tchr. Covenant Presbyn. Ch., 1983-92, Grace Bible Ch., 1995, mem. adult choir, 1983-92, mem. Christian edn. com., 1985-91, Christian edn. dir., 1984-86; v.p. Women in Ch., 1984-86; organizer Fall Festival as alternative to Trick. Mem. Hospice Nurses Assn. Presbyterian. Home: 3709 Dauphine St Sebring FL 33872 Office: Good Shepherd Hospice Mid Fla Inc PO Box 1884 Sebring FL 33871

KOEHN, PATRICIA A., financial planner; b. Menominee, Mich., Nov. 11, 1950; d. Gerald O. and Marion J. Blohm; m. Dean B. Koehn, June 24, 1972; children: Matthew, Christopher. BA, Mich. State U., 1972. Cert. fin. planner. Mgr. rsch. and devel. NN Investors Life, Milw., 1973-75; mgr. group mktg. Conn. Mut., Milw., 1975-76; fin. planner Fin. Planning Inc., Milw., 1977-80; pres. Assoc. Fin. Planners Am., Inc., Milw., 1981-84; v.p. Security Capitol Adv., Inc., Atlanta, 1987-89; CEO Fin. Strategies, Inc., Atlanta, 1990—; program speaker various women's assns., 1978—. Co-author: Separate Purchase Life Insurance Marketing Manual, 1979; contbr. fin. articles to women's mags. Chmn. fin. com. St. Ives Homeowners Assn., Atlanta, 1992-94; educator Piedmont Hosp. Women's Day, Atlanta, 1991; bd. dirs. Atlanta Women's Network, 1993—, chair Gala, 1994; chair Habitat for Humanity, 1993; mem. women's guild St. Benedict's Ch. Mem. Nat. Assn. Life Underwriters, Atlanta Assn. Life Underwriters, Women Bus. Owners, Internat. Assn. Fin. Planners, The Women's CEO Support Group (founder), St. Ives Country Club (fin. com. 1992—). Home: 3027 Shinnecock Hills Dr Duluth GA 30136-2045 Office: 570 Colonial Park Dr Roswell GA 30075

KOELLING, CATHERINE WILLIAMS, restaurant owner; b. Grosse Pointe, Mich., Nov. 5, 1960; d. James Park and Catherine Ann (Candler) Williams; m. David Cameron Koelling, Sept. 24, 1983; children: Jessen, Marjorie. BA in Mktg., Mich. State U., 1982. With sales dept. Proctor & Gamble, Milw., 1982-83; with mktg. dept. Commander's Palace Restaurant, New Orleans, 1983-85; with sales in wine Judge & Dolph, Chgo., 1985-86; owner The Greenery, Barrington, Ill., 1986—. Co-chairperson Chicago Fund for Aging and Disability, 1992-95. Republican. Episcopalian. Office: The Greenery 117 North Ave Barrington IL 60010

KOENIG, BONNIE, non-profit organization administrator; d. Bruce D. and Florence (Englander); m. Gerald N. Rosenberg; children: Rachel Rosenberg, Joshua Koenig. BA, Dickinson Coll., 1979; MA, Yale U., 1983. Program assoc. U.S. Dept. Commerce/ITA, Washington, 1983-85; exec. dir. Coun. Great Lakes Govs., Chgo., 1986-90, Zonta Internat., Chgo., 1990—. Mem. Com. Fgn. Affairs Chgo. Coun. Fgn. Rels., 1986—. Mem. Am. Soc. Assn. Execs. (internat. sect.). Office: Zonta International 557 W Randolph St Chicago IL 60661-2206

KOENIG, ELIZABETH BARBARA, sculptor; b. N.Y.C., Apr. 20, 1937; d. Hayward and Selma E. (Rosen) Ulman; m. Carl Stuart Koenig, Sept. 10, 1961; children: Katherine Lee, Kenneth Douglas. BA, Wellesley Coll., 1958; MD, Yale U., 1962; postgrad., Art Students League N.Y., 1963-64, Corcoran Sch. Art, 1964-67. Exhibited one-woman shows including St. John's Coll., Annapolis, Md., 1974, also solo retrospectives Lyman Allyn Mus., New London, Conn., 1978, Rotunda of Pan-Am. Health Orgn., Washington, 1978; group shows include Internat. Dedication Nat. Bur. Standards, Gaithersburg, Md., 1966, No. Va. Mus., Alexandria, 1975, Textile Mus., Washington, 1974-75, Meridian House Internat., Washington, 1980; commd. works include: Free Spirit marble carving Washington Hebrew Congregation, 1978, Monumental Torso bronze for grounds George Meany Ctr. for Labor Studies, 1982; represented in many pvt. collections, U.S. and Europe, 1965—. Recipient 1st prize sculpture Tri-State Regional Exhbn., Md., 1970, 2d and 3d prize sculpture, 1971. Mem. Artists Equity Assn. (v.p. Washington 1977-83), Art Students League N.Y. (life), Internat. Sculpture Ctr., New Arts Ctr. Avocations: reading, gardening. Home: 9014 Charred Oak Dr Bethesda MD 20817-1924

KOENIG, GINA LEE, microbiologist; b. Scranton, Pa., July 3, 1962; d. Leon Henry Koenig and Carmela Ann (Romolo) Koenigsberg; m. John Henry Carter III, Feb. 11, 1989 (div. 1995). BS, Pa. State U., 1984; MA with honors, San Francisco State U., 1993. Rsch. asst. Ctr. for Air Environ. Studies, State College, Pa., 1983-84; fisheries biologist Nat. Marine Fisheries Service, Seattle, 1984-85; rsch. asst. Monterey Mushrooms, Watsonville, Calif., 1985-87; microbiologist Genencor, Internat., South San Francisco, 1987-92; rsch. scientist, curator culture collection dept. Roche Molecular Systems, Alameda, Calif., 1992—, mem. instnl. biol. safety com., 1992—. Contbr. articles to profl. jours. Recipient 1st pl. award Calif. State U. Biology Student Rsch. Competition, 1992. Mem. Am. Soc. Microbiology (com. for culture collections 1994—), Soc. for Cryobiology, U.S. Fedn. Culture Collections (program com. 1992, convenor ann. meeting 1992, chmn. publicity com. 1992-94, exec. bd. dirs.-at-large 1993-96), World Fedn. Culture Collections, Pa. State U. Alumni Assn., Soc. for Indsl. Microbiol. Democrat. Mem. Christian Ch. Office: Roche Molecular Systems Inc 1145 Atlantic Ave Alameda CA 94501-1145

KOENIG, JUDITH ELLEN, broadcasting company executive; b. Morehead City, N.C., Apr. 3, 1954; d. Charlie Perry and Dorothy Ellen (Hardesty) Dyess; m. Dominic John Pardio Jr., Sept. 12, 1970 (div. 1974); children: Charles Perry, Regina Antonette; m. Danny Carl Koenig, May 23, 1975 (div. 1992). Office mgr. S.E. State Broadcasting Corp., Havelock, N.C., 1977-78, Musicradio of N.C., Inc., Havelock, N.C., 1978-80; credit/traffic mgr. Holiday Radio Inc., Salem, Oreg., 1980-81; prog./ops. mgr. Greater Willamette Vision Ltd., Salem, Oreg., 1981-85, Emerald City Broadcasting Inc., Salem, Oreg., 1985-87; prog. mgr. Silver King Broadcasting of Oreg., Inc., Salem, Oreg., 1987-88; prog. mgr. Blackstar Communications of Oreg., Inc., Salem, Oreg., 1988-89, gen. mgr., 1989—. Mem. Oreg. Assn. Broadcasters, Nat. Assn. Broadcasters, Nat. Assn. TV Programming Execs., Salem C. of C., Salem Conv. and Visitors Assn., West Salem Rotary. Office: KBSP TV22 4923 Indian School Rd NE Salem OR 97305-1128

KOENIG, MARIE HARRIET KING, public relations director, fund raising executive; b. New Orleans, Feb. 19, 1919; d. Harold Paul and Sadie Louise (Bole) King; m. Walter William Koenig, June 24, 1956; children: Margaret Marie, Susan Patricia. Major in Voice, La. State U., 1937-39; Pre-law, Loyola U., 1942-43; BS in History, U. LaVerne, 1986. Adminstrv. asst. to atty. gen. State of La., New Orleans, 1940-44; contract writer MGM Studios, Culver City, Calif., 1944-46; asst. sec., treas. Found. for Ind., L.A., 1950-56, Found. for Social Rsch., L.A., 1950-56; dir. communications Incentive Rsch. Corp., L.A., 1969-78; rsch. supr., devel. dept. Calif. Inst. Technology, Pasadena, Calif., 1969; dir. funding devel. Rep. Party of L.A. County, South Pasadena, 1989-92. Author: Does the National Council of Churches Speak for You?, 1978; delivered lecture series on U.S. fgn. policy. Hon. citizen Colonial Williamsburg Found., 1987; active Nat. Soc. Historic Preservation, 1986, Gene Autry Western Heritage Mus., 1986, Friends of the Huntington Libr., 1986, Town Hall of L.A., 1986—, Pasadena City Women's Club, 1982-84, The Masquers Club; bd. mem. nominating com. Coun. Women's Clubs; charter mem. Nat. Mus. of Women in Arts; bd. mem. Pasadena Opera Guild; contbg. mem. L.A. World Affairs Coun., 1990, L.A. County Mus. Art, 1990; pres. Pasadena Rep. Women Federated. Recipient Cert. Recognition Calif. State Assembly, 1989, Recognition of Excellence, Achievement and Commitment U.S. Ho. Reps., 1989, Cert. Merit Rep. Presdl. Task Force, 1986, Cert. Appreciation U.S. Def. Com., 1984, Hon. Freedom Fighter award U.S. Def. Com., 1985, Cert. Appreciation Am. Conservative Union, 1983, Cert. Commendation Rep. Cen. Com. L.A. County, 1972, Cert. Appreciation Eisenhower-Nixon So. Calif. Com., 1952. Mem. Greater L.A. Press Club, Freedoms Found. at Valley Forge (charter L.A. chpt.). Republican. Home: 205 Madeline Dr Pasadena CA 91105-3311

KOENIGS, RITA SCALES, judge; b. Milw., May 5, 1952; d. John J. and Gertrude M. (Kendall) S. BA, Am. Internat. Coll., 1974; JD, Western New Eng. Coll. 1977. Bar: Mass. 1977, U.S. Dist. Ct. Mass. 1977. Assoc. Joseph & Manganaro, Springfield, Mass., 1977-79, Oberg, Linial & Scales, Springfield, 1979-80; staff trial atty. Mass. Defenders Com., Pittsfield, 1980—; atty.-in-charge Com. for Pub. Counsel Svcs., Pittsfield, 1987-90, Springfield, 1990—; judge Trial Ct. of Commonwealth of Mass. Dist. Ct. Dept., 1990—. Mem. planning bd. and capital outlay com. City of Pittsfield, 1988-90. Office: Pittsfield Dist Ct 24 Wendell Ave Pittsfield MA 01201-6306

KOENIGSBERG, JUDITH Z. NULMAN, clinical psychologist; b. Bklyn., Apr. 21, 1951; d. Macy and Sarah (Rosenberg) Nulman; m. David I. Koenigsberg, June 18, 1972; children: Benjamin, Rachel. Grad. summa cum laude, Yeshiva U. Tchrs. Inst., New York City, 1971; BA with honors, Bklyn. Coll., 1972; MA, Northeastern Ill. U., 1980; postgrad., U. Chgo., 1980-82; MEd, Loyola U., Chgo., 1985; PhD in Psychology, Northwestern U., 1990. Lic. and reg. clin. psychologist, Ill.; Nat. Register of Health Service Providers in Psychology. Clin. specialist Charter Barclay Hosp., Chgo., 1985-86; psychology extern Luth. Gen. Hosp., Park Ridge, Ill., 1987-88; psychol. testing extern Evanston (Ill.) Hosp., 1988-89, psychology intern, 1989-90; psychology postdoctoral resident Loyola U. Chgo., 1991-92; clin. psychologist U. Chgo., 1993-94; pres., psychol. cons. Ednl. Corp., 1995; Tutors Unlimited, Inc., pres. Contbr. articles to profl. jours. Recipient Outstanding Achievement award Nat. Culture Coun., 1972; scholarship award dept. modern langs. Bklyn. Coll., 1972, Kappa Delta Pi, 1972. Mem. APA, Ill. Psychol. Assn., Chgo. Soc. for Psychotherapy Rsch., Prescribing Psychologists' Register, Northwestern U. Alumni Assn. Sch. Edn. and Social Policy (dir. bd. 1993-94). Office: 708 Church St Suite 243 Evanston IL 60201 also: The Barclay 166 E Superior St Suite 201 Chicago IL 60611

KOENIGSMARK, JOYCE ELYN SLADEK, women's health nurse; b. Chgo., Sept. 29, 1938; d. John E. and Elsie (Volman) Sladek; m. Jerry Koenigsmark, Sept. 12, 1959; children: Jeffrey, Joy, Jocelyn, Joletta, Janine. Diploma in nursing, Presbyn.-St. Lukes Hosp., Chgo., 1959. RN, Ill. Staff nurse Parkway Terrace Nursing Home, Wheaton, Ill., 1977-78; staff nurse med./surg. Cen. DuPage Hosp., Winfield, Ill., 1978-80, staff and charge nurse well baby nursery, 1980-85; staff and charge nurse, advanced clinician well baby nursery, mother-baby care, spl. care nursery Edward Hosp., Naperville, Ill., 1985-94; prin. Joyce Koenigsmark, Document Examiner, 1978-84, Joyce Koenigsmark, Master Graphoanalyst, 1978-86; co-owner Hawthorne Pharmacy and Gift Shop, Wheaton, Ill., 1978—. Mem. AWHONN, Internat. GraphoAnalysis Soc. (life, sec. Ill. chpt. 1980, v.p. 1981, pres. 1982, cert. GraphoAnalyst 1978, Master Graphoanalyst 1983, Ill. GraphoAnalyst of Yr. 1983, Pres.'s citation of merit 1983). Home: 1510 Center Ave Wheaton IL 60187-6102

KOENKER, DIANE P., history educator; b. Chgo., July 29, 1947; m. Roger Koenker; 2 children. AB in History, Grinnell Coll., 1969; AM in Comparative Studies in History, U. Mich., 1971, PhD in History, 1976. From asst. prof. to assoc. prof. in history Temple U., Phila., 1976-83; asst. prof. history U. Ill., Urbana-Champaign, 1983-86, assoc. prof., 1986-88, prof. history, 1988—, dir. Russian and East European Ctr., 1990—; vis. lectr. history U. Ill., Urbana-Champaign, 1975; vis. fellow Australian Nat. U., 1989; Fulbright-Hays Faculty Rsch. Abroad, 1993; active Study Group on Russian Revolution, Study Group on Internat. Labor and Working-Class History; lectr. in field. Author: Moscow Workers and the 1917 Revolution, 1981, paperback edit., 1986, (with William G. Rosenberg) Strikes and Revolution in Russia 1917, 1989, editor: Tret'ya Vserossiiskaya Konferentsiya Professional'nykh Soyuzov 1917, 1982, (with William G. Rosenberg and Ronald Grigor Suny) Party, State and Society in the Russian Civil War: Explorations in Social History, 1989; editor, translator: (with S.A. Smith) Notes of a Red Guard, 1993; mem. editl. bd. Cambridge Soviet Paperbacks; mem. adv. bd. Soviet Studies in History, 1986-89; book reviewer to numerous jours.; contbr. articles to profl. jours. Rsch. fellow Temple U., 1977, 82, Sr. fellow Russian Inst.-Columbia U., 1977-78, Individual fellow NEH, 1983-84, Rsch. fellow NEH, 1984-85, MUCIA Exch. fellow Moscow State U., 1991; grantee Am. Coun. Learned Socs.-Social Sci. Rsch. Coun., 1977-78, Temple U., 1979-81, 82-83, William and Flora Hewlett Internat. Rsch. grantee, 1986, Nat. Coun. for Soviet and East European Rsch. grantee, 1989, IREX Travel grantee, 1993; recipient Fulbright-Hays Faculty Rsch. award for USSR, 1989, Arnold O. Beckman Rsch. Bd. award, 1990-91. Mem. Am. Hist. Assn. (mem.

George Louis Beer Prize com. 1993-95), Am. Assn. Advancement Slavic Studies, Midwest Workshop of Russian and Soviet Historians, Assn. Women in Slavic Studies. Office: U Ill Russian and East European Ctr 104 Internat Studies Bldg 910 S 5th St Champaign IL 61820 also: U Ill Dept History 309 Gregory Hall 810 S Wright St Urbana IL 61801

KOEPP, DONNA PAULINE PETERSEN, librarian; b. Clinton, Iowa, Oct. 8, 1941; d. Leo August and Pauline Sena (Outzen) Petersen; m. David Ward Koepp, June 5, 1960 (div. June 1984). BS in Edn., U. Colo., 1967; MA in Libr., U. Denver, 1974; postgrad., U. Colo., 1984-85. Subject specialist govt. publs., map dept. Denver Pub. Libr., 1967-85; head govt. documents, map libr. U. Kans., Lawrence, 1985—. Prodn. mgr. Meridian Jour., 1988-93. Mem. Map & Geography Round Table of Am. Libr. Assn. (chmn. 1986-87, Outstanding Contbn. to Map Librarianship 1991), Govt. Documents Round Table of Am. Libr. Assn., Western Assn. Map Librs. (sec. 1983-84). Office: Univ Kans Librs 6001 Malott Hall Lawrence KS 66045

KOEPPE, PATSY PODUSKA, internist, educator; b. Memphis, Nov. 18, 1932; d. Ben F. and Lily Mae (Reid) Poduska; m. Douglas F. Koeppe Sr., Sept. 8, 1967; 1 child, Douglas F. Jr. BA, Tex. Woman's U., 1954; MD, U. Tenn., 1957. Intern Roanoke (Va.) Meml. Hosp., 1960-61; resident in internal medicine VA Teaching Group Hosp., Memphis, 1961-62, Lahey Clinic, Boston, 1962-63; fellow in endocrinology and metabolism U. Tex. Med. Br., Galveston, 1963-65; pvt. practice Kingsville, Tex., 1972-73; dir. Women's Health Care Ctr., College Park, Md., 1974-77; instr. internal medicine and endocrinology U. Tex., Galveston, 1965-69; asst. prof. endocrinology Med. Br., U. Tex., Galveston, 1969-72, asst. prof. internal medicine, 1969-72, 78-87; assoc. prof. U. Tex., Galveston, 1987-93, prof., 1994—; mem. grad. faculty biomed. sci. Med. Br., U. Tex., Galveston, 1983—, acting dir. div. geriatrics, 1991-92. Mem. Am. Geriatric Soc., Tex. Med. Assn., Tex. Med. Found., So. Assn. Geriatric Medicine, Galveston County Med. Soc. Presbyterian. Home: 323 Brookdale Dr League City TX 77573-1668 Office: Univ Tex Med Br 30325 Jennie Sealy Hosp D60 Galveston TX 77555-0460

KOEPSELL, PAMELA ANN, neonatal nurse; b. Brookings, S.D., Nov. 9, 1959; d. Paul Loel and Delores Lillian (Johnson) K. Diploma, Sioux Valley Hosp., Sioux Falls, S.D., 1981; BSN, S.D. State U., 1989. Nursing case mgr. Midwestern Home Health Care Sioux Valley Hosp., Sioux Falls, 1988-91, charge nurse, 1982-87, neonatal flight nurse, 1982-93, primary nurse, 1986-93; clin. care coord., 1987—. Mem. Nat. Assn. Neonatal Nurses, S.D. Perinatal Assn., Sioux Valley Hosp. Nurses Alumni Assn. (2d v.p. 1985-86, 1st v.p. 1990-91), Sigma Theta Tau. Presbyterian. Home: 909 S Lowell Ave Sioux Falls SD 57103-2347 Office: Sioux Valley Hosp 1100 S Euclid Ave Sioux Falls SD 57117-5039

KOERBER, MARILYNN ELEANOR, gerontology educator, consultant, nurse; b. Covington, Ky., Feb. 1, 1942; d. Harold Clyde and Vivian Eleanor (Conrad) Hilge; m. James Paul Koerber, May 29, 1971. Diploma, Christ Hosp. Sch. Nursing, Cin., 1964; BSN, U. Ky., 1967; MPH, U. Mich., 1970. RN, Ohio, S.C.; cert. gerontologist. Staff nurse premature and newborn nursery Cin. Gen. Hosp., 1964-65; staff nurse, hosp. discharge planner Vis. Nurse Assn., Cin., 1967-69; asst. dir. Vis. Nurse Assn., Atlanta, 1976-78; instr. Coll. Nursing, U. Ky., Lexington, 1970-71; supr. Montgomery County Health Dept., Rockville, Md., 1971-74; asst. prof. Coll. Nursing, U. S.C., Columbia, 1979-86, instr., 1987-89; alzheimer's project coord. S.C. Commn. on Aging, Columbia, 1988-90; dir. edn. and tng. Luth. Homes S.C., White Rock, 1988-91; grad. asst. U. S.C. Sch. of Pub. Health, 1991-94; trainer for homemakers home health aides S.C. Divsn. on Aging, 1991—; coord. to train homemakers home aides nursing assts. State Pilot Program, DSS and Divsn. on Aging, 1993—; mem. utilization rev. bd. Palmetto Health Dist., Lexington, 1984—; test item writer, nurse aide cert. Psychol. Corp., San Antonio, 1989, 91, 92; bd. examiners Nursing Home Adminstrn. and Community Residential Call Facility Adminstr., chmn. of edn. com., Columbia, S.C., 1990-93; presenter gerontol. workshops and residential care facilities adminstrn. Contbg. editor: (handbook) Promoting Caregiver Groups, 1984; reviewer gerontology textbooks, 1983-91; contbr. tng. video and manuals on Alzheimers, 1988 (hon. mention Retirement Rsch. Found. 1989). Del. S.C. Gov. White House Conf. on Aging, Columbia, 1981; chmn. ann. mtg. S.C. Fedn. for Older Ams., Columbia, 1989-91. USPHS trainee, 1965-67, Adm. on Aging trainee, 1969-70. Mem. ANA (recert. gerontol. nurse 1988, 92, community health nurse 1989, 93), S.C. Nurses Assn., Am. Pub. Health Assn., So. Gerontol. Soc., Gerontol. Soc. Am., S.C. Gerontol. Soc. (treas. 1989-91, Rosamond R. Boyd award 1986, Pres. award Mid State Alzheimers Chpt., 1993), Coun. Gerontol. Nursing, Soc. for Pub. Health Edn., Am. Soc. on Aging, Alzheimers Assn. (bd. dirs. Columbia chpt. 1988-93, sec. 1992, chmn. nominating com. 1991-92; bd. dirs. S.C. combined health appeal 1991-93), Nat. Coun. on Aging, Nat. Gerontol. Nursing Assn. Democrat. Unitarian Universalist.

KOERING, MARILYN JEAN, anatomy educator, researcher; b. Brainerd, Minn., Jan. 7, 1938; d. Clement J. and Vi K. (Holtkamp) K. B.A., Coll. St. Scholastica, Duluth, 1960; M.S., U. Wis.-Madison, 1963, Ph.D., 1967, post-grad., 1968. Instr. dept. anatomy U. Wis., 1963-64; asst. prof. George Washington U., Washington, 1969-73, assoc. prof., 1973-79, prof. anatomy, 1979—, dir. neurosci. program, 1990-94; vis. assoc. div. biology Calif. Inst. Tech., 1976; affiliate scientist Wis. Primate Research Ctr., Madison, 1975-78; guest worker Pregnancy Research br. Nat. Inst. Child Health and Devel., 1977-84; vis. prof. Jones Inst. for Reproductive Medicine, Eastern Va. Med. Sch., 1985-92. Mem. editorial bd. Biology of Reproduction, 1974-78; contbr. articles to profl. jours. Recipient Alumni award Coll. of St. Scholastica, 1989; NIH fellow, 1967-68; NIH grantee, 1969—. Mem. AAAS, Am. Assn. Anatomists, Soc. Study Reproduction. Office: George Washington U Med Ctr Dept Anatomy 2300 I St NW Washington DC 20037-2337

KOERPER, MARION ALLEN, medical educator; b. Washington, 1943; m. Robert Blumberg, 1973; children: Marc, Andrew. BA, Stanford U., 1965; MD, U. Calif., San Francisco, 1970. Diplomate Am. Acad. Pediatrics, Sub-Specialty Bd. Pediatric Hematology-Oncology. Intern in pediats. San Francisco Gen. Hosp., 1970-71; resident in pediats. Kaiser Hosp., San Francisco, 1971-72; sr. resident in pediats. U. Calif., San Francisco, 1972-73, fellow in pediat. hematology/oncology, 1973-76; asst. clin. prof. U. Calif. Med. Sch., San Francisco, 1976-86, assoc. clin. prof., 1986—, dir. Hemophilia Treatment Ctr., 1976—. Founder, med. dir. Hemophilia Summer Camp, 1978—. Fellow Am. Acad. Pediatrics; mem. Nat. Hemophilia Found. (med. v.p. 1994—, med. and sci. adv. com. 1987—), Am. Soc. Hematology, Northern Calif. Hemophilia Found. (med. advisor, med. dir. 1977—), World Fedn. Hemophilia. Office: U Calif Dept Pediatrics Box 0106 San Francisco CA 94143-0106

KOESTNER, LAURIE A., nurse; b. Appleton, Wis., Nov. 6, 1958; d. Kenneth H. and Geraldine A. (Dunn) Kiser; m. Bruce R. Koestner, Sept. 28, 1985; children: Alison Jo, Marty, Evan. EMT, Fox Valley Tech. Coll., 1976, ADN, 1984. CCRN, CEN; cert. BLS, ACLS, PALS, neonatal resuscitation. Emergency med. technician St. Elizabeth Hosp., Appleton, 1976-90, LPN emergency dept., 1976-84, RN emergency dept., 1984-89; RN, staff charge emergency dept. St. Vincent Hosp., Green Bay, Wis., 1989-91; RN, supr. emergency dept. New London (Wis.) Family Med. Ctr., 1991—. Treas. Fox Valley EMT Assn., 1978. Mem. AACN, Emergency Nurses Assn., Am. Heart Assn. Lutheran. Home: 1424 N Graceland Ave Appleton WI 54911-3883

KOETTER, LEILA LYNETTE, administrator; b. McCook, Nebr., June 12, 1963; d. Larry Wayne and Leanna Lois (Leibrandt) H.; m. Darin Koetter, May 29, 1993; children: Michaela Nichole, Logan Walter. BS in Elem. Edn., U. Nebr., 1985, BS in Early Childhood, 1985; postgrad. in early childhood, U. Nebr. Lincoln at Kearney, 1987—. Asst. volleyball coach McCook (Nebr.) Community Coll., 1985-88; dir. nature camp YMCA, McCook, 1985-89; dir. nature camp child devel. ctr. McCook Community Coll., 1985-94, master tchr. child devel. ctr., 1985-90, faculty, instr., 1985—, adminstr. child devel. ctr., 1985—; adv. bd. head child devel. ctr. McCook Community Coll., 1985—; advisor, instr. Coun. for Early Childhood Profl. Recognition, Washington, 1990—. Coord. Week of Young Child, McCook; youth coach YMCA, McCook, 1987—. Mem. ASCD, Nat. Assn. Edn. Young Children, Nat. Coalition for Campus Childcare, Nebr. Assn. Edn. Young Children, Nebr. Edn. Assn. Home: 306 W D St Mc Cook NE 69001-3639 Office: McCook Community Coll 1205 E 3rd St Mc Cook NE 69001-2631

KOFFEL, BETTY LOU, anesthesiologist, educator; b. Sellersville, Pa., Oct. 23, 1952; d. Jay Roland and Vera Louise (Heath) K.; m. Walter Mokriski, Aug. 17, 1974 (div. Dec. 1993); children: Janet Keny, Claudia Christina. BA, Keuka Coll., 1974; MD, Med. Coll. Pa., 1978. Intern in internal medicine Abington (Pa.) Meml. Hosp., 1978-79; sr. asst. surgeon USPHS, Balt., 1979-83; resident in anesthesiology U. Md. Med. System, Balt., 1983-85, fellow in anesthesiology, 1985-86; instr. U. Md. Sch. of Medicine, Balt., 1986-88, asst. prof., 1988-94; assoc. prof., 1994—. Contbr. articles to profl. jours. Grantee ICI Pharms., 1989, Am. Soc. Regional Anesthesia, 1991. Mem. Am. Soc. Anesthesiologists, Md. Soc. Anesthesiologists (chair Balt. Anesthesia Study Com.), Soc. Obstetric Anesthesia and Perinatology. Office: U Md 22 S Greene St Baltimore MD 21201

KOH, CHRISTA M., technical translator, realtor, physical therapist; b. Berlin, Germany, Apr. 18, 1941; came to U.S., 1965; d. Hans Wolfgang and Maria Theresia Heinrich; m. Kwan S. Koh, July 1, 1972; children: Kimberly Kristen, Alexis Korene, Karsten Kwan. Cert., Phys. Therapy Sch., Berlin, 1961; lic. in phys. therapy, Chgo., 1969. Lic. realtor, Fla.; lic. phys. therapist, Ill., Germany. Intern in phys. therapy Evang. Hosp., Saarbricken, Germany, 1962-63; staff phys. therapist Walton Hosp., Liverpool, Eng., 1963-64, St. Joseph Hosp., Guelph, Ont., Can., 1964-65, Schwab Rehab. Hosp., Chgo., 1965-68, Kostner Manor Nursing Home, Chgo., 1968-69; dir. phys. therapy St. Elizabeth's Hosp., Chgo., 1969-81, Bethesda Hosp., Chgo., 1981-85; realtor Century 21, Country Hills, Pitts., 1986-88; systems analyst Columbia Healthcare Corp., Ft. Myers, Fla., 1991-92; realtor Coldwell Banker McFadden & Sprowls, 1993-95, Guaranteed Real Estate Svcs., Inc., 1995—; technical translator Fischer Internat. Systems Corp., Naples, Fla., 1994—. Symphony usher, vol. S.W. Fla. Symphony Soc., 1993—; mem. Ft. Myers Women's Network, 1993—, Chicagoland Phys. Therapy Dirs. Forum, 1975-85; vol. usher Barbara M. Mann Hall, 1994—. Mem. Am. Phys. Therapy Assn., Am. Translators Assn., Nat. Assn. Realtors, Ft. Myers Assn. Realtors.

KOHL, JEANNE ELIZABETH, state senator, sociologist, educator; b. Madison, Wis., Oct. 19, 1942; d. Lloyd Jr. and Elizabeth Anne (Sinness) K.; m. Kenneth D. Jenkins, Apr. 15, 1973; children: Randall Hill, Brennan Hill, Terra Jenkins, Kyle Jenkins, Devon Jenkins; m. Alexander Sumner Welles, Nov. 10, 1985. BA, Calif. State U., Northridge, 1965, MA, 1970; MA, UCLA, 1973, PhD, 1974. Tchr. L.A. Sch. Dist., 1965-74; lectr. Calif. State U., Long Beach, 1973-78; vis. asst. prof. U. Calif., Irvine, 1974-77; So. Calif. mgr. Project Equity/U.S. Dept. Edn., 1978-84; asst. dean, coord. women's programs U. Calif., Irvine, 1979-82; lectr. Calif. State U., Fullerton, 1982-85, U. Wash., Seattle, 1985—; asst. prof. Pacific Luth. U., Tacoma, Wash., 1986-88; state legislator from 36th dist. Wash. Ho. of Reps., Olympia, 1992-94, majority whip, 1993-94; mem. Wash. Senate, Olympia, 1994—. Author: Explorations in Social Research, 1993, Student Study Guide-Marriage and the Family, 1993; contbr. articles to profl. jours. Bd. dirs. Com. for Children, Seattle, 1986-91, Queen Anne Cmty. Coun., Seattle, 1988-93, Stop Youth Violence, Wash., 1993—, Queen Anne Helpline, Seattle, 1992-94. Grantee U.S. Dept. Edn., 1988-89, 90-91. Home: 301 W Kinnear Pl Seattle WA 98119-3732 Office: Wash State Senate PO Box 40436 Bldg Olympia WA 98504-0436

KOHLHORST, GAIL LEWIS, librarian; b. Phila., Dec. 5, 1946; d. Richard Elliott and Lucille (Lampkin) Lewis; m. Allyn Leon Kohlhorst, Feb. 14, 1974; 1 dau., Jennifer Marion. B.A. in Govt, Otterbein Coll., Westerville, Ohio, 1969; M.S. in L.S, Cath. U. Am., 1977. Info. classifier U.S. Ho. of Reps. Commn. on Internal Security, Washington, 1969-70; adminstrv. asst. Office of Gen. Counsel, GSA, Washington, 1971-76; chief tech. services sect. GSA Libr., Washington, 1976-79; chief GSA libr., 1979-88; acting chief, div. info. and libr. svcs. U.S. Dept. Interior, Washington, 1988-89; chief libr. svcs. br. GSA, Washington, 1989—. Author: Art and Architecture: An Annotated Bibliography, 1986, Total Quality Management: An Annotated Bibliography, 1990, 91, 93, Federal Librarians Round Table, ALA, Yearbook, 1989, Federal Librarian, 1991-94; contbr. Calendar Commn. on the Bicentennial for the U.S. Constn. Outreach com. Dulin United Methodist Ch., 1994-95. Recipient Outstanding Performance awards, 1973, 75, 76, 79, 81-86, 88, 89, 91-94, Sol. Achievement awards, 1982-84, Dept. of Interior Achievemet award, 1989, Commendable Svc. award, 1984, Nat. Capital Performance award, 1985, Meritorious Svc. award, 1992. Mem. ALA, Fed. Librs. Round Table (pres. 1990-91, membership chair 1994—), Fed. Libr. and Info. Ctr. (observer 1984—, exec. bd. 1992-94, chair, 1994—, mem. membership and governance com.), Fed. Pre-Conf. on the White House Conf. on Librs. and Scis. (del. 1990), Fedlink Adv. Coun. (chair exec. adv. coun. 1990), Pub. Employees Roundtable (bd. dirs. 1994—), D.C. Libr. Assn., United Meth. Women (mem. Dulin outreach com. 1994-95, pres. Joshua's Way 1995), Beta Phi Mu. Methodist. Home: 1721 Linwood Pl McLean VA 22101 Office: GSA Libr 18th & F St NW Washington DC 20405-0002

KOHLSTEDT, SALLY GREGORY, history educator; b. Ypsilanti, Mich., Jan. 30, 1943. BA, Valparaiso U., 1965; MA, Mich. State U., 1966; PhD, U. Ill., Urbana, 1972. Asst. prof. Simmons Coll., Boston, 1971-75; assoc. prof. to prof. Syracuse (N.Y.) U., 1975-89; prof. history of sci. U. Minn., Mpls., 1989—, assoc. dean Inst. Tech., 1989-95; vis. prof. history of sci. Cornell U., 1989; lect. univs. in U.S. and abroad; mem. nat. panels. Author: The Formation of the American Scientific Community: AAAS, 1848-1860, 1976; editor: (with Margaret Rossiter) Historical Writing on American Science, Osiris, 2d Series, 1, 1985, (with R.W. Home) International Science and National Scientific Identity: Australia between Britain and America, 1991, The Origins of Natural Science in the United States: The Essays of George Brown Goode, 1991; contbr. articles to profl. jours.; mem. editoral bd. Signs, 1980-88, 90-93, Sci., 1980-81, News and Views: History of Am. Sci. Newsletter, 1980-86, Sci., Tech. and Human Values, 1983-90, Syracuse Scholar, 1985-88, chair, 1988; assoc. editor Am. Nat. Biography, 2d edit., 1988; reviewer books, aricles, proposals for NSDF, NEH, U. Chgo. Press, numerous other pub. cos. NSF grantee, 1969, 78-79, 84, 93-95, Smithsonian Instn. predoctoral fellow, 1970-71, Danforth Assoc., 1975-82, Syracuse U. grantee, 1976, 82, Am. Philos. Soc. rsch. grantee, 1977, Haven fellow Am. Antiquarian Soc., 1982, Fulbright Sr. fellow U. Melbourne, Austaalia, 1983, Woodrow Wilson Ctr. fellow, 1986, Smithsonian Instn. Sr. fellow, 1987. Fellow AAAS (nominating com. 1980-83, sect. chair 1986), Am. Hist. Assn. (profl. com. 1974-76, rep. U.S. Nat. Archives Adv. Coun. 1974-76), Berkshire Conf. Women Historians (program com. 1974), Forum on the History Sci. in Am. (coord. com. 1980-86, chair 1985, 86), History of Sci. Soc. (sec. 1978-81, coun. 1982-84, 89-91, com. on publs. 1982-87, chair nominating com. 1985, women's com. 1972—, vis. lectr. 1988-89, chair edn. com. 1989, pres. 1992, 93), Internat. Congress for History of Sci. (U.S. del. 1977, 81, vice chair 1985), Orgn. Am. Historians (chair com. on status of women, 1983-85, endowment fund dr., auction subcom. 1990-91). Lutheran. Home: 4140 Edmund Blvd Minneapolis MN 55406-3646 Office: U Minn 123 Pillsbury Hall Minneapolis MN 55455

KOHN, JEAN GATEWOOD, medical facility administrator, physician; b. Chgo., July 8, 1926; d. Gatewood and Esther Lydia (Harper) Gatewood; m. Martin M. Kohn, Feb. 10, 1951; children: Helen, Joel, Michael, David. BS, U. Chgo., 1948, MD, 1950; MPH, U. Calif., Berkeley, 1973. Diplomate Am. Bd. Pediatrics. Physician Permanente Med. Group, San Leandro, Calif., 1953-60; pediatric cons. Calif. Children Svcs., 1961-72; lectr. maternal and child health U. Calif., 1973-91; med. advisor rehab. engring. ctr. Packard Children's Hosp. at Stanford, Calif., 1976—, med. dir. child prosthetic clinic, 1977—; assoc. neurologic diagnostic ctr. U. Calif. San Francisco, 1960-72; pediatric cons. Project HOPE, Nicaragua, 1966, Sri Lanka, 1968, Navajo Indian Reservation, Ganado, Ariz., 1970, Brazil, 1972, Peru, 1972; pediatric cons. sch. pub. health U. Hawaii, Okinawa, 1975. Contbr. chpts. to books and articles to profl. jours. Mem. adv. panel State of Calif. Dept. Spl. Edn., Calif. Children Svcs.; bd. dirs. Mental Health Assn., United Cerebral Palsy Assn., Head Start, San Mateo County, 1993—. Recipient Lyda M. Smiley award Calif. Sch. Nurses Orgn., 1987. Fellow Am. Acad. Pediatrics, Am. Acad. Cerebral Palsy and Devel. Medicine; mem. Assn. Child Prosthetic and Orthotic Clinics (bd. dirs. 1993—), Project HOPE Alumni Assn. (pres. 1988-92). Home: 1 Baldwin Ave # 616 San Mateo CA 94401-3850 Office: Packard Children's Hosp at Stanford Rehab Engring Ctr 725 Welch Rd Palo Alto CA 94304

KOHN, JULIEANNE, travel agent; b. Detroit, Apr. 15, 1946; d. Ralph Merwin and Jane Tacke (Meyers) K.; BA, Heidelberg Coll., Tiffin, Ohio, 1968; postgrad. Eastern Mich. U., 1969-70; diploma Inst. Cert. Travel Agts., 1979. Travel agt. Am. Express Co., Detroit, 1970-73, Thomas Cook Inc., Detroit, 1973-75; mgr. Island Traveller, Grosse Ile, Mich., 1975-76; pres., owner Flying Suitcase, Inc., Grosse Ile, 1976—; ptnr. Tri-Kohn Investments, Grosse Ile, Mich., 1983—; pres., owner FSI Tours, Ltd., Grosse Ile, Mich., 1990—; pres., ptnr. From Rags to Riches, Ltd., Grosse Ile, 1991; owner JK Enterprises, 1993—; ptnr. Gifts of the World, Gross Ile, Mich., 1993—. Mem. Am. Soc. Travel Agts., Inst. Cert. Travel Agts. (life). Episcopalian. Club: Grosse Ile Golf and Country, Grosse Ile Exchange Club. Home: 9781 Hawthorne Glen Dr Grosse Ile MI 48138-1687 Office: JK Enterprises 8117 Macomb St Grosse Ile MI 48138-1565

KOHN, KAREN JOSEPHINE, graphic and exhibition designer; b. Muskegon, Mich., Jan. 8, 1951; d. Herbert George and Catherine Elizabeth (Johnson) K.; m. Robert Joseph Duffy Jr. , July 10, 1982; children: Megan Kathleen, Sarah Evelyn. BFA, cum laude, U. Mich., 1973; MFA, Sch. Art Inst. Chgo., 1975. Free-lance designer, Chgo., 1976-77; designer Stevens Exhibits, Chgo., 1977-78; artist-in-residence Chgo. Council on Fine Arts, 1978-79; designer Chgo. Hist. Soc., 1979-81, dir. design, 81-84; prin. Karen Kohn & Assocs. Ltd., Chgo., 1985—. Work appeared in Mus. News, Kraft Gen. Foods hdqrs. Recipient Superior Achievement award for temporary exhbn. Congress of Ill. Hist. Socs. and Mus., 1985, Superior Achievement award for permanent exhbn., 1989, Cert. Excellence Strathmore Graphics Gallery, 1990, award of Merit Ill. Assn. Bus. Comm., 1993, Motorola Pinnacle award, 1994. Mem. Am. Assn. Mus. (Distinctive Merit awards 1982, 84, 85, Highest Honor awards 1982, 83, 84, 92), Nat. Assn. Mus. Exhibitors (Midwest regional rep. 1983-84), Am. Assn. Mus., Am. Ctr. Design, Am. Inst. Graphic Artists.

KOHN, MARY LOUISE BEATRICE, nurse; b. Yellow Springs, Ohio, Jan. 13, 1920; d. Theophilus John and Mary Katharine (Schmitkons) Gaehr; m. Howard D. Kohn, 1944; children: Marcia R., Marcia K. Epstein. AB, Coll. Wooster, 1940; M.Nursing, Case Western Res. U., 1943. Nurse, 1943-44, Atlantic City Hosp., 1944, Thomas M. England Gen. Hosp., U.S. Army, Atlantic City, 1945-46, Peter Bent Brigham Hosp., Boston, 1947, Univ. Hosps., Cleve., 1946-48; mem. faculty Frances Payne Bolton Sch. Nursing Case Western Res. U., 1948-52; vol. nurse Blood Svc., ARC, 1952-55; office nurse, Cleve., part time 1955-94; free-lance writer. Author: (with Atkinson) Berry and Kohn's Operating Room Technique, 5th edit., 1978, 6th edit., 1986, 7th edit., 1992; asst. editor Cleve Physician Acad. Medicine, 1966-71. Bd. dirs. Aux. Acad. Medicine Cleve., 1970-72, officer, 1976; mem. Cleve. Health Mus. Aux., Am. Cancer Soc. vol.; mem. women's com. Cleve. Orch., 1970; mem. women's coun. WVIZ-TV. Mem. Am., Ohio, Greater Cleve. nurses assns., alumni assns. Wooster Coll., Frances P. Bolton Sch. Nursing (pres. 1974-75), Assn. Operating Rm. Nurses, Antique Automobile Assn. Am., Western Res. Hist. Soc., Am. Heart Assn., Cleve. Playhouse Aux., Internat. Fund for Animal Welfare, Cleve. Animal Protective League, U.S. Humane Soc., Friends of Cleve. Ballet, Smithsonian Instn., Council World Affairs, Orange Community Arts Council, Cleve. Art Mus., Cleve. Children's Mus., Cleve. Racquet Club, Women's City Club. Home: 28099 Belcourt Rd Cleveland OH 44124-5615

KOHRING, DAGMAR LUZIA, fundraiser, consultant; b. Lage, Fed. Republic Germany, Mar. 8, 1951; came to U.S., 1966; d. Wilfried and Luzia W. (Knichel) K.; m. Arthur Gingrande Jr., Dec. 29, 1976 (div. June 1982). BA, Am. U., 1972, MA, 1974. Cert. fundraising exec. Asst. dir. devel. Harvard Art Mus., Cambridge, 1981-83; campaign officer Harvard U., Cambridge, 1983-85; sr. cons., campaign dir. C.H. Benz Assocs., Westfield, N.J., 1985-88; v.p., sen. cons. Brakeley, John Price Jones, Inc., Stamford, Conn., 1988-93; pres., CEO Internat. Fundraising & Mgmt. Cons., Inc., Boston/Bonn, 1993—. Nat. Endowment for the Arts fellow, 1983. Mem. Nat. Soc. Fundraising Execs., Women in Devel., Rotary, Harvard Club. Home and Office: 36 Hancock St Boston MA 02114 also: Eltviller Strasse 14, 53175 Bonn Germany

KOHRS, DIANA JOYCE, genealogist; b. St. Charles, Mo., Oct. 18, 1929; d. George Albert Button and Fern Viva (Lockwood) DeSchamps; m. Rodney Pemberton, Feb. 4, 1949 (div. 1954); 1 child, Randall Grant; m. Lloyd F. Kohrs, Mar. 14, 1960 (dec. June 1988); 1 child, Charmaine L. Kohrs Seavy. BA, U. Calif., Sacramento, 1952. Author: Braget of America and Norway, 1989, Standeford of America, 1992. Mem. Md. Genealogy Soc., Mo. Genealogy Soc., Old Fort Genealogy Soc.-Kans. Democrat. Home: 3 Pretoria Ct Saint Charles MO 63303-3124

KOKKIN, KIRSTEN KNOWLTON, sculptor; b. Oslo, Norway, Aug. 23, 1951; arrived in U.S., 1987; d. Sverre and Tutte (Pinsle) K.; m. James Arthur Knowlton, June 6, 1987. Student, State Sch. of Arts and Crafts, Oslo, 1969-73, State Acad. of Art, 1973-77, Royal Acad. of Art, Stockholm, 1977-79. Portrait sculptor Mr. P.E.A. Wright, Australia, 1979-80; rsch. assistance profl. state Acad. of Art, Oslo, 1981-82; editor western region Nat. Sculpture Rev. Mag., N.Y.C., 1989-93; tchr. Art Students League, Denver, 1993—; field faculty tchr. Norwich Sch. of Design, Montpelier, Vt., 1993; juror Loveland High Plaines Art Coun., Loveland, 1993—. One woman show includes Saks Gallery, Denver, Kunstnerforbundet, Oslo, Sante Fe, N.Mex., 1993; exhibited in group shows at Autumn Salon of the State, Norway, 1992, Nat. Sculpture Soc., N.Y.C., 1992, Sculpture in the Park, Loveland, Colo., 1990-92, Jubilee Ball Show at Lincoln Ctr., Fort Collins, Colo., 1991, Nat. Acad. of Design, 165th Ann. Exhibition, N.Y.C., 1990, 163rd Ann. Exhibition, 1988, Nat. Sculpture Soc., N.Y.C., 1988; prin. works include Monumental Fountain Bamble Hall, Norway, 1992, The Lincoln Ctr., Colo., 1992, Life Size Fountain, The Beverly Hills Peninsula Hotel, Calif., 1991, Life Size Sculputre Fountain Cherry Creek Pedestrian Mall, Colo., 1990, Mem'l Monument for Fisherman Lost at Sea, Norway, 1989, Life Size Sculpture Oslo Shopping Mall, Norway, 1989, Baptistery Sculpture for Church in Lofoten, Norway, 1989, The State Acad. Athletic Sports, Oslo, Norway, 1987. Recipient The Franklin Mint award for Excellence in the Arts, Loveland, 1991, First prize for monumnetal fountain , Ulstein, Norway, 1990, First prize for meml. to Fishermen losta at sea in Aalesund, Norway. Fellow Nat. Sculpture Soc., Norwegian Sculpture Soc. Home: 179 S Lafayette St Denver CO 80209-2521 Office: 179 S Lafayette St Denver CO 80209-2521

KOKOLA, MELODY BACSKO, library director; b. New Brunswick, N.J., Dec. 1, 1947; d. Albert B. and Helen Geczy Bacsko; divorced; children: John Christopher, Carolee Alison. BA, Rutgers U., 1970; MS, Grad. Sch. Library Service, Columbia U., 1977. Librarian Bayonne (N.J.) Pub. Library, 1977-86; library dir. Metuchen (N.J.) Pub. Library, 1986—; treas. Libraries of Middlesex County, N.J., 1987-91, N.J. Library Compact Disc Cir., Woodbridge, 1987—; v.p. Libraries of Middlesex Automation Consortium, 1988-90. Sec. Meml. Park Commn., Metuchen, 1987—, Cable TV Adv. Commn., Metuchen; lt. gov. N.J. Dist. Kiwanis Internat., 1994-95. Mem. ALA, N.J. Libr. Assn., Pub. Libr. Assn., Columbia U. Libr. Sch. Alumni Assn. (alumni bd. dirs. 1988-90), Kiwanis (publicist Metuchen chpt. 1988-90, 1st v.p. 1988-91, pres. 1991-93). Mem. Reformed Ch. Am. Home: 43C Middlesex Ave Metuchen NJ 08840-1117 Office: Metuchen Pub Libr 480 Middlesex Ave Metuchen NJ 08840-1412

KOLAR, MARY JANE, association executive; b. Benton, Ill., Aug. 9, 1941; d. Thomas Haskell and Mary Jane (Sanders) Burnett; m. Otto Michael Kolar, Aug. 13, 1966; children: Robin Lynn, Deon Michael. B.A. with high honors, So. Ill. U., 1963, M.A. with highest honors, 1964. Tchr. pub. schs. Benton and Zeigler, Ill., 1960-63; grad. asst. and grad. fellow So. Ill. U., Carbondale, 1963-64; instr. Ridgewood High Sch., Norridge, Ill., 1964-67, Maine Twp. High Sch., Des Plaines, Ill., 1967-70; freelance writer Chgo., 1970-71; cons. Contractor Promotions, Chgo., 1970-71; ednl. coord. Am. Dietetic Assn., Chgo., 1971-72; dir. profl. devel. Am. Dental Hygienists Assn., Chgo., 1972-78; dir. Learning Ctr. div. Am. Coll. Cardiology, Bethesda, Md., 1978-80; dir. edn. Nat. Moving and Storage Assn., Alexandria, Va., 1980-82; exec. dir. Women in Communications, Inc., Austin, Tex., 1982-84, Altrusa Internat., Chgo., 1984-87, Assn. Govt. Accts., Alexandria, 1987-90, Bus./Profl. Advt. Assn., Alexandria, 1991-92; exec. dir. Am. Assn. Family and Consumer Scis., Alexandria, 1992—, dir. project taking charge

Pregnancy Prevention Program, dir. Project Taking Courage, Pregnancy Prevention Program; cons. spkr. various profl. assn., ednl. instns. and fed. ays.; dir. project taking change pregnancy prevention program. Contbr. articles to profl. jours., chpts. to books. Mem. adv. council Accrediting Commn. Assn. of Ind. Colls. and Schs., 1980-88; treas. Pub. Employees Roundtable, 1988-90, Hollin Hills Civic Assn., 1989-90. Fellow Am. Soc. Allied Health Professions (dir. 1978-79), Am. Soc. Assn. Execs. (mem. Key Profl. Assn. coun. 1994—, awards com. 1992-93, cert., univ. affairs commn. 1986-92, chair 1990-91, found. bd. 1987-91, chmn. edn. sect. 1982-83, bd. dirs. 1983-86, chair higher edn. task force 1990-91, chair fellows 1987, Educator of Yr. award 1978, Key award 1990, mentor Key Profl. Assn. Council 1994—), Greater Washington Soc. Assn. Execs. (edn. com. 1979-82, CEO com. 1990-92, mem. strategic planning coun. 1994—); mem. Future Home Makers Am. (bd. dirs. 1992—, strategic planning com. 1994—), Alexandria C. of C. (assn. coun. 1990—, steering com. 1993—), Women in Comm. (newsletter editor, legis. and career reentry chmn., chmn. ERA task force, dir. Washington profl. chpt. 1981-82, program com. Chgo. chpt. 1984-86), So. Ill. U. Alumni Assn. (bd. dirs. 1984-89, v.p. 1986-89, presdl. search com. 1986-87). Office: 1555 King St Alexandria VA 22314

KOLASA, KATHRYN MARIANNE, food and nutrition educator, consultant; b. Detroit, July 26, 1949; d. Marion J. and Blanche Ann (Gasiorowski) K.; m. Patrick Noud Kelly, Jan. 3, 1983. BS, Mich. State U., 1970; PhD, U. Tenn., 1974. Test kitchen home economist Kellogg Co., 1971; instr. dept. food sci. and food systems adminstrn. U. Tenn.-Knoxville, 1973-74; asst. prof. dept. food sci. and human nutrition Mich. State U., East Lansing, 1974-76, assoc. prof., 1976-82; prof., chmn. food, nutrition and instn. mgmt. Sch. Home Econs., East Carolina U., Greenville, N.C., 1982-86, prof., head nutrition edn. and svcs. sect. Dept. Family Medicine, Sch. Medicine, 1986—; mem. subcom. food and nutrition bd. NAS on Uses of the RDA, 1981-83; cons. food and nutrition; vice chmn. edn. subcom. Am. Heart Assn. Consumer Nutrition, 1992-93. Recipient grants in nutrition and food service and med. nutrition edn., 1974—; Kellogg nat. fellow, 1985-88. Mem. Soc. Nutrition Edn. (pres. 1984), Am. Instn. Nutrition, Inst. Food Technologists, Am. Dietetic Assn., Soc. Tchrs. Family Medicine. Roman Catholic. Author: (with Ann Bass and Lou Wakefield) Community Nutrition and Individual Food Behavior, 1978, (interactive video disc, with Ann Jobe) Cardiovascular Health: Focus on Nutrition, Fitness and Smoking Cessation.

KOLB, BERTHA MAE (BERTHA MAE RAGSDALE), travel agency administrator; b. Dumas, Ark., Nov. 3, 1925; d. Harold Dewey and Hallie Eugenia (Muskelley) Ragsdale; m. Charles Rudolph Kolb, Oct. 9, 1951 (dec. 1982); 1 child, Charles Harold. Student, La. State U., 1959-61. Sec. Le Tourneau Co., Vicksburg, U.S. Govt. Waterways Experiment Sta.; travel agt. Am. Internat. Travel, Inc., 1983-. Pres. Vicksburg Coun. of Garden Clubs, 1972; bd. dirs. Garden Clubs of Miss., 1977-89; active numerous Vicksburg civic svc. clubs, 1953-. Mem. Vicksburg Country Club (pres. ladies orgn. 1969-70), Town and Country Garden Club (pres. Vicksburg chpt. 1973-75). Episcopalian.

KOLB, DOROTHY GONG, elementary education educator; b. San Jose, Calif.; d. Jack and Lucille (Chinn) Gong; m. William Harris Kolb, Mar. 22, 1970. BA (with highest honors), San Jose State U., 1964; postgrad., U. Hawaii, Calif. State U., L.A.; MA in Ednl. Tech., Pepperdine U., 1992. Cert. life elem. educator, mentally retarded educator K-12, learning handicapped pre-sch., K-12, adult classes. Tchr. Cambrian Sch. Dist., San Jose, Calif., 1964-66, Cen. Oahu (Hawaii) Sch. Dist., Wahiawa, 1966-68, Montebello (Calif.) Unified Sch. Dist., 1968—. Named to Pi Lambda Theta, Kappa Delta Pi, Pi Tau Sigma, Tau Beta Pi; recipient Walter Bachrodt Meml. scholar.

KOLB, REBECCA JANE, customer service executive; b. Newark, Ohio, Sept. 9, 1959; d. Robert Edward and Marjorie Ruth (Evans) Pfeffer; m. James Charles Kolb, Nov. 15, 1986; 1 child, Kendell Meredith. BA, Miami U., Oxford, Ohio, 1981. Office mgr. Info. People, Newark, 1982-84, Hartford Computer Exch., Glastonbury, Conn., 1987, Chase Enterprises, Hartford, Conn., 1988; customer svc. coord. Wasserstrom Co., Columbus, Ohio, 1984-86; staff supr. Ohio Tuition Trust Authority, Columbus, 1990, customer rels. mgr., 1990-93, customer svc. mgr., 1994—. Vol. River Round-Up/Arbor Day, City of Newark, 1992-94, A Call to College, Newark, 1993-94, I Know I Can, Columbus, 1993-94; mem. rental property com. St. Paul's Evang. Luth. Ch., 1993-94, mem. fin. com., 1994. Mem. Soc. for Consumer Affairs Profls. (program chair 1993-94), Ohio Assn. Student Fin. Aid Adminstrs. (outreach com. 1993-94, needs analysis com. 1993-94), Licking County Patriots Club. Republican. Office: Ohio Tuition Trust Auth 62 E Broad St Fl 4 Columbus OH 43215-3515

KOLB, VERA M., chemistry educator; b. Belgrade, Yugoslavia, Feb. 5, 1948; came to U.S., 1973; d. Martin A. and Dobrila (Lopicic) K.; m. Cal Y. Meyers, 1976 (div. 1986). BS, Belgrade U., 1971, MS, 1973; PhD, So. Ill. U., 1976. Postdoctoral fellow So. Ill. U., Carbondale, 1977-78, mem. faculty, 1978-85; assoc. prof. chemistry U. Wis., Parkside, 1985-90, prof. chemistry, 1990—; vis. scientist The Salk Inst. for Biol. Studies, U. Calif.-San Diego, 1992-94. Editor: Teratogens, Chemicals Which Cause Birth Defects, 1988, 2d edit., 1993; contbr. articles to sci. pubs.; patentee in field. Violinist Racine (Wis.) Symphony Orch., Civic Orch. Milw. Fulbright grantee, 1973-76, grantee NIH, 1984-87, Am. Soc. Biochemistry and Molecular Biology, 1988; NASA fellow, 1992-94. Mem. Am. Chem. Soc. (task force on occupational safety and health 1980—). Office: Univ Wis Parkside Dept Chemistry PO Box 2000 Kenosha WI 53141-2000

KOLBE, JANE BOEGLER, state librarian; b. Olivet, S.D., Mar. 17, 1944; d. Stanley and Grace (Schoepke) Boegler; m. Robert E. Kolbe, June 24, 1967. BA in Math., Westmar Coll., 1966; MLS, U. Minn., 1968; postgrad. bus. adminstrn., Sioux Falls Coll., 1974-76; EdD in Adult and Higher Edn., U. S.D., Vermillion, 1986. Catalog librarian I.D. Weeks Library, U. S.D., Vermillion, 1967-68, circulation librarian, 1968-69; library dir., assoc. prof. Norman B. Mears Library, Sioux Falls (S.D.) Coll., 1969-86; state librarian State of S.D., Pierre, 1986—; trustee Sioux Falls Pub. Library, 1973-79, chmn. bd., 1978-79; mem. S.D. State Library Commn., 1973-80, pres. 1977-78; faculty mem. Sioux Falls Coll. Bd. Trustees, 1979-81, 84-86; bd. trustees N. Cen. Univ. Ctr., Sioux Falls, 1982-84; adv. bd. Bibliog. Ctr. for Research, Denver, 1977-79, trustee, 82-84. NIH fellow U. Minn., 1966-67. Mem. ALA, PLA, S.D. Libr Assn. (chair acad. sect. 1971-72, 84-85), Mountain Plains Libr. Assn. (v.p. 1979-80, pres. 1980-82, Disting. Svc. award 1981), Western Coun. State Librs. (sec. 1989-90, pres. 1991-92), Chief Officers of State Libr. Agys. (sec. 1992—), Bus. and Profl. Women's Club (Pierre treas. 1988-90, pres. 1990-91), Zonta (pres. Sioux Falls 1972-74). Democrat. Methodist. Office: SD State Libr 700 Governors Dr Pierre SD 57501-2294

KOLBESON, MARILYN HOPF, advertising executive, organization and management consultant, educator; b. Cin., June 9, 1930; d. Henry Dilg and Carolyn Josephine (Brown) Hopf; children: Michael Llen, Kenneth Ray, Patrick James, Pamela Sue Kolbeson Lang, James Allan. Student U. Cin., 1947, 48, 50. Sales and mktg. mgr. Cox Patrick United Van Lines, 1977-80; sales mktg. mgr. Creative Incentives, Houston, 1980-81; pres. Ad Sense, Inc., Houston, 1981-87, M.H. Kolbeson & Assocs., Houston, 1987, Seattle, 1987—, The Phoenix Books, Seattle, 1987-90; cons. N.L.P. Communications; lectr., cons. in field. Mem. adv. bd. Alief Ind. Sch. Dist., 1981-87, pres., 1983-84; bd. dirs. Santa Maria Hostel, 1983-86, v.p., 1983-84; founder, pres. Mind Force, Houston, 1978-87 and Seattle, 1987—; founder META Group, Seattle, 1991—. Mem. citizen's adv. bd. Arcola (Ill.) Sch. Bd., 1966-67; mem. Greater Houston Conv. and Visitors Coun., loaned exec., 1986-87; mem. adv. bd. Am. Inst. Achievement, 1986-87; vol. Seattle Pub. Schs., 1992—; charter mem. Rep. Task Force. Mem. Internat. Platform Assn., Houston Advt. Splty. Assn. (bd. dirs. 1984-87, treas. 1985, v.p. 1986-87), Inst. Noetic Scis. (charter), Galleria Area C. of C. (bd. dirs. 1986-87), Toastmasters (area gov. 1978), Grand Club (v.p. 1986), Lakewood Seward Park Community Club (bd. dirs. 1992—). Republican. Christian Scientist. Office: 5247 S Brandon St Seattle WA 98118-2522

KOLE, JANET STEPHANIE, lawyer, writer, photographer; b. Washington, Dec. 20, 1946; d. Martin J. and Ruth G. (Goldberg) K. AB, Bryn Mawr Coll., 1968; MA, NYU, 1970; JD, Temple U., 1980. Bar: Pa. 1980. Assoc. editor trade books Simon & Schuster, N.Y.C., 1968-70; publicity dir. Am. Arbitration Assn., N.Y.C., 1970-73; freelance photojournalist, N.Y.C., 1973-76; law clk. Morgan Lewis & Bockius, Phila., 1977-80; assoc. Schnader, Harrison, Segal & Lewis, Phila., 1980-85; ptnr. Cohen, Shapiro, Polisher, Shiekman & Cohen, Phila., 1985—. Author: Post Mortem, 1974; editor Environmental Litigation, 1991; contbr. numerous articles to gen. interest publs., profl. jours.; past mem. bd. editors New Am. Rev. Mem. Mayor's Task Force on Rape, N.Y.C., 1972-77; adv. Support Ctr. Child Advs., Phila., 1980—; mem. Phila. Vol. Lawyers for the Arts; steering com. Lawyers for Reproductive Rights. Fellow Acad. Advocacy; mem. ABA (coun. mem. sect. litigation, former dir. publs., former co-div. dir. substantive areas of litigation, former editor litigation news, former chmn. com. on monographs and unpublished papers, com. spl. pubs.), Assn. Trial Lawyers Am. Democrat. Office: Cohen Shapiro Polisher Shiekman & Cohen 12 S 12th St Fl 22 Philadelphia PA 19107-3836

KOLENIAK ROLD, BARBARA DONNA, nurse; b. N.Y.C., Feb. 20, 1950; d. William Zazula and Catherine Sheridan (Quigley) Koleniak; m. James Lee Rold, Dec. 29, 1974 (div. June 1991); children: Christopher, William, Cara. Nursing Diploma, St. Vincent's Sch. Nursing, Richmond, 1971; BA, Marymount Manhattan Coll., N.Y.C., 1973. RN; cert. HIV/AIDS testing and counseling. Staff nurse N.Y. Med. Coll., N.Y.C., 1971-72; pvt. duty nurse N.Y. Nurse Registry, N.Y.C., 1972-73; staff nurse U. Nebr. Med. Ctr., Omaha, 1973-74, Children's Hosp., Omaha, 1975, ENCOR Med. Support Unit, Omaha, 1987-89; nurse mgr. St. Clare's Home A.R.F., Neptune, N.J., 1990; clin. coord. pediat. HIV/AIDS program Jersey Shore Med. Ctr., Neptune, 1990—; pub. speaker on pediat. HIV/AIDS. Reviewer curriculum manual The Best Parent I Can Be, 1989. Recipient Starfish award Starfish Soc. N.J., 1992. Democrat. Roman Catholic. Office: Jersey Shore Med Ctr 1945 Rte 33 Neptune NJ 07754

KOLICH, CYNTHIA LOUISE, emergency nurse; b. Kansas City, Mo., July 4, 1949; d. Roy Arnold and Vivian Louise (Boettcher) Stroup; m. Michael James Kolich, Jan. 15, 1977; children: Sean Michael, Aaron Russell. Diploma in nursing, Trinity Luth. Hosp Sch Nursing, Kansas City, 1972; BS, Kans. State U., 1974; BSN, Avila Coll., 1983; MSN, U Mo., Kansas City, 1992. Staff nurse ICU, Sacred Heart Hosp., Eugene, Oreg., 1972-74; staff nurse cardiothoracic ICU, U. Kans. Med. Ctr., Kansas City, 1974-76; from staff nurse to asst. head nurse surg. ICU, St. Luke's Hosp., Kansas City, Mo., 1976-77; physician asst.to cardiothoracic surgeon Kansas City, Kans., 1977-78; charge nurse office practice Old Westport Ear, Nose and Throat Group, Kansas City, Mo., 1978-80; instr. edn. dept. Olathe (Kans.) Med. Ctr., 1980-81, staff nurse ICU, 1981-85, staff nurse emergency rm., 1985-91, mgr. patient care emergency room and gastrointestinal lab., 1991—. HHS Profl. Nurse Traineeship grantee U. Mo. Kansas City Sch. Nursing, 1991-92. Mem. Emergency Nurse's Assn., Sigma Theta Tau. Republican. Methodist. Home: 15840 W 144th St Olathe KS 66062

KOLITZ, SALLY LYNN, clinical and neuropsychologist; b. Jersey City, Mar. 31, 1943; d. Norman and Sylvia (Goldstein) Ostrow; m. Elbert W. Russell, Apr. 2, 1989; 1 child, Brent Kolitz. BA, Vanderbilt U., 1965; MEd, U. Fla., 1967; PhD in Clin. Psychology, U. Miami (Fla.), 1986. Lic. psychologist, Fla.; diplomate Am. Bd. Profl. Disability Cons. Tchr. Bronson (Fla.) High Sch., 1965-66; dir. counseling Chamberlayne Jr. Coll., Boston, 1967-68; indsl. psychologist Gillette Co., Boston, 1968-69; dir. family life edn. Family Svc., Miami, 1971-75; researcher, grantee Am. Heart Assn., Miami, 1978-80; pvt. practice psychology Miami, 1986—. Author: Psychology of the Cardiac Patient, 1980, 88. Mem. APA, Nat. Acad. Neuropsychologists, Internat. Neuropsychology Soc., Sigma Xi. Office: 6262 Sunset Dr Ph 228 Miami FL 33143-4843

KOLKER, SONDRA G., fund raising/special events executive; b. N.Y.C., Nov. 30, 1943; d. Morris Henry and Alice (Cohen) Budow; m. Justin William Kolker, Aug. 23, 1963 (div.); children: Lawrence Paul, David Brett. Student, Hofstra U. Dir. N.Y.C. Office N.Y. State Dem. Com., 1977-79; v.p., exec. dir. Fund for Higher Edn., N.Y.C., 1980-88; pres. Sondra Kolker & Assocs., Halesite, N.Y., 1988—; spl. cons. Internat. Devel. Svcs. subs NMP of Am., Inc., 1989-90; dist. rep. Congressman Robert J. Mrazek, 1990-93. Speechwriter for numerous speakers at corp. banquets, 1980-88. Bd. dirs. Huntington (N.Y.) Townwide Fund, 1978—; active Huntington Hosp. Aux., 1965—, Great Gatsby Soc. for Multiple Sclerosis, 1988-90, Marble Hills Civic Assn., Halesite, 1958—; committeewoman Huntington Dem. Com., 1974-82; fundraiser/dist. rep. Congressman Robert J. Mrazek, L.I., N.Y., 1991-93. Recipient Meritorious Svc. award Huntington Twp. C. of C., 1974, 76, 77, 78, Bicentennial Citation Town of Huntington, 1977. Mem. NAFE, MOMA, Nat. Mus. Women in the Arts, L.I. Crafts Guild, Huntington Twp. C. of C., Women's Econ. Round Table, Huntington Bus. and Profl. Women. Jewish. Home and Office: Sondra Kolker & Assocs 4 Everett Pl Halesite NY 11743-2211

KOLKEY, GILDA P., artist; b. Chgo.; d. David and Evelyn (Jacobson) Cowan; widowed; children: Daniel, Sandor, Eric. BA in Painting, U. Ill., Champaign; postgrad., Art Inst. Chgo., 1978-79. Art tchr. Highland Park (Ill.) Recreational Ctr., 1976. Exhibited in group shows at Art Inst., Chgo., 1949, 50, 56; contbr. paintings to Rainbow House for Battered Women, Traveler's Aid, Art Resources in Tchg. Recipient award of Excellence, North Shore Art League, 1965-66, painting awards New Horizons in Painting, 1959, Scan Members Show, 1992, hon. mention Women's Club of Evanston, 1972. Mem. Arts Club Chgo., Mid.-Am. Club, Chgo. Soc. Artists. Republican. Home: 1100 N Lake Shore Dr # 21B Chicago IL 60611

KOLLER, KAREN KATHRYN, social services administrator; b. Lorain, Ohio, June 23, 1949; d. Harry Charles and Lavonne Rita (Ball) K. BA, Adrian (Mich.) Coll., 1971; MBA, Baldwin Wallace Coll., Berea, Ohio, 1977. Mgr. Harry C. Koller, Acct., Lorain, Ohio, 1974-79; sec.-treas. Credit Bur. of Lorain, Inc., 1971-79, Haytotter, Inc., 1979-80; ops. mgr. Lorain br. Credit Bur. Toledo, 1979-83; owner Karen Koller Bookkeeping, Lorain, 1979—; ptnr. Crackabee Shelties, Lorain, 1980—, K & K Co., Lorain, 1979-88; comptroller Neighborhood House Assn. of Lorain County, Inc., 1985—. Treas. Erie Shores council Girl Scouts U.S., Lorain, 1987-93, bd. dirs., 1982-93; chmn. City of Lorain Adv. Bd. for Disabled, 1988; campaign chmn. Mem. Lorain Bus. and Profl. Women (treas. 1979-80), AAUW, Quota, Delta Mu Delta. Home: 1132 W 7th St Lorain OH 44052-1461 Office: Neighborhood House Assn 1536 E 30th St Lorain OH 44055-1695

KOLLER, MARITA ANN, accountant; b. Chgo., June 6, 1955; d. Frank J. and Jean J. Koller. BA, Western Ill. U., 1976; MPA, Am. U., 1980; AAS, Oakton Coll., 1989. Acct. UOP, Des Plaines, Ill., 1986—; computer specialist Baxter Labs., Deerfield, Ill., 1985-86; actuarial asst. Towers, Perrin, Foster and Crosby, Chgo., 1981-85; instr. computer tech. Oakton Coll., Des Plaines, 1985—. U. Ill. scholar. Mem. Am. Mgmt. Assn., Am. Soc. Profl. and Women Execs., Nat. Soc. Pub. Accts. Home: 934 E Forest Ave Des Plaines IL 60018-1476

KOLLMANN, HILDA HANNA, banker; b. Tinley Park, Ill., Dec. 12, 1913; d. Ernest A. and Rosalie (Blume) K. Ed., Bryant and Stratton Bus. Coll. Asst. cashier State Bank of Blue Island (became County Bank & Trust Co. 1962), Ill., 1945-53; cashier State Bank of Blue Island (became County Bank & Trust Co. 1962), 1953-60, asst. sec., 1953-54, sec., 1954-55, v.p., 1955-70, dir., 1956—, trust officer, 1959-66; v.p. Pullman Bank & Trust Co., Chgo., 1969-70, Standard Bank & Trust Co., Chgo., 1969-70, First Nat. Bank of Lockport, 1969-70, Heritage Bancorp., 1970—; bd. dirs. Heritage Fin. Svcs. Sec.-treas. Blue Island Pub. Welfare Assn., 1956-60, pres., 1961-63; chmn. indsl. and expansion com. Blue Island Planning Commn. Mem. Nat. Assn. Bank Women (pres. 1961-62), Assn. Chgo. Bank Women (pres. 1956-57). Club: Blue Island Woman's (pres. 1985-87). Home: 12761 Gregory St Blue Island IL 60406-2126 Office: 12015 Western Ave Blue Island IL 60406-1118

KOLLSTEDT, PAULA LUBKE, communications executive; b. Cin., Aug. 27, 1946; d. Elmer George and Mary Margaret (Kelly) Lubke; m. Stephen Leonard Kollstedt, Jan. 21, 1968; children: Kelly, Lance, Stacey, Jonathan. BA, Xavier U., 1968, MEd, 1982. Cert. secondary tchr., Ohio. Editor, writer Shillito's Dept. Store, Cin., 1966-69; freelance writer, Cin., 1969-74; pub. info. coord. Prince William County Parks and Recreation Com. (Va.), 1974-75; communications coord. City of Cin. Recreation Com., 1975-78; cons. Warner Amex Cable Television, Cin., 1982-84, Moellers Assocs., Cin., 1982-84; writer Cin. Enquirer, 1982-83; executive communication specialist Gen. Electric Aircraft Engines, 1984-87, employee communication specialist 1987-90, mgr. communication 1990—; speaker Cin. Preschool Coops., 1981, Cin. Women's Conf., 1984, lectr., presenter workshops on self-esteem for parents, 1975-86; lectr. bus. communications, 1992—. Author: Surviving the Crisis of Motherhood, 1982; contbr. articles to newspapers; writer, producer multimedia presentation Communication Cincinnati, (Unique Program award Ohio Parks and Recreation), 1978. Mem. Women in Communications (v.p. programs 1981-82; Gt. Lakes regional 1st pl. award 1984, 86, 87, 88, recipient Nat. Clarion award, 1990, Gem award, 1992). Recipient Prism award Pub. Rels. Soc. Am., 1983, 85, 86, 87, 88, 92, Bronze Quill award Internat. Assn. Bus. Communicators, 1986, 87, 88, Silver Quill award Internat. Assn. Bus. Communicators, 1989. Roman Catholic. Home: 5391 Haft Rd Cincinnati OH 45247-7419 Office: GE Aircraft Engines 1 Neumann Way MD-N4 Evendale OH 45215

KOLMAN, ANITA SUE, evaluation research consultant; b. Lakewood, N.J., Feb. 26, 1948; d. Irvin Oscar and Lillian (Muskatt) K.; m. Marvin Lloyd Marshak, Sept. 24, 1972; children: Rachel, Adam. BA in Sociology, U. Md., 1970; MA in Sociology, U. Minn., 1974, PhD in Sociology, 1977. Asst. prof. Augsburg Coll., Mpls., 1977-84; rsch. scientist Amherst H. Wilder Found., St. Paul, 1984-93; asst. prof. Coll. St. Catherine, St. Paul, 1985-86; evaluation rsch. cons. pvt. practice, St. Louis Park, Minn., 1993—. Contbr. rsch. reports to profl. publs. Vol. arts educator St. Louis Park Pub. Schs., 1988—; youth softball coach City of St. Louis Park, 1990-92; bd. dirs. Minn. Com. Prevention of Child Abuse, St. Paul, 1990-92. Recipient Regents award Augsburg Coll., 1983. Mem. Am. Sociol. Assn. (session organizer annualmeeting 1972—), , Am. Evaluation Assn., Sociologists Minn. (pres., sec., newsletter editor, program chair annual meeting 1983—), Sociologists Women in Soc., Phi Beta Kappa. Jewish. Home and office: 2855 Ottawa Ave S Saint Louis Park MN 55416

KOLODZIEJ, KAREN ANN, insurance underwriter; b. Pawtucket, R.I., July 18, 1966; d. Stanley Kazmierz and Mary (Gilbert) K. BS, Bryant Coll., 1988. Adminstrv. asst. to v.p. Merrill Lynch, Providence, 1987-88; asst. product analyst Pawtucket (R.I.) Mut. Ins., 1988-89, system analyst, 1989-92, ins. underwriter, 1992—. Vol. R.I. Spl. Olympics, 1993, 94. Mem. Nat. Assn. Ins. Women, Mut. Underwriters Assn. New England. Independent. Roman Catholic. Office: Pawtucket Mut Ins PO Box 820 Pawtucket RI 02862-0820

KOLPAKOVA, IRINA, dancer, educator, coach; b. Leningrad, USSR, May 22, 1933; m. Vladilen Semenov. Student, Leningrad Choreographic Sch.; studies with Agrippina Vaganova. Mem. Leningrad-kirov Ballet; ballet mistress, instr., coach Am. Ballet Theatre, N.Y.C., 1990—. Leading roles include Cinderella, Coast of Hope, Ala and Lolly, Don Quixote, Creation of the World; roles with the Leningrad-Kirov Ballet include Chopiniana (Les Sylphides), The Creation of the World; title roles include Giselle, The Fountain of Bakhchiserai, The Nutcracker, Othello, Pushkin, Romeo and Juliet, The Sleeping Beauty, La Sylphide, Raymonda; created roles include The Stone Flower, The Legend of Love, Fairy of the Rhone's Mountains. Named Merited Artist R.S.F.S.R., 1957, People's Artist, 1960, First prize Gold Etoile Internat. Dance Festival, 1965. Office: Am Ballet Theatre 890 Broadway New York NY 10003

KOMANDO, KIMBERLY ANN, computer company executive, radio and television host, news anchor; b. Union, N.J., July 1, 1964. BS in Computer Info. Systems, Ariz. State U., 1985. Mktg. rep. IBM, Phoenix, 1984-85; major account rep. AT&T, Phoenix, 1985-87; exec. v.p. Nationwide Auto Care Ctrs., Phoenix, 1987-88; pres. The Komando Corp., Ariz./Fla., 1988—; mgr. UNISYS, Phoenix, 1988-91; domestic and internat. mktg. cons.; speaker in field. Author: How to Cash In On Auto Malls, 1988, 401 Great Letters, 1993; talkshow and daily radio show host; internationally weekly syndicated columnist; contbr. articles to profl. jours. Home: Ste 5160 4455 E Camelback Rd Phoenix AZ 85018 Office: The Komando Corp 4332 N Wells Fargo Ste 200 Scottsdale AZ 85251

KOMOROWSKI, CHERYL ANN, librarian; b. Buffalo, Nov. 11, 1956; d. Donald and Carol (Brown) Hoffman; m. Frank Komorowski, Oct. 1, 1976; children: Justine, Alan. BS, Buffalo State Coll., 1976. Lic. real estate profl., 1986. Libr. Boylan, Brown, Code, Fowler, Randall and Wilson, Rochester, 1986-88, Arthur Andersen & Co., Rochester, N.Y., 1988—; asst. libr. Harter Secrest and Emery, Rochester. vol. Rochester Philharm. Orch., 1982—.

KOMP, BARBARA ANN, technical publications executive; b. La Porte, Ind., Nov. 3, 1954; d. Gerald Lee and Betty Mae (Schelin) K. BA in Elem. Edn., Ball State U., 1977. Cert. in lang. arts & reading competencies, 1977. Quality control insp. Foreman Mfg. Co., Rolling Prairie, Ind., 1978-80; quality control insp. Weil-McLain Co., Michigan City, Ind., 1980-81, jr. quality control engr., 1981-84, tech. writer, 1984-88. Advisor Jr. Achievement, Michigan City, 1982-84; mem. bd. dirs. Mich. City YMCA, 1992-93, Christman-in-April, Michigan City, chair in-kind donations com., 1993—, bd. sec., 1994—. Mem. Soc. for Tech. Communication (Tech. Manual Achievement award 1986, Tech. Manual Merit award 1990, 92), Women in Mgmt. Avocations: jazz aerobics, photography, volleyball. Office: Weil-McLain A Marley Co 500 Blaine St Michigan City IN 46360-2387

KONA, MARTHA MISTINA, librarian, freelance information consultant; b. Banovce, Slovakia; came to U.S., 1950; d. Albert and Anna (Kubrican) Mistina; m. William Kona, Aug. 6, 1955 (dec. Dec. 1989); children: Olivia, Lindy Anne; m. William P. Mihalovic, Apr. 30, 1992. Student, U. Salzburg, 1950; BA, Rosary Coll., 1953, MA, 1958; postgrad., Roosevelt U., 1980. Libr. instr., prof. Univ. Ill., Chgo., 1958-63; rsch. libr. Cen. Soya Chemurgy, Chgo., 1965-73; asst. dir. Rush Univ. Libr., Chgo., 1973-78; pvt. practice cons., info. specialist Wilmette, Ill., 1980; pvt. practice author and lectr. Wilmette, 1985—; cons., liaison Matica Slovenska, Slovak Nat. Libr. and Archives, Martin, Slovak Republic, 1990—. Author: Soybean Proteins, 1969, Multi Media Catalog, 1975, Health Science Librarians of Illinois, 1977; Slovak Americans and Canadians, 1985; co-author, editor: Archbishop Dr. Karol Kmetko, 1989; contbr. articles to profl. jours. Bd. dirs. Slovak Am. Found. Edn. and Sci., Inc., 1994—. Mem. AAUW, AAUP (chair bylaws com.1975-77), Health Sci. Librs. Ill. (co-founder, archivist 1970-77), Slovak World Congress (chair heritage commn. 1990—), First Cath. Slovak Union, Ill. Audio Visual Assn. (pres. 1975-77), Slovak Inst. (Rome), Sovereign and Mil. Order of Temple Jerusalem (bd. dirs. 1974—), Imperial Order of Constantine the Great and St. Helen (bd. dirs. 1977—), Dames of the Order in U.S.A. (Lady Comdr.), Order St. John Jerusalem, Woman's Club Wilmette Philanthropy (chair 1991-93), Pi Gamma Mu. Home: 600 3rd St Wilmette IL 60091-1921

KONDRATAS, SKIRMA ANNA, policy analyst; b. Vilkaviskis, Lithuania, Jan. 26, 1944; d. Bronius and Gražina (Starinskas) Makaitis; m. Ramunas Antanas Kondratas, June 27, 1970; children: Vidmas Antanas, Rimga Alena. BA, Harvard U., 1965; MA, Boston U., 1969; MBA, George Mason U., 1981. Dep. dir. rsch. Rep. Nat. Com., Washington, 1981-84; sr. policy analyst Heritage Found., Washington, 1984-86; dir. Office of Analysis & Evaluation Food and Nutrition Svc., USDA, Alexandria, Va., 1986-87, adminstr., from 1987; asst. sec. community planning and devel. Housing and Urban Devel. Dept., Washington, 1989-92; exec. dir. Nat. Commn. Am. Urban Families, Washington, 1992; sr. fellow Hudson Inst., Washington, 1992—. Author: (with Stuart Butler) Out of the Poverty Trap, 1987; contbr. articles to profl. jours. Fulbright fellow, 1965-66, Nat. Def. Fgn. Lang. fellow, 1966-67, sr. fellow Hudson Inst., Washington, 1992—. Mem. Phi Beta Kappa. Office: Hudson Inst 1015 18th St NW Ste 200 Washington DC 20036

KONECNY, KAREN ANDREA, administrator; b. Bridgeport, Conn., July 5, 1957; d. Andrew Anthony and Emma Florence (Zedlewski) K.; m. Herbert Ronald Cornet, July 28, 1990. Student, Waterbury State Tech. Coll., 1991—. Office mgr. Stratford (Conn.) Surg. Assn., 1981-92; office, bus. mgr. Bridgeport (Conn.) Internat. Medicine Assn., 1992-94; office sec. New Haven Orthopedic Group, 1994—. Mem. NAFE, Ladies of Hog, Phi Theta Kappa. Democrat. Roman Catholic. Home: 55 Raymond St Stratford CT 06497-5228

KONEFF, MARY ELLEN, artist; b. Akron, Ohio, Mar. 4, 1953; d. John and Genevieve Mary (Mikolajczyk) K.; m. Jorge Manuel Saralegui, Mar. 6,

1953. BA, Antioch Coll., Yellow Springs, Ohio, 1976. lectr. Long Beach (Calif.) State U., Manhattan Beach (Calif.) Pub. Arts Program. One and two person shows include Source Gallery, San Francisco, 1982, Isis Galley, Larkspur Landing, Calif., 1983, Isis Gallery, Mill Valley, Calif., 1985, L.A. Artcore Gallery, 1991; exhibited in numerous group shows, including Ruth Bachofner Gallery, Santa Monica, Calif., 1991, Century Gallery, Sylmar, Calif., 1992, NCJW/L.A.'s Women's Ctr., 1993, Middlebury (Vt.) Coll. Mus. of Art, 1993, Albany (N.Y.) Inst. History and Art, 1994, Owensboro (Ky.) Mus. Fine Art, 1994, Westmoreland Mus. Art, Greensburg, Pa., 1994, Babcock Galleries, N.Y.C., 1993, and others; represented in permanent collections including Chevron USA, San Francisco, Federal Home Loan Bank, San Francisco, Loews Hotel, Santa Monica, Calif., Simi Valley (Calif.) Hosp., Union Bank Switzerland, L.A., and others. Mem. So. Calif. Women's Caucus for Art. Home: 2243 Cloverfield Blvd Santa Monica CA 90405

KONER, PAULINE, dancer, choreographer; b. N.Y.C., June 26, 1912; d. Samuel and Ida (Ginsberg) K.; m. Fritz Mahler, May 23, 1939 (dec. 1973). Student, Columbia U., 1928-30; studies with Michel Fokine, studies with Michio Ito, studies with Angel Cansino; DFA (hon.), R.I. Coll., 1985. Faculty dance div. Juilliard Sch., 1986—; mem. faculty Sch. Performing Arts, N.Y.C., N.C. Sch. Arts, Winston-Salem; adj. prof. Bklyn. Coll., 1975-79; guest tchr. modern dance Internat. Ballet Seminar, Copenhagen, 1971, 72, Am. Dance Ctr., N.Y.C., 1972; lectr. and guest artist many leading univs. in U.S.; performed under auspices State Dept. in Mexico, S.Am., Europe; artist-in-residence N.C. Sch. Arts, Winston-Salem, 1965-76; tchr. choreographer workshop Cultural Ctr. of Philippines, 1973; nat. adjudicator Am. Coll. Dance Festival, Kennedy Ctr., 1981; guest lectr. U. Arts., Phila., 1991, 92, 93. Performed at White House, 1967; conducted choreography workshops Nat. Assn. Regional Ballets, 1968; staged ballet Dayton (Ohio) Civic Ballet, 1969, Alvin Ailey Repertory Co., 1969, Atlanta Ballet Co., 1969; filmed TV broadcasts of numerous performances; premiere: The Farewell, 1962, Solitary Songs, Am. Dance Festival, 1975, Pauline Koner Dance Consort, 1976-82, A Time of Crickets, Am. Dance Festival, 1976, Mosaic, Dance Umbrella Series, 1977, Cantigas, Am. Dance Festival, 1978, Flight Riverside Festival, 1980; resident dancer Riverside Dance Festival, 1979-81; solo concerts in N.Y.C., 1930—, Near East, 1932, Russia, 1935, Riverside Co., 1980-82; guest artist Jose Limon Co., 1945-60; guest artist, tchr. Jacob's Pillow Dance Festival, intermittently 1945-70; dir. Pauline Koner Dance Co., 1947-64; guest choreographer Nat. Sch. Dance, Rome, 1960-63, Nat. Ballet Chile, 1961; performer, tchr. Conn. Coll. Sch. Dance, 1948-60; pioneer TV dance CBS, 1946; artist-in-residence: U. Ill., 1984, Alvin Ailey Repertory Co., 1984; choreographer: Solitary Songs at Alvin Ailey Repertory Co., 1984; author: (autobiography) Solitary Song, 1989, Elements of Performance, 1993; contbr. articles to books and mags.; State Dept. tour of India, Singapore and Korea, 1967; restaged Poéme for N.C. Sch. Art, 1991, Concertino for Dance-Fusion, Phila., 1991; spl. coaching Jacobs Pillow, 1991; solo performance The Farewell for Margie Gillis, 1995. Recipient Dance Mag. award, 1963, Citation award De La Torre Bueno Awards Com., 1990; Nat. Endowment of Arts grantee, 1969, 75, 77-78, 79.

KONG, LAURA S. L., seismologist; b. Honolulu, July 23, 1961; d. Albert T.S. and Cordelia (Seu) K.; m. Kevin T.M. Johnson, Mar. 3, 1990. ScB, Brown U., 1983; PhD, MIT/Woods Hole Oceanog. Inst., 1990. Grad. rschr. Woods Hole (Mass.) Oceanog. Instn., 1984-90; postdoctoral fellow U. Tokyo, 1990-91; geophysicist Pacific Tsunami Warning Ctr., Ewa Beach, Hawaii, 1991-93; seismologist U.S. Geol. Survey Hawaiian Volcano Obs., 1993—; mem. grad. faculty dept. geology & geophysics U. Hawaii; mem. Hawaii State Earthquake Avd. Bd., 1993—; mem. equal opportunity adv. bd. Nat. Weather Svc. Pacific Region, Honolulu, 1992-93, Asian-Am./Pacific Islander spl. emphasis program mgr., 1992-93. Contbr. articles to profl. jours.; spkr., editl. reviewer in field. Rsch. fellow Japan Govt.-Japan Soc. for Promotion of Sci., 1990; recipient Young Investigator grant Japan Soc. for Promotion of Sci., 1990. Mem. Am. Geophys. Union, Seismol. Soc. Am., Hawaii Ctr. for Volcanology, Assn. Women in Sci., Sigma Xi. Office: US Geol Survey Hawaiian Volcano Obs PO Box 51 Hawaii National Park HI 96718-0051

KONG, TRUDITH ANN, engineer; b. Oakland, Calif., May 7, 1955; d. Robert and Emma Kong. BS in Chem. Engring., U. Calif., Berkeley, 1977. Registered engr., Wash. Engr. Battelle-PNL, Richland, Wash., 1977-79; engr. Monsanto, Seattle, 1979-82, sr. prodn. engr., 1982-84; engr. instrumentation Zurn/Nepco, Woodinville, Wash., 1984-90; chief engr. instrumentation Zurn/Nepco, Redmond, Wash., 1990—. Mem. Instrument Soc. Am., Tau Beta Pi. Office: Zurn/Nepco PO Box 747 Redmond WA 98073

KONIECKO, MARY ANN, elementary education educator; b. Canton, Ohio, Aug. 29, 1952; d. Alexander Joseph and Mary Therese (Jaglowski) K. BS in Edn., Kent State U., 1974. Cert. tchr., Ohio. Tchr. elem. sch. Louisville (Ohio) City Schs., 1974—. Republican. Roman Catholic. Home: 714 E 1st St Minerva OH 44657-1104

KONIECZNY, SHARON LOUISE, insurance company executive; b. Madison, Minn., July 2, 1952; d. Frank H. and Elenore A. (Mikkelson) K. Student, Dakota Wesleyan U., 1970-71, U. Minn., 1971-72. Sales rep. Advance Schs., Bloomington, Minn., 1972; sales agt. ITT Life Ins., Mpls., 1973-75, mktg. auditor, 1975-76, supr. new bus., 1976-79, mgr. UND Issue, 1979-81, asst. v.p. new bus., 1981-83, asst. v.p.sales support, 1983-87, v.p., sales mktg., 1987-94; nat. dir. new bus. devel. UND Issue, 1994—. Mem. United Way, Mpls. (vice chmn. 1984-85, chmn. 1985). Mem. Nat. Assn. Life Underwriters (gen. agy. mgmt. conf.), Am. Mktg. Assn., Nat. Assn. Ins. Women, Soc. Ins. Trainers and Educatores, Internat Assn. Fin. Planners. Democrat. Lutheran. Home: 12610 50th Ave N Minneapolis MN 55442-2060

KONNER, JOAN WEINER, university administrator, educator, broadcasting executive, television producer; b. Paterson, N.J., Feb. 24, 1931; d. Martin and Tillie (Frankel) Weiner; children: Rosemary, Catherine; m. Alvin H. Perlmutter. Student, Vassar Coll., 1948-49; BA, Sarah Lawrence Coll., 1951; MS, Columbia U., 1961. Editorial writer, columnist, reporter Hackensack (N.J.) Record, 1961-63; producer, reporter WNDT Ednl. Broadcasting Corp., N.Y.C., 1963-65; producer, writer, reporter NBC News, N.Y.C., 1965-77; exec. producer nat. pub. affairs programs WNET Ednl. Broadcasting Corp., N.Y.C., 1977-78, v.p. programming WNET, 1981-84, exec. producer, 1984-86; exec. producer Bill Moyers' Jour., 1978-81; pres. Pub. Affairs TV, Inc.; exec. producer Bill Moyers' series for PBS, 1986-88; prof. broadcast and journalism, dean Grad. Sch. Journalism Columbia U., N.Y.C., 1988—, pub. Columbia Journalism Rev. Past trustee Columbia U. Rockland Ctr. for Arts, Sarah Lawrence Coll. Recipient 12 Emmy awards NATAS, Columbia-du Pont award, Peabody award, Gavel award ABA, Edward R. Murrow award, others. Mem. Dirs. Guild, Writers Guild, Soc. Profl. Journalists, Pulitzer Prize Bd., Ctr. for Media Studies, Freedom Forum, Newspaper Women's Club of N.Y.C., Century Assn., Cosmopolitan Club. Office: Columbia U Grad Sch Journalism Journalism Bldg New York NY 10027

KONNER, MARGARET ANNE, management consultant; b. Livingston, N.J., June 12, 1965; d. Michael Stephen Konner and Joan Ellen (Segal) Erath. BS in Math. and Computer Sci., Tufts U., 1986; MS in Mgmt., MIT, 1993. Software engr. ITP Buston, Inc., Cambridge, Mass., 1986-88; mgr. Unix rsch. Internat. Data Corp., Framingham, Mass., 1988-91; assoc. Booz, Allen & Hamilton, 1992—; various positions Knudsen Erath Winery, Dundee, oreg., 1991—, Preston Vineyard, Healdsburg, Calif., 1993—. Vol. Rafael House, San Francisco, 1994—, Inner City Outings, 1994—; mem. World Affairs Coun. Mem. Commonwealth Club. Democrat. Home: 1750 Vallejo St San Francisco CA 94123

KONO, JEAN E., nursing educator; b. Marshalltown, Iowa, Oct. 20, 1941; d. Harold and Helen I. (Melton) Bailey; m. Frederick L. Kono, June 8, 1963; children: Matthew D., Kristine H. Diploma, Mercy Hosp., 1962; BSN, Mary Crest Coll., 1977; postgrad., U. Iowa, Coll. nursing. Head nurse, mental health St.Luke's Hosp., Cedar Rapids, Iowa; child therapist Vera French Mental Health Ctr., Davenport, Iowa; nurse mgr., mental health Mercy Hosp., Davenport, Iowa; clin. instr. Eastern Iowa Coll., Bettendorf, Iowa. Mem. APNA, Iowa Nurses Assn. (bd. dirs., dist. 6 pres.).

KONON, NEENA NICHOLAI, interior designer; b. Chgo., Dec. 4, 1951; d. Nicholas Alexander and Marie G. (Korotkoff) K. BFA cum laude, Ohio U., 1973. Interior designer Architectonics, Inc., Chgo., 1973-75, sr. interior designer, 1978-82; interior designer Space Mgmt. Assoc., Inc., Chgo., 1975-78; design prin. Borkon & Konon Assoc., Inc., Chgo., 1982-84; dir. interiors Perkins & Will, Chgo., 1984-91; assoc. Womon Bus. Enterprise, Chgo., 1984-91; pres. Nicholai Ltd., Chgo., 1991—; interiors cons. WBE (Woman Bus. Enterprise), Chgo., 1991—. Liaison restoration Holy Trinity Russian Orthodox Cathedral, Chgo., 1987, millenium com., 1988, Synergy Orthodox Laity Assn., Chgo. Mem. Chgo. Real Estate Exec. Women, Internat. Facilities Mgrs. Assn., Chgo. Real Estate Exec. Women. Republican.

KONRAD, AGNES CROSSMAN, retired real estate agent, retired educator; b. Rutland, Vt., Nov. 26, 1921; d. Warren Julius and Susan Anna (Cain) Crossman; children: Suzanne Martha, Dianna Marie; m. Henry Konrad, Nov. 27, 1954. Assoc. degree in Edn., Castelton Coll., 1943; BS in Edn., Castelton State Coll., 1952; postgrad., SUNY, New Paltz, 1969-70, Fla. Atlantic U., 1973. Cert. realtor-assoc. Tchr. Pittsford (Vt.) Pub. Schs., 1943-44, tchr. 1st grade, 1950-52; tchr. 3d grade Hyde Park (N.Y.) Elem. Schs., 1952-73; realtor assoc. Four Star Realty of Boca Raton (Fla.), 1973-93; ret., 1993; tchr. 3d grade Violet Ave. Sch., Hyde Park (N.Y.) Sch. System, 1969-73. Mem. AAUW, N.Y. State Ret. Tchrs. Assn. (life), Castleton Vt. State Coll. Alumni. Home: 1229 SW 13th St Boca Raton FL 33486-5307

KONSTANTINOVSKAIA, VALERIA, puppeteer, puppet maker, sculptor, educator; b. Kirovo, Russia, Aug. 23, 1934; came to U.S., 1991; d. Konstantin Konstantinovsky and Lidia Mironovich Mikhilova; m. Boris Belov, Jan. 4, 1960 (dec. Oct. 1991); 1 child, Anton. EdM, Tchr. Coll., Moscow, 1955. Cert. tchr. Tchr. ESL U. Samarkand, Uzbekistan, 1955-58, Saratov, Russia, 1958-66; translator, editor Moscow, 1966-76, tchr. ESL, 1976-80; tchr. ESL Moscow Arts U., 1980-84; puppet theater dir., mgr., tchr. Cultural Ctr., Moscow, 1980-91; ESL tchr. Westbrook (Maine) Schs., Maine, 1993—; puppeteer, puppet maker, instr., founder Puppets 'R' Us Theater, Portland, Maine, 1991—; pres. Arts for All Ednl. Internat. Non-Profit Corp., Portland, 1993—. Sculptor, vis. artist to schs., hosps., group homes, cmty. ctrs. Home and Office: Puppets 'R' Us Theater 37 Dorset St Portland ME 04102-1101

KOO, GRACE, artist; b. Riverside, Calif., Jan. 5, 1921; d. Chung Sup and Ai Joo (Park) Koo; m. William F. Donoghue Jr., Jan. 26, 1974. BFA, U. Calif., Irvine, 1977. Mgr., owner Koo's Cafe, Santa Ana, Calif., 1942-61; clk. typist Civil Svc. U.S. Dept. Army, Korea, 1961-62; sec. Ford Aeronutronic, Newport Beach, Calif., 1962-65; adminstrv. asst., dept. math. U. Calif., Irvine, 1965-73; artist freelance, 1974—. Mem. U. Calif. Faculty Assocs., 1974—. Home: 22 Perkins Ct Irvine CA 92715-4043

KOOLOIAN, ELIZABETH, construction company executive; b. Providence, Dec. 24, 1931; d. Anthony Antranig and Noyemzar (Mardigian) Krikorian; m. Azarig Kooloian Sr., Apr. 25, 1954; children: Julie Ann, Elizabeth Marguerite, Nina Lori, Kim Elaine, Azarig Jr. Grad., Armenian Lang. Sch., 1945; cont. edn. student, Providence Coll., 1982. Registered apt. mgr. Exec. sec. State of R.I., Providence, 1950-55; v.p. A. Kooloian Constrn. Co., Inc., North Providence, R.I., 1956—, Kooloian Realty, North Providence, R.I., 1978—; partner Bay Tower Nursing Ctr., Providence, 1984—. Mem. Norton Art Gallery, Palm Beach, Fla. Mem. NAFE, Armenian Students Assn. Am. (donar), Armenian Gen. Benevolent Union (pres. club, donar), Met. Mus. Art (assoc.), Women in the Arts (charter). Armenian Apostolic Ch.

KOONS, ELEANOR (PEGGY), clinical social worker; b. Sarasota, Fla., July 26, 1927; d. James Lee and Odessa (Dobbs) Swafford; m. Nelson A. Koons, Dec. 27, 1945. BA in Human Resources, Eckerd Coll., 1986; MSW, U. So. Fla., 1988. Lic. clin. social worker. Indsl. nurse Electro-Mech. Rsch. Co., Sarasota, Fla., 1963-65; office mgr. Koons Constrn. Co., Sarasota, 1970-80; day treatment counselor Manatee Community Mental Health Ctr., Bradenton, Fla., 1980-81, day treatment counselor geriat. residential treatment sys., 1981-82, community liaison, counselor, 1982-83; office mgr. Koons Constrn. Co., 1983-88; hospice intern Hospice S.W. Fla., 1987-88, sr. social svc. counselor, 1988-92; pvt. practice Sarasota, 1992—; presenter Nat. Hospice Assn. Conf., Detroit, Fla. Hospice Symposium, Ocala, Fla. Assn. Pediatric Tumor Programs, State Conf., Clearwater, others. Contbr. articles to Bereavement Mag., 1992, 94. Recipient Retired Social Worker of Yr. award Tampa Bay (Fla.) Unit; Grad. record fellow U. So. Fla. Mem. NASW (co-chairperson 1993-94), ACA, Assn. Pediatric Oncology Social Workers, Fla. Assn. Oncology Social Workers, Coalition for Children and Youth of Sarasota. Home: 5117 Circled Oak Dr Sarasota FL 34233-2236

KOONTZ, CHERYL L., insurance executive, business owner; b. Dallas, Oct. 10, 1955; d. Sherwood Otis and Margaret Frances (Pyles) Koontz; m Doyle Wayne Coker (div.). Student, Eastfield Jr. Coll. Spl. corr. Bankers Life and Casualty Co., Dallas, 1975-78; exec. sec. Trinity Abstract and Record Co., Dallas, 1979-80; group ins. mgr. Lee Mgmt. Inc., Irving, Tex., 1980-85; group ins. dir. World-Wide Ins. Mgmt. Corp., Dallas, 1985-94; ins. adminstrn. cons. Koontz Cons., Inc., 1994—. Mem. NAFE. Home: 2823 Blanton St Dallas TX 75227-7214

KOONTZ, EVA ISABELLE, medical technologist; b. Jetmore, Kans., Feb. 3, 1935; d. Vernon Ward and Lillian Mae (Bell) K. BS in Natural Scis., Sterling (Kans.) Coll., 1957; cert. in med. tech., U. Kans. Med. Ctr., 1958. Office technologist Group Practice, Mission, Kans., 1958-60; chemistry supr. Bethany Hosp., Kansas City, Kans., 1960-64; rsch. asst. pediatric hematology and metabolic rsch. U. Kans. Med. Ctr., Kansas City, Kans., 1964-72, R&D Tech., Providence-St. Margaret's Health Care Ctr., Kansas City, Kans., 1972-74; staff technologist St. Lukes Hosp., Kansas City, Mo., 1974-79; clin. lab. mgr. and supr. Quincy Rsch. Ctr., Kansas City, Mo., 1979-80; staff technologist Lakeside Hosp., Kansas City, Mo., 1980-82; med. technologist supr. Midwest Rsch. Inst., Kansas City, Mo., 1982-88; cert. toxicology scientist Clin. Reference Labs., Inc., Lenexa, Kans., 1988—. Mem. Am. Soc. for Med. Tech., Am. Assn. for Clin. Chemistry, Mo. Soc. Med. Technologists. Republican. Presbyterian. Home: 10251 Cedarbrooke Ln Kansas City MO 64131-4209 Office: Clin Reference Labs Inc 11844 W 85th St Shawnee Mission KS 66214-1518

KOOPMANN, RETA COLLENE, sales executive; b. Oklahoma City, Feb. 27, 1944; d. Henry William and Hazel (Rollins) Singleton; m. Fred F. Koopmann, June 1, 1963 (div. 1974); 1 child, Rebecca Dawn; m. Walter J. Parrish, Jan 3, 1987 (div. 1990). BS, Calif. Coast U., 1987, postgrad. in bus. adminstrn., 1987—. Front end mgr. Kroger Co., Cleve., 1969-72; with acctg. dept. Johns Manville, Denison, Tex., 1972-74; bakery/deli merchandiser Kroger Co., Columbia, S.C., 1974-83; v.p. bakery, deli ops. Kash n' Karry div. Lucky's Inc., Tampa, Fla., 1983-88, Kash n' Karry Food Stores Inc., Tampa, 1988-90; LBO, corp. dir. bakery/deli/sea food ops. United Supermarkets, Inc., Lubbock, Tex., 1990-91; mgr. regional supermarket accounts Tenneco-Packaging Corp. Am., Northbrook, Ill., 1991—. Author tng. manuals, 1984, 86, 87. Bd. trustees Jim Borck Ednl. Found., Inc., 1988—, pres. elect, 1993, chairperson of bd., 1994, chair com. for deli skills tng. program; vol. Spl. Olympics, Tampa, 1986, 87, 88; bd. govs. Am. Biog. Inst. Rsch. Assn., 1989—. Mem. NAFE, Internat. Deli/Bakery Assn. (exec. bd. 1986-89), Internat. Platform Assn., Retail Bakers Assn. (bd. dirs. 1989—, chmn. deli com., deli dir.), Eagles. Republican. Lutheran. Home: 3010 Ridge Run Dr Hiram GA 30141-3337 Office: Packaging Corp Am PO Box 891 Hiram GA 30141-0891

KOPACK, PAMELA LEE (PAMELA LEE MACMINN), business services executive; b. Portland, Maine, July 25, 1951; d. Everett John Foye and Lois Florence (Loveland) MacMinn; student Sears, Roebuck Extension Inst., 1969-73, Newspaper Inst. Am., 1979-85; m. Charles Thomas Kopack, Apr. 2, 1971. Sales staff Sears Roebuck & Co., Cleve., 1966-69, credit collector, 1972-75; exec. sec., asst., Cole Nat. Corp., Cleve., 1976-79; pres. Kopack Svc. Bur., Cleve., 1979—. Author poetry pub. in Poetry-People, 1975, other publs., 1974—, lyrics for songs recorded on single records and albums, 1974-79; author greeting cards, articles, short stories. Recipient poetry award for Facets of a Housewife, 1977. Mem. NAFE, Career Guild (New Feature award 1982), Secs. Workshop, P.S. for Profl. Secs. (Bur. Bus. Practice, article award 1979), Internat. Platform Assn., Ohio Women Bus. Leaders. Clubs: Women's Opportunity Workshop. Office: PO Box 81573 Cleveland OH 44181-0573

KOPACZ, KATHLEEN PATRICIA, public relations executive; b. Newburgh, N.Y., Nov. 16, 1961; d. Richard F. and Grace I. (Weyant) K. BS, Sacred Heart U., Bridgeport, Conn., 1983; MS, St. Thomas U., Miami, Fla., 1985. Asst. to sports inform. U.S. Naval Acad., Annapolis, Md., 1986; mgr. AMC Theatres, Gainesville, Fla., 1986-87, Clearwater, Fla., 1988-89, Orlando, Fla., 1988-89; dir. promotions Daytona Internat. Speedway, Daytona Beach, Fla., 1989—. Chmn. spl. events com. Destination Daytona. Recipient scholarship N.Mex. Highlands U., 1979, Sacred Heart U., 1981. Mem. NAFE (1st v.p. Oceanshore Women's Network chpt. 1992—), Daytona Beach Advt. Fedn. (first v.p.). Republican. Roman Catholic. Home: 420 Lake Bridge Plz #407 Ormond Beach FL 32174-9518 Office: Daytona Internat Speedway 1801 Volusia Ave Daytona Beach FL 32114-1215

KOPALA, CAROLE JEAN, analyst; b. Franklin, Ky., Aug. 21, 1948; d. George Donald and Ruby Elizabeth (Harper) Arney; m. Philip Stephen Kopala, Apr. 5, 1975 (div. Jan. 1991); 1 child, Ashley Elizabeth. BA, Vanderbilt U., 1970, MA, 1972. Rsch. asst. Nashville Outpatients Clinic, 1970-72; rsch. assoc. Tenn. Dept. Youth, Nashville, 1972-73; commd. 2d lt. USAF, 1974, advanced through grades to maj., 1985; occupational test psychologist USAF, Lackland AFB, Tex., 1975-78, occupational analyst, 1975-78; sr. exptl. psychologist Flight Dynamics Lab. USAF, Wright Patterson AFB, Ohio, 1979-81, program mgr. Flight Dynamics Lab., 1981-83, acquisitions mgr. Office Dep. Chief of Staff Systems, 1983-87; acquisitions mgr. Office Asst. Sec. Pentagon USAF, Washington, 1987-91; recording sec., archivist Congl. Panel for Acquisition Reform, Newington, Va., 1991-93; ret. USAF, 1993; sr. acquisition analyst Analytical Svcs. (ANSER), Arlington, Va., 1993—. Contbr. articles to profl. jours. Republican. Home: 6110 Scotch Dr Alexandria VA 22310-1534 Office: Ste 700 1215 Jefferson Davis Hwy Arlington VA 22202

KOPENHAVER, PATRICIA ELLSWORTH, podiatrist. Student, Columbia U., 1950-53; BA, George Washington U., 1954; MA, Columbia U., 1956; Dr. Podiatric Medicine, N.Y. Coll. of Podiatric Medicine, 1963; postgrad., N.Y. Coll. Podiatric Medicine, 1980. Diplomate Nat. Bd. Podiatry Examiners. Pvt. practice podiatry Greenwich, Conn., 1964—; mem. staff Laurelton Convalescent Hosp., Greenwich. Bd. dirs. Monmouth Opera Guild, 1965; trustee Monmouth Opera Festival, 1966, v.p., 1964; mem. Greenwich Arts Coun.; program chmn. Greenwich Women's Rep. Club, 1983-84, 4th dist. rep., 1984-85, 87—. Recipient Hosp. Fund award for med. research translations ARC. Mem. AAUW (v.p. 1991, pres. Greenwich br. 1992-94), NOW, Conn. Podiatric Med. Assn., Hist. Soc., Asian Soc., Fairfield Podiatry Assn., Am. Assn. Women Podiatrists (charter pres. 1969-78), Acad. Podiatry, Am. Podiatry Coun., UN Assn. U.S.A., Acad. Podiatric Medicine (chmn. nominating com. 1981, 1st v.p. 1983-84, chmn. fundraising 1984-85, chmn. women's issues 1985, chmn. community edn. 1989), Am. Acad. Sports Medicine, Am. Acad. of Podiatric Sports Medicine (assoc. 1989), George Washington U. Alumni Assn., Columbia Alumni Assn., Fairfield County Alumni Assn. Columbia U., Nat. Fedn. Rep. Women, Bruce Mus., Nature Conservancy, Federated Garden Clubs Conn., St. Mary Ladies Guild, Greenwich Gardeners, Womans' Club (ways and means com. 1989), English Speaking Union, Soroptimists Internat. Am. (pres. Greenwich br. 1990—, bd. dirs. 1995—), Inc. (vice-chmn. program com. 1985—, regional med. scholarship chmn. 1987, med. scholarship chmn. N.E. region 1988, program dir. 1988—, pres. Greenwich br. 1990-92), Toastmasters, Travel Club (program com. 1984—, Indian com.), Pi Epsilon Chi. Home: 2 Sutton Pl S New York NY 10022-3070 Office: 8 Dearfield Dr Greenwich CT 06831-5348

KOPETZ, VINETTE NICKEL, editor; b. Bainbridge, Ohio, May 3, 1935; d. Victor Kenneth and Martha Marie (Kinske) Nickel; m. Raymond Kopetz, Apr. 24, 1964; children: Stephanie Victoria, Peter James. BA, Valparaiso U., 1960. Editorial asst. Encyclopedia Britannica, Chgo., 1960-62; asst. editorial mgr. Am. Vet. Med. Assn., Chgo., 1962-66; dir. Wilmette (Ill.) Youth Employment Ctr., 1980-85; program coord. Northwestern U., Evanston, Ill., 1985-89; assoc. dir. publs. Inst. Environ. Scis., Mt. Prospect, Ill., 1989—. Bd. dirs. PTA, Vol. Pool Assn., Parents Against Drug and Alcohol Abuse, Wilmette, 1975-86; mem. Wilmette Sch. Bd. Caucus. Recipient Cert. of Appreciation Village of Wilmette, Ill., 1985. Mem. AAUW, Am. Soc. Assn. Execs., Chgo. Soc. Assn. Execs. Democrat. Lutheran. Office: Inst Environ Scis 940 E Northwest Hwy Mount Prospect IL 60056-3422

KOPLEY, CATHERINE S., investment company executive; b. Passaic, N.J., Sept. 15, 1948; d. Alex W. and Rita M. Sudol; m. James M. Kopley, May 27, 1970; children: Anne, Michael. BS, St. Peter's Coll., 1970; JD, Seton Hall U., 1974. Bar: N.J. 1974, Pa. 1976. Pres. Pruco Securities, Prudential Ins. Co., Newark, N.J., 1974-94; v.p. strategic initiatives Prudential Ins. Co., South Plainfield, N.J., 1995—. Office: Prudential Ins Co 1111 Durham Ave South Plainfield NJ 07080

KOPLOVITZ, KAY, communication network executive; b. Milw., Apr. 11, 1945; d. William E. and Jane T. Smith; m. William C. Koplovitz Jr., Apr. 17, 1971. BS, U. Wis., 1967; MA in Communications, Mich. State U., 1968. Radio and TV producer, dir. Sta. WTMJ-TV, Milw., 1967; editor Communications Satellite Corp., Washington, 1968-72; dir. community services UA Columbia Cablevision, Oakland, N.J., 1973-75; v.p., exec. dir. UA Columbia Satellite Services Inc., Oakland, 1977-80; founder, pres., CEO USA Network and Sci-Fi Channel, N.Y.C., 1980—. Mem. bd. overseers NYU Grad. Sch. Bus., 1984-87; bd. dirs. Nat. Jr. Achievement, 1986—. Recipient Outstanding Alumnus award Mich. State U. Grad. Sch. Bus., 1985, Outstanding Corp. Social Responsibility CUNY, 1986, Women Who Run the World award Sara Lee Corp., 1987, Muse award N.Y. Women in Film and TV, 1992, Ellis Island medal of honor, 1993, Crystal award Women in Film, 1993; named to Broadcasting Mag. Hall of Fame, 1992. Mem. Nat. Cable TV Assn. (bd. dirs. 1984—), Advt. Coun. Inc. (chmn. 1992-93, bd. dirs. 1985—), Internat. Coun., Nat. Acad. TV Arts and Scis. (chmn. 1994-95, bd. dirs. 1984-93), Women in Cable (founding bd. dirs., membership chmn. 1979-80, v.p. 1981-82, pres. 1982-83), Cable Advt. Bur. (bd. dirs., exec. com., treas. 1981-87, Chmn.'s award for leadership 1987), Nat. Acad. Cable Programming (bd. dirs. 1984-87), Com. of 200, Womens Forum, N.Y.C. Partnership (bd. dirs. 1987—). Office: USA Network 1230 Avenue Of The Americas # 18th New York NY 10020-1513

KOPNICK, LYNN ARSHT, lawyer, accountant; b. Detroit, Mar. 3, 1961; d. Saul P. and Shirley Edith (Stahl) Arsht; divorced. BA, Kalamazoo Coll., 1983; JD, Wayne State U., 1986; LLM in Taxation, NYU, 1987. Bar: Ill. 1987, U.S. Dist. Ct. (no. dist.) Ill. 1987. Atty. tax dept. Ernst & Young, Chgo., 1987-91; tax counsel CBI Industries, Inc., Oak Brook, Ill., 1991—; bd. arbitrator Cook County Mandatory Arbitration, Chgo., 1991—. Mem. AIDS Legal Council of Chgo., 1988—; classroom instr. Jr. Achievement, Hinsdale, Ill., 1995. Mem. ABA, Chgo. Bar Assn. (state and local tax com., fed. tax com.), Com. on State Taxation, Ill. State Bar Assn., Kalamazoo Coll. Chgo. Alumni Assn. (steering com. 1987—). Jewish. Office: CBI Industries Inc 800 Jorie Blvd Oak Brook IL 60521

KOPP, NANCY KORNBLITH, state legislator; b. Coral Gables, Fla., Dec. 7, 1943; d. Lester and Barbara M. (Levy) Kornblith; m. Robert E. Kopp, May 3, 1969; children: Emily, Robert E. III. BA with honors, Wellesley Coll., 1965; MA, U. Chgo., 1968; LittD (hon.) Hood Coll., 1988. Instr. polit. sci. U. Ill., 1968-69; staff spl. subcom. on edn. U.S. Ho. of Reps., Washington, 1970-71; legis. staff Md. Gen. Assembly, Annapolis, 1971-74; mem. Md. Ho. of Dels., 1974—, speaker Pro Tem, 1991-93, chmn. appropriations subcom. on edn. and human resources, 1981-91; mem. exec. com. Nat. Conf. State Legislators; exec. com. So. Reg. Edn. Bd. Mem. LWV, AAUW, Common Cause. Democrat. Jewish. Office: Md Ho of Reps State Capitol Annapolis MD 21401

KOPPELMAN, DOROTHY MYERS, artist, consultant; b. N.Y.C., June 13, 1920; d. Harry Walter and May (Chalmers) M.; m. Chaim Koppelman, Feb. 18, 1943; 1 child, Ann. Student Bklyn. Coll., 1938-42, Am. Artists Sch., 1940-42, Art Students League, 1942; student of Aesthetic Realism with Eli Siegel, 1942-78, Ellen Reiss, 1978—. Instr. Art Bklyn. Coll., 1952-75; dir. Terrain Gallery, N.Y.C., 1955-83; dir. Visual Arts Gallery, Sch. Visual Arts,

1961-62; pres. Aesthetic Realism Found., 1973-85, cons., 1973—; instr. Nat. Acad. Sch. of Design, 1988-89. One woman shows include Terrain Gallery, 1961, Rina Gallery, Jersey City, 1963; exhibited in group shows at Mus. Modern Art, N.Y.C., 1962, Balt. Mus., 1962, Bklyn. Mus., 1962, N.J. State Mus., Jersey City, Butler Art Inst., Youngstown, Ohio, San Francisco Art Inst., 1961-62, 65, Nat. Acad. Ann., 1986, 90; group shows incl. Swiss Inst., N.Y.C., Susan Teller Gallery, N.Y.C., 1993, 95, Drawing Ctr., N.Y.C.; represented in permanent collections Hampton Inst. Author: (with others) Aesthetic Realism: We Have Been There - Six Artists, 1969. Illustrator Children's Guide to Parents, 1971. Tiffany grantee for painting, 1965. Home: 498 Broome St New York NY 10013-2213 Office: Aesthetic Realism Found Inc 141 Greene St New York NY 10012-3201

KOPPER, BEVERLY ANN, psychologist, educator, social worker; b. Syracuse, N.Y., Feb. 3, 1954; d. Richard Ervin and Elizabeth Barbara (Kozlowski) K.; m. Carroll Dudley Roland, Aug. 5, 1983. BA, SUNY, Buffalo, 1976; MSW, U. Wis., 1979; MS, Iowa State U., 1986, PhD, 1988. Lic. psychologist, social worker, Iowa. Sch. social worker Area Edn. Agy. 6, Marshalltown, Iowa, 1979-89; social worker Profl. Counseling Svcs., Marshalltown, 1980-86; social worker Family Health Care Ctr., Iowa Falls, Iowa, 1989—, psychologist, 1990—; social worker Ctr. for Child and Family Svcs., Marshalltown, 1987—, psychologist, 1990—; asst. prof. U. No. Iowa, Cedar Falls, 1990—; lectr. U. No. Iowa, Cedar Falls, 1988-90; social worker Ellsworth Mcpl. Hosp., Iowa Falls, 1989—. Contbr. articles to profl. jours. Mem. APA, NASW, Acad. Cert. Social Workers, Iowa Psychol. Assn. Home: 3291 220th St Marshalltown IA 50158-8955 Office: Univ No Iowa 446 Baker Cedar Falls IA 50613

KOPPUS, BETTY JANE, retired savings and loan association executive; b. Toledo, June 14, 1922; d. Carl Emerson and Hilda Sarah (Semlow) K.; student pub. schs. With United Savs. and Loan Assn. (now Standard Fed.), Toledo, 1940—, asst. sec., 1943, treas., 1943-73, sec., 1973-78, v.p. 1978-84. Former trustee, sec. Lutheran Social Service Northwestern Ohio; mem. St. Mark's Luth. Ch. Mem. Toledo C. of C. (past treas., trustee), Toledo Area Govt. Research Assn. (past treas., dir.), Twin Mgmt. Forum, Beta Sigma Phi. Clubs: Zonta (Toledo I), Brandywine Country, River Road Garden. Address: 5709 Chardonnay Dr Toledo OH 43615-7312

KOPRIVICA, DOROTHY MARY, management consultant, real estate and insurance broker; b. St. Louis, May 27, 1921; d. Mitar and Fema (Guzina) K. B.S., Washington U., St. Louis, 1962; cert. in def. inventory mgmt. Dept. Def., 1968. Mgmt. analyst Transp. Supply and Maintenance Command, St. Louis, 1954-57, Dept. Army Transp. Materiel Command, St. Louis, 1957-62; program analyst Dept. Army Aviation System Command, St. Louis, 1962-74, spl. asst. to comdr., 1974-78; ins. broker D. Koprivica, Ins., St. Louis, 1978—; real estate broker, St. Louis, 1978—. Mem. Bus. and Profl. Women (pres. 1974-75). Eastern Orthodox. Lodge: Order Eastern Star.

KOPROWSKA, IRENA, cytopathologist, cancer researcher; b. Warsaw, Poland, May 12, 1917; came to U.S., 1944; d. Henryk and Eugenia Grasberg; m. Hilary Koprowski, July 14, 1938; children: Claude, Christopher. BA, Popielewska/Roszkowska, Warsaw, 1934; MD, Warsaw U., 1939. Cert. Am. Bd. Pathology, Internat. Bd. Cytology. Intern in medicine Villejuif Lunatic Asylum, Seine, France, 1940; asst. pathologist Rio De Janeiro City Hosp., Miguel Couto, Brazil, 1942-44; rsch. fellow dept. pathology Cornell U. Med. Coll., N.Y.C., 1945-46, rsch. asst. dept. pharmacology, 1949-50, rsch. fellow dept. of anatomy, 1949-54; rsch. fellow applied immunology Pub. Health Rsch. Inst. of The City of N.Y., 1946-47; asst. pathologist N.Y. Infirmary for Women and Children, N.Y.C., 1947-49; asst. prof. dept. pathology SUNY Downstate Med. Ctr., N.Y.C., 1954-57; assoc. prof. pathology, dir. cytology lab./Sch. Cytotech. Hahnemann Med. Coll., Phila., 1957-64, prof. pathology dir. cytology lab., sch. cytotechnology, 1964-70; prof. pathology, dir. cytology lab. Temple U. Sch. Med., Phila., 1970-87, prof. emerita, 1987—; cons. WHO, Switzerland, Egypt, Iran, Latin Am., India, 1960-85, Armed Forces Inst. Pathology, Air Force Cytology Rescreen Project, 1979-80. Contbr. articles on cancer rsch. to profl. and sci. jours. Named Woman Physician of Yr., Polish Am. Med. Assn., 1977; grantee USPHS-Nat. Cancer Insts., 1954-75, rsch. grantee Bender Co., Vienna, Austria, 1983-89. Fellow Am. Soc. Clin. Pathologists (emeritus), Coll. Am. Pathologists (emeritus), Coll. Physicians of Phila., Internat. Acad. Cytology (hon.), Internat. Acad. Pathology (emeritus); mem. Am. Assn. for Cancer Rsch. Inc. (emeritus), Am. Assn. Pathologists Inc. (emeritus), Am. Med. Women's Assn., Am. Soc. Cytology (life, Papanicolaou award 1985), Am. Soc. Exptl. Pathology, Argentinian Soc. Cytology (hon.), Path. Soc. Phila. Home: 334 Fairhill Rd Wynnewood PA 19096-1804

KORANDO, DONNA KAY, journalist; b. Chester, Ill., Mar. 31, 1950; d. Samuel L. and Dorothy L. (Meyer) K.; m. James J. Heidenry, Nov. 28, 1981; children: Reid Samuel, Rachel. BA, So. Ill. U., 1972; MSL, Yale U., 1980. Tchr. journalism Lincoln High Sch., Manitowoc, Wis., 1972-73; copy editor St. Louis Post-Dispatch, 1973-77, editorial writer, 1977-86, editor commentary page, 1986—. Mem. Lafayette Square Restoration Com., St. Louis, 1981—. Mem. Assn. Opinion Page Editors (pres.), Media Club of St. Louis. Roman Catholic. Office: St Louis Post Dispatch 900 N Tucker Blvd Saint Louis MO 63101-1069*

KORBY, BETH ANDREA, pediatric occupational therapist; b. Detroit, Apr. 20, 1964; d. Albert R. and Nancy J. (Jacobs) K. BS in Occupational Therapy, Ea. Mich. U., 1987; postgrad., NYU, 1994—. Registered occupational therapist. Staff therapist Hinsdale (Ill.) Hosp., 1988-91; pediatric clin. specialist Rush-Presbyn.-St. Luke's Med. Ctr., Chgo., 1991-94; instr., faculty Rush U., Chgo., 1992-94; teaching fellow NYU, N.Y.C., 1994—; contract occupational therapist Therapists Unltd., N.Y.C., 1994—; per diem therapist Children's Meml. Home Health Care, Deerfield, Ill., 1992-94, pediatric study group, Chgo., 1991-94. Mem., co-v.p. Hadassah Health Profl. Group, Chgo., 1992-94. Grantee U. Ill. Partnership Project, 1993. Mem. Am. Occupational Therapy Assn., Neurodevelopmental Treatment Assn., Sigma Delta Tau Alumnus. Jewish.

KORCHA, LYNDA LEE, educator; b. Wichita, Kans., June 19, 1952; d. Rodney Roy and Gloria June (Ross) Brosius; m. Brian Eugene McClintock, Dec. 19, 1976 (div. 1984); children: Ericka Lynn, Malinda Angeline, Alexis Antoinette; m. Kyle Anthony Korcha, July 15, 1989. AA, Antelope Valley Jr. Coll., Lancaster, Calif., 1972; BS in Kinesiology, UCLA, 1974; postgrad., Calif. State U., Chico, 1976. Recreation leader/coach L.A. County Parks and Recreation, Lancaster, Calif., summers 1972-74; trach coach Paradise (Calif.) Unified Sch. Dist., 1975-76; tchr./coach Fall River (Calif.) Joint Unified Sch. Dist., 1976-79, Morongo Unified Sch. Dist., 29 Palms, Calif., 1979-84, Palm Springs (Calif.) Unified Sch. Dist., 1984-91, Eddy Middle Sch., Columbus, Ga., 1991—; dept. coord. phys. edn. Nellie N. Coffman Middle Sch., Cathedral City, 1988-91. Recipient Exemplary Teaching award Nellie N. Coffman Middle Sch., 1990. Mem. NEA, Calif. Tchrs. Assn., UCLA Alumni Assn., Calif. Assn. Health, Phys. Edn. and Recreation, Alpha Chi Omega. Republican. Presbyterian. Home: 5421 Susan Ln Columbus GA 31907-4269 Office: Eddy Middle Sch 2100 S Lumpkin Rd Columbus GA 31903-2730

KORCINSKY, CHRISTINE, accountant; b. Greenville, Pa., May 2, 1967. BSBA in Acctg., Gannon U., 1989. CPA. Office asst. Gannon U., Erie, Pa., 1985-86, Dormitory asst. Porter Hall, 1986-87, lab. asst. computer ctr., 1987-88; acct. intern DeMarco Wachter & Co., Erie, Pa., 1988-89, staff acct., 1989-90; supr., mgr. Pashke Twargowski & Lee, Erie, Pa., 1990—; office mgr. Cardo Elec., Erie, Pa., 1991—; bookkeeper asst., computer specialist YWCA, Meadville, Pa., summers 1987, 88. Bessemer scholar, 1985-88. Mem AICPA, Pa. Inst. CPA's (organizer govtl. edn. courses 1992, coord. mentor program 1992—), Inst. Mgmt. Accts., Pannbriar Athletic Club.

KORDELSKI, KATHLEEN MARIA, psychiatric-mental health nurse; b. Abington, Pa., Aug. 25, 1953; d. Edward Alexander Kordelski and Clare Joan (Howlett) Hilbert; m. Stephen Fendelman, Oct. 7, 1977; children: Sara Larissa Fendelman, Melissa Anne Fendelman. Diploma in nursing, Med. Coll. of Pa., 1977. RN cert.; cert. in psychiat. and mental health nursing ANA, chem. dependency nursing RN, Chem. Dependency Nat. Consortium of Chem. Dependency Nurses. Staff nurse Eugenia Hosp., Lafayette Hills, Pa., 1984-86; charge nurse Chestnut Hill Hosp., Phila., 1986-88; charge nurse Horsham Clinic, Ambler, Pa., 1988-90, nursing coord., 1988-90, program adminstr. adult II dual diagnosis svc., 1992—, program adminstr. adult psychiatry svc., 1993—, program adminstr. short term assessment and treatment svc., 1993—, clin. dir. inpatient svcs., 1994—, dir. adult treatment svcs. inpatient and partial hosps., 1995—; presenter FHC Hosp. Pan Americano, P.R., 1991. HIV-AIDS cert. instr. ARC, 1992. Mem. Drug and Alcohol Nurses Assn. (bd. dirs. 1991-93, membership com. chairperson 1991—, nat. conf. com. chair 1994), Nat. Consortium Chem. Dependency Nurses, Am. Psychiat. Nurses Assn. Democrat. Office: Horsham Clinic 722 E Butler Pike Ambler PA 19002-2310

KOREMAN, DOROTHY GOLDSTEIN, physician, dermatologist; b. Bklyn., Nov. 1, 1940; d. Benjamin and Ida (Krenick) Goldstein; m. Neil M. Koreman, Aug. 16, 1964; children: Elizabeth Koreman Landau, Robert Stephen. BA, Bklyn. Coll., 1961; MD, SUNY, Bklyn., 1965. Diplomate Am. Bd. Dermatology. Intern pediatrics Kings County Hosp. Ctr., Bklyn., 1965-66; resident dept. dermatology Wayne State U. Sch. Medicine, Detroit, 1966-69; clin. instr. dermatology Sch. Medicine Wayne State U., Detroit, 1969-71; asst. clin. prof. dermatology U. Miami, 1971-75, assoc. clin. prof. dermatology, 1975-82, clin. prof. dermatology and cutaneous surgery, 1982—; chief of staff Ami Palmetto Gen. Hosp., Hialeah, 1990-91. Mem. North Dade bd. dirs. Greater Miami Jewish Fedn., 1975—. Mem. Miami Dermatol. Soc. (pres. 1978-79). Office: 7100 W 20th Ave Ste 107 Hialeah FL 33016-1813

KORETZ, JANE FAITH, biophysicist; b. N.Y.C., Aug. 12, 1947; d. Norman Joseph and Natalie (Cromer) K. BA with high honors, Swarthmore Coll., 1969; PhD in Biophysics, U. Chgo., 1974. Postdoctoral fellow MRC Cell Biophysics Unit King's Coll., London, 1974-76; rsch. assoc. Coll. Med. and Dentistry of N.J., Newark, 1976-77; asst. prof. dept. biology Rensselaer Poly. Inst., Troy, N.Y., 1977-83; assoc. prof. Rensselaer Poly. Inst., Troy, 1983-90, prof., 1990—; assoc. dir. ctr. for biophysics Dept. Biology Rensselaer Poly. Inst., Troy, 1989-91; dir., 1991—, head biochemistry and biophysics program, 1992—; cons. in field; reviewer NIH, 1989—, NSF, 1977—. Contbr. articles to profl. jours. Reader, program producer RISE, Schenectady, N.Y., 1984-91. Fellowship Muscular Dystrophy Assn., 1974-76; grantee Nat. Eye Inst.; Fulbright scholarship Ctr. for Internat. Exchange of Scholars, 1991; recipient Henry Fukui Travel award Nat. Found for Eye Rsch., 1989. Mem. Assn. for Women in Sci., Internat. Soc. for Eye Rsch., Optical Soc. Am., Am. Soc. Biochemistry and Molecular Biology, Biophys. Soc. (coun. mem. 1988-91), Assn. for Rsch. in Vision and Ophthalmology. Office: Ctr for Biophysics/Biology Rensselaer Poly Instit Troy NY 12180

KORN, IRENE ELIZABETH, elementary education educator, consultant; b. Wellston, Mo., May 28, 1937; d. Nicholas Anthony and Myrtle Marie (Knowles) Kuntz; m. Dale Stanley Korn, Sept. 12, 1959; children: Kurt Lawrence, Kenneth Dale, Nancy Ann. BS in Edn., U. Mo., St. Louis, 1969, MS in Edn., 1972, MS in Spl. Edn., 1985. Cert. K-12 reading, social studies tchr., learning disabilities, behavior disorders, Mo. Elem. tchr. N.W. R-1 Sch. Dist., House Springs, Mo., 1969—; tchr. cons. geography program adv. coun. U. Mo., 1989—, Advanced Summer Inst., summer 1990; writer test items Mo. Mastery Achievement Test, fall 1990; mem. social studies work group to write state stds. edn. Mo. Dept. Elem. and Sec. Edn., 1994. Named Woman of Yr., George Khoury Baseball Leagues, St. Louis, 1987. Mem. ASCD, Nat. Coun. Social Studies, Nat. Coun. for Geographic Edn., Am. Geographical Soc., Mo. Tchrs. Assn. (professorial rights and responsibilities com. 1987-91, pres. N.W. 1984-86), Mo. Coun. Social Studies, Jefferson County Dist. Edn. Assn. (pres.-elect 1988-89, 91-92), Mo. Geog. Alliance (steering com. 1991—, chmn. elem. curriculum materials 1991-92, tchr. cons. Columbia 1988—, Advanced Inst. P.R. 1992), Phi Delta Kappa. Home: 37 Black Oak Ln Fenton MO 63026-3409

KORNBLEET, LYNDA MAE, insulation, fireproofing and acoustical contractor; b. Kansas City, Kans., June 15, 1951; d. Seymore Gerald Kornbleet and Jacqueline F. (Hurst) Kornbleet Malka. BA, U. St. Thomas, Houston, 1979. Lic. real estate salesperson; cert. women/disadvantaged bus. enterprise, City of Houston, 1985, Dallas/Fort Worth Airport. Temporary counselor Lyman's Personnel, Houston, 1974-75; real estate salesperson Coldwell Banker, Houston, 1975-77; sales, office mgr. Acme Insulation, Dallas, also Houston, 1977-79; owner, pres. Payless Insulation, Houston, 1979—; contractor City of Houston, 1985—. Bd. dirs. Disadvantaged Bus. Cert. State of Tex., 1989—; vender Houston Bus. Coun. Named Contractor of the Yr., Sears Home Improvement, 1988; active Houston Ind. Sch. Dist., 1989—. Awarded and completed acoustical treatment of Astrodome for Rep. Nat. Conv. 1992. Mem. Insulation Contractors Assn Am., Nat. Assn. Remodeling Industry (bd. dirs. Houston 1982-84), Houston Air Conditioning Coun. (bd. dirs. 1982-83), Cellulose Insulation Contractors (chmn. Houston 1981-82), Houston Bus. Coun., 1987-88, Insulation Contractors Assn. Greater Houston (pres. 1991—). Democrat. Jewish. Avocations: bridge, golf, baseball. Office: Payless Insulation 207 Reinerman St Houston TX 77007-7228

KORNBLIT, SANDRA COHEN, lawyer; b. Bronx, N.Y., July 15, 1949; d. Theodore and Ethel Hass Cohen; m. Mitchell L. Kornblit, June 24, 1973; 1 child, Elizabeth Ann. BA, Goucher Coll., 1971; JD, Hofstra U., 1974. Bar: N.Y. Assoc. Gottesman Wolgel & Smith, N.Y.C., 1974-78, 81-82, Rycken Burlian & Houben, Brussels, 1978-81; v.p., corp. counsel ITOCHU Internat. Inc., N.Y.C., 1982—. Mem. Assn. Bar of the City of N.Y., Am. Corp. Counsel. Republican. Office: ITOCHU International Inc 335 Madison Ave New York NY 10017

KORNEL, ESTHER, psychologist; b. Basel-Stadt, Switzerland, Dec. 16, 1928; came to U.S., 1958; d. Salomon and Perla (Muller) Muhlrad; m. Ludwig Kornel, May 27, 1952; children: Ezriel Edward, Amiel Mark. BA, Roosevelt U., 1971, MA, 1973; PsyD, Ill. Sch. Profl. Psychology, 1979. Fellow and diplomate Am. Bd. Med. Psychologists. Clin. psychologist Luth. Gen. Hosp., Park Ridge, Ill., 1973-74; unit coordinator Luth. Gen. Hosp., Park Ridge, 1974-82; pvt. practice psychologist Des Plaines, Ill., 1974—; clin. assoc. Dept. Psychiatry, Abraham Lincoln Sch. Medicine, U. Ill., 1974-82; cons. oncology, group leader oncology staff Luth. Gen. Hosp., 1975-82, coord. psychology tng., 1981-82; group leader mastectomy counseling project, Northwestern U. Cancer Ctr., Chgo., 1981-82; clin. tng. cons. Forest Inst. Profl. Psychology, Des Plaines, Ill., 1985-90. Mem. Amnesty Internat., N.Y.C., Women's Am. Orgn. for Rehab. through Tng., N.Y.C., Women's Internat. Zionist Orgn., N.Y.C., Common Cause, Washington. Recipient Experimental Family Therapist award Inst. Juv. Research State of Ill., 1984. Mem. Am. Psychol. Assn., Assn. for Advancement of Psychology, Am. Soc. Clin. and Exptl. Hypnosis (assoc.),. Democrat. Jewish. Office: Landings Profl Ctr 2604 Dempster Ste 409 Des Plaines IL 60016

KORNREICH, SHARON, art therapist, educator; b. Queens, N.Y., Apr. 20, 1963; d. Ivan and Bernice Martha (Hilsenrath) K. BA, CUNY, 1985; Master of profl. studies, Pratt Inst., 1987. Recreation leader Eastchester Park Nursing Home, Bronx, N.Y., 1982-86; recreation/art therapist Manhattan Psychiat. Ctr., N.Y.C., 1986-87; asst. dir. recreation therapy New Rochelle (N.Y.) Hosp., 1989; art therapist, group therapist N.Y. Psychotherapy & Counseling Ctr., Queens, 1987-91; assoc. dir. activities therapy Dewitt Nursing Home, N.Y.C., 1990-91; art educator, therapist N.Y.C. Bd. Edn./Pub. Sch. 12 Community Day Hosp., Bronx, 1991—; art educator Academies Program (Drug Prevention), Bronx, 1993. Mem. Am. Art Therapy Assn., N.Y. Art Therapy Assn. (program coord. 1988-90). Home: 26426 Langston Ave Floral Park NY 11004-1043 Office: PS 12 Community Day Hosp 2555 Tratman Ave Bronx NY 10461-3460

KORSGAARD, CHRISTINE MARION, philosophy educator; b. Chgo., Apr. 9, 1952; d. Albert and Marion Hangaard (Kortbek) K.; m. Timothy David Gould, June 1980 (div. Sept. 1984). BA, U. Ill., 1974; PhD, Harvard U., 1981. Instr. Yale U., New Haven, 1979-80; asst. prof. U. Calif., Santa Barbara, 1980-83; from asst. prof. to prof. U. Chgo., 1983-91; prof. Harvard U., Cambridge, Mass., 1991—; vis. assoc. prof. Berkeley, 1989, UCLA, 1990; Tanner lectr. human values, 1992. Contbr. book chpts., articles to profl. jours. Whiting fellow, 1978-79. Mem. Am. Philos. Assn., N.Am. Kant Soc., Hume Soc., Am. Soc. for Polit. and Legal Philosophy.

KORSHAK, YVONNE, art historian; b. Chgo., May 30, 1936; d. Donald Korshak and Irma B. Jaffe; m. Robert J. Ruben; 1 child, Karin. BA cum laude, Radcliffe Coll., Cambridge, Mass., 1958; MA, U. Calif. Berkeley, 1966; PhD, U. Calif., 1973. Asst. prof. U. Md., College Park, 1972-74, Fordham U., N.Y.C., 1974-75; from asst. prof. to prof. Adelphi U., Garden City, N.Y., 1975—, chairperson Dept. Art and Art History, 1978-81, dir. honors program, dir. mus. studies, 1979—; project dir. seminar on the modern condition NEH, 1990. Author: Frontal Faces in Attic Vase Painting, 1987, co-editor: Selections from Permanent Collection, 1983. Recipient Pres.'s award for excellence in teaching, 1990. Mem. Coll. Art Assn. Am., Archaeological Inst. Am., Long Island Art Historians Assn., American Soc. for Eighteenth Century Studies, American Philological Assn. Office: Adelphi U Dept Art And History Garden City NY 11530

KORTH, CHARLOTTE BROOKS, furniture and interior design firm executive; b. Milw.; d. Lewis C. and Marguerite Peil Brooks; m. Robert Lee Williams, Jr., Oct. 25, 1944 (dec.); children: Patricia Williams, Melissa Williams O'Rourke, Brooks Williams; m. Fred Korth, Aug. 23, 1980. Student, U. Wis., 1941. Owner Charlotte's Inc., El Paso, Tex., 1951—, chmn., CEO, 1979—; pres. Paso del Norte Design, Inc., El Paso, 1978-81, 83—; mem. adv. com. for interior design program El Paso C.C., 1981—; mem. adv. bd. Southwest Design Inst., 1982—; ptnr. Wilko Partnership, 1981—; mem. adv. bd. Mountain Bell Telephone Co., 1976-79; mem. Sch. Architecture Found. Adv. Coun. U. Tex. Austin, 1985-91. Charter mem. Com. of 200, 1982—, Nat. Mus. Women in the Arts, 1985—; mem. Renaissance 400, El Paso, El Paso Women's Symphony Guild, El Paso Mus. Art. Recipient of Silver plaque Gifts and Decorative Accessories Mag., 1978; named Woman of Yr. by El Paso Am. Bus. Women's Assn., 1978, Outstanding Woman of Yr. by Women's Polit. Caucus, 1979. Mem. Am. Soc. Interior Designers (bd. dirs. Tex. chpt. 1977-82), El Paso Women's C. of C. (hon.), El Paso C. of C. (dir. 1976-82), Coronado Country Club (El Paso), Internat. Club (El Paso), Santa Teresa Country Club (N.Mex.). Avocations: travel, antiques, collectibles. Home: 6041 Torrey Pines El Paso TX 79912-6041 also: 4200 Massachusetts Ave # 101 Washington DC 20016 Office: Charlotte's Inc 5411 N Mesa St El Paso TX 79912-5420

KORTH, PENNE PERCY, ambassador; b. Hattiesburg, Miss., Nov. 3, 1942; m. Fritz-Alan Korth, Dec. 15, 1965; children: Fritz Jr., Maria, James. Student, U. Tex. Sr. Washington assoc., client liaison and rep. trust and estate div. Sotheby's, 1986-89; amb. to Mauritius, Port Louis, 1989-92; pres., CEO Firestone and Korth Ltd., Washington, 1993—; bd. dirs. Chevy Chase Bank. bd. dirs. Chevy Chase Bank, Meridian Internat. Ctr., Coun. of Am. Ambs., Van Cliburn Found. Co-chmn. Am. Bicentennial Presdl. Inauguration, 1988-89; mem. Meridian Internat. Ctr. Mem. Coun. Am. Ambassadors, Van Cliburn Found., Sulgrave Club, Chevy Chase Club. Office: Firestone and Korth Ltd 1910 24th St NW Washington DC 20008-1635

KORTH, SALLY KATHLEEN, nurse, technology specialist; b. Detroit, June 11, 1950; d. John Francis and Bertha Marie (Oleyar) K.; m. Douglas Lee McDonnell, May 7, 1977; children: Patricia, Lucas, Rose. ADN, Kalamazoo Valley C.C., 1976; BS, Western Mich. U., 1977. Cert. emergency nurse, advanced cardiac life support. Emergency dept. staff nurse Borgess Med. Ctr., Kalamazoo, 1973-77, clin. nurse preceptor emergency dept., 1981-93, info. tech. specialist, 1993—; emergency dept. staff nurse Conway (S.C.) Gen. Hosp., 1979-81; optical imaging task force chair Borgess Med. Ctr., Kalamazoo, 1993—. Contbr. articles to profl. jours. Leader sibling support group Compassionate Friends, Kalamazoo, 1989-92; computer tutor, leader Kalamazoo Pub. Schs., 1988-94; peer team mem. Critical Incident Stress Debriefing Team, Kalamazoo, 1989-94. Recipient Outstanding Vol. Svc. award Bd. of Edn., Kalamazoo, 1989. Mem. NOW, Emergency Nurses Assn., Mich. Nurses Assn., Kalamazoo Inst. of Arts. Office: Borgess Med Ctr 1521 Gull Rd Kalamazoo MI 49001-1640

KORWIN, LISA, social services administrator; b. N.Y.C., Oct. 31, 1959; d. Bert and Barbara (Levine) K. BA, SUNY, Oswego, 1981; MPA, Calif. State U., Hayward, 1992. Exec. dir. A Safe Place, Oakland, Calif., 1982-86; program developer ECHO Housing, Hayward, Calif., 1986-90; exec. dir. Echo Housing, Hayward, Calif., 1990-92; orgnl. cons. The Ctr. Applied Local Rsch., Richmond, Calif., 1992—. Active Alameda County Battered Women's Network, Calif., 1985; bd. mem. No. Calif. Battered Women's Coalition, 1986; chair Alameda County Homeless Coalition, 1987. Democrat. Jewish.

KORY, MARIANNE GREENE, lawyer; b. N.Y.C.; d. Hyman Louis and Belle (Rome) Greene; children: Erich Marcel, Lisa. BA, CCNY; JD, N.Y. Law Sch., 1976; LLM in Law and Marine Affairs, U. Wash., 1986. Bar: Ohio 1977, D.C. 1979, N.Y. 1983, Vt. 1994, U.S. Dist. Ct. (so. and ea. dists.) N.Y. 1983. Hearing examiner Ohio Bd. Employee Compensation, Columbus, 1977; atty. advisor Office Hearings and Appeals, Social Security Adminstrn., Cin. and N.Y.C., 1977-78; gen. atty. labor Office of Solicitor, U.S. Dept. of Labor, N.Y.C., 1978-82; sole practice, N.Y.C., 1983-89, Seattle, 1989-91, Burlington, Vt., 1994—. Founder Cin. chpt. Amnesty Internat., 1977. Alvin Johnson fellow. Mem. Phi Beta Kappa. Office: 3 Northshore Dr Burlington VT 05401

KORZELIUS, LINDA DIANE, church lay worker, financial specialist, artist; b. Teaneck, N.J., June 8, 1955; d. Joseph Robertson and Beatrice (Hoyt) K. BFA, Ramapo Coll. N.J., 1977. Mem. parish coun. and pastor's adv. coun. St. Joseph's Ch., Oradell, New Milford, N.J., 1985—; eucharistic min., mem. various coms. St. Joseph's Ch., Oradell/New Milford, N.J., 1985—; catechist St. Joseph's Ch., Oradell/New Milford, 1985-87, St. Theresa Ch., Cresskill, N.J., 1987—; chairperson spiritual life com. St. Joseph Ch., Oradell, New Milford, 1991—; loan payoff specialist Alliance Funding Co., Montvale, N.J., 1990-91; asst. to treas. Yegen Assocs., Paramus, N.J., 1991; accounts receivable dept. clk. Mokrynski & Assocs., Hackensack, N.J., 1993—; instr. Christian Founds. for Ministry Program Archdiocese of Newark, 1993. Exhibiting artist, 1973—. Mem. Ladies of Knights Bowling League (pres. Northvale, N.J. club 1991—). Home: 153 River Rd New Milford NJ 07646-1703

KOSHLAND, MARIAN ELLIOTT, immunologist, educator; b. New Haven, Oct. 25, 1921; d. Waller Watkins and Margaret Ann (Smith) Elliott; m. Daniel Edward Koshland, Jr., May 25, 1945; children: Ellen R., Phyllis A., James M., Gail F., Douglas E. B.A., Vassar Coll., 1942, M.S., 1943; Ph.D., U. Chgo., 1949. Research asst. Manhattan Dist. Atomic Bomb Project, 1945-46; fellow dept. bacteriology Harvard Med. Sch., 1949-51; asso. bacteriologist biology dept. Brookhaven Nat. Lab., 1952-62, bacteriologist, 1963-65; assoc. research immunologist virus lab. U. Calif., Berkeley, 1965-69, lectr. dept. molecular biology, 1966-70, prof. dept. microbiology and immunology, 1970-89, chmn. dept., 1982-89, prof. dept. molecular and cell biology, 1989—; mem. Nat. Sci. Bd., 1976-82; mem. adv. com. to dir. NIH, 1972-75; mem. coun. Nat. Inst. Allergy and Infectious Diseases NIH, 1991—. Contbr. articles to profl. jours. Mem. NAS, Nat. Acad. Arts and Scis., Am. Acad. Microbiology, Am. Assn. Immunologists (pres. 1982-1983), Am. Soc. Biol. Chemists. Home: 3991 Happy Valley Rd Lafayette CA 94549-2423 Office: U Calif Dept Molecular/Cell Biology 439 LSA Berkeley CA 94720

KOSINSKY, BARBARA TIMM, librarian; b. St. Louis, July 4, 1942; d. Paul E. and Virginia L. (Borcherding) T.; m. John P. Kosinsky, July 25, 1964; children: James Alan, Bethany Anne. BS in Edn., Concordia Coll., River Forest, Ill., 1964; BA in Computer Sci., North Cen. Coll., Naperville, Ill., 1986; MLS, SUNY, Buffalo, 1972. Cert. tchr., Ill., N.Y. Tchr. St. Paul Luth. Sch., North Tonawanda, N.Y., 1964-67; libr. Trinity Luth. Sch., West Seneca, N.Y., 1971-80, North Cen. Coll., Naperville, 1981-89; regional mktg. rep. Online Computer Libr. Ctr., Dublin, Ohio, 1990—; free-lance writer West Seneca and Naperville, 1978—. Contbr. articles to religious mags. and general interest publs. Mem. ALA, Am. Soc. Info. Sci., Nat. Writers Club, Wis. Libr. Assn. Home: 225 Carlin Ct Hartland WI 53029 Office: PO Box 138 Hartland WI 53029

KOSKI, JENNIFER LYNCH, finance educator; b. Madison, Wis., Jan. 15, 1961; d. Wayne Montgomery and Carolyn Sue (Andrew) Lynch; m. Mark Ray Koski, Aug. 19, 1990; 1 child, Helen Maija. BS magna cum laude, Brown U., 1983; MBA, Harvard U., 1987; PhD, Stanford U., 1991. Analyst Goldman, Sachs & Co., N.Y.C., 1983-85; assoc. Brown Bros. Harriman &

Co., N.Y.C., 1985; asst. prof. fin. U. Washington Sch. Bus. Adminstrn., Seattle, 1991—. Mem. Am. Fin. Assn., Western Fin. Assn., Phi Beta Kappa. Office: Univ Washington Dept Finance Dj # 10 Seattle WA 98195

KOSLOW, SALLY, editor-in-chief. Editor-in-chief McCall's mag., N.Y.C., 1994—. Office: McCalls 110 Fifth Ave New York NY 10011*

KOSS, ROSABEL STEINHAUER, retired educator; b. Phila., Sept. 3, 1913; d. Arthur H. and Agnes (Temple) Steinhauer; m. Franklyn C. Koss, July 6, 1947 (dec. 1987); children: C. Lynn Knauff, Susan Kreiner, Carolyn Ruef, Rosalind Diehl. BS, Trenton State Coll., 1935; MA, Teachers Coll., N.Y.C., 1942; DEd, Columbia U., 1964. Cert. health edn. specialist, 1989. Supr. health and phys. edn. Flemington (N.J.) Pub. Schs., 1935-37; tchr. health and phys. edn. Ridgewood (N.J.) High Sch., 1937-40, Passaic Valley Regional High Sch., Little Falls, N.J., 1940-48; asst. prof. Montclair State Coll., Upper Montclair, N.J., 1958-61, Upsala Coll., East Ornge, N.J., 1964-71; assoc. to full prof. Ramapo Coll of N.J., Mahwah, N.J., 1971-84; dir. tchr. edn. Ramapo Coll of N.J., Mahwah, 1974-79, prof. emeritus, 1985; adj. prof. Stockton State Coll., Pomona, N.J., 1985—; asst. sport attachee Royal Swedish Embassy, N.Y.C., 1964-74. Author: (with others) Dance for Older Adults, 1988, Mature Stuff. Physical Activity for Older Adults, 1989; contbr. articles profl. jours. Mem. Little Falls (N.J.) Bd. Edn., 1954-63, N.J. Commn. on Aging, 1991; trustee, treas. Bergen County (N.J.) Ret. Sr. Vol. Program, 1979-84; mem. recreation adv. com. Stone Harbor Bd. Health; mem. Cape May County Freeholders Adv. Commn. on Women, 1986—, Cape May County Human Svcs. Adv. Coun., 1989—; del. White House Conf. on Aging, 1995; vestrywoman St. Mary's Episcopal Ch., Stone Harbor. Recipient Work Study grants to Sweden The Royal Swedish consulate, 1968, 70, 72, Athletic Alumni Women's award Trenton State Coll., 1976, State of N.J. Senate and Gen. Assembly citation, 1994; named to Trenton State Coll. Alumni Athletic Hall of Fame, 1987, Seneca Falls Women's Hall of Fame, 1994, Nat. Women's Hall of Fame, 1994; named Gerontologist of Yr. Soc. on Aging N.J., 1993; Rosabel Koss ann. award in her honor AAPHERD. Mem. Am. Alliance Health, Phys. Edn., Recreation and Dance (life mem., profl. achievement award, N.J., 1973, honor award fellow 1979, merit award Ea. Dist. 1980, coun. on aging and adult devel.), Gerontol. Soc. N.J. (parliamentarian 1988-89), AAUW, Nat. Coun. on the Aging, Assn. Gerontology in Higher Edn., Internat. Soc. of Comparative Phys. Edn. and Sport, Cape May County LWV, Garden Club, Wetlands Isnt. (docent). Home: 150 91st St Stone Harbor NJ 08247-2016

KOSTAKOS, CASS CHRISTY, computer consultant; b. Miami, Fla., Oct. 16, 1967; d. Kenneth Constantine and Marcia Kay (Loy) K. BA in Polit. Sci. summa cum laude, Fla. Internat. U., 1993. Asst. mgr. Mishawaka Canoe Supplies, Chgo., 1984-86; computer cons. Ctr. for Instrl. Tech., North Miami, Fla., 1991—; asst. mgr. Ednl. Equipment Media, North Miami, 1992. Mem. Amnesty Internat., Greenpeace, Phi Kappa Phi.

KOSTAS, ELENA MARIE, industrial engineer; b. San Diego, July 24, 1961; d. Gregory Nicholas and Dorothy Anastasia (Stavros) K. BSME, Calif. Poly, 1984; MBA, U. Redlands, 1992. Cert. integrated resource mgmt. Mfg. activity assoc. Solar Turbines, Inc., San Diego, 1984-86, design engr., 1986-87, sr. indsl. engr., 1987—. Fund raising account rep. United Way/Chad, San Diego, 1993, 94; facilitator, trainer Inroads, Inc., San Diego, 1994. Mem. Am. Prodn. and Inventory Control Soc., Solar Teaming Coun., Pi Tau Sigma (life), Tau Beta Pi (life). Home: 14891 Summerbreeze Way San Diego CA 92128 Office: Solar Turbines Inc 2200 Pacific Hwy San Diego CA 92101

KOSTER, ELAINE LANDIS, publishing executive; b. N.Y.C.. BA, Barnard Coll., 1962. Exec. v.p., pub. Dutton Signet, N.Y.C., now exec. v.p., pub.; also sr. v.p. Penguin USA, N.Y.C. Office: Dutton Signet 375 Hudson New York NY 10014-3672

KOT, MARTA VIOLETTE, artist, art educator; b. Hartford, Conn., Nov. 27, 1963; d. Edward Anthony and Maria Czermak Kot. BA in Graphic Design/Art, Ctrl Conn. State U., 1985, MS in Adminstrn., Supervision and Curriculum Devel., 1988; cert. in Polish art history, Jagiellonian U., Cracow, Poland, 1988; MA in Studio Art and Environ. Art, NYU, 1990; student, Acad. de la Grande Chaumiere, Paris, 1990-92; cert. French lang. and Civilization, U. Paris - Sorbonne, 1992; cert. Polish lang., Cath. U. of Lublin, Poland, 1993; postgrad., Columbia U., 1994—. Art cons. gifted and talented programs Consol. Sch. Dist. of City of New Britain, Conn., 1987-88; pvt. art tchr. Studio of Antoine Camilleri, Valletta, Malta, 1985, Studio of Zbylut Grzywacz, Cracow, 1988, Studio of Adam Wsiotkoswki, Cracow, 1988; selected participant Internat. Student Exch. Program, Georgetown U., Washington, 1985, host country Malta-Royal U. of Malta. One woman shows include 80 Washington Sq. East Galleries, N.Y.C., 1990; exhibited in group shows at Ctrl. Conn. State U., New Britain, 1982, 85, 87, 88, Slocumb Gallery, Tenn., 1985, Macy Art Gallery, N.Y., 1994, Columbia U., N.Y., 1994. Corp. mem. Boys and Girls Club, New Britain; bd. dirs. Camp Schade Program Affiliated United Way, New Britain. Recipient award for graphic design Advt. Club Greater Hartford, 1984. Home: PO Box 2697 New Britain CT 06050-2697

KOTAKIS, KATHLEEN THERESA, wholesale industrial and commercial distributor; b. Bronx, N.Y., Feb. 6, 1962; d. George and Mary Grace (Ruddy) K. BBA, Baruch Coll., 1987. Sales assoc. Met. Mus. Art, N.Y.C., 1982-85, sales supr., 1985-87; account exec. Leslie Supply, N.Y.C., 1987-88; sales rep. Grainger Inc., N.Y.C., 1988-89, market specialist, 1989-90, sales tng. supr., 1990-91, nat. accounts mgr., 1991—. Democrat. Roman Catholic. Office: Grainger Inc 1930 Eastchester Rd Bronx NY 10470

KOTARA, PAMELA KATHERINE, accountant; b. Karnes City, Tex., Feb. 4, 1955; d. Vincent Francis and Joyce (Heinen) Liska; m. Louis Francis Kotara, July 17, 1953; children: Kristen Rachelle, Duane Francis. BBA, U. Tex., 1976. CPA, Tex.; CIA; CFE. Sr. mgr. audit KPMG Peat Marwick, San Antonio, 1977-89; dir. acctg. policy USAA, San Antonio, 1989-90, exec. dir. acctg. policy, 1990-92, exec. dir. internal audit, 1992—. Treas. Boy Scout Troop 157, San Antonio, 1994—. Mem. AICPA, Tex. Soc. CPAs (mem. com. chair 1984-89, Young CPA of Yr. 1989), Inst. Internal Auditors, Inst. Mgmt. Accts., Assn. Cert. Fraud Examiners. Home: 8426 Littleport San Antonio TX 78239

KOTCHER, SHIRLEY J. W., lawyer; b. Bklyn.; d. Irving and Violet (Miller) Weinberg; m. Harry A. Kotcher; children: Leslie Susan, Dana Anne. BA, NYU; JD, Columbia U. Bar: N.Y. In-house counsel Booth Meml. Med. Ctr., Flushing, N.Y., 1975-83, gen. counsel, 1983-91; v.p., gen. counsel The N.Y. Hosp. Med. Ctr. Queens (formerly Booth Mem. Med. Ctr.), 1991—; advisor health care Borough Pres. Queens, N.Y., 1978. Author: Hidden Gold and Pitfalls in New Tax Law, 1970. Mem. ABA (health law forum com.), Nat. Health Lawyers Assn., Am. Acad. Hosp. Attys., Am. Soc. Law and Medicine, Am. Soc. Health Care Risk Mgmt., Assn. for Hosp. Risk Mgmt. N.Y., Greater N.Y. Hosp. Assn. (legal adv. com. 1976—). Office: Booth Meml Med Ctr NY Hosp And Med Ctr Flushing NY 11355

KOTECKI, JOANNA KRYSTYNA EMERLE, parochial school educator; b. Chgo., Apr. 16, 1953; d. Joseph and Maria (Jazwinski) Emerle; m. Jeffrey David Kotecki, July 1, 1978; children: Andrew James, Elizabeth Anne. Student, U. Madrid, 1973-74; BA in Tchr. Edn. in Spanish, U. Ill., Chgo., 1974, MA in Hispanic Lit., 1980. Cert. 7-12 Spanish tchr., Conn. Tchr. Spanish, Elk Grove (Ill.) High Sch., 1975-79, Maine-Oakton-Niles (Ill.) Adult Continuing Edn., 1975-77; tchr. Spanish Brookfield (Conn.) High Sch., 1990-91; adj. instr. Sacred Heart U., Fairfield, Conn., 1980-82; tchr. Stratford (Conn.) Cath. Regional Sch. System, 1992-93, West Shore Mid. Sch., Milford, Conn., 1993—; translator, 1986—. Mem., corr. sec. Stratford Newcomers Club, 1980-88; rep. Internat. Hospitality Com., Fairfield County, Conn., 1985—; mem. hospitality com. Newtown (Conn.) Welcome Wagon, 1988-92, Head O'Meadow PTA, Newtown Middle Sch. PTA. Mem. Am. Translators Assn. (assoc.), Am. Coun. on Teaching Fgn. Langs. Roman Catholic. Home: 111 Head O'Meadow Rd Newtown CT 06470

KOTEFF, MARY ELIZABETH, accountant; b. Harvey, Ill., Oct. 14, 1965; d. Walter and Florence Leona (Walz) K. BS in Acctg., U. Fla., Gainesville, Fla., 1987; M in Acctg., Fla. Atlantic U., Boca Raton, Fla., 1988. CPA. Project acct. JC Penney Co., Plano, Tex., 1988-90; acctg. info. systems mgr. Mixit, divsn. JC Penney, Plano, Tex., 1990-91, fin. ctrl. mgr., 1991-94; acctg. mgr. custom decorating divsn. JC Penney, Plano, 1994—; total quality mgmt. tgn. leader JC Penney Co., Plano, Tex., 1993—; guest speaker East Tex. State U., 1994. Vol. acctg dept George Bush Re-election Campaign, Dallas, 1992; corp. coord. The Family Pl., Dallas, 1994; vol. Time for Dallas, 1994. Mem. Inst. Mgmt. Assts. (dir. advt. 1990-91 Stevenson trophy, dir. tech. programs 1991-92, dir. mem. 1992-93, dir. manuscripts, 1993-94, sec. 1994—,), JC Penney Running Club (treas. 1991-94), Retail Fin. Execs. Assn., Tex. Soc. CPA's (com. mem. 1994—). Republican. Roman Catholic. Home: 3883 Turtle Creek #312 Dallas TX 75219 Office: JC Penney Co 6501 Legacy Dr MS 5102 Plano TX 75024

KOTHERA, LYNNE MAXINE, clinical psychologist; b. Cleve., Dec. 18, 1938; d. Leonard Frank and Lillian (Shackleton) Kothera; m. Richard Litwin, Oct. 24, 1965. BA with hons., Denison U., Granville, Ohio, 1960; MA, NYU, 1983; PhD, L.I. U., Bklyn., 1989; postgrad. psychotherapy/psychoanalysis, NYU, 1992—. Dancer Martha Graham Dance Co., N.Y.C., 1961-62, Carmen DeLavallade Dance Co., N.Y.C., 1965-68, Glen Tetley Dance Co., N.Y.C., 1965-69; prin. dancer John Butler's, N.Y.C., 1971; artist-in-residence Boston High Schs. - Title III, 1969-71, Hobart-Smith Coll./Denison U., 1973; auditor N.Y. State Council of the Arts, N.Y.C., 1974-78; predoctoral fellow clin. psychology Yale-New Haven Hosp., 1987-88; postdoctoral fellow neuropsychology Inst. of Living, Hartford, Conn., 1989-91; with dept. rehab. medicine Mt. Sinai Med. Ctr., N.Y.C., 1991—. Mem. APA (divsn. 39, 40 and 42), Internat. Neuropsychol. Soc. Democrat. Home: 23 E 11th St New York NY 10003-4450 Office: Mt Sinai Med Ctr/Rehab Medicine 1 Gustave Levy Pl PO Box 1241 New York NY 10029

KOTKIN, LINDA SHARON, professional speaker; b. Bklyn., June 12, 1946; d. Louis and Claire (Weiss) K. BS, Cortland (N.Y.) U., 1968; MEd, Boston U., 1970; MBA, L.I. U., 1978. Tchr. math. Scituate (Mass.) Pub. Schs., 1968-71, Bellmore/Merrick (N.Y.) Pub. Schs., 1971-78; asst. store mgr. Richards, Miami, Fla., 1978-80; dir. tng. Jefferson Ward, Miami, Fla., 1980-87; mgr., tng. adminstr. Radio Shack, Ft. Worth, 1987—; prof. speaker Kotkin Comms., Ft. Worth, 1993—; cons. Stage West, Ft. Worth, 1989-93, United Way, Ft. Worth, 1989-91, Bus. Vols. for the Arts, Ft. Worth, 1989-93. Contbr. articles to profl. jours. Mem. Am. Soc. for Tng. and Devel. (pres. 1992, Profl. Award for Disting. Achievement 1989, 90, 92), Nat. Speakers Assn. Office: Kotkin Communications PO Box 330997 Fort Worth TX 76163-0997

KOTNOUR, MARY MARGARET, elementary physical education educator; b. Winona, Minn., Jan. 28, 1956; d. Thomas and Maxine (Herber) K. BS in Phys. Edn., Winona State U., 1978; MEd in Counseling, U. Idaho, 1983. Cert. tchr. Minn., Idaho, Wash. Elem. phys. edn. specialist Sch. Dist. #211, Coeur d'Alene, Idaho, 1979-85; elem. phys. edn. coord. Sch. Dist. #271, Coeur d'Alene, 1985-86, elem. phys. edn. specialist, 1986—; Reviewer of Phys. Edn. Books, Prentice Hall, Inc., Englewood, N.J. Author: Physical Fitness Games and Activities Kit, 1990. Bd. dirs. Big Brothers and Big Sisters, Coeur d' Alene; coach, clinician, tng. chmn. Spl. Olympics, Coeur d' Alene; vol. chaplain County Jail. Recipient Disting. Young Alumni award Winona State U., 1987; named to Outstanding Young Women of Am., 1984. Mem. AAHPERD, NEA, Idaho Assn. Health Phys. Edn., Recreation and Dance (nominated for Outstanding Phys. Edn. Tchr. of Yr., 1986, '92), Idaho Edn. Assn., Coeur d' Alene Edn. Assn. (negotiating team 1988—), Delta Kappa Gamma. Office: Ramsay Elem Sch 1351 W Kathleen Ave Coeur D Alene ID 83814-8307

KOTOWSKI, CHRISTINE ANNE, legal nurse consultant; b. Buffalo, Feb. 8, 1947; d. Leonard Michael and Irene (Jedrzejewski) Zmozynski; m. David M. Kotowski, Oct. 26, 1968; children: Jeffrey, Jennifer, Kenneth, Gregory. AAS cum laude Trocaire Coll., 1981; BSN cum laude, Daemen Coll., N.Y., 1983. RN, N.Y. Nurse's asst. St. Joseph Inter-Community Hosp., Cheektowaga, N.Y., 1978-80; camp nurse Jewish Ctr., Greater Buffalo, Amherst, 1981; charge nurse Williamsville Suburban Nursing Home, N.Y., 1981, day supr., 1982, asst. DON, 1982-84; nurse cons. Brown and Kelly Law Offices, Buffalo, 1984; cons. and lectr. in field. Pre-Cana sponsor Our Lady of Blessed Sacrament Ch., Depew, N.Y., 1985-88; supporter Bowmansville Vol. Fire Dept; sec. alumni bd. dirs. Daemen Coll. Nursing, 1988-94. Mem. Am. Assn. Legal Nurse Cons. (chair by-laws com. we. N.Y. chpt.), Profl. Nurses Assn. Western N.Y., Western N.Y. Paralegal Assn. (co-founder med. splty. sect. 1990, chair med. splty. sect. 1991-92), Delta Epsilon Sigma. Republican. Roman Catholic. Avocations: choir, church projects, travel, music, reading. Office: Brown and Kelly 1500 Liberty Building Bldg Buffalo NY 14202-3615

KOTROUS, MONTE MARIE, information systems specialist; b. Nebr., Aug. 4, 1956; d. Leslie Corwin and Fern Marie (Russell) Wills; m. Val Edward Kotrous, May 22, 1978. BA in Psychology, U. Nebr., 1978. Jr. geophysicist Bore Hole Exploration, Tulsa, 1978-81; geosci. technician Dowling Petroleum, Midland, Tex., 1981-82; geol. technician Barnes, Eimers and New Kumet, Midland, Tex., 1982-83; geophys. technician Union Oil Calif., Midland, Tex., 1983-89, database adminstr., tech., 1989-90, regional computer coord., 1990-92, mainframe adminstr., 1992—; mem. database steering team Union Oil Calif., Midland, 1993—, geographix user group, Midland, 1993—, office vision user group, Brea, Calif., 1990-91. Designer Cross Stitch Quick & Easy, 1990. Vol. Christmas in April, Midland, 1988-93, Permian Basin Soup Kitchen Food Drive, Midland, 1991; walker March of Dimes, Midland, 1988-89. Methodist. Home: 301 Wilcrest # 7404 Houston TX 77042 Office: Union Oil Calif 14141 South West Fwy Sugar Land TX 77048

KOTT, BEVERLY PARAT, financial counselor; b. Chgo., Sept. 7, 1936; d. Louis Joseph and Marie Elizabeth (Katich) Parat; m. Russell Kott; children: Vinson V., Donna M., James L., Michael A. Grad., Life Underwritr Tng. Coun., Washington, 1977. Mem. mgmt. ea. region Met. Life Ins. Co., Balt., 1977; ins. broker, 1979-85; pres. Kott & Assocs. Fin. Counseling Svc., Joppa, Md., 1985—; fin. counselor coop. extension svc. U. Md., Bel Air, 1987—, mem. Harford extension adv. coun., 1988-93; dir. Padre Rio RM, 1993—. Commr. Harford County Commn. for Women, Bel Air, 1981-87; v.p. Joppa Friends of the Libr., 1988—; dir. Joppatowne Civic Assn., Joppa, 1990—; mem. Rumsey Island Civic Assn., 1980—; dir. Padre Rio Rosary Makers, 1993—; mem. Prison Ministry, 1983—; lay min. Roman Cath. Ch., 1995—. Named one of Most Beautiful People, Harford County, 1990. Mem. Hunt Valley Bus. and Profl. Woman's Club (charter), Aux. VFW (pres. 1988-90, legis., youth, publicity and cancer aid coms. 1989, 90), Mensa Internat. Roman Catholic. Home: 661 Towne Center Dr Joppa MD 21085-4439 Office: PO Box 349 Joppa MD 21085-0349

KOTUK, ANDREA MIKOTAJUK, public relations executive, writer; b. New Brunswick, N.J., Oct. 19, 1948; d. Michael and Julia Dorothy (Muka) Mikotajuk. BA, Douglass Coll., Rutgers U., 1970. Pub. relations asst. Wall St. Jour. Newspaper Fund, Princeton, N.J., 1970; editorial asst. Redbook mag., N.Y.C., 1970-71; asst. pub. relations dir. Children's Aid Soc., N.Y.C., 1971-75; assoc. pub. relations dir. Planned Parenthood, N.Y.C., 1975-80; pres. Andrea & Assocs., N.Y.C., 1980—. Writer publicist for non-profit agys.; contbg. editor Arts Mag., 1970-75. Office: Andrea & Assocs 112 E 23rd St New York NY 10010-4518

KOTVAS, KAREN ELAINE, screenwriter, tree farmer; b. Rahway, N.J., June 24, 1942; d. Joseph Kotvas and Ida Wilhelmina Gruss. BA in English, Rutgers U., 1964; MS in Edn., U. Pa., 1965. Tchr. 2d grade Wrightstown, Pa., 1964-65; tchr. 6th grade Rahway, 1965; tchr. 1st grade Westfield, N.J., 1966; tchr. kindergarten Fanwood, N.J., 1966-69; mktg. rep. Polaroid Corp., Cambridge, Mass., 1969-76; tour guide Fred Harvey, Grand Canyon, Ariz., 1969-70; Keno salesperson Sahara Hotel, Las Vegas, Nev., 1969-70; exec. dir., lobbyist L.E.G.A.L., Trenton, N.J., 1976-90; tree farmer Valle Crucis, N.C., 1980—; writer Colonia, N.J. Author: Bred in the Bone, 1985; screenwriter: Shakedown on State Street, 1992, Ropin', 1992; contbr. articles to mags. Home: 131 East St Colonia NJ 07067

KOURIDES, IONE ANNE, endocrinologist, researcher, educator; b. N.Y.C., Sept. 1, 1942; d. Peter T. and Anne E. (Spetseris) K.; m. Charles G. Zaroulis, Nov. 30, 1974; children: Anna Larisa, Andrew, Christina, Peter. BA, Wellesley Coll., 1963; MD, Harvard U., 1967. Diplomate Am. Bd. Internal Medicine, Am. Bd. Endocrinology and Metabolism. Intern Jewish Hosp., Wash. U., St. Louis, 1967-68; resident Montefiore, Albert Einstein Med. Sch., Bronx, N.Y., 1968-69; fellow Beth Israel, Harvard U., Boston, 1970-72; assoc. prof. medicine Cornell U. Med. Coll., N.Y.C., 1981—; sr. assoc. med. dir. Pfizer Pharms., N.Y.C., 1990—. Mem. editorial bd. Endocrinology, Jour. Clin. Endocrinol Metabolism, also others; contbr. over 100 articles to sci. jours., chpts. to books. Mem. nat. campaign Harvard Med. Sch., Boston, 1986—; nat. bd. dirs. Philoptochos Soc. Greek Orthodox Archdiocese. Grantee NIH, 1979-84. Fellow ACP; mem. Am. Soc. Clin. Investigation, Am. Assn. Physicians, Am. Thyroid Assn. (coms.), Endocrine Soc. (coms.). Home: 1070 Park Ave New York NY 10128-1000 Office: Pfizer Pharms 235 E 42nd St New York NY 10017

KOVACH, BARBARA ELLEN, management and psychology educator; b. Ann Arbor, Mich., Dec. 28, 1941; d. Harry Arnold and Margaret Mayne (Buell) Lusk; m. Craig Randall Duncan, Dec. 28, 1963 (div. 1973); children: Deborah Louise, Mark Randall; m. Randall Louis Kovach, May 2, 1981; 1 child, Jennifer Elizabeth. BA magna cum laude, Stanford U., 1963, MA, 1964; PhD, U. Md., 1973. Asst. prof. psychology U. Mich., Dearborn, 1973-77, assoc. prof., 1977-82, prof., 1982-84, chair Dept. Behavioral Scis., 1980-83; dean Univ. Coll. Rutgers U., New Brunswick, N.J., 1984-88, prof. mgmt. and psychology, 1984—, dir. leadership devel. program, 1988—; pres. Leadership Devel. Inst., Princeton, N.J., 1990—; cons. Rochester (N.Y.) Products-Gen. Motors, Grand Rapids, Mich., 1982-87, Ford Motor Co., Dearborn, 1981-82, Mich. Bell Telephone, 1980-81, Rockwell Internat., Troy, Mich., 1993—. Author: Sex Roles and Personal Awareness, 1978, 90, Power and Love, 1982, Organizational Sych, 1983, Adolescent Experience, 1983, Teh Flexible Organization, 1984, Survival on the Fast Track, 1988, 93, Organization Gameboard, 1989, Leaders-In-Place, 1994; prodr. (videotape series) Keys to Leadership I, 1991-93, II, 1993-94; contbr. articles to profl. jours. Daniel E. Prescott fellow U. Md., 1972; recipient Susan B. Anthony and Faculty Recognition awards U. Mich., 1980. Mem. Am. Psychol. Assn., Acad. Mgmt., Organizational Devel. Network, Phi Beta Kappa. Republican. Episcopalian. Home: 95 Cuyler Rd Princeton NJ 08540-3460 Office: Rutgers U Sch of Bus New Brunswick NJ 08903

KOVACHEVICH, ELIZABETH ANNE, federal judge; b. Canton, Ill., Dec. 14, 1936; d. Dan and Emilie (Kuchan) Kovachevich. AA, St. Petersburg Jr. Coll., 1956; BBA in Fin. magna cum laude, U. Miami, 1958; JD, Stetson U., 1961. Bar: Fla. 1961, U.S. Dist. Ct. (mid. and so. dists.) Fla. 1961, U.S. Ct. Appeals (5th cir.) 1961, U.S. Supreme Ct. 1968. Research and adminstrv. aide Pinellas County Legis. Del., Fla., 1961; assoc. DiVito & Speer, St. Petersburg, Fla., 1961-62; house counsel Rieck & Fleece Builders Supplies, Inc., St. Petersburg, 1962; pvt. practice law St. Petersburg, 1962-73; judge 6th Jud. Cir., Pinellas and Pasco Counties, Fla., 1973-82, U.S. Dist. Ct. (mid. dist.) Fla., St. Petersburg, 1982—; chmn. St. Petersburg Profl. Legal Project-Days in Court, 1967; chmn. Supreme Ct. Bicentennial Com. 6th Jud. Circuit, 1975-76. prodr., coord. TV prodn. A Race to Judgement. Bd. regents State of Fla., 1970-72; legal advisor, bd. dirs. Young Women's Residence Inc., 1968; mem. Fla. Gov.'s Commn. on Status of Women, 1968-71; mem. Pres.'s Commn. on White House Fellowships, 1973-77; mem. def. adv. com. on Women in Service, Dept. Def., 1973-76; Fla. conf. publicity chmn. 18th Nat. Republican Women's Conf., Atlanta, 1971; lifetime mem. Children's Hosp. Guild, YWCA of St. Petersburg; charter mem. Golden Notes, St. Petersburg Symphony; hon. mem. bd. of overseers Stetson U. Coll. of Law, 1986. Recipient Disting. Alumni award Stetson U., 1970, Woman of Yr. award Fla. Fedn. Bus. and Profl. Women, 1981, ann. Ben C. Willard Meml. award, Stetson Lawyers Assn., 1983, St. Petersburg Panhellenic Appreciation award, 1964, Mrs. Charles Ulrick Bay award, St. Petersburg Rotary award, St. Petersburg Quarterback Club award, Pinellas United Fund award in recognition of concern and meritorious effort, 1968, Woman of Yr. award Beta Sigma Phi, 1970, Am. Legion Aux. Unit 14 Pres. award cmty. svc., 1970, Dedication to Christian Ideals award and Man of Yr. award KC Dists. 20-21, 1972. Mem. ABA, Fla. Bar Assn., Pinellas County Trial Lawyers, Assn. Trial Lawyers Am., Am. Judicature Soc., St. Petersburg Bar Assn. (chmn. bench and bar com., sec. 1969). Office: US Dist Ct US Courthouse 611 N Florida Ave Rm 108 Tampa FL 33602-4501*

KOVACS, DIANE KAYE, librarian, researcher; b. Denver, Oct. 3, 1962; d. Robert Joseph and Jean Ann (Finch) Engelbrecht; m. Michael J. Kovacs, June 23, 1984. BA in Anthropology, U. Ill., 1985, MS in Libr. and Info. Sci., 1989; MEd, 1993. Social scis. reference libr. Bucknell U., Lewisburg, Pa., 1989-90; assoc. prof., reference libr. Kent (Ohio) State U., 1990—. Editor: Directory of Scholarly Electronic Conferences, 1992; contbr. articles to profl. jours. Mem. ALA. Office: Kent State U Librs And Media Svcs Kent OH 44242

KOVANDA, JANET LOUISE, financial planner; b. Chgo., Aug. 12, 1946; d. John James and Irene Theresa (Salczencko) Pavlick; m. Robert James Kovanda, Apr. 20, 1968; children: Jeffrey Robert, Kristy Jannae. Cert. fin. planner. Asst. to v.p. R.E. Hauert Fin. Svcs., Oak Brook Terr., Ill., 1980-82; registered rep. Francis Manzo Co., Lisle, Ill., 1983-85, Dreher & Assocs., Oak Brook Terr., 1985—; ptnr., tchr. Fin. Planning Teaching Assn., Streamwood, Ill., 1984—; owner, fin. planner Birmingham Fin. Svcs., Westmont, Ill., 1983—; adj. faculty Coll. for Fin. Planning, Denver, 1984—. Trustee Westmont Police Pension Fund; past pres. Farmingdale Cove Homeowners Assn., Westmont. Mem. Internat. Assn. for Fin. Planning (past chmn. south suburban Chgo. chpt. 1992-93, pres. 1991-92, dir. ethics 1989-90, bd. dirs.), Inst. for Cert. Fin. Planners. Office: Birmingham Fin Svcs 825 N Cass Ave Ste 201 Westmont IL 60559

KOVELESKI, KATHRYN DELANE, retired special education educator; b. Detroit, Aug. 12, 1925; d. Edward Albert Vogt and Delane (Bender) Vogt; BA, Olivet (Mich.) Coll., 1947; MA, Wayne State U., Detroit, 1955; m. Casper Koveleski, July 18, 1952; children: Martha, Ann. Tchr. schs. in Mich., 1947-88; tchr. Garden City Schs., 1955-56, 59-88, resource and learning disabilities tchr., 1970-88, ret. 1988. Sec. bd. Christian edn. Congl. Ch., 1988-89, chmn., 1988-90, mem. Mem. BPW (Woman of Yr. 1985-86 Garden City), Mich. Assn. Ret. Sch. Pers. , Wayne Lit. Club (past pres., treas. 1988-89), Sch. Masters Bowling League (v.p. 1984-88), Odd Couples Bowling League (pres. 82-83).

KOVITZ, NANCY R., sales promotion agency executive; b. Chgo.; d. Samuel Harold Freed and Julia (Silverman) Stone; m. Alan David Kovitz, Apr. 16, 1961; children: Samuel Howard, Kathryn Ann. BA, U. Chgo., 1960; MLS, Rosary Coll., 1983. Rsch. asst. Newberry Libr., Chgo., 1979-82; info. specialist Peat Marwick Main, Chgo., 1982-84; mgr. info. ctr. Frankel and Co., Chgo., 1984—; lectr. Columbia Coll., Chgo. Contbr. articles to profl. jours.; editor abstracting newsletter. Bd. mem. Internat. Comm. for Women Mus., Chgo., 1983-85. Mem. Spl. Librs. Assn., Am. Librs. Assn., AMA, Chgo. Calligraphy Collective. Office: Frankel & Co 111 E Wacker Dr Chicago IL 60601-4208

KOVNER, KATHLEEN JANE, civic worker, portrait artist; b. Cambridge, Mass., Nov. 25, 1919; d. David Leo and Kathleen Elizabeth (Lalley) Lane; m. Benjamin Kovner, June 20, 1938; children: Kathleen Barbara (dec.), Michael Anthony, Peter Christopher. Student, Art Students League, N.Y.C., 1937-40. Owner, CEO Helen Bennett Ltd., Stamford, Conn., 1948-59; cons. Bride's Mag., N.Y.C., 1967-70; co-chair membership com. Women's Nat. Republican Club, N.Y.C., 1980-81, chmn. membership com., 1981-87, v.p., 1986-87, bd. dirs., 1981-87; ltd. ptnr. 519 8th Ave Corp., N.Y.C., 18-19th St. Corp., N.Y.C., Kaufman Arcade Bldg., N.Y.C., 19th St. Assn., N.Y.C. Portrait artist in oils, with various portraits in pvt. collections. Fundraiser St. Ignatius Loyola, N.Y.C., 1960-61, Jeanine Pirro-Campaign for Dist. Atty., Westchester County, N.Y., 1993. Roman Catholic. Home: 1445 Flagler Dr Mamaroneck NY 10543 also: 923 5th Ave New York NY 10021

KOWAL, RUTH ELIZABETH, library administrator; b. Amherst, Mass., Mar. 16, 1948; d. Alfred Alexander and Mary Arandale (Tomlinson) Brown; m. Harold F. Kowal, June 19, 1989; children: Elizabeth Ann, Susannah Terry. BS, Syracuse U., 1970; MLS, Simmons U., 1971. Reference libr. Falmouth (Mass.) Pub. Libr., 1971-74; sch. libr. Nauset High Sch., Eastham, Mass., 1974-75; asst. dir. Plymouth (Mass.) Pub. Librs., 1975, dir., 1976-83; exec. dir. Southeastern 3R's, Highland, N.Y., 1983-86; regional adminstr. Ctrl. Mass. Libr. System, Worcester, 1987-91, Ea. Mass. Libr. System,

Boston, 1991—; instr. Northeastern U., Boston, 1980-83, SUNY, Albany, 1984-86. Mem. ALA. Office: Ea Mass Reg Libr Boston Pub Libr Boston MA 02117

KOWALCZYK, JEANNE STUART, biology educator; b. Atlanta, Dec. 22, 1942; d. A. Sidney and Martha Ross (Hart) Jones; m. Alex W. Stuart, Sept. 9, 1961 (dec. 1981); m. Bruno Kowalczyk, Jan. 15, 1983. BS, Jacksonville State U., 1966, MS, 1968; PhD, Auburn U., 1972. Head biology dept. Belmont (N.C.) Abbey Coll., 1972-78; prof. biology U. S.C., Spartanburg, S.C., 1978—. Contbr. articles to profl. jours. NSF fellow, 1968-72. Mem. Appalachian Region Electron Microscopist Soc., South East Parasitologist Soc., Sigma Xi, Gamma Sigma Delta, Gamma Beta Phi. Democrat. Roman Catholic. Home: Paradox Farm Gaffney SC 29340

KOWALESKI, JANE ELIZABETH, real estate executive; b. Stamford, Conn., Nov. 7, 1948; d. Stanley Francis and Sally Sophie (Wolak) K. AA, Norwalk Community Coll., 1969; AS in Fashion Merchandising, U. Bridgeport, 1985; postgrad., So. Conn. State Coll., 1990—. Retail mgr. and buyer Bob's Sports Inc., Stamford, 1966-84; realtor G. Stanton Properties, Stamford, 1984—; 1990-93. Pre-sch. tchr. Downtown Children's Ctr. for Champion Internat. Mem. Nat. Bd. Realtors, Conn. Bd. Realtors, Stamford Bd. Realtors, Real Estate Inst. (grad., v.p. bus. brokerage div.). Home: 24 Benstone St Stamford CT 06905-3516 Office: G Stanton Properties 1074 Hope St Stamford CT 06907-2110

KOWALEWSKY, KAREN JEAN, meteorologist, consultant; b. Paterson, N.J., Mar. 6, 1963; d. Andrew and Ruth Ann (Patterson) K. BS, SUNY, Oswego, 1985; MS, U. Wash., 1988. Rsch. meteorologist Applied Rsch. Corp., Landover, Md., 1988-89; air quality meteorologist Galson Corp., Syracuse, N.Y., 1989-92; staff atmospheric sci. Radian Corp., Rochester, N.Y., 1992—; adj. faculty SUNY, Oswego, 1991. Mem. Am. Meteorol. Soc. (cert. cons. meteorologist), Am. Geophys. Union, Air and Waste Mgmt. Assn., Sigma Xi (assoc.). Home: 248 Surrey Hill Way Rochester NY 14623 Office: Radian Corp 155 Corporate Woods Ste 100 Rochester NY 14623-1458

KOWALICK, SUSAN GOLDENBERG, physical therapist; b. Detroit, Nov. 8, 1956; d. Edwin and Gloria (Comisar) Goldenberg; children: Ariel, Kassia, Michael. BS in Phys. Therapy, Old Dominion U., 1982; AAS in Phys. Therapy, Nassau Community Coll., 1977. Lic. phys. therapist, N.C. Phys. therapy asst. Riverside Hosp., Newport News, Va., 1977-79; asst. phys. therapist Judy Saperstein, Norfolk, Va., 1979-82, Hillhaven, Norfolk, 1979-82; phys. therapist Moore Regional Hosp., Pinehurst, N.C., 1982-83; owner, phys. therapist Sandhills Phys. Therapy, Pinehurst, 1983-88; owner, phys. therapist, adminstr. Pinehurst Rehab. Ctr., 1988—; pres. Bod Carolina Affiliated Phys. Therapist Network, 1994—. Leader Brownie Girl Scouts U.S., Pinehurst, 1989-90; dir. Sandhills Soccer League, Southern Pines, N.C., 1990—, coach, 1990—. Mem. Am. Phys. Therapy Assn. (ho. of dels. 1991, 92, 94), N.C. Phys. Therapy Assn. (chmn. task force 1989—, chmn. fiscal intermediary com. 1990, pres. 1990-92, v.p. 1993, chair task force healthcare reform 1994—, mem. legis. com. 1990—, chief del. 1995—). Office: Pinehurst Rehab Ctr PO Box 3850 Pinehurst NC 28374-3850

KOWALSKI, LYNN MARY, podiatrist; b. Passaic, N.J., Aug. 15, 1955; d. George J. and Gladys L. (Kucera) K.; m. Donald Storbeck, Feb. 9, 1975 (div. Mar. 1982); children: Jason, Jessica. BSN, William Paterson Coll., 1984; DPM, N.Y. Coll. Podiatric Medicine, 1988. RN, N.J.; diplomate Am. Podiatric Med. Examiners, Am. Bd. Podiatric Orthopedics & Primary Podiatric Medicine; lic. physician N.Y., N.J. Resident in podiatric surgery N.Y. Coll. Podiatric Medicine & Affiliated Hosps., 1988-89; pvt. duty nurse Bergen County, N.J., 1989; pvt. practice podiatrist Brick, N.J., 1990—; guest speaker Eldermed, Brick, 1991, Diabetes Support Group, Point Pleasant, N.J., 1991, 92, Arthritis Support Group, 1991, Garden State Rehab. Hosp., Toms River, N.J., Community Svcs., Toms River and Brick, 1992, Laurelton Village Community Edn., Brick, 1992, Lions Head North, 1992, Family Wellness Fair, Toms River, 1992, Green briar 2, 1992, Post Polio Support Group-Garden State Rehab. Hosp., Toms River, 1992, Treat Your Feet-Med. Ctr. Ocean County Health Edn. Network, 1992, Parkinsons Support Group-Med. Ctr. Ocean County, 1992. Contbr. articles to profl. jours. Mem. Toms River-Ocean (N.J.) County C. of C., 1990, Brick, 1991, Community Svcs., Toms River, 1992; vol. women's health day Med. Ctr. Ocean County, 1992, elder med. screening Sr. Citizen Villages, 1993. Fellow Am. Coll. Foot Orthopedics & Medicine; mem. Am. Diabetes Assn. (Tour de Cure 1992), Am. Coll. Foot Surgeons (assoc.), Am. Running and Fitness Assn., Am. Podiatric Med. Assn., N.J. Podiatric Med. Soc., Kiwanis, Manasquan Elks (health fair 1992), Sigma Theta Tau (charter), Psi Chi. Office: 1608 Route 88 Ste 118 Brick NJ 08724-3009

KOWALSKI, S. MARIA, pediatrician; b. Janow, Podlaski, Poland, Feb. 2, 1924; came to U.S., 1971; d. Stanislaw and Josefa (Naliwafko) Rossa; m. Henryk Kowalski, Jan. 23, 1956 (dec. Jan. 1982); children: Henryk Mariufs, Michael Adam. MD, Med. Acad., Warsaw, Poland, 1950. Diplomate Am. Bd. Pediatrics, Am. Bd. Emergency Medicine; lic. Poland, Israel, R.I., Mass. Asst. to Prof. Szenajch and Prof. Bogdanovicz Children's Clinic U. Warsaw, 1949-54, head dept. liver diseases Children's Clinic, 1954; rschr. infectious hepatitis Polish Min. Health, Czechoslovakia, 1954; pediatrician, gen. practitioner Israeli Health Ctr., Haifa and Tele Aviv, 1957; physician respiratory dept. Zeuderziekenhuis Hosp., Rottendam, 1962-63; rotating intern Miriam Hosp., Providence, 1971-72; clin. fellow dept. clin. nutrition Children's Hosp. Med. Ctr., 1972-74, asst. clin. nutrition, mem. staff, 1974-76; pvt. practice pediatric and family medicine Providence, 1976—; affiliated with R.I. Hosp., Providence, Miriam Hosp., Providence, St. Joseph's Hosp., Providence, Women and Infants Hosp., Providence, Morton Hosp., Tauton, Mass. Fellow Am. Coll. Emergency Physicians. Home: 70 Humboldt Ave Providence RI 02906-4533 Office: 68 Humboldt Ave Providence RI 02906

KOWLESSAR, MURIEL, retired pediatric educator; b. Bklyn., Jan. 2, 1926; d. John Henry and Arene (Driver) Chevious; m. O. Dhodanand Kowlessar, Dec. 27, 1952; 1 child, Indrani. AB, Barnard Coll., 1947; MD, Columbia U., 1951. Diplomate Am. Bd. Pediatrics. Instr. Downstate Med. Ctr., Bklyn., 1958-64, asst. prof., 1965-66; asst. prof. clin. pediatrics Temple U., Phila., 1967-70; assoc. prof. Med. Coll. Pa., Phila., 1971-83, dir. pediatric group svcs., 1975-90, acting chmn. pediatrics dept., 1981-83, vice chair pediatrics dept., 1982-91, prof., 1983-91, prof. emeritus, 1991—. Contbr. articles to med. jours. Mem. Pa. Gov.'s Task Force on Spl. Supplemental Food Program for Women, Infants and Children, Harrisburg, 1981-83, Phila. Bd. Health, 1982-86; vol. Phila. Com. for Homeless, 1991-92, Gateway Literacy Program, YMCA, Germantown Bridge, Pa., 1992-93. Fellow Am. Acad. Pediatrics (emeritus); mem. Phila. Pediatric Soc., Phi Beta Kappa. Democrat.

KOYM, ZALA COX, elementary education educator; b. San Antonio, July 21, 1948; d. Bruce Meador and Ruby Esther (Jordan) Cox; m. Charles Raymond Koym, July 5, 1969; children: Carol Ann, Cathy Lynn, Suzie Kay. BS in Edn., SW Tex. State U., 1970. Cert. supervision of tchr. effective practices. Elem. tchr. Schertz-Cibolo Ind. Sch. Dist., Schertz, Tex., 1970-71; substitute tchr. Alamogordo (N.Mex.) Pub. Schs., 1973-75; tchr. 5th grade Round Rock (Tex.) Ind. Sch. Dist., 1983-90, asst. prin., 1988-91, tchr. 2d grade, 1990—; textbook advisor State of Tex., 1989; chairperson/coord. 5th grade level Round Rock Ind. Sch. Dist., 1986-90, 2d grade level chairperson, 1990-93; sci. lab. coord. Robertson Elem., Old Town Elem, 1983-89; presenter Sci. Workshop Round Rock Ind. Sch. Dist., 1993, 94. mem. PTA, 1981—, v.p. programs, 1994—; vacation Bible sch. dir. FUMC, 1985-86, 86-87, scholarship com., 1992-94; neighborhood capt. March of Dimes, 1990, Am. Heart Assn., 1994; mem. Campus Student Assistance Program Team, 1990-94, Old Town Bldg. Leadership Team, 1991-92. Mem. ASCD, Assn. Tex. Profl. Educators, Phi Delta Kappa (sec. 1991-93, assoc. hist. 1994—). Home: 3806 Curtis Dr Round Rock TX 78681-1644 Office: Old Town Elem Sch 2001 Old Settlers Blvd Round Rock TX 78681-2160

KOZA, JOAN LORRAINE, fabric manufacturing company executive; b. Berwyn, Ill., Apr. 28, 1941; d. Frank Louis and Lorraine Frances (Thomas) K.; BS in Communications, U. Ill., 1963. Office mgr. Dwan Med. Ctr., Summit, Ill., 1959-64; law office mgr. firm Gordon, Reicin & West, Chgo., 1964-73; sales mgr. Ambassador Hotels, Chgo., 1973-76; exec. v.p. MPC Industries, Inc. & subs., indsl. and recreational fabrics, Chgo., 1976—; owner, mgr. JK Advt., 1977—; pres. Chgo. Legal Secs. Assn., 1970-72; v.p. Ill. Assn. Legal Secs., 1970-73. Pres., chmn. bd. Children's Research Found., 1963-66. Contbg. author: New American Poetry Anthology (Golden Poet award 1988, 89). Named Chgo. Legal Sec. of Yr., 1972, Ill. Legal Sec. of Yr., 1972. Mem. Alpha Lambda Delta, Theta Sigma Pi. Roman Catholic. Home: 546 Banyon Ln La Grange IL 60525-1962 Office: 4834 S Oakley Ave Chicago IL 60609-4094

KOZAK, ELLEN LISA, painter; b. N.Y.C., Oct. 14, 1955; d. Aaron and Lillian (Weiss) K. BFA, Mass. Coll. Art, 1977; MS in Visual Studies, MIT, 1979. Lectr. dept. art U. Mass., Boston, 1979, asst. prof. dept. art., 1979-80; lectr. Princeton (N.J.) U., 1993; rsch. affiliate MIT, Cambridge, Mass., 1979-80; artist-in-residence Mass. Coll. of Art, Boston, 1980-82, Blue Mountain Ctr., 1988, Va. Ctr. for Creative Arts, 1992; artist residency fellow Yaddo Colony, 1986, 90; vis. artist Seian Art U., Kyoto, Japan, 1982-84, Parsons Sch. Design, N.Y.C., 1991, 92, 94-95, Pratt Inst., N.Y.C., 1993—; studio instr. drawing and painting Art Ctr. 92nd St Y, N.Y.C., 1988-92. Solo exhbns. include Ctr. Advanced Visual Studies MIT, Cambridge, Mass., 1980, Osaka (Japan) Contemporary Art Ctr., 1983, Tochigi Prefectural Mus. Fine Art, Japan, 1983, Gallery Amelia, Tokyo, 1985, Van Buren, Brazelton, Cutting Gallery, Cambridge, 1986, Jay Gallery, N.Y.C., 1986, South Huntington (N.Y.) Pub. Libr., 1987, Port Washington (N.Y.) Pub. Libr., 1988, 55 Mercer Gallery, N.Y.C., 1992, Carolyn J. Roy Gallery, N.Y.C., 1994; group exhbns. include Decordova Mus., Lincoln, Mass., 1977, Koelnischer Kunstverein, Colonge, Germany, 1981, Am. Ctr. for Artists and Students, Centre Pompidou, Paris, 1981, Tochigi Prefectural Mus. Fine Art, Utsunomia, Japan, 1983, Jay Gallery, 1984, 86, van Stratten Gallery, Chgo., 1986, Sragow Gallery, N.Y.C., 1988, Cork Gallery at Lincoln Ctr., N.Y.C., 1989, 90, Nat. Mus. Women in Arts, Washington, 1991, Evehjem Mus., 1991, Kathryn Sermas Gallery, N.Y.C., 1992, Michael Walls Gallery, N.Y.C., 1992, Trenkman Gallery, N.Y.C., 1992, Geoffrey Young Gallery, Great Barrington, Mass., 1992, Bill Bace Gallery, N.Y.C., 1992, Chassie Post Gallery, Atlanta, 1993, The Painting Ctr., N.Y.C., 1993, E.S. Vandam Gallery, N.Y.C., 1993, Boston Pub. Libr., 1994; permanent collections include Met. Mus. Art, N.Y.C., Bklyn. Mus., N.Y. Pub. Libr., Tochigi Prefectual Mus. Fine Art, Utsunomia, Boston Pub. Libr., others; artist (book) Orpheus Eurydice Hermes by Rainier Maria Rilke, 1995. Artists' grantee Cambridge Arts Coun., 1978, Sloan Found., 1979, Japan Victor Corp., 1983. Studio: 284 Lafayette St # 4D New York NY 10012

KOZAK, HARLEY JANE, actress; b. Wilkes-Barre, Pa., Jan. 28, 1957; d. Joseph Aloysius and Dorothy (Taraldsen) K. Cert., NYU, 1980. Appeared in films Parenthood, 1989, Arachnophobia, 1990, The Taking of Beverly Hills, 1990, The Favor, 1990, Necessary Roughness, 1991, All I Want for Christmas, 1991, Glenorky, 1995, TV series Harts of the West, 1993-94, Bringing Up Jack, 1995. Office: United Talent Agy 9560 Wilshire Blvd Beverly Hills CA 90212-9999

KOZAR, MARTHA CECILE, corporate executive; b. Davenport, Iowa, May 4, 1963; d. Albert Eugene and Carol Margaret (Sejrup) Lorenz; m. Paul J. Kozar, June 30, 1990. BA in Computer Sci., Lewis U., Romeoville, Ill., 1985; MBA, U. Notre Dame (Ind.), 1989. Systems analyst GE, Morris, Ill., 1984-86; MIS supr. Blistex Inc., Oak Brook, Ill., 1986-87; mktg. intern Whirlpool Corp., LaPorte, Ind., 1988; mktg. asst. Miles Inc., Elkhart, Ind., 1989-90, asst. product mgr., 1990-91; asst. brand mgr. The Dial Corp., Phoenix, 1991-93, brand mgr., 1993—.

KOZBERG, DONNA WALTERS, rehabilitation administration executive; b. Milford, Del., Jan. 1, 1952; d. Robert Glyndwr and Gailey Ruth (Bedorf) Walters; m. Ronald Paul Kozberg, June 8, 1974. BA, U. Fla., 1973, M in Rehab. Counseling, 1974; MFA, CUNY, 1979; MBA, Rutgers U., 1986. Cert. rehab. counselor. Rehab. counselor Office Vocat. Rehab., N.Y.C., 1975-81; area dir. Lift, Inc., Staten Island, N.Y., 1981-83; ea. region dir. pub. relations, advt. Lift, Inc., Mountainside, N.J., 1983-85, v.p., 1985—, v.p., chief fin. officer, 1988, exec. v.p., 1991-93, pres., 1993; co-founder, mng. dir. Expert Strategies, Inc., Mountainside, N.J., 1992—; self-employed writer, editor, 1975—; adv. bd. Rutgers Exec. Master Bus. Adminstrn. Contbr. articles to profl. jours.; assoc. editor Parachute mag., 1978; editor-in-chief (newsletter) Counselor Adv, 1980. Pres. Com. on Employment of People with Disabilities; trustee Ctr. for Creative Living; bd. dirs. N.J. Adv. Coun. for Independent Living, adv. panel NYU. Mem. Nat. Rehab. Assn. (Spl. citation 1974, grantee 1973), Nat. Rehab. Adminstrs. Assn., Nat. Rehab. Counselors Assn., Poets and Writers. Home: 45 Dug Way Watchung NJ 07060 Office: Lift Inc PO Box 1072 Mountainside NJ 07092-0072

KOZIOL, DELORIS ELIZABETH, epidemiologist, researcher; b. Alexandria, Va., Apr. 29, 1949; d. Edward Stephen and Joyce Kathleen (Helm) K. BA, U. Del., 1971; MPH, Johns Hopkins U., 1986, PhD, 1990. Med. technologist NIH, Bethesda, Md., 1972-73, rsch. med. technologist, 1973-83, infection control specialist, 1983-89, acting dep. hosp. epidemiologist, 1989, dep. hosp. epidemiologist, 1989—. Author: (with others) Infectious Diseases, 5th edit., 1994; contbr. articles to profl. jours. Sec., bd. dirs. Palisades Assn., Inc., Kensington, Md., 1990—. Mem. APHA, Am. Soc. Clin. Pathologists (registered med. technologist), Soc. for Healthcare Epidemiology Am., Soc. for Epidemiologic Rsch. Roman Catholic. Office: NIH Bldg 10 Rm 4A21 Bethesda MD 20892

KOZLIK, EMILY C., association executive; b. Omaha, Sept. 13, 1952; d. Robert George and Clare Eleanor (O'Hearn) Cunningham; m. Michael D. Kozlik, Sept. 30, 1983; children: John Edward, Caroline Clare. BA, Creighton U., 1974. Staff houseparent United Cath. Social Svcs., Omaha, 1973-75; social svc. worker Douglas County, Omaha, 1975-76; program dir. YWCA, Omaha, 1976-78, exec. dir., 1978—. Bd. dirs. Womens Fund of Greater Omaha, 1992—, Pvt. Industry Coun., Omaha, 1993—; mem. United Way Roundtable 2000, Omaha, 1994. Named one of Ten Outstanding Young Omahans by Jaycees, 1981, 82, one of 75 Women of Achievement by Great Plains Girl Scouts, 1987. Mem. Agy. Execs. Assn., Leadership Omaha Alumni, CEO Network (chair membership 1994), Jr. League, Alpha Sigma Mu. Home: 5122 Nicholas St Omaha NE 68132-1434 Office: YWCA of Omaha 222 S 29th St Omaha NE 68131-3543

KOZLOVA, VALENTINA, ballerina; b. Moscow, Aug. 26, 1957; came to U.S., 1979; d. Vladimir Koslov and Anna (Shuvanova); m. Carlo Montali, Aug. 8, 1991; 1 child, Clelia Maria. Ballet diploma, Bolshoi Ballet Acad. Sch., Moscow, 1973. Soloist Bolshoi Ballet, Moscow, 1974-76, prin., 1976-79; prin. Australian Ballet, Melbourne and Sydney, 1981-83; prin. appearing in all major internat. dance galas N.Y. City Ballet, 1983—; asst. choreographer Miami Ballet Concerto, Fla., 1980, N.J. Closter Ballet, 1980-81, Santiago Ballet, Chile, 1981-82, Australian Ballet, 1982. Classical repertory includes: Swan Lake, La Bayadere, Giselle, Sleeping Beauty, Romeo and Juliet, Spartacus, Don Quixote; modern repertory includes works by Western choreographers including: Jerome Robbins, Glen Tetley, Roland Petit, John Cranko, Alvin Ailey, Peter Martins, George Balanchine, Helgi Tomasson, Elliott Feld, Margo Sappington, Bill Soleau; starred on Broadway and at Kennedy Ctr. in: On Your Toes, 1983; dance videos include Tribute to Anna Pavlova, 1982, La Fille Mal Gardée, 1986. Office: NYC Ballet Inc NY State Theater Lincoln Ctr Pla New York NY 10023*

KOZLOWSKI, BETTE MARIE, accountant; b. Camden, N.J., Apr. 2, 1959; d. Joshua Ashley and Doris Annette (Saunders) T. BS with honors in Acctg., Pa. State U., 1981. CPA, Conn. Staff acct. Ernst and Whinney, Hartford, Conn., 1981-83; sr. mgr. KPMG Peat Marwick, Phila., 1983—. Mem. AIPCA, Jules Link Inst. Accts., Beta Gamma Sigma, Beta Alpha Psi, Phi Mu. Republican. Methodist. Office: KPMG Peat Marwick 1600 Market St Philadelphia PA 19103-7240

KOZLOWSKI, JANIECE RAE, accountant; b. Dayton, Ohio, June 25, 1959; d. Gerald Ray and Joann (Davis) Moore; m. Richard Ernest Kozlowski, May 23, 1981; children: Kristen Rae, Joanna Elaine. BS in Bus. and Acctg., Wright State U., Fairborn, Ohio, 1981. CPA, Ohio. Gen. acct. Lucas Ledex, Inc., Vandalia, Ohio, 1982-85, asst. to acct., 1986-88, acctg. specialist, 1988—. Home: 290 Essex Dr Tipp City OH 45371-2238

KRA, PAULINE SKORNICKI, foreign language educator; b. Lodz, Poland, July 30, 1934; came to U.S., 1950, naturalized, 1955; d. Edward and Nathalie Skornicki; m. Leo Dietrich Kra, Mar. 10, 1955; children: David Theodore, Andrew Jason. Student Radcliffe Coll., 1951-53; BA, Barnard Coll., 1955; MA, Columbia U., 1963, PhD, 1968; MA, Queens Coll., 1990. Lectr., Queens Coll., City U. N.Y., 1964-65; asst. prof. French, Yeshiva U., N.Y.C., 1968-74, assoc. prof. French, 1974-82, prof., 1982—. Mem. MLA, Am. Assn. Tchrs. French, Am. Soc. 18th Century Studies, Société française d'étude du XVIII siècle, Soc. Montesquieu, Assn. for Computers and Humanities, Assn. for Literary and Linguistic Computing, Phi Beta Kappa. Author: Religion in Montesquieu's Lettres persanes, 1970; contbr. articles to profl. jours. Home: 10914 Ascan Ave Forest Hills NY 11375 Office: 500 W 185th St New York NY 10033-3201

KRACKE, JUDY SUTTON, sculptor; b. Amarillo, Tex., Jan. 18, 1940; d. W.M. and Zuma Vance Sutton; children: Kristen, Kurtis. AA, Christian Coll., 1960; BS, U. Tex., 1962; MA, West Tex. A&M U., 1985, MFA, 1986. Tchr. Spring Br. Ind. Sch. Dist., Houston, 1962-66, Tex. Children's Hosp., Houston, 1964-66, Galveston (Tex.) Sch. Dist., 1974-75; tchr. dept. psychiatry Baylor Coll. Medicine, Houston, 1964-66; tchr. Amarillo Mus. Art, 1977-79, Amarillo Coll., 1978-91; part-time instr. West Tex. A&M U., 1984—; dir. One Sun, One Earth, One Peace, 1992—, Tritotems, Scottsdale C.C., 1994, Passages, Scottsdale C.C., 1994; vis. artist Ea. N.Mex. U., Clovis, 1989, Midwestern State U., Wichita Falls, Tex., 1990, Tex. Christian U., Ft. Worth, 1990, Calif. State U., Bakersfield, 1992, Nat. U. Cordoba, 1992-93; subject various interviews. One woman shows include Brookhaven Coll., Dallas, 1990, White Chapel, Tempe (Ariz.) Art Ctr., 1991, Quadome II, Tex. Christian U., Ft. Worth, 1991, Spirit Mount, Calif. State U., Bakersfield, 1992, Jaime Conci Art Gallery, Cordoba, Argentina, 1993, Mildura (Australia) Arts Centre, 1995, Union Artists Ukraine, Charnigov, 1995, Mildura Project Sculpture, 1995; exhibited in group show at Dallas Mus. of Art, 1991, Nelson Park, Abilene, 1993, Presbyn. Home for Children, Amarillo, 1993, Radford (Va.) U., 1994, Scottsdale (Ariz.) C.C., 1994, numerous others; sculptures commd. by various orgns. Pres. Galveston Fine Art Assn., 1973-74. Recipient Purchase award Shreveport Art Guild, Barnwell Mus., 1974, Design award 7 Who Care Award, KVII, Amarillo, 1985, 2d place award Amarillo Gateway Design, 1991, Achievement award AAUW, 1994; grantee Amarillo C. of C., 1993, Tex. Commn. on Arts, 1991, Abilene (Tex.) Cultural Affairs Coun., 1991-92. Office: 4019 Montage Amarillo TX 79109

KRAEMER, LILLIAN ELIZABETH, lawyer; b. N.Y.C., Apr. 18, 1940; d. Frederick Joseph and Edmee Elizabeth (de Watteville) K.; m. John W. Vincent, June 22, 1962 (div. 1964). BA, Swarthmore Coll., 1961; JD, U. Chgo., 1964. Bar: N.Y. 1965, U.S. Dist. Ct. (so. dist.) N.Y. 1967, U.S. Dist. Ct. (ea. dist.) N.Y. 1971. Assoc. Cleary, Gottlieb, Steen & Hamilton, N.Y.C., 1964-71; assoc. Simpson Thacher & Bartlett, N.Y.C., 1971-74, ptnr., 1974—; mem. vis. com. U. Chgo. Law Sch., 1988-90, 91-94, chmn. ea. region capital fund drive, 1983-86. Bd. mgrs. Swarthmore Coll., 1993—. Fellow Am. Coll. Bankruptcy; mem. Assn. of Bar of City of N.Y. (mem. various coms.), Coun. on Fgn. Rels., N.Y. State Bar Assn., Order of Coif, Phi Beta Kappa. Democrat. Episcopalian. Home: 2 Beekman Pl New York NY 10022-8058 also: 62 Pheasant Ln Stamford CT 06903 Office: Simpson Thacher & Bartlett 425 Lexington Ave New York NY 10017-3903

KRAEMER, SYLVIA KATHARINE, government official, historian; b. Neisse, Silesia, Germany, Feb. 24, 1944; came to U.S., 1948; d. Thomas Paramore and Dorothea Freihube (Kraemer) Doughty; m. Russell Inslee Fries, Apr. 11, 1970 (div. Nov. 1991); children: Thomas Mount, Gwyneth Buchanan. BA in English, Hollins Coll., 1965; PhD in History, Johns Hopkins U., 1969. Instr. Johns Hopkins U., Balt., 1969; asst. prof. history Vassar Coll., Poughkeepsie, N.Y., 1969-70, So. Meth. U., Dallas, 1970-73; rsch. assoc. prof. U. Maine, Orono, 1975-78; mem. vis. faculty Bangor (Maine) Theol. Sem., 1981-83; chief historian NASA, Washington, 1983-89, dir. Office Spl. Studies, 1989—, mem. adv. coun., 1981-83. Author: Urban Idea in Colonial America, 1977, NASA Engineers in the Age of Apollo, 1992; also essays. Mem. Maine Humanities Coun., 1979-83; cons. on edn. issues, Va., 1993—. Fellow Coun. Humanities, So. Meth. U., 1973; rsch. grantee NSF, 1978-80. Fellow Internat. Acad. Astronautics; mem. Women in Aerospace, Exec. Women in Govt., Soc. for History in Fed. Govt. (exec. coun. 1988-91, James Madison award 1989), AAUW. Office: NASA 300 E St SW Washington DC 20546

KRAETZER, MARY C., sociologist, educator, consultant; b. N.Y.C., Sept. 12, 1943; d. Kenneth G. and Adele L. Kraetzer; m. Kestas E. Silunas. AB, Coll. New Rochelle, 1965; MA, Fordham U., 1967, PhD, 1975. Instr. Mercy Coll., Dobbs Ferry, N.Y., 1969-70, asst. prof., 1970-75, assoc. prof., 1975-79, prof., 1979—; research asst. Fordham U., Bronx, N.Y., 1965-67, teaching asst., 1967-68, teaching fellow, 1968-69, adj. instr., 1971-75, adj. asst. prof., 1975-76; adj. assoc. prof. L.I. U. Grad. Br. Campus Mercy Coll., 1976-79, adj. prof., 1979-81, coordinator M.S. in Community Health Program, 1976-81, adj. prof. Westchester campus, 1988—; rsch. cons. elem. schoolbooks Nat. Council of Chs./Church Women United Task Force on Global Consciousness, N.Y.C., 1971; mem. adv. com. edn. and society div. Nat. Council Chs., 1975-78; mem. evaluation team Middle States Assn. Colls. and Secondary Schs. Commn. on Higher Edn., Monmouth, N.J., 1976. Contbr. chpts. to books, articles to profl. jours. Recipient citation Am. Men and Women of Sci., 1978; Bd. Regents scholar, 1961-65, Fordham U. scholar, 1965-68; Fordham U. fellow, 1968-69; grantee Mercy Coll., 1984, 85, 86, 88, 92; NSF summer intern, 1967. Mem. Am. Sociol. Assn., Am. Pub. Health Assn. Office: Mercy Coll 555 Broadway Dobbs Ferry NY 10522-1189

KRAFCISIN, TERESA M., food products executive; b. Chgo., July 11, 1962. BBA, Loyola U., Chgo., 1984; MBA, U. Chgo., 1993. CPA, Ill. Sr. acct. Ernst & Young, Chgo., 1984-87; mgr. Ernst & Young, Paris, 1987-90; project mgr. Coca-Cola Beverages, Paris, 1990-91; region fin. mgr. Coca-Cola Poland, Warsaw, 1993—. Office: The Coca-Cola Co P-Warsaw Poland PO Drawer 1734 Atlanta GA 30301

KRAFKA, KRISTINE KAROLINE, technical writer; b. Waterloo, Iowa, Sept. 3, 1964; d. Richard Kay and Caroline Elizabeth (Wehrman) K.; m. Martin George Edleman, Mar. 20, 1993. BS, Iowa State U., 1987. Cert. tchr. agriculture and secondary English 7-12, Iowa. Advt. account exec. Gazette Co. Iowa Farmer Today divsn., Cedar Rapids, 1987-88; dir. biol. regulatory affairs Ft. Dodge (Iowa) Labs. divsn. Am. Home Products Corp., 1988—. Recipient Iowa Farmer degree Iowa Future Farmers Am., 1981, Am. Farmer degree Nat. Future Farmers Am., 1985; named Iowa Jr. Master Lamb Prodr., Iowa Dept. Agriculture, 1982, Nat. Suffolk Sheep Queen, Nat. Suffolk Sheep Assn., 1982-83. Mem. AAUW (v.p. 1991-92), U.S. Animal Health Assn., Animal Health Inst. (mem. vet. biologics sect., chair regulatory com. working group 1990-93), Iowa Suffolk Sheep Assn. (bd. dirs. 1984—).

KRAFT, CARI, computer company director; b. Bklyn., Nov. 16, 1963; d. Stanley and Elaine Gail (Pierce) Silverman; m. Todd Alan Kraft, May 27, 1990. BS in Decision Scis., U. Pa., The Wharton Sch., 1985; BAS in Econs., U. Pa., 1985. Cons., co-founder Computer Synergetix, Huntingdon Valley, Pa., 1985; dir. program devel. Strategic Mgmt. Group, Phila., 1985-87; tech. mgr. Packard Press Corp., Phila., 1987-89; tech. dir. Omicron (co. of PBR Cons. Group), Phila., 1989-93; dir. bus. devel. Omicron, Phila., 1994—; bd. dirs. Group Motion Dance Co.; cons. Bklyn. Bagels Inc., Phila., 1990—. Office: Omicron Con 23d Flr West Tower 1500 Market St Philadelphia PA 19102

KRAFT, DONNA LEE, accountant; b. Norristown, Pa., Apr. 20, 1957; d. Walter Eugene and Marguerite (Elmer) Williams; m. Jeffrey Lang Kraft, Dec. 22, 1986; 1 child, Jennifer Leigh. BS in Acctg., Towson State U., 1992. Tax acct. Fashion Bug/Charming Shoppes, Phila., 1986-88; acct. Growth Systems, Inc., Balt., 1992-93, Bon Secours Health Systems Inc., Mariottsville, Md., 1993—. Mem. Inst. Mgmt. Accts., Towsontown Women's Bus. and Profl. Assn. Republican. Office: Bon Secours Health Systems 1505 Marriottsville Rd Marriottsville MD 21104-1399

KRAFT, ELAINE JOY, community relations and communications official; b. Seattle, Sept. 1, 1951; d. Harry J. and Leatrice M. (Hanan) K.; m. Lee Somerstein, Aug. 2, 1980; children: Paul Kraft, Leslie Jo. BA, U. Wash., 1973; MPA, U. Puget Sound, 1979. Reporter Jour. Am. Newspaper, Bellevue, Wash., 1972-76; editor Jour./Enterprise Newspapers, Wash. State,

1976; mem. staff Wash. State Senate, 1976-78, Wash. Ho. of Reps., 1978-82, pub. info. officer, 1976-78, mem. leadership staff, asst. to caucus chmn., 1980—; ptnr., pres. Media Kraft Communications; mgr. corp. info., advt. and mktg. communications Weyerhaeuser Co., 1982-85; dir. communications Weyerhaeuser Paper Co., 1985-87; dir. community rels. N.W. region Coors Brewing Co. 1987—. Recipient state and nat. journalism design and advt. awards. Mem. Nat. Fedn. Press Women, Women in Communications, Wash. Press Assn. Home: 14329 SE 63rd St Bellevue WA 98006-4802 Office: PO Box 5921 Bellevue WA 98006

KRAFT, KAREN ANN, secondary school educator; b. Bklyn., June 27, 1964; d. Michael John and Barbara Ann (DeMaio) Miele; m. John L. Kraft, June 17, 1989; children: Taylor Michael, Mason Genaro. BS, North Tex. State U., 1986; MA in Edn., U. North Tex., 1990. Lic. provisional tchr. English and Spanish, gifted and talented, Tex. Tchr. Westwood H.S., Palestine, Tex., 1987-88, Allen (Tex.) H.S., 1988-93, Coppell (Tex.) H.S., 1993—; tchr. Nat. Honor Soc. Faculty Coun., Allen, 1989-93; mem. poetry soc. Coppell H.S., 1994—, also mentor program facilitator. Mem. ASCD, Nat. Coun. Tchrs. English, Tex. Assn. for Gifted and Talented, Coppell High Sch. Poetry Soc. Roman Catholic. Home: 1303 Laguna Vista Way Grapevine TX 76051

KRAFT, LISA DIANE, mechanical engineer; b. Canton, Ohio, Feb. 9, 1954; d. William Carl and Barbara Jean (Brower) Dawson; m. Richard Clayton Andrus Jr., Dec. 4, 1976 (div. June 1988); 1 child, William Clayton; m. Robert L. Kraft, Oct. 14, 1988; 1 child, Natalie Claire. BSME, Memphis State U., 1983. Warrenty clk. Diesel Recon Co., divsn. Cummins Engine Co., Memphis & L.A., 1978-79, engrng. tech., 1979-82, divsn. engr., 1984-85, project engr., 1985-87, mktg. mgr. engines, 1987-90, project engrng. mgr., 1990, mgr. mfg., engrng & maintenance, 1991-94; v.p. ctrl. support Cummins Cal Pacific, Inc., Irvine, Calif., 1994—. Tenn. State Bd. scholar, 1972. Mem. ASME, Am. Soc. Metals, Soc. Mfg. Engrs. (sr. mem., chmn. local chpt. 1986-87, Outstanding Young Mfg. award 1987), Tau Beta Pi.

KRAG, OLGA, interior designer; b. St. Louis, Nov. 27, 1937; d. Jovica Todor and Milka (Slijepcevic) Golubovic. AA, U. Mo., 1958; cert. interior design UCLA, 1979. Interior designer William L. Pereira Assocs., L.A., 1977-80; assoc. Reel/Grobman Assocs., L.A., 1980-81; project mgr. Kaneko/Laff Assocs., L.A., 1982; project mgr. Stuart Laff Assocs., L.A., 1983-85; restaurateur The Edge, St. Louis, 1983-84; pvt. practice comml. interior design, L.A., 1981—, pres., R.I., 1989—. Mem. invitation and ticket com. Calif. Chamber Symphony Soc., 1980-81; vol. Westside Rep. Coun., Proposition 1, 1971; asst. inaugural presentation Mus. of Childhood, L.A., 1985. Recipient Carole Eichen design award U. Calif., 1979. Mem. Am. Soc. Interior Designers, Inst. Bus. Designers, Phi Chi Theta, Beta Sigma Phi. Republican. Serbian Orthodox. Home and Office: 700 Levering Ave Apt 10 Los Angeles CA 90024-2797

KRAHNKE, BETTY ANN, county official; b. Washington, Sept. 27, 1942; d. Richard George Jr. and Mary (McLaughlin) Fletcher; m. Wilson Norris Krahnke, July 11, 1964; children: Carolyn, Catherine, Margaret. BA in Political Sci. with highest honors, U. Calif., Santa Barbara, 1964; postgrad., Johns Hopkins U., 1964-65. Columnist The Planning Game, The Montgomery Jour.; moderator Montgomery Week in Review, Montgomery Cmty. TV. Mem. Montgomery County Planning Bd., 1979-87; vol. coord. Congresswoman Connie Morella's re-election campaign, 1988; Bush del. Rep. Nat. Conv., 1988, 92; chmn. Citizen's Coord. Com. on Friendship Heights; active mem. LWV; former exec. v.p. Montgomery County Hist. Soc.; mem. coun. Montgomery United Way; elected mem. Montgomery County Coun., 1990, 94, chair Coun. pub. safety com., coun. health & human svcs. com., coun. govt's. com. on noise abatement at Nat. and Dulles Airport; mem. land use and environ. com.; treas., mem. bd. dirs. Nat. Orgn. to Insure a Sound-Controlled Environment. Office: Office County Coun Coun Office Bldg 6th Fl 100 Maryland Ave Rockville MD 20850

KRAINIK, ARDIS, opera company executive; b. Manitowoc, Wis., Mar. 8, 1929; d. Arthur Stephen and Clara (Bracken) K. BS cum laude, Northwestern U., 1951, postgrad., 1953-54, DFA (hon.), 1984; LHD (hon.), DePaul U., 1985, Loyola U., 1986, U. Wis., 1986; DFA (hon.), St. Xavier Coll., 1986, Knox Coll., 1987, Columbia Coll., Chgo., 1988, Lake Forest Coll., 1989, Roosevelt U., 1989; LLD (hon.), Albion Coll., 1990; D Mus. Arts (hon.), U. Ill., Chgo., 1990; LHD (hon.), No. Ill. U., 1990; HHD (hon.), Lewis U., 1991; MusD (hon.), Ind. U. N.W., 1992, Barat Coll., 1993; LHD honoris causa, Lawrence U., 1993; DFA (hon.), St. Mary's Coll., 1994. Tchr. drama, pub. speaking Horlick High Sch., Racine, Wis., 1951-53; exec. sec., office mgr. Lyric Opera, Chgo., 1954-59; asst. mgr. Lyric Opera, 1960-75, artistic adminstr., 1975-80, gen. mgr., 1981—, gen. dir., 1987—; St. mary's Coll., DFA, 1994; bd. dirs. No. Trust Co. Trustee Northwestern U., mem. women's bd., mem. adv. coun. Kellogg Sch. Mgmt.; mem. governing bd. Ill. Arts Alliance; bd. dirs. Opera Am.;. Recipient Commendatore Italian Order Merit, 1983, Ill. Order Lincoln, 1985, Apptd. Rector, 1993, Grand Decoration of Honor in Silver, Republic of Austria, 1994, Alumni Merit award Northwestern U., 1986, award of Achievement Girl Scouts U.S., 1987, Dushkin Svc. award Music Ctr. of North Shore, 1987, Thomas De Gaetani award U.S. Inst. for Theatre Tech., 1990, Bravo award Rosary Coll., 1991, Career Svc. award Arts Mgmt. News Svc., 1992, Edward Moss Martin award Union League Club, 1993, Crystal award Chgo. Drama League, 1994, Exemplary Woman award Women in Charge, 1994, Sara Lee Frontrunner award, 1994, Friendship award European Union, 1994, Grand Decoration in Silver Svcs., Republic of Austria, 1994, European Unio Friendship award, 1995; named Tribute to Chgo. Women Honoree Midwest Women's Ctr., 1986, one of Chicagoans of Yr. Boys and Girls Club, 1987, Exec. of Yr. Crain's Chgo. Bus., 1990. Mem. Ill. Arts Alliance (governing bd.), Internat. Assn. Opera Dirs., Opera Am. (bd. dirs.), Chgo. Hist. Soc. Guild, Northwestern U. Women's Bd., Northwestern U. Assocs., Northwestern U. Kellogg Sch. Mgmt. (adv. coun.), Mortar Bd., Econ. Club (bd. dirs.), Comml. Club (past pres.), Lake Geneva Country Club, Pi Kappa Lambda. Christian Scientist. Office: Lyric Opera of Chgo 20 N Wacker Dr Ste 860 Chicago IL 60606-2805

KRAKORA-LOOBY, JANICE MARIE, pediatrician; b. Chgo., Jan. 14, 1951; d. Joseph George and Marie Adele (Doleshek) Krakora; m. John Augustus Looby III, July 21, 1979; children: Eileen Loretta, John Augustus IV, James Patrick. BS with honors, Mich. State U., 1972, DVM with honors, 1973; MD with honors, Rush Med. Coll., Chgo., 1987. Diplomate Am. Bd. of Pediatrics. Assoc. vet. Kohn Animal Hosp., Highland Park, Ill., 1973-75; assoc. vet. Libertyville (Ill.) Animal Hosp., 1976-77, hosp. dir., 1977-82; assoc. vet. Mundelein (Ill.) Animal Hosp., 1982-85; intern and resident in pediatrics Rush-Presbyn.-St. Luke's Med. Ctr., Chgo., 1987-90; pediatrician Vernon Hills (Ill.) Pediatric Assoc. Ltd., 1990—; bd. dirs. Sun Room, Inc., Lake Forest, Ill. Active St. Mary Parish Coun., editor newsletter, 1991-94, sch. parents club. Paul Harris fellow Rotary, 1988. Fellow Am. Acad. Pediatrics; mem. AMA, AVMA, Am. Med. Women's Assn., Chgo. Med. Soc., Ill. Med. Assn., Chgo. Pediatric Soc., Lake County Pediatric Soc., Aerospace Medicine Assn., Rotary Club Lake Forest/Lake Bluff. Home: 1764 Bowling Green Dr Lake Forest IL 60045-3504 Office: Vernon Hills Pediatric Assocs Inc 10 W Phillip Rd Vernon Hills IL 60061-1730 also: 36100 N Brookside Dr Gurnee IL 60031

KRAKOW, AMY GINZIG, advertising and marketing executive, writer; b. Bklyn., Feb. 25, 1950; d. Nathan and Iris (Minkowitz) Ginzig. BA, Bklyn. Coll., 1971, postgrad. in TV prodn., 1974. Copy mgr. U.S. News & World Report, N.Y.C., 1977-80; promotion mgr. Sta. WINS-Radio, N.Y.C., 1980-82; promotion dir. CBS Mags., N.Y.C., 1982-84, The Village Voice, N.Y.C., 1984-85, N.Y. Woman (Am. Express Pub.), N.Y.C., 1987-89; cons. Silverman Collection, Santa Fe, 1985—; sem. leader Radcliffe Pub. workshop, 1986-92, Mag. Pubs. Congress, 1989. Author: Total Tattoo Book, 1994; prodr. Festival of Street Entertainers, N.Y.C., 1984-93, Albuquerque, 1980, Obies-Off-Broadway Theater Awards, 1984-86; creator, prodr. Ann. Coney Island Tattoo Festival, 1986-93, The Psychedelic Festival, 1988; exec. dir. Radio Creative Mercury Awards, 1991-93; curator American Style: New York's Tattoo Roots, South St. Seaport Mus., 1995. Bd. dirs. Sideshows by the Seashore, Coney Island, U.S.A., Bklyn., 1985-92, Bond St. Theater Coalition, 1985—, City Lore, N.Y.C., 1987—, Princeton Bio Ctr., 1991-93. Recipient BPA award, 1981, Addy award, 1985, AAF Crystal Prism award, 1994. Mem. Advt. Women N.Y., Delta Phi Epsilon.

KRAKOW, BARBARA LEVY, art gallery executive; b. Boston, June 9, 1936; d. Daniel and Frances (Wermont) Levy; m. Alvin Krakow, Aug. 23, 1959; children: David, Lisa. BA summa cum laude, Boston U., 1958. Treas. HKL, Ltd., Boston and N.Y.C., 1967-74; pres. Four Art Svcs., Boston, 1972-76, Harcus Krakow Gallery, Boston, 1964-83, Barbara Krakow Gallery, Boston, 1983—; mem. vis. com. Worcester (Mass.) Art Mus., 1988, panelist, 1989; panelist The Art Show, N.Y., 1990, 92, "On Collecting," The Danforth Mus., Framingham, 1990, "Boston: Regional Art Mecca of New York's Shadow," Boston Ctr. for Arts, 1990, "The Contemporary Scene," Worcester Art Mus., 1992; advisor The New Provincetown Print Project, The Fine Arts Wk. Ctr., 1990—; moderator "Voices at Major Institutions," Inst. of Contemporary Art, Boston, 1991; curator 9th drawing show Boston Ctr. Arts, 1988. Mem. Boston Mayor's Mgmt. Rev. Com., 1985-86; hon. chmn. AIDS Action Com. Art Auction, Boston, 1988, 90, 92; mem. Cultural Dist. Task Force, Boston, 1988-89, Pub. Art Policy Task Force, Boston, 1988-89; bd. overseers Inst. of Contemporary Art, Boston, 1992—. Recipient Outstanding Woman in Bus. award Boston YWCA, 1986. Mem. Art Dealers Assn. Am. (membership com. 1987—), Internat. Fine Print Dealers Assn. (bd. dirs. 1987). Office: 10 Newbury St Boston MA 02116

KRAKOWSKI, LINDA S., computer coordinator, consultant; b. Chgo., May 23, 1949; d. Edward J. and Geraldine (Prohaska) Tesarek; children: Ian, Olivia. BA, U. Ill., 1971; Cert. Advanced Studies, Lewis U., 1977; MA, Nat. Coll. Edn., 1985, EdD, 1987. Tchr. English High Sch. Dist. 230, Palos Hills, Ill., 1976-87, coord., instr. computers, 1987—; owner, cons. Ill. Computing Educators Consortium, Palos Hills, 1987—; presenter Ill. Gifted Edn. Coun., 1984-87; designer computer systems Banco Argentina, Buenos Aires, 1988; mem. strategic planning com. and intervention team High Sch. dist. 230, Palos Hills, 1989—; judge Educationis Lumen award com., Lewis U., 1991—. Vol. Crisis Ctr. for South Suburbia, 1985—; active Hartigan for Gov. campaign, Chgo., 1989-90, Clinton/Gore Presdl. Campaign, Ill., Carol Moseley Braun for Senator Campaign, Chgo.; del. Dem. Nat. Conv., N.Y.C., 1992; mem. Fourth Presbyn. Ch. of Chgo., Legion of Young Polish Women. Ill. Dept. Edn. grantee, 1984-85; named Suburban Educator of Yr., Lewis U., 1990. Mem. AAUW (bd. dirs., past pres.), NEA (bd. dirs. 1979—, adv. pub. rels. 1979—, Excellence in Gifted Edn. Design award 1985), Ill. Edn. Assn. (bd. dirs. 1979—). Office: Ill Computing Educators Consortium 10705 S Roberts Rd Ste 21 Palos Hills IL 60465

KRAL, NANCY BOLIN, political science educator; b. St. Louis, Oct. 4, 1958; d. Alpha E. Jr. and Shirley Judith (Wiseman) Bolin; m. Kenneth Joseph Kral, June 12, 1982; 1 child, Kelly Ann. BS, U. Tex., 1979; MA, U. Houston, 1989. Tchr. govt. Round Rock Ind. Sch. Dist., Austin, Tex., 1980-84, Spring Ind. Sch. Dist., Houston, 1984-85, Klein Ind. Sch. Dist., Houston, 1985-88; instr. polit. sci. Houston Community Coll., 1987-88; prof. polit. sci., program coord. North Harris Montgomery Coll. Dist., Tomball, Tex., 1988—; asst. to chancellor North Harris Montgomery Coll. dist., Tomball, Tex., 1993; edn. chair Tomball Regional Arts Coun., 1991-93, bd. dirs.; bd. dirs. Tri-Magna Industries, Waco. Co-author: Texas Government. Bd. dirs. Champion Forest Civic Assn., Houston, 1986-88, North Area chpt. Houston Symphony League, 1989-92, Performing Arts Coun. North Houston, 1994—; chair Tomball Coll. Law Day; pres. Northampton Homeowners Assn., 1985-86; del. Tex. Rep. Conv., Ft. Worth, 1990, Dallas, 1992; faculty advisor Coll. Reps., Tomball Coll.; panelist Nat. Inst. Staff and Orgnl. Devel. Conf., 1992. Taft fellow Abilene Christian U., 1988. Mem. NOW, Am. assn. Women in C.C., Tex. Jr. Coll.Tchrs. Assn. (chair govt., sect. 1991-92, legis. com. 1992—, sec. 1994, 95), Tex. Abortion Rights Action League, Tex. Women's Pol. Caucus, Soc. Prevention Cruelty to Animals, March of Dimes Guild, Midwest Polit. Sci. Assn., Ctr. for Study of Presidency, Univ. Houston Alumni Assn., Univ. Tex. Austin Ex-Students' Assn., N.W. Rep. Women (legis. chair 1988-90, campaign chair 1990-92), League of Women Voters, Alpha Xi Delta North Houston Alumnae (pres. 1990-92). Presbyterian. Home: 9319 Appin Falls Dr Spring TX 77379 Office: North Harris Montgomery Coll Dist 30555 Tomball Pkwy Tomball TX 77375

KRAM, SHIRLEY WOHL, federal judge; b. N.Y.C., 1922. Student, Hunter Coll., 1940-41, CUNY, 1940-47; LLB, Bklyn. Law Sch., 1950. Atty. Legal Aid Soc. N.Y., 1951-53, 1962-71; assoc. Simons & Hardy, 1954-55; pvt. practice law, 1955-60; judge Family Ct., N.Y.C., 1971-83; judge U.S. Dist. Ct. (so. dist.) N.Y., N.Y.C., 1983-93, sr. judge, 1993—. Author: (with Neil A. Frank) The Law of Child Custody, Development of the Substantive Law. Office: US Dist Ct US Courthouse 40 Foley Sq Rm 2601 New York NY 10007-1551*

KRAMER, CAROL GERTRUDE, marriage and family counselor; b. Grand Rapids, Mich., Jan. 14, 1939; d. Wilson John and Katherine Joanne (Wasdyke) Rottschafer; m. Peter William Kramer, July 1, 1960; children: Connie R. Kramer Sattler, Paul Wilson Kramer. AB, Calvin Coll., 1960; MA, U. Mich., 1969; PhD, Holy Cross Coll., 1973; MSW, Grand Valley State U., 1985. Diplomate Internat. Acad. Profl. Counseling and Psychotherapy; cert. addictions/substance abuse counselor, Mich., hypnotist/psychotherapist, N.Y. Elem. tchr. Jenison (Mich.) Pub. Sch., 1960-64; sch. social worker Grand Rapids Pub. Sch., 1964-81; pvt. practice marriage and family counselor Grand Rapids, 1973—; v.p. Human Resource Assocs., Grand Rapids, 1983-88; guest lectr. Calvin Coll., Mich. State U., Grand Valley State U., 1975-85. Ruling elder 1st Presbyn. Ch., Grand Rapids, 1975-78; mem. Gerald R. Ford Rep. Women, Grand Rapids, 1980-87; mem. Mich. Bd. of Licensing Marriage Counselors, 1985-88, co-chair pastoral rels. com. Gun Lake Community Ch., 1989-91, v.p. consistory, 1991-93. Named one of Outstanding Young Women in Am., 1974. Fellow Am. Assn. Marriage and Family Therapists; mem. Mich. Assn. Marriage Counselors (awards com. 1988, chmn. 1991, nominations com. 1992—), NASW, Kent County Family Life Coun. (pres. 1975), Voters Against Sexual Abuse (pres. 1992—, pres. bd. dirs.). Home: 12622 Park Dr Wayland MI 49348-9322 Office: Psychology Ctr 2059 Lake Michigan Dr NW Grand Rapids MI 49504-4742

KRAMER, CECILE E., retired medical librarian; b. N.Y.C., Jan. 6, 1927; d. Marcus and Henrietta (Marks) K. B.S., CCNY, 1956; M.S. in L.S., Columbia U., 1960. Reference asst. Columbia U. Health Scis. Library, N.Y.C., 1957-61, asst. librarian, 1961-75; dir. Health Scis. Libr. Northwestern U., Chgo., 1975-91; asst. prof. edn. Northwestern U., 1975-91, prof. emeritus, 1991—; instr. library and info. sci. Rosary Coll., 1981-85 ; cons. Francis A. Countway Library Medicine, Harvard U., 1974. Pres. Friends of Libr., Fla. Atlantic U., Boca Raton. Fellow Med. Libr. Assn. (chmn. med. sch. librs. group 1975-76, editor newsletter 1975-77, instr. continuing edn. 1966-75, mem. panel cons. editors Bull. 1987-90, disting. mem. Acad. Health Info. Profls. 1993—); mem. Biomed. Comm. Network (chmn. 1979-80). Home: 9184 Flynn Cir Apt 4 Boca Raton FL 33496-6675

KRAMER, DIANA R., human resources executive; b. N.Y.C., Mar. 10, 1949; d. Joseph and Gloria S.; m. Steven Kramer, May 7, 1975. BA, Glassboro (N.J.) State Coll., 1972; MA, New Sch. Social Research, N.Y.C., 1975; PhD, Fordham U., 1979. Tchr. N.Y.C. Bd. Edn., 1972-80; mgr. human resources and tng. AT&T, Basking Ridge, N.J., 1980-87; mgr. human resources, planning and devel. BASF Corp., Parsippany, N.J., 1987-90; dir. human resources and tng. Miles Inc., Ridgefield Park, N.J., 1990-93; pres. Kramer Cons. Solutions, Chatham, N.J., 1993—. Mem. APA, ASTD, Am. Psychol. Soc., Exec. Women N.J., N.J. Human Resource Planning Soc., N.Y. Human Resource Planning Soc., N.Y. Assn. Applied Psychology, Met. N.Y. Assn. for Applied Psychology, Orgn. Devel. Network of Greater N.Y., Soc. for Human Resource Mgmt., Soc. for Indsl. and Organizational Psychology. Home and Office: Kramer Consulting Solutions 1 Colonial Way Chatham NJ 07928-2757

KRAMER, ELISSA LIPCON, nuclear medicine physician, educator; b. N.Y.C., Feb. 22, 1951; d. Jules and Esther Ruth (Wagner) L.; children: Rachel, Aaron. BA, U. Pa., 1973; MD, NYU, 1977. Diplomate Am. Bd. Nuc. Medicine, Am. Bd. Radiology. Ob-gyn. intern Bellevue Hosp. Ctr./NYU Med. Ctr., 1977-78, resident in radiology, 1978-80, fellow in nuc. medicine, 1980-82; asst. prof. clin. radiology NYU, 1982-89, assoc. prof. clin. radiology, 1989—; assoc. prof. radiology Cornell U. Med. Ctr., Ithaca, N.Y., 1989-90; assoc. Sloan-Kettering Cancer Ctr., N.Y.C., 1989-90; assoc. dir. nuc. medicine Tisch Hosp., N.Y.C., 1989—; assoc. attending physician Tisch Hosp., 1990—, Bellevue Hosp., N.Y.C., 1990—. Author, editor: (book) Clinical SPECT Imaging, 1995; contbr. articles to profl. jours. Nat. Cancer Inst./NIG Rsch. grantee, 1993—. Mem. Am. Coll. Radiology, Am. Assn. Women Radiologists, Radiology Soc. N.Am., Soc. Nuc. Medicine (mem. brain imaging coun. 1982—, mem. bd. dirs. 1992-93). Office: NYU Med Ctr Divsn Nuc Med 560 1st Ave New York NY 10016-6497

KRAMER, JANICE KAY, real estate marketing executive; b. Boonville, Mo., Jan. 16, 1944; d. Stanley Monroe and Jewel Mary (Enderlin) K. Student, U. Mo., U. Ill-Chgo. Urban planner Environetic Rsch. Corp., Chgo., 1969-72; sr. analyst Real Estate Rsch. Corp., Chgo., 1972-76; mkt. feasibility cons. J. K. Kramer Real Estate, Chgo., 1976-78; real estate mktg. supr. to. mgr. McDonald's Corp., Oak Brook, Ill., 1978-81, staff dir., 1981-84, dir. mkt. devel., 1984—; educator, mkt. evaluation Internat. Mkts. McDonald's Corp., 1981—, Women's Career Devel., 1983—; bus. advisor INROADS, Chgo., 1984-89; steering coun. co-chair com. Women's Leadership Network, McDonald's Corp., 1993-94, sec., 1994-95; mem. Corp. Learning Adv. Coun., 1994—. Recipient Leadership awards YWCA, 1986, 88. Mem. Chgo. Coun. on Fgn. Rels., Columbia Yacht Club. Home: 1501 N State Pky Chicago IL 60610-1502 Office: McDonald's Corp Kroc Dr Oak Brook IL 60521

KRAMER, JOYCE L., lawyer. BA with distinction, U. Rochester, 1973; JD, Emory U., 1976. Bar: Ga. 1976, N.Y. 1980, D.C. 1980. Staff atty. SEC, Washington, 1976-79; assoc. Skadden, Arps, Slate, Meagher & Flom, N.Y.C., 1979-81; mng. dir., dep. gen. counsel Oppenheimer & Co., N.Y.C., 1981—; mem. adj. faculty Am. U. Washington Coll. Law, Washington, 1978-79. Mem. Nat. Assn. Securities Dealers, Inc. (mem. dist. 10 com.), Securities Industry Assn. (exec. com., compliance and legal divsn.). Office: Oppenheimer & Co Inc Oppenheimer Tower World Financial Center New York NY 10281

KRAMER, KAREN SUE, mind-body psychologist; b. L.A., Sept. 6, 1942; d. Frank Pacheco Kramer and Velma Eileen (Devlin) Moore; m. Stewart A. Sterling, Dec. 30, 1965 (div. 1974); 1 child, Scott Kramer Sterling. BA, U. Calif., Berkeley, 1966; MA, U.S. Internat. U., 1976; PhD, Profl. Sch. Psychology, 1980. Psychometrist U. Calif. Counseling Ctr., Berkeley, 1966-67; social worker Alameda County Welfare Dept., Oakland, Calif., 1967-69; vol. coord. San. Diego County Probation Dept., 1971-73; officer San Diego County Probation Dept., 1973-76; counselor and coord. clin. and outreach programs Western Inst., San Diego, 1976-77; program coord. and counselor Women's Resource Ctr., Oceanside, Calif., 1977-78; pvt. practice psychology San Diego, 1978-81; planner analyst San Diego County Dept. Health Svcs., 1979-81; social svcs. program cons. Calif. Dept. Social Svcs., Emeryville, 1981-83; affirmative action officer State Compensation Ins. Fund, San Francisco, 1983-87; regional property mgr. Compensation Ins. Fund, San Francisco, 1991—; community psychologist Calif. Dept. Mental Health, 1987-89; pvt. practice psychology Berkeley, 1990—; prof. Nat. U. San Diego, 1979-81; pres. North County Coun. Social Concerns, Vista, Calif., 1977-78; advisor USMC Camp Pendleton Human Svcs., 1978-87; mem. adv. bd. Chinatown Resources Devel. Ctr., San Francisco, 1984-87, San Francisco Rehab., 1984-87; bd. dirs. Network Cons. Svcs., Napa Calif.; founder Qi Gong China, 1994. Mem. Peer Counselors Assn. (adv. bd. 1987-90), Calif. Prevention Network (bd. dirs. 1989-93, editorial advisor jour. 1992-93).

KRAMER, LINDA LEE, assistant superintendent; b. San Jose, Aug. 25, 1954; d. John Graves Ricker and Yvonne Marie (Arbios) Jackson. BA, Calif. State U., Chico, 1976; MA, Calif. State U., Sacramento, 1985. Cert. tchr., Calif. Kindergarten tchr. Wasco (Calif.) Union Elem. Sch. Dist., 1976-78; 1st grade tchr. Pleasant Ridge Union Sch. Dist., Grass Valley, Calif., 1978-81, vice prin., kindergarten tchr., 1981-82, prin., kindergarten tchr., 1982-84, prin., 1984-89, asst. supt., 1989—; participant Adminstr. Tng. Ctr., 1986-87, prin. coord., trainer, 1987-88, 88-89, 89-90, 92—, trainer, 1990—; participant in workshops, seminars Nevada County Curriculum Coun. Recipient Regional Merit award Calif. Sch. Leadership Acad., 1992; Region 2/Nevada County Adminstr. of Yr. award ACSA, 1992. Mem. Assn. Sch. Adminstrs. (state bd. dirs. 1993—, mem. awds. com. chairperson 1991-92, past pres. 1989-90, pres. 1988-89, pres.-elect 1987-88, sec. 1986-87, Nevada County pres. 1984-86, v.p., program chairperson 1983-84, sec./treas. 1982-83). Episcopalian. Home: 5715 Tudor Way Loomis CA 95650 Office: Pleasant Ridge Union Sch Dist 22580 Kingston Ln Grass Valley CA 95949-7706

KRAMER, MARY ELIZABETH, health services executive, state legislator; b. Burlington, Iowa, June 14, 1935; d. Ross L. and Geneva M. (McElhinney) Barnett; m. Kay Frederick Kramer, June 13, 1958; children: Kent, Krista. BA, U. Iowa, 1957, MA, 1971. Cert. tchr., Iowa. Tchr. Newton (Iowa) Pub. Schs., 1957-61; tchr. Iowa City Pub. Schs., 1961-67, tchr., asst. supt., 1971-75; dir. pers. Younkers, Inc., Des Moines, 1975-81; v.p. human resources IASD Health Svcs Inc., Des Moines, 1981—; mem., asst. minority leader Iowa State Senate, Des Moines, 1990—. Bd. dirs. Polk County Child Care Rsch. Ctr., Des Moines, 1986—, YWCA, Des Moines, 1989-94; mem. Olympic adv. com. Blue Cross and Blue Shield Assn., Chgo., 1988-92. Named Mgr. of Yr. Iowa Mgmt. Assocs., 1985, Woman of Achievement YWCA, 1986, Woman of Vision Young Women's Resource Ctr., 1989. Mem. Soc. Human Resource Mgmt., Iowa Mgmt. Assn. (pres. 1988), Greater Des Moines C. of C. (bd. dirs. 1986—), Nexus, Rotary Internat. Republican. Presbyterian. Home: 1209 Ashworth Rd West Des Moines IA 50265-3546 Office: IASD Health Svcs Corp 636 Grand Ave Des Moines IA 50309 also: Iowa State Senate State Capitol Des Moines IA 50319

KRAMER, MARY VINCENT, information specialist; b. Rochester, N.Y., Sept. 30, 1957; d. Leonard Patterson and Ruth Helen (Farrell) Vincent; m. Dusty Kramer, Nov. 4, 1989; children: Morgan Lindsay, Matthew Aaron. AS in Bus. Adminstrn., Monroe Community Coll., Rochester, 1981; BS in Mgmt., St. John Fisher Coll., 1989. Tech. info. asst. Xerox Corp., Rochester, N.Y., 1979-89; tech. info specialist Xerox Corp., Rochester, 1989—; steering com. Treas. Employee Involvement, 1987-94. Recipient cert. of appreciation Assn. Info. and Image Mgmt., 1985. Mem. Assn. for Quality and Participation, Xerox Mgmt. Assn., Am. Mgmt. Assn., Alpha Sigma Lambda. Roman Catholic. Office: Xerox Corp 800 Phillips Rd Bldg 105-66C Webster NY 14580-9791

KRAMER, NANCY JOAN, calligrapher, designer, educator; b. Kew Gardens, N.Y., July 5, 1953; d. Franklin and Barbara (Richter) K.; m. Steven Craig Goldman, June 18, 1978; children: Allison, Eric. AB, Goucher Coll., 1975; MBA, Northeastern U., 1980; postgrad., Eastern Nazarene Coll. Cert. tchr., Mass.; engr. trainee. Owner, mgr., designer Notes Unltd., Randolph, Mass., 1984—; with Randolph Pub. Sch., 1985—; calligraphy instr. M.E. Young P.T.O. Elem. Sch., Randolph, 1987—; tchr., tchrs. aide Randolph Pub. Sch. System, 1991—; calligraphy instr. Massasoit Community Coll., Brockton, Mass., 1988—. Reporter (Goucher quarterly) Class Rep., 1987—. Mem. AAUW (v.p. 1987—). Home: 8 Bonnie Ln Randolph MA 02368-5227 Office: Notes Unltd Randolph MA 02368

KRAMER, REBECCA ANN, artist; b. Adrian, Minn., June 28, 1953; m. Richard P. Kramer, Dec. 27, 1975. BS, S.D. State U., 1977; postgrad., U. Mont., 1988-91. Freelance painter, sculptor Missoula, Mont., 1980—; exhbn. curator Greater Missoula Visual Artists Gallery Tours, 1989-91, Missoula Sister City Art Exhibit for Neckergemund, Germany, 1994; curator Missoula Cultural Exch., 1992-94. Exhibited in shows at No. Pacific Gallery, Missoula, 1990, Allistar Gold Gallery, Missoula, 1991, Gallery of Visual Arts/U. Mont., Missoula, 1991, Missoula Mus. Arts, 1992, 93, Ruggero Maggi, Milan, 1992, Mont. State U., Bozeman, 1992, Pacific Art Ctr., Seattle, 1993, Missoula Cultural Exch., 1994, Alt Rathaus Mus., Neckargemund, Germany, 1994, Ea. Wash. U., Cheney, 1994, others; represented in collections, including U. Mont. Bd. dirs., v.p. Bitterroot Homeowner's Assn., Lolo, Mont., 1985-92. Senator Pat Williams/Fell-Oskins grantee U. Mont., 1990. Mem. Women's Caucus Art (founder Mont. chpt. 1994), Greater Missoula Visual Artists (mem. steering com. 1989-91). Home: 6200 Delarka Dr Lolo MT 59847

KRAMER, RUTH, accountant; b. N.Y.C., June 20, 1925; d. Isidore and Sarah (Heller) Kleiner; m. Paul Kramer, Oct. 27, 1946; children: Stephen David, Lynne Adair. BA, Bklyn. Coll., 1946. Registered pub. acct., N.Y. Tchr. elem. sch. N.Y.C. Bd. Edn., 1946-50; acct. Lichtenstein & Kramer, N.Y.C., Lynbrook, N.Y., 1954; jr. ptnr. Paul Kramer & Co., Lynbrook, 1954-56, ptnr., 1956-65, mng. ptnr., 1965—; cons. Nassau County (N.Y.) Dist. Attys. Office, 1956-65; expert witness acctg. matters Nassau County

Grand Juries, 1956-65; bd. dirs. Flinch & Bruns Funeral Home, Inc.; mem. IRS liaison com. Bklyn. Dist., 1965-76; mem. N.Y. State Bd. for Pub. Accountancy, 1982-89. Troop leader Girl Scouts U.S., 1947-48; chmn. Tri-Town sect. Anti Defamation League, 1952-53; active Heart Fund; pres. Lynbrook Women's Rep. Club, 1956-58; treas. Assembly Candidates Campaign Com., 1964; mem. Nassau County Fedn. Rep. Women, Syosset Woodbury Rep. Club. Named Woman in Acctg., local TV channel, 1974. Mem. Nat. Soc. Pub. Accts. (del.), Empire State Assn. Pub. Accts. (Meritorious Service award, 2d v.p., 1975-76, 1st v.p. 1977-78, pres. 1978-79, Pres.'s award, 2d past pres. exec. bd. 1979-80, 1st past pres. exec. bd. 1981-82, pres. Nassau County chpt. 1962-63, 75-76, state bd. dirs. 1980—, Woman of Yr. award 1982), Tax Inst. C.W. Post Coll., Acctg. Inst. C.W. Post Coll. Clubs: Am. Jewish Congress, Lynbrook Pythian Sisters (past chief). Home and Office: 23 Hilltop Dr Syosset NY 11791-2002

KRAMER, TERESA LEE, clinical psychologist, educator; b. Dayton, Ohio, Sept. 13, 1956; d. Howard Clarence and Beverly Lee (Bane) K.; m. Kim Allen Jones, Oct. 5, 1991. BA in Comm. Arts, U. Cin., 1978, MA in Clin. Psychology, 1986, PhD in Clin. Psychology, 1989. Rsch. asst. to clin. dir. psychology dept. U. Cin., 1982-83, therapist walk-in clinic, 1983-84, intern dept. psychology, 1984-87; rsch. asst. dept. psychiatry Traumatic Stress Study Ctr. U. Cin. Coll. Medicine, 1987-88; psychology intern Med. U. S.C.-VA Med. Ctr., 1988-89; postdoctoral resident, co-instr. psychology Wright State U. Sch. Profl. Psychology, 1989-90; asst. prof. clin. psychiatry, assoc. dir. Traumatic Stress Study Ctr. U. Cin. Coll. Medicine, 1990—, instr. psychiatry residents, clin. supr. psychology students, 1990—, clin. coord. child and adolescent svcs., dir. rsch., 1992—; therapist Rollman Psychiat. Inst., Psychol. Svcs. Ctr. U. Cin., Juvenile Ct. Intervention Unit Hamilton County, Mental Hygiene Clinic VA Med. Ctr., Crime Victims Rsch. & Treatment Ctr.; with alcohol/drug treatment program VA Med. Ctr.; psychol. cons. Consultation/Liaison Svc.; pub. rels. dir. Kahn's & Co./ Hillshire Farms, 1981-82; mem. disaster response com. Dept. Psychiatry U. Cin. Coll. Medicine, 1993; mem. dissertation and master's thesis com. Union Inst. and U. Cin. Coll. Nursing, 1993; bd. dirs., mem. program devel., evaluation com. Women Helping Women, 1993; speaker various profl. confs. Editorial reviewer: Jour. Traumatic Stress, 1992—; contbr. articles to profl. jours. Organizer, co-facilitator support group for single mothers, 1982-83; vol. counselor Women Helping Women/Rape Crisis Ctr., 1981-82; mem. sexual assault care network Univ. Hosp., 1990—. Scripps-Howard scholar, 1977-78; rsch. grantee NIH, 1987. Mem. APA, Internat. Soc. for Traumatic Stress Studies, Ohio Psychol. Assn., Phi Beta Kappa. Presbyterian. Office: U Cin Dept Psych Sch Medicine M L 559 Cincinnati OH 45267

KRAMM, DEBORAH ANN, data processing executive; b. Pasadena, June 24, 1949; d. Donald F. and Mary (Roach) Coonan; m. Kenneth R. Kramm, Dec. 20, 1969; children: Deidre Lyn, Jonathan Russel. BA, U. Calif.-Irvine, 1971; MS, Mich. Tech. U., 1981. Math. asst. NASA-Jet Propulsion Lab., Pasadena, 1967-70; library asst. U. Calif. Irvine Libr., 1967-71; rsch. assoc. animal behavior lab. Mich. Tech. U. , Houghton, 1971-80; programmer/ analyst Shell Oil Co., Houston, 1981-85, corp. auditor EDP, 1985-87, team leader systems analyst, 1987-88, group leader SLA, 1988-90, supr. resource planning and adminstrn., 1990-91, adminstrv. coord. product devel. ctr.-design ctr., 1991-93, bus. analyst sr. systems analyst, 1993—; chmn. bd. MMARK, Houston, 1983-85. Contbr. articles to profl. jours.; Designer (program application software) Shell Point-of-Sale Terminal, 1982-85. Treas. KFHS Orch., 1986-88; co-leader Boy Scouts Am., Houston, 1981-83. AAUW scholar, 1980, Calif. State scholar, 1967-71. Mem. NAFE, AAUW (pres. br. 1975-81). Club: Shell Data Processors, Houston Bus. Forum (bd. dirs.). Home: 5814 Pinewilde Dr Houston TX 77066-2324 Office: Shell Oil Info Ctr 1500 Old Spanish Trl Houston TX 77054-1818

KRAMM, DEBORAH LUCILLE, lawyer; b. Milw.; d. Hartzell McDonald and Alice Lucille (Johnson) K.; m. Gary Baiz, June 19, 1988. Student, Trinity Coll., Deerfield, Ill., 1971-73; BS, Bradley U., 1974; JD, New Eng. Sch. of Law, 1977; postgrad., Georgetown U., 1978. Bar: N.Y. 1982, Ill. 1980, Mass. 1978. Trademark atty. U.S. Trademark Office, Washington, 1977-78; assoc. Hume, Clement, Willian, Brinks & Olds, Chgo., 1978-81; atty. Avon Products, Inc., N.Y.C., 1981-84; atty. Tiffany & Co., N.Y.C., 1981-84, v.p., sec., 1984-85; counsel Am. Brands, Inc., Old Greenwich, Conn., 1986—. Bd. dirs. Nat. Found. for Advancement for Arts, 1987-91; chmn. Martha Graham Guild, 1988—; trustee Martha Graham Ctr. for Contemporary Dance, Inc., N.Y.C., 1989—. Curt Tiege scholar, 1973. Mem. U.S. Trademark Assn. (bd. dirs. 1984-87), Cosmetic, Toiletry and Fragrance Assn. (chmn. trademark com. 1984). Office: Am Brands Inc 1700 E Putnam Ave Old Greenwich CT 06870-1300

KRANITZKY, MARY LISA, finance company executive; b. Schenectady, N.Y., July 20, 1955; d. Charles William Kranitzky, and Shirley Ann (Thomas) Ballou. BS in Fin., U. Ala., 1982. Fin. specialist GE Co., Birmingham, Ala., 1981-83, supv. acctg. adminstrn., Atlanta, 1984-85, corp. auditor, Schenectady, 1985-87; mgr. fin. analysis and auditing GE Constrn. Svcs., Burkville, Ala., 1988-90; mgr. fin. Manheim Auctions Inc., Atlanta, 1990-92; program fin. mgr. Latin Am. sales Gen. Electric Indsl. & Power Systems, Schenectady, 1992-94; dir. fin. GE Capital/PT Astra Sedaya Finance, Jakarta, Indonesia, 1995—. Bd. dirs. Birmingham Opera Theater, 1980—. Recipient Acad. Excellence medal Fin. Execs. Inst., 1982. Mem. Beta Gamma Sigma, Phi Kappa Phi, Omicron Delta Epsilon. Episcopalian. Avocations: music; water skiing; reading. Home: 73 Appletree Ln Clifton Park NY 12065 Office: PT Astra Sedaya Finance, JL R.S. Fatmawati No 9, Jakarta 12420, Indonesia

KRANJAC, PAULETTE LISA, advertising executive; b. Newark, N.J., Mar. 6, 1953; d. Sylvia Dorothy Tunis; m. Thomas Kranjac, Nov. 28, 1982. BA, CUNY, 1975, MA, 1978. Pres. List Process Co., Inc., N.Y.C., 1983—, List Process Mgmt., Inc., N.Y.C., 1983—, List Process Alternative Media, Inc., N.Y.C., 1989—, List Process Direct, Inc., N.Y.C., 1992—. Contbr. articles to profl. jours. Mem. Direct Mktg. Assn. (membership chair alternate response 1993), Advt. Women of N.Y., Women's Direct Mktg. Assn. Office: List Process Co Inc 420 E 79th St New York NY 10021

KRANKING, MARGARET GRAHAM, artist; b. Florence, S.C., Dec. 21, 1930; d. Stephen Wayne and Madge Williams (Dawes) Graham; BA summa cum laude (Clendenin fellow), Am. U., 1952; m. James David Kranking, Aug. 23, 1952; children: James Andrew, Ann Marie Kranking Eggleton, David Wayne. Asst. to head publs. Nat. Gallery Art, Washington, 1952-53; profl. artist, 1966—; tchr. art Woman's Club Chevy Chase (Md.), 1976-88; guest instr. Amherst Coll., 1985; one-woman shows: Spectrum Gallery, Washington, 1974, 76, 78, 79, 83, 85, 87, 90, 92, Philip Morris U.S.A., Richmond, Va., 1982, 83, 86, Florence (S.C.) Mus., 1991, Lombardi Cancer Treatment Ctr., Washington, 1992, Spectrum Gallery, 1995; group shows include: Balt. Mus., 1974, 76, Corcoran Gallery Art, Washington, 1952, 72, USIA Traveling Exhibit, C. Am., 1978-79, AARP Traveling Exhibition, 1986; represented in permanent collection U. Va., 1979, Philip Morris U.S.A., 1982, 83, USCG, 1986-93, AT&T, 1986, 88, Freddie Mac, 1987, 88, Florence Mus., S.C., 1994; traveling exhbn. Nat. Watercolor Soc., 1985-86, Watercolor U.S.A., 1987, 92, Am. Watercolor Soc., 1988, Am. Artist mag., 1988, 91, 92, North Light Mag., 1990, Adirondacks Nat. Exhbn. of Am. Watercolor, 1988, 89, Artitude 7th Internat. Art Competition, N.Y., 1989, Shada Gallery, Riyadh, Saudi Arabia, 1991, Belle Grove Plantation Invitational, Middletown, Va., 1994; ofcl. artist USCG. Mem. Spectrum Gallery Washington, So. Watercolor Soc., Artists Equity, Washington Watercolor Assn., M.W. Watercolor Soc., Potomac Valley Watercolorists (pres. 1981-83), Nat. Watercolor Soc, Southwestern Watercolor Soc. Roman Catholic. Home: 3504 Taylor St Bethesda MD 20815-4022

KRANTZ, JUDITH TARCHER, novelist; b. N.Y.C., Jan. 9, 1927; d. Jack David and Mary (Brager) Tarcher; m. Stephen Falk Krantz, Feb. 19, 1954; children: Nicholas, Anthony. B.A., Wellesley Coll., 1948. Fashion publicist Paris, 1948-49; fashion editor Good Housekeeping mag., N.Y.C., 1949-56; contbg. writer McCalls, 1956-59, Ladies Home Jour., 1959-71; contbg. west coast editor Cosmopolitan mag., 1971-79. Author: Scruples, 1978, Princess Daisy, 1980, Mistral's Daughter, 1982, I'll Take Manhattan, 1986, Till We Meet Again, 1988, Dazzle, 1990, Scruples Two, 1992, Lovers, 1994.

KRANTZ, MELISSA MARIANNE, public relations company executive; b. Cornwall, N.Y., Sept. 19, 1954; d. Abraham and Jane (Steinheimer) K.; m. David Michael Fleisher, Nov. 19, 1978; children: Jenny Rachel, Sara Rose. BA in Polit. Sci., SUNY Coll., Purchase, 1976. Account exec. Pub. Interest Pub. Relations, Inc., N.Y.C., 1975-77; assoc. Kekst & Co., N.Y.C., 1977-83, ptnr., 1983-91; v.p. corp. comm. JWP Inc., 1991-92; pres. Krantz Group, Inc., 1992—. Trustee Beth Am Shalom Synagogue, White Plains, N.Y., 1985-87, Mazon; bd. dirs. Project Ezra, N.Y.C., 1986—; bd. dirs. Better Bus. Bur. Met. N.Y., Inc., 1988—, mem. exec. com., 1989—. Democrat. Jewish. Home: 15 Franklin Ln Harrison NY 10528

KRANZ, DIANE ANNETTE, accountant; b. Williamsport, Pa., Oct. 4, 1966; d. James Albert and Ruth Ann (Nuss) K.; children: Anthony Mercaldo. BSBA in Acctg., Lycoming Coll., 1994. Fin. reporting acct. Brodart Co., Williamsport, Pa., 1987-94, supr. retail acctg., 1994—. Mem. Williamsport Mgmt. Club, Jr. League (Williamsport membership devel. 1992-93). Republican. Roman Catholic. Home: PO Box 4033 Williamsport PA 17701-0633 Office: Brodart Co 500 Arch St Williamsport PA 17705

KRASCHNESKE, MARGARETHE REGINA (MARGE SANERA), artist, educator; b. Pitts., June 23, 1911; d. Leo and Regina (Salzer) Sanera; m. John Herman Kraschneske, Aug. 31, 1940 (dec. 1971); children: Carol Joan Kraschneske Ford, Beth Kraschneske Fisher. Student, Art Inst. Pitts., 1930-31, John Huntington Inst., Cleve., 1933-34. Art dir. Ladies Day Out program Erie (Pa.) YWCA, 1950-63; art dir. Erie Day Sch., 1956-60; adminstr. art edn. Art Ctr. of Erie, 1957-67; artist-in-residence, tchr. The Summit, Austin, Tex., 1991; ind. artist Sanera Creative Portraits, Lakewood, Ohio; judge children's arts and crafts shows, Erie area, 1948-67; judge, chair art shows art clubs, Erie area, 1948-67; art. dir. Am. Women's Vol. Svcs., Erie, 1943-44; art tchr. Jr. ARC, Erie, 1949. Solo exhbns. include Erie Pub. Mus., 1949; paintings displayed in Bus. and Industry Art Ctr., Erie; represented in numerous pub. and pvt. collections in 34 cities of U.S. Winner 1st prize in oil Chautauqua (N.Y.) Art Assn., 1954, Oil Portrait prize Erie Art Club, 1961, 2d prize in water color May show Erie Art Club, 1955. Mem. Nat. Mus. Women in Arts (Washington) (charter), Art Club Erie (bd. dirs. 1950-57), Fedn. Erie Artists, Internat. Soc. Artists, Am. Portrait Soc. Republican. Lutheran. Home and Studio: Ste 111 The Carlyle 12900 Lake Ave Lakewood OH 44107-1577

KRASNER, DIANE LEE, enterostomal therapy nurse; b. Cleve., Apr. 8, 1953; d. Morton H. and Florence (Schermer) K.; m. George Krotkoff, Dec. 15, 1975. MA in Egyptology, Johns Hopkins U., 1976, MS in Adult Edn. with honors, 1985; BSN with honors, U. Md., 1979, MSN, 1994, postgrad., 1994—. Cert. enterostomal therapy nurse. Staff nurse, asst. head nurse Sinai Hosp. of Balt., 1979-81, enterostomal therapy nurse clinician, 1986-89; staff nurse surg. unit Greater Balt. Med. Ctr., 1981-82; instr. med.-surg. nursing Md. Gen. Hosp., 1982-85; enterostomal therapy nurse West Balt. Home Health Care, 1985, Harbor Hosp. Ctr., Balt., 1989-91; adj. faculty, mem. curriculum com. Harrisburg Area Enterostomal Therapy Nursing Edn. Program; mem. Nat. Pressure Ulcer Adv. Panel, 1992-94. Editor: Chronic Wound Care: A Clinical Source Book for Healthcare Professionals, 1990; author ednl. materials; mem. editorial adv. bd. Ostomy/Wound Mgmt., 1987—, rev. editor, 1989—, contbg. editor, 1991—; contbr. chpts. to books, articles to profl. jours. Mem. Wound Ostomy Continence Nurses Soc., World Coun. Enterostomal Therapy, Wound Healing Soc., United Ostomy Assn., Friends of Ostomates worldwide, Simon Found., Am. Cancer Soc., Md. Educators for Staff Devel., Johns Hopkins U. Alumni Assn., U. Md. Alumni Assn., Sigma Theta Tau, Pi Lambda Theta, Phi Kappa Phi. Home: 106 Armagh Dr Baltimore MD 21212

KRASNER, JENNY, sculptor; b. N.Y.C., Apr. 12, 1961; d. Oscar and Joanna (Vanterpool) K.; m. Erik Mitchell Quam, Sept. 12, 1992. BA, Hamilton Coll., 1983; BFA, Oxford (Eng.) U., 1986, MA, 1990; MFA, Columbia U., 1988. artist marketplace program Bronx Mus., 1992. One person show at Johnson & Johnson Gallery, New Brunswick, N.J., 1994; exhibited in group shows at Quietude Garden Gallery, East Brunswich, N.J., 1991, Nabisco Gallery, East Hanover, N.J., 1992, Ben Shahn Gallery, Wayne, N.J., 1992, Bronx (N.Y.) Mus., 1992, Progressive Culture Works, Jersey City, 1992, Art Ctr. on First, Jersey City, 1990, N.J. State Mus., Trenton, N.J., 1994, Jersey City Mus., 1994. J.B. Moore scholar, 1983, Trinity Coll. scholar to Oxford U., 1986, Vt. Studio Sch. scholar, 1987. Democrat. Home and Office: 380 Mountain Rd # 1706 Union City NJ 07087

KRASNOW, MARCIA LEE, early childhood education administrator; b. Denver, Feb. 25, 1947; d. Joseph Frank and Gladys (Davidson) Kauffman; m. Willard Krasnow, June 15, 1969. BS, Boston U., 1969; MEd, R.I. Coll., 1974, Tufts U., 1978; CAGS, Northeasthern U., 1984; EdD, U. Mass., 1995. Cert. tchr., tchr. young children with spl. needs, tchr. of moderate spl. needs, generic specialist, sch. counselor, elem. prin., supr./dir., Mass.; lic. mental health counselor, Mass. Primary grade tchr. Norwood (Mass.) Pub. Schs., 1969-77, early childhood specialist, 1978—, dir. Chpt. 188 grant, 1986—, dir. Even Start grant, 1991—; cons. in field, 1978—; adj. faculty Lesley Coll., Cambridge, Mass., 1978-85, Mass. Bay C.C., Wellesley, 1978-85; mem. policy coun. Head Start, Avon, Mass., 1990-92. Author: Triumph Teachers Guide, 1979. Bd. dirs. Dept. Social Svcs., South Area, Norwood, 1985-89, Office for Children, Norwood, 1978-82, Neponset Valley Nursing Assn., Norwood, 1980-93, Norfolk-Bristol Home Health Agy.; trustee Southwood Hosp.-Neponset Valley Health System, 1983-86. HEW grantee, 1977-78. Mem. NEA, Mass. Tchrs. Assn., Am. Counseling Assn., Delta Kappa Gamma. Office: Norwood Pub Schs 100 Westover Pkwy Norwood MA 02062

KRASSA, KATHY BOLTREK, molecular biologist; b. N.Y.C., Dec. 6, 1946; d. Henry and Gloria Beatrice (Poliakoff) Boltrek; m. Robert Frederick Taylor Krassa; children: Josh Boltrek, Vicky Krassa. BS, Cornell U., 1968; postgrad., L.I. U., 1973-74; PhD, U. Colo., 1987. Lab. tech. U. Colo., Boulder, 1968-70; teaching asst. C.W. Post Coll., L.I. U., Glen Cove, N.Y., 1973-74; rsch. assoc. Nassau County Med. Ctr., East Meadow, N.Y., 1975-79; teaching asst. U. Colo., Boulder, 1980-81, rsch. asst., 1981-87, postdoctoral rschr., 1988-91; CEO Molecular Jeanetics, Boulder, 1991—. Author: Structure and Function of the Single-Stranded DNA Binding Protein of the Bacteriophage T4, 1987; contbr. articles to profl. jours. NIH grantee, 1974, 82, Am. Cancer Soc. rsch. grantee, 1988, 89.

KRAUS, JEAN ELIZABETH GRAU, insurance agent; b. New Orleans, June 8, 1932; d. Adolph Eugene and Katherine Caroline (O'Nion) Grau; divorced; children: Steven, Marilyn, Laurence, Lorraine. BEd, Loyola U. of New Orleans, 1953, MS, 1972. Cert. tchr., La. Tchr. French and English Notre Dame Acad., Washington, 1954-55; tchr. French Orleans Parish Pub. Sch. Dist., New Orleans, 1953-54, 72-86; pvt. ins. agt., New Orleans, 1980—; tchr. gifted students Plaquemines Parish Pub. Schs., 1987-89; tchr. French East Baton Rouge, La., 1989-90, St. Charles Parish, La., 1990-91; registered rep. Jackson Nat. Fin. Svcs., New Orleans, 1993—. Author numerous poems, contbr. poetry to Scimitar and Song, Yearbook Modern Poetry, Reflections of Light Anthology, newspapers, mags. Pres. Aurora-Hyman-Kabel Civic Orgn., New Orleans, 1982—, del. Pres.' Council of Civic Orgns., 1984—; adv. bd. Algiers Community Network, 1985—; active Algiers Priorities Conv., 1986—, Non-Pack Police Support Group, West Bank Action Com. Mem. AAUW (past pres. Crescent City chpt.), Codofil, France-Amerique, Am. Assn. Tchrs. French, La. Edn. Assn., L'Athenee Louisinais, Internat. Platform Assn. Kappa Kappa Iota, Delta Epsilon Sigma, Kappa Delta Pi. Republican. Roman Catholic. Home and Office: 1601 Kabel Dr New Orleans LA 70131-3633

KRAUS, MARGERY, consultant; b. Franklin, N.J., May 20, 1946; d. Soland Lily (Cvern) Rosen; B.A. in Polit. Sci., Am. U., 1967, M.A. in govt., 1970; m. Stephen Kraus, Sept. 4, 1966; children—Lisa, Evan, Mara. With Close Up Found., Arlington, Va., 1971-84, v.p., 1976-84; exec. v.p. Arnold & Porter Consulting Group, Washington, 1984-86 , pres., 1987—; pres., CEO APCO Assocs. GCI Group Co., divsn. Grey Advt., 1994—; bd. dirs. Internat. Mgmt. and Devel. Inst.; cons., speaker in field. Chmn. bd. Children's Rsch. Inst., Children's Nat. Med. Ctr.; bd. dirs. Close Up Found., End Hunger Network, Pub. Affairs Coun., The Acad. Marshall Found., The Internat. Mgmt. and Devel. Inst. Home: 9609 Whitecedar Ct Vienna VA 22181-5423 Office: APCO 1155 21st St NW Ste 1000 Washington DC 20036-3308

KRAUS, NORMA JEAN, industrial relations executive; b. Pitts., Feb. 11, 1931; d. Edward Karl and Alli Alexandra (Hermanson) K. BA, U. Pitts., 1954; postgrad. NYU , 1959-61, Cornell U., 1969-70. Pers. mgr. for several cos., 1957-70; corp. dir. personnel TelePrompter Corp., N.Y.C., 1970-73; exec. asst., speech writer to lt. gov. N.Y. State, Office Lt. Gov., Albany, 1974-79; v.p. human resources, labor relations and stockholder relations Volt Info. Scis., Inc., N.Y.C., 1979—. Co-founder, Manhattan Women's Polit. Caucus, 1971, N.Y. State Women's Polit. Caucus, 1972, vice chair N.Y. State Women's Polit. Caucus, 1978; bd. dirs. Ctr. for Women in Govt., 1977-79. Lt. (s.g.) USNR, 1954-57. Pa. State Senatorial scholar, 1950-54. Mem. Women's Econ. Roundtable, Indsl. Relations Research Assn. Democrat. Avocations: politics, women's rights. Office: Volt Info Scis Inc 4th Fl 1221 Avenue of the Americas New York NY 10020-1579

KRAUS, PANSY DAEGLING, gemology consultant, editor, writer; b. Santa Paula, Calif., Sept. 21, 1916; d. Arthur David and Elsie (Pardee) Daegling; m. Charles Frederick Kraus, Mar. 1, 1941 (div. Nov. 1961). AA, San Bernardino Valley Jr. Coll., 1938; student Longmeyer's Bus. Coll., 1940; grad. gemologist diploma Gemological Assn. Gt. Britain, 1960, Gemological Inst. Am., 1966. Clk. Convair, San Diego, 1943-48; clk. San Diego County Schs. Publs., 1948-57; mgr. Rogers and Boblet Art-Craft, San Diego, 1958-64; part-time editorial asst. Lapidary Jour., San Diego, 1963-64, assoc. editor, 1964-69, editor, 1970-94, sr. editor, 1984-85; pvt. practice cons., San Diego, 1985—; lectr. gems, gemology local gem, mineral groups; gem & mineral club bull. editor groups. Mem. San Diego Mineral & Gem Soc., Gemol. Soc. San Diego, Gemol. Assn. Great Britain, Mineral. Soc. Am., Epsilon Sigma Alpha. Author: Introduction to Lapidary, 1987; editor, layout dir.: Gem. Cutting Shop Helps, 1964, The Fundamentals of Gemstone Carving, 1967, Appalachian Mineral and Gem Trails, 1968, Practical Gem Knowledge for the Amateur, 1969, Southwest Mineral and Gem Trails, 1972, Introduction to Lapidary, 1987; revision editor Gemcraft (Quick and Leiper), 1977; contbr. articles to Lapidary jour., Keystone Mktg. catalog. Home and Office: PO Box 600908 San Diego CA 92160-0908

KRAUS, SHERRY STOKES, lawyer; b. Richmond, Ky., Aug. 11, 1945; d. Thomas Alexander and Callie (Ratliff) Stokes; m. Eugene John Kraus, Aug. 27, 1966. Student, U. Ky., 1962-64; BS, Roosevelt U., 1966; JD cum laude, Albany Law Sch., 1975; LLM in Taxation, NYU, 1981. Bar: N.Y. 1976, U.S. Dist. Ct. (we. dist.) N.Y. 1976, U.S. Tax Ct. 1986. Law clk. U.S. Tax Ct., Washington, summer 1974, 4th dept. Appellate div. N.Y. State Supreme Ct., Rochester, 1975-77; assoc. Nixon, Hargrave, Devans & Doyle, Rochester, 1977-81, 83-84, Harter, Secrest & Emery, Rochester, 1984-86; pvt. practice Rochester, 1986—; faculty grad. tax program Sch. Law, NYU, N.Y.C., 1981-82; prin. tech. adv. to assoc. chief counsel - tech. IRS, Washington, 1983-84. Articles editor ABA Tax Articles Periodical, The Tax Lawyer, 1984-88; mng. editor NYU Tax Articles Periodical, NYU Tax Law Rev., 1981-82; lead articles editor Tax Articles Periodical, Albany Law Rev., 1973-75; contbr. articles to profl. jours. David J. Brewer scholar Albany Law Sch., 1973. Mem. ABA, N.Y. State Bar Assn. (tax sect. exec. com. 1984—), Monroe County Bar Assn. (treas. 1990-92), Monroe County Bar Found. (pres. 1994—), Justinian Soc. Office: 513 Times Square Building Bldg Rochester NY 14614-2078

KRAUSCHE-MARTIN, KAREN, social services administrator, clinical social worker; b. N.Y.C., Sept. 2, 1947; d. John Francis and Gladys Rose (Cure) K.; m. John Charles Martin, Oct. 16, 1977; children: Stacey Elizabeth, Sean Patrick. BA, Sacred Heart U., 1984, MAT, 1993; MSW, Fordham U., 1985; cert. family therapy, Smith Coll., 1989; MAT, Sacred Heart U., 1993. Cert. social worker, N.Y., Conn.; cert. sch. social worker, tchr., Conn. Social worker United Cerebral Palsy, Bridgeport, Conn., 1983, Norwalk (Conn.) Sch. Sys., 1983-84, Cath. Family Services, Bridgeport, 1984-89; pvt. practice social work Ctr. Family Guidance, Stratford, Conn., 1986-90; social worker Fairfield (Conn.) Bd. Edn., 1993—; cons. Apple Tree Nursery Sch., Trumbull, Conn., 1989-91, Shelton (Conn.) Bd. Edn., 1989-92; social worker Olsten-Kimberly Quality Care, 1994—; substitute tchr. Norwalk Sch. Sys., 1994—. Bd. dirs. Trumbull Counseling Ctr., 1984-89; mem. Regional Youth Substance Abuse Prevention Coun., Trumbull, 1988-89. Mem. Nat. Assn. Social Workers (register of clin. social work), Conn. Assn. Sch. Social Workers, Acad. Cert. Social Workers. Roman Catholic. Home: 50 Friar Ln Trumbull CT 06611-4014

KRAUSE, HEATHER DAWN, data processing executive; b. Kansas City, Kans., May 6, 1956; d. Jack E. Firth and Bonnie Jo (Reeves) Cupps; m. Kerry Murray Krause, May 23, 1981. Cert., Kansas City Skill Ctr., 1980. Cert. drafting tchr.; cert. in bus. supervision; cert. in Novell Netware system adminstrn. Assoc. drafter Black & Veatch, Kansas City, Mo., 1980; technician mech. design Wilcox Electric, Kansas City, 1980; coord. CAD design systems Smith & Loveless, Inc., Lenexa, Kans., 1980—; owner Digital Design Technologies, Kansas City, Mo., 1989—; tech. editor Que Books Macmillan Computer Pub., 1994—; instr. Longview C.C., Lee's Summit, Mo., 1987-93. Mem. NAFE, Kansas City Area AutoCAD Users Group, Heartland Windows User Group, Phi Theta Kappa. Democrat. Home: PO Box 11319 Kansas City MO 64112-0319

KRAUSE, HELEN FOX, physician, otolaryngologist; b. Boston, Mar. 20, 1932; d. Nathan and Frances Lena (Rich) Fox; children: Merrick-Eli, Beth Reva Krause-Harper, Kim Debra. BS, U. Maine, 1954; MD, Tuft U., 1958. Diplomate Am. Bd. Otolaryngology. Intern Health Ctr. Hosps. Pitts., 1958-59; resident Eye & Ear Hosp., Children's Hosp., VA Hosp., 1959-62; pvt. practice Pitts., 1962—; pres. Am. Acad. of Otolaryngic Allergy, 1984-85, Pa. Acad. of Otolaryngology, 1989-90; pres. Pitts. Otological Soc., 1983-85; cons. U.S. Pharmacopea, 1991—; bd. govs. Am. Acad. Otolaryngology H & N Surgery, 1982-89, 90—; clin. assoc. prof. U. Pitts. Sch. Medicine, Pa. State U. Hershey Med. Coll. Author, editor: Otolaryngic Allergy and Immunology, 1989; lectr., vis. prof. Singapore, Bangkok, Hong Kong (multiple tng. programs 1990); contbr. chpts. to books and articles to profl. jours. Pres. North Hills Jewish Community Ctr., Pitts., 1973-74; cons. North Allegheny Sch. Bd., Pitts., 1977; lectr. North Allegheny Sr. High Sch., Wexford, 1979-84; chmn. Desert Storm Project, North Hills Bus. and Profl. Women, 1991. Rsch scholar Jackson Meml. Labs., Bar Harbor, Maine, 1954; recipient Disting. Svc. award Pa. Acad. Otolaryngology, 1993, Hon. Achievement award Am. Acad. Otolaryngology and Surgery, 1993. Fellow Am. Coll. Surgeons, Am. Acad. Otolaryngologic Allergy (Svc. award 1990, cert. appreciation 1991), Am. Acad. Facial Plastic and Rsch. Surgery; mem. Phi Beta Kappa, Phi Kappa Phi. Office: 9104 Babcock Blvd Ste 4110 Pittsburgh PA 15237-5884

KRAUSE, LOIS RUTH BREUR, chemistry educator, engineer; b. Paterson, N.J., Mar. 26, 1946; d. George L. and Ruth Margaret (Farquhar) Breur; m. Bruce N. Pritchard, 1968 (div. May 1982); children: John Douglas, Tiffany Anne,; m. Robert H. Krause, June 16, 1990. Student, Keuka Coll., 1964-65; BS in Chemistry cum laude, Fairleigh Dickinson U., 1980, MAT summa cum laude, 1994; postgrad., Stevens Inst. Tech., Clemson U., 1994—. With dept. R & D UniRoyal, Wayne, N.J., 1966-68, Jersey State Chem. Co., North Haledon, 1968-69, Inmont, Clifton, N.J., 1969; from chemist to sr. analyst Lever Bros., Edgewater, N.J., 1976-80; process engr. Bell Telephone Labs., Murray Hill, N.J., 1980-84, RCA, Somerville, N.J., 1984-86; sr. engr. electron beam lithography ops. Gain Electronics Corp., Somerville, 1986-88; ind. tech. cons. Pritchard Assocs., Budd Lake, N.J., 1988-92; tchr. of math. and scis. Mt. Olive Bd. Edn. (temporary assignments), 1990-92; tchr. chemistry Morris Hills Regional Dist., 1992-93; instr. in chemistry Clemson U., 1994—; presenter profl. papers for profl. confs. Patentee package design. Troop leader, trainer, cons. Bergen County council Girl Scouts U.S., 1969-80, troop leader Morris Area council, 1980-83, head com. Mt. Olive twp., 1980-81; den leader, den leader coach, trainer Boy Scouts Am., 1973-76. Peter Sammartino scholar, 1994. Fellow Am. Inst. Chemists; mem. IEEE (sr.), NEA, NRA (life), AAAS, ASCD, Components, Hybrids and Mfg. Tech. Soc. (semicondr. tech. subcom. Electronic Components Conf. program com. 1981-86), Am. Soc. Quality Control, Soc. Women Engrs., Am. Chem. Soc., Assn. Women in Sci., Nat. Woodlot Owners Assn., Arbor Day Found., Mensa, Marine Corps League Aux., Phi Omega Epsilon, Phi Delta Kappa. Republican. Episcopalian. Home and Office: 303 Cherokee Hills Dr Pickens SC 29671

KRAUSE, SUSAN RUTH, artist; b. Fond du Lac, Wis., Feb. 25, 9140; d. Arnold Frank and Meta Firle; m. Kurth Werner Krause, June 15, 1963;

children: Scott Alan, Sheryl Lynn. BS, U. Wis., 1962; student, Houston Mus. Fine arts, 1974-75, Laguna Sch. Art, Laguna Beach, Calif., 1982. Cert. occupational therapist. Staff occupational therapist Milw. County Mental Health, 1963-65; tchr. art St. Thomas Day Sch., Nassau Bay, Tex., 1970-74; pres., gen. mgr. Art-A-Fair Festival, Laguna Beach, 1988-90; ptnr. Back Door Gallery, Laguna Beach, 1990-92; staff Occupl. Therapist Sundance Rehab., 1993; acting dir. of Occupl. Therapy Beverly Manor, Costa Mesa, Calif., 1994—. Numerous one woman and group shows throughout Ariz. Calif., Wis. and Tex. Bd. dirs. Tourism, Arts and Promotion, Costa Mesa, Calif., 1989-90; pres. Barnraisers - Discovery Mus. of Orange County, Santa Ana, Calif., 1985—; parks commr. City of El Lago, Tex., 1972-74; bd. dirs. El Lago Pool and Recreation Assn., 1972-74; pres. Costa Mesa Art League, 1978-80, Clear Creek Art League, 1977-78; mem. Punch and Judy Guild of Children's Hosp. of Orange County, 1977-95, pres., 1983-84, mem. All Guilds Fashion Show adv. bd., 1984-95, gen. chmn., 1992. Mem. Laguna Mus. Art, Costa Mesa C. of C., Newport Harbor C. of C., bd. dirs. of Dolphins Group.

KRAUS-FRIEDMANN, NAOMI, biochemistry educator; b. Budapest, Hungary, July 4, 1933; came to U.S., 1965; d. Jacob and Vilma Krausz; divorced; 1 child, Daphna Friedmann. MS, Hebrew U., Jerusalem, 1960; PhD, Hebrew U., 1965. Instr. sch. medicine U. Pa., Phila., 1968-74; asst. prof. sch. medicine U. Tex., 1974-76, assoc. prof. sch. medicine, 1976-86; prof. sch. medicine U. Tex., Houston, 1986—. Editor: Hormonal Regulation of Gluconeogenesis, 1986; contbr. over 100 sci. papers to profl. jours. Mem. Assn. Women in Sci. (pres. Houston Gulf chpt. 1975-77, v.p. Houston Gulf chpt. 1989-90). Office: U Tex Sch Medicine Dept Physiol Cell Biol Houston TX 77225

KRAUSS, BEATRICE JOY, psychology researcher, educator; b. Portland, Oreg., Dec. 26, 1943; d. Edwin Eugene and Mable Maru (Wilhelm) Osgood; m. Herbert Harris Krauss, Aug. 28, 1965; children: Michael Conal, Daniel Avram. MusB, Northwestern U., 1965; MA, U. Kans., 1967; PhD, CUNY, 1979. Dir. rsch. Community Sch. Dist. 18, Bklyn., 1978-79; asst. prof. Coll. of New Rochelle, N.Y., 1979-87, assoc. prof., 1987-90, dir. coll. ctr., dir. women's studies, 1989-90; mgr. rsch. group Eric Marder Assocs., N.Y.C., 1986-89; sr. rsch. assoc. Meml. Sloan Kettering Cancer Ctr., N.Y.C., 1990-93; sr. project dir., prin. investigator Nat. Devel. and Rsch. Inst., Inc., N.Y.C., 1993—; treas. Internat. Orgn. for Study Group Tensions, N.Y.C., 1987—; mem. Jacob's Inst. for Women's Health. Reviewer Jour. Health and Social Behavior, Psycho-Social Oncology, (with others) Living with Anxiety and Depression, 1974; contbr. articles to profl. jours. Cons. Com. on Alcohol and Drug Abuse, Irvington, N.Y., 1983-84; pres. Sleepy Hollow Concert Assn., Tarrytown, N.Y., 1983-85, 90-92. Grantee Coll. of New Rochelle, 1985, NIMH, 1990, 94, SPSSI, 1992, N.Y. State Legis., 1993, N.Y. State AIDS Inst., 1993. Mem. AAAS, APA (task force on teaching psychology of women 1982-84), Am. Evaluation Assn., Assn. for Women in Psychology (assoc. editor newsletter 1988), N.Y. Acad. Scis., Sigma Xi, Psi Chi. Home: 6 Downing Ct Irvington NY 10533-2330

KRAUSS, JUDITH BELLIVEAU, nursing educator; b. Malden, Mass., Apr. 11, 1947; d. Leo F. and Dorothy (Conners) Belliveau; m. Ronald L. Krauss, Sept. 5, 1970; children: Jennifer Leigh, Sarah Elizabeth. BS, Boston Coll., 1968; MSN, Yale U., 1970. RN, Conn. Clinical specialist Conn. Mental Health Ctr., New Haven, 1971-73; instr., clin. specialist Yale Sch. Nursing, New Haven, 1971-73; asst. prof. rsch. Yale U. Sch. Nursing, New Haven, 1973-78, assoc. dean, 1978-85; prof., dean Yale U. Sch. Nursing, New Haven, Conn., 1985—; cons. pharm. and pub. cons., schs., govt. agys. Author: The Chronically Ill Psychiatric Patient and the Community, 1982 (Am. Jour. Nursing Book of Yr. 1982); editor Archives of Psychiat. Nursing, 1986—; mem. edit. bd. Issues in Mental Health Nursing, Psycholsocial Rehab., Psychiat. Nursing Forum, Hosp. and Cmty. Psychiatry; contbr. articles to profl. jours. Am. Nurses Found. scholar, 1978; recipient Chamberlain award Soc. Edn. and Rsch. in Nursing, 1994; named Disting. Alumna Yale Sch. Nursing, 1984. Mem. ANA (psychiat. nursing coun., Disting. Contbn. to Psychiat. Nursing award 1992), Am. Acad. Nursing, Conn. Nurses Assn. (mem. cabinet on edn. 1987-89, bd. dirs. 1988-91, rep. to ANA house of dels. 1988-91, Josephine Dolan award 1989), Sigma Theta Tau (Disting. Lectr. award 1987), Delta Mu (Founders award 1987). Office: Yale U Sch Nursing PO Box 9740 New Haven CT 06536-0740

KRAUSS, SUE ELIZABETH, radiologist technologist, medical management; b. Poplar Bluff, Mo., Oct. 29, 1951; d. Raymond Harry and Wanda Elizabeth (Randol) Gibson; 1 child, Emily Sue. AS in Radiol. Tech., Santa Fe Jr. Coll., 1971. Radiol. technologist U. Fla., Gainesville, 1971-73; sect. chief Mt. Sinai Hosp., Miami Beach, Fla., 1973-76; asst. chief Miami Heart Inst., 1976-80; radiol. technologist Casa Grande (Ariz.) Regional Med. Ctr., 1983—; CEO AMMAN, Inc., Casa Grande, 1986—. Mem. Am. Soc. Radiol. Technologists, Am. Registry Radiol. Technologists, Radiology Bus. Mgrs. Assn., Rural Health Care Clinics Assn., Assn. Physician Hosp. Orgns., Casa Grande Regional Med. Aux., Am. Cancer Soc., Am. Mgmt. Assn., Nat. Parks and Conservation Assn., Audobon Soc., World Wildlife Fedn., World Wildlife Fund, Sierra Club. Republican. Baptist. Office: AMMAN Inc 900 E Florence Blvd Ste D Casa Grande AZ 85222-4673

KRAUT, JOANNE LENORA, computer programmer, analyst; b. Watertown, Wis., Oct. 29, 1949; d. Gilbert Arthur and Dorothy Ann (Gebel) K.; BA in Russian, U. Wis., Madison, 1971, MS in Computer Sci., 1973. Computer programmer U. Wis. Sch. Bus., Madison, 1969-72, Milw. Ins. Co., 1973-74; tech. coord. Wis. Dept. Justice, Madison, 1974-83; tech. svcs. supr. CRC Telecommunications (formerly Benchmark Criminal Justice Systems), New Berlin, Wis., 1983-89; sr. programmer/analyst Info. Communications Corp., Pub. Safety Software, Inc., 1989-91; advanced systems engr. EDS, 1991-93; technical specialist Time Ins., Milw., 1993—. Mem. Lakewood Gardens Assn. (dir. 1981-83), Dundee Terrs. Condominium Assn. (officer 1983—). Mem. Phi Beta Kappa. Home: 609 Dundee Ln Hartland WI 53029-2722 Office: Time Ins 501 W Michigan Milwaukee WI 53201

KRAVEC, CYNTHIA VALLEN, microbiologist; b. Newark, Sept. 8, 1951; d. William George and Elizabeth Irene (VanAllen) K. BS, Syracuse (N.Y.) U., 1974; MS, Seton Hall U., S. Orange, N.J., 1980; MBA, Monmouth Coll., W. Long Branch, N.J., 1986. Registered microbiologist. Sr. technician GIBCO/Invenex, Millburn, N.J., 1974-79; rsch. scientist Wampole Labs. div. Carter-Wallace Inc., East Windsor, N.J., 1979-90; scientist Roche Diagnostic Systems subsidiary Hoffmann-LaRoche, Inc., Nutley, N.J., 1990—. Contbr. articles to profl. jours. Mem. Am. Soc. Microbiology, Tissue Culture Assn., Soc. of Indsl. Microbiology. Home: 1006 Coolidge St Westfield NJ 07090-1215 Office: Roche Diagnostic Systems 1080 US Hwy 202 North Branch NJ 08876-1760

KRAVITCH, PHYLLIS A., federal judge; b. Savannah, Ga., Aug. 23, 1920; d. Aaron and Ella (Wiseman) K. B.A., Goucher Coll., 1941; LL.B., U. Pa., 1943; LL.D. (hon.), Goucher Coll., 1981. Bar: Ga. 1943, U.S. Dist. Ct. 1944, U.S. Supreme Ct. 1948, U.S. Ct. Appeals (5th cir.) 1962. Practice law Savannah, 1944-76; judge Superior Ct., Eastern Jud. Circuit of Ga., 1977-79, U.S. Ct. Appeals (5th cir.), Atlanta, 1979-81, U.S. Ct. Appeals (11th cir.), 1981—. Trustee Inst. Continuing Legal Edn. in Ga., 1979-82; mem. Bd. Edn., Chatham County, Ga., 1949-55; mem. coun. Law Sch., Emory U., Atlanta, 1986-91; mem. vis. com. Law. Sch., U. Chgo., 1990-93. Recipient Hannah G. Solomon award Nat. Coun. Jewish Women, 1978, James Wilson award U. Pa. Law Alumni Soc., 1992. Fellow Am. Bar Found.; mem. ABA (Margaret Brent award 1991), Savannah Bar Assn. (pres. 1976), State Bar Ga., Am. Judicature Soc., Am. Law Inst, U. Pa. Law Soc. Office: US Ct Appeals 11th Circuit 56 Forsyth St NW # 202 Atlanta GA 30303

KRAVITZ, KATHY, English language educator; b. Phila., June 13, 1949; d. Jordan Kravitz and Betty (Schane) Shore. BS, Millersville State Coll., 1972; MA, Villanova U., 1976. Cert. tchr., Pa. Tchr., coach Souderton (Pa.) Sch. Dist., 1972—; advisor Youth to Youth, Souderton, Pa., 1987—; trainer Youth to Youth Internat., Columbus, Ohio, 1991—; tchr., coach Beaver Coll., Glenside, Pa., 1983—; coach Chestnut Hill (Pa.) Coll., 1989-91; cons. Health Promotion Coun., Phila., 1993—. Recipient Gov.'s Highway Safety award for Alcohol Edn. Pa. Highway Dept., 1993, Drug Educators award Montgomery County, 1990; named Coach of Yr. by Pa. Athletics Conf., 1994. Mem. PAAWARE (com. chair 1991-93), Drug/Alcohol Resistance Team (bd. dirs. 1992-93), Pa. State Edn. Assn. Democrat. Mem. Soc. of Friends. Home: 325 Britt Rd North Wales PA 19454-2417 Office: Indian Crest Mid Sch 139 Harleysville Pike Souderton PA 18964-2095

KRAY, ANTOINETTE, actress; b. Chgo., June 13, 1911; d. Meyer and Lizaveta Markovna (Taranova) Krawitz. Student, Art Inst., Chgo., 1928-30. Children's illustrator Jr. Life, Chgo., 1930-31, Hygeia, Chgo., 1930-31. Actress (off broadway plays) The Chief Thing, Marouf, The Glass Menagerie, Slow Night in Elk City, Widower's Houses, The Blue Bird, Don Perlimplin; (TV shows) The Doctors, Search for Tomorrow, World Apart, East Side, West Side, The Reporter, The Defenders, For the People, Trials of O'Brien, Consumer Survival Kit, Lucky Pup (commls.) Bell Telephone, Sylvania, WXYZ-TV (News Promo), Balt. Fed. Loan (cable TV) Well Hello Fanny; author: Isn't it a Lovely Day, 1978, Mother Bickerdyke & Me, 1988. Mem. Actors Equity Assn., Screen Actors Guild, Am. Fedn. of TV and Radio Actors, Dramatists Guild, Inc.

KRAY, ELAINE LOUISE, auditor; b. Pitts., Oct. 31, 1943; d. Richard Lewis and Elizabeth Barbara (Carrola) Reese; m. Roger W. Kray, May 8, 1965 (dec. 1983); children: Arlene Erickson, Jason Reese. AS, Pitts. Bus. Acad., 1962. Info. systems/staff mem. Allegheny Power Svcs., Greensburg, Pa., 1966-74; asst. to the pres. O.S.I. Inc., Pitts, 1987-89; auditor Aqua Marine Resort and Country Club, Avon Lake, Ohio, 1989-92, Holiday Inn, Westlake, Ohio, 1993—; owner Well Pleased Co., Avon Lake, Ohio, 1992—; cons. rooms divsn. Heaven on Earth Inn, Avon Lake, Ohio, 1993-94; hotel/restaurant evaluator OSI Inc., 1987—. Creator coupon filing system "Clipper Sheet", 1992. Found. Young Widowed Parents, Pitts., 1984-89; cert. grief counselor South Hills Health Sys., Pitts., 1986-89; cert. bereavement counselor New Life Hospice of Greater Lorain County, Elyria, Ohio, 1994—; coach Odyssey of the Mind, Avon Lake, 1992; vol. Lorain County Blood Bank, Avon Lake, 1991—. Mem. Am. Inst. of Wine and Food, Wine Tasters Guild, Intertel, Soc. for Creative Anachronism, DAR, Mensa (gifted children coord. 1986-88). Republican. Home: 32682 Carriage Ln Avon Lake OH 44012

KREAGER, EILEEN DAVIS, administrative consultant; b. Caldwell, Ohio, Mar. 2, 1924; d. Fred Raymond and Esther (Farson) Davis. B.B.A., Ohio State U., 1945. With accounts receivable dept. M & R Dietetic, Columbus, Ohio, 1945-50; complete charge bookkeeper Magic Seal Paper Products, Columbus, 1950-53, A. Walt Runglin Co., Los Angeles, 1953-54; office mgr. Roy C. Haddox and Son, Columbus, 1954-60; bursar Meth. Theol. Sch. Ohio, Delaware, 1961-86; adminstrv. cons. Fin. Ltd., 1986—; ptnr. Coll. Administrv. Sci., Ohio State U., 1975-80; seminar participant Paperwork Systems and Computer Sci., 1965, Computer Systems, 1964, Griffith Found. Seminar Working Women, 1975; pres. Altrusa Club of Delaware, Ohio, 1972-73. Del. Altrusa Internat., Montreal, 1972, Altrusa Regional, Greenbrier, 1973. Mem. AAUW, Assoc. Am. Inst. Mgmt. (exec. council of Inst., 1979); Am. Soc. Profl. Cons., Internat. Platform Assn., Ohio State U. Alumna Assn., Columbus Computer Soc., Innovation Alliance, Toastmasters Internat., Ohio State U. Faculty Club, Univ. Club of Columbus, Delaware Country Club, Columbus Met. Club, Kappa Delta. Methodist. Home: PO Box 214 Columbus OH 43085-0214

KREAR, GAIL RICHARDSON, elementary education educator, consultant; b. Little Rock, July 24, 1942; d. Floyd E. Richardson and Selmarie (Hart) VanDerGriff; m. Bill J. Eason, May 17, 1963 (dec. 1985); 1 child, Kari V.; m. J. David Krear, Feb. 14, 1993. BA, U. Ark., 1964; MS, George Washington U., 1974; PhD in Elem. Edn., Montgomery County Pub. Schs., 1976. Ednl. cons., 1976-77, 85—; acting prin. Montgomery County Pub. Schs., Rockville, Md., 1974-76; tchr. in an award sch. State Sch. of Excellence, Rockville, Md., 1991-92; tchr. Nat. Sch. Excellence, 1994-95. Coach Montgomery County Recreational Dept., Rockville, 1978-81, Olney Boys & Girls Club, 1982. Mem. Am. Contract Bridge League (life master), Washington Bridge League, Alpha Delta Pi. Republican. Office: Montgomery County Pub Schs Rockville MD 20850

KREBILL, KERRY LORRAINE, conductor; b. Ames, Iowa, Mar. 23, 1947; d. Lyle Darwin and Leila Eleanor (Lander) Inskeep; m. John Robert Krebill, Sept. 3, 1967 (ec. Dec. 1985); children: Kristin Liesbeth Krebill McCabe, Peter Frederick Inskeep. BA in Music Edn., Drake U., 1970; M of Music in Choral Conducting, Cath. U. Am., 1981. Dir. music Cottage Grove Presbyn. Ch., Des Moines, 1969-75, St. Patrick's Roman Cath. Ch., Cambridge, Mass., 1975-77, Lexington (Mass.) United Meth. Ch., 1976-77, Colesville United Meth. Ch., Silver Spring, Md., 1977-78, Gaithersburg (Md.) Presbyn. Ch., 1983-84; mem. profl. choir Nat. Shrine Immaculate Conception, Washington, 1979-82; music dir., founder Musikanten Chamber Ensemble, Bethesda, Md., 1979—; artistic dir. Alexandria (Va.) Choral Soc., 1982—; dir. chorus Trinity Coll., Washington, 1980-82; adj. prof. music U. D.C., 1989—; guest conductor Salzburg (Austria) Ch. Music Festival, 1991, Am. Guild Organists, Annapolis, Md., 1977, Cmty. Schs., Arlington, Va., 1977, Interfaith Concert, Washington, 1977, organizer, conductor Ednl. Travel, Inc., Poland, Italy, Flanders, 1990, 92, 93; tchr. piano, pvt. practice, Bethesda, 1991—. Am. Field Svc. scholar, Netherlands, 1965-66, Cath. U. Bd. Trustees scholar, Washington, 1979-81; recipient Alexandria (Va.) C. of C. Woman-to-Woman citation, 1992, Louise Goucher Meml. award Am. Choral Found., 1993, Adventuresome Programming of Contemporary Music award ASCAP. Mem. Am. Choral Dirs. Assn. (Md. state pres. 1989-90), Chorus Am., Conductors Guild, Sigma Alpha Iota, Phi Kappa Phi, Pi Kappa Lambda. Democrat. Presbyterian. Home: 9307 Wadsworth Dr Bethesda MD 20817-2413

KREBS, CAROL MARIE, architect; b. St. Louis, May 6, 1958; d. Festus John and Virginia (Klohr) K. B in Environ. Design, U. Kans., 1982; MA in Edn. Counseling, St. Louis U., 1995. Archtl. intern GSA, Kansas City, Mo., 1980-81, Old Post Office Renovation, St. Louis, 1980-81; free-lance archtl. designer St. Louis, 1981-84; archtl. designer Interior Space, St. Louis, 1984, Gina Ward and Assoc., St. Louis, 1984-85, Michael Fox and Assoc., St. Louis, 1985-86; mgr. facility design and constrn. Southwestern Bell Telephone, St. Louis, 1986-88; mgr. int. arch. and design exec. facilities Southwestern Bell Corp. Asset Mgmt., St. Louis, 1989-90; psychiat. therapist DePaul Health Ctr., St. Louis, 1994—. Big sister Big Bros./Big Sisters of Greater St. Louis, 1986—; mem. Operation Food Search. Mem. AIA. Home: 965 Cleveland Ave Saint Louis MO 63122-2606

KREBS, HOPE PAULA, lawyer; b. Phila., Feb. 13, 1961; d. Robert Krebs and Lois Sheila (Ponnock) Krebs Panitch.; m. Kim R. Kinser, May. 17, 1992. BS in Acctg., Drexel U., 1984; JD, Villanova (Pa.) U., 1987; LLM in Taxation, N.Y.U., 1992. Bar: N.Y. 1988, U.S. Tax Ct. 1988. Part-time acct. Morris J. Cohen & Co., Phila., 1980-84; law clerk Frank & Pollack, Phila., 1985-86; lawyer Gordon, Hurwitz, Butowsky et al, N.Y.C., 1987-90, Varet & Fink P.C., N.Y.C., 1990—; adjunct prof. of law Villanova U. Sch. of Law, 1995—; adj. prof. law Villanova U. Sch. Law, 1995—. Contbr. articles to profl. jours. Mem. ABA, NAFE, Internat. Fiscal Assn., Internat. Tax Inst., Am. Women's Econ. Devel. Corp., Network Enterprising Women, N.Y. State Bar Assn., N.Y. Women's Bar Assn., Wall St. Tax Assn. Democrat. Jewish. Office: Varet & Fink PC 53 Wall St New York NY 10005-2834

KREBS, LINDA UREN, oncology nurse; b. Schenectady, N.Y., May 22, 1946; d. Donald Eveleth and Emily Chandler (Whittredge) Uren; children: William Douglas V, Robin Elizabeth. BSN, U. Vt., 1968; MSN, U. Colo., 1977, postgrad. Cert. oncology nurse. Staff nurse Hartford (Conn.) Hosp., 1968-69; staff and charge nurse 5th Ave. Gen. Hosp., Huntsville, Ala., 1969-71, NIH, Bethesda, Md., 1973-74; oncol. nurse specialist Denver Gen. Hosp., 1978, Colo. Regional Cancer Ctr., Denver, 1978-80, Univ. Hosp., Denver, 1980-88; nursing oncol. program leader Univ. Colo. Cancer Ctr., Denver, 1988—; instr. J.F. Drake State Tech. Trade Sch., Huntsville, 1971; sr. instr. Univ. Colo. Sch. Nursing, Denver, 1983—; lectr. Cancer Info. Svc., Colorado Springs, 1989—; cons. Am. Cancer Soc., Denver, 1980—, Cancer Rsch. Ctr., Lakewood, Colo., 1993—. Contbr. articles to profl. jours. and chpts. in books. Bd. dirs. Am. Cancer Soc. Colo. Divsn., Denver, 1988—; adv. bd. mem. Colo. Mammography Trust, Denver, 1990—. Mem. Oncology Nursing Soc. (chpt. com. 1987-91, membership com. 1991-94, v.p. Metro Denver chpt. 1983-84, pres. 1984-88, rsch. chair 1988—, bd. dirs. 1994—, Pres.'s award 1992), Sigma Theta Tau (nominating com. 1984). Office: Univ Colo Health Scis Ctr Box B 189 4200 E 9th Ave Denver CO 80262

KREBS, MARGARET ELOISE, publishing company executive; b. Clearfield, Pa., Apr. 20, 1927; d. Henry Louis and Delia Louise (Beahan) K.; grad. high sch. With Progressive Pub. Co., Inc., Clearfield, 1945—, bus. office mgr., 1956-60, bus. mgr., 1960-63, asst. to pub., 1963-69, asso. pub., 1981—, dir., exec. v.p., 1969-77, pres., 1977—; v.p./sec. Clearfield Broadcasters, Inc., Stas. WCPA-AM and WQYX-FM, 1965—, dir., 1971—. Mem. Pa. Newspaper Women's Assn., Clearfield Bus. and Profl. Women's Club (pres. 1952-53, dist. membership chmn. 1952-53), Sigma Delta Chi. Democrat. Roman Catholic. Club: Lake Glendale Sailing (sec. 1966—). Home: 526 Ogden Ave Clearfield PA 16830-2146 Office: 206 E Locust St Clearfield PA 16830-2423

KREBS, MARTHA, physicist, federal agency administrator. Ph.D., theoretical physics, Catholic U. of America, Washington, D.C., 1966. Staff dir. House subcommittee on energy development and applications, Washington, D.C., 1977-83; assoc. dir. planning and development Lawrence Berkeley Lab., 1983-93; dir., office of energy research Dept. of Energy, 1993—. Office: Office of Energy Rsch Dept Energy 1000 Independence Ave SW Washington DC 20585

KREBSBACH, RENITA ALLENE, software engineer, systems analyst; b. Billings, Mont., Mar. 30, 1960; d. Kevin Peter and Allene Roberta (Small) K. BS in Computer Sci., Mont. State U., 1983. Software engr. Boeing Def. and Space Group Boeing Co., Kent, Wash., 1983-89, systems analyst Computer Svcs., 1989-92; software test engr. Boeing Def. and Space Group Boeing Co., Seattle, 1992-93, Hughes Info. Tech. Corp., Aurora, Colo., 1994—. Mem. Nat. Geog. Soc., Soc. Women Engrs. (sect. sec. 1987, sect. rep. 1988-90, dir. 1990-92), Enological Soc. (Seattle chpt.), Mont. State U. Alumni Assn., Cascade Bicycle Club, Hughes Leadership Club, AAA Club. Republican. Presbyterian. Home: # 302 12734 E Asbury Cir Aurora CO 80014

KREEK, MARY JEANNE, physician; b. Washington; d. Louis Francis and Esperance (Agee) Kreek; BA, Wellesley Coll., 1958; MD, Columbia, 1962; m. Robert A. Schaefer, Jan. 24, 1970; children: Robert A., Esperance Anne. Med. researcher NIH, Bethesda, Md., 1957-62; intern, resident Cornell N.Y. Hosp. Med. Ctr., N.Y.C., 1962-65, fellow, 1965-67; instr. medicine Cornell Med. Coll., 1966-67; acad. medicine specializing in internal medicine, endocrinology, gastroenterology, clin. pharmacology, N.Y.C., 1966—; mem. staff N.Y. Hosp.-Cornell U., 1968-77, clin. asst. prof., asst. attending physician, now assoc. attending physician, adj. assoc. prof.; asst. prof. Rockefeller U., 1967-72, sr. rsch. assoc., physician, 1972-83, assoc. prof., physician, 1983-94, prof., sr. physician, head of lab., 1994—; head Ind. Lab. on Biology of Addictive Diseases, 1975-94, head Lab., 1994—; sr. physician Rockefeller U. Hosp., 1994—; mem. gen. medicine study sect. NIH, 1973-77; co-chmn. John E. Fogarty (NIH) Internat. Conf. Hepatotoxicity Due to Drugs and Chems., 1977; vis. prof. Pahlavi U., Shiraz, Iran, summer 1977; spl. adv. Nat. Inst. Drug Abuse, 1976-86, mem. Nat. Adv. Coun., 1991—, prin. investigator Rsch. Ctr. Biol. Bass Addictive Diseases, 1987—; mem. gastroenterology adv. com. FDA, 1975-79, 92-96, NIH Gen. Clin. Recipient Borden Rsch. award, 1962; Career Scientist award Health Rsch. Council City N.Y., 1974-75; Dole/Nyswander award; Outstanding Rsch. Svc. in Addictive Diseases award, NIH-NIDA, 1984—; Rsch. Scientist award, NIH Gen. Clin. sect., 1978—. NIH Gen. Rsch. Ctr. Study Sect., 1979-83, chmn., 1982-83; mem. exec. com. Coll. Problems Drug Dependence, 1982-87, 89-94, chmn. exec. com., 1985-87, chair sci. program com., 1991—; fellow CPDD 1992—; dir. NIH-NIDA Rsch. Ctr., 1987—. Soc Fellow ACP, Am. Coll. Neuropsychopharmacology, Am. Fedn. for Clin. Rsch.; mem. Shakespeare Soc. of Wellesley, Am. Gastroent. Assn., N.Y. Gastroent. Assn. (pres. 1987), Endocrine Soc., Am. Assn. Study Liver Diseases, Internat. Assn. Study Liver, Internat. Narcotic Research Conf. Group (exec. com. 1993—), Research Soc. on Alcoholism, Soc. on Neurosciences, Phi Beta Kappa, Sigma Xi. Home: 1175 York Ave New York NY 10021-7169 Office: Rockefeller U New York NY 10021

KREGG, JUDITH LYNNE, accountant; b. Miami, Fla., June 1, 1947; d. Edward and Vernon Margurite (Davis) Malm; m. Gene Robert Kregg, Dec. 11, 1971 (div. Mar. 1977). A in Bus., Miami-Dade C.C., 1980. Staff acct. SONY Corp., N.Y.C., 1968-72, First Mortgage Investment, Miami Beach, Fla., 1975-78; regional controller Smith Barney, Miami, Fla., 1978; staff acct. Fininvest Internat., Key Biscayne, Fla., 1979; chief acct. Transway Internat., Coral Gables, Fla., 1980-81; constrn. acct. Senior Corp., Miami Beach, 1981-85; dir. acctg. The Continental Cos., Coconut Grove, Fla., 1985-90; controller Ireland Cos., North Miami, Fla., 1990; comml. acctg. mgr. Harbour Realty, Bay Harbor, Fla., 1991-94; sr. acct. Grand Bay Resort & Residencies, Coconut Grove, Fla., 1994—. Editor The SandDollar, 1991—. Bd. dirs., 2d v.p., community coun. WLRN, South Fla.'s Pub. Radio & TV Sta., Miami, 1992—. Recipient Cert. of Appreciation, WLRN, 1993. Mem. Inst. Mgmt. Accts. Miami Chpt. (pres. 1993-94, bd. dirs. 1991-92, cert. of appreciation 1995), Am. Orchid Soc., Coral Gables Orchid Soc., PEO Sisterhood (Miami Lakes Chpt. treas. 1992-93, pres. 1995—). Home: 2620 SW 23 Ave Miami FL 33133

KREIN, GRACE DUNCAN, retired educator; b. Calvin, N.D., Dec. 6, 1911; d. Merritt Smith and Margaret Mary (Higgins) Duncan; m. Alvin Roger Krein, June 6, 1937 (dec.); children: Carol Grace, Rodney, Sylvia, Elaine, Annelle. BA, State U., 1935; postgrad., N.D. State U., 1973. Life cert. secondary tchr. Rural edn. tchr. Wyndmere (N.D.) Sch. Dist., 1930-35; English tchr. Wishek (N.D.) Pub. Sch., 1935; high sch. prin. Lehr (N.D.) Pub. Sch., 1935-37; English tchr., drama and debate coach Ashly (N.D.) Pub. Schs., 1957-60; English tchr., libr. Tappen (N.D.) High Sch., 1960-62; instr. in libr. sci. and architecture lib. N.D. State U., Fargo, 1966-77; tutoring disadvantaged children Phoenix Washington Sch. Dist., 1978—. Author: (poetry) Reveries, 1994; contbr. poetry to anthologies and mags. Sec. Rep. Party, Morris, Minn., 1964; interim pastor Congregational Ch., 1960-61. Mem. AAUW.

KREINBROOK, MARY LUDY, tax collector; b. Berlin, Pa., Sept. 20, 1942; d. James Erwin and Emma Edith (DeLozier) Ludy; m. Homer Henry Kreinbrook, Nov. 16, 1962; children: Homer H. Jr., Pamela Sue, Parke Erwin. Diploma, Berlin Brothersvalley. Salesperson Bittner's Gas and Appliance, Somerset, Pa., 1960-63; mfr. Sumers Fertilizer, Somerset, 1963-64; with water authority Borough of Berlin, Pa., 1964-67, tax collector, 1973—. With Boy Scouts Am., Berlin, Pa.; leader 4-H. Mem. Somerset Tax Collectors Assn., Pius Spring Women's Club. Lutheran. Home: 207 Main St Berlin PA 15530

KREINER, LYNNE BARTHOLOMEW, human resources executive; b. Hanover, N.H., Mar. 9, 1948; d. Lloyd G. and Elisabeth (Thrall) Bartholomew; m. H. George Kreiner II, Jan. 23, 1993; children: Daniel B. Graham, Hadley Graham. BA, U. Vt., 1970. Pers. adminstr. Fairbanks Weighing div. Colt Industries, Inc., St. Johnsbury, Vt., 1974-76; pers. dir. Fassetts Bakery, Inc., South Burlington, Vt., 1978-85; human resources mgr. Semicon Electronics, Inc., South Burlington, Vt., 1986, Univ. Health Ctr., Burlington, Vt., 1986-87; sr. v.p., human resources Bank of Vt., Burlington, 1987-91; v.p. human resources Bombardier Capital, Inc., Burlington, 1991-92; cons. The Kreiner Co., Buffalo, 1992-93, Burchfield Penney Art Ctr., Buffalo, 1993—; mem. coun. Burchfield Penney Art Ctr. Assoc. bd. dirs. Med. Ctr. Hosp. of Vt., Burlington, 1992; adv. com. human resources program Trinity Coll., Burlington, 1992; active United Way dr., Bank of Vt., 1990. Mem. Soc. Human Resource Mgrs. (Niagara chpt.), Vt. Pers. Assn. (treas. 1987-91), Vt. Bankers Assn. (pers. com. 1987-91), Variety Club Buffalo. Home and Office: 72 Middlesex Rd Buffalo NY 14216

KREISMAN, BARBARA A., federal agency administrator; m. Raymond Banoun; 1 child, Annick. Bar: Md., D.C. Atty. advisor complaints and compliance div., trial atty. hearing divsn. FCC, Washington, 1980-82, chief renewal br., renewal and transfer divsn., 1982-85, chief low power TV br., video svcs. divsn., 1985-87, chief legal br., policy and rules divsn., 1987-89, asst. chief audio divsn., 1989, chief video svcs. divsn., mass media bur., 1989—. Office: Fed Comm Commn Video Svcs Divsn 1919 M St NW Rm 702 Washington DC 20554*

KREITZ, HELEN MARIE, retired elementary education educator; b. Taylor, Tex., Aug. 22, 1929; d. Joseph Jr. and Mary Lena (Miller) K. BA, Baylor U., 1950; MEd, U. Tex., 1959. Cert. tchr., Tex. Bookkeeper Singer

Sewing Machine Co., Taylor, 1950-51; advt. salesperson Taylor Times, 1951-52; tchr. Temple (Tex.) Ind. Sch. Dist., 1952-88. Lector, lay minister St. Mary's Cath. Ch., Temple, 1974—. Mem. Tex. Ret. Tchrs. (life, treas. Temple chpt. 1991—), Tex. State Tchrs. Assn. (life, treas. Temple chpt. 1954-55), Tex. Classroom Tchrs. Assn. (life, pres. Temple chpt. 1967-69), U. Tex. Execs. (life), Pi Lambda Theta. Roman Catholic. Home: PO Box 3446 Temple TX 76505-3446

KREJCSI, CYNTHIA ANN, textbook editor; b. Chgo., Dec. 28, 1948; d. Charles and Dorothea Bertha (Hahn) K.; m. Daniel Neil Ehlebracht, May 16, 1986 (div. Nov. 1988). BA, North Park Coll., 1970; postgrad. Nat. Coll. Edn., 1989—. Prodn. editor Ency. Brit., Chgo., 1970-71, style editor, 1971-72; asst. editor Scott, Foresman & Co., Glenview, Ill., 1972-77, assoc. editor, 1977, editor, 1978-84, sr. editor, 1984-95; sr. editor Benefic Press, Westchester, Ill., 1977-78; editorial mgr. Ligature, Chgo., Ill., 1995—. Mem. ASCD, Nat. Council of Tchrs. of English, Internat. Reading Assn. (bd. dirs. suburban coun.), Nat. Reading Conf., Assn. Ill. Mid. Schs. Home: 1425 Partridge Ln Arlington Heights IL 60004-7988 Office: Ligature 165 N Canal St Chicago IL 60606

KREKORIAN, ELIZABETH ANNE, nursing college administrator; b. East St. Louis, Ill., Sept. 20, 1928; d. George and Paskalia Esther (Pagourakis) K. Diploma, Christian Welfafre Hosp., 1949; BSN, St. Louis U., MA, 1970, PhD, 1974. RN, Ill., Mo., Ariz. Assoc. coord. Lewis & Clark Coll., Godfrey, Ill.; chair Lindenwood Colls., St. Charles, Mo.; pres., CEO Deaconess Coll. Nursing, St. Louis. Mem. AACN, NLN, Sigma Theta Tau. Office: Deaconess Coll Nursing 6150 Oakland Ave Saint Louis MO 63139-3215

KREMENTZ, JILL, photographer, author; b. N.Y.C., Feb. 19, 1940; d. Walter and Virginia (Hyde) K.; m. Kurt Vonnegut, Jr., Nov. 1979; 1 child, Lily. Student, Drew U., 1958-59; attended Art Students League, Columbia U. With Harper's Bazaar mag., 1959-60, Glamour mag., 1960-61; pub. relations staff Indian Industries Fair, New Delhi, 1961; reporter Show mag., 1962-64; staff photographer N.Y. Herald Tribune, 1964-65, staff photographer Vietnam, 1965-66; assoc. editor Status-Diplomat mag., 1966-67; contbg. editor N.Y. mag., 1967-68; corr. Time-Life Inc., 1969-70; contbg. photographer People mag., 1974—. Contbr. photography numerous U.S. and fgn. periodicals.; one-woman photography shows Madison (Wis.) Art Center, 1973, U. Mass., Boston, 1974, Nikon Gallery, N.Y.C., 1974, Del. Art Mus., Wilmington, 1975, Newark Mus., 1994; represented in permanent collections Mus. Modern Art, Library of Congress; photographer: The Face of South Vietnam (text by Dean Brelis), 1968, Words and Their Masters (text by Israel Shenker), 1974; photographer, author: Sweet Pea: A Black Girl Growing Up in the Rural South (foreword by Margaret Mead), 1969, A Very Young Dancer, 1976, A Very Young Rider, 1977, A Very Young Gymnast, 1978, A Very Young Circus Flyer, 1979, A Very Young Skater, 1979, The Writer's Image, 1980, How It Feels When a Parent Dies, 1981, How It Feels to be Adopted, 1982, How It Feels When Parents Divorce, 1984, The Fun of Cooking, 1985, Lily Goes to the Playground, 1986, Jack Goes to the Beach, 1986, Katherine Goes to Nursery School, 1986, Jamie Goes on an Airplane, 1986, Tanya Goes to the Dentist, 1986, Benjy Goes to a Restaurant, 1986, Holly's Farm Animals, 1986, Zachary Goes to the Zoo, 1986, A Visit to Washington, D.C., 1987, How It Feels to Fight For Your Life, 1989, A Very Young Skier, 1990, A Very Young Musician, 1990, A Very Young Gardener, 1990, A Very Young Actress, 1991, How It Feels to Live With a Physical Disability, 1992. Recipient Nonfiction award Washington Post/Children's Book Guild, 1984, ACCH Joan Fassler Meml. Book award, 1990, Equality, Dignity, Independence award Nat. Easter Seals, 1992. Mem. PEN. Address: care Alfred A Knopf Inc 201 E 50th St New York NY 10022

KREMER, HONOR FRANCES (NOREEN KREMER), real estate broker, small business owner; b. Ireland, Aug. 9, 1939; came to U.S., 1961; m. Manny Kremer, May 17, 1963; 1 child, Patrick David. BS, CUNY; MS, Baruch Coll. Group sec. Bentalls, Ltd., Kingston-On-Thames, Surrey, Eng., 1954-58, Cen. Secondary Sch., Hamilton, Ont., Can., 1959-61; office mgr. Aschner Assocs., N.Y.C., 1961-63; pub. rels. asst. McMaster U., Hamilton, 1963-64; office mgr. Packaging Components, N.Y.C., 1965-67; head acctg. Shaller Rubin Assocs., N.Y.C., 1967-72, v.p. fin. and adminstrn., 1972-79, sr. v.p., 1979-82, sr. v.p., mem. exec. com., 1982—, sec.-treas. multi-media div., 1972-75; pvt. practice bus. cons., 1986-89; sr. v.p., exec. v.p., fin. officer Lewis & Gace Med. Advt., N.Y.C., 1989-91; broker, owner Malone Kremer Realty, Leonia, N.J., 1991—; bus. cons., 1991—. Mem. Nat. Fedn. Bus. and Profl. Women (bd. dirs., v.p.), Advt. Fin. Mgmt. Group. Roman Catholic.

KRENEK, DEBBY, newspaper editor; d. Ernest Reed and Elizabeth Pendleton (Brown) K.; m. James C. Roberts Jr., Feb. 28, 1987; children: Christine Elizabeth Roberts, Taylor James Roberts. BJ, Tex. A&M Univ., 1978. Copy editor Corpus Christi (Tex.) Caller-Times, 1978-81; news editor Dallas Times Herald, 1981-85, asst. bus. editor, 1985-86, exec. news editor, 1986-87; dep. news editor N.Y. Daily News, 1987-88, dep. mng. editor, 1988-91, mng. editor, 1991-93, exec. editor, 1993—. Named to Acad. of Women Achievers YWCA, N.Y., 1992. Office: New York Daily News 220 E 42nd St Ste 817 New York NY 10017*

KREPKY, CYNTHIA D., technical publishing administrator; b. Columbus, Ohio, Apr. 1, 1956; d. Donald Rex, Jr., and Nancy May (Dawson) Barnes; m. David Morris Krepky, June 1, 1991. BS in Botany and Marine Sci., U. Wash., 1981, MPA, 1985; cert. exec. mgmt. U. Wash., 1990. Water quality technician Ohio EPA, Columbus, 1978; exec. sec. Dan A. Carmichael, AIA, Columbus, 1978-79; supr. publs. Vitro Corp., Silverdale, Wash., 1982-85; sr. tech. writer water pollution control dept. Municipality Met. Seattle (Metro), 1985-87, supr. 1987—; bd. dirs. Hood Canal Environ. Council, Seabeck, Wash., 1985-88; chmn. conservation com. Kitsap Audubon, Poulsbo, Wash., 1982-84; mem. adv. bd. dirs. U. Washington Extension Tech. Writing Cert. Program, Green River C.C. Multimedia Design Program. Author: Citizen's Guide to Municipal Incorporation in the State of Washington, 1985. Tech. advisor and publicity co-chmn. Silverdale Inc. Com., 1983-85. Mem. Am. Soc. Pub. Adminstrn. (student rep. Evergreen chpt. Council 1984-85, coun. mem. Evergreen chpt. 1986-90), Water Environ. Fedn., Am. Mgmt. Assn., Cityclub (Seattle). Avocations: backpacking, canoeing, scuba diving, gardening, stained glass. Home: 2245 E Crescent Dr Seattle WA 98112-3415 Office: Metro 821 2nd Ave Seattle WA 98104-1519

KREPPS, ETHEL CONSTANCE, lawyer; b. Mountain View, Okla., Oct. 31, 1937; d. Howard Haswell and Pearl (Moore) Goomda. R.N., St. John's Med. Center, 1971; B.S., U. Tulsa, 1974, J.D., 1979; m. George Randolph Krepps, Apr. 10, 1954; children: George Randolph, Edward Howard Moore. Nurse St. John's Med. Ctr., Tulsa, 1971-75. Bar: Okla., 1979. pvt. practice law, Tulsa, 1979—; mem. Indian law alumni com. U. Tulsa Coll. Law; atty., dir. Indian Child Welfare Program, 1981—; nat. v.p. A.I.L.S.A.; sec. bd. dirs. Okla. Indian Legal Svcs, 1986—; administrative law judge, Dept. Health Enforcement Unit, Okla; bd. dirs. North Am. Coun. on Adoption of Children; mem. Okla. adv. commn. civil rights; atty. Native Am. Coalition, Inc., Kiowa Tribe Okla., Tulsa Indian Youth Council, Legal Rsch. Okla. Indian Affairs Commn. Chmn., Okla. Indian Child Welfare Orgn., 1981—; tribal sec. Kiowa Tribe Okla., 1979-81; atty. nurse aide registry Okla. Dept. Health, 1994—. Mem. ABA, Fed. Bar Assn., Tulsa Women Lawyers Assn., Am. Indian Bar Assn., Okla. Indian Bar Assn., Okla. Bar Assn., Tulsa County Bar Assn., Oklahoma County Bar Assn., Am. Indian Nurses Assn. (v.p.), Okla. Women Lawyers Assn., Nat. Indian Social Workers Assn. (pres. 1984—), Assn. Trial Lawyers Am., Phi Alpha Delta, Nat. Native Am. C. of C. (sec. 1980—), Internat. Indian Child Conf. (founder, chair). Democrat. Baptist. Author: A Strong Medicine Wind, 1979; Oklahoma Memories, 1981. Home: 3000 NW 12th St Oklahoma City OK 73107-5306 Office: PO Box 53551 1000 NE Tenth Oklahoma City OK 73104

KREPS, JUANITA MORRIS, economics educator, former government official; b. Lynch, Ky., Jan. 11, 1921; d. Elmer M. and Cenia (Blair) Morris; m. Clifton H. Kreps, Jr., Aug. 11, 1944; children: Sarah, Laura, Clifton. AB, Berea Coll., 1942; MA, Duke U., 1944; PhD, 1948; hon. degrees, Bryant Coll., 1972, U. N.C. at Chapel Hill, Denison U., Cornell Coll., 1973, U. Ky., Queens Coll., St. Lawrence U., 1975, Wheaton Coll., 1976, Claremont Grad. Sch., Berea Coll., 1979, Tulane U., Colgate U., 1980, Trinity Coll., 1981, U. Rochester, Grove City Coll., 1984, Davidson Coll., 1990; hon. degree, Lenoir-Rhyne Coll., 1991, U. Notre Dame, 1992, Duke U., 1993. Instr. econs. Denison U., 1945-46, asst. prof., 1948-50; mem. faculty Duke U., 1955-77, assoc. prof., 1962-68, prof. econs., 1968-77, James B. Duke prof., 1972-77, James B. Duke prof. emerita, 1979—, asst. provost, 1969-72, v.p., 1973-77, v.p. emerita, 1979—; sec. U.S. Dept. Commerce, 1977-79; mem. adv. com. Congl. Commn. for the Future of Worker Mgmt. Rels., Secs. of Commerce and Labor, 1993-94. Author: (with C.E. Ferguson) Principles of Economics, 2d rev. edit, 1965, Lifetime Allocation of Work and Income, 1971, Sex in the Marketplace: American Women at Work, 1971, Women and the American Economy, 1976; co-author: (with Richard Perlman and Gerald Somers) Contemporary Labor Economics, 1973; Editor: Employment, Income and Retirement Problems of the Aged, 1963, Technology, Manpower and Retirement Policy, 1966, Sex, Age and Work, 1975. Bd. dirs. Am. Coun. on Germany, Rsch. Triangle Found., Ednl. Testing Svc., 1972-77; mem. Nat. Manpower Policy Task Force; trustee Berea Coll., Duke Endowment, nat. Humanities Ctr., 1983-86, U. N.C., Wilmington, 1993—, HumRRO, 1980-83, Coun. of Fgn. Rels., 1983-86; pres. bd. overseers Tchrs. Ins. and Annuity Assn. and Coll. Retirement Equities Fund, 1985—. named to Presdl. Commn. on Nat. Agenda for the 80's, 1979; recipient N.C. Pub. Service award, 1976; Stephen Wise award, 1978, Woman of Yr. award Ladies Home Jour., 1978, Duke U. Alumni award, 1983, Haskins award Coll. Bus. and Pub. Adminstrn., NYU, 1984, first Corp. Governance award Nat. Assn. Corp. Dirs., 1987, Dir.'s Choice Leadership award Nat. Women's Econ. Alliance Found., 1987, Disitng. Meritorious Service medal Duke U. Alumni, 1987. Fellow Gerontol. Soc. (v.p. 1971-72), Am. Acad. Arts and Scis.; mem. AAUP, AAUW (Achievement award 1981), Am. Econ. Assn. (v.p. 1983-84), So. Econ. Assn. (pres. 1975-76), Indsl. Rels. Rsch. Assn. (exec. com.). Office: Duke U 115 E Duke Bldg Durham NC 27708-0768

KRESCH-HAGLER, SANDRA DARYL, consulting firm executive; b. N.Y.C., Sept. 13, 1945; d. Howard and Jean (Goldsmith) Gleich; m. Samuel H. Hagler, Jan. 6, 1973. BS, U. Pa., 1966. Rsch. assoc. Simat, Helliesen & Eichner, Inc., N.Y.C., 1966-67; study dir. Nat. Analysts, Inc., Phila., 1968-69; pres. Sandra D. Kresch Cons. Svcs., Calif., 1969-70; v.p., mgr. market rsch. Nat. Analysts, Inc., Chgo., 1970-75; v.p. Booz, Allen Venture Mgmt., N.Y.C., 1976-78; v.p. corp. devel. Booz Allen & Hamilton, Inc., N.Y.C., 1978-80, v.p. mgmt. cons., 1980-83; sr. v.p. mktg. Time Video Info. Svcs., Inc., 1983-84; dir. strategic planning Mag. Group, Time Inc., 1984-86; dir. internat. devel. Time Mag., 1986-88; mng. dir. internat. pub. CMP Publs., Inc., Manhasset, N.Y., 1988-89; pres. Sandra D. Kresch Cons. Assocs., N.Y.C., 1989-90; chief exec. officer TransData Corp. subs. Am. Banker Bond Buyer, Wayne, Pa., 1990-91; pres. ISC Assocs., Inc. N.Y.C., 1990-93; pres. PSD Internat. Inc., 1994—. Bd. dirs. YWCA of USA; chmn. strategic planning com., 1991; bd. dirs. Spence-Chapin Svcs. to Families, exec. com., chmn. program and policy com.; bd. dirs. Utopia Pkwy. Arts. Recipient Tribute to Women in Internat. Industry award, 1978. mem. Fin. Woman's Assn., Advt. Women N.Y., Pub. Investors Am. (adv. bd.). Democrat. Jewish. Home: 14 E 75th St New York NY 10021-2657 Office: 78 Roxbury Rd Washington Depot CT 06793

KRESLER, FRANCES PERROTTET, watercolorist, educator; b. Wheaton, Ill., May 1, 1917; d. William Pelatiah and Frances Mary (Miles) Armstrong; m. Leon Edward Kresler, May 16, 1945 (dec. Oct. 1979); children: Stacey, Philip, Ann. Student, Mary Baldwin Coll., Staunton, Va., 1936-38, Rollins Coll., 1939-40. Sec. art dept. Rollins Coll., Winter Park, Fla., 1940-41; sec. to engring. officer Mil. Air Base, Orlando, Fla., 1941-44; sec. to Dr. Leon E. Kresler, Kentland, Ind., 1945-79; tchr. watercolor painting, Williamsport, Ind., 1992-93. Pres. St. Joseph's Hosp. Aux., Tucson, 1986. Mem. So. Ariz. Watercolor Guild, Santa Cruz Valley Art Assn., Tri Kappa of Ind. (pres. 1964), Kappa Kappa Gamma. Republican. Episcopalian. Home: 301 Bluff St Williamsport IN 47993-1303

KRESS, HEATHER GABRIELLE, lawyer; b. Port-of-Spain, West Indies, Trinidad & Tobago, Oct. 22, 1944; came to U.S., 1963; d. Gabriel Bernardo and Violet Ayesha (Lalla) Rodrigues; m. Kenneth I. Kress, Mar. 8, 1968; 1 child, Kimberly Stacy. BA in French, Spanish cum laude, Holy Family Coll., 1967; MA Philosophy summa cum laude, U. Dayton, 1969; JD, Georgetown U., 1977. Bar: N.Y. 1978, U.S. Dist. Ct. (so. and ea. dists.) N.Y. 1978. Instr. philosophy U. Dayton, Ohio, 1967-69; legal personnel coord. Cleary, Gottlieb, Steen & Hamilton, N.Y.C., 1969-71; fin. analyst Traveler's Ins. Co., Garden City, N.Y., 1971-74; intern City Coun., Washington, 1975-76; clerk Washington Sqaure Legal Svcs., 1976-77; staff atty. Fed. Reserve Bank, N.Y., 1977-79; asst. gen. counsel CIT Fin. Corp., N.Y.C., 1979-80; assoc. counsel Irving Bank Corp., N.Y.C., 1980-83, Irving Trust Co., N.Y.C., 1983-86; with Buckley Kremer O'Reilly Pieper Hoban & Marsh, Mineola, N.Y., 1986; banking atty. Certilman Haft Balin Buckley Kremer & Hyman, N.Y.C., 1986-88, Rivkin, Radler & Kremer, Uniondale, N.Y., 1986—; lectr. in field. Contbr. articles to profl. jours. Mem. environ. com. Oldfield Middle Sch., Greenlawn, N.Y., 1992; mem. counsel vestry St. John's Ch., Huntington, N.Y., 1992—; mem. The Town of Hempstead Minority & Women Revolving Loan Com., 1993—. Scholar St. Thomas Aquinas Soc., Port-of-Spain, Trinidad, 1963. Mem. N.Y. State Bar Assn., N.Y. County Lawyers Assn. Avocations: travel, arts, reading, skiing, walking. Home: 1 Partridge Ln Huntington NY 11743 Office: Rivkin Radler & Kremer EAB Plz Uniondale NY 11556-0111

KRESS, JILL CLANCY, human resources professional; b. Washington, Oct. 11, 1949; d. John William and Barbara Lois (Smith) Costello; m. Patrick Thomas Kress, Dec. 22, 1972 (div. 1987); 1 child, Jason Patrick. BS in Edn., Jacksonville U., 1971; MA in Adminstrn., U. No. Fla., 1973. Tchr. Duval County Pub. Sch., Jacksonville, Fla., 1971-74; dir. adminstrn. Nat. Exec. Search, Washington, 1974-83; dir. adminstrn., placement The Stradford Schs., Rockville, Md., 1983-84; cons. human resources Concepts, Inc., Montgomery Village, Md., 1984-87; dir. pers. Cellmark Diagnostics, Germantown, Md., 1987-89; mgr. staffing and coll. rels. Life Technologies, Inc., Gaithersburg, Md., 1989—; workshop trainer Va. Tech., Blacksburg, 1992—, Md. U., College Park, 1991—, Hood Coll., Frederick, 1994—; biotech. adv. bd. Montgomery Coll. Mem. Soc. for Human Resources Mgmt., Biotechnology Indsl. Orgn. (steering com. mem.), Montgomery County High Technology Coun. (steering com., author newsletter 1993), Middle Atlantic Placement Assn. (adv. bd.). Republican. Roman Catholic. Home: 10024 Stedwick Rd # 303 Gaithersburg MD 20879-2710 Office: Life Technologies Inc 8400 Helgerman Ct Gaithersburg MD 20884-9980

KRETSCHMER, INGRID BUTLER, elementary education educator; b. Port Jefferson, N.Y., Apr. 19, 1936; d. Arthur David and Clara (Anderson) Butler; m. Fred Kretschmer, Apr. 10, 1955; children: Arthur Frederick, Susan Elizabeth Kretschmer Leining, Cory. BA, Adlephi Suffolk Coll., 1966; MEd, Dowling Coll., 1977. Cert. elem. tchr., N.Y. Tchr. k-6 Rocky Point (N.Y.) Sch. Dist., 1966-86, tchr. compensatory math., 1986—; grade level coord. Rocky Point Sch. Dist., 1975-80, co-creator, instr. in-svc. math course k-6, 1992—. Co-author: Developmental Reading Skills Record, 1969. Mem. Rocky Point PTA, 1966—; pres. bd. Trinity Nursery Sch., Rocky Point, 1978-80; mem. Ch. Coun. Trinity Luth. Ch., Rocky Point, 1978-83, Riverhead (N.Y.) Rep. Club, 1983—. Mem. Am. Fedn. Tchrs., N.Y. State United Tchrs. (del. 1983—, Svc. award 1990), Rocky Point Tchrs. Assn. (sec. 1967-69, bldg. rep. 1973-83, pres. 1983-94), L.I. Pres.' Coun. (treas. 1989-91). Home: 333 E Woodland Dr Wading River NY 11792-9604

KREVIT, RITA RECHA, alderwoman, retired business owner; b. Leipzig, Saxony, Germany, Nov. 26, 1920; came to U.S., 1946.; d. Hans Hermann and Charlotte (Mislowitzer) Hartwich; divorced; 1 child, Hilary Toby Converse. Attended coll., Manchester, Eng., 1940-41. Bus. owner, mgr. Spectra, Inc., Milford, Conn., to 1981, Bristol Kow Mats, Inc., Milford, to 1972; alderwoman Bd. of Aldermen, New Haven, Conn., 1987—. Pres. Tower One-Tower East Residents Assn., 1984—. Democrat. Jewish. Home: 18 Tower Ln New Haven CT 06519 Office: Office Board of Aldermen City Hall 165 Church St New Haven CT 06510

KREYER, VIRGINIA, minister; b. Bklyn., Apr. 24, 1925; d. Louis Frederick and Adrienne L. (Decker) K. BA, Westhampton Coll., 1948; MDiv, Union Theol. Seminary, N.Y.C., 1952; MSW, Adelphi U., 1960. Ordained to min., Ch. of Christ, 1952. Social worker United Cerebral Palsy Assn. of Nassau County, Inc., Roosevelt, N.Y., 1952-84; cons. on disabilities United Ch. Bd. for Homeland Ministries, N.Y.C., 1978-91, Cleve., 1991—; del. to World Coun. of Churches, Cabberra, Australia, 1991; deacon Garden City (N.Y.) Community Ch., 1991—. Guest editor: Pastoral Psychology, 1965. Bd. dirs. Coord. Ctr. for Women in Ch. and Soc., United Ch. of Christ, 1979-90; bd. dirs. Geneva Point Ctr., Center Harbor, N.H., 1978-89, 91—. Mem. AAUW (Garden City branch), local ministerial groups. Home: 366 Stewart Ave Garden City NY 11530-4533

KRIBBS, NANCY BARONE, psychologist; b. Cleve., Apr. 17, 1956; d. Dominic D. and Emily Therese (Citino) Barone; m. Gary M.B. Kribbs, Oct. 2, 1982; 1 child, Elizabeth. BS Psychology, Xavier U., 1977; MA Psychology, U. Toledo, 1982, PhD Psychology, 1983. Grad. rsch. asst. Henry Ford Hosp., Detroit, 1980-83; asst. prof. psychology Pa. State, Harrisburg, 1983-87; rsch. assoc. U. Pa., Phila., 1987-91, rsch. asst. prof., 1991—; cons. Unit for Exptl. Psychiatry, Phila., 1991—, Ctr. for Sleep and Respiratory Neurobiology, Phila., 1993—, VA Med. Ctr., Phila., 1987—. Contbr. articles to profl. jours., chpts. to books in field. Biomed. rsch. support Pa. State U., Harrisburg, 1986; recipient Spl. Ctr. of Rsch.-co-investigator award NIH, 1988-93, 93—. Mem. APA, Am. Psychol. Soc., Sleep Rsch. Soc., Soc. Psychophysiol. Rsch. Roman Catholic. Office: Ctr for Sleep/U Pa 991 Maloney 3600 Spruce St Philadelphia PA 19104-4211

KRIDER, MARGARET YOUNG, art educator; b. Pitts., Aug. 20, 1920; d. Thomas Smith and Josephine Bridget (Connolly) Y.; m. Robert Arthur Krider, May 12, 1945; children: Karen L., Ann Noel, Darcie Ellen Robbins. BFA in Art Edn., Carnegie-Mellon U., 1942; MEd in Art Edn., Edinboro U., 1969. Tchr. art West Homestead (Pa.) Pub. Sch., 1942-44, Mt. Oliver (Pa.) Pub. Sch., 1942-44; recreational worker Valley Forge Gen. Hosp. ARC, Phoenixville, Pa., 1944-45; assoc. prof. Villa Maria Coll., Erie, Pa., 1950-87; adj. instr. Pa. State U. Behrend Campus, Erie, Pa., 1981-87; presenter papers Ea. Arts Convention, N.Y.C., 1962, Kutztown (Pa.) State U., 1967, U. Pa. Art Conference, Pitts., 1980. Exhibited in one and two-man shows incl. Chautauqua Art Gallery, William Penn Meml. Mus., Butler Mus., Patterson Gallery, Glass Growers Gallery, Sycamore Gallery, Cummings Gallery, Schuster Gallery, juried and invitational shows incl. Erie Art Mus., Erie Summer Festivals, Agnon Fine Art and Crafts, Carlow Coll. Pa. Women's Art, Bruce Gallery, Forum Gallery; contbr. articles to art jours. Bd. dirs., sec. Arts Coun. Erie, Pa., 1974-76, Erie Civic Ballet Co., 1970-75; bd. dirs. Erie County Hist. Soc., 1988-94; active LWV, 1950s; Girl Scout leader Cathedral Grade Sch., Erie, 1956-66; hist. restoration advisor Battles Mus., Girard, Pa., 1993—. Recipient Community award Florence Crittenton Home, 1991; named Outstanding Tchr. Villa Maria Coll. Presdl. Award, 1987, Outstanding Art Educator PAEA, 1989. Mem. AAUW (bd. dirs., chair 1967-90, Found. Ednl. award 1984, Outstanding Woman finalist 1992), Women's Round Table, Nat. Art Edn., Northwestern Pa. Artists Assn. (chair membership), Pa. Soc. Art Edn., Delta Kappa Gamma (chmn. Book Alive). Republican. Roman Catholic. Home: 6130 Mistletoe Ave Fairview PA 16415-2702

KRIDLER, JAMIE BRANAM, children's advocate, social psychologist; b. Newport, Tenn., Jan. 23, 1955; d. Floyd A. and Mary Leslie (Carlisle) Branam; m. Thomas Lee Kridler, Mar. 19, 1989; children: Brittani Audra, Houston Scott, Clark Eaton, Sabrina Morrow. BS, U. Tenn., 1976, MS, 1977; PhD, Ohio State U., 1985; cert. retailing, profl. modeling, Bauder Fashion Coll., Atlanta, 1973. Fashion coord. Bill's Wear House, Gatlinburg, Tenn., 1969-77; buyer Shane's Boutique, Gettysburg, Tenn., 1977-78; instr. Miami U., Oxford, Ohio, 1978-81; asst. prof. U. Tenn., Knoxville, 1985-89; mktg. dir. Profitt's Dept. Stores. Alcoa, Tenn., 1989-90; mktg. cons. Kridler & Kridler Mktg., Newport, Tenn., 1990-93; children's advocate Safe Space, Newport, Tenn., 1993—; adj. faculty U. Tenn., Knoxville, 1990—, Walters State Coll., Morristown, Tenn., 1990—, Carson Newman Coll., Jefferson City, Tenn., 1993—; chair Children's Com. Tenn. Task Force Against Domestic Violence, Nashville, 1993—; participant Children's Defense Fund, Washington, 1992—. Costume designer Newport Theatre Guild: Guys and Dolls, Carousel, Fiddler on the Roof, Music Man, Crimes of the Heart, Rumors, Come Back to the Five and Dime, Jimmy Dean, 1991—; Miami U. Dance Theatre, Ice Show. Bd. dirs. Safe Space, 1991-92; v.p. Newport Theatre Guild, 1991-92, pres. 1992—. Named Outstanding Tchr., Miami U., Oxford, 1981, Outstanding Educator, U. Tenn., Knoxville, 1989; recipient numerous grants from univ. and non-profit orgns. Mem. NAACP, Lioness Club, Kappa Omicorn Nu. Democrat. Episcopalian. Home: 112 Woodlawn Ave Newport TN 37821-3031

KRIEGER, DOLORES ESTHER, retired elementary education educator; b. Ft. Dodge, Iowa, Oct. 22, 1935; d. James William and Grace Dolores (Donovan) Carpenter; m. Duane Art Krieger, June 14, 1958; children: Danette Marie, Diane Ellen, Douglas Arthur. BS, Coll. St. Francis, Joliet, Ill., 1971; MS, No. Ill. U., 1975; student, Alfred Adler Inst., Chgo., 1984-88. Tchr. Jefferson (Iowa) Grade Sch., 1956-58; tchr. Rockdale Grade Sch., Joliet, Ill., 1971—, ret., 1994; creative dramatics tchr. Coll. St. Francis, 1970-72, cooperating tchr., 1980—, adult edn., 1987—; lectr. in field. Author video Successful Parenting Skills. Chairperson Franciscana/Jubilation, St. Francis Acad., 1980's. Fellow AAUW; mem. St. Joseph Med. Ctr. Aux. (sec. 1965-66), Delta Kappa Gamma (corres. sec. 1988-90, membership chmn. 1990—). Democrat. Roman Catholic. Home: 617 N William St Joliet IL 60435-5939

KRIEGER, KATHY L., lawyer; b. Detroit, May 19, 1953; d. Douglas R. Krieger and Marion (Case) Smith. AB, Yale U., 1974; postgrad., U. Mich. Law Sch., 1974-75; JD, NYU, 1977. Bar: N.Y. 1978, D.C. 1985, U.S. Ct. Appeals (2d, 6th, 7th, 9th and D.C. cirs.). Atty. appellate ct. br. NLRB, Washington, 1977-79; asst. gen. counsel United Brotherhood Carpenters, Washington, 1979-84, assoc. gen. counsel, 1984—, now gen. counsel. Mem. ABA, Women's Bar Assn., Nat. Lawyers Guild. Office: United Brotherhood Carpenters 101 Constitution Ave NW Washington DC 20001-2133*

KRIEGER, MARCIA S., judge; b. Denver, Mar. 3, 1954; d. Donald P. Jr. and Marjorie Craige (Gearhart) Smith; m. Michael S. Krieger, Aug. 26, 1976 (div. July 1988); children: Miriam Anna, Matthias Edward. BA, Lewis & Clark Coll., 1975; postgrad., U. Munich, 1975-76; JD, U. Colo., 1979. Bar: Colo. 1979, U.S. Dist. Ct. Colo., U.S. Ct. Appeals (10th cir.). Assoc. Mason, Reubner & Peek, P.C., Denver, 1976-83, Smart, DeFurio Brooks, Eklund & McClure, Denver, 1983-84; ptnr. Brooks & Krieger, P.C., Denver, 1984-88, Wood, Ris & Hames, P.C., Denver, 1988-94; judge U.S. Bankruptcy Court, 10th Circuit, Denver, 1994—; lectr. U. Denver Grad. Tax Program, 1987—, Colo. Soc. CPA's, Denver, 1984-87, Colo. Continuing Legal Edn., Denver, 1980—, Colo. Trial Lawyers Assn., Denver, 1987—. Contbr. articles to profl. publs. Mem. Denver com. on fgn. relations, 1986—; vestry person Good Shepherd Episcopal Ch., Englewood, 1986—. Mem. Colo. Bar Assn., Arapahoe Bar Assn., Denver Bar Assn., Colo. Women's Bar Assn., Comml. Law League, Zonta Club. Republican. Office: US Custom House 721 19th St Denver CO 80202-2508*

KRIENKE, CAROL BELLE MANIKOWSKE (MRS. OLIVER KENNETH KRIENKE), realtor; b. Oakland, Calif., June 19, 1917; d. George and Ethel (Purdon) Manikowske; student U. Mo., 1937; BS, U. Minn., 1940; postgrad. UCLA, 1949; m. Oliver Kenneth Krienke, June 4, 1941 (dec. Dec. 1988); children: Diane (Mrs. Robert Denny), Judith (Mrs. Kenneth A. Giss), Debra Louise (Mrs. Ed Paul Davalos). Demonstrator, Gen. Foods Corp., Mpls., 1940; youth leadership State of Minn. Congl. Conf., U. Minn., Mpls. 1940-41; war prodn. worker Airesearch Mfg. Co., Los Angeles, 1944; tchr. L.A. City Schs., 1945-49; realtor DBA Ethel Purdon, Manhattan Beach, Calif., 1949; buyer Purdon Furniture & Appliances, Manhattan Beach, 1950-58; realtor O.K. Krienke Realty, Manhattan Beach, 1958—. Manhattan Beach bd. rep. Community Chest for Girl Scouts U.S., 1957; bd. dirs. South Bay council Girl Scouts U.S.A., 1957-62, mem. Manhattan Beach Coordinating Coun., 1956-68, South Coast Botanic Garden Found., 1989—; v.p. Long Beach Area Childrens Home Soc., 1967-68, pres. 1979; charter mem. Beach Pixies, 1957-93, pres. 1967; chmn. United Way, 1967; sponsor Beach Cities Symphony, 1953—, Little League Umpires, 1981-91. Recipient Longstanding Local Bus. award City of Manhattan Beach, 1993. Mem. DAR (life, citizenship chmn. 1972-73, v.p. 1979, 83—), Calif. Retired Tchrs. Assn. (life), Colonial Dames XVII Century (charter mem. Jared Eliot chpt. 1977, v.p., pres. 1979-81, 83-84), Friends of Library, South Bay Bd. Realtors, Nat. Soc. New England Women (life, Calif. Poppy Colony), Internat. Platform Assn., Soc. Descs. of Founders of Hartford (life), Friends of Banning Mus., Hist. Soc. of Centinela Valley, Manhattan Beach Hist. Soc., Manhattan Beach C. of C. (Rose and Scroll award 1985), U. Minn. Alumni (life). Republican.

Mem. Community Ch. (pres. Women's Fellowship 1970-71). Home: 924 Highview Ave Manhattan Beach CA 90266-5813 Office: OK Krienke Realty 1716 Manhattan Beach Blvd Manhattan Beach CA 90266-6220

KRIENKE, KENDRA CLIVER, art dealer, artist; b. Plainfield, N.J.; d. Edwin Kendall Cliver and Estelle (Blaine) Hufnagel; m. Douglas Elliot Krienke (div. 1991); m. Allan L. Daniel, June 1, 1993. BAA, Drew U., 1969. Owner, portrait painter, frame designer, art dealer Whistler's Daughter Art Gallery, Basking Ridge, N.J., 1974-84; owner, frame designer, art dealer Whistler Gallery, Basking Ridge, 1985-90; dealer in original vintage art by illustrators for children and fantasy N.Y.C., 1989—. Contbg. author: American Illustrator Art, 1991; prepared 10 exhbns. and catalogues, 1978-84; curator Childhood Enchantments—British and American Illustration for Children, Mus. Cartoon Art, 1989, Johnson & Johnson, 1990. Mem. Soc. Illustrators. Address: 230 Central Park W New York NY 10024

KRIER, CYNTHIA TAYLOR, state legislator, lawyer; b. Beeville, Tex., July 12, 1950; m. Joseph Krier, 1982. B.J., U. Tex., 1971, J.D., 1975. Bar: Tex. 1975. Of Counsel Matthews & Branscomb, San Antonio; mem. Tex. State Senate from 26th dist., 1985—; judge Bexar County Courthouse, San Antonio. Mem. ABA, Tex. Bar Assn., San Antonio Bar Assn., Omicron Delta Kappa, Phi Kappa Phi, Phi Delta Phi. Republican. Office: Office County Judge County Courthouse 5th Fl 100 Dolorosa San Antonio TX 78205-3036 also: 301 S Frio St San Antonio TX 78207-4421*

KRIGSMAN, NAOMI, psychologist, consultant, photographer; b. Haifa, Israel; came to U.S., 1953, naturalized, 1961; d. Bezalel and Regina (Yacobi) Goussinsky; m. Ruben Krigsman; children—Michael W., Richard G., Jonathan H. MS, CCNY; PhD, Hofstra U.. Lic. psychologist, N.Y. State. Psychologist Mental Retardation Clinic, Flower-Fifth Avenue Hosp., N.Y.C., Children's Ctr., N.Y.C. Dept. Welfare, Rehab. Clinic, St. Barnabas Hosp., Newark, United Cerebral Palsy Ctr., Roosevelt, N.Y., Burke Rehab. Ctr., White Plains, N.Y., New Rochelle City Sch. Dist., N.Y.; v.p. Devel. Research Assocs. Inc.; cons. on employment selection, career devel., employee relocation, quality circles, U.S. and Israel; psychol. evaluations and consultation in custody disputes; feature writer N.Y. Womensweek, 1978-79; mem. bus. adv. com. dept. rehab. medicine, Mt. Sinai Med. Ctr., 1991—. Co-author tng. materials for quality circles; also author articles; exhibited in 2-person photography shows, 1990, 91, 1-person show, 1993, Israel, 1994; Fellow N.Y. State Mental Health Dept., 1958-59. Mem. Am. Psychol. Assn., Westchester County Psychol. Assn. (chmn. profl. edn. com. sch. psychology div. 1976-78, founder, pres. div. indsl./orgnl. psychology 1988-90, bd. dirs 1990), Westchester Photographic Soc. Home: 13 Dupont Ave White Plains NY 10605-3537

KRIM, MATHILDE, medical educator; b. Como, Italy, July 9, 1926; came to U.S.; BS, U. Geneva, Switzerland, 1948, PhD, 1953; DSc (hon.), Long Island U., 1987; LLD (hon.), Columbia U., 1988; DSc (hon.), Brandeis U., 1989; DHL (hon.), Southeastern Mass. U., 1990; DSc. (hon.), Tulane U., 1990; DHL (hon.), SUNY, Stonybrook, 1991; DSc(hon.), Columbia Coll., 1992. Asst. genetic sect., dept. exptl. biology Weizmann Inst. Sci., Rehovot, Israel, 1953-54, jr. scientist, 1954-57, rsch. assoc., 1957-59; rsch. assoc.divsn. virus rsch. Cornell Med. Coll., N.Y.C., 1959-62; rsch. assoc. Sloan Kettering Inst. Cancer Rsch., N.Y.C., 1962-68, assoc., 1968-75, assoc. mem., 1975-85, co-head interferon evaluation program, 1975-81, head interferon lab, 1981-85; assoc. rsch. scientist dept. pediatrics St. Luke's-Roosevelt Hosp. Ctr. and Columbia U., N.Y.C., 1986-90; adjunct prof. pub. health Columbia U., N.Y.C., 1990—; founding co-chair, chmn. bd., CEO Am. Found. for AIDS Rsch., L.A.; bd. dirs. AIDSFILMS, Am. Com. for Weizmann Inst. Sci., Nat. Biomed. Rsch. Found.; trustee Scientists' Inst. for Pub. Information, Feinberg Grad. Sch. Weizmann Inst. Sci., African-Am. Inst.; mem. adv. panel on higher edn., New York, 1965, President's Com. on Mental Retardation, 1966-69, jury Albert D. Lasker Rsch. awards 1968-71, 78—, adv. bd. Health Profls. for Polit. Action, 1968-70, adv. com. to Sec. of HEW on Health Proteciton and Disease Prevention, 1969-70, Coun. NEH, 1969-73, Panel of Cons. on Cancer, Com. Labor and Pub. Welfare, U.S.Senate, 1970-71, adv. com. Nat. Colorectal Cancer Program NIH, 1971-73, working group develo. rsch. segment Virus Cancer Program NIH, 1971-74, review com. "A" Virus Cancer Program NIH, 1974-77, adv. com. Inst. Internat. Edn., 1974—, adv. com. Program of Sci., Tech., and Human Values NEH, 1974-78, U.S. Nat. Commn. for UNESCO, 1979-80, adv. com. World Rehabilitation Fund, 1978-82, Interferon Clin. Adv. Com. Schering-Plough Corp., 1980-85, Bristol Labs. Adv. Panel on Biological Response Modifiers, 1981-84, sci. adv. com. Am. Found. AIDS Rsch., 1985—, Com. of 100 for Nat. Health Ins., AIDS task force Am. Assn. Sex Educators, Counselors and Therapists, 1985—, rsch. adv. coun. Nat. Orgn. for Rare Disorders Inc., 1985—, AIDS Health Edn. Risk Reduction Consultation, Ctrs. for Disease Control, 1986, task force on Chemotherapeutics, Nat. Inst. of Allergy and Infectious Diseases, NIH, 1986, met. area adv. com. Lower Manhattan AIDS consortium, 1986—, scientific adv. bd. Nat. Coalition on Immune System Disorders, 1986—, adv. com. The Village Nursing Home, 1986—, sect. for the study of ethical, legal and social issues HIV Ctr. for Clin. and Behavioral Studies, 1987—, AIDS Rsch. Ctr., 1987—, bd. advisors Nat. Lawyers Guild AIDS Network, 1987—, AIDS adv. panel Planned Parenthood Fed. Am., 1988—, nat. adv. com. Nat. Communtiy AIDS Partnership, 1988—, adv. com. Women and AIDS Resource Network, 1988—; commr. Pres.'s Commn. for the Study of Ethical Problems in Medicine and Biomedical and Behavioral Rsch., adv. bd. LOVE HEALS, 1989—, adv. bd. Internat. Alliance for Haiti, 1989—, adv. bd. AIDS-AUF-KLARUNG, Frankfurt, Germany, 1990—, internat. com. Lottare Informare Formare Educare, Rome, Italy, 1990—, adv. coun. Columbia Sch. Pub. Health, 1990—, AIDS adv. panel, Med. Soc. State of New York, 1992—. Editor (with others) Mediation of Cellular Immunity in Cancer by Immune Modifiers: Progress in Cancer Research and Therapy, 1981;mem. editorial bd. The Aids Record; assoc. editor Cancer Investigation, Interferon Newsletter, Aids Care; contbr. articles to profl. jours. Bd. dirs. Nat. Med. Assn. Found., 1968-69, Inst. of Soc., Ethics, and the Life Scis. (The Hastings Ctr.), 1979-89; trustee Nat. Urban League, 1966-72, The Rockefeller Found., 1971-84, AIDS Med. Found. 1983-89, chairperson; vice chmn. Citizens Organized Against Drug Abuse, 1966; exec. sec. Am. Com for Assistance to Tunisia, 1968-69; dir. at large Am. Cancer Soc., 1970-72. Fellow NAS 1977; s47-52; recipient Spirit of Achievement award Nat. Women's Divsn. Albert Einstein Coll. Medicine, 1972, Humanitarian award Fund for Human Dignity, 1985, award for contbns. to civic life Women's City Club, 1986, John and Samuel Bard award in medicine and sci., 1986, Human Rights Campaign Fund award, 1986, Elizabeth Cutter Morrow award, City of New York YWCA, 1986, Jack Dempsey Humanitarian award St. Clare's Hosp. and Health Ctr., 1986, 10 Ams. Who've Made a Difference award Better Health and Living Mag., 1987, Eleanor Roosevelt Leadership award NOW, 1987, Achievement award Am. Assn. of Physicians for Human Rights, 1987, Humanist Disting. Svc. award Am. Humanist Assn., 1987, Hall of Fame award Internat. Women's Forum, 1987, Commitment to Life award, AIDS project L.A., 1987, Frontrunner award Sara Lee Corp., 1988, Exceptional achievement award, Women's Project and Prodns., 1988, Pres.'s award Am. Equity Assn., 1988, Medical award Hassadah, New York, 1988, award for Pioneering Achievements in Health and Higher Edn. Charles A. Dana Found., 1988, gold medal of honor Casita Maria, 1988, Caring award Stewart McKinney Found., 1988, Outstanding Mother award Nat. Mother's Day Com., 1989, Myrtle Wreath Humantiarian award Nat. Hassadah, 1991, Edwin C. Whitehead award Nat. Ctr. Health Edn., 1991, M. Carey Thomas award Bryn Mawr Coll., 1991, Scientic Freedom and Responsibility award Am. Assn. for Advancement of Science, 1994; named Woman of Distinction Birmingham (Ala.) So. Coll., 1987, Dallas Cares Benefit honoree, 1989, 100 New York Women Barnard Coll., 1989. Mem. NAS, NAACP, Am. Assn. Advancement of Sci., Soc. Biological Therapy, Am. Soc. Microbiology, Internat. Soc. for Interferon Rsch., Am. Humanists Assn. Office: Am Found AIDS Rsch East Satellite 5900 Wilshire Blvd Fl 2 Los Angeles CA 90036-5013*

KRIMSKY, KAREN NORMA, paint contractor; b. Norman, Okla., Nov. 29, 1953; d. Martin L. and Arline R. (Orzack) K. BFA in Art, U. Okla., 1977. Registered ins. rep. Owner Karen Krimsky Painting, Norman, 1979—; tchr. Firehouse Art Ctr., Norman, 1993, Oklahoma City (Okla.) C.C., 1993. Exhibitor 1st Annual Ring Competition, Tenn., 1976, Okla. Designer/Craftsman, Oklahoma City, 1976; solo photography show Norman, 1994. Collector Leukemia Soc., Oklahoma City, 1991-93; remodel cons., vol. Jacobson House Am. Indian Mus. Recipient 1st place Am. Color Photo, Firehouse Biennial, Norman, 1989, 3d place, 1991. Mem. Norman Women's Entrepreneurs Network, Toastmasters Internat. (treas. 1993-94), Oklahoma City Alumni Assn.

KRINER, SALLY GLADYS PEARL, artist; b. Bradford, Ohio, Jan. 29, 1911; d. Henry Walter and Pearl Rebecca (Brubaker) Brant; m. Leo Louis Kriner, Feb. 28, 1933; children—Patricia Staab, Jane Palombo. Grad. Arsenal Tech. sch. Indpls.; student Ind. U.-Indpls., 1954, Herron Sch. Art, Indpls., 1958. Exhibited in one woman shows Hoosier Salon, Indpls., 1960, Village Art Gallery, Southport, Ind., 1967, 70, 73, Brown County Art Guild, Nashville, Ind., 1970, 74, 77, 80, 83, 87, 92; group shows include South Side Art League, Indpls., 1959-74, Indpls. Art League, 1959-64, Brown County Art Guild, 1974—, Hoosier Salon, 1961, 65, 67, 68, 73, 75, 76, 77, 82, 86, 87, 91; represented in permanent collections Riley Hosp., Indpls., others. Founder Southside Women's Symphony Com., Indpls., 1958; treas. Perry Twp. Republican Club, Ind., 1960-65; pres. State Assembly Women's Club, 1965-67; bd. dirs. ARC, Indpls., 1942-45, Southside Civic Orgn., Indpls., 1954, Clowes Hall Women's Com., Indpls., 1963. Recipient citation ARC, 1946; citation Marion County Meritorious Service Award, 1959; citation Greater Southside Civic Orgn., 1961; Art award Kappa Kappa Kappa, 1967, 68, 70, 71. Fellow Indpls. Art League Found. (numerous awards 1960-66); mem. Southside Art League, Inc. (pres. 1964-65, numerous awards 1964-75, founder), Ind. Artists Club, Inc. (Purchases award 1978), Ind. Heritage Arts, Inc., Rutland Art Assn., Brown County Art Guild (pres. 1980-83, v.p. 1983—), Ind. fedn. Arts Clubs (bd. dirs. 1963-73), Ind. Artist (chmn. prize fund 1974-75), Consignment and appraisal of fine arts, Hoosier Salon, Indpls. Mus. Arts, Nat. Soc. Arts and Letters, Nat. Mus. Women in Arts, Hoosier Group Women in Arts. Presbyterian. Avocation: growing flowers. Home and Studio: 394 E Freeman Ridge Rd Nashville IN 47448-8871

KRINEY, MARILYN WALKER, publishing executive; b. Montclair, N.J., June 12, 1938; d. James Griffin and Grace Dagnall (Scott) Walker; m. Gordon Arthur Kriney, 1966; 1 child, Alexander Walker. AB in English, Douglass Coll., 1960; MBA in Fin., NYU, 1986. Editor T.Y. Crowell Publishers, N.Y.C., 1967-77; sr. editor Children's Books HarperCollins, N.Y.C., 1977-83, editor-in-chief Harper Trophy, 1983-89, sr. v.p., publisher, 1989—. Office: HarperCollins Pub 10 E 53rd St New York NY 10022-5244

KRINSKY, CAROL HERSELLE, art history educator; b. N.Y.C., June 2, 1937; d. David and Jane (Gartman) Herselle; m. Robert Daniel Krinsky, Jan. 25, 1959; 2 children. BA, Smith Coll., 1957; MA, NYU, 1960, PhD, 1965. Mem. faculty NYU, 1965—, assoc. prof. art history, 1973-78, prof., 1978—. Author: Vitruvius de Architectura 1521, 1969, Rockefeller Center, 1978, Synagogues of Europe, 1985, Gordon Bunshaft of Skidmore, Owings & Merrill, 1988, Europas Synagogen, 1988; contbr. articles to profl. jours. Bd. dirs. Internat. Survey Jewish Monuments, Urbana, Ill., 1981—, Soc. Archtl. Historians, 1978-80, 86-89, The Mac Dowell Colony, Inc., 1989—, Jewish Heritage Coun. World Monuments Fund.; co-chair seminar on the city Columbia U., 1993—. Am. Coun. Learned Socs. grantee, 1981, Nat. Endowment for the Arts grantee, 1993; recipient Arnold Brunner award N.Y.C. chpt. AIA, 1990. Mem. Soc. Archtl. Historians (pres. 1984-86, pres. N.Y.C. chpt. 1977-79), Coll. Art Assn., Planning History Group, Am. Urban History Assn, Women's City Club, Phi Beta Kappa. Office: NYU Dept Fine Arts 100 Washington Sq E New York NY 10003

KRIPKE, EVA (EVE KRIPKE), counselor; b. Buer Erle, Germany, July 21, 1932; came to U.S., 1936; d. Edgar and Hildegard (Mendel) Kadden; m. Sidney Seward Kripke, June 27, 1954; children: Susan Kripke Byers, David L., Daniel T. BA, U. Mich., 1954; MA, U. Iowa, 1970. Lic. profl. counselor, Ohio; nat. cert. counselor. Counselor Univ. H.S., Iowa City, 1971-72, West H.S., Iowa City, 1972-76, Anthony Wayne H.S., Whitehouse, Ohio, 1976—; mem. part-time faculty U. Toledo, 1986; counselor, therapist E. Cintron & Assocs., Perrysburg, Ohio, 1986—; counselor Youth for Understanding, Columbus, Ohio, 1990—; svc. provider Resource Careers, Toledo, 1994—. Author: Where Are you Going?, 1980; editor: Single Parent Family, 1976; also articles. Pres. bd. dirs. West Ctr., Toledo, 1990-91, mem. advocacy com., 1993-94. Scholar Jennings Found., 1985. Mem. ACA, NEA, Am. Mental Health Counselors Assn., N.W. Ohio Assn. for Counseling and Devel. (pres. 1986), Ohio Counseling Assn., Phi Delta Kappa, Phi Lambda Theta. Jewish. Office: E Cintron & Assocs 139 W Indiana Ave Perrysburg OH 43551

KRIPKE, MARGARET LOUISE, immunologist; b. Concord, Calif., July 21, 1943; d. Clyde Charles and Vivian Faith (Leighter) Cook; m. Bernard Kripke, Dec. 28, 1966 (div. 1974); 1 child, Katharine; m. Isaiah J. Fidler, Oct. 18, 1975; children: Morli, Daniel. AB, U. Calif., Berkeley, 1965, MA, 1967, PhD, 1970; postdoctoral, Ohio State U., 1970-72. Asst. prof. dept. pathology Coll. Medicine, U. Utah, Salt Lake City, 1972-75; head immunobiology of phys. and chem. carcinogenesis sect. Cancer Biology Program, NCI-Frederick Cancer Rsch. Facility, Frederick, Md., 1975-82; assoc. dir. Cancer Biology Program, NCI-Frederick (Md.) Cancer Rsch. Facility, 1979, dir., 1979-82; dir. immunobiology of phys. and chem. carcinogenesis lab. NCI-Frederick (Md.) Cancer Rsch. Facility, 1982-83; chmn. dept. immunology U. Tex. M.D. Anderson Cancer Ctr., Houston, 1983—; Kathryn O'Connor rsch. prof. U. Tex. Med. Sch., Houston, 1983-86, rsch. prof. dept. pathology, 1984-87, rsch. prof. dept. dermatology, 1984—, Vivian L. Smith chair in immunology, 1986—; Edna Roe Meml. lectr. VIIIth Internat. Congress on Photobiology, Strasbourg, 1980, Chancellor's Disting. lectr. U. Calif., Berkeley, 1980; chmn. Gordon Conf. on Cancer, New London, N.H., 1983; Warner-Lambert lectr. U. Mich., Ann Arbor, 1983; dir. program in immunology U. Tex., Grad. Sch. Biomedical Scis., Houston, 1989-92; bd. sci. counselors div. cancer biology and diagnosis and ctrs. Nat. Cancer Inst., Bethesda, Md., 1989-93; mem. exec. com. sci. adv. bd. EPA, Washington, 1991—; mem. subcom. to review Nat. Cancer Program Nat. Cancer Adv. Bd.; Estee Lauder lectureship Johns Hopkins Univ., Balt., 1983; Grace Faillace lectureship Northridge Hosp., Ft. Lauderdale, Fla., 1985; Meyerhoff Professorship, Weizmann Inst. Sci., Rehovot, Israel, 1985; Pharma-Medica lecture, Danish Dermatological, Arhus, Denmark, 1987; spl. lecture 17th World Cong. Dermatology, Berline, 1987; Maruice S. Segal lecture, Tufts Univ. Sch. Medicine, Boston, 1989. lectr. in field. Contbr. chpts. to books and articles to profl. jours. Recipient Calif. Alumni Assn. scholarship, 1961, Lila Gruber award for cancer rsch. Am. Acad. Dermatology, 1984, Past State Pres.'s award Tex. Fedn. of the Bus. and Profl. Women's Club, 1992. Mem. Am. Soc. for Photobiology (sec. coun. 1991—), Am. Assn. for Cancer Rsch. (pres.-elect 1992, pres. 1993-94), Am. Assn. Immunologists, Soc. for Leukocyte Biology (coun. 1985-89), Soc. for Investigative Dermatology. Office: M D Anderson Cancer Ctr 1515 Holcombe Blvd Houston TX 77030-4009

KRISE, PATRICIA LOVE, automotive industry executive; b. Indpls., July 28, 1959; d. John Bernard and Ann (Emmons) Love; m. Thomas Warren Krise, Sept. 5, 1987. BA magna cum laude, Hanover Coll., Ind., 1981; MBA with hons., Miami U., Oxford, Ohio, 1982. Substitute tchr. Henry County Sch. Dist., Knightstown, Ind., 1982-83; project mgr. Servaas Labs., Inc., Indpls., 1983-84; sales analyst Ford Motor Co., Mpls., 1984, outstate field mgr., 1984-86, met. field mgr., 1986-87, truck merchandising mgr., 1987-88, merchandising mgr., 1988-89; met. field dir. Denver dist. Ford Motor Co., 1989, market representation specialist Denver dist., 1990-91; regional mkt. rep. mgr. Infiniti Div. Nissan, Naperville, Ill., 1991-92; regional merchandising mgr. Infiniti divsn. Nissan Motor Corp., Naperville, Ill., 1992-93, dealer ops. cons., 1993—; advisor/presenter Ford Dealer Advt. Fund, Mpls., 1987-88. Tutor adult literacy. Recipient Outstanding Mktg. award Ctrl. Region Ford Motor Co., 1987, Wall St. Jour. award, 1982; named Internat. Woman of Yr., 1992. Mem. Twin Cities Sales Mgrs. Club, Hanover Coll. Alumni Assn., Women's Athletic Assn. (treas. 1979-80), Pre-Law Club (pres. 1980-81), Nat. Assn. Female Execs., Alpha Delta Pi. Republican. Roman Catholic.

KRISSLER, SUZANNE PIERCE, office technologies educator; b. Binghamton, N.Y., Sept. 5, 1951; d. Melvin John and Helen (Toth) Pierce; married, 1980. AAS, Broome C.C., Binghamton, N.Y., 1971; BS in Bus. Edn., SUNY, Albany, 1973, MS, 1975, EdS in Counseling and Pers. Svcs., 1976. Cert. edn. specialist; cert. notary public; permanent cert. bus. edn. Mem. faculty Broome C.C., 1973-74; mem. faculty Orange County C.C., Middletown, N.Y., prof., 1981—; exec. dir. Ridley-Lowell Sch. of Bus., Binghamton, N.Y., 1976-79; chair Middle States Evaluation Com., Middletown, 1991-93; organizer various seminars. Author: Employment Techniques Handbook, 1978, Job & Career Fair Manual, 1994; contbr. articles to profl. jours. Mem. Nat. Bus. Edn. Assn., Eastern Bus. Edn. Assn., N.Y. State Bus. Tchrs. Assn., Inst. Mgmt. Accts. Office: Orange County CC 115 South St Middletown NY 10940

KRISSOFF, SYLVIA GITTLEN, artist, art historian, retired educator; b. Grand Rapids, Mich., Mar. 17, 1919; d. Alex and Ruth (Armour) Gittlen; m. Abraham Krissoff, Dec. 29, 1940; children: Joel Edward, William Bruce. Student, Art Inst. Chgo., 1939-40; BA with teaching cert., Calvin Coll., Grand Rapids, 1966; MA in Art Edn., Western Mich. U., 1968; MA in Art History, U. Mich., 1970. Tchr. art Riverside Jr. High Sch., 1966-68; instr. Grand Rapids Jr. Coll., 1971-80, Grand Valley State U., 1976-81, U. Mich. Ext., 1971-80, Kendall Sch. Design, 1981-87; instr. Aquinas Coll., 1968-69, emeritus, 1988—; instr. history of sculpture Grand Rapids Art Mus., 1993; freelance art reviewer Grand Rapids Press, 1982—; guest curator Gerald Mast Exhbn. and Catalogue, 1991, Walter and Lois McBride Exhbn., 1992; lectr. art history Women's City Club, Grand Rapids, Grand Valley Artists, Friends of Art, Holland, Mich., Muskegon Art Mus., also others. One-woman shows Calvin Coll., 1974, Grand Rapids Art Mus., 1976-77, Gallery Luisa, 1979, 81, 82, 85, Cascade Art Gallery, 1987, 91, Breton Village Art Gallery, 1988, 1st United Meth. Ch., 1990, T.C. Downtown, 1993; exhibited in group shows Aquinas Coll., Calvin Coll., 1974, Hackley Gallery, U. Mich., Grand Haven Christian Art Show, 1973, 74; represented in permanent collection Grand Rapids Art Mus., Butterworth and Blodgett hospitals, also pvt. collections; contbr. exhbn. catalogs Artists of Grand Rapids, 1981, Artists of Michigan of 19th Centruy, 1987. Past pres. Grand Rapids chpt. Hadassah, past v.p. Mich. region; past pres. Sisterhood, Temple Emanuel; chmn. accessions com. Grand Rapids Art Mus. Recipient hon. mention Grand Haven Christian Art Show. Mem. Coll. Art Assn., Mich. Watercolor Soc. Home and Studio: 1916 San Lu Rae Dr SE Grand Rapids MI 49506-3458

KRISTL, CLAIRE ANN SIMMINGER, physical therapist; b. Ft. Huachuca, Ariz., Nov. 9, 1959; d. Raymond Louis and Dorothy Mae (Gratto) Kervahn; m. Frederick David Simminger, Dec. 12, 1981 (div. Oct. 1986); m. Roman Kristl, Sept. 4, 1991; children: Sean David, Jakub Aaron, Roman Raymond. BS cert. in phys. therapy, No. Ariz. U., 1982. Registered phys. therapist, Calif. Dir. phys. therapy U.S. Army Med. Activity, Bremerhaven, Germany, 1983-85, Kathy Kram Phys. Therapy, Watsonville, Calif., 1985-86; staff phys. therapist St. Francis Hosp., Columbus, Ga., 1985, Craig Phelps Phys. Therapy, Salinas, Calif., 1986; dir. rehab. Casa Serena, Salinas, 1986; owner, mgr. Phelps & Simminger Phys. Therapy, Salinas, 1986—. Community speaker, 1986—; area treas. Cub Scouts Am., Carmel Valley, Calif., 1993. Mem. Am. Phys. Therapy Assn., Calif. Phys. Therapy Assn. (rep. 1987), Zonta. Home: 39 Miramonte Rd Carmel Valley CA 93924 Office: 321 E Romie Ln Ste B Salinas CA 93901-3129

KROEGER, SUSAN JEAN, accountant; b. Glenridge, N.J., July 3, 1961; d. John Alfred and Patricia Ann (ferrante) Kroeger; m. George Clarence Merrill, June 18, 1983; children: C.J., B.J., G.J., P.J. BA, William Paterson Coll., 1986. CPA, N.J., notary pub., ins. broker; lic. real estate sales person, N.J. Clk. Crum & Foster, Parsippany, N.J., 1980-86; internal auditor Crum & Foster, Parsippany, 1986-87; sr. acct. Ernst & Young & Co., Iselin, N.J., 1987-89; pvt. practice Parsippany, 1989—; real estate sales assoc. Scura Realtors, 1993—. Mem. AICPA, N.J. Soc. CPAs. Republican. Roman Catholic.

KROGER, ALTHEA, state legislator; b. Chgo., Oct. 9, 1946; m. Joseph W. Kroger; 1 child. BA, St. Louis U., 1969; MA, U. Vt., 1985; JD, Vt. Law Sch., 1988; MPA, Harvard U., 1989. Mem. Vt. Ho. Reps., 1977-84; asst. whip, 1979-84; mem. Vt. Senate, 1991—. Democrat. Roman Catholic. Home: 10 Church St Essex Junction VT 05452 Office: Vt State House State Capitol Montpelier VT 05602*

KROGMANN, JOAN L., horse trainer, writer; b. Queens, N.Y., Oct. 12, 1936; d. Milton Irving and Hazel Darling (Diefenbacher) Andres; divorced; 1 child, Kimberley. Studied with Vladimer Littauer, Luis de La Vellette, George Brush, Frank Collins, others, 1958-75. Lic. real estate agent, N.Y. Owner Little Plains Stable and Little Plains Breeding Farm, L.I., N.Y., 1957-94; lic. real estate agent Century 21, N.Y., 1984-88; freelance writer N.Y., 1980-94; owner La Petite Cheval Farm, Loxahatchee, Fla., 1994—; organizer, creator L.I. High Score Awards, 1959-94; tchr. phys. edn., L.I., 1980-90; organizer L.I. Mini Circuit, 1984-90, Showcase Series, 1992 Galaxy Champions. Contbr. articles to various publs. Tchr., advisor Girl Scouts U.S., L.I., 1970-94, Boy Scouts Am., L.I., 1970-94; mem. bd. advisors Bd. Coop. Edn. Spl., L.I., 1979-94; pk. steward Town of Huntington, L.I., 1988-94, mem. conservation bd., 1988-94; active intensive care program Suffolk County Handicapped, L.I., 1993-94. Named Trainer of Yr., L.I. Mini Circuit, 1989-90, Pleasure Horse Champion, Nassau Suffolk Horsemans, 1991, 92, 93, 94, Trainer of Yr., North Shore Horse Shows, 1994. Mem. Am. Horse Show Assn. (show mgr.), Nat. Hunter Jumper Assn. Home: 13678 14th Pl N Loxahatchee FL 33470

KROHLEY, PATRICIA ANNE, realtor, artist; b. N.Y.C., Feb. 13, 1954; d. Casper and Ann Marie (Calise) Inzerillo; m. Richard John Krohley Sr., June 10, 1977 (separated Mar. 1994); 1 child, Richard John Jr. Student, Bklyn. Mus. Art Sch., 1971, Queens Coll., 1974. Lic. real estate salesperson, N.Y. Realtor Century 21 Bonus RE, Woodhaven, N.Y., 1988-93, Re/Max Bonus Realty, Woodhaven, N.Y., 1993—; mem. agt. adv. panel Century 21 Broker's Coun., L.I., N.Y., 1990; key communicator Re/Max Bonus Realty, Woodhaven, 1993—. Recipient scholarship Bklyn. Mus. Art, 1971. Mem. Nat. Assn. Realtors, N.Y. State Assn. Realtors, L.I. Bd. Realtors, Women in Transition (founder, pres. 1993—). Office: Re/Max Bonus Realty 94-19 Jamaica Ave Woodhaven NY 11421

KROL, ROSEMARY, librarian; b. Turners Falls, Mass., Jan. 3, 1955; d. Walter John and Agnes Helen (Kallins) K. BA in Sociology, U. Mass./Dartmouth, 1976; M. Libr. and Info. Sci., Simmons Coll., 1986; MPA, Govs. State U., 1989. Dir. Montague Pub. Librs., Turners Falls, Mass., 1979-86; prof. libr. sci. and info. Govs. State U., University Park, Ill., 1986-90; info. specialist C. Berger & Co., Carol Stream, Ill., 1990-91; tech. libr. Argonne (Ill.) Nat. Lab., 1991—. Co-compiler: Sourcebook of Library Technology, 1988, 90; indexer Libr. Tech. Newsletter, 1988-90. Mem. ALA, Franklin County Libr./Media Assn. (pres. 1985-86). Office: Argonne Nat Lab 9700 Cass Ave Lemont IL 60439-4801

KROLL, EMILY T., nursing administrator; b. Pitts., Dec. 19, 1944; d. Richard J. and Emily (Troianowski) Schick; m. Robert Regis Kroll, May 4, 1965; children: Robert, William, Michael, Melissa. Diploma, Mercy Hosp. Sch. Nursing, Pitts., 1965; BSN, La Roche Coll., 1985; MSEd, Duquesne U., 1989; cert. gestalt therapist, Ctr. for Human Devel., Pitts., 1992. RN, Pa.; cert. instr. nonviolent crisi intervention. Rehab. auditing cons. Worldwide Rehab. Cons., Inc., Lansdale, Pa.; psychometrician Paul Bernstein, PhD, Pitts.; mgr. No. and S.W. Communities Mental Health Svcs., Pitts.; clin. specialist adutl psychiat. and mental health nursing, 1991; pvt. therapy practice Pitts. Mem. Mercy Hosp. Alumni Assn., Sigma Theta Tau. Home: 145 Hornaday Rd Pittsburgh PA 15210-4219

KROLL, KARIN ALLISON, disability consultant; b. Chgo., Aug. 10, 1966; d. Seymour and Dorine Mae (Ellisen) K. BA in Sociology, U. Iowa, 1988; MA in Rehab. Psychology, U. Wis., Madison, 1990. Cert. rehab. counselor. Case mgr. Anixter Ctr., Chgo., 1990-93, rsch. trainer, 1993-94. Vol. Mus. of Sci. and Industry, Chgo., 1993-94. Mem. Nat. Rehab. Assn., Nat. Rehab. Counseling Assn., Am. Counseling Assn., Am. Rehab. Counseling Assn., Chi Sigma Iota. Office: Anixter Ctr 2001 N Clybourn Ave Chicago IL 60614-4036

KROMINGA, LYNN, cosmetic and health care company executive, lawyer; b. L.A., May 16, 1950; d. Dale E. and Phyllis M. Krominga; m. Amnon Shiboleth, Apr. 9, 1992; 1 child, Karen Lee Shiboleth. B.A. in German, U. Minn., 1972, J.D., 1974. Bar: Minn. 1974, N.Y. 1976. Assoc. firms in Mpls. and N.Y.C., 1974-77; assoc. counsel Am. Express Co., N.Y.C., 1977-80; sr. internat. counsel Revlon, Inc., N.Y.C., 1981-92, v.p. law, 1988-92, gen. counsel to exec. com., 1991-92, pres. licensing div., 1992—, mem. exec. com.,

1993—. Mem. ABA, Internat. Bar Assn., Cosmetic, Toiletry and Fragance Assn. (vice chmn. govt. rels. com. 1991-92), Am. Arbitration Assn. corp. counsel com. 1986-92; panel of arbitrators for large complex cases 1993—, Phi Beta Kappa. Home: 333 E 57th St New York NY 10022 Office: Revlon Inc 625 Madison Ave New York NY 10022-1801

KRONE, IRENE, product consultant; b. N.Y.C., Oct. 12, 1940; d. Frederick Wilhelm and Gertrude (Gottschlich) Beckmann; m. Helmut Krone, Nov. 14, 1970; 1 child, Kathryn Maria. BS, Chestnut Hill Coll., 1962; postgrad., Sch. Visual Arts and Interior Design, 1962-64, NYU, 1967-68. Market rsch. analyst, then licensing mgr. Celanese Corp., N.Y.C. and Brussels, 1962-67; v.p. product devel. Doyle Dane Bernbach, N.Y.C., 1967-79; pres. I. Krone Assocs. Inc., N.Y.C., 1979—. Pres., founder Stop Traffic Offenses Program, N.Y.C., 1982—. Mem. Fashion's Inner Circle. Home: 1 E 62d St New York NY 10021 Office: 737 3d Ave New York NY 10017

KRONE, JULIE, jockey; b. Benton Harbor, Mich., July 24, 1963; d. Don and Judy Krone. Began as profl. jockey Tampa Bay (Fla.) Downs, 1980; leading woman jockey in U.S., 1986-88. Races won include Cornhusker Handicap, AK-Star-Ben racetrack, Omaha, 1988, Flower Bowl Handicap, Belmont Park, 1988, Modesty Stakes, Arlington Park, Ill., 1989, Budweiser Md. Classic, Pimlico, 1989, Belmont Stakes, 1993; first rode in Kentucky Derby, 1992; recipient Comeback award Am. Sportscasters Assn., 1994. Office: care Jockeys' Guild 250 W Main St Ste 1820 Lexington KY 40507*

KRONEN, JERILYN, psychologist; b. N.Y.C., July 17, 1947; d. Morris and Hester (Engel) Levy; m. Kenneth Kronen, Apr. 11, 1976; children: Ari, Joshua. PhD, Yeshiva U., 1982; cert. in psychotherapy & psychoanalysis, N.Y.U., 1988. Lic. psychologist, N.Y. Tchr. Pub. Sch. 119, N.Y.C., 1969-72; sch. psychologist Bd. Coop. Edn. Svc., N.Y.C., 1972-82; pvt. practice N.Y.C., 1982—; mem. faculty Resolve, N.Y.C., 1989—; adj. clin. supr. Ferkauf-Yeshiva U., N.Y.C., 1989—; lectr. in field. Bd. dirs. Couples Club Kehilat Jeshurun Synagogue, N.Y.C., 1989-91, adoption resource person, 1990—; liaison mem. Lower Sch. Ramaz, N.Y.C., 1990-92. Mem. APA, Div. 39 Psychoanalysis. Home and Office: 137 E 36th St Ste 14 New York NY 10016-3528

KRONENBERG, JACALYN, oncological and pediatrics nurse, administrator; b. N.Y.C., July 21, 1949; d. Martin Jerome and Joyce (Weinberg) Jacobs; m. Robert Kronenberg, Jan. 23, 1971 (div.); 1 child, Joshua Louis. BA, William Paterson Coll. of N.J., 1971; ADN, Phoenix Coll., 1977. RN, Calif.; cert. IV nurse, chemo, ACLS, pediatric advanced life support. Asst. charge nurse Phoenix Gen. Hosp.; nurse Ariz. State Crippled Children's Hosp., Tempe; maternal, child nurse Desert Samaritan Hosp., Mesa, Ariz.; nurse mgr. PPS Inc., Phoenix, Med-Pro 2000, Phoenix; clin. nurse II Phoenix Children's Hosp.; nurse mgr. adolescent unit Shriners Hosp., L.A.; nurse mgr. pediatrics, oncology, gynecology, med./surg. Santa Monica (Calif.) Hosp. Med. Ctr., 1993-94; dir. nurses, dir. patient care svcs. NMC Homecare, Anaheim, Calif., 1994; dir. med./surg. Midway Hosp. Med. Ctr., L.A., 1995—. Nursing Lab. Tech. scholar, 1976. Mem. Oncology Nursing Soc., Pediatric Oncology Nurse Soc., Nursing Diagnosis Assn. of N.Am., IV Nursing Soc., Pediatric Nursing Soc. Office: Midway Hosp Med Ctr 5925 San Vincente Blvd Los Angeles CA 90019

KRONHOLM, MARTHA MARY, elementary educator; b. Wisconsin Rapids, Wis., July 28, 1952; d. Donald Edward and Ruth Marie (Albert) K. BS, U. Wis., LaCrosse, 1974; MEPD, U. Wis., Stevens Point, 1980; PhD, So. Ill. U., 1993. Elem. tchr. grades 4-6 Wisconsin Rapids Pub. Schs., 1974-88, sci. coord., 1986-88; ad hoc faculty U. Wis., Stevens Point, 1986-88; instr. sci. methods So. Ill. U., Carbondale, 1989-91; 6th grade tchr. Wisconsin Rapids (Wis.) Pub. Schs., 1992—, action rsch. team, 1993—; mem. environ. edn. task force Wis. Dept. Pub. Instrn., Madison, 1983-85; rsch. asst. Earthwatch, Ethiopia, 1984, Borneo, 1985, Minn., Alaska, 1987; mem. bd. visitors U. Wis., Stevens Point, 1987—; mem. tchr. certification rev. com. Wis. Environ. Edn., State of Wis., 1981-83. Co-author: (curriculum guides) Wisconsin Environmental Education Curriculum Planning Guide, 1985, Wisconsin Rapids Environmental Education Guide, 1989, Wisconsin Rapids Science Guide, 1988; author articles, abstracts in field. Mentor; mem. Habitat Restoration Com., 1992—; edn. chairperson Aldo Leopold chpt. Audubon Soc., Stevens Point, 1983-88; tchr. amb. Russian Expedition, 1995. Christa McAuliffe fellow U.S. Dept. Edn., 1987; Delta Kappa Gamma Soc. Internat. scholar, 1989; Lifetouch Enrichment grantee, 1994; recipient Kohl fellowship award, 1994; named Wisconsin Rapids Tchr. of Yr., 1994. Mem. Wis. Assn. for Environ. Edn. (sec., Aldo Leopold award 1990), AAUW (newsletter co-editor Wisconsin Rapids chpt. 1986-88, Project Renew scholar 1990), Ruffed Grouse Soc. (banquet com. 1983-87, Edn. and Conservation award 1986), Delta Kappa Gamma (sec. Gamma chpt., Golden award 1988), Phi Kappa Phi, Kappa Delta Pi, Phi Delta Kappa (Howard M. Soule Ednl. Leadership fellow 1992). Democrat. Lutheran. Home: 1430 23rd St N Ste G Wisconsin Rapids WI 54494-2192

KRONKE, DORENE EMMA, pharmaceutical executive; b. Tyler, Minn., May 20, 1950; d. Arthur John and Elaine Irene (Wendorff) K.; m. Jonathan Krim, June 21, 1980 (div. Oct. 1983); m. Michael William Rossi, Nov. 19, 1983 (separated). BA in Bus. Adminstrn., SW State U., 1973; MBA, Ariz. State U., 1981. Unit mgr. Good Samaritan Hosp., Phoenix, 1973-75; waitress Phoenix Country Club, 1976-77; sales rep. Treasure Chem. Co., Billings, Mont., 1977; profl. rep. Merck Sharp & Dohme, Missoula, Mont., 1978-80; program coord. Merck Sharp & Dohme, West Point, Pa., 1981-83; dist. mgr. Merck Sharp & Dohme, San Diego, 1983-86; product mgr. Merck Sharp & Dohme, West Point, 1986-88; region dir. Merck Sharp & Dohme, Mpls., 1988-91; v.p. sales and mktg. MGI Pharma, Inc., Mpls., 1991-92; exec. dir. info. edn. and svcs. Astra Merck, Inc., Wayne, Pa., 1992—. Bd. dirs. Nat. Soc. for Prevention of Blindness, Orange, Calif., 1986; trustee First Unitarian Soc., Mpls., 1990; mem. Phila. Mus. Art, Nat. Parks & Conservation Assn., Washington, Nat. Mus. of Women in the Arts, Washington. Mem. NOW, Ariz. State U. Alumni Assn., S.W. State U. Alumni Assn. Office: 725 Chesterbrook Blvd Wayne PA 19087-5677

KRONMAN, CAROL JANE, lawyer; b. Passaic, N.J., Mar. 25, 1944; d. Robert M. and Helen (Harris) K.; children: Audrey Jane, Heather Sue. AB, Cornell U., 1965; MA, Columbia U., 1966; JD, Yeshiva U., 1980. Bar: N.Y. 1981, N.J. 1981, Fla. 1981, U.S. Dist. Ct. N.J. 1981, U.S. Dist. Ct. (so. dist.) N.Y. 1984, U.S. Supreme Ct. 1990, U.S. Dist. Ct. (ea. dist.) N.Y. 1991. Asst. prof. William Paterson Coll., Wayne, N.J., 1967-69; treas. Capital Theatre Inc., N.J., 1977-83; coord. paralegal studies Montclair State Coll., N.J., 1982-83, prof., 1982-85; ptnr. Kronman & Kronman P.A., Totowa, N.J., 1981-85; ptnr. N.J. office Max E. Greenberg, Cantor & Reiss, South Hackensack, N.J., 1986-87; ptnr. Blodnick, Pomeranz, Reiss, Schultz & Abramowitz, P.C., N.Y. and N.J., 1987-89; of counsel Budd, Larner, Gross, Rosenbaum, Greenberg & Sade, 1989-90; pvt. practice Caldwell, N.J., 1990-93; gen. counsel office of Mayor Office of Constrn. City of N.Y., 1991-94; lectr. N.J. Inst. for Continuing Legal Edn., 1987, Constrn. Failure and Disaster Super conf. Conf. Mgmt. Corp., N.Y.C., 1988; assoc. Hosp. Joint Diseases, N.Y.C. Author: Different Types of Contracts, 1987; editor, pub. The Kronman Letter, Surety and Fidelity News, 1995—; contbr. articles to profl. jours. Recipient Svc. award in engring. and industry Am. Orgn. Rehab. through Tng. Fedn., 1993, Svc. award in real estate and constrn., 1994, Spl. Recognition award Profl. Women in Constrn., 1993; noted for Spl. Presentation for Committment to Excellence in Rsch., Hosp. for Joint Diseases, N.Y. Hosp. Mem. Orgn. Rehab. through Tng. (bd. dirs. real estate and constrn. industry chpt., svc. award), N.J. Bar Assn., N.Y. State Bar Assn., Fla. Bar Assn., Profl. Women in Constrn. Address: 2 Sutton Pl S Apt 3A New York NY 10022 Office: 227 Jackson Pines Rd Jackson NJ 08527 also: 2 Sutton Pl Ste 3A New York NY 10022

KROPAS, CLAUDIA VICTORIA, electronic engineer; b. Boston, Nov. 11, 1957; d. George C. and Virginia M. (Tuinila) K. BS in Applied Math., Fla. Inst. Technology, 1979; BEE, U. Dayton, 1984; MEE, Calif. State U., Sacramento, 1988. Cert. engr.-in-tng. Equipment design engr. So. Bell Telephone & Telegraph Co., Ft. Lauderdale, Fla., 1979-83; electronic engr. McClellan AFB, Sacramento, Calif., 1984-85; sr. engr. Aerojet Solid Propulsion Co., Sacramento, 1985-88; rsch. and devel. engr. Wright Lab., Wright-Patterson AFB, Ohio, 1989—; Contbr. articles to profl. jours. Contbr. articles to profl. jours. Mem. IEEE, ASTM, Am. Soc. for Nondestructive Testing, Soc. Women Engrs.

KROPF, JOAN R., museum curator; b. Cleve., Aug. 4, 1949; d. Joseph and Irene (Verderber) K. BA, Eckerd Coll., 1994. Co-dir., curator Salvador Dali Mus., St. Petersburg, Fla., 1971—. Editor, co-author: (book) Dali's Animal Crackers, 1993, (show catalogs) The Secret Life Drawings, 1983, Galacid...Catalog, 1992, (mus. catalog) Dali's Graphic Art, 1993. Rep. arts adminstr. com. Pub. Arts Commn., St. Petersburg, 1993; festival/art show judge for various orgns., Fla., 1982—. Office: Salvador Dali Mus 1000 3d St S Saint Petersburg FL 33701

KROPIDLOWSKI, DONNA LEE, hospital administrator; b. Ashville, N.C., Aug. 20, 1945; d. Robert John and Robbie Lee (Marlor) Beaumont; m. Henry J. Kropidlowski, Sept. 24, 1964; children: Denise, Scott, Jason. BS in Human Svcs., Medaille Coll., 1985; MA in Pastoral Ministry, Christ the King Seminary, 1990; mgmt. studies cert., Cornell U., 1993. Cert. chaplain. Coord. vol. svcs. Haven House Domestic Violence Shelter, Buffalo, 1978-80; ombudsman, youth counselor Nat. Conf. Christians and Jews, Buffalo, 1980-82; dir. pastoral care Kenmore (N.Y.) Mercy Hosp., 1990—; guest speaker Roman Cath. Diocese Buffalo, 1991. Trustee Christ the King Sem., 1993—; vol. Kairos Prison Ministry, local chair, 1983-90; chair exec. com. Diocesan Pastoral Coun. Buffalo, 1988-94; mem. Hospice Quality Assurance Com., 1994—. Recipient Vol. Svc. award Albion Correctional Facility, 1987, 86, 85, 84. Mem. Nat. Cursillo (regional chair 1991-93). Office: Kenmore Mercy Hosp 2950 Elmwood Ave Kenmore NY 14217

KROPILAK, DELPHINE ALICE, maternal-child nurse; b. Montclair, N.J., Feb. 27, 1954; d. Alfred Anderson and Ann (DuBoyce) Jensen; m. Gregory Kropilak Sr., May 31, 1980; children: KellyAlice, Erin Elizabeth, Gregory Joseph II. AAS, Felician Coll., 1976, BSN, 1994. RNC; cert. low risk neonatal nursing NAACOG, NALS, BLS, Neonatal IV. Staff nurse Children's Hosp., Newark, 1976-80, Meadowlands Hosp. Med. Ctr., Secaucus, N.J., 1985-89; maternal child staff St. Mary's Hosp., Hoboken, N.J., 1989—; sen. staff nurse Columbus Hosp., Newark, 1980-93; staff pediat. intensive care unit St. Barnabas Med. Ctr., Livingston, N.J., 1993—, staff nurse pediat. ICU, 1992—. Mem. Orgn. for Obstetric Gynecol. and Neonatal Nurses, Jersey Area Nursing Diagnosis Assn. Roman Catholic. Home: 258 Devon St Kearny NJ 07032-2504

KROWN, SUSAN ELLEN, physician, researcher; b. Bronx, N.Y., Sept. 8, 1946; d. Frederick B. and Paula (Hauser) K.; m. Roger E. Pitt, May 18, 1980 (div. 1988); 1 child, Catherine Krown Pitt. AB, Barnard Coll., 1967; MD, SUNY, Bklyn., 1971. Diplomate Am. Bd. Internal Medicine. Intern, then jr. and sr. resident in internal medicine Mt. Sinai Hosp., N.Y.C., 1971-74; with Meml. Sloan-Kettering Cancer Ctr., N.Y.C., 1974—, assoc. mem., 1984-94, mem., 1994—; clin. asst. Meml. Hosp., N.Y.C., 1977-78, asst. attending physician, 1978-82; assoc. attending physician Meml. Sloan-Kettering Cancer Ctr., N.Y.C., 1982-94, attending physician, 1994—; asst. prof. Med. Coll. Cornell U., N.Y.C., 1977-83; assoc. prof. Med. Coll. Cornell U., N.Y.C., 1983—; mem. oncologic drugs adv. com. FDA, Rockville, Md., 1986-90, cons., 1990—; chair oncology com. AIDS Clin. Trials Group, Bethesda, Md., 1990-92, mem. exec. com., 1992—; chair task force on Kaposi's Sarcoma staging Am. Joint Com. on Cancer, Chgo., 1991-93. Mem. editorial bd. Jour. Interferon Rsch., 1985—, Jour. AIDS, 1988—; contbr. numerous articles to profl. jours. NIH Rsch. grantee; Am. Cancer Soc. Jr. Faculty fellow, 1978-81. Mem. Internat. Soc. for Interferon Rsch. (coun. 1986-92), Soc. for Biol. Therapy (bd. dirs. 1987-89), AIDS Task Force (chmn. Meml. Sloan Kettering Cancer Ctr. 1989—), Alpha Omega Alpha. Office: Meml Sloan Kettering Ctr 1275 York Ave New York NY 10021-6007

KRUCK, DONNA JEAN, special education educator, consultant; b. Peoria, Ill., Jan. 26, 1930; d. Walter George and Lois Irene (Newburn) Hagemeyer; m. Michael Roy Kruck Jr., June 27, 1948; children: Pamela Ann Kruck Hokanson, Michael Roy III, Quentin Robert. BS, Ill. State U., 1961; MEd, U. Ill., 1968. Cert. spl. edn. tchr. and adminstr., Ill. Tchr. New Lenox Dist. 122, Ill., 1956-61; tchr. spl. edn. Lincoln Way Area Joint Agreement, New Lenox, 1961-66; tchr. spl. edn., coord. Joliet Twp. High Sch. Dist. 204, Ill., 1966-86; pvt. practice cons. and diagnostician New Lenox, 1986-92; instr. Chapel Christian U., 1994—; child adv. New Lenox Dist. 122, 1986-88; instr. Chapel Christian U., 1994—. Author: Let's Learn to Cook, 1971. Pres. Joliet Twp. Edn. Assn., 1971-76; donar Aurora Area Blood Bank, Joliet, 1974-90. Mem. AAUW, NEA (life), Nat. Ret. Tchr. Assn., Am. Assn. Retired Persons, Am. Assn. Mental Retardation, Am. Bus. Women's Assn., Coun. Exceptional Children (life), Coun. Adminstrs. Spl. Edn., Christian Edn. Assn., Ill. Edn. Assn. (life), Ill. Div. Learning Disabilities, Coun. for Ednl. Diagnostic Svcs. (div. learning disabilities), Lutherans for Life, Kappa Delta Pi, Delta Kappa Gamma. Lutheran.

KRUECKEBERG, SUZANNE MARIE, psychologist, family therapist; b. Evanston, Ill., Mar. 18, 1963; d. Dan William and Maryanne (Sahr) K. BA, UCLA, 1985; MA, DePaul U., 1988, PhD, 1992. Lic. clin. psychologist, Ill. Practicum therapist DePaul Community Mental Health Ctr., Chgo., 1985-87, mental health trainee, 1987-88; neuropsychol. ttechnician U. Ill. Hosp. Phys. Med. and Rehab., Chgo., 1988-89; student intern Midwest Family Resources, Chgo., 1988-89; psychol. intern Inst. for Juvenile Rsch., Chgo., 1989-90; psychologist in pvt. practice Ctr. for Family Change, Oakbrook Terrace, Ill., 1993—; staff psychologist U. Ill. Chgo. Craniofacial Ctr., 1990—; asst. prof. psychology, dept. pediatrics U. Ill. Chgo. Coll. Medicine, 1993—. Contbr. articles to profl. jours. Mem. APA, Am. Cleft Palate Assn., IJR Family Systems Alumni (pres. 1993—). Democrat. Lutheran. Office: Craniofacial Ctr 808 S Wood St Chicago IL 60612-7300

KRUEGER, BONNIE LEE, editor, writer; b. Chgo., Feb. 3, 1950; d. Harry Bernard and Lillian (Soyak) Krueger; m. James Lawrence Spurlock, Mar. 8, 1972. Student Morraine Valley Coll., 1970. Adminstrv. asst. Carson Pirie Scott & Co., Chgo., 1969-72; traffic coord. Tatham Laird & Kudner, Chgo., 1973-74; traffic coord. J. Walter Thompson, Chgo., 1974-76; prodn. coord., 1976-78; editor-in-chief Assoc. Pubs., Chgo., 1978—; editor-in-chief Sophisticate's Hairstyle Guide, 1978—, Sophisticates Beauty Guide, 1978—, Complete Woman, 1981—; pub., editorial svcs. dir. Sophisticate's Black Hair Guide, 1983—, Sophisticate's Soap Star Styles, 1994. Mem. Statue of Liberty Restoration Com., N.Y.C., 1983; campaign worker Cook County State's Atty., Chgo., 1982; poll watcher Cook County Dem. Orgn., 1983; mem. Chgo. Architecture Found. Mem. Soc. Profl. Journalists, Nat. Assn. Female Execs., Am. Health and Beauty Aids Inst. (assoc. mem.), Lincoln Park Zoological Soc., Landmarks Preservation Coun. of Ill., Art Inst. Chgo., Sigma Delta Chi. Lutheran. Clubs: Sierra, Headline Club. Office: Complete Woman 875 N Michigan Ave Chicago IL 60611-1901

KRUEGER, KATHERINE KAMP, lawyer; b. Chgo., Apr. 7, 1944; d. Rudolph Pollay and Josephine Yvette (Marland) Kamp. Student U. Paris, Sorbonne, 1963-64; B.S. magna cum laude, Tulane U., 1965, M.S., 1968; J.D., Northwestern U., 1980. Bar: Tex. 1980, Ill. 1988. Micropaleontologist, Gulf Oil Corp., New Orleans, 1967-68; custodian collections geology Field Mus., Chgo., 1968-76, lectr., 1975-76; lectr. earth sci. Northeastern Ill. U., Chgo., 1977; atty. oil and gas Gulf Oil Corp., Houston, 1980-81, Amoco Prodn. Co., Houston, 1981-87, atty. environ. law Amoco Corp., Chgo., 1987-89; atty. litigation Amoco Prodn. Co., Houston, 1989-90; atty. legal dept. Dow Chem. Co., Freeport, Tex., 1990-92; atty. legal dept. City of Houston, Tex., 1992-93, adminstr. dept. pub. works and engring., 1993-94; regulatory analyst Environ. Resource Ctr., Houston, 1994—; bd. dirs. The Eureka Soc., Escondido, Calif., 1974—; vol. lectr. Desk and Derrick, Houston, 1983. Contbr. articles to profl. jours. Campaign vol., poll watcher Ind. Democratic candidate for Ill. Constl. Conv., Chgo., 1968; poll watcher Ind. Democratic candidate for Ill. Rep., Chgo., 1978; del. Dem. Senatorial Dist. 7 Conv., Tex., 1984, Moscow Conf. on Law and Bilateral Econ. Rels., 1990. NSF Student grantee microbiol. dept. U. Miami Marine Lab., 1960-64; grantee La. Heart Found., Sophie Newcomb Coll. Botany Dept., 1962-63, Grad. Sch. Tulane U. Scholars and Fellows Orgn., 1965-66; named Steinmayer Best Geol. Student, Tulane U., 1965; Houston Bar Found. fellow, 1982—. Fellow Houston Bar Found. (life); mem. ABA, State Bar Tex., Houston Bar Assn., Chgo. Bar Assn., Phi Beta Kappa, Sigma Gamma Epsilon, Eta Sigma Phi. Home: 4607 Nasa Road 1 Apt 315 Seabrook TX 77586-5484

KRUEGER, NANCY ASTA, physical therapist; b. Manhattan Beach, Calif., Jan. 8, 1947; d. Henry Adolph and Asta Ida (Harrison) Graef; m. Gary Patrick Krueger, June 14, 1969. Student, Lewis & Clark Coll., 1964-66; BS, U. So. Calif., L.A., 1969; postgrad., U. So. Calif., Downey, 1980-81. Staff phys. therapist Los Angeles County-U. So. Calif. Med. Ctr., L.A., 1969-71, Stockton (Calif.) State Hosp., 1971; pediatric phys. therapist Calif. Childrens Svcs.-San Joaquin County, Stockton, 1972-73; sr. phys. therapist Calif. Childrens Svcs.-San Diego County, San Diego, 1974-80; mng. dir. therapy svcs. Sharp-Cabrillo Hosp., San Diego, 1981-83; sr. phys. therapist El Cajon (Calif.) Valley Hosp., 1983-84; prin. El Cajon Therapy Assocs., 1984—; cons. Teledyne Ryan Aero., San Diego County, 1984—; speaker in field. Singer Old Globe Madrigal Singers, 1983; vice chair adv. com. Maternal, Child and Adolescent Health, San Diego County, 1987-89; active local polit. campaigns; advisor Mesa Coll., 1985—; mem. edn. and sci. com. Arthritis Found., 1986-87; chairperson adv. com. Mesa Coll., 1994. Fellow Am. Acad. Sports Medicine, Orthopedic Soc.; mem. Am. Phys. Therapy Assn. (chmn. San Diego dist. 1977-78, bd. dirs. Calif. chpt. 1983-84, mem. nominating com. 1989-91, chmn. 1991, v.p. 1994-96, fin. com. Orthopedic sect. 1993-96), Aux. Am. Optometric Assn., Arthritis Health Profls. Assn. (v.p. 1991-93), Jrs. of Social Svc. (treas. 1991-93), Soroptimists (sec. El Cajon chpt. 1982, chmn. 1994). Democrat. Episcopalian. Home: 4657 Rancho Park Ave San Diego CA 92120 Office: El Cajon Therapy Assocs 590 S Magnolia Ave El Cajon CA 92020-6011

KRUG, KAREN-ANN, healthcare financial executive, accountant; b. Riverdale, N.D., Apr. 22, 1951; d. C. and Elsie (Eide) K.; m. C. Scott James, Aug. 19, 1978. BS, N.D. State U., 1980; MBA, U. Phoenix, 1994. CPA, Calif. Mgr. proof transit 1st Nat. Bank Grand Forks (N.D.); sr. acct. Leo E. Bell & Assocs., Grand Forks, 1978-80; dir. project rev. Agassiz Health Systems Agy., Grand Forks, 1980-82; sr. adminstrv. asst. St. Mary's Hosp., Reno; dir. planning and devel. St. Mary's Health Care Corp., Reno, 1982-87; contr. Pacific Presbyn. Med. Ctr., San Francisco, 1987-89; corp. contr. Daughters of Charity Nat. Healthcare System Seton Med. Ctr., Daly City, Calif., 1989-93; CFO, v.p. fin. Howard Cmty. Hosp., Kokomo, Ind., 1994—. Vol. Jr. Achievement, Reno, 1984-87, Project Literacy U.S., San Francisco, 1987-88. Fellow Healthcare Fin. Mgmt. Assn.; mem. AICPA (bd. trustees Benevolent Fund 1993—), Calif. Soc. CPA's (healthcare com. 1989-93, chmn. 1991-93), Delta Gamma (treas. San Francisco alumni chpt. 1992-93).

KRUGER, MOLLEE COPPEL, writer; b. Bel Air, Md., Mar. 28, 1929; d. Benjamin and Mary (Hoffman) Coppel; m. Jerome Kruger, Feb. 20, 1955; children: Lennard Gideon, Joseph Avrum. BA, U. Md., 1950. Columnist The Harford Gazette, Bel Air, Md., 1945-47; advt. copywriter Joseph Katz Co., Balt., 1951-55; TV scriptwriter Jewish Community Coun., Washington, 1960-72; columnist, feature writer various newspapers, Washington and N.Y.C., 1967-88; freelance writer various nat. publs., 1980—; condr. writing workshop Montgomery County Community Svcs., Rockville, Md., 1982; cons. Buddemeir Co., Balt., 1958-59; pres. Maryben Books, Rockville, 1970—; tchr. creative writing Jewish Community Ctr., Rockville, 1974-78, cons. editor sr. adult publs., 1975, 76, 77; cons. editor Standards Alumni Assn., 1992. Author: Unholy Writ, 1970, More Unholy Writ, 1973, Yankee Shoes, 1975 (Gold Ribbon Bicentennial award 1976), Daughters of Chutzpah, 1983, Admiral of the Mosquitoes, 1990, Ladies First, 1995; editor Standard newsletter Nat. Bur. Standards, 1978-80 (award of excellence 1979); playwright, prodr. hist. show for Md. 350 Com., Montgomery County, Rockville, 1982-84. Founding mem. Humanities Commn. Montgomery County, 1984-91; judge Md. Writing Contest for Sr. Citizens, Annapolis, 1987-91, Montgomery County Bd. Elections, 1990-92. Recipient Cert. of Recognition U.S. Dept. Commerce, Washington, 1979, Alice Sherry Meml. award Poetry Soc. Va., Charlottesville, 1988; profiled as Outstanding Md. Woman Writer Md. State Dept. Edn., Md. Commn. for Women, Balt., 1989. Mem. Nat. League Am. Pen Women (Md. state letters chmn. 1990-92, br. pres. elect 1992-94, nat. letters bd. 1992-94, chmn. nat. letters com. 1994—, nat. membership chmn. 1994—, nat. exec. bd. 1994—, awards 1983, 85, 87, 89, 1st prize Nat. Adult Short Story contest 1994, 1st prize Nat. Catherine Leach Poetry competition 1994), Mortar Bd. Alumni Club (pres. 1977-78). Democrat. Jewish.

KRULESKI, KATHY MARIE, highway designer; b. Harrisburg, Pa., Oct. 8, 1961; d. William Frederick Sr. and Jessie Marie (Conrath) Finkbone; m. John Peter Kruleski, Oct. 22, 1983 (div. 1990). Student, Dauphin County Technical, Harrisburg, 1979, Harrisburg Area C.C., 1985, 91. Draftsperson Gannett Fleming Inc., Camp Hill, Pa., 1979-83; geotechnical draftsperson F.T. Kitlinski & Assocs., Harrisburg, 1984-85; highway technician Baker Engrs., Inc., Harrisburg, 1985-90; highway designer Sheladia Assocs., Inc., Camp Hill, 1992-95, McCormick, Taylor & Assocs., Inc., 1995—. Active Rep. State Com., Harrisburg, 1980—, Ctrl. Pa. Ashtray Assn., Harrisburg, 1985—, Penbrook Fire Co., Harrisburg, 1990—. Mem. VFW, Venture Clubs of Am. (sec. 1992—), Am. Soc. of Hwy. Engrs., Harrisburg. Lutheran. Home: 611 Blue Bell Ave Harrisburg PA 17112-2304

KRULFELD, RUTH MARILYN, anthropologist, educator; b. N.Y.C., Apr. 15, 1931; d. Leon and Frances (Rosenberg) Pulwers; m. Jacob Mendel Krulfeld, Aug. 28, 1964; 1 child, Michael David. BA cum laude, Brandeis U., 1956; PhD, Yale U., 1974. Field rschr. micro-geog. rsch. farms, Singapore, Malaya, 1951-53; anthropol. rsch. Jamaica, 1957, Costa Rica, Nicaragua, Panama, 1958, Lombok, Indonesia, 1960-62, 93, N.E. Thailand, 1993; asst. prof. anthropology, dir. grad. students George Washington U., Washington, 1964-72, 93—, assoc. prof., 1973-76, prof., 1976—, chmn. dept. anthropology, 1984-87, founder, grad. advisor spl. grad. program in 3d world devel.; mem. Judaic studies com. George Washington U.; v.p., bd. dirs. Ctr. Multicultural Human Resources; rschr. S.E. Asian refugees, 1981—, Laotian refugees in U.S., 1981—, also rsch. on culture change in villages in Indonesia. Contbr. articles to profl. jours.; co-author several books. Bd. dirs. No. Va. Regional Humanities Coun. Currier scholar Yale U., 1958; Ford fellow, 1960-62; grantee Found. for Study of Man, 1957, Am. Coun., 1963, Cotlow faculty rsch. grantee, 1992-93, faculty rsch. grantee George Washington U., 1992-93. Mem. Anthrop. Soc. Washington, Am. Athrop. Assn. (nominating com., com. on refugee issues gen. anthropology divsn., vice chair com. on refugee issues gen. anthropology divsn. 1993-94, Cori award for best paper on refugees issues 1992, Pedigogical Rsch. and Innovative Devel. in Edn. award 1994). Jewish. Office: George Washington U Dept Anthropology Washington DC 20052

KRULIK, BARBARA S., director, curator; b. N.Y.C., June 13, 1955; d. Herbert Arnold and Irene Sylvia (Lichterman) K. BA in Art History, Pa. State U., 1976. Asst. to dir. NAD, N.Y.C., 1976-77, acting dir., 1977-78, coord. exhbns., 1978-83, asst. dir., 1983-89, interim dir., 1989-90, dep. dir., 1990-92; cons., assoc. dir. Forum Gallery, 1992-94; dir. grad. sch. figurative art New York Acad. Art, N.Y.C., 1994—. Author, editor exhbn. catalogues. Mem. Am. Assn. Mus. (curators and registrars coms.), Internat. Coun. on Mus. Office: NY Acad Art 111 Franklin St New York NY 10013

KRULWICH, TERRY ANN, biochemistry researcher; b. N.Y.C., Apr. 7, 1943; d. Lester S. and Beatrice (Cohen) K.; m. S. Paul Posner, June 10, 1973; children: Jeremy Michael, Adam Jared, Amos Allen. BA, Goucher Coll., 1964; MS, U. Wis., 1966, PhD, 1968; DSc (hon.), Goucher Coll., 1987. Postdoctoral fellow in molecular biology Albert Einstein Coll. Medicine, Bronx, 1968-70; asst. prof. biochemistry Mount Sinai Sch. Medicine CUNY, N.Y.C., 1970-74, assoc. prof., 1974-81, prof. biochemistry, 1981—, dean, grad. sch. biol. sci., 1981—; mem. cellular and molecular com., basis of disease review com. NIH, 1978-81, mem. microbiology, physiology and genetics study sect., 1983-87, mem. nat. gen. med. scis. adv. coun., 1991-94. Editor: The Bacteria, Vol. XII, 1990; mem. editorial bd. Jour. Bacteriology, 1985—, Microbiol. Revs., 1983-88, Jour. Bioenergetic Biomembranes, 1991—, BBA Revs. Bioenergetics, 1992—. Trustee Ramaz Sch., N.Y.C., 1981-91, Heschel Sch., N.Y.C., 1991—. Predoctoral fellow NSF, 1964-68, postdoctoral fellow NSF, 1968-70; recipient Rsch. Career Devel. award NIH, 1975-80. Mem. Am. Soc. Microbiology (div. chmn. physiol. 1990-91), Am. Soc. for Biochemistry and Molecular Biology, Biophys. Soc., N.Y. Acad. Scis., Harvey Soc. Office: Mt Sinai Sch Dept Biochem 1 Gustave L Levy Pl New York NY 10029-6504

KRUPNICK, ELIZABETH RACHEL, insurance company executive; b. N.Y.C., Oct. 21, 1949; d. Julius Michael and Doris (White) K.; children: Tobias Perse, Jacob. BA in Art History, Colby Coll., 1973; MA, U. Mo., 1976. Instr. journalism Emerson Coll., Boston, 1976-78; asst. prof. journalism U. Maine, Orono, 1978-79, Portland Oreg. State U., 1979-83; asst. v.p. Aetna Life & Casualty, Hartford, Conn., 1985-89, v.p. corp. affairs, 1989—, now sr. v.p. corp. affairs. Co-author: From Despair to Decision,

1982. Mem. Women in Communications, Ins. Info. Inst. communications com., 1987, pub. relations com., 1986. Office: Aetna Life & Casualty 151 Farmington Ave Hartford CT 06156-0002*

KRUPNIK, VEE M., financial company executive; b. Chgo.; d. Phillip and Jane (Glickman) K.; m. Melvin Drury, Sept. 24, 1978. BS, Northwestern U., CPA, cert. fin. planner, real estate broker, ins. broker, Ill. Assoc. dir. corp. fin. Weis, Voisin, Cannon, Chgo., 1967-68; pres. PEC Industries Inc., Ft. Lauderdale, Fla., 1969-71; acct., real estate and ins. broker Vee M. Krupnik & Co., Chgo., 1971-73; sales cons. Baird & Warner Inc., Chgo., 1973-81, asst. v.p. comml.-investment div., 1981-85, v.p. corp. group, 1985-89; comml./investment specialist, 1990-91; v.p. comml. investment sales, 1992—. Mem. Internat. Assn. Fin. Planning (bd. dirs. 1985-87), Internat. Council Shopping Ctrs., Nat. Assn. Corp. Real Estate Execs., Nat. Assn. Securities Dealers, Women's Exec. Network, Nat. Assn. Realtors (bd. dirs. 1983-84, comml. investment council), Cert. Comml. Investment Mems. (pres. Ill. chpt. 1983-84), Ill. Assn. Realtors (bd. dirs. 1983-84), Chgo. Bd. Realtors (bd. dirs. 1982-85, 88-91), Chgo. Assn. Realtors (bd. dirs. 1992-94), Chgo. Assn. Realtors Multiple Listing Svc. (bd. dirs. 1992—), Chgo. Assn. Commerce and Industry, Chgo. Assn. Realtors Comml. Investment Multiple Listing Svc. (chmn. 1991-94), Comml. Investment Multiple Listing Service (pres. 1982-84), Comml. Real Estate Orgn., Chgo. Real Estate Exec. Women. Home: 5757 N Sheridan Rd #7A Chicago IL 60660-4751 Office: Baird & Warner Inc 4040 N Lincoln Ave Chicago IL 60618-3038

KRUPP, RENEE ANDREA, billing administrator; b. Chgo., Feb. 25, 1962; d. Ben and Lydia Krupp. BA, U. Chgo., 1984; MBA, DePaul U., 1990. Cert. procedural coder. Rsch. technologist Med. Sch. Northwestern U., Chgo., 1984-90; billing coord. Northwestern Med. Faculty Found., Chgo., 1990—. Contbr. articles to profl. jours. Mem. Am. Acad. Procedural Coders.

KRUPSKA, DANYA (MRS. TED THURSTON), theater director, choreographer; b. Fall River, Mass., Aug. 13, 1921; d. Bronislaw and Anna (Niementowska) Krupski; m. James M. Hanrihan (div. 1953); 1 child, Brion; m. Ted Thurston, May 27, 1954; 1 child, Tina Lyn. Student, Lankenau Sch. for Girls, Phila.; studied with, Ethel Phillips Dance Studio, Catherine Littlefield Ballet Studio, L. Egorova, Paris, Mikhail Mordkin, N.Y.C. and Phila.; studied, Aubrey Hitchens Studio, N.Y.C., Bobby Lewis Dir.'s Studio, N.Y.C. Performed concerts and toured in Poland, Roumania, Balkan Countries, Hungary, Vienna, Palestine, 1929-36; joined Phila. Ballet (Littlefield) for European tour, 1937, Chgo. Opera Season, 1938, Am. Ballet (Ballanchine), N.Y.C., 1938; soloist Broadway prodn.: Frank Fay Show, Radio City Music Hall Ballet; leading role on nat. tour: Johnny Belinda 1941; soloist in: Chouve Souris, 1943; dancer in role of Dream Laurie, 1st Nat. Co. of Okla., later Broadway Co., 1945; asst. to choreographer Agnes de Mille on Rodgers and Hammerstein prodn.: Allegro; asst. to choreographer on ballet prodn.: Fall River Legend, opera prodn.: Rape of Lucrece, Broadway prodns.: Girl in Pink Tights, Gentlemen Prefer Blonds, Paint Your Wagon; assisted Michael Kidd on Broadway prodn.: Can Can; choreographer Broadway prodn.: Most Happy Fella (Tony award nomination), Seventeen, 1st Shoestring Revue, Carefree Heart, Happiest Girl in the World (Tony award nomination), Her First Roman, 1968, Apollo and Miss Agnes; choreographer Met. Opera prodn.: The Gypsy Baron; choreographer Italian mus.: Rugantino, 1962; choreographer: TV Salute to the Peace Corps, 1965; guest choreographer: Zorba, Nat. Theatre, Reykjavik, Iceland, 1971, Company for Stora Teatern, Gothenburg, Sweden, 1971, Fantastiks, Little Theatre, Gothenburg, 1971, Okla. Nat. Theatre, Reykjavik, 1972, No No Nanette, Malmö Stadsteater, Sweden, 1973, Richard Rodger's Prodn. of Rex, Broadway, N.Y.C., 1976, Showboat, Malmö Stadsteater, 1976, Empress of China, Cin. Playhouse, 1984; dir., choreographer: Porgy and Bess, Malmö Stadsteater, Sweden, 1973, Bernstein's The Mass, Malmö Stadsteater, 1975, Chicago, Det Danske Teater, Denmark, 1977, Our Man in Havana, Poland, 1977, Cabaret, Helsingborg Stadsteater, Sweden, 1978, Guys and Dolls, Aarhus Teater, Denmark, 1978, Once Upon a Mattress, Nat. Theater Reykjavik, Iceland, 1981, Animalen, Malmö Stadsteater, Sweden, 1985, Papushko, Colonade Theatre, N.Y.C., 1985; producer, dir.; choreographer: The King and I, Malmö Stadsteater, Sweden, 1984; produced, directed, choreographed Sound of Music, Malmo Stadsteater, Sweden, 1990; directed, choreographed Lerner and Loewe lost musical Day before Spring, N.Y.C., 1990; dance and mus. staging How it Was Done in Odessa, Walnut St. Theatre, Phila., 1991; dir. mus. prodns., N.Y. City Center; Most Happy Fella, 1959, Showboat, 1961, Fiorello, 1962 (also White House prodn. for gov.'s conf. 1968), Oklahoma; choreographer for Buick Hour, 1952, Colgate Comedy Hour, 1953, Omnibus; dir. U.S. Steel Theatre Guild Prodns; Ballets Outlook for Three (Ellington), Pointes on Jazz (Brubeck), Am. Ballet Theatre. Mem. Actors Equity Assn., Soc. Stage Dirs. and Choreographers (exec. bd. mem.), Actors Studio (playwrights and dirs. unit), Dramatist's Guild. Office: 564 W 52d St New York NY 10019

KRUSE, ANN GRAY, computer programmer; b. Oklahoma City, Jan. 4, 1941; d. Floyd and Bernice Florence (Follansbee) Gray; A.B., Randolph Macon Woman's Coll., 1963; M.B.A., U. Chgo., 1973; m. Roy Edwin Kruse, Mar. 20, 1971 (dec.). Programming mgr. Ind. Info. Controls, Valparaiso, Ind., 1966-67; systems programmer Nat. Bus. Lists, Inc., Chgo., 1968-69, Am. Steel Foundries, Hammond, Ind., 1970-73; engr. applications programming Bell Helicopter Textron, Fort Worth, 1974-76; lead systems programmer Harris Data Communications, Dallas, 1976-81; sr. systems programmer Lone Star Gas Co., Dallas, 1981-82; sr. software specialist E-Systems, Dallas, 1982—. Republican. Episcopalian. Home: 6128 Black Berry Ln Dallas TX 75248-4909 Office: PO Box PO Box 660023 Dallas TX 75266-0023

KRUSE, NANCY CLARSON, elementary education educator; b. Flushing, N.Y., Aug. 19, 1946; d. Robert LeRoy Jr. and Julie (Batten) Clarson; m. William Franz Kruse, Feb. 4, 1984. BS in Elem. Edn., Adelphi U., 1968, MA in Elem. Edn., 1970; student, postgrad., Nat. U. Ireland, U. Coll. Dublin, 1966-69. Cert. tchr., N.Y. Rschr., developer use of microcomputers in elem. classroom Syosset (N.Y.) Ctrl. Sch. Dist., 1980-81; tchr. 4th grade South Grove Sch., Syosset;, 1966, 69; Leader Children's Internat. Summer Villages, 1979, 80; bd. dirs. Goudreau Mus. Math. in Art and Sci., New Hyde Park, store buyer, 1987—, store mgr., 1988-92; instr. calligraphy. Speaker, workshop presenter in field. Mem. Nat. Assn. to Advance Fat Acceptance, N.Y.S. Union of Tchrs., Apples in Edn. Users Group (founder), Wives Info. Network of N.Y.S. Park Police (co-founder), Mac Users Group. Home: 68 Ketcham Rd Hicksville NY 11801-2023 also: 3427 Pinetree St Port Charlotte FL 33952 Office: South Grove Sch Colony Ln Syosset NY 11791

KRUSE, PAMELA JEAN, lawyer; b. Miami, Fla., June 3, 1950; d. Robert Emil and Irma G. Kruse. BS, Mich. State U., 1973, MA, 1975, PhD, 1979; JD, U. Mich., 1985. Bar: Mich. 1986. Grad. asst. Mich. State U., East Lansing, 1976-77, asst. intramural dir., 1977-79, labor rels. rep., 1979-81, asst. dir. labor rels., 1981-82; resident mgr. 719 Oakland, Ann Arbor, Mich., 1982-83; rsch. asst. Law Sch. U. Mich., Ann Arbor, 1982-85; jud. clk. U.S. Dist. Ct. (we. dist.) Mich., 1985-86; assoc. Clary, Nantz, Wood, Hoffius, Rankin & Cooper, Grand Rapids, Mich., 1986-91; with Village Bike Shops, 1991—. Bd. dirs. Babe Zaharias Golf Tournament, Am. Cancer Soc., 1987-91. Recipient Gold and Silver medals U.S. Pan Am. Team, Winnipeg, Man., Can., 1967, Silver medal U.S. Olympic Team, Mexico City, 1968; holder world records swimming 400 meters freestyle, 1967, 200 meters freestyle, 1967, 440-yard freestyle, 1966; inducted to Greater Fort Lauderdale Sports Hall of Fame, 1979. Mem. ABA, State Bar Mich. (exec. coun. young lawyers sect. 1987-90), Grand Rapids Bar Assn. (chairperson, exec. bd. dirs. young lawyers sect. 1987-91), Mich. Pub. Employer Labor Rels. Assn. (bd. dirs. 1981-82, chmn. manual revision com. 1982), Mich. State U. Alumni Assn. (1st v.p., bd. dirs. 1988—), U.S. Olympians, Phi Delta Kappa, Kappa Alpha Theta.

KRUSE, ROSALEE EVELYN, accountant; b. Muscatine, Iowa, Aug. 23, 1953; d. Burr Arthur Beeding and Mary Ellen (Phillips) McGourty; m. Michael Raymond Kruse, May 20, 1972; children: Lauretta Kathleen, Matthew William. A in Gen. Studies, Muscatine C.C., 1986; BBA, U. Iowa, 1988; M of Acctg., St. Ambrose U., 1993. CPA, Iowa. Acct. Rock Island (Ill.) Arsenal, 1989—. Mem. AICPA, Am. Soc. Mil. Comptrs. (chairperson chpt. competition 1991-92, treas. 1993-94, 1st v.p. 1994—), Iowa Soc. CPAs, Inst. Mgmt. Accts. Methodist. Home: 324 Fletcher Ave Muscatine IA 52761 Office: Rock Island Arsenal Attn SMCRI-RMB Bldg 390 Rock Island IL 61299

KRUSICK, MARGARET ANN, state legislator; b. Milw., Oct. 26, 1956; d. Ronald J. and Maxine C. K. BA, U. Wis., 1978; postgrad., U. Wis., Madison, 1979-82. Legal asst. Milw. Law Office, 1973-78; teaching asst. U. Wis., Milw., 1978-79; staff mem. Govs. Ombudsman Program for the Aging & Disabled, Madison, Wis., 1980; administrv. asst. Wis. Higher Ednl. Aids Bd., Madison, 1981; legis. aide Wis. Assembly, Madison, 1982-83, state rep., 1983—. Author: Wisconsin Youth Suicide Prevention Act, 1985, Wisconsin Nursing Home Reform Act, 1987, Wisconsin Truancy Reform Act, 1988, Elder Abuse Fund, 1989, Lyme Disease Fund, 1989, Stolen Goods Recovery Act, 1990, Fair Prescription Drug Pricing Act, 1994. Mem. St. Gregory Great Cath. Ch., Milw., 1960—, Dem. Party, Milw., 1980—, Layton Park Assn.; bd. dirs. Alzheimer's Disease Assn., 1986-88. Named Legislator of Yr. award Wis. Sch. Counselors, Madison, 1986; recipient Sr. Citizen Appreciation Allied Coun. for Sr. Milw., 1987, crime Prevention award Milw. Police Dept., Milw., 1988, Cert. Appreciation, Milw. Pub. Sch., 1989, Friends of Homecare award, 1989, Environ. Decades' Clean 16 award, 1986-90. Mem. Jackson Park Neighborhood Assn., U. Milw. Alumni Assn. (trustee 1986-90). Home: 3426 S 69 St Milwaukee WI 53219 Office: Wis Assembly State Capital Madison WI 53702

KRZYNA, TINA MARIE, wood scientist; b. Bridgeport, Conn., Oct. 10, 1962; d. Joseph Edward and Mary (Koshi) K. BS in Wood Sci. and Tech., U. Maine, 1984. Tech. dir. Swain Industries, Seymour, Ind., 1984-86; from structure wood specialist to product support mgr. Weyerhaeuser, Elkin, N.C., 1986-93; tech. mgr. Weyerhaeuser, Elkin, 1993—. Mem. bldg. com. Habitat for Humanity, Mooresville, N.C., 1992—; lector St. Theresa Ch., Mooresville, 1992—. Mem. NAFE, Am. Bus. Woman's Assn. (v.p. 1990-91), Am. Plywood Assn. (tech. com. 1993—), Forest Products Soc., Charlotte Profl. Women. Roman Catholic. Office: Weyerhaeuser PO Box 590 Elkin NC 28621-0590

KRZYZAN, JUDY LYNN, automotive executive; b. Buffalo, Sept. 1, 1951; d. James Lambert and Janet Lucille (Grabau) McKellar; m. Ronald Edward Krzyzan, Dec. 21, 1974 (div. Jan. 1989); 1 child, Brian Edward. Student, Erie Community Coll., 1969-70. With counter and delivery M & H Auto Supply, Orchard Park, N.Y., 1973-75; parts counter person Crest Dodge Inc., Orchard Park, 1975-81; parts mgr. Case Chrysler Plymouth, Hamburg, N.Y., 1981-87, Mancuso Chrysler Plymouth, Hamburg, 1987-91, Transitowne Dodge, Williamsville, N.Y., 1991—; supr. Profl. Inventory Assn., N.H., 1976-85. Mem. Chrysler Parts and Svc. Mgrs. Guild (v.p., sec. 1986-87, 89-92), The Greater Buffalo Auto Body Guild. Home: 2801 Creek Rd Hamburg NY 14075 Office: Transitowne Dodge 7408 Transit Rd Williamsville NY 14221-6091

K-TURKEL, JUDITH LEAH ROSENTHAL (JUDI K-TURKEL), writer, editor, publisher; b. N.Y.C., Jan. 3, 1934; d. Samuel S. and Pauline (Turkel) Rosenthal; divorced; children: Joseph, Jeffrey Kesselman, David, Kevin Peterson. BA, Bklyn. Coll., 1955. Story and mng. editor Dell Publs., N.Y.C., 1955-58, 62-65; editor-in-chief Sterling, Stearn & KMR Publs., N.Y.C., 1959-62; sr. editor Macfadden-Bartell Publs., N.Y.C., 1966-68; freelance writer N.Y.C. and Wis., 1968-89; pres. P/K Assocs., Inc., Madison, Wis., 1977—; instr. adult edn. Great Neck (N.Y.) Pub. Schs., 1973-76, U. Wis., Madison, 1977-82; instr. journalism Madison Area Tech. Coll., 1984-87; lectr. nonfiction writing CW Post Ctr., L.I. U., Manhasset, N.Y., 1976-77; tchr.-in-residence Rhinelander (Wis.) Sch. Arts, 1984-86. Author: (writing as Judi Kesselman) Stopping Out, 1976, (writing as Judi Kesselman-Turkel with Franklynn Peterson) The Do-It-Yourself Custom Van Book, 1977, Vans, 1979, (with others) Eat Anything Exercise Diet, 1979, Snowmobile Maintenance and Repair, 1979, I Can Use Tools, 1981, (textbook) Good Writing, 1980, Test Taking Strategies, 1981, Study Smarts, 1981, Homeowner's Book of Lists, 1981, How to Improve Damn Near Everything Around Your Home, 1981, The Author's Handbook, 1982, rev., 1986, The Grammar Crammer, 1982, Research Shortcuts, 1982, Note-Taking Made Easy, 1982, The Vocabulary Builder, 1982, Getting it Down: How to Get Your Ideas on Paper, 1983, Spelling Simplified, 1983, The Magazine Writer's Handbook, 1983, rev. edit., 1986; syndicated computer newspaper columnist, 1983—; editor (newsletter) CPA Micro Report, 1985-92, CPA's PC Network Advisor, 1991-92; pub. CPA Computer Report, 1994—; contbr. articles to profl. jours. Chmn. non-partisan Citizens Nominating Com., Great Neck, 1972-75. Recipient Bus. Press. award, 1977, Nat. Press Club award, 1984, 85. Mem. Am. Soc. Journalists and Authors, Coun. Wis. Writers (pres. 1982-85), Authors Guild, Authors League, Nat. Press Club, Pen & Brush Club (Madison, publ. chmn. 1978-89). Home and Office: P/K Assocs Inc 3006 Gregory St Madison WI 53711-1847

KUBA, DEBORAH IRENE, sales director; b. Bridgeport, Conn., Mar. 26, 1955; d. Richard Wallace and Doris Irene (Feher) K. BS in Math., Fairfield U., 1977, Georgetown U., 1977; MBA in Fin., Am. U., 1985. Nat. sales mgr. Aztech Corp., Washington, 1977-79, Audyxx Corp., Washington, 1979-82; dir. sales Martin Marietta Corp., Bethesda, Md., 1982-87; nat. sales mgr. Western Union, McLean, Va., 1987-89; v.p. sales and mktg. Centel Corp., Reston, Va., 1989-92; sales dir. Wiltel Inc., Beltsville, Md., 1992—; v.p. Broadview Estates, Annapolis, Md., 1986-88. Mem. SOS Sailing Club. Home: 2806 Broadview Ter Annapolis MD 21401-7233 Office: Wiltel Inc Virginia Manor Beltsville MD 22091-5302

KUBASEK, NANCY KATHERINE, law educator; b. Sandusky, Ohio, Nov. 1, 1956; d. Joseph Verland and Nancy Carol (Billings) K.; m. M. Neil Browne, Nov. 1, 1980. BS in Edn., Bowling Green State U., 1978; JD, U. Toledo Coll. Law, 1982. Bar: Ohio. Supr. Gen. Motors, Toledo, 1980-82; prof. legal studies Bowling Green (Ohio) State U., 1982—. Author: (books) The Legal Environment of Business, 1986, Environmental Law, 1994; contbr. over 30 articles to legal jours. Democrat. Office: Bowling Green State U Bowling Green OH 43402

KUBBY, KAREN LYNNE, municipal official, artist; b. Ft. Belvoir, Va., Aug. 8, 1960; d. Robert Stanley and Marilyn Myers Kubby; m. Joseph Lloyd Bolkcom, Oct. 22, 1994. B in Gen. Studies, U. Iowa, 1982. Model U. Iowa, Iowa City, 1980-84; sci. tchr. Upward Bound, Iowa City, 1983-84; sci. learning asst. New Dimensions in Learning, Iowa City, 1983-85; artist Iowa City, 1985—; mem. coun. City of Iowa City, 1989—. Lifeguard, water safety instr. Iowa City Recreation Divsn., 1979-84; vol., first aid instr. ARC, Iowa City, 1987—; collaborative idea bldg. trainee Nat. League of Cities, Washington, 1989; bd. dirs., treas. Free Med. Clinic, Iowa City, 1988—; vol. Free Lunch Program, Iowa City, 1986—; treas. Iowa Socialist Party, 1984—; mem. Johnson County Art Coun. Recipient Irv Koth award Socialist Party U.S.A., 1985. Mem. Women in Mcpl. Govt. Jewish. Office: PO Box 924 Iowa City IA 52244-0924

KUBIC, SARAH ELIZABETH, aeronautical production engineer; b. Danville, Va., Aug. 6, 1965; d. Fred Kenneth and Lessie Owen (Emerson) Webb; m. Daniel William Kubic, Jan. 7, 1989; 1 child, Jennifer Marie. AA in Sci. and Engring., Danville (Va.) C.C., 1985; BS in Aerospace and Ocean Engring., Va. Poly. and State U., 1988. Mech. engr. fleet support divsn. Naval Ordnance Sta. Cartridge Actuated Device, Indian Head, Md., 1989-90; prodn. engr. Comml. Flight Systems Divsn. Honeywell Inc., Mpls., 1991—. Mem. Honeywell Women's Coun. (programs chair 1994-95), Industry Vols. Encouraging Sci. and Tech. (rep.). Office: Honeywell Inc 8840 Evergreen Blvd Minneapolis MN 55433

KUBIDA, JUDITH ANN, museum administrator; b. Chgo., Aug. 29, 1948; d. William and Julia Ann (Kun) K.; m. Benjamin Kocolowski, Nov. 22, 1980. Attended, Southeast Coll. Adminstrn. asst. in Visitor Svcs. Dept. Mus. Sci. and Industry, Chgo. Columnist monthly community newspaper Pullman Flyer. Dir. Historic Pullman Found., Historic Pullman Dist., Chgo., editor quarterly newsletter Update, create publicity brochures, liaison with Ill., Chgo. Film Offices, publicity chmn., mem. annual house tour com., produce commemorative plate. Democrat. Home: 11334 S Langley Ave Chicago IL 60628-5126 Office: Hist Pullman Found Hotel Florence 11111 S Forrestville Ave Chicago IL 60628-4649

KUBISTAL, PATRICIA BERNICE, educational consultant; b. Chgo., Jan. 19, 1938; d. Edward John and Bernice Mildred (Lenz) Kubistal. AB cum laude, Loyola U., Chgo., 1959, AM, 1964, AM, 1965, PhD, 1968; postgrad. Chgo. State Coll., 1962, Ill. Inst. Tech., 1963, State U. Iowa, 1963, Nat. Coll. Edn., 1974-75. With Chgo. Bd. Edn., 1959-93, tchr., 1959-63, counselor, 1963-65, adminstrv. intern, 1965-66, asst. to dist. supt., 1966-69, prin. spl. edn. sch., 1969-75, prin. Simpson Sch., 1975-76, Brentano Sch., 1975-87, Roosevelt High Sch., 1987, Haugan Sch., 1989, Cook County Juvenile Temporary Detention Ctr. Sch., Jones Met. High Sch. Bus. and Commerce, 1988-89, Cook County Juvenile Temporary Detention Ctr., 1989-90, adminstr. dept. spl. edn., 1990-93; supr. Lake View Evening Sch., 1982-92, ednl. cons. 1993—; lectr. Loyola U. Sch. Edn., Nat. Coll. Edn. Grad. Sch., Mundelein Coll., 1982-91; coord. Upper Bound Program of U. Ill. Circle Campus, 1966-68. Book rev. editor of Chgo. Prins. Jour., 1970-76, gen. editor, 1982-90. Active Crusade of Mercy; mem. com. Ill. Constnl. Conv., 1967-69; mem. Citizens Sch. Com., 1969-71; mem. edn. com. Field Mus., 1971; ednl. advisor North Side Chgo. PTA Region, 1975; gov. Loyola U., 1961-87. Recipient Outstanding Intern award Nat. Assn. Secondary Sch. Prins., 1966, Outstanding Prin. award Citizen's Shc. Com. of Chgo., 1986; named Outstanding History Tchr., Chgo. Pub. Schs., 1963, Outstanding Ill. Educator, 1970, one of Outstanding Women of Ill., 1970, St. Luke's-Logan Sq. Community Person of Yr., 1977; NDEA grantee, 1963, NSF grantee, 1965, HEW Region 5 grantee for drug edn., 1974, Chgo. Bd. Edn. Prins.' grantee for study robotics in elem. schs.; U. Chgo. adminstrv. fellow, 1984. Mem. Ill. Personnel and Guidance Assn., NEA, Ill. Edn. Assn., Chgo. Edn. Assn., Am. Acad. Polit. and Social Sci., Chgo. Prins. Club (pres. aux.), Nat. Council Adminstrv. Women, Chgo. Council Exceptional Children, Chgo. Council Fgn. Relations, Chgo. Urban League, Loyal Christian Benevolent Assn., Kappa Gamma Pi, Pi Gamma Mu, Phi Delta Kappa, Delta Kappa Gamma (parliamentarian 1979-80, pres. Kappa chpt. 1988-90, Lambda state editor 1982-92, chmn. Lambda state comm. com. 1992, Internat. Golden Gift Fund award), Delta Sigma Rho, Phi Sigma Tau. Home and Office: 5111 N Oakley Ave Chicago IL 60625-1829

KÜBLER-ROSS, ELISABETH, physician; b. Zurich, Switzerland, July 8, 1926; came to U.S., 1958, naturalized, 1961; d. Ernst and Emma (Villiger) K.; m. Emanuel Robert Ross, Feb. 7, 1958; children: Kenneth Lawrence, Barbara Lee. M.D., U. Zurich, 1957; D.Sc. (hon.), Albany (N.Y.) Med. Coll., 1974, Smith Coll., 1975, Molloy Coll., Rockville Centre, N.Y., 1976, Regis Coll., Weston, Mass., 1977, Fairleigh Dickinson U., 1979; LL.D., U. Notre Dame, 1974, Hamline U., 1975; hon. degree, Med. Coll. Pa., 1975, Anna Maria Coll., Paxton, Mass., 1978; Litt.D. (hon.), St. Mary's Coll., Notre Dame, Ind., 1975, Hood Coll., 1976, Rosary Coll., River Forest, Ill., 1976; L.H.D. (hon.), Amherst Coll., 1975, Loyola U., Chgo., 1975, Bard Coll., Annandale-on-Hudson, N.Y., 1977, Union Coll., Schenectady, 1978, D'Youville Coll., Buffalo, 1979, U. Miami, Fla., 1976; D.Pedagogy, Keuka Coll., Keuka Park, N.Y., 1976. Rotating intern Community Hosp., Glen Cove, N.Y., 1958-59; rsch. fellow Manhattan State Hosp., 1959-62; resident Montefiore Hosp., N.Y.C., 1961-62; fellow psychiatry Psychopathic Hosp., U. Colo. Med. Sch., 1962-63; instr. psychiatry Colo. Gen. Hosp., U. Colo. Med. Sch., 1962-65; mem. staff LaRabida Children's Hosp. and Rsch. Ctr., Chgo., 1965-70; asst. prof. psychiatry, asst. dir. psychiatric consultation and liaison service Billings Hosp., U. Chgo., 1965-71; chief cons. and rsch. liaison sect. LaRabida Children's Hosp. and Rsch. Ctr., 1969-70; med. dir. Family Service and Mental Health Ctr. S. Cook County, Chicago Heights, Ill., 1970-73; pres. Ross Med. Assos. (S.C.), Flossmoor, Ill., 1973-77; pres., chmn. bd. Shanti Nilaya Growth and Health Ctr., Escondido, Calif., 1977—; consulting psychiatrist Chicago Lighthouse for the Blind, 1965-71; consultant Peace Corps, 1965-71, Illinois State Psychiatric Inst., 1965-71; mem. numerous adv., cons. bds. in field. Author: On Death and Dying, 1969, Questions and Answers on Death and Dying, 1972, Death: The Final Stage, 1974, To Live Until We Say Goodbye, 1978, Working It Through, 1981, Living With Death and Dying, 1981, Remember The Secret, 1981, On Children and Death, 1985, AIDS: The Ultimate Challenge, 1988, On Life After Death, 1991, Death is of Vital Inportance: On Life, Death and Life After Death, 1994; contbr. chpts. to books, articles to profl. jours. Recipient Teilhard prize Teilhard Found., 1981; Golden Plate award Am. Acad. Achievement, 1980; Modern Samaritan award Elk Grove Village, Ill., 1976; named Woman of the Decade Ladies Home Jour., 1979; numerous others. Mem. AAAS, Am. Holistic Med. Assn. (founder), Am. Med. Women's Assn., Am. Psychiat. Assn., Am. Psychosomatic Soc., Assn. Cancer Victims and Friends, Ill. Psychiat. Soc., Soc. Swiss Physicians, Soc. Psychophysiol. Research, Second Attempt at Living. Address: 33613 N 83d St Scottsdale AZ 85262*

KUBY, BARBARA ELEANOR, personnel executive, management consultant; b. Medford, Mass., Sept. 1, 1944; d. Robert William and Eleanor (Frasca) Asdell; m. Thomas Kuby, July 12, 1969. BS in Edn./Psychology, Kent State U., 1966, MEd, 1987. Tchr. Nordonia/Euclid (Ohio) Pub. Schs., 1966-78; mgr. tng. and devel. United Bldg. Factories, Manama, Bahrain, 1979-81, Norton Co., Akron, Ohio, 1981-85; v.p. Kuby and Assocs. Inc., Chagrin Falls, Ohio, 1973-91, pres., 1992—; corp. dir. human resource devel. and systems TransOhio Savs. Bank, Cleve., 1985-88; asst. v.p. human resources and adminstrv. systems Leasing Dynamics, Inc., Cleve., 1988-90; dir. human resources, organizational devel. 60J0 Industries, Akron, 1990-93; v.p. human resources and orgnl. devel. Go-Jo Industries, Akron, 1993—; adj. faculty, cons. Buffalo State U., 1972-92, Lake Erie Coll., Cleve., 1985—; lectr., cons. Cleve. State U., 1978—; program dir. Ctr. Profl. Adv., East Brunswick, N.J., 1978—. Cons., lectr. Girl Scouts U.S.A., Cleve., 1981-90; colleague Creative Edn. Found.; cons. project bus. Jr. Achievement, 1992-93. Mem. Am. Mgmt. Assn., Human Resource Planning Soc., Soc. for Human Resource Mgmt., Gestalt Inst. of Cleve., Greenpeace, ACLU. Home: 7236 Chagrin Rd Chagrin Falls OH 44023-1102

KUBY, PATRICIA ANN WILLIAMS, early childhood educator; b. Mobile, Ala., Aug. 19, 1944; d. Percy Lafayette and Bertha Ross (Ledbetter) Williams; m. Carl Joseph Kuby Jr., Aug. 30, 1965; children: Kathryn Amelia, Candace Ross, Carl Joseph III. BA in Elem. Edn., La. Coll., Pineville, 1966; MA in Reading, N.E. La. U., Monroe, 1972; PhD in Early Childhood Edn. and Devel., U. Ala., Birmingham, 1994. Cert. in elem. edn., early childhood edn., reading, principalship, Ala. Tchr. 4th grade Orleans Parish Schs., New Orleans, 1966-70, 7th grade remedial reading tchr., 1972-74; tchr. 5th grade Franklin Parish Schs., Winnsboro, La., 1970-71; reading specialist Franklin Parish Schs., Winnsboro, 1971-72, Etowah County Schs., Gadsden, Ala., 1974-76; instr. devel. reading Calhoun Coll., Decatur, Ala., 1987-88; instr. child care Decatur City Schs. Continuing Edn., 1989-90; grad. asst. U. Ala., Birmingham, 1989-93; asst. prof. early childhood/elem. edn. Athens (Ala.) State Coll., 1993—; cons. early childhood edn. Headstart, Morgan County, Ala., 1989, Women's Missionary Union, Birmingham, 1992; cons. Dept. Human Resources, Ala., 1988-89; cons. pre-sch. Ala. Bapt. Conv., Montgomery, 1981—. Contbr. articles to profl. jours. Key communicator Westlawn Elem. Sch. Decatur, 1992-94. U. Ala. at Birmingham grantee, 1989-93. Mem. Nat. Assn. for Edn. Young Children, Ala. Assn. for Edn. Young Children, Tennessee Valley Assn. for Edn. Young Children (pres. 1989-91, 93-94), So. Early Childhood Assn., Assn. for Childhood Internat., Internat. Reading Assn., Tennessee Valley Reading Coun., Kappa Delta Epsilon, Kappa Delta Pi. Baptist. Home: 2214 Essex Dr SW Decatur AL 35603-1015

KUCERA, EDNA LEE, hospital administrator; b. Key West, Fla., Mar. 23, 1948; d. Jasper William and Jeanne Marie (McSorley) Newcomer; m. Gerald Frances Abramowski, May 4, 1968 (div. 1984); children: Kenneth Richard, Debra Lee, Mary Beth; m. Richard Charles Kucera, May 25, 1991; 1 stepchild, Valerie Gail. AAS, Suffolk County Community Coll., Selden, N.Y., 1971; BS, St. Joseph's Coll., Patchogue, N.Y., 1989; MS, SUNY, Stony Brook, 1994. Staff nurse St. Charles Hosp., Port Jefferson, N.Y., 1966-72; supr. Woodhaven Nursing Home, Port Jefferson, N.Y., 1974-76; asst. nursing care coord. St. Charles Hosp., Port Jefferson, N.Y., 1976-78, nursing care coord., 1978-87, quality assurance coord., 1987-89; dir. quality mgmr. Brookhaven Meml. Hosp., Patchogue, 1989-94; asst. adminstr. U. Hosp., Stony Brook, 1994—; lectr. Suffolk County Arthritis Found., Huntington, N.Y., 1980-85. Brownie troop leader Girl Scouts U.S.A., Miller Place, N.Y., 1975-79. Mem. Nat. Assn. Quality Assurance Profls. (cert.), Nat. League Nursing, N.Y. State Nurses Assn. Republican. Roman Catholic. Office: Univ Hosp at Stony Brook Stony Brook NY 11772

KUCHAREK, SUSAN LYNN, marketing educator, consultant; b. Wurtzberg, Germany, Dec. 23, 1964; came to U.S., 1966; d. Edmond Walter and Maria Ann (Brandstetter) Gardner; m. Martin Edward Kucharek, June 5, 1993. BSBA, Miami U. of Ohio, 1987; BS in Edn., Ohio State U., 1989. Cert. vocat. tchr. Sales mgr. Lazarus Dept. Stores, Columbus, Ohio, 1987-88; office mgr. Dr. Gardner's Office, Columbus, Ohio, 1980-89; mktg. educator Napoleon (Ohio) City Schs., 1989—, mem. faculty assn., 1989—. Nominated for Outstanding New Mktg. Educator Ohio Mktg. Edn. Assn. Mem. NEA, Am. Vocat. Assn., Ohio Vocat. Assn., Ohio Mktg. Edn. Assn., Ohio DECA (trustee 1992—, dist. chairperson 1991-92). Republican. Roman Catholic. Home: 2624 Marla Ln Maumee OH 43537 Office: Napoleon City Schs Briarheath Dr Napoleon OH 43545

KUCHARSKI, KAREN ANN, artist, educator; b. Nanticoke, Pa., Aug. 5, 1958; d. Eugene H. and Arlene H. (Fedorchak) K. BA in Studio Art with honors, SUNY, Binghamton, 1980; cert. teaching, Elmira Coll., 1981; MFA in Printmaking, Syracuse U., 1986. Tchr. art N.Y. State Pub. Schs., 1981-91; com. mem. Studio Sch. and Art Gallery, Johnson City, N.Y., 1982-84; printmaking studio asst. Syracuse (N.Y.) U., 1985-86; tchr. drawing and painting Met. Sch. for the Arts, Syracuse, 1985-86; tchg. asst. Syracuse U., 1984-86; mentor Empire State Coll., 1989; vis. asst. prof. physiology dept. Cornell U., Ithaca, N.Y., 1989—; asst. prof. fine arts Elon Coll., N.C., 1991-94; adj. asst. prof. Binghamton U., N.Y., 1994,. One-woman shows include: Waterman Wildlife Ctr., Apalachin, N.Y., 1979, Studio Sch. & Art Gallery, Johnson City, 1983, Binghamton U., 1986, Coll. of William and Mary, Williamsburg, Va., 1989; exhibited in group shows at U. Art Gallery, Binghamton, 1981, Townhouse Gallery, Owego, N.Y., 1982, Cazenovia Coll., N.Y., 1985, City Hall, Syracuse, 1986, Lowe Art Gallery, Syracuse U., 1987, Hunterdon Art Ctr., Clinton, N.J., 1988, Cornell U., N.Y., 1988, Waterworks Art Ctr., Salisbury, N.C., 1992, Fridholm Fine Arts Bldg., Asheville, N.C., 1993, Bixler Gallery, Stroudsburg, Pa., 1994; represented in pub. collections at Sheraton Inn, Liverpool, N.Y., 1986, Cornell Univ., 1991, Elon Coll., 1991; represented in various pvt. collections. Summer fellow Syracuse U., 1986, vis. fellow Cornell U., 1987, resident fellow, Vt. Studio Colony, 1988; grantee N.Y. State Coun. on the Arts, 1991; vis. scholar U. N.C., 1992-93. Office: Art and Art History Dept Binghamton U Vestal Pkwy East Binghamton NY 13901

KUCHTYAK, GALE MARIE LOUISE, pharmacist; b. New Brunswick, N.J., Oct. 19, 1949; d. John Vincent and Edna Barbara (Pisinski) K. BS in Pharmacy, Rutgers U., 1972, BA, 1972; postgrad., St. Joseph's Coll., 1992—. Registered pharmacist, N.J. Pharmacist Devine's Pharmacy, Dunellen, N.J., 1972-73; staff pharmacist Middlesex Gen. Hosp., New Brunswick, N.J., 1973-79; pharmacist, narcotic coord. Riverview Med. Ctr., Red Bank, N.J., 1979—. Organist, St. Mary's Cath. Ch., 1974-75. Mem. N.J. Soc. Hosp. Pharmacists (sec. South Ctrl. chpt. 1993-94, pres. elect 1994—), Am. Soc. Hosp. Pharmacists, Union of Polish Women (sec. South River, N.J. chpt. 1990—, v.p. 1988-90). Roman Catholic. Office: Riverview Med Ctr 1 Riverview Plaza Red Bank NJ 07701

KUCK, MARIE ELIZABETH BUKOVSKY, retired pharmacist; b. Milw., Aug. 3, 1910; d. Frank Joseph and Marie (Nozina) Bukovsky; Ph.C., U. Ill., 1933; m. John A. Kuck, Sept. 20, 1945 (div. Nov. 1954). Pharmacist, tchr. Am. Hosp., Chgo., 1936-38, St. Joseph Hosp., Chgo., 1938-40, Ill. Masonic Hosp., Chgo., 1940-45; chief pharmacist St. Vincent Hosp., Los Angeles, 1946-48, St. Joseph Hosp., Santa Fe, 1949-51; dir. pharm. services St. Luke's Hosp., San Francisco, 1951-76; pharmacist Mission Neighborhood Health Center, San Francisco, 1968-72; docent Calif. Acad. Sci., 1977—, DeYoung Mus., 1989—; mem. peer rev. com. Drug Utilization Com., Blue Shield Calif. and Pharm. Soc. San Francisco. Recipient Bowl of Hygeia award Calif. Pharm. Assn., 1966. Mem. No., Calif. (legis. chmn. aux. 1967-69, chmn. fund raising luncheon 1953-71, pres. San Francisco aux. 1974), Nat., Am., No. Calif. (pres. 1955-56, pres. San Francisco aux. 1965-66, editor ofcl. publ. 1967-70), San Francisco (sec. 1977-79, treas. 1979-80, pres. 1982-83; Pharmacist of Yr. award 1978) pharm. socs., Am. Pharm. Assn. (pres. No. Calif. br. 1956-57, nat. sec. women's aux. 1970-72, hon. pres. aux. 1975—), Calif. Council Hosp. Pharmacists (organizer 1962, sec.-treas. 1962-66), Am. Soc. Hosp. Pharmacists, Assn. Western Hosps. (gen. chmn. hosp. pharmacy sect. conv. San Francisco 1958), Internat. Pharmacy Congress (U.S. del. Brussels 1958, Copenhagen 1960), Fedn. Internationale Pharmaceutique, Lambda Kappa Sigma. Home: 2261 33d Ave San Francisco CA 94116

KUCZMARSKI, SUSAN SMITH, marketing strategy consulting company executive; b. Portland, Oreg., Apr. 24, 1951; d. Fernando Martin and Bula Grace (Weddle) Smith; m. Thomas Dale Kuczmarski, Aug. 21, 1976; children: John Thomas, James Smith, Thomas Michael. BA, Colo. Coll., 1973; MIA, Columbia U., 1975, MEd, 1978, EdD, 1979. Instr. U. Ill., Chgo., 1976-77, Nat.-Louis U., Evanston, Ill., 1986-88; lectr. Rosary Coll., River Forest, Ill., 1977-78; asst. prof. Concordia U., River Forest, 1977-79; edn. dir. Constl. Rights Found., Chgo., 1979-81; assoc. dir. devel., instr. Northwestern U., Evanston, 1981-84; exec. v.p. Kuczmarski & Assocs., Chgo., 1984—; adv. Edward Lowe Found., Cassopolis, Mich., 1986-94. Author, editor: Youth and Society: Rights and Responsibilities, 2d edit., 1980; co-author: Values-Based Leadership: Rebuilding Employee Commitment, Performance, and Productivity, 1995; book rev. editor Jour. Internat. Affairs, 1973-75. Vol. Harlem Tutorial Program, N.Y.C., 1973-74. Internat. House fellow, 1974, Columbia U. Sch. Internat. Affairs fellow, 1974-75, Columbia U. internat. fellow, 1975-76. Mem. Com. on Fgn. Affairs, Kappa Alpha Theta. Republican. Roman Catholic. Office: 1165 N Clark St Chicago IL 60611

KUDRONOWICZ, JUANITA HELEN, occupational health nurse; b. Culdesac, Idaho, Feb. 19, 1935; d. Leonard Augustine and Christine Mae (Funnemark) Yochum; m. Ambrose Andrew Kudronowicz, June 11, 1955; children: Doloris, Kevin, Kathleen, Sharon, Ambrosine, Allen. AA, Lewis and Clark State Coll., 1969. Occupational health nurse Potlatch Corp., Lewiston, 1969-90, lead nurse, 1990—. Vol. ARC, Lewiston, 1989—. Mem. Emergency Dept. Nursing Assn. (publicity chmn. 1971-73), Nat. League Nursing, Idaho Nurses Assn. (sec. dist. 4 1970-71), Women of Moose (Acad. of Friendship, Coll. of Regents, recorder). Roman Catholic. Home: 3129 7th St Lewiston ID 83501 Office: Potlatch Corp 805 Mill Rd Lewiston ID 83501

KUEHNE, HELENIRENE ANNE, art educator; b. Douglasville, Pa., Nov. 7, 1941; d. John Julius Dusco and Helen Kathryn Rogosky; m. Paul Howard Kuehne, June 28, 1980; 1 child, John Paul. BS, Kutztown U., 1964, MEd, 1968; postgrad., U. No. Colo., 1978, LaSalle U., 1994. Tchr. elem. art Kutztown (Pa.) Area Schs., 1964-83, tchr. secondary art, 1983—, chair fine arts dept., mem. curriculum coun., 1993—; tchr. coop. tchr. program Kutztown U., 1970—, mem. program adv. com., 1972. Works exhibited in various art shows, 1978-81. Sec. Muhlenberg Twp. Arts Bd., Laureldale, Pa., 1991—; merit badge counselor Boy Scouts Am., Laureldale, 1993—; active Friends of Reading Pub. Mus., 1991. Grantee Pa. Coun. Arts, 1993-94. Mem. AAUW (chair 1979-80, 88-89), Wyomissing Inst. Fine Arts, Delta Gamma. Home: 3512 Kent Ave Laureldale PA 19605 Office: Kutztown Area Sr High 50 Trexler Ave Kutztown PA 19530

KUEHNER, BARBARA LOUISE, nursing educator, physiology educator; b. Lebonan, Oreg., Mar. 19, 1943; d. Joseph Wykoff and Jeanne Elizabeth (Abraham) Nadal; m. Richard Andrew Kuehner, May 28, 1966; children: Kristy Elizabeth, Heather Jeanne. BA, Pomona Coll., 1964; MA, U. Mich., 1966; BSN, Oreg. Health Sci. U., 1983. RN, Oreg.; cert. staff devel. ANA. Biology instr. Coll. of the Redwoods, Eureka, Calif., 1966-70; anatomy and physiology instr. Am. River Coll., Sacramento, Calif., 1970-73; biology and physiology instr. Calif. State Coll., San Bernardino, 1974-78, numerous colls., Portland, Oreg., 1979-83; RN King City Convalescent Ctr., Tigard, Oreg., 1983-84; home health RN Staff Builders, Portland, Oreg., 1984-85; oncology nurse, educator St. Vincent Hosp. and Med. Ctr., Portland, Oreg., 1985—. Editor The Interpreter, 1976-78 (merit award 1978), Nursing Newsletter, 1988—; co-editor Regional Nursing Newsletter, 1993—. Asst. leader Explorer Scouts, Portland, 1990-91. Grantee Am. River Coll., 1972. Mem. AAUW (program v.p. 1980-81), Sigma Theta Tau (rsch. awards 1988—, book dr. 1992—). Office: St Vincent Hosp & Med Ctr 9205 SW Barnes Rd Portland OR 97225-6622

KUEHNERT, DEBORAH ANNE, medical center administrator; b. Raleigh, N.C., Nov. 21, 1949; d. Eldor Paul and Lila Catherine (Gilbert) K. Student, Valparaiso (Ind.) U., 1967-69; BS in Biology, Lenior Rhyne Coll., Hickory, N.C., 1977. Cert. med. technologist. Rsch. asst. Strong Meml. Hosp., Rochester, N.Y., 1967-68; lab. technician Richard Baker Hosp., Hickory, N.C., 1969-76; med. technician, shift supr. Glenn R. Frye Hosp., Hickory, 1977-83; lab. tech. dir. Frye Regional Med. Ctr., Hickory, 1983-85, adminstrv. dir. lab. svcs., 1986-92; sr. tech. dir. lab. svcs. Al-Fanateer Hosp., Jubail, Saudia Arabia, 1993; med. technologist lab. Chinle (Ariz.) Health Care Facility, Navajo Indian Reservation USPHS Hosp., 1993; instr. microbiology Catawba Valley Tech. Coll., Hickory, 1977-94, Lenior Rhyne Coll., Hickory, 1978-94; chief tech. lab. No. Area Armed Forces Hosp., Hafr Al Batin, Saudi Arabia, 1994—; cons. Frye Physicians, Hickory, 1985—; lab. cons. Am. Med. Internat., New Orleans, 1986, Lake City, Fla., 1984-85; cons. Med. Lab. Observer, Chgo., 1989. Mem. Am. Soc. Clin. Pathologists, N.C. Soc. Blood Bankers. Lutheran. Home: 34 Penny Ln Hickory NC 28601-9341

KUENY, TRACY LEE, accountant; b. Media, Pa., Mar. 14, 1969; d. Charles Joseph and Margaret Esther (Lowe) Corace; m. Matthew David Kueny, Oct. 15, 1994. BS in Acctg., U. Del., 1991. Sr. acct. Beneficial Tax Masters, Inc., Peapack, N.J., 1991—. Mem. Inst. Mgmt. Accts. (Raritan Valley chpt.). Home: J2 East Garden Way Dayton NJ 08810 Office: Beneficial Tax Masters Inc 200 Beneficial Ctr Peapack NJ 07977

KUEST, MARILYN SIBYL, school nurse; b. Seattle, Feb. 24, 1938; d. Richard Austin and Bernadette (McMahon) Smith; m. Harold LeRoy Kuest, Oct. 1, 1960; children: Carole Kiele, Kristi Drake, Coleen Arndt, Karen, Cathie, Kelly. BSN, Seattle U., 1960; M Edn. Guidance and Counseling, City U., Bellevue, Wash., 1993. RN, Wash. Nurse delivery rm. Providence Hosp., Seattle, 1960; pub. health nurse Seattle-King County Health Dept., 1960-61; sch. nurse Sequim (Wash.) Sch. Dist., 1980—. Active High Priority Infant Tracking, Child Devel. Screening, Adolescent Access to Health Care, AIDS task force Clallam County, Wash., Teenage Pregnancy Prevention Coalition, Clallam County Interagy. Coord. Coun. Bd., cmty. clubs and orgns.; instr. First Aid-CPR, 1976—; bd. dirs. Umbrella Svcs., United Way; com. chair United Way; eucharistic min., lector, parish coun., v.p. Altar Soc. v.p. and treas., Guild chair, stewardship com. chair St. Joseph's Ch. Mem. Nat. Assn. Sch. Nurses (cert.), Sch. Nurse Orgn. Wash. (v.p. 1988-89, chair scholarship com., adv. bd. profl. edn. Pacific Luth. U. 1989—, mem. legis. com. 1989—, alt. area III rep. 1990, area III rep. 1993—, Sch. Nurse Yr. 1992), Am. Sch. Health Assn., Sch. Health Assn. Wash., Ft. Worden Alumni Assn., Delta Kappa Gamma. Roman Catholic. Home: 1079 Finn Hall Rd Port Angeles WA 98362-8115 Office: Sequim Sch Dist 503 N Sequim Ave Sequim WA 98382-3199

KUESTEN, CARLA LYNN, research scientist; b. California, Mo., June 16, 1957; d. Carl Louis and June Frisch (Kellner) K. Student, Ctrl. Mo. State U., 1976; BS, U. Idaho, 1981; MS, Oreg. State U., 1983; PhD, Cornell U., 1992. Lab. asst. food rsch. dept. U. Idaho, 1980-81; grad. rsch. asst. food sci. and tech. Oreg. State U., 1981-83; evaluation specialist product evaluation dept. S. C. Johnson & Son, Inc., 1983-87; grad. rsch. asst. food sci. and tech. Cornell U., 1987-92; scientist R&D product evaluation divsn. Philip Morris, Richmond, Va., 1992-93; assoc. rsch. svcs. mgr. rsch. svcs. S.C. Johnson Wax, Racine, Wis., 1994—; presenter in field. Contbr. rsch. articles to sci. jours. R&D grantee S. C. Johnson and Son, Inc. Mem. Am. Chem. Soc., Inst. Food Technologists, Assn. for Chemoreception Scis., Sigma Xi. Office: SC Johnson Wax Rsch Svcs Racine WI 53402

KUETHE, MARIA, psychologist; b. N.Y.C., Aug. 3, 1934; d. Albert and Olga (Kenin) Meiff; m. Robert Arthur Gordon, May 21, 1955 (div. 1966); 1 child, Benjamin David Gordon; m. James Louis Kuethe, Jan. 25, 1967; 1 child, Sarah Leah Kuethe. BA, Bard Coll., 1957; MA, U. Chgo., 1958; PhD, U. Albany, 1987. Lic. psychologist, N.Y. Lectr. in Russian U. Chgo., 1962-63, Johns Hopkins U., Balt., 1966-67; ct. psychologist Saratoga County Mental Health Ctr., Saratoga Springs, N.Y., 1987-89; supervising psychologist Saratoga County Mental Health Ctr., Saratoga Springs, 1989-92, pvt. practice in psychology, 1991—; cons. Project Head Start, N.Y.C., 1992-93. Translator (with H. McLean) Nervous People and Other Satires. Mem. Am. Psychol. Assn. Office: 6 Franklin Square Saratoga Springs NY 12866

KUGLER, DAWN MARIE, clinical psychologist; b. Red Wing, Minn., June 22, 1963; d. Kenneth Herman Quade and Barbara Jean (Gehrke) Steffenhagen; m. David Edward Kugler, June 3, 1983; children: Alyssa, Andrew. BS in Psychology, U. N.D., 1985, MA in Psychology, 1988, PhD in Clin. Psychology, 1991. Lic. clin. psychologist, S.D. Psychology intern Wichita (Kans.) Guidance Ctr., 1990-91; clin. psychologist Psychol. Assocs. of the Black Hills, Rapid City, S.D., 1992—, pres. exec. com., 1993. Cadet USAF, 1981-83. Mem. APA, Assn. for Retarded Citizens (bd. dirs. 1989-90), S.D. Psychol. Assn., Inc. (pres.-elect 1992—, pres. 1994). Office: Psychol Assocs Black Hills Ste 102 2630 Jackson Blvd Rapid City SD 57702

KUHAR, JUNE CAROLYNN, retired fiberglass manufacturing company executive; b. Chgo., Sept. 20, 1935; d. Kurt Ludwig and Dorothy Julia (Lewand) Stier; m. G. James Kuhar, Feb. 5, 1953; children: Kathleen Lee, Debra Suzanne. Lic. real estate salesperson. Student William Rainey Harper Coll., Chgo. Engaged in fiberglass mfg., 1970—; sec.-treas. Q-R Fiber Glass Industries Inc., Rolling Meadows, Ill., 1970—. Leader Girl Scouts U.S.; mem. Civil Def. Disaster and Rescue Team, 1965-70, Rolling Meadows Golden Yrs. Coun., Arlington Heights Concerned People Helping to Understand Multiple Sclerosis; chmn. benefit fashion show William Rainey Harper Coll.- Sch. of Fashion Design, 1983. Mem. Multiple Sclerosis Soc., Nat. Fedn. Ileitis and Colitis, Bus. and Profl. Women N.W., Bus. and Profl. Woman's Club (pres. 1984—), Am. Legion Aux., Women in the Arts (charter). Home: 2303 Meadow Dr Rolling Meadows IL 60008-1546

KUHLER, DEBORAH GAIL, grief counselor, former state legislator; b. Moorhead, Minn., Oct. 12, 1952; d. Robert Edgar and Beverly Maxine (Buechler) Ecker; m. George Henry Kuhler, Dec. 28, 1973; children: Karen Elizabeth, Ellen Christine. BA, Dakota Wesleyan U., 1974; MA, U. N.D., 1977. Cert. grief counselor; lic. profl. counselor, S.D. Outpatient therapist Ctr. for Human Devel., Grand Forks, N.D., 1975-77; mental health counselor Community Counseling Services, Huron, S.D., 1978-88, 91-93; owner, dir. bereavement svcs. Kuhler Funeral Home, Huron, 1978—; adj. prof. Huron U., 1979-83, 90—; mem. from dist. 23 S.D. Ho. Reps., Pierre, 1987-90; mem. House Judiciary com., chair House Health and Welfare Com., Pierre, 1990. Active Beadle County Rep. Women, 1st United Meth. Ch. Named Young Alumnus of the Yr., Dakota Wesleyan U., 1989, Bus. and Profl. Women, 1989. Mem. ACA, AAUW (Achievement in Politics award 1987), Am. Mental Health Counselors Assn., Women Execs. and Adminstrs., Assn. for Death Edn. and Counseling, Phi Kappa Phi. Home: 1360 Dakota Ave S Huron SD 57350-3660

KUHLMAN, KIMBERLY ANN, clinical dietician; b. Toledo, June 30, 1954; d. James Gilbert and Jane Marie (Konczal) Schramm; m. Carl Edwin Kuhlman Jr., May 23, 1981; children: Eric, Christopher. BS in Pub. Health, U. Toledo, 1977; BS in Dietetics, Bowling Green State U., 1978; MEd in Health Edn., U. Toledo, 1988. Cert. diabetes educator. Dietetic intern Good Samaritan Hosp., Cin., 1979; dietitian, tchr. The Toledo Hosp., 1980, clinical dietitian, 1981-83, nutrition support dietitian, 1983-86; dietitian Alcohol Treatment Ctr., Toledo, 1986-87; clin. dietitian Coop. Care Unit, Toledo Hosp., 1987-88; mem. faculty W.W. Knight Family Practice, Toledo, 1988—; guest lectr. Toledo Pub. Schs., 1983-84, guest speaker pvt. industry coun., 1989—; instr. Health Aware program Toledo Hosp. Community Health Project, 1980-83. Author: (fact sheet) Home Prental Nutrition; (booklet) Pediatric Nutrition, A Guide to Sensible Eating. Mem. Toledo Art Mus., Toledo Zoo, Toledo Bot. Garden; treas. Presch. Nutrition Coun. N.W. Ohio, Toledo, 1986-89, Am. Cancer Soc. Babe Zaharias Classic; Cub Scout leader Boy Scouts Am. Recipient Patient Care award, 1994. Mem. Nutrition Educators of Health Profls. Practice Group, Sports and Cardiovascular Nutritionists Practice Group of Am. Dietetics Assn., Toledo Dietetic Assn. (chmn. regulations com. 1986-88, co-chmn. membership com. 1983-84, chmn. 1984-85), Toledo Hosp. Corp. Wellness Planning Com., Ann. Conf. on Patient Edn. for AAFP (planning com.), Soc. Tchrs. of Family Medicine. Lutheran. Home: 4264 River Rd Toledo OH 43614-5528

KUHN, ANNE NAOMI WICKER (MRS. HAROLD B. KUHN), foreign language educator; b. Lynchburg, Va.; d. George Barnett and Annie (Hicks) Wicker; m. Harold B. Kuhn. Diploma Malone Coll., 1933, Trinity Coll. Music, London, 1937; AB, John Fletcher Coll., 1939; MA, Boston U., 1942, postgrad., 1965-70; postgrad. (fellow) Harvard U., 1942-44, 66-68; hon. grad. Asbury Coll., 1978. Instr., Emmanuel Bible Coll., Birkenhead, Eng., 1936-37; asst. in history John Fletcher Coll., University Park, Iowa, 1938-39; librarian Harvard U., 1939-44; tchr. adult edn. program U.S. Armed Forces, Fuerstenfeldbruck Air Base, Germany, 1951-52; prof. Union Bibl. Sem., Yeotmal, India, 1957-58; lectr. Armenian Bible Inst., Beirut, Lebanon, 1958; prof. German, Asbury Coll., Wilmore, Ky., 1962—, co-dir. coll. study tour to East Germany and West Germany, 1976, 77, 78, co-dir. acad. tours, 1979, 80; dir. acad. tour, Russia, 1981, 85, Scandanavia, 1982, Indonesia, Singapore, 1983, Hong Kong and Thailand, 1983, 85, East Germany, West Germany, France and Austria, 1983, Russia and Finland, 1984, 85, 89, China, 1979, 84, 85, 89, Estonia, Latvia, 1985, 89, Poland, 1989, 91, 92, Portugal, Spain, France, Ireland, Scotland, Norway, England, 1987, The Balka, Hungary, Czech Republic, Slovak Republic, Bulgaria, Romania and Turkey, 1992; tchr. Seoul Theol. Sem., fall 1978. Author: (pamphlet) The Impact of the Transition to Modern Education Upon Religious Education, 1950; The Influence of Paul Gerhardt upon Wesleyan Hymnody, 1960, Light to Dispel Fear, 1987; transl. German ch. records, poems, letters; contbr. articles to profl. jours. Del. Youth for Christ World Conf., 1948, 50, London Yearly Meeting of Friends, Edinburgh, Scotland, 1948, World Council Chs., Amsterdam, 1948, World Friends Conf., Oxford, Eng., 1952, World Methodist Conf., Oslo, Norway, 1961, Deutscher Kirchentag, Dortmund, Germany, 1963, German Lang. Congress, Bonn, W. Ger., 1974, Internat. Conf. Religion, Amsterdam, Netherlands, Poland, West Berlin, Fed. Republic Germany, 1986, Internat. Missionary Conf., Eng., 1987, Congress on the Bible II, Washington, 1987; participant Internat. Congress World Evangelization, Lausanne, Switzerland, 1974; del., speaker Internat. Conf. on Holocaust and Genocide, Oxford and London, 1988; speaker Founders Week Malone Coll., Ohio, 1989, Nat. Quaker Conf., Denver; mem. acad. tour Poland, 1988. Recipient German Consular award, Boston, 1965, Thomas Mann award Boston U., 1967; named Ky. Col., 1978. Fellow Goethe-Institut for Germanisten, Munich, 1966-68, 70-71. Mem. AAUW, Am. Assn. Tchrs. German, NEA, Ky. Ednl. Assn., Lincoln Lit. Soc., Protestant Women of Chapel, Harvard Univ. Faculty Club (Cambridge, Mass.), Harvard Univ. Club Eastern and Ctrl. Ky. (Lexington), United Daughters of the Confederacy, Delta Phi Alpha (award 1963, 65). Mem. Soc. of Friends. Home: 406 Kenyon Ave Wilmore KY 40390-1033

KUHN, JOSEPHINE M. KELLER, interior decorating business owner; b. Davenport, Iowa, Sept. 27, 1937; d. George Antone and Olive Katherine Keller; m. James Paul, Dec. 27, 1958; children: Christine, Cynthia, George. Student, Am. Inst. Commerce, Davenport, 1958, Coll. DuPage, Glenn Ellyn, 1972, U. Conn., Stamford, 1976, Harvard U., 1990. Pres., owner Timeless Designs, Inc., Lake Forest, Ill., 1984—. Mem. Women's Archtl. League (bd. dirs. 1985-91, 1st v.p. 1989-91).

KUHN, KATHLEEN JO, accountant; b. Springfield, Ill., Aug. 9, 1947; d. Henry Elmer and Norma Florene (Niehaus) Burge; m. Gerald L. Kuhn, June 22, 1968; children: Gerald Lynn, Brett Anthony. BS in Bus., Bradley U., 1969. CPA, Ill. Controller Byerly Music Co., Peoria, Ill., 1969-70; staff acct. Clifton Gunderson & Co., Columbus, Ind., 1970-71; acct. Dept. of Transp., State of Ill., Springfield, 1972-76; acct. Gerald L. Kuhn & Assocs., Springfield, 1976-78, ptnr., 1979—, quality control mgr., 1990—; grad. asst. in Dale Carnegie courses, 1979-80. Writer, editor co. policy guideline, 1979-80; editor co. quality control manual, 1990. Recipient Attendance award Continuing Profl. Edn. for Accts., 1979—. Mem. Am. Inst. CPAs, Springfield Art Assn., Ill. Soc. CPAs, Am. Woman's Soc. CPAs, Nat. Bus. & Motivational Assn. Lutheran. Clubs: Olympic Swim, Metro. Federated Jr. Women's. Home: 2511 Westchester Blvd Springfield IL 62704-5406 Office: 2659 Farragut Dr Springfield IL 62704-1462

KUHN, LUCILLE ROSS, retired naval officer; b. Washington, July 19, 1927; d. Lilburn Joseph and Flora Lee (Perry) K.; A.A. with distinction, George Washington U., 1959, B.A., 1960. Ins. clk. Southwestern Life Ins. Co., Richmond, Va., 1945-48; joined U.S. Navy, 1949, advanced through grades to capt., 1975; woman officer rep. 2d Navy Recruiting Area, Washington, 1963-65; U.S. Naval Security Group, Washington, 1965-68; dir. mil. personnel 12th Naval Dist., San Francisco, 1968-70; mem. staff Office Asst. Sec. Def. for Legis. Affairs, Washington, 1971-74; dir. Officer Candidate Sch., Newport, 1975-77; dir. pay/personnel adminstrv. support system Bur. Naval Personnel, Washington, 1977-79; comdg. officer Recruit Tng. Command, Orlando, Fla., 1979-81; dep. comdr. Navy Recruiting Command, Washington, 1981-84. Aide de camp to Va. govs., 1960—. Decorated Legion of Merit with gold star, Meritorious Service medal with gold star, Nat. Def. Service medal with bronze star. Mem. Naval Hist. Found., Psi Chi. Home: 2302 Kenmore Rd Richmond VA 23228-6037

KUHN, MARGARET (MAGGIE KUHN), organization executive; b. Buffalo, 1905; d. Samuel Frederick and Minnie Louise (Kooman) K. BA, Case-Western Res. U., 1926; hon. degree, Swarthmore Coll., Simmons Coll., Albright Coll., U. Pa., Beaver Coll., U. Mass., 1988, Case Western Res. U., 1989, No. Ill. U., 1990. Formerly with YWCA, Cleve., Phila.; Gen. Alliance Unitarian Women, Boston; later with United Presbn. Ch. U.S.A., N.Y.C.; editor, writer for ch. mag. Social Progress; alt. observer for Presbyns. at UN; ret., 1970; a founder Gray Panthers, Phila., 1971; now nat. convener; cons. nat. task force on women United Presby. Ch., past 3d v.p. health, edn. and welfare assn.; lectr.; mem. nat. adv. bd. Hospice, Inc.; adv. TV series Over Easy; former mem. Fed. Jud. Nominating Com. Pa. Author: Get Out There and Do Something about Injustice, 1972, Maggie Kuhn on Aging, 1977. Recipient 1st ann. award for justice and human devel. Witherspoon Soc., 1974, Disting. Service award in consumer advocacy Am. Speech and Hearing Assn., 1975, Freedom award Women's Scholarship Assn. Roosevelt U., 1976, ann. award Phila. Soc. Clin. Psychologists, 1976, Peaceseeker award United Presbyn. Peace Fellowship, 1977, Humanist of Yr. award Am. Humanist Assn., 1978. •

KUHNER, ARLENE ELIZABETH, English language educator, reviewer, academic administrator; b. Victoria, B.C., Can., May 1, 1939; d. Theodore Foort and Gladys Virginia (Evans) Huggins; m. Robert Henry Kuhner, Dec. 17, 1971; children: Mary Kathleen, Gwynne Elizabeth, Benjamin David. BA in English, Seattle U., 1960; postgrad., U. Calif., Berkeley, 1960-61; MA in English, U. Wash., 1966, PhD in English, 1978. Editor English dept. U. Wash., Seattle, 1964-66; instr. Seattle U., 1966-69, asst. prof., 1969-71; mem. adj. faculty Anchorage Community Coll., 1971-81, tchr., 1981-87; assoc. prof. U. Alaska, Anchorage, 1987-90, chair women's studies dept., 1989-93, prof., chair English dept., 1990-93, assoc. dean for acad. program & curriculum, prof. English, 1993—. Contbr. numerous papers to profl. confs. Contbg. mem. Oreg. Shakespeare Festival; nat. assoc. Folger Shakespeare Libr., Washington, 1987—; ptnr. in conscience Amnesty Internat., 1985—; bd. dirs. Tudor Community Sch., Anchorage, 1975-77. Woodrow Wilson Found. fellow, 1960; Western State Project grantee, 1986, 87, various others. Mem. MLA, Women's Caucus for Modern Langs., Nat. Coun. Tchrs. of English, Renaissance Soc. Am., Nat. Women's Studies Assn., N.W. Women's Studies Assn., Philos. Assn. of the Pacific Coast, Assn. for Can. Studies in U.S., Marlowe Soc. Am., Margaret Atwood Soc., Phi Kappa Phi. Democrat. Roman Catholic. Office: U Alaska Coll Arts and Scis 3211 Providence Dr Anchorage AK 99508-4614

KUHR, KATHLEEN ANN, principal; b. Chgo., Dec. 25, 1949; d. Leonard Anthony and Loretta T. (Sarat) K.; m. Walter E. Langosch, July 1, 1984. BA, Dominican Coll., 1971; MS, U. Wis., 1973; EdS, No. Ill. U., 1987, EdD, 1988. Cert. supt. K-12, tchr. 6-12, supr. K-12, guidance K-12. Tchr. English Jerstad-Agerholm Jr. High Sch., Racine, Wis., 1971-74; tchr., counselor Highland Park (N.J.) Mid. Sch., 1974-81; guidance counselor Zion (Ill.)-Benton High Sch., 1981-82, Maple Sch., Northbrook, Ill., 1982-86; prin. Orchard St. Sch., Fox River Grove, Ill., 1986-88, Mechanics Grove Sch., Mundelein, Ill., 1988—; mem. Adminstrv. Acad. Adv. Coun., Lake County, Ill., 1990—, sec., 1990-93, McHenry County Curriculum Coun. Contbr. articles to profl. jours. Dir. Metuchen (N.J.) Hot Line, 1979-80, trainer, counselor, 1974-81. Mem. NAESP, Whole Lang. Assn., Ill. Prins. Assn. (dir. 1990-91), Kappa Delta Pi. Home: 38591 N Arbor Ct Wadsworth IL 60083-9551 Office: Mechanics Grove Sch 1200 N Midlothian Rd Mundelein IL 60060-1146

KUHRT, SHARON LEE, nursing administrator; b. Denver, July 20, 1957; d. John Wilfred and Yoshiko (Ueda) K. BS in Nursing, Loretto Heights

Coll., 1982; MS in Nursing, Regis U., 1992. RN, Colo., Hawaii,. Mass., Maine. RN level III Porter Meml. Hosp., Denver, 1981-87; transport supr. Kapiolani Med. Ctr. for Women & Children, Honolulu, 1987-89; dir. patient care unit Aspen Valley Hosp., Colo., 1989-91; dir. Nursing Edn. Ctrl. Maine Med. Ctr., Lewiston, 1991—. Mem. ANA (cert. in pediatric nursing and nursing adminstrn.). Home: RR 1 Box 356B New Gloucester ME 04260-9749

KUJAWSKI, ELIZABETH SZANCER, art curator, consultant; b. N.Y.C., Feb. 7, 1951; d. Henryk and Irene (Zilz) Szancer; m. Nathan Kujawski, Mar. 25, 1973; children: Melissa, Stephanie. BA in Art History and Italian, Douglas Coll., 1972; MA in Art History, Queens Coll., 1975. Asst. curator Collection of Nelson A. Rockefeller, N.Y.C., 1975-79; asst. dir. SKT Galleries, Inc., N.Y.C., 1979-82; prin., art curator, cons. Elizabeth S. Kujawski-Curatorial Cons., N.Y.C., 1982—. Mem. Nat. Assn. Corporate Art Mgmt., Assn. Profl. Art Advisors. Office: 767 Fifth Ave Ste 4200 New York NY 10153

KUKLA, CYNTHIA MARY, artist; b. Chgo., June 23, 1952; d. Stanley A. and Eugenia (Markowski) Cukla; children: Glenn D., Garth A. BFA, Sch. of Art Inst. Chgo., 1973; MFA, U. Wis., 1983. Asst. prof. art No. Ky. U., Highland Heights, 1983-89, assoc. prof. art, 1989-93; assoc. prof. art Ill. State U., Normal, 1993—; lectr. art U. London, 1985, 87, All Hallows Coll., Dublin, 1993; art reviewer Dialogue, Arts in the Midwest, Columbus, Ohio, 1989-92; book reviewer Prentice-Hall, Inc., also Harcourt Brace, 1985—; art juror Regional Art Exhibits, 1984—; chmn. ann. conf. panel Nat. Coll. Art Assn., 1989, Mid-Am. Coll. Art Assn., 1986, S.E. Coll. Art Assn., 1988. One woman shows at Kent State U., Canton, Ohio, 1992, Liberty Gallery, Louisville, 1992, Market Gallery, Rockford, Ill., 1991, Rosewood Art Ctr., Kettering, Ohio, 1990, Headley-Whitney Mus., Lexington, 1987, Cin. Commn. on Arts, 1986, Armory Art Gallery, Blacksburg, Va., 1985, others; exhibited in group shows at Arrowmont Ctr. for Arts & Crafts, Gatlinburg, Tenn., 1993-94, Kharkov (Ukraine) Art Mus., 1993, Liberty Gallery, Louisville, 1993, Carnegie Art Ctr., Covington, Ky., 1993, Canton Art Inst., 1992, Galerie Hertz, Louisville, Ohio, 1992, Mus. Ctr. at Union Terminal, Cin., 1991, Zephyr Gallery, Louisville, 1991, Mayor's Office Commn. on Culture and Arts, Honolulu, 1991, Solway Coll. Complex, Cin., 1991, Grand European Nat. Ctr. of Arts and Letters, Nationale des Arts, Nice, France, 1990, Am. Embassy, Quito, Ecuador, 1989, Fine Arts Acad., Warsaw, Poland, 1988, Knox Coll. Gallery, Galesburg, Ill., 1988, U. Tenn. travelling exhbn., Knoxville, 1987-89, Ctr. for Contemporary Art, U. Ky., Lexington, 1987, Watertower Art Ctr., Louisville, 1987, Laguna Beach (Calif.) Art Mus., 1983, Springfield (Mo.) Art Mus., 1980, 83, 86, numerous others; works reviewed in (art jour.) New Art Examiner, 1994, Dialogue, 1989, 90, Cin. Enquirer, 1986, 88, 89, Atlanta Art Papers, 1988, Montgomery Ala. Jour., 1987, Louisville Courier-Jour, 1987, 91, 92, Lexington Herald-Leader, 1987, St. Louis Post-Dispatch, 1986, others. Conf. developer, panel chair Gender and Ethnicity in Art, Cin. Art Mus., 1992; mem. exec. bd. Women's Studies program No. Ky. U., 1985-92. Grantee Ky. Found. for Women, 1987, 90, Ky. Art Coun., 1988, No. Ky. U., 1985, 87, 90-91, 93; Millay Colony/Studios Midwest fellow, 1986, 88; named One of Outstanding Young Women Am., Jaycees, 1983. Mem. Nat. Women's Caucus for Art, Contemporary Connection of the Contemporary Art Ctr. (founding mem.), Coll. Art Assn., Nature Conservancy, Wilderness Soc., World Wildlife Fund, Greenpeace Action League. Office: Dept Art 5620 Ill State U Normal IL 61790-5620

KUKLA, DOLORES LOUISE, nurse; b. Detroit, Nov. 23, 1930; d. Edward Joseph and Anna (Loula) K. Diploma, Grace Hosp. Sch. Nursing, 1952; BSN, Wayne State U., 1960; BA in Social Svcs., Madonna Coll., 1976; MEd in Adult Edn., Marygrove Coll., 1977. Staff nurse Henry Ford Hosp., Detroit, 1952-58; pool nurse Staff Builders, Detroit, 1959-62; instr. Grace Hosp. Sch. of Nursing, Detroit, 1963-77; staff nurse various hosps., St. Petersburg, Fla., 1978-92; lab. facilitator St. Petersburg Jr. Coll., Pinellas Park, Fla., 1992—. Mem. AAUW, Am. Holistic Nurses Assn. Home: 8400 49th St N Apt 309 Pinellas Park FL 34665 Office: St Petersburg Jr Coll 7400 66th St Pinellas Park FL 34647

KUKLINSKI, JOAN LINDSEY, librarian; b. Lynn, Mass., Nov. 28, 1950; d. Richard Jay and M. Claire (Murphy) Card; B.A. cum laude, Mass. State Coll., Salem, 1972; M.L.S., U. R.I., 1976; m. Walter S. Kuklinski, June 17, 1972. Classified librarian U. R.I. Extension Div. Library, Providence, 1974-75, U. R.I. Cataloging Dept., Kingston, 1975-79; original cataloger Tex. A&M U. Library, College Station, 1979-82; cataloger Goldfarb Library, Brandeis U., Waltham, Mass., 1982-83; automation coordinator, 1983-85; exec. dir. Minuteman Library Network, Framingham, Mass., 1985—. Mem. Town of South Kingstown (R.I.) Women's Adv. Commn., 1977-79; trustee Princeton (Mass.) Pub. Libr., 1994—; mem. strategic planning com. for libr. svc. in yr. 2000 Mass. Bd. Libr. Commrs. Mem. ALA (resources and tech. services div. 1980—), Mass. Librs. Assn., New Eng. Libr. Assn., Libr. Info. Tech. Assn., Assn. Specialized Librs. and Coop. Groups, Am. Contract Bridge League, Delta Tau Kappa. Office: Minuteman Library Network 4 California Ave Framingham MA 01701-8218

KUKURA, RITA ANNE, elementary school educator; b. Tulsa, July 18, 1947; d. James Albert and Carmen Alberta (Parsons) Hayden; m. Joel Richard Graft, Oct. 28, 1967 (dec. Apr. 1969); m. Raymond Richard Kukura, Dec. 18, 1971 (div. 1981); children: Tiffany Carmen Noel, Austin Raymond. BS, Kent State U., 1971; MS, Okla. State U., 1991. Cert. early childhood, nursery, elem. tchr., Okla., spl. edn. tchr. for emotionally disturbed. Tchr. kindergarten Southlyn Elem. Sch., Lyndhurst, Ohio, 1971-73; elem. tchr. Wakefield Acad., Tulsa, 1981-83, tchr. kindergarten, 1983-87; reg. early intervention coord. Okla. Dept. Edn., Tulsa, 1990-92; tchr. devel. delayed children, coord. integrated program Child Devel. Inst. Children's Med. Ctr., Tulsa, 1992-93; tchr. elem. sch. Prue (Okla.) Schs., 1994—; manuscript reviewer for profl. orgns., 1989-91; presenter confs. in field; lectr. in field; presenter Internat. Soc. for Study of Behavioral Devel. meeting, 1991. Den leader Cub Scouts Am., Tulsa, 1984-88; com. mem. Boy Scouts Am., Tulsa, 1984-88; vol. officer worker Met. Tulsa Citizen Crime Commn., 1986; adv. com. Latchkey Project, Tulsa County, 1985; area coord. Nat. Tourette Syndrome Assn., fundraiser, 1988-90; ad hoc task force on day care Interagy. Coord. Coun., 1989-91; nat. rep. Tourette Syndrome Assn. to Nat. Broadcasting Assn. AERho, 1990-93; mem. resource com. Ronald McDonald House, 1990-92, vol. Tulsa area, 1991—, STARBASE, 1993-94, Drug Edn. for Youth, 1994; mem. adv. bd. Tulsa Regional Coordinating Coun. for Svcs. to Children and Youth and Families, 1991-92; planning com. symposium Magic Coun. Girl Scouts Am.; lt. sr. mem. Tulsa Composite Squadron CAP, 1992—; active Human Rights Com. for Ind. Opportunities, 1995—; presenter numerous confs. Recipient Den Leader Tng. award Boy Scouts Am., 1988. Mem. AAUW (bd. dirs. Tulsa County chpt. 1991-93), Assn. for Childhood Edn. Internat., Fedn. of Families for Children's Mental Health, Assn. for Care of Children's Health, Nat. Assn. Early Childhood Tchr. Educators, Friends of Spl. Children, Nat. Tourette Syndrome Assn. (state pres. 1987-92, state dir. 1992-93, hon. mem. bd. dirs. 1993), Gold Star Wives Am., Kappa Delta Pi, Omicron Nu, Alpha Epsilon Rho (hon. mem. S.W. region). Roman Catholic. Office: Prue Schs PO Box 130 Prue OK 74060-0130

KULA, JUDITH CHRISTINA, printing company executive; b. Boston, May 18, 1958; d. Eric Bertil and Gulli Ingegerd (Ahs) K. BA, Middlebury Coll., 1980; postgrad., Radcliffe U., 1980, Harvard U., 1991. Sales rep. R.R. Donnelley & Sons Co., N.Y.C., 1980-87; sales rep. Maxwell Communication Corp., N.Y.C., 1987-88, v.p. sales, 1988, sr. v.p. sales, 1988-90; sr. v.p. sales Quebecor Printing (USA) Corp., N.Y.C., 1990-93, sr. v.p. strategic planning, 1994—. Recipient Luminaire award Women In Prodn., N.Y.C., 1990. Mem. Mag. Publishers Assn., Graphic Communications Assn., Gravure Assn. Am. Office: Quebecor Printing USA Corp 125 High St 23rd Fl Boston MA 02110

KULAWAT, SUCHADA, Thai diplomat; b. Chumporn, Thailand, Aug. 19, 1958; d. Wallop and Laddawan (Sanidvono) K. BA, Chulalongkorn U., Bangkok, 1980; cert. in French lit. and civilization, U. Paris, Sorbonne, 1983; M in Journalism, North Tex. State U., 1988. Sr. writer The Nation, Bangkok, 1988-89; joined Thai Fgn. Svc., 1989—; first sec. Thai Mission to UN, N.Y.C., 1989—. Contbr. numerous revs. to profl. jours. Mem. Pub. Rels. Soc. Am., Nat. Geog. Soc., Italian Cultural Soc., Asia Soc. Office: Thai Mission to UN 351 E 52nd St New York NY 10022

KULBACK, JANET L. KLANCNIK, counselor; b. Wayne, Mich.; d. Frank and Agnes (Zyzneski) K.; m. Edwin F. Kulback, Nov. 15, 1975; 1 child, John Andrew. BA, Mich. State U., 1967, MA, 1968, EdS, 1983. Nat. cert. counselor, sch. psychologist; lic. sch. psychologist, cert. tchr., Mich. Counselor Madison Dist., Madison Heights, Mich., 1968-83, social studies tchr., 1984-93, sch. psychologist, 1985-86, counselor, 1993—; sch. psychologist Troy (Mich.) Sch. Dist., 1984. Mem. Madison Heights Youth Assistance Parent Edn. Com., 1993-94. Mem. Am. Counseling Assn., Oakland Counselors Assn., Nat. Sch. Psychologists Assn. Roman Catholic. Office: Wilkinson Mid Sch 26524 John R Rd Madison Heights MI 48071-3612

KULIK, ROSALYN FRANTA, food company executive, consultant; b. Wilmington, Del., Aug. 29, 1951; d. William Alfred and Virginia Louise (Ellis) Franta. BS in Voc. Home Econs. Edn., Purdue U., 1972, MS in Foods and Nutrition, 1974. Registered dietitian. Home economist Kellogg Co., Battle Creek, Mich., 1974-75, nutrition and consumer specialist, 1975-77, mgr. advt. to children, 1977-79, corp. adminstrv. asst., 1979, dir. nutrition, 1979-82, dir. nutrition and analytical services, 1982, v.p. nutrition and chemistry, 1983, v.p. quality and nutrition, 1983-87, v.p., asst. to chmn., 1987-88; exec. v.p., gen. mgr. Fearn Internat., Franklin Park, Ill., 1988-90; cons., 1991—; chmn. tech. com. Grocery Mfrs. Am., Washington, 1985-87, mem. tech. com. planning group, 1982-88; trustee Internat. Life Scis. Inst., Washington, 1982-88; v.p. Internat. Life Scis. Inst. Nutrition Found., Washington, 1985-88, exec. com., 1985-88; mem. of corp. Culinary Inst. Am. Contbr. articles on food sci. and nutrition to profl. jours. Bd. dirs. State Arthritis Found., County Vol. Ctr. Recipient Ada Decker Malott Meml. scholarship, Purdue U., 1970. Mem. Inst. Food Technologists, Am. Dietetic Assn., Phi Kappa Phi, Gamma Sigma Delta, Omicron Nu, Alpha Omicron Pi (mem. Phi Upsilon chpt.). Republican. Lutheran.

KULMATISKI, PHYLLIS GENEVIEVE, art educator, sculptor; b. Bklyn., Sept. 10, 1949; d. Philip Lanson and Jean (Graczyk) Zysk; m. Andrew J. Kulmatiski, July 10, 1971; children: Andrew, Anna. BS cum laude, SUNY, New Paltz, 1970; MS in Art Edn., Coll. St. Rose, 1991. Cert. art tchr., N.Y. Elem. art tchr. Mohonasen Ctrl. Schs., Rotterdam, N.Y., 1970-72; art tchr. Voorheesville (N.Y.) Ctrl. Schs., 1981; H.S. art tchr. Scotia (N.Y.) Glenville Ctrl. Schs., 1981—, arts in edn. bldg. chair, 1990—, interage class dir., 1988—, environment club dir., 1989—, art club dir., 1981-94; vis. artist Girls' Inc., Schnectady, N.Y., 1992. Shows include Schenectady Mus., 1991 (first place award), 1994, Skidmore Invitational Show, 1992. Dir., advisor Amnesty Internat., Scotia-Glenville H.S., 1988-91, yearbook adv. 1, 1994-95; bldg. rep. Scotia-Glenville Tchrs. Assn., 1990-94; mem. Coll. of St. Rose BFA Adv. Bd. Art tchrs. fellow, Skidmore Coll., 1982, 84. Mem. Nat. Art Edn. Assn., N.Y. State Art Tchrs. Assn., Christians in Visual Arts. Democrat. Home: 5 Wildwood Ave Scotia NY 12302-3215 Office: Scotia Glenville HS 1 Tartan Way Scotia NY 12302-1200

KULP, EILEEN BODNAR, social worker; b. Glens Falls, N.Y., Sept. 25, 1941; d. Joseph and Bertha (Choquette) Bodnar; m. Randolph Heath Kulp, June 5, 1961; children: Kimberly, Randolph Heath II, Kevin Joseph. B in Sociology, Hampton (Va.) U., 1978; MSW, Norfolk (Va.) State U., 1981. Lic. clin. social worker, Va.; diplomate in clin. social work Nat. Bd. Examiners; cert. addictions specialist. Social worker II adult chem. dependency Peninsula Hosp., Hampton, 1981-82, leader treatment team adolescent chem. dependency unit, 1982-84, sr. clinician adult chem. dependency unit, 1984-86, program coord. adult chem. dependency unit, 1986-88, dir. adult treatment programs, 1988-92; pvt. practice Newport News, Va., 1986-93; dir. new founds drug and alcohol programs Riverside Regional Med. Ctr., Newport News, 1994—; mem. addictions profls. team People Exch. Program, Norway, Sweden, Germany, 1989—; dir. intensive outpatient treatment programs Chesseh & Assocs., 1993-94. Bd. dirs Hampton Count PTA's, pres., 1979-80; bd. dirs. Hamtpon City Schs. Bd. Edn., 1981-85, Safe Haven Home for Abused Children, 1993—, Commonwealth Va. Citizens Adv. Bd. Youth and Family Svcs., Dept. Corrections, 1989—; chmn. adv. bd. Hampton Juvenile and Domestic Rels. Ct., bd. dirs., 1984—. Mem. Va. Coun. Social Welfare (pres. Tidewater chpt. 1987-88), Nat. Assn. Social Workers, Va. Assn. Alcoholism and Drug Abuse Counselors, Am. Coun. Alcoholism, Hampton Mental Health Bd. (pres. 1988-89), Va. Soc. Clin. Social Workers, Va. Coun. PTA's (life), Acad. Cert. Social Workers (cert.), Alpha Kappa Mu. Roman Catholic. Home: 26 Sarfan Dr Hampton VA 23664-1760

KUMAGAI, DENICE JEAN, actress; b. San Jose, Calif., Sept. 3, 1956; d. Henry Shigeru and Mae Haruko (Ohara) K. Artistic dir. Cold Tofu (Asian Am. Improvisational Comedy Group), L.A., 1989—. Appeared in (films) Clear & Present Danger, 1994, Suburban Commando, 1990, The Room Upstairs, 1987, Go Tell the Spartans, 1978, (TV series) And the Soul Shall Dance, 1977, M*A*S*H*, 1980, Highway to Heaven, 1984, Nighcourt, 1984-91, The Room Upstairs, 1987, Head of the Class, 1990, Empty Nest, 1991, Major Dad, 1991, Murphy Brown, 1992, Full House, 1992, Columbo, 1993, (theatre) Tofu on the Rampage, 1990, Living Tofu, 1989, Tofurama, 1988, M. Leroy in Greenland, 1984, Estonia You Fall, 1982, A Christmas Carol, 1980, The Grapevine, 1993, Comedy One Act Festival, 1993.

KUMAR, MARTHA JOYNT, educator; b. Washington, July 4, 1941; d. John Howard and May Aberdeen (Lepley) Joynt; m. Vijayendra Kumar, June 12, 1970; 1 child, Zal Alexander. BA, Conn. Coll., 1963; MA, Columbia U., 1965, PhD, 1972. Researcher NBC, News Dept., Election Unit, N.Y.C., 1965-66; instr. Tenn. State U., Nashville, 1967, U. Md., Balt., 1970-71; instr. Towson State U., Balt., 1971-72, asst. prof., 1972-75, assoc. prof., 1975-81, prof., 1981—; cons. in field. Co-author: Portraying the President: The White House and the News Media, 1981; assoc. editor Presdl. Studies Quar., 1986-89, co-chair editorial bd., 1994—; editorial bd. mem. Am. Jour. Polit. Sci.; contbr. articles to profl. jours. Mem. City Mgmt. Com., New Castle, Del., 1990-91. Ford Found. grantee, 1978-80. Mem. Am. Polit. Sci. Assn. (Kirkpatrick fund bd. 1990—), Presidency Rsch. Group (sec., treas. 1989-93, v.p. 1993—), Phi Beta Kappa. Home: 53 The Strand New Castle DE 19720 Office: Towson State U Dept Polit Sci Towson State U Baltimore MD 21204

KUMIN, LIBBY BARBARA, speech language pathologist, educator; b. Bklyn., Nov. 11, 1945; d. Herbert H. and Berniece (Shuch) K.; m. Martin J. Lazar, Jan. 18, 1969; 1 child, Jonathan Kumin. BA summa cum laude, LIU, 1965; MA, NYU, 1966, PhD, 1969. Lic. speech pathologist, Md.; cert. clin. competence in speech-lang. pathology. Asst. prof. speech pathology U. Md., College Park, 1972-76; cons., 1976-80; adj. prof. Loyola Coll., Balt., 1976-80, assoc. prof., 1980-88, chmn. dept. speech and lang. pathology, 1983—, prof., 1988—; specialist in speech and language in Down Syndrome; mem. profl. adv. bd. Nat. Down Syndrome Cong; mem. Speech/Lang./Hearing Commn., Howard County Bd. Edn., Columbia, Md., 1982-89. Author: Aphasia, 1978, Communication Skills in Children with Down Syndrom, 1994; editor: Communicating Together; contbr. articles on Down Syndrome, others. Vol. cons. Howard County Office on Aging, 1977-83. Recipient Outstanding Individual of Year award Howard County Assn. Retarded Citizens, Nat. Meritorious Service award Nat. Down Syndrome Congress, 1987. Aaron and Lillie Straus Found. grantee, 1983-89; Columbia Found. grantee; recipient summer research award Loyola Coll., 1983, 91. Mem. Am. Speech/Lang./Hearing Assn. (cert.), Md. Speech and Hearing Assn., ARC, Sigma Tau Delta, Pi Lambda Theta. Office: Loyola Coll Dept Speech Pathology 4501 N Charles St Baltimore MD 21210-2601

KUMIN, MAXINE WINOKUR, author, poet; b. Phila., June 6, 1925; d. Peter and Doll (Simon) Winokur; m. Victor Montwid Kumin, June 29, 1946; children: Jane Simon, Judith Montwid, Daniel David. A.B., Radcliffe Coll., 1946, M.A., 1948. cons. in poetry Library of Congress, 1981-82; elector The Poet's Corner, The Cathedral of St. John the Divine, 1990—. Author: (poems) Halfway, 1961, The Privilege, 1965, The Nightmare Factory, 1970, Up Country, 1972 (Pulitzer prize for poetry 1973), House, Bridge, Fountain, Gate, 1975, The Retrieval System, 1978, Our Ground Time Here Will Be Brief, 1982, The Long Approach, 1985, Nurture, 1989, Looking for Luck, 1992; (novels) Through Dooms of Love, 1965, The Passions of Uxport, 1968, The Abduction, 1971, The Designated Heir, 1974; (essays) To Make A Prairie, 1979, In Deep, 1988, Women, Animals and Vegetables: Essays and Stories, 1994; (short stories) Why Can't We Live Together Like Civilized Human Beings?, 1982; author 20 children's books; contbr. poems to nat. mags. Recipient Am. Acad. and Inst. Arts award, 1989, Levinson award Poetry mag., 1987, The Poets' prize, 1994; fellow Woodrow Wilson, 1979-80, 91-93. Fellow Am. Acad. Poets; mem. Poetry Soc. Am., PEN Am., Authors Guild, The Writers Union. Address: Curtis Brown Assoc 10 Astor Pl New York NY 10003-6903

KUMOR, CHARLOTTE LORRAINNE, library administrator; b. Akron, Colo., Feb. 21, 1936; d. Louis John and Velma Rose (Ireland) Gebauer; m. Leon Joseph Kumor, June 30, 1958; children: Ronald, Maureen Kumor Johnson. BS, Colo. State U., 1957. Dir. Goodall City Libr., Ogallala, Nebr., 1985—. Pres. Grant (Nebr.) Bd. Edn., 1974-86. Named Woman of Yr., Bus. and Profl. Women, Ogallala, 1993. Mem. Nebr. Libr. Assn. Roman Catholic. Office: Goodall City Libr 203 W A St Ogallala NE 69153-2544

KUNCEL, RUTH BOUTIN, psychologist; b. Chgo., Aug. 24, 1945. BA, U. Chgo., 1967, MA, 1970, PhD, 1970. Lic. clin. psychologist, Ill. Rsch. assoc. U. Chgo., 1970-75; sr. rsch. assoc. Internat. Pers. Mgmt. Assn., Chgo., 1975-77; sr. rsch. psychologist Merit Employment Assessment Svcs., Flossmoor, Ill., 1977-84; lectr. Roosevelt U., Chgo., 1974-75; asst. rsch. analyst Leo Burnett, U.S.A., Chgo., 1984-85; rsch. analyst United Way/Crusade of Mercy, Chgo., 1985-89; psychology extern Ill. State Psychiat. Inst., Chgo., 1989-90, U. Chgo. Hosps., 1990-91; psychology intern West Side VAMC, Chgo., 1991-92; clin. psychologist Assocs. in Psych Care-Wheaton, Wheaton, Ill., 1992—; mem. DuPage County Conciliation Program; lectr. dept. psychiatry U. Chgo. Hosps., 1994—; allied health profl. Good Samaritan Hosp., Downers Grove, Ill., 1993—, MacNeal Hosp., Berwyn, Ill., 1993—. Contbr. chpt. to books, articles to profl. jours.; author pers. selection tests. USPHS fellow, 1968-70; U. Chgo. fellow, 1967-68; recipient Woodrow Wilson Letter of Commendation, 1967. Mem. Am. Psychol. Assn., Midwest Neuropsychology Group.

KUNDERT, ALICE E., state legislator; b. Java, S.D., July 23, 1920; d. Otto J. and Maria (Rieger) K. Elem. tchr.'s cert., No. State Coll., Aberdeen, S.D., state tchr. cert. Tchr. elem. grades, 1939-43, 48-54; clk., mgr., buyer Gates Dept. Store, Beverly Hills, Calif., Clifton Dress Shop, Hollywood, Calif., 1943-48; dep. supt. schs. Campbell County, S.D., 1954; county cts. clk., 1955-60, register deeds, 1955-69; town treas. Mound City, 1965-69; auditor State of S.D., Pierre, 1969-79; sec. of state, 1980-87; dir. sch. programs S.D. Dept. Edn. and Cultural Affairs, 1987-89; state rep. State of S.D., 1991—. Leader 4-H Club, 1949-53, county project leader in citizenship, 1963-64; sec. Greater Campbell County Assn., 1955-57; organizer, leader Mound City Craft and Recreation Club, 1955-60; chmn. Heart Fund, March Dimes, Red Cross, Mental Health drs.; mem. S.D. Gov.'s Study Commn., 1968—; mem. state and local adv. com. region VIII Office Econ. Opportunity; bd. mem., chmn. Black Hills Recreation Lab., 1956-61; exec. sec. Internat. Leaders Lab., Ireland, 1963; Polit. co. vice chmn. Rep. Com., 1964-69, sec-treas. fin. chmn., 1968; mem. State Rep. Adv. Com., 1966-68; state and nat. counselor Teen Age Rep. Club Campbell County, 1964—. Named Outstanding Teenage Rep. adv. in nation, 1970, 71, 76; Recipient Disting. Alumni award No. State Coll., 1975. Home: PO Box 67 Mound City SD 57646-0067 Office: Office Sec of State State Capital Bldg Pierre SD 57501*

KUNG, ALICE HOW KUEN, high tech company executive; b. Kowloon, Hong Kong, Nov. 26, 1956; d. Yam Sang and Yuet Shoung (Lew) K. BA in with honors-distinction in Econs., Stanford U., 1978; MBA, Harvard U., 1983. CPA, Calif. Staff auditor audit div. Arthur Andersen & Co., San Francisco, 1978-79, sr. cons. cons. div., 1980-81; cons. strategy mgmt. group Arthur D. Little, Inc., San Francisco, 1982; mgr. customer mktg. Gould AMI Semicondrs., Santa Clara, Calif., 1983-84; product mgr. voice messaging products IBM/Rolm Systems, Santa Clara, 1985-86, market and bus. planning mgr. Far East and L.Am., 1987-89; internat. mktg. dir. Minx Software, Inc., San Jose, Calif., 1989-92; dir. for Asia and Pacific SuperMac Tech., Sunnyvale, Calif., 1992-93; mng. dir. Radius Hong Kong, 1994—; owner Orient Express, Mountain View, Calif., 1986-90. Vol. Harvard Community Ptnrs., Oakland, Calif., 1993. Scholar Harvard U., 1981-83. Mem. Asian Am. Mfrs. Assn., Sources 91 (organizing com., officer 1992), Asian Bus. League, Internat. Bus. Club, Phi Beta Kappa. Democrat. Office: Radius Hong Kong Emperor Group Ctr, 208 Hennessy Rd Unit 2002, Wanchai Hong Kong

KUNICK, PAMELA ELYSE, marketing director; b. Detroit, May 18, 1963; d. Frederick Leonard and Sandra Barbara (Rosenthal) K. BBA with honors, U. Mich., 1985; MBA, Harvard U., 1990. From advt. mgmt. trainee to acct. mgr. Lintas: Campbell-Ewald, Warren, Mich., 1985-88; mktg. cons. Gen. Cinema Theaters, Chestnut Hill, Mass., 1989; asst. mktg. mgr.- dir. mktg. Buena Vista Home Video, Burbank, Calif., 1990—. Grad./participant Leadership Devel. Group of the Jewish Fedn., L.A., 1993; mem. exec. com. Access: The Young Adult Program of the Jewish Fedn. Coun., 1994—. Merit scholar U. Mich. Birmingham Alumni Assn., 1983-85. Democrat.

KUNIN, MADELEINE MAY, federal agency administrator, former governor; b. Zurich, Switzerland, Sept. 28, 1933; came to U.S., 1940, naturalized, 1947; d. Ferdinand and Renee (Bloch) May; m. Arthur S. Kunin, June 21, 1959; children—Julia, Peter, Adam, Daniel. B.A., U. Mass., 1956; M.S., Columbia U., 1957; M.A., U. Vt., 1967; numerous hon. degrees. Newspaper reporter Burlington Free Press, Vt., 1957-58; guide Brussels World's Fair, Belgium, 1958; TV asst. producer Sta. WCAX-TV, Burlington, 1960-61; freelance writer, instr. English Trinity Coll., Burlington, 1969-70; mem. Vt. Ho. of Reps., 1973-78; lt. gov. State of Vt., Montpelier, 1979-82, gov., 1985-91; disting. vis. in Pub. Policy Bunting Inst., Cambridge, Mass., 1991-92, Dartmouth Coll., Hanover, N.H., 1992; deputy sec. of education Dept. Education, Washington, D.C., 1993—; fellow Inst. Politics, Kennedy Sch. Govt., Harvard U., 1983; lectr. middlebury Coll., St. Michael's Coll., 1984; disting. pub. policy visitor Rockefeller Ctr., Dartmouth Coll., 1992; pub. policy fellow Bunitn gInst., Radcliffe Coll., Harvard U., 1991029; Vt. Joint Fiscal Com., 1977-78; mem. exec. com. Nat. conf. Lt. Govs., 1979-80; founder and pres. Inst. Sustainable Communities, Montpelier, Vt., 1990-93. Author: Living a Political Life: A Memoir, 1994, (with Marilyn Stout) The Big Green Book, 1976; contbr. articles to profl. jours., mags. and newspapers. Named Outstanding State Legislator, Eagleton Inst. Politics, Rutgers U., 1975; Montgomery fellow Dartmouth Coll., 1991. Mem. Nat. Gov.'s Assn. (mem. exec com.), Nat. Govs.' Conf. (chair com. on energy and the environ.), New Eng. Gov.'s Conf. (chairperson). Democrat. Office: Office of Dep Sec Edn 400 Maryland Ave SW Washington DC 20202-0001

KUNKEL, BARBARA, psychotherapist, consultant; b. Garfield, N.J., Mar. 17, 1945; d. Everett Edward and Florence Hilda (Davidsen) K.; children: Tasha Jade Decker, Lara Ashley Decker. BA in Psychology and Pre-Theology, Elmira Coll., N.Y., 1966; MA in Human Devel., Fairleigh Dickinson U., 1983; PhD in Transpersonal Psychology and Alcholism Studies, Union Inst., 1988; grad. Postdoctoral Tng. Program N.E. Soc. Group Psychotherapy, 1993. Mgmt., human relations cons. pvt. practice, N.J., Mass., Maine, N.Y., 1983—; co-founder, psychologist Carr Counseling, Waltham, Mass., 1989—, teacher of A Course in Miracles, 1991—; clk. Supreme Jud. and Superior Cts., York County, Maine, 1985-88; clin. supr. Mass. Correctional Inst., Shirley, Mass., 1992-93; cons. Ctr. for Addictive Behaviors, Inc., Salem, Mass., 1988-91; mem. faculty Nasson Coll., Springvale, Maine, 1986-87. Teaching fellow Fairleigh Dickinson U., 1983-84. Recipient Beyond Excellence award, 1993. Mem. Am. Psychol. Practitioners Assn. (founding mem.), Am. Acad. Healthcare Provides in Addictive Disorders, Northeastern Soc. for Group Psychotherapy (affiliate mem.). Avocations: carpentry, photography, study Krishnamurti, furniture restoration. Home: 264 Delaware Dr Narrowsburg NY 12764 Office: Carr Counseling 371 Moody St Ste 102 Waltham MA 02154-5208

KUNKEL, GEORGIE MYRTIA, writer, retired school counselor; b. Chehalis, Wash.; d. George Riley and Myrtia (McLaughlin) Bright; m. Norman C. Kunkel, Apr. 25, 1946; children: N. Joseph D.C., Stephen Gregory, Susan Ann, Kimberly Jane Waligorska. BA in Edn., Western Wash. U., 1944; MEd, U. Wash., 1968. Typist, clk. FHA, Seattle, 1940; tchr. pub. schs. Vader, Centralia, Wash., Seattle, 1941-67; pvt. cons., Seattle, 1970—; counselor Highline Pub. Schs., Seattle, 1967-82; sch. counselor rep.

State of Art Conf., Balt., 1980. Editor Women and Girls in Edn., 1972-75. Author 3 Grandma Mini-books; contbr. articles to profl. jours. Organizer Women and Girls in Edn., Wash. state, 1971; pres. Wash. State NOW, 1973; mem. West Seattle Community Council, 1980. Grantee Women Adminstrs. Wash. State, 1971, Edn. Service Dist., Seattle, 1980. Mem. NEA (sec. pub. relations), Am. Assn. Counseling and Devel. (pres. state br. 1982-83), Am. Sch. Counseling Assn. (pres. state div. 1980-81), Seattle Counselors Assn. (organizer, past pres. office exec., Counselor of Yr. 1990), Holmes Harbor Homeowners Assn. (organizer and pres.), West Seattle C. of C., Past Pres. Club (Seattle), West Seattle Dem. Women's Club (pres.). Unitarian Universalist. Club: Past Presidents (Seattle). Avocation: singing. Home and Office: 3409 SW Trenton St Seattle WA 98126-3743

KUNKEL, REBECCA ANNE, mental health nurse; b. Evansville, Ind., Nov. 18, 1950; d. John Tapley and Mildred Louise (Tummin) Brown; m. Michael James Kunkel, June 13, 1970; children, Andrew Michael, Kristine LeAnne. LPN, Sch. of Health Occupations, 1970; AS in Nursing, U. Evansville, 1981, BSN, 1989. RN, Ind.; LPN. Staff nurse Deaconess Hosp., Evansville, 1969-71, 1972-82; charge nurse Bethel Manor, Evansville, 1971-72; nurse St. Mary's Med. Ctr., Evansville, 1982-88; nurse, office mgr. Dr. Romulus B. Thomas, Evansville, 1988-92; nurse mgr. Arbor Hosp. of Evansville, 1992-93, dir. health care coordination, 1993-95; nursing supr. behavioral health scis. Jasper (Ind.) Meml. Hosp., 1995—. Roman Catholic. Office: Jasper Meml Hosp 900 9th St Jasper IN 47546

KUNS, NANCY LEE, office manager, pharmacist; b. Ashtabula, Ohio, Apr. 16, 1960; d. Frank Joseph Nappi Jr. and Wanda Gay (Britton) Mackey; m. Bryan P. Kuns, July 30, 1983; children: Kaitlyn, Brianne, Derek. BS, U. Toledo, 1983. Office mgr. Kuns Family Medicine, Inc., Castalia, Ohio, 1987—; pharmacist Firelands Community Hosp., Sandusky, Ohio, 1989-91, Walmart Pharmacy, Sandusky, 1991—. Com. chmn. Aux. to 5th Dist. Ohio Osteo. Assn., 1990—, treas., 1987-90, pres., 1991-93, v.p., 1993—. Mem. Ohio Pharmacists' Assn., N.W. Ohio Hosp. Pharmacists, Ohio Soc. Hosp. Pharmacists, Beta Sigma Phi (v.p. Xi Iota Eta chpt. 1990-91, pres. 1994—). Roman Catholic. Home: 6105 Deyo Rd Castalia OH 44824-9741

KUNSMAN, CYNTHIA LOUISE MULLEN, critical care nurse; b. Allentown, Pa., Sept. 29, 1966; d. Donald Lee and Phyllis Ann (Herbert) Mullen; m. Gary Wayne Kunsman, May 5, 1990. ASN, Gwynedd-Mercy Coll., Gwynedd Valley, Pa., 1986; BSN, Gwynedd-Mercy Coll., 1987; MMin, Chesapeake Bible Seminary, 1994; ND, Clayton Sch. Natural Healing, 1995. CCRN. Staff nurse oncology/urology med./surg. Lehigh Valley Hosp. Ctr., Allentown, 1986; staff nurse PCCU Lehigh Valley Hosp. Ctr., 1987-88, staff nurse ICU, 1989; staff nurse MICU La. State U., Shreveport, La., 1990-91; asst. head nurse cardiovascular svcs. HCA Presbyn. Hosp., Oklahoma City, 1992-93; staff nurse cardiothoracic ICU U. Md., Balt., 1993—; prof. biological sci. Chesapeake Bible Coll., 1993—; staff nurse cardio thoracic ICU U. Md. Med. Sys., 1993—. Author: (book) Arrhythmia Interpretation: A Guide for Nurses, 1991; contbr. articles to profl. jours. Mem. Pa. Nurses Assn. (chair nominations com. local dist. 1988-90), AACN, Orgn. for the Advancement of ASN, Ctr. for Bioethics and Human Dignity.

KUNSTADTER, GERALDINE SAPOLSKY, foundation executive; b. Boston, Jan. 6, 1928; d. Harry Herman and Nettie Sapolsky; m. John W. Kunstadter, Apr. 23, 1949; children: John W., Lisa, Christopher, Elizabeth. Student, MIT, 1945-48. Draftsman U. Chgo. Cyclotron Project, 1948; engring. asst. Gen. Electric Corp., Lynn, Mass., 1948-49; pres. Capricorn Investments Corp., 1971—; chmn., dir. A. Kunstadter Family Found., N.Y.C., 1966—; host family program dir. N.Y.C. Commn. for UN, 1971-86; pres. Nat. Inst. Social Scis., 1979-81. Bd. dirs. Friends of N.Y.C. Commn. for UN and Consular Corps, Bridge to Asia Found., Menninger Found., Topeka, Nat. Com. on U.S.-China Rels., Yale-China Assn., Feld Ballets, N.Y.C., Ctr. U.S.-China Arts Exch., Inst. World Affairs, Am. Forum; mem. resource coun. Ptnrs. of Ams., Washington; mem. adv. coun. East Asian studies program MIT Sch. Architecture; mem. Peace Links Leadership Network, Nat. Coun. Women (internat. hospitality com.), Overseas Devel. Coun., Atlantic Coun., N.Y.-Beijing Friendship City Com. Recipient Windham award, 1970, silver medal Nat. Inst. Social Sci., 1981. Mem. Inst. Current World Affairs, Coun. on Fgn. Rels., Am. Women's Club, Hurlingham Club, Lansdowne Club (London).

KUNTZ, LILA ELAINE, secondary business education educator; b. Decorah, Iowa, July 13, 1931; d. Arthur Lloyd and Alice Elene (Thompson) Dahle; m. Darrell Wayne Kuntz, Dec. 26, 1959 (div. 1979); 1 child, Barbara Lynn. BA, Luther Coll., 1954; postgrad., U. Iowa, 1957-58, U. Minn., 1961-75, Mankato State Coll., 1966-76. Cert. tchr., Minn. Tchr. business Flat Rock (Mich.) High Sch., 1954-55, Springville (Iowa) High Sch., 1955-58, Spring Lake Park (Minn.) High Sch., 1958-60, Lincoln High Sch., Bloomington, Minn., 1961-70, Jefferson High Sch., Bloomington, 1970—. Rep. del., Edina, Minn., 1979-95; active Norwegian-Am. Mus., Decorah, Iowa, 1987—. Mem. NEA, Minn. Edn. Assn., Minn. Bus. Edn. Assn., Bloomington Edn. Assn., Delta Pi Epsilon. Lutheran. Home: 5221 Abercrombie Dr Edina MN 55439-1466 Office: Jefferson High Sch 4001 W 102nd St Bloomington MN 55437-2699

KUNTZ, MARION LUCILE LEATHERS, classicist, historian, educator; b. Atlanta, Sept. 6, 1924; d. Otto Asa and Lucile (Parks) Leathers; m. Paul G. Kuntz, Nov. 26, 1970; children by previous marriage: Charles, Otto Alan (Daniels). BA, Agnes Scott Coll., 1945; MA, Emory U., 1964, PhD, 1969. Lectr. Latin Lovett Sch., Atlanta, 1963-66; mem. faculty Ga. State U., 1966—, assoc. prof., 1969-73, prof. Latin and Greek, 1973—, Regents' Prof., 1975—, chmn. dept. fgn. langs., 1975-84, research prof., 1984—, Fuller E. Callaway disting. prof., 1985—, alumni disting. prof., 1994. Author: Colloquim of the Seven About Secrets of the Sublime of Jean Bodin, 1975, Guillaume Postel, Prophet of the Restitution of All Things: His Life and Thought, 1981, Jacob's Ladder and the Tree of Life: Concepts of Hierarchy and the Great Chain of Being, 1987, Postello, Venezia e Il Suo Mondo, 1988; also scholarly articles; mem. editorial bd. Library of Renaissance Humanism. Named Latin Tchr. of Yr. State Ga., 1965; Semple scholar, 1965, Am. Classical League scholar, 1966, Gladys Krieble Delmas scholar, 1991; Am. Coun. Learned Socs. grantee, 1970, 73, 76, 81, 87, 90; recipient medal for excellence in Renaissance studies Pres. of Coun. Gen., Tours, France, 1995. Mem. Am. Philol. Assn., Renaissance Soc. Am. (coun. 1994—), Am. Soc. Aesthetics, Am. Cath. Philos. Assn., Soc. for Values in Higher Edn., Philosophy and Religion, Am. Soc. Ch. History, Am. Histo. Assn., Internat. Soc. Neo-Platonic Studies, Internat. Soc. Neo-Latin Studies, Soc. Christian Philosophers (mem. exec. bd. 1987—), Société des Seiziémistes, Medieval Acad., Société de Culture Européenne, Soc. Medieval and Renaissance Philosophy (mem. exec. bd. 1988—), Soc. di Philosophique Medievale, Archaeol. Inst. Am., Classical Assn. Midwest and South (Semple award 1965), Am. Acad. Rome (sec.-treas. 1970-74), Friends of the Vatican Libr., Italian Cultural Soc., Nat. Trust Hist. Preservation, DeKalb Hist. Soc. (v.p. 1977-80), Hellenic Study Club (pres. Atlanta 1974), Atlanta Preservation Soc., Ga. Trust for Hist. Preservation, Atlanta Hist. Soc., High Museum of Art (patron), Friends of the Warburg Inst., World Monuments Fund, Phi Beta Kappa, Phi Kappa Phi, Omicron Delta Kappa. Roman Catholic. Home: Villa Veneziana 1655 Ponce De Leon Ave Atlanta GA 30307 also: Dorsoduro, 714 Venice Italy

KUNTZ, MARY M. KOHLS, corporate treasurer; b. Chgo., Nov. 25, 1928; d. George William and Myrtle Hansen K.; m. Earl Jeremy Kuntz, July 28, 1957; children: Karen A., Bradford G. Student, Northwestern U., 1946-50. Pvt. practice acctg. Chgo., 1951-63; owner Chgo. Tax Service, 1954-63; controller Gen. Bus. Services, Chgo., 1960-68; v.p., treas. Gen. Tele-Communications, Inc., Chgo., 1968—. Leader Girl Scouts U.S., 1968-71; pres. Wilmette (Ill.) PTA, 1971-75. Mem. Assn. Telemessaging Svcs. Internat., Nat. Soc. Pub. Accts., Chgo. Soc. Clubs, Women's Club Wilmette (bd. dirs. 1975). Office: Gen Tele-Communications Inc 69 W Washington St Chicago IL 60602-3004

KUNZ, MARGARET MCCARTHY, realtor; b. Woodbury, N.J.; m. Lyle Bernard Kunz, July 31, 1965; children: Carolyn Louise, Elizabeth Anne, Paul Bernard. BA, U. Miami, 1957; MSW, Tulane U., 1962. Realtor Byrne-Rinehart & Co., South Miami, Fla., 1990—. Past pres., bd. mem. The Villagers, Inc., Miami; bd. dirs. Theatre Arts League, Miami. Mem. Miami Bd. Realtors, Med. Faculty Assn. U. Miami (bd. dirs.), Women's Guild U. Miami, Powerhouse Miami. Home: 7245 SW 142nd Ter Miami FL 33158-1610

KUNZE, DOLORES JOHANNA, veterinarian; b. Waltham, Mass., Mar. 29, 1950; d. John Herman and Dorothy (Angiulo) K.; m. Morrow Bradford Thompson, Mar. 20, 1976 (div. 1985). BS in Agriculture, U. Ga., 1972, DVM, 1976; MS, Mich. State U., 1980. Lic. veterinarian, N.C., S.C. Resident large animal dept. Coll. Vet. Medicine, Mich. State U., Lansing, 1977-80, asst. prof. vet. medicine, 1980-81; asst. prof. vet. medicine N.C. State U., Raleigh, 1981-84; staff veterinarian Aiken (S.C.) Animal Hosp., 1985-87, East Side Vet. Clinic, Spartanburg, S.C., 1987-88; pvt. practice Boiling Springs Animal Clinic, P.A., Inman, S.C., 1988—; bd. dirs. Spartanburg Vet. Emergency Clinic, sec., 1990-91, pres., 1994—. Contbr. articles to profl. publs., 2 chpts. to books. Mem. AVMA, S.C. Vet. Med. Assn., Phi Zeta (Zeta chpt.). Presbyterian. Home: PO Box 16014 Spartanburg SC 29316 Office: Boiling Springs Animal Clin 4370 Hwy 9 Inman SC 29349

KUPCINET, ESSEE SOLOMON, performing arts producer; b. Chgo., Dec. 7; d. Joseph David and Doris (Schoke) Solomon; m. Irv Kupcinet, Feb. 12, 1939; children: Karyn (dec.), Jerry S. PhB, Northwestern U., 1937. Asst. to dir. psychology dept. Michael Reese Hosp., Chgo., 1939-41; exec. producer eight Jefferson Award Shows; producer 1st Literary Arts Ball, Cultural Center, Chgo., 1979; talent coordinator Kup's Show, Chgo., 1964-84; producer for spl. events, 1978—. Mem. adv. bd., bd. dirs. Free St. Theater; prodn. chmn. Acad. Honors, 1984-87; chmn. bd. trustees Acad. Sch. Performing Arts, 1984-86, hon. lifetime chair, 1986—; prodn. chmn. Variety Club Telethon, 1984, 85; bd. dirs. Mus. Broadcasting Commn.; exec. com. Chgo. Tourism Coun., 1984-88; exec. bd. Internat. Theatre Festival, 1985-86; mem. sponsors com. Chgo. Pub. Libr., 1985-86; co-founder Chgo. Acad. Arts. Decorated Knight of Orange Nassau (The Netherlands); recipient Spl. award Jefferson Com., 1976; Cliff Dwellers award, 1975; Emmy award CBS, 1977, 79; Artisan award Acad. Theatre Arts and Friends, 1977; Prime Minister's medal for service to Israel, 1974; Woman of Yr. award Facets Multimedia, 1982, Mass Media award NCCJ, 1988, others; named (with Irv Kupcinet) Mr. and Mrs. Chgo., Greater North Michigan Ave. Assn., 1987, Chgo. Acad. for the Arts, 1988, Woman of Yr., Variety Club #26, 1988; honored by Mus. Brekest, Conn., 1989; honored (with Irv Kupcinet) 10th Anniversary Chgo. Acad. for Arts, 1992. Mem. NATAS (governing bd., program chmn. 1982-91, Govs. awards 1986, 91), Arts Club. Jewish.

KUPFERSCHMID, MARY S., librarian; b. Berwyn, Ill., Apr. 19, 1940; d. George Franklyn and Arline Elizabeth (Carlsten) Wahl; m. Frank Goodale Stearns, Aug. 26, 1961 (div. Aug. 1985); children: Laura Christine, Katherine Arline, David Kenneth; m. Steven W. Kupferschmid, Oct. 12, 1985. BA in Econs., Brown U., 1961; MS in Libr. Sci., Villanova U., 1977. Librarian Wissahickon Valley Pub. Libr., Ambler, Pa., 1977-79; librarian, head of interlibr. loan Bethlehem (Pa.) Area Pub. Libr., 1979—. Mem. Pa. Libr. Assn., Pa. IDS Bd. Dirs. (v.p. 1987-92), Phi Beta Kappa, Phi Kappa Phi. Home: 401 1st Ave Bethlehem PA 18018 Office: Bethlehem Area Pub Libr 11 W Church St Bethlehem PA 18018

KUPPERMAN, HELEN SLOTNICK, lawyer; b. Boston; d. Morris Louis and Minnie (Kaplan) Slotnick; B.A., Smith Coll.; postgrad. Royal Acad. Dramatic Art, London; J.D., Boston Coll., 1966; m. Robert H. Kupperman, Dec. 23, 1967; 1 dau., Tamara. Bar: Mass. 1966, D.C. 1986. Atty., advisor NASA, Washington, 1966-73, sr. atty., 1973-77, asst. gen. counsel for gen. law, 1977-86, assoc. gen. counsel, 1986, spl. asst. gen. counsel space station, 1986-87, chairperson contract adjustment bd., 1974-87, exec. v.p. Robert H. Kupperman & Assocs. Inc., 1987—; adj. fellow space policy study Ctr. Strategic and Internat. Studies, 1987-88; rep. on U.S. delegation to legal subcomittee of UN Com. on Peaceful Uses of Outer Space, 1977-87. Recipient NASA Sustained Superior Performance award, 1977, Exceptional Service medal, 1983, NASA Ses Bonus, 1980, 85, Space Station Task Force Group Achivement award NASA, 1984. Mem. U.S. Assn. of Internat. Inst. Space Law (sec. 1981, bd. dirs. 1989—), ABA, Fed., Mass., D.C., Boston bar assns., Internat. Women Lawyers Assn., Am. Astronautical Assn. (gen. counsel 1986-87). Jewish. Bus. editor Boston Coll. Indsl. and Comml. Law Rev., 1965-66. Home: 2832 Ellicott St NW Washington DC 20008-1019

KUPST, MARY JO, psychologist, researcher; b. Chgo., Oct. 4, 1945; d. George Eugene and Winifred Mary (Hughes) K.; m. Alfred Procter Stresen-Reuter Jr., Aug. 21, 1977. BS, Loyola U., 1967, MA, 1969, PhD, 1972. Lic. psychologist, Ill., Wis. Postdoctoral fellow U. Ill. Med. Ctr., Chgo., 1971-72; rsch. psychologist Children's Meml. Hosp., Chgo., 1972-89; assoc. prof. psychiatry and pediatrics Northwestern U. Med. Sch., Chgo., 1981-89; prof. pediatrics Med. Coll. Wis., Milw., 1989—; practice clin. psychology, Chgo., 1975-89, McHenry, Ill., 1987-89. Editor: (with others) The Child with Cancer, 1980; contbr. articles to profl. jours. Mem. APA, Wis. Psychol. Assn., Soc. Pediatric Psychology. Office: Med Coll Wis Dept Pediatrics 8701 W Watertown Plank Rd Milwaukee WI 53226-4801

KURAS, JEAN MARY, educator; b. Jersey City, Jan. 30, 1944; d. Stanley Richard and Ann (Tyra) K. BA, N.J. State Tchrs. Coll., 1960, MA, 1966. Tchr. Bloomfield (N.J.) Bd. Edn., 1962—. Pres. Big Bros.-Big Sisters Essex and Newark, Bloomfield, 1982-84, Bloomfield Hist. Soc., 1981—; vol. office staff Senator Bradley, N.J., 1984; trustee League for Family Svc., Bloomfield, 1988—, v.p., 1990-94. Art for Kids grantee Sta. WOR-TV, N.J., 1990. Mem. NEA, N.J. Edn. Assn., Essex County Edn. Assn., Bloomfield Edn. Assn. (sec. 1987-90, v.p. 1990—). Home: 11 Hawthorne Ave Glen Ridge NJ 07028-2010 Office: Oak View Sch 150 Garrabrant Ave Bloomfield NJ 07003-4510

KURCZYNSKI, ELIZABETH MICKELSEN, pediatrician; b. Mpls., Apr. 6, 1943; d. Olaf and Edith L. (Nielsen) Mickelsen; m. Thaddeus W. Kurczynski, June 22, 1963 (div. Oct. 1979); children: Peter, Karen. BS, U. Wis., 1964; MD, Case Western Res. U., 1968. Diplomate Am. Bd. Pediatrics, Am. Bd. Hematology/Oncology. Intern Univ. Hosp., Cleve., 1968-69, resident, 1969-70; resident, fellow in hematology/oncology U. Mich., Ann Arbor, 1970-73; instr. pediatrics Mott Childrens Hosp., Ann Arbor, Mich., 1973-74; asst. prof. pediatrics Albert Einstein Med. Sch., N.Y.C., 1974-76, Case Western Res. Sch. Medicine, Cleve., 1976-80; dir. pediatrics Kaiser Found. Hosp., Parma, Ohio, 1980-85; physician-in-charge Permanente Med. Group, Atlanta, 1985-88; dir. pediatric hematology/oncology Med. Ctr., Atlanta, 1988—; dir. comprehnsive hemophilia ctr. Scottish Rite Childrens Med. Ctr., Atlanta, 1988—, responsible investigator children's cancer group, 1990—. Fellow Am. Acad. Pediatrics; mem. Am. Soc. Hematology, Am. Soc. Clin. Oncology, Am. Soc. Pediatric Hematology/Oncology. Office: Scottish Rite Childrens Med Ctr 5455 Meridian Mark Rd NE Atlanta GA 30342-1613

KUREK, DOLORES BODNAR, physical science and mathematics educator; b. Toledo, Dec. 14, 1935; d. James J. and Veronica Clara (Gorajewski) Bodnar; m. Arnold John Kurek, Aug. 30, 1958; children: Kerry, Darrah, Michele, James, Ursula. BS, Mary Manse Coll., 1958; MEd, U. Toledo, 1968, doctoral candidate. Chemistry, physics and math. tchr. St. Ursula Acad., Toledo, 1961-75; sci. tchr. McAuley High Sch., Toledo, 1975-78; chemistry tchr. St. Francis de Sales High Sch., Toledo, 1978-83; instr. math. and chemistry Owens Tech. Coll., Toledo, 1980-86; instr. chemistry, physics and astronomy Lourdes Coll., Sylvania, Ohio, 1983-86, assoc. prof. phys. sci., 1986—; instr. math. U. Toledo, 1986—; pres., chmn. judging, co-dir. N.W. Dist. Sci. Day, Toledo, 1975—; regional dir. Women of Sci., Toledo, 1987—; bd. dirs. Toledo Jr. Sci. Humanities Symposium, Toledo; dir. Copernicus Planetarium, Lourdes Coll., 1990—; v.p. edn. Tech. Soc. Toledo, 1989—; pres. Tech. Found. Toledo, 1991—; dir. field-based earth sci. program for mid. sch. tchrs. grant Ohio Bd. Regents, 1992. Inventee in field; contbr. articles to profl. jours. Mem. Toledo Mus. of Art, 1987—, Toledo Zool. Soc., 1988—. Grantee Internat. Conf. on Chem. Edn., 1994; Mary Manse scholar, 1954-58; named One of 100 Women Sci. Exemplars in Ohio, Women in Sci., Engring. and Math. Consortium Ohio, 1988, Woman of Toledo, St. Vincent Med. Ctr., 1988; recipient award for tchg. excellence and campus leadership Sears Roebuck Found., 1991. Mem. Am. Chem. Soc. (James Conant Bryant award 1980, 81), Ohio Acad. Sci. (Acker award 1980), Nat. Sci. Tchrs. Assn., Soc. for Coll. Sci. Tchrs., Am. Assn. Physics Tchrs., Mensa, Astron. Soc. Pacific, Gt. Lakes Planetarium Assn., Phi Delta Kappa (newsletter editor 1984-86). Roman Catholic. Home: 624 Arcadia Ave Toledo OH 43610-1108 Office: Lourdes Coll 6832 Convent Blvd Sylvania OH 43560-2898

KUREPA, ALEXANDRA, mathematician; b. Zagreb, Yugoslavia, Dec. 31, 1956; came to U.S., 1985; d. Svetozar and Zora (Lopac) K.; m. Rodney Anthony Waschka II, June 24, 1988; children: Andre Kurepa Waschka, Lana Kurepa Waschka. BS, U. Zagreb, 1978, MS, 1982; PhD, U. North Tex., 1987. Asst. prof. math. U. Zagreb, 1987-88, Tex. Christian U., Ft. Worth, 1988-93, N.C. A&T State U., Greensboro, 1993—. Author: Matematica 2, 1989; contbr. articles to profl. jours. Rsch. grantee UNESCO, 1988, 89. Mem. Am. Math. Soc., Math. Assn. Am., Assn. for Women in Math. Office: NC A&T State U Dept Math Greensboro NC 27411

KURIANSKY, JUDY, television and radio talk show host, reporter, psychologist, writer, lecturer; b. N.Y.C., Jan. 31, 1947; d. Abraham and Sylvia (Feld) Brodsky; m. Edward Kuriansky, Aug. 24, 1969. BA, Smith Coll., 1968; MEd, Boston U., 1970; PhD, NYU, 1980. Reporter Sta. WABC-TV, N.Y.C., 1980-82, Sta. WBZ-TV, Boston, 1981-82, Sta. WCBS-TV, 1982-86, CBS-TV, N.Y.C., 1986-88, Sta. WPIX-TV, N.Y.C., 1987-89, Sta. CNBC-TV, Ft. Lee, N.J., 1989—; host Total Wellness for Women program Sta. WDBB-TV, Birmingham, Ala., 1988-89; program host Sta. WABC-AM, N.Y.C., 1980-87, Sta. WOR-AM, 1987-88; temp. program host ABC Talk Radio, N.Y.C., 1988-90; host Modern Satellite Network, 1981; TV host J.C. Penney Golden Rule Network, Dallas, 1988-90; feature contbr. Attitudes Show LifeTime, 1992—; host Love Phones Sta. WHTZ Radio, N.Y.C., 1992—; cons. Lily of France, Val Mode Lingerie, Charles of the Ritz, The Rolland Co., Taylor-Gordon Arons Advt., Clairol; tchr. Columbia U. Med. Sch., 1974-79, Inst. for Health and Religion, 1980-82; adj. prof. psychology NYU, 1989-90; judge Most Unforgettable Women contest Revlon, 1990; therapy coord. Nat. Inst. for Psychotherapists, 1977-79; therapist Ctr. for Marital and Family Therapy, 1986—; v.p. Quezon Corp., 1978-79; sr. rsch. scientist N.Y. State Psychiat. Inst., 1970-78; lectr. Blanton Peale Inst., 1979-81. Author: Sex, Now That I've Got Your Attention, Let Me Answer Your Questions, 1984, How to Love a Nice Guy, 1990, Italian and Japanese translations; columnist Family Circle mag., 1984-89, Whole Life Times, 1986-87, King Features Newspaper, 1984-86, N.Y. and L.I. Newsday, 1993—; writer New Woman, Ad Age, Boardroom Reports, Am. Advt. Fedn. mag., Chgo. Tribune Woman News; contbg. editor Beauty Mag., 1989-90. Bd. dirs. Scientists Com. for Pub. Info., 1977-79; mem. adv. bd. N.Y. City Self Help Orgn., 1983-85; mem. benefits com. Mental Health Svcs. for Deaf, 1980-82. Recipient Civilian Commendation, N.Y.C. Police Dept., 1984, Cert. for Unique Pub. Svc., AWRT, 1984, Maggie award Planned Parenthood, 1985, 93, Freedoms Found. award Children for a Better Soc., 1986, Olive award Coun. of Chs., 1986, Mercury award Larimi Communications, 1987. Fellow Am. Psychol. Assn.; mem. Am. Women in Radio and TV (pres. N.Y. chpt. 1988-89, nat. found. vice chair 1988-90—), Soc. Sex Therapy and Rsch. (charter) TV Acad. of N.Y. (gov. 1987—), Friars Club. Office: CNBC 244 W 72nd St Apt 14D New York NY 10023-2815

KURIC, JUDI LYNN POPPLEWELL, clinical nurse specialist, consultant; b. Muncie, Ind., Aug. 31, 1961; d. Charlie D. and Berniece Marie (Fowler) Popplewell; m. Steven P. Kuric, May 22, 1982; children: Katelyn, Kyle. BSN, Ind. U., Indpls., 1983; MSN, Wayne State U., 1990. Cert. critical care nurse, rehab. nurse, neuro nurse. Staff nurse Detroit Receiving Hosp.; system coord. S.E. Mich. Spinal Cord Injury System, Detroit; clin. nurse specialist/cons. Evansville, Ind.; coor. continuing edn. U. So. Ind. Contbr. articles to profl. jours. Mem. ANA, AACN, Am. Assn. Spinal Cord Injury Nurses (bd. dirs. 1986-91, pres. 1989-90), Am. Assn. Neurol. Nurses (chmn. health policy com. 1989-91), Assn. Rehab. Nurses (founding pres. Heartland chpt., nat. nominating com. 1994—), Nat. Spinal Cord Injury Assn. (bd. dirs. 1985-89, exec. com. bd. dirs. 1987-89, sec.-treas. S.E. Mich. chpt. 1985-87), Am. Spinal Injury Found. (bd. dirs. 1988-90), Nat. Fedn. Splty. Nursing Orgns. (v.p. 1990, pres. 1991), Sigma Theta Tau. Home: 8450 Remington Dr Evansville IN 47711-6321

KURITA, DEBRA LYNN, city official; b. Salt Lake City; d. Ikuya and Rosemary (Baer) K.; m. Keene N. Wilson, Oct. 1, 1983; 1 child, Skyler E. Ba in Polit. Sci., U. Calif., Davis, 1976; MPA, U. So. Calif., 1981. Adminstrv. intern small bus. L.A. Mayor's Office, 1979-80; with mcpl. svcs. dept. City of Lawndale, Calif., 1980-81; adminstrv. specialist fin. dept. City of Torrance, Calif., 1981-84; adminstrv. asst. I and II community devel. agy City of Santa Ana, Calif., 1984-86, mgr. adminstrv. svcs., 1986-89, asst. city mgr., 1989—. Mem. Am. Soc. Pub. Adminstrn., Mcpl. Mgmt. Assts. So. Calif. (treas. 1984-85). Office: City of Santa Ana 20 Civic Center Plz # 25M Santa Ana CA 92701-4023

KURTZ, CAMILLE LOUISE, medical nurse; b. Ottawa, Ont., Can., Aug. 2, 1959; came to U.S., 1982; d. Emile Joseph and Georgette Rita Proulx Latreille; m. William John Kurtz, Mar. 20, 1982. BSN, Ottawa U., 1981; MA in the Orgnl. Nurse Exec. Role, Columbia U., 1991. Cert. BLS instr. ARC. Staff nurse neurosurgery Ottawa Civic Hosp., 1981-82; staff nurse spl. care Norwalk Conn. Hosp., 1983-84; founder, pres. Fgn. Nurses Assn. of Japan, Tokyo, 1987-88; asst. dir. nursing Homestead Health Ctr., Stamford, Conn., 1988-89; homedialysis program coord. Dialysis Assocs., Stamford, 1990-92; transplant coord. N.Y. Regional Transplant Program, 1992-93, dir. donor svcs., 1993-94, dir. planning and devel., 1994—. Scholar dept. nursing edn. Tchrs. Coll., Columbia U., 1991. Mem. ANA, Am. Nephrology Nurses' Assn., Fgn. Nurses Assn. in Japan (guest spkr. 1991), Sigma Theta Tau. Home: 69 Toilsome Ave Norwalk CT 06851-2421

KURTZ, DOLORES MAY, civic worker; b. Reading, Pa., Oct. 27, 1933; d. Harry Claude and Ethel Gertrude (Fields) Filbert; m. William McKillips Kurtz, Oct. 26, 1957. Cert. secretarial program, Pa. State U., 1980. Legal sec. Snyder, Balmer & Kershner, Reading, 1951-53; head teletype operator E.I. duPont de Nemours, Reading, 1953-56; exec. sec. Ford New Holland (Pa.) Inc. (formerly Sperry New Holland div. Sperry Corp.),, 1956-91, ret., 1991. Mem. Lancaster County Rep. Com., 1983-85; pres. New Holland Area Woman's Club, 1982-84; bd. dirs. Lancaster County Fedn. Women's Clubs, 1982—, 2d v.p., 1984-86, 1st v.p., 1986-88, pres. 1988-90; founding mem. Summer Arts Festival, New Holland, 1980—, bd. dirs., 1985-91; membership chmn. S.E. dist. Pa. Fedn. Women's Clubs, 1984-86; bd. dirs. Community Meml. Park Assn., New Holland, 1957-82; area rep., bd. dirs. Woman's Rep. Club Lancaster County, 1982-84; committeewoman New Holland Boro 1983-85; v.p. Lancaster-Lebanon Arthritis Found. Guild, 1992, pres., 1993. Recipient Outstanding Vol. for Pa. award Pa. Fedn. Women's Clubs, 1984. Methodist. Avocations: arts and crafts, travel, photography.

KURTZ, JOAN HELENE, pediatrician; b. N.Y.C., Apr. 23, 1937; d. Joseph G. and Catherine (Jacobs) Kurtz; m. Anthony M. Suriano, Oct. 15, 1960; children: Michael J., Anthony C., Catherine M. BA cum laude, NYU, 1958, MD, 1962. Diplomate Am. Bd. Pediatrics. Intern in pediatrics Bellevue Hosp., N.Y.C., 1962-63; resident in pediatrics Bronx Mcpl. Hosp. Ctr., N.Y., 1963-65; pvt. practice Carmel, N.Y., 1965-80; pediatrician Cigna Healthcare of Ariz., Phoenix, 1980—. Recipient Physicians Recognition award AMA. Fellow Am. Acad. Pediatrics; mem. Phoenix Pediatrics Soc., Ariz. Med. Assn., Phi Beta Kappa. Roman Catholic. Office: CIGNA Healthcare 12635 N 42nd St Phoenix AZ 85032-7601

KURTZ, KAREN BARBARA, writer, editor, administrator, consultant; b. Ft. Dodge, Iowa, July 21, 1948; d. Clifford Wenger and Eleanor Marie (Ulrich) Swartzendruber; m. Mark Allen Kurtz, June 25, 1977. AA, Hesston Coll., 1968; BA in Edn., Goshen (Ind.) Coll., 1970; MA in Elem. Edn., Ind. U., 1975. Lifetime cert. elem. tchr. First grade tchr. Fairfield Community Sch., Goshen, 1970-79; asst. editor and advt. copywriter Barth and Assocs., Middlebury, Ind., 1986-87; freelance writer, editor, cons. Kurtz Lens and Pen, Inc., Goshen, 1979-94, pres., 1994—; asst. dir. info. svcs. Goshen Coll., 1987-89; dir. found. rels., 1990-93. Author: Paper, Paint and Stuff, 1984, More Paper, Paint and Stuff, 1989; asst. editor Heritage Country Mag., 1986-87; regular contbr. to Doll World; contbr. articles to various mags. Ch. bd. dirs. Goshen City Ch. of Brethren, 1977, 94, also chmn. stewardship dr., coord. art in the ch. Mem. NEA, NAFE, Ind. State Tchr.'s Assn., Fairfield Educators Assn., Soc. Children's Book Writers and Illustrators. Republican.

KURTZ, MAXINE, personnel executive, lawyer; b. Mpls., Oct. 17, 1921; d. Jack Isadore and Beatrice (Cohen) K. BA, U. Minn., 1942; MS in Govt. Mgmt., U. Denver, 1945, JD, 1962; postdoctoral student, U. Calif., San Diego, 1978. Bar: Colo. 1962; U.S. Dist. Ct., Colo., 1992. Analyst Tri-County Regional Planning, Denver, 1945-47; chief rsch. and spl. projects Planning Office, City and County of Denver, 1947-66, dir. tech. and evaluation Model Cities Program, 1966-71; pers. rsch. officer Denver Career Service Auth., 1972-86, dir. pers. svcs., 1986-88, sr. pers. specialist, 1988-90; pub. sector pers. cons., 1990—, atty., 1990—; expert witness nat. com. on urban problems U.S. Ho. of Reps., U.S. Senate. Author: Law of Planning and Land Use Regulations in Colorado, 1966; co-author: Care and Feeding of Witnesses, Expert and Otherwise, 1974; bd. editors: Pub. Adminstrn. Rev., Washington, 1980-83, 88-92; editorial adv. bd. Internat. Pers. Mgmt. Assn.; prin. investigator: Employment: An American Enigma, 1979. Active Women's Forum of Colo.; Denver Dem. Com.; chair Colo. adv. com. to U.S. Civil Rights Commn., 1985-89, mem. 1989—. Sloan fellow, U. Denver, 1944-45; recipient Outstanding Achievement award U. Minn., 1971, Alumni of Notable Achievement award, 1994. Mem. ABA, Am. Inst. Planners (sec. treas. 1968-70, bd. govs. 1972-75), Am. Soc. Pub. Adminstrn. (nat. council 1978-81, Donald Stone award), Colo. Bar Assn., Denver Bar Assn., Order St. Ives., Pi Alpha Alpha. Jewish. Home: 2361 Monaco Pky Denver CO 80207-3453 Office: 2361 Monaco Pky Denver CO 80207-3453

KURTZ, ROBIN SUE, psychologist; b. Boston, May 4, 1960; d. Joseph Ronald and Hinda Rosalyn (Weener) Kurtz; m. Gilbert F. Rivera, Oct. 24, 1992. BA, Boston U., 1982; MA, U. West Fla., 1986; EdD, North Ariz. U., 1992. Lic. psychologist, Ala., Ariz. Counselor drug and alchohol USN, Pensacola, Fla., 1983-85; instr. No. Ariz. U., Flagstaff, 1988-92; psychologist Auburn (Ala.) U., 1992—; cons. Bay Area Health Clinic, Pensacola, 1983-84; residential counselor Lakeview Ctr., Pensacola, 1983-84; instr. Coconino C.C., Flagstaff, 1991-93; presenter in field. Mem. APA, Am. Coun. Exercise, Nat. Dance Exercise Instr. Tng. Assn., Soc. Clin. and Exptl. Hypnosis, Boston U. Alumni Band, Phi Beta Phi (advisor). Home: 803 Choctaw Ave Auburn AL 36830 Office: Auburn U Drake Health Ctr Auburn AL 36849

KURTZ, SWOOSIE, actress; b. Omaha; d. Frank and Margo (Rogers) K. Student, Acad. Music and Dramatic Arts, London, U. So. Calif. Appeared on TV series Mary, 1978, Love, Sidney, 1981-83, Sisters, 1991—(Emmy award nominee for Lead Actress in Drama, 1993, 94, SAG award nominee for Lead Actress in Drama 1995); TV specials include Uncommon Women and Others, Ah, Wilderness!, Fifth of July, The House of Blue Leaves, The Visit, Walking Through the Fire, The Mating Season; TV films include Guilty Conscience, A Time to Live, Terror on Track 9, Baja, Oklahoma, The Image, The Positively True Adventures of the Alleged Texas Cheerleader-Murdering Mom, And the Band Played On (Emmy award nominee for Supporting Actress in Special, 1994, Ace award nominee), Truman Capote's One Christmas, Betrayed; TV guest appearances on Kojak, Carol and Company (Emmy award); film appearances include Slap Shot, 1977, The World According to Garp, 1982, Against All Odds, 1984, Wild Cats, 1986, True Stories, 1986, Vice Versa, 1988, Bright Lights, Big City, 1988, Baja, Oklahoma, 1988, Dangerous Liaisons, 1988, Stanley and Iris, 1989, A Shock to the System, 1989, The Image, 1989, Reality Bites, 1994; theatrical appearances include: Ah, Wilderness!, 1975, Tartuffe, 1977, A History of the American Film, 1978 (Drama Desk award), Fifth of July, 1980-81 (Tony award, Drama Desk award, Outer Critics Circle award), Michael Bennett's Scandal, 1985, The House of Blue Leaves, 1986 (Tony award, Obie award), The Effect of Gamma Rays on Man in the Moon Marigolds, Uncommon Women and Others, 1977 (Obie award), Who's Afraid of Virginia Woolf?, 1980, Children, 1976, Summer, 1980, Beach House, 1986, The Middle Ages, 1980, Hunting Cockroaches, 1987 (Drama Logue award), Love Letters, 1989, Lips Together, Teeth Apart, Six Degrees of Separation. Recipient Emmy award Outstanding Guest Performer in Comedy or Drama series. Office: The Sterling/Winters Co Agy for the Performing Arts 9000 Sunset Blvd West Hollywood CA 90069 Address: Agency for the Peforming Arts 900 Sunset Blvd. West Hollywood CA 90069

KURTZE, CRYSTAL CATHERINE, creative director; b. Sioux City, Iowa, Dec. 30, 1949; d. Lowell Emery and Frances Mary (Gasink) G.; m. John Wiliam Kurtze, Sept. 18. 1969; Div. 1972; 1 Child: Jennifer Kurtze. Student, Wayne State Coll., 1968-69; BFA, Morningside Coll., Sioux City, Neb., 1972-75. Artist Fairall & Co., Sioux City, 1972-74; advt. mgr. Tompkins Constrn., Sioux City, 1974-78; prin. Crystal Kurtze Advt., South Sioux City, Iowa, 1978-81, Creative Design & Mktg., Valley, Nebr., 1981-87; gen. mgr. Meta Mktg., Omaha, 1987-91, owner, pres., 1991—. Creative dir. Eagle Window, 1988 (Addy and Merit award 1988); contbr. articles to profl. jours. Mem. Am. Soc. Advt. and Promotion, C. of C., Omaha Press Club. Republican. Methodist. Office: Ste 430 7905 L St Omaha NE 68127

KURZ, CAROLYN JANE HEPPLER, medical society executive; b. Owensboro, Ky., Dec. 1, 1946; d. Leonard Allen and Beverly Euleen (Miller) Heppler; m. James Arthur Kurz, May 9, 1987. Student, U. Ky., 1964-66, 72-80, U. Md., 1967, 69, George Washington U., 1969-70. Asst. comptroller Sears, Roebuck & Co., Owensboro, 1965-67; sec. DOD Schs., Seoul, People's Republic of Korea, 1968; asst. to fin. mgr. Am. Soc. Microbiology, Washington, 1968-69; adminstrv. asst. George Washington U., Washington, 1969-70; v.p., chief exec. officer Fayette County Med. Soc., Lexington, Ky., 1971—; mem. Ky. Medicare Adv. Com., 1992—. Mem. ethics and edn. com. Better Bus. Bur., 1990—. Mem. Am. Assn. Med. Soc. Execs. (chmn. CAE task force 1993-94, chmn. profl. execellence task force 1994—), Greater Lexington C. of C., Am. Soc. Assn. Execs. (cert.), Congressman Hopkins Woman's Conf. (mem. adv. com. Lexington chpt. 1988, mem. steering com. 1989-92), Congressman Hopkins Srs. Conf. (steering com. Lexington chpt. 1989, Ky. Woman 90, Ky. Woman 94, exhibits chair). Office: Fayette County Med Soc 2628 Wilhite Dr Lexington KY 40503-3302

KURZWEIL, BETTE GRAYSON, lawyer; b. Newark, July 10, 1947; d. Sidney and Joan (Rosenman) Grayson; children: Jeremy Scott, Cynthia Joan. BA in History with honors, NYU, 1969; JD, Bklyn. Law Sch., 1977. Bar: N.J. 1977. Tchr. Newark Bd. Edn., 1969, Boston Bd. Edn., 1970-71; social worker Mt. Sinai Hosp., N.Y.C., 1971-74; pvt. practice Springfield, N.J.; mem., chmn. Fee Arbitration in Union County, Union, N.J., 1984-92. V.p. membership program Hadassah, Millburn, N.J., 1985-89. Mem. Women Lawyers in Union County (treas., sec., v.p., pres. 1980-92), Union County Bar Assn. (activities com. 1984-89). Office: 155 Morris Ave Springfield NJ 07081

KURZWEIL, EDITH, sociology educator, editor; b. Vienna; d. Ernest W. and Wilhelmine M. (Fischer) Weiss; m. Charles H. Schmidt, June 24, 1945 (div. 1958); children: Ronald J., Vivien A.; m. Mr. Kurzweil, Aug. 2, 1958 (dec. 1966); 1 child, Allen J. B.A., Queens Coll., CUNY, 1967; M.A., New Sch. Social Rsch., 1969, Ph.D., 1973. Asst. prof. sociology Hunter Coll., N.Y.C., 1972-75, Montclair State Coll., Upper Monclair, N.J., 1973-78; assoc. prof. sociology Rutgers U., Newark, 1979-85, prof. sociology, chmn., 1985-92; Disting. Olin. Prof. Adelphi U., 1993, univ. prof., 1994—; vis. prof. Goethe U., 1984. Author: The Age of Structuralism, 1980, Italian Entrepreneurs, 1983, The Freudians: A Comparative Perspective, 1989, Freudians and Feminists, 1995; editor: (with others) Literature and Psychoanalysis, 1983, Writers and Politics, 1983, Cultural Analysis, 1984; exec. editor Partisan Rev., Boston, 1978-94, editor, 1994—. Rockefeller Humanities fellow, 1982-83, NEH fellow, 1987-88; NEH grantee, 1989-90, 91-92. Mem. Am. Sociol. Assn., Tocqueville Soc., Internat. Assn. History of Psychoanalysis, Internat. Sociol. Assn., Women's Freedom Network (bd. dirs. 1994), P.E.N. Home: 1 Lincoln Plz New York NY 10023 Office: Partisan Review 236 Bay State Rd Boston MA 02215-1403

KUSCH, KELLY ANN, educator; b. Chgo., Jan. 8, 1966; d. Gregory R. and Marilyn (Wetterstrom) K.; m. Larry D. Kavanagh III, Mar. 24, 1990; 1 child, Madeline Y. BA & BS, U. Chgo., 1987; MEd, Xavier U., 1989. Cert. tchr. Ohio, Ky. Tchr. Greek, Latin Covington (Ky.) Latin Sch., 1990—; volleyball coach Covington Latin Sch., 1992—. Vol. publicity chair, edn. chair Friends of Cin. Art Mus., 1989—. Mem. Am. Classical League, Cin. Area Tchrs. Classics, NOW.

KUSEK, CAROL JOAN (JOAN KUSEK), genealogist, publisher, distribution executive; b. Ottawa, Kans., Feb. 1, 1955; d. Ronald Eugene and Veda Doris (Geiss) Elliott; m. Gary Gerard Kusek, Sept. 10, 1977; children: Jacquelyn Ruth, David Michael. Student, Johnson County Community Coll., Overland Park, Kans., 1973-76, 88. Cert. geneal. records specialist. Office mgr. Lenexa (Kans.) Animal Hosp., 1973-82; journeyman, sign painter Elliott Custom Signs, Overland Park, 1982-92; owner Kusek Geneal. Svcs., Overland Park, 1985—; instr. Johnson County Community Coll., Overland Park, 1989—; researcher; contbr. gen. publs. Contbr. articles to geneal. publs. Mem. Johnson County Geneal. Soc. (pres. 1991-92), Assn. of Profl. Genealogists. Home: 9640 Walmer St Shawnee Mission KS 66212-1554

KUSHEN, BETTY SANDRA, writer, educator; b. N.Y.C., Nov. 8, 1933; d. Moses and Betty (Cohen) Cohen; m. Allan Stanford Kushen; children: Annette Joyce, Robert Allan. BEd, U. Miami, 1954; MA, NYU, 1959, PhD, 1969. Author: (biography) Virginia Woolf and The Nature of Communion; assoc. editor Jour. Evolutionary Psychology; contbr. articles to Early Am. Lit., Lit. and Psychology, Am. Imago, Am. Writers Before 1800, Jour. Evolutionary Psychology. Mem. MLA, Virginia Woolf Soc. Jewish. Home: One Raynor Rd West Orange NJ 07052

KUSHMAUL, JANET F., social welfare coordinator; b. Marion, Ohio, Feb. 15, 1939; d. John Garold and Nellie Mae (Foos) Benge; m. Thomas Richard Kushmaul, July 28, 1962; children: Thomas Richard Jr., Timothy Alan, Daniel Lee. BS, Wittenberg U., 1967; MS, Wright State U., 1988. Tchr. elem. sch. New Carlisle-Bethel Dist., Clark County, Ohio, 1960-65; substitute tchr. Mad River Green Dist., Clark County, 1975-77; coord. leader tng. La Leche League Internat., Springfield, Ohio, 1972-79; sec. Highlands United Ch. of Christ, Springfield, 1977-79, Wittenberg U., Springfield, 1981-83; dir. edn. Planned Parenthood WCO, Springfield, 1984-88; program coord. Early Intervention, Clark County, 1988-91, Parents and Children Together, Clark County, 1991—; mem. Child Protection Team, Springfield, 1993—; chair Cluster Adv. Coun., Springfield, 1989-92, Headstart Health Adv., Springfield, 1988-91, Teenage Pregnancy Prevention, Springfield, 1985-89. Activist Metro Ministry, Springfield, 1975-85; grad. Springfield Leadership Acad., 1991. Mem. ACA, Midwest Ohio Counseling Assn. (pres. 1989-90), Ohio Counseling Assn. (bd. dirs. 1989-90), Am. Mental Health Counselors, Ohio Mental Health Counselors, World Assn. for Infant Mental Health, Zero to Three Nat. Ctr. for CLin. Infant Programs, Zonta Internat. (bd. dirs. 1989-92). Democrat. Home: 5400 Penny Pike Springfield OH 45502 Office: Parents & Children Together 206 O'Connor Ln Springfield OH 45504

KUSHNER, AILEEN, medical/surgical nurse; b. Bklyn., Jan. 26, 1947; d. Harold and Gloria (Ostrofsky) Jarashow; divorced; Michelle, Adam, Brad. AS, SUNY, Farmingdale, 1983; postgrad., SUNY, Stony Brook, 1988-89, student, 1993—; student, Adelphi U., 1990-91, SUNY Regents Coll., 1993—. RN, N.Y. Staff nurse medicine, surgery Nassau County Med. Ctr., East Meadow, N.Y., 1983-89, med. head nurse, 1989—. Home: 3042 Lowell Ave Wantagh NY 11793-3221

KUSHNER, EVA, academic administrator, educator, author; b. Prague, Czechoslovakia, June 18, 1929; d. Josef and Anna (Kafkova) Dubsky; m. Donn Jean Kushner, Sept. 15, 1949; children: Daniel Peter, Roland Joseph, Paul Joel. B in Philosophy, Coll. Marie de France, Montreal, 1946; BA, McGill U., 1948, MA, 1950, PhD in French Lit., 1956; D (hon.), Acadia U., 1988, United Theol. Coll., 1992, St Michael's U., 1993. Lectr. French McGill U., Montreal, 1952-55, instr. French, 1956, 58, 61-62, 67-69, prof. French lang. and lit., 1976-87, chair dept. French, 1976-80; pres., vice chancellor Victora U. U. Toronto, 1987-94, dir. ctr. comparative lit., 1994—; sessional lectr. philosophy Sir George Williams U., 1952-53; lectr. U. Coll., London, 1958-59; lectr. Carleton U., 1961; asst. prof. French & comparative lit., 1963, assoc. prof., 1965, prof., 1969-76, chmn. comparative lit., 1965-69, 70-72, 75-76, adj. prof. lit., 1976-79; mem. exec. com. Can. Coun., 1975-81; v.p. Social Scis. & Humanities Rsch. Coun. Can., 1983-86; mem. adv. bd. Nat. Libr. Can.; pres. Humanities Rsch. Coun. Can. 1970-72; vice-chmn. George R. Gardiner Mus. Ceramic Arts, 1990-94. Author: Patrice de La Tour de Pin, 1961; Le mythe d'Orphée dans la littérature française contemporaine, 1961; Chants de Bohême, 1963; Rina Lasnier, collection Ecrivains canadiens d'aujourd'hui, 1964; Poètes d'aujourd'hui, 1969; Saint-Denys Garneau, 1967; François Mauriac, 1972, Japanese transl., 1976; co-author anthology Que. poetry, transl. into Hungarian, 1978, Polish, 1985; editor Renewals in the Theory of Literary History; co-editor/co-author: L'avènement de l'esprit nouveau (1400-80), 1988, Théorie littéraire: problèmes et perspectives, 1989; co-dir. rsch. Renaissance vols. Histoire comparée des littératures de langues européennes; mem. editorial com. Can. Comparative Lit. Rev., Dalhousie French Studies, Etudes Montaignistes; mem. internat. adv. bd. Synthesis, Literary Rsch.; contbr. articles to profl. publs. Fellow Royal Soc. Can. (v.p. 1980-82); mem. Academie Européenne des lettres, des sciences et des arts, Am. Comparative Lit. Assn. (adv. bd.), Internat. Comparative Lit. Assn. (pres. 1979-82, co-editor proc. 7th, 9th, 10th, 11th Congresses, vols. IV-V, 1991, VI, 1992, VII-VIII, 1993, IX 1994), Internat. Fedn. for Modern Langs. and Lits. (v.p. 1987-93), MLA (del. assembly, chmn. 16th century French lit. div., mem. exec. coun. 1983-86, nominating com. 1986-88), Assn. internat. des études françaises, Assn. des profs. de français des univs. canadiennes, Assn. canadienne de littérature comparée (v.p. 1969-71), Internat. Assn. Neo-Latin Studies, Soc. canadienne d'études de la Renaissance, Assn. des littératures canadienne et québecoise, Can. Soc. Semiotic Research. Office: Victoria Coll, 73 Queen's Park, Toronto, ON Canada M5S 1K7

KUSHNER, PAMELA RHODA, family physician, educator; b. N.Y.C., Dec. 15, 1955; d. Joseph and Dolores Kushner; m. Myles Lenhoff (dec. June 1993); children: Maxwell, Samuel. BA and MA in Biology, UCLA, 1979; MD, U. Calif., Irvine, 1983. Lic. physician, Calif., Hawaii, cert. drug enforcement adminstr. Mgr. amino acid chromatography lab. Neuropsychiat. Inst. UCLA, 1977-79; family physician Family Health Plan, Inc., Long Beach, Calif., 1985-86, Hawthorne (Calif.) Med. Group, 1986-87; clin. instr. family medicine U. Calif., Irvine, 1987-90; pvt. practice Long Beach, 1987—; med. dir. Health Care Mgmt. Utilization Rev., 1989—; clin. faculty family medicine program for osteopaths Pacific Hosp., 1989—; asst. clin. prof. family medicine U. Calif., Irvine, 1990—; physician advisor So. Calif. Physician Exch. Ins. Co., 1989—, Calif. Med. Rev., 1989—; chair utilization rev. Palmcrest North Convalescent, 1988-89; chair dept. family practice Long Beach Meml. Med. Ctr., 1990—, mem. utilization rev. com., 1988-91—, chair utilization rev. com., 1991—; del. for Meml. Med. Ctr. AMA-Hosp. Med. Staff Sect., 1992—; staff Millers Children's Hosp., Long Beach, Women's Hosp., Long Beach, Charter Suburban Hosp., Long Beach. Reviewer editorial bd. Family Practice Recert.; contbr. articles to med. jours. Media spokesperson Am. Cancer Soc., L.A. Sta., 1988—, instr. Long Beach bd. dirs. Mem. AMA (alt. del. young physician's sect. 1990-91), Am. Acad. Family Physicians (media spokesperson issues for better health network 1987—, publs. com. 1985-86), Am. Acad. Pediatrics (liaison profl. liability com. 1990-91, profl. liability com. 1986-90), Calif. Med. Assn. (chair tobacco free Calif. com. 1987—, profl. liability com. 1991—, del. 1992—, chair com. resident and community comm. Long Beach chpt. 1988-89, com. health edn. of pub. 1986-88, quality of patient care subcom. 1985-93), Calif. Acad. Family Physicians (new physicians com. 1990-91, Calif. congress dels. 1987—, alt. del. 1986-87, bd. dirs. 1985-86, risk mgmt. com. 1985-89, L.A. chpt. pres. elect 1991—, chpt. sec./treas. 1988-90, chpt. young physicians com. 1987-89, Long Beach chpt. pres. pres. 1991-92, chpt. v.p. 1989-90, chpt. sec./treas. 1988-89), Long Beach Med. Assn. (pres. 1992—, pres. elect 1991-92, chair pub. liaison com. 1990—, bd. dirs. 1987—), L.A. County Med. Assn. (issues task force coun. 1991—, new physician rep. 1990-91, biomed. ethics com. 1989—), Soroptimist Internat. (Woman of Distinction 1994), Phi Delta Epsilon. Office: 2865 Atlantic Ave Ste 207 Long Beach CA 90806-1711

KUSKIN, KARLA, writer, illustrator; b. N.Y.C., July 17, 1932; d. Sidney T. and Mitzi (Salzman) Seidman; m. Charles Kuskin, Dec. 4, 1955 (div. August 1987); children: Nicholas, Julia; m. William L. Bell Jr., July, 1989. Student, Antioch Coll., 1950-53; B.F.A., Yale U., 1955. tchr. cons. schs. at elem. and univ. levels. Author, illustrator: Roar and More, 1956 (A.I.G.A. best children's books), rev. edit., 1990, James and the Rain, 1957, The Animals and the Ark, 1958, In the Middle of the Trees, 1958 (A.I.G.A. best 50 books), Just Like Everybody Else, 1959, Which Horse is William?, 1959, Square as a House, 1960, The Bear Who Saw the Spring, 1961, All Sizes of Noises, 1962, Alexander Soames: His Poems, 1962, (as Nicholas J. Charles) How Do You Get from Here to There?, 1962, ABCDEFGHIJKLMNOPQRSTUVWXYZ, 1963, The Rose on My Cake, 1964, Sand and Snow, 1965, (as Nicholas J. Charles) Jane Anne June Spoon and Her Very Adventurous Search for the Moon, 1966, The Walk the Mouse Girls Took, 1967, Watson, the Smartest Dog in U.S.A., 1968, In the Flaky Frosty Morning, 1969, Any Me I Want to Be: Poems, 1972, What Did You Bring Me?, 1973, Near the Window Tree: Poems and Notes, 1975, A Boy Had a MOther Who Bought Him a Hat, 1976, Herbert Hated Being Small, 1979, Dogs & Dragons, Trees and Dreams: A Collection of Poems, 1980, Night Again, 1981, Something Sleeping in the Hall, 1985, Soap Soup, and other verses, 1992, A Great Miracle Happened Here: A Chanukah Story, 1993, Patchwork Island, 1994, City Dog, 1994; illustrator 16 books other authors; author 3 books illustrated by Marc Simont; author: Jerusalem Shining Still, 1987, Soap Soup (Parenting Reading award 1992), A Great Miracle Happened There, 1993 (Parents' Choice Honor Book 1993), Patchwork Island, 1994, (with illustrator Milton Avery) Paul, 1994, City Dog, 1994, City Noise, 1994; contbg. author: The State of the Language, 1980; author: filmstrips What Is Design?, 1971, An Electric Talking Picture, 1972, Karla Kuskin, 1979, Poetry Explained by Karla Kuskin, 1980; contbg. editor: Saturday Review, 1973; author video tapes: A Talk with Karla Kuskin, Poetry for Children, 1991; book reviewer: Record-Poetry Parade; contbr. articles to publs. including, New York mag., House and Garden, N.Y. Times, Wilson Library Bull., Horizon mag. Recipient awards Nat. Coun. Tchrs. English, 1979, awards N.Y. Acad. Scis., 1979, awards New Eng. Book Show, 1961, CBC Showcase award for A Boy Had a Mother Who Bought Him a Hat, 1976, Notable Books awards ALA, 1980, 82, 92, Best Picture Book award for the Philharmonic Gets Dressed, N.Y. Times, 1982, Parents' Choice award book for lit., 1986, Parents' Choice award, 1987; named Outstanding Bklyn. Author 1981. Jewish. Home and Office: 96 Joralemon St Brooklyn NY 11201-4000

KUSLANSKY, LAURIE RACHEL, cognitive psychologist, linguist; b. N.Y.C., Mar. 2, 1955; d. Harry and Rose (Halpern) K. BA in Linguistics, Queens Coll., 1979; MA in Linguistics, Columbia U., 1979, MPhil in Psychology, 1989, PhD in Psychology, 1992. Interpreter, expert witness U.S. Depts. of Justice and the Treasury, Immigration and Naturalization Svc., N.Y. State Supreme Ct., N.Y. and N.J., 1983-93; dir. rsch., trial cons. strategy, witness preparation and jury selection DecisionQuest, Inc., N.Y.C., 1993—; instr. ESL Yeshiva U., 1982-84; tchr. asst. cognitive psychology Tchrs. Coll. Columbia U., 1989; adj. asst. prof. ednl. psychology Manhattan Sch. of Music, 1982-92; cons., trainer in lang., psychology and edn. Sta. WNET-TV, Ednl. Testing Svc./The Coll. Bd., R.A. Assocs., Assessment Systems, Inc., Manhattan Sch. Music. Recipient Cert. of Appreciation Drug Enforcement Adminstrn. U.S. Dept. Justice, 1986, Cert. of Appreciation U.S. Customs Svc., 1989. Mem. APA (law and psychology divsn. 41 1991—), Nat. Assn. Judiciary Interpreters and Translators. Democrat. Office: DecisionQuest Inc 310 Madison Ave Ste 303 New York NY 10017

KUSMA, KYLLIKKI, lawyer; b. Tartu, Estonia, Dec. 8, 1943; came to U.S., 1951, naturalized, 1958; d. August and Helju (Traat) K.; B.F.A., Ohio U., 1966; M.A. (Vets. Rehab. Adminstrn. fellow), Ohio State U., 1967; J.D., Ohio No. U., 1976; M.L.T., Georgetown U., 1980. Bar: Ohio 1977, D.C. 1978. Speech and hearing therapist Lima (Ohio) Meml. Hosp., 1967-70, Tipp City (Ohio) Schs., 1970-74; atty.-adv. Office Chief Counsel, IRS, Washington, 1977-81; v.p., asso. tax counsel Security Pacific Nat. Bank, Los Angeles, 1981-83; ptnr. Brownstein Zeidman & Lore, Washington, 1983—; instr. Wright State U., 1972-76. Author: (with others) Mortgage-Backed Securities Special Update: REMICs, 1988. Vol. local civic, polit. activities; contbr. articles to profl. jours. Mem. ABA, D.C. Bar Assn., Ohio Bar Assn., D.C. Women's Bar Assn., Phi Kappa Phi. Democrat. Office: Brownstein Zeidman & Lore 1401 New York Ave NW Ste 900 Washington DC 20005-2190

KUSSMAN, ELEANOR (ELLIE KUSSMAN), educational superintendent; b. Bklyn., Mar. 17, 1934; d. Mortimer Joseph and Eleanor Mary (O'Brien) Gleeson; m. Karl Kussman, June 30, 1956 (dec. Oct. 1988); children: Katherine Ann, Kristine Sue Kussman MacDonald. BA, Wheaton Coll., Norton, Mass., 1955; MS, LaVerne Coll., Claremont, Calif., 1974. Cert. tchr. K-C.C., cert. in pupil pers. and adminstrn., Calif. Tchr. sci. and math. Norwood (Mass.) Jr. High Sch., 1955-56; tchr. phys. edn. Brawley (Calif.) Union High Sch., 1956-58; tchr. phys. edn. Ctrl. Union High Sch., El Centro, Calif., 1958-74, tchr. health careers, 1974-80, state and fed. project dir., 1980-85; instr. horse husbandry and equitation Imperial Valley Coll., Imperial, Calif., 1974-76; supr. Imperial Valley (Calif.) Regional Occupational Program, 1985—; cons. E.E. Kussman Cons., El Centro, 1992—, Calif. Joint Gender Equity Com., Sacramento, 1991—, State of Calif. Gender Equity, Sacramento, 1986—; instr. program in counseling and guidance U.Calif., Redlands, 1989. Mem. fin. com. United Way, El Centro, 1987-93; sec.-treas. Pvt. Industry Coun., El Centro, 1985—; past sec.-treas. Calif. Regional Occupational Ctrs./Programs, 1986-88. Mem. AAUW, ASCD, Assn. Calif. Sch. Adminstrs. (past local and regional officer), Rotary Internat. (bd. dirs. 1994—), Phi Delta Kappa. Home: PO Box 83 El Centro CA 92244 Office: Imperial Valley ROP 1398 Sperber Rd El Centro CA 92243

KUTNER, JANET, art critic, book reviewer; b. Dallas, Sept. 20, 1937; m. Jonathan D. Kutner, Jan. 15, 1961. Student, Stanford U., 1955-57; BA in English, So. Meth. U., 1959. Asst. dir. Dallas Mus. Contemporary Arts, 1959-61; art critic, book reviewer Dallas Morning News, 1970—; Dallas/Ft. Worth corr. ARTnews Mag., 1975—; arts adv. panel Dallas Mcpls. Libr., 1981-91; adv. bd. Arts Magnet High Sch. of Dallas, 1980-92; mem. adv. com. Sch. Architecture and Environ. Design, U. Tex., Arlington, 1985-87; mem. long range planning com. Dallas Mus. Art, 1985-86; visual arts and architecture adv. panel Tex. Com. on Arts, 1980-82. Contbg. editor Art Gallery Mag., 1971-73; contbr. articles to profl. jours.; juror various art exhbns. Bd. trustees Greenhill Sch., Dallas, 1980-81. Art critic's grantee Nat. Endowment for Arts, 1976-77, art critic's fellow Nat. Gallery Art, 1991—. Mem. Am. Assn. Museums, Dallas Mus. Art, Internat. Coun. Museums, ArtTable. Office: Dallas Morning News Dallas TX 75265

KUTSCHER, KATHLEEN ANN, social welfare administrator, social worker; b. Springfi.ld, Mass., Dec. 1, 1955; d. Henry W. and Gloria R. (Gallegos) Stepanik; m. William Lee Kutscher, Dec. 15, 1979 (div. Dec. 1987). BA in Sociology, U. Colo., 1983; MSW, U. Denver, 1985. Dir. ret. sr. vol. program Vols. of Am., Denver, 1985-86; coord. exceptional family mem. program U.S. Army/Fitzsimons Med. Ctr., Aurora, Colo., 1986-87; coord. state family program Colo. Army N.G., Denver, 1987-89; mgr. family advocacy program U.S. Army, Wildflecken, Germany, 1989-91, dir. army community svc., 1990-91; supervising social worker U.S. Army, Vilseck, Germany, 1991-94; utilization mgr. behavioral health scis. Madigan Army Med. Ctr., Tacoma, Wash., 1994—. Mem. allocation com. Mile High United Way, Denver, 1986-87. Sgt. U.S. Army, 1976-82, ETO. Mem. NASW. Democrat. Roman Catholic. Home: 10907 62d St E Puyallup WA 98372 Office: Madigan Army Med Ctr Tacoma WA 98431

KUVSHINOFF, BERTHA HORNE, painter, sculptor; b. Dungeness, Wash., Aug. 29, 1915; d. Mellon Tobias and Mariamagdalena (Volnagel) Horne; m. Nicolai V. Kuvshinoff. Represented in numerous mus., pvt. and pub. collections, including Evansville (INd.) Art Mus., Miami Mus. Modern Art, Seattle Art Mus., World's Fair, Seattle, 1962-63; exhibited in group and one-woman shows in France and England. Recipient Diploma of Merit of Univ. of Arts, Univ. Delle Arti, Rome, Italy. Studio: 121 1/2 Yale Ave N Seattle WA 98109

KUYKENDALL, PATRICIA MCCRAW, accountant, consultant; b. West Point, Miss., Oct. 11, 1958. AA in Acctg., Richland Coll., 1985; BA in Acctg., Mgmt., U. Tex., Dallas, 1987. CPA, Tex. Assoc. Coopers & Lybrand, Dallas, 1988-90; sr. internal auditor E Sys., Dallas, 1990-91; mgr. acctg. Fox Meyer, Carrollton, Tex., 1991-94; CFO, cons. Computer Sys. Authority, Dallas, 1994—. Chancel choir Univ. Park Meth. Ch., Dallas, 1988—; mem. Richland Coll. Acctg. Edn. Adv. Com., Dallas, 1989—. Mem. AICPAs, Tex. State Soc. CPAs (Dallas chpt.).

KUYPER, JOAN CAROLYN, foundation administrator; b. Balt., Oct. 22, 1941; d. Irving Charles and Ethel Mae (Pritchett) O'Connor; m. L. William Kuyper, Dec. 20, 1964; children: Susan Carol, Edward Philip. BA in Edn., Salisbury State U., 1963; postgrad. Columbia U., 1978; MA in Arts Mgmt. and Bus., NYU, 1988. Elem. sch. tchr. Prince Georges County Schs., Md.,

1963-68; free lance singer, opera, oratorio, chamber music Amato Opera, N.Y.C., 1967-80; owner, mgr. Privette Artists' Registry, Placement Service for Singers, Teaneck, N.J., 1969-78; exec. dir. Teaneck Artists Perform-Chamber Music Series, 1975-80; program dir. Vols. in Arts & Humanities, Vol. Bur. Bergen County, N.J., 1978-81; dir. Bergen Mus. Art and Sci., 1981-83; cons. Am. Soc. Prevention Cruelty to Animals, 1984, Am. Council for the Arts, 1987; dir. ops. Isabel O'Neil Found. and Studio, 1984-85. Dir. vol. services March of Dimes Birth Defects Found. of Greater N.Y., 1985-88; dir. chpt. devel. Huntington's Disease Soc. Am., 1988-91; bd. dirs Pro Arte Chorale and adv. bd. on the arts, Teaneck, 1976-81; mgmt. cons. mid-size cities Girl Scouts U.S., 1992—. Mem. N.Y. Soc. Assn. Execs. (membership com. 1991-94), Am. Soc. Assn. Execs. (cert. 1992), Assn. Mus., Mus. Coun. N.J., Am. Mktg. Assn. (bd. dirs. 1990—), Assn. for Vol. Adminstrn. (author handbook). Democrat. Presbyterian. Clubs: Altrusa (bd. dirs. 1984-86, 90—, pres. 1986-88), P.E.O., Phi Alpha Theta. Home: 345 W 58th St Apt 14X New York NY 10019-1142 also: 1275 Pebble Beach Rd Tobyhanna PA 18466-9119

KUZIOR, LINDA E., safety engineer; b. Springfield, Ohio, Dec. 28, 1963; m. Kenneth J. Kuzior, Dec. 19, 1987. BE in Chem. Engrng & Chemistry, Youngstown State U., 1987. Lab. technician Electrochems., Youngstown, Ohio, 1987-88; sales engr. Struthers Wells, Inc., Warren, Pa., 1988-90; project engr. Gilbert/Commonwealth, Library, Pa., 1991-92; safety engr. Gilbert/Commonwealth, Library, 1992—; cons. Redex Industries, Inc., Salem, Ohio, 1990-92. Vol. Pitts. Energy Tech. Ctr. Sci. Bowl, 1992-93. Republican. Roman Catholic. Office: Gilbert Commonweath Inc PO Box 618 Library PA 15129-0618

KUZNESOF, ELIZABETH ANNE, history educator. BA, U. Wash., 1961, MA, 1968; PhD, U. Calif., Berkeley, 1976. Vis. prof. history U. Kans., Lawrence, 1976-77, asst. prof. history, 1977-80, assoc. prof., 1980-85, prof., 1985—, assoc. prof. history, 1981-87, prof. history, 1987—, dir. L.Am. studies, 1992—. Author: Household Economy and Urban Development in Sao Paulo 1765 to 1836, 1986; guest editor, author Jour. Family History, 1985; contbr. articles to profl. jours. Numerous fellowships and grants NEH, 1980, 91, Social Sci. Rsch. Coun., 1991-92, Fulbright/S.Am. Today Grant, 1986, Fulbright Tchg. Rsch. Grant to Brazil, 1988, Tinker, John Carter Brown Libr., Hall Found. for Humanities, 1985-86, Utah Eccles Fellowship, 1991-92. Office: Univ of Kansas Ctr Of Latin Am Studie University Of Kansas KS 66045

KWIK-KOSTEK, CHRISTINE IRENE, physician; b. Lvov, Poland, Sept. 12, 1939; d. Karol Stanislaus and Leonarda Fryderica (Seniuk) Kostek; widowed; children: Catherine, Christine. Grad. summa cum laude, Med. Acad. Cracow, Poland, 1956-62; student primary aerospace medicine course, Brooks AFB, Tex., 1985; student chief of profl. staff course, Sheppard AFB, Tex., 1988. Diplomate Am. Bd. Emergency Medicine; cert. Bd. Internal Medicine, Poland; cert. Ednl. Coun. Fgn. Med. Grads.; recert. Extended Allergy Care Provider. Intern. Med. Acad. Cracow, Poland, 1962-63; residency in internal medicine II-Clinic of Internal Diseases, Cracow, Poland, 1963-66, staff mem., 1966-69; gen. med. officer Gen. Hosp., Sokoto, Nigeria, 1969-72; intern. Frankford Hosp., Phila., 1972-73; house physician Holy Redeemer Hosp., Meadowbrook, Pa., 1973-74; emergency room physician John F. Kennedy Hosp., Phila., 1974-76, emergency room dir., 1976-78; commd. capt. USAF Med. Corps, 1978, advanced through grades to col., 1993; emergency room and primary car physician USAF Clinic, Ramstein, West Germany, 1978-81; officer in charge Emergency Room and Gen. Practice Clinic, Peterson Field, Colo., 1981-84; primary care physician Malcolm Grow Med. Ctr., Andrews AFB, Md., 1984-88; chief clinic svcs. 63d Med. Group/SGH, Norton AFB, Calif., 1988-93; staff physician 60th Med. Group, Travis AFB, Calif., 1993—; asst. tchr., sr. asst. tchr. Inst. Descriptive Anatomy, Cracow, 1963-69; emergency physician on call First Aid Sta., Cracow, 1966-69. Fellow Am. Coll. Emergency Physicians; mem. AMA, Am. Coll. Emergency Physicians, World Med. Assn., Am. Coll. Physician Execs. Office: 60th Med Group DGMC Travis A F B CA 94535

KWONG, KATY MEI-KUEN, school bilingual guidance counselor, association executive; b. Hong Kong, Feb. 24, 1964; Came to U.S., 1979; d. Jones Siu-Fu and Wai Ping (Ng) K. BA in Engrng. and Econs., Brown U., 1986; MA in Bilingual Edn., U. Mass., 1991. Chinese bilingual tchr. Malden (Mass.) Pub. Schs., 1986-93, bilingual guidance counselor, 1993—; ind. workshop facilitator, 1986—. Mem. Human Rights Adv. Coun., 1992-93, Healthy 2000 Steering Com., 1993, Asian Am. Civil Rights Task Force, 1993—; organizer Conf. Asian Pacific Am. Youth, 1993; pres., bd. dirs. YWCA Malden, 1993—. Recipient Multicultural Recognition award Commonwealth Mass., 1992. Mem. Mass. Assn. Bilingual Edn., Mass. Asian Am. Edn. Assn. (v.p.), Coalition for Asian Pacific Am. Youth (adv. coun. 1994—). Democrat. Home: 12 Noble St Malden MA 02148 Office: YWCA 54 Washington St Malden MA 02148

KYLE, CORINNE SILVERMAN, management consultant; b. N.Y.C., Jan. 4, 1930; d. Nathan and Janno (Harra) Silverman; m. Alec Kyle, Aug. 29, 1959 (div. Feb. 1969); children: Joshua, Perry (dec.), Julia. BA, Bennington Coll., 1950; MA, Harvard U., 1953. Assoc. editor Inter-Univ. Case Program, N.Y.C., 1956-60; co-founder, chief editor Financial Index, N.Y.C., 1960-63; rsch. analyst McKinsey & Co., N.Y.C., 1963-64; sr. rsch. assoc. Mktg. Sci. Inst., Phila., 1964-67; founding ptnr. Phila. Group, 1967-70; sr. assoc. Govt. Studies and Systems, Phila., 1970-72, cons. program planning and control, Phila., 1972-78, sr. assoc. Periodical Studies Svc., 1978-81; v.p., dir. rsch. Total Rsch. Corp., Princeton, N.J., 1981-82; mgr. social rsch. The Gallup Orgn., Princeton, 1982-86; v.p., Response Analysis Corp., 1986-91; dir. rsch. Gallup Internat. Inst., 1991—; lectr. rsch. methods Temple U., 1981-82; vis. prof. Fairleigh Dickinson U., 1990-91, 93; dir. Verbena Corp., N.Y.C. Contbr. numerous articles to profl. publs. Mem. adv. coun. to 8th Dist. city councilman, Phila., 1971-79; mem. 22d Ward Dem. Exec. Com., 1971-78, State Dem. Com., 1974-76; mem. Pa. Gov.'s Council on Nutrition, 1974-76; v.p. Miquon Upper Sch. Bd., Phila., 1977-78; trustee Princeton Regional Scholarship Found., 1982-85, pres., 1984-85; mem. bd. edn. Princeton Regional Sch. Dist., 1984-93, pres. 1987, 89; mem. exec. bd. Mercer County (N.J.) Sch. Bds. Assn., 1987-92, v.p., 1991-92; v.p. Princeton Community Dem. Orgn., 1992—; mem. Princeton Regional Planning Bd., 1994—. Mem. Am. Polit. Sci. Assn., Am. Assn. for Pub. Opinion Rsch. Home: 156A Spruce St Princeton NJ 08542

KYLE, GENE MAGERL, merchandise presentation artist; b. Phila., Oct. 11, 1919; d. Elmer Langham and Muriel Helen (Magerl) K. Student Center for Creative Studies, Detroit, 1938-45. Mdse. presentation artist D. J. Healy Shops, Detroit, 1946-50, Saks Fifth Ave., Detroit, 1950-58, J.L. Hudson Co., Detroit, 1958-84; freelance merchandise presentations for windows, Grosse Pointe, Mich., 1989—; tchr. workshop classes. Exhibited in group shows at Mich. Water Color Soc., 1944, 53, 74, Mich. Artists Exhbn., 1962, 64, Scarab Club, 1948, 49, 52, Detroit Artists Market, 1946—, Michigan Gallery, 1989, 90, 91, 92, Coach House Gallery, 1980, 90, Cmty. House, Birmingham, Mich., 1993-94. Vol. presentation work. Recipient various art awards. Mem. Detroit Inst. Arts Founders Soc., Mich. Water Color Soc., Windsor Art Gallery.

KYLE, PENELOPE WARD, state administrator, lawyer; b. Hampton, Va., Aug. 6, 1947; d. Lanny Astor and Penelope (Ward) K.; m. Charles L. Menges, Oct. 10, 1981; children: Kyle Ward, Penelope Whitley, Patricia Lee. BA, Guilford Coll., 1969; postgrad., So. Meth. U., 1969-71; JD, U. Va., 1979; MBA, Coll. William & Mary, 1987. Bar: Va. 1979, U.S. Ct. Appeals (4th cir.) 1979. Asst prof. Thomas Nelson C.C., Hampton, 1970-76; assoc. McGuire, Woods Battle & Boothe, Richmond, Va., 1979-81; assoc. counsel CSX Realty, Inc., Richmond, 1981-83, asst. v.p. and asst. to pres., 1987-89, v.p., 1989-92; asst. corp. sec. CSX Corp., Richmond, 1983-87, v.p., 1993-94; exec. dir. Va. Lottery, Richmond, 1994—. Trustee Hist. Richmond Found., 1983-94, 1st v.p., 1987-89, pres., 1989-91, chmn., 1991-93; bd. visitors James Madison U., Harrisburg, Va., 1984-92; mem. Port of Richmond Commn., 1985-94; bd. dirs. Ctrl. Richmond Assn., 1988—, vice chmn., 1991-93, chmn., 1993—; mem. Indsl. Devel. Authority City of Richmond, 1990-94, vice chmn., 1991-93, chmn., 1993-94; bd. mem. Richmond Childrens Mus., 1992—, Cornerstone Real Estate Investment Trust, 1993—; commr. Richmond Devel. and Housing Authority, 1994—. Mem. ABA, Va. Bar Assn. (pres. young lawyers conf. 1984-85, mem. coun. 1984-85), Richmond Bar Assn., Jr. League Richmond, Bear and Bull Club (bd. dirs. 1986-89, sec. bd. dirs. 1987-88), The Country Club of Va. Home: 4706 Charmian Rd Richmond VA 23226-1706 Office: Va Lottery 901 E Main St Richmond VA 23219

KYMAN, WENDY, sex therapist, health educator; b. N.Y.C., Mar. 29, 1947; d. Jack and Tess (Starman) K.; 1 child, Jesse. BS, CCNY, 1968; MS, Bklyn. Coll., 1971; PhD, NYU, 1984. Diplomate, cert. sex therapist and educator Am. Bd. Sexology. Tchr. N.Y.C. Bd. Edn., 1968-74; coord., supr. YWCA Women's Ctr., 1977-78; instr. health edn. SUNY, Old Westbury, 1980-81; instr. allied health SUNY, Nanuet, 1982; family planning counselor NYU Health Svc., N.Y.C., 1984; asst. prof. health edn. CUNY Hunter Coll., 1984-85; sr. pub. health educator Gouverneur Hosp., 1984-87; asst. prof. health edn. CUNY Baruch Coll., 1985—; pvt. practice sex therapy and sex educator, cons., N.Y.C.; teaching fellow NYU, 1980. Contbr. articles to profl. jours. Profl. Staff Congress of CUNY rsch. grantee, 1988-89. Mem. Am. Assn. Sex Educators, Counselors and Therapists (cert. sex educator), Nat. Coun. Women in Medicine, Am. Pub. Health Assn., Nat. Women's Health Network. Home: 272 6th Ave Brooklyn NY 11215-2547 Office: CUNY Baruch Coll 17 Lexington Ave New York NY 10010

KYRIAKOU, LINDA GRACE, communications executive; b. N.Y.C., Dec. 5, 1943; d. Frank T. and Dolores Helen (Coscia) Lagamma; m. Konstantinos G. Kyriakou, May 7, 1967; 1 child, Christina Elena. BA, Hunter Coll., 1965. Acct. exec., dir. rsch. Booke and Co., N.Y.C., 1969-75; mgr. pub. rels. CIT Fin. Corp., N.Y.C., 1975-79; dir. corp. comm. Sequa Corp., N.Y.C., 1979-88, v.p. corp. comm., 1988—. Recipient Twin award, 1985. Mem. Pub. Rels. Soc. Am., Nat. Investor Rels. Inc. (bd. dirs. 1981-82), Women's Bond Club N.Y. (bd. govs. 1978-80). Office: Sequa Corp 200 Park Ave New York NY 10166

KYTE, BONNIE (FRANCES ANN), realtor; b. Washington, May 24, 1944; d. Homer and Irene Margaret (Lynch) Grizzard; div.; children: Cynthia Ann, James Ronald. AA, Montgomery Coll., 1964; BA, U. Md., 1966. Social worker Montgomery County Dept. Social Svcs., Rockville, Md., 1966-69; from travel agt. to mktg. specialist USAIR Travel Agy., 1970-88; realtor RE/MAX Choice, Fairfax, Va., 1987—; owner, fashion cons. Working Woman Affordable Silks, Fairfax, 1985-87; dir. child care program Pr. Wm. County Dept. Social Svcs., Manassas, Va., 1982-87; chair, bd. dirs. No. Va. Assn. Realtors Housing Opportunities Found., 1991—. Advisor, vol. Women's Ctr., Vienna, Va., 1988—; election bd. officer, Fairfax, 1990—; vol. Am. Heart Assn., Nat. Diabetes Found., 1990—. Recipient oratorical award Am. Legion, Wheaton, Md., 1958. Mem. Prince William C. of C. (membership dir. 1987-88), Va. Assn. Realtors (cmty. resdl. com. 1991), No. Va. Assn. Realtors (conv. com. 1991), Homeowners Assn. (archtl. review com. 1988-89), Va. Assn. Female Execs. (treas. 1989-90), Nat. Assn. Profl. Saleswomen, New Beginnings, Parents Without Ptnrs., YWCA (ann. conf. chair 1987), AAUW (pres. Manassas chpt. 1982-84, chair internat. affairs com. 1980-82), Bus. and Profl. Women (ways and means com. 1985-87). Roman Catholic. Office: RE/MAX Choice 10511 Braddock Rd Ste A Fairfax VA 22032-2242

KYTE, LYDIANE, botanist; b. L.A., Jan. 6, 1919; d. Aurele and Helen Scott (Douglas) Vermeulen; m. Robert McClung Kyte, June 2, 1939; children: Katherine Liu, Bobbin Cave, William Robert Kyte. BS, U. Wash., 1964. Supt. Weyerhaeuser Co., Rochester, Wash., 1972-77; lab mgr. Briggs Nursery, Olympia, Wash., 1977-80; owner Cedar Valley Nursery, Centralia, Wash., 1980—; cons. Internat. Exec. Service Corps, Brazil, 1987, Egypt, 1990. Author: Plants From Test Tubes: An Introduction to Micropropagation, 1983, 2d rev. edit., 1988. Mem. Internat. Plant Propagators' Soc., Tissue Culture Assn., Internat. Assn. Plant Tissue Culture, Am. Assn. for Hort. Sci., Am. Assn. Univ. Women. Home and Office: Cedar Valley Nursery 3833 Mcelfresh Rd SW Centralia WA 98531-9510

LA, ANNE A., compensation accounting analyst; b. Saigon, Vietnam, July 3, 1966; came to U.S., 1975; d. Binh Cong Nguyen and Agnes Dang; m. Steven M. La, Nov. 24, 1990. AS, De Anza Coll., 1990; BS in Fin., San Jose State U., 1992. Lic. real estate, fire & casualty, life & disability, Calif. Registered rep. Waddell & Reed Fin., San Jose, Calif., 1987-89; asst. mgr. ITT Fin. Svcs., Milpitas, Calif., 1989-90; internat. order mgmt. analyst Tandem Computers, Inc., Cupertino, Calif., 1990-94, U.S. compensation acctg. analyst, 1994—. Mem. NAFE, Toastmasters. Republican. Office: Tandem Computers Inc 10600 Ridgeview Ct Cupertino CA 95014

LAARTZ, ESTHER ELIZABETH, interior designer; b. Adair, Iowa, May 28, 1913; d. Christian Henry and Pearl Ethel (Hardenbrook) L. BA, Riverside Jr. Coll., 1933; grad., N.Y. Sch. Design, 1943, Parsons Sch. Interior Design. Designer, mgr. studio interior design Bloomingdales, N.Y.C., 1944-51; mgr. studio interior design Gimbel Bros., Pitts., 1951-61; pvt. practice interior design Los Angeles, 1963-70; interior designer Ross Thiele & Son, La Jolla, Calif., 1970-74, Wiseman & Gale, Scottsdale, Ariz., 1977-88; pvt. practice Phoenix, 1988—; mem. faculty Scottsdale Coll. Docent mem. Phoenix Art Mus., 1986—. Fellow Am. Inst. Interior Designers (pres. Western Pa. chpt. 1955-59, N.E. regional v.p. 1958, pres. Los Angeles chpt. 1967-69, nat. sec. 1959, regional v.p. southern Calif. 1968-70); mem. Am. Soc. Interior Designers (life). Republican. Home and Office: 811 W Indianola Ave Phoenix AZ 85013-3338

LABALME, PATRICIA HOCHSCHILD, educational administrator; b. N.Y.C., Feb. 26, 1927; d. Walter and Kathrin (Samstag) Hochschild; m. George Labalme, Jr., June 6, 1958; children: Jennifer R., Henry G., Lisa G., Victoria A. B.A. magna cum laude, Bryn Mawr Coll., 1948; M.A., Harvard U., 1950, Ph.D., 1958. Instr. history Wellesley Coll., Mass., 1952-57; tchr. history Brearley Sch., N.Y.C., 1957-59; lectr. Barnard Coll., N.Y.C., 1961-77; adj. assoc. prof. history Hunter Coll., N.Y.C., 1979; lectr. NYU, N.Y.C., 1980-82; adj. prof. history NYU, 1986-87; assoc. dir. Inst. for Advanced Study, Princeton, N.J., 1982-88; sec. corp. Inst. for Advanced Study, Princeton, 1982-92, asst. to dir., 1992—; mem. adv. bd. G. K. Delmas Found., N.Y.C., 1976-79, trustee, 1979; trustee Am. Acad. in Rome, N.Y.C., 1979—; exec. dir. Renaissance Soc. Am., N.Y.C., 1982-85, trustee, 1982-89; bd. dirs. Quantum Chem. Corp., 1990-93. Author: Bernardo Giustiniani: A Venetian of the Quattrocento, 1969; contbg. editor: Beyond Their Sex: Learned Women of the European Past, 1980, A Century Recalled: Essays in Honor of Bryn Mawr College, 1987; contbr. articles to profl. jours. and publs. Trustee Brearley Sch., 1975-83, pres., 1978-82, hon. trustee, 1983—; trustee Lawrenceville Sch., 1986—. Recipient Caroline A. Wilby prize Radcliffe Coll., 1958. Mem. Am. Hist. Assn., Soc. for Renaissance Studies, Renaissance Soc. Am., Ateneo Veneto, Cosmopolitan Club, Harvard Club (N.Y.C.), Cream Hill Lake Assn. (West Cornwall, Conn.), Phi Beta Kappa. Office: Inst for Advanced Study Olden Ln Princeton NJ 08540-4920

LABARGE, MARGARET WADE, medieval history educator; b. N.Y.C., July 18, 1916; arrived in Can., 1940; d. Alfred Byers and Helena (Mein) Wade; m. Raymond C. Labarge, June 20, 1940 (dec. May 1972); children: Claire Labarge Morris, Suzanne, Charles, Paul. BA, Radcliffe Coll., 1937; LittB, Oxford (Eng.) U., 1939; LittD (hon.), Carleton U., Ottawa, Ont., Can., 1976; LLD (hon.), U. Waterloo, Ont., Can., 1993. Lectr. history U. Ottawa, Carleton U., 1950-62; adj. prof. history Carleton U., Ottawa, 1983—. Author: Simon de Montfort, 1962, A Baronial Household, 1965, Gascony, 1980, A Small Sound of the Trumpet, 1987, others; contbr. articles to profl. jours. Chmn. bd. dirs. St. Vincent's Hosp., Ottawa, 1969-81; pub. rep. bd. dirs. Can. Nurses Assn., 1980-83; bd. dirs. Carleton U., 1984-93, Coun. on Aging, 1986-93 (pres., 1989-91). Recipient Alumnae Recognition award Radcliffe Coll., 1987. Fellow Royal Soc. Can.; mem. Medieval Acad., Order of Can., Phi Beta Kappa. Roman Catholic. Home and Office: 402-555 Wilbrod St, Ottawa, ON Canada K1N 5R4

LABELLE, ANN D., legislative staff member; b. Chelmsford, Mass., Jan. 23, 1950. BSN, D'Youville Coll., 1970; BS in Biology, Southeastern Mass. U., 1974; MS in Health Policy and Mgmt., Harvard U., 1976; DDS, U. Md., 1983. Health svcs. cons. Johns Hopkins U. Ctr. Hosp. Fin. and Mgmt., 1980-86; sr. health policy advisor to sec. Dept. Health and Human Svcs., 1986-89; mem. staff House Ways and Means Com., Washington, 1989-90, minority health counsel, 1993—; exec. dir. Adv. Coun. Social Security, 1990-92; chief health counsel, staff dir. Senate Labor and Human Resources Com., 1992-93. Office: Com Ways and Means 1106 Longworth House Office Bldg Washington DC 20515*

LABELLE, PATTI, singer; b. Phila., Oct. 4, 1944; d. Henry Holte; m. Armstead Edwards; children: Zuri, Stanley, Dodd. Singer Patti LaBelle and the Bluebelles, 1962-70; lead singer musical group LaBelle, 1970-76; solo performer, 1977—. Albums include Over the Rainbow, 1967, La Belle, 1971, Moon Shadows, 1972, Pressure Cookin', 1974, Chameleon, 1976, Patti LaBelle, 1977, Live at the Apollo, 1980, Gonna Take A Miracle-The Spirit's in It, 1982, I'm in Love Again, 1984, Winner in You, 1986, The Best of Patti LaBelle, Patti, Be Yourself, Live (Apollo Theater), 1993, Gems, 1994; appeared in films A Soldier's Story, 1985, Beverly Hills Cop, 1985; appeared in TV movie Unnatural Causes, 1986, TV series A Different World, Out All Night, 1992. Recipient award of Merit, Phila. Art Alliance, 1987.Recipient Grammy award: best Rhythm & Blues vocal for "Burnin'", 1991, Grammy nomination (Best Rhythm & Blues Female Vocal, 1994) for "All Right Now". Home: 8730 Sunset Blvd & PH-W Los Angeles CA 90069 Office: care MCA Records Inc 100 Universal City Plz Universal Cty CA 91608-1014*

LABODA, AMY SUE, writer; b. Phila., Sept. 10, 1962; d. Gerald and Sheila Lois (Plasky) L.; mem. Barry Lee Marz, Mar. 5, 1987; children: Rose Marie, Leah Ann. BA, Sarah Lawrence Coll., 1984. Vol. U.S. Peace Corps, Togo, 1985; flight instr., pilot Redwood Aviation, Santa Rosa, Calif., 1986, Qualiflight Tng., Ft. Worth, 1987-88; depts. editor Flying mag., N.Y.C., 1988-90; free-lance writer, mktg. cons. Ft. Myers, Fla., 1990—; mem. selection com. Am. Flyers Scholarship, Pal-Walkee, Ill., 1990—. Cons. editor textbook series: The Pilot's Manual, 2nd edit., 1993; contbr. articles to various mags. Mem. Exptl. Aircraft Assn., Aircraft Owners and Pilots Assn., Women in Aviation (internat. exec. bd. dirs.), Women's Scuba Assn.

LABOUSIER, SUSAN EVELYN, choreographer, dancer; b. Boston, Mar. 25, 1954; d. Harry E. and Evelyn M. (Durant) Neeves; m. Richard L. Labousier, June 16, 1973; children: Michelle Lee, Wendy Ann. Student, MIT, Boston Conservatory, Boston Sch. Ballet, Brookline (Mass.) Ballet, Natick (Mass.) Sch. Ballet and Theatre Arts, Le Ctr. De Danse, Newton, Mass.; studies with Mme. Tatiana Ouroussoff and Pamela E. Feri; student in psychology and theatercraft, MIT, 1970-71; student, Boston Sch. Ballet, 1968-70, Natick Sch. Ballet, 1973, Le Centre de Dance, 1973-79. Cert. to teach, Dance Masters of Am., 1979, cert. for studies in prevention of dance injuries, Boston Children's Hosp., Div. Sports Medicine, 1979. Owner, dir. Susan Neeves Dance Studio, Roxbury, Mass, 1968-70, Fidelis Way Dance Workshop, Brighton, Mass., 1970-73; founder Franklin (Mass.) Dance Workshop, 1977—, Fla. Dance Workshop, 1991—. Dir./choreographer numerous Showtime prodns., 1968-92, A Family Affair, Brighton, Mass., 1970, Christmas Prodn., Franklin, 1984; choreographer The Unsinkable Molly Brown, Roxbury, Mass., 1968, TheDrunkard, Franklin, 1979, My Fair Lady, South Boston, 1971, Franklin, 1987, Peter Pan, Summer Arts Sch., Port Charlotte, Fla., 1992; appeared in ballets Swan Lake, Coppelia, Giselle, Les Sylphides, Orpheus of the Underworld, Rodeo. Choreographer Summerthing, Boston, 1968; dir./choreographer benefit prodn. Arthritis Found., 1983; founder, operator Susan Neeves Dance Studio, Mission Ch., Boston, 1968-70, Fidelis Way Dance Workshop, Brighton, Mass., 1970-73; model, dancer Mayor's Youth Activity Commn. Fashion Show, Boston, 1972; bd. dirs. Dance Masters Am., 1986-87; founder The Franklin Dance Co. Inc. as a charitable performing troupe, 1979—; active Franklin Arts Coun., 1986-87. Recipient Outstanding Citizenship award DAR, 1972, Brotherhood award Jewish War Vets. Am., 1972; recipient Award for Outstanding Performance at Boston City Hall, Mayor Kevin White, 1972. Mem. ASCAP, Charlotte County Arts & Humanities Coun., Charlotte County C. of C. Home and Office: 3357 Vassar St Port Charlotte FL 33980-8560

LABUS, MARTA HAAKE, analyst, writer; b. Huntington, W.Va., Sept. 13, 1943; d. Donald Robert and Constance Edith (Hay) Haake; m. Otto P. Labus, May 10, 1982 (div. July 1990). AAS in Paralegal Studies, Am. Inst., 1991; BA summa cum laude, Ohio U., 1965; MA, U. Ill., 1966, PhD, 1971. Asst. prof. English Westminster Coll., New Wilmington, Pa., 1971-78; novelist, lectr. Phoenix, 1982—; analyst U.S. Bankruptcy Ct., Phoenix, 1991-94, San Francisco, 1994—. Author: (under pen name Claire McCormick) Resume for Murder, 1982, The Club Paradis Murders, 1983, Murder in Cowboy Bronze, 1985. Fellow Woodrow Wilson Found., 1965, NEH, 1976, U. Ill., 1969. Mem. Nat. Conf. Bankruptcy Clks., Phi Beta Kappa, Phi Kappa Phi. Home: 601 Van Ness Ave # 429 San Francisco CA 94102 Office: US Bankruptcy Ct 235 Pine St San Francisco CA 94104

LACEY, BEATRICE CATES, psychophysiologist; b. N.Y.C., July 22, 1919; d. Louis Henry and Mollie (Libowitz) Cates; m. John I. Lacey, Apr. 16, 1938; children: Robert Arnold, Carolyn Ellen. Student, Columbia U., 1935-38; A.B. with distinction, Cornell U., 1940; M.A., Antioch Coll., 1958. Mem. staff Fels Research Inst., Yellow Springs, Ohio, 1953-82; sr. investigator Fels Research Inst., 1966-72, sr. scientist, 1972-82; instr. Antioch Coll., Yellow Springs, 1956-63, asst. prof., 1963-68, assoc. prof., 1968-73, prof., 1973-82; Fels prof. psychiatry Wright State U. Sch. Medicine, 1977-82, clin. prof. psychiatry, 1982-89, Fels prof. emeritus, 1989—; acting sci. dir. Fels Research Inst., 1979-82. Assoc. editor Psychophysiology, 1975-78; reviewer Jour. Abnormal Psychology, Psychophysiology, Biol. Psychology, Cognitive Psychology, Sci.; contbr. articles to profl. jours.; researcher, author numerous publs. in psychophysiology of the autonomic nervous system. Recipient Disting. Sci. Contbn. award, Am. Psychol. Assn., 1976, Psychol. Sci. Gold Medal award, Am. Psychol. Found., 1985. Fellow Acad. Behavioral Medicine Research, Soc. Exptl. Psychologists, Am. Psychol. Soc. (William James fellow 1989); mem. Soc. Psychophysiol. Research (dir. 1972-75, pres. 1978-79), Soc. Neurosci., Phi Kappa Phi. Home: 1425 Meadow Ln Yellow Springs OH 45387-1221

LACEY, SHERRY KAY, accountant, tax specialist; b. Walla Walla, Wash., Feb. 22, 1959; d. Elvin William and Ruby Ina (Klein) Sievers; m. Gordan Ray Lacey, Sept. 17, 1978; children: Janelle Lanae, Jillian Larae. AS in Acctg., Everett C.C., 1989; BS in Acctg., Ctrl. Wash. U., 1993. Office mgr. Walla Walla Coll. Ch., College Place, Wash., 1984-87; acct. Acctg. Force, Seattle, 1990; sole propr. Sound Tax and Acctg., Everett, Wash., 1987—; vol. income tax assistance coord. IRS, Everett, 1992. Treas. Forest Pk. Elem., Everett, 1988-90, PTA co-leader, 1993; bd. dirs. Pathfinder Youth Club, Everett, 1992-93. Recipient Outstanding Svc. award IRS, 1992. Mem. Soc. Student Accts. Home and Office: 118 76th St SW Everett WA 98203

LACH, ALMA ELIZABETH, food and cooking writer, consultant; b. Petersburg, Ill.; d. John H. and Clara E. (Boeker) Satorius; diplome de Cordon Bleu, Paris, 1956; m. Donald F. Lach, Mar. 18, 1939; 1 dau., Sandra Judith. Feature writer Children's Activities mag., 1954-55; creator, performer TV show Let's Cook, children's cooking show, 1955; hostess weekly food program on CBS, 1962-66, performer TV show Over Easy, PBS, 1977-78; food editor Chgo. Daily Sun-Times, 1957-65; pres. Alma Lach Kitchens Inc., Chgo., 1966—; dir. Alma Lach Cooking Sch., Chgo.; lectr. U. Chgo. Downtown Coll., Gourmet Inst., U. Md., 1963, Modesto (Calif.) Coll., 1978, U. Chgo., 1981; resident master Shoreland Hall, U. Chgo., 1978-81; food cons. Food Bus. Mag., 1964-66, Chgo.'s New Pump Room, Lettuce Entertain You, Bitter End Resort, Brit. V.I., Midway Airlines, Flying Food Fare, Inc., Berghoff Restaurant, Hans' Bavarian Lodge, Unocal '76, Univ. Club Chgo.; columnist Modern Packaging, 1967-68, Travel & Camera, 1969, Venture, 1970, Chicago mag., 1978, Bon Appetit, 1980, Tribune Syndicate, 1982. Recipient Pillsbury award, 1958; Grocery Mfrs. Am. Trophy award, 1959, certificate of Honor, 1961; Chevalier du Tastevin, 1962; Commanderie de l'Ordre des Anysetiers du Roy, 1963; Confrerie de la Chaine des Rotisseurs, 1964; Les Dames D'Escoffier, 1982, Culinary Historians of Chgo., 1993. Mem. Am. Assn. Food Editors (chmn. 1959). Clubs: Tavern, Quadrangle (Chgo.). Author: A Child's First Cookbook, 1950; The Campbell Kids Have a Party, 1953; The Campbell Kids at Home, 1953; Let's Cook, 1956; Candlelight Cookbook, 1959; Cooking a la Cordon Bleu, 1970; Alma's Almanac, 1972; Hows and Whys of French Cooking, 1974; contbr. to World Book Yearbook, 1961-75, Grolier Soc. Yearbook, 1962. Home and Office: 5750 S Kenwood Ave Chicago IL 60637-1744

LACHANCE, JANICE RACHEL, federal agency administrator, lawyer; b. Biddeford, Maine, June 17, 1953; d. Ralph L. and Rachel A. (Desnoyers) L. BA, Manhattanville Coll., 1974; JD, Tulane U., 1978. Bar: Maine 1978, D.C. 1982. Staff dir. subcom. on antitrust Ho. of Reps., Washington, 1982-83; adminstrv. asst. Congresswoman Katie Hall, 1983-84; asst. pres. sec. Mondale-Ferraro Campaign, Washington, 1984; press sec. Congressman

Tom Daschle, 1985; ptnr. Lachance and Assocs., Washington, 1985-87; dir. communications and polit. action Am. Fedn. Govt. Employees (AFL-CIO), Washington, 1987-93; dir. policy and communications U.S. Office Pers. Mgmt., Washington, 1993—; vis. scholar Cornell U., 1972-73. Editor newsletter Govt. Standard, 1987-93. Mem. Delta Delta Delta, Phi Alpha Delta. Democrat. Roman Catholic. Office: US Office Pers Mgmt 1900 E St NW Ste 5F12 Washington DC 20415-0001

LACHENICHT-BERKELEY, ANGELA MARIE, marketing professional; b. St. Louis, Feb. 3, 1955; d. Bernard J. and Dolores B. (Vaughn) L.; m. David L. Fuller, Sept. 6, 1974 (div. Mar. 1987); m. John Berkeley, Apr. 22, 1991. A in Bus. Adminstrn., Meremac Community Coll., St. Louis, 1983; chancellor cert., U. Mo., St. Louis, 1989; cert. of tng. in employment law, U. Mo. St. Louis, St. Louis, 1990. P.B.X. operator Arthur Enterprises, St. Louis, 1971-73; credit mgr. Watson Furniture, St. Louis, 1973-80; owner, operator Action Video World, St. Louis, 1980-85; regional telemktg. mgr. Crown Cable TV, St. Louis, 1985—; coord. Am. Cablevision, St. Louis, 1988; cons. Thomas Construction, St. Louis, 1987-90. Author, editor: (guide) Cencom Insider, 1989-91. Telemarketing coord. Comic Relief/Health Care for Homeless Coalition, St. Louis, 1988-92; cons. Non-Profit Employment Liaison Com., St. Louis, 1989-90. Recipient Emmy award, St. Louis chpt. NATAS, 1988, Civic Commendation, Health Care for the Homeless Coalition, St. Louis, 1989, 90, 91, 92. Mem. Women in Cable, Nat. Cable TV Assn. Democrat. Roman Catholic. Office: Crown Cable TV 9358 Dielman Industrial Dr Saint Louis MO 63132-2205

LACKEY, MARY MICHELE, physician assistant; b. Johnson City, N.Y., Dec. 22, 1955; d. Joseph Charles and Jane Ann (Weston) Reardon; m. Donald V. Lackey Jr., Oct. 27, 1979. AAS in Nursing, Broome Community Coll., Binghamton, N.Y., 1978; cert. family nurse practitioner, Albany Med. Coll., 1982; BS in Psychology and Sociology, U. State of N.Y., Albany, 1989. Cert. physician asst., family nurse practitioner, nurse midwife; RN, N.Y., Conn. Physician asst. Streit, Hickey & Lasky MD, P.C., Saratoga Springs, N.Y., 1982-85, Litchfield Hills Ob/Gyn., Sharon, Conn., 1986-89, Foothills Family Health Ctr., Amenia, N.Y., 1991—; physican asst. Vassar Coll. Health Svcs., Poughkeepsie, N.Y., 1990—. Leader, instr. Girl Scouts U.S.A., Dutchess County, N.Y., 1990—. Lt. col. U.S. Army, 1975—. Fellow Am. Acad. Physician Assts., Am. Coll. Nurse Midwives; mem. Nat. Guard Assn. U.S., Malitia Assn. N.Y., Phi Theta Kappa. Roman Catholic. Home: RR 1 Box 222 Salt Point NY 12578-9801

LACOMB, ROBBIE DAYLE, art educator; b. Sinton, Tex., Oct. 27, 1948; d. Lawrence Robert and Dorthy Audrey (Vickers) L.; m. Michael Nathaniel Hugh Roach, July 28, 1990; children from previous marriage: Robert Eric Lacher, Amie Melissa Lacher. BFA, Stephen F. Austin State U., 1987, MA, 1989, MFA, 1990. Artist Arts in Edn. Shreveport (La.) Regional Arts Coun., 1979-88; substitute tchr. Ctr. Ind. Sch. Dist., Center, Tex., 1982-86; grad. teaching asst. Stephen F. Austin State Coll., Nacogdoches, Tex., 1987-90; tchr.'s instr. Tex. Arts Coun. Summer Program, Austin, 1991, 92; instr. art Angelina Coll., Lufkin, Tex., 1993—; adj. faculty art Panola Coll.-Shelby Coll. Ctr., 1989-91, art history Lon Morris Coll., Jacksonville, Tex., 1991-92; rschr. Illustrated Herbals Woodson Rsch. Ctr. Rice U., Houston, 1992, Huntington Libr., San Marino, Calif., 1990, 92. One-woman shows include Centenary Coll., Shreveport, La., 1989, La. State U., Shreveport, 1991, Houston, 1993; pub.: Bert Long Jr., The Rome Series, 1993; illustrator: Christmas Memories: Lon Morris Coll., 1990. Vol. ednl program Mus. East Tex., Lufkin, 1991—; troop leader Girl Scouts Am., Center, 1983-87; cub scout asst. den mother Boy Scouts Am., Martinsville, Tex., 1978-79, merit badge counselor, 1983-87; mem. Friends Angelina Coll., 1994.

LACOMB-WILLIAMS, LINDA LOU, community health nurse; b. Galion, Ohio, Oct. 1, 1948; d. Horace Allen and Roberta May (Black) Braden; m. Robert Earl LaComb, Feb. 1, 1970 (div. Aug. 1984); children: Robin Marie, Patrick Alan; m. Robert Allen Williams, Aug. 30. 1991; children Erin, Megan. BSN, Capital U., 1970. RN, Fla., Ohio. Staff nurse St. Anne's Hosp., Columbus, Ohio, 1970; pub. health nurse Hillsborough County Dept. Health, Tampa, Fla., 1970-80, community health nurse supr., 1980-87; sr. community health nurse Polk County Dept. Health, Lakeland, Fla., 1987-88; sr. RN supr. Children's Med. Svcs., Tampa, 1988-91, Lakeland, 1991—. 1st lt. flight nurse res. USAF, 1971-75. Recipient Boss of Yr. award Stawberry Chpt. of Am. Bus. Women's Assn., 1985. Mem. ANA, ARC, Fla. Nurses Assn. (grievance rep. state employees profl. bargaining unit 1976-87, pres. 1984-87, 1st v.p. 1989-91, Undine Sams award 1987, Nurse of Yr. award Dist. Four 1987), Sigma Theta Tau (Delta Beta chpt.). Republican. Presbyterian. Home: 502 Shamrock Rd Brandon FL 33511-5548 Office: Children's Med Svcs 1417 Lakeland Hills Blvd Lakeland FL 33805-3200

LACY, ANN MATTHEWS, geneticist, educator, researcher; b. Boston, May 29, 1932; d. Clive Willoughby and Mona Bellingham (Matthews) L. BA in Botany, Wellesley Coll., 1953; MS in Microbiology, Yale U., 1956, PhD in Microbiology, 1959. Rsch. asst. Carnegie Inst. Washington, Cold Spring Harbor, N.Y., 1953-54; instr. genetics Goucher Coll., Towson, Md., 1959-61, asst. prof. genetics, 1961-67, assoc. prof. genetics, 1967-73, prof. genetics, 1973—, Elizabeth Connolly Todd prof., 1994—, chmn. dept. biol. sci., 1969-72, 86-87, 89, chmn. faculty natural sci. & math., 1988-91; sr. rsch. fellow U. Glasgow, Scotland, 1968-69; sr. investigator NSF rsch. grants Goucher Coll., 1960-70. Contbr. articles to profl. jours. Mem. AAAS, Genetics Soc. Am., Am. Inst. Biol. Scis., Sigma Xi. Unitarian. Office: Goucher Coll Dept Biol Scis Dulaney Valley Rd Baltimore MD 21204

LACY, CAROLYN JEAN, elementary education educator, secondary education educator; b. Marshall, Ark., Apr. 6, 1944; d. Charles Ira Bolch and Edna Rebecca Cherry; 1 child, Kelli Jean. AA with distinction, Riverside City Coll., 1980; BA, U. Calif., Riverside, 1982, postgrad., 1983; MEd, U.S. Internat. U., 1993. Cert. social sci. tchr., Calif. Educator Perris (Calif.) Elem. Sch. Dist., 1984-89, Rialto (Calif.) Unified Sch. Dist., 1989—; instr. Developing Capable People, Riverside, Calif., 1986-89; presenter, lectr. Jurupa Unified Sch. Dist., Riverside, 1990, Rialto Unified Sch. Dist., 1990; developer peer tutor program Perris Elem. Sch. Dist., 1989. Editor: (newsletter) Perris Lights, 1989. Active Students in Environ. Action, Riverside, 1978. Named Mentor Tchr. State of Calif., 1988. Mem. Riverside County Task Force for Self-Esteem, Nat. Coun. for Self Esteem, AAUW, NEA, Calif. Tchrs. Assn., U. Calif. Alumni Assn., Phi Delta Kappa, Alpha Gamma Sigma. Democrat. Mem. LDS Ch. Home: 4044 Wallace St Riverside CA 92509-6809

LACY, ELIZABETH BERMINGHAM, state supreme court justice; b. 1945. BA cum laude, St. Mary's Coll., Notre Dame, Ind., 1966; JD, U. Tex., 1969; LLM, U. Va., 1992. Bar: Tex. 1969, Va. 1977. Staff atty. Tex. Legis. Coun., Austin, 1969-72; atty. Office of Atty. Gen., State of Tex., Austin, 1973-76; legis. aide Va. Del. Carrington Williams, Richmond, 1976-77; dep. atty. gen. jud. affairs div. Va. Office Atty. Gen., Richmond, 1982-85; mem. Va. State Corp. Commn., Richmond, 1985-89; justice Supreme Ct. Va., Richmond, 1989—. Office: Va Supreme Ct PO Box 1315 100 N 9th St Richmond VA 23210

LADANYI, BRANKA MARIA, chemist, educator; b. Zagreb, Croatia, Sept. 7, 1947; came to U.S., 1969; d. Branko and Nevenka (Zilic) L.; m. Marshall Fixman, Dec. 7, 1974. BSc, McGill U., Montreal, Can., 1969; M in Philosophy, Yale U., 1971, PhD, 1973. Vis. prof. of chemistry U. Ill., 1974; postdoctoral research assoc. Yale U., 1974-77, research assoc., 1977-79; asst. prof. chemistry Colo. State U., Ft. Collins, 1979-84, assoc. prof. chemistry, 1985-87, prof. chemistry, 1987—; vis. fellow Joint Inst. for Lab. Astrophysics, 1993-94. Assoc. editor Jour. Chem. Physics, 1994—; referee and contbr. articles to profl. jours. Fellow Sloan Found., 1982-84, Dreyfus Found., 1983-87; vis. fellow JILA, 1993-94; grantee NSF, NATO, 1983-89. Mem. AAAS, Am. Chem. Soc. (PRF grantee 1979-82, 1989-91), Am. Phys. Soc., NOW, Sigma Xi. Home: 1100 E Pitkin St Fort Collins CO 80524-3909 Office: Colo State U Dept Chemistry Fort Collins CO 80523

LADD, DIANE, actress; b. Meridian, Miss., Nov. 29, 1943; m. Bruce Dern (div.); 1 child, Laura; m. William Shay, Jr. (div.). Grad., St. Aloysius Acad. Appearances include (films) The Wild Angels, 1966, The Reivers, 1969, Macho Callahan, 1970, Rebel Rousers, 1970, WUSA, 1970, White Lightning, 1973, Alice Doesn't Live Here Anymore, 1974, Chinatown, 1974, Embryo, 1976, All Night Long, 1981, Something Wicked This Way Comes, 1983, Black Widow, 1987, Plain Clothes, 1988, National Lampoon's Christmas Vacation, 1989, Wild at Heart, 1990, A Kiss Before Dying, 1991, Rambling Rose, 1991, Cemetery Club, 1992, Carnosaur, 1993, Fatherhood, 1993, Spirit Realm, 1993, Obsession, 1994, Mrs. Milnck (also dir.), 1994. Recipient award Brit. Acad., Spirit award, Golden Globe award, 3 Acad. award nominations, 4 Golden Globe nominations, Emmy nomination for Guest Actress in a Comedy Series (Grace Under Fire), 1994. Office: Diane Ladd Prodns Inc PO Box 17111 Beverly Hills CA 90209-3111*

LADD, MARCIA LEE, staffing services executive; b. Bryn Mawr, Pa., July 22, 1950; d. Edward Wingate and Virginia Lee (McGinnes) Mullinix; children: Joshua Wingate, McGinnes Lee. BA, U. Pa., 1972; MEd, U. Va., 1973; MA, Emory U., 1979. Rsch. assoc. N.C. Tng. and Standards Coun., Raleigh, 1973-75; dir. counseling svc. N.C. State Youth Svcs. Agy., Raleigh, 1975-76; acad. dean Duke U., Durham, N.C., 1976-77; prin. Ladd & Assocs. Mgmt. Cons., Chapel Hill, N.C., 1979-88; v.p. adminstrn. CompuChem Corp., Research Triangle Park, N.C., 1988-91; v.p. mktg. Prentke Romich Co., Wooster, Ohio, 1991-94; v.p. ops. Exec. Staffing Svcs., Inc., Cary, N.C., 1994—. Bd. visitors Wayne County Arts Coun., Wooster, 1992, Carolina Friends Sch., Durham, 1986-89; bd. dirs. Stoneridge/Sedgefield Swim/Racquet Club, Chapel Hill, N.C., 1985-88, Oakwood Hist. Soc., Raleigh, 1981-84. Decorated Order of Long Leaf Pine Gov. of N.C., 1976. Presbyterian. Office: Executive Staffing Svcs Inc 130 Edinburgh S Ste 105 Cary NC 27511

LADD-POWELL, ROBERTA KAY, horsebreeder, marketing executive; b. Clearwater Beach, Fla., July 24, 1953; d. F. Robert and Marguerite Elizabeth (Ethier) Ladd; m. Michael Moore Powell, Jan. 13, 1992. BA in Indsl. Pyschology, Calif. State U., Long Beach, 1975. Lic. seminar facilitator. Sales trainer western region GTE Directories Corp., Los Alamitos, Calif., 1977-84; breeder, mktg. dir. Liberty West Arabians, Calif., 1978—; dir. mktg., tng. and promotions Guam Cable TV, Yellow Pages Ink, 1990—. Pub. Desert Horse Directory, 1984-86; editor Arabian Horse Jour., 1982-83, Animal Air Transport mag., 1988-89; contbr. articles to trade jours. and newspapers. Dir. promotions Ride Across Am. Benefit, Tucson, 1988-89; fund raiser Rainforest Action Network, San Francisco, 1988-89; supporter Orange County Riders, 1980-81, Therapeutic Riding Orgn. Tucson, 1988-89. Mem. NAFE, Internat. Arabian Horse Assn. (conf. del. 1987, 88), Am. Horse Shows Assn., Arabian Racing Assn. Calif. (Top 10 Arabian Race Mare award for LWA Khlassy Lady 1988, region 2 res. Champion Mare 1989, Can. Top 20 Mare 1989), Arabian Jockey Club (vice chmn., mem. exec. com. 1988—), So. Ariz. Arabian Horse Assn. (racing chmn. Tucson chpt. 1988-89), Sierra Pacific Arabian Racing Coun. (pres. 1987-88), Guam Equestrian Fedn. (bd. dirs. 1990-93), Hawaii Combined Tng. Assn., Arabian Horse Registry, U.S. Dressage Fedn. Methodist. Home and Office: 970 S Marine Dr Apt 10303 Tamuning GU 96911-3403

LADEWIG GOODMAN, JEANNE MARGARET, artist; b. Grand Rapids, Mich., June 26, 1923; d. Roland Adolph and Margaret Francis (Palmer) Ladewig; m. Larry Goodman, June 1963 (div. 1966). BEd, Concordia Coll., 1945; MS in Art Edn., Ill. Inst. Tech., 1970; postgrad., Chgo. Art Inst., 1959-68. Tchr. Luth. Schs., Chgo., 1952-62; tchr. art Park Ridge (Ill.) Pub. Sch. Dist. 64, 1962-74, Art coord., 1974-86; artist, exhibitor Abney Gallery, N.Y., 1993—, Contemporary Art Workshop, Chgo., 1993—; workshop presenter NAEA-IAEA; guest lectr. U. Ill., 1971-72; adv. bd. Contemporary Art Workshop, Chgo.; hiring cons. Evanston (Ill.) Schs., 1985. Exhibited in group shows at Ditmar Gallery Northwestern, 1972, Abney Galleries, 1973; contbr. articles to profl. jours. Vol. free meals Luth. Ch., Chgo., 1990—; vol. Terra Mus. of Art, Chgo., 1989—. Grantee Helene Wurlitzer Found., 1972; 1st prize water color show Artist Guild of Chgo., 1986. Mem. AAUW, Chgo. Soc. of Artists, Chgo. Artists Coalition. Lutheran.

LADIGES, LORI JEAN, learning disabilities specialist; b. Sheboygan, Wis., Feb. 25, 1956; d. Donald William and Marion Margaret (Henning) L. BS in Edn., U. Wis., 1978; MA in Learning Disabilities, Cardinal Stritch Coll., 1984. Cert. tchr. elem. (grades 1-8), Cognitive disorders (K-12) and learning disabilities (K-12). Learning disabilities specialist Kohler (Wis.) Pub. Sch., 1978—; instr. (part-time) Silver Lake Coll., Manitowoc, Wis., 1984-92, Cardinal Stritch Coll., Milw., 1989—; sch. evaluation consortium chairperson spl. edn. Kohler Pub. Schs., 1989—, learning disabilities specialist, rep. long-range planning com., 1992—, cheerleading advisor, 1981-84, yearbook advisor, 1985-86. Mem. Alpha Sigma (Grace Alvord award 1978). Lutheran. Home: 2236 N 23rd St Sheboygan WI 53083-4443

LADNER, JOYCE A., academic administrator; b. Hattiesburg, Miss.. BA in Sociology, Tougaloo Coll.; MA, PhD in Sociology, Washington U., St. Louis. Assoc. prof. dept. sociology Howard U., Washington, 1971-73, v.p. acad. affairs, 1990—, interim pres., 1994—; prof. Hunter Coll. CUNY, 1973-81. Author: Tomorrow's Tomorrow: The Black Woman, 1971, Mixed Families: Adoption Across Racial Boundaries; editor The Death of White Sociology, 1973, Adolescence and Poverty: Challanges for the 1990s, 1991; contbr. chpts. to over 20 books and articles to Washington Post, N.Y. Times, Ebony, others. Chair Mayor's Blue Ribbon Panel on Teenage Pregnancy Prevention for D.C, 1984-85; past chair Bd. Trans Africa Forum; past sec. Twenty-First Century Found.; bd. dirs. Recording for the Blind. Recipient DuBois-Johnson-Frazier Outstanding Scholarship award Am. Sociol. Assn., Joseph S. Himes Disting. Career award Assn. Black Sociologists, Acad. Excellence award Nat. Congress Black Faculty. Mem. Coalition of 100 Black Women (bd. dirs.). Office: Howard Univ Office of Pres 2400 Sixth St NW Ste 402 Washington DC 20059*

LADUKE, NANCIE, lawyer, corporate executive; b. Mayfield, Ky.; m. Daniel E. LaDuke, 1978. BA, Wayne State U., 1962; JD, U. Detroit, 1976. Pvt. practice Detroit, 1976; atty. KMart, Troy, Mich., 1977-84, comml. law counsel, 1984-90, v.p., sec., 1991—. Office: KMart Corp 3100 W Big Beaver Troy MI 48084

LADWIG, PATTI HEIDLER, lawyer; b. Harleysville, Pa., Aug. 28, 1958; d. L. Donald and Joan E. (Wright) Heidler; m. Manfred Friedrich Ladwig, July 30, 1983; 1 child, Brittney Nichole. BA in Psychology, U. Miami, 1980, JD, 1988. Bar: Fla. 1988, U.S. Dist. Ct. (so. dist.) Fla. 1988. Assoc. atty. Taplin, Howard & Shaw, West Palm Beach, Fla., 1988-92; ptnr. Shaw, St. James, & Ladwig, West Palm Beach, Fla., 1992, St. James & Ladwig, P.A., West Palm Beach, Fla., 1992-93; pvt. practice Patti Heidler Ladwig, P.A., West Palm Beach, 1993—; bd. dirs. Cmty. Assns. Inst., West Palm Beach, First Wellington, Inc. Pres., bd. dirs. Treasure Coast Communities Assn., West Palm Beach, 1990—, Pine Lake Condominium Assn. Inc., Pembroke Pines, Fla., 1986-88; mem. community appearance com. ACME Improvement Dist., Wellington, Fla., 1990—, Condominium Owners Fla., 1991—, Fedn. Mobile Home Owners Fla., 1990—; del. Fla. Legis. Action Com., 1989-91. Mem. Interamerican Assn. Profl. Women, Fla. Assn. Women Lawyers, Fla. Bar Assn. (bus. law sect., mem. condominium and planned devel. com. real property, probate and trust law sect.). Lutheran. Office: Ste 1060 1645 Palm Beach Lakes Blvd West Palm Beach FL 33401

LA FACE, FRANCINE MARIE, geriatric services professional, travel agent; b. Hialeah, Fla., Nov. 5, 1962; d. Bruno and Mary La Face. AAS, Suffolk C.C., Selden, N.Y., 1984; postgrad., St. Joseph's Coll. P.C.A Midpoint Home Healthcare, Hauppauge, N.Y., 1985-87; counselor Madonna Heights, Dix Hills, N.Y., 1987-88; travel agt. Distant Travel Inc., Deer Park, N.Y., 1991—; recreation asst. Islandia (N.Y.) Home for Adults, 1993; vol. Little Flower Nursing Home, East Islip, N.Y., 1980-81, Pederson-Krag, St. James, N.Y., 1994—. Vol. VA Hosp., Northport, N.Y., 1984; coord. singles group Faith Tabernacle, West Babylon, N.Y., 1993-94. Mem. Long Island Leisure Svc. Assn. Office: Distant Travel Inc 61 E Industry Ct Deer Park NY 11729

LAFARGE, CATHERINE, dean; b. Paris, May 22, 1935. BA, Mt. Holyoke Coll., 1957; PhD in French, Yale U., 1966. Acting instr. French Yale U., 1964-66, instr. to asst. prof., 1966-74, assoc. prof., 1974-80; prof. French Bryn Mawr Coll., 1980—, chmn. dept. French, 1979-84; dean Grad. Sch. Arts and Scis., Bryn Mawr Coll., 1985—. Author: The Emergence of the Bourgeoisie, 1964, Reverie et Realite dans les Nuits de Paris de Restif de la Bretonne, 1975, Paris and Myth: One Vision of Horror, In: Studies in Eighteenth Century Culture, vol. V, 1976, L'Anti-Fete dans le Nouveau Paris de L S Mercier, La Fete Revolutionnaire, 1977; author: (with J.P. Bouler) Les emprunts de mme Dupin L'Infortune litteraire des Dupin: Essai de bibliographie critique, Vol. CLXXXII, 1979, Studies on Voltaire & 18th Century: Catalogue topographique partiel des papiers Dupin-Rousseau disperse de 1951 à 58, Annales de la Societe Jean-Jacques Rousseau, Vol. XXXIX, 1980; editor: Dilemmes du Roman. Essays in Honor of Georges May, 1989. Bd. dirs. Grad. Record Examination, Test of English as a Fgn. Lang.; chmn. com. on langs. and lit. Yale U. Mem. Internat. Soc. 18th Century Studies, Am. Soc. 18th Century Studies, Soc. Francaise d'Etude 18th Siecle, Am. Assn. Tchrs. of French, Assn. Internat. Studies. Office: Bryn Mawr Coll Bryn Mawr PA 19010*

LAFAVE, LEANN LARSON, lawyer; b. Ramona, S.D., May 31, 1953; d. Floyd Burdette and Janice Anne (Quist) L.; m. Richard Curtis Finke, May 19, 1973 (div. Jan. 1978); 1 child, Timothy; m. Dwayne Jeffery LaFave, May 31, 1981 (div. 1992); children: Jeffrey, Allison. BS, U. S.D., 1974, JD with honors, 1977. Bar: S.D. 1977, U.S. Dist. Ct. S.D. 1977, U.S. Ct. Appeals (8th cir.) 1977, N.D. 1978, U.S. Dist. Ct. N.D. 1978. Asst. atty. gen. State of S.D., Pierre, 1977-78, 79-81; assoc. Bjella, Neff, Rathert & Wahl, Williston, N.D., 1978-79, Tobin Law Offices, P.C., Winner, S.D., 1981-83; assoc. dean, asst. prof. U. S.D. Sch. Law, Vermillion, 1983-86, dir. continuing legal edn., 1983-89, assoc. prof. law, 1986-89; ptnr. Aho & LaFave, Brookings, S.D., 1990-91; pvt. practice Brookings, 1991-92; asst. U.S. atty. U.S. Dist. S.D., 1992—; mem. S.D. Bd. Pardons and Paroles, 1987-90, chmn., 1989-90; comml. arbitrator Am. Arbitration Assn., 1985—; prof. Kilian C.C. Contbr. articles to profl. jours. Mem. planning coun. Nat. Identification Program for Advancement Women in Higher Edn. Adminstrn., Am. Coun. on Edn., S.D., 1984-90; bd. dirs. Mo. Shores Women's Resource Ctr., Pierre, 1980, W.H. Over Mus., Vermillion, 1986-87, S.D. Vol. Lawyers for Arts, 1987—, Brookings Interagy. Coun., 1990-91, Brookings Women's Ctr., 1990-94; sec. Mediation Ctr., Inc. Named S.D. Woman Atty. of Yr. Women in Law U. S.D., 1985. Mem. S.D. Bar Assn. (bd. govs. young lawyers sect. 1983-84), S.D. Mediation Assn., Epsilon Sigma Alpha (S.D. coun. sect. 1985-86). Republican. Episcopalian. Home: 1808 S Jefferson Ave Sioux Falls SD 57105-2415 Office: PO Box 1073 Sioux Falls SD 57101

LAFAYE, CARY DUPRE, librarian; b. Horry County, S.C., June 22, 1945; d. Moffatt Barmore and Helen Elizabeth (Cappelmann) DuPre; m. Angus Bird Lafaye, Mar. 21, 1970; 1 dau., Helen Cary. B.A. cum laude, U.S.C., 1967, M. Librarianship, 1973. Reading, history tchr. Moultrie Jr. High Sch., Mount Pleasant, S.C., 1967-69; tchr. French, history Irmo High Sch. (S.C.), 1969-71; library asst. U.S.C., Columbia, 1971-72; librarian Richland County Pub. Library-Cooper Br., Columbia, S.C., 1973-74; reference librarian Midlands Tech. Coll., Beltline Library, Columbia, 1975—; teaching asst., reader Coll. Libr. Info. Sci., U. S.C., 1992, 94. Mem. Ala, S.C. Library Assn., Southeastern Library Assn., U. S.C. Coll. Library and Info. Sci. Assn. (v.p. 1987-88), Phi Beta Kappa, Beta Phi Mu (chpt. pres. 1983-84), Kappa Delta. Home: 1412 Haynesworth Rd Columbia SC 29205-1536 Office: Midlands Tech Coll Beltline Library PO Box 2408 Columbia SC 29202-2408

LAFFERTY, BEVERLY LOU BROOKOVER, physician; b. Newark, Ohio, Aug. 15, 1938; d. Lawrence William and Rosie (Rey) Brookover; B.S., Ohio State U., 1959, M.D., 1963; diplomate Am. Bd. Family Practice; children—Marla Michele, William Brookover, Wesley Voris, Latour Rey. Intern Grant Hosp., Columbus, Ohio, 1963-64; practice medicine, West Union, Ohio, 1964-75, Sun City Center, Fla., 1975-79, Brandon, Fla., 1979-95; mem. staff Adams County Hosp., v.p., 1971-72, chief of staff, 1973-75; mem. staff Humana Hosp., Brandon, 1977-95, chmn. dept. family practice, 1984-86, hosp. trustee, 1984-92, chief of staff elect, 1986-88, chief of staff, 1988-90. Mem. AMA, Fla., Hillsborough County med. assns., Am. Acad. Family Physicians, Fla. Acad. Family Physicians, Alpha Lambda Delta, Alpha Epsilon Iota, Alpha Epsilon Delta (sec. 1958-59). Mem. Order Eastern Star. Home: 3913 John Moore Rd Brandon FL 33511-8020

LA FLARE, MARY J. DICKINSON, librarian; b. N.Y.C., Apr. 12, 1929; d. Lambert Francis and Mary Catherine (Mosher) Dickinson; m. Joseph P. La Flare, 1951 (div. 1969); children: Joseph P., Mary Ellen, Lizanne La Flare Krol, Patricia La Flare Santella. BA, Coll. Mt. St. Vincent, Riverdale, N.Y., 1950; MLS, St. John's U., Queens, N.Y., 1971. Cert. pub. libr., N.Y. Libr., rschr. Info. and Retrieval Ctr. Levittown (N.Y.) Union Free Sch. Dist., 1969-71; grad. asst. dept. L.S. St. John's U., 1969-71; mktg. rsch. libr. Sperry & Hutchinson, N.Y.C., 1971-76, project mgr. mktg. rsch., 1977-82; reference libr. Uniondale (N.Y.) Pub. Libr., 1985-86; reference libr., community libr. Farmingdale (N.Y.) Pub. Libr., 1986—; adj. prof. Nassau C.C., Garden City, N.Y., 1982-92, Hofstra U., Hempstead, N.Y., 1983-85; reading cons. Daleview Nursing Home, Farmingdale, 1993-94. St. Johns U. fellow, 1969-71. Mem. Coll. Mt. St. Vincent Alumnae (mem. capital fund com. 1985), Acad. St. Joseph Alumnae. Republican. Roman Catholic. Home: 142 Jervis Ave Farmingdale NY 11735 Office: Farmingdale Pub Libr 116 Merritts Rd Farmingdale NY 11735

LAFONT, LYDIA ANN, nurse manager; b. New Orleans, Mar. 13, 1955; d. Darwin Michael and Geraldine Marie (Terrebonne) L. Diploma, Charity Hosp. Sch. Nursing, 1977. RN, La. Staff nurse Charity Hosp., New Orleans, 1977-81, 97th Gen. Hosp., Frankfurt, Germany, 1981-85, Charity Hosp., New Orleans, 1985-87; staff nurse South La. Med. Ctr., Houma, 1987-90, RN mgr., 1990—. Sponsor Christian Children's Fund, Richmond, Va., 1990—. Mem. AACCN, Charity Hosp. Sch. Nursing Alumni Assn. Republican. Roman Catholic.

LAFOREST, LANA JEAN, lawyer, real estate broker; b. Providence, Apr. 14, 1952; d. Harold Joseph Ecker and Nettie Jean (Starks) Page; children: Timothy Charles, Tisha DeAnne. AA in Humanities and Social Scis., Niagara County C. C., 1989; BA in English Lit. magna cum laude, Buffalo State Coll., 1990, MA in English Lit., 1992; JD, SUNY Buffalo Sch. Law, 1994; doctoral student, SUNY, Buffalo, 1994—. Lic. real estate broker. Property mgr. Personal Income Property Mgmt., Lockport, 1976—; sales assoc. John F. Collins Realty, Lockport, 1979-83, Town Crier Clark Nodine Realty, Lockport, 1983-90, McKnight, Hogan & Noonan, Lockport, 1990-91, H. Potter Realty, Lockport, 1991-93; lawyer Family Court Resource Project Haven House, 1994—; instr. domestic violence clinic U. Buffalo Law Sch., 1994; pvt. practice Amherst, N.Y., 1994—; owner, operator Custom Crafts by Lana, Lockport, 1975-79; adv. domestic violence clinic U. Buffalo Law Sch., 1994. Editor: (lit. mag.) Writer's Revue, 1989; corr. Union-Sun and Jour., summer 1989. Girl scouts coord. Niagara County Coun. Girl Scouts, Sanborn, N.Y., 1978-84; clover clan 4-H club leader Niagara County Coop. Extension, Lockport, 1984-87; with Project Dandelion, Neighborhood Legal Svcs., 1994—. Mem. ABA, MLA, N.Y. State Bar Assn., Niagara Linguistics Soc., Nat. Assn. Realtors, Univ. Buffalo Law Sch. Alumni Assn., Buffalo State Coll. Alumni Assn., Niagara County Community Coll. Alumni Assn., U. Buffalo Assn. Women Law Students, Erie County Bar Assn., Women's Bar Assn. Erie County, Phi Alpha Delt. Office: P O Box 406 East Amherst NY 25062

LAFOUREST, JUDITH ELLEN, editor, publisher, lecturer, writer, educator; b. Indpls., Jan. 10; d. Edward Elston and Dorothy Jeanette (Parker) LaFourest; BA, Ind. U.-Purdue U., Indpls., 1972; MAT, Ind. U., 1980; m. William E. Lugar; children: Beth Anne Gruner, Paul Christopher Stewart Pitts Lugar. Lead pre-vocat. instr., ednl. adminstr. Opportunities Industrialization Ctr., Indpls., 1972-76; part-time English and human rels. instr. Profl. Careers Inst., Indpls., 1975-78; editor, pub. Womankind, Indpls., 1977-83; co-dir. Womankind Ctr., 1981-82; editor, creative writer, photographer Bio-Feed-Back Bio Dynamics/BMC, Indpls., 1977-80; mem. assoc. faculty, creative writing inst. and composition Ind. U.-Purdue U., Indpls., 1979-87, supr. student tchrs. of English, 1983-89; adj. faculty dept. English, Butler U., 1984—; also lectr., free-lance editor. Editor The Pen Woman, 1994—. Ind. sec. NOW, 1978-80. Recipient Disting. Alumni award Ind. U.-Indpls., 1980; Jessamyn West scholar. Mem. Nat. League Am. Pen Women (Ind. br., co-pres. 1990-92, pres. 1992-94, nat. 2nd v.p. 1994—), Ind. U.-Indpls. Liberal Arts Alumni Assn. (pres. 1982), Internat. Platform Assn., Sigma Tau Delta. Office: Butler U Dept English 4600 Sunset Ave Indianapolis IN 46208-3443

LAFSER, NATALIE GLADYS, school district administrator; b. St. Louis, Dec. 7, 1939; d. Frank Joseph and Gladys Isabel (Geck) L. BA, Fontbonne Coll., 1962; MS in Edn., Ind. U., 1972. Cert. k-8 tchr., k-12 counselor, Mo. Elem. tchr. Diocese of Green Bay, Shawano, Wis., 1962-64, Diocese of

Marquette, Kingsford, Mich., 1964-65; jr. high sch. tchr. St. Louis Archdiocese, 1965-71, elem. sch. counselor, 1971-79, secondary sch. counselor, 1979-89, dir. oiffice of learning styles, 1989—. Author: (booklets) Manual for Parents, 1987, Practitioner's Guide to Learning Styles, 1994; producer (video) Learning Styles, 1990. Mem. Nat. Catholic Edn. Assn. Roman Catholic. Office: St Louis Archdiocesan Office of Learning Styles 4449 S Spring Ave Saint Louis MO 63116-4322

LAGANGA, DONNA BRANDEIS, sales and marketing executive; b. Bklyn., June 27, 1949; d. Sidney L. and Sylvia (Herman) Brandeis; B.S. in Bus. Edn., Central Conn. State Coll., New Britain, 1972, M.S., 1975; m. Thomas LaGanga, Aug. 11, 1974. Various secretarial positions, 1969-72; tchr. bus. Lewis S. Mills Regional High Sch., Burlington, Conn., 1972-78; cons. nat. accounts Southwestern Pub. Co., Pelham Manor, N.Y., 1978-84, dist. sales mgr., 1984-89; pres. DBL Industries, Inc., 1989—; nat. accounts mgr. South-Western Pub. Co., Cin., 1989-93, from sr. sales and mktg. mgr. to nat. career sch. mgr., 1993-95; dir. admissions and records Tunxis Cmty. Tech. Coll., Farmington, Conn., 1995—; co-owner Colonial Welding Svc.; seminar condr., 1980—; pres. DBL Industries, Inc. Mem. adv. bd. secretarial sci. dept. LaGuardia Community Coll., Long Island City, N.Y., 1982—; adv. bd. Krissler Bus. Inst. EDPA grantee, 1973; mem. non-partisan ednl. reform task force Pres. George Bush; cert. profl. sec. Mem. NAFE, Assn. Info./Systems Profls., Am. Mgmt. Assn., Nat. Bus. Edn. Assn., Profl. Secs. Internat., Eastern Bus. Edn. Assn., Conn. Bus. Edn. Assn., New Eng. Bus. Edn. Assn., Profl. Secs. Assn. N.Y., Nat. Assn. Cert. Profl. Secs., U.S. Golf Assn., Delta Pi Epsilon. Avocations: knitting, sewing, reading, bicycling, golf. Home: 2929 Torringford St Torrington CT 06790-2332

LAGON, CYNTHIA BOSTIC, librarian; b. Jackson Springs, N.C., July 8, 1949; d. William Andrew and Thelma Ester (Ewings) Bostic; children: Chante, Cheronda. BA, N.C. Ctrl. U., 1971, MLS, 1975. Libr. I Duke U., Durham, N.C., 1971-75; asst. libr. U. Ill., Chgo., 1985-87, Coll. of Chiropractic, Lombard, Ill., 1988-89; ref. libr. Triton Coll., River Grove, Ill., 1990—, prof. coll. 101, 1993, mem. acad. senate, 1992—. Sec. Hist. Soc. Original Bapt. Ch., Chgo., cons., 1991—. Mem. ALA, Ill. Libr. Assn. (mentor networks program 1992-95). Office: Triton Coll 2000 Fifth Ave River Grove IL 60171

LAGORIA, GEORGIANNA MARIE, curator, writer, editor, visual art consultant; b. Oakland, Calif., Nov. 3, 1953; d. Charles Wilson and Margaret Claire (Vella) L.; m. David Joseph de la Torre, May 15, 1982; 1 child, Mateo Joseph. BA in Philosophy, Santa Clara U., 1975; MA in Museology, U. San Francisco, 1978. Exhbn. coordinator Allrich Gallery, San Francisco, 1977-78; asst. registrar Fine Arts Mus., San Francisco, 1978-79; gallery coordinator de Saisset Mus., Santa Clara, Calif., 1979-80, asst. dir., 1980-83, dir., 1983-86; dir. Palo Alto (Calif.) Cultural Ctr., 1986-91; ind. writer, editor and cons. mus. and visual arts orgns., Hawaii, 1992—; V.p. Non-Profit Gallery Assn., San Francisco, 1980-82; bd. dirs. Fiberworks, Berkeley, Calif., 1981-85; field reviewer Inst. Mus. Services, Washington, 1985-87; adv. bd. Hearst Art Gallery, Moraga, Calif., 1986-89, Womens Caucus for Art, San Francisco, 1987—; mem. adv. bd. Weigand Art Gallery, Notre Dame Coll., Belmont, Calif. Curator exhbns. The Candy Store Gallery, 1980, Fiber '81, 1981; curator, author exhbn. catalogue Contemporary Hand Colored Photographs, 1981, Northern Calif. Art of the Sixties, 1982, The Artist and the Machine: 1910-1940, 1986; author catalogue, guide Persis Collection of Contemporary Art at Honolulu Advertiser, 1993; co-author: The Little Hawaiian Cookbook, 1994; coord. exhbn. selections Laila and Thurston Twigg-Smith Collection and Toshiko Takaezu ceramics for Hui No'eau Visual Arts Ctr., Maui, 1993; editor Nuhou (newsletter Hawaii State Mus. Assn.); spl. exhbn. coord. Honolulu Acad. Arts. Mem. Arts Adv. Alliance, Santa Clara County, 1985-86; grant panelist Santa Clara County Arts Council, 1987. Exhbn. grantee Ahmanson Found., 1981, NEA, 1984, Calif. Arts Coun., 1985-89. Mem. Am. Assn. Mus., ArtTable, 1983—, Calif. Assn. Mus. (bd. dirs. 1987-89), Hawaiian Craftsmen (bd. dirs. 1994—), Honolulu Jr. League, Key Project (bd. dirs. 1993-94). Democrat. Roman Catholic. Home and Office: 47-665 Mapele Rd Kaneohe HI 96744

LAGRANGE, CLAIRE MAE, special education educator; b. Tarkio, Mo., Oct. 11, 1937; d. Floyd Gerald and Phyllis Geneva (Wilson) McElfish; m. Irving Joseph LaGrange, May 20, 1955; children: Raymond, Robert, Rhonda, Roger. BA, U. Southwestern La., 1983; MEd, Northwestern State U., 1990. Cert. English, spl. edn., K-12 mild and moderate, assessment tchr., libr. sci., La. Tchr.'s aide St. Martin Parish Sch. Bd., Cecilia, La., 1979-82; tchr. English Florien (La.) High Sch., 1984-86; tchr. Zwolle (La.) High Sch., 1986-90, Cecilia Jr. High Sch., 1990-92, Cecilia High Sch., 1992—; mem. La. Tchr. Assessment Team. Den mother Cub Scouts-Boy Scouts Am., Spokane, Wash., 1967-69; Sunday sch. tchr. First Friends Ch., Spokane, 1968-69. Fellow U. S.W. La Alumni Assn., Northwestern State U. Alumni Assn.; mem. ASCD, Coun. Exceptional Children, Nat. Educators Am., Nat. English Honor Soc., Internat. Reading Assn., La. Assn. Educators, La. Ednl. Assessment Tchrs. Assn., La. Reading Assn., St. Martin Assn. Educators. Home: 1052 Charles Marks Rd Arnaudville LA 70512-3820

LAGRONE, LAVENIA WHIDDON, chemist, real estate broker; b. Conroe, Tex., Feb. 27, 1940; d. James Lewis and Cora Lee (DeLuish) Whiddon; A.A., Kilgore Coll., 1960; B.S., North Tex. State U., 1962; grad. med. tech. Baylor U. Med. Center, 1962; m. Doyle W. LaGrone, June 26, 1959 (div. Sept. 1965); 1 child, Russell Randal. Sr. technologist in spl. chemistry Baylor U. Med. Center, Dallas, 1962-63; research chemist, supr. labs., cardiovascular surgery Southwestern Med. Sch., Dallas, 1964-69, Upstate Med. Center, SUNY, Syracuse, 1969-70; research assoc., supr. lab., dept. surgery U. Tex. Med. Br., Galveston, 1970-74, research assoc., supr. labs., pediatric nephrology, 1974—, mem. chem. safety com., 1984-87; real estate broker DeLanney & Assocs., realtors, 1979-83; owner La Grone & Assocs., Realtors, 1983—. Chmn. student activities PTA Galveston, Tex., 1976-77. Recipient Top Real Estate Sales award, Top Real Estate Producer award, DeLanney & Assocs., 1979, also named Broker's Excellence award and Top Real Estate Commn. award, 1980, also Million Dollar Producer 1980-91. Mem. Am. Soc. Clin. Pathologists (registered med. technologist), Nat. Assn. Realtors, Tex. Assn. Realtors, Galveston Bd. Realtors, Multiple Listing Service (budget com., MLS com.), Phi Theta Kappa. Club: Bus. and Profl. Women's (pub. relations officer 1985-86, chmn. Young Careerist Award 1987, chmn. Woman of Yr. Award 1989, scholarship com. 1988). Contbr. articles to chemistry and med. jours. Home: 142 San Fernando Dr Galveston TX 77550-5712 Office: U Tex Med Br 301 University Blvd Galveston TX 77550-2708

LAHIFF, JEANNE, lawyer; b. Morristown, N.J., May 11, 1960; d. Thomas Martin Sr. and Grace Therese (Brady) L. Diploma, U. Francois Rabelais, Tours, France, 1980; BA magna cum laude, Boston Coll., 1981; JD, U. Pa., 1987. Bar: N.Y., 1989, N.J., 1988, U.S. Dist. Ct. (so. dist., ea. dist. 1989), N.Y., U.S. Dist. Ct. N.J., 1990. Assoc. Cahill, Gordon & Reindel, N.Y.C., 1987-88; law clk. Supreme Ct. N.J., Hackensack, 1988-89; assoc. Paul, Weiss, Rifkind, Wharton & Garrison, N.Y.C., 1989-91, McCarter & English, Newark, N.J., 1991-94; asst. atty. gen. Office Atty. Gen., State of N.Y., N.Y.C., 1994—; adj. prof. Seton Hall U. Sch. Law, 1992-93. Recipient N.J. Hist. Soc. award. Mem. N.J. Bar Assn., Essex Inn of Ct., Phi Alpha Theta.

LAHR, SHERRILL KAY, school system administrator; b. Norman, Okla., June 23, 1944; d. John Galen and Helen Rachel (Smith) Saylor; m. John Stephen Lahr, Dec. 22, 1966; children: Lisa, Jeffrey. BS in Home Econs., U. Nebr., 1967; MEd, Valdosta State U., 1991. Supr. U. Nebr., Lincoln, 1978-79, Omaha Pub. Schs., 1979-80; mgr. U. Mo., Columbia, 1980-86; dietitian Parkwood Devel. Ctr., Valdosta, Ga., 1986-89; sch. nutrition dir. Brooks County Schs., Quitman, Ga., 1989—; mem. Ga. Sch. Fund and Svc. Assn., Am. Sch. Fund and Svc. Assn., 1989—. Pres. Sunday Sch. class. Mem. PEO (treas. 1993-94), Omicron Nu, Lambda Chi Alpha, Phi Upsilon Omicron. Office: Brooks Co Bd Edn PO Bos 511 Quitman GA 31643

LAHTI, CHRISTINE, actress; b. Detroit, Apr. 5, 1950; d. Paul Theodore and Elizabeth Margaret (Tabar) L.; m. Thomas Schlamme, Sept. 4, 1983; 1 child, Wilson Lahti. BA in Speech, U. Mich., 1972; postgrad., Fla. State U., 1972-73; studies with William Esper, Uta Hagen, Herbert Berghof Studios. Actress: (stage prodns.) The Woods, 1978 (Theater World award 1979), Division Street, 1980, Loose Ends, 1981, Present Laughter, 1983, Landscape of the Body, 1984, The Country Girl, 1984, Cat on a Hot Tin Roof, 1985, Little Murders, 1987, The Heidi Chronicles, 1989, Three Hotels, 1993; regular mem. cast (TV series) Dr. Scorpion, 1978, The Harvey Korman Show, 1978, (TV films) The Last Tenant, 1978, The Henderson Monster, 1980, The Executioner's Song, 1982, Single Bars, Single Women, 1984, Love Lives On, 1985, Amerika, 1987, No Place Like Home, 1989, Crazy from the Heart, 1991, The Fear Inside, 1992, The Good Fight, 1985 (feature films) And Justice For All, 1979, Whose Life Is It, Anyway?, 1981, Swing Shift, 1984 (N.Y. Film Critics Circle award for best supporting actress 1985, Acad. award nomination 1985, Golden Globe award nomination 1985), Ladies and Gentlemen: The Fabulous Stains, 1985, Just Between Friends, 1986, Housekeeping, 1987, Season of Dreams, 1987, Stacking, 1988, Running on Empty, 1988, Gross Anatomy, 1989, Miss Firecracker, 1989, Funny About Love, 1990, The Doctor, 1991, Leaving Normal, 1992, Hideaway, 1995. Recipient Golden Globe award for Best Actress in a Miniseries or Motion picture Made for TV. Office: ICM 8942 Beverly Blvd Los Angeles CA 90048*

LAI, SHU-YUAN, banker; b. Taiwan, July 9, 1952; came to U.S., 1976; d. Chin-Sui and Yee-Lee L.; m. Tsong-Yue, Apr. 5, 1975; children: Sharon, Irving. BS, Nat. Taiwan U., 1974; MBA, SUNY, Buffalo, 1979. CPA, Kans. V.p., loan officer Gen. Bank, L.A., 1991—. Bd. dirs. Formosa Assn. for Pub. Affairs, Washington, 1994-95, Taiwanese Assn. in USA, L.A., 1993-94, N. Am. Taiwanese Women Assn., 1992-94, Taiwanese Am. Citizen League, L.A. chpt. 1993. Mem. Chia-Yee Girls' High Alumni Assn. (pres. 1994).

LAINE, KATIE MYERS, communications consultant; b. Bluffton, Ohio, Oct. 2, 1947; d. George Emerson and Elanore (Keeney) Myers; m. Donald Edward Laine (div. Feb. 1990); 1 child, Brett Edward. BS in Edn., S.W. Tex. State U., 1970. Dir. vols. Austin (Tex.) Ctr. for Attitudinal Healing, 1983-86; talk show host Austin Cablevision, 1986-89; community rels. officer Laguna Gloria Art Mus., Austin, 1989-90; spl. events mgr. Ann Richards for Gov. Campaign, Austin, 1990—. Profl. TV talk show host Katie Laine and Friends. Mem. Mayor's Adv. Coun., Austin, 1989—, Austin Women's Polit. Caucus, 1989—, Emily's List, 1989—; vol. Mayor Lee Cooke Campaign, 1988, Ann Richards Campaign for Gov., 1989; tchr. Divorce Recovery Clinic. Mem. NOW, Women in Communications, Nat. Assn. for Corp. Speaker Activities, Paramount Producers. Home: 8703 United Kingdom Austin TX 78748 Office: Divorce Recovery & Family Resources Ctr Austin TX 78759

LAING, BEVERLY ANN, sports association administrator; b. Newark, Mar. 13, 1959; d. Gustave Raymond Hicks and Gloria Mildred (Bellina) Hicks-Prestinari; m. James Thomas Laing Sr., Mar. 10, 1979; children: Christina Marie, James Thomas Jr. A degree, Lab. Inst. Merchandising, N.Y.C., 1979. Pension adminstr. Prudential Ins. Co., Florham Park, N.J., 1976-79; med. asst. Anthony Rossi, M.D., Cedar Grove, N.J., 1983-85; legal asst., paralegal O'Donnell, Kennedy, Esqs., West Orange, N.J., 1986-90; paralegal Greenberg, Mellinger, Esqs., Morris Plains, N.J., 1991; asst. mgr. U.S. Golf Assn., Far Hills, N.J., 1991—. Vol. player registration Children's Miracle Network for golf tournament at Essex County Country Club, West Orange, N.J., 1992. Recipient 1st pl. ribbon N.J. Ceramic Show, 1984. Mem. U.S. Golf Assn. Republican. Roman Catholic. Office: US Golf Assn Golf House Liberty Corner Rd Far Hills NJ 07931

LAING, JOAN RAE, psychologist; b. Delta, Iowa, Dec. 10, 1938; d. George and Dorothea (Walker) Jones; m. Earl John Laing, Aug. 12, 1961 (div. July 1979); children: Catherine, John, Patricia. BA with honors, Cen. Coll., Pella, Iowa, 1958; MA, U. Iowa, 1960; MS, Iowa State U., 1977, PhD, 1979. Lic. psychologist, Iowa. Teaching asst. U. Iowa, Iowa City, 1958-60; tchr. Iowa Pub. Schs., 1960-63; rsch. asst. U. Iowa, Iowa City, 1964-67; intern in psychology U. Cin., 1978-79; psychologist Vassar Coll., Poughkeepsie, N.Y., 1979-80; rsch. psychologist Am. Coll. Testing, Iowa City, 1980-88; dir. psychol. svcs. St. Anthony Regional Hosp., Carroll, Iowa, 1988-91; clin. faculty behavioral scis. dept. U. Osteo. Medicine and Health Scis., Des Moines, 1991—. Editor: Newsnotes, Assn. for Measurement and Evaluation in Counseling and Devel., 1984-87, mem. editorial bd., 1986-89; mem. editorial bd. Jour. nat. Assn. Women Deans, Adminstrs. and Counselors, 1983-87; contbr. articles to profl. jours. Mem. Friends Iowa City Pub. Libr., 1980-88, Friends Carroll Pub. Libr., 1988-91. Mem. APA, Assn. for Measurement and Evaluation in Counseling and Devel. (mem. exec. coun.), Iowa Psychol. Assn. (pres. 1991, sec. divsn. 1990-91, pres. divsn. 1994). Episcopalian. Office: Tower Med Clinic 3200 Grand Ave Des Moines IA 50312-4104

LAING, KAREL ANN, magazine publishing executive; b. Mpls., July 5, 1939; d. Edward Francis and Elizabeth Jane Karel (Templeton) Hannon; m. G. R. Cheesebrough, Dec. 19, 1959 (div. 1969); 1 child, Jennifer Read; m. Ronald Harris Laing, Jan. 6, 1973; 1 child, Christopher Harris. Grad., U. Minn., 1960. With Guthrie Symphony Opera Program, Mpls.,, 1969-71; account supr. Colle & McVoy Advt. Agy., Richfield, Minn., 1971-74; owner The Cottage, Edina, Minn., 1974-75; salespromotion rep. Robert Meyers & Assocs., St. Louis Park, Minn., 1975-76; cons. Webb Co., St. Paul, 1976-77, custom pub. dir., 1977-89; pres. K.L. Publs., Inc., Bloomington, Minn., 1989—. Contbr. articles to profl. jours. Community vol. Am. Heart Assn., Am. Cancer Soc., Edina PTA; charter sponsor Walk Around Am., St. Paul, 1985. Mem. Bank Mktg. Assn., Fin. Instn. Mktg. Assn., Advt. Fedn. Am., Am. Bankers Assn., Direct Mail Mktg. Assn., St. Andrews Soc. Republican. Presbyterian. Office: KL Publs 2001 Killebrew Dr Minneapolis MN 55425-1820

LAING, PENELOPE GAMBLE, art educator; b. Dallas, July 24, 1944; d. William Oscar and Beth (Robertson) G.; m. Richard Harlow Laing, June 29, 1970; children: Scott Emerson, Lindsey Elizabeth. BA in Art, N. Tex. State U., 1966; MFA, Edinboro State Coll., 1979. Cert. tchr., Tex. (life), N.C. (Art all-level). Art cons. Lawrence (Kans.) Unified Sch. Dist., 1966-68; instr. art Ball State U., Muncie, Ind., 1969-71, Edinboro (Pa.) State U., 1976-77, Pitt C.C., Greenville, N.C., 1980-83; exec. dir. Pitt-Greenville Arts Coun., Greenville, 1983-84; free-lance designer, 1984-90; art tchr., head dept. art Pitt County Schs., 1990—; seminar participant N.C. Ctr. for Advancement of Tchg., 1993, tchr.-scholar, 1994. Bd. dirs., v.p. Pitt-Greenville Arts Coun., 1979-82; mem. adv. bd. Pitt County Schs., Greenville, 1985-87; pres. PTA S. Greenville Sch., 1986-87. Named Fellow, Tchr. Exec. Inst., Pitt County Edn. Found., Greenville, 1992; grantee Pitt County Edn. Found., 1991, 92, 93, N.C. Ctr. for Advancement Teaching, 1993, Tchr./scholar, 1994. Mem. Nat. Art Edn. Assn., N.C. Art Edn. Assn. (bd. dirs. 1992-94, chmn. elem. divsn. 1992-94), Surface Design Assocs. (N.C. rep.). Democrat. Home: 204 Pineview Dr Greenville NC 27834 Office: 1325 Red Banks Rd Greenville NC 27858

LAIOU, ANGELIKI EVANGELOS, history educator; b. Athens, Greece, Apr. 6, 1941; came to U.S., 1959; d. Evangelos K. and Virginia I. (Apostolides) Laios; m. Stavros B. Thomadakis, July 14, 1973; 1 son, Vassili N. B.A., Brandeis U., 1961; M.A., Harvard U., 1962, Ph.D., 1966. Asst. prof. history Harvard U., Cambridge, Mass., 1969-72, Dumbarton Oaks prof. Byzantine history, 1981—; assoc. prof. Brandeis U., Waltham, 1972-75; prof. Rutgers U., New Brunswick, N.J., 1975-79, disting. prof., 1979-81; chmn. Gennadeion com. (Am. Sch. Classical Studies), Athens, Greece, 1981-84; dir. Dumbarton Oaks, 1989—. Author: Constantinople and the Latins, 1972, Peasant Society in the Late Byzantine Empire, 1977, Mariage, amour et parenté à Byznace, XIe-XIIIe siècles, 1992, Gender, Society and Economic Life in Byzantium, 1992, Consent and Coercion to Sex and Marriage in Ancient and Medieval Societies, 1993. Guggenheim Found. fellow, 1971-72, 79-80, Dumbarton Oaks sr. fellow, 1983-88, Am. Coun. Learned Socs. fellow, 1988-89. Mem. Am. Hist. Assn., Medieval Acad. Am., Societa Ligure di Storia Patria, Greek Com. Study of South Eastern Europe. Office: Dumbarton Oaks 1703 32nd St NW Washington DC 20007-2961

LAIRD, JEAN ELOUISE RYDESKI (MRS. JACK E. LAIRD), author, adult education educator; b. Wakefield, Mich., Jan. 18, 1930; d. Chester A. and Agnes A. (Petranek) Rydeski; m. Jack E. Laird, June 9, 1951; children: John E., Jayne E., Joan Ann P., Jerilyn S., Jacquelyn T. Bus. Edn. degree Duluth (Minn.) Bus. U., 1948; posgrad. U. Minn., 1949-50. Tchr. Oak Lawn (Ill.) High Sch. Adult Evening Sch., 1964-72, St. Xavier Coll., Chgo., 1974—; lectr., commencement address cir. Writer newspaper column Around The House With Jean, A Woman's Work, 1965-70, Chicagotown News column The World As I See It, 1969, hobby column Modern Maturity mag., travel column Travel/Leisure mag., beauty column Ladycom mag., Time and Money Savers column Lady's Circle mag., consumerism column Ladies' Home Jour. Mem. Canterbury Writers Club Chgo. (past. pres.), Oak Lawn Bus. and Profl. Women's Club (Woman of Yr. award 1987), St. Linus Guild, Mt. Assisi Acad., Marist, Queen of Peace parents clubs. Roman Catholic. Author: Lost in the Department Store, 1964; Around The House Like Magic, 1968; Around The Kitchen Like Magic, 1969; How To Get the Most From Your Appliances, 1967; Hundreds of Hints for Harrassed Homemakers, 1971; The Alphabet Zoo, 1972; The Plump Ballerina, 1971; The Porcupine Story Book, 1974; Fried Marbles and Other Fun Things To Do, 1975; Hundreds of Hints for Harassed Homemakers; The Homemaker's Book of Time and Money Savers, 1979; Homemaker's Book of Energy Savers, 1981; also 348 paperback booklets. Contbr. numerous articles to mags. Home: 10540 Lockwood Ave Oak Lawn IL 60453-5161 also: 1 Magnificent Mile Bldg Chicago IL 60600 also: Vista De Lago Lake Geneva WI 53147

LAIRD, MARY See WOOD, LARRY

LAIRD-LAGASSEE, JANET, artist; b. Lewiston, Maine, Nov. 27, 1947; d. Arthur Gustavus and Alice Beatrice (Nelson) Laird; m. J. Arthur Lagassee, Aug. 23, 1969; 1 child, Nicholas Arthur. Student, Portland Sch. Art, 1967-69. Solo exhbns. include Arcady Mus. Festival Concert Series, Hupper Gallery, Hebron, Maine, Water St. Gallery, Newburyport, Mass., Lewiston-Auburn (Maine) Coll.; juried group shows include Miniature Art Soc., Fla., 1986—, Miniature Painters, Sculptors & Gravers Art Soc. of Washington, 1986—, Miniature Art Soc. N.J., 1986-93, Del Bello Gallery, Toronto, 1986-91, Ga. Miniature Art Soc., 1986—, Jane Law Art Studios and Gallery, Surf City, N.J., 1987— (Best in Show award), La. Watercolor Soc., 1988, 93, New Eng. Watercolor Soc. Nat. Open, 1988, 90, 94, Mont. Miniature Art Soc., 1988—, Redding (Calif.) Mus. and Art Ctr., 1990, Cape Cod Art Assn., 1992—, North East Watercolor Soc., 1993, 94, Nev. Artists Assn., 1993, 94, Acad. Artists Assn., Mass., 1993, Parklane Gallery, Seattle, 1993, 94, So. Vt. Artists Assn., 1992, 93, 94, Art Gallery of Fells Pt. Md., 1988, 89, 90, 92, 93, 94, Am. Nat. Miniature Show, Laramie, Wyo., 1989—, New Eng. Watercolor Soc. New Eng. Show, 1994; permanent collections include Ga. Miniature Art Soc., corporate and private collections, others. Recipient Watson-Guptill award Acad. Artists Assn., 1993, Strathmore Artists Excellence award Still River Artists Guild, 1993, Best in Show award Nev. Artists Assn., 1993, First Overall award, 1994, Best in Show award Mont. Miniature Art Soc. Internat., 1989, award N.E. Watercolor Soc., 1993, First Overall award Parklane Gallery, Kirkland, Washington, 1994, Best of Show award Art Gallery of Fells Point, Balt., 1994. Mem. Miniature Artists Am. (assoc.), Ga. Miniature Art Soc., Miniature Painters, Sculptors and Gravers Soc. (elected assoc.), Cider Painters Am., New England Watercolor Soc. (elected). Home and Studio: 43 Elmwood Rd Auburn ME 04210-6509

LAKAH, JACQUELINE RABBAT, political scientist, educator; b. Cairo, Apr. 14, 1933; came to U.S., 1969, naturalized, 1975; d. Victor Boutros and Alice (Mounayer) Rabbat; m. Antoine K. Lakah, Apr. 8, 1951; children: Micheline, Mireille, Caroline. BA, Am. U. Beirut, 1968; MPh, Columbia U., 1974, cert. Mid. East Inst., 1975, PhD, 1978. Assoc. prof. polit. sci. and world affairs Fashion Inst. Tech., N.Y.C., 1978—, asst. chairperson social scis. dept., 1989—; asst. prof. grad. faculty polit. sci. Columbia U., N.Y.C., summer 1979, vis. scholar, 1982-83, also mem. seminar on Mid. East; guest faculty Sarah Lawrence Coll., 1981-82; cons. on Mid. East; faculty rsch. fellow SUNY, summer 1982. Fellow Columbia Faculty, 1970-73, NDEA Title IV, 1971-72; Mid. East Inst. scholar, 1976; Rockefeller Found. scholar, 1967-69. Mem. European Cmty. Studies Assn., Am. Polit. Sci. Assn., Fgn. Policy Assn., Internat. Studies Assn., Internat. Polit. Sci. Assn. Roman Catholic. Home: 41-15 94th St Queens NY 11373-1745 Office: 7th Ave At 27th St New York NY 10001-5992

LAKATTA, PATRICIA LOUISE, former nurse, public relations and marketing executive; b. Scranton, Pa., Dec. 5, 1946; d. Edward David and Pauline Ann (Lucas) L.; m. Joseph B. Sakaduski, Apr. 27, 1968 (div. June 1982); children: Joseph, Jill. RN, Nesbitt Hosp. Sch. Nursing, 1967; BA in Communications cum laude, Goucher Coll., 1980; MS in Mktg., Johns Hopkins U., 1994. RN, Pa., Md. Nurse various hosps., Balt., 1967-77; health educator Goucher Coll., Towson, Md., 1979-80; adminstrv. coord. Telesis Inc., Balt., 1980-81; project dir. Ashton-Worhington Inc., Balt., 1981-84; dir. pub. rels. St. Joseph Hosp., Towson, 1984-86; dir. pub. affairs Homewood Hosp. Ctr./John Hopkins Health System, Balt., 1986-89; pres. Mktg. Communications, Inc., Towson, 1989; v.p. mktg. and pub. rels. Farrar Network, Balt., 1989-91; pres. Mktg. Communications Inc., Towson, 1991—; editor Nursing Spectrum Mag., 1992-94; radio cons., Balt., 1987; writing cons. Glenelg (Md.) Country Sch., 1988, Children's Hosp., Balt., 1988—; mem. faculty Goucher Coll., Towson, 1986—; med. writer U. Md., Johns Hopkins, Kernan Hosp.; part-time nurse Va. Hosp., Balt., 1992. Writer, prodr.: (film) One Voice, 1982 (1st pl. award Nat. AFL/CIO); writer, supr.: Personal Delivery, 1985 (1st pl. award), (newsletter) Housecall, 1987; writer, prodr.: A Living Spirit, 1984; pub. children's cassette Sunny Side Up, 1995. Bd. dirs. Am. Heart Assn., Balt., 1986—, chair comm., 1987—; mem. exec. com. Acad. Health Svcs. Met., 1987-88; mem. adv. bd. Goucher Coll., 1984—; bd. dirs. Balt. Choral Arts; dir. comm. ARC, Greater Chesapeake and Potomac region; comm. officer ARC, 1994. Recipient Presl. award Am. Heart Assn., All Star award. Fellow Balt. Pub. Rels. Soc.; mem. Pub. Rels. Soc. Am., Md. Hosp. Soc. (bd. dirs. 1986-88), Am. Hosp. Assn., APHA (nat. media campaign com.), Md. Press Assn., Md. Found. Nursing (bd. dirs.), Am. Mktg. Assn. Democrat. Roman Catholic.

LAKE, BONNIE JOSEPHINE, flutist, educator; b. Cleve., Apr. 22, 1930; d. Frederic Cleland and Clara Josephine (Haskins) L. Studied with William Kincaid, 1946-48, studied with Jean-Pierre Rampal, 1951-53; MusB, MusB in Edn., Oberlin Coll. Conservatory, 1952, MusM, 1955; studied with Robert Willoughby, 1954-62; cert. in flute, Mozarteum Somer Acad., Salzburg, Austria, 1958; cert. in flute, chamber music, Acad. Internat. d'Ete, Nice, France, 1961; studied with Maurice Sharpe. With Akron (Ohio) Symphony, 1952-54; flutist, piccolo Indpls. Symphony, 1955-57; flutist Balt. Symphony, 1957—, piccoloist, 1957-62, asst. 1st flute, 1962-76, 2d flute, 1976—; prof. flute Peabody Inst. Music, Balt., 1958—, Goucher Coll., Towson, Md., 1962—; adj. tchr. flute Oberlin (Ohio) Conservatory, 1952-54, Jordan Coll. Music, Indpls., 1955-57; flutist La d'Oro Trio, Balt., 1967-70, Md. Quintet, Balt., 1966-70, Phila. Composers Forum, 1968-69, Res Musica, Balt., 1979-86; judge, tchr. master classes Flute Socs. Balt. and Washington. Solo recitals in U.S. and western Europe. Mem. Music Tchrs. Nat. Assn., Women in the Arts, Am. Fedn. Music (scholar 1948), Nat. Flute Assn., Mu Phi Epsilon, Pi Alpha Lambda. Presbyterian. Home: 1101 N Calvert St Baltimore MD 21202-3840 Office: Balt Symphony 1212 Cathedral St Baltimore MD 21201

LAKE, KATHLEEN C., lawyer; b. San Antonio, Jan. 11, 1955; d. Herschel Taliaferro and Virginia Mae (Hylton) Cooper; m. Randall Brent Lake, Apr. 9, 1977; 1 child, Ethan Taliaferro. AB magna cum laude, Middlebury Coll., 1977; JD with high honors, U. Tex., 1980. Bar: Tex. 1980, U.S. Ct. Appeals (5th cir.) 1981, U.S. Ct. Appeals (D.C. and 3d cirs.) 1984. Assoc. atty. Vinson & Elkins, Houston, 1980-88; ptnr. Vinson & Elkins, LLP, Houston, 1989—. Fellow Tex. Bar Found., Houston Bar Found.; mem. ABA, Fed. Energy Bar Assn., State Bar Tex., Tex. Law Rev. Assn. (life), Houston Bar Assn., Middlebury Coll. Alumni Assn. (com. mem. 1980—), Phi Beta Kappa, Phi Kappa Phi, Order of the Coif. Office: Vinson & Elkins LLP 2300 First City Twr 1001 Fannin Houston TX 77002-6760

LAKE, SUZANNE PHILENA, singer, teacher; b. Palisade, N.J., June 26, 1929; d. Mayhew Lester and Suzanne Louise (Robin) L.; m. George A. De Vos, Nov. 19, 1974. pvt. tchr., Oakland, Calif., 1976-86, univ. extension U. Calif., Sacramento State U., 1981-84. Featured roles opera, N.Y.C., 1948-51; appeared in Broadway plays The King and I, 1951-54, Flower Drum Song, 1960-61; concert and supper club appearances in U.S., Can., Carribbean, Japan, and Europe, 1955-86, also TV appearances. Mem. Actors Equity, AFTRA, Am. Guild Mus. Artists, Am. Guild Variety Artists. Home: 2835 Morley Dr Piedmont CA 94611-2547

LAKE, TINA SELANDERS, artist, educator; b. London, Sept. 12, 1953; came to U.S., 1956; d. Leslie Martin Selanders and Doris Kirk; m. Paul Saunders Lake III, Dec. 30, 1971; children: Rachel, Alexander. BS, Towson State U., 1977; MFA, San Francisco Art Inst., 1980; postgrad., Ark. Arts Ctr., 1985. Teaching asst. Towson State U., Balt., 1977; grad. teaching asst. San Francisco Art Inst., 1979; instr. drawing and painting, summer arts camp, adult drawing Ark. River Valley Art Ctr., Russellville, 1986, instr. beginning drawing for children, painting and drawing, 1991; vis. instr. U. Ozarks, 1987, Ark. Tech. U., Russellville, 1987; part-time instr. Ark. Tech. U., 1986, vis. lectr., 1982, 83; guest speaker 3d Ann. Young Author's Conf., Ark. Tech. U., 1991; pub. rels. asst. San Francisco Art Inst., 1980; lectr. Berkeley (Calif.) Art Ctr., 1981, Ark. Arts Ctr., 1992. Exhibited in group shows at Holtzman Gallery, Balt., 1976, Balt. Arts Festival, 1977, San Francisco Art Inst., 1979, The Woman's Bldg., L.A., 1980, The Goodman Bldg., San Francisco, 1981, Ark. River Valley Arts Ctr., Russellville, 1981, 91, Ark. Arts Ctr., Little Rock, 1985, 86, 89, 91, 92, 93, 94, U. Ark. Fine Arts Ctr. Gallery, Fayetteville, 1986, Ark. Tech. U., 1991, Ark. Territorial Restoration Exhbn., Little Rock, 1992, 93, Russell Fine Arts Ctr., Henderson State U., Arkadelphia, Ark., 1992, 94, Treishmann Gallery Hendrix Coll., Conway, Ark., 1993, Springfield (Mo.) Art Mus., 1994, Ark. Art Ctr., Little Rock, 1995; represented in Ctrl. Ark. Libr. Sys., and numerous pvt. collections; graphic designer: (design and layout literary mag.) Occident, 1980-81; art adv. (literary mag.) Nebo, 1984-86. Recipient numerous Best of Show awards and Purchase awards. Home and Studio: 400 S Commerce Ave Russellville AR 72801-5935

LAKEY, JOYCE F., therapist; b. Ft. Wayne, Ind., June 7, 1930; d. Keith E. and Florence (Polak) Lakey; m. James W. Shanks, May 8, 1953 (div. May 1984); children: Jeff, Michael, Paula, Laurie (dec.). AB, Ind. U., 1952; MS, Ind. State U., 1972. Cert. nat. counselor; cert. clin. social worker, Ind. Editorial asst. Sun-Times, Chgo., 1952-53; copywriter Wabash Advt. Co., Terre Haute, Ind., 1953-55; part-time counselor Terre Haute, 1977-89; therapist Gibault Sch. for Boys, Terre Haute, 1987—; freelance photojournalist, Terre Haute, 1952—; instr. tchr.-parenting classes Family Edn. Assn., 1978-90. Contbr. articles to profl. jours., mags., newspapers. Bd. dirs. Covered Bridge Coun. Girl Scouts U.S., 1965, Vigo County Hist. Soc., Terre Haute, 1984; pres. bd. dirs. Girls Club of Terre Haute, 1979; active PTA, Vigo County Assn. for Mental Health, Cancer Soc., others. Recipient Disting. Svc. award Girls Club Am., 1973, Girls Club of Terre Haute, 1981, others; E.H. Kilbourne scholar, 1948-52. Mem. ACA, NASW, Internat. Assn. Addictions and Offender Counselors, Ind. Counseling Assn., Midwest Regional Network for Intervention with Sex Offenders (founding mem., adv. bd.). Home: 3121 Oak St Terre Haute IN 47803-2648

LAKNER, JEAN DIANE, counselor; b. Huron, S.D., Sept. 13, 1948; d. Joy Chase and Lois May (NcNeil) Duxbury; m. John William Lakner, Aug. 24, 1968; children: Gregory, Kimberly, Sara, Katie. BS, Black Hills State U., 1969, MS, 1976. Lic. profl. counselor S.D. Tchr. phys. edn. Sundance (Wyo.) Schs., 1969-71; tchr. elem. sch. Draper (S.D.) Schs., 1971-73, Crazy Horse Sch., Wanblee, S.D., 1973-76; prin. elem. sch. Roscoe (S.D.) Pub. Schs., 1976-78; counselor elem. sch. Pierre (S.D.) Pub. Schs., 1978-90; counselor mental health Profl. Counseling Assocs., Pierre, 1990—. Mem., officer Pierre-Ft. Pierre Child Protection Team, 1978—; hon. mem. S.D. PTA, 1986. Mem. Am. Counselors Assn., S.D. Counselors Assn. (Sch. Counselor of Yr. 1986). Democrat. Roman Catholic. Office: Profl Counseling Assocs 125 W Dakota Ave Pierre SD 57501-4501

LALE, CISSY STEWART (LLOYD LALE), freelance writer; b. Port Arthur, Tex., Jan. 15, 1924; d. Lloyd M. and May (Cowart) Stewart; m. Max Sims Lale, Oct. 9, 1983. BJ, U. Tex., 1945. Reporter Record-News, Wichita Falls, Tex., 1945, News-Messenger, Marshall, Tex., 1945-47; editor Times-Rev., Cleburne, Tex., 1947-49; women's editor Star-Telegram, Ft. Worth, 1949-87; freelance writer, columnist mag. Ft. Worth mag., 1987-90, 90—. Bd. dirs. Trinity Terr. Retirement Community, 1991-94. Cissy Stewart Day proclaimed by Ft. Worth City Coun., 1987, portrayed in outdoor mural City of Ft. Worth, 1987. Mem. Women in Comm. Inc. (nat. pres. 1968-71), Tex. State Hist. Assn. (2d v.p. 1994), East Tex. Hist. Assn. (pres. 1994), Tex. Heritage, Inc. (bd. dirs. Ft. Worth chpt. 1990), Womans Club Ft. Worth, Ft. Worth Garden Club (v.p. 1992-93). Episcopalian. Home: Apt 101 3900 White Settlement Rd Fort Worth TX 76107-7822

LA LIBERTE, ANN GILLIS, graphic artist, consultant, designer, educator; b. St. Paul, Nov. 10, 1942; d. Edward Robert and Frances Caroline (Sullivan) Gillis; m. Paul Henry La Liberte, Aug. 22, 1964; children: Paul E., Elizabeth A., Stephen A., Helen C., Peter N., Marc H. Student, Am U., 1963-64, Cardinal Stritch Coll., Milw., 1960-63; BA, Coll. St. Catherine, St. Paul, 1985. Artist, owner Ann La Liberte Papers and Posters, Minnetonka, Minn., 1968-71, A.L. Graphic Design and Drawings, Minnetonka, Minn., 1983—; artist Arts in the Schs., Minn., 1985—. Liturgical designer Christian Chs., Mpls. and St. Paul, 1977—; paintings, drawings, photography and sculpture exhibited Mpls. and St. Paul area, 1983—; sculpture Life Exhibit, Paul VI Inst. for the Arts, Washington, 1988, on tour Vt., Ohio, Mo., Ill., Wis., 1988. Del. Minn. Ind. Reps., 1969, vice chair, 1970; promotional artist, Soc. Preservation Human Dignity, Palatine, Ill., 1973, Minn. Citizens Concerned for Life, 1980-88, Secular Franciscans, St. Paul, 1985; deanery rep. Pastoral Coun. Archdiocese of St. Paul, Mpls., 1978-82; chair devel. task force Out-Reach program Resurrection Ch., Mpls., 1980-81, cons. artist 1983—, pvt. art tchr., dir. creativity and problem solving seminars, 1991—; mem. worship bd. Ch. of Immaculate Heart of Mary, Minnetonka, 1991—; liturgical art and environ. cons. Mem. Nat. Assn. Liturgical Ministers, Mpls. Soc. Fine Arts, Nat. Mus. Women in the Arts (charter), Walker Art Ctr., Coll. St. Catherine Alumna Assn., Artists for Life Nat. Slide Registry, Delta Phi Delta. Roman Catholic. Home: 13418 Excelsior Blvd Minnetonka MN 55345-4910

LALIM-FALCONE, PATRICIA JEANNE, administrative assistant; b. Montevideo, Minn., Oct. 12; d. Clarence I. and Eva (Corneliusen) Lalim; m. Alfonso Benjamin Falcone, Oct. 22; children: Christopher L., Steven B. BS, U. Minn., 1956; MS, U. Wis., 1958, PhD, 1962. Libr. asst. U. Minn., St. Paul, 1953-54; singer/performer Mpls., 1949-55; asst. prog. dir. U. Wis. Meml. Union, Madison, 1957-58; instr. U. Wis., Madison, 1965-66; adminstrv. asst. A.B. Falcone, M.D., Ph.D., Fresno, Calif., 1968—; pvt. investor Patricia Lalim Falcone, Ph.D., Fresno, 1968—; lectr. in field; contbr./presenter various conf., seminars. Contbr. articles to profl. jours.; author various ednl. and profl. pamphlets; artist/craftsman textile designs for U. Wis. Traveling exhibit, 1965-66. Bd. dirs. Fresno/Madera Polit. Action Com., 1985-89, 1990—; mem. Supts. Roundtable, Fresno Unified Sch. Dist., 1989; chmn. U. Calif., Fresno com. to bring UC campus to Fresno area, 1987—; chmn. Parent Adv. Com. for Gifted and Talented, 1985, mem. 1984—; citizens adv. coun. U. Calif., San Joaquin, 1991—; active Anti Defamation League. U. Wis. fellow, 1958-59, scholar, 1959-62. Mem. AAUW, Med. Aux. of Fresno County Med. Soc. (exec. bd. 1989—), Assn. for Acad. Excellence (chmn. 1988-91), Edison Computech Assn., Am. Scandinavian Found., Norwegian Am. Hist. Assn., Fresno Art Mus., Kappa Omicron Nu, Pi Lambda Theta, Phi Delta Gamma. Office: 2240 E Illinois Ave Fresno CA 93701-2118

LALLI, CELE GOLDSMITH, editor; b. Scranton, Pa., Apr. 8, 1933; d. Arthur Langfeld and Viola Catherine (Wolfort) Goldsmith; m. Michael Anthony Lalli, Apr. 4, 1964; children—Francesca Ann, Erica Catherine. BA, Vassar Coll., 1955. From asst. editor to editor Amazing Sci. Fiction Stories, N.Y.C., 1955-65; mng. editor Modern Bride's Guide to Decorating Your First Home, N.Y.C., 1965-69; exec. editor Modern Bride, N.Y.C., 1969-81, editor-in-chief, v.p., 1982—. Co-author: Modern Bride Guide to Your Wedding and Marriage, 1984, Wedding Celebrations, 1992. Bd. dirs. Conn. Assn. for Children with Learning Disabilities, 1984—. Recipient Invisible Little Man award West Coast Sci. Fiction Orgn., 1961; named to YWCA Acad. of Women Achievers, 1986. Mem. Am. Soc. Mag. Editors, Fashion Group. Republican. Roman Catholic. Office: Modern Bride Cahners Pub Co 249 W 17th St New York NY 10011-5300*

LALLI, MARY SCHWEITZER, writer, artist; b. Newark, Ohio, June 24, 1925; d. Clemence Sylvester and Ethel Ann (Deem) Schilling; m. Francis Edward Schweitzer, Aug. 23, 1947 (div. Oct. 1974); children: Dale Francis, Darrell Charles, David Edward; m. Joseph G. Lalli, June 21, 1975. BA, Denison U., 1947. Lic. tchr. English. Tchr. English Ctrl. Jr. High, Newark, 1947-48; profl. artist Nat. Forum Profl. Artists, Phila., 1968-75; dir. art shows Nat. Forum of Profl. Artists, 1968—; Art Alliance. Writer Doll Castle News, Doll Times, Doll Reader, Antique Doll World, Doll Collector's Price Guide, Doll World, 1983—; photojournalist Doll Times; columnist Doll Designs. Recipient 125 art awards Phila. Plastic Club, 1972, 73, 78, award of honor Inst. Pub. Edn., Drexel Hill, Pa., 1980. Mem. Nat. League Am. Pen Women (1st v.p. 1985-89), DaVinci Art Alliance (pres., v.p. 1968-77), Plastic Club, Chester County Art Assn.

LALLY, NORMA ROSS, federal agency administrator, retired; b. Crawford, Nebr., Aug. 10, 1932; d. Roy Anderson and Alma Leona (Barber) Lively; m. Robert Edward Lally, Dec. 4, 1953 (div. Mar. 1986); children: Robyn Carol Murch, Jeffrey Alan, Gregory Roy. BA, Boise (Idaho) State U., 1974, MA, 1976; postgrad., Columbia Pacific U., 1988—. With grad. admissions Boise State U., 1971-74; with officer programs USN Recruiting, Boise, 1974; pub. affairs officer IRS, Boise and Las Vegas, 1975-94; ret., 1994; speaker in field, Boise and Las Vegas, 1977—. Contbr. articles to newspapers. Mem. task force Clark County Sch. Dist., Las Vegas. Staff sgt. USAF, 1950-54. Mem. NAFE, Internat. Assn. Bus. Communicators, Mensa, Toastmasters (Las Vegas), Marine's Meml. Club (life), Am. Legion. Home: 3013 Hawksdale Dr Las Vegas NV 89134-8967

LALLY-GREEN, MAUREEN ELLEN, legal educator; b. Sharpsville, Pa., July 5, 1949; d. Francis Leonard and Charlotte Marie (Frederick) Lally; m. Stephen Ross Green, Oct. 5, 1979; children: Katherine Lally, William Ross, Bridget Marie. BS, Duquesne U., 1971, JD, 1974. Bar: Pa. 1974, D.C., U.S. Dist. Ct. (we. dist.) Pa. 1974, U.S. Ct. Appeals (3d cir.) 1974, U.S. Supreme Ct. 1978. Atty. Houston Cooper, Pitts., 1974-75, Commodity Futures Trading Commn., Washington, 1975-78; counsel Westinghouse Electric Corp., Pitts., 1978-83; adj. prof. law Duquesne U., Pitts., 1983-86, prof. law in criminal, employment discrimination labor law, profl. responsibility law, legal writing, environ. law, 1986—; fed. dist. ct. arbitrator; mem. criminal procedure rules com. Supreme Ct. of Pa., 1994—; dir. European Union Law Conf., Dublin. Chaiperson, mem. Cranberry Twp. Zoning Hearing Bds., Mars, Pa., 1983—; counsel Western Pa. Ptnrs. of Ams., 1987—, pres. 1993—; active Elimination of World Hunger Project, 1977—. Fellow Kellogg Found. (for Ptnrs. of Ams.), 1990-92. Mem. Pa. Bar Assn. (ethics com. 1987—, commn. on women in the law 1994—), Allegheny County Bar Assn. (women in law com., professionalism com., ethics com., sec. bd. dirs. 1992-94), Duquesne U. Alumni Assn. (bd. dirs. 1982-89, sec. 1988-89, gov. of bd. 1995—), Duquesne U. Law Alumni Assn. (bd. dirs. 1987—, treas. 1991—, v.p. 1992—). Republican. Roman Catholic. Office: Duquesne U Sch Law G-11 Pittsburgh PA 15282

LAMAR, MARTHA LEE, chaplain; b. Birmingham, Jan. 2, 1935; d. Alco L. and Anne Lee (Morris) Lee; m. William Fred Lamar, Jr., June 7, 1986; children: Barbara Gayle Martin, Owen Parker Jr. BS, Auburn U., 1955; MA, Christian Theol. Sem., Indpls., 1992. From adminstv. asst. to rsch. coord. Ala. Affiliate Am. Heart Assn., Birmingham, 1977-86; adminstrv. asst. alumni office De Pauw U., Greencastle, Ind., 1986-89; nursing home chaplain Heritage House Health and Rehab. Ctr., Greencastle, 1989—; nursing home chaplain Garfield Park Health Facility, Indpls., 1992-94, Heritage Ho. Health and Rehab. Ctr., Martinsville, Ind., 1992—; chaplain cons. Oakwood Corp., Indpls., 1991—. Vol. chaplain's office De Pauw U., 1986—, community work for homeless, Greencastle, 1986—, Fountain Sq. Devel. Corp., Indpls., 1992. Mem. ACA, Nat. Interfaith Coalition on Aging, Am. Soc. on Aging, Mental Health and Aging Network and Forum on Religion, Spirituality and Aging. Methodist. Office: Heritage House Health & Rehab Ctr 1601 Hosp Dr Greencastle IN 46135

LAMB, ANN MARIE, research scientist; b. N.Y.C., Oct. 14, 1938; d. Leonard Joseph Cammalleri and Angela Marie (Mirandi) Stein; m. Jackson L. Lamb, 1964 (div. Sept. 1980); children: Judith Mirandi, Angela Holladay. BS, SUNY, Cortland, 1960; MS in Edn., Miss. State U., University, 1969, PhD, 1989; certificate, U. Ga. Drug and Alcohol Studies, Athens, 1977. Cert. psychometrist, tchr., counselor, Miss. Dir. special programs Noxubee County Schs., Macon, Miss., 1968-74; rep. region Div. Alcohol and Drugs Mental Health Agy. St. Miss., Jackson, 1974-76; dir. program Mental Health Services Sch. Age Children Amory (Miss.) Pub. Schs., 1976-78; exec. dir. 3 Rivers Area Health Services Inc., Amory, Miss., 1978-81; grad. asst. Rehabilitation Research and Tng. Ctr. Low Vision Blind Miss. State U., University, 1982-83; counselor student fin. aid Miss. Sate U., University, 1983-87; asst. research Rehabilitation Research and Tng. Ctr. Low Vision/Blind Miss. State U., University, 1987—; test adminstr. Standardized Testing Program Miss. State U. 1985—. Contbr. articles to profl. jours. Mem. Concerned Citizens Clay County, pres., sec., 1980-84; mem., vice chmn. Clay County 3d Dist. Dem. Exec. Com., 1984—; trustee East Miss. C.C. Mem. Miss. Counselor Assn., Coun. Exceptional Children, Faculty and Profl. Women's Assn. (sec. 1985, chair scholarship com. 1994), Phi Delta Kappa. Roman Catholic. Office: Rehab Tng Ctr LOw Vision 48-50 Magruder St Mississippi State MS 39762

LAMB, DARLIS CAROL, sculptor; b. Wausa, Nebr.; d. Lindor Soren and June Berniece (Skalberg) Nelson; m. James Robert Lamb; children: Sherry Lamb Sobh, Michael, Mitchell. BA in Fine Arts, Columbia Pacific U., San Rafael, Calif., 1988; MA in Fine Arts, Columbia Pacific U., 1989. Exhibited in group shows at Nat. Arts Club, N.Y.C., 1983, 85, 89, 90, 91, 92 (Catherine Lorillard Wolfe award sculpture 1983, C. L. Wolfe Horse's Head award 1994), N.Am. Sculpture Exhibit, Foothills Art Ctr., Golden, Colo., 1983, 84, 86, 87, 90, 91, Pub. Svc. Colo. award 1990), Nat. Acad. Design, 1986, Nat. Sculpture Soc., 1985, 91 (C. Percival Dietsch Sculpture Prize 1991), Loveland Mus. and Gallery, 1990, 91, Allied Artists of Am., 1992, others; represented in permanent collections: Nebr. Hist. Soc., Am. Lung Assn. of Colo., Benson Park Sculpture Garden, Loveland, others. Mem. Am. Artists Profl. League, Catherine Lorillard Wolfe Art Club, N.Am. Sculpture Soc. Office: PO Box 9043 Englewood CO 80111-0301

LAMB, DEBORAH A., federal and state government lawyer; b. Missoula, Mont., May 31, 1953; d. George E. and Ingeburg (Teckenburg) L.; m. Joseph Valenza, 1989. BA summa cum laude, Lewis and Clark Coll., 1975; MA with distinction, John Hopkins Sch., 1977; JD cum laude, Georgetown U., 1988. Bar: D.C., 1989. Economist Bur. of East West Trade, Dept. Commerce, Washington, 1978-82; dir. Korea and Taiwan Internat. Trade Adminstrn., Dept. Commerce, 1982-88; atty. Steptoe & Johnson, Washington, 1988-90; internat. trade counsel Senate Com. on Fin., Washington, 1990—. Mem. ABA, D.C. Bar Assn., Amnesty Internat. Office: Com on Finance 205 Senate Dirksen Office Bldg Washington DC 20510*

LAMB, IRENE HENDRICKS, medical researcher; b. Ky., May 9, 1940; d. Daily P. and Bertha (Hendricks) Lamb; m. Edward B. Meadows. RN, Ky. Bapt. Hosp., Louisville; student, Berea (Ky.) Coll., Calif. State U., L.A. RN, Calif., Ky. Charge nurse, head nurse acute medicine, med. ICU, surgical ICU, emergency room various med. ctrs., 1963-67; staff nurse rsch. coronary care unit, 1968; asst. nurse coord., nurse coord. clin. rsch. ctr. U. So. Calif./L.A. County Med. Ctr., L.A., 1969-74; sr. rsch. nurse cardiology Stanford (Calif.) U. Sch. Medicine, 1974-85, rsch. coord. pvt. clin., 1988, dir. clin. rsch. pvt. cardiology group, 1989-92; clin. rsch. cons., community health nurse, 1993-94. Co-author numerous articles to med. jours.; contbr. articles to nursing jours. and chpts. to med. books. Mem. Am. Heart Assn. (cardiovascular nursing sect.). Home: 208 Rockcastle St Berea KY 40403-1243

LAMB, MARY ANGELA, patient educator; b. Cin., June 17, 1939; d. Harry C. and Victoria Rose (Wich) Vogelsang; div.; children: Ronald, Catherine, Rod. Diploma in Nursing, Mercy Sch. Nursing, 1960; BSN, Thomas More Coll., 1985. RN, Ohio; cert. CDE, CETN. Staff nurse St. Francis Hosp., Cin., 1960-61, Flagler Hosp., St. Augustine, Fla., 1961, St. Vincent Hosp., Jacksonville, Fla., 1961-63, North Miss. Community Hosp., Tupelo, 1963, Moline (Ill.) Pub. Hosp., 1964-66; staff nurse, head nurse Good Samaritan Hosp., Cin., 1966-72, patient educator, 1973—; cons. United Ostomy Assn., Cin., 1975—. Vol., speaker Am. Cancer Soc., Cin., 1975—; vol. Am. Diabetic Assn., Cin., 1970—. Mem. Am. Assn. Diabetic Edn., Diabetic Educators of Cin. Area (treas. 1992), Internat. Assn. Enterstomal Therapists. Roman Catholic. Home: 5611 Old Blue Rock Rd Cincinnati OH 45247 Office: Good Samaritan Hosp 375 Dixmyth Ave Cincinnati OH 45220

LAMB, STACIE THOMPSON, elementary school educator; b. Abilene, Tex., Nov. 9, 1965; d. George Lyman and Shirley Elizabeth (Burton) T.; m. Dennis A. Lamb; children: Lane, Logann. BS in Edn., Lubbock Christian Coll., 1986; postgrad., Tex. Tech U. Elem. Edn. grades 1-6, Tex. 1st grade tchr. Lubbock (Tex.) I.S.D. Brown Elem., 1986-87; 3rd grade tchr., chairperson Morton (Tex.) I.S.D., 1987-89; 5th grade lang. arts tchr. Whiteface (Tex.) C.I.S.D., 1990—. Mem. ASCD, Classroom Tchrs. Assn. (sec. 1988-89, elem. rep. 1991-92). Home: 2104 Tech Dr Levelland TX 79336-6706 Office: PO Box 117 Whiteface TX 79379

LAMBERG, JOAN BERNICE, purchasing agent; b. St. Paul, July 5, 1935; d. Gustave William and Anna Marie (Steinhilpert) L.; 1 child, Mary Lamberg King. Student, U. Mo., Rolla, 1971. Payroll clk. Continental Baking Co., Mpls., 1953-54; mgr. prodn. scheduling, purchasing and inventory control Stewart Paint Mfg. Co., Mpls., 1954-72; with purchasing, accounts payable and sales dept. Horton-Earl Co., South St. Paul, Minn., 1972—. Mem. Northwestern Soc. for Coatings Tech. (treas. 1984-85, sec. 1985-86, v.p. 1986-87, pres. 1987-88, tech. com. 1985-90, membership chmn. 1985—, advt. mgr. 1988—, symposium com. 1985—, monthly meeting notice editor 1988—, Trigg award 1986), Fedn. Socs. for Coatings Tech. (bd. dirs. 1987-89). Home: 6949 Macbeth Cir Saint Paul MN 55125-2408 Office: Horton-Earl Co 949 Concord St S South Saint Paul MN 55075-5912

LAMBERSON, MARY JANE, artist, educator; b. Logan, Iowa, Aug. 10, 1944; d. James Perry and Emma Jane (Skinner) Laughrey; m. Robert Ray Lamberson, Aug. 30, 1964; children: Courtney Kaye, Robert Russell. BFA, Kearney (Nebr.) State Coll., 1988; MA in Edn., U. Nebr., Kearney, 1991. Teaching asst. U. Nebr., Kearney, 1989-91, adj. art instr., 1991; com. chair Dannebrog, Nebr., 1991—; com. chair Art Exit 305, 1991—. Creator Dannebrog Outdoor Hist. Mural, 1991, Kearney's Mayor's Art Project Outdoor Mural, 1993; designer, cons. Cedar Rapids High Sch. Indoor Hist. Mural, 1992. Recipient art awards. Mem. Impact II, Women Artists of Nebr., Kansas City Artist Coalition, Kans. Sculpture Assn., Nebr. Crafts Coun. (bd. dirs. 1988—), Assn. Nebr. Art Club. Home: 688 Liberty Rd Dannebrog NE 68831-9756

LAMBERT, DEBORAH KETCHUM, public relations executive; b. Greenwich, Conn., Jan. 22, 1942; d. Alton Harrington and Robyna (Neilson) Ketchum; m. Harvey R. Lambert, Nov. 23, 1963 (div. 1985); children: Harvey Richard Jr., Eric Harrington. BS, Columbia U., 1965. Researcher, writer The Nowland Orgn., Greenwich, Conn., 1964-67; model Country Fashions, Greenwich, Conn., 1964-67; freelance writer to various newspapers and mags., 1977-82; press sec. Va. Del. Gwen Cody, Annandale, Va., 1981-82; assoc. editor Campus Report, Washington, 1985—; adminstrv. asst. Accuracy in Media, Inc., Washington, 1983-84, dir. pub. affairs, 1985—; TV producer weekly program The Other Side of the Story, 1994—; bd. dirs. Accuracy in Academia, Washington; film script cons. The Seductive Illusion, 1988-89. Columnist: The Eye, The Washington Inquirer, 1984—, Squeaky Chalk, Campus Report, 1985—; contbr. articles to various mags.; producer: The Other Side of the Story, 1993—. Co-founder, mem. Va. Rep. Forum, McLean, 1983—; mem. Rep. Women's Fed. Forum. Mem. Am. Bell Assn., Pub. Rels. Soc. Am., DAR., World Media Assn., Am. Platform Assn. Republican. Presbyterian. Home: 1945 Lorraine Ave Mc Lean VA 22101-5331 Office: Accuracy in Media Inc 4455 Connecticut Ave NW Washington DC 20008-2328

LAMBERT, EDYTHE RUTHERFORD, retired language educator, civic volunteer; b. Candler, N.C., Oct. 6, 1921; d. John William and Addie Bell (Holcombe) Rutherford; m. Robert Stansbury Lambert, Mar. 7, 1946; children: Margaret Anne, Dorothy Lee (dec.). BA, U. N.C., Greensboro, 1942; MA, Clemson U., 1970. Tchr. French Linden (N.C.) High Sch., 1942-43; lab. tech. Am. Enka (N.C.) Corp., 1943-44; reporter Asheville (N.C.) Citizen-Times Co., 1944-46; with pub. relations dept. Shorter Coll., Rome, Ga., 1955; instr. Clemson (S.C.) U., 1966-68. Docent hist. house mus. Pendleton Hist. Found., 1974—; pres. Clemson Area Arts Council, 1978-79, Pickens County Friends of the Arts, S.C., 1981-82, Clemson Council Human Relations, 1987; bd. dirs. Clemson Child Devel. Ctr., 1976—. Recipient Algernon Sydney Sullivan award for community svcs. Clemson U., 1990, Human Rights award Baha'is of Pickens County, 1991. Mem. AAUW (pres. 1985—, Named Gift Recipient 1979, 86, fellow 1964, editor The Palmetto Leaf, 1984-86), Phi Kappa Phi. Democrat. Methodist. Club: Clemson U. Woman's (v.p. membership 1984-85).

LAMBERT, ELAINE L., surgical nurse, administrator; b. West Chester, Pa., Dec. 17, 1938; d. Lewis Robert and Grace Elma (Matlack) Beard; m. Dennis John Lambert, Jan. 2, 1989; children: Bruce Lewis, Brenda Elaine. Diploma, Presbyn. Hosp., Phila., 1959; B in Profl. Sci., U. Sys. of N.H., 1993. Cert. operating room nurse. Staff nurse operating room and emergency room Chester County Hosp., West Chester, 1959-71; night supr., charge nurse ICU Pa. Valley Regional Hosp., 1972-79, relief oper. rm. mgr., 1979-81; nurse mgr. of surg. svcs. Valley Regional Hosp., Claremont, N.H., 1982-91, 1979-82; sr. nurse mgr. oper. rm./cen. supply Rutland (Vt.) Regional Med. Ctr., 1991-94; dir. Ortho. Surgery Ctr., Concord, N.H., 1994—. Mem. NAFE, N.H. Orgn. Nurse Execs., N.H.-Vt. Oper. Rm. Mgrs., Vt. Orgn. Nurse Execs., Assn. Oper. Rm. Nurses.

LAMBERT, JEAN MARJORIE, health care consultant; b. Bay City, Mich., Mar. 19, 1943; d. Richard William and Fidelis Rena (LeVasseur) L. BA, Madonna U., Livonia, Mich., 1967; MA, Eastern Mich. U., 1975. Dir. religious edn. Archdiocese of Detroit, 1970-75, dir. of evaluation, 1975-77; assoc. dir. programming Intermedia Found., Santa Monica, Calif., 1977-78; acad. dean St. John Provincial Sem., Plymouth, Mich., 1978-84; asst. dir. quality mgmt. Sisters of Mercy Health Corp., Farmington Hills, Mich., 1984-87; sr. cons. Mercy Collaborative, Livonia., Mich., 1987-88; v.p. Mission Mercy Health System, Cin., 1988-91; v.p. Mission Sisters Providence Health System, Springfield, Mass., 1991—; asst. prof. homiletics St. John Sem., Plymouth, Mich., 1978-85, St. Mary of the Woods Coll., Terre Haute, Ind., summer 1985, St. Meinrad Sem., Ind., summer 1984; bd. dirs. Combined Health Appeal of Mass. Editor Religious Edn., 1975-77. Nat. Cath. Edn. Assn.-Assn. Theol. Schs. for U.S. and Can. grantee, 1983. Mem. NAFE, Groundwork, Network, Am. Hosp. Assn., Am. Mgmt. Assn., Mental Health Assn., Cath. Health Assn. (bd. dirs. New Eng. Conf.), Acad. Leadership in Cath. Health Care. Roman Catholic. Avocations: woodcarving, photography, continuing education. Office: Sisters of Providence Health System 146 Chestnut Springfield MA 01103

LAMBERT, JOAN DORETY, elementary education educator; b. Trenton, N.J., Oct. 21, 1937; d. John William and Margaret (Fagan) Dorety; m. James E. Lambert Sr., June 25, 1960; children: Margi, Karen, James E., Kevin. BA, Georgian Ct. Coll., Lakewood, N.J., 1958. Cert. tchr., Pa., N.J. Tchr. 2d and 3d grades combined Washington Elem. Sch., Trenton, 1958-61; tchr. kindergarten music St. Genevieve Sch., Flourtown, Pa., 1968-78, tchr. 3d grade, 1978—; producer, dir. musical shows for St. Genevieve Sch., 1970-78; demonstration classroom for writing process on computers Chestnut Hill Coll. Mem. Jr. League of Trenton, 1960-68, Jr. League of Phila., 1968-70. Teleflex Internat. grantee, 1989-92, Anna B. Stokes Meml. scholar, 1960, Met. Opera grantee, 1958-60. Mem. NEA. Republican. Roman Catholic. Home: 33 Coventry Ct Blue Bell PA 19422-2528 Office: St Genevieve Sch 1237 Bethlehem Pike Flourtown PA 19031-1902

LAMBERT, JUDITH A. UNGAR, lawyer; b. N.Y.C., Apr. 13, 1943; d. Alexander Lawrence and Helene (Rosenson) Ungar; m. Peter D. Leibowits, Aug. 22, 1965 (div. 1971); 1 child, David Gary. BS, U. Pa., 1964; JD magna cum laude, U. Miami, 1984. Bar: N.Y. 1985, Fla. 1990. Assoc. Proskauer Rose Goetz & Mendelsohn, N.Y.C., 1984-86, Taub & Fasciana, N.Y.C., 1986-87, Hoffinger Friedland Dobrish Bernfeld & Hasen, N.Y.C., 1987-88; pvt. practice N.Y.C., 1988—. Mem. ABA, N.Y. State Bar Assn., Assn. Bar of City of N.Y., N.Y. Women's Bar Assn. (family law and trusts and estates com.), N.Y. County Lawyers Assn. Office: 245 E 54th St New York NY 10022-4707

LAMBERT, LYN DEE, law librarian, lawyer; b. Fitchburg, Mass., Jan. 5, 1954; m. Paul Frederick Lambert, Aug. 11, 1979; children: Gregory John, Emily Jayne, Nicholas James. BA in History, Fitchburg State Coll., 1976, MEd in History, 1979; JD, Franklin Pierce Law Ct., 1983; MLS, Simmons Coll., 1986. instr. parelegal studies courses Fisher Coll., Fitchburg, 1989-94,

Anna Maria Coll., Paxton, 1995—. Law libr. Fitchburg Law Libr., Mass. Trial Ct., 1985—; instr. paralegal studies courses Fisher Coll., Fitchburg, 1989-94, Anna Marie Coll., Paxton, Mass., 1995—. Mem. Am. Legion Band, Fitchburg, 1959—, Westminster (Mass.) Town Band, 1965—. Recipient Community Leadership award Phi Delta Kappa-Fitchburg State Coll. chpt., 1993. Mem. ALA, Am. Assn. Law Librarians (copyright com. 1987-89, publs. rev. com. 1990-92, state, ct. and county law librs. spl. interest sect. publicity com. 1993—), Law Librarians New Eng. (conf. com. 1988), Mass. Libr. Assn. (edn. chair 1991-93, freedom of info. com., legislation com.), New Eng. Libr. Assn., New Eng. Microcomputer Users Group (profl. assoc.), North Cen. Mass. Libr. Alliance (newsletter editor 1990—), Spl. Libr. Assn., Beta Phi Mu, Phi Alpha Delta. Office: Fitchburg Law Libr Mass Trial Ct Superior Courthouse 84 Elm St Fitchburg MA 01420-3232

LAMBERT, MARTHA LOWERY, state legislator; b. Douglasville, Ga., Mar. 27, 1937; d. Edmond Davis and Mary (Daniel) Lowery; m. Paul Dean Lambert, June 13, 1959; children: Melanie Lynn, Kurt Phillip, Brett Cameron, Matthew Dean. Mem. N.Mex. Ho. of Reps., Santa Fe, 1981—; part-owner Premier Foods Inc., Albuquerque, 1989—. Pres. Albuquerque Dist. Dental Aux., 1971, Albuquerque Fed. Rep. Women, 1975; alt. del. Nat. Rep. Conv., Kansas City, Mo, 1976, Houston, 1992. Home: 616 Running Water Cir SE Albuquerque NM 87123-4162 Office: N Mex Ho of Reps State Capitol New Mexico State Capitol NM 87503

LAMBERT, OLIVIA SUE, commercial artist, writer; b. Philippi, W.Va., July 10, 1939; d. Curtis Truman and Olive Virginia (Cox) L. BA in History, Alderson Broaddus Coll., 1961. Interim pub. rels. officer Alderson Broaddus Coll., Philippi, 1965; clk. Barbour County Ct. House, Philippi, 1966; free lance artist, writer Philippi, 1965—. Artist: (book jackets) History of Barbour County, 1965, History of Calhoun County, 1982; illustrator: (book) Wappatomaka, 1971; cartographer: Blue-Gray Reunion Map, 1993. Mem. Rep. Nat. Com., Philippi Sesquecentennial Com., Blue-Gray Reunion Com., Nature Conservancy. Mem. AAUW, Coll. Club, W.Va. Filmmakers Guild, W.Va. Writers Inc., Barbour County Writers Workshop, Order Eastern Star. Methodist. Home and Office: 4 Woodsboro Dr Rte 3 Philippi WV 26416

LAMBERT, PEGGY LYNNE BAILEY, lawyer; b. Seattle, Oct. 15, 1948; d. John Thomas and Doris Mae (Lindgren) Bailey; m. Tom Kenneth Newton, May 25, 1975 (div. 1980); m. Allan Gregory Lambert, Aug. 3, 1980 (separated); children: Eli Raven, Joshua Alec. BA in Psychology, Beloit Coll., 1970; MS in Counseling Psychology, Ill. Inst. Tech., 1973; JD, Syracuse (N.Y.) U., 1978. Bar: D.C. 1983. Mental health specialist Ill. Dept. Mental Health, Chgo., 1971-72; research faculty Cornell U., Ithaca, N.Y., 1973-75; assoc. O'Connor, Sovocool, Pfann and Greenburg, Ithaca, 1978, Dacy, Richin & Meyers, Silver Springs, Md., 1979-81; ins. adminstr. Nat. Assn. Broadcasters, Washington, 1981-86, dir. ins. programs, 1986-90; assoc. Architect of the Capitol, Washington, 1990—. Co-author, editor: Broadcaster's Property and Liability Insurance Buying Guide, 1989. Mem. ABA, D.C. Bar Assn. (steering com. of arts entertainment, sports law sect. 1989-90, sect. editor newsletter 1989-90). Democrat. Jewish. Office: Architect of the Capitol Office of Gen Coun Rm H2-265A Ford House Office Bldg Washington DC 20515

LAMBERT, WILLIE LEE BELL, mobile equipment company owner, educator; b. Texas City, Tex., Oct. 23, 1929; d. William Henry and Una Oda (Stafford) Bell; m. Eddie Roy Lambert, July 2, 1949; (dec. Mar. 1980); children: Sondra Kay Lambert Bradford, Eddie Lee. Degree in bus., Met. Bus. Coll., 1950; AAS, Coll. of Mainland, 1971; BS, Sam Houston U., 1976. Cert. hand and foot reflexologist, Hatha Yoga instr. Sec. Judges Reddell & Hopkins, Texas City, 1945-47, Charles Martin Petroleum, Texas City, 1948-50; acct. Goodyear Co., La Marque, Tex., 1968-70; serials libr. Coll. of the Mainland, Texas City, 1970-77, instr., 1971—; exec. dir., office mgr. Mobile Air Conditioning, La Marque, 1977-80; owner Kivert, Inc., La Marque, 1982—; ptnr., exec. dir. A/C Mobile Equipment Corp., La Marque, 1988—; owner Star Bell Ranch, 1985—. Vol. Union Carbide Chems., Texas City, 1970—, Carbide Retiree Corp., Inc., Texas City, 1980—, Hospice, Galveston, Tex., 1985—, various polit. campaigns, Texas City, 1951-62; v.p. Coalition on Aging Galveston County, Texas City, 1990—; mem. adv. coun. bd. Galveston County Sr. Citizens, Galveston, 1990—; mem. planning bd. Heart Fund and Cancer Fund, Texas City, 1953-62, Santa Fe (Tex.) Sr. Citizens, 1990—; sec. YMCA, 1947-55; sec. Ladies VFW, 1950-59; leader Girl Scouts Am., 1958-65; v.p. PTA, 1957-60; counselor Bapt. Ch. Camp, 1960-64; v.p. Santa Fe Booster Club, 1963-67. Named Mother of Yr. Texas City/La Marque C. of C., 1990, Vol. of Yr. Heights Elem. Sch., Texas City Sch. Dist., 1959, Unsung Hero award Tex. City, 1995. Republican. Baptist. Home: 3422 K1/2 PO Box 1253 Santa Fe TX 77510

LAMBERTI, MARJORIE, history educator; b. New Haven, Sept. 30, 1937; d. James and Anna (Vanacore) L. B.A., Smith Coll., 1959; M.A., Yale U., 1960, Ph.D., 1965. Prof. history Middlebury Coll., Vt., 1964—, Charles A. Dana prof., 1984—. Author: Jewish Activism in Imperial Germany, 1978, State, Society and the Elementary School in Imperial Germany, 1989; mem. editorial bd. History of Edn. Quar., 1992—; contbr. articles to profl. jours. NEH fellow, 1968-69, 81-82; German Acad. Exch. Svc. rsch. grant, 1988. Fellow Inst. for Advanced Study (Princeton 1992-93); mem. Am. Hist. Assn., Conf. Group for Ctrl. European History, Leo Baeck Inst., Phi Beta Kappa. Home: 37 Gorham Ln Middlebury VT 05753-1016 Office: Middlebury Coll Dept History Middlebury VT 05753

LAMBERTON, VICKY J., accountant; b. Scranton, Pa., June 30, 1964; d. Dwight J. and Shirley M. (Strada) Chapman; m. Robert D. Lamberton, Sept. 30, 1989; 1 child, Emma C. B, Cedar Crest Coll., 1986. CPA, Pa. Acct., mem. audit staff Parente, Randolph, Orlando, Carey & Assocs., Wilkes-Barre, Pa., 1986-92; controller, acct. John T. Howe Inc., Lake Ariel, Pa., 1992—. Treas. Centenary Meth. Ch., Lake Ariel, 1988—; committee woman Wayne County Rep. Com., Honesdale, Pa., 1992—. Mem. AICPA. Office: John T Howe Inc PO Box 125 Lake Ariel PA 18436

LAMBIRD, JENNIFER SALYER, strategic planning professional; b. Balt., July 11, 1966; d. Perry Albert and Mona Sue (Salyer) L. AB in Computational Linguistics, Stanford U., 1988; M in Mgmt., Northwestern U., 1993. Sr. cons. Andersen Consulting, San Francisco, 1988-90; dir. World Orgn. China Painters, Oklahoma City, 1990-91; cons. Ministry of Privatization, Warsaw, Poland, 1992; strategic planning mgr. AT&T Network Sys., Berkeley Heights, N.J., 1993—; adv. bd. mem. Map Info., Albany, 1994. Home: 292 Maple St New Providence NJ 07974-2616 Office: AT&T Network Systems 1WC113 One Oakway Berkeley Heights NJ 07922

LAMBIRD, MONA SALYER, lawyer; b. Oklahoma City, July 19, 1938; d. B.M. Jr. and Pauline A. Salyer; m. Perry A. Lambird, July 30, 1960; children: Allison Lambird Watson, Jennifer Salyer, Elizabeth Gard, Susannah Johnson. BA, Wellesley Coll., 1960; LLB, U. Md., 1963. Bar: Okla. 1968, Md. Ct. Appeals 1963, U.S. Supreme Ct. 1967. Atty. civil div. Dept. Justice, Washington, 1963-65; sole practice law Balt. and Oklahoma City, 1965-71; mem. firm Andrews Davis Legg Bixler Milsten & Price, Inc. and predecessor firm, Oklahoma City, 1971—; minority mem. Okla. Election Bd., 1984—, vice-chmn., 1990—; mem. profl. responsibility tribunal Okla. Supreme Ct., 1984-90; Master of Bench, sec.-treas. Luther Bohanan Am. Inn of Ct., Oklahoma City, 1986—, pres., 1994—. Editor: Briefcase, Oklahoma County Bar Assn., 1976. Profl. liaison com. City Oklahoma City, 1974-80; mem. Hist. Preservation of Oklahoma City, Inc., 1970—; del. Oklahoma County and Okla. State Republican Party Conv., 1971—; Okla. City Orch. League Inc., legal advisor, 1973—, bd. dirs., 1973—; incorporator, bd. dirs. R.S.V.P. of Oklahoma County, pres., 1982-83; bd. dirs. Congregate Housing for Elderly, 1978—, Vis. Nurses Assn., 1983-86, Oklahoma County Friends of Library, 1980-91, The Support Ctrs., Inc., 1989—. Mem. ABA, Okla. Bar Assn. (pres. labor and employment law sect., bd. govs. 1992-94, pres.-elect 1995), Oklahoma County Bar Assn. (bd. dirs. 1986—, pres. 1990), Oklahoma County Bar Found. (pres. 1988), Jr. League Oklahoma City (bd. dirs. 1973-76, legal advisor), Oklahoma County and State Med. Assn. Aux. (dir.), Seven Sisters Colls. Club (pres. 1972-76), Women's Econ. Club (steering com. 1981-86). Methodist. Home: 419 NW 14th St Oklahoma City OK 73103-3510 Office: 500 W Main St Oklahoma City OK 73102-2220

LAMBOWITZ, SHEILA, state agency administrator; b. Bklyn., June 22, 1947; d. Jack J. and Florence (Lehrman) Mintz; m. Alan M. Lambowitz, Dec. 24, 1968 (div. 1994). BA in Comparative Lit., Bklyn. Coll., 1969; MBA in Mgmt., St. Louis U., 1981; postgrad., Ohio State U., 1986—. Customer svc. rep. Conn. Blue Cross, North Haven, 1969-72; customer relations mutual fund specialist Delaware Mgmt. Co., Phila., 1972-73; HMO coord. Blue Cross & Blue Shield of Greater N.Y., N.Y.C., 1974-75; rsch. analyst Blue Cross Hosp. Svcs., Inc., St. Louis, 1976-78, mgr. product devel. then mgr. govt. programs div., 1978-83, 83-86; hosp. rates & audits chief Ohio Dept. of Human Svcs., Columbus, 1986-90, surveillance & utilization rev. chief, 1990-91; mgr. long term care mgmt. info. system project Dept. Human Svcs., Columbus, Ohio, 1991-93, chief case mix and sys. adminstrn., 1993—; mem. HCFA joint applications devel. com. Health Stds. Quality Bur., Ohio Time Study Dept. Human Svcs., 1993—, coord. HCFA nurse facility case mix demonstration project Office Rsch. and Devel., 1994—. Mem. Orgn. of Am. Historians, Am. Hist. Assn., Phi Alpha Theta. Democrat. Jewish. Office: Ohio Dept of Human Svcs 30 E Broad St 33d Fl Columbus OH 43266-0423

LAMBRO, HOLLY KATHERINE, publishing company executive, writer; b. Wellesley, Mass.; d. Pascal and Mary (Lapery) Lambro; 1 child, Melissa Lambro. Student, Boston U., 1962, 64-65. Mem. staff U.S. Rep. Gene Snyder of Ky., Washington; with Human Events, Washington; sec. U.S. Rep. Thomas J. Meskill of Conn., Washington; asst. to bur. chief London Daily Mirror, N.Y.C.; prin. Holly Ltd., Ridgefield, Conn. Author: Safe Places, 1972, Safe Places for the 80s, 1984. Mem. Albanian Orthodox Ch.

LAMEL, LINDA HELEN, insurance company executive, former college president, lawyer; b. N.Y.C., Sept. 10, 1943; d. Maurice and Sylvia (Abrams) Treppel; 1 child, Diana Ruth Sands. BA magna cum laude, Queens Coll., 1964; MA, NYU, 1968; JD, Bklyn. Law Sch., 1976. Bar: N.Y. 1977, U.S. Dist. Ct. (3d dist.) N.Y. 1977. Mgmt. analyst U.S. Navy, Bayonne, N.J., 1964-65; secondary sch. tchr. Farmingdale Pub. Sch., N.Y., 1965-73; curriculum specialist Yonkers Bd. Edn., N.Y., 1973-75; program dir. Office of Lt. Gov., Albany, N.Y., 1975-77; dep. supt. N.Y. State Ins. Dept., N.Y.C., 1977-83; pres., chief exec. officer Coll. of Ins., N.Y.C., 1983-88; v.p. Tchr.'s Ins. and Annuity Assn., N.Y.C., 1988—; dir. Seneca (N.Y.) Ins. Co. Contbr. articles to profl. jours. Campaign mgr. lt. gov.'s primary race, N.Y. State, 1974. Mem. ABA (tort and ins. sect. com. chmn. 1985-86), N.Y. State Bar Assn. (exec. com. ins. sect. 1984-88), Assn. of Bar of City of N.Y. (chmn. med. malpractice com. 1989-91), Am. Mgmt. Assn. (ins. and risk mgmt. council), Fin. Women's Assn., Assn. Profl. Ins. Women (Woman of Yr. award 1988), Phi Beta Kappa (v.p. Phi Beta Kappa Assoc. 1992—), Kappa Delta Pi, Phi Alpha Theta. Office: 730 3rd Ave New York NY 10017-3206

LAMM, CAROLYN BETH, lawyer; b. Buffalo, Aug. 22, 1948; d. Daniel John and Helen Barbara (Tatakis) L.; m. Peter Edward Halle, Aug. 12, 1972; children: Alexander P., Daniel E. BS, SUNY Coll. at Buffalo, 1970; JD, U. Miami (Fla.), 1973. Bar: Fla., 1973, D.C., 1976, N.Y. 1983. Trial atty. frauds sect. civil div. U.S. Dept. Justice, Washington, 1973-78, asst. chief comml. litigation sect. civil div., 1978, asst. dir., 1978-80; assoc. White & Case, Washington, 1980-84, ptnr., 1984—; mem. Sec. State's Adv. Com. Pvt. Internat. law, 1988-91; arbitrator U.S. Panel of Arbitrators, Internat. Ctr. Settlement of Investment Disputes. Mem. bd. editors Can./U.S. Rev. Bus. Law, 1987-92; mem. editorial adv. bd. Inside Litigation; contbr. articles to legal publs. Fellow Am. Bar Found.; mem. ABA (chmn. young lawyers div., rules and calendar com., chmn. house membership com., chmn. assembly resolution com., sec. 1984-86, chmn. internat. litigation com. coun. 1991-94, sect. litigation, ho. dels. 1982—, nominating com. 1984-87, D.C. Cir. mem. standing com. fed. judiciary 1993—, com. scope and correlation of work), Am. Arbitration Assn. (arbitrator, com. on fed. arbitration act), Fed. Bar Assn. (chmn. sect. on antitrust and trade regulation), Bar Assn. D.C. (bd. dirs., sec.), D.C. Bar (bd. govs. 1987-93, steering com. litigation sect.), Am. Law Inst., Women's Bar Assn. D.C., Am. Soc. Internat. Law, Internat. Bar Assn. (bus. law sect., internat. litigation com.), Am. Turkish Friendship Coun. (bd. dirs., chair comml. com.), Am. Uzbekistan C. of C. (bd. dirs., sec., gen. counsel), Nat. Women's Forum, Columbia Country Club. Democrat. Home: 2801 Chesterfield Pl NW Washington DC 20008-1015 Office: White & Case 1747 Pennsylvania Ave NW Washington DC 20006-4604

LAMM, CINDY MAE, counselor; b. Lynchburg, Va., Aug. 19, 1957; d. Wallace Bishop and Erma Rachel (Campbell) L. AS, Ferrum Coll., 1977, BS, 1979; MEd, James Madison U., 1981; EdS, U. Va., 1987. Resident dir. Emory (Va.) and Henry Coll., 1981-83; asst. dir. housing U. N.C., Asheville, 1983-85; victim svcs. coord. Sexual Assault Resource Agy., Charlottesville, Va., 1987-92, assoc. dir. and client svcs. coord., 1992—. Mem. Virginians Aligned Against Sexual Assault, Am. Counseling Assn. Office: Sexual Assault Resource Agy PO Box 6705 Charlottesville VA 22906-6705

LAMM, DONNA LEE, journalist; b. Hoxie, Kans., Aug. 17, 1960; d. Dean Leroy and Willa Dalene (Sewell) Gawith; m. Freddie Ray Lamm, Dec. 31, 1983; children: Elaine MaDonna, Henry Silas, Rachel Alison. AA, Colby (Kans.) C.C., 1980; BS, Kans. State U., 1982. Disc jockey Mr. K's, Manhattan, Kans., 1981, Aggie Sta., Manhattan, Kans., 1981-82; announcer KXXX-FM, Colby, Kans., 1980-81, KMAN-KMKF, Manhattan, 1981, KXXX-AM-FM, Colby, 1982; sales rep. KZMC-FM, McCook, Nebr., 1983; co-editor Thomas County Herald, Colby, 1983-88; layout, reporter/photographer Colby Free Press, 1988; free-lance writer/photographer Colby, 1992; advt./layout instr. Colby C.C., 1987, journalism instr. and publs. advisor, 1988-92; judge newswriting classes 1993 Kans. Scolastic Press Assn. regional contest. Accompanist, Sun. sch. tchr., com. mem. College View Bapt. Ch.; vol. Easter Seals, 1987-89, 91-93, Colby Diplomats, 1986; hostess for two Miss Troia contestants, 1983; co-chair USD 315 Kids Voting Kans., 1994. Secrest Ann. scholar, 1978-79, Bob Harris Meml. scholar, 1980, Dane G. Hansen scholar, 1981; recipient numerous awards Kans. Press Assn., Kans. Press Women. Mem. Kans. Press Women (sec. 1987-88, 2d v.p., 1988-90, 1st v.p., 1990-92, pres. 1992-94, dir. budget 1994—), Colby Press Women (charter, pres. 1985-86, 87, 90-91, sec.-treas. 1984-85, v.p. 1987-88), Gold Key, Phi Theta Kappa, Alpha Epsilon Rho. Baptist. Home: 970 W 5th St Colby KS 67701-1803

LAMM, HARRIET A., mathematics educator; b. Beeville, Tex., Dec. 4, 1948; d. James R. and Dorothy D. (Kendall) L. BA, Tex. Christian U., 1971; BS in Edn., S.W. Tex. State U., 1973, MEd, 1976; PhD, Tex. A&M U., 1993. Cert. secondary tchr., Tex. Instr. math. South San Antonio Ind. Sch. Dist., San Antonio, 1973-74; teaching asst. in math. S.W. Tex. State U., San Marcos, 1974-76; tchr. math. Seguin (Tex.) Ind. Sch. Dist., 1976-78, George West (Tex.) Ind. Sch. Dist., 1978-83, Lingleville (Tex.) Ind. Sch. Dist., 1983, Northside Ind. Sch. Dist., San Antonio, 1984-87, Beeville (Tex.) Ind. Sch. Dist., 1987-88; teaching asst. Tex. A&M U., College Station, 1991-92; instr. math. Bee County Coll., Beeville, 1988-91, 1992—; instr. math. Tarleton State U., Stephenville, Tex., 1983. Mem. ASCD, Am. Ednl. Rsch. Assn., Nat. Coun. Tchrs. Math., Tex. Coun. Tchrs. Math., Sch. Sci. and Math. Assn., Math. Assn. Am., Assn. Tex. Profl. Educators, Rsch. Coun. for Diagnostic and Prescriptive Math.

LAMMERS, NITZIA I., geriatrics nurse, administrator; b. Panama City, Panama, Jan. 25, 1947; d. Raul R. and Dora (Paz) Alvarado; m. Dieter H. Lammers, Aug. 19, 1967; children: Roland, Monica, Yvette. Diploma, Akron Sch. Practical Nursing, 1975; BSN, U. Akron, 1981; MSN in Gerontol. Adminstrn., Case Western Res. U., 1986. Cert. gerontol. nurse. Staff nurse, med.-surg. unit St. Thomas Med. Ctr., Akron, Ohio, health educator, coord. patient edn.; mgr. for hosp.-based skilled nursing facility Grant Med. Ctr., Columbus, Ohio; nurse mgr. Akron (Ohio) Gen. Med. Ctr., 1991-92; dir. nursing Rockynol Retirement Community, Akron, 1992-94; dir. long-term care svcs. for hosp.-based skilled nursing Edwin Shaw Hosp., Akron, 1994—. Mem. ANA, Gerontol. Soc. Am., Internat. Soc. Nursing, Sigma Theta Tau, Alpha Mu.

LAMOND, SHARON ANN, administrator; b. Providence, Sept. 23, 1948; d. John and Alice M. (Ulczukiewicz) Dec; m. William F. Lamond, Jr., Nov. 18, 1972; 1 child, Kristin. AS in Nursing, Community Coll. R.I., 1969; BSN, Stonehill Coll., 1987. Pub. health nurse Town Carver Mass., 1980-85; branch mgr., supr. Southeastern Mass. Health Care, Plymouth, Mass., 1985-87; quality assurance mgr. Staff Builders Home Care, Boston, 1987-90; dir. profl. svcs., adminstr. Kimberly Quality Care, Providence, 1990-92; supr. family practice Harvard Community Health Plan of N.E., Swansea, Mass., 1992; mem. triage Dept. Pediatrics, Harvard Community Health Plan of N.E., Warwick, R.I., 1993—. Recipient Stonehill Coll. Student Recognition award, 1987. Mem. ANA (cert. cmty. health nurse), Am. Assn. for Continuity of Care, Continuing Care Profls. R.I. (treas. 1990-96), Alpha Sigma Lamdba. Home: 110 Colonial Rd North Attleboro MA 02760-2837

LAMONT, ALICE, accountant, consultant; b. Houston, July 19; d. Harold and Bessie Bliss (Knight) L. BS, Mont. State U.; MBA in Taxation, Golden Gate U., 1983; CPA. Tchr. London Central High Sch., 1971-80; acct. Signetics, Sunnyvale, Calif., 1980-82; propr. Alice Lamont Ltd., 1985—. Mem. Atlanta Hist. Soc., High Mus. Art, Atlanta Botanical Garden, Brit. Amer. Bus. Group, also membership com., 1993—, Friend of Atlanta Opera, Atlanta Opera Guild, St. Philips Planned Giving Com. Fellow Ga. Soc. CPAs; mem. AAUW (life, audit chmn. 1993—, mem. scholarship com. 1994—), Atlanta Tax Study Assn., Inst. Internal Auditors, English Speaking Union, Women Bus. Owners, Buckhead Bus. Assn., Atlanta Woman's Club (co-chair ways and means com. 1985-86, asst. treas. 1986-88, treas. 1990, 92-94), Women's Commerce Club.

LAMONT, BARBARA GIBSON, librarian; b. Huntington, Ind., Nov. 8, 1925; d. Herbert Donald and Edith (VanAntwerp) LaM. A.B., Coll. William and Mary, 1947; M.A., Radcliffe Coll., 1952; M.S. in L.S, Simmons Coll., 1954. With Harvard Library, 1951-64; head librarian Douglass Coll., Rutgers U., 1964-67; head librarian Vassar Coll., 1967-83, head librarian emeritus, 1983—. Trustee Southeastern (N.Y.) Library Resources Council, 1967-73. Home: Andrews Rd Rural Route 2 Box 358 Lagrangeville NY 12540

LAMONT, LEE, art management executive; b. Queens, N.Y.; m. August Tagliamonte, Apr. 30, 1951; 1 child, Leslie Lamont. With Nat. Concerts & Artists Group, N.Y.C., 1955-58; asst. Sol Hurok Concerts, N.Y.C., 1958-67; person rep. for concerts, rec. and TV Isaac Stern, N.Y.C., 1968-76; v.p. ICM Artists Ltd., N.Y.C., 1976-85; pres. ICM Artists Ltd. and ICM Artists (London) Ltd., N.Y.C., 1985-95, chmn. bd. dirs., 1995—; Mem. adv. com. Hannover (Germany) Internat. Violin Competition. Mem. US/USSR Trade and Econ. Coun., Am. Coun. on the Arts, Japan Soc., Asia Soc., Am. Symphony Orch. League (bd. dirs.), Bohemian Club. Office: ICM Artists Ltd 40 W 57th St 16th Fl New York NY 10019

LAMONT, MICHELE, sociologist, educator; b. Toronto, Ont., Can., Dec. 15, 1957; came to U.S., 1983; d. Jacques and Jeanine (Page) L.; m. Frank Richardson Dobbin, June 6, 1987. BA, Ottawa U., Ont., 1977, MA, 1978; Doctorate, U. Paris, 1983. Postdoctoral fellow Stanford (Calif.) U., 1983-85; asst. prof. U. Tex., Austin, 1985-87; asst. prof. Princeton (N.J.) U., 1987-93, assoc. prof., 1993—. Author: Money, Morals and Manners, 1992, Cultivating Differences, 1992; co-editor: Cultivating Differences: Symbolic Boundaries and the Making of Inequality, 1992. Grantee NSF, 1992-94, German Marshall Funds U.S., 1992-93. Mem. Am. Sociol. Assn. (chair cultural sect. 1993-94). Home: 7 Hart Ave Hopewell NJ 08525-1405 Office: Princeton U Sociology Dept Princeton NJ 08544

LAMONT, ROSETTE CLEMENTINE, Romance languages educator, theatre journalist, translator; b. Paris; came to U.S., 1941, naturalized, 1946; d. Alexandre and Loudmilla (Lamont) L.; m. Frederick Hyde Farmer, Aug. 9, 1969. B.A., Hunter Coll., 1947; M.A., Yale U., 1948, Ph.D., 1954. Tutor Romance langs. Queens Coll., CUNY, 1950-54, instr., 1954-61, asst. prof., 1961-64, assoc. prof., 1965-67, prof., 1967—; mem. doctoral faculties, comparative lit., theatre, French and women's studies cert. program CUNY, 1968—; State Dept. envoy Scholar Exch. Program, USSR, 1974; rsch. fellow, 1976; lectr. Alliance Francaise, Maison Francaise of NYU; vis. prof. Sorbonne, Paris, 1985-86; vis. prof. theatre Sarah Lawrence Coll., 1994. Author: The Life and Works of Boris Pasternak, 1964, De Vive Voix, 1971, Ionesco, 1973, The Two Faces of Ionesco, 1978, Ionesco's Imperatives: The Politics of Culture, 1993, Women on the Verge, 1993; translator: Days and Memory, 1990; also contbr. to various books; mem. editorial bd. Western European Stages, also contbg. editor; European corr. Theatre Week; Columbia Dictionary of Modern European Literature; fgn. corr. Stages. Decorated chevalier, then officier des Palmes Academiques, officier des Arts et Lettres (France); named to Hunter Coll. Hall of Fame, 1991; Guggenheim fellow, 1973-74; Rockefeller Found. humanities fellow, 1983-84. Mem. PEN, MLA, Am. Soc. Theatre Research, Internat. Brecht Soc., Drama Desk (voting mem.), Internat. Assn. Theatre Critics, Phi Beta Kappa, Sigma Tau Delta, Pi Delta Phi. Club: Yale. Home: 260 W 72nd St New York NY 10023-2817 also: 51 W Chester St Nantucket MA 02554 Office: CUNY Queens Coll Dept Romance Langs Flushing NY 11367

LA MONT, TAWANA FAYE, video director, public relations executive; b. Ft. Worth, May 12, 1948; d. Jerry James and Roberta Ann (Wilkinson) La M. AA, Antelope Coll., Lancaster, Calif., 1979; BA in Anthropology, UCLA, 1982. Forest technician region #9, trail constrn. supr. U.S. Forest Svc., Pear Blossom, Calif., 1974-79; trail constrn. supr., maintenance asst. Calif. State Parks, 1979-81; cable TV installer Sammons Comm., Glendale, Calif., 1982-84; camera operator Sammons Comm., San Fernando, Calif., 1984—; video studio and ENG remotes dir., mgr., program mgr. channels 6 and 21 Sammons Comm., Glendale, Calif., 1987—; video dir. LBW & Assocs. Internat., Ltd., 1988—; mem. ednl. access channel satellite program evaluation com., Glendale and Burbank, 1990—; mem. Foothill Community TV Network, Glendale and Burbank, 1987—. Prodr., dir. (homeless video) Bittersweet Streets, 1988; cameraperson Rockin in A Hard Place, 1988—; dir., editor over 1000 videos. Active Glendale Hist. Soc., 1992—; bd. dirs. Am. Heart Assn., 1992—, comms. chair; bd. dirs. ARC, 1993—, cultural diversity chair, 1994—; mem. mktg. com. Burbank YMCA, 1994—. Recipient award of appreciation Bur. Census, 1990, LBW and Assocs. Internat., 1988, USMC, 1991, award of outstanding pub. svc. Social Security Adminstrn. HHS, 1989, dedicated svc. award Am. Heart Assn., 1992, cert. of appreciation, 1994. Mem. NFA, Am. Women in Radio and TV, Wildlife Waystation, Alpha Gamma. Democrat. Home: PO Box 142 Lake Hughes CA 93532-0142

LA MONTE, ANGELA MAE, painter; b. New Britain, Conn., May 19, 1944; d. James Michael and Angeline (D'Agata) La M. MFA, CCNY, 1977; MS, Bank St. Coll., 1982. Instr. of painting and drawing Malcolm-King Coll., N.Y.C., 1979-89, chair dept. of arts, 1984-89; lectr. in field. Exhibite din group shows at Multi-Media Arts Gallery, N.Y.C., 1991, 92, 93, 94, Boniface Gallery of Cathedral of St. John the Divine, N.Y.C., 1986, Atlantic Gallery, N.Y.C., 1990, 92, 93, Castillo Gallery, N.Y.C., 1987, Galley M., N.Y.C., 1988, Gallery Art 54, N.Y.C., 1988, Adelphi U., Garden City, N.Y., 1977, Harlem State Office Bldg. Gallery, 1981, Malcolm-King Coll., N.Y.C., Art '84 Tobago, 1984; represented in pvt. collections. Louis Comfort Tiffany Found. scholar, 1968-69; recipient Louis La Beaume prize Nat. Acad. Fine Arts, 1969.

LAMOTHE, IRENE ELISE, television producer, distributor; b. Berlin, N.H., Sept. 13, 1949; d. Wilfred J. and Estelle Bertha (Lefevre) L.; divorced. Diploma/Med. Lab. Tech., Naval Med. Sch., Bethesda, Md., 1971; Diploma/Communications, Leland Powers Sch., Boston, 1973. Pvt. pilot airplane, 1974, comml. pilot rotorcraft-helicopter, 1982. Owner, operator New Eng. Security Agy., Milan, N.H., 1974-78; adminstr., instr. Kahana's Stunt Sch., Chatsworth, Calif., 1980-83; project devel. specialist Galaxy Mountain Music Prodns., Van Nuys, Calif., 1984-87; writer, prodr. Lance-Cara Pub. Co./Wilby Records, Mission Hills, Calif., 1988—; exec. producer LCJ Prodns., Studio City, Calif., 1989—; chief exec. officer Zemoz Entertainment, 1992—; ind. stunt woman, major studios, 1978-85. Producer: (ednl. video) Discover Yourself In Hollywood, 1992 (Angel award for Excellence in Media 1993); producer, co-writer, Safety is No Accident, 1991; producer (TV series) Hollywood Structured, 1989—, Inside California Country, 1986; writer/producer: (Christmas songs) Wilby the X-mas Tree, 1988, A Christmas Waltz, 1988; co-creator: (multi-media project) GB the Cosmic Snoball, 1985. With USN, 1967-72. Recipient Angel Award for Excellence in Media Hollywood Structured, 1991, 92, Angel Award for Ednl. Video, 1993, Bronze award Worldfest Houston, 1992. Mem. SAG, AAUW, Women in Film, Whirly-Girls. Office: LCJ Prodns 3841 Eureka Dr Studio City CA 91604-3107

LAMOUREUX, GLORIA KATHLEEN, nurse, air force officer; b. Billings, Mont., Nov. 2, 1947; d. Laurits Bungaard and Florence Esther (Nielsen)

Nielsen; m. Kenneth Earl Lamoureux, Aug. 31, 1973 (div. Feb. 1979). BS, U. Wyo., 1970; MS, U. Md., 1984. Staff nurse, ob-gyn DePaul Hosp., Cheyenne, Wyo., 1970; enrolled USAF, 1970, advanced through grades to col.; staff nurse ob-gyn dept. 57th Tactical Hosp., Nellis AFB, Nev., 1970-71, USAF Hosp., Clark AB, Republic Philippines, 1971-73; charge nurse ob-gyn dept. USAF Regional Hosp., Sheppard AFB, Tex., 1973-75; staff nurse ob-gyn dept. USAF Regional Hosp., MacDill AFB, Fla., 1976-79; charge nurse ob-gyn dept. USAF Med. Ctr., Andrews AFB, Md., 1979-80, MCH coord., 1980-82; chief nurse USAF Clinic, Eielson AFB, Alaska, 1984-86, Air Force Systems Command Hosp., Edwards AFB, Calif., 1986-90; comdr. San Vito Dei Normanni Air Station, Italy, 1990-92, 42d Med. Group, Loring AFB, Maine, 1992-94; 37th Med. Group, Moody AFB, Ga., 1994—. Mem. Assn. Women's Health, Obstetric, and Neonatal Nurses (sec.-treas. armed forces dist. 1986-88, vice-chmn. armed forces dist. 1989-91), Air Force Assn., Assn. Mil. Surgeons U.S., Bus. and Profl. Women's Assn. (pub. rels. chair Prince George's County chpt. 1981-82), Assn. Healthcare Execs., Sigma Theta Tau. Republican. Lutheran. Home: 3109 Robinson Rd Valdosta GA 31602

LAMPE, HARRIETT RICHMOND, retired educator, artist; b. Pitts., June 5, 1906; d. David Philip and Harriet Calhoun (Colwell) Richmond; m. William Seth Lampe, Apr. 12, 1930; children: Keith, Elin, Seth, Karen. BA, Carnegie-Mellon U., 1927; postgrad., Columbia U., 1926, 27, 28, Fairleigh Dickinson U., 1959, U. Mich., Dearborn, 1961. Cert. art tchr., Pa., N.J., Mich. Tchr. elem. art Bavard Sch., Pitts., 1927-29; tchr. art Frick Tchr.'s Tng., Pitts., 1929-31, Tenafly (N.J.) High Sch., 1959-61; tchr. art, English, French jr. and sr. high schs. Birmingham, Mich., 1962-71. One-woman shows include Maitland Gallery of Art and the Ormond War Meml. Art Gallery; exhibited in group shows at U. Miami Lowe Gallery, Winter Park Art Festival, Halifax Art Festival, Images and others; represented in pvt. collections, Fla., Mich., Pa., N.Y. Mem. AAUW, Detroit Women Painters and Sculptors, Detroit Fine Arts Alliance, Birmingham Art Assn., Pitts. Art League, Nat. League of Am. Pen Women, Art League of Volusia County (Fla.), Artist Group, Beaux Art of Volusia. Republican. Presbyterian. Home: 9 Hialeah Dr Apt 102 Daytona Beach FL 32117-2531

LAMPEL, ANITA KAY, psychologist; b. L.A., May 25, 1946; d. Jack Murray and Rose (Maltun) L.; m. Stanley David Mishook, Dec. 21, 1975; children: Jacob, David. PhD, Stanford U., 1969. Diplomate Am. Bd. Profl. Psychology; lic. psychologist, Calif. Staff psychologist Children's Meml. Hosp., Chgo., 1970-73; mgr. children's program San Bernardino (Calif.) County Dept. of Mental Health, 1973-79; pvt. practice San Bernardino, 1979—; instr. various univs., Calif., 1973—. Author: (with others) Group Psychotherapy with Children and Adolescents, 1987; contbr. articles to profl. jours. Chair Gifted Edn. Adv. Commn., San Bernardino, 1988-90; mem. Family Life Edn. Adv. Commn., San Bernardino, 1988-91. Mem. Am. Psychology Assn., Calif. State Psychology Assn., Inland Counties Psychol. Assn. (sec. 1988-89), Am. Bd. Profl. Psychology (western regional bd. dirs. 1988-93).

LAMPERT, ELEANOR VERNA, employment development specialist; b. Porterville, Calif., Mar. 23; d. Ernest Samuel and Violet Edna (Watkins) Wilson; student in bus., fin. Porterville Jr. Coll., 1977-78; grad. Anthony Real Estate Sch., 1971; student Laguna Sch. of Art, 1972, U. Calif.-Santa Cruz, 1981; m. Robert Mathew Lampert, Aug. 21, 1935; children—Sally Lu Winton, Lary Lampert, Carol R. John. Bookkeeper, Porterville (Calif.) Hosp., 1956-71; real estate sales staff Ray Realty, Porterville, 1973; sec. Employment Devel. Dept., State of Calif., Porterville, 1973-83, orientation and tng. specialist CETA employees, 1976-80. Author: Black Bloomers and Han-Ga-Ber, 1986. Sec., Employer Adv. Group, 1973-80, 81—; mem. U.S. Senatorial Bus. Adv. Bd., 1981-84; charter mem. Presdl. Republican Task Force, 1981—; mem. Rep. Nat. Congl. Com., 1982-88; pres. Sierra View Hosp. Vol. League, 1988-89 ; vol. Calif. Hosp. Assn., 1983-89, Calif. Spl. Olympics Spirit Team. Recipient Merit Cert., Gov. Pat Brown, State of Calif., 1968. Mem. Lindsay Olive Growers, Sunkist Orange Growers, Am. Kennel Club, Internat. Assn. Personnel in Employment Security, Calif. State Employees Assn. (emeritus Nat. Wildlife Fedn., NRA, Friends of Porterville Library, Heritage Found., DAR (Kaweah chpt. rec. sec. 1988—), Internat. Platform Assn., Dist. Fedn. Women's Clubs (recording sec. Calif. chpt. 1988—), Ky. Hist. Soc., Women's Club of Calif. (pres. Porterville chpt. 1988-89, dist. rec. sec. 1987-89), Mo. Rep. Women of Taney County, Internat. Sporting and Leisure Club, Ladies Aux. VFW (No. 5168 Forsyth, Mo.), Ozark Walkers League.

LAMPERT, MIRIAM TUTTLE, marketing professional; b. La Grange, Ill., Jan. 4, 1965; d. Frederick G. Tuttle and Jeanne A. (Dondanville) Brown; m. William W. Lampert, July 6, 1991. BS in Bus. and Mtkg., Ea. Ill. U., Charleston, 1987. Cert. prof. in direct mktg. Project coord. HHC Direct, San Diego, 1989-91; mktg. coord. IDEA, internat. assn. fitness profls., San Diego, 1991-92, prodn. mgr., 1992-93, mktg. mgr., 1993—; direct mail cons. Pinpoint Mktg., San Diego, 1991—. Vol. North County Conv. and Visitors Bur., Escondido, Calif., 1990-92. Mem. San Diego Direct Mktg. Club.

LAMPKIN, M. MARTHA, architect, city planner; b. Decatur, Ill., Sept. 25, 1952; d. Louis William and Mary Estelle (Hayes) L. BArch, U. Notre Dame, 1975; MArch, M City Planning,, MIT, 1981. Registered arch., Ill., Mass.; cert. Nat. Coun. Archtl. Registration Bds. Arch. Metz, Train & Youngren, Inc., Chgo., 1975-77; asst. prof. architecture La. Tech U., Ruston, 1088-78; arch., planner Skidmore, Owings & Merrill, Boston, 1981-83, Chgo., 1985; urban designer Lane, Frenchman and Assocs., Inc., Boston, 1984-85; prin., v.p. Sasaki Assocs., Inc., Watertown, Mass., 1985—, also bd. dirs.; guest lectr., studio critic MIT, Harvard Grad. Sch. Design, Boston Archtl. Ctr., U. Notre Dame, Kent State U., Wentworth Inst. Tech., 1981—; bd. dirs. Nat. Archtl. Accrediting Bd., 1980-83, mem. accreditation team, 1979—. Co-author master plans for numerous univs., including Case Western Res. U., Ga. Inst. Tech., U. Ill., Iowa State U., Harvard U., U. Colo. Health Scis. Ctr., U. Lowell, Mass., U. Mass., Lowell, also Univ. Circle Master Plan, Cleve., Bank of Boston, Housatonic Corp. Ctr., Milford, Conn., Va. Ctr., Fairfax County, Campustown Revitalization Plan, Ames, Iowa, Ctrl. Area Circulator, Chgo., Ames Townscape Plan, Boston Common Garage Renovation, numerous others. Mem. design and engring. com. Artery Bus. Com., 1989—; mem. designer selection panel Mass. Turnpike Authority; trustee 1000 Friends of Mass., 1992; mem. Rotch Travelling Scholarship Com., 1990-95. Recipient 1st award in design Commonwealth of Mass., 1986; Loeb fellow Harvard UGrad. Sch. Design, 1991-92. Fellow AIA (chmn. regional and urban design com. 1992-94); mem. Boston Soc. Architects (bd. dirs. 1983—, co-chmn. ctrl. artery task force 1988—, mem. Hrleston Parker award jury 1993, chmn. nominating com. 1992, bd. dirs., commr. design 1988-90, chmn. urban design citation com. 1984, 87, design excellence in housing awards jury, 1990), New Eng. Women in Real Estate (steering com. 1991-94). Office: Sasaki Assocs Inc 64 Pleasant St Watertown MA 02172

LAMROUEX, DAWN MARIE, accounting and mathematics educator; b. Saginaw, Mich., Aug. 7, 1958; d. Donald Duane and Doris Julia (Kilburn) Cole; m. Randy Gilbert Wildermuth, Feb. 20, 1976 (div. 1988); children: Ryan Scott, Beth Anne, Troy Alan; m. Jody Ken Lamroueux, Oct. 16, 1993; stepchildren: Jody Ken Jr., Cory Alan, Adam Christopher. AB in Data Processing, Baker Coll., Owosso, Mich., 1986, BBA in Acctg./CIS, 1992. Computer sales person ICON Tech. Corp., Owosso, 1986-88; independent acct. Owosso, 1988—; instr. acctg., math. Baker Coll., Owosso, 1992-94; acct. Crown Leisure divsn. C.C.I., 1995—. Contbr. articles to profl. jours. Mem. Inst. Mgmt. Accts. (Saginaw Valley chpt. Acctg. award 1991).

LAMSON, EVONNE VIOLA, therapist, computer software company executive, consultant, pastor, Christian education administrator; b. Ithaca, Mich., July 8, 1946; d. Donald and Mildred (Perdew) Guild; m. James E. Lamson, Nov. 2, 1968; 1 child, Lillie D. Assoc. in Math., Washtenaw C.C., Ypsilanti, Mich., 1977; BS, Ea. Mich. U., 1989; MA in Pastoral Counseling Ashland (Ohio) Theol. Sem., 1993. Lic. profl. counselor, Mich. Data base mgr. ERIM, Ann Arbor, Mich., 1978-91; mgr. product svcs. Comshare, Ann Arbor, 1981-90, project leader, tng. course designer info. techs., 1991-93; founder, pres. G & L Consultants, Brighton, Mich., 1982—; tng. specialist ComShare, Ann Arbor, 1990-93; Assoc. Pastor, dir. Christian edn. Keystone Community Ch., Saline, Mich., 1993—; founder Living Waters Counseling, 1993—. Study leader Brighton Wesleyan Ch., 1981-93; lic. minister Weseleyan Ch. Am., 1993—; program dir. Wesleyan Womens Assn. of Brighton, 1983-91; clin. staff counselor Women's Resource Ctr., Howell, Mich., 1991-94; clin. counselor Livingston Counseling and Assessment, 1994—. Mem. AACD, NAFE, AACC, Am. Mgmt. Assn., Fairbanks Family of Am., Internat. Platform Assn. Avocations: skiing, motivational speaking, reading. Home: 6708 Calfhill Ct Brighton MI 48116 Office: Living Waters Counseling 3457 E Grand River Howell MI 48843

LAMY, M(ARY) REBECCA, land developer, former government official; b. Ft. Bragg, N.C., Nov. 21, 1929; d. Charles Joseph and Sarah Esther (Koonce) L.; B.A., U. N.C., Greensboro, 1952. Procurement analyst Air Force MIPR Mgmt. Office, Washington, 1958-60, procurement and fiscal officer, 1960-68; budget analyst Naval Air Systems Command, Washington, 1968-69, indsl. specialist, 1969-71; indsl. specialist A.D.T.C., Eglin AFB, Fla., 1971-74, Def. Logistics Agy., Alexandria, Va., 1974-81; logistics mgmt. specialist Strategic Systems Project Office, Dept. Navy, Washington, 1981-82; procurement analyst Hdqrs. Dept. Army, Washington, 1982-85. Mem. Onslow Mus. Found. Bd. (emeritus), Onslow Meml. Hosp. Aux., 1985-91. Recipient Outstanding Performance awards U.S. Air Force, 1956, 65, 72, 73; Quality award Def. Logistics Agy., 1979, Outstanding Performance award, 1978, 79, Exceptional Service award, 1983, 84, 85; Comdr.'s award Hdqrs. Dept. Army, 1985; others. Mem. U. N.C. at Greensboro. Alumni Assn.

LANAHAN, MARIA J., secondary education educator; b. Newark, Sept. 15, 1947; d. Apolinario M. and Mary J. (Fonseca) De Oliveira; divorced; children: James John, Tara Lynn. BA in Spanish, Montclair State Coll., 1969, MA in Sociology, 1973, supr./prin. cert., 1988. Cert. Spanish tchr. grades K-12, fgn. lang. area coord. Tchr. Spanish H.B. Whitehorne Mid. Sch., Verona, N.J., 1969-86, coord. gen. arts area, 1975-86; tchr. Spanish, coord. fgn. lang. area grades 5-12 Verona High Sch., 1986—; adj. prof. teaching and curriculum Montclair (N.J.) State U., 1992—; student travel leader NETC/EF, Verona, 1987—; mem. critical thinking network Montclair State Coll., 1990—; mem. and com. leader Mid. States Evaluation Team, 1987, 89, 93. Mem. ASCD, Am. Assn. Tchrs. Spanish and Portugese. Office: Verona High Sch 151 Fairview Ave Verona NJ 07044

LANAM, LINDA LEE, lawyer; b. Ft. Lauderdale, Fla., Nov. 21, 1948; d. Carl Edward and Evelyn (Bolton) L. BS, Ind. U., 1970, JD, 1975. Bar: Ind. 1975, Pa. 1979, U.S. Dist. Ct. (no. and so. dists.) Ind. 1975, U.S. Supreme Ct. 1982, Va. 1990. Atty., asst. counsel Lincoln Nat. Life Ins. Co., Ft. Wayne, Ind., 1975-76, 76-78; atty., mng. atty. Ins. Co. of N.Am., Phila., 1978-79, 80-81; legis. liaison Pa. Ins. Dept., Harrisburg, 1981-82, dep. ins. commr., 1982-84; exec. dir., Washington rep. Blue Cross and Blue Shield Assn., Washington, 1984-86; v.p. and sr. counsel Union Fidelity Life Ins. Co., Am. Patriot Health Ins. Co., etc., Trevose, Pa., 1986-89; v.p., sr. counsel, corp. sec. Life Ins. Co. Va., Richmond, 1989—, also bd. dirs.; chmn. adv. com. health care legis. Nat. Assn. Ins. Commrs., 1985-87, chmn. long term care, 1986-87, mem. tech. resource com. on cost disclosure and genetic testing, 1993-94; mem. tech. adv. com. Health Ins. Assn. Am., 1986-89. Contbr. articles to profl. jours. Pres. Phila. Women's Network, 1980-81; chmn. city housing code bd. appeals Harrisburg, 1985-86. Mem. ABA, Richmond Bar Assn. Republican. Presbyterian. Office: Life Ins Co Va/Aon Corp 6610 W Broad St Richmond VA 23230-1702

LANCASTER, ALDEN, educational consultant; b. Balt., Feb. 25, 1956; d. Henry Carrington and Martha (Roe) L. BA magna cum laude, Duke U., 1977; MA, George Washington U., 1979. Program designer, coord. Duke U., Durham, N.C., 1977-79; mgr. profl. devel. programs Nat. Assn. Coll. and Univ. Bus. Officers, Washington, 1979-80; assoc. dir. refugee relief agy. Ch. of the Saviour, Bangkok, Thailand, 1980-81; dir. community svcs. U.S. Cath. Conf. Refugee Resettlement Agy., San Diego, 1981-82; nat. project dir. Bread for the World Ednl. Fund, Washington, 1982-83; edn. dir., exec. dir. Ptnrs. for Global Justice, Washington, 1983-85; dir. adult edn. programs, tchr. Spanish Ednl. Devel. Ctr., Washington, 1983-86; exec. dir., cons. Samaritan Ministry Greater Washington, 1985-87; career counselor, tng. cons. Rockport Inst., Washington, 1985—; dir. nat. literacy tng., ednl. cons. Assn. for Community Based Edn., Washington, 1987—; ednl. cons. George Washington U., Washington, 1989-93; ednl. cons. Pub./Pvt. Ventures, Phila., Savannah, Ga., Ft. Lauderdale, Fla., 1990-91; ednl. cons., dir. nat. literacy projects Wider Opportunities for Women, Washington, 1991-94; mgmt. cons. Women's Tech. Assistance Project, Ctr. Cmty. Change, 1988-89; ednl. cons. United Way Am., 1992—, Eckerd Family Youth Alternatives, Clearwater, Fla., 1993—; adj. assoc. prof. George Washington U., 1993—; grant evaluation and literacy staff devel. cons. Nat. Inst. Literacy, 1993—; staff devel. cons. Ranch Navajo Sch. Bd., Pine Hill, N.Mex., 1993—, Centro de Estudios Pop Wuj, Quetzaltenango, Guatemala, 1995; cons. Utah State Office of Edn., 1994; contextual literacy cons. Friends of the Family, Inc., Balt., 1994—; instr. tchr. tng. Essex C.C., 1995—; lit. sys. and staff devel. capacity-bldg. evaluation cons. State of Maine, 1995—. Author: An Introduction to Intergenerational Literacy, 1992; co-author: (with Thomas g, Sticht) Functional Context Education: A Primer for Program Providers, 1992; editor, primary author: Literacy for Empowerment: A Resource Handbook for Community Based Educators, 1989. Mem. nat. adv. bd. Project Lifelong Learning Pa. State U., 1992-93. Mem. Assn. Community Based Edn. Home and Office: 6706-A Poplar Ave Takoma Park MD 20912

LANCASTER, BARBARA MAE, management consulting company executive; b. Stafford Springs, Conn., Feb. 18, 1930; d. Harold D. and Ruth (Bristol) Stebbins; m. Colin T. Lancaster, June 5, 1948 (div. July 1979); children: Wayne, Sharon, Kevin, Karen, Kim. BS in Commerce, Rider Coll., 1981, MBA, 1984. CPA, N.J.; cert. fin. planner, life underwriter; chartered fin. cons. Acct. Electro Mech. Research, Princeton Junction, N.J., 1963-70; treas. Raritan Valley Ceilings, Inc., Monmouth Junction, N.J., 1970-78; adminstrv. asst. Total Enterprises, Princeton, N.J., 1979-81; pres. Lancaster Mgmt., Inc., Monmouth Junction, 1981—; tchr. Adult Sch., South Brunswick, N.J., 1986—; adj. prof. Rutgers U., 1989, vis. prof.; speaker Mercer County Coll., Trenton, N.J., 1986—, Women Life Underwriters, Freeport, Bahamas, 1988. Author: Entrepreneurial Training Institute Course I-Business Plan, 1994, Guide to Living Styles for Retirees-Professional Education, 1995. Mem. small bus. adv. Princeton C. of C., 1984—; mem. adv. bd. Small Bus. Devel. Ctr., Newark, 1986—, Nat. Coun. Aging, 1995—; chair J. Devel. Authority for Small Bus., Minorities and Women's Ent., 1991—. Named Advocate of Yr., U.S. SBA, N.J., 1987. Mem. Nat. Assn. Women Bus. Owners (treas. N.J. chpt. 1987—), N.J. Assn. Women Bus. Owners (pres. 1986-88), Women Life Underwriters Conf. (pres. 1987-88, nat. pres. 1991-92), Bus. and Profl. Women, Mid-Atlantic Venture Capital (v.p. 1988). Democrat. Home and Office: 112 Appletree Ct Monmouth Junction NJ 08852-2102

LANCASTER, KAREN MARIE, accountant; b. Perth Amboy, N.J., Sept. 6, 1969; d. James Peter and Sandra Ellen (Auman) Williams; m. George Edgar Lancaster, June 1, 1991. BBA, U. Mich., 1991. CPA, Mich. Sr. assoc. Coopers & Lybrand, Detroit, 1991-93; chief acct. City of Ann Arbor, Mich., 1993—. Treas. Huron Valley Alumna Assn., Ann Arbor, 1992—; ch. clk. United Ch. of Christ, Clinton, Mich., 1994—; fin. advisor Alpha Gamma Delta, Ann Arbor, 1992-94. Mem. AICPAs, Mich. Assn. CPAs, Mich. Mcpl. Fin. Officers, Govt. Officers Fin. Officers. Republican. Congregationalist. Office: City of Ann Arbor PO Box 8647 100 N 5th Ave Ann Arbor MI 48107

LANCASTER, KENDELL RENÉ QUESENBERRY, floral designer, business manager, administrator; b. Radford, Va., Oct. 24, 1956; d. William Clarence and Evelyn Allene (Young) Quesenberry; m. Ted Allen Carter, Sept. 20, 1974 (div. Dec. 1979); 1 child, Jesika Allene; m. Michael Bernard Lancaster, Nov. 29, 1985; stepchildren: Michael J., John David, Melanie A., Matthew O. AAS in Mktg., New River C.C., 1994; BS, Bluefield Coll., 1996. Designer, trainee Sun City (Fla.) Florist, 1975; designer Pulaski (Va.) Flower Shop, 1976-77; owner, designer Blue Ridge Flowers & Gifts, Pulaski, 1981; designer The Village Flower Shop, Radford, Va., 1982-84; instr., designer New River Community Coll., Dublin, Va., 1984-85; owner, designer The White Horse, Max Meadows, Va., 1985-92; designer Dublin Flower Shop, 1987-88, The Wicker Basket, Wytheville, Va., 1988-90, Flowers by Mary, Max Meadows, Va., 1988-90; designer, buyer The Draper (Va.) Mercantile, 1989—; office mgr. Rowland Express (Va.) Inc., 1994—; instr.designer New River C.C., 1994; guest speaker Christian Women's Club, Wytheville, 1989, Rural Retreat (Va.) Lit. Club, 1990, Profl. Bus. Women's Club, Pulaski, 1981; judge Chautauqua Festival, Wytheville, 1989; designer Fine Arts Showcase of Home, Pulaski, Va., 1990; youth group leader, vol. notetaker New River C.C., 1992—; guest designer Teleflora Design Show, 1992. Baptist. Home: PO Box 392 Max Meadows VA 24360-0392

LANCASTER, LISA MARIE, law enforcement officer; b. Worcester, Mass., Nov. 13, 1966; d. William Peter Ben and Willie Mae (Blyther) L.; m. James T. Spencer, Jr., July 15, 1987 (div. July 1988). Student, Lincoln U., 1984-85, U. S.C., 1986; B, Community Coll., Dover, Del., 1991; A in Criminal Justice, C.C. of the Air Force, Wilmington Coll., 1990; postgrad., Wesley Coll., 1991—. E-1 3743 BMTS USAF, Lackland AFB, Tex., 1985-86; E-2, E-3 363 SPS USAF, Shaw AFB, S.C., 1986-88; E-4 8th SPS USAF, Kunsan Air Base, Korea, 1989-90; E-5 436 SPS USAF, Dover, 1990—; pres. dorm coun. 363 SPS, Shaw AFB, 1986-88; K-55 radar cert. 436 SPS, Dover, 1991—; drug identifier Del. State Police Acad., Dover, 1991—. Rep. Worcester (Mass.) Youth Games, 1982-84; counselor Worcester City Boys & Girls Camp, 1983-84; social worker Shelter for Abused Children, Sumter, S.C., 1987-88; vol. Shelter for Homeless, Kunsan, 1989-90; tchr. Drug Abuse Resistance Edn., 1993; active Big Sister program. Mem. NAACP (Del. charter), 436 Security Policy Booster Club (sec. 1990—). Democrat. Baptist. Home: Newtowne Village 106 Victoria Blvd Newark DE 19702 Office: 436 Sps Dover A F B DE 19902

LANCASTER, PEGGY, advertising agency executive. Prin., creative dir. Scott/Lancaster (formerly Scott Lancaster Mills Atha), L.A., 1976—. Recipient numerous creative awards; named Woman of Yr., Am. Advt. Fedn., 1973. Office: Scott/Lancaster Ste 125 27520 Hawthorne Blvd Rolling Hills Estate CA 90274

LANCASTER, SALLY RHODUS, philanthropy consultant; b. Gladewater, Tex., June 28, 1938; d. George Lee and Milly Maria (Meadows) Rhodus; m. Olin C. Lancaster Jr., Dec. 23, 1960; children: Olin C. III, George Charles, Julie Meadows. BA magna cum laude, So. Meth. U., 1960, MA, 1979; PhD, East Tex. State U., 1983. Tchr. English, Tex. pub. schs., 1960-61, 78-79; sr. advisor Meadows Found., Inc., Dallas, 1979-94, also trustee and dir.; cons. to philanthropy sector, 1994—. Trustee So. Meth. U., 1980-88, East Tex. State U., regent 1987-93; Tex. del. White House Conf. on Tourism, 1995; adv. dir. Los Caminos del Rio Inc.; dir. Inst. Nautical Archaeology; mem. adv. bd. Communities Found. Tex. Recipient Disting. Alumni award So. Meth. U., 1986, East Tex. State U., 1994, Citizenship Excellence award in philanthropy Dallas Hist. Soc., 1984. Mem. Am. Evaluation Assn., Conf. S.W. Founds., Council on Founds., Philos. Soc. of Tex., Phi Beta Kappa (assoc. pres. 1980-82, nat com. on assns. 1983-85), Am. Assn. Continuing Edn., World Future Soc. Presbyterian. Office: Meadows Foundation Inc Wilson Historic Block 3003 Swiss Ave Dallas TX 75204-6090

LANCE, CHRISTINA MARIE, marketing professional; b. Erie, Pa., Feb. 2, 1960; d. James W. and Helen Jayne (Williams) Tipton; m. John Peter Lance, Feb. 8, 1992; 1 child, Joshua Daniel Turner. Student in Psychology and Journalism, Pa. State U. Tchr. Ctrl. Clear, Philipsburg, Pa., 1980-85; asst. dir. Svcs. Inc., Gettysburg, Pa., 1986-90; dir. LSS-SR Hospice, Gettysburg, 1990-93; owner, pres. PR Assocs., Gettysburg, 1991—, pres., owner, 1992—. Cons. Take Pride in Your Country, Gettysburg, 1993; active AIDS quilt project, South Central, Pa., 1992—. Mem. NAFE, Gettysburg C. of C. (com. mem. 1992—). Democrat. Russian Orthodox. Office: PR Assocs 334 York St Ste D Gettysburg PA 17325

LANCOUR, KAREN LOUISE, secondary education educator; b. Cheboygan, Mich., June 2, 1946; d. Clinton Howard and Dorothy Marie (Passeno) L. AA, Alpena Community Coll., 1966; BA, Ea. Mich. U., 1968, MS, 1970. Teaching asst. Ea. Mich. U., Ypsilanti, 1968-70; tchr. sci. Utica (Mich.) Community Schs., 1970—. Nat. event supr. Sci. Olympiad, 1986—, nat. rules com., 1987—, state event supr., 1986—, regional dir., 1987. Mem. Nat. Sci. Tchrs. Assn., Mich. Sci. Tchrs. Assn., Nat. Assn. Biology Tchrs., Met. Detroit Sci. Tchrs. Assn., Smithsonian Inst., Nat. Geographic Soc., Edison Inst., Mortar Bd., Internat. Biograph. Soc., Am. Biograph. Inst. Rsch. Assn. (dep. gov.), Internat. Platform Assn., Phi Theta Kappa, Kappa Delta Phi. Home: 8378 18 Mile Rd Apt 202 Sterling Heights MI 48313-3034 Office: Henry Ford II High Sch 11911 Clinton River Rd Sterling Heights MI 48313-2420

LAND, JUDITH BROTEN, stockbroker; b. Newark, July 27, 1951; d. Robert Allan and Marjorie (Frederickson) Broten; m. Andre Paul Land, Jan. 6, 1973; children: Ian Sherard, Margo Caryn. Student, Hood Coll., 1969-70, Denver U., 1970-71, Monmouth Coll., 1971-72, Fla. Atlantic U., 1976-77. Lic. ins. agt., Fla. Ops. dept. Fahnestock & Co., Red Bank, N.J., 1973; with ops. dept. Thomson McKinnon, South Orange, N.J., 1973-75; br. ops. rep. Thomson McKinnon, Boca Raton, Fla., 1977-80; sales asst., trainee Butcher & Singer Inc., Boca Raton, 1980-81, stockbroker, 1981-85; stockbroker A.G. Edwards & Sons, Inc., Boca Raton, 1985—; lectr. Palm Beach County Schs., Boca Raton, 1987-95, Palm Beach County Librs., 1990-91; daily stock market radio reporter Sta. WDBF-AM, Delray Beach, Fla., 1979-81. Community theatre performer; song composer. Mem. Whispering Pines PTA, 1986—, Singing Pines Children's Mus., Boca Raton, 1985-89, Young Women of the Arts, Boca Raton, 1989, C. of C., 1990-92. Republican. Episcopalian. Office: AG Edwards & Sons Inc 1900 Glades Rd Ste 451 Boca Raton FL 33431

LANDAU, LAURI BETH, accountant, tax consultant; b. Bklyn., July 21, 1952; d. Jack and Audrey Carolyn (Zuckernick) L. BA, Skidmore Coll., 1973; postgrad., Pace. U., 1977-79. CPA, N.Y., Oreg. Mem. staff Audrey Z. Landau, CPA, Suffern, N.Y., 1976-78; mem. staff Ernst & Whinney, N.Y.C., 1979-80, mem. sr. staff, 1980-82, supr., 1982-84; mgr. Arthur Young & Co., N.Y.C., 1984-87, prin., 1987-89; sr. mgr. Ernst & Young, N.Y.C., 1989-92; prnt. Landau & Landau, New City, N.Y., 1992—; speaker World Trade Inst., N.Y.C., 1987—, Nat. Fgn. Trade Coun., N.Y.C., 1989—. Composer songs. Career counselor Skidmore Coll., Saratoga Springs, N.Y., 1977—; mem. leadership com. Class of 1973, 83-85, pres., 1985-93, fund chmn., 1987-88, mem. planned gift com., 1989—. N.Y. State Regents scholar, 1970. Mem. Nat. Conf. CPA Practitioners, N.Y. State Soc. CPAs, Skidmore Coll. Alumni Assn. (mem. nominating com. 1989-92). Skidmore Alumni Club, German Shepherd Dog Am. Club. Democrat. Office: 17 Squadron Blvd Ste 303 New City NY 10956

LANDAU-CRAWFORD, DOROTHY RUTH, local social service executive; b. S.I., N.Y., Oct. 5, 1957; d. Robert August and Dorothy Faith (Schaut) Landau; m. John W. Crawford, Oct. 21, 1989. AS in Applied Sci., SUNY-Farmingdale, 1977; BS in Biology, Wagner Coll., 1979. Sci. tchr. Bais Yaakov, S.I., 1979-81; dental asst. Dr. Marvin Freeman, S.I., 1981-82; office mgr. Dr. Bennett C. Fidlow, S.I., 1982-85; polit. aide to S.I. Borough Pres., 1985-89; exec. dir. Richmond Sr. Svcs. Project Share, 1990—. Environ. chmn. S.I. League for Better Govt., 1984—; pres. Tottenville Improvement Council Inc., Staten Island, 1985—; exec. dir. Richmond Sr. Svcs. Project Share, 1990—; Dem. candidate for N.Y. State Assembly 60th dist., 1986, dist. leader; dir. community bds. S.I. Borough Pres.' Office; founder, pres. environ. group S.I.L.E.N.T., S.I., 1985; 1st v.p. 123d Community Council, S.I., 1986; social chmn. S. Shore Democratic Club; founding mem. Friends of Clay Pit Pond Park; mem. Protectors of Pine Oak Woods Inc., Roserio Alliotta Dem. Club, Dem. Orgn. of Richmond; trustee S.I. Bd. Leukemia Soc. Am., 1988—, chair Celebrity Waiters Luncheon; spl. election candidate for 51st Councilmatic Dist., 1994. Recipient Community Activist Award Office of Pres. S.I. Borough, 1987. Mem. NAFE, Bus. and Profl. Women (Young Careerist for S.I.). Roman Catholic. Avocations: photography, sports, ceramics, youth programs. Home: 168 Bedell Ave Staten Island NY 10307-2057 Office: 500 Jewett Ave Staten Island NY 10302-1538

LANDAUER, JERAMY LANIGAN, publishing company executive; b. Medford, Mass., Dec. 27, 1939; d. William Nicholas and Marion Elizabeth (Dorman) L. BA, Trinity Coll., Washington, 1961; cert., Harvard U., 1962; MBA, Columbia U., 1964. From mgr. direct mktg. to sr. v.p. direct mktg. Funk & Wagnalls, Inc., Ramsey, N.J., 1973-80; pres. Book Div. Times-Mirror Mags., N.Y.C., 1980-87; v.p., gen. mgr. Book Group Meredith Corp., Des Moines, 1987-88, pres. Book Group, 1988-91; pres. Landauer Corp., Des Moines, 1991—; bd. dirs. D.M.I.X., N.Y.C. Pres., bd. dirs. Girls' Club N.Y.C., 1986-87; bd. dirs. Trinity Coll., Washington, 1981-87, Des Moines

Met. Opera, 1988—, Des Moines Symphony, 1989-91. Mem. Direct Mktg. Assn. (bd. dirs. 1984-91), Rotary.

LANDBERG, ANN LAUREL, nurse, psychotherapist; b. Chgo., June 20, 1926; d. Carl Ryno and Ebba Sadie Elvira (Engstrom) Granlund; m. Harry Morton Landberg, Apr. 1, 1953 (dec. Feb. 1967); stepchildren: Rosabel, Marcene. RN, Swedish Hosp. Sch. Nursing, Seattle, 1948. Asst. head nurse Halcyon Hosp., Seattle, 1948; doctor's asst. Office of H.M. Landberg, M.D., Seattle, 1948-50, psychotherapist, 1950-67; pvt. practice psychotherapy, Seattle, 1967—; cons. Good Shepherd Sch. for Disturbed Girls, Seattle, 1954—, bd. dirs., 1954-60. Mem. Am. Psychotherapy Assn., King County Med. Aux., Stevens Hosp. Aux. (life), Swedish Hosp. Alumni (pres. 1952-53), Nat. Council Jewish Women, City of Hope, Edmonds Arts Assn. (life patron), Seattle Forensic Inst. (charter). Club: Swedish (Seattle). Home: 16900 Talbot Rd Edmonds WA 98026-5051 Office: 1007 Spring St Seattle WA 98104-1235

LANDEN, SANDRA JOYCE, psychologist, educator; b. L.A., May 8, 1960; m. Bernard B. Reifkind, Aug. 15, 1981. BA, UCLA, 1982, MA, 1984, PhD, 1988. Lic. clin. psychologist, Calif. Rsch. asst. UCLA Autism Clinic, 1980-82, UCLA Teaching Homes for Devel. Disabilities Project, 1981-82; rsch. assoc. UCLA Project for Devel. Disabilities, 1982-87; co-coord. parent tng. program UCI-UCLA Program for ADHD Children, 1984; teaching assoc. psychology dept. UCLA, 1984-87; psychology intern Hathaway Home for Children, Lakeview Terrace, Calif., 1985-86, clin. staff, 1986-87; clin. postdoctoral fellow Childrens Hosp. L.A., 1987-88; adj. faculty Grad. Sch. Edn. and Psychology Pepperdine U., L.A., 1988—; psychologist L.A., 1987—; dir. Westside Parenting Ctr., L.A., 1992—. Contbr. articles to profl. jours. Recipient scholarship UCLA, 1978-82, fellowship UCLA, 1982-85, dissertation rsch. grant UCLA, 1985-87. Mem. APA (div. psychoanalysis), Calif. Psychol. Assn., L.A. Psychol. Assn., Am. Assn. Mental Retardation, L.A. Child Devel. Ctr. Office: 11340 W Olympic Blvd Ste 245 Los Angeles CA 90064

LANDER, LEILA ASHER, sales executive; b. Glendale, Calif., July 23, 1949; d. Martin and Betty (Gurian) Asher; m. Richard C. Lander, Nov. 30, 1975; children: Melissa, Emily, Adam. BS in Bus. Adminstrn., Woodbury U., 1970. Ops. officer Union Bank, L.A., 1970-75; sales exec. US Leasing Corp., San Francisco, 1975-77, Titmus Optical, Petersberg, Va., 1977-79; nat. account sales mgr. Scott Worldwide, Phila., 1979—. Founding mem. Irvine (Calif.) Women's Assistence League, 1991. Recipient Blazer award for outstanding sales. Mem. Alpha Xi Delta Alumni. Democrat. Home: 48 Emerald Irvine CA 92714-7520

LANDERS, ANN (MRS. ESTHER P. LEDERER), columnist; b. Sioux City, Iowa, July 4, 1918; d. Abraham B. and Rebecca (Rushall) Friedman; m. Jules W. Lederer, July 2, 1939 (div. 1975); 1 dau., Margo Lederer Howard. Student, Morningside Coll., 1936-39, LHD (hon.), 1964; hon. degree, Wilberforce (Ohio) Coll., 1972, Am. Coll. Greece, 1979, Meharry Med. Coll., 1981, Jacksonville U., 1983, St. Leo Coll., 1984, Fla. Internat. U., 1984, Med. Coll. Pa., 1985, New Eng. Coll., 1985, U. Wis., 1985, Lincoln Coll., 1986, Nat. Coll. Edn., 1986, Southwestern Adventist Coll., 1987, Duke U., 1987, Rosary Coll., 1989, U. Hartford, 1989, L.I. U., 1989, Med. Coll. Ohio, 1989, Roosevelt U., 1991, Ind. U., 1991, Howard U., 1991, Bellevue U., 1992, DePaul U., 1992, Ursinus Coll., 1992, Hillsdale Coll., 1993, St. Xavier U., 1993, Chgo. Theol. Sem., 1993, Barry U., 1993, Northwestern U., 1994. Syndicated columnist Chgo., 1955—; pres. Eppie Co., Inc., Chgo. Author: Since You Asked Me, 1962, Ann Landers Talks to Teen-agers about Sex, 1964, Truth is Stranger, 1968, Ann Landers Speaks Out, 1975, The Ann Landers Encyclopedia, 1978; also pub. svc. booklets and numerous mag. articles; syndicated columnist Los Angeles Times-Creators Syndicates. Chmn. Eau Claire (Wis.) Gray-Lady Corps, ARC, 1947-53; chmn. Minn.-Wis. council Anti-Defamation League, 1945-49; asst. Wis. chmn. Nat. Found. Infantile Paralysis, 1951-53; hon. nat. chmn. 1963 Tb Christmas Seal Campaign; bd. sponsors Mayo Clinic, 1970; mem. sponsors com. Mayo Found.; nat. adv. bd. Dialogue for the Blind, 1972; adv. com. on better health services AMA; county chmn. Democratic Party Eau Claire; bd. dirs. Rehab. Inst. Chgo.; nat. bd. dirs. Am. Cancer Soc., Nat. Cancer Inst.; vis. com. bd. overseers Harvard Med. Sch.; mem. Pres.'s Commn. Drunk Driving; trustee Menninger Found., Nat. Dermatology Found., Am. Coll. Greece, Deree-Pierce Coll., Athens, Meharry Med. Sch., Hereditary Disease Found.; dirs. adv. bd. Yale Comprehensive Cancer Ctr. Recipient award Nat. Family Service Assn., 1965, Adolf Meyer award Assn. Mental Health N.Y., 1965, Pres.'s Citation and nat. award Nat. Council on Alcoholism, 1966, 2d nat. award, 1975, Golden Stethoscope award Ill. Med. Soc., 1967, Humanitarianism award Internat. Lions Club, 1967; plaque of honor Am. Friends of Hebrew U., 1968, Gold Plate award Acad. Achievement, 1969; Nat. Service award Am. Cancer Soc., 1971, Robert T. Morse award Am. Psychiat. Assn., 1972; plaque recognizing establishment of chair in chem. immunology Weizmann Inst., 1974, Jane Addams Public Service award Hull House, 1977, Health Achievement award Nat. Kidney Found., 1978, Nat. award Epilepsy Found. Am., 1978, James Ewing Layman's award Soc. Surg. Oncologists, 1979, citation for disting. service AMA, 1979, Thomas More medal Thomas More Assn., 1979, NEA award, 1979, Margaret Sanger award, 1979, Stanley G. Kay medal Am. Cancer Soc., 1983, 1st William C. Menninger medal for achievement in mental health, 1984, Albert Lasker pub. service award, 1985, Edwin C. Whitehead award, 1988, Community Svc. award Gateway Found.'s Citizen's Coun., 1989, Pub. Svc. award NIMH, 1989, award for outstanding pub. edn. Nat. Alliance for the Mentally Ill, 1990, Outstanding Pub. Svc. to Sci. award Nat. Assn. for Biomed. Rsch., 1990. Fellow Chgo. Gynecol. Soc. (citizen hon.); mem. LWV (pres. 1948), Brandeis U. Women (pres. 1960), Chgo. Econs. Club (dir. 1975), Harvard Club (Award 1994), Sigma Delta Chi. Clubs: Chgo. Econs. (dir. 1975), Harvard, Sigma Delta Chi. Office: Chgo Tribune 435 N Michigan Ave Chicago IL 60611*

LANDERS, SUSAN MAE, psychotherapist; b. Houston; d. James Edward and Frances Pauline (Braunagel) L. BS in Advt., U. Tex.; MS in Psychol. Counseling, U. Houston, Clearlake, 1994; cert. in sales, Dale Carnegie Inst. Mktg. rep. K.C. Products, Houston, 1981-83; account exec. Williamson County Express, Austin, Tex., 1984; advt. cons. Stas. KMMM/KOKE, Austin, 1985; key account sales rep. GranTree Furniture Rental, Austin, 1986-89; individual habilitation counselor Ctr. for the Retarded Inc., Houston, 1990; case mgr. Mental Health and Mental Retardation Authority Harris County, Houston, 1991-92; primary therapist Riceland Psychiat. Hosp., 1994—. Mem. NAFE. Home: 4605 N Braeswood # 108CC Houston TX 77096 Office: MHMRA 2850 Fannin Houston TX 77002

LANDERS, VERNETTE TROSPER, writer, educator, association executive; b. Lawton, Okla., May 3, 1912; d. Fred Gilbert and LaVerne Hamilton (Stevens) Trosper; m. Paul Albert Lum, Aug. 29, 1952 (dec. May 1955); 1 child, William Tappan; m. 2d, Newlin Landers, May 2, 1959 (dec. Apr. 1990); children: Lawrence, Marlin. AB with honors, UCLA, 1933, MA, 1935, EdD, 1953; Cultural doctorate (hon.) Lit. World U., Tucson, 1985. Tchr. secondary schs., Montebello, Calif., 1935-45, 48-50, 51-59; prof. Long Beach City Coll., 1946-47; asst. prof. Los Angeles State Coll., 1950; dean girls Twenty Nine Palms (Calif.) High Sch., 1960-65; dist. counselor Morongo (Calif.) Unified Sch. Dist., 1965-72, coordinator adult edn., 1965-67, guidance project dir., 1967; clk.-in-charge Landers (Calif.) Post Office, 1962-82; ret., 1982. V.p., sec. Landers Assn., 1965—; sec. Landers Vol. Fire Dept., 1972—; life mem. Hi-Desert Playhouse Guild, Hi-Desert Meml. Hosp. Guild; bd. friends Copper Mountain Coll., 1990-91; bd. dirs., sec. Desert Emergency Radio Service; mem. Rep. Senatorial Inner Circle, 1990-92, Regent Nat. Fedn. Rep. Women, 1990-92, Nat. Rep. Congl. Com., 1990-91, Presdl. Task Force, 1990-92; lifetime mem. Girl Scouts U.S., 1991. Recipient internat. diploma of honor for community service, 1973; Creativity award Internat. Personnel Research Assn., 1972, award Goat Mt. Grange No. 818, 1987; cert. of merit for disting. svc. to edn., 1973; Order of Rose, 1978, Order of Pearl, 1989, Alpha Xi Delta; poet laureate Center of Internat. Studies and Exchanges, 1981; diploma of merit in letters U. Arts, Parma, Italy, 1982; Golden Yr. Bruin UCLA, 1983; World Culture prize Nat. Ctr. for Studies and Research, Italian Acad., 1984; Golden Palm Diploma of Honor in poetry Leonardo Da Vinci Acad., 1984; Diploma of Merit and titular mem. internat. com. Internat. Ctr. Studies and Exchanges, Rome, 1984; Recognition award San Gorgonio council Girl Scouts U.S., 1984—; Cert. of appreciation Morongo Unified Sch. Dist., 1984, 89; plaque for contribution to postal service and community U.S. Postal Service, 1984; Biographee of Yr. award for outstanding achievement in the field of edn. and service to community Hist. Preservations of Am.; named Princess of Poetry of Internat. Ctr. Cultural Studies and Exchange, Italy, 1985; community dinner held in her honor for achievement and service to Community, 1984; Star of Contemporary Poetry Masters of Contemporary Poetry, Internat. Ctr. Cultural Studies and Exchanges, Italy, 1984; named to honor list of leaders of contemporary art and lit. and apptd. titular mem. of Internat. High Com. for World Culture & Arts Leonardo Da Vinci Acad., 1987; named to honor list Foremost Women 20th Century for Outstanding Contbn. to Rsch., IBC, 1987; ABI medal of honor 1987, Golden Acad. award, Presdl. Order of Merit Pres. George Bush-Exec. Coun. of Nat. Rep. Senatorial Com., Congl. cert. of Appreciation U.S. Ho. of Reps.; other awards and certs. Life fellow Internat. Acad. Poets, World Lit. Acad.; mem. Am. Personnel and Guidance Assn., Internat. Platform Assn., Nat. Ret. Tchrs. Assn., Calif. and Nat. Assn. for Counseling and Devel., Am. Assn. for Counseling and Devel. (25 yr. membership pin 1991), Nat. Assn. Women Deans and Adminstrs., Montebello Bus. and Profl. Women's Club (pres.), Nat. League Am. Pen Women (sec. 1985-86), Leonardo Da Vinci Acad. Internat. Winged Glory diploma of honor in letters 1982), Landers Area C. of C. (sec. 1985-86, Presdl. award for outstanding service, Internat. Honors Cup 1992-93), Desert Nature Mus., Phi Beta Kappa, Pi Lambda Theta (Mortar Bd., Prytanean UCLA, UCLA Golden Yr. Bruin 1983), Sigma Delta Pi, Pi Delta Phi. Clubs: Whittier Toastmistress (Calif.) (pres. 1957); Homestead Valley Women's (Landers). Lodge: Soroptimists (sec. 29 Palms chpt. 1962, life mem., Soroptimist of Yr. local chpt. 19, Woman of Distinction local chpt. 1987-88). Author: Impy, 1974, Talkie, 1975, Impy's Children, 1975; Nineteen O Four, 1976, Little Brown Bat, 1976; Slo-Go, 197Owls Who and Who Who, 1978; Sandy, The Coydog, 1979; The Kit Fox and the Walking Stick, 1980; contbr. articles to profl. jours., poems to anthologies. Guest of honor ground breaking ceremony Landers Elem. Sch., 1989, dedication ceremony, 1991. Home: 632 N Landers Ln PO Box 3839 Landers CA 92285

LANDI, DIANE MARIE, graphic designer, consultant; b. Paterson, N.J., Apr. 27, 1952; d. Mario Gustave and Josephine (Ryba) L. Cert. media completion, Sch. Visual Arts, N.Y.C., 1972. Ptnr. R-Art Corp., N.Y.C., 1972; chief designer Medallion Industries, Paterson, 1972-77; designer Equitable Bag, L.I. City, N.Y., 1977-82; owner Landi Graphics, N. Bergen, N.J., 1982—. Mem. Nat. Assn. Self-Employed, Amnesty Internat., MENSA, Humane Soc. U.S., Beethoven Soc. Libertarian.

LANDIS, DONNA MARIE, nursing administrator, women's health nurse; b. Lebanon, Pa., Sept. 5, 1944; d. James O.A. and Helen Joan (Fritz) Muench; m. David J. Landis, 1967 (div. 1985); children: Danielle M. Landis Farley, David J., Derek J.; m. John C. Broderick, 1990 (div. 1995). Diploma, St. Joseph's Hosp. Sch. Nursing, Reading, Pa., 1965. RN, Md. Head nurse med.-surg. unit Hosp. of U. Pa., 1965-67; nurse various hosps. and physician's offices, Md., Pa., 1965-85; clin. dir., clin. study coord. Osteoporosis Assessment Ctr., Wheaton, Md., 1985-95; clin. dir. Osteoporosis Diagnostic and Monitoring Ctr., Laurel, Md., 1985—. Mem. Balt. Bone Club, Soc. Clin. Densitometry (steering com. 1993—, assoc. editor SCAN 1994—), Nat. Osteoporosis Found., Sandoz Women's Speakers Bur., Allied Health Profls./Arthritis Found., St. Joseph's Hosp. Alumni Assn. Office: 14201 Laurel Park Dr Ste 226 Laurel MD 20707

LANDIS, LORI RAE, programmer/analyst; b. Akron, Ohio, Oct. 18, 1959; d. Gary Allen and Judith Rae (Foth) L. BS in BA, Jacksonville State U., 1981. Assoc. systems analyst Pan Am World Svcs., Arnold AFS, Tenn., 1981-84; programmer/analyst Rich's Dept. Store, Atlanta, 1984-86, Magnum Comms. Ltd., Atlanta, 1986-88; software systems cons. Am. Software, USA, Atlanta, 1988—; lectr. in field. Office: American Software Ste 40 470 E Paces Ferry Rd NE Atlanta GA 30305-3300

LANDIS, MICHELE, executive; b. Warren, Ohio, May 1, 1947; d. Sullivan and Elaine Christine (Cantelmo) Santucci; m. Russell M. Landis, Dec. 19, 1970 (div. 1995); 1 child, Julie Lee. Grad. high sch., Warren, Ohio. Pres., co-founder Upper St. Clair Tennis Devel. Program, Inc., Pitts., 1983—. Vol. Family House, Pitts., 1987-91, Hospice, Pitts., 1987-92, U.S. Tennis Assn., White plains, N.Y., 1993. Republican. Roman Catholic. Home: 1807 Tilton Dr Upper Saint Clair PA 15241-2636

LANDIS, SARA MARGARET SHEPPARD, editorial consultant; b. Badin, N.C., May 20, 1920; d. Thomas Coates and Ouida (Watson) Sheppard; m. Williard Griffith Landis, Dec. 7, 1945; children: Susan Sheppard, Timothy Joseph, Margaret Carol. Student, Flora MacDonald Coll. Women, 1937-38, Rice Bus. Coll., 1939; AB in Journalism, U. N.C., 1942. Editorial asst. Redbook Mag., N.Y.C., 1942-43; with Doubleday and Co., N.Y.C., 1944-46, Eagle Pencil Co., N.Y.C., 1953-54; mgr. personnel Workman Service, N.Y.C., 1955-56, Clay Adams Co., N.Y.C., 1957-58; job analyst Bigelow Carpet Co., N.Y.C., 1959-60; asst. to guidance dir. Childrens Village, Dobbs Ferry, N.Y., 1960-61; dir. promotions, advt. Oceans Publs., Dobbs Ferry, 1961-66; mgr. promotions Reinhold Pub. Co., N.Y.C., 1967-68, Watson Guptil Pub. Co., N.Y.C., 1968, Chilton Book Co., Phila., 1968-69; cons. editorial, promotions Sheppard-Landis Ink, N.Y.C., 1969—. Mem. St. George Episc. Ch. Mem. English Speaking Union (head book discussion group 1989—), Friends Epiphany chpt. N.Y. Pub. Library, United Daughters Confederacy. Home and Office: 271 Ave C Peter Cooper-Stuyvesant Town New York NY 10009

LANDIS, SHARYN BRANSCOME, educator; b. New Castle, Pa., Feb. 13, 1942; d. Maynard R. and Irene (Calderwood) Branscome; m. Kenneth R. Landis, Feb. 17, 1961; children: Kenneth R. Jr., Michelle Landis Nielsen, Jonathan A. BS in Edn., Youngstown U., 1967; MBA, U. Phoenix, 1984. Cert. secondary tchr., Colo. Tchr. Butler (Pa.) Community Coll., 1979-81, Barnes Bus. Coll., Denver, 1981-82, Arapahoe Community Coll., Little, Colo., 1981-82, Met. State Coll., Denver, 1982-84; dean of students Nat. Coll., Aurora, Colo., 1984-86; dist. resource tchr. Aurora (Colo.) Pub. Schs., 1986-93; tchr. bus. edn. Highlands Ranch (Colo.) H.S., 1993—. Bd. dirs. Children's Diabetes Assn., Denver, 1981-85. Named Hon. Life Mem. PTA, Pa., 1980-81. Mem. AAUW, Nat. Bus. Edn. Assn., Colo. Vocat. Assn. (state sec. 1991-94), Colo. Educators for and about Bus., Mt. Plains Bus. Assn., Phi Delta Kappa, Delta Pi Epsilon. Republican. Methodist. Home: 9245 S Mountain Brush Ct Highlands Ranch CO 80126 Office: Highlands Ranch H S Peoria St 9375 Cresthill Ln Highlands Ranch CO 80126

LANDMAN, BETTE EMELINE, academic administrator; b. Piqua, Ohio, July 18, 1937; d. Wilson Richard and Lois (Wilson) L. BS, Bowling Green State U., 1959; MA, Ohio State U., 1961, PhD, 1972. From instr. to asst. prof. anthropology Springfield (Mass.) Coll., 1963-67; asst. prof. Temple U., 1967-71; asst. prof. anthropology Beaver Coll., Glenside, Pa., 1971-76, dean, 1976-85, v.p. acad. affairs, 1980-85, acting pres., 1982-83, 85, pres., 1985—. Bd. dirs. Abington (Va.) Meml. Hosp., 1986-93, Abington Meml. Hosp. Found., 1993—; mem. blood doner champaign ARC, chair Pa.-Jersey Region Higher Edn., 1990-91; mem. bd. advisors Coll. Physicians of Phila., 1994—. Recipient Disting. Teaching award Christian R. and Mary F. Lindback Found., 1973; NSF fellow, 1961-63, Wenner-Gren Found. for Anthrop. Rsch. fellow, 1965-66; named Disting. Dau. of Pa., 1992; Ann. Pa. Am. Coun. on Edn.-NIP award established in her honor, 1992. Mem.. Am. Coun. Edn. (state coord. 1980-84, commn. on leadership devel. 1989-94, chmn. 1991-92, bd. dirs. 1993—), Assn. Am. Colls. (bd. dirs. 1986-91, vice chair 1989-90, chair 1990-91), Assn. Presbyn. Colls. and Univs. (exec. com. 1988-93, sec. 1989-90, v.p. 1990-91, pres. 1991-92), Pa. Assn. Colls. and Univs. (exec. com. 1992-93), Nat. Assn. Ind. Colls. and Univs. (commn. on campus concerns 1991—, vice chmn. 1992, chmn. 1993), Sigma Xi, Phi Kappa Phi, Kappa Delta Pi. Office: Beaver Coll Office of Pres 450 S Easton Rd Glenside PA 19038-3295

LANDON, JENNIFER FARHA, psychologist; b. Wichita, Kans., Sept. 27, 1962; d. Floyd E. and Janet Joy Farha; m. Patrick Leo Landon, Oct. 6, 1990; 1 child, Melanie Gaye. BS, U. Okla., 1984; MA, U. Mo., 1987, PhD, 1989. Lic. psychologist, Mo. Clin. psychologist Kansas City (Mo.) VA Med. Ctr., 1989—; adj. asst. prof. psychiatry Kans. U. Med. Ctr., Kansas City, 1992—. Contbr. articles to profl. jours. Bd. dirs. Epsicopal Ch. of Resurrection, Blue Springs, Mo., 1992—. Mem. APA, Nat. Orgn. VA Psychologists (membership chair 1992—), Soc. for Personality Assessment. Office: Kansas City VA Med Ctr 4801 E Linwood Blvd Kansas City MO 64128-2226

LANDOVSKY, ROSEMARY REID, figure skating school director, coach; b. Chgo., July 26, 1933; d. Samuel Stuart and Audrey Todd (Lyons) Reid; m. John Indulis Landovsky, Feb. 20, 1960; children: David John, Linette. BA in Psychology, Colo. Coll., 1956. Profl. skater Holiday on Ice Touring Show, U.S., Mex., Cuba, 1956-58; skating dir. and coach Paradice Arena, Birmingham, 1958-62, Les Patineurs, Huntsville, Ala., 1960-62; coach competitive (Ice Skating Inst. Am., U.S. Figure Skating Assn.) Michael Kirby and Assocs., River Forest, Chgo., Ill., 1962-63; rink mgr., skating dir. Lake Meadows Ice Arena, Chgo., 1963-68; coach (ISIA, USFSA) Rainbo Arena, Chgo., 1968-73; skating dir. Northwestern U. Skating Sch., Evanston, Ill., 1968-73, Robert Crown Ice Ctr., Evanston, 1973-75; dir. instl. programs Skokie (Ill.) Park Dist., 1975-87; competition dir. ISIA All America Competition, 1985-86. Dir., producer, choreographer Ice Show: Nutcracker Ballet, 1973, Ice Extravaganza III, 1985, Ice Lights '86, '87. Election judge, worker, Ind. Dems., Chgo., 1964-68. Mem. Profl. Skaters Guild, Ice Skating Inst. Am., Coll. Coll. Alumni Assn. (mem. Chgo. area com.), Gamma Phi Beta. Office: Skokie Skatium 9300 Bronx Ave Skokie IL 60077-1261

LANDRAM, CHRISTINA LOUELLA, librarian; b. Paragould, Ark., Dec. 10, 1922; d. James Ralph and Bertie Louella (Jordan) Oliver; m. Robert Ellis Landram, Aug. 7, 1948; 1 child, Mark Owen. BA, Tex. Woman's U., 1945, B.L.S., 1946, M.L.S., 1951. Preliminary cataloger Library of Congress, Washington, 1946-48; cataloger U.S. Info. Ctr., Tokyo, Japan, 1948-50, U.S. Dept. Agr., Washington, 1953-54; librarian Yokota AFB, Yokota, Japan, 1954-55; librarian St. Mary's Hosp., West Palm Beach, Fla., 1957-59; librarian Jacksonville (Ark.) High Sch., 1959-61; coord. Shelby County Libraries, Memphis, 1961-63; head catalog dept. Ga. State U. Library, 1963-86, librarian, assoc. prof. emeritus, 1986—. Contbr. articles to library jours. Mem. Ga. Library Assn. (chmn. resources and tech. services sect. 1969-71), Metro-Atlanta Library Assn. (pres. 1967-68), ALA (chmn. cataloging norms 1979-80, nominating com. 1977-78), Southeastern Library Assn. (mem. govtl. rels. com. 1975-78, intellectual freedom com. 1984-86, mem. Rothrock awards com. 1987-90). Presbyterian. Home: 1478 Leafmore Rdg Decatur GA 30033-2110

LANDRE, DEBRA ANN, mathematics educator; b. Quantico, Va., Sept. 15, 1955; d. Thomas F. and Joy L. (Carstens) L. BA in French and Math., Bradley U., 1976, MS in Edn., 1977; MS in Math., Ill. State U., 1979. Math. instr. Bradley U., Peoria, Ill., 1977-79, Ill. Valley Community Coll., Peru, 1980, Ill. Wesleyan U., Bloomington, 1981; computer sci. instr. Lincoln Coll., Bloomington, 1981-85; math. instr. Ill. State U., Normal, 1979-85; pres. Quality Input Inc., Normal, 1983-85; dir. acad. computing San Joaquin Delta Coll., Stockton, Calif., 1985-88; math. instr. San Joaquin Delta Coll., Stockton, 1988—. Author: Explorations in Elementary Algebra, 1992, Explorations in Intermediate Algebra, 1992, Explorations in College Algebra, 1992, Explorations in Statistics and Probability, 1992; co-author: Mathematics: Theory into Practice, 1980, Microprocessor-Based Operations: Systems Software, 1985, Microprocessor-Based Operations, 1985, Data Acquisition, 1985, Explorations in Elem. Algebra, 1992, Explorations in Intermediate Algebra, 1992, Explorations in Coll. Algebra, 1992, Explorations in Statistics and Probability 1992; contbr. articles to profl. jours. Mem. Calif. Assn. Dirs. Acad. Computing (pres. 1988-90), Calif. Ednl. Computer Consortium (bd. dirs. 1987-90, editor 1988-90), No. Calif. Cmty. Coll. Computer Consortium (sec./editor 1986-91), Calif. Math. Coun. (editor exec. bd. 1990—, pres. elect 1991-93, pres. 1994-95), Am. Math. Assn. of Two Yr. Colls. (editor 1994—), Calif. Tchrs. Assn. (pres.-elect 1994—). Office: San Joaquin Delta Coll 5151 Pacific Ave Stockton CA 95207-6370

LANDRIEU, MARY L., state treasurer; b. Nov. 23, 1955; m. E. Frank Snellings. BA, La. State U. Real estate agt., La. state rep. from dist. 90, 1979-89, La. state treas., 1987—; del., Dem. Nat. Conv., 1980. Mem. LWV, Women Execs. in State Govt., Fedn. Dem. Women, Delta Gamma. Roman Catholic. Office: Treasury Dept PO Box 44154 Baton Rouge LA 70804-4154*

LANDRY, BRENDA LEE, securities analyst; b. Wolfboro, N.H., June 24, 1942; d. Christopher Lee and Barbara F. (Sullivan) L. B.A., Vassar Coll., 1964. Sales analyst Polaroid Co., Cambridge, Mass., 1966-70; 1st v.p. White Weld, N.Y.C., 1970-78, Merrill Lynch, N.Y.C., 1978-80; prin. Morgan Stanley & Co., Inc., N.Y.C., 1980—. Contbr. articles to profl. jours.; various TV appearances. Mem. N.Y. Soc. Security Analysts, Women's Fin. Assn., Photo Mfrs. Assn., Vassar Club. Republican. Home: PO Box 10 Water Mill NY 11976-0010 Office: Morgan Stanley 1251 Ave Of The Americas New York NY 10020-1104*

LANDRY, DEBBY ANN, computer programmer; b. Tacoma, July 27, 1963; d. Israel Joseph and Joyce Ann (Franzella) L.; 1 child, Jessica Elizabeth. BS, S.E. La. U., 1987; postgrad., U. So. Miss., 1994. Computer programmer Lockheed Engring. and Scis., Bay St. Louis, Miss., 1988-92; programmer/analyst I Sverdrup Techs., Inc., 1992-94; computer assoc. sr. Lockheed Engring. & Scis., Stennis Space Center, Miss., 1994—. Democrat. Roman Catholic. Home: 213 Coronet Dr Slidell LA 70460-5105 Office: Lockheed Engring & Scis Co Bldg 2105 Stennis Sp Ct MS 39529

LANDRY, SARA GRIFFIN, social worker; b. Thomaston, Ga., Sept. 17, 1920; d. John Carl and Mary Thelma (Abercrombie) Griffin; m. Thomas Leonard Perkins, Dec. 22, 1939 (dec. Jan. 27, 1945); 1 child, Thomas Leonard Perkins Jr.; m. George Kimball Landry, Dec. 19, 1949 (dec. Aug. 30, 1971). AB in Social Work magna cum laude, Wesleyan Coll., 1980; MS in Family Counseling, Mercer U., 1981. Receptionist Social Security Adminstrn., Macon, Ga., 1945-50, clerical, 1960-65, svc. rep., 1965-78; dir., organizer Bibb County Foster Grandparent Program, Macon, Ga., 1981-84; coord. rsch. project Med. Ctr. of Cen. Ga., Macon, Ga., 1986-87; social worker, bd. dirs. Bibb County Sr. Citizens Inc., Macon, Ga., 1984—; sec. bd. dirs. Bibb County Sr. Citizens, Inc., Macon, Ga., 1989-90, pres. bd. dirs., 1990-91; bd. dirs. grant chmn. Family Counseling Ctr., Macon, 1986-92, 94—. Contbr. articles, poems and various short stories to profl. jours. Bd. dirs., v.p., com. chmn. Am. Cancer Soc., Macon, 1956—, hon. life mem., 1993—; sec., com. chmn. Dem. Women Bibb County, 1979—; mem., sec. Civic Woman's Club, Macon, 1955-61; mem. Coun. Cath. Women, St. Joseph's Parish, pres., 1956-58; mem., bd. dirs. Savannah Diocesan Coun. Cath. Women, 1957-59; bd. dirs. Macon Little Theatre, 1994—. Named Vol. of Yr., Bibb County Sr. Citizens, Inc., 1988, Am. Cancer Soc., 1987-88, Cherry Blossom Sr. Queen for Cmty. Svc., 1986, Fundraiser Honoree, Am. Cancer Soc., 1991; Sara Landry Day proclaimed in her honor Mayor of Macon, 1991. Mem. LWV, AAUW (pres. 1991-93), Wesleyan Coll. Alumnae Assn. (Sara Griffin Perkins Landry scholarship established for non-traditional age students 1994), Nat. Honor Soc., Macon Little Theatre. Democrat. Roman Catholic. Home: 3807 Drury Dr Macon GA 31204-1313

LANDRY, TANNIE HAMILTON, career officer; b. Hazleton, Pa., July 8, 1944; d. Elwood Hamilton and Helen Geraldine (Schwartz) Jones; m. Roland Albert Landry, Jan. 2, 1979; 1 child, Jessica Tomiko. BS, E. Stroudsburg Coll., 1966; MA, Cen. Mich. State U., 1974. Cert. acquisition/logistics profl. level III, aircraft maintenance officer/master level, personnel and adminstrv. officer. Commd. 2d lt. USAF, 1968, advanced through grades to col., 1990; various to aircraft maintenance officer McGuire AFB, Scott AFB, Clark AFB, N.J., Ill., Philippines, 1974-83; comdr. 314th Avionics Squadron Little Rock AFB, 1983-85; asst. dep. comdr. for maintenance prodn. Dover AFB, Del., 1985-88; chief Air Force Corrosion Office Air Force Logistics Command, Robins AFB, Ga., 1988-89; dep. base comdr. Robins AFB, Ga., 1989-90, dir. space and spl. systems, 1990-93; dir. logistics engring. and acquistion mgmt. Air Force Tech. Applications Ctr., Fla., 1993—. Sunday Sch. tchr. Trinity United Meth. Ch., Warner Robins, Ga., 1990-93, trustee adminstr., 1990-92, 92-93; Sunday Sch. tchr. Clark Air Base Chapel, Philippines, 1980-83; mem. Civilian/Mil. Affairs, Brevard County, Fla., 1993-94. Decorated Vietnam Svc. medal with 5 oak leaf clusters, Gallantry Cross, Rep. of Vietnam, Campaign medal, Rep. of Vietnam, others. Mem. The Retired Officers Assn., Christian Deaf Assn., NAFE, Nat. Geographic Soc., Nat. Arbor Soc. Home: 356 Country Walk St Melbourne FL 32940-1804 Office: Air Force Tech Appls Ctr PO Box 4711 Patrick AFB FL 32925-4711

LANDSMAN, SANDRA GILBERT, psychologist, transactional analyst, hypnotherapist; b. Detroit, Jan. 5, 1933; d. Arthur Bernard (dec.) and Ida Myra (Finkelstone) (dec.) G.; BS, Wayne State U., 1955, MA, 1970, PhD, 1984. Ordained to ministry, 1994; cert. hypnotherapist, spiritual healer. m.

Rodney Glenn Landsman, Apr. 3, 1955; children: Victoria Louise Landsman Peterson, Jonathan Gilbert, Faith Susan, Jill Barbara. Cons., counselor Continuum Center for Women, Oakland U., Rochester, Mich., 1970-77; pvt. practice Transactional Analysis, Farmington Hills, Mich., 1966-87; clin. cons., U.S., Can., Europe, South Am.; Transactional Analysis, clin. supr. North Metro & Dearborn Downriver Growth Centers, Rochester and Allen Park, Mich., 1975-78; mem. faculty Macomb County (Mich.) Community Coll., 1976-79; dir. clin. and edn. services Landsman/Foner & Assocs., West Bloomfield, Mich., 1977-82; disting. lectr. Sch. Social Work, Mich. State U., 1975-78; dir. Coastal Hypnosis Ctr.; cons. in field; mem. faculty dept. psychology Columbia Pacific U.; internat. lectr. on psychopathology and pre and peri-natal psychology and metaphysics, U.S., Can., Europe, S.Am., 1966—. Cert. social worker, Mich.; trustee Temple Beth Am; nat. women's com. Brandeis U. Mem. NOW, Am. Counseling Assn., Nat. Mus. Women in the Arts, Orgn. Rehab. and Tng., U.S. Power Squadrons, Universal Holistic Healers Assn., Assn. Pastlife Rsch. and Therapies Internat. Transactional Analysis Assn. (mem. editorial bd.), U.S. Transactional Analysis Assn. (clin. teaching mem.), Nat. Guild Hypnotists, Am. Coun. Hypnotist Examiners, Women's Am. Orgn. for Rehab. and Tng., Alternative Edn. Assn., European Transactional Analysis Assn., Pre & Peri-Natal Assn. N.Am., Nat. Assn. Social Workers, Am. Coll. Personnel Assn., Fla. Soc. Profl. Hypnotists, Assn. Specialists in Group Work, Mich. Assn. for Counseling and Devel., Mich. Coll. Personnel Assn., Mich. Assn. Specialist Group Work (past pres.), Mich. Assn. Women Deans, Adminstrs. and Counselors, New Directions in Edn. and Psychotherapy (charter, trustee), Pre and Perinatal Assn. of N.Am. Author: Affective Disorders: The Assessment, Development, and Treatment Strategies of Manic-Depressive Structure; I'm Special: An Experiential Workbook for the Child in Us All, Found: A Place for Me-the Development Diagnosis and Treatment of Manic-Depressive Structure, (with others) Secret Places; contbr. articles to profl. publs. Office: Ste 16 810 Saturn St Jupiter FL 33477-4398

LANE, ADELAIDE IRENE, computer systems specialist, researcher; b. Bronx, N.Y., Sept. 27, 1939; d. Anton John and Constance Mary (Fogle) Pospisil; m. Robert Walton Lane, Sept. 26, 1964; children: Frank Anton, Miriam Helen, Robin Ann. BS in Edn. cum laude, SUNY, Oneonta, 1961; MS in Edn., Hofstra U., 1963; MS in Computer Sci., Rensselaer Poly. Inst., 1983. Cert. tchr., N.Y., Vt. Tchr. Island Trees Jr. High Sch., Levittown, N.Y., 1961-64; copy editor, typesetter Pennysaver & Press, Bennington, Vt., 1976-77; tchr. Mt. Anthony Jr./Sr. High Sch., Bennington, 1977-80; computer operator Rensselaer Poly. Inst., Troy, N.Y., 1981-82, graphics application programmer, 1982-87, sr. graphics application programmer, 1987-92, mgr. instrnl. computing, 1992-94, mgr. instrn. multimedia, 1994—; tchr. computer sci. Russell Sage Coll., Troy, 1984-85; cons. Union Coll., Schenectady, 1990. Editor: The Rock Ribs of Bennington Town, 1977; contbr. articles to profl. jours. Asst. coach Bennington Swim Team, 1972-75; troop leader Girl Scouts U.S., Hoosick Falls, N.Y., 1973-79; tchr. Hoosick Falls Ice Skating Club, 1975-80. Interuniv. Consortium for Ednl. Computing fellow, 1984. Mem. IEEE (affiliate), Nat. Computer Graphics Assn., Ednl. Uses of Info. Tech./EDUCOM (mem. Joe Wyatt Challenge selection com. 1990-91). Republican. Roman Catholic. Office: Rensselaer Poly Inst ITS CII 3157 Troy NY 12180

LANE, ALETA CECILE, real estate agent; b. Boston, June 24, 1954; d. Walter John Jeffress and Dorothea Cecile (Dyett) Rowling; m. James Frederick Saunders, May 1979 (div. June 1984); 1 child, Amber Cecile; m. Oscar Lane Jr., Apr. 24, 1994. Student, Simmons Coll., 1972-75. Fin. mgr., leasing mgr. Robinson Cadillac, Morrow, Ga., 1983-86; pres. Leaseport, Inc., Atlanta, 1986-89; v.p., gen. mgr. Robinson Volkswagon, East Point, Ga., 1987-88; buyer's agt. Purchasers Rep., Alpharetta, Ga., 1988-90, Re/Max Imperial, Atlanta, 1990-91, Re/Max Execs., Atlanta, 1991—. Bd. dirs., sec. Last Days Revival Worship Ctr. Mem. Am. Bus. Women Assn., Altanta (Ga.)/Dekalb Bd. Realtors, Atlanta C. of C. Home: 4183 Windermere Dr Lithonia GA 30038 Office: Re/Max Execs Inc 2260 N Druid Hills Rd NE Atlanta GA 30329-3107

LANE, ANN JUDITH, history and women's studies educator; b. N.Y.C., July 27, 1931; d. Harry A. and Elizabeth (Brown) Lane; children: Leslie Patricia, Joni Alexandra. BA, Bklyn. Coll., 1952; MA, NYU, 1958; PhD, Columbia U., 1968. Mng. editor Challenge Mag., NYU, 1953-56; asst. prof. Douglass Coll., Rutgers U., New Brunswick, N.J., 1968-71; prof. John Jay Coll., SUNY, 1971-83; vis. prof. Wheaton Coll., Norton, Mass., 1981-82; prof. history, dir. women's studies Colgate U., Hamilton, N.Y., 1983-90, U. Va., Charlottesville, 1990—. Author: To Herland and Beyond, 1990, Mary Ritter Beard: A Sourcebook, 1977, 2d edit., 1988, The Brownsville Affair, 1971; editor: Charlotte Perkins Gilman Reader, 1980, Herland: A Lost Utopian Novel, 1979. Chair Com. on Status of Women in the Profession, Orgn. of Am. Historians, 1992-95; dir. History Tchr. Inst., N.Y. Coun. for Humanities, summer 1985; mem. historians adv. com. Nat. Women's Hall of Fame, 1986—; bd. dirs. Louis M. Rabinowitz Found., 1972-76. Fellow, Berkshire Conf. Women Historians, 1988, Ford Found., 1981-82, Nat. Endowment for Humanities, 1980-81, Lilly Endowment, Inc., 1977-79, AAUW, 1959-60. Mem. AAUP (mem. com. on women 1987—), Orgn. Am. Historians (mem. Frederick Jackson Turner prize com. 1979), Women in Hist. Profession (exec. bd., coordinating com. 1971-74). Home: 2603 Jefferson Park Cir Charlottesville VA 22903-4133

LANE, DOROTHY SPIEGEL, physician; b. Bklyn., Feb. 17, 1940; d. Milton Barton and Rosalie (Jacobson) Spiegel; m. Bernard Paul Lane, Aug. 5, 1962; children: Erika, Andrew, Matthew. BA, Vassar Coll., 1961; MD, Columbia U., 1965, MPH, 1968. Diplomate Am. Bd. Preventive Medicine, Am. Bd. Family Practice. Resident preventive medicine N.Y.C. Dept. Health Dist., 1966-68; project dir. children and youth project Title V, HHS N.Y.C. Dept. Health Dist., Rockaway, N.Y., 1968-69; med. cons. Maternal and Child Health Svc. HHS, Rockville, Md., 1970-71; asst. prof. preventive medicine Sch. Medicine SUNY, Stony Brook, 1971-76, assoc. prof., 1976-92; prof., 1992—; assoc. dean Sch. Medicine SUNY, Stony Brook, 1986—; chair dept. community medicine, dir. med. edn. Brookhaven Meml. Hosp. Med. Ctr., Patchogue, N.Y., 1972-86. Contbr. numerous articles to profl. jours. Mem. exec. com. Am. Cancer Soc., L.I. div., 1975—; corp. mem. Nassau Suffolk Health Systems Agy., L.I., 1977—; bd. dirs. Community Health Plan Suffolk, Hauppauge, 1986-91. Grantee HHS-USPHS, 1977-85, 83—, Nat. Cancer Inst., 1987—. Fellow APHA, Am. Coll. Preventive Medicine (regent 1988—), Am. Acad. Family Physicians, N.Y. Acad. Medicine, Am. Bd. Preventive Medicine (trustee). Office: SUNY Sch Medicine Health Scis Ctr L-4 Stony Brook NY 11794-8437

LANE, ELISABETH ANN, interior designer; b. Orange, N.J., Mar. 5, 1942; d. William Spurrier and Ruth (Hoehle) L.; B.F.A., Ohio Wesleyan U., 1963; grad. Brera Acad., Milan, Italy, 1964. Dir. interior design, buyer O'Neill & Bishop Inc., Haverford, Pa., 1969—; tchr. interior design schs., 1966—. Mem. Am. Soc. Interior Design (regional dir.), Nat. Home Fashions League, Kappa Kappa Gamma. Republican. Quaker. Home: 7 Hopeton Ln Villanova PA 19085-1113 Office: O'Neill & Bishop Inc 338 Lancaster Ave Haverford PA 19041-1309

LANE, GLORIA JULIAN, foundation administrator; b. Chgo., Oct. 6, 1932; d. Coy Berry and Katherine (McDowell) Julian; m. William Gordon Lane (div. Oct. 1958); 1 child, Julie Kay Rosewood. BS in Edn., Cen. Mo. State U., 1958; MA, Bowling Green State U., 1959; PhD, No. Ill. U., 1972. Cert. tchr. Assoc. prof. William Jewell Coll., Liberty, Mo., 1959-60; chair forensic div. Coral Gables (Fla.) High Sch., 1960-64; assoc. prof. No. Ill. U., DeKalb, 1964-70; prof. Elgin (Ill.) Community Coll., 1970-72; owner, pub. Lane and Assocs, Inc., San Diego, 1972-78; prof. Nat. U., San Diego, 1978-90; pres., chief exec. officer Women's Internat. Ctr., San Diego, 1982—; founder, dir. Living Legacy Awards, San Diego, 1984—. Author: Project Text for Effective Communications, 1972, Project Text for Executive Communication, 1980, Positive Concepts for Success, 1983; editor Who's Who Among San Diego Women, 1984, 85, 86, 90—, Systems and Structure, 1984. Named Woman of Accomplishment, Soroptimist Internat., 1985, Pres.'s Coun. San Diego, 1986, Center City Assn., 1986, Bus. and Profl. Women, San Diego, 1991, Woman of Yr., Girls' Clubs San Diego, 1986, Woman of Vision, Women's Internat. Ctr., 1990, Wonderwoman 2000 Women's Times Newspaper, 1991; recipient Independence award Ctr. for Disabled, 1986. Home and Office: 6202 Friars Rd Apt 311 San Diego CA 92108-1008

LANE, HANA UMLAUF, editor; b. Stockholm, Mar. 14, 1946; came to U.S., 1951, naturalized, 1957; d. Karel Hugo Antonin and Anatolia (Spitel) Umlauf; m. John Richard Lane, Feb. 16, 1980; 1 stepchild, Matthew John. A.B. magna cum laude, Vassar Coll., 1968; A.M. in Russian and East European Studies, Yale U., 1970. Asst. to exec. editor Newspaper Enterprise Assn., N.Y.C., 1970-72, sr. asst., asst. editor World Almanac div., 1972-75, assoc. editor World Almanac, 1975-80, spl. project editor, 1977-80; editor World Almanac and World Almanac Publs., N.Y.C., 1980-85; editor in chief Pharos Books, N.Y.C., 1984-91; editor Pharos Books, 1991-93; sr. editor John Wiley & Sons, 1993—. Editor: World Almanac Book of Who, 1980, World Almanac and Book of Facts, 1981-85; (with others) The Woman's Almanac, 1977. Democrat. Home: 140 Fairview Ave Stamford CT 06902-8040

LANE, JULIA A., nursing educator; b. Chgo., June 29, 1927; d. James and Julia (Ivins) L. BSN, DePaul U., 1956; MSN, Cath. U. Am., 1961; PhD, Loyola U., Chgo., 1974. Cert. nurse midwife. Staff nurse St. Joseph Hosp., 1954-55, Chgo. Bd. of Health, 1955-57; instr. South Chgo. Hosp. Sch. Nursing, 1957-58, dir. edn., 1960-63; prof. Loyola U. Sch. Nursing, 1963—, dean, 1974-91; prof., 1992-94, ret., 1994. Home: 300 N State St Apt 4532 Chicago IL 60610-4807 Office: Loyola U Marcella Neihoff Sch Nursing 6525 N Sheridan Rd Chicago IL 60626-5311

LANE, KATHLEEN MARGARET, optical company administrator; b. Mpls., Oct. 25, 1946; d. Bernard Melvin and Margaret (Beck) Aanerud; m. Kenneth LeRoy Lane, Sept. 1, 1979; 1 child, Dennis Leon. Cost acct. Honeywell, Mpls., 1964-66; bank bookkeeper Columbia Heights State Bank, Minn., 1968-71; inventory control mgr. Hodes Optical Inc., Torrance, Calif., 1972-75, office mgr., 1975-79; lens supr. Coburn Optical Industries, Inc., Carson, Calif., 1979-85, br. mgr., St. Paul, 1985-93; office mgr. J.M. Refrigeration, St. Croix Falls, Wis., 1993; customer rels. Opti Fair, Aneheim, Calif., 1978-83. Mem. Am. Inst. Banking, NAFE. Avocations: restoring old furniture, camping, knitting. Office: JM Refrigeration 132 Middle Sch Dr Saint Croix Falls WI 54024

LANE, MARCIA, marriage and family therapist, consultant; b. Chgo., July 6, 1931. M in Pub. Svc. Counseling, Western Ky. U., 1972; PhD in Marriage and Family Therapy, Columbia Pacific U., 1990; postgrad., U. Louisville, 1992-94. Cert. marriage and family therapist. Social worker Ky. Dept. Child Welfare, Owensboro, 1970-71, community resource developer, 1971-72, supr., 1972-74; dir. Day Treatment & Group Home Delinquent Youth, Hopkinsville, Ky., 1974-77; social svcs. supr. juvenile svcs., foster care, adoptions Jefferson County, Louisville, 1977-79; supt. Owensboro Treatment Ctr. Delinquent Youth, 1979-81; supr. Hopkins County Dept. Social Svcs., Madisonville, Ky., 1981-87; family treatment specialist Dept. Social Svcs., Hopkinsville, 1987—; clin. internship supr. Kent sch. social work U. Louisville, 1992-93, clin. supr. cerily therapy program of Louisville, sex offender counselor cert. program, 1992—; clin. internship supr. sch. social work U. Tenn., Nashville, 1992-93; gov. appointee and vice chair Ky. Bd. Cert. Marriage & Family Therapists, Frankfort, 1994—. Author, presenter (workshop) Empowering Survivors of Ritualistic Child Abuse, 1992; co-author, presenter (workshop) A Therapeutic Response to Cultural Diversity-Juvenile Sex Offenders, 1994. Chair-del. Regional Interagency Coun. Severely Emotionally Disturbed Children, Hopkinsville, 1992—, Pennyrile Family Preservation Dist. Com., Hopkinsville, 1994—; bd. dirs. Family Preservation Project, Princeton, Ky., 1990—. Named Disting. Citizen, Action Child Abuse, 1980, Ky. Col., Commonwealth of Ky., 1981. Mem. NAACP, NASW (chair Pennyrile chpt. 1981-83), Am. Assn. Marriage & Family Therapy (clin., approved supr.), Ortho Psychiat. Assn. (clin.). Office: Ky Dept Social Svcs 115 Hammond Plz Hopkinsville KY 42240

LANE, MARGARET ANNA SMITH, property manager developer; b. Aspinwall, Pa., Nov. 26, 1918; d. Max Charles and Mary Ann (Jones) Smith; m. Frank A. Lane Jr., Feb. 7, 1954; 1 child, Alan Michael. AB, UCLA, 1940; MS, U. So. Calif., 1949. Cert. secondary tchr., Calif. Demonstration and tng. tchr. UCLA and U. Calif., Northridge, 1948-74; pvt. practice Cottonwood, Ariz., 1975—; tchr. dept. chmn. L.A. City Schs., 1948-74; sec.-treas. Silver Hoof, Inc., Sedona, Stone Pine Gallery, Ltd., Sedona. Mem. Pi Gamma Mu. Home: PO Box I-I West Sedona AZ 86340

LANE, MARGARET BEYNON TAYLOR, librarian; b. St. Louis, Feb. 6, 1919; d. Archer and Alice (Jones) Taylor; B.A., La. State U., 1939, J.D., 1942; B.S. in Library Sci., Columbia U., 1941; m. Horace C. Lane, Jan. 6, 1945; children—Margaret Elizabeth, Thomas Archer. Reference and circulation asst. Columbia Law Library, N.Y.C., 1942-44; law librarian, asst. prof. U. Conn. Sch. Law, Hartford, 1944-46; law librarian La. State U. Law Sch., Baton Rouge, 1946-48; recorder documents La. Sec. of State's Office, Baton Rouge, 1949-75; law librarian Lane Fertitta, Lane Janney & Thomas, 1976—. Author: State Publications and Depository Libraries, 1981, Selecting And Organizing State Government Publications, 1987. Mem. depository library council to Pub. Printer, 1972-77; mem. plan devel. com. La. Fed. Depository Library, 1982-83. Treas. Delta Iota House Bd. of Kappa Kappa Gamma, 1965-68; mem. La. Adv. Coun. State Documents Depository Program, 1991—. Inducted into La. State U. Law Ctr. Hall of Fame, 1987. Mem. ALA (interdivisional com. public documents 1967-74, chmn. 1967-70; govt. documents round table, state and local documents task force 1972—, coordinator 1980-82; James Bennett Childs award 1981), La. Library Assn. (Essae M. Culver Disting. Service award 1976; chmn. documents com. 1982-83, Lucy B. Foote award subject specialist sect. 1986, Named in Her honor Margaret T. Lane Award 1994), La., Baton Rouge Bar Assns., Mortar Bd., Phi Delta Delta, Kappa Kappa Gamma. Club: Baton Rouge Library. Home: 7545 Richards Dr Baton Rouge LA 70809-1547 Office: PO Box 3335 Baton Rouge LA 70821-3335

LANE, PATRICIA PEYTON, nursing consultant; b. Danville, Ill., Oct. 5, 1929; d. Louis Weldon Sr. and Ruth Jeanette (Meyer) Peyton; m. H.J. Lane, Dec. 23, 1950 (div.); children: Jennifer Lane-Carr, Peter Lane, Amelia Ozog. Diploma, St. Elizabeth Hosp., 1950; BA in Psychology magna cum laude, Rosary Coll., 1974; postgrad., Lakeview Coll. of Nursing, Danville, Ill., 1987-88; student, Triton Jr. Coll., River Grove, Ill., 1969-72. Staff nurse St. Elizabeth Hosp., Danville, Ill., 1950; staff nurse nursery Ill. Rsch. and Ednl. Hosp., Chgo., 1951, charge nurse tumour clinic, 1951-54; res. sch. nurse elem. schs., Oak Park, Ill., 1969-78; sta. mgr. Oak Park-River Infant Welfare, Cicero, Ill., 1972-76; vision and hearing screener suburban elem. schs., Ill., 1980-82; sch. nurse West Subrban Assn. Spl. Edn., Cicero, 1978-80; caseworker, counselor Vermilion County Mental Health and Devel. Disabilities, Inc., Danville, 1983-86; case coord., nurse cons. Crosspoint Human Svcs., Danville, 1986-88; staff nurse psychiat. acute care unit Community Hosp. of Ottawa, Ill., 1988-89; dir. social svcs. Pleasant View Luther Home, Ottawa, 1989-93; clin. case coord. Access Svcs., Inc., Mendota, Ill., 1993—; cmty. ombudsman LaSalle County Alternatives for the Older Adult, Peru, Ill., 1993—; cons. in field. Mem. ANA, Ill. State Nurses Assn. (cert. psychiat./mental nurse). Office: Alternatives for the Older Adult 2000 Luther Dr Peru IL 61350

LANE, PATRICIA S., nursing home administrator, media specialist; b. Louisville, July 3, 1932; d. Ransom Grady and Jessie Marie (Lee) Snowden; m. Fred Arlo Lane, Jan. 30, 1953; children: Pat, Freda, Cameron. BA, Stetson U., 1953, MA, 1975. Tchr. City High Sch., Chattanooga, 1953; sec. to dean So. Bapt. Theol. Sem., Louisville, 1954; tchr. Waggener Jr. High Sch., Louisville, 1955-56; church sec. Arlington Bapt. Ch., Jacksonville, Fla., 1957; librarian Lumberton (N.C.) High Sch., 1965; media specialist Mainland Sr. High Sch., Daytona Beach, Fla., 1966-72, DeLand High Sch., 1973-81; adminstr. DeLand Convalescent Ctr., 1982-90, Fairview Manor Ltd., Daytona Beach, FL, 1990—; chmn. Missions Devel. Coun., 1991-92. Sunday sch. sec. 1st Bapt. Ch., DeLand, Fla., 1989-93, mem. pers. com., 1987-90. Mem. Fla. Health Care Adminstrs. Assn. (sec. local dist. 1986-87). Democrat. Baptist. Home: 231 W Minnesota Ave Deland FL 32720-3477 Office: Fairview Manor Ltd Wilder Blvd Daytona Beach FL 32114

LANE, ROBIN, lawyer; b. Kerrville, Tex., Nov. 28 1947; d. Rowland and Gloria (Benson) Richards; m. Stanley Lane, Aug. 22, 1971 (div. 1979); m. Anthony W. Cunningham, Nov. 22, 1980; children: Joshua Lane, Alexandra Cunningham. BA with honors in Econs., U. Fla., 1969; MA, George Washington U., 1971; JD, Stetson U. Coll. Law, 1978. Bar: Fla. 1979, U.S. Ct. Appeals (11th cir.) 1981, U.S. Supreme Ct. 1986, U.S. Ct. Appeals (D.C. cir.) 1992, U.S. Ct. Appeals (3rd cir.) N.Y. 1993. Mgmt. trainee internat. banking Gulf Western Industries, N.Y.C.; internat. rsch. specialist Ryder Systems, Inc., Miami, Fla., 1973, project mgr., 1974; assoc. Wagner, Cunningham, Vaughan & McLaughlin, Tampa, Fla., 1979-85; pvt. practice law, 1985—; guest lectr. med. jurisprudence Stetson U. Coll. Law, 1982-91, also mem. exec. coun. law alumni bd. Contbr. articles to various revs. Recipient Am. Jurisprudence award-torts Lawyers Co-op. Fla., 1979; Scottish Rite fellow, 1968-69. Mem. ABA, Acad. Fla. Trial Lawyers (mem. com. 1983-84), Assn. Trial Lawyers Am., Fla. Bar Assn., Fla. Women's Alliance, Omicron Delta Epsilon. Home: 914 S Golf View St Tampa FL 33629-5222 Office: PO Box 10155 Tampa FL 33679-0155

LANE, SARAH MARIE CLARK, elementary education educator; b. Conneaut, Ohio, July 27, 1946; d. Robert George and Julia Ellen (Sanford) Clark; m. Ralph Donaldson Lane, May 28, 1977; children: Richard, Laura. BS in Edn., Kent State U., 1977; MS in Edn., Coll. Mt. St. Joseph, 1988. Cert. tchr., Ohio. Coord. newspaper in edn. Tribune Chronicle, Warren, Ohio, 1986-89; tutor MacArthur Found. Project, Warren, Ohio, 1988-89; tchr. chpt. I Lakeview Local Schs., Cortland, Ohio, 1989—. Author: A Walk Through Historic Cortland, 1994; free-lance writer newspaper Conn. News Herald, 1963-64, Tribune Chronicle, 1980-89; contbr. articles to profl. jours. V.p. Bazetta Cortland Hist. Soc., 1983-85; chmn. com. local history project Lakeview Schs., Cortland, 1992—. George Record Found. scholar, 1964-66. Mem. Internat. Reading Assn. (Ohio coun.), Cortland Community Concert Band (pres. 1991-92),. Mem. Christian Ch. (Disciples of Christ). Home: 298 Corriedale Dr Cortland OH 44410-1622 Office: Cortland Elem Sch 264 Park Ave Cortland OH 44410-1047

LANE, SHARI, psychotherapist, consultant; b. Cleve., July 13, 1945; d. William A. and Vera Olga (Leibersberger) Piekney; 1 child, Tara Chandra Limpert. B.A., U. S.C., 1967; cert. secondary English, U. N.C., 1968; M.Ed., U. Houston, 1976. Cert. alcoholism and drug abuse counselor, Tex. Instr., co-developer, adult communications lab., instr. lit., composition Central Piedmont Community Coll., Charlotte, N.C., 1969-71; tchr. curriculum design Montrobac Montessori Sch., Stamford, Conn., 1974-75; trainer, counselor Victoria Women's Ctr., Tex., 1975-78; women's editor, broadcaster, pub. relations Sta. KNAL and KVIC, Victoria, 1975-78; instr. interdisciplinary and humanities dept. U. Houston-Victoria, 1975-78; dir. new options pilot program State of Tex., 1977-79; coordinator mgmt. and planning Austin Mental Health/Mental Retardation Ctr., Tex., 1979-81; dir. cons. services MOHR Devel., 1982; counselor, adminstrv. coordinator APLE Found., 1982-83; psychotherapist, cons. interpersonal conflict resolution for individuals and instns., specializing in substance abuse and co-dependency, Houston, 1983—; speaker Mental Health Assn., Houston, 1983—. Contbr. articles to profl. publs.; author: For Giving, 1983. Mem. LWV, NOW, Am. Assn. for Counseling and Devel.

LANE, TERESA POPE, accountant; b. Raleigh, N.C., July 17, 1966; d. Waeford Randel and Bonita Kay (Owen) Pope; m. Ralph Randolph Lane, Sept. 17, 1988; 1 child, Emily Ann. BS in Acctg., Meredith Coll., 1988. Cost acct. Miles Inc., Clayton, N.C., 1988-91, cost analyst, 1991-92, acctg. supr., 1992—. Mem. Inst. Mgmt. Accts., Smithfield Jr. Woman's Club. Methodist. Office: Miles Inc Hwy 70 E Clayton NC 27520

LANE, VIRGINIA YVONNE, family counselor, educator; b. Hereford, Tex., Mar. 29, 1930; d. Arthur Bryant Clark and Zeta Loraine (Clements) Carstens; m. Robert Eugene Epple, Oct. 25, 1947 (div. June 1968); children: Robert David, John Curtis, Elizabeth Ann, Debra Alison; m. Brad William Lane. AA with highest honors, Cerritos C.C., 1966; BA, Calif. State U., Fullerton, 1973, MS in Counseling, 1978. Lic. marriage, family and child counselor. Parenting educator aide Norwalk (Calif.)-La Mirada Unified Sch. Dist., 1960-63, parent educator, 1963-78; parenting instr., psychology instr. North Orange County C.C., Fullerton, 1964—; marriage, family and child counselor Norwalk, 1982-88. Vol. psychotherapist Olive Crest Group Homes, Orange County, 1979-80; mem. La Casa shelter, L.A. County, 1982—, ACLU, L.A., 1980-90. PTA scholar, 1970. Mem. Nat. Assn. Parent Educators, Assn. for Early Childhood Edn., Assn. for Humanistic Psychology, Calif. Assn. Marriage Family Counselors, Calif. Tchrs. Assn. Democrat. Unitarian Universalist. Office: Cypress Coll 9200 Valley View Cypress CA 90630

LANE, WENDY SUE, human resources professional, artist; b. St. Paul, Nov. 10, 1955; d. Wesley David and Margaret Ann (Mullaney) L. Student, Coll. Assoc. Arts, St. Paul, 1974-77; BA in Arts Adminstrn., Met. State U., St. Paul, 1988; postgrad., Mpls. Coll. Art and Design, 1993—. Office mgr. Mpls. YMCA Camp Warren, 1984-86; mgr. human resources, affirmative action officer Walker Art Ctr., Mpls., 1986-93, benefits and HRIS mgr., 1994—; tour guide Walker Art Ctr., 1982-83; instr. Contemporary Arts Seminar, 1992-95; artist-in-residence Yellowstone Nat. Park, 1993; spkr. in field. Exhibited in group shows including The Northwestern Gallery, 1994, Bloomington (Minn.) Art Ctr., 1989-92, Md. Pastel Soc., Bethesda, 1989, Mpls. Coll. Art and Design, 1989, Lowertown Lofts Artists Coop., St. Paul, 1989, 91, 93, WARM Gallery, Mpls., 1990, Wilensky Arts, Mpls., 1991, U. Minn. Paul W. Larson Gallery, St. Paul, 1993, North Hennepin C.C., Brooklyn Park Minn., 1993. Vol. mem. edn. subcom. ARTS over AIDS Task Force, 1988-93. Jerome Found. fellow Women's Art Registry Minn. Mentor/Protegee Program, Mpls., 1992; career opportunity grantee Minn. Arts Bd., 1993. Mem. ASTD, Women's Caucus for Art, Coll. Art Assn., Women's Art Registry Minn., St. Paul Art Collective, Lowertown Lofts Artists Coop., Bloomington Art Ctr., Mpls. Inst. Art. Office: Walker Art Ctr Vineland Pl Minneapolis MN 55403 Studio: 275 4th St E Ste 820 Saint Paul MN 55101-1628

LANE-MAHER, MAUREEN DOROTHEA, marketing educator, consultant; b. West Point, N.Y., June 26, 1943; d. John Joseph and Dorothea (Fennell) L. BA, St. Louis U., 1965; MEd, U. Va., 1972, EdD, 1977. High sch. history tchr. Va., Okinawa, Japan, 1965-69; published products coord. 3M Bus. Products Sales, Inc., Springfield, Va., 1969-71; program mgr. U. Va., Charlottesville, 1971-77, asst. prof., 1977-78; mktg. svcs. mgr. Westinghouse, Iowa City, 1978-83; mktg. mgr. Nat. Computer Systems, Washington, 1983-87; prof. Nat.-Louis U., McLean (Va.) Acad. Ctr., 1989—; gen. ptnr. The ML Group, Washington, 1987—; spl. asst. USIA, Washington, 1982-83. Contbg. editor, contbr. Ednl. IRM Quar., 1990-92. Exch. exec. class XIII Pres.'s Commn. on Exec. Exch., 1982. Mem. Global Bus. Assn., Am. Mktg. Assn., Mid-Atlantic Women Studies Assn. Roman Catholic. Office: Nat Louis U 8000 Westpark Dr Mc Lean VA 22102-3105

LANE-OREIRO, LAVERNE TERESA, former tribal official; b. Bellingham, Wash., Aug. 29, 1951; d. Vernon Adrian and Nancy Ann (Solomon) Lane; m. David William Cagey Oreiro, Oct. 27, 1979; children: Tyson Hawk, Cody Lane. Student, Grenoble, France, 1972-73; BA in Humanities, Seattle U., 1974. Asst. dir. social svcs. Lummi Indian Tribe, Bellingham, 1974-77, dir. fed. contracts, 1977-78, exec. dir., 1978-81; real estate agt. Ron Bennett & Assocs., Bellingham, 1982-86; Indian edn. coord. Ferndale (Wash.) Pub. Schs., 1984—; vice-chairperson Lummi Indian Nation, 1991-93; pub. spkr. and presenter for local confs., media press confs., talk shows and cmty. functions; bd. chmn. Lummi Tribal Enterprises, Bellingham, 1978-80; bd. dirs. minority sci. and engring. adv. bd. U. Wash., Seattle, 1987-91; mem. minority cmty. adv. bd. Western Wash. U., Bellingham, 1989-93; Wash. state del.-at-large White House Conf. on Indian Edn., Washington, 1992. Writer eulogies for variety of tribal mems. including tribal leaders, elders, etc. Co-chairperson Nat. Indian Women's Fast Pitch, Lummi Indian Reservation, 1978, co-MC Nat. Indian Edn. Opening Rec., Spokane, Wash., 1985; mem. cmty. adv. bd. U. Wash. Women's Ctr., 1995—. Recipient Cmty. Svc. Diversity award Western Wash. U., 1994. Mem. Wash. State Indian Edn. Assn. (bd. sec. 1985-86, 1st v.p. 1986-87), Western Wash. Native Am. Edn. Consortium (vice-chairperson 1985-86, chairperson 1986-87). Democrat. Roman Catholic. Home: 2210 Lummi View Dr Bellingham WA 98226-9208 Office: Ferndale Sch Dist # 502 PO Box 428 Ferndale WA 98248-0428

LANE STONE, NANCY ANN, hospice official, educator; b. Montague, Mass., Oct. 23, 1945; d. John Henry Adams and Helen Ann (Yez) Lane; m. Richard F. Koscinski, June 8, 1968 (dec. June 1980); children: Todd Lane Koscinski, Michael Lane Koscinski; m. David Lewis Stone, Feb. 26, 1984. BA, U. Mass., 1981; M. Human Svcs., Keene State Coll., 1990. Cert.

tchr., Mass.; cert. experienced educator, N.H. Substitute tchr. Montague Pub. Schs., 1981-84, Keene (N.H.) Pub. Schs., 1985-86; v.p. Beck Mfg., Keene, 1986—; dir. Good Mourning Children, Keene, 1988—; dir. children's svcs. Hospice of Monadnock Region, Keene, 1992—, vol., 1994—; cons. to staff adv. com. Franklin County Tech. Sch., Turners Falls, Mass., 1977-84; intern, vol. Hospice of Cheshire County, Keene, 1989-90; mem. adj. clin. faculty Antioch New Eng. Grad. Sch., 1993—; mem. adj. faculty Keene State Coll., 1990—. Dir. Big Bro./Big Sister Orgn. Recipient Sch. Vol. award Symonds Sch., Keene, 1984-85. Mem. AAUW, Assn. for Death Edn. and Counseling, Keene Woman's Club (v.p. 1986-88), Keene Bus. and Profl. Women's Club, N.H. Hospice Orgn., Children's Hospice Internat. Roman Catholic. Office: Good Mourning Children Program 54 Blackberry Ln Keene NH 03431-2120

LANEY, SANDRA EILEEN, chemical company executive; b. Cin., Sept. 17, 1943; d. Raymond Oliver and Henrietta Rose (Huber) H.; m. Dennis Michael Laney, Sept. 30, 1968; children: Geoffrey Michael, Melissa Ann. AS in Bus. Adminstrn., Thomas More Coll., 1988. Adminstrv. asst. to chief exec. officer Chemed Corp., Cin., 1982, asst. v.p., 1982-84, v.p., 1984-91, v.p., chief adminstrv. officer, 1991-93, sr. v.p., chief adminstrv. officer, 1993—, bd. dirs., 1986—; bd. dirs. Roto-Rooter, Cin., Nat. San. Supply Co., L.A., Omnicare, Inc., Cin., Chemed Corp., Cin. Bd. advisors Sch. Nursing and Health U. Cin., 1992. Mem. Cin. Club. Roman Catholic.

LANG, CATHERINE LOU, small business owner; b. Hugo, Okla., June 12, 1946; d. John Wilburn Sr. and Velma Lou (Evans) Freeman; m. Laurence Larry Lang, Nov. 20, 1974; children: Tana Louise, Henry Nathan, Gina Elise; 1 stepchild, Michael. BA in Sociology and Econs., Northeastern State U., 1970. Co-owner C&L Jewelry, Waterford, Mich., 1980—; landlord of rental home, Novi, Mich., 1977-93. Active Northwest Child Rescue Women Jr. League, 1975—, League of Women of Detroit; mem. PTA Mercy Sch. for Girls, Farmington, Mich., 1981—, Walled Lake Mich. Schs.; mem. Great Decisions, active in leadership, 1988; team parent Team Elan Skating Team, 1991-92; mem. Lakes Assn., Novi, 1992; mem. Covenant Bapt. Ch., 1977—, Am. Bapt. Women. Recipient (with son) Arrow of Light pin Cub Scouts. Mem. AAUW (charter Novi-Northville br.), Internat. Fedn. Univ. Women, Nat. Assn. Investors Corp., Detroit Skating Club, Top Stock Stock Club. Democrat. Home: 1369 E Lake Dr Novi MI 48377-1442 Office: C&L Jewelry 924 W Huron St Waterford MI 48328-3726

LANG, JEAN MCKINNEY, editor, educator; b. Cherokee, Iowa, Nov. 6, 1921; d. Roy Clarence and Verna Harvey (Smith) McKinney; BS, Iowa State U., 1945; MA, Ohio State U., 1969; postgrad. U. South Fla., 1972; m. Thomas E. Greef; 1 dau., Barbara Jean Wilcox; step-children: Mary McDonald, Daniel A. Greef. Merchandiser, jewelry buyer Rike-Kumler Co., Dayton, Ohio, 1952-59, Met. Co., Dayton, 1959-64; tchr. DeVilbiss High Sch., Toledo, 1966-67; chmn. dept. retailing Webber Coll., Babson Park, Fla., 1967-72; assoc. editor Wet Set Illustrated, 1972-75; sr. editor Pleasure Boating, Largo, Fla., 1975-84; tchr. bus. adminstrn. St. Petersburg (Fla.) Jr. Coll., 1974-88; adj. prof. bus. adminstrn., 1988—, securities arbitrator, 1992—; editor Suncoast Woman, 1986-88. Mem. U.S. Senatorial Bus. Adv. Bd.; mem. Nat. Boating Safety Adv. Council, 1979-81; Recipient recognition Nat. Retail Mchts. Assn., 1971, certs. of appreciation U.S. Power Squadron, 1976, Webber Coll., 1972. Mem. AAWU, Fla. Women's Alliance, Greater Tampa C. of C., Tampa Aux. Power Squadron, USCG Aux., Sales and Mktg. Execs. of Tampa (pres.'s award 1973), Fla. Freelance Writers Assn., Am. Mktg. Assn., Gulf Coast Symphony, Internat. Platform Assn., The Fashion Group, Fla. Coun. Yacht Clubs, Toledo Yacht Club (hon.), Tampa Yacht and Country Club, Chi Omega. Republican. Presbyterian. First woman to cruise solo from Fla. to Lake Erie in single-engine inboard, 1969, to be accepted into Fla. Council Yacht Clubs; yachting accomplishments published in The Ensign, Lakeland Boating, Yachting, Boote mags. Office: PO Box 402 Largo FL 34649-0402

LANG, K. D. (KATHERINE DAWN LANG), country music singer, composer; b. Consort, Alta., Can., 1961; d. Adam and Audrey L. Lang. Mem. Tex. swing fiddle band, 1982—; formed band The Reclines. Albums include A Truly Western Experience, 1984, Angel with a Lariat, 1986, Shadowland, 1988, Absolute Torch and Twang, 1990 (Can. Country Music Awards album of the yr.), Ingenue, 1992, Even Cowgirls Get the Blues (soundtrack), 1993; actress (film) Salmonberries, 1991. Recipient Can. Country Music awards, including Entertainer of Yr., 1989, Grammy award, 1990, 1993, Best Pop Female Vocal for Constant Craving, Grammy nomination Best Pop Female Vocal for Miss Chatelaine, 1994, William Harold Moon award Soc. of Composers, Authors and Music Publishers of Can., 1994. Office: Sire Records 75 Rockefeller Plz New York NY 10019-6989*

LANG, LILLIAN OWEN, accountant; b. Yorkville, Tenn., Oct. 8, 1915; d. Hugh Preston and Susan (Davis) Owen; 1 child, John Sanford Lang. Student U. Tenn. Extension, 1956-62, Memphis State U., 1963-64, Memphis Acad. Arts, 1965-66. CPA, Tenn. Shipping clk. Buckeye Cellulose Corp., 1943-46; x-ray technician Memphis and Shelby County Health Dept., 1948-56; acctg. clk. Purex Corp., 1957-59; bookkeeper Electrolock, Inc., 1959-62; sec.-treas. Allied Bruce Terminix Cos., Inc., Mobile, Ala., 1962-80, v.p., 1980-86, also dir.; pvt. practice acctg., Memphis, 1986—; former dir. dir. affiliated corps. Leasing of Mobile, Inc., Terminix Services of Tupelo (Miss.). Mem. DAR, Tenn. Soc. CPAs (Memphis chpt.), Am. Soc. Women Accts. (pres. Mobile chpt. 1977-78, dir. S.E. area 1979-81). Mem. Disciples of Christ. Home and Office: 1960 N Pkwy # 601 Memphis TN 38112

LANG, PEARL, dancer, choreographer; b. Chgo., May 1922; d. Jacob and Frieda (Feder) Lack; m. Joseph Wiseman, Nov. 22, 1963. Student, Wright Jr. Coll., U. Chgo. Formed own co., 1953; faculty Yale, 1954-68; tchr., lectr. Juilliard, 1953-69; tchr., lectr. Jacobs Pillow, Conn. Coll., Neighborhood Playhouse, 1963-68, Israel, Sweden, Netherlands. Soloist, Martha Graham Dance Co., 1944-54; featured roles on Broadway include Carousel, 1945-47, Finian's Rainbow, 1947-48, Danced Marth Graham's roles in Appalachian Spring, 1974-76, Primitive Mysteries, 1978-79, Diversion of Angels, 1948-70, Herodiade, 1977-79; role of Solvieg opposite John Garfield Broadway include, ANTA Peer Gynt; choreographer: TV shows CBC Folio; co-dir. T.S. Eliot's Murder in the Cathedral, Stratford, Conn., Direction, 1964-66, 67, Lamp Unto Your Feet, 158, Look Up and Live TV, 1957; co-dir., choreographer: full length prodn. Dybbuk for CBC; dir. numerous Israel Bond programs; assumed roles Emily Dickinson: Letter to the World, 1970; Clytemnestra, 1973; Jocasta in: Night Journey, 1974, for Martha Graham Dance Co.; choreographer: dance works Song of Deborah, 1952, Moonsung and Windsung, 1952, Legend, 1953, Rites, 1953, And Joy Is My Witness, 1954, Nightflight, 1954, Sky Chant, 1957, Persephone, 1958, Black Marigolds, 1959, Shirah, 1960, Apasionada, 1961, Broken Dialogues, 1962, Shore Bourne, 1964, Dismembered Fable, 1965, Pray for Dark Birds, 1966, Tongues of Fire, 1967, Piece for Brass, 1969, Moonways and Dark Tides, 1970, Sharjuhm, 1971, At That Point in Place and Time, 1973, The Possessed, 1974, Prairie Steps, 1975, Bach Rondelays, 1977, I Never Saw Another Butterfly, 1977, A Seder Night, 1977, Kaddish, 1977, Icarus, 1978, Cantigas Ladino, 1978, Notturno, 1980, Gypsy Ballad, 1981, Hanele The Orphan, 1981, The Tailor's Megilleh, 1981, Bridal Veil, 1982, Stravinsky's opera Oedipus Rex, 1982, Song of Songs, 1983, Shiru L'adonay, 1983, Tehillim, 1983, Sephardic Romance and Tfila, 1989, Koros, 1990, Eyn Keloheynu, 1991. Founder Pearl Lang Dance Found.; mem. Boston Symphony, Tanglewood Fest. Recipient 2 Guggenheim fellowships; recipient Goldfadden award Congress for Jewish Culture, Achievement award Artists and Writers for Peace in the Middle East, Cultural award Workmen's Circle, Queens Coll. award, 1991, Jewish Cultural achievement award Nat. Found. for Jewish Culture, 1992. Mem. Am. Guild Mus. Artists. Home: 382 Central Park W New York NY 10025-6054

LANGA, JANE ANNE, beverage company creative administrator; b. St. Louis, July 8, 1959; d. Robert Ray and Jesse Darlene (Hinchcliff) L. AFA, St. Louis C.C., 1979; BFA, U. Kans., 1981. Jr. designer Hellmuth, Obata & Kassabaum, St. Louis, 1981-82; designer KPLR-TV, St. Louis, 1982-84, Eastman Advt., St. Louis, 1984-86; art dir. Busch Creative Svcs., St. Louis, 1986-89; prodn. mgr. Louis London, St. Louis, 1989-91; sr. creative mgr. Anheuser Busch, Inc., St. Louis, 1991—. Vol. St. Louis Zoo, 1994, St. Louis Olympic Festival, 1994. Recipient cert. of excellence Print Magazine, 1988. Mem. Point of Purchase Advt. Inst. (judge 1991—, Gold award 1992, 93), Not Just An Art Dirs. Club (pres.). Home: 1520 High School Dr Brentwood MO 63144-1131 Office: Anheuser Busch Inc 1 Busch Pl Saint Louis MO 63118

LANGBORT, POLLY, retired advertising executive; b. N.Y.C.; d. Julius and Nettie (Berman) L. BA, Adelphi U. Sec. Young & Rubicam, Inc., N.Y.C., media buyer, media planner, 1960-65, planning supr., 1965-70, v.p. group supr., 1970-75, v.p. dir. planning devel., 1975-80, sr. v.p., dir. planning, 1980-85, sr. v.p. direct mktg. and media services Wunderman, Worldwide div., 1985-86, exec. v.p. dir. mktg. & media services Wunderman, Worldwide div., 1986-90; assoc. pub. Lear's Mag., N.Y.C., 1990-91; ret., 1991. Author: DMA Factbook, 1986; contbr. articles to profl. jours. Spl. gifts chairperson Am. Cancer Soc., N.Y.C., 1985-90. Jewish. Home: Peconic Hills Dr Southampton NY 11968

LANGDON, GLENDA JEAN, accountant; b. Alma, Mich., Oct. 20, 1950; d. Vivian E. and Helen Lois (Brown) Hall; m. Bruce Allen Langdon, Dec. 14, 1968; children: Allen, Troy, LeAnn. Diploma, Ithaca H.S., 1968; student, Baker Coll. Factory staff Toledo Communator, Owosso, Mich., 1977-83; tax preparer H & R Block, Durand, Mich., 1983-89; acctg. and tax staff Langdon's Tax Ctr., Owosso, Mich., 1989-94; payroll clk. Pines Country House, Owosso, 1994—. treas. St. John's United Ch. of Christ, 1988-93. Mem. Inst. Mgmt. Accts. Office: Langdon Tax Ctr 315 W Juddville Rd Owosso MI 48867

LANGDON, VICKI N., public information coordinator; b. Sherman, Tex., Apr. 22, 1960; d. Sue N. (Campbell) L. BS in Journalism with acad. distinction, East Tex. State U., 1982. Asst. news dir. Sta. KSEO/KLBC Radio, Durant, Okla., 1982-83, news dir., 1983; entertainment editor, staff writer The Denison (Tex.) Herald, 1983-93; coord. pub. info. Denison (Tex.) Ind. Sch. Dist., 1993—. Publicist (documentary) Mother Maybelle's Carter Scratch, 1989-90; photographer (cover videocassette tape) Johnny Cash Live in London, 1985, (souvenir concert program) Johnny Cash, 1985, (cookbook) Mother Maybelle's Cookbook, 1989, (feature story) Country Music People mag., 1991, (album cover) Helen Carter Clinch Mountain Memories, 1993, (album cover) Anita Carter Yesterday, 1995. Recipient award Tex. State Teachers Assn., Tex. Classroom Teachers Assn., Am. Cancer Soc. Tex. Div., Galveston County Press Club, Texoma Music Assn. Mem. Carter Family Fan Club (area rep.), John and June Cash Fan Club (Tex. co-rep.), Marty Stuart Fan Club, Alpha Chi. Office: Denison Ind Sch Dist 1201 S Rusk Ave Denison TX 75020

LANGE, BILLIE CAROLA, aquatic exercise video specialist; b. Cullman, Ala.; d. John George and Josephine (Richard) Luyben; m. Harry E. Lange (div.); children: JoAnne Lange Graham, Linda Jean Lange Reeve. Grad., Long Beach City (Calif.) Coll.; BMus, U. So. Calif. Chief piano accompanist Long Beach Civic Opera Assn.; tchr./creator aquatic exercise program U. Ala., Huntsville, 1984-87; advisor Aquatic Exercise Assn., Port Washington, Wis., 1988—; creator, prodr. aquatic video exercise tapes Billie C. Lange's Aquatics, Palm Beach, Fla., 1979—. Creator: (aquatic execise video tapes) Slim and Trim Yoga with Billie In and Out of Pool, 1979, Slim and Trim with Billie In Pool, 1994; pianist various audio tapes; instrumental, audio Tranquility, 1992. Mem. Nat. Acad. Recording Arts and Scis. Office: PO Box 822 Umatilla FL 32784-0822

LANGE, JEANNE MICHELLE, film producer; b. Summit, N.J., Aug. 29, 1948; d. Howard Francis and Doris Mae (Sandnes) L.; m. David M. Haskell, May 22, 1972 (div. Aug. 1990); 1 child, Alexandrea. Student, Am. Acad. Dramatic Arts, N.Y.C., 1950-52, Juilliard Sch. Music, 1950-54, Syracuse U., 1966-68, New Sch. for Social Rsch., 1966-68. Actress on Broadway, TV, films, 1965-82, various film prodn. positions,, 1983-85; prodr., ptnr. Journey Prodns., Burbank, Calif., 1985-91; CEO, StoneRoad Prodns., Inc., Studio City, Calif., 1991—; co-founder, mng. prodr. Advent Theatre, 1981-85. Prodr. film Wrestling with God, 1990, (Cine Golden Eagle award, awards Houston Film Festival, N.Y. Film Festival, Chgo. Film Festival). Bd. dirs. Studio City Residents Assn., 1986-90, Ecumedia, L.A., 1990-92; v.p. bd. dirs. Stone-Campbell Found., North Hollywood, Calif., 1986—; mem. adminstrv. com. of gen. bd. Christian Ch. Disciples of Christ, Indpls., 1989-91; mem. comm. task force World Coun. Chs., 1992—; chmn. adv. bd. 1st Christian Ch. North Hollywood, 1992—. Recipient Citizen's Contbn. award State of Calif., 1982, Cindy award Internat. Audio Visual Communicators, 1991, Angel award L.A. Internat. Film Com., 1991. Mem. Women in Film, Ind. Film Prodrs. Democrat. Office: StoneRoad Prodns Inc 11288 Ventura Blvd Ste 909 Studio City CA 91604-3135

LANGE, JESSICA, actress; b. Minn., Apr. 20, 1949; d. Al and Dorothy Lange; m. Paco Grande, 1970 (div. 1982); 1 child with Mikhail Baryshnikov, Alexandra; children with Sam Shepard: Hannah Jane, Samuel Walker. Student, U. Minn.; student mime, with Etienne DeCroux, Paris. Dancer Opera Comique, Paris; model Wilhelmina Agy., N.Y.C. Film appearances include King Kong, 1976, All That Jazz, 1979, How to Beat the High Cost of Living, 1980, The Postman Always Rings Twice, 1981, Frances, 1982 (Acad. award nominee 1982), Tootsie, 1982 (Acad. award 1983), Country, 1984, Sweet Dreams, 1985, Crimes of the Heart, 1986 (Acad. award nominee 1987), Everybody's All American, 1988, Far North, 1988, Men Don't Leave, 1988, Music Box, 1989 (Acad. award nominee 1990), Cape Fear, 1991, Night and the City, 1992, Blue Sky, 1994 (Golden Globe award Best Actress in a Drama 1995, Acad. award for Best Actress 1995), Losing Isaiah, 1995, Rob Roy, 1995; TV movies: Cat on a Hot Tin Roof, 1984, O' Pioneers!, 1992; in summer stock prodn. Angel on My Shoulder, N.C., 1980, Streetcar Named Desire, 1992. Office: Creative Artists Agy care Ron Meyer 9830 Wilshire Blvd Beverly Hills CA 90212*

LANGE, JOAN C., hypnotherapist; b. Chgo., Dec. 2, 1944; d. Leon Louis and Dorothy Mae (Morehead) Sadowski; m. William C. Lange, Aug. 4, 1986; 1 child, Erika Riewe. B. Coll. Ozarks, 1966; M of Hypnotherapy, Southwest Coll. Hypnotherapy, 1992. Cert. Am. Bd. Hypnotherapy, Nat. Bd. Hypnotherapy and Hypnotic Anaesthesiology. Bus. mgr. Otis Assocs., Northbrook, Ill., 1986-89; asst. to dir. Med. Ctr. Libr. U. N.Mex., Albuquerque, 1990-93; owner Bradley County Hypnotherapy Clinic, Cleveland, Tenn., 1993—. Mem. NAFE, Tenn. Assn. Clin. Hypnotherapists (sec.-treas. 1993—), Cleveland C. of C.

LANGE, KATHERINE JOANN, writer; b. Wyandotte, Mich., Feb. 8, 1957; d. James DiDi and Margaret Ann (Kirk) Putman. Student, Normandale Coll., 1980-82. V.p., artist mgr. The T.S.J. Prodns. Inc., Richfield, Minn., 1975—; mgr., agt. The T.S.J. Booking Agy., Richfield, 1980—; asst. editor, author Songwriter U.S.A. mag., Atlanta, 1986-87; staff writer Music Mgmt. and Internat. Promotion mag., Copenhagen, 1983—; pres. Katherine's Greetings, 1994—. Contbr. articles to Sun Newspapers, Songwriter Connection, Woman's Press. Mem. ASCAP, NAFE, Am. Fedn. Musicians. Democrat. Lutheran. Home and Office: The TSJ Prodns Inc 422 Pierce St NE Minneapolis MN 55413-2514

LANGE, LYNETTE PATRICIA, real estate agent, marketing professional; b. St. Cloud, Minn., Sept. 20, 1964; d. Daniel Herbert and Patricia Barbara (Berg) Schulist. Student, Bemidji State U., 1982, Anoka Ramsey Community Coll., 1982—; student in nursing, Anoka Ramsey Community Coll., 1993—. Contract security specialist Hannon Security Svcs., Golden Valley, Minn., 1988-91; real estate agt. Sundial Realty, Mpls., 1990—; prin. Lange Enterprises, Inc., Golden Valley, 1991—. Fundraiser, vol. Am. Heart Assn./Diabetes Found. Home: 13987 Silverod St NW Anoka MN 55304-3668

LANGE, MARILYN, social worker; b. Milw., Dec. 6, 1936; d. Edward F. and Erna E. (Karstaedt) L.; divorced; children: Lara McKelvie, Gregory Cash. B of Social Work, U. Wis., Milw., 1962, MSW, 1974. Cert. ind. clin. social worker. Recreation specialist Dept. Army, Europe, 1962-63; social worker Family Svc. Milw., 1967-75, dir. homecare divsn., 1975-85; nat. field rep. Alzheimers Assn., Chgo., 1986-90; exec. dir. Village Adult Day Ctr., Milw., 1991—. Mem. Nat. Coun. Aging, Wis. Adult Daycare Assn. (pres.-elect), Dementia Care Network, Older Adult Svc. Providers Consortium, West Allis Bus. & Profl. Women, U. Wis.-Milw. Alumni Assn. Home: 5727 W Fillmore Dr Milwaukee WI 53219 Office: Village Adult Day Ctr Inc 130 E Juneau Ave Milwaukee WI 53202

LANGE, SUSAN ALICE See **STOESSER, SUSAN ALICE**

LANGE, WENDY KAY, chemical engineer; b. Warren, Mich., Jan. 2, 1966; d. William Walter and Barbara Joyce (Ables) Kotelniski; m. Paul Michael Lange, June 15, 1991. BSChemE, Mich. Tech. U., 1988; MSChemE, U. Detroit, 1990. Coord. of materials testing Composites Dept. GM, Warren, Mich., 1988-92, recycling support to divsn., 1992-94, N.Am. ops. recycling person, 1994. Mem. Engring. Soc. Detroit, Soc. Automotive Engrs. Office: GM Engring Ctr N1-N57 30200 Mound Rd Warren MI 48090

LANGENHEIM, JEAN HARMON, biology educator; b. Homer, La., Sept. 5, 1925; d. Vergil Wilson and Jeanette (Smith) H.; m. Ralph Louis Langenheim, Dec. 1946 (div. Mar. 1961). BS, U. Tulsa, 1946; MS, U. Minn., 1949, PhD, 1953. Rsch. assoc. botany U. Calif., Berkeley, 1954-59, U. Ill., Urbana, 1959-61; rsch. fellow biology Harvard U., Cambridge, Mass., 1962-66; asst. prof. biology U. Calif., Santa Cruz, 1966-68, assoc. prof. biology, 1968-73, prof. biology, 1973—; academic v.p. Orgn. Tropical Studies, San Jose, Costa Rica, 1975-78; mem. sci.adv. bd. EPA, Washington, 1977-81; chmn. com. on humid tropics U.S. Nat. Acad. Nat. Research Council, 1975-77; mem. com. floral inventory Amazon NSF, Washington, 1975-87. Author: Botany-Plant Biology in Relation to Human Affairs.; Contbr. articles to profl. jours. Grantee NSF, 1966-88; recipient Disting. Alumni award U. Tulsa, 1979. Fellow AAAS, AAUW, Calif. Acad. Scis., Bunting Inst.; mem. Bot. Soc. Am., Ecol. Soc. Am. (pres. 1986-87), Internat. Soc. Chem. Ecology (pres. 1986-87), Assn. for Tropical Biology (pres. 1985-86), Soc. for Econ. Botany (pres. 1993-94). Home: 191 Palo Verde Ter Santa Cruz CA 95060-3214 Office: U Calif Dept Biology Sinsheimer Labs Santa Cruz CA 95064

LANGENKAMP, CHRISTINE YVONNE, human resources professional; b. Bedford, Ohio, Nov. 26, 1957; d. Jay Edward Berman and Elizabeth Marie (Cadek) Giambrone; m. Michael John Langenkamp, May 21, 1988; children: Cortney, Megan, Allison. BS, Miami U., Oxford, Ohio, 1979. Cert. sr. profl. in human resources. Mgr. human resources Federated Dept. Stores, Inc., Columbus, Ohio, 1983-85, Eddie Bauer Inc., Columbus, 1987-89; dir. human resources Childress Klein Properties, Charlotte, N.C., 1989-91; mgr. human resources Sharonview Fed. Credit Union, Charlotte, 1991—. Mem. Soc. for Human Resources Mgmt., Charlotte Area Pers. Assn. (bd. dirs.-at-large 1993-94, membership chair 1994, cert. chair 1995). Republican. Roman Catholic. Office: Sharonview Fed Credit Union 13504 South Point Blvd Charlotte NC 28273

LANGEN KAMP, SANDRA CARROLL, healthcare policy executive; b. St. Joseph, Mo., Feb. 10, 1939; d. William Harry Minger and Beverly (Carroll) Lee; m. R. Hayden Downie, June 1, 1963 (div. Feb. 1979); children: Whitney, Timothy, Allyson. BS, Tex. Women's U., 1960. Adjunctive therapist Menninger Meml. Hosp., Topeka, 1960-66; asst. adminstr. Hillcrest Med. Ctr., Tulsa, 1977-82; dir. Vol. Action Agy., Tulsa, 1982-83; exec. dir. Tulsa Bus. Health Group, 1983—; v.p. Met. Tulsa C. of C., 1985—; exec. dir. Tulsa Program for Affordable Health Care, 1986—; cons. mem. Okla. Employment Security Commn., Oklahoma City, 1988—; exec. dir. Tulsa Cmty. Found. for Indigent Health Care, 1986—; officer State of Okla. Basic Health Benefits Bd., 1985-90, chmn., 1992-93; exec. dir. Tulsa Program for Affordable Health Care, 1989—; mem. health benefit com. State of Okla. Ins. Commn., 1994—; Gov. Com. Health Care, 1993. Author: editorial column Point of View, 1985—, Tulsa mag., 1985—. Count commn. appointee Tulsa Met. Area Planning Commn., 1973-81; mayor's appointee Tulsa Housing Authority, 1985-88; pres. Tulsa Met. Ministry, 1980-83; bd. dirs. ARC, Tulsa, 1971-73, 84-85. Mem. Am. C. of C. (exec. dir. Okla. chpt.), Met. Tulsa C. of C. (v.p. 1983—), Tulsa Tennis Club. Democrat. Roman Catholic. Office: Met Tulsa C of C 616 S Boston Ave Tulsa OK 74119-1222

LANGER, ELAINE RUTH, computer programmer, consultant; b. N.Y.C.; d. Abraham and Goldie (Lusher) Goldsmith; m. Andre Langer; children: Karen G., Joseph. BA, NYU, 1948, postgrad., 1948-50. With systems svc. IBM Corp., N.Y.C., 1951-54; cons. N.Y.C., 1955-62; instr. computer programming Empire Tech. Sch., N.Y.C., 1968-81, Cope Vocat. Inst., N.Y.C., 1981-83; faculty dir. Internat. Computers and Comm. Sys., Inc., N.Y.C., 1984-87; sr. data processing cons. N.Y. Life Ins. Co., N.Y.C., 1987-88; mgr. computer programs divsn. continuing studies Baruch Coll., CUNY, N.Y.C., 1988—. Mem. ACM, Ams. for Israel and Torah Women (life). Office: Baruch Coll 17 Lexington Ave New York NY 10010

LANGER, ELLEN JANE, psychologist, educator, writer; b. N.Y.C., Mar. 25, 1947; d. Norman and Sylvia (Tobias) L. BA, NYU, 1970; PhD, Yale U., 1974. Cert. clin. psychologist. Asst. prof. psychology The Grad. Ctr. CUNY, 1974-77; assoc. prof. psychology Harvard U., Cambridge, Mass., 1977-81; prof. Harvard U., 1981—; cons. NAS, 1979-81, NASA; mem. div. on aging Harvard U. Med. Sch., 1979—, mem. psychiat. epidemiology steering com., 1982-90; chair social psychology program Harvard U., 1982—, chair Faculty Arts and Scis. Com. of Women, 1984-88. Author: Personal Politics, 1973, Psychology of Control, 1983, Mindfulness, 1989; editor: (with Charles Alexander) Higher Stages of Human Development, 1990; contbr. articles to profl. and scholarly jours. Guggenheim Fellow, grantee NIMH, NSF, Soc. for Psychol. Study of Social Issues, Milton Fund, Sloan Found., 1982. Fellow Computers and Soc. Inst., Am. Psychol. Assn. (Disting. Contributions to Psychology in the Public Interest award 1988); mem. Soc. Expl. Social Psychology, Phi Beta Kappa, Sigma Xi. Democrat. Jewish. Office: Harvard U Dept Psychology 33 Kirkland St Cambridge MA 02138-2044

LANGEREIS-BACA, MARIA, speech-language pathologist; b. Hoorn, Netherlands, Dec. 16, 1930; came to U.S., 1956; d. Jan and Ditje (Schollée) Langereis; m. Stanley H. Skigen (dec.); 1 child, Michelle Arlene; m. Wilhelm Voebel (div.); children: George L., Helene Patimah; m. Gregorio Baca. BS, N.Mex. State U., 1982, MS in Speech, MS in Ednl. Mgmt. Devel., 1985, EdD in Ednl. Mgmt. Devel., 1989. Cert. elem. tchr., ednl. adminstr., speech-lang. pathologist. Asst. personnel mgr. D.M. Read Inc., Bridgeport, Conn., 1960-62; order librarian U. Bridgeport (Conn.), 1962-65; dir. community house Nichols Improvement Assn., Trumbull, Conn., 1960-65; speech-lang. pathologist Las Cruces (N.Mex.) Pub. Schs., 1984-88, Hatch (N.Mex.) Pub. Schs., 1985-89, Albuquerque Pub. Schs., 1989—; cons. Hospice Inc., Las Cruces, 1985-89, Associated Health Service, Las Cruces, 1986-89; ednl. cons., 1988—. Leader Girl Scouts Am., Las Cruces, 1976-77; leader 4H Club, Las Cruces, 1978-80; vol. Las Cruces Pub. Schs., 1978-79. Mem. Am. Speech Hearing and Lang. Assn., N.Mex. Speech Hearing and Lang. Assn., Assn. Supervision and Curriculum Devel., Phi Kappa Phi, Phi Delta Kappa. Republican. Roman Catholic. Club: Singles Scene (bd. dirs. 1985—). Home: 6309 Loftus Ave NE Albuquerque NM 87109-2717

LANGFIELD, HELEN ELION, artist, radio commentator; b. New London, Conn., July 6, 1924; d. Harry Robert and Ida Fannie Elion; m. Raymond Lee Langfield, Oct. 6, 1952; 1 child, Joanna Langfield Rose. BA in English, Ohio State U., 1946; MA in Studio Art, Conn. Coll., 1972. Interviewer, commentator Sta. WNLC/WTYD, Waterford, Conn., 1971-88; instr. Lyman Allyn Mus., New London, Conn., 1984-86; chmn., art instr. Conn. Coll. Summer Program in Humanities, New London, 1968-72; TV interviewer, New London, 1970. Columnist New London Day, 1972; exhibited in one-woman and group shows at Wadsworth Atheneum, Hartford, 1974, Aldrich Mus. of Art, Ridgefield, Conn., 1976, 55 Mercer, N.Y.C., 1977, Whitney Counterweight, N.Y.C., 1981, Pastel Soc. Am., N.Y.C., 1982, Adam Gimbel Gallery, N.Y.C., 1982, 83, Cummings Art Ctr., New London, 1979, 83, 85, Brouhaha Gallery, Providence, 1986, Vangarde Gallery, New London, 1986, 87, 88, NOHO Gallery, N.Y.C., 1981, 85, 88, Conn. Commn. on Arts Showplace, Hartford, 1987, Lyman Allyn Mus., New London, Conn., 1988, 92, Conn. Coll., New London, 1988, MS Gallery, Hartford, 1988, Mark Humphrey Gallery, Southhampton, N.Y., 1991, Boca Raton (Fla.) Mus. Art, 1992; represented in permanent collections Michael DeSantis, Inc., N.Y.C., Radisson Hotel, New London, 1st Nat. Bank Danbury, Conn., Conn. Savings Bank, New Haven, Suisman, Shapiro, Wool, Brennan, Gray and Faulkner, P.C., New London, Citicorp, Boston, Otis Elevator, Hartford, State Ct. House, New London, pvt. collections. Commr. Conn. Commn. on the Arts, Hartford, 1983-85. Jewish. Home: 23362 Torre Cir Boca Raton FL 33433

LANGHAM, NORMA, playwright, educator, poet, composer, inventor; b. California, Pa.; d. Alfred Scrivener and Mary Edith (Carter) L. BS, Ohio State U., 1942; B in Theatre Arts, Pasadena Playhouse Coll. Theatre Arts, 1944; MA, Stanford U., 1956; postgrad., Summer Radio-TV Inst., 1960,

Pasadena Inst. Radio, 1944-45. Tchr. sci. California High Sch., 1942-43; asst. office pub. info. Denison U., Granville, Ohio, 1955; instr. speech dept. Westminster Coll., New Wilmington, Pa., 1957-58; instr. theatre. California U., Pa., 1959, asst. prof., 1960-62, assoc. prof., 1962-79, prof. emeritus, 1979—, co-founder, sponsor, dir. Children's Theatre, 1962-79; founder, producer, dir. Food Bank Players, 1985, Patriot Players, 1986, Noel Prodns., 1993. Writer: (plays) Magic in the Sky, 1963, Founding Daughters (Pa., Nat. DAR awards 1991), Women Whisky Rebels (Pa., Nat. DAR awards 1992), John Dough (Freedomes Found. award 1968), Who Am I?, Hippocrates Oath, Gandhi, Clementine of '49, Soul Force, Dutch Painting, Purim, Music in Freedom, The Day the Moon Fell; composer, lyricist (plays) Why Me, Lord?, (text) Public Speaking; co-inventor computer driving game. Mem. Calif. Ctr. in the Woods, Calif. Cmty. Choir, Whisky Rebellion Task Force. Recipient Exceptional Acad. Svc. award Pa. Dept. Edn., 1975, Appreciation award Bicentennial Commn. Pa., 1976, Gregg award Calif. U. of Pa. Alumni Assn., 1992; Henry C. Frick Ednl. Commn. grantee. Mem. AAUW (co-founder Calif. br., 1st v.p. 1971-72, pres. 1972-73, Outstanding Woman of Yr. 1986), DAR, Theatre Assn. Pa., Internat. Platform Assn. (poetry awards 1993, 94), Calif. U. of Pa. Assn. Women Faculty (founder, pres. 1972-73), Calif. Cmty. Choir, Calif. Ctr. in the Woods, Dramatists Guild, Whisky Rebellion Task Force, Mensa, Alpha Psi Omega, Omicron Nu. Presbyterian (elder). Home: PO Box 459 California PA 15419-0459

LANGHOUT-NIX, NELLEKE, artist; b. Utrecht, The Netherlands, Mar. 27, 1939; came to U.S., 1968, naturalized, 1978; d. Louis Wilhelm Frederick and Geertruida Nix; m. Ernst Langhout, July 26, 1958; 1 child, Klaas-Jan Marnix. MFA, The Hague, 1958. Head art dept. Bush Sch., Seattle, 1969-71; dir. creative projects Project Reach, Seattle, 1971-72; artist-in-residence Fairhaven Coll., Bellingham, Wash., 1974, Jefferson Community Center, Seattle, 1978-82, Lennox Sch., N.Y.C., 1982; dir. NN Gallery, Seattle, 1970—; guest curator Holland-U.S.A. Bicentennial show U. Wash., 1982; project dir. Women in Art Today, Wash., 1989, Wash. State Centennial Celebration; Washington to Washington traveling exhibition, 1989; mem. nat. adv. bd. Nat. Mus. Women in Arts. Executed wall hanging for King County Courthouse, Seattle, 1974; one-woman shows include: Nat. Art Center, N.Y.C., 1980, Gail Chase Gallery, Bellevue, Wash., 1979, 80, 83, 84, Original Graphics Gallery, Seattle, 1981, Bon Nat. Gallery, Seattle, 1981, Kathleen Ewing Gallery, Washington, 1986, Ina Broerse Laren, Holland, 1992, Charlotte Daneel Gallery, Holland, 1992, Christopher Gallery, Tucson, 1992, Mercer Island Community Arts Ctr., 1992, Lisa Harris Gallery, Seattle, 1994; group shows include: Cheney Cowles Mus., Spokane, 1977, Bellevue Art Mus., 1978, 86, Renwick Gallery, Washington, 1978, Kleinert Gallery, Woodstock, N.Y., 1979, Artcore Meltdown, Sydney, Australia, 1979, Tacoma Art Mus., 1979, 83, 86, 87, Ill. State Mus., Springfield, 1979, Plener Sandomierz, Poland, 1980, Plener Kielce, Poland, 1980, Western Assn. Art Museums traveling show, 1979-80, Madison Square Garden, N.Y.C., 1981, Exhbn. Space, N.Y.C., 1982, Lisa Harris Gallery, 1985, 87, 88, Wash. State Centennial, Tacoma, 1989, Nordic Heritage Mus., Seattle, 1994; represented in permanent collections Plener Collection, Sandomierz, Poland, Bell Telephone Co. Collection, Seattle, Wash. U., Seattle, Children's Orthopedic Hosp., Seattle, Nat. Mus. Women in Arts, Washington; installations Tacoma Art Mus. Bd. dirs. Wing Luke Mus., Seattle, 1978-81, Wash. State Trust Hist. Preservation, 1990-93; v.p. Denny Regrade Community Council, 1978-79; mem. Seattle Planning Commn., 1978-84. Author (with others) Step Inside th Sacred Circle, 1989, an Artist's Book 1940-45 Remembered, 1991. Recipient Wallhanging award City of Edmonds (Wash.), 1974; Renton 83 merit award, 1984; Merit award Internat. Platform Assn. Art Exhibit, 1984, Silver medal 1st place, 1985, 87, Gold medal, Internat. Platform Assn., 1989. Mem. Denny Regrade Arts Council (co-founder), Internat. Platform Assn., Women in Arts N.Y.C., Nat. Mus. Women in Arts (founding mem., Libr. fellow, chairperson Wash. State com. 1988-89, mem. nat. adv. com. 1993—), Internat. Platform Assn., Seattle-King County Community Arts Network (bd. dirs. 1983-85, chmn. 1984-85), Nat. Artist Equity Assn. Address: PO Box 375 Mercer Island WA 98040

LANGLEY, CHERYL STRANGE, non-profit administrator; b. Washington, Jan. 4, 1946; d. Claude Burbon and Shirley Lorraine (Comstrock) Strange; m. Joseph Richard Langley, July 30, 1966 (div. July 1985); 1 child, Andrea Lauren. BA in Mgmt., U. Md., 1989. Legis. aide Hon. M.L. Sprague, Annapolis, 1974-79; personal aide Hon. Claude Pepper, Washington, 1979-83, legis. aide, 1983-87; program coord. Teamster Retiree Housing Corp. and subsidiary, Washington, 1990-92, asst. dir., 1992—; dir., trustee Teamster Retiree Housing of Worcester, Inc., Washington, 1991—. Recipient Presdl. scholarship U. Md., 1989. Mem. AAUW, Nat. Ctr. for Housing Mgmt., U. Md. Alumni Assn., Alpha Sigma Lambda. Republican. Home: 556 Quince Ct La Plata MD 20646

LANGLEY, PATRICIA ANN, lobbyist; b. Butler, Pa., Feb. 13, 1938; d. F.J. and Ella (Serafine) Piccola; m. Harold D. Langley, June 12, 1965; children: Erika, David. BA, U. Pitts., 1961; postgrad., Georgetown U., 1967, Cath. U. Am., 1985, George Mason U., 1990—. Legis. staff U.S. Congress, Washington, 1961-63; dir. social studies Am. Polit. Sci. Assn., Washington, 1963-65; legis. specialist U.S. Congress, Washington, 1965-67, caseworker, 1967-68; polit. staff Dem. Study Group U.S. Congress, Washington, 1969; Washington rep. Family Services Am., 1975-82, dir. Washington hdqrs., 1989-92, v.p. for govt. rels., 1992; pres. Policy Directions, Arlington, Va., 1992—; instr. George Mason U., 1994—; bd. dirs. Coalition for Children and Youth, Washington, 1977-78; chmn. steering com. for the Coalition on White House Conf. on Families, 1979-80, Ad Hoc Coalition on A.F.D.C., 1981-82. Mem. Donaldson Run Civic Assn., Arlington, Va., 1980—. Recipient Service Recognition U.S. Dept. Health and Human Services, 1980. Mem. Am. Soc. Assn. Execs., Women in Govt. Rels., Nat. Coun. Family Rels., North Va. Assn. Female Execs., Arnova, Groves Conf. Roman Catholic. Home and Office: 2515 N Utah St Arlington VA 22207-4031

LANGSAM, IDA S., press agent, consultant; b. N.Y.C., Apr. 5, 1951; d. Sydney and Mary (Goldberg) L. AAS in Photography, Fashion Inst. Tech., 1971; BA in Mass Communications, Queens Coll., 1973. Publicity dir. Mike's Artist Mgmt., N.Y.C., 1978-79; sr. account exec. Howard Bloom Orgn., N.Y.C., 1979-81; publicity dir. Aucoin Mgmt., N.Y.C., 1981-82; pres. Pub. I Publicity Svcs., N.Y.C., 1982-91; exec. v.p. music divsn. Middleberg & Assocs., N.Y.C., 1991—; guest panelist New Music Seminar, N.Y.C., 1985-88, CMJ/MM Seminar, N.Y.C., 1987-88, Founds. Forum, L.A., 1989, Platinum Seminar, Hoboken, N.J., 1990; instr. Discovery Ctr., N.Y.C., 1988-90; adj. profl mus. bus. profls. program grad. level NYU, 1995. Office: Middleberg & Assocs 130 E 59th St 12th Fl New York NY 10022

LANGSLEY, PAULINE ROYAL, psychiatrist; b. Lincoln, Nebr., July 2, 1927; d. Paul Ambrose and Dorothy (Sibley) Royal; m. Donald G. Langsley, Sept. 9, 1955; children: Karen Jean, Dorothy Ruth Langsley Runman, Susan Louise. BA, Mills Coll., 1949; MD, U. Nebr., 1953. Cert. psychiatrist, Am. Bd. Psychiatry and Neurology. Intern Mt. Zion Hosp., San Francisco, 1954; resident U. Calif., San Francisco, 1954-57; student health psychiatrist U. Calif., Berkeley, 1957-61, U. Colo., Boulder, 1961-68; assoc. clin. prof. psychiatry U. Calif. Med. Sch., Davis, 1968-76; student health psychiatrist U. Calif., Davis, 1968-76; assoc. clin. prof. psychiatry U. Cin., 1976-82; pvt. practice psychiatry Cin., 1976-82; cons. psychiatrist Federated States of Micronesia, Pohnpei, 1984-87; resident in geriatric psychiatry Rush-Presbyn./St. Luke Hosp., Chgo., 1989-91. Trustee Mills Coll., Oakland, 1974-78; bd. dirs. Evanston Women's Club. Fellow Am. Psychiat. Assn. (chair continuing med. edn. 1990—); mem. AMA, Am. Med. Womens Assn., Acad. Medicine Cin., Ohio State Med. Assn., Ill. Pediat. Assn. (sec. 1993-95). Home: 9445 Monticello Ave Evanston IL 60203-1117

LANGSTON, CYNTHIA MAE, environmental engineer, consultant; b. Casper, Wyo., Nov. 5, 1962; d. Jesse Conrad and Judie Mae (Hinton) L. AS in Gen. Engring., Casper Coll., 1983; BSChemE, U. Wyo., 1985; MS in Ecol. Engring., Colo. Sch. Mines, 1993. Environ. engr., staff cons. TechLaw, Inc., Denver, 1987-94; health and safety mgr. Ageiss Environ., Inc., Denver, 1995—. Mem. Am. Soc. Safety Engrs., Nat. Environ. Health Assn. Office: Ageiss Environ Inc 1900 Grant St Ste 1130 Denver CO 80203

LANGSTON, JOANN, advocate general; b. Staten Island, N.Y.; d. William J. and Lillian J. (Evans) Hawkes; m. William Greenwood Langston (dec.); children: Lee Langston Harrison, Susan Langston Ames, William G. Jr., Nancy E., Joy K. BA in Math., Coll. New Rochelle; JD, U. Md., PhD in Econs. Industry v.p., program mgr. GEOMET, Inc.; dep. dir. office of budgeting, program planning and evaluation, assoc. exec. dir. hazard identification and econ. analysis Consumer Product Safety Commn.; army dir. contract adv. and assistance svcs., mgmt. agy. dir. army study program, dir., army chair Def. Systems Mgmt. Coll., Ft. Belvoir, Va.; competition adv. gen. Office of Asst. Sec. of Army, Falls Church, Va. Fellow Washington Acad. Sci.; mem. ABA, Md. Bar Assn., Ops. Rsch. Soc. Am., Mil. Ops. Rsch. Soc. Office: 5109 Leesburg Pike Sky 6 Ste 302 Falls Church VA 22041-3201*

LANGUM, W. SUE, civic worker; b. Kennett, Mo., Jan. 10, 1934; d. Howard S. and Lucille (Hubble) Walker; m. Norman H. Nelson, June 22, 1957 (dec. Sept. 1969); 1 child, Kirby Walker Nelson; m. John K. Langum, Dec. 28, 1972. Student, Northwestern U., 1952-53, Crane Jr. Coll., 1953-54. Svc. rep. Ill. Bell Tel. Co., Chgo., 1956-57; receptionist Tri-City Animal Hosp., Elgin, Ill., 1967-69; rsch. asst. Bus. Econs. Inc., Chgo., 1969-73, dir., 1973—. V.p. Elgin Coun. PTA, 1969-73; bd. dirs. OEO, 1972-73, Meals on Wheels, Elgin, 1972-93, Coloquy Coffee House, 1968-70, Judson Coll. Friends, 1976-87, Elgin Area Hist. Soc., 1982—, Elgin Symphony Orch. Assn., 1984-93, Elgin Symphony League, 1982-93, pres. 1984-86; bd. dirs. United Meth. Women, 1978-93, pres., 1980-84; vol. Fish, 1974-76; bd. dirs., treas. Easter Seal Assn. for Crippled Children, 1977-90; mem. Elgin Beautification Commn., 1986-88, Tuesday Morning Bible Study Club. Mem. Sister Cities Assn. Elgin (bd. dirs. 1990), LWV (v.p. Elgin Club 1965), Tucson Women's Club, Current History Forum Club. Republican. Home: Diamond T Ranch 9820 E Old Spanish Trl Tucson AZ 85748-7547 also: Balsam Bay Is Manitowish Waters WI 54545

LANGWORTHY, AUDREY HANSEN, state legislator; b. Grand Forks, N.D., Apr. 1, 1938; d. Edward H. and Arla (Kuhlman) Hansen; m. Asher C. Langworthy Jr., Sept. 8, 1962; children: Kristin H., Julia H. BS, U. Kans., 1960, MS, 1962; postgrad., Harvard U., 1989. Tchr. jr. high sch. Shawnee Mission Sch. Dist., Johnson County, Kans., 1963-65; councilperson City of Prairie Village, Kans., 1981-85; mem. Kans. State Senate, 1985—; del. Midwestern Conf. State Legislatures, 1989; alt. del. Nat. Conf. State Legislatures, 1985-87, del., 1987—, nominating com., 1990-92. City co-chmn. Kassebaum for U.S. Senate, Prairie Village, 1978; pres. Jr. League Kansas City, Mo., 1977, Kansas City Eye Bank, 1982-85; mem. bd. Greater Kansas City ARC, 1975—, pres., 1984, chmn. midwestern adv. coun., 1985-86, nat. bd. govs., 1987-93; mem. Johnson County Community Coll. Found., 1989—; mem. Leadership Kans., Germany Today Program, 1991; bd. dirs. Kans. Wildlife & Parks Fund; trustee Found. on Aging, 1992—; mem. nat. adv. panel Child Care Action Campaign, 1988—. Recipient Outstanding Vol. award Cmty. Svcs. Award Found., 1983, Confidence in Edn. award Friends of Edn., 1984, Pub. Svc. award as Kans. Legislator of Yr., Hallmark Polit. Action Com., 1991, Clara Barton honor award Greater Kansas City ARC, Intergovtl. Leadership award League Kans. Municipalities, 1994. Mem. LWV, Women's Pub. Svc. Network, U. Kans. Alumni Assn. Episcopalian. Home: 6324 Ash St Shawnee Mission KS 66208-1369

LANIER, ANITA SUZANNE, musician, piano educator; b. Talladega, Ala., May 21, 1946; d. Luther Dwight and Elva (Hornsby) L. BS in Music Edn., Jacksonville (Ala.) State U., 1969. Elem. music tchr. Talladega City Schs., 1969-81; librarian, elem. music tchr. Talladega Acad., 1981-84; tchr. piano and organ Talladega, 1981—. Organist Trinity United Meth. Ch., Talladega, 1981—. Recipient Commemorative Honor medallion, 1990, World Decoration of Excellence medallion, 1990; named Woman of the Yr., 1990, Rsch. Adv. of Yr., 1990, ABI, 1990. Mem. NAFE, AAUW, Am. Pianists Assn., Pilot Club (sec. 1977-78), World Inst. Achievement, Women's Inner Circle Achievement, Internat. Platform Assn., Delta Omicron. Home: 601 North St E Talladega AL 35160-2525

LANIS, VIOLET ANN, business educator; b. Gary, Ind., Sept. 10, 1948; d. Steve and Danica (Arbutina) Bayus; m. Barry S. Lanis, Dec. 1, 1973. BS, Ball State U., 1970, MEd, 1972. Tchr. Thornton Twp High Schs., Harvey, Ill., 1970-73; lectr. Katharine Gibbs Secretarial Sch., Norwalk, Conn., 1974-78; adj. lectr. Sacred Heart U., Bridgeport, Conn., 1974-79; adj. asst. prof. U. Bridgeport, 1974-81; tchr. Darien (Conn.) Pub. Schs., 1981-83; instr. Norwalk Community Coll., 1983-87; adj. lectr. Dekalb Coll., Dunwoody, Ga., 1988; lectr., asst. to dir. student teaching supervision and field experience Ind. U. N.W., Gary, 1989—. Author secretarial procedures manual, 1979. Mem. NEA, Norwalk Jr. Woman's Club (v.p. 1980-81), Delta Pi Epsilon, Kappa Delta Pi (pres. 1993—). Roman Catholic. Office: Ind U NW Divsn Edn 3400 Broadway Gary IN 46408-1197

LANK, ANNA BESS, actress; b. Rochester, N.Y., Nov. 22, 1954; d. Norman Emanuel and Edith Stella (Handleman) Lank; m. Michael David Mortenson, Sept. 6, 1992. BA in Theatre Arts, UCLA, 1976. Performed in off-Broadway and regional shows, films, TV series, and stock and dinner theatre, including Shmulnik's Waltz, The Witch, A Country Doctor, Candide, The Heidi Chronicles, A Christmas Carol, Cop Gives Waitress $2 Million, The Secretary, The Babysitter's Club, Guiding Light, Music Man, Kismet, Three Penny Opera, Annie, Man of La Mancha, many others. V.p. Opera Bd. Dirs., N.Y.C., 1991—. Mem. Actors Equity Assn. SAG, NATAS. Jewish.

LANK, EDITH HANDLEMAN, columnist, educator; b. Boston, Feb. 27, 1926; m. Norman Lank; children: Avrum, David, Anna. BA magna cum laude, Syracuse U., 1947. Columnist L.A. Times Syndicate, 1976—; TV host Sta. WOKR-TV, Rochester, N.Y., 1983-84; radio host Sta. WBBF-AM, Rochester, 1984-85; lectr. St. John Fisher Coll., Rochester, 1977-89; commentator Sta. WXXI-FM, Rochester, 1977—; guest Am. Pub. Radio, St. Paul, 1987—; speaker in field. Author: Home Buying, 1981, Selling Your Home, 1982, Modern Real Estate Practice in New York, 1983, rev. 4th edit. 1992, The Complete Home Seller's Kit, 1988, rev. 3rd edit. 1994, The Complete Home Buyer's Kit, 1989, rev. 3rd edit., 1994, Dear Edith, 1990, Essentials of New Jersey Real Estate; co-author: Your Home as a Tax Shelter, 1993; contbr. articles to Time, New Yorker, McCall's, Real Estate Today, Persuasions, Modern Maturity, others. Recipient media award Bar Assn. Monroe County, 1982, Matrix award Women in Ommunications, 1984, Woman of Distinction award Gov. Mario Cumo, N.Y., 1985; named Communicator of Yr., SUNY, Brockport, 1986. Mem. Real Estate Educators Assn. (bd. dirs., Consumer Edn. award 1982, 83, 86, Real Estate Educator of Yr. 1984), Nat. Assn. Real Estate Editors (bd. dirs), Jane Austen Soc. N.Am. (dir.), Phi Beta Kappa. Home and Office: 240 Hemingway Dr Rochester NY 14620-3399

LANMAN, BRENDA KAY, operating room nurse; b. Ottumwa, Iowa, June 9, 1962; d. Edwin Clair and Mildred Lucille (Davis) Burkhiser; m. Roger E. Lanman, July 7, 1984; children: Andrew, Matthew. BSN, Iowa Weselyan Coll., Mt. Pleasant, Iowa, 1984. Instr. community health nurse USN, Sigonella, Sicily, 1984-86; staff nurse Ottumwa Regional Med. Ctr., 1986-93; nursing preceptor Ottumwa Regional Health Ctr., 1988-93; chmn. nursing quality improvement coun. Ottumwa Regional Med. Health Ctr., 1992-93; staff nurse oper. rooms Lester E. Cox Med. Ctr., South Springfield, Mo., 1993—. Home: 800 E Loren Springfield MO 65807

LANPHER, LUCILLE MARLENE, auditor; b. Oceanside, N.Y., Sept. 30, 1946; d. George Edward and Arline Lucille (Stewart) Tucker; m. Charles Andrew Kyme, Sept. 23, 1967 (div. Sept. 19, 1988); children: Kimberly Ann, Heather Arline, Matthew Charles; m. James Francis Lanpher, Nov. 24, 1989. AS in Acctg. summa cum laude, Nassau C.C., 1973; BS in Acctg. summa cum laude, L.I. U., 1979. Pvt. practice acct. North Babylon, N.Y., 1980-84; tax auditor N.Y. Dept. Taxation and Fin., Hempstead, 1985-91, Fla. Dept. Revenue, West Palm Beach, 1992—. Mem., leader Girl Scouts U.S., North Babylon, 1978-85; pres. PTA Grace Episcopal Day Sch., Massapequa, N.Y., 1983; mem. vestry Ch. of Good Shepherd, Tequesta, Fla., 1993-95, jr. warden, 1994. Mem. Sierra Club, Bus. and Profl. Womens Club. Office: Fla Dept Revenue 2468 Metrocentre Blvd West Palm Beach FL 33407

LANSBURY, ANGELA BRIGID, actress; b. London, Oct. 16, 1925; came to U.S., 1940; d. Edgar and Moyna (Macgill) L.; m. Peter Shaw, Aug. 12, 1949; children: Anthony, Deirdre. Student, Webber-Douglas Sch. Drama, London, 1939-40, Feagin Sch. Drama, N.Y.C., 1940-42; LHD (hon.), Boston U., 1990. Host 41st, 42d and 43d Ann. Tony Awards, 45th Ann. Emmy Awards. Actress with Metro-Goldwyn-Mayer, 1943-50; films include: Gaslight, 1944 (Acad. award nomination), National Velvet, 1944, The Picture of Dorian Gray, 1944 (Golden Globe award, Acad. award nomination), The Harvey Girls, 1946, The Hoodlum Saint, 1946, Till the Clouds Roll By, 1946, The Private Affairs of Bel Ami, 1947, If Winter Comes, 1948, Tenth Avenue Angel, 1948, State of the Union, 1948, The Three Musketeers, 1948, The Red Danube, 1949, Samson and Delilah, 1949, Kind Lady, 1951, Mutiny, 1952, Remains to be Seen, 1953, A Life at Stake, 1955, The Purple Mask, 1956, A Lawless Street, 1956, Please Murder Me, 1956, The Court Jester, 1956, The Long Hot Summer, 1958, Reluctant Debutante, 1958, Summer of the 17th Doll, 1959, A Breath of Scandal, 1960, Dark at the Top of the Stairs, 1960, Season of Passion, 1961, Blue Hawaii, 1961, All Fall Down, 1962, Manchurian Candidate, 1962 (Golden Globe award, Acad. award nomination), In the Cool of the Day, 1963, Dear Heart, 1964, The World of Henry Orient, 1964, Out of Towners, 1964, The Greatest Story Ever Told, 1965, Harlow, 1965, The Amorous Adventures of Moll Flanders, 1965, Mister Buddwing, 1966, Something for Everyone, 1970, Bedknobs and Broomsticks, 1971, Death on the Nile, 1978, The Lady Vanishes, 1980, The Mirror Crack'd, 1980, The Pirates of Penzance, 1982, The Company of Wolves, 1983, Beauty and the Beast, 1991; star TV series Murder She Wrote, 1984— (Golden Globe awards 1984, 86, 91, 92, 10 Emmy nominations, Lead Actress - Drama); appeared in TV mini-series Little Gloria, Happy at Last, 1982, Lace, 1984, Rage of Angels, part II, 1986; other TV movies include: The First Olympics-Athens 1896, A Talent for Murder, Gift of Love, 1982, Shootdown, 1988, The Shell Seekers, 1989, The Love She Sought, 1990, Mrs. 'Arris Goes to Paris, 1992; appeared in plays Hotel Paradiso, 1957, A Taste of Honey, 1960, Anyone Can Whistle, 1964, Mame (on Broadway), 1966, 83 (Tony award for Best Mus. Actress 1966), Dear World, 1968 (Tony award for Best Mus. Actress 1969), All Over (London Royal Shakespeare Co.), 1971, Gypsy, 1974 (Tony award for Best Mus. Actress 1975, Sarah Siddons award), The King and I, 1978, Sweeney Todd, 1979 (Tony award for Best Mus. Actress 1979, Sarah Siddons award), Hamlet, Nat. Theatre, London, 1976. Named Woman of Yr., Harvard Hasty Pudding Theatricals, 1968, Comdr. of British Empire by Queen Elizabeth II, 1994; inducted Theatre Hall of Fame, 1982; recipient British Acad. award, 1991. Office: Bldg 426 100 Universal City Plz Universal Cty CA 91608-1014

LANSDOWNE, KAREN MYRTLE, retired English language and literature educator; b. Twin Falls, Idaho, Aug. 11, 1926; d. George and Effie Myrtle (Ayotte) Martin; B.A. in English with honors, U. Oreg., 1948, M.Ed., 1958, M.A. with honors, 1960; m. Paul L. Lansdowne, Sept. 12, 1948; children: Michele Lynn, Larry Alan. Tchr., Newfield (N.Y.) High Sch., 1948-50, S. Eugene (Oreg.) High Sch., 1952; mem. faculty U. Oreg., Eugene, 1958-65; asst. prof. English, Lane Community Coll., Eugene, 1965-82, ret., 1982; cons. Oreg. Curriculum Study Center. Rep., Cal Young Neighborhood Assn., 1978—; mem. scholarship com. First Congl. Ch., 1950-70. Mem. MLA, Pacific N.W. Regional Conf. Community Colls., Nat. Council Tchrs. English, U. Oreg. Women, AAUW (sec.), Jaycettes, Pi Lambda Theta (pres.), Phi Beta Patronesses (pres.), Delta Kappa Gamma. Co-author: The Oregon Curriculum: Language/Rhetoric, I, II, III and IV, 1970. Home: 15757 Rim Dr La Pine OR 97739-9412

LANSING, SHERRY LEE, motion picture production executive; b. Chgo., July 31, 1944; d. Norton and Margo L. BS summa cum laude in Theatre, Northwestern U., 1966. Tchr. math. public high schs. Los Angeles, 1966-69; model TV commls. Max Factor Co., 1969-70, Alberto-Culver Co., 1969-70; story editor Wagner Internat. Prodn. Co., 1972-74, dir. west coast devel., 1974-75; story editor MGM, 1975-77, v.p. creative affairs, 1977; v.p. prodn. Columbia Pictures, 1977-80; pres. 20th Century Fox Prodns., 1980-82; founder Jaffee-Lansing Prodns., 1982—; chmn. Paramount Pictures' Motion Picture Group, 1992—. Appeared in movies Loving, 1970, Rio Lobo, 1970; exec. story editor movies, Wagner Internat., 1970-73; v.p. prodn., Heyday Prodns., Universal City, Calif., 1973-75; exec. story editor, then v.p. creative affairs, MGM Studios, Culver City, Calif., 1975-77; sr. v.p. prodn., Columbia Pictures, Burbank, Calif., 1977-80, pres., 20th Century-Fox Prodns., Beverly Hills, Calif., 1980-83; ind. producer., Jaffe-Lansing Prodns., Los Angeles, 1983-91; producer Racing With the Moon, 1984,Firstborn, 1984, Fatal Attraction, 1987, The Accused, 1988, Black Rain, 1989, School Ties, 1992, Indecent Proposal, 1993; TV exec. producer When the Time Comes,1987, Mistress, 1992. Office: Paramount Pictures Corp 5555 Melrose Ave Los Angeles CA 90038-3197*

LANSKY, JUDITH CAROL, lawyer; b. Milw., Nov. 11, 1950; d. Leo and Esther Louise (Kahn) L. BS, U. Wis., 1972, MS, 1978, JD, 1980. Bar: Wis. 1980, Tex. 1982, Ark. 1982, U.S. Dist. Ct. (ea. and we. dists.) Ark. 1982, U.S. Ct. Appeals (8th cir.) 1983. Assoc., examiner EEOC, Houston, 1981-82; assoc. Mays and Crutcher, Little Rock, 1982-84; lectr. in law U. Ark., Little Rock, 1984-86; law clk. Hon. Judge George Howard Jr. U.S. Dist. Ct., Little Rock, 1986—. Bd. dirs. Advocates for Battered Women, Little Rock, 1984-86, Ark. chpt. ACLU, 1985-86, YMCA, Little Rock, 1991-94. Mem. ABA. Office: US Dist Ct 600 W Capitol Ave Ste 276 Little Rock AZ 72201-3325

LANSKY, ZENA, surgeon; b. Phila., Apr. 18, 1942; d. Jacob and Thelma Lansky. BA summa cum laude, U. Pa., 1963; MD, Med. Coll. Pa., 1967. Diplomate Am. Bd. Surgery, 1975. Intern Montefiore Hosp., 1968-69; resident in surgery Bellevue Hosp., 1968-72, chief resident in surgery, 1971-72, instr. surgery, 1971-72; teaching asst. NIH, 1970, 71; mem. med. staff Morton F. Plant Hosp., Largo Med. Ctr., Clearwater Community Hosp.; med. dir. Gulf Coast Home Health Care, 1990; pres. Metabolic Cons. Inc. Infusion Co., pharmacy; mem. nat. med. adv. bd. New Eng. Critical Care, 1985; mem. adv. bd. Ind. Home Health Care, 1984-91. Mem. editorial bd. Nutritional Support mag., 1987; contbr. articles to profl. jours.; inventor gastrostomy tube, long term venous catheter repair kit, gastrostomy tube and percutaneous endoscopic kit. Bd. dirs. Pinellas County chpt. Am. Cancer Soc., 1980-85. Fellow ACS, Southeastern Surg. Congress; mem. Am. Soc. Parenteral and Enteral Nutrition (bd. dirs. 1989), Fla. Med. Assn., Fla. Assn. Nutritional Support (pres. 1986-87), Pinellas County Med. Soc. Office: Metabolic Cons Inc 412 S Missouri Ave Clearwater FL 34616

LANTRIP, SANDRA TYNES-LEBLANC, realtor; b. Baton Rouge, Dec. 9, 1948; d. Otis Calvin Tynes and Mable (Brown) Hudgins; m. Terry L. Lantrip; children: Stacey Ann, William Heath, Lawrence Lloyd LeBlanc. Student, La. State U., 1966-67, SE La. U., 1967-68. Lic. real estate agent, La.; cert. mineral lease and royalty broker. Co-owner, v.p. Unltd. Properties Inc., Ethel, La., 1978-82; co-owner Unltd. Mgmt. Inc., Zachary, La., 1979-82, Sandia Properties, Ethel, 1982-86; corp. recruiter, acct. exec. Sales Cons., Baton Rouge, 1986-87; corp. recruiter, acct. exec. mgr. Armon's Career Ctr., Baton Rouge, 1987-88; pvt. practice cons., 1988-89; agt. Farms and Acreage Real Estate, 1986-89, Town & Country Properties, 1990—; owner The Real McCoy, 1988—. Bd. dirs. Battered Womens' League. Mem. NAFE, Baton Rouge Bd. Realtors, Realtors Land Inst. (state treas. ALC designation 1994), C. of C. of Baton Rouge. Democrat. Roman Catholic. Home: 8618 Highway 955 E Ethel LA 70730-9801 Office: PO Box 135 Ethel LA 70730-0135

LANTZ, JOANNE BALDWIN, university chancellor emerita; b. Defiance, Ohio, Jan. 26, 1932; d. Hiram J. and Ethel A. (Smith) Baldwin; m. Wayne E. Lantz. BS in Physics and Math., U. Indpls., 1953; MS in Counseling and Guidance, Ind. U., 1957; PhD in Counseling and Psychology, Mich. State U., 1969; LittD (hon.), U. Indpls., 1985; LHD (hon.), Purdue U., 1994; LLD (hon.), Manchester Coll., 1994. Tchr. physics and math. Arcola (Ind.) High Sch., 1953-57; guidance dir. New Haven (Ind.) Sr. High Sch., 1957-65; with Ind. U.-Purdue U., Fort Wayne, 1965—, interim chancellor, 1988-89, chancellor, 1989-94, chancellor emerita, 1994—. Contbr. articles to profl. jours. Mem. Ft. Wayne Econ. Devel. Adv. Bd. and Task Force, 1988-91, Corp. Coun., 1988-94; bd. advisors Leadership Ft. Wayne, 1988-94; mem. adv. bd. Ind. Sml. Bus. Devel. Ctr., 1988-90; trustee Ancilla System, Inc., 1984-89, chmn. human resources com., 1985-89, exec. com., 1985-89; trustee St. Joseph's Med. Ctr., 1983-84, pers. adv. com. to bd. dirs., 1978-84, chmn., 1980-84; bd. dirs. United Way Allen County, sec., 1979-80; bd. dirs. Anthony Wayne Vocat. Rehab. Ctr., 1969-75. Mem. Fort Wayne Ind.-Purdue Alumni Soc. (hon. mem. 1987), Am. Psychol. Assn., AAUW (internat. fellowship com. 1986-88, prog. com. 1981-83, Am. women fellowship com. 1978-83, chmn. 1981-83, trust rsch. grantee 1980), Southeastern Psychol. Assn. (referee conv. papers 1987, 88), Ind. Sch. Women's Club (v.p.

prog. chair 1979-81), Pi Lambda Theta, Sigma Xi, Delta Kappa Gamma (editorial bd. 1986-88, gen. chair conv. 1985-86, dir. N.E. region 1982-84, adminstrv. bd., exec. bd. 1982-84, leadership devel. com.).

LANZA, DENISE MARIE, park and recreation administrator; b. Paterson, N.J., Aug. 24, 1959; d. Michael Anthony Sr. and Florence Henrietta (Carabello) L.; m. Robert Henry Rizzie, Sept. 7, 1986; 1 child, Alissa Rose Rizzie. BS cum laude, Montclair State Coll., 1981. Cert. leisure profl., cert. recreation supr. Recreation supr. Morris County Park Commn., Morristown, N.J., 1981-83, dir. visitor svcs., 1983-92, dir. recreation, 1993—; speaker various seminars in field, 1990—. Sec. Alamac Assn., Mt. Arlington, N.J., 1992—. Mem. N.J. Recreation and Park Assn. (mem.-at-large 1994-95, trade show coord. 1991—, Supr. of Yr. 1990). Office: Morris County Park Commn PO Box 1295 Morristown NJ 07962-1295

LANZA, SHELLEY BROWN, lawyer; b. Toledo, July 19, 1956; d. Charles Leo and Rose (Milano) Brown; m. Gregg Lanza, July 26, 1980; children: Angelina, Lauren, Giuliana. BA in Acctg. summa cum laude, Adrian Coll., 1977; JD, U. Calif., Berkeley, 1982. Bar: Ohio 1982. Assoc. Vorys, Sater, Seymour & Pease, Columbus, Ohio, 1982-86; v.p., gen. counsel Honda of Am. Mfg. Inc., Marysville, Ohio, 1986—. Mem. Child Conservation League, Powell, Ohio, 1986; chmn. devel. com., bd. trustees Columbus Zoo. Mem. ABA, Ohio Bar Assn., Columbus Bar Assn., Union County Bar Assn., Am. Corp. Coun. Assn., Am. Mgmt. Assn., Motor Vehicle Mfrs. Assn. (mem. various coms.), Columbus Womens Mentoring Program, Alpha Chi. Republican. Roman Catholic. Home: 1745 White Oak Dr Delaware OH 43015-9272 Office: Honda of Am Mfg Inc Legal Dept 24000 Honda Pky Marysville OH 43040-9251

LANZONE, DEBORAH VON HOFFMANN, state legislative staff member; b. Montclair, N.J., Apr. 23, 1952; d. Robert Ferdinand and Anne Marie (Perdue) von Hoffmann; m. Dale Martin Lanzone, Oct. 17, 1981; 1 child, Dominic Peter. BA in Liberal Arts, Colgate U., 1974. Legis. aide Mass. Legislature, Boston, 1975; mem. advance staff Nat. Dem. Com., Washington, 1976; congrl. liaison officer Land Use Planning Commn., Washington, 1977-79, Heritage Conservation Recreation Svc., Washington, 1979-81; planner natural resources Nat. Park Svc., Washington, 1981-86; spl. asst. to dir. Fish and Wildlife Svc., Washington, 1986-88; sr. regulatory analyst Bur. Land Mgmt., Washington, 1988-89, congrl. liaison officer, 1989-91; staff dir. subcom. energy and natural resources U.S. Ho. Reps., Washington, 1992-94, mem. legis. staff Com. on Resources, 1994—. Del. Mass. Nat. Dem. Conv., 1976; mem. advance staff Nat. Dem. Campaign, 1976, inaugural staff Nat. Dem. Com., 1977. Episcopalian. Office: US Ho Reps Com on Resources 1329 Longworth HOB Washington DC 20515

LAPADOT, SONEE SPINNER, automobile manufacturing company official; b. Sidney, Ohio, Apr. 19, 1936; d. Kenneth Lee and Helyn Kathryn (Hobby) Spinner; m. Jan. 13, 1955 (div. Apr. 1970); 1 child, Douglas Cameron Proud; m. Robert Stephen Lapadot, May 4, 1974 (div. Mar. 1994). Student, U. Cin., 1954-56, U. Akron, 1966; BS in Mgt. Human Resources, Spring Arbor Coll., 1991. Mgr. engring. change implementation Terex div. GM, Hudson, Ohio, 1975-77, mgr. prodn. scheduling, 1977-78, gen. adminstr. product purchasing, 1978-79; sr. staff asst. non-ferrous metals GM, Detroit, 1979-80, mgr. tires and wheels, 1980-83, mgr. staff purchasing, 1983-85, mgr. corp. constrn. contracting, 1985-86; mfg. techs. adminstr. Chrysler Motors, Detroit, 1986-87, mgr. mfg. prodn. control adminstrn. and svcs., 1988, mgr. advanced planning and prodn. systems, 1988-89, mgr. advanced planning and control power train, 1989-90, mgr. Mound Rd. Engine Prodn. Control, 1990—. Active fund-raising Boy Scouts Am., Grosse Pointe, Mich., 1980-82, Detroit, 1985-94, United Fund, Detroit, 1980-94, Jr. Achievement, Detroit, 1984, 90-94. Mem. NAFE, Soc. Automotive Engrs., Am. Soc. Profl. and Exec. Women, Am. Prodn. and Inventory Control Soc., Automotive Industry Action Group (returnable containers and packaging team), Mensa, Women's Econ. Club of Detroit. Home: 1941 Squirrel Rd Bloomfield Hills MI 48304-1162 Office: Chrysler Motors Corp Mound Rd Engine Plant 20300 Mound Rd Detroit MI 48234

LAPCEK, BARBARA NEOGY, arts educational executive; b. Yonkers, N.Y., Nov. 24, 1933; d. Joseph and Elizabeth (Sarubbi) Lapchick; m. Roy E. Brown; 1 child, Jeffrey D. Brown; m. 2d Rajat Neogy; 1 child, Tayu Lapcek Neogy. BA cum laude with honors, Barnard Coll., 1955; postgrad., Columbia U., 1955-56. Founder, exec. dir. Nommo Art Gallery, Kampala, Uganda, 1964-69; cultural columnist The People, Uganda, 1965-68; asst. editor, advt. mgr. Transition Mag., Accra, Ghana, 1966-72; dir. N.Y. State Arts in Prison Program, N.Y.C., 1974-77; editor Jackson's Excerpta, N.Y.C., 1973-75; dir. N.Y. State Artists Fellowship Program, N.Y.C., 1977-82; exec. dir. Musica Sacra, N.Y.C., 1982-84; exec. dir. program Skowhegan Sch. Art, N.Y.C., 1984—; mem. adv. bd. Culture Coun. Found., N.Y.C., 1979-82, Bob Blackburn's Printmaking Workshop, N.Y.C., Women Explorers: Oral History, N.Y.C., Dieu Donne Paper Workshop, N.Y.C.; panelist N.Y.C. Dept. Cultural Affairs, 1979-82; nominator Louis Comfort Tiffany Found., N.Y.C. Author: Hear the Rock, 1961. Named Woman of Yr., Uganda Hist. Soc., 1967; recipient Svc. to the Arts award Maine Art Dealers Assn., 1990. Office: Skowhegan Sch Rm 1116 200 Park Ave S New York NY 10003

LAPIN, SHARON JOYCE VAUGHN, interior designer; b. Lagrange, Mo., July 28, 1938; d. John Nolan and Wilma Emma (Huebotter) Vaughn; BA summa cum laude, U. Wash., Seattle, 1960; m. Byron Richard Lapin, Oct. 14, 1972. Appeared in various Broadway shows, TV commls. and TV shows, 1962-72; mgr. arts and crafts div., convenience products Clayton Corp., Fenton, Mo. Bd. dirs. St. Louis Conservatory and Schs. for Arts, 1977—, v.p., 1982-87; chmn. bd. Studio Set, 1978-81, pres., 1975-78, bd. dirs., 1975-83; bd. dirs. Friends of Sci. Mus., 1980-90, v.p., 1984-85; pres. Assocs. Bd. Dirs., St. Louis Sci. Ctr., Inc., 1986-87; bd. dirs. Jr. Div., St. Louis Symphony Women's Assn., 1973-75; bd. dirs. Womens Assn. St. Louis Symphony, 1988-90. Mem. AFTRA, SAG, AEA, Am. Soc. Interior Designers, Pi Beta Phi, Mu Phi Epsilon.

LA PLANTE, PATRICIA ANN, counselor, radio broadcaster; b. Bklyn., Feb. 13, 1955; d. Kenneth Charles and Patricia Ann (Duffy) La P. BA in Comms., Va. Tech., 1982; postgrad., Dallas Theol. Sem., 1989; MA in Bib. Counseling, Colo. Christian U., 1990; postgrad., Denver Sem. Radio announcer Pillar of Fire Ch., Zarephath, N.J. & Denver, 1987-90, 91-94; radio coord. Hope for the Heart, Dallas, 1990-91; counselor Crossroads Bapt. Ch., Northglenn, Colo., 1992—; dir. cmty. rels. Sta. KPOF, Westminster, Colo., 1991—; owner, dir. Anchor Counseling and Comm., Northglenn, 1990-92; guest lectr. Denver Sem., 1992-94. Crisis intervention pers. dir. Drop-in Ctr./The RAFT, N.J. and Va., 1974-77, 80-82; coord. blood drs. Crossroads Bapt. Ch., Northglenn, 1992—; active Share Colo., 1991—. Mem. Am. Counseling Assn., Am. Assn. Christian Counselors, Nat. Religious Broadcasters. Home: 1057 C W 112th Ave Westminster CO 80234-3318 Office: KPOF Radio 3455 W 83d Ave Westminster CO 80030

LAPOINTE, LISA, social worker; b. New Orleans, Oct. 31, 1955; d. Jon Strauss; m. Marc J. LaPointe, May 17, 1980; children: Elise, Elizabeth, Stephanie. Diploma, Newman Sch., 1973; BA, Tulane U., 1977, MSW, 1979. Social worker Orleans Parish Sch. Bd., New Orleans, 1980-82, Lloyd Noland Hosp., Birmingham, Ala., 1982-87, Cypress Hosp., Lafayette, La., 1987-88; pvt. practice social worker Opelousas, La., 1988—; con. Cypress Hosp., 1988—. Mem. Nat. Assn. Social Workers, Acad. Cert. Social Workers, La. Bd. Cert. Social Workers. Office: PO Box 880 Opelousas LA 70571-0880

LAPOINTE-PETERSON, KITTIE VADIS, choreographer, ballet school director, educator; b. Chgo., June 4, 1915; d. Samuel Joseph and Katie (Parbst) Andrew; m. Arthur Joseph LaPointe, Dec. 17, 1938 (dec. Apr. 1985); children: Janice Deane, Suzanne Meta; m. Ray Burt Peterson, Feb. 2, 1992. Studies with, Marie Zvolanek, Chgo., 1921-28, Laurent Novikoff, Chgo., 1928-35, Edward Caton, Chgo., 1928-35; student, Royal Danish Ballet, Copenhagen, 1926. Dancer Chgo. Civic Opera, 1929-32, Century of Progress, Chgo., 1933-34, Stone-Camryn Ballet, Chgo., 1934-35, Mary Vandas Dancers, Chgo., 1935-38, Balaban-Katz Theaters, Chgo., 1935-36; tchr., choreographer Studio of Dance Arts, Chgo., 1952-68, Herrstrom Sch., Chgo., 1968-72; dir. Le Ballet Petit Sch., Chgo., 1972-92. Soloist in Michael Fokine's Co., 1935. Mem. Danish Brotherhood and Sisterhood (pres. 1962-65, 72-75, Midwest dist. pres. 1972-74), Chgo. Outdoor Art League (sec. 1975-79, Manor Garden Club. Home: 5843 W Peterson Ave Chicago IL 60646-3907

LAPON, DIANE ARLENE, financial planner; b. Boston, Oct. 27, 1944; d. Peretz and Ruth G. (Wolman) Singer; m. Stanley Robert Lapon, Apr. 7, 1968 (div. 1981); children: Jeremy, Jennifer, Elizabeth. BS, U. Pitts., 1966; MS, U. Pa., 1967; MBA, Babson Coll., 1982; MST, Bentley Coll., 1987. Tchr. Drexel, Lesley, Mass. Bay and Middlesex C.C.s, 1966-82; personal fin. planner Shory Huntington, Concord, Mt. Harman Fin. Mgmt., Newton, Mass., 1982-86, Seidman Fin. Svcs., Boston, 1986-89; tax mgr. Arthur Andersen, Boston, 1989—; tchr. fin. planning Harvard U., Arthur Anderson & Co. Mem. AICPA (PFP divsn.), Internat. Assn. Fin. Planners (exec. bd. 1986-88, mem. Boston chpt.), Inst. Cert. Fin. Planners, Mass. Soc. CPAs (chair fin. and estate planning com.), Boston Bar Assn., Boston Estate Planning Coun. Home: 10 Rutgers Rd Wellesley MA 02181-2513

LAPP, SUSAN BOLSTER, learning disability educator; b. Washington, Nov. 23, 1945; d. Robert Fay and Nona (Peifly) Bolster; m. Richard Gordon Lapp, Apr. 22, 1967. BS in Edn., Miami U., Oxford, Ohio, 1967; MEd, Xavier U., Cin., 1977. Cert. tchr. English; cert. in learning disabilities and behavior disorders K-12. Sec. Penta Tech. Coll., Perrysburg, Ohio, 1965-67; tchr. 3d grade Toledo Pub. Schs., 1966-67; thcr. 7th and 8th grades Fairfield (Ohio) City Schs., 1967-78, 6th, 7th and 8th grade learning disabilities tchr., 1978—, spl. svcs. coordinator, 1984—, career edn. coordinator, 1987—; career edn. coordinator Butler County Joint Vocat. Sch., Hamilton, Ohio, 1987—; student vol. dir. Fairfield Middle Sch., 1990—. Vice chair S.W. Ohio Profl. Devel. Ctr., 1993—, co-sec., 1994. Named Spl. Edn. Tchr. of Yr., S.W. Ohio Spl. Edn. Regional Resource Ctr., 1989, Ohio Career Educator of Yr., Career Edn. Assn., 1991, Outstanding Sch. Vol./Ptnr. award, 1991. Mem. NEA, S.W. Ohio Edn. Assn., Fairfield Classroom Tchrs. Assn., Ohio Mid. Sch. Assn., Nat. Assn. for Career Edn., Career Edn. Assn. (Ohio Career Planning Team of Yr. 1994), Orton Soc. Home: 900 Harrison Ave Hamilton OH 45013-3511 Office: Fairfield Middle Sch 255 Donald Dr Fairfield OH 45014-3085

LAPPE, FRANCES MOORE, author, lecturer; b. Pendleton, Oreg., Feb. 10, 1944; d. John and Ina (Skrifvars) Moore; m. Marc Lappe, Nov. 11, 1967 (div. 1977); children: Anthony, Anna; m. J. Baird Callicott, Dec. 1, 1985 (div. 1991); m. Paul Martin DuBois, Aug. 19, 1991. BA in History, Earlham Coll., 1966; PhD (hon.), St. Mary's Coll., 1983, Lewis and Clark Coll., 1983, Macalester Coll., 1986, Hamline U., 1987, Earlham Coll., 1988, Kenyon Coll., 1989, U. Mich., 1990, Nazareth Coll., 1990, Niagara Coll., 1993. Co-founder, mem. staff Inst. for Food and Devel. Policy, Oakland, 1975-90; co-founder, co-dir. Ctr. for Living Democracy, Brattleboro, Vt., 1990—. Author: Diet for A Small Planet, 1971, 75, 82, 91, Mozambique and Tanzania: Asking the Big Questions, 1979, What To Do After You Turn Off the T.V., 1985, Rediscovering America's Values, 1989; (with Joseph Collins) Food First: Beyond the Myth of Scarcity, 1977, Aid as Obstacle, 1980, Now We Can Speak, 1984, Nicaragua: What Difference Could a Revolution Make?, 1984, World Hunger: Twelve Myths, 1986; (with Rachel Schurman and Kevin Danaher) Betraying the National Interest, 1987, (with Schurman) Taking Population Seriously, 1990, (with Paul Martin Du Bois) The Quickening of America: Rebuilding Our Nation, Remaking Our Lives, 1994. Named to Nutrition Hall of Fame Ctr. for Sci. and Pub. Interest, 1981; recipient Mademoiselle Mag. award, 1977; World Hunger Media award, 1982, Right Livelihood award, 1987. Office: Ctr Living Democracy RR 1 Black Fox Rd Brattleboro VT 05301-9801

LAQUER, MARY JANE WINIARSKI, speech/language pathologist; b. Phila., June 29, 1956; d. Eugene Anthony and Constance Mary (Rdesinski) Winiarski; m. David Edward Laquer, Sept. 27, 1980; children: Julie, Carolyn. BS, Pa. State U., 1978; MEd, U. Va., 1980. Cert. clin. competence speech/lang. pathology, Pa. Speech/lang. pathologist Montco Vis. Nurse Assn., Norristown, Pa., 1980-81, In Speech Inc., Valley Forge, Pa., 1981-82; speech/lang. pathologist and cognitive remediator Bryn Mawr Rehab., Malvern, Pa., 1982-87, Doylestown (Pa.) Rehab. & Vis. Nurse Home Care, 1986—; pvt. practice speech lang. pathology & cognitive remediating North Wales, Pa., 1986—; cons. Main Line Rehab. Assocs., Malvern, 1987—, Speech (Lang.) Pathology Cons., Conshohocken, Pa., 1990—, North Penn Vis. Nurses, Lansdale, Pa., 1992—. Mem. AAUW, Am. Speech Lang. Hearing Assn., Soc. Cognitive Rehab., Keystone Head Injury Found. Democrat. Home and Office: 207 S 5th St North Wales PA 19454-2903

LARA, VELMA CECILIA, social worker; b. Edinburg, Tx., Mar. 8, 1953; d. David Michael and Catalina (Dela Rosa) Ceballos; 1 child, Rebecca. BA in Social Welfare, Tex. Tech U., 1975; MS in Social Work, U. Tex., Arlington, 1984. Lic. social worker, Tex. Eligibility worker Tex. Dept. Human Resources, Lubbock, 1975-78, social worker, 1978-80, child protective worker, 1980-82, 84-87; dir. social svcs. St. Mary of the Plains Hosp., Lubbock, 1987—; condr. pvt. home studies for pending adoptions, including contracted svcs. for Tex. Dept. Protective Regulatory Svcs.; asst./assessor families Lubbock Ind. Sch. Dist. Bd. dirs. Ronald McDonald House, Lubbock, 1992—, Cath. Family Svcs., Lubbock, 1993—; cert. leader Weight Watchers. Mem. NASW (nat., local affiliate), Tex. Hosp. Assn. Home: 3403 101st St Lubbock TX 79423-5122

LARABEE, MARCIA RAND, counselor, writer; b. Melrose, Mass., Mar. 21, 1939; d. Roger Glade and Muriel Henley (Foster) Rand; m. John Edgar Larabee, June 14, 1959 (div. June 1981); children: Jacqueline Chenot, John Robert (dec.), Michael Rand, Kyle Foster, David James. BA in English, Ohio Wesleyan U., 1960; MA in Human Devel., Fairleigh Dickinson U., 1978. Lic. clin. profl. counselor; cert. tchr., N.Y. Tchr. Cleve. Pub. Schs., 1960-61, Montessori Sch., Chatham Twp., N.J., 1976-78; tchr. Voorheesville (N.Y.) Cen. Schs., 1978-81, 82-85, sch. treas., 1981-82; counselor Al-Care, Albany, N.Y., 1985-89, pvt. practice, Schenectady, N.Y., 1989-90, Safe Harbor Miles Hosp., Newcastle, Maine, 1990-91, pvt. practice, Damariscotta, Maine, 1991-94; pvt. practice Schenectady & Saratoga Springs, N.Y., 1994—; mem. focus com., women's events com. Women's Ctr., Miles Hosp., Damariscotta, 1993-94. Researcher and writer in field; contbr. articles to profl. jours. Mem. Am. Assn. Grief Counselors, Inc., Assn. for Humanistic Psychology, Internat. Women's Writing Guild, Maine Hist. Soc., C.G. Jung Ctr. Studies in Analytical Psychology. Home: 3 Rip Van Ln Ballston Spa NY 12020 Office: Tuttle Assocs 1375 Union St Schenectady NY 12308

LARAMÉE, EVE ANDRÉE, artist, educator; b. L.A., Jan. 6, 1956; d. Yves André and Ann Mary (Franq) L. BA, San Diego State U., 1978; MFA, San Francisco Art Inst., 1980. Represented by TZ'Art and Co. Gallery, N.Y.C.; founder, dir. Art/Media, Albuquerque and Santa Fe, 1983-86; adj. prof. NYU, 1989—; vis. prof. MIT, Cambridge, Mass., 1992, Md. Inst. Coll. Art, Balt., 1993-94, Cooper Union Sch. Art, N.Y.C., 1995; sculptor-in-residence Guggenheim Mus., Chesterwood, Mass., 1992. Exhibited in shows at Albuquerque Mus., 1983, Contemporary Arts Mus., Houston, 1989, New Mus. Contemporary Art, N.Y.C., 1989, Hudson River Mus., Yonkers, N.Y., 1990, Islip Art Mus., East Islip, N.Y., 1991, Artists Mus., Berlin, 1992, Mus. Contemporary Art, Chgo., 1992, 93, Internat. Artists Mus., Lodz, Poland, 1993, High Mus. Art, Atlanta, 1994, Katonah (N.Y.) Mus., 1995, New Mus. Contemporary Art, N.Y.C., 1995. Studio fellow Inst. Contemporary Art - the Clocktower, N.Y.C., 1987-88; fellow N.Y. Found. Arts, 1989; sculptor-in-residence grantee Guggenheim Mus., 1992. Office: Frederieke Taylor TZ'Art & Co Gallery 28 Wooster St New York NY 10013

LARAYA-CUASAY, LOURDES REDUBLO, pediatric pulmonologist, educator; b. Baguio, Philippines, Dec. 8, 1941; came to U.S., 1966; d. Jose Marquez and Lolita (Redublo) Laraya; m. Ramon Serrano Cuasay, Aug. 7, 1965; children: Raymond Peter, Catherine Anne, Margaret Rose, Joseph Paul. AA, U. Santo Tomas, Manila, Philippines, 1958, MD cum laude, 1963. Diplomate Am. Bd. Pediatrics. Resident in pediatrics U. Santo Tomas Hosp., 1963-65, Children's Hosp. Louisville, 1966-67, Charity Hosp. New Orleans-Tulane U., 1967-68; fellow child growth and devel. Children's Hosp. Phila., 1968-69; fellow pediatric pulmonary and cystic fibrosis programs St. Christopher's Hosp. for Children, Phila., 1969-71, rsch. assoc., 1971-72; clin. instr. Tulane U., New Orleans, 1967-68; asst. prof. pediatrics Temple Health Scis. Ctr., Phila., 1972-77; assoc. prof. pediatrics Thomas Jefferson Med. Sch., Phila., 1977-79; assoc. prof. pediatrics U. Medicine & Dentistry N.J., Robert Wood Johnson Med. Sch., New Brunswick, 1980-85, prof. clin. pediatrics, 1985—; dir. pediatric pulmonary and cystic fibrosis program U. Medicine and Dentistry, Robert Wood Johnson Med. Sch., New Brunswick, 1981—. Co-editor: Interstitial Lung Diseases in Children, 1988. Recipient Pediatric Rsch. award Mead Johnson Pharm. Co., Manila, 1965. Fellow Am. Coll. Chest Physicians (steering com., chmn. cardiopulmonary diseases in children 1976—), Am. Acad. Pediatrics (tobacco free generation rep. 1986-92); mem. Am. Ambulatory Pediatric Soc., Am. Thoracic Soc., Am. Sleep Disorder Assn., N.J. Thoracic Soc. (chmn. pediatric pulmonary com. 1986-91, governing coun. mem. 1981—), Am. Coll. Physician Execs., Lung Club. Home: 100 Mercer Ave Spring Lake NJ 07762 Office: UMDMJ Robert Wood Johnson Med Sch CN19 New Brunswick NJ 08903

LARCH, BILLIE BENTLEY, nursing administrator; b. Texarkana, Tex., Aug. 26, 1919; d. William Calvin and Lula Marie (Cowley) Bentley; m. Monroe P. Larch, Mar. 26, 1936; children: James Monroe, Michael B. BSN, U. Ark., Little Rock, 1962; MSN, U. Cen. Ark., Conway, 1971; MA in Gerontology, U. Little Rock, 1987. Cert. gerontol. nurse and psychiat. clin. specialist nurse. Nurse cons. Ark. Dept. Mental Health, Little Rock, 1978-89; assoc. chief nursing svc. for edn. John L. McClellan VA Hosp., Little Rock, 1972-85; exec. dir. Ark. State Nurses Assn., Little Rock, 1989-92; nurse cons. Larch Cons. Svcs., 1992—; health care specialist Children and Family Divsn. Ark. Dept. Human Svcs., 1993—; mem. nursing faculty Allied Health, U. Ark., 1973-76; med. rschr. for pros. and def. trial lawyers, 1992—. Developer small group work program Chronically and Mentally Ill, Ark., 1966—; organizer Ark. affiliate chpt. Am. Diabetes Assn., 1973; healthcare specialist Ark. Dept. Human Svcs., Children's and Family Divsn., 1993—. Recipient Gold Star award Atty. Gen.'s Office, 1989; named to Hall of Fame in Nursing, Ark. State Nurses Assn., 1988. Mem. Nat. League for Nursing (Linda Richards award 1969). Home: 8422 Kling Rd Mabelvale AR 72103-3614 :

LARDIERE, MARIE KATHLEEN, insurance representative; b. Hunterdon, N.J., Mar. 11, 1951; d. Joseph William and Ninette (Tarantini) L. Student, County Coll. Morris, 1970-71, Felician Coll., 1971-73. Svc. rep. Smith Kline Biosci., East Orange, N.J., 1978-89; ins. specialist Blue Cross/Blue Shield, Newark, 1989—. Vol. West Orange (N.J.) Animal League, Our Lady of the Lake Ch., Verona. Republican. Roman Catholic. Home: 52 Seaman Rd West Orange NJ 07052

LARDIERI, JACQUELINE MARIE, elementary school educator; b. Newark, Dec. 31, 1940; d. John and Geraldine (Genuario) Ricca; m. Vincent Gerard Lardieri, June 29, 1963; children: Anthony Gerard, John Ricca, Gerald Patrick. BA, Kean Coll., 1963. Tchr. Fairview Sch., Bloomfield, N.J., 1963-67; tchr., activities coord., yearbook editor, religion coord. Holy Spirit Sch., Pequannock, N.J., 1986—; liaison faculty adv. coun. Holy Spirit Sch., 1993—. Mem. Nat. Cath. Edn. Assn. Republican. Roman Catholic.

LARIN, PAT NOEL, interior designer; b. N.Y.C., Dec. 8, 1941; d. Howard Albert and Shirley (Yohann) Fausty; m. David J. Larin, Jan. 1978; children: Pamela Thompson, Mark Goldby. BS, Cornell U., 1963. Lic. gen. contractor, Calif.; cert. interior designer, Calif. Prin. interior designer Butterfield, Kits and Baths, Palo Alto, Calif., 1978-80; pres. Pat Larin Interiors, Los Altos Hills, Calif., 1980—. Contbr. articles and projects to profl. jours. Mem. ASID (various offices including bd. dirs. Calif. chpt. 1989, 93-94).

LARK, M. ANN, management consultant, strategic planner; b. Denver, Feb. 28, 1952; d. Carl Eugene and Arlena Elizabeth (Bashor) Epperson; m. Larry S. Lark, Apr. 1, 1972 (div. 1979). Cert. seminar leader. Asst. corp. sec., savs. dir. Imperial Corp. dba Silver State Savs. & Loan, Denver, 1972-75; client svcs. mgr. 1st Fin. Mgmt. Corp., Englewood, Colo., 1977-81; regional account mgr. Ericsson Info. Systems, Chatsworth, Calif., 1981-82; ind. cons. Denver, 1982-84; regional account mgr. InnerLine/Am. Banker, Chgo., 1984-85; chief info. officer Security Pacific Credit Corp., San Diego, 1985-88; prin. The Genessee Group, Thousand Oaks, Calif., 1988—. Home and Office: 1144 El Monte Dr Thousand Oaks CA 91362-2117

LARKIN, MARY SUE, financial planner; b. Kansas City, Kans., Sept. 29, 1948; d. Claude Dewey Jr. and Mildred Elaine (Foster) Wyrick; m. James Donald Larkin, June 5, 1971; children: Michael James, David Kirk. BA in Elem. Edn., Baker U., 1970; MA in Edn., Ariz. State U., 1980. Tchr. Bonner Springs (Kans.) Unified Sch. Dist., 1970-71, Finney County Unified Sch. Dist., Garden City, Kans., 1971-73, Deer Valley Unified Sch. Dist., Phoenix, 1974-80; fin. planner Larkin & Assocs., Sun City, Ariz., 1980—. Co-author: The Larkin Guide-Enjoying the Riches of Retirement, 1987. Recipient creative programming award Nat. Univ. Continuing Edn. Assn., 1994. Mem. Internat. Assn. Fin. Planning (pres. greater Phoenix chpt. 1994-95), Inst. CFPs, Altrusa (pres. Sun City 1987-89). Republican. Roman Catholic. Office: 17220 N Boswell Blvd Ste L200 Sun City AZ 85373-2000

LARKIN, MOSCELYNE, retired artistic director, dancer; b. Miami, Okla., Jan. 14, 1925; d. Reuben Frances and Eva (Matlogova) L.; m. Roman Jasinski, Dec. 24, 1943 (dec. 1991); 1 child, Roman. Studied with Serge Grigorieff, Lubov Tchernicheva, Mikhail Mordkin, Anatole Vilzak, Vincenzo Celli; hon. doctorate of Fine Arts, U. of Tulsa, 1991. With Ballet Russe, 1941-47, Ballet Russe de Monte Carlo, 1948-52; prima ballerina Radio City Music Hall, N.Y.C., 1951-52; with Alexandra's Danilova's Great Moments of Ballet touring co., 1952-54; established Tulsa Sch. Ballet, from 1956; artistic dir. Tulsa Civic Ballet, 1956-76, Tulsa Ballet Theater, 1976-91; artistic dir. emerita Tulsa Civic Ballet, 1991—. Dance performances include Mikhail Forkine's Paganini and Les Sylphides; Leonid Massine's Le Beau Danube, Symphonie Fantastique, Les Presages; George Balanchine's Concerto Barocco, Night Shadow, Cotillion; Agnes De Mille's Rodeo; David Lichine's Graduation Ball; Michael Maule's The Carib Peddler. Recipient Dance Mag. award, 1988, Gov. Arts award, 1988, Rogers State Coll. Lynn Riggs award, 1989, award of Am.,1992; named to Tulsa Press Clubb Headliner award, Okla. Hall of Fame, 1979, Tulsa Hall of Fame, 1988, Okla. Womens Hall of Fame, 1993, and numerous others. Mem. Southwestern Regional Ballet Assn. (exec. v.p. 1963-76), Nat. Assn. Regional Ballet. Home: 5414 S Gillette Ave Tulsa OK 74105-6434 Office: Tulsa Ballet Theatre 4512 S Peoria Ave Tulsa OK 74105-4563*

LARKIN, NELLE JEAN, computer programmer, analyst; b. Ralston, Okla., July 4, 1925; d. Charles Eugene and Jennivea Pearl (Lane) Reed; m. Burr Oakley Larkin, Dec. 28, 1948 (div. Aug. 1969); children: John Timothy, Kenneth James, Donald Jerome, Valerie Jean Larkin Rouse. Student, UCLA, 1944, El Camino Jr. Coll., 1946-49, San Jose (Calif.) City Coll., 1961-62. Sr. programmer, analyst III Santa Clara County, San Jose, Calif., 1963-69; sr. analyst, programmer Blue Cross of No. Calif., Oakland, 1971-73; sr. programmer, analyst Optimum Systems, Inc., Santa Clara, Calif., 1973-75, Crocker Bank, San Francisco, 1975-77, Greyhound Fin. Service, San Francisco, 1977-78; analyst, programmer TRW, Mountain View, Calif., 1978-79; sr. programer analyst Memorex, Santa Clara, 1979-80; staff mgmt. cons. Am. Mgmt. System, Foster City, Calif., 1980-82; sr. programmer, analyst, project leader Tymeshare, Cupertino, Calif., 1982-83; sr. programmer, analyst Beckman Instruments, Palo Alto, Calif., 1983-89; analyst, programmer U.S. Postal Svc., San Mateo, Calif., 1989—. Mem. Calif. Scholarship Fedn. (life mem. 1943), Alpha Sigma Gamma. Home: 3493 Londonderry Dr Santa Clara CA 95050-6632 Office: US Postal Svc 2700 Campus Dr San Mateo CA 94497-0001

LARKIN, SARA ANN, artist; b. Quincy, Mass., Dec. 28, 1946; d. Sydney S. and Myrtle (Harriman) Larkin; m. Richard Preston Lacey, Dec. 29, 1972 (dec. 1974). BFA, U. Pa., 1969; Cert. of Completion, Pa. Acad. Fine Arts, 1969; student, Cornell U., Syracuse U., 1964-65. Women's style editor Bangkok World Newspaper, 1970-71; owner, cons. artist Sara Larkin Gallery, Hong Kong, 1972-76; artist, art investor, cons. Sara Larkin Fine Art, Washington, 1978—; vis. artist St. John's Coll., Annapoli, Md., summer 1992; artist/pvt. tutor Sara Larkin Studio, Annapolis, 1992—. One woman shows include Fashion Moda, NYC, 1982, NASA Hdqrs., Washington, 1982, Langley Rsch. Ctr., Hampton, Va., 1983, Alpha Gallery, Rockville, Md., 1980-90, Covington-Burling, Washington, 1993; group exhibits include Danforth Mus., Framingham, Mass., 1984, El Paso (Tex.) Mus. Art, 1986, Expo '86, Tokyo, 1986, Mitsukoshi Gallery, Tokyo, 1986, Govinda Gallery, Washington, 1986, John F. Kennedy Space Ctr., Spaceport USA, 1987, Mass. Bay C.C., 1989 ; included in permanent collection in John F. Kennedy Ctr., Okla. Air & Space Muse, Fed. Res. Collection, Washington; painting series include Spacescapes-An American Landscape, 1980s, Baseball, 1990s.

Vol. C.R.A.B. Sailing for Disabled Charity, Annapolis, 1993. Ford Found. scholar, 1968, 69; Nat. Endowment Arts grantee, 1982; recipient N.Y. State Initiative award, 1969, Commendation, Gov. Hong Kong and U.S. Consul Hong Kong, 1974, Popular prize Arts Club of Washington, 1992. Mem. Nat. Arts Club. Home: 239 Prince George St Apt 3R Annapolis MD 21401-1633 Office: Sara Larkin Fine Art 2301 E St NW Washington DC 20037-2829

LA ROCCA, ISABELLA, artist; b. El Paso, Apr. 14, 1960; d. Remo and Alicia Estela (Gonzalez) La R. BA, U. Pa., 1984; MFA, Ind. U., 1993. Freelance photographer N.Y.C., 1986-90; assoc. instr. Ind. U., Bloomington, 1991-93; instr. Herron Sch. Art, Indpls., 1992; vis. asst. prof. Ind. U., 1994—; asst. prof. DePauw U., 1994—. One-woman shows include The Ctr. Photography Woodstock, N.Y., Moore Coll., Pa., 1994; exhibited in group shows at Bellevue Gallery, 1992, 494 Gallery, N.Y.C., 1993. Ind. U. CIC Minority fellow, 1990-91; Jewish Found. Edn. Woman scholar, 1990; recipient Friends Photography Ferguson award, 1993.

LAROCCA, PATRICIA DARLENE MCALEER, mathematics educator; b. Aurora, Ill., July 12, 1951; d. Theodore Austin and Lorraine Mae (Robbins) McAleer; m. Edward Daniel LaRocca, June 28, 1975; children: Elizabeth S., Mark E. BS in Edn./Math., No. Ill. U., 1973, postgrad., 1975. Tchr. elem. sch. Roselle (Ill) Sch. Dist., 1973-80; instr. math. Coll. DuPage, Glen Ellyn, Ill., 1980—; pvt. cons., Downers Grove, Ill. Bd. dirs. PTA, Hillcrest Elem. Sch., Downers Grove; active Boy Scouts Am.; mem. 1st United Meth. Ch. Ill. teaching scholar, 1969. Methodist. Home and Office: 5648 Dunham Rd Downers Grove IL 60516-1246

LAROCCO, PATRICIA CREA, physician; b. Woodbury, N.J., July 29, 1949. BS, Immaculata Coll., 1971; MD, U. N.C., 1986. Resident in ob-gyn. Cooper Hosp., Camden, N.J., 1986-87; transitional medicine resident Albert Einstein Med. Ctr., Phila., 1992-93; resident in pathology Temple U. Hosp., Phila., 1993—. V.p. Bd. Edn., Willingboro, N.J., 1992-93, pres., 1993-94. Home: 22 North Pl Willingboro NJ 08046-1323

LA ROCHE, MARIE-ELAINE, investment banker; b. N.Y.C., Aug. 17, 1949; d. Andre and Madeleine (Hanin) LaR.; 3 children. BS in Internat. Affairs, Georgetown U., 1971; MBA, Am. U., 1978. With equity sales dept. Morgan Stanely Investment Banking Co., N.Y.C., 1978-81, v.p. investment banking, 1981-84; v.p. investment banking Morgan Stanely Investment Banking Co., London, 1984-85; prin. mktg. dir. fixed income div. Morgan Stanely Investment Banking Co., N.Y.C., 1985-86, mng. dir. fixed income div., 1986—, mng. dir., dir. worldwide fixed income mktg., 1986-89, mng. dir., dir. pub. fin. dept., 1989-94, firm mgr. Nat. co-chair Women's Campaign Fund; mem. Com. of 200, 1991—; founder WISH List. Named to YWCA Acad. Women Achievers, 1983. Mem. Forum for Women Dirs., Fin. Womens Assn. of N.Y. Republican. Roman Catholic. Office: Morgan Stanley & Co Inc 1251 Ave of the Americas New York NY 10020-1001

LAROSE, NANCY JEAN, fiberglass manufacturer; b. Lowell, Mass., Nov. 9, 1949; d. George Michael and Jean E. (Coffin) LaR.; m. Michael W. Marks, Jan. 5, 1970 (div. Feb. 1972). Grad., high sch., 1967. Night supr. Swim Industries, Largo, Fla., 1980-86; asst. plant mgr. Blue Dolphin Pools, Largo, 1986-92; field cons. Fibretech, Largo, 1992-94; owner LaRose Fiberglass, St. Petersburg, Fla., 1994—. Mem. NAFE, AARP, Nat. Parks and Conservation, Smithsonian Instn., Police Benevolence Assn. Christian. Home and Office: 3237 Prescott St N St Petersburg FL 33713

LARREY, INGE HARRIETTE, jazz and blues freelance photographer; b. Freiburg, Germany, Jan. 21, 1934; came to U.S., 1983; d. Friedrich W. and Claerle I. (Mueller) Luger; m. Toni Halter, Aug. 5, 1967 (div. 1977); m. Louis A. Larrey, June 13, 1981. Student, N.Y. Inst. Photography, Saudi Arabia, 1983. Au Pair, Finland, 1952; Various assignments Federal Republic of Germany in Turkey, Spain, Belgium, England, 1956-82; audit student in journalism, photography U. Houston, 1984; substitute employee with consulate gen. Federal Republic of Germany, Houston, 1985; visitors' Relations German real estate company, Houston, 1985—. Works shown in more than a dozen exhbns., 1986-91; photographs in pvt. collections, in various publs., on cassette, record covers. Vol. Houston FotoFest, Women's Caucus for Art. Mem. Nat. Mus. of Women in the Arts (charter), Am. Image News Svc., Cultural Arts Coun. of Houston, Friends of Photography, Houston Ctr. for Photography, Jazz Heritage Soc. Tex., Milt Larkin Jazz Soc. (founding). Office: Sueba USA Corp 1800 W Loop S # 1323 Houston TX 77027

LARRIMORE, PATSY GADD, nursing administrator; b. Knoxville, Tenn., Feb. 18, 1933; d. Harry Collins and Frances (Irwin) Gadd; m. Walter Eugene Larrimore; children: Patricia J. Titus, Walter Eugene Jr., Beverly Calderon. BS, Johns Hopkins U., 1976, MEd, 1977. RN. Pediatric supr. Johns Hopkins Hosp., Balt., 1960-68; supr. critical care South Balt. Gen. Hosp., 1968-78; DON Hosp. for Sick Children, Washington, 1978-84; field rep. Joint Commn. Accreditation Hosp., Chgo., 1984—; dir. nursing Bon Secours Hosp., Balt., 1987-88; assoc. dir. clin. affairs Paralyzed Vets. Am., Washington, 1989-92; pres. Diabetes Action Rsch. and Edn. Found., Inc., Washington, 1991-92; asst. prof. nursing and allied health Catonsville Community Coll., Balt. Contbr. articles to profl. jours. Bd. dirs. Christian Relief Svcs., Alexandria, Va., 1987-92. Recipient Bronze Svc. award Am. Heart Assn., 1981, Md. affiliate Silver Disting. Svc. award, 1980, Cen. Md. chpt. Bronze Svc. Recognition medallion, 1982, Md. chpt. Founder's award Am. Heart Assn., 1978, D.C. Hosp. Svc. award, 1982. Mem. Am. Heart Assn. (bd. dirs. Balt. chpt. 1972-84, Md. chpt. 1978-85, Bronze Service award Md. affiliate 1981, Silver Disting. Service Cen. Md. chpt. 1980, Bronze Service Recognition award, 1979), Am. Assn. Critical Care Nurses, Am. Nurses Assn., Advanced Nursing Adminstrn., Assn. Care Children's Health (bd. dirs. 1981-82), Am. Soc. Nursing Service Adminstrs., Am. Assn. Spinal Cord Injury Nurses, Phi Delta Kappa. Home: 108 Mountain Rd Linthicum Heights MD 21090-1736

LARROCA, MELEAH STEPHENS, accountant; b. Bolivar, Mo., May 8, 1964; d. Gerald Frank and Helen Marie (Talley) Stephens; m. Raymond Gil Larroca, Aug. 14, 1988. BA, U. Mo., 1986. Acctg.mgr. Nat. Capital Mgmt., San Francisco, 1986-88; controller The Gordon Group, San Francisco, 1988-91, v.p. fin., CFO, 1992—. Office: The Gordon Group 901 Battery St San Francisco CA 94111-1301

LARSEN, ELIZABETH B. (LIBBY LARSEN), composer; b. Wilmington, Del., Dec. 24, 1950; m. James Reece, Sept. 6, 1975; 1 child. BA, U. Minn., 1971, MA, 1975, PhD, 1978. co-founder Minn. Composers Forum. Composer operas Silver Fox, 1979, Tumbledown Dick, 1980, Clair de Lune, 1984, Frankenstein, The Modern Prometheus, 1990, A Wrinkle in Time, 1992, Mrs. Dalloway, 1993; orchestral and chamber works Symphony: Water Music, 1985, Four on the Floor, 1983, Overture: Parachute Dancing, 1983; choral and solo vocal works: Coming Forth into Day, 1986, Missa Gaia, 1992. RecipientDisting. Alumni award U. Minn., 1987, Catherine Steward award, 1991, Grammy award, 1994; named Exxon/Rockefeller composer in residence, Minn. Orch., 1983-87. Address: 2205 Kenwood Pkwy Minneapolis MN 55405

LARSEN, ETHEL PAULSON, retired secondary school educator; b. Superior, Wis., Jan. 24, 1918; d. Ole Peter Paulson and Petra Marie (Boardsen) Gilbertson; m. James Eugene Larsen, June 13, 1943; children: Robert, Karen Larsen DePalermo, Deborah Larsen Farmer, Candice Larsen Herrera. AA, Kendall Coll., 1940; student, U. Wis., 1940-44; BS, SW Tex. U., 1960; postgrad., U. Tex., 1961-67. Tchr. Lakefield (Minn.) Pub. Schs., 1944-46; credit mgr. Sagebiel's Automotive Parts, Seguin, Tex., 1948-49; supervisory clk. supply Edward Gary AFB, San Marcos, Tex., 1951-56; property/acctg. chief Gary Army Air Field, San Marcos, 1956-59; tchr. Seguin High Sch., 1960-80; substitute tchr. Seguin Pub. Schs., 1981-83; reporter, photographer Seguin Citizen newspaper, 1981; now ret.; developer speech-journalism curriculum, Minn. State Bd. Edn., 1945; pres. AAUW, Seguin, 1965-66, Seguin Classroom Tchrs., 1971-72; del. to Tex. State Tchrs. Assn., Austin, 1970. Founding mem. York Creek Flood Prevention Dist. for Hays, Comal and Guadalupe counties, 1953-54; Voice of Democracy chair VFW Aux., Geronimo, Tex., 1970-78; writer radio scripts for improved farm-city rels., 1956; vol. tax aide, Seguin, 1987-90; Circle leader 1st United Meth. Ch., Seguin, 1989—; mem. T.B. Bd. Guadalupe County, 1954-57. Mem. Nat. Writers Club, Seguin Garden Club, Seguin-Guadalupe County Ret. Tchrs. (pres. 1990—), Nat. Coun. State Garden Clubs, Inc. (life), Tex. Garden Clubs, Inc. (life), Tex. State Garden Clubs (life, Tex. dist. VII), Tex. Agrl. Ext. Svc. (master gardener), Order Ea. Star, Oakwood Art Group, Delta Kappa Gamma (Theta Kappa chpt. pres. 1978-80). Home: 1619 Driftwood St Seguin TX 78155-5211

LARSEN, PAULA ANNE, operating room nurse; b. Norfolk, Va., Oct. 2, 1962; d. Larry Gene and Sue Frances (Williams) P. ADN, Labette C.C., 1982. RN, Mo.; CNOR, TNCC. Lab. asst. Labette County Med. Ctr., Parsons, Kans., 1979-82; RN operating rm. St. John's Regional Med. Ctr., Joplin, Mo., 1982-85, RN oper. rm., shift coord., 1989-94; head nurse Mason Gen. Hosp., Shelton, Wash., 1994—; with Mo. Lions Eye Bank, 1989-94. Mem. adv. coun. Organ and Tissue Donation. Mem. Assn. Operating Rm. Nurses (del. 1991). Republican. Baptist. Office: Mason Gen Hosp 901 Mountain View Dr Bldg 1 Shelton WA 98584

LARSON, DIANE LAVERNE KUSLER, principal; b. Fredonia, N.D., July 28, 1942; d. Raymond Edwin and LaVerne (Mayer) Kusler; m. Donald Floyd Larson, Aug. 14, 1965. BS, Valley City (N.D.) State U., 1964; MS, Mankato (Minn.) State U., 1977; EdS, U. Minn., 1987. Cert. tchr., Minn. Tchr. elem. Cokato (Minn.) Elem. Sch., 1962-64, Lakeview Elem. Sch., Robbinsdale, Minn., 1964-66; vocal tchr. Wheaton (Minn.) High Sch., 1966-67; tchr. Owatonna (Minn.) Elem. Sch., 1967-88, prin., 1988—; v.p. Cannon Valley Uniserv, Mankato, 1981-83; NEA del. World Confederation of Orgns. of the Teaching Professions, Melbourne, 1988. Named Woman of Yr., Owatonna Bus. and Profl. Women, 1990. Mem. NEA (bd. dirs. 1986-88), Minn. Edn. Assn. (bd. dirs. 1983-88, Outstanding Woman in Leadership award 1983), Minn. Reading Assn. (bd. dirs. 1983—, Pres. award 1984), Internat. Reading Assn. (coord. for Minn. 1990—), Minn. Elem. Prins. Assn., Delta Kappa Gamma (legis. chmn. 1986—, pres. 1992, Woman of Achievement award 1989, Tau leadership chair). Congregationalist. Home: 19654 Bagley Ave Faribault MN 55021-7732 Office: Washington Sch 338 E Main St Owatonna MN 55060-3696

LARSON, GAYLE ELIZABETH, public relations professional; b. Vancouver, Wash., Nov. 5, 1942; d. Edwin Ellis and Lois Marguerite (Wilson) L. Student, U. Mex., 1963; BA in Spanish lang. and lit., Wash. State U., 1964; cert. in Hispanic studies, U. Madrid, 1970; postgrad., City U. Portland, 1983. Flight attendant, purser Pan Am. Airlines, N.Y.C., 1965-69; bilingual asst. Touche, Ross Internat., Madrid, 1969-73; mgr. sales and pub. rels. Westin Hotels, Portland, Oreg., 1979-84; dir. pub. rels. Columbia River coun. Girl Scouts U.S., Portland, 1986-89; freelance writer, cons. Vancouver, 1989—; workshop presenter Women in Communications, 1984; pub. rels. cons. Make a Wish Found., Portland, 1989; mentor talented and gifted program Portland Pub. Schs., 1989; tchr. English as 2d lang. Mangold Inst., Madrid, 1970. Novelist: Senorita Blonde, 1989, The Fraudulent Monk, 1991. Mem. Pub. Rels. Soc. Am. (Silver Anvil commendation 1989), Women in Communications (v.p. spl. events 1987), Willamette Writers, Quill and Scroll. Home: 2808 S St Vancouver WA 98663

LARSON, JACQUELYNNE BORST (PENNY LARSON), real estate auction executive; b. Glens Falls, N.Y., Nov. 3, 1938; d. Jacque Becker and Madeline (Edmunds) Borst; m. Donald F. Larson, Apr. 4, 1957 (div. Feb. 1981); children—Daniel, David, Christy. Student U. Ill., 1956-57. Lic. real estate salesperson. Sole propr. Larson Enterprises, Glenview, Ill., 1960-72; controller Ada S. McKinley Community Services, Chgo., 1973-82; exec. v.p. Kaufman Lasman Assocs., Inc., Chgo., 1982-86; chief exec. officer Fed. Auction Service Corp., 1986-88; chief ops. officer Larry Latham Auctioneers, 1988-90; dir. nat. auction programs Resolution Trust Corp, 1990—. Officer, bd. dirs. LWV, Glenview, 1973-74, North Shore Assn. for Retarded, Evanston, 1969-71; mem. East Maine Dist. 63 Sch. Bd., Des Plaines, Ill., 1974-79; deacon Presby. Ch. of Glenview, 1974. Recipient $25 Million Sales award Kaufman Lasman Assocs., 1985, Silver Anvil award Pub. Rels. Soc. Am., 1992. Mem. Nat. Assn. Realtors, Chgo. Real Estate Bd. (Salesperson of Yr. 1985, 86). Home: 4342 Redwood Ave Apt 216 Pacific Palisades CA 90272

LARSON, JANE RUTH SCHAEDIGER, non-profit organization administrator; b. Englewood, N.J., Sept. 27, 1939; d. Alvin Henry and Ruth Louise (Otterbein) S.; m. James Roderick Larson, Oct. 21, 1961; children: Linda Jane Larson Daniel, Debra Jane Larson. BS in Edn., Wittenberg U., 1961; postgrad., U. Toledo, 1970. p. 6th grade classroom tchr. Toledo Pub. Schs., 1961-63; elem. sch. music tchr. Sylvania (Ohio) City Schs., 1970-86; staff aide part-time Nat. Abortion and Reproductive Rights Action League of Ohio, Columbus, 1986-88, interim exec. dir., 1992, data organizer, office mgr., 1988—. Recipient Dedicated Svc. award Nat. Abortion and Reproductive Rights Action League, 1989. Mem. NOW, LWV, AAUW (program and policy chair, Ohio campaign for choice coord. 1989-91, testified for women's reproductive rights 1991, Community Svc. award 1990), Ohio Women, Inc. (exec. bd., equality day award com. 1992—), Religious Coalition for Reproductive Rights. Home: 3111 Rivermill Dr Columbus OH 43220 Office: NARAL Ohio 760 E Broad St Columbus OH 43205

LARSON, JANE WARREN, ceramist; b. San Francisco, June 2, 1922; d. Stafford Leak and Viola (Lockhart) Warren; m. Clarence Ernest Larson, Apr. 21, 1957; children: Lawrence Ernest, Lance Stafford. Student, Swarthmore Coll., 1939-41; BA with honors, U. Rochester, 1943; MFA in Ceramics, Antioch Coll., 1982. Tech. editor Tenn. Eastman Corp., Oak Ridge, 1943-46; chief Tech. Info. Ctr. Carbide & Carbon Chem. Corp., Oak Ridge, 1946-51; tech. editor physics div. Rand Corp., Santa Monica, Calif., 1954-55; tech. editor libr. Rand Corp., Washington, 1955-57; ceramist Janeware, Santa Monica, 1953-55; pres., bldg. founder Oak Ridge Community Art Ctr., 1963-66, ceramic tchr., 1965-69; ceramic tchr. Inst. Learning in Retirement Am. U., Washington, 1985-88, 94. One-person shows at AAAS, Washington, 1990, Studio Gallery, Washington, 1992, others 1973—; group shows at Bader Gallery and others, 1971—, Internat. Sculpture Conf., Washington, 1990; mural artist Guest Quarters Hotel gardens, Bethesda, Md., 1987, Oak Ridge Com. Art Ctr. garden, 1992, Fed. City Shelter, Washington, 1988; sculptor Johns Hopkins Ctr. Internat. Studies, Washington, 1990, Nat. Acad. Engring., Beckman Ctr., Irvine, Calif., 1990, U. Md., College Park, 1994—, Asia Nora Restaurant, Washington, 1994; contbr. articles and reviews to profl. jours.; commns. include 4 murals 20 vases Germaines Restaurant, Washington, 1978, lobby mural Nat. Milk Producers Assn., Rosslyn, Va., 1983, Office Tech. Assessment, 1994, others. Commr. Cable TV Commn., Montgomery County, Rockville, Md., 1989-90. Mem. Ind. Agy. Women (pres. 1964-65), Kiln Club Washington (1st prize ann. show 1993), Achievement Rewards Coll. Sci., Inc. (v.p. 1980-81), Artists Equity, Internat. Sculpture Ctr., Bethesda Ceramic Guild, Studio Gallery (1st prize ann. show 1994), Phi Beta Kappa. Home and Office: 6514 Bradley Blvd Bethesda MD 20817-3248

LARSON, JEANETTE CAROLYN, library consultant; b. Ft. Dix, N.J., Sept. 16, 1952; d. Wilbur Arthur and Carolyn Linda (Baker) Pawson; m. James Warren Larson, Jan. 31, 1975. BA, U. N.Mex., 1974; MS in Libr. Sci., U. So. Calif., 1979. Libr. Anaheim (Calif.) Pub. Libr., 1977-79; children's libr. Irving (Tex.) Pub. Libr., 1979-80; children's libr. Mesquite (Tex.) Pub. Libr., 1980-85, supr. pub. svc., 1985-91; mgr. continuing edn. and cons. Tex. State Libr., Austin, 1991—; cons. Larson Assocs., Austin, 1991—. Author: Animal Antics, 1987, Secret Code is READ, 1990; reviewer Booklist, 1985; contbr. articles to libr. jours. Bd. dirs. Prodrs.: Vols. for USA, Film Fest Dallas, 1989-91; vol. Reading is Fundamental, Austin, 1992-95, Humane Soc. Austin, 1991-93. Mem. ALA (Shirley Olofson award 1982), AAUW, Tex. Libr. Assn. (Outstanding New Libr. award 1987), Dallas County Libr. Assn. (pres. 1985-86), Beta Phi Mu. Democrat. Home: 7300 Geneva Dr Austin TX 78723 Office: Tex State Libr 1201 Brazos St Austin TX 78701

LARSON, KATHERINE ELIZABETH, elementary school counselor; b. Kenmare, N.D., Aug. 13, 1948; d. Robert Merton and Ruby Mary (Peterson) H.; m. Allen Lynn Larson, June 24, 1973; children: Chantel Justine, Paige Katherine, Brady Allen. BS, N.D. State U., 1970; MEd in Guidance and Counseling, No. State U., 1993. Jr. high home econs. tchr. Hardin (Mont.) Pub. Sch., 1970-71; home econs./social sci. tchr. Burke Ctrl. Pub. Sch., Lignite, N.D., 1971-91; elem. sch. counselor Kenmare (N.D.) Pub. Sch., 1991—; regional cons. N.D. Sch. Counselor, Kenmare, 1994. Mission/community rep. Christ Luth. Ch. Women, Lignite, N.D., 1994, alter com., work group leader, Sunday sch. tchr. Mem. Am. Sch. Counselors Assn., N.D. Sch. Counselors Assn., Kenmare Edn. Assn. (past pres. local chpt.), Am. Legion Aux. (past sec.), Internat. Curling Club. Home: PO Box 227 Lignite ND 58752-0227 Office: Kenmare Pub Sch PO Box 667 Kenmare ND 58746-0667

LARSON, LEONE ADRIENNE, funeral director, embalmer; b. Oelwein, Iowa, Aug. 29, 1964; d. Adrian Spencer Larson and Genevieve Ann (Schnuelle) Milbrandt. Student in pre-mortuary studies, William Penn Coll., 1986-88; A in Applied Funeral Svc., New England Inst. Applied Arts & Scis., 1989. Cert. lic. funeral dir., embalmer, life ins. agt. Asst. to funeral dir. Garland-Van Arkle Langkamp, Oskaloosa, Iowa, 1986-88; apprentice to funeral dir. James f. O'Donnell & Sons, Inc., Lowell, Mass., 1988-90; funeral dir., embalmer John S. Rhodes Funeral Home, St. Petersburg, Fla., 1990-91; pre-need advisor Harris-Martin-Burke Funeral Home, Pontiac, Ill., 1991-93; field rep. The Forethought Group, St. Louis, 1993-94; family svc. counselor Doane, Beal & Ames Funeral Home, South Yarmouth, Mass., 1994—. Vol. Big Brother/Big Sister, Lowell, Mass., 1988-90, County Coronors campaign, Bloomington, Ill., 1992, Emergency Rm. and Health Care Proxy Cape Cod Hosp. Recipient Alumni award New England Inst., 1989; scholar Am. Bd. Funeral Svc., 1988, Iowa Funeral Dirs.' Assn., 1988. Mem. Am. Bus. Women's Assn. (co-chair), Talisman Internat. (founding bd. dirs., sec. 1993—), Jr. Women's Club. Republican. Lutheran. Home: 25 Waterfield Rd Osterville MA 02655 Office: Doane Beal & Ames Funeral Home 1372 Bridge St South Yarmouth MA 02664

LARSON, LORALEE, fiscal officer; b. St. Louis, July 2, 1933; d. Karl Ferdinand and Josephine Irene (Biggs) Jenz; m. Tony J. Larson, Sept. 3, 1993; children: Melvin K. Rosner, Stephen M. Rosner. AA, Laramie County C.C., 1971; BSBA, Chapman U., 1987. Asst. to dist. mgr. P. Lorillard Co., Cheyenne, Wyo., 1957-77; sec. Wyo. Agr. Dept. Plant Sci. Divsn., Cheyenne, 1976, Wyo. House Appropriations Com., Cheyenne, 1975-76, Wyo. Legis. Svc. Office, Cheyenne, 1976-87; fiscal officer Wyo. Legis., Cheyenne, 1988—; job coach Magic City Enterprises, Cheyenne, 1987-92. Treas. Laramie County Rep. Womens Club, Cheyenne, 1963-75, X-JWC, Cheyenne, 1968, Civic League, Cheyenne, 1972-73; sec. Laramie County Rep. Ctrl. Com., Cheyenne, 1975-76. Roman Catholic. Home: 3521 Cleveland Ave Cheyenne WY 82001-2140 Office: State of Wyo Legis Svc Rm 213 State Capitol Bldg Cheyenne WY 82002

LARSON, MARY BEA, elementary education educator; b. Brookings, S.D., Apr. 19, 1946; d. Theodore Orville and Doris Rose (Conway) Larson; children: Christie DiRé, Corey DiRe. BA, Wash. State U., 1968, Portland State U., 1973; MA, U. Guam, 1975; postgrad., Seattle Pacific U. Cert. tchr., Wash. Tchr. early childhood and creativity Chemeketa C. C., Salem, Oreg.; tchr. kindergarten-1st grade Govt. Guam, Agana; tchr. kindergarten, 3rd grade Canal Zone Govt., Balboa; tchr. kindergarten, 2d and 3d grades, elem. art specialist Marysville (Wash.) Sch. Dist.; mem. profl. adv. bd. coll. edn. Western Wash. U., 1989—. Active Snohomish County Arts Coun. Mem. NEA (del. to Nat. Rep. Assembly, Washington 1992, San Francisco 1993), Wash. Edn. Assn., Marysville Edn. Assn. (pres. 1990-92), Nat. Mus. Women in Arts, Seattle Art Mus. (landmark), Alpha Delta Kappa (state sgt.-at-arms 1990-92, state chaplain 1992-94, state v.p. 1994—). Home: 15605 N Spring Tree Ct SE Mill Creek WA 98012-5825

LARSON, NANCY CELESTE, computer systems analyst, music educator; b. Chgo., July 17, 1951; d. Melvin Ellsworth and Ruth Margaret (Carlson) L. BS in Music Ed., U. Ill., 1973, MS in Music Edn., 1976; postgrad., Purdue Univ., 1982-86. Vocal music educator Consol. Sch. Dist., Gilman, Ill., 1975-77; elem. vocal music tchr. Sch. Dist. 161, Flossmoor, Ill., 1977-87; instr. Vander Cook Coll., Chgo., 1980-88; systems programmer analyst Sears, Roebuck & Co., Chgo., 1987-92, tech. instr., 1989-90, project leader, 1990-91, sr. systems analyst, 1991-92; sr. systems analyst Trans Union Corp., Chgo., 1992—, project mgr., 1994, mgr., 1994—; tchr. adult computer edn. Homewood-Flossmoor High Sch., 1986-90. Chmn. Faith Luth. Ch., 1982-87, pres. bd., 1988-91, vocal soloist and voice-over performer. Mem. Ill. Music Educators Assn., Music Educators Nat. Conf., Ill. Educators Assn., Nat. Educators Assn., Am. ORFF Schulwerk Assn., Flossmoor Edn. Assn. (negotiator 1983-86). Republican. Lutheran. Office: Trans Union Corp 555 W Adams Chicago IL 60606

LARWOOD, LAURIE, psychologist; b. N.Y., 1941; PhD, Tulane U., 1974. Pres., Davis Instruments Corp., San Leandro, Calif., 1966-71, cons., 1969—; asst. prof. organizational behavior SUNY, Binghamton, 1974-76; assoc. prof. psychology, chairperson dept., assoc. prof. bus. adminstrn. Claremont (Calif.) McKenna Coll., 1976-83, Claremont Grad. Sch., 1976-85; prof., head dept. mgmt. U. Ill.-Chgo., 1983-87; dean sch. bus. SUNY, Albany, 1987-90; dean Coll. Bus. Adminstrn., U. Nev., Reno, 1990-92; dir. Inst. Strategic Bus. Issues, 1992—; mem. western regional advisory coun. SBA, 1976-81; dir. The Mgmt. Team; pres. Mystic Games, Inc. Mem. Acad. Mgmt. (editorial rev. bd. Rev. 1977-82, past chmn. women in mgmt. div., managerial consultation-tech. and innovation div.); chair Am. Psychol. Assn., Assn. Women in Psychology. Author: (with M.M. Wood) Women in Management, 1977; Organizational Behavior and Management, 1984, Women's Career Development, 1987, Strategies-Successes-Senior Executives Speak Out, 1988, Women's Careers, 1988, Managing Technological Development, 1988; mem. editorial bd. Sex Roles, 1979—, Consultation, 1986-91, Jour. Organizational Behavior, 1987—, Group and Orgn. Mgmt., 1982-84, editor, 1986—; founding editor Women and Work, 1983, Jour. Mgmt. Case Studies, 1983-87; contbr. numerous articles, papers to profl. jours. Home: 2855 Sagittarius Dr Reno NV 89509-3885 Office: U Nev Coll Bus Adminstrn Reno NV 89557

LASALLE, JOAN MARIE, design engineer; b. Johnstown, Pa., Sept. 18, 1957; d. Richard Philip and Barbara Ann (Knapp) Chiappelli; m. Charles LaSalle, Jr., Sept. 29, 1984; 1 child, Richard Anthony. BS in Civil Engring. Tech., U. Pitts., Johnstown, Pa., 1984. Registered profl. engr., Pa. Tow truck operator, bookkeeper Breezewood (Pa.) Garage, 1975-79; press rm. helper Std. Register Corp, Bedford, Pa., 1979-80; summer intern Pa. Dept. Transp., Hollidaysburg, 1984; constrn. inspector Larsen Engrs./Architects, Rochester, N.Y., 1985; constrn. inspector Eads Group, Altoona, Pa., 1985, 86, jr. hwy. engr., constrn. inspector, 1986-87; project engr. JLG Industries Inc., McConnellsburg, Pa., 1987—. Ch. organist Breezewood United Meth. Ch., 1992-94. Home: PO Box 69 Breezewood PA 15533 Office: JLG Industries Inc JLG Dr McConnellsburg PA 17233

LASATER, SANDRA JO, nurse; b. Cookeville, Tenn., Jan. 20, 1948; d. Herbert Hershel and Bunola Christine (Jones) Garrett; m. Richard Lee Lasater Jr., July 21, 1973; children: Becky, Beth, Bonnie, Lee, Scott. Diploma, St. Thomas Sch. Nursing, 1970; BSN, Vanderbilt U., 1972, MSN, 1973. Cert. urology registered nurse. Child psychiatry head nurse, coord. Vanderbilt Univ. Hosp., Nashville, 1970-73; clin. instr. Univ. Tenn., Nashville, 1975-77; asst. dir. nursing, RN operating rm. Cookeville (Tenn.) Gen. Hosp., 1977-81; adminstrv. dir., drug info. and treatment Cumberland Med. Ctr., Crossville, Tenn., 1981-82; DON White County Community Hosp., Sparta, Tenn., 1982-84; clin. instr. Columbia (Tenn.) State Community Coll., 1984-85; supr. operating rm. Bedford County Hosp., Shelbyville, Tenn., 1984-85; RN ambulatory care Alvin C. York VA Med. Ctr., Murfreesboro, Tenn., 1985—; nursig cons. to Spl. Projects/Guardcare, Tenn. Army N.G. Contbr. articles to profl. jours. Vol. nurse ARC, Nashville, 1973. Lt. col. Army Nurse Corp., 1979—, with Operation Desert Storm, 1991. Mem. Tenn. Army Nat. Guard Officer Assn. Home: 705 Cason Ln Murfreesboro TN 37129-4832

LASHER, ESTHER LU, minister; b. Denver, June 1, 1923; d. Lindley Aubrey and Irma Jane (Rust) Pim; m. Donald T. Lasher, Apr. 9, 1950 (dec. Mar. 1982); children: Patricia Sue Becker, Donald T., Keith Alan, Jennifer Luanne Oliver. Assoc. Fine Arts, Colo. Women's Coll., 1943; BA, Denver U., 1945; MA Religious Edn., Ea. Bapt. Sem., 1948; MA, Denver U., 1967. Ordained to ministry Bapt. Ch., 1988. Christian edn. dir. 1st Bapt., Evansville, Ind., 1948-52; minister Perrysburg Bapt. Ch., Macy, Ind., 1988—; libr. Peru (Ind.) Pub. Schs., 1990-91; sec. Ind. Ministerial Coun., Indpls., 1990-92; chairperson Women in Ministry, Indpls., 1988-93; chmn. Fellowship Mission Circle, Rochester, Ind., 1988-93; mem. Partnership in Ministry, Indpls., 1990-94; bd. mgrs. Am. Bapts./Ind., 1991-93. Pres. Toastmasters,

Rochester, 1991-92, edn. v.p., 1992-93; asst. dir. Greenwood Pub. Libr., 1977-85; dir. Fulton County Pub. Libr., 1985-90; bd. dirs. Manitau Tng. Ctr., Rochester, 1988-90; v.p. Mental Helath Ctr., Rochester, 1987-90; founder Fulton County Literacy Coalition, Rochester, 1989-90; tutor/trainer Peru Literacy Coalition of Peru Pub. Libr., 1994—; sec. Northwest Area ABC/IN, 1994—; sec.-treas. North Miami County Mins. Fellowship, 1993—; bd. dirs. Peru Civic Ctr., 1995—. Named Outstanding Libr., Biog. Inst., 1989. Mem. Leadership Acad. (bd. dirs. 1988-90), Ministers Coun. Ind. (bd. dirs., sec.), Bus. and Profl. Women (pres. Greenwood, Ind. chpt. 1984-86), Rochester Women's Club (pres. 1989-92), Fulton County Mins. Assn. (treas. 1993—), Logansport Assn. Bapt. Women (pres. 1992-94), Peru Bus. and Profl. Women, Peru Lit. Club, CASA Miami County, Rotary, Sigma Alpha Iota (advisor). Republican. Home: 1117 Rosewood Dr Peru IN 46970-3020 Office: Perrysburg Bapt Ch PO Box 196 Macy IN 46951-0196

LASHGARI, DEIRDRE EBERLY, English literature educator, editor, translator; b. Ann Arbor, Mich., Apr. 7, 1941; d. Ralph Dunbar and Katherine (Causey) Eberly; m. Woody Nance. BA in English and French, U. Calif., Berkeley, 1963, MA in English, 1965, MA in Near Ea. Langs., 1968, PhD in Comparative Subjects Lit., 1987. Freelance writer, translator, editor Berkeley, 1970-89; asst. prof. English Calif. State Poly. U., Pomona, 1989-92, assoc. prof., 1992—; freelance writer, translator, editor, Pomona, 1989—. Co-editor: The Other Voice: 20th Century Women's Poetry in Translation, 1976, women Poets of the World, 1983, Violence, Silence, and Anger: Women's Writing as Transgression, 1995; contbr. articles and essays to profl. jours. Fulbright Rsch. fellow Fulbright Agy., U.S. Govt., 1969-70. Mem. MLA, Nat. Coun. Tchrs. English, Nat. Assn. Ethnic Studies, Am. Lit. Translators Assn., Soc. Multi-Ethnic Lits. U.S., Philol. Assn. Pacific Coast. Office: Calif State Poly U Dept English & Fgn Langs 3801 W Temple Ave Pomona CA 91768

LASHNER, MARILYN AUERBACH, communication content analyst, forensic expert; b. Phila., Dec. 11, 1929; d. Jacob and Mildred (Goodrich) Auerbach; m. Melvin Lashner, Aug. 19, 1951; children: Bret Auerbach, Jane Leslie, William Mark, Suzanne. BS in English and Edn., U. Pa., 1950, MS in English and Edn., 1954; PhD in Communications., Temple U., 1979. Cert. secondary English tchr., Pa. Tchr. English, dir. dramatics Cheltenham High Sch., Elkins Park, Pa., 1951-54; instr. English, Pa. State U., Abington, 1967-75; tchr. effective English communication Tng. div. U.S. Civil Svc., Phila., 1974; pres., dir. rsch. Inst. for News Media Analysis, Meadowbrook, Pa., 1979-84; asst. prof. communications Temple U., Phila., 1980-81; prin. researcher Media Analysis & Communicaitons Rsch., Meadowbrook, 1984—; forensic expert on meaning and interpretation of communication content in cases of libel, slander, invasion of privacy, prejudicial publicity, product liability, change of venue, fraudulent advertising, copyright infringement, contract interpretation. Author: The Chilling Effect in TV News: Intimidation by the Nixon White House, 1984; also articles. Recipient 1st place nat. award for First Amendment essay Nat. Assn. Broadcasters, 1977; fellow Temple U., 1976-79. Mem. Nat. Forensic Ctr. for Disting. Experts, Pi Delta Theta. Office: Media Analysis & Comm Rsch PO Box 3165W Meadowbrook PA 19046

LASHOF, JOYCE C., public health educator; b. Phila.; d. Harry and Rose (Brodsky) Cohen; m. Richard K. Lashof, June 11, 1950; children: Judith, Carol, Dan. AB, Duke U., 1946; MD, Women's Med. Coll., 1950; DSc (hon.), Med. Coll. Pa., 1983. Dir. Ill. State Dept. Pub. Health, 1973-77; dep. asst. sec. for health programs and population affairs Dept. Health, Edn., and Welfare, Washington, 1977-78; sr. scholar in residence NAS, Washington, 1978; asst. dir. office of tech. assessment U.S. Congress, Washington, 1978-81; dean sch. pub. health U. Calif., Berkeley, 1981-91, dean emeritus, prof. pub. health Sch. Pub. Health, 1991-94; co-chair Commn. on Am. after Roe vs. Wade, 1991-92; mem. Sec.'s Coun. Health Promotion and Disease Prevention, 1988-91. Recipient Alumni Achievement award Med. Coll. Pa., 1975. Mem. editl. bd. Wellness Letter, 1983—, editl. com. Ann. Rev. of Pub. Health, 1987-90. Home: 601 Euclid Ave Berkeley CA 94708-1331 Office: U Calif-Berkeley Sch Pub Health 19 Earl Warren Hall Berkeley CA 94720

LASKEY, DEBORAH ANN, health systems administrator, consultant; b. Toledo, Nov. 5, 1952; d. Robert C. and Dorothy G. (Miller) L. BBA, U. Toledo, 1991, postgrad., 1991—. Clin. technician Med. Coll. Hosp., Toledo, 1975-81; clin. technician, acute specialist Symed Care, Inc., Toledo, 1981-84; clin. technician Greenfield Health Systems, Toledo, 1984-86, tech. advisor, 1986-89, adminstrv. mgr., 1989—; cons. Doctors Hosp., Columbus, Ohio, 1989—, Aultman Hosp., Canton, Ohio, 1989—, Lima (Ohio) Meml. Hosp., 1989-92, Desert Cities Dialysis, Victorville, Calif., 1991. Contbr. articles to profl. jours. Mem. Maumee Valley Save a Pet, Toledo, 1991—. Mem. Nat. Renal Adminstrs. Assn., Tri State Renal Network, Bd. Nephrology Examiners (regional rep. 1992—). Lutheran. Office: Greenfield Health Systems 3401 Glendale Toledo OH 43614

LASKIN, BARBARA VIRGINIA, legal association administrator; b. Chgo., July 2, 1939; d. Cyril Krieps and Gertrude Katherine (Kujawa) Szymanski; children: Dawn Katherine Doherty, Amy Lynn Anderson. BA, U. Ill., Chgo., 1967; MA, Am. U. Beirut, 1978, Georgetown U., 1985. Asst. buyer Carson, Pirie, Scott & Co., Chgo., 1967-69; fgn. svc. officer Dept. State, Washington, 1969-79; mgr. gift shops Marriott Hotels, Washington, 1979-81; office mgr. Robt Schwinn & Assoc., Bethesda, Md., 1983-85; exec. dir. Internat. Acad. Trial Lawyers, San Jose, Calif., 1985—. Fellow Rotary Club San Jose; mem. AAUW (v.p. 1987), Am. Soc. Assn. Execs., Meeting Planners Internat., Internat. Spl. Events Soc. (v.p. edn. 1995), Profl. Conservation Mgrs. Assn. Roman Catholic. Office: Internat Acad Trial Lawyers 4 N 2nd St Ste 175 San Jose CA 95113-1306

LASLO, LAURA ELIZABETH, security manager, artist; b. Cleve., June 27, 1953; d. George Edward and Elizabeth Ann Laslo. AA, Grossmont Jr. Coll., El Cajon, Calif., 1974; BA, San Diego State U., 1976, cert. in tchg. Art tchr. Cajon Valley Sch. Dist., El Cajon, 1978-79; San Diego County sr. clk. Registrar of Voters, 1979-82; security mgr. Nat. Advanced Sys., San Diego, 1982-83; tech. libr. IVAC Corp., San Diego, 1983-86; tech. libr., security mgr. Logicon, Inc., San Diego, 1987—. One-women shows include All Media Student Art Exhibit, 1976, Bastille Gallery, 1977, Extra Ordinaire Gallery, 1981, San Diego and Mex. Art Exchange, 1982, The Right Bank Art Gallery, 1983, 1620 Lewis St. Gallery, 1986. Hist. commr. La Mesa (Calif.) City, 1990—; mem. San Diego Mus. of Art. Recipient commendation City of La Mesa, 1991. Mem. San Diego Artist Guild. Office: Logicon Inc 200 Catalina Blvd San Diego CA 92147

LASSESEN, CATHERINE AVERY CLAY, small business owner, manager/trainer; b. Corte Madera, CA, Nov. 8, 1961; d. Ralph Kindel Boyland Clay and Susan Avery (Kendall) Clay; m. B. Rune Lassesen, Mar. 2, 1991. BA in Hotel Adminstrn., U. Nev., 1985. Promotions asst. Tropicana Hotel, Las Vegas, Nev., 1985; front desk mgr. Marriott Corp., various locations, 1986-88; mgr. Six Ravens Ranch, Boonville, Calif., 1988—, CEO, 1988-92; owner/mgr. Custom Engraving by Catherine, Boonville, Calif., 1989—; co-owner, trainer Bridgegate Stables & Tack Barn One, Boonville, 1991-93; owner, instr. Flying Colors An Equine Edn. Svc. Six Ravens Ranch, Boonville, Calif., 1994—. Publicity dir. Mendocino County Fair and Apple Show, 1992-94. Named one of the Women of Yr., Clark County, Las Vegas, Nev., 1986. Mem. Ind. Career Women (historian 1991-92, v.p. 1992-93), U. Nev. Las Vegas Alumni Assn., Delta Zeta (province alumnae dir. 1991-93), Am. Vaulting Assn., Am. Quarter Horse Assn., N.Am. Horseman Assn., Am. Horse Show Assn., Calif. Gymkhana Assn. (judge 1992—, dist. 37 pres. 1992-93, co-chmn. 1993-94), N.Am. Riding for the Handicapped Assn., Inc. Office: Six Ravens Ranch Box 298 19500 Mountain View Rd Boonville CA 95415-0298

LASSITER, PAMELA MARIA, equal employment opportunity manager; b. Norfolk, Va., Nov. 19, 1960; d. Mary Magdeline Reid. BA in Econs. & Sociology, CUNY, 1982; JD, U. Va., 1985. Law clk. U.S. Dept. Transp./ Nat. Hwy. Traffic Safety Office, Washington, 1985, Akin, Gump, Strauss, Haver & Feld, Washington, 1986, Fried, Frank, Harris, Shriver & Jacobson, Washington, 19876; EEO compliance officer U.S. Dept. Labor/Employment Stds. Adminstrn., N.Y.C., 1988-89; EEO complaint officer N.Y.C. Bd. Edn./ Human Resources/Office of Equal Opportunity, Bklyn., 1989; sr. EEO rep. Empire Blue Cross/Blue Shield Human Resources/EEO, N.Y.C., 1989-91; EEO adminstr. The CIT Group, Inc., Livingston, N.J., 1991—. Author seminars, 1991-92. Mem. Nat. Assn. Exec. Women. Democrat. Roman Catholic. Office: The CIT Group Inc 650 Cit Dr # 1150 Livingston NJ 07039-5703

LASSITER, SYBIL MAE, nursing educator, consultant; b. Chgo., Apr. 24, 1928; D. Aubrey and Lillian (Thomas) Pollard; m. Vincent P. James, June 28, 1958 (div. June 1978); children: Yasmine James Evans, Viviene James Mott, Courtney. RN, Bellevue Sch. Nursing, 1951; BSN, CUNY, 1956; MS in Edn., St. John's U., 1969; PhD in Nursing Theory, NYU, 1985. Cert. nurse tchr., health tchr., N.Y. Asst. head nurse Bellevue and N.Y. Hosp., N.Y.C., 1951-53; pub. health nurse N.Y.C. Dept. Health, 1953-56; nursing sci. instr. St. John's Episcopal Sch. Nursing, N.Y.C., 1956-60; med.-surg. instr. Flushing Hosp. Sch. Nursing, N.Y.C., 1962-65; pub. sch. tchr., dean N.Y.C. Bd. Edn., 1965-70; sch. nurse tchr. Herricks Pub. Sch. System, Nassau, N.Y., 1970-73; assoc. prof. nursing Adelphi U., Garden City, N.Y., 1974-90, East Tenn. State U., Johnson City, 1992—; health and drugs cons. N.Y. State Dept. Edn., N.Y.C., 1973-74; tchr., supr. NYU Hosps., 1962-85; regents coll. degree examiner SUNY, Albany, 1986-89; cons. doctoral students Adelphi U., Garden City, 1985-91; leader health discussions Indigent Mothers-Roosevelt (N.Y.) Sch., 1989-91; presenter seminars on assertiveness Headstart tchrs., Nassau, 1988-90. Contbr. articles to profl. jours. Mem. steering com. Breast Cancer project Dept. Health, Nassau, 1988-90; vol. Dem. Orgn., Hempstead, N.Y., 1988-91; bd. dirs. Unity Ch. of Christianity, Valley Stream, N.Y., 1989-92. Recipient doctoral scholarship Helena Rubenstein, 1979-80, Art Merit award Town of Hempstead, 1990, Rsch. award Nursing Rsch. Project, Adelphi U., 1984; rsch. grantee Sigma Theta Tau, 1986. Mem. Assn. Black Nursing Faculty in Higher Edn., L.I. Black Artists, One Hundred Black Women of L.I. Home: 112 Heather Ln Stanmore Estates Johnson City TN 37601

LASSUS, JOANN CAROL, comedienne; b. Huntington, N.Y., Aug. 8, 1960; d. Edmund Menvielle and Audrey Katherine (Vickerman) L. BA in Comm./English, Hofstra U., 1982. Copywriter WLIR-FM, Hempstead, N.Y., 1984-86; pers. liaison Ally & Gargano, N.Y.C., 1986-87; asst. dean admissions Hofstra U., Hempstead, 1987-91; self-employed comedienne, writer, 1990—. Author: (screenplay) A Quiet Summer Waltz, 1993. Featured on cover of Newsday mag., 1993. Mem. United Uterine Front, Eastside Players. Home: 234 Mallard Rd Carle Place NY 11514

LAST, MARIAN HELEN, social services administrator; b. L.A., July 2, 1953; d. Henry and Renee (Kahan) Last. BA, Pitzer Coll., 1975; postgrad., U. So. Calif., 1975-84; MS, Long Beach State U., 1980. Lic. marriage therapist. Coordinator City of El Monte, Calif., 1975-76, project dir., 1976—; pvt. practice psychotherapist Long Beach, Calif., 1982—; div. mgr. City of El Monte, 1982—; cons. U. So. Calif. Andrus Ctr., L.A., 1977-78; bd. dirs. Coord. Coun., City of El Monte, 1975—, Sr. Pres.'s Coun., 1982—; Congl. del. White House Conf. on Aging, 1995. Co-author rape survival guide, 1971. Dir., co-founder Rape Response Program, Pomona, San Gabriel Valley, Calif., 1971-80; cons. on sexual assault Pitzer Coll., Claremont, Calif., 1975-78; past pres. El Monte-South El Monte Coord. Coun. Recipient Susan B. Anthony award NOW, Pomona, 1976. Mem. Am. Soc. on Aging, Calif. Assn. Sr. Ctr. Dirs. (dist. dir. XIII), Calif. Parks and Recreation Soc. (Profl. Citation award 1993), Calif. Assn. Marriage and Family Therapists, Emergency Resources Assn. (bd. dirs.), Women's Club, Civitan, Chi Kappa Rho Gamma. Democrat. Jewish. Office: City of El Monte 3120 N Tyler Ave El Monte CA 91731-3354

LAST, SUSAN WALKER, curriculum developer; b. Waterbury, Conn., Sept. 26, 1962; d. Harold Alfred and Mary (Alferie) Hull; m. Michael Allen Walker, Feb. 11, 1984 (div. July 1988); 1 child, Cassandra Mary; m. Robert Lee Last, Sept. 26, 1992. BS, Ind. U., 1983. Ctr. dir. Sylvan Learning Corp., Arlington, Tex., 1984-88, franchise cons., 1988-89, dist. mgr., 1989-90; coord. of program devel. Sylvan Learning Systems, Arlington, 1991—; trainer, cons. Charles R. Hobbs Corp., Salt Lake City, 1989—; cons. Highpointe, Arlington, 1988—. Author: (curriculum) Study Skills Program, 1990, Study Power Video, 1991, Basic Math Program (K-8), 1994, Adult Reading Program, 1993. Mem., speaker Parents Without Ptnrs., Arlington, 1991. Mem. ASCD, Children with Attention Deficit Disorders, Nat. Coun. Tchrs. of English, Nat. Coun. Tchrs. of Math. Home: 3902 Wrentham Dr Arlington TX 76016 Office: Sylvan Learning Systems 4101 W Green Oaks Blvd Ste 327 Arlington TX 76016

LATHAM, ELEANOR RUTH EARTHROWL, neuropsychology therapist; b. Enfield, Conn., Jan. 12, 1924; d. Francis Henry and Ruth Mary (Harris) Earthrowl; m.Vaughan Milton Latham, July 20, 1946; children: Rebecca Ann, Carol Joan, Jennifer Howe, Vaughan Milton Jr. BA, Vassar Coll., 1945; MA, Smith Coll., 1947, Clark U., Worcester, Mass., 1974; EdD, Clark U., Worcester, Mass., 1979. Lic. psychologist, Mass. Guidance counselor Worcester Pub. Schs., 1967-74, sch. psychologist, 1975-80; pvt. practice neuropsychology Worcester, 1981—; postdoctoral trainee Children's Hosp.-Harvard Med. Sch., Boston, 1980-81; med. staff Hahnemann Hosp., Worcester, St. Vincent Hosp., Worcester, The Med. Ctr. Cen. Mass., Worcester; assoc. in pediatrics U. Mass. Med. Ctr. and Med. Sch., Worcester, 1982—. Author: Neuropsychological Impairment in Duchene Muscular Dystrophy, 1985, Motor Coordination and Visual-Motor Development in Duchenne Muscular Dystrophy, Developmental Considerations in Educational Planning for Boys with Duchenne Muscular Dystrophy; contbr. chpt.: Children and Death, 1987. Mem. Internat. Neuropsychology Soc., Am. Psychol. Assn. Republican. Unitarian. Home: 59 Berwick St Worcester MA 01602-1442 Office: Vernon Med Ctr 10 Winthrop St Worcester MA 01604-4435

LATHAM, JOSEPHINE EVILINE, sales executive; b. Kelford, N.C., Nov. 11, 1947; d. John A. and Catherine (Hoggard) Ruffin; m. William Alfred Latham, Nov. 27, 1981. BA, N.C. Ctrl. U., 1970. Community organizer Community Action Against Poverty, Indpls., 1969-71; pub. rels. dir. Community Action Against, Indpls., 1971-72; edn. specialist City of Indpls., 1972-73; quality supr. Allison Trans. div. GM, 1978-85, engring. coord., 1985—; sr. sales dir. Mary Kay Cosmetics, Carmel, Ind., 1989—. Mem. Nat. Coun. Negro Women. Democrat. Baptist. Home: 803 Cedar Wd Carmel IN 46032 Office: Mary Kay Cosmetics 2511 E 46th St Indianapolis IN 46202

LATHAM, PATRICIA HORAN, lawyer; b. Hoboken, N.J., Sept. 5, 1941; d. Patrick John and Rosemary (Moller) Horan; m. Peter Samuel Latham, June 12, 1965; children: John Horan, Kerry Patricia. BA, Swarthmore Coll., 1963; JD, U. Chgo., 1966. Bar: D.C. 1967, U.S. Dist. Ct. D.C. 1967, U.S. Ct. Appeals 1967, U.S. Supreme Ct. 1970, Va. 1989, U.S. Dist. Ct. (ea. dist.) Va. 1989, U.S. Dist. Ct. Md. 1991. Assoc. Fried Frank Harris Shriver & Kampelman, Washington, 1966-69; atty. Office of Gen. Counsel, SEC, Washington, 1969-71; assoc. Martin & Smith, Washington, 1971—, ptnr., 1974-85; ptnr. Latham & Latham, Washington, 1986—; lectr. Columbus Sch. of Law, Cath. U. Am., Washington, 1978—; panel of arbitrators N.Y. Stock Exchange; co-founder, co-dir. Nat. Ctr. Law and Learning Disabilities, 1992—. Co-author: Attention Deficit Disorder and the Law, 1992, Learning Disabilities and the Law, 1993, ADD and the College Student, 1993, Succeeding in the Workplace, 1994, Higher Education Services for Students with Learning Disabilities and Attention Deficit Disorder: A Legal Guide, 1994. Legal advisor League of Rep. Women of D.C., 1988-90; co-founder, trustee Beacon Coll., 1989-93, chmn. bd. trustees, 1990-92; mem. nat. adult issues com. Children and Adults with Attention Deficit Disorders. Mem. ABA, D.C. Bar, Am. Arbitration Assn. (panel of arbitrators and mediators), N.Y. Stock Exchange (panel of arbitrators), City Tavern Club. Roman Catholic. Home: 7000 Loch Edin Ct Potomac MD 20854

LATHROP, ANN, librarian, educator; b. L.A., Nov. 30, 1935; d. Paul Ray and Margaret (Redfield) W.; divorced; children: Richard Harold, John Randolph, Rodney Grant. BA in History summa cum laude, Ea. N.Mex. U., 1957; MLS, Rutgers U., 1964; PhD, U. Oreg., 1988. Cert. elem. tchr., Calif.; cert. libr., Calif; adminstrv. credential, Calif. Elem. sch. tchr. Chalfont (Pa.) Boro Sch., 1960-61, Livingston Elem. Sch., New Brunswick, N.J., 1961-63, Rosedale Elem. Sch., Chico, Calif., 1964-65; libr. Chico (Calif.) H.S., 1965-72, Princeton (Calif.) H.S., 1972-73, Santa Maria (Calif.) H.S., 1973-77; libr. coord. San Mateo County Office Edn., Redwood City, Calif., 1977-89; assoc. prof. Calif. State U., Long Beach, 1989-92, prof., 1993—; dir. Calif. Software Clearinghouse, Calif. State U. Long Beach. Author: Online Information Retrieval as a Research Tool in Secondary School Libraries, 1988; co-author: Courseware in the Classroom, 1983; editor: Online and CD-ROM Databases in School Libraries, 1989, the 1988-89 Educational Software Preview Guide, 1988, Technology in the Curriculum Recource Guides, 1988; editor, founder: (jours.) The Digest of Software Reviews: Education, 1983-86, Software Reviews on File, 1985-86; editor: (database) California Online Resources in Education, 1989—; contbr. chpts. to books, articles to prof. jours. Mem. ALA, NEA, Am. Assn. Sch. Libs., Assn. State Tech. Using Tchr. Educators, Calif. Faculty Assn., Calif. Media and Libr. Educators Assn., Calif. Reading Assn., Computer Using Educators, Internat. Soc. for Tech. in Edn., Phi Delta Kappa. Office: Calif State U 1250 Bellflower Blvd Long Beach CA 90840-1402

LATHROP, GERTRUDE ADAMS, chemist, consultant; b. Norwich, Conn., Apr. 28, 1921; d. Williams Barrows and Lena (Adams) L. B.S., U. Conn., 1944; M.A., Tex. Woman's U., 1953, Ph.D., 1955. Devel. chemist on textiles/Alexander Smith & Sons Carpet Co. Yonkers, N.Y., 1944-52; research assoc. textiles Tex. Woman's U., 1952-56; chief chemist Glasgo Finishing Plant div. United Mchts. & Mfrs., Inc., Conn., 1956-57; chief chemist Old Fort Finishing Plant div. United Mchts. & Mfrs., Inc., N.C., 1957-63; research chemist United Mchts. Research Ctr., Langley, S.C., 1963-64; lab. mgr. automotive div. Collins & Aikman Corp., Albemarle, N.C., 1964-78; chief chemist, lab. mgr. Old Fort Finishing Plant div. United Mchts., 1979-82. Treas. 1st Congl. Ch., Asheville, N.C., 1985-87, bd. deacons, 1990-93; tax-aide counselor to elderly IRS, 1984—, Am. Assn. Ret. Person, Widowed Person Svcs., Asheville-Buncombe County, Inc., 1990-91, pres. Widowed Persons Svcs., 1992—; active RSVP Land of Sky, 1989-92; pub. Rels. com. Swannanoa Valley, N.C., Am. Assn. Ret. Persons, 1984-92, v.p., 1992, treas., 1993-94. Recipient Disting. Alumni award U. Conn. Sch. Family Studies, 1980-81. Mem. ASTM (chmn. transp. fabrics on flammability com. 1973-75), Am. Chem. Soc. (emeritus), Am. Assn. Textile Chemists and Colorists (emeritus, sec., rsch. chmn., treas., vice chmn. 1962-64, chmn. edn. com. Piedmont sect. 1977-78), Bus. and Profl. Women's Club (chpt. pres. 1974-76, Woman of Yr. award 1979, 80), Iota Sigma Pi (emeritus mem.-at-large). Home and Office: PO Box 1166 Black Mountain NC 28711-1166

LATIFF-BOLET, LIGIA, psychologist; b. Colon, Panama, Sept. 10, 1953; came to the U.S., 1971; d. Antonio and Graciela (Whittaker) L.; m. Celso Goicoechea. Bolet, Aug. 1991; 1 child, Ligia Alanna. BA, Loyola U., New Orleans, 1975; MA, Caribbean Ctr. Advanced Study, Santurce, Puerto Rico, 1979, PhD, 1982. Lic. clin. psychologist. Staff psychologist Puerto Rico State Psychiat. Hosp., Rio Piedras, 1980-82; project dir. Secretariat Aux. Mental Health, Rio Piedras, 1982-83; chief psychologist U.S. Army MEDDAC Panama, Panama City, 1983-88; dir. dept. psychology 1st Hosp. Panamericano, Cidra, Puerto Rico, 1988-91; coord. family preservation program Aiken-Barnwell Mental Health Ctr., 1993—; lectr. various agys., 1982—. Trainer Crisis Line Cath. Ch. Santuario Nacional, Panama City, 1987-88; coord. workshops program Un Mensaje al Corazon, Panama City, 1987-88. NIMH scholar, 1978-79. Mem. APA, World Fedn. Mental Health, Internat. Platform Assn. Roman Catholic. Home: 9 Myer Dr Fort Gordon GA 30905

LATIMER, ALLIE B., lawyer, government official; b. Coraopolis, Pa.; d. Lawnye S. and Bennie Latimer. BS, Hampton Inst., 1947; JD, Howard U., 1953, MDiv, 1986, DMin, 1988; LLM, Cath. U., 1958; postgrad., Am. U., 1960-61. Bar: N.C. bar 1955, D.C. bar 1960. Vol. in projects Am. Friends Service Com., N.J. and, Europe, 1948-49; correctional officer Fed. Reformatory for Women, Alderson, W.Va., 1949-51; personnel clk. NIH, Bethesda, 1953-55; realty officer Mitchell AFB, N.Y., 1955-56; with Office Gen. Counsel, GSA, Washington, 1957-76; chief counsel Office Gen. Counsel, GSA, after 1966, asst. gen. counsel, 1971-76, gen. counsel, 1977-87; asst. gen. counsel NASA, 1976-77; spl. counsel Gen. Svcs. Adminstrn., Washington, 1987—; past chmn. central office com. Fed. Women's Program, GSA; mem. membership and budget com. Health and Welfare Council, 1967-72. Bd. dirs. D.C. Mental Health Assn., pres., 1977-79; bd. dirs. Friendship House, Washington; elder Presbyn. Ch.; pres. Interacial Council, 1964-75; chmn. Presbyn. Econ. Devel. Corp., 1975-81; mem. governing bd. Nat. Council Chs. of Christ in U.S.A. Recipient GSA Sustained Superior Service award, 1959, Meritorious Service award, 1964, Commendable Service award, 1964, Pub. Service award, 1971, Outstanding Performance award, 1971, Presdl. Rank award, 1983, Disting. Service award, 1984. Mem. ABA, Nat. Bar Assn. (sec. 1966-74), Fed. Bar Assn., Washington Bar Assn., N.C. Bar Assn., Nat. Bar Found. (dir. 1970-71, pres. 1974-75), Hampton Alumni Assn. (pres. Washington chpt. 1970-71), Howard Law Alumni Assn. (v.p. 1962-63) alumni assns), Links (pres. Washington chpt. 1971-74, nat. v.p. 1976-80), Federally Employed Women (founder, 1st pres.). Home: 1721 S St NW Washington DC 20009-6117

LATIMER, HELEN, information resource manager, writer, researcher; b. Elizabeth, N.J.; d. Raymond O. and Minna A. Mercner; divorced; children: Alexander, Victoria. AB, Duke U.; MS in Journalism, Columbia U.; cert. in bus. adminstrn., Harvard-Radcliffe; MBA in Mktg., Am. U.; postgrad., U. Calif., Berkeley, Rutgers U. Instr. mktg. Am. U., Washington; mgr. info. resources Burdeshaw Assocs., Ltd., Bethesda, Md., 1985-94, assoc., 1994—; initiated publ. specialists program George Washington U., Washington; officer alumni bds. Harvard-Radcliffe Program in Adminstrn., Am. U.; comm., info. resource mgmt. cons., tech. editor MIT Servomechanisms Lab.; AA to editor Reinhold Pub. (former subs. McGraw-Hill); facilitator, subgroup on mktg. The White House Conf. on Libr. and Info. Svcs., 1991. Contbr. articles to newspapers and mags. Past leader Troop 1907, Girl Scouts Am.; mem. Troop 100 com. Boy Scouts Am. Mem. Spl. Librs. Assn., Harvard Bus. Sch. Club D.C. (initiated admission of women, v.p., bd. dirs.).

LATIMER, MARGARET PETTA, nutrition and dietetics educator; b. Sacramento, Aug. 17, 1932; d. Rosario and Helen (Sclafani) Petta; m. Westford Ramos Latimer, June 18, 1978. BS, U. Calif., Berkeley, 1954; MA, Calif. State U., Sacramento, 1982. Registered dietitian, Calif.; life teaching credential, Calif. Therapeutic dietitian U. Calif. Med. Ctr., San Francisco, 1955-65; dietitian Roseville (Calif.) Community Hosp., 1966-67, Mercy San Juan Hosp., Carmichael, Calif., 1967-69; substitute tchr. San Juan Unified Sch. Dist., Sacramento, 1970-75, tchr. adult edn., 1971-74; instr. dietetics American River Coll., Sacramento, 1975-77, San Joaquin Delta Coll., Stockton, Calif., 1975—; cons. dietitian, Sacramento, 1973-78. Mem. Am. Dietetic Assn., Soc. for Nutrition Edn., Nutrition Today, Calif. Dietetic Assn. (pres. Golden Empire dist. 1974-75), AAUW (gourmet chmn. 1981-82, editor AAUW Book of Favorite Recipes 1982). Republican. Roman Catholic. Office: San Joaquin Delta Coll 5151 Pacific Ave Stockton CA 95207

LATIOLAIS, MINNIE FITZGERALD, nurse, hospital administrator; b. Vivian, La., Dec. 26, 1921; d. Thomas Ambrose and Mildred Surita (Nagle) Fitzgerald; m. Joseph C. Latiolais Jr., July 19, 1947; children: Felisa, Diana, Sylvia, Mary, Amelia, Joseph Clifton III. RN, New Orleans, 1943. Asst. night supr. Touro Infirmary, New Orleans, 1943; orthopedic surg. nurse Ochsner Clinic, New Orleans, 1943-47; asst. dir. nursing, Ochsner Found. Hosp., 1947; supr. Lafayette (La.) Gen. Hosp., 1960-64; adminstrv. asst., supr. oper. rm. Abbeville (La.) Gen. Hosp., 1964-68; gen. mgr., neurol. surg. nurse J. Robert Rivet, neurol. surgeon, Lafayette, 1968-78; hosp. cons. assoc. B.J. Landry & Assocs., hosps. cons., Lafayette, 1979—; dir. nursing Acadia St. Landry Hosp., Church Point, 1981-82; supr. supplies, processing and distbn. Univ. Med. Ctr., Lafayette, 1982-90; bd. dirs. SW La. Rehab. Assn., 1975-89, pres., 1979-80; mem. Mid-La. Health Systems Agy., 1977-82, project rev. chmn., 1978-80; vice chmn. Acadica Regional Clearing House, 1984-86; mem. crafts and practical nurse com. Lafayette Regional Vocat.-Tech. Inst., 1980-84, chmn. 1983-84. Mem. Am. Nurses Assn. (past), La. State Nurses Assn., Lafayette Dist. Nurses Assn. (pres. 1967-69, Nurse of Yr. 1991). Roman Catholic.

LATOURETTE, DANIELLE, accountant; b. New Brunswick, N.J., Sept. 9, 1967; d. Donald George and Diane Elizabeth (Molnar) LaT. BS in Bus. and Econ., Lehigh U., 1989; postgrad., Brenau U. Cert. mgmt. acct. Jr. acct.-fin. acctg. Johnson & Johnson Consumer Products, Skillman, N.J., 1989-91, jr. acct.-contract mfg., 1991-92, sr. acct.-materials mgmt., 1992; sr. cost acct.

Johnson & Johnson Consumer Products, Royston, Ga., 1993-94, purchasing mgr., 1994—. Mem. Inst. Mgmt. Accts. Office: Johnson & Johnson Consumer Products Inc Old Elbert Rd Royston GA 30662

LATSIOS, BARBARA LYNN, government official; b. Phila., Jan. 25, 1954; d. Stephen and Helen Valentina (Matweychuk) Sameruck; m. George Latsios, Aug. 29, 1976; 1 child, Cassandra. Clk., stenographer Nat. Park Svc., Phila., 1971-72, park ranger, 1972-79, supervisory park ranger, 1979-85, purchasing agt., 1985-87; contract specialist EPA, Phila., 1987-90, program analyst, 1990—. Mem. Nat. Contract Mgmt. Assn., AFL-CIO (sec. Local 2058 Phila. 1973-75, 2d v.p. 1976-79). Republican. Russian Orthodox. Office: EPA Region III 841 Chestnut St Bldg Philadelphia PA 19107-4414

LATZA, BEVERLY ANN, accountant; b. Pompton Plains, N.J., June 10, 1960; d. George and Helen Mae (Ryan) L. BA in Acctg., Bus. Adminstrn., Thiel Coll., 1982. Internal auditor Monroe Systems for Bus., Morris Plains, N.J., 1983-85; acct. Am. Airlines, Tulsa, 1985-86, Accountemps, Tulsa, 1986-87; credit investigator Denrich Leasing, Inc., Kansas City, Mo., 1987-89; tax examining asst. IRS, Kansas City, Mo., 1989—. Lutheran. Home: 13148 W 88th Ct Apt 141 Lenexa KS 66215-4923 Office: IRS 2306 E Bannister Rd Kansas City MO 64132

LAU, CHERYL A., former state official. BM, Ind. U.; JD, U. San Francisco. Bar: 1986. Formerly dep. atty. gen. Nev. Motor Vehicles and Pub. Safety Dept., Carson City, Nev.; sec. of state, State of Nev. State of Nev., Carson City, 1991-94; gen. coun. U.S. Ho. of Reps., Washington, 1995—. Office: House of Reps 219 Cannon House Office Bldg Washington DC 20515

LAU, ELIZABETH KWOK-WAH, clinical social worker; b. Hong Kong, Jan. 7, 1940; m. Edmond Y. Lau, June 5, 1965; children: Melissa, Ernest. BA, Brigham Young U., 1963; MSW, U. Kans., 1965. Supr. N.E. Community Mental Health Ctr., San Francisco, 1968-73; clin. dir. Chinatown Child Devel. Ctr., San Francisco, 1973-75; program specialist Kai Ming Head Start Program, San Francisco, 1975-77; clin. social worker VA Hosp., Palo Alto, Calif., 1977—; social work coord. nursing home VA Hosp., San Francisco, 1986—; host, interviewer Sta. KTSF-TV, San Francisco, 1982—; bd. dirs. Kai Ming Head Start Program. Author: Innovative Parenting, 1980, How to Love Your Children, 1983, How to Raise a Successfull Child, 1984, How to Train a Bright Child, 1985, Understanding Your Children, 1987, The Art of Child Rearing, 1989, Getting to Know Americans, 1990, Providing Guidance to Teenagers, 1991, The Art of Parenting I & II, 1994. V.p. Parents-Tchrs. League Zion Luth. Sch., San Francisco, 1981-83. Recipient Performance award VA Med. Ctr., Palo Alto, 1979, 83, Social Wokr Research award VA Med. Ctr., Palo Alto, 1985. Mem. Nat. Assn. Social Workers (cert.). Home: 470 Ortega St San Francisco CA 94122-4622 Office: VA Med Ctr 4150 Clement St San Francisco CA 94121

LAU, MICHELE DENISE, advertising consultant, sales trainer, television personality; b. St. Paul, Dec. 6, 1960; d. Dwyane Udell and Patricia Ann (Yri) L. Student, U. Minn., 1979-82. Pub. rels. coord. Stillwater (Minn.) C. of C., 1977-79; asst. mgr. Salkin & Linoff, Mpls., 1982, store merchandiser, sales trainer, 1982-83; rental agt. Sentinel Mgmt. Co., St. Paul, 1983-84; account exec. Community Svc. Publs., Mpls., 1984-85, frwy. news supr., 1985, asst. sales mgr., 1985-86; asst. sales mgr. St. Paul Pioneer Press Dispatch, 1986-91; pres. Promotional Ptnrs., Eden Prairie, Minn., 1991—; on-air personality Sta. WCCO II Cable TV Mpls., 1988-89, co-host Afternoon Midwest, 1989—; co-host Home Shopping Show, host Minn. Voices, Fox 29; cons. U. Minn. Alumni mag., 1986-89. Author mechandising and sales tng. manuals. Fund-raiser sustaining program YMCA, Mpls., 1986, Jr. Achievement, St. Paul, 1988; cons. Muscular Dystrophy Assn., St. Paul, 1988-89; bd. dirs. St. Paul Jaycees. Mem. NAFE, Nat. Assn. Home Builders, Mpls. Builder Assn. (amb.), Metro-East Profl. Builders Assn. (spl. events com.), Advt. Fedn., The Newspaper Guild, Internat. Platform Assn., Speakeasy Club. Lutheran. Home and Office: Promotional Ptnrs 8033 Belair Ln Eden Prairie MN 55347

LAUBER, MIGNON DIANE, food processing company executive; b. Detroit, Dec. 21; d. Charles Edmond and Maud Lillian (Foster) Donaker. Student Kelsey Jenny U., 1958, Brigham Young U., 1959; m. Richard Brian Lauber, Sept. 13, 1963; 1 child, Leslie Viane (dec.). Owner, operator Alaska World Travel, Ketchikan, 1964-67; founder, owner, pres. Oosick Soup Co., Juneau, Alaska, 1969—. Treas., Pioneer Alaska Lobbyists Soc., Juneau, 1977—. Mem. Bus. and Profl. Women, Alaska C. of C. Libertarian, Washington Athletic Club. Author: Down at the Water Works with Jesus, 1982; Failure Through Prayer, 1983, We All Want to Go to Heaven But Nobody Wants to Die, 1988. Home: 321 Highland Dr Juneau AK 99801-1442 Office: PO Box 1625 Juneau AK 99802-0078

LAUBER, PATRICIA GRACE, writer, juvenile prose; b. N.Y.C., Feb. 5, 1924; d. Hubert Crow and Florence (Walker) L.; m. Russell Frost III, Apr. 11, 1981. BA, Wellesley Coll., 1945. Rsch., writer Look Mag. Book Dept., N.Y.C., 1945-46; staff writer Scholastic Mags., N.Y.C., 1946-48, editor, 1948-54, freelance editor, 1954-56; freelance editor Challenge Books, Coward-McCann, N.Y.C., 1955-59; founding editor, editor-in-chief Science World, Street & Smith, N.Y.C., 1956-59; chief editor Science and Mathematics, The New Book of Knowledge, Grolier, N.Y.C., 1961-67; freelance editor Good Earth Books, Garrard, Scarsdale, N.Y., 1973-79; cons. editor Sci. Am. Books, N.Y.C., 1977-80; cons. Nat. Sci. Resources Ctr., NAS-Smithsonian Instn., 1992-94. Author numerous children's books including Volcano: The Eruption and Healing of Mount St. Helens, 1986 (Newbery Honor Book 1987, N.Y. Acad. Scis. Hon. Mention 1987), From Flower to Flower: Animals and Pollination, 1986 (N.Y. Acad. Scis. Hon. Mention 1988), Dinosaurs Walked Here and Other Stories Fossils Tell, 1987, Snakes Are Hunters, 1988, Lost Star, the Story of Amelia Earhart, 1988, Yellowstone, 1988, Meteors and Meteorites: Voyagers from Space, 1989, The News About Dinosaurs, 1989 (N.Y. Acad. Scis. Hon. Mention 1990), Living with Dinosaurs, 1989 (Orbis Pictus hon. mention Nat. Coun. Tchrs. English 1990), Seeing Earth from Space, 1990 (Orbis Pictus hon. mention Nat. Coun. Tchrs. English 1991), Summer of Fire, 1991, Great Whales-The Gentle Giants, 1991, Fur, Feathers, and Flippers, 1994, What Do You See?, 1994, others. Recipient award for Overall Contbn. to Children's Lit., Washington Post/Children's Book Guild, 1983, Eva L. Gordon award Am. Nature Study Soc., 1988, Lit. award Cen. Mo. State U., 1989, Lifetime Achievement commendation Nat. Forum on Children's Sci. Books, Carnegie-Mellon U., 1992. Mem. PEN, The Authors Guild, Soc. Children's Book Writers. Democrat. Congregationalist. Office: care Scholastic Trade Books 555 Broadway New York NY 10012-3999

LAUDADIO, MARILYN GRACE, theater educator; b. N.Y.C., Aug. 17, 1951; d. Albert Charles and Marie A. L. BA, Barry Coll., 1972; MA, U. Miami, Coral Gables, Fla., 1974; postgrad., Fla. Atlantic U., 1989—, Fla. State U., 1979-80. Dance program coord. U. Miami Theatre, Coral Gables, 1973-74; asst. prof. Barry U., Miami, Fla., 1974-89; theatre dir. in residence Sch. Bd. Broward County, Ft. Lauderdale, Fla., 1989-90; artistic dir., pres. Mimic Theatre Co., Inc., Hollywood, Fla., 1974—; movement cons. Player's State Theatre, Miami, 1974-76; guest artist in residence N.Y.C. Ballet, 1976; guest dir. Fla. Shakespeare Festival, Miami, 1980—; mime and comedia cons. Walt Disney EPCOT Ctr., Orlando, Fla., 1981-82; cons. Am. Stage Co., St. Petersburg, Fla., 1981-84; cons. Internat. Thespian Soc. Actress TV series Miami Vice, 1988, documentary Way of the Humanist, 1978 (Emmy award), numerous plays and musicals; choreographer: A Midsummer Night's Dream, 1988, TV movie B.L. Strykker, 1989; dir. plays, musicals including: As You Like It, 1988, The Tempest, 1988, My Fair Lady, 1990, The Mikado, 1989. Project dir. Broward County Office Environ. Svcs. Recycling Campaign. Mem. SAG, Actors Equity Assn., Am. Theatre in Higher Edn., Fla. Assn. Theatre Educators, Broward Tchrs. Union. Republican. Roman Catholic. Home: 3909 SW 58th Ter Hollywood FL 33023-6146

LAUDE, ISABELLA C., investment administrator; b. Sagamore, Pa., Apr. 16, 1931; m. Walter Laude, May 11, 1957; 5 children. BSN, Case Western Res. U., 1956; MS in Rehab. Counseling, Va. Commonwealth U., 1966; PhD in Health Edn., Columbia-Pacific U., 1986. RN; cert. counselor psychologist, cert. tree farmer; notary public; registered parliamentarian. Supr., dir. Cleve. Clinic, 1953-57; investor, adminstrv. dir. Babson Park, Fla., 1957—; tree farmer Boxwood Farm, Ashland, Va., 1970—; owner, mgr. Seminole Hotel, Lake Wales, Fla., 1972-78; adminstrv. dir. for various profl. assns. Lake Wales, 1972-86, health educator for various profl. assns., 1972-86; citrus mgr. Pine Knoll, Babson Park, 1978—; health cons. Richmond (Va.) Diocesan Sch. Bd., 1967-70. Author: Enjoying Road to Fatherhood, 1966, family life curriculum for Cath. schs., Richmond, 1967; editor: (monthly column) Jour. Fla. Med. Assn., 1980-84, (newsletter) Med. Aux. Music Club, 1978-86, (mag.) Music Club Mag., 1991—. Bd. dirs. ARC, Richmond, 1957-72, Sr. Ctr., Richmond, 1970-72; govt. appointee White House Confs. on Children and Youth, Richmond, 1970; presdl. appointee Women in Svc. to Handicapped, 1970; founding mem. Lake Wales Arts Coun., 1973, Lake Wales Little Theater, 1978; mem. election bd., election official Polk County, 1989—; life mem. Va. Assn. for Hist. Preservation, 1975—. Named Nurse of Yr., ARC, 1966. Fellow Rose Fay Thomas Fellows; mem. AAUW (life), So. Med. Assn. (aux. v.p. 1982-86), Nat. Fedn. Music Clubs (life, exec. com. 1991—), Fla. Fedn. Music Clubs (pres. 1987-89, Mem. of Yr. 1989). Republican. Roman Catholic. Office: PO Box 161 Lake Wales FL 33859-0161

LAUDER, ESTEE, cosmetics company executive; b. N.Y.C.; m. Joseph Lauder (dec.); children: Leonard, Ronald. LLD (hon.), U. Pa., 1986. Chmn. bd. Estee Lauder Inc., 1946—. Author: Estee: A Success Story, 1985. Named One of 100 Women of Achievement Harpers Bazaar, 1967, Top Ten Outstanding Women in Business, 1970; recipient Neiman-Marcus Fashion award, 1962; Spirit of Achievement award Albert Einstein Coll. Medicine, 1968; Kaufmann's Fashion Fortnight award, 1969; Bamberger's Designer's award, 1969; Gimbel's Fashion Forum award, 1969; Internat. Achievement award Frost Bros., 1971; Pogue's Ann. Fashion award, 1975, Golda Meir 90th Anniversary Tribute award, 1988; decorated chevalier Legion of Honor France, 1978; medaille de Vermeil de la Ville de Paris, 9, 1979; 4th Ann. award for Humanitarian Service Girls' Club N.Y., 1979; 25th Anniversary award Greater N.Y. council Boy Scouts Am., 1979; L.S. Ayres award, 1981; Achievement award Girl Scouts U.S.A., 1983; Outstanding Mother award, 1984; Athena award, 1985; Pres. award Cosmetic Exec. Women, 1989, Neiman-Marcus Fashion award, 1992; honored Lincoln Ctr., World of Style, 1986; 1988 Laureate Nat. Bus. Hall of Fame. Office: Estee Lauder Inc 767 Fifth Ave New York NY 10153-0002

LAUDER, VALARIE ANNE, editor, educator; b. Detroit, Mar. 1; d. William J. and Murza Valerie (Mann) L. AA, Stephens Coll., Columbia, Mo., 1944; postgrad. Northwestern U. With Chgo. Daily News, 1944-52, columnist, 1946-52; lectr. Sch. Assembly Service, also Redpath lectr., 1952-55; freelance writer for mags. and newspapers including N.Y. Times, Yankee, Ford Times, Travel & Leisure, Am. Heritage, 1955—; editor-in-chief Scholastic Roto, 1962; editor U. N.C., 1975-80, lectr. Sch. Journalism, 1980—; gen. sec. World Assn. for Pub. Opinion Rsch., 1988—; nat. chmn. student writing project Ford Times, 1981-86; pub. rels. dir. Am. Dance Festival, Duke U., 1982-83, lectr., instr. continuing edn. program, 1984; contbg. editor So. Accents mag., 1982-86. Mem. nat. fund raising bd. Kennedy Ctr., 1962-63. Recipient 1st place award Nat. Fedn. Press Women, 1981; 1st place awards Ill. Women's Press Assn., 1950, 1951. Mem. Pub. Rels. Soc. Am. (treas. N.C. chpt. 1982, sec. 1983, v.p. 1984, pres.-elect 1985, pres. 1986, chmn. council of past pres., chmn. 25th Ann. event 1987, del. Nat. Assembly 1988-94, S.E. dist. officer, nat. nominating com. 1991), Women in Communications (v.p. matrix N.C. Triangle chpt. 1984-85), N.C. Pub. Rels. Hall of Fame Com., DAR, Soc. Mayflower Desc. (bd. dir. Ill. Soc. 1946-52), Chapel Hill Hist. Soc. (bd. dir. 1981-85, 94—, chmn. publs. com. 1980-85), Chapel Hill Preservation Soc. (bd. trustees 1993—, nominating com. 1994), N.C. Press Club (3d v.p. 1981-83, 2d v.p. 1983-85, pres. 1985, 1st pl. awards 1981, 82, 83, 84), Univ. Woman's Club (2d v.p. 1988), The Carolina Club, The Nat. Press Club. Office: U NC Sch Journalism and Mass Comm CB 3365 Chapel Hill NC 27599-3365

LAUDERDALE, KATHERINE SUE, lawyer; b. Wright-Patterson AFB, Ohio, May 30, 1954; d. Azo and Helen Ceola (Davis) L. BA in Soviet Studies, Ohio State U., 1975; JD, NYU, 1978. Bar: Ill. 1978, U.S. Dist. Ct. (no. dist.) Ill. 1978, Calif. 1987. Assoc. Schiff, Hardin & Waite, Chgo., 1978-82; dir. bus. and legal affairs Sta. WTTW-TV, Chgo., 1982-83, gen. counsel, 1983—, also v.p., sr. v.p., gen. counsel legal and bus. affairs, 1993—; acting sr. v.p. Prodn. Ctr., 1994. Mem. Lawyers Com. for Harold Washington, Chgo., 1983; bd. dirs. Midwest Women's Ctr., Chgo., 1985-94; active Chgo. Coun. Fgn. Rels., 1981—, mem. fgn. affairs com., 1985—. mem. ABA, Chgo. Bar Assn. (bd. dirs. TV Prodns., Inc. 1986—), Lawyers for Creative Arts (bd. dir. 1984—), ACLU (bd. dirs. 1987-94), Nat. Acad. TV Arts and Scis., NYU Law Alumni Assn. Midwest (mem. exec. bd. 1982—). Democrat. Office: Sta WTTW-TV 5400 N St Louis Ave Chicago IL 60625-4698

LAUENSTEIN, ANN GAIL, librarian; b. Milw., Nov. 8, 1949; d. Elmer Lester Herbert and Elizabeth Renatta (Bovee) Zaeske; m. Mark Lauenstein, Aug. 16, 1986; 1 child, Maria. MA, U. Wis., 1972. Asst. libr. U. Wis., Wausau, 1972-73; cataloger, libr. MacMurray Coll., Jacksonville, Ill., 1973-76; corp. libr. Anheuser-Busch Cos. Inc., St. Louis, 1976—; facilitator Anheuser-Busch Quality Circle, St. Louis, 1984—. Treas. Friends of Kirkwood Libr., 1986—; mem. adv. coun. Sch. Info. Sci. U. Mo., 1987—. Mem. AAUW (editor jour. 1981-84, publicitiy chmn. 1985-87, scholar 1984), Spl. Librs. Assn. (network liaison 1981-83, chmn. employment com. 1983-84, chmn. hospitality com. 1984-85, membership chmn. 1988-89, newsletter editor 1992—), St. Louis Regional Libr. Network (coun. 1981-83), St. Louis Online Users Group, Women in Bus. Network (adv. panel 1980-82, 86-87, programs planner 1987-88, asst. coord. 1988-89), Ohio Coll. Libr. Consortium Acquisitions Users Coun. Office: Anheuser-Busch Co Inc 1 Busch Pl Saint Louis MO 63118-1852

LAUER, JEANETTE CAROL, history educator, author; b. St. Louis, July 14, 1935; d. Clinton Jones and Blanche Aldine (Gideon) Pentecost; m. Robert Harold Lauer, July 2, 1954; children: Jon, Julie, Jeffrey. BS, U. Mo., St. Louis, 1970; MA, Washington U., St. Louis, 1973, PhD, 1975. Assoc. prof. history St. Louis Community Coll., 1974-82; assoc. prof. history U.S. Internat. U., San Diego, 1982-90, prof., 1990-94; dean Coll. of Arts and Scis., San Diego. Author: Fashion Power, 1981, The Spirit and the Flesh, 1983, Til Death Do Us Part, 1986, Watersheds, 1988, The Quest for Intimacy, 1991, 2nd edit., 1993, No Secrets, 1993, The Joy Ride, 1993, For Better or Better, 1995. Woodrow Wilson fellow, 1970, Washington U. fellow, 1971-75. Mem. Am. Hist. Assn., Orgn. Am. Historians. Democrat. Presbyterian. Home: 18147 Sun Maiden Ct San Diego CA 92127-3102

LAUFMAN, LESLIE RODGERS, hematologist, oncologist; b. Pitts., Dec. 13, 1946; d. Marshall Charles and Ruth Rodgers; m. Harry B. Laufman, Apr. 25, 1970 (div. Apr. 1984); children: Hal, Holly; m. Rodger Mitchell, Oct. 9, 1987. BA in Chemistry, Ohio Wesleyan U., 1968; MD, U. Pitts., 1972. Diplomate Am. Bd. Internal Medicine and Hematology. Intern Montefiore Hosp., Pitts., 1972-73, resident in internal medicine, 1973-74; fellow in hemotology and oncology Ohio State Hosp., Columbus, 1974-76; dir. med. oncology Grant Med. Ctr., Columbus, 1977—; practice medicine specializing in hemotology and oncology Columbus, 1977—; bd. dirs. Columbus Cancer Clinic; prin. investigator Columbus Cmty. Clin. Oncology Program, 1989—. Contbr. articles to profl. jours. Mem. AMA, Am. Women Med. Assn. (sec./treas. 1985-86, pres. 1986-87), Am. Soc. Clin. Oncology, Southwest Oncology Group, Nat. Surg. Adjuvant Project for Breast and Bowel Cancers. Office: 393 E Town St # 109 Columbus OH 43215-4741 also: 8100 Ravin 248S Edge Ct S Worthington OH 43235

LAUGHLIN, BARBARA L., bank executive. Past exec. v.p. Seaman's Bank for Savs., N.Y.C.; now exec. v.p. First Empire State Corp., Buffalo, N.Y. Office: First Empire State Corp 1 Montana Ave Buffalo NY 14211-1638*

LAUGHTON, KATHARINE L., career officer; b. L.A., Dec. 9, 1942; d. Herman and Mary-Alice (McCunniff) H.; m. Robert James Laughton, Oct. 16, 1972. Attended, Vassar Coll., 1960-61; BA, U. Calif., Riverside, 1964; dist. grad., Navy War Coll., 1986. Dep. dir. mgmt. info. svcs. Military Sealift Command, 1977-79; commdg. officer Military Sealift Command, Pt. Canaveral, 1979-82; program mgr. Naval Data Automation Command, 1982-84; spl. asst. inspector gen. U.S. Navy, 1984-86; head ADP svcs. commdr. n chief U.S. Atlantic, Norfolk, Va., 1986-87. Recipient medal of merit for excellence in tech. Armed Forces Communications & Elecs. Assn., 1991, Parsons award for scientific and Tech. progress Navy League, 1990. Mem. AFCEA (internat. v.p.), Vassar Club. Episcopalian. Office: Navy Department Washington DC 20350-2000

LAULE, ALICE RICHARDS, ophthalmologist; b. Riverside, Calif., Aug. 24, 1947; d. John Robert and Margaret Alice (Rogers) Richards; m. Stephen Fletcher Laule, Dec. 14, 1991; stepchildren: Stephen Patrick, Cynthia Marie, Jacob Earl. BA magna cum laude, Calif. Luth. U., 1969; MD with honors, U. Ark., 1976. Diplomate Am. Bd. Ophthalmology. Asst. prof. rehab. dept. U. Ark., Little Rock, 1978-80; pvt. practice Harrison, Ark., 1981—; active staff North Ark. Med. Ctr., Harrison, 1981—; regional trustee Am. Holistic Med. Assn., Raleigh, N.C., 1991—; pres. Harrison Optical Inc., 1988—. Author: (novel) Diary of a Ghost, 1991; author in field. Pres. Future Visions Found., Inc., 1994—. Mem. AMA, Am. Acad. Ophthalmology, Am. Motorcyclist Assn., Ark. Med. Soc., Alpha Omega Alpha.

LAUNDER, YOLANDA MARIE, graphic design manager; b. Columbus, Ohio, Mar. 21, 1957; d. Wilbur Winfield and Julia Mary (Moretti) Reifein; m. David Paul Launder, Oct. 14, 1989; 1 child, Jonathan David. BFA in Design Comm., Tex. Tech. U., 1979. Graphic designer Perception, Inc., Chgo., 1980-81; graphic designer Source, Inc., Chgo., 1982-83, assoc. design mgr., 1983-84; sr. graphic designer Oscar Mayer Foods Corp., Madison, Wis., 1984-85, design mgr., 1986-88, group design mgr., 1989—; lectr. Wis. Dept. Agriculture, Madison, 1988, Design Mgmt. Inst., Martha's Vineyard, Mass., 1991, Oscar Mayer Foods Corp., Women Career Devel., Madison, 1993-94. Co-inventor in field of Oscar Mayer Lunchables Packaging, 1989—. Sunday sch. tchr. St. Bernard's Ch., Dallas, 1973-75; evaluated high sch. portfolios Tex. Tech. U., Chgo., 1982-83; poll watcher David Patt Alderman campaign, Chgo., 1982; graphic design vol. Mental Health Assn. Dane County, 1986, United Way of Wis., Madison, 1992. Recipient Snack Food Package of the Yr. award Food & Drug Packaging Mag., 1989, Sial D'or award Salon International de L'alimentation, Paris, 1990, Bronze award for Excellence in Packaging for Oscar Mayer Lunchables, The Nat. Paperboard Packaging Coun., 1990, Mktg. Creativity award Kraft U.S.A., 1992, 93. Mem. Women in Design/Chgo. (program dir. 1982-83, membership dir. 1983-84, pres. 1984-85), Madison Advt. Fedn. (Addy awards com. 1985, voluntary action com. 1986), Design Madison (programs com. 1989-92), Package Designers Coun., Design Mgmt. Inst. Avocations: travel, theater, reading, art galleries, exercising. Office: Oscar Mayer Foods Corp 910 Mayer Ave Madison WI 53704

LAU-PATTERSON, MAYIN, psychotherapist; b. N.Y.C., May 13, 1940; d. Justin S. and Susan (Lee) Lau; m. Oscar H. L. Bing, Dec. 26, 1962 (div. Dec. 1974); children: David C., Michael H.; m. Michael Morrow Patterson, Nov. 8, 1989. BA, Goucher Coll., 1962; MA, George Wash. U., 1966; postgrad., Boston Coll., 1977. Lic. psychologist, Mass.; lic. profl. counselor, Tex.; cert. chem. dependency specialist, marriage, and family therapist, clin. hypnosis, Tex. Psychologist children's unit Met. State Hosp., Waltham, Mass., 1966-67, clin. psychologist, 1967-68, prin. psychologist, 1968-70, chief psychologist, 1970-76; chief psychologist South Cove Community Health Ctr., Boston, 1976-78; pvt. practice Newton, Mass., 1974-77, Gateway Counseling, Framington, Mass., 1975-78, Alamo Mental Health, San Antonio, 1978-92, The Patterson Relationship and Counseling Ctr., San Antonio, 1992—; clin. instr. psychology Dept. Psychiatry Harvard U. Med. Sch., Cambridge, MAss., 1974-76; instr. Tufts New Eng. Med. Ctr. Hosp., Boston, 1975-78; presenter Am. Acad. Child Psychiatry, 1973, 74. Contbr. articles to profl. jours. Office: 3510 N Saint Marys St Ste 310 San Antonio TX 78212-3164

LAURENCE, JANICE HENDERSON, psychologist and researcher; b. Phila., Apr. 1, 1957; d. Howard Robert and Dolores Jenny (Dinote) Henderson; m. Michael Tripucka Laurence, June 7, 1980; children: Julia, Danielle. BA magna cum laude, Temple U., 1979, MA, 1984; MA, George Mason U., 1990, PhD, 1993. Rsch. asst. Temple U., Phila., 1979-80, McFann-Gray & Assocs., Arlington, Va., 1981; rsch. assoc. Human Resources Rsch. Orgn., Alexandria, Va., 1981-83, rsch. scientist, 1983-86, sr. scientist, 1986-91, sr. staff scientist, 1991—; cons. Naval Postgrad. Sch., Monterey, Calif., 1983—, Dept. Edn., Washington, 1990, U. Pa., Phila., 1993. Author: Low-aptitude Men in the Military, 1991; editor/author: Adaptability Screening for the Armed Forces, 1993; author chpts. to books. Fellow Inter-Univ. Seminar on Armed Forces and Soc.; mem. APA, divsn. mil. psychology, treas. 1994—), Mil. Testing Assn., Pers. Testing Coun., Phi Beta Kappa. Home: 3902 Adrienne Dr Alexandria VA 22309-2600 Office: HUMRRO 66 Canal Center Plz Ste 400 Alexandria VA 22314-1591

LAURENT, JERRY SUZANNA, technical communications company executive; b. Oklahoma City, Okla., Dec. 28, 1942; d. Harry Austin and M. LaVerne (Barker) Minick; m. Leroy E. Laurent, July 2, 1960; children: Steven, Sandra, David, Debra. AS in Tech. Writing, Okla. State U., 1986. With Technically Write, Mustang, Okla., 1960-75, acctg. adminstr., 1976-80, retail bus. mgr., 1981-87, owner, CEO, 1989—. Mem. Soc. Tech. Communication (Superscript editor 1985, feature editor 1986, v.p. 1985, student chpt. pres. 1986, program coord. Okla. chpt. 1992-93, sec. Okla. chpt. 1993-94, v.p. 1994-95, state pres.-elect 1995—), Am. Bus. Women's Assn. (dist. III v.p. 1988-89, conf. gen. chair 1992, Bulletin award 1977, 81, 83, 84, 93, 94, Woman of Yr. 1977, Bus. Assoc. of the Yr. 1983-84, v.p. 1994-95, editor Smoke Signals, 1993-94, v.p. HUGS, 1993, chmn. bd. dirs. Help Us Grow Spiritually, 1993-95). Democrat. Baptist. Home: 347 W Forest Dr Mustang OK 73064-3430

LAURENTI, SANDRA DESANTIS, middle school educator; b. Syracuse, N.Y., Apr. 23, 1948; d. Lawrence Francis and Anne Louise (Belvito) DeSantis; m. Vincent John Laurenti, Aug. 9, 1969; separated; children: David John, Daniel Joseph. BS, Syracuse U., 1969, MS, 1973. Cert. tchr., N.Y. Tchr. Lyncourt Sch., Syracuse, 1969—; spl. cons. to Onondage County Dist. Atty. for Program F.U.T.U.R.E. Campaign worker mayoral candidate Joseph Nicoletti, Syracuse, 1993; chairperson Drug Alcohol Com., 1990-93. Grantee Mobil Oil, 1993, Bristol/Squibb, 1993. Democrat. Roman Catholic. Home: 108 Ausable Run Liverpool NY 13088 Office: Lyncourt Sch 2707 Court St Syracuse NY 13208

LAURIA, MARGARET MUNRO, secondary education educator; b. Princeton, N.J., Dec. 17, 1949; d. David D. III and Elizabeth Vroman (Munro) Dunwoody; m. Peter F. Lauria, June 19, 1981; children: Kevin D. Pirko, Brian J. Pirko. AS, Tompkins-Cortland C.C., 1977; BA in Secondary Edn. English, SUC, Cortland, 1980, MEd in English, 1983. English tchr. Homer (N.Y.) High Sch., 1979-80, Dryden (N.Y.) Ctrl. Schs., 1980—. Mem. NEA, Dryden Faculty Assn. (v.p. 1986-87). Home: PO Box 237 60 Mill St Dryden NY 13053-0237 Office: Dryden Ctrl Schs RR 38 Dryden NY 13053

LAURICELLA, JANET MAY, association administrator; b. Fitchburg, Mass., Dec. 9, 1944; d. Ronald George and Pauline Janet (Perodeau) LeClair; m. David Lauricella, Apr. 3, 1987; children: Thomas II, Kristine, Beth, Robert, Heather, Cheryl. BA in Biology, Fitchburg State Coll., 1974, postgrad., 1974-80. Owner, operator nursery sch. Westminster, Mass., 1980-82; assoc. dir. Mental Health Assn. North Cen. Mass., Fitchburg, 1982-83; job specialist Jobs for Bay State Grads., Fitchburg, 1983-84; state dir. student activities Jobs for Bay State Grads., Boston, 1984-87; pres., chief profl. officer United Way Greater Gardner, Mass., 1987—. Contbr. articles to profl. jours. Mem., past pres. Oakmont Music Parents Assn., Ashburnham, Mass.; bd. dirs. Montachusett Coun. Girl Scouts U.S., 1987-90; dir. Emanuel Singers. Mem. NAFE, Rotary (pres. Gardner Club 1992), Greater Gardner C. of C. (Cmty. Svc. award for Leadership in AIDS). Lutheran. Office: United Way of Greater Gardner 161 Chestnut St # A Gardner MA 01440-2703

LAURIE, MARILYN, communications and computer company executive; b. N.Y.C.; d. Abraham and Irene Gold; m. Robert Laurie; children: Amy, Lisa. BA in English, Barnard Coll., 1959; MBA, Pace U., 1975. Responsible for environ. programs AT&T, N.Y.C., 1971-75, established electronic media program, 1975-78, exec. speeches, policy statements, 1978-79, advt. mgr., 1979-80; exec. dir. AT&T Bell Labs., 1980-83; v.p. AT&T Bell Labs., N.J., 1983-84, AT&T, N.J., 1984-85; group v.p. AT&T, 1986-87; sr. v.p. AT&T, Basking Ridge, N.J., 1987—; chmn. AT&T Found., N.Y.C. Author articles on environ. issues. Co-founder Environ. Action Coalition, 1970; co-originator Earth Day, 1970; bd. dirs. N.Y.C. Ballet, N.Y.C. Pub. Edn. Fund.

Recipient Gold Key award Pub. Relations News, 1985, 87, 88, WEAL award Women's Equity Action League, 1985, Women in Communications Matrix award, 1988; named to YWCA Acad. Women Achievers, 1984; named Pub. Rels. All Star, Inside Pub. Rels. Mag., 1993. Mem. Pub. Rels. Seminar (sec./treas.), Arthur Page Soc. (bd. officer), Catalyst (bd. dirs.), N.Y.C. Partnership, Women's Forum, Am. Bd. Advisors Russian-Am. Press and Info. Ctr. Office: AT&T 295 N Maple Ave RM 434213 Basking Ridge NJ 07920 also: AT&T Foundation 1301 Ave of the Americas New York NY 10019

LAURIE, PIPER (ROSETTA JACOBS), actress; b. Detroit, Jan. 22, 1932; m. Joseph Morgenstern, 1962; 1 child. Motion picture debut in Louisa; other motion pictures include The Milkman, Francis Goes to the Races, Prince Who Was A Thief, Son of Ali Baba, Has Anybody Seen My Gal, No Room for the Groom, Mississippi Gambler, Kelly and Me, Golden Blade, Dangerous Mission, Johnny Dark, Dawn at Socorro, Smoke Signal, Ain't Misbehavin', Until They Sail, The Hustler (Acad. award nominee 1962), Carrie, 1976 (Acad. award nominee 1976), Tim, 1978, Return to Oz, 1985, Children of a Lesser God, 1986, Appointment with Death, 1988, Other People's Money, 1990, Storyville, 1992, Rich in Love, 1992, Trauma, 1993, Wrestling Ernest Hemingway, 1993; TV appearances include Days of Wine and Roses, Playhouse 90, The Deaf Heart, The Ninth Day, G.E. Theatre, Play of the Week, Hallmark Hall of Fame, Nova: Margaret Sanger, The Woman Rebel, In the Matter of Karen Ann Quinlan, Rainbow, Skag, The Thorn Birds, 1983; TV films include The Bunker, 1981, Love, Mary, 1985, Mae West, 1985, Promise, 1986, Toughlove, 1985, Lies and Lullabies, 1993, Shadows of Desire, 1994, Fighting for My Daughter, 1995; TV series: Twin Peaks, 1990-91, Traps, 1994; appeared Broadway play Glass Menagerie, 1965, off-Broadway plays Rosemary and the Alligators, 1961. Recipient Emmy award Acad. TV Arts and Scis., 1987; named Woman of Yr., Harvard U. Hasty Pudding, 1962. Mem. Acad. Motion Picture Arts and Scis. Address: William Morris Agy care Jonathan Howard 151 S El Camino Dr Beverly Hills CA 90212-2704*

LAUTENSCHLAGER, PEGGY ANN, prosecutor; b. Fond du Lac, Wis., Nov. 22, 1955; d. Milton A. and Patsy R. (Oleson) L.; m. Rajiv M. Kaul, Dec. 29, 1979 (div. Dec. 1986); children: Joshua Lautenschlager Kaul, Ryan Lautenschlager Kaul; m. William P. Rippl, May 26, 1989; 1 child, Rebecca Lautenschlager Rippl. BA, Lake Forest Coll., 1977; JD, U. Wis., 1980. Bar: Wis., U.S. Dist. Ct. (we. dist.). Pvt. practice atty. Oshkosh, Wis., 1981-85; dist. atty. Winnebago County Wis., Oshkosh, 1985-88; rep. Wis. Assembly, Fond du Lac, 1988-92; U.S. attorney U.S. Dept. of Justice, Madison, Wisc., 1992-93; apptd. mem. Govs. Coun. on Domestic Violence, Madison, State Elections Bd., Madison. Active Wis. and Fond du Lac County Dem. Parties, 1976—, Dem. Nat. Com., Washington, 1992-93; mem. com. U. Wis., 1989—. Named Legislator of Yr., Wis. Sch. Counselors, 1992, Legislator of Yr., Wis. Corrections Coalition, 1992. Mem. Wis. Bar Assn., Fond du Lac County Bar Assn., Fond du Lac Assn. for Retarded Citizens, Fond du Lac Women in Mgmt., Fond du Lac Morning Optimists, Fond du Lac LWV, Phi Beta Kappa. Home: 1 Langdon St # 211 Madison WI 53702

LAVAIL, JENNIFER HART, neurobiologist, educator, researcher; b. Evansville, Ind., Apr. 2, 1943; d. L. Paul and Ruth (Lensing) Hart; children: Matthew H., Katherine H. BA, Trinity Coll., Washington, 1961-65; PhD, U. Wis., 1970. Postdoctoral fellow dept. neuropathology Harvard Med. Sch., Cambridge, Mass., 1970-73, instr., 1973-74, asst. prof., 1974-76; assoc. prof. anatomy U. Calif., San Francisco, 1976-83, prof., 1983—; bd. sci. counselors Nat. Inst. Neurol. and Communicative Disorders and Stroke, NIH, 1988-92. Woodrow Wilson fellow Ford Found., 1965-66; Alfred P. Sloan fellow Sloan Found., 1976-79. Mem. Am. Assn. Anatomists (v.p. 1988-90, Charles Judson Herrick award 1975). Office: U Calif Dept Anatomy PO Box 452 San Francisco CA 94143

LAVALLEE, DEIRDRE JUSTINE, marketing professional; b. Woonsocket, R.I., June 14, 1962; d. Albert Paul and Margaret Justine (O'Brien) L. BS in Chem. Engring., U. R.I., 1984. Sales engr. NGS Assocs. Inc., Canton, Mass., 1985-87; mgr. dist. sales MKS Instruments Inc., Andover, Mass., 1987—. V.p., bd. dirs. Nat. Conf. Standards Labs.; mem. adv. bd. Tex. State Tech. Coll. Mem. AIChE (sec. chpt.), Am. Soc. Materials, Am. Inst. Physics, Am. Vacuum Soc. Home: 845 13th St Boulder CO 80302-7503 Office: MKS Instruments Inc 5330 Sterling Dr Boulder CO 80301-2309

LAVALLEE, KATHERINE LYNN FRIEDRICH, physical therapist; b. Syracuse, N.Y.; d. George Alanson and Janice Lee (Young) F.; m. Robert Lawrence Lavallee, Oct. 12, 1991. AA, Maria Regina Coll., Syracuse, N.Y., 1983; BS, Daemen Coll., Amherst, N.Y., 1988. Staff phys. therapist Good Samaritan Hosp., Lebanon, Pa., 1988-89; phys. therapist Regain Sports Medicine Clinic, Lebanon, 1988-89; cons. phys. therapist Lebanon County Life Support Facility, Lebanon, 1989; asst. head phys. therapist Syracuse Sports Medicine, P.C., Liverpool, N.Y., 1989-92; lead phys. therapist Rose Med. Ctr., Denver, 1992—. Mem. NAFE, Am. Phys. Therapy Assn., Internat. Platform Assn. Office: Rose Med Ctr 4955 N Peoria Ste C Denver CO 80239

LAVALLEE, MAUREEN MADELINE, psychologist; b. Bradford, Mass., June 10, 1955; d. Donald Alfred and Barbara Mary (McCarron) L.; m. Christopher Van Kleeck, Sept. 1, 1985; children: Alexander, Andrew. BA, Clark U., 1977; MEd, Boston U., 1983; D of Psychology, Mass. Sch. Profl. Psychology, 1987. Psychotherapist Human Resource Inst., Franklin, Mass., 1986-88; consulting psychologist Bur. Instutional Schs., Westborough, Mass., 1987-89; psychologist Eastern Shore Assocs., Shrewsbury, Mass., 1988-91, Lancaster Assocs., Shrewsbury, 1988-91, pvt. practice, Worcester, Mass., 1991—; clin. cons. Devereaux Ctr., Rutland, Mass., 1993—, Mentor Program, East Brookfield, Mass. Mem. APA, Am. Soc. Clin. Hypnosis, Nat. Register Health Svc. Providers, New Eng. Soc. for the Study of Dissociation, Internat. Soc. Study of Dissociation, Mass. Psychol. Soc. Office: 131 Lincoln St Worcester MA 01605-2403

LAVALLEY, JUDY TUCKER, cardiology critical care nurse; b. Birmingham, Ala., Oct. 6, 1954; d. James Melvin and Clytee (Whitman) Tucker; divorced. Lic. practical nurse, Itawamba Jr. Coll., Tupelo, Miss., 1974, ADN, 1982; BSN, Miss. U. for Women, Tupelo, Miss., 1994. RN, Miss.; cert. in ACLS. Physician's asst. in cardiology Internal Medicine Assocs. Ltd., Tupelo; critical care nurse North Miss. Med. Ctr., Tupelo, staff nurse cardiac catheterization lab., noninvasive cardiol supr. Mem. Am. Acad. Med. Adminstrs., Sigma Theta Tau.

LAVANDIER, JESSICA LUZ, urban planner; b. N.Y.C., Feb. 22, 1966; d. Federico Lavandier and Martha (Brouse) Devernoe. BS, Eckerd Coll., 1987; cert. in heritage preservation, Ga. State U., 1991; M of City Planning, Ga. Inst. Tech., 1991. Biol. scientist U. South Fla., St. Petersburg, 1987-88; grad. asst. U. Nice, France, 1989; grad. asst. Ga. Tech., Atlanta, 1989-91, project planner, 1991-92; project planner Urban Design Ctr., Atlanta, 1991-92; urban planner City of Marietta, Ga., 1992-94; planner III Dept. Planning and Econ. Devel., Fulton County, Atlanta, 1994—. Watch leader Eckerd Coll. Search and Rescue, St. Petersburg, 1983-86; bd. dirs. CIRCA, Atlanta Preservation Ctr., 1993—, Atlanta Bicycle Campaign, 1992-94; chair Cobb Bicycle Transp. Com., Cobb County, Ga., 1993-94; tour guide Atlanta Preservation Ctr., 1989—. Scholar Eckerd Coll., 1983-87, grad. scholar Rotary Internat., 1988-89, Nat. Hispanic scholar, 1991. Mem. Am. Planning Assn., Nat. Trust for Historic Preservation, Ga. Planning Assn., Atlanta Preservation Ctr. Home: 390 9th St Atlanta GA 30309 Office: Fulton County Dept Planning/Econ Devel 141 Pryor St Ste 5001 Atlanta GA 30303

LAVANE, LOUISE M., medical/surgical nurse; b. Lufkin, Tex.; d. Lewis J. and Mae L. (Perry) Menefee; m. Eldridge LaVane Jr., May 4, 1983; children: Katrinka M. Jenkins, Lintonette L. Acliese. Grad., Meml. Hosp. Vocat. Nursing, Lufkin, 1971; ADN, Angelina Coll., Lufkin, 1976; BSN, Stephen F. Austin State U., 1994; MS in Nursing, U. Tex., Tyler. LVN, RN, Tex.; cert. emergency nurse, me.-surg. nurse; cert. ACLS, CPR instr. Dir. emergency svcs. Meml. Med. Ctr. East Tex., Lufkin; asst. nurse mgr. Woodland Hts. Med. Ctr., Lufkin. Mem. ANA (med. surg. coun.), Tex. Nurses Assn., Nat. Black Nurses Assn., Emergency Dept. Nurses Assn.

LAVE, JUDITH RICE, economics educator; came to U.S., 1961; d. J.H. Melville and G.A. Pauline (Lister) Rice; m. Lester Bernard Lave, June 21, 1965; children: Tamara Rice, Jonathan Melville. BA in Econs., Queen's U., Kingston, Ont., Can., 1957-61; MA in Econs., Harvard U., 1964, PhD, 1967; LLD, Queen's U., 1994. Lectr., asst. prof. econs. Carnegie Mellon U., Pitts., 1966-73, assoc. prof., 1973-78; dir. econ. analysis Office of Sec., Dep. of Asst. Sec. Planning and Evaluation, Washington, 1978-79; dir. office of rsch. Health Care Fin. Adminstrn., Washington, 1980-82; prof. health econs. U. Pitts., 1982—; cons. Nat. Study Internal Medicine Manpower, Chgo., 1976, Wash. State Hosp. Assn., 1984, Horty, Springer & Mattern, Pitts., 1984, Hogan and Hartson, Washington, 1989, Ont. Hosp. Assn., Conn. Hosp. Assn., 1991; cons. various agys. U.S. HHS (formerly U.S. HEW), 1971-89; mem. adv. panel Robert Wood Johnson Found., Princeton, N.J., 1983-84, Leonard Davis Inst., Phila., 1984, U.S. Congress, 1977, 82, 83—; com. mem. Inst. Medicine Coms., Washington, 1975-91, Project 2000 Commn. on Future of Podiatry, Washington, 1985-86. Editl. bd. Wiley Series in Health Svcs., 1989-90, Health Svcs. Rsch., 1970-74, Inquiry, 1979-82, AUPHA Press, 1986, Jour. of Health Policy Politics and Law; co-author: Hospital Construction Act - An Evaluation of the Hill Burton Program, 1948-73, 74, Health Status, Medical Care Utilization and Outcome: A Bibliography of Empirical Studies (4 vols.) 1989, Providing Hospital Services, 1989; contbr. numerous articles to profl. jours. Mem. Prospective Payment Assessment Commn., 1993—, planning com. ARC, Pitts., 1986—; mem. rev. com. United Way, Pitts., 1988-90; bd. dirs. Craig Ho., Pitts., 1976-77. Woodrow Wilson fellow, 1961-62. Mem. Assn. Health Svcs. Rsch. (pres. 1977-88, bd. dirs. 1983-93), Found. for Health Svcs. Rsch. (pres. 1988-89, bd. dirs. 1983—), Am. Pub. Health Soc., Am. Econ. Soc. (com. mem.), Inst. Medicine, Nat. Acad. Social Ins. Democrat. Home: 1008 Devonshire Rd Pittsburgh PA 15213-2914 Office: U Pitts A649 Pub Health Pittsburgh PA 15213

LAVELLE, AVIS, federal administration official; b. Chgo., Mar. 5, 1954; d. Adolph Eugene and Mai Evelyn (Hicks) Sampson. BS in Comms. cum laude, U. Ill., 1975. Announcer, pub. affairs dir. Sta. WTAX Radio, Springfield, Ill., 1977-78; news dir., anchor Sta. WLTH Radio, Gary, Ind., 1978-79; reporter, anchor Stas. WJJD/WJEZ, Chgo., 1979-84; chief polit. reporter Sta. WGN-Radio/TV, Chgo., 1984-88; campaign press sec. Richard M. Daley for Mayor, Chgo., 1988-89; mayoral press sec. Officer of the Mayor, Chgo., 1989-92; nat. press sec. Clinton/Gore for Pres., Little Rock, Ark., 1992; spl. asst. to chmn. Vernon Jordan Presdl. Transition, Washington, 1992-93; asst. sec. pub. affairs U.S. Dept. Health and Human Svcs., Washington, 1993—. Bd. dirs. Project Image, Inc., Chgo., 1988-89, Human Resources Devel. Inst., Chgo., 1988; mem. steering com. Black Adoption Taskforce of Ill., Chgo., 1987; mem. Delta Sigma Theta Pub. Svc., Chgo., 1973—. Recipient African Am. Bus. and Profl. Women award Dollars and Sense Mag., 1989, Women at Work award Nat. Commn. Working Women, 1980, First Place Team award AP, 1984. Democrat. Office: Dept of Health & Human Services Public Affairs 200 Independence Ave SW Washington DC 20201

LAVELLE, MARY LEE DEMETRE, psychiatric nursing educator; b. Charleston, S.C., May 30, 1945; m. John L. Lavelle Jr., Aug. 4, 1973; children: Paul, Rachelle. Diploma nursing with honors, Med. Coll. S.C., 1966, BSN with highest honors, 1974, MSN in Psychiat. Nursing with honors, 1990. RN, S.C.; cert. BCLS. Various nursing positions, 1966-68; staff nurse Charleston County Hosp., Charleston, S.C., 1969, head nurse med. fl., 1969-72, supr., 1972-75; coord. alumni affairs Med. U. of S.C., Charleston, 1974-76; with Family Planning Clinic, Charleston County Health Dept., Charleston, 1975-76; instr. med. terminology Trident Tech. Coll., Palmer Campus, Charleston, 1975-76; emergency med. system auditor Palmetto Lowcountry Health System, 1986; coord. alumni affairs Med. U. of S.C., Coll. of Nursing, Charleston, 1982-88; curator Ruth Chamberlin Hist. Libr. Ruth Chamberlin Hist. Nursing Libr., Charleston, 1988-92; asst. intern coord. staff devel. dept., diabetic instr. patient edn. dept. Roper Hosp., Charleston, 1985; staff nurse nursing pool Inst. of Psychiatry, Med. U. S.C., Charleston, 1985; instr. nursing LPN program Trident Tech. Coll., Charleston, 1991—, instr. psychiat. nursing ADN program, 1990—; instr. psychiat. nursing Med. U. S.C., 1994—; bd. dirs. Med. U. S.C. Assn., 1992-95; mem. nursing pool psychiatry Charleston Meml. Hosp., 1992—; presenter in field. Mem. S.C. Heart Assn., 1967-78. Saul Alexander Ednl. scholar, 1973, scholar Bus. and Profl. Women's Club, 1972, Am. Bus. Women's Assn., 1972. Fellow Nightingale Soc. (hons.); mem. Coll. of Nursing Alumni Assn. Med. U. of S.C. (v.p. 1967-69, pres. 1969-74, bd. dirs. 1974-75, ex-officio bd. mem. 1982-88, nominating com. 1992-93), Med. U. of S.C. Alumni Assn. (councilor 1971-74, sec. 1974-75, v.p. 1977-79, pres. 1979-80, bd. dirs. 1981-88, 92). Home: 694 Fort Sumter Dr Charleston SC 29412

LAVELLE-NICHOLS, ROBIN ANN, accountant; b. Tacoma, Wash., Nov. 27, 1959; d. Gregory Henry and Shirley Ann (Heggen) L.; m. Gordon L. Nichols, Aug. 20, 1983; children: Melinda Ann, Angela Elizabeth, Lindsey Katherine. BBA cum laude, Pacific Luth. U., 1985. CPA, Wash. V.p. acctg. and fin. Sorrento Enterprises, Inc., Spanaway, Wash., 1980-85; accountant, audit mgr. Ernst & Young, Seattle, 1985-90; audit. mgr. Dwyer, Pemberton & Coulson, Tacoma, Wash., 1990-92; pvt. practice Tacoma, Wash., 1992—. Mem. AICPA, Wash. Soc. CPAs, Inst. Mgmt. Accts. (dir. acquisition 1985-87, dir. tech. programs 1989-90, v.p. profl. devel. 1990-91, Outstanding Achievement Mem. Acquisition award 1985-86, v.p. membership and mktg. 1991-92, v.p. fin. and adminstrn., 1993-94, chair corp. and acad. devel.), Pacific Luth. U. Bus. Alumni Assn. (founding bd. dirs.), Wash. State Horseman Assn., Beta Alpha Psi (pres. Delta Rho chpt.). Home and Office: 4104 145th St E Tacoma WA 98446-1674

LAVENAS, SUZANNE, writer, editor, consultant; b. Buenos Aires, Dec. 17, 1942; came to U.S., 1955; d. Carlos Fernando and Mary (Sharp) Lavenas; m. Wesley First, Jan. 9, 1982. Student, Antioch Coll., 1960-64, 65-66. Computer programmer N.Y. Telephone, N.Y.C., 1966-68; prodn. editor, then copy editor Travel Weekly, N.Y.C., 1968-76, chief copy editor, 1976-79; mng. editor Indsl. Chem. News, N.Y.C., 1981-82; editor, writer, cons. N.Y.C., 1986—. Author numerous articles. Mem. Overseas Press Club, Soc. Silurians. Republican. Episcopalian. Home: 236 Edgemere St Montauk NY 11954-5249

LAVENSON, SUSAN BARKER, corporate executive, consultant; b. L.A., July 26, 1936; d. Percy Morton and Rosalie Laura (Donner) Barker; m. James H. Lavenson, Apr. 22, 1973; 1 child, Ellen Ruth Stanclift. BA, Stanford U., 1958, MA, 1959; PhD (hon.), Thomas Coll., 1994. Cert. gen. secondary credential tchr., Calif. Tchr. Benjamin Franklin Jr. High Sch., San Francisco, 1960; tchr. French dept. Lowell High Sch., San Francisco, 1960-61; v.p. Monogram Co., San Francisco, 1961-62; creative dir. Monogram Co., N.Y.C., 1973-76; pres. SYR Corp., Santa Barbara, Calif., 1976-89; ptnr. Lavenson Ptnrs., Camden, Maine, 1989—; mem. commn. on co-edn. Wheaton Coll., Norton, Mass., 1985-87; mem. Relais et Chateaux, Paris, 1978-89; cons. World Bank Recruitment Divsn., 1993; chmn. bd. dirs. Pinetree Computer Sys., Rockport, Maine. Author: Greening of San Ysidro, 1977 (Conf. award 1977). Trustee Camden Pub. Libr., 1989—, v.p., 1991-93; trustee Thomas Coll., Waterville, Maine, Atlantic Ave. Trust; founding pres. Maine chpt. Internat. Women's Forum, 1991—. Mem. Camden Yacht Club, Stanford Alumni Assn., Com. of 200 (treas. 1985-86), Phi Delta Kappa. Home and Office: 12 Norumbega Dr Camden ME 04843-1746

LAVENTHAL, LISA DENISE, elementary and secondary educator; b. Little Neck, N.Y., Nov. 1, 1963. BA in Comm., SUNY, Albany, 1985; MS in Edn., English, Long Island U., 1993. Clk. Avis Rent-a-Car, Garden City, N.Y., 1983-84; pub. rels. coord. N.Y. State Dept. Tax & Fin., Albany, 1985; account exec., pub. rels. coord. Harriett Ruderman, Bertin Design, Port Washington, N.Y., 1985-87; mktg. and advt. specialist, editor Computer Assocs., Islandia, N.Y., 1988-92; tchr. Nassau County Pub. Schs., Long Island, N.Y., 1992—; elem. and secondary English tchr. Home: 170 Heathcote Rd Elmont NY 11003-2006

LAVID, JEAN STERN, school director; b. Roanoke, Va., Jan. 4, 1943; d. Ernest George and Marianne (Stamm) Stern; m. Aug. 26, 1968 (div. 1989); children: Nathan, Eric, Craig, Brian, Laura. BA, Coll. William and Mary, 1965; MA, Wichita State U., 1986, specialist degree, 1989. Cert. permanent tchr. German, N.Y.; cert. supt., bldg. adminstr., Kans., Colo., N.Y., Va., N.H., Ohio, Ariz., Pa., Ky. Rural community devel. vol. Peace Corps, Turkey, 1965-67; tchr. German, Spanish and English Kenmore (N.Y.)-Tonawanda Sch. Dist., 1967-70; tchr. German Grand Island (N.Y.) Sch. Dist., 1978-82, coord. adult edn., prin., 1982; grad. rsch. asst. Wichita (Kans.) State U., 1984-86, instr. German, 1985; asst. prin. Unified Sch. Dist. 259, Wichita, 1986-88; supt., high sch. prin. Unified Sch. Dist. 314, Brewster, Kans., 1988-91; supt. Unified Sch. Dist. 271, Stockton, Kans., 1991-93; dir. edn. Computer Learning Ctr., Alexandria, Va., 1993; sr. dir. distbr. Nat. Safety Assocs., Lofton, Va., 1993—; dir. KinderCare Learning Ctr., Alexandria, 1994; dir. edn. Gesher Jewish Day Sch. of No. Va., Fairfax, 1994; dir. Kinder Care Learning Ctr., Vienna, Va.; mem. sch. community adv. coms., N.Y., Kans., 1975-86; chmn. Com. To Revise Fgn. Lang. Curriculum, Grand Island, 1981-83; judge Kans. Fgn. Lang. Competition, 1987. Contbr. numerous articles on ednl. leadership to profl. jours. Pres. Grand Island Food Coop., 1978-83, Waterford Food Coop., Wichita, 1983-88. mem. Am. Assn. Sch. Adminstrs., Assn. for Supervision and Curriculum Devel., Nat. Assn Secondary and Elem. Sch. Prins., Am. Assn. Tchrs. German, Kans. Assn. Sch. Adminstrs., Kans. Unitied Sch. Adminstrs., AAUW (active local, regional and state levels 1973—), Phi Kappa Phi, Phi Delta Kappa, Nat. Supts. Acad. Home: 9734 Hagel Cir Lorton VA 22079 Office: Kinder Care Learning Ctr 437 Knoll St NW Vienna VA 22180

LAVIN, AUDREY ANN PERLMAN, education consultant, English language educator; b. Chgo., Dec. 2, 1927; d. Mandel and Blanch R. (Bloom) Perlman; m. Carl H. Lavin, Feb. 22, 1953; children: Maud K., Carl H., Jr., Franklin L., Douglas B. BS, Northwestern U., 1949; MA, U. Akron, 1976; PhD, Case Western Reserve U., 1984. Cert. bus. and tech. writer. Lectr. English Case Western Reserve U., Cleve., 1978-80; asst. prof. English Coll. Wooster, Ohio, 1980-83, 86-87; Fulbright prof. U. Alcalá de Hanares, Madrid, 1987-89; internat. edn. cons., vis. prof. U. Nacional P. H. Ureña Santo Domingo, Dominican Republic, 1990, Am. U., San Salvador, El Salvador, 1990, Internat. Exec. Svc. Corps, Guatemala City, Guatemala, 1991, Budapest U. Econs., Hungary, 1992, Pontifica Universidad Javeriana, Bogotá, Colombia, 1993, U. P. J. Sefarik, Presov, Slovakia, 1993, Am. U. and Fulbright Com., Cairo, 1993, Far Eastern State U., Vladivostock, Russia, 1994, U. Transylvania, Brasov, Romania, 1994; tchr., Kiryat Ekron, Israel, 1986; cons. bus. writing, Canton, Ohio, 1990—; organizer exec. com. comm. consortium Edn. Enhancement Partnership Ohio, 1990-93; lectr. in field. Author: Aspects: E. M. Forster, Pattern and Rhythm, 1989, Aspects of the Novelist: E. M. Forster, 1994; editor (jour.) Revista Española de Estudios Norteamericanos, 1989; asst. editor Etc., Jour. Gen. Semantics, 1950-53; contbr. articles to profl. jours. Mem. Temple Isreal, 1953—, Canton Jewish Ctr., 1953—, The Wilderness Ctr., 1960—; organizer Nat. Feminist Conf., Madrid, 1987; past pres. YMCA Camp Tippecanoe, Canton Country Day Sch. Parents Assn.; fellow exec. com. YMCA, Canton, 1985—; bd. dirs. Canton Planning Comm., Canton, 1991—; bd. dirs., chair legis. com. Ohio Humanities Coun., Colombus, 1991—. Recipient Nat. Program award Jewish Fedn. Montreal, 1993; Faculty grantee Case Western Reserve U., 1980, Coll. Wooster, 1983, 86, 87, Book grantee U. de Alcalá de Henares, 1989; Inst. Gen. Semantics scholar, 1949. Mem. MLA, Nat. Coun. Tchrs. English. Home and Office: 5240 Plain Center Rd NE Canton OH 44714

LAVIN, BERNICE E., cosmetics executive; b. 1925; m. Leonard H. Lavin, Oct. 30, 1947; children: Scott Jay, Carol Marie, Karen Sue. Student, Northwestern U. Dir., v.p., sec.-treas. Alberto-Culver Co., Alberto-Culver U.S.A., Inc., 1961-93; sec.-treas., dir. Alberto-Culver Internat., Inc., Draper Daniels Media Svcs., Inc.; v.p., sec.-treas. Sally Beauty Co., Inc. Office: Alberto-Culver Co 2525 Armitage Ave Melrose Park IL 60160-1163

LAVIN, LINDA, actress; b. Portland, Maine, Oct. 15, 1937; d. David J. and Lucille (Potter) L. BA, Coll. William and Mary, Williamsburg, Va., 1959. Debut: (Off-Broadway) Oh, Kay!, 1960, (Broadway) A Family Affairs, 1962; appearances in revues Wet Paint, 1965, The Game Is Up, 1965, The Mad Show, 1966; with nat. touring company On a Clear Day You Can See Forever, 1966-67; mem. acting company Eugene O'Neil Playwrights' Unit, 1968; other stage appearances include It's a Bird... It's a Plane... It's Superman, 1966, Something Different, 1967, Little Murders, 1969, Cop-Out, 1969, The Last of the Red Hot Lovers, 1969 (Tony nominee), Story Theatre, 1970, The Enemy is Dead, 1973, Love Two, 1974, The Comedy of Errors, 1975, Dynamite Tonite!, 1975, Six Characters in Search of an Author, Am. Repertory Theatre, Cambridge, Mass., 1983-84 season, Broadway Bound, 1986 (Tony award 1987), Gypsy, 1990, The Sisters Rosensweig, 1993, Death Defying Acts, 1995; film appearances: See You In The Morning, 1989, I Want to Go Back Home, 1989; star: (TV series) Alice, 1976-85 (Golden Globe award 1979); star and prodr.: (TV series) Room for Two, 1992—; prodr.: (PBS TV miniseries) The Sunset Gang, 1991; other TV appearances on Phyllis, Family, Rhoda, Harry O; TV movies include: The Morning After, 1974, Like Mom, Like Me, 1978, A Matter of Life and Death, 1981, Another Woman's Child, 1983, A Place To Call Home, Lena: My One Hundred Children. Recipient Sat. Rev., Outer Critics Circle awards for Little Murders, Theater World award for Wet Paint. Office: Metropolitan Talent Agy 4526 Wilshire Blvd Los Angeles CA 90010*

LAVIN, ROXANNA MARIE, finance executive; b. San Antonio, Sept. 8, 1952; d. Teddy Harold and Cora Ann (Ames) Maddox; m. Michael Paul Lavin, July 11, 1971; children: Sharon Renai, Christopher Michael, Katherine Marie. Student, Ea. Mich. U., 1985, 86, 70; BBA magna cum laude, Cleary Coll., 1992; postgrad, Ctr. Mich. U., 1993, Madonna Univ., 1994. Sales clk. Children's Fashion Shop, Livonia, Mich., 1970; bookkeeping clk. Ypsilanti (Mich.) Savs. Bank, 1970-73; receptionist, acctg. clk. Maize & Blue Properties, Ann Arbor, Mich., 1986-87; acctg. clk. Sensors, Saline, Mich., 1987; office supr., fin. mgr. Great Lakes Coll. Assn., Ann Arbor, 1988-94; fin., pers. mgr. Jackson (Mich.) Libr., 1994—. Sec., treas. Old Mill Hills Assn., Pinckney, Mich., 1990-93; mem. Pinckney High and Mid. Sch. Parents, 1990-92; parent vol. Lincoln Cons. Schs., Ypsilanti, 1985-86. Recipient scholarship Ea. Mich. U., 1970. Mem. AAUW. Office: Jackson Dist Libr 244 W Michigan Ave Jackson MI 49201

LAVIN-CORTI, ROSE MAUREEN, artist; b. Perth Amboy, N.J., Oct. 16, 1952; d. James V.P. and Emma (Kiblosh) Lavin; m. Franco Casentini, Feb. 14, 1974 (div. 1984); 1 child, Franco K. Casentini; m. Stefano Corti, Oct. 24, 1984; 1 child, Sandro J. Corti. Student, Georgian Ct., 1970-72, U. Florence (Italy), 1972-73. Saleswoman Correges, Rome, 1977-78; sec. McDonnell-Douglas, Rome, 1978-80, McCann-Erickson, Rome, 1980-82, RAI TV and Radio Corp., N.Y.C., 1983-84; mgr. Benetton, Woodbridge, N.J., 1984-85; sole proprietor Art Studio LC, Woodbridge, 1990—. Artist drawing logo contest, Tarquinia, Italy (Silver medal 1978). Directress St. Peter's Altar Guild, Perth Amboy, 1991-94; mem. NOW, 1991—. Mem. Nat. Mus. of Women in the Arts, Nat. Assn. Women Bus. Owners. Democrat. Episcopalian. Home: 677 Parker St Perth Amboy NJ 08861-2913 Office: Art Studio LC 76 Main St Woodbridge NJ 07095-2816

LAVIOLETTE, CAREY LEBLANC, assistant principal; b. Norfolk, Va., Nov. 3, 1956; d. Nedier Jr. and Madge (LeBlanc) LeBlanc; m. Kirk Anthony Laviolette, Apr. 8, 1977; children: Kal, Laurie. BS cum laude, U. Southwestern La., 1978, MS in Guidance and Counseling, 1984, SpED, 1989. Lic. profl. counselor, adminstr., supr., La. Middle sch. tchr. earth sci. and life sci. Iberia Parish Sch. Bd., New Iberia, La., 1979, tchr. secondary phys. sci. and physics, 1979-85, guidance counselor, 1985-89, drug free schs. and communities facilitator, 1989-94; asst. prin. Delcambre (La.) H.S., 1994—; 4-Mat learning style trainer Iberia Parish Sch. Bd., 1992—; mem. drug free curriculum writing team La. State Dept. Edn., Baton Rouge, 1990-92. Active Am. Heart Assn., New Iberia, 1989-92; bd. dirs., sec. Iberia Parish Teen Ct., New Iberia, 1992—. Mem. Am. Assn. Counseling and Devel., La. Assn. Counseling and Devel., New Iberia C. of C. (health and safety com. 1989-93), Phi Kappa Phi. Democrat. Roman Catholic. Office: Delcambre HS 601 W Main St Delcambre LA 70528

LAVOIE, NOELLA, advertising agency executive; b. Rimouski, Que., Can., Dec. 25, 1953; d. Gerard Lavoie and Emma Ruest. Cert. in mktg., Ecole Hautes Etudes Comml., Montreal, 1985; BA, U. Laval, Québec, Que., 1986. Media dir. Publim, Québec, 1981-85, account supr., 1985-87; rep. Radio Can., Québec, 1987-89, sales mgr., 1989; v.p. client svcs. Marketel, Québec, 1989-91, v.p., gen. mgr., 1991-94; pres., gen. mgr. Cargo Marketel, Québec, 1994—; cons. Theatre du Gros Mecano, Québec, 1990-91, Québec 2002, 1992. Mem. Ste-Foy C. of C., Québec Met. C. of C., Cercle de la Garnison,

Lions (v.p. Québec Centre club 1989-92). Office: Cargo Marketel, 871 Chemin Saint-Louis, Québec, PQ Canada G1S 1C1

LAW, CAROL JUDITH, medical psychotherapist; b. N.Y.C., May 1, 1940; d. Aldo and Jennie (Feldman) Settimo; m. Perry J. Koll, Dec. 26, 1967 (div. Nov. 1974); 1 son, Perry J.; m. Edwin B. Law, June 1, 1979. BA, Upsala Coll., 1962; postgrad., Rutgers U., 1964-66; MA, Columbia Pacific U., 1982, PhD, 1984. Diplomate Am. Bd. Med. Psychotherapy. Pers. dir. Hotel Manhattan, N.Y.C., 1961; supr. social work Essex County, Newark, 1962-67; exec. dir. USO, Vung Tau, South Vietnam, 1967-68; dir. Dept. Health and Rehab. Svcs., Pensacola, Fla., 1968-79; therapist, tchr. Franciscan Renewal Ctr., Scottsdale, Ariz., 1982-92; pvt. practice Scottsdale, 1982-92; drug free workforce cons. Pensacola C. of C., Fla., 1992—; pres. Drug Free Workplaces, Inc., 1993—; mem. Healthy Start of N.W. Fla.; dist 1 chmn. Alcohol, Drug Abuse and Mental Health Planning Coun. Mem. state adv. bd. Parents Anonymous, Phoenix, 1982; chmn. Gov.'s Adv. Commn. Drugs and the Elderly, Tallahassee, 1978; pres. Jaycettes, Pensacola, 1969; chmn. social com. United Way Fund, Pensacola, 1977; mem. adv. bd. USO, Pensacola, 1973, H.R.S. Dist. 1 Community Collaboration Project; trustee ORME Sch. Fellow Am. Acad. Polit. and Social Sci.; mem. Am. Assn. Pub. Adminstrs., Pensacola Country Club, Escambia County Drug Court Coalition, Fla. State C. of C. (drug issues com.), Nat. Drugs Don't Work (Fla. rep.). Roman Catholic. Home: 3386 Chantarene Dr Pensacola FL 32507-3586

LAW, CLARENE ALTA, innkeeper, state legislator; b. Thornton, Idaho, July 22, 1933; d. Clarence Riley and Alta (Simmons) Webb; m. Franklin Kelso Meadows, Dec. 2, 1953 (div. July 1973); children: Teresa Meadows Jillson, Charisse Meadows Haws, Steven Riley; m. Creed Law, Aug. 18, 1973. Student, Idaho State Coll., 1953. Sec., sub. tchr. Grand County Schs., Cedar City, Utah, 1954-57; UPI rep. newspaper agy. Moab, Utah Regional Papers, Salt Lake City and Denver; auditor Wort Hotel, Jackson, Wyo., 1960-62; innkeeper, CEO Elk Country Motels, Inc., Jackson, Wyo., 1962—; rep. Wyo. Ho. of Reps., Cheyenne, 1991—, chmn. house travel com., 1993—, mem. bank bd. State of Wyo., 1991—; bd. dirs. Jackson State Bank, Snow King Resort. Chmn. sch. bd. dirs. Teton County Schs., Jackson, 1983-86. Named Citizen of Yr. Jackson C. of C., 1976, Bus. Person of Yr. Jackson Hole Realtors, 1987, Wyo. Small Bus. Person SBA, 1977. Mem. Wyo. Lodging and Restaurant Assn. (pres., chmn. bd. dirs. 1988-89, Big Wyo. award 1987), Internat. Leisure Hosts (bd. dirs. Phoenix chpt. 1991-94), Soroptimists (charter), BPW (Woman of Yr. 1975). Republican. Mem. LDS Ch. Home: Box 575 43 W Pearl Jackson WY 83001 Office: Elk County Motels Inc 43 W Pearl Jackson WY 83001

LAW, FLORA ELIZABETH (LIBBY LAW), retired community health and pediatrics nurse; b. Biddeford, Maine, Sept. 11, 1935; d. Arthur Parker and Flora Alma (Knutti) Butt; m. Robert F. Law, 1961; children : Susan E., Sarah F., Christian A., Martha F.; m. John F. Brown, Jr., 1982. BA, Davis and Elkins (W.Va.) Coll., 1957; postgrad., Cornell U.-N.Y. Hosp., N.Y.C., 1960; BSN, U. Nev., Las Vegas, 1976, MS in Counseling Edn., 1981. RN, Nev.; cert. sch. nurse. Staff nurse So. Nev. Community Hosp. (now Univ. Med. Ctr.), Las Vegas; relief charge nurse Valley Psychiat. Inst., Las Vegas; pub. health nurse Clark County Dist. Health Dept., Las Vegas; sch. nurse Clark County Sch. Dist., Las Vegas; ret., 1994. Chair task force on sch. nursing Nev.'s Commn. for Profl. Standards in Edn.; mem. nurse practice act revision com. Nev. State Bd. Nursing. Mem. Nat. Assn. Sch. Nurses (past state dir., sch. nurse liaison Clark County Tchrs. Assn.), NEA, Clark County Assn. Sch. Nurses (past pres.), Sigma Theta Tau. Home: 3420 Clandara Ave Las Vegas NV 89121

LAW, JANET MARY, music educator; b. East Orange, N.J., Mar. 8, 1931; d. Charles and Mary Ellen (Keavy) Maitland; m. William Howard Law, Dec. 13, 1952; children: Robert Alan, Gail Ellen. Lic. Practical Nurse, St. Barnabas Sch., 1971; BA magna cum laude, Fairleigh Dickinson U., Rutherford, N.J., 1981; tchr. tng. course, Westminster Choir Coll., 1990—, Queens U., Canada, 1993. Registered Suzuki tchr., Suzuki piano tchr., traditional piano tchr. Staff nurse psychiat. unit St. Barnabas Med. Ctr., Livingston, N.J., 1972-78; office nurse, asst. to pvt. physician North Arlington, N.J., 1978-79; dir., owner B Sharp Acad., Rutherford, N.J., 1979-83; founder, tchr. piano music preparatory div. Fairleigh Dickinson U., Rutherford, 1983-89; founder, coord. piano divsn. Garden State Acad. Music, Rutherford, N.J., 1989-94; tchr. piano divsn. Garden State Acad. Music, Rutherford, 1989—; Suzuki piano coord., tchr. Suzuki piano program, coord. Suzuki piano divsn. Montclair (N.J.) State U., 1994—. Author: Keyboard Kapers, 1983; inventor music games, 1983. Mem. Music and Performing Arts Club, Profl. Music Tchrs. Guild N.J. Inc., Suzuki Assn. of the Ams. Home: 169 Hillcrest Dr Wayne NJ 07470-5629 Office: Garden State Acad Music 88 Park Ave Rutherford NJ 07070-1957 Office: Montclair State University Music Prep Divsn Upper Montclair NJ 07043

LAWHON, TOMMIE COLLINS MONTGOMERY, child development/family living educator; b. Shelby County, Tex., Mar. 15; d. Marland Walker and Lillian (Tinsley) Collins; m. David Baldwin Montgomery, Mar. 31, 1962 (dec. Aug. 1964); m. John Lawhon, Aug. 27, 1967; 1 child, David Collins. B.S., Baylor U., 1954; M in Home Econs. Edn. in Home Econs., Tex. Woman's U., 1964, Ph.D., 1966. Cert. tchr., Tex., home economist, family life educator. Tchr., Victoria Pub. Schs. (Tex.), 1954-55; stewardess, supr. Am. Airlines, Dallas/Fort Worth, 1955-62; prof. home econs. Ea. Ky. U., Richmond, 1966-67, U. North Tex., Denton, 1968—; profl. presenter Profl. Devel. Inst., U. North Tex., 1981—, mem. faculty senate 1984—, chmn. on coms., 1987-88, com. status of women, 1984-87, mem. faculty salary study com., 1989—, chmn., 1989-90, mem. tradition com., 1989—, recorder, 1989—; bd. dirs. Univ. union, 1985-88, mem. Status of Women Com., 1984-87, mem. Com. on Coms., 1986—, chmn. 1987-88, vice chmn., 1988-89. Co-author: Children are Artists, 1971; Hidden Hazards for Children and Families, 1982; editor: What to do with Children, 1974; Field Trips for Children, 1984; contbr. articles to profl. jours. Chmn., United Way North Tex. State U., 1980-81; chmn. crusade Am. Cancer Soc., Denton County, 1982-83; chmn. nominating com. First Bapt. Ch., Denton, 1983-84, 84-85. Recipient Presdl. award Tex. Council on Family Relations, 1979; Fessor Graham award North Tex. State U., 1980; Recipient Service award Am. Cancer Soc., 1983; Outstanding Home Economists Alumni award Baylor U., 1985, named Honor Prof. North Tex. State U., 1975. Mem. Tex. Council on Family Relations (pres. 1977-79, chmn. policy advisor com. 1986-88, nominating com. 1986-88), Denton Assn. for Edn. of Young Children (pres. 1970-72, 84-85, 85-86, v.p. 1986-87), Tex. Assn. Coll. Tchrs. (nominating com. 1988-89, 89-90, v.p. 1990-92, v.p. U. North Tex. chpt. 1987-88, pres. 1988-89, 89-90), Tex. Home Econs. Assn. (chmn. FLCD nominating com. 1983-84, chmn. child devel. and family relations sect. 1988-90, sect. rep. THEA bd. 1989-90), Nat. Council on Family Relations (com. 1982-83), North Tex. Home Econs. Inter-orgnl. Council (adviser 1983-85), Phi Delta Kappa (pres. local chpt. 1991-92), Alpha Iota/Phi Upsilon Omicron (advisor 1970-82, chmn. nat. com. 1984-87, nat. bd. dirs. 1990—, com. pubs. 1991—). Democrat. Clubs: Tri D (v.p. Baylor U. 1953-54); Univ. Grad. (pres. Tex. Woman's U. 1965-66). Office: U North Tex Coll Edn Denton TX 76203

LAWLAH, GLORIA GARY, state legislator, educator; b. Newberry, S.C., Mar. 12, 1939; d. Eugene Calvin and Erline (Guess) Gary; m. John Wesley Lawlah III, 1960; children: John Wesley IV, Gloria Gene, Gary McCarrell. BS, Hampton U., 1960; MA, Trinity Coll., Washington, 1970; postgrad., George Washington U., 1968-81. Formerly mem. Md. Ho. of Dels.; mem. Md. State Senate, Annapolis, Md., 1991—; mem. Dem. State Cen. Com., 1982-86; mem. coordinating com. 26th Legis. Dist., Prince Georges, Md., 1982-87; mem. Black Dem. Council, Md. Bd. dirs. Nat. Polit. Congress Black Women, 1984-87, Coalition on Black Affairs, 1980-82, Pub. Access Cable Corp., Prince Georges City, 1980-85, Hillcrest-Marlow Planning Bd., Prince Georges City, 1982-87, Family Crisis Ctr., Prince Georges City, 1982-84; co-chair Rev. Task Force for Pub. Safety, Prince Georges City, 1982; del. Dem. Nat. Conv.; co-chair Prince Georges City Exec. 7th Councilmanic Dist. Campaign, 1982; mem. Ctr. for Aging Greater S.E. Community Found. Mem. Nat. Council Negro Women (life), NAACP (3d v.p. Prince Georges City chpt. 1980-82). Club: Links. Home: 3801 24th Ave Temple Hills MD 20748-3003 Address: State House Senate Annapolis MD 21401*

LAWLER, MARY LEE, construction executive; b. Shelbyville, Ill., Nov. 16, 1943; d. Earl Franklin and Minnie Beatrice (Weiger) Fought; m. James Richard Lawler, Apr. 27, 1963; children: Teri Ann, John Richard. Student, Visalia Coll. Beauty, 1979. Lic. cosmotologist. Hairdresser Rosalie's Hair Styles, Exeter, Calif.; hairdresser, shop owner Mary Lee's Hair Styles, Exeter, Calif.; data entry, credit researcher Synanon, Badger, Calif.; co-owner, office mgr. LAwler Constrn., Exeter. Pres. Band Boosters, Exeter, 1981-82; advisor Keywanettes, Exeter, 1979-83. Mem. Rebekah Lodge (warden 1976-77, 83-84, v.p. 1994—). Roman Catholic. Home and office: 1577 W Visalia Rd Exeter CA 93221-9614

LAWLEY, KAREN R., health and safety officer; b. Lakehurst, N.J., July 24, 1947; d. Marsden Jr. and Ruth (Nichols) L.; m. Steven A. Coval, July 20, 1985; 1 child, Elick M. BS, Pa. State U., University Park, 1969. Sr. rsch. technician Mass. Gen. Hosp., Boston, Mass., 1973-81; sr. rsch. asst. Harvard U., Cambridge, Mass., 1981-84; lab. coord. Harvard U., Cambridge, 1984-87, facilities coord. and safety officer, 1987-92, health and safety officer, 1992—. Contbr. articles to profl. jours. Office: 16 Divinity Ave Rm 151 Cambridge MA 02138-2020

LAWLIS, PATRICIA KITE, air force officer, computer consultant; b. Greensburg, Pa., May 5, 1945; d. Joseph Powell, Jr., and Dorothy Theresa (Allshouse) Kite; m. Mark Craig Lawlis, Sept. 17, 1976 (div. 1983); 1 child, Elizabeth Marie. BS, East Carolina U., 1967; MS in Computer Sci., Air Force Inst. Tech., 1982; PhD in Computer Sci., Ariz. State U., 1989. Cert. secondary math. tchr. Employment counselor Pa. State Employment Service, Washington, Pa., 1967-69; math. tchr. Fort Cherry Sch. Dist., McDonald, Pa., 1969-74; commd. 2d lt. USAF, 1974, advanced through grades to lt. col., 1994, data base mgr. Air Force Space Command, Colorado Springs, Colo., 1974-77, computer systems analyst, USAF in Europe, Birkenfeld, Germany, 1977-80, prof. computer sci. Air Force Inst. Tech., Wright-Patterson AFB, Ohio, 1982-86, 89-94, ret. 1994; computer cons., pres. C.J. Kemp Systems, Inc., Huber Heights, Ohio, 1983—; Ada cons., Ada Joint Program Office, Washington, 1984-94. State treas. NOW, Pa., 1973-74. Recipient Mervin E. Gross award Air Force Inst. Tech., 1982, Prof. Ezra Kotcher award, 1985. Mem. Computer Soc. of IEEE, Assn. Computing Machinery, Tau Beta Pi (v.p. Ohio Eta chpt. 1981-82), Upsilon Pi Epsilon. Office: CJ Kemp Systems Inc PO Box 24363 Huber Heights OH 45424

LAWRENCE, ALICE LAUFFER, artist, educator; b. Cleve., Mar. 2, 1916; d. Erwin Otis and Florence Mary (Menough) Lauffer; m. Walter Ernest Lawrence, Sept. 27, 1941; 1 child, Phillip Lauffer. Diploma in art, Cleve. Inst. Art, 1938; BS in Art Edn., Case Western Res. U., 1938. Grad. asst. in art edn. Kent (Ohio) State U., 1939-40; art tchr. Akron (Ohio) and Cleve. Pub. Schs.; comml. artist B.F. Goodrich Co., Akron, 1942-44; sub. art tchr. Akron Pub. Schs.; sketch artist numerous events Akron, 1945-91. Author numerous poems. Mem. Cuyahoga Valley Art Ctr., Women's Art Mus., Akron Art Mus., 1963-94. Recipient 1st pl., 2d pl. in drawing, Butler Mus. Am. Arts, 1940-41, Cleve. Mus. Art, 1944. Mem. Woman's Art League Akron (sec. 1962), Ohio Watercolor Soc., Internat. Soc. Poets (life). Republican. Home: 861 Clearview Ave Akron OH 44314-2969

LAWRENCE, BARBARA CORELL, insurance company director, real estate investor; b. Binghamton, N.Y., Nov. 19, 1927; d. Archibald G. and Helen (Smith) C.; m. Albert Lawrence, June 28, 1950; children: David C., Janet H., Elizabeth A. BS, Cornell U., 1949. Tchr. Johnson City, N.Y., 1949-50, Schenectady, N.Y., 1957-58; prop. owner, mgr. Lawrence Props., Schenectady, 1955—; bd. dirs., sec. United Community Ins. Co., N.Y.C., Lawrence Ins. Group, Albany, N.Y., Lawrence Agy. Corp., Albany, Lawrence Group, Inc., Schenectady, Senate Ins. Co. Ariz.; dir. Northeast Savings. Founder Lawrence Inst.; mem. Jr. League; elder, First Reformed Ch., chmn. Chanel Guild; mem. women's aux. Schenectady Boys and Girls Club, The Schenectady Found.; bd. dirs. Ind. Living in the Capital Dist., Schenectady County Humane Soc.; patron Saratoga Performing Arts Ctr.; trustee Ellis Hosp., Proctor's Guild; co-chair Schenectady 300th Anniversary; trustee Union Coll.; patroon of Schenectady; mem. Regents Select Commn. on Disabilities, Met. Opera Assn.; bd. dirs. Adirondack Conservancy. Recipient Julliet Lowe Woman of Achievement award Mohawk Pathways Girl Scout Coun., 1990. Mem. Schenectady Panhellenic Assn. (past pres.), Delta Gamma, PEO Sisterhood, Garden Club Schenectady, Gardeners Wookshop, Cornell Club of the Capital Dist. and N.Y.C., Northern Lake George Yacht Club, Mohawk Golf Club. Home: 708 Riverview Rd Rexford NY 12148-1433

LAWRENCE, DEAN GRAYSON, retired lawyer; b. Oakland, Calif.; d. Henry C. and Myrtle (Grayson) Schmidt; A.B., U. Calif.-Berkeley, 1934, J.D., 1939. Admitted to Calif. bar, 1943, U.S. Dist. Ct., 1944, U.S. Ct. Appeals, 1944, Tax Ct. U.S., 1945, U.S. Treasury Dept., 1945, U.S. Supreme Ct., 1967; asso. Pillsbury, Madison & Sutro, San Francisco, 1944, 45; gen. practice Oakland, 1946-50, San Jose, 1952-60, Grass Valley, 1960-63, 66—; county counsel Nevada County, 1964-65. Nevada County Bd. Suprs., 1969-73, chmn., 1971. Vol. animal welfare movement; sec. Nev. County Humane Animal Shelter Bd., 1966-86; state humane officer, 1966-82; pres. Nev. County Humane Soc., 1974-86, mem. Humane Soc. U.S., Fund for Animals; pres. Humane Information Svc., 1992—; bd. dirs. Nevada County Health Planning Council, Golden Empire Areawide Health Planning Council, 1974, 75; trustee Grass Valley Pub. Libr., 1962-64. Mem. People for Ethical Treatment of Animals, Doris Day Animal League, Farm Animal Reform Movement, Performing Animal Welfare Soc., Pet Adoption League, Bus. and Profl. Women's Club, AAUW, Animal Protection Inst. Am. (Humanitarian of Yr. 1986), Animal Legal Defense Fund, Golden Empire Human Soc. (Lifetime Achievement award 1990), League Unbiased Women, Phi Beta Kappa, Sigma Xi, Kappa Beta Pi, Pi Mu Epsilon, Pi Lambda Theta. Episcopalian. Office: PO Box 66 Grass Valley CA 95945-0066

LAWRENCE, DEBORAH GLENN, maternal/child nurse; b. Monroe, La., July 24, 1955; d. John Walter and Lillie Marie (Speir) Glenn; m. Marion Alvin Lawrence, Jan. 25, 1974 (div. July 1981); 1 child, Stephen. BS in Nursing, N.E. La. U., 1976; MSN, N.W. State U., 1983. RN, La.; cert. neonatal intensive care nurse. Staff RN, newborn nursery St. Francis Med. Ctr., Monroe, 1977-78, staff RN, neonatal intensive care unit, 1978-80, transports, neonatal intensive care unit, 1978-86, head nurse, newborn, spl. care nursery, 1980-86; maternal/child dir. HCA No. Monroe Hosp., 1988-91; asst. prof. N.E. La. U., Monroe, 1990—; maternal/child clin. nurse HCA North Monroe Hosp., 1991-94; dir. neonatal ICU and pediatric ICU St. Francis Med. Ctr., Monroe, 1994—; clin. instr. Grambling State U., Monroe, 1986; dir. nursing Bowden Pediatric Nursing Service, Monroe, 1986-88. Mem. NAACOG, Sigma Theta Tau. Republican. Baptist. Home: St Francis Med Ctr 309 Jackson St Monroe LA 71201 Office: HCA North Monroe Hosp 3421 Medical Park Dr Monroe LA 71203-2355

LAWRENCE, DEBORAH JEAN, statistician; b. San Jose, Calif., June 25, 1960. BA in Math., San Jose State U., 1982; MS in Stats., Stanford U., 1985. Math. aide Info. Mgmt. Internat., Moffet Field, Calif., 1980-82; group engr. Lockheed Missiles and Space Co., Sunnyvale, Calif., 1982-89; total quality mgmt. mgr. Analog Devices, Inc., Santa Clara, Calif., 1989—; reengring. spl. interest group leader Coun. for Continuous Improvement, 1994—. Author tech. papers. Mem. Am. Soc. for Quality Control (sr. mem., cert. engr.), Am. Statis. Assn. Office: Analog Devices Inc. M/S 431 1500 Space Park Dr Santa Clara CA 95052-8020

LAWRENCE, DEIRDRE ELIZABETH, librarian, coordinator research services; b. Lawton, Okla., Mar. 15, 1952; d. Herbert Thomas and Joan Roberta (McDonald) L. BA in Art History, Richmond Coll., 1974; MLS, Pratt Inst., 1979; postgrad., Harvard U., 1981-82. Prin. libr. mus. librs. and archives, coord. rsch. svcs. Bklyn. Mus., 1983—; head cataloging and tech. scvs. Mus. Fine Arts, Boston, 1980-83; mem. preservation task force Rsch. Librs. Group, 1985-91, steering com. 1986-88, art and architecture com.; mem. conservation/preservation adv. coun. Met. Reference and Rsch. Agy., N.Y., 1988-92; grant reviewer fed. and state agys.; cons. in field. Author: New York and Hollywood Fashion, 1986, Dressing the Part: Costume Sket, 1989, Modern Art--The Production, 1989, Culin: Collector and Documentor of the World He Saw, Fashion and How It Was Influenced by Ethnographic Collections in Museums, Native American Art and Culture: Documentary Resources, Access to Visual Images-Past and Present; contbr. articles to profl. jours. Mem. Art Librs. Soc. N.Am., Spl. Librs. Assn., Native Am. Art Studies Assn., Internat. Fedn. Libr. Assns. Office: Brooklyn Mus 200 Eastern Pky Brooklyn NY 11238-6052

LAWRENCE, ESTELENE YVONNE, transportation executive, musician; b. Lynch, Ky., Aug. 10, 1933; d. Samuel Coleridge and Florence Estelle (Gardner) Taylor; m. Otto Lee Lawrence, Sept. 14, 1957; children: Stuart, Neil, Adelbert. Student Fenn Coll., 1953-60, Cleve. Inst. Music, 1955-56, John Carroll U., 1977-78, Northeastern U., 1979-80; BA Cleve. State U., 1993. Stenographer Cleve. Transit System/Regional Transit Authority, 1951-76, tng. asst., 1976-78, pers. devel. asst., 1978-82, dist. adminstr., 1983-86; supr./mgmt. skills instr. RTA, 1976-86, dir. tng. and career devel., 1986-88. Dir. music Friendly United Baptist Ch., 1947—; piano tchr., 1953-73; asst. minister of music Mt. Nebo Baptist Ch., 1994—; pianist/organist Nat. Bapt. Conv., 1971, 80. Publicity chmn. Moses Cleve. Sch. PTA, 1965-75; audit chmn. RTA Main Office Credit Union, 1980-83; dist. sec. Boy Scouts Am., 1982-83; chmn. adv. bd. Baldwin Wallace Coll., 1984-88; mem. adv. bd. Cleve. Mgmt. Devel. Consortium, 1985-88; chief musician RTA Choir; mem. Cleve. Choral Union, 1992—. Mem. Am. Choral Dirs. Assn., Cleve. Mgmt. Seminars (treas. 1979-81, pres. 1981-83), Conf. Minority Transp. Ofcls., Phi Kappa Gamma (pres. 1966-69), Mu Phi Epsilon (historian 1990-91, chorister 1991-92, pres. 1992-93). Mem. A.M.E. Ch. Clubs: East 153d St. (v.p. 1980—), East Ky. Social. Home: 4066 East 153d St Cleveland OH 44128

LAWRENCE, EVELYN THOMPSON, retired educator, researcher; b. Marion, Va., Nov. 13, 1919; d. John Emmett and Susie Barnett (Madison) Thompson; m. Joseph John Lawrence, Oct. 5, 1946; 1 child, Sheila Ann (dec.). BS in Edn., W. Va. State Coll., 1941; M of Music, U. Mich., 1952; continuing edn., U. Va., 1960s, 70s. Elem. sch. tchr., music tchr. Carnegie High Sch., Marion, Va., 1941-65; tchr. Marion Primary Sch., 1965-84; judge art, storytelling, and creative writing Smyth County Schs., Marion, Chilhowie, Va., 1984-94; rocking reader Smyth County Schs., Marion, 1994—; producer, dir. plays Supporters Enriched Edn. and Knowledge, Marion, 1983-92; music and recreation dir. Douglass Ctr., Toledo, Ohio, summer, 1953; instr. ch. music Va. Union U., Richmond, summer 1960, 61. Author: History of Blacks in Smyth County, 1991-92, Edn. Dir. of Smyth County Blacks: 1906-65, 1994; (docudrama) Lady with the Torch, 1985. Organist and choir dir. Mt. Pleasant Meth. Ch., Marion, 1994—; bd. dirs. Blue Ridge Job Corps, Marion, 1994—; v.p., past pres. Church Women United, Marion, 1994. Recipient 2 nominations Tchr. of Yr. award, S.W. Va. Coun. of Internat. Reading Assn., Abingdon, Va., 1981, 82, Svc. to Youth award Carnegie Sch. Alumni, Marion, 1983, Citizen of Yr. award Marion Rotary Club. Mem. AAUW (chmn. cultural rels. com. 1994), Alpha Kappa Alpha, Alpha Delta Kappa. Home: 312 Broad St Marion VA 24354-2804

LAWRENCE, JANICE SHARPE, controller; b. Nashville, May 12, 1961; d. James Eskew and Dorthey (Ryan) Sharpe; m. William Lloyd Lawrence, Sept. 11, 1984 (div. Sept. 30, 1989); 1 child, Kristin Nicole. BS in BA in Acctg., Tenn. Tech. U., 1983. Auditor I Dept. Mental Health, State of Tenn., Nashville, 1984-85, auditor II, 1985-86; contr. Alcohol and Drug Coun. of Middle Tenn., Inc., Nashville, 1986—; mem. com. to review fiscal manual State of Tenn. Dept. Health, Nashville, 1992-94. Mem. Inst. Mgmt. Accts., Bus. Mgrs. Network (sec. 1993-94). Roman Catholic. Office: Alcohol and Drug Coun 2612 Westwood Dr Nashville TN 37204-2710

LAWRENCE, JEAN HOPE, writer, marketing consultant; b. Waukegan, Ill., Mar. 5, 1944; d. George Herbert and Hope Delinda (Warren) L.; 1 child, Kelsey Hope. BA, George Washington U., 1966. Tech. editor, Am. Chem. Soc., Washington, 1966; proposal writer Krohn-Rhodes Inst., Washington, 1966-67; legislative counsel Aerospace Industries Assn., Washington, 1967-82; v.p., co-owner Data Specific, Washington, 1985-86; editorial adviser Am. C. of C. Execs., Alexandria, Va., 1983-86, lectr., 1984—; founder, pres. Angel Watch Prodn., 1992. Contbg. editor: Communications Concepts, 1983-86; editor, pub., creator: (newsletters) Get It Done!, 1987-88, Cheap Relief, 1988—; film prodr. OMNIFAX, 1994. Washington Film & Video Coun. Mem. Washington Ind. Writers, Women's Direct Response Group, Women in Film and Video. Democrat. Methodist. Avocation: essayist. Address: 3217 Connecticut Ave NW Washington DC 20008-2515

LAWRENCE, KATHY, medical/surgical nurse, radiology nurse; b. Searcy, Ark., Dec. 9, 1949; d. S.V. and Pearl (Bolden) Smith; children: Ryan, Damon. ADN, Odessa (Tex.) Coll., 1977; BSN, U. Tex., Galveston, 1992. Cert. med. asst., diabetes educator. Head nurse, acting supr. Med. Ctr. Hosp., Odessa, 1978-80; asst. head nurse Meml. Gen. Hosp., Elkins, W.Va., 1980-81; staff nurse United Hosp. Ctr., Clarksburg, W.Va., 1981-83; field supr. Upjohn/Healthcare Svcs., Midland, Tex., 1983-85; primary nurse, physician's office Naidu Clinic, Odessa; nursing supr. U. Tex. Med. Br., Galveston. Mem. Am. Assn. Diabetes Educators, Am. Assn. Med. Assts. (sec. local chpt.), Am. Assn. Intravenous Therapists, Am. Radiological Nurses Assn., Am. Assn. Neurosci. Nurses, Intravenous Nurses Soc., Alpha Nu Chi. Home: 6315 Central City Blvd # 820 Galveston TX 77551

LAWRENCE, LINDA HIETT, writer, administrator; b. Phoenix, July 26, 1939; d. Lydle and Hazeldell (Sutton) Hiett; children: Pamela Lee Reardon, Annabel Virginia Urrea. BA, U. Ariz., 1961; MA, Ariz. State U., 1985, EdD, 1986. Cert. sch. supt., prin., tchr., Ariz. Prin. Washington Elem. Sch. Dist. 6, Phoenix, 1980-83; prin. Dysart Unified Sch. Dist. 89, Peoria, Ariz., 1985-87, asst. supt., 1987-88; supt. Cottonwood Ariz. Oak Creek Sch. Dist. 6, 1988-91; cons., writer, 1991—; adj. prof. No. Ariz. U., 1990-91. Author: Adventures in Arizona, 1991; co-author: History of Jerome and Verde Valley, 1991. Trustee Marcus J. Lawrence Hosp. NSF grantee for Math; recipient USC's 100 Outstanding Supts. award. Mem. Sacred Heart Alumni Assn., Ariz. State U. Alumni Assn. (chpt. pres.), Ariz. Humanities Coun. Assn., Phoenix Zoo, Friends of Our Brothers and Sisters, Scared Heart Alumni Assn., Ariz. State U. Alumni Assn., Phi Delta Kappa.

LAWRENCE, LORI LOUISE, restaurateur; b. Brockton, Mass., Oct. 12, 1950; d. Hallett Thompson and Dorothy Mae (McElroy) L.; m. David John Forrest, 1994; 1 child, Cameron Stuart Forrest. AA, Canada Coll., Redwood City, Calif., 1970; postgrad., Chapman Coll., 1971-72, Foothill Coll., 1973-74. Owner, operator The Natural Gourmet, Palo Alto, Calif., 1974-76, Quiche Lori, Palo Alto, 1976-81; sales assoc Williams-Sonoma, Palo Alto, 1981-86; owner, operator Lori's Kitchens, Palo Alto, 1982-91; sales assoc. Neiman-Marcus Epicure, Palo Alto, 1986-91; owner, operator The Rose & Crown, Palo Alto, 1991—; Contbr. articles to publs. Recipient award dessert category Cook Your Way to France Profl. Chef's Contest, 1990. Mem. San Francisco Profl. Food Soc. Office: The Rose & Crown 547 Emerson St Palo Alto CA 94301

LAWRENCE, MARY JOSEPHINE (JOSIE LAWRENCE), library official, artist; b. Carbondale, Pa., Mar. 9, 1932; d. Domenick Anthony and Teresa Rose (Zaccone) Gentile; m. John Paul Lawrence, Apr. 25, 1953 (dec. June 1977); children: Mary Josephine, Jane Therese, Susan Michele. BFA, Mass. Coll. Art, 1989; postgrad, Chelsea (Eng.) Sch. Art, 1989, San Pancrazio Art Sch., Tuscany, Italy, 1990, 91, 92; cert. in grad. studies, Guangzhou Acad. Fine Arts, China, 1993. Sales clk. Gorins, 5&10, Jordan Marsh, Boston, 1946-49; clk.-typist, sec. John Hancock Ins. Co., Boston, 1950-53; machine operator, quality control supr. Rust Craft Greeting Cards, Dedham, Mass., 1961-69; restaurant hostess Tony's Villa, Waltham, Mass., 1972-73; mus. sales clk., artist John F. Kennedy Libr., Boston, 1979-87, mgr. mus. store, supr., 1988—; tchr.'s asst. San Pancrazio Art Sch., 1992. One woman shows include de Havilland Fine Art Gallery, Boston, 1993; exhibited in group shows including South Shore Arts Ctr., Cohasset, Mass., 1991, North River Arts Soc., Marshfield Hills, Mass. Recipient outstanding achievement awards Nat. Archives and Rsch. Adminstrn., 1989, 94, Svc. award, 1990, Honorable Mention award South Shore Arts Ctr., 1991, Best of Show award de Havilland Fine Art Gallery, 1992, Best of Show North River Arts Soc., 1994. Mem. Boston Visual Artist Union, de Havilland Fine Art Gallery, South Shore Art Ctr., North River Arts Soc. Democrat. Roman Catholic. Office: John F Kennedy Libr and Mus Columbia Pt Boston MA 02125

LAWRENCE, PAMELA MARIE, investment advisor; b. Mt. Kisco, N.Y., May 3, 1952; d. Vincent L. and Mary H. (Santelli) Cascioli; m. William F. Lawrence, Apr. 3, 1993. BA, Marymount Coll., 1974; MBA in Fin., Pace U., 1980. Adminstrv. asst. Bessemer Trust Co., N.Y.C., 1975-76; trader/jr. analyst Grumman Pension Fund, N.Y.C., 1976-78; analyst/trader W. R. Family Assocs., N.Y.C., 1978-87; rsch. analyst David J. Greene and Co., N.Y.C., 1987-88; mng. dir., portfolio mgr. Magten Asset Mgmt., N.Y.C.,

1988-92; mng. dir., v.p., portfolio mgr. Whippoorwill Assocs., Inc., White Plains, N.Y., 1992—. V.p. Cath. Big Bros., N.Y.C., 1991—. Mem. Fin. Women's Assn. N.Y., N.Y. Soc. Security Analysts. Office: Whippoorwill Assocs Inc 11 Marine Ave White Plains NY 10606

LAWRENCE, PATRICIA ANN, obstetrician-gynecologist; b. Rocky Mount, N.C., Mar. 31, 1926; d. Graham Vance and Vera Lynn (Burnette) L. Student, Queens Coll., 1942-43, U. N.C., Chapel Hill, 1943-46; MD, U. Va., 1950. Diplomate, Am. Bd. Ob.-Gyn. Resident in ob.-gyn. Ind. U. Med. Ctr., Indpls., 1950-54; pvt. practice Charlotte, N.C., 1955—; mem. staff Carolinas Med. Ctr., exec. com. dept. ob.-gyn., 1983-87, chmn. search com., 1988. Contbr. articles to med. jours. Pres. Mecklenburg unit Am. Cancer Soc., Charlotte. Named Outstanding Career Woman, Cen. Charlotte Assocs., 1968. Fellow Am. Coll. Obstetricians and Gynecologists, South Atlantic Assn. Obstetricians and Gynecologists; mem. AMA, N.C. Med. Assn., Mecklenburg County Med. Soc., So. Med. Assn., N.C. Ob-Gyn Soc., Raintree Country Club, Tower Club, Jefferson Club, Farmington Country Club. Democrat. Baptist. Home: 1908 Sterling Rd Charlotte NC 28209-1610 Office: 1001 Blythe Blvd Ste 402 Charlotte NC 28203-5866

LAWRENCE, PATRICIA I., financial manager; b. East Chicago, Ind., Mar. 22, 1964; d. Aron W. Farmer and Vada M. (Noch) Lyle; m. Mark E. Lawrence, Sept. 20, 1986. Diplôme de Langue, Alliance Francaise, France, 1985; BS in Acct., Ind. U., 1986. Cert. mgmt. acct., 1991. Asst. to comptr. Agy. For Instr. Tech., Bloomington, Ind., 1984-86; acct. R.R. Donnelley & Sons, Inc., Crawfordsville, Ind., 1986-88; sr. acct., acctg. specialist Thomson Consumer Electronics, Inc., Indpls., 1988-90; fin. analyst Thomson Consumer Electronics, Inc., Syracuse, N.Y., 1990-92; mgr., fin. planning and analysis Thomson Consumer Electronics, Inc., Lancaster, Pa., 1992—. Mem. Nat. Assn. Female Execs., Inst. Mgmt. Accts., Alpha Kappa Psi. Home: 163 Ridings Way Lancaster PA 17601 Office: Thomson Consumer Electronics MS048 1002 New Holland Ave Lancaster PA 17601

LAWRENCE, PAULA DENISE, physical therapist; b. Ft. Worth, May 21, 1959; d. Roddy Paul and Kay Frances (Spivey) Gillis; m. Mark Jayson Lawrence, Apr. 20, 1985. BS, Tex. Women's U., 1982. Lic. phys. therapist, Tex., Calif. Sales mgr. R. and K Camping Ctr., Garland, Tex., 1977-82; staff physical therapist Longview (Tex.) Regional Hosp., 1982-83, dir. phys. therapy, 1983-87, dir. rehab. svcs., 1987-88; staff phys. therapist MPH Home Health, Longview, Tex., 1983-84; owner, pres. Phys. Rehabil. Ctr., Hemet, Calif., 1988—; mem. adv. com. div. health occupations Kilgore (Tex.) Coll., 1985-88; mem. profl. adv. bd. Hospice Longview, 1985-88. Mem. NAFE, Am. Phys. Therapy Assn., Calif. Phys. Therapy Assn., Am. Bus. Women's Assn. (v.p. 1987, 89, pres. 1990, Woman of Yr. 1988, 91), Assistance League Aux., Soroptomist (corres. sec. 1992, dir. 1993-95), Psi Chi, Omega Rho Alpha. Home: 899 Kristin Ln Hemet CA 92545-1645 Office: 901 S State St Ste 500 Hemet CA 92543-7127

LAWRENCE, RUTH ANDERSON, pediatrician, clinical toxicologist; b. N.Y.C.; d. Stephen Hayes and Loretta (Harvey) A.; m. Robert Marshall Lawrence, July 4, 1950; children, Robert Michael, Barbara Asselin, Timothy Lee, Kathleen Ann, David McDonald, Mary Khalil, Joan Margaret, John Charles, Stephen Harvey. BS in Biology summa cum laude, Antioch Coll., 1945; MD, U. Rochester, 1949. Internship and residency in pediatrics Grace New Haven (Conn.) Hosp., 1949-50; asst. resident in Medicine Grace New Haven (Conn.) Community Hosp., 1950-51; postdoctoral fellow Yale New Haven Hosp., 1951, chief resident newborn svc., 1951; cons. in medicine U.S. Army, Ft. Dix, N.J., 1952; from clin. instr. to sr. instr. in pediatrics U. Rochester, N.Y., 1952-64, assoc. resident, 1957-58, asst. prof., 1964-70, assoc. prof., 1970-85, prof. pediatrics, ob.-gyn., 1985—; rsch. pediatrician, Monroe County Health Dept., Rochester, 1952-58; dir. Finger Lakes Regional Poison Control Ctr., 1958—; chief nursery svc. Strong Meml. Hosp., Rochester, 1960-73, chief dept. pediatrics, The Highland Hosp., Rochester, 1960-91; rsch. in field. Author: (book with others) Caring for Your Baby and Young Child, 1991, Breastfeeding: A Guide for the Medical Profession, 4th edit. 1994, What to Expect in the First Year, 1989, Breastfeeding: A Guide for the Medical Profession, 4th edit. 1994; editor various periodicals; contbr. numerous articles to profl. publs. Recipient Gold Medal award, U. Rochester Alumni Assn., 1979, William Keeler award Rochester Safety Coun., 1982, Civic Contribution citation Rochester Safety Coun., 1984, Career Achievement award Girl Scouts U.S. of Genesee Valley, 1987, Rochester Diocesan award for women, St. Bernard's Inst., 1989, Albert David Kaiser Medal, 1991, numerous svc. awards; named Woman of Yr. Girl Scouts U.S. of Monroe County, 1968; hon. fellow Am. Sch. Health Assn., 1960, rsch. fellow Jackson Meml. Rsch. Labs., 1945. Fellow Am. Pediatric Soc., Am. Acad. Clin. Toxicology (trustee, chair com. on rsch. fellowship, com. sci. rev.); mem. Human Milk Banking Assn. N.Am. (adv. bd.), Nat. Acad. Sci. (subcom. on nutrition during lactation), Physicians for Social Responsibility, Acad. Breastfeeding Medicine (founding bd. dirs. 1994—), Safety Coun. Rochester and Monroe County (past pres.), Bd. of Life Line (past pres.), Alpha Omega Alpha. Roman Catholic. Office: U Rochester Sch Medicine 601 Elmwood Ave Rochester NY 14642-0001

LAWRENCE, SALLY CLARK, academic administrator; b. San Francisco, Dec. 29, 1930; d. George Dickson and Martha Marie Alice (Smith) Clark; m. Henry Clay Judd, July 1, 1950 (div. Dec. 1972); children: Rebecca, David, Nancy; m. John I. Lawrence, Aug. 12, 1976; stepchildren: Maia, Dylan. Docent Portland Art Mus., Oreg., 1958-68; gallery owner, dir., Sally Judd Gallery, Portland, 1968-75; art ins. appraiser, cons. Portland, 1975-81; interim dir. Mus. Art. Sch., Pacific Northwest Coll. Art, Portland, 1981, asst. dir., 1981-82, acting dir., 1982-84, dir., 1984-94, pres., 1994—; bd. dirs. Art Coll. Exch. Nat. Consortium, 1982-91, pres., 1983-84. Bd. dirs. Portland Arts Alliance, 1987—, Assn. Ind. Colls. of Art and Design, 1991—. Mem. Nat. Assn. Schs. Art and Design (bd. dirs. 1984-91, treas. bd. dirs. 1994—), Oreg. Ind. Coll. Assn. (bd. dirs. 1981—, exec. com. 1989—, pres. 1992—). Office: Pacific NW Coll of Art 1219 SW Park Ave Portland OR 97205-2430

LAWRENCE, SYLVIA YVONNE, critical care nurse; b. Danville, Pa., July 11, 1937; d. John Jacob and Florence Rebecca (Fenstermacher) Tanner; m. Davey Leon House, Oct. 4, 1958 (div. 1980); children: Susan D., Gayle Y. House Troxell; m. William C. Lawrence (div.). Diploma, Thomas Jefferson U., 1958; BSN, Lycoming Coll., 1991. RN, Pa.; cert. emergency nurse. Nurse various med. facilities, Pa., 1958-70; ho. supr. Sycamore Manor Nursing Home, Williamsport, Pa., 1970-71; gen. duty staff nurse Evangelical Community Hosp., Lewisburg, Pa., 1971-82, surg. staff nurse, 1983-87; surg. staff nurse Twelve Oaks Hosp., Houston, 1982-83; staff nurse emergency dept. Muncy Valley Hosp., 1985-91; patient care mgr. asst. Geisinger Med. Ctr., Danville, 1987—. Mem. Sigma Theta Tau. Republican. Home: PO Box 338 Riverside PA 17868

LAWRENCE, TELETÉ ZORAYDA, speech and voice pathologist, educator; b. Worcester, Mass., Aug. 5, 1910; d. James Newton and Cora Valeria (Hester) Lester; A.B. cum laude, U. Calif., Berkeley, 1932; M.A., Tex. Christian U., 1963; pvt. study voice with Edgar Schofield, N.Y.C., 1936-41, drama with Enrica Clay Dillon, N.Y.C., 1937-40; m. Ernest Lawrence, Oct. 9, 1939; children—James Lester, Valerie Alma. Lic. speech-lang. pathologist. Mem. Am. Lyric Opera Co., 1939—; instr. speech Sch. Fine Arts, Tex. Christian U., Fort Worth, 1959-66, asst. prof., 1966-71, assoc. prof., 1971-75, prof., 1975-76, emeritus, 1976—, speech pathologist specializing voice disorders Speech and Hearing Clinic, 1959—, faculty research leave, Gt. Britain, Western Europe, Hungary, 1968; pvt. practice speech and voice pathology, 1960—. Mem. bd. Sunshine Haven, home for retarded children, 1957-59; gen. chmn. Ft. Worth and Tarrant County, Nat. Retarded Children's Week, 1954; mem. family and child welfare div. Community Council Ft. Worth and Tarrant County, 1955-57, mem. health and hosp. div., 1959-60; mem. women's com. Ft. Worth chpt. NCCJ, 1956-59; exec. v.p. Fine Arts Found. Guild of Tex. Christian U., 1955-56, past exec. sec., past fin. sec. Recipient Faculty Research grant Tex. Christian U., 1961. Fellow Internat. Soc. Phonetic Scis.; mem. Nat. Council Chs. (bd. joint com. missionary edn. Pacific Coast area, 1952-55), United Ch. Women of Ft. Worth (chmn. Christian world missions dept. 1955-57, pres. 1957-59). Ft. Worth Area Council Chs. (v.p. 1955-57, exec. com. 1957-59, bd. dirs. 1959-60), U. Calif. Alumni Assn. (life), Am. Speech-Lang.-Hearing Assn. (life; cert. clin. competence in speech pathology), Tex. Speech-Lang.-Hearing Assn. (cert.), Ft. Worth Council for Retarded Children, Speech Communication Assn. (sec. speech and hearing disorders interest group 1962-63, mem. com. 1961-64), Am. Dialect Soc., Internat. Assn. Logopodics and Phoniatrics, Phonetic Soc. Japan (hon.), AAUP (emeritus), Lambda Ma'ams of Lambda Chi Alpha (pres. Ft. Worth 1962-63), Phi Beta Kappa Assn. (Ft. Worth chpt.), Phi Beta Kappa (Alpha of Calif. chpt.; charter mem., v.p. Delta of Tex. chpt. 1971-73, pres. 1973-74), Delta Zeta, Psi Chi, Sigma Alpha Eta. Republican. Mem. Christian Ch. Clubs: Woman's of Fort Worth, Women of Rotary. Participant, 13th Congress of Internat. Assn. Logopedics and Phoniatrics, Vienna, 1965, 14th Congress, Paris, 1968, 15th Congress, Buenos Aires, 1971, 16th Congress, Interlaken, Switzerland, 1974, 17th Congress, Copenhagen, 1977, 18th Congress, Washington, 1980, 19th Congress, Edinburgh, Scotland, 1983; participant 10th Internat. Congress of Linguists, Bucharest, 1967; participant 6th Internat. Congress of The Internat. Soc. Phonetic Scis., Prague, 1967, 7th Internat. Congress, Montreal, 1971, 8th Internat. Congress, Leeds, Eng., 1975; participant 1st Congress Internat. Assn. Sci. Study Mental Deficiency, Montpellier, France, 1967, Semmelweis Ann. Week, Budapest Acad. Scis., 1968, 3d World Congress Phoneticians, Tokyo, 1976. Author: Handbook for Instructors of Voice and Diction, 1968; contbr. articles to profl. jours. Home: 3860 S Hills Cir Fort Worth TX 76109-2757

LAWS, PRISCILLA WATSON, physics educator; b. N.Y.C., Jan. 18, 1940; d. Morris Clemens and Frances (Fetterinan) Watson; m. Kenneth Lee Laws, June 3, 1965; children: Kevin Allen, Virginia. BA, Reed Coll., 1961; MA, Bryn Mawr Coll., 1963, PhD, 1966. Asst. prof. physics Dickinson Coll., Carlisle, Pa., 1965-70; assoc. prof. Dickinson Coll., Carlisle, 1970-79, prof. physics, 1979—, chmn. dept. physics and astronomy, 1982-83; cons. in field. Author: X Rays: More Harm than Good?, 1977, The X-Ray Information Book, 1983; contbr. numerous articles to profl. jours.; assoc. editor Am. Jour. Physics, 1989—. Vice-pres. Cumberland Conservancy, 1972-73, pres. 1973; bd. dirs. Pa. Alliance for Returnables, 1974-77; asst. sec., treas. Carlisle Hosp. Authority, 1973-76; pres. bd. Carlisle Day Care Ctr., 1973-74. Fellow NSF, 1963-64, grantee, 1989-95, Commonwealth of Pa., 1985-86, U.S. Dept. Edn. Fund for Improvement of Post-Secondary Edn., 1986-89, 89-93, AEC; recipient Innovation award Merck Found., 1989, Educom Incriptal award for curriculum innovation in sci. labs., 1989, award Sears Roebuck and Co., 1990, award Outstanding Software Devel. Computers in Physics Jour., 1991, Pioneering Achievement in Edn. award Dana Found., 1993. Mem. Am. Assn. Physics Tchrs. (Disting Svc. citation 1992), Fedn. Am. Scientist, Sigma Xi, Sigma Pi Sigma, Omicron Delta Kappa. Democrat. Home: 10 Douglas Ct Carlisle PA 17013-1714 Office: Dickinson Coll Dept of Physics & Astronomy Carlisle PA 17013

LAWSON, ANN MARIE MCDONALD, librarian; b. Jersey City; d. William and Mary Agnes (Dolan) McDonald; student Columbia, 1947, N.Y. U., 1949, City Coll. N.Y., 1959, Pratt Inst., 1963; m. Philip James Lawson, Apr. 26, 1952. Methods analyst Rueben H. Donnelley Corp., N.Y.C., 1953-57; librarian chems. div. Union Carbide Corp., N.Y.C., 1957-65, Tatham Laird & Kudner, N.Y.C., 1965-67, Met. Transp. Authority, N.Y.C., 1967-80; cons., 1980—; active library tng. program Ballard Sch. (YWCA), 1949—; cons. WHO, Geneva, Switzerland, 1950; lectr. Pratt Inst. Grad. Library Sch., 1967. Mem. Assn. Records Mgrs. and Adminstrs. (pres. 1948-50); Spl. Libraries Assn. Republican. Contbr. articles to mags. Home and Office: 119 Washington Pl New York NY 10014-3837

LAWSON, ARRITA ELIZABETH, geriatrics, nephrology nurse; b. Oak Hill, W.Va., Feb. 23, 1958; d. James William and Inez Faye (Combs) Gordon; m. Robert Eugene Lawson, Oct. 18, 1978 (div. Oct. 1990); children: Melissa Elizabeth Lawson, Robert Ryan Lawson; m. Steven Bryan Waybright, Aug. 22, 1992 (annulled 1993). Student, W.Va. U., 1976-78; ASN, Fla. Jr. Coll., Jacksonville, 1981; postgrad., Memphis State U., 1991. RN, S.C.; cert. CPR, nephrology nurse. Unit supr. Garden Grove Artificial Kidney Ctr., Inc., Glendora, Calif., 1985-87; PRN staff mem. Glendora Artificial Kidney Ctr., Inc., 1985-87; RN coord. mobile acute hemodialysis So. Calif. Acute Dialysis Svc., Inc., Glendora, 1985-87; staff RN acute and chronic hemodialysis East Memphis Kidney Clinic, Inc., 1987; staff RN outpatient hemodialysis Meth. Hosps. Memphis, 1987-89; asst. dir. renal svcs. Crittendon Meml. Hosp., West Memphis, Ark., 1989; clin. coord. Kings Dau.'s & Son's Nursing Home, Memphis, 1989-90; asst. DON ADON Hillhaven Raleigh Nursing Home, Memphis, 1990-91; DON Meadowbrook Manor Columbia, S.C., 1991-92; case mgr. coord. Blue Cross Blue Shield, Columbia, 1992—; legal nurse cons., owner PN-PRN, Inc., Elgin, S.C., 1994—. Mem. Long Term Care Nurses, Am. Soc. Law Medicine and Ethics, Health Lawyers Assn. Home: 220 Cherrywood Dr Elgin SC 29045

LAWSON, BETH ANN REID, strategic planner; b. N.Y.C., Jan. 9, 1954; d. Raymond Theodore and Jean Elizabeth (Frinks) Reid; m. Michael Berry Lawson, Jan. 29, 1983; children: Rayna, Sydney. BA, Va. Tech., 1976; MPA, Golden Gate U., 1983. From systems analyst I to support ops. asst. City of Virginia Beach, Va., 1977-93; water conservation coord. City of Virginia Beach, 1993-94; owner Strategic Planning and Teamwork, Virginia Beach, 1993—; cons. Virginia Beach Rescue Squad, 1992-93, Virginia Beach Mcpl. Employees Fed. Credit Union, 1992-93, Virginia Beach Resort Area Adv. Commn., 1993, Virginia Beach Conv. and Visitors Devel. Bur., 1991-93. Sun. sch. tchr. Wycliffe Presbyn. Ch., Virginia Beach, 1991-92. Mem. NAFE, Va. Assn. Ednl. Data Systems, Deming Quality Group, Virginia Beach Rotary Club (Outstanding Employee 1993), Va. Tech. Alumni Assn. (pres. 1982-83). Home: 701 Earl of Warwick Ct Virginia Beach VA 23454 Office: Strategic Planning and Teamwork 701 Earl of Warwick Ct Virginia Beach VA 23454

LAWSON, CAROLE JEAN, educator, author; b. San Antonio, June 18, 1944; d. Albert Joseph and Pearl Nettie (Garner) Fuller; m. James Ray Lawson, Sept. 7, 1962; children: Regina Anne (Lawson) Kacho, Clinton Ray. Founder Love Makes the World Go Around in Peace, Ft. Worth, Tex., 1988—; founder, dir. Healing Thru Love Seminars, Ft. Worth, Tex., 1988—; founder Sunshine 'n Rainbows Stress Overcomers, Ft. Worth, 1985-87; founder, head Omni-Vision Pub. and Prodns., Ft. Worth, 1990-93. Pub. editor Omni Vision newsletter, 1985-93; author: To God Be the Glory, poetry collection, 1988-90, My Rocky Mountain High, 1989, The Reflection of God's Smile, 1991. Sec. Lightly Speaking Forum, Ft. Worth, 1987-89; supporter of publicity Campaign for the Earth, 1990-91; founder, pres. Universal World Investments. Named Honorary Mayan Centurian. Mem. NAFE. Home and Office: 1112 Edney St Fort Worth TX 76115-4317

LAWSON, JANE ELIZABETH, bank executive; b. Cornwall, Ont., Can.; d. Leonard J. and Margaret L. BA, LLB, U. N.B., Can., 1971. With law dept. Royal Bank Can., Montreal, Que., Can., 1974-78, sr. counsel, 1978-84; v.p., corp. sec. Royal Bank Can., Montreal, Que., 1988-92, sr. v.p., sec., 1992—. Mem. Can. Bar Assn., N.B. Bar Assn., Que. Bar Assn., Inst. Chartered Secs. and Adminstrs., Inst. Corp. Dirs., Inst. Donations and Pub. Affairs Rsch. (fin. com.), Am. Soc. Corp. Secs., Mt. Royal Tennis Club. Office: Royal Bank Can PO Box 6001, 1 Place Ville Marie, Montreal, PQ Canada H3C 3A9

LAWSON, JEAN KERR, fund raising executive, consultant; b. Chgo., Oct. 31, 1941; d. Andrew Leslie and Dorothy Helen (Hayes) L.; m. Thomas Edward Miller, Aug. 4, 1962 (div.); children: Galen Elizabeth Miller Block, Andrew C., Colin P. Student, U. Colo., 1959-61, Marquette U., 1962; MA, St. John's Coll., Annapolis, Md., 1979; postgrad., Marquette U., 1992—. Cert. fund raising exec. Reorgn. analyst Office of the Gov. State of N.Mex., Santa Fe, 1976-78; litigation case supr. Kirkland & Ellis, Chgo., 1980; legal analyst Clausen, Miller, Gorman, Caffrey & Witous, Chgo., 1980-81; dir. alumni ann. fund U. Wis.-Milw. Found., Milw., 1983-88; dir. devel. and alumni programs U. Md., College Park, 1988-90; devel. cons. White Plains, N.Y., 1990-91; v.p. public affairs Aiglon Coll. Trusts, Chesieres-Villars, Switzerland, 1991-92; fund raising exec., cons., 1992—; intern Fisher Trust Co., 1994—. Author: (with others) N.Mex. State Government Reorganization, 1976, Executive Branch of N.Mex. State Government, 1976, Responsive Government in New Mexico, 1977, 78. Vol. scholarship run U. Wis. Alumni Assn., Milw., 1984-87, Jr. League Am., 1967—; founder, pres. Iowa chpt. Nat. Cystic Fibrosis Found., Waterloo, 1968-70; bd. dirs. Am. Cancer Soc., No. N.Mex., 1978-79; hon. fellow dept. edn. adminstrn. U. Wis., Madison, 1991-92. St. John's Coll. fellow, 1978, 79. Mem. AAUW, Nat. Soc. Fundraising Execs., Coun. for Advancement and Support Edn. Episcopalian. Home: 6803 Wandawega Cir Mequon WI 53092-8514

LAWSON, J(ENICE) EVELYN, quality assurance professional, pharmacist; b. Ozark, Mo., Jan. 20, 1952; d. Robert Evelyn and Jenice Gemima (Spiess) L. AA, East Cen. Coll., 1972; BS in Pharmacy, U. Mo., Kansas City, 1975; BS in Chemistry, Northwest Mo. State U., 1979; MS in Pharmaceutics and Pharm. Chemistry, Ohio State U., 1985. Registered pharmacist, Mo. Pharmacy intern Federmann Drug Store, Kansas City, 1974; staff pharmacist The Corner Drug, Maryville, Mo., 1975, St. Francis Hosp., Maryville, Mo., 1976-78, Easter's Ben Franklin Pharmacy, Maryville, Mo., 1979; grad. rsch., teaching assoc. Ohio State U., Columbus, 1980-84; pharmacist Boehringer Ingelheim, Ingelheim, Fed. Rep. Germany, 1985; computer programmer, cons., coll. pharmacy Ohio State U., Columbus, 1986-87; mgr. Lynn Drug Co., Columbus, 1987-88; regulatory compliance specialist Clorox Tech. Ctr., Pleasanton, Calif., 1989—; preposition 65 coord., 1989-94, monitor of upcoming legis. pertaining to co., rev. materials for compliance with regulations, submit documents to fed. EPA, Clorox Tech. Ctr., Pleasanton, 1989—. Tutor Laubach Literacy Action, Livermore, Calif., 1989; adult choir, handbell choir, children's choir, pianist, single adult min. worker Trinity Bapt. Ch., Livermore. Mem. Am. Pharm. Assn. Contra Costa German-Am. Club, Soc. Risk Analysis and Exposure Assessment, Diamond Toastmasters (sec. dist. 57 club 4582, 1991, treas. 1991—, pres. 1991, Competent Toastmaster award 1991, Able Toastmaster award 1993), Kappa Epsilon (Nellie Wakeman award 1983). Southern Baptist. Office: Clorox Tech Ctr PO Box 493 Pleasanton CA 94566-0803

LAWSON, JENNIFER, broadcast executive; b. Birmingham, Ala., June 8, 1946; d. Willie DeLeon and Velma Theresa (Foster) L.; m. Elbert Sampson, June 1, 1979 (div. Sept. 1980); m. Anthony Gittens, May 29, 1982: children: Kai, Zachary. Student, Tuskegee U., 1963-65; MFA, Columbia U., 1974; LHD (hon.), Teikyo Post U., Hartford, Conn., 1991. Assoc. producer William Greaves Prodns., N.Y.C., 1974-75; asst. prof. film studies Bklyn. Coll., 1975-77; exec. dir. The Film Fund, N.Y.C., 1977-80; TV coord. Program Fund Corp. for Pub. Broadcasting, Washington, 1980-83, assoc. dir. TV Program Fund, 1983-89, dir. TV Program Fund, 1989; exec. v.p. programming PBS, Alexandria, Va., 1989—; v.p. Internat. Pub. TV, Washington, 1984-88; panelist Fulbright Fellowships, Washington, 1988-90. Author, illustrator: Children of Africa, 1970; illustrator: Our Folktales, 1968, African Folktales: A Calabash of Wisdom, 1973. Coord. Nat. Coun. Negro Women, Washington, 1969. Office: PBS 1320 Braddock Pl Alexandria VA 22314

LAWSON, JOYCE ANN, human resources executive; b. Piscataway, N.J., Aug. 16, 1929; d. Edward Albert and Elisa Iola (Gamba) L. BS, NYU, 1959, MBA, 1961. From placement rep. to compensation analyst GE Co., Phila., 1961-67, cons. pers. rsch., 1968-72; mgr. employee rels. GE Co., Valley Forge, Pa., 1967-68; cons. corp. employee rels. GE Co., Fairfield, Conn., 1972-85; cons., owner Human Resource Mgmt. Consulting, Stamford, Conn., 1985—; ad hoc industry group on selection guidelines com. mem. Equal Employment Adv. Coun., Washington, 1980-85. Author: (with others) Management Handbook, 1981. Bd. dirs. Soc. Human Resource Mgmt. Found. Inc., 1984-92, v.p., 1990-92, sec.-treas., 1992, archivist/internal auditor, 1993-94. Recipient Founders Day certificate NYU, 1959. Mem. Soc. for Human Resources Mgmt., Nat. Human Resources (pres. 1980-81, chair ann. conf. 1984, mem. of yr. 1978), Beta Gamma Sigma. Office: Human Resources Mgmt Cons 444 Bedford St # 5E Stamford CT 06901

LAWSON, M. JULIET, lawyer; b. Mobile, Ala., May 26, 1959; d. William Max Lawson and Perina Juliet (Barich) Franc. BA, U. Miss., 1981, JD, 1987. Bar: Miss. 1988, U.S. Dist. Ct. (no. and so. dists.) Miss. 1988. Tchr. Ocean Springs (Miss.) Sch. System, 1981-85; atty. Ronald W. Lewis & Assocs., Oxford, Miss., 1988-89; atty. occupl. hearing loss and hand-arm vibration syndrome Scruggs, Millette, Lawson & Dent, P.A., Pascagoula, Miss., 1989—; cons. Occupational Hearing Loss, P.A., 1989—. Contbr. articles to profl. jours. Mem. Walter Anderson Players, Ocean Springs, 1973-94. Mem. ABA, ATLA (chmn. occupational hearing loss litigation group 1990-94), Miss. Trial Lawyers Assn. (editor 1990-92), Magnolia Bar Assn. Democrat. Roman Catholic. Office: Scruggs Millette Lawson & Dent PA 934 Jackson Ave Pascagoula MS 39568

LAWSON, MARGUERITE PAYNE, small business owner; b. Detroit, Apr. 30, 1935; d. LeRoy and Marguerite Lenore (Archambeau) Payne; m. William Allen Stanke, Sept. 4, 1954 (div. Sept. 1962); children: Elizabeth Susan Hankey, Elaine Kathryn Dinwiddie; m. Vernon Arthur Lawson, Aug. 15, 1975. BA in Social Sci., Mich. State U., E. Lansing, 1957. Lic. real estate assoc.; cert. tax preparer. Tchr. El Segundo Unified Sch. Dist., Calif., 1957-58, Las Virgenes Unified Sch. Dist., Calif., 1962-66, Timber Unified Sch. Dist., Thousand Oaks, Calif., 1966-72, Muroc Unified Sch. dist., Edwards, Calif., 1972-78; store owner Margie Lawson's Gourmet Ctr., Lancaster, Calif., 1978—; tour leader Royal Cruise Line voyages, 1987-92; speaker various local clubs, TV sta., Lancaster and Palmdale, Calif., 1977—. Contbr. newspaper articles to Antelope Valley Press, 1975—, also photojournalist; pub. travel writer. Candidate Lancaster (Calif.) City Coun., 1977, Antelope Valley Hosp. Bd., 1982; pres. College Terrace Park Condo Assn., 1987-92; founder, chmn., judge Curtain Call, 1989—; judge Gourmet Products Show, 1992—; patron to 4 local theatrical groups, 1986—. Mem. AAUW, Mensa, Intertel, Am. Booksellers Assn., Asst. League Antelope Valley, Desert Amigas-Domestic Violence (affiliate), Alpha Charter Guild. Republican. Home: 2849 W Avenue J4 Lancaster CA 93536-6016 Office: Margie Lawson's Gourmet Ctr 906 W Lancaster Blvd Lancaster CA 93534-2306

LAWSON, SHIRLEY ANN, food service executive; b. Gardena, Calif., Oct. 11, 1940; d. Andrew Jason and May Louise (Hudson) Rutherford; m. Gilbert Lee Anderson, May 5, 1961 (div. Aug. 10, 1986); children: Johnny Gilbert, Bret Michael, Bruce David, Richard Glen; m. Ted E. Lawson, Mar. 19, 1990. Student in history, U. Md., Spain, 1964; student in sociology, U. Alaska, 1974. Prin. sec. Pennell Elem. Sch., Fairbanks, Alaska, 1972-79; student office mgr. Shadle Park High Sch., Spokane, Wash., 1981-89; office mgr. St. Mary's Sch., Medford, Oreg., 1991-92; food svc. dir. Camp Colman, Lakebay, Wash., 1993—. Home and Office: 127 S Keene Way Dr Medford OR 97504

LAWSON DONADIO, CAROLINA ANNA, foreign language educator, translator; b. Naples, Italy, Mar. 11, 1920; d. Joseph and Concetta (Bartolomeo) Donadio; m. Allan Leroy Lawson, Sept. 15, 1945; 1 child, John. Laurea in European langs., lit., instns., Western Group Instituto Universitario Orientale, Naples, Italy, 1946; PhD in French and Italian, Tulane U., 1971. Lectr. overseas div. U. Md., Leghorn, Italy, 1952; tchr. Warren Easton High Sch., New Orleans, 1958-61; teaching asst. Tulane U., New Orleans, 1961-64; instr. Tex. Christian U., Ft. Worth, 1964-65; lectr. Downtown ctr., U.Chgo., 1967-73, U. Akron, Ohio, 1975-76; pvt. practice lectr., translator, ind. scholar, freelance writer Moncks Corner, S.C., 1985—; vis. prof. Kent (Ohio) State U., 1977-84. Author: (textbook) Nuove Letture di Cultura Italiana, 1975; fgn. lang. editorial reviewer Ency. Brit. Chgo., 1971; review editor: Italian Culture, 1981-84; contbr. many articles in lit. criticism, art history, textbooks of fables, fairy tales, and biographies to profl. and fgn. lang. publs. Recipient cert. of proficiency in Japanese lang. and culture Tokyo Coll., 1958. Mem. MLA, Am. Assn. Tchrs. of Italian, Am. Assn. Italian Studies, Am. Assn. Tchrs of French, Nat. Italian-Am. Found. Republican. Roman Catholic.

LAWTON, JACQUELINE AGNES, retired communications company executive, management consultant; b. Bklyn., June 9, 1933; d. Thomas G. and Agnes R. (McLaughlin) Maguire; m. George W. Lawton, Feb. 14, 1954; children: George, Victoria, Thomas. With N.Y. Telephone, 1954-82, mktg. mgr. govt., edn. and med. Mid State, 1978-81, mktg. mgr. health care, N.Y.C., 1981-82; dist. field market mgr. health care and lodging; region 1 N.E. and Region 2 Mid Atlantic, AT&T-Am. Bell, N.Y.C., 1982-83; ea. region mgr. pers., mktg. and sales AT&T Info. Systems, Parsippany, N.J., 1983-86, pvt. practice mgmt. and travel cons., Cornish Flat, N.H., 1986—; diocesan dir. Medjugirje in Am., Manchester, N.H. Republican. Roman Catholic. Home and Office: PO Box 385 Cornish Flat NH 03746-0385

LAWTON, LORILEE ANN, pipeline supply company owner, accountant; b. Morrisville, Vt., July 17, 1947; d. Philip Wyman Sr. and Margaret Elaine (Ather) Noyes; m. Lee Henry Lawton, Dec. 6, 1969; children: Deborah Ann,

Jeffrey Lee. BBA, U. Vt., 1969. Sr. acct., staff asst. IBM, Essex Junction, Vt., 1969-72; owner, pres., chmn. bd. Red-Hed Supply Inc, Colchester, Vt., 1972—; owner, treas. Firetech Sprinkler Corp., Colchester, 1992—; treas. Greater Burlington Indsl. Corp.; bd. dirs. Cynosure, Burlington, Vt.; mem. small bus. adv. bd. State of Vt. Bd. dirs. Vt. Environ. Coun. Mem. Assn. Gen. Contractors Am., Assn. Gen. Contractors Vt., Am. Water Works Assn., Vt. Water Works Assn., New Eng. Water Works Assn., No. Vt. Homebuilders Assn., Water and Sewer Distbrs. Am., Am. Fire Sprinkler Assn., Nat. Fire Protection Assn. Republican. Home: 53 Middle Rd Colchester VT 05446-1118 also: Firetech Sprinkler Corp 1720 Hegeman Ave Colchester VT 05446

LAWTON, NANCY, artist; b. Gilroy, Calif., Feb. 28, 1950; d. Edward Henry and Marilyn Kelly (Boyd) L.; m. Richard Enemark, Aug. 4, 1984; children: Faith Lawton, Forrest Lawton. BA in Fine Art, Calif. State U., San Jose, 1971; MFA, Mass. Coll. Art, 1980. artist-in-residence Villa Montalvo Ctr. Arts, Los Gatos, Calif., 1971, Noble & Greenough Sch., Dedham, Mass., 1990. One-woman shows include The Bklyn. Mus., 1983, Victoria Munroe Gallery, N.Y.C., 1993; group shows include San Francisco Mus. Modern Art, 1973, The Bklyn. Mus., 1980, 83, Staempfli Gallery, N.Y.C., 1984, The Ark. Art Ctr. Mus., Little Rock, 1984, 88, 92, 93, Victoria Munroe Gallery, 1985, 87, 88, 92, Butler Inst. Am. Art, Ohio, 1988, Smith Coll. Mus. Art, Mass., 1988, NAD, N.Y.C., 1988, Reynolds Gallery, Richmond, 1994; public collections include The Ark. Art Ctr. Mus., Art Inst. Chgo., Bklyn. Mus., Nat. Mus. Am. Art, Smithsonian Inst., Washington. Scholar Mellon Found., 1982; N.Y. State Creative Artists grantee, 1983, N.Y. State Arts Devel. Fund grantee, 1989. Home and Office: 49 Monument Rd Orleans MA 02653

LAWYER, ALECIA LYNN, professional oboist, educator; b. Paris, Tex., June 25, 1968; d. Kenneth Lee and Norma Jean Griffin; m. Lawrence Mark Lawyer. BM cum laude, So. Meth. U., 1990; MM, Juilliard Sch., 1992. Substitute oboist Houston Symphony Orch., Houston Grand Opera, %D, Houston Oratorio Soc.; oboist West End Chamber Players, Dallas, 1994—; solo engagement Juilliard Sch., Banff Centre for the Arts, Can., others. Orchestral ensemble performances include Juilliard Orch., Bloomingdale Chamber Orch., Garland (Tex.) Symphony Orch.; chamber performances include Quintet Cantabile, Trio Trouvere, Juilliard Chamber Orch. Recipient numerous scholarships and music awards. Mem. Internat. Double Reed Soc., DAR, LWV, Mortar Board, Golden Key Honor Soc. Episcopal. Home: 9701 Meyer Forest # 14205 Houston TX 77096

LAWYER, VIVIAN JURY, lawyer; b. Farmington, Iowa, Jan. 7, 1932; d. Jewell Everett Jury and Ruby Mae (Schumaker) Brewer; m. Verne Lawyer, Oct. 25, 1959; children: Michael Jury, Steven Verne. Tchr.'s cert. U. No. Iowa, 1951; BS with honors, Iowa State U., 1953; JD with honors, Drake U., 1968. Bar: Iowa 1968, U.S. Supreme Ct. 1986. Home econs. tchr. Waukee High Sch. (Iowa), 1953-55; home econs. tchr. jr. high sch. and high sch., Des Moines Pub. Schs., 1955-61; pvt. practice law, Des Moines, 1972—; chmn. juvenile code tng. sessions Iowa Crime Commn., Des Moines, 1978-79, coord. workshops, 1980; assoc. Lawyer, Lawyer & Assocs., Des Moines, 1981—; co-founder, bd. dirs. Youth Law Center, Des Moines, 1977—; mem. com. rules of juvenile procedure Supreme Ct. Iowa, 1981-87, adv. com. on costs of ct. appointed counsel Supreme Ct. Iowa, 1985-88; trustee Polk County Legal Aid Svcs., Des Moines, 1980-82; mem. Iowa Dept. Human Svcs. and Supreme Ct. Juvenile Justice County Base Joint Study Com., 1984—. Mem. Iowa Task Force permanent families project Nat. Coun. Juvenile and Family Ct. Judges, 1984-88; mem. substance abuse com. Commn. Children, Youth and Families, 1985—; co-chair Polk County Juvenile Detention Task Force, 1988. Editor: Iowa Juvenile Code Manual, 1979, Iowa Juvenile Code Workshop Manual, 1980; co-editor: 1987 Cumulative Supplement, 1993 supplement, Iowa Academy of Trial Lawyers Trial Handbook; author booklet in field, 1981. Mem. Polk County Citizens Commn. on Corrections, 1977. Iowa Dept. Social Svcs. grantee, 1980. Mem. Iowa Bar Assn., Assn. Trial Lawyers Am., Purple Arrow, Phi Kappa Phi, Omicron Nu. Republican. Home: 5831 N Waterbury Rd Des Moines IA 50312-1339 Office: 427 Fleming Building Des Moines IA 50309-4011

LAX, KATHLEEN THOMPSON, federal judge. BA, U. Kans., 1967; JD, U. Calif., L.A., 1980. Law clk. U.S. Bankruptcy Ct., L.A., 1980-82; assoc. Gibson, Dunn & Crutcher, L.A., 1982-88; judge U.S. Bankruptcy Ct., L.A., 1988—; bd. dirs. L.A. Bankruptcy Forum, 1988—; bd. govs. Fin. Lawyers Conf., L.A., 1991-92, 94—. Bd. editors: Calif. Bankruptcy Jour., 1988—. Office: US Bankruptcy Court Rm 1334 255 E Temple St Los Angeles CA 90012

LAY, ELIZABETH MARIAN, financial systems development administrator; b. Reading, Eng., Oct. 11, 1949; d. John Hunter and Brigid Mary (Maas) L. BS in Biology, SUNY, Albany, 1976; Cert. in Exec. Devel., George Washington U., 1989. mem. adv. coun. No. Va. Mental Health Inst.; puppeteer Smithsonian Instn., 1970-71. Sec. Touche Ross & Co., Washington, 1971-73, para-cons., 1974-75, assoc. cons., 1975-82; fin. systems liason Student Loan Mktg. Assn., Washington, 1982-84, mgr. fin. systems, 1985-87, dir. fin. systems, 1988—. Mem. Nat. Mental Health Assn. (life), Alexandria Mental Health Assn. (pres. 1984-86, treas. 1993-94, Disting. Svc. award 1994), Am. Mensa. Democrat. Office: Student Loan Mktg Assn 1050 Thomas Jefferson St NW Washington DC 20007

LAYBOURNE, GERALDINE, broadcasting executive; b. Plainfield, N.J., 1947; married; 2 children. BA, Vassar Coll., 1969; MS, U. Pa., 1971. Former high sch. tchr.; with Nickelodeon, 1980—, creator Nick at Nite, 1985—, pres.; also vice chmn. MTV Networks. Office: MTV Networks 1515 Broadway New York NY 10036-5702*

LAYCOCK, ANITA SIMON, psychotherapist; b. Cheyenne, Wyo., Dec. 17, 1940; d. James Robert and Dorothy (Dearmin) Simon; m. Maurice Percy Laycock, June 18, 1965(dec. 1976); 1 child, (dec.). BA, U. Wyo., 1962, MA, 1971. Lic. counselor, Wyo., nationally cert. addiction specialist. Grad. student counselor, psychometrist Wyo. State Prison, Rawlins, 1971-73; counselor, trainer Dept. of Insts. State of Colo., Denver, 1973-75; counselor, tchr. supr. Jefferson County Evaluation-Diagnostic Ctr., Rawlins, 1975-78; psychometrist Wyo. State Penitentiary, Rawlins, 1978-79; counselor, therapist Rocky Mountain Arts and Scis., Cheyenne, 1979-81; counselor, therapist supr., dir. SWARA, Rock Springs, Wyo., 1981-85; therapy dir. St. Joseph Residential Treatment, Torrington, Wyo., 1985-88; dir. psychiatric unit Nat. Med. Enterprises Hill-Haven-Pk. Manor, Rawlins, 1988-89; chief exc. officer Simon-Laycock & Assocs., Rawlins, 1989—; cons. Kids in Distressed Situations, Rawlins, 1990-91, Child Devel. Ctr., Rawlins, 1991—; dir. Pub. Offender and Forensic Mental Health Program, Rawlins, 1988-91. Author: (programs) related to sex offenders. Pres. Cheyenne City Panhellenic, 1965-68. Named Miss Wyo.-Miss Universe, 1960; named Miss Wool of Wyo., 1965. Mem. ACA, Nat. Sex Offenders Counselors, Nat. Assn. Drug and Alcohol Counselors, Pub. Offenders Counselors Assn., Western Corrections Assn., Wyo. Assn. Addiction Specialists (pres. 1988—). Home: PO Box 3027 Cheyenne WY 82009 Office: Simon Laycock & Assocs 1716 Yellowstone hwy Cheyenne WY 82009

LAYER, MEREDITH MITCHUM, financial services company executive, public responsibility professional; b. Rutherfordton, N.C., July 26, 1946; d. Lee Wallace and Ellie (Saine) Mitchum; m. Charles Layer, 1990. BS, U. N.C., Greensboro, 1968; MS, U. Md., 1972. Tchr. home econs. Prince Georges County pub. schs., Md., 1968-72; assoc. dir. market research H.J. Kaufman Advt., Washington, 1972-74; dir. consumer edn. Washington Consumer Affairs Office, 1974-76; dir. consumer affairs U.S. Dept. Commerce, Washington, 1976-80; v.p. consumer affairs Am. Express Co., N.Y.C., 1980-82, sr. v.p.-pub. responsibility, 1982—; former mem. consumer adv. coun. Fed. Res. System, Washington; bd. dirs. Nat. Consumers League, Washington, N.Y. Met. Better Bus. Bur., N.Y.C. Contbr. articles to profl. jours. Trustee Inst. for Future, 1986—; bd. dirs. Women's Forum N.Y., 1987-88; former bd. overseers Malcolm Baldridge Nat. Quality Award; commr. Nat. Commn. Working Women, 1987—. Recipient Consumer Edn. award Nat. Found. Consumer Credit Fedn., 1981, Disting. Woman award Northwood Inst., 1985, Matrix award N.Y. Women in Communications, Inc., 1986, Acad. Women Achievers award N.Y.C. YWCA, 1989, N.Y. Women's Agenda Star award, 1992. Mem. Soc. Consumer Affairs Profls. (pres. 1985, individual achievement award 1990), Advt. Women N.Y. (Advt. Woman of the Yr. award 1987), Fin. Women's Assn., Am. Home Econs. Assn., Internat. Credit Assn. (bd. dirs. 1984—). Office: Am Express Co Am Express Tower World Fin Ctr New York NY 10285

LAYTON, MAE-ELLEN ALBRIGHT, client support consultant; b. Anchorage, Alaska, Oct. 21, 1965; d. Mabry O'Neal and Marion Janet (Rooney) L. BS in Mktg., N.H. Coll., 1987. Mktg. sec. energy sys. divsn. Thermo Electron, Waltham, Mass., 1987-89; adminstrv. asst. Project Software & Devel., Inc., Cambridge, Mass., 1989-90, quality assurance analyst, 1990-92, tech. support analyst, 1992-93; client support cons. Collaborative Med. Sys., Waltham, 1993—. Home: 90 Highland Ave Arlington MA 02174-7839 Office: Collaborative Med Sys 50 Sawyer Rd 2 Univ Park Waltham MA 02154

LAYTON, VIVIAN, special event consultant; b. Memphis, Oct. 24, 1960; d. Elbert A. and Dorothy L. (Davis) L. BS in Mktg., U. South Fla., 1983. Catering mgr. Westin Hotels, Atlanta; corp. sales mgr., food svcs. by mgr. Mgr. Food Svcs., Atlanta; asst. dir. catering Altanta Hilton Hotel; dir. catering Penta Hotel, Altanta; pres. distinctive events The Layton Group, Inc., Altanta. Active Young Republicans. Mem. Nat. Assn. Catering Execs., Meeting Planners Internat., Internat. Spl. Events Soc., Hands on Atlanta. Lutheran. Office: The Layton Group Inc 205 15th St NW Atlanta GA 30318

LAZARIAN, TINA JERI, court reporter; b. Oceanside, N.Y., Jan. 19, 1962; d. Charles John and Margaret (Marashlian) L. BA in Polit. Sci., Molloy Coll., 1980; cert. in court reporting, Stenotype Acad., N.Y.C., 1988. Cert. shorthand reporter, N.Y. Flight attendant Saudi Arabian Airlines, Jeddah, Saudi Arabia, 1981-83, Gulf Air, Bahrain, 1984-86; ct. reporter Tina J. Lazarian Court Reporting Agy., N.Y.C., 1988—. Mem. Nat. Ct. Reporters Assn., N.Y. State Ct. Reporters Assn., NAFE. Democrat. Home: 309 Park Ave Hoboken NJ 07030-3805

LAZARIS, PAMELA ADRIANE, municipal agency administrator; b. Dixon, Ill., Oct. 13, 1956; d. Michael Constantine and Ellen Euridice (Eftax) L.; m. Eugene Dale Monson, Oct. 17, 1987; children: Anthony Edward, Anna Adriane. BFA in Fine Arts, U. Wis., Milw., 1978; MS in Urban and Regional Planning, U. Wis., 1982; MBA, U. St. Thomas, 1992. Analyst planning Wis. Dept. Natural Resources, Madison, 1979-82; asst. city planner City of Albert Lea, Minn., 1982-83; specialist community devel. City of Winona, Minn., 1983-85; dir. community devel. City of Waseca, Minn., 1985—. Vol. spl. events Farmam-Minn. Agrl. Interpretive Ctr., Waseca, 1985-86; sec., comm. dir. Waseca Area Cmty. Fund, 1989-95; mem. Waseca County Econ. Devel. Commn., 1988-95. Named one of Oustanding Young Women of Am., 1986. Mem. Am. Inst. Cert. Planners (cert.), Am. Planning Assn. (chpt. bd. dirs. 1986-89), Minn. Planning Assn. (v.p. 1989-90, dist. bd. dirs. 1985-89), Toastmasters (chpt. sgt.-at-arms 1987, ednl. v.p. 1988, 91-95). Home: PO Box 325 110 6th Ave NE Waseca MN 56093 Office: City of Waseca 508 S State St Waseca MN 56093-3097

LAZARUS, ROCHELLE BRAFF, advertising executive; b. N.Y.C., Sept. 1, 1947; d. Lewis L. and Sylvia Ruth (Eisenberg) Braff; m. George M. Lazarus, Mar. 22, 1970; children: Theodore, Samantha, Benjamin. AB, Smith Coll., 1968; MBA, Columbia U., 1970. Product mgr. Clairol, N.Y.C., 1970-71; account exec. Ogilvy & Mather, N.Y.C., 1971-73, account supr., 1973-77, mgmt. supr., 1977-84, sr. v.p., 1981—, account group dir., 1984-87; gen. mgr. Ogilvy & Mather Direct, N.Y.C., 1987-88, mng. dir., 1988-89, pres., 1989-91; pres. Ogilvy & Mather, N.Y.C., 1991-94, pres. N. Am., 1994—. Mem. Smith Coll. Career Counseling Bd., Northampton, Mass., 1978; bd. dirs. Ann Taylor, Advt. Edn. Found., YMCA, Nat. Women's Law Ctr.; mem. Com. of 200; mem. bus. com. Solomon R. Guggenheim Mus.; mem. bd. overseers Columbia Bus. Sch.; trustees Columbia Presbyn. Hosp. Recipient YWCA Women Achievers award 1985; named Advertising Woman of the Yr., Advertising Women of N.Y., 1994. Mem. Am. Assn. Advt. Agys. (bd. dirs.), Advt. Women N.Y. (Woman of Yr. 1994), Women's Direct Mktg. Group, Direct Mktg. Assn. Home: 106 E 78th St New York NY 10021 Office: Ogilvy & Mather Direct Worldwide Plz 309 W 49th St New York NY 10019-7316

LAZARUS, SARA LOUISE, theatre director and educator; b. Bklyn., Apr. 15, 1948; d. Laurence and Bella (Sollender) L.; m. David Seader, June 5, 1988. BS, Northwestern U., 1968; cert. in acting, Royal Acad. Dramatic Art, London, 1975. Actress, singer Broadway, Off-Broadway, nat. tours, regional theatre, 1968-78; actor, instr. Durham (N.H.) Summer Theatre, U. N.H., 1978; announcer, moderator New Eng. Forum, Sta. WHEB-AM-FM, Portsmouth, N.H., 1979; dir. Hangar Theatre, Cornell U., Ithaca, N.Y., 1981; founder, tchr. Sara Lazarus Studio for Mus. Theatre Studies, N.Y.C., 1982—; dir. 137th and 138th Ann. Hasty Pudding Shows, Harvard U., Cambridge, Mass., 1985, 86, Centenary Stage Co., Hackettstown, N.J., 1987, 89, Yale U. Dramatic Assn., New Haven, 1988, guest instr. master classes, 1991; instr. Am. Mus. and Dramatic Acad., N.Y.C., 1985-86, 92. Dir. Babes in Arms concert, Avery Fisher Hall, Lincoln Ctr., N.Y.C., 1989 (Back Stage Bistro award 1989), Ridin' High, Eighty-Eights (Back Stage Bistro award 1990), Hollywood Opera, The Ballroom, 1990, The 1959 Broadway Songbook, The Oak Room, Algonquin Hotel, 1991, Cabaret Comes to Carnegie, Weill Recital Hall, 1991, Oliver, Chiswick Park Theatre, Sudbury, Mass., 1992, Plaisir D'Amour, 1992, Dancing in the Dark Oak Room Alqonquin Hotel, 1993, Weill at Weill Carnegie Weill Recital Hall, 1992, Shauna Hicks and Her 60's Chicks, 1993-94 (Bistro award, Manhattan Assn. Cabarets award), Havana BC, 1993-94 (Bistro award), Hoagy On My Mind-A Carmichael Revue-The Ballroom, 1994, The Blindfold-Working Lights Unlimited, 1994; (recordings) The 1959 Broadway Songbook, Live at the Algonquin, Babes in Arms. Outstanding Dir. award CAB Mag., 1992, Outstanding Dir. award Cabaret Hotline, 1992. Mem. Soc. Stage Dirs. and Choreographers, Actors Equity Assn., Manhattan Assn. Cabarets (Outstanding Dir. 1991), League of Profl. Theatre Women. Home and Office: 535 Cathedral Pky New York NY 10025-2086

LAZECHKO, D.M. (MOLLY LAZECHKO), former state legislator; b. Innisfail, Alta., June 3, 1926; came to U.S., 1960; d. Archibald Donald and Violet Georgina (Adams) Manuel; m. Walter Vladmir Lazechko, Apr. 16, 1960; children: William Donald, Robert James. BA, Boise State U., 1976. Cert. elem. tchr. Tchr. Olds Sch. Dist., Stewart Sch., Alta., 1945-46, Innisfail (Alta.) Sch. Dist., 1946-50; tchr., vice prin. Calgary (Alta.) Sch. Dist., 1950-59; exchange tchr. Edinburgh, Scotland, 1954-55; math tutor mgr. Title I, Boise, Idaho, 1974-76; elem. tchr. Boise (Idaho) Sch. Dist., 1976-87; jr. high tchr. Chpt. I, Boise, 1987-88; ret., 1988-90; mem. Idaho Ho. of Reps., Boise, 1991, 92; pres. div. I Alta. Tchrs. Assn., Calgary, 1958-59, Whittier PTA, Boise, 1969-70, 73-74; pres., 3d v.p. Dist. 8 Idaho State PTA, 1973-75; sec., elem. dir. Boise (Idaho) Edn. Assn., 1978-81. Treas. LWV, Boise, 1988-90, House Dems. Campaign. Com., Boise, 1991-92; precinct capt. Ada County Dems. Dist. 16, Boise, 1988-90; sec. Boise Ret. Tchrs., 1989-90, pres., 1993-94; bd. mem. Boise Neighborhood Housing Svcs., 1990-92, Cmty. Contbn. Ctr., 1991-92, Idaho Housing Coalition, 1991-92; gov. appt. to bd. of Idaho Coun. on Domestic Violence, 1994—; bd. dirs. Epilepsy League of Idaho, 1993-94; candidate Idaho Legis. Ho. Reps., 1994. Mem. NEA, Idaho Edn. Assn., Idaho Conservation League, Idaho Women's Network, Grassroots Women's Lobby, Idaho Citzen's Network. Episcopalian.

LAZENBY, GAIL R., library director; b. Charlotte, N.C., May 6, 1947; d. James Yates and Marian Elizabeth (Church) Rogers. BA, Salem Coll., 1969; MLS, U. N.C., 1971. Cert. libr., Ga. Br. libr. Atlanta Pub. Libr., 1970-77; br. coord. Dekalb Libr. System, Decatur, Ga., 1977-82; asst. dir. West Ga. Regional Libr., Carrollton, 1982-83; asst. dir. Cobb County Pub. Libr., Marietta, Ga., 1983-90, dir., 1991—. Mem. Leadership Cobb, Cobb County, 1985-86. Mem. ALA, Ga. Libr. Assn. (2d v.p. 1987-89), Southeastern Libr. Assn. (v.p.-pres. elect. 1990-92, pres. 1992-94), Kiwanis Club Marietta (bd. dirs. 1991-92), sec. 1992-93, sec.-treas. 1993-94, pres.-elect 1994-95). Office: Cobb County Public Lib 266 Roswell St SE Marietta GA 30060-2005

LAZEROV, FRANCES CALDERON, realtor, commercial property owner; b. Indpls., Nov. 18, 1938; d. Albert Samuel and Florence (Sarfaty) Calderon; m. Israel Samuel Lazerov, May 31, 1959; children: David Albert, Florence Elise. Student, Ind. U., 1956=59. Lic. realtor, broker; cert. residential specialist, relocation specilist. Real estate sales assoc. Carriage Estates, Indpls., 1968-78, F.C. Tucker Co., Indpls., 1978—. Recipient various real estate sales awards. Mem. Residential Sales Coun., Residential Adv. Coun., Indpls. Aero Club. Office: FC Tucker Co 9277 N Meridian St Indianapolis IN 46260-1875

LAZERSON, ELEANOR MARIE, psychiatric/mental health nurse, administrator; b. Chgo.; d. Ettore A. and Lena A. (Plastine) Ianniccari; m. Jack Lazerson, Mar. 24, 1962 (div.); children: David, Deborah, Darlene, Donna. Diploma, Presbyn. Hosp. Sch. Nursing, Chgo., 1954; BA, Northeastern U., Chgo., 1976; MS, No. Ill. U., 1978. Cert. psychiat./mental health nurse, clin. nursing supr.-adminstr. Clin. nursing supr./adminstr. Dept. Mental Health and Developmental Disabilities, Chgo.; staff nurse, patient educator VA Hosp., Chgo.; lectr. in field. Author script for audiovisual presentation on manic-depressive illness. Fellow Am. Orthopsychiat. Assn.; mem. ANA, Ill. Nurses Assn., Chgo. Nurses Assn., Am. Psychiat. Nurses Assn., Am. Nurses Found.

LAZERWITZ, ROBERTA JOYCE, primary school educator; b. Paterson, N.J., Jan. 25, 1943; d. Gerald and Eve (Grossman) Joff; m. Bud Lazerwitz, Mar. 16, 1969; children: Jennifer, Elyse, Ian. Bachelor's degree, William Paterson Coll., 1964, M in Elem. Edn., 1968. Tchr. East Rutherford (N.J.) Bd. Edn., 1964—. Recipient Gov.'s award State of N.J., 1985. Mem. NEA, N.J. Edn. Assn., Bergen County Edn. Assn., Assn. Kindergarten Educators. Home: 15 Longwood Ct Wayne NJ 07470

LAZINSKY, JO ANNE MARIE, advertising executive; b. Bklyn.; d. Guy A. and Lillian (Chiarello) Cimino. Student, Duquesne U., 1960-62; BA cum laude, St. John's U., Jamaica, N.Y., 1964. Cert. in secondary edn. English tchr. Wantagh (N.Y.) High Sch., 1964-65; advt. media analyst Advt. Info. Services, N.Y.C., 1965-66; editor, copywriter J.C. Penney Co., Inc., N.Y.C., 1973-76; editor Avon Products, Inc., N.Y.C., 1976-79; advt. copywriter Conklin, Labs & Bebee, Syracuse, N.Y., 1980-83; advt. mgr. Will & Baumer Candle Co., Syracuse, 1983-84; sales promotion supr. Carrier Corp. div. United Techs., Syracuse, 1984-85; advt. cons. Liverpool, N.Y., 1985-87; copy chief New England Bus. Svc., Inc., Groton, Mass., 1987-91, assoc. advt. mgr. div. mktg. products, 1991-94; acct. mgr. Image Products, 1994—. Contbg. editor style guide for Avon Products Co., Inc., 1977-78; contbr. articles to newspapers and various trade jours. Mem. bd. mgrs. North Area Syracuse YMCA, 1981-86, mem. mktg. com., 1984-85. Recipient Advt. award Assn. of Advt. Agys. Internat., 1982. Mem. New England Direct Mktg. Assn. Home: 13L Bonnie Ln Derry NH 03038-4009 Office: New England Bus Svc Inc Divsn Mktg Products 500 Main St Groton MA 01471-0002

LAZIO, SISTER MARY MARGARET, healthcare facility executive; b. Grand Rapids, Mich., Oct. 13, 1945. Student, Fontbonne Coll., St. Louis, 1963-68, Penn Valley C.C., Kansas City, 1968; BSN, Avila Coll., Kansas City, 1970; MSN, Cath. U. Am., 1978. RN, Mo. Staff nurse various units St. Joseph Hosp., Kansas City, Mo., 1970-74; head nurse med.-surg. unit St. Joseph Hosp., Kansas City, 1974-76, summer relief nursing supr., 1977, primary nursing coord., 1978-79, clin. dir. med.-surg. nursing, 1979-83, asst. adminstr. mission and values, 1983-85, assoc. adminstr. mission, nursing and support svcs., 1985-87; interim CEO Carondelet Health Corp., St. Joseph Hosp., Kansas City, 1986; v.p., DON St. Joseph Health Ctr., Kansas City, 1987-90, COO, 1990—; adj. faculty Avila Coll., Kansas City, 1979-83, preceptor for sr. nursing leadership students, 1975; nursing adminstrn. practicum Washington (D.C.) Hosp. Ctr., 1978; trustee St. Joseph Health Ctr. Found. Bd., 1985-87, Avila Coll. Bd., 1992—; lectr. in field. Mem. Am. Orgn. Nurse Execs., Mo. Orgn. Nurse Execs., Kansas City Area Hosp. Assn. (com. on nursing 1987, subcom. on retention 1987, nursing svc. adminstrs. 1987-90, coun. on human resources 1988-92), Am. Coll. Healthcare Execs. (diplomate), Sigma Theta Tau (chpt. pres. 1985-86). Home: 9930 McGee St Kansas City MO 64114 Office: Saint Joseph Health Ctr 1000 Carondelet Dr Kansas City MO 64114

LAZOR, PATRICIA ANN, interior designer; b. Bound Brook, N.J., Feb. 3, 1936; d. Charles A. and Grace E. (Siegrist) LaGattuta; m. E. Alexander Lazor, Aug. 22, 1959; children: Pamela A., Carolyn L., Charles L., Peter A. BA, Chestnut Hill Coll., 1957; MEd, Rutgers Coll., 1962; cert., N.Y. Sch. Interior Design, 1972. Tchr. Bridgewater (N.J.) Raritan Schs., 1958-69; designer Patricia A. Lazor Interior Design, Bernardsville, N.J., 1975-85; pres. Alexander Abry, Inc., Washington, 1985-87; owner, designer Patricia A. Lazor Interior Design Antiques, Inc., Bernardsville, N.J., 1985—. Com.-woman Rep. Party, Somerset County, N.J., 1978; chmn. Family Counseling Service Somerset County, 1972-78. Mem. Essex Hunt Club (Peapack, N.J.), Somerset Hills Country Club (Bernardsville), Garden Club of Morristown, The Morristown Club, Kappa Delta Phi. Republican. Home and Office: Interior Design/Antiques Inc Roebling Rd Bernardsville NJ 07924

LAZRUS, ABBE SUE, mental health consultant; b. Takoma Park, Md., Feb. 10, 1961; d. Sherman and Charlotte (Dunyer) L. BA in Psyhology, U. Md., 1983; MA in Clin. Psychology, Towson State U., 1986. Cert. profl. counselor, Md. Adminstrv. asst. First Cambridge Corp., Rockville, Md., 1986; clerical unit supr. Montgomery House, Gaithersburg/Kensington, Md., 1986-88, vocat. coord., 1994; counselor, quality assurance-intake coord., asst. dir. Vesta, Inc., Landover Hills, Md., 1988-92, cons., 1992-93; utilization mgmt. coord. Pathways, Annapolis, Md., 1992-93; cons. Am. Med. Capital Corp., Washington, 1992, 93-94; vocat. coord. Montgomery House, Gaithersburg, 1994-95; rehab. specialist divsn. rehab. svc. Md. State Dept. Edn., 1995—. Mem. APA (assoc.). Home: PO Box 4083 Silver Spring MD 20914-4083

LAZZARA, BERNADETTE See PETERS, BERNADETTE

LEA, ELEANOR LUCILLE, retired state agency administrator; b. Diller, Nebr., Nov. 6, 1916; d. Edward Richard and Gertrude (Loock) Henrichs; m. Stanley Guy Lea, Mar. 6, 1936; children: Dianna Evenson, Cylesta Peters, Jeffrey, Chad. Student, Fairbury State Coll. Owner Modern Furniture Store, Fairbury, Nebr., 1945-80; dist. mgr. Field Enterprises, Chgo., 1966-80; libr. resource person Fairbury Pub. Libr., 1982-85; job coord. Blue River Area Agy. on Aging, Lincoln, Nebr., 1985-87; Bd. mem. Operation ABLE, Lincoln, 1987-92, Nat. Grandparent Program, Beatrice, Nebr., 1985-87. Pres., dist. v.p. United Meth. Women; Sunday Sch. supt. Meth. Ch., Fairbury; v.p. sch. bd. Fairbury Pub. Sch. Bd., 1956-62; bd. mem. Girl Scouts U.S.A., 1950-56. Mem. Toastmasters (v.p. pub. rels. Lincoln 1992-94). Republican. Home: 2920 S 72d St # 85 Lincoln NE 68506

LEA, PAMELA WARREN, real estate appraiser; b. South Charleston, W.Va., June 3, 1947; d. George Herbert Warren and Eileen Kathel (Ellis) Warren Hoflich; m. Ted Mann Lea, Aug. 21, 1971 (div. Nov. 1982); children: Lisa Dawn, Robert Christopher, Andrea Elizabeth. Student, U. N.C., Greensboro, 1965-67, 69-71, Ga. State U., Atlanta, 1984. Data entry operator Ticor Mortgage Ins. Co., Atlanta, 1983-84; underwriting asst. United Guaranty, Atlanta, 1984-85; real estate appraiser Arnold M. Schwartz & Assocs., Atlanta, 1985-91; pvt. practice real estate appraiser Atlanta, 1991—. Baptist. Home and Office: Apt 2403 34181 Lakeside Dr Atlanta GA 30326

LEACH, CHRISTINE ELAINE, technical support executive; b. Riverside, Calif., Aug. 25, 1957; d. Kenneth Orvis and Gwendolyn Eloise (Belew) T.; m. Robert Gary Leach, June 11, 1983; children: Robert Arlan, Jonathan Abraham. Enlisted USAF, 1977, advanced through grades to tech. sgt., 1980, asst. mgr., 1983, adminstrv. supr. battle staff sect., 1984, mgr. force applications adminstrn., 1984-90, resigned, 1988; facility security officer Logicon, Inc., 1990—, assoc. program asst., 1990—; instr. for software Logicon, Inc., Bellevue, Nebr., 1988—. Mem. Air Force Assn. (life). Republican. Baptist. Office: 1408 Ft Crook Rd S Bellevue NE 68005-2969

LEACH, DEBRA ANN, alcohol beverage association executive; b. Kokomo, Ind., Dec. 27, 1952; d. William Thomas and Mary Ellen (Clarke) L.; m. Gary Simpkins Widdowson, Aug. 9, 1974 (dec. Feb. 1980). BS, U. Md., 1975. Home econs. tchr. Wicomico County Schs., Salisbury, Md., Balt. City Schs., 1976-81; bartender, cocktail server Md., Va., 1982-88; nat. program dir. Techniques of Alcohol Mgmt., Alexandria, Va., 1988—; exec. dir. Nat. Licensed Beverage Assn., 1992—. Contbr. articles to profl. jours. Mem. adv. bd. Nightclub and Bar mag.; active Sky Ranch for Boys, N.Am. Responsible Hospitality Partnership. Mem. NOW, Am. Soc. Assn. Execs., Assn. Chief Exec. Coun., World Assn. Alcohol Beverage Industries, Nat.

Lic. Beverage Assn. (exec. dir. 1992—), Nat. Abortion Rights Action League, Nat. Wildlife Fedn., World Wildlife Fund, Responsible Hospitality Inst. Home: 5120 Maris Ave # 401 Alexandria VA 22304-1961 Office: NLBA/TAM 4214 King St Alexandria VA 22302-1507

LEACH, LYNNE E., nursing educator; b. Ridley Park, Pa., 1949; d. David J. and Mildred Elizabeth (Wynn) Fleming; m. Joseph P. Leach. RN, Bryn Mawr Hosp. Sch. Nursing, Pa., 1970; BS in Edn., Millersville (Pa.) U., 1975; MS in Nursing, U. Del., Newark, 1983; EdD, Widener U., Chester, Pa., 1994. Staff nurse Queen's Med. Ctr., Honolulu, 1972, Crozer-Chester Med. Ctr., Upland, Pa., 1970-71, 72-76; instr. nursing Bryn Mawr Hosp. Sch. Nursing, 1976-80; asst. prof. nursing Widener U., Chester, 1983—. Mem. AWHONN (edn. coord. Pa. Sect. 1985-87, coord. Delco chpt. 1987-88, sec. treas. Pa. sect. 1988-90, chair Pa. sect. 1991-92, dist. III adv. coun. 1988—, chairperson dist. III 1993-95, nat. exec. bd. 1993-95), NAFE, Sigma Theta Tau (Eta Beta chpt.), Pi Lamba Theta (Phila. chpt.). Office: Widener U Sch of Nursing Chester PA 19013

LEACH, MARIA LOPEZ, accountant, educator; b. Acapulco, Guerrero, Mex., May 7, 1956; came to U.S., 1974; d. Praxedis Lopez and Antonieta (Rodriguez) Migala; m. J. Michael Leach, May 3, 1975; children: Heather, Megan. BA in Acctg., Miss. U. for Women, 1987; M in Profl. Acctg., Miss. State U., 1988. Cert. mgmt. acct.; CPA, Miss. Real estate salesman Century 21, Columbus, Miss., 1977-79; sec., bookkeeper Mike Leach Constrn., Columbus, 1980-85; ins. salesman Wigger's Ins., Columbus, 1981-89; instr. acctg. Miss. U. for Women, Columbus, 1990, Miss. State U., Starkville, 1990-92; fin. analyst United Technologies Motor Sys., Columbus, 1992-93, sr. cost acct., 1994—. Mem. Inst. Mgmt. Accts. (bd. dirs. 1988, 89). Republican. Home: PO Box 8938 Columbus MS 39705 Office: United Technologies Motor Sys PO Box 2228 Columbus MS 39704

LEACH, SHAWNA, food service director; b. Lehi, Utah, July 9, 1949; d. Lloyd D. and Dawna Mae (Marrott) Boren; m. Micheal Merrell Wiley, Feb. 11, 1967 (div.); children: Shannon Wiley Espinoza, Cyndie Wiley Anderson, Michael Shane, Stacie Lee; m. Calvin Donald Leach, Feb. 18, 1983. Cert. in dietary managing, Ctrl. Ariz. Coll., 1993. Mgr. cafeteria Provo (Utah) Sch. Dist., 1976-86; supply clk. Bur. of Reclamation, Page, Ariz., 1987-88; dir. food svc. Page Unified Sch. Dist., 1988—. Mem. Am. Sch. Food Svc. Assn. (dir., adminstr. I 1992—, instr. 1993—), Am. Sch. Bus. Officials, Ariz. Sch. Bus. Officials, Ariz. Sch. Food Svc. Assn. (chair certification 1992, state officer), Dietary Mgrs. Assn., Page Recycles. Democrat. LDS. Home: PO Box 3618 Page AZ 86040-3618 Office: Page Unified Sch Dist PO Box 1927 Page AZ 86040-1927

LEACH, SHERYL, television show character creator; b. Athens, Tex.; d. B.J. Stamps; m. Jim Leach; 1 child. Sch. tchr. Tex.; writer DLM Inc., Allen, Tex.; devel. The Backyard Show (now Barney & Friends) PBS-TV, 1987. Creator of Barney the Dinosaur TM, 1987; devel. Barney and the Backyard Gang video series and numerous others. Office: Lyons Group Ste 1600 2435 N Central Expy Richardson TX 75080-2722*

LEACHMAN, CLORIS, actress; b. Des Moines, June 30, 1930; m. George England, 1953 (div. 1979); 5 children. Ed., Northwestern U. Actress: (films) including Kiss Me Deadly, 1955, Butch Cassidy and the Sundance Kid, 1969, W.U.S.A., 1970, The People Next Door, 1970, Lovers and Other Strangers, 1970, The Steagle, 1971, The Last Picture Show, 1971 (Acad. award for best supporting actress 1971), Charles and the Angel, 1972, Happy Mother's Day...Love, George, 1973, Dillinger, 1973, Daisy Miller, 1974, Young Frankenstein, 1974, Crazy Mama, 1975, High Anxiety, 1977, The Mouse and His Child, 1977 (voice), Foolin' Around, 1979, The North Avenue Irregulars, 1979, The Muppet Movie, 1979, Scavenger Hunt, 1979, Yesterday, 1979, Herbie Goes Bananas, 1980, History of the World, Part 1, 1982, Shadow Play, 1986, My Little Pony, 1986 (voice), Walk Like a Man, 1987, Hansel and Gretel, 1987, Prancer, 1989, Love Hurts, 1990, Texasville, 1990, Walter and Emily, 1991, My Boyfriend's Back, 1993, The Beverly Hillbillies, 1993, A Troll in Central Park, 1994 (voice), Storytime, 1994, Nobody's Girls, 1994; TV series including Lassie, 1957, Route 66, Laramie, Trials of O'Brien, Mary Tyler Moore Show, Phyllis, 1975-77, Facts of Life, The Nutt House, 1989; (TV movies) including Silent Night, Lonely Night, 1969, Suddenly Single, 1971, Haunts of the Very Rich, 1972, Brand New Life, 1973, Dying Room Only, 1973, Crime Club, 1973, Death Sentence, 1974, Thursday's Game, 1974, Hitchhike!, 1974, The Migrants, 1974, A Girl Named Sooner, 1975, Ladies of the Corridor, The New Original Wonder Woman, 1975, Death Scream, 1975, Someone I Touched, 1975, It Happened One Christmas, 1977, Long Journey Back, 1978, Mrs. R.'s Daughter, 1979, Willa, 1979, S.O.S. Titanic, 1979, The Acorn People, 1981, Advice to the Lovelorn, 1981, Miss All-American Beauty, 1982, Dixie: Changing Habits, 1983, The Demon Murder Case, 1983, Ernie Kovacs, Between the Laughter, 1984, Deadly Intentions, 1985, Love is Never Silent, Danielle Steele's Fine Things, 1990, In Broad Daylight, 1991, A Little Piece of Heaven, 1991, Fade to Black, 1993, Without a Kiss Goodbye, 1993, Spies, 1993, Miracle Child, 1993, Double, Double, Toil and Trouble, 1993 (TV miniseries) Backstairs at the White House, 1979; theater appearance in Grandma Moses: An American Primitive, Washington, 1990; guest appearance: The Love Boat, 1976. Recipient 6 Emmy awards. Address: Met Talent Agy 4526 Wilshire Blvd 3d Fl Beverly Hills CA 90212*

LEADER, DORIS MORRELL, association executive, human rights activist; b. Oak Park, Ill., Feb. 15, 1923; d. Jacque Cyrus and Mildred (Newmark) Morrell; m. Henry Boyer Leader, June 8, 1946; children: Martha Lois, Elizabeth Anne, Emily Jane, Julia Morrell. BA, Swarthmore Coll., 1944; MA, Syracuse U., 1946. Program dir. indsl. women YWCA, New Haven, Conn., 1946-47; pres. YWCA, York, Pa., 1953-57; bd. dirs. nat. bd. YWCA of the U.S.A., N.Y.C., 1958-76, commd. rschr. YWCA as Christian Movement, 1964-67, v.p., 1973-76, chmn. nat. nominating com., 1979-82, mem. World Svc. Coun., 1977—; bd. trustees YWCA, York, 1975—; commr. Pa. Human Rels. Commn., Harrisburg, 1972-86, vice chmn., 1974-86, sec. adv. coun., York, 1963-72; sec., co-chair Community Audit Human Rights, York, 1960-63, 80-90. Treas., vice chair Community Progress Coun., York, 1969-79; chair state pub. affairs com. Jr. Leagues Pa., Harrisburg, 1963-65; life mem. PTA, program and human rels. chair, 1950s; dir. York City Sch. Bd., 1987—, pres., 1993—; mem. York County Hist. Soc., 1980—. Recipient Golden Deeds award Exchange Club, 1974, Disting. Pennsylvanian award Greater Phila. C. of C., 1980, Legion of Honor, Chapel of Four Chaplains, 1982, Legacy award AAUW, 1984, Community Svc. award City of York, 1987, Disting. Daughter of Pa. award Gov. Robert Casey, 1990. Mem. NAACP (Freedom award 1982), LWV. Democrat. Unitarian. Home: 448 Linden Ave York PA 17404

LEAF, KAREN, lawyer; b. Berkeley, Calif., May 10, 1955; d. David McPherron and Claire Anderson (Tapley) L.; m. Timothy Elgin Ainsworth, Sept. 8, 1985; children: Colin Elgin, Robert McPherron. BA, Williams Coll., Williamstown, Mass., 1977; JD, Columbia U., 1982. Bar: Calif. 1983, U.S. Dist. Ct. (ea. dist.) Calif. 1983, U.S. Dist. Ct. (no. dist.) Calif. 1984, U.S. Ct. Appeals (9th cir.) 1987, U.S. Dist. Ct. (cen. dist.) Calif. 1992. Instr. English Chinese U. Hong Kong, 1977-79; law clk. U.S. Dist. Ct., Sacramento, Calif., 1982-84; litigation assoc. Dinkelspiel Donovan & Reder, San Francisco, 1984-89; dep. atty. gen. Calif. Atty. Gens. Office, Sacramento, 1989-92, 95—; litigation assoc. Eisen & Johnston, San Francisco, 1992-94; instr. legal writing Sch. Law U. Calif. Davis, 1995. Harlan Fiske Stone scholar Columbia U. Law Sch., N.Y.C., 1980-81, 81-82. Office: Eisen & Johnston 980 9th St Sacramento CA 95814

LEAHY, NOREEN MARIE, nursing clinician; b. Boston, July 28, 1955; d. Michael John and Dorothea Ellen (Norton) Pembroke; m. Thomas Michael Leahy, June 5, 1976; children: Sean, Colleen, Michael, Sarah. BSN, Salem State Coll., 1977; MS, Boston U., 1984. CNRN. Staff nurse Mass. Gen. Hosp., Boston, 1977-79, unit tchr., 1979-84, supr., 1984-85; clin. nurse specialist Boston U. Med. Ctr., 1985-94, Boston Specialty and Rehab. Hosp., 1995—; clin. instr. Somerville (Mass.) Hosp. Sch. Nursing, 1991-92; cons. in field, Dorchester, Mass., 1983—. Author: Quick Reference to Neuroscience Critical Care Nursing, 1990; contbr. articles to profl. jours. Den leader St. Ann's Cub Scouts, Dorchester, 1989—. Mem. AACN, ANA, Mass. Nurses Assn., Am. Assn. Neurosci. Nurses, Mass. Conf. Group for Classification of Nursing Diagnoses, Greater Boston Assn. Neurosci. Nurses (past pres. 1983-84), Sigma Theta Tau. Democrat. Roman Catholic. Home: 35 Oakton Ave Dorchester MA 02122

LEAK, MARGARET ELIZABETH, insurance company executive; b. Atlanta, Sept. 9, 1946; d. William Whitehurst and Margaret Elizabeth (Whitsitt) L. BS in Psychology, Okla. State U., 1968; postgrad., U. Okla., 1968-69, Cornell U., 1976-78; grad. advanced mgmt. program, Harvard U., 1983-84. Editor communications Eastern State Bankcard Assn., N.Y.C., 1969-71; sr. edn. specialist Citibank, N.Y.C., 1971-73; adminstr. orgn. devel. NBC, N.Y.C., 1973-74; mgr. tng. and devel. Atlantic Mut. Cos., Property/Casualty Ins., N.Y.C., 1974-76, sec. human resources, 1976-78, v.p. human resources, 1978-84, v.p. human resources and corp. communications, 1984-86, sr. v.p. adminstrv. services, 1987—. Office: Atlantic Mut Cos 3 Giralda Farms Madison NJ 07940-1004

LEAL, BARBARA JEAN PETERS, fundraising executive; b. Hartford, Ala., Oct. 24, 1948; d. Clarence Lee and Syble (Simmons) Peters; m. Michael Wayne Foster, 1966 (div.); children: Michaelle, Jonathan; m. Ramon Leal, 1991. AA, Enterprise State Jr. Coll., 1970; BA, U. South Fla., 1974; MA, Trinity U., San Antonio, 1975; postgrad. Universidad Nacional Autonoma de Mexico, 1982. Cert. fund raising exec. Instr., San Antonio Coll., 1975; planner Econ. Opportunities Devel. Corp., San Antonio, 1976, Alamo Area Council Govts., San Antonio, 1977-82; dir. planned giving Oblate Missions, San Antonio, 1982—; spkr. in field. Author: Paratransit Provider Handbook, 1978; contbg. author: Human Responses to Aging, 1976; Transportation for Elderly Handicapped Programs and Problems, 1978; contbr. articles to profl. pubs. Named one of Outstanding Young Women of Am., 1985. Founding mem. Nat. Soc. Fund Raising Execs. (past pres. San Antonio chpt.), Am. Coun. on Gift Annuities, Coun. Advancement and Support Edn., San Antonio Planned Giving Com. Democrat. Roman Catholic. Office: Oblate Missions PO Box 96 San Antonio TX 78291-0096

LEAPLEY, PATRICIA MURRAY, dietitian; b. Lowell, Mass.; d. Henry J. and Ruth (Slipp) Murray; m. Robert A. Leapley; children: Robert Jr., Deborah, John. BS in Nutrition and Edn., Framingham State Coll., 1959; MS in Allied Health Services, U. North Fla., 1986. Registered dietitian, Washington, cert. diabetes educator; lic. dietitian, Fla. Chief nutrition clinic Walter Reed Army Med. Ctr., Washington, 1976-79; coordinator diabetes program U. South Fla., Tampa, 1979-80; dir. nutrition BLD Nutrition Mgmt. Systems, Clearwater, Fla., 1980-84, Health Care Assocs., Rockville, Md., 1984; clin. nutrition specialist Riverside Hosp., Jacksonville, Fla., 1985-87; dir. nutrition services The Drs. Clinic, Jacksonville, 1987-88; diabetes and lipid nutrition specialist Dept. Vets. Affairs Lake City (Fla.) Med. Ctr. Author (book and slides): Food Facts for Diabetes and Weight Control, 1979; contbr. numerous articles to profl. jours. Served as capt. U.S. Army, 1959-64. Recipient Alumni Achievement award Framingham State Coll., 1979; first dietitian to develop diet for treatment of Phenylketonuria in children, Walter Reed Med. Amry Med. Ctr., 1960. Mem. Am. Assn. Diabetes Educators (bd. dirs. 1980-83, program chair VA/AADE diabetic educators group 1994-95), Am. Dietetic Assn. (exec. bd. 1972-79), Am. Diabetes Assn. (Jacksonville bd. dirs. 1985—, Washington bd. dirs. 1973-79, coun. on epidemiology sec. 1982-89). Home: PO Box 23398 Jacksonville FL 32241-3398

LEAR, DOROTHY BENNETT, biomedical services professional; b. Mpls., Jan. 15, 1935; d. Howard Waite and Beatrice Helen (Carmichael) Bennett; m. James Richard Lear, Feb. 18, 1965; children: Catherine Dorothy, Stuart James, Alan Duncan, Lynne Anne, Elizabeth Anne. BS, Syracuse U., 1956; postgrad., Vt. Tech. Coll., 1991-93. Copy editor Vt. Sunday News and St. Albans (Vt.) Messenger, 1971-76; freelance writer, editor St. Albans, 1976-88; owner, mgr. Comptext Co., St. Albans, 1980—; sr. processor IBM, Burlington, Vt., 1988-93; mem. staff ARC Biomed. Svcs., Burlington, Vt., 1994—; pres. League Vt. Writers, 1988-91. Editor-in-chief Scot mag., 1986-87; contbr. to Vt. Woman mag., 1987. Instr. Am. Heart Assn., Burlington, 1975-89; bd. dirs. ARC, Burlington, 1974-75, instr. 1975—; bd. dirs. Hardack Ski Area, St. Albans, 1975-86, Vt. Ambulance Dist. 3, Burlington, 1977-87; educator Vt. Emergency Med. Svcs., 1976-86; 1st lt. Milton (Vt.) Rescue Squad, 1976-88; sect. chief Nat. Ski Patrol, No. Vt., 1981-82. Mem. AAUW (bd. dirs. 1985—), St. Andrew's Soc. Vt. (bd. dirs. 1985—). Republican. Episcopalian. Home: 180 N Main St Saint Albans VT 05478-1552 Office: ARC Biomed Svcs Vt/NH Blood Svcs 32 N Prospect St Burlington VT 05401

LEAR, EVELYN, soprano; b. Bklyn., Jan. 8, 1930; m. Thomas Stewart; children: Jan, Bonni. Vocal student in, N.Y.C.; student, N.Y. U., Hunter Coll. Song recitals, Phillips Gallery, Washington; mem. Juilliard Sch. Music Workshop; recital, Town Hall, N.Y.C., 1955; lead in Marc Blitzstein's Reuben, Reuben; performed Strauss's Four Last Songs with London Symphony Orch., 1959; mem. Deutsche Opera, 1959, appeared in Lulu at Vienna Festival, 1962, The Marriage of Figaro at Salzburg Festival, 1962, debut, Vienna State Opera, 1964, Frankfurt Opera, 1965, Covent Garden, 1965, Kansas City (Mo.) Performing Arts Found., 1965, Chgo. Lyric Opera, 1966, La Scala Opera, 1971, also in Brussels, San Francisco, Los Angeles, Buenos Aires, debut at Met. Opera as Lavinia in Mourning Becomes Electra, 1967, mem. co., 1967—; roles include Tosca, Manon, Marshallin, Desdemona, Mimi, Dido, Donna Elvira, Marina, Tatiana: TV appearance in La Boheme, 1965; numerous solo appearances, 1960—; appeared in film Buffalo Bill, 1976; rec. artist Angel Records, Deutsche Grammophon. Recipient Concert Artists Guild award 1955, Liederabend, Salzburg Festival 1964, Grammy award for best operatic recording (Marie in Wozzeck) 1965; Fulbright scholar, 1957. Address: care Zemsky/Green Divsn Columbia Artists Mgmt Inc 165 W 57th St New York NY 10019*

LEAR, FRANCES LOEB, television executive; b. Hudson, N.Y., July 14, 1923; d. Herbert Adam and Aline (Friedman) Loeb; m. Norman Milton Lear, 1956 (div. 1985); children: Kate, Maggie. Grad. high sch., Northampton, Mass. Asst. buyer Bloomingdales, N.Y.C., 1945-51; buyer Lord & Taylor, N.Y.C., 1952-59; owner Woman's Pl., Inc., L.A., 1965-84; founder Lear's Mag., N.Y.C., 1988-94; editor-in-chief Lear's Magazine, 1992-94; pres. Lear Television, N.Y.C., 1994—. Author: (autobiography) The Second Seduction, 1992; appeared video Take Control of Your Money, 1995; contbr. articles to jours. Office: Lear Television 110 E 59th St New York NY 10022-8043*

LEARN, DORIS LYNN, school district purchasing director; b. Long Beach, Calif., May 11, 1949; d. Rowe Francis and Annie Mae (Tunstill) Christopher; m. Thomas Robert Learn, Oct. 17, 1987. Student Foothill Coll., 1966-67, DeAnza Coll., 1969-71, Rider Coll., 1988-90. Cashier Navy Exchange, China Lake, Calif., 1965-66, Navy Exchange, Moffett Field, Calif., 1966-67; exec. sec. Varian Assocs., Palo Alto, Calif., 1967-75; salesperson Jorgensen Steel, Langhorne, Pa., 1976; exec. sec. Pennsbury Sch. Dist., Fallsington, Pa., 1976-82, dir. purchasing, 1982—. Mem. Pa. Assn. Sch. Bus. Ofcls. (Pa. registered sch. bus. specialist 1986, mem. conf. com. 1986, 91, bd. dirs. 1994—), Assn. Sch. Bus. Ofcls., Pa. Sch. Bds. Assn., Nat. Assn. Female Execs., Govt. Fin. Officers Assn., Pennsbury Assn. Suprs. and Adminstrs., Nat. Purchasing Assn., Delaware Valley Assn. Sch. Bus. Officials (pres. 1992-93). Republican. Presbyterian. Avocations: needlecrafts, golf, spectator sports. Home: 1365 Brook Ln Jamison PA 18929-1403 Office: Pennsbury Sch Dist 134 Yardley Ave Box 338 Levittown PA 19058-0338

LEARY, CAROL ANN, academic administrator; b. Niagara Falls, N.Y., Mar. 29, 1947; d. Angelo Andrew and Mary Josephine (Pullano) Gigliotti; m. Noel Robert Leary, Dec. 30, 1972. BA, Boston U., 1969; MS, SUNY, Albany, 1970; PhD, Am. Univ., 1988. Asst. to v.p. for student affairs, dir. women's programs Siena Coll., Loudonville, N.Y., 1970-72; asst. dir. housing Boston U., 1972-78; dir. residence Simmons Coll., Boston, 1978-84, assoc. dean, 1984-85; assoc. dir. The Washington Campus, Washington, 1985-86; adminstrv. v.p., asst. to pres. Simmons Coll., Boston, 1988-94; pres. Bay Path Coll., Longmeadow, Mass., 1995—. Chair, coll. and univ. devel. com. St. Francis Homeless Shelter, Boston, 1990—. Fellow SUNY, Albany, 1969-70, Am. U., 1986-88; Ednl. Policy Fellowship Program fellow, 1990-91. Mem. Coun. for the Advancement and Support of Edn., Am. Assn. Higher Edn., Am. Coun. Edn. (rep. Mass. div. 1991—), Phi Beta Kappa. Office: Bay Path Coll Office of the President 588 Longmeadow St Longmeadow MA 01106

LEARY, NANCY JANE, marketing professional, educator; b. Natick, Mass., Mar. 25, 1952; d. Norman Leslie and Dorothy (Holmquist) Pidgeon; m. Patrick J. Leary, Sept. 17, 1977 (div. May 1984). AA, Mass Bay Coll., Wellesley, Mass., 1979; BS, Lesley Coll., Cambridge, Mass., 1988; MA in Edn., U. South Fla., 1992. Cert. tchr., Fla. Sec. GTE Corp., Needham, Mass., 1973-78; coord. edn. Cullinet Software Inc., Westwood, Mass., 1983-84, adminstrv. asst., 1984-85, mgr. adminstrn., 1985-86; specialist product mktg. Cullinet Co., Westwood, Mass., 1986-88; v.p. mktg. and adminstrn. Jonathan's Landscaping, Bradenton Beach, Fla., 1988-89; supr. tech. support staff A Plus Tax Product Group, Arthur Andersen, Inc., Sarasota, Fla., 1989-90; cons. Palmetto, Fla., 1990—; tchr. Manatee County, 1992—. Contbr. articles to profl. jours. Mem. Fla. Community Assn. Mgrs., NAFE, AAUW, Nat. Coun. for the Social Studies, Phi Kappa Phi. Office: 5011 Baystate Rd Palmetto FL 34221

LEARY, ROBIN JANELL, administrative secretary; b. Hudson, Wis., July 9, 1954; d. Edward James and Marlys Marie (Ensign) L. BA in History, U. Wis., Eau Claire, 1976. From stenographer I to program asst. 3 U. Wis., Eau Claire, 1977—; elected sec. 3rd Congl. Dist./Dem. Party of Wis., 1993—. Chmn. Eau Claire County Dem. Com., 1990-92, sec., 1986-90, mem. ex-officio county exec. bd., 1993—; mem. credentials com. Wis. Dem. Com., 1990-94, chmn. com., 1990-92; del. Nat. Dem. Conv., Atlanta, 1988, N.Y.C., 1992. Named Female Dem. Vol. of Yr., Eau Claire County Dem. Party, 1989. Mem. AFL-CIO (Eau Claire area labor coun., treas. 1986-94, trustee 1994—, sec. 3d congl. dist. com. on polit. edn. 1993—), AFSCME Pub. Employees Organized to Promote Legis. Equality (vice chmn. 3d congl. dist. 1992-93, chmn. 1993—, coun. 24 family and gender com. 1990—, tri-coun. state women's com.). Home: 2104 Providence Ct Eau Claire WI 54703-4103 Office: U Wis 105 Garfield Ave Eau Claire WI 54701-4800

LEASE, JANE ETTA, librarian; b. Kansas City, Kans., Apr. 10, 1924; d. Joy Alva and Emma (Jaggard) Omer; B.S. in Home Econs., U. Ariz., 1957; M.S. in Edn., Ind. U., 1962; M.S. in L.S., U. Denver, 1967; m. Richard J. Lease, Jan. 16, 1960; children—Janet (Mrs. Jacky B. Radifera), Joyce (Mrs. Robert J. Carson), Julia (Mrs. Earle D. Marvin), Cathy (Mrs. Edward F. Warren); stepchildren—Richard Jay II, William Harley. Newspaper reporter Ariz. Daily Star, Tucson, 1937-39; asst. home agt. Dept. Agr., 1957; homemaking tchr., Ft. Huachuca, Ariz., 1957-60; head tchr. Stonebelt Council Retarded Children, Bloomington, Ind., 1960-61; reference clk. Ariz. State U. Library, 1964-66; edn. and psychology librarian N.Mex. State U., 1967-71; Amway distbr., 1973—; cons. solid wastes, distressed land problems reference remedies, 1967; ecology lit. research and cons., 1966—. Ind. observer 1st World Conf. Human Environment, 1972; mem. Las Cruces Community Devel. Priorities Adv. Bd. Mem. ALA, Regional Environ. Edn. Research Info. Orgn., NAFE, P.E.O., D.A.R., Internat. Platform Assn., Las Cruces Antique Car Club, Las Cruces Story League, N.Mex. Library Assn. Methodist (lay leader). Address: 2145 Boise Dr Las Cruces NM 88001-5149

LEASE, JUDY ELLEN, communications educator; b. Amarillo, Tex., Nov. 20, 1941; d. Charles H. Sr. and Nola Imogene (Baker) Gifford; m. Ronald Charles Lease, Aug. 24, 1962; 1 child, Tracy Rene. BA, U. Northern Colo., Greeley, 1963; MA, Purdue U., 1971. English, speech. secondary sch. tchr. Wenatchee Pub. Schs., Wash., 1963-65, 66-69; grad. instr. Purdue U., West Lafayette, Ind., 1969-73; instr. comm. U. Utah, Salt Lake City, 1974-78; adj. instr. U. Chgo., Ill., 1978-79; adj. dir. oral comm. U. Utah, Salt Lake City, 1980-85; vis. lectr. U. Mich., Ann Arbor, 1985-86; dir., mgmt. comm. ctr. Tulane U., New Orleans, 1986-90; sr. assoc., cons. Spectra Comm. Assocs., New Orleans, 1990—; clin. assoc. prof. U. Utah, Salt Lake City, 1990—; cons. in field, 1981—. Contbd. articles to profl. jours. Mem. Speech Comm. Assn., Assn. Bus. Comm., Mgmt. Com. Assn. (founding mem.). Office: U Utah David Eccles Sch Bus Salt Lake City UT 84112

LEASE, LINDA ZALOKAR, psychologist; b. Cleve., July 24, 1945; d. John Edward and Florence A. (Legat) Zalokar; m. John Richard Lease, Apr. 30, 1971; children: Jessica, Elizabeth, Hilary, Alyson, Amanda, Richard. BA, U. Dayton, 1967; MA, U. Cin., 1969; PhD, U. Mich., 1976. Lic. psychologist, Pa.; cert. sch. psychologist. Rehab. counselor Mass. Rehab. Commn., Boston, 1969-71; staff psychologist Children's Svc. Ctr., Wilkes Barre, Pa., 1979-84; psychologist pvt. practice, Hazleton, Pa., 1984—; cons. Luth. Life Enrichment, Hazleton, 1984-93. Literary agt.: (book) Cecil, 1992. Bd. dirs. United Way of Greater Hazleton, 1990-93, Parents Assn. for Gifted Edn., Hazleton, 1988—, Child Advocacy Com., Hazleton, 1990-93. Mem. APA, Pa. Psychol. Assn. Roman Catholic. Office: 1710 E Broad St Hazleton PA 18201

LEASOR, JANE, religion and philosophy educator, musician; b. Portsmouth, Ohio, Aug. 10, 1922; d. Paul Raymond Leasor and Rana Kathryn (Bayer) Leasor-McDonald. BA, Wheaton Coll., 1944; MRE, N.Y. Theol. Sem., 1952; PhD, NYU, 1969. Asst. prof. Belhaven Coll., Jackson, Miss., 1952-54; dept. chmn. Beirut Coll. for Women, 1954-59; asst. to pres. Wheaton (Ill.) Coll., 1961-63; dean of women N.Y. Theol. Sem., N.Y.C., 1963-67; counselor CUNY, Bklyn., 1967-74; assoc. prof. Beirut U. Coll., 1978-80; tchr. internat. sch., Les Cayes, Haiti, 1984-85; pvt. tutor, 1985—; tchr. Fayette County (W.Va.) Schs., 1993—. Author religious text for use in Syria and Lebanon, 1960; editor books by V.R. Edman, 1961-63, Time and Life mags. Mem. Am. Assn. Counselors, Am. Guild Organists. Republican. Episcopalian. Home and Office: 4403 Malden Dr Charleston WV 25306-6445

LEASURE, JUDITH ANN, engineering company executive; b. Wilmington, Del., Sept. 19, 1947; d. Charles Granville and Margaret Magdelaine (Lindell) McVey; m. Charles Mitchell Leasure, Dec. 6, 1969. BA, U. Del., 1969; MA, Coll. Notre Dame of Md., 1987. Tchr. Lake Forest Sch. Dist., Felton, Del., 1969-70, Talbot County Pub. Schs., Easton, Md., 1970-75, Escola Graduada, Sao Paulo, Brazil, 1975-77; testing technician Princess Anne and Balt., 1979-81; programmer/analyst WMAR-TV, Balt., 1982-84; mgr. data processing EA Engring., Sci. & Tech., Hunt Valley, Md., 1984, mgr. corp. info. svcs., 1984-90, dir. facilities svcs., 1990—. Mem. NAFE, Exec. Women's Network, Internat. Facilities Mgrs. Assn. Avocations: reading, needlework, music, travel. Office: EA Engring Sci & Tech 11019 McCormick Rd Hunt Valley MD 21031

LEATHER, VICTORIA POTTS, college librarian; b. Chattanooga, June 12, 1947; d. James Elmer Potts and Ruby Lea (Bettis) Potts Wilmoth; m. Jack Edward Leather; children: Stephen, Sean. BA cum laude, U. Chattanooga, 1968; MSLS, U. Tenn., 1978. Libr. asst. East New Orleans Regional Libr., 1969-71; libr. Erlanger Nursing Sch., Chattanooga, 1971-75; chief libr. Erlanger Hosp., Chattanooga, 1975-77; dir. Eastgate Br. Libr., Chattanooga, 1977-81; dir. libr. svcs. Chattanooga State Tech. Community Coll., 1981—. Mem. Allied Arts, Hunter Mus., High Mus. Art. Mem. ALA, Southeastern Libr. Assn., Tenn. Libr. Assn. (chair legislation com.), Chattanooga Area Libr. Assn. (pres. 1978-79), Tenn. Bd. Regents Media Consortium (chair 1994-95), Phi Delta Kappa. Episcopalian.

LEATHERBERRY, ANNE KNOX CLARK, interior designer, architectural designer; b. Geneva, Ill., Jan. 19, 1953; d. Donald William and Margaret Lorraine (Johnson) Clark; m. David Boyd Leatherberry, Aug. 5, 1978; children: Elizabeth Anne, Laura Knox. BS in Bus., Miami U., Oxford, Ohio, 1975. With Carson, Pirie, Scott & Co., Chgo., 1975-77; health care sales specialist Gen. Foods Corp., Northlake, Ill., 1977-78; account mgr. Cin., 1978-79; pres., owner Annie's Originals/Kids Collectables, Ltd., Waukesha, Wis., 1979—; mktg. rep./demonstrator mktg. Waukesha, 1988-91; owner Dreamhouse Designs, Waukesha, 1990—, Creative Enterprises Inc., 1990—; cons. Lamb's Quarters, Hartford, Wis., 1982-83, Ungerwear, West Alexandria, Ohio, 1982-84, Little Bits, Waukeshaw, 1984-90, Evelyn's Creations, East Troy, Wis., 1986-90, The Queen's Empire, Inc., Pitts., 1989-90, DRC Co., Mukwonago, Wis., 1990—, Don Belman Builders, 1991-92, Millikin Homes, 1992—, Opportunity Homes, 1993—, Affordable Homes, 1993—, Gemini Homes, 1993, Nelson Remodeling, 1993. Active Waukesha Area Symphonic Band, 1979—, sec. bd. dirs. 1987-89, Carroll Coll. Community Orch., 1985-86; vol. tchrs. aide Clarendon Ave. Sch., Mukwonago, 1988-89; asst. leader Girl Scouts Am., 1988, leader, 1988-89; vol. staff aide Jim Thompson for Gov. campaign, 1975-76; dir. Children's Choir, 1986; summer music dir. Luth. Ch., 1986, 88; events chair Edgewood Golf League, 1988-92; vol. Rose Glen Reading Rams, Waukesha, 1990—, Health Rm., 1990-91, tchrs. aid, 1991—. Mem. NAFE, PEO (officer 1980-82), Direct Mktg. Assn., Soc. Craft Designers, Met. Builders Assn., Nat. Assn. of Remodeling

Industry, Kappa Kappa Gamma. Republican. Lutheran. Home and Office: W241 S 5910 Autumn Haze Ct Waukesha WI 53186

LEATHERMAN, CAROLYN HALL, librarian, educator; b. Richmond, Va., July 17, 1946; d. Jennings Andy and Ruby Dean (Stephenson) Hall; m. William Jacob Leatherman III, June 10, 1969. BA, Madison Coll., Harrisonburg, Va., 1969; MLN, Emory U., 1970; PhD, Va. Commonwealth U., 1992. Reference libr. Atlantic Co., N.J. Pub. Libr., 1970-71; libr. Carter G. Woodson Sch., Hopewell, Va., 1971—; adj. faculty Va. State U., 1974-75, Va. Commonwealth U., Richmond, 1987-88, 92—; libr. Bur. Econ. Rsch. and Devel., 1975-80. Mem. NEA, Hopewell Edn. Assn., Va. Edn. Assn., Va. Ednl. Media Assn., Intertel, Mensa, Phi Kelta Kappa. Methodist. Home: PO Box 213 Hopewell VA 23860-0213

LEATHERS, MARGARET WEIL, foundation administrator; b. Princeton, Ind., Dec. 22, 1949; d. Albert J. and Nora Jewel (Franklin) Weil; m. Charles L. Leathers, June 19, 1971 (div. Dec. 1987); children: Julianna L., Kevin Sean. AB, U. Ill., 1971; MS, Russell Sage Coll., 1979. Cert. tchr., N.Y., health edn. specialist. Employment counselor Snelling & Snelling, Schenectady, N.Y., 1972-76; substitute tchr. Monahasen High/Jr. High Sch., Schenectady, 1978-79; grant abstractor State of N.Y., Albany, 1979; program coordinator Am. Lung Assn. Santa Clara-San Benito Counties, San Jose, Calif., 1982-84, dir. programs, 1984-87, nat. clinic leader trainer, 1986—, acting exec. dir., 1987-88, exec. dir., 1988—. Author: Camp Superstuff Workbook and Teachers Manual, 1983; contbr. articles to profl. publs. and mags. Bd. dirs., officer Santa Clara Valley Coun. Parent-Participating Nursery Schs., 1980-81; resource vol. Lyceum Santa Clara Valley, 1983-87; leader Explorer post Boy Scouts Am., San Jose, 1988; mem. adminstrv. bd. coun. ministries United Meth. Ch.; mem. staff 1st asthma camp Young Tchrs. of Health, Soviet Union, 1989, Seattle, 1990; mem. citizen's oversight com. Local Transp. Commn. for Santa Clara County, 1993—; mem. steering com. for Measure A., 1992. Mem. APHA, Soc. Pub. Health Educators, Am. Sch. Health Assn., Assn. of United Way Agys. (exec. bd. 1993), ALA Calif. Coun. Execs. (v.p. 1994). Democrat. Home: 341 Springpark Cir San Jose CA 95136-2144 Office: Am Lung Assn 1469 Park Ave San Jose CA 95126-2530

LEATON, MARCELLA KAY, insurance representative, business owner; b. Eugene, Oreg., Oct. 9, 1952; d. Robert A. and Wanda Jo (Garner) Boehm; m. Michael G. Schlegel, Aug. 9, 1975; children: Kaellen June, Krystalynn Michele. Grad. high sch., Springfield, Oreg. Sales rep. The Prudential, Novato, Calif., 1973—; bus. owner Marcella Enterprises, Novato, 1983—; owner, operator Meetings Extraordinaire, 1987—; owner Mastermind Escapes, 1990—. Contbr. articles to profl. jours. Mem. Nat. Assn. Life Underwriters (nat. quality award 1978, 80, 84), Marin Life Underwriters, Nat. Assn. Profl. Saleswomen (founder Marin chpt., pres. 1982-85, 91-93, chmn. 1985-87, nat. v.p. 1985-86, awards and recognition chmn. 1985-88, nat. pres. 1987-90, exec. dir. 1988-91, regional v.p. 1991-92, N.W. region conf. chmn. 1993), Leading Life Producers No. Calif., Million Dollar Round Table (qualifying), Marin Rowing Assn. (travel chmn. 1992-93), President's Club, Western Star Club. Office: Marcella Enterprises 7595 Redwood Blvd Ste 200 Novato CA 94945-7700

LEATTO, RENNE, director, writer; b. Evergreen Park, Ill., Oct. 28, 1952; d. Anthony Gino and Patricia (Bays) L.; m. Matt Ross, June 14, 1974 (div. 1984); m. Lee Sommie, June 27, 1986. Student, L.A. City Coll., 1970-71, So. Oreg. State Coll., 1981-82. Freelance dir., writer, producer, 1982—; guest lectr. film classes So. Oreg. State Coll., Ashland, 1987. Dir. numerous documentaries, dramatic, animated and info. films which are distributed worldwide and translated into several langs., including Peer Intervention, 1990, The Causes and Effects of Drug Abuse, 1990, Make the Right Decision, 1990, Alcohol, Drugs and Kids, 1988, Anger: Handle with Care, 1982; scriptwriter for numerous films including Dolphins: Our Friends From the Sea, 1984, It Could Never Happen to Me, 1984, Why Wellness?, 1986, Sexual Harassment Awareness, 1992; writer feature film Kelly, 1991, workplace violence series, 1994, Aids and Kids: A Bridge to Compassion, 1994. Grantee Oreg. Arts Commn., 1989; Media award Nat. Safety Coun., Silver medal Internat. Film & TV Festival of N.Y., Houston Internat. Film and Video Festival. Mem. Women in Film Cen. Fla.

LEAVELL, LAURA DEBORAH, medical/surgical nurse, consultant; b. Savannah, Ga., Oct. 2, 1951; d. Arvelle Benson Leavell and Lola Elaine (Moore) Erhardt. BA, Columbia Coll., 1986; BSN, U. Mo., 1992. RN, Mo. Various positions U. Mo., Columbia, 1969-76; keypunch supr. EDS, Inc., Columbia, 1976-78; various positions Centerre Bank, Columbia, 1978-85; unit sec. Ellis Fischel State Cancer Ctr., Columbia, 1986-90; tax preparer H&R Block, Columbia, 1988-90; various positions Daybreak RTC, Inc., Columbia, 1990-93, cons., 1993—; RN VA Hosp., Columbia, 1993—; mem. self-care deficiency theory steering com. VA Hosp., 1993-94. Bd. dirs. Mid-Mo. AIDS Project, Columbia, 1994—. Health Profl. scholar VA, 1991-92. Mem. Am. Philatelic Soc. Home: 151 Sun Glow Ct Columbia MO 65201 Office: VA Hosp 600 Hospital Dr Columbia MO 65201

LEAVENS, PATRICIA ANN, director of chapter I; b. Webster, Mass., June 14, 1933; d. Charles Nelson and Mary Ann (Foley) L. BA, Coll. Our Lady of the Elms, 1957; MA, North Adams State Coll., 1981. Tchr. elem. St. Ann's Acad., Worcester, Mass., 1957-59, St. Joseph's Sch., North Brookfield, Mass., 1959-61; elem. tchr. Cathedral Elem. Sch., Springfield, Mass., 1961-63, St. Joseph's, North Adams, Mass., 1963-72; chpt. I dir. North Adams Pub. Schs., 1972—; vis. prof. Westfield (Mass.) State Coll., 1982-84, North Adams State Coll., 1988. Contbr. articles to profl. jours. Coordinator Cath. Christian Doctrine, North Adams, 19792-90; mem. Alzheimers Support Group, North Adams; troop leader Girl Scouts Am., North Adams; trustee Northern Berkshire Assn. for Retarded Citizens, North Adams. Mem. Cath. Daus. Am. (sec. Mass. chpt. 1990—, vice regent 1991—), Internat. Reading Assn. (state coord. Mass. chpt. 1981-83), Mass. Reading Assn. (pres. 1979-80), Berkshire Reading Coun. (pres. 1976-78), Delta Kappa Gamma (pres. Sigma chpt. 1989-92). Democrat. Office: North Adams Pub Schs 191 E Main St North Adams MA 01247-4496

LEAVER, JUDY KAY, mental health services professional; b. West Plains, Mo., Feb. 20, 1947; d. Otho A. and Margaret A. (Piper) Jones; m. S.C. Leaver, Dec. 21, 1968 (div. Mar. 1980); children: Chris, Kevin. BA in Social Work, U. Mo., 1969; MA in Counseling, U. Tulsa, 1981. Lic. profl. counselor, Okla; lic. social work assoc., Okla. Family life educator Family and Children's Svc., Tulsa, 1977-84, dir. skills for living, counselor, 1979-84; counselor Associated Psychologists, Tulsa, 1983-87; instr. Tulsa Jr. Coll., 1986-87, 92; therapist Brookhaven Hosp., 1986-87; exec. dir. Mental Health Assn. Tulsa, 1987-93; dir. community edn., dir. affiliate rels. Nat. Mental Health Assn., Alexandria, Va., 1993—. Contbg. writer monthly pubs. Single Spirit, 1982-85, Tulsa Kids, 1989—. Chairperson United Way Agy. Execs., Tulsa, 1991-92; mem. Mayor's City-County Com. on Homelessness, Tulsa, 1991-92, Legis. Task Force on Rights of Mentally Ill, Tulsa, 1990-92; chiarperson Okla. State Bd. Lic. Social Workers, Oklahoma City, 1986-91; bd. dirs. Leadership Tulsa, 1986-88, Tulsa Alliance for Mentally Ill, 1989-92; ruling elder John Knox Presbyn. Ch., Tulsa, 1988-91. Named Mental Health Provider of Yr., Tulsa Alliance for Mentally Ill, 1989. Mem. NASW, ACA, Nat. Alliance for Mentally Ill, Am. Soc. Mental Health Assn. Profls. Democrat. Home: 630 G St SE Apt 1 Washington DC 20003-2763

LEAVITT, MARY JANICE DEIMEL, special education educator, civic worker; b. Washington, Aug. 21, 1924; d. Henry L. and Ruth (Grady) Deimel; B.A., Am. U., Washington, 1946; postgrad. U. Md., 1963-65, U. Va., 1965-67, 72-73, 78-79, George Washington U., 1966-67; tchr.'s cert. spl. edn., 1968; m. Robert Walker Leavitt, Mar. 30, 1945; children: Michael Deimel, Robert Walker, Caroline Ann Leavitt Snyder. Tchr., Rothery Sch., Arlington, Va., 1947; dir. Sunnyside, Children's House, Washington, 1949; asst. dir. Coop. Sch. for Handicapped Children, Arlington, 1962, dir., Arlington, Springfield, Va., 1963-66; tchr. mentally retarded children Fairfax (Va.) County Pub. Schs., 1966-68; asst. dir. Burgundy Farm Country Day Sch., Alexandria, Va., 1968-69; tchr., substitute tchr. specific learning problem children Accotink Acad., Springfield, Va., 1970-80; substitute tchr. learning disabilities Children's Achievement Center, McLean, Va., 1973-82, Psychiat. Inst., Washington and Rockville, Md., 1976-82, Home-Bound and Substitute Program, Fairfax, Va., 1978-84; asst. info. specialist Ednl. Research Service, Inc., Rosslyn, Va., 1974-76; docent Sully Plantation, Fairfax County (Va.) Park Authority, 1981-87, 88—, Childrens Learning Ctrs., vol. Honor Roll, 1987, Walney-Collections Fairfax County (Va.) Park Authority, 1989—; sec. Widowed Persons Service, 1983-85, mem., 1985—. Mem. edn. subcom. Va. Commn. Children and Youth, 1973-74; Den mother Nat. Capital Area Cub Scouts, Boy Scouts Am., 1962; troop fund raising chmn. Nat. Capitol coun. Girl Scouts U.S.A., 1968-69; capt. amblyopia team No. Va. chpt. Delta Gamma Alumnae, 1969; vol. Prevention of Blindness, 1980—; fund raiser Martha Movement, 1977-78; mem. St. John's Mus. Art, Wilmington, N.C., 1989—, Corcoran Gallery Art, Washington, 1989-90, Brunswick County Literacy Coun., N.C., 1989—. Recipient award Nat. Assn. for Retarded Citizens, 1975, Sully Recognition gift, 1989, Ten Yr. recognition pin Honor Roll, 1990. Mem. AAUW (co-chmn. met. area mass media com. D.C. chpt. 1973-75, v.p. Alexandria br. 1974-76, fellowship co-chmn., historian Springfield-Annandale br. 1979-80, 89-94, 94—, name grantee ednl. found. 1980, cultural co-chmn. 1983-84), Assn. Part-Time Profls. (co-chmn. Va. local groups, job devel. and membership asst. 1981), Older Women's League, Nat. Mus. of Women in the Arts (charter mem.), Delta Gamma (treas. No. Va. alumnae chpt. 1973-75, pres. 1977-79, found. chmn. 1979-81, treas. Beta Epsilon chpt. 1994—, Katie Hale award 1989). Club: Mil. Dist. of Washington Officer's Clubs (Ft. McNair, Ft. Myer). Episcopalian. Home: 7129 Rolling Forest Ave Springfield VA 22152-3622

LEAVITT KOST, MEREDITH B., printing company executive; b. Hartford, Conn., Mar. 31, 1964; d. Robert R. and Betty B. (Shortleff) Leavitt; m. Samuel J. Kost, Sept. 25, 1993. AS in Graphic Arts Tech., Springfield (Mass.) Tech. C.C., 1984; AS in Printing Mgmt., Rochester Inst. Tech., 1986, BS in Printing Mgmt., 1987. Prodn. planner Case-Hoyt Corp., Rochester, N.Y., 1987-92; mfg. systems coord. Case-Hoyt Corp., Rochester, 1992—; customer svc. rep. Upstate Litho, Inc., Rochester, 1994—; EMT Henrietta (N.Y.) Vol. Ambulance, 1988—. Mem. Rochester Club of Printing House Craftsmen (co-chairperson Gallery of Superb Printing awards 1989-92). Office: Upstate Litho Inc 1500 Brighten Henrietta Townline Rd Rochester NY 14623

LEBEDOFF, RANDY MILLER, lawyer; b. Washington, Oct. 16, 1949; m. David Lebedoff; children: Caroline, Jonathan, Nicholas. BA, Smith Coll., 1971; JD magna cum laude, Ind. U., 1975. Assoc. Faegre & Benson, Mpls., 1975-82, ptnr., 1983-86; v.p., gen. counsel Star Tribune, Mpls., 1989—; asst. sec. Star Tribune Cowles Media Co., Mpls., 1990—. Bd. dirs. Minn. Opera, 1986-90, YWCA, 1984-90, Planned Parenthood Minn., 1985-90, Fund for Legal Aid Soc., 1988—, Abbott-Northwestern Hosp., 1990-94. Mem. Newspaper Assn. (legal affairs com. 1991—, mem. history com. U.S. Dist. Ct.), Order of Coif. Home: 1738 Oliver Ave S Minneapolis MN 55405 Office: Star Tribune 425 Portland Ave Minneapolis MN 55488

LEBENBOM, ELAINE FRIEDMAN, composer, poet, lecturer; b. Detroit, Mar. 12, 1933; d. Isidore Harold and Gertrude Shayne (Silverman) Friedman; m. David Lebenbom, May 30, 1957; children: Miriam, Sallie, Matthew, Michael. MusB in Composition, U. Mich., 1955, MusM in Composition, 1982. Tchr. pvt. schools Detroit, 1956-85; tchr. Women's Aux. Brandeis U., Detroit, 1965-66; dir. spl. music program Friend's Sch., Detroit, 1974; mem. faculty Detroit Community Mus. Sch., 1974-77; composer-in-residence Jefferson Elem. Sch., Royal Oak, Mich., 1977; lectr. Mich. Music Tchrs. Assn., East Lansing, 1975-76, Midrasha Coll. Jewish Studies, Southfield, Mich., 1985; speaker Sta. WDET-FM, Detroit, 1986; invited participant West Coast Writer's Conf., Kalamazoo, 1992. Contbr. poetry to Wayne Lit. Rev., 1993. Bd. dirs. Birmingham Bloomfield Cultural Commn., 1990—, Midrasha Coll. Jewish Studies, 1981-83. Recipient 1st prize Mich. Composers' Club, 1955, Nat. Fedn. Music Clubs; Mich. Coun. for Arts grantee, 1988. Mem. ASCAP, Internat. League Women Composers, Am. Music Ctr., Detroit Tuesday Musicale (judge manuscripts 1979—), Jewish Women in Arts (chairperson 1988). Democrat.

LEBLANC, JEANETTE AMY, psychotherapist, educator, writer; b. Blytheville, Ark., Mar. 31, 1968; d. Bob Gene and Joan Ann (Hall) Ash; m. Robert Louis LeBlanc, May 27, 1987. BS in Liberal Arts and Psychology, USNY, Albany, 1989; MS in Community Counseling, Ga. State U., 1991; PhD in Adminstrn. and Mgmt., Walden U., 1994. Libr. technician Civil Svc., Munich, 1988-89; crisis counselor U.S. Army Community Svc., Munich, 1988-89; adolescent counselor Bradley Ctr. Hosp., Inc., Columbus, Ga., 1990-91; group therapist children of alcoholics, 1991-92; social svcs. coord., therapist Anne Elizabeth Shepherd Home, Inc., Columbus, 1991-93; instr. Upper Iowa U., Ft. Polk, La., 1993—; group therapist for womens group Vernon Cmty. Action Coun., Leesville, La., 1994—. With U.S. Army, 1986-88. Mem. ACA, NAFE, Assn. for Counselor Edn. and Supr., Internat. Assn. Marriage and Family Counselors, Sierra Club, Toastmasters.

LEBLANC, LAUREEN ALISON, service company administrator; b. Santa Ana, Calif., Feb. 25, 1964; d. Thomas Albert and Kathleen Mary (Thompson) Cox; m. Mark J. LeBlanc, July 17, 1992; children: Katherine Morgan, (from a previous marriage) Robert Daniel, Alicia Michelle. Grad. high sch., Oakland Park, Fla., 1982. Horse trainer, mgr. various show horse stables, U.S. and Europe, 1975-84; office mgr. Land Title Ins. Co., Ft. Lauderdale, Fla., 1979-82; gen. mgr. Boca Travel Trailer Resort, Boca Raton, Fla., 1982-85; asst. mgr. credit Boca Raton Hotel and Country Club, 1985-90; credit and accounts receivable mgr. Callaway Gardens Resort, Pine Mountain, Ga., 1990-94; contr. Holiday Inn Denver Internat. Airport Hotel Trade & Conv. Ctr., 1994—. Mem. NAFE, Internat. Assn. Hospitality Accts., U.S. Dressage Assn., Nat. Assn. Credit Mgrs.

LEBLANC, PATRICIA JOHAN, librarian, educator, technology coordinator; b. Tacoma, Wash., Apr. 16, 1953; d. Alfred R. and Margaret J. (Douglas) LeB.; m. Nikolai Kristensen, Aug. 5, 1977; 1 child, Cassidy Alexander Kristensen. BA, U. Puget Sound, 1975; MEd, St. Martin's Coll., 1985. Cert. tchr.; cert. libr.; cert. adminstr. Elem. tchr. Enumclaw (Wash.) Sch. Dist. 216, elem. libr., tech./staff devel. coord.; presenter ednl. tech. topics. Contbr. articles to profl. jours. Mem. ASCD (staff devel. coun., project leader), N.W. Coun. Computers in Edn., Wash. Assn. Sch. Adminstrs., Phi Delta Kappa. Home: 702 N J St Tacoma WA 98403-2020

LEBLANC, TINA, dancer; b. Erie, Pa.; m. Marco Jerkunica, May 1988. Trained, Carlisle, Pa. Dancer Joffrey II Dancers, N.Y.C., 1982-83, The Joffrey Ballet, N.Y.C., 1984-92; prin. dancer San Francisco Ballet, 1992—. Work includes roles in (with San Francisco Ballet) Con Brio, Bizet Pas de Deux, Swan Lake, Nanna's Lied, Handel -- A Celebration, La fille mal gardée, Rubies, Tchaikovsky Pas de Deux, Seeing Stars, The Nutcracker, La Pavane Rouge, Company B; (with other companies) The Green Table, Les Presages, Le sacre du printemps, Les Noces, Light Rain, Romeo and Juliet, Runaway Train, Empyrean Dances, La Vivandière. Recipient Princess Grace award, 1988. Office: San Francisco Ballet 455 Franklin St San Francisco CA 94102

LEBOUTILLIER, JANET ELA, real estate investment asset manager, writer; b. Marshfield, Mass., May 10, 1936; d. Preston Carleton and Barbara (Higgins) Ela; m. John Walter McNeill, Oct. 10, 1959 (div. 1970); children: Duncan Davis, Sarah McNeill Treffry; m. Martin LeBoutillier, May 10, 1986. AA, Briarcliff Jr. Coll., 1956; BA in English Lit., U. Colo., 1958; postgrad. Real Estate/Mortgage Banking, NYU, 1973-78. Lic. N.Y. and Conn. real estate broker; cert. property mgr. Sales, leasing agt. L.B. Kaye Assocs., Ltd., N.Y.C., 1969-74; comml. leasing agt. Kenneth D. Laub & Co., N.Y.C., 1975; dir. leasing, asst. bldg. mgr. Douglas Elliman Gibbons & Ives Co., N.Y.C., 1975-76; adminstr. REIT adv. unit Chase Manhattan Bank, N.A., N.Y.C., 1976-78; asst. dir. real estate investments Mass. Mut. Life Ins. Co., Springfield, Mass., 1978-80; dir. real estate investments Yale U., New Haven, Conn., 1980-81; ind. cons. N.Y.C., 1981-83; sr. analyst, equity mgmt., sales and devel. Aetna Realty Investors, Inc., Hartford, Conn., 1983-84; dir. pub. involvement unit Aetna Realty Investors, Inc., 1984-86; sr. asset mgr. Cigna Investments, Inc., Hartford, 1986-87; v.p. Wm. M. Hotchkiss Co., New Haven, Conn., 1987-88; pres., prin. LeBoutillier & LeBoutillier, Inc., Lyme, Conn., 1989-93. Author: Meditations on Joy, 1995. Mem. Grace Episcopal Ch., mem. pastoral care and healing commn., coord. prayer team ministry. Mem. Internat. Coun. Shopping Ctrs., Nat. Coun. for Urban Econs. Devel., Inst. Real Estate Mgmt. (chpt. 51 pres., sec., treas., nat. asset mgmt. com.), Fin. Women's Assn., The Real Estate Exch., Urban Land Inst., Internat. Order of St. Luke the Physician (founder, convener Old Saybrook, Conn. area chpt. 1993). Democrat. Episcopalian. Home and Office: 8 Laurel Dr Old Lyme CT 06371-1462

LEBOW, LAUREL MARY LAVIN, real estate developer, real estate asset manager; b. Newport, R.I., Feb. 5, 1956; d. Charles Vincent and Barbara (Hofheins) Lavin; m. Jeffrey A. Lebow, May 29, 1988. BS, Emory U., 1977. Gen. mgr. Source Enterprises, New Orleans, 1980-81; exec. Johnstown Am. Co., Atlanta, 1981-86; dir. asset mgmt. Club Properties, Inc., Atlanta, 1986-90; v.p. Mgmt. Solutions, Inc., Atlanta, 1990-92, CPA Realty, Inc., Atlanta, 1992—. Mem. Inst. Real Estate Mgmt., MENSA, Jr. League of Atlanta. Republican. Episcopalian. Office: CPA Realty Inc 2951 Flowers Rd S Ste 220 Atlanta GA 30341-5533

LEBOWITZ, CATHARINE KOCH, state legislator; b. Winchester, Mass., June 30, 1915; d. William John and Carolyn Sophia (Kistinger) Koch; m. Murray Lebowitz, Sept. 21, 1971 (dec. Oct. 1978). Student Northeastern U., 1948-49, Boston Coll., 1949-52. Sec. ERA, Bangor, Augusta, Maine, 1935-38, WPA, Portland, Maine, 1938-42; personnel officer, exec. sec. USN, Portland, 1942-47; exec. sec. Clark Babbitt, Boston, 1947-48; adminstrv. asst. Moore Bus. Forms, Boston, 1948-52; apt. mgr., wholesale appliance div. Coffin-Wimple Inc., 1952-62, clerk U.S. Dist. Ct. Bangor (No. dist), 1962-79; sec. Portland Credit Bur., 1980-86; mem. Bangor City Council, 1985-87; mem. Maine State Legislature, 1982-92; bd. dirs. Eastern Transportation, 1989-94; mem. Bus. Adv. Coun., 1991—; active Program Rev. Subcom., 1991—; mem. adv. com. RSVP, 1987—, bd. dir., bus. adv. coun., and chmn. sub com. project with industry RSVP, 1992—; mem. adv. coun. Eastern Maine Tech. Coll., 1992—; bd. dirs. Rural Health Ctrs. Maine, Inc., 1992—; adv. bd. Maine Ctr. for the Arts, U. Maine, 1992—. Sec. Symphony Women, Bangor, 1964-84; bd. dirs. Opera House Com., Bangor, 1978-94; del. Rep. Nat. Conv., 1984, 88; mem. Spl. Task Force to Study Child Abuse, 1985-92; legis. com. United Way of Penobscot Valley, 1988-93, bd. mem., 1993—; adv. com. Maine Devel. Found., 1984-92; adv. bd. Aftercare, 1990, planning bd. St. Joseph Hosp., 1987-92, dir., v.p. St. Joseph Hosp. Aux., 1994—, Bangor City Hosp. Aux., 1988—; bd. dirs. Penobscot Theater, 1990; accredited Beauty Pageant judge, 1986—. Recipient Civilian Meritorious Service award USN, Portland Maine, 1946; named Hon. Alumnus Secretarial Sci., Husson Coll., 1980. Mem. Credit Women Internat. (treas. 1975-77, Credit Woman of Yr. 1969), Credit Profls., 1988-92, Bangor Community Theater (treas. 1973—, award 1973), U. Maine Maine Masque Theater (judge 1983-90), Maine N.G. Assn. (hon.), Maine Air N.G. (hon.), Nat. Assn. Retired Fed. Employers (v.p. bd. dirs. 1993—, sec. 1994), Credit Women Bangor (sec. 1965-67), Bangor Dist. Nursing Assn. (corp. mem. at large), Bangor C. of C. (mem. consumer rels. coun. 1981-90, coord. 150th anniversary prodn. Music Man 1984), Bangor Hist. Soc. (bd. dirs. 1993—, exec. bd. sec. 1994—), Penobscot County Extension Svc. (bd. dir. 1995), Penobscot County Republicans, Penobscot County Rep. Women's Club (sec. 1979), Bangor City Rep. Club (bd. dirs., treas. 1993—), Newcomb Soc., Ret. Fed. Employees (v.p. 1994), Zonta Club (pres. Bangor 1962-64, 80-82, v.p. 1994, Outstanding Leader 1991), Mgmt. Club.

LEBOWITZ, WENDY ANN, psychologist; b. Framingham, Mass., Feb. 9, 1952; d. Marshall and Charlotte Lily (Meyersohn) L.; m. Joel Theodore Nowak, Dec. 22, 1973; children: Dov Lebowitz-Nowak, Maxim M. Lebowitz-Nowak. AB, Clark U., 1974; MPH, Columbia U., 1981; MA, Adelphi U., 1983, PhD, 1988. Lic. psychologist, N.Y. Counselor, instr. N.Y. Inst. Tech., N.Y.C., 1978-82; psychology intern St. Luke's Med. Ctr., N.Y.C., 1984-85; v.p. Multimedia Amusements of Boston, Inc., Huntington, N.Y., 1985-87; psychologist Interfaith Med. Ctr., Bklyn., 1987—; ind. cons., Bklyn., 1992—. Contbr. chpt. to book: Sterilization Abuse, 1978; appeared on radio program Health in Inner Cities, 1991. Mem. choir Brooklyn Heights Synagogue, 1991—, leader AIDS support group, 1991-93, also officer. Mem. APA, N.Y. State Psychol. Assn. (mem. coun. 1993—), Bklyn. Psychol. Assn. (sec. 1992—). Jewish. Office: Interfaith Med Ctr 555 Prospect Pl Brooklyn NY 11238

LEBRECHT, THELMA JANE MOSSMAN, reporter; b. Indpls., Feb. 21, 1946; d. Elmore Somerville and Lois Thelma (Johnson) Mossman; m. Roger Dublon LeBrecht, May 4, 1968. BS in Journalism, U. Fla., 1968. Pub. affairs reporter WBT and WBTV, Charlotte, N.C., 1967-72; freelance reporter Toronto and N.Y.C., 1972-76; reporter KYW Newsradio, Phila., 1976-80; editor ABC Radio Network, N.Y.C., 1980-81; reporter AP Broadcast, Washington, 1981—. Mem. Radio and TV Corrs. Assn. in U.S. Capitol (chmn. 1991). Office: AP Broadcast 1825 K St NW Washington DC 20006-1202

LECHTMAN, PAMELA JOY, travel writer; b. St. Paul, Apr. 29, 1943; d. Ben L. and Leona Betty (Cell) Price; B.S., U. Minn., 1965; m. Allen Lee Lechtman, June 16, 1967; children—Arthur Thomas, Anthony Grant. Cert. travel counselor. Tchr. art St. Paul Ind. Sch. Dist., 1966-67; tchr. Alameda (Calif.) Unified Sch. Dist., 1967-68; with public rels. dept. Fitness, Inc., 1976-79; travel writer, 1979—; travel editor Shape mag., Woodland Hills, Calif., 1981-89; travel columnist News Chronicle, Thousand Oaks, Calif., 1980-83; instr. tourism Ventura (Calif.) Coll., 1978-80; producer radio program Update, Sta. KVEN-AM, Ventura, 1974-80; spa editor Total Health; contbg. West Coast editor Connections, 1981-84; author broadcasting guide You're On The Air, 1979; travel editor Ventura County Mag.; travel writer Jewish Jour., L.A.; contbr. Health and Fitness News Service Los Angeles Times Syndicate, Passions Internat. Mag.; travel editor Malibu Times, Calif., 1990—; guest lectr. UCLA Extension Travel Journalism; editor (newsletter) Calif. for Nonsmoker's Rights, Westside Br.; travel columnist Century City News, L.A. Hon. mem. bd. dirs. Ams. for Nonsmokers' Rights. Mem. AAUW (life, fellow Ventura County Br. 1976, grantee 1980), Internat. Assn. of Food, Wine and Travel Writers (bd. dirs., regional dir. So. Calif.). Home: 4261 Cresthaven Dr Thousand Oaks CA 91362-4279

LECKIE, CAROL MAVIS, retired state government administrator; b. Watertown, Wis., Feb. 25, 1929; d. Arthur Walter Bessel and Effie Vada (Squires) Downs; m. Ralph Junior Judd, Sept. 27, 1947 (div. Dec. 1952); children: Russell Howard, Barbara Rae; m. Leonard John Leckie, Sept. 30, 1977 (dec. May. 1990); stepchildren: Leonard John, Gordon Armstrong, Lorna Jean. Grad. high sch. Madison, Wis. Mgr. data processing Dept. Justice, State of Wis., Madison, 1971-79, mgr. Records Mgmt. Program, 1979-83, mgr. Typography Sect., 1983-90; ret. Mem. com. State of Wis. Employees Combined Campaign, Madison, 1986, 88-91, co-chair, 1987. Mem. Assn. Records Mgrs. and Adminstrs. (pres. 1983-84), Bus. Forms Mgmt. Assn. Lutheran. Avocations: travel, aerobics. Home: 810 Ziegler Rd Madison WI 53714-1342

LECLAIR, SUSAN JEAN, clinical laboratory scientist; b. New Bedford, Mass., Feb. 17, 1947; d. Joseph A. and Beatrice (Perry) L.; m. James T. Griffith; 1 child, Kimberly A. BS in med. tech., Stonehill Coll., 1968; postgrad., Northeastern U., Boston, 1972-74; MS in Med. Lab. Sci., U. Mass., Dartmouth, 1977. Cert. clin. lab. scientist; cert. med. technologist. Med. technologist Union Hosp., New Bedford, Mass., 1968-70; supr. hematology Morton Hosp., Taunton, Mass., 1970-72; edn. coord., program dir. Sch. Med. Tech. Miriam Hosp., Providence, 1972-79; hematology technologist R.I. Hosp., Providence, 1979-80; asst. prof. med. lab. sci. U. Mass., Dartmouth, 1980-84, assoc. prof. med. lab. sci., 1984-92, prof. med. lab. sci., 1992—; instr. hematology courses Brown U., Providence, 1978-80; cons. Bd. R.I. Schs. Med. Tech., R.I. Hosp. Div. Clin. Hematology, Cardinal Cushing Gen. Hosp., Charlton Meml. Hosp., St. Luke's Hosp., VA Med. Ctr., Providence, 1984—, Nemasket Group, Inc., 1984-87, Gateway Health Alliance, 1985-87; chair hematology/hemostasis com. Nat. Cert. Agy. for Med. Lab. Pers. Exam. Coun., 1994—. Contbr. articles to profl. jours.; contbr. articles to jours and chpts. to books; author computer software in hematology. Reviewer Nat. Commn. Clin. Lab. Scis., 1986-89; chairperson Mass. Assn. Health Planning Agys., 1986-87; bd. dirs. Southeastern Mass. Health Planning Devel. Inc., (1975-88, numerous other offices and coms.); planning subcom. AIDS Edn. (presentor Info Series). Mem. Am. Soc. Clin. Lab. Sci., Nat. Cert. Agy. for Med. Lab. Pers. (chair Hematology Com. of Exam Coun. 1994—), Am. Soc. Med. Tech. Edn. and Rsch. Fund, Inc. (chairperson 1983-85), Mass. Assn. for Med. Tech. (pres. 1977-78), Southeastern Mass. Soc. Med. Tech. (pres. 1975-76), Alpha Mu Tau (pres. 1993-94). Office: U Mass Dept Med Lab Sci Dartmouth MA 02747

LECOCKE, SUZANNE ELIZABETH, lawyer; b. Nuremburg, Germany, Nov. 3, 1958; came to U.S., 1959; d. Frank Joseph and Carolyn Elizabeth (Partain) L. BS magna cum laude, U. Tex., 1981; JD, U. Houston, 1987. Bar: Tex. 1987, U.S. Dist. Ct. (so. and no. dists.) Tex. 1987, U.S. Ct. Appeals (5th and fed. cirs.) 1992, U.S. Dist. Ct. (no. dist.) Calif. 1993. Supr. systems support Southwestern Bell Telephone, San Antonio, 1981-82; engr. Mitre Corp., Houston, 1982-84; law clk. to judges DeAnda, Bue and Hoyt U.S. Dist. Ct. (so. dist.) Tex., Houston, 1986-89; assoc. Liddell, Sapp, Zivley, Hill & Laboon, Houston, 1989-91, Arnold, White & Durkee, Houston, 1991—. Co-author: Patent Law Handbook, 1992-93, 93-94, 94-95. Mem. ABA, Am. Intellectual Property Law Assn., Tex. Bar Assn., Houston Intellectual Property Law Assn., Houston Young Lawyers Assn., Upsilon Pi Epsilon. Roman Catholic. Office: Arnold White & Durkee 750 Bering Dr Houston TX 77057-2104

LECOCQ, KAREN ELIZABETH, artist; b. Santa Rosa, Calif., Nov. 4, 1949; d. Maynard Rodney and Lois May (Lessard) LeC. BA, Calif. State U., Fresno, 1971, MA, 1975; postgrad., Calif. Inst. of the Arts, L.A., 1971-72. Founding mem. Feminist Art Program, Fresno, Calif., 1971, Calif. Inst. of the Arts, L.A., 1972; One woman shows include Calif. State U. Art Gallery, Fresno, 1970, 76, Merced (Calif.) Coll., 1969, 77, 91, Coll. Green, Merced, 1969, Calif. Inst. of the Arts, L.A., 1972, Recent Sculptures, Fresno, 1977, 78, Studio Opening, Fresno, 1979, Womanart Gallery, N.Y.C., 1980, Merced, 1987, Arts Coun. Gallery, Merced, 1989, Amos Eno Gallery, N.Y.C., 1994, others; commissions include Absolut Vodka, 1993; vis. artist Merced County Schs., 1977-78, 79-82, 88-91; grad. instr. Calif. State U., Fresno, 1976-78, Merced Coll., 1973-76. Group shows include Womanhouse, L.A., 1972, Off Centre Centre, Calgary, Alta., Can., 1985, 86, Ryosuke Gallery, Osaka, Japan, 1986, Carnegie Ctr. for the Arts, Turlock, Calif., 1988, 89, Gallery Six Oh One, San Francisco, 1989, Fresno Art Mus., 1989, Two Penny Gallery, Sacramento, 1990, Ann Saunders Gallery, Jamestown, Calif., 1991, Pro arts Gallery, Oakland, Calif., 1991, Calif. Mus. Art, Santa Rosa, 1991, Harbs Gallery, Lexington, Va., 1992, Russell Sage Gallery, Troy, N.Y., 1992, Amos Eno Gallery, 1992, 93, many others. Docent Gallery Guide Art Train, Merced, 1983; artistic dir. Black and White Ball, Merced Regional Arts Coun., 1989-94. Cora T. McCord scholar; CETA grantee, Merced, 1978, Fresno, 1977; Calif. Inst. Arts scholar, 1972. Mem. Internat. Sculpture Source, No. Calif. Women's Caucus for Art, Pro Arts of Oakland, San Francisco Mus. Art. Democrat. Home and Office: 2408 King Way Merced CA 95340

LECOMPTE, PEGGY LEWIS, secondary school educator, columnist, consultant, association executive; b. St. Louis, Oct. 7, 1939; d. Obadiah and Winnie Louise (Penquite) Lewis; m. Larry F. LeCompte Sr., Nov. 22, 1968; 1 child, Larry F. Jr. BS, Lincoln U., 1960; MS, Nat. Coll. Edn., 1991. Tchr. Dist. 189, E. St. Louis, 1962-67, tchr. and dept. head, 1969—; bd. dirs. and pres. YWCA St. Clair County, 1993—; nat. bd. dirs. YWCA; columnist (newspapers) Crusader, E. St. Louis, 1970-77, Monitor, 1977-88, E. St. Louis News Jour., Belleville, 1988—, Pure News, Springfield, Ill., 1991—; pres. Impact Assocs., Belleville, 1991—; cons. So. Ill. U. Edwardsville, 1993, 94, Koman Group, E. St. Louis, 1994—. Nat. bd. dirs. Top Ladies Distinction, 1987—; bd. dirs. GEMM Media Ctr., 1989—, pres., 1991; bd. dirs. and mem. rels. chmn. St. Mary's Hosp., 1990—; bd. dirs. Riverbluffs Girl Scouts, 1991—, sec., 1991; bd. dirs. Comprehensive Mental Health, 1992-94, past pres., 1993; campaign mgr. Com. to Elect Braun, Belleville, 1992-93; mem. Women's Leadership Team for Roland W. Burris, statewide, 1993-94. Named Woman of Achievement, YWCA/Belleville News-Democrat, 1985; recipient svc. medallion Boys Clubs Am., 1986, Leadership award Top Ladies Distinction, 1994, Kimmell Leadership award So. Ill. U. Edwardsville, 1991. Mem. Alpha Kappa Alpha (life, chair internat. membership 1994—). Home: 212 Bunker Hill Rd Belleville IL 62221-5764

LE COUNT, VIRGINIA G., communications company executive; b. Long Island City, N.Y., Nov. 22, 1917; d. Clifford R. and Luella (Meier) LeCount. BA, Barnard Coll., 1937; MA, Columbia U., 1940. Tchr. pub. schs. P.R., 1937-38; supr. HOLC, N.Y.C., 1938-40; translator Guildhall Publs., N.Y.C., 1940-41; office mgr. Sperry Gyroscope Co., Garden City, Lake Success, Bklyn. (all N.Y.), 1941-45; billing mgr. McCann Erickson, Inc., N.Y.C., 1945-56; v.p., bus. mgr., bd. dirs. Infoplan Internat, Inc., N.Y.C., 1956-69; v.p., bus. mgr. Communications Affiliates Ltd., Communications Affiliates (Bahamas) Ltd., N.Y.C., 1964-69; mgr. office services Interpublic Group of Cos., Inc., N.Y.C., 1971-72; bus. mgr. Jack Tinker & Ptnrs., Inc., N.Y.C., 1969-70; corp. records mgr. Interpublic Group of Cos., Inc., N.Y.C., 1972-83, mktg. intelligence data mgr., 1975-83. Mem. Alumnae Barnard Coll. Mem. Marble Collegiate Ch. Club: Atrium. Home: 136 E 55th St Apt 10Q New York NY 10022-4534

LECRON, MARY FRAZER See FOSTER, MARY FRAZER

LECUYER, ELLEN DELPHINE, publishing company executive; b. Montreal, Que., Can., May 10, 1956; d. Lucien and Doris (Daly) L.; m. Michael S.L. Levesque, Dec. 30, 1983. B in Commerce, Concordia U., Montreal, 1977. Research analyst Reader's Digest, Montreal, 1977-79, asst. mgr. mktg. research, 1979-81, mgr. mktg. research, 1981-87, asst. product mgr. spl. books div., 1987-88, mgr. list acquistion, new subscriber mailings mag. div., 1988—. Mem. Am. Mktg. Assn., Canadian Direct Mktg. Assn., Profl. Market Research Soc. Avocations: cross country skiing, curling. Home: 4554 Royal Ave, Montreal, PQ Canada H4A 2M8 Office: Reader's Digest Assn Can, 215 Redfern Ave, Westmount, PQ Canada H3Z 2V9

LEDBETTER, GAIL YVONNE, assistant principal; b. Petersburg, Va., Apr. 22, 1949; d. Leonard Spencer and Evelyn (Jones) L. BS, Va. State U., 1972, MEd, 1974. Tchr. Midlothian High Sch., Richmond, Va., 1973-85; dept. chair vocat. Matoaca High Sch., Petersburg, 1986-91, asst. prin., 1992—. Bd. dirs., sec. Petersburg Boys Choir, 1993. Named Tchr. of Yr., Chesterfield County Pub. Schs., Chester, Va., 1976-77, 2d runner-up Tchr. of Yr., State of Va., 1976-77. Mem. ASCD, Alpha Kappa Alpha, Phi Delta Kappa. Baptist. Home: 320 S West St Petersburg VA 23803-4054 Office: Matoaca High Sch 6001 Hickory Rd Ettrick VA 23803-1527

LEDBETTER, RANDI RAE, obstetrician/gynecologist; b. Portland, Oreg., June 24, 1952; d. James Edward Wagenblast and Shiela Faye (Mathis) Rhyne; m. Gordon Kirk Ledbetter, Feb. 14, 1971. BA in Biology, Linfield Coll., 1974; MD, Ohio State U., 1978. Diplomate Am. Bd. Ob-Gyn., Am. Bd. Family Practice. Intern, resident Family Practice Residency of Idaho, Boise, 1978-81; pvt. practice Boise Family Practice, 1981-88; resident in ob-gyn. Kaiser Found. Hosp., San Francisco, 1988-91; pvt. practice Women's Healthcare Assocs., Portland, Oreg., 1991—; chmn. laparoscopy com. ob-gyn. dept. St. Vincent's Hosp., Portland, 1993—. Mem. women's task force Women's Life, Boise, 1985-88. Fellow Am. Coll. Ob-Gyn.; mem. Oreg. Med. Assn., Washington County Med. Soc. (bd. dirs.), Porsche Club Am., Sports Car Club Am., Team Continental (dir. med.). Republican. Home: 12929 NW Laidlaw Rd Portland OR 97229 Office: Women's Healthcare Assocs 9155 SW Barnes Rd Ste 340 Portland OR 97225

LEDBETTER, SHARON FAYE WELCH, educational consultant; b. L.A., Jan. 14, 1941; d. James Herbert and Verdie V. (Mattox) Welch; m. Robert A. Ledbetter, Feb. 15, 1964; children: Kimberly Ann, Scott Allen. BA, U. Tex.-Austin, 1963; learning disabilities cert. Southwestern U., Tex., 1974; MEd, Southwest Tex. State U., 1979, prin. cert., 1980, supt. cert., 1984. Speech pathologist Midland Ind. Sch. Dist., Tex., 1963, Austin Ind. Sch. Dist., Tex., 1964-72; speech pathologist, asst. prin. Round Rock Ind. Sch. Dist., Tex., 1972-84; prin. Hutto Ind. Sch. Dist., 1984-88; asst. dir. div. mid. sch. edn. Tex. Edn. Agy., 1989-94; educational cons. 1994—. Pres. Berkman PTA, 1983-84; sponsor Jr. Woman's Club, 1980-82; mistress ceremonies Hutto Beauty Pageant, 1986, 87. Recipient Appreciation award Round Rock Sch. Dist., 1984, St. Judes Children's Research Hosp., 1985, Soc. Disting. Am. High Sch. Students, 1985, Disting. Svc. award Tex. Edn. Agy, 1994. Mem. Nat. Mid. Sch. Assn., Tex. Mid. Sch. Assn., Tex. Assn. Community Schs., Tex. Assn. Secondary Sch. Prins., Phi Delta Kappa, Delta Kappa Gamma. Avocations: horses, spectator sports. Home: 43 Woodland Loop Round Rock TX 78664-9776

LEDBURY, DIANA GRETCHEN, adult education educator; b. Denver, Mar. 7, 1931; d. Francis Kenneth and Gretchen (Harry) Van Ausdall; m. Chander Parkash Lall, Dec. 26, 1953 (div. Aug. 1973); children: Anne, Neil, Kris; m. Eugene Augustus Ledbury, Sept. 13, 1976; stepchildren: Mark, Cindy, Rob. BA in Sociology, Colo. U., 1953. Instr. Home, and family life Seattle Pub. Schs. Adult Edn., 1957-62, Seattle C.C., Seattle, 1962-69, Green River C.C., 1969-71; asst. tchr. Renton Sch. Dist., Wash., 1974-83; adult edn. tchr. Mental Health Network, Renton, 1984—; coord. Inter-Study, Renton, 1985—, program dir. Crossroads Child Care, 1985-86, family svcs. coord. , 1986-87, program supr. Candyland Too Child Care Ctr., 1987—, Candyland Also, 1987-90; coord. child care staff Washington Fitness Ctr., 1991-93. Mem. Renton Area Youth Svcs. Bd., Sch. and Community Drug Prevention Program, Renton dist. coun. PTA, Renton Citizen's Com. on Recreation; vol. Griffin Home for Boys; coord. Modern Dance Prodn., Carco Theater; adult leader Camp Fire Girls' Horizon Club; mem. bd. Allied Arts of Renton; mem. Bicentennial Com. for a Cultural Arts, Edn. and Recreation Ctr.; PTA rep. Dimmit Jr. High Sch.; mem. Sch. and Community Recreation Com.; founder Handicapped Helping Themselves, Mental Health Network; precinct committeeperson 11th dist. Republican party, Wash., 1976-85. Recipient Golden Acorn award Wash. State Congress PTA, Renton, 1972. Mem. AAUW (legis. chair 1983-87, mem. com. on strategic sch. policy safety in schs. 1993-94, com. on getting parents involved. 1994-95, pub. policy chair 1994-95), Assn. Social and Health Services (mem. com. 1984-85). Episcopalian. Club: Campfire Horizon (leader). Avocations: arts; culture; recreation; child and family advocate.

LEDDY, SUSAN, nursing school educator; b. N.J., Feb. 23, 1939; d. Bert B. and Helen (Neumann) Kun; children: Deborah, Erin. BS, Skidmore Coll., 1960; MS, Boston U., 1965; PhD, NYU, 1973; cert., Harvard U., 1985. Chair dept. nursing Mercy Coll., Debbs Ferry, N.Y.; dean sch. nursing U. Wyo., Laramie, dean coll. health scis.; dean Sch. Nursing Widener U., Chester, Pa., 1988-93; postdoctoral fellow U. Pa., 1994-95. Author: (with M. Pepper) Conceptual Bases of Professional Nursing, 1985, 3d edit., 1993. Bd. dirs. Springfield Hosp., 1992-94. Mem. NLN (bd. dirs. and 1st v.p. 1985-87).

LEDER, SANDRA JUANITA, elementary school educator; b. Stuttgart, Ark., Apr. 17, 1942; d. Everett Samuel and Lorene (Payer) L. BS, U. Cen. Ark., 1963; MEd, McNeese State U., 1976, EdS, 1979; PhD, Fla. State U., 1984. Cert. tchr. grades 1-8, supr., prin., aerospace edn., supr. student tchrs., La.; cert. pvt. pilot. Elem. tchr. DeWitt (Ark.) Pub. Schs., 1963-66, Gillett (Ark.) Pub. Schs., 1966-69; math. tchr. Tulsa County, Tulsa, Okla., 1970; tchr. Calcasieu Parish, Lake Charles, La., 1971-94, Episcopal Day Sch., Lake Charles, La., 1994—; condr., dir. numerous aerospace camps, 1980—; chmn., judge sci. fairs; com. mem. and chmn. self-study com. So. Assn. Colls. and Schs., 1985-86; arranger numerous tours and workshops in field. Manuscript rev. panel Sci. Scope, 1988-91, writer, 1992; TV interviews, 1991—; radio and ednl. TV appearances, Tchr. in Space applicant, 1985; contbr. Metric Curriculum Guide for La., 1978; presenter in field; contbr. articles to profl. jours. Vol. reader NEA, 1990; active outreach com. Episcopal Ch. of Good Shepherd, 1994; pres. Lake Charles Regional Airport Authority, 1991, 95, sec., 1993, v.p., 1994; mem. gen. adv. coun. Sowela Tech. Inst., 1990; active Mayor's Commn. for Women, 1986-91, fall conf. chmn. resource fair, 1988; founder Lake Charles Ninety-Nines Challenger Ctr. Recipient S.W. Region Frank Brewer Aerospace Edn. award CAP, 1990, Excellence in Aviation Edn. Championship award S.W. region FAA, 1989, Acad. Edn. award Women's History Month, Lake Charles, Great Expectations Tchr. award Sta. KPLC-TV, 1993, Pinnacle award, 1993, NEWMAST award NASA, 1986, STEP award, 1993, Outstanding Young Astronaut Chpt. Leader award 1993; grantee Space Acad., 1988, South Ctrl. Bell, 1991, 93, Olin Corp., 1994. Mem. NEA (vol. reader 1990), NSTA, Nat. Space Soc., La. Assn. Educators (del. to convs. 1977-79, 84, 86), Aircraft Owners and Pilots Assn., Delta Kappa Gamma (pres. 1992-94, legis. com. 1985-86, chair social com. 1987-89, comm. com. chair 1990—), Kappa Kappa Iota, Phi Delta Kappa. Republican. Episcopalian. Office: Episcopal Day Sch Ch of Good Shepherd 715 Kirkman St Lake Charles LA 70601

LEDERBERG, VICTORIA, state judge, former state legislator, lawyer, psychology educator; b. Providence, July 7, 1937; d. Frank and Victoria (Marzilli) Santopietro; m. Seymour Lederberg, 1959; children: Tobias, Sarah. AB, Pembroke Coll., 1959; AM, Brown U., 1961, PhD, 1966; JD, Suffolk U., 1976. Mem. R.I. Ho. of Reps., 1975-82, chmn. subcom. on edn., fin. com., 1975-82, subcom. on mental health, retardation and hosps. and health, spl. legis. commns pub. sch. funding and funding handicapped edn. programs; chmn. nat. adv. panel on financing elem. and sec. edn., Washington, 1979-82; mem. R.I. State Senate, 1985-91, chmn. fin. com. subcom. on social svcs., 1985-89, dep. majority leader, 1989-91; prof. psychology R.I. Coll., 1978-93; pvt. practice, Providence; mcpl. ct. judge, Providence, 1991-93; justice R.I. Supreme Court, Providence, 1993—. USPHS Fellow physiol. psychology, 1964-66. Trustee Brown U., 1983-89, Roger Williams U., 1980—, vice chmn. corp., dir. Sch. Law, Butler Hosp., 1985-93, also sec. of corp. Mem. New Eng. Psychol. Assn., ABA, R.I. Bar Assn., Sigma Xi. Office: 250 Benefit St Providence RI 02903-2719

LEDERER, MRS. ESTHER P. See LANDERS, ANN

LEDERER, MARION IRVINE, cultural administrator; b. Brampton, Ont., Can., Feb. 10, 1920; d. Oliver Bateman and Eva Jane (MacMurdo) L.; m. Francis Lederer, July 10, 1941. Student, U. Toronto, 1938, UCLA, 1942-45. Owner Canoga Mission Gallery, Canoga Park, Calif., 1967—; cultural heritage monument Canoga Mission Gallery, 1974—; Vice pres. Screen Smart Set women's aux. Motion Picture and TV Fund, 1973—; founder sister city program Canoga Park-Taxco, Mexico, 1963; Mem. mayor's cultural task force San Fernando Valley, 1973—; mem. Los Angeles Cultural Affairs Commn., 1980-85. Mem. Los Angeles Cultural Affairs Commn., 1980-85. Recipient numerous pub. service awards from mayor, city council, C. of C. Mem. Canoga Park C. of C. (cultural chmn. 1973-75, dir. 1973-75). Presbyn. Home: PO Box 32 Canoga Park CA 91305-0032 Office: Canoga Mission Gallery 23130 Sherman Way Canoga Park CA 91307-1402

LEDERMAN, ARLINE J., art gallery director, educator; b. N.Y.C., May 29, 1937; d. Irving I. and Evelyn Helen (Freedman) L.; m. Edward A. Friedman, Jan. 13, 1963; children: Millard Timur, Philip Kerim. BA, NYU, 1958, MA, 1969, PhD, 1989; degree in fine arts, Cooper Union Inst., 1968. Prin. Lederman-Horch, Fine Art Works, A.J. Lederman Fine Arts, N.Y.C., 1981-93; instr. Kabul (Afghanistan) U., 1970-73; chairperson visual arts Middlesex County Coll., Edison, N.J., 1976-78; dir. art edn. Montclair (N.J.) State Coll., 1978-87; dir. Fine Art Works, Hoboken, N.J., 1994—; pres., CEO A.J. Lederman Fine Art, Hoboken, N.J., 1990—; adj. asst. prof. F.I.T., NY.C., 1990—; vis. dir. El Museo del Barrio, N.Y.C., 1980-81; cons. Royal Govt. Afghanistan, Kabul, 1970-72, 75-77, Montclair (N.J.) Sch. Sys., 1980-81. Author: (with others) Art Education: An International Perspective, 1984, (catalog) Paterson Museum/Carol Arber, 1994. Bd. dirs. Printmaking Workshop, 1969—, Afghanistan Relief Com., N.Y.C., 1978—. Recipient Alumni award for Excellence, Cooper Union Inst., 1968, Gov.'s award State of N.J., 1987, Tchr. of Yr. Art Educators of N.J., 1987; Fulbright fellow, 1977-78. Mem. Internat. Soc. Art Dealers (founder, pres. 1990—), Univ. Coun. Art Edn. (bd. dirs. 1978—, past pres.), Hudson County C. of C., Hajji Baba Club (bd. dirs. 1973—, pres.). Jewish. Home: 901 Hudson St Hoboken NJ 07030 Office: AJ Lederman Fine Art 309 Court St Hoboken NJ 07030

LEDERMAN, STEPHANIE BRODY, artist; b. N.Y.C.; d. Maxwell and Ann (Rockett) Brody. Student, U. Mich.; BS in Design, Finch Coll.; MA in Painting, L.I. U., 1975. One-person exhbns. Franklin Furnace, N.Y.C., 1979, Kathryn Markel Fine Arts, N.Y.C., 1979, 81, 83, Katzen/Brown Gallery, N.Y.C., 1988, 89, Real Artways, Hartford, Conn., 1984, Alfred U., 1990, Hal Katzen Gallery, N.Y.C., 1992, Hillwood Art Mus., Brookville, N.Y., 1992, Casements Mus., Ormond Beach, Fla., 1994, Broward Cmty. Coll., Ft. Lauderdale, Fla., 1994, Hebrew Home for the Aged, N.Y.C., 1994-95, Galerie Caroline Corre, Paris, 1995; exhibited in numerous group shows including Newark Mus., 1983, Met. Mus. Art, N.Y.C., 1986, Queens Mus., 1989, Basel Art Fair, 1989, Caroline Corre, Paris, 1991, R.I. Mus. Art, 1991, Am. Acad. Arts & Letters, N.Y.C., 1992, Guild Hall Mus., East Hampton, N.Y., 1993, Ind. Mus. Art, Terre Haute, 1993, Jewish Mus., N.Y.C., 1993; represented in permanent collections Newark Mus., Mus. Modern Art, Prudential Ins., Bertelsmann Music Group, Guild Hall Mus., East Hampton, L.I., Chase Manhattan Bank, N.Y. Health and Hosp. Corp., Victoria & Albert Mus., London, Doubleday Books. Recipient Hassam and Speicher purchase award Am. Acad. and Inst. Arts and Letters, 1988; grantee Creative Artists Pub. Svc., 1977, Ariana Found. for Arts, 1985, Artists Space, 1987, E.D. Found., 1991, Lancaster Group, U.S.A. Comm. award, 1991, Spl. Opportunity stipend N.Y. State Coun. Arts, 1992, 94, Heuss Ho. project Lower Manhattan Cultural Coun., 1992. Studio: 85 N 3d St 5th Fl Brooklyn NY 11211

LEDFORD, HANNA MAY, state official; b. Athens, Ga., Sept. 11, 1946. AB in Journalism, U. Ga., 1964. Reporter Marietta (Ga.) Daily Jour., 1968-69; info. specialist Ga. Dept. Industry Trade and Tourism, Atlanta, 1969-76, asst. dir. tourist divsn., 1976-83, dir. tourist divsn., 1983—, dep. commr., 1986—; pres. Welcome South Ctr., Atlanta, 1993—; bd. dirs. Cecil B. Day Sch. Hospitality Adminstrn. Recipient Unity Appreciation award Travel Industry Ga. Assn., 1989, Disting. Achievement in Journalism John E. Drewry award Henry W. Grady Coll. Journalism U. Ga., 1994; named Resolution Outstanding Leader, Ga. Ho. of Reps., 1987, Top Ten Atlanta Businesswomen, Atlanta Bus. Chronicle, 1990. Mem. Ga. Hospitality and Travel Assn. (bd. dirs., Travel Industry Leader of Yr. 1985), Southeast Tourism Soc. (bd. dirs., Travel Dir. of Yr. 1986, Pres. award 1993), Travel South USA (bd. dirs., chmn. 1991-93). Office: State of Ga Industry Trade & Tourism Dept PO Box 1776 Atlanta GA 30301

LEDFORD, MARIE SMALLEY, real estate appraiser, consultant; b. Willimantic, Conn., June 1, 1951; d. Harold Eugene and Elizabeth Louise (Loehr) Smalley; m. Timothy Eugene Ledford, Jan. 23, 1988. AA, Young Harris (Ga.) Coll., 1971; BS, W. Ga. Coll., 1973; MEd, U. Ga., 1978. Math. tchr. secondary schs., Atlanta and, V.I., 1973-82; assoc. appraiser Childers Assoc., Atlanta, 1985-87, Am. Realty Concepts, Atlanta, 1987-88; owner, appraiser, cons. Ledford & Assoc., Atlanta, 1988—. Office: 2064 Peachtree Industrial Ct Atlanta GA 30341-2240

LEDLEY, TAMARA SHAPIRO, earth system scientist, climatologist; b. Washington, May 18, 1954; d. Murray Daniel and Ina Harriet (Gordon) Shapiro; m. Fred David Ledley, June 6, 1976; children: Miriam Esther, Johanna Sharon. BS, U. Md., 1976; PhD, MIT, 1983. Rsch. assoc. Rice U., Houston, 1983-85, asst. rsch. scientist, 1985-90, sr. faculty fellow, 1990—; mem. Alaska SAR facility archive working team NASA, Pasadena, Calif., 1988; McMurdo SAR facility sci. working team, 1990; participant workshop of Arctic leads initiative Office Naval Rsch., Seattle, 1988, 1st DeLange Conf. on Human Impact on Environ., Houston, 1991; cons. Houston Mus. Natural Sci., 1989-90, Broader Perspectives, Houston, 1989; dir. weather project for tchr. tng. program George Obs., Rice U., 1990-92; co-dir. Rice Houston Mus. Natural Sci. Summer Solar Inst., 1993. Contbr. articles to profl. publs. Spl. judge Houston Area Sci. and Engring. Fair, 1985; judge S.W. Tex. Region High Sch. Debates, 1986, Houston Area Sci. and Engring. Fair, 1990, 91; guest expert Great Decisions '88 Polit. Discussion Group, 1988. Fellow sci. computing Nat. Ctr. for Atmospheric Rsch., Boulder, Colo., 1978, Fed. Jr. fellow, 1972-74; senatorial scholar State of Md., 1972-76; grantee NSF, 1985-87, 87-88, 89-92, 90-93, 92-94, 94—, Tex. Higher Edn. Coordinating Bd., 1988-90, 90-92, Univ. Space Rsch. Assn., NASA, 1990—, 1991-93, 94—. Mem. AAAS, Am. Geophys. Union (com. global environ. change 1993—, assoc. editor Jour. Geophys. Rsch.-Atmospheres 1993-96), Am. Meteorol. Soc., Oceanography Soc., Sigma Xi, Phi Beta Kappa, Phi Kappa Phi, Alpha Lambda Delta. Office: Rice U Dept Space Physics & Astronomy 6100 Main St Houston TX 77005-1827

LEDONNE, DEBORAH JANE, secondary education educator; b. Darby, Pa., Mar. 4, 1956; d. Peter Anthony and Camella Jean (Perrone) LeD. Undergrad. credits in Spanish, U. Madrid, 1977; BA in Modern Langs., BS in Edn., Villanova U., 1978; Sorbonne U. Paris, U. Paris, 1979; MA in Modern Langs., Villanova U., 1982. Tchr. French/Spanish Marple Newtown Sch. Dist., Newtown Square, Pa., 1978—; tutor Phila. area, 1978—; sec. Faculty Adv. Coun., 1990—. Mem. Phila. Mus. Art, Annenberg Ctr. of Phila. Recipient Maria Rosa award for Excellence Am. Inst. Italian Culture, 1978; chosen to attend Nat. Debutante Ball, N.Y.C., 1974, Internat. Debutante Ball, Vienna, 1975; named a Woman of Yr. Am. Biog. Inst., 1993, one of 2,000 Notable Am. Women, 1994. Mem. NEA, Pa. State Edn. Assn., Alliance Francaise, Pa. State Modern Lang. Assn., Bally's Holiday Fitness Club, Kappa Delta Pi. Roman Catholic. Office: Marple Newtown Sch Dist 120 120 Media Line Rd Newtown Square PA 19073-4696

LEE, ALDORA G., social psychologist; b. Schenectady, N.Y.; d. Alois W. and M. Dorothy (Swigert) Graf. AB, Ind. U.; MA, Stanford U.; PhD, U. Colo. Dir. women studies Wash. State U., Pullman, 1976-78, dir. unit on aging, 1976-81; cons. in market research Syva, Palo Alto, Calif., 1982; staff market rsch. analyst Allstate Rsch. and Planning Ctr., Menlo Park, Calif., 1983—; rep. Wash. Assn. Gerontol. Edn., N.W. region rep. Nat. Women's Studies Assn., 1978-81. Contbr. articles to profl. jours. Mem. Menlo Park Libr. Commn., 1984-92, chmn., 1985-87; instr. Career Action Ctr., Palo Alto, 1984-87; Menlo Park rep. system adv. bd. Peninsula Libr. System, 1992—. Recipient Allstate Good Hands award for Cmty. Svc., 1994. Mem. Am. Mktg. Assn., Am. Psychol. Soc., Am. Sociol. Assn., Western Psychol. Assn., SRI Organon, Toastmasters (Toastmaster of Yr. 1989, Able Toastmaster, Competent Toastmaster), Phi Beta Kappa, Sigma Xi.

LEE, ALEXANDRA SAIMOVICI, civil engineer; b. Negrest, Vaslui, Romania, Nov. 6, 1932; came to U.S., 1969; d. Leonidas and Etlea (Schreibman) Saimovici; m. Jack Lee, July 14, 1972. Grad. in constrn. engring., Constrn. Inst., Bucharest, Romania, 1956. Registered profl. engr., S.C. Structural engr. Energo Constructia, Bucharest, 1956-61, Elcora Constrn. Metalicas, Buenos Aires, 1961-69, Walter Kidde, N.Y.C., 1969-70, John Kassner, N.Y.C., 1970-72; civil engr. I, City of Columbia, S.C., 1972-77, design engr., 1977-82, civil engr. II, 1982—. Mem. NSPE, Am. Pub. Works Assn. Home: 3733 Greenbriar Dr Columbia SC 29206-3323 Office: City of Columbia PO Box 147 Columbia SC 29202-0147

LEE, ANN MCKEIGHAN, secondary school educator; b. Harlan, Iowa, Nov. 18, 1939; d. Earl Edward and Dorothy Elizabeth (Kaufman) McK.; m. Duane Edward Compton, Aug. 13, 1960 (div. 1985); children: Kathleen, David, Anne-Marie, John. Cert. in med. tech., Creighton U., 1960; BA in Art History, Ind. U., 1984; MA, U. South Fla., 1992, postgrad. Cert. secondary tchr., Fla.; cert. med. technologist. Realtor Savage/Landrian Realty, Indpls., 1978-84; lectr. Marian Coll., Indpls., 1987-88; tchr. Sarasota (Fla.) County Schs., 1989-92, rep. faculty coun., 1991-92; lectr. curriculum & instrn. U. South Fla., 1993—; docent Historic Spanish Point, Osprey, Fla., 1989-93, Ringling Mus. Art, 1993—; presenter panel Bibliographic Intstruction in Art History. Contbr. articles to profl. jours. V.p. fin. LWV, Indpls., 1971-73; v.p. dist. IV aux. ADA, 1976-78, comptroller, 1978-89; coord. Gold Coun. and Ambs. U. South Fla., 1990-92. Recipient Silver Svc. award Crossroads Guild, 1981. Mem. AAUW, Coll. Art Assn., Soc. Archtl. Historians, Gulf Coast Heritage Assn. (co-chmn. pub. rels.), Sarasota Arts Coun. (tchr. rep. 1990), Phi Kappa Phi, Phi Delta Kappa. Roman Catholic. Home and Office: 3617 Shady Brook Ln Sarasota FL 34243-4840

LEE, ANNE NATALIE, nurse; b. Bklyn.; d. Taras Pavlovich and Maria (Jukovskaya) Dubovick; B.A., Hunter Coll., 1940; M.A., N.Y.U., 1948; R.N., McLean Hosp. Sch. Nursing, Waverly, Mass., 1946; M.S., Boston U., 1958; m. Henry Lee, Feb. 20, 1945; adopted children: Alice, Jennifer, Philip. Pvt. duty nurse, N.Y.C., 1946-48; staff nurse Vis. Nurse Service, 1947-48; staff nurse health dept. Schoharie Co., N.Y., 1948-51; supervising nurse N.Y. Dept. Health, Syracuse, 1951-53, cons. hosp. nursing, Albany, 1958-63, cons. nurse in epidemiology, 1963-65, cons. nurse in svc. edn., 1965-72, cons. nursing svcs. and adminstrn., 1972-75, dir. Office Hosp. Nursing Svcs. N.Y. State Dept. Health, 1975-80; dir., coord. nursing service instr. program cosponsored N.Y. State Dept. Health, N.Y. State Hosp. Assn., N.Y. State League Nursing, N.Y. State Nurses Assn., 1954-57; sometimes lectr. Mem. Am. Nurses Assn. (cert. advanced nursing adminstrn.), Sigma Theta Tau. Contbr. articles to profl. jours. Home and Office: 1149 Hillsboro Mile Pompano Beach FL 33062-1724

LEE, BARBARA A., federal magistrate judge. AB, Boston U., 1959; LLB, Harvard Law Sch., 1962. Bar: Conn. 1962, N.Y. 1966. Atty. Poletti Freidin Prashker Feldman & Gartner, 1968-74, ptnr., 1974-82; pvt. practice N.Y.C., 1983-87; U.S. magistrate judge U.S. Dist. Ct. (so. dist.), N.Y., 1988—; adj. prof. law Seton Hall U., So. Orange, N.J., 1984-87. Mem. com. on ecumenical and inter-religious affairs of Roman Cath. Archdoicese of N.Y., 1983—.

Mem. Fed. Magistrate Judges Assn., Assn. Bar City of N.Y. (mem. adminstrv. law com. 1973-74, mem. fed. cts. com. 1981-84, mem. com. on state cts. of superior jurisdiction 1984-87, mem. libr. com. 1989-92), Nat. Assn. Women Judges, N.Y. Assn. Women Judges, N.Y. County Lawyers Assn. Office: US Courthouse 40 Foley Sq New York NY 10007-1581

LEE, BARBARA CATHERINE, career counselor; b. Augusta, Ga., Apr. 30, 1931; d. Walter Charles and Dorothy Fulgum (Sasser) L.; married, Dec. 23, 1951 (div. Feb. 1959); 1 child, William Lee Hooton. BS in Vocat. Hom Econs., Winthrop Coll., 1952; MEd, U. Ga., 1960, MS in Family and Child Devel., 1968; EdS in Counselor Edn., Ga. Southern U., 1991. Cert. NBCC. Vocat. hom econs. tchr. Evans (Ga.) High Sch., 1955-56; vocat. home econs. tchr. Murphey Jr. High Sch., Augusta, Ga., 1956-63; vocat. consumer home econs. tchr. Butler High Sch., Augusta, 1963-75, Josey High Sch., Augusta, 1975-81; vocat. child devel. tchr. Hephzibah High Sch., Augusta, 1981-85; elem. and middle sch. counselor Ridge Spring-Monetta Elem. and Middle schs., 1986-87; part-time grad. rsch. asst. Ga. Southern U., Statesboro, 1990; career counselor St. John's High Sch., Charleston, S.C., 1991—; part-time tchr. Augusta Coll., 1972-73; part-time child devel. tchr. Augusta Tech. Sch., 1985-86; part-time edl. dir. adolescent program Human Hosp., 1988-89. Recipient Ga. Six-Yr. Study scholarhips Richmond County Bd. Edn., 1958; recipient Augusta Woman's Club scholarship, 1990. Mem. AAUW (scholarship chmn. Ga. chpt. 1983), AACD, Am. Sch. Counselor Assn. Am. Vocat. Assn., Nat. Career Devel. Assn., S.C. Assn. Counseling Devel., S.C. Career Devel. Assn., Kappa Delta Pi, Phi Upsilon Omicron, Phi Kappa Phi. Office: St Johns High Sch 1518 Main Rd Johns Island SC 29455-3436

LEE, BETTE GALLOWAY, accountant; b. Charlotte, N.C., Oct. 5, 1927; d. William Lawson and Bertha (Christenbury) Galloway; m. Joe Lee, June 11, 1949 (div. Sept. 1968); children: Carolyn Jean, William Patterson, Perry Galloway. AA, Carolina Bus. Coll., Charlotte, 1948; student, Cen. Piedmont Community Coll., Charlotte, 1974—. Clk. accounts receivable Associated Transport, Charlotte, 1948-49; bookkeeper J.E. Elrod Lumber Co., Charlotte, 1949-54; acct. F.W. Faires Co., Charlotte, 1954-56, Boise-Cascade Bldg. Materials, Charlotte, 1971-74, D.W. Flowe & Son Grading Co., Charlotte, 1974-83; office mgr. and acct. BBC Tax Svcs., Charlotte, 1963-71; prin. B.G. Lee Bookkeeping Svc., Charlotte, 1983—; cons. various small bus.'s, 1985—; leader seminars fin. analyses, 1985—. Asst. leader local troop U.S. Girl Scouts, 1963-70; active on Rep. Presdl. Task Force, Washington, 1989. Mem. Am. Soc. Women Accts., Women Bus. Owners, Charlotte C. of C. (BG Network), Beta Sigma Phi (Iota chpt.). Presbyterian. Home and Office: 2600 Commonwealth Ave Charlotte NC 28205-5305

LEE, BETTY REDDING, architect; b. Shreveport, La., Dec. 6, 1919; d. Joseph Alsop and Mary (Byrd) Redding; m. Frank Cayce Lee, Nov. 22, 1940 (dec. Aug. 1978); children: Cayce Redding, Clifton Monroe, Mary Byrd (Mrs. Kent Ray). Student La. State U., 1936-37, 37-38, U. Calif. War Extension Coll., San Diego, 1942-43; student Centenary Coll., 1937; attended Roofing Industry Ednl. Inst., 1980-82, 84, 86-88, 89-90, 93, Better Understanding Roofing Systems Inst., 1989. Sheetmetal worker Consol.-Vultee, San Diego, 1942; engring. draftsman, 1943-45; jr. to sr. archtl. draftsman Bodman & Murrell, Baton Rouge, 1945-55; sr. archtl. draftsman to architect Post & Harelson, Baton Rouge, 1955-58; assoc. arch. G. Ross Murrell, Jr., Baton Rouge, 1960-66; staff arch. Charles E. Schwing & Assos., Baton Rouge, 1966-71, Kenneth C. Landry, Baton Rouge, 1971, 73-74; design draftsman Rayner & McKenzie, Baton Rouge, 1972-73; cons. arch. and planner Office Engring. and Cons. Svcs., La. Dept. Health and Human Resources, Baton Rouge, 1974-82; arch. La. Dept. Facility Planning and Control, 1982—. Author Instructions to Designers for Roofing Systems for Louisiana Public Buildings; co-author: Building Owners Guide for Protecting and Maintaining Built-Up Roofing Systems, 1981; designed typical La. country store for La. Arts and Sci. Ctr. Mus. Recipient Honor award Schuller BURSI Group, 1989, 90, 91, 92, 93. Mem. La. Assn. Children with Learning Disabilities, 1967-69, Multiple Sclerosis Soc., 1963—, CPA Aux., 1960-69, PTA, 1953-66; troop leader Brownies and Girl Scouts U.S.A., 1959-60; asst. den mother Cub Scouts, 1955-57. Licensed architect. Mem. ASTM, Nat. AIA, AIA La., AIA Baton Rouge (first woman mem.), DAR, Constrn. Specifications Inst. (charter mem. Baton Rouge chpt.) So. Bldg. Code Congress Internat., Miss. Roofing Contractors Assn. (first woman hon.), Nat. Roofing Contractors Assn., La. Inst. Bldg. Scis. (founding mem. 1980), Roof Cons. Inst. (govt. liaison mem.), Jr. League Baton Rouge., Le Salon du Livre Club, Kappa Delta. Democrat. Episcopalian. Home: 1994 Longwood Dr Baton Rouge LA 70808-1247 Office: Capitol Sta PO Box 94095 Baton Rouge LA 70804-9095

LEE, CARLA ANN BOUSKA, nursing educator; b. Ellsworth, Kans., Nov. 26, 1943; d. Frank J. and Christine Rose (Vopat) Bouska; m. Gordon Larry Lee, July 8, 1967. RN, Marymount Coll., Salina, Kans., 1964; BSN, U. Kans., 1967; MA, Wichita State U., 1972, EdS, 1975, M in Nursing, 1984; PhD, Kans. State U., 1988. RN; cert. family and adult nurse practitioner, advanced nurse adminstr., med.-surg. nurse, health edn. specialist. Staff, charge nurse Ellsworth (Kans.) County Vet. Meml. Hosp., 1964-65; critical, coronary, and surg. nurse Med. Ctr. U. Kans., Kansas City, 1966-67; asst. dir., chief instr. sch. nursing Wesley Sch. Nursing, Wichita, Kans., 1967-74; asst. prof. Wichita State U., 1974-92; asst. prof., dir. nurse practitioner program Ft. Hays State U., Hays, Kans., 1992—; lectr. Wichita State U., 1972-74; cons. Hays Med. Ctr./Family Healthcare Ctr., 1993—, Baker U., Northeastern U., Boston; mem. adv. coun. Kans. Newman Coll.; adv. bd. Kans. Originals, Kans. Dept. Econ. Devel. Project, Wilson; mem. grad. faculty U. Kans., 1993—, Wichita State U., 1993—; rschr. in field. Author: (with Barrett) Fluids & Electrolytes: A Basic Approach, 3d edit., 1984 (poetry) Seasons: Marks of Life, 1991 (Golden Poet award 1991), (booklet) Czechoslavakian History, 1988; author, editor History of Kansas Nursing, 1987; contbr. articles to profl. jours. Co-founder Kans. Nurses Found., pres., trustee; vol. ARC, 1967-90, bd. dirs., 1977-90; mem. researcher Gov.'s Commn. Health Care, Topeka, 1990; city coord. campaign Sec. State, 1986; vol., lectr. Am. Heart Assn., Am. Cancer Soc., 1967—; election judge Sedgwick County, Kans., 1989—. Nurse Practitioner Tng. grantee U.S. Health and Human Svcs.; named Outstanding Community Leader, Jaycees, Alumnus of Yr., Kansas U., Marymount Coll.; recipient Tchr. award Mortar Bd. Fellow Am. Acad. Nursing; mem. ANA (credentialing ctr.), Kans. State Nurses Assn. (bd. dirs., treas.), Kans. Alliance of Advanced Nurse Practitioner's (founder, pres.), Great Plains Nurse Practitioner's Soc. (founder, pres.), Alpha Eta (Wichita State U. chpt. pres.). Republican. Roman Catholic. Home: 1367 N Westlink St Wichita KS 67212-4238 Office: Ft Hays State U 600 Park St Hays KS 67601-4059

LEE, CAROL FRANCES, lawyer; b. Montreal, Que., Can., Sept. 17, 1955; came to U.S., 1966; d. Frank B. and Mary Lee; m. David John Seipp, Sept. 10, 1994. BA, Yale U., 1976, JD, 1981; BA, Oxford (Eng.) U., 1978. Bar: D.C. 1982, U.S. Ct. Appeals (D.C. cir.) 1982, U.S. Dist. Ct. D.C. 1984, U.S. Supreme Ct. 1986. Law clk. to judge U.S. Ct. Appeals (D.C. cir.), Washington, 1981-82; law clk. to justice U.S. Supreme Ct., Washington, 1982-83; assoc. Wilmer, Cutler & Pickering, Washington, 1983-88, ptnr., 1989-93; gen. counsel Export-Import Bank U.S., Washington, 1993—; lectr. law Harvard U., Cambridge, Mass., 1989-90, 92, Yale U., New Haven, Conn., 1991. Contbr. articles to profl. jours. Marshall scholar U.K., Oxford, 1976. Fellow Am. Bar Found.; mem. ABA, Am. Soc. Internat. Law, Am. Soc. Legal History, Phi Beta Kappa. Office: Export-Import Bank US 811 Vermont Ave NW Washington DC 20571-0002

LEE, CAROLINE DURED, art appaiser, consultant, curator; b. Ft. Worth, Nov. 27, 1934; d. Willis Frank and Virginia C. (McIntyre) L.; m. Tom T. Adams, Aug. 25, 1956 (div. 1971); children: Holly, Erin; m. Robert M. Ellis, Dec. 22, 1990. Student, Stephens Coll., 1952-53, U. Ariz., 1953-55, Tex. Christian U., 1955, U. Tex., Austin and San Antonio, 1955, 78-79, San Antonio Art Inst., 1968-70, Trinity U., San Antonio, 1970-71, U. Mex., San Antonio, 1979, No. C.C., Taos, N.Mex., 1992, Lindenwood Coll., 1992. Dir. Southwest Craft Ctr. Gallery, San Antonio, 1971-75; owner, dir. Objects Gallery, San Antonio, 1980-84, Exvoto Gallery, San Antonio and Houston, 1985-86; owner, dir. Caroline Lee Gallery, San Antonio, 1984-87, Houston, 1986-88; owner, dir. Caroline Lee Gallery and Consulting Office, Taos, N.Mex., 1990-92, Caroline Lee Fine Art Appraising, Taos, 1991—; hon. instr. art segment Integration of Abilities Trinity U., San Antonio, 1970-71; juror, curator numerous Tex. art exhbns., 1973—; pvt. cons. various collectors, architects, designers, 1988-95; cons., art curator Taos Inn, 1992—; lectr., panel participant various mus. and orgns. One-woman show: San Antonio Art Inst., 1969; group shows: The Hand and the Spirit Gallery, Scottsdale, Ariz., 1979, Hadler-Rodriguez Gallery, Houston, 1979, Houston Designer/Craftsmen Exhbn., 1979 (award of excellence), Tex. Women Artists, 1980 (2d prize mixed media); invitational exhbns.: Of Paper and Porcelain, The Hand and Spirit Gallery, Scottsdale, 1980, 80 Texans, Galveston Arts Ctr., 1980; permanent collections: Archives of Am. Art, Smithsonian Inst., Washington, Mountain Bell Telephone Co., U. Tex. Health Sci. Ctr., pvt. individuals; author essays for catalogue and newsletter. Bd. mem. Santa Rosa Children's Hosp. Vol. Orgn., San Antonio, McNay Mus. Art, San Antonio, San Antonio Art League, Witte Mus. Art, San Antonio, Tex. Sculpture Symposiums, San Antonio; mem. Com. for Benefit for N.Mex. AIDS Svcs., Santa Fe, Com. for Friends of Santa Fe Opera-Apprentice Program, Com. for Vis. Nurse Svcs. Benefit, Santa Fe; mem. adv. bd. Rio Grande Planned Parenthood of Taos; chairwoman Fundraiser Benefits for the Harwood Mus., Taos. Named Accredited Sr. Appraiser, Am. Soc. Appraisers, 1993. Democrat. Home and Office: PO Box 1449 Taos NM 87571

LEE, CHARLYN YVONNE, chemical engineer; b. Washington, May 1, 1960; d. James Charles and Beverly Mae (Williams) L. BSChemE, MIT, 1982; MSChemE, Ga. Inst. Tech., 1984. Engring. intern Naval Surface Weapons Ctr., Silver Spring, Md., 1977-78; engring. aid VA, Washington, 1978-81; engr. Dupont Savannah River Lab, Aiken, S.C., 1982-83, Dupont Exptl. Sta., Wilmington, Del., 1984-86; mfg. engr. Dupont Spruance Plant, Richmond, Va., 1986-89; rsch. engr. Dupont Jackson Lab., Deepwater, N.J., 1989-91; process engr. Dupont Pontchartrain Works, LaPlace, La., 1991-93. Bd. mem. Richmond Area Program for Minorities in Engring., 1987-89; corp. advisor Nat. Action Coun. for Minorities in Engring., Wilmington, 1991; mem. D.C. Youth Adv. Bd. for Mental Health, Washington. Proctor and Gamble grantee, 1981; Gem fellow Nat. Consortium for Grad. Degrees for Minorities in Engring., Inc., 1982. Mem. AIChE, NAFE. Home: 4812 Illinois Ave NW Washington DC 20011

LEE, CORINNE ADAMS, retired educator; b. Cuba, N.Y., Mar. 18, 1910; d. Duston Emery and Florence Eugenia (Butts) Adams; m. Glenn Max Lee, Oct. 30, 1936 (dec. Feb. 1964). BA, Alfred U., 1931. Cert. tchr., N.Y. Tchr. English Lodi (N.Y.) High Sch., 1931-36, Ovid (N.Y.) Cen. Sch., 1936-67. Author: (light verse) A Little Leeway, 1983, (anecedotes, light verse, quips) A Little More Leeway, 1984, (essays, short stories, poems) Still More Leeway, 1986. Mem. life PTA. Mem. Nat. Ret. Tchrs. Assn., N.Y. State Ret. Tchrs. Assn., Schuyler County Ret. Tchrs. Assn., Elmira and Area Ret. Tchrs. Assn., LWV. Avocations: reading, travel, writing.

LEE, DIANE WEBSTER, nurse practitioner; b. Brownfield, Tex., July 17, 1952; d. Loren Clay and Virginia Maxine (Stephens) Webster; m. W.R. Lee, June 12, 1976; children: Ronald, Kaytlin. Diploma in nursing, Northwest Tex. Hosp. Sch., 1973; cert. pediatric nurse practitioner, U. Tex. Med. Br., Galveston, 1974. RN, Tex.; cert. neurosi. nurse. Staff nurse, team leader Northwest Tex. Hosp., Amarillo, 1973; nurse practitioner with pvt. practice physician Amarillo, 1974-77, 86—; supr., clin. dir. St. Anthony's Hosp., Amarillo, 1977-86; coord. radiol. assistance team Mason & Hanger-Silas Mason Pantex Plant, Amarillo, 1981-86. Loaned exec. United Way, Amarillo, 1987; troop health and safety officer Amarillo area Boy Scouts Am., 1992-93, troop com. chmn., 1993. Mem. AACN, Nat. Assn. Pediatric Nurse Assocs. and Practitioners (cert.), Am. Assn. Neurosci. Nurses, Am. Acad. Nurse Practitioners, Tex. Nurse Practitioners, Nat. Assn. Physician Nurses. Office: Neurol Surgery 1901 Medi-Park Ste 2026 Amarillo TX 79106

LEE, DONNA JEAN, retired hospice and respite nurse; b. Huntington Park, Nov. 12, 1931; d. Louis Frederick and Lena Adelaide (Hinson) Munyon; m. Frank Bernard Lee, July 16, 1949; children: Frank, Robert, John. AA in Nursing, Fullerton (Calif.) Jr. Coll., 1966; extension student, U. Calif., Irvine, 1966-74; student, U. N.Mex., 1982. RN, Calif. Staff nurse Orange (Calif.) County Med. Ctr., 1966-71, staff and charge nurse relief ICU, CCU, Burn Unit, ER, Communicable Disease, Neo-Natal Care Unit, 1969-71, charge nurse communicable disease unit, 1969-70; staff and charge nurse ICU, emergency rm., CCU, med./surg. units Anaheim (Calif.) Meml. Hosp., 1971-74; charge and staff nurse, relief Staff Builders, Orange, 1974-82; agy. nurse Nursing Svcs. Internat., 1978-89; asst. DON Chapman Convalescent SNF, Orange, 1982; geriatric and pedicatrics nurse VNASS, 1985-93; hospice/respite nurse VIA Upjohn Home Healthcare Svcs and VNA Support Svcs. of Orange, 1985-93; ret.; staff relieve nurse ICU/CCU various hosps. and labs, including plasmapheresis nurse Med. Lab. of Orange, 1978. Life mem. Republican, pres. task force, 1982—; past mem. Republican adv. com., Rep. Presdl. Trust; mem. Rep. Presdl. Legion of Merit. Mem. AACN, RNCC, RNSC, ADA, Inst. Noetic Scis., The Heritage Found., Aria, Intravenous Therapy Assn. U.S.A. (cert.), Am. Cancer Soc., Am. Lung Assn., Am. Heart Assn., Nat. Multiple Sclerosis Soc., Easter Seal Soc., Internat. Platform Assn. Baptist. Home: 924 S Hampstead St Anaheim CA 92802-1740

LEE, DORA FUGH, artist; b. Beijing, China, Aug. 16, 1930; arrived in U.S., 1957; d. Philip and Sarah F.; m. Richard Wen-han Lee; children: April, Sarah, Handel, Helen. Student, Chow Yang Law Sch., Peking, China, 1947; studied Chinese traditional painting, western watercolor, sculpture. Art tchr. Chinese Sch., Tokyo, 1950-53; illustrator CIE Visual sect. U.S. Army, Tokyo, 1953-56; tchr. Chinese calligraphy George Washington U., 1982; tchr. Chinese traditional painting Smithsonian Instn., 1983. One-person exhbns. in Chinese Cultural Ctr., Washington, 1958, Swan Gallery, Plainfield, N.J., 1963, China Inst., N.Y.C., 1964, Stoneman Gallery, Washington, 1966, 70, 72, 74, Franz Bader Gallery, Washington, 1976, 80, 82, 83, 84, 85, 87, 88, 92, 94, Johns Hopkins, Balt., 1985, Pacific Art Club, Hong Kong, 1989; permanent collections include Smithsonian Inst., Washington, NIH, Nat. Cathedral, Washington, Nat. Portrait Gallery, Washington, Nat. Mus. Women in Arts, Washington, Nat. League Am. PEN Women, numerous others. Mem. Nat. League Am. PEN Women, Am. Watercolor Soc., Washington Watercolor Assn. Home: 6305 Orchid Dr Bethesda MD 20817

LEE, EDNA PRITCHARD, education educator; b. Windsor, N.C., Oct. 6, 1923; d. Peter Bernard and Edna (Smith) Pritchard; m. Mack Lloyd Lee Sr., May 17, 1945 (dec. Nov. 1970); 1 child, Mack Lloyd Jr.; m. Lee Cross, June 1, 1991. BS, State U. N.C., Elizabeth City; MA, NYU, N.Y.C. Cert. N.Y. Adminstr.-Supr. Tchr. elem. schs. Windsor, N.C., 1944-61; tchr. elem. schs. Mohegan Lake, N.Y., 1961-68, asst. prin. elem. sch., 1968-82; dir. basic edn. Peekskill (N.Y.) High Sch., 1969-80; adj. prof. Mercy Coll., Peekskill, 1985—; vice chmn. bd. dirs. Peekskill Area Health Ctr.; bd. dirs. Family Resource Ctr., Montrose Child Care Ctr. Co-author: Syllabus for 4th Grade Social Studies, 1972. Named Woman of Yr., NAACP, Peekskill, 1976, Woman Engr. of Yr., Bus. and Profl. Women, Peekskill, 1980; recipient Louis Gregory award Bahai Religion, Peekskill, 1988. Mem. AAUW (v.p. 1970-72), Blacks in Govt., Delta Kappa Gamma, Alpha Kappa Alpha, Tee-Ettes (sec. 1982-88). Home: 101 Dutch St Montrose NY 10548-1517

LEE, ELIZABETH BOBBITT, architect; b. Lumberton, N.C., July 9, 1928; d. William Osborne and Catharine Wilder (Bobbitt) Lee. Student Salem Coll., 1945-47; B.Arch. with honors, N.C. State Coll., 1952. Registered architect, N.C., 1955, S.C., 1964. Assoc. William Coleman, Architect, Kinston, N.C., 1952-55; Skidmore, Owens & Merrill, N.Y.C., 1955-56; prin. Elizabeth B. Lee, FAIA, Architect, Lumberton, N.C., 1956-73, 82—; sr. ptnr. Lee & Thompson, Architects, Lumberton, 1973-82. Bd. dirs. Robeson Little Theatre, Lumberton, 1977-80, N.C. Dance Theatre, Winston-Salem, N.C., 1980-85, Robeson County Community Concerts, Lumberton, 1980-87; trustee N.C. State U., Raleigh, 1983-92; mem. bd. endowment N.C. State U., 1993—. Recipient cert. recognition Randolph E. Dumont Design Program, 1970, Disting. Alumna award, Salem Coll., 1989. Fellow AIA (nat. dir. 1983-85; officeholder N.C. chpt., 1959, v.p., 1978, pres. 1979, bd. dirs. 1980, pres. eastern sect. N.C. chpt., 1975, bd. dirs. S. Atlantic Regional Council, 1977-79); mem. Jr. League (pres. Lumberton chpt., 1968), Robeson County Heart Assn. (pres. 1970), N.C. Design Found., N.C. Archtl. Found. (pres. 1982-83), Lumberton Jr. Service League (pres. 1968), N.C. State Alumni Assn. (bd. dirs. 1982-85, chmn. Robeson county chpt.), Phi Kappa Phi. Democrat. Presbyterian. Home: 906 N Chestnut St Lumberton NC 28358-4801 Office: 407 Elm St PO Box 1067 Lumberton NC 28359

LEE, EMMA MCCAIN, social worker; b. McCormick, S.C., July 8, 1948; d. John Walker and Emma Eliza (Nealous) McCain; m. Lannis Bernard Lee, Dec. 27, 1986; children: Nefertiti McCain, Jasmine Lee; stepchildren: LaTonia, LaStacia, Lannis Bernard Jr., Laterra. BS in Sociology, Paine Coll., 1970; MA in Sociology, Am. U., 1975; postgrad., U. S.C., 1991—. Caseworker II Phila. County Bd. Assts., 1972-75; social worker II, human svcs. sr. provider Ga. Dept. Human Resources, Augusta, 1976—. Mem. AACD, Nat. Orgn. Forensic Social Work, So. Sociol. Soc., Alpha Kappa Mu. Democrat. Office: Ga Dept Human Resources Ga Regional Hosp 3405 Old Savannah Rd Augusta GA 30906-3815

LEE, ESTHER MARIE WHITE, elementary education educator; b. Little Rock, Dec. 16, 1941; d. Elbert and Velma (Wyatt) White; div.; 1 child, Erika Valise Lee. BA, Philander Smith Coll., 1964; MA, Gov.'s State U., 1975. Tchr. Little Rock Pub. Sch., 1964-66, Chgo. Pub. Sch., 1968—. Mem. Local Sch. Coun., 1989—, treas., 1989. Recipient Scope Educator award, 1990; named Outstanding Educator of Mexican Cmty., Com. of South Chgo., 1991. Mem. Alpha Kappa Alpha Sorority Inc. Democrat. Roman Catholic. Home: 17686 Hillcrest Dr Country Club Hills IL 60478

LEE, EUN KYUNG, telecommunications professional; b. Seoul, Nov. 1, 1959; came to the U.S., 1992; d. Chan-Bok and Jin Sil (Park) L. B in Info. Sci., Yonsei U., Seoul, 1982. Dir. Dacom Corp., Seoul, 1982-91; exec. dir. Dacom Am., Fort Lee, N.J., 1992—. Recipient award Ministry of Comm., Seoul, 1986. Office: Dacom America Inc 1 Executive Dr Fort Lee NJ 07024

LEE, EVELYN MARIE, secondary education educator; b. Germantown, Ohio, Dec. 17, 1931; d. Robert Orlandus and Edna Cathern (Durr) Stump; m. John Henry Lee, Dec. 16, 1956; children: Mark Douglas, David Matthew, Lori Ann Lee Delehoy. BS in Edn., Otterbein Coll., 1954; MA in Edn., U. Alaska, 1979. Dept. store tng. supr., asst. mdse. mgr. The Home Store, Dayton, Ohio, 1954-55; tchr. Parma (Ohio) Pub. Schs., 1955-56; math aide civil svc. Nat. Adv. Com. for Aeros. Ames Lab., Moffett Field, Calif., 1956-57; substitute tchr. Warren (Ohio) Pub. Schs., 1957-59, tchr., 1969-60; tchr. Gwinn (Mich.) Pub. Schs., 1960-64; tchr. Anchorage Sch. Dist., 1964-65, 68-87, substitute tchr., 1987—; cons. Lakeshore Curriculum Materials Co., 1990—. Life mem. Alaska PTA; vol. Ushering in the Arts; performer Anchorage Community Theatre and Opera Co. Mem. NEA (life, ret.), NEA-Alaska (life, ret., bd. dirs.), Alaska Hist. Soc. (life), Anchorage Concert Assn. (coun. of dirs.). United Methodist. Home: 6911 Gemini Dr Anchorage AK 99504-4519

LEE, FRANCES HELEN, editor; b. N.Y.C., Jan. 6, 1936; d. Murray and Rose (Rothman) Lee; BA, Queens Coll., 1957; MA, NYU, 1962. Editorial asst. Christian Herald Family Bookshelf, N.Y.C., 1957-62; with Gordon and Breach Sci. Pubs., Inc., N.Y.C., 1964-66, Am. Electric Power Svc. Corp. AEP Operating Ideas, N.Y.C., 1966-69, Indsl. Water Engring. Mag., N.Y.C., 1969-71; directory editor Photographic div. United Bus. Publs., N.Y.C., 1971-80; editor Am. Druggist Blue Book, Hearst Books/Bus. Publs. Group, 1980-81, spl. projects coord. motor manuals Hearst Book div., 1981-82, editor New Price Report, 1982-84; editor Am. Druggist Blue Book, 1982-88; freelance editor, cons., 1988—. Supr. Bronx div. N.Y. State CD, 1953-59. Mem. com. on N.Y.C. charter revision Citizens Union, 1975, com. on city personnel practices, 1975-76, com. on city mgmt., 1977—, bd. dirs., 1978—, co-chmn. com. on N.Y.C. Cultural Concerns, 1979—; vol. N.Y. Opera Guild, 1990—; vol. N.Y.C. Opera, 1992—. Recipient cert. of honor NYU Alumni Fedn., 1985, Meritorious Serv. award, 1986. Mem. N.Y. Bus. Press Editors (bd. dirs. 1988-90, sec. 1990-91), Women's Equity Action League (chmn. rsch. com.), NYU Alumnae Club (dir. 1976-78, rec. sec. 1978-80, v.p. 1980-82, pres. 1982-84, rep. to bd. dirs. fedn. 1984-86), NYU Alumni Fedn. (dir.-at-large 1986—), Villa-Lobos Music Soc. (sec. 1989-91, treas. 1992—), NYU Club (bd. govs. 1987-89.) Home: 170 2d Ave New York NY 10003

LEE, GENEVIEVE BRUGGEMAN, publishing company executive; b. Mahnomen, Minn., May 23, 1928; d. Joseph William and Mary Martha (Bastain) Bruggeman; m. Joel Kenneth Lee, Aug. 23, 1946; children: Rebecca Marie, Joel Gregory. Clk. Family Svc. Assn., N.Y.C., 1946-47; counselor Cin. Employment Svc., 1968-70; exec. sec. Ch. Bulls. of Buffalo, Inc., 1970-73, v.p., 1973—; bd. dirs. Woodgate Assn., East Amherst, N.Y.; mem. adv. bd. Schofield Residence, Buffalo, 1983-85, now chmn. bd. dirs., mem. exec. bd., sec., 1985-90, vice chmn./sec., 1991-94. Mem. Ken-Ton C. of C., Zonta (pres. Kenmore 1984-86, bd. dirs. area 3, 1986-88, sec. dist. IV 1988-90). Republican. Roman Catholic. Home: 258 Old Meadow Dr East Amherst NY 14051-2405 Office: Ch Bulls of Buffalo Inc 745 Englewood Ave Buffalo NY 14223-2406

LEE, JANE PILLOW RIGHTOR, association executive; b. Helena, Ark., Mar. 10, 1908; d. Henry Haskell and Jennie (Pillow) Rightor; m. Frederick Billings Lee, May 7, 1939 (dec. Oct. 1992); children; Jane Lee Wolfe, Frederick B. Jr., Laura Lee Kent. BA, Smith Coll., 1930. Pres. YWCA of Nat. Capital Area, Washington, 1958-60; mem. nat. bd. YWCA of the U.S.A., N.Y.C., trustee, mem. exec. com., chmn. world svc. coun. Recipient Ambassador award YWCA of the U.S.A., 1993. Democrat. Episcopalian. Home: 1327 Potomac School Rd Mc Lean VA 22101

LEE, JANET WASHBURN, health products executive; b. Tucson, Apr. 2, 1955; d. Benton Charles and Thelma Louise (Pritchett) Washburn. BA, Ariz. State U., 1976. Electronics buyer Motorola SG, Phoenix, 1976-78; mgr. communications and tng. Honeywell PMSD, Phoenix, 1978-80; stockbroker Kidder, Peabody and Co., Phoenix, 1980-88; banker Comml. Bus. Mktg. Valley Bank, Phoenix; cons., pres. Desert West Med. Compliance, Phoenix, 1990—; pres. Heflin Health & Safety Inc., Phoenix, 1993—; instr., conducts bus. and fin. seminars; bd. Samaritan Poison Control Ctr. Bd. mem. YMCA Fin. Devel., Phoenix, 1986—; mem. Phoenix Art Mus., 1984—; past chmn. Spina Bifida Celebrity Tennis, Scottsdale, 1984; com. mem. Symington for Gov. Campaign, Fiesta Bowl com., 1994. Named Women of the Year Bus. and Profl. Women, Phoenix 1981, Young Career Woman , 1979. Mem. Phoenix C. of C., Scottsdale C. of C., Phoenix City Club. Republican. Office: Heaflen Health Safety Inc Desert West Med Compliance PO Box 13449 Phoenix AZ 85002

LEE, JANIS K., state legislator; b. Kensington, Kans., July 11, 1945; m. Lyn Lee; children: David, Brian, Daniel. BA, Kans. State U., 1970. Mem. from dist. 36 Kans. State Senate, 1988—. Mem. Kappa Delta Pi, Phi Kappa Phi. Democrat. Home: RR 1 RR 1 Box 145 Kensington KS 66951-9745 Office: State Senate State Capital Topeka KS 66612*

LEE, JEANNE KIT YEW, administrative officer; b. N.Y.C., July 31, 1959; d. Tat Yuen and Yow Seum (Chu) Lee. BBA, Baruch Coll., 1982. Clk. typist U.S. Dept. Health and Human Svcs., N.Y.C., 1980-83; clk. typist U.S. Consumer Product Safety Commn., N.Y.C., 1983-85, adminstrv. asst., 1985-90; sys. adminstr. U.S. Consumer Product Safety Commn., 1986-93; adminstrv. officer U.S. Consumer Product Safety Commn., N.Y.C., 1990—. Mem. NAFE, Humane Soc., Nat. Wildlife Fedn. (assoc.), Am. Humane, DAV (Commanders Club 1988—).

LEE, JEANNINE ANNE, law librarian; b. Buffalo, Mar. 18, 1957; d. Jennie Josephine (Sciortino) Lee; m. Richard S. Geer, 1988; 1 child, Matthew. BA, SUNY, Buffalo, 1978, MLS, 1980. Reference libr. SUNY, Buffalo, 1980-81, Buffalo and Erie County Pub. Libr., 1981-85; sr. law librarian Supreme Ct. Libr., Buffalo, 1985—; guest lectr. Sch. Info. and Libr. Studies SUNY, 1988—. Mem. Am. Assn. Law Librs. (tech. svcs. com., Upstate N.Y. chpt. nominating com. 1988, editor newsletter 1989-91, bd. dirs. 1990-91, local arrangements chmn. 1993, chmn. grants and scholarships 1994—), N.Y. Unified Ct. Law Librs. Assn. (v.p., pres. elect 1988-89, program chmn. edn. and tng. seminar 1988, sec. 1993-94). Democrat. Roman Catholic. Office: Supreme Ct Libr 92 Franklin St Buffalo NY 14202-3991

LEE, JOLI FAY EATON, educator; b. Holdredge, Nebr., Sept. 24, 1951; d. Ray Lee and Lois Illeen (Willoughby) Larkins; m. James Edward Eaton, Aug. 16, 1969 (div. Jan. 1979); children: Threva, James, Beth; m. Chris Lee, Aug. 13, 1991; stepchildren: Michael Lee, Robyn Lee. BS in Elem. Edn., N.Mex. State U., Las Cruces, 1980, MA in Curriculum and Instruction, 1984. Cert. elem. tchr., N.Mex. Tchr. elem. Alamogordo (N.Mex.) Pub. Schs., 1980—; co-chmn. City Elem. Sci. Fair, Alamogordo, 1989-90, chmn.,

1990-92; with Summer Sci. Pilot Program, 1992-94. Contbr. articles to profl. jours. Nat. conv. co-chmn. Nat. Speleological Soc., Tularosa, N.Mex., 1986; joint venturer Cave Rsch. Found., 1983—; person. dir., Guadalupe Area Cave Rsch. Found., N.Mex., 1987-90; del. Cave Exploration Del. to People's Republic of China, 1993. Crimson scholar N.Mex. State U., 1980. Mem. NEA, Nat. Speleological Soc. (sec. Southwestern region 1984, 91-92, 93, Southwestern regional chmn. 1985-86). Republican. Episcopalian. Home: 406 Sunrise Ave Alamogordo NM 88310-4141 Office: North Elem Sch 1300 Florida Alamogordo NM 88310-6331

LEE, JOYCE A., administrative assistant; b. Safford, Ariz., Sept. 18, 1942; d. Roy and Minnie R. (Mobley) Brewer; m. Eugene W. Gaddy Jr., Mar. 16, 1970 (div. 1985); children: Carol, Kevin, Aaron; m. Glenn A. Lee, Oct. 16, 1992. AA, Ea. Ariz. Coll., 1980, AAS, 1993; postgrad., U. Phoenix, 1993—. Dispatcher Mohave County Sheriff's Office, Kingman, Ariz., 1969-74; sec. Globe (Ariz.) Mobile Home Sales, 1975-83; data entry supr. SMC & Assocs., Globe, 1985-88; tax preparer H&R Block Co., Globe, 1992; adminstrv. asst. Am. Pub. Co., Globe, 1994—. Girls camp dir. LDS Ch., Globe, 1985-90; mem. com. Boy Scouts Am., Globe. Mem. NAFE, Phi Theta Kappa. Democrat. Home: Rte 1 CC # 179 Globe AZ 85501 Office: Am Pub Co Omni Care Ctr 1100 Monroe Globe AZ 85501

LEE, JUDITH C., writer, editor; b. Myrtle Point, Oreg., 1936; d. Ralph F. and Lola M. (Greene) Milne; m. Myron E. Lee, 1967. BA, U. Oreg., 1959; MLS, San Jose State U., 1981. Tech. writer GTE Sylvania, Mountain View, Calif., 1962-66, sr. tech. writer, 1968-73; sr. tech. writer Microelectronics div. Philco-Ford, Santa Clara, Calif., 1966-67; sr. publs. writer Lockheed Corp., Sunnyvale, Calif., 1974; adminstr. tech. communications Catalytica Assocs., Santa Clara, 1977-80; mgr. info. resources Hydro Rsch. Sci., Santa Clara, 1982-83; staff editor Bus. Software Mag., Redwood City, Calif., 1984-85, mng. editor, 1985-86; mng. editor SandCastles, Inc., Mountain View, 1986-87; editorial cons. Alcatel Info. Systems, Milpitas, Calif., 1987-88; mng. editor NewsFaces, Inc., Los Gatos, Calif., 1988; sr. tech. writer-editor SRI Internat., Menlo Park, Calif., 1989-90, specialist tech. writer, editor, 1991—; mem. steering com. Silicon Valley Tech. Communications Sem., 1985. Book reviewer Sci. and Tech. Ann. Ref. Rev., 1989-91. Recipient Award of Merit No. Calif. Tech. Communication Competition, 1979, Distinction in Corp. Advt. award, 1989. Mem. IEEE, AAUW (com. chmn. 1970), Soc. Tech. Communication (sec. Silicon Valley chpt. 1968), Assn. Tchrs. Tech. Writing, Spl. Libraries Assn., Internat. Platform Assn., Sigma Delta Pi, Alpha Lambda Delta, Beta Phi Mu. Home: 3322 Saint Michael Dr Palo Alto CA 94306-3057 Office: SRI Internat 333 Ravenswood Ave Menlo Park CA 94025-3493

LEE, JUNE WARREN, dentist; b. Boston, Feb. 24, 1952; d. Earl Arnold and Rosemary Regina (Leary) Warren; m. William Lee, July 25, 1976; children: Jaime Michelle, Daniel William. BA, Brandeis U., 1973; DDS, Georgetown U., 1977; student, U.S. Dental Inst., 1985-87. Pvt. practice, Boston, 1977—; chair gen. arrangements YDC 21, Yankee Dental Congress. Mem. Altrusa Club of Quincy, Mass., 1979—, Cunningham Sch. PTO, Milton, Mass, 1987—, Parent-Adv. Coun., Collicot Elem. Sch., Milton, 1986-87; dental instr. Cunningham Sch., 1987—; dental screening, Healthworks, Neponset Health Ctr., Boston, 1981-84. Master Acad. Gen. Denistry (coun. ann. meetings and internat. confs., past pres. New Eng. Mastertrack program, pres.-elect Mass chpt., past chmn. editl. rev. bd. Audiodent); fellow Am. Coll. Dentists, Internat. Coll. Dentists, Acad. Dentistry Internat.; mem. ADA, Mass. Dental Soc., South Shore Dist. Dental Soc. (chmn.-elect 1991, chmn. 1992), Am. Orthodontic Soc., Am. Acad. Gnathologic Orthopedics, Am. Assn. for Functional Orthodontics, Am. Assn. Women Dentists (sec. 1987, v.p. 1988, pres.-elect 1989, pres. 1990, A.T. Cross Co. Women of Achievement award 1985), Women's Dental Soc. Mass. (sec. 1978, v.p. 1979-81, pres. 1981-83), Mass. Dentists Interested in Legislation, Chestnut Hill Rsch. Study Club. Roman Catholic. Office: 383 Neponset Ave Dorchester MA 02122-3197

LEE, KAMEE ANGELA, financial analyst; b. Hong Kong, Sept. 4, 1961; d. Yick-Kun and Fan-Yuk (Ho) L.; m. Hei-Wai Lee, May 23, 1988; 1 child, Jonathan. BA magna cum laude, Whittier Coll., 1984; MS in Fin., U. Ill., 1986, M of Acctg. Sci., 1989. CPA, Fla.; cert. mgmt. acct. Tax assoc. Price Waterhouse, Miami, Fla., 1989-90; staff acct. Humana Health Care Plans, Tampa, Fla., 1990-92; mgr. finance and accounting Humana Health Care Plan, Tampa, Fla., 1992-94; mgr. data analysis and reporting Access Care, Tampa, 1994—. Recipient Wall Street Journ. Student Achievement award, 1984, Barr scholar, Moss scholarship in acctg., 1987, Whittier Coll. scholarship, 1981-84, Acad. Achievement award, 1983. Mem. AICPA, Fla. Inst. CPA, Inst. of Mgmt. Accts., Phi Kappa Phi. Home: 15607 Knollwood Dr Dearborn MI 48120-1346

LEE, KATE LEARY, financial adviser; b. Hastings, Nebr., Dec. 13, 1946; d. Robert Michael and Alyce Rita (Popp) Leary; widowed; children: Modie Alexander Lee, Marni Sue Lee. AA, Mesa Jr. Coll., 1968; BA in Spl. Edn., U. No. Colo., 1970, MA in Learning Disabilities, 1977, MBA, 1982. Lic. tchr., Colo. Speech pathologist, audiologist Unit 13, Scottsbluff, Nebr., 1971-76; tchr. spl. edn. Sch. Dist. 13, Greeley, Colo., 1977-78; master spl. edn. Havern Ctr., Inc., Denver, 1978-80; v.p. R.M. Leary & Co., Inc., Denver, 1980-84, pres., 1984—; sr. arbitrator BBB, 1988—; broker rep. Titan Value Equities Group, Inc., 1983-94. Fin. coun. Notre Dame Cath. Parish, Denver, 1989—; vol. coord. for State of Colo. gubernatorial candidate, 1994. Mem. Western Div. Conf. Pensions and Benefits, Colo. Harvard Bus. Sch. Club, Soc. Asset Allocators and Fund Timers, Inc. (dir. 1990-93), Ambassador Club Greater Denver C. of C. Office: RM Leary & Co Inc 3300 E 1st Ave # 290 Denver CO 80206

LEE, KATHRYN ELLEN, corporate lawyer; b. Highland Park, Mich., Sept. 2, 1958; d. Brendan Joseph and Elise Alexandra (Worobetz) L.; m. Albert E. Bender, May 1, 1993. BA in Econs., U. Mich., 1980; JD, U. Ga., 1985. Law assoc. Shumacker & Thompson, Chattanooga, 1985-88, Altman, Kritzer & Levick, Atlanta, 1989-92; corp. counsel real estate The Home Depot, Inc., Atlanta, 1992—. Office: Home Depot 2727 Paces Ferry Rd NW Atlanta GA 30339

LEE, LAURIE NEILSON, lawyer; b. Portland, Oreg., Jan. 22, 1947; d. Duncan Reese and Lilian (Schwichtenberg) Neilson; m. Douglas Caldwell, Sept. 13, 1968 (div. Aug. 1987); children: Jessica, Ashley; m. Alan M. Lee, Jan. 1, 1988; stepchildren: Erin Lee, Sam Lee. BA, U. Oreg., 1969; JD, Lewis & Clark Coll., 1980. Bar: Oreg. 1980, U.S. Dist. Ct. Oreg. 1980. Assoc. Urbigkeit, Hinson & Abele, Oregon City, Oreg., 1980-85, Gleason, Scarborough, McNeese, O'Brien & Barnes, P.C., Portland, Oreg., 1985-88; ptnr. Bullivant, Houser, Bailey, Pendergrass & Hoffman, Portland, 1989-94, Foster Pepper & Shefelman, Portland, 1994—; speaker legal seminars Oreg. State Bar, 1984-86, 88, 90, 92, 93, 94, Oreg. Law Inst., 1989, Oreg. Soc. CPAs, 1986-90, 92, Nat. Bus. Inst., 1990, Portland Tax Forum, 1991. Contbr. articles to profl. jours.; contbg. author: Administering Trusts in Oregon, 1994. Mem. activities coun. Portland Art Mus., 1989-91, Nature Conservancy, Portland, 1990; bd. dirs. The Dougy Ctr., Portland, 1989-91; mem. N.W. Planned Giving Roundtable, 1992—; past chair, past sec., com. mem. exec. com. estate planning and adminstrn. sect. Oreg. State Bar, Lake Oswego, 1982-88. Fellow Am. Coll. Trust and Estate Coun.; mem. ABA, Oreg. Women Lawyers (charter), Estate Planning Coun. Portland Inc. (bd. dirs. 1992—, chair planning com. 22d Ann. Estate Planning Seminar 1992), Oreg. State Bar, Multnomah County Bar Assn. Office: Foster Pepper & Shefelman 1 Main Pl 15th flr 101 SW Main St Portland OR 97204-3223

LEE, LILLIAN VANESSA, microbiologist; b. N.Y.C., June 1, 1951; d. Wenceslao and Ada (Otero) Cancel; B.S. in Biology, St. Johns U., 1972; M.S. in Microbiology, Wagner Coll., 1974; m. Thomas Christopher Lee, June 11, 1972; children—Tovan, John-Peter, Phillip-Michael. Grad. lab. asst. in microbiology Wagner Coll., S.I., N.Y., 1972-74; clin. microbiology technologist Queens Hosp. Center, Jamaica, N.Y., 1974-81, clin. microbiology supr., 1981-84; sect. head microbiology Nyack (N.Y.) Hosp., 1984-93, acting lab. mgr., 1992-93; microbiology mgr. Beth Israel Med. Ctr., N.Y., 1994—. Cert. registered microbiologist and specialist in microbiology, clin. lab. specialist. Mem. Am. Soc. Clin. Pathologists, Am. Soc. Microbiology (N.Y.C. br. coun. mem. 1992—, program com. chair 1993—), Am. Acad. Microbiology, Med. Mycology Soc., N.Y., N.Y. Acad. Scis., N.Y.C. Soc. Infectious Diseases. Home: 14 Continental Dr West Nyack NY 10994-2803 Office: Beth Israel Med Ctr 1st Ave at 16th St New York NY 10003

LEE, LILY KIANG, scientific research company executive; b. Shanghai, China, Nov. 23, 1946; came to U.S., 1967, naturalized, 1974; d. Chi-Wu and An-Teh (Shih) Kiang; m. Robert Edward Lee; children: Jeffrey Anthony, Michelle Adrienne, Stephanie Amanda, Christina Alison. BS, Nat. Cheng-Chi U., 1967; MBA, Golden Gate U., San Francisco, 1969. Acct., then acctg. supr. Am. Data Systems, Inc., Canoga Park, Calif., 1969-73; sr. acct. Pertec Peripheral Equipment div. Pertec Corp., Chatsworth, Calif., 1973-76; mgr. fin. planning and acctg., then mgr. fin. planning, program and internal control Sci. Ctr. div. Rockwell Internat. Corp., Thousand Oaks, Calif., 1976—. Mem. NAFE, Am. Mgmt. Assn., Nat. Mgmt. Assn., Nat. Property Mgrs. Assn. Republican. Baptist. Office: Rockwell Internat Corp PO Box 1085 1049 Camino Dos Rios Thousand Oaks CA 91358

LEE, LINDA TOM, apparel executive; b. Mt. Vernon, N.Y., Sept. 16, 1950; d. Wing Sing and Ying Hi (Ng) Tom; m. Charles I. Lee, June 17, 1978; children: Christopher, Jessica. BFA, Pratt Inst., 1972. Designer Whatever Wear, Inc., N.Y.C., 1975-78, Empire Shield, N.Y.C., 1983-85, Allison Mfg., N.Y.C., 1985-87; dir. design Gear Holding Co., N.Y.C., 1987-88; sr. designer Kleinert's Inc. Ala., N.Y.C., 1988—. Office: Kleinerts INc Ste 1711 112 W 34th St New York NY 10120

LEE, MARGARET ANNE, social worker, psychotherapist; b. Scribner, Nebr., Nov. 23, 1930; d. William Christian and Caroline Bertha (Benner) Joens; m. Robert Kelly Lee, May 21, 1950 (div. 1972); children: Lawrence Robert, James Kelly, Daniel Richard. AA, Napa Coll., 1949; student, U. Calif., Berkeley, 1949-50; BA, Calif. State Coll., Sonoma, 1975; MSW, Calif. State U., Sacramento, 1977. Diplomate clin. social worker; lic. clin. social worker, Calif.; lic. marriage and family counselor, Calif.; tchr. Columnist, stringer Napa (Calif.) Register, 1946-50; eligibility worker, supr. Napa County Dept. Social Services, 1968-75; instr. Napa Valley Community Coll., 1978-83; practice psychotherapy Napa, 1977—; oral commr. Calif. Dept. Consumer Affairs, Bd. Behavioral Sci., 1984—; bd. dirs. Project Access, 1978-79. Trustee Napa Valley C.C., 1983—, vp. bd., 1984-85, pres. bd., 1986, 90, 95, clk., 1988-89; bd. dirs. Napa County Coun. Econ. Opportunity, 1984-85, Napa chpt. March of Dimes, 1957-71, Mental Health Assn. Napa County, 1983-87; vice chmn. edn. com. Calif. C.C. Trustees, 1987-88, chmn. edn. com., 1988-89, legis com., 1985-87, bd. dirs., 1989—, 2d v.p., 1991, 1st v.p., 1992, pres., 1993; mem. student equity rev. group Calif. C.C. Chancellors, 1992; bd. dirs. C.C. League Calif., 1992—, 1st v.p., 1992. Recipient Fresh Start award Self mag., award Congl. Caucus on Women's Issues, 1984. Mem. NASW, Mental Health Assn. Napa County, Calif. Assn. Physically and Handicapped, Women's Polit. Caucus, Calif. Elected Women's Assn. Edn. and Rsch., Am. Assn. Women in Community and Jr. Colls. Democrat. Lutheran. Office: 1100 Trancas St Napa CA 94558-2908

LEE, MARGARET NORMA, artist; b. Kansas City, Mo., July 7, 1928; d. James W. and Margaret W. (Farin) Lee; PhB, U. Chgo., 1948; MA, Art Inst. Chgo., 1952. Lectr., U. Kansas City, 1957-61; cons. Kansas City Bd. Edn., Kansas City, Mo., 1968-86; guest lectr. U.Mo.-Columbia, 1983, 85, 87, 89, 91, 93; one-woman shows Univ. Women's Club, Kansas City, 1966, Friends of Art, Kansas City, 1969, Fine Arts Gallery U. Mo. at Columbia, 1972, All Souls Unitarian Ch. Kansas City, Mo., 1978; two-Woman show Rockhurst Coll., Kansas City, Mo., 1981 exhibited in group shows U. Kans., Lawrence, 1958, Chgo. Art Inst., 1963, Nelson Art Gallery, Kansas City, Mo., 1968, 74, Mo. Art Show, 1976, Fine Arts Gallery, Davenport, Iowa, 1977; represented in permanent collections Amarillo (Tex.) Art Center, Kansas City (Mo.) Pub. Library, Park Coll., Parkville, Mo. Mem. Coll. Art Assn. Roman Catholic. Contbr. art to profl. jours.; author booklet. Home and Studio: 4109 Holmes St Kansas City MO 64110-1127

LEE, MARIANNA, editor; b. N.Y.C., Aug. 23, 1930; d. Isaac and Charlotte (Steiner) Lubow; m. Edward Lee, June 17, 1968 (div. 1978); 1 child, Susanna. BA, Smith Coll., 1952; postgrad, Columbia U., 1952-53; postgrad., Oxford (Eng.) U., 1957-58. Asst. editor Watson-Guptill Publs., N.Y.C., 1958-59; chief copy editor Grolier, Inc., N.Y.C., 1960-61; mng. editor Portfolio & Art News Ann., N.Y.C., 1961-62; assoc. editor Parade Publs., N.Y.C., 1962-66; mng. editor The Johns Hopkins Press, Balt., 1966-68, U. Tex. Press, Austin, 1968-69; sr. publs. mgr. Scripps Inst. of Oceanography, La Jolla, Calif., 1979-82; mng. editor Harcourt Brace and Co., San Diego, 1982—. Contbr. articles to profl. jours. Democrat. Jewish. Office: Harcourt Brace and Co 525 B St San Diego CA 92101

LEE, MARILYN (IRMA) MODARELLI, law librarian; b. Jersey City, Dec. 8, 1934; d. Alfred E. and Florence Olga (Koment) Modarelli; m. Alfred McClung Lee III, June 8, 1957 (div. July 1985); children: Leslie Lee Ekstrand, Alfred McClung IV, Andrew Modarelli. BA, Swarthmore (Pa.) Coll., 1956; JD, Western New Eng. Sch. of Law, 1985. Bar: Mass. 1986. Claims rep., supr. region II Social Security Adminstrn., Jersey City, 1956-59; law libr. County of Franklin, Greenfield, Mass., 1972-78; libr. I Franklin Law Libr. Mass. Trial Ct., Greenfield, 1978—; mem. Franklin County Futures Lab Task Force (Mass. Cts.), 1994—. Chmn. Franklin County (Mass.) Regional Tech., Turners Falls, 1974-76, Sch. Bldg. Com., 1974-76; mem. Franklin County Planning Bd., 1988-93, mem. exec. bd., 1993—; clk. Franklin County Tech. Sch., 1976-81; vice chmn. Greenfield Planning Bd., 1987—; mem. Greenfield Sch. Bldg. Com., 1995—. Mem. Mass. Bar Assn., Franklin County Bar Assn. (chmn. lawyer referral com. 1992-94, vice chmn. 1994—, chmn. libr. com. 1992—), Law Librs. of New Eng. (treas. 1993—), Am. Assn. Law Librs., Greenfield Charter (com. clk. 1979-83), Swarthmore Alumni Coun. Office: Mass Trial Ct Franklin Law Libr 425 Main St Greenfield MA 01301-3313

LEE, MARTHA, artist, writer; b. Chehalis, Wash., Aug. 23, 1946; d. William Robert and Phyllis Ann (Herzog) L.; m. Peter Reynolds Lockwood, Jan. 25, 1974 (div. 1982). BA in English Lit., U. Wash., 1968; student, Factory of Visual Art, 1980-82. Reporter Seattle Post-Intelligencer, 1970; personnel counselor Theresa Snow Employment, 1971-72; receptionist Northwest Kidney Ctr., 1972-73; proprietress The Reliquary, 1974-77; travel agt. Cathay Express, 1977-79; artist, 1980—; represented by Pulliam Deffenbaugh Gallery, Portland, Oreg., Uppertown Antiques, Astoria, Oreg. Painter various oil paintings; exhibitor group and one-person shows. Home and Studio: 24409 Pacific Hwy Ocean Park WA 98640-3823

LEE, MARY KATHRYN, banker; b. Santa Clara, Calif., Feb. 3, 1964; d. Paul Ralph and Sue Ella (French) L. BA in Econs., Stanford U., 1985; MBA, UCLA, 1990. Fin. analyst Goldman, Sachs & Co., N.Y.C., 1985-87, L.A., 1987-88; assoc. in bus. credit Continental Bank, L.A., summer 1989; assoc. in corp. fin. Chase Manhattan Bank, L.A., 1990-93; pvt. practice fin. cons. L.A., 1993-94; v.p. bus. devel. Imperial Bank, L.A., 1994—. Bd. dir. Kids at Heart Olive Crest Found., L.A., 1993—. Mem. L.A. Area C. of C. (growing co. com. 1995—), Santa Monica Area C. of C. (all cities resource group, 1995—, profl. network group, 1995—). Republican. Episcopalian. Home: 451 San Vicente Blvd. #4 Santa Monica CA 90402 Office: Imperial Bank Ste 1010 9920 S La Cienega Blvd Inglewood CA 90301

LEE, MICHELE, actress; b. L.A., June 24, 1942; d. Jack and Sylvia Helen (Silverstein) Dusick; m. James Farentino, Feb. 20, 1966 (div. 1983); 1 son, David Michael; m. Fred Rappoport, Sept. 27, 1987. Actress roles include (Broadway play) How to Succeed in Business Without Trying, 1962-64, Seesaw, 1973, (movies) How to Succeed in Business With Really Trying, 1967, The Love Bug, 1969, Dark Victory, 1975, Bud and Low, 1976, A Letter to Three Wives, 1985, Single Women, Married Men, 1989, The Fatal Image, 1990, My Son Johnny, 1991, (TV movie) Broadway Bound, 1992, When No One Would Listen, 1993, Big Dreams Broken Hearts: The Dottie West Story, 1995, (TV series) Knots Landing, 1979-93 (Outstanding Lead Actress award Soap Opera awards 1992). Recipient Top Star of Tomorrow award Motion Picture Exhibitors of U.S. and Can., 1967, Drama Desk award Broadway Critics, 1973, Outer Critics Circle award, 1973; nominated for Antoinette Perry award, 1973-74, Emmy for Knots Landing, 1981-82.

LEE, NANCEE, health care administrator; b. Santa Monica, Calif.; d. Monroe Lee and Marie (Wilkinson) Thompson. BA, Bklyn. Coll., 1983; MA, Antioch U., L.A., 1989. Asst. media dir. Gay Men's Health Crisis, N.Y.C., 1983-84; tchr. L.A. Unified Sch. Dist., 1985-89; HIV educator Hemophilia Coun., Pasadena, Calif., 1989-92; HIV prevention specialist Health Quarters, Beverly, Mass., 1992-94; coord. health resources Women, Inc., Dorchester, Mass., 1993-94; with AIDS program County of L.A., 1995—. Host radio program series on HIV Human Sexuality, 1992. Vol. dir. Rock Angel Fund Raising, Boston, 1990—; mem. L.A. AIDS Edn. Bd., L.A., 1989-92; mem. North Shore AIDS Collaborative, Salem, Mass., 1993. Unitarian. Office: County of LA AIDS Program 600 S Commonwealth Ave Los Angeles CA 90005

LEE, NAOMI PEARL, academic administrator; b. Moorhead, M.N., Nov. 28, 1948; d. Cecil Allen and Marcella Esther (Tweten) B.; m. Gary Ralph Lee, Jan. 6, 1968; 1 child, Laura Annabelle. BA, Wash. State U., 1976, MA, 1981, PhD, 1984. Counselling asst. Career Devel. Prog./WSU, Pullman, Wash., 1981-83; visiting asst. prof. WSU, Pullman, 1984-85; acad. counselor Dept. Athletics, Wash. State U., Pullman, 1983-87, Coll. Liberal Arts & Sci., U. Fla., Gainesville, 1987—; cons. Wash. State Dept. Labor, 1983. Editor: Research & Pub. Service with the Rural Elderly, 1980. Gen. mgr. Palouse Empire Cougars Semi-pro Baseball Team, Pullman, 1985-87. Mem., Nat. Acad. Adv. Assn., Am. Coll. Pers. Assn., Commn. XVI, Phi Kappa Phi. Democrat. Lutheran.

LEE, NELDA S., art appraiser and dealer, film producer; b. Gorman, Tex., July 3, 1941; d. Olan C. and Onis L.; A.S. (Franklin Lindsay Found. grantee), Tarleton State U., Tex., 1961; B.A. in Fine Arts, N. Tex. State U., 1963; postgrad. Tex. Tech. U., 1964, San Miguel de Allende Art Inst., Mexico, 1965; 1 dau., Jeanna Lea Pool. Head dept. art Ector High Sch., Odessa, Tex., 1963-68. Bd. dirs. Odessa YMCA, 1970, bd. dirs. Am. Heart Assn., Odessa, 1975; fund raiser Easter Seal Telethon, Odessa, 1978-79; bd. dirs. Ector County (Tex.) Cultural Center, 1979—, Tex. Bus. Hall of Fame, 1980-85; bd. dirs., mem. acquisition com. Permian Basin Presdl. Mus., Odessa, 1978; bd. dirs., chairperson acquisition com. Odessa Art Mus., 1979—; pres. Mega-Tex. Prodns., TV and movie producers; pres. Ector County Democratic Women's Club, 1975, Nelda Lee, Inc., Odessa; appointee Tex. Commn. Arts, 1993—. Group exhbns. include El Paso, Tex., New Orleans. Recipient Designer-Craftsman award El Paso Mus. Fine Arts, 1964. Mem. Am. Soc. Appraisers (sr.), Nat. Tex. Assn. Art Dealers (pres. 1978—), Odessa C. of C. Contbr. articles to profl. jours. Office: Nelda Lee Inc PO Box 4268 Odessa TX 79760-4268

LEE, NORA R., social worker, administrator; b. Hattiesburg, Miss., Oct. 17, 1953; d. Walter G. and Sarah (Reedy) Robillard; 1 child, Grant W. Lee Jr. BA in Libr. Sci., Miss. U. Women, 1975; MLS, U. Miss., 1977. Media specialist Ella Darling Elem., Greenville, Miss., 1976; grad. teaching asst. U. Miss., Oxford, 1976-77; catalog libr. CBN U., Virginia Beach, Va., 1977; resident mgr. Bush Realty & Great Atlantic Realty, Virginia Beach, 1979-82; catalog specialist SOLINET, Atlanta, 1984-86; sr. caseworker Fulton County (Ga.) Dept. Family and Children Svcs., Atlanta, 1986-88, prin. caseworker, 1988-92, casework supr., 1992—. Vol. Project Open Hand, Atlanta, 1990—. Mem. AAUW, NAFE, Ga. County Welfare Assn. (state bd. dirs. 1994—, local co-chair constn. and bylaws 1994, publicity 1994, state mem. budget and fin. 1994—). Home: 1838 Georgiana Dr NE Atlanta GA 30329 Office: Fulton County Dept Family & Children Svcs 225 James P Brawley Dr NW Atlanta GA 30314

LEE, PALI JAE (POLLY JAE STEAD LEE), retired librarian, writer; b. Nov. 26, 1929; d. Jonathan Everett Wheeler and Ona Katherine (Grunder) Stead; m. Richard H.W. Lee, Apr. 7, 1945 (div. 1978); children: Lani Catherine Kain, Karin Lee Robinson, Ona G., Laurie B., Robin Louise Lee Halbert; m. John K. Willis, 1979 (dec. 1994). Student, U. Hawaii, 1944-46, Mich. State, 1961-64. Cataloguer and processor U.S. Army Air Force, 1945-46; with U.S. Weather Bur. Film Library, New Orleans, 1948-50, FBI, Wright-Patterson AFB, Dayton, Ohio, 1952, Ohio Wholesale Winedealers, Columbus, Ohio, 1956-58, Coll. Engring., Ohio State U., Columbus, 1959; writer tech. manual Annie Whittenmeyer Home, Davenport, Iowa, 1960; with Grand Rapids (Mich.) Pub. Library, 1961-62; dir. Waterford (Mich.) Twp. Libraries, 1962-64; acquisition librarian Pontiac (Mich.) Pub. Libraries, 1965-71, dir. East Side br., 1971-73; librarian Bishop Mus., Honolulu, 1975-83. Author: Mary Dyer, Child of Light, 1973, Giant: Pictorial History of the Human Colossus, 1973, History of Change: Kaneohe Bay Area, 1976, English edit., 1983, Na Po Makole-Tales of the Night Rainbow, 1981, rev. edit., 1988, Mo'olelo O Na Pohukaina, 1983, Ka Ipu Kukui, 1994; contbr. articles to profl. jours. Chmn. Oakland County br. Multiple Sclerosis Soc., 1972-73, co-chmn. Pontiac com. of Mich. area bd., 1972-73; sec. Ōhana o Kokua, 1979-83, Paia-Willis Ōhana, 1982-91, Ōhana Kame'ekua, 1988-91; bd. dirs. Detroit Multiple Sclerosis Soc., 1971; mem. Mich. area bd. Am. Friends Svc. com., 1961-69; mem. consumer adv. bd. Libr. for Blind and Physically Handicapped, Honolulu, 1991—; pres. consumer 55 plus bd. Honolulu Ctr. for Ind. Living, 1990-94; pres. Honolulu chpt. Nat. Fedn. of Blind, 1991-94, 1st v.p. #93 state affiliate, 1991-94, editor Na Na Maka Aloha newsletter, 1990-94; 1st v.p. Hawaii chpt. Talking Book Readers Club, 1994—. Recipient Mother of the Yr. award Quad City Bus. Men, 1960, Bowl of Light award Hawaiian Community of Hawaii, 1989. Mem. Internat. Platform Assn., Soc. Friends. Office: PO Box 10706 4462 Sierra Dr Honolulu HI 96816-4022

LEE, PAMELA ANNE, accountant, financial analyst; b. San Francisco, May 30, 1960; d. Larry D. and Alice Mary (Reece) L. BBA, San Francisco State U., 1981. CPA, Calif. Typist, bookkeeper, tax acct. James G. Woo, CPA, San Francisco, 1979-85; tutor bus. math. and statistics San Francisco State U., 1979-80; teller to ops. officer Gibraltar Savs. and Loan, San Francisco, 1978-81; sr. acct. Price Waterhouse, San Francisco, 1981-86; corp. acctg. mgr. First Nationwide Bank, Daly City, Calif., 1986-89, v.p., 1989-91, v.p., project mgr., 1991-92, sr. conversion and bus. analyst, 1992-93; sr. bus. analyst, asst. v.p. Bank of Am., 1993—; acctg. cons. New Performance Gallery, San Francisco, 1985, San Francisco Chamber Orch., 1986. Founding mem., chair bd. trustees Asian Acctg. Students Career Day, 1988-89. Mem. NAFE, Am. Inst. CPA's, Calif. Soc. CPA's, Nat. Assn. Asian-Am. CPA's (bd. dirs. 1986, news editor 1987, pres. 1988). Republican. Avocations: reading, music, travel, personal computing, needlework. Office: 50 California St Fl 11 San Francisco CA 94111-4624

LEE, PEARL, investment company executive; b. Cambridge, Md., Jan. 12, 1950; d. Bon Yue and Toy Yow (Fong) L. BFA, Phila. Coll. Art, 1974. Artist in residence Pa. Coun. Arts, Phila. and Shippensburg, Pa., 1975-77; with sales staff Exxon Office Systems, Phila., 1979-81; owner Pearl Lee Designs, Phila., 1978-84; account exec. Sears Bus. Systems, Wilmington, Del., 1984-87; assoc. v.p. Dean Witter Reynolds, Phila., 1987—. Mem. Phila. Mus. Art. Mem. World Affairs Coun., Asian Am. Women's Coalition, Zool. Soc. Phila., Found. for Architechture. Methodist. Office: Dean Witter Reynolds Inc 2 Logan Sq Philadelphia PA 19103

LEE, QWIHEE PARK, plant physiologist; b. Republic of Korea, Mar. 1, 1941; came to U.S., 1965; d. Yong-sik and Soon-duk (Paik) Park; m. Ick-whan Lee, May 20, 1965; children: Tina, Amy, Benjamin. MS, Seoul Nat. U., Republic of Korea, 1965; PhD, U. Minn., 1973. Head dept. plant physiology Korea Ginseng and Tobacco Inst., Seoul, 1980-82; instr. Sogang U., Seoul, 1981, Seoul Women's U., 1981; research assoc. U. Wash., Seattle, 1975-79. Exec. dir. Korean Community Counseling Ctr., Seattle, 1983-86. Named one of 20 Prominent Asian Women in Wash. State, Chinese Post Seattle, 1986. Mem. AAAS. Buddhist. Home: 13025 42nd Ave NE Seattle WA 98125-4624 Office: U Wash Dept Pharm SJ-30 1959 NE Pacific St Seattle WA 98195-0004

LEE, ROBIN S., surgeon, researcher; b. Pitts., Nov. 28, 1957; d. Lamont and Patricia Anne (Flaherty) S.; 1 child, Zoe Bryson Mayfield. BA, Swarthmore Coll., 1980; MD, Harvard U., 1990. Intern U. Calif., San Francisco, 1990-91, resident gen. surgery, 1991-93; rsch. fellow Mass. Gen. Hosp., Boston, 1993—. Resident scholar Am. Coll. Surgeons, 1994. Office: Mass Gen Hosp TBRC 149 13th St Boston MA 02129

LEE, ROSALYN SANDRA, computer professional; b. Columbus, Ohio; d. Russell Woodward and Olga Viola (Smith) L. A in Archtl. Tech., CCNY, 1979; BArch, Pratt Inst., 1983. Archtl. designer Pratt Inst., Bklyn., 1979-82; project coord. Home Life Ins., N.Y.C., 1982-86; archtl. designer, CAD operator Design Technologies, N.Y.C., 1986-88; project coord., CAD operator Facilities Mgmt., White Plains, N.Y., 1988-89; project mgr., CAD mgr. Continental Ins., N.Y.C., 1989—. Democrat. Home: PO Box 1303 Bronx NY 10452-1303 Office: Continental Ins Co 180 Maiden Ln New York NY 10038-4925

LEE, ROSEALEE MARIE, business and marketing executive; b. Ottumwa, Iowa, Feb. 2, 1951; d. William Anthony and Mildred Mae (Dimmitt) Tallman; m. David James Lee, Oct. 17, 1976; children: Jessica Anne, Jaymi Marie. Formerly exec. v.p. Associated Cos., Inc., St. Louis Park, Minn.; pres. Profl. Assistance Plus, Mpls., 1978-87; exec. dir. Soc. for Biomaterials, Mpls., 1986—; pres. ARDEL, Inc., Mpls., 1987—. Editor: Shortcuts in the Kitchen, 1983. Pres. Heritage Assn., Buffalo Grove, Ill., 1988-90. Mem. Assn. Exec. Assn. Office: ARDEL Inc 6518 Walker St Ste 150 Minneapolis MN 55426-4244

LEE, SABRINA KAY, manufacturer's representative; b. Dallas, Dec. 10, 1957; d. Robert Arlen Lee and Sandra Louise Houghtaling; m. Gaylord Gutierrez, Mar. 25, 1978 (div. 1982). Grad. high sch., Irvine, Calif. Cashier Camping World of Calif., Valencia, 1980-92, svc. writer, svc. advisor, store mgr., 1983-92; tng. dir. Camping World of Calif., Fairfield, Calif., 1982-83; mfrs. rep. Rogers & Rogers Enterprises, Middletown, Calif., 1992—.

LEE, SANDRA ANN, investment company executive; b. Houston, Nov. 28, 1942; d. Herman and Lillian (Bily) Sporn; m. Kenneth Phillip Veit, June 2, 1962 (div. June 1989). BA, U. Tex., 1963; MS, Am. U., Washington, 1971; MBA, U. Conn., 1979. CFA. Programmer GE, Bethesda, Md., 1963-64; assoc. mem. tech. staff Rsch. Analysis Corp., McLean, Va., 1964-66; mem. tech. staff MITRE Corp., McLean, 1966-72; systems mgr. Travelers Ins. Cos., Hartford, Conn., 1972-74; data base adminstr. Mass. Mut. Life Ins. Co., Springfield, Mass., 1974-75; investment mgr. cons. West Hartford, Conn., 1975-79, 87-92; trust officer Shawmut Bank, Hartford, 1979-87; sr. v.p. investments The T.O. Richardson Co., Farmington, Conn., 1992—. Mem. Hartford Soc. Fin. Analysts (pres., bd. mem. 1982-89). Republican. Congregationalist. Office: The T O Richardson Co 11 Main St Farmington CT 06032-2229

LEE, SANDRA DALE, insurance accounting and finance executive; b. Hamilton, Bermuda, May 13, 1952; came to U.S., 1954; d. Edward Dale and Enid Virginia (Bachman) Cochran; m. Richard Gerald Lee, Jr., Sept. 22, 1973; children: Richard G., III, Patricia K., Scott C., John P. BA in Math. magna cum laude, U. West Fla., 1977, BA in Acctg. magna cum laude, 1977; MBA, Queens Coll., 1992. CPA, Wash.; CPCU; cert. mgmt. acct.; assoc. in rsch. and planning. Asst. contr. Bapt. Hosp., Pensacola, Fla., 1975-77; internal auditor Sacred Heart Hosp., Pensacola, 1977-78; acctg. mgr. Safeco Ins., Seattle, 1978-82; fin. analyst, forecasting dir. United Pacific Ins., Federal Way, Wash., 1982-87; corp. planning mgr. Royal Ins., Charlotte, N.C., 1988—. Vol., mem. PTA, Seattle and Charlotte, 1985—; pheresis donor ARC, Charlotte, 1989—; leader, vol. Boy Scouts Am., Charlotte, 1992—, Girl Scouts U.S., Charlotte, 1990—. Mem. AICPA, Inst. Mgmt. Accts., CPCU Soc., Ins. Acctg. and Systems Assn. (treas. 1985-87). Home: 12001 Wych Ln Charlotte NC 28273 Office: Royal Ins PO Box 1000 MS-2212 Charlotte NC 28201-1000

LEE, SANDY KARON, program director. BFA, Valdosta State U., 1989. Coll. work study program asst. Griffin Corp., Inc., Valdosta, Ga., 1987-88; mktg. intern Valdosta (Ga.) Mall, 1989; account mgr. Howard Comm., Inc., Macon, Ga., 1989-91; program coord. Ames (Iowa) C. of C., 1991; membership svcs. dir. Waycross (Ga.)-Ware County C. of C., 1991-93; dir. grants and projects Brewton-Parker Coll., Mount Vernon, Ga., 1994—, active mentor program. mem. Am. Cancer Soc., 1991-93, bd. dirs., 1992-93, pub. info. spokesperson annual Phone-A-Thon, 1991-93; grad. Leadership Waycross, 1991, steering com. mem., 1992-93; mem. Leadership Waycross Alumni Assn., 1991-93, sec.-treas., 1993; active Waycross-Ware County Drug Action Coun., 1992-93. Mem. Ga. Edn. Advancement Coun. Home: 100 E Sixth St #B Vidalia GA 30474 Office: Brewton Parker Coll Mount Vernon GA 30445-0197

LEE, SARAH CHUNG, systems analyst; b. Taejon, Korea, Apr. 15, 1953; d. Pokchae and Dosum L. BSBA, Western New Eng. Coll., Springfield, Mass., 1988, MBA, 1993. Contract adminstr. Hanscom AFB, Bedford, Mass., 1989, ops. rsch. analyst, 1990—. Roman Catholic. Home: 158 Concord Rd Apt G28 Billerica MA 01821-4634 Office: Hanscom AFB Bedford MA 01731

LEE, SUSAN JOYE, educator, minister; b. Pensacola, Fla., Apr. 2, 1947; d. C.M. and Joyce (Mahanay) Biederstadt; m. Ralph B. Lee Jr., June 11, 1966; children: Ryan B., Jennifer Joyce. BA in Edn., Baylor U., 1968; MRE, Southwestern Bapt. Theol. Sem., 1978. Cert. tchr. Tchr. Spring Br. Ind. Sch. Dist., Houston, 1968-71; curriculum developer West Meml. Bapt. Ch., Houston, 1970; spl. edn. min. Tallowood Bapt. Ch., Houston, 1971-74; leadership trainer Minn.-Wis. Baptist Ch., Rochester, Minn., 1979-84; dir., counselor Christian Lifestyle Counseling, Pewaukee, Wis., 1979-85; min. to mid. schs. Westburg Bapt. Ch., Houston, 1985-87; presch.-children's-women's min. Harpeth Heights Bapt. Ch., Nashville, 1987-92; presch.-children cons. Bapt. Sunday Sch. Bd., Nashville, 1992—. Vol. New Hope FBC, Cedar Park, Austin Health Svcs.; friend Cedar Park Libr. Named Southwesterner of Yr., Southwestern Bapt. Theol. Sem., 1982. Mem. Christian Women's Club (Nashville bd. dirs. 1991-92), Nat. Assn. for Edn. of Young Child, Tenn. Assn. for Young Child. Home: 116 Bamboo Trl Cedar Park TX 78613-3451

LEE, TERESA CHRISTINE, sales executive; b. Napoleon, N.D., Dec. 14, 1937; d. Peter Joseph and Dorothea (Hauck) Draeger; m. Arwood Lawton Lee, Feb. 16, 1957 (div.); children: Jeri Kim, Tracy Ann, Kathryn Michelle, Kristeen Doreen. AA, Orange Coast Coll., 1972; BS, U. Phoenix, 1984. Cert. presch. adminstr., vocat. tchr. Asst. mgr. collection Catalina, Inc., L.A., 1957-60; rep. inside sales U.S. Plywood Corp., L.A., 1960-63; instrnl. aide Edison High Sch., Huntington Beach, Calif., 1971-75, technician career ctr., 1975-79; adminstrv. asst. Am. Hosp. Supply, Irvine, Calif., 1979-80; owner Terry Lee and Assocs., Huntington Beach, Calif., 1979-84; office mgr., coord. contracts Am. Hosp. Supply, Irvine, Calif., 1980-85; mgr. customer svc. Pepsico Food Systems, Irvine, 1985, rep. sales, 1985-89, mgr. equipment sales, 1989-92; mktg. cons., Fountain Valley, Calif., 1992—; owner Graphix One, Fountain Valley, 1994—. Commr. Huntington Beach High Sch. Dist., 1980-87, Garden Grove Sch. Dist., 1988—vol., 1994—; pres. Orange County Pers. Com., 1983-84; lay Min. St. Simon and Jude Ch., 1982-84; ednl. lobbyist, Sacramento, 1986. Mem. Am. Bus. Women's Assn. (sec./treas. 1984-86), Toastmasters, Scrabble Club (asst. dir. chpt. 34 1993—). Roman Catholic.

LEE, TONĪA RENEÉ, entertainer, former government agent; b. Colorado Springs, Mar. 27, 1963; d. Ernest and Claudine (Brunt) L. BA in Oral Communication, Cen. (Okla.) State U., 1983; postgrad., Tex. So. U., 1983, Oral Roberts U., 1984-85; MPA, U. So. Calif., 1987, cert. in jud. adminstrn., 1987; postgrad., Saybrook Inst., 1988-89, U. West Los Angeles, 1986-87, U. La Verne, 1990-92. Cert., registered hypnotherapist. Spl. agt. U.S. Dept. Def., Gardena, Calif., 1986-93; vol. cons. Tulsa County Juvenile Bur., 1985; black per rep. counselor, Cen. State U., 1982-83; libr. asst., 1981; admission and records clk., 1982, mem. High Sch.-Coll. rels. bd. (award of merit for outstanding svc. 1981), student senate 1981-83, student senate housing chmn. 1981-82, recruiter, 1981-83; housing mayor Oral Roberts U., 1982. Author: Slavery Without Chains and Other Selected Poems. Vol. ARC, 1980; mem. Young Democrats, 1981-83, NAACP (L.A. chpt. 1990-92). Recipient Editor's Choice award Nat. Libr. of Poetry, 1994; named to Outstanding Young Women of Am., 1985. Mem. NAFE, Pre-Law Club (sec.-treas. 1982-83), Am. Bus. Women's Assn., SAG, NCO Wives Club (ednl. scholarship 1980), Ctrl. State U. Alumni Assn., U. So. Calif. Alumni Assn., Kappa Delta Pi, Delta Sigma Theta (golden life mem., ednl. scholarship 1980). Democrat. Baptist.

LEE, VIRGINIA DIANE, lay worker; b. Hackensack, N.J., Sept. 3, 1939; d. Harold Ehler and Marion Estelle (Pierrez) True; m. Jerald Dana Lee, June 7, 1962; children: Diana, Tara, James. BS, Albright Coll., 1961; MS, Ohio U., 1963. Deacon Presbyn. Ch. of Kennett Square, Pa., 1981-84, elder, 1988-91, asst. clk. of session, 1989-91, co-chmn. personnel com., 1989-90, chmn. personnel com., 1990-91; v.p. Presbyn. Women's Assn., Kennett Square, 1983-85; dressmaker, Mendenhall, Pa., 1984-94. Mem. Winterthur (Del.) Guild, 1990, 91; alumna rep. for student recruitment Albright Coll., Reading, Pa., 1990, 91; mem. membership com. Westminster Presbyn. Ch., Wilmington, Del., 1991, 92, food svc. chmn., 1993, Communion com., 1994, co-chmn. Circle, 1994. Mem. AAUW (mem. scholarship com. Wilmington, Del. chpt. 1980, 81), Phi Upsilon Omicron. Republican. Home: PO Box 4 Mendenhall PA 19357-0004

LEE, YEU-TSU MARGARET, surgeon, educator; b. Xian, Shensi, China, Mar. 18, 1936; m. Thomas V. Lee, Dec. 29, 1962 (div. 1987); 1 child, Maxwell M. AB in Microbiology, U. S.D., 1957; MD, Harvard U., 1961. Cert. Am. Bd. Surgery. Assoc. prof. surgery Med. Sch., U. So. Calif., L.A., 1973-83; commd. lt. col. U.S. Army Med. Corps, 1983, advanced through grades to col., 1989; chief surg. oncology Tripler Army Med. Ctr., Honolulu, 1983—; assoc. clin. prof. surgery Med. Sch., U. Hawaii, Honolulu, 1984-92, clin. prof. surgery, 1992—. Author: Malignant Lymphoma, 1974; author chpts to books; contbr. articles to profl. jours. Pres. Orgn. Chinese-Am. Women, L.A., 1981; active U.S.-China Friendship Assn., 1991—. Recipient Chinese-Am. Engrs. and Scis. Assn., 1987; named Sci. Woman Warrior, Asian-Pacific Womens Network, 1983. Mem. ACS, Soc. Surg. Oncology, Assn. Women Surgeons. Office: Tripler Army Med Ctr Dept Surgery Honolulu HI 96859

LEEBER, SHARON CORGAN, art consultant; b. St. Johns, Mich., Oct. 1, 1940; d. Michael Henry and Virginia Eileen (Robinson) Corgan; children: Mark, Tracy, Greg. Student, U. Wyo., 1958-61; BFA in Sculpture, Am. U., 1961; MFA in Sculpture, U. Colo., 1962, postgrad., 1970-72. Instr. sculpture El Centro Coll., Dallas, 1971-77, instr. and developer dept. photography, 1977-81; instr. sculpture U. Tex., Dallas, 1976-77; pres. Archtl. Arts Co., Dallas, 1980—; ptnr. Art Assets, a N.Y. Corp., 1993—; lectr. Nat. Campus Planning Symposium, Baylor U., Waco, Tex., 1982, Am. Soc. Landscape Architects, Tex., 1983, 84, Nat. Soc. Campus and Univ. Planners, New Orleans, 1982, Wash. State Arts Alliance Forum, Seattle, 1985, Les Femmes du Monde, Dallas, 1988, West Palm Beach Devel. Seminar, 1990, Architects and Landscape Architects, Johannesburg, South Africa, 1990, Wyo. Econ. Devel. Sesion, Denver, 1990, Young Pres. Assn., Pasadena, Calif., Urban Land Inst., Boston, 1993, Nucleo Radio Mill, 1993; curator/juror a traveling exhbn. of The Contemporary Artists of Mont. for 1993—; curator Ted Waddell and a Few Friends, 1994—; reviewer Nat. Grad. Fellow, 1987; curator/co-curator various mus. shows. Author: Selecting and Acquiring Art for Your Development Project, 1987; one-woman shows include Barnwell Art Ctr., Shreveport, La.; permanent collections include Dallas Mus. Fine Arts, Barnwell Art Ctr., Shreveport, La., Del Mar Coll., Corpus Christi, Tex., Incarnate Word Coll., San Antonio, U. Tex., Dallas, U. Tex., Arlington, Brookhaven Coll., Dallas, Renaissance Ctr., Detroit, Arlington (Tex.) City Libr., Internat. Sculpture Park, Liberty Hill, Tex.; contbr. articles to profl. jours. Curriculum advisor Dallas Magnet Sch. Sys., 1975; bd. dirs. Program for Talented and Gifted Children, Dallas, 1978-79, Tex. Sculpture Symposium, 1984-85, also fundraising chmn., City of Dallas Parks and Recreation/The Bathhouse Cultural Ctr., 1984-85, Florentine Art Found., 1985-86; membership com. Internat. Women's Forum, 1992-93, global com., 1993-94; mem. adv. com. Dallas Pub. Art, 1992-94; mem. small scale devel. coun. Urban Land Inst., 1985-92; active Dallas Forum, 1991—, others. Mem. Dallas Women's Forum (membership com. 1994), Internat. Women's Forum (global com. co-chmn. 1993-94, spring retreat art tour presentation 1993, membership com. 1992-92).

LEEDER, ELLEN LISMORE, language, literature educator, literary critic; b. Vedado, Havana, Cuba, July 8, 1931; came to U.S., 1959; d. Thomas and Josefina (Jorge) Lismore; m. Robert Henry Leeder, Dec. 20, 1957; 1 child, Thomas Henry. Doctora en Pedagogía, U. Havana, Cuba, 1955; MA, U. Miami, 1966, PhD, 1973. Lang. tchr. St. George's Sch., Havana, 1952-59; from part-time instr. to full prof. Spanish Barry U., Miami Shores, Fla., 1960-75, prof. Spanish, 1975—, chmn. dept. for lang., 1975-76, coord. of Fgn. Lang., 1976-89; dir. Spanish immersion program, 1986-88; part-time prof. Miami-Dade C.C., 1974-75; vis. prof. U. of Madrid, 1982; prof. Forspor Program Studies Abroad, 1989, 90; cons. HEH, 1981-83; judge Assiacion Criticos y Comentariastas del Arte, Miami, 1985—; judge Silver Knight Awards, 1979-83; oral examiner juror Dade County Pub. Schs., Miami, 1986-87. Author: El Desarraigo en Las Novelas de Angel Maria de Lera, 1978, Justo Sierra y el Mar, 1979, Dimension Existencial en la Narrativa de Lera, 1992. Bd. dirs. Vis. Nurse Assn., 1978-80. Mem. MLA, South Atlantic MLA, Am. Coun. Teaching Fgn. Langs., Am. Assn. Tchrs. Spanish and Portuguese (pres. 1978-84, v.p. 1984-87), Fla. Fgn. Assn., Circulo de Cultura Panamericano, Assn. Internat. Hispanistas, Assn. Cubana de Plojeres Universitarias (orricer), Cuban Women Assn., Phi Alpha Theta, Kappa Delta Pi, Sigma DXelta Pi, Alpha Mu Gamma, Coral Gables Country Club. Home: 830 SW 101st Ave Miami FL 33174-2836 Office: Barry Univ 11300 NE 2nd Ave Miami FL 33161-6628

LEEDS, ELIZABETH LOUISE, miniature collectibles executive; b. L.A., July 24, 1925; d. Charles Furnival and Etta Louise (Jackson) Mayes; m. Walter Albert Leeds, Jan. 20, 1973 (dec.); children: Pam Ravey Lewis, Linda Ravey McCallam, Diane Ravey Lathrop, Tom Ravey. Student pub. sch., Prescott, Ariz. Lic. real estate agt., Ariz., cert. motel mgr. Real estate agt., Prescott, Ariz., 1962-64; sec. to mgr. Kon Tiki Hotel, Phoenix, 1964-65; draftsman Goleta Water Dist., Calif., 1965-68; asst. to vp research and design House of Mosaics, Santa Barbara, Calif., 1968-69; exec. chmn. poster design, dept. music U. Calif.-Santa Barbara, 1969-74; v.p. Colorform West, Inc., Santa Barbara, 1974-75; pres. Leeds Miniatures, Inc., Lincoln City, Oreg., 1975-86, Leed's Co., Inc., 1989—; cert. instr. Technologies for Creating, DMA, Inc., 1986—; lamp and silk screen designer Colorform West, Inc.; ind. assoc. The Environ. Network. Illustrator: Just A Story by Gustav Coenod, 1964. Active Global Vols., 1993, Oceanic Soc. Expeditions, 1993. Mem. Hobby Industry Am., Miniatures Industry Assn. Am., Nat. Assn. Female Execs., Eugene C. of C., Eugene Bus. and Profl. Women (cert. practitioner neuro-linguistic programming, trainer values realization). Republican. Clubs: Assn. Humanistic Psychology, Internat. New Thought Alliance, Assn. Transpersonal Psychology. Home: 2290 Arthur Ct Eugene OR 97405-1525

LEEDS, NANCY BRECKER, sculptor, lyricist; b. N.Y.C., Dec. 22, 1924; d. Louis Julius and Dorothy (Faggen) Brecker; m. Richard Henry Leeds, May 9, 1945; children: Douglas Brecker, Constance Leeds Bennett. Grad. Pine Manor Jr. Coll., 1942-44. Pres. Roseland Ballroom, N.Y.C., 1977-81. One-woman shows: Andrew Crispo Gallery, N.Y.C., 1979, Jeannette McIntyre Gallery Fine Arts, Palm Springs, Calif., 1987-88; exhibited in group shows at Bond Street Gallery, Great Neck, N.Y., Gallery Ranieri, N.Y.C., 1978, Country Art Gallery, 1984, Nature Conservatory Show, Country Art Gallery, 1985, Bonwit Teller, Manhasset, N.Y., 1985, Jeanette C. McIntyre Gallery, Palm Springs, Calif., 1987, The Empire Collection, N.Y.C., 1988, 89, Nassau County Mus. of Art, 1992; permanent collections include New Orleans Mus. of Art. Writer lyrics for musical Great Scot, 1965, score for Scrooge Musical Theatre of Ariz., 1989; lyricist for popular music. Trustee The Floating Hosp., N.Y.C., 1975—, v.p. Mem. ASCAP, The Dramatist Guild, The Songwriters Guild. Avocations: tennis; skiing.

LEEDS, ROBIN LEIGH, transportation executive; b. Athens, Ohio, Jan. 4, 1942; d. Clarence Thomas and Jean B. (Foster) Flowers; m. John A Cornwell, Oct. 28, 1957 (div. Jan. 1968); children: Michael John, Brian Arthur; m. Barry H. Leeds, Apr. 20, 1968; children: Brett Ashley, Leslie Robin. BS in Edn., Ohio U., 1967. Cultural arts dir. Regional Sch. Dist. # 10, Burlington, Conn., 1978-81; exec. dir. Conn. Sch. Transp. Assn., West Hartford, Conn., 1982—; exec. sec. N.E. Sch. Transp. Safety Inst., West Hartford, 1987—; chmn. Conn. Sch. Transp. Safety Commn., 1990—; state del. Nat. Standards Congress, Warrensburg, 1990, 95; mem. Gov.'s Motor Carrier Adv. Com., Conn., 1989—, Dept. Motor Vehicles Safety Task Force, Conn., 1991—. Mem. adv. bd. Sch. Transp. News, 1994—. Chmn. gifted edn. task force, Regional Sch. Dist., 1976-78. Named Contractor of Yr., Sch. Bus Fleet Mag., 1990, Exec. of Yr., Conn. Soc. Assn. Execs., 1993. Mem. Nat. Sch. Transp. Assn., Nat. Assn. Pupil Transp., Nat. Safety Coun., Conn. Soc. Assn. Execs. (Assn. Exec. of Yr. award). Home: 133 Jerome Ave Burlington CT 06013-2433 Office: Conn Sch Transp Assn 630 Oakwood Ave Ste 406 West Hartford CT 06110-1505

LEEDY, EMILY L. FOSTER (MRS. WILLIAM N. LEEDY), retired education educator, consultant; b. Jackson, Ohio, Sept. 24, 1921; d. Raymond S. and Grace (Garrett) Foster; MEd, Ohio U., 1957; postgrad. Ohio State U., 1956, Mich. State U., 1958-59, Case Western Res. U., 1963-65; m. William N. Leedy, Jan. 1, 1943; 1 son. Dwight A. tchr. Frankfort (Ohio) schs., 1941-46, Ross County Schs., Chillicothe, Ohio, 1948-53; elem. and supervising tchr. Chillicothe City Schs., 1953-56; dean of girls, secondary tchr. Berea City Schs., 1956-57; vis. tchr. Parma City Schs., 1957-59; counselor Homewood-Flossmoor High Sch., Flossmoor, Ill., 1959-60; teaching fellow Ohio U., 1960-62; asst. prof. edn., 1962-64; assoc. prof., counselor Cuyahoga Community Coll., 1964-66; dean of women Cleve. State U., 1966-67, assoc. dean student affairs, 1967-69; guidance dir. Cathedral Latin Sch., 1969-71; dir. women's service div. Ohio Bur. Employment Svcs., 1971-83; cons. in edn., 1983-87. Mem. adv. com. S.W. Community Info. Svc., 1959-60; youth com. S.W. YWCA, 1963-70, chmn., 1964-70, bd. mgmt., 1964-70; group svcs. coun. Cleve. Welfare Fedn., 1964-66; chmn. Met. YWCA Youth Program study com., 1966, bd. dirs., 1966-72, v.p., 1967-68; chmn. adv. coun. Ohio State U. Sch. Home Econs., 1977-80, chmn., 1978-80. Named Cleve. area Woman of Achievement, 1969; named to Ohio Women's Hall of Fame, 1979, Chillicothe Ross Women's Hall of Fame, 1988; recipient Outstanding Contbn. special award Nat. Assn. Commns. for Women, 1983, Meritorious Svc. award Nat. Assn. Women Deans, Adminstrs. and Counselors, 1984. Mem. AAUW, Am., Northeastern Ohio (sec. 1958-59, exec. com. 1963-64, pub. rel. chmn. 1962-64, newsletter chmn., editor 1963-64, del. nat. assembly 1959-63) personnel and guidance assns., LWV, Am. Assn. Retired Persons (Ohio women's initiative spokesperson 1987-89, state legis. com. 1989-90, AARP/VOTE state coord. Ohio 1990-94), Nat. Assn. Women Deans and Counselors (publs. com. 1967-69, profl. employment practices com. 1980-82, Meritorious Svc. award 1984), Ohio (program chmn. 1967, editor Newsletter 1968-71), Cleve. Counselors Assn. (pres. 1966), Zonta Internat. (exec. bd. 1968-70, treas. 1970-72, chmn. dist. V Status of Women 1980-81), Nat. Assn. Commns. for Women (dir. 1980-81, sec. 1981-83), Rio Grande Coll. Alumni Assn. (Atwood Achievement award 1975), Bus. and Profl. Women's Club (Nike award 1973), Ohio Retired Tchrs. Assn., Svc. Corps of Retired Execs. Delta Kappa Gamma, Women's City Club (Cleve.). Home: 580 Lindberg Blvd Berea OH 44017-1418 Office: 699 Rocky Rd Chillicothe OH 45601

LEE-LAMPSHIRE, WENDY LYNNE, philosophy educator, writer; b. Colorado Springs, Colo., Oct. 23, 1959; d. Jack Everett and Gloria Francis (Rohrbach) Lee; m. William Allen Orwin, June 17, 1977 (div. Dec. 1980); twins: Nickolaus Allen Orwin, Benjimin Scott Orwin; m. Douglas Eugene Lee-Lampshire, Dec. 28, 1981; children: Lindsay Andrei, Carley Aurora. BA, U. Colo., 1986; PhD, Marquette U., 1992. Lab. tech. Descret Pharm., Salt Lake City, 1977-79; student advisor U. Colo., Colorado Springs, 1983-84; rsch. asst. Marquette U., Milw., 1987-88, teaching asst., 1988-91, teaching fellow, 1991-92; asst. prof. philosophy Bloomsburg (Pa.) U., 1992—; presenter in field. Book reviewer, cons.; contbr. articles to profl. jours. Recipient grant Marquette U., 1987-88, 88, 88-91, 91-92. Mem. AAUW, Assn. Pa. State Coll. and Univ. Faculty, Am. Philos. Assn., Soc. for Analytic Feminism, Ea. Soc. Women in Philosophy, Ea. Pa. Philos. Assn., Bloomsburg/Lycoming Philosophy Consortium, Commn. on Status of Women Bloomsburg. Home: 2936 Whitebirch Ln Bloomsburg PA 17815 Office: Bloomsburg Univ Dept Philosophy 219 Bakeless Ctr Bloomsburg PA 17815

LEEMAN, SUSAN EPSTEIN, neuroscientist, educator; b. Chgo., May 9, 1930; d. Samuel and Dora (Gubernikoff) Epstein; m. Cavin Leeman (div.); children: Eve, Raphael, Jennifer. BA, Goucher Coll., 1951; MA, Radcliffe Coll., 1954, PhD, 1958; DS (hon.), SUNY, Utica, 1992; hon. degree, Goucher Coll., 1993. Instr. Harvard Med. Sch., Boston, 1958-59; postdoctoral fellow Brandieis U., Waltham, Mass., 1959-62, 62-66, rsch. assoc., adj. ast. prof., asst. rsch. prof., 1966-68, 68-71; asst. prof. Harvard Med. Sch., 1972-73, assoc. prof., 1973-80; prof. U. Mass. Med. Ctr., Worcester, 1980-92, dir. interdept. neurosci. program, 1984-92; prof. Boston U. Sch. Medicine, 1992—. Recipient Burroughs Wellcome Vis. Professorship award U. Ky., 1992, Women's Excellence in Scis. award Fedn. Am. Socs. for Exptl. Biology, 1993, Fred Conrad Koch award 1994. Mem. NAS (197th Lilly lectr. 1994, Fred Conrad Koch award 1994). Office: Boston U Sch Medicine Dept Pharmacology 80 E Concord St Boston MA 02118

LEEPER, KATHIE ALICE, speech communication educator; b. Sioux Rapids, Iowa, Jan. 28, 1944; d. Delford Allen and Dorothy A. (Krusenstjerna) Benson; m. Michael G. Webster, June 10, 1967 (div. 1986); children: Byron G. Webster, Daniel Q. Webster, Matthew B. Webster, Kirstin S. Webster; m. Roy V. Leeper, July 14, 1987. BS, Iowa State U., 1966; PhD in Exptl. Pub. Addr., Ind. U., 1974. Instr. Our Lady of the Lake Coll., San Antonio, 1969; instr. Incarnate World Coll., San Antonio, 1971-74, asst. prof., 1974-76; asst. prof. N.W. Mo. State U., Maryville, 1976-80, assoc. prof., 1980-84, prof., 1984—; cons. New Eng. Bur. Systems, Maryville, 1990-91; presenter profl. confs. Reviewer: Introduction to Speech (William J. Seiler), 1988, Communicating in Small Groups, 3d edit. (Steven A. Beebe and John T. Masterson), 1990. Pub. info. officer Am. Cancer Soc., Maryville, 1988—, chairperson communication com. Mo. divsn., 1992—. Recipient Gaspar award Am. Cancer Soc., Atlanta, 1990, 91, Communications Day grant Mo. Com. for Humanities, 1985. Mem. AAUW (pres. 1986-88), Internat. Comm. Assn., Pub. Rels. Soc. Am., Internat. Pub. Rels. Assn., Assn. for Edn. in Mass Comm., Ctrl. States Comm. Assn., Speech Comm. Assn. Methodist. Home: 161 White Ridge Dr Maryville MO 64468-1142 Office: NW Mo State U Dept Speech 148 Wls Maryville MO 64468

LEET, MILDRED ROBBINS, corporate executive, consultant; b. N.Y.C., Aug. 9, 1922; d. Samuel Milton and Isabella (Zeitz) Elowsky; m. Louis J. Robbins, Feb. 23, 1941 (dec. 1970); children: Jane, Aileen; m. Glen Leet, Aug. 9, 1974. BA, NYU, 1942; LHD (hon.), Coll. Human Svcs., 1988; LLD honoris causa, Marymount Coll., Tarrytown, N.Y., 1991; HHD, Lynn U., 1993; D Humanitarian Svc. (hon.), Norwich U., 1994. Pres. women's div. United Cerebral Palsy, N.Y.C., 1951-52; bd. dirs. United Cerebral Palsy, 1953-55; rep. Nat. Coun. Women U.S. at UN, 1957-64, 1st v.p., 1959-64, pres., 1964-68, hon. pres., 1968-70; sec., v.p. conf. group U.S. Nat. Orgns. at UN, 1961-64, 76-78, vice chmn., sec., 1962-64, mem. exec. com., 1961-65, 75—, chmn. hospitality info. svc., 1960-66; vice chmn. exec. com. NGO's UN Office Public Info., 1976-78, chmn. ann. conf., 1977; chmn. com. on water, desertification, habitat and environment Conf. NGO's with consultative status with UN/ECOSOC, 1976—; mem. exec. com. Internat. Coun. Women, 1960-73, v.p., 1970-73; chmn. program planning com., women's com. OEO, 1967-72; chmn. com. on natural disasters N.Am. Com. on Environment, 1973-77; N.Y. State chmn. UN Day, 1975; ptnr. Leet & Leet (cons. women in devel.), 1978—; co-founder Trickle Up Program, 1979—, co-pres., 1991—. Contbr. articles to profl. jours.; editor UN Calendar & Digest, 1959-64, Measure of Mankind, 1963; editorial bd.: Peace & Change. Co-chmn. Vols. for Stevenson, N.Y.C., 1956; vice chmn. task force Nat. Dem. Com., 1969-72; commr. N.Y. State Commn. on Powers Local Govt., 1970-73; chmn. Coll. for Human Svcs., 1985—; former mem. bd. dirs. Am. Arbitration Assn., New Directions, Inst. for Mediation and Conflict Resolution, Spirit of Stockholm; bd. dirs. Hotline Internat.; v.p. Save the Children Fedn., 1986-93; rep. Internat. Peace Acad. at UN, 1974-77, Internat. Soc. Community Devel., 1977—; del. at large 1st Nat. Women's Conf., Houston, 1977; chmn. task force on internat. interdependence N.Y. State Women's Meeting, 1977; mem. Task Force on Poverty, 1977—; chmn. Task Force on Women, Sci. and Tech. for Devel., 1978; U.S. del. UN Status of Women Commn., 1978, UN Conf. Sci. and Tech. for Devel., 1979, co-dir. Trickle Up Program, Inc, 1979—; Brazzaville Centennial Celebration, 1980; mem. global adv. bd. Internat. Expn. Rural Devel., 1981—; mem. Coun. Internat. Fellows U. Bridgeport, 1982-88; trustee overseas edn. fund LWV, 1983-91; v.p. U.S. Com. UN Devel. Fund for Women, 1983—; mem. Nat. Consultative Com. Planning for Nairobi, 1984-85; co-chmn. women in devel. com. Interaction, 1985-91; mem. com. of cooperation Interam. Commn. of Women, 1986; bd. dirs. Nat. Women's Conf. Com., 1986-87; adv. com. Am. Assn. Internat. Aging, 1986-90; mem. Overseas Devel. Bd., 1988—; bd. dirs Internat. Devel. Conf., 1991—. Recipient Crystal award Coll. Human Svcs., 1983, ann. award Inst. Mediation and Conflict Resolution, 1985, Woman of Conscience award Nat. Coun. Women, 1986, Temple award Inst. Noetic Scis., 1987, Presdl. End Hunger award, 1987, Giraffe award Giraffe Project, 1987, Woman of the World award Eng.'s Women Aid, 1989; co-recipient Rose award World Media Inst., 1987, Human Rights award UN Devel. Fund for Women, 1987, (with Glen Leet) Pres.'s medal Marymount Manhattan Coll.,

1988, Leadership award U.S. Peace Corps, Woman of Vision award N.Y.C. NOW, 1990, Matrix award Women in Communications, Inc., Spirit of Enterprise award Rolex Industries, 1990, ann. award Interaction, 1990, citation Pres.'s Bush Ann. Points of Light Award, 1992, Internat. Humanity award ARC Overseas Assn., 1992, Excellence award U.S. Com. for UNIFEM, 1992, Champion of Enterprise award Avon, 1994. Mem. AAAS, Women's Nat. Dem. Club, Women's Forum Inc., Cosmopolitan Club, Princeton Club. Home and Office: 54 Riverside Dr New York NY 10024

LEFCOWITZ, BARBARA FREEDGOOD, English educator, writer; b. N.Y.C., Jan. 15, 1935; children: Marjorie, Eric. BA, Smith Coll., 1956; MA, SUNY, Buffalo, 1964; PhD, U. Md., 1970. Instr. English SUNY, Buffalo, 1962-64, Am. U., Washington, 1965-67; prof. English Anne Arundel C.C., Arnold, Md., 1971—. Author: (poetry books) Shadows and Goatbones, 1992, The Queen of Lost Baggage, 1986, The Wild Piano, 1981, A Risk of Green, 1978, (novel) Red Lies and White Lies, 1994. Writing fellow Nat. Endowment for the Arts, 1984, Rockefeller Found., 1985, Md. Arts Coun., 1986. Jewish. Home: 4989 Battery Ln Bethesda MD 20814-2634 Office: Anne Arundel C C Dept English 101 College Pky Arnold MD 21012-1857

LEFEBVRE, PEGGY ANDERSON, advertising executive; b. Springfield, Mo., Dec. 2, 1951; d. Paul William and Norma Jean (Turk) Anderson; m. Donald E. Lefebvre, July 25, 1980. BA in Graphic Arts cum laude, U. Ill., 1974; MBA, Pacific Western U., 1993. Coord. advt. and trade show Bell & Howell, Salt Lake City, 1971-74; designer, prodn. asst. Sta. KUTV, Salt Lake City, 1974; art dir. Associated Advt., Salt Lake City, 1977-80; owner, creative dir. Lefebvre Advt., Anaheim, Calif., 1980—; freelance designer various advt. agys., Chgo.; bd. dirs. Delmark Corp.; past guest lectr. advt. copywriting and bus. devel. Nat. U., Inc. Mag., Orange Coast Coll. One woman shows Ward Gallery, Chgo., 1974, Atrium Gallery, Salt Lake City, 1976. Past bd. dirs. MADD, Orange County Sexual Assault Network; mem. Anaheim Area Visitor and Conv. Bd., WSAAA. Recipient Excellence in Creative Direction award, Bus. and Profl. Advt. Assn., 1989, Outstanding Achievement in Advt. award Western Assn. Conv. & Visitor Burs. Republican. Office: Lefebvre Advt 1547 E La Palma Ave Anaheim CA 92805-1624

LEFELHOCZ, IRENE HANZAK, nurse, business owner; b. Cleve., Nov. 10, 1926; d. Joseph J. and Gisella Elizabeth (Biro) Hanzak; m. Joseph R. Lefelhocz, Aug. 7, 1948; 1 child, Joseph R. III. RN, St. Luke's Hosp. Sch. Nursing, 1948; BSN, Case Western Res. U., 1963; MEd, John Carroll U., 1971. RN, Ohio, Ala. Pres., mgr. The Joseph House, Gadsen, Ala.; adminstrv. cons. The Episcopal Kyle Home, Gadsen; nurse cons. Ala. Dept. Health, Montgomery, Ala.; supr. Holy Name of Jesus Hosp., Gadsden; nurse cons., pres., dir. Physician Choice Vis. Nurse Agy.; counselor Sch. Nursing, Holy Name of Jesus Med. Ctr. Mem. allocations com. United Way, Etowah County; active numerous other community orgns.; bd. dirs., vice chmn. Etowah County chpt. ARC. Mem. NEA, Ohio Edn. Assn., ARC (past pres.). Home: 173 Lake Shore Dr Gadsden AL 35906-8570 Office: Physician Choice Home Care Svc Inc 173 Lakeshore Dr Gadsden AL 35906

LEFEVRE, PATRICIA LOUISE LUKOMSKI, psychiatric social worker; b. Detroit, Sept. 3, 1944; d. Leo Edward and Louise Nettie (Gajewski) Lukomski; m. Robert Leo LeFevre (dec.); children: September Louise, Danielle Leanne. BS, Mich. State U.; MSW, U. Mich. Psychiat. social worker Hawaii Dept. Pub. Health, Wahiawa; supr. State of Mich., Detroit; psychotherapist Inst. for Human Potential, Huntington Beach, Calif.; clin. social worker U. Calif.-Irvine Med. Ctr., Martin Meml. Hosp., Stuart, Fla.; psychotherapist Indian River Community Mental Health Ctr., Stuart; psychiat. social worker S.C. Dept. Corrections, Greenville, U.S. Dept. Vets. Affairs, McAllen, Tex.; currently assoc. regional mgr. U.S. Dept. Vets. Affairs, Providence, R.I. Fundraising organizer YMCA, Huntington Beach, Sct. Kjaeld's Kapel, Viborg, Denmark. Mem. NASW (bd. advisors), Am. Assn. Orthopsychiatry.

LEFF, ILENE J(OAN), management consultant, corporate and government executive,; b. N.Y.C., Mar. 29, 1942; d. Abraham and Rose (Levy) L.; BA cum laude, U. Pa., 1964; MA with honors, Columbia U., 1969. Statis. analyst McKinsey & Co., N.Y.C., 1969-70, rsch. cons., 1971-74, mgmt. cons., N.Y.C. and Europe, 1974-78; dir. exec. resources Revlon, Inc., N.Y.C., 1978-81, dir. human resources, 1981-83, dir. personnel, 1983-86; cons. APM Inc., 1986-88, ind. mgmt. cons., 1988-93, 95—; dep. asst. sec. for mgmt. HUD, Washington, 1993-94; rsch. asst. U. Pa., Phila., 1964-65; employment counselor State of N.J., Newark, 1965-66; tchr., Newark, 1966-69; lectr. Grad. Program in Pub. Policy, New Sch. for Social Rsch., Wharton Sch., Duke U.; chmn. com. on employment and unemployment, mem. exec. com. Bus. Rsch. Adv. Coun., U.S. Bur. Labor Stats., 1980; sr. del. econ. rels. and trade Sino-U.S. Conf., 1986. Ops. coun. Jr. Achievement Greater N.Y., 1975-78; cons. Com. for Econ. Devel., N.Y. Hosp., Regional Plan Assn., Am. Cancer Soc.; vol. for dep. mayor for ops. N.Y.C., 1977-78. Mem. N.Y. Human Resource Planners (treas. 1984), Fin. Women's Assn. N.Y. (exec. bd., 1977-78, 83-84), The Fashion Group (treas. 1989). Contbr. issue papers and program recommendations to candidates for U.S. Pres., U.S. Senate and Congress, N.Y. State Gov., mayor N.Y.C.

LEFF, SANDRA H., gallery director, consultant; b. N.Y.C., Dec. 24, 1939; d. I. Bernard and Rose (Kupfer) L. BA, Cornell U., 1960; MA, Inst. Fine Arts, N.Y.C., 1969. Editorial asst. Indsl. Design Mag., N.Y.C., 1960-61; instr., asst. Mus. of City of N.Y., 1962-65; assoc. print dept. Sotheby Parke Bernet, N.Y.C., 1969-73; rsch. asst. Daniel Chester French Exhibit, Washington, 1975-77; dir. Am. painting Graham Gallery, N.Y.C., 1977-93. Author: (exhbn. catalogs) Thomas Anshutz: Paintings, Watercolors and Pastels, 1979, Guy Pène du Bois: Painter, Draftsman and Critic, 1979, Helen Torr, 1980, John White Alexander: Fin-de-Siècle American, 1980, Jan Matulka & Vaclav Vytlacil, 1992. Ford Found. fellow, 1967. Mem. Phi Beta Kappa.

LEFFEL, PAULA MARIE, school financial aid administrator; b. Columbus, Ohio, Mar. 12, 1959; d. Paul Edward and Pauline (Draculich) L. B in Acctg. and Bus. Adminstrn., Otterbein Coll., Westerville, Ohio, 1984. Bookkeeper Brown Labs., Columbus, 1977-78; acctg. mgr. Chemlawn Corp., Columbus, 1978-85; owner restaurant All Am. Hero, Columbus, 1985-90; fin. aid dir. Churchman Bus. Sch., Easton, Pa., 1990—; scuba diving instr.; medic first aid instr. Pub. notary Franklin County Ct., Columbus, 1979-87; mem. Drivers Alert Network, Minn., 1988—; mem. PADI, Santa Ana, Calif., 1987—; v.p. Lehigh Valley Crimestoppers (v.p. 1991—); active Mini Trails dist. Boy Scouts Am., 1991-93. Recipient Gold medal Nat. Tae Kwon Do Assn., 1988. Mem. Nat. Assn. Fin. Aid Adminstrs., Ea. Assn. Fin. Aid Adminstrs., Pa. Assn. Fin. Aid Adminstrs., Lehigh Valley Fin. Aid Adminstrs., Easton Kiwanis (bd. dirs. 1990-93). Home: 2609 Liberty St Easton PA 18042-2618 Office: Churchman Bus Sch 355 Spring Garden St Easton PA 18042-3532

LEFFLER, CAROLE ELIZABETH, mental health nurse, women's health nurse; b. Sidney, Ohio, Feb. 18, 1942; d. August B. and Delores K. Aselage; children: Veronica, Christopher. ADN, Sinclair Community Coll., Dayton, Ohio, 1975. Cert. psychiat. nurse coord. Nurse Grandview Hosp, Dayton, 1961-76; substitute sch. nurse Fairborn (Ohio) City Schs., 1981-82; dir. nursing Fairborn Nursing Home, 1983; psychiat. nurse coord. Dayton Mental Health Ctr., 1984—; mem. exec. bd. 1199. Vol., instr., disaster health nurse ARC; officer, leader, camp nurse for Girl Scouts, Boy Scouts; Ch. Parish Coun. Recipient Fleur de Lis award Girl and Boy Scouts, Svc. award ARC, Fairborn Mayors Cert. Merit for civic pride, Ohio Govs. award Through Innovation. Mem. ANA, Ohio Nurses Assn. Home: 29 W Bonomo Dr Fairborn OH 45324-3407

LEFFLER, PAULA ZAGARIS, real estate developer; b. Modesto, Calif., Sept. 18, 1956; d. Paul Mike and Liberty (Grillos) Zagaris; m. Duke Thomas Leffler, Sept. 29, 1979; children: Libby, Duke, Hilary. BA, U. Calif., Berkeley, 1978; MBA, Calif. State U., Stanislaus, 1987. Cert. property mgr., gen. bldg. and engring. contractor; lic. real estate broker. V.p. Steven Paul Zagaris Devel. Co. Inc., Modesto, 1979-82; v.p., CFO Paul M. Zagaris Realtor, Inc., Modesto, 1982-86; pres. Liberty Property Mgmt., Modesto, 1987—; bd. dirs. Direct Line Techs., Modesto. Bd. dirs. BRAVO! Repertoire Dance Theatre, Modesto, 1987, 88. Mem. Nat. Assn. Realtors, Inst. Real Estate Mgmt., Calif. Assn. Realtors, Modesto Bd. Realtors, Omega Nu (treas. 1991, 92, bd. dirs. 1992). Republican. Greek Orthodox. Office: Liberty Property Mgmt Ste 102 1230 E Orangeburg Ave Modesto CA 95350

LEFKOW, JOAN HUMPHREY, judge; b. Kans., Jan. 9, 1944; d. Otis L. and Donna Grace (Glenn) Humphrey; m. Michael F. Lefkow, June 21, 1975; children: Maria Aithne, Helena Claiborne, Laura Bethany, Margaret Frances. AB, Wheaton Coll., 1965; JD, Northwestern U., 1971. Bar: Ill. 1971, U.S. Dist. Ct. (no. dist.) Ill. 1972, U.S. Ct. Appeals (7th cir.) 1972, U.S. Ct. Appeals (5th cir.) 1980. Law clerk to Hon. Thomas E. Fairchild U.S. Ct. Appeals (7th cir.), 1971-72; atty. Lega Assistance Found. Chgo., 1972-75; adminstrv. law judge Ill. Fair Employment Practices Commn., 1975-77, chief adminstrv. law judge, 1977-79; instr. sch. law U. Miami, Fla., 1980-81; exec. dir. Cook County Legal Assistence Found., 1981-82; now magustrate judge U.S. Dist. Ct. (no. dist.) Ill. Editor Northwestern U. Law Rev. Active PTA. Mem. Chgo. Bar Assn. (legal aid com. 1982), Chgo. Coun. Lawyers (gov. bd. 1975-77), 7th Cir. Bar Assn. Episcopalian. Office: Everett McKinley Dirksen Bldg 219 S Dearborn St Rm 2402 Chicago IL 60604*

LEFKOWITS, MARJORIE DEE, motion picture advertising writer/producer; b. New Brunswick, N.J., Oct. 1, 1949; d. Stuart Jacob and Elaine (Rashkind) L. BA cum laude, U. Mich., 1971. Copywriter Andrew Curcio Advt., Boston, 1972-74; mgr. promotion and publicity Sta. WSBK-TV, Boston, 1974-76; writer/producer Sta. WJZ-TV, ABC, Balt., 1976-77, HBO, Inc., N.Y.C., 1978-79; creative dir. HBO/Cinemax, N.Y.C., 1980-84; ind. writer/producer TV advt. L.A. and N.Y.C., 1984-90; creative dir. Craig Murray Prodns., Burbank, Calif., 1990-91. Accounts include Schindler's List, Jurassic Park, Beauty and the Beast. Mem. Am. Lupus Soc., Lupus Found. Am., 1992—. Recipient awards Internat. Film and TV Festival N.Y., N.Y.C., 1981, 82, 83, award Broadcasters Design Assn., 1982, Clio award, N.Y.C., 1984, Key Art award Hollywood Reporter, L.A., 1993, Key Art, 1994. Mem. Women in Film. Home and Office: 1433 Barry Ave # 101 Los Angeles CA 90025

LEFKOWITZ, ROSE FRANCES, medical records administrator, educator, author; b. Detroit, July 24, 1954; d. Charles and Miriam (Pollack) L.; m. Harold Greenberger, Nov. 6, 1983; children: David Jay, Susan Erica. BA cum laude, Bklyn. Coll., 1975; BS cum laude, Downstate Med. Ctr., 1977; M in Pub. Adminstrn., NYU, 1981, postgrad., 1987—. Dir. med. records sect., Trafalgar Hosp., N.Y.C., 1977-78; asst. dir. med. records sect., Maimonides Med. Ctr., Bklyn., 1978-80; instr. Downstate Med. Ctr. SUNY, Bklyn., 1981-83, asst. prof. Downstate Med. Ctr., 1983—; cons. Jr. Coll. Health Sci., Daejeon, Republic of Korea, 1983-85, St. Mary's Hosp., Bklyn., 1984-86, Mary Immaculate Hosp., Queens, N.Y., 1984-86, Woodhull Med. Ctr., Bklyn., 1986—, Parkway Hosp., Queens, 1986—; bd. dirs. Bklyn. Hospice Program; mem. clin. preceptors com. Downstate Med. Ctr., 1978—, mem. adv. com., 1981—, clin. site coordinator, 1982—; preceptor Borough of Manhattan Community Coll. Med. Record Tech. Program, 1977-80, Downstate Med. Ctr.-SUNY Med. Record Adminstrn. Program, 1978-80. Author: (with I. Topor) Comparative Health Recordkeeping Systems in Health Care Facilities, 1989; producer videotape presentation Examination Before Trial: Guide for Health Care Professionals, 1987; contbr. articles to profl. jours. Mem. numerous SUNY governing coms., 1981-87. Mem. Am. Soc. of Law and Medicine (mem. speaker's bur. 1986—), Health Care Fin. Mgmt. Assn., Nat. Assn. Female Execs., Am. Med. Record Assn., Med. Record Assn. of N.Y. State (mem. speaker's bur. 1986—, mem. cons.'s listing 1986—, mem. edn. com. 1986, coding arbitration subcom. 1985-86, pub. relations com. 1982-83), Greater N.Y. Med. Record Assn. (bd. dirs., exec. council 1982—, chmn. publicity com. 1982-83, editor newsletter 1984-85, subcom. on edn. Bklyn. and S.I. chpt. 1986-87, editor jour. 1984-87, scholarship and ednl. fund com. 1986), Met. N.Y. Tumor Registrars Assn. (v.p. 1986-87, co-dir. edn. com.). Office: Health Scis Ctr 450 Clarkson Ave Box 105 Brooklyn NY 11203

LEFLER, LISA JANE, anthropologist and social sciences educator; b. Gastonia, N.C., Jan. 21, 1959; d. Buddy Allen and Jean (Nations) L. AA in Liberal Arts, Montreat-Anderson Coll., 1979; BA in Psychology, Appalachian State U., 1981; MA in Edn., Western Carolina U., 1988, EDS, 1991; postgrad., U. Tenn. Instr. social scis. Southwestern C.C., Sylva, N.C., 1988-93, Haywood C.C., Clyde, N.C., 1990—; instr. history Western Carolina U., Cullowhee, N.C., 1989, 93, vis. instr. anthropology Dept. Continuing Edn., 1990, instr. dept. anthropology, continuing edn. instr., 1990—, instr. regional history, 1990—, lectr. new beginning program, 1989-92, instr. anthropology, 1991—; also counselor asst. upward bound program Western Carolina U., 1989, lectr. new beginning program, 1989-92; chem. dependency curriculum writer, grant writer, lectr. Unity Regional Treatment Ctr./Indian Health Svc., Cherokee, N.C., 1990, 93—; mem. subcom. Project Healthy Cherokee. Chair Mountain Heritage Ctr. Mus. Vols.; former bd. dirs. Catch the Spirit of Appalachia, Inc. Tennis scholar Montreat-Anderson Coll., 1977-79. Mem. Am. Anthrop. Assn., Southeastern Anthrop. Soc., Appalachian Studies Assn. Mem. Worldwide Ch. of God. Home: Rt 1 Box 204C Whittier NC 28789

LEFLEY, HARRIET PHILLIPS, psychologist, educator; b. Boston, Mar. 21, 1924; d. Frederick and Bella (Schapira) Phillips; m. John A. Lefley, Mar. 16, 1958; children: Keith, Carla. BA, Roosevelt U., 1964, MA, 1967; PhD, U. Miami, 1973. Lic. psychologist, Fla. Resident cons. in social rsch. Govt. of the Bahamas, 1967-70; dir. U. Miami (Fla.)/Jackson Meml. Cmty. Mental Health Ctr., 1974; asst. prof. dept. psychiatry and anthropology U. Miami, 1977-88, assoc. prof. psychiatry Sch. Medicine, 1980-85, prof. psychiatry and behavioral sci. Sch. Medicine, 1985—; assoc. dir., dir. rsch. and evaluation New Horizons Cmty. Mental Health Ctr., Miami, 1977-88; dir. Cross Cultural Tng. Inst. for Mental Health Profls., Miami, 1979-82; cons. St. Luke's Drug Abuse Program, Miami, 1985-86; program evaluator Miccosukee Tribe of Fla., 1973-76; cons., trainer Ministry of Labour and Welfare and Ministry of Edn., Govt. of Bahamas, 1970-72; founder, mem. exec. com. Fla. Alliance for Mentally Ill, 1985—; mem. adv. bd. Fla. Mental Health Inst., Tampa, Fla., 1985—; bd. dirs. Fla. Protection and Advocacy Ctr., Tallahassee, Fla. Author, editor: Cross-Cultural Training for Mental Health Professionals, 1986, Families of the Mentally Ill: Coping and Adaptation, 1987, Familes as Allies in Treatment of the Mentally Ill, 1990, Clinical Training for Serious Mental Illness, 1990, Helping Families Cope With Mental Illness, 1994; author: Surviving Mental Illness, 1993; contbr. over 100 articles to profl. jours., chpts. to books. Chair curriculum and tng. Nat. Alliance for the Mentally Ill., Arlington, Va., 1981-88; co-chair blue ribbon jury Mental Health Assn. Miami, 1982-83. Mary Switzer scholar Nat. Rehab. Assn., 1988; recipient Disting. Contbn. award Dade County Psychol. Assn., 1987, honor award Miami Commn. on Status of Women, 1989-90, Steven V. Logan award for Outstanding Psychologist, Nat. Alliance for Mentally Ill, 1992. Mem. APA (co-chmn. task force on clin. tng. 1992—, Spl. Achievement award 1992), Soc. for Cross-Cultural Rsch. (exec. com., rep. for psychol. scis. 1978-80), Am. Psychiat. Assn. (cons., com. on chronic mental illness 1986—, nat. com. on state systems 1990 and cmty. psychiatry 1990—, nat. com. on homelessness 1993—), Am. Assn. Cmty. Psychiatrists (hon.), Internat. Coun. Psychologists, World Assn. for Psychosocial Rehab., Internat. Assn. Cross-Cultural Psychology. Home: 5841 SW 63d Ct Miami FL 33143 Office: U Miami Sch Medicine Dept Psychiatry PO Box 016960 Miami FL 33101

LEFLY, DIANNE LOUISE, research psychologist; b. Denver, July 17, 1946; d. Gordon Eugene Boen and Elizabeth (Welsh) Tuveson. AB, U. No. Colo., 1968; MA, U. Colo., 1980; PhD, U. Denver, 1994. Classroom tchr. Adam County Sch. Dist. #12, Thornton, Colo., 1968-77; rschr. John F. Kennedy Child Devel. Ctr., Denver, 1979-81, U. Colo. Health Scis. Ctr., 1981-89, U. Denver, 1989—; cons. Colo. State Dept. Edn., Denver, 1993—. Contbr. articles to profl. jours. Mem. Colo. Rep. Party, Denver, 1968—. Scholarship U. No. Colo., 1964-68; fellowship U. Denver, 1989. Mem. Am. Ednl. Rsch. Assn., Mensa. Republican. Home: 8650 W 79th Ave Arvada CO 80005-4321 Office: U Denver 2155 S Race St Denver CO 80210-4633

LEGER, LINDA SUE, transportation company executive; b. Cin., Mar. 4, 1951; d. Walter and Allie Marie (Steele) Osborne; m. Dennis Ray Leger, May 29, 1969 (div. Sept. 1991); 1 child, Russell. BS Edn. in Chemistry/Math., Cumberland Coll., 1973. Lab. technician Am. Enka, Clemson, S.C., 1973-76, shift chemist, supr., 1976-78; wastewater treatment plant operator City Utilities Commn., Corbin, Ky., 1978-81; environ. specialist CSX Transp., Inc., Corbin, 1981-90; environ. mgr. CSX Transp., Inc., Huntington, W.Va., 1990—; indsl. rep. Wastewater Operators Cert. Bd., Frankfort, Ky., 1982-90. Baptist. Office: CSX Transp PO Box 5840 Huntington WV 25703-0840

LEGER, PAMELA DENISE, secondary education educator; b. Ft. Lee, Va., Aug. 20, 1966; d. Daniel Joseph and Donna (Regan) L.; m. Darryl Mark Morgan, July 8, 1989 (div.); children: Tybor Mark, MeLani Suzette. BS, La. Tech. U., 1988. Summer sch. tchr. Lincoln Parish, Ruston, La., 1988; geometry/algebra tchr. Springhill (La.) High Sch., 1988-89; algebra and 8th grade tchr. East Beauregard Sch., Drycreek, La., 1990; tchr. math., chair dept. Fairview Sch., Grant, La., 1990-94; gifted math. tchr. Fairview Sch./Elizabeth Sch., Grant, 1994—. Tchr. Ruston Cath. Ch., 1985-86. Named High Sch. Math. Tchr. of Yr., Fairview Sch., 1992; Fairview H.S. Tchr. of Yr., 1993. Mem. ASCD, Math. Assn. Am., Assn. of Profl. Educators of La., Nat. Coun. Tchrs. Math., La. Assn. Tchrs. Math. Roman Catholic.

LEGG, HAROLYN LEE, librarian; b. Crawley, W.Va., Aug. 17, 1955; d. Harold Lee and Emma Irene (Miller) L. BS in Edn., Bowling Green State U., 1976, MEd, 1980, postgrad., 1990-91. Cert. 7-12 English tchr., K-12 ednl. media, Ohio. Dist. libr. Liberty-Benton High Sch., Findlay, Ohio, 1977—. Contbr. articles to profl. jours.; book reviewer The Book Report, 1982—. Recipient Cable in Classroom award Continental Cablevision, 1992. Mem. ALA, Ohio Ednl Libr. Media Assn. (co-chmn. intellectual freedom dept. 1988-91, chmn. 1992-93, Social Issues Resource Series Intellectual Freedom award 1987), Hancock County Librs. Assn. (chmn. 1985—), Nat. Coun. Tchrs. English, ASCD. Democrat. Methodist. Home: 1715 Southshore Dr Findlay OH 45840 Office: Liberty-Benton High Sch 9050 State Rt 12 W Findlay OH 45840

LEGGE, JEAN MARY, secondary school educator; b. Jamestown, N.D., Apr. 26, 1951; d. Alvin Joseph and Caroline Lucille (Peters) Steckler; m. Edwin H. Hassler, Dec. 1976 (div. Dec. 1985); children: Jennifer, Zachary, Erin; m. Lewis J. Legge, Jan 15, 1988. BS in Edn., Valley City (N.D.) State U., 1987. Legal sec. Bruce Britton Law Office, Jamestown, 1973-74; bookkeeper, vol. coord. South Ctrl. Mental Health, Jamestown, 1974-75; high sch. sci. tchr. Kathryn (N.D.) Pub. Sch., 1987-89, Marion (N.D.) Pub. Sch., 1989—; mem. breeding bird survey U.S. Fish & Wildlife, Valley City, 1988—, vol. neotropical migrant bird census on Arrowwood Nat. Wildlife Refuge, 1994; outdoor skills workshop facilitator N.D. Game & Fish Dept., Bismarck, 1992—; HIV/AIDS workshop facilitator N.D. Dept. Pub. Instrn., Bismarck, 1991—; sci. educator, panelist insvc. Valley City State U., 1989—; reviewer Nat. Sci. Edn. Standards, 1995. Author curriculum material to use newspapers in class. Coach 4-H Wildlife Judging Team-Barnes County, Valley City, 1989; com. chair camp registratsion Barnes County Wildlife Fedn., Valley City, 1991—, com. chair poster contest, 1993. Recipient 1st pl. N.D. Wildlife Judging Team - 4H, 1989, Commendation U.S. Dept. Army C.E., Mpls., 1992; named N.D. Outstanding Biology Tchr. Nat. Assn. Biology Tchrs., 1992. Mem. NSTA, N.D. Sci. Tchrs. Assn., N.D. Orienteering Alliance (sec. 1993—), Marion Edn. Assn. (v.p. 1990, sec. 1993, pres. 1994), N.D. Birding Soc., Am. Birding Assn., Barnes County Wildlife Fedn., Shevenne Valley Natural Sci. Soc., Water Edn. Tchrs. (curriculum field tchr. 1994). Home: 3212 115th Ave SE Valley City ND 58072-9492

LEGGETT, NANCY PORTER, university executive assistant; b. Greenville, N.C., Aug. 14, 1952; d. Earl Lindeburgh and Louise (Adams) Porter; m. Ted Clayton Johnston, Nov. 19, 1971 (div. Dec. 1979); 1 child, Clayton Porter; m. Donald Yates Leggett, Aug. 17, 1980. Student, East Carolina U., 1971-73, Pitt C.C., Greenville, 1975-76. Sec./coord. grad. ext. and tchr. edn. programs Divsn. Continuing Edn., East Carolina U., Greenville, 1971-80; sect. sec. ambulatory pediatrics Sch. Medicine, East Carolina U., Greenville, 1981-83; adminstrv. sec. to chmn. dept. pediatrics Esat Carolina U., Greenville, 1983-94; exec. asst. to chmn. dept. pediatrics Sch. Medicine, East Carolina U., Greenville, 1994—, resource person dept. pediatrics, 1984-94; mem. benefits com. East Carolina U. Mem. Cmty. Appearance Commn., City of Greenville, 1990—; mem. com. N.C. Symphony, Greenville, 1988-89; mem. Greenville Mus. Art, 1980-92; mem./steering com. Children's Miracle Network Telethon, Greenville, 1986-90; vol. Friends of the Children's Hosp. of Greenville, 1986-88; mem. Nat. Scleroderma Found., 1987-88; mem. Hist. Hope Found., Windsor, N.C., 1980—; bd. dirs. Rose High Sch. Acad. Boosters, 1994—. Recipient Bus. Edn. Award for shorthand East Carolina U., 1971, Outstanding Young Women of Am. award, 1981. Mem. Greenville Country Club, Kiwanis (charter mem., bd. dirs. 1990-91). Baptist. Home: 110 Kimberley Dr Greenville NC 27858 Office: East Carolina Univ Sch of Medicine Dept Pediatrics Greenville NC 27858

LEGGITT, MITZI LEE, business manager; b. Denver, Jan. 19, 1968; d. Edward Jerome and Helen Darlene (Fullenwider) Powszukiewicz; m. Scotty Walter Leggitt, Sept. 5, 1992; children: Megan Marie, Brenna Lee. Student, Pikes Peak C.C., 1989-90; Associates degree, Blair Jr. Coll. Mem. audit personnel Thimgan & Assocs., Inc., Lakewood, Colo., 1991-93; road clk., sec. Saguache County Road Dept., Saguache, Colo., 1991-92; data entry tech. Fremont County Sheriff's Dept., Canon City, Colo., 1992-93; quality assurance/quality control tech. Environ. Chem., Del Norte, Colo., 1993-94; office mgr. Creede (Colo.) C. of C., 1994—; owner, operator Creede Western Wear, 1992-94; owner, trainer, handler Red Rock Chows, 1987—. Phys. therapist Acts 19:11 Sertoma, Black Forest, Colo., 1989-90; notary pub., 1989—; Rep. candidate Mineral County clk./recorder, Creede, 1994. Baptist. Home: PO Box 382 Creede CO 81130

LEGINGTON, GLORIA R., middle school educator. BS, Tex. So. U, Houston, 1967; MS, U. So. Calif., L.A., 1973. Cert. adminstr. (life). Tchr., mentor L.A. Unified Sch. Dist., 1991-93; grade level chair L.A. Unified Schs., 1975-78, faculty chairperson, 1978, 80, 84, Black history/Martin Luther King program chair, 1978, 80, 83, 86, 88, 90-92, social chair, bus coord., svc. club sponsor, 1978-80, Indian edn. chair, 1980-84, opportunity chair, 1976-78, grade level chair, 1984; Black edn. commn. liaison, 1989-90, impact tchr., 1991-92, human rels. sponsor, 1991-92, coun. Black adminstrs.-student conf. facilitator, 1992, tchr. inservice classes for area colloqium, parents, tchrs., faculty shared decision making coun., 1993-94, mem. faculty senate, 1992-93, mem. shared decision-making coun., 1993-94, mem. sch. improvement, 1993-94, mem. discipline com., 1993-94. Chair United Way, 1988, 90; sponsor, 8th Grade, 1994-95. Mem. NEA, Internat. Reading Assn., United Tchrs. L.A., Calif. League of Mid. Schs., Delta Epsilon.

LEGUE, LAURA ELIZABETH, resort and recreational facility executive; b. Towanda, Pa., Oct. 11, 1954; d. William Frederick and Frances Lorraine (Cease) Goeckel; m. Stephen Wheeler, Nov. 9, 1974 (div. June 1989); m. Brian E. Legue, Mar. 17, 1990. AA, Mt. Ida Jr. Coll., Newton Ctr., Mass., 1974. Lic. community assn. mgr. Gen. mgr. Towanda Motel & Restaurant, Inc., 1974-82; mgr. Wilson's Suede & Leather, Lawrenceville, N.J., 1982-83; front office mgr. Park Shore Resort Hotel, Naples, Fla., 1985-87; property mgr. World Tennis Ctr. and Resort, Naples, 1987—; pres. World Tennis Club, Inc., Naples, 1991—; notary pub. State of Fla., 1987—. Mem. Collier County Hotel Assn. (sec. 1988, v.p. 1989). Office: World Tennis Ctr. 4800 Airport Rd Naples FL 33942

LE GUIN, URSULA KROEBER, author; b. Berkeley, Calif., Oct. 21, 1929; d. Alfred Louis and Theodora (Kracaw) Kroeber; m. Charles A. Le Guin, Dec. 22, 1953; children: Elisabeth, Caroline, Theodore. B.A., Radcliffe Coll., 1951; M.A., Columbia, 1952. Vis. lectr. or writer in residence numerous workshops and univs., U.S. and abroad. Author: Rocannon's World, 1966, Planet of Exile, 1967, City of Illusion, 1967, A Wizard of Earthsea, 1968, The Left Hand of Darkness, 1969, The Tombs of Atuan, 1971, The Lathe of Heaven, 1971, The Farthest Shore, 1972, The Dispossessed, 1974, The Wind's Twelve Quarters, 1975, A Very Long Way from Anywhere Else, 1976, Orsinian Tales, 1976, The Language of the Night, 1978, Leese Webster, 1979, Malafrena, 1979, The Beginning Place, 1980, Hard Words, 1981, The Eye of the Heron, 1981, The Compass Rose, 1982, King Dog, 1985, Always Coming Home, 1985, Buffalo Gals, 1987, Wild Oats and Fireweed, 1988, A Visit from Dr. Katz, 1988, Catwings, 1988, Solomon Leviathan, 1989, Fire and Stone, 1989, Catwings Return, 1989, Dancing at the Edge of the World, 1989, Tehanu, 1990, Searoad, 1991, Blue Moon Over Thurman Street, 1993, Wonderful Alexander and the Catwings, 1994, Going Out With Peacocks, 1994, A Fisherman of the Inland Sea, 1994;

also numerous short stories, poems, criticism, screenplays. Recipient Howard D. Vursell award, Am. Acad. of Arts and Letters, 1991, Pushcart prize, 1991, Boston Globe-Hornbook award for excellence in juvenile fiction, 1968, Nebula award (novel) 1969, (novel and story) 1975, (novel) 1990, (story) 1975, Hugo award (novel) 1969, (story) 1973, (novella) 1973, (novelette) 1988, Gandalf award 1979, Kafka award, 1986, Newbery honor medal, 1971, Nat. Book award 1973; Fulbright fellow, France, 1953-54. Mem. Sci. Fiction Research Assn., Sci. Fiction Writers Assn., Authors League, PEN, Writers Guild West, NOW, NARAL, Phi Beta Kappa. Office: c/o Virginia Kidd PO Box 278 Milford PA 18337-0278 also: c/o Matthew Bialer William Morris Agy 1350 Ave of the Americas New York NY 10019

LEHMAN, BARBARA ALBU, foreign language educator, translator; b. Vineland, N.J., July 7, 1950; d. Kurt Gunther and Ruth (Landau) Albu; divorced; children: David, Kara. BA, Douglass Coll., 1972; MS, Rutgers U., 1983; degree in Holocaust Edn. (hon.), Hebrew U., Jerusalem, 1994. Cert. educator French and German. French/German lang. educator Mount Olive Township Schs., Flanders, N.J., 1973-81; French lang. educator Upper Freehold Schs., Allentown, N.J., 1984—; translator Internat. Congress on Glass, Albuquerque, 1980, Hamburg, Germany, 1983; travel guide EF Tours, Europe, 1984—. Vice-chmn. Somerset County Commn. on Women, Somerville, N.J., 1985—. Meml. scholar Lihn Family, 1968, Grauel scholar Brookdale Holocaust Studies, 1994. Mem. Kappa Delta Pi. Home: 107 Ridgeview Dr Belle Mead NJ 08502

LEHMAN, BARBARA ALICE, language arts educator; b. Newton, Kans., May 16, 1952; d. Frederick Stauffer and Millie Elizabeth (Page) B.; m. Daniel Wayne Lahman, Aug. 15, 1971; 1 child, Hadley Frances. Student, Ea. Mennonite Coll., 1972; BS in Elem. Edn., George Mason U., 1974; MA in Early Childhood/Elem. Edn., NYU, 1978; EdD in Curriculum and Instrn., U. Va., 1986. Kindergarten aide Falls Church (Va.) Pub. Sch., 1974-75; elem. tchr. Arlington (Va.) Pub. Schs., 1975-77, Charlottesville (Va.) City Schs., 1982-83; tchr. Spence Sch., N.Y.C., 1978-82; grad. instr. U. Va., Charlottesville, 1983-86; asst. prof. Ohio State U., Mansfield, 1986-92, assoc. prof. children's lit., lang. arts, reading, 1992—; cons. Children's Lit. Inst., U. Va., 1990, 91; mem. editorial adv. bd. Reading Tchr., Newark, Del., 1993—, Nat. Reading Conf. Yearbook, 1990-91. Contbr. articles to profl. publs. Bd. dirs. Children's Theater Found., Mansfield, 1988—. Dean's fellow Curry Sch. Edn., U. Va., 1985-86; grantee Curry Sch. Edn., 1986, Ctr. for Teaching Excellence, Ohio State U., 1987. Mem. Internat. Reading Assn. (chair Arbuthnot award com. 1994—, past pres. Children's Lit. and Reading Spl. Interest Group 1993-94), Nat. Coun. Tchrs. English, Children's Lit. Assn., Nat. Reading Conf., U.S. Bd. on Books for Young People, Phi Delta Kappa. Democrat. Mennonite. Office: Ohio State U Mansfield Campus 1680 University Dr Mansfield OH 44906-1547

LEHMAN, DEANA DURON, college program administrator; b. Vernon, Tex., Sept. 3, 1956; d. Roy Dean and Ilanon Grason (Turner) Wright; m. Mark L. Lehman, Aug. 23, 1980; children: Weston Mark, Roy Edward. BA, Tex. Tech U., 1979, MA in French, 1980; MA in English, Midwestern State U., Wichita Falls, Tex., 1986. Dir. devel. studies Vernon Regional Jr. Coll., 1989-91, spl. svcs. coord., 1991—; grant writing cons. Coach, Boys Club Basketball Team, Vernon, 1992—. Mem. AAUW, Com. of Practitioners. Lutheran. Office: Vernon Regional Jr Coll 4400 College Dr Vernon TX 76384-4005

LEHMAN, LOIS JOAN, medical librarian; b. Danville, Pa., Apr. 25, 1932; d. Harold M. and Leona (Shuey) L. B.A., Pa. State U., University Park, 1954; M.S., Columbia U., 1959. Librarian Lankenau Hosp., Phila., 1959-66; reference librarian Sch. Medicine, U. Pa., Phila., 1966-68; asst. librarian head pub. services Coll. Medicine, Pa. State U., Hershey, 1968-71, acting librarian, 1971-72, librarian, 1972—. Mem. Med. Libr. Assn., Assn. Acad. Health Scis. Libr. Dirs., Health Scis. Librs. Consortium (bd. dirs.), Interlibr. Delivery Svc. of Pa. (bd. dirs.), Quentin Riding Club. Office: Pa State U Coll Medicine George T Harrell Libr The Hershey Med Ctr Hershey PA 17033

LEHMANN, ESTHER STRAUSS, investment company executive; b. Binghamton, N.Y., Apr. 19, 1944; d. Julius and Betty (Lind) Strauss; m. Aaron Lehmann, Feb. 27, 1966; children: Shanna, Shira, Marc, David. BS, Cornell U., 1966; cert. in vol. and non-profit orgn. mgmt., U. Conn., 1976; cert. employee benefits specialist, U. Pa., 1983. V.p. Fairway Mgmt., West Hartford, Conn., 1976-80; investment exec. Herzfeld & Stern, Paramus, N.J., 1980-86; assoc. v.p. Gruntal & Co., Inc., Ft. Lee, 1988—. Home: 1632 Dover Ct Teaneck NJ 07666-2965

LEHMANN, KATE, television producer; b. Rolla, Mo., May 20, 1956; d. Ernest Karl and Sarah Ann (Willius) L. BA, Smith Coll., 1978; MA, Coll. of St. Catherine, 1991. Prodn. mgr. Sta. KTCA-TV, St. Paul, 1979-88; mng. dir. Film in The Cities, St. Paul, 1988-90; dir. prodn. ITVS, St. Paul, 1991-92; owner Lehmann Prodn. Svcs., Mpls., 1992—; cons. Pub. Radio Internat., Mpls., 1994; bd. dirs. Film in The Cities, St. Paul. Mem. Assn. Ind. Video and Film, Ind. Feature Project. Home and Office: Lehmann Prodn Svcs 3317 Garfield S Minneapolis MN 55408

LEHMANN-CARSSOW, NANCY BETH, educator, coach; b. Kingsville, Tex., Sept. 9, 1949; d. Valgene William and Ella Mae (Zajicek) Lehmann; m. William Benton Carssow, Jr., Aug. 1, 1981. BS, U. Tex., 1971, MA, 1979. Freelance photographer, Austin, Tex., 1971—; geography tchr., tennis coach Austin Ind. Sch. Dist., Tex., 1974—; salesperson, mgr. What's Going On Clothing, Austin, 1972-78; area adminstr. Am. Inst. Fgn. Study, Austin, 1974-81; area rep. World Encounters, Austin, 1981—, tour guide, Egypt, Kenya, 1977, 79, 81, 87, 92; participant 1st summer inst. Nat. Geog. Soc., Washington, 1986; tchr. Leader for People in Soviet Union, 1989, 90; vol. First Internat. Environ. Exposition to Antarctica. Author curriculum materials; photographer (book) Bobwhites, 1984. Recipient Merit award Nat. Coun. Geog. Edn., 1975, Creative Teaching award Austin Assn. Tchrs., 1978; Fulbright scholar, Israel, 1983; recipient study grant to Malaysia & Indonesia, 1990. Mem. NEA, Nat. Coun. Social Studies, Nat. Coun. Geog. Edn., East African Wildlife, Earthwatch (participant archaeol. dig. in Swaziland 1984), World Wildlife Fund, Rotary, Delta Kappa Gamma (pres. 1986-88), Phi Kappa Phi. Democrat. Roman Catholic. Avocations: stained glass, photography, tennis, gardening, needlepoint. Home: 1025 Quail Park Dr Austin TX 78758-6749 Office: Lanier High Sch 1201 Peyton Gin Rd Austin TX 78758-6699

LEHMKUHL, MARGIE MAE, family practice nurse; b. Falls City, Nebr., Aug. 21, 1950; d. Arthur E. and Dora W. (Harper) Jimeson; m. Ronald Joseph Lehmkuhl, June 1, 1968; children: Darcie G., Joseph B. AA with honors, Johnson County C.C., Overland Park, Kans., 1977; BSN with highest distinction, U. Kans., Kansas City, 1979. RN, Kans., Mo. Pediatric and float nurse Humana Hosp., Overland Park, 1979-81, unit mgr., 1981-85; utilization rev. coord. Blue Cross/Blue Shield, Kansas City, Mo., 1985-86; joint venture liaison Blue Cross/Blue Shield and Managed Healthcare Resources, Kansas City, Mo., 1986-87; continuing care provider Managed Healthcare Resources, Overland Park, 1987-88; nursing supr. Hickman Mills Clinic, Kansas City, Mo., 1988-91; asst. adminstr., clin. Hickman Mills Clinic, Kans. City, Mo., 1991-92; dir. occupational health Vis. Nurse Assn. Greater Kansas City, 1993—. V.p. Kans. State Sigma Phi Epsilon Mothers Club, 1992-94; mem. ways and means com. Shawnee Mission West Booster Club, 1983-91; coord. Holy Trinity Religious Edn. Pre-sch., Lenexa, Kans., 1975, 76, instr., 1973-75, bd. dirs., 1975-76. Arthur S. and Leora J. Peck scholar, 1977; Allstate Found. nursing scholar, 1977. Mem. ANA, Kans. State Nurses Assn., U. Kans. Nursing Alumni Assn. (Alumni award 1979), Assn. Occupational Health Nurses, Sigma Theta Tau, Phi Kappa Phi. Home: 14912 W 89th St Lenexa KS 66215 Office: Vis Nurse Assn Corp 527 W 39th St Kansas City MO 64111

LEHR, BARBARA AUGUSTA, sales executive; b. New Haven, July 1, 1924; d. Frederick Lincoln and Julia Elizabeth (Mattson) L. Student, Vassar Coll., 1941-43; BS in Religious Edn., NYU, 1964. Comml. mgr. Sta. WBIB-FM, New Haven, 1943-45; record librarian OWI, N.Y.C., 1945-47; with CBS, N.Y.C., 1947-49, R.H. Donnelley, N.Y.C., 1949-86; sales rep. for AM commls. Sta. WMCA-AM, N.Y.C., 1987—; freelance writer N.Y.C., 1987-94. Lay mem. to ann. conf. N.Y.C. Meth. Ch., 1978-86; mem. Marble Collegiate Ch. Mem. Telephone Pioneers Am., Order Eastern Star. Republican. Home: 7 Stuyvesant Oval Apt 1H New York NY 10009-1902

LEHR, SUZANNE, guidance counselor; b. Bicknell, Ind., Dec. 22, 1939; d. Lewis Albert and Dorothy Lucille (Roberts) Staker; m. James A. Lehr, May 29, 1982; children: Rebecca Lynne Bowlin, Rhett Lyndal Bowlin. AA, Stephens Coll., 1959; BA, U. Evansville, 1962; MS in Edn., N.W. Mo. State U., 1986. Cert. biology tchr., counselor, Mo. Sec. A&H Truck Line, Evansville, Ind., 1957-60; supr. product info. Mead Johnson & Co., Evansville, 1962; tchr. Ctrl. High Sch., Tulsa, 1963-65, Chas. W. Eliot Jr. High Sch., Cleve., 1965-66, St. Veronica Elem. Sch., Milw., 1967, Muskego (Wis.) High Sch., 1967-68; tchr. Savannah (Mo.) Jr. High Sch., 1976-84, counselor, 1984-89; counselor Bode Middle Sch., St. Joseph, Mo., 1989—; instr., facilitator Active Parenting, St. Joseph, 1993-94; adj. instr. N.W. Mo. State U., Maryville, 1985—. Contbr. articles and revs. to profl. jours. Named one of Twenty Who Count St. Joseph News-Press, 1993, Outstanding Young Women Am., 1972; recipient Outstanding Counselor award Mo. Sch. Counselor Assn., 1992-93. Mem. Mo. Peer Helpers Assn. (treas. 1988-93), N.W. Mo. Sch. Counselor Assn. (sec.-treas., v.p., pres. 1988-92, Middle Sch. Counselor of Yr. 1991), Mo. State Tchrs. Assn., PEO (pres. 1990-92), Delta Kappa Gamma, Phi Delta Kappa. Baptist. Home: 2502 Gene Field Rd Saint Joseph MO 64506

LEHRMAN, MARGARET MCBRIDE, news executive, producer; b. Spokane, Wash., Sept. 25, 1944; d. John P. and Ruth A. (Score) McBride; m. Michael Lloyd Lehrman, June 27, 1970. BA, U. Oreg., 1966; MS, Columbia U., 1970. Dir. coll. desk Peace Corps, Washington, 1966-69; asst. to exec. editor The Morning News Co., Washington, 1970-72; reporter Albright Communications, Washington, 1973-74; tv assignment editor ABC News, Washington, 1974; press asst. Senator Robert P. Griffin, Washington, 1975-79; researcher Today Show, NBC News, Washington, 1979, assoc. producer, 1979-83, Washington producer, 1983-89, dep. bur. chief, 1989—. Trustee U. Oreg. Found., 1990—. Recipient George Hood award for diplomatic reporting (China) adv. bd. Internat. Women's Media Found. Office: NBC News 4001 Nebraska Ave NW Washington DC 20016-2795

LEHTINEN, MERJA HELEN, journalist, researcher, publisher; b. N.Y., Feb. 25, 1954; d. Osmo Ilmari and Hilkka Annikki (Kokkonen-Lind) L. AB in American Studies, Mount Holyoke, 1976; student, Dartmouth, 1975; cert. in Finnish and Scandinavian, U. Helsinki, 1978. Assoc. tech. writer The Travelers Ins. Co., Hartford, 1976-78; mng. editor Am. Soc. Heating, Refrigerating and Air Conditioning Engrs., N.Y., 1979-81; internat. editor Am. Soc. Civil Engrs., N.Y., 1981-83; dir. publs. Am. Assn. Engring., N.Y., 1983-84; mng. editor Bill Comms., Inc., N.Y., 1984; news editor McGraw Hill Co., N.Y., 1984-85; exec. editor Mng. Automation Mag., N.Y., 1986-87; editor-in-chief, publisher Indsl. Computing Mag. Kruger, McCarthy & Lehtinen, N.Y., 1987-93; pres. Westisle Pub. Co., Westford, Mass., 1993; owner, pub. Discover Connecticut Magazine and The Connecticut Chronicles, 1993—; intern for Sen. Strom Thurmond U.S. Senate, Washington, 1973; dir. career guidance Am. Assn. Engring. Scis., N.Y., 1983-84; commr. Econ. Devel. Commn. of Colchester, Conn., 1992—, hearing officer, 1994—; bd. dirs. Indsl. Computing Soc., Rsch. Triangle Park, N.C., 1993—. Author (book) Quality Control, 1977 (recipient award of excellence Soc. Tech. Comms., 1977); contbr. articles to profl. jours. and mags. Vice chmn. Rep. Town Com., 1993—; Rep. candidate for nomination to U.S. Congress 2d dist., 1992. Recipient rsch. fellow Rep. National Com., Washington, 1975. Mem. Instrument Soc. Am., Indsl. Computing Soc. (founder, mem. bd. dirs. 1993-95). Republican.

LEIBOVITZ, ANNIE, photographer; b. Conn., Oct. 2, 1949. Student, San Francisco Art Inst. Chief photographer Rolling Stone, from 1973, photographer, 1970-83; photographer Vanity Fair, 1983—; photographer for advertisements, 1987—; proprietor Ann Leibovitz Studio, N.Y.C. Works exhibited various galleries; author: Photographs 1970-90, 1992. Recipient Innovation in Photography award Am. Soc. Mag. Photographers, 1987. Office: Annie Leibovitz Studio 55 Vandam St New York NY 10013-1104 also: Annie Leibovitz Studio 101 W 18th St New York NY 10011*

LEIBOVITZ, BARBARA LYNN, filmmaker, television producer; b. Ft. Worth, Oct. 12, 1960; d. Samuel and Marilyn Edith (Heit) L. BA, U. Miami, 1982. Broadcast assoc. CBS News/48 Hours, N.Y.C., 1987-89; rschr. Today-Nine Network, Sydney, Australia, 1990; freelance prodr. Entertainment Tonight, Washington, 1990-91, E! Entertainment TV, L.A., 1991, VH-1, L.A., 1993-95; prodr., dir. Leibovitz Projects, L.A., 1992—. Roy Webster Dean award Studio Film & Tape, 1993. Mem. Internat. Documentary Assn., Women in Film, Ind. Feature Project. Democrat. Jewish.

LEIBOW, LOIS MAY, educator; b. Newark, Jan. 4, 1937; d. Samuel and Sada (Rothman) Applebaum; m. Sheldon G. Leibow, Aug. 11, 1963; children: Philip, Frances, Brian. BA, Douglass Coll., 1959; MA in Sociology, CCNY, 1962. Substitute tchr. Monmouth County Registry, N.J., 1983—; telemarketer Target Teleconcepts, Inc., Hazlet, N.J., 1991—, Prudential Ins. Co., Red Bnnk, N.J., 1991—. Newspaper columnist Atlanticville, Long Branch, N.J., 1984—; contbr. Am. String Tchr., 1979. Mem. Hadassah (life, program v.p. Woodbridge, N.J. chpt. 1972-74), Sisterhood of Temple Beth El (bd. dirs.), Jewish War Vets., Woman's Club Perth Amboy N.J. Republican. Office: Target Teleconcepts Village Ct Hazlet NJ 07730

LEIBOWITZ, ANN GALPERIN, lawyer; b. Balt., Oct. 11, 1940; d. Harold Marcy and Dorothy Rebecca (Trivas) Galperin; m. Howard Marvin Leibowitz, July 3, 1960; children: Ellen Ann, Katherine Leibowitz Kotkin. AB, Goucher Coll., 1960; LLB, U. Md., 1964. Bar: Mass. 1964, U.S. Ct. Appeals (1st cir.) 1984. Patent agt. W.R. Grace & Co., Clarksville, Md., 1960-63; patent atty. Polaroid Corp., Cambridge, Mass., 1963-72, corporate atty., 1972-77, sr. corporate atty. and labor counsel, 1977—; lectr. Coun. Edn. in Mgmt., Walnut Creek, Calif., 1987—; mem. faculty Mass. Continuing Legal Edn., Boston, 1991—. Bd. trustees Goucher Coll., Towson, Md., 1983-89; chmn. fin. com. Town of Weston, 1989-91, active, 1984-91, chmn. bd. selectmen, 1993—, active, 1991—; mem. exec. adv. bd. Ctr. House, Boston, 1990—. Mem. ABA, Am. Corporate Counsel Assn. (bd. dirs. N.E. chpt. 1988-91), Mass. Bar Assn. (lectr. 1987—), Boston Bar Assn., Indsl. Rels. Rsch. Assn. Office: Polaroid Corp 575 Technology Sq Cambridge MA 02139

LEIGH, BARBARA ANNE, child therapist; b. Chgo., Jan. 4, 1966; d. William Hunt and Elizabeth Anne (Sicher) L. BA, Hollins Coll., 1987; MS in Edn., Ind. U., 1989. Lic. profl. counselor and therapist, Oreg. Archeologist Mus. of London, 1979; intern Ill. Dept. Edn., Springfield, 1982; page Ill. Ho. of Reps., Springfield, 1982; admissions hostess Hollins Coll., Roanoke, Va., 1984-87; therapist Ctr. for Human Devel., John Day, Oreg., 1989-91; child therapist Family Friends, Grants Pass, Oreg., 1991-93, supr., 1993—; train attendant Amtrak, Chgo., 1984-89; news reporter, staff therapist, announcer, D.J. Stas. KAJO, KLDR, Grants Pass, 1993—; cons. in field. Contbr. articles to profl. jours. Rep. Children and Youth Svcs. Com., John Day, 1990-91; vol. Rogue AIDS Awareness Network, Grants Pass. Mem. APA (assoc.), ACA, Omicron Delta Kappa, Psi Chi (pres. 1986), Pi Lambda Theta. Office: Family Friends 322 NW F St Grants Pass OR 97526

LEIGH, JENNIFER JASON (JENNIFER LEIGH MORROW), actress; b. L.A., Feb. 5, 1962; d. Barbara Turner and Vic Morrow. Student, Lee Strasberg Inst. Appearances include (films) Eyes of a Stranger, 1980, Fast Times at Ridgemont High, 1982, Wrong is Right, 1982, Easy Money, 1983, Grandview U.S.A., 1984, Flesh + Blood, 1985, The Hitcher, 1986, The Men's Club, 1986, Sister, Sister, 1987, Under Cover, 1987, Heart of Midnight, 1988, The Big Picture, 1989, Last Exit to Brooklyn, 1989, Miami Blues, 1990, Crooked Hearts, 1991, Backdraft, 1991, Rush, 1992, Single White Female, 1992, Short Cuts, 1993, The Hudsucker Proxy, 1994, Mrs. Parker and the Vicious Circle, 1994, Dolores Claiborne, 1994; (TV movies) Angel City, 1980, The Killing of Randy Webster, 1981, The Best Little Girl in the World, 1981, The First Time, 1982, Girls of the White Orchid, 1983, Buried Alive, 1990. Office: ICM 8899 Beverly Blvd West Hollywood CA 90048-2412 also: care Elaine Rich 2400 Whitman Pl Los Angeles CA 90068*

LEIGH, LINDA DIANE, psychologist, clinical neuropsychologist; b. Miami, Fla., June 12, 1946; Lic. psychologist, Fla. BA, Brown U., 1977; MA, Mich. State U., 1984, PhD, 1987. Lic. psychologist, Conn., Fla., Mich. Postdoctoral fellow Fairfield Hills Hosp., Newtown, Conn., 1988-89; clin. neuropsychologist Datahr Rehab. Inst., Brookfield, Conn., 1989-90; pvt. practice psychologist East Lansing, Mich., 1990-92; pvt. practice Ft. Myers, Fla., 1992—; cons. neuropsychologist Tamarack, Inc., Sparrow Hosp., East Lansing, 1992; mem. staff Lee Meml. Hosp., Charter Glade Hosp., Ft. Myers, 1994. Mem. APA, Nat. Acad. Neuropsychologists, Coun. for Nat. Register Health Svc. Providers in Psychology. Democrat. Office: 8192 College Pkwy # 12 Fort Myers FL 33919

LEIGH, SHARI GREER, software consulting firm executive; b. Reading, Pa., Mar. 1, 1959; d. Martin and Francine Rita (Gross) Rothenstein; m. Martin Brad Greer, Dec. 31, 1979; children: Shannon Leigh, Krista Heather. BA in Biochemistry, Wellesley Coll.-MIT, 1980; postgrad. in bus. adminstrn., Colo. State U., 1982-83. Lead thermal engr. Rockwell Internat. Space div., Downey, Calif., 1980-81; systems engr. Martin Marietta Aerospace, Denver, 1981-82, aerospace new bus. analyst, 1982-84; v.p. Miaco Corp. (Micro Automation Cons.), Englewood, Colo., 1984-87, pres., chief exec. officer, 1987—. Co-designer life systems monitor for Sudden Infant Death Syndrome, 1980. Exec. bd. dirs. Mile High chpt. ARC, 1991—. Recipient Recognition award for 500 fastest growing cos. Inc. Mag., 1990, 91, Blue Chip Enterprise award Am.'s Best Small Bus., U.S. C. of C., 1991; named Bus. Leader to Watch in the 90's Corp. Connection; finalist Colo. Small Bus. of the Yr. award C. of C., 1992-93, Person of Yr., U.S. Small Bus. Bus. Adminstrn., South Metro Small Bus. Person of Yr., 1992-93. Mem. Greater Denver Chamber (coun. mem. small bus. bd. 1991-93), So. Met. C. of C. (bd. dirs. 1994—). Office: Miaco Corp 6300 S Syracuse Way Ste 415 Englewood CO 80111-6724

LEIGH, SHERREN, communications executive, editor, publisher; b. Cleve., Dec. 22, 1942; d. Walter Carl Maurushat and Treva Eldora (Burke) Morris; m. Norman J. Hickey Jr., Aug. 23, 1969 (div. 1985). BS, Ohio U., 1965. Communications dir. Metal Lath Assn., Cleve., 1965-67; creative dir. O'Toole Inc., Chgo., 1967-69; sr. v.p. RLC Inc., Chgo., 1969-77; pres. Leigh Communications Inc., Chgo., 1978—; chmn. Today's Chgo. Woman mag., 1982—; pres. Ill. Ambassadors, Chgo., 1985-86; bd. dirs. Chgo. Fin. Exchange, 1985-87. Author: How to Write a Winning Resume, How to Negotiate for Top Dollar, How to Find, Get and Keep the Job You Want. Bd. dirs. Midwest Women's Ctr., Chgo., 1984-86, Girl Scouts Chgo., 1985-87, Black Women's Hall of Fame Found., Chgo., 1986—, Apparel Industry Bd., Chgo., 1988. Recipient Corp. Leadership award YWCA Met. Chgo., 1979, Entrepreneurship award, 1988, Media Advocate of Yr. award U.S. SBA, 1994; named one of 10 Women of Achievement Midwest Women's Ctr., Chgo., 1987, Advt. Woman of Yr. Women's Advt. Club, Chgo., 1988; inducted City of Chgo. Women's Hall of Fame, 1988. Mem. Chgo. Network, Econ. Club Chgo., Execs. Club Chgo., Com. of 200 (founding mem.). Office: Leigh Communications 233 E Ontario St Ste 1300 Chicago IL 60611-3214

LEIGHTON, FRANCES SPATZ, writer, journalist; b. Geauga County, Ohio; m. Kendall King Hoyt, Feb. 1, 1984. Student, Ohio State U. Washington corr. Am. Weekly; corr. and Washington editor This Week Mag.; Washington corr. Met. Group Sunday Mags.; contbg. editor Family Weekly; free-lance journalist Metro Sunday Group, Washington; lectr. summer confs. Dellbrook-Shenandoah Coll., Georgetown U., Washington. Author over 30 books on hist. figures, celebrities, Hollywood, psychiatry, the White House and Capitol Hill, 1957—; (with Louise Pfister) I Married a Psychiatrist, 1961, (with Francois Rysovy) A Treasury of White House Cooking, 1968, (with Frank S. Caprio) How to Avoid a Nervous Breakdown, 1969, (with Mary B. Gallagher) My Life with Jacqueline Kennedy, 1969, (with Traphes Bryant) Dog Days at the White House, 1975, (with William Fishbait Miller) Fishbait—the Memoirs of the Congressional Doorkeeper, 1977, (with Lillian Rogers Parks) My 30 Years Backstairs at the White House (made into TV mini-series), 1979, (with Hugh Carter) Cousin Beedie, Cousin Hot--, My Life with the Carter Family of Plains, Georgia, 1978, (with Jerry Cammarata) The Fun Book of Fatherhood-or How the Animal Kingdom is Helping to Raise the Wild Kids at Our House, 1978, (with Natalie Golos) Coping with Your Allergies, 1979, (with Ken Hoyt) Drunk Before Noon—The Behind the Scenes Story of the Washington Press Corps, 1979, (with Louis Hurst) The Sweetest Little Club in the World, The Memoirs of the Senate Restaurateur, 1980, (with John M. Szostak) In the Footsteps of Pope John Paul II, 1980, (with Lillian Rogers Parks) The Roosevelts, a Family in Turmoil, 1981, (with June Allyson) June Allyson, 1982, (with Beverly Slater) Stranger in My Bed, 1985 (made into TV movie, 1987), (with Oscar Collier) How to Write and Sell Your First Novel, 1986, The Search for the Real Nancy Reagan, 1987, (with Oscar Collier) How To Write and Sell Your First Nonfiction Book, 1990, (with Stephen M. Bauer) At Ease at the White House, 1991; contbr. numerous feature stories on polit., social and govtl. personalities to various publs. Bd. dirs. Nat. Found., from 1963. Recipient Edgar award, 1961. Mem. Senate Periodical Corr. Assn., White House Corr. Assn., Am. News Women's Club, The Writers Club, Nat. Press Club, Writers League of Washington (pres.), Washington League Am. Pen Women (pres.), Smithsonian Assocs., Nat. Trust Historic Preservation, Lake Barcroft Woman's Club, Delta Phi Delta, Sigma Delta Chi. Unitarian. Office: Lake Barcroft 6336 Lakeview Dr Falls Church VA 22041

LEIGHTON, MIRIAM, artist, consultant; b. N.Y.C.; d. Nathan and Rose (Unger) Kaback; m. Bruce Leighton, Feb. 22, 1965 (dec.); children: Elayne Joyce, Jo-Ann Helene. Student, NYU, 1934, 45. Cons. Saks Fifth Ave., N.Y.C., 1954-56; freelance cons. Ft. Lee, N.J., 1973-80; cons. in field; rep. Artists and Sculptors, N.J., 1984—. Active vol. various charitable orgns. Honored by Am. Cancer Soc., Technion, Univ. of Tech., United Jewish Community of Bergen County, Holly Ctr. (adv. for abused children), others.

LEIGL, KATHLEEN ANN, human resource administrator; b. Mayville, Wis., Oct. 26, 1952; d. Philip Alphonse and Mary Jane (Caine) L. BS, U. Wis., Oshkosh, 1975, MS in Indsl. Relations, 1984. Corp. personnel supr. Siecor Corp., Hickory, N.C., 1984-87; corp. human resources supr. Harris Corp., Melbourne, Fla., 1987-92; rep. employee rels. James River Co., Menesha, Wis., 1992-94; mgr. human resources sci. protein labs. Viobin Am. Home Products Corp., Waunakee, Wis., 1994—. Mem. NAFE, Soc. Human Resrouces, High Yield Investment Care. Roman Catholic. Home: 205 Marguerite Ct Mayville WI 53050 Office: James River Corp 160 Washington St Menasha WI 54952

LEIN, HEBE BEATRIZ, psychologist; b. Rosario, Argentina, Mar. 18, 1945; came to U.S., 1979; d. Adolfo and Debora (Slepoy) L.; m. Leonardo Berezovsky, Nov. 13, 1968 (div. Nov. 1987); children: Karen, Sonia. M in Psychology, U. Rosario, 1967; PhD in Psychology, U.S. Internat. U., San Diego, 1982. Lic. psychologist, Calif. Cons. psychologist Regional Ctrs., L.A., 1985-87; mem. panel of experts L.A. Superior Ct., Calif., 1986—; pvt. practice psychologist L.A., 1986—; cons. psychologist Mc Laren Hall, El Monte, Calif., 1990—. Mem. Am. Psychol. Assn. Office: 3407 W 6th St Ste 803 Los Angeles CA 90020-2555

LEIN, LAURA, social anthropologist, researcher; b. Nashville, Jan. 31, 1947; d. Allen and Teresa (LaFratta) L.; m. Benjamin Jack Kuipers, June 28, 1975; children: Anna, Rebecca, David. BA in Social Anthropology, Swarthmore Coll., 1969; MA, Harvard U., 1970, PhD, 1973. Project dir. Wellesley (Mass.) Coll., 1977-85, assoc. dir., 1977-80, acting dir., 1980-81, dir., 1981-85; sr. lectr., rsch. scientist sch. social work U. Tex., Austin, 1985—, sr. lectr. dept. anthropology, 1985—, dir. women's studies program, 1987-91. Author: Families Without Villians, 1984; co-author: Children, 1984. Mem. Soc. for Applied Anthropology Assn., Am. Anthropology Assn., Nat. Coun. for Rsch. (chair 1982-83), Northeastern Anthrop. Assn., Groves Conf., Phi Kappa Phi. Office: U Tex Sch Social Work Austin TX 78712

LEINAAR, KAREN SUE, athletic director; b. Dowiagac, Mich., Aug. 14, 1959; d. Arlen Glen and Suzanne (Reed) L. BS, Mich. State U., 1982; MA, Western Mich. U., 1994. Coord. night programs Delton (Mich.)-Kellogg Schs., 1982-84, in-sch. suspension tchr., 1984-88, tchr. physical edn., 1988-91, dist. athletic dir., 1988—, tchr. driver edn., 1986—; recreation dir. SW Barry Recreation Dept., Delton, 1982-87; coach volleyball, track Delton-Kellogg Schs., 1985-93; volleyball, track official Mich. H.S. Athletic Assn., East Lansing, 1985—. Exec. mem. WBA Ruster Found., Sturgis, Mich.,

1991, student leadership trainer, 1987—; mem. com. Delton Area Founders Weekend, 1988—. Mem. Nat. Interscholastic Athletic Adminstrs. Assn., Mich. Interscholastic Athletic Adminstrs. Assn. (5 yr. svc. award 1990), Mich. Health Physical Edn. Assn., Mich. Traffic Safety Edn. Assn. Office: Delton-Kellogg Schs 327 N Grove St Delton MI 49046

LEINBACH, NANCY YOCOM, psychologist; b. Urbana, Ohio, Apr. 9, 1936; d. David Clyde and Kathryn Elizabeth (Brinnon) Yocom; m. Philip Eaton Leinbach, July 27, 1957; children: Jonathan Eaton, David Timothy. AB, San Diego State Coll., 1958; MS in Edn., Wheelock Coll., 1973; PhD, Boston Coll., 1988. Lic. psychologist, La. Head tchr. Children's House Lesley Coll., Cambridge, Mass., 1973-74; lectr. Boston Coll., Wheelock Coll., Lesley Coll., Boston, 1974-83; psychoeducator Parents with Toddlers Program, Boston, 1974-81, Parenting Ctr. of Children's Hosp., New Orleans, 1985-86; psychol. asst. to psychologists in pvt. practice Metarie, La., 1985-89; lectr. Loyola U., New Orleans, 1989; counselor Tulane U. Counseling Ctr., New Orleans, 1988-90; cons., adminstr. Mental Health Network, Inc., Gretna, La., 1990; psychologist II Southeast La. Hosp., Mandeville, 1990—; intern Coastal Community Counseling Ctr., Braintree, Mass., 1983-84; cons. Early Childhood Programs, Boston, 1977-82. Author handbooks in field. Adv. com. Crisis Care Ctr., YWCA, New Orleans, 1987-88; bd. dirs. Early Childhood Project, Children's Mus., Boston, 1981-84, Infant-Toddler Ctr., Brookline, Mass., 1979-82, Child Care Resource Ctr., Cambridge, Mass., 1977-79. Staff devel. grantee Inst. of Mental Hygiene, New Orleans, 1993; mem. action grantee Nat. Assn. for Edn. of Young Children, 1978. Mem. APA, La. Psychol. Assn., Nat. Assn. Edn. Young Children(bd. dirs., co-pres. Boston chpt. 1972-80), Tulane U. Women's Assn. Democrat. Home: 7530 Saint Charles Ave # J New Orleans LA 70118-3874 Office: Southeast La Hosp PO Box 3850 Mandeville LA 70470-3850

LEINEN, MARGARET SANDRA, oceanographic researcher; b. Chgo., Sept. 20, 1946; d. Earl John and Ester (Louis) Leinen; m. Denzel Earl Gleason, 1984; 1 child, Daniel Glenn Whaley. BS, U. Ill., 1969; MS, Oreg. State U., 1975; PhD, U. R.I., Kingston, 1980. Marine scientist U. R.I., Kingston, 1980-82, asst. rsch. prof., 1982-86, assoc. prof., 1986-88, prof., 1988—, assoc. dean, 1988-92, dean and vice provost, 1992—. Office: U RI Grad Sch Oceanography Narragansett RI 02882-1197

LEINO, DEANNA ROSE, educator; b. Leadville, Colo., Dec. 15, 1937; d. Arvo Ensio Leino and Edith Mary (Bonan) Leino Malenck; adopted child, Michael Charles Bonan. BSBA, U. Denver, 1959, MS in Bus. Adminstrn., 1967; postgrad. Community Coll. Denver, U. No. Colo., Colo. State U., U. Colo., Met. State Coll. Cert. tchr., vocat. tchr., Colo. Tchr. Jefferson County Adult Edn., Lakewood, Colo., 1963-67; retired tchr. bus., coordinator coop. office edn., Jefferson High Sch., Edgewater, Colo., 1959-93, ret., 1993; sales assoc. Joslins Dept. Store, Denver, 1978—; mem. ea. team, clk. office automation Denver Svc. Ctr. Nat. Park Svc, 1993-94, U.S. Dept. Labor, 1994—; instr. Community Coll. Denver, Red Rocks, 1967-81, U. Colo. Denver, 1976-79, Parks Coll. Bus. (name now Parks Jr. Coll.), 1983—; dist. adviser Future Bus. Leaders Am. Active City of Edgewater Sister City Project Student Exchange Com.; pres. Career Women's Symphony Guild; treas. Phantoms of Opera, 1982—; active Opera Colo. Assocs. & Guild, I Pagliacci; ex-officio trustee Denver Symphony Assn., 1980-82. Recipient Disting. Svc. award Jefferson County Sch. Bd. 1980, Tchr. Who Makes A Difference award Sta. KCNC/Rocky Mountain News, 1990, Youth Leader award Lakewood Optimist Club, 1993; inducted into Jefferson High Sch. Wall of Fame 1981 Mem. NEA (life), Colo. Edn. Assn., Jefferson County Edn. Assn., Colo. Vocat. Assn., Am. Vocat. Assn., Colo. Educators for and about Bus., Profl. Secs. Internat., Career Women's Symphony Guild, Profl. Panhellenic Assn., Colo. Congress Fgn. Lang. Tchrs., Wheat Ridge C. of C. (edn. and scholarship com.), Federally Employed Women, Delta Pi Epsilon, Phi Chi Theta, Beta Gamma Sigma, Alpha Lambda Delta. Republican. Roman Catholic. Club: Tyrolean Soc. Denver. Avocations: decorating wedding cakes, crocheting, sewing, music, world travel. Home: 3712 Allison St Wheat Ridge CO 80033-6124

LEIS, WINOGENE B. (MRS. HENRY PATRICK LEIS, JR.), professional association executive; b. Clay, W.Va., Feb. 27, 1919; d. Gruder L. and Daisy M. (Young) Barnette; R.N. cum laude, Kanawha Valley Hosp., 1939; m. Henry Patrick Leis, Jr., Jan. 8, 1944; children: Henry Patrick III, Thomas Frederick. Nurse, Kanawha Valley Hosp., 1939-43. Decorated lady comdr. Equestrian Order Holy Sepulchre Jerusalem. Mem. Woman's Aux. Internat. Coll. Surgeons (corr. sec. N.Y. State surg. div. 1955-57, v.p. 1961-63, pres. 1963-67; pres. U.S. sect. 1970, dir. 1970—, pres. Internat. Body 1977-78, bd. govs. 1978—, chairperson rsch. and scholarship com. 1990—), Flower Fifth Avenue Hosp. Woman's Aux. (dir. 1956-59, 69—), Woman's Aux. N.Y. Acad. Scis., Woman's Aux. N.Y. State Med. Soc., Woman's Aux. Cabrini Med. Ctr., Woman's Aux. Westchester County Med. Ctr., Woman's Aux. Lenox Hill Hosp., Woman's Aux. So. Med. Assn., Cath. Women's Guild, Ocean Dunes Club, Surf Golf and Beach Club. Republican. Roman Catholic.

LEISING, JEAN, state legislator. Farm owner and operator; indls. nurse Good Samaritan Hosp. Sch. Nursing; state senator from dist. 42 Ind. Senate, 1988—. Trustee Cath. Community Found. Mem. Ind. Corn Growers Assn., Batesville (Ind.) C. of C., Soybean Assn., Pork Producers and Cattlemen's Assn. Republican. Home: 5268 Stockpile Rd Oldenburg IN 47036 Office: Ind State Senate State Capitol Indianapolis IN 46204*

LEIST, ELISABETH PASEK, retail executive, retired; b. Hastings, Nebr., July 1, 1927; d. Joseph Edwin and Ethel (Anderson) Pasek; m. Frederick Morris Leist Sr., Nov. 26, 1949 (dec. 1976); children: Frederick Morris, Laurette Elisabeth. AA, Stephens Coll., 1947; BS, Ind. U., 1949. Ordained elder Presbyn. Ch., 1984. Electronics and camera merchandiser treasury div. J.C. Penney, Niles, Ill., 1974-79; with K-Mart, Des Plaines, Ill., 1979-94, camera and jewelry dept. mgr., 1981-88, jewelry and cosmetic dept. mgr., 1988-91; jewelry dept. mgr. K-Mart, Des Plaines, 1991-94; ret., 1994. Chmn. pub. rel. coun. Girl Scouts Am., LaPorte, Ind., 1950-52, from organizer to svc. unit chmn., Ill., 1968-84, alt. del., publicity chmn., 1984-88.

LEISTNER, MARY EDNA, retired chemistry educator; b. Evanston, Ill., Apr. 13, 1929; d. Joseph W. and Edna C. (Moe) Cox; m. Delbert L. Leistner, Sept. 30, 1950; children: David, Martha, Joseph. BS in Chemistry, Purdue U., 1950; MEd, Miami U., Oxford, Ohio, 1964. Tchr. sci. and math. Cen. Jr. High Sch., Sidney, Ohio, 1962-66; tchr. chemistry, biology, advanced chemistry Sidney High Sch., 1966-93; mem. high sch. chemistry test com. Nat. Sci. Tchrs. Assn. Am. Chem. Soc., 1983-85. Mem. exec. com. Ohio Dist. Luth. Women's Missionary League, Columbus, 1978-82, convention chmn., 1988; pres. Miami Valley zone, 1985-87; pres. Redeemer Ladies Soc., Sidney, 1980-91; auxiliary gift shop com. mem. Wilson Meml. Hosp., Sidney, 1994—. Mem. Nat. Sci. Tchrs. Assn. (Cadre 100 award), Western Ohio Sci. Tchrs. Assn. (pres. 1972-73), Sci. Edn. Council Ohio (dist. rep. exec. bd. 1984-86, treas. 1986-90, pres. elect 1991-92, pres. 1992-93, immediate past pres. 1993-94), Sidney Edn. Assn. (treas. 1980-82, 85-86, tchr. of Yr., 1988), Ohio Acad. Scis. (Jerry Acker Outstanding Tchr. of Yr. 1988-89, Exemplar 1993). Republican. Lutheran.

LEITCH, SHELLY M., neonatal critical care, maternal-women's health, and pediatric rehabilitation nurse; b. Guam, Nov. 24, 1954; d. Dougald A. and B. Claire (MacGregor) L. BSN cum laude, No. Mich. U., 1975. RN, Mich., Tex.; cert. high risk neonatal nurse. Float pool staff nurse Bay Med. Ctr., Bay City, Mich., 1979-80; staff nurse II infant spl. care unit U. Tex. Med. Br., Galveston, 1980-83, staff nurse III infant spl. care unit tng., 1983-87, tng. specialist II infant spl. care unit, 1987-91, staff nurse III spl. projects infant spl. care unit AHN children's extended care unit, 1992; nurse clinician IV, children's extended care unit Children's Hosp.-U. Tex. Med. Br., Galveston, 1992—. Mem. Nat. Assn. Neonatal Nurses.

LEITZE, ANNETTE EMILY RICKS, mathematics educator; b. Jacksonville, Ill., May 31, 1951; d. William Brown and Rachel Emily (Husted) Ricks; m. Harold Dean Leitze, Aug. 19, 1972; children: Jason Matthew, Jeremy Michael. BS in Math., Western Ill. U., 1972; MA in Math., Ind. U., 1988, PhD in Math. Edn., 1992. Cert. 6-12 math. tchr., Ill. Tchr. math. Triopia Jr.-Sr. High Sch., Concord, Ill., 1975-80; assoc. instr. dept. math. Ind. U., Bloomington, 1986-88, rsch. asst., assoc. instr. Sch. Edn., 1989-92, instr. math. Sch. Continuing Studies, 1992; prof. Ball State U., Muncie, Ind., 1992—. Contbg. editor: Projects for Real World Problem Solvers, 1991; author software Problem-Solving Data Bank; also articles. Mem. restructuring task force Monroe County Community Sch. Corp., Bloomington, 1989, mem. math. textbook adoption com., 1992. Grad. fellow Ind. U. Sch. Edn., 1989, 90. Mem. Am. Ednl. Rsch. Assn., Spl. Interest Group, Ind. Coun. Tchrs. Math., Math. Assn. Am., Nat. Coun. Tchrs. Math., Psychology of Math. Edn., Sch. Sci. and Math. Assn., Kappa Mu Epsilon, Phi Delta Kappa. Office: Ball State U Dept Math Scis Muncie IN 47306

LEKAS, MARY DESPINA, otolaryngologist; b. Worcester, Mass., May 13, 1930; d. Spyridon Peter and Merciny S. (Manoliou) L.; m. Harold William Picozzi. BA, Clark U., 1949; MD, Athens (Greece) U., 1957; MA, Brown U., 1986; student, Boston U. Diplomate Am. Bd. Otolaryngology. Sci. instr. Hahnemann Hosp. Sch. Nursing; rotating intern Meml. Hosp., Worcester, 1957-58; resident in otolaryngology R.I. Hosp., Providence, 1958-62; resident in otolaryngology and otorhinolaryngology U. Pa. Grad. Sch. Medicine, 1960; surgeon in chief, dept. otolaryngology R.I. Hosp., 1984—; pvt. practice Providence, 1962—; chmn. dept. otolaryngology Brown U., Providence, 1984—; cons. Cleft Palate Clin. and Craniofacial of R.I. Hosp., 1964—, VA Hosp., Providence, 1967—, St. Joseph Hosp., Providence, 1983—, Miriam Hosp., Providence, 1984—; lectr. profl. orgns. Europe, U.S. Mem. editorial bd. Am. Jour. Rhinology, 1987—; contbr. articles to profl. jours. Mem. alumni coun. Clark U. Clark V./Jonas Clark fellow; named R.I. Woman Physician of Yr., 1992. Fellow ACS, Soc. Univ. Otolaryngologists-Head and Neck Surgeons, Triological Soc. (ea. sect. sec., Presdl. Citation 1993), Am. Acad. Otolaryngology-Head and Neck Surgeons, Am. Acad. Facial Plastic and Reconstructive Surgeons, Am. Acad. Broncho-Esophagology (treas., v.p. 1990); mem. AMA, Assn. Acad. Dept. Otolaryngology-Head and Neck Surgery, Deafness Rsch. Found., Am. Cleft Palate Assn., Am. Med. Women's Assn. (R.I. Woman Physician of Yr. 1992), Centurian Club, New Eng. Otolaryng. Soc. (pres. 1987-88). Greek Orthodox. Home: 129 Terrace Ave Riverside RI 02915-4726 Office: Physicians Office Bldg 110 Lockwood St Providence RI 02903-4801

LEKUS, DIANA ROSE, librarian; b. Washington, Feb. 5, 1948; d. Max and Eleanor (Kruger) L. Student, Hofstra U., 1965-66; BA, Emerson Coll., 1969; MLS, U. Pitts., 1970. Asst. dept. head. search dept. Temple U., Phila., 1970-71; cataloging supr. weekly record sect. R.R. Bowker, N.Y.C., 1972-75; cataloger, asst. prof. U. Ill., Champaign-Urbana, Ill., 1975-78; customer svc. rep. Res. Fund, N.Y.C., 1979-81; list libr. Kleid Co., N.Y.C., 1981-94. Sr. editor Am. Book Pub. Record, 1974; book reviewer Libr. Jour., 1979. Mem. Editorial Freelancer's Assn., N.Y. Sheet Music Soc., Hadassah (life). Democrat. Jewish. Home: 28-05 37th St Astoria NY 11103

LELAND, JO (JOSEPHINE LELAND), former secondary school educator; b. Bklyn., Sept. 19, 1917; d. Nayef Joseph and Bahria (Jabbour) Mosleh; m. Mitchell Kayatta, Apr. 13, 1941 (dec. 1974); children: George, Jerome, Jane; m. Sigmunt Leland (dec.) May 30, 1983. BA, Bklyn. Coll., 1941; MA, Syracuse U., 1963. Cert. art tchr. Dist. mgr. Avon, Bklyn., Utica, N.Y., 1954-60; art instr. Bd. of Edn., Utica, N.Y., 1960-62, Whitesboro, N.Y., 1962-64; art instr. Bd. of Edn., Frankfort, N.Y., 1965-81, ret., 1981—; expeditor USN Dept., 1942-44. Mem. AAUW (pres. 1988-91, endowment 1992). Republican. Roman Catholic. Home: 10198 SW 88th Ct Ocala FL 34481-8916

LELAND, PAULA SUSAN, educational administrator, educator; b. Duluth, Minn., Feb. 10, 1953; d. Clarence Henry and Agnes Gudrun (Feiring) L. BS in Elem. Edn. and Music with honors, U. Minn., Duluth, 1975, BS in English, Lang. Arts and Sec. Edn. with honors, 1979; MS in Edn. Adminstrn. and Edn. summa cum laude, U. Wis., Superior, 1982, MEd in Profl. Devel., English and Language Arts summa cum laude, 1984, Spl. degree in Edn. Adminstrn. summa cum laude, 1988, postgrad., 1988—; postgrad., U. St. Thomas, 1989, U. Minn., Mpls. Tchr. elem. gifted children U. Minn., Mpls., 1980; tchr. Hermantown (Minn.) Cmty. Schs. Dist. 700, 1975—, substitute adminstr., 1982-92; mem. staff devel. com. Hermantown (Minn.) Cmty. Schs. Dist. 700, Hermantown, 1987—; dist. coord. and chairperson, planning, evaluating and reporting com., adminstrv. rep. State Dept. of Edn. for Minn. #700, Hermantown, 1984-86; supr. student tchrs. U. Wis., Superior, 1977—, adminstr. practicum, 1981-82; supr. student tchrs. U. Minn., Duluth, 1977—; mem. faculty community adv. com. for student tchrs., 1985—; Coll. St. Scholastica, 1977—; supr. tchr. aides, parent vols., and interpreters, 1980—; fgn. exch. tchr. host, 1982-83; profl. edn. tutor, 1989-90; mem. textbook com. Hermantown Schs., 1977—; writer, reporter Hermantown Star, 1978. Curriculum writer Hermantown Community Schs.; music arranger, composer, lyricist. Mem. Dem. Nat. Conv. supporter, Dem. Party Local Affiliation, Duluth, 1972—, Lake Superior Ctr. Non-Profit Orgn.; choir dir., dir. music Zion Luth. Ch., 1980—, dir./coord. music and handbell, 1983—, asst. dir. 1976-79, co-chair music and co-author music tape for Centennial Celebration, 1988, mem. nominating and worship coms. chairperson, 1992-94, recorder, sec. and choir sec., pastor-selected com. for assoc. in ministry, 1980—, vocalist, 1967—, Sunday Sch. tchr., Bible sch. tchr. 1968-75, substitute asst. dir., 1976-80, coun. mem. 1992—, v.p. 1993-94, pres. 1994—, chair call com. pastor-elect, 1994—, bd. dirs found., 1994—; supporter Reading is Fundamental, 1975—, United Way of Greater Duluth, 1975—; mem. Dairy Coun., Hermantown Arts Coun.; active Goodwill Industries, Salvation Army, Clean Water Action, Minn. Dept. Natural Resource-Wildlife, U. Minn. Legis. Network, 1992—; Archtl. Planner Ednl. Facilities and Creative Activity, 1984; bd. dirs. Duluth Fed. Employees Credit Union, 1994-95. Named to The Nat. Women's Hall of Fame, 1995; Alworth scholar, 1971-75, Denfeld scholar, 1968-71. Mem. AAUW, NAFE, Am. Mus. Nat. Hist., Assn. Lutheran Ch. Musicians (invited), Future Tchrs. Orgn., Red Cross Club (pres, former v.p., svc. award), Sons of Norway (Viking Ship Project), N.Am. Assn. for Environ. Edn., Norwegian Am. Heritage Fund, Minn. Valley Nat. Wildlife Refuge, N.D. Parks and Recreation, Friends of Deep Portage, Arrowhead Reading Coun., Minn. Reading Assn., Hermantown Fedn. Tchrs., Hermantown Sch. Dist. Cont. Edn. (co-chair, former sec., cert. of appreciation 1990), Hermantown Fedn. Tchrs., Minn. Hist. Soc., Midwest Fed. Banking Consortium, U. Minn.-Duluth Alumni Assn., U. Wis.-Superior Alumni Assn., Minn. Naturalists Assn., Tweed Mus. Art, Mpls. Soc. of the Arts, Mpls. Soc. of Fine Arts, Minn. Inst. Art, Internat. Platform Assn., Smithsonian Nat. Assocs., Smithsonian Inst., Charles F. Menninger Soc., Laura Ingalls Wilder Meml. Soc., Midwesterners Club, Alpine Club, Zoofari Club, Queen Mary and Spruce Goose Voyager Club, Kappa Delta Pi, Sigma Alpha Iota, Phi Kappa Phi, Phi Delta Kappa, Delta Kappa Gamma, Beta Sigma Phi, Alpha Delta Kappa. Home: 2237 W 11th St Hermantown MN 55806-1201 Office: 4289 Ugstad Rd Hermantown MN 55811-3615

LELAND, SARA, ballet dancer; b. Melrose, Mass., Sept. 2, 1941; m. Arthur Kevorkian. Student with, E. Virginia Williams, Melrose, Mass. Dancer New England Civic Ballet, Joffrey Ballet, 1959-60; dancer N.Y.C. Ballet, 1960-83, asst. ballet mistress, 1983—. Dancer: (ballets) Les Biches, 1960, Don Quixote, Jewels, 1967, Symphony in Three Movements, 1972, Union Jack, 1976, Vienna Waltzers, Dances at a Gathering, 1969, The Golberg Variations, 1971, Illuminations, The Concert, 1971, Gaspard de la Nuit, 1973, Lost Sonata, 1972, Choral Variations on Bach's Von Himmel Hoch, 1972, Scherzo Fantastique, 1972; ballet master staged works for the Joffrey Ballet, Boston Ballet, the Dance Theater of Harlem. Office: NYC Ballet Inc NY State Theater Lincoln Ctr Plz New York NY 10023*

LELYVELD, GAIL ANNICK, actress; b. Boston, May 22, 1948; d. Edward I. and Beatrice Elizabeth (Hewitt) L. BA in Polit. Sci., Boston U., 1970; MA in Polit. Sci., Goddard Coll., 1974; studies with Paul Barry, Peter Donat, Ray Reinhardt, Darrell Lauer, others. Actress, 1970—; tech. staff USA Prodns. and Midseason, Hempstead, N.Y., 1986-87, prodn. stage mgr., 1987—; tech. staff Gray Wig, Hempstead, 1986, 87; cons. Talking With prodn. M.A., C.W. Post. Appeared in numerous films including Frances, Halloween III, Children on Their Birthdays, Project 1917, Rocky II, Happy Endings, Seeds of Innocence, Bonfire of the Vanities, The Bird's Eye View, Insomnia; (TV shows): Archie Bunker's Place, Mister Clown Says, White Noise, The Gentle Creature, (ABC Afterschool Spl.) Summer Stories: The Mall, Mathnet, Bill Cosby Murder Mystery; actor (theatre) Alice in Wonderland, Not so Grimm Fairytale Players; actress (Littletop Theatre Co.) Toby Tyler, Marmalade Gumdrops, (theatre) Bohemian Lights, King Lear - Tenant, doctor, & knight Plainedge Playhouse, The Hostage, USA Prodns.; singer Musicum Collegium Hofstra U., Pala Opera Assn., St. Patrick's Cathedral Choir, Temple Emanual New Hyde Park Choir; theatre tech. involvement includes stage mgr., sound asst. Wings; sound asst. Danton's Death; asst. stage mgr. Endgame, Breaker Morant; lighting, stage mgr. The Foreigner; lighting asst. Midnight Waltz. Mem. AFTRA, Toastmasters. Jewish. Home: 291 Saville Rd Mineola NY 11501-1345

LEMA, JO-ANNE S., academic administrator; b. Worcester, Mass., Nov. 5, 1947; d. James Patrick and Florence Marie (Howard) Sullivan; m. Luis E. Lema, Sept. 25, 1971; children: Maria, James. BA, Merrimack Coll., 1969; EdM, Boston U., 1975; EdD, Harvard U., 1981. Researcher MIT, Cambridge, Mass., 1969-71, 79-81; tchr. Colegio Bolivar, Cali, Columbia, 1971-73; contracts adminstr. Educators Cons. Svc., Shrewsbury, Mass., 1973-75; tchr., rsch. asst. Harvard Univ., Cambridge, 1977-79; dir. inst. rsch. Bryant Coll., Smithfield, R.I., 1982-89; asst. v.p. Bryant Coll., Smithfield, 1989—. Rep. town mtg. mem. Town Govt., North Attleboro, Mass., 1990-93; scholarship com. mem. Harvard Radcliffe Club of R.I., Providence, 1991—, exec. com., 1992—; trustee, chmn., North Attleboro Heights Assn. Mem. Soc. for Coll. and Univ. Planning (regional rep. 1991—, bd. dirs. 1991—), Harvard Radcliffe Club of R.I. (scholarship com. 1991—, exec. com.). Home: 106 Blackberry Rd North Attleboro MA 02760-3504 Office: Bryant Coll 1150 Douglas Pike Smithfield RI 02917-1220

LEMASTER, SHERRY RENEE, fundraising administrator; b. Lexington, Ky., June 25, 1953; d. John William and Mary Charles (Thompson) LeM.; BS, U. Ky., 1975, MS, 1984. Cert. fund raising exec. Lab. technician in virology, serology Cen. Ky. Animal Disease Diagnostic Lab., Lexington, 1975-76; grant coord., environ. specialist Commonwealth Ky. Dept. for Natural Resources and Environ. Protection, Frankfurt, 1976-78; coord. residence hall program Murray (Ky.) State U., 1978-80; dean students Midway (Ky.) Coll., 1980-81, v.p. devel., alumnae affairs, 1981-86; dir. devel. Wilderness Road Coun. Girl Scouts U.S., Lexington, 1986-88, Coll. of Agr. and Life Scis. Va. Poly. Inst. and State U., Blacksburg, Va. 1988-94; sr. major gifts officer Bowman Gray Sch. Medicine Wake Forest U. and N.C. Baptist Hosp., Inc., Winston-Salem, N.C., 1994—. amb. U. Ky. Coll. Agr.; cons. U.S. Dept. Edn., 1987—; chmn. Midway chpt. Am. Heart Assn., 1981, Woodford County chpt., 1983; mem. adminstrv. bd. First United Meth. Ch., Lexington, 1982-84, 87; mem. Coun. for Advancement and Support Edn., 1981—, chmn. Ky. conf., 1982; planning com. Nat. Disciples Devel. Execs. Conf., 1984; mem. East Ky. First Quality of Life Com., 1987-88. Recipient Young Career Woman award Bus. and Profl. Women's Club, Frankfort, 1981; named to Hon. Order of Ky. col., 1977, hon. sec. state, 1984. Mem. Am. Coun. on Edn., Nat. Soc. Fund Raising Execs. (bd. dirs. Lexington chpt. 1986), Advancement Women in Higher Edn. Adminstrn. (former state planning com. Ky.), Ky. Assn. Women Deans Adminstrs. and Counselors (editor Newsletter 1981), U. Ky. Alumni Assn. (life), Gen. Fedn. Womens Clubs, P.E.O. (charter, chpt. X-Ky., sec. chpt. AU-Va. 1991-93, Va. state chpt., amendments and accommendation com. 1990-92), Ninety-Nines Internat. Assn. Women Pilots (vice chmn. Ky. Bluegrass chpt. 1986-87, chmn. and chmn. bd. 1987-88), Lexington Jaycees, Kentuckians N.Y., Jr. League Roanoke Valley, Inc., Nat. Agriculture Alumni and Devel. Assn., Pi Beta Phi Nat. Alumnae Assn. (alumnae province pres. 1980-81, sec. bd. dirs. Ky. Beta chpt. 1982-84, pres. Va. Zate chpt. house corp. 1991-94), Alpha Kappa Psi Alumnae Assn. (charter Murray chpt.). Avocations: private pilot, needlecrafts, swimming, equitation, racquetball. Office: Bowman Gray Baptist Hosp Wake Forest U The Med Ctr Medical Center Blvd Winston Salem NC 27157

LEMASTER, SUSAN M., marketing consultant, writer; b. Cody, Wyo., May 9, 1953; d. Floyd Morris and Virginia Kristena (Renner) LeM.; B.A., U. Wyo., Casper, 1979; A.A., Casper Coll., 1977. Reporter, night editor Casper Star Tribune, 1972-76; copy editor, editor In Wyo. mag., Casper, 1979; info. dir. Wyo. Rural Electric Assn., Casper, 1980-81; story editor Wyo. Horizons mag., Casper, 1981-82; asst., instr. English lab. Casper Coll., 1982-84; mktg. mgr. Chen & Assocs., Inc., 1984-87; mktg. cons., 1987-90; dir. mktg. KaWES and Assocs., Inc., 1990-91, pub. rels./mktg. cons., 1992—; freelance writer and editor, 1982—; night sch. instr. Casper Coll., 1983-84, summer sch. instr., 1984. Editor Casper Jour., 1983-84. Recipient First Place News Story, Wyo. Press Assn., 1973; first pl. Editing award Wyo. Press Women, 1980. Mem. Soc. Mktg. Profl. Svcs. (bd. dirs. L.A. chpt. 1990-94), L.A. Press Club, Phi Theta Kappa, Phi Kappa Phi, Alpha Mu Gamma. Democrat. Home: 1940 N Highland Ave Apt 54 Los Angeles CA 90068-3292

LEMAY, HELEN SCHNEIDER, advertising, public relations and conference management executive; b. Stamford, Conn., July 10, 1947; d. George William and Wilhelminia Helen (Bellmar) Meier; m. Lester G. Lemay; children: Christopher Mitchell, Mark Robert. AA, Brian McMahon Community Coll., 1965-67; student, U. Wash., 1967-69. Asst. personnel mgr. W. H. Brady Co., Milw., 1976-78; mgr. mktg. Cornwell Services, Milw., 1978-80; pres. Schneider & Assocs., Waco and Dallas, Tex., 1981—. Communications chmn. United Way, 1992; mem. Tex. Quality Consortium. Named one of Outstanding Young Women Am., Jr. Woman's Clubs Am., 1984, 85, Outstanding Vol. of Yr., Tex. Jr. Woman's Clubs, 1985. Mem. Advt. Club Am., Pub. Rels. Soc. Am., Am. Soc. for Quality Control, Waco Advt. Club (bd. dirs. 1984—), Waco C. of C. (communications com. 1986—), Rotary, Jr. Woman's Club (pres. 1983-84), Brown Deer Jr. Women's Club (Milw., pres. 1979-80). Lutheran. Home: 4458 Cabot Dr Grand Prairie TX 75052-3384 Office: 6701 Sanger Ave Ste 106 5400 Bosque Blvd # 680 Waco TX 76710

LEMAY, NANCY, graphic designer, painter; b. N.Y.C., Sept. 7, 1956; d. Michael and Mary (Lombardozzi) Potenzano; m. Harry Adrian LeMay, Jan. 24, 1986. BFA with honors, Sch. Visual Arts, 1978; postgrad., NYU, 1981-84. Admissions counselor Sch. Visual Arts, N.Y.C., 1979-81, acad. advisor, 1981-84; asst. art dir. NYU, N.Y.C., 1984-87; graphic designer J. C. Penney, N.Y.C., 1987-89; art dir. Catch A Rising Star, N.Y.C., 1989; graphic designer WNBC TV News Graphics, N.Y.C., 1989-90; graphics engr. NBC Network News Graphics, N.Y.C., 1990-91; graphics engr. KCOP TV News, L.A., 1991-94, art dir., 1994—; adv. commn. High Sch. Art and Design, N.Y.C., 1984-91; judge Washington and Balt. Area Emmy Awards for Graphics. Exhibited in group show Wings N Water Festival (poster winner), 1990; designer: (logotype design) Art Direction Mag. (Award of Merit), 1985; contbr. MacWeek Mag., 1989. Recipient Sch. Art League full scholarship, 1974, Rhodes Family award, 1978, Master Eagle Gallery Award of Merit, 1976, 77, 78. Home: 357 S Curson Ave Los Angeles CA 90036-5201 Office: KCOP TV 915 N La Brea Ave Los Angeles CA 90038-2383

LEMEN, DEBORAH JEAN, sales and marketing executive; b. Neodesha, Kans., May 28, 1959; d. Carl James Reece and Oma Jean (Boehme) Hurlson; m. Dennis Wayne Lemen, Dec. 17, 1977; children: Travis Wayne, Branden Lee. Student, Adela Hale Bus., Hutchinson, Kans., 1977-78. Typist Hutchinson News, 1978, with telephone sales, 1980, with outside sales, 1981, nat. mgr., 1985, mktg. dir., 1991—. Bd. dirs. Big Sisters of Hutchinson, 1991, Hutchfest, 1992—; vol. Casa, 1993. Mem. Am. Bus. Women's Assn. (prs. 1991-92, Woman of Yr. award 1991), Kans. Press (bd. dirs. mktg. com. 1991-92), Kans. Newspaper Assn. (bd. dirs. 1991-92). Democrat. Presbyterian. Home: 211 W 27th Ave Hutchinson KS 67502-3425 Office: The Hutchinson News 300 W 2nd Ave Hutchinson KS 67501-5211

LEMIEUX, LINDA DAILEY, museum director; b. Cleve., Sept. 6, 1953; d. Leslie Leo LeMieux Jr. and Mildred Edna (Dailey) Tutt. BA, Beloit Coll., 1975; MA, U. Mich., 1979; assoc. cert., Mus. Mgmt. Program, Boulder, Colo., 1987. Asst. curator Old Salem, Inc., Winston-Salem, N.C., 1979-82; curator Clarke House, Chgo., 1982-84; curator Western Mus. Mining and Industry, Colorado Springs, Colo., 1985-86, dir., 1987—. Author: Prairie Avenue Guidebook, 1985; editor: The Golden Years--Mines in the Cripple Creek District, 1987; contbr. articles to mags. and newspapers. Fellow Hist. Deerfield, Mass., 1974—. Research grantee Early Am. Industries Assn., 1978. Mem. Am. Assn. Mus., Am. Assn. State and Local History, Colo.-Wyo. Mus. Assn., Colo. Mining Assn., Nev. Mining Assn., Mountain Plains Assn. Mus., Women in Mining. Republican. Presbyterian. Home: 1337 Hermosa Way Colorado Springs CO 80906-3050 Office: Western Mus of Mining & Industry 1025 N Gate Rd Colorado Springs CO 80921-3018

LEMKE, BETH GIBSON, city planning manager; b. Petersburg, Va., Feb. 16, 1967; d. William Pierce and Viola (Jackson) Gibson; m. Richard Warren

Lemke, June 30, 1990; 1 child, Kendrick Jackson. AS in Psychology and Sociology, Richard Bland Coll., 1986; BS in Urban Studies, Va. Commonwealth U., 1987; MBA, Embry-Riddle, 1990. Planning analyst Dept. Econ. Devel., State of Va., Chesterfield County, 1987; neighborhood profiles project mgr. Housing Opportunities Made Equal, Inc., Richmond, Va., 1987; regional planner Ctrl. Fla. Regional Planning Coun., Bartow, Fla., 1988; sr. planner, acting planning adminstr. Planning Dept., State of Fla., Titusville, 1988-91; prin. planner Dept. Planning and Redevel., State of Fla., Daytona Beach, 1991-93, planning mgr., 1994—; active I-4 Master Plan Project Adv. Group, Airport Master Plan Land Use Com. Active Cmty. Wide Safety Program. Mem. Am. Planning Assn. (treas., coord. profl. devel. 1992-94), Am. Inst. Cert. Planners, Inst. Transp. Engrs., Fla. Planning and Zoning Assn., Met. Planning Orgn. (vice chmn. tech. coordinating com. 1992-94, also chmn.). Office: City of Daytona Beach 301 S Ridgewood Ave Daytona Beach FL 32115

LEMMEY, TARA LYNN, marketing professional; b. Bayonne, N.J., Feb. 4, 1964; d. Robert Lemmey and Diana M. (Lorenston) Caldarola. BA, Rutgers U., 1987. Mktg. staff People Express Airline, Newark, 1983-87; account mgr. Douglas Turner Advt., Newark, 1987; dir. communications United Way, Newark, 1987-88; account mgr. Hammond Farrell, Inc., N.Y.C., 1988—, Young and Rubicam, N.Y.C.; account exec. print campaign, Corning telecommunicaitons, Benjamin Moore paint, UNISYS, Anderson Cons. Mem. N.Y. Ad Club, Bus. and Profl. Advt. Assn., Rutgers Alumni Assn. Office: Young and Rubicam 285 Madison Ave New York NY 10017-6401

LEMMON, JEAN MARIE, editor-in-chief; b. Duluth, Minn., Nov. 11, 1932; d. Lawrence Howard and Marie Julien (Gunderson) H.; m. Richard LuVerne LemMon, Apr. 17, 1965 (div. 1976); 1 child, Rebecca Jean. BA, U. Minn., 1954. Editor Better Homes and Gardens Mag., Des Moines, 1961-63, dept. head crafts, 1985-86, editor-in-chief, 1993—; women's editor Successful Farming, Des Moines, 1963-68; pres. Jean LemMon & Assocs., Des Moines, 1968-84; project editor Meredith Pub. Svcs., Des Moines, 1984-85; editor-in-chief Country Home Mag., Des Moines, 1986-93; adv. bd. Drake U. Journalism Sch., 1991—. Mem. ASCAP, Mensa Internat., Am. Soc. Interior Designers. Office: Better Homes and Gardens 1716 Locust St Des Moines IA 50309*

LEMOINE, GRETCHEN ANNE, legal secretary; b. Ft. Worth, Oct. 16, 1950; d. Evart W. Hedlund and Elizabeth Janet (Rocker) Pereira; m. David E. Lemoine, Apr. 2, 1977 (div. May 1993); children: Mark A., Brooke E. Student, U. Wyo., 1968-69, Calif. Polytechnic U., 1969-72. Sec. Kovac Equipment Co., Fresno, Calif., 1987-89; legal sec. Airport Law Ptnrs., Fresno, 1989-91; adminstrv. asst. Millerton New Town Devel. Co., Friant, Calif., 1991-93; legal sec. Lozano, Smith, Smith, Woliver & Behrens, Fresno, 1994—. Active Children's Home Soc., Yuba City, Calif., 1983-86, Am. Cancer Soc., Yuba Ctiy, 1983-86; bd. mem. Yuba Sutter Soccer League, Yuba City, 1983-85; bd. rep. Boy Scouts Am., Yuba City, 1983-86.

LEMPERT, SUSAN G., agency administrator; b. N.Y.C., Aug. 2, 1931; d. Louis and Evelyn (Hamburger) Goodstein; m. Arthur Lempert, July 1, 1955; children: Robert, Edward Tad, Elizabeth. AB in Journalism, Stanford U., 1952; MA in Pub. Law & Govt., Columbia U., 1955; MPA, San Francisco State U., 1983. Pub. rels. GE, San Francisco, 1952-54; researcher Coun. on Fgn. Rel., N.Y.C., 1954-56; editorial staff U.S. News & World Report, San Francisco, 1956-57; housing dir. Human Investment Program, San Mateo, Calif., 1983-88; exec. dir. Age Ctr. Alliance, Inc., Menlo Park, Calif., 1989—. City coun. mem. City of San Mateo, 1993—; bd. dirs. San Mateo Union H.S. Dist., 1983-93; San Mateo City Elem. Sch. Dist., 1973-83. Mem. LWV (pres. 1968), Calif. Elected Womens Orgn., League Calif. Cities (policy com. 1993—).

LEMR, SANDRA J., geriatrics nurse, administrator; b. Painesville, Ohio, Aug. 31, 1951; d. Charles J. and Dorothy J. (Vasinosky) Nagy; m. James C. Lemr, May 10, 1974; children: Melissa Ann, James Robert. AAS, Lakeland Community Coll., Mentor, Ohio, 1971; student, Lake Erie Coll., Painesville, Ohio. Nursing supr. Lake Hosp. Systems, Painesville, 1971-86, Heartland of Mentor, 1986-91; asst. dir. nursing Madison (Ohio) Health Care, 1991—. Home: 90 Woodworth Ave Painesville OH 44077-3842

LEN, TATYANA, computer engineer; b. Leningrad, USSR, Feb. 4, 1956; came to U.S., 1980; d. Jacob Abram and Sophia (El) Mazo; m. Leon Efim Len, Apr. 8, 1977; children: Marina Nataly, Jacklina Alice. MA in Music, Conservatory Music, 1979; BS in Computer Sci., U. Akron, 1982. Tchrs. asst. U. Akron, Ohio, 1981-82; database analyst TTI Citicorp, L.A., 1982-86; sr. database analyst CCH, L.A., 1986-90; sr. system architect L.A. Times, 1990—; asst. conductor Belarus Opera House, Minsk, USSR, 1979. Author: The Youth of Ancient Profession, 1979. Mem. Software AG User Group. Republican. Jewish. Office: LA Times 207 N Broadway Fl 4 Los Angeles CA 90012-3203

LENARD, MARY JANE, accounting and information systems educator; b. York, Pa., July 8, 1955; d. Martin and Anne Ruth (Zimmerman) Kondor; m. Robert Louis Lenard; children: Kevin, Kelsey. BS in Econ. and Adminstrv. Sci., Carnegie Mellon U., 1977; MBA in Fin., U. Akron, 1982; PhD in Bus. Adminstrn., Kent State U., 1995. Cert. mgmt. acct. Mgmt. trainee Equibank, N.A., Pitts., 1977-78; acct., auditor The Goodyear Tire & Rubber Co., Akron, Ohio, 1978-86; instr. U. Akron, 1986-93; mem. adj. faculty Cleve. State U., 1994—. Pres. Hillcrest Elem. PTA, 1992-93; v.p. Summit County PTA, 1994—; active Revere Schs. Computer Curriculum Com., 1994-95. Mem. Am. Acctg. Assn., Inst. Mgmt. Accts. (dir. mem. retention 1994—), Inst. Ops. Rsch. and the Mgmt. Scis., Decision Scis. Inst., Akron Women's Network. Office: Cleveland State Univ Cleveland OH 44115

LENG, MARGUERITE LAMBERT, regulatory consultant, biochemist; b. Edmonton, Alberta, Canada, Sept. 25, 1926; came to the U.S., 1950; d. Joseph Edouard and Marie (Kiwit) Lambert; m. Douglas Ellis Leng, June 18, 1955; children: Ronald Bruce, Janet Elaine, Douglas Lambert. BS in Honours Chemistry, U. Alberta, 1947; MSc, U. Saskatchewan, 1950; PhD, Purdue U., 1956. Rsch. asst. U. Mich. Med. Rsch. Inst., Ann Arbor, 1950-53; sr. rsch. chemist bioproducts Dow Chem. Co., Midland, Mich., 1956-59, sr. registration specialist, product registration mgr., 1966-73, rsch. assoc. for internat. registration agrochems., 1973-86, mgr. internat. regulatory affairs, 1986-90; pres., cons. Leng Assocs., Midland, 1991—. Editor: Pesticide Chemist and Modern Toxicology, 1981, Agrochemical Environmental Fate Studies: State of the Art, 1995; contbr. articles to profl. jours., chpts. to books. Life ins. med. rsch. fellow Equitable Life Assurance Co., 1949-50. Fellow Am. Inst. Chemists (bd. dirs. 1992—, vice chmn. bd. dirs., exec. com. 1993—), Am. Chem. Soc. (agrochems. div. fellow 1976, chmn. 1981, program chmn. 1980, alt. councilor 1984-91, councilor 1992—), N.Y. Acad. Scis.; mem. Internat. Soc. for Study Xenobiotics, Assn. Analytical Chemists Internat., Soc. Environ. Toxicology and Chemistry, Internat. Soc. Regulatory Toxicology and Pharmacology, Sigma Xi. Home and Office: 1714 Sylvan Ln Midland MI 48640-2538

L'ENGLE, MADELEINE (MRS. HUGH FRANKLIN), author; b. N.Y.C., Nov. 29, 1918; d. Charles Wadsworth and Madeleine (Barnett) Camp; m. Hugh Franklin, Jan. 26, 1946; children: Josephine Franklin Jones, Maria Franklin Rooney, Bion. A.B., Smith Coll., 1941; postgrad., New Sch., 1941-42, Columbia U., 1960-61; holder 19 hon. degrees. Tchr. St. Hilda's and St. Hugh's Sch., 1960—; mem. faculty U. Ind., 1965-66, 71; writer-in-residence Ohio State U., 1970, U. Rochester, 1972, Wheaton Coll., 1976—, Cathedral St. John the Divine, N.Y.C., 1965—. Author: The Small Rain, 1945, Ilsa, 1946, Camilla Dickinson, 1951, A Winter's Love, 1957, And Both Were Young, 1949, Meet the Austins, 1960, A Wrinkle in Time, 1962, The Moon by Night, 1963, The 24 Days Before Christmas, 1964, The Arm of the Starfish, 1965, The Love Letters, 1966, The Journey with Jonah, 1968, The Young Unicorns, 1968, Dance in the Desert, 1969, Lines Scribbled on an Envelope, 1969, The Other Side of the Sun, 1971, A Circle of Quiet, 1972, A Wind in the Door, 1973, The Summer of the Great-Grandmother, 1974, Dragons in the Waters, 1976, The Irrational Season, 1977, A Swiftly Tilting Planet, 1978, The Weather of the Heart, 1978, Ladder of Angels, 1980, A Ring of Endless Light, 1980, Walking on Water, 1980, A Severed Wasp, 1982, And It Was Good, 1983, A House Like a Lotus, 1984, Trailing Clouds of Glory, 1985, A Stone for a Pillow, 1986, Many Waters, 1986, Two-Part Invention, 1988, A Cry Like a Bell, 1987, Sold Into Egypt, 1989, From This Day Forward, 1988, An Acceptable Time, 1989, The Glorious Impossible, 1990, Certain Women, 1992, The Rock That Is Higher: Story As Truth, 1993, Anytime Prayers, 1994, Troubling a Star, 1994. Pres. Crosswicks Found. Recipient Newbery medal, 1963, Sequoyah award, 1965, runner-up Hans Christian Andersen Internat. award, 1964, Lewis Carroll Shelf award, 1965, Austrian State Lit. award, 1969, Bishop's Cross, 1970, U. South Miss. medal, 1978, Regina medal, 1985, Alan award Nat. Coun. Tchrs. English, 1986, Kerlan award, 1990; collection of papers at Wheaton Coll. Mem. Authors Guild (pres., mem. council, mem. membership com.), Authors League (mem. council), Writers Guild Am., Colonial Dames. Episcopalian. Home: 924 West End Ave New York NY 10025 Office: care Farrar Straus & Giroux Inc 19 Union Sq W New York NY 10003-3304

LENNON, MARILYN ELLEN, environmentalist; b. Paterson, N.J., Feb. 7, 1954; d. George Henry and Florence (Buczek) L. BA, Ramapo Coll., 1976; M in City Regional Planning, Rutgers U., 1978. Environ. and land use planner Bergen County Planning Bd., Hackensack, N.J., 1975-78; project planner Pandullo Quirk Assoc., Wayne, N.J., 1978-80; environ. planning cons. Enviro Resource, Inc., Allendale and Atlantic City, N.J., 1980-81, Lennon Assoc., Inc., Atlantic City, 1981-83; sr. v.p., prin.-in-charge Paulus Sokolowski & Sartor, Inc., Warren, N.J., 1983—. Author: (chpt. in book) Advances in Environmental Science and Engineering, 1986. Bd. dirs. Liberty Sci. Mus., 1991—; mem. adv. bd. Paramus Cath. Girls H.S., 1992—; mem. Gov. Christine Todd Whitman's Transition Team. Named one of Outstanding Young Women in Am., 1982, Pioneer Woman of the 90's Bergen County, 1990. Mem. Am. Planning Assn. (legis. com. N.J. chpt. 1986), Atlantic City C. of C. (v.p. 1982, bd. dirs. 1984). Democrat. Roman Catholic. Home: 484 Lanza Ave Garfield NJ 07026-2035 also: 126 9th Ave Seaside Park NJ 08752-1816 Office: Paulus Sokolowski & Sartor Inc 67A Mountain Boulevard Ext Warren NJ 07059-5626

LENNOX, ANNIE, rock musician; b. Aberdeen, Scotland, Dec. 25, 1954; m. Radha Raman, Mar. 1984 (div. 1985). Student, Royal Acad. Music, London. Mem. musical group Catch, Tourists, 1977-80; founding mem. Eurythmics. Albums: (with Eurythmics) In The Garden, 1980, Sweet Dreams, 1983, Touch, 1984, 1984 (For the Love of Big Brother), 1984, Be Yourself Tonight, 1985, Revenge, 1986, Savage, 1988, We Too Are One, 1989, Greatest Hits, 1991, Eurythmics Live, 1993; (solo) Diva, 1992; actress (film) Revolution. Office: RCA Records 1133 Ave Of The Americas New York NY 10036-6710*

LENNOX, GLORIA (GLORIA DEMEREE), real estate executive; b. Baden, Pa., Feb. 14, 1931; d. Gilbert and Marion (Slosson) Whetson; m; William Lennox, June 19, 1954 (div. 1985); children: Cheryl Lennox Watson, Lynda Lennox Huerta, Jim; m. Philip Demeree, July 4, 1985. BS in Edn., Kent State U., 1954; MA in Spl. Edn., Ariz. State U., 1968; grad., Realtor's Inst. Grad. Realtor Inst.; cert. residential specialist, cert. residential broker state and nat. Tchr. Maple Leaf Sch., Garfield Heights, Ohio, 1954-55, Madison (Ind.) Dist. Elem. Sch., 1958, Scottsdale (Ariz.) Schs., 1961-68, Devereux Sch., 1968-70, Tri-City Mental Health Sch., Mesa, Ariz., 1970-71; br. mgr. M. Leslie Hansen, Scottsdale, 1972-74; v.p., gen. mgr. John D. Noble and Assocs., Scottsdale, 1974-83; pres., broker Gloria Lennox & Assocs., Inc., Scottsdale, 1983—. Chmn. bd. Interfaith Counseling Svc., 1988, 89; trustee Scottsdale Congl. United Ch. of Christ, 1986-88, 92; chmn. leadership com. Logos Ch., 1994. Kent State U. scholar, 1950-54. Mem. Nat. Assn. Realtors, Ariz. Assn. Realtors (Realtor Assoc. of Yr. 1975), Scottsdale Assn. Realtors (life, Hall of Fame award 1992, Disting. Career award 1994), Women's Coun. Realtors, Realtor Nat. Mktg. Inst., Scottsdale Bd. Realtors (pres. 1981-82, Realtor of Yr. 1982), Ariz. Town Halls, Ariz. Country Club. Republican. Home: 7561 N Via Camello Del Sur Scottsdale AZ 85258-3005 Office: Gloria Lennox and Assocs 4533 N Scottsdale Rd Ste 200 Scottsdale AZ 85251-7618

LENOIR, GLORIA CISNEROS, small business owner, business executive; b. Monterrey, Nuevo Leon, Mex., Aug. 18, 1951; came to U.S., 1956, naturalized; d. Juan Antonio and Maria Gloria (Flores) Cisneros; m. Walter Frank Lenoir, June 6, 1975; children: Lucy Gloria, Katherine Judith, Walter Frank IV. Student, Inst. Am. Univs., 1971-72; BA in French Art, Austin Coll., 1973, MA in French Art, 1974; MBA in Fin., U. Tex., 1979. French tchr. Sherman (Tex.) High Sch., 1973-74; French/Spanish tchr, dept. chmn. Lyndon Baines Johnson High Sch., Austin, 1974-77; legis. aide Tex. State Capitol, Austin, Tex., 1977-81; stock broker Merrill Lynch, Austin, 1981-83, Schneider, Bernet and Hickman, Austin, 1983-84; bus. mgr. Holleman Photographic Labs., Inc., Austin, 1984-87, 88-90; account exec., stock broker Eppler, Guerin & Turner, 1987-88; ind. distbr. Austin, 1990-93; owner, cons. Profl. Cons. Svcs., Austin, 1991—; adj. faculty Spanish , internat. bus. St. Edwards U., 1991--; group counselor, organizer Inst. Fgn. Studies, U. Strasbourg, France, summer 1976; mktg. intern IBM, Austin, summer 1978; mktg. cons. Creative Ednl. Enterprises, Austin, 1980-81; hon. speaker Mex.-Am. U. of Tex., Austin, 1984; speaker various orgns., bus. classes, Austin, 1981-84; speaker, coord. small bus. workshops, 1985. Photographs pub. in Women in Space, 1979, Review, 1988; exhibited in group shows throughout Tex., 1979, 88-89. Neighborhood capt. Am. Cancer Soc., Austin, 1982-86, 90, Am. Heart Assn., 1989; active PTA, 1989—, mem. Bryker Woods Elem. PTA Bd., 1990-92, pres., 1990-91, mem. Kealing Jr. High Sch. PTA Bd., 1992-94, chair 50th anniversary celebration com., 1990, hospitality chmn., 1st grade coord., Austin, 1986, mem. legis. com. Tex. State, 1990-92; vol. liaison leads program Austin Coll., 1983—; mem. Advantage Austin, 1988; peer panelist Major Art Insts. Austin, 1989-90; co-chair fin. Cen. Presbyn. Ch., elder, 1988-90, session clk., 1989, chair membership com. 1990, mem. staff com., 1991-92, coord. women's breakfast series, 1991-92; mem. Austin City Coun. of PTAs Bd., 1991—; megaskills leader Austin Ind. Sch. Dist., 1991—; mem. Kealing Jr. High Sch. PTA, 1992-94. Recipient Night on the Town award IBM, 1978. Mem. Photo Mktg. Assn. Republican. Home and Office: 1202 W 29th St Austin TX 78703-1917

LENOIR, MARIA ANNETTE, management consultant; b. St. Louis, June 11, 1950; d. Jack and Beatrice (Brown) Doyle; m. Howard L. Williams, Sept. 29, 1969 (div. Aug. 1981); 1 child, Howard L. Jr.; m. Aguinaldo Alphonse Lenoir Jr., June 28, 1985; 1 stepchild, Aguinaldo Alphonse III. Student, Florissant (Mo.) Valley Community Coll., 1974-76; BA in Mgmt., Webster U., 1980. Stenographer Internat. Shoe Co., St. Louis, 1968-69; office mgr. Chemplastics Inc., St. Louis, 1969-71; advt./media coord. Ralston Purina Co., St. Louis, 1971-73, sec., 1973-76, adminstrv. asst., 1976-79, sales/mktg. adminstr., 1979-84; pres., chief exec. officer, owner Corp. Image, Inc., St. Louis, 1984—; instr. St. Louis Univ., 1987, St. Louis Community Coll.; pub. rels. advisor Mo. White House Conf. Small Bus., St. Louis, 1986; mem. adv. panel Omni Internat. Hotel, St. Louis, 1986. Contbr. articles to profl. jours. Mktg. advisor Jr. Achievement of Miss. Valley, Hazelwood, Mo., 1983—; mem. Women's Assn. St. Louis Symphony, 1984—, ACE (div. of SCORE), St. Louis, 1985—; role model St. Louis Pub. Schs., 1987; bd. dirs. Community Commitment, Greeley Community Ctr. Youth Emergency Svcs. (YES), St. Louis, 1988—. Named Outstanding Young Women Am., 1987. Mem. Meeting Planners Internat., Nat. Speakers Assn., Am. Soc. Tng. and Devel., Assn. Ind. Meeting Planners (adv. com., bd. dirs.), Florissant Valley Community Coll. Alumni Assn. (v.p. 1985-86, sec./treas. 1987, Alumna of Yr. award 1986 Hall of Fame), Women in Leadership Alumni, NAFE, St. Louis Regional Commerce & Growth Assn., Boulder Yacht Club. Democrat. Pentecostal. Office: Corp Image Inc 4825 Lockwig Trl Florissant MO 63033-7521

LENOX, ANGELA COUSINEAU, quality assurance professional; b. Vergennes, Vt., Dec. 12, 1946; d. Romeo Joseph and Colombe Mary (Gevry) C.; m. Donald Allen Lenox, Oct. 5, 1969 (div.); 1 child, Tiffanie Jae. RN diploma, Albany Med. Ctr. Sch. Nursing, 1969; BS, Barry U., 1982; M of Health Mgmt., St. Thomas U., 1990. Cert. in profl. healthcare quality. Intravenous therapist Holy Cross Hosp., Ft. Lauderdale, Fla., 1979-91; utilization review coord. North Borward Hosp., Pompano Beach, Fla., 1984-89; med. staff quality mgr. Humana Bennett, Plantation, Fla., 1990-91; med. resource analyst Hermann Hosp., Houston, 1991-93; assoc. mgr. quality improvement The Prudential, Sugarland, Tex., 1993—. Contbr. articles to profl. jours. 1st lt. U.S. Army res., 1991—. Mem. Tex. Gold Coast Quality Assurance Profls., Tex. Soc. Quality Assurance, Nat. Assn. Healthcare Quality. Home: 8523 Dawnridge Dr Houston TX 77071 Office: The Prudential 24 Greenway Plaza Houston TX 77046

LENTS, PEGGY IGLAUER, marketing executive; b. St. Louis, Apr. 14, 1950; d. Hank S. and Elizabeth Ruth (Metzger) Iglauer; m. Don G. Lents, Aug. 27, 1972; children: Stacie Lee, Kelsey Lynn. BA magna cum laude, Tufts U., 1971; MPA, Harvard U., 1974. Legis. aide Congressman Symington, Washington, 1971; adminstrv. mgr. May Co., London, 1974; buyer Famous Barr subs. May Co., St. Louis, 1976-78; gen. mdse. mgr. Roman Co., St. Louis, 1978-80, mktg. dir., 1981-82, v.p., 1982; mktg. cons., 1983-86; ptnr. Andrews & Lents, St. Louis, 1987-89; pres. Lents & Assocs., St. Louis, 1990—; cons. Human Resources Adminstrn., N.Y.C.; teaching fellow Tufts U., 1971-72. Bd. dirs. Lucky Land Sch., 1980-81, Springboard to Learning, 1987—, UN Assn., 1987-88, Mo. Bot. Garden, 1988-92, Ctr. Contemporary Arts, 1989—; mem. adv. bd. Alzheier's Assn., 1993—, St. louis conservatory and Sch. for the Arts, 1992-93; v.p. planning and devel. NCJW, 1986-90; adv. bd. Metro Link Arts in Transit; chmn. NCD Nat. Leadership Program, 1974; cons., Washington, 1972, polit. campaigns N.D., Iowa; mem. Adv. bd. Synchronia Mus. Soc., 1993—. Univ. fellow Tufts U., 1971; fellow Harvard U., 1974. Mem. Am. Mgmt. Assn., Fashion Group, Jewish Hosp Sch. Nursing Alumni Assn. (hon. life), Pioneers, Direct Mail Club St. Louis, Women in Bus., Directory Group (U.K.), Westwood Country Club. Home: 1166 Hampton Park Dr Saint Louis MO 63117-1424

LENTZ, CONSTANCE MARCHAND, accountant; b. Tampa, Fla., May 6, 1948; d. George Ray and Allie Mae (Renner) L. BSBA, Calif. State U., Northridge, 1970, MSBA, 1974. CPA, Nev. Staff acct. Laventhol & Horwath CPA, Las Vegas, Nev., 1981-84; sr. mgr., acct. Deloitte, Haskins & Sells, Las Vegas, 1984-90; acct., pres. Constance M. Lentz, CPA, Ltd., Las Vegas, 1990—. Treas., bd. dirs. Warm Springs Res. Homeowners Assn., Henderson, Nev., 1990—; trustee New Vista Ranch, Las Vegas, 1990—; treas. bd. trustees Las Vegas Natural History Mus., 1989-94; treas., bd. dirs. Clark County unit/Nev. divsn. Am. Cancer Soc., Las Vegas, 1978-85. Mem. AICPA, Nev. Soc. CPAs, Las Vegas C. of C. (Leadership Las Vegas grad. 1991), Leadership Las Vegas Alumni Assn. Office: 930 S 3d St Ste 100A Las Vegas NV 89101

LENTZ, DEBORAH LYNN, telemetry/thoracic surgery nurse; b. Greenport, N.Y., Oct. 24, 1971; d. Stanley Antone Jr. and Linda Ann (Bernhard) C.; m. Stephen C. Lentz III, Dec. 1993; 1 child, Stephen C. Lentz IV. Cert. LPN, Harry Ward Tech. Ctr., Riverhead, N.Y., 1989; ADN, SUNY, Alfred, 1991. RN, N.Y.; cert. BLS, ACLS. LPN San Simeon By the Sound, Greenport, 1989-91; RN Meml. Sloan Kettering Cancer Ctr., Manhattan, N.Y., 1991-92, L.I. Jewish Hosp., New Hyde Park, N.Y., 1992-94, Ctrl. Suffolk Hosp., 1994—. Roman Catholic. Home: 68750 Rt 48 Greenport NY 11944

LENZEN, LAURA ELAINE, civil engineer; b. Lincoln, Nebr., Apr. 6, 1947; d. George Harry and Esther Ruth (Gies) DeBus; divorced; children: Timothy A., Amy L.; m. Louis W. Lenzen, Feb. 15, 1980. Registered profl. engr., Nebr.; cert. profl. mgr. From sec. to traffic engr. supr. Nebr. Dept. Rds., Lincoln, 1969-89, wetlands engr. unit head, 1989—. Mem. Nebr. Mgrs. Assn., Engrs. Club Lincoln (bd. dirs., sec.-treas.). Home: 2017 N 57th St Lincoln NE 68505-1107 Office: Nebr Dept Roads PO Box 94759 Lincoln NE 68509-4759

LEO, KAREN ANN, library administrator; b. Akron, Ohio, June 5, 1945; d. Ellsworth John and Flonnie Ada (Dykes) Hunter; m. Louis J. Leo, May 23, 1970. BA, Baldwin-Wallace Coll., 1967; AM in Libr. Sci., U. Mich., 1968. Fiction libr. Cleve. Pub. Libr., 1968-69; ref. libr. San Jose State Coll., Calif., 1969-70; head ref. libr., asst. to county libr. Stanislaus County Free Libr., Modesto, Calif., 1970-77; asst. city libr. Pomona Pub. Libr., Calif., 1977-81; head cen. libr. Riverside City & County Pub. Libr., Calif., 1981-85; libr. dir Orange (Calif.) Pub. Libr., 1985-92, libr. dir. Corona Pub. Libr., Calif., 1992—. Community adviser Jr. League of Riverside, 1982-85. Mem. community video adv. bd., Orange, 1985-92. Mem. ALA (membership com.), AAUW, Calif. Libr. Assn. (community rels. com., Calif. Inst. Librs.), Pub. Libr. Execs. So. Calif. Democrat. Methodist. Office: Corona Public Libr 650 S Main St Corona CA 91720-0090

LEON, LYDIA ANN, religious studies educator; b. Montebello, Calif., Dec. 2, 1959; d. Ruben and Lydia Ann (Montoya) L. Student, Cerritos Coll., 1983-89; AA in biblical studies, Evang. Bible Inst., 1994; student, Evang. Christian U., 1995—. Ordained to ministry Assn. Evang. Gospel Assemblies, 1989. With customer svc. dept. C.T.S., Commerce, Calif., 1978-83; freight biller, data entry clk. Pro Express, Montebello, Calif., 1983-86; with accounts payable dept. Lubricating Specialties, Pico River, Calif., 1986—; dir., founder, Bible studies educator Praise Hymn Ministries, Bellflower, Calif., 1986—. Songwriter various compositions; author: (curriculum) Doctrines of Demons, 1994; editor, staff writer: Praise Hymn Newsletter, 1993-94. Bible studies educator, musician One Way Family Ministries, Downey, Calif., 1984-85, mem. ministry to prison inmates, 1984-85, mem. ministry to convalescent homes, 1984-85, mem. ministry to women's shelters, 1984-85, mem. ministry to homeless Fred Jordan Missions, 1984-85. Named Best Alto El Rancho H.S. Choraleers, Pico Rivera, 1976, named most talented choraleer, 1977. Mem. Assn. Evang. Gospel Assemblies. Office: Praise Hymn Ministries PO Box 4191 Downey CA 90241

LEÓN, TANIA JUSTINA, composer, music director, pianist; b. Havana, Cuba, May 14, 1943; came to U.S., 1967; d. Oscar and Dora (Ferran) L. BA in Piano and Theory, Peyrellade Conservatory Music, Havana, 1963; MA in Music Edn., Nat. Conservatory Music, Havana, 1965; BA in Acctg., U. Havana, 1965; BS Music Edn., NYU, 1973, BS in Music Edn., 1973, MA in Composition, 1975. Prof. Bklyn. Coll. Conservatory of Music, 1994—; vis. prof. Yale U., New Haven, 1993; vis. lectr. Harvard U., Cambridge, Mass., 1994; resident composer Lincoln Ctr. Inst., 1985, teaching artist, 1982-88; composer in residence Nat. Black Music Festival, 1990, Cabrillo Music Festival, 1990, Yaddo, 1991, Ravinia Festival, 1991, Cleve. Inst., 1992, Bellagio Ctr., Italy, 1992, Cornish Coll., Seattle, 1993, Billings Symphony, 1993, Carnegie Mellon U., Pitts., 1993, Harvard Coll., Cambridge, Mass., 1993, Voices of Change, Dallas, 1993; panelist N.Y. State Council on the Arts, 1980, 81, 86, NEA composing program, 1980-82, recording program, 1985-87; mem. adv. bd. Bklyn. Coll. Conservatory, 1982-84, Meet the Composer, 1983—, Children TV Workshop; artistic dir. Composers Forum Inc., N.Y.C., 1987—; assoc. prof. composition Bklyn. Coll., 1987—; bd. dirs. Am. Music Ctr., N.Y. Found. for Arts; with Cin. Symphony Orch., 1991—, Revson Composer fellow N.Y. Philharmonic, 1993—; U.S. rep. U.S.-Mex. Fund for Culture, 1994. Piano soloist, Cuba, 1964-67; piano soloist, N.Y. Coll. of Music Orch., N.Y.C., 1967, NYU Orch., N.Y.C., 1969, Buffalo Symphony Orch., 1973; staff pianist, condr., Dance Theatre of Harlem, N.Y.C., 1968—, assoc. condr., 1983—, music dir., 1968-79; founder, Dance Theatre of Harlem Orch., 1975; concert series Meet the Performer, 1977; music dir. concert series Dance in Am. Spl., Sta. WNET-TV; guest condr. concert series, Genova (Italy) Symphony Orch., 1972, Juilliard Orch., Festival Two Worlds, Spoleto, Italy, Symphony New World, 1974, Royal Ballet Orch., 1974, 76, BBC Orch., 1974, 76, Halle Orch., 1974, Buffalo Philharm. Orch., 1975, Concert Orch. of L.I., 1979, Sadler's Wells Orch., 1979, London Universal Symphony, 1979, Composer's Forum, 1979, Lincoln Ctr. Outdoor Festival, 1980, Bklyn. Coll. Symphony, 1981, J. F. Kennedy Ctr. Opera House Orch., 1981, 82, Radio City Music Hall, 1982, Spoleto Festival, Charleston, 1983, Orch. of Our Time, N.Y., N.Y. Grand Opera, Colonne Orch., Paris, Mich. Opera, Human Comedy, Royale Theatre, Broadway, Pasadena Orch., P.R. Symphony, Met. Opera Orch., Phoenix Symphony, Columbus Symphony Orch., Fund. Latinoamericana Musica Contemporanea P.R., Am. Women Condr./Composer Symposium, Eugene, Oreg., New Music Am., Houston, New Music in Am., 1989 and Concert in the Pk., 1990 both with Bklyn. Philharm., Cabrillo Festival, 1990, Nat. Black Arts Festival, Atlanta, 1990, La Crosse Symphony, Wis., 1991, Dance Theatre of Harlem, 1991, 92, 93, 25th Anniversary Season-94, Celebrate Bklyn. Festival, 1991, Bklyn. Philharm., 1991, New World Symphony, Miami, Fla., 1991, 94, Cosmopolitan Symphony Orch., N.Y.C., 1991, Beethovenhalle Symphony Orch., Bonn, Germany, 1992, Opera Orch. of Johannesburg, 1992, Nat. Symphony Orch., Johannesburg, 1992, Louisville Symphony, 1992, RIAS Orch., Berlin, 1992, Billings Symphony, 1993, Dance Theater of Harlem, 1993, 94, Carnegie Mellon Orch., 1993, Alvin Ailey 35th Anniversary Season, 1993, Am. Composers Orch. Chamber Ensemble, 1994, Munich Biennale, 1994, others; royal command performer concert series, London Palladium, 1974, 76, Concert Orch. L.I., 1976, concert pianist, Sta. WNYC-FM, 1968-70; conductor coord.: concert series Music by Black Composers Series, Bklyn. Philharmonia, 1978-79; music dir., condr., Bklyn. Philharm. Community Concert Series, 1977—; mus. dir., condr. The Wiz, Broadway Theatre, 1978; music dir. Death, Destruction and Detroit, 1979, Alvin Ailey Am. Dance Theatre, 1983—, Whitney Mus. Contemporary Music Concert Series, 1986, 87; mus. dir., composer: Maggie Magalita, J.F. Kennedy Ctr. Performing Arts, 1980, TWindows, 1982; apptd. music dir. concert series, Intar Theatre, N.Y.C.; condr., mus. dir. concert series Godspell, NYU, 1978, Carmencita, 1978; composer (ballet music) Haiku, 1974, (piano concerto) Tones, 1970, Sailor's Boat, (score for musical) Dougla, 1974, (African ballet) La Ramera de la Cueva, 1974, (score for musical) Namiac Poems, 1974, (for voice, chorus and orch.) Spiritual Suite, 1975, (2 sopranos, chorus and mixed ensemble with narrator), Concerto Criollo, 1976, (concerto for piano, 8 timpanies and orch.) Pet's Suite, 1979, (for flute and piano) I Got Ovah, 1980, (for soprano, piano and percussion, based on poems by Carolyn M. Rodgers) Concerto Criollo, 1980, Four Pieces for Cello, 1981, De-Orishas, 1982, Ascend, Fanfare for Brass and Percussion, 1983, (for solo piano) Momentum, 1984, Bata, 1985, Permutation Seven, 1985, A La Par, 1986, Ritual, 1987, Pueblo Mulato, 1987, Heart of Ours, a piece, 1988, Parajota Delaté, 1988, Kabiosile, 1988, Latin File, 1988, Indigena for instrumental ensemble, 1991, Solisti Chamber Orch N.Y., 1991, Carabali for orch., 1992, Crossings for brass ensemble, 1992, Arenas d'un Tempo for clarinet, cello and piano, 1992, Son Sonora for flute and guitar, 1993, Scourge of Hyacinths: chamber opera, 1994, Para Viola y Orquesta for viola and orch., 1994, Sin Normas Ajenas for chamber orch., 1994; records on CRI, WesternWind, Albany Records, Newport Classics, Leonarda Records. Bd. dirs. Am. Composers Orch. Recipient Young Composers prize Nat. Council Arts, Havana, 1966, Alvin Johnson award Am. Council Emigres in the Profession, 1971, Cintas award in composition, 1974-75, 78-79, Achievement award Nat. Council Women of U.S., 1980, Byrd Hoffman Found. award, 1981, Key to City of Detroit, 1982, Queens Council on Arts award, 1983, Meet The Composer awards, 1978-94, Manhattan Arts award, 1985, Dean Dixon Achievement award, 1985, N.Y. State Coun. on Arts award, 1988, Mayor's citation, City of N.Y., 1989, Celebrate Bklyn. Achievement award, 1990, award in music Am. Acad. and Inst. of Arts and Letters, 1991; Nat. Endowment for Arts fellow, 1975. Mem. ASCAP (Composers award 1978-94), French Soc. Composers, Am. Acad. Poets (bd. dirs.), Am. Composers Orch. (bd. dirs.), Am. Fedn. Musicians, Ctr. New Music, Am. Music Ctr. (bd. dirs. 1985—), Internat. Artists Alliance, Am. Women Composers, AFL-CIO.

LEONARD, ANGELINE JANE, psychotherapist; b. McKeesport, Pa., Dec. 9, 1940; d. Paul James Franklin and Jane Angeline (McKee) L.; m. Tom L. Kregel, Aug. 25, 1962 (div. 1970). BFA, U. Okla., 1962; MA in Art History, UCLA, 1965; MA in Clin. Art Therapy, Immaculate Heart Coll., 1980; PhD in Clin. Psychology, Cambridge Grad. Sch., 1991. Lic. marriage, family, child counselor, Calif., marriage and family counselor, N.C.; registered art therapist; cert. hypnotherapist, guided imagery. Tchr. San Gabriel (Calif.) Mission High Sch., 1964-66, L.A. Valley Coll., Van Nuys, 1966-90, L.A. Unified Sch. Dist., 1980-90; pvt. practice psychotherapy, Reseda, Calif., 1982—; spkr. in field. Author: California Art Therapy Trends, 1993; author of poems. Bd. dirs., v.p. Ch. of Religious Sci., North Hollywood, Calif., 1989-93. Mem. Am. Art Therapy Assn., Am. Assn. Marriage and Family Therapists, Artist Equity Assn. (sec.), Calif. Assn. Marriage and Family Therapists, So. Calif. Art Therapy Assn. (bd. dirs.), No. Calif. Art Therapy Assn. Democrat. Home and Office: 19520 Vose St Reseda CA 91335-3637

LEONARD, CLAIRE OFFUTT, pediatric geneticist educator; b. Rochester, N.Y., Apr. 1, 1945; d. Edward Preble and Virginia Leoma (Williams) Offutt; divorced; children: Christopher Edward, Kathleen. BA, Mount Holyoke Coll., 1967; MD, John Hopkins U., 1971. Diplomate Am. Bd. Pediatrics, Am. Bd. Genetics. Intern and resident in pediat. U. Colo., 1971-74, fellow in genetics and birth defects, 1974-75; fellow in genetics Johns Hopkins Hosp., Balt., 1978-80; asst. prof. pediatrics John Hopkins U., Balt., 1980-81; asst. prof. pediatrics U. Utah, Salt Lake City, 1981-87, assoc. prof. pediatrics, 1987—. Mem. Am. Soc. Human Genetics, Am. Acad. Pediatrics, Am. Coll. Human Genetics, Soc. Inherited Metabolic Disorders. Mem. Soc. of Friends. Office: U Utah Dept Peds 50 N Medical Dr Salt Lake City UT 84112

LEONARD, DOROTHY LOUISE, environmental analyst; b. Newark, Aug. 30, 1932; d. Joseph Peter and Charlotte Mary (Dinkel) L.; m. Gary Lawrence Fellows, Sept. 4, 1954 (div. Mar. 1978); children: Mark Leonard, Paige Charlotte Wright, Scott Lawrence, Joy Dorothy. BA, Syracuse U., 1954; postgrad., SUNY, Brockport, 1976, George Washington U., 1982-84. Asst. planner Monroe County Dept. Planning, Rochester, N.Y., 1975-77; specialist coastal resources N.Y. Dept. State, Albany, 1977-80; program analyst Office Coastal Zone Mgmt. Nat. Oceanic & Atmospheric Adminstrn. div. U.S. Dept. Commerce, Washington, 1980-83, specialist fisheries devel. Nat. Marine Fisheries Svc., 1983-86; program mgr. shellfish water quality projects Nat. Ocean Svc., Washington, 1986—; pres. Dorothy Leonard Assocs., Washington, 1985—; program mgr. molluscan shellfish projects Nat. Marine Fisheries Svc., 1991—; bd. dirs. Charleston Maritime Inst.; cons. Charleston Harbor Project. Mem. com. N.Y. Legis. Com. on Women, Albany, 1975-77; pres. Washington Area Waterfront Action Group, 1986—; mem. bd. advisors Inst. for Coastal and Marine Recovery, 1988—. Mem. Am. Fisheries Soc., Nat. Fisheries Assn., World Aquaculture Soc., Am. Soc. Limnology and Oceanography, AIA (urban design com. 1986—), Chesapeake Bay Citizen Adv. Com., Waterfront Washington Assn., Survival of the Sea Soc. (bd. advisors 1987-89), LWV, Phi Kappa Phi. Republican. Presbyterian. Home: 776 Rolling View Dr Annapolis MD 21401 Office: NOAA Strategic Environ Assessment Divsn NORCA1 SSMC4 1305 E West Hwy Silver Spring MD 20910

LEONARD, ELIZABETH LIPMAN, psychologist; b. Phila., Sept. 5, 1947; d. M. Irvin and Natalie Claire (Seidmann) Lipman; m. Sept. 5, 1969; children: Noah, Emily. BS, Boston U., 1969; MS, Va. Commonwealth U., 1975; PhD, Tufts U., 1986. Lic. phys. therapist, psychologist. Dir. phys. and occupational therapy Crotched Mountain Rehab. Ctr., Greenfield, N.H., 1977-80; dir. child devel. unit Child Health Svcs., Manchester, N.H., 1980-85; rsch. assoc. Cath. Med. Ctr., Manchester, 1985-87; psychologist Barrow Neurol. Inst./St. Joseph's Hosp. and Med. Ctr., Phoenix, 1987—; cons. biomed. engring. MOCO, Inc., Scituate, Mass., 1986—. Editorial bd.: Phys. and Occupational Therapy in Pediatrics; contbr. articles to profl. jours. Recipient traineeship Vocat. Rehab. Adminstrn., Boston U., 1967-68; scholarship award Found. for Phys. Therapy, 1982; grantee March of Dimes, N.H. Devel. Disabiliies Coun., 1981, Div. Health and Human Svcs.-Maternal and Child Health, State of N.H., 1980, Bur. for Health Promotion, State of N.H., 1986, Ariz. Disease Rsch. Control Commn., 1990. Mem. APA, Internat. Soc. for Infant Studies, Internat. Neuropsychol. Soc., Soc. for Rsch. in Child Devel., Soc. Pediatric Psychology, Nat. Acad. Neuropsychology. Office: Barrow Neurol Inst Ste 412 222 W Thomas Phoenix AZ 85013

LEONARD, JANET TONKA, management consultant; b. Indpls., July 31, 1952; d. Clarence and Marjorie (Tuley) Tonka; m. Kenneth Carl Leonard, Mar. 7, 1981. BA, Duke U., 1974; MBA, Columbia Grad. Sch. of Bus., 1983. Sales rep. to dist. account mgr. to asst. nat. account mgr. Gen. Foods Corp., Atlanta, Dallas and White Plains, N.Y., 1974-81; mgmt. cons. Touche Ross, N.Y.C., 1983-85; corp. planning mgr. PepsiCo, Purchase, N.Y., 1985-86; sr. mgmt. cons. The Alexander Group, Inc., N.Y.C., 1987-89; pres., founder Canaan Fin. Mgmt., Inc., New Canaan, Conn., 1989—, JTL Enterprises, New Canaan, Conn., 1988—. Site coordinator IRS Vol. Income Tax Assistance Program, New Canaan, 1989; alumni admissions adv. bd. Duke U., Fairfield County, Conn., 1988-89. Mem. Young Women's League (New Canaan chpt.), Assn. of Am. Univ. Women, Kappa Kappa Gamma (Delta Beta chpt.). Home: 213 Old Stamford Rd New Canaan CT 06840-6605

LEONARD, SUSAN RUTH, psychologist, consultant; b. Mineola, N.Y., June 15, 1955; d. Donald Edward Leonard and Jane (Solomon) Hertzberg. BA, L.I. U., 1977; MA, U. N.C., 1980, PhD, 1985. Lic. psychologist, N.C. From instr. to asst. prof. psychology dept. Wake Forest U., Winston-Salem, N.C., 1984-86, staff psychologist counseling ctr., 1985-89; clin. psychologist Manoogian Psychol. Assocs., Winston-Salem, 1986—; cons. Ctr. for Creative Leadership, Greensboro, N.C., 1985-92. Vol. United Way, Winston-Salem, 1989-90, Mental Health Assn., Winston-Salem, 1990-91; mem. adv. com. Family Svcs., Family Violence, Winston-Salem, 1987-89; trustee Resource Ctr. for Women and Ministry in South, 1989-91; bd. dirs. AIDS Task Force, Winston-Salem, 1989-92, Crisis Control Ministry, Winston-Salem, 1990-92, 93—, AIDS Care Svc., Winston-Salem, 1991—. Mem. APA, AAUW, Assn. Women in Psychology, N.C. Psychol. Assn. Office: Manoogian Psychol Assocs 1338 Ashley Sq Winston-Salem NC 27103-2949

LEONARD, VIRGINIA KATHRYN, public finianical manager; b. Street, Md., Aug. 31, 1944; d. Elbert Monroe and Mildred Rudolph (Patrick) Joines; m. James Richard Leonard, Aug. 31, 1963; children: James Richard II, Raymun Bradley. Student, Ea. Nazarene Coll., 1962-63; AA, Harford Community Coll., 1976; BS in Bus. Mgmt., U. Md., 1983; grad., U.S. Army Mgmt. Staff Coll., 1988, Fed. Exec. Inst., 1992. Sec. with U.S. Army, Aberdeen Proving Ground, Md., 1965-75; program analyst Facilities Engring., Aberdeen Proving Ground, Md., 1976-79; budget analyst Aberdeen Proving Ground Command, 1980; program analyst officer Facilities Engring., Aberdeen Proving Ground, Md., 1981; budget analyst Test and Evaluation Command, Aberdeen Proving Ground, Md., 1982-83; budget analyst, budget officer Dept. of Army, Washington, 1984; budget officer test and evaluation command U.S. Army, Aberdeen Proving Ground, Md., 1985-89; fin. mgr. test and evaluation command U.S. Army, Aberdeen Proving Ground, 1989-94, dir. resource mgmt. test and evaluation command, 1994—. Mem. Am. Soc. Mil. Comptrollers, Assn. U.S. Army, Fed. Exec. Inst. Alumni Assn. Office: Test and Evaluation Command AMSTE-RM Dept of Army Aberdeen Proving Ground MD 21005

LEONE, GINA, artist, editor; b. Astoria, N.Y., June 29, 1966; d. Leo F. and Patricia Leone. Cert. in Comml. Art., Somerset County Tech. Inst., Sommerville, N.J., 1988; BFA in Illustration with honors, Pratt Inst., 1990. Computer artist Digital Learning Systems, Parsipanny, N.J., 1987-88, Einstein & Sandom, Inc., N.Y.C., 1989-90; freelance artist Califon, N.J., 1987—. Artist; exhibits include Manhattan Savings Bank, N.Y.C., 1990, Dog Fanciers Club, 1988-94 (hon. mention, Westminster award 1992), Creative Newspaper (award of merit 1989) St. Hubert's Giralda Animal Imagery Exhibit, Madison, N.J., 1991, 92 (1st place award 1991) Art Show at the Dog Show, Wichita, Kans. 1991, Wildlife Art Exhibit School of Vet. Medicine, La. State U., 1991, Twp. of Lebanon Mus., 1993, Dog Mus., St. Louis, 1991, 94-95; commns. include Am. Kennel Club Gazette, N.Y.C., Fancy Pubs., Inc., Mission Viejo, Calif.. 1988-91; pub., editor (quarterly) The Dachshund Rev., 1991-94, advisory editor, 1995—. Finalist Dog Writers' Assn. Am., Inc. Competition, 1994. Mem. Dachshund Club Am. (top owner and handler 1992), Dachshund Club of N.J. (bd. dirs. 1992-94), Dachshund Fanciers Assn. Berks County, N.J. Office: Animal Portraits & Illustrations RD 1 Box 357 Califon NJ 07830

LEONE, JANET ROSEMARIE, critical care nurse; b. Miami, Fla., Sept. 25, 1958; d. Anthony Daniel and Josephine Marie (Danzo) Leone. BSN summa cum laude, Fla. State U., 1980. RN, Fla.; cert. ACLS, adminstrn. chemotherapy agts. Staff nurse Doctors Hosp. Sarasota, Fla., 1981, Tampa (Fla.) Gen. Hosp., 1981-88; supr. sr. utilization mgmt. Aetna Health Plans, Tampa, 1988-93, med. case mgr., 1993—; seminar speaker, 1987. Vol. Muscular Dystrophy Assn., Tampa, 1991, Health Care Reform Com., 1993. Fellow AACN; mem. Flight Angels. Roman Catholic. Home: 1914 Plantation Key Cir Apt 201 Brandon FL 33511

LEONE, JAYNE MARIE, quality assurance professional; b. Farmington, Conn., Sept. 8, 1959; d. Thomas J. and Justine (Mastrofilippo) L. BS, Bentley Coll., 1981; MBA, St. John's U., 1987. Cert. paralegal in employee benefits. Statis. analyst Chiquita Brands Inc., N.Y.C., 1982-84, asst. mgr. quality info., 1984-87; mgr. quality info. Chiquita Brands Inc., Cin., 1987—. Mem. Am. Soc. Quality Control, Am. Statis. Assn., Beta Gamma Sigma. Office: Chiquita Brands Inc 250 E 5th St Cincinnati OH 45202

LEONE, JUDITH GIBSON, educational media specialist, video production company executive; b. Toms River, N.J., Sept. 27, 1945; d. James Delaney and Louise Gertrude (Eberhardt) Gibson; m. Stephan Robert Leone, Nov. 27, 1971; stepchildren: Cheryl, Debra. BA, Kean Coll., 1970; MLS, Rutgers U., 1980. Cert. edn. media specialist. Tchr. Toms River Schs., 1970-84, media specialist, 1984-89; v.p., owner Prodn. House, Toms River, 1985-94; libr. coord. Amb. Christian Acad., Toms River, 1989-95; exec. dir. Designer Showcase, 1995—; mem. region 5 book evaluation com. N.J. State Libr. System, 1986—. Sec., bd. dirs. The Shelter, Inc., Bricktown, N.J., 1979—; pres. Open Arms, Inc.; pres., bd. dirs. Harbor House; v.p., bd. dirs. Ocean County chpt. United Way; bd. dirs. Garden State Philharm., Italian-Am. Cultural and Heritage Soc. Mem. N.J. Ednl. Assn., Ednl. Media Assn. N.J., Ocean County Libr. Assn., Internat. Assn. Sch. Librarianship, Toms River Country Club. Democrat. Home: 143 Cranmoor Dr Toms River NJ 08753-6805

LEONG, JO-ANN CHING, microbiologist, educator; b. Honolulu, May 15, 1942; d. Raymond and Josephine Ching; m. Oren T.H. Leong; children: Kara Elise, Jonathan Raymond. BA in Zoology, U. Calif., Berkeley, 1964; PhD in Microbiology, San Francisco Sch. Medicine, 1971. Postdoctoral rsch. assoc. dept. biochemistry U. Calif., San Francisco, 1971-75, asst. rsch. virologist Cancer Rsch. Inst., 1975; asst. prof. Oreg. State U., Corvallis, 1975-80, assoc. prof., 1980-86, prof., 1986-92, disting. prof., 1992—; grant reviewer Sea Grant, NSF, CRIS, USDA, NIH; cons. Am. Microscan, 1986. Co-author: Retroviruses and Differentiation, 1982, Molecular Approaches to Bacteria and Viral Diseases of Fish, 1983, Fish Vaccination, 1988, Viral Vaccines for Aquaculture, 1993, Human Endogenous Retroviruses, 1994. Coord. Women in Sci. Career Workshop, Portland (Oreg.) State U., 1977. Recipient Dernham Rsch. Fellowship, Am. Cancer Soc., 1973-75, fellowship Giannini Found. for Med. Rsch., 1973, Rsch. award Sigma Xi, 1990; named NORCAS prof. Batelle NW Labs, 1976, Disting Prof. Oreg. State U. Alumni Assn., 1991. Fellow Am. Acad. Microbiology; mem. AAAS, AAUP (exec. bd. 1982), European Assn. of Fish Pathologists, Am. Soc. Microbiology, Am. Soc. Virology, Am. Fisheries soc. (fish health sect.), Assn. Women in Sci., Am. Assn. Cancer Rsch. Office: Oreg State U Dept Microbiology Corvallis OR 97331

LEONG, SUE, community health and pediatrics nurse; b. Alameda, Calif., Feb. 15, 1930; d. Leong Dai Sun and Leong San See. BS, U. Calif., San Francisco, 1953; MPH, U. Mich., 1963; MA, San Francisco Theol. Sem., 1958. Cert. sch. nurse, sch. nurse practitioner, nurse specialist. Head nurse Lafayette Clinic, Detroit; pub. health nurse San Francisco Health Dept.; assoc. dir. Ecumenical Campus Ctr., Ann Arbor, Mich.; sch. nurse practitioner Ann Arbor Pub. Schs.; exec. dir. Mich. Assn. Sch. Nurses; adj. asst. prof. U. Mich. Contbr. articles to profl. jours. Mem. NEA, Nat. Assn. Pediatric Nurse Assocs. and Practitioners, Am. Sch. Health Assn., Nat. Assn. Sch. Nurses, Mich. Assn. Sch. Nurses (Disting. Svc. award 1990, Dorothy Christy award 1993). Home: 1506 Golden Ave Ann Arbor MI 48104-4327

LEPAGE, CANDYCE RUTH, school psychologist; b. Springfield, Mass., Aug. 5, 1951; d. Stephen Edward and Ina Ruth (Melenek) LeP. BS in Edn., Am. Internat. Coll., 1973; MEd, CAGS, Springfield Coll., 1974. Cert. sch. psychologist; NCSP., lic. ednl. psychologist. Home tchr. Springfield (Mass.) Pub. Schs., 1975; substitute tchr. Springfield and Chicopee (Mass.) Pub. Schs., 1975-77; substitute sch. psychologist Chicopee Pub. Schs., 1975, counselor-examiner, 1977-78, counselor, examiner, chair chpt. 766, 1978-80; sch. psychologist Ralph C. Mahar Regional Sch., Orange, Mass., 1980—. Bd. dirs. membership Human Resource Ctr. for Rural Communities, Athol, Mass., 1985-86. Mem. Nat. Sch. Psychologists Assn., Mass. Sch. Psychologists Assn., We. Mass. Sch. Psychologists Assn., Franklin/Hampshire Guidance Assn., Athol-Orange Health and Human Svcs. Coalition, Athol-Orange Community Devel. Corp., Psi Chi.

LEPAGE, EILEEN MCCULLOUGH, financial consultant, educator; b. Phila., Oct. 16, 1946; d. Charles Norman and Marie Teresa (Inglesby) McCullough; m. Clifford Bennett LePage Jr., May 17, 1969; children: Clifford Bennett III, Alexander Pierce. BA in English and Secondary Edn., George Washington U., 1969; MEd, Temple U., 1972. Cert. secondary sch. tchr.; registered securities rep. Record-keeper child growth and devel. program Children's Hosp. of Phila., 1965; with advt. dept. Phil. Inquirer, 1966-67; with ops. control U.S. Civil Svc. Commn., Washington, 1967-69; mgr. N.J. Bell Telephone, Trenton, 1969; researcher Temple U., Phila., 1969-71; tchr. Wyomissing (Pa.), 1972-77; fin. cons. various orgns., 1984-93; cons. EML Consulting, Reading, 1994—; adj. instr. Reading (Pa.) Area Community Coll., 1978-81; lectr. English Albright Coll., Reading, 1981-84; founding mem. Common Cents Investment Club, 1983-93. Author: The Clue in the Snow, 1957; editor: 1st Complete Pocket Guide to Atlantic City Casinos, 1984, The Autobiography of Capt. Michael Kevolic, 1986. Bd. dirs. Nat. Found. March of Dimes, Reading, 1969-75, chmn., 1974-75; bd. sch. dirs. Wyomissing Area Sch. Dist., 1984-92; bd. dirs. Wyomissing Pub. Libr., Reading, 1980-85; asst. chmn Region 8 Pa. Sch. Bds. Assn., 1989-91; dir. Saturday Morning Sch., Assn. for Children with Learning Disabilities, Reading, 1970; acting sec. Berks County Commn. for Women, Reading, 1993; active Reading Community Players, 1980. Mem. AAUW (topic chmn.), Am. Assn. Individual Investors (life). Home and Office: EML Cons 10 Phoebe Dr Reading PA 19610-2857

LEPOME, PENELOPE MARIE, rehabilitation counselor, educator; b. Buffalo, Dec. 17, 1945; d. Raymond Arthur and Mildred Evelyn (Johnson) Kramer; m. Robert Charles LePome, May 26, 1966 (div. Jan. 1982); children: Lisa Anne, Kathryn Jane, Robert Charles II. BA in Biology, SUNY, Buffalo, 1967; MS in Vocat. Rehab., U. Nev., Las Vegas, 1984, postgrad., 1993—. Cert. rehab. counselor, substance abuse counselor, ins. rehab. specialist; lic. substitute tchr. and sch. counselor, Nev. Co-owner, salesman Flamingo Realty, Las Vegas, Nev., 1974-76; substitute tchr. Clark County Sch. Dist., Las Vegas, 1969-74, 1982-84; adj. faculty Clark County Community Coll., Las Vegas, 1984-86, Truckee Meadows Community Coll., Reno, 1987; bus. and industry field specialist, Tng. Inst. Clark County Community Coll., 1985-86; probation officer on call Clark County Juvenile Services, Las Vegas, 1984; counselor Nike House, Las Vegas, 1984; mental health techician III, State of Nev., 1984-86; rehab. coord. I, Nev. Bur. Vocat. Rehab., Reno, 1986-92; pvt. practice rehab. counseling, 1984-86; rehab. counselor GENEX Svcs. Inc. (formerly Gen. Rehab. Svcs., Inc.), Reno, 1992—. Active Nev. Womens Polit. Caucus, Las Vegas, 1983-85; carnival chmn. Rex Bell PTA, Las Vegas, 1974-75, treas., 1975-76; leader Frontier Area Girl Scouts U.S., Las Vegas, 1975-76, cookie sale chmn., 1980; treas., bd. dirs. Young Audiences, Las Vegas, 1979-80; mem. Reno City Coun. Adv. Com. Persons With Disabilities, 1991-93. N.Y. State Regents scholar, 1963. Mem. AACD, AAUW (div. officer Nev. 1983-85, pres. 1982-83, v.p. programming 1981-82, v.p. membership 1980-81, life mem.), Assn. Part-time Profls. (bd. dirs.). Republican. Office: 1325 Airmotive Way # 175X Reno NV 89502-3201

LEPOW, JACQUELINE VOIGT, chemist; b. Sheboygan, Wis., Jan. 5, 1953; d. Carlton William and Caroline Jean (Koeppe) Voigt; m. Michael James LePow, Sept. 2, 1986. BA in Chemistry, Alverno Coll., Milw., 1992, BA in Maths., 1992. Environ. chemistry technician Wis. Electric Power Co., Milw., 1981-90; rsch. asst. Miller Brewing Co., Milw., 1990-92; analyt. chemist Hydrite Chem. Co., Milw., 1992—. Mem. Women in Sci. So. Wis. (v.p. 1993-94), Fedn. Environ. Technologists (chmn. 1994), Great Lakes Leadership Network (mem. steering com. 1994), League Women Voters. Office: Hydrite Chem Co 300 Patrick Blvd Brookfield WI 53045-5831

LEPPIK, MARGARET WHITE, state legislator; b. Newark, N.J., June 5, 1943; d. John Underhill and Laura Schaefer White; m. Ilo Elmar Leppik, June 18, 1967; children: Peter, David, Karina. BA, Smith Coll., 1965. Rsch. asst. Wistar Inst., U. Pa., Phila., 1967-68, U. Wis., Madison, 1968-69; mem. Minn. Ho. Reps., St. Paul, 1990, 92, 94. Commr. Golden Valley (Minn.) Planning Com., 1982-90; active Golden Valley Bd. Zoning Appeals, 1985-87. Recipient Citizen of Distinction award Hennepin County Human Svcs. Planning Bd., 1992. Mem. LWV (v.p., dir. 1984-90), Minn. Opera Assn. (pres. 1986-88), Rotary Internat., Optimists Internat. Republican. Home: 7500 Western Ave Golden Valley MN 55427 Office: 393 State Office Bldg Saint Paul MN 55155

LEPPO, TAMARA ELIZABETH MARKS, former sales representative; b. San Jose, Costa Rica, Dec. 12, 1962; came to U.S., 1968; d. Russell Edward and Patricia (Hunt) Marks; m. Michael Leppo, Apr. 23, 1994. Student, Wheaton Coll., Norton, Mass., 1981-83; BA in Spanish Lang. and Lit., Boston U., 1985. Research analyst Coopers & Lybrand, N.Y.C., 1985-87; project coordinator Healthcare Communications, Inc., Princeton, N.J., 1987-88, product mgr., 1988-89; electronic product rep. Commerce Clearing House, Inc., Boston, 1990-91; sales rep., 1991-94. Pres. Boston U. South Campus Govt., 1984-85; mem. June Opera Festival N.J., Princeton, 1986-90. Mem. Am. Mus. of Natural History, Boston U. Alumni Assn., Wheaton Coll. Alumni. Republican. Home: 35-11 Briarwood Ln Marlborough MA 01752

LERMAN, EILEEN R., lawyer; b. N.Y.C., May 6, 1947; d. Alex and Beatrice (Kline) L. BA, Syracuse U., 1969; JD, Rutgers U., 1972; MBA, U. Denver, 1983. Bar: N.Y. 1973, Colo. 1976. atty. FTC, N.Y.C., 1972-74; corp. atty. RCA, N.Y.C., 1974-76; corp. atty. Samsonite Corp. and consumer products div. Beatrice Foods Co., Denver, 1976-78, assoc. gen. counsel, 1978-85, asst. sec., 1979-85; ptnr. Davis, Lerman, & Weinstein, Denver, 1985-92, Eileen R. Lerman & Assocs., 1993—; bd. dir. Legal Aid Soc. of Met. Denver, 1979-80. Bd. dirs., vice chmn. Colo. Postsecondary Ednl. Facilities Authority, 1981-89; bd. dirs., pres. Am. Jewish Com., 1989-92; mem. Leadership Denver, 1983. Mem. ABA, Colo. Women's Bar Assn. (bd. dir. 1980-81), Colo. Bar Assn. (bd. govs.), Denver Bar Assn. (trustee), N.Y. State Bar Assn., Rhone Brackett Inn (sec. 1994), Denver Law Club, Rutgers U. Alumni Assn., University Club. Home: 1018 Fillmore St Denver CO 80206-3332 Office: Eileen R Lerman & Assocs 50 S Steele St Ste 420 Denver CO 80209-2809

LERMAN, RUTH, sculptor; b. N.Y.C., July 17, 1922; d. Isadore and Rose (Marachnick) L.; m. Joseph Gans; 1 child, Adrienne. One woman shows include Creative Gallery, N.Y.C., 1951, 52, Madison Gallery, N.Y.C., 1961, Sculpture Ctr., N.Y.C., 1969, 74, 81, Jewish Cmty. Ctr. on the Palisades, Tenafly, N.J., 1989, Albany (N.Y.) Ctr. Galleries, 1991, Broome St. Gallery, N.Y.C., 1993; exhibited in group shows at Lincoln Ctr., N.Y.C., 1985, Park Row Gallery, Chatham, N.Y., 1985, Berkshire Artisans, Pittsfield, Mass., 1987, Five Points Gallery, East Chatham, N.Y., 1987, N.Y.C. Arsenal Gallery, N.Y.C., 1989, many others; corp. collections include Chiba Bank, Gen. Elec., Euro-Properties, Inc. (France), Hooker Chem. Co., Nico Constrn. Co., Pines Publs., Young & Rubican Internat. Recipient Bronze medal for stone sculpture Knickerbocker Arts, 1965, Purchase award Chem. Bank, 1979, merit award Universita Della Arti, Italy, 1981, award Millay Colony for Arts, Austerlitz, N.Y., 1983, Elliot Liskin award for Sculpture, Yaddo, N.Y., 1984, award for casting a bronze N.Y. Foundry, 1985. Home: 365 Rte 24 East Chatham NY 12060

LERNER, LINDA JOYCE, human resources executive; b. N.Y.C., Aug. 19, 1944; d. Morris and Victoria (Mizrahi) L. BS in Bus., U. Bridgeport, 1966. Asst. dir. pers. Bridgeport (Conn.) Hosp., 1969-73; dir. pers. Tufts U., Boston, 1973-80; sr. v.p. human resources Provident Instn. Savs., Boston, 1981-88; sr. v.p. UST Corp. Bank Holding Co., Boston, 1988—. Mem. allocations com. Combined Jewish Philanthropies; v.p. bd. dirs. Horizons for Youth, Boston, 1991—; bd. dirs. Operation A.B.L.E. Fellow Internat. Mktg. Inst., Boston, 1978. Mem. ASTD, N.E. Human Resources Assn., Am. Bankers Assn. (human resources exec. com. 1991—), Mass. Bankers Assn. (human resources com. 1989—, chmn. human resources com. 1993-94), Fin. Women Internat., Boston Human Resources Assn. (chmn. sr. practitioners, bd. dirs.), The Boston Club. Office: UST Corp 40 Court St Boston MA 02108-2202

LERNER, PAULA MARIE, photographer; b. N.Y.C., Nov. 16, 1959; d. Bernard and Dorothy (Simon) L.; m. Thomas James Dunlap, June 5, 1988; children: Maia Lerner Dunlap, Eliana Lerner Dunlap. BA in Philosophy, Harvard U., 1983. Freelance photographer, 1985—. Recipient Excellent Portfolio award Maine Photog. Workshop, Rockport, 1989, Pictures of Yr. award U. Mo. Sch. Journalism, 1993. Mem. Am. Soc. Media Photographers (Silver medal/Big Picture award 1993), Nat. Press Photographers Assn. Office: 30 Selwyn Rd Belmont MA 02178-3556

LEROY, CATHERINE A., legislative counsel; b. Houston, Oct. 26, 1946. BA, Smith Coll., 1968; JD, U. Mich., 1973. Staff atty. U.S. Equal Employment Opportunity Commn., 1973-75, asst. counsel, 1975-80; chief counsel subcom. on civil and constitutional rights, com. on the judiciary, 1980—. Office: Subcom Civil & Constl Rights 806 O'Neill House Office Bldg Washington DC 20515*

LEROY, ELIZABETH REICHELT, adult education educator; b. Chgo., Dec. 17, 1939; d. Walter Glen and Dorothy Catherine (Hoffman) Reichelt; m. Robert Edward LeRoy, June 8, 1963; children: Robert Scott, Mary Beth, Linda Ann, Jeffrey Alan. BS in Edn., Ball State U., 1961, MA in Spl. Edn., 1965. Tchr. St. Victor's Sch., Calumet City, Ill., 1958-59, Hoover Sch., Calumet City, 1961-63, Michigan City (Ind.) Schs., 1964, LaPorte (Ind.) Comty. Schs., 1973-75, Dept. Corrections, Westville, Ind., 1977—; coord. Promising Practices Adult Edn., Indpls., 1992—. Fellow AAUW (br. pres. 1977-79, 91-93, state chair women's issues 1977-81, state chair cultural issues 1981-83, br. chair ednl. found. 1985—), Am. Assn. Adult Continuing Edn. (charter), Ind. State Tchrs. Assn. (pres. 1986—, instnl. tchr. task force 1989—), Correctional Edn. Assn., Correctional Edn. Assn. Ind. Roman Catholic. Home: 701 W 11th LaPorte IN 46350 Office: Westville Correctional Ctr Box 473 Westville IN 46391

LERSCH, DELYNDEN RIFE, computer engineering executive; b. Grundy, Va., Mar. 22, 1949; d. Woodrow and Eunice Louise (Atwell) Rife; m. John Robert Lersch, May 9, 1976; children: Desmond, Kristofer. BSEE, Va. Poly. Inst. and State U., 1970; postgrad. Boston U., 1975—. With Stone & Webster Engrng. Corp., 1970-91, elec. engr., supr. computer applications, Boston, 1978-80, mgr. computer graphics, 1980-84, mgr. engrng. systems and computer graphics, 1984-87, div. chief info. techs., 1987-90, v.p., 1990-91; chief A.D.P. officer Univ. Rsch. Assocs., 1991-94; CARE account mgr. Perot Sys. Corp., Dallas, 1994—. Named Stone and Webster's Woman Engr. of Yr., 1976, 79; Mass. Solar Energy Research grantee, 1978; honored by Engrng. News Record mag. for contbns. to constrn. industry, 1983. Mem. IEEE (sr.), Assn. Women in Sci., Soc. Women Engrs. (sr.), Women in Sci. and Engrng., Energy Communicators, Nat. Computer Graphics Assn., Profl. Council New Eng., Women in Energy (dir. Mass. chpt. 1978, New Eng. region 1979), LWV, Rotary (Rotarian of Yr. 1993-94). Congregationalist. Club: Boston Bus. and Profl. Women's. Author: Cable Schedule Information Systems As Used in Power Plant Construction, 1973, 2d edit., 1975; Information Systems Available for Use by Electrical Engineers, 1976; contbr. articles in field of computer aided design and engrng. Home: 1106 Bristol Cir De Soto TX 75115-2818 Office: Perot Sys Corp 12377 Merit Dr Ste 1100 Dallas TX 75251

LERUD, JOANNE VAN ORNUM, library administrator; b. Jamestown, N.D., Nov. 21, 1949; d. Elbert Hiel and Dorothy Arlene (Littrick) Van Ornum; m. Gerald Henry Groenewold, Jan. 15, 1971 (div. Nov. 1978); 1 child, Gerd Heil Groenewold; m. Jeffrey Craig Lerud, Aug. 30, 1980; 1 child, Jesse Currier. BS in Geology, U. N.D., 1971, MS in Geology, 1979; MA in Librarianship and Info. Mgmt., U. Denver, 1979. Assoc. tech. info. specialist Marathon Oil Co., Littleton, Colo., 1980-86; libr. dir. Mont. Coll. Mineral Sci. and Tech., Butte, 1986-89, Colo. Sch. Mines, Golden, 1989—; report investigator in field. NSF grantee, 1970. Mem. Geosci. Info. Soc. (v.p. 1988, pres. 1989). Office: Colo Sch Mines Arthur Lakes Libr Golden CO 80401

LESCHINSKI, DAWN CAROL, pilot; b. Elizabeth, N.J., Oct. 13, 1960; d. Adam and Virginia June (Price) L. A, Mercer C.C., Trenton, N.J., 1983. Lic. pilot. Reservationist People Express Airlines, Newark, 1984-85; flight instr. Aviation Career Acad., Lumberton, N.J., 1985-86; multi-engine pilot D-W Transp., Lumberton, 1986-87; co-pilot So. Jersey Airways, Atlantic City, 1987-89; jet pilot Allied-Signal, Southbend, Ind., 1990—. Vol. pilot Spl. Olympics, St. Paul, 1992. Recipient 1st Place award Garden State 300, 1985, Safety award Nat. Bus. Aircraft Assn., 1994. Home: 3506 N Main St Apt 17 Mishawaka IN 46545

LESHER, MARGARET LISCO, newspaper publisher, songwriter; b. San Antonio, Tex., May 4, 1932; d. Lloyd Elmo Lisco and Dovie Deona (Maynard) Lisco Welch; m. William Jarvis Ryan (dec.); children: Patricia Ryan Simmonds, Wendi Ryan Alves, Jill Ryan Heidt, Roxanne Ryan Gibson; m. Dean Stanley Lesher, Sr., Apr. 2, 1973 (dec.); children: Dean S. II, Melinda K., Cynthia A. Student Coalinga (Calif.) Jr. Coll. Dir. sales Chatmar, Inc., Concord, Calif., 1970-73; dir. cmty. svcs. Contra Costa Times Newspaper, Walnut Creek, Calif., 1973-94; chmn. bd. Lesher Comm., Inc., Walnut Creek, 1974—, Calif. Delta Newspapers, Inc., Antioch, 1975—, No. Calif. Publs., Inc., Telegraph.-News Publs., Inc., Inc.; pres., exec. dir., dean Margaret Lesher Found. Composer, lyricist gospel song Margaret Lesher Album, 1976 (So. Calif. Motion Picture Coun. Bronze Halo award 1982); author 14 published poems. Pres., exec. dir. Dean and Margaret Lesher Found.; regent Holy Names Coll., Oakland, Calif., 1979-86; chief of protocol Contra Costa County, 1980—; dir. Bay Area Sports Hall of Fame, San Francisco, 1982—; bd. overseers U. Calif., San Francisco, 1983-90; mem. San Francisco Host Com., 1983—, Internat. Host Com. of Calif., 1983-86, Nat. Reading Initiative Coordinating Coun., 1988—; developed Citizen Recognition Awards Program with County Police Chiefs Assn.; founded Contra Costa Literacy Alliance; commr. Port of Richmond, Calif., 1983-86; chmn. adv. bd. Crisis Nursery of Bay Area, Concord, 1983-86; adv. bd. Oakland A's Baseball Team, 1984-85, Battered Women, 1983—; pres. bd. dirs. Mt. Diablo Hosp. Found., 1980-81; bd. dirs. Contra Costa Council, 1984-90; mem. adv. bd. Las Trampas Sch. Mentally Retarded, chmn., 1984-90; trustee Oakland Symphony Orch., 1985-86; host Informed Viewer pub. svc. program Sta. KFCB-TV. Recipient Spl. Merit award State of Calif., 1982, Internat. Silver Angel award, 1st pl. for lit. program Calif. Newspaper Pub.'s Assn.; named Calif. Assembly Woman of Yr. Mem. Am. Newspaper Pub. Assn. (ednl. svcs. com. 1988—), Gospel Music Assn., ASCAP, Nat. TV Acad. Arts & Scis., Blackhawk Country Club. Republican. Christian. Avocation: horses. Office: Contra Costa Times Lesher Comm Inc 2640 Shadelands Dr Walnut Creek CA 94598-2513

LESIAK, LUCILLE ANN, graphic designer; b. Chgo., Dec. 31, 1946; d. Walter Joseph and Anna (Cachur) L. BS, Ill. Inst. Tech., 1968. Designer Scott, Foresman & Co., Glenview, Ill., 1968-79, McDougal, Littell & Co., Evanston, Ill., 1979-80; prin. Image Concepts Ltd., Chgo., 1980-82; pres. Lucy Lesiak Design Ltd., Chgo., 1982-91; prin. Lesiak/Crampton Design, Inc., Chgo., 1991—. Mem. Am. Inst. Graphic Arts, Nat. Assn. Women Bus. Owners, Chgo. Book Clinic (cert. of award 1974, 78, 79, 85-90, 94, Desi award 1987, 89). Roman Catholic. Home: 575 W Madison St Apt 2809 Chicago IL 60661

LESLIE, LOTTIE LYLE, retired secondary education educator; b. Huntsville, Ala., Aug. 5, 1930; d. James Peter and Amanda Lacy Burns; children: Thomas E. Lyle Jr., Theodore Christopher Leslie, DeMarcus Miller Leslie. BS, Ala. A and M U., 1953, student, 1960-83; training cert., Learning Ctrs. of Am., 1985. Cert. secondary tchr. Social studies, English, Music. Tchr. Madison County Bd. Edn., Huntsville, Ala. Author: Teaching the Importance of Character Through Poetry, 1968-69, Ways to Teach Language Composition and Literature, Versatility Versus Violence, Families and Foreign Relationships, Musical Instruments of the World From K-12 and Undergraduate to Graduate; contbr. poetry to profl jours. Recipient Miss Liberty trophy, 1986, Victory pin, 1987, Medal of Honor Commemorating Disting. Lifelong Achievements, 1993, cert. appreciation Indian Creek P.B. Ch., 1994. Mem. NEA, ASCD, Ala. Edn. Assn., Madison County Music Edn. Assn., Internat. Black Writers and Artists, Inc., N.Y. Poetry Soc., Am. Poetry Assn. (vol. IV no. 2 summer 1985). Home: 3207 Farris Dr NW Huntsville AL 35810-3342

LESONSKY, RIEVA, editor in chief; b. N.Y.C., June 20, 1952; d. Gerald and Muriel (Cash) L. BJ, U. Mo., 1974. Researcher Doubleday & Co., N.Y.C., 1975-78; researcher Entrepreneur Mag., L.A., 1978-80, rsch. dir., 1983-84, mng. editor, 1985-86, exec. editor, 1986-87; editor Entrepreneur Mag., Irvine, Calif., 1987-90; editor-in-chief Entrepreneur Mag. Bus. Start-Ups Entrepreneur Group, Irvine, Calif., 1990—; rsch. dir. LFP Inc., L.A., 1980-82; speaker, lect. in field. Editor: 184 Businesses Anyone Can Start, 1990, Complete Guide to Owning a Home-based Business, 1990, 168 More Businesses Anyone Can Start, 1991, 111 Businesses You Can Start for Under $10,000, 1991; contbr. articles to mags. Apptd. SBA Nat. Adv. Coun., 1994-96. Named Dist. Media Advocate of Yr., Small Bus. Adminstrn. Mem. Women's Network for Entrepreneurial Tng. (bd. dirs., advisor, nat. steeri. Office: Entrepreneur Mag Group 2392 Morse Ave Irvine CA 92714-6234

LESSARD, LINDA ANN, accountant; b. Port Huron, Mich., June 21, 1954; d. Willis John and Marie (Susalla) Dean; m. Arthur Gordon Lessard, Aug. 23, 1974; children: David, Jonathan. AA, St. Clair City C. C., Port Huron, 1974; BA, Mich. State U., 1977. CPA, Mich. Systems operator Danielson, Schultz & Co., Lansing, Mich., 1975-77, Ward & Ward, CPA, Detroit, 1977-79; systems mgr. Heemer, Klein, Grainer & Lamb, Warren, Mich., 1979-80, Grainer & Rossi, CPA, Warren, 1980-83; systems supr. Arthur Andersen & Co., Detroit, 1983-90; legal adminstr. Bigler, Berry, Johnston, Sztykiel & Hunt, Troy, Mich., 1990—; v.p. Metro Sml. Systems Mgmt., Detroit, 1979-83. Team walk leader March of Dimes, Detroit, 1989; auditor Miss Am. Scholarship Pageant, Macomb County, Mich., 1990-93; mem. St. Thecla Home and Sch. Assn., treas., 1993-95, vice chairperson parish coun., 1994—. Office: Bigler Berry Johnston Sztykiel & Hunt 1301 W Long Lake Ste 250 Troy MI 48098

LESSER, DEENA P., town clerk; b. Bklyn., Apr. 11, 1930; d. Benjmain M. and Zelda E. (Goldstein) Lynn; m. Frank Lesser, Dec. 17, 1950; children: Steven Charles, Laura Lesser Lane, Julie Lesser Barkan. BA, Adelphi U., 1950. Dir. design, treas. Vintage Prints, Inc., Port Washington, N.Y., 1969-84; trustee Village of Thomaston, N.Y., 1981-87; mayor Village of Thomaston, 1989-92; cons. Claire Stern Assocs., N.Y.C., 1984-86; real estate sales Frank Lesser Realty, Great Neck, N.Y., 1986-92; town clk. Town of North Hempstead, Manhasset, N.Y., 1992—; mem. Great Neck Cable Commn., pub. access com., 1982-85; bd. dirs. Water Authority of Great Neck North. Mem. Great Neck Village Ofcls. Assn. (vice-chair 1989-91). Democrat. Jewish. Office: Town of North Hempstead 200 Plandome Rd Manhasset NY 11030-2326

LESSER, JOAN L., lawyer; b. L.A.. BA, Brandeis U., 1969; JD, U. So. Calif., 1973. Bar: Calif. 1973, U.S. Dist. Ct. (cen. dist.) Calif. 1974. Assoc. Irell and Manella, L.A., 1973-80, ptnr., 1980—; mem. planning com. Ann. Real Property Inst., Continuing Edn. of Bar, Berkeley, 1990—; speaker at profl. confs. Trustee Windward Sch.; mem. Grad. Leadership, L.A., 1992. Mem. Orgn. Women Execs. (past pres., bd. dirs.), Order of Coif. Office: Irell and Manella Ste 40 1800 Avenue Of The Stars Los Angeles CA 90067-4211

LESSER, WENDY, literary magazine editor, writer, consultant; b. Santa Monica, Calif., Mar. 20, 1952; d. Murray Leon Lesser and Millicent (Gerson) Dillon; m. Richard Rizzo, Jan. 18, 1985; 1 stepchild, Dov Antonio; 1 child, Nicholas. BA, Harvard U., 1973; MA, Cambridge (Eng.) U., 1975; PhD, U. Calif., Berkeley, 1982. Founding ptnr. Lesser & Ogden Assocs., Berkeley, 1977-81; founding editor The Threepenny Rev., Berkeley, 1980—; vis. lectr. U. Calif., Santa Cruz, 1983, 86, 90; Bellagio resident Rockefeller Found., Italy, 1984. Author: The Life Below the Ground, 1987, His Other Half, 1991, Pictures at an Execution, 1994; editor: Hiding in Plain Sight, 1993. Fellow NEH, 1983, 92, Guggenheim fellow, 1988. Democrat. Office: The Threepenny Rev PO Box 9131 Berkeley CA 94709

LESSICK, MIRA LEE, nursing educator; b. Hazleton, Pa., Jan. 25, 1949; d. Jack H. and Shirley E. (Frumkin) L. Diploma in nursing, Albany (N.Y.) Med. Ctr., 1969; BSN, Boston U., 1972; MS, U. Colo., 1973; PhD, U. Tex., 1986. Staff nurse Boston City Hosp. and Mass. Gen. Hosp., 1969-72; instr. to asst. prof. nursing, genetics clinician U. Rochester, N.Y., 1973-79; asst. prof. nursing, practitioner Rush U., Chgo., 1986-91, assoc. prof. nursing, 1992—. Contbr. articles to profl. jours. Recipient Bd. of Govs. award, Excellence in Pediatric Nursing award Albany Med. Ctr., 1969, Outstanding Nurse Recognition award March of Dimes Birth Defects Found., 1991, Recognition award for Individual Contbn. to Maternal-Child Health Nat. Perinatal Assn., 1993. Mem. AAAS, ANA, APHA, Internat. Soc. Nurses in Genetics (chair rsch. com.), Assn. Women's Health, Obstetric, and Neonatal Nurses, Am. Soc. Human Genetics, Chgo. Nurses Assn. (legis. com. 1990-91), N.Y. Acad. Scis., Midwest Nursing Rsch. Soc., Sigma Theta Tau (Luther Christman award for excellence in published writing 1993), Phi Kappa Phi. Home: 4180 N Marine Dr Apt 610 Chicago IL 60613-2210 Office: Rush U Coll Nursing 301 SSH Chicago IL 60612

LESSLEY, LORI BURKHALTER, real estate referral broker; b. Petersburg, Va., June 20, 1959; d. Donald R. and Dolores (Kell) Burkhalter; m. John C. Lessley, Nov. 28, 1986; 1 child, Helen. Student, Millsaps Coll., 1977-78, Memphis State U., 1978, U. S.C., 1991—. Real estate sales agt. Northside Realty, Atlanta, 1984-90; real estate referral broker RAL Referral, Inc., Columbia, S.C., 1991—. Pres. Chattahoochee Sta. Homeowners Assn., Norcross, Ga., 1989. Mem. La Leche League Internat., Golden Key Honor Soc. Presbyterian.

LESTER, ANGELA LAVONE, contractor; b. Memphis, Jan. 14, 1948; d. Irby Earl and Hilda Anita (Barr) Smith; m. Richard Allen Demott, Aug. 21, 1970 (div. 1981); children: Brian Allen, Christopher Richard; m. David Lee Lester, July 14, 1984. Archtl. cert., Polk C.C., Lakeland, Fla., 1978. Cert. building contractor, real estate broker, Fla., 1986. Residential designer, owner So. Drafting and Design, Winter Haven, Fla., 1978-82; real estate agt., sales dir. Lakeside Realty, Lakeland, 1981-87; real estate agt., owner Lester & Assocs., Lakeland, 1988-93; builder, owner All Fla. Homes Inc., Lakeland, 1993—; builder, owner Lester Properties Inc., Lakeland, 1986-92. Baptist. Home and Office: 8409 Maid Marion Tr Lakeland FL 33809

LESTER, PAMELA ROBIN, lawyer; b. N.Y.C., Aug. 5, 1958; d. Howard M. and Patricia Barbara (Briger) L. Student, Princeton U., 1978-79; BA cum laude, Amherst Coll., 1980; JD, Fordham U., 1983. Bar: N.Y. 1984, D.C. 1985. With Advantage Internat., Inc., Washington, 1984-89, gen. counsel, 1987-89; assoc. Akin, Gump, Strauss, Hauer & Feld, Washington, 1989-90; v.p. bus. affairs and gen. counsel Time Warner Sports, N.Y.C., 1991—; adj. lectr. sports law Am. U. Law Sch., 1989-91; adj. faculty sports law Fordham U. Law Sch., 1992—. Contbr. chpt. to: The Law of Professional and Amateur Sports, 1989. Mem. ABA (program and sports divsn. chair forum entertainment and sports industries' governing com., 1992-94, governing com. standing com. on forum-coms., 1994—), Assn. Bar City N.Y. (sports law com. 1991—), Sports Lawyers Assn. (bd. dirs.), N.Y. State Bar Assn., Women's Sports Found. (mem. bd. adv.). Office: Time Warner Sports 1100 Ave Of The Americas New York NY 10036-6712

LESTHA, CHRISTINE ANN, nurse practitioner; b. Worcester, Mass., June 16, 1961; d. Donald William and Dorothy Mary Ellen (Miller) L. BSN, Northeastern U., 1986; MSN, Simmons Coll., 1990. Cert. adult nurse practitioner. Staff nurse New Eng. Med. Ctr., Boston, 1986-90; nurse practitioner, employee health coord. Somerville (Mass.) Hosp., 1991-92; nurse practitioner Marlborough (Mass.) Hosp., 1992—. Sponsor Nat. Abortion Rights Action League, Mass. Choice, Marlborough Emergency Svcs. Found, Northeastern U. Alumni Fund (mem. exec. com.), Planned Parenthood, Delta Phi Epsilon Alumnae; mem. Sudbury Valley Trustees; founder Marlborough Area Advanced Practice Nurses Group. Mem. Am. Coll. Nurse Practitioners, Nurse Pertinent Legislation Affecting Nurses (PLAN), Mass. Nurses Assn., Mass. Coalition Nurse Practitioners, Boston Area Employee Health Adminstrs. (co-chair 1991-93), Appalachian Mountain Club. Roman Catholic. Home: 2 Elm Pl Marlborough MA 01752 Office: Marlborough Hosp 57 Union St Marlborough MA 01752

LETENDRE, MARY JEAN, federal agency administrator; b. Chippewa Falls., Wis.; m. Andre LeTendre; children: Jeanne Marie, Jacqueline Doyle, Robert, Jon, Andre. Student, Northland Coll.; BS summa cum laude, Coll. St. Scholastic; MA, U. No. Colo.; LLD (hon.), Coll. St. Scholastica, 1992. Elem. tchr. Chippewa Falls, Wis.; title I tchr. Wausau, Wis.; homebound instr. Tulsa; cons. Wausau Pub. Schs.; spl. asst. to sec. Dept. of Edn.; acting asst. sec. office elem. and secondary edn. Office Elem. and Secondary Edn., Dept. of Edn., now dir. compensatory edn. programs. Trustee Bakers Scholars, Georgetown U.; mem. Confraternity of Christian Doctrine; mem. edn. com. N.S.O., Kennedy Ctr. Recipient Disting. Svc. award Nat. Assn. Fed. Edn. Program Adminstrs., 1989, Humanitarian award Nat. Coalition Chpt. 1 Parents. Office: Compensatory Edn Progs Dept of Edn 1280 Maryland Ave SW Rm 4400 Washington DC 20224*

LETIZIA, DOROTHY, nursing educator; b. Dover, N.J., Dec. 20, 1938; d. Max and D. Marie (McManus) Meichsner; m. Carl Letizia, July 2, 1960; children: Karen, Janie. BSN, U. Pa., 1960, MSN, 1970; EdD, Rutgers U., 1989. RN, N.J. Clin. adj. faculty mem. Gloucester County Coll., Sewell, N.J., 1982-88; clin. assoc. prof. Camden County Coll., Blackwood, N.J.; assoc. dean, curriculum coord. Our Lady of Lourdes Sch. Nursing, Camden, N.J., 1992—; mem. adv. bd. coop. programs in nursing Camden County Coll., 1990—. Mem. ANA, AACN, AAUW, Nat. League Nursing, Am. Assn. Adult and Continuing Edn., Sigma Theta Tau. Home: 209 Crest Rd Atco NJ 08004-2738

LETOURNEAU, TANYA MISNER, college director; b. Grand Haven, Mich., Dec. 4, 1963; d. Wilbur Dean Misner and Maria Borden. BA in Psychology, St. Michael's Coll., 1987; MA in Counseling Psychology, U. Mo., Columbia, 1992. Tchr. Readak Ednl. Svcs., Acton, Mass., 1987-88; guidance counselor Wentworth Mil. Acad., Lexington, Mo., 1988-90; grad. asst. U. Mo., Columbia, 1990-92; dir. career svcs. Delaware Valley Coll., Doylestown, Pa., 1992—. Mem. Coll. Placement Coun. Office: Delaware Valley Coll 700 E Butler Ave Doylestown PA 18901

LETT, CYNTHIA ELLEN WEIN, marketing executive; b. Takoma Park, Md., Dec. 24, 1957; d. Arthur Benjamin and Mary Louise (Barker) Wein; m. Gerald Lee Lett, June 1, 1991. BS, Purdue U., 1979; M, Antioch Sch. Law, 1982-83. Mktg. researcher Sheraton, Washington, 1979-80; sales mgr. Sea Pines Plantation Co., Hilton Head Island, S.C., 1980-81; dir. sales Sheraton Potomac Hotel, Rockville, Md., 1981-82, Ritz Carlton Hotel, Washington, 1982-83; pres. Creative Planning Internat., Washington, 1983—; dir. mem. Great Inns Am., Annapolis, 1987-89; etiquette cons., 1989—; dir. meetings Am. Healthcare Inst., 1991-92; corp. affairs mgr. MCI Telecom Corp., 1992—. Author: Getaway Innstyle, America's Fifty Best Inns, 1990; editor Travel Inn Style Newsletter, 1990-91. Mem. Meetings Planners Internat., Washington Conv. and Visitors Assn., Greater Washington Soc. Assn. Execs., Found. for Internat. Meetings (bd. govs. 1985-86), Purdue Club (1982-93). Office: Creative Planning Internat 13116 Hutchinson Way Ste 100 Silver Spring MD 20906-5947

LETZ, EILEEN KORBER, community health nurse; b. Custer, Mont., Dec. 31, 1916; d. Louis Charles and Gertrude Helen (Jackman) Korber; m. Arthur P. Letz, May 17, 1941 (dec.); children: Philip, Richard, Nancy. RN, Bozeman Deaconess Hosp., 1939; BSN, Mont. State U., 1964; MPH, U. Hawaii, 1968. RN, Mont. Supr. surg. fl. Billings (Mont.) Deaconess Hosp., 1952-56; community health nurse Yellowstone County, Billings, 1964-67, 68-70; community health nurse Ft. Peck reservation Indian Health Svc., Poplar, Mont., 1970-72; community health nurse Crow reservation Indian Health Svc., Crow Agency, Mont., 1972-75; nursing cons., program mgr. commun. helath nursing Indian Health Svc., Billings, 1975-82, ret., 1982. Mem. Mont. league for Nursing (bd. dirs. 1980-84, 91-92, v.p. 1984-91), Am. Assn. Ret. Persons. Democrat. Seventh Day Adventist. Home: 2316 Miles Ave Billings MT 59102-4705

LETZIG, BETTY JEAN, association executive; b. Hardin, Mo., Feb. 18, 1926; d. Robert H. and Alina Violet (Mayes) L. BA, Scarritt Coll., 1950, MA, 1968. Ednl. staff The Methodist Ch., Ark., Okla. Tex., 1953-60; with Internat. Deaconess Exchange Program, London, 1961-62; staff exec. Nat. Div. United Meth. Ch., N.Y.C., 1962-95, ret. 1995; coord. Mission Pers. Support Svcs., 1984-88; exec. sec. Deaconess Program Office, 1989-95. Contbr. articles to profl. jours. Bd. dirs. Internat. Svcs. Assn. for Health, Inc., Atlanta, 1974-88, Vellore Christian Med. Coll., N.Y.C., 1984-94; mem. U.S. com. Internat. Coun. Social Welfare, Washington, 1983-89; active Nat. Interfaith Coalition on Aging, Athens, Ga. and Washington, 1972—, pres., 1981-85. Recipient Deaconess Exch. award Commn. Deaconess Work, 1961-62. Mem. Nat. Coun. Aging, Nat. Voluntary Orgns. Ind. Living for Aging (exec. com. 1978-84), Nat. Coun. Social Welfare, Older Women's League. United Methodist. Avocations: travel, beachcombing, photography, needlework. Home: 235 E 22d St Apt 1U New York NY 10010 Office: Nat Program Divsn Gen Bd Global Ministries 475 Riverside Dr Rm 300 New York NY 10115-0099

LEUNG, BETTY BRIGID, nursing administrator; b. Shanghai, People's Rep. China, Oct. 28, 1949; d. Chek Sang and Si Iun (Vong) L. Diploma, St. James Sch. Nursing, 1974; BSN, Hunter-Bellevue Sch. Nursing, 1985; MS in Nursing, CUNY, 1989. Nurse ICU St. James Mercy Hosp., Hornell, N.Y., 1974-80; sr. staff ICU NYU Med. Ctr., N.Y.C., 1980-81, nurse clinician, 1981-85, asst. clin. coord., 1985-88, clin. coord., 1988-91, nursing supr., 1991—. St. James Sch. Nursing scholar, 1972-74; recipient Women's Bd. award, 1974, Therese Cornell Meehan Nursing Rsch. award 1990. Mem. AACN, Am. Orgn. Nurse Execs. Roman Catholic. Office: NYU Med Ctr 560 1st Ave New York NY 10016-6497

LEUPP, EDYTHE PETERSON, retired educator, administrator; b. Mpls., Nov. 27, 1921; d. Reynold H. and Lillian (Aldridge) Peterson; m. Thomas A. Leupp, Jan. 29, 1944(dec.); children: DeEtte, Patrice, Stacia, Roderick, Braden. BS, U. Oreg., 1947, MS, 1951, EdD, 1972. Tchr. various pub. schs. Idaho, 1941-45, Portland, Oreg., 1945-55; dir. tchr. edn. Northwest Nazarene Coll., Nampa, Idaho, 1955-61; sch. adminstr. Portland Pub. Schs., 1963-84; dir. tchr. edn. George Fox Coll., Newberg, Oreg., 1984-87; ret., 1987; vis. prof. So. Nazarene U., Bethany, Okla., 1988—; pres. Portland Assn. Pub. Sch. Adminstrs., 1973-75; dir.-at-large Nat. Coun. Adminstrv. Women in Edn., Washington, 1973-76; state chmn. Oreg. Sch. Prins. Spl. Project, 1978-79; chair Confdn. Oreg. Sch. Adminstrs. Ann. Conf.; rschr. 40 tchr. edn. programs in colls. and univs.; designer tchr. edn. progra, George Fox Coll. Author tchr. edn. materials. Pres. Idaho State Aux. Mcpl. League, 1957, Nampa PTA, 1958, Nampa unit AAUW, 1956; bd. dirs. Portland Fedn. Women's Clubs, 1963. Idea fellow Charles Kettering Found., 1978, 80, 87, 91, 92, 93, 94. Mem. ASCD, Am. Assn. Colls. Tchr. Edn., Delta Kappa Gamma (state pres. 1986-88, Golden Gift award 1984), Phi Delta Kappa, Pi Lambda Theta. Republican. Nazarene. Home: 8100 SW 2nd Ave Portland OR 97219 Office: So Nazarene U Bethany OK 73008

LEVA, MARISA, occupational therapist; b. Schenectady, N.Y., Feb. 12, 1954; d. Donald Leva. BA in Spanish magna cum laude, SUNY, Brockport, 1976; BS in Occupational Therapy magna cum laude, Temple U., 1984. Cert. hand therapist. Occupational therapist Fitzgerald Mercy Hosp., Darby, Pa., 1984, St. Agnes Med. Ctr., Phila., 1984-86; clin. specialist in hand therapy Delaware County Meml. Hosp., Drexel Hill, Pa., 1986—. Mem. Soc. Am. Magicians, Internat. Brotherhood Magicians.

LEVALLEY, JOAN CATHERINE, accountant; b. Decatur, Ill., Nov. 27, 1931; d. Clarence and Pearl Mae (McClure) Krall; m. Charles R. LeValley, Apr. 13, 1958 (div.); children: Curtis Ray, Cara Marie. BA in Bus., Manchester Coll., 1957. Accredited tax advisor, Ill. Acct. with various firms, 1960-76; pvt. practice acctg., Park Ridge, Ill., 1964-79; pres., dir. LeValley & Assocs., Inc., Park Ridge, 1979—; mem. tax adv. com. Chgo. IRS Dirs.; mem. com. United Way of Park Ridge, 1991, co-chmn., 1992. Mem. Nat. Assn. Pub. Accts., Ind. Acct. Assn. Ill. (2d woman pres. 1987-88, Person of Yr. award 1990), Bus. and Profl. Women Park Ridge (pres. 1974-75, Bus. Woman of Yr. 1983), Park Ridge C. of C. (treas. 1985-87). Baptist. Avocations: baking; sewing; gardening. Home: 2200 Bouterse St Apt 101 Park Ridge IL 60068-2367 Office: LeValley & Assocs Inc 841 W Touhy Ave Park Ridge IL 60068-3351

LEVAR, JANE GERALYN, financial analyst; b. Milw., Sept. 10, 1960; d. William Anthony and Elizabeth Rose (Grall) L. BS, Marquette U., 1982. CPA; cert. mgmt. acct., internal auditor. Tax acct. Samson Resources, Tulsa, 1982-84; sr. acct. Kolb Lauwasser, Milw., 1984-86; fin. analyst Wis. Gas Co., Milw., 1986—. Mem. Inst. Mgmt. Accts., Wis. Inst. CPAs. Home: 5900 Oriole Ln Greendale WI 53129 Office: Wis Gas Co 626 E Wisconsin Ave Milwaukee WI 53202

LEVEAR, KAREN LEEANN, financial analyst; b. Gardena, Calif., Apr. 30, 1963; d. Gordon Larry and Kathleen (Rogers) Deedon; m. Simon Levear, Aug. 24, 1984; children: Jennifer Kathleen, Duncan Alexander. BS, Oreg. State U., 1985. Sr. asst. mgr. Household Fin. Corp., Portland, Oreg., 1985-87; fin. analyst Willamette Savs. & Loan, Portland, 1987-90; consumer loan portfolio evaluation mgr., asst. v.p. First Interstate Bank, Portland, 1990—. Mem. Inst. Mgmt. Accts., Cascade Sports Car Club (alt. dir., com. chair 1987—).

LEVEL, ALLISON VICKERS, science librarian; b. Cookeville, Tenn.. BSPA, U. Ark., 1981; MEd, Kent State U., 1985; MLS, Emporia State U., 1990. Student svcs. Kent (Ohio) State U., 1983-85, No. Ariz. U.,

Flagstaff, 1985-87; student svcs. U. Ark., Fayetteville, 1988; asst. dean, distance edn. Emporia (Kans.) State U., 1989-90; sci. & tech. libr. Libr. of Congress, Washington, 1990—; co-chmn. Libr. Congress Reference Forum. World Wide Web Team vol. Smithsonian Inst., Washington, 1992. Mem. ALA (mem. legislation com. sci. and tech. sect.), D.C. Libr. Assn. Office: Sci & Tech Divsn Libr Of Congress Washington DC 20540

LEVELT SENGERS, JOHANNA MARIA HENRICA, research physicist; b. Amsterdam, The Netherlands, Mar. 4, 1929; came to U.S., 1963; d. Wilhelmus Henricus and Maria Antonia Josephine (Berger) Levelt; m. Jan V. Sengers, Feb. 21, 1963; children: Rachel Teresa, Adriaan Jan, Maarten Willem, Phoebe Josephine. BS, Municipal U., Amsterdam, 1950, MS, 1954, PhD in Physics, 1958; hon. doctorate, Delft U. Tech., 1992. Rsch. asst. Municipal U., Amsterdam, 1954-63; postdoctoral assoc. U. Wis., Madison, 1958-59; rsch. physicist Nat. Bur. Standards, Gaithersburg, Md., 1963—; group leader Nat. Bur. Standards, Gaithersburg, 1978-88; vis. prof. U. Louvain, Belgium, 1971; vis. scientist Municipal U., Amsterdam, 1974-75; Regent's prof. U. Calif., L.A., 1982; sr. fellow Nat. Inst. Standards and Tech., Gaithersburg, 1983—. Contbr. 12 chpts. to books and over 100 articles to profl. jours. Recipient DOC silver medal, 1972, DOC gold medal, 1978, WISE award U.S. Interagy. Com., Women in Sci. and Engring., Washington, 1985, A.V. Humboldt Rsch. award Ruhr-U., Bochum, Germany, 1991. Fellow Am. Phys. Soc.; mem. ASME (nat. del. rsch. com. water and steam 1988—), AIChE, AAAS, NAE, Royal Netherlands Acad. Scis. (corr.), Internat. Assn. Properties Water and Steam (v.p. 1988-90, pres. 1990-91), European Phys. Soc. , Am. Chem. Soc. (divsn. phys. chemistry), Sigma Xi. Democrat. Home: 110 N Van Buren St Rockville MD 20850-1861 Office: Nat Inst Standards & Tech Gaithersburg MD 20899

LEVENSTEIN, DEBRA M. H., financial executive; b. N.Y.C., Apr. 9, 1956; d. Stanley Norman and Lillian Anna (Adoff) Hertz. BA in Acctg., CUNY, 1977; MBA in Fin., St. John's U., 1989. CPA, N.Y. Staff acct. various cos., 1977-79; sr. acct. KPMG Peat Marwick, N.Y.C., 1979-81; budget mgr. Ogilvy & Mather Advt., N.Y.C., 1981-87; dir. budgets and taxes AC&R Advt., N.Y.C., 1989-90; contr. McCaffrey and McCall Advt., N.Y.C., 1991-94; CFO Berlin Wright Cameron Advt., N.Y.C., 1994—. Pres. Thornton-Burns Owners, Inc., Forest Hills, N.Y., 1986-92. Mem. AICPA, N.Y. State Soc. CPAs.

LEVENSTEIN, ROSLYN M., advertising consultant, writer; b. N.Y.C., Mar. 26, 1920; d. Leo Rapoport and Stella Schimmel Rosenberg; m. Justin Seides, June 7, 1943 (div. 1948); 1 child, Leland Seides.; m. Lawrence Levenstein, June 25, 1961. BA in Advt., NYU, 1940. Sr. v.p., assoc. creative dir. Young and Rubicam, Inc., N.Y.C., 1962-79; cons. Young and Rubicam, Inc., Los Angeles and San Diego, 1979-83; advt. cons., writer mag. articles La Jolla, Calif., 1979—. Creator: Excedrin Headache comml. (Andy awards 1967, 68, 69), I'm Only Here for the Beer (Cannes award 1970, Clio Jury award 1970). Recipient: Silver Lion award Cannes Film Festival, 1968, multiple advt. awards U.S. and Eng.; named one of YWCA Women of Yr., 1978. Mem. Charter 100, Women's Com. Brandies U., Nat. Pen Women, San Dieto Writers & Editors Guild. Home: 5802 Corral Way La Jolla CA 92037-7423

LEVENTHAL, ELLEN IRIS, portfolio manager, financial services executive; b. N.Y.C., Feb. 17, 1949; d. Harry and Laura (Schapira) L. BA, Barnard Coll., N.Y.C., 1971; MA, Columbia U., 1973; MBA, NYU, 1978; student, Harvard U., 1968. Registered rep. NASD. Sr. investment analyst Comptrollers Office City of N.Y., 1978-79; asst. investment officer Chem. Bank, N.Y.C., 1980-81; v.p., portfolio mgr. E.F. Hutton, N.Y.C., 1981-87, Shearson Lehman Bros., N.Y.C., 1987-89, Ellaure Corp., N.Y.C., 1989—; portfolio mgr. Delta Capital Mgmt., 1993—. Mem. Investment Tech. Assn., N.Y. Soc. Security Analysts, NYU Bus. Forum, NYU Fin. Club, Money Marketeers of NYU, Princeton Club of N.Y., Barnard Coll. Club of N.Y., City Club of N.Y., Women's City Club of N.Y., Kappa Delta Pi.

LEVENTHAL, RUTH, university provost and dean, educator; b. Phila., May 23, 1940; d. Harry Louis Mongin and Bertha (Rosenberg) Mongin Blai; children—Sheryl Anne, David Alan. B.S., U. Pa., 1961, Ph.D., 1973, M.B.A., 1981. Cert. med. technologist, clin. lab. scientist. Trainee NSF, 1971; trainee USPHS, 1969-70, 73; asst. prof. med. tech. U. Pa., Phila., 1974-77; acting dean U. Pa., 1977-81; dean Hunter Coll., N.Y.C., 1981-84; provost, dean, prof. biology Capitol Coll. Pa. State U., Middletown, 1984—; site visitor Middle State Assn. Colls. and Secondary Schs., Phila., 1983—. Author: (with Cheadle) Medical Parasitology: A Self Instructional Text, 1979, 2d edit., 1985; contbr. chpt. to book and articles to profl. jours. Chmn. pub. service div. Tri-County United Way, South Central Pa., 1985—; mem. health found. bd. Harrisburg Hosp., Pa., 1984—; bd. dirs. Tri-County Planned Parenthood, 1984—, Harrisburg Acad., Wormleysburg, Pa., 1984—, Metro Arts of Harrisburg, 1984—. Recipient Alice Paul award Women's Faculty Club, U. Pa., 1981; Recognition award NE Deans of Schs. of Allied Health, 1984; fellow U. Pa., 1972. Mem. Am. Soc. Parasitologists, Am. Assn. Higher Edn., N.Y. Soc. Tropical Medicine, N.J. Soc. Parasitology, AAUW (bd. dirs. Pa. br. 1985—), Sigma Xi. Office: Pa State U-Harrisburg Capital Coll 777 W Harrisburg Ave Middletown PA 17057-4846*

LEVERTOV, DENISE, poet; b. Ilford, Essex, Eng., Oct. 24, 1923; came to U.S., 1948, naturalized, 1955; d. Paul Philip and Beatrice A. (Spooner-Jones) Levertoff m. Mitchell Goodman, Dec. 2, 1947 (div. 1975); 1 child, Nikolai. Ed. privately; Litt.D. (hon.), Colby Coll., 1970, U. Cin., 1973, St. Lawrence U., 1984, Bates Coll., 1984, Allegheny Coll., 1987, St. Michael's Coll., 1987, Mass. Coll. of Art, 1989, U. Santa Clara, 1993. Tchr. YMCA-YWCA Poetry Ctr., N.Y.C., 1964; vis. lectr. Drew U., Madison, N.J., 1965, CCNY, 1965, Vassar Coll., Poughkeepsie, N.Y., 1966-67, U. Calif., Berkeley, 1969; vis. prof. MIT, Cambridge, 1969-70; scholar Radcliffe Inst. Ind. Study, 1964-65, 66-67; artist-in-residence Kirkland Coll., Clinton, N.Y., 1970-71; Elliston lectr. U. Cin., spring 1973; prof. Tufts U., Medford, Mass., 1973-79, Stanford U., Calif., 1981—; poet-in-residence Brandeis U., Waltham, Mass., 1981-94; A.D. White Prof. at Large Cornell U., Ithaca, N.Y., 1993—. Author: The Double Image, 1946, Here and Now, 1957, Overland to the Islands, 1958, Five Poems, 1958, With Eyes at the Back of Our Heads, 1959, The Jacob's Ladder, 1961, O Taste and See, 1964, City Psalm, 1964, Psalm Concerning the Castle, 1966, The Sorrow Dance, 1967, A Tree Telling of Orpheus, 1968, A Marigold from North Vietnam, 1968, Three Poems, 1968, In the Night: A Story, 1968, The Cold Spring and Other Poems, 1969, Embroideries, 1969, Relearning the Alphabet, 1970, Summer Poems, 1969, A New Year's Garland for My Students, 1970, To Stay Alive, 1971, Footprints, 1972, The Poet in the World, 1974, The Freeing of the Dust, 1975, Chekov on the West Heath, 1977, Modulations for Solo Voice, 1977, Life in the Forest, 1978, Collected Earlier Poems 1940-60, 1979, Pig Dreams: Scenes from the Life of Sylvia, 1981, Wanderer's Daysong, 1981, Light Up the Cave, 1981, Candles in Babylon, 1982, Poems 1960-1967, 1983, Oblique Prayers, 1984, El Salvador: Requiem and Invocation, 1984, The Menaced World, 1984, Selected Poems, 1986, Poems 1968-1972, 1987, Breathing the Water, 1987, A Door in the Hive, 1989, Evening Train, 1992, New and Selected Essays, 1992, Tesserae, 1995; translator: Selected Poems of Guillevic, 1969, Poets of Bulgaria, 1985, Black Iris: Selected Poems of Jean Joubert, 1988; translator, editor: (with Edward C. Dimock, Jr.) In Praise of Krishna: Songs from the Bengali, 1967; editor: Out of the War Shadow: An Anthology of Current Poetry, 1967, (with Kenneth Rexroth and William Carlos Williams) Penguin Modern Poets 9, 1967. Recipient Bess Hokin prize Poetry mag. 1959, Longview award 1961, Harriet Monroe Meml. prize 1964, Inez Boulton prize Poetry mag. 1964, Morton Dauwen Zabel Meml. prize Poetry mag., 1965, Lenore Marshall Poetry prize 1976, Elmer Holmes Bobst award in poetry 1983, Shelley Meml. award Poetry Soc. of Am., 1984, Robert Frost medal, 1990, Lannan award, 1993; Am. Acad. and Inst. of Arts and Letters grantee, 1965; Guggenheim fellow, 1962; NEA Sr. Fellowship, 1990. Mem. Am. Inst. Arts and Letters, Académie Mallarmé (corr.). Office: care New Directions 80 8th Ave New York NY 10011-5126*

LEVI, BARBARA GOSS, physicist, editor; b. Washington, May 5, 1943; d. Wilbur H. and Mildred C. (Wallin) Goss; m. Ilan M. Levi, Sept. 10, 1966; children: Daniel S., Sharon R. BA, Carleton Coll., 1965; MS, Stanford U., 1967, PhD, 19711. Assoc. editor Physics Today Am. Inst. Physics, N.Y.C., 1969-70, cons. editor Physics Today, 1970-89, assoc. editor Physics Today, 1987-88; sr. assoc. editor Physics Today, N.Y.C., 1989-93, sr. editor, 1993—; mem. tech. staff Bell Labs, Holmdel, N.J., 1982-83; mem. rsch. staff Ctr. for Energy and Environ. Studies Princeton U., 1981-82, 83-87; lectr. Ga. Tech., Atlanta, 1976-80, Fairleigh Dickinson U., Madison, N.J., 1970-75; vis. prof. Rutgers U., Piscataway, N.J., 1988-89; cons. U.S. Office Tech. Assessment, Washington, 1976-93. Editor: (with others) Energy Sources: Conservation and Renewables, 1985, The Future of Land-Based Strategie Missiles, 1989, Global Warming: Physics and Facts, 1992. Treas. LWV, Holmdel and Colts Neck, N.J., 1983-94. Fellow AAAS, Am. Phys.Soc. (edn. com. 1989-91, chmn. forum on physics and soc. 1988-89, forum councilor, 1992-95, mem. exec. bd. 1994-95); mem. AAUW (nuclear energy task force 1975-77), Fedn. Am. Scientists (gov. bd. 1985-89), Am. Assn. Physics Tchrs.

LEVIEN, JOY, corporate lawyer; b. N.Y.C.; d. Edward and Augusta (Cohen) L. BA, Cornell U., 1954, JD cum laude, 1957. Bar: N.Y. 1957. With Corp. Trust Co., 1958-62, Levien & Penn, 1963-64, Inst. of Internat. Edn., 1964-67; corp. sec., licensing atty. The Singer Co., 1967-79; v.p. legal R.H. Macy & Co. Inc., N.Y.C., 1980—. Trustee, 1st v.p. David and Minnie Berk Found., 1980—. Named to YWCA Acad. Women Achievers. Mem. Assn. Bar City N.Y., Am. Soc. Corp. Secs., Order of Coif, Phi Beta Kappa. Home: 333 East 79 St New York NY 10021 Office: R H Macy & Co Inc 151 W 34th St New York NY 10001-2124

LE VIEUX, JANE STUART, pediatrics nurse; b. Washington, May 1, 1956; d. Richard Stuart and Jane Marie (O'Connell) Le V.; m. Gary B. Elliott, Sept. 4, 1982; children: Julianne, Aimée. BSN, U. South Ala., 1979; MS in Child Devel., U. North Tex., 1989, MEd in Counseling and Play Therapy, 1991. Lic. profl. counselor; registered play therapist, Tex. Staff nurse ICU Children's Med. Ctr., Dallas, 1979-81, RN cardiac cath lab., 1981-84, bone marrow transplant child life specialist, 1991—; supr. cardiac cath lab. Humana Hosp.-Medical City, Dallas, 1984-86, pediatric clin. nurse educator, 1986-87; child and family therapist The Caring Ctr., Dallas, 1992—. Active Weekend to Wipe Out Cancer, Dallas, Children's Cancer Fund, Jr. League of Dallas; mem. adv. bd. Trinity Ministry to Poor, El Tesora De La Vida. Author: (with others) A Handbook for Practitioners, 1993. Mem. Assn. for Play Therapy, ANA, Tex. Nurses Assn., Child Life Coun., Assn. for Care of Children's Health, Phi Delta Kappa. Roman Catholic. Home: 4815 Royal Ln Dallas TX 75229 Office: The Caring Ctr 8222 Douglas Ave Ste 777 Dallas TX 75225

LEVIN, BETSY, lawyer, educator, university dean; b. Balt., Dec. 25, 1935; d. M. Jastrow and Alexandra (Lee) L. AB, Bryn Mawr (Pa.) Coll., 1956; LLB, Yale U., 1966. Bar: D.C. 1967, Colo. 1982. Research geologist U.S. Geol. Survey, Washington, 1956-63; law clk. to judge U.S. Ct. Appeals (4th cir.), Balt., 1966-67; spl. asst. to U.S. Amb. to UN, Arthur J. Goldberg N.Y.C., 1967-68; dir. edn. studies Urban Inst., Washington, 1968-73; prof. law Duke U., Durham, N.C., 1973-80; gen. counsel U.S. Dept. Edn., Washington, 1980-81; dean, prof. law U. Colo., Boulder, 1981-87; exec. v.p. Assn. Am. Law Schs., Washington, 1987-92; Arch T. Allen vis. disting. prof. law U. N.C. Sch. Law, Chapel Hill, 1993; vis. prof. law Am. U. Washington Coll. Law, 1994, Georgetown U. Law Ctr., Washington, 1994; disting. vis. prof. sch. law U. Balt., 1995; mem. Nat. Coun. Ednl. Rsch., 1978-79; mem. civil rights reviewing authority HEW, 1979-80. Co-author: Educational Policy and the Law, 2d edit., 1982, 3d edit., 1991; editor: Future Directions for School Finance Reform, 1975; co-editor: The Courts, Social Science and School Desegregation, 1977, School Desegregation: Lessons of the First 25 Years, 1979. White House fellow, 1967-68. Fellow Am. Bar Found., Colo. Bar Found.; mem. ABA, Nat. Assn. Women Judges (program com. 1985-92), Am. Law Inst. (coun.), Order of Coif. Office: U Balt Sch Law 1420 N Charles St Baltimore MD 21201

LEVIN, CAROL ARLENE, educator; b. L.A., Apr. 4, 1945; d. Harold Allen and Sally (Salter) L. AA, Santa Monica Coll., 1965; BA, UCLA, 1967; MS, Pepperdine U., 1990. Cert. tchr., 1969, bilingual tchr., 1977. Tchr. L.A. Unified Sch. Dist., 1969-89; master tchr. UCLA, 1985-89; tchr., adviser bilingual editor newspaper D.A.R.E. to Read, 1989-94; adviser drug, alcohol and tobacco edn., 1994—; pres., v.p. Calif. Assn. Childhood Edn., Los Angeles, 1977-81; chmn. workshop Calif. State Assn. for Childhood Edn. Internat. Conf., Universal City, 1979; invited observer Assn. for Childhood Edn. Internat. White House Conf.-Families, Los Angeles, 1980; tchr., adviser elem. news Sta. KTTV, Los Angeles, 1980-82. Editor: (with others) Our Los Angeles, 1976; contbr. articles to profl. jours. Treas. Dickens Towers Homeowners Assn., Sherman Oaks, Calif., 1978-80; sec. Sherman Villas Homeowners Assn, Sherman Oaks, 1981-83; mem. Sherman Oaks Homeowners Assn., 1986—, Palm Springs (Calif.) Tennis Club Owners Assn., 1981—; mem. Los Angeles Music Ctr. Theatre Group Vols., 1987—. Recipient P.I.E. award Los Angeles Schs., 1978, 79, 80, 81. Mem. NEA, Calif. Tchrs. Assn., Women in Ednl. Leadership, Delta Kappa Gamma (sec. Epsilon chpt.), Unihi Edn. Found. (bd. dirs., sec.). Office: LA Unified Sch Dist Office Instrn 2151 N Soto St Los Angeles CA 90012

LEVIN, DEBBE ANN, lawyer; b. Cin., Mar. 11, 1954; d. Abram Asher and Selma Ruth (Herlands) L. BA, Washington U., St. Louis, 1976; JD, U. Cin., 1979; LLM, NYU, 1983. Bar: Ohio 1979. Staff atty. U.S. Ct. Appeals (6th cir.), Cin., 1979-82; shareholder Schwartz, Manes & Ruby, Cin., 1983—; lectr. tax conf. U. Cin., 1984-86, adj. prof. coll. of bus., 1987-89. Editor: U. Cin. Law Rev., 1972-79. Mem. ABA, Ohio Bar Assn., Cin. Bar Assn., Women Entrepreneurs, Inc., Cin. Bus. & Profl. Women's Club, Order of Coif. Jewish. Office: Schwartz Manes & Ruby 2900 Carew Tower Cincinnati OH 45202

LEVIN, JILL SUSAN, real estate company officer, broker; b. Albany, N.Y., Feb. 7, 1962; d. Richard Martin and Claire Miriam (Friedenburg) L. AS, Roane State U., 1988; BS in Bus., U. Tenn., 1991. Lic. realtor, Tenn. Partial owner, broker Realty Mgmt. Co., Knoxville, 1982—. Fred M. Roddy scholar U. Tenn., 1988. Mem. Knoxville Bd. Realtors, Nat. Home Builders Assn., Internat. Coun. Shopping Ctrs., Apt. Coun. Greater Knoxville (bd. dirs. 1993—), Pierre Moran Mchts. Assn. (bd. dirs. 1992—), Golden Key Nat. Honor Soc., Phi Kappa Phi, Beta Gamma Sigma. Office: Realty Mgmt Co 5410 Homberg Dr Knoxville TN 37919

LEVIN, KAREN PAULA, convention planner; b. Balt., Mar. 27, 1958; d. Joseph and Shirley (Toback) L. BA, Johns Hopkins U., 1980. Circulation mgr., prodn. mgr. Times Publ. Group, Balt., 1980-85; mgr. exhibits and ops. Rosen Group, Inc., Balt., 1985—; reunion planner Camp Louise, Cascade, Md., 1989—; site coord. Craft Bus. Inst., Balt., 1994. Editor, publ. Gettin' Old Gazette newsletter, 1988—. Mem. Nat. Assn. Exposition Mgrs., Phi Beta Kappa. Democrat. Jewish. Home: 6101 Stuart Ave Baltimore MD 21209 Office: The Rosen Group Inc 3000 Chestnut Ave Ste 300 Baltimore MD 21211-2751

LEVIN, LAUREN (LO LEVIN), artist, teacher, designer; b. Framingham, Mass., June 8, 1949; d. Abraham and Ida Rena (Cohen) L. Grad., Art Inst. Boston, 1971; postgrad., Sch. Fashion Design, Boston, 1976, Parsons Sch. Design, 1979. Owner, creator Struck of Loke (improvisational theater and cafe), Worcester, Mass., 1971-75; designer, 'Lo'Scapes Fashion Art, Honolulu, 1983—; artist portraits and impressions Faces by 'Lo', Honolulu, 1969—, Cape Code, 1969—, Ibiza, Spain, 1969—; owner, operator, artist Artspace Gallery, Honolulu, 1990-91; tchr. Very Spl. Arts, Hawaii, 1983—. Mem. Pacific Handcrafters Guild (bd. dirs.), Hawaii Handcrafters Ednl. Found. (bd. dirs. 1992—). Home: PO Box 61820 Honolulu HI 96839-1820

LEVIN, LINDA ROSE, mental health counselor; b. Des Moines, June 29, 1951; d. Morris Sam and Betty Francis (Burns) Nemirovski; m. Michael Arthur Levin, Feb. 25, 1971; children: David Bradley, Shane Michael. Student, Grandview Jr. Coll., 1969-70; BS in Psychology, Ottawa Univ., 1992, MA in Counseling, 1994. Cert. hypnotherapist, advanced hypnotherapist. Asst. dir. trade practice Better Bus. Bur., Phoenix, 1980-83; program coord. Carnation Health and Nutrition Ctr., Phoenix, 1983-85; v.p. AAA Telephone Answering Svc., Phoenix, 1985-90; past state of Ariz. rep. Toughlove, Phoenix, 1988-90; counselor level II, resident advisor Wayland Family Ctrs., Phoenix, 1990-91; case mgr. for the serious mentally ill Community Care Network, Phoenix, 1991-92; pvt. practice in hypnotherapy Counseling Ctr. for Personal Growth, Phoenix, 1992—. Vol. arbitrator Better Bus. Bur., 1983—. Mem. Am. Arbitration Assn. Democrat. Jewish. Office: Counseling Ctr for Personal Growth 10430 N 19th Ave Ste 8 Phoenix AZ 85021

LEVIN, MARLENE, human resources executive, educator; b. Detroit, Oct. 7, 1934; d. Louis and Cele (Drapkin) Bertman; m. Jerome J. Goodman, Apr. 4, 1954 (dec. Mar. 1962); children: Bennett J., Marc R.; m. Herbert R. Levin, June 7, 1967. Student U. Miami, 1952-53; BA, Coll. of New Rochelle, 1975; MPA, NYU, 1978. Cert. human resource mgr. Asst. administr. Richmond Children Ctr., Yonkers, N.Y., 1973-74; research assoc. Westchester Country Dept. Mental Health, N.Y., 1975-80, clinic adminstr., 1980-82; founder, pres. The Phoenix Group, Armonk, N.Y., 1982-88; v.p. human resources and adminstrn. Ensign Bank, N.Y.C., 1988-92; adj. prof. Iona Coll., New Rochelle, N.Y., 1978-88; cons. Social Area Research, Scarsdale, N.Y., 1983-84; lectr./trainer Volvo of Am., Inc., Rockleigh, N.J., 1983-84, Lederle Labs., Spring Valley, N.Y., 1984-88. Contbr. articles on sociol. subjects to profl. jours. Mem. Mental Health Council, Mount Kisco, N.Y., 1981-83, Council for Youth, Armonk, 1984-92; mem. legis. adv. com. N.Y. State 37th Dist., 1991. Mem. Nat. Staff Devel. Council, NOW (v.p. White Plains 1978-80). Democrat. Jewish. Avocation: stamp collecting. Home: 2576 NW 63 St Boca Raton FL 33496

LEVIN, PAMELA JEAN, counselor; b. Rockford, Ill., Oct. 26, 1942; d. Clifton Elgin and Zola Brenice (Griffith) Backus; children: Eric Daniel, Jennifer Jean Levin-Landheer. BS, U. Ill., 1964. RN. Staff nurse, med. nursing Boston VA Hosp., 1964-65; chief nursing dept. Washingtonian Hosp., Boston, 1965-66; staff nurse Highland, Cowell and Alta Bates Hosps., Oakland and Berkeley, Calif., 1967-70; asst. dir. Day Treatment Ctr. Gladman Hosp., Oakland, 1970; pvt. practice transactional analysis San Francisco Bay Area and No. Calif., 1971—; internat. lectr. Transactional Analysis & Devel.; co-pres., v.p. Eric Berne Seminars of San Fransisco, 1977-78; co-founder Group House Inc., Berkeley, 1971; coodinator N.W. Fla. Alcoholic Rehab. Clinic, 1966; co-founder Orr's Hot Springs Healing Retreat Community, Ukiah, Calif., 1974-79. Author: Becoming The Way We Are, An Introduction to Personal Development in Recovery and In Life, 1988, Cycles of Power, A Users Guide To The Seven Seasons of Life, 1988, French transl., 1986, How to Develop Your Personal Powers, A Workbook for your Life's Time, 1982, (children's book) The Fuzzy Frequency, 1978; author, founder Experiencing Enough, human potential tng. course, 1984; founding mem., editorial bd. quar. jour. Women & Therapy, 1982-86; contbr. numerous articles to profl. jours.; developer instructional aids including blocks, cymbals, devel. cycle and deviations chart, growth and devel. chart, series of comparative charts of psychol. theory; featured commentator/analyst in film Hello Up There, Eric!, Rogers Prodns., Inc., 1979. Recipient Eric Berne Sci. award for article The Cycle of Development, 1984. Mem. Internat. Transactional Analysis Assn. (cert. Level I and II, 1st woman teaching and clin. mem., co-founder women's caucus 1970, bd. trustees 1973, 74, 75, chair pub. info. and profl. relations com. 1987—, press screeing com. 1976-78, women's editorial bd. jour. 1977, editor Script, internat. newsletter 1983-85, co-editor 1986), Can. Assn. for Transactional Analysis, Am. Assn. Counselling & Devel., Inst. Devel. Edn. and Psychotherapy, Nat. Assn. Female Execs., AAUW, New Directions in Edn. & Psychotherapy, Internat. Soc. for Study of Innovative Psychotherapies, Media Alliance, Feminist Writer's Guild, Author's Guild, Author's League. Home and Office: PO Box 1429 Ukiah CA 95482-1429

LEVIN, PATRICIA OPPENHEIM, special education educator, consultant; b. Detroit, Apr. 5, 1932; d. Royal A. and Elsa (Freeman) Oppenheim; m. Charles L. Levin, Feb. 21, 1956; children: Arthur David, Amy Ragen, Fredrick Stuart. AB in History, U. Mich., 1954, PhD, 1981; MEd, Marygrove Coll., 1973. Tchr. reading and learning disabled, cons., Detroit, 1967-76, Marygrove Coll.; coord. spl. edn., Marygrove Coll., 1976-86; adj. prof. Oakland U., 1987-90, U. Miami, 1989—; edn., curriculum cons. Lady Elizabeth Sch., Jávea (Alicante) Spain, 1988-91; dir. Oppenheim Tchr. Tng. Inst., Detroit; mem. adv. bd. Eton Acad., Birmingham, Mich., 1991-93; internat. conf. presenter; workshop presenter Dade City Schs., 1992—. Mem. Mich. regional bd. ORT, 1965-68, 86—; mem. youth svcs. adv. com. S.E. Mich. chpt. ARC Bd., 1973-79; v.p. women's aux. Children's Hosp. Mich.; bd. dirs. women's com. United Cmty. Svcs., 1968-73; women's com. Detroit Grand Opera Assn., 1970-75; mem. coms. Detroit Symphony Orch., Detroit Inst. Arts; torch drive area chmn. United Found., 1967-70; bd. dirs. Greater Miami Opera Guild Bd., 1994—, active, 1992—, Fla. Concert Assn. Cresendo Soc., 1993—. Mem. Internat. Reading Assn., Nat. Coun. Tchrs. of English, Assn. Supervision and Curriculum Devel., Nat. Assn. Edn. of Young Children, Mich. Assn. Children with Learning Disabilities (edn. v.p., exec. bd. 1976-80), Coun. Exceptional Children, Williams Island Club, Westview Country Club, Phi Delta Kappa, Pi Lambda Theta.

LEVIN, SUSAN BASS, lawyer; b. Wilmington, Del., July 18, 1952; d. Max S. and Harriet C. (Rubin) Bass; children: Lisa, Amy. BA, U. of Rochester, 1972; JD, George Washington U., 1975. Bar: D.C. 1975, U.S. Ct. Claims 1975, N.J. 1976, Pa. 1981, U.S. Ct. Appeals (3d cir.) 1983, U.S. Supreme Ct. 1984. Law clk. to assoc. justice U.S. Ct. Claims, Washington, 1975-76; assoc. Covington & Burling, Washington, 1976-79; pvt. practice Cherry Hill, N.J., 1979-87; counsel Ballard, Spahr, Andrews & Ingersoll, Phila., Camden (N.J.), 1994—; mayor Cherry Hill, 1988—. Pres. Cherry Hill (N.J.) Twp. Council, 1986-88; trustee N.J. Coalition of Small Bus. Orgns., 1985-87; del. Dem. Presdl. Conv., 1992; chair Pam's List; trustee N.J. Alliance for Action, South Jersey Devel. Coun. Recipient Woman of Achievement award Camden County Girl Scouts, 1986. Mem. Tri County Women Lawyers (pres. 1984-85), N.J. Assn. Women Bus. Owners (state pres. 1984-85 named Woman of Yr. 1985). Office: Ballard Spahr Andrews & Ingersoll 1735 Market St Philadelphia PA 19135

LEVIN, VEDA MARA, middle school educator, writing consultant; b. Miami Beach, Fla., Aug. 10, 1949; d. Louis Levin and Lynne Helen (Jaffe) Levin Martin. BA, U. Miami, 1970; MS, Fla. Internat. U., 1984. Cert. secondary sch. tchr. Occupational specialist Model Cities Manpower Agy., Miami, Fla., 1971-72; tchr. Brownsville Jr. High Sch., Miami, 1972-76, McMillan Jr. High Sch., Miami, 1976-77; tchr. English Southwood Middle Sch., Miami, 1977—; supt. creative writing Dade County Youth Fair, Miami, 1987-93. Editor, adviser Illusions mag., 1981-94. Grantee NEH, 1984. Mem. United Tchrs. Dade, Columbia Scholastic Press Assn. (judge 1986-90), So. Interscholastic Press Assn., Delta Kappa Gamma. Democrat. Jewish. Office: Southwood Middle Sch 16301 SW 80th Ave Miami FL 33157-3730

LEVINE, AMY FELDMAN, art educator; b. N.Y.C., Oct. 10, 1956; d. Bernard Robert and Janice Ruby (Dworsh) Feldman; m. Ramon Levine, Sept. 10, 1978; children: Alyssa, Sara. BA, SUNY, Binghamton, 1978; MFA, L.I. U., 1985. Cert. art tchr., N.Y., N.C. Artist's asst. Carole Jean Feverman Studio, Port Washington, N.Y., 1979; freelance illustrator ECL Art Assocs., Huntington, N.Y., 1978-85; art tchr. Massapequa (N.Y.) Pub. Schs., 1986-93, Wake County Schs., Raleigh, N.C., 1993—; represented by Primavera Gallery, Huntington, 1984—. Teamster's Union scholar, 1974. Mem. NEA, N.C. Mus. Art, Wake Visual Arts Assn. Democrat. Jewish.

LEVINE, BARBARA GERSHKOFF, early childhood educator, consultant; b. Providence, June 2, 1950; d. Aaron and Miriam Charlotte (Blackman) Gershkoff; m. Alan Marshal Levine, Aug. 22, 1971 (div. Sept. 1986); children: Adam Jonathan, Matthew Corey Gershkoff; m. H. Michael Mogil, Feb. 6, 1988. BS in Early Childhood Edn., Wheelock Coll., 1972. Head tchr. Town & Country Schs., College Park, Md., 1973-74, head tchr., supr., 1974-75; head tchr. Early Childhood Ctr., Rockville, Md., 1987—; cons. How the Weatherworks, Rockville, 1987—; co-chair Project Sky Awareness Week, Think Weather, Inc., Rockville, 1991—. Co-author: (videotape, tchr.'s guide) Our Sea of Clouds, 1992, A Hurricane: Through the Eyes of Children, 1993, (videotape, tchrs. manual) Weather Study Under a Newspaper Umbrella, 1989, (book) The Amateur Meteorologist, 1993; contbr. articles to profl. jours. Mem. Nat. Assn. for Educating Young Children, Nat. Sci. Tchrs. Assn. Home and Office: How the Weatherworks 1522 Baylor Ave Rockville MD 20850-1025

LEVINE, BERYL JOYCE, state supreme court justice; b. Winnipeg, Man., Can., Nov. 9, 1935; came to U.S., 1955; d. Maurice Jacob and Bella (Gutnik) Choslovsky; m. Leonard Levine, June 7, 1955; children: Susan Brauna, Marc Joseph, Sari Ruth, William Noah, David Karl. BA, U. Man., Winnipeg, 1965; JD with distinction, U. N.D., 1974. Assoc. Vogel, Branther, Kelly, Knutson, Weir & Bye, Ltd., Fargo, N.D., 1974-85; justice N.D. Supreme Ct., Bismarck, 1985—, chmn. jud. planning com. Bd. dirs. Fargo Youth Commn., 1974-77, Hospice of Red River Valley, Fargo; chmn. Gov.'s

Commn. on Children at Risk, 1985. Named Outstanding Woman in N.D. Law, U. N.D. Law Women's Caucus, 1985. Mem. Cass County Bar Assn. (pres. 1984-85), N.D. State Bar Assn., Burleigh County Bar Assn., Order of Coif. Office: ND Supreme Ct State Capitol Judicial Wing 1st Fl 600 E Blvd Ave Bismarck ND 58504

LEVINE, ELLEN R., magazine editor; b. N.Y.C., Feb. 19, 1943; d. Eugene Jack and Jean (Zuckman) Jacobson; m. Richard U. Levine, Dec. 21, 1964; children: Daniel, Peter. Student, Wellesley Coll. Reporter The Record, Hackensack, N.J., 1964-70; editor Cosmopolitan mag., N.Y.C., 1976-82; editor in chief Cosmopolitan Living mag., N.Y.C., 1980-81, Woman's Day mag., N.Y.C., 1982-91, Redbook mag., N.Y.C., 1991-94, Good Housekeeping, N.Y.C., 1994—; dir. N.J. Bell, Newark; commr. U.S. Atty. Gen.'s Commn. on Pornography, 1985-86. Author: Planning Your Wedding, Waiting for Baby, Rooms That Grow With Your Child. Mem. exec. com. Senator Bill Bradley, 1984—. Named to Writers Hall of Fame, 1981, Acad. Women Achievers, YWCA, 1982; recipient Outstanding Profl. Achievement award N.J. coun. Girl Scouts U.S., 1984, Woman of Achievement award N.J. Fedn. Women's Clubs, 1984, Matrix award N.Y. Women in Communications, Inc., 1989, honor award Birmingham So. Coll., 1991. Office: Good Housekeeping 959 Eighth Ave New York NY 10019*

LEVINE, GAVRIELLE, mathematics educator, psychologist; b. N.Y.C., Apr. 8, 1948; d. Saul Charles and Pauline Ann (Rosenzweig) L. BA, Barnard Coll., 1969; MA, Columbia U., 1977, MPhil, 1982, PhD, 1991. Lic. psychologist, N.Y. Math. tchr. N.Y.C. Bd. Edn., 1969-79; rsch. coord. Reading Rainbow-PBS TV Series, N.Y.C., 1982-83; ednl. developer ednl. software Children's TV Workshop, N.Y.C., 1982-84; math. instr. Hunter Coll., N.Y.C., 1985-91; asst. prof. math. edn. C.W. Post Campus, L.I. U., Brookville, N.Y., 1989—; mem. adv. bd. Tchr. Edn. Equity Project, N.Y.C., 1993—; cons. Children's TV Workshop, N.Y.C., 1988-94. Author: (chpt.) Mathematics Teacher Resource Handbook, 1993. Recipient Dean's grant for student rsch. Tchrs. Coll., Columbia U., 1988-89, Rsch. grant C.W. Post Rsch. Com., 1990-95. Mem. APA, Am. Ednl. Rsch. Assn. (Outstanding Dissertation Award Program 1991), Nat. Coun. Tchrs. Math., N.E. Ednl. Rsch. Assn. (editor Researcher), Phi Delta Kappa (rsch. rep.). Office: CW Post Campus LI Univ School of Education Brookville NY 11548

LEVINE, JANIS E., financial analyst; b. Akron, Ohio, Apr. 7, 1953; d. Paul and Sarah (Levin) L.; student U. Cin., 1971-73; B.S. in Acctg., U. Akron, 1975; M.B.A., Xavier U., 1978. Acctg. intern Price Waterhouse & Co., Cleve., 1974-75; systems acct. Mead Corp., Cin., 1975-77; internal auditor, sr. capital expenditures analyst Champion Internat. Corp., Stamford, Conn., 1977—. Vol., Headstart and ARC; adv. Jr. Achievement. Recipient Young Citizens Achievement award for Headstart, 1969. Mem. AAUW, NAFE, Jewish Fedn. Stamford (cmty. rels. coun., leadership devel. divsn., programs com., events com., Israel com., Washington conf. com.), Bus. and Profl. Women, Young Leadership Council, Stamford Forum for World Affairs, Assn. MBA Execs., Inst. Mgmt. Accts. (community programs dir.), Am. Jewish Congress, B'nai B'rith Women, Beta Alpha Psi (sec.). Office: Champion Internat Corp 1 Champion Plz Stamford CT 06921-6001

LEVINE, JULIE GORCHOW, career planning administrator, consultant; b. Mpls., June 24, 1956; d. Neil N. and Roslyn Diane (Wein) Gorchow; m. Robert G. Levine, Nov. 28, 1981; 2 children. BA in Anthropology, Northwestern U., 1978; MEd, U. Pa., 1986. Group sales mgr., asst. buyer Hecht's Dept. Store, Washington, 1978-81; exec. recruiter Sweeney Cons., Denver, 1982; asst. store mgr. Casual Corner, Denver, 1983-84; assoc. dir. career devel. and placement U. Pa. Wharton Grad. Sch., Phila., 1984-90; pvt. practice Phila., 1991—; presenter in field. Leadership trainer Fedn. Jewish Agys., Phila., 1988-90; bd. observer Hillel Greater Phila., 1990; bd. dirs. Home and Sch. Assn., co-chair adult edn., 1994; treas. HarZion Home and Sch. Assn., 1994—. Mem. Pa. Counseling Assn., Nat. Career Devel. Assn., Nat. Assn. Women Educators, Counselors, Am. Coll. Personnel Assn., Am. Assn. for Counseling and Devel. Home and Office: 758 Cornerstone Ln Bryn Mawr PA 19010-2074

LEVINE, MADELINE GELTMAN, Slavic literatures educator, translator; b. N.Y.C., Feb. 23, 1942; d. Herman and Nettie (Kritman) Geltman; m. Steven I. Levine; children: Elaine, Daniel. B.A., Brandeis U., 1962; M.A., Harvard U., 1964, Ph.D., 1971. Asst. prof. Grad Sch. CUNY, N.Y.C., 1971-74; assoc. prof. U. N.C., Chapel Hill, 1974-80, prof., 1980-94, Wm. R. Kenan, Jr. prof. Slavic lits., 1994—, chmn. dept. Slavic langs., 1979-87, 94—, Wm. R. Kenan Jr. Prof., 1994—; chmn. joint com. on Ea. Europe, Am. Coun. Learned Socs.-Social Sci. Rsch. Coun., 1989-92. Translator: A Memoir of the Warsaw Uprising (Miron Bialoszewski), 1977, 2d edit. 1991, The Poetry of Osip Mandelstam: God's Grateful Guest (Ryszard Przybylski), 1987, Beginning With My Streets: Essays and Recollections (Czeslaw Milosz), 1992, A Year of the Hunter (Czeslaw Milosz), 1994; translator with Francine Prose: A Scrap of Time and Other Stories (Ida Fink), 1986; author: Contemporary Polish Poetry, 1925-75, 1981. NEH fellow, 1984; recipient (with Francine Prose) award for lit. translation PEN-America, 1988. Mem. Am. Assn. for Advancement of Slavic Studies, Polish Inst. of Arts and Scis. Am., Am. Assn. Tchrs. of Slavic and East European Langs., Am. Literary Translators Assn., Pen-Am. Home: 5001 Whitehorse Rd Hillsborough NC 27278-9399 Office: U NC 421 Dey Hall CB # 3165 Chapel Hill NC 27599

LEVINE, MARILYN MARKOVICH, lawyer, arbitrator; b. Bklyn., Aug. 9, 1930; d. Harry P. and Fannie L. (Hymowitz) Markovich; m. Louis L. Levine. June 24, 1950; children: Steven R., Ronald J., Linda J. Morgenstern. BS summa cum laude, Columbia U., 1950; MA, Adelphi U., 1967; JD, Hofstra U., 1977. Bar: N.Y. 1978, U.S. Dist. Ct. (so. and ea. dists.) N.Y. 1978, D.C. 1979, U.S. Supreme Ct. 1982. Sole practice Valley Stream, N.Y., 1978—; contract arbitrator bldg. svc. industry, N.Y.C., 1982—; panel arbitrator retail food industry, N.Y.C., 1980—; arbitrator N.Y. dist. cts., Nassau County, 1981—; mem. Nat. Acad. Arbitrators, 1992—. Panel arbitrator Suffolk County Pub. Employee Relations Bd., 1979—, Nassau County Pub. Employee Relations Bd., 1980—, Nat. Mediation Bd., 1986—, N.Y. State Pub. Employee Relations Bd., 1984—; mem. adv. council Ctr. Labor and Industrial Relations, N.Y. Inst. Tech., N.Y., 1985—; counsel Nassau Civic Club, 1978—. Mem. ABA, N.Y. State Bar Assn., D.C. Bar Assn., Nassau County Bar Assn., N.J. Bd. Mediation (panel arbitrator), Am. Arbitration Assn. (arbitrator 1979—), Fed. Mediation Bd. (arbitrator 1980—). Home and Office: 1057 Linden St Valley Stream NY 11580-2135

LEVINE, NAOMI BRONHEIM, university administrator; b. N.Y.C., Apr. 15, 1923; d. Nathan and Malvina (Mermelstein) Bronheim; m. Leonard Levine, Apr. 11, 1948; 1 dau., Joan. B.A., Hunter Coll., 1941; LL.B., Columbia, 1946, J.D., 1970. Bar: N.Y. bar 1946. With firm Scaadrett, Tuttle & Chalaire, N.Y.C., 1946-48, Charles Gottleib, N.Y.C., 1948-50; with Am. Jewish Congress, 1950-78, exec. dir., 1972-78; v.p. to sr. v.p. external affairs NYU, 1978—; asst. prof. law and police sci. John Jay Coll., N.Y.C., 1969-73, L.I. U., 1965-69. Author: Schools in Crisis, 1969, The Jewish Poor-an American Awakening, 1974, Politics, Religion and Love, 1990; mem. editorial staff Columbia Law Rev., 1945-46. Bd. dirs. Interracial Council Bus. Opportunities, Am. Women's Econ. Devel. Council; trustee N.Y. UJA-Fedn. Recipient Constl. Law prize Hunter Coll., 1944; named to Hall of Fame, 1972. Office: 70 Washington Sq S New York NY 10012-1091

LEVINE, NINA BETH, school librarian; b. Islip, N.Y., Aug. 6, 1954; d. Jerome Paul and Arline Leah (Kosofsky) L.; m. Ronny Martin Faber, July 6, 1986 (div. July 1991); 1 child, Benjamin Lewis Faber. BA magna cum laude, SUNY, Geneseo, 1975, MLS, 1976. Cert. sch. libr. media specialist, pub. librarian. Dir. of libraries Salamanca City Schs., N.Y., 1977-79; libr., media specialist Cornwall Ctrl. Schs., N.Y., 1979-82, Blue Mt. Middle Sch., Hendrick Hudson Schs., Montrose, N.Y., 1982—; cons. Kingston (N.Y.) Schs., 1987, Pittsford (N.Y.) Schs., 1988, Putnam-North Westchester Bd. Coop. Ednl. Svcs., Yorktown Heights, N.Y., 1986, 93; regional turnkey trainer N.Y. State Ednl. Dept., Yorktown Heights, 1989; instr. Bedford Tchrs. Ctr., North Salem, N.Y., 1992. Youth group leader Assn. for Retarded Citizens, Suffolk County, N.Y., 1970-72; community vol. Proyecto Amistad, Arequipa, Peru, 1974; bd. dir., trainer Sarah Wells Girl Scout Coun., Middletown, N.Y., 1980-82. Recipient Outstanding Leadership award Assn. for Retarded Citizens, Suffolk County, N.Y., 1972. Mem. ALA, ASCD, Westchester Libr. Assn., People for the Am. Way, Putnam-North Westchester Tchr. Bank, Psi Chi. Democrat. Jewish. Home: 922 Parkway Pl Yorktown Heights NY 10598-1020 Office: Blue Mt Middle Sch 7 Furnace Woods Rd Montrose NY 10548

LEVINE, RHEA JOY COTTLER, anatomy educator; b. N.Y.C., Nov. 26, 1939; d. Zachary Robert Cottler and Hildreth (Abramson) Cottler Rosenfeld; m. Stephen Maxwell Levine, June 16, 1960; children: Elizabeth, Michael Gordon, Zachary Thomas. AB summa cum laude, Smith Coll., 1960; MS, NYU, 1963, PhD, 1966. Lab. instr. NYU Sch. Commerce, N.Y.C., 1963-64; postdoctoral fellow, instr. histology Yale U. Sch. Medicine, New Haven, 1966-68; rsch. assoc. U. Pa. Sch. Medicine, Phila., 1968-69; asst. prof. anatomy Med. Coll. Pa., Phila., 1969-74, assoc. prof. anatomy, 1974-80, prof. anatomy, 1980—, vice chmn., 1988-89; manuscript reviewer numerous sci. journals, Washington and N.Y.C., 1975—; reviewer grant proposals NSF, Washington, 1975—, mem. NIH Study Sect., 1980-84. Contbr. sci. articles to profl. jours. Trustee Stockton State Coll., Pomona, N.J., 1983—, chmn. bd. trustees, 1991-94; bd. dirs. The Hollybush Festival, Glassboro, N.J., 1987-91, Smith Coll. Friends of Libr., Northampton, Mass., 1968-72. NYU Sch. Medicine summer rsch. fellow, 1960, NSF grad. fellow, 1960-65, A.H. Robins rsch. fellow, 1966, USPHS fellow, 1966-68; grantee Women's and Program project NIH, NSF, 1973—; recipient Founder's Day award NYU, 1966, Smith Coll. medal, 1994. Mem. AAAS, Coalition Jewish Profl. Women South N.J. (steering com.), Am. Assn. Anatomists, Am Soc. Cell Biology, Biophys. Soc. (coun. 1991-94, chair pub. sci. policy com. 1992-94), Histochem. Soc., Soc. Gen. Physiology, Wilderness Med. Soc., N.Y. Acad. Scis., Smith Coll. Club, Woodcrest Country Club (house chair 1983-84), Phi Beta Kappa, Sigma Xi. Jewish. Office: Med Coll Pa Dept Anatomy Neurobiology EPPI Divsn 3200 Henry Ave Philadelphia PA 19129-1187

LEVINE, RHONDA JOY, writing educator; b. Bklyn., Mar. 3, 1951; d. Samuel and Hilda (Chachkes) L. BA in English, SUNY, Buffalo, 1973; MA in English and Am. Lit., U. Calif., San Diego, 1981, PhD in English and Am. Lit., 1985. Teaching asst. U. Calif., San Diego, 1973-78, 81-85, co-dir. 3rd coll. composition program, 1975-76; vis. asst. prof. U. Minn. Twin Cities, Mpls., 1985; coord. English Component- Summer Transitional Enrichment Program, Santa Barbara, 1987-91; assoc. dir. program of intensive English U. Calif., Santa Barbara, 1986-88, dir. ESL program, 1990-92, lectr. writing program, 1985—; CEO Triangle Cons. and Profl. Writing Svcs., Santa Barbara, 1993—. Co-author: 3rd College Writing Resource Text and Theoretical Framework for Teaching Writing, 1975; reviewer: (profl. anthology) Face to Face, 1991; co-author: (with J. Kirscht. and J. Reiff) article for College Composition and Communication jour., 1994. Pub. policy chairperson of bd. dirs. Gay and Lesbian Resource Ctr., Santa Barbara, 1986-92, exec. dir., 1992-93; mem. Greater Santa Barbara Community Assn., 1985—. Recipient Humanitarian award Greater Santa Barbara Community Assn., 1991; named Outstanding Women of Yr., 2nd dist. Santa Barbara Community Commn. on Women, 1992. Mem. MLA, NOW, Nat. Coun. Tchrs. of English (co-founder lesbian and gay caucus, coll. divsn. 1987—), Wellspring Found. (bd. dirs. 1993—, grant writer 1993—). Jewish. Office: Univ Calif Writing Program Santa Barbara CA 93106

LEVINE, SHEREE FAITH, lawyer; b. Springfield, Mass., May 21, 1956; d. Irving H. and Lillian I. (Sugarman) L. BA, U. Pa., 1976; JD, Boston Coll., 1979. Bar: N.Y. 1980, Mass. 1980. Intern U.S. Atty. for the So. Dist. of N.Y. bus. frauds section, N.Y.C., 1978; atty. U.S. Securities & Exchange Commn., N.Y.C., 1979-82, br. chief, 1982-85; atty. Securities Industry Assn., N.Y.C., 1985-86, asst. gen. counsel, 1986-87, asst. v.p., asst. gen. counsel, 1988-89, asst. and assoc. v.p., 1990—, v.p., sec., assoc. gen. counsel. Editor: looseleaf jour. Uniform Commercial Code, 1977-79. Mem. ABA, Assn. Bar City N.Y. Office: Securities Industry Assn 120 Broadway Fl 35 New York NY 10271-0080

LEVINE, SUZANNE BRAUN, magazine editor; b. N.Y.C., June 21, 1941; d. Imre and Esther (Bernson) Braun; m. Robert F. Levine, Apr. 2, 1967; children: Joshua, Joanna. BA with honors, Radcliffe Coll., 1963. Reporter Seattle mag., 1963-65; reporter, researcher Time/Life Books, N.Y.C., 1965-67; features editor Mademoiselle, N.Y.C., 1967-68, McCalls mag., N.Y.C., 1968-69; free-lance writer, 1970; mng. editor Sexual Behavior mag., 1971-72, MS. mag., N.Y.C., 1972-88; editor Columbia Journalism Rev., N.Y.C., 1989—; adj. prof. Columbia Grad. Sch. Journalism. Co-editor: The Decade of Women, A Ms History of the Seventies, 1980; exec. producer: Ms. HBO TV spl., 1981, She's Nobody's Baby, TV documentary, 1981 (Peabody award). Woodrow Wilson guest lectr. coord. Chautauqua Conf. on Families. Mem. Am. Soc. Mag. Editors (exec. com.), Women's Media Group. Office: Columbia U Columbia Journalism Rev 700 Journalism Bldg New York NY 10027

LEVINE, YARI, artist, jewelry designer; b. Minsk, Russia; came to U.S. 1927; d. Samuel and Lillian (Lapidus) Turboff; m. Samuel S. Levine, June 10, 1945; children—Steven Robert, Mark Eric. Cert. in Fine Arts, Pratt Inst., 1939; student Am. Artists Sch., 1941, New Sch. Social Research, 1942-43. One-woman shows at: Ward Egleston Galleries, 1964, Washington Hebrew Congregation, N.Y.C., 1959, Brandeis U., 1966, U. Wis., 1969, Union of Am. Hebrew Congregations, 1953, 66, Nassau Community Coll., 1970, Art and Design Atelier, 1980, Hebrew Tabernacle, 1981; exhibited in group shows at: Creative Gallery, John Myers Gallery, 1952, A.C.A. Gallery, 1954, 55, 56, Nat. Acad. Galleries, 1953-78, Internat. Jewish Conf. Exhibit, Los Angeles, 1955, Suffolk Mus., 1957, 300th Houston Commemorative Exhibit, 1957, Art League of L.I., 1957, Heckscher Mus., 1962, Lido Gallery, 1970, Harbor Gallery, 1974, Hudson Guild Gallery, 1980, Artists Equity of N.Y., 1980, Lever House, 1983, Jacob K. Javits Fed. Bldg., 1984, 85; works represented in permanent collections at House of Living Judaism of Union of Am. Hebrew Congregations, N.Y.C., Westchester Reform Temple, Temple Sinai of Washington, U. Wis., others. Named Artist of Jewish Yr., Union of Am. Hebrew Congregations, 1966. Fellow Internat. Inst. Arts and Letters; mem. Artists Equity of N.Y., Nat. Assn. Women Artists, Jewish Visual Artists Assn. of Nat. Council on Arts in Jewish Life, Internat. Platform Assn. Address: 63 Hamlet Rd Levittown NY 11756 Studio: 24 Fifth Ave Suite 214 New York NY 10011

LEVINSON, JOAN SUSAN, artist; b. St. Louis, June 8, 1956; d. Marvin and Marilyn (Yezner) L. Student, Washington U., St. Louis, 1974-76; BFA, U. Kans., 1978; MFA, Cranbrook Acad. Art, Bloomfield Hills, Mich., 1981. Exhbn. artist Mus. Bellerive, Zurich, 1994, Jack Shainman Gallery, 1993, Mid-Am. Biennial-Nelson Atkins Mus., 1991, Stux Gallery, 1990; one-person shows Nicholas Davies Gallery, N.Y., 1994, Nevertheless Press Gallery, St. Louis, 1989, Locus Gallery, St. Louis, 1987, Timothy Burns Gallery, 1985, Bonsack Gallery, St. Louis, 1984; numerous pvt. collections. Mem. organizing com. An Affair of the Arts AIDS Benefit, St. Louis, 1988, Artists for Nuclear Disarmament, St. Louis, 1985. Art grantee Mid-Am. Arts Alliance/NEA, 1990.

LEVIN-WIXMAN, IRENE STAUB, librarian; b. Bklyn., Sept. 30, 1928; d. Harry and Regina (Klein) Staub; BA, Hunter Coll., CUNY, 1949; MLS, L.I. U., 1969; m. Harold E. Levin, Nov. 19, 1950 (dec. June 1984); children: Alan, Leslie, Kim, Paula; m. Lee Wixman, June 5, 1989.. Reference librarian and young adults Henry Waldinger Library, Valley Stream, N.Y., 1969-87, program coordinator public relations, 1976-87; free-lance info. specialist, Boynton Beach, Fla., 1988—; cons. on Jewish books and libraries; librarian Judaica Libr. Temple Emanu El, Palm Beach., Fla., 1988—; active Palm Beach Libr. Adv. Bd., 1993—; lectr. books with Judiac themes. Trustee, Sisterhood Temple B'nai Israel of Elmont, 1969-71, 87, Temple B'nai Israel of Elmont, 1982; libr. Temple Emanuel, Palm Beach, Fla., 1988—. Recipient Library Public Relations Council award, 1973, Fannie Goldstein Merit award, 1992. Mem. Assn. Jewish Libraries (editor Bull., 1973-83, Newsletter, 1978—), Am. Mizrachi Women, Hadassah. Contbr. to Contemporary Literary Criticism, Vol. 13, 1979.

LEVIS, JOAN REGINA, maternal/child health nurse, educator; b. New Haven, Sept. 20, 1941; d. Frederick Ferdinand and Josephine Veronica (Dural) L. Diploma, Mt. Vernon Hosp. Sch. Nursing, 1965; BSN, Pace U., 1982, MSN with distinction, 1985. Cert. child and adolescent nurse, pediatric nurse, ANCC. Staff nurse Mt. Vernon (N.Y.) Hosp., 1965-66, pvt. duty nurse, 1966-67; asst. clin. instr., then clin. instr. Mt. Vernon Hosp. Sch. Nursing, 1967-80, instr. pediatrics, 1980-85, lead instr. pediatrics, 1985—, curriculum chair, 1985-90, clin. instr. psychiat. nursing, 1985—; CPR instr., Totsaver instr. Am. Heart Assn., Mt. Vernon, 1980—; cons. Mt. Vernon Day Care Ctr., 1985—; cons. bereavement support group Monastery of the Sacred Heart, Yonkers, N.Y., 1986—; child abuse prevention instr. N.Y. State Dept. Edn., Mt. Vernon, 1990-94. Mem. N.Y. State Nurses' Assn., Alumnae of Mt. Vernon Hosp. Sch. of Nursing (pres. 1971-73), Pace U.-Leinhard Sch. of Nursing Alumnae, Bus. and Profl. Women's Club Mt. Vernon, Sigma Theta Tau. Roman Catholic. Office: Mt Vernon Hosp Dorothea Hopfer Sch Nursing 53 Valentine St Mount Vernon NY 10550

LEVISAY, SUZANNE BAKER, counselor; b. Oklahoma City, Apr. 15, 1947; d. Robert and Helen (Lischalk) Baker; m. David Levisay, June 1, 1972; 1 child, Michael Ethan. BA, U. North Tex., 1969, MA, 1972; MSSW, U. Tex., Arlington, 1979. Lic. master social worker, advanced clin. practitioner, ind. practitioner in social work, Tex. Treatment coord. children's residential svcs. Tarrant County MHMR, Ft. Worth; outpatient therapist Denton County MHMR, Denton, Tex.; pvt. practice counselor Denton. Mem. NASW, Am. Orthopsychiat. Assn., Acad. Cert. Social Workers. Office: Levisay and McGraw 1305 N Elm St Denton TX 76201-3019

LEVISON-MARCUS, PEGGY LEE, psychologist; b. Mitchell, S.D., June 24, 1942; d. Eugene Keith and Berenice Pauline (Stuart) Snow; m. Stuart Allen Levison, June 3, 1933 (div. 1987); children: Derek, Gregory, Rebecca; m. Peter Colton Marcus, July 19, 1991. BA in Russian Lang., San Diego State U., 1969; MA in Human Behavior, U.S. Internat. U., 1975, PhD in Clin. Psychology, 1978. Counselor LaJolla (Calif.) Pub. Sch., 1976; psychotherapist The Marks Clinic, San Diego, 1976-78; staff psychotherapist Fifth Ave. Ctr. for Counseling and Psychotherapy, N.Y.C., 1978-81, Ctr. for Stress Disorders, Bayside, N.Y., 1978-85; pvt. practice Bayside and N.Y.C., 1985—; cons. in field; pvt. tutor Russian lang., San Diego, 1975-77. Author: Manual for GPI, 1979. Pres. Scripps Clinic and Rsch. Found. Women's Group, LaJolla, 1968-69. Mem. APA, NOW, MADD, Internat. Psychol. Assn., N.Y. State Psychol. Assn., Amnesty Internat., Sierra Club. Office: 35 W 9th St #1B New York NY 10011

LEVIT, EDITHE JUDITH, physician, medical association administrator; b. Wilkes-Barre, Pa., Nov. 29, 1926; m. Samuel M. Levit, Mar. 2, 1952; children: Harry M., David B. BS in Biology, Bucknell U., 1946; MD, Woman's Med. Coll. of Pa., 1951; DMS (hon.), Med. Coll. Pa., 1978; DSc (hon.), Wilkes U., 1990. Grad. asst. in psychology Bucknell U., 1946-47; intern Phila. Gen. Hosp., 1951-52, fellow in endocrinology, 1952-53, clin. instr., assoc. in endocrinology, 1953-57, dir. med. edn., 1957-61, cons. med. edn., 1961-65; asst. dir. Nat. Bd. Med. Examiners, Phila., 1961-67; assoc. dir., sec. bd. Nat. Bd. Med. Examiners, 1967-75, v.p., sec. bd., 1975-77, pres., chief exec. officer, 1977-86, pres. emeritus, life mem. bd., 1987—; cons. in field, 1964—; mem. coun. Coll. Physicians of Phila., 1986—, adv. coun. Inst. for Nuclear Power Ops., Atlanta, 1988-93; bd. dirs. Phila. Electric Co., Germantown Savs. Bank, Phila. Contbr. articles to profl. jours. Bd. dirs. Phila. Gen. Hosp. Found., 1964-70; bd. dirs. Phila. Council for Internat. Visitors, 1966-72; bd. sci. counselors Nat. Library Medicine, 1981-85. Recipient award for outstanding contbns. in field of med. edn. Commonwealth Com. of Woman's Med. Coll., 1970; Alumni award Bucknell U., 1978; Disting. Dau. of Pa. award, 1981; Spl. Recognition award Assn. Am. Med. Colls., 1986; Disting. Service award Fedn. State Med. Bds., 1987; Master A.C.P. Fellow Coll. Physicians of Phila.; mem. Inst. Medicine of Nat. Acad. Scis., AMA, Pa., Phila. County med. socs., Assn. Am. Med. Colls., Phi Beta Kappa, Alpha Omega Alpha, Phi Sigma. Home: The Rittenhouse 210 W Rittenhouse Sq Philadelphia PA 19103

LEVIT, HELOISE B. (GINGER LEVIT), arts administrator, fine arts and media consultant; b. Phila., Apr. 2, 1937; d. Elmer and Claire Frances (Schwartz) Bertman; m. Jay Joseph Levit, July 14, 1962; children: Richard Bertman, Robert Edward, Darcy Francine. BA in French Literature, U. Pa., 1959; MA in French Literature, U. Richmond, 1975; Cert., Alliance Française, Paris, 1991, Chambre de Commerce et d'Industrie de Paris, 1991, La Sorbonne, Paris, 1994. Arts broadcaster Richmond, Va., 1976-82; dir. Fine Arts Am., Inc., Richmond, 1982-84; tchr. Henrico County Pub. Schs., Richmond, 1984-88; dir. devel. Sta. WVST-FM Va. State U., Petersburg, 1987-88; mgr., dir. devel. Richmond Philharm. Orch., 1988-94; fine arts and media cons. Art-I-Facts, Richmond, 1988—. Author: Moments, Monuments & Monarchs, 1986 (Star award 1986); arts writer Richmond Rev., 1989-90; anchor, producer (syndicated radio series) Va. Arts Report, 1978-83, Va. Women, 1984 (Va. Press Women award 1986). V.p. Va. Mus. Collector's Cir., Richmond, 1986-91, mem. steering com.; pres. Richmond Area Dem. Women's Club, 1992-93; mem. Va. Mus. Coun., Richmond; mem. Richmond Symphony Orch. League. Mem. Am. Assn. Tchrs. of French, Va. Capitol Corrs. Assn., Va. Press Women, U. Pa. Alumni Club (v.p. 1980-90, Ben Franklin award 1990), Am. Symphony Orch. League, Amicale Francaise, Alliance Francaise (cert. 1989, 91), Va. Writers Club. Home and Office: Art-I-Facts 1608 Harborough Rd Richmond VA 23233-4720

LEVITAN, KATHERINE D., lawyer; b. Vienna, Austria, July 8, 1933; came to U.S. 1938, naturalized 1942; d. Otto and Hedweega (Saltzer) Lenz; m. Leonard Levitan, Sept. 12, 1952; children—Joel, Jeffrey, Debbie, Diane. B.A. cum laude, N.Y.U. 1952, J.D. cum laude, 1955, LL.M. in Criminal and Family Law, 1977. Bar: N.Y. 1956, U.S. Dist. Ct. (ea. dist.) N.Y. 1972, U.S. Supreme Ct. 1974. Tchr. bus. law N.Y. Inst. Tech., Old Westbury, 1968-69; assoc. Bennett Reiss, Great Neck, N.Y., 1969-70, Malone and Dorfman, Freeport, N.Y., 1970-71; sole practice, Jericho, N.Y., 1971-80; practice with assocs., Mineola, N.Y., 1980—; also lectr.; assoc. prof. Hofstra Law Sch. Bd. dirs., legal counsel For Our Children and Us, Inc., Nassau chpt. ACLU, 1975—; mem. Nassau County Democratic Com., 1969—, law guardian adv. panel 2d dept. Human Rights Adv. Commn. Nassau County; past pres. Nassau chpt. N.Y. Civil Liberties Union. Mem. Nassau Bar Assn. (grievance com., martim com.), Nassau/Suffolk Women's Bar Assn. (past pres., legal counsel), Nassau Civil Liberties Union, L.I. Women's Network, Acad. Matrimonial Lawyers, Contbr. articles to profl. publs. Home: 113 Olive Ln New Hyde Park NY 11040-2333 Office: 200 Old Country Rd Mineola NY 11501-4235

LEVITAN, SUSAN LORI, entertainment development and production executive, consultant, psychotherapist; b. New Hyde Park, N.Y., Aug. 5, 1958. BA, UCLA, 1981; postgrad., Pepperdine U., 1993—. Coord. spls. ABC TV, L.A., 1987-90; ind. producer, 1990—; alumni advisor UCLA. Vol. polit. campaigns and various charities. Mem. Calif. Assn. Marriage and Family Therapists, UCLA Alumni Assn., Psi Chi.

LEVITAS, MIRIAM C. STRICKMAN, events coordinator, realtor associate, television producer, talent; b. Phila., Aug. 3, 1936; d. Morris and Bella (Barsky) Cherrin; m. Bernard Strickman, June 3, 1956 (dec. 1975); children: Andrew, Brian, Craig, Deron; m. Theodore Clinton Levitas, Apr. 25, 1976; children: Steven, Leslie, Anthony. Student Temple U., 1953-56, LaSalle U., Chgo., 1968; cert. in Gerontology Ga. State U., 1988, coord. Intergenerational Connections, State of Ga., 1989—. V.p. programming interior design Nat. Home Fashions League, Atlanta, 1974-75; Ga. Bd. Realtors, 1971—; adminstr. Stanley H. Kaplan Ednl. Ctr., Atlanta, 1974-84; owner, pres. Levitas Svcs., Inc. (Internat. Destinations), Atlanta, 1984-85; owner, v.p. Nat. Travel Svcs. and Internat. Destinations, Atlanta, 1984-85; realtor Philip White Properties Inc./Sotheby's Internat. Realty, 1985-91; realtor Coldwell Banker Previews, 1991—. Exec. producer, host community svc. videos TV cable broadcast, Atlanta, 1988—; solo pianist Paul Whiteman TV, Phila. Youth Orch., Frankford Symphony Orch., 1950. Pres. Ahavath Achim Sisterhood, Atlanta, 1977-79; bd. dirs. Jewish Family Svcs., Atlanta chpt. Nat. Osteoporosis Found., 1990-91, Outings in the Park, 1989-91; chmn. Tea at the Ritz Scottish Rite Children's Med. Ctr., 1987-90, women's div. Israel Bond, Atlanta, 1987, 88, 89, mem. aux.; chmn. Who's Bringing in the Great Chefs Scottish Rite Childrens Med. Ctr., 1990, 91, 92; mem. Atlanta Symphony, High Mus. Art, Nat. Mus. of Women in Arts (charter), Alliance Theater Atlanta. Phila. Bd. Edn. scholar, 1952, Atlanta Hist. Ctr.-Atlanta Hist. Soc., Alliance No. Dist. Dental Soc.; charter mem. U.S. Holocaust Mus.; bd. dirs. Jewish Family Svcs., nat. bd. advisors Brevard Music Ctr., 1993—. Named Woman of Achievement, Atlanta Jewish Fedn., 1993. Mem. Ga. Gerontology Soc., Atlanta Bd. Realtors, Spl. Children of the South (chmn. 1991-93), Internat. Furnishings and Design Assn. (Atlanta chpt.), Women in Film, Am. Women in Radio and TV, Children's Med. Ctr. Aux., Brandeis Nat. Women (life), Hadassah (life), Nat. Council Jewish Women (life), B'nai Brith (life), Scots (life).

LEVITT, B. BLAKE, medical and science writer; b. Bridgeport, Conn., Mar. 25, 1948; d. John Joseph and Beatrice Dolores (Rozanski) Blake; m. Andrew Levitt, Dec. 20, 1968 (div. May 1977); m. Jon P. Garvey, Nov. 19, 1983. BA in English magna cum laude, BA in History summa cum laude, Quinnipiac Coll., 1972; postgrad., Yale U., 1988. Instr. English as fgn. lang. U. Khon Kaen, Thailand, 1968-69; market researcher Lyons Bakeries Ltd., London, summer 1971; traffic mgr., copywriter Provocatives Advt. Agy., Danbury, Conn., 1976-78; tech. writer tng. divsn. Jack Morton Prodns., N.Y.C., 1978-82; freelance feature and med. writer Litchfield County Times, New Milford, Conn., 1982-85, N.Y. Times, N.Y.C., 1985-89; freelance writer med. and sci. books, 1989—. Co-author: Before You Conceive, The Complete Pre-Pregnancy Guide, 1989 (Will Solimene Book award for excellence 1991), Electromagnetic Fields: A Consumer's Guide to the Issues and How to Protect Ourselves, 1995; contbr. articles to N.W. Hills mag., New Eng. Monthly, Conn. Mag. Founding mem., bd. dirs. Warren (Conn.) Land Trust, 1989-91; mem. Dem. Town Com., Warren, 1993—; mem. zoning bd. appeals Town of Warren, 1993—. Mem. Nat. Assn. Sci. Writers, Am. Med. Writers Assn., Author's Guild, Author's League.

LEVITT, ELEANOR SOSNOW, counseling psychologist, volunteer; b. Hackensack, N.J., Mar. 13, 1936; d. Louis U. and Anna Lillian (Miller) Sosnow; m. Harry Levitt, June 15, 1969; 1 child, David Avrum. BA, Cornell U., 1958; MA, NYU, 1965, PhD, 1970. Employment interviewer, counselor N.Y. State Employment Svc. Profl. Placement Ctr., N.Y.C., 1960-65; counseling coord. Hofstra U., Hempstead, N.Y., 1969-71; asst. prof. County Coll. Morris, Dover, N.J., 1975-76; counselor Project Eve Kean Coll., Union, N.J., 1977; asst. dir. Career Counseling and Placement Office William Paterson Coll., Wayne, N.J., 1978-79; vol. advocate for institutionalized elderly Ombudsman Office State of N.J., Trenton, 1993—; adj. instr. psychology Kean Coll., Union, 1976-77. Treas. LWV, Livingston, N.J., 1975-77; vol. Am. Coun. Jewish Women, Livingston, 1992—. NDEA fellow, 1965-67. Mem. Phi Beta Kappa, Psi Chi.

LEVITT, MIRIAM, pediatrician; b. Lampertheim, Germany, June 10, 1946; came to U.S., 1948; d. Eli and Esther (Kingston) L.; m. Harvey Flisser, June 25, 1967; children: Adam, Elizabeth, Eric. AB, NYU, 1967; MD, Albert Einstein Coll. Medicine, Yeshiva U., 1971. Diplomate Am. Bd. Pediatrics. Intern Montefiore Med. Ctr., Bronx, N.Y., 1970-71, resident in pediatrics, 1971-73, attending pediatrician, 1975—; dir. outpatient svcs. pediatrics Bronx-Lebanon Hosp., N.Y.C., 1973-77; instr. pediatrics Albert Einstein Coll. Medicine, N.Y.C., 1973-76, asst. prof. clin., 1976—; med. staff Lawrence Hosp., Bronxville, N.Y., 1978—, dir. pediatrics, 1988—; sch. physician Bronxville Bd. Edn., 1983—. Fellow Am. Acad. Pediatrics; mem. Westchester County Med. Soc. Office: 1 Pondfield Rd Bronxville NY 10708-3706

LEVY, ARTHUR LOUELLA WHITE, oncological/operating room nurse; b. Texarkana, Tex., Nov. 5, 1932; d. David Arthur and Myrtle (Watson) White; 1 child, Dee Anne. BSN, U. Houston, 1954. RN. Staff, head nurse, asst. supr., supr. Meth. Hosp., Houston, 1954-61; head nurse Tex. Inst. Rehab. and Rsch., Houston, 1961-66; asst. dir. operating rm., recovery and outpatient surgery Diagnostic Ctr. Hosp., Houston, 1966-84; head nurse M.D. Anderson Cancer Ctr., Houston, 1985—. Mem. Assn. Oper. Rm. Nurses. Democrat. Methodist. Home: 6843 Chasewood Dr Missouri City TX 77489

LEVY, CAROL SUE, artist; b. Miami Beach, Fla., May 17, 1944; d. Bernard and Sylvia (Rosman) L. Student, Miami-Dade C.C., 1962-64; B of Design, U. Fla., 1967; MFA in Printmaking, U. Miami, 1978. Supr. graphic design Comm. Svc./U. Miami, Fla., 1968-76; instr. Pres. Program Miami-Dade C.C., Fla., 1987; adj. instr. visual arts Miami-Dade C.C., 1979-88; chair ART AGAINST AIDS fundraiser, Miami, 1989, co-chair, 1991; vis. asst. prof. Fla. Internat. U., Miami, 1991-92; adj. instr. Fla. Internat. U. and New World Sch. of Arts, Miami, 1989-90, 92, 94; curator Out of Bounds North Miami Ctr. Contemporary Art, Miami, 1993; vis. artist Pelissippi State Tech. C.C., Knoxville, Tenn., 1993; lectr. multi-media materials Comm. Svcs., U. Miami, Fla., 1968-75; instr printmaking workshop Jr. High Gifted Program, U. Miami, 1978; panelist Women and MFAs/Womens Caucus Art, Miami Beach, 1986; curator S.M. Lurie Meml. Exhibit, Gloria Luria Gallery, Bal Harbour, Fla., 1991. One-woman shows include Greene Gallery, Fla., 1984-88, Books and Books, Coral Gables, Fla., 1995; group shows include Greene Gallery, Fla., 1986, U. West Fla., Pensacola, 1988, North Miami Ctr. Art, 1989, New World Sch. Art Gallery, 1992, Francis Wolfson Art Gallery, 1986, 89, 90, Art of Miami-Secca, N.C., 1985-86, Birmingham (Ala.) Biennial, 1985, Inter-Am. Art Gallery, Miami, 1987, 88. Recipient Merit award Vision of Ourselves, Valencia C.C., 1984, Merit award 26 Hortt Meml., Ft. Lauderdale Mus. Art, 1984, Merit award 27 Hortt Meml., Ft. Lauderdale, 1985, Individual Artist fellowship Fla. Fine Art, 1987-88.

LEVY, DALE PENNEYS, lawyer; b. Phila., Sept. 10, 1940; d. Harry M. and Rosalind (Fried) Penneys; m. Richard D. Levy, Dec. 12, 1970; children: Jonathan D., Michael Z. BA, Wellesley Coll., 1962; JD, U. Pa., 1967. Bar: Pa. 1967, U.S. Ct. Appeals (3rd cir.) 1971. Assoc. Blank, Rome, Comisky & McCauley, Phila., 1967-76, ptnr., 1976—; bd. dirs. Phila. Sch., Phila. Indsl. Devel. Corp. Contbr. articles to profl. jours. Bd. dirs., chair Women in Transition, 1983-85, active adv. bd., 1985—; chair Women's Rights Com., 1978; bd. dirs. Phila. Sr. Ctr., 1994—. Mem. ABA, Pa. Bar Assn., Phila. Bar Assn. (past chair women's rights com.). Mem. ABA (real property, probate and trust law sect., vice chairperson com. on pub.-pvt. ventures/privatization internat. law and practice sect.), Phila. Bar Assn. (real estate, corp., banking and bus. law sect., mem. women's rights com.). Office: Blank Rome Comisky & McCauley 4 Penn Center Plz Philadelphia PA 19103-2521

LEVY, ELLEN S., occupational therapist; b. Takoma Park, Md., July 3, 1955; d. Edward S. and Dorothy M. (Baer) L. BS, U. Pa., 1978; postgrad., Johns Hopkins U. Registered occupational therapist. Occupational therapist Phila. State Hosp., 1979; sr. occupational therapist Phila. Psychiat. Ctr., 1980-81, The Fairmount Inst., Phila., 1983-85; coord. fieldwork, adj. instr. Temple U., Phila., 1981-83; occupational therapy cons., Phila., 1981-89; traveling occupational therapist Pro-Rehab, Inc., 1989-91; occupational therapy asst. mgr. Pro-Rehab, Inc., Va., 1991-92; mgr. occupational therapy Pro-Rehab, Inc., Va., Md., 1992-93; interdisciplinary mgr. Pro-Rehab, Inc., Charlottesville, Va., 1993-94; cons., 1994—; mem. adj. faculty Coll. Health Scis., Roanoke, Va., 1993-94; dir. phys. medicine team Md. chpt. Voluntary Optometric Svcs. to Humanity, 1987—; presenter World Congress Occupational Therapy, 1994. Sec. SANE Edn. Fund, Phila., 1977-78; bd. dirs. Circle L. of Camp Louise, Balt., 1991—. Recipient Cert. of Appreciation Lions Club, San Pedro Sula, Honduras, 1988, 89, Cumyagua, Honduras, 1990, Guatemala City, 1992, Salamá, Guatemala, 1993, San Cristobal, Guatemala, 1994. Mem. Am. Occupational Therapy Assn. (cons. cerft. occupational therapy assts. in groups task force 1990—), World Fedn. Occupational Therapists, Va. Occupational Therapy Assn. (conf. presenter 1993), ACLU. Democrat. Jewish. Home and Office: 806 Brantford Ave Silver Spring MD 20904-2005

LEVY, LEAH GARRIGAN, federal official; b. Miami, Fla., Apr. 29, 1947; d. Thomas Leo and Mary (Flaherty) Garrigan; m. Roger N. Levy, May 2, 1977; children: Philip, Aaron. Student, George Mason U. Mem. legis. staff U.S. Ho. Reps., 1973-75; mem. scheduling staff U.S. Senate, 1975-77, mem. administrv. scheduling staff, 1977-81; staff asst. pub. liaison The White House, 1982-84; spl. asst. U.S Dept. Transport, Washington, 1984-89, U.S. Dept. Housing, Washington, 1989—; scheduling asst. Empower Am., Washington, 1993-94; scheduler majority leader Dick Armey U.S. Ho. of Reps., Washington, 1995—. Contbr. to Rep. Nat. Com., Washington. Contbr. Rep. Nat. Conv. Va. Rep. Party, Washington; del. Va. State GOP Conv., Richmond, 1994. Roman Catholic.

LEVY, MARIAN MULLER, transportation executive; b. N.Y.C., Mar. 10, 1942; d. Arthur Russ and Diana Elise (Ornstein) Muller; m. Richard Dennis Levy, Nov. 16, 1962; children: Dawn, Nicole, Jason, Adam. Student, Bklyn. Coll., 1959-61, 68-70. Sec. ASCAP, N.Y.C., 1959-61; tchr. spl. edn Garden Park Sch., Phoenix, 1974-76; v.p. Pac Expediters, Ltd., Scottsdale, Ariz., 1976—. Bd. dirs. Outreach, Phoenix, 1982-92; co-chmn. Council Jews Spl. Needs, Phoenix, 1987-88; chairperson Hospice of the Valley Art Com. Recipient Paul D. Mahoney Outstanding Svc. award Hospice of the Valley, 1991. Mem. Scottsdale Ctr. for Arts, Fine Art for Fine Causes, Phoenix Art Mus., The Heard Mus. Home: 7850 E Camelback Rd Unit 602 Scottsdale AZ 85251-2291 Office: Pac Expediters Ltd 3020B N Scottsdale Rd Scottsdale AZ 85251-7210

LEVY, MAXINE KESSIE, counselor; b. Waukegan, Ill., Jan. 13, 1939; d. Joseph W. and Jean I. (Shavin) Kessie; m. Stephen Levy, June 25, 1961; children: Allison Dale, William Eric, Phillip Samuel, Daniel Aron. BA in Teaching Lang. Arts, U. Ill., 1961; MA in Counseling, Roosevelt U., Chgo., 1966; MA in Spl. Edn., Northeastern Ill. U., 1981, adminstrv. cert., 1984. Secondary tchr. English, Chgo. Bd. Edn., 1961-62; instr. ice skating Winnetka (Ill.) Park Dist., 1977-78; adminstrv. aide off-campus program Twp. High Sch. Dist. 203, Wilmette, Ill., 1978-80; tchr. learning disabilities Twp. High Dist. 113, Highland Park, Ill., 1979-84; counselor, coord. talented and gifted program Twp. High Dist. 214, Elk Grove Village, Ill., 1985—; mem. adj. faculty dept. edn. Roosevelt U., Chgo., 1990—. Bd. dirs. Willowbrook Sch. PTA, Glenview, Ill., 1970-78, pres., 1975-77; pres. Choral Parents Orgn., Glenbrook North High Sch., Northbrook, Ill., 1983-85; pres. Farno chpt. Women's Am. Orgn. Rehab. Through Tng., 1970-72, sec. Chgo. region, 1972-74, regional v.p., 1974-76, bd. dirs., 1980-85; bd. govs. Millikin Club Chgo., 1987—; mem. Peer Helper Network Greater Chgo., 1989—. Recipient Outstanding Contbn. to Edn. award Twp. High Sch. Dist. 214, 1990. Mem. ACA (pres. N.W. Suburban chpt. 1988-90), Nat. Assn. Gifted Children (treas. divsn. counseling and guidance 1990—), Nat. Assn. Coll. Admissions Counselors, Ill. Assn. Gifted Children, Phi Delta Kappa. Office: Elk Grove High Sch 500 W Elk Grove Blvd Elk Grove Village IL 60007-4296

LEVY, ROCHELLE FELDMAN, artist; b. N.Y.C., Aug. 4, 1937; d. S. Harry and Eva (Krause) Feldman; m. Robert Paley Levy, June 4, 1955; children: Kathryn Tracey, Wendy Paige, Robert Paley, Angela Brooke, Michael Tyler. Student Barnard Coll., 1954-55, U. Pa., 1955-56; BFA, Moore Coll. Art, 1979. Mgmt. cons. Woodlyne Sch., Rosemont, Pa., 1983-84; sr. ptnr. DRT Interiors, Phila., 1983—; ptnr. Phila. Phillies, 1981-94. One-woman shows: Watson Gallery, Wheaton Coll., Norton, Mass., 1977, U. Pa., 1977, Med. Coll. Pa., Phila., 1982, Aqueduct Race Track, Long Island, N.Y., 1982, 68, Phila. Art Alliance, 1983, Moore Coll. Art, Phila., 1984, Phila. Art Alliance, 1994. Pres., League of Children's Hosp., Phila., 1969-70; chmn. bd. trustees Moore Coll. Art, 1988—; bd. overseers Ctr. for Judaic Studies U. Pa., 1993—. Recipient G. Allen Smith Prize, Woodmere Art Gallery, Chestnut Hill, Pa., 1979; Woman honoree Samuel Paley Day Care Ctr., Phila., 1990, Jefferson Bank Declaration award, 1991, Nat. Philanthropy honoree, 1994. Trustee Moore Coll. Art, 1988—, chmn. bd. trustee, 1990—; mem. selections and acquisitions com. Pa. Acad. Fine Arts, 1979—; bd. mgrs., 1975—, chmn. exec. com., 1982—, bd. trustee, 1990—. Mem. Allied Artists Am., Artist's Equity, Phila. Art Alliance, Phila. Print Club. Office: Phila Phillies PO Box 7575 Philadelphia PA 19101-7575

LEVY, (ALEXANDRA) SUSAN, construction company executive; b. Rockville Centre, N.Y., Apr. 26, 1949; d. Alexander Stanley and Anna Charlotte (Galasieski) Jankoski; m. William Mack Levy, Aug. 12, 1977. Student, Suffolk Community Coll., Brentwood, N.Y., 1976. Cert. constrn. assoc. Supr. N.Y. Telephone Co., Babylon, 1970-74; v.p. Aabbacco Equipment Leasing Corp., Lindenhurst, N.Y., 1974-81; pres., owner Femi-9 Contracting Corp., Lindenhurst, 1981—. Mem. affirmative action adv. coun. N.Y. State Dept. Transp., Albany, 1984-88, human resources adv. panel Long Island Project 2000; mem. Presdl. Task Force, Washington, 1982—; mem. Leadership Am., 1994—. With U.S. Army, 1967-69. Recipient Henri Dunant Corp. award ARC Suffolk County, 1986, Race to the Top award Bridgestone Tire Corp., 1992, Nawbo award Nat. Assn. Women Bus. Owners, 1993; named honoree Women on the Job, 1989. Mem. Nat. Assn. Women in Constrn. (founder L.I. chpt., pres. 1983-85, regional chmn. woman-owned bus. enterprise com., nat. chmn. pub. rels. and mktg. com., nat. dir. Region 1 1988-89, Mem. of Yr. L.I. chpt. 1987, Exec. of Yr. L.I. chpt., nat. dir., 1988-89, nat. treas. 1991-93, nat. v.p. 1993-94, nat. pres.-elect 1994-95, pres. 1995—), Nassau Suffolk Contractors Assn. (sec. 1984-87, sec.-treas. 1987—, bd. dirs.), Nat. Assn. Women Bus. Owners (charter, Top Woman Bus. Owner award 1993), Am. Plat Form Assn. Republican. Roman Catholic. Avocations: reading, writing, golf. Home: 133 Hollins Ln East Islip NY 11730-3006 Office: Femi-9 Contracting Corp 305 E Sunrise Hwy Lindenhurst NY 11757-2521

LEVY, SUSAN NAOMI, librarian; b. Elmhurst, N.Y., Aug. 26, 1948; d. David J. and Gertrude (Stern) L. AB, Hunter Coll., 1970; MA, Boston U., 1972; MLS, SUNY, Albany, 1972. Cert. Libr. Coll. off ice asst. CUNY, 1973-77; adult svc. libr. Bklyn. Pub. Libr., 1977-78, libr. telephone reference, 1978-83, asst. div. chief, telephone reference, 1983—. Recording sec. AAUW, Bklyn. Branch, 1980-85. Mem. ALA, Mensa, Lambda Ind. Dems., Phi Beta Kappa. Democrat. Jewish. Office: Brooklyn Public Library Grand Army Pla Brooklyn NY 11238

LEW, FRAN, artist. BA in Art with honors, Bklyn. Coll., 1966; MFA, Boston U., 1968; postgrad., Internat. Ctr. Painting and Costume Design, Venice, Italy, 1978, Art Student's League, N.Y.C., 1978-79, Reilly League of Artists, White Plains, N.Y., 1979-84. One-man shows include Grand Ctrl. Art Galleries, N.Y.C., 1990, Manhattan Borough Pres.'s Art Gallery, N.Y.C., 1989, Pen and Brush Club, N.Y.C., 1989, Columbus Club, N.Y.C., 1982; group shows include John Pence Gallery, San Francisco, 1987, Salmagundi Club, Nat. Arts Club, Am. Artists Profl. League; represented in public collections Gov.'s Mansion, Albany, N.Y., Consulate of Israel, N.Y.C.; represented in permanent collection Cornell Mus.; portraits include Gov. Mario M. Cuomo, First Lady Matilda Cuomo, Nobel Laureate Dr. Vincent duVigneaud, Philip H. Geier Jr., Daniel Damiano, trilogy Golda Meir, David Ben Gurion, and Moshe Dayan. Artist, cons. Westchester 2000, White Plains, 1989. Recipient Crescent Cardboard Corp. prize Am. Artist Mag., 1987. Mem. Art Students' League (life), Reilly League Artists, Knickerbocker Artists (Gold medal 1984), Hudson Valley Art Assn. (Mrs John Newington award 1989), Catherine Lorillard Wolfe Art Club (Margaret Dole award 1988), Pen and Brush Club (Solo award 1987). Home and Studio: 150 Lake St # 3F White Plains NY 10604-2436

LEW, GINGER, lawyer; b. San Mateo, Calif., Nov. 3, 1948; d. Bing and Suey Bow (Ng) L.; m. Carl Lennart Ehn, Feb. 2, 1984; children: Melissa, Jeremy. BS, UCLA, 1970; JD, U. Calif.-Berkeley, 1974. Bar: Calif. 1974, D.C. 1980. Dep. city atty. City of Los Angeles, 1974-75; asst. regional counsel Dept. Energy, San Francisco, 1975-77, dep. regional counsel, 1977-78, chief counsel, 1978-80; dep. asst. sec. of state for East Asia, Dept. of State, Washington, 1980-81, spl. adviser, 1981-82; ptnr. Stovall, Spradlin, Armstrong & Israel, Washington, 1983-86, Arthur Young Co., Washington, 1986-93; gen. counsel U.S. Dept. Commerce, Washington, 1993—. Recipient Outstanding Achievement award Dept. of State, 1980, Meritorious Svc. award, 1981. Mem. ABA, Asian Pacific Am. Bar Assn. (bd. dirs. 1981-83), Women's Bar Assn., Orgn. of Chinese-Americans, Pi Sigma Alpha. Clubs: Commonwealth (San Francisco); Nat. Lawyers. Office: US Dept Commerce Office Gen Counsel 14th & Constitution Ave NW Washington DC 20230*

LEW, JOYCELYNE MAE, actress; b. Santa Monica, Calif., Feb. 25, 1962; d. George and Mabel Florence (Lum) L. BA in Theatre Arts, UCLA, 1981, teaching credential, 1982; MA in Urban Edn., Pepperdine U., 1984; bilingual cert., U. So. Calif., 1983; postgrad., Stella Adler Acad., 1988. Appeared in films The Groundlings, 1987, Tai-Pan, 1987, Fatal Beauty, 1989, The Royal Affair, 1993, Shattered Image, 1993, Dr. Boris and Mrs. Duluth, 1994, TV programs The Young and the Restless, 1990, Phil Donahue Show, 1993, Hard Copy, 1994; voice over artist, mag. model, body double, dancer; co-writer film script They Still Call Me Bruce, 1986 (award); song lyricist Nighttime Blues. Mem. judging com. for film grants Nat. Endowment for Arts, 1986; mem. L.A. Beautiful, 1993. Mem. AFTRA, SAG, NATAS (blue ribbon com. for Emmy awards 1986-90), Assn. Asian Pacific Am. Artists (treas. 1983-89), Nat. Asian Am. Telecomms. Assn., Am. Film Inst. Conservatory Workshop, Calif. PTA (life). Home and Office: 1958 N Van Ness Ave Los Angeles CA 90068

LEWALLEN, ELINOR GRACE KIRBY, organization executive, lay church worker; b. Miltonvale, Kans., May 17, 1919; d. Osbourn Eddy and Grace Dale (Gorrell) Kirby; m. Thomas Monroe Lewallen, Jr., Aug. 14, 1948; children: Janet, Dean, Gary, Kent, Bonnie. AA, Coffeyville Jr. Coll., 1939; BA, Baker U., 1943; postgrad., U. Colo., 1969-70, Iliff Sch. Theology, Denver, 1986, 90, 94. Youth pres. Kans. Conf. United Meth. Youth, Baldwin, Kans., 1940-41; program dir. for young adults YWCA, Rockford, Ill., 1943-46; program dir. Bus. and Profl. Girls Club of YWCA, Denver, 1946-48; program dir. for young adults YWCA, Denver, 1943-48; nat. pres. Fedn. Parents and Friends of Lesbians and Gays, Denver, 1987-88, chmn. Fedn. Parents-FLAG Religious Issues Task Force, 1988-91; rsch. sec. values study Little Sch. of Iliff Sch. of Theology, 1977-84; numerous leadership roles Park Hill United Meth. Ch., Denver, 1953—; del. to ann. conv. Colo., 1979-88; mem. conf. task force on AIDS, Rocky Mt. Conf., 1986-92, com. on sexuality ministries, 1981—; mem. steering com. John Wesley Iliff Group; presenter United Meth. Gen. Conf. Com. to Study Homosexuality, St. Louis, 1991; mem. adminstrv. coun. Parkhill United Meth. Ch., 1993-94. Chmn. impact neighborhood task force Denver Anti-Crime Coun., 1972-80; election judge, Denver 1981—; mem. Colo. Gov.'s Adv. Coun. on AIDS, 1987-88. Recipient award of recognition Denver Anti-Crime Coun., 1980, Outstanding Leadership award Nat. Parents, Families, and Friends of Lesbians and Gays, 1988, 92, Hall of Honor and Swan award Denver Parents, Families and Friends of Lesbians and Gays, 1994. Mem. LWV, Assn. Group Workers (charter Colo. chpt.). Democrat. Home: 2258 Krameria St Denver CO 80207-3931

LEWANDOWSKI, CANDACE LYNN, public accountant; b. Trenton, Mich., Mar. 21, 1959; d. James Mervin and Sally Jean (Williams) Barnes; m. Thomas Francis Lewandowski, Oct. 24, 1980; children: Thomas James, Samantha Ann. BS in Acctg., Oakland U., 1982; MS in Fin., Walsh Coll., Troy, Mich., 1992. CPA. Sr. acct. Ernst & Whinney, Detroit, 1983-85; acct. Grey & Trepeck, CPAs, P.C., Birmingham, Mich., 1987-88; v.p. Lewandowski Brothers, Troy, Mich., 1980—; sr. fin. analyst Kelly Svcs., Troy, 1993-94; mgr. pricing and contracts N000, 1994—; adj. instr. Walsh Coll., 1992-93. Republican. Roman Catholic. Office: Kelly Svcs 999 W Big Beaver Rd Troy MI 48084

LEWANDOWSKI, MICHALENE MARIA, human service consultant, lecturer; b. Hamilton, Ont., Can., June 2, 1920; d. Stanley Casmere and Winifred (Kolodziejski) Doskotch; m. Henry Adam Schultz, Aug. 30, 1939 (dec. July 1940); m. Matthew John Lewandowski, July 27, 1941 (dec. Jan. 1987); children: Adrian, Christopher. Student, Wayne State U. Cert. med. asst.; cert. Am. Coll. Nursing Home Adminstrs., Mich. Health Facilities Assn., various other state health assns. Activity-patient affairs dir. Abbey Nursing Home, Warren, Mich., 1963-70; designated social worker Good Shepherd Nursing Home, Detroit, 1970, Rose-Villa Nursing Home, Roseville, Mich., 1970-81; instr. rehab. and devel. various nursing homes, Warren, 1976—; originator Day Care Ctrs., Macomb County, Mich., 1990-91; cons. various nursing homes, Mich., 1984-87; profl. lectr., 1990—; instr. rehab. and human rels. devel. in nursing homes Macomb County Community Coll., 1976; pres. Macomb County Activity Dirs. Assn., 1975; panelist in field. Author: The Human Island, 1970 (Outstanding Cultural Achievement award, 1976); contbr. articles to profl. pubns. Del. White House Conf. on Aging, Lansing, Mich., Washington, 1971; state commr. on aging State of Mich., Lansing, 1975-80; bd. dirs. Macomb County (Mich.) Coun. on Aging, 1973, spl. cons., 1976. Recipient citation for Care and Therapy of Aged, City of Warren, 1964, Polish Nat. Alliance for Complete Dedication to the Aged, 1970, Spl. Tribute State of Mich., 1974; named Citizen of Week WBRB, 1970; honored for Contbns. to Mankind, Macomb County Commrs., 1973; recipient personal letter from Pres. Nixon for her work; documentary on her work with elderly presented on Sta. WXYZ-TV.

LEWARK, CAROL ANN, special education educator; b. Fort Wayne, Ind., Mar. 8, 1935; d. Lloyd L. and Elizabeth J. (Arthur) Meads; m. Paul N. Lewark, Aug. 20, 1955; children: David P., Laura, Beth, Daniel A. BA, St. mary of Woods, 1978; MS, Ind. U., 1981. Cert. elem. educator, spl. educator mentally retarded K-12, learning disabilities K-12, Ind.; cert. home tng. specialist, Wis. Home tng. specialist Madison Wis. ARC, Madison, 1968-70; nursery sch. cons. Allen County ARC, Ft. Wayne, Ind., 1971-73; early childhood spl. edn. dir. Allen County ARC, Ft. Wayne, 1973—; cons. in field; presenter in field; apptd. by Ind. Gov. to State Interagy. Coordinating Coun. for Infants and Toddlers, 1992-95; apptd. to Higher Ed Coun. for Early Childhood and Spl. Edn. Contbr. articles to profl. jours. Apptd. to Leadership Ft. Wayne, 1994. Named Model Project Site 99-457 Early Intervention Ind. State Dept. Mental Health, 1987; Tech. Assistance grantee Georgetown U., 1991-93. Mem. Ind. Coun. for Exceptional Children (sec. 1990-94), First Steps of Allen County (facilitator 1989—), Leadership Fort Wayne. Home: 910 Kensington Blvd Fort Wayne IN 46805-5312 Office: ARC of Allen County 2542 Thompson Ave Fort Wayne IN 46807-1099

LEWENT, JUDY C., pharmaceutical executive; b. Jan. 13, 1949. BA, Goucher Coll., 1970; MS in Mgmt., MIT, 1972. With corp. fin. dept. E.F. Hutton & Co., Inc., 1972-74; asst. v.p. for strategic planning Bankers Trust Co., 1974-75; sr. fin. analyst corp. planning Norton Simon, 1975-76; div. contr. Pfizer, Inc., 1976-80; dir. acquisitions and capital analysis Merck & Co., Inc., Whitehouse Sta., N.J., 1980-83, asst. contr., 1983-85; exec. dir. fin. evaluation and analysis Merck & Co. Inc., Whitehouse Sta., N.J., 1985-87, v.p., treas., 1987-90, v.p. fin., CFO, 1990-92, sr. v.p., CFO, 1993—. Office: Merck & Co Inc One Merck Dr PO Box 1000 Whitehouse Station NJ 08889-0100

LEWICKE, CATHERINE PEARL, retired education educator; b. Lowell, Mass., Aug. 29, 1917; d. John P. and Anna G. (O'Reilly) Cryan; m. Edward Lewicke, Apr. 8, 1945 (dec. Mar. 1991); children: Edward Thomas, John Arthur, Jane Frances, Peter Paul, Anna Maria. BS in Edn., Lowell Tchrs. Coll., 1939; EdM, Boston U., 1956, CAGS, 1964; EdD, U. Lowell (Mass.), 1991. Cert. tchr., sch. psychologist, reading cons., Mass. Prin. elem. sch., Wilmington, Mass., 1941-44; tng. specialist U.S. Army, Ft. Devens, Mass., 1944-45; reading and test cons. pub. schs., Uxbridge, Mass., 1956-61; reading supr. pub. schs., Westford, Mass., 1961-66; assoc. prof. edn. Worcester (Mass.) State Coll., 1966-82, supr. student tchrs., 1967-82, prof. emerita, 1982—; adj. prof., grad. program Children's Literature, Linguistics, undergrad. supervision of student tchrs., Worcester (Mass.) State Coll., 1982—, supervision practicum for grad. students, 1990—; storyteller pub. schs. Mem. Internat. Reading Assn., Nat. Coun. Tchrs. English, Assn. Tchr. Educators, Assn. Supervision and Curriculum. Roman Catholic.

LEWIN, DEBRA DAPHNA, model agency owner; b. Poughkeepsie, N.Y., Sept. 4, 1966; d. Shallom and Henia (Wisgardisky) Lewin. BS in Bus., U. Vt., Burlington, 1988. Varsity coach South Burlington (Vt.) High Sch., 1984-86; mktg. dir. No. Lights, Burlington, 1988; co-owner Promark Models, Burlington, 1989-92; owner Debra Lewin Prodns. & Talent, Burlington, 1992—, Miami, Fla., 1994—; producer Miss Vt./Am., 1992—; guest cons. Champlain Coll., Burlington, 1993. Named Miss Vt., Miss. Am. Orgn., 1990. Jewish. Office: Debra Lewin Prodns & Talent 269 Pearl St Burlington VT 05401

LEWIN, PEARL GOLDMAN, psychologist; b. Bklyn., Apr. 25, 1923; d. Frank and Anna (Simon) Goldman; m. Seymour Z. Lewin, Oct. 17, 1943; children: David, Jonathan. BA, Hunter Coll., 1943; MS, U. Mich., 1947; PhD, NYU, 1980. Lic. psychologist, N.Y. Insp. chemist quarter master corps U.S. Army, 1943-45; chemist chem. warfare U.S. Army, Edgewood Arsenal, Md., 1945; asst. psychologist Bur. Psychol. Svcs., U. Mich., Ann Arbor, 1947-48; freelance rsch. asst. chemistry N.Y.C., 1955-71; adj. lectr. CUNY, Bklyn., 1973-74, instr., 1974-79, asst. prof., 1979-80; psychologist Creedmore Psychiat. Ctr., N.Y.C., 1980-82; sr. psychologist Manhattan Family Ct., N.Y.C., 1982-87; cons., 1987—; mentor Peer Counseling Orgn., Bklyn. Coll., 1976-80, coord. student svcs. New Sch. Liberal Arts, 1974-76, adminstr. acad. regulations, 1974-76. Author: Sexist Humor, 1979. Mem. APA, Pi Lambda Theta, Phi Kappa Phi. Home and Office: 4231 N Walnut Ave Arlington Heights IL 60004-1302

LEWIN, SUSAN GRANT, creative director advertising and public relations; b. Phila., Feb. 25, 1939; d. Benj Gerald Winig and May (Lipsky) Feman; m. Chester Grant, Aug. 7, 1960 (div. 1966); m. Harold F. Lewin, June 4, 1967; children: Adam, Gabrielle. BA, U. Pa. Reporter and columnist Home Furnishing Daily, 1962-65, design editor, 1965-70; sr. editor architecture House Beautiful Mag. Hearst Publs., 1970-82; creative dir. Formica Corp., N.Y.C., 1982—; pres. Design Communications Internat., N.Y.C., 1988—, global creative dir., 1994; exhbn. curator Surface and Ornament, 1983-88, Table to Tablescape, Kansas City Art Inst., et al, 1988-91, Found Futures,

1992; bd. dirs. Archtl. League. Author: Formica and Design, 1991, One Of A Kind American Art Jewelry Today, 1994. Recipient Disting. Editorial award Am. Soc. Interior Designers, 1967, Nat. Endowment for Arts, 1978, Pres.' award Inst. Bus. Designers, 1983, Circle of Excellence award Internat. Furnishings & Design Assocs., 1993. Mem. AIA (com. on design), Archtl. League, World Design, Am. Inst. Graphic Arts, Indsl. Designers Soc., Mcpl. Arts Soc., IFDA. Office: Formica Corp 250 W 57th St New York NY 10107

LEWINSOHN, JODIE, federal agency administrator; b. Okla., Mar. 26, 1931; d. Milton Mark and H. Maree (Myer) L. AB, Stanford U., 1952; MA, Johns Hopkins U., 1954. With Fgn. Svc., 1958; mem. U.S. Embassy, Cambodia, 1958-59; dir. office E. Asian and Pacific affairs U.S. Info. Agy., 1959—. Office: E Asia & Pacific Affairs US Info Agy 301 4th St SW Rm 766 Washington DC 20547-0009*

LEWIS, ANITA JANET, graphic designer; b. Welch, W.Va., Mar. 30, 1964; d. Rush Toliver Justice and Mary Anne (Creed) Baker; m. William Clint Lewis. BA, Concord Coll., Athens, W.Va., 1976. Art dir. Mediad Advt., Bluefield, W.Va., 1976-80; adj. instr. Concord Coll., Athens, W.Va., 1979-80; part owner The Art Dept., Bluefield, W.Va., 1981; art dir. Geol. Cons. Svcs., Bluefield, 1981-89; art dir. Marshall Miller & Assocs., Bluefield, 1989-92, adminstrv. officer, 1992-94; dir. advt. Turner Vision, Bluefield, 1994—. Vol. United Way of the Virginias, Bluefield, 1993. Mem. Greater Bluefield C. of C. (editor newsletter 1992—). Episcopalian. Home: 302 Crabapple St Bluefield VA 24605-9648 Office: Turner Vision PO Box 169 Bluefield WV 24701

LEWIS, ANN FRANK, social welfare association executive, columnist; b. Jersey City, Dec. 19, 1937; d. Samuel and Elsie (Golush) Frank; student Radcliffe Coll., 1954-55; m. Myron Sponder, 1989; children from previous marriage: Patricia Fay, Beth Ellen, Susan Jane. Asst. to mayor of Boston, 1968-75; dep. campaign mgr. Bayh for President, 1975-76; adminstrv. asst. to cong. Stan Lundine, 1976-81; adminstrv. asst. to Congresswoman Barbara Mikulski, 1978-81; polit. dir. Dem. Nat. Com., 1981-85; nat. dir. Ams. for Dem. Action, 1985-87; nat. affairs columnist MS mag., 1988-92; analyst Monitor Radio and WHDH TV 1992; v.p. for pub. policy Planned Parenthood Fedn. Am.; pres. Politics, Inc. Co-chair Back to Bus. com., 1994. Inst. Politics of Kennedy Sch. Govt. fellow Harvard U., 1989. Office: 1120 Connecticut Ave # 461 Washington DC 20036-5004

LEWIS, ANNE MCCUTCHEON, architect; b. New Orleans, Oct. 15, 1943; d. John Tinney and Susan (Dart) McCutcheon; m. Ronald Burton Lewis, Oct. 2, 1971; children: Matthew, Oliver. BA magna cum laude, Radcliffe Coll., 1965; MArch, Harvard U., 1970. Registered architect, D.C. Designer and planner Skidmore, Owings & Merrill, Washington, 1969-72, Keyes, Lethbridge & Condon, Washington, 1972-75; prin. Anne McCutcheon Lewis AIA, Washington, 1976-81; ptnr. McCartney Lewis Architects, Washington, 1981—. Mem. Harvard U. Grad. Sch. Design Alumni Coun., Cambridge, Mass., 1979-82; bd. dirs. Friends Non-Profit Housing, Washington, 1981—, Washington Humane Soc., 1990—. Mem. AIA (Design awards 1979, 83, 89, 90, 91, 92, 93, dir.-at-large Washington chpt. 1982-84). Mem. Soc. of Friends. Office: McCartney Lewis Architects 1503 Connecticut Ave NW Washington DC 20036-1103

LEWIS, AUDREY GERSH, financial marketing consultant; b. Phila., Dec. 1, 1933; d. Benjamin and Augusta (Fine) Gersh; divorced; children: Jamie Lewis Keith, Ruth-Ellen. Student, Temple U., 1951-53. Asst. mgr. accounts payable/receivable Turner Constrn. Co., Louisville, 1953-55; rep. sales, mktg., fin. depts. Benjamin Gersh Wholesaler Jeweler, Wyncote, Pa., 1955-69; registered rep. Seaboard Planning Corp. (formerly B.C. Morton Broker Del.), Greenwich, Conn. and Wyncote, 1969-72; placement counselor sales and mktg. dept. Greyhound Permanent Pers. subs. Greyhound Corp., Stamford, Conn., 1974-77; asst. v.p. Am. Investors Corp., Greenwich, 1977-85; founder, pres. Audrey Gersh Lewis Cons. Ltd., Greenwich, 1985—. Chair Cancer Fund, Wyncote, United Fund Leadership Award, Wyncote; asst. treas. Republican Town Com., Greenwich, 1981-82; mem. Greenwich Town Alarm Appeals Bd., 1985—. Mem. Assn. Corp. Growth (bd. dirs., v.p. mktg. and pub. rels. N.Y. chpt. 1989-92, mem. nat. ann. meeting planning com. 1992, 93, 94), Fin. Women's Assn., Women's Econ. Round Table, Greenwich C. of C. (mem. pub. rels. com. 1990—, corp. devel. com. 1991—), Centre for the Study of the Presidency (nat. adv. coun.), N.Y. Hong Kong Assn., Am. C. of C. in Hong Kong, World Trade Centres in Can. Office: Audrey Gersh Lewis Cons Ltd PO Box 4644 Greenwich CT 06830-8644

LEWIS, DEBBIE DEE, marketing executive; b. Fort Wayne, Ind., May, 1955; d. Kenneth R. and M. Irene Miller; m. Charles D. Lewis (div. 1981); children: David R., Carrie A... Store activities rep. McDonald's Systems, Newport News, Va., Fort Wayne, Ind., 1978, community relations rep. Fort Wayne, Columbus, Ohio, 1979-81; regional mktg. mgr. Arby's, Inc., Ohio region, 1982-83; mktg. dir. McNeill Enterprises, Inc., Chillicothe, Ohio, 1984-86; project mgr./mktg. dept. Mid-Am. Fed., Columbus, 1987-88; dir. advt. Record Herald, Washington Court House, Ohio, 1988-91; program mgr. Hopewell Jobs for Ohio Grads., Hillsboro, Ohio, 1991-92; acct. exec. Cox. Enterprises/Dayton Daily News, 1993-94; account exec. Ohio Mag., Columbus, 1994—; trainer regional mktg. mgrs. Arby's, Columbus, 1982-83; mktg. cons. MEI Franchises, 1984-86. Fund raiser Ronald McDonald House, Columbus, Indpls., 1980-81; pres. Alliance for a Prosperous Downtown Washington Ct. House, 1990. Recipient Best Bets awards McDonald's Indpls. region, 1980, 81, BPW Young Careerist Yr. award, local and regional, 1990-91, Jobs for America's Graduates Phenominal Growth award 1992. Mem. Dayton Advt. Club. Methodist. Avocations: reading, bicycling, crafts. Office: Ohio Mag 62 E Broad St Columbus OH 43215

LEWIS, DIANE PATRICIA, finance executive; b. Elizabeth, N.J., Oct. 9, 1956; d. Walter Charles and Ethel Alida (Worth) L. Assocs. of Bus., Union Coll., 1976; B of Psychology, Rutgers Coll., 1979. Br. mgr. Household Fin. Corp., Wayne, N.J., 1979-85; asst. treas., budget coord., security adminstr. electronic funds transfer Chase Manhattan Bank, N.Y.C., 1985-92, 2d v.p. tech. svc. ctr., fin. planning and adminstrn., trading floor, risk mgmt., 1992—; pres. Dreams & Visions, Making Them a Reality, 1993—; dir. seminars, workshops, classes Eckankar, Rahway, N.J., 1979-89; lectr. in field. Mem. Phi Theta Kappa. Home and Office: PO Box 303 Fanwood NJ 07023-1501 Office: Chase Manhattan Bank 4 Chase MetroTech Ctr 4th Flr Brooklyn NY 11245

LEWIS, ELEANOR ROBERTS, lawyer; b. Detroit, Jan. 5, 1944; d. David Edward and Patricia Mary (Easterbrook) Roberts; m. Roger Kutnow Lewis, June 24, 1967; 1 child, Kevin Michael. B.A., Wellesley Coll., 1965; M.A.T., Harvard U., 1966; J.D., Georgetown U., 1974. Bar: D.C. 1975, U.S. Dist. Ct. D.C. 1975, U.S. Ct. Appeals (D.C. cir.) 1975, U.S. Ct. Appeals (10th cir.) 1976, U.S. Supreme Ct. 1980. cert. tchr. Tchr., Waltham (Mass.) High Sch., 1966-67, Holton-Arms Sch., Bethesda, Md., 1967-71; atty. HUD, Washington, 1974-76, asst. gen. counsel, 1979-82; atty. Brownstein Zeidman & Schomer, Washington, 1976-79; chief counsel internat. commerce U.S. Dept. Commerce, Washington, 1982—. Author, editor (with others) Street Law, 1975. Contbr. chpts. to books, articles to legal and fin. jours. Bd. dirs. Dana Place Condominium, Washington. Wellesley Coll. scholar, 1963-65. Mem. ABA (U.S. govt. liaison to internat. sect.), D.C. Bar Assn., Sr. Execs. Assn. (pres. dept. commerce chpt.). Home: 5034 1/2 Dana Pl NW Washington DC 20016 Office: US Dept Commerce 14th & Constitution Ave NW Washington DC 20230-0002*

LEWIS, ELENA DAWN, programmer analyst; b. South Bend, Ind., July 13, 1964; d. Joseph Paul Lewis and Helen Paulette (King) Pyles; 1 child, Jocelyn Janelle. BBA, Ohio U., 1986. Jr. programmer Centerior Energy, Cleve., 1987-89; tech. cons. Datronics Inc./Alcoa Aluminum, N.Y., Tenn., 1989-91; sr. programmer, analyst Allen Bradley Co., Cleve., 1992—. Career beginnings mentor Urban League, Cleve., 1993; career beginnings tutor Urban League/Allen Bradley, Cleve., 1993-94. Mem. Black Data Processing Assn., Approve Workman Are Not Ashamed. Baptist. Office: Allen Bradley Co 747 Alpha Dr Cleveland OH 44143

LEWIS, ELISAH B., university official; b. Coral Gables, Fla., Feb. 14, 1961; d. Jean Sara (Mechlouitz) L. BFA, EdB, U. Miami, 1983, MEd, 1985, PhD, 1990. Art tchr. U. Miami, Coral Gables, Fla., 1979-89, Lowe Art Mus.; grad. asst. fin. assistance dept. U. Miami, Coral Gables, 1983-88, grad. asst. to acad. advisor, 1985-88, master tutor coord., 1988-89, testing examiner, 1988—, coord. transfer, jr. acad. advisor, 1989—. Mem. Fairchild Tropical Garden, Parrot Jungle and Garden, Lowe Art Mus. Recipient Silver Knight award in Art, 1979, Hibiscus award Fairchild Tropical Garden, 1993, Rose award, 1994; named Outstanding Young Women in Am., 1988. Mem. Nat. Acad. Adv. Assn. (grantee 1990, award 1991), Winterthur Mus., Nat. Geog. Soc., Audubon Soc., Omicron Delta Kappa, Rho Lamda, Alpha Epsilon Phi (officer 1980-83, award 1983). Office: U Miami Coll Arts & Scis PO Box 248004 Coral Gables FL 33124-8004

LEWIS, EVELYN, management consultant; b. Goslar, Germany, Sept. 19, 1946; came to U.S. 1952, naturalized 1957; d. Gerson Emanuel and Sala (Mendlowicz) L. BA, U. Ill.-Chgo., 1968; MA, Ball State U., 1973, PhD, 1976. Rsch. analyst Comptr. State Ill., Chgo., 1977-78; lectr. polit. sci. dept. Loyola U., Chgo., 1977; asst. to commr. Dept. Human Svcs., Chgo., 1978-81; group mgr. communications Arthur Andersen & Co., Chgo., 1981-84; dir. communications and pub. rels. Heidrick and Struggles, Inc., Chgo., 1984-88; assoc. ptnr. change mgmt. svcs. practice Andersen Cons., 1989—; adj. faculty sch. bus. adminstrn. Roosevelt U., 1988. Mem. Children of the Holocaust, Chgo., 1982; bd. dirs. Internat. Children's Benefit Fund. Mem. Internat. Communication Assn., Coun. of Communication Mgmt, B'nai Brith. Jewish. Avocations: writing, poetry, bicycling, hiking. Office: Andersen Cons Arthur Andersen & Co 69 W Washington St Chicago IL 60602-3004

LEWIS, FELICE FLANERY, lawyer, educator; b. Plaquemine, La., Oct. 5, 1920; d. Lowell Baird and E. Elizabeth (Lee) Flanery; m. Francis Russell Lewis, Dec. 22, 1944. BA, U. Wash., 1947; PhD, NYU, 1974; JD, Georgetown U., 1981. Bar: N.Y. 1982. Dean L.I. Univ., Liberal Arts & Scis., Bklyn., 1974-78; assoc. Harry G. English, Bklyn., 1983-85, 91—; adj. prof., polit. sci. L.I. Univ., Bklyn., 1983—. Author: Literature, Obscenity and Law, 1976; co-editor: Henry Miller, Years of Trial & Triumph, 1962-64, 1978. Home: 28 Whitney Cir Glen Cove NY 11542-1316 Office: Harry G English 7219 3rd Ave Brooklyn NY 11209-2131

LEWIS, GLADYS SHERMAN, nurse, educator; b. Wynnewood, Okla., Mar. 20, 1933; d. Andrew and Minnie Elva (Halsey) Sherman; R.N., St. Anthony's Sch. Nursing, 1953; student Okla. Bapt. U., 1953-55; AB, Tex. Christian U., 1956; postgrad. Southwestern Bapt. Theol. Sem., 1959-60, Escuela de Idiomas, San Jose, Costa Rica, 1960-61; MA in Creative Writing, Central (Okla.) State U., 1985; PhD in English Okla. State U. 1992; m. Wilbur Curtis Lewis, Jan. 28, 1955; children: Karen, David, Leanne, Cristen. Mem. nursing staff various facilities, Okla., 1953-57; instr. nursing, med. missionary Bapt. mission and hosp., Paraguay, 1961-70; vice-chmn. edn. commn. Paraguay Bapt. Conv., 1962-65; sec. bd. trustees Bapt. Hosp., Paraguay, 1962-65; chmn. personnel com., handbook and policy book officer Bapt. Mission in Paraguay, 1967-70; trustee Southwestern Bapt. Theol. Sem., 1974-84, chmn. student affairs com., 1976-78, vice-chmn. bd. 1978-80; ptnr. Las Amigas Tours, 1978-80; writer, conference leader, campus lectr., 1959—; adj. prof. English Cen. State U., Okla. (name changed to U. Cen. Okla.), 1990-91; faculty mem., asst. prof. English U. Cen. Okla., 1991—. Active Dem. com., Evang. Women's Caucus, 1979-80; leader Girl Scouts U.S.A., 1965-75; Okla. co-chmn. Nat. Religious Com. for Equal Rights Amendment, 1977-79; tour host Meier Internat. Study League, 1978-81. Mem. AAUW, Internat. and Am. colls. surgeons women's auxiliaries, Okla. State, Okla. County med. auxiliaries, Am. Nurse Assn., Nat. Women's Polit. Caucus, 1979-80. Author: On Earth As It Is, 1983; Two Dreams and a Promise, 1984, Message, Messenger and Response, 1994; also religious instructional texts in English and Spanish; editor Sooner Physician's Heartbeat, 1979-82; contbr. articles to So. Bapt. and secular periodicals. Home: 14501 N Western Ave Edmond OK 73013-1828

LEWIS, GOLDY SARAH, real estate developer, corporation executive; b. West Selkirk, Man., Can., June 15, 1921; d. David and Rose (Dwor) Kimmel; m. Ralph Milton Lewis, June 12, 1941; children: Richard Alan, Robert Edward, Roger Gordon, Randall Wayne. B.S., UCLA, 1943; postgrad., U. So. Calif., 1944-45. Pvt. practice acctg. L.A., 1945-57, law office mgr., 1953-55; dir., exec. v.p. Lewis Homes, Upland, Calif., 1955—, Lewis Construction Co. Inc., Upland, 1959—, Lewis Bldg. Co., Inc., Las Vegas, 1960—, Republic Sales Co., Inc., 1956—, Kimmel Enterprises, Inc., 1959—; mng. partner Lewis Homes of Calif., 1973—; mng. ptnr. Lewis Homes of Nev., 1972—, Western Properties, 1972—, Foothill Investment Co., 1971—, Republic Mgmt. Co., 1978—. Contbr. articles to mags., jours. Mem. Dean's Coun. UCLA Grad. Sch. Architecture and Urban Planning; mem. UCLA Found., Chancellor's Assocs.; endowed Ralph and Goldy Lewis Ctr. for Regional Policy at UCLA, 1989, Ralph and Goldy Lewis Hall of Planning and Devel. at U. S.C., 1989, others. Recipient 1st award of distinction Am. Builder mag., 1963, Homer Briggs Svc. to Youth award West End YMCA, 1990, Spirit of Life award City of Hope, 1993; co-recipient Builder of Yr. award Profl. Builder Mag., 1988, Housing Person of Yr. award Nat. Housing Conf., 1990, Entrepreneur of Yr. award Inland Empire, 1990; Ralph and Goldy Lewis Sports Ctr. named in their honor City of Rancho Cucamonga, 1988, also several other parks and sports fields including Lewis Park in Claremont.; named one of Woman of Yr. Calif. 25th Senate Dist., 1989, (with husband Ralph M. Lewis) Disting. Chief Exec. Officer, Calif. State U., San Bernadino, 1991, Mgmt. Leaders of the Yr. Univ. Calif., Riverside, 1993. Mem. Nat. Assn. Home Builders, Bldg. Industry Assn. So. Calif. (Builder of Yr. award Baldy View chpt. 1988), Internat. Coun. Shopping Ctrs., Urban Land Inst. Office: Lewis Homes PO Box 670 Upland CA 91785-0670

LEWIS, HELEN, librarian; b. Chgo., Apr. 12, 1945; d. William and Helen (Kovel) Fiala; children: Geoffrey, Samuel. AA, U. Fla., 1967; BA, U. Md., 1969; MLS, U. R.I., 1973. Ref. libr. Homer Babbidge Libr. U. Conn., Storrs, 1974-87, instrn. coord., 1990—; 1st v.p. Conn. State Fedn. Tchrs., Berlin, 1987-90. Contbr. articles to profl. jours. Mem. Am. Fedn. Tchrs. Women's Issues Com., Washington, 1987-89, pres. Local 3695, Storrs, 1984-88. Mem. ALA (pay equity com. 1985-87, union task force 1982-87), Nat. Com. on Pay Equity, Assn. Coll. and Rsch. Librs., Libr. and Info. Tech. Assn. Democrat. Home: 1 Eastwood Rd Storrs CT 06268 Office: U Conn Homer Babbidge Libr U-SRI Storrs CT 06268

LEWIS, JANIE CAROL, tax preparer, accounting consultant; b. Hollandale, Miss., Mar. 20, 1957; d. Elijah Elbert and Josephine (Clay) Lewis. BBA, Delta State U., 1978. Data entry supr. II Hughes Aircraft Co., El Segundo, Calif., 1980-89; pvt. practice tax preparer Inglewood, Calif., 1989—; beauty cons. Aloette Cosmetics of Long Beach, Calif. Mem. Alpha Kappa Alpha (charter). Democrat. Mem. Pentecostal Ch. Home: 536 Evergreen St Apt 4 Inglewood CA 90302-1959

LEWIS, JEANNE M., nurse educator, emergency trauma, pediatrics nurse; b. Escanaba, Mich.. BS in Biology, Fine Arts, Mt. Mary Coll., 1976; BSN, U. Md., Balt., 1985; MSN, Villanova U., 1990. RN, Pa., N.J.; cert. advanced pediats. nurse, instr. ACLS, instr./trainer BCLS, instr. pediat. advanced life support, Am. Heart Assn. Staff nurse burn ctr. St. Christopher's Hosp. for Children, Phila., 1985-86; staff nurse emergency dept. Osteo. Med. Ctr. Phila., 1986-88, nursing edn. coord., 1988-89; emergency dept. pool nurse Chestnut Hill Hosp., Phila., 1989-90; ednl. nurse specialist Children's Hosp. of Phila., 1989-90; emergency trauma relief nurse emergency trauma ctr. Abington (Pa.) Meml. Hosp., 1991—; faculty Meth. Hosp. Sch. Nursing, Phila., 1990-92; critical care edn. coord./CNS Cooper Hosp., Camden, N.J., 1992—; lectr. MidAtlantic Regional Assn. Burn Care Facilities, 1985; discussion leader roundtable Nat. Pediatric Conf., 1989. Contbr. articles to profl. jours. Mem. edn. task force Nat. Emergency Nurse's Assn., 1994. Mem. AACN, Emergency Nurses Assn., Sigma Theta Tau, Phi Kappa Phi. Home: 654 Summit Ave Philadelphia PA 19128-2981 Office: Cooper Hosp U Med Ctr Camden NJ 08103

LEWIS, JOAN PATRICIA MONTAGUE, pain management physician; b. N.Y.C., Jan. 27, 1949; m. Victor Lewis, Feb. 10, 1966 (div. Nov. 1966); 1 child, Brian. AA, East L.A. Coll., 1969; BS, Calif. State U., 1981; MD, UCLA, 1985. RN, Calif. Intern in gen. surgery UCLA-King/Drew, 1985-86, head and neck surgeon, 1986-89, critical care fellow, 1989-90; anesthesiologist UCLA-Harbor, Torrance, 1990-93, pain fellow, 1993-94; founder Pain Mgmt. Clinics of N.Mex., Albuquerque, 1994—. Mem. AMA, Am. Assn. Otolaryngol. Allergy, Am. Pain Soc. Office: 4401 N 4th NW Albuquerque NM 87107

LEWIS, JOCELYA (GRO MAMBO ANGELA NOVANYON IDIZOL), ethnologist, religious leader, choreographer, dancer, playwright; b. Phila., June 9, 1953; d. Joseph and Bertha (Hack) Smith; m. Ahmed Lewis, Dec. 2, 1977; 1 child, Ahmed Jr. Bus. student, C.C. Phila., 1971-72; dance student, Arthur Hall Dance Ensemble, Phila., 1971; studied under Nana Parabia, 1977-78; studied under Papa Hilaire Michel, Mariane, Haiti, 1978-83; studied under Mambo Josephine, Delmas, Haiti, 1978-83; studied under Hungan Rejje', Kenscoff, Haiti, 1978-83; studied under Hungan Daniel, St. Louis, Haiti, 1978-83; studied under Hungan Marcell, Mais Jace, Haiti, 1978-83; studied under Hungan Lieonells, Haiti, 1978-83. Cert. master dancer. Instr. Arthur Hall Dance Ensemble, Phila., 1973-77; founder, dir. Spirit Cultural Dance Ensemble, Phila., 1975—; founder, high priestess LePeristyle Haitian Sanctuary, Phila., 1982—; dir. African Dance Dept. Lacher Latari, 1976; bd. dirs. Le Peristyle Sanctuary, Mariane, 1990—, Ctr. African Culture, Phila., 1991—; dance instr. various colls. and univs. Author: Divine Messages of the Loas, 1990, Vol. II, 1991, The African Way, 1992; presented dance recitals Walnut St. Theatre, 1976; appeared in Ayida, Acad. of Music, Phila., 1974, Aqua Suite, Robin Hood, Dell Theatre, 1982, Aqua Suite, The Play Germantown Friends Theatre, 1991; first pub. voodoo ceremonies held in the U.S., Afro-American Hist. and Cultural Mus., Phila., 1992, 93, 94. Tour condr., lectr. Ile Ife Mus., 1974. Recipient J.J. Desslaine award J.J. Desslaine Soc., 1990, Spl. Achievement award Level Movement, 1990; Choreographer grantee Pa. Coun. Arts, 1991.

LEWIS, JOSEPHINE VICTORIA, marketing executive; b. Chgo., Dec. 3, 1936; d. Wincenty and Helena (Francysczak) Gurbacki; m. Laurence Warren Lewis, Jan. 8, 1955; children: Laurence Michael, Michaleen Kay, Gregory Michael. AS, Triton Coll., 1979. Sec. Marsh & McLennan, Chgo., 1953-57; with factory prodn. Motorola, Franklin Park, Ill., 1969-70; with inventory control Reflector Hardware, Melrose Park, Ill., 1970-71; distbn./inventory supr. Jewel Imports (Osco Drug, Inc.), Oakbrook, Ill., 1971-83; Midwest regional mgr. Port of Seattle, 1983—. Leader Dupage County Girl Scouts U.S.A., 1968-71; den mother Thatcher County Boy Scouts Am., 1974-75; fundraiser United Way Northlake, Ill., 1972-74; active Christian Family Movement, Marriage Encounter. Mem. Women in Internat. Trade, Internat. Trade Assn. Greater Chgo., Customs Brokers and Fgn. Freight Forwarders Assn., Ocean Freight Agts. (sec. 1993, treas. 1994, v.p. 1995), Piggyback Assn. Chgo., Midwest Fgn. Commerce Club, Chgo. Transp. Club. Office: Port of Seattle 184 Shuman Blvd Ste 200 Naperville IL 60563-8475

LEWIS, JULIETTE, actress; b. Fernando Valley, Calif., June 21, 1973; d. Geoffrey and Glenis Batley L. TV appearences include Homefires (Showtime miniseries), I Married Dora, 1988, A Family For Joe, 1990; TV Movies include Too Young To Die, 1989; films include My Stepmother is an Alien, 1988, Meet the Hollowheads, 1989, National Lampoons Christmas Vacation, 1989, Cape Fear, 1991 (Academy Award nomination best supporting actress 1991), Crooked Hearts, 1991, Husbands and Wives, 1992, Kalifornia, 1993, That Night, 1993, What's Eating Gilbert Grape, 1993, Romeo is Bleeding, 1994, Natural Born Killers, 1994, Mixed Nuts, 1994. Office: William Morris Agy 151 El Camino Blvd Beverly Hills CA 80212*

LEWIS, LANIGHTA WEST, rehabilitation nurse; b. Johnson, Vt., Feb. 9, 1932; d. Trefley W. and Emma (Wildes) West; m. Donald E. Lewis, Nov. 9, 1955; children: Eric Patrick, Paula Lewis Hegner, Anita Lewis Carlsson, Scott Christopher. Diploma, Gifford Meml. Hosp., Randolph, Vt., 1955; cert. in drug/alcohol rehab., St. Louis U.; student, Orlando (Fla.) Tech. Coll.; cert. in profl. counseling, Internat. Loss Control Inst., St. Paul. Lic. risk mgr., Fla.; cert. ins. rehab. specialist, Fla.; cert. case mgr., ins. rehab. specialist. With Gifford Meml. Hosp., 1955-63; house supr. Holiday Hosp., Orlando, 1964-68; nurse Ctr. for Nursing, 1968-73; with Mid Fla. Ctr. Alcoholism, Orlando, 1971-73; asst. adminstr. Extendicare Subacute Facility, 1971-73; with Orlando Regional Hosp. and Kissimee (Fla.) Meml. Hosp., 1973-75; health care risk mgmt./rehab. specialist St. Paul Fire & Marine Ins. Co., Maitland, Fla., 1975-88; founder, pres., CEO, rehab. specialist Caduceus Cons., Inc., Orlando, 1988—. Author: (with others) Nursing Skills Text Book, 1975; contbr. articles to nursing jours. Mem. adv. bd. Lucerne Spinal Cord Ctr. Named to Nat. Disting. Svc. Registry, 1989. Mem. ANA, Rehab. Nurses Assn., Women for Responsible Legislation, Fla. Nursing Assn. (ho. of dels.), Case Mgmt. Soc., Fla. Nurses Assn., Ctrl. Fla. Rehab. Nurses Assn. (mem. govtl. affairs com.), Physician Nurses Assn. Home: 410 Bywater Dr Orlando FL 32839-2961

LEWIS, LAURA HESTER SHEPHERD, clinical psychologist, consultant; b. Rulo, Nebr., Nov. 18, 1921; d. Ernest Charles and Marian Eloise (Cook) Shepherd; divorced, 1978; 1 child, Ellen Lewis Anderson. RN, NE Methodist Hosp., Omaha, 1942; BS, Nebr. Wesleyan U., 1959; PhD, U. Nebr., 1967. Lic. psychologist, Nebr., N.Mex.; diplomate Am. Bd. Profl. Psychology. Asst. staff psychologist U. Nebr. Psychol. Clinic, Lincoln, 1961-64; from asst. clin. psychologist to staff psychologist Lincoln State Hosp., 1964-65; intern Nebr. Psychiatric Inst., Omaha, 1964-65; practicum supr. field placement child psychiatry fellows and residents Lincoln Regional Ctr. Nebr. Psychiat. Inst., Omaha, 1966-67; dir. training for paraprofessionals children's and adolescent psychiat. unit Lincoln Regional Ctr., Nebr., 1966-70; psychology practicum supr. dept. psychology U. Nebr., Spring 1967; coord. clin. svcs. children's/adolescent psychiat. unit Lincoln Regional Ctr., 1966-69, acting dir., 1969-70; dir. inpatient psychiatric svcs. Children's Meml. Hosp., Chgo., 1972-74, dir. tng. psychology divsn. of child psychiatry, 1970-74; asst. prof. clin. psychiatry & pediatrics Northwestern U. Med. Sch., Chgo., 1973-74; dir. Harbor City (Calif.) Outpatient Clinic, 1974-78; clin. adminstr., clin. child psychologist So. Calif. Permanente Med. Group-Kaiser Divsn., Lomita, 1974-78; pvt. practice, cons. Calif., 1978-92, Las Vegas, Nev., 1992-94; contract instr. Calif. Sch. Profl. Psychology, L.A., 1978-79; instr. clin. psychology Calif. State U., Dominguez Hills, Spring 1978; asst. clinical prof. dept. psychiatry L.A. Harbor Gen. Hosp. L.A. Harbor-UCLA Sch. Medicine, Torrance, Calif., 1980-89; clinical prof. psychology Fuller Theol. Sem., Pasedena, Calif., 1981; N.Mex.; mem. med. staff Northeastern Regional Hosp., 1993—; vis. lectr. psychology Nebr. Wesleyan U., Lincoln, 1969-70; cons. telephone hot line, Village of Oak Park, Ill., 1974, UCLA Sch. Medicine, 1976, Rivera Hall, Redondo Beach, Calif., 1978, Rehab. Svcs., Bay Harbor Hosp., Harbor City, Calif., 1993, Project for Prevention of Sexual Abuse of Presch. Children, Children's Svcs. Dept. Psychiatry, Harbor-UCLA Sch. Medicine, Torrance, 1993; bd. dirs. Harbor View House, San Pedro, Calif.; delegate People-to-People Program, People's Rep. of China, 1989, USSR, 1991; speaker presentations and seminars at hospitals, religious centers, corps., 1973-91. Author: (with others) Group Therapy with Children and Adolescents: A Treatment Manual, 1985; contbr. articles to profl. jours. Mem. Nebr. Little White House Conf. on Children and Youth, 1968; mem. health svcs. task force Village of Oak Park, Ill., 1974. 1st lt. U.S. Army Nurse Corps, 1942-45, PTO. Fellow Acad. Clin. Psychologists; mem. APA (disvn. 12, sect. 1), Soc. Personality Assessment, N.Mex. Psychol. Assn., Nebr. Psychol. Assn. (com. legis. affairs and profl. relationships 1969), Sigma Xi. Democrat. Methodist. Home: PO Box 2956 1214 6th St Las Vegas NM 87701

LEWIS, LINDA CHRISTINE, sales executive; b. St. Paul, Oct. 7, 1949; d. Richard Lewis and Gloria Christine (Dickey) Williams; m. John T. Housladen, Dec. 12, 1971 (div. Dec. 1978); children: Matthew, Joshua; m. Douglas Scott Lewis, July 21, 1979. BS with honors, Southwest Tex. State U., 1971. Area sales mgr. AM Internat., Austin, Tex., 1978-82; nat. sales mgr. Auscom Inc., Austin, 1982-85, v.p. sales, 1985; v.p. sales KMW Systems Corp., Austin, 1985-89; original equipment mfr. sales mgr. Intel Corp., Austin, 1989-90; dir. of sales Tadpole Tech. Inc., Austin, 1990-92; dist. sales mgr. Rocal-Datacom, 1992—. Asst. scoutmaster, Boy Scouts Am. Mem. Am. Contract Bridge League. Republican. Lutheran. Home: 3509 Carla Dr Austin TX 78754-4917

LEWIS, L(INDA) MAUREEN, publishing executive; b. Culver City, Calif., May 22, 1948; d. Richard Harold and Nada Maureen (Kimball) Eastwood; m. James T. Mayer, Apr. 29, 1970 (div. Mar. 1985); children: Theodore Duke, Kirk Ryan; m. John S. Lewis, July 23, 1988. BA, UCLA, 1969; elem. teaching credential, Calif. State U., Northridge, 1972; postgrad., Calif. State U., Fullerton, 1986. Instr. journalism Saddleback Community Coll., Mission

Viejo, Calif., 1981-83; mgr. advt. and mktg. communications Kim Lighting, Industry, Calif., 1985-87; adminstr. mktg. dir. Approved Products, Santa Ana, Calif., 1987-88; asst. to pres., mgr. advt. and spl. projects Republic Capital Holding Corp., Burbank, Calif., 1988-89; exec. dir. The Dalton Press, Corona del Mar, Calif., 1989-90; mgr. Forensic Publs. L.A. County Bar Assn., 1990—; assoc. editor Preface mag., Laguna Hills, Calif., 1982, Saddleback Alive mag., Laguna Hills, 1983. Mem. AAUW (publs. editor Mission Viejo br. 1979-80, chmn. pub. info. 1980-81, 1st v.p. 1981-82, pres. 1982-83, named grant honoree 1981, communications officer publs. and pub. info. Calif. div. 1981-83).

LEWIS, LORRAINE, general counsel; b. Springfield, Mass., Feb. 25, 1956; d. Richard N. and Janet Claire (Howard) Pratte; m. Jacob M. Lewis, Sept. 28, 1985; 2 children. BA in History magna cum laude, Yale Coll., 1978; JD, Harvard Law Sch., 1981. Bar: D.C., Ill., 1982. Field atty. NLRB, Chgo., 1982-84; assoc. Feder & Edes, Washington, 1984-85; vol. atty. Washington Lawyer's Com. for Civil Rights, 1986; staff asst. Sen. John Glenn, 1986; asst. counsel then counsel and gen. counsel sen. com. on govtl. affairs, 1987-93; gen. counsel Office of Personnel Mgmt., 1993—. Office: Office Personnel Mgmt 1900 E St NW Rm 7353 Washington DC 20415*

LEWIS, MARGARET MARY, marketing professional; b. Bridgeport, Conn., Sept. 27, 1959; d. Raymond Phillip and Catherine Helen (Gayda) Palovchak; m. William A. Lewis Jr., Oct. 4, 1980. BS summa cum laude, Sacred Heart U., 1986; postgrad., U. Bridgeport; AS, Katherine Gibbs Sch., 1980. Program mgr. sales svc. group Newspaper Coop. Couponing, Inc., Westport, Conn., 1985-87; sales adminstr. Supermarket Communication Systems, Inc., Norwalk, Conn., 1987-88, mgr. mktg. support, 1988-89; asst. project mgr. sales promotion Mktg. Corp. Am., Westport, 1989-91, account exec., 1991-92; mgr. program svcs. Ryan Partnership, Westport, 1992-93, sr. program mgr., 1993—. Mem. NAFE, Direct Mktg. Assn., Am. Mgmt. Assn. Democrat. Roman Catholic. Home: 16 Nickel Pl Monroe CT 06468-3005 Office: 55 Post Rd W Westport CT 06880-6425

LEWIS, MARTHA NELL, expressive arts therapist, massage therapist, counselor; b. Atlanta, Mar. 4, 1944; d. Clifford Edward and Nell (Shropshire) Wilkie; m. Jeffrey Clark Lewis, Aug. 20, 1966 (div. Aug. 1986); children: John Martin, Janet Michelle. BA, Tex. Tech. U., 1966; massage therapy, The Winters Sch., 1991; MA, Norwich U., 1994. Registered massage therapist, Tex. Geophys. analyst Shell Oil Co., Houston, 1966-68; photogravity specialist Photogravity, Inc., Houston, 1972-80; tchr. music Little Red Sch. House, Houston, 1974-75; sec., treas. Lewis Enterprises, Inc., Houston, 1976-83; regulatory supr. Transco Energy Co., Houston, 1983-92; founder, massage therapist The Winters Sch. Care Team, Houston, 1991—; exec. dir. Music for Healing and Transition Program, 1994—. Advisor youth Corpus Christi Ch., Houston, 1970-80; vocalist, instrumentalist Sounds of Faith Folk Group, Houston, 1978—; harpist Houston Harpers Harp Ensemble, 1990-92; instr. exercise, body awareness Transco Energy Co. Fitness Ctr., Houston, 1990-92; vol. The Inst. for Rehab. and Rsch., Houston, 1989-90, Houston Hospice, 1992—, St. Luke's Episc. Hosp. Healing Health Com., 1993—, lay chaplain, 1994—, Houston Healing Healthcare Project, 1993—. Mem. Am. Massage Therapy Assn., Space City Ski Club (asst. trip coord. 1991-92), Houston Sigma Kappa Found., Sigma Kappa Alumnae Assn. (pres. Houston chpt. 1974-76, nat. collegiate province officer 1981-85, Houston Alumnae of Yr. 1981, Tex. Alumnae of Yr. 1980, Pearl Ct. award 1991). Roman Catholic. Home: 910 B W 23rd St Houston TX 77008 Office: 3100 Richmond Ave Ste 213K Houston TX 77098

LEWIS, MARY-FRANCES, civic volunteer; b. Westminster, Md., May 14, 1940; m. William Ervin Lewis; children: John, Angela, Mary Sue, Rob, Amie, Clint, Derek. Student, Johns Hopkins U., 1960-61, Ariz. State U., 1966-69. Tech. sec. Johns Hopkins U., Balt., 1959-62; grant sec. Northwestern U., Evanston, Ill., 1962-66. Bd. dirs., chmn. and v.p. Ariz. Supreme Ct. Foster Care Rev. Bd., 1979-82; bd. dirs. Tempe Ctr. for Habilitation, 1979-92; elected to governing bd. Tempe Union High Sch., 1978—; foster parent State of Ariz., Phoenix, 1971-94. Named Woman of Distinction, Tempe St. Luke's Hosp., 1992, All Am. Woman, City of Tempe, 1985. Mem. Ariz. Sch. Bd. Assn., Nat. Sch. Bd. Assn., Kiwanis (sec. 1989-91). Republican. Methodist. Home: 1213 E Loyola Dr Tempe AZ 85282-3945 Office: Tempe Union High Sch Dist 500 W Guadalupe Rd Tempe AZ 85283-3521

LEWIS, NANCI VICEDOMINI, investment advisor; b. Springfield, Mass., Apr. 26, 1962; d. Roland Benito and Ann Ernestine (Desmone) Vicedomini; m. Jonathan Joseph Lewis, May 20, 1990. BA in Econs., Boston Coll., 1984; MBA, Rollins Coll., 1986. Fin. analyst Sikorsky Aircraft div. United Technologies, Stratford, Conn., 1986-87, fin. program analyst, 1987-88; corp. planning analyst Sprague Technologies, Stratford, 1988; cons. Total Planning Concept, East Haven, Conn., 1989—; v.p. ROANN Electronics, Wolcott, Conn., 1989—. Fundraising New Haven Symphony Orch., New Haven, 1991. Mem. Women in Sales.

LEWIS, NANCY PATRICIA, speech and language pathologist; b. Miami, Fla., Sept. 23, 1956; d. James and Sara (Gilman) L. BS, U. Fla., 1978; MS, U. Ariz., 1980. Postgrad. fellow U. Tex. Med. Br., Galveston, 1979-80, speech lang. pathologist, 1980-81; speech lang. pathologist Albuquerque Pub. Schs., 1982-84; child devel. specialist Albuquerque Spl. Presch., 1984—; pvt. practice speech-lang. pathology Albuquerque, 1985—; coord. Project Ta-kos, 1987—; artist Trash Warrior wearable art; instr. Express Ability in movement, 1992—; speaker in field. Author (dianostic procedure) Khan-Lewis Phonological Analysis, 1986; (therapeutic materials) Familiar Objects and Actions, 1985. Labor coord. Lama Found., San Cristobal, 1988, fundraiser, 1988-91, speech pathology cons., 1990—, bd. dirs., 1990—; bd. dirs. Vol. for Outdoors, Albuquerque, 1984—; cmty. vol. mediator N.Mex. Ctr. for Dispute Resolution, 1993—; cons. Robert Wood Johnson Found. City of Santa Fe Carino Children's Project, 1993—; developer, instr. Conflict Resolution Curriculum, 1993—. Fellow U. Tex. Med. Br., Galveston, 1981. Mem. Am. Speech Lang. and Hearing Assn., N.Mex. Speech Lang. and Hearing Assn. Democrat.

LEWIS, NATALIE PUTNAM, government official; b. Boston; d. Arthur Barnard and Carrie (Webber) B; m. George W. Lewis (dec. June 1965); children: G. Webber, Lochlain Putnam. BA, MA, 1969, PhD, 1971. Editorial asst. Harvard, Cambridge, Mass., 1952-60; rsch. dir. U.S. Govt., Boston, 1969-81, Norfolk, Va., 1982—. Author Firelite Farm, 1963, To My Sons, 1966, Poems for My Husband, 1955. Office: PO Box 68011 Virginia Beach VA 23455-9110

LEWIS, RITA HOFFMAN, plastic products manufacturing company executive; b. Phila., Aug. 6, 1947; d. Robert John and Helen Anna (Dugan) Hoffman; 1 child, Stephanie Blake. Student Jefferson Med. Coll. Sch. Nursing, 1965-67, Gloucester County Coll., 1993—; Gen. mgr. Sheets & Co., Inc. (now Flower World, Inc.), Woodbury, N.J., 1968-72; dir., exec. v.p., treas. Hoffman Precision Plastics, Inc., Blackwood, N.J., 1973—; ptnr. Timber Assocs.; commr. N.J. Expressway Authority, 1990—, sec., 1990-91, treas., 1991—, chmn. pers., 1991—; apptd. mem. N.J. Senate Forum on Budget and Revenue Alternatives, 1991; guest speaker various civic groups, 1974; poetry editor SPOTLIGHTER Innovative Singles Mag. Author: That Part of Me I Never Really Meant to Share, 1979; In Retrospect: Caught Between Running and Loving; columnist Innovative Singles mag., 1989—. Mem. Com. for Citizens of Glen Oaks (N.J.), 1979—, Gloucester Twp. Econ. Devel. Com., 1981—, Gloucester Twp. Day Scholarship Com., 1984—; chairperson Gloucester Twp. Day Scholarship Found., 1985—; bd. dirs. Diane Hull Dance Co. Recipient Winning Edge award, 1982, Mayor's award for Womens' Achievement, 1987, Outstanding Community Service award Mayor, Council and Com., 1987. Mem. NAFE, Sales Assn. Chem. Industry, Blackwood Businessmen's Assn., Soc. Plastic Engrs. Roman Catholic.

LEWIS, SHARI, puppeteer, entertainer; b. N.Y.C., Jan. 17, 1934; d. Abraham B. and Ann (Ritz) Hurwitz; m. Jeremy Tarcher, Mar. 15, 1958; 1 child, Mallory. Star weekly NBC-TV show The Shari Lewis Show, 1960-63, weekly syndicated series Lambchop's Play-Along (named TV Guide's Best of Best for Children), 1975-77, weekly TV show BBC, London, 1969-75, weekly TV show for ind. network in Gt. Britain, (1970); writer, producer, star NBC spl. A Picture of Us, 1971; condr. over 100 symphonies in U.S., Can., Japan, 1977—; command performances, London, 1970, 73, 78; author 59 pub. books including 15 One Minute Bedtime Stories (bestselling series); 18 home video cassettes: including 101 Things for Kids to do Shari's Christmas Concert, Don't Wake Your Mom, 1992, Let's Make Music, 1994. Past mem. nat. bd. dirs. Girl Scouts U.S.; past internat. bd. dirs. Boy Scouts Am.; past pres. Am. Ctr. Films for Children; past hon. chmn. bd. trustees Internat. Reading Found.; trustee Greater L.A. Zoo Assn. Recipient 10 Emmy awards, including award for best program and outstanding female personality, 1989, for outstanding performer in a children's program, 1992, outstanding writing in children's series, 1993, outstanding performer in a children's series, 1993, 94; Peabody award, 1960, 50th Anniversary Dir.'s award Ohio State Award Com., 1988, Monte Carlo Internat. TV award, 1963, Radio-TV Mirror award, 1960, Kennedy Ctr. award for excellence in arts for young people, 1986, Video Choice award, 1988, Parents Choice award, 1992, Calif. Media award, 1992, Dir. Choice Recognition award, 1992, Assn. Visual Communicators Gold Cindy award, 1992, Parents Mag. prize, 1993, Gemini award for LambChop's Play Along, 1994; TV Guide Top Ten Children's Shows, 1993. Office: care Jim Golden 3128 Cavendish Dr Los Angeles CA 90064-4743

LEWIS, SHEILA MURIEL, retired communications management specialist; b. Glendive, Mont., Sept. 23, 1937; d. John Edward and Muriel Christine (Johnson) O'Neil; m. Lyndell W. Lewis, Dec. 14, 1957 (div. 1973); children: Sheri Lynne, Debra Lynne, Linda Marie, Valerie Jean. AA, Colo. Women's Coll., 1957; BS, U. No. Colo., 1976; postgrad., Stanford U. Adminstrv. asst. DAFC/Dept. Defense DOT/FAA, Denver, 1956-64; substitute tchr. Portland (Oreg.) Public Schs., 1964-72; communications operator Denver Air Rt. Traffic Control Ctr., 1972-78, communications specialist, 1978-80, computer programmer, 1980-82, air traffic controller, 1982-86; communications specialist Air Force Space Command, Falcon AFB, Colo., 1986-95, retired, 1995. Troop leader Campfire Girls, Las Vagas, 1964-72, pres. PTA, Las Vagas, 1964-72. . Mem. AAUW, Armed Forces Communications and Electronics Assn., Aviation Space Edn. Assn., Civil Air Patrol, Univ. Aviation Assn., Order of Eastern Star, Order of White Shrine Jerusalem, Chi Omega. Democrat. Lutheran. Home: 4934 Daybreak Cir Colorado Springs CO 80917-2657

LEWIS, SHERYL RAE, marketing executive; b. Atlanta, May 9, 1945; d. Abe L. and Ida (Keel) L. Student, Sophie Newcomb Coll., New Orleans, 1963-65; BS in Journalism, Boston U., 1967. Creative dir. Williams Whittle, Alexandria, Va., 1978-80, Lauer Assocs. Advt., McLean, Va., 1981-85; mktg. dir. Potomac Mills Mall, Woodbridge, Va., 1985-89, Springfield (Va.) Mall, 1990—. Mem. task force on bus. and aging Coun. of Govts.; chmn. pub. rels. com. Nat. Kidney Found., Washington, 1983-86, exec. com. mem., 1983-86, bd. dirs., 1987-92; mem. Women's Health Task Force, 1991. Recipient Maxi award Internat. Coun. Shopping Ctrs., 1987, Maxi award nominee, 1991, 92, 93, 94, Merit award, 1986, 88, Norma award Nat. Retail Merchants Assn., 1986, 87, Retail Advt. Conf. award, 1986, 87, Addy award Advt. Club Washington, 1974, 78, 80. Mem. NAFE, Internat. Platform Assn., Fairfax County Mktg. Edn. Adv. Bd. (bd. dirs. 1990—), No. Va. Women's Ctr. (career counselor 1989—), Internat. Coun. Shopping Ctrs., Coun. of Govts. (task force on bus. and aging). Jewish. Office: Springfield Mall 6500 Springfield Mall Springfield VA 22150-1701

LEWIS, SHIRLEY JEANE, psychology educator; b. Phoenix, Aug. 23, 1937; d. Herman and Leavy (Hutchinson) Smith; AA, Phoenix C.C., 1957; BA, Ariz. State U., 1960; MS, San Diego State U., 1975, MA, 1986; MA, Azusa Pacific U., 1982; PhD, U. So. Calif., 1983. Cert. Tchr., Calif.; m. Edgar Anthony Lewis, June 25, 1966 (div. May 1980); children: Edgar Anthony, Roshaun, Lucy Ann Jonathan. Recreation leader Phoenix Parks and Recreation Dept., 1957-62; columnist Ariz. Tribune, Phoenix, 1958-59; tchr. phys. edn. San Diego Unified Schs., 1962—; adult educator San Diego C.Cs., 1973—, instr. psychology, health, Black studies, 1977—, counselor, 1981—; community counselor S.E. Counseling and Cons. Svcs. and Narcotics Prevention and Edn. Systems, Inc., San Diego, 1973-77; counselor educator, counselor edn. dept. San Diego State U., 1974-77; marriage, family, child counselor Counseling and Cons. Ctr., San Diego, 1977—; inservice educator San Diego Unified and San Diego County Sch. Dists., 1973-77; Fulbright Exch. counselor, London, 1994—; lectr. in field. Girl Scout phys. fitness cons., Phoenix, 1960-62; vol. community tutor for high sch. students, San Diego, 1963; sponsor Tennis Club for Youth, San Diego, 1964-65; troop leader Girl Scouts U.S., Lemon Grove, Calif., 1972-74; vol. counselor USN Alcohol Rehab. Center, San Diego, 1978; mem. sch. coun.'s adv. bd. San Diego State U. Named Woman of Year, Phoenix, 1957, One of Outstanding Women of San Diego, 1980; recipient Phys. Fitness Sch. award and Demonstration Sch. award Pres.'s Coun. on Phys. Fitness, Taft Jr. High Sch., 1975, Excel award Corp. Excellence Edn., 1989; Delta Sigma Theta scholar, 1957-60; Alan Korrick scholar, 1956. Mem. NEA, Calif. Tchrs. Assn., San Diego Tchrs. Assn., Assn. Marriage and Family Counselors, Am. Personnel and Guidance Assn., Calif. Assn. Health, Phys. Edn. and Recreation (v.p. health), Am. Alliance of Health, Phys. Edn. and Recreation, Assn. Black Psychologists (corr. sec. 1993), Assn. African-Am. Educators, Delta Sigma Theta (Delta of Yr. 1987). Democrat. Baptist. Contbr. articles to profl. jours. Home: 1226 Armacost Rd San Diego CA 92114-3307 Office: 2630 B St San Diego CA 92102-1022

LEWIS, SUSAN JANE, psychiatric and mental health nurse; b. Ashland, Ky., Nov. 21, 1946; d. James Ottis and Elizabeth Toka (McKee) L.; 1 child, John Lewis Schneider. ADN, Lexington Tech. Inst., 1968; BA in Rehab. Counseling, Marshall U., 1975, MA in Counseling, 1978, BS in Nursing, 1979; PhD in Health and Human Svcs., Columbia Pacific U., 1989. Cert. psychiat. mental health nurse, clin. specialist. Team leader Albert B. Chandler Med. Ctr., U. Ky., Lexington, 1968-72; nurse counselor Bluegrass East Mental Health Ctr., Lexington, 1972-74; instr. nursing Marshall U., Huntington, W.Va., 1975-77; psychiat. nurse St. Mary's Hosp., Huntington, 1978-79; instr. nursing Marshall U., Huntington, 1979; psychiat. nurse practitioner VA Med. Ctr., Huntington, 1979-86; psychiat. nurse clin. specialist VA Med. Ctr., Louisville, Ky., 1986—. Author: (with others) Manual of Psychosocial Nursing Interventions-Promoting Mental Health on Medical-Surgical Units, 1989; co-author, editor: Managing the Violent Patient: A Clinician's Guide, 1993; contbr. articles to profl. jours. Named Disting. Lectr., Soc. Gastrointestianl Assts., N.Y.C., 1985; recipient Books of Yr. award Am. Jour. Nursing, 1989. Home: 203 N Hubbards Ln Louisville KY 40207-2250 Office: VA Med Ctr Louisville KY 40206-1433

LEWIS, VIRGINIA MARIE, psychologist; b. San Rafael, Calif., June 21, 1942; d. Lyle C. Lewis and Juanita Marie (Nelson) Smith. BA, Calif. State U., San Francisco, 1968, MA, 1971; PhD, Pacific Sch. of Psychology, Palo Alto, Calif., 1986. Lic. psychologist, ednl. psychologist, marriage, family and child counselor; cert. sch. psychologist, Calif. Counselor Haight Ashbury Med. Clinic, San Francisco, 1969-71; counselor/edn. coord. EOC Program, San Francisco, 1971-72; sch. psychologist San Francisco Unified Sch. Dist., 1972-78; assoc. Mental Rsch. Inst., Palo Alto, 1978-90, sr. rsch. fellow, 1990—; pvt. practice psychologist/therapist Palo Alto, 1980—; instr. dept. edn. psychology Calif. State U., Hayward, 1985-87, Western Grad. Sch. of Psychology, Palo Alto, 1987—; cons., com. mem. doctoral dissertations, 19876; cons. Evergreen Ctr., San Leandro, Calif., 1983-85; founding mem. Soterial Alt. Family Edn. Clinic, 1978-80; external assessor Calif. Commn. for Tchr. Prep. and Licensing, 1979; co-prin. investigator rsch. on recovery process alcoholic families, 1989—; prin. investigator, author Devel. of Family Goal Attainment Scales, 1980—; co-author grants in fielsr. facilitator, therapist in eye movement desentization and reprocessing, 1990—. Resource cons. Friends for Youth, Redwood City, Calif., 1989-90. Recipient Don D. Jackson Meml. award Mental Rsch. Inst., Palo Alto, 1980. Mem. APA, Calif. Psychol. Assn., Santa Clara County Psychol. Assn., Calif. Assn. Sch. Psychologists and Psychometrists, Psychologists Assn. San Francisco (exec. sec., editor, 1974-77), EPIC (founder, chair eye movement desentization and reprocessing profl. issues com. 1991-94). Office: 555 Middlefield Rd Palo Alto CA 94301-2124

LEWIS-BRENT, LANA JANE, art publishing and distribution company executive; b. Panama City, Fla., May 29, 1946; d. Luther Darius and Leona Mae (Jhonson) Lewis; m. Paul Richard Brent, Sept. 5, 1971; children: Jensen Lewis, Anders Paul. Student, Stetson U., 1966-68. Payroll bookkeeper, data processing coordinator Sunshine-Jr. Stores, Inc., Panama City, Fla., 1968-71, pub. relations dir., 1971-75, sr. v.p., 1975-82, pres., chief exec. officer, 1982-92, also vice chairperson, dir., ret., 1992; pres. Paul Brent Designer, Inc., 1992—; dir. First Nat. Bank, Panama City, Fla., 1980-87. Mem. Bay Arts and Humanities Coun., Panama City, Fla., 1980—; mem. Fla. Gov.'s Pub. Facilities Financing Commn., 1983-84, mem. Fla. Gov.'s Regional Interstate Banking Adv. Com., 1984-85; vice chmn. Seven and Eight to Build Fla., 1984-85; bd. dirs. United Way of Bay County, Fla., 1981-84, Bay Med. Ctr. Found., Panama City, 1985-92, Jacksonville Br. Fed. Reserve Bank Atlanta, 1987—, Tootsie Roll Industries, 1988—. Mem. Nat. Grocers Assn. (Woman Grocer of Yr. 1983), Food Mktg. Inst., Nat. Assn. Convenience Stores, Com. of 200, Fla. Women's Network, Retail Grocers Assn. Fla. (bd. dirs. 1976-86), Fla. C. ofC. (bd. dirs. 1983-88), LWV Bay County (founding). Clubs: St. Andrew's Yacht, Bay Point Country (Panama City, Fla.). Home: 1216 Dewitt St Panama City FL 32401-4041

LEWITZKY, BELLA, choreographer; b. Los Angeles, Jan. 13, 1916; d. Joseph and Nina (Ossman) L.; m. Newell Taylor Reynolds, June 22, 1940; 1 child, Nora Elizabeth. Student, San Bernardino Valley (Calif.) Jr. Coll., 1933-34; hon. doctorate, Calif. Inst. Arts, 1981; PhD (hon.), Occidental Coll., 1984, Otis Parsons Coll., 1989, Juilliard Sch., 1993. Chmn. dance dept., chmn. adv. panel U. So. Calif., Idyllwild, 1956-74; founder Sch. Dance, Calif. Inst. Arts, 1969, dean, 1969-74; vice chmn. dance adv. panel Nat. Endowment Arts, 1974-77, mem. artists-in-schs. adv. panel, 1974-75; mem. Nat. Adv. Bd. Young Audiences, 1974—, Joint Commn. Dance and Theater Accreditation, 1979; com. mem. Am. chpt. Internat. Dance Coun. of UNESCO, 1974—; bd. dirs. Am. Arts Alliance, 1974-88; trustee Nat. Found. Advancement Arts, 1982-90, 92-95, Calif. Arts Coun., 1983-86; trustee Calif. Assn. Dance Cos., 1976—, Idyllwild Sch. music and Arts, 1986—, Dance/USA, 1988—, Calif. State Summer Sch. of Arts, 1988—; cons. the dance project WNET, 1987—. Co-founder, co-dir., Dance Theatre, Los Angeles, 1946-50; founder, dir., Dance Assocs., Los Angeles, 1951-55; founder 1966, since artistic dir. Lewitzky Dance Co., Los Angeles; choreographer, 1948—; founder, former artistic dir. The Dance Gallery, Los Angeles; contbr. articles in field.Works choreographed include Trio for Saki, 1967, Orrenda, 1969, Kinaesonata, 1971, Pietas, 1971, Ceremony For Three, 1972, Game Plan, 1973, Five, 1974, Spaces Between, 1975, Jigsaw, 1975, Inscape, 1976, Pas de Bach, 1977, Suite Satie, 1980, Changes and Choices, 1981, Confines, 1982, Continuum, 1982, Walking/Falling, 1982, 1990, The Song of the Woman, 1983, Nos Duraturi, 1984, 8 Dancers/8 Lights, 1985, Facets, 1986, Impressions #1, 1987, Impresssions #2, 1988, Agitime, 1989, Impressions #3, 1989, Episode #1, 1990, Glass Canyons, 1991, Episode #2, 1992, Episode #3, 1992, Episode #4, 1993. Mem. adv. com. Actors' Fund of Am., 1986—, Women's Bldg. Adv. Council, 1985-91, Calif. Arts Council, 1983-86, City of Los Angeles Task Force on the Arts, 1986—; mem. artistic adv. bd. Interlochen Ctr. for Arts, 1988—. Recipient Mayoral Proclamation, City of L.A., 1976, 1982, ann. award Dance mag., 1978, Dir.'s award Calif. Dance Educators Assn., 1978, Plaudit Award, Nat. Dance Assn., 1979, Labor's Award of Honor for Community Svc., L.A. County AFL-CIO, 1979, L.A. Area Dance Alliance and L.A. Junior C. of C. Honoree, 1980, City of L.A. Resolution, 1980, Distguished Artist Award, City of L.A. and Music Ctr., 1982, Silver Achievement award YWCA, 1982, California State Senate Resolution, 1982, 1984, Award of Recognition, Olympic Black Dance Festival, 1984, Distinguished Women's Award, Northwood Inst., 1984, California State U. Distinguished Artist, 1984, Vesta Award, Woman's Bldg, L.A., 1985, L.A. City Council Honors for Outstanding Contributions, 1985, Woman of the Year, Palm Springs Desert Museum, Women's Committee, 1986, Disting. Svc. award Western Alliance Arts Adminstrs., 1987, Woman of Achievement award, 1988, Am. Dance Guild Ann. award, 1989, So. Calif. Libr. for Social Studies & Rsch. award, 1990, Am. Soc. Journalists & Authors Open Book award, 1990, Internat. Soc. Performing Arts Adminstrs. Tiffany award, 1990, Burning Bush award U. of Judaism, 1991, 1st recipient Calif. Gov.'s award in arts for individual lifetime achievement, 1989; honoree L.A. Arts Coun., 1989, Heritage honoree, Nat. Dance Assn., 1991, Vaslav Nijinsky award, 1991, Hugh M. Hefner First Amendment award, 1991, Artistic Excellence award Ctr. Performing Arts U. Calif., 1992, Lester Horton Lifetime Achievement award Dance Resource Ctr. of L.A., 1992, Occidental Coll. Founders' award, 1992, Dance/USA honor, 1992, Visual Arts Freedom of Expression award Andy Warhol Found., 1993, Artist of Yr. award L.A. County High Sch. Arts, 1993, Freedom of Expression honor Andy Warhol Found. Visual Arts, 1993, Calif. Alliance Edn. award, 1994; grantee Mellon Found., 1975, 81, 86, Guggenheim Found., 197EA, 1969-94. Mem. Am. Arts Alliance (bd. dirs. 1977), Internat. Dance Alliance (adv. council 1984—), Dance/USA (bd. dirs. 1988). Office: Lewitzky Dance Co 1055 Wilshire Blvd Ste 1140 Los Angeles CA 90017

LEWKOWITZ, KAREN HELENE, orthodontist; b. Bklyn., Dec. 26, 1956; d. William A. and Janet B. (Kagan) L.; m. Robert Louis Shpuntoff, Dec. 18, 1983; children: Hilana Megan, Ariana Elizabeth. BA magna cum laude, CUNY, 1978; DDS, Columbia U., 1982; cert. in orthodontics, NYU, 1984. Researcher W. M. Krogman Ctr., Children's Hosp. Phila., Pa., 1976; ptnr. Bayside (N.Y.) Orthodontic Assocs., 1984—; pres. med. awareness com. Queens Coll.-CUNY, 1977-78; attending orthodontist, lectr. Jamaica (N.Y.) Hosp., 1984—. Mem. Temple Torah, Little Neck, N.Y., 1988-94, Temple Israel, Great Neck, N.Y., 1994—, Hadassah, Great Neck, 1990—; v.p. of programming Orgn. Rehab. Thru Tng., Lake Success, N.Y., 1991. Mem. ADA, Acad. Gen. Dentistry, Am. Assn. Women Dentists, Am. Assn. Orthodontists, Queens County Dental Soc. (trustee 1985—, historian 1990, treas. 1991, sec. 1992, v.p. 1993, pres.-elect 1994, pres. 1995), Alpha Omega (pres. Columbia U. chpt. 1980-82, pres. Queens-Nassau chpt. 1984-87, Presdl. citation 1986, regent N.Y. met. area 1990, 91). Office: Bayside Orthodontic Assocs 59-01 Springfield Blvd Bayside NY 11364

LEY, LINDA SUE, employee benefits company executive; b. Franklin, Ind., Nov. 27, 1949; d. Jiles Rex and Naomi Katherine (Van Horn) Riggs; m. Thomas Alan Ley, Feb. 28, 1987. BS in Edn. with distinction, Ind. U.-Purdue U., 1971, MS in Edn. with highest distinction, 1975. Cert. paralegal; lic. life, accident, health, property and casualty ins. agt., Ind. Elem. tchr. Indpls. Pub. Schs., 1972-74, Center Grove Community Schs., Greenwood, Ind., 1974-81; dir. adminstrn. Brougher Agy., Inc., Greenwood, 1981-84; mgr. claims/customer svc. The Associated Group, Inc., Indpls., 1984-89; v.p. team ops. Key Benefit Adminstrs., Inc., Indpls., 1989-92; regional mgr. ops. rev. Anthem Benefit Svcs. Corp., Indpls., 1992—. Mem. cotillion com. Humane Soc. Indpls., 1991; vol. Riley Run for Children, Indpls., 1985-92. Recipient Good Girl Citizenship award Women's Aux. of Am. Legion, 1968. Mem. Am. Mgmt. Assn., Nat. Assn. Life Underwriters, Nat. Assn. Health Underwriters, Inst. Internal Auditors, Indpls. Paralegal Assn., Toastmasters Internat. Republican. Episcopalian. Home: 6358 Bluff Acres Dr Greenwood IN 46143 Office: Anthem Benefit Svcs Corp 120 Monument Cir Indianapolis IN 46204

LEY, MARIA, cytotechnologist; b. Hong Kong, May 6, 1959; came to U.S., 1992; d. Julio Chung Ching and Sui Ching (Lam) Ley. Diploma in Med. Lab. Sci., Hong Kong Poly., 1980; Higher Cert. in Med. Lab. Sci., Hong Kong U., 1986; BAAS, Midwestern State U., Wichita Falls, Tex., 1993. Cert. cytotechnologist. Med. lab. technician II Hong Kong Govt., 1980-86, med. lab. technician I, 1986-87, med. technologist, 1987-92; cytotechnologist Pathology Assocs., Wichita Falls, 1992-93, Damon Met-West, Dallas, 1993—. Mem. Internat. Acad. Cytology (cert.), Am. Soc. Clin. Pathologists (cert.).

LEYBOURN, CAROL, musician, educator; b. Toledo, Dec. 15, 1933; d. Charles Wilson and Esther Lenore (McCaughey) L.; m. Donald Herbert Kenney, Aug. 21, 1954 (div. 1981); children: James Herbert, Paul McLean, Laura Elizabeth, Matthew McLean; m. Jerry Frederick Janssen, May 26, 1984. MusB, U. Mich., 1955, MusM, 1957. Tchg. asst. U. Mich., Ann Arbor, 1955-57; concert pianist USIA, Kaiserslautern, Germany, 1957-61; dir., instr. Leybourn Studios, Ann Arbor, 1961-90; solo pianist, harpsichordist Ann Arbor, 1961-90; keyboardist, mgr. Sterling Chamber Players, Ann Arbor, 1975-90; keyboardist Ann Arbor Chamber Orch., 1980-90, Ann Arbor Symphony, 1980-90; pianist Leybourn Trio, 1986—, Janssen Trio, 1986—; solo pianist, harpsichordist Libertyville, Ill., 1990—; pianist Camerata Singers, Lake Forest, Ill., 1990-91; lectr., cons. various piano tchr. groups, 1975—; dir. Jr. Chamber Players, Ann Arbor, 1978-90, Junior Dixieland Jazz Players, Ann Arbor, 1984-90, St. Gilbert's Elem. Sch. Grayslake, Ill., 1990-91; performer Nat. Conf. Women in Music, U. Mich., 1981, 83; adj. music instr. Ann Arbor Community Edn., 1984-90; instrumental music dir. Greenhills Sch., Ann Arbor, 1988-90; mem. piano faculty David Adler Cultural Ctr., Libertyville, Ill., 1990—; adj. piano faculty Coll. of Lake County, 1993—. Arranger (Dixieland music books) for 6th Graders--

Combo!, 1987. Bd. dirs. Ann Arbor Soc. Mus. Arts, 1962-90; dir. chamber music and jazz workshops David Adler Cultural Ctr., Libertyville, 1991—; founder, chmn. bd. dirs. Lake County Youth Orch., 1994—. Regents scholar U. Mich., 1951-55. Mem. Nat. Music Tchrs. Assn., Mich. Music Tchrs. Assn., Ill. Music Tchrs. Assn., Washtenaw Coun. for Arts, Women's City Club (Ann Arbor), Mu Phi Epsilon (pres. Ann Arbor alumnae chpt. 1964-66), Pi Kappa Lambda. Republican. Presbyterian. Home: Leybourn Studios 316 Mainsail Dr Grayslake IL 60030-2613 Office: David Adler Cultural Ctr Libertyville IL 60048

LHERMITTE, REBECCA GOODSELL, librarian; b. Niles, Mich., Mar. 25, 1943; d. Robert Louis and Sarah (Stafford) Goodsell; m. Joseph Glenn Mason, May 13, 1967 (div. June 1975); m. Patrick Roger Lhermitte, May 1, 1984. AB, U. Mich., 1965, AM Libr. Sci., 1966. Libr. Flint (Mich.) Pub. Libr., 1966-67, U. Mich., Ann Arbor, 1967-68, U. Calif., Oakland, 1968-92, Continuing Edn. of Bar, Berkeley, 1992—. Bd. dirs. Big Sisters of the East Bay, Oakland, 1979-82, Univ. Art Mus. Coun. Berkeley, Calif., 1990-93. Mem. Librs. Assn. U. Calif. Berkeley (chair 1991-92, sec.-treas. 1988-89). Office: Continuing Edn of Bar 2300 Shattuck Berkeley CA 94704-1576

L'HEUREUX-DUBE, CLAIRE, judge; b. Quebec City, Que., Can., Sept. 7, 1927; d. Paul H. and Marguerite (Dion) L'H.; m. Arthur Dubé (dec. 1978); children: Louise Dubé, Pierre Dubé (dec. 1994). BA magna cum laude, Coll. Notre-Dame de Bellevue, Que., 1946; LLL cum laude, Laval U., Que., 1951, LLD (hon.), 1984; LLD (hon.), Dalhousie U., 1981, Montreal U., 1983, Ottawa U., 1988, U. Que., 1989, U. Toronto, 1994. Bar: Que. 1952. Ptnr. Bard, L'Heureux & Philippon, 1952-73; sr. ptnr. L'Heureux, Philippon, Garneau, Tourigny, St.Arnaud & Assocs., from 1969; Puisne judge Superior Ct. Que., 1973-79, Ct. Appeal of Que., 1979-87, Supreme Ct. Can., Ottawa, 1987—; commr. Part II Inquiries Act Dept. Manpower and Immigration, Montreal, 1973; del. Gen. Council Bar of Que., 1968-70, com. on adminstrn. justice, 1968-73, others; pres. family law com., Family Ct. com. Que. Civil Code Revision Office, 1972-76; pres. Can. sect. Internat. Commn. Jurists, 1981-83; participant Internat. Invitational Conf. on Matrimonial and Child Support, Inst. Law Research and Reform, Edmonton, Alta., 1981; adminstr., mem. Que. founding com. of Judges' Conf., 1982-83; lectr. in family law. Editor: (with Rosalie S. Abella) Family Law - Dimensions of Justice, 1983; chmn. editorial bd. Can. Bar Rev., 1985-88; author articles, conf. proc., book chpt. Bd. dirs. YWCA, Que., 1969-73, Ctr. des Loisirs St. Sacrement, 1969-73, Ctr. Jeunesse de Tilly-Ctr. des Jeunes, 1971-77; v.p. Can. Consumers Council, 1970-73; v.p. Vanier Inst. of the Family, 1972-73; lifetime gov. Fondation Univ. Laval, 1980, bd. dirs., 1984-85; mem. Comité des grandes orientations de l'Univ. Laval, 1971-72; mem. nat. council Can. Human Rights Found., 1980-82, 82-84; mem. Can. del. to Peoples Republic China on Status of Women, 1981; pres. Can. sect. Internat. Commn. Jurists, 1981-83, v.p. internat. bd., 1992—. Apptd. Queen's Counsel, 1969; recipient Medal of the Alumni, U. Laval, 1986, Medaille du Barreau de Que., 1987. Mem. Can. Bar Assn., Can. Inst. Adminstrn. Justice, Internat. Soc. Family Law (bd. dirs. 1977-88, v.p. 1981-88), Internat. Fedn. Woman Lawyers, Fedn. Internat. des Femme Juristes, L'Assn. des Femmes Diplômées d'Univ., Assn. Québécoise pour l'Étude Comparative du Droit (pres. 1984-90), Internat. Commn. Jurists (pres. Can. sect., 1981-83, v.p. internat. bd. 1992—), Phi Delta Phi. Roman Catholic. Office: Supreme Ct Can, Wellington St, Ottawa, ON Canada K1A 0J1

LI, GRACE CHIA-CHIAN, strategic management consultant; b. Taipei, Taiwan, Republic of China, Aug. 7, 1963; came to U.S., 1987; d. Chuan-Chun and Yu-Lin (Hsueh) L.; m. Michael H. Chang, Dec. 21, 1993. BA, Nat. Cheng Chi U., Taipei, 1985; MBA, Wash. U., 1989. Acct. Cosa Libermann LTD, Taipei, 1985-86; cost acctg. supr. Johnson & Johnson, Taipei, 1988; planning and control specialist IBM Corp., Taipei, 1986-87; fin. analyst Ameritech Cellular, St. Louis, 1989-92; mgr. market planning Ameritech Internat., Hoffman Estates, Ill., 1992-94; internat. mktg. mgr. Pactel Internat., Walnut Creek, Calif., 1994; bus. cons. Decision Consulting, San Ramon, Calif., 1994—; guest spkr. on China telecom. industry devel. Nat. Comm. Forum, Chgo., 1993. Mem. NAFE, Chgo. Com. Fgn. Rels. Office: Decision Consulting 42 Victory Ct San Ramon CA 94583

LI, PEARL NEI-CHIEN CHU, information specialist, executive; b. Jiangsu, China, June 17, 1946; came to U.S., 1968; d. Ping-Yung and Yao-Hwa (Li) Chu; m. Terry Teng-Fang Li, Sept. 20, 1969; children: Ina Ying, Ping Li. BA, Nat. Taiwan U., Taipei, 1968; MA, W.Va. U., 1971; cert. advanced study in info. studies, Drexel U., 1983. Cert. sr. libr., N.J. Instr. Nat. Tchr.'s Coll., Chang-Hua, Taiwan, 1977-78; reference libr. Camden County Libr., Voorhees, N.J., 1981-82; libr. Kulzer and Dipadova, P.A., Haddonfield, N.J., 1982-87; libr. dir. Am. Law Inst., Phila., 1987-92; gen. mgr., info. specialist Unitek Internat. Corp. (Am.), Mt. Laurel, N.J., 1992—; tchr. South Jersey Chinese Sch., Cherry Hill, N.J., 1978-82. Editor: CLE Around the Cuontry (annually), 1988-92; contbr. articles to profl. jours. Bus. mgr. Chinese Community Ctr., Voorhees, 1981. Mem. NAFE, N.J. Entrepreneurial Network, Inc., Spl. Librs. Assn., Soc. Competitive Intelligence Profls. Home: 1132 Sea Gull Ln Cherry Hill NJ 08003-3113 Office: Unitek Internat Corp 520 Fellowship Rd Ste A-114 Mount Laurel NJ 08054-3406

LI, QIONG, mechanical engineering researcher; b. Taigu, Shanxi, China, Apr. 26, 1954; came to U.S., 1984; d. Yizhou Li and Jinfeng Guo; m. Mingfa Yang, Aug. 6, 1982; children: Samson X. Yang, Edward X. Yang. BS, Taiyuan U. Tech., Shanxi, China, 1981; MS, U. Ill., 1987, PhD, 1992. Instr. Taiyuan U. Tech., 1982-84; vis. scholar U. Ill. Urbana-Champaign, Urbana, 1984-85, rsch. asst., 1985-92; rsch. asst. Ohio State U., Columbus, 1992-94; sr. rsch. engr. Caterpillar Co., 1994—. Mem. Am. Soc. Mech. Engring. (assoc.), Soc. Automotive Engring. Office: Caterpillar Co Tech Ctr Bldg L PO Box 1875 Peoria IL 61656-1875

LI, YING, economist, computer scientist; b. Kunming, Peoples Republic of China, Apr. 5, 1964; came to U.S., 1987; d. Juexian and Shude (Xu) L.; m. Xingxiang Li, Jan. 1, 1989. BS in Math., Sichuan U., Peoples Republic of China, 1984; MS in Computer Sci., Wash. State U., 1992, PhD in Econs., 1993. Lectr. Sichuan U., Republic of China, 1984-87; teaching asst. Wash. State U., Pullman, 1988-90, rsch. asst., 1990-93; economist Fannie Mae, Washington, 1993—. Contbr. articles to profl. jours. NSF grantee, 1991-92. Mem. Internat. Neural Network Soc., Chinese Economists Soc., Beta Gamma Sigma. Office: Fannie Mae 3900 Wisconsin Ave NW Washington DC 20016-2892

LIANG, VERA BEH-YUIN TSAI, psychiatrist, educator; b. Shanghai, China, July 29, 1946; came to U.S., 1970, naturalized, 1978; d. Ming Sang and Mea Ling Chu Tsai; m. Hanson Liang, Nov. 6, 1971; children: Eric G., Jason G. MBBS, U. Hong Kong, 1969. Diplomate Am. Bd. Psychiatry and Neurology. Intern Cambridge Hosp. (Mass.), 1970-71; resident Hillside div. L.I. Jewish Med. Ctr., New Hyde Park, N.Y., 1971-73; fellow Albert Einstein Coll. Medicine, Bronx, N.Y., 1973-75, asst. clin. prof., 1989—; instr. SUNY, Bklyn., 1975-79; asst. prof. SUNY, Stony Brook, 1979-89; med. dir. Hillside Ea. Queens Ctr., Queens Village, N.Y., 1977-90, 91-92; staff child psychiatrist Schneider Children's Hosp., New Hyde Park, N.Y., 1990-92; sr. psychiatrist South Oaks Hosp., Amityville, N.Y., 1992—; cons. in field. Contbr. articles to profl. jours. Mem. Am. Psychiat. Assn., Am. Acad. Child Psychiatry. Office: South Oaks Hosp 400 Sunrise Hwy Amityville NY 11701-2508

LIAO, MEI-JUNE, biopharmaceutical company executive; came to U.S., 1974; BS, Nat. Tsing-Hua U. Taiwan, 1973; MPh, Yale U., 1977, PhD, 1980. Tchg. asst. Nat. Taiwan U., 1973-74, Temple U., Phila., 1974-75; tchg. asst. Yale U., New Haven, 1975-76, rsch. asst., 1976-79; postdoctoral assoc. MIT, Cambridge, 1980-83; sr. scientist Interferon Scis. Inc., New Brunswick, N.J., 1983-84, group leader, 1984-85, dir. cell biology, 1985-87, dir. R&D, 1987—. Contbr. articles to profl. jours.; inventor in field. Mem. Am. Soc. Biochemistry and Molecular Biology, Internat. Soc. Interferon and Cytokine Rsch., Soc. Chinese Bioscientists in Am. Office: Interferon Sci Inc 783 Jersey Ave New Brunswick NJ 08901-3605

LIAS, BARBARA IRENE, principal; b. Punxsutawney, Pa., Jan. 19, 1944; d. Francis Alexander and Barbara Deloris (Bulka) Rutkosky; m. Edward Ethber Lias Sr., June 6, 1964; children: Edward Ethber Jr., Christopher Francis. BS, Ind. U. of Pa., 1965, MS, 1970; adv. cert. adminstrn. ednl. curriculum & supervision, St. Bonaventure U., 1980. Elem. tchr. Port Allegheny (Pa.) Sch. Dist., 1965-85; elem. prin. Johnsonburg (Pa.) Sch. Dist., 1985-89, H.S. prin., 1989—, chmn. profl. devel. com., 1988—, chmn. drug and alcohol com., 1986—; chmn. Tech.-Prep. Assn. with Penn State Dubois, Johnsonburg, 1994. Mem. Quad County H.S. Prins. Assn. (pres. 1992-94), Port Allegany Women's Club (pres. 1973), Rotary, Delta Kappa Gamma. Republican. Roman Catholic. Home: RD Box 340 Port Allegany PA 16743 Office: Johnsonburg Sch Dist Elk Ave Johnsonburg PA 15845

LIBBEY, DARLENE HENSLEY, artist, educator; b. La Follettee, Tenn., Jan. 9, 1952; d. Charles Franklin and Geneva (Chitwood) Hensley; children: Michael Damon McLaughlin, Marina Auston. BFA in Painting, San Francisco Art Inst., 1989; MFA in Painting/Drawing, U. Tenn., 1994. Grad. asst. Alliance of Ind. Colls., N.Y.C., 1989; gallery asst. Holley Solomon Gallery, N.Y.C., 1989; teaching assoc., instr. U. Tenn., Knoxville, 1991-94; lectr., instr. U. Tex.-Pan Am., 1994—; curator Belleza Salon, Knoxville, 1993—; invitational rep. San Francisco Art Inst., N.Y. Studio Program, Alliance Ind. Colls., 1989; organizer Multi-Media Group Exhbn. One-woman shows include U. Tex.-Pan Am., 1995; exhibited in group shows at San Francisco Art Inst., 1985, 86, 87, 88, 89, Pacific Ctr., San Francisco, 1988, Alliance of Ind. Colls., N.Y.C., 1989, San Francisco Mus. Modern Art, 1990, Bluxom Studios, San Francisco, 1991, Gallery 1010, Knoxville, 1991, 92, Ewing Gallery, U. Tenn., Knoxville, 1991, 92, 93, 94, SUNY, Syracuse, 1992, Printers Mark, Knoxville, 1993, Unitarian Ch., Knoxville, 1993, Tomato Head, Knoxville, 1994, Belleza Salon, Knoxville, 1994. Vol. San Francisco Mus. Modern Art, 1990-91; founding mem. Grad. Student Union, U. Tenn., Knoxville, 1993; vol. instr. Knox County Schs., Knoxville, 1992-93; vis. artist Marin County Schs., San Anselmo, Calif., 1989. Tuition scholar San Francisco Art Inst., 1987; materials grantee U. Tenn., 1993, grantee Buck Found., 1987-89. Mem. Coll. Art Assn. Democrat. Unitarian. Home: 2112 N 12th St Mcallen TX 78501 Office: U Tex-Pan Am Art Dept 1201 W University Dr Edinburg TX 78539-2999

LIBBIN, ANNE EDNA, lawyer; b. Phila., Aug. 25, 1950; d. Edwin M. and Marianne (Herz) L.; m. Christopher J. Cannon, July 20, 1985; children: Abigail Libbin Cannon, Rebecca Libbin Cannon. AB, Radcliffe Coll., 1971; JD, Harvard U., 1975. Bar: Calif. 1975, U.S. Dist. Ct. (cen. dist.) Calif. 1977, U.S. Dist. Ct. (no. dist.) Calif. 1979, U.S. Dist. Ct. (ea. dist.) Calif. 1985, U.S. Ct. Appeals (2d cir.) 1977, U.S. Ct. Appeals (5th cir.) 1982, U.S. Ct. Appeals (7th cir.) 1976, U.S. Ct. Appeals (9th cir.) 1976, U.S. Ct. Appeals (D.C. cir.) 1978. Appellate atty. NLRB, Washington, 1975-78; assoc. Pillsbury, Madison & Sutro, San Francisco, 1978-83, ptnr., 1984—; dir. Alumnae Resources, San Francisco. Mem. ABA (labor and employment sect.), State Bar Calif. (labor law sect.), Bar Assn. San Francisco (labor law sect.), Nat. Women's Health Network, No. Calif. Field Hockey Assn., Radcliffe Club (San Francisco). Office: Pillsbury Madison & Sutro 235 Montgomery St San Francisco CA 94104-2902

LIBBY, SANDRA CHIAVARAS, educator; b. Clinton, Mass., Apr. 8, 1949; B.S. in Spl. Edn., Fitchburg (Mass.) State Coll., 1970, M.Ed. in Reading, 1976; postgrad. (fellow) Clark U., 1981-83; 2 children. Tchr. spl. class Webster (Mass.) Schs., 1970-73, asst. coord. program materials, resource room, 1974, tchr./coord. primary spl. needs program, 1975-78, tchr. jr. high English, 1978-79, reading tchr. jr. high, 1979-80 adminstrv. asst. intern Shepherd Hill Regional Sch., Dudley, Mass., 1980-81; dir., owner Teddy Bear Day Care Ctr., Dudley, Mass., 1983-85; devel. specialist Ft. Devens Post Learning Ctr., Shirley, Mass., 1985-86; resource room tchr. Murdock High Sch., Winchendon, Mass., 1986; tchr. behavioral modification Middle Sch., Winchendon, 1986-87; coord., tchr. gifted and talented Lancaster Pub. Schs., 1987-90; tchr. learning disabilities Leominster Pub. Sch., 1990-91, tchr. primary level behavior modification, 1991—. Mem. Nat. Edn. Assn., Mass. Tchrs. Assn., Leominster Tchrs. Assn. (bldg. rep. 1992—, negotiating com. 1993—), Internat. Reading Assn. (v.p. 1994—, chairperson celebrate literacy award 1994—), Mass. Reading Assn. (mem. North Worcester County coun. 1994—), Webster Emblem Club (pres. 1984-85), Phi Delta Kappa (Horace Mann grant 1989-90). Cert. in elem. and spl. edn., reading, reading supervision, learning disabilities, English (secondary), Mass. Home: 59 Wilker Rd # 3rr Ashburnham MA 01430-1301

LIBERMAN, LEE SARAH, lawyer, educator; b. N.Y.C., Aug. 19, 1956; d. James Benjamin and Deen (Freed) L.; m. William Graham Otis, Oct. 24, 1993. BA, Yale U., 1979; JD, U. Chgo., 1983. Bar: N.Y. 1985, D.C. 1994. Law clk. U.S. Ct. Appeals (D.C. cir.), Washington, 1983-84; spl. asst. to asst. atty. gen., civil div. U.S. Dept. Justice, Washington, 1984-86; dep. assoc. atty. gen. U.S. Dept. Justice, 1986, assoc. dep. atty. gen., 1986; law clk. to Justice Antonin Scalia U.S. Supreme Ct., Washington, 1986-87; asst. prof. law George Mason U., Arlington, Va., 1987-89; assoc. counsel to the Pres. Exec. Office of the Pres., Washington, 1989-92; assoc. Jones, Day, Reavis & Pogue, Washington, 1993-94; adj. prof. law Georgetown Law Sch., 1995. Mem. Federalist Soc. for Law & Pub. Policy (founder, dir., nat. co-chmn.). Republican. Jewish.

LIBKA, BONNIE RAE, guidance counselor; b. Davenport, Iowa, Feb. 20, 1951; d. Gerald Carl and Vera Margarette (Scheer) Borcher; m. Robert John Libka, June 16, 1973; children: Michelle Andrea Libka Hunt, Kimberly Ann, Jennifer Krisin. BA, Concordia U., 1973, MA, 1984. Cert. K-9 tchr., guidance counselor, Ill. Kindergarten tchr., ch. sec. Holy Cross Luth. Sch. and Ch., Chgo., 1973-74; tchr., libr. asst. Am. Embassy Sch., New Delhi, India, 1988-89; GED instr. Morton Coll., Cicero, Ill., 1989-92; English as second lang. instr. Triton Coll., River Grove, Ill., 1984-93; guidance counselor, tchr. Walther Luth. High Sch., Melrose Park, Ill., 1992—; dir. guidance, fgn. exch. student coord., Walther Luth. H.S. Block leader North Maywood, 1980—; mem. St. Paul Luth. Ch., 1974—. Mem. ASCD, Luth. Edn. Assn., No. Maywood Cmty. Orgn. Office: Walther Luth High Sch 900 Chicago Ave Melrose Park IL 60160

LIBKIND, JEAN SUE JOHNSON (JEAN SUE JOHNSON-LIBKIND), publishing executive; b. Racine, Wis., Apr. 4, 1944; d. John Bert and Loretta Laura (Richards) Johnson; m. D.M. Spradling, June 5, 1966 (div. Nov. 1971); 1 child, Eric David (dec.); m. Robert Lawrence Libkind, Oct. 13, 1991. Student, U. Oslo, Norway, 1965; BA in Journalism, U. Wis., 1966. Libr. asst. Racine (Wis.) Pub. Libr., 1962-64; mng. editor Daily Cardinal, Madison, 1965-66; project assoc. U. Wis.-Journalism Extension, Madison, 1966-68; office mgr. Senrac Enterprises, Madison, 1968-71; prodn. mgr. U. Wis. Press, Madison, 1971-72; asst. jours. mgr. U. Wis. Press, Racine, 1972-77, ast. mktg. mgr., 1977-80; mktg. mgr. U. Ga. Press, Athens, 1980-84; sales, mktg. mgr. U. Penn Press, Phila., 1984-88; mktg. dir. Jewish Publ. Soc., Phila., 1988-91, mktg. dir. pub. ops., 1991-94; owner Johnson Libkind Pubs.' Agy.; speaker and cons. in field. Program chair Unitarian Universalist Fellowship, Athens, 1982-84; active Compassionate Friends. Recipient Svc. award USMC, 1966, Svc. award After Sch. Day Care Assn., 1976; named Hon. Lt. Col., Ga. Militia, 1985. Mem. Women in Comm. (treas. 1990-91, sec. 1989-90, pres. 1970-71), Phila. Pub. Group (pres. 1990-92), Women in Scholarly Pub. (newsletter editor 1981-83, mentoring co-chair 1993-94), Religious Pub. Group. Home: 837 N Woodstock St Philadelphia PA 19130

LIBOT, ELIZABETH MARIA, computer programmer; b. Utrecht, The Netherlands, July 28, 1932; came to U.S., 1957; d. Albertus Johannus Petrus and Jacoba Maria (Henkelman) Van Der Vliet. Assoc. in Pre-Medicine, Bonifacius Coll., Utrecht, 1951; postgrad., Front Range C.C., Denver, 1985. Sr. programmer Owens-Corning Fiberglass, Toledo, 1968-72; lead programmer Potomac Rsch., Inc., Denver, 1978-79; programmer/analyst Petro-Lewis Corp., Denver, 1979-84; prin. programmer State of Colo., Denver, 1985—. 2d lt. Royal Dutch Navy, 1951-55. Democrat. Home: 6769 Hillridge Pl Parker CO 80134

LIBRETTO, ELLEN VIRGINIA, librarian, consultant; b. N.Y.C., Feb. 7, 1947; d. George Émile and Virginia Dorothea (MacPherson) Stauffer; m. John C. LiBretto, May 27, 1972 (div. 1984). BA, CUNY, 1968, MLS, 1970. Libr. N.Y. Pub. Libr., N.Y.C., 1968-78; libr. cons. Queens (N.Y.) Borough Pub. Libr., 1978—; cons. to pub. librs., pubs., schs. Author: High/Low Handbook, 1981, 2d edit., 1985, New Directions for Young Adult Services, 1983, High/Low Handbook: Encouraging Literacy in the 1990s, 3d edit., 1990; contbr. articles to periodicals. Mem. ALA (bd. dirs. 1979-82, chair Hi/Lo com. 1976-80), Young Adult Libr. Svcs. Assn. (bd. dirs. 1979-82), N.Y. Libr. Assn., Authors Guild, N.Y. Libr. Club (pres., bd. dirs. 1986-91). Episcopalian. Home: 29-29 167th St Flushing NY 11358 Office: Queens Borough Pub Libr 89-11 Merrick Blvd Jamaica NY 11432

LIBRIZZI, ROSE MARIE MEOLA, library administrator, counselor; b. Newark, Apr. 15, 1940; d. Salvatore J. and Marie (Consoli) Meola; m. Vincent F. LiBrizzi, June 25, 1965 (div. 1983); children: Vincent, Steve. BA in History and Pre-law magna cum laude, Bloomfield (N.J.) Coll., 1965; MLS, Rutgers U., 1967; JD, Seton Hall U., 1989; MA in Counseling, MontclairState U., 1992. Cert. tchr., N.J.; cert. sch. libr.; profl libr. cert. Acting children's libr. Newark Pub. Libr., 1965-66; head children's svcs. Belleville (N.J.) Pub. Libr., 1966-68; asst. dir. Kearny (N.J.) Pub. Libr., 1969; mem. adj. faculty Kean Coll., Union, N.J., 1969-73; supr. children's svcs. Jersey City Pub. Libr., 1973-87, asst. dir., 1987-90, 91—, libr. dir., 1990-91. Mem. ABA, ALA, N.J. Libr. Assn. (v.p. 1988, mem.-at-large 1982, sec. 1981, pres. and founder adminstr. sect. 1978, chairperson pers. adminstrn. com., chairperson resolutions, nominations and honor and awards coms., chairperson NJLA Centennial Celebration com. 1984-89, Adminstrn. section award), Hudson County Libr. Dirs. Assn. (pres. 1990—), Exxex-Hudson Region Exec. Bd. (mem-at-large, sec. 1990—, chairperson continuing edn. com. 1986-88), Rutgers Alumni Assn. (pres., senator, mem. alumni fedn. bd. 1990—). Home: 5 Squier Ct Livingston NJ 07039 Office: Jersey City Pub Libr 472 Jersey Ave Jersey City NJ 07302-3499

LICHT, ALICE VESS (ALICE O'NEILL), publishing executive, journalist; b. Caroleen, N.C., May 28, 1937; d. Troy Cleet Vess and Clara Ella Lee (Johnson) Littleton; m. Gennaro Pietro Di Biase, Nov. 12, 1955 (div. 1971); children: Stephen Eugene, Michael Antonio; m. Raymond Licht, Feb. 11, 1989. BA in English, Theatre, R.I. Coll., 1969, MA in English, 1976; postgrad., Emerson Coll., 1982-83, Southwestern U., 1984. Cert. secondary sch. English tchr. English tchr. Scituate (R.I.) High Sch., 1969-83; actress films and TV L.A., 1984-86, freelance journalist, 1984-86; pres., journalist Los Angeles Features Syndicate, 1986—. Mem. AAUW, NAFE, Internat. Platform Assn., Chgo. Internat. Press Club. Home: 650 Winnetka Mews Winnetka IL 60093-1967

LICHTENBERG, MARGARET KLEE, publishing company executive; b. N.Y.C., Nov. 19, 1941; d. Lawrence and Shirley Jane (Wicksman) Klee; m. James Lester Lichtenberg, Mar. 31, 1963 (div. 1982); children: Gregory Lawrence, Amanda Zoe. BA, U. Mich., 1963; postgrad., Harvard U., 1963. Book rev. editor New Woman mag., 1972-73; assoc. editor children's books Parents Mag. Press, 1974; editor, rights dir. Books for Young People, Frederick Warne & Co., N.Y.C., 1975-78; sr. editor Simon & Schuster, N.Y.C., 1979-80; dir. sales promotion Grosset & Dunlap, N.Y.C., 1980-81; ednl. sales mgr. Bantam Books, N.Y.C., 1982-84; dir. mktg. and sales Grove Press, N.Y.C., 1984-86; dir. of sales Grove Press, 1986-87; dir. sales Weidenfeld & Nicolson, N.Y.C., 1986-87; mktg. dir. Beacon Press, Boston, 1988—; writer, freelance critic, 1961—. Contbr. articles, essays, stories, poetry, revs. to mags., newspapers and anthologies. Bd. dirs. Children's Book Council, 1978. Recipient 2 Avery Hopwood awards in drama and fiction, 1962, 2 in drama and poetry, 1963; coll. fiction contest award Mademoiselle mag., 1963; Woodrow Wilson fellow, 1963. Mem. Women's Nat. Book Assn. (past pres. N.Y. chpt.). Home: 130 Appleton St Apt 5D Boston MA 02116-6045 Office: Beacon Press 25 Beacon St Boston MA 02108-2892

LICHTENSTEIN, NATALIE G., lawyer; b. N.Y.C., Sept. 17, 1953; d. Abba G. and Cecile (Geffen) L.; m. Willard Ken Tom, June 10, 1979. AB summa cum laude, Radcliffe Coll., 1975; JD, Harvard U., 1978. Bar: D.C. 1978. Atty., advisor U.S. Dept. Treasury, Washington, 1978-80; prin. counsel World Bank, Washington, 1980-94, chief counsel East Asia and Pacific divsn. Legal Dept., 1995—; adj. prof. Chinese law Georgetown U., Washington, 1982-86. Contbr. articles on Chinese and Vietnamese law to profl. jours.

LICHTMAN, SUSAN C., television news broadcaster, reporter; b. Pittsfield, Mass.; d. Robert W. and Vivien Carole (Mayer) L. BS, Boston U. Producer Commonwealth Games Com., Edmonton, Alta., Can., 1978; reporter ITV, Edmonton, Alta., Can., 1978-79; producer Sta. WFSB-CBS News, Hartford, Conn., 1979-81; news anchor Sta. WFAA-ABC News, Dallas, 1981-82; news anchor, reporter Sta. KFMB-CBS News, San Diego, 1982-86, Sta. WTVJ-NBC News, Miami, Fla., 1987-92; news anchor Sta. KTTV-Fox News, L.A., 1993—; media cons., Miami, 1990-92, L.A., 1992—. Photojournalist numerous newspapers and mags. Bd. dirs. South Fla. Leukemia Soc., Miami, 1991-92; fundraiser Muscular Dystrophy, Miami, 1987-92, New World Sch. of the Arts, Miami, 1990. Recipient Emmy award, 1994, NATAS, 1985, Golden Mike award, 1994. Office: Sta KTTV News 5746 W Sunset Blvd Los Angeles CA 90028-8588

LIDE, NEOMA JEWELL LAWHON (MRS. MARTIN JAMES LIDE, JR.), poet; b. Levelland, Tex., Apr. 1, 1926; d. Charles Samuel and Juel (Yeager) Lawhon; Secretarial cert. Draughon's Bus. Coll., 1943; student U. Tex., 1944-46; R.N., Jefferson-Hillman Sch. Nursing, 1950; m. Martin James Lide, Jr., Nov. 12, 1950; children—Martin James, III, Brooks Nathaniel, Gardner Lawhon. Writer column Baldwin Times, Bay Minette, Ala., 1964-68, Shades Valley Sun newspapers, Birmingham, Ala., 1974-75; v.p., sec. Martin J. Lide Assocs., Inc., Birmingham, 1977-81; R.N. supr. St. Martin's in the Pines, 1984. Mem. def. adv. com. Women in Services, for Ala., 1961-63; coordinator women's activities Nat. Vets. Day, Birmingham, 1961-68; mem. exec. com., 1968-70; exec. bd. Women's Com. of 100 for Birmingham, 1964-65, 84-85; spkr. Arlington Hist. Assn., 1983; mem. Gorgas bd. U. Ala., Tuscaloosa, 1959. Recipient citation Merit, Muscular Dystrophy Assn. Am., 1961. Mem. Christian Women's Soc. Mountain Brook (bd. dirs. 1993), Nat. Soc. DAR (regent Princess Sehoy chpt. 1983-85, 91-92, chpt. spkr. 1988, 92, chpt. exec. bd. 1991-94), Cauldron Club (spkr. 1989, 2d v.p. 1992-93). Author: (poetry) Instead of Sunset, 1973; (narrative) Life of Service-These are My Jewels, 1979; Music in the Wind - The Story of Lady Arlington, 1980; Brother James Bryan-Hope Lives Eternal, 1981; Music of the Soul, 1982; The Past and Psyche of Arlington, 1983, The Light Side of Life in the American Colonies, 1988, The American Woman, 1989, revised, 1992. Home: 3536 Brookwood Rd Birmingham AL 35223-1446

LIDELL, MARCIA HICKLIN, customer service executive; b. Hilliard, Ohio, Jan. 25, 1958; d. John Ryland Jr. and Alma May (Lowe) Hicklin. AA, Kennesaw Coll., 1978, Assoc. in Bus. Adminstrn., 1979, BS, 1980; MBA, Mercer U., 1988. Field examiner Gen. Electric Capital, Atlanta, 1981-84; ops. officer audit Citicorp, N.A., Atlanta, 1984-85; audit staff mgr. Citicorp, N.A., Atlanta, Ga., 1985-86, sr. loan officer, 1986-89; sr. fin. analyst Sprint, Atlanta, 1989, gen. mgr. carrier svc. ctr., 1989-94, gen. mgr. ops. strategic planning and analysis, 1994—. Kennesaw Found. scholar, 1976-80. Mem. DAR. Republican.

LIDTKE, DORIS KEEFE, computer science educator; b. Bottineau County, N.D., Dec. 6, 1929; d. Michael J. and Josephine (McDaniels) Keefe; m. Vernon L. Lidtke, Apr. 21, 1951. BS, U. Oreg., 1952; MEd cum laude, Johns Hopkins U., 1974; PhD, U. Oreg., 1979. Programmer analyst Shell Devel. Co., Emeryville, Calif., 1955-59, U. Calif., Berkeley, 1960-62; asst. prof. Lansing (Mich.) Community Coll., 1963-68; ednl. specialist Johns Hopkins U., Balt., 1968; assoc. program mgr. NSF, Washington, 1984-85; program dir., 1992-93; sr. mem. tech. staff Software Productivity Consortium, Reston, Va., 1987-88; asst. prof. Towson State U., Balt., 1968-80, assoc. prof., 1980-90, prof. computer sci., 1990—. Named Outstanding Educator, Assn. for Ednl. Data Systems, 1986. Mem. Assn. for Computing Machinery (coun. 1984-86, 94—, spl. interest group bd. 1985—, edn. bd. 1980—, chair 1994—, recognition Svc. award 1978, 83, 85, 86, 90, 91), Computer Soc. of IEEE (Outstanding Contbn. award 1986, 92), Nat. Edl. Computer Conf. (steering com., chmn. 1985-89, vice chmn. 1983-85, recognition award 1988, 92), Computing Scis. Accreditation Bd. (v.p. 1993—). Home: 4806 Wilmslow Rd Baltimore MD 21210-2328 Office: Towson State U Computer & Info Scis Baltimore MD 21204

LIE, PENELOPE JANE, healthcare associate; b. Melbourne, Victoria, Australia, Nov. 28, 1963; d. J. T. and Margaret Ruth (Macfarlane) L. AB, Harvard U., 1985; postgrad., U. Calif., Berkeley, 1993—. Cons Agribus. Assocs., Inc., Waltham, Mass., 1986-89; analyst Palo Alto (Calif.) Med. Found., 1990-93; summer assoc McKinsey & Co., Inc., 1994. Bd. dirs.

Community Rowing, Inc., Cambridge, Mass., 1986-89. Mem. Am. Coll. Healthcare Execs.

LIEBELER, SUSAN WITTENBERG, lawyer; b. New Castle, Pa., July 3, 1942; d. Sherman K. and Eleanor (Klivans) Levine; BA, U. Mich., 1963, postgrad. U. Mich., 1963-64; LLB (Stein scholar), UCLA, 1966; m. Wesley J. Liebeler, Oct. 21, 1971; 1 child, Jennifer. Bar: Calif. 1967, Vt. 1972, D.C. 1988. Law clk. Calif. Ct. of Appeals, 1966-67; assoc. Gang, Tyre & Brown, 1967-68, Greenberg, Bernhard, Weiss & Karma, L.A., 1968-70; assoc. gen. counsel Rep. Corp., L.A., 1970-72; gen. counsel Verit Industries, L.A., 1972-73; prof. of law law sch. Loyola U., L.A., 1973-84; spl. counsel, chmn. John S. R. Shad, SEC, Washington, 1981-82; commr. U.S. Internat. Trade Commn. Washington, 1984-88, vice chmn., 1984-86, chmn., 1986-88; ptnr. Irell & Manella, L.A., 1988-94; sr. v.p. Legal Rsch. Network, Inc., L.A., 1994—; vis. prof. U. Tex., summer 1982; cons. Office of Policy Coordination, office of Pres.-elect, 1981-82; cons. U.S. Ry. Assn., 1975, U.S. EPA, 1974, U.S. Price Commn., 1972; mem. Adminstrv. Conf. U.S., 1986-88. Mem. editorial adv. bd. Regulation mag. CATO Inst. Mem. ABA, State Bar Calif. (treas., vice chair, chair exec. com. internat. law sect.), L.A. County Bar Assn., D.C. Bar Assn., Practicing Law Inst. (internat. law adv. com.), ITC Trial Lawyers Assn., Washington Legal Found. (acad. adv. bd.), bd. dirs. Century City Hosp., adv. bd. U. Calif. Orientation in U.S.A. Law, Order of Coif. Jewish. Sr. editor UCLA Law Review, 1965-66; contbr. articles to legal publ.

LIEBENSON, GLORIA KRASNOW, interior design executive; b. Chgo., Apr. 6, 1922; d. Henry Randolph and margaret (Rivkin) Krasnow; m. Herbert Liebenson, Mar. 11, 1944; children: Lauren Ward, Lynn Liebenson Green. Student, Int. Inst. Interior Design, Washington, 1961; B Am. Studies, Dunbarton Coll., Washington, 1974. Lic. Interior Designer, D.C. Numerous positions Journalism, Advt., editing, 1942-62; interior design exec. Creative Interiors, 1962—; tchr. interior design YMCA, Washington, 1980-82. Mem. editorial staff Champlin Encyclopedia, 1945-47; journalist Shreveport Jour., 1944. Bd. Dirs. Jewish Social Svc. Agy., Washington, 1983-85, Nat. Coun. Jewish Women. 1982-84; pres. Friends Nat. Museum African Art, 1983-85, D.C. Mental Health Assn., 1986-88. Mem. Womens Nat. Dem. Club. Democrat. Jewish. Home and Office: 2703 Unicorn Ln NW Washington DC 20015-2233

LIEBERMAN, ANNE MARIE, financial executive; b. Jersey City, Aug. 28, 1946; d. Ralph Norman and Kathleen Celestine (Dooris) L.; m. Stephen Bruce Oshry, Sept. 21, 1986. BA, Sonoma State U., 1968; MLS, U. Calif., 1970, MBA, 1977. Cert. fin. planner; cert. fund specialist. V.p. Bank of Am., San Francisco, 1977-81, Lawrence A. Krause & Assocs., San Francisco, 1982-86; pres. Lieberman Assocs., Larkspur, Calif., 1986—. Author: Marketing Your Financial Planning Practice, 1986, Mastering Money, 1987; contbg. author: Financial Planning Can Make You Rich, 1987, The Expert's Guide to Managing a Successful Financial Planning Practice, 1988, About Your Future, 1988; columnist The Bus. Jour. Bd. dirs. Marin Gen. Found. Hosp., 1995. Mem. Inst. Cert. Fin. Planners (Fin. Writer's award 1986), Internat. Assn. Fin. Planning, Nat. Ctr. for Fin. Edn. (trustee 1994). Office: Lieberman Assocs 100 Smith Ranch Rd San Rafael CA 94903-1900

LIEBERMAN, CAROL COOPER, healthcare marketing communications consultant, city planning administrator; b. St. Louis, June 14, 1938; d. Norman Leonard and Ethel (Silver) Mistachkin; m. Malcolm P. Cooper, Aug. 25, 1962 (div. June 1977); children: Lawrence, Edward, Marcus; m. Edward Lieberman, Apr. 1992. BS, U. Wis., 1959; MA, N.Y. Inst. Tech., 1992. Media buyer Lennen and Newell, Los Angeles, 1959-61; advt. mgr. Hartfield-Zodys, Los Angeles, 1961-62, Haggarty's, L.A., 1962-63; sales rep. Abbott Labs., Bklyn., 1974-75; edn. dir. N.Y. and N.J. Regional Transp. Program, N.Y.C., 1975-78; account exec. Med. Edn. Dynamics, Woodbridge, N.J., 1978-79; dir. program devel. Kallir, Phillips & Ross Info. Media, N.Y.C., 1979-81; exec. v.p. sales and mktg. Audio Visual Med. Mktg., N.Y.C., 1981-85; exec. v.p. Park Row Pubs./John Wiley & Sons Med. Div., N.Y.C., 1985-88; pres., prin. Park Row Pubs., N.Y.C., 1988-91; healthcare mktg. communications cons., Southampton, N.Y., 1991—; cons., prof. comms. and speech N.Y. Inst. Tech., 1991—; exec. dir. Bus. Improvement Dist., Riverhead, N.Y., 1994—; cons. Am. Acad. Physician Assts., Washington, 1986-87, Am. Soc. Anesthesiologists, Chgo., 1986-88, Am. Acad. Family Physicians, 1987-91, Am. Psychiat. Assn., 1988, Am. Coll. Gen. Practitioners, 1988, N.Am. Soc. Pacing and Electrophysiology, 1988-91. Editor pub. med. papers, med. films, med. jours. for pharmaceutical cos. Mem. Am. Women in Radio and TV, Soc. Tchrs. Family Medicine (cons.), Pharm. Advt. Council, Nat. Council Jewish Women, Hadassah. Home and Office: 41 Barkers Island Rd Southampton NY 11968

LIEBERMAN, GAIL FORMAN, financial executive; b. Phila., May 26, 1943; d. Joseph and Rita (Groder) Forman. BA in Physics and Math., Temple U., 1964, MBA in Fin., 1977. Dir. internat. fin. Standard Brands Inc., N.Y.C., 1977-79; staff v.p. fin. and capital planning RCA Corp., 1979-82; CFO, exec. v.p. Scali McCabe Sloves, Inc., 1982-93; v.p. finance, CFO, mng. dir. Moody's Investors Svc., N.Y.C., 1994—; bd. dirs. Allied Devices, Inc. Bd. dirs. Vineyard Theater Group, N.Y.C. Mem. Fin. Execs. Inst. Office: Moody's Investor Svcs 99 Church St New York NY 10007-2701

LIEBERMAN, ILENE STIFELMAN, mayor, lawyer; b. Bklyn., May 30, 1947; d. Herbert and Evelyn (Magoon) Stifelman; children: Adam, Jeffrey, Stacy. BA, SUNY, Cortland, 1968; 2MA, NYU, 1974; JD summa cum laude, Nova U., Davie, Fla., 1989. Bar: Fla. 1990. Councilwoman City of Lauderhill, Fla., 1984-88, coun. pres., 1984, 86, coun. pres. protem, 1985, coun. treas., 1987, mayor, 1988—. Mem. Consumer Protection Agy., Lauderhill, 1980-82, Lauderhill Code Enforcement Bd., 1982-84, Adv. Coun. Intergovernmental Rels., Tallahassee, 1993—, Growth Mgmt. Adv. Commn., Tallahassee, 1993, Census 2000, 1993—, Environ. Land Mgmt. Study Commn., Tallahassee, 1991-92; hon. v.p. B'nai Zion, 1984-93; bd. dirs. Shotrim Soc., 1989-91, JCC, 1989-93; mem. Broward County Resource Recovery Bd.; pres., co-founder N.W. Lauderhill Homeowners Assn., 1980-83; precinct leader Lauderhill Dem. Exec. Com., 1981-88; active Gwen Cherry Women's Polit. Caucus, Fin. Adminstrn. and Intergovtl. Rels., Adv. Coun. Intergovtl. Rels.; vice-chair Fla. Sesquicentennial Commn., 1994. Recipient Outstanding Svc. award Early Childhood Devel. Assn., Israel Freedom award, 1990, Mother of Yr. award Temple Beth Israel, 1990, Disting. Community Svc. award UN Assn., 1992, Woman of Distinction award Assn. Retarded Citizens, 1992. Mem. Nat. League Cities (bd. dirs. 1993-94, mem. Census 2000 com. 1994), Fla. League Cities (2nd v.p. 1991-92, 1st v.p. 1992-93, pres. 1993-94), Broward League Cities (vice chairperson legis. com. 1989, chairperson 1990-93, Pres.'s award 1992), Lauderhill-Lauderdale Lakes C. of C., B'nai Brith Women, Armond Hadassah, Lauderhill Women's Club, United Dem. Club (bd. dirs. 1990), Kiwanis (Kiwanian of Yr. award 1991), Optimists. Home: 8300 NW 49th St Lauderhill FL 33351-5545 Office: City of Lauderhill 2000 City Hall Dr Lauderhill FL 33313-7706

LIEBERMAN, ROCHELLE PHYLLIS, relocation company executive; b. Bklyn., June 27, 1940; d. Solomon and Freda (Shapiro) Beller; m. Melvyn Lieberman, June 10, 1961; children—Eric Neil, Marc Evan. B.A., Bklyn. Coll., 1961; M.Ed., Duke U., 1977. Tchr., Bklyn. pub. schs., 1961-64; instr. Carolina Friends, Durham, N.C., 1967-70; grad. intern Duke U., Durham, 1974-75, faculty adviser, 1975-76; sales assoc. Kelly Matherly, Durham, 1978-81; pres. Shelli, Inc., Durham, 1981—. Treas. Duke Forest Assn., Durham, 1980-85. Mem. LWV, Durham and Chapel Hill Bd. Realtors, Women's Council of Realtors (sec. 1980-81), Duke U. Eye Ctr. adv. bd., Kappa Delta Pi. Republican. Jewish. Clubs: Duke Faculty, Duke Campus (Durham). Avocations: piano; walking; knitting; writing; reading. Office: Shelli Inc 1110 Woodburn Rd Durham NC 27705-5738

LIEBES, RAQUEL, import/export company executive, educator; b. San Salvador, El Salvador, Aug. 28, 1938; came to the U.S., 1952, naturalized, 1964; d. Ernesto Martin and Alice (Philip) L.; m. Richard Paisley Kinkade, June 2, 1962 (div. 1977); children: Kathleen Paisley, Richard Paisley Jr., Scott Philip. BA, Sarah Lawrence Coll., 1960; MEd, Harvard U., 1961; MA, Yale U., 1965, PhD, 1991; PhD in English, Oxford (Eng.) U., 1994. Teaching fellow in Spanish Sarah Lawrence Coll., Bronxville, N.Y., 1958-60; econ. teaching fellow Yale U., New Haven, 1964-65, instr. Spanish, 1964-66; exec. stockholder Import Export Co., San Salvador, 1968—, also bd. dirs.; adj. prof. Am. U., Washington, 1989-91; instr. dept. fgn. lang. and linguistics, dept. fgn. studies Georgetown U., Washington, 1990-93. Contbr. glossary of Spanish med. terms. Hon. consul Govt. of El Salvador, 1977-80; docent High Mus. of Art, Atlanta, 1972-77; vol. Grady Hosp., Atlanta, 1966-71; instr. Spanish for med. drs. Tucson Med. Ctr., 1966-71; chmn. Atlanta Coun. for Internat. Visitors, 1966-71; mem. Outreach Group on Latin Am., Washington, 1982-86; founding mem. John Kennedy Ctr. for Performing Arts, 1980—; mem. Folger/Shakespeare Libr., Smithsonian Inst., Agape, El Salvador. Fellow Yale U., 1963, econ. fellow Yale U., 1964-65; fellow Corcoran Mus. of Art, 1984-85. Mem. MLA, Am. Biog. Inst. Rsch. Assn. (hon. consul of El Salvador, dep. gov. 1978-80, bd. advisors 1994), Jr. League of Washington, Harvard Club, Yale Club. Republican. Home: 700 New Hampshire Ave NW Washington DC 20037-2406

LIEBHABER, ROBERTA GAYLE, secondary education educator; b. N.Y.C., Nov. 5, 1959; d. Arnold and Selma (Mermey) L. BA, Queens Coll., 1981, MS, 1985. Cert. secondary education tchr., N.Y. English tchr. N.Y.C. Pub. Sch. 204, 1983-86, Rochester Pub. Sch. System, N.Y., 1986-88, The Young Mother's Program, The Family Learning Ctr., Rochester Pub. Sch. System, N.Y., 1988—. Author: (poetry anthology) Anthology of Contemporary Poetry, 1987, Perceptions-Vol. II, 1991; (short story) City Newspaper of Rochester, 1988; editor: (poetry anthology of students writing) You Don't Know Me, 1994. Election inspector League of Women Voters Election Bd., Rochester, N.Y., 1993—. Grantee Ctr. Ednl. Devel., Rochester, 1990, Project UNIQUE, 1990-94. Mem. Writers and Books, Am. Assn. U. Women, Arts and Lectures, United Fedn. Tchrs. Democrat. Jewish. Office: The Young Mothers Program The Family Learning Ctr 30 Hart St Rochester NY 14605

LIEBICH, MARCIA TRATHEN, community volunteer; b. Troy, N.Y., Mar. 10, 1942; d. Roland Henry and Ida Mae (Horsfall) Trathen; m. Donald Herbert Liebich, May 13, 1941; children: Kurt Roland, Mark Christian. BA, Elmira Coll., 1964. With Sunnyview Hosp. and Rehab. Ctr., Schenectady, 1982—, dir. devel., 1992-94; CEO Sunnyview Hosp. Found., 1994—. Co-founder Parent Anonymous Lay Therapy, Schenectady, 1974-80; trustee Elmira (N.Y.) Coll., 1978-94; bd. dirs. United Way, Schenctady, 1980-81, pres. 1985, bd. dirs. United Way, N.Y., 1991—, Sunnyview Rehab. Hosp., Schenectady, 1982, pres. 1988-91; social svcs. Women's Legis. Forum, Albany, 1984-91; bd. dirs. Leadership Schenectady, 1987-92, Schenectady C. of C., 1987-90, YMCA Capital Dist., 1991-94, WMHT Pub. Radio and TV, 1991—; pres. Samaritan Counseling Ctr., Schenectady, 1988-91; bd. dirs., treas. Bridge Ctr. Drug Treatment, Schenectady, 1988-91. Recipient YWCA Community Vol. award, 1986, K.S. Rozendaal award Community Svc. Schenectady, 1987, Liberty Bell award Schenectady Bar Assn., 1990, Women of Vision Betty Bean award YWCA, 1990. Mem. AAUW (pres. 1978), Jr. league Schenectady (Vol. of Yr. award 1981), Phi Beta Kappa. Republican. Lutheran. Home: 6 Brian Dr Rexford NY 12148-1415

LIEBMAN, JUDITH RAE STENZEL, operations research educator; b. Denver, July 2, 1936; d. Raymond Oscar and Mary Madelyn (Galloup) Stenzel; m. Jon Charles Liebman, Dec. 27, 1958; children: Christopher Brian, Rebecca Anne, Michael Jon. BA in Physics, U. Colo., Boulder, 1958; PhD in Ops. Rsch., Johns Hopkins U., 1971. Successively asst. prof., head indsl. systems, assoc. prof. U. Ill., Urbana, 1972-84, prof., 1984—, chmn. bd. Ill. Resource Network, 1987-90, acting vice chancellor for rsch., 1986-87, vice chancellor for rsch., 1987-92, acting dean Grad. Coll., 1987-92, dean, 1987-92, prof. ops. rsch., 1992—; vis. prof. Tianjin (China) U., 1985; charter mem. Ill. Gov.'s Sci. Adv. Com., Ill. Exec. Com., 1989-92; mem. adv. com. for engring. NSF, 1988-92, chmn., 1991-92. Author: Modeling and Optimization with GINO, 1986; author numerous articles in field. Bd. dirs. United Way, Champaign, Ill., 1986-91; bd. dirs. East Cen. Ill. Health Systems Agy., Champaign, 1977-82, pres., 1980-82. Mem. Ops. Rsch. Soc. Am. (pres. 1987-88), Nat. Assn. State Univs. and Land Grant Colls. (exec. bd. 1990-92), Rotary, Sigma Xi, Sigma Pi Sigma, Alpha Pi Mu, Phi Kappa Phi. Home: 113 W Whitehall Ct Urbana IL 61801-6664 Office: U Ill 1206 W Green St Urbana IL 61801

LIEBMAN, NINA R., economic developer; b. Toledo, Ohio, May 27, 1941; d. Jules Jay and Phyllis Gertrude (Kasle) Roskin; m. Theodore Liebman, Oct. 27, 1968; children: Sophie, Hanna, Tessa. Student, U. Marseilles, Aix-en-Provence, France, 1959-60, Skidmore Coll., 1960-61, NYU, 1961-63; cert. labor negotiator, Cornell U., 1993. Pub. info. officer Young Adult Inst., N.Y.C., 1978-81; U.S.A. dir. Rhone-Alps Econ. Devel. Assn., N.Y.C. and Lyon, France, 1981-85; internat. mktg. specialist N.Y. State Dept. Econ. Devel., N.Y.C., 1985-89, chief internat. programs, 1989—; mem. U.S. Com. for UN Devel. Fund for Women. Co-author: Biz Speak: A Dictionary of Business Terms, Slang and Jargon, 1986. Vol., trained mediator Bklyn. Mediation Ctr. Fellow Eisenhower Exch. Fellowship Program, 1993. Mem. Fellow Eisenhower Exch. Fellowship Program; mem. Alliance Am. and Russian Women, Minority Internat. Network for Trade, Bklyn. C. of C. (bd. dirs., internat. advisor), Bklyn. Heights Assn., Mcpl. Arts Soc., Grace Choral Soc. (bd. dirs. 1993—). Democrat. Jewish.

LIEBMANN, MARTHA SCHREIBER, psychotherapist; b. Bklyn., Apr. 13, 1938; d. Edward M. and Elsa (Henner) Heyman; m. Jordan C. Schreiber, Dec. 25, 1958 (div. Dec. 1971); children: Eric, Nancy; m. Richard O. Liebmann, Aug. 25, 1990. BA, Queens Coll., 1957; MSW, Columbia U., 1959; PhD, Union Inst., Cin., 1989. Cert. social worker, N.Y.; lic. marriage and family counselor, N.J. Staff therapist group and indivdual therapy Washington Square Inst., N.Y.C., 1968—, dir. psychiat. social svcs., sr. supr., mem. faculty, 1980—; pvt. practice, 1974—. Mem. Am. Group Psychotherapy Assn., Nat. Assn. for Advancement Psychoanalysis, Coun. Psychoanalytic Psychotherapists. Jewish. Home: 229 Franklin St Haworth NJ 07641-1411 Office: Washington Square Inst 41 E 11th St Fl 4 New York NY 10003-4678 also: Psychotherapy Assocs 253 S Washington Ave Bergenfield NJ 07621

LIEBOW, JOANNE ELISABETH, marketing communication coordinator; b. Cleve., May 15, 1926; d. Arnold S. and Rhea Eunice (Levy) King; m. Irving M. Liebow, June 30, 1947 (div. Jan. 1972); children: Katherine Ann Liebow Frank, Peter. Student, Smith Coll., 1944-47; BA, Case Western Res. U., 1948. Cleve. reporter Fairchild Publs., N.Y.C., 1950-51; freelance pub. rels., Cleve., 1972-78; pub. info. specialist Cuyahoga Community Coll., Cleve., 1979—. Founder, pres. Mt. Sinai Hosp. Jr. Women's Aux., Cleve., 1948-50; pres. PTA, Bryden Elem. Sch., Beachwood, Ohio, 1964; mem. bd., pres. Beachwood Bd. Edn., 1968-76. Recipient Exceptional Achievement award Coun. for Advance Edn., 1982, Citation award, 1982, Grand Prize, 1983; Sophia Smith scholar Smith Coll., 1946, Cleve. Communicator's award Women in Communications, Inc., 1982. Home: 23511 Chagrin Blvd Apt 211 Cleveland OH 44122-5538 Office: Cuyahoga Community Coll Ea Campus 4250 Richmond Rd Cleveland OH 44122-6195

LIEFERT, PATRICIA LYNN, foreign service officer; b. Mpls., Nov. 10, 1963; d. Jerome Melvin and Mary Teresa (Grehan) L. BA, Bryn Mawr Coll., 1985; MA, U. Minn., 1988. Joined Fgn. Svc., Dept. State, Washington, 1988; program analyst AID, Washington, 1988-91; project officer AID, Ecuador, Ukraine, 1991—. Roman Catholic. Office: Am Embassy Kiev 5850 Washington DC 20523-5850

LIEM, ANNIE, pediatrician; b. Kluang, Johore, Malaysia, May 26, 1941; d. Daniel and Ellen (Phuah) L. BA, Union Coll., 1966; MD, Loma Linda U., 1970. Diplomate Am. Bd. Pediatrics. Intern Glendale (Calif.) Adventist Hosp., 1970-71; resident in pediatrics Children's Hosp. of Los Angeles, 1971-73; pediatrician Children's Med. Group, Anaheim, Calif., 1973-75, Anaheim Pediatric Med. Group, 1975-79; practice medicine specializing in pediatrics Anaheim, 1979—. Fellow Am. Acad. Pediatrics; mem. Los Angeles Pediatric Soc., Orange County Pediatric Soc., Adventist Internat. Med. Soc., Chinese Adventist Physicians' Assn. Office: 1741 W Romneya Dr # D Anaheim CA 92801-1805

LIER, NANCY JEAN, medical educator, administrator; b. Breckenridge, Mich., Sept. 21, 1942; d. Joseph and Lucinda Martha (Feltman) Smolek; m. James William Lier, June 20, 1964; 1 child, Thomas James. BS, Madonna U., 1964; postgrad., U. Kans., 1976-77; MS in Sci. Adminstrn., Cen. Mich. U., 1985. Supr. immunohematology St. Mary's Med. Ctr., Saginaw, Mich., 1964-66, 67-68, supr. bacteriology, 1968-69, dir. sch. med. tech., 1967—; staff technologist Flint (Mich.) Med. Lab., 1966-67; acad. appointments include Grad Valley State U., Allendale, Mich., 1967—, Cen. Mich. U. Mt. Pleasant, 1967—, Saginaw Valley State U., University Center, Mich., 1967—, Aquinas Coll., Grand Rapids, Mich., 1967—, Lake Superior State U., Sault Ste. Marie, Mich., 1967—, Madonna U., Livonia, Mich., 1967—, Mich. Tech. U., Houghton, 1967—. Vol. Boy Scouts Am., Frankenmuth, Mich., 1972-83. Mem. Am. Soc. Clin. Pathologists (cert. med. technologist), Am. Soc. Med. Technologists. Republican. Roman Catholic. Home: 9112 E Curtis Rd Frankenmuth MI 48734-9507 Office: St Mary's Med Ctr 830 S Jefferson Ave Saginaw MI 48601-2594

LIFE, BRENDA JOY, adult nurse practitioner; b. Salem, Ohio, May 11, 1953; d. Charles Keith and Donna (Phillips) Hobart; m. James Harrison Life, Sept. 14, 1974; 1 child, Charles Jamison. LPN, St. Joseph Hosp. Sch. Nursing, 1974; ADN, Lorain C.C., 1978; BSN, Bowling Green State U., 1985; MSN, Case Western Res. U., 1992. RN, Ohio, N.Y.; cert. adult nurse practitioner; cert. stress test technologist Am. Coll. Sports Medicine. Critical care nurse St. Joseph Hosp., Lorain, Ohio, 1974-80, head nurse ICU, 1980-81; critical care nurse Lorain Community Hosp., 1981-88, adult nurse practitioner, 1988—; adult nurse practitioner Cleve. Metro Health Ctr., 1992-93, North Ohio Heart Ctr., Lorain, 1993—. Mem. ANA, Am. Acad. Nurse Practitioners, N.E. Ohio Nurse Practitioners Group, Ohio Coalition Nurses with Splty. Cert. (v.p. membership), Sigma Theta Tau. Democrat. Home: 1215 State St Vermilion OH 44089-1246

LIFER, SUSAN RUTH, rehabilitation administrator, physical therapist; b. N.Y.C., Dec. 28, 1952; d. Mervin and Doris Florence (Kraus) Meyer; children: Benjamin, Sarah, Daniel. BS in Phys. Therapy magna cum laude, Northeastern U., 1974. Registered phys. therapist, Maine. Staff phys. therapist New Eng. Bapt. Hosp., Boston, 1974-75; staff phys. therapist Easton (Pa.) Hosp., 1975-76, chief phys. therapist, 1976-77; supr. phys. therapy Hunterdon State Sch., Clinton, N.J., 1977-78; pvt. practice Stewartsville, N.J., 1980-85; dir. phys. therapy Penobscot Valley Hosp., Lincoln, Maine, 1985-88, dir. rehab. svcs., 1988-91; dir. phys. rehab. Millinocket (Maine) Regional Hosp., 1991—, Facility for Occupational and Rehab. Medicine, Millinocket, 1991—; ergonomic cons. Lincoln (Maine) Pulp and Paper, 1986—, Bowater/Great No. Paper, Millinocket, 1986—; adj. instr. Am. Lung Assn., Bethlehem, Pa., 1983, 84; phys. therapy cons. Warren Haven, Oxford, N.J., 1979-85, Project First Step, Washington, N.J., Project Sunshine, Phillipsburg (N.J.) Pub. Schs.; phys. therapist Lehigh Valley Easter Seal Soc., Bethlehem, Elizabeth Levinson Ctr., Bangor, Maine; acting supr. phys. therapy Hunterdon State Sch., Clinton. Recipient Dr. Frith Humanitarian award, 1986. Mem. Am. Phys. Therapy Assn., Phi Kappa Phi. Office: Millinocket Regional Hosp 200 Somerset St Millinocket ME 04462-1298

LIFF, DIANE R., general counsel; b. June 4, 1944; d. Ben W. and Sylvia (Elman) L. BA, Coll. of Wooster, 1966; JD, U. Chgo., 1971. Bar: D.C. Atty. Ohio State Legal Svcs. Assn., 1971-72; asst. atty. gen. State of Ohio, 1972-74; adj. prof. of law Ohio State U. Coll. of Law, 1973-75; chief consumer protection divsn. Ohio Dept. Commerce, 1974-75; law dir. Pub. Utilities Commn. of Ohio, 1975-76; atty. Columbia Gas Distbn. Cos., 1976-78; asst. gen. counsel for litigation Dept. of Transp., 1978-90, spl. counsel office of gen. counsel, 1990—. Recipient Urban fellow, 1970, Reginald Herber Smith Cmty. Lawyer fellow, 1971-72; award for excellence Transp. Gen. Counsel, 1978; Silver medal for Meritorious Svc. Sec. Transp., 1979, Sr. Exec. Svc. award for Outstanding Performance, 1982, 84. Office: Office of the Gen Coun Dept of Transp 400 7th St SW Washington DC 20590*

LIFKA, MARY LAURANNE, history educator; b. Oak Park, Ill., Oct. 31, 1937; d. Aloysius William and Loretta Catherine (Juric) L. B.A., Mundelein Coll., 1960; M.A., Loyola U., Los Angeles, 1965; Ph.D., U. Mich., 1974; postdoctoral student London U., 1975. Life teaching cert. Prof. history Mundelein Coll., Chgo., 1976-84, coordinator acad. computer, 1983-84, prof. history Coll. St. Teresa, Winona, Minn., 1984-89, Lewis U., Romeoville, Ill., 1989—; chief reader in history Ednl. Testing Service, Princeton, N.J., 1980-84; cons. world history project Longman, Inc., 1983—; cons. in European history Coll. Bd., Evanston, Ill., 1983—; mem. Com. on History in the Classroom. Author: Instructor's Guide to European History, 1983; contbr. articles to publs. Mem. Am. Hist. Assn., Ednl. Testing Service Devel. Com. of History. Democrat. Roman Catholic. Office: Lewis U RR 53 Romeoville IL 60441

LIGARE, KATHLEEN MEREDITH, strategy and marketing executive; b. Providence, Aug. 29, 1950; d. Kenneth MacAllister and Carol (Smith) Ligare. BA, Carleton Coll., 1972; MS, Yale U., 1976; MBA, Northwestern U., 1982. Sr. assoc. Booz, Allen & Hamilton, Chgo., 1978-82; mgr. mktg. and product devel. GE Capital Corp., Barrington, Ill., 1982-83, planning mgr., 1983-84, region mgr., 1984-85; sr. v.p. sales and mktg. Gen. Electric Capital Corp., Barrington, Ill., 1992-93, region mgr., 1984-85, sr. v.p. sales and mktg., 1992-93, sr. v.p. internat., 1993—; prin. KML Enterprises, Inc., Chgo., 1985-92. Author: Illinois Women's Directory, 1977. Bd. dirs. Midwest Women's Ctr., Chgo., 1978-89; chair, bd. dirs. alumni ann. fund Carleton Coll., 1990-93, bd. dirs., 1987-94, mem. alumni bd., 1989, trustee, 1993—. Mem. Chgo. Fin. Exch. Office: Gen Electric Capital Corp 600 Hart Rd Barrington IL 60010

LIGGETT, TWILA MARIE CHRISTENSEN, public television company executive, academic administrator; b. Pipestone, Minn., Mar. 25, 1944; d. Donald L. Christensen and Irene E. (Zweigle) Christensen Flesher. BS, Union Coll., Lincoln, Nebr., 1966; MA, U. Nebr., 1971, PhD, 1977. Dir. vocal and instrumental music Sprague (Nebr.)-Martell Public Sch., 1966-67; tchr. vocal music, pub. schs., Syracuse, Nebr., 1967-69; tchr. Norris Pub. Sch., Firth, Nebr., 1969-71; cons. fed. reading project, pub. schs., Lincoln, 1971-72; curriculum coord. Westside Community Schs., Omaha, 1972-74; dir. State program Right-to-Read, Nebr. Dept. Edn., 1974-76; asst. dir. Nebr. Commn. on Status of Women, 1976-80; asst. dir. project adminstrn./devel. Great Plains Nat. Instructional TV Libr., U. Nebr., Lincoln, 1980—; exec. prodr. Reading Rainbow, PBS nat. children's series, 1980— (8 Emmy awards 1990, 91, 92, 93, 94); cons. U.S. Dept. Edn., 1981; Far West Regional Lab., San Francisco, 1978-79; panelist, presenter AAAS, NEA, NEH, NSF, Corp. Pub. Broadcasting, Internat. Reading Assn., Blue Ribbon panelist, Acad. TV Arts & Scis., 1991-94, final judge Nat. Cable Programming Awards, 1991-92. Author: Reading Rainbow's Guide to Children's Books: The 101 Best Titles, 1994. Bd. dirs. Planned Parenthood, Lincoln, 1979-81. Recipient Grand award N.Y. Internat. Film and TV Festival, 1993. Mem. NATAS, Internat. Reading Assn. (Spl. award Contbns. Worldwide Literacy 1992), Am. Women in Film and TV,Phi Delta Kappa. Presbyterian. Home: 649 S 18th St Lincoln NE 68508-2681 also: 301 E 79th St Apt 23P New York NY 10021-0944 Office: PO Box 80669 Lincoln NE 68501-0669 also: Reading Rainbow 301 E 79th St Apt 23P New York NY 10021-0944

LIGGIO, JEAN VINCENZA, artist, educator; b. N.Y.C., Nov. 5, 1927; d. Vincenzo and Bernada (Terrusa) Verro; m. John Liggio, June 6, 1948; children: Jean Constance, Joan Bernadette. Student, N.Y. Inst. Photography, 1965, Elizabeth Seton Coll., 1984, Parsons Sch. of Design, 1985. Hairdresser Beauty Shoppe, N.Y.C., 1947-65; freelance oil colors and portraits N.Y.C., 1958-75; instr. watercolor N.Y. Dept. Pks., Recreation and Conservation, Yonkers, 1985-89, Bronxville (N.Y.) Adult Sch., 1989—; substitute tchr. cosmetology Yonkers Bd. Edn., 1988-89. Paintings pub. by Donald Art Co., C.R. Gibson Greeting Card Co.; 12 watercolor paintings for Avon Calendar, Avon Cosmetics Co., 1994. Recipient numerous awards. Mem. Mt. Vernon Art Assn. (pres. membership com. 1983—), Mamaroneck Artist's Guild, Hudson River Contemporary Artist's, Scarsdale Art Assn. (publicity chmn. 1984-89), New Rochelle (N.Y.) Art Assn. Home and Office: 166 Helena Ave Yonkers NY 10710-2524

LIGHON, BRENDA M., safety and loss control representative; b. Ann Arbor, Mich., Dec. 12, 1957; d. Hoyd Phillip and Anna Mae (Kelly) Hardwick; m. David Nelson Lighon, July 28, 1984; children: William Ivan Jackson III, James Phillip Jackson. BA in Communication Disorders, U. Colo., 1980; MA in Mgmt, U. Phoenix, 1989; A in Loss Control Mgmt., Ins. Inst. Am., 1993. Group leader Child Opportunity Program, Denver, 1979-81; med. rec. tech. Childrens Hosp., Denver, 1981-82; divsn. clk. IBM Corp., Newport, R.I., 1984; ins. analyst West Marc Communications, Inc., Denver, 1985-89; safety & loss control rep. State of Colo., Divsn. Risk Mgmt., Denver, 1989—; cons. in field. Author: Alien Sands, 1993. Mem. NAFE,

Nat. Assn. Ins. Women Internat., Nat. Environ. Health Assn., Met. Ins. Profls. (v.p. 1987—, pres.-elect 1994). Democrat. Baptist. Office: State Colo Divsn Risk Mgmt 225 E 16th Ave Ste 600 Denver CO 80203-1610

LIGHT, BETTY JENSEN PRITCHETT, former college dean; b. Omaha, Sept. 14, 1924; d. Lars Peter and Ruth (Norby) Jensen; m. Morgan S. Pritchett, June 27, 1944 (dec. 1982); children: Randall Wayne, Robin Kay Pritchett Church, Royce Marie Pritchett Creech; m. Kenneth F. Light, Nov. 23, 1985. B.S., Portland State U., 1965; M.B.A., U. Oreg., 1966; Ed.D., Oreg. State U., 1973. Buyer Rodgers Stores, Inc., Portland, Oreg., 1947-62; chmn. bus. div. Mt. Hood Community Coll., Gresham, Oreg., 1966-70, dir. evening coll., 1970-71, assoc. dean instn., 1972-77, dean humanities and behavioral scis., 1977-79, dean devel. and spl. programs, 1979-83; dean communication arts, humanities and social scis. Mt. Hood Community Coll., 1983-86; mem. state com. for articulation between community colls. and higher edn., 1976-78; mem. Gov.'s Council on Career and Vocat. Edn., 1977-86. Author: Values and Perceptions of Community College Professional Staff in Oregon, 1973; contbg. author: (case study) The Pritchett Study in Retailing, An Economic View, 1969. Mem. Gresham City Council, 1983-86. Mem. Oreg. Bus. Edn. Assn., Am. Assn. Higher Edn., Nat. Assn. Staff and Oreg. Devel., Oreg. Women's Polit. Caucus, Am. Vocat. Assn., Oreg. Vocat Assn., Danish Heritage Soc. Club: Soroptimist (pres. 1974-75, 81-82). Home: 1635 NE Country Club Ave Gresham OR 97030-4432

LIGHT, CHERYL ELLEN, lawyer; b. Kingsport, Tenn., June 24, 1958; d. Bob Leonard and Juanita Irene (Dykes) L.; m. Michael Jarrell Searcy, Oct. 15, 1983; children: Cameron Light, Aaron Michael. BS, East Tenn. State U., 1980; JD, Wake Forest U., 1983. Assoc. Campbell and Hooper, Newport, Tenn., 1984-88, Morton, Lewis, King & Krieg, Knoxville, Tenn., 1989; assoc. gen. coun. 1st Am. Nat. Bank, Knoxville, 1989—; mem. moot ct. bd. Sch. Law Wake Forest U., Winston-Salem, N.C., 1981-83. Mem. ABA, Tenn. Bar Assn., Omicron Delta Kappa. Methodist. Office: 1st Am Nat Bank 505 S Gay St Knoxville TN 37902

LIGHT, DOROTHY KAPLAN, lawyer, insurance executive; b. Alden, Iowa, May 20, 1937; d. Edward T. and Bessie (Nachazel) Kaplan; m. Ernest Isaac Light, Dec. 28, 1959; children: Christina, William, Samuel, David (twins). B.A., U. Iowa, 1959, J.D., 1961, hon. degree Georgian Ct. Coll., 1991. Bar: Iowa 1961, N.J. 1973; C.P.C.U., CLU. Pvt. practice, Marshalltown, Iowa, 1962-63, Iowa City, 1963-71; with U.S. Army, N.J., 1972-74; asst. gen. counsel Prudential Property & Casualty Ins. Co., Holmdel, N.J., 1974-77, assoc. gen. counsel, dir. corp. services, 1977-82, dir. pub. affairs mktg. dept., 1979-82, dir. pub. affairs, 1982-83, v.p. govt. affairs, 1982-87; v.p. The Prudential Ins. Co. Am., Newark, 1987-90, v.p. and corp. sec., 1990—; chmn. Prudential Found.; bd dirs. Ctr. for N.J. Resources, trustee N.J. Ctr. Analysis of Public Issues, N.J. Supreme Ct. adv. comm. Profl. ethics; Mem. N.J. govs'. transition team, N.J. econ. master plan commn.,, N.J. econ. devel. task force, Am. Soc. Corp. Secs. Republican. Roman Catholic. Office: Prudential Ins Co Am 751 Broad St Newark NJ 07102-3777

LIGHT, MARION JESSEL, retired elementary education educator; b. San Antonio, Dec. 5, 1915; d. Marion Jackson and Kate Jessel (Cox) Parr; m. Marion Russell Light, Nov. 8, 1958 (dec. July 1983); children: Russell Jeffers, Paul Love. BA, So. Meth. U., 1936; MA, U. Tex., 1947. Cert. elem. and secondary sch. tchr., Tex. Elem. tchr. Dallas Ind. Sch. Dist., 1936-72; 1st v.p. The Cosmos Rev. Class, 1991-92. Del. to 16th Senatorial Dist. Dem. Conv., 1988; moderator Presbyn. Women 1st Ch. , Dallas, 1989-90, vice moderator, 1994-95. Mem. AAUW (chmn. hobbies and crafts Dallas br. 1970s), Dallas Ret. Tchrs. Assn. (corr. sec. 1984-92), Dallas Women's Forum (rec. sec. Friday study 1987-89), Bay View Century Club (corr. sec. 1988-89, pres. 1993-95), Dallas Symphony Orch. League, Delta Kappa Gamma (pres. Delta Sigma chpt. 1956-58, Chpt. Achievement award 1979, Marion Parr Light Recruitment grantee named in her honor Delta Sigma chpt. 1958). Democrat.

LIGHT, PATRICIA KAHN, university official, psychologist; b. Elizabeth, N.J., Mar. 29, 1939; d. Perry M. Kahn and Thelma Kurtz; m. Richard J. Light, June 27, 1965; children: Jennifer Susan, Sarah Elizabeth. AB, Bennington (Vt.) Coll., 1960; EdM, Harvard U., 1966, EdD, 1973. Lic. psychologist, Mass. Tchr. math. Elizabeth pub. schs., 1961-65; counselor Newton (Mass.) High Sch., 1967-68; staff psychologist Powell Assocs., Cambridge, Mass., 1969-74; dir. counseling, chief psychologist Harvard Bus. Sch., Boston, 1974-94, dir. MBA program devel. and faculty support, 1994—; invited speaker in field. Author: Let the Children Speak, 1975; author cassette: Dual Career Families, 1979. Mem. adv. com. Radcliff Coll., 1987-90; parent advisor Buckingham, Brown & Nichols Sch., 1980-91, trustee, 1994—. Fellow Mass. Psychol. Assn.; mem. APA, Pi Lambda Theta. Office: Harvard Bus Sch Baker East 215 Boston MA 02163

LIGHT, WILMA CHARLEAN, physician; b. Darby, Pa., June 7, 1945; d. Frederick Haak and Margaret (Robinson) L. BS, Buckness U., 1967; MD, Thomas Jefferson U., 1971. Diplomate Am. Bd. Pediats., Am. Bd. Allergy and Immunology. With Children's Hosp. of Buffalo, 1971-74, fellow, 1974-76; pvt. practice Latrobe, Pa., 1976—. Mem. AMA, Am. Acad. Allergy and Immunology, Pa. Med. Soc. Republican. Mem. Christian and Missionary Alliance Ch. Office: 1100 Ligonier St Latrobe PA 15650

LIGHTFOOT, JAN LINDA, artist, photographer; b. Middletown, Conn., Dec. 3, 1949; d. Francis St. Martin and Isabella Carta-Fairfield Me. AS, U. Maine at Orono, 1977. Freelance artist, photographer Maine, 1978-83; bd. coordinator Hospitality House Inc., Fairfield, Maine, 1982—; program coordinator Hospitality House Inc., Hickley, Maine, 1986—; speaker in field. Impressionistic artist; photographer wildlife. Adv. for civil rights and better life for the poor. Office: Hospitality House Inc PO Box 62 Hinckley ME 04944-0062

LIGHTFOOT, TEDDI, music school director, composer, singer; b. Poteau, Okla., Apr. 29, 1946; d. Charles Fredrick and Frances Mary (Stucin) Zirbel; m. Jon Charles Lightfoot, Feb. 5, 1970 (div. June 1978). MusB, San Francisco State Coll., 1968, MA, 1972; postgrad., Conservatorio, Florence, Italy, 1968-69. Designer mfg. Lightfoot Fyne Leather Clothing, San Francisco, 1970-88; supr. Police Fire Communications, South San Francisco, Calif., 1977-85; dir., tchr. Yamaha Music Sch., South San Francisco, 1986-90; co-owner Lightweight Music Pub. Co., San Francisco and L.A., 1990—, Radical Prodns. Rec. Co., San Francisco and L.A., 1990—; sr. exec. v.p. Hello Tomorrow Music Group, 1991-92; dir., artist and repetoire Growing Up Music, 1991-92; music dir. Ctr. Stage U.S.A., San Francisco, 1994, Burlingame Enrichment Acad., 1994, Into the Woods, San Mateo, Calif., 1994; choral dir. Bayside Mid. Sch., San Mateo, 1985-86; dir. sch. for music and mus. entertainment Lightfoot Studio, South San Francisco, 1984—; actress in commls. and TV, San Francisco, 1978—, Italy, 1968-69; dir. Razzle Dazzle Kids Performance Troupe, South San Francisco, 1985—; creative/mus. cons. schs. and orgns., Bay Area, Calif., 1984—. Composer, arranger shows, original works, prodns., San Francisco, 1978—; composer, singer: Let Me Sing, 1989; composer Heroes Are Just Ordinary People, Eyes of God; coproducer, mus. dir. albums P.J. Ford and Something New, 1992, Children Care, 1992; music dir. rock opera Love's Destiny, 1990; lead actor, singer theatrical prodn. Stroll Down Broadway, San Mateo, 1994. Dir. Barbara Neal Prodns., San Francisco, 1987; lay min. Unity Christ Ch., San Francisco, 1988—, dir. Unity Angels Choir, 1985—; tchr. musical theatre San Mateo High Sch., 1992—. Named State Grand Champion Calif. State Talent Assn., 1986-94; inducted into Calif. Youth Hall of Fame, 1993. Mem. Nat. Assn. Tchrs. Singing, Music Tchrs. Assn. Calif., No. Calif. Songwriters Assn., Theatre Bay Area, Internat. New Thought Music Alliance Com. Democrat. Office: Lightfoot Studio 574 Commercial Ave South San Francisco CA 94080-3410

LIGHTNER, CANDACE LYNNE, advocate, government relations consultant; b. Pasadena, Calif., May 30, 1946; d. Dykes Charles and Katherine (Karrib) Doddridge; children: Serena, Travis. Student pub. schs., Fairfield, Calif.; hon. D.Humanities, St. Francis Coll., Johnstown, Pa., 1984; D in Pub. Service (hon.), Kutztown U., Johnstown, Pa., 1987; HHD (hon.), Marymount Coll., Johnstown, Pa., 1987. With various pvt. offices, 1964-70; real estate salesperson Calif., 1972-80; founder, pres., chmn. bd. Mothers Against Drunk Driving, Hurst, Tex., 1980-85; cons. Mothers Against Drunk Driving, Arlington, Tex., 1985-87; govt. rels. cons. Berman and Co., Washington, 1993—. Co-author: Giving Sorrow Words; contbr. articles to profl. jours. Mem. Sacramento County Task Force on Drunk Driving, Presdl. Commn. on Drunk and Drugged Driving; bd. dirs. Nat. Commn. on Drunk Driving, 1984-86, Nat. Partnership for Drug Free Use, Nat. Hwy. Safety Adv. Com., Love is Feeding Everyone, 1988-89, others; judge Gleitsman Found.; bd. advisors Bhopal Justice Campaign; founder, legis. advocate Victims in Action, Victims in Action Polit. Action Com., 1992; founder, pres. Am. Against Crime, 1992—. Named to Good Housekeeping's Most Admired Woman's Poll, 1986; ranked in top 25 of Am. most influential people World Almanac and Book of Facts, 1986, one of the original thinkers of the eighties, Life mag., 1990; recipient Pres.'s Vol. Action award, 1983, Jefferson award Am. Inst. Pub. Service, 1983, Testimonial award Civitan Internat., 1984, Epilepsy Found. award, 1984, Woman of Year award Mortar Bd. Soc., Baylor U., 1985, Anti-discrimination award Am. Anti-discrimination Com., 1985, YWCA Woman of Year award, 1986, Commonwealth award U. Del., 1986, Black and Blue award Thomas Jefferson U. Hosp. Emergency Medicine Soc., Human Dignity award Kessler Inst. for Rehab., Woman of Distinction award Third Nat. Congress Coll. Women Student Leaders and Woman of Achievement, 1987, Disting. Leadership award World Congress of Victimology, 1987, Living Legacy award Women's Internat. Ctr., 1988, Friends of Children award Assn. Childhood Edn. Internat., 1988; selected by Johns Hopkins U. to participate in Anglo-Am. Successor Generation program, 1985; honored as one of Seven Who Succeeded, Time Mag., 1985; honored by Esquire mag. as mem. Am.'s New Leadership Class, 1985, others. Office: 1331 Pennsylvania Ave NW # A Washington DC 20004-1703

LIGON, PATTI-LOU E., real estate investor, educator; b. Riverside, Calif., Feb. 28, 1953; d. Munford Ernest and Patsy Hazel (Bynum) L. BS, San Diego State U., 1976; BBA, Nat. U., San Diego, 1983, MA in Bus. Adminstrn., 1984; Clear Profl. Credential, Nat. U., 1986. Cert. profl. counselor. Escrow asst. Cajon Valley Escrow, El Cajon, Calif., 1978-79; escrow asst. Summit Escrow, San Diego, 1979-81; escrow officer Fidelity Nat. Title, San Diego, 1982-84, Dawson Escrow, San Diego, 1984; owner, property mgr., investment adviser Ligon Enterprises., San Diego, 1980—, cons., 1982—. Chmn. com., alumnae and assocs. San Diego State U., 1983, 84, 85; com. chmn. San Diego Zool. soc., 1985; pres. Friends of Symphony, Riverside, Calif., 1978. Recipient commendation City and County of Honolulu, 1981. Mem. Nat. Notary Assn., Calif. Escrow Assn., Am. Home Econs. Assn., Nat. Assn. Female Execs, Internat. Platform Assn., Calif. Bus. Edn. Assn., Jr. League of San Diego, Sigma Kappa (pres. 1974, v.p. sorority corp. 1976—). Republican. Methodist. Club: Spinster (pres. 1981), Univ. (San Diego). Avocations: racquetball; clothing design; photography; travel. Home and Office: Ligon Enterprises 7937 Wetherley St La Mesa CA 91941-6335

LIKENS, SUZANNE ALICIA, physiologist, researcher; b. Chgo., Nov. 12, 1945; d. Harry Ross and Sibyle Lovelett (Butler) L. BS in Biology, U. N.Mex., 1969, MS in Physiology, 1982. Research asst. biology dept. U. N.Mex., Albuquerque, 1969; sr. research technologist Inhalation Toxicology Research Inst., Albuquerque, 1974-93; lab. scientist II state lab. divsn. N.Mex. Dept. Pub. Health, Albuquerque, 1994—; mgr. dressage horse shows Am. Horse Show Assn./U.S. Dressage Fedn. Contbr. sci. papers and articles to profl. jours. Mem. N.Mex. Mus. Natural History & Sci. Found. Mem. AAAS, N.Mex. Natural History and Sci. Mus. Found. (docent, operator planetarium, lectr. on astronomy), N.Mex. Zool. Soc., N.Mex. Herpetol. Soc. (charter), Cousteau Soc., Women in Sci. and Engring., Am. Horse Show Assn., U.S. Dressage Fedn., N.Mex. Dressage and Combined Tng. Assn., S.W. Dressage Assn. (bd. dirs. 1989-94), N.Y. Acad. Scis., Sigma Xi. Republican. Presbyterian. Home: 1311 Dartmouth Dr NE Albuquerque NM 87106-1803

LIKINS, ROSE MARIE, foreign service officer; b. Andrews AFB, Md., Jan. 22, 1959; d. Eugene Aloysius and Merlyn (Houghland) McCartney; m. John Foster Likins, MAy 30, 1981; children: James, Kevin. BA in Internat. Affairs, Mary Washington Coll., Fredericksburg, Va., 1981, BA in Spanish, 1981. Joined Fgn. Svc., U.S. Dept. State, Washington, 1981—. Rm. mother Tuckahoe Elem. Sch., Arlington, Va., 1993-94. Mem. Am. Fgn. Svc. Assn., Mortar Board (pres. chpt. 1980-81), Phi Beta Kappa. Roman Catholic.

LILLESTOL, JANE MARIE, academic administrator; b. Jamestown, N.D., July 20, 1936; d. Harper J. and Doris (Mikkelson) Brush; m. Harvey Lillestol, Sept. 29, 1956; children: Kim, Kevin, Erik. BS, U. Minn., 1969, MS, 1973, PhD, 1977; grad. Inst. Ednl. Mgmt., Harvard U., 1984. Dir. placement, asst. to dean U. Minn., St. Paul, 1975-77; assoc. dean, dir. student acad. affairs N.D. State U., Fargo, 1977-80; dean Coll. Human Devel. Syracuse (N.Y.) U., 1980-89, v.p. for alumni rels., 1989—, project dir. IBM Computer Aided Design Lab., 1989-92; charter mem. Mayor's Commn. on Women, 1986-90; NAFTA White House Conf. for Women Leaders, 1993. Co-author: Textile Fabrics and Their Selection, 9th edit. Bd. dirs. Univ. Hill Corp. Syracuse, 1983-93; mem. steering com. Consortium for Cultural Founds. of Medicine, 1980-89; trustee Pebble Hill Sch., 1990-94, N.D. State U., Archbold Theatre. Recipient award U.S. Consumer Product Safety Commn., 1983, Woman of Yr. award AAUW, 1984, svc. award Syracuse U., 1992. Roman Catholic. Office: Syracuse U Office Alumni Rels 820 Comstock Ave Syracuse NY 13244-5040

LILLEY, MILI DELLA, insurance company executive, entertainment management consultant; b. Valley Forge, Pa., Aug. 29; d. Leon Hanover and Della Beaver (Jones) L. MBA, Tex. Christian U., 1957, PhD, 1959. Various positions G & G Cons. Inc., Ft. Lauderdale, Fla., 1971-75; v.p. AMEX, Inc., Beverly Hills, Calif. and Acapulco, Mex., 1976-80; pres. The Hanover Group, Ft. Lauderdale, 1981—; personal and bus. mgr. entertainers including Ink Spots and Del-Vikings, Ft. Lauderdale, 1984—, Lanny Poffo, Ft. Lauderdale, 1990—; mgr. Lanny Poffo; dist. agt. ITT LIfe Ins. Corp. and other leading cos. Named to All Stars Honor Roll Nat. Ins. Sales Mag., 1989. Mem. Fla. Assn. Theatrical Agents, Fla. Guild of Talent Agts., Mgrs., Producers and Orchestras. Office: The Hanover Group PO Box 70218 Fort Lauderdale FL 33307-0218

LILLICH, ALICE LOUISE, retired secondary education educator; b. East Cleveland, Ohio, Aug. 18, 1940; d. Robert Earl and Charlotte Louise (Stewart) L. BS in Home Econs. Edn., Ohio U., 1968. Cert. tchr., Ohio. Quality control Stouffer's Frozen Foods, Cleve., 1961-67; head home econs. dept. Wellston (Ohio) City Schs., 1969-94; Ohio reference person Wagons West tours of Afton, Wyo. Mem. AAUW (2d vice chair 77-80, publicity chair 1985-86, issue chair 1987-90), Ohio Ret. Tchrs. Assn. (Jackson County chpt.), Cleve. Audubon Soc., Republican Optimist Club (flag chair 1987-88, 2d v.p. 1989-90), Phi Delta Kappa (found. rep. 1986-87), Delta Kappa Gamma (v.p. 1992—, pres. 1994). Methodist. Home: 37570 Milann Dr Willoughby Hills OH 44094

LILLIE, CATHY COMER, mechanical engineer; b. Stockton, Calif., Oct. 22, 1958; d. Howard Richard and Doris Hilda (MEssing) Comer; m. Ross Carter Lillie, Oct. 17, 1981; 1 child, Reed Andrew. BSME, Mich. Tech. U., 1980, MSME, 1986. Project engr. Martin Marietta Energy Systems, Paducah, Ky., 1980-84, GM Corp., Warren, Mich., 1986-89; sr. project engr. GM Corp., Detroit, 1989-90; sr. application engr. Robert Bosch Corp., Farmington Hills, Mich., 1990-94, engring. supr., 1994—. Patentee in field. Mem. ASME, Soc. Automotive Engrs.

LILLIE, CHARISSE RANIELLE, lawyer, educator; b. Houston, Apr. 7, 1952; d. Richard Lysander and Vernell Audrey (Watson) L.; m. Thomas L. McGill, Jr., Dec. 4, 1982. B.A. cum laude, Conn. Wesleyan U., 1973; J.D., Temple U., 1976; LL.M., Yale U., 1982. Bar: Pa. 1976, U.S. Dist. Ct. (ea. dist.) Pa. 1977, U.S. Ct. Appeals (3d cir.) 1980. Law clk. U.S. Dist. Ct. (ea. dist.) Pa., Phila., 1976-78; trial atty., honors program, civil rights div. Dept. Justice, Washington, 1978-80; dep. dir. Community Legal Services, Phila., 1980-81; asst. prof. law Villanova U. Law Sch., Pa., 1982-83, assoc. prof., 1983-84, prof., 1984-85; asst. U.S. atty. U.S. Dist. Ct. (ea. dist.) Pa., 1985-88; gen. counsel Redevel. Authority City of Phila., 1988-90; city solicitor Law Dept. City of Phila., 1990-92; ptnr. litigation dept. Ballard, Spahr, Andrew and Ingersoll, 1992—, exec. com. bd. dirs., 1994—; mem. 3d Cir. Lawyers Adv. Com., 1982-85, legal counsel Pa. Coalition of 100 Black Women, Phila., 1983-88; bd. dirs. Juvenile Law Center, Phila., 1982—, Pa. Intergovernmental Coop. Authority, 1992—; commr. Phila. Ind. City Charter Commn., 1991-94; trustee Women's Law Project, Phila., 1984—; mem. Mayor's Commn. on May 13 MOVE Incident, 1985—. Bd. dirs. Women's Way, Phila. Davenport fellow, 1973; Yale Law Sch. fellow, 1981; recipient Equal Justice award Community Legal Svcs., Inc, 1991, J. Austin Norris award Barristers Assn., 1991, Outstanding Alumna award Wesleyan U., 1993, Elizabeth Dole Glass Ceiling award ARC, Phila. chpt., 1994; named One of the Top Three Phila. Labor Mgmt. Attys. Phila. Mag., 1994. Mem. ABA, Nat. Bar Assn., Fed. Bar Assn. (1st v.p. Phila. chpt. 1982-84, pres. Phila. chpt.1984-86, 3rd cir. rep. 1991—), Nat. Conf. Black Lawyers (pres. 1976-78, Outstanding Service award 1978), Am. Law Inst., Phila. Bar Assn. (vice chair bd. govs. 1994, chair, bd. of govs., 1995—), Hist. Soc. U.S. Dist. Ct. (ea. dist.) Pa. (dir. 1983—), Barristers Assn. (J. Austin Norris award 1991). Home: 7000 Emlen St Philadelphia PA 19119-2601 Office: Ballard Spahr Andrews Ingersoll 1735 Market St 51st Fl Philadelphia PA 19103-7599

LILLIE, HELEN, journalist, novelist; b. Glasgow, Scotland, Sept. 13, 1915; came to U.S., 1938; d. Thomas and Helen Barbara (Lillie) L.; m. Charles S. Marwick, Sept. 20, 1956. MA, U. Glasgow, 1938; postgrad., Yale U., 1938-40. Rsch. asst. info. divsn. Brit. Info. Svcs., N.Y.C., 1942-45, Brit. Security Coord., N.Y.C., 1945-46; asst. U.S. mgr., writer Media Reps., Inc., N.Y.C., 1947-54; with advt. dept. Family Cir. Mag., N.Y.C., 1955-56; Am. corr. The Glasgow Herald (name now The Herald), 1956—; freelance feature writer, book reviewer Detroit Free Press, 1965-66. Author: The Listening Silence, 1970, Call Down the Sky, 1973, Home to Strathblane, 1993, (columns) Inside USA, Helen Lillie's Washington Letter. V.p., acting pres. Cosmopolitan B PM Club of DC, 1972-73. Mem. Am. News Women's Club D.C., Soc. Women Geographers, Advt. Women of N.Y. (various coms.). Presbyterian. Home and Office: 3219 Volta Pl NW Washington DC 20007-2732

LILLY, ELIZABETH GILES, mobile park executive; b. Bozeman, Mont., Aug. 5, 1916; d. Samuel John and Luella Elizabeth (Reed) Abegg; m. William Lilly, July 1, 1976; children: Samuel Colborn Giles, Elizabeth Giles. RN, Good Samaritan Hosp., Portland, Oreg., 1941; student, Walla Walla Coll., Lewis and Clark Coll. Bus., Portland. ARC nurse area high schs., Portland; owner Welton Studio Interior Design, Portland; in pub. rels. Chas. Eckelman, Portland, Fairview Farms-Dairy Industry; owner, builder Mobile Park Plaza, Inc., Portland. Del. platform planning com. Rep. Party; mem. Sunnyside Seventh Day Adventist Ch. Recipient Svc. award Multnomah County Commrs., 1984. Mem. Soroptimist Internat. (local bd. dirs., bd. dirs. Women in Transition), Rep. Women's Club (pres.), C. of C., World Affairs Coun., Toastmistress (pres.), Oreg. Logging Assn. (pres. bd. dirs.), Rep. Inner Circle (life). Address: 19825 SE Stark St Portland OR 97233-6039

LILLY, SHANNON JEANNE, dancer; b. Alexandria, Va., Feb. 18, 1966; d. John Howard Lilly and Barbara Lynn (Root) Graham. Student, Contra Costa Ballet Centre, San Francisco Ballet Sch. Dancer Phoenix Ballet Co., 1985-86; mem. of Corps de Ballet San Francisco Ballet, 1986-88, soloist, 1988-91, prin. dancer, 1991-94; prin. dancer Northern Ballet Theatre, Birmingham, England, 1994—; Performed with San Francisco Opera, 1993; performed at the Reykjavik Arts Festival, Iceland, 1990. Performed with Jean Charles Gil and Friends, Paris, 1988, Tanantella, 1989, In the Middle Somewhat Elevated, 1990, Rubies, 1991, Bagaku, 1991, Sleeping Beauty, 1991; ballets include New Sleep, Connotations, Narcisse, Interplay, The Concert, Handel-a Celebration, Ballet d'Isoline, Menuetto, Giuliani: Variations on a Theme, Contredanses, Concerto in d: Poulenc, Con Brio, Intimate Voices, Calcium Light Night, Krazy Kat, Serenade, Swan Lake, Flower Festival at Genzano, Dark Elegies, Who Cares?, Theme and Variations, Airs de Ballet, Pulcinella, The Wanderer Fantasy, The Sons of Horus, Ballo Della Regina, The Theme Variations, Dreams of Harmony, Nutcracker, La Fille mal gardee, Rodeo, La Sylphide, The Sleeping Beauty, Meistens Mozart, Bugaju, Rubies, Symphony in C, The Four Temperaments, Star and Stripes, In the middle, somewhat elevated, Seeing Stars, Company B, La Pavane Rouge, Job, Harvest Moon, Tagore, Romeo and Juliet, Il Distratto, Divertissement d'Auber, Sinfonia, Scarlatti, Portfolio, The Comfort Zone, Dreams of Harmony, The End, Forgotten Land, Napoli. Episcopalian. Office: Northern Ballet Company, Spring Hall Huddersfield Rd, Halifax HX3 0AQ, England*

LILLY-HERSLEY, JANE ANNE FEELEY, nursing researcher; b. Palo Alto, Calif., May 31, 1947; d. Daniel Morris Sr. and Suzanne (Agnew) Feeley; children: Cary Jane, Laura Blachree, Claire Foale; m. Dennis C. Hersley, Jan. 16, 1993. BS, U. Oreg., 1968; student, U. Hawaii, 1970; BSN, Sacramento City Coll., 1975. Cert. ACLS, BCLS. Staff and charge nurse, acute rehab. Santa Clara Valley Med. Ctr., San Jose, Calif., staff nurse, surg. ICU and trauma unit; clin. project leader mycophenolate mofetil program team Syntex Rsch., Palo Alto. Co-founder, CFO and dir. scientific rsch. CURE (Citizens United Responsible Environmentalism), Inc. Mem. AACN, NAFE.

LIM, CHI LO, export company executive; b. Kowloon, Hong Kong, May 16, 1962; came to U.S., 1983; d. Dy and Mei-Chung (Tsoi) L. BS in Bus., U. Santo Tomas, Manila, 1983; MS in Bus., U.S. Internat. U., 1984, D of Bus. Adminstrn., 1994. Asst. mgr. Everwealth Hardware, Manila, 1981-83; dir. Transray Corporation, L.A., 1984—; gen. mgr. Synex Internat., San Diego, 1992—. Mem. NAFE. Office: Synex Internat 9225 Dowdy Dr # 220-221 San Diego CA 92126

LIMACHER, MARIAN CECILE, cardiologist; b. Joliet, Ill., May 4, 1952; d. Joseph John and Shirley A. (Smith) L.; m. Timothy C. Flynn, May 17, 1980; children: Mary Katherine Flynn, Brian Patrick Flynn. AB in Chemistry, St. Louis U., 1973, MD, 1977. Diplomate Am. Bd. Internal Medicine, Am. Bd. Cardiovascular Diseases. Resident in internal medicine Baylor Coll. Medicine, Houston, 1977-80, cardiology fellow, 1980-83, instr. medicine, 1983-84; dir. cardiology non-invasive labs. Ben Taub Hosp., Houston, 1983-84; asst. prof. medicine U. Fla., Gainesville, 1984-91, assoc. prof., 1991—; dir. non-invasive labs. Gainesville VA Med. Ctr., 1984—, chief cardiology, 1994—; dir. preventive cardiology program U. Fla., 1987—. Author: (with others) Cardiac Transplantation: A Manual for Health Care Professionals, 1990, Geriatric Cardiology, 1992, The Role of Food in Sickness and in Health, 1993, Clinical Anesthesia Practice, 1994, Primary Care, 1994; mem. editorial bd. Clin. Cardiology, 1990—; contbr. articles to profl. jours. Mem. bioethics commn. Diocese of St. Augustine, Jacksonville, Fla., 1990-94. Recipient Preventive Cardiology Acad. award NIH, 1987-92; grantee NIH, 1994—. Fellow ACP, Am. Coll. Cardiology (chair ad hoc com. women cardiology 1994—), Coun. Geriatric Cardiology; mem. Am. Soc. Preventive Cardiology (v.p. 1994—), Am. Heart Assn. (fellow coun. clin. cardiology, bd. dirs., pres. Alachua County divsn. 1986-89). Roman Catholic. Office: U Fla Coll Medicine PO Box 100277 Gainesville FL 32610-0277

LIMBURG, PATRICIA DIANNE, school counselor; b. Hamtramck, Mich., Apr. 23, 1948; d. Arthur Hugh and Oneida (De Bord) Smith; m. James Alan Limburg, June 6, 1970; children: Christopher James, Stephen Patrick. BA, Oakland U., 1970; MS, U. Wis., 1972; postgrad., U. Wis., Madison, 1972-75, U. Wis., Milw., 1993-94. Cert. sch. counselor, Wis. Rsch. asst. Rsch. and Guidance Lab Superior Students, Madison, 1972-74; dir. counseling Middleton (Wis.)-Cross Plains Schs., 1974-77; counselor youth svc. bur. Youth Svc. Bur., Mesa, Ariz., 1977-78; counselor social svc. Family Planning, Racine, Wis., 1982-85; dir. Womansplace, Racine, 1985-88; psychotherapist Lakeside Family Therapy, Racine, 1988—; sch. counselor Racine Unified Sch. Dist., 1990—. Mem. Wis. Sch. Counselor Assn. Unitarian-Universalist. Home: 203 Eldorado Dr Racine WI 53402

LIMBURG MANCINI, BARBARA ANN, pharmacist; b. Chgo., Feb. 7, 1952; d. Thomas George and Cathleen Joan (Chandler) Limburg; m. Alan Mark Mancini, Sept. 19, 1981. BS in Pharmacy, U. Ill., Chgo., 1976, PharmD, 1993. Registered pharmacist; cert. nutritional support pharmacist. Staff pharmacist U. Chgo. Med. Ctr., 1976-78, Loyola U. Med. Ctr., Maywood, Ill., 1978-79; staff/nutritional support, team pharmacist Olympia Fields (Ill) Osteo. Med. Ctr., 1979-84; clin. pharmacist Caremark, Elmhurst, Ill., 1984-87; mgr. pharmacy and patient svs. Caremark, Homewood, Ill., 1987-89; clin. pharmacist CareTech LTD Partnership, Elmhurst, 1989-91; pres. Infusion Solutions, Inc., Indian Head Park, Ill., 1993—; cons. pharmacist surveyor Joint Commn. on Accreditation of Healthcare Orgns.,

Oak Brook Terrace, Ill., 1990—. Mem. Am. Pharm. Assn., Am. Soc. of Hosp. Pharmacists, Am. Soc. for Parenteral and Enteral Nutrition, Ill. Coun. of Hosp. Pharmacists (chmn. home care com. 1994), No. Ill. Soc. of Hosp. Pharmacists, Chgo. Area Soc. for Parenteral and Enteral Nutrition, Ill. Pharmacists Assn. Office: Infusion Solutions Inc 23 Westwood Dr Indianhead Park IL 60525-9007

LIMMROTH, KARIN LEIGH, international design consultant, TV correspondent; b. New Orleans, Oct. 4, 1949; d. Weldon Eugene and Cora Elizabeth (Graby) L. BA, Bryn Mawr Coll., 1969; BFA, Sch. Visual Arts, N.Y.C., 1970. Designer, assoc. art dir. Essence mag., N.Y.C., 1973-74; designer RCA Records, N.Y.C., 1970-72; asst. art dir. Seventeen mag., N.Y.C., 1970-72; designer CBS Records, N.Y.C., 1974-75, Fantasy Records & Filmworks, Berkeley, Calif., 1975-76; asst. art dir., set designer CBS TV, L.A., 1979-8l; art dir. CBS News, N.Y.C., 1981-83, CBS Entertainment, L.A., 1981-83; art dir., design cons. Ogilvy & Mather, N.Y.C., L.A., 1983-87; assoc. creative dir. E&J Gallo Winery, Modesto, Calif., 1987-89; dir. Image Assocs., Paris and N.Y.C., 1989—; mktg. cons. U.S. Embassy, Paris, 1991—; design cons. San Francisco Opera, 1975-76, U.S. Olympic Com., Boulder, Colo., 1978-79, Internat. Olympic Com., Barcelona, Spain, 1989—; art dir., design cons. Ogilvy & Mather, N.Y.C. and L.A., Young & Rubicom, L.A., Saatchi & Saatchi/Compton, N.Y.C., Scali McCabe Sloves, N.Y.C., 1983-87; field prodr.-dir. VOX-TV, Germany, 1993—. Co-star talk show La 5 TV, Paris, 1990-92; European corr./prodr. TV show MediaTV (seen in 68 countries), 1992—; European music corr. BET Network (USA), 1993—; French corr. NBC Super Channel, 1993-94, RTL-TV Germany, 1994, Worldwide TV News EYE-TV and Agenda 21, 1995—; field prodr./dir. Nat. Geog. TV Explorer. Fundraiser Martha Graham Dance Co., N.Y.C., 1985, Amnesty Internat., Paris, 1989. Recipient award N.Y. Art Dirs. Club, 1977-78; nomination Internat. Emmy, 1993, N.Y. Festival, 1993. Mem. NARAS (bd. dirs. 1976-78, Grammy nomination 1973, Internat. Emmy nomination 1993, N.Y. Festival nomination 1993), Am. Film Inst. (art direction fellow 1976, 77), Am. Inst. Graphics Arts, La Maison des Artists (France), La Donne Vino (Italy), Internat. Design and Advt., Women in Film, Cinefilles (France), Anglo-am. Press Assoc. (Paris). Office: Image Assocs, 5 Rue du Foin, 75003 Paris France

LIMON, LAVINIA, social services administrator; b. Compton, Calif., Mar. 5, 1950; d. Peter T. and Marie W. Limon; m. Mohamed Hanon. BA in Sociology, U. Calif., Berkeley, 1972. Asst. dir., office mgr. Ch. World Svc., N.Y.C., 1975-77; chief Vietnamese refugee sect. Internat. Rescue Com., N.Y.C., 1977-79; dir. Internat. Rescue Com., L.A., 1983-86, 1983-86; asst. dir. ops. Am. Coun. for Nationalities Svcs., L.A., 1979-83; exec. dir. Internat. Inst. L.A., Washington, 1986-93; dir. office refugee resettlement and office family assistance Adminstrn. for Children and Families Dept. HHS, Washington, 1993—; bd. dirs. Am. Coun. for Nationalities Svc., 1992, chair standing com. of profl. coun., 1992; organizer U.S. refugee conf. Am. Coun. Vol. Agys., Manila, 1982; cons. Dept. of State, 1979, 80. Mem. bd. human rels. hate violence response alliance City of L.A., 1992; chair corp. coun. execs. United Way of L.A., 1992, mem. task force fund on devel., 1990; mem. citizen's adv. com. Eastside Neighborhoods Revitilazation Study, 1992; mem. steering com. Coalition for Humane Immigration Rights of L.A., 1992; mem. steering com. Jerusalem Coop. Cities Project, 1991; chair Refugee Forum L.A. County, 1984-85, chair vol. agy. com., 1983-84; treas. Calif. Refugee Forum, 1985-86. Democrat. Home: 4508 Flintstone Rd Alexandria VA 22306 Office: Refugee Resettlement Office 370 L'Enfant Promenade SW Washington DC 20447

LIN, ALICE LEE LAN, physicist, researcher, educator; b. Shanghai, China, Oct. 28, 1937; came to U.S., 1960, naturalized, 1974; m. A. Marcus, Dec. 19, 1962 (div. Feb. 1972); 1 child, Peter A. AB in Physics, U. Calif., Berkeley, 1963; MA in Physics, George Washington U., 1974. Statis. asst. dept. math. U. Calif., Berkeley, 1962-63; rsch. asst. in radiation damage Cavendish Lab. Cambridge (Eng.) U., 1965-66; info. analysis specialist Nat. Acad. Scis., Washington, 1970-71; teaching fellow, rsch. asst. George Washington U., Catholic U. Am., Washington, 1971-75; physicist NASA/Goddard Space Flight Ctr., Greenbelt, Md., 1975-80, Army Materials Tech. Lab., Watertown, Mass., 1980—. Contbr. articles to profl. jours. Mencius Ednl. Found. grantee, 1959-60. Mem. AAAS, N.Y. Acad. Scis., Am. Phys. Soc., Am. Ceramics Soc., Am. Acoustical Soc., Am. Men and Women of Sci., Optical Soc. Am. Democrat. Home: 28 Hallett Hill Rd Weston MA 02193-1753 Office: Army Materials Tech Lab Mail Stop MRS Bldg 39 Watertown MA 02172

LIN, SUE-JEAN, financial services executive; b. Taiwan, China, Nov. 29, 1958; d. Su-Chou and Chin-Len (Chen) L.; m. Steven Shou-han Wang, Nov. 29, 1986; children: Lawrence Wang, Imbert Wang. BS, U. Nev., 1980, MBA, 1983. Cert. mgmt. acct. Acct. Sierra Pacific Power Co., Reno, Nev., 1980-83, supr., acctg. system, 1983-86; fin. systems specialist Northrop Corp., Anaheim, Calif., 1986-89; mgr. fin. systems Allergan, Inc., Irvine, Calif., 1989-90, mgr. info. systems, 1991-92, sr. project mgr., 1993-94, dir. fin. shared svcs., 1994—; cert. mgmt. acct. program dir., NAA/Reno chpt., 1985. Home: 20962 Calle Celeste Lake Forest CA 92630-2233 Office: Allergan Inc 2525 Dupont Dr Irvine CA 92715-1531

LINCLAU, DENISE MARIE, nursing administrator; b. Detroit, Oct. 1, 1951; d. Adolph Francis and Marie Yvonne (DeWolf) L.; m. Donald M. Miller, Apr. 11, 1975 (div.); children: Martin Linclau-Miller, Russell Linclau-Miller. BSN, Wayne State U., 1974; MSA, Cen. Mich. U., 1985; student, Wharton Sch. Exec. Mgmt./, Leonard Davis Inst. Health Care Mgmt., U. Pa., 1988, 94. RN, Mich.; cert. nurse adminstr., critical care, trauma nurse. Instr. nursing edn. St. John Hosp., 1973-85; dir. ednl. svcs. Holistic Health Care, Inc., Warren, Mich., 1985-86; clin. mgr. critical care div. Hutzel Hosp. Detroit Med. Ctr., 1986-88; adminstrv. mgr. critical care div. Harper Hosp. Detroit Med. Ctr., 1988-95; dir. critical care nursing svcs. Detroit Receiving Hosp., Detroit Med. Ctr., 1989-95; asst. v.p. critical care and emergency svcs. Sinai Hosp., Detroit, 1995—; instr. advanced courses (ACLS) Am. Heart Assn., 1982—, instr. basic courses BCLS, 1985—. Instr. and mem. U.S. Power Squadron Grosse Pointe, Mich., 1984—; del. People to People Ambassadors Program to People's Republic of China, 1991. Recipient Nat. Disting. Svc. award Registry Nursing Am. Nurses Assn., 1988. Mem. AAUW, ANA, AACN (Pres. award 1975), Am. Assn. Nursing Execs., Am. Orgn. Nurse Execs., Am. Burn Assn., Am. Assn. Female Execs., Sigma Theta Tau, Sigma Iota Epsilon. Roman Catholic. Home: 1375 Grayton Rd Grosse Pointe Park MI 48230

LINCOLN, LOUISE HASSETT, museum curator, art historian, writer; b. Balt., Mar. 23, 1947; d. Charles Clifford and Martha Julia (Ludlum) Hassett; m. Bruce K. Lincoln, Apr. 17, 1971; children: Martha Louise, Rebecca Anne. BA, Bryn Mawr Coll., 1969; MA, U. Del., 1972. Editor Mpls. Inst. Arts, 1977-80, asst. curator, 1980-84, assoc. curator, 1984-87, curator African, Oceanic and New World Cultures, 1988—; adj. prof. art history U. St. Thomas, St. Paul, 1994—; mem. rev. panel Nat. Endowment for the Arts, Washington, 1993; cons., writer World Book Ency., Chgo., 1992. Author: Finished in Beauty, Southwest Indian Silver, 1983, Assemblage of Spirits: Idea and Image in New Ireland, 1987, Visions of the People: A Pictorial History of Plains Indian Life, 1992 (Wittenborn award 1993); contbr. articles to profl. jours. Recipient Scholarly Contbn. award Am. Assn. Mus. Curators, 1993. Mem. Am. Anthropol. Assn., Native Am. Art Studies Assn., Pacific Arts Assn., African Studies Assn. Office: Mpls Inst Arts 2400 3rd Ave S Minneapolis MN 55404-3506

LINCOLN, SANDRA ELEANOR, chemistry educator; b. Holyoke, Mass., Mar. 11, 1939; d. Edwin Stanley and Evelyn Ida (Mackie) L. BA magna cum laude, Smith Coll., 1960; MSChem, Marquette U., 1970; PhD in Inorganic Chemistry, SUNY, Stony Brook, 1982. Tchr., prin. Oak Knoll Sch., Summit, N.J., 1964-74; tchr. Holy Child High Sch., Waukegan, Ill., 1974-76; lectr. chemistry, dir. fin. aid Rosemont (Pa.) Coll., 1976-78; teaching asst. SUNY, Stony Brook, 1978-82; assoc. prof. chemistry U. Portland, Oreg., 1982—; researcher Oreg. Grad. Ctr., Beaverton, 1982—. Contbr. articles to profl. jours. Cath. sister Soc. Holy Child Jesus, 1963—. Recipient Pres.'s award for Teaching, SUNY, Stony Brook, 1981; Burlington No. Outstanding scholar, 1987. Mem. Am. Chem. Soc., Phi Beta Kappa, Sigma Xi. Democrat. Home: 5431 N Strong St Portland OR 97203-5711 Office: U Portland 5000 N Willamette Blvd Portland OR 97203-5750

LIND, TERRIE LEE, social services administrator; b. Spokane, Wash., June 5, 1948; d. Clifford and Edna Mae (Allenbach) Presnell; m. Stephen George Lind, Aug. 29, 1970 (div. Mar. 1981); children: Erica Rachel, Reid Christopher. BA cum laude, Wash. State U., 1970, MA, 1971. Cert. tchr., Wash., Ariz.; cert. in Porch Index Communicative Ability. Specialist communication disorders U. Tex., Houston, 1971-73; clin. supr. The Battin Clinic, Houston, 1973-76; specialist communication disorders Spokane Guilds Sch., 1980-82; program coord. Fresno (Calif.) Community Hosp., 1982-87; program adminstr. Advantage 65* sr. access program Health Dimensions, Inc., San Jose, Calif., 1987-90; dir. patient svcs. San Jose Med. Ctr., 1990-92; dir. cmty. svcs. Planned Parenthood of Mar Monte, San Jose, 1992—; cons. Adolescent Chem. Dependency Unit, Fresno, 1984-87. Mem. AAUW (officer 1976-82), Am. Speech and Hearing Assn. (cert., Continuing Edn. award 1985-86), Wash. Speech and Hearing Assn. (co-chmn. state conv. program com. 1981-82), Soc. Consumer Affairs Profls. in Bus., Wash. State U. Alumni Assn. Home: 1717 Don Ave San Jose CA 95124 Office: Planned Parenthood 1691 The Alameda San Jose CA 95126

LINDBERGH, ANNE SPENCER MORROW (MRS. CHARLES AUGUSTUS LINDBERGH), author; b. Englewood, N.J., 1906; d. Dwight Whitney and Elizabeth Reeve (Cutter) Morrow; m. Charles Augustus Lindbergh, May 27, 1929 (dec. 1974); children: Charles Augustus (dec.), Jon Morrow, Land Morrow, Anne Spencer, Scott Morrow, Reeve Morrow. Grad., Miss Chapin's Sch., N.Y.C., Smith Coll., Northampton, Mass., 1928; MA (hon.), Smith Coll., Northampton, Mass., 1935; LLD (hon.), Amherst Coll., 1939, Univ. Rochester, 1939. Author: North to the Orient, 1935, Listen! The Wind, 1938, The Wave of the Future, 1940, The Steep Ascent, 1944, Gift from the Sea, 1955, The Unicorn and Other Poems, 1935-1955, 1956, Dearly Beloved, 1962, Earth Shine, 1969, Christmas in Mexico: 1972, 1971, Bring Me a Unicorn: Diaries and Letters of Anne Morrow Lindbergh, 1972, Hour of Gold, Hour of Lead: Diaries and Letters of Anne Morrow Lindbergh, 1929-2932, 1973, Locked Rooms and Open Doors: Diaries and Letters of Anne Morrow Lindbergh, 1932-1935, 1974, The Flower and the Nettle: Diaries and Letters of Anne Morrow Lindbergh, 1936-1939, 1976, War Within and Without: Diaries and Letters of Anne Morrow Lindbergh, 1939-1944, 1980, The People in Pineapple Place, 1982, Bailey's Window, 1984, The Worry Week, 1985, The Hunky-Dory Diary, 1986, The Shadow on the Dial, 1987, Nobody's Orphan, 1987, The Prisoner of Pineapple Place, 1988, Next Time, Take Care, 1988, Tidy Lady, 1989, Travel Far, Pay No Fare, 1992, Three Lives to Live, 1992, Nick of Time, 1994. Recipient two prizes for lit. work Smith Coll.; cross of honor (for part in survey of trans-Atlantic air route) U.S. Flag Assn., 1933; Hubbard gold medal (for work as co-pilot and radio operator in flight of 40,000 miles over five continents) Nat. Geog. Soc., 1934. *

LINDBLOM, MARJORIE PRESS, lawyer; b. Chgo., Mar. 17, 1950; d. John E. and Betty (Grace) P.; m. Lance E. Lindblom, June 13, 1971; children: Derek, Ian. AB cum laude, Radcliffe Coll., 1971; JD with honors, U. Chgo., 1978. Bar: Ill. 1978, U.S. Dist. Ct. (no. dist.) Ill. 1978, U.S. Ct. Appeals (7th cir.) 1978, U.S. Ct. Appeals (10th cir.) 1983, U.S. Supreme Ct. 1983, U.S. Ct. Appeals (5th cir.) 1984. Assoc. Kirkland & Ellis, Chgo., 1978-84, ptnr., 1984-94; N.Y.C., 1994—; asst. dir. fiscal affairs Ill. Bd. Higher Edn., 1973-75; budget analyst Ill. Bur. Budget, Office of Gov., 1972-73; admissions officer Princeton U., 1971-72; adj. prof. Northwestern U., Evanston, Ill., 1994. Comment editor U. Chgo. Law Rev., 1977-78. Bd. dirs. Chgo. Lawyers Com. for Civil Rights Under Law, 1989-94, Pub. Interest Law Initiative, 1989-94. Mem. ABA, Chgo. Coun. Lawyers (bd. govs. 1987-91, legal counsel 1986-87), 7th Cir. Bar Assn., Women's Bar Assn. of Ill. Office: Kirkland & Ellis Citicorp Ctr 153 East 53rd St New York NY 10022

LINDBORG, SUSAN ELIZABETH, artist, tattooist, educator; b. Redwood City, Calif., Mar. 15, 1954; d. Clarke B. and Roxie C. (Warren) Pierce; (div. Sept. 1981); children: Ryan Robert, Shannon Elizabeth. Student, Brooks Coll. for Women, 1973. Artist Golden Hills Art Assn., Milpitas, Calif., 1970-74; tattooist Modified Motorcycle Assn., Calif., 1980-89; tchr. tattoo The Art of Cosmetic Tattoo, Campbell, Calif., 1992-94; artist Calif. Artists, 1968—, Pacific Art Festivals, Pine Grove, Calif., 1993—. Artist: (book) Washing the Saints Feet, 1992; author: The Art of Cosmetic Tattoo, 1993. Recipient award in home econs. Bank of Am., Milpitas, 1972; named Tattooist of the Yr., Nat. Tattoo Conv., L.A., 1991. Home: 53-601 Kam Hwy Hauula HI 96717

LINDBURG, DAYTHA EILEEN, physician assistant; b. Emporia, Kans., June 24, 1952; d. Kenneth Eugene and Elsie Eileen (Smith) L. BS cum laude, Kans. State U., 1974; BS magna cum laude, Wichita State U., 1976. Registered cert. physician asst. Physician asst. in family practice Fredrickson Clinic, Lindsborg, Kans., 1976-93; physician asst. in ob/gyn. Mowery Clinic, Salina, Kans., 1993—; cons. McPherson County (Kans.) Health Dept., 1983—. Bd. dirs. McPherson County Humane Soc., 1989-93; choir mem. Messiah Luth. Coun., Lindsborg, 1981—, liturgist, 1991—, mem. Altar Guild, 1976—. Kans. Bd. Regents scholar, 1970-71, Kans. State U. scholar, 1972, 73. Mem. Assn. of Physician Assts. in Obstetrics and Gynecology, Kans. Acad. Physician Assts., Am. Acad. Physician Asst.

LINDE, LUCILLE MAE (JACOBSON), motor-perceptual specialist; b. Greeley, Colo., May 5, 1919; d. John Alfred and Anna Julia (Anderson) Jacobson; m. Ernest Emil Linde, July 5, 1946 (dec. Jan. 1959). BA, U. No. Colo., 1941, MA, 1947, EdD, 1974. Cert. tchr. Calif., Colo., Iowa, N.Y.; cert. ednl. psychologist; guidance counselor. Dean of women, dir. residence C.W. Post Coll. of L.I. Univ., 1965-66; asst. dean of students SUNY, Farmingdale, 1966-67; counselor, tchr. West High Sch., Davenport, Iowa, 1967-68; instr. grad. tchrs. and counselors, univ. counselor, researcher No. Ariz. U., Flagstaff, 1968-69; vocat. edn. and counseling coord. Fed. Exemplary Project, Council Bluffs, Iowa, 1970-71; sch. psychologist, counselor Oakdale Sch. Dist., Calif., 1971-73; sch. psychologist, intern Learning and Counseling Ctr., Stockton, Calif., 1972-74; pvt. practice rsch. in motor-perceptual tng. Greeley, 1975—; researcher ocumeter survey, Lincoln Unified Sch. Dist., Stockton, 1980, 81, 82, Manteca (Calif.) High Sch., 1981; motor perceptual tng. LUSD, 1981, 82, YMCA, Stockton, 1983, 84, others; spkr. Social Sci. Edn. Consortium, Colo. U., 1993; presenter seminars in field. Author: Psychological Services and Motor Perceptual Training, 1974, Guidebook for Psychological Services and Motor Perceptual Training (How One May Improve In Ten Easy Lessons!), 1992, Manual for the Lucille Linde Ocumeter: Ocular Pursuit Measuring Instrument, 1992, Motor-Perceptual Training and Visual Perceptual Research (How Students Improved in Seven Lessons!), 1992, Effects of Motor-Perceptual Training on Academic Achievement and Ocular Pursuit Ability, 1992; inventor ocumeter, instrument for measuring ocular tracking ability, 1989, and target for use with ocumeter, 1991. Mem. Rep. Presdl. Task Froce, 1989-90, trustee, 1991, life and charter mem., 1994—; mem. Rep. Nat. Com., 1990, 93-94, Rep. Nat. Com. on Am. Agenda, 1993, Nat. Rep. Congrl. Com., 1990, 92, 93, 95. Recipient Presdl. Medal of Merit and lapel insignia, 1988, Nat. Rep. Senatorial Com., 1991-94, Appreciation cert. Nat. Rep. Congl. Com., 1991, cert. of recognition Rep. Nat. Com., 1992, lapel pin Rep. Senatorial Inner Cir., 1992, Rep. Presdl. Commemorative Honor Roll, 1993, award Nat. Fedn. Rep. Women, 1989-94, Rep. Senatorial Freedom medal, 1994, Rep. Legion of Merit medallion and lapel pin, 1994; named to Rep. Nat. Hall of Honor, 1992. Mem. AAUP, NAFE, Nat. Assn. Sch. Psychologists and Psychometrists (speaker at conf. 1976), Nat. Fedn. Rep. Women, The Smithsonian Assocs., Nat. Trust for Hist. Preservation, Am. Pers. and Guidance Assn., Nat. Assn. Student Pers. Adminstrs., Nat. Assn. Women Deans and Counselors, Calif. Tchrs. Assn., Internat. Platform Assn., Independence Inst., Learning Disabilities Assn. (speaker internat. conv. 1976), Rep. Senatorial Inner Circle (senatorial commn. & cert. 1991, 93), Greeley Rep. Women's Club, Pi Omega Pi, Pi Lambda Theta. Home: 1954 18th Ave Greeley CO 80631-5208

LINDELL, ANDREA REGINA, college dean, nurse; b. Warren, Pa., Aug., 21, 1943; d. Andrew D. and Irene M. (Fabry) Lefik; m. Warner E. Lindell, May 7, 1966; children—Jennifer I., Jason M. B.S., Villa Maria Coll., 1970; M.S.N. Catholic U., 1975, D.N.Sc., 1976; diploma R.N., St. Vincent's Hosp., Erie, Pa. Instr. St. Vincent Hosp. Sch. Nursing, 1964-66; dir. Rouse Hosp., Youngsville, Pa., 1966-69; supr. Vis. Nurses Assn., Warren, Pa., 1969-70; dir. grad. program Cath. U., Washington, 1975-77; chmn., assoc. dean U. N.H., Durham, 1977-81; dean, prof. Oakland U., Rochester, Mich., 1981-90, dean, Schmidlapp prof. nursing U. Cin., 1990—; bd. dirs. CHEMED Corp.; cons. Moorehead U., Ky., 1983. Editor; Jour. Profl. Nursing, 1985; contbr. articles to profl. jours. Mem. sch. bd. Strafford Sch. Dist., N.H., 1977-80; Gov.'s Blue Ribbon Commn. Direct Health Policies, Concord, N.H., 1979-81; vice chmn. New England Commn. Higher Edn. in Nursing, 1977-81; mem. Mich. Assn. Colls. Nursing, 1981—. Named Outstanding Young Woman Am., 1980. Mem. Nat. League Nursing, Am. Assn. Colls. Nursing, Sigma Theta Tau. Democrat. Roman Catholic. Avocations: water skiing; roller skating; reading; fishing; camping; Office: Univ Cincinnati Main Campus Cincinnati OH 45221

LINDEMANN, CORRINE E., technical writer, editor; b. Rush City, Minn., Dec. 17, 1933; d. Walter Alec and Elsie Elizabeth (Rodbom) Erickson; m. A. Willis Lindemann, May 15, 1954 (div. Jan. 1981); children: James, David, Brad. AS in Interior Design, St. Petersburg Jr. Coll., 1975; BA in Liberal Studies, Antioch U. West, 1982; cert. in Technical Writing, DeAnza Coll., 1990, cert. in Elec. Pub., 1993. Co-dir. Scene II Mag., Clearwater, Fla., 1968; co-owner Scene II Boutique, Clearwater, Fla., 1968-70; sec. GE, Sunnyvale, Calif., 1977-84; interior designer freelance, San Jose, Calif., 1986-87; writer, editor freelance, Silicon Valley, Calif., 1990—. Treas. Upper-Pinnellas County Young Rep. Club., 1968. Mem. NAFE, Commonwealth Club of Conn., Nu Omega (pres. 1971-72), Beta Sigma Phi (recording sec. 1978-79).

LINDEMULDER, CAROL ANN, interior designer, artist; b. San Diego, May 2, 1936; d. Franklin Geert and Leone Augusta (Oltman) L. BA in Decorative Arts, U. Calif., Berkeley, 1959; postgrad. in fine arts, San Diego State U., 1965-67. Tchr. interior design and fine arts adult edn. divsn. San Diego City Schs., 1960-67; with Milo of Calif., Inc. subs. Milo Electronics Corp., 1968-73, corp. staff asst., 1972, asst. to dir. mktg., 1972-73; with Frazee Industries, 1975-77; owner, designer-artist Call Carol, San Diego, 1976--; former instr. U. Calif. Extension, San Diego, instr. San Diego landscape painting, 1993—. One-woman show Point Loma Art Assn., 1967, Scandia Interiors, 1977, Cen. Fed. Savs. & Loan, 1978, John Duncan Interiors, 1979, Villa Montezuma Mus., 198l; exhibited in group shows Calif. Western U., 1963, Jewish Community Ctr., 1963-64, So. Calif. Expn., 1964, San Diego Mus. Art, 1966, 7l, 75, San Diego State U., 1974, Spectrum Gallery, 1985, A.R.T. Beasley Gallery, 1985, Atrium Gallery, Mich., 1989, San Diego Artist Showcase, 1991. Coord. Christmas program San Diego Community Vol. Bur., 196l; a founder, treas., bd. dirs. Save Our Heritage Orgn., 1969-7l, pres., 1974-75, 79-81; mem. San Diego Hist. Sites Bd., 1985-93, vice chmn., 1985-92; founder, pres. Save the Coaster Com., 1981-83; co-founder San Diego Hist. Preservation Endowment Fund, 1990; mem. Calif. Preservation Found. Named Vol. of Month, San Diego Community Vol. Bur., 196l; recipient President's commendation Save Our Heritage Orgn., 1984. Mem. Nature Conservancy, Jr. League San Diego. Republican. Office: PO Box 81718 San Diego CA 92138

LINDEN, LYNETTE LOIS, bioelectrical engineer; b. Cheyenne, Wyo., Feb. 5, 1951; d. Byron Nels and Mary Ann (Savage) L. BA with honors, U. Calif., Santa Cruz, 1972; MS, MIT, 1974, PhD, 1988. Asst. engr. Burroughs Corp., Pasadena, Calif., 1969-70; engr., cons. Burroughs Corp., La Jolla, Calif., 1971-73; teaching asst. U. Calif., Santa Cruz, 1974-76; teaching asst. MIT, Cambridge, Mass., 1973-75, tutor, 1976-79; engr. Lincoln Labs., Lexington, Mass., 1979-80; asst. prof. engring. Boston U., 1980-90; ind. rsch. sci. Watertown, Mass., 1990—. Contbr. articles to profl. jours. Mem. AAAS, N.Y. Acad. Scis., Soc. Women Engrs., Sigma Xi. Office: PO Box 138 Watertown MA 02272-0138

LINDERMAN, JEANNE HERRON, priest; b. Erie, Pa., Nov. 14, 1931; d. Robert Leslie and Ella Marie (Stearns) Herron; m. James Stephens Linderman; children: Mary Susan, John Randolph, Richard Webster, Craig Stephens, Mark Herron, Elizabeth Stewart. BS in Indsl. and Labor Rels., Cornell U., 1953; MDiv magna cum laude, Lancaster Theol. Sem., 1981; postgrad., clin. pastoral edn., Del. State Hosp., New Castle, 1981. Ordained priest, Episcopal Ch. Mem. pers. staff Hengerer Co., Buffalo, 1953-55; chaplain Cathedral Ch. St. John, Wilmington, Del., 1981-82; priest-in-charge Christ Episcopal Ch., Delaware City, Del., 1982-87; vicar Christ Episcopal Ch., 1987-91; assoc. rector St. Andrew's Episcopal Ch., Wilmington, Del., 1991-95, priest in charge, 1995—; chair human sexuality task force, Diocese of Del., 1981-82, mem. clergy compensation com. and diocesan coun., 1982-86, pres. standing com., 1991—, com. on constitution and canons, 1989. Author, editor hist. study papers. Bd. dirs. St. Michael's Day Nursery, Wilmington, 1985-88; mem. secondary schs. com. Cornell U.; bd. dirs., chmn. pers. com. Geriatrics Svcs. of Del., 1989—, sec. bd., 1993—. Mem. Episcopal Women's Caucus, Del. Episcopal Clergy Assn., Nat. Assn. Episcopal Clergy, DAR, Mayflower (elder, surgeon 1983—), Dutch Colonial Soc. Del., Stoney Run Questers (pres.), Cornell Women's Club Del. (pres. 1966), Women of St. James the Less (pres. 1972-73), Women's Witnessing Community at Lambeth, Patriotic Soc. in Del. (sec.-treas. conv. 1965-68), Chi Omega. Republican. Home: 307 Springhouse Ln Hockessin DE 19707-9691 Office: St Andrews's Episcopal Ch Eighth And Shipley St Wilmington DE 19801

LINDGREN, JENNIFER GOUX, business executive, financial planner, educator; b. L.A., Jan. 10, 1946; d. Warren Goux and Violet (Louis) Goux Knupp; m. Larry E. Lindgren, July 1, 1967; children: Todd E., Kristen E., Kurt W. BA in Psychology, UCLA, 1967. Cert. tchr., Calif.; CFP; gen. securities lec., Calif.; lic. ins. agt., Calif. Elem. tchr. L.A. City Schs., 1968-72; art tchr. Sierra Canyon Day Camp, Newhall, Calif., summer 1975,76; co-owner Lindgren's Jewelry, Porterville, Calif., 1978—; instr. Porterville Adult Sch., 1988-94; investment exec. Baraban Securities/Volker Ins., Woodland Hills, Calif., 1989-94, Fin. West Group, Tarzana, Calif., 1994, Investment Ctrs. of Am., Bank of Sierra, Porterville, 1995—. Troop co-leader Girl Scouts U.S., Porterville, 1984-86; student host family Rotary Internat., Porterville, 1990-91; sec.-treas. Porterville Edn. Found., 1988—. Mem. AAUW (pres., v.p., other offices 1987—, Named Gift honoree 1991), Inst. CFPs, Central Valley Soc. CFPs, UCLA Alumni Assn., Porterville C. of C., Zonta Club. Republican. Office: 90 N Main St Porterville CA 93257

LINDH, PATRICIA SULLIVAN, banker, former government official; b. Toledo, Oct. 2, 1928; d. Lawrence Walsh and Lillian Winifred (Devlin) Sullivan; m. H. Robert Lindh, Jr., Nov. 12, 1955; children: Sheila, Deborah, Robert. B.A., Trinity Coll., Washington, 1950, LL.D., 1975; LL.D., Walsh Coll., Canton, Ohio, 1975, U. Jacksonville, 1975. Adoption case worker Cath. Charities, Chgo., 1954-55; editor Singapore Am. Newspaper, 1957-62; spl. asst. to counsellor to Pres., 1974, spl. asst. to Pres., 1975-76; dep. asst. sec. state for ednl. and cultural affairs Dept. State, 1976-77; v.p., dir. corp. communications Bank Am., Los Angeles, 1978-84, World Banking P.R. Bank Am., San Francisco, 1985—. Trustee La. Arts and Sci. Center, 1970-73, Calif. Hosp. Med. Ctr., 1979-84; bd. dirs. Jr. League of Baton Rouge, 1969, Children's Bur. Los Angeles, 1979, 84, USO Northern Calif.; Rep. state vice chairwoman La., 1970-74; Rep. nat. committeewoman, La., 1974; mem. pub. affairs com. San Francisco World Affairs Coun., 1985; adv. bd. Jr. League Los Angeles, 1980-84; bd. visitors Southwestern U. Sch. Law. Roman Catholic. Home: 850 Powell St San Francisco CA 94108-2051

LINDLEY, PAMELA GAY, educator; b. Danville, Ill., Mar. 23, 1949; d. Paul Coolidge and Mildred Loujean (Trent) Garland. BS, Lincoln Meml. U., Harrogate, Tenn., 1972; MS, Radford U., 1975; EdD, Tex. Woman's U., 1991. Cert. 1-6 tchr., nursery sch., pre-kindergarten, spl. edn., learning disabilities tchr., Md. Libr. technician Civilian Pers. Office, Wildflecken, Germany, 1979-80; customer clk. Chesapeake & Potomac Tel. Co., Forestville, Md., 1981-82; tchr. adults Ctrl. Tex. Coll., Killeen, 1983-85; substitute tchr. Alexandria (Va.) City Schs., 1987-90; elem. tchr. Prince George's County Schs., Temple Hills, Md., 1989-90; tchr. reading and math. Ednl. Inroads, Hyattsville, Md., 1991; tchr. high sch. math. Potomac Job Corps, Washington, 1992; tchr. King George (Va.) County Schs., Md., 1993—. Maj. USAR, 1975—. Mem. AAUW, Tex. Assn. for Edn. Young Children, Orton Dyslexia Assn., Res. Officers Assn. (scholar 1987), Tex. N.G. Assn. (life, scholar 1988), Pi Lambda Theta. Democrat. Baptist. Home: PO Box 259 Welcome MD 20693 Office: King George High Sch King George VA 22485

LINDLEY, PATRICIA S., employment manager; b. Columbus, Ohio, Jan. 28, 1957; d. Ed and Jean Lindley. BS, Ohio State U., 1979. Employment rep. Bank One, Columbus, Ohio, 1983-85; sr. employment rep. Bank One, Columbus, 1985-86, staffing coord., 1986-91, employment mgr., 1991-92, sr.

employment mgr., 1992—. Vol. Canine Companions, Inc., Delaware, Ohio, 1993. Mem. Pers. Assn. Ctrl. Ohio. Office: Bank One Columbus 800 Brooksedge Blvd Columbus OH 43271-0610

LINDNER, PATRICIA REID, state representative, lawyer. BS in Speech, Northwestern U., 1961; MS in Polit. Sci., U. Colo., 1966; JD, No. Ill. U., 1980. Bar: Ill. 1981, Fed. Trial Bar, 1981. Asst. pub. defender Kane County, Ill., 1981-84; ct. apptd. atty. Kane County, 1984-86; pvt. practice Aurora, Ill., 1986—; state rep. State of Ill., Springfield. Bd. dirs. Aurora Found., Gary Wheaton Bank of Fox Valley, YWCA, chair pers. com., Community Div. for Capital Campaign, Legal Aid Vol., co-chair Women of Distinction Luncheon, 1991; active Rep. Women's Club and numerous coms. Mem. Ill. State Bar Assn., Kane County Bar Assn. (chair legis. com.), Women in Mgmt., Kane County Family Law Com. Home: PO Box 661 Densmore Rd Aurora IL 60506*

LINDQUIST, BARBARA ANN, design company executive; b. Jackson Heights, N.Y., May 21, 1951; d. Rudolph Daniel and Josephine Marie (Papay) Kuchman; 1 child, Lisa Marie. BS in Home Econs., Calif. State U., Northridge, 1974. V.p. Bullock's Dept. Store, Palm Desert, Calif., 1975-91, R.H. Macy's Store, Calif. and Ariz., Carter Hawley Hall Dept. Store, Las Vegas, Nev., 1991-93; pres., CEO Feature Presentation, Las Vegas, 1993—. Bd. dirs. Scottsdale (Ariz.) Symphony, 1990-91; active Childhelp USA, 1987—, Tiempo de los Niños, 1987—, United Way Bd., 1987, 94. Mem. Las Vegas C. of C., Fashion Group Inc., Network Exec. Women in Hospitality, Delta Delta Delta (scholar 1973). Republican. Office: Feature Presentation 1005 S Cimarron Rd Las Vegas NV 89128

LINDQUIST, MARSHA, financial executive; b. N.Y.C.; d. Seymour Bookstaber and Jessie Lehmann. BS, Am. U., 1971; MBA, Frostburg U., 1981. Mgr. mgmt. info. Bechtel Corp., Gaithersburg, Md.; bus. mgr. Martin Marietta, Greenbelt, Md.; mgr. fin. analysis McDonnell Douglas, Rockwell, Md.; controller Mgmt. Systems Designers, Vienna, Va.; dir. contracts META, Arlington, Va. Mem. Inst. Mgmt. Accts., Nat. Contract Mgmt. Assn., Am. U. Alumni Assn. (pres.). Home: 8400 Harron Valley Ct Gaithersburg MD 20879-4917

LINDQUIST, SUSAN PRATZNER, museum executive; b. San Francisco, Dec. 20, 1940; d. Carleton Edward Pratzner and Edith Crane (Johnson) Cox; m. Philip George Lindquist, Oct. 27, 1962; children: Tucker D., Travis C. BS in Edn., Lesley Coll., 1962; MEd, Northeastern U., Boston, 1979; postgrad., U. Calif., Berkeley, 1994. Tchr. local sch. Marshfield, Mass., 1962-63, Peabody, Mass., 1963-66; coord. early intervention Dept. Mental Health, Hyannis, Mass., 1976-79; supr. Dept. Social Svcs., Hyannis, 1981; program dir. Latham Sch., Brewster, Mass., 1982-85; vol. coord. Cape Cod Mus. Natural History, Brewster, 1986—, assoc. dir., 1987, pres., 1987—; corporator Cape Cod Five Bank, 1994, trustee. Bd. dirs. Cape Cod C. of C., 1993, Mus. Inst. for Teaching Sci., Boston; trustee Cape Cod Acad., 1994; mem. Brewster Bd. Appeals, 1977-87. Office: Cape Cod Mus Natural History PO Box 1710 Rte 6A Brewster MA 02631

LINDSAY, ANNE WOLFE, lawyer; b. Elizabeth, N.J., Apr. 2, 1934; d. Sidney G. and Lenore (Weinberg) Wolfe; m. Robert A. Lindsay, June 13, 1954 (div. Nov. 1974); children: Ellen, David, Joshua, Adam, Peter; m. Robert V. Edwards, Dec. 31, 1985. BA in Sociology, Syracuse U., 1955; JD, Cleve. State U., 1977. Bar: Ohio 1977. Asst. dir. law City of Cleve., 1977-79; staff atty. Chessie System R.R.s, Cleve., 1979-84; pres. Iris Inc. (Mfr.), Cleve., 1984—; pvt. practice Cleveland Heights, Ohio, 1984—; legal cons. Productive Solutions, Euclid, Ohio, 1992—. V.p. bd. dirs. Ams. United for Separation of Ch. and State, Washington, 1978-82; bd. dirs. Ams. for Religious Liberty, Silver Spring, Md., 1982—. Home and Office: Iris Inc and Law Office 2525 Edgehill Rd Cleveland Hts OH 44106-2403

LINDSAY, DIANNA MARIE, educational administrator; b. Boston, Dec. 7, 1948; d. Albert Joseph and June Hazelton (Mitchell) Raggi; m. James William Lindsay III, Feb. 14, 1981. BA in Anthropology, Ea. Nazarene Coll., 1971; MEd in Curriculum and Instrn., Wright State U., 1973, MEd in Social Studies Edn., 1974, MEd in Edn. Adminstrn., 1977; EdD in Edn. Adminstrn., Ball State U., 1976. Supr. social edn. Ohio Dept. Edn., Columbus, 1976-77; asst. prin. Orange City Schs., Pepper Pike, Ohio, 1977-79; prin. North Olmsted (Ohio) Jr. High Sch., 1979-81; dir. secondary edn. North Olmsted City SChs., 1981-82; supt. Copley (Ohio)-Fairlawn City Schs., 1982-85; prin. North Olmsted High Sch., 1985-89, New Trier High Sch., Winnetka, Ill., 1989—; bd. dirs. Harvard Prins. Ctr., Cambridge, Mass. Contbr. articles to profl. jours. Bd. dirs. Nat. PTA, Chgo., 1987-89 (Educator of Yr. 1989). Named Prin. of Yr. Ohio Art Tchrs., 1989, one of 100 Up and Coming Educators, Exec. Educator Mag., 1988; recipient John Vaughn Achievements in Edn. North Cen. Assn., 1988. Mem. AAUW, Ill. Tchrs. Fgn. Lang., Rotary Internat., Phi Delta Kappa. Methodist. Office: New Trier High Sch 385 Winnetka Ave Winnetka IL 60093-4295

LINDSAY, DORIS WHITE, recording industry executive, publishing executive; b. Cagayan, Misamis, Philippines, Sept. 3, 1937; d. M.J.W. and Rita (Rothgeb) W.; children: John, Jean Lindsay Ingraham, Mark R. BA, Elon Coll., 1957; postgrad., U. N.C., 1960. Pres. Fountain Records, High Point, N.C., 1979—. Mem. Nat. Acad. Recording Artists Soc., Country Music Assn., Coun. of Garden Clubs (pres. High Point chpt.), Civitan (Citizen of Yr. 1968). Home: 1203 Biltmore Ave High Point NC 27260-3613

LINDSAY, ELENA MARGARET, nurse; b. Evansville, Ind., Oct. 6, 1941; d. Gordon Graham and Irma Louise (Berkemeier) Kuhn; m. Robert Dean Lindsay Jr., Dec. 29, 1988; children: Maria, Robert. BS in Nursing, U. Evansville, 1963. RN. Evening coord., head nurse Welborn Meml. Bapt. Hosp., Evansville, 1969-74; dir. nurses Warrick Hosp., Boonville, Ind., 1975-76; head nurse St. Mary's Med. Ctr., Evansville, 1976-87; staff nurse, HIV counselor, BCLS instr., ACLS VA Med. Ctr., Salt Lake City, 1987-94. 2d lt. U.S. Army, 1961-64. Mem. DAV (life aux. mem.), AACN, Soc. Orthopedic Nurses (past pres.). Republican. Mem. United Ch. of Christ. Home: 5064 South Heath Ave Kearns UT 84118-6972 Office: 500 Foothill Dr Salt Lake City UT 84148-0001

LINDSAY, JUNE CAMPBELL MCKEE, communications executive; b. Detroit, Nov. 14, 1920; d. Maitland Everett and Josephine Belle (Campbell) McKee; BA with honors in Speech (McGregor Fund Mich. grantee), U. Mich., 1943; Electronics Engring. certificate Signal Corps Ground Signal Svc., 1943; postgrad. (Inst. Gen. Semantics grantee), U. Chgo., 1944-45, N.Y. U. (Armour grantee), 1945-46, Columbia U., 1946-47, Wayne State U., 1960-64, U. Mich., 1964-70, 78—; MA, Specialist-in-Aging Cert., Inst. of Gerontology, 1982; m. Powell Lindsay, Nov. 25, 1967; 1 child, Kristi Costa-McKee. Coord., activator McKee Prodns., Detroit, 1943-56, Being Unltd., 1957—, InterBeing, Inc., 1979—, M.U.T.U.A.L. A.I.D., 1981—; info. dir. Suitcase Theatre, Inc., Lansing and Ann Arbor, Mich. Cons. Cornelian Corner Detroit, Inc., 1957-63, Islamic Ctr. Found. Soc., Detroit, 1959-62, City Ann Arbor Human Rels. Commn., 1966-68, Urban Adult Edn. Inst., Detroit, 1968-69, Mich. Bell Tel. Co., Detroit, 1969, African Art Gallery Founders, Detroit Inst. Arts, 1964, WKAR-TV, Mich. State U., 1971—. Mem. Nat. Caucus, Ctr. for Black Aged; bd. dirs. Mus. Youth Internat., Saline, Mich., Ann Arbor Community Devel. Corp. Chaplain's asst. Univ. Hosp., Ann Arbor, 1971-72; program dir. People-to-People, Ann Arbor, 1971-72; Suitcase Theatre tour coord. Brit. Empire's Leprosy Relief Assn., 1972—; assembly cons. Baha'i Faith, 1960—; mem. Comprehensive Health Planning Coun. S.E. Mich., Baha'i Internat. Health Agy., Inst. for Advancement of Health, Catherine McAuley Health Ctr. Share and Care Support Group. Recipient Award for Excellence Mich. Ednl. Assn., 1971, Mich. Assn. Classroom Tchrs., 1972; exec. dir. Powell Lindsay Meml. Program in Theatre and Communications, Louhelen Baha'i Sch. and Residential Coll., U. Mich., Flint, Mott Community Coll., 1988—. Mem. ACLU, Soc. for Individual Responsibility, Am. Women in Radio and TV, Broadcast Pioneers, Am. Fedn. Advt., Internat. Platform Assn., Gray Panthers, Planetary Citizens, Am. Assn. Adult and Continuing Edn., Am. Pub. Health Assn., Wellness Assocs., Mich. Assn. Holistic Health, Internat. Health Found., Inst. Study Conscious Evolution, Am. Soc. on Aging, Mich. Health Coun., Nat. Coun. on Aging, U.S., Assn. Humanistic Psychology, Assn. Holistic Health, Internat. Soc. for the Study of Subtle Energies and Energy Medicine, Nat. Inst. for the Clin. Application of Behavioral Medicine, Assn. Baha'i Studies, Mental Health Assn. in Mich., Mich. Soc. Gerontology, Washtenaw County Council on Aging, Nat. Coun. Sr. Citizens, Am. Assn. Ret. Persons, People's Med. Soc., Giraffe Soc., World Future Soc., Nat. Trust for Hist. Preservation, Orgn. Devel. Inst. (registered orgn. devel. profl. 1988), UN Assn. of the U.S.A. Home: 2339 S Circle Dr Ann Arbor MI 48103-3442

LINDSAY, SHARON WINNETT, lawyer, consultant; b. N.Y.C., Apr. 10, 1949; d. William Richardson and Rosemary (Walton) Winnett; m. George Peter Lindsay, Sept. 8, 1973; children: William Charles, Kimberly Michelle. BA, MA, Fordham U., 1970; JD, Harvard U., 1973. Bar: N.Y. 1974, U.S. Dist. Ct. (fed. dist.), U.S. Ct. Appeals 1974. Atty. Milbank, Tweed, Hadley & McCloy, N.Y.C., 1973-83; v.p., asst. gen. counsel J.P. Morgan & Co., Inc., N.Y.C., 1983—. Trustee Fordham U., Bronx, N.Y., 1994—; bd. dirs. Scarsdale Middle Sch., N.Y., 1990—. Mem. ABA, N.Y. State Bar Assn., Bar Assn. City of N.Y., Scarsdale Golf Club, Stockbridge Golf Club, Phi Beta Kappa. Roman Catholic. Home: 25 Mamaroneck Rd Scarsdale NY 10583 Office: Morgan & Co 60 Wall St New York NY 10260

LINDSAY-HARTZ, JANICE, clinical psychologist, researcher; b. Sioux City, Iowa, Dec. 4, 1947; d. Charles Douglas and Margaret Gertrude (Barbour) Lindsay; m. Steven Edward Marshall Hartz, June 12, 1976. ScB summa cum laude, Brown U., 1970; MA, Clark U., 1975, PhD, 1980. Lic. clin. psychologist, marriage and family therapist. Psychology rsch. asst. U. Pa., Phila., 1970-72; biology and sci. tchr. Germantown Friends Sch., Phila., 1971-73; family therapy trainee The Nathan Ackerman Inst. for Family Therapy, N.Y.C., 1976-78; psychotherapist Bklyn. Ctr. for Psychotherapy, 1978-79; clin. psychologist Psychiat. Assocs. at Grant Ctr. Hosp., Miami, Fla., 1980-82; pvt. practice Miami, 1982—; asst. prof. Sch. Profl. Psychology, Nova U., Ft. Lauderdale, Fla., 1982-84. Author chpts. to books; contbr. articles to profl. jours. Activist Save Sunset Cove, Key Largo, Fla., 1987-89. NSF fellow, 1974-78; scholar Clark U., 1973-74. Mem. APA, Fla. Psychol. Assn., Dade County Psychol. Assn. (newsletter editor 1985-88, social responsibility chair 1993—), Fla. Psychoanalytic Soc. (friend), Psychologists for Social Responsibility, Sigma Xi. Democrat. Office: 1570 Madruga Ave PH2 Miami FL 33146

LINDSEY, ANNE LOVELL, management consultant; b. Mpls., June 26, 1950; d. Ray Warren and Louise Lovell (Randall) L. BA, Mt. Holyoke Coll., 1972; MBA, Harvard U., 1977. CPA, Ill. Underwriter Aetna Ins. Co., Hartford, Conn., 1972-75; acct. Arthur Andersen & Co., Chgo., 1977-80, mgmt. cons., 1980-87; mgmt. cons. Andersen Cons., London, 1987-90, assoc. ptnr., 1990-93; assoc. ptnr. Andersen Cons., Chgo., 1993—. Office: Andersen Cons 69 W Washington Chicago IL 60602

LINDSEY, BONNIE JOAN, vocational school educator; b. Oklahoma City, May 4, 1935; d. David DeWitt and Genevieve Catherine (Rucinski) Bevans; m. Donald G. Lindsey, Apr. 3, 1963 (div. 1974): 1 child, Jon Erik. AS, Mt. San Jacinto Coll., 1973; BA Vocat. Edn., Long Beach State U., 1975, MA Vocat. Edn., 1977. Tchr. Riverside (Calif.) Regional Occupation program, 1972-74, mem. adv. com., 1983-85; supr. Colton-Redlands-Yucaipa Regional Occupation Program, Redlands, Calif., 1974-75; assoc. prof. Riverside Community Coll., 1975-89, prof. emeritus, 1989—; tchr. Idaho State U., Pocatello, 1990-93, chmn. dept. health occupations, 1990—. Author: Medical Assisting, 1974, 75, 89; co-author Professional Medical Assistant: Clinical Assisting, 1990. Mem. Am. Assn. Med. Transcription (pres. Orange Empire chpt. 1985-88), Am. Assn. Med. Assts., Calif. Assn. Med. Assisting Instrs., Vocat. Indsl. Clubs of Am. (named Advisor of Yr. 1974), Epsilon Pi Tau. Democrat. Roman Catholic. Home: 1504 Sierra Dr Pocatello ID 83201-5946 Office: Idaho State U Campus Box 8380 Pocatello ID 83209-8380

LINDSEY, D. RUTH, physical education educator; b. Kingfisher, Okla., Oct. 26, 1926; d. Lewis Howard and Kenyon (King) L. BS, Okla. State U., 1948; MS, U. Wis., 1954; PEd, Ind. U., 1965. Cert. kinesiotherapist, 1970. Instr. Okla. State U., Stillwater, 1948-50, Monticello Coll., Alton, Ill., 1951-54, DePauw U., Greencastle, Ind., 1954-56; prof. Okla. State U., Stillwater, 1956-75; vis. prof. U. Utah, Salt Lake City, 1975-76; prof. phys. edn. Calif. State U., Long Beach, 1976-88; prof. emeritus phys. edn. Calif. State U., 1988—; freelance author, cons. Westminster, Calif. Co-author: Fitness for the Health of It, 6th edit., 1989, Concepts of Physical Fitness, 8th edit., 1993, Fitness for Life, 4th edit., 1992, Concepts of Physical Fitness and Wellness, 1993, The Ultimate Fitness Book, 1984, Survival Kit for Those Who Sit, 1989; editor: Perspectives: Jour. of Western Soc. for Phys. Edn. Coll. Women, 1988—. Amy Morris Homans scholar, 1964; recipient Disting. and Meritorious Svc. Honor award Okla. Assn. Health, Phys. Edn. and Recreation, 1970, Meritorious Performance award Calif. State U., 1987, Julian Vogel Meml. award Am. Kinesiotherapy Assn., 1988. Fellow AAHPERD, Am. Kinesiotherapy Assn., Calif. Assn. Health, Phys. Edn., Recreation and Dance, Nat. Coun. Against Health Fraud, Orange County Nutrition Coun., Tex and Acad. Authors Assn., Phi Kappa Phi. Republican. Baptist.

LINDSEY, DOTTYE JEAN, marketing executive; b. Temple Hill, Ky., Nov. 4, 1929; d. Jesse D. and Ethel Ellen (Bailey) Nuckols; m. Willard W. Lindsey, June 14, 1952 (div.). BS, Western Ky. U., 1953, MA, 1959. Owner, Bonanza Restaurant, Charleston, W.Va., 1965; tchr. remedial reading Alice Waller Elem. Sch., Louisville, 1967-75, tchr., 1953-67, 1975-84, contact person for remedial reading, 1968—; regional mgr. A.L. Williams Fin. Mktg. Co., 1988—; profl. model Cosmo/Casablancas Modeling Agy., Louisville, 1984-89; with Primerica Fin. Svcs. (formerly A.L. Willams Fin. Svcs.), Louisville, 1988—; model, 1984-89; regional mgr. Primerica Fin. Svcs., 1988—. Treas. Met. Louisville Women's Polit. Caucus, 1980-88, Ky. Women's Polit. Caucus, 1988-91; bd. sponsor ROTC Western Ky. U., 1950; local precinct capt., 1987—; election officer, 1984—; treas. Ky. Women's Polit. Caucus, 1988-91. Named Miss Ky., 1951. Mem. NEA, Ky. Edn. Assn., Jefferson County Tchrs. Assn., various polit. action coms., Internat. Reading Assn., Am. Childhood Edn. Assn. Democrat. Baptist.

LINDSEY, JACQUELYN MARIA, editor; b. Buffalo, June 6, 1952; d. George Henry and Patricia Ann (Rott) Bilkey; m. Timothy Paul Murphy, Jan. 29, 1970 (div. May 1981); children: Paul Jeffrey, Jeremy Michael; m. Warren Lee Eckert, Dec. 5, 1987 (div. June 1992); m. Donald J. Lindsey, Nov. 5, 1994. Student, Ind. U., 1984. Adminstrv. asst. Western N.Y. Cath. Visitor, Buffalo, 1979-81; sec. religious edn. Our Sunday Visitor, Huntington, Ind., 1981-84, editorial asst. periodicals dept., 1985, staff editor periodicals and books, editor My Daily Visitor, 1985-91, coord. Diocesan edits., 1986-88, assoc. editor books, 1987-90, editor trade books, 1990-93, acquisitions editor trade books, 1991—, acquisitions editor religious edn., 1991—. Editor, compiler: Photo Directory of U.S. Catholic Hierarchy, 1987, 90, 93; editor Leaves Marianhill Missionaries, 1991—. Candidate for rep. Ind. Gen. Assembly 21st Dist., 1984; mem. LaFontaine Arts Coun., Huntington County, 1985-88; mem. Huntington County Dems., 1986-88. Mem. Cath. Press Assn. Office: Our Sunday Visitor Pub 200 Noll Plz Huntington IN 46750-4304

LINDSEY, JOHANNA, writer; b. 1952. Writings include (romance novels) Captive, 1977, A Pirate's Cove, 1978, Fires of Winter, 1980, Paradise Wild, 1981, Glorious Angel, 1982, So Speaks the Heart, 1983, The Heart of Thunder, 1983, A Gentle Feuding, 1984, Brave the Wild Wind, 1984, Love Only Once, 1985, Tender is the Storm, 1985, A Heart So Wild, 1986, When Love Awaits, 1986, Hearts Aflame, 1987, Secret Fire, 1987, Tinder Rebel, 1988, Silver Angel, 1988, Defy Not the Heart, 1989, Savage Thunder, 1989, Warrior's Woman, 1990, Gentle Rogue, 1990, Once a Princess, 1991, Keeper of the Heart, 1991, Prisoner of My Desire, 1991, Man of My Dreams, 1993, Angel, 1993, Surrender My Love, 1994. Office: Avon Books 105 Madison Ave New York NY 10016-7418*

LINDSEY, RETHA F., college official; b. Snyder, Tex., June 15, 1949; d. Joe W. and Muriel (Hammons) Vincent; 1 child, Kevin W. AA, Western Tex. Coll., 1980; BA, U. Tex., Odessa, 1984. Asst. editor Sweetwater (Tex.) Reporter, 1976-79; corr. Abilene Reporter News, Sweetwater, 1979-81; account exec. Adams-Shelton Communications, Abilene and Odessa, Tex., 1981; reporter Odessa American, 1981-82; news dir. Odessa Coll., 1982, dir. news and info., 1982-89; dir. coll. rels. Keene (N.H.) State Coll., 1992—; bd. dirs. Dist. IV Council Advancement and Support of Edn., 1986-88. Bd. dirs. Permian Basin Ctr. Battered Women, Midland, Tex., 1985-89, pres. bd. 1989. Recipient Excellence award Coun. Advancement and Support Edn., 1985, 87, 88, 89. Mem. Permian Basin Advt. Fedn. (pres. 1990, Gold Addy award Midland-Odessa 1986, 87, 88, 89). Office: Keene State Coll 229 Main St Keene NH 03435

LINDSEY, SUSAN BUSH, accountant; b. Joliet, Ill., June 13, 1936; d. Robert E. and Marie (Schwartz) Bush; m. John Marshall Lindsey, Aug. 13, 1961; children: Elizabeth Rebecca Lindsey Locke, Rebecca Susan. BA, Ind. State U., 1958; MS, U. Ill., 1959; student, Thomas More Coll., 1977-80, Temple U., 1980. CPA, Pa. Asst. libr. U. Sch. So. Ill. U., Carbondale, 1959-61; instr. libr. sci. U. Ill., Urbana, 1961-63; acquisitions dept. U. Ill. Libr., Urbana, 1962-64; vol. libr. Silvergate Elem. Sch., San Diego, 1973-75; sub. tchr. Beechwood Sch., Fort Mitchell, Ky., 1976-77; staff acct. Rainer and Co., Newtown Square, Pa., 1982, Stein, Goldberg & Co., Phila., 1982-85; owner, sole practice Swarthmore, Pa., 1985—. Vol. Community Accts., Phila., 1985; treas. Swarthmore Pub. Lib., 1985-88; mem. Swarthmore Bus. and Profl. Assn., 1986-93. Mem. Am. Libr. Assn., Am. Soc. Women Accts., Am. Woman's Soc. CPAs, Pa. Inst. CPAs (exec. com. Phila. chpt. 1993—, various state and local coms.). Presbyterian. Office: 200 Yale Ave Swarthmore PA 19081-2202

LINDSEY, TRACY WALKER, accountant; b. Florence, Ala., June 7, 1962; d. Howard Turner and Virginia Estelle (Cox) Walker; m. Gaythor Durant Lindsey, May 16, 1987. BS in Bus. Adminstrn., U. Ala., Tuscaloosa, 1984, MA in Fin., 1988. Assoc. cert. profl. mgr. Staff acct. Jamison, Money, Farmer and Co., Tuscaloosa, 1984-86; in-charge acct. Blue Cross and Blue Shield Ala., Birmingham, 1988—. Cons. applied econs. Jr. Achievement, Birmingham, 1988—. Mem. Inst. Mgmt. Accts. (editor newsletter Footnotes 1993, projects coord. 1994—), Leadership Devel. Assn. (treas. 1993-94).

LINDSTEDT-SIVA, (KAREN) JUNE, marine biologist, oil company executive; b. Mpls., Sept. 24, 1941; d. Stanley L. and Lila (Mills) Lindstedt; m. Ernest Howard Siva, Dec. 20, 1969. Student, U. Calif.-Santa Barbara, 1959-60, U. Calif.-Davis, 1960-62; B.A., U. So. Calif., 1963, M.S., 1967, Ph.D., 1971. Asst. coordinator Office Sea Grant Programs U. So. Calif., 1971; environ. specialist So. Calif. Edison Co., Rosemead, 1971-72; asst. prof. biology Calif. Luth. U., 1972-73; sci. advisor Atlantic Richfield Co., Los Angeles, 1973-77, sr. sci. advisor, 1977-81, mgr. environ. scis., 1981-86, mgr. environ. protection, 1986—; mem. Nat. Sci. Bd., 1984-90; mem. panels on environ. issues Nat. Rsch. Coun.; mem. Polar Rsch. Bd., 1994—; mem. EPA Panel on Environ. Risk Reduction, 1992-94; mem. NAS Alaska Panel; mem. biology adv. coun. Calif. State U.-Long Beach, 1980-92; bd. dirs. So. Calif. Acad. Scis., 1983-93, pres., 1990-92; mem. Marine Scis.; adv. coun. U. So. Calif. Inst. Coastal and Marine Scis.; trustee Bermuda Biol. Sta. for Rsch.; chmn. Oil Spill Conf., San Antonio, 1989, API Oil Spills Com. Contbr. articles to profl. jours. Recipient Calif. Mus. Sci. and Industry Achievement award, 1976, Trident award for Marine Scis., 11th Ann. Rev. Underwater Activites, Italy, 1970, Achievement award for Advancing Career Opportunities for Women, Career Planning Council, 1978; research grantee; distg. scholar biology Calif. Lut. U. Colloquim Scholars, 1988. Fellow ASTM (award of merit 1990), So. Calif. Acad. Scis.; mem. AAAS, Soc. Petroleum Industry Biologists (pres. 1976-80), Marine Tech. Soc., Calif. Native Plant Soc., Am. Inst. Biol. Sci., Phi Beta Kappa, Sigma Xi, Phi Kappa Phi. Office: Atlantic Richfield Co 515 S Flower St Los Angeles CA 90071-2200

LINDSTROM, CATHERINE CAUTHORNE, psychologist, management consultant; b. Roanoke, Va., June 6, 1949; d. Edward Tolton and Margaret Louise (Mutter) Via; m. Jon C. Lindstrom, Apr. 11, 1987. BSN, Med. Coll. Va., 1971; MS, Old Dominion U., 1983, PhD, 1987. Lic. psychologist, Ariz. Rsch. assoc. Ctr. for Applied Psychol. Studies, Norfolk, Va., 1983-85, Ea. Va. Med. Authority, Norfolk, Va., 1984-86; mgmt. cons. Orgnl. Devel. Tidewater, Virginia Beach, 1984-87; corp. dir. health sys. Samaritan Health Svc., Phoenix, 1987-90; dir. patient centered care project John C. Lincoln Hosp. and Health Sys., Phoenix, 1990—; spkr. Internat. Nursing Sci. Congress, Washington, 1992, Nat. Assn. Hosp. Radiology Adminstrs., San Francisco, 1992, Nat. Assn. Rehab. Nurses, Denver, 1993, Am. Assn. Nurse Execs., 1994. Contbr. articles to profl. jours. Vol. mediator Cmty. Mediation Svcs., Phoenix, 1989—; mem. gov.'s task force emergency med. svc. tng. State of Va., Richmond, 1975-77. Fellow Old Dominion U., 1983-84. Mem. APA, Assn. Nurse Execs., Patient Centered Care Network (chair 1993—), Coun. Health Profls., Ariz. Hosp. Assn. Office: John C Lincoln Hosp 250 E Dunlap Phoenix AZ 85020

LINDULA, PAMELA O'HARA, lawyer; b. St. Cloud, Minn., Dec. 7, 1962; d. Cecil Alvin and Delores Evelyn (Henry) O'Hara; m. Mark Elvin Lindula, May 4, 1993; 1 child, Katherine Anna. BS, Coll. St. Benedict, St. Joseph, Minn., 1984; JD, U. Minn., 1988. Bar: Minn. Law clk. Court of Appeals, State of Minn., St. Paul, 1988-89; sr. atty. Bankers Systems, St. Cloud, Minn., 1989—. Mem. NOW. Office: Bankers Systems Inc PO Box 1457 Saint Cloud MN 55302

LINEBERGER, BARBARA JO, association executive; b. Lincolnton, N.C., July 20, 1938; d. Yates Webb and Grace Elizabeth (Keever) L. BS in Math., Guilford Coll., 1960; MSW, U. N.C. Chapel Hill, 1978. Diplomate Acad. Cert. Social Workers. Math. tchr. Harford County (Md.) Bd. Edn., Bel Air, 1960-62; tchr. Lincolnton City Schs., 1962-63; tchr. math. New Hanover County (N.C.) Bd. Edn., Wilmington, 1963-64; youth program dir. YWCA, Wilmington, N.C., 1964-78, program coorelator, 1978-81, exec. dir., 1981—; mem. com. to involve local assns. with World Coun. meeting YWCA USA-World Coun., N.Y.C., 1987. Editor 30 various booklets on parliamentary law, 1992-93. Treas. and personnel chair Task Force Against Family Violence, Wilmington, 1978-83; chair day in the park Cape Fear United Way, Wilmington, 1982; bd. dirs. Women's Shelter, Wilmington, 1984-85; pres. and treas. Domestic Violence Shelter and Svcs., Wilmington, 1986, 87-89, bd. tnr., 1989—. Recipient Dir.'s award Cape Fear United Way, 1982. Mem. NASW, Nat. Assn. YWCA Execs. (bd. dirs. and conf. chair 1993), Nat. Assn. Parliamentarians (chair editing com. 1992-93), Delta Kappa Gamma. Office: YWCA of Wilmington 2815 S College Rd Wilmington NC 28412-6826

LINERT, SUSAN MARIE, oil company executive; b. Seattle, May 18, 1949; d. Edwin Joseph and Gilda Leah (Taylor) L. Diploma, Skagit Valley Coll., Mt. Vernon, Wash., 1969; BS in Petroleum Engring., N.Mex. Inst. Mining and Tech., 1984. Rsch. and devel. equipment operator Petroleum Tech. Corp., Redmond, Wash., 1977-79; well completion supr. William Perlman Co., Ignacio, Colo., 1985; asst. dept. mgr. Best Products, Lynnwood, Wash., 1986-87; prodn. supt. Kimbell Oil Co. Tex., Farmington, N.Mex., 1987—. Mem. Soc. Petroleum Engrs. Home: 1218 Mccoy Ave Aztec NM 87410-1732 Office: Kimbell Oil Co Tex 300 W Arrington St Ste 220 Farmington NM 87401-8433

LINFORD, MARY SUZANNE (SUE LINFORD), food distibrution executive; b. Indpls., Apr. 15, 1935; d. Robert William and Mary Catherine (Madden) Schmutte; widowed; children: Christopher, Douglas, Mark, Paul, Julie. Student, U. Alaska, 1959-80. Lic. real estate agt., Alaska. Various positions Indpls. and Anchorage, 1949-1973; acct., treas., gen. mgr., pres. Linford of Alaska Wholesale Food Distbr., Anchorage, 1973-83; pres., gen. mgr. Linford of Alaska, Anchorage, 1985—; exec. dir. Common Sense for Alaska, Anchorage, 1984-86; property mgr. Sue Linford Investments, Anchorage, 1983—; pvt. practice real estate, Anchorage, 1985—. Editor State PTA Bulletin, 1969-71. Mem. Alaska Blue Ribbon Commn., 1979-80, various city commns. City of Anchorage, 1979-92, budget commr., 1988-89; commr. Port of Anchorage, 1989-92; chmn. libr. bds. City of Anchorage, Greater Anchorage Borough and Municipality of Anchorage, 1969-77; founding mem., officer Anchorage Arts Coun., 1971-74; bd. dirs. Anchorage Symphony, 1990—, Alaska Zoo, 1989—; vice chmn., mem. Archdiocesan Fin. Coun.; pres. Anchorage Sch. Bd., 1974-77; active Anchorage PTA; mem. Anchorage Concert Chorus, 1981—. Mem. Alaska C. of C., Anchorage C. of C. (sec.-treas., v.p., bd. dirs. 1977-81, treas., bd. dirs. 1992—, Outstanding Cmty. Svc. Gold Pan award 1981), Ruralcap (cert. of appreciation 1981, outstanding contbn. award 1985), Chaine des Rotisseurs, Bailliage U.S.A., Petroleum Club Anchorage, San Francisco Tennis Club (life), Capt. Cook Athletic Club, Zonta (bd. dirs. 1968-80), Rotary. Office: Linford of Alaska Inc 135 Cordova St Anchorage AK 99501

LING, KATHRYN WROLSTAD, health association administrator; b. Watertown, Wis., Aug. 3, 1943; d. Jeffrey Harold and Constance Devina (Egre) Wrolstad; stepchildren: Renee Rainey, Roz Harper. BS in History and Polit. Sci., U. Wis., 1965. Supr. recreation ARC, DaNang, Cam Ran Bay, VietNam, 1968; assoc. exec. dir. Am. Cancer Soc., Evanston, Ill., 1968-71, exec. dir., 1971-73; exec. dir. Montgomery County Unit Am. Cancer Soc., Md., 1973-76, cons. income devel., 1976, dir., profl. edn. cancer incidence and end results, 1976-78, dir. income devel., 1978-82; exec. dir. Am. Cancer Soc., Chgo., 1982-84; assoc. exec. dir. Alzheimer's Disease and Related Disorders Assn., Chgo., 1985-87, v.p. community svcs., 1988-91, sr. v.p. chpt. Family Svcs. and Edn. divsn., 1991-93; cons. Nat. Aphasia Assn.; pres. The Leadership Edge, Chgo. Home: 1255 N Sandburg Ter Chicago IL 60610-2258

LING, LILY HSU-CHIANG, real estate executive, accountant; b. Taipei, Republic of China, May 29, 1952; came to U.S., 1974; d. John Y. and Sophia (Siu-ho) Liu; m. William Chong-Seng Ling, Dec. 23, 1976; 1 child, Johnathan. B of Bus., Chengchi U., Republic of China, 1974; MBA, Fla. State U., 1975. CPA, Tex. Acct. The Lummus Co., Houston, 1978-79; gen. ledger acct. Black, Sivalls & Bryson Inc., Houston, 1979-81; pres. Lily H. Ling & Co., Houston, 1981—; sales mgr. Robert William Homes, Inc. and L. William Homes, Houston, 1991—. Bd. dirs. Tex. Buddhist Assn., Houston, 1985-90. Mem. AICPA, Tex. Soc. CPAs, Houston Bd. Realtors, Houston Soc. Chinese-Am. CPAs, Chengchi U. Alumni Assn. (pres. Houston chpt. 1984). Office: Lily H Ling & Co Ste 178 7011 Harwin Houston TX 77036

LINGER, ELOISE LAVONNE, political scientist; b. Washington, July 9, 1944. BA in History, Fed. City Coll., 1972; MA in Polit. Sci., New Sch. for Social Rsch., 1992, postgrad. in sociology and hist. studies, 1988—. Neurology rsch. tech. Children's Hosp., Boston, 1964-68; mem. nat. staff Student Mobilization Com. to End War in Vietnam, Washington, 1969-71; Boston area and New England regional coord. Student Mobilization Com. to End War in Vietnam, 1965-69; mem. nat. staff Women's Nat. Abortion Action Coalition, Washington, 1971-72; lab. tech. Tex. Air Control Bd., Austin, 1972-74; speech writer Amb. Sabah Qabbani, editor all English lang. materials Syrian Arab Republic Embassy, Washington, 1974-75; tchr. world history and social studies Riyadh (Saudi Arabia) Internat. Community Sch., 1975-77; rank and file worker activist UAW, Internat. Assn. Machinists, Internat. Ladies' Garment Workers Union, Internat. Union Elec. Workers, Mass. and N.J., 1979-87; adminstr. Ctr. for Studies Social Change New Sch. Social Rsch., N.Y.C., 1987-93; tchr. U. Havana, Cuba, 1993-94; polit. sociologist. Contbr. articles to profl. jours. Recipient Davis Putter award, 1990, Rsch. awards New Sch. for Social Rsch., 1992, Improvement of Doctoral Dissertations award NSF, 1994; Elinor Goldmark Black Dissertation fellow New Sch. for Social Rsch., 1993. Office: New Sch for Social Rsch Ctr for Studies Social Change 64 University Pl # 400 New York NY 10003

LINGG, BARBARA ANN, statistician; b. Bklyn.. BA, Queens Coll., 1964; MA, U. Md., 1970. Claims examiner Social Security Adminstrn., Flushing, N.Y., 1964-67; statistician Social Security Adminstrn., Balt., 1970-80, supervisory statistician, 1980—; grad. asst. U. Md., College Park, 1968-69; social worker Prince Georges County, Md., 1970. Contbr. articles to profl. publs. Vol. Pets on Wheels, Balt., 1988—. Mem. Am. Statis. Assn., Am. Sociol. Assn.

LINGLE, KATHLEEN MCCALL, consultant, marketing executive, entrepreneur; b. Berea, Ohio, Aug. 24, 1944; d. Arthur Vivian McCall and Mary M. (Maxwell) Miller; m. John Hunter Lingle, Sept. 3, 1968 (div. 1991); 1 child, Michael Cameron; m. Sam F. Serrapede, Aug. 15, 1993. BA, Occidental Coll., 1966; MS, Ohio State U., 1977. Project dir. Ohio State U. Hosp., Columbus, 1977-78; rsch. assoc. Ednl. Testing Service, Princeton, N.J., 1978-82; mgr. mktg. services Gulton Industries, Princeton, 1982-84; rsch. dir. Rsch. 100, Princeton, 1984-85; dir. mktg. planning and rsch. Applied Data Research, Princeton, 1985-88; Western European sales mgr. Heuristics Software, Inc., Sacramento, 1988-89; pres., chief exec. officer Princeton Leadership Dynamics, 1989-90; rsch. dir. Families & Work Inst., N.Y.C., 1990-91; dir. tng. Families & Work Inst., 1991-93; cons. Wyatt Co., N.Y.C., 1994—. Vice pres. ops. Unitarian Ch. of New Brunswick (N.J.), 1983-84; served with Peace Corps, Chile and Venezuela, 1966, 69-72. Mem. NAFE, Am. Mktg. Assn., Am. Mgmt. Assn., Bus. and Profl. Women (chairperson membership com., 1990-91), N.J. Assn. Women Bus. Owners, Princeton Network Profl. Women, Princeton Area C. of C. (mem. membership com.), Am. Field Svc. (Princeton chpt.). Democrat. Home: 50 Coriander Dr Princeton NJ 08540-9434

LINGLE, MARILYN FELKEL, freelance writer, columnist; b. Hillsboro, Ill., Aug. 16, 1932; d. Clarence Frederick and Anna Cecelia (Stank) Felkel; m. Ivan L. Lingle, Oct. 4, 1950; children: Ivan Dale, Aimee Lee Lingle Galligan, Clarence Craig. Sec. Ill. State Police, 1950; with welfare dept. Ill. Pub. Aid, Hillsboro, 1951-52; researcher Small Homes Council, Champaign, 1952-53; sec. Hillsboro Schs., 1954; office, payroll clk. Eagle Picher Zinc, Hillsboro, 1955-56; continuity dir. Sta. WSMI, Litchfield, Hillsboro, 1966-87; adv. bd. Am. Savs. Bank/Citizens Savs. Bank, vice chmn., 1986-93. Contbr. poetry to profl. jours. Fin. chmn. Hillsboro Hosp. Aux., 1972; literacy vol. Graham Correctional Ctr., Hillsboro, 1986—; pres., bd. dirs. Montgomery Players and Encore Play Theatre, 1954-70; child sponsor through World Vision. Mem. Cousteau Soc., Internat. Wildlife Fedn., Nat. Wildlife Fedn., Phi Theta Kappa Internat. Democrat. Lutheran. Club: Hillsboro Country. Avocations: bridge, golf, gardening, travel, reading.

LINGLE, MELINDA HAGGERTY, public relations executive; b. Wichita Falls, Tex., Sept. 2, 1964; d. Carl Walter and Rebecca Irene (Worsham) Haggerty Bennett; m. Joey Ric Lingle, May 30, 1987; 1 child, Chandler Ross. BA in Communications, Cameron U., 1993. Sales assoc. Estee Lauder/Dillards, Lawton, Okla., 1983-87; radio announcer KMGZ-Magic 95, Lawton, 1985-86; co-owner Joey Lingle Greyhounds, Blair, Okla., 1987—; acct. exec. Altus (Okla.) TV Prodn., 1990-91; v.p. pub. affairs Shortgrass Arts & Humanities Coun., Altus, 1991-93; cons. recruiting video We. Okla. State Coll., 1992-93; cons. publications Main Street Altus, Inc., 1994. prodr., writer (TV comml.) "Drive You Wild", 1990 (MIDI award). Reporter-historian Beta Mothers, Altus, 1991—. Recipient State Media award Am. Cancer Soc., 1991, Phi Theta Kappa We. Okla. State Coll., 1992, Lambda Pi Eta Cameron U., 1993. Mem. Okla. Greyhound Assn. (sec. treas. 1994—), Speech Communications Assn. Republican.

LINHART, LETTY LEMON, editor; b. Pittsburg, Kans., Sept. 22, 1933; d. Robert Sheldon and Lois (Wise) Lemon; m. Robert Spayde Kennedy, June 8, 1955 (div. 1978); children: Carole Shea, Nancy Schrimpf, Nina Kennedy; m. Daniel Julian Linhart, June 9, 1986. BS, BA in English and Journalism, U.Kans., 1955; MS in Journalism, Boston U., 1977. Reporter Leavenworth (Kans.) Times, 1954; editor Human Resources Rsch. Office George Washington U., Washington, 1955-56; editor Behavior Rsch. Lab. Harvard Med. Sch., Boston, 1956-58; instr. Boston YMCA, 1960-64; freelance writer and columnist, 1975—; editor Somerville (Mass.) Times, 1975-77; pub. rels. dir. Lettermen of Lexington, Mass., 1978; instr. English Rollins Coll., Winter Park, Fla., 1978-79, Valencia Community Coll., Orlando, Fla., 1978-82, U. Cen. Fla., Orlando, 1979-82; editor Fla. Specifier, Winter Park, 1982-85, Mobile Home News, Maitland, Fla., 1985-86; instr. English Seminole C.C., Sanford, Fla., 1986-94; Elderhostel instr. Canterbury Rsch. Ctr., 1994—; editor Oviedo (Fla.) Voice, 1994—. Author: Are These Extravagant Promises, 1989; contbr. articles to profl. jours. Pres. MIT Dames Boston, 1958-59, Boston Alumnae of Delta Delta Delta, 1959-62; dist. pres Delta Delta Delta, Tex., 1962-65; mem. Friends of Cornell Mus., Winter Park, Fla. Named Outstanding Collegiate Delta Delta Delta, 1955. Mem. NAFE, Ctrl. Fla. Jazz Soc. (bd. dirs. 1983-93), Internat. Platform Soc., Soc. of Women Execs., Altrusa Club (publicity com. 1980-83), Univ. Club of Winter Park, Mortar Bd., Phi Beta Kappa (Belmont, Mass. pres. 1965-78), Theta Sigma Phi, Sigma Delta Chi, Delta Sigma Rho. Home: PO Box 1131 Oviedo FL 32765-1131 Office: Oviedo Voice 169 W Broadway Oviedo FL 32765

LINK, MAE MILLS (MRS. S. GORDDEN LINK), space medicine historian and consultant; b. Corbin, Ky., May 14, 1915; d. William Speed and Florence (Estes) Mills; m. S. Gordden Link, Jan. 11, 1936. B.S., George Peabody Coll. for Tchrs., Vanderbilt U., 1936; M.A., Vanderbilt U., 1937; Ph.D., Am. U., 1951; grad., Air War Coll., 1965. Instr. social sci. Oglethorpe U., 1938-39; instr. English Drury Coll., 1940-41; assoc. dir. edn. Ga. Warm Springs Found., 1941-42; mil. historian Hdqrs. Army Air Forces, 1943-45, Office Mil. History, Dept. of Army, 1945-51; spl. asst. to surgeon gen., sr. med. historian U.S. Air Force, Washington, 1951-62; cons. in documentation and space medicine historian NASA, Washington, 1962-64; coord. documentation, life scis. historian NASA, 1964-70; rsch. assoc. Ohio State U. Found., 1970-72. Author: Medical Support of the Army Air Forces in World War II, 1955, Annual Reports of the U.S. Air Force Medical Service, 1949-62, Space Medicine in Project Mercury, 1965; (with others) USA/USSR Joint Publ. Foundations of Space Biology and Medicine, 1976; Editor: U.S. Air Force Med. Service Digest, 1957-62; contbr. to Collier's Ency., Ency. Brit., Funk and Wagnall's New Ency., profl. jours. Recipient Meritorious Service award U.S. Air Force, 1955, Ann. Outstanding Performance awards, 1956-62, Outstanding Alumna award Sue Bennett Coll., 1977. Fellow Am. Med. Writers Assn. (past pres. Middle Atlantic region); mem. Aerospace Med. Assn., Air Force Hist. Found. (charter), Internat. Congress History Medicine, Societe Internat. d'Histoire de la Medecine, Planetary Soc. (charter). Republican. Episcopalian.

LINK, PADDY, legislative staff member; married; 2 children. BA, Mary Washington Coll., 1972. Legis. dir. to Rep. Larry Pressler, 1975-81, then spl. asst. to Rep. Larry Pressler; congl. liaison officer Office of Sec. NOAA Dept. of Commerce, 1981, dep. then dir. Office Legis. Affairs NOAA, 1982-89; cons. subcom. on tech., environment and aviation House Com. on Sci., Space and Tech., 1989-92, Rep. legis. asst. subcom. on tech., environment and aviation, 1992-93; staff dir. to Senator Larry Pressler, 1993—. Office: Sen Larry Pressler R-SD 283 Senate Russell Office Bldg Washington DC 20510*

LINK, SHIRLEY ANN, telecommunications executive; b. Cleve., Apr. 22, 1946; d. Walter John and Margaret Irene (Kurtz) Korniet; m. Charles H. Martin, Sept. 10, 1965 (div. 1969); m. Gerald Smelko, Dec. 26, 1970 (div. 1979); children: Brian Martin, James Martin, Paul Smelko; m. Steven William Link, Nov. 15, 1985 (div. 1993). Student, Cuyahoga Community Coll., 1979-80, 82, Cleve. State U., 1981, 83. Sales mgr. Grolier, Strongsville, Ohio, 1978-80; sec. Lessem Glass, Cleve., 1980-82; interior designer Cleve., 1981-83; bookkeeper N&H, Inc., Cleve., 1983-84; asst. to project mgr. DeBartolo Corp., Northfield, Ohio, 1984-86; v.p. Clifton Phone Systems, Cleve., 1986-93; with Vista Communications, Garfield Heights, Ohio, 1993—. Mem. NAFE, Soc. Telecommunications Profls., Smithsonian Instn. (assoc.). Democrat. Office: Vista Communications 4720 Warner Rd Garfield Hts OH 44125-1117

LINKKILA, LESLIE ELIZABETH, marketing professional, microbiologist; b. Putnam, Conn., Aug. 11, 1959; d. Peter Henry and Eleanor Jean (Csiki) L.; m. Philip Joseph DiNuovo, Oct. 8, 1988. BS, U. Conn., 1980; MS, U. N.H., 1983. Rsch. asst. Dept. Microbiology, Univ. N.H., Durham, 1980-83; rsch. scientist Jackson Estuarine Lab., Univ. N.H., Durham, 1983-84; tech. assoc. Mass. Inst. of Tech., Cambridge, Mass., 1984-85; tech. svcs. filtration and molecular biology mktg. mgr. Schleicher & Schuell, Inc., Keene, N.H., 1985-90; original equipment mfg. accounts mgr./v.p. dir. corp. accts. OWL Scientific, Woburn, Mass., 1990—. Group leader United Way, Keene, 1987. Mem. AAAS, NAFE, Bus. and Profl. Women (named Young Career Woman 1987), Assn. Women in Sci., Sigma Xi.

LINKLATER, ISABELLE STANISLAWA YAROSH-GALAZKA (LEE LINKLATER), secondary education educator; b. Chgo., Sept. 15, 1939; d. Baron Stanislaw and Isabelle Lydia (Yarosh) Galazka. BE, Chgo. State U., 1959. Cert. secondary tchr., Ill. Pub. rels. coord. Kelling Co., Chgo., 1955-57; tchr. Chg. Bd. Edn., 1957-89, coord. computer lab., 1989—; founder, pres., exec. dir. Assisi Animal Found. Edn. writer, coord. Elsa Internat. Wild Animal Appeal, Ill., 1985—; writer Lakeland Press, 1992. Bd. dirs. Townsquare Players, Woodstock (Ill.) Opera House, 1989-91. Recipient Outstanding Citizen award CBS Broadcasting, 1992. Mem. McHenry County Defenders (bd. dirs. 1989-91), East African Wildlife Soc. (U.S. rep.). Office: Assisi Animal Found PO Box 143 Crystal Lake IL 60039-0143

LINKONIS, SUZANNE NEWBOLD, case manager, counselor; b. Phila., Aug. 24, 1945; d. William Bartram and Kathryn (Taylor) Newbold; m. Bertram Lawrence Linkonis, May 29, 1966; children: Robert William, Deborah Anne, Richard Anthony. AA in Psychology, Albany (Ga.) Jr. Coll., 1979; BA in Psychology, Albany (Ga.) State Coll., 1981; MS in Indsl. Psychology, Va. Commonwealth U., 1986. Office mgr. Long Advt. Agy., Richmond, Va., 1981-84; media mgr. Clarke & Assocs., Richmond, Va., 1984-85; human resources asst. Continental Ins., Richmond, Va., 1985; rsch. assoc. Signet Bank, N.A., Richmond, Va., 1986-87; program coord. Med. Coll. Va., Richmond, 1988; personnel mgr. Bur. Microbiology, Richmond, 1988; personnel specialist Va. State Dept. Corrections, Richmond, 1989-90; human rights advocate Va. State Dept. Youth & Family Svcs., Richmond, 1990-92, rehab. counselor, 1992-94; sr. rehab. counselor, 1994; pre-trial case mgr./counselor Henrico County Govt., 1995—; future dir., cons. Mary Kay Cosmetics, Springfield, Va., 1975-77. Mem. NAFE, AAUW. Republican. Roman Catholic. Home: 401 Saybrook Dr Richmond VA 23236 Office: 8700 Dixon Powers Dr Richmond VA 23273

LINN, CAROLE ANNE, dietitian; b. Portland, Oreg., Mar. 3, 1945; d. James Leslie and Alice Mae (Thorburn) L. Intern, U. Minn., 1967-68; BS, Oreg. State U., 1963-67. Nutrition cons. licensing and cert. sect. Oreg. State Bd. Health, Portland, 1968-70; chief clin. dietitian Rogue Valley Med. Ctr., Medford, Oreg., 1970—; cons. Hillhaven Health Care Ctr., Medford, 1971-83; lectr. Local Speakers Bur., Medford. Mem. ASPEN, Am. Dietetic Assn., Am. Diabetic Assn., Oreg. Dietetic Assn. (sec. 1973-75, nominating com. 1974-75, Young Dietitian of Yr. 1976), So. Oreg. Dietetic Assn., Alpha Lambda Delta, Omicron Nu. Democrat. Mem. Christ Unity Ch. Office: Rogue Valley Med Ctr 2825 E Barnett Rd Medford OR 97504-8332

LINN, TERE, advertising and marketing company executive; b. Columbus, Ohio, Sept. 27, 1956; d. William Dean Linn and Norma Ann (Vermillion) Linn Murphy; m. Daniel L. Hostetler, Oct. 17, 1981. B.F.A., Bowling Green State U., 1978. Jr. designer Bowling Green State U., Ohio, 1977-79, graphic design supr., 1979, asst. dir. pub. relations, 1980-81; art dir. Miller/Pelton/Bellone, Schenectady, 1982-84; sr. art dir., v.p. H. Linn Cushing, Inc., Albany, N.Y., 1984—. Mem. Ad Club Northea. N.Y. (bd. dirs. 1985—, Nori award 1985), Univ. and Coll. Designers Assn. (Silver award 1979), Am. Women in Radio and TV, Nat. Assn. Female Execs., Art Dirs. Club Greater Boston, Advt. Club Greater Boston. Democrat. Methodist. Avocations: bicycling; tennis; racquetball; sewing. Office: H Linn Cushing Inc 4 Corporate Pla Washington Ave Albany NY 12203

LINNAN, JUDITH ANN, psychologist; b. Pasadena, Calif., July 11, 1940; d. Robert Emmet Linnan and Jane Thomas (Shutz) H.; m. Ralph Theodore Comito, Feb. 1, 1964 (div. Mar. 1975); children: Matthew, Andrew, Kristine. BA, U. Portland, 1962; MS, Calif. State U., Long Beach, 1974; PhD, CCI Internat. U., 1982; postgrad., Newport Inst., 1984-87, 95—. Probation officer L.A. County Probation Dept., 1962-63; social worker L.A. County Dept. Probation and Social Svcs., 1963-69; counselor Huntington Beach (Calif.) Free Clinic, 1970-73, counseling ctr., Calif. State U., Long Beach, 1973-74; psychologist Fullerton (Calif.) Union High Sch. Dist., 1975-80, Psychiat. Med. Group, Orange County, Calif., 1981-82; psychologist, dir. Berkeley Psychol. Svcs., Placentia, Calif., 1982—; pvt. practice psychotherapist Huntington Beach, 1975—; founder, dir. Pacific Acad., Fullerton, 1981-82; dir. human resources So. Calif. Coll. Optometry, Fullerton, 1986—; pvt. provider Orange County Social Svcs., 1992—; dir. single parent program Placentia Unified Sch. Dist., 1994—. Democrat. Roman Catholic. Office: Berkeley Psychol Svcs 101 N Kraemer Blvd Ste 124 Placentia CA 92670-5000

LINNANSALO, VERA, engineer; b. Helsinki, Finland, Oct. 9, 1950; came to U.S., 1960, naturalized, 1969; d. Boris and Vera (Schkurat-Schkuropatsky) L. BS in Computer and Info. Sci., Cleve. State U., 1974, BME, 1974; MBA, U. Akron, 1983. Engring. assoc. B.F. Goodrich Co., Akron, Ohio, 1974-75, assoc. product engr., 1975-77, tire devel. engr., 1977-79, advanced tire devel. engr., 1979-84, quality devel. engr., 1984-85, sr. quality devel. engr., 1985-86; coordinator GM-10 Uniroyal Goodrich Tire Co., Akron, 1986-88, sr. tire devel. scientist, 1988-89; mgr. design and product quality Pirelli Armstrong Tire Corp., New Haven, 1989-90; product design engr. truck ops. Ford Motor Co., Dearborn, 1990-93, vehicle quality and process specialist, corp. quality office, 1993-94, supr. econoline quality and reliability comml. truck vehicle ctr., 1995—. Mem. Am. Soc. Quality Control (sr., cert. quality engr.), Soc. Automotive Engrs., Mensa. Home: 9234 Mayflower Plymouth MI 48170 Office: Ford Motor Co 1179 Town Ctr Dr Dearborn MI 48124-3900

LINNEMEYER, ANNIE, library director; b. Joplin, Mo., Jan. 6, 1947; d. George Lee and Margaret Eleanor (Williams) Chancellor; 1 child, William Andrew Keller. BA, Mo. U., 1969, MA, 1976. Br. mgr. St. Charles (Mo.) City Coun. Libr., 1977-84; br. mgr. Springfield/Greene County (Mo.) Libr., 1985-89, exec. dir., 1989—; exec. bd. Mo. Libr. Network Corp., St. Louis, 1991—. Mem. adv. bd. Springfield Pub. Sch. Found., 1992-94; pres. Ozarks Regional Info. On-Line Network, Springfield, 1993—; mem. Gov.'s Commn. on Informational Tech.; mem. exec. bd. Mo. Rsch. and Edn. Network; bd. dirs. Ozarks Pub. TV, 1994—; mem. task force Mo. Goals 2000, 1995. Mem. ALA, Mo. Libr. Assn. (pres. 1993-94, exec. bd. 1990-94), Forum, Pub. Libr. Assn., Rotary (treas. Springfield Club 1994). Office: Springfield-Greene Cty Libr 620 W Republic Rd Springfield MO 65807-5818

LINSALATA, JOANNA MARIE, artist, editor; b. Dayton, Ohio, Dec. 29, 1922; d. Russel Lowell and Marie (Teeter) Stoner; m. Carmine Rocco Linsalata, Mar. 22, 1942 (dec. Aug. 1980); children: Maria, Laura, Lisa, Philip, Nicholas. Student, Ohio State U., 1939-42, U. Tex., 1944; BA, Oakland U., 1970; postgrad., Mich. State U., Lansing, 1982. Instr. Italian adult edn. Oakland U., Rochester, Mich., 1967-70; exhbn. chair Pontiac Art Ctr., 1979-81; critic Newart Examiner, Washington, Oakland Press, Pontiac, Mich., 1979-80; lectr. in field. One-woman shows include Gallery 140, Lake Orion, Mich., Southfield (Mich.) Art Coun., Hope Coll., Saginaw (Mich.) Mus., Winchester Invitational, Rochester, Ctrl. Mich. U., Macomb Coll., Pontiac Art Ctr., Front Rm. Gallery, Detroit, Spazio Immagine, Milan, Showplace Sq., San Francisco; exhibited in group shows at Oakland U., U. Ill., Midland Mich., Dayton Art Inst., Detroit Focus, Pontiac Art Ctr.; outdoor sculpture exhibited at Rep. Conv., Chene Park Parking Lot, Orion Art Ctr. Bd. dirs. Orion Art Ctr., Lake Orion, 1970—, Orion Hist. Soc., Lake Orion, 1994. Grantee Mich. Coun. Arts, Detroit, 1980, Detroit Coun. Arts, 1982. Mem. NOW. Democrat. Home and Studio: 940 W Clarkston Lake Orion MI 48362

LINSCOTT, SUSAN ELLEN, scientist; b. La Salle, Ill., June 17, 1958; d. Jacob and Ann Hildred (Wisniewski) Gondeck; m. Christopher William Linscott, Sept 21, 1979. BS with distinction, U. Minn., 1981, MS with distinction, 1989. Food scientist Doyle Pharm. Co., Mpls., 1981-86; sr. sci. Amway Corp., Grand Rapids, Mich., 1986-91; assoc. prin. sci. Gen. Mills, Inc., Mpls., 1991—; supv. Gen. Mills Intern Program, Mpls., 1991—; active Gen. Mills Sr. Tech. Group, 1991—. Big sister YMCA Project Motivation, Mpls., 1982-85; coord. Gen. Mills United Way Campaign, Mpls., 1993. Best New Food Product award State of Mich., 1989. Mem. Inst. Food Techs., Minn. Inst. Food Techs. (chmn. edn. com. 1992-94, mem. long range planning com. 1991-920, Arabian Horse Registry, Phi Kappa Phi. Roman Catholic. Office: Gen Mills Inc 9000 Plymouth Ave N Minneapolis MN 55427

LINTON, BARBARA J., state legislator; b. Ashland, Wis., June 27, 1952; d. Charles H. and Marie (Lucloff) Hanninen; m. Michael F. Linton; children: Michelle, Sara. Student bus. adminstrn., Northland Coll., 1987. Farmer Linton's North York Farms, Highbridge, Wi, 1972-82; acct. Drummond Water Utility, Drummond, Wis., 1974-78; fin. aid planner Northland Coll., Ashland, Wis., 1984-85; mem. Wis. Assembly, 1986—; mem. Ashland County Bd. Suprs., 1984-88, chmn. fin. com., vice chmn. exec. com.; sgt.-at-arms Majority Caucus, 1989; co-chair joint com. on fin., 1991—, joint com. on audit, joint com. on employment rels. and other coms. Wis. Assembly. Bd. dirs. 4-H Found. Recipient Alumni award 4-H, Legislative Wxcellence award Tavern League Wis., Excellence award State Emergency Response Bd., Appreciation award DAV, Spl. award from Dept. Natural Resources for Advocacy of State Parks and Trails, Dedication award Lake States Women in Timber Industry, award Nat. Farmers Assn., award ABLE coalition, award for dedication to advancement of small business Wis. Fin. Svcs. Assn., Legislator of Yr. award Vocat. and Tech. Adult Edn., 1994, Fraternal Congress, 1994, VTAE Bds. Assn. Mem. Mellen Area C. of C., Friends of the Vaughn Libr., Ashland County 4-H Leaders, Veritas Honor Soc., Alpha Chi. Democrat. Lutheran. Home: RR 1 Box 299 High Bridge WI 54846-9713 Office: Wis State Assembly State Capital Madison WI 53702

LIONE, GAIL ANN, lawyer; b. N.Y.C., Oct. 22, 1949; d. James G. and Dorothy Ann (Marsino) L.; 1 child, Margo A. Peyton. BA, U. Rochester, 1971; JD, U. Pa., 1974. Bar: Pa. 1974, Ga. 1975, D.C. 1990. Atty. Morgan, Lewis & Bockius, Phila., 1974-75, Hansell & Post, Atlanta, 1975-80; v.p. 1st Nat. Bank of Atlanta, 1980-86; sr. v.p., corp. sec., gen. counsel Sun Life Group of Am., Inc., Atlanta, 1986-89; v.p. Md. Nat. Bank, Balt., 1989-90; gen. counsel, sec. U.S. News & World Report, L.P., Applied Graphics Technologies, Atlantic Monthly Co., Washington, 1990—; bd. mgrs. U. Pa. Law Sch., 1982-85. Chmn. bd. Spl. Audiences, Inc., 1983-85, bd. dirs., 1975-89; vice chmn. Metro Atlanta United Way Campaign, 1986-87; chmn. bd. Atlanta Ballet, 1985-86, bd. dirs., 1975-89; mem. U. Rochester Trustee Coun., 1994—; bd. dirs. YMCA Balt., 1989-90; past bd. dirs. Metro YMCA, Sudden Infant Death Syndrome Inst., Atlanta Cmty. Food Bank; mem. Leadership Atlanta, 1988. Named Top 20 Women in Atlanta by Atlanta Bus. Chronicle, 1987, Top 40 Under 40 Atlanta Mag., 1984; teaching fellow Salzburg Inst., 1989. Mem. ABA (co-chair litigation sect. com. fed. legis. 1994—, standing com. comm. 1993—, ho. dels. 1980-84), State Bar Ga. (sec., dir., chair com. young lawyer's sect. 1976-84, trustee client security fund 1985-89). Office: U S News & World Report 2400 N St NW Washington DC 20037

LIONE, SUSAN GARRETT, sales executive; b. Boston, May 23, 1945; d. Charles Gerard and Josephine (Galgano) Garrett; m. Gerald Frederick Lione, Nov. 9, 1968; children: Mark Garrett, Christina Marie. BA in Econs., Immaculata Coll., 1966. Investment asst. Morgan Guaranty Trust, N.Y.C., 1966-69; portfolio mgr. Union Trust Co., Stamford, Conn., 1969-72; sales coord. Japan Air Lines, Hong Kong, 1977-84; mktg. coord. Hong Kong Tennis Patron Assn., 1982-84; ind. study on schs. Cen. Pk. Task Force, N.Y.C., 1990; sales assoc. Preferred Properties, New Canaan, Conn., 1991—; pres. Am. Women's Assn., Hong Kong, 1977-78; sec. New Canaan CARES, 1989-90, v.p., 1990-91, pres., 1991-93. Bd. dirs. United Way New Canaan, 1994—, allocations com., 1994—; lay adv. bd. St. Aloysius Ch., New Canaan, 1994. Mem. AAUW. Office: Preferred Properties 170 Main St New Canaan CT 06840-5526

LIOTTA, BARBARA JOSEPHS, sculptor; b. Cleve., July 20, 1952; d. Sidney D. and Nina (Warady) Josephs; m. Robert Case Liotta, Oct. 16, 1983; children: Benjamin Isaac, Joseph Case. BFA, Sarah Lawrence Coll., 1974. Researcher Washington Post, 1978-79, Johns Hopkins Sch. of Advanced Internat. Studies, Washington, 1979-80; cons. Arnold & Porter, Washington, 1980-82. Exhibited in group shows at Dumbarton Gallery, 1988, 90. Bd. dirs., music devel. com. Corcoran Gallery, Washington; bd. dirs. Washington Rev. Home and Studio: 3726 Harrison St NW Washington DC 20015

LIPE, LINDA BON, lawyer; b. Clarksdale, Miss., Jan. 10, 1948; s. William Ray and Gwendolyn (Strickland) Lipe. BBA in Accountancy, U. Miss., 1970, JD, 1971. Bar: Miss. 1971, Ark. 1976, U.S. Dist. Ct. (no. dist.) Miss. 1971, U.S. Dist. Ct. (ea. dist.) Ark. 1976, U.S. Ct. Appeals (8th cir.) 1985. Sr. tax acct. Arthur Young & Co., San Jose, Calif., 1971-74, A.M. Pullen & Co., Knoxville, Tenn., 1975; legal counsel to gov. State of Ark., Little Rock, 1975-79; dep. pros. atty. 6th Jud. Dist. Ark., Little Rock, 1979-80; chief counsel Ark. Public Service Commn., Little Rock, 1980-83; asst. U.S. atty. Eastern Dist. Ark., Dept. Justice, Little Rock, 1983—. Mem. ABA, Miss. State Bar, Ark. State Bar Assn., Ark. Bar Assn. Episcopalian. Office: US Attys Office PO Box 1229 Little Rock AR 72203

LIPINSKI, ANN MARIE, newspaper editor. Assoc. mng. editor for met. news. Chgo. Tribune, now dep. mng. editor. Recipient Pulitzer prize for series on politics and conflicts of interest Chgo. City Coun., 1988. Office: Chgo Tribune PO Box 25340 435 N Michigan Ave Chicago IL 60611*

LIPINSKI, BARBARA JANINA, psychotherapist, psychology educator; b. Chgo., Feb. 29, 1956; d. Janek and Alicja (Brzozkiewicz) L.; m. Bernard Joseph Burns, Feb. 14, 1976 (div. 1985). B of Social Work, U. Ill., Chgo., 1978; MFCC, MA, U. Calif., Santa Barbara, 1982; PhD, U. So. Calif., 1992. Cert. tchr., Calif., psychology tchr., Calif.; cert. adminstrn.; cert. non-pub. agt.; lic. marriage, family and child therapist. Police svc. officer Santa Barbara (Calif.) Police Dept., 1978-79; peace officer Airport, Santa Barbara, 1979-80; emergency comms. Univ. Police, Santa Barbara, 1980-82; facilitator, instr. Nat. Traffic Safety Inst., San Jose, Calif., 1981-87; assoc. dir. Community Health Task Force on Alcohol and Drug Abuse, Santa Barbara, 1982-86; instr. Santa Barbara C.C., 1987-88; patients' rights adv. Santa Barbara County Calif. Mental Health Adminstrn., 1986-89; pvt. practice psychotherapist Santa Barbara, 1985—; faculty mem., clin. coord. Pacifica Grad. Inst., Carpinteria, Calif., 1989—; intern clin. psychology L.A. County Sheriff's Dept., 1991-92; cons. Devereux Found., Santa Barbara, 1993, Ctr. for Law Related Edn., Santa Barbara, 1986; cons., trainer Univ. Police Dept., Santa Barbara, 1982, 89. Vol. crisis work Nat. Assn. Children of Alcoholics, L.A., 1987; crisis intervention worker Women in Crisis Can Act, Chgo., 1975-76; vol. counselor Santa Barbara Child Sexual Assault Treatment Ctr.-PACT, Santa Barbara, 1981-82. Recipient Grad. Teaching assistanship U. So. Calif., 1990-92. Mem. APA, Am. Assn. Marriage and Family Therapy, Am. Profl. Soc. on Abuse of Children, Calif. Psychol. Assn., Calif. Assn. Marriage and Family Therapists, Internat. Soc. for Traumatic Stress Studies. Home: 1911 Bath St Santa Barbara CA 93101-2812 Office: Pacifica Grad Inst 249 Lambert Rd Carpinteria CA 93013-3019

LIPINSKY, CAROL, business owner; b. Miami, Fla., Dec. 30, 1957; d. Murray and Helaine (Levine) L. Student, Guilford Coll., 1975-76; AA in Liberal Arts and Recreation, 1977; cert., Brown Coll. of Ct. Reporting, 1979. Owner, ct. reporter Lipinsky Reporting, Atlanta, 1982-86; sales rep. Atlantic Equipment Co., Miami, Fla., 1986-89; owner, tennis instr. The First Bounce, Inc., Atlanta and N.Y., 1989—. Named Profl. of Yr. Ga. Profl. Tennis Assn.

LIPITZ, ELAINE KAPPEL, fine arts educator; b. N.Y.C., Oct. 5, 1924; d. Herman Kappel and Ceil (Friedson) Ferester; m. Elliott Alan Lipitz, Mar. 20, 1945; children: Linda Marsha Schreiber, Alice Lynn Lindholm. BFA, Pratt Coll., 1946; MA, Columbia U., 1955; MA in Adminstrn., St. Johns U., 1974. Fine art tchr. Art & Design High Sch., N.Y.C., 1946-47; fine art tchr. Jamaica High Sch., Queens, N.Y., 1949-70, fin art supr., 1970-75; coord. student affairs John Bowne High Sch., Queens, 1979-90, dir. community rels., 1990—; interior design cons., 1950-80; jewelry designer, 1950-62. One woman shows include Gallery of Manhasset, 1968, Booth Meml. Art Gallery, Queens, 1989; exhibited in group shows at Ctr. Kew Gardens Hills, 1966, Bklyn. Mus. Art, 1969, Park Ave. Christian Ch., 1969, N.Y. Regional Exhbn. Painting and Sculpture, 1969, Newsday Fed. Art Show, 1969 (1st Prize), 70 (2d Place award), Norfolk Mus., 1970, Gallery North, Setauket, N.Y., 1994. Recipient Mayor's Honor award for Cmty. Svc., 1989, 1st prize sculpture Govt. Ctr. Art Guild of Coconut Creek, Fla., 1994. Home: 3 Princess Tree Ct Port Jefferson NY 11777-1742

LIPKE, SANDRA LOUISE, legislative aide, alderwoman. BS, U. Wis., 1985. Registered rep. Offerman & Co., Inc., Stevens Point, Wis., 1986-87, Olde Discount Stockbrokers, Inc., Milw., 1987-88; back office mgr. Investment Designers, Inc., Brookfield, Wis., 1988-89; leasing agt. Sierra Investment Co., Milw., 1990-92; legis. aide Wis. State Assembly, Madison, 1992—. State Conv. com. Dem. Party, 1987, 2d vice chair, 1986-87, membership com. chair, 1986-87, resolution com. chair, 1985; active many dem. polit. campaigns; organizer Dem. Party Sponsored Forum, Indian Hunting and Fishing Rights, 1987; fin. com. City of Oak Creek, 1989-91, alderwoman, 1994—; exec. com. Wis. Women's Network.

LIPKIN, MARY CASTLEMAN DAVIS (MRS. ARTHUR BENNETT LIPKIN), retired psychiatric social worker; b. Germantown, Pa., Mar. 4, 1907; d. Henry L. and Willie (Webb) Davis; m. William F. Cavenaugh, Nov. 8, 1930 (div.); children: Molly C. (Mrs. Gary Oberbillig), William A.; m. Arthur Bennett Lipkin, Sept. 15, 1961 (dec. June 1974). Student, Pa. Acad. Fine Arts, 1924-28; grad. in Social Work, U. Wash., 1946-48. Nursery sch. tchr. Miquon (Pa.) Sch., 1940-45; caseworker Family Soc. Seattle, 1948-49, Jewish Family and Child Service, Seattle, 1951-56; psychiat. social worker Stockton (Calif.) State Hosp., 1957-58; supr. social service Mental Health Research Inst., Fort Steilacoom, Wash., 1958-59; engaged in pvt. practice, Bellevue, Wash., 1959-61. Former mem. Phila. Com. on City Policy. Former diplomate and bd. mem. Conf. Advancement of Pvt. Practice in Social Work; former mem. Chestnut Hill women's com. Phila. Orch; mem. Bellevue Art Mus., Wing Luke Mus. Mem. ACLU, LWV, Linus Paul Inst. Sci. and Medicine, Inst. Noetic Scis., Menninger Found., Union Concerned Scientists, Physicians for Social Responsibility, Center for Sci. in Pub. Interest, Asian Art Council, Seattle Art Mus., Nature Conservancy, Wilderness Soc., Sierra Club.Women's Univ. Club Seattle, Friday Harbor Yacht Club Washington). Home: 10022 Meydenbauer Way SE Bellevue WA 98004-6041

LIPMAN, CAROL KOCH, designer; b. Lincoln, Nebr., Mar. 23, 1960; d. Robert Carl and Gertrude Evelyn (Kornmuller) Koch; m. Ken Lipman, Dec. 16, 1989. B.S., Drexel U., 1982. Design asst. Sydney Carvin Milliken, N.Y.C., 1981, 82-83, Jones New York, N.Y.C., 1983-84; sales rep., designer Asymmetry, N.Y.C., 1984-85; designer Rayman/Ridless, N.Y.C., 1985-87; designer Echo Design Group, Albert Nipon Belts, 1987-88; designer Philip Sand Belts, 1988; designer, mgr. product devel. Karl Lagerfeld Bijoux div. Victoria Internat., 1988-89; designer The 1928 Jewelry Co., 1989-91; brand mgr. Hair Jewelry divsn. Crystals, 1991-92; brand mgr. Aurora R.S.V.P. Collection, 1993, vice pres. design, 1994; mgr. design dept. Leegin Creative Leather Products, Inc., 1994—. Mem. NAFE, Phi Eta Sigma, Phi Kappa Phi, Omicron Nu. Avocations: art, art history, jewelry making.

LIPMAN, DEBORAH S., federal agency administrator; b. Pitts., Sept. 20, 1953; d. Lawrence and Helene Swartz; m. Andrew D. Lipman, Jan. 7, 1982; children: Abigail, Elyse. BA, U. Pa., 1975; MA in City and Regional Planning, U. N.C., 1977. Transp. planner Dept. Transp., 1977; sr. cons. Ernst & Whinney, 1977-79; prof. staff subcom. on commerce, transp. and tourism House com. on energy and commerce, 1979-81; group leader nat. resources, sr. transp. analyst Sen. com. on budget, 1981-86; pres. Women's Transp. Seminar, 1986—. Recipient Mellon fellow, 1975-77. Office: Office of Govt Relations Wash Metro Area Transit Authority 600 5th St NW Rm 2A12 Washington DC 20001*

LIPMAN, WYNONA M., state legislator; b. Ga.; children: Karyne Anne, William (dec.). BA, Talladega Coll.; MA, Atlanta U.; Ph.D., Columbia U.; LL.D. (hon.), Kean Coll., Bloomfield Coll. Former high sch. tchr., lectr. Seton Hall U., Assoc. prof. Essex County Coll.; mem. N.J. State Senate, 1971—, Human Svcs. com., budget and appropriation com., Women, Children Family Svcs com. chmn., Commn. on Sex Discrimination in the Statutes. Mem. NAACP, Nat. Coun. Negro Women, Women's Polit. Caucus, Essex County Urban League. Recipient Outstanding Woman award Assn. Women Bus Owners, 1983. Democrat. Home: Ste 1035 50 Park Pl Newark NJ 07102-4301 Office: NJ State Senate State Capitol Trenton NJ 08625*

LIPNER, ROBYN, legislative staff director. BA, Evergreen State Coll., 1978; MA, U. Calif., Berkeley, 1983. Fellow Women's Rsch. and Edn. Inst. Office of Rep. Patricia Schroeder, 1985-86, legis. asst., 1986-89; policy assoc. Am. Pub. Welfare Assn., 1989-90; mem. profl. staff Sen. Brock Adams, 1990-93; staff dir. Subcom. Aging Senate Labor & Human Resources Com., 1993—; mem. health and human svcs. cluster Clinton-Gore Transition Team, 1992. Office: Subcommittee on Aging 615 Senate Hart Office Bldg Washington DC 20510*

LIPPINCOTT, LAURENE ALICE, electron device technician, artist; b. Phila., Feb. 9, 1950; d. Arthur Noel and Mabel Alice (Williams) Gardiner; m. Robert A. Roll, Nov. 28, 1970 (div. June 1982); m. Alan Jaye Lippincott, June 22, 1985 (dec. Nov. 1985); children: Kevin B., Christine M. Student, Raritain Valley C.C., North Branch, N.J., 1975; cert., Rutgers Labor Edn. Ctr., 1983, Amray Sem. Sch., Bedford, Mass., 1980, Cornell Leadership Acad., 1984. Sculptor Waylande Gregory, Bound Brook, N.J., 1964-70; lab. technician I and II Towne Labs., Somerville, N.J., 1968-70; sr. electron device mechanic, failure mode analysis microscopist ATT Bell Labs., Murray Hill, N.J., 1970—; artist Anatoly Ivanov, Bridgewater, N.J., 1982—; v.p. Alexandra, Inc., Flemmington, N.J., 1986—. Illustrator: My First Birthday, 1990; prin. works include Mountain Lion (2d prize 1969), Fight for Life (1st prize 1973); contbr., developer, co-author: Spin on Glass. Mem. Microscopy Soc. Am., Microbeam Analysis Soc., Internat. Fedn. Socs. for Electron Microscopy, Women of ATT Bell Labs., Comm. Workers Am. (exec. bd. 1986-87, legis. chair 1987-90), Hunterdor Art Ctr., ATT/CWA Allliance Com., Plainfield Musical Club (assoc., hospitality chair 1986-90). Democrat. Episcopalian.

LIPPITT, ELIZABETH CHARLOTTE, writer; b. San Francisco; d. Sidney Grant and Stella L. Student Mills Coll., U. Calif.-Berkeley. Writer, performer own satirical monologues, nat. and polit. affairs for 85 newspapers including Muncie Star, St. Louis Globe-Dem., Washington Times, Utah Ind., Jackson News, State Dept. Watch. Singer debut album Songs From the Heart; contbr. articles to 85 newspapers including N.Y. Post, L.A. Examiner, Orlando Sentinel, Phoenix Rep., The Blue Book; author: 40 Years of American History in Published Letters 1952-1992. Mem. Commn. for Free China, Conservative Caucus, Jefferson Ednl. Assn., Presdl. Adv. Commn. Recipient Congress of Freedom award, 1959, 71-73. Mem. Amvets, Nat. Trust for Hist. Preservation, Am. Security Coun., Internat. Platform Assn., Am. Conservative Union, Nat. Antivivisection Soc., High Frontier, For Our Children, Childhelp U.S.A., Free Afghanistan Com., Humane Soc. U.S., Young Ams. for Freedom, Coun. for Inter.-Am. Security, Internat. Med. Corps, Assn. Vets for Animal Rights, Met. Club, Olympic Club, Commonwealth Club. Home: 2414 Pacific Ave San Francisco CA 94115-1238

LIPPITT, MARY ELIZABETH JORDAN, counselor; b. Butler, Ga., Oct. 20, 1953; d. Frank J. and Elizabeth (Olive) Jordan; m. Nathaniel W. Lippitt, Feb. 23, 1980; children: Elizabeth, Margaret. BA, Wesleyan Coll., Macon, Ga., 1974; MS, Columbus (Ga.) Coll., 1993. Nat. bd. cert. counselor. In pub. rels. Macon (Ga.) C. of C., 1975-76; litigation paralegal Lee & Clark, Savannah, Ga., 1976-79; farm mgr., retail mkt. mgr. Jordan Farms, Inc., Talbotton, Ga., 1986-91; office asst. Ga. State U., Columbus, 1992; intern counseling and placement ctr. Columbus Coll., 1992. Mem. Talbot County (Ga.) Child Abuse Protocol Com., 1993-94. Mem. Phi Kappa Phi, Chi Sigma Iota, Am. Counseling Assn., Nat. Career Devel. Assn., Am. Mental Health Counselors Assn., Ga. Mental Health Counselors Assn. Unitarian. Home: PO Box 87 Talbotton GA 31827-0087

LIPPMAN, MURIEL MARIANNE, biomedical scientist; b. N.Y.C., Oct. 16, 1930; d. Louis George and Erna (Hirsch) L. BA, Syracuse U., 1951; MS, U. Pa., 1955; postgrad., Tufts U., 1965-66, Yale U., 1966-67; PhD, U. Chgo., 1970. Chmn. sci. dept. St. Agnes High Sch., Roshester, N.Y., 1957-59, Nazareth Acad., Rochester, 1959-63; asst. prof. biology, research dir. Nazareth Coll., Rochester, 1963-65; scientist Retina Found., Boston, 1965-66; vis. scientist Karolinska Inst., Stockholm, 1967; assoc. prof. biology Seton Hall U., South Orange, N.J., 1970-71; sr. staff fellow Nat. Cancer Inst., Bethesda, Md., 1971-76; sr. scientist Food and Drug Adminstrn. Bur. Med. Devices, Silver Spring, Md., 1976-77; sr. staff scientist Nat. Acad. Scis., Washington, 1977-78; dir. scientific planning and review Clement Assocs., Washington, 1978-79; pres. ERNACO, Inc., Silver Spring, 1979—; adj. prof. biology Am. U., Washington, 1981-83; vis. prof. Cook Coll., Rutgers State U., N.J., 1985-86; adj. prof. anatomy Frederick (Md.) C.C., 1991, No. Va. C.C., Sterling, 1992—. Contbr. articles to profl. jours. Commr. Human Relations Commn. Montgomery County, Md., 1982-83. Recipient numerous grants and fellowships including Cancer Rsch. grantee Damon Runyon Found., 1964, Am. Cancer Soc. grantee, 1969-70, Biomedical rsch. grantee Evans Found., 1984-91, Nat. Heart, Lung and Blood Inst. NIH, 1986-87; U.S. Pub. Health fellow, 1965-66, KC Rsch. fellow, 1967, Danforth Teaching fellow U. Chgo., 1970; Teaching Excellence award Rochester Acad. Scis., 1963. Mem. N.Y. Acad. Scis., Soc. for Complex Carbohydrates, Soc. Toxicology Nat. Capital Br. Culture Assn., Sigma Xi. Home: 3740 Capulet Ter Silver Spring MD 20906-2644 Office: ERNACO Inc PO Box 6522 Silver Spring MD 20906-6522

LIPPY, KAREN DOROTHY FETHE, nursing administrator; b. Balt., July 2, 1946; d. Vernon Harold and Dorothy Margaret (Wirth) Fethe; m. Robert Eugene Lippy, July 29, 1972; 1 child, Jarrod Blaire. BS in Nursing, U. Md., Balt, 1972, MS in Nursing, 1975. Cert. clin. specialist in adult psychiat./mental health nursing; cert. in nursing adminstrn.-advanced. Clin. nurse specialist Springfield Hosp. Ctr., Sykesville, Md., 1975-79, asst. dir. nursing, 1979-86, dir. nursing, 1986—; clin. nurse specialist Reentry Mental Health Svcs., Westminster, Md., 1983—; mem. task force on RN standards of practice Md. State Bd. Nursing; mem. patient rights, classification and RN job specification task forces Md. Mental Hygiene Adminstrn. Recipient Gov.'s Citation for Excellence, State of Md., Achievement in Nursing Adminstrn., Md. Dept. Mental Hygiene. Mem. ANA, Md. Nurses Assn. (dist. bd. dirs.), Sigma Theta Tau, Phi Kappa Phi. Home: 2519 Bird View Rd Westminster MD 21157-8309

LIPSCOMB, ANNA ROSE FEENY, small business owner, arts organizer, fundraiser b. Greensboro, N.C., Oct. 29, 1945; d. Nathan and Matilda (Carotenuto) L. Student langs., Alliance Francaise, Paris, 1967-68; BA in English and French summa cum laude, Queens Coll., 1977; diploma advanced Spanish, Forester Instituto Internacional, San Jose, Costa Rica, 1990; postgrad. Inst. Allende San Miguel de Allende, Mex., 1991. Reservations agt. Am. Airlines, St. Louis, 1968-69, ticket agt., 1969-71; coll. rep. CBS, Holt Rinehart Winston, Providence, 1977-79, sr. acquisitions editor Dryden Press, Chgo., 1979-81; owner, mgr. Historic Taos (N.Mex.) Inn, 1981-89, Southwest Moccasin and Drum, Taos; pres., co-owner Southwest Products, Ltd., 1991—; fundraiser Taos Arts Celebrations, 1989—; bd. dirs. N.Mex. Hotel and Motel Assn., 1986—; sem. leader Taos Women Together, 1989; founder All One Tribe Found., 1994, All One Tribe Fall Drumming Workshop Series, 1992—. Editor: Intermediate Accounting, 1980; Business Law, 1981. Contbr. articles to profl. jours.; patentee in field. Bd. dirs., 1st v.p. Taos Arts Assn., 1982-85; founder, bd. dirs. Taos Spring Arts Celebration, 1983—; founder, dir. Meet-the-Artist Series, 1983—; bd. dirs. and co-founder Spring Arts N.Mex., 1986; founder Yuletide in Taos, 1988, A Taste of Taos, 1988; bd. dirs. Music from Angel Fire, 1988—; founding mem. Assn. Hist. Hotels, Boulder, 1983—; organizer Internat. Symposium on Arts, 1985; bd. dirs. Arts in Taos, 1983, Taoschool, Inc., 1985—; mem. adv. bd. Chamisa Mesa Ednl. Ctr., Taos, 1990—; founder All One Tribe Found., 1994. Recipient Outstanding English Student of Yr. award Queens Coll., 1977; named Single Outstanding Contbr. to the Arts in Taos, 1986. Mem. Millicent Rogers Mus. Assn., Taos Lodgers Assn. (mktg. task force 1989), Taos County C. of C. (1st v.p. 1988-89, bd. dirs. 1987-89, advt. com. 1986-89, chmn. nominating com. 1989), Internat. Platform Assn., Phi Beta Kappa. Democrat. Home: Talpa Rte Taos NM 87571 Office: PO Drawer N Taos NM 87571

LIPSCOMB-BROWN, EDRA EVADEAN, retired childhood educator; b. Marion, Ill., Aug. 3, 1919; d. Edgar and Anna Josephine (Wiesbrodt) Turnage; m. July 5, 1939 (div. Sept. 1950); 1 son, H. Alan; m. Mark S. Brown, 1981. B.S., So. Ill. U., 1955; M.A., U. Mich., 1955; Ed.D., Ind. U., 1962; postgrad., U. Minn. Tchr. Benton (Ill.) Elem. Schs., 1939-54, DeKalb (Ill.) Consol. Schs., 1955-56; mem. faculty No. Ill. U., DeKalb, 1956-81; prof. elem. edn. No. Ill. U., 1967-81, chmn. elem. and childhood edn., 1978-81, ret., 1981; ednl. cons. to various schs., No. Ill.; mem. vis. accreditation com. Nat. Council Accreditation Tchr. Edn., Kent State U., 1974, U. Wis.-Stout, 1975; co-author, director numerous projects sponsored by U.S. Office Spl. Edn., 1979-81. Author: Lipscomb Teacher Attitude Scale; Contbr. articles to profl. jours. Research grantee No. Ill. U., 1965, 73; Research grantee State of Ill., 1972-73. Mem. Internat. Reading Assn., Internat. Assn. Supervision and Curriculum Devel., NEA, Ill. Edn. Assn., Assn. Higher Edn., Am. Ednl. Research Assn., Pi Lambda Theta. Democrat.

LIPSHUTZ, LAUREL SPRUNG, psychiatrist; b. Easton, Pa., Dec. 11, 1946; d. Joseph A. and Helen A. (Rochlin) S.; m. Robert M. Lipshutz, June 15, 1975; 1 child, Jonathan. BA, U. Pa., 1968; MD, Albany Med. Coll. of Union U., 1972. Diplomate Am. Bd. Psychiatry and Neurology. Resident in psychiatry Johns Hopkins Hosp., Balt., 1972-75; unit chief psychiatric inpatient unit Phila. Gen. Hosp., 1975-77; dir. psychiatric inpatient svc. Pa. Hosp., Phila., 1977—; assoc. dir. residency tng. Inst. of Pa. Hosp., Phila., 1983—; coord. psychiatric clerkship for U. Pa. med. students Pa. Hosp., Phila., 1982—; sr. examiner Am. Bd. Psychiatry and Neurology, 1979—; sr. attending psychiatrist Inst. Pa. Hosp., 1989—, psychiatrist, 1984—; clin. assoc. prof. psychiatry U. Pa. Sch. Medicine, 1987—. Mem. Am. Psychiatric Assn., Pa. Psychiatric Assn., Phila. Psychiatry Soc., Assn. Acad. Psychiatry (region III Excellence in Teaching award 1995). Office: Penn Hospital 800 Spruce St Philadelphia PA 19107-6130

LIPSINSKY, BETTE ELAINE, fine artist, secretary; b. St. Louis, June 24, 1943; d. Owen Paul Davis and Wilma Alma (Filsinger) Ingalls; m. Erwin Richard Lipsinsky, Aug. 1, 1964; children: Rebecca Ann, Jennifer Sue. Student, Washington U., 1963-64, Jefferson Coll., 1985-86, 89-92. Bookkeeper Southwest Bank, St. Louis, 1961-64; various svc. positions St. Louis, 1977-82; bookkeeper Pioneer Bank & Trust, Maplewood, Mo., 1983-87; underwriter Safeco Ins., St. Louis, 1987; sec. Laudry Dryer and Equipment Co., St. Louis, 1987-88, Mo. Goodwill Industries, St. Louis, 1988—; owner, mgr. Image Creations, Arnold, Mo., 1990—. Artist: (mural) Faces of the Services, 1976, Maxville, Mo. 1913; illustrator: (books) Messin' Around in the Kitchen, 1991, The Rainbow of Love, 1992; author religious Christian paintings and portraits in pencil or oil. Dir. day camp Girl Scouts U.S., Arnold, 1974-76; mem. Concerned Women for Am., 1993. Republican. Home and Office: Image Creations 466 Oye Dr Arnold MO 63010-1749

LIPSKY, JOY-ELLEN, software engineer, project manager; b. St. Louis, Mar. 5, 1952; d. William and Pauline (Aldridge) L. BA in Math., San Jose (Calif.) State U., 1974, MS in Computer and Info. Sci., 1979. Cert. systems profl., cert. computer programmer. Asst. systems engr. Santa Clara Valley Water Dist., San Jose, 1974-80; sr. systems programmer Mohawk Data Scis., Los Gatos, Calif., 1980-82; sr. software engr., assoc. Assoc. Applied Engring. Assocs., Los Gatos, Calif., 1982-83; program mgr. DB/Access, Cupertino, Calif., 1983-89; product mgr., application and database cons. Tandem Computers, San Jose, 1989—; cons. Images By Suzie, San Francisco, 1986—, Personnel Impressions, San Francisco, 1987—. Named one of Outstanding Young Women Am., 1985. Mem. ACM (chmn. San Francisco Peninsula chpt. 1984-85, 91-92, mem.-at-large com. on chpts. 1985-87, mem. membership bd. 1987—), Am. Bus. Women's Assn. (pres. Los Gatos chpt. 1985-86, chair Bay Area Coun. 1990-91), Phi Kappa Phi, Upsilon Pi Epsilon. Democrat.

LIPSKY, LINDA ETHEL, business executive; b. Bklyn., June 2, 1939; d. Irving Julius and Florence (Stern) Ellman; m. Warren Lipsky, June 12, 1960 (div. Sept. 1968); 1 child, Phillip Bruce; m. Jerome Friedman, Jan. 17, 1988. BA in Psychology, Hofstra U., 1960; MPS in Health Care Adminstrn., Long Island U., 1979. Child welfare social worker Nassau County Dept. Social Service, N.Y., 1960-64; adminstr. La Guardia Med. Group of Health Ins. Plan of Greater N.Y., Queens, 1969-72; cons. Neighborhood Service Ctr., Bronx, N.Y., 1973-78; dir. ODA Health Ctr., Bklyn., 1978-82; pres. Millin Assocs., Inc., Nassau, N.Y., 1982—. Mem. Health Care Fin. Mgmt. Assn., Nat. Assn. Community Health Ctrs., Nat. Assn. Female Execs., Hofstra U. Alumni Assn. (mem. senate 1984—, chairperson membership com. 1985—), Pi Alpha Alpha. Republican. Jewish. Avocations: cooking, writing, reading. Office: Millin Assocs Inc 521 Chestnut St Cedarhurst NY 11516-2223

LIPSON, GRETA BARCLAY, author, education educator; b. Toronto, Jan. 6, 1925; d. Joseph and Rachel Barclay; m. William Allen Lipson, Mar. 12, 1942; children: Eric, Mark, Stefan. BS, Wayne State U., 1964, MEd, 1969, EdD, 1973. Tchr. elem. schs. various orgns., Berkley, Mich., 1964-68; lectr. Grad. Sch., Wayne State U., Detroit, 1968-69; dir. student tchr. placement U. Mich., Dearborn, 1973-80, assoc. prof. edn., 1969-88, assoc. prof. emeritus, 1988—; coord. Ctr. Alternative Tchg. Strategies, Oak Park, Mich., 1973-75. Author: Fact, Fantasy & Folklore, 1977, Calliope, 1981, Extra! Extra!, 1981, Mighty Myth, 1982, Ethnic Pride, 1983, Famous Fables for Little Troupers, 1984, Romeo & Juliet Plainspoken, 1985, Everyday Law for Young Citizens, 1988, Fast Ideas for Busy Teachers, 1989, A Book for All Seasons, 1990, Tales with a Twist, 1991, Audacious Poetry, 1992, A Leash on Love, 1992, The Scoop on Frogs & Princes, 1993, More Fast Ideas for Busy Teachers, 1994, Hard Choices, 1995. Recipient Downer award for ednl. leadership, 1972; named Disting. Faculty Mem., Mich. Assn. Governing Bds., 1987. Home: 12740 Ludlow Huntington Woods MI 48070

LIPTAK, IRENE FRANCES, retired business executive; b. Clifton, N.J., Feb. 22, 1926; d. George J. and Anna J. (Strelec) L. Student, U. Newark, 1944-45; BS, Rutgers U., 1950, MBA, 1955, EdM, 1964; postgrad., Montclair State Coll., 1960-61, Fairleigh Dickinson U., 1963-64. Exec. sec., adminstrv. asst. to pres. and chmn. bd. Botany Mills, Inc., Passaic, N.J., 1942-53; treas., sec. Rowland-Johnson Co., Clifton, 1953-80; exec. sec. to chief exec. officer Edison Parking Corp., Newark, 1983; bldg. adminstr. Hippodrome Bldg., N.Y.C., 1984; office mgr. Decor Structure, Inc., Carlstadt, N.J., 1984-85. Editor: Ch. News, 1958-68. Mem. conf. planning com. N.J. Commn. on Women, 1972; treas. Slovak Nat. Cath. Cathedral, Passaic, 1976-77; sec., dir., trustee Charles Jr. and Dorothy Johnson Found., 1957-80. Mem. AAUW (life, corr. sec. Nutley br. 1972-74, treas. 1974-76, pres. 1979-81, dir. N.J. divsn. 1975-76), Grad. Sch. Edn. Alumni Assn. Rutgers, Rutgers U. Coll. Honor Soc. (life), Rutgers U. Coll. Alumni Assn. (life, mem. ctrl. coun. 1971-74, v.p. Paterson regional coun. 1986-94), Am. Soc. Notaries (life), Am. Friends Arts, S.W. Bergen Stroke and Disabled Club (founder, pres. 1987-88), Phi Chi Theta (chmn. nat. conv. 1972). Republican. Home: 106 Ridge Rd Rutherford NJ 07070-2422

LIPTON, AMY N., lawyer; b. Flushing, N.Y., July 9, 1954; d. Mortimer J. and Lucille (Goldberg) Natkins; m. Richard B. Lipton; children: Lianna, Justin. BA, Brandeis U., 1976; JD, Boston U., 1979. Bar: Ill. 1979, N.Y. 1981. Assoc. Baker & McKenzie, Chgo. and N.Y., 1979-87; gen. counsel, sr. v.p. CUC Internat., Inc., Stamford, Conn., 1987—. Trustee, dir. Am. Craft Mus., N.Y.C., 1994—. Office: CUC International Inc 707 Summer St Stamford CT 06901

LIPTON, BARBARA, museum director, curator; b. Newark, N.J.; m. Milton Lipton; children: Joshua, Sara, Beth. BA, U. Iowa; MA, U. Mich.; MLS, Rutgers U. Library dir. Newark Mus., 1970-75, spl. projects cons., 1975-82; asst. dir. Castle Gallery Coll. of New Rochelle, N.Y., 1982-83; guest curator Dept. Indian and No. Officers, Ottawa, Ont., Can., 1983-85; dir. Jacques Marchais Mus. Tibetan Art, S.I., N.Y., 1985—; tchr., lectr. various schs. and mus. including Mus. Natural History, Smithsonian Inst., Washington, 1976—; former guest curator many mus. Author: (catalogs) Survival Art Life of the Alaskan Eskimo, 1976, Arctic Vision, 1984, Treasures of Tibetan Art, 1995; (bibliography) Westerners in Tibet, 1972; exec. producer, writer documentary film: Village of No River, 1981. Grantee NEH, 1976, 79, 80, 87, 91. Mem. Am. Assn. Museums. Home: 282 Scotland Rd South Orange NJ 07079-2041 Office: Jacques Marchais Mus Tibetan Art PO Box 060198 Staten Island NY 10306

LIPTON, BRONNA JANE, marketing communications executive; b. Newark, May 10, 1951; d. Julius and Arlene (Davis) L.; m. Sheldon Robert Lipton, Sept. 23, 1984. BA in Spanish, Northwestern U., 1973. Tchr. Spanish Livingston (N.J.) High Sch., 1973-78; profl. dancer Broadway theater, film, TV, N.Y.C., 1978-82; v.p., mgr. Hispanic mktg. svcs. Burson-Marsteller Pub. Rels., N.Y.C., 1982-89; exec. v.p. Lipton Communications Group, Inc., N.Y.C., 1989—; mem. minority initiatives task force Am. Diabetes Assn., Alexandria, Va., 1987-90, mem. pub. rels. com., 1990-91, mem. visibility and image task force, 1991-92, bd. dirs. N.Y. Downstate affiliate, chmn. visibility and image com., 1992-93. Mem. rev. panel Hispanic Designers, Inc. Recipient Pinnacle award Am. Women in Radio and TV (N.Y. Chpt.), 1984, Value Added awards Burson-Marsteller, N.Y.C., 1982, 83, 84. Mem. Hispanic Pub. Rels. Assn. Home: 1402 Chapel Hill Mountainside NJ 07092

LIPTON, DONNA KATHY, psychologist; b. Bklyn., June 23, 1958; d. Howard Stanley and Estelle Beatrice (Schaber) Nissman; m. Stanley Lipton, June 1, 1986. BA, Hunter Coll., 1981; MS, St. Johns U., 1988; PsyD, Yeshiva U., 1992. Lic. psychologist; cert. sch. psychologist. Tchr. Bd. of Edn., Queens, N.Y., 1985-87; psychology intern Glen Cove (N.Y.) Schs., 1987-88; psychologist Brentwood (N.Y.) Sch. Dist., 1988-93; pvt. practice Roslyn Heights and Northport, N.Y., 1993—; psychologist Herricks Union Free Sch. Dist., New Hyde Park, N.Y., 1993—. Mem. APA, Nat. Cert. Sch. Psychologists. Office: 70 Glen Cove Rd East Hills NY 11577 also: 55 Sandy Hollow Rd Northport NY 11768

LIPTON, JOAN, art historian, consultant; b. N.Y.C., Feb. 19, 1938; d. Theodore and Roslyn (Levine) Weissman; m. Gerald M. Lipton, 1960; 1 child, Julie Ann. BA summa cum laude, Adelphi U., 1959; MA, Hunter Coll., 1970; MS in Philosophy, CUNY, 1985, PhD, 1986. Cert. supr./prin., N.J. Tchr., supr. Rumson-Fair Haven High Sch., Rumson, N.J., 1968-92; art historian, lectr. Rumson Community Edn., 1986—, Brookdale Coll. Adult Edn., Lincroft, N.J., 1990—; cons., lectr. to schs., colls., museums, librs., charity groups and adult retirement communities; ednl. lectr. in Italy, 1994. Mem. NAD, Met. Mus., Mus. Modern Art, Whitney Mus., Guggenheim Mus., Monmouth Hist. Soc., Coll. Art Assn., Phi Beta Kappa, Sigma Delta Pi. Home: 41 Sunset Ave Long Branch NJ 07740

LIPTON, LEAH, art historian, educator, museum curator; b. Kearny, N.J., Mar. 22, 1928; d. Abraham and Rose (Berman) Shneyer; m. Herbert Lipton, Sep. 19, 1951 (dec. 1979); children: David, Ivan, Rachel. BA, Douglass Coll. Rutgers U., New Brunswick, N.J., 1949; MA, Harvard U., Cambridge, Mass., 1950; postgrad., Harvard U., 1970-73, Wellesley Coll., 1970-73. Photo, library researcher Mus. Fine Arts, Boston, 1950-53, lectr., division edn., 1965-70; instr. Boston Coll., 1968-69; faculty, full prof. Framingham State Coll., Mass., 1969-94; ret., 1994; interim dir. Danforth Mus. Art, 1994-95; mem. bd. trustees Danforth Mus. Art, Framingham Mass., 1975—; curator Am. art Danforth Mus. Art, Framingham Mass., 1994—; chair exhibitions Com.; Collections Com. Danforth Mus., Framingham Mass., 1988, guest curator Nat. Portrait, Wash., 1985. Author: Book, 1985, Exhibition Catalogues, 1988-94; contbr. articles to profl. jours., 1981—. Co-Founder Danforth Mus. Art., Mass. 1973-75. Recipient Distinguished Service award Framingham State Coll., Mass. 1978, 87. Mem. Coll. Art Assn., Am. Studies Assn. Office: Danforth Mus of Art 123 Union Ave Framingham MA 01701

LIPTON, NINA ANNE, marketing executive; b. N.Y.C., Oct. 6, 1959; d. Robert and Rita Kay (Wolfman) L. BA in Econs., Wellesley Coll., 1981; postgrad., London Sch. Econs., 1981-82. Rsch. asst. Nat. Econ. Rsch. Assocs., White Plains, N.Y., 1983-84; cons. A.T. Hudson and Co., Paramus, N.J., 1984; asst. economist Dean Witter Reynolds, N.Y.C., 1984-89; dir. market rsch. Platinum Guild Internat., N.Y.C., 1989-94; pres. Alternative Med. Ctrs., Inc., N.Y.C., 1995—; bd. dirs. RRI Industries, Boca Raton, Fla., Aztec Mgmt. Co. Writer This Week in Platinum weekly, 1989-94; contbr. articles to profl. jours. Recruiter, fundraiser, reunion com. chair Wellesley (Mass.) Coll. Alumnae Assn.,1982—. Mem. Internat. Precious Metals Inst., Nat. Assn. Bus. Economists, Futures Industry Assn.

LISA, ISABELLE O'NEILL, mergers and acquisitions company executive, law firm administrator; b. Phila., Mar. 12, 1934; d. Thomas Daniel and Margaret Marie (Hayes) O'Neill; m. Donald Julius Lisa, June 15, 1957; children: Richard Allan, Steven Gregory. Student, Harper Community Coll., Rolling Meadows, Ill., 1976, Scottsdale Community Coll., 1980, Ariz. State U., 1981-82. Cost control clk. Curtis Pub. Co., Phila., 1952-56; sec. United Ins. Co., Annapolis, Md., 1956-57; firm adminstr., legal sec. Law Offices Donald J. Lisa, Bloomingdale, Ill., 1987; legal sec. Lisa & Kubida, P.C., Phoenix, 1987-88, firm adminstr., 1987-89; firm adminstr. Lisa & Assocs., Phoenix, 1989-90, Lisa & Lisa, Phoenix, 1990-91, Lisa & Assocs., 1991—; v.p. adminstrn. Lisa & Co., Phoenix, 1987—. Den mother Cub Scouts Am., Millburn, N.J., 1965; founder, pres. Pro-Tem Rutgers U. Law Wives Assn., 1962-63; bd. advisors Am. Inst., Phoenix, 1991—. Mem. NAFE, Maricopa County Bar Assn. (legal adminstrs. sect. 1992—), Internat. Platform Assn., Rotary. Republican. Roman Catholic. Home: 8661 E Carol Way Scottsdale AZ 85260 Office: Gainey Ranch Corp Ctr Ste 239 8777 N Gainey Center Dr Scottsdale AZ 85258-2106

LISALDA, SYLVIA ANN, primary educator; b. San Diego, Oct. 14, 1949; d. Joseph and Irene (Valdez) Lisalda; m. Robert Holguin Marquez, Sept. 1, 1979 (div. 1986). AA, Valley Coll., Van Nuys, Calif., 1964; BA in English, Calif. State U., Northridge, 1971. Tchr. kindergarten L.A. Unified Schs., 1965—. Democrat. Roman Catholic. Office: Sylmar Elem Sch 13291 Phillippi Ave Sylmar CA 91342

LISBOA-FARROW, ELIZABETH OLIVER, public and government relations consultant; b. N.Y.C., Nov. 25, 1947; d. Eleuterio and Esperanza Oliver; student pvt. schs., N.Y.C.; m. Jeffrey Lloyd Farrow, Dec. 31, 1980; 1 child, Hamilton Oliver Farrow; 1 stepson, Maximillian Robbins Farrow. With Harold Rand & Co. and various other public relations firms, N.Y.C., 1966-75; dir. pub. rels. N.Y. Playboy Club and Playboy Clubs Internat., 1975-79; pres., CEO Lisboa Assocs., Inc., N.Y.C., 1979—; founder, pres. Lisboa Prodns., Inc., Washington, 1994—; counselor Am. Woman's Devel. Corp. Sec. Nat. Acad. Concert and Cabaret Arts; mem. nat. adv. council SBA, 1980-81, apptd., 1994—; exec. dir. Variety Club of Greater Washington, Inc., 1985-90, Children's Charity; bd. dirs. Variety Myoelectric Limb Bank Found., 1990-91; mem. Women and Heart Disease Task Force. Recipient Disting. award of Excellence SBA, 1992, Women Bus. Enterprise award U.S. Dept. Transp. NHTSA, 1994; named Pub. Rels. Woman of Yr. Women in Pub. Rels. Mem. SAG, NATAS, U.S. Hispanic C. of C. (Blue Chip Enterprise award 1993), Small Bus. Advisory Coun., U.S. C. of C., Advt. Coun., Am. Heart Assn., Hispanic Bus. and Profl. Women's Assn., Ibero-Am. C. of C. (Small Bus. award 1993, bd. dirs. 1995—), City Club Washington. Office: 1317 F St NW Washington DC 20004-1105

LISI, MARY M., federal judge. BA, U. R.I., 1972; JD, Temple U., 1977. Tchr. history Prout Meml. High Sch., Wakefield, R.I., 1972-73; hall dir. U. R.I., 1973-74; law clerk to Prof. Jerome Sloan Temple U., Phila., 1975-76; law clerk U.S. Atty., Providence, R.I., 1976, Phila., 1976-77; asst. pub. defender R.I. Office Pub. Defender, 1977-81; asst. child advocate Office Child Advocate, 1981-82; also. pvt. practice atty. Providence, 1981-82; dir. office ct. appointed spl. advocate R.I. Family Ct., 1982-87; dep. disciplinary counsel office disciplinary counsel R.I. Supreme Ct., 1988-90, chief disciplinary counsel, 1990-94; mem. Select Com. to Investigate Failure of R.I. Share and Deposit Indemnity Corp., 1991-92. Recipient Providence 350 award, 1986, Meritorious Svc. to Children of Am. award, 1987. Office: Fed Bldg and US Courthouse One Exchange Terrace Rm 113 Providence RI 02903*

LISK, PAMELA KONIECZKA, lawyer; b. Chgo., Oct. 8, 1959; m. Thomas Joseph Lisk; 1 child, Sarah. BA, Northwestern U., 1980; M of Pub. Policy, JD, Harvard U., 1984. Staff atty. SEC, Washington, 1984-86; assoc. Lord, Bissell & Brook, Chgo., 1986-89; sr. atty. Sundstrand Corp., Rockford, Ill., 1989—. Mem. Ill. Bar Assn., Phi Beta Kappa.

LISKA, MARGARET NAYLOR (PEGGY LISKA), retired small business owner; b. Callaway, Nebr., July 27, 1922; d. James Corban and Ruth Frances (Snodgrass) Naylor; m. Arthur Joseph Liska, Apr. 5, 1946; children: Jo, A. James. BS, U. Denver, 1944. Auditor Conn. Gen. Life Ins., Hartford, 1944-45; mgr. Conn. Gen. Life Ins., Denver, 1945-46; co-owner Broadview (Ill.) Hardware, 1946-60, Ben Franklin Store, Batavia, Ill., 1962-93; pres. Liska Enterprises, Inc., Batavia, 1962-93; owner Wedding Wisdom, Batavia, 1982-93. Mem. AAUW (Rsch. and Project Endowment namee 1986), AARP, PEO (pres.), Am. Needlework Guild, Embroiders Guild of Am., St. Charles Country Club, Order of Eastern Star. Home: 310 B Woodridge Circle South Elgin IL 60177

LISKOV, BARBARA HUBERMAN, software engineering educator; b. Los Angeles, Nov. 7, 1939. BA in Math., U. Calif., Berkeley, 1961; MS in Computer Sci., Stanford U., 1965, PhD, 1968. With applications programming sect. Mitre Corp., Bedford, Mass., 1961-62, mem. tech. staff, 1968-72; with Harvard U., Cambridge, Mass., 1962-63; grad. research asst. dept. computer sci. Stanford U., Palo Alto, Calif., 1963-68; prof. computer sci. and engring. MIT, Cambridge, 1972—, NEC prof. software sci. and engring., 1984—. Author: (with others) CLU Reference Manual, Lecture Notes in Computer Science 114, 1981; (with J. Guttag) Abstraction and Specification in Program Development, 1986; assoc. editor Transactions on Programming Langs. and Systems; contbr. articles to profl. jours. Mem. IEEE, Am. Acad. Arts and Scis., Assn. Computing Machinery (spl. interest groups on databases, oper. systems and programming langs.), Nat. Acad. Engring.

LISNEK, MARGARET DEBBELER, artist, educator; b. Covington, Ky., Sept. 26, 1940; d. Aloysius Frank and Mary Elizabeth (Haubold) Debbeler; m. Schiller William Lisnek, June 26, 1966; 1 child, Kimberly Anne. AA with honors, Mt. San Antonio Coll., 1985; BA in Art with honors, Calif. State U., Fullerton, 1991. Cert. substitute tchr. Freelance artist, 1985—; tchr. art Rorimer Elem. Sch., La Puente, Calif., 1992-93, City of Walnut (Calif.) Recreation Svcs., 1992—, Christ Luth. Sch., West Covina, Calif., 1993—, Los Molinos Elem. Sch., Hacienda Heights, Calif., 1993—, Los Altos Elem. Sch., Hacienda Heights, 1993—; mem. Getty Inst. Insvc. Resource Team. One-woman shows include Calif. State U., Fullerton, 1990; exhibited in group shows. Sec., treas., social chair PTA, Los Altos Elem. Sch., Hacienda Heights, 1972-73; membership and social chair Friends of Libr., Hacienda Heights, 1974-75; active Nat. Mus. Women in the Arts, L.A. County Art Mus., Norton Simon Mus., Pasadena, Calif. Mem. Calif. Art Edn. Assn.

LISSAKERS, KARIN MARGARETA, federal agency administrator; b. Aug. 16, 1944; married; 2 children. BA in Internat. Affairs, Ohio State U., 1967; MA in Internat. Affairs, Johns Hopkins U., 1969. Mem. staff com. fgn. rels. U.S. Senate, Washington, 1972-78, mem. staff subcom. multinat. corps., 1972, staff dir. subcom. fgn. econ. policy, 1977; dep. dir. econ. policy planning staff U.S. Dept. State, Washington, 1978-80; sr. assoc. Carnegie Endowment for Internat. Peace, N.Y.C., 1981-83; lectr. internat. banking, dir. internat. bus. and banking program Sch. Internat. Pub. Affairs Columbia U., N.Y.C., 1985-93; U.S. exec. dir. Internat. Monetary Fund, Washington, 1993—. Author: Banks, Borrowers and the Establishment, 1991; contbr. articles to profl. jours. Office: Internat Monetary Fund 700 19th St NW Rm 13-320 Washington DC 20431

LISSENDEN, CAROLKAY, pediatrician; b. Newark, Aug. 22, 1937; d. George Cyrus Sr. and Irene Elizabeth (Hempel) L.; m. Bart Albert Barré, June 13, 1964; children: Lisa Kim Barré-Quick, Bart Christopher Barré. BA, U. Pa., 1959; MD, Med. Coll. Pa., 1964. Pediat. intern St. Luke's Hosp., N.Y.C., 1964-65; pediat. resident Columbia-Presbyn. Hosp., N.Y.C., 1965-67; pvt. practice Mountainside, N.J., 1967—. Fellow Am. Acad. Pediats.; mem. AMA, N.J. Med. Assn., Union County Med. Assn. Republican. Presbyterian. Home and Office: 135 Wild Hedge Ln Mountainside NJ 07092

LIST, CARA ANN, artist; b. Milw., Oct. 21, 1962; d. Walter Reinhold and Barbara Lucille (Shipman) L. BA, Scripps Coll., 1984; postgrad., Oreg. Sch. Arts and Crafts, Portland, 1986, Pacific N.W. Coll. Art, 1986; post baccalaureate studio cert., Sch. Art Inst. Chgo., 1987; MFA, Sch. Visual Arts, N.Y.C., 1990. One-woman shows at Quartersaw Gallery, Portland, 1991, 92, 93; exhibited in group shows at Scripps Coll., Claremont, Calif., 1983, 84, Sch. Art Inst. Chgo. Gallery, 1987, Visual Arts Gallery, 1989, 90, Quartersaw Gallery, 1991, 92, Westbeth Gallery, N.Y.C., 1993. Grantee Sch. Art Inst. Chgo., 1987. Mem. Coll. Art Assn. Home and Studio: 134 Dean St Brooklyn NY 11201-6311

LISTON, HEATHER CECELIA, controller; b. Champaign, Ill., Sept. 23, 1961; d. William T. and Phyllis Marion (Hurd) L. AB, Princeton U., 1983; MS, NYU, 1984. Auditor Coopers and Lybrand, N.Y.C., 1983-85; acct. N.Y. Philharmonic, N.Y.C., 1985-86; mgmt. fellow Am. Symphony Orchestra League, Washington, 1986-87; bus. mgr. Orchestra of St. Luke's, N.Y.C., 1987-90; controller Am. Youth Hostels, N.Y.C., 1990; spl. asst. to pres. Edwin Schlossberg Inc., N.Y.C., 1990—. Vol. Big Sisters, Inc. Mem. ACLU. Democrat. Home: 214 E 83rd St Apt 5A New York NY 10028-2841 Office: Edwin Schlossberg Inc 641 6th Ave New York NY 10011

LISTON, MARY FRANCES, retired nursing educator; b. N.Y.C., Dec. 17, 1920; d. Michael Joseph and Ellen Theresa (Shaughnessy) L. BS, Coll. Mt. St. Vincent, 1944; MS, Catholic U. Am., 1945; EdD, Columbia, 1962; HHD (hon.), Allentown Coll., 1987. Dir. psychiat. nursing and edn. Nat. League for Nursing, N.Y.C., 1958-66; prof. Sch. Nursing, Cath. U. Am., Washington, 1966-78; dean Sch. Nursing, Cath. U. Am., 1966-73; prof. Marywood Coll., 1984-87; spl. assignment Imperial Med. Center, Tehran, Iran, 1975-78; dep. dir. for program affairs Nat. League for Nursing, N.Y.C., 1978-84. Mem. Sigma Theta Tau. Home: 182 Garth Rd Scarsdale NY 10583-3863

LISTROM, LINDA L., lawyer; b. Topeka, Kans., Mar. 17, 1952. BA magna cum laude, U. Houston, 1974; JD, Harvard U., 1977. Bar: Ill. 1977. Ptnr. Jenner & Block, Chgo. Bd. dirs. Cook County Court Watching Project, Inc., 1983-92. Mem. ABA. Office: Jenner & Block 1 IBM Plz Chicago IL 60611*

LIT, JUDITH EVELYN, film producer, director; b. Norwich, N.Y., Jan. 8, 1945; d. Nathan Bernard and Miriam Leah (Stone) Golub; m. Peter Lit, June 28, 1969 (div. July 1973); 1 adopted child, Kyra S. BA in Art History, Syracuse U., 1966; MA in Theatre, U. Colo., 1976. Cert. tchr., Calif. Social worker Contra Costa County, Richmond, Calif., 1966-68; tchr. Mendocino Unified Schs., San Francisco, 1969-71; dancer, choreographer Studio 210, James Tyler Dancers, San Francisco, 1970-79; producer, dir. San Francisco, 1979-86; festival dir. On Screen Women's Film Festival, San Francisco, 1986-88; owner, ptnr. Cinema Cons., San Francisco, 1988—; cons. in field. Prodr./dir. (film) Vaces From the Classroom, 1986; assoc. prodr. (film) Dark Circle, 1982, others. Bd. dirs. Citizens Policy Ctr., Oakland, 1983-86, No. Calif. Women in Film and TV, 1986-88, Ind. Documentary Group, 1990—; jury chair San Francisco Internat. Film Festival, 1989, 93. Recipient Cert. of Spl. Merit Acad. Motion Picutre Art and Scis., 1983, First Pl. Nat. Ednl. Film Festival, 1985, Nat. Emmy Outstanding Individual Achievement in News and Documentary, 1990. Mem. Assn. Ind. Video and Filmmakers, Film Arts Found. Office: Cinema Cons 325 27th St San Francisco CA 94131

LITCHFIELD, JEAN ANNE, nurse; b. Gary, Ind., Oct. 6, 1942; d. Donald Kleine and Helen Louise (Sweet) Eller; m. Norman E. Stone, Dec. 27, 1965 (div. Aug. 1973); children: Diana, David, Julie; m. Frank Litchfield, Jan. 26, 1974. Lic. practical nurse, Ind. U. Vocat. Tech. Coll., 1973; AS in Biology, Richland Community Coll., 1991; BSN, Millikin U., 1993. Nurse asst. St. Anthony Hosp., Terre Haute, Ind., 1960-73, nurse, 1973-74; nurse St. Mary's Hosp., Decatur, Ill., 1974—; mem. student welfare com. Millikin U., Decatur, 1991-92. Recipient 1st place art award 1984, 85, 86, 2d place art award 1984, 85, 2d place County Fair, 1985, Gold Poet award World of Poetry, 1989, Silver Poet award, 1990; named Most Caring Nurse St. Mary's Hosp. 1990, Clara Compton scholar, St. Mary's Hosp., 1993, 94, scholar Am. Legion, 1992. Mem. Internat. Platform Assn., Barn Colony Artists (treas. 1986-88), Phi Theta Kappa, Beta Sigma Phi (treas. 1976-78), Alpha Tau Delta (treas. 1991-92, pres. 1992-93), Sigma Theta Tau Internat. Home: 1680 N 30th St Decatur IL 62526-5416

LITERATI, MARIANNE MITCHELL, technical engineer; b. Billings, Mont., Apr. 4, 1959; d. Porter Hayward and Barbara Rose (Falk) Mitchell; m. Alan Jay Literati, July 2, 1983; children: Alex Mitchell, Eric Alan. BS in Computer Sci., U. Okla., 1981; MS in Computer Engring., Stanford U., 1983. Mem. tech. staff AT&T Bell Labs., Denver, 1982-89, disting. mem. tech. staff, 1990—. Home: 3756 W 102d Ave Westminster CO 80030 Office: AT&T Bell Labs Rm 30L53 11900 N Pecos Denver CO 80234

LITMAN, DELAINE, retail executive, public relations administrator; b. Houston, May 7, 1953; d. Eugene H. and Jeanette (Furstenfeld) Worley. Owner N.O.W., Austin, Tex., 1984—. Mem. Mary Martha Guild, Bethany Luth. Ch., Austin, 1990—; vol. Brooke Elem. Sch., Austin Adopt-A-Sch. Program. Mem. NAFE, AAUW, Phi Theta Kappa (pres. 1993—, Outstanding Provisional mem. 1993, 3d pl. poetry award Creative Writing Contest 1993, Outstanding Svc. award 1993, PTK scholarship 1993). Republican. Home: 3105 S I H 35 Apt 1052 Austin TX 78741-6930

LITMAN, HELENA D., lawyer; b. Wroçlaw, Poland, July 24, 1948; French citizen; came to U.S., 1968, permanent resident, 1968; d. Ignacy and Barbara (Katz) Dunica; children: Sacha, Benjamin. Student, NYU, 1971, JD, 1979. Bar: N.Y. Assoc. Kaye, Scholer, Fierman, Hayes & Handler, N.Y.C., 1979-83; assoc. counsel Citibank, N.A., N.Y.C., 1983—. Contbg. editor NYU Jour. Internat. Law, 1977-78. Woodrow Wilson Dissertation fellow, 1971. Mem. ABA, N.Y. State Bar Assn. Home: 350 Central Park West New York NY 10025

LITRELL, BARBARA, publishing executive. Sr. v.p., pub. McCall's mag., N.Y.C. Office: McCalls 110 Fifth Ave New York NY 10011*

LITRENTA, FRANCES MARIE, psychiatrist; b. Balt., June 25, 1928; d. Frank P. and Josephine (DeLuca) L. AB, Coll. Notre Dame Md., 1950; MD, Georgetown U., 1954. Diplomate Am. Bd. Psychiatry and Neurology. Rotating intern St. Agnes Hosp., Balt., 1954-55, asst. resident in psychiatry, 1955-56; fellow in psychiatry Univ. Hosp., Balt., 1956-57; fellow in child psychiatry Georgetown U. Hosp., Washington, 1957-59; clin. instr. psychiatry Med. Ctr. Georgetown U., Washington, 1959-63; clin. asst. prof. Med. Ctr. Georgetown U., 1963-72, clin. assoc. prof. psychiatry Med. Ctr., 1972-87; pvt. practice Balt., 1959—; cons. St. Vincent's Infant Home, Balt., 1965-75; mem. coun. to dean Georgetown U. Sch. Medicine, 1977-93. Fellow Am. Acad. Child and Adolescent Psychiatry, Am. Orthopsychiat. Assn.; mem. Am. Psychiat. Assn. (life), Md. Psychiat. Soc., Georgetown Med. Alumni Assn. (nat. communications chmn. 1987-90, bd. dirs. 1989—, class co-chmn. 1974-87, class communications chmn. 1988—). Office: 6110 York Rd Baltimore MD 21212-2600

LITT, IRIS F., pediatrics educator; b. N.Y.C., Dec. 25, 1940; d. Jacob and Bertha (Berson) Figarsky; m. Victor C. Vaughan, June 14, 1987; children from previous marriage: William M., Robert B. AB, Cornell U., 1961; MD, SUNY, Bklyn., 1965. Diplomate Am. Bd. Pediat. (bd. dirs. 1989-94). Intern, then resident in pediat. N.Y. Hosp., N.Y.C., 1965-68; assoc. prof. pediat. Stanford U. Sch. Medicine, Palo Alto, Calif., 1982-87, prof., 1987—, dir. divsn. adolescent medicine, 1976—, dir. Inst. for Rsch. on Women and Gender, 1990—; bd. dirs. Youth Law Ctr., San Francisco. Editor Jour. Adolescent Health. Mem. Soc. for Adolescent Medicine (charter), Am. Acad. Pediatrics (award sect. on adolescent health), Western Soc. Pediatric Rsch., Soc. Pediatric Rsch., Am. Pediatric Soc. Office: Stanford U Sch of Medicine 300 Pasteur Dr Stanford CA 94305

LITT, MARGOT WILLIAMSON, art consultant, designer; b. Chgo., Feb. 13, 1933; d. George Joseph Jaeger and Ellen Douglas Williamson; m. Nathaniel Litt, Mar. 23, 1962; children: Andrew J., Jessica A. BA, Sarah Lawrence Coll., Bronxville, N.Y., 1955; postgrad., Inst. of Fine Arts, NYU, N.Y.C., 1955-56, U. Pa., 1991-94, Univ. of the Arts, Phila., 1990-91. Tchr. U.S.I.S., Santiago, Chile, 1955; designer Univ. Players, Princeton, N.J., 1957-59; costume designer, asst. to Theoni V. Alchedge N.Y.C., 1958-64; owner Pennsauken Flower World, Pennsauken, N.J., 1982-84; owner antique business Rancocas, N.J., 1985-87; art cons. Phila., 1989—; cons. and mem. Playwrights Workshop, Phila., 1990—. Bd. dirs. Theatre Ctr. of Phila., 1987-91, Haddonfield (N.J.) Bd. Edn., 1978-87; vol. U. Pa. Mus., Phila., 1988-90. Recipient Svc. award Haddonfield Bd. Edn., 1987. Mem. LWV (bd. dirs. 1974-87). Home and Office: 413-15 Gaskill St Philadelphia PA 19147

LITTELL, PHYLLIS MAUREEN, counselor; b. Albuquerque, N.Mex., Oct. 15, 1941; d. Maurice William Robinson and Hazel Maureen (Billings) Wood; m. Danny Lane Littell, June 15, 1963; children: Tammy Littell Boser, Linda Littell Boser. AB, Hanover Coll., 1963; BS, Ind. U., 1977. Tchr. Sch. Town of Clarksville, Ind., 1963-65; high sch. counselor Mooresville (Ind.) High Sch., 1977-79, Plainfield (Ind.) High Sch., 1979-84; ind. individual & family counselor Greenwood, Ind., 1984—. Contbr. articles to various mags. Pres. Hendricks County Coun. Prevention of Child Abuse, Ind., 1990-91. Mem. ACA, Kappa Kappa Kappa (v.p. 1991-92). Mem. Ch. of Christ. Office: 512 S Madison Ave Greenwood IN 46142

LITTKE, LAEL JENSEN, author; b. Mink Creek, Idaho, Dec. 2, 1929; d. Frank George and Ada Geneva (Petersen) Jensen; m. George Charles Littke, June 29, 1954 (dec. Feb. 1991); 1 child, Lori Sue Littke Fry. BS, Utah State U., 1952. Sec. Gates Rubber Co., Denver, 1952-54, Life Ins. Assn. of Am., N.Y.C., 1954-63; instr. Pasadena (Calif.) City Coll., 1978-84; tchr. UCLA, 1988. Author: There's A Snake at Girls Camp, 1994, The Bridesmaid's Dress Disaster, 1994, Star of the Show, 1993, The Watcher, 1994, Blue Skye, 1991, also 24 other books. Bd. dirs. PTA, 1976-78, Save the Libr. Com., Pasadena, 1993. Mem. PEN Internat. (treas. 1982-84), Soc. of Childrens Book Writers, Authors Guild, Mystery Writers of Am., So. Calif. Coun. on Lit. for Children and Young People. Democrat. Mem. Ch. of LDS. Home: 1345 Daveric Dr Pasadena CA 91107-1645

LITTLE, ANNA DENISE, marketing professional; b. Montclair, N.J., May 2, 1956; d. Jethro Craven and Verneader (Wright) L. BA, Fla. State U., 1980. Researcher, tech. asst. Sta. WFSU-TV, Tallahassee, 1979-80; with editorial staff Burrelle's Press Clipping Service, Livington, N.J., 1981-82; customer service and sales rep. Funk and Wagnalls, Inc., L.I., 1982-84; editor, media coordinator Murdoch Mags., N.Y.C., 1984-86; promotional and editorial mgr. Direct Response Group div. Hearst Mags., N.Y.C., 1986-88; sales rep. Good Housekeeping Mag., Hearst Mag., 1988-89; key account specialist The Faxon Co., N.Y.C., 1989; programming operator Gateway Cable, Newark, N.J., 1991—. Mem. NAFE, Acad. TV Arts and Scis. (mem. Blue Ribbon Panel). Democrat. Mem. Pentecostal Ch.

LITTLE, DIANA DICKSON, oncology clinical nurse specialist; b. Mobile, Ala., Dec. 14, 1950; d. James David Jr. and Lillian (Johnston) Dickson; m. James E. Little, June 18, 1971 (dec. Mar. 1990); 1 child, Amy Yvonne; m. Jake William Heard, Aug. 29, 1991. ADN, Hinds Jr. Coll., Raymond, Miss., 1975; BSN, William Carey Coll., Hattiesburg, Miss., 1981; MS, U. So. Miss., Hattiesburg, 1991. RN, Miss.; cert. oncology nurse. Staff and charge nurse emergency rm. Miss. Bapt. Med. Ctr., Jackson, 1975-76; staff nurse genitourinary, ear, nose, throat and eye units VA Med. Ctr., Jackson, 1976-79, hematology-oncology nurse, 1979-91, oncology clin. nurse specialist, 1991—. Contbr. articles to profl. jours. Mem. adv. bd. Hospice of Cen. Miss., Jackson, 1990—; bd. dirs. Miss. div. Am. Cancer Soc., 1986—, chair nursing sub-com. for profl. edn., Miss. div., 1985-87, 91—; vol. ARC, Jackson, 1987—. Recipient Lane Adams award Am. Cancer Soc., 1989. Mem. Nat. Oncology Nursing Soc., Miss. Oncology Nursing Soc., Nat. Orgn. VA Nurses, S.W. Oncology Group, Am. Cancer Soc. (adv. group on nursing 1993—). Baptist. Home: 240 Dona Ave Jackson MS 39212-4813 Office: Dept Vet Affairs 1500 E Woodrow Wilson Ave Jackson MS 39216-5199

LITTLE, SYLVIA FORD, oil industry executive. Student, So. Meth. U., Scottsdale Community Coll., Ariz. Owner, operator gas and oil properties San Juan Basin, N.Mex., 1977—; pres. Little Oil & Gas, Inc., San Juan Basin, N.Mex. Founder Farmington (N.Mex.) Totah Festival of Authentic Indian Art; chmn. residential com. Town Forum 2000, 1980; mem. exec. com., state ctrl. com. N.Mex. Rep. Com., 1984-86; bd. dirs. N.Mex. Fedn. Rep. Women, 1984-90, Farmington LWV; mem. industry adv. com. to N.Mex. Dept. Energy, 1993; mem. N.Mex. Bd. Econ. Devel. Commrs., 1994—. Mem. Ind. Petroleum Assn. N.Mex. (pres.-elect 1990, pres. 1991-93), N.Mex. Oil and Gas Assn. (exec. com. 1993—), Assn. Commerce and Industry N.Mex. (bd. dirs. 1988-92), Farmington C. of C. (redcoats amb. com., pres.-elect 1995), Rotary. Office: 2346 E 20th St Farmington NM 87401-8906

LITTLEFIELD, VIVIAN MOORE, nursing educator, administrator; b. Princeton, Ky., Jan. 24, 1938; children: Darrell, Virginia. B.S. magna cum laude, Tex. Christian U., 1960; M.S., U. Colo., 1964; Ph.D., U. Denver, 1979. Staff nurse USPHS Hosp., Ft. Worth, Tex., 1960-61; instr. nursing Tex. Christian U., Ft. Worth, 1961-62; nursing supr. Colo. Gen. Hosp., Denver, 1964-65, pvt. patient practitioner, 1974-78; asst. prof. nursing U. Colo., Denver, 1965-69, asst. prof., clin. instr., 1971-74, asst. prof., 1974-76, acting asst. dean, assoc. prof. continuing edn., regional perinatal project, 1976-78; assoc. prof., chair dept. women's health care nursing U. Rochester Sch. Nursing, N.Y., 1979-84; clin. chief ob-gyn., nursing U. Rochester Strong Meml. Hosp., N.Y., 1979-84; prof., dean U. Wis. Sch. Nursing, Madison, 1984—; cons. and lectr. in field. Author: Maternity Nursing Today, 1973, 76, Health Education for Women: A guide for Nurses and Other Health Professionals, 1986; mem. editorial bd. Jour. Profl. Nursing; contbr. articles to profl. jours. Bur. Health Professions Fed. trainee, 1963-64; Nat. Sci. Service award, 1976-79. Mem. MAIN, AACN, NLN (bd. dirs.), Am. Acad. Nursing, Am. Nurses Assn., Consortium Prime Care Wis. (chair), Health Care for Women Internat., Midwest Nursing Research Soc., Sigma Theta Tau (pres. Beta Eta chpt., co-chair coun nursing practice and edn. 1995). Avocations: golf, biking. Office: U Wis Sch Nursing 600 Highland Ave H6/150 Madison WI 53792-2455

LITWIN, LINDA JOAN, laboratory executive, medical illustrator; b. Hartford, Conn., Aug. 18, 1944; d. Robert Davis and Greta (Westerfeld) Moses; m. Paul Gary Litwin, Apr. 12, 1969 (dec. Apr. 1986); children: Seth Eaton, Jared Stix. Diploma, Mt. Ida Jr. Coll., Boston, 1965; BS, U. Ky., 1968. Med. illustrator U. Ky. Med. Ctr., Lexington, 1966-68, U. Cin. Coll. Medicine, 1969-72, Mayo Inst. of Jewish Hosp., Cin., 1970-76, USDA, 1978—; pvt. swimming instr., 1960-90; freelance horse trainer, instr., 1966—; instr., trainer obedience Capitol Dog Tng. Club, Washington, 1979-85; v.p., co-owner Orthodyne Lab., Inc., Rockville, Md., 1982—. Mem. Jr. Women's Club, Wyoming, Ohio, 1972-77. Recipient awards U.S. Dressage Fedn., 1969-87, U.S. Kennel Club, 1978-85, Pvt. Pilot lic. Airplane SEL, 1986, Instrument Rating, 1992, Wings I award FAA, 1988, Wings II, 1991, Wings III, 1993, Wings IV, 1994, Cert. of Recognition FAA, 1989. Mem. NAFE, Aircraft Owners and Pilots Assn., Internat. Women Pilots Assn. (membership chmn., vice chmn., chmn. Washington chpt. 1993—), Montgomery County Airport Assn. (bd. dirs. 1995—), U.S. Hunter, Jumper Assn., Am. Horse Show Assn., Potomac Valley Dressage Assn. (treas. 1984-86). Office: Orthodyne Lab Inc 771 E Gude Dr Rockville MD 20850-1329

LIU, ALICE YEE-CHANG, biology educator; b. Hunan, China, July 12, 1948; came to U.S., 1970; d. Tin-Kai and Te-Ming (Young) L.; m. Kuang Yu Chen, Aug. 26, 1978; children: Andrew T-H, Winston T-C. BS, Chinese U., Hong Kong, 1969; PhD, Mount Sinai Sch. Med., 1974. Postdoctoral fellow Yale U. Med. Sch., New Haven, Conn., 1974-77; asst. prof. Harvard Med. Sch., Boston, 1977-84; assoc. prof. Rutgers U., Piscataway, N.J., 1984-89, prof., 1989—; dir. grad. program in cell and devel. biology Rutgers U.-U. Medicine-Dentistry N.J.-R.W. Johnson Med. Sch., 1994—; mem. pharmacological scis. rev. com. NIH, 1984-88; mem. cell biology panel NSF, 1989-93, 94-95; mem. basic rsch. adv. group N.J. Commn. on Cancer Rsch., 1989-93, 94—. Author: Receptors Again, 1985; editorial bd. Biol. Signals, 1991—. Recipient N.Y.C. Bd. of Higher Edn. award, 1972, Am. Cancer Soc. Scholar award, Boston, 1982-85; NIH postdoctoral fellow, 1974-77, Medical Found. fellow, Boston, 1977-79. Mem. Am. Soc. Biochemistry and Molecular Biology, Am. Soc. Pharmacology and Experimental Therapeutics. Home: 20 Woodlake Dr Piscataway NJ 08854-5148 Office: Rutgers U PO Box 1059 Nelson Biology Labs Piscataway NJ 08855-1059

LIU, KATHERINE CHANG, artist, art educator; b. Kiang-si, China; came to U.S., 1963; d. Ming-fan and Ying (Yuan) Chang; m. Yet-zen Liu; children: Alan S., Laura Y. MS, U. Calif., Berkeley, 1965. Lectr. N.J., Oreg., Tex., Ohio, N.C., S.C., New Eng., Fla., Okla., Ky. Northwestern and Midwest Watercolor Socs., Rocky Mountain Nat. Watermedia Workshop, U. Va. Ext., Longwood Coll.; mem. teaching staff master class Hill Country Arts Found., Tex., 1995; mem. invited L.A. Artcore Reviewing and Curatorial Bd., 1993; invited juror, lectr. more than 75 exhibits and orgns., 1980—. One-woman shows include Harrison Mus., Utah State U., Riverside (Calif.) Art Mus., Ventura (Calif.) Coll., Fla. A&M U., Louis Newman Galleries, L.A., L.A. Artcore, Lung-Men Gallery, Taipei, Republic of China, State of the Arts Invitational Biennial, Parkland Coll. Ill., 1989, 91, Watercolor U.S.A. Hon. soc. Invitational, Springfield Art Mus., 1989, 91, 94, Hunter Mus. Art, Tenn., 1993, Bakersfield Art Mus., 1994, Chgo. Navy Pier Internat. Art Expo, 1994, Sandra Walters Gallery, Hong Kong, 1994; Invitational, U. Brit. Columbia Art Gallery, 1992, U. Sydney Art Mus., 1992, Ruhr-West Art Mus., Wise, 1992, Macau Art Mus., 1992, Rosenfeld Gallery, Phila., 1994, Mandarin Oriental Fine Arts, Hong Kong, 1994, Horwitch-Newman Gallery, Scottsdale, Ariz., 1995, Watercolor USA Honor Soc. Biennial, 1995; contbr. works to 20 books and 31 periodicals. Co-curator Taiwan-USA-Australia Watermedia Survey Exhbn., Nat. Taiwan Art Inst., 1994; sole juror San Diego Watermedia Internat., 1993, Triton Mus. Open Competition, 1994, Northern Nat. Art Competition, 1994, Watercolor West Nat., 1993, Tenn., Utah, Hawaii, N.C. Watercolor Socs.; co-juror Rocky Mountain Nat., San Diego Internat. and West Fedn. Exhibits; sole juror N.Am. Open, Midwest, Southwest and over 30 state-wide competitions in watermedia or all-media. Recipient Rex Brandt award San Diego Watercolor Internat., 1985, Purchase Selection award Watercolor USA and Springfield (Mo.) Art Mus., 1981, Gold medal, 1986, Mary Lou Fitzgerald meml. award Allied Arts Am. Nat. Arts Club, N.Y.C., 1987, Achievement award of Artists Painting in Acrylic Am. Artists Mag., 1993; NEA grantee, 1979-80. Mem. Nat. Watercolor Soc. (life, chmn. jury 1985, pres. 1983, Top award 1984, cash awards 1979, 87), Watercolor U.S.A. Honor Soc., Nat. Soc. Painters in Casein and Acrylic (2nd award 1985), Rocky Mountain Nat. Watermedia Soc. (juror 1984, awards 1978, 80, 86).

LIVENGOOD, CHARLOTTE LOUISE, employee development specialist; b. L.A., June 18, 1944; d. James Zollie and Zela (Cogburn) L. BS in Secondary Edn., Tex. A & I U., 1968; MEd in Pers. Guidance and Counseling, North Tex. U., 1971. Cert. secondary teaching, Tex.; cert. counselor, Tex. Counselor Gus Grissom High Sch., Huntsville, Ala., 1971-72; tchr. West Springfield High Sch., Springfield, Va., 1972-73; edn. specialist U.S. Dept. Def., El Paso, Tex., 1975-78; instr. El Paso (Tex.) C.C., 1977-78; employee devel. specialist U.S. Office Pers. Mgmt., Dallas, 1978-79; pers. mgmt. specialist Dept. Vets. Affairs, Houston, 1979-87; labor rels. specialist Dept. Vets. Affairs, VA Med. Ctr., Houston, 1987-89; pers. staffing specialist Dept. Vets. Affairs, Houston, 1989-90; employee devel. specialist, acad. tng. officer HUD, Ft. Worth, 1990—; EEO investigator Dept. Vet. Affairs, 1984-87; speaker in field. Editor: (monthly office newspaper) Pipeline, 1980-87. Chairperson, forensics coach Jr. High Sch. Speech Dept., 1968-69; tchr. S. Brand Prarie H.S., 1969-71; mem. Dallas/Ft. Worth Quality Control Coun., Tex. War on Drugs Com., 1990—; hon. mem. Dallas/Ft. Worth Fed. Exec. Bd., 1993-94. Recipient Future Secs. of Am. scholarship, 1962. Mem. Am. Pers. and Guidance Assn., Internat. Transactional Analysis Assn., Tex. State Tchrs. Assn., Tex. Classroom Tchrs. Assn., Fed. Bus. Assn., VA Employee Assn., Intergovernmental Tng. Assn., Intergovernmental Tng. Coun. (chairperson 1993-94). Mem. Church of Christ. Office: US Dept Housing & Urban PO Box 2905 1600 Throckmorton Fort Worth TX 76113-2905

LIVENGOOD, VICTORIA ANN, opera singer; b. Thomasville, N.C., Aug. 8, 1959; d. Gerald Winston and Carolyn Ann (Young) L. MusB in Voice, U. N.C., 1983; MusM in Opera, Boston Conservatory, 1985. tchr. master classes Pittsburg U., Kans., 1990, Temple U., Phila., 1993, U. N.C., Chapel Hill, 1994. Appeared as Queen Gertrude in Hamlet, Greater Miami (Fla.) Opera Co., 1987, Beauty in Beauty and the Beast, Opera Theater St. Louis, 1987, Mercy Kirke in Hazel Kirke, Lake George (N.Y.) Opera, 1987, Giulietta in Les Contes d'Hoffmann, Cleve. Opera Co., Charlotte in Werther, Seattle Opera Co., 1989, Dalila in Samson and Dalila, Lyne Opera, Kansas City, 1990, Dorabella in Cosi Jan Tutte, Hawaii Opera Theater, 1990, Carmen in Carmen, Conn. Opera Co., Hartford, 1990, Dalila in Samson and Dalila, Lyric Opera, Kansas City, 1990, Dorabella in Cosi Fan Tutti, Hawaii Opera Theater, 1990, Oper der Stadt Köln, Cologne, Germany, 1992, Meg Page in Falstaff, Calgary (Can.) Opera Co., 1991, Idamante in Idomeneo, and Sesto in La Clemenza, L'Opera de Nice, France, 1991, Laura in Louisa Miller, Met. Opera Co., N.Y.C., 1991, Mrs. Grose in Turn of the Screw, Edmonton Opera, Can., 1993, Isolier in Il Conte Ory with Charleston's Spoleto Festival, 1993, Maddalena in Rigoletto, Oper der Stadt Köln and Edmonton Opera, 1994, Desideria in the Saint of Bleeker Street, Kansas City Lyric Opera, 1994, Lola in Cavalleria Rusticana, Met. Opera, 1994, Sonetka in Lady Macbeth of Mtsensk, Met. Opera, 1994, Carmen in Carmen, Oper der Stadt Köln, 1995; soloist at J.F. Kennedy Ctr., Washington, 1986; performed with Am. Symphony Orch., Carnegie Hall, N.Y., 1986, N.C. Symphony Orch., Carnegie Hall, 1987, Nat. Symphony Orch., Washington, 1990, Atlanta Symphony Orch., 1991, Balt. Symphony Orch., 1991, Cologne Symphony, Germany, 1992, Minn. Symphony, 1992, Columbus Symphony, 1993, Buffalo Philharm., 1994, Northwest Chamber Mus. Soc., Portland, Oreg., 1994, others; solo recitalist in numerous locations including Boston, N.Y., N.C., Kans., Mo., others; EMI recs. include Oberon (soloist), 1992; subject of article Mus. Am. mag., 1986, Opera News Mag., 1987, 94, 95. Min. music Mills Home Bapt. Ch., Thomasville, 1980-81; recitalist Hosp. Guild, Thomasville, 1980-82, 87, 92, Epilepsy Benefit, Kansas City, Mo., 1989, Aids Benefit-Buffalo Philharmonic N.Y., 1994. Recipient Nat. award Met. Opera Auditions, N.Y.C., 1985, Internat. award Rosa Ponselle Competition, N.Y.C., 1987, Luciano Pavarotti Competition, Phila., 1988, Key to City of Thomasville, 1992; grantee Sullivan Found., 1987, Nat. Inst. Music Theater, 1989. Office: care Herbert Barrett Mgmt 1776 Broadway Ste 1610 New York NY 10019-2002

LIVESAY, CORINNE RYDER, developmental editor, educator; b. Detroit, Apr. 3, 1955; d. George Arthur and Violet Marie (LaVenture) Ryder; m. Stephen Dwight Livesay, Dec. 18, 1978; children: Stephen Brent, Kara Marie, Kathryn Elyse. BS, Bob Jones U., 1978; MBA, Oakland U., 1982. Adult edn. instr. Roseville (Mich.) Cmty. Schs., 1978-82; bus. comm. instr. Macomb Cmty. Sch., Warren, Mich., 1982-86; asst. prof. Liberty U., Lynchburg, Va., 1986-93; devel. editor, writer Austen Press, Homewood, Ill., 1993—; adj. faculty Belhaven Coll., Jackson, Miss., 1994—; tng. cons. Ross Labs., Altavista, Va., 1990-91; trainer Am. Mgmt. Assn. Extension Inst., Lynchburg, Va., 1991-92. Author: Getting and Staying Organized, 1994, Study Guide for Management and Organizational Behavior, 1994, Supervision: Lecture Supplements, 1994, Supervision: Transparency Masters, 1994, Strengthen Your Skills, 1995, Study Guide for Management Comprehension Analysis and Application, 1995. Mem. ASTD. Baptist. Home and Office: 117 Lake Forest Ln Clinton MS 39056

LIVESAY, VALORIE ANN, lead security analyst; b. Greeley, Colo., Sept. 9, 1959; d. John Albert and Mary Magdalene Yurchak. BA in Edn., U. No. Colo., 1981; M in Computer Info. Sys., U. Denver, 1991. Drafter Computer Graphics, Denver, 1981, Advanced Cable Sys., Inc., Denver, 1981-82, Am. TV Comm. Corp., Englewood, Colo., 1982-83; janitor Rockwell Internat., Golden, Colo., 1983-84, analytical lab tech., 1984-86, metall. operator, 1986-88; nuclear material coord. EG&G Rocky Flats Inc., Golden, 1988-92, lead security analyst, 1992—. Active Channel 6, Denver, 1985, World Wildlife Fund, Westminster, Colo., 1987, Denver Dumb Friends League, 1987, The Nature Conservancy, Boulder, Colo., 1989. Mem. NAFE. Home: 6344 W 115th Ave Westminster CO 80020 Office: EG&G Rocky Flats Inc PO Box 464 Rocky Flats Plant Golden CO 80402-0464

LIVINGSTON, ANN CHAMBLISS, lawyer; b. Mpls., July 25, 1952; d. Johnston Redmond and Patricia A. Livingston. BA, Trinity U., San Antonio, 1974; JD, St. Mary's U., San Antonio, 1979. Bar: Tex. 1979, U.S. Ct. Appeals (5th cir.) 1981, U.S. Patent and Trademark Office, 1986, Ct. Appeals (fed. cir.) 1988. Briefing atty. Supreme Ct. of Tex., Austin, 1979-80; assoc. Groce, Locke & Hebdon, San Antonio, 1980-85; ptnr. Gunn, Lee & Jackson, San Antonio, 1985-89; assoc. Baker, Mills & Glast, San Antonio, 1989-90, Baker & Botts, San Antonio, 1990—. Exec. editor St. Mary's U. Law Jour., 1978-79. Mem. Tex. Bar Assn., San Antonio Intellectual Property Law Assn., Phi Delta Phi. Home: HC01 Box 77C Dripping Springs TX 78620 Office: Baker & Botts 98 San Jacinto Blvd Austin TX 78701

LIVINGSTON, BARBARA, educator. BA in Elem. Edn., Bklyn. Coll., 1955; MA in Early Childhood Edn., Adelphi U., 1975. Cert. elem. edn. tchr., N.Y., early childhood edn., N.Y., spl. edn., N.Y. Reading tchr. P.S. 182, Dist. 19, Bklyn., 1974-76; spl. edn. tchr. self-contained classroom P.S. 13, East N.Y.., Bklyn., 1976-81; resource room tchr. P.S. 128, Middle Village, Queens, N.Y., 1981-86; spl. edn. lang. coor./tchr. trainer/ staff developer Dist. Office 24Q, Middle Village, N.Y., 1986-90; VAKTS (reading system)/lang. coord. Dist. 24 Queens, Corona, N.Y., 1988-90; resource room tchr., staff developer Intermediate Sch. 61Q, Corona, N.Y., 1990—. Author: VAKTS (Visual Auditory Kinesthet Tactile, Social-emotion)- A Multi-Sensory Approach to Beginning Reading based on OrtonGillingham Method, 1988. Pres. alumni chpt. Children's Centre for Creative Arts, Adelphi U., Garden City, N.Y., 1974-75; bd. dirs. Alumni Assn., Adelphi U., Garden City, 1974-75; group leader Centre for Creative Arts Saturday Morning Program, Adelphi U., Garden City, 1972-75; dir. adult edn. program Temple Judea Howard Beach, 1974-76. Recipient Educator of Yr. award Assn. Tchrs. of N.Y., 1985. Mem. Orton Dyslexia Soc., Coun. for Exceptional Children (Master Tchr. 1987), ASCD, Internat. Reading Assn., United Fedn. Tchrs., Am. Fedn. Tchrs., Jewish Tchrs. Assn. Home: 15506 86th St Howard Beach NY 11414-2404

LIVINGSTON, MARGARET GRESHAM, civic leader; b. Birmingham, Ala., Aug. 16, 1924; d. Owen Garside and Katherine Molton (Morrow) Gresham; m. James Archibald Livingston, Jr., July 16, 1947; children: Mary Margaret, James Archibald, Katherine Wiley, Elizabeth Gresham. Grad. The Baldwin Sch., Phila., 1942; AB, Vassar Coll., 1945; MA, U. Ala., 1946. Acting dir. Birmingham Mus. Art, 1978-79, 81, chmn. bd. dirs., 1978-86; bd. dirs. Birmingham Civic Ctr. Authority, 1988—; bd. dirs. Altamont Sch., Birmingham, 1963—, chmn. bd. 1986. Named Woman of Yr., Birmingham, 1986; named to Ala. Tennis Hall of Fame, 1994. Mem. Am. Assn. Mus. Episcopalian. Clubs: Jr. League, Ala. State Tennis Assn.

LIVINGSTON, MYRA COHN, poet, writer, educator; b. Omaha, Aug. 17, 1926; d. Mayer L. and Gertrude (Marks) Cohn; m. Richard Roland Livingston, Apr. 14, 1952 (dec. 1990); children: Joshua, Jonas Cohn, Jennie Marks. BA, Sarah Lawrence Coll., 1948. Profl. horn player, 1941-48; book reviewer Los Angeles Daily News, 1948-49, Los Angeles Mirror, 1949-50; asst. editor Campus Mag., 1949-50; various public relations positions and pvt. sec. to Hollywood (Calif.) personalities, 1950-52; tchr. creative writing Dallas (Tex.) public library and schs., 1958-63; poet-in-residence Beverly Hills (Calif.) Unified Sch. Dist., 1966-84; sr. instr. UCLA Extension, 1973—; cons. to various sch. dists., 1966-84, cons. poetry to publishers children's lit., 1975—. Author: Whispers and Other Poems, 1958, Wide Awake and Other Poems, 1959, I'm Hiding, 1961, See What I Found, 1962, I Talk to Elephants, 1962, I'm Not Me, 1963, Happy Birthday, 1964, The Moon and a Star and Other Poems, 1965, I'm Waiting, 1966, Old Mrs. Twindlytart and Other Rhymes, 1967, A Crazy Flight and Other Poems, 1968, The Malibu and Other Poems, 1972, When You Are Alone/It Keeps You Capone: An Approach to Creative Writing with Children, 1973, Come Away, 1974, The Way Things Are and Other Poems, 1974, 4-Way Stop and Other Poems, 1976, A Lollygag of Limericks, 1978, O Sliver of Liver and Other Poems, 1979, No Way of Knowing: Dallas Poems, 1980, A Circle of Seasons, 1982, How Pleasant to Know Mr. Lear!, 1982, Sky Songs, 1984, A Song I Sang to You, 1984, Monkey Puzzle, 1984, The Child as Poet: Myth or Reality?, 1984, Celebrations, 1985, Worlds I Know and Other Poems, 1985, Sea Songs, 1986, Earth Songs, 1986, 1987, Higgledy-Piggledy, 1986, Space Songs, 1988, There Was a Place and Other Poems, 1988, Up in the Air, 1989, Birthday Poems, 1989, Remembering and Other Poems, 1989, My Head Is Red and Other Riddle Rhymes, 1990, Climb Into the Bell Tower: Essays on Poetry, 1990, Poem-making: Ways to Begin Writing Poetry, 1991, Light and Shadow, 1992, I Never Told and Other Poems, 1992, Let Freedom Ring: A Ballad of Martin Luther King, Jr., 1992, Abraham Lincoln, A Man for All the People, 1993, Platero Y Yo/Platero and I (trans. 1994, Flights of Fancy and other poems, 1994, Keep on Singing: A Ballad of Marian Anderson, 1994; The Writing of Poetry, film strips; co-editor: The Scott-Foresman Anthology, 1984; editor 36 anthologies of poetry; contbr. articles on children's lit. to ednl. publs., essays on lit. and reading in edn. to various books; mem. editorial adv. bd. The New Advocate, The Reading Teacher. Officer Beverly Hills PTA Council, 1966-75; pres. Friends of Beverly Hills Public Library, 1979-81; bd. dirs. Poetry Therapy Inst., 1975—, Reading is Fundamental of So. Calif., 1981—. Recipient honor award N.Y. Herald Tribune Spring Book Festival, 1958, excellence in poetry award Nat. Coun. Tchrs. of English, 1980, Commonwealth Club award, 1984, Nat. Jewish Book award, 1987, Kerlan award U. Minn., 1994. Mem. Authors Guild, Internat. Reading Assn., Soc. Children's Book Writers (honor award 1975), Tex. Inst. Letters (awards 1961, 80), So. Calif. Council on Lit. for Children and Young People (Comprehensive Contribution award 1968, Notable Book award 1972, Poetry Quartet award 89), PEN. Address: 9308 Readcrest Dr Beverly Hills CA 90210-2533

LIVINGSTON, PAMELA ANNA, corporate image and marketing management consultant; b. Richmond Hill, N.Y., Nov. 21, 1930; d. Paul Yount and Anna Margaret (Altland) L.; B.A., Adelphi U., 1951; postgrad. NYU, 1952, Columbia U., 1959, Am. Acad. Dramatic Art, 1954, IBM Systems and Mktg. Schs., 1967-70, Brandon Sch. Electronic Data Processing, 1973, Penn State U., 1993. Personnel and public relations depts. Am. Can Co., N.Y.C., 1951-60; exec. sec. to pres. York (Pa.) div. Borg-Warner Corp., 1962-65; freelance writer, 1965-67; mktg. ofcl. IBM Corp., 1967-70; research analyst, dir. new EDP bus. Ins. Co. N. Am., 1971-74; asst. to v.p. corp. affairs IU Internt., Phila., 1974-75; communications and mktg. mgmt. cons. specializing in corp. identity, 1975—; corp. image cons., 1984—; freelance writer, speaker on identity, 1994—. Recipient various journalism awards, award in mktg. and sales IBM, 1969-70, award for innovative product application, 1969. Mem. Sales/Mktg. Execs. Internat., Art Alliance, Public Relations Soc. Am., Econs. Club of York C. of C., Phila. Club Advt. Women, AAUW, Phila. Acad. Fine Arts, World Affairs Council, English-Speaking Union, Kappa Kappa Gamma. Contbr. articles to tech. jours. Home and Office: 108 S Rockburn St York PA 17402-3467

LIVINGSTON, PATRICIA ANN, marine biologist, researcher; b. Detroit, Dec. 10, 1954. BS, Mich. State U., 1976; MS, U. Wash., 1980, M in Pub. Adminstrn., 1987. Ecosystem modeller Nat. Marine Fish Svc., Seattle, 1977-82, trophic interactions program leader, 1983—; mem. sci. and tech. bd. The Sea Use Council, Seattle, 1986—. Contbr. articles on ecosystem modelling and marine fish trophic interactions to profl. jours. Bd. dirs. Little Anchor Child Care Ctr., 1992-93, treas., 1992, pres. bd., 1993. Mem. Am. Fisheries Soc. (officer and regional fish corr. Marine Fish sect. 1982-84, membership chair internat. sect. 1992, soc. membership com. 1991-92). Office: NW and Alaska Fisheries Ctr Bldg 15700 7600 Sand Point Way NE Seattle WA 98115-6349

LIVINGSTONE, CHARLEEN THOMPSON, furniture manufacturer; b. Utica, N.Y., Dec. 13, 1929; d. Charles Alva and Edith Elizabeth (Wagner) Thompson; m. James Richard Livingtone, Apr.12, 1952; children: Charleen E. Steers, Edith A., Jane Roberts. Grad., Mohawk Valley Community Coll., 1949. Asst. prodn. Time Inc., N.Y.C., 1951-52; advt. prodn. Hoag & Provandie, Boston, 1953-55; sales cons. Guy P. Livingstone Co., Winchester, Mass., 1964-95; v.p. Livingstone Mfg. Co. Mass. Inc., Winchester, 1978-95. Apptd. mem. Wellington Sch. Bldg. Com., Belmont, Mass., 1968, elected sec., 1969, elected. chmn. Pro Tem, 1972. Episcopalian. Home: 90 Agassiz Ave Belmont MA 02178-1324 Office: Livingstone Mfg Co Mass Inc 28 Church St Winchester MA 01890-2502

LIVINGSTONE, SUSAN MORRISEY, nonprofit administrator; b. Carthage, Mo., Jan. 13, 1946; d. Richard John II and Catherine Newell (Carmean) Morrisey; m. Neil C. Livingstone III, Aug. 30, 1968. AB, Coll. William and Mary, 1968; MA, U. Mont., 1973; postgrad., Tufts U., 1973, Fletcher Sch. Law and Diplomacy, 1973—. Researcher Senator Mark O. Hatfield, Washington, 1969-70; chief legis. and press asst. Congressman Richard H. Ichord, Washington, 1973-75, adminstrv. asst., 1975-81; cons. Congressman Wendell Bailey, Washington, 1981; exec. asst. VA, Washington, 1981-85, assoc. dep. adminstr. logistics and mgmt., 1985-86, sr. procurement exec., 1985-89, assoc. dep. adminstr. logistics, 1986-89; asst. sec. Army Dept. of Def., Washington, 1989-93; v.p. health and safety svcs. ARC, Washington, 1993—; mem interagy. com. on women's bus. enterprise The White House, 1985-89; mem. Pres.'s Coun. on Mgmt. Improvement, 1985-86. NDEA fellow. Mem. Exec. Women in Govt., Procurement Round Table (bd. dirs. 1994), Assn. U.S. Army (bd. dirs. 1994—), Women in Internat. Security (adv. bd. 1994—). Republican. Episcopalian. Office: ARC 8111 Gatehouse Rd Falls Church VA

LIVINGSTONE, TRUDY DOROTHY ZWEIG, dancer, instructor; b. N.Y.C., June 9, 1946; d. Joseph and Anna (Feinberg) Zweig; m. John Leslie Livingstone, Aug. 7, 1977; 1 child, Robert Edward. Student, Charles Lowe Studios, N.Y.C., 1950-52, Nina Tinova Studio, N.Y.C., 1953-56, Ballet Russe de Monte Carlo, N.Y.C., 1956-57, Bklyn. Coll., 1964-66; BA in Psychology cum laude, Boston U., 1968, MEd, 1969; postgrad., Serena Studios, Carnegie Hall Ballet Arts, N.Y.C., 1973-74. Tchr. Millis (Mass.) Pub. Schs., 1969-72, Hebrew Acad. Atlanta, 1974-76; profl. dancer various orgns. including Rivermont Country Club, Jewish Community Ctr., Callanwolde Performing Arts Ctr., Atlanta, 1974-84; founder, owner, instr. dance Sasha Studios, Atlanta, 1974-77; owner Trudy Zweig Livingstone Studios, Wellesley, Needham, Mass., 1987-88, Palm Beach, Fla., 1989—; judge dance competition Atlanta Council Run-Offs, 1976. Vol. League Sch., Bklyn., 1965, Kennedy Meml. Hosp., Brighton, Mass., 1969, Nat. Affiliation for Literacy Advances, Santa Monica, Calif., 1982. Mem. Am. Alliance for Health, Phys. Edn., Recreation and Dance, Poets of the Palm Beaches, L.A. Athletic Club, Wellesley Coll. Club, Governor's Club (West Palm Beach). Jewish.

LIZANICH-ARO, SUZANNE, health care consultant; b. Newark, Sept. 17, 1953; d. Frank and Natalie Ann Lizanich; m. Karl Stephen Aro, July 1, 1978; 1 child, Stephen Christopher. AAS in Nursing, County Coll. Morris, 1973; BA in English, Fairleigh Dickinson U., 1975; MA in Am. Studies, Seton Hall U., 1976; MPH in Health Svcs. Adminstrn., Johns Hopkins U., 1982. RN, Md., D.C., N.J. Relief charge nurse, staff nurse Dover (N.J.) Gen. Hosp., 1973-76; student health nurse Student Health Ctr. Fairleigh Dickinson U., Madison, N.J., 1973-75; chief occupational health nurse Nat. Health Svcs., Inc., Washington, 1976-77; community health nurse Vis. Nurse Assn., Washington, 1977-78; program asst., ambulatory care mgr. Nat. Capital Med. Found., Inc., Washington, 1978-81; program mgr., project mgr., rev. specialist United Mineworkers Health & Retirement Funds, Washington, 1982-85; dir. utilization rev. Am. PsychMgmt. Inc., Washington, 1985-86; health systems cons. SLA Cons., Inc., Silver Spring, Md., 1986—; progam devel. cons. Green Spring Health Svcs., Columbia, Md., 1989-94; system design cons. Medecision Inc., Berwyn, Pa., 1987—. Office: SLA Cons Inc 1008 Balmoral Dr Silver Spring MD 20903-1303

LIZIK, ANDREA NOREEN, elementary education educator; b. Pitts., Mar. 28, 1953; d. Andrew Thomas and Leona Geraldine (Biesuz) L. BS in Elem. Edn., Edinboro State Coll., 1974; MS in Edn., Duquesne U., 1977. Cert. elem. edn. tchr., Pa. Tchr. St. James Elem. Sch., Apollo, Pa., 1975-78; tchr. Kiski Area Sch. Dist., Vandergrift, Pa., 1978—, head tchr., 1980—, mentor, 1991—. Fellow Marconi Ladies Aux., 1985—, Assumption Ladies Guild, 1982—. Fellow NEA, Pa. State Edn. Assn., Kiski Area Edn. Assn. (rep. coun. 1978—), Delta Kappa Gamma. Home: 194 Fitzgerald St Leechburg PA 15656 Office: Kiski Area Sch Dist 200 Poplar St Vandergrift PA 15690

LLANA, VICKI D., community health/public health nurse; b. Concord, Mass., Sept. 19, 1954; d. John A. and Bonnie C. (Pyles) Harrison; m. Rob Llana, Nov. 15, 1986. BSN, Simmons Coll., 1985; postgrad., NYU, 1994. RN, Mass., N.Y., Vt.; cert. community health nurse. Pub. health nurse Rensselaer County Health Dept., Hoosick Falls, N.Y., 1986-89; hospice home care nurse St. Peter's Hospice, Troy, N.Y., 1988-94; clin. supr. CompCare, Adams, Mass., 1989-91, MCH clin. supr., 1992-93; per diem primary nurse Leonard Home Care, Troy, N.Y., 1991—; psychiat. nurse Samaritan Hosp., Troy, N.Y., 1994; co-owner organic vegetable and sheep farm. Mem. Town Planning Bd.

LLANSA, MARIA ELENA, broadcast executive; b. Havana, Cuba, May 1, 1955; d. Juan Antonio and Odina (Barcala) L. BA in Psychology, U. P.R., 1972; BA in Comm., Loyola U., 1974; MA in Journalism and Comm., U. Fla., 1980. With promotions and mktg. Sta. WTVJ-TV, Miami, 1976-78; coord. franchise Miami Cablesystems, 1980-81; mgr. broadcast system Dynamic Cable Colony Comm., Hialeah, Fla., 1981-83; acct. exec. Sta. WQBA-AM, Miami, 1984; mgr. sales Sta. WQBA-FM, Miami, 1985-91, mgr. sta., 1991-93; pres. Capitalvision Talent & Promotions Inc., Miami, 1993—; v.p. mktg. Capitalvision Prodns., Miami, 1993, 94. Participant Leadership Miami, 1980-81. Roman Catholic. Home: 110 Salamanca Ave Apt P H Miami FL 33134 Office: Capitalvision Talent & Promotions 2490 Coral Way Ste 501 Miami FL 33145

LLOYD, CELESTE SCALISE, lawyer; b. San Antonio, May 15, 1959; d. Robert and Edna (King) Scalise; m. James S. Boyd Jr., Oct. 6, 1984 (div. Dec. 1988); m. Marshall Bruce Lloyd, May 13, 1989. BA, U. Tex., San Antonio, 1979; JD, Tex. Tech U., 1983. Bar: Tex. 1984, U.S. Ct. Appeals (5th cir.) 1984, U.S. Dist. Ct. (so. dist.) Tex. 1985, U.S. Dist. Ct. (no. dist.) Tex. 1990, U.S. Dist. Ct. (we. dist.) Tex. 1991, U.S. Dist Ct. (ea. dist.) Tex. 1992. Field ops. asst. Bur. of Census U.S. Dept. of Commerce, San Antonio, 1980; title examiner, law clk. Lubbock (Tex.) Abstract & Title Co., 1982-83; assoc. Bonilla & Berlanga, Corpus Christi, Tex., 1983-89; sr. assoc. Heard, Goggan, Blair & Williams, San Antonio, 1989-90; assoc. Denton & McKamie, San Antonio, 1990, Joe Weiss and Assocs., San Antonio, 1990; assoc. field litigation office Cigna Law Offices of Sean P. Martinez, San Antonio, 1990—; mem. adv. group Camino Real Health Systems Agy., Inc., San Antonio, 1978-80. Mem. substance abuse adv. com. Planned Parenthood Bd., Corpus Christi, 1983-85; vice chair Nueces County Mental Health/Mental Retardation Substance Abuse Com., San Antonio, 1987-89. Mem. ABA (urban, state and local govt. sect., labor law sect.), Tex. Bar Assn., San Antonio Bar Assn., Bexar County Women's Bar Assn., U. Tex. at

San Antonio Alumni Assn. (v.p.), Delta Theta Phi. Episcopalian. Home: 2130 W Gramercy San Antonio TX 78201 Office: Law Offices Sean P Martinez 300 Convent St Ste San Antonio TX 78205-3713

LLOYD, DEBRA WOOD, banker; b. Anderson, Ind., Apr. 21, 1951; d. Wilburn H. and Mary L. (Robbins) Wood; m. Stephen Michael Lloyd, Oct. 9, 1992. BA, Anderson (Ind.) U., 1973; MBA, Butler U., Indpls., 1982. Comml. lender Merchants Nat. Bank, Indpls., 1976-85, Irving Trust Co., N.Y.C., 1985-86; v.p., comml. real estate lender Peoples Bank & Trust Co., Indpls., 1986—; part-time instr. comml. lending U. Indpls., 1991. Vol. Conner Prairie, Noblesville, Ind., 1985—, Pan Am Games, Indpls., 1987, U.S. Rowing, Indpls., 1988—; del. 1st Japan-Am. Grassroots Summit, Tokyo, 1991; bd. dirs. YWCA of Indpls., grad. Exec. Women's Leadership Program; mem. adv. coun. Bus. Women's Ctr. Mem. Japan Am. Soc., Columbia Club (new dimensions com.), Robert Morris Assocs., English Speaking Union, Contemporary Club. Republican. Office: Peoples Bank & Trust Co 130 E Market St Indianapolis IN 46204-3204

LLOYD, JACQUELINE, English language educator; b. N.Y.C., Aug. 21, 1950; d. R.G. and Hortense (Collins) L. BA, Fisk U., 1972; MEd, U. North Fla., 1989. Adj. prof. Edward Waters Coll., Jacksonville, Fla., 1983, 90—. Mem. Nat. Coun. Tchrs. English. Democrat. Presbyterian. Home: 5006 Andrew Robinson Dr Jacksonville FL 32209-1002

LLOYD, LEONA LORETTA, judge; b. Detroit, Aug. 6, 1949; d. Leon Thomas and Naomi Mattie (Chisolm) L.; 1 stepson, Joseph Andersen. BS, Wayne State U., 1971, JD, 1979. Bar: Mich. 1981, U.S. Dist. Ct. (ea. dist.) 1981, U.S. Supreme Ct. 1988, U.S. Cir. Ct. (6th cir.) 1983. Speech, drama tchr. Detroit Bd. Edn., 1971-75; instr. criminal justice Wayne State U., Detroit, 1981; sr. ptnr. Lloyd and Lloyd, Detroit, 1982-92; prin. asst., corp. counsel City Detroit Law Dept., 1992-94; judge 36th Dist. Ct., Detroit, 1994—. Co-author, dir. (gospel musical) Freedom Song, 1991. Wayne State U. scholar, 1970, 75; recipient Fred Hampton Image award, 1984, Kizzy Image award, 1985, Nat. Coalition of 100 Black Women Achievement award, 1986, Community Svc. award Wayne County exec. William Lucas, 1986, Merit Black Law Student Assn. cert. U. Detroit, 1986, Spirit of Detroit award, 1991, Keep This Dream Alive award Martin Luther King Assn., 1995, Special Tribute award State of Mich., 1995, Resolution award County of Wayne, 1995, Appreciation cert. City of Detroit, 1995, Bar Assn. award B'nai B'rith Barristers, 1995, Testimonial Resolution award Detroit City Coun., 1995; named to Black Women Hall of Fame. Mem. ABA, Wolverine Bar Assn., Mary McLeod Bethune Assn., Nat. Acad. of Recording Arts & Scis., Mich. State Bar. Office: 421 Madison Ste 3067 Detroit MI 48226

LLOYD, SUSAN ELAINE, middle school educator; b. Sioux Falls, S.D., Aug. 25, 1942; d. Travis Monroe and Lois Elaine (Herridge) Hetherington; m. Jerry Glynn Lloyd, Mar. 13, 1982; children: Joseph Sanders Rogers III, Melissa Elaine Rogers. BS in Edn., SW Tex. State U., 1965; MA, U. Tex., San Antonio, 1979; AA, Stephens Coll., 1962. Cert. reading specialist, supervisory, art (all levels), secondary English, elem. edn. Art tchr. South Park Ind. Sch. Dist., Beaumont, Tex., 1965-68; reading specialist John Jay High Sch., San Antonio, 1979-84; reading dept. coord. Sul Ross Mid. Sch., Northside Ind. Sch. Dist., San Antonio, 1984—, remedial reading tchr., 1990; developer reading curricula, cons.; advisor Scholastic TAB Book Club, 1992—. Author: Reading Education in Texas, 1992, 93. Named Sul Ross Middle Sch. Tchr. of Yr., 1993, Trinity U. Disting. Educator, 1993. Mem. ASCD, Internat. Reading Assn. (hon. chmn. 14th ann. SW regional meeting, presenter 19th 1991, 20th 1992), Tex. Reading Coun., Alamo Reading Assn., Assn. Tex. Profl. Educators, San Antonio Watercolor Group. Home: 7614 Tippit Trl San Antonio TX 78240-3627 Office: Sul Ross Mid Sch 3630 Callaghan Rd San Antonio TX 78228-4323

LLOYD, THERESA ANN, intensive care nurse; b. Bklyn., Nov. 13, 1956; d. Edward J. and Dorothy H. (Motyka) Linnick; m. Kevin R. Lloyd, Oct. 15, 1983; children: Darren, Curtis. Diploma, Pilgrim Psychiat.Ctr., Brentwood, N.Y., 1977; BSN, SUNY, 1988. Staff nurse Franklin Gen. Hosp., Valley Stream, N.Y., 1978-79, charge nurse cardiac step down, 1980-81, ICU staff nurse, 1981-87, ICU head nurse, 1987-88, ICU staff nurse, 1988-93; obstetrics staff nurse, 1993—, maternity nurse, 1994—; CPR instr. Am. Heart Assn., Mincola, N.Y., 1983-88. Mem. Am. Heart Assn. Methodist. Home: 139 Oakley Ave Elmont NY 11003 Office: Franklin Hosp Med Ctr 900 Franklin Ave Valley Stream NY 11580

LLOYD, WANDA SMALLS, newspaper editor; b. Columbus, Ohio, July 12, 1949; d. Gloria Walker; m. Willie Burk Lloyd, May 25, 1975; 1 child, Shelby Renee. BA, Spelman Coll., Atlanta, 1971. Copy editor Providence Evening Bull., R.I., 1971-73, Miami Herald, Fla., 1973-74, Atlanta Jour., Ga., 1974-75, Washington Post, 1975-76; instr. program for minority journalists Columbia U., N.Y.C., summer 1972; dep. Washington editor Times-Post News Service, 1976-86; dpt. mng. editor cover stories, USA Today, 1986-87, mng. editor/adminstrn., 1987-88, sr. editor, 1988—; cons. So. Regional Press Inst., Savannah State Coll., Ga., 1973—; mem. adv. bd. urban journalism workshop Howard U., Washington, 1983—. Mem., bd. dirs. Nation's Capital council, Girl Scouts U.S., Washington 1985; trustee Spelman Coll., 1988—; mem. adv. com. Alfred Friendly Found., 1992—; bd. dirs. The Newspaper Fund, 1992—. Mem. Washington Assn. Black Journalists, Nat. Assn. Black Journalists, Washington Spelman Alumnae Assn. (v.p. 1984-86; Named Alumna of Yr. 1985), Delta Sigma Theta. Baptist. Office: USA Today 1000 Wilson Blvd Arlington VA 22209-3991*

LLOYD-JONES, JEAN G. HALL, state legislator; b. Washington, Oct. 14, 1929; d. John and Lucille Thurston Hall; m. Richard Lloyd-Jones, 1951; children: Richard A., Mary, John D., Jeffrey. Student, U. N.Mex., 1946-49; BA, Northwestern U., 1951; MA, U. Iowa, 1970. Mem. Iowa Ho. of Reps., 1979-86; mem. Iowa Senate, 1987-91, pres. pro tempore, 1991—. Mem. LWV (pres. Iowa state league 1972-76), NOW, Iowa Assn. R.R. Passengers, UN Assn., Iowa Peace Inst. Democrat. *

LO, THERESA NONG, health science administrator; b. Hai Phong, Vietnam, Mar. 16, 1945; d. Dang Van and Boi Thuy (Lam) Nong; m. Chu Shek Lo, Dec.27, 1969; 1 child, Francesca Che Lo. Student, Ottumwa Heights Coll., 1964-65; BA, Clarke Coll., 1968; PhD, Ind. U., Indpls., 1974. Lab. asst. Clarke Coll., Dubuque, Iowa, 1966-68; teaching/rsch. asst. Med. Ctr. Ind. U., Indpls., 1968-73; USPHS postdoctoral trainee U. Calif., San Francisco, 1973-75; vis. fellow Nat. Heart, Lung & Blood Inst., Bethesda, Md., 1975-77; vis. fellow Nat. Cancer Inst. NIH, Bethesda, 1977-78; rsch. chemist Lab. of Cellular Metabolism, Nat. Heart, Lung & Blood Inst., Bethesda, 1979-82, Lab. Chem. Pharmacology, Nat. Heart, Lung & Blood Inst., Bethesda, 1982-88; health sci. adminstr. trainee div. blood diseases & resource Nat. Heart, Lung & Blood Inst., Bethesda, 1988-89; chemist rev. logistics br. NIH, Bethesda, 1989-91; scientific review adminstr., review br. Nat. Inst. Arthritis & Musculoskeletal & Skin Diseases, Bethesda, Md., 1991—; liaison to Drug Enforcement Adminstrn., U.S. Dept. Justice, lab. chem. pharmacology Nat. Heart, Lung and Blood Inst., Bethesda, 1982-83, coord. sci. seminar program lab. chem. pharmacology, 1982-83; role model NIH career day div. equal opportunity NIH, Bethesda, 1988, 90, 91; U.S. savs bond canvasser, 1989; exec. sec. NIH Asian/Pacific Islander Am. Adv. Com., 1991, vice chair, 1992—, NIAMS EEO Adv. Com., 1992—; invited speaker Chinese Acad. Med. Scis., Beijing, 1982, Ottumwa Quota Club, 1964,. Contbr. articles and abstracts to profl. jours. Sec. Orgn. Chinese Ams., Inc., Greater Washington, 1984, woman rep. White House briefing, Washington, 1985; participant women's mgmt. tng. initiative HHS Pers. Adminstrn., 1987-88; bd. dirs. Orgn. of Chinese Ams., Greater Washington, 1991-92. Ottumwa Quota Club scholr, 1965, Clarke Coll. scholar, 1965-68; named hon. citizen City of Indpls., 1968, hon. speedway ambassador Civil Town of Speedway (Ind.), 1972; recipient Spl. Achievement award Nat. Cancer Inst., div. extramural activities, 1990. Mem. Am. Soc. for Biochemistry and Molecular Biology, Am. Soc. for Pharmacology and Exptl. Therapeutics, Am. Soc. for Cell Biology, Inflamation Rsch. Assn., Cardiovascular Rsch. Inst. Alumni Assn., Ind. U. Alumni Assn, Clarke Coll. Alumni Assn., Sigma Xi. Home: 5304 Elsmere Ave Bethesda MD 20814-1647 Office: NIAMS Review Br Natcher Bldg Rm 5AS-37B Bethesda MD 20892-6500

LOAN, LORI ALICE, neonatal nurse, nurse researcher; b. Tacoma, Wash., May 27, 1960; d. Norman Wayne and Carlene Alice (Van Houten) Stanke; m. Bradley Jay Loan, June 27, 1981; children: Alia Marie, Tana Jay. BSN, Pacific Luth. U., 1982; MS, U. Wash., 1992, PhD, 1995. RN, Wash.; cert. neonatal ICU nurse. Clin. nurse neonatal ICU Madigan Army Med. Ctr., Tacoma, 1982-86, nurse specialist neonatal ICU, 1986-89, project dir. nursing rsch. svc., 1989-93; sr. nurse researcher, 1994—; test item writer CCRN neonatal, 1992-93, exam devel. com., 1994—. Bd. dirs. Puget Sound Sch. Gymnastics, Puyallup, Wash., 1981—; speakers bur. Western Wash. chpt. March of Dimes, 1989—. Bristol-Myers Squibb Found. scholar ANA and Bristol-Myers Squibb Found., 1991; recipient Nat. Rsch. Svc. award Nat. Inst. Nursing Rsch., 1992. Mem. AACN, Nat. Assn. Neonatal Nurses (Rsch. grantee 1991), Pacific N.W. Assn. Neonatal Nurses, NCC, Sigma Theta Tau. Lutheran. Home: 2313 Tacoma Point Dr E Sumner WA 98390-9486 Office: Madigan Army Med Ctr Dept Nursing Nursing Rsch Svc Tacoma WA 98431-5383

LOBER, IRENE MOSS, education educator; b. N.Y.C., Aug. 1, 1927; d. David and Beckie Moss; BS in Edn., CCNY, 1948; MA, George Washington U., 1967; EdD, Va. Poly. Inst. and State U., 1974; m. Solomon William Lober, Oct. 25, 1947; children: Clifford Warren, Richard Wayne, Lori Ann. Registered sch. bus. adminstr. Formerly tchr., librarian; prin. staff devel. Fairfax County (Va.) Pub. Schs., 1965-77; supt. University City (Mo.) Pub. Schs., 1977-81, Danbury (Conn.) Pub. Schs., 1981-85; prof. SUNY Coll. at New Paltz, 1985—, chmn. dept. ednl. adminstrn., 1990—, dir. EdD program, 1993—; guest lectr. Washington U., George Washington U., Va. Poly. Inst., U. Va., Fordham U., C.W. Post Coll., L.I. U.; mem. bus. adv. council Datahr, Inc., 1982-85; pres. N.Y. State Coun. for Advancement of Depts. of Ednl. Adminstrn., 1994; cons. in field; founding incorporator Sci. Horizons Inc., Danbury, 1984-85; founding incorporator COMPUtourney Inc., 1990—; designated disting. expert and peer reviewer Asst. Sec. Edn. Chester finn, 1987-89; speaker/presentor various internat., nat. and state confs. and convs. Author: Promoting Your School, 1993; contbr. articles to profl. jours. Chairperson Mo. Instructional TV Council, 1981; mem. legal and govt. studies group Nat. Inst. Edn. Dept HEW, nat. adv. bd. U. Wis. Rsch. and Devel. Ctr., 1978-80, lay adv. bd. St. Louis Met. Med. Soc., 1980-81; bd. advisors St. Josephs Inst. for the Deaf, 1980-81; pres. adv. cabinet Greater St. Louis Council Girl Scouts U.S., 1980-81, bd. dirs. Southwestern Conn. Council, 1981-85; bd. dirs. Fairfield council Boy Scouts Am., Danbury region Jr. Achievement, 1981-86, Regional Hospice, Danbury, 1984-86, Danbury Conn. Am. Heart Assn., 1985-86; apptd. supt. in residence, Western Conn. State U., 1984; exec. bd., trustee United Way No. Fairfield County; div. chairperson United Way campaign, 1982-86; trustee, bd. dirs. United Way, Danbury, 1982-85; elected mem. bd. edn. Poughkeepsie City Sch. Dist., 1993—. Recipient Townsend Harris medal CCNY Alumni Assn.; IDEA fellow; Ford Found. grantee, 1977-78. Mem. ASCD, Am. Assn. Sch. Adminstrs. (nat. chmn. higher edn com. 1987-89, mem. membership svcs. com.), Am. Mgmt. Assn., Sch. Adminstrs. Assn. N.Y. State, Ednl. Rsch. Svc., N.Y. State Coun. Sch. Supts., N.Y. State Assn. Sch. Bus. Ofcls., Assn. Sch. Bus. Ofcls. Internat. (nat. chmn. maintenance and ops. research com. 1985-89), Nat. Assn. Secondary Sch. Prins. (chair profs. secondary sch. adminstrn. com.), NEA (profs. of higher edn. commn.), Authors Guild, Authors League, Nat. Assn. Elem. Sch. Prins., Phi Delta Kappa (pres. New Paltz chpt. 1991-93), Phi Kappa Phi, Pi Lambda Theta (publs. adv. bd. 1981-84). Office: SUNY-New Paltz 101 Old Main New Paltz NY 12561

LOBIG, JANIE HOWELL, special education educator; b. Peoria, Ill., June 10, 1945; d. Thomas Edwin and Elizabeth Jane (Higdon) Howell; m. James Frederick Lobig, Aug. 16, 1970; 1 child, Jill Christina. BS in Elem. Edn., So. Ill. U., 1969; MA in Spl. Edn. Severely Handicapped, San Jose State U., 1989. Cert. elem. tchr., Calif., Mo., Ill., handicapped edn., Calif., Mo.; ordained to ministry Presbyn. Ch. as deacon, 1984. Tchr. trainable mentally retarded children Spl. Luth. Sch., St. Louis, 1967-68; tchr. trainable mentally retarded and severly handicapped children Spl. Sch. Dist. St. Louis, 1969-80, head tchr., 1980-83; tchr. severly handicapped children San Jose (calif.) Unifed Sch. Dist., 1983-86; tchr. autistic students Santa Clara County Office Edn., San Jose, 1986—; tchr. Suzanne Dancers, 1991-92. Vol. Am. Cancer Soc., San Jose, 1986-89, 92, St. Louis Reps., 1976-82, Am. Heart Assn., 1985—, Multiple Sclerosis Soc., 1990—; troop leader Camp Fire Girls, San Jose, 1984-85; moderator bd. deacons Evergreen Presbyn. Ch., 1986-89; mem. exec. bd. Norwood Creek Elem. Sch. PTA, 1983-86. Mem. Council for Exceptional Children, Assn. for Severly Handicapped, Nat. Edn. Assn., Calif. Tchrs. Assn. Republican. Home: 3131 Creekmore Way San Jose CA 95148-2805 Office: Fred Marten Spl Sch 14265B Story Rd San Jose CA 95127-3823

LOBRON, BARBARA L., writer, editor, photographer; b. Phila., Mar. 19, 1944; d. Martin Aaron and Elizabeth (Gots) L.; student Pa. State U., 1962-63; B.A. cum laude, Temple U., Phila., 1966; student photography Harold Feinstein, N.Y.C., 1970, 79-80; student art therapy Erika Steinberger, N.Y.C., 1994—. Reporter, writer Camden (N.J.) Courier-Post, 1966-68; editorial asst. Med. Insight mag., N.Y.C., 1970-71; mng. editor Camera 35 mag., N.Y.C., 1971-75, also asso. editor photog. anns. for U.S. Camera/ Camera 35, 1972, 73; freelance editor as Word Woman, N.Y.C., 1975-77, 79—; acct. exec. Bozell & Jacobs, N.Y.C., 1977-79; copy editor Camera Arts mag., N.Y.C., 1981-83; editorial coord. Center mag., Nat. Ctr. Health Edn., 1985; editorial coord. Popular Photography mag., 1986-95; contbg. editor Photograph; Photographs: group exhbns. include Internat. Women's Art Festival, N.Y.C., 1975, Rockefeller Ctr., N.Y.C., 1976, Photograph Gallery, N.Y.C., 1981 ; acrylic painting exhbns. at Tchrs. Coll., N.Y.C., 1994; represented in collection Library of Calif. Inst. Arts, Valencia. Tchr. Sch. Vol. Program, N.Y.C., 1994—. Recipient 1st pl. honors Dist. 1, Internat. Assn. Bus. Communicators, 1977. Copy editor: The Complete Guide to Cibachrome Printing, 1980, The Popular Photography Question and Answer Book, 1979, The Photography Catalog, 1976, Strand: Sixty Years of Photography, 1976, You and Your Lens, 1975; contbr. articles to comml. publs., chpts. to books. Dist. leader SGI-USA. Buddhist. Avocations: acting, ceramics, reading, photography, singing. Home: 85 Hicks St Apt 7 Brooklyn NY 11201-6825

LOCALIO, MARCIA JUDITH, medical/surgical nurse; b. Phila., June 14, 1947; d. Herman Julius and Mildred Barbara (Brown) Bandarsky; m. Anthony Bernard Localio, Feb. 25, 1967; children: Jennifer Hope, David Anthony. Diploma in nursing, Bucks County Vocat. Tech. Sch., 1984; ADN, Bucks County Community Coll., 1989; student, Ctr. for Nursing Excellence, Thomas Edison State Coll. RN, N.J., Pa.; cert. EMT, instr. CPR, first aid; cert. phlebotomist Am. Soc. Clin. Pathology. Instr. CPRand EMT State of N.J., Princeton; nurse instr. IV therapy and venipuncture State of N.J., North Princeton Devel. Ctr. Recipient nursing scholarship, State of N.J., Sustained Achievement award N.J. Dept. Human Svcs., 1991-92. Mem. Am. Soc. Clin. Pathologists (assoc.), N.J. Nursing Assn., Intravenous Nurses Soc.

LOCHANKO, ELIZABETH ALEXANDRA, communications executive; b. Toronto, Ontario, Can., Apr. 30, 1957; came to U.S., 1960; d. Adam and Alexandra (Zabuga) L. BA, Rutgers U., 1979; M of Music, Johns Hopkins U., 1982. Office mgr. Simos C. Dimas Esquire, N.Y.C., 1982-84; pub. rels. mgr. 'K' Lines/Cloud Tours, N.Y.C., 1984-86; sr. acct. exec. Peter Martin Assocs., N.Y.C., 1986-88; sr. v.p. corp. communications Sony Pictures Entertainment, L.A., 1988—. Mem. NAFE, Johns Hopkins Alumni Assn., Douglass Rutgers Alumni Assn., Phi Beta Kappa.

LOCKART, BARBETTA, counselor, jeweler, artwear designer, artist; b. Sacramento, Calif., Feb. 28, 1947; d. Bernard Elwood and Naomi Joyce (Wilson) L.; m. Michael Stanley Ray, Dec. 29, 1982 (div). AA in English, Southwestern Coll., Chula Vista, Calif., 1974; BA, San Diego State U., 1975; MA in Edn. Adminstrn., N.Mex. State U., Las Cruces, 1979, MA in Counseling and Guidance, 1981. Sec., interim coord., tchr. Indian Edn. Project, Palm Springs (Calif.) Unified Sch. Dist., 1976-79; outreach counselor Tecumseh House/Boston Indian Coun., 1980-81, asst. dir., 1981; acad. counselor, coord. native Am. affairs Ea. N.Mex. U., Portales, 1981-82; ind. researcher in field of counseling, Albuquerque, 1982-89, Sacramento, Calif., 1989—; pres., Sacramento, 1989—; owner Dearwater Designs, Albuquerque, 1985-88, Sacramento, 1988-90, Barbetta's Beads & Art, Sacramento, 1990—; speaker in field of community edn., alcoholism, urban native Am. women. Rockefeller Found. fellow, 1978-79; Nat. Inst. Edn. fellow, 1979-80. Author: Resolving Discipline Problems for Indian Students: A Preventative Approach, 1981, Auctions and Auction-Going: Make Them Pay Off for You; contbr. articles to profl. jours.

LOCKBAUM, MARIE CAROL, flight attendant; b. Ridley Park, Pa., July 10, 1948; d. George Earl and Marie Ann (Hyland) L. Grad. h.s., Darby, Pa. Sec. for law firm Miami, Fla., 1967-68; sec. ARA Svcs., Phila., 1968-70; flight attendant Am. Airlines, Chgo., 1970—; instr. Am. Airlines, N.Y.C., 1975-76, supr., 1976. Chair Wings Found., Dallas, 1988—. Home: # E-309 5350 Toscana Way Apt 309 E San Diego CA 92122-5663

LOCKE, ELIZABETH HUGHES, foundation administrator; b. Norfolk, Va., June 30, 1939; d. George Morris and Sallie Epps (Moss) Hughes; m. John Rae Locke, Jr., Sept. 13, 1958 (div. 1981); children—John Rae III, Sallie Curtis. B.A. magna cum laude with honors in English, Duke U., 1964, Ph.D., 1972; M.A., U. N.C., 1966. Instr. English, U. N.C., Chapel Hill, 1970-72; vis. prof. English, Duke U., Durham, N.C., 1972-73, dir. univ. pubs., 1973-79; corp. contbns. officer Bethlehem Steel Corp., Pa., 1979-82; dir. edn. div. and communications Duke Endowment, Charlotte, N.C., 1982—; past pres. Communications Philanthropy, Washington; cons. to communication community Coun. on Founds., Washington, 1985—; mem. Ind. Sect. bd. com. on pub. edn. Editor: Duke Encounters, 1977, Prospectus for Change: American Private Higher Education, 1985, (mag.) Issues, 1985—. Pres., Jr. League, Durham, 1976, Hist. Preservation Soc., Durham, 1977, Pub. Rels. Soc. Am., Charlotte chpt., 1988, Charlotte Area Donors Forum; past pres. Sch. of Arts, Charlotte; bd. visitors Davidson Coll., Charlotte Country Day Sch., Duke U., Johnson C. Smith U. Recipient Leadership award Charlotte C. of C., 1984; Danforth fellow, 1972. Mem. Nat. Task Force, English Speaking Union, Phi Beta Kappa. Democrat. Episcopalian. Club: Tower. Office: 100 N Tryon St # 3500 Charlotte NC 28202-4012

LOCKE, LINDA HAUTAU, elementary school teacher; b. Detroit, Aug. 8, 1944; d. Llewellyn Alwin Hautau and Madlyn Irene (Hitchings) Hautau Hanton; m. Ronald Floyd Locke, Sept. 11, 1965; children: Rhonda Faye Locke Oldford, Ann Marie. BS, Wayne State U., 1965, MA, 1985, post-grad., 1989. Life cert. provisional tchr. elem. and mid. sch., Mich. Tchr. Port Huron (Mich.) Area Sch. Dist., 1965-70, 76—; tchr. mem. instrnl. devel. coun. Port Huron Area Sch. Dist.; tchr. cons. Learning Resources, Port Huron, 1990—. Tchr. Sunday sch. Faith Luth. Ch., Port Huron, 1973-80; active Lakeport Elem. Sch. PTA; mem. Bluewater Math./Scis. Coun., treas., 1991—. Runner up Tchr. of Yr. award Jaycees, Port Huron, 1978; nominated Presdl. Sci. Tchr., Washington, 1991. Mem. NEA, AAUW (treas. Port Huron br. 1992), Mich. Edn. Assn. Office: Lakeport Elem Sch 3835 Franklin St Lakeport MI 48059-1930

LOCKE, MARY ESTHER, psychologist; b. Hartford, Conn., July 21, 1949; d. Philip and Esther (Brainard) L.; m. Robin Christian Shear, July 16, 1983; children: Sarah Merrill, Philip Christian. BA, Wellesley Coll., 1971; MA, San Francisco State U., 1972, Loyola U., Chgo., 1985; PhD, Loyola U., Chgo., 1986. Lic. clin. psychologist, Ind. Clinician Tipton (Ind.) Cmty. Counseling Ctr., 1984-86, dir., 1986-87; dir. psychology New Medico at Visitors Hosp., Buchanan, Mich., 1987-89; rehab. psychologist N.E. Ind. Rehab. Inst., Ft. Wayne, 1991-93; pvt. practice, Ft. Wayne, 1988—. Bd. dirs. Ft. Wayne Dance Collective, 1990-92; bd. dirs. Three Rivers Montessori, Ft. Wayne, 1990-94, v.p., 1991-92. Mem. APA, Ind. Psychol. Assn., Nat. Register Health Svc. Providers in Psychology. Home: 9921 Woodstream Dr Fort Wayne IN 46804-7005

LOCKE, VIRGINIA OTIS, textbook editor, behavioral sciences writer; b. Tiffin, Ohio, Sept. 4, 1930; d. Charles Otis and Frances Virginia (Sherer) L. BA, Barnard Coll., 1953; postgrad., Duke U. Program officer, asst. corp. sec. Agrl. Devel. Coun., N.Y.C., 1954-66; staff psychologist St. Luke's-Roosevelt Med. Ctr., N.Y.C., 1973-75; freelance writer and editor N.Y.C., 1976-85; writer-editor Cornell U. Med. Coll./N.Y. Hosp. Med. Ctr., N.Y.C., 1986-89; sr. editor humanities and social scis. coll. divsn. Prentice Hall divsn. Simon & Schuster, Englewood Cliffs, N.J., 1989—. Co-author: (coll. textbook) Introduction to Theories of Personality, 1985, The Agricultural Development Council: A History, 1989. Founder Help Our Neighbors Eat Year-round (H.O.N.E.Y.), Inc., N.Y.C., chmn., 1983-87, vol., 1987—, newsletter editor, 1992—; reader Recording for the Blind, N.Y.C., 1978-84; vol. Reach to Recovery program Am. Cancer soc., Bergen County, N.J., 1990—. Recipient Our Town Thanks You award, N.Y.C., 1984, Mayor's Vol. Svc. award, N.Y.C., 1986, Cert. of Appreciation for Community Svc. Manhattan Borough, 1986, Jefferson award Am. Ins. Pub. Svc., Washington, 1986.

LOCKE-MATTOX, BERNADETTE, athletic administrator; b. Rockwood, Tenn., Dec. 31, 1958; d. Alfred M. and Nola (Gillespie) Locke; m. Vincent Mattox, July 6, 1991. Assoc. Degree, Roane State Coll., 1979; Bachelor Degree, U. Ga., 1981. Tchr. Danielsville (Ga.) High Sch., 1982; acad. advisor U. Ga., Athens, 1982-83, asst. coach, 1985-90; customer svc. rep. Xerox Corp., Atlanta, 1984-85; asst. coach U. Ky., Lexington, 1990-94, asst. athletic dir., 1994—; with broadcasting Sta. WKYT-TV/Host Com., Lexington, 1994—. Hon. chair Children's Miracle Network, 1994—; bd. dirs. Jobs Am. Grads., 1994—. Named Outstanding Sports Figure, Complex Women's Sports Hall of Fame, 1990, Oustanding Female, No Nonsense Panty Hose, Tex., 1992, Woman of Yr., Women's Ctr. Ky., 1994, Master's Sports Woman of Yr., Women's Sports Found., 1994, Outstanding Young Lexingtonian, C. of C., 1994. Office: Univ of Ky Memorial Coliseum Lexington KY 40506-0032

LOCKETT/GARZA, CAROL DENISE, graphic designer, photographer; b. Memphis, July 25, 1959; d. Calvin Coolidge Miller and Betty Lee (Lockett) Scott; m. David Ramirez Garza, Mar. 24, 1983 (div. Oct. 1992); children: David Ramirez Garza II, Taylore Lauren. AA in Visual Comms., Md. Coll. Art and Design, 1991; BA in Graphic Design, Coll. Notre Dame of Md., 1993. Illustrator Urban Profile Mag., Balt., 1991; intern Patuxent Pub. Co., Columbia, Md., 1992; designer, illustrator Morrese, Inc., N.Y.C., 1993; freelance graphic designer, illustrator CLGraphics, Columbia, 1993—. Artist: calendar for Montgomery County Equal Housing Commn., 1991; artist, designer inauguration quilt for pres. of Coll. of Notre Dame of Md., 1992. Active Jeffers Hill Elem. Sch. PTA, Columbia, 1990-92; vol. Girl Scouts Am., Columbia, 1991-92. Mem. Nat. Mus. for Women in the Arts, Nat. Geographic Soc., Am. Mus. Natural History, Nat. Trust for Hist. Preservation, Graphic Artists Guild, Advt. and Graphic Arts Soc. Howard County, Alumnae Assn. Coll. Notre Dame of Md. Home: 8953 Footed Ridge Columbia MD 21045-5418

LOCKHART, AILEENE SIMPSON, retired dance, kinesiology and physical education educator; b. Atlanta, Mar. 18, 1911; d. Thomas Ellis and Aileene Reeves (Simpson) L. B.S., Tex. Woman's U., 1932; M.S., U. Wis., 1937, Ph.D., 1942; D.Sc. (hon.), U. Nebr., 1967. Mem. faculty Mary Hardin Baylor Coll., Belton, Tex., 1937-42, U. Wis., 1941-42; asst. prof., then assoc. prof. phys. edn. and pharmacology U. Nebr., 1942-49; assoc. prof., then prof. U. So. Calif., 1949-73; dean Coll. Health, Phys. Edn., Recreation and Dance Tex. Woman's U., 1973-78, prof. dance and phys. edn., chmn. dept. dance, 1978-83, adj. prof., 1983-88; Clare Small lectr. U. Colo., 1975; Ethel Martus Lawther lectr. U. N.C., 1978; Amy Morris Homans lectr., Milw., 1976; Donna Mae Miller Humanities scholar/lectr. , U. Ariz., Tucson, 1989; vis. prof./lectr. Iowa State U., univs., Wash., Oreg., Wis., Mass.; N.H., Calif. State U., Long Beach, Springfield (Mass.) Coll., Smith Coll., Wellesley Coll., U. Maine-Presque Isle, Dunfermline Coll., Edinburgh, Scotland, U. Brazil, Brasilia; cons. editor William C. Brown Publishing Co., Dubuque, Iowa, 1954—. Author or co-author 12 books; contbr. numerous articles profl. jours.; cons. editor or editor over 200 books. Recipient Disting. Alumnae award Tex. Woman's U., 1971, Disting. Alumnae award U. Wis.-Madison, 1981, Cornaro award, 1980, Honor award Ministry Edn., Taiwan, 1981, Minnie Stevens Piper Found. award State of Tex., 1983, Nat. Dance Assn. Heritage award, 1985; Amy Morris Homans fellow, 1961-62; honra ao Merito Ministerio de Educato and Cultura Brazilia, Brazil, 1977; Nat. Dance Assn. scholar, 1986; Tex. Assn. Health, Phys. Edn., Recreation and Dance scholar, 1986. Fellow Am. Coll. Sports Medicine, Am. Alliance Health, Phys. Edn., Recreation and Dance (Honor award 1963, Luther Halsey Gulick award 1980), Am. Acad. Phys. Edn. (pres. 1980-81, Hetherington award 1992); mem. Nat. Assn. Girls and Women in Sports (honor award 1991), Nat. Dance Assn., So. Assn. Phys. Edn. Coll. Women, Nat. Assn. Phys. Edn. in Higher Edn., Phi Kappa Phi. Presbyterian.

LOCKHART, GEMMA, television producer, writer; b. Rapid City, S.D., Dec. 5, 1956; d. Jim and Teena L.; children: Mica, Nakca, Aaron. BA in English, Creative Writing, Dartmouth Coll., 1979. TV news reporter Duhamel Broadcasting Enterprises, Rapid City, S.D., 1974-80; TV producer Rural Ethnic Inst., Rapid City, 1981-83; instr. Oglala Lakota Coll., Kyle, S.D., 1983-86; horse rider Black Hills, S.D.; TV producer S.D. Pub. TV, Vermillion, 1989-90; ind. producer, 1990—; CEO Wambli Win Prodns., 1994—; auditor Lakota Elders, Dakota Land, 1975—; freelance columnist various publs. including USA Today, 1992—; CEO Wambli Win Prodns., 1994. Mem. NAFE, Dartmouth Coll. Alumni Coun. (editorial bd. alumni mag.). Republican. Home: PO Box 8044 Rapid City SD 57709-8044 also: Dark Canyon Rapid City SD 57702

LOCKHART, MADGE CLEMENTS, educational organization executive; b. Soddy, Tenn., May 22, 1920; d. James Arlie and Ollie (Sparks) Clements; m. Andre J. Lockhart, Apr. 24, 1942 (div. 1973); children: Jacqueline, Andrew, Janice, Jill. Student, East Tenn. U., 1938-39; BS, U. Tenn., Chattanooga and Knoxville, 1955, MEd, 1962. Elem. tchr. Tenn. and Ga., 1947-60, Brainerd High Sch., Chattanooga, 1960-64, Cleveland (Tenn.) City Schs., 1966-88; owner, operator Lockhart's Learning Ctr., Inc., Cleveland and Chattanooga, 1975—; co-founder, pres. Hermes, Inc., 1973-79; co-founder Dawn Ctr., Hamilton County, Tenn., 1974; apptd. mem. Tenn. Gov.'s Acad. for Writers. AuthAor poetry, short stories and fiction; contbr. articles to profl. jours. and newspapers. Pres. Cleveland Assn. Retarded Citizens, 1970, state v.p., 1976; pres. Cherokee Easter Seal Soc., 1973-76, Cleveland Creative Arts Guild, 1980; bd. dirs. Tenn. Easter Seal Soc., 1974-77, 80-83; chair Bradley County Internat. Yr. of Child; mem. panel for grants Coun. Govts. S.E. Tenn. Devel. Dist., 1990-92; mem. Internat. Biog. Centre Adv. Coun., Cambridge, Eng., 1991-92; mem. mayor's com. Mus. for Bradley County, Tenn., 1992—. Recipient Service to Mankind award Sertoma, 1978, Gov.'s award for service to handicapped, 1979; mental health home named in her honor, Tenn., 1987. Mem. NEA (life), Tenn. Edn. Assn., Am. Assn. Rehab. Therapy, S.E. Tenn. Arts Coun., Cleveland Edn. Assn. (Service to Humanity award 1987). Mem. Ch. of Christ. Clubs: Byliners, Fantastiks. Home: 3007 Oakland Dr NW Cleveland TN 37312-5281

LOCKLEAR, HEATHER, actress; b. L.A., Sept. 25, 1961; d. Bill and Diane L.; m. Tommy Lee, 1986 (div. 1994); m. Richie Sambora, 1994. Appeared in (TV series) Dynasty, 1981-89, T.J. Hooker, 1982-87, Going Places, 1990, Melrose Place, 1992—, (films) Firestarter, 1986, Return of the Swamp Thing, 1990, Waynes World 2, 1993, (TV movies) Twil, 1981, City Killer, 1984, Blood Sport, 1986, Texas Justice, 1995. Office: William Morris Agy 151 El Camino Blvd Beverly Hills CA 90212*

LOCKNER, VERA JOANNE, farmer, rancher, legislator; b. St. Lawrence, S.D., May 19, 1937; d. Leonard and Zona R. (Ford) Verdugt; m. Frank O. Lockner, Aug. 7, 1955; children: Dean M., Clifford A. Grad., St. Lawrence (S.D.) High Sch., 1955. Bank teller/bookkeeper First Nat. Bank, Miller, S.D., 1963-66, Bank of Wessington, S.D., 1968-74; farmer/rancher Wessington, 1955—. Sunday sch. tchr. Trinity Luth. Ch., Miller, 1968-72; treas. PTO, Wessington, 1969-70; treas., vice chmn., chmn., state com. woman Hand County Dems., Miller, 1978—. Named one of Outstanding Young Women of Am., Women's Study Club, Wessington, 1970. Mem. Order of Ea. Star (warder, marshall, chaplain 1970—). Home and Office: RR 2 Box 102 Wessington SD 57381

LOCKWOOD, HELSHI, advertising executive; b. East Orange, N.J., May 18, 1941; d. Warren Sewell and Ann Frances (Gleason) L.; m. Bertram A. Tunnell Jr., Dec. 13, 1969 (div. Oct. 1976); children: Bertram A. III, Tory Lockwood; stepchildren: John, Mark, Tracy, Wendy, Jan, Kate; m. William B. Hewson Jr., May 30, 1981; 1 child, Charles W.; stepchildren: William B. III, Andrew L., Elizabeth S. BA, Pa. State U., 1963. Promotion asst. Vogue Mag., London, 1963-64; advt. sales rep. Brides Mag., London, 1964-65; west coast mgr. Status Mag., L.A., 1965-67; asst. advt. mgr. Status Mag., N.Y.C., 1968-69; advt. sales rep. Eye Mag., N.Y.C., 1967-68; N.Y. mgr. Phil. and Boston Mags., N.Y.C., 1969-76; v.p. Metro Mag., N.Y.C., 1976-78; exec. v.p., ptnr. Catalyst Communications, N.Y.C., 1978-80; account mgr. Dun's Rev., N.Y.C., 1980-82; ea. advt. dir. Dun's Bus. Month, N.Y.C., 1982-84, advt. dir., 1984-85; dir. nat. accounts Chgo. Mag., N.Y.C., 1986; ea. advt. mgr. Mediatex Nat. Sales, N.Y.C., 1987-88, v.p., nat. sales dir., 1989-94, v.p., mng. dir., 1994—. Deacon Brick Ch., N.Y.C., 1983. Mem. Advt. Women N.Y. Republican. Episcopalian. Home: 8 Hanson Rd Darien CT 06820-2502 Office: Mediatex Nat Sales 420 Lexington Ave Ste 1908 New York NY 10170-0156

LOCKWOOD, LINDA PICKHARDT, accountant, financial planner; b. Chgo., Sept. 19, 1944; d. Frederick Oswald and Lillian (Sadowski) Pickhardt; m. Frank Stephen Lockwood, June 25, 1966 (div. Dec. 1991); children: Amy Helen, Rebecca Elizabeth. BA, Ripon (Wis.) Coll., 1965; MEd, No.Ill. U., 1973. CPA, Ill.; CFP. Elem. tchr. Warrenville (Ill.) Sch. Dist., 1965-67, Fulton County Schs., Atlanta, 1967-68, DeKalb County Schs., Atlanta, 1968-69; adminstrv. asst. Oddessy Press, N.Y.C., 1969-70; elem. tchr. Lake Zurich (Ill.) Sch. Dist., 1971-73; acct. JPB & Assocs., Barrington, Ill., 1989-90, Dow, Wood & Co., Barrington, Ill., 1990—. Mem. AICPA, Ill. Soc. CPAs, Internat. Bd. of Cert. Fin. Planners. Office: Dow Wood & Co 44 N Walkup Ave Crystal Lake IL 60014

LOCKWOOD, LOIS MINIELY, animal hospital executive; b. Boise, Idaho, Nov. 23, 1924; d. Howard John and Margaret E. (Danielson) Miniely; m. Robert W. Lockwood, Jan. 19, 1945; children: Linda K. Lockwood Johnson, Craig H. BA in Social Welfre, U. Calif., Berkeley, 1949. V.p. Diversified Baby Products, Covina, Calif., 1984-88; prin. Commonwealth Animal Hosp., Fullerton, Calif., 1987—. Pres. H.S. and grade sch. PTA, West Covina, Calif., 1966-70, LWV, West Covina, 1966-68; leader Girl Scouts U.S.A. and Boy Scouts Am., West Covina, 1960-65; fund raiser Dorothy Chandler Pavilion; mem. West Covina Planning Coun., 1965. Named Citizen of Yr., West Covina C. of C., 1964. Mem. AAUW (pres. West Covina 1966-68). Home: 2136 E Vine Ave West Covina CA 91791 Office: Commonwealth Animal Hosp 1941 W Commonwealth Ave Fullerton CA 92633

LOCKWOOD, MOLLY ANN, communications company executive; b. London, Sept. 19, 1936; d. Warren Sewell and Ann Frances (Gleason) L.; BS, Pa. State U., 1958. With exec. tng. program Lord & Taylor, N.Y.C., 1958-60; assoc. merchandising editor House & Garden Mag., N.Y.C., 1960-65; advt. dir. Status Mag., N.Y.C., 1965-70; merchandising dir. Holiday Mag., N.Y.C., 1970; account mgr. Ladies' Home Journal Mag., N.Y.C., 1970-72; adv. dir. Girl Talk Mag., N.Y.C., 1972-74; mktg. dir./assos. pub. East/West Network Mag., N.Y.C., 1974-77; pres., chief exec. officer, ptnr. Catalyst Communications, Inc., N.Y.C., 1977—; pres. Catalyst Pub. Inc., 1987—; sec. bd. 244 Madison Realty Corp., 1984—; mktg. and sales dir. Mus. Mag., 1979-83. Mem. Advt. Women N.Y., Am. Soc. Travel Agts., Rear Guard, Kappa Kappa Gamma Alumnae Assn. Home: 1133 Park Ave New York NY 10128-1246 Office: Catalyst Comm Inc 260 Madison Ave New York NY 10016-2401

LOCKWOOD, RHONDA J., mental health services professional; b. Jacksonville, N.C., Apr. 4, 1960; d. George Barton and Sally Lynn (Hassell) L. BA, Newberry Coll., 1982; MS in Edn., Youngstown State U., 1988. nat. cert. counselor. Corrections/tng. officer Geauga County Sheriff's Dept., Chardon, Ohio, 1982-87; forensic counselor Human Svcs. Ctrs., Inc., New Castle, Pa., 1987-89; dir. children & family svcs. Marion Citrus Mental Health Ctrs., Inc., Ocala, Fla., 1989—; founder Sexual Abuse Intervention Network, Ocala, 1990—, chair, 1990-92, Family Svcs. Planning Team, 1992-94; mem. Svc. Assessment Team Dist. 13, 1993-94; cons. Health & Human Svcs. Bd. Dist. 13, 1993-94. Pol. vol. state campaigns Democratic Party, Warren, Ohio, 1978-85; mem. Sexual Abuse Prevention Edn. Network, New Castle, 1987-88; cons. Mad Dads Orgn., Ocala, 1993; mem. Juvenile Justice Coun., Ocala, 1993-94. Recipient Outstanding Teen Vol. award Am. Red Cross, 1977. Fellow N. Eastern Ohio Police Benevolent Assn.; mem. Nat. Mus. for Women in the Arts, Nat. Bd. Cert. Counselors, Chi Sigma Iota, Phi Kappa Phi. Democrat. Home: 201 E Main St Archer FL 32618 Office: Marion Citrus Mental Health Emerald Ctr 324 SE 24th St Ocala FL 34471

LODOWSKI, RUTH ELLEN, physician; b. Dallas, Feb. 15, 1951; s. Charles Harry and Genevieve (Gowaty) L. BS, U. Tex., 1972; MBA, North Tex. State U., Denton, 1976; MD, U.Tex.-San Antonio, 1986. Resident asst., then head resident Castilian Dormitory, Austin, Tex., 1971-73; singer self-employed band, Austin, 1972-74; teller Greenville Ave. Bank, Dallas, 1974-75; employment interviewer Tex. Employment Commn., Grand Prairie, 1975-76; personnel intern U.S. Dept. Justice, Seagoville, Tex., 1976-77; personnel asst. Army and Air Force Exchange Service, San Antonio, 1977-78; staffing adminstr., personnel adminstr. Tex. Instruments Inc., Dallas, 1978-81, U. Tex. Med. Sch. at San Antonio, 1982-86; intern, then resident Parkland Meml. Hosp., Dallas, 1986-90; pvt. practice medicine specializing in psychiatry, Dallas, 1990—; clin. faculty psychiatry dept. U. Tex. Southwestern Med. Sch., Dallas, 1991—. Mem. AMA, Am. Psychiat. Assn., Tex. Med. Assn., Tex. Soc. Psychiat. Physicians, Dallas County Med. Soc., Kiwanis Internat. (top ten medal of honor). Address: 12201 Merit Dr Ste 660 Dallas TX 75251-2262

LOEB, DEANN JEAN, nurse; b. West Union, Iowa, Aug. 1, 1960; d. Dale Alfred and Annagene Helen (Suhr) Ungerer; m. Thomas Allan Loeb, Sept. 1, 1985; children: Ryan, Jennifer, Andrea, Cody. Diploma in nursing, NE Iowa Tech. Inst., 1982. Lic. practical nurse, Iowa. Laundry aide Good Samaritan Ctr., West Union, 1977, kitchen aide, cook, 1977-79, nurses asst., 1979-81, practical nurse, 1982-84; practical nurse Ind. (Ind.) Care Ctr., 1985-89, Dr. Jose C. Aguiar, Waterloo, Iowa, 1989-93, Dr. John Musgrave-Dr. Mary O'Connell, Waterloo, Iowa, 1993-94; nurse Waterloo Asthma and Allergy Clinic, 1994—. Leader Brownies, asst. leader Girl Scouts U.S.; tchr. Bible, Sunday sch., mem. parish bd. edn., mem. parish life com. Zion Jubilee Luth. Ch., Jesup, Iowa. Republican. Home: 7144 Spring Creek Rd Jesup IA 50648-9568

LOEB, FRANCES LEHMAN, civic leader; b. N.Y.C., Sept. 25, 1906; d. Arthur and Adele (Lewisohn) Lehman; student Vassar Coll., 1924-26; L.H.D. (hon.), NYU, 1977; m. John L. Loeb, Nov. 18, 1926; children: Judith Loeb Chiara, John L., Ann Loeb Bronfman, Arthur Lehman, Deborah Loeb Brice. N.Y.C. commr. for UN and Consular Corps, 1966-78. Exec. com. Population Crisis Com., Washington; life mem. bd. Children of Bellevue, Inc., 1974—; bd. dirs. Internat. Presch., Inc., N.Y. Landmarks Conservancy; chmn. bd. East Side Internat. Community Ctr., Inc.; mem. UN Devel. Corp., 1972-94; life trustee Collegiate Sch. for Boys, N.Y.C.; trustee Cornell U., 1979-88, trustee emeritus, 1988—; trustee Vassar Coll., 1988—; bd. overseers Cornell U. Med. Coll., 1983-88 (life mem. 1988—), Inst. Internat. Edn. (life). Mem. UN Assn. (dir.). Clubs: Cosmopolitan, Vassar, Women's City (N.Y.C.). Home: 730 Park Ave New York NY 10021-4945 also: Anderson Hill Rd Purchase NY 10577 also: Lyford Cay, Nassau The Bahamas

LOEB, JANE RUPLEY, university administrator, educator; b. Chgo., Feb. 22, 1938; d. John Edwards and Virginia Pentland (Marthens) Watkins; m. Peter Albert Loeb, June 14, 1958; children: Eric Peter, Gwendolyn Lisl, Aaron John. BA, Rider Coll., 1961; PhD, U. So. Calif., 1969. Clin. psychology intern Univ. Hosp., Seattle, 1966-67; asst. prof. ednl. psychology U. Ill., Urbana, 1968-69, asst. coord. rsch. and testing, 1968-69, coord. rsch. and testing, 1969-72, asst. to vice chancellor acad. affairs, 1971-72, dir. admissions and records, 1972-81, assoc. prof. ednl. psychology, 1973-82, assoc. vice chancellor acad. affairs, 1981-94, prof. edn. psychology, 1982—. Author: College Board Project: the Future of College Admissions, 1989. Chmn. Coll. Bd. Coun. on Entrance Svcs., 1977-82; bd. govs. Alliance for Undergrad. Edn., 1988-93; active charter com. Coll. Bd. Acad. Assembly, 1992-93. HEW grantee, 1975-76. Mem. APA, Am. Ednl. Rsch. Assn., Nat. Coun. Measurement in Edn., Harvard Inst. Ednl. Mgmt. Home: 1405 N Coler Ave Urbana IL 61801-1625 Office: U Ill 1310 S 6th St Champaign IL 61820-5796

LOEB, JEANETTE WINTER, investment banker; b. N.Y.C., June 18, 1952; d. Leon and Fay (Rotenberg) Winter; m. Peter Kenneth Loeb, Nov. 1, 1980; 1 child, Alexander Winter. BA, Wellesley Coll., 1974; MBA, Harvard U., 1977. Assoc. Goldman, Sachs & Co., N.Y.C., 1977-81, v.p., 1981—, ptnr. 1986—. Wellesley Coll. Devel. Fund chmn. for N.Y. Mem. Phi Beta Kappa. Club: India House. Office: Goldman Sachs & Co 85 Broad St New York NY 10004-2434

LOEBEL, JANE LOUISE, psychotherapist; b. Milw., Aug. 31, 1927; d. Philip R. and Edith Louise (Kaplan) Brachman; m. Harlan John Blare, Aug. 31, 1949 (dec.); children: Katherine J., John Philip; m. Kurt W. Loebel, June 6, 1970. BA, U. Ill., 1949; MA, U. Chgo., 1961. Lic. marriage, family & child counselor, Calif. Counselor Counseling Ctr. U. Colo., Boulder, 1961-66; counselor, acting dir. Marriage Counselors Office Sacramento Superior Ct., 1966-70; founder, co-dir. Women's Therapy Ctr., Berkeley & El Cerrito, Calif., 1978-86; pvt. practice psychotherapy Berkeley, 1970—. Mem. Assn. Family Therapists No. Calif. (pres. 1971-76, bd. dirs., program dir.). Democrat. Unitarian.

LOEBLICH, HELEN NINA TAPPAN, paleontologist, educator; b. Norman, Okla., Oct. 12, 1917; d. Frank Girard and Mary (Jenks) Tappan; m. Alfred Richard Loeblich, Jr., June 18, 1939; children: Alfred Richard III, Karen Elizabeth Loeblich, Judith Anne Loeblich Covey, Daryl Louise Loeblich Valenzuela. BS, U. Okla., 1937, MS, 1939; PhD, U. Chgo., 1942. Instr. geology Tulane U., New Orleans, 1942-43; geologist U.S. Geol. Survey, Washington, 1943-45, 47-59; mem. faculty UCLA, 1958—, prof. geology, 1966-84, prof. emeritus, 1985—, vice chmn. dept. geology, 1973-75; research assoc. Smithsonian Instn., 1954-57; assoc. editor Cushman Found. Foraminiferal Research, 1950-51, incorporator, hon. dir., 1950—. Author: (with A.R. Loeblich, Jr.) Treatise on Invertebrate Paleontology, part C, Protista 2, Foraminiferida, 2vols., 1964, Foraminiferal Genera and Their Classification, 2 vols., 1987, Foraminifera of the Sahul Shelf and Timor Sea, 1994; author: The Paleobiology of Plant Protists, 1980; mem. editl. bd. Palaeoecology, 1972-82, Paleobiology, 1975-81; contbr. articles to profl. jours., govt. publs. and encys. Recipient Joseph A. Cushman award Cushman Found., 1982; named Woman of Yr. in Sci. Palm Springs Desert Mus., 1987; Guggenheim fellow, 1953-54. Fellow Geol. Soc. Am. (sr., councilor 1979-81); mem. Paleontol. Soc. (pres. 1984-85, patron 1987, medal 1982), Soc. Sedimentary Geology (councilor 1975-77, hon. mem. 1978, Raymond C. Moore medal 1984), UCLA Med. Ctr. Aux. (Woman of Yr. medal), AAUP, Internat. Paleontological Assn., Paleontol. Rsch. Inst., Am. Microscopical Soc., Am. Inst. Biol. Scis., Phi Beta Kappa, Sigma Xi. Home: 1556 W Crone Ave Anaheim CA 92802

LOEB-MUNSON, STELLA MARIE, school system administrator; b. Cleve., Feb. 14, 1943; d. Charles Harold and Beulah Hortense (Franklin) Loeb; children: Charles William, Maisha Kwetu. BS in Elem. Edn., Kent State U., 1969; MS in Ednl. Adminstrn., St. John Coll., 1974. Tchr. Cleve. Pub. Schs., 1969-72; freshman advisor spl. svcs., dir. peer counseling Case Western Res. U., Cleve., 1977-80, asst. dir. spl. svcs., 1977-80; classroom tchr. East Cleveland (Ohio) City Schs., 1981-84, curriculum specialist, 1984-85, bldg. prin., 1985—; mem. adv. bd. Young Audiences of Greater Cleve., Inc.; dist. chair East Cleve. Computer Com., 1988—; facilitator, presenter Ohio Dept. Edn., 1991, Ohio Acad. for Prins., 1987-91; presenter Cleve. State U., Lakeland C.C., 1991. Mem. program adv. com. Young Audiences Greater Cleve., 1991. Stella Loeb-Munson day proclaimed by East Cleve. City Coun. and Mayor, 1991; recipient Disting. Arts Educator award Ohio Arts Edn. Assn., 1994, Ohio N.E. Regional Disting. Arts Educator award, 1994; named Nat. Disting. Prin. U.S. Secondary Edn., 1991, Prin. Leadership Nat. Safety Ctr., Nat. Assn. Elem. Sch. Prins., Nat. Assn. Secondary Sch. Prins., 1992. Mem. N.E. Ohio Computer Consortium (bd. dirs. 1988—), ASCD, Nat. Assn. Elem. Sch. Adminstrs., Ohio Assn. Elem. Sch. Adminstrs. (Disting. Prin. Ohio 1991), Phi Delta Kappa (greater Cleve. inter-univ. chpt., named Disting. Educator of Yr. 1992). Democrat. Office: Caledonia Sch 914 Caledonia Ave Cleveland OH 44112-2319

LOEHRKE, CHRISTINE CAROL, rehabilitation facility administrator; b. Dayton, Ohio, June 9, 1950; d. Eugene Max and Carol Jean (Showalter) L. BA in Psychology, Wittenberg U., 1973. Psychology asst. Vocat. Guidance & Rehab. Services, Cleve., 1973-76, program mgr., 1976-79, tng. specialist, 1979-81; dir. rehab. and planning Goodwill Industries Inc., Dayton, Ohio, 1981-84; assoc. dir. Youth Enrichment Services Inc., Cleve., 1984-87, Epilepsy Found. N.E. Ohio, Cleve., 1987-94; exec. dir. Epilepsy Found. Northeast Ohio, Cleve., 1994—; instr. Cuyahoga Community Coll., Parma, Ohio, 1979-81; co-founder Westside Guidance Ctr., Lakewood, Ohio, 1974-76; vol. counselor Third Legacy Alcoholism Ctr. Inc., Lakewood, 1974-76. Co-author: (bus. plan) Implementation of a Prime Manufacturing subsidiary in a Sheltered Workshop, 1985. Recipient cert. appreciation Council Exceptional Children, 1977, cert. appreciation, Kiwanis, 1978; named Disting. Rehab. Profl., Nat. Disting. Service Registry Med. and Vocat. Rehab. Div., 1987. Mem. Nat. Rehab. Assn., Nat. Rehab. Adminstrs. Assn., Ohio Rehab. Adminstrs. Assn. (bd. dirs. 1982-84, 88—), N.E. Ohio Rehab. Assn. (bd. dirs.), NAFE. Democrat. Lutheran. Home: 1034 E 171st St Cleveland OH 44119-3102 Office: Epilepsy Found of NE Ohio 2800 Euclid Ave #450 Cleveland OH 44115

LOESCH, KATHARINE TAYLOR (MRS. JOHN GEORGE LOESCH), communication and theatre educator; b. Berkeley, Calif., Apr. 13, 1922; d. Paul Schuster and Katharine (Whiteside) Taylor; student Swarthmore Coll., 1939-41, U. Wash., 1942; BA, Columbia U., 1944, MA, 1949; grad. Neighborhood Playhouse Sch. of Theatre, 1946; postgrad. Ind. U., 1953; PhD, Northwestern U., 1961; m. John George Loesch, Aug. 28, 1948; 1 child, William Ross. Instr. speech Wellesley (Mass.) Coll., 1949-52, Loyola U., Chgo., 1956; asst. prof. English and speech Roosevelt U., Chgo., 1957, 62-65; assoc. prof. communication and theatre U. Ill. at Chgo., 1968—; assoc. prof. emerita speech in communication and theater, U. Ill., Chgo., 1987—. Contbr. writings to profl. jours.; poetry performances. Active ERA, Ill., 1975-76. Am. Philos. Soc. grantee, 1970; U. Ill., Chgo., grantee, 1970. Mem. MLA, Speech Communication Assn. (Golden Anniversary prize award 1969, chmn. interpretation div. 1979-80), Celtic Studies Assn. N.Am., Pi Beta Phi. Episcopalian. Office: U Ill Dept Performing Arts PO Box 4348 MC/132 Chicago IL 60680

LOESCH, MABEL LORRAINE, social worker; b. Annandale, Minn., July 1, 1925; d. Rudolph and Hedwig (Zeidler) Treichler; m. Harold Carl Loesch, Oct. 19, 1945; children: Stephen, Gretchen, Jonathan, Frederick. BS, La. State U., 1972, MSW, 1974. Cert. Acad. Cert. Social Worker, bd. cert. diplomate. Tchr. Am. schs. Tegucigalpa, Honduras, 1960-61, Guayaquil, Ecuador, 1962-66, La Ceiba, Honduras, 1966-67; supr. clin. svc. Blundon Home, Baton Rouge, 1974-81; social worker, cons. Dhaka, Bangladesh, 1981-85; social worker Manna Food Bank, Pensacola, Fla., 1986—; adj. instr. social work dept. Southern U., Baton Rouge, 1976-81. Editor: Making Do, 1989, Making Do II, 1994. Mem. adv. com. Luth. Ministries of Fla., 1993—. Mem. NASW, Mensa (local sec. 1986-90, chair scholarships com.), Phi Kappa Phi. Democrat. Lutheran. Home: 2140 E Scott St Pensacola FL 32503-4957

LOESCHER, BARBARA ANN, auditing executive; b. Mauston, Wis., Aug. 20, 1953; d. Arnold John Loescher and Carol Jeanne (Vinopal) Gross. BS in Bus. and Acctg., Edgewood Coll., 1988. CPA, Wis; cert. internal auditor, fraud examiner. Acct. Harco Ins. Co., Milw., 1977-78; corp. acct. Blunt Ellis and Loewi, Milw., 1978-79; fin. technician Cumis Ins. Soc., Inc., Madison, Wis., 1979-81; budget, tax and cost specialist Cumis Ins. Soc., Inc., Madison, 1981-83, risk mgmt. investment specialist, 1983-84, fraud auditing mgr., 1984-90; asst. to sr. v.p. individual life and health mktg. CUNA Mut. Fin. Svcs. Corp., Inc., Madison, 1990-91; pres., COO, Fin. Standards Group, Inc., Boca Raton, Fla., 1991-94; pres. Loescher & Assocs., Boca Raton, 1994—; lectr. seminars on auditing, risk mgmt. and fraud. Author of numerous articles in field. Mem. AICPA, Wis. Inst. CPAs, Inst. Internal Auditors (sec. 1987), Nat. Assn. Cert. Fraud Examiners. Republican. Roman Catholic. Home and Office: 21479 Sweetwater Ln S Boca Raton FL 33428

LOEVINGER, JANE, psychologist, educator; b. St. Paul, Feb. 6, 1918; d. Gustavus and Millie (Strouse) L.; m. Samuel I. Weissman, July 13, 1943; children: Judith, Michael B. BA in Psychology, U. Minn., 1937, MS in Psychometrics, 1938; PhD. in Psychology, U. Calif., Berkeley, 1944. Instr. psychology and edn. Stanford (Calif.) U., 1941-42; lectr. psychology U. Calif., Berkeley, 1942-43; part-time instr. in stats. and sociology Washington U., St. Louis, 1946-47, research psychologist and cons. air force projects, 1950-53, research assoc. prof. child psychiatry, 1960-64, research assoc. prof., Grad. Inst. Edn., 1964-71, research assoc., Social Sci. Inst., 1964-70, research prof., 1971-74, prof., 1974-88, Stuckenberg prof. human values and moral devel., 1984-88, prof. emeritus dept. psychology, 1988—; rsch. assoc. Jewish Hosp., St. Louis, 1954-60; mem. personality and cognition research rev. com. NIMH, 1970-74; ad hoc reviewer U. Witwatersrand, Johannesburg, Republic of South Africa, 1985, NSF, NIMH, various other orgns.; mem. various coms. Washington U.; lectr. in field. Author: (with R. Wessler) Measuring Ego Development 1: Construction and Use of a Sentence Completion Test, 1970, (with R. Wessler and C. Redmore) Measuring Ego Development 2: Scoring Manual for Women and Girls, 1970, Ego Development: Conceptions and Theories, 1976, Scientific Ways in the Study of Ego Development, 1979, Paradigms of Personality, 1987; cons. editor: Psychol. Rev., 1983—, Jour. Personality and Social Psychology, 1984—, Jour. Personality Assessment 1987—; contbr. articles to profl. jours., book revs., letters and abstracts. Recipient Research Sci. award NIMH, 1968-73, 74-79; Ednl. Testing Service Disting. Vis. scholar, 1969; Margaret M. Justin fellow, 1955-56, NIMH grantee, 1956-79. Fellow Am. Psychol. Assn. (pres. Div. 5 1962-63, mem. com. on tests, mem. policy and planning bd. 1969-72, mem. policy task force on psychologists in criminal justice system 1976-77, pres. Div. 24 1982-83, com. on early career award in personality 1985), Phi Beta Kappa, Sigma Xi (assoc.). Democrat. Home: 6 Princeton Ave Saint Louis MO 63130-3136 Office: Washington U Dept Of Psychology Saint Louis MO 63130

LOEWE, BARBARA, religion educator; b. Newark, Nov. 11, 1938; d. Oscar U. and Lillian (Freund) L. BS, Fla. So. Coll., 1960; MA, Western Res. U., 1961; postgrad., U. Denver, Fla. State U. Tchr. Manatee County Schs., Bradenton, Fla., 1960-63; instr. SUNY, Brockport, 1965; asst. prof. Bloomsburg (Pa.) State Coll., 1965-68; prof. Hillsborough C.C., Tampa, 1969—; guest lectr., counselor, minister Universal Ch. of the Master, Santa Clara, Calif., 1979—; real estate investor, Tampa, 1970—. Bd. dirs. Meadowood Condominium Assn., Tampa, 1979-85, pres., 1979-85; bd. dirs. Hillsborough C.C. chpt. Fla. United Svcs., 1988, Stageworks Theatre, 1989-90, Mary Walker Apts. of Tampa Jewish Fedn., 1995—. Mem. Fla. Comms. Assn. (exec. sec., treas. 1986-90), S.E. Regional Minister's Assn. of Universal Ch. of the Master (treas. 1994-95, chair 1995—), Mensa (mem. exec. com. Tampa Bay chpt. 1987—). Home: PO Box 151173 Tampa FL 33684-1173

LOEWENTHAL, NESSA PARKER, educator; b. Chgo., Oct. 13, 1930; d. Abner and Frances (Ness) Parker; m. Martin Moshe Loewenthal, July 7, 1951 (dec. Aug. 1973); children: Dann Marcus, Ronn Carl, Deena Miriam; m. Gerson B. Selk, Apr. 17, 1982 (dec. June 1987). BA in Edn. and Psychology, Stanford U., 1952. Faculty Stanford Inst. for Intercultural Communication, Palo Alto, Calif., 1973-87; dir. Trans Cultural Svcs., San Francisco, 1981-86, Portland, Oreg., 1986—; dir. dependent svcs. and internat. edn. Bechtel Group, San Francisco, 1973-81, internat. edn. cons., 1981-84; mem. adv. com. dept. internat. rels. Lesley Coll., Cambridge, Mass., 1986—; mem. Bay Area Ethics Consortium, Berkeley, 1989-92; mem. Oreg. Ethics Commons, 1993—; chmn. ethics com. Sietar Internat., Washington, 1987—; mem. faculty Summer Inst. for Internat. Comms., Portland, Oreg., 1987—, mem. governing bd., 1992—. Author: Professional Integration, 1987, Update: Federal Republic of Germany, 1990, Update: Great Britain, 1987; author, editor book series Your International Assignment, 1973-81; contbr. articles to profl. jours. Mem. equal opportunity and social justice task force Nat. Jewish Rels. Adv. Coun.; bd. dirs. Kids on the Block, Portland; mem. Lafayette (Calif.) Traffic Commn., 1974-80; bd. dirs. Ctr. for Ethics and Social Policy, 1988—; mem. exec. bd. and planning com. Temple Isaiah, Lafayette, 1978-82; bd. dirs. Calif. Symphony, Orinda, 1988-90; mem. exec. com. overseas schs. adv. com. U.S. Dept. State, 1976-78. Named Sr. Interculturalist, Sietar Internat., 1986. Mem. ASTD, Soc. for Intercultural Edn., Tng. and Rsch. (chmn. 1986-87, nomination com. 1985-86, co-chmn. 1989-90, chmn. ethics com. 1989—, governing bd. 1992—), World Affairs Coun. (exec. bd. internat. profl. performance area 1993—), Am. Women for Internat. Understanding, Portland City Club. Democrat. Home: 712 NW Westover Ter Portland OR 97210-3136

LOFGREN, ZOE, county government official; b. San Mateo, Calif., Dec. 21, 1947; d. Milton R. and Mary Violet L.; m. John Marshall Collins, Oct. 22, 1978; children: Sheila Zoe Lofgren Collins, John Charles Lofgren Collins. BA in Polit. Sci., Stanford U., 1970; JD cum laude, U. Santa Clara, 1975. Bar: Calif., 1975. D.C. Adminstrv. asst. to Congressman Don Edwards, San Jose, Calif., 1970-79; ptnr. Webber and Lofgren, San Jose, 1979-81; mem. Santa Clara County Bd. Suprs., 1981-94; elected to 104th U.S. Congress,

Calif. 16th Dist., 1995—; part-time prof. Law, U. Santa Clara, 1978-80. Exec. dir. Community Housing Developers, Inc., 1979-80; trustee San Jose Community Coll. Dist., 1979-81; bd. dirs. Community Legal Svcs., 1978-81, San Jose Housing Svc. Ctr., 1978-79; mem. steering com. sr. citizens housing referendum, 1978; del. Calif. State Bar Conv., 1979-82, Dem. Nat. Conv., 1976; active Assn. Immigration and Nationality Lawyers, 1976-82, Calif. State Dem. Cen. Com., 1975-78, Santa Clara County Dem. Cen. Com., 1974-78, Notre Dame High Sch. Blue Ribbon Com., 1981-84, Victim-Witness Adv. Bd., 1981-94. Recipient Bancroft-Whitney award for Excellence in Criminal Procedure, 1973. Mem. Santa Clara County Bar Assn. (trustee 1979—), Santa Clara County Women Lawyers Com. (exec. bd. 1979-80), Sanata Clara Law Sch. Alumni Assn. (v.p. 1977, pres. 1978), Nat. Women's Polit. Caucus, Assn. of Bay Area Govts. (exec. bd. 1981-86). Office: US House Reps 2307 Rayburn House Office Bldg Washington DC 20515-0516

LOFT, DEBORAH LYNN, sales and marketing executive; b. Portsmouth, Ohio, Nov. 3, 1965; d. David Lawrence and Mabel Irene (Stillmaker) L. BS in Consumer Sci., Miami U., Oxford, Ohio, 1989; MBA, Xavier U., 1993. Interior designer W.B. Meier, Cin., 1989-91; computer/coop. exec. CBS, Cin., 1991-93; sales/mktg. exec. Human Element, Cin., 1993—. Mentor Big Bros./Big Sisters, Cin., 1993; vol. Friends of Mus., Cin., 1990—. Republican. Methodist. Home: 3026 Gloss Ave Cincinnati OH 45213-2424

LOGAN, APRIL CHARISE, lawyer; b. Wauconda, Ill., Oct. 6, 1952; d. G. Edwin and Virginia June (Walker) L. BS in Biology and Genetics, Aurora (Ill.) U., 1974; MS in Human Med. Genetics, Ind. U., 1977; JD, U. Tulsa Coll. Law, 1985. Bar: Calif. 1985, U.S. Patent Office 1989, U.S. Ct. Appeals (fed. cir.) 1990. Rsch. asst. dept. med. genetics Ind. U., Indpls., 1974-77; geneticist, med. educator Indpls. Sickle Cell Ctr., 1977-78; lectr. histology Marian Coll., Indpls., 1978; vol. technologist genetics dept. Children's Med. Ctr., Tulsa, 1979-82; instr. biology Oral Roberts U., Tulsa, 1978-1984; assoc. Rogers & Wells, San Diego, 1985-86, Adams, Duque & Hazeltine, San Diego, 1986-87, Spensley Horn Jubas & Lubitz, San Diego, 1987-88, Knobbe, Martens, Olson & Bear, San Diego, 1988-91; with Office of Patent Counsel The Scripps Rsch. Inst., La Jolla, Calif., 1991—. Contbr. poetry to lit. mags. Recipient Gold Ivy Leaf award Aurora U., 1974; doctoral tng. grantee Ind. U., 1976. Mem. ABA, Am. Intellectual Property Law Assn., San Diego County Bar Assn., San Diego Intellectual Property Law Assn. (sec.-treas. 1990-91, v.p. 1991-92, pres. 1992-93) Biotech. In Cyte, Fed. Crct. Bar Assn., Women in Bus., Lawyers Club, Mensa, Beta Beta Beta, Phi Delta Phi. Republican. Office: Office of Patent Counsel The Scripps Rsch Inst TPC-8 10666 N Torrey Pines Rd La Jolla CA 92037-1027

LOGAN, LINDA JO, secondary school educator; b. Houston, May 3, 1968; d. Earl Roger and Louise Delphine (Meyer) L. BS in Secondary English Edn., U. Tex., 1990. Cert. English and reading tchr., Tex. Tchr. reading Northside Ind. Sch. Dist., San Antonio, 1990—; counselor Master Sch., Austin, Tex., summers 1989—. Mem. ASCD, NEA, Tex. Mid. Sch. Assn., Ex-Students Assn. U. Tex. Republican. Roman Catholic. Office: HB Zachry Mid Sch 9410 Timber Path San Antonio TX 78250

LOGAN, MARY CALKIN, volunteer director community relations; b. Washington, Jan. 23, 1941; d. Loren Malcolm and Edith Garrison Calkin; m. Richard Lewis Logan, Jan. 6, 1962; children: Ashley Logan Drews, Austin Lewis. BA, U. Tex., 1963. Tchr. Tex. State Sch. for the Deaf, Austin, 1963-64; exec. sec. Dewar, Robertson & Pancoast, Austin, 1964-69; devel. dir. St. Joseph High Sch., Victoria, Tex., 1989-94; vol. dir. comty. rels. Hospice of S. Tex., Victoria, 1994—. Author, producer video; author script. Vice chair Gov.'s Commn. for Women, State of Tex., 1989-90, Victoria County (Tex.) Rep. Orgn., 1988-94; chmn. Tex. Women's Hall of Fame, 1988; v.p. Palmer Drug Abuse Program, 1990-91, Women's Crisis Ctr., Victoria, 1987-89; sec. Boys' Club, Victoria, 1981-83; active steering com. Nat. Pub. Radio, Victoria, 1992—. Mem. Jr. League Victoria (pres. 1985-86), Ct. of Six Flags (sec. 1989-90, treas. 1993-94), Victoria Preservation, Inc. (sec., founding mem., pres. 1994—), Victoria Country Club (pres. 1989-90), Settlement Club of Austin. Episcopalian. Home: 707 W Stayton Ave Victoria TX 77901-6343

LOGAN, PATRICIA JEAN, interior designer; b. Aurora, Ill., Feb. 24, 1926; d. Harley J. and Svea (Andrews) Benjamin; m. Marcel Guillaume, June 21, 1974. BA, MA, UCLA, 1951. Interior designer, 1951—. Author: Maliblue, 1980, (videos) Contemporary American Art, 1993. Bd. dirs. League for Crippled Children. Recipient awards City of Santa Monica, Calif., 1960, City of L.A., 1974, L.A. Times, Chgo. Tribune. Mem. Am. Soc. Interior Designers (historian), Am. Mus. Contemporary Art (pres. 1989—).

LOGAN, SANDRA JEAN, economics and business educator; b. Dayton, Ohio, Jan. 3, 1940; d. Max B. and Edna E. (Sanderson) Parrish; m. John E. Logan, Apr. 25, 1964. BA, Drew U., 1962; MBA, Columbia U., N.Y.C., 1964; PhD, U. S.C., 1976. Piano tchr. Whippany, N.J., 1957-64; lab. analyst Bear Creek Mining Co., Morristown, N.J., summer 1957, 58; rsch. asst. Drew U., Madison, N.J., summer 1962; staff asst. N.J. Bell Telephone Co., Newark, summer 1963, 64-67; instr. bus. U. Toledo, 1967-69; asst. prof. econs. and bus. S.C. State Univ., Orangeburg, 1970-76; prof. econs. and bus. Newberry (S.C.) Coll., 1976—, acting v.p. acad. affairs, 1993—; cons. econs., Ohio and S.C., 1967—, N.J. Bell Telephone Co., Newark, 1968; lectr. bus. Ea. Mich. U., Ypsilanti, spring 1969. Active Coldstream Home Owners Assn., Columbia, S.C., 1972-80; officer St. Andrews Woman's Club, Columbia, 1969-76. Rsch. grantee U. S.C. and S.C. State U., 1974-75. Mem. Am. Econs. Assn., So. Econs. Assn. Republican. Presbyterian. Home: 112 Smiths Market Ct Columbia SC 29212-1923 Office: Newberry Coll College St Newberry SC 29108

LOGAN, SHARON BROOKS, lawyer; b. Easton, Md., Nov. 19, 1945; d. Blake Elmer and Esther N. (Statum) Brooks; children: John W. III, Troy Blake. BS in Econs., U. Md., 1967, MBA in Mktg., 1969; JD, U. Fla., 1979. Bar: Fla. 1979. Ptnr. Raymond Wilson, Esq., Ormond Beach, Fla., 1980, Landis, Graham & French, Daytona Beach, Fla., 1981, Watson & Assocs., Daytona Beach, 1982-84; prin. Sharon B. Logan, Esq., Ormond Beach, 1984—; legal advisor to paralegal program Daytona Beach Community Coll., 1984—. Sponsor Ea. Surfing Assn., Daytona Beach, 1983—, Nat. Scholastic Surfing Assn., 1987—; bd. dirs. Ctr. for Visually Impaired, Daytona Beach, 1991—; mem. Fla. Supreme Ct. Hist. Soc. Recipient Citizenship award Rotary Club, 1962-63; Woodrow Wilson fellow U. Md., 1967. Mem. ABA, Fla. Bar Assn. (real property and probate sect.), Volusia County Bar Assn. (bd. dirs.), Volusia County Real Property Council, Inc. (bd. dirs. 1987—, sec. 1987-88, v.p. 1988-89, pres. 1989-90, sec. 1990-91), Ducks Unlimited, Mus. Arts ans Scis., Volusia County Estate Planning Council, Daytona Beach Area Bd. Realtors, Ormond Beach C. of C., Gator Club, Halifax Club, Tomola Oaks Country Club, Daytona Boat Club, Md. Club, Beta Gamma Sigma, Alpha Lamba Delta, Phi Kappa Phi, Omicron Delta Epsilon, Delta Delta Delta (Scholarship award 1964), Sigma Alpha Epsilon. Democrat. Episcopalian. Avocations: cooking, sewing, golf, tennis, aerobics. Office: Sharon B Logan Esq 400 S Atlantic Ave Ste 110 Ormond Beach FL 32176-7142

LOGAN, TINA, sculptor, painter; b. Phila., Sept. 16, 1929; d. Harold O'Driscol Hunter and Mary Ernestine (Appleton) Goodrich; m. John Thomas Logan, June 24, 1949; children: Karen, Tom, Hunter, Susan, Dave. Student, Bennington Coll., 1947-48, U. Hartford, 1977-80. lectr. kaleidoscope and wood carving, lectr. sculpture New Britain Mus.; lectr. paper sculpture Berkshire Mus.; lectr. sculpture Ethel Walker Sch., Landings Art Guild; artist in residence Glastonbury Pub. Sch. One-woman shows include Arts Exclusive, Simsbury, Conn., Wiley Gallery, Hartford, Conn., Ferguson Gallery, Simsbury; exhibited in group shows, including Lily Pad, Charleston, R.I., Greene Gallery, Guilford, Conn. (Sculpture hon. mention, Becker award), Taylor-Wexford, Hilton Head, S.C., Internat. Oasis, Savannah, Ga., Gallery Alexou, Savannah; represented in permanent collections at Shawmut Bank, Hartford, many pvt. collections. Recipient sculptors hon. mention Mystic Art 26th Regional Show, hon. mention Pump House Gallery Spring Show, Sculpture award Conn. Painters and Sculptors. Mem. Conn. Women Artists (Best of Show award), Conn. Acad. Fine Arts. Home: 11 Marsh Haven Ln Savannah GA 31411-2718

LOGAN, VERYLE JEAN, retail executive, realtor; b. St. Louis, Oct. 24; d. Benjamin Bishop and Eddie Mae (Williams) Logan. BS, Mo. U., 1968; postgrad. Wayne State U., 1974, 76, U. Mich.-Detroit, 1978, 80. Cert. residential specialist. With Hudson Dept. Store, Detroit, 1968-84, Dayton Hudson, Mpls., 1984-86, div. mdse. mgr., 1983-84, retail exec. div. mdse. mgr. Coats and Dresses, 1984-86; pres. Ultimate Connection, Inc., Mpls., 1987—. Mem. Golden Valley Black History Month Com., 1987—, co-chair, 1991-92, also bd. dirs., 1993—; trustee Harry Davis Found., 1988-94, mem. exec. bd., 1990, v.p., 1991-92; chair equal opportunity com. Mpls. Bd. Realtors, also bd. dirs., 1993—. Named Woman of Yr., Am. Bus. Women, 1984. Mem. Grad. Realtors Inst., Am. Bus. Womens Assn. (v.p. 1983-84, named Woman of Yr. 1984), Minn. Black Networking (exec. bd. 1985—), Delta Sigma Theta (life, Mpls.-St. Paul alumnae chpt., recording sec. 1985-87, chmn. arts and letters, corresponding sec. 1987-88, chmn. heritage and archives 1988-89, 1st v.p. 1991-93, pres. 1993—, named Delta of the Yr., 1988), Grad. Realtors Inst., M.L. King Tennis Buffs Club. Office: Burnet Realty Lakes 3033 Excelsior Blvd Minneapolis MN 55416-4665

LOGGANS, SUSAN VON BROCKHOEFT, nurse; b. New Orleans, June 29, 1955; d. George Emmett and Dorothy Claire (Castellano) Von Brockhoeft; m. Joseph Stewart Loggans, May 12, 1977. BS in Nursing La. State U., New Orleans, 1977. Cert. rehab. nurse. Staff nurse Oktibbeha County Gen. Hosp., Starkville, Miss., 1977-78, Lowndes County Gen. Hosp., Columbus, Miss., 1978-79, F.E. Hebert Hosp., New Orleans, 1979-81; asst. unit dir. East Jefferson Hosp., Metairie, La., 1981-87; charge nurse Health South Rehabilitation Ctr., 1987-88, Touro Infirmary Rehabilitation Unit, 1989-93; staff nurse SW Wash. Med. Ctr., 1993-94; clin. mgr. Covington Med. and Rehab. Ctr., Vancouver, Wash., 1995—. Republican. Home and Office: 14706 SE 5th Cir Vancouver WA 98684-7417

LOGGIE, JENNIFER MARY HILDRETH, medical educator, physician; b. Lusaka, Zambia, Feb. 4, 1936; came to U.S., 1964, naturalized, 1972; d. John and Jenny (Beattie) L. M.B., B.Ch., U. Witwatersrand, Johannesburg, South Africa, 1959. Intern Harare Hosp., Salisbury, Rhodesia, 1960-61; gen. practice medicine Lusaka, 1961-62; sr. pediatric house officer Derby Children's Hosp., also St. John's Hosp., Chelmsford, Eng., 1962-64; resident in pediatrics Children's Hosp., Louisville, 1964, Cin., 1964-65; fellow clin. pharmacology Cin. Coll. Medicine, 1965-67; mem. faculty U. Cin. Med. Sch., 1967—, prof. pediatrics, 1975, assoc. prof. pharmacology, 1972-77. Contbr. articles to med. publs.; editor Pediatric and Adolescent Hypertension, 1991. Grantee Am. Heart Assn., 1970-72, 89-90. Mem. Am. Pediatric Soc. (elected), Midwest Soc. Pediatric Research. Episcopalian. Home: 1133 Herschel Ave Cincinnati OH 45208-3112 Office: Children's Hosp Rsch Found Elland And Bethesda Ave Cincinnati OH 45229

LOGIUDICE, ELAINE A., nursing administrator; b. Sellersville, Pa.; d. William and Miriam (Yoder) Anders; m. Guy LoGiudice. BS, Columbia U., 1961; MSN, Cath. U. Am., 1982. Cert. nurse adminstr., advanced. Dept. chairperson, instr. Washington Hosp. Ctr. Sch. Nursing, Washington, 1974-82; asst. dir. nursing Prince George's Gen. Hosp., Cheverly, Md., 1982-85; dir. maternal/child health D.C. Gen. Hosp., Washington, 1986—. Mem. ANA (item writer for cert. exam in nursing adminstrn., advanced), Coun. on Computer Applications in Nursing.

LOGSDON, PATRICIA DAVIDSON, strategic planning professional; b. Aberdeen, Md., Sept. 1, 1960; d. Robert Bailey and Jacqueline (Thiery) Davidson; m. Dan L. Logsdon, Mar. 14, 1987. BS in Mktg. and French, Ill. State U., 1982; MBA, Tex. A&M U., 1985. Grad. asst. Tex. A&M U., College Station, 1985; demand analyst GTE, Houston, 1985-87; adminstr. sales support project GTE, Dallas, 1987-89, product mgr., 1989-90, mgr. bus. market strategy, 1990-92; sr. mgr. market planning GTE-Cantv Caracas, Venezuela, 1992-94; dir. strategic planning GTE-Cantv Venezuela, Caracas, 1994—. Vol. Spl. Olympics, Arlington, Tex., 1992. Scholar Tex. A&M U. Coll. Bus., 1984. Republican. Home: GTE/CANTV Venezuela PO Box 599003 Miami FL 33159 Office: GTE-CANTV Venezuela, Edificio Impres Avenida Tamanaco, Caracas Venezuela

LOGUE, JUDITH R., psychoanalyst, educator; b. Phila., Aug. 21, 1942; d. Martin and Laura (Goldman) Kirshenbaum; AB in Govt., Wheaton (Mass.) Coll., 1963; MSW, Rutgers U., 1966, PhD, Rutgers U. Grad. Sch. Arts and Scis., 1983; grad. N.Y. Center for Psychoanalytic Tng., 1978; m. Stephen Felton, Feb. 8, 1966 (div. Aug. 1989); 1 dau., Jane Jennifer; m. A. Douglas Logue, Feb. 14, 1990. Clin. social worker VA, Newark, 1967; psychotherapist Santa Barbara (Calif.) Mental Health Services, 1967-69; supr. Santa Barbara Counselling Center, 1967-69; pvt. practice psychoanalysis, 1969—; psychoanalyst, therapist Fifth Ave. Center for Psychotherapy, N.Y.C., 1969-72; instr. Marymount Manhattan Coll., 1971; psychotherapy supr. clin. faculty, dept. psychiatry Rutgers U. Med. Sch., New Brunswick, N.J., 1972-75, teaching asst. Grad. Sch. Social Work, 1974-76; vis. lectr. Bryn Mawr Coll. Sch. Social Work and Social Research, 1980; mem. faculty N.Y. Center for Psychoanalytic Tng., 1980—, N.J. Inst. Psychoanalysis and Psychotherapy, 1982—. Bd. dirs. N.Y. Ctr. for Psychoanalytic Tng., Inst. for Psychoanalysis and Psychotherapy N.J. Faculty, 1982—. NIMH fellow, 1965; diplomate Am. Bd. Psychotherapy. Recipient Disting. Faculty award Atlantic County Psychoanalytic Soc., 1987. Fellow N.J. Soc. for Clin. Social Work; mem. AAUP, APA (div. 39, sect. 1), NASW, Conf. Psychoanalytic Psychotherapists, Nat. Assn. for Advancement Psychoanalysis, Groves Conf. on Family, Acad. Cert. Social Workers, Soc. for Psychoanalytic Tng. (bd. dirs. 1983—, dir. social sci. program 1983-86). Mem. editorial bd. jour. Current Issues in Psychoanalytic Practice, 1983—; contbr. articles to profl. jours. Home and Office: 159 Valley Rd Princeton NJ 08540-3442

LOGUE-KINDER, JOAN, government official; b. Richmond, Va., Oct. 26, 1943; d. John T. and Helen (Harvey) Logue; m. Lowell A. Henry Jr., Oct. 6, 1963 (div. Sept. 1981); children: Lowell A. Henry III, Catherine D. Henry, Christopher Logue Henry; m. Randolph S. Kinder, Dec. 13, 1986. Student, Wheaton Coll., 1959-62; BA in Sociology, Adelphi U., 1964; cert. in edn., Mercy Coll., Dobbs Ferry, N.Y., 1971; postgrad., NYU, 1973; cert. in edn., St. John's U., 1974. Asst. to dist. mgr. U.S. Census Bur., N.Y.C., 1970; tchr. and adminstr. social studies Yonkers (N.Y.) Bd. Edn., 1971-75; dir. pub. rels. Nat. Black Network, N.Y.C., 1976-83; corp. v.p. NBN Broadcasting (formerly Nat. Black Network), N.Y.C., 1984-90; sr. v.p. The Mingo Group/Plus, N.Y.C., 1990-91; v.p. Edelman Pub. Rels. Worldwide, N.Y.C., 1991-93; dep. asst. sec. pub. affairs U.S. Dept. Treasury, Washington, 1993-94, asst. sec. pub. affairs, 1994—; cons. in field. Mem. alumnae recruitment coun. Wheaton Coll.; mem. Nigerian-Am. Friendship Soc., 1978-81; bd. dirs. Westchester Civil Liberties Union, 1974-77, Greater N.Y. coun. Girl Scouts U.S., 1985—, Operation PUSH, 1985—; del. White House Conf. on Small Bus.; active polit. campaigns, including Morris Udall for U.S. Pres, Howard Samuels for Gov.; sr. black media advisor Dukakis/Bentsen presdl. campaign, 1988; conv. del. N.Y. State Women's Polit. Caucus, 1975, pres. Black caucus, 1976-77. Recipient Excellence in Media award Inst. New Cinema Artists, 1984. Mem. World Inst. Black Comm. (bd. dirs. 1983-91), Women in Comm., Inc., Advt. Women of N.Y., 100 Black Women. Home: 1080 Wisconsin Ave NW Apt 204W Washington DC 20007 Office: Dept of Treasury 1500 Pennsylvania Ave Washington DC 20220

LOHMAN, LORETTA CECELIA, social scientist, consultant; b. Joliet, Ill., Sept. 25, 1944; d. John Thomas and Marjorie Mary (Brennan) L. BA in Polit. Sci., U. Denver, 1966, postgrad., 1985—; MA in Social Sci., U. No. Colo., 1975. Lectr. Ariz. State U., Tempe, 1966-67; survey researcher Merrill-Werthlin Co., Tempe, 1967-68; edn. asst. Am. Humane Assn., Denver, 1969-70; econ. cons. Lohman & Assocs., Littleton, Colo., 1971-75; rsch. assoc. Denver Rsch. Inst., 1976-86; rsch. scientist Milliken Chapman Rsch. Group, Littleton, 1986-89; owner Lohman & Assocs., Littleton, 1989—; affiliate Colo. Water Resources Rsch. Inst., Ft. Collins, Colo., 1989-91; tech. adv. com. Denver Potable Wastewater Demo Plant, 1986-90; cons. Constrn. Engrng. Rsch. Lab., 1984—; peer reviewer NSF, 1985-86, Univs. Coun. Water Resources, 1989—; WERC consortium reviewer N.Mex. Univs.-U.S. Dept. Energy, 1989—; course cons. Regis Coll., Denver, 1992—. Contbr. articles to profl. jours. Vol. Metro Water Conservation Projects, Denver, 1986-90; vol. handicapped fitness So. Suburban Parks and Recreation. Recipient Huffsmith award Denver Rsch. Inst., 1983; Nat. Ctr. for Edn. in Politics grantee, 1964-65. Mem. ASCE (social and environ. objectives com.), Am. Water Works Assn., Am. Water Resources Assn., Orgn. Am. Historians, Colo. Water Congress, Water Environ. Fedn., Sigma Xi, Pi Gamma Mu, Phi Alpha Theta. Democrat. Home and Office: 3375 W Aqueduct Ave Littleton CO 80123-2903

LOIGMAN, DORIS, insurance agent; b. Bklyn., July 10, 1933; d. Martin M. and Sally (Rosenthal) Meyer; m. Bernard Loigman, Apr. 6, 1952; children: Larry Scott, Gail Ann, Mark David. Grad. high sch., Lakewood, N.J. CPCU; cert. profl. ins. woman. Owner Loigman Ins. Agy., Middletown, N.J., 1975—. Mem. CPCU, Ind. Agts. Am., C. of C., Hadassah (exec. bd. Red Bank chpt. 1970). Jewish. Office: Loigman Ins Agy 79 Oak Hill Rd Ste B Red Bank NJ 07701

LOKEN, BARBARA, marketing educator, social psychologist; b. Owatonna, Minn., Aug. 22, 1951; d. Gordon Keith and June Rosaline (Iverson) Anderson; m. B. Michael Diebel, Apr. 7, 1991; 1 child, Elizabeth Loken Diebel. B.A. in Psychology magna cum laude, U. Minn., 1973; M.A., NYU, 1976; Ph.D. in Social Psychology, U. Ill., 1981. Research and statis. asst. Nat. Soc. Prevention Blindness, N.Y.C., 1974-76; research asst. dept. psychology U. Ill., 1976, 78-80, instr., 1977-78; NIMH trainee in measurement, 1979-80, asst. prof. dept. mktg. U. Minn., 1980-86, assoc. prof., 1986-92, prof., 1992—, co-dir. edn. evaluation Minn. heart health project Sch. Pub. Health, 1982-88, adj. assoc. prof. dept. psychology, 1987-92, adj. prof., 1992—; vis. assoc. prof. mktg. UCLA, 1988. Research grantee Sch. Mgmt., U. Minn., 1981-84, 86, 88-93. Mem. Am. Psychol. Assn., Am. Mktg. Assn., Assn. Consumer Research. Contbr. articles to profl. jours. Office: U Minn Carlson Sch Mgmt 271 19th Ave S Minneapolis MN 55455-0430

LOKIS, MARIANNA, advertising and marketing executive; b. Manchester, N.H., June 29, 1967; d. Demetrios and Sophie (Yanakis) L. BBA magna cum laude, Baruch Coll., 1989. Mktg. asst. Eigen Software, N.Y.C., 1988-89; advt. asst. Travers, Inc., Flushing, N.Y., 1989-90; account mgr. Lazar Stricker & Assocs. Advt. Inc., N.Y.C., 1990-93; mktg. mgr. Travers Inc., Flushing, N.Y., 1993—; cons. various firms, N.Y.C., 1990-93. Mem. Beta Gamma Sigma. Office: Travers Inc 128-15 26th Ave Flushing NY 11354

LOKMER, STEPHANIE ANN, public relations counselor; b. Wheeling, W.Va., Nov. 14, 1957; d. Joseph Steven and Mary Ann (Mozney) L. BA in Comm., Bethany Coll., 1980; cert., U. Tübingen, Germany, 1980, Sprach Inst. Tübingen, Germany 1980. V.p., Wheeling Coffee and Spice, W.Va., 1981—; pharm. mktg. rep. Bristol Labs., Wheeling, 1982-84, pharm. hosp. mktg. rep., 1984-85; pharm. mktg. rep. Boehringer Ingelheim, Nashville, 1985-87; owner, pres. Lokmer & Assocs. Inc. Pub. Relations, 1986—. Mem. Pub. Rels. Soc. Am. (accredited), Counselors Acad., Zeta Tau Alpha. Republican. Roman Catholic. Avocations: flying, traveling, tennis, reading.

LOLLAR, KATHERINE LOUISE, social worker, therapist; b. Cin., Nov. 1, 1944; d. Robert Miller and Dorothy Marie L.; div.; 2 children. BA, U. Kans., 1966; MSW, Loyola U., 1971. Lic. clin. social worker, Oreg.; cert. social worker, Wash.; bd. cert. diplomate clin. social work. Head activity therapy dept. Fox Children's Ctr., Dwight, Ill., 1966-68; child care worker Madden Mental Health Ctr., Hines, Ill., 1968-69, social worker, 1971-74; pvt. practice therapy Wheaton and Oakbrook, Ill., 1977-82; intern Monticello Care Unit alcohol and drug treatment program, 1983; cons. Residential Facility for Developmentally Disabled Adults, Battle Ground, Wash., 1983-85; therapist Cath. Community Svcs., Vancouver, Wash., 1983-88; outsta. mgr. Wash. Div. Devel. Disabilities, Vancouver, 1987—; pvt. practice therapy Vancouver, 1988—. Troop cons. Columbia River coun. Girl Scouts Am., 1984-86, internat. trip leader, 1993, life mem.; com. mem. Friends of Sangam Internat. Com., 1994—; mem. Internat. Field Selection Team, 1994—; mem., Sunday sch. tchr. Unity of Vancouver. Mem. NASW (sec. Vancouver chpt. 1982-84, co-chair 1985-87, unit rep. Wash. state unit 1990-92), Singles on Sat. Sq. Dance Club, Fun Lovers Sq. Dance Club (v.p. 1994-95). Office: 650 Officers Row Vancouver WA 98661-3836

LOMAN, MARY LAVERNE, retired mathematics educator; b. Stratford, Okla., June 10, 1928; d. Thomas D. and Mary Ellen (Goodwin) Glass; m. Coy E. Loman, Dec. 23, 1944; 1 child, Sandra Leigh Loman Easton. BS, U. Okla., 1956, MA, 1957, PhD, 1961. Grad. asst., then instr. U. Okla., Norman, 1956-61; asst. prof. math. U. Ctrl. Okla., Edmond, 1961-62; assoc. prof. U. Cen. Okla., Edmond, 1962-66, prof., 1966-93; prof. emeritus U. Ctrl. Okla., Edmond, 1993—; ret., 1993. NSF fellow, 1965-67. Mem. Math. Assn. Am., Nat. Coun. Tchrs. Math., Okla. Coun. Tchrs. Math. (v.p. 1972-76), Higher Edn Alumni Coun. Okla., VFW Aux., Delta Kappa Gamma. Home: 2201 Tall Oaks Trl Edmond OK 73003-2325

LOMBARDI, CELESTE, zoological park administrator; b. Columbus, Ohio, Feb. 16, 1955; d. Adam Dominic and Frances Elizabeth (Varda) L.; m. Terence Lawrence Smith, Mar. 26, 1990; 1 child Matthew Peachey. BS in Zoology, Ohio State U., 1978. Zoo keeper Children's Zoo Columbus Zoo, 1978-83, supr. Children's Zoo, 1983-90, asst. curator mammals, 1990-93, gen. curator, 1993—. TV appearances include David Letterman Show, Good Morning America, PM Magazine, and various local news shows. Mem. Am. Assn. Zool. Parks and Aquariums, Am. Assn. Zoo Keepers. Roman Catholic. Home: 4190 Rutherford Rd Powell OH 43065-9733 Office: Columbus Zoo PO Box 400 9990 Riverside Dr Powell OH 43065-9606

LOMBARDI, JENNIFER ANN, lawyer; b. Bklyn., May 3, 1963; d. Anthony and Harriet (Krasowski) L. BA, Trenton State Coll., 1985; JD, Seton Hall U., 1988. Law clk. County of Monmouth, Freehold, N.J., 1988-89; assoc. Pogarsky, Louis & Santagleo, Toms River, N.J., 1989-92, Law Offices of Kevin W. Kelly, Brick, N.J., 1993—. Mem. Ocean County Bar Assn. (chair women's lawyers 1994), N.J. State Bar Assn. Office: 514 Brick Blvd Brick NJ 08723-6006

LOMBARDI, KAREN L., psychotherapist, psychoanalyst, educator; b. Rochester, N.Y., Sept. 10, 1945; d. Louis Norman and Theresa Rosemary (Ferro) L.; m. Michael A. Civin, Sept. 11, 1976; 1 child, Chloe Antonia. BA, Sarah Lawrence Coll., 1967; MA, NYU, 1973, PhD, 1980. Lic. psychologist, N.Y.; cert. sch. psychologist. Asst. rsch. scientist Inst. for Devel. Studies, NYU, 1967-71, assoc. rsch. scientist, 1972-73; teaching fellow Sch. Psychology Program, NYU, 1973-75; psychology field work supr. Medgar Evers Coll., Bklyn., 1975-76; psychology intern Kings County Hosp. Ctr., Bklyn., 1975-76; cons. psychologist Marymount Manhattan Coll., N.Y.C., 1977-78; NIMH fellow Psychology in the Schs., 1978-79; psychologist Early Childhood Screen Program, Long Beach (N.Y.) Pub. Schs., 1979-81; supervising psychologist Project Pryme, Rockaway, N.Y., 1981; pvt. practice in psychotherapy and assessment, 1981—; assoc. prof. Derner, Inst. Advanced Psychol. Studies, Adelphi U., 1984—; adj. asst. prof. NYU, 1981-82, Fordham Univ., 1982-84; faculty and supr. Postdoctoral Program in Psychotherapy and Psychoanalysis, Derner Inst. of Advanced Psychol. Studies, Adelphi Univ., Garden City, 1992—; rep. postdoctal exec. bd. 1983-85, tng. com., 1984-87, faculty search com., 1984—, dir. sch. psychology program, 1986—, playroom com., 1987, scholarship com., 1987—, chairperson dissertation awards com., 1987—. Reviewer Jour. of Cons. and Clin. Psychology, Readings: A Journal of Reviews and Commentary on Mental Health; assoc. editor Jour. of Cen. Nassau Guidance and Counselling Svcs. Fellow Am. Orthopsychiat. Assn.; mem. Am. Psychol. Assn., Nassau County Psychol. Assn., Adelphi Soc. for Psychoanalysis and Psychotherapy. Office: Derner Inst Adelphi Univ Garden City NY 11530

LOMBARDINI, CAROL ANN, lawyer; b. Framingham, Mass., Dec. 29, 1954; d. Harry and Sarah (Scarano) L. m. William L. Cole, Apr. 23, 1983; children: Kevin Daniel, Kristin Elizabeth. BA, U. Chgo., 1976; JD, Stanford U., 1979. Bar: Calif. 1979. Assoc. Meserve, Mumper & Hughes, L.A., 1979-80, Proskauer Rose Goetz & Mendelsohn, L.A., 1980-82; from counsel to sr. v.p. legal and bus. affairs Alliance of Motion Picture and TV Prodrs., Encino, Calif., 1982—; trustee Dirs. Guild Contract Adminstrn., Encino, 1982—, Prodr.-Writers Guild Pension & Health Plans, Burbank, Calif., 1983—, SAG-Prodr. Pension & Health Plans, Burbank, 1986—, Dirs. Guild-Prodr. Pension & Health Plans, L.A., 1987—. Office: Alliance Motion Picture & TV Prodrs 15503 Ventura Blvd Encino CA 91436

LOMMATSCH, I. LAVON, business administration, consultant; b. Denver, June 6, 1940; d. William Theodore and Iro (Watenpaugh) Fisher; m. Lynn Lommatsch, June 1, 1985; children: James Waldorf, Lance Waldorf, Stacy Waldorf, Eric, Keith. Student, U. Colo., 1960-61, Front Range C.C., Denver, 1984, Don Kagy Real Estate Sch., Denver, 1985. Lic. realtor, Colo. With juvenile divsn. Adams County Dist. Atty., Brighton, Colo., 1983-86; with Adams County Parks and Cmty. Resources, Brighton, 1986—. Charter mem. bd. dirs. Women In Crisis, Adams County, 1983; prodr., dir. walk-a-thons Adams County Trails and Greenway Found.; active fundraising Amaranth Diabetes Found., Alternatives to Domestic Violence, Cmty. Health Svcs., Hearing/Seeing Dogs, Santa's Workshop, Shriner's Burn Ctrs. Recipient Excellence award Nat. Assn. County Info. Officers, 1986, State Recognition award Heart Assn. Mem. Order Ea. Star (worthy matron 1977-78), Order Amaranth, Inc. (grand royal matron 1991-92), White Shrine Jerusalem. Lutheran. Avocations: music, outdoors, wildlife.

LOMPA, SUSAN JOYCE, printing and lithograph company owner, concert artist; b. Albany, Calif., Apr. 25, 1941; d. Coulter Morgan and Zorah Alice (Bassett) Bowers; m. Richard M. Lompa, Feb. 17, 1962 (div. Oct. 1989); children: Ernest Frederic, John Paul. Grad. high sch., Oakland, Calif., 1959. Catalog clk. Montgomery Ward & Co., Oakland, 1959-61; underwriting clk. Blue Cross/No. Calif., Oakland, 1961-64; owner Lompa Printing and Lithograph Co., Albany, 1967—; soloist, concert artist D&S Music Ministry, No. Calif. Soloist, profl. Christian concert artist at chs. of numerous denominations and prisons, No. Calif.; recorded Someone Up There Loves Me, 1989. Affiliate mem. Live Oak Br., Children's Hosp., Oakland, Calif.; mem. Richmond (Calif.) Art Ctr., 1967—. Mem. Printing Industries of No. Calif., Printing Industries Am., Soroptimist Internat. of the Ams. (founder region, pres., dist. dir., regional sec., gov., Woman of Distinction, 1984, numerous certs.), Richmond Club. Republican. Methodist. Office: Lompa Printing & Lithograph 600 Cleveland Ave Berkeley CA 94710-1008

LONDON, ALICE, lawyer; b. El Paso, Tex., May 25, 1958; d. Clarence and Ruth (Lasky) Oppenheim; m. Jack London, May 4, 1991. BA, Tulane U., 1980; JD, U. Tex., 1983. Bd. cert. personal injury trial law. Assoc. Law Office of Windle Turley, Dallas, 1983-84, Kidd, Whitehurst & Harkness, Austin, Tex., 1984-86, Kidd, Whitehurst, Harkness & Watson, Austin, 1986-92; ptnr. Whitehurst, Harkness, Watson, London, Ozmun & Galow, Austin, 1992—. Named Outstanding Young Lawyer, Austin Young Lawyers Assn., 1990, Outstanding Woman Litigator, Travis County Women Lawyers Assn., 1993. Mem. Travis County Women Lawyers Assn., Travis County Bar Assn. (bd. dirs. 1991-93), Capital Area Trial Lawyers (pres. 1993-94). Democrat. Jewish. Office: PO Box 1802 Austin TX 78767-1802

LONDON, CHARLOTTE ISABELLA, reading specialist; b. Guyana, S.Am., June 11, 1946; came to U.S., 1966, naturalized, 1980; d. Samuel Alphonso and Diana Dallett (Daniels) Edwards; m. David Timothy London, May 26, 1968 (div. May 1983); children: David Tshombe, Douglas Tshaka. BS, Fort Hays State U., 1971; MS, Pa. State U., 1974, PhD, 1977. Elem. sch. tch., Guyana, 1962-66, secondary sch. tchr., 1971-72; instr. lang. arts Pa. State U., University Park, 1973-74; reading specialist/ednl. cons. N.Y.C. Community Coll., 1975; dir. skills acquisition and devel. center Stockton (N.J.) State Coll., 1975-77; reading specialist Pleasantville (N.J.) Public Schs., 1977—; ind. specialist United Nations Devel. Programme , Guyana, 1988—; v.p. Atlantic County PTA, 1980-82; del. N.J. Gov.'s Conf. Future Edn. N.J., 1981; founder, pres. Guyana Assn. Reading and Lang. Devel., 1987. Sec. Atlantic County Minority Polit. Women's Caucus. Mem. Internat. Reading Assn., Nat. Council Tchrs. English, Assn. Supervision and Curriculum Devel., NEA, N.J. Ednl. Assn., AAUW, Pi Lambda Theta, Phi Delta Kappa (sec.). Mem. African Methodist Episcopal Ch. Home: 6319 Crocus St Mays Landing NJ 08330-1107 Office: Pleasantville Pub Schs W Decatur Ave Pleasantville NJ 08232

LONDRÉ, FELICIA MAE HARDISON, theater educator; b. Ft. Lewis, Wash., Apr. 1, 1941; d. Felix M. and Priscilla Mae (Graham) Hardison; m. Venne-Richard Londré, Dec. 16, 1967; children: Tristan Graham, Georgianna Rose. BA with high honors, U. Mont., 1962; MA, U. Wash., 1964; PhD, U. Wis., 1969. Asst. prof. U. Wis. at Rock County, Janesville, 1969-75; asst. prof., head theatre program U. Tex. at Dallas, Richardson, 1975-78; assoc. prof. U. Mo., Kansas City, 1978-82, prof. theatre, 1982-87; women's chair in humanistic studies Marquette U., 1995; curator's prof. U. Mo., Kansas City, 1987—; dramaturg Mo. Repertory Theatre, Kansas City, 1978—, Nebr. Shakespeare Festival, 1990—; guest dramaturg Gt. Lakes Theatre Festival, 1988; mem. archives task force Folly Theatre, 1982-83; artistic advisor New Directions Theatre Co., 1983-90; hon. lectr. Mid-Am. State Univs. Assn., 1986-87; mem. U.S.-USSR Joint Commn. on Theatre Historiography, 1980; fgn. vis. prof. Hosei U., Tokyo, 1993; mem. adv. bd. Contemporary World Writers, 1991—; lectr. univs. Budapest, Pécs, Debrecen, Hungary, 1992—. Author: Tennessee Williams, 1979, Tom Stoppard, 1981, Federico Garcia Lorca, 1984, (play) Miss Millay Was Right, 1982 (John Gassner Meml. Playwriting award 1982), The History of World Theater: From the English Restoration to the Present, 1991 (Choice Outstanding Academic Bokk award, 1991); (opera libretto) Duse and D'Annunzio, 1987; book rev. editor: Theatre Jour., 1984-86; assoc. editor: Shakespeare Around the Globe: A Guide to Notable Postwar Revivals; mem. editorial bd. Theatre History Studies Jour., 1981-87, 89—, Studies in Am. Drama, 1945-present, 1984—, 19th Century Theatre Jour., 1984—, Bookmark Press, Tennessee Williams Rev., 1985-87, Jour. Dramatic Theory and Criticism, 1986—, Theatre Survey, 1991—, On-Stage Studies, The Elizabethan Review, 1992—, Theatre Symposium, 1994—; contbr. articles and book and theatre revs. to profl. publs. Hon. co-founder, bd. dirs. Heart of Am. Shakespeare Festival, 1991—; bd. dirs. Edgar Snow Meml. Fund, 1993—. Fulbright grantee U. Caen, Normandy, France, 1962-63, faculty rsch. grantee U. Mo., 1985, 86, 90, 91, tchr. seminar grantee Mo. Humanities Coun., 1993; grad. fellow U. Wis., 1966-67, Trustees fellow U. Kansas City, 1987-88. Mem. MLA, Am. Soc. for Theatre Rsch. (mem. exec. com. 1984-90), Shakespeare Theatre Assn. Am. (sec. 1991-93), Internat. Fedn. for Theatre Rsch. (del. gen. assembly 1985), Am. Theatre Assn. (commn. on theatre rsch. 1981-87, chmn. 1984-86), Theatre Libr. Assn., Dramatists Guild, Literary Mgrs. and Dramaturgs Am., Am. Drama Soc., Shakespeare Oxford Soc., Mid-Am. Theatre Conf. (chair grad. rsch. paper competition 1985), Internat. Panorama and Diorama Soc. Roman Catholic. Home: 528 E 56th St Kansas City MO 64110-2769 Office: Mo Repertory Theatre 4949 Cherry St Kansas City MO 64110-2229

LONERGAN, LAUREN ELIZABETH, lawyer; b. New Milford, Conn., Apr. 2, 1957; d. Leo Edward and Yvonne Althea (Gero) Reap; m. David Paul Lonergan, July 12, 1977. Student, Carleton Coll., 1975-77; BA, Macalester Coll., 1979; JD, U. Minn., 1982. Atty. O'Connor & Hannan, Mpls., 1982-87, Hart, Bruner, O'Brien & Thornton, Mpls., 1987-88; atty., shareholder Briggs & Morgan, P.A., Mpls., 1988—. Mem. ABA, Minn. State Bar Assn. Office: Briggs & Morgan 2400 IDS Towers Minneapolis MN 55402

LONEY, LINDA CHRISTINE, pediatrician; b. Herington, Kans., Mar. 29, 1949; d. James Monroe and Leonella Marie (Vinduska) L.; m. Thomas Warren Cooper, Sept 28, 1974; children: Rachel, Nathan. BA, U. Kans., 1971; MD, Wash. U., 1976. Diplomate Nat. Bd. Med. Examiners. Chief resident St. Louis Children's Hosp., 1978-79, founder, cons. sexual abuse clinic, 1978-83; instr. pediatrics Washington U. Sch. Medicine, St. Louis, 1980-83; pediatrician Med. Care Group, St. Louis, 1983, Bur. Spl. Med. Services, Concord, N.H., 1984-86; chief clin. pediatrics Mass. Hosp. Sch., Canton, 1986-90; staff pediatrician Mass. Hosp. Sch., 1991—, Watertown Health Ctr., 1994—; med. cons. Cole Harrington Children's Ctr., Canton, 1986—; speaker in field, 1977-85; instr. pediatrics Harvard Med. Sch., 1990-91; mem. staff Children's Hosp., Boston, Mass., 1990-91. Mem. adv. bd. Raphael House, St. Louis, 1980-83, Parents Anonymous, Boston, 1986. Fellow Am. Acad. Pediatrics, Mass. Acad. Pediatrics (com., cons. 1986—); mem. Phi Beta Kappa. Democrat. Jewish. Home: 30 Hamlin Rd Newton MA 02159-1002 Office: Watertown Health Ctr 85 Main St Watertown MA 02172

LONEY, MARY ROSE, airport administrator. Dir. aviation Phila. Internat. Airport. Office: Phila Pa Dept Comm Div Aviation 3751 Island Ave Phila Airport Philadelphia PA 19153

LONG, ANN MARIE, health facility administrator; b. Hartford, Conn., Oct. 9, 1945; d. John and Bridie (Griffin) O'Connell; m. Michael T. Long, Sept. 9, 1967; children: Michael, Maura, Deirdre. Diploma, St. Francis Hosp., Hartford, 1966; BSN magna cum laude, U. Hartford, 1978; M. in Health Care Mgmt., The Hartford Grad. Ctr., 1987. RN, Conn.; cert. in advanced continuity of care; cert. in nursing adminstrn. Critical care staff nurse St. Francis Hosp. and Med. Ctr., Hartford, 1966-67, continuing care coord., 1978-83, nursing supr., 1983-90, dir. continuing care, 1990—; dir. continuing care Mt. Sinai Hosp., Hartford, 1992—; nursing instr. St. Francis Sch. Nursing, Hartford, 1967-68; dir. of continuing care St. Francis Hosp. and Med. Ctr., Mt. Sinai Hosp., 1992—; profl. adv. com. Vis. Nurses Assn. Farmington Valley. Justice of the Peace, Simsbury, Conn. Mem. ANA (cert. nursing adminstrn.), Conn. Nurses Assn., Conn. Hosp. Assn. (continuing care coords. conf.), Conn. Assn. Continuity Care, Sigma Theta Tau, Alpha Chi. Home: 9 Metacom Dr Simsbury CT 06070

LONG, ANNA MARIBETH, electrical engineer; b. Nashville, Aug. 18, 1960; d. George William and Martha Elizabeth (Love) L.; m. Arvind M. Parikh, June 11, 1988. BS in Applied Sci., U. Louisville, 1982, M in Elec. Engring., 1983. Policy analyst intern U.S. Govt., Washington, 1980-81; master control programmer Sta. WKPC-TV, Louisville, 1982-83; system devel. engr., network analyst, lead system engr., adv. engr. IBM, Gaithersburg, Md., 1983—; treas. RDS Systems, Inc., Rockville, Md., 1989—; prin. CG Consulting, Gaithersburg, Md., 1989—; del. Internat. Student Pugwash Conf., Ann Arbor, Mich., 1983; instr. Montgomery Coll., Germantown, Md., 1984-86; adj. asst. prof. U. Md., College Park, 1986—. Counselor Montgomery County Fin. Counseling Svc., 1986-87. Named Hon. Ky. Colonel. Mem. IEEE, Omicron Delta Kappa, Tau Beta Pi, Eta Kappa Nu. Office: IBM Software Solutions Divsn 6700 Rockledge Dr Bethesda MD 20817

LONG, BARBARA ELLIS, psychologist; b. St. Louis, Mar. 8, 1923; d. Oliver Everett and Melva Augusta (Westcott) Ellis; m. Richard Rodne Long, June 18, 1946 (dec. 1975); children: Susan Long Hood, Roger Ellis. Student, Washington U., St. Louis, 1941-42; BS with honors, U. Ill., Urbana, 1945, MA, 1846; PhD, Union Inst., Cin., 1973. Lic. clin. psychologist, Calif. Clin. psychologist Community Child Guidance Ctr., Yale Child Study Ctr., Portland and New Haven, 1948-49, 51-52, Thurston County Child Guidance Ctr., Olympia, Wash., 1952-56, St. Louis County Child Guidance Clinic, Clayton, Mo., 1958, Richland County Mental Health Clinic, Columbia, S.C., 1959-61; pvt. practice Columbia and St. Louis, 1959-65, 71-73; project dir., methodologist St. Louis County Health Dept., Clayton, Mo., 1965-67; instr., rsch. psychologist Webster Coll., Webster Groves, Mo., 1967-68; clin. and rsch. psychologist St. Louis State Hosp., 1968-71; children's svc. coordinator Dept. Pub. Health and Welfare, San Mateo County, San Mateo, Calif., 1973-75; pvt. practice San Carlos, Calif., 1976—; cons. mental health agys. and schs., U.S.A., Gt. Britain, Denmark, UNESCO, Indonesia, 1970—; mem. adj. faculty U. Calif. Santa Cruz Extension, 1974, U. San Francisco, 1978-79, Palo Alto Sch. of Profl. Psychology, 1982; expert witness San Mateo County (Calif.) Family Ct. Svcs. Author: The Journey to Myself, 1978; editor People Watching, 1969-72, Jour. Clin. and Child Psychology, 1976-77; contbr. articles to profl. jours. Fellow Am. Psychol. Assn., Am. Orthopsychiat. Assn.; mem. San Mateo County Psychol. Assn., Calif. State Psychol. Assn., Soc. Personality Assessment, Bay Area Multiple Personality Soc., Assn. Family and Conciliation Cts., Profl. Acad. Custody Evaluators, Psi Chi, Alpha Kappa Delta. Episcopalian. Office: 1622 San Carlos Ave Ste D San Carlos CA 94070-2022

LONG, CYNTHIA ANNE P. (CINDY LONG), nurse; b. Oak Ridge, Tenn., July 2, 1953; d. Edwin S. and Beulah B. (Burgess) Prigmore; m. Rodger W. Long, May 31, 1975; children: Jennifer S., Kathryn A. Diploma in nursing, Ida V. Moffett Sch. Nursing, 1973. Registered vascular technolgist; cert. nurse operating rm.; cert. RN 1st asst. Staff nurse Bapt. Med. Ctr., Birmingham, Ala., 1973-75, Sacred Heart Hosp., Pensacola, Fla., 1975-77; staff nurse Physicians and Surgeons Hosp., Shreveport, La., 1977-79, dir. vascular lab., 1989-94; 1st asst. nurse Dr. Rod Yeager, Shreveport, 1979—. Mem. Soc. Vascular Technology, Vascular Nurses Assn., Soc. Diagnostic and Med. Sonographers, Assn. Operating Rm. Nurses. Republican. Methodist. Home: 3706 Eddy Pl Shreveport LA 71101 Office: Dr Rod M. Yeager 1534 Elizabeth Ste 340 Shreveport LA 71101

LONG, DEE, state legislator; b. 1939; m. Nicholas Long; 2 children. BA, Northwestern U.; postgrad., U. Minn. Legislator State of Minn., St. Paul, 1978—; speaker of House; mem. rules and legis. adminstrn. com., taxes com., ways and means com. Home: 2409 Humboldt Ave S Minneapolis MN 55405-2540 Office: Minn Ho of Reps State Capitol Saint Paul MN 55155*

LONG, ELIZABETH ANN, physical therapist; b. Indpls., Nov. 28, 1961; d. Alfred and Irene (Prost) Schoepf; m. Bradford Keith Long, June 22, 1985. BS, U. Md., 1984. Registered phys. therapist, Md. Staff phys. therapist Greater Washington Ortho. Group, Silver Spring, Md., 1984-85, Kensington Phys. Therapy, Wheaton, Md., 1985-87; chief phys. therapist Office of Drs. Ghovanlou & Townsend, Greenbelt, Md., 1987-89; staff phys. therapist Potomac Home Health Care, Rockville, Md., 1986-90, clin. rehab. supr., 1991—. Mem. Honors Admission Com., U Md., 1980-82. Recipient Malinoski award Md. Assn. Home Care, 1994. Mem. Am. Phys. Therapy Assn. (Md. chpt. 1984—, sect. on orthopedics 1985-90, sect. on geriatrics 1988—, sect. on cmty. health 1992—, reimbursement com. mem. 1994—), U. Md. Alumni Bd. Republican. Presbyterian. Home: 15037 Joshua Tree Rd North Potomac MD 20878-2548

LONG, ELIZABETH VALK, magazine publisher; b. Winston-Salem, N.C., Apr. 29, 1950; d. Henry Lewis and Elizabeth (Fuller) V. BA, Hollins Coll., 1972; MBA, Harvard Bus. Sch., 1979. Clin. adminstr. Mass. Gen. Hosp., Boston, 1973-77; asst. to circulation dir. Time Mag.-Time Inc., N.Y.C., 1979-80, 81-82; circulation dir. Fortune Mag.-Time Inc., N.Y.C., 1982-84, Sports Illustrated-Time Inc., N.Y.C., 1984-85, Time Mag.-Time Inc., N.Y.C., 1985-86; publisher Life Mag.-Time Inc., N.Y.C., 1987-93; pres. Time Mag., 1993—. Trustee Hollins Coll., 1987—; mem. bus. com. Mus. Modern Art, N.Y.C.; mem. bd. visitors Wake Forest U., Winston-Salem, N.C.; bd. dirs. Hanover Direct, Inc., Weehawken, N.J.; mem. Com. of 200. Recipient Matrix award N.Y. Women in Comms., 1992, Silver Medal award Am. Advt. Fedn., 1993. Mem. Phi Beta Kappa. Office: Time Inc Time & Life Bldg 1271 Ave of Americas New York NY 10020-1393*

LONG, JEANINE HUNDLEY, state legislator; b. Provo, Utah, Sept. 21, 1928; d. Ralph Conrad and Hazel Laurine (Snow) Hundley; m. McKay W. Christensen, Oct. 28, 1949 (div. 1967); children: Cathy Schuyler, Julie Schulleri, Kelly M. Christensen, C. Brett Christensen, Harold A. Christensen; m. Kenneth D. Long, Sept. 6, 1968. AA, Shoreline C.C., Seattle, 1975; BA in Psychology, U. Wash., 1977. Mem. Wash. Ho. of Reps., 1983-87, 93-94, mem. bd. joint com. pension policy, Inst. Pub. Policy; mem. Wash. Senate, 1995—. Mayor protem, mem. city coun. City of Brier, Wash., 1977-80. Republican. Office: PO Box 40482 Olympia WA 98504-0482

LONG, MARGARET KAREN, art educator; b. Bridgeport, Conn., Mar. 18, 1950; d. Felix Joseph and Clayda Erna (Town) Petko; m. James Ray Long, July 1, 1977 (div. May 1991); children: Mason Douglas, Megan Elizabeth. AA in Photography & Comml. Art, L.A. Harbor Coll., 1973; BFA in Human Svcs., Calif. State U., Fullerton, 1976; MA in Philosophy & Art History, Calif. State U., Dominguez Hills, 1982; MA in Counselor Edn., Calif. State U., San Bernadino, 1993. Cert. secondary tchr. Calif. Photographer, artist pvt. practice, San Pedro, Calif., 1968-73; photographer Blalack Studios, Fullerton, Calif., 1973-76; artist 110 Wilshire Studios, Fullerton, Calif., 1974-77; med. recs. tech. Long Beach (Calif.) Meml. Hosp., 1977-80; instr. photography S.E.L.A. ROP Adult Edn., Cerritos, Calif., 1980; instr. art, social studies ABC Unified Sch. Dist., Cerritos, Calif., 1980-82; educator art, journalism, yearbook Coachella Unified Sch. Dist., Thermal, Calif., 1983—; mentor tchr. Calif. Dept. Edn., 1989-95; counselor to disturbed teens, Insight, Thermal, 1986-94; pres. faculty forum Coachella Valley H.S., 1993-94; dept. chair Visual and Performing Arts Dept., Thermal, 1983-94, coord., site rep., 1988-91; mem. accreditation and steering coms., Calif. Accreditation for Schs., Thermal, 1976-77, 93-94. Exhibited in group shows Malden Gallery Invitational Show, 1975, Laguna All Calif. Show, 1976. Foster parent State Dept. Social Svcs., Rancho Mirage, Calif., 1991-92; mem. Friends of Coachella Libr., 1986-94. Mem. Calif. Art Edn. Assn., Hi-Desert Artists Coop. (exhibitor 1984-85).

LONG, MARIE KATHERINE, public relations consultant, researcher; b. Cleve., Dec. 8, 1925; d. Mike Kurilich and Katherine (Grasso) Kurilich; m. Elgen Marion Long, May 12, 1946; children: Donna Marie Long Weiner, Harry Elgen. Student, Cleve. Coll., 1943-44, Harbor Jr. Coll., L.A., 1954-55. Lic. real estate agt., Calif. Exec. sec. Fawick Airlfex Co., Cleve., 1943-44, Pillsbury and Globe Mills, L.A., 1944-48; ptnr. Elgen Long, gen. contractor, San Mateo, Calif., 1958-77, Woodside (Calif.) Investment Co., 1964-71; logistics mgr. pub. rels. Crossroads Endeavor, Woodside, 1971—; pub. rels. cons. Elgen Long Enterprises, San Mateo, 1971—; research on Amelia Earhart disappearance, San Mateo, 1972—; adminstrv. coord., project mgr. pub. rels. Internat. Human Potential Orgns., San Francisco, 1977-82; cons. to books and mags., 1971—. Troop leader Girl Scouts U.S.A., San Mateo, 1954-61; fundraiser Woodside High Sch. Band, 1966-68; Am. Heart Assn., also other orgns., San Mateo, 1973—; v.p. Western Aerospace Mus., Oakland, Calif., 1982—, also life mem.; mem. People to People, Hunger Project; adv. com. USN Meml. Found. Mem. Internat. Platform Soc., Peninsula Press Club. Democrat. Home and Office: 11975 Danvers Circle San Diego CA 92128

LONG, MAXINE MASTER, lawyer; b. Pensacola, Fla., Oct. 20, 1943; d. Maxwell L. and Claudine E. (Smith) M.; m. Anthony Byrd Long, Aug. 27, 1966; children: Deborah E., David M. AB, Bryn Mawr Coll., 1965; MS, Georgetown U., 1971; JD, U. Miami, 1979. Bar: Fla. 1979, U.S. Ct. Appeals (5th cir.) 1980, U.S. Dist. Ct. (so. dist.) Fla. 1980, U.S. Ct. Appeals (11th cir.) 1981, U.S. Dist. Ct. (mid. and no. dists.) Fla. 1987. Law clk. to U.S. dist. judge U.S. Dist. Ct. (so. dist.) Fla., Miami, 1979-80; assoc. Shutts & Bowen, Miami, 1980-90, of counsel, 1990-92, ptnr., 1992—. Mem. Fla. Bar Assn. (chair bus. litigation com., exec. coun. bus. law sect.), Dade County Bar Assn. (mem. fed. cts. com., recipient pro bono award/Vol. Lawyers for the Arts 1989). Office: Shutts & Bowen 201 S Biscayne Blvd Miami FL 33131

LONG, MICHELLE, artist; b. Lincoln, Nebr., Sept. 29, 1961. BFA, U. Tex., Arlington, 1989; MFA, Tex. Woman's U., 1992. Operator graphic arts dept. Express Typesetting Co., Dallas, 1981-84; asst. slide libr. U. Tex., 1988-89; custom framer Zak's, Irving, Tex., 1990-91; gallery asst. Tex. Woman's U., Denton, 1991-92; gallery dir., mgr. 3 Day Framing & Gallery, Inc., Dallas, 1992-94; owner Michelle D. Long Gallery & Framing, Coppell, Tex., 1994—; vis. artist John F. Townley Elem. Sch., Irving, 1991; guest lectr. Tex. Woman's U., 1992; instr. Art Daze Sch., Coppell, Tex., 1993—; curator Crossing Over the White Line, Women of the 90's, Dallas Women's Caucus for Art Nat. Open Exhbn., Dallas, 1993, v.p. 1994, 95, Wise Women Speak, 1994. Exhibited in numerous group shows, including Arlington Cmty. Ctr., 1989, Arlington Art Assn., 1989, Mesa (Ariz.) Art Ctr., 1989, D-Art Visual Art Ctr., Dallas, 1992, 93, 94, Hill Country Arts Found. Gallery, Ingram, Tex., 1992, La. State U., Baton Rouge, 1992, So. Meth. U., Dallas, 1993, Navarro Coun. Arts, Corsicana, Tex., 1993, Studio 12 Gallery, Coppell, Tex., 1993, 500X Gallery, Dallas, 1993, U. North Tex., Ft. Worth, 1994; represented in pvt. collections. Mem. Nat. Women's Caucus for Art (v.p. Dallas chpt. 1993—). Gallery and Studio: 509 1/2 W Bethel Rd Irving TX 75109

LONG, NICHOLA Y., technical writer; b. Walnut Creek, Calif., Jan. 4, 1955; d. Shogo and Elizabeth (Hughes) Yamaguchi. BS in Indsl. Tech./Electronics, Tuskegee U., 1978. From spl. tech. asst. to tech. writing specialist Western Electric Corp., Winston-Salem, N.C., 1977-86; sr. tech. documentation specialist AT&T Network Systems, Winston-Salem, 1986—. Friend, The Arts Council, Inc., Winston-Salem, 1984-86. Mem. NAFE, Am. Soc. Profl. and Exec. Women, Tuskegee Nat. Alumni Assn. (pres. Winston-Salem chpt. 1984-85), Alliance Black Telecommunications Employees, Alpha Kappa Mu. Home: 168 Carrisbrooke Ln Winston Salem NC 27104-2528 Office: AT&T Network Systems 2400 Reynolda Rd Winston Salem NC 27106-4606

LONG, RUTH MARY, interior contracting corporation executive; b. Somers Point, N.J., May 10, 1932; d. Lynford Preston and Luella (Golden) Fowles; m. Donald Keith Long, June 30, 1967. B.A., U. Fla., 1953. Mgr. corr. study dept. U. Fla. Bookstore, Gainesville, 1953-54; statistician Jacobs Jewelers, Jacksonville, Fla., 1955-56; claims rep. Social Security Adminstrn., Gastonia, N.C., Washington, 1956-67; adminstrv. coordinator Duncan Long, Inc., Long Island City, N.Y., 1967—; acctg. advisor Great Outdoors Pub. Co., St. Petersburg, Fla., 1979-80. Recipient Hon. Membership Fla. Players, 1955; Fla. Ho. of Reps. scholar, 1949. Democrat. Avocations: reading; collecting cookery books and lit.; Caribbean and Jamaican studies. Home: 531 Main St Apt 122 Roosevelt Island New York NY 10044 Office: Duncan Long Inc 10-40 46th Ave Long Island City NY 11101

LONG, SANDRA ELAINE, accountant, financial analyst; b. Charlotte, N.C., Oct. 25, 1961; d. Howard Asbury and Carol Frances (Abernathy) L.; m. John Sherwood Langdon, June 2, 1984. BA in Acctg., N.C. State U., 1983; postgrad., Queen's Coll., Charlotte, 1991—. CPA, N.C. Cost acct. Pa. House, Monroe, N.C., 1983-84; microcomputer acctg. specialist Interstate Graphics, Charlotte, 1984-85, mgr. data processing, 1985-86, contr., 1986; cons. Price Waterhouse, Charlotte, 1986-87, sr. cons., 1987-88; fin. analyst BASF, Charlotte, 1988-89, sr. fin. analyst, 1989-91; sr. fin. analyst Hoechst Celanese, Charlotte, 1991—. Blumenthal fellow Queen's Coll., 1991-95. Mem. Inst. Mgmt. Accts. (cert., pres. 1990-91, nat. bd. dirs. 1992-94, Mem. of Yr. award Charlotte 1993), N.C. Assn. CPA's (pres.-elect 1994-95). Democrat. Home: 9919 Dunfries Rd Matthews NC 28105 Office: Hoechst Celanese 2300 Archdale Dr Charlotte NC 28210

LONG, SARAH ANN, librarian; b. Atlanta, May 20, 1943; d. Jones Lloyd and Lelia Maria (Mitchell) Sanders; m. James Allen Long, 1961 (div. 1985); children: Andrew C., James Allen IV; m. Donald J. Sager, May 23, 1987. BA, Oglethorpe U., 1966; M in Librarianship, Emory U., 1967. Asst. libr. Coll. of St. Matthias, Bristol, Eng., 1970-74; cons. State Libr. of Ohio, Columbus, 1975-77; coord. Pub. Libr. of Columbus and Franklin County, Columbus, 1977-79, dir. Fairfield County Dist. Libr., Lancaster, Ohio, 1979-82, Dauphin County Libr. System, Harrisburg, Pa., 1982-85, Multnomah County Libr., Portland, Oreg., 1985-89; system dir. North Suburban Libr. System, Wheeling, Ill., 1989—; chmn. Portland State U. Libr. Adv. Coun., 1987-89. Contbr. articles to profl. jours. Bd. dirs. Dauphin County Hist. Soc., Harrisburg, 1983-85, ARC, Harrisburg, 1984-85; pres. Lancaster-Fairfield County YWCA, Lancaster, 1981-82; vice-chmn. govt. and edn. div. Lancaster-Fairfield County United Way, Lancaster, 1981-82; sec. Fairfield County Arts Coun., 1981-82; adv. bd. Portland State U., 1987-89. Recipient Dir.'s award Ohio Program in Humanities, Columbus, 1982; Sarah Long Day established in her honor Fairfield County, Lancaster, Bd. Commrs., 1982. Mem. ALA (elected coun. 1993—), Pub. Libr. Assn. (pres. 1989-90, chair legis. com.), Ill. Libr. Assn. (pub. policy com. 1991—). Office: N Suburban Libr Systems 200 W Dundee Rd Wheeling IL 60090

LONG, SARAH ELIZABETH BRACKNEY, physician; b. Sidney, Ohio, Dec. 5, 1926; d. Robert LeRoy and Caroline Josephine (Shue) Brackney; m. John Frederick Long, June 15, 1948; children: George Lynas, Helen Lucille Corcoran, Harold Roy, Clara Alice Lawrence, Nancy Carol. BA, Ohio State U., 1948, MD, 1952. Intern Grant Hosp., Columbus, Ohio, 1952-53; resident internal medicine Mt. Carmel Med. Ctr., Columbus, 1966-69, chief resident internal medicine, 1968-69; med. cons. Ohio Bur. Disability Determination, Columbus, 1970—; physician student health Ohio State U., Columbus, 1970-73; sch. physician Bexley (Ohio) City Schs., 1973-83; physician advisor to peer rev. Mt. Carmel East Hosp., Columbus, 1979-86, employee health physician, 1981—; physician cons. Fed. Black Lung Program, U.S. Dept. Labor, Columbus, 1979—. Mem. AMA, Ohio State Med. Assn., Franklin County Acad. Medicine, Alpha Epsilon Delta, Phi Beta Kappa. Home: 2765 Bexley Park Rd Columbus OH 43209-2231

LONG, SHELLEY, actress; b. Fort Wayne, Ind., Aug. 23, 1949; m. Bruce Tyson; 1 child, Juliana. Student, Northwestern U. Writer, assoc. prodr., co-host Chgo. TV program Sorting It Out, 1970s (3 local Emmys 1970); mem. Second City, Chgo.; guest TV appearances various shows including M.A.S.H., Love Boat, Family; regular TV series Cheers, 1982-87, Good Advice, 1993-94; motion pictures include A Small Circle of Friends, 1980, Caveman, 1981, Night Shift, 1982, Losin' It, 1983, Irreconcilable Differences, 1984, The Money Pit, 1986, Outrageous Fortune, 1987, Hello Again, 1987, Troop Beverly Hills, 1989, Don't Tell Her It's Me, 1990, Frozen Assets, 1992, The Brady Bunch, 1995; TV films include The Cracker Factory, 1979, The Promise of Love, 1980, The Princess and the Cabbie, 1981, Memory of a Murder, 1992, A Message from Holly, 1992, The Women of Spring Break, 1995; TV mini-series, Voices Within: The Lives of Trudy Chase, 1990. Recipient Emmy award Outstanding Actress in a Comedy

Series for Cheers, 1983. Office: Creative Artists Agy Ron Meyer 9830 Wilshire Blvd Beverly Hills CA 90212*

LONGAS, MARIA OLIVA, chemistry educator, researcher; b. Medellin, Antioquia, Columbia; came to U.S., 1965; d. Francisco de Paula and Maria Ignacia (Carmona) L. MS, NYU, 1973, PhD, 1978. Rsch. assoc. Columbia U. Coll. of Physicians & Surgeons, N.Y.C., 1979-81; postdoctoral fellow Mt. Sinai Sch. Medicine, N.Y.C., 1982-83, asst. prof., 1983-87; assoc. prof. Purdue U. Calumet, Hammond, Ind., 1990—. Contbr. articles to profl. jours. Recipient Alumni award Hunter Coll., CUNY, 1971; grantee Nat. Inst. Aging, 1983-87; grantee Purdue Rsch. Found., summers 1988, 90-91, travel grantee, 1989, 91, 93. Mem. Am. Chem. Soc., Am. Chem. Soc. for the Biol. Chemist, N.Y. Acad. Sci., Soc. Complex Carbohydrates, Soc. for Applied Spectroscopy. Office: Purdue Univ Calumet 2233 171st St Hammond IN 46323-2094

LONGDEN, CLAIRE SUZANNE, financial planner, investment advisor; b. Sheffield, Yorkshire, Eng., June 2, 1938; came to U.S., 1964; d. John Stewart and Daisy (Heath) L. Diploma in pvt. sec., Coll. Commerce & Tech., Sheffield, 1956; cert. in Fin. Planning, Coll. Fin. Planning, 1979. Sec. Sheffield, 1956-62; G-4 asst. UN/WHO, Geneva, Switzerland, 1962-64; pvt. sec. Arthur Wiesenberger, N.Y.C., 1966-70; v.p. Alex Brown & Sons, N.Y.C., 1970-75; 1st v.p. Butcher & Singer, N.Y.C., 1975-89; pres. Claire Longden Assocs., Rhinebeck, N.Y., 1989—; adj. prof. fin. planning NYU, 1981-82. Conf. speaker 1980-86; contbr. articles to profl. jours. Bd. dirs. No. Dutchess Hosp., Rhinebeck, 1989, pres., 1995—. Named one of Top Planners Nationwide, Money mag., 1987. Mem. Inst. Cert. Fin. Planners (nat. bd. dirs. 1984-86, founder, N.Y.C. chpt. 1982-86, N.E. regional dir. 1985-86, bd. of ethics 1993-95, Cert. Fin. Planner of Yr. 1984), Womens Bond Club N.Y. (pres. 1982-84), Inst. Am. Fin. Planners (bd. dirs. 1983-85), Registry Fin. Planning Practitioners, Rotary (pres. Rhinebeck chpt. 1993-94). Office: Claire Longden Assocs 30 E Market St Rhinebeck NY 12572-1606

LONGLEY, ALICE BEEBE, financial analyst; b. Kalamazoo, Mich., June 6, 1948; d. Clifford Deming and Mildred (Dunn) Beebe; m. Frank Alan Longley, Aug. 22, 1981; children: Jonathan Thatcher, Andrew Deming, Clifford Alan. BA, Wellesley Coll., 1970; MA, Columbia U., PhD, 1981. Prof. Columbia U., N.Y.C., 1978-80; v.p. research Donaldson, Lufkin & Jenrette, N.Y.C., 1982—. Mem. N.Y. Soc. Security Analysts, Phi Beta Kappa. Office: Donaldson Lufkin & Jenrette 140 Broadway New York NY 10005-1285

LONGLEY, MARJORIE WATTERS, newspaper executive; b. Lockport, N.Y., Nov. 2, 1925; d. J. Randolph and Florence Lucille (Craine) Watters; m. Ralph R. Longley, Oct. 1, 1949 (dec.). B.A. in English with highest honors cum laude, St. Lawrence U., 1947. Sports editor, feature writer Lockport Union Sun and Jour., 1945; with N.Y. Times, N.Y.C., 1948-88, asst. to v.p. consumer mktg., 1975-78, circulation sales mgr., 1978-79, sales dir., 1979-81, dir. pub. affairs, 1981-88; pres. Gramercy Internat., Inc. (mktg. and pub. rels.), N.Y.C., 1988—; dir. pub. affairs and pub. info., N.Y.C. Off-Track Betting Corp., 1990-94; mem. Nat. Newspapers' Readership Coun., 1979-82; mem. adv. coun. API, 1980-85. Author: America's Taste, 1960. Trustee St. Lawrence U., 1969-75, 77—; chmn. bd. dirs. Am. Forum for Global Edn., 1977—; pres. N.Y. State Adult Edn. Coun., 1974-77; mem. N.Y. State Adv. Coun. for Vocat. Edn., 1976-81, postsecondary edn., 1978-81, Mayor's Coun. Environment of N.Y.C., 1983—; bd. dirs. Nat. Charities Info. Bur.; chmn. 42d St. Edn., Theatre, Culture, 1984-88, chmn. emeritus, 1988—. Mem. Nat. Inst. Social Scis., Am. Mgmt. Assn. (nat. mktg. coun. 1972-89, bd. dirs. 1986-88), Nat. Arts Club, Overseas Press Club, Phi Beta Kappa. Democrat. Baptist. Office: Gramercy Internat Inc 34 Gramercy Park E New York NY 10003-1731

LONGO, KELLY PORTER, research scientist; b. New London, Conn., Sept. 24, 1961; d. Louis McCullough and Patricia Ann (Holland) Porter; m. Michael Joseph Longo, Apr. 25, 1987. BA, Conn. Coll., 1993. Technician Pfizer, Inc., Groton, Conn., 1982-88, asst. scientist, 1988-91, assoc. scientist, 1991-95, sci., 1995—. Contbr. articles to sci. jours. Advisor-liaison SMART Orgn., Pfizer, Inc., Groton, 1992—. Roman Catholic. Home: 87 Hewitt Rd Mystic CT 06355

LONGSWORTH, ELLEN LOUISE, art historian, consultant; b. Auburn, Ind., Aug. 21, 1949; d. Robert Smith and Alice Louise (Whitten) L.; m. Frederic Sanderson Stott, Sept. 1, 1973 (div. 1981); m. Joseph Nicholas Teta, June 15, 1991. BA, Mt. Holyoke Coll., 1971; MA, U. Chgo., 1976; PhD, Boston U., 1987. Trainer, designer Polaris Enterprises Corp., Quincy, Mass., 1981-82, asst. v.p., 1982-84, cons., 1989-93; asst. prof. Merrimack Coll., N. Andover, Mass., 1985—, assoc. prof., 1990—, chmn. dept., 1993—; adj. instr. art and art history Bradford Coll., Haverhill, Mass., 1975-80; vis. lectr. art history Lowell (Mass.) U., 1981-82, Boston U., 1982-86, 88, 91, Babson Coll., Wellesley, Mass., 1984-85. Mem. Merrimack Valley Coun. on the Arts and Humanities, Haverhill, 1975-78, Friends of Kimball Tavern, Bradford Coll., Haverhill, 1975-80; bd. dirs. Winnekenni Found., Haverhill, 1990—. Grantee Faculty Devel., Merrimack Coll., 1989-90, 92-93, Kress Summer Travel, Boston U., summers 1980, 86; fellowship Boston U., 1980-82, 85; recipient internship Isabella Stewart Gardner Mus., Boston, 1979-80. Mem. AAUW, Coll. Art Assn., South-Ctrl. Renaissance Conf., Am. Assn. Italian Studies, Italian Art Soc., Renaissance Soc. Am. Republican. Methodist. Home: 62 Arlington St Haverhill MA 01830-5922 Office: Merrimack Coll North Andover MA 01845

LONKART, GEORGIA FAITH, banker; b. Trenton, N.J., Jan. 17, 1947; d. George W. and Laura L. (Tilghman) Balles; m. Robert S. Lonkart, Apr. 8, 1967; children: Kevin. L., Scott C. Student, Rutgers U., Camden, 1972-75; BA in English, U. R.I., 1982. Fin. aid officer Brown U., Providence, 1980-84; ops. mgr. R.I. Hosp. Trust Nat. Bank, Providence, 1984-85, ops. officer, 1985-86, asst. v.p., 1986-87, v.p., 1987-89; mgr. sr. ops. Bank of Boston, 1989-90; 1st v.p. R.I. Hosp. Trust (subs. Bank of Boston), Providence, 1990-91; dir. cons. fin. ops. Bank of Boston, 1991-93; sr. cons. banking and investment svcs. KPMG Peat Marwick, Boston, 1994—. Mem. Am. Inst. Bankers, Consumer Bankers Assn. Home: 62 Carue Dr North Scituate RI 02857-1013 Office: KPMG Peat Marwick One Boston Pl Boston MA 02108

LOO, MINNIE, lawyer; b. Hong Kong, Oct. 1, 1957; came to the U.S., 1963; d. York Yuk Wah and Lily Lai King (Hung) L. AS, City Coll. of San Francisco, 1977; AB in Polit. Sci., U. Calif., 1978, AB in Journalism, 1978; JD, Georgetown U. Law Ctr., 1981. Bar: Calif., U.S. Dist. Ct. (no. dist. Calif.), U.S. Ct. Appeals (9th cir.), U.S. Supreme Ct.; real estate broker, Calif. Law clerk to Hon. Jack R. Rainville U.S. Bankruptcy Ct., San Francisco, 1981-83; owner, officer, dir. Etiquette, a Calif. Corp., San Francisco, 1983-84; lawyer Law Office of Minnie Loo, San Francisco, 1983-91; aide to Hon. Willie B. Kennedy, Bd. Suprs., San Francisco, 1985-91; atty.-advisor Office of U.S. Trustee, San Francisco, 1991—. judge pro tem Municipal Ct., San Francisco; mem. NASD Bd. Arbitrators; arbitrator State Bar Calif.; atty. Vol. Legal Svcs. Program; legal advisor Yee on Tong Benevolent Assn. Office: Office of the US Trustee 250 Montgomery St Ste 1000 San Francisco CA 94104-3401

LOOK, ALICE, television producer; b. N.Y.C., Aug. 2, 1952; D. Walter F. W. and Soak Har (Ho) L.; m. Donald (Sandy) Forbes McGill, May 26, 1984; 1 child, Ian Look McGill. BA, NYU, 1974. Producer, news writer NBC Radio, N.Y.C., 1976-77; producer, news writer WNBC TV, N.Y.C., 1977-87, reporter, 1987; owner Look TV, Darien, Conn., 1989—; bd. dirs. YWCA of Darien (Conn.)-Norwalk, pub. rels. cons., 1990—. Bd. trustees Darien Libr., 1994—; TV host Darien Dateline, 1991; coord. Christmas In April Program, Darien YWCA, 1992. Recipient Emmy for best news broadcast NATAS, 1983-84. Home and Office: 36 Walmsley Rd Darien CT 06820-5129

LOOK, JANET K., psychologist; b. Bklyn., Mar. 11, 1944; d. Harry and Isabelle (Chernoff) Kaplan; divorced; children: Howard, Erika (dec.). AB, NYU, 1964; EdM, Rutgers U., 1967, EdD, 1976. Lic. psychologist; cert. sch. psychologist. Asst. examiner Ednl. Testing Svc., Princeton, N.J., 1964-66; instr. Rutgers U., New Brunswick, N.J., 1968-69; psychologist Seattle Pub. Schs., 1991—; pvt. practice Kirkland, Wash., 1993—; adj. instr. U. Conn., Waterbury, 1973-91; appearances on various TV and radio shows including the Today Show; interviews include Litchfield County Times, 1987, Waterbury Rep.-Am., 1983-87, Manchester Jour. Inquirer, 1986, Danbury News-Times, 1985; presenter APA, San Francisco, 1991, Nation's Concern and Its Response, U. Wis., Milw., 1991, Nat. Assn. Sch. Psychologists, Dallas, 1991, Divorce Issues Inst., So. Conn. State U., New Haven, 1989. Author: (with others) The Troubled Adolescent, 1991; contbr. articles to newspapers. Mem. APA, Wash. State Psychol. Assn., Nat. Assn. Sch. Psychologists, Wash. State Assn. Sch. Psychologists (area rep., exec. bd. 1991-93). Office: 1104 Market St Kirkland WA 98033-5441

LOOMIS, CAROL A., educator; b. N.Y.C., Sept. 15, 1938; d. Carroll Furman and Edna (Haunfelder) L. BS, Cornell U., 1960; MA, NYU, 1964; PhD, Columbia U., 1969. Tchr. Pa. State U., State College, 1969-78, Hunterdon, Pittstown, N.J., 1979-81, Maallaien, Macungie, Pa., 1981—. Contbr. articles to profl. jours. Office: Maallaien RD 6 Box 6050 Walker Rd Macungie PA 18062

LOOMIS, CAROL J., journalist; b. Marshfield, Mo., June 25, 1929; d. Harold and Mildred (Case) Junge; m. John R. Loomis, Mar. 19, 1960; children: Barbara, Mark. Student, Drury Coll., 1947-49; B in Journalism, U. Mo., 1951. Editor Maytag News, Maytag Co., Newton, Iowa, 1951-54; rsch. assoc. Fortune mag., N.Y.C., 1954-58, assoc. editor, 1958-68, mem. bd. editors, 1968—. Office: Fortune Mag 1271 Ave Of The Americas New York NY 10020-1300

LOOMIS, JACQUELINE CHALMERS, photographer; b. Hong Kong, Mar. 9, 1930 (parents Am. citizens); d. Earl John and Jennie Bell (Sherwood) Chalmers; m. Charles Judson Williams III, Dec. 2, 1950 (div. Aug. 1973); children: Charles Judson IV, John C., David F., Robert W.; m. Henry Loomis, Jan. 19, 1974; stepchildren: Henry S., Mary Loomis Hankinson, Lucy F., Gordon M. Student, U. Oreg., 1948-50, Nat. Geog. Soc., 1978-79, Winona Sch. Profl. Photography, 1979, Sch. Photo Journalism, U. Mo., 1979. Pres. J. Sherwood Chalmers Photographer, Jacksonville, Fla., 1979—, Windward Corp., Washington, 1984—. Contbr. photos to Nat. Geog. books and mag., Fortune mag., Nat. Newspapers, Ducks Unltd., Living Bird Quar., Orvis News, Frontiers Internat., others, also calendars; one-woman show Woodbury-Blair Mansion, Washington, 1980; rep. in pub. and pvt. collections. Trustee Sta. WJCT-TV, Jacksonville, Fla., 1965-73, mem. exec. com., chmn., 1965-66; co-chmn. Arts Festival, Jacksonville, 1970, chmn., 1971; bd. dirs., mem. exec. com. Nat. Friends Pub. Broadcasting, N.Y.C., 1970-73; bd. dirs. Washington Opera, 1976—, Pub. Broadcasting Svcs., Washington, 1972-73, Planned Parenthood of North Fla., 1968-70; bd. dirs. Jacksonville Art Mus., 1968-70, treas., 1968; bd. dirs. Jacksonville Symphony Assn., 1988-94; mem. bd. Children's Home Soc. of Fla., 1988—. Recipient Cultural Arts award Jacksonville Coun. Arts, 1971, award Easton Waterfowl Festival, 1982, 1st and 2d prizes, 1984. Mem. Profl. Photographers Am. (Merit award 1982), Photog. Soc. Am., Am. Soc. Picture Profls., Jr. League Jacksonville Inc., Fla. Yacht Club (Jacksonville), Amelia Island Plantation Club (Fla.), Timuquana Country Club (Fla.). Republican. Presbyterian. Avocations: travel, golf, sailing, skiing, riding. Home and Office: 4661 Ortega Island Dr Jacksonville FL 32210-7500

LOONEY, CLAUDIA ARLENE, academic administrator; b. Fullerton, Calif., June 13, 1946; d. Donald F. and Mildred B. (Gage) Schneider; m. James K. Looney, Oct. 8, 1967; 1 child, Christopher K. BA, Calif. State U., 1969. Dir. youth YWCA No. Orange County, Fullerton, Calif., 1967-70; dir. dist. Camp Fire Girls, San Francisco, 1971-73; asst. exec. dir. Camp Fire Girls, Los Angeles, 1973-77; asst. dir. community resources Childrens Hosp., Los Angeles, 1977-80; dir. community devel. Orthopaedic Hosp., Los Angeles, 1980-82; sr. v.p. Saddleback Meml. Found./Saddleback Meml. Med. Ctr., Laguna Hills, Calif., 1982-92; v.p. planning and advancement Calif. Inst. Arts, Santa Clarita, Calif., 1992—; instr. U. Calif., Irvine, Univ. Irvine; mem. steering com. U. Irvine. Mem. steering com. United Way, Los Angeles, 1984-86. Fellow Assn. Healthcare Philanthropy (nat. chair-elect, chmn. program Nat. Edn. Conf. 1986, regional dir. 1985-89, fin. com. 1988—, pres., com. chn. 1987—, Give To Life com. chmn. 1987-91, Orange County Fund Raiser of Yr. 1992); mem. Nat. Soc. Fund Raising Execs. Found. (cert., vice chmn. 1985-90, chair 1993—), So. Calif. Assn. Hosp. Devel. (past pres., bd. dirs.), Profl. Ptnrs. (chmn. 1986, instr. 1988—), Philanthropic Ednl. Orgn. (past pres.). Office: Calif Inst of the Arts 24700 McBean Pky Valencia CA 91355-9999

LOPATA, HELENA ZNANIECKA, sociologist, researcher, educator; b. Poznan, Poland, Oct. 1, 1925; d. Florian Witold and Eileen (Markley) Znaniecki; m. Richard Stefan Lopata, Feb. 8, 1946 (wid. July 1994); children: Theodora Karen Lopata-Menasco. B.A., U. Ill., 1946, M.A., 1947; Ph.D., U. Chgo., 1954; DSc (hon.), Guelph U., Can., 1995. Lectr. U. Va. Extension, Langley AFB, 1951-52, DePaul U., 1956-60; lectr. Roosevelt U., 1960-64, asst. prof. sociology, 1964-67, assoc. prof., 1967-69; prof. sociology Loyola U., Chgo., 1969; chmn. dept. sociology Loyola U., 1970-72, dir. Center for Comparative Study of Social Roles, 1972—; mem. NIMH Rev. Bd., 1977-79; mem. Mayor's Council Manpower and Econ. Devel., 1974-79; mem. adv. com., chair tech. com. White House Conf. on Aging, 1979-81; adv. council Nat. Inst. Aging, 1978-83. Author: Occupation: Housewife, 1971, Widowhood in an American City, 1973, Polish Americans: Status Competition in an Ethnic Community, 1976, Women as Widows: Support Systems, 1979; City Women: Work, Jobs, Occupations, Careers, Vol. I, America, 1984, Vol. II, Chicago, 1985, (with Debra Barnewolt and Cheryl Miller) City Women in America, 1986; (with Henry Brehm) Widows and Dependent Wives: From Social Problem to Federal Policy, 1986, Polish Americans, 1994, Circles and Settings: Role Changes of American Women, 1994; adv. editor: Sociological Quar., 1969-72, Jour. Marriage and Family, 1978-82, Symbolic Interaction, 1989—; editor: Marriages and Families, 1973, Research on the Interweave of Social Roles: (with Nona Glazer and Judith Wittner), vol. 1, Women and Men, 1980, (with David Maines), vol. 2, Friendship, 1981, (with Joseph Pleck) vol. 3, Families and Jobs, 1983, vol. 4, Current Research on Occupations and Professions, 1987, vol. 5, 1990, Current Research on Occupations and Professions, 1990, Widows: The Middle East, Asia and the Pacific, 1987, Widows: North America, 1987; (with David Maines) Friendship in Context, 1990; adv. bd. Symbolic Interaction, 1977-89—; contbr. articles to profl. jours. Bd. dirs. Wellesley Center of Research and Women, 1979-84. Recipient Research award Radcliffe Coll., 1982; grantee Chgo. Tribune, 1956, Midwest Coun. Social Research on Aging, 1964-65, Adminstrn. on Aging, 1967-69, 68-71, Social Security Adminstrn., 1971-75, also 1975-79, Indo-Am. Fellowship Program: Coun. for Internat. Exchange Scholars, 1987-88, Rsch. Stimulation grantee Loyola U. Chgo., 1988, 92; named Faculty Mem. of Yr., Loyola U., 1975. Fellow Midwest Council for Social Research on Aging (pres. 1969-70, 91-92, postdoctoral tng. dir. 1971-77), Ill. Sociol. Assn. (pres. 1969-70), Gerontol. Soc. Am. (chmn. social and behavioral sci. sect. 1980-81), Internat. Gerontol. Assn.; mem. Soc. for Study Social Problems (chmn. spl. problems com. 1971, v.p. 1975, council 1978-80, pres. 1983, Disting. Scholar award family div. 1989), Am. Sociol. Assn. (council 1978-81, chmn. sect. family 1976, chmn. sect. sex roles 1975, Sorokin awards com. 1970-73, publs. com. 1972-73, nominations com. 1977, chmn. sect. on aging 1982-83, Cooley-Blumer awards com. 1984, Jessie Bernard awards com. 1984-86, disting. scholarly publ. awards selection com. 1988-89, awards policy com. 1990-92, co-chair com. on internat. sociology, 1992—), Internat. Sociol. Soc. (com. on family rsch. coun. 1991-94, com. rsch. on women, rsch. com. on work 1972—, rsch. com. on aging 1990—), Midwest Sociol. Assn. (state dir. 1972-74, pres. 1975-76, chair 1994—, publs. com. 1992—), Nat. Coun. Family Rels. (Burgess award 1990, chair internat. sect. 1991-93), Polish Inst. of Arts and Scis. in Am. (dir. 1976-82), Polish Welfare Assn. (bd. dirs. 1988-91), Internat. Inst. Sociology, 1994—, Sociologists for Women in Society (mem. task force alternative work patterns, pres. 1993-94, adv. editor Gender and Society 1993-94), Soc. Study Symbolic Interaction (G.H. Mead award 1993). Home: 5815 N Sheridan Rd # 917 Chicago IL 60660-3859 Office: Loyola Univ Dept Sociology 6525 N Sheridan Rd Chicago IL 60626-

LOPER, CANDICE KAY, data processing professional; b. Sublette, Kans., Oct. 29, 1953; d. Robert Franklin and Marion Joyce (Sooby) L.; m. Eugene E. Peake, Aug. 12, 1993. Student, McPherson (Kans.) Coll., 1971-72; lic. in cosmetology, Crums Beauty Sch., Manhattan, Kans., 1974; student, Garden City (Kans.) Community Coll., 1975-76, Diablo Valley Coll., 1988-89. ICCP cert. data processor. Owner, operator Candi's For Beautiful Hair, Garden City, 1974-78; systems project librarian Bank of Am., San Francisco, 1980, analyst, 1981, systems analyst, 1981-82, sr. systems analyst, 1982-83, cons., 1983-84, systems cons., team leader, 1984; project mgr. Wells Fargo Bank, Concord, Calif., 1984-86; systems analyst 1st Nationwide Bank, San Francisco, 1986-88; adv. systems engr. Bank Am., Concord, Calif., 1988-89; owner Candi's Visions, Independence, Mo., 1988—; project mgr. Continuum Co., Kansas City, Mo., 1989—. Home: 3419 S Home Ave Independence MO 64052-1239 Office: Continuum Co 2d Fl 301 W 11th St Kansas City MO 64105-1634

LOPER, CHARLENE MARIE, army officer; b. Allentown, Pa., Mar. 11, 1958; d. Henry Noe and Pauline E.L. (Hubbard) Magnon; m. Leonard J. Loper, Mar. 29, 1985; 1 child, John W. BS, N.E. La. U., 1979; MS, U. So. Calif., 1989. Commd. 2d lt. U.S. Army, 1979, advanced through grades to major, 1993, platoon leader to exec. officer 101st M.I. Bn., 1979-81; assignments officer 1st Inf. Div. U.S. Army, Ft. Riley, Kans., 1981-83; pers. staff officer MS ARNG, 184th Trans Bde, Laurel, Miss., 1983-86; from tng. officer to brigade electronic warfare officer to bn. ops. officer then co. comdr. 103d M.I. Bn. U.S. Army, Wurzburg, Fed. Republic Germany, 1986-90; chief ops. and resource mgmt. Field Sta. Berlin U.S. Army, 1990-91; selected Acquistions Corps U.S. Army, Ft. Leavenworth, 1991; with Combined Arms Command U.S. Army, Ft. Leavenworth, Kans., 1991-93; command gen. staff U.S. Army, Ft. Leavenworth, 1993-94. Decorated Army Achievement medal, Army Commendation medal, Meritorious Svc. medal with 2 oak leaf clusters. Mem. Marne Assn., Assn. Old Crows, Phi Kappa Phi. Roman Catholic. Address: 7853 Michael St Fort George G Meade MD 20755

LOPER, LINDA SUE, learning resources center director; b. Wakefield, R.I., Jan. 28, 1945; d. Delmas Field and Dora Belle (Hanna) Sneed; children: Matthew Lee Mathany, Amanda Virginia Mathany, Morgan Lynnclare Loper. BA, Peabody Coll., Nashville, 1966, MLS, 1979; EdD in Ednl. Adminstrn., Vanderbilt U., Nashville, 1988. Tchr. Parkway Sch., Chesterfield, Mo., 1966-68, Charlotte Mecklenburg Schs., Charlotte, N.C., 1968-71; dir. city libr. Jackson George Regional Libr. System, Pascagoula, Miss., 1979-82; media ctr. specialist Pascagoula Mcpl. Sch. Dist., 1982-83, Moore County Sch. System, Lynchburg, Tenn., 1983-91; ref. libr. Motlow State Community Coll., Tullahoma, Tenn., 1983-85; dir. learning resource ctr. Columbia State Community Coll., Columbia, Tenn., 1991—; exec. dir. Tenn. Bd. Regents Media Consortium, 1993—; presenter TLA Ann. Conv., Knoxville, Tenn., LEAP State Dept. Edn. Conf. for Libr., Chattanooga; career ladder participant Tenn. Edn. Dept. Level II; TIM trainer Dept. Edn., Nashville; exec. dir. Tenn. Bd. of Regents Media Consortium, 1993—. Author: Bibliography for Tennessee Commission on Status of Women, 1979; contbr. article to profl jour. Pres. Moore County Friends of Libr., Lynchburg, Tenn, 1991; bd. mem. Moore County Hist. and Geneal. Soc., Lynchburg, 1991; mem. Tenn. Bicentennial Com., Giles County; mem. exec. bd. Hope House Domestic Violence Shelter; sec., mem. exec. bd. Hope House Domestic Violence Shelter. Recipient Gov.'s Acad. award State Dept. of Edn., U. Tenn., 1988, Inst. for Writing Tenn. History, U. Tenn., 1990, Gov.'s Conf. on Info. Sci., Nashville, 1990. Mem. ASCD, ALA, S.E. Libr. Assn., Tenn. Libr. Assn., Moore County Edn. Assn. (treas., chair tchrs. study coun., chair polit. action commn. 1989-91), Giles County Edn. Found., UDC (historian), DAR, Phi Delta Kappa, Beta Phi Mu, Delta Kappa Gamma. Democrat. Methodist. Office: Columbia State Cmty Coll PO Box 1315 Columbia TN 38402-1315

LOPES, MARIA FERNANDINA, commissioner; b. Ganda, Angola, Portugal, Dec. 12, 1934; came to U.S., 1963; d. Rodrigo do Carmo and Maria Jose Fernandes (Mendes) Marques; m. Fernandes Esteves Lopes, Aug. 11, 1962; children: Lisa Maria Lopes Moss, Mark Esteves. Student, Lisbon (Portugal) Comml. Inst., 1953, Massasoit Community Coll., Brockton, Mass., 1988. With archives dept. Portuguese Govt., Lisbon, 1958-62; congl. aide Congresswoman Margaret M. Heckler, Fall River, Taunton, Mass., 1972-74; mem. Taunton (Mass.) Sch. Com., 1976-93; commr. Bristol County, Mass., 1991—. Founder Day of Portugal, 1974. Home: 28 Worcester St Taunton MA 02780-2041 Office: Office County Commissioners Superior Courthouse Nine Court St PO Box 208 Taunton MA 02780

LOPES, MYRA AMELIA, educational administrator; b. Nantucket, Mass., July 9, 1931; d. Leo Joseph and Mary Ellen (Moriarty) Powers; m. Curtis Linwood Lopes, June 25, 1955; children: Dennis, Sherry, Kathy, Curtis, Becky. BS, Bridgewater, 1954; diploma, Inst. Children's Lit., 1982, N.Y. Inst. Journalism, 1984. Cert. elem. educator, Mass. Tchr. Fairhaven (Mass.) Sch. System, 1954-58; prin. Sheri Ka Kindergarten, Fairhaven, 1960-76; market promotion Store Systems, Greater New Bedford, Mass., 1976-82; writer Fairhaven Sch. System, 1987—, fund raiser, reading promoter, 1987-92. Author: Look Around You, 1990, Looking Back, 1991, Seeing It All, 1992, But Then There Was More, 1993, Captain Joshua Slocum: A Centennial Tribute, 1994. Bd. dirs. Fairhaven Improvement Assn., 1986-94, chmn. membership, 1986-89, pres., 1990-93; bd. dirs. YWCA, Fairhaven, 1982-88, chmn. cmty. rels., 1982-83, nominating chmn., 1983-84, chmn. pers. bd., 1984-88; bd. trustees Millicent Libr., 1993-95. Democrat. Roman Catholic. Home: 71 Fort St Fairhaven MA 02719-2811

LOPEZ, ESTRELLITA COLUMNA, trading company executive; b. Manila, Nov. 20, 1953; came to U.S., 1990; d. Tiburcio Leaban and Dionicia Flores (Madriaga) Columna; divorced; 1 child, Ricci Anne C. A Secretarial Sci., Feati U., Manila, 1972. Office helper Kraft Foods, Inc. (Philippines), Paranaque, 1970-72; office clk. Nestle Philippines, Makati, 1972-76; acctg. clk.-typist Ultra Internat. Trading, Makati, 1976-78; clk.-typist Constrn.-Devel. Corp. of Philippine Internat. Trading Co., Makati, 1979-82, sec., 1982-86; exec. sec. to pres. Duty Free Philippines, Paranaque, 1986-90; exec. asst. Colina Group, Beverly Hills, Calif., 1990-91; mng. dir., buyer internat. sales Asian Am. Trading Co., Ltd., L.A., 1991—. Home and Office: Asian Am Trading Co Ltd 4359 Clayton Ave Los Angeles CA 90027

LOPEZ, JUDITH CARROLL, lawyer; b. Boulder, Colo., Dec. 22, 1945; d. Robert Warren and Irene Caroll (Young) Adams; m. Richard Manuel Lopez, Mar. 19, 1967 (div. Nov. 1975); children: Heather Linn, Amber Elise. BA, Colo. Coll., 1967; JD, U. Wyo., 1979. Assoc. R. Michael Mullikin, Jackson Hole, Wyo., 1979-81; pvt. practice Jackson Hole, 1981-82; atty. KN Energy, Inc., Lakewood, Colo., 1982-88; assoc. Hawley & Vanderwerf, Denver, 1988-89; corp. counsel ANR Freight System, Inc., Golden, Colo., 1990—; bd. dirs. Edit, Inc. Bd. mgrs. Stonebridge Townhomes Homeowners Assn., Lakewood, 1993—. Mem. Transp. Lawyers Assn., Wyo. Bar Assn. Office: ANR Freight System Inc 1819 Denver West Dr Bldg 26 Golden CO 80401

LOPEZ, LOURDES, ballerina; b. Havana, Cuba, 1958; came to U.S., 1959; Studied with, Alexander Nigodoff and Martha Mahr, Miami, Perry Brunson; attended, Sch. of Am. Ballet, N.Y.C. Mem. corps de ballet N.Y.C. Ballet, 1974-80, soloist, 1980-84, prin., 1984—. Created roles in Peter Martins' Sonate di Scarlatti and Rejouissance; other repertory includes: La Sonnambula, Divertimento No. 15, Serenade, Stars and Stripes, Apollo, Kammermusik No. 2, Firebird, The Four Seasons, The Goldberg Variations, Moves, Violin Concerto, Concerto Barocco, Theme and Variations, N.Y.C. Ballet's Balanchine Celebration, 1993, Cortège Hongrois, others; appeared in PBS series Dance in Am. Office: care NYC Ballet Inc NY State Theater Lincoln Ctr Plz New York NY 10023*

LOPEZ, MARIA-ELENA, comptroller, financial consultant; b. Havana, Cuba, May 20, 1956; came to U.S., 1960; d. Manuel and Concepcion (Del Vallado) Lopez Diaz; m. Reinerio A. De Quesada, May 14, 1982 (div. Aug. 1993); children: Francisca Maria Lopez De Quesada, Gabriella Maria Lopez De Quesada. BA, U. Miami, 1975, MA, 1978. Cert. real estate broker. Lang. instr., translator Berlitz, Miami, Fla., 1977-78; asst. ops. mgr. Bank of Boston Internat., Miami, Fla., 1978; credit analyst, adminstr. C&S Internat. Bank, Miami, Fla., 1979-80; asst. treas. Republic Internat. Bank N.Y., Miami, Fla., 1980-84; exec. asst. to CEO Cheezem Devel. Corp., Miami, Fla., 1985-86; comptr., officer Flagler 251, Inc., Miami, Fla., 1984—; fin. con. fgn. investors, 1988—; broker WSF Realty Inc., Miami, 1990—. Legal rep. Guardian Ad Litem, Dade County Family Cts., Miami, 1993—; vol. La Liga Contra El Cancer, League Against Cancer, Miami, 1973—. Republican. Roman Catholic. Home: 430 Gerona Ave Coral Gables FL 33146 Office: Flagler 251 Inc 255 E Flagler St 3d flr Miami FL 33131

LOPEZ, NANCY, professional golfer; b. Torrance, Calif., Jan. 6, 1957; d. Domingo and Marina (Griego) L.; m. Ray Knight, Oct. 25, 1982; children: Ashley Marie, Erinn Shea, Torri Heather. Student, U. Tulsa, 1976-78. Profl. golfer Ladies Profl. Golf Assn., 1978—. Author: The Education of a

Woman Golfer, 1979. First victory at Bent Tree Classic, Sarasota, Fla., 1978; named AP Athlete for 1978; admitted to Ladies Profl. Golf Assn. Hall of Fame, 1987, to PGA World Golf Hall of Fame, 1989. Mem. Ladies Profl. Golf Assn. (Player and Rookie of Yr. 1978). Republican. Baptist. Office: care Internat Mgmt Group Ste 1300 1 Erieview Plz Cleveland OH 44114

LOPEZ, PATRICIA HEMPEY, trademark administrator; b. Chgo., Mar. 22, 1957; d. Cesareo and Mabel Iride (Valente) L.; m. Helio Paulo Ferraz, Apr. 15, 1979 (div. Sept. 1986); 1 child, Graziela Ferraz; m. Daniel Guy Hempey, June 13, 1990. LLB, JD, Cath. U., 1989; LLM in Intellectual Property, Franklin Pierce Law Ctr., 1990. Law clk. Montanry Pimenta & Lioce, Rio de Janeiro, 1986-88, assoc., 1988-89; legal asst. Foley & Lardner, Alexandria, Va., 1990-91, Sys. Ctr., Inc., Reston, Va., 1991-93; trademark adminstr. Visa Internat. Svc. Assn., San Francisco, 1993—. Democrat. Home: 640 Leo Dr Foster City CA 94404 Office: Visa Internat Svc Assn 900 Metro Center Blvd Foster City CA 94404

LOPEZ, SYLVIA ANN, principal; b. San Angelo, Tex., Oct. 25, 1953; d. Vivian C. and Olivia (Trinidad) Dominguez; children: Celina D. Hernandez, Deanna D. Hernandez. BS in Bilingual Edn., Southwest Tex. State U., 1976; MA in Guidance & Counseling, So. Meth. U., 1979; degree in mid-mgmt., East Tex. State U., 1987. Elem. tchr. Dallas Pub. Schs., 1976-83, counselor, 1983-89; counselor Sunset High Sch., Dallas, 1989-90; asst. prin. Edwin J. Kiest Elem., Dallas, 1990-92; dean of instrn. W.W. Samuell High Sch., Dallas, 1992-93; prin. John H. Reagan Elem., Dallas, 1993—. Named One of Top Ten Women-Positive Role Models, Girls Club-West Dallas, 1989. Mem. Assn. Hispanic Sch. Adminstrs., Tex. Elem. Prin. of Sch. Adminstrs., Dallas Assn. Sch. Adminstrs. Democrat. Roman Catholic. Home: 1812 Williams Way Dallas TX 75228 Office: John H. Reagan Elem Sch 201 N Adams Ave Dallas TX 75208

LOPEZ-BEAVER, SYLVIA MARIE, director bilingual program; b. San Antonio, Dec. 29, 1946; d. Floyd Martin and Maria Lucia (Nunez) Lopez; m. Steven Beaver, Mar. 1, 1978; children: Christy Danne, Stacy Marie. BS in Elem. Edn., Tex. A&I U., 1971; MS, So. Meth. U., 1976. Cert. elem. tchr., bilingual, ESL. Elem. tchr. Harlandale Ind. Sch. Dist., San Antonio, 1971-73; elem. pre-kindergarten tchr. Mount Calm County Sch., Sheridan, Mich., summers 1971-73; elem. curriculum tchr. Dallas Ind. Sch. Dist., 1973-76; bilingual cons. Region X Edn. Svc. Ctr., Richardson, Tex., 1976-81; bilingual coord. U. Tex., Tyler, 1981-82; bilingual cons. Multifunctional Resource Ctr., El Paso, 1982-85; elem. tchr. Carrollton (Tex.) Farmers Br. Ind. Sch. Dist., 1985-90; bilingual dir. Waxahachie (Tex.) Ind. Sch. Dist., 1990—; cons. Addison-Wesley Pubs., Dallas, 1980-89, Economy Book Co., Oklahoma City, 1981-84, Regents Book Co., Dallas, 1976-81, Ballard & Tighe Pubs., Calif., 1981-83. Pres. Ellis County Parenting Edn. Coalition, Waxahachie, 1991-93. Mem. Tex. Assn. Bilingual Edn., Nat. Assn. Bilingual Educators, Bilingual Educators Assn. Metroplex (sect. 1992-93), Ellis County Parenting Edn. Coalition (pres. 1991-93), New Focus Waxahachie Inc. (sec. 1993—, bd. dirs. 1990-93). Home: 501 Houston St Apt 101A Waxahachie TX 75165-1302 Office: Waxahachie Ind Sch Dist 101 E Marvin St Waxahachie TX 75165-3035

LOPEZ-BOYD, LINDA SUE, geriatrics nurse; b. Kankakee, Ill.; D. Delven H. and Reina (M. (Soucy) Brandt; m. James D. Boyd; 1 child, Albert B. Diploma, St. Luke's Sch. Nursing, 1967; BSN, Ind. U. Sch. Nursing, 1975, MS in Nursing, 1978, postgrad. Cert. gerontol. nurse ANA. Critical care nurse, 1967-75; lectr. Ind. U. Sch. Nursing, Indpls., 1975-79; dir. Winona Meml. Hosp., Indpls., 1981-86; med./surg. clin. nurse specialist St. Francis Hosp., Indpls., 1986-88; dir. nursing edn. Evergreen Healthcare, Ltd., Indpls., 1988-93; instr. CPR. Mem. Nat. Coun. on Aging. Mem. Ind. State Nurses Assn., Am. Diabetes Assn., Gerontol. Soc. Am., Marion County AIDS Coalition, Intravenous Nurses Soc.

LÔPEZ DE MENDEZ, ANNETTE GISELDA, education educator; b. Santurce, P.R., July 13, 1949; d. Frank and Ana Maria (Vale) López; m. Héctor Méndez, Feb. 15, 1971; 1 child, Nannette. BA in Humanities, U. P.R., Rio Piedras, 1970; MA in Early Childhood Edn., NYU, 1978; EdD, Harvard U., 1994. Rsch. asst. Mt. Sinai Hosp., N.Y.C., 1972-73; founder, elem. educator Humacao (P.R.) Montessori Sch., 1973-76; dir., tchr. Montessori Sch. P.R., San Juan, 1976-78; supr., trainer Head Start Insvc. Program, U. P.R., Rio Piedras, 1978-80; assoc. prof. Coll. Edn. U. P.R., Rio Piedras, 1980-85, 87—; teaching fellow Harvard U., Cambridge, Mass., 1985-86; dir. ednl. rsch. U. P.R., 1992—; cons. Gen. Coun. Edn., San Juan, 1992—, Commn. Women's Affairs, San Juan, 1990-92; dir. Edn. Rsch. Ctr. U. P.R., 1992—; mem. Educators' Forum Harvard U., 1990—; mem. systemwide ednl. reform com. Dept. Edn., P.R., 1992-94; mem. Action Rsch. for Ednl. Change Com., 1993—. Pres. Isla Verde Residence Assn., P.R., 1992—. Mem. ASCD, Am. Montessori Soc., Assn. Childhood Edn. Internat., Nat. Assn. Edn. Young Children, N.Am. Montessori Soc., Montessori Internat. Assn., Am. Ednl. Rsch. Assn. Democrat. Roman Catholic. Home: 44 Venus St Santurce PR 00979 Office: Univ PR Sch Edn PO Box 23304 Rio Piedras PR 00931-3304

LOPEZ-MUNOZ, MARIA ROSA P., land development company executive; b. Havana, Cuba, Jan. 28, 1938; came to U.S., 1960; d. Eleuterio Perfecto and Bertha (Carmenati Colon) Perez Rodriguez; m. Gustavo Lopez-Munoz, Sept. 9, 1973. Student, Candler Coll., Havana, 1951-53; Sch. Langs., U. Jose Marti, Havana, 1954-55. Lic. interior designer, real estate broker. Pres. Fantasy World Acres, Inc., Coral Gables, Fla., 1970-84, pres., dir., 1984—; sec. Sandhills Corp., Coral Gables, Fla., 1978-85, dir., 1978—. Treas. Am. Cancer Soc., Miami, Fla., 1981, sec. Hispanic Bd., 1987, pres. Hispanic div., 1989, bd. dirs., aux. treas.; bd. dirs. Am. Heart Assn., Miami, 1985, chmn. Hispanic div.; bd. dirs. YMCA, Young Patronesses of Opera, Miami, 1985, Lowe Mus. of U. Miami, 1986—, Linda Ray Infant Ctr.; pres. Ladies Aux. Little Havana Child Care Ctr.; trustee Ronald McDonald House, sec. exec. bd., 1992; mem exec. bd. Young Patronesses of the Opera; cabinet mem. Deed Club Bone Marrow Transplant Ctr. Sch. Medicine U. Miami-Jackson Meml. Hosp, 1992. Recipient Merit award Am. Cancer Soc., 1980, 81, 82, 83, 84, Dynamic Woman award, 1992; Woman with Heart Award, Am. Heart Assn., 1985, Merit awards, 1980-84, Women of Yr., 1986, Outstanding Ladry award Greater Miami Opera, 1992; named Woman of Yr., Children's Hosp., 1993; named to Gt. Order of José Marti, 1988; named Leading Golf Couples of Miami by AC5, 1995. Mem. Real Estate Bd. Realtors. Republican. Roman Catholic. Clubs: Ocean Reef (Key Largo, Fla.); Opera Guild (Miami); Key Biscayne Yacht; Regine's Internat. Bath Club (Paris), Jockey, Bath. Avocations: yachting, snow skiing, scuba diving, guitar, piano. Office: Fantasy World Acres Inc 147 Alhambra Cir # 22021 Miami FL 33134-4524

LOPEZ-ROMANO, SYLVIA SILVA, educational program executive; b. Las Vegas, Nev., Dec. 11, 1937; d. Enrique A. Silva and Faustina Flores; m. Peter Paul Lopez, 1954 (div. 1976); children: Peter John, Marie Anne, Henry Matthew, Vincent Martin, Renee Marie; m. Aldo Romano, Apr. 30, 1977. BA in Social Welfare cum laude, Calif. State U., Chico, 1973, BA cum laude in Spanish, 1973, MA in Edn., 1981; EdD, U. San Francisco, 1991. Migrant edn. community aide, 1968-70; case aide counselor Mental Retardation Service, Chico, Calif., 1970-72, elem. sch. tchr., 1973-75; instr., lectr. Calif. State U., Chico, 1975—, adminstrv. fellow, 1982-83; coordinator Upward Bound project, Chico, 1976-80, dir. student affirmative action, 1986; dir. ednl. equity svcs. programs, 1986-89, dir. univ. outreach programs, univ. ednl. equity officer, 1991—; lectr. cross-cultural awareness for counseling program Laverne U., 1984—; mem. adv. bd. Western Assn. Ednl. Opportunity Programs; keynote speaker, workshop presenter in field; cons. workshop for county sch. tchrs. and adminstrs., 1990-91; past mem. adv. bd. Ednl. Equity Svcs.; cons. on early childhood edn. Orcut Sch. Dist., Santa Monica, Calif., 1976. Chmn. student affirmative action adv. bd. Calif. Acad. Partnership Program; co-founder Hispanic Profl. Group; past mem. community adv. bd. Upward Bound; cons. Mendocino Nat. Forest, 1991. Recipient Steve Holman award Western Assn. Ednl. Opportunity, 1988, Outstanding Latina Alumni recognition award Calif. State U., 1992. Mem. Am. Assn. for Higher Edn. (Hispanic caucus), Nat. Assn. for Women in Edn., Hispanic Assn. for Community and Edn. (bd. dirs., past pres.), Calif. Avc. for Re-entry, Chicano/Latino Coun. (founding mem., chair 1993—), Greater Chico C. of C., Phi Delta Kappa, Bambda Theta Nu (founding advisor). Democrat. Roman Catholic. Home: 811 Grass Ct Chico CA 95926-3129 Office: Calif State U Univ Info Ctr Sutler Hall 2nd and Hazel Chico CA 95929-0722

LOPKER, ANITA MAE, psychiatrist; b. San Diego, May 25, 1955; d. Louis Donald and Betty Jean (Sayman-Campbell) L. BA magna cum laude, U. Calif., San Diego, 1978; MD, U. Rochester, 1982. Diplomate Nat. Bd. Med. Examiners. Intern in internal medicine Yale U. Sch. Medicine-Greenwich Hosp., 1982-83; resident in psychiatry Yale U. Sch. of Medicine, 1983-86; postdoctoral fellow Yale U. Sch. Medicine, New Haven, Conn., 1982-86; clin. instr. Yale U. Sch. Medicine, New Haven, 1986-88; pvt. practice specializing in eating disorders Westport, Conn., 1987—; cons. psychiatrist Yale-New Haven Hosp Lyme Disease Study Clinic, 1987—, Yale U. Lyme Disease Rsch. Project, 1986—, Alcoholism and Drug Dependency Coun., Inc., 1989-90; internat. lectr. on Lyme psychiat. syndrome; nat. lectr. on eating disorders, substance abuse. Contbr. articles to profl. jours. Founding mem. Nat. Mus. for Women in the Arts, Washington, 1987; patron Menninger Found.; bd. dirs. The Fairfield Orch. Mem. AAAS, N.Y. Acad. Scis., Am. Psychiat. Assn., Conn. Psychiat. Soc., World Fedn. Mental Health (life), Menninger Found., Alpha Omega Alpha, Phi Beta Kappa. Home: 27 Strathmore Ln Westport CT 06880-4700 Office: 7 Whitney Street Ext Westport CT 06880-3761

LOPP, SUSAN JANE, insurance underwriter; b. Billings, Mont., Feb. 16, 1944; d. Russell and Edith (Trapp) Wallace; m. Robert J. Lopp, June 2, 1963; children: Robert J. Jr., Cheryl J. BA, U. Mont., 1972. CLU, ChFC; registered rep. Reporter Park County News, Livingston, Mont., 1965-66; tchr. Sch. Dist. #5, Kalispell, Mont., 1968-73; planner Areawide Planning Orgn., Kalispell, 1974-77; econ. devel. dir. NW MT HRDC, Inc., Kalispell, 1978-79; ins. underwriter The Equitable, Kalispell, 1979-88, The Prudential, Kalispell, 1989—; mem. Mont. Supreme Ct. Gender Bias Task Force, Helena, 1990—, Mont. Pvt. Industry Coun., Helena, 1988—; commr. Mont. Human Rights Commn., 1993—; dir., sec.-treas. Mont. Life and Health Ins. Guaranty Assn. Bd., 1994—, chair, 1995—; Govs. Coun. for Monts. Future, Helena, 1992; chair Govs. Coun.-Women & Employment, Helena, 1981-83, Mont. Bd. Printing, Helena, 1991-92. Active Flathead City-County Health Bd., Kalispell, 1987—, chair, 1989—; mem. Flathead Coop. Planning Coalition Campaign Bd., 1993-94, Mont. Sch. for Deaf and Blind Found., Great Falls, 1988—, Mont. Rep. Women Bd., 1980-85; exec. com. United Way Flathead County, Kalispell, 1986-92; chair Mont. Womens Prison Site Selection Com., Helena, 1991. Recipient Mont. Centennial Equity award Mont. Depts. Labor and Pub. Instrn. and Higher Edn., 1989, 4-H Silver Clover award Mont. State U./Mont. Ext. Svc., 1980. Mem. AAUW (Mont. pres. 1980-82, Named Gift 1982, 93), N.W. Mont. Life Underwriters (pres. 1988-89), Flathead County Rep. Women (pres. 1985), Am. Soc. CLU and ChFC, Glacier County Pachyderm Club. Republican. Mem. Seventh Day Adventist. Office: The Prudential 295-3d Ave EN Box 7547 Kalispell MT 59904

LORBER, BARBARA HEYMAN, communications executive; b. N.Y.C.; d. David Benjamin and Gertrude (Meyer) Heyman; divorced. AB in Polit. Sci., Skidmore Coll., 1966; MA, Columbia U., 1973, postgrad., 1973-76. Asst. dir. young citizens divsn. Dem. Party, 1966-68; exec. asst. to dean Albert Einstein Coll. Medicine, Bronx, N.Y., 1968-72; exec. asst. to v.p. devel. Vanderbilt U., Nashville, 1976-77; spl. projects dir. Am. Acad. in Rome, N.Y.C., 1977-78; pub. affairs dir., assoc. devel. dir. Met. Opera, N.Y.C., 1978-84; sr. v.p. Hill and Knowlton, N.Y.C., 1985-88; pres. Lorber Group, Ltd., N.Y.C., 1989—; guest lectr. Arts and Bus. Coun., N.Y.C., Internat. Soc. Performing Arts Adminstrs., N.Y.C., NYU Sch. Continuing Edn., Nat. Media Conf., Nat. Soc. Fund Raising Execs., N.Y.C.; exec. prodr., prodr., writer N.Y. Internat. Festival Arts, N.Y.C., 1988. Author chpts. to book; contbr. articles to profl. jours. Office: Lorber Group Ltd 66 Perry St New York NY 10014

LORCH, MARISTELLA DE PANIZZA (MRS. INAMA VON BRUNNENWALD), Romance languages educator, writer, lecturer; b. Bolzano, Italy, Dec. 8, 1919; came to U.S., 1947, naturalized, 1951; d. Gino and Giuseppina (Cristoforetti) de Panizza; m. Claude Bové, Feb. 10, 1944 (div. 1955); 1 dau., Claudia; m. Edgar R. Lorch, Mar. 25, 1956; children: Lavinia Edgarda, Donatella Livia. Ed., Liceo Classico, Merano, 1929-37; Dott. in Lettere e Filosofia, U. Rome, 1942; DHL (hon.), Lehman Coll., CUNY, 1993. Prof. Latin and Greek Liceo Virgilio, Rome, 1941-44; assoc. prof. Italian and German Coll. St. Elizabeth, Convent Station, N.J., 1947-51; faculty Barnard Coll., 1951-90, prof., 1967—, chmn. dept., 1951—, chmn. medieval and renaissance program, 1972-86; founder, dir. Ctr. for Internat. Scholarly Exch., Barnard Coll., 1980-90; dir. Casa Italiana, Columbia U., 1969-76, chmn. exec. com. Italian studies, 1980-90, dir. Italian Acad. Advanced Studies in Am., 1991—. Author: Critical edit. L. Valla, De vero falsoque bono, Bari, 1970, (with W. Ludwig) critical edit. Michaelida, (with K. Hieatt), 1976, On Pleasure, 1981, A Defense of Life: L. Valla's Theory of Pleasure, 1985, (with E. Grassi) Folly and Insanity in Renaissance Literature, 1986, (with F. Colombo, M. Spaziani, Sinisca) All' America, 1990; editor: Il Teatro Italiano del Renascimento, 1981, Humanism in Rome, 1983, La Scuola, New York, 1987; mem. editorial bd. Italian jour. Romanic Review; also articles on Renaissance lit. and theater. Chmn. Am. Ariosto Centennial Celebration, 1974; chmn. bd. trustees La Scuola N.Y., 1986-91; trustee Lyceé Française de N.Y., 1986—. Decorated Cavaliere della Repubblica Italiana, 1973, Commendatore della Repubblica Italiana, 1988; recipient AMITA award for Woman of Yr. in Italian Lit., 1973, Columbus '92 Countdown prize of excellence in humanities, 1990, Elen Cornaro award Sons of Italy Woman of Yr., 1990, Father Ford award, 1994. Mem. Medieval Acad. Am., Renaissance Soc. Am., Am. Assn. Tchrs. Italian, Am. Assn. Italian Studies (hon. pres. 1990-91), Internat. Assn. for Study of Italian Lit. (Am. rep., assoc. pres. 8th Congress 1973), Acad. Polit. Sci. (life), Pirandello Soc. (pres. 1972-78), Arcadia Acad. (Asteria Aretusa 1976). Home: 445 Riverside Dr New York NY 10027-6842

LORD, BETTE BAO, writer; b. Shanghai, China, Nov. 3, 1938; came to U.S., 1946, naturalized, 1964; d. Sandys and Dora (Fang) Bao; B.A., Tufts U., 1959, M.A., 1960, hon. doctorate, 1982; hon. doctorate, U. Notre Dame, 1985, Bryant Coll., Dominican Coll., 1990, Skidmore Coll., 1992, Marymount Coll., 1992; m. Winston Lord, May 4, 1963; children: Elizabeth Pillsbury, Winston Bao. Asst. to dir. East-West Cultural Center, Honolulu, 1961-62; program officer Fulbright Exchange Program for Sr. Scholars, 1962-63; dancer, tchr. modern dance, Geneva and Washington, 1964-73; conf. dir. Assoc. Councils of the Arts, N.Y.C., 1970-71; writer, lectr., 1982—; author: (non-fiction) Eighth Moon, 1964 (Readers' Digest Condensed Books), (novel) Spring Moon, a novel of China (Lit. Guild selection), 1981, In the Year of the Boar and Jackie Robinson (named one of best books for children AIH), 1984, Legacies: A Chinese Mosaic, 1990 (one of 10 best nonfiction books of 1990 Time mag.). Mem. selection bd. White House Fellows, 1979-81; former bds. trustees Asia Found., Com. of 100; chairperson Freedom House; trustee Kennedy Ctr. Community and Friends, Nat. Portrait Gallery; bd. dirs. Nat. Com. U.S.-China Rels., Inc., N.Y.C., 1982; trustee Freedom Forum, Freedom House, Asia Soc., Asia Found., Aspen Inst., Com of 100. Named Woman of Yr., Chinatown Planning Coun., 1982; recipient Disting. Am. award, 1984, Internat. Understanding award, 1988, U.S.I.A. award, 1988, Women's Project & Prodns. Exceptional Achievement award, 1992, Literacy Lion award N.Y. Pub. Libr., 1992, Medal of Distinction, Barnard Coll., 1993; named to Internat. Women's Hall of Fame, 1989. Mem. Coun. on Fgn. Rels., PEN, Freedom Forum Selection Com. Free Spirit Awards, Authors Guild. Address: 740 Park Ave #2A New York NY 10021

LORD, DONNA MARIE, insurance claims professional; b. Hammond, Ind., July 28, 1962; d. Anthony Michael and Patricia Louise (Kaszuba) Lucito; m. Bern A. Lord, Apr. 30, 1994. B in Bus. Mgmt., Western Ill. U., 1984. Claims rep. trainee State Farm Ins., Berwyn, Ill., 1985, claim rep., 1985-87; sr. claim rep. State Farm Ins., Elmhurst, Ill., 1987-89; claim rep. ITT/Hartford Ins., Downers Grove, Ill., 1989-90, claim supr., 1990-92, environ. claims casualty gen. adjuster, 1992-93; account exec. ITT/Hartford Ins., Northfield and Naperville, Ill., 1993-94; sr. litigation cons., spl. account coord. ITT/Hartford, 1994—; arbitrator Arbitration Forums, Deerfield, Ill., 1992—. Mem. Alpha Omicron Pi. Home: 36 Pottowattomie Ct Naperville IL 60563-1235

LORD, EVELYN MARLIN, former mayor; b. Melrose, Mass., Dec. 8, 1926; d. John Joseph and Mary Janette (Nourse) Marlin; m. Samuel Smith Lord Jr., Feb. 28, 1948; children: Steven Arthur, Jonathan Peter, Nathaniel Edward, Victoria Marlin, William Kenneth. BA, Boston U., 1948; MA, U. Del., 1956; JD, U. Louisville, 1969. Bar: Ky. 1969, U.S. Supreme Ct. 1973. Exec. dir. Block Blight Inc., Wilmington, Del., 1956-60; mem. Del. Senate, Dover, 1960-62; administrv. asst. county judge Jefferson County, Louisville, 1968-71; corr. No. Ireland News Jour. Co., Wilmington, 1972-74; legal adminstr. Orgain, Bell & Tucker, Beaumont, Tex., 1978-83; v.p. Tex. Commerce Bank, Beaumont, 1983-84; councilman City of Beaumont, 1980-82, mayor pro tem, 1982-84, mayor, 1990-94; tourism chmn. U.S. Conf. Mayors, 1994, mem. adv. bd., chmn. arts, culture and recreation, 1992-94; bd. dirs. Tex. Commerce Bank. V.p. Symphony Soc. S.E. Tex., 1990—, v.p., 1994—; bd. dirs. Beaumont Comty. Found., 1990—, S.E. Tex. Art Mus., 1990—; bd. dirs. Lincoln Inst. Land Policy; trustee, pres. Beaumont United Way, 1995, v.p., 1994—; v.p. Three Rivers coun. Boy Scouts Am., 1978-84, 89-95; pres. Kentuckiana coun. Girl Scouts U.S., Louisville, 1966-70. Recipient Silver Beaver award Boy Scout Am., Beaumont, 1979, Disting. Alumni award Boston U., 1983, Disting. Leadership award Nat. Assn. Leadership Orgns., Indpls., 1991, Disting. Grad. award Leadership Beaumont, 1993, Rotary Svc. Above Self award 1994; named Citizen of Yr., Sales and Mktg. Assn., 1990, Beaumont "Man of Yr.", 1993. Mem. LWV (Del. state pres. 1960-62, mem. bd. Tex. state 1978-80), Bus. and Profl. Women Assns. (Woman of Yr. 1983), 100 Club (sec.), Girl Scouts Am. (life), Rotary (hon.), Sigma Kappa (life), Phi Kappa Phi, Delta Kappa Gamma (hon.), Sigma Iota Epsilon (hon.). Home: 1240 Nottingham Ln Beaumont TX 77706-4316

LORD, JACKLYNN JEAN, student services representative; b. Sacramento, Feb. 2, 1940; d. Jasper Jackson and Celia (Moreno) Opdyke; m. Brent Andrew Nielsen, Aug. 6, 1966 (dec. Sept. 1974); 1 child, Taumie Celia; m. Mark William Lord, Mar. 5, 1983; 1 child, Jacklynn Michelle. Student, Sacramento State U., 1958-60, Cabrillo Coll., 1962-66, Sacred Coll. of Jamilian Theology and Div. Sch., Reno, 1976—. Ordained Ch. Internat. Community Christ. Communications cons. Pacific Telephone Co., San Jose, Calif., 1966-74, Nev. Bell Co., Reno, 1974-76; student services rep. for extension program Jamilian U. of Ordained, Reno, 1976—; asst. music dir. Internat. Community Christ, Reno, 1980—; choral instr. Jamilian Parochial Sch., Reno, 1976—; sexton Jamilian Handbell Choir, Reno, 1981—; organist Symphonietta, Reno, 1983—. Mem. Nat. League Concerned Clergywomen. Republican. Home: 1990 Humboldt St Reno NV 89509-3645 Office: Internat Community Christ 643 Ralston St Reno NV 89503-4436

LORD, JACQUELINE WARD, accountant, photographer, artist; b. Andalusia, Ala., May 16, 1936; d. Marron J. and Minnie V. (Owen) Ward; m. Curtis Gaynor, Nov. 23, 1968. Student U. Ala., 1966, Auburn U., 1977, Huntingdon Coll., 1980, Troy State U., 1980; B.A. in Bus. Adminstrn., Dallas Bapt. U., 1985. News photographer corr. Andalusia (Ala.) Star-News, 1954-59, Sta. WSFA-TV, Montgomery, Ala., 1954-60; acct., bus. mgr. Reihardt Motors, Inc., Montgomery, 1962-69; office mgr., acct. Cen. Ala. Supply, Montgomery, 1969-71; acct. Chambers Constrn. Co., Montgomery, 1972-75; pres. Foxy Lady Apparel, Inc., Montgomery, 1973-76; acct. Rushton, Stakely, Johnston & Garrett, attys., Montgomery, 1975-81; acctg. supr. Arthur Andersen & Co., Dallas, 1981-82; staff acct. Burgess Co., C.P.A.s, Dallas, 1983; owner Lord & Assocs. Acctg. Service, Dallas, 1983—; tax acct. John Hasse, C.P.A., Dallas, 1984-86; Dallas Bapt. Assn., 1986—. Vol. election law commr. Sec. of State of Ala. Don Siegelman, Montgomery, 1979-80; mem. Montgomery Art Guild, 1964-65, Ala. Art League, 1964-65, Montgomery Little Theatre, 1963-65, Montgomery Choral Soc., 1965. Recipient Outstanding Achievement Bus. Mgmt. award Am. Motors, 1968. Mem. Am. Soc. Women Accts. (pres. Montgomery chpt. 1976-77, area day chmn. 1978, del. any. meeting 1975-78), Nat. Assn. Ch. Bus. Adminstrn., Soroptimists (pres. elect Montgomery chpt. 1975-76). Home: 5209 Meadowside Dr Garland TX 75043-2731

LORD, JANE ANNE, insurance broker; b. Alton, Ill., Oct. 14, 1932; d. H. L. and Cora LaRue (Reeder) Neudecker; widowed; children: Brian B., Jane Elizabeth. BA, So. Ill. U., 1957; MA, Monticello Coll. for Women, 1962; PhD, UCLA, 1982. Ins. broker, 1957—. Bd. dirs. Am. Heart Assn., Found. for Retarded. Named to Lewis and Clark Hall of Fame. Mem. AAUW, Nat. Assn. Life Underwriters, Palm Springs C. of C., Nat. Assn. Ins. Women, Rotary Internat., Order of Eastern Star, Life Champion Circle, Tempo de los Ninos. Home: 2882 Greco Ct Canyon Heights Palm Springs CA 92264

LORD, M. G., writer; b. La Jolla, Calif., Nov. 18, 1955; d. Charles Carroll and Mary (Pfister) L.; m. Glenn Horowitz, May 19, 1985. B.A., Yale U., 1977. Reporter N.Y. Bur. Wall St. Jour., N.Y.C., summer 1976; editorial artist Chgo. Tribune, 1977-78; editorial cartoonist, columnist Newsday, N.Y.C., 1978-94; cartoons syndicated L.A. Times Syndicate, 1984-89; column syndicated Copley News Svc., 1989-94. Author: Mean Sheets, 1982, Prig Tales, 1990, Forever Barbie: The Unauthorized Biography of a Real Doll, 1994. Resident humanities fellow U. Mich., 1986-87. Club: Yale (N.Y.C.). Office: c/o Janis Vallely Literary 320 Riverside Dr New York NY 10025

LORD, MIA W., peace activist; b. N.Y.C., Dec. 2, 1920; m. Robert P. Lord (dec. Nov. 1977); children: Marcia Louise, Alison Jane. BA in Liberal Arts cum laude, Bklyn. Coll., 1940; postgrad., San Francisco State U., 1984—. Hon. sec. Commonwealth of World Citizens, London; membership sec. Brit. Assn. for World Govt., London; sec. Ams. in Brit. for U.S. Withdrawal from S.E. Asia, Eng.; organizer Vietnam Vigil to End the War, London; pres. Let's Abolish War chpt. World Federalist Assn., San Francisco State U.; appointed hon. sec. Commonwealth of World Citizens, London; officially invited to Vietnam, 1973; organizer Vietnam Vigil to End the War, London. Author: The Practical Way to End Wars and Other World Crises: the case for World Federal Government: listed in World Peace through World Law, 1984, and in Strengthening the United Nations, 1987, War: The Biggest Con Game in the World, 1980. Hon. sec., nat. exec. mem. Assn. of World Federalists-U.K.; founder, bd. dirs. Crusade to Abolish War and Armaments by World Law. Nominated for the Nobel Peace Prize, 1975, 92, 93; recipient four Merit awards Pres. San Francisco State U. Mem. Secretariat of World Citizens USA (life), Assn. of World Federalists USA, Brit. Assn. for World Govt. (membership sec.), Crusade to Abolish War and Armaments by World Law (founder, dir.), World Govt. Orgn. Coord. Com., World Fed. Authority Com., Campaign for UN Reform, Citizens Global Action, World Constitution and Parliament Assn., World Pub. Forum, Internat. Registry of World Citizens. Home: 174 Majestic Ave San Francisco CA 94112-3022

LORD, NANCY, pediatrics nurse; b. Abington, Pa., July 26, 1962; d. John Baldwin and Marian (Johannes) Lord. BSN, Villanova U., 1984; MBA Health Adminstrn., St. Joseph's U., Phila., 1993. Cert. pediatric advanced life support, pediatric critical care. Staff nurse Albert Einstein Med. Ctr., Phila., 1984-86, Norrell Home Health Care, Bala Cynwyd, Pa., 1986-87, Vis. Nurses Assn. of Eastern Montgomery County, Abington, Pa., 1987-88; staff nurse U. Med. Ctr. Cooper Hosp., Camden, N.J., 1988-94, nurse mgr., 1994—; lectr. pediatric critical care course Cooper Hosp., Camden, N.J., 1990—. Mem. AACN, Nat. League for Nursing. Home: 17 Hollowell Way Mount Laurel NJ 08054

LORDAHL, JO ANN, writer, therapist; b. Apr. 25; 1 child, Lynn McRee. PhD, Fla. State U., 1970. speaker, appearances on TV, radio and workshops. Author: Those Subtle Weeds, 1974, The End of Motherhood, 1990, Reconnecting the Healing Circle, 1993, Money Meditations for Women, 1994; contbr. poems to profl. publs. Fellow Atlantic Ctr. for the Arts, 1984, Fla. Studio Theatre, 1988, Dorland Mt. Arts Colony in Calif., 1987, 92, 94, Ucross Wyo., 1994. Mem. AAUW, NOW, Toastmasters, PEN Women. Home: PO Box 2666 Gainesville FL 32602

LORDI MARKER, SUSAN MARIE, artist, educator; b. Beaver Falls, Pa., Mar. 13, 1954; d. Tony Carl and Dianne Magdalene (Scuderi) Lordi; m. Dennis Clark Marker, June 17, 1978; children: Sara Lordi Marker, David Clark Marker. BS cum laude, U. Mo., 1976; MFA with honors, U. Kans., 1993. Contract designer various restaurants Kansas City, Mo., 1976-80; workshop leader Creative Art for Children, Kansas City, 1984-87; instr. U. Kans., Lawrence, 1989—. One-woman shows include U. Kans. Regents Gallery, Johnson County, 1993, appalachian Ctr. for Crafts Gallery, Smithville, Tenn., 1994; exhibited in group shows at Fiber Art Internat., Pitts., 1991 (2nd prize), Chautauqua Internat., Dunkirk, N.Y., 1992, Soc. for

Contemporary Crafts, 1993, numerous other nat. and internat. juried and invitational exhbns. Recipient Juror's Choice award Fiber Directions, 1992, Fiber Art Internat., 1993. Mem. Surface Design Assn. (South-Cen. region). Home and Office: 2804 W 121st Ter Leawood KS 66209-1220

LOREE, GRACE CAROLYN, librarian; b. Toronto, Ont., Can., Nov. 20, 1936; came to U.S., 1959; d. Reginald Helier and Margaret Helene (Bridgman) Langlois; m. Paul James Loree, June 27, 1959 (div. 1986); children: Ruth, Howard, Paul. BA, U. Toronto, 1958, B in Libr. Sci., 1959; MLS, SUNY, Buffalo, 1985. Cert. profl. pub. libr., 1985. Libr. Buffalo & Erie County Pub. Libr., 1959-60; libr., cataloger Health Scis. Libr. U. Buffalo, 1960-62; libr. Health Scis. Resource Ctr. Kenmore (N.Y.) Mercy Hosp., 1971-86; acquisitions libr. D'Youville Coll., Buffalo, 1986—. Mem. AAUP, Assn. Coll. and Rsch. Librs., We. N.Y. Libr. Resources Coun. (Continuing Edn. com. 1987-91, 94—, automation com. 1991-94), We. N.Y. Health Scis. Librs. (exec. com. 1983-87), Beta Phi Mu. Home: 3104 E River Rd Grand Island NY 14072-1959 Office: D'Youville Coll Libr 320 Porter Ave Buffalo NY 14201-1084

LOREN, MARY ROONEY, controller; b. Monaghan, Ireland, Nov. 18, 1939; came to U.S., 1957; d. Peter Paul and Mary Alice (McKenna) Rooney; m. Thomas Leroy Loren, Aug. 22, 1959; children: Mary Teresa, Aileen Frances, Susan Marie. AAS in Acctg., Adirondack C.C., 1976; BS in Bus., Skidmore Coll., 1979. Acctg. supr. Neles-Jamesbury, Glens Falls, N.Y., 1979-88; contr. Queensbury Hotel, Glens Falls, 1988-89; mgmt. acct. Ahlstrom Screen Pl., Glens Falls, 1989-92; mill contr. Hollingsworth & Vose, Greenwich, N.Y., 1993—; owner Heritage Heirlooms. Treas. Every Woman's Coun., Glens Falls, 1985—; lectr., eucharistic min. St. Michael's Roman Cath. Ch., Glens Falls, 1980—. Mem. Inst. Mgmt. Accts. (corp., acad. dir. 1993-94, pres. 1992-93, Achievement award 1992-93, Cmty. Svc. award 1993). Republican.

LORENCE, LINDA SUZANNE, music industry executive; b. Santa Barbara, Calif., Sept. 28, 1962; d. Robert John and Joan Lucille (Cook) L. A of Fine Arts, Ferrum Coll., 1982; MusB, Berklee Coll. of Music, 1987. Profl. vocalist Boston, 1985-89; asst. career devel. coord. Berklee Coll. of Music, Boston, 1988-89; affiliate rels. rep. SESAC, Inc., N.Y.C., 1989-91, mgr. affiliate rels., 1991-93, dir. creative dept., 1993—. Recipient Cleo Laine Jazz Masters award Berklee Coll. Music, 1985, 87. Mem. NAFE, NARAS (assoc. gov. 1993—), Nat. Acad. Popular Music (bd. dirs. 1990—), Women in Music (pres., bd. dirs. 1992—), N.Y. Coalition Profl. Women in the Arts and Media (mem. steering com. 1992—), Nat. Music Counsel (bd. dirs. 1993—). Democrat. Methodist. Home: 235 W 22nd St Apt 3J New York NY 10011-2759 Office: SESAC 421 W 54th St New York NY 10019-4405

LORENZ, KATHERINE MARY, banker; b. Barrington, Ill., May 1, 1946; d. David George and Mary (Hogan) L. BA cum laude, Trinity Coll., 1968; MBA, Northwestern U., 1971; grad., Grad. Sch. for Bank Adminstrn., 1977. Ops. analyst Continental Bank, Chgo., 1968-69, supr. ops. analysis, 1969-71, asst. mgr. customer profitability analysis, 1971-73, acctg. officer, mgr. customer profitability analysis, 1973-77, 2d v.p., 1976, asst. gen. mgr. contr.'s dept., 1977-80, v.p., 1980, contr. ops. and mgmt. svcs. dept., 1981-84, v.p., sector contr. retail banking, corp. staff and ops. depts., 1984-88, v.p., sr. sector contr. pvt. banking, centralized ops. and corp. staff, 1988-90, v.p., sr. sector contr. bus. analysis group/mgmt. acctg., 1990-94, mgr. contrs. dept. adminstrn. and tng., 1990-94; v.p., from chief of staff to chief adminstrv. officer Bank of Am. Ill., Chgo., 1994—. Mem. Nat. Assn. for Bank Cost and Mgmt. Acctg., Execs. Club Chgo. Office: Bank of Am Ill 231 S La Salle St Rm 1320 Chicago IL 60697

LORENZ, MARIANNE, curator; b. Denver, Nov. 5, 1949; d. Paul Frederick and Celesta (Johnson) Holscher. BA, U. Colo., 1971, MFA, 1981, MBA in Mktg., 1982. Tchr. French/German Adams County #50, Westminster, Colo., 1972-80; coord. pub. programs Colo. State History Mus., Denver, 1984-85, dir. edn., 1985-87; curator edn. Joslyn Art Mus., Omaha, 1987-89; asst. dir. collections and programs Dayton (Ohio) Art Inst., 1989—. Author: Theme and Improvisation Kandinsky and the American Avant-Garde, 1912-1950, 1992; contbr. Dictionary of Art, 1993. Fulbright grantee, 1975-76. Mem. Am. Assn. Museums, Coll. Art Assn. Home: 347 Triangle Ave Dayton OH 45419-1733 Office: Dayton Art Inst 456 Belmonte Park N Dayton OH 45405-4700

LORENZ, VALERIE CLAIRE, psychotherapist; b. Bremerhaven, Federal Republic of Germany, Oct. 9, 1936; d. Heinrich Friedrich and June Alice (Lofland) L.; (div.); children: Patrice, Pamela, Robert. BS, Penn. State U., 1975, M.Ps.Sc., 1978; PhD, U. Pa., 1983; postgrad., Inst. Cognitive Therapy Md. Psychol. Assn., 1985. Cert. clin. mental health counselor. Md. Rsch. asst. Gov.'s Acton Ctr. Pa., Middletown, 1978; dir. research Gambling Treatment Program Taylor Manor Hosp., Ellicott City, Md., 1983; dir. treatment ctr. Nat. Found. Study and Treatment Path. Gambling, Balt., 1984-86; dir. Forensic Ctr. Compulsive Gambling, Balt., 1984—; exec. dir. Nat. Ctr. Path. Gambling Inc., Balt., 1986—; adv. bd., bd. dirs. Nat. Coun. Compulsive Gamblin, N.Y.C., 1976—; pres. bd. dirs. Alternatives Inc., Pa., 1973-76, Women in Crisis, Harrisburg, Pa., 1973-75; Fla. Coun. on Compulsive Gambling adv. bd., 1988—; qualified expert witness on compulsive gambling in mil., st. and fed. cts.; internationally recognized expert on compulsive gambling. Editorial bd. Jour. Gambing Studies, 1982—; contbr. numerous articles to profl. jours., books and mags.; author annotated bibl. on compulsive gambling; co-editor: Compulsive Gambling and the Law, Lotteries and Compulsive Gambling. Advocate for mentally ill, compulsive gambles; expert testimony state legislature, White House, Congress, 1973—. Mem. Am. Psychol. Assn., Am. Mental Health Counselors Assn., Md. Psychol. Assn. (coordinator legis. dist. 1985—), Ea. Psychol. Assn., Nat. Forensic Ctr., Jr. League Balt., GamAnon, Delta Tau Kappa, Phi Delta Kappa. Office: Nat Ctr Pathological Gambling 92426 E Baltimore St Baltimore MD 21202-4728

LORE-RENFRO, ROBIN DENISE, truck parts company official, small business owner; b. Redlands, Calif., May 24, 1959; d. Dallas Robert and Margaret Josephine (Rigler) Lore; m. Tonnie Lea Renfro, June 10, 1993. Student, Sch. of Ministry, San Diego, 1985, Westech Coll., Pomona, Calif., 1992. Steelworker Luxfer USA Ltd., Riverside, Calif., 1986-92; shipping attendant Kemmer Precision, Cerritos, Calif., 1993; stockroom foreperson Acme Truck Parts, Carson, Calif., 1994—; owner Squeaky Clean, Westminster, Calif., 1993—. With U.S. Army, 1976-82. Baptist. Home and Office: 7822 12th St Apt C Westminster CA 92683-4475

LORIMER, LINDA KOCH, college official; m. Ernest McFaul Lorimer; children: Katharine Elizabeth, Peter Brailler. AB, Hollins Coll., 1974; JD, Yale U., 1977; DHL, Green Mountain Coll., 1981, Washington Coll., 1992, Randolph-Macon Coll., 1992. Bar: N.Y. 1978, Conn. 1982. Assoc. Davis Polk and Wardwell, N.Y.C., 1977-78; asst. gen. counsel Yale U., New Haven, 1978-79, assoc. gen. counsel, 1979-84, assoc. provost, 1983-87, acting assoc. v.p. human resources, 1984-85; prof. law, pres. Randolph-Macon Woman's Coll., Lynchburg, Va., 1987-93; sec. Yale Univ., New Haven, 1993—; lectr. Yale Coll. Undergrad. Seminars, 1980, 83; bd. dirs. Sprint, McGraw Hill; past pres., mem. exec. com. Women's Coll. Coalition; mem. corp. Yale U., 1980-93, chair Virginia Rhodes scholarship com., 1991-93. Chair editorial bd. Jour. Coll. and Univ. Law, 1983-87. Former trustee Hollins Coll., Berkeley Div. Sch.; mem. com. on responsible conduct rsch. Inst. Medicine, NAS, 1988; bd. dirs. Norfolk Acad.; cabinet mem. United Way of Greater New Haven. Mem. Nat. Assn. Coll. and Univ. Attys. (exec. bd. 1981-84), Nat. Assn. Schs. and Colls. of United Meth. Ch. (1st v.p.), Assn. Am. Colls.,(bd. dirs., chmn. bd.), Am. Assn. Theol. Schs. (bd. dirs.), Mory's Assn., Phi Beta Kappa. Episcopalian. Home: 87 Trumbull St New Haven CT 06511 Office: Woodbridge Hall Yale Univ New Haven CT 06520-9999

LORING, GLORIA JEAN, singer, actress; b. N.Y.C., Dec. 10, 1946; d. Gerald Louis and Dorothy Ann (Tobin) Goff; m. Alan Willis Thicke, Aug. 22, 1970 (div. 1986); children: Brennan Todd, Robin Alan; m. Christopher Beaumont, June 18, 1988 (div. 1993); m. René Laglerm, Dec. 20, 1994. Grad. high sch. Owner Glitz Records, L.A., 1984—; pres. Only Silk Prodns., L.A., 1985-90; owner Silk Purse Prodns., 1992—. Began profl. singing, Miami Beach, 1965; appeared in numerous TV shows; featured singer: Bob Hope's Ann. Armed Forces Christmas Tour, 1970; featured several record albums; featured actress: Days of Our Lives, 1980-86; composer: TV themes Facts of Life, 1979, Diff'rent Strokes, 1978; author: Days of Our Lives Celebrity Cookbook, 1981, Vol. II, 1983, Living the Days of Our Lives, 1984, Kids, Food and Diabetes, 1986, Parenting a Diabetic Child, 1991, The Kids Food and Diabetes Family Cookbook, 1991. Celebrity chmn. Juvenile Diabetes Found. Recipient Humanitarian of Yr. award Juvenile Diabetes Found., 1982, 88, Parents of Yr. award, 1984, Woman of Yr. award Jeweler's Assn. Am., 1986. Mem. Nat. Acad. Songwriters (gold mem.).

LORING, HONEY, small business owner; b. Phila.. BA in Psychology, U. Md., 1970; MEd, Wash. U., St. Louis, 1971. Lic. psychologist-master Vt.; directress cert. Assn. Montessori Internat. Counselor Gardenville Diagnostic Ctr., St. Louis, 1971-72; tchr. Early Learning Pre-Sch., St. Louis, 1972-74; music dir., cabin counselor Follow Through Day Camp, Brattleboro, Vt., 1972-74; tchr. Montessori Sch., Dublin, 1974-75; ednl. cons. children's books Left Bank Books, St. Louis, 1975-76; program dir. day camp Brattleboro Child Devel., 1975-79; behavioral therapist Behavioral Medicine Unit, Dartmouth Med. Sch., 1979-84; pvt. therapist Brattleboro, Vt., 1984-85; founder, pres. Gone to the Dogs, Putney, Vt.; dog groomer, 1979-92; founder, dir. Camp Come to the Dogs, 1990—; mfr. dog collars, 1984—; founder The Tails Up Inn, 1995—. Author: (with Jeremy Birch) You're On. . .Teaching Communication Skills, 1984, The Big Good Wolf; contbr. articles to profl. jours. Leader 4-H Dog Club; helper Riding for the Physically Handicapped, St. Louis, 1974. Home and Office: RR 1 Box 958 Putney VT 05346-9801

LORMAN, BARBARA K., state senator; b. Madison, Wis., July 31, 1932; 3 children. Student U. Wis., Whitewater and Madison. Pres. Lorman Iron and Metal Recycling Co., 1979-87; mem. Wis. State Senate from 13th Dist., 1980—; chair edn. com.; mem. health, human svc. and aging com., mem. fin. insts. and cultural affairs com., mem. select com. on healthcare reform; sec. Legis. Coun., also mem. spl. com. on farm safety, mem. spl. com. on women offenders in correctional system; mem. spl. com. study sch. aid formula; commr. Edn. Commn. of States. Bd. dirs. Rainbow Hospice Care, Inc., Ft. Atkinson (Wis.) Devel. Coun., Ft. Atkinson (Wis.) Meml. Hosp.; mem. exec. bd. Sinissippi Coun. Boy Scouts Am.; mem. govs. commn. U.S.S. Wisconsin; active Edn. Block Grant Com., Edn. Comm. Bd., Chronic Renal Disease Adv. Com., Dept. Corrections Community Rels. Bd., Nat. Kidney Foun. Wis., Dept. Devel. Forward Wisconsin, Prison Overcrowding Task Force. Rep. Party Wis. Mem. Rotary Internat. Office: Wis State Senate State Capital Madison WI 53702 also: 1245 Janette St Fort Atkinson WI 53538-1526*

LORO, LAURA JEAN, reporter, writer; b. Phila., Apr. 23, 1959; d. Michael Joseph and Hazel Rose (Catalano) L.; m. Jerry Del Colliano, Feb. 14, 1983 (div. Mar. 1991); 1 child, Daria Rose. BA in Journalism magna cum laude, U. S.C., 1981. Editorial asst. Inside Radio Inc., Cherry Hill, N.J., 1981; asst. editor Radio Only Mag. Inside Radio, Inc., Cherry Hill, N.J., 1982, mng. editor Radio Only Mag., 1983, editor Inside Radio newsletter, 1984, contbg. writer, 1981-87; assoc. editor Inside Radio Inc., Cherry Hill, N.J., editor, 1986; mng. editor Inside Radio and Radio Only, Cherry Hill; Phila. corr. Advt. Age, Chgo., 1987—; freelance writer various publs. Phila., 1987—. Contbr. articles to profl. jours. Mem. Phila. Advt. Club, Phi Beta Kappa. Roman Catholic.

LORO, LAUREN MARGUERITE, secondary educator; b. New Haven, Mar. 14, 1948; d. Anthony S. and Marguerite (Belviso) L. BS, Western Conn. State Coll., Danbury, 1970; MS, U. Bridgeport (Conn.), 1977. Instrumental music dir. Sleeping Giant Jr. High, Hamden, Conn., 1970-77, Hamden High Sch., 1977—; flute with New Haven Symphony Orch., 1971, 72; music dir. Hamden High Sch. Concert Band, Orch., Marching Band, 1977—, Hamden High Sch. Dance Band, 1982—, Theatre Dept., 1972—, Hamden Summer Theatre, 1974—, Michael J. Whalen Theatre Dept., 1975-84, Sleeping Giant Jr. High, Hamden, 1972-83, Quinnipiac Coll., Hamden, 1980, dist. so. region CMEA All Mid. Sch. Band, 1994. Mem. Hamden Edn. Assn., Conn. Music Educators Assn. Office: Hamden High Music Dept 2040 Dixwell Ave Hamden CT 06514-2404

LOSADA-PAISEY, GLORIA, psychologist; b. Havana, Cuba, Apr. 20, 1957; came to U.S., 1962; d. Manuel Benito and Maria del Pilar (Fernandez) Losada; m. Timothy John Henry Paisey, June 4, 1983 (div. June 1989); 1 child, Monica Leigh. BA, Fla. Internat. U., 1980; D Psychology, Nova U., 1984. Lic. psychologist, Conn. Pre-doctoral psychology fellow Yale U., New Haven, 1983-84; clin. psychologist State of Conn. Dept. Mental Retardation Southbury Tng. Sch., Southbury, Conn., 1984-86, State of Conn. Dept. Mental Retardation New Haven Ctr., New Haven, 1986-88; dir. psychol. svcs. State of Conn. Dept. Mental Retardation Region 6, Waterford, Conn., 1988-92; clin. psychologist Conn. Dept. Children and Youth Svcs., Middletown, Conn., 1992—; pvt. practice psychology, Waterbury, 1986—; dir. treatment program for mentally retarded offenders Southbury Tng. Sch., State of Conn., 1984-86. Mem. APA, New Eng. Psychol. Assn. Democrat. Roman Catholic. Office: 265 Meriden Rd Waterbury CT 06705

LOSCHIAVO, LINDA BOSCO, library director; b. Rockville Ctr., N.Y., Aug. 31, 1950; d. Joseph and Jennie (DelRegno) Bosco; m. Joseph A. LoSchiavo, Sept. 7, 1974. BA, Fordham U., 1972, MA, 1990; MLS, Pratt Inst., 1974. Picture cataloguer Frick Art Reference Libr., N.Y.C., 1972-75; sr. cataloguer Fordham U. Libr., Bronx, N.Y., 1975-87, head of retrospective conversion, 1987-90, systems libr., 1990-91, dir. libr. at Lincoln Ctr., 1991—; libr. cons. Mus. Am. Folk Art Libr., N.Y.C., 1985-90; indexer Arco Books, N.Y.C., 1974. Editor: Macbeth, 1990, Julius Ceasar, 1990, Romeo and Juliet, 1990. Mng. producer Vineyard Opera, N.Y.C., 1981-88. Mem. N.Y. Tech. Svcs. Librs., Beta Phi Mu, Alpha Sigma Nu. Home: 317 Collins Ave Mount Vernon NY 10552 Office: Fordham Univ Library 113 W 60th St New York NY 10023

LOSEY-NANDAL, DIANNA LYNN, nurse; b. Sodus, N.Y., Apr. 6, 1965; d. Gary Lawrence and Jeanne Marie (Mayville) Losey; m. Darrell Scott Nandal, Oct. 16, 1993. BSN, Roberts Wesleyan Coll., 1987. RN, N.Y., CCRN. Med.-surg. telemetry nurse —, 1987-89; cardiothoracic ICU nurse Rochester (N.Y.) Gen. HOsp., 1989-91; traveling intensive care nurse Am. Mobile Nurses, 1991—. Mem. AACCN.

LOSSE, ARLYLE MANSFIELD, retired librarian; b. Sheboygan, Wis., Apr. 15, 1917; d. Truman Roy and Emilie (Hildebrandt) Mansfield; m. Carl H. Losse, Jan. 20, 1962. BS, Milw. State Tchrs. Coll., 1939; MS in Libr. Sci., U. Wis., 1960. Asst. to reference libr. Mead Pub. Libr., Sheboygan, 1958-59; libr. Milw. (Wis.) Pub. Libr. System, 1960-82. Contbr. articles and poetry to publs. and jours.; developer (with husband) games for publication in mags. Active mem. Sheboygan (Wis.) Community Players, 1957-58; leader Great Books Discussion Group, Milw., 1963-64. Mem. ALA, Spl. Librs. Assn., Art Librs. Soc. of N.Am., (com. standards for art librs., 1973-75), Wis. Fellowship Poets, Nat. League Am. Pen Women, Acad. Am. Poets, Inc., Beta Phi Mu. Presbyterian. Home: 7240 W Burleigh St Apt 2 Milwaukee WI 53210-1185

LOSSE, CATHERINE ANN, pediatric nurse, critical care nurse, educator; b. Mount Holly, N.J., Mar. 12, 1959; d. David C. and Bernice (Lewis) L. Diploma, Helene Fuld Sch. Nursing, 1980; BS in Nursing, Thomas Jefferson U., 1986; MS in Nursing, U. Pa., 1989. RN, CCRN, pediatric nurse, pediatric advanced life support, ACLS, BLS instr. Staff nurse adult med.-surg. Meml. Hosp. Burlington County, Mount Holly, N.J., 1980-81; staff nurse pediatric home care Newborn Nurses, Moorestown, N.J., 1986-87; clin. nurse II surg. intensive care Deborah Heart & Lung Ctr., Browns Mills, N.J., 1986-87; clin. nurse III pediatric cardiology Deborah Heart & Lung Ctr., Browns Mills, 1981-86, 87—; ednl. nurse specialist critical care The Children's Hosp., Phila., 1992-94; instr. nursing maternal child health-pediat. Burlington County Coll., 1994—; clin. instr. pediatrics Thomas Jefferson U., 1990; clin. instr. adult med. surg. Burlington County Coll., 1991. Mem. AACN, ANA, Assn. for Care of Children's Health, Soc. Pediatric Nurses, N.J. State Nurses Assn. (cabinet on continuing edn. rev. team III), N.E. Pediatric Cardiology Nurses Assn., Sigma Theta Tau. Home: 253 Spout Spring Ave Mount Holly NJ 08060-2041

LOSTY, BARBARA PAUL, college official; b. Norwich, N.Y., June 16, 1942; d. Henry Edward and Mary Frances (Crowell) Paul; m. Thomas August Losty, Nov. 27, 1965; children: Ellen Christine, Amanda Elizabeth. BA, Wellesley Coll., 1964; MA, U. Conn., 1969, PhD, 1971. Asst. prof. psychology Westminster Coll., Fulton, Mo., 1971-73; asst. prof. psychology Stephens Coll., Columbia, Mo., 1973-75, assoc. dir. sch. liberal and profl. studies, 1975-79, assoc. dean of faculty, 1979-85; dean U. Wis. Ctr.-Sheboygan County, Sheboygan, 1985-91; coord. human svcs. degrees Thomas Edison State Coll., Trenton, N.J., 1992-94; assoc. dean human svcs. degrees, 1994—. Home: 4 Blue Spruce Ct Hightstown NJ 08520-9621 Office: Thomas Edison State Coll 101 W State St Trenton NJ 08608-1176

LOTAS, JUDITH PATTON, advertising executive; b. Iowa City, Apr. 23, 1942; d. John Henry and Jane (Vandike) Patton; children: Amanda Bell, Alexandra Vandike. BA, Fla. State U., 1964. Copywriter Liller, Neal, Battle and Lindsey Advt., Atlanta, 1964-67, Grey Advt., N.Y.C., 1967-72; creative group head SSC&B Advt., N.Y.C., 1972-74, asso. creative dir., 1974-79, v.p., 1975-79, sr. v.p., 1979-82, exec. creative dir., 1982-86; founding ptnr. Lotas Minard Patton McIver, Inc., N.Y.C., 1986—. Active scholarship fund raising; bd. dirs. Samuel Eaxman Cancer Rsch. Found., N.Y.C., 1981-88; fundraiser Nat. Coalition for the Homeless, N.Y.C., 1986—. Recipient Clio award, Venice Film Festival award, Graphics award Am. Inst. Graphic Artists, 1970, Effie award, Grad. of Distinction award Fla. State U., 1993; named Woman of Achievement, YWCA, One of Advt. Agys. 100 Best Women Ad Age, 1989. Mem. Advt. Women N.Y. (1st v.p. 1984-87, bd. dirs. 1981-87, Advt. Woman of Yr. 1993), The Ad Coun. (mem. creative rev. bd. 1994—), Kappa Alpha Theta. Democrat. Home: 45 E 89th St New York NY 10128-1232

LOTEMPIO, JULIA MATILD, accountant; b. Budapest, Hungary, Oct. 14, 1934; came to U.S., 1958, naturalized 1962; d. Istvan and Irma (Sandor) Fejos; m. Anthony Joseph LoTempio, Mar. 11, 1958. AAS in Lab. Tech. summa cum laude, Niagara County C.C., Sanborn, N.Y., 1967; BS in Tech. and Vocat. Edn. summa cum laude, SUNY, Buffalo, 1970; MEd in Guidance and Counseling, Niagara U., 1973, BBA in Acctg. summa cum laude, 1983. Sr. analyst, rschr. Gt. Lakes Carbon Co., Niagara Falls, N.Y., 1967-71; tchr. sci. Niagara Falls Schs., 1973-75; tchr. sci. and English Starpoint Sch. System, Lockport, N.Y., 1975-77; instr. acctg. principles Niagara County Community Coll., Sanborn, N.Y., 1989—; club adminstr., acct. Twinlo Racquetball, Inc., Niagara Falls, 1979-81; bus. cons. Twinlo Beverage, Inc., Niagara Falls, 1981-85; staff acct. J.D. Elliott & Co. PC, CPAs, Buffalo, 1986-87; acct., Lewiston, N.Y., 1988—; instr. applied chemistry Niagara County C.C., 1979, instr. acctg. principles, 1989—; bd. dirs. Niagara Frontier Meth. Home Inc., Niagara Frontier Nursing Home Inc., The Blocher Homes Inc., Buffalo. Mem. faculty continuing edn., speaker, chairperson fin. and community rels. coms. United Meth. Ch., Dickersonville, N.Y., 1985-90; guest speaker, counselor, tchr. Beechwood Svc. Guild, Buffalo, 1987-91; bd. dirs. Niagara Frontier Meth. Home, Inc., Getzville, N.Y., 1988—; bd. dirs., mem. fin., investment, pension, ins., and community rels. coms. Niagara Frontier Nursing Home Co., Inc., Getzville, 1988—, Blocher Homes, Inc., Williamsville, N.Y., 1988—; asst. sec., bd. dirs., mem. exec., quality and assurance coms., chmn. community rels. com. Beechwood/Blocher Community, Buffalo, 1990—; mem. Coop. Parish Coun., Sanborn, N.Y., 1991—; mem. adminstrv. bd., chmn. outreach com. Pekin (N.Y.) United Meth. Ch., 1992—; sec. to bd. dirs. Beechwood/Blocher Found., Amherst, N.Y., 1992—, asst. treas., 1993-94, treas., 1994, vice chmn., 1994—. Mem. NAFE, Nat. Soc. Pub. Accts., Nat. Assn. Accts., Nat. Fedn. Bus. and Profl. Women's Club, Internat. Platform Assn., Niagara U. Alumni Assn., SUNY Coll. Buffalo Alumni Assn., Niagara County C.C. Alumni Assn. Home and Office: 1026 Ridge Rd Lewiston NY 14092-9704

LOTSE, ANNE CECILIA, international civil servant; b. Uppsala, Sweden, July 10, 1950; came to the U.S., 1966; d. Erik Gunnar and Maj-Britt (Zaine) L.; m. John Van Houten Dippel, Sept. 30, 1978; children: Stephen, David. BA, U. Maine, 1972; MPhil, Columbia U., 1975. Jr. profl. officer UN Devel. Programme, Gaborone, Botswania, 1976-78; program assoc. The Rockefeller Found., N.Y.C., 1978-80; recruitment officer UN Devel. Programme, N.Y.C., 1980-82; country officer UN Capital Devel. Fund, N.Y.C., 1982-84; coord. devel. rev. The Rockefeller Found., N.Y.C., 1984-86; rsch. officer UN Children's Fund, N.Y.C., 1986-88, programme funding officer, 1988-92, sr. programme funding officer, 1992-94, dep. dir., 1994—. Bd. mem., chairperson bd. dirs. Internat. Womens Tribune Ctr., N.Y.C., 1986—; mem. adv. com. Seeds, N.Y.C., 1987—. Named Grad. fellow of the arts and scis. Columbia U., N.Y.C., 1972-73, Pres.'s fellow Columbia U., N.Y.C., 1973-76. Mem. Phi Beta Kappa. Home: 333 Hudson Terr Piermont NY 10968 Office: UNICEF 3 UN Plaza New York NY 10017

LOTT, MARJORIE GOLDBERG, accountant; b. Ft. Worth, July 23, 1940; d. Abraham Issac and Florene Wilmoth (Richardson) Goldberg; m. Ashburn Richard Piland Jr., Aug. 8, 1959 (div. May 1975); children: Ashburn Richard Piland III, Leslie Piland Sinclair; m. Kenneth Edward Lott, Feb. 25, 1976. BBA in Acctg., U. Houston, 1977. CPA, Tex.; cert. mgmt. acct. Owner Dick Piland Enterprises, Ga., 1969-75; supr. Teneco Oil Co., Houston, 1977-81; contr. Carbonite Oil Co., Houston, 1981-83; contr., dir. fin. Houston Assn. Realtors, 1983-89; prin. Marjorie Lott, CPA, Houston, 1989—; dir. ops. Baca Landata, Houston, 1992. Audit liaison United Way, Houston, 1992-93. Recipient Award of Merit, Am. Fedn. Music Clubs, 1975, Presdl. citation Houston Assn. Realtors, 1984. Mem. Tex. Soc. CPAs (bd. dirs. 1987—, v.p. Houston chpt. 1989, legis. regional coord. polit. affairs Houston and 13 counties 1992—), Houston West C. of C. (chmn. 1994). Office: PO Box 770842 Houston TX 77215

LOTTES, PATRICIA JOETTE HICKS, foundation administrator, retired nurse; b. Balt., Aug. 18, 1955; d. James Thomas and Linda Belle (Cadd) Hicks; m. Jeffrey Grant Gross, Aug. 18, 1979 (div. 1981); m. William Melamet Lottes, Sept. 10, 1983. Diploma in practical nursing, Union Meml. Hosp., 1978. Staff nurse Union Meml. Hosp., Balt., 1978-79, critical care nurse, 1979-81; vis. critical care nurse Balt., 1981-84; head nurse Pharmakinetics, Inc., Balt., 1984-85; dir. Arachnoiditis Info. and Support Network, Inc., Ballwin, Mo., 1991—, dir. nat. support groups, 1992—; nat. support group leader Arachnoid, 1993—. Sec., treas. O'Fallon (Mo.) Elks Ladies Aux., 1989-91, treas., 1991-92, incorporator, 1991, bd. dirs., 1991-94; co-chairperson 303d Field Hosp., U.S. Army Family Support Group, St. Louis, 1990-94. Mem. Nat. Disaster Med. Systems (assoc.), Elks Benevolent Trust, Elks Nat. Home Perpetual Trust. Republican. Baptist. Home: 606 Barbara Dr O'Fallon MO 63366-1306

LOTTES, SUSANNAH INGRAM, food technologist; b. Cleve., June 25, 1965; d. Jack C. and Janet Anne (Steffey) Kern; m. Gerald Raymond Lottes, Aug. 5, 1989. BA in Zoology, Miami U., 1987. Quality technician J.E. Seagrams & Sons, Lawrenceburg, Ind., 1988-89; assoc. food technologist Tastemaker, Cin., 1989-91; food technologist Gold Medal Products, Cin., 1991—. Mem. Warren County Young Reps., Lebonon, Ohio, 1993—. Mem. Ohio Valley Inst. Food Technologists, Inst. Food Technologists. Home: 5269 S Dixie Hwy Franklin OH 45005 Office: Gold Medal Products 2001 Dalton Ave Cincinnati OH 45214

LOTZ, JOAN THERESA, public relations company executive; b. N.Y.C., Feb. 22, 1948; d. Andrew J. and Joan (McCartney) L. BA, Lehman Coll., 1970. Libr. asst. Met. Mus. Art, N.Y.C., 1969-74; office mgr. York Cable Corp., Inc., N.Y.C., 1974-77, Mobile Communications, Inc., N.Y.C., 1977-78; lease mgr. Major Muffler Ctrs., Inc., N.Y.C., 1978-81; v.p., asst. to chmn. Rowland Worldwide, N.Y.C., 1981-93; pres. JL Enterprises, N.Y.C., 1993—. N.Y. State Regent's scholar, 1965-69. Mem. Nat. Scholastic Soc. Democrat. Roman Catholic.

LOTZE, BARBARA, physicist; b. Mezokovesd, Hungary, Jan. 4, 1924; d. Matyas and Borbala (Toth) Kalo; came to U.S., 1961, naturalized, 1967; Applied Mathematician Diploma with honors, Eotvos Lorand U. Scis., Budapest, Hungary, 1956; PhD, Innsbruck (Austria) U., 1961; m. Dieter P. Lotze, Oct. 6, 1958. Mathematician, Hungarian Cen. Statis. Bur., Budapest, 1955-56; tchr. math., Iselsberg, Austria, 1959-60; asst. prof. physics Allegheny Coll., 1963-69, assoc. prof., 1969-77, prof., 1977-90, prof. emeritus, 1990—, chmn. dept., 1981-84; lectr. in history of physics; speaker to civic groups. Mem. Am. Phys. Soc. (mem. com. internat. freedom of scientists 1993—), Am. Inst. Physics (mem. adv. com. history of physics 1994—), Am.

Assn. Physics Tchrs. (coun., sect. rep. Western Pa., chmn. nat. com. on women in physics 1983-84, com. internat. physics edn. 1991-93, Disting. Svc. award 1986, cert. of appreciation 1988), AAUW, N.Y. Acad. Scis., Am. Hungarian Educators Assn. (pres. 1980-82), Wilhelm Busch Gesellschaft (Hanover). Editor: Making Contributions: An Historical Overview of Women's Role in Physics, 1984; co-editor The First War Between Socialist States: The Hungarian Revolution of 1956 and Its Impact, 1984; contbr. articles to profl. jours. Home: 462 Hartz Ave Meadville PA 16335-1325 Office: Allegheny Coll Dept Physics Meadville PA 16335

LOTZE, EVIE DANIEL, psychodramatist; b. Roswell, N.Mex., Mar. 6, 1943; d. Wadsworth Richard and Lee Ora (Norrell) Daniel; m. Christian Dieter Lotze, June 9, 1963; children: Conrad, Monica. BA cum laude, La. State U., 1964; MA, Goddard Coll., 1975; PhD, Union Inst., Cin., 1990. Dir. Casa Alegre, Hogares, Albuquerque, 1979-80; pvt. practice Riyadh, Saudi Arabia, 1980-83, Silver Spring, Md., 1983-85; dir. Gulf States Psychodrama Tng., Houston, 1986-88; founder, dir. Innerstages Psychodrama Tng., Houston, 1988-94; program devel. cons. in tng. Children's Nat. Med. Ctr., Washington, 1994—; supr. Houston Area psychodramatists, 1988—; tng. cons. Assn. Applied Psychologists, Moscow, 1992—; cons. in field. Author: (tng. manual) Clinical Psychodrama Training Manual, 3 vols., 1990. Bd. dirs. Interact Theater, Houston, 1992. Fellow Am. Soc. for Group Psychotherapy and Psychodrama; mem. Am. Group Psychotherapy Assn., Internat. Coun. Psychologists. Democrat. Lutheran. Home: 2016 15th St NW Washington DC 20009 : Innerstages Tng Inst Dept Psychiatry Childrens Nat Med Ctr Childrens Nat Med Ctr Washington DC 20010

LOTZ-KAUTZMAN, VIRGINIA ANN, psychotherapist; b. Pitts., May 19, 1951; d. John and Dorthea (Brinski) Lotz; m. John Anthony Kautzman, Aug. 19, 1978; children: Elizabeth Marie, Bonnie Anna. BA in Sociology, U. Pitts., 1972, MS in Child Devel./Child Care, 1978. Cert. child care worker. Rehab. counselor, disability examiner Pa. Bur. Vocat. Rehab., Harrisburg, 1973; child care worker children's crisis intervention inpatient St. Francis Med. Ctr., Pitts., 1973-78; youth psychotherapist Jefferson County Comprehensive Mental Health, Steubenville, Ohio, 1978-80; child and family psychotherapist No./S.W. Communities Mental Health/Mental Retardation, Pitts. and Wexford, Pa., 1980-92; cons. Louise Child Care, Pitts., 1993, Pa. Psychol. Svcs., Pitts., 1991; field instr. Grad. Sch. Social Work, U. Pitts.; workshop facilitator profl. child care groups, C.C. Allegheny County, YWCA. Active McConnell's Mill Preservation Assn., 1992-93. Mem. Nat. Orgn. Child Care Workers Assn., Child Care Assn. Pa. (newsletter editor 1978—, cons. 1993, Frances Vandivier award 1989). Roman Catholic. Home: RD # 1 Box 295 New Castle PA 16101

LOUCK, LISA ANN, lawyer; b. Davenport, Iowa, July 16, 1963; d. Richard Lane and Jo Ann (Frerkes) L. BS in Bus. Adminstrn., Iowa State U., 1985; JD, South Tex. Coll. Law, 1991. Bar: Tex. 1992. Atty. Bigham & Luttrell, Houston, 1992-93, Woodard, Hall & Primm, Houston, 1994—; mediator Tex. Registry Alt. Dispute Resolution Profls., 1992—. Recipient Am. Jurisprudence award Lawyers Coop. Pub., 1991. Mem. ABA, State Bar Tex., Houston Young Lawyers Assn., Phi Alpha Delta. Office: Woodard Hall & Primm PC 7100 Texas Commerce Tower Houston TX 77002

LOUDEN, SUZANNE LOIS, educational consultant; b. Monroe, Mich., Apr. 3, 1937; d. James Clifford and Pauline Lois (Crumm) Brancheau; m. Roger William Lousen, Sept. 8, 1972; 1 child, Thomas James. BA in Edn./Music, U. Dayton, 1966; MA in Counseling and Guidance, John Carroll U., 1972; MA in Spl. Edn., U. Colo., 1976. Cert. sch. adminstr. Tchr. St. Joseph's (Mo.) Sch., Manteca (Calif.) Schs., St. Anthony's Sch., New Riegel, Ohio; youth dir. Dayton, Ohio; elem. sch. counselor Harrison Sch. Dist., Colorado Springs, Colo.; instr. U. Colo., Colorado Springs; cons. various schs., Colo.; instr. cooking classes, 1985—. Author (lesson plan books) The Sunshine Series, 1980. Mem. govt. team Leave No Child Behind, Denver, 1993. Mem. Am. Sch. Counselors Assn., Colo. Sch. Counselors Assn. (v.p., treas.), Nat. Assn. Mediation in Edn., Nat. Coun. Self-Esteem, Nat. Honor Soc. for Women. Roman Catholic. Home and Office: 14065 Gleneagle Dr Colorado Springs CO 80921-3219

LOUDON, DOROTHY, actress; b. Boston, Sept. 17, 1933; d. James E. and Dorothy Helen (Shaw) L.; m. Norman Paris, Dec. 18, 1971 (dec.). Student, Syracuse U., 1950-51, Emerson Coll., summers 1950, 51, Alviene Sch. Dramatic Art, 1952, 53, The Am. Acad. Dramatic Art. Appeared in nat. repertory cos. of: The Effect of Gamma Rays on Man in the Moon Marigolds, 1970, Plaza Suite, 1971, Luv, 1965, Anything Goes, 1967; appeared in Broadway productions: Nowhere To Go But Up, 1962 (Theatre World award), Sweet Potato, 1968, Fig Leaves Are Falling, 1969 (Tony nominee), Three Men on a Horse, 1969 (Drama Desk award), The Women, 1973, Annie (Tony award, Drama Desk award, Outer Critics Circle award), 1976 (Dance Educators Am. award), Ballroom, 1979 (Tony nominee), Sweeney Todd, 1980, West Side Waltz, 1981 (Sarah Siddons award), Noises Off, 1983 (Tony nomination), Jerry's Girls, 1985 (Tony nomination), Annie 2, 1990, Comedy Tonight, 1994; appeared in film Garbo Talks, 1984; numerous appearances on TV variety and talk shows; star TV show Dorothy, 1979; appeared in supper clubs: The Blue Angel, Le Ruban Bleu, Persian Room. Mem. Actors Equity, Screen Actors Guild, AFTRA. Office: Lionel Larner Ltd 130 W 57th St #10A New York NY 10019-3325

LOUGHERY, CHARLENE KRISTI, public relations specialist; b. Glendora, Calif., Aug. 20, 1966. B in English, San Diego State U., 1988; M in Comm., Calif. State U., Fullerton, 1992. Pub. rels. asst. Los Angeles County Arboretum, Arcadia, Calif., 1988; pub. rels. advisor Adult and Continuing Edn. Baldwin Park (Calif.) Unified Sch. Dist., 1990-94; mktg. asst. Alpha Metals, Inc., 1994—. Editor newsletter Baldwin Park chpt. Calif. Coun. for Adult Edn., 1991-93. Mem. Am. Mktg. Assn., Calif. Coun. Adult Edn. (scholar 1991, Citation Meritorious Svc. South Coast chpt. 1994), Calif. Sch. Pub. Rels. Assn., Calif. Assn. Pub. Info. Officers. Office: Alpha Metals Inc 16772 Von Karman Ave Irvine CA 92714

LOUIE, PAMELA V., comptroller; b. Oakland, Calif., Sept. 10, 1962; d. Peter and Eleanor (Verceles) Louie; 1 child, Robert Louie-Maule. BS in Acctg., U. San Francisco, 1994. Acct. Oryx Capital Corp., San Francisco, 1989-90; fin. cons. Oakland, Calif., 1990-93; comptroller UNARCO/Real Time Solutions, Napa, Calif., 1991—. Treas.-sec. Peninsula Women's Rugby Non-Profit, Oakland, 1989—; treas. Asian Pacifica Sisters, San francisco, 1994—, APLBN Com. of APS, San Francisco, 1992-94. Home: PO Box 10154 Oakland CA 94610-0154 Office: UNARCO/Real Time Solutions 831 Latour Ct Napa CA 94558-6260

LOUIS-DREYFUS, JULIA, actress. TV appearances include Saturday Night Live, 1982-85, Day by Day, 1986-89, Seinfield, 1990— (Emmy nomination Supporting Actress-Comedy, 1993, 94); films include Soul Man, 1986, Troll, 1986, Hannah and Her Sisters, 1986, National Lampoon's Christmas Vacation, 1989, Jack the Bear, 1993, North, 1994. Office: TPEG Mgmt 9150 Wilshire Blvd Ste 205 Beverly Hills CA 90212*

LOUKIDES, REBECCA SUSAN, health services administrator; b. Easton, Md., July 15, 1951; d. John August and Frieda Marie (Schmick) Fuchs; m. Nicholas Allen Loukides, Aug. 4, 1973; children: Alex Nicholas, Nicole Tekla. BA, Salisbury State U., 1973. Addictions counselor Caroline County Health Dept., Denton, Md., 1974-77, dir. of addictions, 1980—; pres. Ea. area dirs. Md. Addictions Dirs. Counsel, Easton, 1990-92, vice-chair, 1992—. Mem. Rotary. Lutheran. Office: Caroline Counseling Ctr PO Box 10 Denton MD 21629

LOUREY, BECKY J., state legislator; b. 1943; m. Gene Lourey; 11 children. Student, Asbury Coll., U. Minn. Mem. Minn. Ho. of Reps., 1990—, mem. various coms., vice-chair health and housing fin. divsn., mem. internat. trade, tech. and econ. devel. divsn., mem. Legis. Commn. Health Care Access. Democrat. Home: Box 100 Star Rte Kerrick MN 55756 Office: Minn Ho of Reps State Capitol Saint Paul MN 55155*

LOVE, BRENDA KAY, administrative assistant; b. Temple, Tex., Dec. 13, 1950; d. Johnnie James Billings and Robbie Erlene (Frazier) Welch; m. Lee James Harwell (div.); 1 child, Clinton Dee; m. Frank Lincoln Leary III, Feb. 14, 1982 (div. 1987). Student, Austin Community Coll., 1978-80, Foothill Coll., 1984-93; AA, BA, Inst. Advanced Study, San Francisco, 1993, post-grad., 1993—. Emergency med. tech.; lic. pilot. Emergency med. tech. Breckenridge Hosp., Austin, Tex., 1979, Santa Clara Valley (Calif.) Med. Ctr., 1980; outside sales rep. Bus. Equipment Co., San Francisco, 1981-82; counselor Nat. Sexually Transmitted Disease Hotline, Palo Alto, Calif., 1984-86, Nat. AIDS Hotline, Palo Alto, 1986-87, San Francisco Sex Information Switchboard, San Francisco, 1987-88; adminstrv. asst. ALZA Corp., Palo Alto, 1983—; lectr., researcher Inst. for Advanced Study of Human Sexuality; bus. mgr. Frank Leary Racing, 1981-83; adminstrv. asst. to chief adminstrv. law judge Tex. Comptroller Pub. Accounts, 1978-80. Author: Encyclopedia of Unusual Sex Practices, 1992; co-producer: (video) 500 Unusual Sex Practices, 1992; contbr. articles to profl. jours. Active Californians Against Censorship Together, San Francisco, 1992—. Mem. Author's Guild, Inst. for Advanced Study of Human Sexuality, Am. Assn. Sex Educators, Counselors and Therapists, Soc. for the Scientific Study of Sex. Libertarian. Jewish. Office: ALZA 950 Page Mill Rd Palo Alto CA 94304

LOVE, CHRISTINE E., fine artist, graphic designer; b. Memphis, Jan. 29, 1953. Studied with Billie Price-Hosmer, 1961-64; student, Memphis Acad. Arts, 1971-72. One-woman shows include Local Color Gallery, Pacific Grove, Calif., 1980, Licsko Gallery, Carmel, Calif., 1992, Three Sisters Gallery, Carmel Valley, Calif., 1993; group exhbns. include Sacramento (Calif.) State Fair, 1981, Licsko Gallery, 1991, Corona del Sol Gallery, Carmel, 1993, Van Gaurd Gallery, Carmel, 1994, Carl Cherry Found., Carmel, 1994, Glamour Con, L.A.; pvt. and pub. collections; illustrator The Masters Manual of Pa Kua Chang, 1984. Recipient 1st prize Gouache Watercolor Fine Arts Competition Monterey County, 1980 and 81. Studio: PO Box 2436 Carmel Valley CA 93924-2436

LOVE, DEBORAH SUE, accountant; b. Milw., Aug. 27, 1952; d. August Lee and Betty Jean (Ralston) Helms; m. Charles Frederick Sage, Apr. 21, 1973 (div. May 1990); children: Charles Herbert, Jennifer Ann; m. Mark Lindsay Love, Aug. 15, 1992. BBA in Acctg. & Fin. summa cum laude, U. Wis., Milw., 1988. Cert. mgmr. acct., CPA. Divsn. acct. Ladish Inc., Cudahy, Wis., 1989; sr. acct. Tetra Pak Processing Systems, Pleasant Prairie, Wis., 1989—. Recipient Wall St. Achievement award Dow Jones, 1990. Mem. Inst. Mgmt. Accts., Wis. Inst. CPA's. Office: Tetra Pak Processing Systems 8400 Lakeview Pky Ste 500 Pleasant Prairie WI 53158

LOVE, EDITH HOLMES, theater producer; b. Boston, Oct. 17, 1950; d. Theodore Rufus and Mary (Holmes) L. Student, Denison U., 1968-72; BFA, U. Colo., 1973. Freelance designer various orgns., Atlanta, 1974-75; costumer Atlanta Children's Theatre, 1975-77; prodn. acct. David Gerber Co., L.A., 1980-81; bus. mgr. Alliance Theatre/Atlanta Children's Theatre, 1977-79, adminstrv. dir., 1981-83, gen. mgr., 1983-85, mng. dir., 1985—; bd. dirs. Midtown Bus. Assocs., 1988-94; adv. bd. Stage Hands, Inc., Atlanta, 1983-89; exec. com. Prodn. Valves, Inc., Atlanta, 1985-89; adv. com. arts mgmt. program Carnegie Mellon U. Mem. Cultural Olympiad Task Force 1996 Summer Olympic Games, 1992—, Met. Atlanta Arts Fund Bd.; bd. dirs. Atlanta Convention and Visitor's Bur., 1993—. Recipient Deca award for Outstanding Bus. Women in Atlanta, 1992. Mem. League Resident Theatres (treas. 1987—), Atlanta Theatre Coalition (exec. com. 1987-91, pres. 1989), Atlanta C. of C. (bd. dirs. bus. coun. for arts 1988—), Leadership Atlanta. Office: Alliance Theatre Co 1280 Peachtree St NE Atlanta GA 30309-3502

LOVE, LAURIE MILLER, science editor; b. Fed. Republic Germany, May 7, 1960; came to U.S., 1961; d. Thomas Walter and Jacquelyn (Jolley) Miller; m. Raymond Lee Love. Student, U. Minn., 1979-80; BA in Psychology, Scripps Coll., 1983; postgrad., UCLA. Programmer specialist Control Data Corp., San Diego, 1982, asst. mgr. software retail store, 1983-84; support technician Ashton-Tate, Torrance, Calif., 1984, editor-in-chief, 1985-87; mgr. tech. pub. Ashton-Tate, Torrance, 1986-87; product mgr. Apple Products, Nantucket Corp., Los Angeles, 1987-88; sr. mktg. cons. Macintosh Market Launch Systems, Rancho Palos Verdes, Calif., 1988; pres. Miller Tech. Pub., Santa Cruz, 1987—; contractor, writer, editor Claris Corp., Santa Clara, Calif., Apple Computer, Cupertino, Calif., FITS Imaging, Soquel, Calif., Aladdin Sys., Watsonville, Calif. Tech. and devel. editor Addison-Wesley, Osborne/McGraw Hill, TAB books; author Using ClarisWorks, 1992, Using ClarisWorks for Windows, 1993; contbr. feature articles to monthly mag., 1985—, computer product manuals, 1987—. Mem. Soc. Tech. Comm. (sr. mem., Silicon Valley chpt.), Sierra Club, Phi Beta Phi (asst. treas. 1980). Democrat. Methodist.

LOVE, MARGARET COLGATE, lawyer; b. Balt., June 9, 1942; d. H.A. and Margaret West (Dennis) L.; 1 child, Jenny West. BA, Sarah Lawrence Coll., 1963; MA, U. Pa., 1969; JD, Yale U., 1977. Bar: Washington, 1977. Lawyer Shea & Gardner, Washington, 1977-79; spl. counsel office of legal counsel U.S. Dept. Justice, Washington, 1979-88, dep. assoc. atty. gen., 1988-89, assoc. dep. atty. gen., 1989-90, pardon atty., 1990—. Mem. ABA (standing com. on ethics and profl. responsibility chair 1994—). Office: Dept Justice 500 1st St NW 4th Fl Washington DC 20530

LOVE, MILDRED ALLISON, retired secondary school educator, historian, writer, volunteer; b. Moultrie, Ga., Mar. 12, 1915; d. Ulysees Simpson Sr. and Susie Marie (Dukes) Allison; m. George Alsobrook Love, Aug. 24, 1956 (dec. 1978). BSEd, U. Tampa (Fla.), 1941; MS in Home Econs., Fla. State U., 1953; MA in History, U. Miami, Coral Gables, Fla., 1969. Cert. tchr., Fla. Vocat. home econs. tchr. Hamilton County Pub. Schs., Jasper, Fla., 1941-43, Pinellas County Pub. Schs., Tarpon Springs, Fla., 1946-51; vocat. home econs. tchr. Dade County Pub. Schs., Miami, Fla., 1951-61, history tchr., 1961-73; supr. food svcs. Ft. Jackson (S.C.), 1944-46. Chmn. subcoun. for crime prevention Brickell Area, City of Miami, 1983-87; mem. Crisis Response Team, Miami Police Dept., 1983—; vol. VA Hosp., Miami, 1987—; historian, vol. vets affairs VFW Auxiliary, Miami, 1988-89; precinct worker presdl. election, 1976, 80; sponsor history honor soc. Miami Edison Sr. High Sch., 1961-73; mem. Mus. of Sci., St. Stephen's Episc. Ch., Coconut Grove, Fla. Named Superior Tchh., Dade County, 1960. Mem. AAUW, VFW ((aux. post 471 Miami, Fla.), Inst. for Retired Profls., Hist. Assn. S. Fla., U. Miami Alumni Assn., Fla. Ret. Educators Assn., Nat. Wildlife Fedn., Am. Legion (aux. post 29 Miami, Fla.), Nat. Trust Hist. Preservation, Coll. of Arts and Scis. Assn. U. Miami, Fla. Vocat. Home Econs. Tchrs. (pres. 1947), Woman's Club of Miami Beach, Sierra Club, Phi Alpha Theta. Democrat. Episcopalian. Home: 2411 S Miami Ave Miami FL 33129-1527

LOVE, PATRICIA SUSAN, commercial lines underwriter; b. Ft. Scott, Kans., Oct. 30, 1956; d. John Carl and Joanna Catherine (Schmitz) Johnson; m. Robert Sherman Love Jr., Oct. 19, 1985; children: Robert Sherman III, Margaret Joanna. AA, Ft. Scott C.C., 1976; cert. gen. ins., Ins. Inst. Am., 1989, Assoc. Underwriting, 1993. Cert. profl. ins. woman. Ins. examiner Western Casualty & Surety, Ft. Scott, 1976-86; comml. lines underwriter Am. States Ins., Ft. Scott, 1986—. Mem. Nat. Assn. Ins. Women (treas. 1990-93, v.p. 1993-94, pres.-elect 1994-95), St. Anne's Altar Soc. (v.p. 1993-94, pres. 1994-95). Roman Catholic. Office: Am State Ins 2801 Horton St Fort Scott KS 66701-3186

LOVE, SANDRA RAE, information specialist; b. San Francisco, Feb. 20, 1947; d. Benjamin Raymond and Charlotte C. Martin; B.A. in English, Calif. State U., Hayward, 1968; M.S. in L.S., U. So. Calif., 1969; m. Michael D. Love, Feb. 14, 1971. Tech. info. specialist Lawrence Livermore (Calif.) Nat. Lab., 1969—. Mem. Spl. Libraries Assn. (sec. nuclear sci. div. 1980-82, chmn. 1983-84, bull. editor 1987-89), Beta Sigma Phi. Democrat. Episcopalian. Office: Lawrence Livermore Nat Lab L-387 PO Box 808 # L387 Livermore CA 94551-0808

LOVE, SUSAN DENISE, accountant, consultant, small business owner; b. Portland, Oreg., Aug. 5, 1954; d. Charles Richard and Betty Lou (Reynolds) Beck; m. Daniel G. Oliveros, Dec. 21, 1979 (div. Nov. 1983); m. Michael Dean Love, Aug. 24, 1984 (div. Mar. 1989); m. Michael Eugene Watson, July 28, 1990 (div. Dec. 1994). BA in Graphic Design, Portland State U., 1976. Office mgr. Rogers Machinery Co., Portland, 1972-77; exec. sec. Creighton Shirtmakers, N.Y.C., 1977-80; dir. adminstrn. Henry Grethel div. Manhattan Industries, N.Y.C., 1980-81; exec. asst. S.B. Tanger and Assocs., N.Y.C., 1981-83; exec. asst., bookkeeper M Life Ins. Co., Portland, 1983-84; acct. cons., owner Office Assistance, Portland, 1984—; owner WE LOVE KIDS Clothing Store, Portland, 1985—; owner, pres. Oreg. Music and Entertainment, 1989—; sec./treas. Designers' Roundtable, Portland, 1985-88; co-owner, The Tuxedo Club, 1992—. Mem. Oreg. State Pub. Interest Rsch. Group, Portland, 1985-90, Oreg. Fair Share,Salem, 1987, mem. adv. bd. career and life options program Clackamas Community Coll., 1989-91. Mem. Women Entrepreneurs Oreg. (bd. dirs. 1988-92, pres. 1992-93, 94-95, Mem. of Yr. award 1991), Brentwood-Darlington Neighborhood Assn. (treas. 1993—), North Clackamas County C. of C., Nat. Fedn. Ind. Bus. Democrat. Office: Oreg Music & Entertainment PO Box 1784 Clackamas OR 97015-1784

LOVEJOY, ANN LOUISE, organizational development consultant; b. Baker, Oreg., Aug. 18, 1949; d. Victor and Norma (Peters) Lovejoy; m. Pierre Ventur, June 9, 1975; 1 child, Conrad Ventur. Bachelors, U. Wash., 1971, Masters, 1975. Bot. field asst. (grant) Yale U., San Luis, Guatemala, 1975-77; editorial asst., micro personal computer trainer Yale U., New Haven, Conn., 1977-86; tech. trainer Bunker Ramo/Allied Signal, Shelton, Conn., 1984-86; sr. training specialist Bank of Boston, Springfield, Mass., 1986-87, MassMutual Life Ins., Springfield, Mass., 1987—. Mem. rep. YMCA Bd. Springfield Metro., 1994—. Mem. ASTD (bd. dirs. Pioneer Valley 1986—), Assn. for Computing Machinery. Office: MassMutual Life Ins 1295 State St Springfield MA 01111-0001

LOVEJOY, JEAN HASTINGS, educator; b. Battle Creek, Mich., July 1, 1913; d. William Walter and Elizabeth (Fairbank) H.; m. Allen Perry, March 27, 1912; children: Isabel L. Best, Linda L. Ewald, Elizabeth L. Fulton, Margaret L. Baldwin, Helen L. Battad. BA, Mt. Holyoke Coll., So. Hadley, Mass., 1935. Traveling sec. Student Volun. Movement, N.Y.C., 1935; bookkeeper Hartford Consumers Co-operative, Conn., 1944; tchr. Pre-School, Congl. Ch., W Hartford, Conn., 1944-45; instr. St. John's U., Shanghai, China; tchr. Edn., 1st Congl. Ch., Berkeley, Calif., 1958-59; instr. Tunghai U., Taiwan, 1960-63; sec. Pres. Tunghai U., Taichung, Taiwan, 1960-63. Pres. ecumenical Assn. for Housing, San Rafael, 1971, 78-80; founding mem. Hospice of Havasu, 1982, pres. bd. dirs., 1985-87, vol. trainer, 1987-92, bereavement coord., 1989-92; bereavement vol. Community Hospice, Tucson, Ariz., vol. referral desk N.W. Interfaith Ctr., Tucson. Recipient OACC Sr. Achievement award, 1991; named Vol. of Yr., Marin County, Calif., 1970, 79; street named "Lovejoy Way", Novato City Coun., Calif., 1980. Mem. LWV (program v.p. Pierce County chpt. 1967, pres. cen. Marin County chpt. 1973-75, legis. analyst land use 1979-80, Calif. chpt.). Mem. United Ch. of Christ. Home: Apt 8208 1500 N Calle Sin Envidia Tucson AZ 85718-7306

LOVEJOY, MARIAN E., state legislator; b. Lawrence, Mass., Feb. 18, 1931; widowed; 5 children. Grad. high sch., North Andover, Mass. Ret. emergency dispatcher; mem. N.H. Ho. of Reps., mem. mcpl. and county govt. com. Supr. of checklist Raymond Sch. Bd., chmn.; mem. Cemetery Adv. Com.; chmn. Raymond Rep. Com.; chair Sch. Bldg. Com.; leader Girl Scouts U.S.; den mother Cub Scouts. Address: NH House of Reps State Capital Concord NH 03301*

LOVELACE, ELAINE COLWELL, psychologist; b. Nordeg, Alta., Can., May 12, 1947; d. Stephen Paul and Hilda Gwendolyn (Miller) Hencley; m. David Wayne Lovelace; children: Caroline, Meredith, Adrian. BSEd with honors, U. Ill., 1968; MS in Edn. Psychology with honors, U. Utah, 1977; PhD in Clin. Psychology, Ga. State U., 1988. Lic. psychologist, Ga., sch. psychologist, Ga. Tchr. Anaheim (Calif.) City Schs., 1968-72, Salt Lake City Schs., 1975-76; therapist The Children's Ctr., Salt Lake City, 1976-77; sch. psychologist Ft. Worth Ind. Sch. Dist., 1977-78; psychologist, tchr. Coweta County Schs., Newnan, Ga., 1978-79, psychologist, therapist, 1979-86, dir. psychology, 1987-90, coord. psychology and counseling, 1990-94; psychology intern VA Med. Ctr., Tuskegee, Ala., 1986-87; pvt. practice Newnan, 1988—; Presentor workshops. Contbr. articles to profl. jours. Edmund J. James scholar U. Ill., 1964-68. Mem. Am. Psychol. Assn., Nat. Assn. Sch. Psychologists, Alpha Lambda Delta (scholastic honorary). Episcopalian.

LOVELACE, ROSE MARIE SNIEGON, federal space agency administrator; b. Sweet Hall, Va., Feb. 19, 1937; d. Adolph and Annie (Mickel) Sniegon; m. William Wayne Lovelace, Aug. 11, 1962. Degree in bus., Longwood Coll., 1957. Adminstrv. aide Dept. of Navy, Washington, 1957-60; adminstrv. asst. Joint Blood Coun.-Pvt., Washington, 1960-63; exec. staff NASA, Washington, 1963-73, program analyst-specialist, 1973-80, chief adminstrv. ops. and Congl. affairs br., 1980-92; ret., 1992; cons. NASA, 1992—. Editor, author: (pamphlet) Space Operations, 1989, (video) Space Communications, 1991. Pres. Jr. Achievement Co., 1953-55, Kettering Recreation Coun., Largo, Md., 1974-76; league coord. U.S. Tennis Assn., Anne Arundel County, Md., 1989-91, team capt., 1985—; active various civic orgns. including LWV, ch., community and county functions, 1957—. Recipient Jr. Achievement Exec. award and Nat. Speakers award, 1954, Gold medal Parks and Planning, Prince Georges County, Md., 1976, Exceptional Svc. award NASA, 1983, Exceptional Svc. medal NASA, 1992. Mem. U.S. Tennis Assn. (county coord. 1989-91), Anne Arundel County Tennis Assn., Big Vanilla Raquet Club. Republican. Office: NASA 600 Independence Ave SW Washington DC 20546-0002

LOVELAND, JACQUELINE JANE, neuroscientist, biologist; b. Point Pleasant Borough, N.J., Feb. 16, 1952; d. George Clark and Virginia Mae (Skimmons) L.; m. Alan Dale Nunes, Aug. 22, 1974 (div. Aug. 1978); 1 child, Emmett Todd Nunes. BA, San Jose State U., 1981, MA, 1987. Rsch. assoc. NASA-Ames Rsch. Ctr., Mt. View, Calif., 1980-83; supr., sr. case mgr. Cmty. Companions, Inc., San Jose, Calif., 1983-85, cons., 1985; neurosci. biologist Syntex Rsch. Inst. of Pharmacology, San Jose, Calif., 1985-93; safety pharmacology biologist Syntex Rsch. Inst. of Pathology, Toxicology & Metalobism, Palo Alto, 1993—. Contbr. articles to profl. jours.; author abstracts. Mem. AAAS, Soc. Neurosci., Psi Chi, Phi Theta Kappa. Office: Syntex Rsch 3401 Hillview Ave Palo Alto CA 94303

LOVELESS, DENISE, fitness professional, health club owner; b. Murray, Utah, June 3, 1963; d. Dennis Joe Loveless and Eleanor Valene Krebs Tillack. BA in Health Edn., Utah State U., 1986. Cert. aerobic instr. Am. Coll. Exercise, also Aerobic Fitness Assn. Am. Trainer, instr. Racquetball & Health Ctr., Rexburg, Idaho, 1981-83, Body Fitness Ctr., Logan, Utah, 1983-86; creator, instr. S.T.A.B. aerobics program Utah State U., Logan, 1983-86; internat. fitness spokesmodel Utah, Calif. and Japan, 1985—; aerobic dir. Salt Lake Fitness Ctr., Salt Lake City, 1986-89; pres. Fitness Factor, Salt Lake City, 1986-89; owner health club Anatomy Acad., Salt Lake City, 1989—; instr. cable TV exercise program Cable Health Club, 1993-94; mem. Utah Gov.'s Coun. for Phys. Fitness, 1992-93. Lead instr. exercise videos Rebound Aerobics, 1986, Step Shaper, 1993; coach, choreographer Team Proform. Recipient Bronze medal Nat. Aerobic Championship, L.A., 1993. Mem. Nat. Health Club Assn. (nat. aerobic dir. 1993-94), Am. Coll. Exercise, Aerobic Fitness Assn. Am., Internat. Dance Exercise Assn. Home: 3393 S 715 E Salt Lake City UT 84106

LOVELESS, KATHY LYNNE, computer specialist; b. Corsicana, Tex., Mar. 7, 1961; d. Vernon Ray and Barbara Alice (Brown) L. BA, Baylor U., 1983. Adminstrv. asst. InterFirst Bank, Dallas, 1983-85; adminstrv. asst. Chaparral Steel Co., Midlothian, Tex., 1985-89, audio/visual coord., 1989-93; freelance computer instr. Duncanville, Tex., 1993-94; tng. specialist U. Tex. Southwestern Med. Ctr., Dallas, 1994—. Pres., v.p. Midlothian Cmty. Theatre, 1990-93, mem. 1987—; v.p. choir Lovers Ln. United Meth. Ch., Dallas, 1994, chmn. worship and membership care com., 1990, 91, mem. adminstrv. bd. comm. com., 1995; bd. dirs. Trinity River Mission, Dallas, 1994, 95, chmn. pub. rels. com., 1995. Mem. NAFE, AAUW, USA Film Festival, Am. Film Inst. Home: 971 Fairbanks Cir Duncanville TX 75137

LOVELESS, PATTY (PATTY RAMEY), country music singer; b. Pikeville, Ky., Jan. 4, 1957; m. Terry Lovelace (div.); m. Emory Gordy, Jr., Feb. 1989. Recording artist MCA, 1985-93, Sony Music, 1993—. Albums: Patty Loveless, 1987, If My Heart Had Windows, 1988, Honky Tonk Angel, 1988 (gold), On Down the Line, 1990, Up Against My Heart, 1991, Only What I Feel, 1993, Why Fallen Angels Fly, 1994; # 1 hit singles Timber, I'm Falling in Love, Chains. Named Favorite New Country Artist by Am. Music Awards, 1989; recipient TNN Music City News Country Award,

Female Artist, 1990; inductee Grand Ole Opry, 1988. Office: PO Box 4450 New York NY 10101-4450*

LOVELL, MARY ANN, secondary education educator; b. Magnolia, Ark., May 30, 1943; d. Dezzy and Priscilla (Glover) Biddle; m. Clearence Edward Lovell, June 4, 1966 (div. 1975); children—Clearesia Ann, Delia Marie, Dezzy Aquib. BA, U. Ark., 1965; MS, Ouachita Bapt. U., 1972. Tchr. high sch., Stutgart, Magnolia, Arkadelphia and Eudora, Ark., 1964-75, Milw., 1981—; tchr. Ethan Allen Sch., Dept. Health and Human Svcs. State of Wis., 1986; job svc. specialist CETA, Wis. Dept. Industry, 1975-76; spl. project, coord. Milwaukee County Civil Svc. Commn., 1976-78. Mem. Internat. Reading Assn., Wis. State Reading Assn., Wis. Edn. Assn. (coun. 1989-90), Milw. Tchrs. Edn. Assn., Milw. Inner City Arts Coun., Inc., Milw. Area Reading Coun., Educators' Politically Involved Coun., Am. Mgmt. Assn., State of Wis. Edn. Profls. (Local 3271). Democrat. Pentecostal. Club: Playboy (Chgo.).

LOVELY, MARY RUTH, consumer packaged goods executive; b. Bridgeport, Conn., May 4, 1961; d. Edward Coughlin and Nancy Ann (Michalka) L. BS in Chemistry, St. Joseph Coll., 1983; postgrad., U. R.I., 1983-84; MBA in Mgmt., Indsl. Relations, U. Bridgeport, 1988. Grad. asst. chemistry dept. U. R.I., Kingston, 1983-84; quality assurance asst. chemist Clairol, Inc., Stamford, Conn., 1984-85, package devel. sr. chemist, 1985-87; assoc. quality specialist quality svcs. hdqrs. PepsiCo, Inc., Valhalla, N.Y., 1987-88, supr. quality svcs. hdqrs., 1988-89; mgr. quality svcs. Cadbury Schweppes Beverages, Trumbull, Conn., 1989-90; mgr. ingredient cert. Cadbury Schweppes Beverages, 1990-91; mgr. standards and specs. Durkee French Foods Inc. divsn. Reckitt & Colman, Inc., Wayne, N.J., 1991-92; mgr. specs, doc, BOM adminstrn. Reckitt & Colman, Inc., Wayne, N.J., 1992-94, sr. mgr. strategic and tech. info. resources, 1994—. Recipient research fellowship Hartford Hosp., 1982. Mem. NAFE, St. Joseph Coll. Alumnae (sec. Fairfield County club 1986-88, co-pres. 1988-90), Am. Mgmt. Assn. Roman Catholic. Home: 3705 Tudor Dr Pompton Plains NJ 07444-1136 Office: Reckitt & Colman Inc 1655 Valley Rd Wayne NJ 07470-8050

LOVEMAN, AURELIA LEFFLER, psychologist, writer; b. N.Y.C., Oct. 31, 1916; d. Louis and Anna (Bush) Leffler; m. Howard Levi, Oct. 5, 1935; m. 2d Joseph Heller Loveman, Nov. 9, 1972; 1 child, Jonathan Levi. PhD, Columbia U., 1961. Chief psychologist Child Devel. Ctr., N.Y.C., 1961-63, Jewish Bd. of Guardians, N.Y.C., 1963-70; pvt. practice Balt., 1970-86; textile designer, 1980—; editor Internat. Old Lace Inc., 1985-87, Chesapeake Region Lace Guild, Balt., 1986-88; cons. textiles Walters Art Mus., Balt., 1986-89, guest curator, 1988. Author: The Good Wife, 1959; contbr. articles to profl. and med. jours. Postdoctoral fellow Albert Einstein Coll. Medicine, 1961-63. Mem. Internat. Old Lace, Embroiderers Guild Am. (editl. bd., tchr. lace corr. course, editor newsletter 1992—), Chesapeake Lace Guild (pres. 1984-86), Fan Soc. N.Am., Pioneer Camellia Soc. (v.p.).

LOVETRI, JEANNETTE LOUISE, voice educator; b. Southampton, N.Y., Apr. 2, 1949; d. James John and Aline Rita (Zimmer) L. Student, Manhattan Sch. Music, 1967-68, Juilliard Sch., 1971-72; pvt. dance, piano and vocal study. Singer opera, cabaret, summer stock, oratorios, jazz, 1966-80; owner voice studio, Greenwich, Conn., 1970-75, N.Y.C., 1975—; tchr. voice music dept. Upsala Coll., East Orange, N.J., 1976-81; founder, dir. The Voice Workshop, pub. speaking seminar, 1983—; guest lectr. Boston Conservatory of Music, 1987-89, Internat. Symposium Care of Profl. Voice, N.Y., 1987—, 1st Internat. Congress Arts Medicine, N.Y.C., 1992, British Voice Assn., Actors Ctr., London, 1993, 1st Internat. Music Theatre Tng., Austraila, Wagner Coll., N.Y., 1994, Loyola Coll. Balt., 1994; lectr., workshop leader, various U.S. cities, Amsterdam, and Copenhagen; sci. rschr. on vocal acoustics Royal Swedish Tech. Inst., 1990, master classes, 1991; guest vocal coach for Meredith Monk at Houston Grand Opera, 1991. Numerous appearances with Bklyn. Contemporary Chorus, Chapman Roberts Singers, Mid-Hudson Opera, others. Mem. N.Y. Singing Tchrs. Assn. (bd. dir., pres., former chmn. Music Theatre Com. Am. Symposium), Nat. Assn. Tchrs. Singing.

LOVETT, CLARA MARIA, university administrator, historian; b. Trieste, Italy, Aug. 4, 1939; came to U.S., 1962; m. Benjamin F. Brown. BA equivalent, U. Trieste, 1962; MA, U. Tex.-Austin, 1967, PhD, 1970. Prof. history Baruch Coll., CUNY, N.Y.C., 1971-82, asst. provost, 1980-82; chief European div. Library of Congress, Washington, 1982-84; dean Coll. Arts and Scis., George Washington U., Washington, 1984-88; provost, v.p. academic affairs, George Mason U., Fairfax, Va., 1988-93; on leave from George Mason U.; dir. Forum on Faculty Roles and Rewards Am. Assn. for Higher Edn., 1993-94; pres. No. Ariz. U., Flagstaff, 1994—; vis. lectr. Fgn. Service Inst., Washington, 1979-85; bd. dirs. Inst. for Research in History, N.Y.C., 1981-82; exec. council Conf. Group on Italian Politics, 1980-83, others; lectr., cons. Fgn. Service Inst. State Dept., 1979—; adv. bd. European program Wilson Ctr., 1986—; bd. dirs. Assn. Am. Colls., 1990—. Author: The Democratic Movement in Italy 1830-1876, 1982 (H.R. Marraro Prize, Soc. Italian Hist. Studies); Giuseppe Ferrari and the Italian Revolution, 1979 (Phi Alpha Theta book award); Carlo Cattaneo and the Politics of Risorgimento, 1972 (Soc. for Italian Hist. Studies Dissertation award), (bibliography) Contemporary Italy, 1985; co-editor: Women, War, and Revolution, 1980, (essays) State of Western European Studies, 1984; contbr. sects. to publs. U.S., Italy. Organizer Dem. clubs Bklyn., 1972-76; exec. com. Palisades Citizens Assn., Washington, 1985-87; vestry mem. St. David's Episc. Ch., Washington, 1986-89. Fellow Guggenheim Found., 1978-79, Woodrow Wilson Internat. Ctr. for Scholars, 1979 (adv. bd. West European program), Am. Council Learned Socs., 1976, Bunting Inst. of Radcliffe Coll., 1975-76, others. Named Educator of Yr., Va. Fedn. of Bus. and Profl. Women, 1992. Mem. Am. Hist. Assn. (officer 1984-87), Am. Assn. Higher Edn. (cons. 1979—), Council for European Studies, Soc. for Italian Hist. Studies, Conf. Group on Italian Politics, others. Avocations: choral singing, swimming. Office: No Ariz U Office of Pres PO Box 4092 Flagstaff AZ 86011

LOVING, SUSAN B., lawyer, former state official; m. Dan Loving; children: Lindsay, Andrew, Kendall. BA with distinction, U. Okla., 1972, JD, 1979. Asst. atty. gen. Office of Atty. Gen., 1983-87, first asst. atty. gen., 1987-91; atty. gen. State of Okla., Oklahoma City, 1991-94; atty. Lester & Bryant, P.C., Oklahoma City, 1995—. Bd. dirs. Bd. for Freedom of Info., Okla. Inc., Boy Scouts of Am., Legal Aid of West Okla., Okla. Com. for Prevention Child Abuse; mem. med. steering com. Partnership for Drug Free Okla., 1993—; adv. bd. Law and You Found. Recipient Nat. Red Ribbon Leadership award Nat. Fedn. Parents, Headliner award, By-liner award Okla. and Tulsa Women in Comm., First Friend of Freedom award Freedom of Info. Okla., Dir. award Okla. Dist. Attys. Assn. Mem. Okla. Bar Assn. (former chmn. administrv. law sect., mem. adminstrn. of justice com., farm crisis task force). Office: Lester & Bryant PC 119 N Robinson Oklahoma City OK 73120-4625

LOVINGER, SOPHIE LEHNER, child psychologist; b. N.Y.C., Jan. 15, 1932; d. Nathaniel Harris and Anne (Rosen) Lehner; m. Robert Jay Lovinger, June 18, 1957; children: David Fredrick, Mark Andrew. BA, Bklyn. Coll., 1954; MS, City Coll., N.Y.C., 1959; PhD, NYU, 1967. Sr. clin. psychologist Bklyn. State Hosp., 1960-61; grad. fellow NYU, N.Y.C., 1961-67; psychotherapy trainee Jamaica (N.Y.) Ctr., 1964-67; asst. prof. Hofstra U., Hempstead, N.Y., 1967-70; prof. Cen. Mich. U., Mt. Pleasant, 1970—; psychotherapist, psychoanalyst N.Y.C. and Mt. Pleasant, Mich., 1964—. Author: Learning Disabilities and Games, 1978, Language-Learning Disabilities, 1991; contbr. articles to profl. jours. Fellow Am. Orthopsychiat. Assn.; mem. Am. Psychol. Assn., Nat. Register Health Svc. Providers. Office: 405 S Main St Mount Pleasant MI 48858-2522

LOVINGOOD, REBECCA BRITTEN, educator; b. Bethlehem, Pa., June 5, 1939; d. Clyde Robert and Helen Cauffiel (Britten) L. BS, Syracuse U., 1961; MA, Guildhall Sch. of Music, London, 1962; cert., Jagiellonian U., Krakow, Poland, 1985. Cert. tchr., N.Y., Pa., N.J. Del. Newspaper reporter The Christian Sci. Monitor, Boston, 1963-65; music tchr. Devereux Found., Devon, Pa., 1965-66; elem. sch. tchr. The Episcopal Acad., Merion, Pa., 1966-90; tchr. Diocese of Wilmington Schs., 1991-92; tchr. 2d grade King of Peace Italian Sch. Archdiocese of Phila., Phila., 1992—; edn. tchr. U. Ala., Tuscaloosa, 1988; dir. children's theater, Saratoga Performing Arts, Saratoga Springs, N.Y., 1969; dir. music events, Aldeburgh Music Festival, Suffolk, Eng., 1970. Author numerous children's plays. Vol. The Musical Fund Soc., Phila., The Coll. of Physicians. Recipient Legion of Honor, Chapel of Four Chaplains, Phila., 1981; travel grant, Kosciuszko Found., N.Y.C., 1985. Mem. Am. Assn. for the History of Medicine. Democrat. Roman Catholic. Home: 1070 Luzerne St Johnstown PA 15905-2542 Office: Westmont-Hilltop Sch Dist Johnstown PA 15905

LOVINS, L. HUNTER, public policy institute executive; b. Middlebury, Vt., Feb. 26, 1950; d. Paul Millard and Farley (Hunter) Sheldon; m. Amory Bloch Lovins, Dept. 6, 1979; 1 child, Nanuq. BA in Sociology, Pitzer Coll., 1972, BA in Polit. Sci., 1972; JD, Loyola U., L.A., 1975; LHD, U. Maine, 1982. Bar: Calif. 1975. Asst. dir. Calif. Conservation Project, L.A., 1973-79; exec. dir., co-founder Rocky Mountain Inst., Snowmass, Colo., 1982—; vis. prof. U. Colo., Boulder, 1982; Henry R. Luce vis. prof. Dartmouth Coll., Hanover, N.H., 1982; pres. Nighthawk Horse Co., 1993, Lovins Group, 1994. Co-author: Brittle Power, 1982, Energy Unbound, 1986, Least-Cost Energy Solving the CO2 Problem, 2d edit., 1989. Bd. dirs. Renew Am., Basalt and Rural Fire Protection Dist., Telluride Inst., E Source, Roaring Park Polocrosse Assn.; vol. firefighter. Recipient Mitchell prize Woodlands Inst., 1982, Right Livelihood Found. award, 1983, Best of the New Generation award Esquire Mag., 1984. Mem. Am. Quarter Horse Assn. Office: Rocky Mountain Inst 1739 Snowmass Creek Rd Snowmass CO 81654-9199

LOW, ANN MARGARET, diplomat; b. Boston, June 1, 1964; d. Alfred Francis and Julia Agnes (Shea) Lyons; m. Kennan Blakely Low, July 22, 1989; 1 child, Patrick Alexander. BS of Fgn. Svc., Georgetown U., 1986; M of Mgmt., Northwestern U., 1994. Asst. to head of global systems and ops. Am. Express Bank, N.Y.C., 1986-88; vice consul U.S. Dept. State, London, 1988-90; asst. treasury attache U.S. Dept. State, Mexico City, 1990-93; advisor U.S. Mission to UN U.S. Dept. State, N.Y.C., 1994—. Office: US Mission to UN 799 United Nations Plz New York NY 10017

LOW, BARBARA WHARTON, biochemist, biophysicist; b. Lancaster, Eng., Mar. 23, 1920; came to U.S., 1946, naturalized, 1956; d. Matthew and Mary Jane (Wharton) L. B.A. (Coll. scholar), Somerville Coll., Oxford (Eng.) U., 1942, M.A., 1946, D.Phil. (AAUW Rose Sidgwick Meml. fellow 1946-47, Spl. Rockefeller Found. fellow 1947), 1948. Research fellow Calif. Inst. Tech., 1946-47; research assoc. in phys. chemistry Harvard U. Med. Sch., 1948, assoc. in phys. chemistry, 1948-50; assoc. mem. Univ. Lab. Phys. Chemistry Related to Medicine and Public Health, 1950-54; asst. prof. phys. chemistry Harvard U., 1950-56; assoc. prof. biochemistry Columbia U. Coll. Physicians and Surgeons, 1956-66, prof., 1966-90, prof. emeritus, 1990—; cons. USPHS; mem. biophysics and biophys. chemistry study sect.; div. rsch. grants NIH, 1966-69; mem. rsch. coun. Pub. Health Rsch. Inst. City N.Y., 1973-78, bd. dirs., 1974-78; to prof. associe U. Strasbourg, France, 1965; vis. prof. Japan Soc. Promotion Sci., Tohoku U., Sendai, Japan, 1975; invited lectr. Chinese Acad. Scis. 1981, Soviet Acad. Scis., 1988; mem. seminar on archaeology of Ea. Mediterranean, Ea. Europe and Near East, Columbia U. Contbr. articles to chem., biochem., biophys., and crystallographic jours., also chpts. in books. Recipient Career Devel. award NIH, 1963-68; NIH sr. research fellow, 1959-63. Fellow Am. Acad. Arts and Scis.; mem. AAAS, Am. Crystallographic Assn., Am. Inst. Physics, Am. Soc. Biol. Chemists, Biophys. Soc., Royal Soc. Chemistry, Harvey Soc., Internat. Soc. Toxinology, Protein Soc., Soc. Neurosci. Office: Columbia U Dept Biochem & Mo Bio 630 W 168th St New York NY 10032-3702

LOW, LOUISE ANDERSON, consulting company executive; b. Saline, Mich., May 1, 1944; d. Harry Linné and Rose Josephine (Chvala) Anderson; m. James Thomas Low, Dec. 30, 1967; children: James William, Eric Linné, Kari Louise, Antony Anderson. BA in Biology, U. Mich., 1966. Permanent teaching cert., Mich.; cert. master gardener Coop. Ext. Svc. Tchr. secondary sci. Novi (Mich.) Community Schs., 1966-67; rsch. asst. U. Mich. Med. Sch., Ann Arbor, 1967-68; tchr. secondary sci. Livonia (Mich.) Pub. Schs., 1968-72; tax preparer H&R Block, Saline, 1991; sr. exec. asst. Low & Assocs., Saline, 1991—. Apptd. mem. long-range planning com. Saline Area Schs., 1990—; mem. youth bd. Zion Luth. Ch., Ann Arbor, 1993—; mem. St. Joseph Hosp. Ball Com., 1994; active Friends of the Saline (Mich.) Dist. Libr. Mem. AAUW (life, bd. dirs., com. chairperson), Washtenaw County Alliance for Gifted Edn. (v.p., bd. dirs.), U. Mich. Conger Alumnae Group (bd. dirs., mem. exec. bd.), Alumni Assn. U. Mich. (life), Interlochen Ctr. for Arts Alumni Orgn. (life), Ann Arbor Area Panhellenic Alumnae (pres. 1976-77), Wayne State U. Faculty Wives, Travis Pointe Country Club, Huron Valley Swim Club, Sigma Kappa (alumnae pres. 1970-72), Alpha Mu Sigma Kappa (mem. corp. bd., mem. adv. bd.). Lutheran. Home and Office: Low & Assocs 3431 Surrey Dr Saline MI 48176-9571

LOW, MARISSA E., health care administrator; b. San Francisco; d. Fred and Winifred L. AA, Fashion Inst. of Design and Mdse., 1979; Cert. Corp. Communications, Calif. State U.-Long Beach, 1987; BSBA, U. Redlands, 1992. Assoc. area mgr. Buffums, Glendale, Calif., 1979-80; asst. buyer Buffums, Long Beach, Calif., 1981-83; mdse. control mgr. Buffums, Long Beach, 1983-86, advt. mgr., 1987-89; account rep. CompuMed, Culver City, Calif., 1989-91; physician recruiter Pioneer Ind. Physician Network, Artesia, Calif., 1991-92; provider rels. mgr. Mullikin Ind. Physician Assn., Long Beach, Calif., 1992-93; dir. provider rels. Mullikin Ind. Physician Assn., Daly City, 1993-94; regional network mgr. AHI Healthcare Systems, Inc., San Mateo, Calif., 1994—. Judge Miss Lakewood Pageant of Beauty, 1987; vol. Long Beach Conv. and Visitors Coun., 1987; pub. rels. chmn. March of Dimes, Calif., 1986; v.p. programs, spl. projects, chmn. bd. dirs., nomination com. chmn. Women's Coun., 1985-91; sec. Women's Bus. Conf., 1985; com. mem. Interval House Le Bal des Papillons. Recipient Cert. Appreciation Orange County Commn. on Status of Women, 1991, Interval House, 1991. Mem. NAFE, Am. Mktg. Assn., Group Health Assn. of Am., Acad. Health Svcs. Mktg. (chmn. managed care com. Health Futures Forum 1992), Healthcare Fin. Mgmt. Assn. Office: 951 Mariners Island Blvd Ste 300 San Mateo CA 94404

LOW, MARY LOUISE (MOLLY LOW), documentary photographer; b. Quakertown, Pa., Jan. 3, 1926; d. James Harry and Dorothy Collyer (Krewson) Thomas; m. Antoine Francois Gagné, Nov. 3, 1945 (div.); children: James L., David W., Stephen J., Jeannie Wolff-Gagné; m. Paul Low, July 11, 1969 (dec. July 1991). Student, Oberlin Conservatory of Music, 1943-44, Oberlin Coll., 1944; cert., Katharine Gibbs Sec. Sch., 1945; degree in psychiat. rehab. work, Einstein Coll. Medicine, 1968-70. Sec. Dept. Store, N.Y.C., 1945; sec., treas. Gagné Assocs., Consulting Engrs., Binghamton, N.Y., 1951-66; psychiat. rsch. asst. Jacobi Hosp., Bronx, 1969-70; asst. to head of sch. Brearley Sch., N.Y.C., 1976-78; pvt. practice documentary photographer San Diego, 1984—. Bd. trustees Unitarian-Universalist Ch. Recipient Dir.'s award for excellence Area Agy. on Aging, San Diego, 1993, Citizen Recognition award County of San Diego, Calif., 1993. Office: Molly Low Photography 5576 Caminito Herminia La Jolla CA 92037

LOW, MERRY COOK, civic worker; b. Uniontown, Pa., Sept. 3, 1925; d. Howard Vance and Eleanora (Lynch) Mullan; m. William R. Cook, 1947 (div. 1979); m. John Wayland Low, July 8, 1979; children: Karen, Cindy, Bob, Jan. Diploma in nursing, Allegheny Gen. Hosp., Pitts., 1946; BS summa cum laude, Colo. Women's Coll., 1976. RN, Colo. Dir. patient edn. Med. Care and Rsch. Found., Denver, 1976-78. Contbr. chpt. to Pattern for Distribution of Patient Education, 1981. Bd. dirs. women's libr. assn., U. Denver, 1982—, vice chmn., 1985-86, chmn., 1986-87, co-chmn. spl. event, 1992, bd. dirs. humanities inst., 1993—, co-chair Founders' Day, 1994, chair Culture Fest Du, 1995; docent Denver Art Mus., 1979—, mem. vol. exec. bd., 1988—, mem. nat. docent symposium com., 1991, chmn. collector's choice benefits, 1988, pres. vols., trustee, 1988-90; mem. alumni assn. bd. U. Denver, 1994—; bd. dirs. Lamont Sch. Music assocs., 1990—; mem. search com. for dir. Penrose Libr., 1991-92; trustee ch. coun., chmn. invitational art show 1st Plymouth Congl. Ch., Englewood, Colo., 1981-84; co-chmn. art auction Colo. Alliance Bus., 1992, 93, com., 1994—. Recipient Disting. Svc. award U. Denver Coll. Law, 1988, King Soopers Vol. of Week award, 1989, Citizen of Arts award Fine Arts Found., 1993, Outstanding Vol. Colo. Alliance of Bus., 1994. Mem. Am. Assn. Mus. (vol. meeting coord. 1990-91), P.E.O. (pres. Colo. chpt. DX 1982-84), U. Denver Alumni Assn. (bd. dirs.). Republican. Congregationalist. Home: 2552 E Alameda Ave Apt 11 Denver CO 80209-3324

LOWDEN, CYNTHIA GAIL, personnel executive; b. Stamford, Conn., May 10, 1958; d. William Herbert and Grace Mildred (Parker) L. BA in English and Econs., Duke U., 1980. Methods analyst The Prudential, New Providence, N.J., 1983-84, assoc. mgr., 1984-85; mgr. mktg. svcs. Prudential Home Mortgages Co., N.Y.C., 1985-87; mgr. planning Prudential Asset Mgmt. Co., Florham Park, N.J., 1987-88, mgr. personnel, 1988-89; mgr. corp. relocation The Prudential, Newark, 1989-90, dir. human resources devel., 1991—. Fellow Life Mgmt. Inst.; mem. Jr. League Summit, Phi Mu (bd. dirs. N.E. alumnae chpt.). Republican. Presbyterian.

LOWDEN, SUZANNE, state legislator; b. Camden, N.J., Feb. 8, 1952; m. Paul W. Lowden; children: Christopher, Jennifer, Paul, William. BA magna cum laude, Am. U.; MA cum laude, Fairleigh Dickinson U. Resort industry exec.; mem. Nev. State Senate, 1993—, majority whip, 1993—. Active Juvenile Diabetes Found., United Way of So. Nev. With USO, 1971, Vietnam. Recipient Woman of Achievement award Women's Coun. of Las Vegas C. of C. Republican. Home: 992 Pinehurst Dr Las Vegas NV 89109 Office: Nev State Senate State Capitol Carson City NV 89710*

LOWE, ANGELA MARIA, telecommunications consultant; b. Newark, Nov. 15, 1963; d. Eleanor Guglioccello; m. Thomas Edward Lowe, Nov. 1, 1986; 1 child, Matthew Richard. BSCE, Pa. State U., 1985; MBA, Rutgers U., 1994. Registered profl. engr., N.J. Engr. Greenhorne & O'Mara, Inc., Greenbelt, Md., 1985-86; structural engr. Goodkind & O'Dea, Inc., Rutherford, N.J., 1986-88; civil engr. Charles Mackie Assocs., Inc., Barnegat, N.J., 1988-90; planning engr. Naval Weapons Sta. Earle, Colts Neck, N.J., 1992-93; v.p., CFO Compro Techs., Inc., Barnegat, 1993—. Admissions vol. Pa. State Alumni Admissions Vol. Program, 1991. Lt. Civil Engring. Corps, USNR, 1990—. Mem. NSPE, NAFE, Pa. State Alumni Assn., Naval Res. Assn. Home: 28 Deer Run Dr S Barnegat NJ 08005-2216

LOWE, CONNIE DELORES, nonprofit association administrator, accountant; b. Brown County, Ind., Aug. 7, 1941; d. Ira W. and Edna Pauline (Loy) Shafer; m. Walter C. Lowe, Oct. 28, 1960; children: Kirk D., Vicki D. Student, Milligan (Tenn.) Coll., 1959, U. Houston, 1960. Acct., contr. Chas. Heyne Co. Inc., Houston, 1973-88; owner K.V.'s Boogies, Willis, Tex., 1986-91; acct., contr. Walsh & Albert Co. Inc., Houston, 1988—; chair bd. dirs., exec. dir. Friends of a Peeper, Inc., Willis, 1993—. Author: (children's books) I Know, I Know, I Know, 1991, My Name Is, 1992, Safety on the Go, 1993. Vol. Tri County Mental Health Mental Retardation, Conroe, Tex., 1986-87.

LOWE, DIANNA BEAMAN, educational administrator; b. Wilson, N.C., May 19, 1950; d. Thomas Lester and Lucille Rebecca (Moore) Beaman; m. Kenneth Nelson Lowe, Dec. 31, 1992. BA, East Carolina U., 1972, MA, 1974. Rsch. assoc., lectr. East Carolina U., Greenville, N.C., 1973-75, asst. dir. instl. rsch., 1975-78, assoc. dir. instl. rsch., 1978-83, asst. to vice chancellor acad. affairs, 1983-92, asst. vice chancellor acad. affairs, 1992—; profl. devel. opportunities presenter Assn. Instl. Rsch. and So. Assn. for Instl. Rsch., 1973—. Mem., officer Free Union F.W.B. Ch. Lydia Circle, Walstonburg, N.C., 1972—. Mem. Assn. Instl. Rsch., So. Assn. Instl. Rsch., N.C. Assn. Instl. Rsch., Phi Kappa Phi (exec. dir. 1987—), Phi Delta Kappa. Office: East Carolina U Acad Affairs 215 Spilman Greenville NC 27858

LOWE, FLORENCE SEGAL, retired public relations executive; b. N.Y.C.; d. Samuel I. and Rose (Cantor) Segal; BS in Edn., U. Pa., 1930; postgrad. Sch. Social Svc., 1935-36; m. Herman Albert Lowe, June 27, 1935; children: Lesley Ellen Lowe Israel, Roger Bernard. Guidance counsellor Phila. Pub. Schs., 1935-41; Washington corr. Variety and Daily Variety, Phila. Daily News, Manchester Union Leader, TV Guide, 1942-58; spl. pub. rels. Radio Sta. WIP, Phila. and Metromedia, 1958-60; coord. spl. projects Metromedia, 1960-70; spl. asst. to chmn. pub. affairs NEA, Washington, 1970-86; sr. cons. arts and cultural comm. Kamber Group, 1986-93, ret., 1994. Mem. pub. rels. and advt. com. Nat. Symphony, 1952-56; mem. Sec. State's Commn. on Travel, 1970-71; mem. Coordinating Com. for Ellis Island, 1982-87; mem. Com. for Nancy Hanks Endowment for Arts, Duke U. Recipient All-Army Entertainment Contest award, 1958; spl. achievement award Nat. Endowment for Arts Chmn., 1983; Spl. Merit award Fed. Govt., 1981, Spl. Achievement award, 1983, Disting. Svc. award, 1985. Mem. Am. Women in Radio and TV (founder, pres. 1954-55), Am. News Women's Club (Woman of Yr. com.), Coun. Jewish Women, Women in Communications (citation for meritorious reporting 1962), Nat. Press Club, Women's Nat. Press Club (treas. 1954, v.p. 1956), Washington Press Club (bd. dirs. 1968-71, 83-84), Am. News Women's Club (v.p. 1969-70), Washington Press Club Found. Home: 2801 New Mexico Ave NW Washington DC 20007-3921 Office: Kamber Group 1920 L St NW Washington DC 20036-5004

LOWE, IDA BRANDWAYN, library administrator, systems administrator; b. Bogota, Colombia, Oct. 5, 1946; came to U.S., 1964; d. Jacobo and Donna (Ghelman) Brandwayn; m. Fredric Robert Lowe, Aug. 16, 1970; children: Evin, Laurence. BA, Cornell U., 1968; MA, New Sch. Social Rsch., 1971; MSLS, Columbia U., 1972; MBA, Baruch Coll., 1988. Cataloger Baruch Coll. Libr., N.Y.C., 1973-80, mgr. info. svcs., 1981-86, asst. dean, 1987, coord. for systems, 1988-94, dep. dir., 1990—, dir. network techs., 1994—; cons. UN Ctr. on Transnational Corp., Ethiopia, 1990-91, UN Devel. Prog., N.Y.C., 1989, Telecom & Network Tng., Colombia and Ecuador, 1993, various librs., 1987— various corps., 1986—, UNDP Mozambique, 1993. Contbr. articles to profl. jours. Recipient Baruch/CUNY award for disting. svc., 1993. Home: 81 Old Rd Westport CT 06880-4145 Office: Baruch Coll 17 Lexington Ave New York NY 10010

LOWE, KATHLENE WINN, lawyer; b. San Diego, Dec. 1, 1949; d. Ralph and Grace (Rodes) Winn; m. Russell Howells Lowe, Oct. 7, 1977; 1 child, Taylor Rhodes. BA in English magna cum laude, U. Utah, 1971, MA in English, 1973, JD, 1976. Bar: Utah 1976, U.S. Dist. Ct. Utah 1976, U.S. Ct. Appeals (10th cir.) 1980, Calif. 1989, U.S. Dist. Ct. (ctrl. dist.) Calif. 1990. Assoc. Parsons, Behle & Latimer, Salt Lake City, 1976-80, ptnr., 1980-84; v.p. law Skaggs Alpha Beta Inc., Salt Lake City; now ptnr. Brobeck, Phleger & Harrison, Newport Beach, Calif. Contbg. editor Utah Law Rev., 1975-76. Mem. ABA, Utah Bar Assn., Salt Lake City Bar Assn., Phi Kappa Phi. Office: Brobeck Phleger & Harrison 4675 MacArthur Ct Ste 1000 Newport Beach CA 92660-1884*

LOWE, MARY JOHNSON, federal judge; b. N.Y.C., June 10, 1924; m. Ivan A. Michael, Nov. 4, 1961; children: Edward H. Lowe, Leslie H. Lowe, Bess J. Michael. BA, Hunter Coll., 1952; LLB, Bklyn. Law Sch., 1954; LLM, Columbia U., 1955; LLD, CUNY, 1990. Bar: N.Y. 1955. Pvt. practice law N.Y.C., 1955-71; judge N.Y.C. Criminal Ct., 1971-72; acting justice N.Y. State Supreme Ct., 1972-74; judge Bronx County Supreme Ct., 1974; justice N.Y. State Supreme Ct., 1977, 1st Jud. Dist., 1978; judge U.S. Dist. Ct. (so. dist.) N.Y., 1978-91, sr. judge, 1991—. Recipient award for outstanding service to criminal justice system Bronx County Criminal Cts. Bar Assn., 1974, award for work on narcotics cases Asst. Dist. Attys., 1974. Mem. Women in Criminal Justice, Harlem Lawyers Assn., Bronx Criminal Lawyers Assn., N.Y. County Lawyers Assn., Bronx County Bar Assn., N.Y. State Bar Assn. (award for outstanding jud. contbn. to criminal justice Sect. Criminal Justice 1978), NAACP, Nat. Urban League, Nat. Council Negro Women, NOW. Office: US Dist Ct US Courthouse Foley Sq New York NY 10007-1501*

LOWENBERG, GEORGINA GRACE, elementary school educator; b. El Paso, Tex., Feb. 15, 1944; d. Eduardo Antonio and Grace Elizabeth (Vletcher) Orellana; m. Edward Daniel Lowenberg, June 14, 1968 (div. 1985); 1 child, Jennifer Anne. BSEd, U. Tex., El Paso, 1965, postgrad., 1965-66; postgrad., U. St. Thomas, 1983. Permanent profl. teaching cert., Tex. Tchr. 5th grade El Paso Pub. Sch. Dist., 1965-70; tchr. 3d grade gifted, talented Ysleta Ind. Sch. Dist., El Paso, 1980—; mem. com. Tex. State Textbook Selection Com., Austin, 1984-85, Tex. State TEAMS Math Adv. Com., Austin, 1986-87; sci. presentor Silver Burdett, Albuquerque, 1985-86; critic reader Scott-Foresman, Dallas, 1986; pres., v.p. Scotsdale Elem. Sch. PTA, El Paso, 1976-83; v.p. Eastwood Middle Sch. PTA, El Paso, 1984-85; mem. Eastwood Heights Elem. Sch. PTA, 1985-87; sec. Eastwood High Sch. Band Boosters, El Paso, 1985-89, Speech Boosters, 1986-88; life mem. Tex. State PTA, 1981—. Troop leader Brownie and Jr. Girl Scouts Am., El Paso, 1977-82. Mem. Assn. Tex. Profl. Educators (regional treas. 1987-88). Roman Catholic.

LOWENBERG, LORRAINE LYNETTE, psychiatric nurse; b. Donnellson, Iowa, Apr. 20, 1940; d. Arnold H. and Frances (Neff) L. BA in Biology, Bluffton (Ohio) Coll., 1962; MBA, Ind. U., South Bend, 1984; ADN, Southwestern Mich. Coll., 1991. RN, Ind. Adminstrv. sec. Miles Labs., Inc., Elkhart, Ind., 1969-86; exec. sec. Elkhart County Health Dept., 1987-88; asst. to the pres. Goshen (Ind.) Coll., 1988-89; staff nurse Oaklawn Hosp., Goshen, 1991, Elkhart Gen. Hosp., 1991-92; staff nurse inpatient unit Otis R. Bowen Ctr. Human Svcs., Warsaw, Ind., 1993—. Mem. Ind. Sheriff's Assn., Chronic Fatigue Immune Dysfunction Syndrome Assn. Am., Am. Soc. for Prevention of Cruelty to Animals, Am. Psychiatric Nurses Assn., Am. Holistic Nurses Assn. Home: 309 1/2 Hackett Rd Goshen IN 46526

LOWENBERG, SUSAN, librarian; b. Bismarck, N.D., Nov. 21, 1957; d. Arthur Lee and Mildred Louise (Schroeder) Eichelberger; m. Anton David Lowenberg, May 21, 1988; children: Derek Arthur, Marissa Emily. BA, Calif. State U., Dominguez Hills, 1979; MLS, UCLA, 1981; MBA, Bradley U., 1986. Bus. libr. Bradley U., Peoria, Ill., 1981-86; chair circulation dept. Calif. State U., Northridge, 1986-89; head access svcs. dept. U. Colo., Boulder, 1989-90, map curator, sci. libr., 1991-92; libr. info. resources and theatre/dance Calif. Inst. Arts, Valencia, 1992—. Author: C.S. Lewis: An Annotated Bibliography, 1993; contbr. articles to profl. jours. Coun. on Rsch. & Creative Work grantee U. Colo., 1990. Mem. ALA, Assn. Coll. Rsch. Librs., Calif. Acad. and Rsch. Librs., Calif. Libr. Assn. Office: Calif Inst Arts 24700 Mcbean Pky Valencia CA 91355-2397

LOWENTHAL, CONSTANCE, art historian; b. N.Y.C., Aug. 29, 1945; d. Jesse and Helen (Oberstein) L. BA cum laude, Brandeis U., 1967; AM, Inst. Fine Arts, NYU, 1969; PhD, Inst. Fine Arts, NYU, N.Y.C., 1976. Mem. faculty Sarah Lawrence Coll., Bronxville, N.Y., 1975-78; asst. mus. educator Met. Mus. Art, N.Y.C., 1978-85; exec. dir. Internat. Found. Art Research, N.Y.C., 1985—; bd. dirs. Internat. Art and Antiques Loss Register Ltd., Ctr. for Edn. Studies, Inc. Regular contbr. Art Crime Update column Wall Street Jour., 1988—; contbr. articles to Mus. News and other profl. publs. Office: Internat Found for Art Rsch 46 E 70th St New York NY 10021-4928

LOWENTHAL, SUSAN, finance company executive; b. Munich, Nov. 30, 1946; came to U.S., 1949; d. Jerry and Gertrude (Wiestreich) L.; m. Alex J. Stolitzka, Oct. ll, 1987. BA, Bklyn. Coll., 1969. Exec. dir. Manhattan Girls Club, N.Y.C., 1969-73; conf. coord. Orton Soc., N.Y.C., 1973-77; v.p. Gemtique, N.Y.C., 1977-81; broker Prudential Bache, N.Y.C., 1981-83, Smith Barney, N.Y.C., 1983-85; pres., chief exec. officer Lowenthal Fin. Svcs., Inc., N.Y.C., 1985-89, fin. cons., money mgr., 1990—. Jewish.

LOWENTHAL, TERRIANN, legislative staff member; b. Portchester, N.Y., Oct. 9, 1958; d. Mort Albert and Eleanor Frances (Levine) L.; 1 child, Joelle Elissa. BA, Cornell U., 1981; JD cum laude, Georgetown U., 1989. Spl. asst. to Hon. Lowell P. Weicker, Jr. Hartford (Conn.) Dist. Office, 1981-83; profl. staff mem. on PO and Civil Svc. Subcommittee on Human Resources Commn., Washington, 1983-84; dep. staff dir. subcom. on Postal Personnel/Modernization U.S. Ho. of Reps., Washington, 1985, legis. analyst com. on edn. and labor, 1985-86, spl. asst. to Hon. Mervyn M. Dymally, 1986, staff dir. subcom. on Census, Stats., and Postal Personnel, 1987—; chief of staff Congressman Tom Sawyer, 1993—; speaker The Sr. Seminar, Fgn. Svc. Inst., U.S. Dept. of State, 1991, Coalition of Minority Policy Profls., 1990, Gen. Acctg. Office Mgmt. Seminar, 1990, Ctr. for Applied Rsch. and Urban Policy, Univ. D.C., 1989, Conf. on Applied Demography, Bowling Green, Ohio, 1988. Nat. coord. Faye Williams for Congress Campaign, 1986. Recipient Stennis Congl. fellowship Coun. for Excellence in govt., Washington. Mem. Nat. Women's Polit. Caucus, Women's Legal Def. Fund, NAACP, Cornell Club of Washington. Democrat. Jewish. Office: Subcom on Census & Stats 515 O'Neill H O B Washington DC 20515*

LOWERS, GINA CATTANI, physicist; b. Evanston, Ill., Oct. 16, 1961; d. Lawrence F. and Arlene Bernice (Phillips) Cattani; m. Robert Judson Lowers, Oct. 10, 1984. BS in Math., U. Calif., Riverside, 1984; BS in Physics, Carnegie-Mellon U., 1987, MS in Physics, 1989; postgrad., W.Va. U. Test systems engr. Aerojet Electrosystems Co., Azusa, Calif., 1983-85; instr. calculus Carnegie Mellon U., Pitts., 1986-88; product devel. engr. Philips Lighting Co., Fairmont, W.Va., 1988—; instr. physics Fairmont State Coll., 1990-91, instr. electronics, 1992—. Judge physics and math. orals and presentations W. Va. State Sci. and Engring. Fair, 1989-91, judge physics projects, 1989, 91, 92; co-chair covenants and restrictions com. Greystone-on-the-Cheat Homeowner's Assn. Mem. Electrochem. Soc., Soc. Mfg. Engrs., Soc. Tech. Comm., Internat. Soc. Optical Engring. Office: Philips Lighting Co RR 3 Box 505 Fairmont WV 26554-9484

LOWERY, MARION MARGARET, rehabilitation counselor; b. Phila., Dec. 19, 1934; d. Harry Galleghar and Margaret (Sauer) R.; children: Pamela A., James D., Stephen L. BA, U. North Colo., Greeley, 1967-70; MEd magna cum laude, Oreg. State U., 1974. Coord.-adult basic Edn. Rogue Com. Coll., Grants Pass, 1971-75; dir.-loaves and fishes Fed. Title VII Programme, Medford, 1975-79; child abuse caseworker State Oregon, Medford, 1979-81; adult caseworker State of Oregon, Medford, employment spec., 1982-87; rehab. counselor State of Oreg., Medford, 1987—; mem. Sch. Transition Team. Author: (pub. rsch.) Changing Status of Women in Middle East. Bd. dirs. Crisis Intervention Svc., Parents Anonymous, Supported Work Coun., Interagy. Coun., Medford, 1980-90. Mem. Regional Vocat. Ednl. Planning Com., Ednl. Svcs. Dist. Representing Vocat. Rehab., Lions (1st v.p.). Democrat. Home: 830 Carol Rae Medford OR 97501-1729 Office: Vocat Rehab 28 W 6th St # A Medford OR 97501-2705

LOWERY, SHARON A., travel industry executive; b. Chgo., Sept. 27, 1943; d. James William and Alice Dorothy (Buckley) L. BA, Knox Coll., 1965. Pres. Expert Visa Svcs. Inc., Chgo. Mem. Nat. Assn. Women Bus. Owners, NAt. Bus. Travel Assn., Ohio Valley Bus. Travel Assn., 410 Club (Chgo.). Home: 1430 Sandstone Dr Wheeling IL 60090-5923 Office: 28 E Jackson Blvd Chicago IL 60604-2215

LOWEY, NITA M., congresswoman; b. N.Y., July 5, 1937; m. Stephen Lowey, 1961; children: Dona, Jacqueline, Douglas. BS, Mt. Holyoke Coll., 1959. Community activist, prior to 1975; asst. sec. state State of N.Y., 1975-87; mem. 101st, 102nd Congresses from 20th N.Y. dist., 1989—, 103rd Congress from 18th N.Y. dist., Washington, D.C., 1993—; mem. appropriations com., 1993—. Democrat. Office: US Ho of Reps 1424 Longworth Ho Office Bldg Washington DC 20515-3218

LOWN, ELIZABETH D., state legislator; b. Portland, Maine, July 14, 1932; m. Robert G. Lown; 3 children. BA, Radcliffe Coll., 1954; MA, Rivier Coll., 1977. Mem. N.H. Ho. of Reps.; chmn. judiciary com. Former selectman City of Amherst, N.H.; past trustee Bean Found. Mem. LWV (past pres. Milford area). Republican. Home: 36 Bloody Brook Rd Amherst NH 03031-3316 Office: NH Ho of Reps State Capitol Concord NH 03301*

LOWRANCE, MURIEL EDWARDS, program specialist; b. Ada, Okla., Dec. 28, 1922; d. Warren E. and Mayme E. (Barrick) Edwards; B.S. in Edn., East Central State U., Ada, 1954; 1 dau., Kathy Lynn Lowrance Gutierrez. Accountant, adminstrv. asst. to bus. mgr. East Central State U., 1950-68; grants and contracts specialist U. N.Mex. Sch. Medicine, Albuquerque, 1968-72, program specialist IV, dept. orthopaedics, 1975-86; asst. adminstrv. officer N.Mex. Regional Med. Program, 1972-75. Bd. dirs. Vocat. Rehab. Center, 1980-84. Cert. profl. contract mgr. Nat. Contract Assn. Mem. Am. Bus. Women's Assn. (past pres. El Segundo chpt., Woman of Yr. 1974), AAUW, Amigos de las Americas (dir.). Democrat. Methodist. Club: Pilot (Albuquerque) (pres. 1979-80, dir. 1983-84, dist. treas. 1984-86, treas. S.W. dist., 1984-86, gov.-elect S.W. dist. 1986-87, gov. S.W. dist. 1987-88). Home: 3028 Mackland Ave NE Albuquerque NM 87106-2018

LOWRANCE, PAMELA KAY, medical/surgical nurse; b. Pensacola, Fla., July 17, 1959; d. Carl Boyce and Sara Mae (Wrenn) L. BSN, U. N.C., 1981. RN, N.C.; cert. in chemotherapy adminstrn. Staff nurse Charlotte (N.C.) Meml. Hosp. and Med. Ctr.; asst. nurse mgr. Carolinas Med. Ctr. Mem. ANA, Oncology Nursing Soc., Soc. of Gynecologic Nurse Oncologists, Sigma Theta Tau. Home: 6014 Rose Valley Dr Charlotte NC 28210-3830

LOWRIE, KATHRYN YANACEK, manufacturing company executive; b. Midland, Mich., Nov. 23, 1958; d. Frank Joseph and Jacqueline Ann (Sipko) Yanacek; m. David Bruce Lowrie, Mar. 14, 1987; 1 child, Alexandra Yanacek. BA in Psychology, Northeastern U., 1980. Psychology tech. Research Inst. of Environ. Medicine, U.S. Army, Natick, Mass., 1980-81, computer programmer, 1981-83; assoc. recruiter Mgmt. Adv. Services, Burlington, Mass., 1983-85, v.p. mgmt. info. systems, 1985-86, exec. v.p., 1986-89; chief exec. officer Computer Careers, Raynham, Mass., 1989-90; v.p. G.R.S.I. Corp., Middleboro, Mass., 1990-94; owner S.B. Industries, Taunton, Mass., 1994—. Bd. dirs. MSPCC. Roman Catholic. Office: 22 Fifth St Taunton MA 02780-4833

LOWRIE, PAMELA BURT, art educator, artist; b. Geneva, Ill., May 12, 1937; d. Morris Nathan and Helyn (Beetlestone) B.; children: Edmund Gale, Matthew Burt; m. Michael Hammer, Aug. 14, 1982. BA, U. Mich., 1959; MS in Edn., No. Ill. U., Dekalb, 1970; MA, Claremont Grad. Sch. (Calif.), 1979. One person shows: Loyola U. Gallery, Chgo., U. Ill. Med. Ctr. Gallery, 1978, Elmhurst (Ill.) Coll. Gallery, 1980, Kankakee (Ill.) Coll. Gallery, 1982, The Edge Gallery, Villa Park, Ill., 1984, Gahlberg Gallery Coll. of DuPage, 1986, 87, 92, Elmhurst Art Mus., 1994, Am. Headquarters of the Theosophical Soc., 1995; group shows include: Five Women Artists from Ill., Notre Dame U., 1979, Springfield (Ill.) Art Assn. Gallery, 1981, Am. Cultural Ctr., Taipei, Taiwan, 1982, Campanille Gallery, Chgo., Limelight-Abstract Art, Riverwalk Gallery, Naperville, Ill., David Adler Cultural Ctr., Libertyville, Ill., Norris Gallery, St. Charles, Ill., Gov. State U., Park Forest, Ill.; represented in permanent collections: Coll. DuPage, Glen Ellyn, Ill., AT&T, Naperville, Eastman Pharms., Malvern, Pa., Getty Synthetic Fuel, Chgo., Monte Christo Condominiums, Fla., Nara Jr. Coll., Japan, No. Trust Bank, Chgo., Plan Corp., Wheaton, Ill.; art cons. Sch. Dist. 41, Glen Ellyn, Ill., 1970-72; prof. art Coll. DuPage, Glen Ellyn, 1972-94; ret. 1994. Dir., staff Nat. Great Tchrs. Seminars, Williams Bay, Wis., 1976-94; staff Calif. Great Tchrs. Seminar, Santa Barbara, 1979, Hawaii Great Tchrs. Seminar, 1990; vis. prof. Christ Ch. Coll., Canterbury, Eng., 1990. Bd. dirs. Fine Arts Rev. Com., DuPage County, Ill., 1982. Home: 926 N Scott St Wheaton IL 60187-3862 Office: Coll DuPage Lambert and 22nd St Glen Ellyn IL 60137

LOWRY, CANDACE ELIZABETH, human resource administrator, consultant; b. Miles City, Mont., Sept. 27, 1950; d. James A. and Nathlee (Azar) Zadick; m. Michael Roy Lowry, June 7, 1980; 1 child, Natalie. BSW with high honors, U. Mont., 1971; MSW with high honors, U. Iowa, 1975; DSW, U. Utah, 1984. Clin. social worker, Utah; cert. marriage and family therapist and supr.; diplomate clin. social work, 1987—. Inpatient social worker II U. Iowa Psychiat. Hosps., Iowa City, 1975-76, inpatient social worker III, 1976-79, coordinator, Iowa Autism Program, 1979-80; coordinator, social work specialist U. Utah Counseling Ctr., Salt Lake City, 1980-86, assoc. dir., 1986; prog. dir. adult unit Wasatch Canyons Hosp., Salt Lake City, 1986—; dir. all adult svcs. Wasatch Canyons Hosp., 1990—; clin. instr. U. Utah, Salt Lake City, 1981—. Co-author: Meeting the Needs of Autistic Children, 1980; contbr. articles to profl. jours. Grantee NIMH, 1986—. Mem. Nat. Assn. Social Workers, Acad. Cert. Social Workers (cert.), Nat. Register Clin. Social Workers, Am. Group Psychotherapy Assn., Salt Lake City C. of C. Home: 2705 Eagle Way Salt Lake City UT 84108-2804 Office: Wasatch Canyons Hosp 5770 S 1500 W Salt Lake City UT 84123-5200

LOWRY, JOAN MARIE DONDREA, broadcaster; b. Weirton, W.Va., June 8, 1935; d. Rudolph and Mary (Telmanik) Dondrea; m. Robert William Lowry, June 15, 1957; 1 child, Christopher Scott. B.S. in Edn., Baldwin-Wallace Coll., 1956; student Ohio Sch. Broadcasting, 1977-79. Gen. mgr., news dir. Sta. WLRO, Lorain, Ohio, 1980-82; host 35 Live, Cinemavidio TV, Elyria, Ohio, 1980-83; TV show host Continental Cable, Cleve., 1983—; pub. relations dir. Sta. WZLE, Lorain, 1982-83; broadcaster, community relations dir. Sta. WRKG, Lorain, 1983—, news dir., 1988—; govt. and pub. affairs mgr. Northwestern Ohio Continental Cablevision, 1991—; treas. bd. dirs. Better Hearing Inst., Washington, 1992—; speaker in field. Appeared in motion pictures: Those Lips Those Eyes, 1982, One Trick Pony, 1982; performer commls. Mem. steering com. Nat. Coun. Better Hearing and Speech, 1985—, mem. coun. better hearing and speech month, Washington, 1985—, Lorain County coun., 1986—; mem. community resource council Leadership Lorain County, 1988-89; nat. pres. Delta Zeta Sorority and Found., 1980—, trustee, 1980—, nat. found. pres., 1987—; active Women in Cable, 1993, Lorain Litter Control Bd., 1981-83; communications and mktg. com. United Way, 1987—; bd. dirs. Lorain Cnty Sr. Citizens Assn., 1982-85, Lorain Consumers Council, 1980—; v.p. Bay Village PTA Council, 1973-75; mem. Martin Luther King Steering Com., 1987—; chmn. adv. bd. Lorain County Heart Assn., 1988; trustee N.E. affiliate Am. Heart Assn., also active Leadership Council, 1988—, trustee; active Multiple Sclerosis Soc., Am. Cancer Soc., Muscular Dystrophy Assn., Founders Meml. Found, others; chair Lorain County Mothers March of Dimes, 1988; grand marshal numerous parades. Named Woman of Achievement, Nat. YWCA and Lorain County Bus. and Industry Assn., 1983, Ohio Delta Zeta Alumnae Woman of Yr.; recipient USAF award, 1982, USN award, 1981, Media award Am. Cancer Soc., 1982, Communication award Easter Seals Soc., 1981, Community Service award Lorain County chpt. Am. Heart Assn., 1981, Service to Mankind award Sertoma Internat., 1988; ofcl. hostess for U.S. Army in Lorain County, 1980-83; Mayor's Proclamation, 1982; hon. recruiter award U.S. Army, 1981; recognition award Ohio House Reps. Mem. Bus. and Profl. Women, Lorain County Arts Council, Leadership Lorain County Alumni Assn. (bd. dirs. 1990—), Baldwin-Wallace Alumni Assn. (nat. pres. 1979-81), LWV (chpt. pres. 1966-67), Cleve. Amateur Fencers (pres. 1965-67), Internat. Platform Assn. Byzantine Catholic. Home: 578 Yarmouth Dr Cleveland OH 44140-1753

LOWRY, LOIS (HAMMERSBERG), author; b. 1937. Author: A Summer to Die, 1977, Find a Stranger, Say Goodbye, 1978, Anastasia Krupnik, 1979, Autumn Street, 1980, Anastasia Again!, 1981, Anastasia at Your Service, 1982, The One Hundredth Thing about Caroline, 1983, Taking Care of Terrific, 1983, Anastasia, Ask Your Analyst, 1984, Us and Uncle Fraud, 1984, Anastasia on Her Own, 1985, Switcharound, 1985, Anastasia Has the Answers, 1986, Anastasia's Chosen Career, 1987, Rabble Starkey, 1987, All About Sam, 1988, Number the Stars, 1989 (John Newbery medal 1990), Your Move, J.P.!, 1990, Anastasia at This Address, 1991, Attaboy, Sam!, 1992, The Giver, 1993 (John Newbery medal 1994). Address: 8 Lexington Ave Cambridge MA 02138-3319 Office: care Houghton Mifflin 222 Berkeley St Boston MA 02116-3748

LOYD, ANN ELDRIDGE, counseling director; b. Macon, Ga., July 7, 1949; d. Clarence W. and Virginia (Bentley) Eldridge; m. J. Russell Loyd, Sr., June 22, 1969; children: J. Russell Loyd, Jr., Jonathan E. AS, Mid. Ga. Coll., 1969; BS in Edn., Ga. Coll., 1971, MEd, 1983; MEd in Counseling Edn., Ga. So. U., 1985. Cert. sch. counselor. Tchr. Mattie Wells Sch., Gray, Ga., 1970-75; dir. mid. sch. Jonesco Acad., Gray, Ga., 1983-85; dir. guidance Stratford Acad., Macon, Ga., 1985-91; dir. counseling Macon Coll., 1991—; bd. dirs. Macon Outreach, 1989-91. Named to Leadership Macon, Macon C. of C., 1992-93. Mem. Ga. Coll. Counseling Assn. (charter treas. 1992—), Am. Counseling Assn., Am. Coll. Counseling Assn., Am. Sch. Counselors Assn. (nat. multi-level sch. counselor 1990), Ga. Sch. Counselors Assn. (post-secondary worksetting chmn. 1985—), Sertoma Internat. (dir. 1991—). Methodist. Office: Macon Coll 100 College St Macon GA 31201-1607

LOZEAU, DONNALEE M., state legislator; b. Nashua, N.H., Sept. 15, 1960; m. David Lozeau; 3 children. Attended, Rivier Coll. Mem. N.H. Ho. of Reps.; mem. corrections and criminal justice com. Chmn. ward five Rep. City Com. Home: 125 Shore Dr Nashua NH 03062-1339 Office: NH Ho of Reps State Capitol Concord NH 03301*

LOZITO, GILDA LELIA, artist, painter; b. N.Y.C., Dec. 20; d. Massimo and Concetta (D'Amico) Greco; m. Rocco Jerome Lozito, Aug. 19, 1941. Student, Bono Hall Acad Fine Arts, 1937-41, Norton Sch. Art, 1949-53, Palm Beach Community Coll., 1960. Art instr. nat. Youth Adminstrn. Art Ctr., N.Y.C., 1939-41; Fed. Civil Svc., Eglin Field, Fla., 1942-45, Morrison Field, Fla., 1946; Architect Agnes Ballard, West Palm Beach, Fla., 1947-52; art instr. pvt. practice West Palm Beach, Fla., 1953—; artist Bagatelle Art Shop, Palm Beach, Fla., 1960-65; art consignments Gallery Gemini, Palm Beach, Fla., 1962-69; art judge City of West Palm Beach, 1968; lectr., cons. Fla., 1953—; cons. in art Pub. Civic Activities, 1970s; dir. exhibitions Nat. League of Am. Pen Women, Palm Beach, 1980s; lectr. in field. One woman shows at Norton Mus. Art, West Palm Beach, 1954, Hobbelink Kaastra Art Gallery, Palm Beach, 1955, Upstairs Art Gallery, Palm Beach, 1959, 1st Nat. in Palm Beach, 1970, February 1994; exhibited in group shows at Palm Beach Coun. Arts; contbr. illustrations to mags. and jours., art reprodns. for book covers, art revs. in Palm Beach Today, Palm Beach's Pictorial P.B. with photograph. Chairperson 20th Anniversary Celebration of Nat. League of Arts & Pen, 1985. Recipient Hon. Diploma awarded in the 2,000 Women of Achievement, 1972, First Prize award Palm Beach Art League Juried Art Exhibition, 1953, First Prize award Lake Worth Art League, 1954, Awards of merit Norton Sch. of Art, 1951, 52, Award of Merit, Palm Beach Nat. League of Art & Pen Women, 1975. Mem. Fla. Artists Group Inc., Soc. Four Arts, Fla. Fedn. Art, Artists Equity Nat., Nat. League Am. Arts and Pen Women (pres.), Palm Beach Quills and Artists, Northwood's Women Aux. in Arts, Nat. Mus. Women Artists, Fla. Watercolor Soc. Home and Office: 307 Cordova Rd West Palm Beach FL 33401-7907

LOZOFF, BETSY, pediatrician; b. Milw., Dec. 19, 1943; d. Milton and Marjorie (Morse) L.; 1 child, Claudia Brittenham. BA, Radcliff Coll., 1965; MD, Case Western Res. U., 1971, MS, 1981. Diplomate Am. Bd. Pediat. From asst. prof. to prof. pediatrics Case Western Res. U., Cleve., 1974-93; prof. pediatrics U. Mich., Ann Arbor, 1993—, dir. Ctr. for Human Growth and Devel., 1993—. Recipient Rsch. Career Devel. award Nat. Inst. Child Health and Human Devel., 1984-88. Fellow Am. Acad. Pediatrics; mem. Soc. for Pediatric Rsch., Soc. Rsch. in Child Devel. (program com. 1988—), Soc. Behavioral Pediatrics (exec. com. 1985-88), Ambulatory Pediatric Soc. Office: Univ Mich Ctr Human Growth and Devel 300 N Ingalls Ann Arbor MI 48109-0406

LU, CATHERINE MEAN HOA, electrical engineer; b. Taipei, Taiwan, China, Oct. 27, 1963; d. Chin Yao and Mei Shan (May) L. BSChemE, Ill. Inst. Tech., 1985, MSEE, 1987, PhD in Elec. and Computer Engring., 1993. Student rsch. engr. Rockwell Internat., Downers Grove, Ill., 1985, summer intern, 1986; summer intern GM Corp., Rochester Hill, Mich., 1987; rsch. asst. Ill. Inst. Tech. (Advanced Telecomm. Rsch. Lab.), Chgo., 1987-89, Ill. Inst. Tech. (Advanced Digital Signal Processing Lab.), Chgo., 1989—; instr. Ill. Inst. Tech. (Elec. and Computer Engring. Dept.), Chgo., 1992—; mem. tech. staff Tellabs, Bolingbrook, Ill., 1993—. Contbr. articles to profl. jours. Recipient Rsch. assistantship IEEE, 1987—; named to Dean's list. Mem. IEEE, Acoustical Soc. Am.. Home: 2755 Windsor Dr Apt 103 Lisle IL 60532 Office: Tellabs Network Access System 1000 Remington Rd Bolingbrook IL 60440

LUBBERS, TERESA S., state senator, public relations executive; b. Indpls., July 5, 1951; d. Richard and Evelyn (Ent) Smith; m. R. Mark Lubbers, Oct. 7, 1978; children: Elizabeth Stone, Margaret Smith. AB, Ind. U., 1973; MPA, Harvard U., 1981. Tchr. English Warren Ctrl. High Sch., 1973-74; pub. info. officer Office of Mayor Richard Lugar, 1974-75; dep. press sec., legis. asst. Office of U.S. Senator Richard Lugar, 1976-78; legis. rep. Nat. Fedn. Ind. Bus., 1978-80; dir. info. INC. Mag., 1981-82; press sec. Dielmann for Congress, 1982-83; pres. pub. rels. firm Capitol Communications, 1983—; state senator State of Ind., Indpls., 1992—; co-founder, v.p. Richard G. Lugar Excellence in Pub. Svc. Series, 1990—; bd. dirs. Young Audiences Ind., Nat. Policy Forum. Bd. deacons Tabernacle Presbyn. Ch.; mem. cultural enrichment com. Immaculate Heart Sch., Meridian Kessler Neighborhood Assn., Rep. Profl. Women's Roundtable; mem. steering com. Forum Series, Girls Inc.; bus. mem. Broad Ripple Village Assn.; vol. Dick Lugar's 1974 Senate Campaign; pub. info. officer Mayor's Office, 1974-75; office mgr., Friends of Dick Lugar, 1976; senate staff Office of Senator Richard Lugar, 1976-78. Republican. Home: 5425 N New Jersey St Indianapolis IN 46220 Office: State Senate State Capitol Indianapolis IN 46204*

LUBER, AMANDA KIMMER, public relations executive, marketing professional; b. Aliquippa, Pa., June 21, 1961; d. William Cephus Jr. and Joan Elizabeth (Phillips) Kimmer; m. Jay Lance Luber, Dec. 10, 1988; 1 child, Matthew William. BA in Pub. Rels., Journalism, Econs., Fla. So. Coll., 1983. Cert. pub. rels. profl. Asst. dir. Ctrl. Fla. Health Fair, Orlando, 1983-84; prodn. editor Harcourt Brace Pub., Orlando, 1984-86; features writer The Independent, Winter Haven, Fla., 1986; pub. rels. dir. Palmview Hosp., Lakeland, Fla., 1986-87, Fantastic Sam's Regional Office, Tampa, Fla., 1987-90; mktg. supr. Manatee Community Blood Ctr., Bradenton, Fla., 1991-94; freelance writer, graphic artist Luber Comms. and Design, Riverview, Fla., 1993—. Founder Reneé Turbeville Meml. Scholarship, Fla. So. Coll., Lakeland, 1984. Mem. Fla. Pub. Rels. Assn. (bd. dirs. 1993-94, newsletter editor 1993-94, Most Improved Chpt. Newsletter state award 1994, PR Profl. of Yr., Judges award 1993, Award of Distinction 1992). Democrat. Roman Catholic. Home and Office: 10408 Deepbrook Dr Riverview FL 33569

LUBETSKI, EDITH ESTHER, librarian; b. Bklyn., July 16, 1940; d. David and Leah (Aronson) Slomowitz; m. Meir Lubetski, Dec. 23, 1968; children: Shaul, Uriel, Leah. BA, Bklyn. Coll., 1962; MS in L.S., Columbia U., 1965; MA in Jewish Studies, Yeshiva U., 1968. Judaica librarian Stern Coll., N.Y.C., 1965-66, acquisitions librarian, 1966-69, head librarian, 1969—; Author: (with Meir Lubetski) Building a Judaica Library Collection, 1983; contbr. articles to profl. jours. Mem. ALA, Assn. Jewish Libraries (corr. sec. 1980-84, pres. N.Y. chpt. 1984-86, nat. v.p. 1984-86, nat. pres. 1986-88, Fanny Goldstein Merit award 1993), N.Y. Library Assn. Home: 1219 E 27th St Brooklyn NY 11210-4622 Office: Yeshiva U Hedi Steinberg Libr 245 Lexington Ave New York NY 10016-4605

LUBETZKY, CAROLE DIANE, elementary education educator, math-science specialist; b. L.A., Oct. 4, 1942; d. Lawrence and Bessie (Gursky) Schneider; m. David H. Lubetzky, Aug. 27, 1967; 1 child, Darren H. BS, San Jose State U., 1965; postgrad., U. Calif., Berkeley, UCLA. Cert. elem. tchr., Md. Tchr. Ascot Elem. Sch., L.A., 1966-67, Greenbelt (Md.) Elem. Sch., 1967—. Recipient 1st Pl Md. State Bicentennial, 1st Pl. Nat. Statistics Contest (grades 4-6), 1992. Mem. NEA, ASCD, Nat. Sci. Tchrs. Assn., Nat. Coun. Social Studies, Nat. Coun. Tchrs. Math., Am. Statis. Soc., Md. Coun. Tchrs. Math. Republican. Office: Greenbelt Elem Sch Greenbelt MD 20770

LUBIC, RUTH WATSON, association executive, nurse-midwife; b. Bucks County, Pa., Jan. 18, 1927; d. John Russell and Lillian (Kraft) Watson; m. William James Lubic, May 28, 1955; 1 son, Douglas Watson. Diploma, Sch. Nursing Hosp. U. Pa., 1955; BS, Columbia U., 1959, MA, 1961, EdD in Applied Anthropology, 1979; Cert. in Nurse Midwifery, SUNY, Bklyn., 1962; LLD (hon.), U. Pa., 1985; DSc (hon.), U. Medicine and Dentistry, N.J., 1986; LHD (hon.), Coll. New Rochelle, 1992; DSc (hon.), SUNY, Bklyn., 1993; LHD (hon.), Pace U., 1994. RN, Pa. Mem. faculty Sch. Nursing, N.Y. Med. Coll.; mem. faculty Maternity Ctr. Assn., SUNY Sch. Nurse-Midwifery, Downstate Med. Ctr.; staff nurse through head nurse Meml. Hosp. for Cancer and Allied Disease, N.Y.C., 1955-58; clin. assoc. Grad. Sch. Nursing N.Y. Med. Coll., N.Y.C., 1962-63; parent educator, cons. Maternity Ctr. Assn., N.Y.C., 1963-67, gen. dir., 1970—; bd. dirs., v.p. Am. Assn. for World Health U.S. Com. for WHO, 1975-94, pres., 1980-81; mem. bd. maternal child and family health rsch. NRC, 1974-80; mem. Commn. on Grads Fgn. Nursing Schs., 1979-83, v.p., 1980-91, treas., 1982-83; bd. govs. Frontier Nursing Svc., 1982-92; bd. dirs. Pan Am. Health and Edn. Found., pres., 1987-88; vis. prof. King Edward Meml. Hosp., Perth, Australia, 1991; Kate Hanna Harvey vis. prof. commun. health nursing Frances Payne Bolton Sch. Nursing, Case Western Res., 1991; Lansdowne lectr. U. Victoria, B.C., Can., 1992. Author: (with Gene Hawes) Childbearing: A Book of Choices, 1987; contbr. articles to profl. jours. Recipient Letitia White award, Florence Nightingale medal, 1955, Alumnae award Sch. Nursing U. Pa., 1986, Rockefeller Pub. Svc. award, 1981, Hattie Hemschemeyer award, 1983, R. Louise McManus award Dept. Nursing Alumni Assn., Tchrs. Coll. Columbia U., 1992, Disting. Svc. award Frances Payne Bolton Sch. Nursing, Case Western Res. U., 1993, McArthur Fellowship award, 1993, Hon. Recognition N.Y. State Nurses Assn., 1993, Spirit of Nursing award Vis. Nurses Svc. of New York, 1994, Mars-MacInnes award NYU, 1994; named Maternal-Child Health Nurse of Yr., ANA, 1985, Hon. Recognition, ANA, 1994. Fellow AAAS, Am. Acad. Nursing, N.Y. Acad. Medicine; mem. APHA (mem. com. on internat. health, sec. maternal and child health coun. 1982, mem. governing coun. 1986-89, mem. nominating com. 1987, mem. action bd. 1988-90), Am. Coll. Nurse-Midwives (v.p. 1964-66, pres.-elect 1969-70), Soc. Applied Anthropology, Inst. Medicine of NAS,

Nat. Assn. Childbearing Ctrs. (pres. 1983-91), Herman Biggs Soc. (sec., treas. 1989-90), Cosmopolitan Club, Sigma Theta Tau. Office: 48 E 92nd St New York NY 10128-1316

LUBIN, JOY KATHLEEN, human resources executive; b. Elizabeth, N.J., July 20, 1943; d. Joseph Andrew and Mary Elizabeth (Hajicek) Silvoy; children: James David, Dawn Marie. Grad. high sch., Clark, N.J. Notary pub. Asst. to pers. mgr. Boyle-Midway div. Am. Home Products Corp., Cranford, N.J., 1961-68; sales rep. Avon Products, Inc., N.Y.C., 1976-81; supr. human resources Glass Products, Inc. subs. AFG Industries, Carbondale, Pa., 1981—; rep. AFG Employee's Credit Union, Kingsport, Tenn., 1986—. Mem. Pa. Employers Adv. Coun. Recipient Outstanding Personal and Profl. Achievement plaque Lackawanna County Pvt. Industry Council, 1986. Mem. Nat. Fedn. Bus. and Profl. Women's Club. Democrat. Roman Catholic. Office: Glass Products Inc Clidco Dr PO Box 313 Carbondale PA 18407-0313

LUBKIN, GLORIA BECKER, physicist; b. Phila., May 16, 1933; d. Samuel Albert and Anne (Gorrin) B.; m. Yale Jay Lubkin, June 14, 1953 (div. Apr. 1968); children: David Craig, Sharon Rebecca. AB, Temple U., 1953; MA, Boston U., 1957; postgrad., Harvard U., 1974-75. Mathematician Fairchild Stratos Co., Hagerstown, Md., 1954, Letterkenny Ordnance Depot, Chambersburg, Pa., 1955-56; physicist TRG Inc., N.Y.C., 1956-58; acting chmn. dept. physics Sarah Lawrence Coll., Bronxville, N.Y., 1961-62; v.p. Lubkin Assocs., electronic cons., Port Washington, N.Y., 1962-68; assoc. editor Physics Today Am. Inst. Physics, N.Y.C., 1963-69; sr. editor Physics Today Am. Inst. Physics, 1970-84, editor, 1985-94, editl. dir., 1994—; cons. in field; mem. Nieman adv. com. Harvard U., 1978-82; co-chmn. search/adv. com. Theoretical Physics Inst., U. Minn., 1987-89, co-chmn. oversight com. 1989—; mem. mng. com. Westinghouse Sci. Writing Prizes, 1988-91; mem. selection com. Knight Fellowships, 1990. Contbr. articles to profl. publs. Gloria Becker Lubkin Professorship of Theoretical Physics established in her honor U. Minn., 1990; Nieman fellow, 1974-75. Fellow AAAS (mem. nominating com. for sect. B physics 1987-89, chair 1989), Am. Phys. Soc. (exec. com. history of physics divsn. 1983-86, 92—, exec. com. forum on physics and soc. 1977-78); mem. N.Y. Acad. Scis. (chair The Scis. pub. com. 1992-93), Nat. Assn. Sci. Writers, Sigma Pi Sigma. Jewish. Office: Am Inst Physics One Physics Ellipse College Park MD 20740

LUBKIN, VIRGINIA LEILA, ophthalmologist; b. N.Y.C., Oct. 26, 1914; d. Joseph and Anna Fredericka (Stern) L.; m. Arnold Malkan, June 6, 1944 (div. 1949); m. Martin Bernstein, Aug. 28, 1949; children: Ellen Henrietta, James Ernst, Roger Joel, John Conrad. BS, NYU, 1933; MD, Columbia U., 1937. Diplomate Am. Bd. Ophthalmology. Intern Harlem Hosp., N.Y.C., 1938-40; asst. resident neurology Montefiore Hosp., N.Y.C., 1940, asst. resident pathology, 1940-41, fellow in ophthalmology, 1941-42; resident ophthalmology Kings County Hosp., Bklyn., 1942-43, Mt. Sinai Hosp., N.Y.C., 1943-44; attending ophthalmologist, assoc. clin. prof. emeritus Mt. Sinai Sch. Medicine, 1944—; pvt. practice N.Y.C., 1945-90; rsch. prof. N.Y. Med. Coll., 1986—; co-creator, now chief of rsch. bioengineering lab. N.Y. Eye and Ear Infirmary (name now The Aborn), N.Y.C., 1978—, now chief rsch.; creator first grad. course in oculoplastics and bi-yearly symposia in devel. dyslexia Mt. Sinai Sch. Medicine; educator courses in psychosomatic ophthalmology Am. Acad. Ophthalmology, 1950-60, educator course in complications of blepharoplasty, 1980-90; bd. dirs. Jewish Guild for the Blind; tchr. surg. ophthalmology in French Cameroon, Presbyn. Mission, 1951; lectr. in numerous countries including India, 1976, 92, Pakistan, 1976, 84, China, 1978, Sri Lanka, 1979, South Africa, 1982, Singapore, 1984, Thailand, 1984, Argentina, 1986, Peru, 1987. Author: (with others) Ophthalmic Plastic and Reconstructive Surgery, 1989; contbr. articles to profl. jours. Pres. N.Y. Soc. for Clin. Ophthalmology, 1979-80. Grantee Intraocular Lens Implant Mfrs., 1989. Fellow AMA, AAAS, Am. Soc. Ophthalmic Plastic and Reconstructive Surgery (founding), Am. Coll. Surgeons, N.Y. Acad. Medicine, N.Y. Acad. Scis., Am. Acad. Ophthalmology, Am. Soc. Cataract and Refractive Surgery, PanAm. Soc. Ophthalmology, N.Y. Soc. Clin. Ophthalmology, Soc. Light Treatment and Biol. Rhythms, Phi Beta Kappa, Alpha Omega Alpha. Home: 1 Blackstone Pl Bronx NY 10471 Office: NY Eye and Ear Infirmary Rm 232 South Bldg 310 E 14th St New York NY 10003

LUCAS, BARBARA B., electrical equipment manufacturing executive; b. 1945. BA, U. Md., 1967; MA, Johns Hopkins U., 1968. V.p., sec. Equitable Bancorp, 1977-85; v.p. pub. affairs, corp. sec. Black & Decker Corp., Balt., 1985—; bd. dirs. Goulds Pumps, Inc. Office: Black & Decker Corp 701 E Joppa Rd Baltimore MD 21286-5559

LUCAS, BETH ANNE, television producer; b. Grand Rapids, Mich., Sept. 15, 1960; d. Gordon Patrick and Phyllis (Sablack) Galka; m. Mark Fordham, Mar. 19, 1982 (div. 1985); m. Gus Lucas, June 3, 1991. Student, Ohio U., 1978, U. Colo., Denver, 1980, Met. State Coll., 1981, U. Colo., 1982, UCLA, 1991-93; BS, Antioch U., 1995. Segment producer Breakaway, Metromedia TV, Hollywood, Calif., 1983; asst. dir. Anything for Money, Paramount TV, Hollywood, 1984; post prodn. supr. Heathcliff DIC, Hollywood, 1984; post prodn. supr. Beauty and the Beast, Witt-Thomas Prodns., Hollywood, 1986-88; assoc. producer Anything But Love, 20th Century Fox, Hollywood, 1989; assoc. producer Easy Street, Viacom Prodns., Hollywood, 1984-85; mgr. post prodn. Matlock, Perry Mason, Father Dowling, Jake and the Fatman, Hollywood, 1990-91. Vol. Children Are Out Future. Mem. NOW, Amnesty Internat., The Nature Conservancy, Nat. Parks and Conservation Assn., Am. Film Inst., Women in Arts, Feminist Majority, Nat. Abortion Rights Action League, Greenpeace, Smithsonian Assocs., Mus. Contemporary Art, L.A. County Mus., Sta. KCET, UCLA Alumni Assn., Child Help USA, Childreach, Mus. of Tolerance.

LUCAS, CONNIE JEAN, artist; b. Detroit, Aug. 6, 1934; d. Thedore and Veronica Kuzma; m. Mike Lucas, May 1, 1953; children: Michael, James, David. BFA in Painting magna cum laude, Eastern Mich. U., 1985, MA in Painting, 1991. Tchr. Plymouth (Mich.) /Canton Schs., 1985—. Detroit Women Painters & Sculptors scholar, 1989; recipient Merit award Saginaw Coun. Arts, 1993, Juror's award Excellence Birmingham Bloomfield Art Assn., 1992. Mem. Mich. Watercolor Soc., Detroit Artists Market, Ann Arbor Women Painters Assn., Farmington Art Club, Wis. Women in Arts.

LUCAS, ELIZABETH COUGHLIN, educator; b. Youngstown, Ohio, May 5, 1918; d. Joseph Anthony and Gertrude Elizabeth (Handel) Coughlin; m. Charles Edward Lucas, Apr. 7, 1945. BS magna cum laude, Notre Dame Coll. of Ohio, 1940; Diploma, Harvard U., 1944; MA in Edn., Calif. State Poly U., 1980. Cert. tchr., Calif. (life), secondary tchr., Pa., Ohio. Tech. sec. for v.p. engring and purchasing Patterson Foundry and Machine Co., East Liverpool, Ohio, 1941-42; tchr. chemistry Point Marion (Pa.) High Sch., 1942, Lincoln High Sch., Midland, Pa., 1942-44; radar specialist Thunderstorm Project U.S. Weather Bur., St. Cloud, Fla., 1946, Wilmington, Ohio, 1947; substitute tchr. math, sci. Chaffey (Calif.) Union High Schs., 1971-75; tchr. math Claremont (Calif.) High Sch., 1975-80; tchr., counselor, head sci. dept. San Antonio High Sch., Claremont, 1980-88; substitute tchr. Claremont Unified Sch. Dist., Claremont, 1988—; mem. dist. adv. com. for math. and sci., Claremont, 1983-85; substitute tchr. San Antonio (Calif.) High Sch., 1988—, Upland (Calif.) High Sch., 1988-89, Hillside High Sch., 1988-89. Author, editor: A Descriptive Study of the Effects of the New Math Syndrome on the Average High School Student, 1980. Lt. (j.g.) USNR, 1944-48. Mem. NAFE, Nat. Coun. of Tchrs. of Math., Nat. Sci. Tchrs. Assn., Assn. for Supervision and Curriculum Devel., Cath. Daus. of the Ams. (regent 1975-77, diocesan chmn. 1979-81). Republican. Roman Catholic. Home and Office: 9185 Regency Way Alta Loma CA 91701-3439

LUCAS, ELIZABETH MARY, marketing professional; b. Chgo., Oct. 9, 1954; d. Joseph John and Elizabeth Mary (Goodwillie) L.; m. Thomas John Sublewski, May 7, 1983; children: Thomas, Juliana. BS in Mktg., Drake U., 1976. Fashion cons. Carson, Pirie, Scott & Co., Chgo., 1976-79; freelance producer Chgo., 1979-84; account exec. Brown & Rosner, Chgo., 1984-86; account supr. Brown, Rosner & Rubin, Chgo., 1986-87, dir. sales, 1987—; mem. Nat. Safety Coun., Chgo., 1987-91, asst. dir. mktg., 1991-92, dir. mktg., 1992—. Mem. Am. Mgmt. Assn., Chgo. Nat. Soc. Performance and Instructional Design, Chgo. Assn. Direct Mktg. Roman Catholic.

LUCAS, GEORGETTA MARIE SNELL, retired educator, artist; b. Harmony, Ind., July 25, 1920; d. Ernest Clermont and Sarah Ann (McIntyre) Snell; m. Joseph William Lucas, Jan. 29, 1943; children:Carleen Anita Lucas Underwood-Scrougham, Thomas Joseph, Joetta Jeanne Lucas Allgood. BS, Ind. State U., 1942; MS in Edn., Butler U., 1964; postgrad. Herron Sch. of Art, Indpls., 1961-65, Ind. U., Indpls. and Bloomington, 1960, 61, 62, 65. Music, art tchr. Jasonville City Schs., Ind., 1942-43, Van Buren High Sch., Brazil, Ind., 1943-46, Plainfield City Schs., Ind., 1946-52, Met. Sch. Dist. Wayne Twp., Indpls., 1952-56, 1959-68; art tchr. Met. Sch. Dist. Perry Twp., Indpls., 1968-81. Illustrator: (book) Why So Sad, Little Rag Doll, 1963; artist (painting) Ethereal Season, 1966, (lithograph) Bird of Time, 1965-66; exhibited in group shows Hoosier Salon Art Exhibit 1956, 60, 62-65, 67, 70, 72, 87, 94, N.Y. Lincoln Ctr., N.Y.C., 1994; represented in permanent collections Ind. State U., Ind.-Purdue U.-Indpls., GM Inst., Detroit; lectr. Art Educators Assn. Ind., Ind. U.-Bloomington, 1976. Mem. NEA (life), Nat. Assn. Women Artist, Ind. Artist Craftsmen, Inc. (hon., pres. 1979-85, 87, 88), Ind. Fedn. Art Clubs (hon., pres. 1986-87, counselor 1988-91, bd. dirs. 1991—, parliamentarian 1992—), Hoosier Salon, Ind. State U. Mortar Bd. 1982, Alumni, 1988, Art Edn. Assn. Ind. (life), Nat. League Am. Pen Women (Ind. state art chmn. 1984—, Best of Show award 1983, pres. Indpls. branch 1994—, front cover drawing Pen-Woman Mag. 1994), Fine Art for State Ind. (Internat. Women's Yr. fine art chmn. 1977), Internat. Platform Assn. (bd. dirs. 1983—, chmn. art com. 1987—, lectr. 1975, 78, 82, 84, Silver award 1978, appointed gov. 1983—), Cen. Ind. Artists (hon.), Alpha Delta Kappa (life, Ind. state chmn. of art 1973-77, pres. 1972-74, represented by painting in nat. hdqrs.-Kansas City, Mo., Fidelis Delta first v.p.), Order of Eastern Star. Republican. Methodist. Avocations: genealogy, travel, numismatics. Home and Office: 10644 E US Hwy 40 Indianapolis IN 46231-2621

LUCAS, JUNE H., state legislator; m. Frank A. Budak; children: Deven Armeni, Adrien. Student, Youngstown State U. Mem. Ohio Ho. of Reps., 1986—, mem. energy and environment, judiciary and criminal justice coms., vice-chairwoman agr. and natural resources com. Contbr. articles to Warren Tribune Chronicle. Active Animal Welfare League. Named Woman of Yr., Coalition Labor Union Women, YWCA, 1988. Mem. NOW (Trumbull County chpt.), LWV, Ohio Bus. and Profl. Women, Ohio Farm Bur., Mosquito Creek Devel. Assn., Farmer's Union, Sierra Club. Democrat. Home: 1435 Locust St Mineral Ridge OH 44440-9721 Office: Ohio House of Reps Office of House Mems Columbus OH 43215*

LUCAS, KAREN ROSE, county official, management analyst; b. Tarrytown, N.Y., July 24, 1948; d. Louis John and Margaret Mary (Jacquin) Zajicek; children: Andrew Burt, Laura Burt; m. Charles E. Lucas, Dec. 6, 1992. BS, Cornell U., 1970. Sr. sanitarian Ulster County Health Dept., Kingston, N.Y., 1972-76, N.Y. State Dept. Health, White Plains, 1976-80; mgmt. analyst Ulster County, Kingston, 1985—; mem. Ulster County Water Adv. Bd., 1987—, Ulster County Labor and Mgmt. Com., 1987—, Ulster County Enhanced 911 Task Force, Kingston, 1988-93, Ulster County AIDS Consortium, 1988—, Ulster County Records Adv. Bd., 1989—; trainer sexual harassment prevention Ulster County, 1988—, mediator Ulster County Worksite Mediation Svc., 1992—; chairperson Ulster County 911 Policies and Procedures Com., 1993-94. Bd. dirs. ARC, Kingston, 1988, Ulster Sullivan Mediation, Inc., 1992—; area chairperson Cornell U. Alumni Admissions Ambs. Network, Ithaca, N.Y., 1993—. Republican. Roman Catholic. Home: 113 Emerson St Kingston NY 12401-4446 Office: Ulster County 244 Fair St Kingston NY 12401-3806

LUCAS, LINDA LUCILLE, community college administrator; b. Stockton, Calif., Apr. 22, 1940; d. Leslie Harold Lucas and Amy Elizabeth (Callow) Farnsworth. BA, San Jose State Coll., 1961, MA, 1969; EdD, U. San Francisco, 1982. Dist. libr. Livermore (Calif.) Elem. Schs., 1962-64; libr. Mission San Jose High Sch., Fremont, Calif., 1964-69; media reference libr. Chabot Coll., Hayward, Calif., 1969-75; asst. dean instrn. Chabot-Las Positas Coll., Livermore, 1975-91; assoc. dean instrn. Las Positas Coll., Livermore, 1991-94, dean acad. svcs., 1994—; participant Nat. Inst. for Leadership Devel., 1991. Bd. dirs. Tri-Valley Community TV, Livermore, 1991—, Valley Choral Soc., 1993—, Chabot-Las Positas Colls. Found., Pleasanton, Calif., 1991-94; mem. needs assessment com Performing Arts Coun., Pleasanton. Mem. ALA, Coun. Chief Librs., Assn. Calif. Community Coll. Adminstrs., Calif. Libr. Assn. Office: Las Positas Coll 3033 Collier Canyon Rd Livermore CA 94550

LUCAS, MELINDA ANN, pediatrician, educator; b. Maryville, Tenn., June 27, 1953; d. Arthur Baldwin and Dorthy (Shields) L. BA, Maryville Coll., 1975; MS, U. Tenn., 1976, MD, 1981. Diplomate Am. Bd. Pediatrics; lic. dr. N.Y., Tenn. Intern in pediatrics U. Rochester, N.Y., 1981-82, resident in pediatrics, 1982-84; pvt. practice, Maryville, 1984-85; emergency room pediatrician U. Tenn. Med. Ctr., Knoxville, 1985-90, dir. child abuse clinic, 1987-90, pediatric intensivist, 1987—, acting dir. pediatric ICU, 1990-92, mem. faculty, 1988—; mem. Pediatric Cons., Inc., Knoxville; physician rep. Project Search Working Symposium, 1990. Contbr. articles to profl. jours. Mem. Blount County Foster Care Rev. Bd., Maryville, Tenn., 1985—, Blount County Exec. Bd. Maryville Coll. Alumni Assn,, 1988-92. Scholar United Presbyn. Ch., 1971, Mary Lou Braly scholar, 1971-73. Fellow Am. Acad. Pediatrics; mem. AMA (Physician Recognition award 1984-87, 88-91, 91-94, 94-97), Am. Profl. Soc. on Abuse of Children, Knoxville Area Pediatric Soc., Soc. Critical Care Medicine (abstract reviewer 1991, 92, 93, 94). Methodist. Home: 1608 Mcilvaine Dr Maryville TN 37801-6230

LUCAS, PATRICIA LYNN, financial executive; b. Memphis, Apr. 22, 1962; d. James Devoughn Harrington and Joyce Marie Horn Raiolo; m. Robert Warren Lucas, May 4, 1957; 1 child, Matthew Robert. Student, DePaul U., 1987. Lic. broker, Ill. Asst. mgr. McDonald's, South Chicago Heights, Ill., 1981, Taco Bell, Chgo., 1982, Brown's Chicken, Chicago Heights, Ill., 1983; customer svc. rep. Am. Nat. Bank, Chgo., 1983-85; bank mktg. rep. Kemper Fin. Svcs., Inc., Chgo., 1985-88; investment exec. Pathway Fin., Chicago Heights, 1988-90; mgr. INVEST Fin. Corp. Calumet Fed. Savs. & Loan, Dolton, Ill., 1990—. Vice pres., treas. Cedarwood Coop., Inc., Park Forest, 1990-92. DePaul U. scholar, 1982-86. Mem. Kemper Exec. Coun., Moose. Home: 3501 Dale Dr Crete IL 60417-1354 Office: Calumet Fed Savs & Loan 1350 E Sibley Blvd Dolton IL 60419-2965

LUCAS, SANDRA ROBERTS, city official, entertainment company executive; b. Riverhead, N.Y., Sept. 18, 1954; d. Newton David and Stella (Garawrecki) Roberts; divorced; 1 child, Gary Joseph. Student, Miami-Dade Jr. Coll., 1972. Gen. mgr., v.p. Parkway Entertainment Ctr, Miramar, Fla., 1981—; vice mayor, commr. City of Miramar, 1993—. Chmn. parks and recreation City of Miramar, 1989-93, mem. Planning and Zoning Commn., 1992-93. Democrat. Home: 3121 SW 65th Ave Miramar FL 33023-3849 Office: City of Miramar 6700 Miramar Pky Miramar FL 33023-4899

LUCAS, SHIRLEY AGNES HOYT, management executive; b. Chgo., Aug. 21, 1921; d. Howard L. and Lucille P. (Von Krippenstapel) Hoyt; m. William H. Lucas, Feb. 2, 1952; 1 child, Lucille Shirley. Student, Northwestern U., 1941-42. V.p. Lucas Co., Chgo., 1980—. Mem. Ill. Hosp. Assn. (Leadership award 1975), Aux. Christ Hosp. and Med. Ctr. (life, past bd. dirs., cotillion chmn., housewalk chmn.). Republican. Lutheran. Office: Lucas Co 9127 S Kedzie Ave Evergreen Park IL 60642-1606

LUCAS, SUZANNE, statistician, entrepreneur; b. Baxter Springs, Kans., Jan. 16, 1939; d. Ralph Beaver and Marguerite (Sansocie) L.; children: Patricia Sue Jennings, Neil Patric Jennings. BA in Math., Calif. State U., Fresno, 1967, MA in Ednl. Theory, 1969; MS in Stats., U. So. Calif., 1979. Asst. to dir. NSF Inst., Calif. State U., Fresno, 1968; Tchr. secondary math. Fresno city schs., 1968-78; statistician corp. indsl. relations Hughes Aircraft Co., Los Angeles, 1979-80; personnel adminstr. Hughes Aircraft Co. Space and Communications Group, Los Angeles, 1981-82, mem. tech. staff in math., 1982-85, staff engr., 1986-87; mem. tech. staff cost analysis The Aerospace Corp., 1987-90; sr. staff engr. Hughes Aircraft Co. Electro Optical Systems, 1990-93, scientist, engr., 1993—; owner, math. cons. Lucas Ednl. Consultants, Manhattan Beach, Calif., 1989—; owner Lucas Enterprises, Manhattan Beach, 1993—; lectr. in biostats. U. So. Calif., 1979. Kiwanis scholar, 1958. Mem. Internat. Soc. Parametric Analysts (pres. So. Calif. chpt. 1991-92), Soc. Cost Estimating and Analysis (cert.), Am. Psychol. Assn., Am. Statis. Assn., U. So. Calif. Alumni Assn. (life), Internat. Platform Assn., Kappa Mu Epsilon. Office: Hughes Aircraft Co EOS PO Box 902 EO/E1/D102 El Segundo CA 90245-0902 also: Lucas Enterprises PO Box 3868 Manhattan Beach CA 90266-1868

LUCCA, LANA KAY, manufacturing analyst; b. North Hornell, N.Y., Aug. 25, 1952; d. Irving Leroy Hazlett and Loraine Jacqueline (Cary) Singleton; m. Mark James Lucca, Jan. 28, 1972 (div. 1977); children: Leilani M., Leslie Kay. Student, Alfred State Coll., 1970-71, Airco Tech. Inst., 1979. Tchr.-model John Robert Powers, Buffalo, 1971-73; mgr., owner Lucca's Pizza, Alfred, N.Y., 1973-76; heavy equipment operator Carborundum Co., Niagara Falls, N.Y., 1977-78; stock room attendant, assembler, prodn. planner Conax Buffalo Corp., 1979—; asst. mgr. Lock, Stock and Barrel, Clarence, N.Y., 1983-86. Leader, assn. rep. Girl Scouts Am., Niagara Falls, Buffalo; chairperson Amherst (N.Y.) Community Intervention, 1988-90; rep. Youth-At-Risk Supts. Adv. Bd., Amherst, 1988-93; vol., conv. rep. PTA, Amherst, 1988-92. Recipient Green Angel award Girl Scouts U.S.A., 1988, Cert. of Appreciation Amherst Community Intervention, 1992. Mem. Am Prodn. and Inventory Control Soc. Episcopalian. Office: Conax Buffalo Corp 2300 Walden Ave Buffalo NY 14225-4740

LUCCHETTI, LYNN L., advertising executive, military officer; b. San Francisco, Calif., Aug. 21, 1939; d. Dante and Lillian (Bergeron) L. AB, San Jose State U., 1961; MS, San Francisco State U., 1967; grad. U.S. Army Basic Officer's Course, 1971, U.S. Army Advanced Officer Course, 1976, grad. U.S. Air Force Command and Staff Coll., 1982, U.S. Air Force War Coll., 1983, Sr. Pub. Affairs Officer Course, 1984. Media buyer Batten, Barton, Durstine & Osborn, Inc., San Francisco, 1961-67; producer-dir. Sta. KTVA-TV, Anchorage, 1967-68; media supr. Bennett, Luke and Teawell Advt., Phoenix, 1968-71; commd. 1st lt. U.S. Army, 1971; advanced through ranks to lt. col., 1985, col., 1989, brig. gen. 1993; officer U.S. Army, 1971-74, D.C. N.G., , 1974-78, U.S. Air Force Res., 1978—, program advt. mgr. U.S. Navy Recruiting Command, 1974-76; exec. coordinator for the Joint Advt. Dirs. of Recruiting (JADOR), 1976-79; dir. U.S. Armed Forces Joint Recruiting Advt. Program (JRAP), Dept. Def., Washington, 1979-91; resources mgr. Exec. Leadership Devel. Program Dept. Def., Washington, 1991-94. Author: Broadcasting in Alaska, 1924-1966. Decorated U.S. Army Meritorious Svc. medal, Nat. Def. medal, U.S. Air Force Longevity Ribbon, U.S. Navy Meritorious Unit Commendation, Dept. Def. Joint Achievement medal, 1984. Sigma Delta Chi journalism scholar, 1960. Mem. Women in Def., Sr. Profl. Wommens Assn. Home: 11401 Malaquena Lane NE Albuquerque NM 87111

LUCCI, SUSAN, actress; b. Scarsdale, N.Y., Dec. 23, 1946; d. Victor and Jeanette L.; m. Helmut Huber, 1969; children: Liza Victoria, Andreas Martin. BA, Marymount Coll., 1968. Portrays Erica in TV series All My Children, 1970—; appearances in other series include: Fantasy Island, The Love Boat, The Fall Guy; TV films: Invitation to Hell, 1985, Mafia Princess, 1985, (mini-series) Anastasia: The Mystery of Anna Anderson, 1986, Haunted by Her Past, 1988, Lady Mobster, 1988, The Bride in Black, 1990, The Women Who Sinned, 1991, Double Edge, 1992, Between Love and Hate, 1993, French Silk, 1994; host of spl. with Tony Danza 99 Ways to Attract the Right Man. Recipient 13 Emmy nominations for best actress in daytime drama series, numerous other awards. Office: All My Children 320 W 66th St New York NY 10023 also: ICM 8942 Wilshire Blvd Beverly Hills CA 90211*

LUCENTE, ROSEMARY DOLORES, educational administrator; b. Renton, Wash., Jan. 11, 1935; d. Joseph Anthony and Erminia Antoinette (Argano) Lucente; BA, Mt. St. Mary's Coll., 1956, MS, 1963. Tchr. pub. schs., Los Angeles, 1956-65, supr. tchr., 1958-65, asst. prin., 1965-69, prin. elem. sch., 1969-85, 86—, dir. instrn., 1985-86, 1986—; nat. cons., lectr. Dr. William Glasser's Educator Tng. Ctr., 1968—; nat. workshop leader Nat. Acad. for Sch. Execs.-Am. Assn. Sch. Adminstrs., 1980; L.A. Unified Sch. Dist. rep. for nat. pilot of Getty Inst. for Visual Arts, 1983-85, 92—, site coord., 1983-86, team leader, mem. supt.'s adv. cabinet, 1987—. Recipient Golden Apple award Stanford Ave. Sch. PTA, Faculty and Community Adv. Council, 1976, resolution for outstanding service South Gate City Council, 1976. Mem. Nat. Assn. Elem. Sch. Prins., L.A. Elem. Prins. Orgn. (v.p. 1979-80), Assn. Calif. Sch. Adminstrs. (charter mem.), Assn. Elem. Sch. Adminstrs. (vice-chmn. chpt. 1972-75, city-wide exec. bd., steering com. 1972-75, 79-80), Asso. Adminstrs. Los Angeles (charter), Pi Theta Mu, Kappa Delta Pi (v.p. 1982-84), Delta Kappa Gamma. Democrat. Roman Catholic. Home: 6501 Lindenhurst Ave Los Angeles CA 90048-4733 Office: Figueroa St Sch 510 W 111th St Los Angeles CA 90044

LUCHSINGER, ARLENE EDITH, librarian; b. Elkhart, Kans., May 7, 1937; d. Orval Jack and Lucille Edith (Byarlay) Abel; m. Dale F. Luchsinger, June 7, 1964; 1 child, Caroline Leslie. AB, U. Kans., 1958; MS, Kans. State U., 1963; A.M.L.S., U. Mich., 1965. Sci. tchr. Hillsdale Sch., Cin., 1958-61; catalog librarian duPont Libr., U. of the South, Sewanee, Tenn., 1965-67, 70-73; reference librarian Ga. State U., Atlanta, 1974-75, head monograph cataloging, 1975-76; biol. sci. bibliographer U. Ga. Univ. Librs., Athens, 1976-78, head sci. collections, 1978-83; asst. dir. for br. librs. U. Ga. Librs., Athens, 1983—. Author: Plant Systematics, 1979, 2d edit., 1986, Smith's Guide to the Literature of the Life Sciences, 1980. Mem. AAAS, ALA, Assn. Coll. and Rsch. Librs., Libr. Adminstrn. and Mgmt. Assn., Ga. Libr. Assn., Southeastern Libr. Assn., Sigma Kappa, Sigma Xi, Internat. Torch Club. Episcopalian. Office: U Ga Sci Libr Athens GA 30602-7412

LUCHT, SONDRA MOORE, state senator; b. Stumptown, W.Va., Dec. 12, 1942; d. Arthur Jackson and Lucille (Cain) Moore; m. William Lucht; 1 child, Carl Joseph. B.A., Glenville State Coll., M.A., Marshall U.; postgrad. James Madison U. Cert. sch. psychologist. Mem. W. Va. State Senate from Dist. 16, 1982—, re-elected, 1986 and 1990; speaker, lectr. on women in politics, other women's issues, child abuse, other youth issues. Co-founder Shenandoah Women's Ctr. Mem. NOW (pres. 1977-82, chair task force on pay equity 1983—, chair commn. on juvenile law 1985—). Democrat. Episcopalian. Office: Senate House State Capitol Charleston WV 25305*

LUCIA, HELEN LOUISE, pathologist, educator; b. Bklyn., Oct. 23, 1942; d. Edward Francis and Helen Quay (Litzenberg) L.; m. Harold A. Dunsford, Oct. 16, 1971; children: Harold A. Jr., William R. BS, CCNY, 1964; MD, NYU, 1968. Diplomate Am. Bd. Pathology. Clin. asst. prof. pathology U. Pitts. Med. Sch., 1974-77; adj. asst. prof. pathology U. Pitts. Grad. Sch. Pub. Health, 1977-80; rsch. assoc. Yale Med. Sch., New Haven, Conn., 1979-82; adj. asst. prof. lab. medicine Yale Med. Sch., New Haven, 1982; pathologist West Haven (Conn.) VA Med. Ctr., 1982; from asst. prof. to assoc. prof. pathology U. Tex. Med. Br., Galveston, 1982-91; prof. pathology U. Miss. Med. Ctr., Jackson, 1992—, dir. med. micro lab., 1992—; presenter in field. Contbr. numerous papers to med. jours. Mem. Binford Dammin Soc. Inf. Dis. Pathology (sec.-treas. 1991—). Office: U Miss Med Ctr 2500 N State St Jackson MS 39216

LUCIA, MARILYN REED, physician; b. Boston; m. Salvatore P. Lucia, 1959 (dec. 1984); m. C. Robert Russell; children: Elizabeth, Walter, Salvatore, Darryl. MD, U. Calif., San Francisco, 1956. Intern Stanford U. Hosps., 1956-57; NIMH fellow, resident in psychiatry Langley Porter, U. Calif., San Francisco, 1957-60; NIMH fellow, resident in child psychiatry Mt. Zion Hosp., San Francisco, 1964-66; NIMH fellow, resident in community psychiatry U. Calif., San Francisco, 1966-68, clin. prof. psychiatry, 1982—; founder, cons. Marilyn Reed Lucia Child Care Study Ctr., U. Calif., San Francisco; cons. Cranio-facial Ctr., U. Calif., San Francisco, No. Calif. Diagnostic Sch. for Neurologically Handicapped Children; dir. children's psychiat. svcs. Contra Costa County Hosp., Martinez. Fellow Am. Psychiat. Assn., Am. Acad. Child Psychiatry; mem. Am. Cleft Palate Assn. Office: 350 Parnassus Ave Ste 602 San Francisco CA 94117-3608

LUCIANO, GWENDOLYN KAYE, planning specialist, rates representative; b. Cleve., Feb. 26, 1954; d. Charles Wayne and Lila (Cole) Rhodes. BA in Math. and Mktg., Lake Erie Coll., 1975, MBA, 1988. cert. project mgmt. profl. Scheduling engr. A.G. McKee & Co., Independence, Ohio, 1975-78; project scheduling supr. Perry Nuclear Plant Raymond Kaiser Engrs., Perry, Ohio, 1978-85; maintenance planning supr. Cleve. Electric Illuminating Co., 1985-89; mgmt. cons. Liberty Cons. Group, Balt., 1989-91; outage planning coord. Cleve. Electric Illuminating, 1991-94; sr. rates rep. Centerior Energy Corp., Independence, Ohio, 1994; instr. Inst. Nuclear Power Ops., Atlanta, 1993-94; mem. bd. dirs. Learning About Bus., 1992-94; chmn. Lake Erie Editorial Adv. Bd., 1991-94. Mem. AAUW, Am. Assn. Cost Engrs., Project Mgmt. Inst., Lake Erie Coll. Nat. Alumni Assn. (v.p. 1994-96). Republican. Episcopalian. Office: Centerior Energy Corp 6200 Oak Tree Blvd Independence OH 44131

LUCID, SHANNON W., biochemist, astronaut; b. Shanghai, China, Jan. 14, 1943; d. Joseph O. Wells; m. Michael F. Lucid; children: Kawai Dawn, Shandara Michelle, Michael Kermit. BS in Chemistry, U. Okla., 1963, MS in Biochemistry, 1970, PhD in Biochemistry, 1973. Sr. lab. technician Okla. Med. Rsch. Found., 1964-66, rsch. assoc., from 1974; chemist Kerr-McGee, Oklahoma City, 1966-68; astronaut NASA Lyndon B. Johnson Space Ctr., Houston, 1979—; mission specialist flights STS-51G and STS-34 NASA Lyndon B. Johnson Space Ctr., mission specialist on Shuttle Atlantis Flight, 1991. First woman to fly on the shuttle three times. Address: NASA Johnson Space Ctr CB-Astronaut Office Houston TX 77058*

LUCIER, TAMARA LYNN, accountant; b. Kenosha, Wis., Oct. 12, 1960; d. Meryle Marvin and Donna Jean (Trust) Pierce; m. Joel Robert Lucier, Nov. 19, 1983; children: Bradley Joseph, Angela Diane. AA in Bus. Adminstrn., Cerritos Coll., 1991; BA in Bus. Adminstrn., Calif. State U., Fullerton, 1993. Bookkeeper Villani & Becker, CPAs, Kenosha, Wis., 1979-83; supr. gen. ledger acctg. Specialty Restaurants Corp., Anaheim, Calif., 1983-85; sr. acct. Masco Bldg. Products Corp., Seal Beach, Calif., 1985-88; supr. gen. acctg. Prestige Stas. Inc., Cerritos, Calif., 1993—; cons. in field. Vol. reading tutor Glazier Elem. Sch., Norwalk, Calif., 1992. Recipient Calif. Grant A award Calif. Student Aid Commn., Sacramento, 1992, Accts award Am. Assn. Women Accts.; Yokohama Tire Corp. scholar Calif. State U. Scholarship Com., Fullerton, 1992. Mem. Inst. Mgmt. Accts. Office: 17215 Studebaker Rd Cerritos CA 90701

LUCKES, MARY HELEN B., mental health nurse; b. Nashville; d. George Armistice and Vivian E. Baum; m. Douglas S. Luckes. ADN, Brunswick Jr. Coll., 1970; BSN, Armstrong State Coll., 1977; MSN, Med. Coll. Ga., 1986. RN, Ga., Fla., S.C.; cert. C.S. in adult psychiat., mental health nursing, ANA. Sr. staff nurse Med. Coll. Ga., Augusta; clin. nurse specialist U. Hosp. Jacksonville (Fla.), William S. Hall Psychiat. Inst., Columbia, S.C. Mem. S.C. Nurses Assn., Sigma Theta Tau (Alpha Xi chpt.). Home: 4824 Smallwood Rd Apt 137 Columbia SC 29223-3237

LUCKEY, DORIS WARING, civic volunteer; b. Union City, N.J., Sept. 17, 1929; d. Jay Deloss and Edna May (Ware) Waring; m. George William Luckey, Mar. 29, 1958; children: G. Robert, Jana Elizabeth, John Andrew. AB, U. Rochester, 1950; CLU, Am. Coll., Bryn Mawr, Pa., 1957. With pers. dept., supr. life dept. Travelers Ins. Co., Rochester, N.Y., 1952-58; agt. asst. life underwriting Mass. Mut. Ins. Co., Rochester, 1958. Chairperson, various past offices Bd. Coop. Edcl. Svcs. and State Edn. Dept., Vocat. Tech. Adv. Com., Rochester and Albany, 1975—, pres., Rochester, 1975-85, Monroe County Sch. Bds. Assn., Rochester, 1980-81; v.p. Penfield (N.Y.) Schs., 1978-81; various fin., ednl. and speaking engagements LWV, 1983—; pres. ch. coun., chair ch. and min. com., co-chair, United Ch. of Christ Denomination in Genesee Valley; vol. numerous other civic, cultural, ch. and artistic orgns. Mem. AAUW (past pres., past bd. dirs., dist. 1 state rep.). Republican.

LUCKOW, ELIZABETH ELLEN, retired nurse; b. Stromsburg, Nebr., Jan. 31, 1934; d. Paul William and Lillian Marcella (Anderson) James; children: Michael, Erin Elizabeth. Diploma in nursing, Lincoln Gen. Hosp., 1954; BS, U. Colo., 1966, cert. pediatric nurse practitioner, 1967, MS, 1970. RN, Colo. Charge nurse sick baby nursery Children's Hosp., Fresno, Calif., 1955-56; pediatric nurse Pediatric Group, Fresno, 1956-62; emer. rm. nurse Gen. Rose Hosp., Denver, 1962; pediatric nurse emer. rm. Children's Hosp., Denver, 1963; pediatric nurse pvt. practice med. office, Denver, 1964; migrant nurse, child care nurse dept. pediatrics U. Colo., Boulder, 1967; clinic coord. Boulder County Devel. Evaluation Clinic, Boulder, 1969-82; child devel. cons. Boulder County Social Svcs., Boulder, 1983-84; staff nurse Boulder Psychiat. Inst., 1985-88; ret., 1988. Mem. Boulder County Child Abuse Team, 1978-79; bd. dirs. Boulder County Bd. Devel. Disabilities, 1980-82; mem., adviser Colo. Subcom. on Mental Retardation, Denver, 1969-78; pres. Colo. Nurses Assn., Boulder, 1973; treas. Boulder Valley Bd. Edn., 1973-76; mem. adv. bd. Boulder Valley Sch. Adv. Bd., 1970-82; mem. Boulder County Mental Health-Child Team, 1978-80. Mem. Non Practicing and Part Time Colo. Nurses Assn. (program com. 1991—), Sigma Theta Tau (life). Methodist. Home: 3111 14th St Boulder CO 80304-2611

LUDGUS, NANCY LUCKE, lawyer; b. Palo Alto, Calif., Oct. 28, 1953; d. Winston Slover and Betty Jean (Brilhart) Lucke; m. Lawrence John Ludgus, Apr. 8, 1983. BA in Polit. Sci. with highest honors, U. Calif., Berkeley, 1975; JD, U. Calif., Davis, 1978. Bar: Calif. 1978, U.S. Dist. Ct. (no. dist.) Calif. 1978. Staff atty. Crown Zellerbach Corp., San Francisco, 1978-80, Clorox Co., Oakland, Calif., 1980-82; staff atty. Nat. Semiconductor Corp., Santa Clara, Calif., 1982-85, corp. counsel, 1985-92, sr. corp. counsel, asst. sec., 1992—. Sec. Nat. Semiconductor Employees Polit. Action Com., Santa Clara, 1992—. Mem. ABA, Am. Corp. Counsel Assn., Calif. State Bar Assn., Phi Beta Kappa. Democrat. Office: Nat Semiconductor Corp 1090 Kifer Rd M/S 16-135 Sunnyvale CA 94086

LUDLOW, BARBARA ANN LANDGRAF, education educator; b. Bklyn., Mar. 23, 1949; d. William Anthony and Helen Marie (Demuth) Landgraf. BA, St. John's U., Jamaica, N.Y., 1966; MA, Cornell U., 1971; MEd, U. Del., 1974; EdD, W.Va. U., 1983. Cert. tchr., W.Va. Tchr. Wilmington (Del.) Pub. Schs., 1971-72, Upshur County Schs., Buckhannon, W.Va., 1973-76; instr. W.Va. U., Mortantown, 1976-83, asst. prof., 1983-87, assoc. prof., 1987—. Recipient Educator of Yr. award W.Va. Assn. for Retarded Citizens, 1987. Fellow Am. Assn. on Mental Retardation (bd. dirs. 1986-91, pres. edn. divsn. 1989-91); mem. Phi Delta Kappa (area coord. W.Va. 1980-88, Outstanding Leadership award 1982). Office: WVa U 504 Allen Hall Morgantown WV 26506

LUDVIG, MARIA MARGARET, research chemist; b. Portland, Oreg., Oct. 17, 1957; d. Imre F. and Ilona Maria Ludvig; m. Marc William Jackson, July 19, 1987; 1 child, Mathieu. BS, Portland State U., 1980, MS, 1983; PhD, Tex. A&M U., 1987. Postdoctoral fellow U. Tex., Austin, 1987-90; rsch. chemist Akzo Chems., Pasadena, Tex., 1990-93; sr. rsch. chemist Akzo-Nobel, Pasadena, 1993—. Contbr. articles to profl. jours. Robert A. Welch predoctoral fellow Tex. A&M U., 1984-87. Mem. Am. Chem. Soc., S.W. Catalysis Soc., Iota Sigma Pi. Office: Akzo Nobel Chems 13000 Bay Park Rd Pasadena TX 77507

LUDWIG, ANN MARIE, women's health care nurse practitioner; b. Providence, Nov. 6, 1958; d. Richard Joseph and Thelma Helen (Muller) Juttner; m. William Arthur Ludwig Jr., May 29, 1982; children: Carissa Marie, Jessica Leigh. BSN, U. Tex. Health Scis. Ctr., Houston, 1982; MSN with honors, U. Tex. Health Scis. Ctr., San Antonio, 1990; student, Southwestern Med. Sch., Dallas, 1992. RN; cert. nurse practitioner; cert. women's health care nurse practitioner. Staff nurse med./surg. St. Luke's Hosp., Kansas City, Mo., 1982-83; charge nurse Med. Ctr. Independence, Mo., 1983-85; edn. coord. Spohn Hosp., Corpus Christi, Tex., 1985-86, maternal-child edn. coord., 1986-91; nursery clin. nurse mgr. Meml. Med. Ctr., Corpus Christi, 1986; women's health care nurse practitioner Coastal Bend Women's Ctr., Corpus Christi, 1991-92; instr. nursing Corpus Christi State U., 1992-93; women's health care nurse practitioner Coastal Bend Women's Ctr., Corpus Christi, 1993—. Mem. NAACOG (chpt. coord. Corpus Christi 1988-89, program coord. 1989-90, 2d rec. sec. 1990-91), Tex. Nurse Practitioners Assn., Sigma Theta Tau. Home: 7817 Charlero Dr Corpus Christi TX 78414 Office: 7121 SPID Ste 206 Corpus Christi TX 78412

LUDWIG, BRENDA JOYCE, elementary school educator; b. Kokomo, Ind., Sept. 13, 1948; d. Ralph Roy and Geraldine Lorraine (Roulston) Shuck; m. John Allen Ludwig, Aug. 29, 1970; children: Derek Jason Aleksandr, Drew Barrett Egon, Trent Randell Dietrich. BA, Mich. State U., 1970. Rsch. asst. Mich. State U., East Lansing, 1967-68; food preparation/sales Schmidt's Supermarket, Okemos, Mich., 1969-70; tchr. N.W. Sch. Dist., Jackson, Mich., 1970-77; dir., tchr. Rainbow Connection Coop. Presch., Pleasant Lake, Mich., 1981-86; tchr. N.W. Sch. Dist., Jackson, 1987—. Registrar, coach N.W. Soccer/Am. Youth Soccer Orgn., Jackson, 1984-90; fin. and facilities com. Jackson Dist. Libr., 1985-87; asst. dir., coach N.W. Odyssey of the Mind, Jackson, 1985-87. Mem. AAUW (treas. 1976—, Ednl. Found. Fellowship honoree 1984), Vested Interest Investment Club (treas., agt. 1983—), Nat. Coun. for Social Studies. Methodist. Home: 8400 Cooper Rd Rives Junction MI 49277

LUDWIG, MARGARET G., state legislator; m. Leland Ludwig; 3 children. BA, Colby Coll. Mem. Maine State Senate. Mem. Maine State Sch. Bd. Assn. Republican. Home: 3 Roger St Houlton ME 04730-1520 Office: Maine State Senate State Capitol Bldg Augusta ME 04330*

LUDWIG, ORA LEE KIRK, coal company executive; b. Morgantown, W.Va., June 25, 1925; d. Thomas Jefferson and Nora Belle (Browning) Johnson; m. Eugene P. Kirk, Dec. 6, 1947 (div. 1957); children: E. Phillip, Lisa Ann Kirk Wiese; m. August J. Ludwig, May 17, 1983. AA, Mt. State Coll., Parkersburg, W.Va. With Rosedale Coal Co., Morgantown, W.Va., 1945—; corp. sec. Rosedale Coal Co., 1954, v.p., 1971, pres., 1980—; with Mon Valley Coal & Lumber Co., Morgantown, 1945—; pres. Mon Valley Coal & Lumber Co., 1983—; with Mon-Valley Mining Co., 1945—, pres., 1980—. Pres. Monongalia Arts Ctr., Morgantown, 1960-83; bd. dirs., com. chmn. W.Va. Hosp. Aux., 1990—; treas. United Way, 1991—; bd. dirs. Lakeview Theatre. Mem. Tri-State Coal Assn., W.Va. Coal Assn., W.Va. Hosp. Assn. (exec. bd. aux., treas. 1991—), Morgantown C. of C. (treas. 1989-90), Women's Alliance, Rotary, White Shrine of Jerusalem, Order Eastern Star. Methodist. Home: 940 Riverview Dr Morgantown WV 26505-4634 Office: Rosedale Coal Co Morgantown WV 26507-0676

LUECKE, ELEANOR VIRGINIA ROHRBACHER, civic volunteer; b. St. Paul, Mar. 10, 1918; d. Adolph and Bertha (Lehman) Rohrbacher; m. Richard William Luecke, Nov. 1, 1941; children: Glenn Richard, Joan Eleanor Ratliff, Ruth Ann. Student, Macalester Coll., St. Paul, 1936-38, St. Paul Bus. U., 1938-40. Author lit. candidate and ballot issues, 1970—; producer TV local issues, 1981—; contbr. articles to profl. jours. Founder, officer, dir., pres. Liaison for Inter-Neighborhood Coop., Okemos, Mich., 1972—; chair countrywide special edn. millage proposals, 1958, 1969; trustee, v.p., pres. Ingham Intermediate Bd. Edn., 1959-83; sec., dir. Tri-County Cmty. Mental Health Bd., Lansing, 1964-72; founder, treas., pres. Concerned Citizens for Meridian Twp., Okemos, 1970-86; mental health rep. Partners of the Americas, Belize, Brit. Honduras, 1971; trustee Capital Area Comprehensive Health Planning, 1973-76; v.p., dir. Assn. Retarded Citizens Greater Lansing, 1973-83; chair, mem. Cmty. Svcs. for Developmentally Disabled Adv. Coun., 1973—; dir., founder, treas. Tacoma Hills Homeowners Assn., Okemos, 1985—; facilitator of mergers Lansing Child Guidance Clinic, Clinton and Easton counties Tri-County Cmty. Mental Health Bd., Lansing Adult Mental Health Clinic, founder. Recipient Greater Lansing Cmty. Svcs. Coun. "Oscar," United Way, 1955, state grant Mich. Devel. Disabilities Coun., Lansing, 1983, Disting. award Mich. Assn. Sch. Bds., Lansing, 1983, Pub. Svc. award C.A.R.E.ing, Okemos, 1988, Earth Angel award WKAR-TV 23, Mich. State U., East Lansing, 1990, Cert. for Cmty. Betterment People for Meridian, Okemos, 1990, 2nd pl. video competition East Lansing/Meridian Twp. Cable Comm. Commn., 1990, 1st pl. award video competition, 1992; Ingham Med. Hosp. Commons Area named in her honor, Lansing, 1971. Home: 1893 Birchwood Dr Okemos MI 48864-2766

LUECKERT, KATHERINE MCMULLEN, assistant city manager; b. Columbia, MO, Jan. 25, 1958; d. John Stuart and Elizabeth Davies (Vincent) McM.; m. Donald Eric Lueckert, Aug. 15, 1981. BA in Polit. Sci., Mary Washington Coll., 1980; MS in Telecomm. Policy, George Washington U., 1984; MPA, George Mason U., 1990. Supr. frames C&P Telephone Co., Falls Church, Va., 1980-83; staff supr. Bell Atlantic, Arlington, Va., 1983-84; telecomm. dir. Prince William County, Va., 1984-89, budget officer, 1989-93; asst. city mgr. City of Plymouth, Minn., 1993—. Vol. Prince William Libr. System, Woodbridge, Va., 1985-88; elder 1st United Presbyn. Ch., Woodbridge, 1989-93. Mem. PEO Sisterhood, Phi Beta Kappa. Office: City of Plymouth 3400 Plymouth Blvd Plymouth MN 55447

LUEKE, DONNA MAE, national retail company manager; b. Toledo, Sept. 18, 1946; d. Herbert Henry and Margery Alberta (Welsh) L. BA, Adrian Coll., 1968. Tchr. Anchor Bay Schs., New Baltimore, Mich., 1968-74; salesperson Jacobson's, Birmingham, Mich., 1974-76; sales rep. Stark & Co., Detroit, 1976-80; regional retail supr. Norwich-Eaton Consumer Pharms., Louisville, 1980-83; territory rep. Procter & Gamble, Louisville, 1983-84; dir. Progressive Retail, Raleigh, N.C., 1984-89; nat. retail mgr. CIBA Consumer Pharms. and CIBA Vision Corp., Wayne, Pa., 1989-92. Student govt. v.p. Adrian Coll., 1966, 67. Mem. Nature Conservancy, Sierra Club, Amnesty Interant., NOW.

LUEPKE, GRETCHEN, geologist; b. Tucson, Nov. 10, 1943; d. Gordon Maas and Janice (Campbell) Luepke; B.S., U. Ariz., 1965, M.S., 1967; U. Colo., summer, 1962. Geol. field asst. U.S. Geol. Survey, Flagstaff, Ariz., 1964; with U.S. Geol. Survey, Menlo Park, Calif., 1967—, geologist, Pacific Br. of Marine Geology, 1976—. Registered geologist, Ore. Mem. U.S. Congress Office Tech. Assessment Workshop, Mining and Processing Placers of EEZ, 1986. Mem. Soc. Econ. Paleontologists and Mineralogists (chmn. com. libraries in developing countries 1988-91), Geol. Soc. Am. (mem. Penrose Conf., 1994), Ariz. Geol. Soc., Peninsula Geol. Soc., Bay Area Mineralogists (chmn. 1979-80), History of the Earth Scis. Soc., Internat. Assn. Sedimentologists, Internat. Marine Minerals Soc. (charter), Geospeakers Toastmasters Club (charter), Sigma Xi. Editor: Stability of Heavy Minerals in Sediments; Econ. Analysis of Heavy Minerals in Sediments; editor book rev. Earth Scis. History, 1989—. Contbr. articles on heavy-mineral analysis to profl. jours. Office: 345 Middlefield Rd Menlo Park CA 94025-3591

LUETH, FAITH MUSKER, music education educator; b. Washington, Feb. 13, 1943; d. Francis and Ellen D. (Parsons) Musker; m. Richard A. Lueth, Dec. 26, 1968; 1 child, Rachel. BA, Boston U., 1964; MA, MM, Boston Conservatory, 1986. Cert. music tchr. K-12. Choral dir. Pollard Middle Sch., Needham, Mass.; asst. prof. music edn. Berklee Coll. Music, Boston, 1988, choral clinician adolescent voice; guest condr. Contbr. chpt. to book. Recipient Disting. Tchr. award, 1990; Mann grantee, 1987. Mem. Am. Choral Dirs. Assn. (Ea. divsn. Reprertoire and Stds. chairperson, mid. sch./Jr. H.S.), Music Educators Nat. Conf., Mass. Music Edn. Assn. (rec. sec.), Mu Phi Epsilon. Address: 8 Irving Dr Walpole MA 02081

LUFT, LORRAINE LEVINSON, clinical psychologist; b. Washington, June 23, 1947; d. Irving and Gladys (Dolgin) Levinson; m. Harold Stephen Luft, May 24, 1970; children: Shira Levinson Luft, Jana Levinson Luft. BA magna cum laude in Econs., Brandeis U., 1969; postgrad., U. Pa., 1969-70; M in City Planning, MIT, 1971; MS, Pacific Grad. Sch. Psychology, 1980, PhD, 1983. Lic. psychologist, Calif. Dir. program evaluation Cambridge-Somerville Mental Health & Retardation Ctr., Cambridge, Mass., 1971-73, Peninsula Hosp. Community Mental Health Ctr., Burlingame, Calif., 1973-86; assoc. dir. Menninger San Francisco Bay Area, Burlingame, Calif., 1986-90; clin. psychologist Peninsula Psychiat. Assocs., San Mateo, Calif., 1986—; mem. clin. faculty Pacific Grad. Sch. Psychology, Palo Alto, Calif., 1989-92, San Mateo County Psychiat. Residency, 1991-93; presenter numerous confs. and mtgs. in field; cons. No. Calif. Psychiat. Soc., CHAMPUS Quality Assurance and Utilization Rev., Alameda County Mental Health Divsn., Health Tng. Ctr., Calif. Dept. Health, Calif. Connection Drug Program, Fla. Consortium Cmty. Mental Health ctrs., Granville Corp., Human Interaction Rsch. Inst., Cmty. Sisters Covenant at St. Albert Ctr. Mem. editorial adv. bd. Community Mental Health Jour., 1979-81; contbr. articles to profl. jours., chpts. to books. Mem. alumni admissions coun. Brandeis U., Waltham, Mass., 1990—; trustee Pacific Grad. Sch. Psychology, Palo Alto, 1990—; mem. site coun. Addison Sch., Palo Alto, 1992-94. Fellow NSF, 1969, HUD, 1970. Mem. APA, Calif. Psychol. Assn., San Mateo County Psychol. Assn. (membership chair 1988-90), Pacific Grad. Sch. Psychology (alumni assoc., pres. 1990-91, Alumnus of Yr. 1993), Peninsula Hosp. Profl. Staff (psychiat. adv. com. 1991—), Jewish Community Fedn. (v.p. 1990-92), Phi Beta Kappa, Omicron Delta Epsilon. Office: 39 N San Mateo Dr Ste 8 San Mateo CA 94401

LUHRS, CARO ELISE, internal medicine physician, administrator, educator; b. Dover, N.J., Jan. 21, 1935; d. Albert Weigand and Ethel Adelaide (Voss) L. BA, Swarthmore Coll., 1956; MD, Harvard U., 1960. Diplomate Am. Bd. Internal Medicine; cert. personal fitness trainer, fitness instr., strength and conditioning specialist. Instr., asst. prof. medicine, dir. hematology labs. Georgetown Univ. Hosp., Washington, 1964-68; White House fellow USDA, Washington, 1968-69, spl. asst. to Sec. of Agr., 1969-73; dir. health and med. divsn. Booz, Allen & Hamilton, Washington, 1973-77; v.p., med. dir. EHE/Nat. Health Svcs., Washington, 1977-78; pvt. practice Washington, 1978—; med. dir. Hummer Assocs., Washington, 1989—; clin. prof. family medicine Georgetown U., Washington, 1991—. Trustee Swarthmore (Pa.) Coll., 1975-79; bd. dirs. USDA Grad. Sch., Washington, 1970-74, The Pillsbury Co., 1973-89, White House Fellow Found., Washington, 1979; bd. regents Uniformed Svcs. U. of Health Scis., Bethesda, Md., 1980-85; cons. Office Sci. and Tech. Policy, The White House, 1977-80; active D.C. Mayor's Adv. Com. on Emergency Med. Svcs., 1980-84. Recipient Disting. Svc. award Uniformed Svcs. U. Health Scis., 1985. Fellow ACP, Royal Soc. Medicine; mem. AMA, Am. Coll. Sports Medicine, Med. Soc. D.C. Office: Caro Luhrs Assocs 1100 Connecticut Ave NW Ste 720 Washington DC 20036

LUHTA, CAROLINE NAUMANN, airport manager, flight educator; b. Cleve., Mar. 26, 1930; d. Karl Henry and Fannie Arletta (Harlan) Naumann; m. Fred Harlan Jones, July 2, 1955 (div. 1961); m. Adolph Jalmer Luhta, Dec. 12, 1968 (dec. 1993); 1 child, Katherine Louise. BA, Ohio Wesleyan U., 1952; BS magna cum laude, Lake Erie Coll., Painesville, Ohio, 1977. Rsch. chemist Standard Oil Co. Ohio, Cleve., 1952-68; office mgr. Adolph J. Luhta Constrn. Co., Painesville, 1968-83; acct. Thomas Y. Ellis, CPA, Painesville, 1978; v.p., bd. dirs. Painesville Flying Svc., Inc., 1968—, flight instr., 1970—, airport mgr., 1983—; v.p., bd. dirs. concord Air Park, Inc., Painesville, 1968—; accident prevention counselor FAA, Cleve., 1975-85. Contbr. articles to profl. jours. Trustee Northeastern Ohio Gen. Hosp., Madison, 1973-83, chmn. bd., 1980-82; trustee Internat. Women's Air and Space Mus., Centerville, Ohio, 1989—, treas., 1991—; trustee Concord Twp., 1992—. Recipient Aerospace award Cleve. Squadron, Air Force Assn., 1966. Mem. Nat. Assn. Flight Instrs., Exptl. Aircraft Assn., Aircraft Owners and Pilots Assn., Ninety-Nines (life, chmn. All-Ohio chpt. 1969-70, Achievement award 1965, Amelia Earhart Meml. scholar 1970), Silver Wings, Order Ea. Star, Alpha Delta Pi (life). Office: Painesville Flying Svc Inc 12253 Concord Hambden Rd Painesville OH 44077-9566

LUKAS, JOAN DONALDSON, mathematics and computer science educator; b. New Haven, June 19, 1942; d. Walter George and Rose (Shor) Donaldson; m. George Lukas, Sept. 1, 1963 (div. 1980); children: David Imre, Jonathan; m. Seamus Edmond Kearney, July 14, 1990. AB, Barnard Coll., 1963; PhD, MIT, 1967. Asst. prof. U. Mass., Boston, 1967-74, assoc. prof. math. and computer sci., 1974-93, prof., 1993—; cons. Bolt, Beranek & Newman, Cambridge, Mass., 1978, 87-90, Intermetrics, Inc., Cambridge, 1981-85, Compass, Inc., Wakefield, Mass., 1984-91, Advanced Compiler & Engring. Techs., Louvain-la-Neuve, Belgium, 1992-93; vis. lectr. Brandeis U., Waltham, Mass., 1970, 79, 94; mem. grad. rev. com. NSF, Washington, 1991-93. Co-author: Learning Mathematics Through Programming, 1977, Logo: Principles, Programming, Projects, 1986; contbr. articles to profl. publs. Vol. for homeless women's advocacy and criminal justice Am. Friends Svc. Com., 1988-94. Mem. IEEE Computer Soc., Assn. for Computing Machinery. Home: 9 Highland Park Malden MA 02148-2429 Office: U Mass 100 Morrissey Blvd Boston MA 02125

LUKASH, BARBARA LYNNE, dermatologist; b. New Hyde Park, N.Y., Aug. 27, 1950; d. Gladys Joyce (Horowitz) L.; m. Ben Zane Cohen, June 18, 1978; children: David, Jesse. BS, U. Wis., 1972; MD, Tulane U., 1976. Diplomate Am. Bd. Dermatology. Intern L.I. Jewish Hosp.; resident U. Chgo. Hosps. and Clinics; pvt. practice dermatology Bronxville, N.Y., 1987—. Fellow Am. Acad. Dermatology; me. Westchester County Med. Soc., N.Y. Med. Soc. Office: 824 Bronx River Rd Bronxville NY 10708

LUKER, JEAN KNARR, administrator; b. St. Petersburg, Fla., May 4, 1944; d. Harry M. Jr. and Mary M. (Insley) Knarr; m. Maurice S. Luker Jr., Mar. 1, 1976; children: Maurice S. III, Amy Luker Cloud, Marc A. AA, Manatee Jr. Coll., 1964; BS in Edn., Fla. State U., 1966; MS in Edn., U. Va., 1982. Tchr., 1st grade Sarasota (Fla.) County Pub. Schs., 1966-70, tchr. emotionally disturbed, 1974-76; tchr. mentally retarded Washinton County Schs., Abingdon, Va., 1978-82; tchr. learning disabled Washinton County Schs., 1982-89, coord. gifted secondary, 1990-91, coord. instructional technology, gifted, 1991—; chair, bd. dirs. Southwest Va. Edn. & Tng. Network, Abingdon, 1993—; mem. Columbia Users Bd., Richmond, Va., 1993—. Co-author, illustrator: Of Clay Metal and Stone: Objects of Ancient Life in Israel, 1977, Objects of Life and Death in Ancient Palestine. Mem. Va. Assn. Edn. of Gifted, Delta Kappa Gamma (scholar com. 1991—), Phi Delta Kappa, Kappa Delta Pi, Phi Theta Kappa. Methodist. Home: 216 Stonewall Hts NE Abingdon VA 24210-2924 Office: Washington County Schs 812 Thompson Dr Abingdon VA 24210-2346

LULAY, GAIL C., human resources and corporative outplacement executive, consultant; b. Evanston, Ill., Feb. 13, 1938; d. Earl Albert and Helen Marie (Blackwell) Minnich; m. Wayne L. Lulay, Aug. 15, 1959; children: Michael Brent, Catherine Marie. BS, Elmhurst Coll., 1970; MS, Roosevelt U., 1972. Cert. counselor, Ill. Instr. Dist. #181, Hinsdale, Ill., 1970-74; corp. bus. devel. Continental Bank, Chgo., 1974-79; pres., owner Lulay & Assocs., Inc., Downers Grove, Ill., 1979—; counselor Crisis Counseling Practice, Hinsdale, 1972-79; instr. Elmhurst Coll. Adult Edn., 1982, Coll. of DuPage, Glen Ellyn, Ill., 1983-86; lectr., consultant in field, 1980—. Author: Nelson Eddy, America's Favorite Baratone, Authorized Biographical Tribute, 1992; contbr. articles to profl. jours. Bd. dirs. Crisis Homes, Des Plaines, Ill., 1984-86. Mem. Am. Assn. Counseling and Devel., Am. Soc. Personnel Adminstrn., Assn. Outplacement Cons. Firms, Inc., Human Resources Mgmt. Assn. of Chgo., Roosevelt U. Alumni Assn., Chi Omega. Office: Lulay & Assocs Inc 1431 Opus Pl Downers Grove IL 60515-1166

LULL, HEIDI MARIE, insurance company executive, agent; b. Benton Harbor, Mich., Mar. 4, 1961; d. David Winston and Susan Ethelyn (Craidon) L. AA, Lake Mich. Coll., 1981; BS, Western Mich. U., 1983. Advt. asst. Hercules Hydraulics, Clearwater, Fla., 1983-85; MIS cons. All-Phase Electric Co., Benton Harbor, Mich., 1985-88; owner, agent State Farm Ins., Benton Harbor, 1988—. Active St. Joseph (Mich.) Mcpl. Band, 1988-91, com. Gilmore Music Festival, Kalamazoo, Mich., 1994; speaker Berrien County Youth Fair, Berrien Springs, Mich., 1991-94; chmn. Flood Relief, Benton Harbor, 1993. Office: State Farm-Heidi Lull Agy 1850 Colfax Ave Benton Harbor MI 49022

LUM, JEAN LOUI JIN, nurse educator; b. Honolulu, Sept. 5, 1938; d. Yee Nung and Pui Ki (Young) L. BS, U. Hawaii, Manoa, 1960; MS in Nursing, U. Calif., San Francisco, 1961; MA, U. Wash., 1969, PhD in Sociology, 1972. Registered nurse, Hawaii. From instr. to prof. Sch. Nursing U. Hawaii Manoa, Honolulu, 1961—, acting dean, 1982, dean, 1982-89; project coordinator Analysis and Planning Personnel Svcs., Western Interstate Commn. Higher Edn., 1977; extramural assoc. div. Rsch. Grants NIH, 1978-79; mem. mgmt. adv. com. Honolulu County Hosp., 1982—; mem. exec. bd. Pacific Health Rsch. Inst., 1980-88; mem. health planning com. East Honolulu, 1978-81; mem. rsch. grants adv. coun. Hawaii Med. Svcs. Assn. Found., Nat. Adv. Coun. for Nursing Rsch., 1990-93. Contbr. articles to profl. jours. Trustee Straub Pacific Health Found., Honolulu. Recipient Nurse of Yr. award Hawaii Nurses Assn., 1982; named Disting. Practitioner in Nursing, Nat. Acads. of Practice, 1986; USPHS grantee, 1967-72. Fellow Am. Acad. Nursing; mem. Am. Nurses Assn., Am. Pacific Nursing Leaders Conf. (pres. 1983-87), Council Nurse Researchers, Nat. League for Nursing (bd. rev. 1981-87), Western Council Higher Edn. for Nurses (chmn. 1984-85), Western Soc. for Research in Nursing, Am. Sociol. Assn., Pacific Sociol. Assn., Assn. for Women in Sci., Hawaii Pub. Health Assn., Hawaii Med. Services Assn. (bd. dirs. 1985-92), Western Inst. Nursing, Mortar Bd., Phi Kappa Phi, Sigma Theta Tau, Alpha Kappa Delta, Delta Kappa Gamma. Episcopalian. Office: U Hawaii-Manoa Sch Nursing Webster 409 2528 The Mall Honolulu HI 96822

LUMBARD, CAROLYN TUCKER, lawyer; b. Union, S.C., Dec. 18, 1942; d. Charles Hubert and Josephine Elizabeth (Thacker) Tucker; m. Dennis Brian Lumbard; children: Lisa Katherine Lumbard Severino, Brian Charles; m. Louis John Wolter, Apr. 29, 1994. BA, Hollins Coll., 1964; MA, Drake U., 1975, MPA, 1978, JD, 1990. Bar: Iowa 1991. Tchr. French. Des Moines Pub. Schs., 1964-67, 75-89; instr. Drake U., Des Moines, 1972-75; pvt. practice, Des Moines, 1991-93; legal counsel Legis. Svc. Bur., Des Moines, 1993—. Coord. art show Iowa Natural Heritage Found., Des Moines; mem. Polk County Conservation Bd., Des Moines, 1987-90; mem., chmn. Iowa Conservation Commn., Des Moines, 1973-83; vice chmn. Greater Des Moines Sister City Commn., 1991—. Home: 2800 Briarwood Pl Des Moines IA 50321 Office: Legis Svc Bur State Capitol Des Moines IA 50319

LUMLEY, SUSAN MCCABE, insurance company executive; b. Bristol, Conn., Mar. 26, 1944; d. James Cornelius and Jean Eleanor (Fucini) McCabe; m. William D. Lumley Jr., Jan. 29, 1984. Student, Ctrl. Conn. State U., 1962-64, Dartmouth Coll., 1983, U. Conn., 1983. Med. underwriter Aetna Life & Casualty, Hartford, Conn., 1964-66; v.p. mgr. Charles G. Marcus Agy., Wethersfield, Conn., 1966—; liaison Ind. Ins. Agts., Wethersfield, 1992. Dir. Better Bus. Bur., Hartford, 1985-89. Mem. Hartford Assn. Ins. Women (pres.-elect 1994—, Ins. Woman of Yr. 1994). Democrat. Roman Catholic. Home: 12 Chestnut Ln East Hartford CT 06118-3507

LUMMIS, CYNTHIA MARIE, lawyer, rancher; b. Cheyenne, Wyo., Sept. 10, 1954; d. Doran Arp and Enid (Bennett) L.; m. Alvin L. Wiederspahn, May 28, 1983; children: Annaliese Alex. BS, U. Wyo., 1976, U. Wyo., 1978; JD, U. Wyo., 1985. Bar: Wyo. 1985, U.S. Dist Ct. of Wyo. 1985, U.S. Ct. of Appeals (10th cir.) 1986. Rancher Lummis Livestock Co., Cheyenne, 1972—; law clk. Wyo. Supreme Ct., Cheyenne, 1985-86; assoc. Wiederspahn, Lummis & Liepas, Cheyenne, 1986—; mem. Wyo. Ho. Judiciary Com., 1979-86, Ho. Agriculture, Pub. Lands & Water Resources Com., 1985-86, Wyo. State Senate, 1993-94, Senate Judiciary Com., 1993-94, Senate Mines, Minerals, Econ. Devel. Com., 1993-94, U. Wyo. Inst. for Environment and Natural Resource Policy and Rsch.; chmn. County Ct. Planning Com., Wyo., 1986-88, Ho. Rev. Com., 1987-92, Joint Revenue Interim Com., 1988-89, 91-92. Sec. Meals on Wheels, Cheyenne, 1985-87; mem. Agrl. Crisis Support Group, Laramie County, Wyo., 1985-87; mem. adv. com. U. Wyo. Sch. Nursing, 1988-90; mem. steering com. Wyo. Heritage Soc., 1986-89. Republican. Lutheran. Club: Rep. Women's (Cheyenne) (legis. chmn. 1982). Office: Wiederspahn Lummis & Liepas 2020 Carey Ave Ste 704 Cheyenne WY 82001-3646*

LUMMIS, MERIAM KATHERINE, human resources manager; b. Perth Amboy, N.J., May 16, 1967; d. Robert Carl and Adair (Trimble) L. BS, Roger Williams U., 1988. Auto rater Covenant Ins., Hartford, Conn., 1988-89; sales assoc. Meier & Frank, Portland, Oreg., 1990-91; from interviewer to human resource mgr. Market Decisions Corp., Portland, Oreg., 1989—. Mem. NAFE, Soc. for Human Resource Mgmt. Republican. Congregationalist. Office: Market Decisions Corp 8959 SW Barbur Blvd Portland OR 97219

LUMPE, SHEILA, state legislator; b. Apr. 17, 1935; m. Gustav H. Lumpe, 1958. AB, Ind. U.; postgrad., Johns Hopkins U.; MA, U. Mo. Mem. Mo. Ho. of Reps. Active Mo. Coun. Women's Econ., Devel. and Tng., Civil Liberties Union; mem. bd. 604 Victims Svc. Coun.; bd. dirs. People to People. Democrat. Home: 6908 Amherst Ave Saint Louis MO 63130-3124 Office: Mo Ho of Reps State Capitol Jefferson City MO 65101*

LUMPKIN, ANNE CRAIG, retired television and radio company executive; b. DeValls Bluff, Ark., Apr. 3, 1919; d. Claude Cleo and Lou (Craig) L. Student, Little Rock Bus. Sch., 1938-39, Patricia Stevens, 1953. Adminstrv. asst. to pres. Sta. KVLC (S.W. Broadcasting), Little Rock, 1949-52, Sta. KGKO (Lakewood Broadcasting), Dallas, 1952-54, Sta. KTLN, Inc., Denver, 1954-58; asst. mgr. Sta. KLRA, Inc., Little Rock, 1958-83; asst. dir. fin. affairs KLRT-TV, Little Rock, 1983-91; retired, 1991. Mem. Ark. Arts Ctr., Little Rock, Fine Arts Club, Little Rock, Nat Audubon Soc., Pulaski County Hist. Soc., Little Rock. Mem. Am. Women in Radio-TV, Am. Bus. Women's Assn., Little Rock Club. Baptist.

LUMPKIN, BETTY STEWART, librarian; b. Anniston, Ala., Apr. 10, 1934; d. Dave Timmons Stewart and Mable Agnes (Stephens) Ogburn; stepfather Davis Leon Ogburn; m. Roy L. Lumpkin Jr., Mar. 20, 1954; 1 child, John Davis. BS in Secondary Edn., U. Chattanooga, 1959; MEd in Aerospace Edn. summa cum laude, Mid. Tenn. State U., 1973. Tchr. Rivermont Elem. Sch., Chattanooga, Tenn., 1966-67; English tchr. Tyner Jr. H.S., Chattanooga, 1967-74; libr. Ooltewah (Tenn.) Mid. Sch., 1974-75, Ooltewah (Tenn.) H.S., 1989—. Author: CD-Rom for Educators and Librarians, 1993. Lyndhurst tchr. grantee Lyndhurst Found., 1988. Mem. Tenn. Libr. Assn. (past bd. dirs., Louise Meredith award 1992), Chattanooga Area Libr. Assn. (past pres.). Republican. Home: 7718 Mahan Gap Rd Ooltewah TN 37363 also: PO Box 659 Harrison TN 37341 Office: OoltewahHS 6123 Mountain View Rd Ooltewah TN 37363

LUNA, PATRICIA ADELE, marketing executive; b. Charleston, S.C., July 22, 1956; d. Benjamin Curtis and Clara Elizabeth (McCrory) L. BS in History, Auburn U., 1978, MEd in History, 1980; MA in Adminstrn., U. Ala., 1981, EdS in Adminstrn., 1984, PhD, ABD in Adminstrn., 1986. Cert. tchr., Ga., Ala. History tchr. Harris County Middle Sch., Ga., 1978-79, head dept., 1979-81; residence hall dir. univ. housing U. Ala., 1981-83, asst. dir. residence life, 1983-85; intern Cornell U., Ithaca, N.Y., 1983; dir. of mktg. Golden Flake Snack Foods, Inc., Birmingham, Ala., 1985-89; sr. v.p. Quest U.S.A., Inc., Atlanta, 1989-90; pres. Promotion Mgmt. Group, Inc., 1990—; cons., lectr. in field. Author: Specialization: A Learning Module, 1979, Grantsmanship, 1981, Alcohol Awareness Programs, 1984; University Programming, 1984; Marketing Residential Life, 1985; The History of Golden Flake Snack Foods, 1986; Golden Flake Snack Foods, Inc., A Case Study, 1987, Cases in Strategic Marketing, 1989, Cases in Strategic Management, 1990, Frequency Marketing, 1992. Fundraiser, U. Ala. Alumni Scholarship Fund, Tuscaloosa, 1983, Am. Diabetes Assn., Tuscaloosa, 1984, Urban Ministries, Birmingham, 1985-88; fundraiser, com. chmn. Spl. Olympics, Tuscaloosa, 1985; fundraiser Am. Cinema Soc., 1988; chmn. Greene County Relief Project, 1982-89; bd. dirs. Cerebral Palsy Found., Tuscaloosa, 1985-86; lay rector and com. chmn. Kairos Prison Ministry, Tutwiler State Prison, Ala., 1986—; lobbyist, com. chmn. task force Justice Fellowship, 1988-91; bd dirs. Internat. Found. Ewha U., Seoul, Korea, 1988-91; chmn. bd. dirs. Epiphany Ministries, 1991—; bd. dir. Hunting Coll. of Fine Arts. Recipient Dir. of Yr. award U. Ala., 1982, 83; Skeets Simonis award, U. Ala., 1984, nat. award Joint Council on Econ. Edn., 1979, rsch. award NSF, 1979; named to Hon. Order Ky. Cols. Commonwealth of Ky., 1985—, Rep. Senatorial Inner Circle, 1986; Com. chmn. Emmaus Ministry, 1985—. Mem. Sales and Mktg. Execs. (chmn. com. 1985-86), Leadership Ala. (pres. 1982-83), Am. Mktg. Assn. (Disting. Leadership award 1987, Commemorative Medal of Honor 1988), Assn. Coll. and Univ. Housing Officers (com. chmn. 1983-85), Nat. Assn. Student Personnel Officers, Snack Food Assn. (mem. mktg. com. and conf. presenter), Internat. Coun. Shopping Ctrs. (Merit award 1991, program com.), Commerce Exec. Soc., Snow Skiing Club, Sailing Club, Omega Rho Sigma (pres. 1983-84), Omicron Delta Kappa, Phi Delta Kappa, Kappa Delta Pi, Phi Alpha Theta. Republican. Methodist. Avocations: skiing, racquetball, tennis, community work, public speaking.

LUNA PADILLA, NITZA ENID, photography educator; b. San Juan, P.R., Mar. 13, 1959; d. Luis and Carmen Iris (Padilla) Luna. BFA, Pratt Inst., 1981; MS, Brooks Inst., 1985. Instr. U. P.R., Carolina, 1981-82, Cultural Inst., San Juan, 1988; asst. prof. photography U. Sacred Heart, Santurce, P.R., 1987—; assoc. dir. communication ctr. U. Sagrado Corazon, Santurce, P.R., 1989-90; juror Avco Fin. Svcs., San Juan, 1988. Contbr. articles to profl. publs.; one-woman shows P.R. Inst. Culture, 1988, Art and History Mus., San Juan, 1989, 94, U. P.R., 1989, 90, Brooks Inst. Photography, Santa Barbara, Calif., 1990, Miriam Walsh Gallery, Glenwood Springs, Colo., 1991, Mus. Ponce, 1991; exhibited in group shows Santa Barbara Mus. Art, 1987, Coll. of Sante Fe, N.Mex., 1988, Durango (Colo.) Arts Ctr., 1988, 90, Laband Art Gallery, L.A., 1989, Cultural Ctr., Vercelli, Italy, 1989, Univ. Union Gallery Calif. Poly. State U, 1990, Durango (Colo.) Arts Ctr., 1990, Coconino Ctr. Arts, Flagstaff, Ariz., 1990, Centro Cultural Washington Irving, Madrid, 1991, L.A. County Fair, 1991, Museo del Grabado Latinoamericano, San Juan, P.R., 1992, 93, 94, also others; in permanent collections; juror Fotografia de prensa "Mandin," 1991-92. MacDowell Colony grantee, Instituto de Cultural Puertorriqueña grantee, 1993, 94. Mem. Soc. Photog. Edn., Friends of Photography. Roman Catholic. Office: U Sagrado Corazón PO Box 12383 San Juan PR 00914-0383

LUND, SISTER CANDIDA, college chancellor; b. Chgo.; d. Fred S. Lund and Katharine (Murray) Lund Heck. BA, Rosary Coll., River Forest, Ill.; MA, Catholic U. Am.; PhD, U. Chgo., 1963; DLitt (hon.), Lincoln Coll., 1968; LLD (hon.), John Marshall Law Sch., 1979; LHD honoris causa, Marymount Coll., 1979; LittD (hon.), St. Mary-of-the Woods Coll., 1994. Pres. Rosary Coll., 1964-81, chancellor, 1981—. Editor: Moments to Remember, 1980, The Days and the Nights: Prayers for Today's Woman, In Joy and in Sorrow, 1984, Coming of Age, 1992, Nunsuch, 1982, God and Me, 1988, Praymates, 1993; author, editor: If I Were Pope, 1987; contbr.: Why Catholic. Mem. women's bd. U. Chgo., 1984—; bd. dirs. The Chgo. Network, 1983-86, The Park Ridge Ctr., 1987—. Recipient Profl. Achievement award U. Chgo. Alumni, 1974, U.S. Catholic award, 1984. Fellow Royal Soc. Arts; mem. Thomas More Assn. (bd. dirs. 1975—), The Arts Club (bd. dirs. 1987—). Home and Office: Rosary Coll 7900 Division St River Forest IL 60305-1099

LUND, CHRISTINE EVA, elementary school counselor; b. East Orange, N.J., Oct. 29, 1956; d. Lowell Dale and Ruth Elizabeth (Carlson) L. BA, Midland Luth. Coll., Fremont, Nebr., 1978; MEd, Boston U., 1982. Cert. elem. tchr. and sch. counselor, Mass. Youth dir. Grace Luth. Ch., LaGrange, Ill., 1978-79; kindergarten tchr. Howard Sch., Fremont, 1979-80; 2d grade tchr. Linden Sch., Fremont, 1980-81; asst. house mgr. South Shore Rehab. Ctr., Quincy, Mass., 1982-83; elem. counselor Meml. Sch., South Natick, Mass., 1983—. Horace Mann grantee, 1988. Mem. Mass. Sch. Counselors Assn. Lutheran. Home: 164 Grant St Framingham MA 01701-8106 Office: Meml Sch 107 Eliot St South Natick MA 01760-5506

LUND, CYNTHIA S., professional society adminstrator; b. Columbus, Ohio, Apr. 11, 1957. AB, Duke U., 1979; MBA, Ohio State U., 1991. Field cons. Am. Heart Assn., Columbus, 1981-84; mgr. ops. Trident Motors, Inc., Columbus, 1984-86; dir. bus. affairs Ohio State Bar Assn., Columbus, 1986-89; dir. comm. and quality review Ohio Soc. CPAs, Columbus, 1989-93; exec. dir. Mo. Soc. CPAs, St. Louis, 1993—. Office: Mo Soc CPAs 275 N Lindberg St 10 Saint Louis MO 63141

LUND, DORIS HIBBS, dietitian; b. Des Moines, Nov. 10, 1923; d. Loyal Burchard and Catharine Mae (McClymond) Hibbs; m. Richard Bodholdt Lund, Nov. 9, 1946; children: Laurel Anne, Richard Douglas, Kristi Jane Lund Lozier. Student, Duchesne Coll., Omaha, 1941-42; BS, Iowa State U., 1946; postgrad., Grand View Coll., Des Moines, 1965; MS, Iowa State U., 1968. Registered dietitian, lic. dietitian. Clk. Russell Stover Candies, Omaha, 1940-42; chemist Martin Bomber Plant, Omaha, 1942-43; dietitian Grand Lake (Colo.) Lodge, 1946; tailoring instr. Ottumwa Pub. Schs., 1952-53; cookery instr. Des Moines Pub. Schs., 1958-62; dietitian Calvin Manor, Des Moines, 1963; home economist Am. Wool Coun./Am. Lamb Coun., Denver, 1963-65, The Merchandising Group of N.Y., 1965-68, Thomas Wolff, Pub. Rels., 1968-70; home economist weekly TV program Iowa Power Co., 1968-70; cons. in child nutrition programs Iowa Dept. Edn., Des Moines, 1970—; Mem. Iowa Home Economists in Bus. (pres. 1962-63), PEO, Pi Beta Phi (Iowa Gamma chpt. pres. 1945-46). Pres. Callanan Jr. H.S. PTA, 1964, Roosevelt H.S. PTA, 1966; pres., mem. Ctrl. Presbyn. Mariners, Des Moines; ruling elder, clk. of session Ctrl. Presbyn. Session, Des Moines, 1972-78; amb. Friendship Force Internat., 1982—. Duchesne Coll. 4 yr. scholar. Mem. Iowa Home Economists in Bus. (pres. 1962-63), PEO, Pi Beta Phi (pres. 1945-46). Republican. Home: 105 34th St Des Moines IA 50312 Office: Iowa Dept Edn Grimes State Office Bldg Des Moines IA 50319

LUND, LOIS A., food science and human nutrition educator; b. Thief River Falls, Minn., Aug. 9, 1927; d. Robert J. and E. Luella (Tosdal) L. BS, U. Minn., 1949, MS, 1954, PhD, 1966. Instr. foods U. Iowa, 1951-55, U. Minn., 1955-63; assoc. prof., dir. core studies program, asst. dir. Sch. Home Econs., 1966-68; research fellow U.S. Dept. Agrl., 1963-66; assoc. dean, dir. Sch. Home Econs. Ohio State U., 1969-72; dean Coll. Human Ecology Mich. State U., East Lansing, 1973-85, prof. food sci. and human nutrition, 1985—; bd. dirs. Consumers Power Co., Jackson, Mich., CMS Energy, Dearborn, Mich. Contbr. articles to profl. jours. Recipient Betty award for excellence in teaching U. Minn., 1958, 63, 68, Hon. Alumni award Mich. State U., 1977, Outstanding Achievement award U. Minn. Alumni Assn., 1977. Mem. Am. Coun. on Consumer Interest, Am. Assn. Cereal Chemists, Inst. Food Technologists, Am. Agrl. Econs. Assn., Soc. for Nutrition Edn., Pi Lambda Theta, Phi Kappa Phi, Phi Upsilon Omicron, Omicron Nu (nat. treas. 1971-74, 84-86), Sigma Delta Epsilon. Lutheran. Home: 5927 Shadowlawn Dr East Lansing MI 48823-2379 Office: Mich State U Dept Food Sci and Human Nutrition East Lansing MI 48824

LUND, RITA POLLARD, aerospace consultant; b. Vallscreek, W.Va., Aug. 28, 1950; d. Willard Garfield and Faye Ethel (Perry) Pollard; m. James William Lund, Dec. 30, 1969. Student, Alexandria Sch. Nursing, 1989-90, Columbia Pacific U., 1989-91. Confidential asst. U.S. Ho. of Reps., Washington, 1975-76; exec. asst. White House Domestic Policy Staff, Washington, 1977-82, White House Sci. Office, Washington, 1982-83; asst. to pres. Telecom Futures Inc., Washington, 1983-84, v.p. for adminstrn., 1985-86; internat. accounts mgr. TFI Ltd., McLean, Va., 1987-89; ind. cons. telecommunications Washington, 1989-90, aerospace cons., 1990—; sec. ELS Corp., 1992. Mem. AIAA, NAFE, Women in Aerospace, Am. Space Transp. Assn., Competitive Alliance Space Enterprise. Republican. Methodist. Home: 9020 Patton Blvd Alexandria VA 22309-3334

LUNDAHL, MARGARET ANN, law librarian; b. Chgo., Nov. 26, 1948; d. John E. and Lois N. (Olausson) L.; m. Gary L. Tucker, June, 1971 (div. 1974). Student, U. Chgo., 1966-68, MBA, 1969, MA, 1976; JD, Ill. Institute Tech., 1980. Bar: Ill. 1980. Asst. bus. librarian U. Chgo. Grad. Sch. Bus., 1969-71; cataloger U. Chgo. Law Library, 1971-76; librarian Isham, Lincoln, & Beale, Chgo., 1976-83; prin. Lundahl Enterprises, Chgo., 1981—. Mem. Am. Assn. Law Libraries, ABA, Spl. Libraries Assn., Chgo. Bar Assn. Home and Office: Lundahl Enterprises 10128 S Avenue J Chicago IL 60617-6009

LUNDBERG, LOIS ANN, property management company executive; b. Tulsa, Sept. 21, 1928; d. John T. and Anna M. (Patterson) McQuay; m. Ted W. Lundberg, Sept. 30, 1954; children: Linda Ann, Sharon Lynn. With Pacific Telephone, 1950-65; gen. ptnr. McLund Co. Property Mgmt., 1972—; realtor Morgan Realty, 1974—; with Nason, Lundberg and Assocs., Orange, Calif., 1983-85, pres., campaign cons., 1985—; pres. NLS Comm. Inc. Bd. dirs. Luth. Ch. of the Master, La Habra, Calif., 1970-75, v.p. of congregation, 1986-87; mem. bd. trustees Nixon Law Office Preservation, Inc., 1972-75, Regional Ctr. of Orange County, 1982; bd. dirs. UCI Med. Ctr./Burn Ctr., 1982; apptd. Council on Criminal Justice Com., 1983—; mem. adv. bd. KOCE-TV, 1976—, La Habra Children's Mus., 1985—. Recipient Gov. Ronald Reagan award, 1967, Woman of Achievement award City of La Habra, 1979; named Outstanding Rep. of Orange County, 1978. Lutheran. Home: 1341 Carmela Ln La Habra CA 90631-3311 Office: Nason Lundberg and Assocs 320 W Whittier Blvd Ste 223 La Habra CA 90631

LUNDBY, MARY A., state legislator; b. Carroll County, Feb. 2, 1948; d. Edward A. and Elizabeth Hoehl; m. Michael Lundby, 1971; 1 child, Daniel. BA in History, Upper Iowa U., 1971. Former staff asst. Senator Roger Jepsen; mem. Iowa State Senate. Active Solid Waste Adv. Com. Republican. Home: 1240 14th St Marion IA 52302-2562 Office: Iowa State Senate State Capitol Des Moines IA 50319*

LUNDE, KATHERINE LAMONTAGNE, educational consultant; b. Kankakee, Ill., May 3, 1947; d. James Armond and Frances Elizabeth (Maas) LaMontagne; m. Walter A. Lunde Jr., June 15,1969; children: Lisa Christine, Walter James. BS, No. Ill. U., 1969; postgrad., Jacksonville (Fla.) U., 1972. Cert. elem., secondary and early childhood educator. Tchr. 1st grade Kenwood Elem. Sch., Ft. Walton Beach, Fla.; kindergarten tchr., supr. Orange Park (Fla.) Kindergarten; asst. dir. Stoneway Sch., Stoneway Pvt. Sch., Plano, Tex.; dir. Westminster Preschool and Kindergarten, Dallas; MNKA workshop design team leader, 1990. Track coach Spl. Olympics, 1981-83; learning disabilities tutor, 1978-85; bd. dirs. Mi Escuelita Preschs., Inc., 1985-90, v.p. bd. dirs., 1989-90. Grantee Sewell Fund, Lard Trust; recipient Christa McAuliffe Outstanding Educator award, 1994. Mem. ASCD, Nat. Assn. Edn. Young Children (life), Dallas Assn. Edn. Young Children, Collin County Assn. Edn. Young Children, Meth. Nursery and Kindergarten Assn. (pres.-elect 1992-93), Kappa Delta Pi. Office: 8200 Devonshire Dr Dallas TX 75209-4425

LUNDEN, JOAN, television personality; b. Fair Oaks, CA, Sept. 19, 1950; d. Erle Murray and Gladyce Lorraine (Somervill) Blunden; children: Jamie Beryl, Lindsay Leigh, Sarah Emily. Student, Universidad de Las Americas, Mexico City, U. Calif., Calif. State U., Am. River Coll., Sacramento, Calif. Began broadcasting career as co-anchor and prodr. at Sta. KCRA-TV and Radio, Sacramento, 1973-75; with Sta. WABC-TV, N.Y.C., 1975—, co-anchor, 1976-80; co-host Good Morning America, ABC-TV, 1980—; host special report TV for Whittle Comm.; host Everyday with Joan Lunden, 1989; film appearances include: Macho Callahan, 1970, What About Bob?, 1991; co-author: (with Andy Friedburg) Good Morning, I'm Joan Lunden, 1986, (with Michael Krauss) Joan Lunden's Mother's Minutes, 1986, Your Newborn Baby; syndicated columnist: Parent's Notes. Recipient Outstanding Mother of Yr. award, Nat. Mother's Day Com., 1982; Albert Einstein Coll. of Yeshiva U. Spirit of Achievement award; Nat. Women's Polit. Caucus award; NJ Divsn. of Civil Rights award; Baylor U. Outstanding Woman of the Year award. Office: Good Morning Am 147 Columbus Ave New York NY 10023-5900*

LUNDERGAN, BARBARA KEOUGH, lawyer; b. Chgo., Nov. 6, 1938; d. Edward E. and Eleanor A. (Erickson) Keough; m. James A. Lundergan, Dec. 29, 1962; children—Matthew K., Mary Alice. B.A., U. Ill., 1960; J.D., Loyola U., Chgo., 1964. Bar: Ill. 1964, U.S. Dist. Ct. (no. dist.) Ill. 1964, U.S. Tax Ct. 1974. With Seyfarth, Shaw, Fairweather & Geraldson, Chgo., 1964—, ptnr., 1971—. Fellow Am. Coll. Trust and Estate Counsel; mem. ABA (com. on fed. taxation), Ill. Bar Assn. (coun. sect. on fed. taxation 1983-91, chair 1989, coun. sect. on trusts and estates sect. coun. 1992—, editl. bd. Ill. Bar Jour. 1993—), Chgo. Bar Assn. (chmn. trust law com. 1982-83, com. on fed. taxation). Office: Seyfarth Shaw Fairweather & Geraldson 55 E Monroe St Chicago IL 60603

LUNDGREN, CLARA ELOISE, public affairs administrator, journalist; b. Temple, Tex., Mar. 7, 1951; d. Claude Elton and Klara (Csirmaz) L. AA, Temple Jr. Coll., 1971; BJ, U. Tex., 1973; MA, Columbia Pacific U., 1986. Reporter Temple Daily Telegram, 1970-72; news editor Austin (Tex.) Am.-Statesman, 1972-75; mng. editor Stillhouse Hollow Pubs., Inc., Belton, 1975-77; pub. affairs officer Darnall Army Community Hosp., Ft. Hood, Tex., 1978-80; editor Ft. Hood Sentinel III Corps, 1980-85; command info. officer Pub. Affairs Office III Corps, Ft. Hood, 1985-87, community relations officer, 1987-88, dep. pub. affairs officer, 1988-94; pub. info. dir. Texas Dept. Transp., Austin, 1994—. Bd. dirs. Helping Our Brothers Out, Inc. Recipient Nat. Observer Journalistic Achievement award Dow Jones & Co., 1971, Superior Civilian Svc. award Dept. Army, 1989, Meritorious Civilian Svc. award, 1992, Exceptional Civilian Svc. award, 1994. Mem. Exec. Women in Tex. Govt., Nat. Assn. Govt. Communicators, Tex. Good Rds./Transp. Assn. Home: 2513 W 45th Austin TX 78756 Office: Pub Info Office Dept Transp 125 E 11th St Austin TX 78701-2409

LUNDGREN, RUTH WILLIAMSON WOOD (RUTH LUNDGREN WILLIAMSON WOOD), public relations executive, writer; b. Bklyn.; d. William and Hanna (Carlson) L.; m. W. F. Williamson, Dec. 17, 1949 (dec.); children: John Ross (dec.), Mark Ward; m. John Earle Wood, Aug. 27, 1988 (dec.). Student, Bklyn. Coll., 1936-41, Columbia U., 1942. Assoc. editor Everywoman's mag., 1940-42; pub. relations staff exec. J.M. Mathes Advt. Agy., 1942-45; dir. pub. relations Pan-Am. Coffee Bur., 1945-48; pres. Ruth Lundgren Ltd., N.Y.C., 1948—. Pub. Ruth Lundgren Newsletter, 1950-58; writer daily column St. Petersburg (Fla.) Times, 1956-60; contbg. editor, writer monthly column Motor Boating and Sailing mag., 1962-80; contbr. to popular profl. publs. Home and Office: 3319 Bayfront Dr Baldwin NY 11510-5103

LUNDQUIST, LINDA ANN JOHNSON, insurance professional; b. Iowa City, Iowa, Aug. 15, 1945; d. Elmer Clinton and Georgia Joan (Molloy) L.; m. Scott Arthur Johnson, Sept. 26, 1981. BA, U. Iowa, 1968. Civil engring. drafter firm Shive-Hattery & Assocs., Iowa City, 1968-78; dir. drafting svcs. firm Shoemaker & Haaland, Profl. Engrs., Coralville, Iowa, 1978-82; mktg. rep. Veenstra & Kimm, Inc., Engineers and Planners, Iowa City and West Des Moines, 1982-86; head mktg. support dept. Stanley Cons. Inc., Muscatine, Iowa, 1986-87; agt. State Farm Ins. Cos., 1988—. mem. spl. appointments Urban Environment Ad Hoc Com., Iowa City, 1985-86, groundwater protection ad hoc adv. com. State Iowa, 1987-88. Recipient Spl. Merit award Cedar Rapids Mus. Art, Iowa, 1979, Svc. award Epsilon Pi, 1993. Mem. Greater Iowa City Area C. of C. (environ. concerns com. 1982-87, chair 1984-86, govt. affairs com. 1988—), Iowa Groundwater Assn. (bd. dirs. 1986-89), Nat. Assn. Life Underwriters (Nat. Sales Achievement award 1991, 93, Louis I. Dublin Nat. Cmty. award 1993-94), Iowa Assn. Life Underwriters, Nat. Wildlife Fedn., Iowa Wildlife Fedn. (conservation issues com. 1987-88), Iowa City Assn. Life Underwriters (bd. dirs. 1993—, chmn. community svc. com. 1993—), Internat. Fund Animal Welfare, Wilderness Soc., World Wildlife Fund, Nature Conservancy, The Humane Farming Assn., The Humane Soc. of USA, Physicians Com. Responsible Medicine, Alpha Gamma Delta (bd. dirs. house assn. 1986—, alumnae advisor 1991—). Avocations: drawing, watercolors, dance. Office: 405 Highway 1 W Iowa City IA 52246-4205

LUNDQUIST, VIRGINIA ARETA, public affairs executive; b. Cleve., Oct. 8, 1949; d. Roger E. and Margaret A. (Grober) Kerr; m. Eric Christopher Lundquist, Apr. 14, 1972. BA in English Lit., U. Detroit, 1971, MBA in Mktg., 1978. Asst. editor FTD news Florists Transworld Delivery Assn., Detroit, 1971-74; copy editor Campbell-Ewald Advt., Detroit, 1974-78; advt. & promotion mgr. Am. Motors Corp., Southfield, Mich., 1978-87; European advt. mgr. Chrysler Motors Corp., Highland Park, Mich., 1987-88; v.p. comm. United Technologies Automotive, Dearborn, Mich., 1988-92; v.p. pub. affairs AlliedSignal Automotive, Southfield, 1992—. Trustee Detroit Symphony Orch., Detroit, 1991—. Mem. Adcraft Club Detroit, Econ. Club Detroit, Pub. Rels. Soc. Am. Office: AlliedSignal Automotive 20650 Civic Center Dr Southfield MI 48076-4110

LUNDSTROM, MARJIE, newspaper editor. Grad., U. Nebr. Columnist, editor, nat. corr. The Denver Post, 1981-89; with The Sacramento Bee, 1989-90, 91—; nat. corr. Gannett News Svc., Washington, 1990-91. Recipient Pulitzer Prize for nat. reporting, 1991. Office: The Sacramento Bee 2100 Q St PO Box 15779 Sacramento CA 95852

LUNDY, BARBARA KILPATRICK, educational supervisor; b. Philadelphia, Miss., Aug. 29, 1946; d. Aubrey Earl and Ester Naomi (Moore) Kilpatrick; m. Charles Edward Lundy, Sr., July 9, 1966; children: Charles Edward, Jr., Jon Patrick, Aubrey Joshua. BS in Edn., North Ga. Coll., 1973, MEd, 1976; EdD, Nova U., 1993. Para-profl. Cherokee County Bd. Edn., Canton, Ga., 1967-73; tchr. Habersham County Bd. Edn., Cornelia, Ga., 1973-80; tchr. Twiggs County Bd. Edn., Jeffersonville, Ga., 1980-87, adminstr., supr., 1987—. Officer PTA, Canton, 1968-72, Cornelia, 1976-79. Scholar PTA, 1972. Mem. NEA, Ga. Edn. Assn. (various local offices 1980—), Ga. Compensatory Edn. Leaders, Internat. Reading Assn. (pres. 1989), Ga. Internat. Reading Assn. (pres. 1989), Middle Ga. Internat. Reading Assn. (pres. 1989), Twiggs Edn. Assn., Alpha Delta Kappa. Baptist. Home: Rt 4 PO Box 143 A1 Cochran GA 31014

LUNDY, SADIE ALLEN, small business owner; b. Milton, Fla., Mar. 29, 1918; d. Stephen Grover and Martha Ellen (Harter) Allen; m. Wilson Tate Lundy, May 17, 1939 (dec. 1962); children: Wilson Tate Jr., Houston Allen, Michael David, Robert Douglas, Martha Jo-Ellen. Degree in acctg., Graceland Coll., 1938. Acct. Powers Furniture Co., Milton, Fla., 1939-40, Lundy Oil Co., Milton, 1941-52; controller First Fed. Savs. & Loan, Kansas City, Mo., 1953-55, Herald Pub. Co., Independence, Mo., 1956-58; mgr. Baird &

Son Toy Co., Kansas City, Mo., 1959-62; regional mgr. Emmons Jewelers of N.Y., Kansas City, 1963-65; owner, pres. Lundy Tax Service, Independence, 1965-85; corporate sec., purchasing mgr. Optimation, Inc., Independence, 1974-85, mgr., 1985—; v.p. Lundy Oil Co., Milton, 1941-52. Contbr. articles to profl. jours. Mem. com. Neighborhood Council, Independence, 1985. Mem. Am. Bus. Women's Assn., Independence C. of C. (mem. com. 1965-85). Republican. Mem. Reorganized Ch. of Jesus Christ of Latter Day Saints. Club: Independence Women's. Home: PO Box 520238 Independence MO 64052-0238 Office: Optimation Inc 300 N Osage Independence MO 64050

LUNENFELD, SUSANNAH VINCENT DYE, construction company executive, consultant; b. Amarillo, Tex., Mar. 20, 1940; d. Everett Lee Jr. and Mary Alice (Ramsdell) Dye; m. Fred Lunenfeld, Aug. 26, 1966; 1 child, Peter Vincent. BA in Econs., U. Tex., 1963; cert. light constrn. and devel. mgmt., U. Calif., Irvine, 1988. Lic. gen. contractor; cert. constrn. document technologist. Tchr. Ysleta Sch. Dist., El Paso, Tex., 1963-75; inspector, constrn. City of Irvine, Calif., 1980-88; project mgr. Conwest Constrn. Inc., Pasadena, Calif., 1989-90; prin., ptnr. Dean Colin Assocs., Sierra Madre, Calif., 1991—. Mem. Constrn. Specifications Inst., Roof Cons. Inst. Home: 2429 Oneida St # 2 Pasadena CA 91107 Office: Dean Colin Assocs 1130 Arno Dr Sierra Madre CA 91024

LUNN, KITTY ELIZABETH, actress; b. New Orleans, Aug. 5, 1950; d. Hugh I. Morrison and Beatrice (McClung) Farrell; m. Andrew Macmillan, Dec. 21, 1989. Student, Washington Sch. Ballet, 1965-68, Neighborhood Playhouse Sch., 1968-70, CUNY, 1991—. Dancer Washington Ballet, 1965-68; radio producer WOR Radio, N.Y.C., 1983-85, WABC Talk Radio, N.Y.C., 1985-87; performer CBS TV, N.Y.C., 1990—. Prin. works include Agnes of God, 1992-94, Fan's False, False Face Soc., 1990, The Waiting, 1990, Sand Dragons, 1990, As the World Turns, 1990-92, Awakenings, 1990, Eyes of a Stranger, 1979, numerous TV appearances, 1978-86; dancer Cleve. Ballet, Dancing Wheels. Bd. dirs. Hosp. Audiences, Inc., N.Y.C., 1990—; dir. svcs. people with disabilities Actors' Work Program, N.Y.C., 1991—; mentor networking project YWCA, N.Y.C., 1991; mem. White House Conf. on Libr. and Info. Svcs., Washington, 1991; N.Y. State Libr. regent advisor; del. Dem. Nat. Conv., 1992. Named Belle Zeller scholar, CUNY, 1993. Mem. SAG, AFTRA (nat. bd. dirs.), Nat. Alliance Broadcast Engrs. and Technicians, Actor's Equity Assn. (councillor Eastern Regional adv. bd. 1990—, chair performers with disabilities com. 1990—), 504 Dem. Club (officer). Roman Catholic. Office: Actors' Equity Assn 165 W 46th St Fl 15 New York NY 10036-2501

LUNZ, NANCY ANN, real estate broker, mortgage broker; b. Buffalo, Apr. 20, 1947; d. Clyde Frederick and Marjorie Marie (Sagerman) Redding; m. David Lunz, 1967 (div. 1973); children: Christopher, Jennifer Robin. Grad., Gold Coast Sch. Real Estate, Miami, Fla., 1989, 91, 92, 93. Lic. cmty. assn. mgr. Security mgr. ISC Security, North Miami, Fla., 1973-77; owner, proprietor Master Maintenance, North Miami, 1977-83; property and condo mgr. PMI Property Mgmt., Inc., Miami, 1983-87; property mgr. Fla. East Coast Properties, North Miami, 1987-89, Cardinal Industries, Miami, 1990-93; broker, owner R.C. Real Estate, Miami, 1993—. Republican. Home: 725 NW 178th Ter Miami FL 33169-4716

LUONGO, LUCILLE FRANCESCA, communications company executive; b. N.Y.C., May 29, 1948; d. Carmine and Jean (Gubitosi) Ariniello. BA in English and Speech, Hofstra U., 1970, MA in Communications, 1975. Tchr. Roosevelt (N.Y.) High Sch.; exec. sec. Katz Communications, Inc., N.Y.C., 1978-79, asst. dir. corp. communications, 1979-81, dir. communication svcs., 1981-82, dir. corp. rels., 1982-85, v.p. corp. rels., 1985-91, sr. v.p. corp. communications, 1991—. Mem. NAFE, Internat. Radio and TV Soc., Am. Women in Radio and TV (pres., trustee found.), Broadcast Promotion and Mktg. Execs., The Caption Ctr. Adv. Bd. Office: Katz Media Corp 125 W 55th St New York NY 10019-5369

LUPOLETTI, CLAUDIA ANN, specialty leasing agent; b. Queens, N.Y., Nov. 11, 1961; d. Richard Mark and Joy E. (Betty) L. BA in English Lit., Gettysburg Coll., 1983. Cert. elem. tchr. Asst. buyer Harris Originals, Inc., Hauppauge, N.Y., 1983-85, TSS Seedmans/Finders Keepers, Bklyn., 1985-86; mktg. dir., account assoc. Sunrise Mall/Mittchell Manning Assocs., N.Y.C. and Massapequa, N.Y., 1986-88; mktg. dir. Kravco, Inc./Green Acres Mall, King of Prussia, Pa., Valley Stream, N.Y., 1988-90, Compass Retail/Green Acres Mall, Atlanta, Valley Stream, 1991; dir. specialty leasing Compass Retail, Inc./Green Acres Mall, Atlanta, Valley Stream, 1991-93, EQK Green Acres Trust/Green Acres Mall Corp., Valley Stream, N.Y., Valley Stream, 1994—. Mem. Pvt. Industry Coun., Hempstead, N.Y., 1989-91. Mem. Internat. Coun. Shopping Ctrs., NY/NJ Coun. Shopping Ctrs., Valley Stream C. of C. Home: 40 Alhambra Dr Oceanside NY 11572-5425 Office: Green Acres Mall Corp 2034 Green Acres Mall Valley Stream NY 11581-1545

LUPONE, PATTI, actress; b. Northport, L.I., N.Y., Apr. 21, 1949; d. Orlando Joseph and Angela Louise (Patti) LuP.; m. Matt Johnston; 1 child, Joshua Luke. BFA, The Juilliard Sch., 1972. Off-Broadway prodns. include: The Woods, School for Scandal, The Lower Depths, Stage Directions; appeared in Broadway prodns.: Next Time I'll Sing to You, The Time of Your Life, The Three Sisters, The Robber Bridegroom (Tony award nominee), The Water Engine, The Beggar's Opera, Edward II, The Baker's Wife, 1976, The Woods, 1977, Working, 1978, Catchpenny Twist, 1978, As You Like It, 1982, The Cradle Will Rock, 1983, Stars of Broadway, 1983, Edmond, 1982, Oliver, 1984; star Broadway musicals Evita, 1979 (Best Actress in Musical Tony award 1980), Anything Goes, 1987; London prodns. Les Miserables, 1985, Sunset Boulevard, 1993; films include: King of the Gypsies, 1978, 1941, 1979, Fighting Back, 1982, Witness, 1985, Wise Guys, 1986, Driving Miss Daisy, 1989; TV Appearances include: Kitty, The Time of Your Life, Lady Bird in LBJ, 1987, The Water Engine, 1992, Family Prayers, 1993; TV series, Life Goes On, 1989-93. Office: Duva-Flack Assocs Inc Ste 1407 200 West 57th St New York NY 10019*

LUPTON, ELLEN, curator, graphic designer; b. Phila., Dec. 1, 1963; d. William La Rue and Mary Jane Laura (Hohman) L.; m. Jerry Abbott Miller, Sept. 22, 1990. BFA, Cooper Union, 1985. Curator Herb Lubalin Study Ctr, The Cooper Union, N.Y.C., 1985-92; curator of contemporary design Cooper-Hewitt Nat. Mus. of Design, Smithsonian Institution, N.Y.C., 1992—; ptnr., cons. Design Writing Rsch., N.Y.C., 1985—. Author: Mechanical Brides: Women and Machines from Home to Office, 1993, (with J.A. Miller) The Bathroom, The Kitchen and The Aesthetics of Waste, 1992; editor: (with Miller) The Bauhaus and Design Theory, 1991. Mem. Am. Inst. Graphic Arts (bd. dirs. 1992—). Democrat. Office: Cooper-Hewitt Mus 2 E 91st St New York NY 10003*

LUPTON, MARY HOSMER, retired small business owner; b. Olympia, Wash., Jan. 2, 1914; d. Kenneth Winthrop and Mary Louise (Wheeler) Hosmer; student Gunston Hall Jr. Coll., 1932-33; BS in Edn., U. Va., 1940; m. Keith Brahe Wiley, Oct. 12, 1940 (dec. Apr. 1955); children: Sarah Hosmer Wiley Guise, Victoria Brahe-Wiley; m. Thomas George Lupton, Nov. 27, 1965 (dec. Feb. 1989); 1 stepson, Andrew Henshaw. Ptnr., Wakefield Press, Earlysville, Va., 1940-55; owner, operator Wakefield Forest Bookshop, Earlysville, 1955-65, Forest Bookshop, Charlottesville, 1965-85, Wakefield Forest Tree Farm, 1955-85. Contbr. articles to profl. mags. Corr. sec. Charlottesville-Albemarle Civic League, 1963-64; sec. Instructive Vis. Nurses Assn., Charlottesville, 1961-62; chmn. pub. info. Charlottesville chpt. Va. Mus. Fine Arts, 1970-77; mem. writers' adv. panel Va. Center for Creative Arts, 1973-75, chmn. pub. info., 1976-77; mem. Albemarle County Forestry Com., 1961-62; bd. dirs. Charlottesville-Albemarle Mental Health Assn., 1980-82, 89-91. Mem. AAUW, DAR (Am. Heritage com. chmn. 1983-85, 89-91), Assns. of U. Va. Libr., New Eng. Hist. Geneal. Soc., Conn. Soc. Genealogists, Geneal. Soc. Va., Albemarle County hist. socs., Va. Soc. Mayflower Descs. (asst. state historian 1979-82), LWV, Soc. Mayflower Descs., Am. Soc. Psychical Research, Brit. Soc. Psychical Rsch., Nature Conservancy, Charlottesville Soc. of Friends, Chi Omega. Unitarian. Address: 2600 Barracks Rd Apt 361 Charlottesville VA 22901-2195

LURIA, ZELLA HURWITZ, psychology educator; b. N.Y.C., Feb. 18, 1924; d. Hyman Hurwitz and Dora (Garbarsky) H.; m. Salvador Edward Luria, Apr. 18, 1945; 1 child, Daniel David. BA, Bklyn., 1944; MA, Ind. U., 1947, PhD, 1951. lic. clin. psychologist, Mass. Ford Found. postdoctoral fellow U. Ill., Urbana, 1951-53, Russell Sage found. fellow, 1953-56, clin. researcher, 1954-58; asst. prof. psychology Tufts U., Medford, Mass., 1958-62, assoc. prof., 1962-70, prof., 1970—; psychiatry lectr. Mass. Gen. Hosp., Boston, 1970-79; vis. scholar Stanford U., 1977, 83; vis. prof. UCLA, 1992, U. Mich., 1993. Sr. author: Psychology of Human Sexuality, 1979, Human Sexuality, 1987. Postdoctoral fellow USPHS, Paris, 1963-64, Bunting fellow Radcliffe Coll., 1989-90; Mellon Found. Faculty grantee Wellesley Coll., 1979-80. Mem. Tufts U. Am. Assn. Univ. Profs. (pres. 1986-87). Home: 221 Mount Auburn Cambridge MA 02138-9999 Office: Tufts Univ Dept Of Psychology Medford MA 02155

LURIE, ALISON, author; b. Chgo., Sept. 3, 1926; children: John, Jeremy, Joshua. AB, Radcliffe Coll., 1947. Lectr. English Cornell U., 1969-73; adj. assoc. prof. English Cornell U., Ithaca, N.Y., 1973-76, assoc. prof., 1976-79, prof., 1979—. Author: V.R. Lang: A Memoir, 1959, Love and Friendship, 1962, The Nowhere City, 1965, Imaginary Friends, 1967, Real People, 1969, The War Between the Tates, 1974, Only Children, 1979, The Language of Clothes, 1981, Foreign Affairs, 1984, The Truth About Lorin Jones, 1988, Don't Tell the Grownups, 1990, Women and Ghosts, 1994. Recipient award in lit. Am. Acad. Arts and Letters, 1978, Pulitzer prize in fiction, 1985; fellow Yaddo Found., 1963-64, 66, Guggenheim Found., 1965, Rockefeller Found., 1967. Office: Cornell U Dept English Ithaca NY 14853

LUSBY, GRACE IRENE, infection control nurse practitioner; b. Huntington Park, Calif., Aug. 20, 1935; d. Fletcher Homer and Charlotte Ione (Hayden) L. BS in Nursing, U. Calif., San Francisco, 1964, MS, 1968; cert. program in epidemiology, U. Calif., San Diego, 1981. RN, pub. health nurse, psychiat. nurse. Staff nurse, head nurse cancer rsch. unit U. Calif., San Francisco, 1964-66; pvt. duty nurse open heart surgery Profl. Registry, San Francisco, 1966-68; infection control coord. San Francisco Gen. Hosp., 1969-92; infection control cons. Oakland, Calif., 1992—; infection control rep. Calif. State Task Force on AIDS, Sacramento, 1983-87, U. Calif.-San Francisco AIDS Task Force, 1983-92; co-establisher 1st infection control program for AIDS San Francisco Gen. Hosp., 1983; infection control-adv. coms. Svc. Employees Internat. Union (Labor), Calif. Nurses Assn., Mayor's Homeless Com., CAL-OSHA, others, San Francisco, 1985—; infection control cons. emergency, home care, skill nursing, psychiatry, San Francisco, 1985—. Contbr. chpts. to books. Recipient Founder's award U. Calif.-San Francisco AIDS/ARC Update, 1988. Mem. Assn. Practitioners of Infection Control (past treas., rec. sec., chair AIDS resource group), PEO Sisterhood (rec. sec., corr. sec.), Women's AIDS Network (charter), Sigma Theta Tau. Home and Office: 5966 Chabolyn Ter Oakland CA 94618

LUSEBRINK, VIJA BERGS, art therapist, educator; b. Riga, Latvia, July 29, 1924; d. Alfreds Egons and Anna (Rozentals) Bergs; children: Ingrid, Karen, Anita. BS, U. Nev., 1951; MA, U. Calif., Berkeley, 1964; PhD, U. Louisville, 1984. Practicing artist Palo Alto, Calif., 1964-69; art therapist Agnews State Hosp., San Jose, Calif., 1969-73; lectr. Calif. State U., Sacramento, 1976; prof. U. Louisville, 1974—, dir. Expressive Therapies, 1986—; guest faculty Coll. Notre Dame, Belmont, Calif., 1980, 89, 92, Fla. State U., Tallahassee, 1991, 93, U. N.Mex., Albuquerque, 1982; pvt. cons., Louisville, 1977—. Author: Imagery and Visual Expression in Therapy, 1990; mem. editl. bd. The Arts in Psychotherapy, 1987—, Art Therapy, 1990—; contbr. articles to profl. jours. Grantee Ky. Humanities Coun., 1987, Flow Fund, N.Y., 1993. Mem. APA, Am. Art Therapy Assn. (rsch. chair 1992), Am. Assn. Study of Mental Imagery (mem. credentials com. 1992), No. Calif. Art Therapy Assn. (hon. life), Ky. Art Therapy Assn. Office: Expressive Therapies U Louisville Louisville KY 40292

LUSHER, JEANNE MARIE, pediatric hematologist, educator; b. Toledo, June 9, 1935; d. Arnold Christian and Violet Cecilia (French) L. BS summa cum laude, U. Cin., 1956, MD, 1960. Lic. physician, Mich.; cert. pediatrics and hematology/oncology Am. Bd. Pediatrics. Resident in pediatrics Tulane divsn. Charity Hosp. La., New Orleans, 1961-64; fellow in pediatric hematology-oncology Child Rsch. Ctr. Mich., Detroit, 1964-65, St. Louis Children's Hosp./Washington U., 1965-66; instr. pediatrics Sch. Medicine Washington U., St. Louis, 1965-66; from instr. to assoc. prof. pediatrics Sch. Medicine Wayne State U., Detroit, 1966-74, prof. pediatrics, 1974—; dir. divsn. hematology-oncology Children's Hosp. Mich., Detroit, 1976—; Marion I. Barnhart prof. hemostasis rsch. Sch. Medicine Wayne State U., Detroit, 1989—; med. dir. Nat. Hemophilia Found., N.Y.C., 1987-94, chmn. med. and sci. adv. coun., 1994—. Author, editor: Treatment of Bleeding Disorders with Blood Components, 1980, Sickle Cell, 1974, 76, 81, Hemophilia and von Willebrand Disease in the 1990's, 1991, Acquired Bleeding Disorder in Children, 1981, F VIII/von Willebrand Factor and Platelets in Health and Disease, 1987, Inhibitors to Factor VIII, 1994, The Science and Politics of Women's Health in America, 1995. Mem. Citizens Info. Com., Pontiac Township, Mich., 1980-82; apptd. mem. Hazardous Waste Incinerator Commn., Oakland County, Mich., 1981. Recipient Disting. Alumnus award U. Cin. Alumni Assn., 1990. Mem. Am. Bd. Pediatrics (chmn. sub-bd. hematology-oncology 1988-90), Am. Soc. Heatology (chmn. sci. com. pediatrics 1991-92), Am. Pediatric Soc., Mich. Humane Soc., Internat. Soc. Thrombosis-Hemostasis (chmn. factor VII/IX subcom. 1985-90, sec., chmn. elect scientific and standardization com. 1994—), Soc. Pediatric Rsch. Office: Children's Hosp Mich 3901 Beaubien Detroit MI 48201

LUSK, GLENNA RAE KNIGHT (MRS. EDWIN BRUCE LUSK), librarian; b. Franklinton, La., Aug. 16, 1935; d. Otis Harvey and Lou Zelle (Bahm) Knight; m. John Earle Uhler, Jr., May 26, 1956; children: Anne Knight, Camille Allana; m. 2d, Edwin Bruce Lusk, Nov. 28, 1970. BS, La. State U., 1956, MS, 1963. Asst. librarian Iberville Parish Library, Plaquemine, La., 1956-57, 1962-68; tchr. Iberville Parish Pub. Schs., Plaquemine, 1957-59, Plaquemines Parish Pub. Schs., Buras, La., 1959-61; dir. Iberville Parish Library, Plaquemine, 1969-89; chmn. La. State Bd. Library Examiners, 1979-89; pres. Camille Navarre Gallery, Ltd., Zachary, La., 1989-94. Mem. Iberville Parish Econ. Devel. Council, Plaquemine, 1970-71; sec. Iberville Parish Bicentennial Commn., 1973—; mem. La. Bicentennial Commn., 1974; bd dirs. McHugh House Mus., 1991-92. Named Outstanding Young Woman Plaquemine, La. Jr. C. of C., 1970. Mem. La. (sect. chmn. 1967-68), Riverland (sec. 1973-74) libraries assns., Capital Area Libraries (chmn. com. 1972-74). Republican. Episcopalian. Author: (with John E. Uhler, Jr.) Cajun Country Cookin', 1966, Rochester Clarke Bibliography of Louisiana Cookery, 1966, Royal Recipes from the Cajun Country, 1969, Iberville Parish, 1970. Home: 22736 Plainsland Dr Zachary LA 70791-9764

LUSK, PEGGY JUNE, mental health counselor, counseling consultant; b. Springfield, Mo., Aug. 31, 1935; d. James G. and Cecile C. (Slagle) L. BA magna cum laude, Drury Coll., 1947; MA, Syracuse U., 1950; postgrad., U. Chgo., 1958-61. Field dir., camp dir. Girl Scouts U.S.A., Springfield, 1946-48; student dean Syracuse (N.Y.) U., 1948-50; resident counselor Winthrop Coll., Rock Hill, S.C., 1950-52; asst. dean women, instr. Ohio Wesleyan U., Delaware, 1952-58; asst. dean students U. Chgo., 1958-61; counselor, asst. prof. Rush Presbyn. St. Luke's Med. Ctr., Chgo., 1961—. Recipient Friend of Nursing award Rush U., Chgo., 1993; Danforth faculty fellow, 1956. Mem. AAUP, Nat. League for Nurisng, Am. Counseling and Pers. Assn., Am. Assn. Mental Health Workers, Nat. Assn. for Women in Edn., Am. Assn. for Higher Edn., Ill. Assn. for Women in Edn. (exec. bd., pres. 1977-79), Alumni Assn. Drury Coll. (pres. Chgo. chpt. 1961-63), Mortar Board. Office: Rush Presbyn St Lukes Med 1743 W Harrison St # 840 Chicago IL 60612-3823

LUSK, RUTH HART, educational administrator; b. Troy, S.C., Sept. 19, 1937; d. James Cline and Lilly May (Robinson) Hart; m. James Albert Lusk, Dec. 10, 1961; children: Laurie Ann, Tracey Leigh, James Kevin. BS in Home Edons., Erskine Coll., Due West, S.C., 1959; MA in Teaching and Elem. Adminstrn., The Citadel, 1976. Cert. tchr. and adminstr., S.C. Tchr. John de le Howe Sch., McCormick, S.C., 1959-61, Mid-Carolina High Sch., Prosperity, S.C., 1962; tchr. Berkeley Elem. Sch., Moncks Corner, S.C., 1970-78, asst. prin., 1978-80, prin., 1980-92; dir. pers. Berkeley County Schs., Moncks Corner, 1992—. Bd. dirs. Am. Cancer Soc., Berkeley County, 1975, Charleston (S.C.) YWCA, 1992—; chmn. Berkeley com. YWCA, Moncks Corner, 1992—; mem. adv. bd. Trident United Way, Moncks Corner, 1993—. Recipient Tribute to Women in Industry award YWCA, Charleston, 1984. Mem. Nat. Adminstrs. Assn., S.C. Adminstrs. Assn., Berkeley County Suprs. and Adminstrs. Assn. (past pres.), Berkeley County Reading Coun., Delta Kappa Gamma, Kappa Kappa Iota (past pres.). Presbyterian. Home: 1224 Old Fort Ave Moncks Corner SC 29461-9269 Office: Berkeley County Schs 227 E Main St Moncks Corner SC 29461-3767

LUSSI, CAROLINE FRANCES DRAPER, motel manager; b. Glen Falls, N.Y., Apr. 5, 1939; d. Arthur Gibb and Lili Caroline (Gadeke) Draper; student U. Colo., 1957-58; A.A.S., Paul Smith's Coll., 1960; grad. Holiday Inn U., 1969; m. Serge Gail Lussi, Feb. 7, 1960; children: Arthur, Cristina, Katrina. Profl. ski instr., 1960—; mgr. Holiday Motor Motel, Wilmington, N.Y., 1961-62; owner, 1962-69; owner, innkeeper Holiday Inn, Lake Placid, N.Y., 1969—; sec. Lake Placid Vacation Corp., 1969—; co-owner, treas. Lake Placid Marina Corp. Mem. adv. bd. Alpine 1980 Olympics; bd. dirs. Lake Placid Meml. Hosp., 1975-81, also mem. aux.; trustee Paul Smiths Coll., 1984-88, Adirondack Nature Conservancy, 1993—. Named Top 10% Innkeeper Holiday Inns, 1972-75. Mem. Lake Placid C. of C., Profl. Ski Instrs. Am. (cert.). Episcopalian. Club: Essex County Adirondack Garden (pres. 1991-92), Shoreowner's Assn. (mem. bd. dirs., 1994), Nature Conservancy (mem. bd. dirs. Adirondack chpt., 1993—). Office: Holiday Inn Lake Placid NY 12946

LUST, BARBARA C., psychology and linguistics educator; d. John Benedict and Virginia (Sleth) L. BA in English Lit., Manhattanville Coll., 1963; postgrad., Fairleigh Dickinson, 1965, The New Sch. for Social Rsch., 1965-66, U. Geneva, Switzerland, 1968-69; MA in English Lit., Fordham U., 1971; PhD Devel. Psychology, CUNY, 1975. Post doctoral fellow dept. linguistics and philosophy MIT, Cambridge, 1974-76; from asst. prof. to prof. dept. human development and family studies Cornell U., Ithaca, N.Y., 1976—, field rep. cognitive studies program, 1987—, co-dir., 1992—, prof. modern langs. & linguistics, 1990—; vis. prof. SUNY, Binghamton, 1977; vis. scientist MIT, 1984, 90; vis. scholar Kelaniya U., Sri Lanka, 1984, U.S. Ednl. Found., 1984; cons. in field, lectr. various colls. and univs. Author: Studies in the Acquisition of Anaphora (vol I 1986, II 1987); co-editor, author: Synthetic Theory & First Language Acquisition, 1994 (vol. I and II); co-author: Studies in the Cognitive Basis of Language Development, 1975; contbr. articles to prof. jours., chpts. to books. Grantee NIMH, 1976, NSF, 1979-88, 92-93; fellow Nat. Inst. Health, 1990, NSF, 1989-91; Smithsonian grant Am. Inst. Indian Studies, 1980-81; recipient Travel award Lingustistic Soc. Am. and NSF, 1982, Rsch. award NSF, 1988-89, James McKeen Cattell award, 1992-93, N.Y. State Coll. Human Ecology award, 1976-79, 83. Fellow AAAS (chair linguistics and the lang. scis. 1993-94); mem. APA, Linguistic Soc. Am. (del. to AAAS psychology sect. 1988—), Am. Psychological Soc., Internat. Assn. Study Child Language, Soc. Rsch. Child Devel., Internat. Soc. Woman in Cognitive Neuroscience, Internat. Soc. Korean Linguistics, New Eng. Child Lang. Assn., N.Y. Acad. Scis., Soc. Philosophy and Psychology, Linguistic Assn. Great Britian, Piaget Soc. Democrat. Office: Cornell U Human Devel & Family Studies Ng 28 Marth Van Rensse Ithaca NY 14853

LUST, ELENORE (NORLIST), artist; b. Chgo.; d. Herbert and Dora (Koumas) Lust; m. Robert Eising, Jan. 7, 1932 (div.). Student, Smith Coll., 1929-30; BA, NYU, 1935, MA, 1957. Cert. tchr., N.Y., N.J. Dir., co-founder Norlyst Art Gallery, N.Y.C., 1940-49; art tchr. Cape of Good Hope Sem., Capetown, South Africa, 1952-55, St. Siprian's Sch., Capetown, 1952-55, N.J. High Schs., 1957-79; art lectr. Herald Tribune N.Y.C., 1944-49, art tchr. Little Red Sch. House, N.Y.C., 1944-49, Bklyn. Mus. Art Sch., 1947-50, Rancocas Valley Region High Sch., 1959-68; spl. edn. tchr. Lenape High Sch. System, 1970-79. Exhibited in one-woman shows at Norlyst Art Gallery, 1944, Stuttaford's Gallery, Capetown, 1952, Cafe Gallery, Burlington, N.J., 1988, Ft. Dix, Pemberton, N.J., 1988; represented in permanent collections at Ft. Dix, Mus. Women in Arts, Washington, and 74 other pvt. and corp. collections. Vol. art asst. tchr. Walter Elem. Sch., Lumber, N.J.; vol. Meml. Hosp., Mt. Holly, N.J. Mem. AAUW, Burlington County Art Guild (pres. 1983-85, v.p. 1989), Atlantic City Art Ctr., Trenton Artists' Workshop Assn., So. N. J. Advocates for Arts, Artworks/Princeton. Democrat. Episcopalian. Studio: PO Box D Mount Holly NJ 08060

LUSTICA, KATHERINE GRACE, publisher, artist, marketing consultant; b. Bristol, Pa., Nov. 20, 1958; d. Thomas Lustica and Elizabeth Delores (Moyer) De Groat. Student, Hussian Sch. Art, Phila., 1976-78, Rider Coll., 1980-82, U. Utah, 1993—. Comml. artist, illustrator Bucks County Courier Times Newspapers, Levittown, Pa., 1978-82; account exec. Trenton (N.J.) Times Newspapers, 1982-84; promotions and account exec. Diversified Suburban Newspapers, Murray (Utah) Printing, 1984-88; pub. Barclays Ltd. Salt Lake City, 1988—; cover artists, illustrator Accent mag., Bristol, 1978-82; freelance artist, 1978—; advt. and creative cons. Everett & Winthrop Products Group, Salt Lake City, 1988-90, Multi Techs. Internat., Salt Lake City, 1990-91. Newcombe scholar, 1981-82. Mem. Art Dirs. Salt Lake City. Presbyterian. Office: 4640 S Stratton Dr Salt Lake City UT 84117

LUSTIG, JOANNE, librarian; b. Newark, July 22, 1952; d. Melvin and Grace Ann (Kertsmar) L.; m. Glenn Seggel, Mar. 26, 1988. BA summa cum laude, Montclair State Coll., 1975; MLS, Rutgers U., 1978. Asst. libr. Sterling Drug Inc., N.Y.C., 1979-80, sr. editor, 1980; info. specialist Knoll Pharms., Whippany, N.J., 1980-82, sr. info. specialist, 1982-84, mgr. med. and sci. info., 1984—; bd. dirs. Highlands Regional Libr. Coop., Chester, N.J., 1990-94, pres. 1991-92; mem. N.J. Libr. Network Strategic Planning Com., 1990-91. Mem. NAFE, N.J. Chpt. Spl. Librs. Assn. (pres. 1987-88, v.p. 1986-87, editor bull. 1984-86), Pharm. Div. Spl. Librs. Assn. (archivist 1989-90, chair regional program planning com. 1985-86), Drug Info. Assn. Jewish. Office: Knoll Pharms 3000 Continental Dr N Mount Olive NJ 07828-1234

LUTES, LINDA DIANE, administrator, Tae Kwon Do educator; b. Alpena, Mich., Nov. 30, 1936; d. Clifton Earl and Ila May (Kilbourne) L.; m. Nelson Scott Moon Howe III, Nov. 13, 1960 (div. 1994). Student, U. Wash., 1955-57, U. Mich., 1959-61; master status 5th Dan, S. Henry Cho's Karate Inst. Inc., N.Y.C., 1989; studied with Yoshiteru Otano Sensi, N.Y.C., 1976-77; studied with, Aikido of Park Slope, Bklyn., 1982-84. Student tchr. Tae Kwan Do S. Henry Cho's Karate Inst., N.Y.C., 1970-79; owner, tchr. Tae Kwan Do Sch. N.Y.C., 1971-79; adminstr., chief instr. Way of Action, Inc., Bklyn., 1981—. Writer, dir., performer: Way of Action Martial Arts Show, 1975-84; numerous exhbns. of prints and paintings in U.S. and Can., 1965—. Mem. United Martial Arts Fedn. (life), Artists Equity, S. Henry Cho Karate Inst., Inc. (affiliate). Office: Way of Action Inc 316 7th St Brooklyn NY 11215

LUTHER, DARLENE, state legislator; b. 1947; m. Bill Luther; 2 children. BA, U St. Thomas. Mem. Minn. Ho. of Reps., 1993—. Home: 6809 Shingle Creek Dr Minneapolis MN 55445-2647 Office: Minn Ho of Reps State Capitol Saint Paul MN 55155*

LUTHER, FLORENCE JOAN (MRS. CHARLES W. LUTHER), lawyer; b. N.Y.C. June 28, 1928; d. John Phillip and Catherine Elizabeth (Duffy) Thomas ; J.D. magna cum laude, U. Pacific, 1963; m. William J. Regan (dec.); children—Kevin P., Brian T.; m. 2d, Charles W. Luther, June 11, 1961. Admitted to Calif. bar; mem. firm Luther, Luther, O'Connor & Johnson, Sacramento, 1964—. Mem. faculty McGeorge Sch. Law, U. Pacific, Sacramento, 1966-88, prof., 1968-88, prof. emeritus, 1988—. Judge Bank Am. Achievement awards, 1969-71. Bd. dirs. Sacramento Suicide Prevention League, 1969-70. Mem. ABA, Calif., Sacramento County bar assns., AAUP, Womens Legal Groups, Am. Judicature Soc., Order of Coif, Iota Tau Tau. Mem. bd. advisors Community Property Jour., 1974—, state decision editor, 1974—. Home: 11101 Fair Oaks Blvd Fair Oaks CA 95628-5136 Office: PO Box 1030 Fair Oaks CA 95628-1030

LUTHER, JODELL LYNN, social worker; b. Long Beach, Calif., Aug. 8, 1967; d. Gary Lynn and Saundra Kaye (Vallance) L. BA in Psychology/Sociology, U. Calif., Riverside, 1989; MA in Forensic Psychology, John Jay Coll., 1992. Adminstrv. asst. U. Calif., Riverside, 1986-90; psychologist intern Kings County Hosp., N.Y.C., 1991-92; social worker Foster Family Network, Long Beach, 1993-94, asst. supr., 1994—. Mem. APA, Long Beach Child Trauma Coun. Democrat. Home: 3695 Farquhar Los Alamitos CA 90720 Office: Foster Family Network 4223 E Anaheim St Long Beach CA 90804-5918

LUTHER, LUANA MAE, editor; b. L.A., Mar. 7, 1939; d. Chester Harry and Mildred P. (Knight) L.; m. O. Solorzano, Sept. 6, 1958 (div. 1974); children: Suzanne, Troy, Stephanie, Paul; m. Edwin J. Salzman, Apr. 4, 1981. BA, Calif. State U., Sacramento, 1974. Law indexer, legis. counsel State Calif., Sacramento, 1975-80, analyst, adminstrv. law, 1981-84; communications dir. Townsend & Co., Sacramento, 1985-87; adminstrv. asst., dept. justice State of Calif., Sacramento, 1987-88; editorial asst. Golden State Report Mag., Sacramento, 1986-88; mktg. cons. Lake Oswego, Oreg., 1989—; editor-in-chief Doral Pub., Wilsonville, Oreg., 1990—. Author: Red Mack Truck Massacre, 1981; contbr. articles to numerous publs.; columnist: Sacramento Bee, 1982-84; editor: (newsletter) Sacramento Youth Band, 1985. Dir. pub. rels., pres. LWV, West Clackamas County, Oreg., 1993—; vol. numerous polit. campaigns, Sacramento; fundraiser Dem. Women's Com., Sacramento, 1986. Mem. Mex.-Am. Ednl. Assn. (treas. 1964, Cert. Appreciation 1971). Democrat. Home: 17701 Blue Heron Way Lake Oswego OR 97034-6619

LUTHER, M. IDA, state legislator. Former mem. Maine Ho. of Reps., past mem. labor com.; mem. Maine State Senate, 1993—. Democrat. Home: 160 Granite St Mexico ME 04257-1733 Office: Maine State Senate State Capital Augusta ME 04333*

LUTHER, VICTORIA JEAN, prevention specialist, school nurse; b. Warren, Ohio, May 17, 1947; d. Albert William and Virginia Jean (Esau) Dyson; m. Hayward B. Luther, July 27, 1968; children: Michelle Luther, William Luther. RN diploma, Youngstown Hosp., 1968; student, Youngstown State U., 1988-91; BSHS, Thomas Edison State Coll., 1993. Cert. prevention cons., Ohio; cert. sch. nurse, Ohio. Sch. nurse Columbiana County JVS, Lisbon, Ohio, 1981-87, South Range Local Schs., North Lima, Ohio, 1987-91; prevention cons. Family Recovery Ctr., Lisbon, 1991—; sch. nurse Salem (Ohio) City Schs., 1992—; prevention cons. in field, 1981—. Recipient Ohio Exemplary Sch. award Ohio Dept. of Alcohol and Drug Addiction Svcs., 1992. Mem. Bus. and Profl. Womens Com. (chair), N.E. Ohio Nurse's Assn., Ohio Nurse's Assn. Home: 4150 W Middletown Rd Canfield OH 44406-9418 Office: Salem City Schs 1226 E State St Salem OH 44460-1757

LUTHER-LEMMON, CAROL LEN, educator; b. Waverly, N.Y., May 8, 1955; d. Carl Ross and Mary Edith (Auge) Luther; m. Mark Kevin Lemmon, June 21, 1986; children: Matthew C., Cathryn M. BS, Ithaca Coll., 1976; MS in Edn., Elmira Coll., 1982. Cert. elem. and secondary tchr., Pa. Reading aide Waverly (N.Y.) Central Schs., 1978-80; tchr. reading N.Y. State Div. for Youth, Lansing, 1981-82; tchr. chpt. I reading, mem. student assistance program and instructional support team Rowe Mid. Sch., Athens (Pa.) Area Sch. Dist., 1982—. Basketball coach Youth Activities Dept., Athens, 1982-85, asst. softball coach, 1990-91; mem. ad hoc com. Waverly Sch. Dist., 1990-91; mem. Goal G parents & edn. Middle Sch. Implementation Team for WINGS-Waverly in a Global Soc. for Waverly Cen. Sch. Dist. Strategic Plan; active Girls' Softball League, Waverly, 1978-80, commr., 1980; bd. dirs. Waverly Community Ch., 1976-78; choir mem. Meth. Ch., Waverly, 1976-90, adminstrv. bd., trustee, chmn. bd. trustees, 1995; mem. Valley Chorus, Pa. and N.Y., 1983-86. With USAR, 1977-83. Mem. ASCD, AAUW (v.p. Waverly br. 1982-83, pres. Waverly br. 1992—), Am. Legion Aux. (girl's state rep. 1972, girl's state chmn. 1976-80 Waverly post, counselor 1977), Chemung Area Reading Coun., N.Y. State Reading Assn. Republican. Home: 490 Waverly St Waverly NY 14892-1102 Office: Athens Area Sch Dist Pennsylvania Ave Athens PA 18810-1440

LUTTRELL, GEORGIA BENA, musician; b. Carbondale, Ill., Oct. 24, 1927; d. George Newton and Phyllis Bena (Gent) Gher; m. Claude Edward Luttrell, Mar. 25, 1964 (dec. Aug. 1987). BA, So. Ill. U., 1947; MusM, Northwestern U., Evanston, Ill., 1948; postgrad., various univs. Asst. prof. music Huntingdon Coll., Montgomery, Ala., 1948-50; music supr. Community Unit Dist. 2 Williamson County, Marion, Ill., 1950-53; music tchr. Dubois Grade Sch., Springfield, Ill., 1953-55; dir. choral music Feitshas High Sch., Springfield, 1955-67; chairperson music dept. Springfield S.E. High Sch., 1967-83; ind. music coord./pianist Springfield, 1983—; accompanist various soloists and choirs, 1944—; accompanist Ill. Music Educators Assn., 1956-66; talent adjudicator Ill. High Sch. Assn., 1957-89, Ill. Elem. Sch. Assn., 1957-89. Pianist Springfield Symphony Orch., 1954-55; author (poet): American Poetry Anthology, 1988, Love's Greatest Treasures, 1989. Dir. choirs Douglas United Meth. Ch., Springfield, 1964-72; choir dir. Unity Ch., Springfield, 1981-85; vol. vocalist Ill. Symphony Chorus, formerly Springfield Symphony Chorus, 1986—. Grantee Carnegie Rsch. Found., 1949, State of Ill., Evanston Twp. High Sch., 1968. Mem. Internat. Platform Assn. (gov., music dir., pianist), Ill. Ret. Tchrs. Assn.

LUTTRULL, SHIRLEY JOANN, protective services official; b. Fordland, Mo., Feb. 26, 1937; d. Thomas Marion and Pauline (Sherrow) Pirtle; m. Leslie Allen Luttrull, June 3, 1956 (div. May 1978); children: Vicki Lynn, Ricki Allen; m. Orben Lowell Clark, Dec. 31, 1982 (div. Oct. 1987); m. Barry Mabe, June 1992 (div. Oct. 1994). Student, Southwest Mo. State U., 1979. Checker person Lea's Market, Fordland, Mo., 1955-56; plant supr. Mellers Photo Lab., Springfield, Mo., 1968-82; shopper Hopper and Hawkins, Dallas, 1982-83; crew leader Sentinal Security, Okla. City, Shrink Control Corp., Houston, 1984-86; sales mgr. Shrink Control Corp., 1986-88; owner Internal Theft Control, Springfield, 1988—. Mem. Mo. Retail Grocers Assn., Springfield C. of C. Republican. Home and Office: 1347 S Airwood Dr Springfield MO 65804-0520

LUTZ, CARLENE, educational association administrator; b. Chgo., Feb. 4, 1946; d. John Calvin Sr. and Helen (Kwast) L. BS in Edn., No. Ill. U., 1967; MA in Edn., U. Conn., 1971; adminstrv. endorsement, Chgo. State U., 1988. Cert. early childhood edn., tchr. kindergarten-grade 9. 2d grade tchr. Chgo. Pub. Schs., 1967-73, reading resource tchr., 1973-79, ESEA coord., 1979-80, upper grade lang. arts, 1980-89, reading resource tchr., 1989-92; asst. dir. Chgo. Tchrs. Union Quest Ctr., 1992—; trainer ednl. rsch. and dissemination and critical thinking programs, Chgo., 1986—. Editor (pamphlet) EPDA Project, Pictorial Report, 1971. Ill. State scholar Ill. State Scholarship Commn., 1964; EPDA fellow U.S. Dept. Edn., 1971. Mem. ASCD, Internat. Reading Assn., Am. Fedn. Tchrs., Chgo. Tchr. Union, Ella Flagg Young Assn., Delta Kappa Gamma, Phi Delta Kappa. Home: 125 Acacia Dr Apt 613 Indianhead Park IL 60525-4409 Office: Chgo Tchrs Union Quest Ctr 222 Merchandise Mart Plz Fl 4 Chicago IL 60654-1016

LUTZ, DONNA SCHULZE, biologist; b. Ames, Iowa, Aug. 24, 1957; d. Donald Kanning and Carol Lee (Grandfield) S.; m. Monte Vernett Lutz, Aug. 13, 1983; children: Katie Lynn, Amanda Lee. BS in Biology and Environ. Studies with distinction, Iowa State U., 1979, MS in Water Resources, 1993. Lab. tech. Iowa State U., Ames, 1980-87, rsch. asst., 1987-93, asst. scientist, 1993—; mgr. projects Des Moines River Water Quality Network. Author: Water Quality Studies: Annual Reports, 1981-84. Recipient honorarium Argonne Nat. Lab., 1978. Mem. Assn. Women in Sci. (sec. ctrl. Iowa chpt. 1992—), Am. Fisheries Soc. (author Transaction article 1994), Phi Kappa Phi. Democrat. Presbyterian. Home: 3211 Lettie Ames IA 50014 Office: Iowa State U 396 Town Eng Bldg Ames IA 50011

LUTZ, EDITH LEDFORD, state legislator; b. Lawndale, N.C., Oct. 20, 1914; d. Curtis and Annie Hoyle Ledford; m. M. Everett Lutz, 1933 (dec.); 1 child, E. Jacob. Farmer, horticulturist; mem. N.C. Ho. of Reps., 1975—, chmn. local and regional govt. II, vice-chmn. agr., forestry, horticulture and wildlife subcom., mem. various coms. Active Sheltered Workshops Rutherford County; bd. dirs. Farm Bur. Named Farm Woman of Yr., S.W. Dist., Woman of Yr., Cleve. Times, Disting. Woman of Cleveland County. Mem. Am. Bus. Women, Cleveland County C. of C. (bd. dirs.), Apple Grower's Assn. Democrat. Methodist. Home: RR 3 Lawndale NC 28090-9803 Office: NC Ho of Reps State Capitol Raleigh NC 27611*

LUTZ, GRETCHEN KAY, English language educator; b. Ft. Worth, Tex., Jan. 6, 1948. BA, Tex. Christian U., 1970; MA, U. Houston, 1974; postgrad., Rice U., Dartmouth Coll., 1994. High sch. and mid. sch. tchr. English Galveston and Deer Park (Tex.) Sch. Dists., 1970-77; instr. ESL and English Schreiner Coll., Kerrville, Tex., 1979-80; instr. English San Jacinto Coll. Ctr., Pasadena, Tex., 1981—. Contbr. articles to profl. jours. Mem. MLA, Nat. Symposium for Coherence in Liberal Arts, C.C. Humanities Assn., Am. Culture and Popular Culture Assn., U.S. European Command Mil. to Mil. Program Conf., Am. Studies Assn. Tex., South Ctrl. MLA, Conf. Coll. Tchrs. English (exec. coun.), S.W. Conf. Christianity and Lit., Western Soc. 18th Century Studies, Tex. Folklore Soc., S.W. Regional Conf. English in Two-Year Colls., Tex. Voices Sesquicentennial Series, Rice English Symposium, San Jacinto Coll. Faculty Symposium. Home: PO Box 30416 Amarillo TX 79120-0416

LUTZ, JULIE HAYNES, astronomy and mathematics educator; b. Mt. Vernon, Ohio, Dec. 17, 1944; d. Willard Damon and Julia Awilda (Way) Haynes; m. Thomas Edward Lutz, July 8, 1967; children: Melissa, Clea. BS, San Diego State U., 1965; MS, U. Ill., 1968, PhD, 1971. Asst. prof. astronomy Wash. State U., Pullman, 1972-78, asst. dean sci., 1978-79, assoc. prof., 1978-84, assoc. provost, 1981-82, prof., 1984—, chair math. and astronomy dept., 1992—; rsch. fellow Univ. Coll. London, England, 1976-77, 82-83; vis. resident astronomer Cerro Tololo Inter-Am. Obs., 1988-89; dir. div. astron. scis. NSF, 1990-92. Contbr. articles on astron. research to profl. jours. Fellow AAAS (mem. com. 1982-85, mem. nominating com. 1992—, chair sect. D 1993—), Royal Astron. Soc.; mem. Am. Astron., Soc. (chair publs. bd. 1986-88), Astron. Soc. Pacific (bd. dirs. 1988—, v.p. 1989, pres. 1990-92), Internat. Astron. Union. Home: 1200 NE Mcgee St Pullman WA 99163-3818 Office: Wash State U Program in Astronomy Pullman WA 99164-3113

LUTZ, LINDA ANN, anesthesiologist; b. Waco, Tex., July 11, 1947; d. Harry Hammen and Anna (Burney) L.; m. John Page, Jan. 1, 1975; children: Patricia Lynette, Jonathan Linden. BA summa cum laude, Trinity U., 1968; MD, U. Tex., 1972. Diplomate Am. Bd. Anesthesiology. Pvt. practice Garland, Tex., 1975—. Capt. U.S. Army, 1972-73. Fellow Am. Coll. Anesthesiologists. Republican. Episcopalian. Office: PO Box 38344 Dallas TX 75238

LUTZ, NANCY FISHBAIN, museum administrator; b. Madison, Wis., Mar. 18, 1948; d. Harold and Marjorie Ann (Dates) Fishbain; m. Wendell Ray Lutz, Aug. 12, 1978. BA in Art History & Photography, U. Mass., 1982; MPA, U. Ariz., 1991. Owner The Art Mart, Springfield, Ohio, 1972-78; freelance photographer Boston, 1981-82; clinic mgr. Brigham Women's Hosp., Boston, 1982-84; mktg., membership dir. Ctr. Creative Photography, Tucson, Ariz., 1986-91, asst. dir., 1991—. Bd. chair Tucson/Pima Arts Coun., 1991-94, chair pub. art com., 1988-91. Mem. Am. Assn. Mus. Office: Ctr Creative Photography U Ariz Tucson AZ 85721

LUTZ, SANDRA JEANIENE, family nurse practitioner; b. Pekin, Ill., Apr. 1, 1937; d. Howard Frederick and Wanda Sue (Weber) Rohrs; m. Eugene Harold Lutz, Jan. 19, 1957; children: Eric H., Karl E., April D., Matthew D., Peter J., Camilia J., Charles W. ADN, Ill. Ctrl. Coll., 1977; BSN, Bradley U., 1986; MSN, U. Ill., Chgo., 1989. Cert. FNP, ANA. Staff nurse/charge nurse ob-gyn. Pekin (Ill.) Meml. Hosp., 1977-81; community health nurse Tazewell County Health Dept., Pekin, 1981-84; staff nurse obstetrics Saint Francis Med. Ctr., Peoria, Ill., 1984-85; dir. home health, DON nursing home Hopedale (Ill.) Med. Ctr., 1985-86; charge nurse nursing home Americana Health Care, Peoria, 1986-87; staff nurse progressive cardiac care unit St. Francis Med. Ctr., Peoria, 1987-89; supr., nurse practitioner med. svcs. Peoria (Ill.) County Jail/Saint Francis Med. Ctr., 1989-92; supr., nurse practitioner Bradley U. Health Ctr./Saint Francis Med. Ctr., Peoria, 1992-94; full-time nurse practitioner St. Francis Community Clinic, 1994—; instr. health sci. Illinois River Correctional Facility, Canton, 1991; part-time nurse practitioner St. Francis Cmty. Clinic, 1992-94. Pres. Tazewell Toastmasters, Pekin, 1990. Mem. Am. Acad. Nurse Practitioners, Am. Holistic Nurses Assn. (north ctrl. regiona dir. 1994—), Ill. Assn. Coun. Nurse Practitioners (exec. sec. 1992-94), Bradley U. Hilltop Nurses Alumni Assn. (v.p. 1985-90, pres. 1990-92, 92-94), Sigma Theta Tau (Epsilon Epsilon sec. 1990-92, pres. elect 1992-94, pres. 1994—), Altrusa Internat. (v.p. 1994), Nurse Healers Profl. Assn. Lutheran. Home: 1514 Summer St Pekin IL 61554 Office: Bradley Univ Health Ctr Heitz Hall Rm 100 Peoria IL 61625

LUTZE, RUTH LOUISE, retired textbook editor, public relations executive; b. Boston, Apr. 19, 1917; d. Frederick Clemons and Louise (Rausch) L. BA with honors, Radcliffe Coll., 1938; postgrad., Boston U., 1938-39. Tchr. Winthrop (Mass.) Pub. Schs., 1938-39; with pub. relations dept. The Boston City Club, Boston, 1939-42; sr. projects editor D.C. Heath & Co., Lexington, Mass., 1942-82; book reviewer, lectr., 1939—; cons. pub. rels. 1991—. Bd. Winthrop Improvement and Hist. Assn., 1980—; vol. tchr. Boston Pub. Schs., 1967-77; mem. Winthrop Rep. Town Com., 1970—. Recipient cert. appreciation for vol. in edn., Kiwanis Club of East Boston, 1972. Mem. Radcliffe Club Boston, First Luth. Ch. Boston (v.p. 1986, deacon 1980-). Home: 110 Circuit Rd Winthrop MA 02152-2819

LUXENBERG, ALISA LYNN, art historian; b. Cleve., June 23, 1960; d. Herbert and Marianna (Dunchack) L. BA in Art History/French Lit., Duke U., 1982; MA in Art History, Boston U., 1984; PhD in Art History, NYU, 1990. Instr. Am. U. in Paris, 1990; Gould Found. fellow Princeton (N.J.) U., 1991-92; vis. asst. prof. Washington U., St. Louis, 1992-93, Ohio State U., Columbus, 1993-94. Contbg. author: (exhbn. catalog) Spain, Espagne, Spanien, 1993. Recipient Kress Summer travel award Boston U., Austin, Tex., 1984. Mem. Coll. Art Assn. (co-chair session at ann. conf. 1995), Assn. Historians of 19th Century Art.

LUZZATTO, ANNE R., federal official; b. Washington, D.C., July 25, 1941. BA, U. Wis., 1963; JD, Am. U., 1978; MA in Internat. Econs., Johns Hopkins Sch. of Adv. Internat. Studies, 1984. Dep. press sec. Mondale-Ferraro Campaign, 1984; v.p. corp. external rels. CBS, Inc., 1985-87; v.p. pub. affairs Citibank, 1987-92, The Investigative Group, Inc., 1992-93; mem. Clinton-Gore Transition Team, Washington, 1992-93; asst. U.S. trade rep. Dept. of Pub. Affairs, Washington, 1993—. Jewish. Office: Office of the Pres 600 17th St NW Rm 100 Washington DC 20506*

LUZZI, LAURA ANN, counselor, consultant; b. Belleville, N.J., Sept. 23, 1962; m. Kevin J. Skotnicki. BA in Psychology and Sociology, Purdue U., 1984; MS in Counseling, Villanova U., 1987. Lic. psychotherapist, Oreg.; cert. counselor. Youth counselor Joint Action in Cmty. Svcs., Phila., 1984-85; counselor Comprehensive Counseling Assn., N.J., 1987-88; sr. clinician S. Bergen Mental Health Ctr., Lyndhurst, N.J., 1987-89; asst. dir. Spectrum for Living, Inc., Hackensack, N.J., 1989-90; children's specialist supr. Psychiat. Emergency Screening Program Bergen County, Inc., Paramus, N.J., 1990; dir. family svcs. The Dougy Ctr. for Grieving Children, Portland, Oreg., 1991-93; workshop presenter for numerous cmty. orgns., Portland, 1993—; cons. cmty. profls., Portland, 1993—; vol., mem. Delta Soc., Rsch. and Pet Ptnrs. Coms., 1990—; freelance illustrator. Vol. edn. com. Wolf Haven, Inc., Wash., 1991-92. Mem. Am. Counseling Assn., Assn. for Play Therapy, Group Specialists and Multi-Cultural Counseling Assn. Home: 2050 NW Glisan Portland OR 97209-1109

LYALL, KATHARINE C(ULBERT), academic administrator, economics educator; b. Lancaster, Pa., Apr. 26, 1941; d. John D. and Eleanor G. Lyall. BA in Econs., Cornell U., 1963, PhD in Econs., 1969; MBA, NYU, 1965. Economist Chase Manhattan Bank, N.Y.C., 1963-65; asst. prof. econs. Syracuse U., 1969-72; prof. econs. Johns Hopkins U., Balt., 1972-77; dir. grad. program in public policy Johns Hopkins U., 1979-81; dep. asst. sec. for econs. Office Econ. Affairs, HUD, Washington, 1977-79; v.p. acad. affairs U. Wis. System, 1981-85; prof. of econ. U. Wis., Madison, 1982—; acting pres. U. Wis. System, Madison, 1985-86, 91-92, exec. v.p., 1986-91, pres., 1992—; bd. dirs. Kemper Ins. Cos.; mem. bd. Carnegie Found. for Advancement of Teaching. Author: Reforming Public Welfare, 1976, Microeconomic Issues of the 70s, 1978. Mem. Mcpl. Securities Rulemaking Bd., Washington, 1990-93. Mem. Am. Econ. Assn., Assn. Am. Univs. (exec. com. 1993—), Phi Beta Kappa. Home: 6021 S Highlands Ave Madison WI 53705 Office: U Wis System Office of Pres 1720 Van Hise Hall 1220 Linden Dr Madison WI 53706

LYBARGER, ADRIENNE REYNOLDS (MRS. LEE FRANCIS), college administrator; b. Boston, Mar. 8, 1926; d. Joseph Anthony and Albertine (Mouton Drevet) Reynolds; BA, Mills Coll., Calif., 1947; cert. Katharine Gibbs Sch., 1948; m. Lee Francis Lybarger, Jr., Sept. 15, 1955 (dec); children: Linda, Lauretta, James (dec.), Lisa, Leslie (dec.), Jeffrey (dec.), Lucia, Lana. Asst. to dir. Mid-Century convocation M.I.T. Cambridge, 1949, asst. to dir. West Coast regional office Mid-Century devel. program, 1949-50, asst. dir. So. regional office, 1950-51; asst. to dir. convocation devel. program Ithaca (N.Y.) Coll., 1951; asst. to dir., devel. program U. Buffalo, 1951-52; asst. to dir. Diamond Jubilee program Case Inst. Tech., Cleve., 1952-54; asst. to dir., expansion and improvement program John D. Archbold Hosp., Thomasville, Ga., 1955-61; ptnr. Lybarger Prodns., comml. films, N.Y.C.; asst. dir., dir. regional campaigns, Ohio, Boston, Mass., N.Y.C., also supr. all other nat. regional campaigns Mount Holyoke Coll. Fund for Future, South Hadley, Mass., 1961-63; fund-raising cons. to capital programs, Vocation Svc. Ctr. and Bronx-Westchester YMCA, YMCA Greater N.Y., 1963-65; dir. devel. and pub. rels. Bank St. Coll. Edn., N.Y.C., 1965-79; cons. S. Bronx Overall Econ. Devel. Corp., 1978-79; v.p. devel. Wells Coll., 1979-92, dir. Wells Capital campaign; ednl. fund-raising cons., 1993—; cons. capital campaign Borough of Manhattan Community Coll., 1979-80; Realtor assoc./mktg. cons. Century 21, Clinton, N.J., 1978-81; Pres., Birch Island (Maine) Corp., 1979; mem. Nat. Women's Hall of Fame, 1987-90, bd. dirs., 1987—. Mem. Am. Prospect Rsch. Assn. Author: (with L. F. Lybarger) Proven Guides to Effective Soliciting (slide film), 1950, rev., 1960, 81; exec. producer, Scriptwriter Now More than Ever, Wells Coll. Home: Kings Manor 272 Pittstown Rd Pittstown NJ 08867

LYBARGER, MARJORIE KATHRYN, nurse; b. Holland, Mich., Apr. 23, 1956; d. Richard Simon and Mary Kathryn (Homan) Denuyl; m. John Steven Lybarger, Aug. 22, 1981; children: Ashley Ann, Ryan Christopher. BA in Psychology, Biola U., Calif., 1979, BS in Nursing, 1984. RN, Calif. Staff nurse Presbyn. Intercommunity Hosp., Whittier, Calif, 1985-86, Healthcare Med. Ctr., Tustin, Calif., 1986-88; staff nurse med.-telemetry unit Friendly Hills Regional Med. Ctr., La Habra, Calif., 1988-90; staff nurse telemetry unit Riverside (Calif.) Community Hosp., 1990-93; staff nurse med. telemetry unit St. Anthony's Ctrl. Hosp., Denver, 1993-94; staff nurse cardiovascular intermediate care unit St. Anthony's Ctr., Denver, Colo., 1994—. Mem. Gamma Phi Beta. Republican. Home: 8489 West 95th Dr Westminster CO 80021

LYBBERT, DIANE LOUISE, material requirements planning specialist; b. South Bend, Ind., Mar. 13, 1951; d. Peter Stanley and Virginia Mae (Houck) Chrapliwy; m. Blair Edward Lybbert, Feb. 21, 1970; children: Jennifer Amy, Jeffrey Blair. B of Bus. and Mktg., Dallas Bapt. U., 1995. Cert. in prodn. and inventory mgmt. Sec. North Tex. State U., Denton, 1970-71; clk., stenographer Volkswagen Products Corp., Ft. Worth, 1971-72, buyer, 1972-74; stenographer Bell Helicopter Textron, Ft. Worth, 1974-78, data release analyst, 1978-85, customer property returns adminstr., 1988-92, material requirements planning specialist, 1985-87, 92—; corp. trainer Bell Helicopter Textron, Ft. Worth, 1991-92, spares project task force, 1993—. Editor newsletters Burleson Ministerial Alliance Aux., 1986-87, Rape Crisis Support of Tarrant County, 1978-80, Morning Toasters, 1993—. Task force mem. Rape Crisis Support of Tarrant County, Ft. Worth, 1975-80; bd. dirs. Burleson (Tex.) Pks. Bd., 1980-85, Burleson Ministerial Alliance Aux., 1985-87; Webelos troop leader Boy Scouts Am., Burleson, 1988. Mem. NAFE, Nat. Mgmt. Assn., Internat. Platform Assn., Toastmasters Internat. (pres. local club 1991, Toastmaster of Yr. 1992, Able Toastmaster-Bronze), Mu Kappa Tau. Republican. Methodist. Home: 7707 Oak Parkway Burleson TX 76028-9586 Office: Bell Helicopter Textron PO Box 482 Fort Worth TX 76101

LYBRAND, THOMASINE LARKINS, tax specialist; b. Greenwood, S.C., Oct. 20, 1953; d. Robert Thomas and Elvena (McCoy) Larkins; m. Bobby Daniel Luker, Feb. 14, 1975 (dec. Mar. 1977); m. John William Lybrand III, Dec. 23, 1977; children: John William IV, Robert Thomas, Patrick Bryce. BS in Acctg., Lander U., 1994; postgrad., Clemson U. Computer oper. Parke-Davis, Greenwood, S.C., 1972-79; instr. data entry Piedmont Tech. Coll., Greenwood, S.C., 1979-82; computer oper. Cin. Milacron, Greenwood, S.C., 1982-85; data processing supr. Abbeville (S.C.) County Meml. Hosp., 1985-87, Hoke, Inc., Spartanburg, S.C., 1987-89; tax preparer, owner The Tax Ctr., Greenwood, 1990—; purchasing acct. GLEAMNS Human Resources Commn., Greenwood. Sharon Jones Williams scholar Lander U., 1992-93, United Saving Bank scholar, 1993-94. Mem. Inst. Mgmt. Accts. Republican. Methodist. Home and Office: 208 Wellington Dr Greenwood SC 29649 also: GLEAMNS Human Resources Commn 237 N Hosp St Greenwood SC 29646

LYCAN, REBECCA TATUM, professional dog handler; b. Atlanta, Oct. 10, 1960; d. Clement Marduke and Ruth (Davenport) Tatum; m. Glenn Eugene Lycan, July 14, 1984. BS in Microbiology, U. Ga., 1982. Lab. technician Optimal Systems, Inc., Norcross, Ga., 1982-84; asst. dog handler Canine Country Club, Chattanooga, 1984-86; profl. dog handler Leading Edge Kennel, Griffin, Ga., 1986—. Nominee for Best New Female Profl. Handler, Kennel Rev. and IAMS, 1989, 90. Mem. Profl. Handlers Assn., Dog Handlers Guild, Griffin Kennel Club, Griffin Kennel Club (show chmn. Fall shows 1990-92), Conyers Kennel Club. Office: Leading Edge Kennel PO Box 849 Griffin GA 30224-0849

LYDICK, BARBARA C., management consultant, strategic planning, negotiation and marketing executive; b. Pitts., Sept. 13, 1944; d. William Duppsdadt and Helen Florence (Walker) Cleeves; m. F. Scott Lydick, June 16, 1968 (div.); 1 child, Nathan Walker Lydick. Student, Western Coll. for Women, Oxford, Ohio, 1962-65; BS, U. Pitts., 1966. Rsch. asst. in chemistry and biology U. Pitts. Sch. Medicine, 1966-67; engr., tech. writer Westinghouse Plant Apparatus Div., Pitts., 1966-71; successively freelance tech. writer, editor Boston, N.Y.C., Washington; freelance proposal mgr. Raytheon Corp., Boston, Arthur D. Little, N.Y.C., Boston, 1971-74; sr. engr., sr. contract analyst, internat. negotiator Westinghouse Nuclear Energy Systems Divs., Pitts., 1974-84; mktg. mgr. Mgmt. Analysis Co., 1984-85; founder, pres. B&A Assocs., Oceanside, Calif., 1985—; dir. strategic planning C F Braun Inc., Alhambra, Calif., 1989-90; dir. internat. licensing InterPacific Capital Corp., L.A., 1991—; condr. numerous seminars in negotiation, women in mgmt.; co-host nat. radio program Women's Bus. Bd. dirs. WFN: tutor Laubach Literacy Coun. San Diego; former advisor sci. & engring. Explorer Scout Post Westinghouse Nuclear Energy Systems Div.; former mem. Mendelssohn Choir/Solist Group, Pitts., Pitts. Chamber Singers, Pitts. Savoyards, World Affairs Coun. Pitts. Mem. Am. Nuclear Soc. Republican. Office: B&A Assocs 1020 Wisconsin Ave Oceanside CA 92054-4241

LYDON, MARY C., physical education educator; b. Boston, May 12, 1931; d. Patrick J. and Annie (O'Neill) L. BS in Edn., Bridgewater State Coll., 1955; EdM, Northeastern U., 1963; EdD, Boston U., 1978. Cert. tchr., Mass. Tchr. phys. edn. Chelsea (Mass.) Pub. Schs., 1955-57, Quincy (Mass.) Pub. Schs., 1959-63, 70—, Buffalo (N.Y.) Pub. Schs., 1963-66; field worker Girl Scouts U.S., Boston, 1957-59; instr. phys. edn. Boston State Coll., 1966-70; adj. prof. Boston State Coll., 1970-74, Boston Coll., 1983-89; clin. instr. U. Mass., Boston, 1994; presenter at profl. confs.; sec. Coun. Sch. Adminstrs. Health & Phys. Edn., 1994—. Trustee Bridgewater Found., 1990-92. Mem. NEA, AAHPERD (conv. planning com. 1988-89, coun. for svcs. Ea. Dist. 1984-88), Mass. Assn. Health, Phys. Edn., Recreation and Dance (pres. 1986-87, exec. bd. 1987—), Quincy Edn. Assn., Mass. Tchrs. Assn., Bridgewater State Coll. Alumni Assn. (pres. 1990-92), Women's Sports Found., Hyannis-Bridgewater Phys. Edn. Alumni Assn. (exec. com. 1980—, pres. 1985-89). Office: Quincy Pub Schs 70 Coddington St Quincy MA 02169-4501

LYERLY, ELAINE MYRICK, advertising executive; b. Charlotte, N.C., Nov. 26, 1951; d. J.M. and Annie Mary (Myrick) L.; m. Marc Rauch, Jan. 17, 1987. AA in Advt. and Comml. Design, Cen. Piedmont Community Coll., 1972. Freelance designer Sta. WBTV, Charlotte, N.C., 1972; fashion illustrator Matthews Belk, Gastonia, N.C., 1972-73; designer Monte Curry Mktg. and Communication Svcs., Charlotte, 1973-74, exec. v.p., 1974-77; pres. Repro/Graphics, Charlotte, 1975-77, Lyerly Agy. Inc., Charlotte, 1977—; bd. dirs. SouthTrust Bank. Illustrator: Mister Cookie Breakfast Cookbook, 1985. Chmn. regional blood ARC, chmn. Greater Carolinas chpt., 1990-93, mem. nat. implementation com., 1991; bd. dirs. United Way, NCCJ; exec. com. Ptnrs. in Quality. Named Bus. Woman of Yr., Shearson Lehman Hutton/Queens Coll., 1989, N.C. Young Careerist Bus. and Profl. Women's Club, 1981; recipient ACE award Women in Comms., 1993. Mem. Women Execs. (bd. dirs.), Women Bus. Owners (adv. coun., Leadership award 1990, Woman Bus. Owner of Yr. award 1994), Pub. Rels. Soc. Am.

(Counselors Acad. 1985—), Charlotte C. of C. (bd. dirs., diversity coun., Bus. Woman of Yr. award 1985), Hadassah. Republican. Jewish. Office: Lyerly Agy Inc 1015 East Blvd Charlotte NC 28203-5713

LYLE, GLENDA SWANSON, state legislator; b. Knoxville, Tenn.; d. Richard and Olivia Swanson; children: Kipp, Elsie, Jennifer, Anthony. BA, U. Denver, 1964; MA, U. Colo., 1973. Former dir. cmty. and personal svcs., instr. early childhood edn., dir. preschool lab C.C. of Denver/Auraria; owner Planners, Inc.; mem. Colo. Ho. of Reps., 1992—, mem. various coms., 1993—. Del. White Ho. Conf. Small Bus., 1980-86; mem. Regional Transp. Dist. Bd., 1986-92, Regulatory Agy. Adv. Bd., Mayor's Planning Bd., Nat. Pub. Lands Adv. Coun., Gov.'s Small Bus. Coun., Colo. Mkt. and Distributive Edn. Adv. Coun., Va Neal Blue Ctr. Mem. Am. Planning Assn., Conf. Minority Transp. Ofcls. (nat. bd. dirs.), Black Women Polit. Action (founding mem.), Black C. of C. (bd. dirs.). Democrat. Office: Colo House of Reps State Capitol Denver CO 80203*

LYLE, JEAN STUART, social worker; b. Rock Hill, S.C., Jan. 13, 1912; d. David and Martha (Nash) L.; B.A., U. S.C., 1949; M.S. in Social Work, Columbia U., 1951. Recreation dir. City of Rock Hill, 1938-44; commd. 1st lt. Med. Service Corps, U.S. Army, 1951, advanced through grades to lt. col., 1966; asst. chief social worker, Ft. Benning, Ga., 1951-55; chief social worker Fort Jay, N.Y., 1955-58, Fort McClellan, Ala., 1958-62, female inpatient service Walter Reed Gen. Hosp., Washington, 1962-66; dir. Army Community Service, U.S. Army, Hawaii, 1966-68, Walter Reed Army Med. Center, 1968-70; cons. group work to Med. Field Service Sch., Fort Sam Houston, Tex., 1969; ret., 1970; dir. vol. services S.C. Dept. Health and Environ. Control, Columbia, 1970-74; pvt. practice social work, Rock Hill, 1974—; tchr. and supr. social work students Catholic U. Am., Washington, 1960-62. Decorated Legion of Merit; recipient Community Service award U.S. Army, 1968. Mem. Nat. Assn. Social Workers, Acad. Cert. Social Workers. Democrat. Address: PO Box 2553 Rock Hill SC 29732

LYLE, VIRGINIA REAVIS, retired archivist, genealogist; b. Nashville, Apr. 19, 1926; d. Damon Ashley and Nellie Alice (Vaughan) R.; m. John Reid Lyle, Sept. 25, 1943; 1 child, Judith L. Haggard. BA, Vanderbilt U., 1974, MLS, 1975. Cert. genealogist, archivist. Administrv. officer Commerce Union Bank, Nashville, 1961-70, 75-78; rsch. asst. R.C.H. Mathews, Jr., Nashville, 1970-75, 78-79; genealogist Nashville, 1980; archivist Metro Nashville-Davidson County Archives, Nashville, 1981-93; ret., 1993. Sec. Homecoming '86 Metro Steering Com. for Tenn., 1986; mem. Pub. Libr. Bd., 1978-81. Mem. Tenn. Archivists, Nat. Geneal. Soc., Mid-State Libr. Assn., DAR, Ladies Hermitage Assn., Soc. Am. Archivists, Acad. Cert. Archivists, Woman's Club of Nashville (adv. bd.). Methodist. Home: 1421 Eastland Ave Nashville TN 37206-2626

LYMAN, PEGGY, dancer, choreographer, educator; b. Cin., June 28, 1950; d. James Louis and Anne Earlene (Weeks) Morner; m. David Stanley Lyman, Aug. 29, 1970 (div. 1979); m. Timothy Scott Lynch, June 21, 1982; 1 child, Kevin Kynch. Grad. high sch., Cin. Solo dancer Cin. Ballet Co., 1964-68, Contemporary Dance Theater, 1970-71; chorus dancer N.Y.C. Opera, 1969-70; Radio City Music Hall Ballet Co., 1970; chorus singer and dancer Sugar, Broadway musical, N.Y.C., 1971-73; prin. dancer Martha Graham Dance Co., N.Y.C., 1973-88, rehersal dir., 1989-90; artistic dir. Martha Graham Ensemble, N.Y.C., 1990-91; faculty Martha Graham Sch., 1975—; head dance div. No. Ky. U., 1977-78; artistic dir. Peggy Lyman Dance Co., N.Y.C., 1978-89; asst. prof. dance, guest choreographer Fla. State U., Tallahassee, 1982-89; guest choreographer So. Meth. U., Dallas, 1986; adjudicator Nat. Coll. Dance Festival Assn., 1983—; co-host To Make a Dance, QUBE cable TV, 1979; mem. guest faculty Am. Dance Festival, Durham, N.C., 1984; site adjudicator Nat. Endowment for Arts, 1982-84; tchr. Hartford Ballet Sch., 1992—, East Conn. Concert Ballet, 1992—; guest faculty Wesleyan U., Middletown, Conn., 1992; guest artist Conn. Coll., 1993; chair dance dept. Hartt sch. U. Hartford, Conn., 1994—; freelance master tch. internat. univs. Prin. dancer Dance in America, TV spls., 1976, 79, 84; guest with with Rudolph Nureyev, Invitation to the Dance, CBS-TV, 1980; guest artist Theatre Choregraphique Rennes, Paris, 1981, Rennes, France, 1983, Adelaide U., 1991; site dir. Martha Graham's Diversion of Angels for student concert U. Mich., 1992, Martha Graham's Panorama, U. Ill., Champaign-Urbana, 1993. Founding mem. Cin. Arts Coun., 1976-78. Mem. Am. Guild Mus. Artists. Office: Hartford Ballet 224 Farmington Ave Hartford CT 06105-3597

LYMAN, RUTH ANN, psychologist; b. Nashville, Ark., Feb. 2, 1948; d. Oren Ernest and Frances Emeline (Urban) Frerking. BS, U. Ala., 1969, MA, 1972, PhD, 1974, MPA, 1986. Lic. psychologist, Ala. Cons. Ohio Coun. Community Mental Health Ctrs., Columbus, 1983, Ellard-Harper Found., Birmingham, Ala., 1983; resource cons. Ala. State Legis. Task Force on Child Abuse & Neglect, Montgomery, 1984-86; chief mental health sect., clin. psychologist U. Ala., Tuscaloosa, 1973-75; exec. dir. Western Mental Health Ctr., Birmingham, 1975-87; pvt. practice clin. psychologist Birmingham, 1988—; bd. dirs. Med. Bus. Mgmt., Inc.; mem. dept. psychiatry steering com. Brookwood HOsp., Birmingham, 1990—; adj. clin. prof. dept. psychology U. Ala., 1973-75, 77—. Author: (with others) Behavior Modification in Children: Case Studies and Illustrations from a Summer Camp, 1974, Outpatient Psychiatry: Progress, Treatment, Prevention, 1985, Administrative Discretion and the Implementation of Public Policy, 1986; contbr. articles to profl. jours. Treas., exec. com. Alcoholism Recovery Svcs., Inc., 1978-87; mem. adv. com. Nat. Alliance for the Mentally Ill., Birmingham, 1986-87, Pers. Bd. Jefferson County, 1978-82, chair, 1982, legis. com. chair, 1980-81; mem. Group Home Adv. Com., 1976-83; bd. dirs. Ala. NCCJ, 1979-82; mem. task force Birmingham Regional Health Systems Agy., Inc., 1977-79, mental health subcom., com. chair, 1979; chair by-laws com. Head Start Policy Coun., Birmingham, 1976-78; v.p. Ala. Coun. Community Health, 1987, stds. com., 1982, planning com., 1980-81, 83-85, sec., treas. and exec. com., 1978-79; bd. dirs., program co-chair Women's Network Birmingham, 1986; adv. com. Mental Health Assn. of Jefferson County, 1976-87. Named Birmingham Career Woman of the Yr., 1981. Mem. APA, NAFE, Southeastern Psychol. Assn., Ala. Psychol. Assn. (chair ad hoc com. for psychologists in pub. agys. 1985-86, chair ethics com. 1990, sec. 1990-92), Birmingham Regional Assn. Lic. Psychologists (co-chair steering com. and cmty. edn. com. 1989-90, pres. 1991), Assn. for Advancement of Psychology, Assn. Lic. Psychologists in Ala., Women's Network of Birmingham (bd. dirs., co-chair program 1986), Zonta Internat.

LYMAN, SHARI LEE WRIGHT, economics educator, analyst; b. Sewart AFB, Tenn., Apr. 12, 1962; d. John B. and Rachel Elaine (Schlarman) Wright; m. G. Robert Lyman, Aug. 17, 1985. BS in Polit. Sci., U. Utah, 1984, MS in Econs., 1990. Cert. tchr. K-12, Nev. Econ. analyst Clark County, Nev., 1987—; adj. faculty econs. C.C. of So. Nev., Las Vegas, 1991—, U. Nev., Las Vegas, 1993—, U. Phoenix, Nellis AFB, Nev., 1993—. Participant, grad. Las Vegas Met. Police Dept. Citizen's Acad., 1991. Mem. NAFE, AAUW, Am. Econ. Assn. (com. on women in econs. 1989—), Brookings Inst. Home: PO Box 729 Moapa NV 89025-0729

LYNCH, BEVERLY PFEIFER, education and information studies educator; b. Moorhead, Minn., Dec. 27, 1935; d. Joseph B. and Nellie K. (Bailey) Pfeifer; m. John A. Lynch, Aug. 24, 1968. B.S., N.D. State U., 1957, L.H.D. (hon.); M.S., U. Ill., 1959; Ph.D., U. Wis., 1972. Librarian Marquette U., 1959-60, 62-63; exchange librarian Plymouth (Eng.) Pub. Library, 1960-61; asst. head serials div. Yale U. Library, 1963-65, head, 1965-68; vis. lectr. U. Wis., Madison, 1970-71, U. Chgo., 1975; exec. sec. Assn. Coll. and Research Libraries, 1972-76; univ. librarian U. Ill.-Chgo., 1977-89; dean Grad. Sch. Libr. and Info. Sci. UCLA, 1989-94, prof. Grad. Sch. Edn. and Info. Studies, 1989—. Author: (with Thomas J. Galvin) Priorities for Academic Libraries, 1982, Management Strategies for Libraries, 1985, Academic Library in Transition, 1989, Information Technology and the University, 1995. Named Acad. Librarian of Yr., 1981. Mem. ALA (pres. 1985-86), Acad. Mgmt., Am. Sociol. Assn., Bibliog. Soc. Am., Caxton Club, The Chicago Network, Grolier Club, Arts Club Chgo., Phi Kappa Phi. Office: UCLA Grad Sch Grad Sch Edn & Info 405 Hilgard Ave Los Angeles CA 90025-1521

LYNCH, CAROL BECKER, academic administrator; b. St. Albans, N.Y., Dec. 3, 1942; d. Milton Taylor and Catherine (Kupsh) Becker; m. G. Robert Lynch, Aug. 19, 1967. AB, Mt. Holyoke Coll., 1964; MA, U. Mich., 1965; PhD, U. Iowa, 1971. NSF postdoctoral fellow U. Colo., Boulder, 1972-73; asst. prof. biology Wesleyan U., Middletown, Conn., 1973-79, assoc. prof. biology, 1979-85, prof. biology, 1985-92, dean of the scis., 1988-90; dean grad. sch. and assoc. vice chancellor for rsch. U. Colo., Boulder, 1992—; prog. dir. population biology, NSF, Washington, 1990-92. Author three book chapters in field; contbr. articles to profl. jours. Recipient career devel. award NIH, 1978-83; rsch. grantee NIH, 1975-88, 78-81, NSF, 1983-87, NATO, U. Edinburgh, 1978-82. Mem. AAAS, Behavior Genetics Assn. (pres. 1989-91), Am. Soc. Naturalists, Soc. Study of Evolution. Office: U Colo Regent Adminstrv Ctr Box 26 Boulder CO 80309

LYNCH, CAROL LEE, director special services, psychologist; b. Passaic, N.J., Sept. 22, 1943; d. Joseph Louis and Ellen (Birish) Dobkowski; m. Carl R. Grant, Feb. 16, 1969 (div. july 1987); m. Mervin Dean Lynch, Aug. 13, 1989; 1 child, Eric Alexander. BA, William Paterson Coll., 1966; MA, NYU, 1970, D Psychology, 1984. Lic. psychologist, N.J., N.Y. Tchr. Bloomfield (N.J.) Pub. Schs., 1966-68, psychologist, 1970-87; dir. spl. svcs. Waldwick (N.J.) Pub. Schs., 1987—; adj. clin. prof. NYU, N.Y.C., 1983-86 adj. prof. Montclair (N.J.) State Coll., 1984-85. Mem. profl. alumni coun. Sch. Edn., Health and Nursing, NYU, 1989-91. NYU fellow, 1981-82. Mem. APA (sch. psychology task force 1989—), N.J. Psychol. Assn. (treas. 1985-86), Nat. Assn. Sch. Psychologists (del. 19840-88), N.J. Assn. Sch. Psychologists (pres. 1982-83), Ea. Ednl. Rsch. Assn. (pres. 1993—), N.J. Coun. Edn., Bergen County Assn. Lic. Psychologists (bd. dirs. 1991-93), NYU SEHNAP Alumni Coun. (chair 1991-93), NYU Sch. Psychology Alumni Assn. (founder 1988-92). Home: 124 Frank Ct Mahwah NJ 07430-2963 Office: Waldwick Pub Schs 155 Summit Ave Waldwick NJ 07463-2133

LYNCH, CAROLE YARD, lawyer; b. Knoxville, Tenn., Aug. 29, 1951; d. Charles R. and Alma (Allred) Yard; 1 child, Allison Kathleen. BA, U. Tenn., 1972, JD, 1977. Bar: Tenn. 1977, Ga. 1982. Assoc. Thomas, Leitner, Mann, Warner & Owens, Chattanooga, 1977-78, Thomas, Mann & Gossett, Chattanooga, 1978-81, ptnr., v.p., 1981-86; ptnr. Grant, Konvalinka, & Harrison, P.C., 1987—. Author: Estate Planning Tennessee Practice, 1992; asst. editor Tenn. Law Rev., 1976-77. Vice chmn. allocations United Way of Chattanooga, 1985, vice chmn. pilot campaign, 1986; active Jr. League of Chattanooga, 1981-92; mem. alumnae adv. coun. U. Tenn. Coll. Law, 1983-92, chair 1990-92, dean's circle, 1989—; bd. dirs. Mental Health Assn. Chattanooga Inc., 1986-92, 1st v.p. 1988-89, sec. 1989-92; trustee St. Nicholas Sch., 1992—. Recipient Alumni Leadership award U. Tenn. Coll. Law, 1988, 92. Fellow Am. Bar Found., Tenn. Bar Found. (hearing com. mem, Tenn. bd. profl. responsibility 1992—, bd. govs. 1994—); mem. ABA (assembly del. 1991—, com. on legal aid and indigent defendants, select com. of the house 1994—), Chattanooga Bar Assn. (bd. govs. 1982-89, sec.-treas. 1985-86, pres. 1987-88), Tenn. Bar Assn. (chair long range planning com. 1989-90, vice chair comml. law, banking and bankruptcy 1988-90, unified bar study com. 1990-91, chair bar leadership conf. 1990, editorial bd. Tenn. Bar Jour. 1991-94, v.p.'s adv. com. 1993-94, bd. govs. 1994—), Ga. Bar Assn., Nat. Conf. Lawyers and Realtors (ABA del. 1990-92), Nat. Conf. Bar Pres.'s (exec. coun. 1989-92, treas. 1992-93, sec. 1993-94, pres. elect 1994—), Phi Alpha Delta. Episcopalian. Home: PO Box 178 Signal Mountain TN 37377-0178 Office: Grant Konvalinka & Harrison PC Republic Ctr Ste 900 633 Chestnut St Chattanooga TN 37450

LYNCH, CATHERINE, history educator; b. Cambridge, Mass., Nov. 7, 1949; d. Kevin and Anne (Borders) L. BA, U. Chgo., 1971; MA, U. Wis., 1973, PhD, 1989; cert. advanced study, Nanjing U., Jiangsu, China, 1981. Instr. history Colby Coll., Waterville, Maine, 1983-84; adj. prof. Asian studies, resident faculty Colby Coll., H. & William Smith-Colby-Bates China Program, Beijing, 1984-85; instr. history Case Western Res. U., Cleve., 1986-89, asst. prof., 1989—; vis. asst. prof. history U. Wis., Madison, 1990; mem. adv. bd. acad. programs China Ednl. Tours-Wellesley, Boston, 1985-86; hon. fellow Ctr. Asian Studies, U. Wis., Madison,1990-91; vis. rschr. Nanjing U., 1991. Mem. editl. bd. H-Asia, 1994—; contbr. articles to profl. jours. Nat. Def. Fgn. Lang. fellow U. Wis., 1972-73, 73-74, Social Coun. Rsch. Coun. fellow, Taiwan and Japan, 1975-77, Fulbright-Hays fellow, 1975-76, Social Sci. Rsch. Coun. fellow U. Wis., 1978, Charlotte W. Newcombe fellow U. Wis., 1981-82; rsch. grantee Case Western Res. U., Cleve., 1990, Nanjing, 1991, Com. on Scholarly Comm. with China and Case Western Res. U., Beijing, 1993. Mem. AAUP, Am. Hist. Assn., Assn. Asian Studies, Midwest Conf. on Asian Affairs (program com. 1992-93, Buchanan prize com. 1993), Soc. Values in Higher Edn., Phi Beta Kappa, Phi Alpha Theta. Office: Case Western Res U Dept History 10900 Euclid Ave Cleveland OH 44106-1712

LYNCH, CATHERINE GORES, social work administrator; b. Waynesboro, Pa., Nov. 23, 1943; d. Landis and Pamela (Whitmarsh) Gores; BA magna cum laude and honors, Bryn Mawr Coll., 1965; Fulbright scholar, Universidad Central de Venezuela, Caracas, 1965-66; postgrad. (Lehman fellow), Cornell U., 1966-67; m. Joseph C. Keefe, Nov. 29, 1981; children: Shannon Maria, Lisa Alison, Gregory T. Keefe, Michael D. Keefe. Mayor's intern, Human Resources Adminstrn., N.Y.C., 1967; rsch. asst. Orgn. for Social and Tech. Innovation, Cambridge, Mass., 1967-69; cons. Ford Found., Bogota, Colombia, 1970; staff Nat. Housing Census, Nat. Bur. Statistics, Bogota, 1971; evaluator Foster Parent Plan, Bogota, 1973; rsch. staff FEDESARROLLO, Bogota, 1973-74; dir. Dade County Advocates for Victims, Miami, Fla., 1974-86; asst. to dep. dir. Dept. Human Resources, Miami, 1986-87, computer liaison, 1987-88, asst. adminstr. placement svcs. program, 1988-89; exec. dir. Health Crisis Network, 1989—; guest lectr. local univs. Participant, co-chmn. various task forces rape, child abuse, incest, family violence, elderly victims of crime, nat., state, local levels, 1974-86; developer workshops in field; participant, chair, co-chair task forces on HIV/AIDS impact, long term care, children and AIDS, AIDS orgnl. issues, 1991—; mem. gov.'s task force on victims and witnesses, gov.'s task force on sex offenders and their victims; mem. ednl. review com. Am. Found. AIDS Rsch.; vice chair Metro-Dade HIV Svcs. Planning Council, 1991-93; active Fla. HIV Svcs. Adv. Coun., 1991-94; review panel Fed. Spl. Projects of Nat. Significance; cert. expert witness on battered women syndrome in civil and criminal cts. Recipient various public svc. awards including WINZ Citizen of Day, 1979, Outstanding Achievement award Fla. Network Victim Witness Svcs., 1982, Pioneer award Metro-Dade Women's Assn., 1989; cert. police instr. Mem. Nat. Orgn. of Victim Assistance Programs (bd. dirs. 1977-83; Outstanding Program award 1984). Fla. Network of Victim/Witness Programs (bd. dirs., treas., 1980-81), Nat. Assn. Social Workers, Am. Soc. Public Adminstrs., Dade County Fedn. Health and Welfare Workers, Fla. Assn. Health and Social Svcs. (Dade County chpt., treas., 1979-80), LWV (bd. dirs. Dade County chpt. 1989-92). Contbr. writings in field to publs. Office: Health Crisis Network 5050 Biscayne Blvd Miami FL 33137

LYNCH, DEBORAH ANN, college administrator; b. Cleve., June 12, 1947; d. Edward John and Dorothy Alice (Le Maitre) Dorony; m. Patrick Michael Lynch, Nov. 16, 1978 (dec. Dec. 11, 1989); 1 child, Ryan Woodward. BA, Kent (Ohio) State U., 1978; MS in Social Sci. Adminstrn., Case Western Res. U., 1980. Senate staff intern Com. on Labor and Human Resources, U.S. Senate, Washington, 1979-80; sr. planning assoc./evaluation assoc. United Way Svcs., Cleve., 1979-84; sr. planning assoc. Fedn. for Community Planning, 1984-85; cons. Mandel Ctr. for Non-Profit Orgn., Case Western Res. U., Cleve., 1986-90; dir. planning, mktg., pub. rels. Ursuline Coll., Pepper Pike, Ohio, 1990-92, dir. instl. planning, rsch. and assessment, 1990—; cons. Inst. for Ednl. Renewal, 1991—; chmn. strategic planning com. Cleve. Commn. Higher Edn., 1992—. Contbr. articles to profl. jours. Trustee Women Infants and Children Program, Cleve., 1981-85, Ohio Conf. for Coll. and Univ. Planning, 1993—. Recipient Ameritech Partnership Award for excellence in mktg. higher edn. Ohio Assn. Independent Colls. and Univs., 1992. Mem. Soc. for Coll. and Univ. Planning (planning com. 1993), Am. Kennel Club (columnist gazette 1985-93), Buckeye Keeshond Club (pres. 1981-83). Soc. of Friends. Home: 6446 Indian Point Rd Painesville OH 44077 Office: Ursuline Coll 2550 Lander Rd Cleveland OH 44124-4318

LYNCH, ELOISE, state legislator; b. Sept. 2, 1927. Student, Kans. Wesleyan; MA, Kans. State U., 1961; PhD, U. Kans., 1981. Former tchr.; mem. Kans. Ho. of Reps. Democrat. Home: 705 S Santa Fe Ave Salina KS 67401-4944 Office: Kans State Senate State Capital Topeka KS 66612*

LYNCH, FRAN JACKIE, investment advisory company executive; b. Bklyn., Dec. 15, 1948; d. William R. and Ruth (Slaiman) Diamondstein; m. James P. Lynch, Jan. 8, 1969; children: Cheryl Ann, Christopher, Kevin. BA, Bklyn. Coll., 1969; student, Suffolk Community Coll., Brentwood, N.Y., 1980-82; postgrad, L.I. U., 1983. V.p. Castle Capital Corp., N.Y.C., 1971-74; agt. Jerome Castle Found., N.Y.C., 1970-74; dir. office services Penn-Dixie Industries, N.Y.C., 1970-74; exec. asst. Med. Fin. Advisor, N.Y.C., 1974; v.p. Sept. Capital Corp., Glen Cove, N.Y., 1977-80; controller Bobgar Inc., Wallweaves Inc. and N.Y. Twine, Syosset, N.Y., 1980-86, The Kapson Group, Commack, N.Y., 1987-91, Westbury Transport ETAL, Astoria, N.Y., 1991-93; ptnr. Econometric Capital Advisors Inc., Miami, Fla., 1992—; bus. mgr. Am-Pro Protective Agy., Columbia, S.C., 1994—; cons. Women's Times, Queens, N.Y., 1987. Sec. Elwood Booster Club, East Northport, N.Y., 1987; mem. Harley Ave. PTA, 1980-87; coach Northport Youth Soccer, 1982; tchr. Confraternity Christian Doctrine Project St. Elizabeth's Ch., 1972-80, bd. dirs. Parish council, S. Huntington, N.Y., 1978-80. Home: 216 Camden Chase Columbia SC 29223

LYNCH, SISTER FRANCIS XAVIER, nun, development director; b. Watertown, N.Y., Oct. 21, 1918; d. George Francis and Sarah Emma (Nicholson) L. BS in Nursing, Cath. U. Am., 1944, MS in Adminstrn., 1948, postgrad. in chemistry, 1949-51; Dr. Humane Letters (hon.), Long Island U., 1967. Tchr. St. Leo Sch., N.Y.C., 1939-40, Holy Angels Sch., Buffalo, N.Y., 1940-41; operating room supr. Champlain Valley Hosp., Plattsburgh, N.Y., 1941-42; instr. Biology & Biol. Scis. D'Youville Coll., Buffalo, N.Y., 1944-48; head dept. Biology D'Youville Coll., Buffalo, 1948-51, dean Sch. of Nursing, 1951-62, pres., 1962-68; initiator expansion program Grey Nuns Motherhouse, Yardley, Pa., 1969-71; dir. devel. Grey Nuns of the Sacred Heart, Yardley, Pa., 1971-92; vol. patient rep. Mercer Med. Ctr., Trenton, N.J., 1993—; cons. to Hosps. operated by Grey Nuns and their schs. of Nursing, 1955-62; mem. N.Y. State Bd. Nurse Examiners (Regents), 1952-64. Bd. dirs. A. Barton Hepburn Hosp., Ogdensburg, N.Y., 1976—. Mem. AAUW, Nat. Cath. Devel. Conf. (charter, v.p., bd. dirs., Disting. Svc. award), Phila. Mus. Art, Mercer Med. Ctr. Aux., Ctr. for Study of the Presidency, World Affairs Coun., Am. Acad. Polit. Sci. Republican. Home: Grey Nuns of Sacred Heart 1750 Quarry Rd Yardley PA 19067

LYNCH, KATHLEEN MARIE, lawyer, real estate executive; b. N.Y.C., Dec. 30, 1949; d. Daniel Francis and Mary Margaret (Flynn) L. BA in Math. cum laude, Coll. of Mt. St. Vincent, 1970; postgrad., U. Pa., 1976-77; JD cum laude, U. Md., 1977; LL.M. in Taxation, NYU, 1991. Bar: Pa. 1977, N.J. 1978, N.Y. 1984, D.C. 1985, Conn. 1995, U.S. Ct. Appeals (3d cir.) 1980, U.S. Supreme Ct. 1981. Research analyst, claims rep. Social Security Adminstrn., Balt., 1973-76; assoc. Drinker, Biddle & Reath, Phila., 1977-84, ptnr., 1984-86; v.p., gen. counsel M. Alfieri Co., Inc., Edison, N.J., 1987-89; v.p., counsel Berwind Property Group, Phila., 1992—; instr. Inst. for Paralegal Tng., Phila. 1984—. Vol. atty. Support Ctr. for Child Advocates, Phila., 1979-86, Queen Village Neighbors Assn., Phila., 1984-86; pres. Soc. Hill Towers Buyers Assn., Phila., 1979-80; bd. dirs. Soc. Hill Civic Assn., 1980. Mem. ABA, Pa. Bar. Assn., Phila. Bar Assn. (chair zoning and land use com. 1985-86), N.J. Bar Assn.

LYNCH, LISA MICHELE, economics educator; b. Waterbury, Conn., Mar. 6, 1956; d. John Povah and Elaine L.; m. Fabio Schiantarelli, July 9, 1988. BA, Wellesley Coll., 1978; MSc, London Sch. Econs., 1979, PhD, 1983. Lectr. U. Bristol, Eng., 1982-83; asst. prof. Ohio State U., Columbus, 1983-85; asst. prof. MIT, Cambridge, 1985-89, assoc. prof., 1989-93; William L. Clayton assoc. prof. internat. econ. affairs Tufts U. Fletcher Sch. Law and Diplomacy, Medford, Mass., 1993—, chmn. econs. and internat. bus. div., 1994—; mem. bd. sr. scholars EQW, Phila., 1991—; rsch. assoc. Nat. Bur. Econ. Rsch., Cambridge, 1993—; mem. nat. adv. com. Nat. Ctr. for Workplace, Berkeley, Calif., 1993—. Editor: Training and the Private Sector: International Comparisons, 1994; editor Jour. Labor Econs., 1993—; contbr. chpts. to books, articles to profl. jours. Recipient grad. student coun. teaching award MIT, 1988. Mem. Indsl. Rels. Rsch. Assn., Am. Econ. Assn., Econometric Soc., Internat. Indsl. Rels. Assn. Office: Tufts U Fletcher Sch Law & Diplomacy Packard Ave Medford MA 02155

LYNCH, MARGARET A., state legislator; b. Keene, N.H., Sept. 10, 1939; 4 children. BA, Keene State Coll., 1979. Ret. coll. adminstr.; mem. N.H. Ho. of Reps., mem. appropriations com. Roman Catholic. Home: 363 Chapman Rd Keene NH 03431-4378 Office: NH Ho of Reps State Capitol Concord NH 03301*

LYNCH, MARY JEAN, art educator, consultant; b. Hillsdale, Mich., Mar. 19, 1948; d. Paul A. and Marie C. (Larson) L.; m. Glenn A. Rowinski, Jan. 24, 1985. BA, Hillsdale Coll., 1970; BFA, Cleve. Inst. Art, 1981. Art tchr. Hillsdale (Mich.) Pub. Schs., 1970-72, Avon (Ohio) Pub. Schs., 1972-77; mus. vol. asst. Am. History Divsn. of Community Life Smithsonian Inst., Washington, 1982-83; art instr. after-sch. program Fairfax County Pub. Schs., Falls Church, Va., 1982-83; arts specialist key after sch.-program Six Schs. Complex, Washington, 1982-83; area coord., arts tchr. fine arts summer program Fine Arts Summer program Chautauqua (N.Y.) Inst., 1981-85; art and art appreciation tchr. St. Mary's Acad., Alexandria, Va., 1983-85; art and art history instr. St. Stephen's Sch., Alexandria, Va., 1983-88; arts and crafts specialist, dir. Panzer Arts and Crafts Shop, Stuttgart, Germany, 1989-91; art cons. Alexandria, 1992—; workshop instr., summer camp instr. resident assocs. program, young assocs. and family activities Smithsonian Inst., Washington, 1983-85, 1991—. Exhibited in group shows inlcuding Anton Gallery, Washington, 1987, Fredonia State Coll., 1983, 84, 85, Chautauqua Art Assn. Gallery, 1983-85 summers, Greater Reston Arts Ctr., 1983, Cleve. Inst. of Art, 1981. Recipient scholarship Cleve. Inst. Art, 1980-81. Mem. NEA, Nat. Arts Edn. Assn. Office: 1100 Belle View Blvd # B1 Alexandria VA 22307-6509

LYNCH, MAUREEN, communications executive; b. Jersey City, N.J., May 28, 1938; d. Thomas Edward and Mary Margaret (Doust) L. AA with honors, Marymount U., 1957; BA with honors, Rosemont Coll., 1959. Beauty and fashion editor Ladies Home Jour. Mag., 1974-82; pres. Maureen Lynch & Co., Inc., 1982—; dir. communications grad. sch. bus. adminstr. Fordham U., 1985—; bd. dirs. Blue Hill Troupe, Ltd., 410-57 Corp. Active Friends of Am. Ballet Theater. Recipient awards N.Y. Art Dirs. Club. Mem. Fashion Group Internat. (v.p. exec. com.), Cosmetic Exec. Women, Trends, West Side Tennis Club, Seabright Lawn Tennis and Cricket Club, NOW, Beta Gamma Sigma.

LYNCH, NANCY ANN, computer scientist, educator; b. Bklyn., Jan. 19, 1948; d. Roland David and Marie Catherine (Adinolfi) Evraets; m. Dennis Christopher Lynch, June 14, 1969; children: Patrick, Kathleen (dec.), Mary. BS, Bklyn. Coll., 1968; PhD, MIT, 1972. Asst. prof. math. Tufts U., Medford, Mass., 1972-73, U. So. Calif., Los Angeles, 1973-76, Fla. Internat. U., Miami, 1976-77; assoc. prof. computer sci. Ga. Tech. U., Atlanta, 1977-82; assoc. prof. computer sci. MIT, Cambridge, 1982-86, prof. computer sci., 1986—; Ellen Swallow Richards chair MIT, 1982-87; cons. Computer Corp. Am., Cambridge, 1984-86, Apollo Computer, Chelmsford, Mass., 1986-89, AT&T Bell Labs, Murray Hill, N.J., 1986-89, Digital Equipment Corp., 1990. Contbr. numerous articles to profl. jours. Mem. Assn. Computing Machinery. Roman Catholic. Office: MIT NE43-525 Cambridge MA 02139

LYNCH, PATRICIA GATES, broadcasting organization executive consultant, former ambassador; b. Newark, Apr. 20, 1926; d. William Charles and Mary Frances (McNamee) Lawrence; m. Mahlon Eugene Gates, Dec. 19, 1942 (div. 1972); children: Pamela Townley Gates Sprague, Lawrence Alan; m. William Dennis Lynch. Student, Dartmouth Inst., 1975. Broadcaster Sta. WFAX-Radio, Falls Ch., Va., 1958-68; pub. TV host Sta. WETA, Washington, 1967-68; broadcaster NBC-Radio, Europe, Iran, USSR, 1960-61; internat. broadcaster, producer Voice of Am., Washington, 1962-69; staff asst. to First Lady The White House, Washington, 1969-70; host Voice of Am. Breakfast Show, Morning show, 1970-86; U.S. ambassador to Madagascar and the Comoros, 1986-89; dir. corp. affairs Radio Free Europe/Radio Liberty, Washington, 1989-94; worldwide lectr., 1968-86; adv. com. Ind. Fed. Savs. and Loan Assn., Washington, 1970-86. Author stories on Am. for English teaching dept. Radio Sweden, 1967-68, others on internat. broadcasting. Chair internat. svc. com. Washington chpt. ARC, 1979-86; bd. visitors Duke U., Durham, N.C. Grantee USIA, 1983; recipient Pub. Service award U.S. Army, 1960. Mem. Coun. Am. Ambs., (bd. dirs.), Assn. Diplomatic Studies and Tng. Dept. State (bd. dirs.), Am. Women in Radio and TV (pres. 1966-67), Am. News Women's Club, Washington Inst. Fgn.

Affairs (bd. dirs.), Internat. Student House, D.C. (bd. dirs.). Republican. Episcopalian.

LYNCH, PAULINE ANN, trust company executive; b. Saginaw, Mich., Mar. 19, 1939; d. Frank H. and Marie A. (Gaertner) Krueger; m. Ralph T. Lynch, Jan. 17, 1959; children: Patrick Thomas, Michael F., Terri Marie. Cert., Am. Inst. Paralegal, Detroit, 1985, Nat. Trust Sch./ Northwestern U, 1988; grad., Nat. Grad. Trust Sch., 1991. Sec. Sun Life Ins. Co., Saginaw, 1956-57; exec. sec. Mich. Bell Telephone, Saginaw, 1957-60; paralegal/probate Polasky, Meisel, Rosenbaum & McLeod, Saginaw, 1964-83; bus. owner Saginaw, 1983-86; v.p., trust officer Second Nat. Bank of Saginaw, 1986—; instr. legal asst. program Delta Coll., Saginaw, 1987-91. Vol. United Way, Saginaw, 1987-91, Voluntary Action, Saginaw, 1987-94; past commentator communion distributor Holy Spirit Cath. Ch., Saginaw, 1980—, mem. parish coun.l bd. dirs. Guardianship Svcs. Saginaw. Mem. Northeastern Estate Planning Coun., Optimist Club. Home: 1200 Curwood Rd Saginaw MI 48609-5224 Office: Second Nat Bank Saginaw 101 N Washington Ave Saginaw MI 48607-1207

LYNCH, PRISCILLA A., nursing educator, therapist; b. Joliet, Ill., Jan. 8, 1949; d. LaVerne L. and Ann M. (Zamkovitz) L. BS, U. Wyo., 1973; MS, St. Xavier Coll., Coll., 1981. RN, Ill. Staff nurse Rush-Presbyn.-St. Luke's Med. Ctr., Chgo., 1977-81, psychiat.-liaison cons., 1981-83, asst. prof. nursing, unit leader, 1985—; mgr. and therapist Oakside Clinic, Kankakee, Ill., 1987—; mem. adv. bd. Depressive and Manic Depression Assn., Chgo., 1986—; mem. consultation and mental health unit Riverside Med. Ctr., Kankakee, 1987—; speaker numerous nat. orgns. Contbr. numerous abstracts to profl. jours., chpts. to books. Bd. dirs. Cornerstone Svcs. Recipient total quality mgmt. award Rush-Presbyn.-St. Luke's Med. Ctr., 1991. Mem. ANA, Ill. Nurses Assn. (coms.), Coun. Clin. Nurse Specialists, Profl. Nursing Staff (sec. 1985-87, mem. coms.). Presbyterian. Home: 606 Darcy Ave Joliet IL 60436-1673

LYNCH, ROSE PEABODY, art gallery executive; b. Dallas, June 6, 1949; d. Russell Vincent and Rose Peabody (Parsons) L.; m. Peter Stuart Milhaupt, Feb. 12, 1972 (div. 1977); m. James Alexander Torrey, Apr. 22, 1989. AAS, Bennett Coll., 1969; BA, Princeton U., 1971; MBA, Harvard U., 1982. Personal asst. Halston, Ltd., N.Y.C., 1975-76; assoc. dir. retail promotion Revlon, Inc., N.Y.C., 1976-80; dir. mktg. devel. Elizabeth Arden, N.Y.C., 1982-85; dir. mktg. Charles of the Ritz, N.Y.C., 1985-87; pres. Danskin, N.Y.C., 1987-89, Trowbridge Gallery, U.S., N.Y.C., 1989-93; cons., acting chief operating officer LeRoi Princeton Inc., 1991-92; v.p. merchandising-fragrance Victoria's Secret, Reynoldsburg, Ohio, 1993—; bd. dirs. Manhattan Theatre Club. Republican. Episcopalian. Office: Victoria's Secret 4 Limited Pky Reynoldsburg OH 43068-5302

LYNCH, SHERRY KAY, counselor; b. Topeka, Kans., Nov. 20, 1957; d. Robert Emmett and Norma Lea Lynch. BA, Randolph-Macon Woman's Coll., 1979; MS, Emporia State U., 1980; PhD, Kans. State U., 1987. Vocat. rehab. counselor Rehab. Services, Topeka, 1980-81, community program cons., 1981-86. Mem. exec. com. Sexual Assault Counseling Program, Topeka, 1983-86, recruitment coordinator, 1983-86, counselor, 1981-86, Nat. Singles Conf. Planning Com., Green Lake, Wis., 1987-90; area admissions rep. Randolph-Macon Woman's Coll., Lynchburg, Va., 1981-87; counseling intern, Winthrop Coll., Rock Hill, S.C., 1986-87; counselor Ripon (Wis.) Coll., 1987-90, Va. Poly. Inst. and State U., 1991—, mem. Student Affairs Staff Devel. Com., 1991-94, chairperson, 1992-94; mem. Student Outreach Svcs. Coun. Northbrooke Hosp., 1988-90, mem. Sexual Assault Victim Edn. Support Com., 1991—, Wellness Com., 1993—, Leadership Resource Team, 1994—; bd. dirs., sec. Ripon Chem. Abuse and Awareness program, 1987-90; bd. dirs. Montgomery County Community Shelter, 1992—, also sec., 1993—, Haymarket Sq. Homeowners Assn., 1992—, also treas., 1993—; chairperson ch. and soc. com. Blacksburg United Meth. Ch., 1992-94, mem. coun. ministries, 1992-94. Recipient Kans. 4-H Key award Extension Service of Kans. State U., 1974; named Internat. 4-H Youth Exchange Ambassador to France, 1977. Mem. Nat. Rehab. Counseling Assn. (bd. dirs. 1982-88, chairperson br. devel. subcouncil 1982-87, chairperson policy and program council 1987-88), Gt. Plains Rehab. Counseling Assn. (newsletter editor 1982-85, bd. dirs. 1983-87, pres. 1984-85, sec. 1986-87), Gt. Plains Rehab. Assn. (bd. dirs. 1983-85, awards chairperson 1984-85), Kans. Rehab. Counseling Assn. (bd. dirs. 1983-86, pres. 1984-85), Kans. Rehab. Assn. (bd. dirs. 1982-85, advt. chairperson 1983-85), Topeka Rehab. Assn. (bd. dirs. 1982-85, sec. 1982-83, pres. 1983-84), Am. Assn. Counseling and Devel., Am. Coll. Personnel Assn. (directorate body counseling and psychol. svcs. commn. VII 1990-93, membership chairperson 1990-93), Wis. Coll. Personnel Assn. (bd. dirs. 1988-90), Assn. for Specialists in Group Work, Va. Coll. Pers. Assn. Republican. Methodist. Avocation: tennis. Home: 2700 Newton Ct Blacksburg VA 24060-4112 Office: Va Tech U Counseling Ctr 152 Henderson Hall Blacksburg VA 24061

LYNCH, SONIA, data processing consultant; b. N.Y.C., Sept. 17, 1938; d. Espriela and Sadie Beatrice (Scales) Sarreals; m. Waldro Lynch, Sept. 18, 1981 (div. Oct. 1983). BA in Langs. summa cum laude, CCNY, 1960; cert. in French, Sorbonne, 1961. Systems engr. IBM, N.Y.C., 1963-69; cons. Babbage Systems, N.Y.C., 1969-70; project leader Touche Ross, N.Y.C., 1970-73; sr. programmer McGraw-Hill, Inc., Hightstown, N.J., 1973-78; staff data processing cons. Cin. Bell Info. Systems, 1978-89; sr. analyst AT&T, 1989-92; lead tech. analyst Automated Concepts Inc., Arlington, Va., 1992-94, cons., 1994—; with Johns Hopkins Applied Physics Lab., Laurel, Md., 1994—. Elder St. Andrew Luth. Ch., Silver Spring, 1992—. Downer scholar CUNY, 1960, Dickman Inst. fellow Columbia U., 1960-61. Mem. Assn. for Computing Machinery, Phi Beta Kappa. Democrat. Home: 13705 Beret Pl Silver Spring MD 20906-3030

LYNCH, STEPHANIE NADINE, clinical psychologist; b. Cambridge, Mass., Apr. 11, 1951; d. Jeremiah and Irma C. (Gauntt) L.; m. Rickey Bernard Silverman, Apr. 17, 1983; children: Jason Frederick, Leonard Jeremiah, Rachel Elizabeth. PhD in Clin. Psychology, Case Western Res. U. 1977. Lic. psychologist, Mass., cert. psychologist, N.H. Staff psychologist Reading (Pa.) Hosp. & Med. Ctr., 1977-79, St. Elizabeth's Hosp., Brighton, Mass., 1979-81; pvt. practice Silverman & Assocs., Plaistow, N.H., 1981—; clin. instr. Tuft U. Sch. Medicine, Boston, 1980-89; cons. Parkland Hosp., Derry, N.H., 1990—, Cath. Med. Ctr., Manchester, N.H., 1990—, St. Elizabeth's Hosp., Brighton, Mass., 1980—, St. John of God Hosp., Brighton, 1981-92, Holy Family Hosp., Methuen, Mass., 1981—. Co-author: (chpt.) Handbook of Innovative Psychotherapies, 1981. Pres. No. New England Down Syndrome Congress, Maine, N.H., Vt., 1988-90. Mem. APA, Mass. Psychol. Assn. Office: Silverman & Assocs 31 Main St Plaistow NH 03865-3002

LYNCH, SUSAN H., state legislator; b. Mpls., July 5, 1943; d. Lewis Mifflin and Helen Hayes; m. Thomas Vincent Lynch, June 14, 1969; children: Brian, Robin, Karen. BA in Biology, Cedar Crest Coll., 1965. Genetic rsch. technician NIH, Bethesda, Md., 1965-67, Children's Hosp., L.A., 1967-69; dir. summer arts and crafts City of Prescott, Ariz., 1976-78, dir. preschool, 1978-82; mem. Prescott City Coun., 1983-87; mem. Ariz. Ho. Reps., Phoenix, 1993—. Bd. dirs. Prescott Fine Arts, Phippen Mus. Western Art; mem. adv. bd. Anytown U.S.A., 1990-93. Mem. AAUW (br. pres. 1990-92), Ariz. Women's End. and Employment, Rep. Women Prescott (treas. 1991). Presbyterian. Office: Ariz State Legislature 1700 W Washington Phoenix AZ 85007

LYNCH, SUSAN KATHRYN, lawyer; b. Calif., June 25, 1951; d. Thomas Joseph and Mary (Kane) Lynch; m. Kim L. Erzinger, July 10, 1982; children: Aaron, Eric. BA, U. Wis., 1975; JD, Hamline U., 1983. Bar: Wis. 1983, Fla. 1984, U.S. Dist. Ct. (we. dist.) Wis. 1983, U.S. Ct. Appeals, 1983. Atty. pvt. practice, Stevens Point, Wis., 1983-87; asst. pub. defender State of Wis., Stevens Point, Wis., 1987-90; dist. atty. Portage County, Stevens Point, Wis., 1991—. Del. Nat. Dem. Conv., N.Y.C., 1992; chair Portage County Dem. Party, Stevens Point, 1985; mem. Wis. Women's Coun., Madison, 1988-90, Wis. Pub. Defender Bd., Madison, 1986-87. Mem. Na. Women's Polit. Caucus, State Bar Wis., State Bar Fla. Office: Portage County Dist Atty 1516 Church St Stevens Point WI 54481

LYNCH, TERESA ANN, state legislator; b. Mpls., Jan. 15, 1954; d. Leslie Alvin Steinberg and Joanne (Pouliot) Brand; m. David C. Lynch, May 18, 1974; children: Emily, Erin, Anna, Tessa. Grad. interpreter tng. program, St. Paul Tech. Coll., 1983. Interpreter Anoka-Hennepin Sch. Dist., Mpls., 1983-87; state rep. Minn. Ho. of Reps. Dist. 50B, Andover, Minn., 1988—. Asst. caucus leader Rep. House Caucus, St. Paul, 1992-94; vice chair Rules & Legislative Adminstrn. Named Legislator of Yr., Assn. of Minn. Counties, St. Paul, 1992; recipient Legis. Recognitive award Nat. Assn. of the Deaf, 1992; named Legislator of Yr., Minn. Assn. Deaf Citizens, 1993. Republican. Office: Minn House of Reps 295 State Office Bldg Saint Paul MN 55155

LYNCH, VIRGINIA LEE, art gallery director; b. Greenville, Tex., May 27, 1915; d. Oscar Roscoe and Catherine Claudine (Cooper) McGaughey; m. Eric Noble Dennard, June 16, 1938 (div. 1960); children: Katherine Fryer, Eric Jr.; m. William Stang Lynch, May 7, 1962 (dec. 1977); stepchildren: F. Bradley, James B., Mrs. Edward T. Barrett. BA, Baylor U., 1937, MA, 1960. Tchr. Tatum (Tex.) High Sch., 1937-38; part-time and substitute tchr. Waco (Tex.) Pub. Schs., Tyler (Tex.) Jr. Coll., 1950-60, Laselle Jr. Coll., Newton, Mass., 1950-60; dir. women Brandeis U., Waltham, Mass., 1960-62; owner Virginia Lynch Gallery, Tiverton, R.I., 1983—; guest curator Newport Art Mus., 1992-94. Trustee R.I. Sch. Design, Providence, 1980—; trustee Newport (R.I.) Art Mus., 1989-93, hon. life trustee, 1993—; mem. R.I. State com. Nat. Gallery Women in Arts, 1987—; mem. Town Planning Bd., Little Compton, R.I., 1980-86, Village Improvement Soc., Little Compton, 1963—, Save the Lighthouse Com., Little Compton; deacon United Congl. Ch., Little Compton, 1980-82; bd. dirs. Little Compton Hist. Soc., v.p., 1980-84. Recipient Citizen of Yr. award R.I. Sch. Design, 1983, State of the Arts award R.I. State Coun. on the Arts, 1992, Best Gallery award R.I. Monthly, 1992-94. Mem. Little Compton Garden Club (pres. 1975-77), Sakonnet Golf Club, Brown U. Faculty Club. Home: 54 S Of Commons Rd Little Compton RI 02837-1522 Office: Virginia Lynch Gallery 3883 Main Rd Tiverton RI 02878-4843

LYNCH-FIRCA, DIANA JOAN, educator; b. Kearny, N.J., Sept. 7, 1954; d. Joseph Daniel and Eleanor L. Lynch; m. John Nicholas Firca, Dec. 18, 1993. BA in Art History and Italian, U. Colo., 1976; MA in Art History, Rosary Coll. at Villa Schifanoia Grad. Sch. of Fine Arts (Italy), River Forest, Ill., 1979; BFA in Painting, Acad. Fine Arts, Milan, Venice, Bari, Italy, 1987; cert. in English as fgn. lang., Internat. House, London, 1990; postgrad., Monmouth Coll., 1990-91, Kean Coll. Cert. art, Italian, elem. edn. tchr. Tchr. English as foreign lang. Am. Inst., Florence, Italy, 1978-79, Brit. Sch., Venice, 1984-85, Am. Lang. Ctr., Matera, Italy, 1986-90; lectr. English U. Inst. Modern Lang., Milan, 1980-84, U. Studi di Bari, 1985-90; tchr. Italian Matawan Regional High Sch., Aberdeen, N.J., 1991—; tchr. art and ESL, Am. Sch., Montagnola, Switzerland, summers 1983-89; tchr. English as fgn. lang. Lord Byron Coll., London, summer 1990, Anglo Continental West Long Branch, N.J., 1990—; mem. adj. faculty ESL, fine art and art history Brookdale C.C., Lincroft, N.J., 1990—. Mem. N.J. Edn. Assn., Nat. Art Edn. Assn., Fgn. Lang. Educators N.J., Guild Creative Art, Art Educators N.J. Roman Catholic. Office: Matawan Regional High Sch Atlantic Ave Matawan NJ 07747

LYNDES GARROT, JOY ERIN, landscape architect; b. Hanover, N.H., Aug. 8, 1957; d. Bryce Burbank and Jeannette Mary (Bickford) Lyndes; m. Donald Jerome Garrot, Jr., June 20, 1981; children: Alexandra Lyndes, Taylor Stephen Martin. BLA, U. Ariz., 1983. Registered landscape architect, Ariz. Rsch. asst. U. Ariz., Tucson, 1980-83; landscape designer Greiner Inc., Tucson, 1983-89; project mgr., pers. dir. Wheat-Gallaher & Assocs., Tucson, 1989—; constrn. supr. Ariz. Dept. Transp., Flagstaff, 1993, cons. landscape architect, project mgr., 1990—; cons. landscape architect, project mgr. U. Ariz./BTA Architects, 1993, City of Tucson, Engring. Div., 1989-91. Contbr. articles to profl. jours. Sec. Tangue Verde Sch. Dist. Ednl. Enrichment Found., Tucson, 1992—; chair Tanque Verde Elem. Sch. Ednl. Enhancers, 1992—, mem. Parent/Tchr. Group, 1990—; vice chair Pima County Design Rev. Com., Tucson, 1992—, Pima County Tech. Rev. Com., 1992—; co-leader Boy Scouts Am., Tucson, 1993. Recipient Mary Miller award for independent study U. Ariz., 1982. Mem. Am. Soc. Landscape Architects, Ariz., Parks and Recreation Assn., Tucson Arts Partnership, Sigma Lambda Alpha. Home: 12350 E Prince Rd Tucson AZ 85749 Office: Wheat-Gallaher & Assocs 377 S Meyer Ave Tucson AZ 85701

LYNE, JUNE D., state legislator; b. 1928. Former bookkeeper, farmer, office mgr.; mem. Ky. Ho. of Reps., 1985—. Active Parents Tchrs. Assn. Mem. Farm Bur., Dem. Club. Mem. Ch. of Christ. Home: 10904 Clarksville Rd Olmstead KY 42265-9110 Office: Ky State Senate State Capital Frankfort KY 40601*

LYNES, (MARY) LINDA CALHOUN, guidance counselor; b. Savannah, Ga., May 9, 1948; d. Malcolm Hoover and Clarice Frances (Whittier) Calhoun; m. Johnie Madison Lynes, Jr., Dec. 18, 1971; children: Brett Madison, Paige Whittier, Abby Louise. BSEd, Ga. So. U., 1970, MEd, 1973, EdS, 1975. Cert. profl. counselor, Ga. Social studies tchr. Beach Jr. High Sch., Savannah, 1970-72; guidance counselor Mercer Jr. High Sch., Savannah, 1972-75, Windsor Forest High Sch., Savannah, 1975—. Recipient Svc. award Windsor Forest High Sch. PTA, 1993. Mem. ACA, Am. Sch. Counselors Assn., Ga. Sch. Counselors Assn., Coastal Area Sch. Counselors Assn., The Landings Club, Delta Kappa Gamma (v.p., pres.). Methodist. Home: 28 Hasleiters Retreat Savannah GA 31411-3108 Office: Windsor Forest High Sch 12419 Largo Dr Savannah GA 31499-6201

LYNN, CAROLYN IRVIN, pediatrics nurse, nursing administrator; b. Marshall, Tex., Feb. 8, 1945; d. Alva J. and Delphia Mae (Irvin); m. John F. Lynn, Mar. 21, 1965; children: John F. Jr., Vaughan Alva, Roseann Denise. Diploma, Tex. Ea. Sch. Nursing, Tyler, 1966. RN, Tex. Sch. nurse Beckville (Tex.) Ind. Sch. Dist.; nursing supr. Henderson (Tex.) Meml. Hosp. Mem. Tex. Nurses Assn. Home: RR 2 Box 236 Beckville TX 75631-9755

LYNN, DONNA MARIA, public relations and marketing executive, writer; b. Hollywood, Calif., Oct. 4, 1945; d. Kane Wallace Lynn and Rita (Piazza) Maxwell; m. Dennis D. Schreffler, 1965 (div. 1973); children: Scott G. Schreffler, Susan M. Schreffler. Student, UCLA, 1963-65, U. Utah, 1965-68; BA, U. Ark., 1970; postgrad. in law, U. Balt., 1973-74. Lobbyist, UniServ dir. NEA, Washington, 1970-77; pres., CEO Lynn Assocs., Inc., Westport, Conn., 1977—; mgr. media rels. Perrier/Great Waters of France, N.Y.C., 1978-79; sr. cons. The Nestle Co., Washington and White Plains, N.Y., 1979-83; dep. dir. sports div. Hill & Knowlton, N.Y.C., 1983-85; mgr. pub. relations Avon Products, Inc., N.Y.C., 1985-86; supr. account group Daniel J. Edelman, N.Y.C., 1979-81. Features editor: Flight Attendant mag., 1986-87; contbr. numerous articles to newspapers and mags. Founder, dir. Earth Day in Ark., 1970; del. White House Conf. on Children and Youth, Washington, 1970; nat. pres. Women's Aux. to Student AMA, 1971-73; liaision White House Press Office, Dem. Nat. Conf., N.Y.C., 1979; mem. Md. Commn. for Women, Annapolis, 1976-77; pres. Annapolis Summer Garden Theatre, 1976-78; mem. bus. adv. bd. Nat. Down Syndrome Soc., N.Y.C., 1985-89. Mem. Am. Mgmt. Assn., Boating Writers Internat., Pub. Rels. Soc. Am., NEA (life, legis. chair Ark. chpt. 1970-73), Rotary Internat., Cedar Point Yacht Club, The Superyacht Soc. (exec. dir. 1989—), Nat. Fedn. Press Women, Conn. Press Club, Phi Alpha Theta. Office: 7 Punch Bowl Dr Westport CT 06880-2126

LYNN, DOROTHY ANN, school counselor; b. Iowa City, Apr. 1, 1947; d. Raymond Louis and Marie Frances (Klouda) Hotz; m. Joseph Ray Lynn, Dec. 26, 1970; children: Debra Ann, Barbara Jo, Joseph Ray. BA in Elem. Edn., U. No. Iowa, 1970; MA in Edn., U. Iowa, 1990. Cert. K-6 and 7-12 counselor, K-6 tchr., Iowa. Tchr. Fredericksburg (Iowa) Community Sch., 1970-71; substitute tchr. Northwood-Kensett and Thompson Community Schs., 1985-87, Iowa City Community Sch. Dist., 1989-91; presch. tchr. Creative World, Iowa City, 1992; K-12 counselor Lone Tree (Iowa) Community Sch., 1992—; vol. and elem. substitute tchr. Lake Mills Community Sch., 1984-88. Contbr. poems to anthologies. Mem. ACA, NEA, Iowa Edn. Assn., Lone Tree Edn. Assn., Iowa Counseling Assn., Am. Sch. Counselors Assn., Iowa Sch. Counselors Assn., Nat. Honor Soc., Kappa Delta Pi. Roman Catholic.

LYNN, ELIZABETH MEAGHER, management educator; b. Oshkosh, Wis., June 13, 1939; d. Joseph Edward and Gertrude Johanna (DeYoung) Meagher; m. Lowell A. Lynn (dec. 1981). BA, Marygrove Coll., Detroit; MA, Villanova U.; MEd, Columbia U.; PhD, Ind. U., 1974. Lectr. CCNY, 1968-71; sr. rsch. assoc. Case Western Res. U. Sch. Nursing, Cleve., 1975-76; staff assoc., mgmt. tng. and devel. Std. Oil Co. (Sohio), Cleve., 1977-82; adj. assoc. prof. dept. bus. comm. Grad. Sch. Bus. Adminstrn., U. So. Calif., L.A., 1982-86; pres. Lynn & Assocs., 1982—; regional mgr. tng. bread divsn. Interstate Brands Corp., Glendale, Calif., 1988-89; assoc. prof. bus. comm. mgmt. dept. GMI Engring. & Mgmt. Inst., Flint, Mich., 1989—; teaching asst. Ind. U., 1971-74; prodn. asst. Villanova U.; environ. advisor Runyan Lake Assn.; adj. prof. Sch. Mgmt. U. Mich.-Flint, 1994—; presenter in field; profl. corr. WESTVACO and Nat. Citizens Com. for Pub. TV. Author: Improving Classroom Communication: Speech Communication, 1976; contbr. articles to profl. jours.; writer instrnl. guides CBS-TV, 21st Century with Walter Cronkhite; manuscript reviewer Addison Wesley, Wadsworth, Acad. Bus. Adminstrn., Eric, World Comm. Jour. Water quality rep. Runyan Lake Assn., Fenton, Mich., 1990—. Fellow Columbia U., 1969-71; dissertation grantee Ind. U., Bloomington, 1974. Mem. Assn. Bus. Comm., Midwest Bus. Adminstrn. Assn., World Comm. Assn., Speech Comm. Assn., Lions. Office: GMI Engring & Mgmt Inst 1700 W 3rd Ave Flint MI 48504

LYNN, EVADNA SAYWELL, investment analyst; b. Oakland, Calif., June 1935; d. Lawrence G. Saywell; m. Richard Keppie Lynn, Dec. 28, 1962; children: Douglas, Lisa. BA, U. Calif., Berkeley, MA in Econs. With Dean Witter, San Francisco, 1958-61, 70-71, Dodge & Cox, San Francisco, 1961-69; v.p. Clark, Dodge & Co., San Francisco, 1971-73; chartered fin. analyst. V.p. Paine Webber, N.Y.C., 1974-77, Wainwright Securities, N.Y.C., 1977-78; 1st v.p. Merrill Lynch Capital Markets, N.Y.C., 1978-90; sr. v.p. Dean Witter Reynolds, N.Y.C., 1990—. Mem. N.Y. Soc. Security Analysts, San Francisco Security Analysts (treas. 1973-74). Mem. Fin. Women's Club of San Francisco (pres. 1967). Office: Dean Witter Reynolds 2 World Trade Ctr New York NY 10048

LYNN, LORETTA WEBB (MRS. OLIVER LYNN, JR.), singer; b. Butcher Hollow, Ky., Apr. 14, 1935; d. Ted and Clara (Butcher) Webb; m. Oliver V. Lynn, Jr., Jan. 10, 1948; children—Betty Sue Lynn Markworth, Jack Benny (dec.), Clara Lynn Lyell, Ernest Ray, Peggy, Patsy. Student pub. schs. Sec.-treas. Loretta Lynn Enterprises; v.p. United Talent, Inc.; hon. chmn. bd. Loretta Lynn Western Stores. Country vocalist with MCA records, 1961—(numerous gold albums); most recent album Just a Woman, 1985, (with Conway Twitty) Making Believe, 1988, Greatest Hits Live, 1992, The Country Music Hall of Fame, 1991, Country's Favorite Daughter (reissue), 1993. Author: Coal Miner's Daughter, 1976. Hon. rep. United Giver's Fund, 1971. Named Country Music Assn. Female Vocalist of Year 1967, 72, 73, Entertainer of Year, 1972, named Top Duet of 1972, 73, 74, 75; recipient Grammy award 1971, Am. Music award 1978, named Entertainer of Decade, Acad. Country Music 1980; inducted into Country Music Hall of Fame, 1988; first country female vocalist to record certified Gold album. Office: care MCA Records Inc 70 Universal City Plz Universal Cty CA 91608-1011*

LYNN, MARJORIE ANNE, association executive; b. Hartford, Conn., Mar. 17, 1940; d. William and Mildred Adele (Perry) Grimm; m. Edwin Charles Lynn, Sept. 20, 1958; children: Bruce Charles, Sharyl Lynn Stropkay. BA, Goddard Coll., 1973. Freelance editor Milford, N.H., 1966-71; tchr. Hamilton (Mass.) -Wenham High Sch., 1972-73; communications specialist MITRE Corp., Bedford, Mass., 1973-77; exec. dir. YWCA, Newburyport, Mass., 1977—; incorporator Inst. Savs., Newburyport, 1992—. Editor: Daysalive, 1990. Bd. dirs., chair Harbor Schs., Newburyport, 1983—. Mem. Rotary, Newburyport C. of C. (bd. dirs., chair). Unitarian. Home: 34 Newbury Rd Ipswich MA 01938-1037 Office: YWCA of Newburyport 13 Market St Newburyport MA 01950-2523

LYNN, NAOMI B., university president, public administration educator; b. N.Y.C., Apr. 16, 1933; d. Carmelo Burgos and Maria (Lebron) Berly; m. Robert A. Lynn, Aug. 28, 1954; children: Mary Louise, Nancy, Judy Lynn Chance, Jo-An. BA, Maryville (Tenn.) Coll., 1954; MA, U. Ill., 1958; PhD, U. Kans., 1970. Instr. polit. sci. Cen. Mo. State Coll., Warrensburg, Mo., 1966-68; asst. prof. Kans. State U., Manhattan, 1970-75, assoc. prof., 1975-80, acting dept. head, prof., 1980-81, head polit. sci. dept., prof., 1982-84; dean Coll. Pub. and Urban Affairs, prof. Ga. State U., Atlanta, 1984-91; pres. Sangamon State U., Springfield, Ill., 1991—; cons. fed., state and local govts., Manhattan, Topeka, Atlanta, 1981-91; bd. dirs. Bank One, Springfield. Author: The Fulbright Premise, 1973; editor: Public Administration, The State of Discipline, 1990, Women, Politics and the Constitution, 1990; contbr. articles and textbook chpts. to profl. pubs. Bd. dirs. United Way of Sangamon County, Springfield Symphony Assn., 1992—. Recipient Disting. Alumni award Maryville Coll., 1986; fellow Nat. Acad. Pub. Adminstrn. Mem. Nat. Assn. Schs. Pub. Affairs and Adminstrn. (nat. pres.), Am. Soc. Pub. Adminstrn. (nat. pres. 1985-86), Am. Polit. Sci. Assn. (mem. exec. coun. 1981-83, trustee 1993—), Am. Assn. State Colls. and Univs. (bd. dirs.), Midwest Polit. Sci. Assn. (mem. exec. coun. 1976-79), Women's Caucus Polit. Sci. (pres. 1975-76), Greater Springfield C. of C. (bd. dirs., accreditation task force 1992); Springfield Urban League (bd. dirs. 1993—), Pi Sigma Alpha (nat. pres.). Presbyterian. Office: Sangamon State U Office of the President Springfield IL 62794-9243

LYNN, PAULINE JUDITH WARDLOW, lawyer; b. Columbus, Ohio, Nov. 14, 1920; d. Charles and Helen P. (Christman) Wardlow; student Wellesley Coll., 1938-40; B.A., Ohio State U., 1942, J.D., 1948; m. Arthur D. Lynn, Jr., Dec. 29, 1943; children—Pamela Wardlow, Constance Karen, Deborah Joanne, Patricia Diane. Admitted to Ohio bar, 1948; practiced in Columbus, 1948-49. Troop leader Girl Scouts U.S.A., 1969-71. Mem. ABA, Columbus Bar Assn., Phi Beta Kappa, Kappa Kappa Gamma (mem. research com. Heritage mus. 1981-87), Pi Sigma Alpha. Republican. Episcopalian. Home: 2679 Wexford Rd Columbus OH 43221-3217

LYNN, PHYLLIS JEAN, entrepreneur; b. Harrisburg, Ill., Feb. 14, 1936; d. Waldo Houston Basham and Ruth Pearl Irvin; m. Vincent Paul Kaduk, Feb. 21, 1958 (div. 1970); children: Kimberly, Tamara, Christopher; m. John M. Lynn, Oct. 8, 1982. AD in Psychology, George Williams Coll., Downers Grove, Ill., 1973. Lic. real estate salesperson. Real estate owner Birdsong Builders, Inc., Downers Grove, 1965-72; owner Charmills Restaurant & Bar, Clearwater, Fla., 1977-82, On Target Co., Indian Head Park, Ill., 1983-92; adminstrv. asst. J.S. James Co., Burr Ridge, Ill.; part owner Atocha Silver Mine, CoChBomba, Bolivia, 1980-81, Cleaves/Lynn, Inc., Western Springs, Ill., 1993—. Lobbyist for ERA, NOW, 1972-73. Home: 6418 Blackhawk Trl La Grange IL 60525-4316 Office: Cleaves/Lynn Inc PO Box 229 Western Springs IL 60558-0229

LYNN, SHEILAH ANN, service executive, consultant; b. Anderson, Ind., Jan. 28, 1947; d. John Benton and Kathleen (Taylor) Bussabarger; m. John Hoftyzer, Dec. 21, 1968 (div. June 1982); children: Melanie Kay, John Theo; m. Guy C. Lynn, May 20, 1984. BS, Ind. U., 1969; MS, Ctrl. Mich. U., Greensboro, 1993; postgrad., Webster U., 1994; diploma, Data Processing Inst., Tampa, Fla., 1983; MS, Cen. Mich. U., 1993. Bookkeeper John Hancock Life Ins. Co., Greensboro, 1970-72; freelance seminar leader and devel. Dhahran, Saudi Arabia, 1978-82; dir. programming Fla. Tech. Inst., Jacksonville, 1983-84, instr. in computer sci., 1984-85; real estate sales assoc. Fla. Recreational Ranches, Gainesville, 1985; instrnl. program coord., workforce tng. coord. Fla. C.C., Jacksonville, 1986—; handwriting analyst, cons. Sheilah A. Lynn & Assocs., Jacksonville, 1989—; cons. programmer, analyst Postmasters Co., Jacksonville, 1986—; pres. Options Cons., Jacksonville, 1986-89, Sheilah A. Lynn & Assocs., Jacksonville, 1989—; 6L cons. assocs. Dacum facilitator and curriculum developer. Mem. Jacksonville Community Council, Inc., 1986-87, Fla. Literacy Coalition, 1986-87. Mem. NAFE, ASTD, Fla. Assn. Ednl. Data Systems, Bus. and Profl. Women, Jacksonville C. of C. (bd. dirs. south coun. 1987, sec. 1989, treas. 1990, v.p. 1991, pres. 1992). Democrat.

LYNN, VIVIAN C., public health administrator; b. Motley, Minn., Dec. 22, 1935; d. Floyd Charles and Anna Katherine (Linn) Cam; m. Wesley Sherrill Lynn, Mar. 17, 1956; children: Ray Charles, Kurt David. BSN, U. Minn., 1958. Staff nurse Owatonna (Minn.) City Hosp., 1958-60, night supr., 1960-61; staff nurse Dickinson County Meml. Hosp., Spirit Lake, Iowa, 1964-66; nurse instr. U. Iowa, Iowa City, 1965-67; pub. health nurse Dickinson Pub. Health, Spirit Lake, 1967-71, nurse adminstr., 1971—. Named Citizen of the Yr. Lake Park C. of C., 1993. Mem. Iowa Pub. Health Assn. (pres. nursing sect. 1992), 15 Dist. Iowa Nurses Assn. (bd. dirs.). Republican. Methodist. Home: Box 424 402 S 1st St Lake Park IA 51347 Office: Dickinson Pub Health Nsg PO Box AB Spirit Lake IA 51360

LYON, BERENICE IOLA CLARK, civic worker; b. Westfield, Pa., June 4, 1920; d. Stephen Artemus and Ruth Gertrude (Tubbs) Clark; m. Robert Louis Lyon, May 28, 1944. Pres., Twin Tiers Geneal. Soc., N.Y. and Pa., 1976-88, pub. jour. Gemini; Pa. state pres. Colonial Dames XVII Century, 1981-83, state chmn. heraldry, 1977-79, hon. state pres., 1983—, organizer-pres. Tyoga Gateway chpt., 1973-75, Treaty Elm chpt., 1975-77, state yearbook-directory compiler, 1979-81, Pa. state chmn. 1988—; N.Y. state chmn. DAR, 1968-71, pres. N.Y. coun. of regents, 1968-71, regent Corning (N.Y.) chpt. 1965-68, Wellsboro (Pa.) chpt., 1977-80, Pa. state vice chmn., 1980-83, Pa. dist. dir., 1983-88, Pa. state chmn., 1987—; N.Y. state chmn. Daus. Am. Colonists, 1965—, Atlantic Coast chmn., 1970-79, organizer-regent Forbidden Trail chpt., 1967-76, regent, 1974-76, 83-88, Pa. state chmn. 1987—; condr. geneal. seminars; speaker to convs., meetings, TV, radio; historian, researcher, writer; lectr., healthful family living, 1991—; contbr. articles on heraldry to 17th Century Rev., 1978-79. Recipient medal of appreciation SAR, 1966. Mem. Ams. of Royal Descent, Descs. Knights of Garter, Magna Carta Dames, Old Plymouth Colony Descs., Order of Crown, Order of Washington, Plantagenet Soc., Mansfield Friends of Library (pres. 1980-81). Clubs: Kiwanis Ladies, Clionian Circle (Corning); Mansfield (Pa.) Garden (pres. 1979-80), N.Y. Fedn. Garden Clubs (sect. chmn. 1969-73). Home: Lowenhof 168A Bailey Creek Rd Millerton PA 16936

LYON, CAROLYN BARTEL, civic worker; b. Richmond, Ind., Mar. 28, 1908; d. Frederick John and Cora Caroline (Eggemeyer) Bartel; m. E. Wilson Lyon, Aug. 26, 1933 (dec.); children: Elizabeth Lyon Webb, John Wilson. BA, Wellesley Coll., 1928; MA, U. Chgo., 1930; LHD (hon.), Pomona Coll., 1974. Editorial asst. U. Chgo. Press, 1930-33. Alumna trustee Wellesley Coll., 1958-65; bd. trustees United Bd. for Christian Higher Edn. in Asia, N.Y.C., 1966-83; mem. women's coun. KCET Pub. TV, L.A., 1965—; active LWV, Claremont, Calif., 1941—, bd. dirs., 1945-50; pres. Foothill Philharmonic Com., L.A. Philharmonic, 1970-72. Mem. UN Assn. U.S. Congregationalist. Home: Apt A-17-18 900 E Harrison Ave Pomona CA 91767

LYON, JEAN COZAD, family nurse practitioner, educator; b. San Francisco, Mar. 6, 1952; d. Charles Earle and Phoebe (LaMunyan) Cozad; m. Robert L. Lyon, Oct. 23, 1976. RN, Sacred Heart Sch. Nursing, 1973; BA in Health Edn., U. Wash., 1975; MS in Health Edn., San Francisco State U., 1980; BSN, Calif. State U., Long Beach, 1984; MSN, San Jose State U., 1986; PhD in Nursing, U. Calif., San Francisco, 1991; family nurse practitioner cert., Sonoma State U., 1994. RN, Calif.; cert. pub. health nurse, clin. nurse specialist, cmty. health nursing, family nurse practitioner. Staff nurse intensive care nursery Washoe Med. Ctr., Reno, 1976; staff nurse, charge nurse cardiopulmonary unit Presbyn. Hosp. Pacific Med. Ctr., San Francisco, 1976-78; staff nurse coronary care unit and emergency dept. Mt. Diablo Hosp. and Med. Ctr., Concord, Calif., 1978-79; clin. instr. nursing edn. dept. Herrick Hosp. and Health Ctr., Berkeley, Calif., 1979-80; asst. DON Peralta Hosp., Oakland, Calif., 1980-84; dir. edn. Hosp. Consortium of San Mateo County, 1984-86; dir. nursing systems and staff devel. Valley Meml. Hosp., Livermore, Calif., 1986-87; dir. edn. Valley Meml. Hosp., Livermore, 1987-90; asst. prof. Samuel Merritt Coll., Oakland, 1990-92, U. Nev., Reno, 1992—; part time faculty statewide nursing program Calif. State U., Dominguez Hills, Calif., 1987—; per diem staff nurse, IV therapy nurse, relief liaison nurse home health care dept. Mt. Diablo Hosp. Med. Ctr., 1988-89; per diem home health nurse Kaiser Martinez Home Health Dept., 1990-94; rsch. coord. Care Continuation Rsch. Project, Kaiser Martinez Med. Ctr., 1991-94; presenter in field. Contbr. articles to profl. jours. Mem. child health improvement task force Hoover Elem. Sch. Coalition, Oakland, 1990-92; mem. profl. adv. bd. Contra Costa County Home Health Agy., 1990-93; mem. State of Nev. Primary Care Com., 1992—. Recipient Outstanding Achievement award Hosp. Consortium of San Mateo County, 1986, scholarship Calif. Soc. for Nursing Svc. Adminstrs., 1988. Mem. APHA, AAUW, Assn. Cmty. Health Nursing Educators (western states rep.), Calif. Pub. Health Assn., Bay Area Soc. for Healthcare Edn. and Tng. (treas. 1984, 85, award of appreciation 1984, 85), Nev. Nurses Assn. (sec.), U. Calif. San Francisco Alumni Assn., Sigma Theta Tau (Nu Iota and Alpha Gamma chpt., Linda Lee Miller scholarship 1986, Linda Lee Miller rsch. award 1991). Democrat. Office: Univ Nev Reno Orvis Sch Nursing # 134 Reno NV 89557-0052

LYON, JOANNE B., psychologist; b. Little Rock, June 2, 1943; d. F. Ike and Marie (Graham) Beyer; m. John M. Lofton, May 22, 1983 (dec. Feb. 1990). BA, Webster U., 1966; MEd, U. Mo., St. Louis, 1976, PhD, 1986. Lic. psychologist, Kans. Reading specialist Rockwood Sch. Dist., St. Louis, 1976-79; psychology cons. handicapped component St. Louis Head Start, 1982-83; intern Topeka State Hosp., 1983-84; dir. partial hosp. programs Family Svc. & Guidance Ctr., Topeka, 1985-89; pvt. practitioner Shadow Wood Mental Health Svcs., Topeka, 1989—; clin. supr. Family Svc. & Guidance Ctr., Topeka, 1989-93. Bd. dirs. Interfaith of Topeka, I Have A Dream Com. Sherman scholar U. Mo., St. Louis, 1982. Mem. Am. Psychol. Assn., Kans. Psychol. Assn., Am. Orthological Assn., Soc. for Personality Assessment. Jewish. Home: 3030 SW Arrowhead Rd Topeka KS 66614-4134 Office: Shadow Wood Mental Health Svcs 2933 SW Woodside Dr Topeka KS 66614-4181

LYON, MARCY B., lawyer; b. Highland Park, Ill., Mar. 13, 1961; d. Martin William and Rita Lee (Cohn) L. Student, U. Calif., Berkeley, 1979-81; BA, UCLA, 1985; JD, Loyola U., L.A., 1991. Bar: Calif. 1991. Pvt. practice San Francisco, 1992-94; legal analyst CCM, Inc., San Rafael, Calif., 1994—. Editor: Television, 1988. Mem. Queen's Bench. Democrat. Office: CCM Inc 1 Thorndale Dr San Rafael CA 94913

LYON, MARTHA SUE, military officer, research engineer; b. Louisville, Oct. 3, 1935; d. Harry Bowman and Erma Louise (Moreland) Lyon. BA in Chemistry, U. Louisville, 1959; MEd in Math., Northeastern Ill. U., 1974. Cert. tchr. Ill., Ky. Rsch. assoc. U. Louisville Med. Sch., 1959-61, 62-63; commd. ensign, USNR, 1965, advanced through grades to comdr., 1983; instr. instrumentation chemistry Northwestern U., Evanston, Ill., 1968-70; tchr. sci., chemistry, gifted math. Waukegan (Ill.) pub. schs., 1970-75; phys. scientist Libr. of Congress, Washington, 1975-76; rsch. engr. Lockheed Missiles & Space Co., Sunnyvale, Calif., 1976-77; instr., assoc. chmn. dept. physics U.S. Naval Acad., Annapolis, Md., 1977-80; analyst Systems Analysis Div., Office of Chief of Naval Ops. Staff, Washington, 1980-81; comdg. officer Naval Res. Ctr., Stockton, Calif., 1981-83; mem. faculty Def. Intelligence Coll., 1983-85; program mgr. Space and Naval Warfare Systems Command, 1985-86, commanding officer PERSUPPACT Memphis, 1986-88; program mgr. Space and Naval Warfare Systems Command, 1988-91; sect. chief Def. Intelligence Agy., 1991—. Chief marching div. Nat. Homecoming Parade and N.Y.C. Regional Parade Task Force Desert Storm. Grantee Am. Heart Assn., 1960-62, NSF, 1971, 72. Mem. Soc. Women Engrs., Am. Statis. Assn., Am. Soc. Photogrammetry, Internat. Conf. Women in Sci. Engring. (protocol chair), Internat. Soc. Bassists, Mensa, Zeta Tau Alpha, Delta Phi Alpha. Club: Order of Ea. Star. Developer processes used in archival photography, carbon-14 analyses; presenter of papers at profl. confs.

LYON, MAXINE LEVERENZ, psychological counselor; b. Enterprise, Oreg., Aug. 23, 1952; d. Roy Martin and Winifred (Jones) Leverenz. BS in Home Econs. and Comms., Oreg. State U., 1975; MA in Psychology, Counseling, Guidance, U. No. Colo., 1981; postgrad., Tex. Woman's U., 1986-88, North Tex. State U., 1986-87. Cert. cmty. coll. instr., Ariz., substance abuse counselor, Ariz., profl. counselor, Ariz., marriage and family therapist, Ariz. Caseworker II Tarrant County Mental Health and Mental Retardation Svcs., Ft. Worth, Tex., 1982-89; owner Active Coping Therapy, Ft. Worth, 1985-89, Scottsdale, Ariz., 1989—; contract counseling and consulting Phoenix area social svc. agencies, 1989—; workshop presenter, guest speaker at civic orgns., Ft. Worth, 1985-89, Phoenix, 1989—. Contbr. articles to mags. Promotion and advt. vol. for Life Saver Saturday, Channel 12 TV, Phoenix, 1989. Named to Outstanding Young Women of Am., 1986; recipient scholarship Jessica Chpt. Oreg. Order Ea. Star, 1980, Silver medal Global USAF XI, 1991, Volksmarch 10K; N.W. Tri-State Grange Assn. scholar, 1970, Union Pacific scholar, 1970, Oreg. scholar Gov. of Oreg., 1970. Mem. NRA, Nat. Parks and Conservation Assn., Nat. Assn. Alcoholism and Drug Abuse Counselors, Am. Counseling Assn., Am. Mental Health Counselor's Assn., Am. Assn. Marriage and Family Therapists (clin.), Internat. Assn. Marriage and Family Counselors, Internat. Assn. Addictions and Offender Counselors, Chi Sigma Iota, Women in Comms. Office: Active Coping Therapy PO Box 31803 Mesa AZ 85275

LYON, PHYLLIS ANN, consultant, retired educator; b. Tulsa, Nov. 10, 1924; life ptnr. Del Martin; 1 surrogate child, Kendra Mon. BA in Journalism, U. Calif., Berkeley, 1946; EdD in Human Sexuality, Inst. for Advanced Study Human Sexuality, San Francisco, 1976. Diplomate Am. Bd. Sexology; ordained to ministry Universal Life Ch., 1969. Reporter Chico (Calif.) Enterprise-Record, 1947-49; assoc. editor Architect and Engr., Seattle, 1949-52; editorial asst. Pacific Builder and Engr., Seattle, 1949-52; traffic mgr. James S. Baker Export Co., San Francisco, 1954-64; adminstrv. asst. operational edn. dept. Glide Urban Ctr., San Francisco, 1965-68; assoc. dir. Nat. Sex Forum, San Francisco, 1968-72, co-dir., 1973-87; prof., registrar Inst. for Advanced Study Human Sexuality, 1976-87; ptnr. LyMar Assocs., San Francisco, 1972—; lectr. San Francisco Theol. Sem., Starr King Sem., Pacific Sch. Religion, U. Calif., Berkeley, U. Calif., Davis, UCLA, San Francisco State U., U. San Francisco, U. Nebr., Kirksville (Mo.) Coll. Osteopathy and Surgery, U. Calif. Sch. Medicine, Stanford U. Sch. Medicine, Sacramento State U., Diablo Valley Coll., Indian Valley Coll., U. Ariz. Med. Sch., Ariz. State U., Iowa State U., U. Oreg., Portland State U., Western Wash. State Coll., U. Wash., Ohio State U., U. Mo. Med. Sch., also others. Author: (with Del Martin) Lesbian/Woman, 1972, updated edit., 1983, repub. updated, 1991 (2d ann. Gay Book award Task Force on Gay Liberation, Social Responsibilities Rountable, ALA 1972), Lesbian Love and Liberation, 1973; contbg. author: Sexual Latitude-For and Against, 1971, The New Sexuality, 1971; contbr. numerous articles to newspapers and mags. Mem. San Francisco Human Rights commn., 1976-87, chmn., 1982-83; founding mem. citizens adv. bd. Ctr. for Spl. Problems, San Francisco Pub. Health Dept., 1973, chmn., 1978; founder, life mem., past co-chmn., bd. dirs. Coun. on Religion and Homosexual; former mem. bd. dirs. Genesis Ch. and Ecumenical Ctr., Friends of San Francisco Deupties and Inmates, San Francisco Women's Ctrs.; former mem. adv. bd. Sr. Action in a Gay Environ., N.Y.C., active polit. campaigns; also others. Recipient numerous awards, including Community United Against Violence, 1981, Alice B. Toklas Lesbian/Gay Dem. Club, 1986, proclamation of honor Human Rights Commn., 1987, cert. of honor San Francisco Bd. Suprs., 1987, Franklin E. Cook Meml. award Long Beach Lambda Dem. Club, 1989, Earl Warren Civil Liberties award No. Calif. chpt. ACLU, 1990; co-recipient appreciation award Lyon-Martin Clinic, 1985, numerous others with Del Martin. Mem. NOW (co-honoree nat. conf. 1988), Daus. of Bilitis (a founder, life, editor The Ladder 1956-60), So. Calif. Women for Understanding (hon.), Bay Area Career Women (hon.), Old Lesbians Organizing for Change, Am. Assn. Ret. Persons, ACLU, Humane Soc. U.S., People for Am. Way, Lesbian Caucus, Lesbian Agenda for Action, Nat. Com. To Preserve Social Security and Medicare, Feminists for Free Expression. Home and Office: 651 Duncan St San Francisco CA 94131

LYONS, JUDE (ANNE LYONS), advertising agency executive; b. Port Chester, N.Y., Oct. 21, 1946; d. William T. and Helen (Covino) L. Grad. high sch., Ridgefield, Conn. V.p. Buddah Records, Inc., N.Y.C., 1970-77, Sire Records, N.Y.C., 1977-78; pres. Cachet Advt., Inc., N.Y.C., 1976—; mktg. dir. Diana Ross Tours, N.Y.C., 1984—; gen. mgr. Muse Records, 1993—; clients include Bottom Line Night Club, Muse Records, Landmark Records, Trix Records, New Audiences Promotors. Office: Cachet Advt Inc 350 Cabrini Blvd Apt 4G New York NY 10040-3629

LYONS, LAURA DONNAWAY, insurance agent; b. Shreveport, La., Dec. 20, 1966; d. William Joseph and Jo-Ann (Thiebaud) Donnaway; m. Jerome William Lyons; 1 child, Amanda C. BA, Loyola U., New Orleans, 1988. Claim rep. Aetna Life and Casualty, Metairie, La., 1989-90, underwriter, 1990-91; account exec. Alvarez-Donnaway-Passons, Metairie, 1991—; bd. dirs. young agts. com. Ind. Ins. Agts. La., Baton Rouge, 1992—. Bd. dirs. jr. com. Women's Guild New Orleans Opera, corr. sec., 1992-93, chmn. theater sales, 1993—; mem. Pres.'s Coun. Loyola U., 1992—, co-chair student affairs com., 1994—. Mem. Soc. Creative Anachronism (chpt. pres. 1994—), Alpha Chi Omega (v.p. alumni chpt. 1993-94). Office: Alvarez-Donnaway-Passons 2301 N Hullen St Metairie LA 70001-6902

LYONS, MARGARET J., electrical engineer; b. Plainfield, N.J., June 10, 1964; d. Edwin William and Teresa (Murphy) L. BSCEE, Purdue U., 1986. Registered engr.-in-tng., N.J. Sr. cons. RAM Comm. Cons., Woodbridge, N.J. Mem. IEEE, Soc. Women Engrs. (pres. N.J. sect. 1989-90, mem. nat. bd. dirs. 1993-95). Home: 184 Kentucky Way Freehold NJ 07728

LYONS, MOIRA K., state legislator; b. Trenton, N.J.. BA, Georgian Ct. Coll.; student, Miami U. Mem. Conn. Ho. of Reps., mem. appropriations com., chmn. transp. com. Democrat. Home: 37 Ocean Dr W Stamford CT 06902-8002 Office: Office of State Senate State Capital Hartford CT 06106*

LYONS, NATALIE BELLER, family counselor; b. Havana, Cuba, Apr. 3, 1926; d. Herman Lawrence and Jennie (Engler) B.; widowed, Apr. 18, 1986; children: Anne, Sara. BS in Surveying, Inst. Vedado, Havana, 1943, BS in Land Appraising, 1943; BA, U. Mich., 1946; MEd, U. Miami, Fla., 1967. Cert. counselor. Family counselor, mem. staff furniture design and mfg. co. Geroge B. Bent, Gardner, Mass., 1953-58; tchr. Winchendon, Mass., parochial high sch., Hollywood/Ft. Lauderdale, Fla., 1963—; family counselor Miami, 1967—; project dir. Ctrl. Am. fisheries Peace Corps, 1972-74; counselor Score, Miami, 1993. Pres. Miami region Hadassah, 1989-91; bd. dirs. Com. for Accuracy in Mid. East REporting in Am., 1990-93, Greater Miami Jewish Fedn., 1985—; co-chair Pro-Israel Rally, Tri County, 1991; tng. dir. Los Amigos de las Ams., 1975—; pres. Am. Soc. for Technion, Miami, 1987-89, bd. dirs., 1992-94; co-chair Joint Action Com., Miami, 1989-91. Recipient Leadership award Hadassah, 1987, honoree Am. Soc. for Technion Scholarship Fund, 1991; named Woman of Yr., Hadassah, 1991. Democrat.

LYONS-CAREL, PAMELA KAY, military officer; b. Houston, Oct. 30, 1962; d. Perry Joseph and Mary Ann Donna (Geffert) L. BS in Aerospace Engring., U. Tex., 1986; MA in Bus. and Mgmt., Webster U., 1990. Licensed comml. pilot, single, multi-engine, and instrument rated. Commd. ens. USN, 1986, advanced through grades to lt., 1990; student pilot VT-6 USN, Whiting, Fla., 1987; student pilot VT-23 USN, Kingsville, Tex., 1987, student pilot VT-22, 1988, instr. pilot VT-23, 1988-90; aggressor pilot VAQ-34 USN, Lemoore, Calif., 1990-93, fleet replacement pilot VFA-125, 1993-94; F/A -18 pilot NAS Lemoore, Calif., 1994—. Decorated Navy Achievement medal; recipient May Trap award Tailhook Assn., 1988. Mem. Women Mil. Aviators, Delta Gamma. Republican. Episcopalian.

LYSTAD, MARY HANEMANN (MRS. ROBERT LYSTAD), sociologist, author, consultant; b. New Orleans, Apr. 11, 1928; d. James and Mary (Douglass) Hanemann; m. Robert Lystad, June 20, 1953; children: Lisa Douglass, Anne Hanemann, Mary Lunde, Robert Douglass, James Hanemann. A.B. cum laude, Newcomb Coll., 1949; M.A., Columbia U., 1951; Ph.D., Tulane U., 1955. Postdoctoral fellow social psychology S.E. La. Hosp., Mandeville, 1955-57; field rsch. social psychology Ghana, 1957-58, South Africa and Swaziland, 1968, Peoples Republic of China, 1986; chief sociologist Collaborative Child Devel. Project, Charity Hosp. La., New Orleans, 1958-61; feature writer African div. Voice Am., Washington, 1964-73; program analyst NIMH, Washington, 1968-78; asso. dir. for planning and coordination div. spl. mental health programs NIMH, 1978-80; chief Nat. Ctr. for Prevention and Control of Rape, 1980-83, Ctr. Mental Health Studies of Emergencies, 1983-89; pvt. cons. specializing on mental health implications social and econ. problems Bethesda, Md., 1990—; cons. on youth Nat. Goals Research Staff, White House, Washington, 1969-70. Author: Millicent the Monster, 1968, Social Aspects of Alienation, 1969, Jennifer Takes Over P.S. 94, 1972, James the Jaguar, 1972, As They See It: Changing Values of College Youth, 1972, That New Boy, 1973, Halloween Parade, 1973, Violence at Home, 1974, A Child's World As Seen in His Stories and Drawings, 1974, From Dr. Mather to Dr. Seuss: 200 Years of American Books for Children, 1980, At Home in America, 1983; editor: Innovations in Mental Health Services to Disaster Victims, 1985, Violence in the Home: Interdisciplinary Perspectives, 1986, Mental Health Response to Mass Emergencies: Theory and Practice, 1988. Recipient Spl. Recognition award USPHS, 1983, Alumna Centennial award Newcomb Coll., 1986. Home and Office: 4900 Scarsdale Rd Bethesda MD 20816-2440

LYTAL, PATRICIA LOU, art educator; b. Ft. Wayne, Ind., Sept. 11, 1936; d. George F. and Geraldine (Beck) Heingartner; m. Wayne Earl Lytal; Sept. 16, 1956; children: Michael Wayne, Patrick Allen (dec.), Terry Lee, Shawn David. Tchr. oil painting Ft. Wayne Park Sch. Bd, 1980-83, Ind. U.- Purdue U. Continuing Edn., Ft. Wayne, 1986—; ind. tchr. oil painting Ft. Wayne, 1976—; instr. Ft. Wayne Sr. Ctr., Decatur (Ind.) Park Bd., Ft. Wayne Park and Recreation Dept.l tchr. oil painting for Chpt. 2 through St. Joseph Med. Ctr.; judge Ft. Wayne Women's Club Ind. Art Contest, 1989-90, 94. Artist: (murals) Diehm Mus. Natural History, 1981, Grace United Meth. Ch. Home, 1983. Recipient 3d pl. china painting State of Ind., Best of Show award Ft. Wayne Woman's Club Ind. Artist Show, award Montpelier Brass Latch Art Show, 1993, 94. Mem. Brown County Art Soc., Park County Art Soc., Ft. Wayne Artist Guild. Democrat. Home and Office: 1625 N Glendale Dr Fort Wayne IN 46804-5851

LYTHCOTT, MARCIA A., newspaper editor. Op-ed editor Chicago Tribune, Ill. Office: Chicago Tribune 435 N Michigan Ave Chicago IL 60611

LYTTON, LINDA ROUNTREE, marriage and family therapist, test consultant; b. Suffolk, Va., Mar. 30, 1951; d. John Thomas and Anne Carolyn (Edwards) Rountree; m. Danny Michael Lytton, June 23, 1973; 1 child, Seth Daniel. BS, Radford U., 1973; MS, Va. Poly. Inst. and State U., 1992. Collegiate profl. cert. Tchr., cons. Fauquier County Pub. Schs., Warrenton, Va., 1973-74, Chesterfield County Pub. Schs., Richmond, Va., 1974-78, Williamsburg (Va.)-James City Pub. Schs., 1979-83, Prince William County Pub. Schs., Manassas, Va., 1983-89; hist. area interpreter Colonial Williamsburg Found., 1978-79; outpatient therapist Prince William County Community Svcs. Bd., 1989-91, emergency svcs. therapist, therapist cons., 1991-93; marriage and family therapist Employee Assistance Svc., Inc., Manassas, 1993—; cons. Horizons for Learning, Inc., Richmond, 1989—; tchr., cons. Ednl. Tutoring Cons., Inc., Manassas, 1989—. Adv. coun. gifted com. Coles Elem. Jr. Great Books Leader, 1993—. Mem. Am. Assn. Marriage and Family Therapy, Va. Assn. Marriage and Family Therapy, Am. Counseling Assn., Internat. Assn. Marriage and Family Counselors, Sigma Kappa (life). Home: 12046 Market Square Ct Manassas VA 22111-3214

MAARBJERG, MARY PENZOLD, office equipment company executive; b. Norfolk, Va., Oct. 2, 1943; d. Edmund Theodore and Lucy Adelaide (Singleton) Penzold; m. John Peder Maarbjerg, Oct. 20, 1966; 1 son, Martin Peder. A.B., Hollins Coll., 1965; M.B.A., Wharton Sch., Pa., 1969. Cons. bus. and fin., Stamford, Conn., 1977-78; corp. staff analyst Pitney Bowes, Inc., Stamford, Conn., 1978-80, mgr. pension and benefit fin. 1980-81, dir. investor relations, 1981-85; v.p. planning and devel. Pitney Bowes Credit Corp., Norwalk, Conn., 1985-86; treas., v.p. planning Pitney Bowes Credit Corp., 1986-94; v.p. mkt. devel. and mgn. dir. Asia Pacific Bowes Fin. Svcs., 1994—. Mem. adv. com. City of Stamford Mcpl. Employees Retirement Fund, 1980-85; mem. fin. adv. com. YWCA, Stamford, 1982-86; bd. dirs. Stamford Symphony, 1985—, Vis. Nurses Assn., 1984-86, Am. Recorder Soc., 1986—. Fellow Royal Statis. Soc.; mem. Fin. Execs. Inst., Phi Beta Kappa. Congregationalist. Office: Pitney Bowes Credit Corp 201 Merritt Seven Norwalk CT 06856

MAAS, CAROL ANN, healthcare advertising administrator; b. Tacoma, Wash., Apr. 4, 1951; d. Wayne LeRoy and Jeanne Maria (Goehler) M. BS, Kans. State U., 1973. Asst. buyer, buyer Macy Dept. Store, Kansas City, Mo., 1974-75; territory mgr. Revlon, Inc., Pitts. and Chgo., 1975-78, Neutrogena Corp., Chgo., 1978-81; mktg. rep. Neutrogena Corp., L.A., 1981-84, sales mgr., 1984-85, gen. mgr., 1986-87, asst. brand mgr., 1987-89, sales/mktg. coord., 1989-91, dir. mktg., 1991-93; dir. consumer healthcare TTA/Newport, Inc., Newport Beach, Calif., 1994—. Vol. Big Sisters of L.A., 1992—; fin. sec. St. Andrew's Luth. Ch., L.A., 1994. Mem. Med. Mktg. Assn. (sr. advisor bd. dirs. 1993—, dep. chair ann. conf. 1994, pres. L.A. chpt. 1994-95), Biomed. Mktg. Assn., Kansas State Alumni Assn. (life mem.). Democrat. Office: TTA/Newport Inc 1201 Dove St Ste 650 Newport Beach CA 92660-2825

MAAS, JANE BROWN, advertising executive; b. Jersey City; d. Charles E. and Margaret (Beck) Brown; m. Michael Maas, Aug. 30, 1957; children: Katherine, Jennifer. BA, Bucknell U., 1953; postgrad., U. Dijon, France, 1954; MA, Cornell U., 1955; LittD, Ramapo Coll., 1986, St. John's U., 1988. Assoc. producer Name That Tune TV Program, N.Y.C., 1957-64; v.p. Ogilvy and Mather Inc., N.Y.C., 1964-76; sr. v.p. Wells, Rich, Greene, Inc., N.Y.C., 1976-82; pres. Muller Jordan Weiss Inc., N.Y.C., 1982-89; pres. Earle Palmer Brown Cos., N.Y.C., 1989-92, chmn., 1992-94, chmn. emeritus, 1994—. Co-author: How to Advertise, 1975, Better Brochures, 1981, Adventures of a Advertising Woman, 1986, The New How to Advertise, 1992, Christmas in Wales: a Homecoming, 1994. Trustee Bucknell U., Lewisburg, 1976-86, Fordham U., N.Y., 1983-91; mem. bd. govs. com. Scholastic Achievement, 1985-92; active Girls Scouts U.S. Greater N.Y., 1970-76; mem. adv. bd. William E. Simon Grad. Sch. Bus., U. Rochester, 1989—; pub. dir. AIA, 1993—. Recipient Matrix award Women in Communications, 1980, N.Y. Advt. Woman of Yr., 1986. Mem. AIA (pub. dir. 1993—), Am. Assn. Advt. Agys. (bd. govs.). Home: PO Box 1109 Westhampton Beach NY 11978-7109

MAAS, JOAN LOUISE, training and development consultant; b. San Jose, Calif., Apr. 26, 1961; d. Elmer Alvin Maas and Betty Lu Rowe. BA, Whitman Coll., 1983; MA in Psychology, U.S. Internat. U. Asst. mgr. New Times Clothing Co., Costa Mesa, Calif., 1984-85; bus. analyst Dun and Bradstreet, Long Beach, Calif., 1985-86; intern McDonnell Douglas, Huntington Beach, Calif., 1986; training and personnel asst. Western Digital, Irvine, Calif., 1986-88; instrl. designer Toastmasters Internat., Rancho Santa Margarita, Calif., 1988-91; prin. Maas Tng. and Devel., Mission Viejo, Calif., 1991-92; staff cons. Richard Chang Assocs., Irvine, 1992; orgnl. devel. specialist Anaheim Meml. Hosp., 1992—. Author Orangespiel newsletter, 1991. Mem. Orange County (Calif.) Young Reps., 1986—, South Orange County Young Reps., 1991. Mem. ASTD (sec. 1992, dir. spl. interest groups 1993, Orange County Merit award 1994), Orange County Nat. Soc. for Performance and Instrn., Toastmasters (v.p. edn. 1991). Home and Office: 612 Poinsettia Ave Corona Del Mar CA 92625

MAAS, MARILYN LOREN, psychologist; b. Detroit, Mar. 22, 1943; d. Morris Jacob and Pauline Ann (Rosenthal) Loren; m. James Weldon Maas, Sept. 15, 1972; children: James, Jonathan. BA, Monteith Coll., 1965; PhD, Northwestern U., 1972. Lic. psychologist, Tex. Staff psychologist Ill. State Psychiat. Inst., Chgo., 1968-72; chief psychologist outpatient dept. Norwich (Conn.) Hosp., 1973-75, cons. dept. psychologist tng. program, 1976-78; pvt. practice clin. psychology San Antonio, 1982—; assoc. clin. prof. U. Tex. Health Sci. Ctr., San Antonio, 1994—; bd. dirs. Catchment Area Coun. Mental Health, State of Conn., 1976-78. Bd. dirs. LWV, San Antonio, 1983-85. Mem. APA, Bexar County Psychol. Assn. Office: 8213 Fredericksburg Rd San Antonio TX 78229

MAATSCH, DEBORAH JOAN, trust administrator, paralegal tax specialist; b. Lincoln, Nebr., Mar. 26, 1950; d. Leon F. Forst and Jarolyn J. Hoffman Forst Conrad; m. Gordon F. Maatsch, Mar. 14, 1969; children: Jason, Diana. BS, U. Nebr., 1976. Acct., supr. U.S. Civil Svc., Heidelberg, Ger., 1971-73; paralegal Mattson Rickets Davies et al, Lincoln, Nebr., 1976-87; tax cons. Lincoln and Denver, 1981—; pres. DGJD Inc.-Bleachers, 1993—; paralegal Wade Ash Woods & Hill, P.C., Denver, 1986-94; sr. trust adminstr. Investment Trust Co., Denver, 1994—; mem. Denver Trust Officers Assocs., bus. adv. bd. Ponderosa H.S., 1994—; officer The "O" Streeters, Lincoln, 1984-87; spkr., coord. Nebr. Continuing Legal Edn. Seminars, 1976-86. Contbr. articles to profl. jours. Officer The Aurorians Synchronized Swim Team Parents Orgn., Rocky Mt. Spash Parents' Corp.; youth edn. staff Ave Maria Cath. Ch., Parker, Colo., 1990-91. Mem. Doane Coll. Alumni Assn. (dir. 1989-93), Rocky Mt. Legal Assts. (dir., sect. chair 1990—), Am. Soc. Women Accts. (officer, dir.), Nebr. Assn. Legal Assts. (officer, dir. 1976-87), Colo. Bar Assn. (computer probate sect.), Phi Chi Theta (treas. 1988-89). Office: Investment Trust Co Ste 180 455 Sherman St Denver CO 80203

MABIE, RUTH MARIE, realtor; b. Pueblo, Colo., Feb. 7; d. Newton Everett and Florence Ellen Allen; M.B.A., La Jolla U., 1980, Ph.D., 1981; m. Richard O. Mabie, Nov. 29, 1946; 1 son, Ward A. Mgr., LaMont Modeling Sch., San Diego, 1962; tchr. Am. Bus. Coll., San Diego, 1964-66; fashion modeling, 1960-72; owner, broker Ruth Mabie Realty, San Diego, 1972—; asst. v.p. Skil-Bilt, Inc., 1976—; dir. Mabie & Mintz, Inc. Mem. San Diego Bd. Realtors, Nat. Assn. Female Execs. Republican. Office: 2231 Camino del Rio So #302 San Diego CA 92108-3605

MABRY, CELIA ELAINE HALES, librarian; b. Ayden, N.C., Sept. 6, 1946; d. Thomas Edwin and Joyce Elaine (Hill) H.; m. Paul Davis Mabry Jr., July 12, 1986. BA, Duke U., 1968, MA, 1970; MLS, East C. U., 1975; PhD, Fla. State U., 1982. Instr. Stratford Coll., Danville, Va., 1970-72; media coord. New Hanover County Pub. Schs., Wilmington, N.C., 1976-78; lectr. East Carolina U., Greenville, N.C., 1980-81; reference libr., English bibliographer U. N.C., Charlotte, 1983-86; reference instr., libr. U. Minn., Mpls., 1986—. Author: (monograph) The World of the Aging: Information Needs and Choices, 1993; contbr. articles to profl. jours. Mem. LWV, Wilmington, 1976-78, Tallahassee, 1978-79; bd. dirs. Mental Health Assn. Minn., 1991—, sec., 1993—; co-pres. U. St. Thomas Women's Assn., 1990-91. Mem. ALA (bd. dirs. reference and adult svcs. divsn. 1988-90, sec. English and Am. lit. discussion group 1986, chmn. libr. svcs. aging population com. 1985-88), Beta Phi Mu, Kappa Delta Pi. Democrat. Methodist. Home: 28 Mississippi River Blvd N Saint Paul MN 55104-5713 Office: U Minn Wilson Libr 309 19th Ave S Minneapolis MN 55455-0414

MACARTHUR, SANDRA LEA, financial services executive; b. Springfield, Mass., July 21, 1946; d. John J. MacArthur and Catherine E. (Lantry) Mason; m. Edgar A. Dunn, June 23, 1973 (div. Mar. 1980); 1 child, Jonathan H.; m. Robert M. Cruickshank, Sept. 15, 1984. AA, Bradford Coll., 1966; BA, Simmons Coll., 1973; MBA, Babson Coll., 1983. Asst. dir. rental properties Wintergreen Resort, Charlottesville, Va., 1978-79; treas., ptnr. Elan, Inc., Boston, 1983-84; agt. State Mut. Am., Newton Center, Mass., 1985-86; sr. account officer Fidelity Investments Instl. Svcs., Boston, 1986-87, mgr. client svcs., 1987-88, assoc. market mgr., 1988-89; market mgr. Fidelity Instl. Retirement Svcs. Co., Boston, 1989-90, v.p. mktg., 1990-92, v.p. comm. prodn., 1992—. Fundraiser Babson Coll., Wellesley, Mass., 1988. Mem. Internat. Assn. Bus. Comm., Internat. TV and Video Assn., New Eng. Employee Benefits Coun., Beta Gamma Sigma. Democrat. Episcopalian. Home: 47 Westchester Rd Jamaica Plain MA 02130-3451 Office: Fidelity Instl Retirement Svcs Co 82 Devonshire St Boston MA 02109-3614

MACAULAY, BARBARA SOLOMON, architect, educator; b. Phila., Apr. 14, 1946; d. Philip Goldman and Dolores (Pomerantz) Solomon; m. James Macaulay (div.); children: Dana L., Lauren. Student, U. Mich., 1964-66; BFA, RISD, 1976, BArch, 1977. Registered architect, Pa. Project architect, staff architect Mitchell/Giurgola Architects, Phila., 1978-86; project architect Bartley Bronstein Long Mirenda, Phila., 1986-88; assoc. ptnr. Extrados Architects, Providence, 1989-94; prin. Barbara Macaulay Architects, Providence, 1992—; teaching asst. RISD, Providence, 1977, vis. critic, 1989—, MA in Tchg. Workshops, 1994, 95; asst. adj. prof. Temple U., Phila., 1988, vis. critic, 1984-88; adj. faculty Roger Williams U., Bristol, R.I., 1990—, vis. critic, 1989—; vis. critic Drexel U., Phila., 1984-88. Exhibited in group shows at RISD, Providence, 1975-77, AIA, Phila., 1984, 86, 88, Am. Coll., 1986, Hunterdon Art Ctr., Clinton, N.J., 1988, The Arcade, Providence, 1993, Spreebogen Internat. Urban Design Exhbn., Berlin, Germany, 1993, Visitors Ctr., Pawtucket, R.I., 1993; works pub. in profl. jours. Mem. Providence Banner Trail Exec. Com., R.I. Arts Advocates. Recipient scholarship U. Mich., 1965-66, AIA scholarship, 1976-77, Firm awards include Pa. Soc. Architects award, 1984, Phila. AIA Silver medal, 1985, Urban Design award Phila. Found. for Architecture, 1989, 2d prize Blackstone River Vis. Ctr. Competition, 1993; Design fellow R.I. State Coun. on the Arts, 1991; Artists Project grantee R.I. State Coun. on the Arts, 1994. Mem. AAUW, Nat. Coun. Archtl. Registration Bds. (cert.). Home and Studio: 135 Williams St Providence RI 02906

MACAUSLAN, MOLLY, facilities director; b. Portland, Maine, May 22, 1959; d. Robert Cubie and Sally Anita (Mirick) MacAuslan; m. Varney Jevan Hintlian, May 2, 1992; 1 child, Julia Goodnow. BA, Mt. Holyoke Coll., 1981. Facilities planner Interleaf Inc., Cambridge, Mass., 1983-87; real estate mgr. Interleaf Inc., Cambridge, 1987-90; facilities mgr. Cole Haan, Yarmouth, Maine, 1990-92; dir. facilities Cole Haan, Yarmouth, 1992—. Republican. Unitarian. Office: Cole Haan 44 N Elm St Yarmouth ME 04096-1173

MACAVINTA-TENAZAS, GEMORSITA, family physician; b. Numancia, Aklan, Phillippines, Dec. 18, 1938; came to U.S., 1967; d. Dominador Zalazar and Georgina Estrada (Tabanera) Macavinta; m. Salvador Torrefiel Tenazas Jr., Apr. 18, 1963; children: Alan, Alex, Albert, Alfred. BA, Far Ea. U., Manila, 1959, D of Medicine, 1964. Diplomate Am. Bd. Family Practice. Intern North Gen. Hosp., Manila, 1963-64; pvt. practice Manila, 1965-67; extern Chinese Gen. Hosp., Manila, 1965-67; with St. Joseph Med. Ctr., Burbank, Calif., 1967-69; chief cytotechnologist Cancer Screening Svcs., North Hollywood, Calif., 1969-73; resident in family practice medicine Health Scis. Ctr., Tex. Tech. U., Lubbock, 1974-75; staff physician VA Outpatient Clinic, L.A., 1975—. Recipient physician recognition awards AMA, 1973-85, 92-94; named Disting. Alumna, Aklan Acad., Philippines, 1991. Fellow Am. Acad. Family Physicians; mem. Calif. Acad. Family Physicians, Filipino Asian-Pacific VA Employees Soc. (pres. L.A. chpt. 1988—), Aklanons of Am. (pres. 1988—, 1st Mrs. Aklan 1986-89), Far Ea. U. Med. Alumni Assn. (asst. sec. 1988—). Roman Catholic. Office: VA Outpatient Clinic 425 S Hill St Los Angeles CA 90013-1110

MACCALLUM, (EDYTHE) LORENE, pharmacist; b. Monte Vista, Colo., Nov. 29, 1928; d. Francis Whittier and Berniece Viola (Martin) Scott; m. David Robertson MacCallum, June 12, 1952; children: Suzanne Rae MacCallum Barslund and Roxanne Kay MacCallum Batezel (twins), Tracy Scott, Tamara Lee MacCallum Johnson, Shauna Marie MacCallum Bost. BS in Pharmacy U. Colo., 1950. Registered pharmacist, Colo. Pharmacist Presbyn. Hosp., Denver, 1950, Corner Pharmacy, Lamar, Colo., 1950-53; rsch. pharmacist Nat. Chlorophyll Co., Lamar, 1953; relief pharmacist, various stores, Delta, Colo., 1957-59, Farmington, N.Mex., 1960-62, 71-79, Aztec, N.Mex., 1971-79; mgr. Med. Arts Pharmacy, Farmington, 1966-67; cons. pharmacist Navajo Hosp., Brethren in Christ Mission, Farmington, 1967-77; sales agt. Norris Realty, Farmington, 1977-78; pharmacist, owner, mgr. Lorene's Pharmacy, Farmington, 1979-88; tax cons. H&R Block, Farmington, 1968; cons. Pub. Svc. Co., N.Mex. Intermediate Clinic, Planned Parenthood, Farmington; one of the first women registered pharmacist apptd. N.Mex. Bd. Pharm., 1982-92. Author numerous poems for mag. Advisor Order Rainbow for Girls, Farmington, 1975-78. Mem. Nat. Assn. Bds. Pharmacy (com. on internship tng., com. edn., sec., treas. dist. 8, mem. impaired pharmacists adv. com., chmn. impaired pharmacists program N.Mex., 1987—, mem. law enforcement legis. com., chmn. nominating com. 1992), Nat. Assn. Retail Druggists, N.Mex. Pharm. Assn. (mem. exec. coun. 1977-81), Order Eastern Star (Farmington). Methodist. Home and Office: 1301 Camino Sol Farmington NM 87401-8075

MACCARIELLA, DEBRA ANNE, social worker; b. Augsburg, Germany, Oct. 31, 1963; d. Salvatore and Diane Mary (Casey) M. AS in Community Svcs., Pa. State U., 1986; BA in Social Work, West Chester U., 1988; postgrad., Pa. State U., 1994—. Intake worker Family Ct., Wilmington, Del., 1987-88; placement coord. Chester County Dept. of Children, Youth and Families, Westchester, Pa., 1989—; post adoption group facilitator Chester County Dept. Children, Youth and Families, Westchester, 1990—, foster parent trainer, 1993—. Mem. Big Bros./Big Sisters of Chester County. Republican. Roman Catholic. Office: Chester County Dept Youth Children & Families 601 Westtown Rd Ste 310 West Chester PA 19382-4504

MACCARTHY, TALBOT LELAND, civic volunteer; b. St. Louis, Jan. 28, 1936; d. Austin Porter Leland and Dorothy (Lund) Follansbee; m. John Peters MacCarthy, June 21, 1958; children: John Leland MacCarthy, Talbot MacCarthy Payne. BA, Vassar Coll., 1958. Sec., treas. Station List Pub. Co., St. Louis, 1979-85, pres., 1985-90. Trustee Robert E. Lee Meml. Assn., Arts and Edn. Coun. Greater St. Louis, pres., 1978-80, emerita; trustee St. Louis Art Mus.; past trustee St. Louis Mercantile Libr. Assn., Family & Children's Svc. Greater St. Louis, Health and Welfare Coun. Greater St. Louis, Jr. Kindergarten St. Louis Page Park YMCA, Scholarship Found. St. Louis, Friends St. Louis Art Mus. Bd., Ch. St. Michael and St. George Sch. Bd.; chmn. Mo. Arts Coun., 1980-85; past chmn. Vol. Action Ctr. Greater St. Louis, ; past vice chmn. bd. dirs. Mary Inst.; past pres. Jr. League St. Louis; mem. Nat. Coun. Arts, 1985-91. Recipient Woman of Achievement citation St. Louis Globe Democrat, 1979, Mo. Citizens for Arts/Arts Advocacy award, 1987, Mo. Arts Award, 1993. Mem. Vassar Club St. Louis (past pres.), Mary Inst. Alumnae Assn. (past pres.), Colonial Dames Am., Garden Club St. Louis. Republican. Episcopalian.

MACCLUER, JEAN WALTERS, geneticist; b. Columbus, Ohio, Mar. 30, 1937; d. Robert Edward and Lucy (Busch) Walters. BS cum laude, Ohio State U., 1959; MS, U. Mich., 1963, PhD, 1968. Asst. prof. dept. biology Pa. State U., University Park, 1972-74; assoc. prof. Pa. State U., 1974-81; assoc. scientist dept. genetics S.W. Found. for Biomed. Rsch., San Antonio, 1981-85, acting chmn., 1993-94, scientist, 1985—; assoc. prof. dept. cellular and structural biology U. Tex. Health Sci. Ctr., San Antonio, 1982-86; prof. U. Tex. Health Sci. Ctr., 1986—; mem. various fed. adv. coms. and editl. bds.; exec. positions in numerous orgns. Co-editor: Computer Simulation in Human Population Studies, 1974, Genetic Epidemiology: Applications and Comparison of Methods, 1987, Genetic Analsis of Complex Traits, 1989, Multipoint Mapping and Linkage Based Upon Affected Pedigree Members, 1989, Issues in Gene Mapping and Detection of Major Genes, 1992, Issues in the Analysis of Complex Diseases and their Risk Factors, 1993; contbr. articles to profl. jours. Mem. med. adv. com. South Tex. Regional Blood Bank, San Antonio, 1988-1992. Ctr. Advanced Study Behavioral Sci. fellow, 1977-78. Mem. Am. Heart Assn. (fellow coun. arteriosclerosis), Am. Soc. Human Genetics (life), Internat. Genetic Epidemiology Soc., Phi Beta Kappa, Sigma Xi. Office: SW Found Biomed Rsch 7620 Northwest Loop 410 San Antonio TX 78227-5301

MACCOBY, ELEANOR EMMONS, psychology educator; b. Tacoma, May 15, 1917; d. Harry Eugene and Viva May (Johnson) Emmons; m. Nathan Maccoby, Sept. 16, 1938 (dec. Apr. 1992); children: Janice Maccoby Carmichael, Sarah Maccoby Bellina, Mark. BS, U Wash., 1939; MA, U. Mich., 1949, PhD, 1950. Study dir. div. program surveys USDA, Washington, 1942-46; study dir. Survey Rsch. Ctr. U. Mich., Ann Arbor, 1946-48; lectr., rsch. assoc. dept. social rels. Harvard U., Cambridge, Mass., 1950-58; from assoc. to full prof. Stanford (Calif.) U., 1958-87, chmn. dept. psychology, 1973-76, prof. emeritus, 1987—; elected Nat. Acad. of Sci., 1993. Author: (with R. Sears and H. Levin) Patterns of Child-Rearing, 1957, (with Carol Jacklin) Psychology of Sex Differences, 1974, Social Development, 1980, (with R.H. Mnookin) Dividing the Child: Social and Legal Dilemmas of Custody, 1992; editor: (with Newcomb and Hartley) Readings in Social Psychology, 1957, The Development of Sex Differences, 1966. Co-chair Carnegie Task Force on Meeting Needs of Children. Recipient Gores award for Excellence in Teaching Stanford U., 1981, Disting. Contbn. to Edn. Research award Am. Ednl. Research Assn., 1984, Disting. Sci. Contbn. to Child Devel. award Soc. for Research in Child Devel., 1987, Disting. Sci. Contbns. award Am. Psychol. Assn., 1988; named to Barbara Kimball Browning professorship Stanford U., 1979—. Fellow Soc. for Rsch. in Child Devel. (pres. 1981-83, mem. governing coun. 1963-66), Am. Psychol. Assn. (div. 7 pres. 1971-72, G. Stanley Hall award 1982), Stanford Ctr. for Studies of Families, Children and Youth; mem. NAS, Western Psychol. Assn. (pres. 1974-75), Inst. for Rsch. on Women and Gender, Social Sci. Rsch. Coun. (chmn. 1984-85), Carnegie Counc. on Adolescence, Inst. of Medicine, Am. Acad. Arts and Scis. Democrat. Home: 729 Mayfield Ave Palo Alto CA 94305-1016 Office: Stanford U Dept Psychology Stanford CA 94305-2130

MACCONKEY, DOROTHY I., academic administrator; b. New Brunswick, N.J.; d. Donald Thurston and Dorothy Bennett (Hill) Ingling; m. Joseph W. MacConkey, June 19, 1949 (dec. Aug. 1975); children: Donald Franklin, Diane Margaret, Dorothy Frances; m. Karl Schmeidler, May 24, 1994. BA, Beaver Coll., 1947; MA, Wichita State U., 1953; PhD, U. Md., 1974; LLD (hon.), Beaver Coll., 1988. Lectr. Wichita (Kans.) State U., 1950-51; rsch.-campaign assoc. United Fund and Council, Wichita, 1951-62; rsch.- com. coordination Health and Welfare Council of Nat. Capital Area, Washington, 1963-65; exec. dir. multi-program agy. Prince Georges County Assn. for Retarded Children, Hyattsville, Md., 1965-66; prof. George Mason U., Fairfax, Va., 1966-76, asst. vice pres., acting dean, 1976-82; v.p., dean of coll. Hiram (Ohio) Coll., 1982-85; pres. Davis & Elkins (W.Va.) Coll., 1985—; bd. dirs. Davis Trust Co., Elkins, 1987—; adv. bd. George Mason U. Found., Fairfax, 1976—; trustee Beaver Coll., Glenside, Pa., 1971-87; cons., evaluator North Cen. Assn., Chgo., 1985—, commr., 1993—; mem. exec. com., pres. Assn. Presbyn. Colls. and Univs.; mem. bd. Svc. Opportunity Colls., Presbyn. Found., trustee, 1993—. Pres. County Chasers of Am., 1985—. Recipient Citizen award for service to handicapped, Fairfax County, 1981, Goddin Women Alumni award, 1985, Woman of Yr. in Edn. award W.Va. Fedn. Women's Clubs, 1986. Mem. Coun. of Pres.', Nat. Assn. Intercollegiate Athletics, Coun. Ind. Colls. (bd. dirs.). Office: Davis and Elkins Coll Office of Pres 100 Campus Dr Elkins WV 26241-3996

MACCONNELL-DAVINROY, IRENE J. H., secondary education educator, consultant; b. Trenton, N.J., Nov. 26, 1936; d. Irving John and Frances Emily (Bentley) MacConnell; m. Thomas Bernard Davinroy, Sept. 17, 1955 (div. 1990); children: Ellise Klaffer, Thomas C., E. Timothy. BA with honors, Pa. State U., 1974, postgrad., 1977-79. Cert. secondary edn. tchr., Pa. Tchr. social studies State College (Pa.) Area Jr. High Sch., 1979—; cons. N.J. Geographic Alliance, Rutgers U., 1986-87, Pa. Geographic Alliance, Indiana U. of Pa., 1987—; tchr. cons. Nat. Geographic Soc., Washington, 1986. Attendant, emergency med. technician Alpha Cmty. Ambulance Svc., State Coll., 1984-92. Fulbright fellow U.S. Dept. Edn., 1983; PGS Disting. Teaching award, 1993. Mem. Nat. Coun. for Geog. Edn. (Disting. Tchg. award 1989), Pa. Geog. Soc. (bd. dirs. 1988—, pres. 1994—, Tchg. award 1993). Home: 246 Mccormick Ave State College PA 16801-6121 Office: State College Area Jr High Sch 2180 School Dr State College PA 16803-1130

MACCRACKEN, MARY JO, physical education educator; b. Akron, Ohio, Oct. 6, 1943; d. Joel Milton and Mary Ellen (Frame) Weaver; m. Alan Lemuel MacCracken Jr., Aug. 23, 1969; 1 child, Alan Lemuel III. BA, Coll. of Wooster, 1965; MA, U. Akron, 1969; PhD, Kent State U., 1980. Tchr., coach Hudson (Ohio) Pub. Schs., 1965-68; instr. U. Akron, 1968-78, asst. prof., then assoc. prof., 1978-88, prof., 1988—, dir. Motor Behavior Lab., 1986—; collaboration tchr. Ritzman Sch., Akron, 1978-93, Mason Sch., Akron, 1978-93, St. Martha's Sch., Akron, 1993-94, Our Lady of Elms, 1994—; presenter at profl. confs. Contbr. articles to refereed jours. Sunday sch. tchr. Christ Ch. Epsicopal, Hudson, 1979-92; vol. Liltin' Leaguers, Jt. League Cleve., 1979-93; faculty mentor Akron High Sch. Drop-Out program, 1989. Grantee Ohio Bd. Regents, 1987-92. Mem. AAHPERD (v.p. health Midwest dist. 1990-92; meritorious honor award Ohio assn. 1988), Am. Psychol. Assn., N.Am. Soc. for Psychology of Sport and Phys. Activity, Nat. Assn. Phys. Edn. in Higher Edn. (sec.), Delta Kappa Gamma (Annie Webb Blanton award 1980). Republican. Home: Box 631 431 N Main St Hudson OH 44236-2247 Office: U Akron Motor Behavior Lab MH 81 Akron OH 44325-5103

MACDONALD, BETTY ANN, artist, educator; b. Bklyn., Aug. 2, 1936; d. Samuel Simon and Stella Anita (Blackton) Kipniss; m. Gordon James MacDonald; divorced; children: Gordon, Maureen, Michael, Bruce. BA, Adelphi U., 1958; MA, Columbia U., 1960. Instr. Montshire Mus., Hanover, N.H., 1979-84, Lebanon (N.H.) Coll., 1984, Smithsonian Instn., Washington, 1985—; Bd. dirs. N.H. Art Assn. Manchester, Ava Gallery, Hanover, N.H.; pres., bd. dirs. Washington Printmakers Gallery. Exhibits in permanent collection at Community for Creative Nonviolence, Washington, 1989, Mus. of Modern Art, Buenos Aires, 1988, Am. Cultural Ctr., New Delhi, India, 1992, Pa. State U., 1992. Grantee Giorgio Cini Found., 1962, NEA, 1981; recipient 1st prize printmakers Washington Women's Art Ctr., 1986, Past Pres.'s award Mus. Fine Arts, Springfield, Mass., 1982, de Cordova Mus., Soc. Am. Graphic Aartists N.Y., Merit award Currier Gallery of Art, 1987. Mem. Nat. League Am. Pen Women, Nat. Assn. Women Artists, L.A. Printmaking Soc. Home: 7222 Vistas Ln Mc Lean VA 22101-5076

MACDONALD, BONNIE LOUISE, psychologist; b. Marblehead, Mass., Mar. 20, 1964; d. George Lawrence and Lois Marie (Selander) MacD.; m. Robert Andrew Gould, July 20, 1991; 1 child, Olivia Lillian MacDonald Gould. BA, Harvard Coll., 1986; MS, Va. Polytechnic Inst., 1989, PhD, 1992. Lic. psychologist. Dir. behavioral medicine North Shore Children's Hosp., Salem, Mass., 1993-94, staff psychologist, 1992-93; dir. Early Childhood Cons. Assocs., Marblehead, 1993—; pvt. pract psychologist Salem, 1993—. Contbg. author: Family Health Psychology, 1992. Mem. APA, Assn. Advancement Behavior Therapy. Democrat. Congregationalist. Office: Ste 500 1 Salem Green Salem MA 01970

MACDONALD, JANICE W., legislative staff member; b. Grand Rapids, Mich., Feb. 8, 1941. Adminstrv. asst. to dir. student activities Aquinas Coll., Grand Rapids, Mich., 1966-69; staff asst. Senator Philip A. Hart, 1969-71; chief clk. Senate Subcom. Antitrust and Monopoly, Com. on Judiciary, 1971-74; exec. asst. Rep. Joseph L. Fisher, 1974-81; office mgr. Seifman & Lechner, Washington, 1981-82; adminstrv. asst. to John G. Milliken Winston & Strawn P.C., Washington, 1982-83; exec. asst. Rep. William D. Ford, 1983-93; chief adminstrv. officer House Com. Edn. and Labor, Washington, 1993—. Office: Dept of Edn & Labor 2181 Rayburn House Office Bldg Washington DC 20515*

MACDONALD, KAREN CRANE, occupational therapist, geriatric counselor; b. Denville, N.J., Feb. 24, 1955; d. Robert William and Jeanette Wilcox (Crane) M.; m. Geno Piacentini, Oct. 22, 1994. BS, Quinnipiac Coll., 1977; MS, U. Bridgeport, 1982; postgrad., NYU, 1983—. Cert. occupational therapist. Occupational therapist, coord. of spl. care unit Jewish Home for the Elderly, Conn., 1987-93, N.Y. Inst., N.Y.C., 1984-86; pvt. practice Fairfield County, Conn., 1977-88; occupl. therapist Rehab. Assocs., Fairfield, Conn., 1993—; instr. NYU, 1985-89, Quinnipiac Coll., 1986-92; lectr., cons. in field. Contbr. articles to profl. jours. Youth leader, deacon Union Meml. Ch., Stamford, Conn., 1980-88; deacon Southport Congl. Ch., 1992-94; chair consumer com. Alzheimer's Coalition of Conn., 1991-92. Teaching fellow NYU, 1983-86. Mem. World Fedn. Occupl. Therapy, Am. Occupl. Therapy Assn. (scholar 1985, coun. edn.), Conn. Occupl. Therapy Assn. (gerontology liaison 1980-83), Pi Lambda Theta. Home: 1 Davenport St Norwalk CT 06851 Office: Rehab Assocs 60 Katona Dr Fairfield CT 06430-3544

MACDONALD, KATHARINE MARCH, journalist, public relations executive; b. Los Angeles, Nov. 12, 1949; d. Ian G. and Eve (March) M. Grad. high sch., Beverly Hills, Calif.; student, Santa Monica Coll., 1971-73, Whittier Law Sch., Los Angeles, 1975-76. Scheduling asst. Jess Unruh for Gov., Los Angeles, 1969-70; dep. press. sec. Jess Unruh for Mayor, Los Angeles, 1973; polit. cons. various local campaigns, Los Angeles, 1973-78; researcher Washington Post-Los Angeles Bur., 1978-86; spl. corr. Washington Post-Los Angeles Bur., Washington, 1980-86; reporter State Capitol Bur. San Francisco Examiner, 1986-89; press dep. to L.A. City Councilman Zev Yaroslavsky, 1990-94; v.p. Hill and Knowlton, Inc., L.A., 1994—; guest lectr. journalism and polit. sci. various colleges and universities, 1984—. Office: 21st Fl 6500 Wilshire Blvd Los Angeles CA 90048

MACDONALD, PATRICIA LILLIG, public relations executive; b. Ridley Park, Pa., Apr. 29, 1941; d. John A. and Sethna Frances (Woods) Lillig; m. Guy W. MacDonald, Aug. 7, 1965; 1 child, Lauren. AB, Immaculata Coll., 1963; MA, Wichita State U., 1979. Analytical chemist McNeil Labs., Ft. Washington, Pa., 1963-65; vol. Peace Corps, Nepal, 1965-68; chemist Frinton Labs., Vineland, N.J., 1968-69; program dir. Am. Lung Assn. So. N.J., Hammonton, 1969-72; program cons. Arthritis Found. Kans., Wichita, 1972-73; health educator Wichita-Sedgwick County Health Dept., 1973-79, dir. health edn., 1979—; adj. instr. Wichita State U., 1979—. Mem. LWV (bd. dirs. 1969—), Pub. Rels. Soc. Am. (sec. 1981, v.p. 1982, pres. 1983, Pub. Rels. Profl. of Yr. 1989), Kans. Pub. Health Assn. (past bd. dirs.), Wichita Press Women (bd. dirs., pres. 1979, v.p., program com. chmn. 1974—). Office: Wichita-Sedgwick Health Dept 1900 E 9th St N Wichita KS 67214-3198

MACDONALD, SARA JEAN, librarian; b. Carmel, Calif., Sept. 9, 1955; d. John Francis and Harriet (Huguenin) MacD. BA, Temple U., 1978; MLS, Drexel U., 1987. Reference libr. Lippincott Libr., U. Pa., Phila., 1987-90, U. of the Arts, Phila., 1987—. Mem. Art Librs. Soc. N.Am. (moderator women and art roundtable), Drexel Coll. of Info. Studies Alumni Assn. (bd. dirs. 1990-91), Phila. Girls' Rowing Club. Office: U of the Arts Libr 320 S Broad St Philadelphia PA 19102-4994

MACDONALD, SHARON ETHEL, dancer, choreographer, administrator; b. Pittsfield, Mass., Mar. 24, 1952; d. Harry and Angeline (Saracco) MacD. BA, Skidmore Coll., 1974; MA, Smith Coll., 1992. Faculty Smith Coll., Northampton, Mass., 1974-76; dancer, tchr. Berkshire Ballet, Pittsfield, 1976-77; dance dir. Becket (Mass.) Arts Ctr., Mass., 1977-80; faculty mem. Williams Coll., Williamstown, Mass., 1979-80; co-artistic dir., owner N.E. Am. Ballet, Northampton, 1980-85; devel. dir., tchr. Berkshire Ballet, Pittsfield, 1984-85; adminstr., tchr. Hartford (Conn.) Ballet, Inc., 1985-90; asst. choreographer Easthampton Mass. Community Theatre Assn., 1981-83, Project Opera, 1982; bd. dirs. Jacob's Pillow Dance Festival, Becket, 1978-81; bd. trustees Becket Arts Ctr., 1979-80; tchr. Trinity Coll., Hartford, Conn., 1990—; dir. mktg., bus. cons. Limelight Prodns., Inc., 1990—; guest artist numerous pub schs., pvt. studios, colls., and univs. Pres. Friends of Jacob's Pillow, Becket, 1978-81, Friends of the Hartford Ballet, 1988-91, Jacob's Pillow Alumnae/Archives Com., 1988—, Dance History Scholars, 1976-79, 91—. Mass. Arts Lottery Grantee Mass. Arts Coun., 1984, Arts Lottery Grantee Northampton Arts Coun., 1984; Smith Coll. Fellow. Mem. AAHPERD, Nat. Dance Assn., Smith Coll. Club. Democrat. Baptist. Home: PO Box 697 Stockbridge MA 01262-0697

MACDONALD, SHEILA DE MARILLAC, energy company executive; b. Santa Monica, Calif., Jan. 17; d. William Alan and M. Jane (Crotty) M. BS, Stanford U.; BA, U. San Francisco; MBA, Harvard U. Prin. Tex. Transaction Mgmt. Co., Houston, 1990-94; exec. v.p. Novus Energy Co., Houston, 1994—. Mem. Harvard Club N.Y., Met. Club, Petroleum Club. Office: Novus Energy Inc 1010 Lamar # 1160 Houston TX 77002

MACDONALD, VIRGINIA BROOKS, architect; b. Denver, July 17, 1918; d. Emmet Earl and Lulu (Gatchel) Stoffel; widowed; m. Russell A. Apple, Oct. 18, 1981; children: Philip Brooks, Anne Brooks Hormann, Bill Brooks, Mike Brooks. BArch, Case Western Res. U., 1946. Registered architect, Hawaii. Dir. Timberline Camp., Honolulu, 1962-67; planner State of Hawaii, Honolulu, 1967-77; pvt. practice architecture Volcano, Hawaii, 1977—. Author: West Hawaii, 1972; (book/report) Na Ala Hele, 1973. Active Volcano Community Assn., 1980—. Recipient Innovative Energy award U.S. Dept. Energy, 1984, Energy Saving award State of Hawaii, 1984, Gov.'s award, 1993. Mem. AIA (past pres. local sect. 1988, dir. state coun., Passive Solar Design award 1994), Sierra Club (past state bd. dirs.), Hawaii Conservation Coun. (past state pres.).

MACDONALD GLENN, LINDA, lawyer; b. Perth Amboy, N.J., Sept. 29, 1955; d. John and Anna (Janocko) Stefanik; m. John Arch MacDonald, Sept. 17, 1983 (dec. Feb. 1984); m. Kim Garrett Glenn, Dec. 31, 1987; stepchildren: Katherine Glenn, Nicole Glenn. AB, Rutgers U., 1977; JD, Western New Eng. Law Sch., 1981. Bar: R.I. 1981, U.S. Dist. Ct. R.I. 1981. Assoc. Manning, West, Santianiello & Pari, Providence, 1981-82; spl. asst. atty., gen. sr. trial atty. Atty. Gen.'s Office State of R.I., Providence, 1982-87; legal counsel sp. legis. com. R.I. Ho. of Reps., Providence, 1986-88; legal counsel R.I. HEW Com., Providence, 1988—; assoc. Saunders, Dumas & Fleury, East Greenwich, R.I., 1987-89; ptnr. Dumas, MacDonald & Holland, East Greenwich, 1988-91, MacDonald and Holland, Ltd., East Greenwich, 1992-94, MacDonald Glenn & Assocs., East Greenwich, 1994—. Mem. Lambda Class Leadership R.I., 1991. Named one of Outstanding Women, YWCA, 1983, Outstanding Bd. Dirs., Leukemia Soc. of R.I., 1984. Mem. ABA, R.I. Bar Assn., R.I. Women's Bar Assn., Assn. Trial Lawyers Am., R.I. Trial Lawyers Assn., Warwick Bus. and Profl. Women's Assn. (Woman of Yr. 1988), R.I. Women's Network, East Greenwich C. of C. (v.p.). Democrat. Greek Catholic. Office: MacDonald-Glenn & Assocs 139 Main St East Greenwich RI 02818-3808

MACDONNELL, JOANNE CAPELLA, writer, editor, editorial consultant; b. Santa Rosa, Calif., Jan. 26, 1937; d. Joseph Lawrence and Mabel Alida (Strome) Capella; m. S.J. Cogliandro, Feb. 23, 1957 (div. 1963); 1 child,

Cory; m. Ignacio Plancarte Lopez, June 2, 1964 (dec. 1971); children: Kenneth Lopez, Lauren Lopez; m. John Faust MacDonnell, Sept. 6, 1981. Student, U. Calif., Berkeley, 1955-56, San Jose (Calif.) State U., 1956-57. Advt. Palo Alto Times, Calif., 1960-62; columnist San Jose Mercury News, Calif., 1962-83; clk. Santa Clara County Superior Ct., San Jose, 1984—. Author six-part series on unsafe toys, 1968; humor columnist San Jose Mercury News, 1977-81. Writer fund-raising brochure Valley Med. Ctr., San Jose, 1964; vol. Alexian Bros. Hosp., San Jose, 1967; TV appearances local pub. TV, San Jose, 1967-70. Recipient 2nd Place feature series award San Francisco Press Club 1968, Achievement in writing award Santa Clara County Pen Women Los Gatos Calif. 1965. Mem. San Francisco Press Club, San Jose Newspaper Guild. Democratic. Roman Catholic. Home: 3514 El Grande Dr San Jose CA 95132-3110

MACDOUGALL, INGEBORG R., mental health nurse; b. Orange, N.J., June 3, 1927; d. August Gottlieb and Heidi Ericka (Muller) Reibling; m. Hollis Blenus MacDougall, Apr. 1, 1950; children: Linda D., Jo Ann, Glen D. BA in Nursing Edn., Bates Coll., 1950; MS, Boston U., 1980. RN, Mass.; cert. psychiat. clin. specialist. Psychiat. clin. specialist VA, Mass.; coord. employee assistance program VA, Bedford, Mass.; cons. in field; chem. dependency educator; lectr. on impaired practice, addictions, leadership devel., and employee assistance. Fellow Am. Orthopsychiat. Assn.; mem. ANA, Mass. Nurses Assn. (Staff Devel. award, co-chair addictions coun., mem. peer assistance com.), Soc. for Family Therapy, Nat. Nurses Soc. on Addiction, Sigma Theta Tau.

MACDOUGALL, PRISCILLA RUTH, lawyer; b. Evanston, Ill., Jan. 20, 1944; d. Curtis Daniel and Genevieve Maurine (Rockwood) MacDougall; m. Lester H. Brownlee, July 5, 1987. BA, Barnard Coll., 1965; grad. with honors, U. Paris, 1967; JD, U. Mich., 1970. Bar: Wis. 1970, Ill. 1970. Asst. atty. gen. State of Wis., 1970-74; lectr. law U. Wis., 1973-75; staff counsel Wis. Edn. Assn. Council, Madison, 1975—; instr. Columbia Coll., Chgo., 1988—; litigator, writer, speaker, educator women's and children's names and women's rights and labor issues. Mem. ABA, Wis. State Bar (founder sect. on individual rights and responsibilities, chairperson, 1973-75, 78-79), Legal Assn. Women Wis. (co-founder). Author: Married Women's Common Law Right to Their Own Surnames, 1972, (with Terri P. Tepper) Booklet for Women Who Wish to Determine Their Own Names After Marriage, 1974, supplement, 1975, The Right of Women to Name Their Children, 1985; contbr. articles to profl. jours. Home: 502 Engelhart Dr Madison WI 53713-4742 Office: 33 Nob Hill Dr Madison WI 53713-2198

MACE, AUDRA JILL, accountant, consultant; b. Port Chester, N.Y., July 20, 1970; d. John Paul Mace and Beverly Phyllis Sage Carnahan and Rory Robert Carnahan. BBA, Pace U., Pleasantville, N.Y., 1992. Registered rep. Account exec. South Richmond Securities Inc., Melville, N.Y., 1992; credit analyst Pepsi Cola Co., Somers, N.Y., 1993; adminstrv. asst. Fowler & Keith Supply Co., Kingston, N.Y., 1993; cost acct. Bird Environ. Techs., Cold Spring, N.Y., 1993; staff acct. Mormac Marine Group, Stamford, Conn., 1993—; ind. account rep. World Telecom Group, 1993. Mem. Inst. Mgmt. Accts., Am. Soc. Women Accts., U.S. Amateur Ballroom Dance Assn. Home: 40 Tina Ln Hopewell Junction NY 12533-5117 Office: Mormac Marine Group Three Landmark Sq Stamford CT 06901

MACE, MARY ALICE, coal company administrator; b. Charleston, W.Va., Nov. 21, 1949; d. John Robert Leake and Georgia Alice (Wilhelm) Crist; m. Charles Michael Mace, May 20, 1968; 1 child, Christina Michelle. Student, U. Charleston, 1990—. Sec. Capitol Paper Supply, Inc., Charleston, 1967-68, Persingers, Inc., Charleston, 1968-77; benefits coordinator Elk Run Coal Co., Inc., Sylvester, W.Va., 1981—; notary public. Sec. PTA, Pettus, W.Va., 1981-83, pres. 1983-85. Mem. NAFE, Health Benefits Group, Women of Moose. Democrat. Home: 2741 Rose Lane Dr Charleston WV 25302-4923 Office: Elk Run Coal Co Inc PO Box 497 Sylvester WV 25193-0497

MACEK, ANNA MICHAELLA, cosmetics executive; b. Lancashire, Eng., Aug. 10, 1950; came to U.S., 1974; d. Wasyl and Maria (Litynska) Flaszczak; m. Frank Macek, Aug. 18, 1977. MA, U. Manchester, Eng., 1973; grad., Ecole des Estheticiennes Inst. de Beaute, Geneva, 1974. Asst. to pres., chief exec. officer Reed-Ingram Corp., N.Y.C., 1974-77; coordinator corp. pub. relations Northrop Corp., Los Angeles, 1978-82; pres. Annastasia Cosmetics, Gardena, Calif., 1983—. Contbr. articles to profl. jours. Mem. Beauty and Barber Supply Inst.

MACER-STORY, EUGENIA ANN, writer, artist; b. Mpls., Jan. 20, 1945; d. Dan Johnstone and Eugenia Loretta (Andrews) Macer; divorced; 1 child, Ezra Arthur Story. BS in Speech, Northwestern U., 1965; MFA, Columbia U., 1968. Writing instr. Polyarts, Boston, 1970-72; theater instr. Joy of Movement, Boston, 1972-75; artistic dir. Magik Mirror, Salem, Mass., 1975-76, Magick Mirror Comm., 1977—. Author: Congratulations: The UFO Reality, 1978, Angels of Time, 1982, Project Midas, 1986, Dr. Fu Man Chu Meets the Lonesome Cowboy: Sorcery and the UFO Experience, 1991, 3d edit., 1994, Gypsy Fair, 1991, The Strawberry Man, 1991, Legacy of Daedalus, 1995; (short stories) Battles with Dragons: Certain Tales of Political Yoga, 1993, 2d edit., 1994; (plays) Fetching the Tree, Archeological Politics, Strange Inquiries, Divine Appliance, 1989, The Zig Zag Wall, 1990, The Only Qualified Huntress, 1990, Telephone Taps Written Up for Tabloids, 1991, Wars with Pigeons, 1992, Conquest of the Asteroids, 1993, Commander Galacticon, 1993, Meister Hemmelin, 1994, Six Way Time Play, 1994, others; philosophy writer; contbr. articles to profl. jours.; author poetry in Woodstock Times, Lamia Ink!, Manhattan Poetry Rev., Sensations, Kore, Smiling Dog Press Anthology, others; feature writer Borderlands Mag., 1994; editor MUFON Newsletter. Shubert fellow, 1968. Mem. Dramatists Guild, U.S. Psychotronics Assn., Internat. Guild of Occult Scis. Democrat. Office: Magick Mirror Comm PO Box 741 New York NY 10116-0741

MACEWAN, BARBARA ANN, middle school educator; b. Adams, Mass., Apr. 22, 1938; d. Thomas Lawrence and Vera (Ziemba) Gaskalka; m. George Louie MacEwan, Feb. 16, 1963; children: Rebecca, Debra. BS in Edn. cum laude, North Adams State Coll., 1959; MEd with honors, Plymouth State Coll., 1994. Cert. K-8, secondary social studies tchr., sch. libr., Mass. Tchr. Town of Valatie, N.Y., 1959-61, 62-63, Dept. Def., Aschefensburg, Germany, 1961-62, Town of East Longmeadow, Mass., 1964; asst. children's libr. Springfield (Mass.) Libr., 1964; tchr. history Southwick (Mass.)-Tolland Regional Schs., 1971—; state coord. Nat. History Day, 1989-92. Author: The Old Cemetery: Southwick, 1977, Shays Rebellion, 1987. Sec. Southwick Hist. Soc., 1976-79, treas., 1979-86, pres., 1986-94; trustee Moore House, Southwick, 1989—; chair Southwick Hist. Commn., 1994—. Recipient recognition New Eng. League Mid. Schs., 1991; Horace Mann grantee Southwick Sch. Com., 1982. Mem. ASCD, NEA, Mass. Tchrs. Assn., Hampden County Tchrs. Assn., Southwick Edn. Assn., New Eng. History Tchrs. Assn., New Eng. Oral History Assn., Nat. Coun. for Social Studies, Mass. Coun. for Social Studies (recognition 1992), Western Mass. Coun. for Social Studies (bd. dirs. 1987—), Mass. Assn. Ednl. Media, Nat. Mus. Am. Indian, New Eng. Native Am. Inst., Phi Delta Kappa. Roman Catholic. Office: Powder Mill Mid Sch 94 Powder Mill Rd Southwick MA 01077-9324

MACFADYEN, CORNELIA VERA, financial executive; b. N.Y.C., Aug. 3, 1953; d. Cornelia Ann Netter. BFA, Pratt Inst., 1976. Art dir. Trout & Ries Advt., N.Y.C., 1977-80; graphic designer CVM Designs, N.Y.C., 1980-84; office mgr. Netter Real Estate, N.Y.C., 1984-86; asst. to pres., chmn. Urban Capital Corp., N.Y.C., 1986-92; v.p. customer svc., product devel. mgr. Viatel, Inc., N.Y.C., 1991—. Artist oil painting, Blue Nude, 1979, The Inferno, 1976, Man On the Move, 1985, Alone, 1987. Founding mem. Manhattan Women's Polit. Caucus, 1969-70, Christopher St. West Block Assn., N.Y.C., 1984; mem. Am. Ballet Theatre. Mem. Soc. Illustrators, Soc. Profl. and Exec. Women, Nat. Assn. Female Execs., New Sch. for Social Research. Republican. Home: 5 E 22d St New York NY 10010

MACFARLANE, ANNETTE ROWANE, writing project assistant, educator; b. Brigham City, Utah, Aug. 10, 1952; d. Ted D. and Lynette Irene (Gardner) M. BS, Utah State U., 1982, MA, 1984, postgrad., 1992—. Cert. secondary tchr., middle sch. tchr., speech, drama and lang. arts. Sales profl. JC Penney, Orem, Utah, 1971; property mgr. Village Green Realty, Provo, Utah, 1971-74; acct. Fred Sands, Realtors, L.A., 1974-76; office mgr. Southwick Realty, Tremonton, Utah, 1976-77; acct. mgr. Thiokol, Inc., Promentary, Utah, 1977-80; editor Thiokol, Inc., Promentary, 1985-87; tchr. Box Elder Sch. Dist., Brigham City, 1987-92; adj. faculty, asst. Utah Writers Project Utah State U., Logan, 1992—; owner Renaissance Publs., Collinston, Utah, 1986—. Author: (mag.) Y-Vector, 1974; author, editor: (mag.) Aerospace Facts, 1985-87. Mem. rules and policy com. Utah Dem. Com., 1984—; campaign mgr. Eli Anderson, Utah Ho. of Reps., 1992, 94. Mem. Nat. Conf. Tchrs. English, Utah Coun. Tchrs. English, Sigma Tau Delta. Home: 3470 W Highway 30 Collinston UT 84306 Office: Utah State Univ UMC 3200 Logan UT 84322-3200

MACGILLIVRAY, LOIS ANN, academic administrator; b. Phila., July 8, 1937; d. Alexander and Mary Ethel (Crosby) MacG. BA in History, Holy Names Coll., 1966; MA in Sociology, U. N.C., 1971, PhD in Sociology, 1973. Joined Sisters of Holy Names of Jesus and Mary, 1955. Research asst. U. N.C., Chapel Hill, 1969-70, 71-72, instr. sociology, 1970-71; sociologist Rsch. Triangle Inst., Durham, N.C., 1973-75, sr. sociologist, 1975-81; dir. Ctr. for Population and Urban-Rural Studies, Research Triangle Inst., Durham, N.C., 1976-81; pres. Holy Names Coll., Oakland, Calif., 1982-92; mem. steering com. Symposium for Bus. Leaders Holy Names Coll., 1982-92; vis. scholar dept. sociology U. N.C., Chapel Hill, 1992-94; pvt. cons. 1992—; mem. policy bd. Univ. Oakland Met. Forum, co-convenor panel on edn. and youth. Bd. dirs. Oakland Coun. Econ. Devel., 1984-86; bd. dirs. Bay Area Biosci. Ctr., 1990-92, mem. adv. com., 1992-94. Mem. Am. Sociol. Assn., Assn. Ind. Calif. Colls. and Univs. (exec. com. 1985-92, vice chmn. 1989-92), Regional Assn. East Bay Colls. and Univs. (past pres., bd. dirs. 1982-92). Home and Office: 101 Hamilton Rd Chapel Hill NC 27514

MACGILLIVRAY, MARYANN LEVERONE, marketing consultant; b. Mpls., Oct. 18, 1947; d. Joseph Paul and Genevieve Gertrude (Ozark) Leverone; B.S., Coll. of St. Catherine, St. Paul, 1969; Med. Technologist, Hennepin County Gen. Hosp., 1970; M.B.A., Pepperdine U., 1976; m. Duncan MacGillivray, Apr. 28, 1973; children—Duncan Michael, Catherine Mary and Monica Mary (twins), Andrew John. Med. technologist Mercy Hosp., San Diego, 1970-72; with Diagnostics div. Abbott Labs., South Pasadena, Calif., 1972-79, tech. service rep., 1972-74, sr. tech. service rep., 1974-75, product coordinator, mktg., 1975-77, mktg. product mgr., 1977-79; clin. diagnostic mktg. cons., Sierra Madre, Calif., 1979-88; founder, mktg. dir. Health Craft Internat., Pasadena, Calif., 1988—; elected council woman City of Sierra Madre, 1990-94, mayor, 1994—. Recipient Pres.'s award Abbott Diagnostics Div., 1975. Mem. Biomed. Mktg. Assn., Am. Assn. Clin. Chemistry, Am. Assn. Clin. Pathologists, Am. Soc. Med. Tech., Calif. Assn. Med. Lab. Technologists, Pasadena Symphony Assn. Roman Catholic. Home: 608 Elm Ave Sierra Madre CA 91024-1245

MAC GOWAN, MARY EUGENIA, lawyer; b. Turlock, Calif., Aug. 4, 1928; d. William Ray and Mary Bolling (Gilbert) Kern; m. Gordon Scott Millar, Jan. 2, 1970; 1 dau., Heather Mary. A.B., U. Calif., Berkeley, 1950; J.D., U. Calif., San Francisco, 1953. Bar: Calif. 1953; cert. family law specialist Calif. State Bar Bd. Legal Specialization. Research atty. Supreme Ct. Calif., 1954, Calif. Ct. Appeals, 1955; partner firm MacGowan & MacGowan, Calif., 1956-68; pvt. practice law San Francisco, 1968—. Bd. dirs. San Francisco Speech and Hearing Center, San Francisco Legal Aid Soc., J.A.C.K.I.E. Mem. Am., Calif., San Francisco bar assns., Queen's Bench. Clubs: San Francisco Lawyers, Forest Hill Garden. Office: 685 Market St San Francisco CA 94105-4212

MACGOWAN, SANDRA FIRELLI, publishing executive, publishing educator; b. Phila., Nov. 9, 1951; d. William Firelli and Barbara (Gimbel) Kapalcik. BS in Biology, BA in English, Pa. State U., 1973, MA in English Lit., 1978. Cert. supervisory analyst N.Y. Stock Exchange. Editor McGraw-Hill Pub. Co., N.Y.C., 1979-81; sr. acquisitions editor Harcourt Brace Jovanovich, Inc., N.Y.C., 1981-82; sr. editor The Coll. Bd., N.Y.C., 1982-88; v.p., head editorial CS First Boston Corp., N.Y.C., 1988-94; v.p. supervisory analyst internat. rsch. S.G. Warburg, N.Y.C., 1994—; part time asst. prof. pub. NYU Sch. Continuing Edn., N.Y.C., 1985—. Author: 50 College Admission Directors Speak to Parents, 1988. Democrat. Office: SG Warburg Park Ave Plz 787 Seventh Ave New York NY 10019

MACGUINNESS, ROSEMARY ANNE, lawyer, real estate broker; b. Newry, County Down, No. Ireland, June 26, 1957; came to U.S., 1981.; d. Michael Gerard and Maureen Rosemary (Leavy) MacG.; m. Philip Martin Bellber, Dec. 5, 1987; children: Sam Martin Belllber, Rhys Patrick Bellber, Mason Philip Bellber. B in Civil Law, U. Coll. Dublin, 1978, diploma in European Law, 1979; MS in Criminal Justice, Northeastern U., 1982. Bar: Ireland 1981, Calif. 1994. Legal asst. Bronson, Bronson & McKinnon, San Francisco, 1983; atty. McInerney & Dillon, Oakland, Calif., 1984-87; sr. counsel Pacific Stock Exch., San Francisco, 1987-90, sr. counsel, dir. arbitration, 1990—. Mem. Queen's Bench. Office: Pacific Stock Exch 301 Pine St San Francisco CA 94104

MACHIN, BARBARA E., lawyer; b. Kansas City, Mo., Mar. 26, 1947; d. Roger H. and Doris D. (Dunkel) Elliott; m. Peter A. Machin, June 1, 1969; 1 child, Andrew D. BS in Sec. Edn., U. Kans., 1969, MA in Curriculum Devel./Anthropology, 1973; JD, U. Toledo Coll., 1978. Bar: Ohio, U.S. Dist. Ct. (no. dist.) Ohio, U.S. Ct. Appeals (6th cir.), U.S. Supreme Ct. Instr. rsch. and writing U. Toledo Coll. of Law, 1978-79; law clerk Lucas County Ct. of Common Pleas, Toledo, 1979-80; assoc., ptnr. Doyle, Lewis & Warner, Toledo, 1980-87; assoc. Shumaker, Loop & Kendrick, Toledo, 1987-92; gen. counsel U. Toledo, 1993—; pres., v.p., mem. bd. trustees Toledo Legal Aid Soc., 1983—; pres. Toledo Civil Trial Attys., 1990-93. Contbr. articles to profl. jours. Mem. house corp. bd. Gamma Phi Beta Sorority, 1985—; mem. bd. trustees Epworth Found., 1993—, St. Luke's Hosp., 1994—. Mem. Ohio State Bar Assn., Toledo Bar Assn., Toledo Women's Bar Assn., Toledo Civil Trial Attys. (pres. 1983-92). Home: 5034 Dauber Dr W Toledo OH 43615 Office: U of Toledo Office of the Gen Counsel 1014 Driscoll 2801 W Bancroft Toledo OH 43606

MACHIORLETE, PATRICIA ANNE, artist, publisher; b. Jersey City; m. Donald W. Machiorlete. BS, Fairleigh Dickinson U., 1967; postgrad., William Paterson Coll., 1968, N.J. Ctr. for Visual Arts, Summit, 1981. Cert. tchr., N.J. Tchr. Wayne (N.J.) Bd. Edn., 1967-69, West Milford (N.J.) Bd. Edn., 1969-71, Clark Sch., East Orange, N.J., 1978-81; artist Essex Fells, N.J., 1982-87, Bedminster, N.J., 1987—; art pub. Peachcroft Collection, Inc., Bedminster, N.J., 1987—. Contbd. articles to profl. mags. Recipient Best in Show award Leonardo Da Vinci Soc., 1982, first prize Essex Water Color Club, 1993. Mem. Nat. Assn. Women Artists (bd. dirs. 1992-93), N.J. Watercolor Soc. (newsletter editor 1991—, Monmouth Mus. award 1988, bd. dir. 1991-94), Garden State Watercolor Soc., Miniature Art Soc. N.J., Essex Watercolor Soc. (1st prize 60th Anniversary Show 1993). Home and Office: Peachcroft Collection Inc 133 Autumn Ridge Rd Bedminster NJ 07921

MACHKOVITZ, SUSAN JEAN, psychologist, mental health consultant, educator; b. Beaver Dam, Wis.; d. Harold John and Lovine Carol Marie (Knorr) Schmidt; m. David Allen Machkovitz, July 11, 1970 (dec. Dec. 1976). BS in Elem.-Spl. Edn. magna cum laude, U. Wis., Whitewater, 1980; MS in Behavior Disabilities, U. Wis., Madison, 1987, PhD in Rehab. Psychology, 1993. Lic. life spl. edn. tchr., lic. elem. edn. tchr., Wis. Instr. behavior modification program Bethesda Luth. Home, Watertown, Wis., 1975-79, spl. educator, 1980-86, diagnostician, edn. specialist, mental health cons., 1986-87; tng. specialist, cons. Tng. Plus, Watertown, 1988; instr. Madison Area Tech. Coll., Watertown, 1988; tchg. and rsch. asst. U. Wis., Madison, 1988-91, supr. student tchrs., 1988-89; psychology intern Ethan Allen Sch. for Boys, State of Wis., Wales, 1991-92; instr. Edgewood Coll., Madison, 1993; psychotherapist River City Psychol. Svcs., Watertown, 1993-94; family therapist, post-doctoral psychology trainee Luth. Social Svcs. Wis. and Upper Mich., 1994—; lectr. U. Wis., Madison, summer, 1991; mental health cons. Head Start Dodge County, Wis., 1994. Contbg. author: Treatment of the Mentally Disabled Offender, 1993. Mem. APA, Wis. Psychol. Assn., Soc. Clin. and Cons. Psychologists, Chi Sigma Iota. Democrat. Roman Catholic. Home: 1409 E Main St Watertown WI 53094 Office: Luth Social Svcs Wis & Upper Mich 1010 DeClark St Beaver Dam WI 53916

MACHTIGER, HARRIET GORDON, psychoanalyst; b. N.Y.C., July 27, 1927; d. Michael J. and Miriam D. (Rand) Gordon; B.A., Bklyn. Coll., 1947; dipl. with distinction, U. London, 1966, Ph.D., 1974; m. Sidney Machtiger, Feb. 7, 1948; children: Avram Coleman, Marcia Gordon, Bennett Rand. Tchr., Phila. Pub. Schs., 1962-64; ednl. therapist Child Guidance Tng. Center, London, 1966-68; ednl. therapist Sch. Psychol. Svc., Inner London Edn. Authority, 1968-70; therapist Paddington Day Hosp., London, 1970-71, London Centre for Psychotherapy, 1971-74, Staunton Clinic, U. Pitts., 1974-78; pvt. practice psychoanalysis, Pitts., 1976—; pres. C.G. Jung Ctr., Pitts., 1976-81; cons. in field. Mem. S.W. Pitts. Community Mental Health, 1976-78; past dir. Pitts. program Inter-Regional Soc. Jungian Analysts, 1975-85. Recipient award for Disting. Contributions to Advancement in Edn., Pa. Dept. Edn., 1962; Social Sci. Rsch. Coun. award, 1973; cert. psychologist, Pa. Fellow Am. Orthopsychiat. Assn.; mem. Am. Psychol. Assn., N.Y. Assn. Analytical Psychologists, Pa. Psychol. Assn., Brit. Psychol. Soc., Brit. Assn. Psychotherapists, Assn. Child Psychology and Child Psychiatry, Nat. Assn. for Advancement Psychoanalysis. Home: 207 Tennyson Ave Pittsburgh PA 15213-1415 Office: 123 Cathedral Mansions 4716 Ellsworth Ave Pittsburgh PA 15213-2851

MACIAS-WYCOFF, SUSAN ELLEN, counselor, educator; b. Santa Ana, Calif., June 1, 1962; d. Donald James Sheldon-Wycoff and Angelina Marie (Heredia) Macias. AA in Child Devel., Sacramento City Coll., 1982; BA in Child Devel., Calif. State U., Sacramento, 1985, MS in Counselor Edn., 1989; PhD in Counselor Edn., U. N.Mex., 1994. Cert. counselor. Lang. tchr. Casa de los Niños, Lima, Peru, 1981-82, Nichibei Gakuin, Matsuyama, Japan, 1985-86; retention counselor coll. migrant program Calif. State U., Sacramento, 1983-87; counseling cons. Woodland (Calif.) Unified Sch. Dist., 1988-89; asst. prof. Humboldt State U., Arcata, Calif., 1989-90; diagnostician U. N.Mex., Albuquerque, 1991-92, teaching assoc., researcher, 1991-94; rsch. assoc. S.W. Hispanic Rsch. Inst., Albuquerque, 1992-93; asst. prof. counselor edn. Calif. State U., Fullerton, 1994—; collaborative researcher Ctr. for Collaboration on Children, Fullerton, 1994—. Contbr. articles to profl. jours. Nat. Hispanic Soc. scholar, 1994; Ford Found. grantee, 1992; fellow Calif. Office Univ. Chancellor, 1991-94. Mem. ACA, Assn. Multicultural Counseling and Devel., Internat. Assn. Marriage and Family Counselors. Democrat. Buddhist. Office: Calif State U Dept Counseling Edn Bldg Fullerton CA 92634

MACIEL, PATRICIA ANN, hospital administrator; b. Providence, Jan. 13, 1940; d. Raymond Wallace Sr. and Elizabeth Josephine (Kelly) Ross; m. John Maciel Jr., July 24, 1963; children: Kelly Patricia, Christopher John. BEd, R.I. Coll., 1961, MA in Teaching, 1976. Cert. tchr., R.I. 3d grade tchr. Pawtucket (R.I.) Pub. Schs., 1961-62; 5th and 6th grade tchr. Providence Pub. Schs., 1962-63; tchr. Pawtucket and Providence Pub. Schs., 1963-72; tchr., curriculum coord. Holy Name Sch., Providence, 1972-80; dir. ednl. programming Basic Skills, Inc., Providence, 1980-83; dir. devel./pub. rels. IN-SIGHT, Warwick, R.I., 1983-88; spl. asst. to sr. v.p. for devel. St. Joseph Hosp., North Providence, R.I., 1988—. Editor, author newsletter IN-SIGHT News, 1980-83. Sec. exec. bd. Holy Name Sch., 1972-80; pres. employee activities com. St. Josephs Hosp., 1991-93; founding mem., pres. Friends of the Pawtucket Pub. Libr., 1966; pres. Pawtucket Jr. Woman's Club, 1965; publicity chair Middlebridge Assn., South Kingstown, R.I., 1989-90; mem. Narrow River Preservation Assn., South Kingstown, 1976—; mem. Save the Bay, State of R.I., 1987—; ex officio mem. R.I. Coll. Found., 1992-94. Recipient Alumna of Yr award Rhode Island Coll., 1992. Mem. R.I. Coll. Alumni Assn. (treas. exec. bd. 1990-92, chair ann. fund dr. 1990-92, chair class reunion 1981, 86, 91, class news sec. 1972-78, pres. 1992-94). Roman Catholic.

MACINTOSH, BETTY ARLENE, state community services administrator; b. Dover, Ohio, July 14, 1938; d. Brady Burrell and Juanita (Scott) Ballard; m. Thomas Eugene Ellwood, Nov. 2, 1957 (div. Sept. 1976); children: Sharon Kay Mahaffey, Scott Thomas; m. Larry David Macintosh, Dec. 23, 1976. BS in Edn., Ohio State U., 1970, MA in Edn., 1975. Social worker Franklin County Welfare Dept., Columbus, Ohio, 1970-71; dir. day care ctr. Amerikid, Columbus, 1971-72; supr. day care unit Ohio Dept. of Welfare, Columbus, 1972-74, mgr. child care unit, 1974-79; early childhood and supportive home svcs. specialist State of Ohio, Columbus, 1979-81; chief Office Early Childhood/Sch. Age Programs Ohio Dept. Mental Retardation/Devel. Disabilities, Columbus, 1986-88, dep. dir., 1988—. Chairperson bd. Action for Children, Columbus. Mem. Profl. Assn. for the Retarded. Methodist. Office: Ohio Dept Mental Retardation Devel Disability 30 E Broad St Fl 12 Columbus OH 43266-0002

MACINTYRE, PATRICIA COLOMBO, middle school educator; b. San Diego, Jan. 20, 1955; d. Vincent Christopher Colombo and Ellen Louise (Johnson) David; m. John Malcolm MacIntyre, July 25, 1981; children: Ann Marie, Katherine Christine. BA, San Diego State U., 1977; MA in Computer Edn., U.S. Internat. U., 1987. Cert. tchr., Calif. Math. and art tchr. Adams Jr. High Sch., Richmond, Calif., 1979-80; math. and computer tchr. Piedmont (Calif.) Middle Sch., 1980-81, La Jolla (Calif.) Country Day Sch., 1982-85; adminstrv. asst. to headmaster St. Michael's Sch., Newport, R.I., 1981-82; math. tchr. Kubasaki High Sch., Dept. Def. Dependents Sch., Okinawa, Japan, 1989-90; math. and computer tchr., tech. coord. Palm Middle Sch., Lemon Grove, Calif., 1985—; speaker, presenter in field. Grantee San Diego Industry-Edn. Coun. 1991, Lemon Grove Sch. Dist. 1990, 91,92; recipient Founder's Day Svc. award Palm Middle Sch. PTA, 1992; Calif. Math. Coun. Scholar 1976; named Tchr. of Yr., Lemon Grove Sch. Dist., 1994-95. Mem. San Diego Computer-Using Educators (grantee 1991), Pi Lambda Theta, Phi Kappa Phi. Republican. Roman Catholic. Office: Palm Middle Sch 8425 Palm St Lemon Grove CA 91945

MACISAAC, ANN MARIE HENRIETTA, adult nurse practitioner; b. Lackawanna, N.Y., Nov. 2, 1952; d. Henry Joseph and Marie Edith (Lindstrom) Dempsey; m. James Joseph MacIsaac, June 12, 1976; children: Katherine Ann, Maureen Ellen. BSN cum laude, Niagara U., 1974; MSN, SUNY, Buffalo, 1982. RN N.Y.; cert. adult nurse practitioner ANA, N.Y., nurse practitioner in adult health, N.Y. Staff nurse U.S. Army Nurse Corps., 1974-75, head nurse, 1975-76; staff nurse primary care St. Joseph's Hosp., Towson, Md., 1978-79; staff nurse, charge nurse St. Joseph Intercommunity Hosp., Buffalo, N.Y., 1979-80; instr. nursing Buffalo Bd. Edn., 1980-82; nurse practitioner drug and alcohol detoxification & rehab Buffalo VA Med. Ctr., 1982-83, nurse practitioner hosp. based home care program, 1983-87, coord., nurse practitioner, head nurse adult day care program, 1987-89, nurse practitioner div. rheumatology, 1989—; clin. instr. SUNY Sch. Nursing, Buffalo, 1983-88, asst. prof., 1989—, clin. instr. SUNY Sch. Medicine, Buffalo, 1989; lectr. in field; cons. in field. Contbr. articles to profl. jours. Asst. coach Amherst (N.Y.) Girls Softball League, 1992; religious tchr. St. Gregory the Great Parish, 1992—; patient svcs. com. Arthritis Found. Western N.Y., 1990—. Capt. U.S. Army, 1973-77. Mem. AMVETS, Nurse Practitioner Assn. Western N.Y. (chmn. pub. rels. 1984, chmn. edn. com. 1984, treas. 1985-86, pres. 1986-88, mem. nominating com. 1989-90, legis. activities com. 1994—), N.Y. State Coalition Nurse Practitioners, Communique (mem. editl. bd. 1990-92, chair/co-chair legis. com. 1990—), Am. Coll. Rheumatology Health Profls. (practice com. 1993-95, membership com. 1995). Independent. Roman Catholic. Home: 21 Scarbora Dr Williamsville NY 14221-3414 Office: Buffalo VAMC-118 3495 Bailey Ave Buffalo NY 14215-1129

MACIUSZKO, KATHLEEN LYNN, librarian, educator; b. Nogales, Ariz., Apr. 8, 1947; d. Thomas and Stephanie (Horowski) Mart; m. Jerzy Janusz Maciuszko, Dec. 11, 1976; 1 child, Christinia Alexsandra. BA, Ea. Mich. U., 1969; MLS, Kent State U., 1974; PhD, Case Western Res. U., 1987. Reference libr. Baldwin-Wallace Coll. Libr., Berea, Ohio, 1974-77, dir. Conservatory of Music Libr., 1977-85; dir. bus. info. svcs. Harcourt Brace Jovanovich, Inc., Cleve., 1985-89; staff asst. to exec. dir. Cuyahoga County Pub. Libr., Cleve., 1989-90; dir. Cleve. Area Met. Library System, Beachwood, Ohio, 1990; media specialist Cleve. Pub. Schs., 1991-93, Berea (Ohio) City Sch. Dist., 1993—. Author: OCLC: A Decade of Development, 1967-77, 1984; contbr. articles to profl. jours. Named Plenum Pub. scholar, 1986. Mem. Spl. Librs. Assn. (pres. Cleve. chpt. 1989-90, v.p. 1988-89, editor newsletter 1988-89), Baldwin-Wallace Coll. Faculty Women's Club (pres. 1975).. Office: Midpark HS 7000 Paula Dr Middleburg Heights OH 44130

MACIVER, LINDA B., information services administrator; b. Manchester, N.H., Apr. 7, 1946; d. George Donald and Vera B. (Arlin) MacI. BA in History, U. N.H., 1968; MEd, Boston U., 1981; MS, Simmons Coll., Boston, 1982. Tchr. social sci. Meml. High Sch., Manchester, 1968-72, libr.-media specialist, 1972-80; media svcs. libr. Simmons Coll., Boston, 1981-82; info. specialist Schneider Parker Jakuc, Inc., Boston, 1982-85; mgr. info. svcs. Ingalls, Quinn & Johnson (formerly Ingalls Assocs.) Boston, 1985-89; with govt. documents dept. Boston Pub. Libr., 1990—; ind. info. broker, 1990—; sr. cons. Growth Strategies Group. Mem. Am. Soc. Info. Sci. (treas. New Eng. chpt. 1984-86), Spl. Libraries Assn., ALA, NELA, NE Online Users, Beta Phi Mu (pres. Beta Beta chpt. 1993-94). Unitarian-Universalist. Home: 123 Commonwealth Ave Apt 3 Boston MA 02116-2334 Office: Boston Pub Libr Copley Sq Boston MA 02117 also: Growth Strategies Group 1 Kennedy Sq Ste 2200 Cambridge MA 02138

MACIVOR, HAZEL JUDITH ARNOLD, genealogist, retired secondary school educator; b. Holly Creek, Ga., Nov. 18, 1921; d. Charles Dewey and Vergia Plummer Paralee (Teem) Arnold; m. Lenwood Wilson Elliott, Sept. 24, 1938 (div. 1940); m. Angus Stewart MacIvor Jr., Dec. 7, 1940; children: Angus Stewart III, Sandra Susan, Charlene Margaret MacIvor Burns, Victoria Dion MacIvor Carson, Catherine Jane. BS, Wayne State U., 1958, MA. Cert. secondary edn. tchr., Mich.; cert. genealogist. History tchr. Detroit Bd. Edn., 1958-63, S. Macomb Community Coll., Warren, Mich., 1961-62, Oak Park (Mich.) Bd. Edn., 1963-66; sec., cons. MacIvor Cons., Inc., Marshfield, Mass., 1984-87; pvt. practice genealogy Marshfield, 1971—. Author: Benjamin Arnold of New Kent County, Va. and Greenville, S.C., 1974; editor Arnold Family of the South jour., 1971-84; contbr. articles on genealogy to profl. publs. Chmn. Dem. Party, Royal Oak, Mich., 1953, fundraiser, 1950's; active Oakland County coun. Camp Fire Girls, 1950's, leader, 1958-59; sponsor Future Tchrs. of Am., Chadsey High Sch., Detroit, 1962-63; vol. tchr. Adult Illiteracy Program, Gainesville, Ga., 1989—. Recipient Red Feather award Father Weinman Settlement Ho., Detroit, 1949. Fellow London Huguenot Soc., Nat. Huguenot Soc. (Mich. chpt.); mem. Nova Scotia Genealogical Soc., United Daus. of Confederacy, U.S. Daus. of War of 1812, DAR (vice regent Ezra Parker chpt. 1976-78, regent Col. Thomas Lothrop chpt. 1982-83, regent Col. William Candler chpt. 1989-91, chmn. bicentennial com. 1976-78), U.S. Daus. War of 1812, Daus. of Founders and Patriots, Soc. Descents Colonial Clergy, Daus. Colonial Wars, Dames of Court of Honour, Daus. of Am. Colonists, Colonial Dames of XVIIth Century, Colonial Daus. of Seventeenth Century, Flagon and Trencher, Order of Soc. of Colonial Physicians and Chirurgiens, Jamestowne Soc., Sons and Daus. of Pilgrims, Magna Carta Dames, Order of Ams. of Armorial Ancestry, Order of the Crown of Charlemagne, Colonial Soc. Ams. of Royal Descent, Order of Three Crusades, Daus. of Barons of Runnemede. Descent of Illegitimate Sons and Daus. Kings of Britain, Nat. Soc. Ams. Royal Descent, Knights of Most Noble Order Bath, Pi Lambda Theta. Episcopalian. Home: 2900 Holster Way Orlando FL 32822-3614

MACK, BRENDA LEE, sociologist, public relations consulting company executive; b. Peoria, Ill., Mar. 24; d. William James and Virginia Julia (Pickett) Palmer; m. Rozene Mack, Jan. 13 (div.); 1 child, Kevin Anthony. AA, L.A. City Coll.; BA in Sociology, Calif. State U., L.A., 1980. Ct. clk. City of Blythe, Calif.; partner Mack Trucking Co., Blythe; ombudsman, sec. bus facilities So. Calif. Rapid Transit Dist., L.A., 1974-81; owner Brenda Mack Enterprises, L.A., 1981—; conflict mediator, cultural sensitivity cons.; lectr., writer, radio and TV personality; cons. European community; co-originator advt. concept View/Door Project; pub. News from the United States newsletter through U.S. and Europe; Cultural Sensitivity Cons.; Conflict Mediator. Past bd. dirs. Narcotic Symposium, L.A. With WAC, U.S. Army. Mem. Women For, Calif. State U. L.A. Alumni Assn., World Affairs Coun., German-Am. C. of C., European Community Studies Assn. Home: 8749 Cattaraugus Ave Los Angeles CA 90034-2558 Office: Brenda Mack Enterprises/Mack Media Presents PO Box 5942 Los Angeles CA 90055-0942

MACK, CRISTINA IANNONE, accountant; b. Olean, N.Y., Sept. 25, 1940; d. Angelo M. and Rose M. (Sirianni) Iannone; m. John O. Mack, Nov. 19, 1967; children—Elizabeth, Andrew. B.A. in Math., U. Calif.-Santa Barbara, 1962; postgrad. U. San Francisco, 1978—, Golden Gate U., 1983. Exec. dir. Bar Assn. San Francisco, 1966-68; owner, acct. CIM Assocs., San Francisco, 1978—; pres. Pacific Staff Inc., 1987—. Treas. Mothers Milk Bank, 1977-87; vice-chmn. Rep. County Central Com., 1991-93; San Francisco co-chair Citizens for Law & Order; v.p. Justice for Murder Victims. Coro Found. fellow, 1963. Mem. Calif. Agrl. Assn. (bd. dirs. dist. 1-A 1986—), Nat. Assn. Women Bus. Owners, Chi Omega Sorority (pres. 1962, treas. 1984-93). Roman Catholic. Club: San Francisco Lawyers Wives (pres. 1974, auditor 1978—). Avocations: tennis. Home: 2963 23d Ave San Francisco CA 94132 Office: 5 Thomas Mellon Cir San Francisco CA 94134-3823

MACK, ELLIE JOHNSON, oncology clinical nurse specialist; b. Newark, Jan. 22, 1944; d. Fleming Peter and Lucille (Green) Johnson; divorced; 1 child, Tracy Lauren. Diploma nursing, Newark Beth Israel Hosp., 1965; B in Health Edn., Jersey City Coll., 1975; M. in Health Edn., Beavers Coll., 1987, M. in Psychology, 1992. Staff nurse Newark Beth Israel Med. Ctr., 1965-70, head nurse, 1970-72; nursing instr. East Orange (N.J.) Gen. Hosp., 1972-75; patient care coord. Albert Einstein Med. Ctr., Phila., 1975-78, nursing instr., 1978-87, dir. outreach, coord. breast cancer program, 1987—. Co-author: (booklet) Patient Education: The Key to Health, 1981; contbr. articles to profl. jours. Educator Breast Cancer Support Com., Phila.; mem. LWV, North Wales, Pa., 1980; speaker Women at Work, Freedom Valley coun. Girl Scouts U.S., Valley Forge, Pa., 1992; mem. disting. speakers bur. Am. Cancer Soc., Phila., 1987—; mem. nat. nursing adv. com. Nat. Am. Cancer Soc., Atlanta, 1990—; mem. cancer in socioeconomically disadvantaged Am. Cancer Soc., Phila., 1989—, mem. nat. reach to recovery rev. and revision, 1991—, breast cancer detection and awareness task force, 1991—. Recipient Vol. Achievement award Am. Cancer Soc., 1991, Cert. of Excellence ARC, 1991, Cert. of Appreciation U. Pa., 1990, Community Svc. award Bright Hope, William Gray, III, Minister, 1992. Mem. Oncology Nursing Soc. (speakers bur. 1988—). Home and Office: Albert Einstein Med Ctr 5401 Old York Rd Philadelphia PA 19141-3030

MACK, FLOSSIE PHILLIPS, elementary educator; b. Mayodan, N.C., Aug. 22, 1944; d. Lewis H. and Hattie O. Phillips. BS, N.C. A&T State U., Greensboro, 1969; MEd, Rutgers U., 1973. Cert. early childhood tchr., bus. edn. tchr. Typist Capitol Collection Bur., 1964-65; receptionist U. N.C., Greensboro, 1969-70; legal sec. Smith & Patterson Law Firm, 1970-71; tchr. Greensboro City Schs., 1973—. State Tuition grantee; Work-Aid scholar; recipient LCH Civil award. Mem. NANBPWC, Tau Gamma Delta.

MACK, JANE LOUISE, early childhood educator, administrator; b. Drexel Hill, Pa., Nov. 23, 1926; d. George Schober and Estelle Marie (Heyland) Cridland; m. Charles Lawrence Mack, June 10, 1950; children: Jacqueline Judith, Nancy David. BS in Nursing, U. Pa., 1949. Instr. nursing arts U. Pa. Hosp., Phila., 1949-53; nurse Mass. Gen. Hosp., Boston, 1953-55; instr. in nursing Emerson Hosp., Concord, Mass., 1954-55; tchr. kindergarten Reading Clinic, Concord, 1959-62; tchr. 3d grade Bartlett Pvt. Elem. Sch., Arlington, Mass., 1962-63; asst. tchr. Lexington (Mass.) Montessori Sch., 1963-64, tchr., administr., 1964-80, prin., 1980-91, tchr., 1991—, headmistress emerita, 1991—; advisor to elem. newspaper, 1991—. Contbr. articles to profl. jours. Tchr. mother and baby care ARC, Lexington, 1970-72; pres. Lexington Family Counseling Bd., 1976-81; bd. dirs., admissions chair Dana Home of Lexington, 1992—. Jane Mack Bldg. named in her honor Lexington Montessori Sch., 1990. Mem. Am. Montessori Soc. (chairperson Montessori tchrs. 1972-76), N.Am. Montessori Tchrs. Assn., Montessori Schs. Mass. (pres. 1987-91). Republican. Home: 7 Parker St Lexington MA 02173-4906

MACK, JUDITH COLE SCHRIM, political science educator; b. Cin., Aug. 9, 1938; d. James Douglass and Cathleen (Cole) Schrim; m. Thomas H. Mack, Jan. 3, 1968; children: Robert Michael, Cathleen Cole. AB with high distinction, U. Ky., 1960; AM, Radcliffe Grad. Sch., 1962; MPhil, Columbia U., 1988, postgrad., 1986—. Tchr. The Lexington (Ky.) Sch., 1962-63; instr. Russian Emory U., Atlanta, 1963-64, Kent (Ohio) State U., 1964-65; instr. Hunter Coll., N.Y.C., 1988-90; adj. lectr. Barnard Coll., N.Y.C., spring 1991, 92; instr. Douglass Coll. Rutgers U., 1992-93; rsch. asst. sociology dept. U. Ky., summer 1961; rsch. asst. Russian and East European Studies Ctr., UCLA, 1965-67; rsch. asst. security studies ctr. UCLA, 1967-68; adj. lectr. Hunter Coll., N.Y.C., spring 1988; presenter in field. Chmn. State Pub. Affairs Com., N.J. Jr. Leagues, 1979-80; bd. dirs. Children's Aide Adoption Soc., Hackensack, N.J., 1979-90, v.p. 1985-90; bd. dirs. Assn. for Children N.J., Newark, 1982—, v.p. 1983-88; bd. trustees Div. of Youth and Family Svcs., Trenton, 1982-91, v.p. 1983-88, others. Recipient Woodrow Wilson fellowship Radcliffe Coll., 1960-61, Nat. Def. fellowship Radcliffe Coll., 1961-62. Mem. Phi Beta Kappa, Phi Sigma Iota, Mortar Bd. Episcopalian. Home: 47 Knollwood Rd Short Hills NJ 07078

MACK, JULIA COOPER, judge; b. Fayetteville, N.C., July 17, 1920; d. Dallas L. and Emily (McKay) Perry; m. Jerry S. Cooper, July 30, 1943; 1 dau., Cheryl; m. Clifford S. Mack, Nov. 21, 1957. B.S., Hampton Inst., 1940; LL.B., Howard U., 1951. Bar: D.C. 1952. Legal cons. OPS, Washington, 1952-53; atty.-advisor office gen. counsel Gen. Svcs. Adminstrn., Washington, 1953-54; trial appellate atty. criminal div. Dept. Justice, Washington, 1954-68; civil rights atty. Office Gen. Counsel, Equal Employment Opportunity Commn., Washington, 1968-75; assoc. judge Ct. Appeals, Washington, 1975-89; sr. judge, 1989—. Mem. Am., Fed., Washington, Nat. Bar Assns., Nat. Assn. Women Judges. Home: 1610 Varnum St NW Washington DC 20011-4206 Office: DC Ct Appeals 500 Indiana Ave NW 6th Fl Washington DC 20001

MACK, KIRBIE LYN, municipal official; b. Chgo., Jan. 3, 1953; d. Robert Lee and Luvonia (Cheatham) Green; m. Jeffery Frazier Mack, Aug. 10, 1974; children: Maaina, Jeffery Jr., Anisha. BA in Psychology, Northeastern Ill. U., 1975; postgrad., U. Wis., 1993—. Pers. specialist City of Madison, Wis., 1975-76; program asst. planning budget analysis dept. natural resource State of Wis., Madison, 1976-79, dir. conservation corps, 1979-80, equal opportunity officer, mgr., 1980-85, chief negotiator employment rels., 1985-89; dir. affirmative action dept. City of Madison, 1989—. Co-host, prodr. (cable TV program) Focus On Equality, 1989—. Pres. Southside Raiders Football Booster Club, Madison, 1995. Recipient Gov.'s Orchid award State of Wis. Gov. Lee Dreyfus, 1987, Exemplary Leadership in Affirmative Action award ASPA, 1992, 93, Outstanding Cmty. Svc. award Prevention & Intervention Alcohol & Drug Abuse, 1992, Spirit of the Am. Woman award Sta. WISC-TV, 1994, Pub. Svc. for Students award Links, Inc. and Madison Pub. Schs., 1994. Mem. NAACP (life, 1st v.p. 1993—, 2d v.p., Outstanding Svc. award Madison br. 1990, 92, Unsung Heroine award 1993), Am. Contract Compliance Assn., Wis. Assn. Black State Employees (past pres. 1985, Pres.'s award 1989-90). Office: City of Madison Ste 130/MMB 215 Martin Luther King Jr Blvd Madison WI 53701

MACK, PAMELA RENEÉ, service recognition awards company executive, personal development consultant; b. Indpls., June 30, 1967; d. Norman Errol and Gail Elizabeth (Green) Graves; m. Anthony Dewayne Mack, Nov. 21, 1987; children: Anthony Jr., Jade, James, Kristen. Student, Butler U., 1985. Cert. make-up technician. Customer svc. rep. Brylane, Inc., Indpls., 1985-87, RCA/BMG, Indpls., 1987-89; adminstrv. asst. Light of the World, Indpls., 1989-93, Nat. City Bank, Indpls., 1993-94; regional asst. O.C. Tanner Co., Indpls., 1994—; owner, pres., cons. Dynamic Image Co., Indpls., 1989—. Author: The Successful Woman, 1990, The Total Christian Woman, 1994; author, editor: (manual) Dynamic Image Consultants, 1991. Fashion show cons. Light of the World, Indpls., 1993, bible study tchr., 1994; image cons. Young Christian Ladies, Indpls., 1994. Mem. NAFE, LWCC. Mem. Diciples of Christ Ch. Home: 9283 E 30th St Indianapolis IN 46229

MACK, PATRICIA JOHNSON, newspaper editor; b. New Brunswick, N.J., Oct. 4, 1942; d. Henry Francis and Ann May (Monahan) Johnson; m. Parker Horton Moore, July 22, 1961 (div. 1971); m. Lonnie Burnell Mack, May 23, 1973; children: Tevis Ann, Kelaine Dorothy, Aidan Ruth. Student, Alderson-Broaddus Coll., 1960-61, U. W.Va., 1961, Harvard U., 1961-62, U. Ky., 1962-64. Reporter The Sentinel Greater Media Newspapers, East Brunswick, N.J., 1971-77; reporter, food editor, restaurant critic News Tribune, Woodbridge, N.J., 1977-92; food editor News Tribune/Record, Woodbridge and Hackensack, N.J., 1992—. Bd. dirs. Parents for Deaf Awareness, 1985-87; active Ctrl. Jersey Health Planning Commn., Woodbridge, 1987, Middlesex County Commn. for Handicapped, New Brunswick, 1987-89. Recipient 7 awards N.J. Press Assn., 1987-92, Cardiac Reporting award N.J. divsn. Am. Heart Assn., 1987, Nutrition Writing award Nestle, 1992, Disting. Svc. award N.J. Dietetic Assn., 1993. Mem. Assn. Food Journalists (Best Food Sect. awards 1987, 92, 93). Office: The Record 150 River St Hackensack NJ 07601-7110

MACK, SUSAN CAMILLE, veterinarian; b. Ponca City, Okla., Sept. 13, 1956; d. Floyd Arnold and Ida Camille (Foss) M. BS in Phys. Therapy, U. Okla., 1980; DVM, Okla. State U., 1987. Registered phys. therapist. Staff phys. therapist Veteran's Hosp., Oklahoma City, 1980-83; assoc. vet. Davis. (Okla.) Vet. Hosp., 1987-89; dir. phys. therapy Cushing (Okla.) Regional Hosp., 1989-91; staff phys. therapist Stillwater (Okla.) Med. Ctr., 1991-93; ptnr., veterinarian Thunderbird Vet. Hosp., Norman, Okla., 1993—. Mem. AVMA, Okla. Vet. Med. Assn. Office: Thunderbird Vet Hosp 1250 156th Ave NE Norman OK 73071

MACKAY, PATRICIA MCINTOSH, counselor; b. San Francisco, Sept. 12, 1922; d. William Carroll and Louise Edgerton (Keen) McIntosh; A.B. in Psychology, U. Calif., Berkeley, 1944, elem. teaching credential, 1951; M.A. in Psychology, John F. Kennedy U., Orinda, Calif., 1979; Ph.D. in Nutrition, Donsbach U., Huntington Beach, Calif., 1981; m. Alden Thorndike Mackay, Dec. 15, 1945; children—Patricia Louise, James McIntosh, Donald Sage. Cert. marriage, family and child counselor. Elem. tchr. Mt. Diablo Unified Sch. Dist., Concord, Calif., 1950-60; exec. supr. No. Calif. Welcome Wagon Internat., 1960-67; wedding cons. Mackay Creative Services, Walnut Creek, Calif., 1969-70; co-owner Courtesy Calls, Greeters and Concord Welcoming Services, Walnut Creek, 1971—; marriage, family and child counselor, nutrition cons., Walnut Creek, 1979—; coordinator Alameda and Contra Costa County chpts. Parents United, 1985—, pres. region 2; bd. dirs. New Directions Counseling Center, Inc., 1975-81, founder, pres. aux., 1977-79. Bd. dirs. Ministry in the Marketplace, Inc.; founder, dir. Turning Point Counseling; active Walnut Creek Presbyn. Ch.; bd. dirs. counseling dir. Shepherd's Gate-shelter for homeless women and children, 1985-92, Contra Costa County Child Care Coun., 1993, 94. Recipient Individual award New Directions Counseling Center, 1978, awards Neo-Life Co. Am. Prestige Club, yearly, 1977-86, Community Svc. award Child Abuse Prevention Coun., 1990, 92, 94. Mem. Assn. Marriage and Family Therapists, Parents United Internat. (pres. region 2, bd. dirs. 1992), U. Calif. Berkeley Alumni (sec. 1979-94), C. of C., Prytanean Alumnae, Delta Gamma. Republican. Club: Soroptomist (dir. 1976, 86) (Walnut Creek). Home: 1101 Scots Ln Walnut Creek CA 94596-5432 Office: 1399 Ygnacio Valley Rd Ste 34 Walnut Creek CA 94598-2831

MACKENZIE, DORIS LAYTON, psychologist, educator, researcher, criminologist; b. Riverton, N.J., June 20, 1943; d. H. Grandon and Ellen S. Layton; m. David Robert MacKenzie, June 29, 1963; children: Wendy, Scott, Todd. BS in Psychology, Pa. State U., 1976, MS in Psychology, 1978, PhD, 1983. Asst. prof. La. State U., Baton Rouge, 1983-89, assoc. prof., 1989-90; assoc. prof. U. Md., College Park, 1990-93, rsch. scholar, 1993—; vis. sci. Nat. Inst. Justice, Washington, 1988-92; co-chair conf. The Am. Prison, Nags Head, N.C., 1987; prin. investigator U. Md., College Park, 1990—; cons. Nat. Inst. Corrections, Washington, 1993. Co-editor: The American Prison, 1989, Measuring Crime, 1990, Drugs and Crime, 1994. Mem. Am. Soc. Criminology, Am. Correctional Assn. (mem. rsch. coun.), Acad. Criminal Justice Scis. Office: U Md Dept Criminal Justice 2220 Lefrak Hall College Park MD 20742

MACKENZIE, LINDA ALICE, computer company executive, consultant telecommunications; b. Bronx, N.Y., June 24, 1949; d. Gino Joseph and Mary J. (Damon) Arale; m. John Michael Lassourreille, Aug. 7, 1968 (div. 1975); 1 child, Lisa Marie Lassourreille; m. Donald John Mackenzie, July 2, 1978 (div. 1982). Student Richmond Coll., 1967-68, West L.A. Community Coll., 1978-81. Spl. rep. N.Y. Telephone Co., White Plains, 1968-71; asst. mgr. Paul Holmes Real Estate Inc., Richmond, N.Y., 1974-77; telcom applications specialist engring. Continental Airlines, L.A., 1977-83; data transmission specialist Western Airlines, Los Angeles, 1983-87; owner Computers on Consignment, El Segundo, Calif., 1984-94; cons. Farwest Brokers, L.A., 1984-85, Caleb Feb. Credit Union, Las Vegas, Nev., 1985, Nat. Dissemenators, Las Vegas, 1985, Vega & Assocs. Prodn. Div., 1987, Uptech/Downtech, 1986, Dollar Rent-a-Car, 1987, Pomona Sch. Dist., 1987, Advanced Digital Networks, 1987, State Senate, 1988, Nordstroms, 1988, Flying Tigers, 1988, Fed. Express, 1989, Sita/ITS, 1990-92, Neutrogena, 1991, B & B Computers, 1992; mktg. cons. AT&T, L.A., 1984-85, Creative Bus. Mktg., Manhattan Beach, Calif., 1994—. Author: The World Within, 1983. Active Calif. Lobbyists for Conservation, 1986. Contbr.: Am. Anthology Poetry, 1987, 88., Poetic Voices of America, 1988. Recipient Alexander award Met. Mus. Art, N.Y., 1967. Mem. Nat. Assn. Female Execs., El Segundo C. of C., Mgmt. Assocs. (assoc.). Republican. Clubs: Marina City, Manhattan Beach Women's. Avocations: painting, creative writing, aerobic dance, skiing, travel.

MACKENZIE, WENDY E., marketing consultant, business owner; b. State College, Pa., Oct. 8, 1964; d. David R. and Doris (Layton) MacK. BA, Pa. State U., 1985. Lic. real estate broker Calif. Sales rep Corp. Health & Productivity, Alamo, Calif., 1986-88; sales cons. R.W. Lynch & Co., San Ramon, Calif., 1987; mktg. mgr. First We. Med. Group, Oakland, Calif., 1988-91; mktg. cons., owner MacKenzie Connections, Lafayette, Calif., 1991-94. Vol. tutor Youth Homes, Walnut Creek, Calif., 1989-91; vol. tutor ESL Diablo Valley Literacy Coun., Walnut Creek, 1994. Named Member of Yr. Walnut Creek Jaycees, 1988. Mem. Indsl. Claims Assn. (eedn. com. 1991-94), Diablo Valley Indsl. Claims Assn., Women Like Us. Home: 1504 Siskiyou Dr Walnut Creek CA 94598-2117 Office: MacKenzie Connections 1080 Carol Ln Ste 101 Walnut Creek CA 94598

MACKETY, CAROLYN JEAN, laser medicine and nursing consultant; b. Chgo., Feb. 27, 1932; d. Gerald J. and Minnette (Buis) Kruyf; m. Robert Martin, Oct. 3, 1952 (div.); m. Armand Mackety, Apr. 15, 1972 (div.); children: Daniel, David, Steven, Martin, Laura Fitzgerald. RN, Hackley Hosp., Muskegon, Mich., 1969; BA, Coll. St. Francis, Joliet, Ill., 1977; MA, Columbia Pacific U., San Rafael, Calif., 1987. Dir. surg. svcs. Grant Med. Ctr., Columbus, Ohio, 1981-84; pres. Laser Cons., Inc., Chgo., 1984-86; v.p. Laser Ctrs. Am., Cin., 1986-88; nursing adminstr. Med. Ctr. Hosp., Burlington, Vt., 1988-91; cons. Colan, Inc., Holland, Mich., 1991—; dir. perioperative svcs. Mercy Hosp., Muskegon, Mich., 1991—, COI instr.; MIS workgroup Sister O Mery Corp., Farmington, Mich. Contbr. articles to profl. jours. Deacon 1st Reformed Ch., Holland, Mich., 1992—, parish nurse. Recipient nursing excellence award Am. Soc. for Lasers Medicine and Surgery, 1991. Mem. Assn. Operating Rm. Nurses (mem. nursing practice com.), Am. Soc. Laser Medicine (nursing excellence award 1992), Mich. Orgn. Nurse Execs.

MACKEY, MYRA, early childhood educator; b. Jesup, Ga., Dec. 9, 1951; d. Theral Eugene Sr. and Ditha (Brewer) M. BS, Ga. Coll., 1973; MEd, U. Ga., 1991; postgrad., U. Sarasota. Tchr. Telfair County Bd. Edn., McRae, Ga., 1973-74, Tattnall County Bd. Edn., Collins, Ga., 1974-75, Crisp County Bd. Edn., Cordele, Ga., 1977-80, Morgan County Bd. Edn., Madison, Ga., 1980-81, 1985-91, coord., 1991—; tchr. Dept. Def. Dependents Sch., Bitburg, Germany, 1981-85. Mem. Edn. Task Force, Morgan C. of C., Madison, 1991—; mem. Morgan Meml. Hosp. Aux., Madison, 1992—; active Madison-Morgan Cultural Ctr., Madison, 1985—, Morgan Interagy. Coun., Morgan County Friends of the Libr., ASPCA, MADD. Ga. Coll. scholar, Milledgeville, 1969, Home Econs. scholar, Ga. Home Econs. Assn., 1972, others. Mem. AAUW (pres. 1989—), ASCD, So. Early Childhood Assn., Nat. Trust Hist. Preservation, Nat. Mus. of Women in the Arts, Nat. Assn. Edn. of Young Children, Ga. Assn. Young Children, Assn. Childhood Edn. Internat., Profl. Assn. Ga. Educators, Coun. Exceptional Children, Internat. Reading Assn., Smithsonian Assocs., Phi Sigma, Delta Kappa Gamma, Phi Kappa Phi, Kappa Delta Pi. Home: 2230 Lions Club Rd Madison GA 30650-9511 Office: Morgan County Primary Sch 993 East Ave Madison GA 30650

MACKEY, SALLY SCHEAR, retired religious organization administrator; b. Seattle, Feb. 17, 1930; d. Rillmond Weible and Helen Annajane (Bovee) Schear; m. Hallie Willis Mackey, May 22, 1953; children: Melinda Kay, John Mark, Heather Lynn. BA, U. Wash., 1951; postgrad., San Francisco Theol. Sem., 1951-53. Teenage program dir., camp dir. YWCA, Seattle, 1953-55; sponsor, devel. Wash. Assn. Chs. Immigration and Refugee Program (affiliate Ch. World Svc.), Seattle, 1979-85, dir., 1985-90; bd. dirs., v.p. Ch. Coun. Greater Seattle, 1974-84; bd. dirs. Wash. Assn. Chs., 1976-79; mem. Gen. Assembly Mission Coun. Presbyn. Ch., N.Y.C., 1979-83, adv. com. on ecumenical rels., Presbyn. Ch. (U.S.A.), Louisville, 1989-92; Presbyn. Ch. (U.S.A.); del. to Caribbean Area Coun. World Alliance Reformed Chs., 1987-92. Home: 2127 SW 162nd St Seattle WA 98166-2654

MACKIEWICZ, ANNE LISA, computer company official; b. Scituate, Mass., Sept. 25, 1950; d. Henry Michael and Martha Mary (Lavoine) M. BA cum laude, Salem State Coll., 1972; postgrad., North Adams State Coll., 1974, Leslie Coll., 1975, Wesleyan U., Middletown, Conn., 1975. Cert. secondary English, French and history tchr., Mass. Tchr. English, Drury High Sch., North Adams, Mass., 1972-76, Silver Lake Jr. High Sch., Halifax, Mass., 1977-78, Marlboro (Mass.) High Sch., 1978-81; substitute tchr. South Shore area Mass., 1976-78; tchr. drama Braintree (Mass.) High Sch., summer 1977; tech. writer Digital Equipment Corp., Littleton, Mass., 1982-89; product tng. mgr. Digital Equipment Corp., Stow, Mass., 1989—. Recipient merit award Soc. for Tech. Communications, 1985; Mass. Bd. Higher Edn. scholar, 1970. Mem. Sterling Inst. (team leader 1988), Smithsonian Assocs., Ea. Interclub Ski League (race mem. 1978-89, club rep. 1979-81), Wedeln Ski Club (Lowell, Mass., social chmn. 1978, tri-club sec. 1984-86, 89-90, editor yearbook 1978, 79). Office: Digital Equipment Corp 40 Old Bolton Rd Stow MA 01775-1299

MACKIEWICZ, LAURA, advertising agency executive. Formerly with D'Arcy Advt.; with BBDO, Chgo., 1973—, now sr. v.p., dir. broadcast and print svcs. Office: BBDO Chgo 410 N Michigan Ave Chicago IL 60611*

MACKINNON, CATHARINE A., law educator, legal scholar, writer; d. George E. and Elizabeth V. (Davis) MacKinnon. BA in Govt. magna cum laude with distinction, Smith Coll., 1969; JD, Yale U., 1977, PhD in Polit. Sci., 1987. Vis. prof. U Chgo., Harvard U., Stanford U, Yale U., others, Osgoode Hall, York U., Canada; prof. of law U. Mich., 1990—. Author: Sexual Harassment of Working Women, 1979, Feminism Unmodified, 1987, Toward a Feminist Theory of the State, 1989, Only Words, 1993. Office: U Michigan Law School Ann Arbor MI 48109-1215

MACKINNON, PEGGY LOUISE, public relations executive; b. Florence, Ariz., June 18, 1945; d. Lacy Donald Gay and Goldie Louise (Trotter) Martin; m. Ian Dixon Mackinnon, Oct. 20, 1973. BA, San Jose State U., 1967, postgrad., 1968. Cert. secondary tchr., Calif. Tchr. Las Lomas High Sch., Walnut Creek, Calif., 1968-69; edn. officer Ormond Sch., Sydney, Australia, 1970-72; tchr. Belconnen High Sch., Canberra, Australia, 1972-73; temp. exec. sec. various orgns., London, 1973-75; mktg. mgr. Roadtown Wholesale, Tortola, British Virgin Islands, 1975-80; sr. v.p., gen. mgr. Hill & Knowlton Inc., Denver, 1981—. Bd. dirs. Rocky Mountain Poison and Drug Found., Denver, 1984-87, Denver C. of C., Boy Scouts Am., Denver coun. Mem. Pub. Relations Soc. Am. (accredited). Home: 9200 Cherry Creek Dr S #21 Denver CO 80231 Office: Hill & Knowlton 999 18th St Ste 2450 Denver CO 80202

MACKLIN, RUTH, bioethics educator; b. Newark, Mar. 27, 1938; d. Hyman and Frieda (Yaruss) Chimacoff; m. Martin Macklin, Sept. 1, 1957 (div. June 1969): children: Meryl, Shelley Macklin Taylor. BA with distinction, Cornell U., 1958; MA in Philosophy, Case Western Res. U., 1966, PhD in Philosophy, 1968. Instr. in philosophy Case Western Res. U., Cleve., 1967-68, asst. prof., 1968-71, assoc. prof., 1971-76; assoc. for behavioral studies The Hastings Ctr., Hastings-on-Hudson, N.Y., 1976-80; vis. assoc. prof. Albert Einstein Coll. Medicine, Bronx, N.Y., 1977-78, assoc. prof., 1978-84, prof. dept. epidemiology and social medicine, 1984—; cons. NIH, 1986—; advisor WHO, Geneva, 1989: apptd. mem. White House Adv. Com. on Human Radiation Experiments, Washington, 1994—. Author: Man, Mind and Morality, 1982, Mortal Choices, 1987, Enemies of Patients, 1993, Surrogates and Other Mothers, 1994; contbr. articles to ethics, law and med. jours. Fellow The Hastings Ctr., Inst. Medicine of NAS, Am. Philos. Assn. (life), Am. Pub. Health Assn., Am. Soc. Law, Medicine and Ethics, Phi Beta Kappa. Democrat. Office: A Einstein Coll Medicine Dept Epidemiology & Social Medicine 1300 Morris Park Ave Bronx NY 10461-1926

MACKNIGHT, CAROL BERNIER, educational administrator; b. Quincy, Mass., Apr. 12, 1938; d. Harold Nelson and Marguerite (Norris) Bernier; m. William J. MacKnight, Aug. 19, 1967. BS, Ithaca Coll., N.Y., 1960; MM, Manhattan Sch. Mus., N.Y.C., 1961; Dipl., Fontainebleau Sch. Music/Art, France, 1963; EdD, U. Mass., 1973. Asst. to supt. Falmouth (Mass.) pub. schs., 1975-76; dir. bus., mgmt., engring. prog. Sch. Bus. Adminstrn. U. Mass., Amherst, 1976-79; assoc. dir. continuing edn. U. Mass., 1979-82, dir. Office Instructional Tech., 1982—; mem. exec. bd. trustees New Eng. Regional Computer Program, Inc., 1986-92; bd. dirs. Info. Sys. and Bus. Exch., 1992—. Editor Jour. Computing in Higher Edn., 1988—, Jour. Info. Sys. for Mgrs., 1992—; mem. editorial rev. bd. Jour. of Computer-Based Instrn., 1988—; author/editor computer progs.; contbr. articles to profl. jours. CDC grantee, 1986, Regents of Boston grantee, 1988, Lilly Fellow Mentor, 1991-92. Mem. ACM, Assn. for Computing Machinery, Educom, Soc. Applied Learning Tech., Assn. for Devel. of Computer Based Instrnl. Systems. Home: 127 Sunset Ave Amherst MA 01002-2019 Office: Office Instructional Tech A115 Lederle Grad Res Ctr Amherst MA 01003

MACKO, NANCY, artist, educator; b. Oceanside, N.Y., Apr. 29, 1950; d. Emil E.M. and Arline (Walker) Kelly; m. Jan Blair, Dec. 24, 1985. BS in Liberal Arts, U. Wis., River Falls, 1977; MA, U. Calif., Berkeley, 1980, MFA in Painting and Printmaking, 1981, Ma in Edn. Psychology, 1989. Assoc. registrar Asian Art Mus., San Francisco, 1985-86; asst. prof. art Scripps Coll., Claremont, Calif., 1986-92, assoc. prof. art, 1992—; vis. lectr. U. Calif., Davis, 1983-84; vis. artist, prof. La Corte della Miniera, Urbino, Italy, 1990; adj. prof. Claremont Grad. Sch., 1986-91; dir. Scripps Copper Art Program, 1990—; cons. in field. Mem. exhbn. com. L.A. Ctr. Photographic Studies, 1994. Rsch. fellow Scripps Coll., 1989. Mem. Calif. Soc. Printmakers (pres. 1984-85), Coll. Art Assn. N.Y. (bd. dirs. 1994—, exec. bd. 1995—). Democrat. Home: 2965 Waverly Dr Los Angeles CA 90039 Office: Scripps Coll 1030 Columbia Claremont CA 91711

MACKSOUD, MONA SALIM, clinical psychologist; b. Beirut, Oct. 31, 1955; d. Salim and Samia (Nassar) M.; m. Abdallah H. Nauphal, Aug. 27, 1993; 1 child, Maya. BA in Psychology with distinction, U. Calif., Davis, 1978; MS in Clin. Psychology, U. Surrey, Eng., 1980; PhD in Clin. Psychology, Columbia U., 1987. Chartered clin. psychologist, Eng.; lic. psychologist, N.Y. Clin. psychologist St. Francis Hosp., Haywards Heath, Eng., 1980-81; tng. psychotherapist Ctr. for Psychol. Svcs. Columbia U., N.Y.C., 1982-85, fellow psychology Ctr. for Infants and Parents, Tchrs. Coll., 1984-85; fellow psychology Am. U. Beirut Med. Ctr., 1985-86, rsch. assoc., 1988-89; vis. fellow Ctr. Ctr. for Lebanese Studies, Oxford, Eng., 1989; rsch. dir. Ctr. for Study of Human Rights Columbia U., N.Y.C., 1990—; hon. clin. psychologist St. George's Hosp., London, 1980-81; cons. UNICEF, 1990, 91, 92, 93; presenter in field. Contbr. articles to profl. jours. Mem. APA, Internat. Soc. for Traumatic Stress Studies, Brit. Psychol. Soc. (chartered clin. psychologist). Greek Orthodox. Office: Columbia U Project on Children & War 1108 Internat Affairs Bldg New York NY 10027

MACLACHLAN, PATRICIA, author; b. Cheyenne, Wyo., Mar. 3, 1938; d. Philo and Madonna (Moss) Pritzkau; m. Robert MacLachlan, Apr. 14, 1962; children: John, Jamie, Emily. BA, U. Conn., 1962. Tchr. English Bennett Jr. High Sch., Manchester, Conn., 1963-79; vis. lectr. Smith Coll., Northampton, Mass., 1986—. Author: The Sick Day, 1979, Arthur, For the Very First Time, 1980 (Golden Kite award 1980), Moon, Stars, Frogs, and Friends, 1980, Through Grandpa's Eyes, 1980, Mama One, Mama Two, 1982, Tomorrow's Wizard, 1982, Cassie Binegar, 1982, Seven Kisses in a Row, 1983, Unclaimed Treasures, 1984 (Horn Book award Boston Globe 1984), Sarah, Plain and Tall, 1985 (Golden Kite award 1985, Scott O'Dell Historical Fiction award 1985, Newbery medal 1986, Jefferson Cup award Va. Libr. Assn. 1986, Christopher award 1986, Garden State Children's Book award N.J. Libr. Assn. 1988), The Facts and Fictions of Minna Pratt, 1988 (Parent's Choice award Parent's Choice Found. 1988), Three Names, 1991, Journey, 1991, All the Places to Love, 1993, Baby, 1993, Skylark, 1994. Bd. dirs. Children's Aid Family Svc. Agency, 1970-80. recipient numerous awards for children's fiction. Office: Dept of Edn Smith Coll Northampton MA 01063*

MACLAINE, SHIRLEY, actress; b. Richmond, Va., Apr. 24, 1934; d. Ira O. and Kathlyn (MacLean) Beatty; m. Steve Parker, Sept. 17, 1954 (div.); 1 child, Stephanie Sachiko. Ed. high sch. Appearances include (Broadway plays) Me and Juliet, 1953, Pajama Game, 1954, (films) The Trouble With Harry, 1954, Artists and Models, 1954, Around the World in 80 Days, 1955-56, Hot Spell, 1957, The Matchmaker, 1957, The Sheepman, 1957, Some Came Running, 1958 (Fgn. Press award 1959), Ask Any Girl, 1959 (Silver Bear award as best actress Internat. Berlin Film Festival), Career, 1959, Can-Can, 1959, The Apartment, 1959 (Best Actress prize Venice Film Festival), Children's Hour, 1960, The Apartment, 1960, Two for the Seesaw, 1962, Irma La Douce, 1963, What A Way to Go, The Yellow Rolls Royce, 1964, John Goldfarb Please Come Home, 1965, Gambit and Woman Times Seven, 1967, The Bliss of Mrs. Blossom, Sweet Charity, 1969, Two Mules for Sister Sara, 1969, Desperate Characters, 1971, The Possession of Joel Delaney, 1972, The Other Half of the Sky: A China Memoir, 1975, The Turning Point, 1977, Being There, 1979, A Change of Seasons, 1980, Loving Couples, 1980, Terms of Endearment, 1983 (Acad. award 1984, Golden Globe-Best Actress), Cannonball Run II, 1984, Madame Sousatzka, 1988 (Best Actress Venice Film Festival, Golden Globe-Best Actress), Steel Magnolias, 1989, Waiting For the Light, 1990, Postcards From the Edge, 1990, Defending Your Life, 1991, Used People, 1992, Wrestling Ernest Hemingway, 1993, Guarding Tess, 1994; (TV shows) Shirley's World, 1971-72, Shirley MacLaine: If They Could See Me Now, 1974-75, Gypsy in My Soul, 1975-76, Where Do We Go From Here?, 1976-77, Shirley MacLaine at the Lido, 1979, Shirley MacLaine...Every Little Movement, 1980 (Emmy award 1980), (TV movie) Out On A Limb, 1987; prodr., co-dir. documentary: China The Other Half of the Sky; star U.S. tour stage musical Out There Tonight, 1990; author: Don't Fall Off the Mountain, 1970, The New Celebrity Cookbook, 1973, You Can Get There From Here, 1975, Out on a Limb, 1983, Dancing in the Light, 1985, It's All in the Playing, 1987, Going Within: A Guide for Inner Transformation, 1989, Dance While You Can, 1991; editor: McGovern: The Man and His Beliefs, 1972. Office: MacLaine Enterprises Inc 201 Santa Monica Blvd Ste 410 Santa Monica CA 90401-2214*

MAC LAM, HELEN, editor, periodical; b. N.Y.C., Aug. 17, 1933; d. Forrest Mearl and Bertha Margaret (Herzberger) Keen; m. David Carlyle MacLam, Feb. 7, 1953; children: Timothy David, David Andrew. AMLS, U. Mich., 1967; AB Sociology, Heidelberg Coll., 1961; MA African Am. Studies, Boston U., 1978. Dep. clerk Mcpl. Ct., Tiffin, Ohio, 1962-64; subprofessional asst. Heidelberg Coll. Libr., Tiffin, Ohio, 1964-66; collection devel. libr. social scis. Dartmouth Coll. Libr., Hanover, N.H., 1967-83; social scis. editor Choice Mag., Middletown, Conn., 1983—; cons. in field; spkr. in field. Editorial bd. Multicultural Review, 1992-95; contbr. articles to profl. jours. Bd. dirs. Headrest, 1976-80, Hanover Consumer Coop. Soc., 1969-72. Recipient Grant award Rsch. Program for Ethnic Studies Librarianship Fisk U., 1975. Mem. Nat. Assn. Ethnic Studies (pres. 1985-87, assoc. editor publs. 1980-83), African Studies Assn., Africana Libs. Coun. (exec. bd. 1989-91), Am. Soc. Indexers, Freelance Editorial Assn., Women in Scholarly Publishing, Assn. Coll. and Rsch. Librs. (New England chpt.). Home: Rt 2 Box 92 Norwich VT 05055 Office: Choice Mag 100 Riverview Ctr Middletown CO 06457

MACLAUGHLIN, MARIA THOMPSON, educational specialist; b. Balt., Mar. 29, 1952; d. John Bernard and Felicisima (Picart) Thompson; m. Matthew Charles MacLaughlin, Sept. 6, 1975; children: Matthew Charles Jr., Timothy Sean. AA, Richard Bland Coll., 1972; BS, Longwood Coll., 1974; MEd, Va. State U., 1985; postgrad., U. Va., 1988—. Cert. adminstr. Tchr. St. James Sch., Petersburg, Va., 1974, Hopewell, Va., 1981-84; tchr. Petersburg (Va.) Pub. Schs., 1986-91; lead reading tchr. Dinwiddie (Va.) County Schs., 1991-92, chpt. I, gifted coord., 1992—. Contbr. articles to profl. jours. Fundraiser Cystic Fibrosis, Hopewell, Va., 1979-83; mem. troop com. Boy Scouts Am., Prince George and Dinwiddie, Va., 1982—, ednl. cons., Richmond, Va., 1991—; vol. Kennedy Ctr. for the Performing Arts, Washington, 1987—; amb. parent WTVR-TV6, Richmond, 1987—; dir. Thompson Creativity Award, Petersburg, 1988—; bd. dirs. Am. Lung Assn., Richmond, 1991—; mem. metrotown com. NCCJ, Richmond, 1994—. Named Outstanding Young Woman of Am., Jaycees, 1983, 87. Mem. NEA, ASCD, Va. Edn. Assn., Dinwiddie Edn. Assn. (pres. 1992-93), Kappa Delta Pi (sec. 1985). Republican. Roman Catholic. Home: 9023 Boydton Plank Rd Petersburg VA 23803-7325

MACLEAN, DEBRA LYNN, accountant; b. Detroit, Feb. 24, 1961; d. Wallace Edwin Flesher and Margaret Bernice (Mee) Kleino; m. Michael David MacLean, Oct. 25, 1980 (div. Apr. 1989); 1 child, David Scott. Acctg. clk. Buss, Bernock, Wilt, Dryer & Thomas, CPAs, P.C., Mt. Clemens, Mich., 1979-81; fin. reporting clk. DME Co., Madison Heights, Mich., 1989-91, cost acct., 1991-93; cost acctg. mgr., physical inventory mgr. Post and Co., Madison Heights, 1993-94; cost acct. MascoTech-Forming Technologies Divsn., Fraser, Mich., 1994—. Mem. Mich. Assn. CPAs, Inst. Mgmt. Accts., Wheel Masters Car Club (treas. 1986-89). Republican. Episcopalian. Office: MascoTech-Forming Technologies Divsn 18450 15 Mile Rd Fraser MI 48026

MACLEAN, EILEEN PANIGEO, state legislator; b. Barrow, Alaska, June 12, 1949; d. Henry and May (Ahmaogak) Panigeo; m. Bryan MacLean, 1969 (div.); children: Tara, Apayang. BA in Edn., U. Alaska, 1975; MEd, U. Alaska/U. Copenhagen, 1984. Tchr. North Slope Borough Sch. Dist., Wainwright, Alaska, 1975-77, curriculum developer, 1977-80; coord. Inupiat hist., culture and lang. North Slope Borough, Barrow, Alaska, 1980-82; pers. officer North Slope Borough, Barrow, 1985-86; dir. Alaska Eskimo Whaling Commn., Barrow, 1982-83, coord. media, 1988-89; liaison Inuit circumpolar conf. Alaska Native Commn., Anchorage, 1984-85; mem. Alaska Ho. Reps., Juneau, 1989—; bd. dirs. Artic Slope Regional Corp; co-chair finance com. Alaska Ho. Reps., Juneau, 1991—, chair econ. task force, 1992—; pres. Inuit Circumpolar Conf., Alaska, Can., Greenland, Russia, 1992—. Co-author: Inuit Curriculum 1977-80. Bd. dirs. North Slope Borough Sch. Dist., 1980-83; mem. assembly North Slope Borough, 1987-90. Recipient Shareholder of Yr. award Ukpeagvik Village Corp., Barrow, 1990, Appreciation award Alaska Fedn. Natives for Youth, Anchoragem 1992. Democrat. Presbyterian. Home: 4490 N Star St Barrow AK 99723 Office: State of Alaska Ho Reps State Capital # 507 Juneau AK 99811*

MACLEOD, CHARLOTTE, author; b. Bath, N.B., Can., Nov. 12, 1922; d. Edward Philips and Mabel Maude (Hayward) MacL. Mem. advt. firm N.H. Miller & Co., Inc., Boston, 1952-82. Author: Astrology for Skeptics, 1972, Rest You Merry, 1978, The Family Vault, 1979, The Luck Runs Out, 1979, The Withdrawing Room, 1980, The Palace Guard, 1981, Wrack and Rune, 1982, The Bilbao Looking Glass, 1983, Something the Cat Dragged In, 1984, The Convivial Codfish, 1984, The Curse of the Giant Hogweed, 1985, The Plain Old Man, 1985, The Corpse in Oozak's Pond, 1987, The Recycled Citizen, 1988, The Silver Ghost, 1988, Vane Pursuit, 1989, The Gladstone Bag, 1990, An Owl Too Many, 1991, The Resurrection Man, 1992, Something in the Water, 1994, Had She But Known: A Biography of Mary Roberts Rinehart, 1994, The Odd Job, 1995; (works for juveniles) Mystery of the White Knight, 1964, Next Door to Danger, 1965, The Fat Lady's Ghost, 1968, Mouse's Vineyard, 1968, Ask Me No Questions, 1971, Brass Pounder, 1971, King Devil, 1978, We Dare Not Go A-Hunting, 1980, Cirak's Daughter, 1982, Maid of Author, 1984; (short stories) Grab Bag, 1987; (as Matilda Hughes) The Food of Love, 1965, Headlines for Caroline, 1967; (as Alisa Craig) A Pint of Murder, 1980, The Grub-and-Stakers Move a Mountain, 1981, Murder Goes Mumming, 1981, The Terrible Tide, 1983, The Grub-and-Stakers Quilt a Bee, 1985, A Dismal Thing to Do , 1986, The Grub-and-Stakers Pinch a Poke, 1988, Trouble in the Brasses, 1989, The Grub-and-Stakers Spin a Yarn, 1990, The Wrong Rite, 1992, The Grub-and-Stakers House a Haunt, 1993; editor: Mistletoe Mysteries, 1989, Christmas Stalkings, 1991; contbr. articles and stories to mags. Recipient Lifetime Achievement award Bouchercon 23, 1992, 5 Am. Mystery awards, Nero Wolfe award. Office: Jed Mattes Inc 200 W 72nd St # 50 New York NY 10023-2824*

MACMANUS, SUSAN ANN, political science educator, researcher; b. Tampa, Fla., Aug. 22, 1947; d. Harold Cameron and Elizabeth (Riegler) MacM. BA cum laude, Fla. State U., 1968, PhD, 1975; MA, U. Mich., 1969. Instr. Valencia Community Coll., Orlando, Fla., 1969-73; rsch. asst. Fla. State U., 1973-75; asst. prof. U. Houston, 1975-79, assoc. prof., 1979-85, dir. M of Pub. Adminstrn. program, 1983-85, rsch. assoc. Ctr Pub. Policy 1982-85; prof., dir. PhD program Cleve. State U., 1985-87; prof. pub. adminstrn. and polit. sci., U. South Fla., Tampa, 1987—, chairperson dept. govt. and internat. affairs, 1987-93; vis. prof. U. Okla., Norman, 1981—; field rsch. assoc. Brookings Instn., Washington, 1977-82, Columbia U., summer 1979, Princeton (N.J.) U., 1979—, Nat. Acad. Pub. Adminstrn., Washington, summer 1980, Cleve. State U., 1982-83, Westat, Inc., Washington, 1983—. Author: Revenue Patterns in U.S. Cities and Suburbs: A Comparative Analysis, 1978, Federal Aid to Houston, 1983, (with others) Governing A Changing America, 1984, (with Francis T. Borkowski) Visions for The Future: Creating New Institutional Relationships Among Academia, Business, Government, and Community, 1989, Reapportionment and Representation in Florida: A Historical Collection, 1991, Doing Business with Government: Federal, State, Local and Foreign Government Purchasing Practices for Every Business and Public Institution, 1992; writer manuals in field; mem. editorial bds. various jours.; contbr. articles to jours. and chpts. to books. Bd. dirs. Houston Area Women's Ctr., 1977, past pres., v.p. fin., treas.; mem. LWV, Gov.'s Coun. Econ. Advisers, 1988-90, Harris County (Tex.) Women's Polit. Caucus, Houston; bd. dirs. USF Rsch. Found., Inc. Recipient U. Houston Coll. Social Scis. Teaching Excellence award, 1977, Herbert J. Simon Award for best article in 3d vol. Internat. Jour. Pub. Adminstrn., 1981, Theodore & Venette Askounes-Ashford Disting. Scholar award U. South Fla., 1991, Disting. Rsch. Scholar award, 1991; Ford Found. fellow, 1967-68; grantee Valencia Community Coll. Faculty, 1972, U. Houston, 1976-77, 79, 83; Fulbright Rsch. scholar, Korea, 1989. Mem. Am. Polit. Sci. Assn. (program com. 1983-84, chair sect. intergovtl. rels., award 1989, mem. exec. coun. 1994—, pres.-elect sect. urban politics 1994—), So. Polit. Sci. Assn. (v.p. 1990-91, pres.-elect 1992-93, pres. 1993-94, V.O. key award com. 1983-84, best paper on women and politics 1988), Midwest Polit. Sci. Assn., Western Polit. Sci. Assn., Southwestern Polit. Sci. Assn. (local arrangements com. 1982-83, profession com. 1977-80), ASPA (nominating com. Houston chpt. 1983, bd. mem. Suncoast chpt., pres.-elect 1991, Lilly award 1992), Policy Studies Orgn. (mem. editorial bd. jour. 1981—, exec. coun. 1983-85), Women's Caucus Polit. Sci. (portfolio pre-decision rev. com. 1982-83, projects and programs com. 1981, fin.-budget com. 1980-81), Acad. Polit. Sci., Mcpl. Fin. Officers Assn., Phi Beta Kappa, Phi Kappa Phi, Pi Sigma Alpha (mem. exec. coun. 1994—), Pi Alpha Alpha. Republican. Methodist. Home: 2506 Collier Pky Land O'Lakes FL 34639-5228 Office: U South Fla Dept Govt & Internat Affairs Soc 107 Tampa FL 33620

MACMANUS, YVONNE CRISTINA, editor, videoscripter, writer, consultant; b. L.A., Mar. 18, 1931; d. Daniel S. and Josefina Lydia (Pina) MacM. Student, NYU, U. So. Calif., U. London. Assoc. editor Bobbs-Merrill, N.Y.C., 1960-63; TV producer Leo Burnett Ltd., London, 1965-66; founding editor, editor-in-chief Leisure Books, L.A., 1970-72; tchr. pub. course UCLA Extension, 1972; sr. editor Major Books, 1974-77; co-pub., editor in chief Timely Books, Chattanooga, 1977; co-owner Write On...!, Chattanooga, 1977—; corp. video PR & video tng., 1983—. Author: Better Luck Elsewhere, 1966, With Fate Conspire, 1974, Bequeath Them No Tumbled House, 1977, Deadly Legacy, 1981, The Presence, 1982, You Can Write a Romance, 1983, (play) Hugo, 1990; contbr. articles to profl. publs. Home and Office: 4040 Mountain Creek Rd Ste 1304 Chattanooga TN 37415-6025

MAC MASTER, HARRIETT SCHUYLER, retired educator; b. Maxbass, N.D., Nov. 5, 1916; d. Hugh Riley and Christine (Park) Schuyler; m. Jay Myron Mac Master, May 27, 1944; children: Jay Walter, Robert Hugh, Anne Schuyler Mac Master. BS, Trenton State Coll., 1971; grad., Inst. for Children's Lit., 1993. Tchr. Woodfern Elem. Sch., Neshanic, N.J., 1972-87; ret., 1987; freelance writer elem. sci. program Silver Burdett Co., 1983. Organizer, vol. Phone Friend for Latchkey Children, Somerset County; elder local Presbyn. Ch. Fellow AAUW, LWV, Older Women's League. Republican. Home: 24 Meadowbrook Dr Somerville NJ 08876-4810

MACMILLAN, CATHERINE COPE, restaurant owner; b. Sacramento, Mar. 3, 1947; d. Newton A. Cope and Marilyn (Jacobs) Combrink; m. Thomas C. MacMillan, Dec. 18, 1967 (div. Jan. 1984); children: Corey Jacobs, Andrew Cope. BA, U. Calif., 1969; MBA, Calif. State U., Sacramento, 1978; JD, McGeorge Sch. Law, 1993. Pub. health microbiologist County of Sacramento, 1969-74; pres., gen. mgr. The Firehouse Restaurant, Sacramento, 1980—; bd. dirs. Westamerica Bank, San Rafael, Calif. Chmn. Sacramento Conv. and Visitors Bur., 1987-88; pres. Old Sacramento Propery Owners Coun., 1987; mem. Sacramento Sports Commn, 1988-89. Mem. Calif. Restaurant Assn. (bd. dirs.), Sacramento Restaurant Assn. (restaurateur of yr. 1983), Old Sacramento Citizens and Merchants Assn. (chmn. bd. dirs. 1984), Sacramento Met. C. of C. (bus. woman of yr. 1992), Calif. State U.-Sacramento Alumni Assn. (sch. of bus. alumna award 1992), Sacramento Capital Club (pres. 1995). Office: The Firehouse Restaurant 1112 2nd St Sacramento CA 95814-3204

MACMINN, PAMELA LEE See KOPACK, PAMELA LEE

MACMULLEN, JEAN ALEXANDRIA STEWART, nurse, administrator; b. N.Y.C., Feb. 21, 1945; d. John Douglas and Isabella Stewart (Park) MacM. Diploma in nursing, Lenox Hill Hosp., N.Y.C., 1965; BS in Nursing, Adelphi U., 1969, MS in Nursing, 1971; MA in Anthropology, U. South Fla., 1978. Nurse renal disease unit N.Y. Hosp., N.Y.C., 1971-72; clin. nurse specialist VA Hosp., Tampa, Fla., 1972-76, med./surg. coord., 1976-82; assoc. chief nurse VA Med. Ctr., Gainesville, Fla., 1982-93; chief nurse VA Med. Ctr., Montgomery, Ala., 1993—. Jour. editor Am. Assn. Nephrology Nurses, Pitman, N.J., 1980-82, referee, adviser, 1983—; contbr. numerous articles to profl. pubs. Mem. Fla. Nurses Assn. Republican. Episcopalian. Office: VA Med Ctr 215 Perry Hill Rd Montgomery AL 36109

MACMURREN, MARGARET PATRICIA, learning consultant; b. Newark, Nov. 4, 1947; d. Kenneth F. and Doris E. (Lounsberry) Bartro; m. Harold MacMurren, Nov. 21, 1970. BA, Paterson State U., 1969; MA, William Paterson Coll., 1976; postgrad., Jersey City State Coll., 1976—. Tchr. Byram (N.J.) Twp. Schs., 1969-77; learning cons., child study team coord. Andover Regional Schs., Newton, N.J., 1977—. Mem. NEA, N.J. Edn. Assn., N.J. Assn. Learning Cons., Sussex Coutny Assn. Learning Cons. (pres. 1982-83, 93-94, sec.-treas. 1991-92, v.p. 1992-93), Andover Regional Edn. Assn. (pres. 1986-87). Home: 4 Systema Pl Sussex NJ 07461-2833 Office: Andover Regional Schs 707 Limecrest Rd Newton NJ 07860-8801

MACNEIL, KATHRINE JEAN, librarian; b. Geary, Okla., Oct. 2, 1943; d. Otto Louis and Helen Mary (Haradon) Krehbiel. BA, Okla. U., 1964, MLS, 1968; MA, Okla. State U., 1975. Vet. libr. Okla. State U., Stillwater, 1968-80; animal, dairy, poultry and vet. scis. libr. Va. Tech., Blacksburg, 1980-82; info. svcs. libr. Med. Scis. Libr. Tex. A&M U., College Station, 1982—. Mem. AAUP (sec. Okla. State U. chpt. 1978-80, sec. VPI 1982), Med. Libr. Assn. (chair vet. med. libr. sect. 1978-79, 93-94, union list com. 1975—). Democrat. Presbyterian. Office: Tex A&M U Med Scis Libr College Station TX 77843-4462

MACNEILL, DEBRA JEAN, education director; b. Attleboro, Mass., Apr. 16, 1954; d. Brainard Hall and Beatrice Verna (Trulson) MacN.; m. Dionisis Sourbis, June 28, 1986 (div. 1989). BS in Edn. magna cum laude, U. Mass., 1976; MEd, Cambridge Coll., 1989. Cert. travel counselor, health educator. Curriculum specialist Inst. Cert. Travel Agts., Wellesley, Mass., 1988-89, mgr. ops., 1989-90, dir. edn., 1993—; sr. tng. specialist Bank of Boston, 1990-91, state tng. mgr., 1991-92; adj. instr. So. Conn. State U., New Haven, 1978-80, Fisher Coll., Boston, 1992; cons. Wilton (Conn.) Pub. Schs., 1979-80, GE Investments, Stamford, Conn., 1993. Author: (texts) Destination Specialist Western Europe, 1993, Customer Service Excellence, 1994; co-author: (texts) Travel Sales and Customer Service, 1995. Mem. adv. bd. Fisher Coll., 1994—; active Charlestown (Mass.) Preservation Soc., 1990—. Office: Inst Cert Travel Agts 148 Linden St Wellesley MA 02181

MACO, TERI R., secondary school educator; b. Allentown, Pa., Nov. 4, 1953; d. Francis M. and Jacqueline K. (Becker) Regan; m. Bruce F. Maco, Oct. 1, 1983; children: Adam S., Alex M. BSChemE with honors, Lehigh U., 1975; MBA with distinction, U. New Haven, 1979; cert. in sci., West Chester U., 1994. Supr. Ivory, Procter & Gamble Mfg. Co., S.I., N.Y., 1975-77; asst. mgr. processing Chesebrough-Ponds, Inc., Clinton, Conn., 1977-81, sec. and bd. dirs. credit union, 1980; group supr. Johnson & Johnson, Ft. Washington, Pa., 1981-83, mgr. processing, 1983-84, mgr. nat. planning, 1984-87; group mgr. acctg. McNeil Computer Products, Inc., Ft. Washington, 1987-93; pres. Child Placement Network, Inc., Norristown, Pa., 1989-93; tchr. Phoenixville (Pa.) H.S., 1993—; developer computer-based tng. program. Author: Capital Asset Pricing Model: Capital Budgeting Applications (NAA Manuscript award 1979). Recipient Johnson & Johnson Achievement awards, 1989, 92. Mem. Nat. Sci. Tchrs. Assn., Nat. Acctg. Assn. Democrat. Roman Catholic. Home: 4183 Ironbridge Dr Collegeville PA 19426-1189

MACON, CAROL ANN GLOECKLER, micro-computer data base management company executive; b. Milw., Mar. 25, 1942; d. William Theodore and Gwendolyn Martha (Rice) Gloeckler; m. Jerry Lyn Macon, Aug. 28, 1981; children: Christian, Marie. BS in Edn. cum laude, U. Wis., Milw., 1969; postgrad., Midwestern State U., Wichita Falls, Tex., 1977, U. Tex., San Antonio, 1978, U. Colo., Colorado Springs. Tchr. Lubbock, Tex.; patient affairs coord. Cardiac Assocs., Colorado Springs; founder, CFO Macon Systems, Inc., Colorado Springs. Artist, Australia, Tex., Colo. Mem. Colorado Springs Symphony Coun., Colorado Springs Fine Arts Ctr., Colorado Springs Rose Soc. (pres.), DaVinci Quartet Assn. (bd. dirs.), Colo. Mountain Club, Phi Kappa Phi, Kappa Delta Pi, Sigma Tau Delta, Psi Chi. Mem. Software Pubs. Assn., Colorado Springs Symphony Coun., Colorado Springs Fine Arts Ctr., Colorado Springs Rose Soc. (pres.), DaVinci Quartet Assn., Colo. Mountain Club, Phi Kappa Phi, Kappa Delta Pi, Sigma Tau Delta, Psi Chi.

MACON, IRENE ELIZABETH, interior designer, consultant; b. East St. Louis, Ill., May 11, 1935; d. David and Thelma (Eastlen) Dunn; m. Robert Teco Macon, Feb. 12, 1954; children: Leland Sean, Walter Edwin, Gary Keith, Jill Renee Macon Martin, Robin Jeffrey, Lamont. Student Forest Park Coll., Washington U., St. Louis, 1970, Bailey Tech. Coll., 1975, Lindenwood Coll., 1981. Office mgr. Cardinal Glennon Hosp., St. Louis, 1965-72; interior designer J.C. Penney Co., Jennings, Mo., 1972-73; entrepreneur Irene Designs Unltd., St. Louis, 1974—; vol. liaison Pub. Sch. System, St. Louis, 1980-82; cons. in field. Inventor venetian blinds for autos, 1981, T-blouse and diaper wrap, 1986; Author 26th Word newsletter, 1986, (songs) My God's Child Teach Free Will, God is Hiring Now, 1993. Committeewoman Republican party, St. Louis, 1984; vice chair 4th Senatorial Dist. of Mo., 1984, vol. St. Louis Assn. Community Orgns., 1983; instr. first aid Bi-State chpt. ARC, St. Louis, 1984, mem. speakers bur., 1991; cubmaster pack #80 Keystone dist. Boy Scouts Am.; block capt. Operation Brightside, St. Louis, 1984; co-chair status and role of women Union Meml. United Meth. Ch., 1986—, program resource sec., 1990—; trustee Wofit Found., 1989; spokesperson Minority Affairs Initiative Program Am. Assn. Retired Persons, 1991; sec. to block Fedn. Block Units St. Louis Urban League, 1994; mem. Notary Pub. Commn., 1994—; Rep. election judge 26.8 pct Ward, 1994; pub. speaker, story teller prayer breakfast Grace Chapel Ministries, 1994. Composer religious music. Named One of Top Ladies of Distinction St. Louis, 1983. Mem. NAACP, Am. Soc. Interior Designers (assoc.), Nat. Mus. Women in the Arts (charter), Nat. Stroke Assn., Internat. Platform Assn., Nat. Coun. Negro Women (1st v.p. 1984), Invention Assn. of St. Louis (subcom. head 1985), Coalition of 100 Black Women, St. Louis Assn. Fashion Designers, Pres. Club. Methodist. Achievements include invention of Irene's Autoshade, an accordian type of pleated material designed to adhere to automobile windows for the purpose of protecting it from the sun. Avocations: reading, designing personal wardrobe, modeling, horseback riding, boating. Home and Office: PO Box 20370 Saint Louis MO 63112-0370

MACON, JANE HAUN, lawyer; b. Corpus Christi, Tex., Sept. 26, 1946; d. E.H. and Johnnie Mae (De Mauri) Haun; m. R. Laurence Macon, Sept. 6, 1969. B in Internat. Studies, U. Tex., 1967, JD, 1970. Bar: Tex. 1971, Ga. 1971, U.S. Dist. Ct. (we. dist.) Tex. 1973, U.S. Ct. Appeals (5th and 11th cirs.) 1973. Legal staff Office Econ. Opportunity, Atlanta, 1970-71; trial atty. City of San Antonio, 1972-77, city atty., 1977-83; ptnr. Fulbright & Jaworski, LLP, San Antonio, 1983—; pres. Internat. Women's Forum, Washington, 1987-89; bd. dirs. Thousand Oaks Nat. Bank, San Antonio. Legal counsel Nat. Women's Polit. Caucus, 1981—; bd. dirs. Alamo council Boy Scouts Am., San Antonio, 1977—. Named to San Antonio Hall of

Fame, 1984; named one of Rising Stars, 1984. Fellow Tex. Bar Found., Tex. Bar Assn. (chmn. women and the law 1984-85, client security fund com.), Southwest Research Found.; mem. San Antonio Bar Assn., San Antonio Young Lawyers Assn., Women Lawyers Tex. (pres. 1984-85), Tex. Banking Bd., Bexar County Women's Bar Assn. Democrat. Baptist. Home: 230 W Elsmere Pl San Antonio TX 78212-2349 Office: Fulbright & Jaworski LLP 300 Convent St Ste 2200 San Antonio TX 78205-3792

MACON, MYRA FAYE, library director; b. Slate Springs, Miss., Sept. 29, 1937; d. Thomas Howard and Reba Elizabeth (Edwards) M. BS in Edn., Delta State U., 1959; MLS, La. State U., 1965; postgrad., U. Akron, Ohio; EdD, Miss. State U., 1977. Librarian Greenwood (Miss.) Jr. High Sch., 1959-62, Greenwood High Sch., 1962-63, Grenada (Miss.) High Sch., 1963-64; library supr. Cuyahoga Falls (Ohio) City Schs., 1964-71; assoc. prof. U. Miss., Oxford, 1971-83; dir. libraries Delta State U., Cleve., 1983—. Editor: School Library Media Services for Handicapped; editor: ANRT Newsletter, Miss. Libraries; contbr. articles to profl. jours. Mem. ALA, Southeastern Library Assn., Miss. Library Assn., Exch. Club, Phi Delta Kappa, Beta Phi Mu, Delta Kappa Gamma, Omicron Delta Kappa. Home: 307 S Fifth Ave Cleveland MS 38732-3153 Office: WB Robers Library Delta State U Cleveland MS 38733

MACQUARRIE, LYNDA DIANE, primary school educator; b. Great Falls, Mont., Oct. 18, 1944; d. Russell B. and Revelyn Maxine (Spores) Arnold; m. Harvey Bruce MacQuarrie, Sept. 18, 1965 (div. Sept., 1980); children: Russell Bruce, Patrick Ryan. BA in Edn., Ea. Wash. U., 1983, MA in Early Childhood Edn., 1986. Cert. tchr. elem., secondary, Wash., Idaho. Kindergarten tchr. Rosalia (Wash.) Sch. Dist., 1983-85; 2nd grade tchr. Plummer (Idaho) Sch. Dist., 1985-86; tchr. grades k-3 Spokane (Wash.) Sch. Dist., 1986—; mem. sci. adoption com. Spokane Sch. Dist. #81, 1991-92, participant in dist. sci. video, 1993-94; instr. for other tchrs. in dist., 1993-94; mem. Subject Adv. Com. State Wash. Commn. on Student Learning Sci., 1994—. Recipient Christa MacAuliffe award Gov. and Office of Supt. Pub. Instrn., Wash., 1992. Mem. Delta Kappa Gamma (recording sec. local chpt. 1992-94). Office: Wilson Elem Sch Spokane Sch Dist # 81 911 W 25th Ave Spokane WA 99203

MACQUEEN, ELIZABETH, sculptor; b. Birmingham, Ala., Nov. 21, 1948; d. Giles Edwards II and Ruth (Brooks) MacQ.; m. Don Baxter, May 20, 1989; 1 child, Mary Elizabeth MacQueen Baxter. BA, UCLA, 1974, postgrad., 1976-77; student, Sch. of Michelangelo, Florence, Italy, 1977-79. Sculptures include Mudra, 1985, Puck Torso, 1987, Ibis, 1989, Persephone, 1993, also Puck, Dos á Dos, numerous sculptures of dancers; sculptures acquired by Place Des Arts, Montreal, Que., Sauza Tequila, Mexico, City Hall Rotunda, Mountain View, Calif., Carolyn Blount Theater, Montgomery, Ala., Ariz. Renaissance Festival, Apache Junction, also pvt. collection Gene Kelly, Beverly Hills, Calif., others. Recipient award for contbns. to states cultural heritage Gov. of Ala., 1989, Gold award Art of Calif. mag., Napa, 1991. Mem. Nat. Sculpture Soc., Internat. Sculpture Ctr. (profl. mem.), Allied Artists Am. (affiliate), San Luis Obispo C. of C. Studio: PO Box 12414 San Luis Obispo CA 93406

MACRI, KATHLEEN, chemical engineer; b. Endicott, N.Y., Oct. 18, 1963; d. Frank Joseph and Jeanne Loise (Griffiths) M. AS in Engring. Sci., Broome C. C., 1983; BSChemE, Clarkson U., 1985. Project engr. Polaroid, Waltham, Mass., 1985-87, project mgr., 1987-89; sr. staff engr. Anitec divsn. Internat. Paper, Binghamton, N.Y., 1989—; dir. proactive equalizing partnership Anitec and Binghamton Schs., 1993—; tutor Broome C.C., Binghamton, 1994—. Author: Food for Thought...An Overview of Chemical Engineering, 1990. Mem. Sch. and Bus. Alliance (bd. dirs., dir. activities 1990—). Office: Anitec 40 Charles St Binghamton NY 13905

MACRO, LUCIA ANN, editor; b. Rhinebeck, N.Y., May 15, 1959; d. Virgil Jordan and Jeannette Anastasia (Jakelski) M.; m. Richard Marchione, 1992. BA, Fordham U., Bronx, 1981. Asst. editor, editor Silhouette Books, N.Y.C., 1985—, sr. editor, 1989—; speaker in field nat. convs. Romance Writers Am., 1985—; interviewed Bus. Week, 1987, CNN, 1991, Sta. WNBC, various newspapers including N.Y. Daily News, Washington Post. Author articles Romantic Times, 1988-89, 93, Romance Writers Report, 1988-89. Recipient Rita award Romance Writers Am., 1990, 92, 94. Democrat. Office: Silhouette Books 300 E 42nd St New York NY 10017-5947

MACULAITIS, JEAN D'ARCY, language educator, researcher, consultant; b. N.Y.C.; d. Peter Anthony D'Arcy and Lillie (Tossas) Favorito; m. Joseph Patrick Maculaitis, Dec. 10, 1966 (div. 1985); children: Martine, Alexis, Maria Elena; foster children: Matthew, David; 1 adopted child, Theresa; m. John W. Cooke, June 7, 1986; 1 stepchild, John Jr. BA in English magna cum laude, Jersey City State Coll., 1966; MA in TESOL, NYU, 1973, PhD, 1978; postdoctorate in neurolinguistics, Princeton U., 1986—. Tchr. English, ESL pub. schs., N.J., 1966-77; adj. instr. tchr. training, ESL, bilingual edn. colls. and univs., N.Y., N.J., P.R., 1978—; leader workshops in ESL, tchr. training pub. schs., Calif., Nev., Ill., N.Y., P.R., 1987—; pres. Career Wise Inc., Sea Bright, N.J., 1986—, MAC Testing and Cons. Inc., Sea Bright; ednl. cons. Prentice Hall, Oxford U. Press, Macmillan Pubs., Longman Pubs., Georgetown Bilingual Svc. Ctr., others; Coll. Commencement speaker, Georgian Ct., 1989. Author: Desarollando Habilidades de Comprehensión en la Lectura: Lectura de Interpretación, 1981, MAC Guidelines for Evaluating, Designing and/or Improving ESL and BE K-12 Programs, 1981, MAC Checklist for Evaluating, Preparing and/or Improving Standardized Tests for Limited English Speaking Students, 1981, Standards for the Preparation and Certification of International Studies Teachers in the United States, 1983, Maculaitis Assessment Program: A Coordination Series of Test Batteries for ESL Students in Grades K-12 (Mac:K-12), 1985, rev. edit., 1990, Centennial Celebration of the Death of Venerable Father Ludovico, 1985, Odyssey: Assessment Component, 1986, Hello, English: Assessment Component, 1988, Viva el Español!: Assessment Component, 1989, Exciting Writing Workbook: Discovering, Imagining and Navigating Series, 1989; (with Mona Scheraga) What to Do Before the Books Arrive (and After), 1982, Declaration of Rights of the Limited English Proficient Child, 1988, (with Mona Scheraga) The Complete ESL/EFL Resource Book: Strategies, Activities and Units for the Classroom, 1988, MAC S.A.T. Grammarworks, 1990; contbr. articles to profl. jours. Trustee Georgian Ct. Coll., 1982, Dominican Acad., 1988—; active Bd. Edn. Holy Cross Sch., 1986—. Miss America contestant, State of N.J., 1964; Dayton Ball scholar Jersey City State Coll., 1964; named An Outstanding Am. Educator NCCJ, 1978. Mem. International Assn. Tchrs. English to Speakers of Other Langs. (chair secondary sch. spl. interest sect., 1972-78, 82-84, bd. execs., 1972-78), NYU Alumnae Assn. (fund raiser, rep. local chpt., 1980-85), Assn. for Supervision and Curriculum Devel., Acad. Guidance Svcs., Am. Entrepreneurs Assn., N.J. Assn. Women Bus. Owners, Nat. Assn. Women Bus. Owners, Nat. Assn. Women Cons. Inc., Am. Booksellers Assn., Soroptimist Internat., Phi Delta Kappa, Kappa Delta Pi. Home: 103 S Ward Ave Rumson NJ 07760-2032 Office: MAC Testing & Cons Inc PO Box 3056 Rumson NJ 07760-3056

MAC WATTERS, VIRGINIA ELIZABETH, singer, music educator, actress; b. Phila.; d. Frederick-Kennedy and Idoleein (Hallowell) Mac W.; m. Paul Abée, June 10, 1960. Grad., Phila. Normal Sch. for Tchrs., 1933; student, Curtis Inst. Music, Phila., 1936. With New Opera Co., N.Y.C., 1941-42; artist-in-residence Ind. U. Sch. Music, 1957-58; assoc. prof. U. Ind. Sch. Music, 1958-68, prof. voice, 1968-82, prof. emeritus, 1982—. Singer: leading roles Broadway mus. Rosalinda, 1942-44, Mr. Strauss Goes to Boston, 1945, leading opera roles New Opera Co., N.Y.C., 1941-42, San Francisco, 1944, N.Y.C. Ctr., 1946-51; leading soprano for reopening of Royal Opera House, Covent Garden, London, 1947-48, Guatemala, El Salvador, Cen. Am., 1948-49; debut at Met. Opera, N.Y.C., 1952; TV spls. on NBC include Menotti's Old Maid and the Thief, 1949, Would-be Gentleman (R. Strauss), 1955; leading singer with Met. Opera Co. on coast to coast tour of Die Fledermaus, 1951-52,, Met. Opera debut, N.Y.C., 1952, leading soprano Cen. City Opera Festival, Colo., 1952-56; performed with symphony orchs. in U.S., Can., S.Am.; concert recitalist U.S., Can., 1950-62; opened N.Y. Empire State Music Festival in Ariadne auf Naxos (Strauss), 1959; soloist Mozart Festival, Ann Arbor, Mich. Recipient Mile award Album Familiar Music, 1949, Ind. U. Disting. Teaching award, 1979; named One of 10 Outstanding Women of the Yr.; Zeckwer Hahn Phila. Mus. Acad. scholar, 1941-42. Mem. Nat. Fedn. of Music Clubs, Nat. Soc. Arts and Letters, Nat. Soc. Lit. and Arts, Soc. Am. Musicians, Nat. Assn. Tchrs. of Singing, Internat. Platform Assn., Sigma Alpha Iota. Club: Matinee Musical (hon. mem. Phila., Indpls. chpts.). Home: 3800 Arlington Rd Bloomington IN 47404-1347 Office: Ind U Sch Music Bloomington IN 47401

MACZULSKI, MARGARET LOUISE, corporate executive; b. Detroit, Apr. 1; d. Bohdan Alexander and Olga Louise (Martinuick) M. BS, Mich. State U. Mgr. meetings Nat. Assn. Realtors, Mktg. Inst., Chgo., 1977-82, mgr. mktg., 1982-83; regional sales mgr. Fairmont Hotels, Chgo., 1982; dir., mgr. trade shows and confs. Am. Broadcasting Co./Pub. Div., Wheaton, Ill., 1983-85; mgr. meeting and conf. planning Am. Soc. Personnel Adminstrn., Alexandria, Va., 1985-90; mgr. meeting and conv. planning Kraft Gen. Foods, Glenview, Ill., 1990—. Mem. Meeting Planners Internat., Greater Washington Soc. Assn. Execs. (past chmn. site inspection com.), Am. Soc. Assn. Execs., Nat. Assn. Exposition Execs., Mich. State U. Alumni Assn. (treas. D.C. chpt. 1987-90). Republican. Roman Catholic. Avocations: piano, swimming. Home: 3150 N Sheridan Rd 24C Chicago IL 60657 Office: Kraft Gen Foods 1 Kraft Ct Glenview IL 60025-5066

MADDALENA, LUCILLE ANN, management executive; b. Plainfield, N.J., Nov. 8, 1948; d. Mario Anthony and Josephine Dorothy (Longo) M.; m. James Samonte Hohn, Sept. 7, 1975; children: Vincent, Nicholas, Mitchell. AA, Rider Coll., 1968; BS, Monmouth Coll., 1971; EdD, Rutgers U., 1978. Newscaster, dir. pub. relations Sta. WBRW, Bridgewater, N.J., 1971-73; editor-in-chief Commerce mag., New Brunswick, N.J., 1973-74; dir. pub. relations Raritan Valley Regional C. of C., New Brunswick, N.J., 1973-74; aide pub. relations to mayor City of New Brunswick, 1974; dir. communications United Way Cen. Jersey, New Brunswick, 1974-77; mgmt. cons. United Way Am., Alexandria, Va., 1977-78; pres., owner Maddalena Assocs., Chester, N.J., 1978—; sr. cons. United Research Co., Morristown, N.J., 1980-81; sr. ptnr., dir. OCD Group, Parsippany, N.J., 1984-87; chmn. bd. dirs. OCD Group (subs. Xicom Inc.), Morristown, N.J., 1988; pres. Morris Bus. Group, Chester, 1989—; adj. faculty Somerset County Coll., Bridgewater, N.J., 1970, Fairleigh Dickinson U., 1980; guest lectr. Rutgers U., New Brunswick, N.J., 1975-80; designer publicly offered seminars for Bell Atlantic, 1992—; cons. change Howmet, Alloy, Dover, N.J., 1993; consortium trainer Johnson & Johnson, 1988—. Author: A Communications Manual for Non-Profit Organizations, 1980; editor New Directions for Instl. Advancement, 1980-81. Chmn. pers. com., police com. Chester Borough Coun., 1984-87; pres. Chester Consolidation Study Commn., 1990. Recipient Mayor's Commendation City of New Brunswick, 1973, Chester Borough, N.J., 1988. Mem. AAUW, LWV, Nat. Assn. Press Women, N.J. Elected Women Officials, Kappa Delta Pi. Republican. Roman Catholic. Club: N.J. Sled Dog Assn. Home: 75 Melrose Dr Chester NJ 07930-2304 Office: Morris Bus Group 415 Rt 24 Chester NJ 07930-2626

MADDEN, ELLEN KOPPERSMITH, auditor; b. Fairhope, Ala., July 18, 1965; d. Arthur Joseph and Leah Mae (Smith) Koppersmith; m. Michael Carl Madden, Nov. 18, 1989. BA, Birmingham So. Coll., 1987. CPA; cert. mgmt. acct. Staff auditor Price Waterhouse and Co., Birmingham, 1987-89; sr. auditor Walter Industries, Inc., Birmingham, 1989—. Mem. jr. bd. Birmingham Music Club; active United Meth. Women, First United Meth. Ch., Birmingham, Birmingham-So. Coll. Alumni Choir. Recipient Area D rep.-Adams Cup Regatta U.S. Sailing Assn., 1990, 91, 93. Mem. AICPA, Inst. of Mgmt. Accts., Ala. Soc. of Pub. Accountancy, Birmingham Sailing Club (former treas., jr. sailing dir., Svc. award 1992), Birmingham So. Alumni Assn. (area II coord.), Phi Beta Kappa. Home: 4638 Round Forest Dr Birmingham AL 35213-1832

MADDEN, HEATHER ANN, aluminum company executive; b. Sharon, Pa., Dec. 20, 1967; d. Edward Arthur and Mary Ann (McWilliams) M. BS in Bus., Salisbury (Md.) State U., 1991; MS in Bus., Johns Hopkins U., 1994. With Delmarva Aluminum Co., Inc., Delmar, Del., 1984—, exec.'s asst., 1987—, also dir., 1990—; computer and fin. cons. Vol. The Holly Ctr., Salisbury, 1992-94. Recipient Holly Svc. award The Holly Found., Salisbury, 1994. Home: 8300 Robin Hood Dr Salisbury MD 21801

MADDEN, JANE PATRICIA, political scientist; b. Orange, N.J., Mar. 17, 1965; d. Edward George and Mary Bernadette (Haveron) M. BA, Fordham U., 1987; MA, Am. U., 1992. Fgn. rights asst. Bantam Doubleday Dell, N.Y.C., 1987-88; planned giving officer CARE, Inc., N.Y.C., 1988-90; acad. affairs intern European Econ. Community, Washington, 1991-92; cons. The World Bank, Washington, 1993—. Tutor Washington Lit. Coun., 1993—; vol. D.C. Cares, Washington, 1994. Mem. Fordham Club Washington (bd. dirs., corr. sec. 1994-95). Office: The World Bank 1818 H St NW Washington DC 20433

MADDEN, KATHRYN I., quality assurance professional; b. Racine, Wis., July 30, 1950; d. Robert John Sr. and Glora M. (Reacek) Merriman; m. Donald H. Madden Sr. (div. 1978); children: Shawn I., Donald H. Jr. Grad., Hamilton High Sch., Sussex, Wis., 1968. Assembly line worker Briggs & Stratton, Milw., 1968-69; accts receivable Sears, Milw., 1969-70; lab tech. Universal Optical, Milw., 1974-77, sales rep., 1979; lab tech. Coca-Cola Bottling, Dallas, 1978, 80-81, quality supv., 1981-91, quality mgr., 1991—. Designer computer program QA Statistical Analysis, 1993. Mem. Southwest Quality Assurance Mgrs. Assn. Democrat. Roman Catholic. Home: 1816 Seminole Trl Mesquite TX 75149-6664 Office: Coca-Cola Bottling North Tex 8161 Moberly Ln Dallas TX 75227-2322

MADDEN, LINDA HINKELMAN, secondary school educator; b. Williamsport, Pa., Feb. 7, 1955; d. William Joseph and Catharine (Cochran) Hinkelman. BA in Spl. Edn., Ctrl. Wash. U., 1977; MA in Rehab. Counseling, U. No. Colo., 1987. Nat. cert. rehab. counselor; cert. vocat. evaluator; lic. tchr., Colo. Tchr. Baker (Oreg.) Sch. Dist., 1977-79; spl. edn. tchr. Byers (Colo.) Sch. Dist., 1984-85; vocat. evaluator Resource Devel. and Mgmt. Sys., Inc., Aurora, Colo., 1986-87; vocat. counselor for physically injured adults Internat. Rehab. Assocs./The Rehab. Team, Englewood, Colo., 1987-88; multiply disabled/trainable mentally disabled adoles. tchr. Robert G. Weiland Sch./Jefferson County Cmty. Ctr., Lakewood, Colo., 1988-89; severe/profound multiply disabled adoles. tchr. Margaret Walters Sch./Jefferson County Cmty. Ctr., Arvada, Colo., 1989-92; trainable mentally disabled adoles. tchr. Denver Pub. Schs.-Merrill Mid. Sch., 1992-93, Denver Pub. Schs.-Baker Mid. Sch., 1993—. With U.S. Army, 1980-84. Mem. Am. Fedn. Tchrs. (com.), Assn. for Cmty. Living (advocate, com. Foothills chpt.), Nat. Parks and Conservation Assn. Office: Baker Mid Sch 574 W Sixth Ave Denver CO 80204

MADDEN, ROBERTA MARGARET, association program developer; b. Council Bluffs, Iowa, Nov. 9, 1936; d. Charles Theodore and Mary Elizabeth (Moffatt) Young; m. Jerry David Madden, Sept. 6, 1956; 1 child, Blake Dana. BA in Govt. summa cum laude, Ohio U., 1968. Editor Ky. Labor News, Louisville, 1962-64, La. State U. Press, Baton Rouge, 1969-72; dir. Consumer Protection Ctr., Baton Rouge, 1972-76; agt. Mut. Benefit Life Ins. Co., Baton Rouge, 1977-79; dist. mgr. U.S. Census Bur., Baton Rouge, 1979-80; exec. dir. YWCA, Baton Rouge, 1980-83, program devel., 1994—; field dir. Common Cause, Baton Rouge, 1983-90; exec. dir. Am. Diabetes Assn., Baton Rouge, 1990-93; mem. adv. com. U.S. Consumer Product Safety Commn., 1973-75; mem. Pub. Affairs Rsch. Coun., Baton Rouge, 1992—. Editor/dir. (oral history project) Remembering the Struggle, 1983; freelance writer/editor, 1966-71. Candidate La. State Senate, Baton Rouge, 1979; mem. state adv. com. U.S. Civil Rights Commn., La., 1981—; founding mem. Capital Area Network, Baton Rouge, 1978—; mem. Early Risers Kiwanis Club, Baton Rouge, 1993—; chmn. race rels. Baton Rouge Coun. on Human Rels., 1993—; grad. Leadership Greater Baton Rouge, 1992. Recipient Advancement of Women award NOW, 1975, Humanitarian award Baton Rouge Human Rels., 1985. Mem. LWV, Kiwanis, Phi Beta Kappa. Democrat. Unitarian. Home: 614 Park Blvd Baton Rouge LA 70806-5331 Office: YWCA PO Box 66435 Baton Rouge LA 70896-6435

MADDEN, TERESA DARLEEN, insurance agency owner; b. Dallas, Aug. 4, 1960; d. Tommy Joe Frederick Dodd and Mary Helen (Sterner) Smith; m. Kim Ashley Madden, June 2, 1989. Student, Tex. Tech U., 1978-81. Cert. ins. counselor. With personal lines svc. Charles R. Ervin Ins., Midland, Tex., 1981, Bryant Scalf Ins., Richardson, Tex., 1981-82; with comml. ins. svc. Street & Assocs. Inc., Dallas, 1982-84; with comml. ins. sales/svc. Hotchkiss Ins., Dallas, 1984-85; mgr. sales Abbott-Rose Ins. Agy., Dallas, 1985-89; owner Glenn-Madden & Assocs. Ins., Dallas, 1990—. Methodist. Office: Glenn Madden & Assocs Inc Ste 1470 9330 Lyndon B Johnson Fwy Dallas TX 75243-3448

MADDEN, THERESA MARIE, education educator; b. Phila., Feb. 12, 1950; d. James Anthony and Marie Margaret (Clark) M. BA in Social Sci., Neumann Coll., 1977; postgrad., Beaver Coll. Cert. tchr., Pa. Tchr. elem. grades St. Anthony Sch., Balt., 1971-73, St. Mary-St. Patrick Sch., Wilmington, Del., 1973-74, Queen of Heaven Sch., Cherry Hill, N.J., 1974-77, St. Bonaventure Sch., Phila., 1977-78, 79-83, St. Stanislaus Sch., Lansdale, Pa., 1978-79; substitute tchr. various schs. Phila., 1983-84; tchr. 8th grade math. St. Cecilia Sch., Phila., 1984-94; tchr. 6th grade math., sci. and reading Corpus Christi Sch., Lansdale, Pa., 1994—; mem. visiting team Mid. States Assn., Phila., 1992; presenter workshops. Mem. Nat. Coun. Tchrs. Math., Pa. Coun. Tchrs. Math., Assn. Tchrs. Math. of Phila. and Vicinity. Roman Catholic. Office: Corpus Christi Sch 920 Sumney Town Pike Lansdale PA 19446

MADDEN, WANDA LOIS, gerontology nurse; b. Augusta, Kans., Apr. 26, 1929; d. George W. and Lillian B. (Dobyns) Provost; m. Laurence R. Madden, June 3, 1947 (div. 1961); children: Matthew, Mark, Luke, John, Michele. ADN, Pasadena City Coll., 1970; postgrad., Calif. State U. Consortium, 1986. RN, Calif. CCU nurse Huntington Meml. Hosp., Pasadena, Calif., 1970-71; ICU Community Hosp., Pico Rivera, Calif., 1971-72; CCU nurse Queen of the Valley Hosp., West Covina, Calif., 1973-74; ICU supr. Visalia (Calif.) Community Hosp., 1974-77, 89-90, ICU nurse, 1978; ICU nurse San Miguel Hosp. Assn., San Diego, 1978-79; supr. Casa Blanca Corp., San Diego, 1979-80; dir. nursing Visalia Convalescence Hosp., 1981-89, Westgate Gardens Convalescent Ctr., Visalia, 1990; psychiat. staff nurse Mill Creek Hosp., Visalia, 1990-91; AIDS case mgr. Tulare County Health Svcs., 1993—; Met. Cmty. Ch. of the Sequoias. Assoc. lay pastor M.C.C. of The Sequoias in Visalia. Home: 2725 N Canary Dr Visalia CA 93291-1719

MADDEX, DIANE REITEMEIER, publishing executive; b. Riverside, Calif., June 14, 1943; d. Robert Francis and Dorothea Jean (Kupfer) Reitemeier; m. Robert Lucien Maddex Jr., June 11, 1965; 1 child, Alison Alexandra. Student, Antioch Coll., 1961-62; BA in English, Northwestern U., Evanston, Ill., 1965. Editorial asst. Nat. Assn. Mut. Ins. Agts., Washington, 1965-67; index editor Bur. Nat. Affairs, Inc., Washington, 1967-68; campaign asst. Dem. Nat. Com., Washington, 1968; mng. editor Nat. Trust for Hist. Preservation, Washington, 1968-72; reporter Pacific Daily News-Guam (Gannett), Saipan, Mariana Islands, 1973; dir. Preservation Press Nat. Trust for Hist. Preservation, Washington, 1974-90; pres., founder Archetype Press, Inc., Washington, 1990—; dir. pub. seminars Nat. Trust for Hist. Preservation, 1970s; lectr. Denver Pub. Inst., 1983; lectr. landscape architecture U. Pa., 1991; juror Washington Ad Club, 1985, Blue Pencil Awards, Washington, 1988, Am. Assn. Mus. Pubs. Competition, 1990-92; chairperson U.S./Internat. Coun. on Monuments and Sites Gen. Assembly Pubs. Com., Washington, 1987. Author: Historic Buildings of Washington, D.C., 1973, Architects Make Zigzags: Looking at Architecture from A to Z, 1986; editor: America's Forgotten Architecture, 1976, All About Old Buildings, 1985, I Know That Building!, 1989, The Wright Style, 1992, Picturing Wright, 1994, The Wright Style Engagement Calendar, 1994—, Wright at a Glance series, 1994—, StyleBooks series, 1994—; others; developer, editor, prodr. and marketer numerous books. Founding mem. D.C. Preservation League, 1971; mem. Design Rev. Bd., Reston, Va., 1981-86; active Preservation Roundtable, Washington; staff mem. Citizens for Humphrey-Mondale, Washington, 1968; vol. various Dem. election campaigns, Washington, 1961—. Recipient Fed. Design Achievement award, Leipzig Internat. Book Fair Design Show award, 1985, Am. Inst. Graphic Arts awards, 1985—, Type Dirs. Club award, 1985, Choice Outstanding Reference of Yr. award, 1985, Art Dirs. Club. Met. Washington awards, Pick of the Lists award Am. Bookseller, 1986, 89, Am. Soc. Assn. Execs. award , 1987, Comm. Arts Design Ann. awards, ASID awards, Am. Soc. Landscape Architects award, others. Mem. Am. Book Prods. Assn. (editor 1990—), Soc. for Comml. Archeology, Washington Book Pubs. (lectr. 1991, awards), Nat. Trust for Hist. Preservation. Office: Archetype Press Inc Ste 407 4201 Connecticut Ave NW Washington DC 20008

MADDOX, ANNIE LAURIE, nursing educator, administrator; b. Quitman, Ga., Dec. 30, 1945; d. Frank H. Sr. and Ina Mae (Carpenter) McElroy; children: Laurie, Matt. Grad., Ga. Baptist Sch Nursing, 1966; BS, Valdosta State Coll., 1988, MEd, 1989, postgrad., 1991; PhD, Ga. State U., 1994. Health aid, then head nurse Presbyn. Home, Quitman, 1960-63, 68-70; owner, bookkeeper Maddox Drugstore, Quitman, 1970-80; instr. health occupations Brooks County High Sch., Quitman, 1981-88, instr. nurses aides, 1983; instr. health occupations Lowndes High Sch., Valdosta, Ga., 1988-89; instr. dept. vocat. edn. Valdosta State Coll., 1989-92; dir. practical nursing program Thomas Tech. Inst., Thomasville, Ga., 1992—. Mem. ASCD, NEA, Ga. Edn. Assn., Nat. Assn. Educators, Ga. Assn. Educators, Am. Vocat. Assn., Ga. Vocat. Assn., Assn. Indsl. and Tech. Tchr. Educators, Internat. Tech. Edn. Assn., Phi Delta Kappa, Phi Kappa Phi. Home: 607 N Laurel St Quitman GA 31643-1221

MADDOX, IRIS CAROLYN CLARK, secondary education educator; b. Wardell, Mo., Apr. 20, 1936; d. Newman Walter and Mary Elizabeth (Edney) Clark; m. James P. Maddox, June 4, 1954; children: James Steven, Sandra Jean. BS cum laude, Prairie View A&M U., 1983, MEd in Indsl. Edn., 1984, MEd in Counseling., 1990. Cert. counselor and tchr., Tex. Tchr. Spring Branch Ind. Sch. Dist., Houston, 1982—; sec. Bus. Office Svcs. Adv. Com., Houston, 1991-92. Mem. Am. Vocat. Assn., Tex. Assn. Continuing Adult Edn., Nat. Assn. Classroom Educators in Bus. Edn., Chi Sigma Iota. Home: PO Box 430791 Houston TX 77243

MADDOX, UTRICIA ANTOINETTE, educator; d. Curtis Anthony and Penolope Rotha (Sabusan) M. BA, New Rochelle Coll.; MA, Herbert H. Lehman U.; cert. advanced study, NYU. Cert. sch. dist. adminstr., sch. adminstr., supr., English tchr. Spl. asst. to deputy supt. N.Y.C. Bd. Edn.; prof. English SUNY, Westchester, 1985—; trainer communication skills GM, Westchester, 1987—; mem. Mid. States Rev. Fin. Com., Westchester, Fgn. Born Program Com., Westchester, policy making com. Learning Disabled Students, Westchester, freshman study skills Coll. Success Com., Westchester; speaker in field. Producer, host (radio broadcast mag.) Platinum Plus, 1986—. Mgr. advt. SSACIA, Westchester; co-host tv program Parenting, N.Y.C.; mem. Senate Homelessness Fact Finding Com., Westchester. Mem. ASCD, Nat. Pub. Radio, Nat. Coun. of Tchrs. of English, Lit. Soc. (past v.p.). Office: PO Box 95 Bronx NY 10467-0095

MADICH, BERNADINE MARIE HOFF, savings and loan executive; b. Duluth, Minn., Mar. 4, 1934; d. Palmer and Esther (Anderson) Hoff; m. Michael Madich, May 23, 1955 (div. 1986); children: Michael R.H., Tina B. Watts, Rory G. (dec.). Student, Inst. Fin. Edn., 1972, 73, 77-78, 83-84, 86-87, cert. real estate law, 1984. Teller St. Louis County Fed. Savs. and Loan, 1972-73, sec., ins. mortgage counselor, 1973-83, loan servicing specialist, 1983-86, asst. mgr. loan servicing dept., 1986—. Pack leader Boy Scouts Am., Duluth, 1964-68; leader Girl Scouts U.S., Duluth, 1972-74; chmn. Duluth Hall of Fame, 1983—; doscent Glensheen U. Minn., 1979-85; vol. St. Luke's Hosp., Duluth, 1968-72; asst. treas. Port Cities Luncheon, Duluth, 1984-86, treas., 1987—, co-chair, 1989—, chmn., 1989-90; chairperson Duluth East High Sch. All-Sch. Reunion, 1986; active Lakeside Presbyn. Ch. Mem. Duluth Area Ins. Women (treas. 1977-79, v.p. 1979-80, pres. 1980-82, advisor 1991—), Duluth Bus. and Profl. Women (treas. 1976-88, 2d v.p. 1986, 1st v.p. 1987, pres. 1988—), Ambassadors of Duluth, Duluth C. of C., Duluth Curling Club, Duluth Figure Skating Club, Altrusta Internat. Home: 6520 W Hunter Lake Rd Duluth MN 55803-9424 Office: St Louis Bank for Savs Fed Savs & Loan PO Box 115 Duluth MN 55801-0115

MADIGAN, DEBRA JEAN, gerontology, psychiatric/mental health nurse; b. Troy, Mo., May 30, 1962; d. James S. and Betty Zane (Vaughn) Burgess; m. Richard E. Madigan. BAS med./surg. nurse, Pike-Lincoln Tech. Ctr., Eolia, Mo., 1986. Lic. practical nurse, Mo.; lic. in intravenous therapy, clin. supr. nurse's assts. Charge nurse, coord. residential care Wentzville (Mo.) Park Care Ctr., 1987-89; charge nurse Medicalodge, Troy, 1988; med.-surg. nurse Lincoln County Meml. Hosp., Troy, 1989; dir. nurses Silex (Mo.) Nursing Ctr., 1989-90; nurse Pheasant Wood Nursing Home, Peterborough,

N.H., 1990-91, Scott-Farrar Home, Peterboro, N.H., 1991-92, Delmar Gardens, Chesterfield, Mo., 1992, 94—, Troy Nursing Ctr., Troy, Mo., 1992—; clin. supr. nurse assts., 1989—; care plan coord. Troy Nursing Ctr., 1992—; med./surg. nurse Barnes St. Peters Hosp., 1993-94. Mem. NAPNES, Mo. State Assn. LPNs. Home: 898 Elm Tree Rd Moscow Mills MO 63362-1308

MADIGAN, MARTHA, photographer, artist, photography educator; b. Milw.; d. Daniel Francis and Margaret Mary (Breen) M.; m. Jeffrey P. Fuller, Oct. 13, 1979; children: Daniel Fuller, Claire Fuller, Grace Fuller. BS in Art Edn., U. Wis., 1972; postgrad., Ariz. State U., 1972-73; MFA, Sch. Art Inst. Chgo., 1978. Photography, printmaking, art instr. North Shore Country Day Sch., Winnetka, Ill., 1973-78; asst. prof.photography, dept. art, art history Wayne State U., Detroit, 1978-79; prof., chairperson dept. photography Tyler Sch. Art Temple U., Phila., 1979—. Solo exhbns. include Hayes Gallery, Milw., 1977, Phila. Coll. Art, 1979, Cranbrook Acad. Art, 1981, Univ. of Arts, Phila., 1990, RISD, 1993, Michael Rosenfeld Gallery, N.Y.C., 1994, others; group exhbns. include Union Gallery, U. Wis., 1971-72, Camerawork Gallery, San Francisco, 1977, Hyde Park Art Ctr., Chgo., 1977Artists Market, Detroit, 1978, Chgo. Ctr. Contemporary Photography, 1978, Nat. Coll. Edn., Chgo., 1978, Ill. State Mus., 1978, New Mus., N.Y.C., 1979, So. Ill. Univ., 1979, Jeffrey Fuller Fine Art, Phila., 1980, 81, 82, 83, 84, Beaver Coll., Pa., 1980, Phila. Mus. Art, 1981, Print Club, 1982, U. Colo., Boulder, 1982, Va. Commonwealth Mus., 1982, Bard Coll., N.Y., 1982, L.A. Ctr. Photographic Studies, 1982, Phila. Coll. Art, 1983, Art Inst. Phila., 1983, Franklin Inst., Phila., 1983, Denver Art Mus., 1983, Painted Bride Art Ctr., Phila., 1984, 85, Md. Inst. Coll. Art, Balt., 1984, IBM Gallery, N.Y.C., 1984, Hong Kong Arts Ctr., 1984, Allentown (Pa.) Art Mus., 1985, 93, James Madison U., Harrisonburg, Va., 1985, Ohio State U., 1985, Santa Barbara Mus. Art, 1986, Md. Art Place, Balt., 1986, Rockwell Mus., Corning, N.Y., 1986, Coll. Notre Dame, Balt., 1987, Fine Arts Mus. L.I., 1988, Bucks County (Pa.) C.C., 1988, The Athenaeum No. Va. Fine Art Assn., 1988, Ctr. Contemporary Arts of Sante Fe, 1989, Carnegie Mellon Art Gallery, Pitts., 1989, Moravian Coll., 1989, Moore Coll. Art, Phila., 1990, Pyramid Art Ctr., Rochester, N.Y., 1990, James Danziger Gallery, N.Y.C., 1991, Midtown Payson Gallery, N.Y.C., 1992, Univ. of Arts, Phila., 1992, Acad. Fine Arts, Bratislava, Czechoslovakia, 1992, numerous others; represented in permanent collections Met. Mus. Art, N.Y.C., Phila. Mus. Art, Art Inst. Chgo., Detroit Inst. Arts, Calif. Mus. Photography, Milw. Art Ctr., Madison (Wis.) Art Ctr., Ill. State Mus., Colo. Mountain Coll., K-Mart Collections, Bloomfield Hills, Mich., McDonald's Corp., Oak Brook, Ill., Goldman/Sachs Collections, N.Y.C., Isabel Munoz, Madrid, Spain, David C. Ruttenberg, others; invited lectr., panelist, jurist; workshops in field. Office: Tyler Sch Art Beech and Penrose Aves Elkins Park PA 19027

MADIGAN, RITA DUFFY, career education coordinator; b. N.Y.C., Jan. 22, 1919; d. Mary (Feichter) Duffy; m. John Callanan Madigan, May 1, 1943; children: John C., James A., Paul F. BA in English History, Our Lady of Good Counsel Coll., 1940; M of Adminstrn., U. Bridgeport, 1963, postgrad., 1970. Tchr. English City of Bridgeport (Conn.), 1961-63, Birkshire Jr. High Sch., Birmingham, Mich., 1963-66; career counselor East Side Med. Sch., Bridgeport, 1969-71; coord. career edn. Ctrl. High Sch., Bridgeport, 1972—. Recipient State SCOVE award, 1986, CCCA Meritorious award, 1993. Mem. AAUW, NEA, Conn. Edn. Assn., Conn. Career Counselors Assn. chmn. 1989-94), Bridgeport Edn. Assn. (del. 1992-94), CCCA, St. Joseph's Ladies League (bd. dirs. 1992-94), Bridgeport Alumnae Assn. Republican. Roman Catholic. Home: 44 Chatham Dr Trumbull CT 06611-3262

MADISON, OCTAVIA DIANNE, mental health services professional; b. Lynchburg, Va., Mar. 28, 1960; d. Raymond Barlow Sr. Madison and Doreatha Madison Anderson. BA, Hampton U., 1982; MEd, Lynchburg Coll., 1983; postgrad., George Mason U., Fairfax, Va., 1989-94, Va. Poly. Inst. and State U., 1994—. Lic. profl. counselor, addiction counselor. Resource counselor Lynchburg Community Action Group, 1983, placement specialist, 1984; program mgr. Lynchburg 70001 Program, 1985; therapist, case mgr. Cen. Va. Community Svcs., Lynchburg, 1985-88; substance abuse counselor II Fairfax County Govt., 1988—; therapist Women's Ctr. No. Va., Vienna, 1990—; psychotherapist Dr. Carolyn Jackson-Sahni-Assocs., 1993; mental health therapist Arlington County Dept. Human Svcs., 1994—. Asst. sec. So. Christian Leadership Conf., Lynchburg, 1983-84; mem. single ministry, asst. chair youth adv. bd. Mt. Pleasant Bapt. Ch., Alexandria, Va., 1991—; bd. examiners Profl. Counselors, 1991—. Recipient 2-Star award United Way (coord.), 1989. Mem. Am. Assn. for Counseling and Devel., Women's Ctr. Career Network, Advs. for Infants and Mothers, Inc., Nat. Black Alcoholism Coun., Va. Counselor's Assn., Washington Met. Area Addictions Counselors, Nat. Bd. Cert. Counselors, Psi Chi, Beta Kappa Chi. Home: 3890 Lyndhurst Dr # 303313 Fairfax VA 22031-3722

MADISON, ROBERTA ELEANOR, epidemiologist, educator, consultant; b. Bklyn., Feb. 10, 1932; d. A.I. and Grace (Weinstein) M.; children: Jerry Solomon, Sue Vann. AB in History, UCLA, 1966, MA, 1969, MSPH in Environ. Health, 1972, DrPH, 1974. Chief epidemiological analyst Los Angeles County, L.A., 1972-75; from asst. prof. to assoc. prof. Calif. State U., Northridge, 1975-83, prof. epidemiology and biostatistics, 1983-89; part-time epidemiologist City of Hope, Duarte, Calif., 1977-85; instr. biostatistics UCLA Sch. Pub. Health, 1978-84; v.p. Enrich; cons., biostatistician Northridge Hosp., 1983—; cons. epidemiology and biostats. Thrasher & Assocs., Northridge, 1988-91, Cytosystems, Cupertino, Calif., 1988-90; cons. epidemiology Warner Day Care Ctr., Woodland Hills, Calif., 1988-90; cons. to phys. therapy masters program Coll. Osteo Medicine of Pacific, 1992-93. Mem. editorial rev. bd. Alzheimers Disease and Assoc. Disorders, 1985—; contbr. articles to profl. jours.; cons. editor: Informed Consent mag., 1994—. Bd. dirs. Basehart Theatre, Woodland Hills, 1986-94. Grantee Am. Lung Assn., others. Fellow Am. Coll. Epidemiology, Cancer Rsch. Ctr.; mem. Am. Statis. Assn. (sec. state edn. sect. 1982, workshop organizing com. State Calif. chpt. 1986—), Golden Key Honor Soc. (hon.), Sigma Xi (sec. chpt. 1982). Office: Calif State U 18111 Nordhoff St Northridge CA 91330-0001

MADONIA, VALERIE, dancer; b. Buffalo. Dancer Nat. Ballet of Can., 1979-81, Am. Ballet Theater, 1981-86, The Joffrey Ballet, N.Y.C., 1987—; mem. Baryshnikov and Co. Tour 1985; guest artist with The Armitage Ballet, 1987, Lines Contemporary Ballet, 1994. Office: 111 E 14th St # 385 New York NY 10019-3818*

MADONNA (MADONNA LOUISE VERONICA CICCONE), singer, actress; b. Bay City, Mich., Aug. 16, 1958; d. Sylvio and Madonna Ciccone; m. Sean Penn, Aug. 16, 1985 (div. 1989). Student, U. Mich., 1976-78. Dancer Alvin Ailey Dance Co., N.Y.C., 1979. Albums include Madonna, 1983, Like a Virgin, 1985, True Blue, 1986, (soundtrack)Who's That Girl, 1987, (with others) Vision Quest Soundtrack, 1983, You Can Dance, 1987, Like a Prayer, 1989, I'm Breathless: Music From and Inspired by the Film Dick Tracy, 1990, The Immaculate Collection, 1990, Erotica, 1992, Bedtime Stories, 1994; film appearances include A Certain Sacrifice, 1980, Vision Quest, 1985, Desperately Seeking Susan, 1985, Shanghai Surprise, 1986, Who's That Girl, 1987, Bloodhounds of Broadway, 1989, Dick Tracy, 1990, Truth or Dare, 1991, Madonna, 1992, Body of Evidence, 1992, Dangerous Game, 1993; Broadway theater debut in Speed-the-Plow, 1987; author: Sex, 1992. Roman Catholic. Office: Sire Records 75 Rockefeller Plz New York NY 10019*

MADORE, SISTER BERNADETTE, academic administrator; b. Barnston, Que., Can., Jan. 24, 1918; came to U.S., 1920, naturalized; d. Joseph George and Mina Marie (Fontaine) M.; A.B., U. Montreal, 1942, B.Ed., 1943; M.S., Cath. U. Am., 1949, Ph.D., 1951. Joined Sisters of St. Anne, Roman Cath. Ch., 1935. Instr. math. and English, Marie Anne Coll., Montreal, Que., 1943-44; prof. biology, dean of coll. Anna Maria Coll., Paxton, Mass., 1952-76, v.p., 1975-77, pres., 1977-93, chancellor, 1993—; fund-raising cons.; corporator YWCA. Past bd. dirs. Central Mass. chpt. ARC; past bd. dirs. Worcester Coll. Consortium; former trustee Worcester Boys Club. Mem. AAAS, Am. Soc. Microbiology, Nat. Assn. Biology Tchrs., Am. Assn. Higher Edn., Worcester C. of C. Home and Office: Anna Maria Coll Office of the Chancellor Sunset Ln Worcester MA 01612-1198

MADORE, JOYCE LOUISE, gerontology nurse; b. Madison, Kans., Dec. 15, 1936; d. Lionel Wiedmer and Mary Elizabeth (Piley) Murphy; m. Robert Madore, Aug. 15, 1969; children: Carl, Clay. BS, Emporia State U., 1980; diploma, Newman Hosp., 1981. RN, Kans., Mo.; cert. gerontol. nurse, non profit adminstr. Med. charge nurse St. Mary's Hosp., Emporia, Kans., 1971-72; dir. nursing Madison (Kans.) Manor, 1974-81, 82-83; staff nurse Newman Meml. Hosp., Emporia, 1981-82; dir. Daybreak Adult Day Svcs. Springfield (Mo.) Area Coun. of Chs., 1983—; mem. Gov.'s Com. to Establish Rules and Regulations on Adult Day Care Patients State of Mo.; cons. U. Mo. Coop. Extension Svc. Program Guides on Adult Day Care. Contbr. video Understanding Aging Program. Named one of Outstanding Nurses in Mo. St. Louis U., 1989. Mem. NAFE, Adult Day Care Assn. (past sec., exec. past v.p. 1989-91), Mo. Nurses Assn., Mo. Adult Day Care Assn. (pres. 1991—). Home: 171 Hilltop Oaks Ln Sparta MO 65753-9801

MADRID, OLGA HILDA GONZALEZ, retired elementary education educator, association executive; b. San Antonio, May 4, 1928; d. Victor A. and Elvira Ardilla Gonzalez; m. Sam Madrid, Jr., June 29, 1952; children: Ninette Marie, Samuel James. Student, U. Mex., San Antonio, St. Mary's U., San Antonio; BA, Our Lady of Lake U., 1956, MEd, 1963. Cert. bilingual tchr., adminstr., Tex. Sec. Lanier High Sch. San Antonio Ind. Sch. Dist., 1945-52, tchr. Collins Garden Elem. Sch., 1963-92; tutor Dayton, Ohio, 1952-54; bd. dirs., sch. rep. San Antonio Tchr.'s Coun., 1970-90; chair various coms. Collins Garden Elem., 1970-92. Elected dep. precinct, senatorial and state Dem. Convs., San Antonio, 1968—; apptd. commr. Keep San Antonio Beautiful, 1985; life mem., past pres. San Antonio YWCA; bd. dirs. Luth. Gen. Hosp., NCCJ, Cath. Family and Children's Svcs., St. Luke's Luth. Hosp.; nat. bd. dirs. YWCA, 1985—, also mem. exec. com.; mem. edn. commn. Holy Rosary Parish, 1994—; mem. bus. assocs. com. Our Lady of the Lake U., 1995—. Recipient Outstanding Our Lady Lake Alumni award Our Lady Lake U., 1975, Guadalupana medal San Antonio Cath. Archdiocese, 1975, Yellow Rose Tex. citation Gov. Briscoe, 1977; Olga H. Madrid Ctr. named in her honor, YWCA San Antonio and San Antonio City Coun., 1983; Lo Mejor De Lo Nuestro honoree San Antonio Light, 1991. Mem. San Antonio Bus. and Profl. Women, Inc. (mem. exec. com.), Salute Quality Edn. (honoree 1993), Delta Kappa Gamma (Theta Beta chpt., mem. exec. com.). Home: 2726 Benrus San Antonio TX 78228

MADRIL, LEE ANN, writer; b. Burbank, Calif., Sept. 16, 1944; d. George Mathew McDougall; 1 child, Francis Michael. Student, Granada Hills (Calif.) Coll., 1962. Freelance writer, 1986-90; shoot out artist, life mem. Bad Co., Auburn, Calif., 1990—; writer Idaho State Newspaper, Just Horses, Indian Valley, 1994—; cons. in authenticity, Calif. State Horsemen, Santa Rosea, 1988-90, Bad Co., 1990. Writer Idaho State Newspaper Just Horses; contbr. articles to profl. jours. Vol. Red Cross, Soques, Calif., 1982, Salinas (Calif.) Valley Meml. Hosp., 1979, Greenpeace, Humane Soc. U.S. Recipient Kodak KINSA award, 1989, winner County and State photo awards, 1993. Mem. Calif. State Horseman's Assn. (state champion 1989-90), Silver Spurs. Republican. Roman Catholic.

MADSEN, DOROTHY LOUISE (MEG MADSEN), writer; b. Rochester, N.Y.; d. Charles Robert and Louise Anna Agnes Meyer; B.A., Mundelein Coll., Chgo., 1978; m Frederick George Madsen, Feb. 17, 1945. Public relations rep. Rochester Telephone Corp., 1941-42; feature writer Rochester Democrat & Chronicle, 1939-41; exec. dir. LaPorte (Ind.) chpt. ARC, 1964; dir. adminstrv. services Bank Mktg. Assn., Chgo., 1971-74; exec. dir. Eleanor Assn., Chgo., 1974-84; founder Meg Madsen Assocs., Chgo., 1984-88; women's career counselor; founder, Clearinghouse Internat. Newsletter; founder Eleanor Women's Forum, Clearinghouse Internat., Eleanor Intern Program Coll. Students and Returning Women. Served to lt. col. WAC, 1942-47, 67-70. Decorated Legion of Merit, Meritorious Service award. Mem. Res. Officers Assn., Mundelein Alumnae Assn., Phi Sigma Tau (charter mem. Ill. Kappa chpt.). Home and Office: 1030 N State St Chicago IL 60610-2844

MADSEN, SANDRA ARLENE, speech communication educator; b. Milw., Dec. 1, 1943; d. Robert W. and Evelyn J. (Curry) George; m. John A. Madsen, June 18, 1966; children: Kaaren B., Michael D. BA, U.Wis., Whitewater, 1965, MAT, 1971; PhD, U. Kans, 1975; JD, U. Iowa, 1993. Bar: Iowa 1993. Asst. instr. U. Kans., Lawrence, 1969-73; instr. assoc. Buena Vista Coll., Storm Lake, Iowa, 1973-91, prof. speech comm., 1991—, dean Sch. Comm. and Arts, 1988-90, assoc. dean faculty, 1984-87, dir. Japanese exch., 1981—; acad. humanist Iowa Bd. Pub. Programs in the Humanities, Iowa City, 1975-78. Mayor City of Storm Lake, 1994—. Danforth assoc. Danforth Found., 1979-85. Office: Buena Vista Coll 610 W 4th St Storm Lake IA 50588-1798

MADY, MARY ANN, special education director, educator; b. Rochester, N.Y., Jan. 29, 1937; m. Kenneth D. Mady, July 12, 1958 (div. June 1983); children: Susan, Donald, Paul, Sarah. BS, SUNY, Brockport, 1957, CAS, 1989; MS, Nazareth Coll., 1987. Cert. sch. adminstr. Tchr. Manchester Shortsville (N.Y.) Ctrl. Sch. Dist., 1957—, chair spl. edn., 1987—, dir. spl. programs, 1989—; mem. Early Intervention Coun., Canandaigua, N.Y., 1991-94, Ont. County Cmty. Svcs. Bd., 1994. Named Rotarian of Yr. by Red Jacket Rotary Club, 1992. Mem. Camp Onseyawa (bd. dirs. 1989—), Coun. Adminstrs. Spl. Edn., Rotary Internat. (trustee 1994). Republican. Roman Catholic. Home: 7190 Lane Rd Victor NY 14564 Office: Manchester-Shortsville Ctrl Sch Dist Rte 21 Shortsville NY 14548

MAEDA, J. A., data processing executive; b. Mansfield, Ohio, Aug. 24, 1940; d. James Shunso and Doris Lucille Maeda; m. Robert Lee Hayes (div. May 1970); 1 child, Brian Sentaro Hayes. BS in Math., Purdue U., 1962, postgrad., 1962-63; postgrad., Calif. State U., Northridge, 1968-75; cert. profl. designation in tech. of computer operating systems and tech. of info. processing, UCLA, 1971. Cons., rsch. asst. computer ctr. Purdue U., West Lafayette, Ind., 1962-63; computer operator, sr. tab operator, mem. faculty Calif. State U., Northridge, 1969, programmer cons., tech. asst. II, 1969-70, supr. acad. applicatons, EDP supr. II, 1970-72, project tech. support coord. programmer II, office of the chancellor, 1972-73, tech. support coord. statewide timesharing tech. support, programmer II, 1973-74, acad. coord., tech. support coord. instrn., computer cons. III, 1974-83; coord. user svcs. info. ctr., mem. tech. staff IV CADAM INC subs. Lockheed Corp., Burbank, Calif., 1983-86, coord. end user svcs., tech. specialist computing dept., 1986-87; v.p. bd. dirs. Rainbow Computing, Inc., Northridge, 1976-85; dir. Aki Tech./Design Cons., Northridge; mktg. mgr. thaumaturge Taro Quipu Cons., Northridge, 1987—; tech. cons. Digital Computer Cons., Chatsworth, Calif., 1988; cons. computer tech., fin. and bus. mgmt., system integration, 1988-90; tech. customer s/w support Collection Data Sys., Westlake, Calif., 1991; tech. writer Sterling Software Engring. Mgmt. Divsn., 1992—. Author, editor more than 250 user publs., BASIC programming lang. tutorials, ref. manuals, user guides; contbr. articles, papers, and photos to profl. jours. Mem. IEEE, SHARE, Digital Equipment Computer Users Soc. (DECUS) (author papers and presentations 1977-81, ednl. spl. interest group 1977-83, steering com. Resource Sharing Timesharing System/Extended (RSTS/E), 1979-82, Steering Software Silver Achievement award 1993). Office: Sterling Software Engring Mgmt Divsn 5900 Canoga Ave Woodland Hills CA 91367-5036

MAERSCH, NANCY KAY, laboratory manager; b. Norfolk, Nebr., May 11, 1942; d. Ambrose Pryor and Angela Gertrude (Goergen) Jordan; m. Frank C. Maersch, May 11, 1968; 1 child, Todd F. BS in Med. Tech., Mt. Marty Coll., 1963; MA in Health Care Adminstrn., Cen. Mich. U., 1981. Diplomate of Lab. Medicine; cert. med. tech.; specialist in hematology. Med. technologist Madison (Wis.) Gen. Hosp. Lab., 1963-64, hematology sect. head, 1964-72, hematology specialist, 1973-79, hematology sect. head, 1979-80, lab. customer svc. rep., 1980-82, mgr. adminstrv. svc. and mktg., 1982-85; mgr. mobile diagnostics Meriter Gen. Med. Labs., Madison, 1985-87, mgr. client svcs., 1987-89, mgr. lab. ops., 1990—; bd. dirs. Dane County Cytology Ctr., Madison; bd. dirs. Wis. chpt. Clin. Lab. Mgrs. Assn., pres.-elect Wis. chpt., 1995-96. Chair Edgefest event Edgewood H.S. Aux., 1987-92; mem. Bus. Forum, Madison, 1989—; vol. Ronald McDonald House; bd. dirs. parents assn. Marquette U., 1993—. Mem. Am. Soc. for Clin. Lab. Sci., Wis. Soc. for Clin. Lab. Sci. (sec. 1967-70, 76-80), Clin. Lab. Mgrs. Assn., Wis. chpt. Clin. Lab. Mgrs. Assn., Madison Area Lab. Suprs., Madison Civics Club. Roman Catholic. Home: 3105 Nottingham Way Madison WI 53713-3457 Office: Gen Med Labs 36 S Brooks St Madison WI 53715-1304

MAETZOLD, LINDA ANN DORE, women's health nurse; b. Sidney, Mont., Oct. 1, 1951; d. Robert Lincoln and Barbara Jean (Wicklund) Dore; m. William Arthur Maetzold, May 26, 1973; children: Christopher, Connie. BSN, U. N.D., 1973; MS in Nursing, U. Okla., 1979. Cert. in inpatient obstetric nursing, high risk obstetrics, critical care obstetrics, ASPO Lamaze. Instr. Wichita State U.; staff nurse Overlake Hosp., Bellevue, Wash.; lectr. SUNY, Binghamton; perinatal clin. specialist LDR & high risk perinatal units, clinician LDR unit Fairfax Hosp., Falls Church, Va., also clinician in labor and delivery room unit. Mem. NAACOG, Va. Nurses Assn., Sigma Theta Tau. Home: 5405 Harrow Ct Fairfax VA 22030-7236

MAFFRE, MURIEL, ballet dancer; b. Enghien, Val D'Oise, France, Mar. 19, 1966; came to U.S., 1990; d. Bernard and Monique (Berteaux) M. Diploma, Paris Opera Ballet Sch., 1981; Baccalauréat (hon.), France, 1984. Dancer Hamburg Ballet, Fed. Republic Germany, 1983-84; soloist Sarragoza Ballet, Spain; premiere danseuse Monte Carlo Ballet, Monaco, 1985-90; prin. dancer San Francisco Ballet, 1990—; guest artist with Berlinor Staatsoper. Recipient 1st prize Nat. Conservatory, Paris, 1983, Grand prize and Gold medal Paris Internat. Ballet Competition, 1984, Isadora Duncan award, 1990. Office: San Francisco Ballet 455 Franklin St San Francisco CA 94102-4471*

MAFNAS, ISABEL IGLESIAS, computer lab specialist, computer consultant; b. Austin, Tex., Sept. 21, 1965; d. Juan Crisostomo and Isabel (Iglesias) M. BA in Statistics, U. Calif., Berkeley, 1987; postgrad., Chabot Coll., 1989-91, Merritt Coll., 1991-92. Stats. tutor, stats. reader U. Calif., Berkeley, 1986-87; stats. reader U. Calif. Extension, Berkeley, 1987-89; instrnl. asst. II Chabot Coll., Hayward, 1988-92, computer lab. specialist, 1992—; tchr. computers Eureka!-Girls Inc., San Leandro, 1993-95. Author: (Software user's guide) Academic Session Time Keeper, 1990, 91, 92, 94. Recipient Newspaper Carrier scholarship Gannett Found., Inc., Guam, 1983, Gannett Spl. scholarship Gannett Found., Inc., Guam, 1983. Office: Chabot College 25555 Hesperian Blvd Hayward CA 94545-2400

MAGAFAS, DIANIA LEE, geriatrics nurse consultant, administrator; b. Chgo., Oct. 17, 1963; d. Alec and Jacqueline Magafas; 1 child, Jason. BS, St. Xavier Coll., Chgo., 1986, MSN, 1991. Staff nurse Ingalls Meml. Hosp., Harvey, Ill., 1986-88; asst. DON Wedgewood Nursing Pavilion, Chgo., 1988-90; nursing cons. long term care Dynamics Healthcare Cons., Inc., Skokie, Ill., 1990—. Mem. Sigma Theta Tau.

MAGEE, BETTY LOU, realtor; b. Oklahoma City, July 28, 1942; d. Jack Lawrence and Edna Lee (Childers) Mackey; m. James Randall Magee, May 15, 1971; children: Jennifer L., Amanda L. BS, Abilene Christian Coll., 1964; MEd, Tex. Tech. U., 1967. Lic. realtor. Tchr. elem. edn. Lubbock, Tex., 1964-67, Richardson, Tex., 1967-73; realtor Fenwick Realtors, Plano, Tex., 1981-89, Re/Max of Plano, 1989—; mem. Residential Sales Coun., 1991-92, Women's Coun. Realtors Collin County, 1985-92. Mem. Tex. Assn. Realtors (mem. polit. action com. 1993), Plano C. of C. (amb.'s club 1991-93, chair newsletter women's divsn. 1988-90, historian women's divsn. 1991). Republican. Home: 3913 Promontory Point Plano TX 75075 Office: Re/Max of Plano 5501 Independence Plano TX 75023

MAGGIO, THERESA GRIFFIN, librarian, consultant; b. Shreveport, La., May 27, 1952; d. James Henry and Annie Laurie (Rosenblath) Griffin; m. Edward James Maggio, July 2, 1977; 1 child, Kelli Suzanne. BS in Social Studies Edn., La. State U., 1975, MLS, 1980; PhD in Libr. and Info. Studies, Fla. State U., 1988. Librarian La. State Library, Baton Rouge, 1980-82; med. library cons. 7th Ward Hosp., Hammond, La., 1984-86; med. librarian Lallie Kemp Hosp., Independence, La., 1982-85; reference libr. Roddenbery Meml. Libr., 1988-89; dep. dir., pub. svcs. libr. SW Ga. Regional Libr., Bainbridge, 1989—. Recipient Baker and Taylor Grassroots award, 1980; La. Library Assn. scholar, 1979, Title IIB fellow, 1985-86. Mem. ALA. Democrat. Roman Catholic. Avocation: horse racing. Home: 3255 Capital Cir NE Apt 8A Tallahassee FL 32308-3746 Office: SW GA Regional Library Shortwell & Monroe Sts Bainbridge GA 31717

MAGGIORE, SUSAN, geophysical oceanographer; b. Newark, Mar. 14, 1957; d. John James and Marietta Nancy (Testa) M.; m. Stephen P. Garreffa, Oct. 21, 1989; 1 child, Julianna Garreffa. BS in Geosci., Montclair State Coll., 1978; postgrad., U. So. Miss., 1981-84. Supr. rsch. and communications The Cousteau Soc., N.Y.C. and Norfolk, Va., 1979-81; geophysicist Naval Oceanographic Office, Bay St. Louis, Miss., 1981-85, NE Consortium Oceanographic Research, Narragansett, R.I., 1985-86; mem. tech. staff AT&T Bell Labs., Whippany, N.J., 1986—; writer, creative cons. The Cousteau Soc., Los Angeles, 1981-89. Researcher book The Cousteau Almanac of the Environment, 1981; contbr. articles to profl. jours. Vol. Dover (N.J.) Gen. Hosp., 1987-88. Mem. Am. Geophys. Union, Marine Tech. Soc., Nat. Assn. Female Execs. Roman Catholic. Office: AT&T Bell Labs 67 Whippany Rd Whippany NJ 07981-1425

MAGILL, DIANNE KAY, foundation administrator; b. Kansas City, Kans., Feb. 16, 1944; d. Francis Glenn and Marjorie Maxine (Gosper) Smith; m. Garry Allen Magill, June 26, 1965 (div. July 1977); children: Kellie Kristen, Erin Alisa. Student, Kans. State U., 1962-64, Moorhead State U., 1978; BS in Polit. Sci., U. Oreg., 1981. Legis. aide Ho. of Reps., Salem, Oreg., 1980; campaign coord. Re-Elect Campbell, Eugene, Oreg., 1981; from dir. pub. rels. to dir. pub. rels. and mktg. ARC, Kansas City, Mo., 1982-87, dir. CMD, 1987-89, dir. pub. support, 1989-92; devel. mgr. Am. Acad. Family Physicians Found., Kansas City, Mo., 1993—; adj. prof. Rockhurst Coll., Kansas City, 1987-89; cons. South Kansas City C. of C., 1992-93. Editor: Hot Stuff!, 1992-93 (Prism award 1993). Campaign advisor Rep. Ctrl. Com., Eugene, 1980. Scholastic scholar U. Oregon, 1981. Mem. Pub. Rels. Soc. Am. (pres. 1988-89, bd. dirs. 1985-88, bd. dirs. social svcs. sect. sec. 1992, v.p. 1993, Banner award 1989, Prism award 1985, 87, 89, 91), NSFRE (cert.), Friends of Art, Ctrl. Exch. (mktg. com. mem. 1987). Home: 8698 W 108th Pl Overland Park KS 66210-1606 Office: Am Acad Family Physicians 8880 Ward Pky Kansas City MO 64114-2756

MAGILL, DODIE BURNS, early childhood education educator; b. Greenwood, S.C., July 10, 1952; d. Byron Bernard and Dora Curry B.; m. Charles Towner Magill, May 4, 1974; children: Charles Towner II, Emily Curry. BA, Furman U., 1974; MEd, U. S.C., 1978. Cert. tchr., early childhood, elementary, elementary principal, supv., S.C. Kindergarten tchr. Sch. Dist. Greenville County, 1974-83; early childhood edn. instr. Valdosta (Ga.) State Univ., 1983-84; dir. lower sch. Valwood Sch., Valdosta, 1984-86; kindergarten tchr. Sch. Dist. Greenville County, 1986—; tchr.-in-residence S.C. Ctr. for Tchr. Recruitment, Rock Hill, 1993, mem. policy bd.; workshop presenter and lectr. in various schs. and sch. dists. throughout U.S., 1974—; chmn. S.C. Pub. Kindergarten Celebration, 1994; giv. S.C. State Readiness Policy Group; mem. Southeastern Region Vision for Edn. Adv. Bd., S.C. Coun. Ednl. Collaboration. Demonstration tchr. S.C. ETV (TV show) Sch. Begins with Kindergarten. Mem. Gov. of S.C.'s State Readiness Policy Group, Southeastern Regional Vision for Edn. Adv. Bd., South Carolina Ctr. Tchr. Recruitment Policy Bd. Recipient Ralph Witherspoon award S.C. Assn. for Children Under Six; named Tchr. of Yr., Greenville County, 1992, 93, State of S.C., 1993, S.C. Tchr. of Yr. Coun. of Chief State Sch. Officers, 1993, 94. Mem. Assn. for Childhood Edn. Internat., S.C. Tchr. Forum (chmn. 1993-94), S.C. Early Childhood Assn., Alpha Delta Kappa. Presbyterian. Office: Mountain Park Elem Sch 1500 Pounds Rd SW Lilburn GA 30247

MAGNER, RACHEL HARRIS, banker; b. Lamar, S.C., Aug. 5; d. Garner Greer and Catherine Alice (Cloaninger) Harris; m. Fredric Michael Magner, May 14, 1972. BS in Fin., U. S.C., 1972; postgrad. UCLA, 1974, Calif. State U., 1975. Mgmt. trainee Union Bank, L.A., 1972-75, comml. loan officer, 1975-77; asst. v.p. comml. fin. Crocker Bank, L.A., 1978, asst. v.p., factoring account exec. subs. Crocker United Factors, Inc., 1978-81; v.p. comml. services div. Crocker Bank, 1981-82, v.p., sr. account mgr. bus. banking div., 1982-83; v.p. and mgr. corporate banking Office of Pres., Sumitomo Bank Calif., 1983—. Home: 2200 Pine Ave Manhattan Beach CA 90266-2207 Office: Sumitomo Bank Calif 101 S San Pedro St Ste 500 Los Angeles CA 90012-3883

MAGNESS, RHONDA ANN, microbiologist; b. Stockton, Calif., Jan. 30, 1946; d. John Pershing and Dorothy Waneta (Kelley) Wetter; m. Barney LeRoy Bender, Aug. 25, 1965 (div. 1977); m. Gary D. Magness, Mar. 5, 1977; children: Jay D. (dec.), Troy D. BS, Calif. State U., 1977. Lic. clin. lab. technologist, Calif., med. technologist; cert. clin. lab. scientist. Med. asst. C. Fred Wilcox, MD, Stockton, 1965-66; clk. typist Dept. of U.S. Army, Ft. Eustis, Va., 1967, Def. Supply Agy., New Orleans, 1967-68; med. asst. James G. Cross, MD, Lodi, Calif., 1969, Arthur A. Kemalyan, MD, Lodi, 1969-71, 72-77; med. sec. Lodi Meml. Hosp., 1972; lab. aide Calif. State U., Sacramento, 1977; phlebotomist St. Joseph's Hosp., Stockton, 1978-79; supr. microbiology Dameron Hosp. Assn., Stockton, 1980—. Active Concerned Women Am., Washington, 1987—. Mem. AAUW, Calif. Assn. Clin. Lab. Technologists, San Joaquin County Med. Assts. Assn., Nat. Geog. Soc., Nat. Audubon Soc. Baptist. Lodge: Jobs Daus. (chaplain 1962-63). Home: 9627 Knight Ln Stockton CA 95209-1961 Office: Dameron Hosp Lab 525 W Acacia St Stockton CA 95203-2484

MAGNOTTO, JOYCE NEFF, English language educator; b. Washington, Mar. 1, 1944; d. Jack David and Goldie (Lev) Neff; m. Antonio Magnotto III, Jan. 31, 1965 (div. Nov. 1993); children: Jana, Julie. BA in English cum laude with honors, Western Md. Coll., 1966; MA in English Lit., U. Md., 1978; postgrad., Westbrook Coll., 1980, Loyola Coll., Balt., 1984-86; Phd, U. Pa., 1991. Tchr. English Oxon Hill (Md.) High Sch., 1967-73, Crossland Evening High Sch., Camp Springs, Md., 1973-78; home and hosp. tchr. Prince George's County Bd. Edn., Upper Marlboro, Md., 1979-80; prof. English and humanities Prince George's C.C., Largo, Md., 1980-93, coord. Writing Across the Curriculum program, 1983-91, chair writing dept., 1991-93; asst. prof. English, coord. profl. writing Old Dominion U., Norfolk, Va., 1993—; writing cons. Tng. Inst. U.S. Gen. Acctg. Office, Washington, 1987—; bd. cons. Nat. Network Writing Across the Curriculum Programs, 1985-92; invited panelist PBS Nat. Teleconf. on Writing Across the Curriculum, 1992; mem. writing adv. bd. Nat. Ctr. Postsecondary Teaching, Learning and Assessment, 1993; elected mem. nat. nominating com. Conf. on Coll. Composition and Comm.; presenter in field. Contbr. articles to profl. jours. Recipient Disting. Program award Md. Assn. Higher Edn., 1985; NEH fellow, 1989, Fulbright-Hays fellow, 1993; merit scholar U. Pa., 1991. Mem. MLA, Assn. Profl. Writing Cons., Nat. Coun. Tchrs. English, Rhetoric Soc. Am. Office: Old Dominion U English Dept Norfolk VA 23529

MAGNUS, ERICA (ERICA MAGNUS THOMAS), painter, author, illustrator; b. Waterbury, Conn., Aug. 14, 1946; d. Paul Gerhard and Hermine Adelaide Magnus; m. David Owen Thomas, Aug. 12, 1972; children: Peter David (dec.), Krista Mary, Karen Roslyn. Student, Atelier, Haarlem, Netherlands, 1966-67, 67-68; BFA in Painting, Mpls. Coll. Art and Design, 1970; MFA in Painting, So. Ill. U., 1974. Freelance graphic designer Winona, Minn., 1972-87; pvt. tchr. drawing gifted children Winona, 1978-79, Athens, Ga., 1980-81; tchr. drawing adult edn. Winona Area Tech. Sch., 1972-79, Communiversity, Ohio U., Athens, 1987-91; author, illustrator Carolrhoda Books Inc., Mpls., 1984-86, Lothrop, Lee & Shepard Books, N.Y.C., 1990—; lectr./workshops kindergarten-12th grade, coll., univ., Ohio, Ky., Tenn., 1986-93; mem. planning com. Dairy Barn Cultural Arts Ctr., Illustrator's Art Show, Athens, 1991-92, Dairy Barn Cultural Arts Ctr., Illustrator's Art Show, Athens, 1994. Author, illustrator: Old Lars, 1984 (Parents Choice award 1984), The Boy and the Devil, 1986, Around Me, 1992, My Secret Place, 1994; art editor Great River Rev., 1977-79; exhibited in group shows at Deans Gallery, Mpls., 1970, Art Gallery St. Mary's Coll., Winona, 1975, Dairy Barn Art Open, 1988, 89, Biennale Internationale, Bratislava, Czechoslovakia, 1985, Master Eagle Gallery, NYC, 1987, The Dairy Barn, Athens, Ohio, 1990, 93, Buckeye Book Fair, Wooster, Ohio, 1992. Recipient Ohio Citizens award Ohio Assn. Edn. Young Children, 1988. Mem. Authors Guild Inc., Authors League Am. Inc., Soc. Childrens Book Writers and Illustrators.

MAGNUSEN, OLGA CRISTINA, director career planning and placement; b. Havana, Cuba, Oct. 24, 1949; came to U.S., 1961; d. Pedro Jose and Olga (Wolter) Talavera; m. Karl Owen Magnusen, Aug. 7, 1982. BA in Spanish, Old Dominion U., 1971; MS in Guidance and Counseling, St. John's U., 1972. Counselor Bishop Kearney High Sch., Bklyn., 1972-73; career counselor Fla. Internat. U., Miami, 1974-77, coop. counselor, 1977-79, assoc. dir. career resource ctr., 1979-88, dir. career planning & placement, 1988—; presenter in field. Hispanic Leadership fellow Woodrow Wilson Found., 1986; named to The Nat. Disting. Svc. Registry, 1989-90, Leadership Miami, 1987. Mem. Fla. Coop. Edn. Placement Assn. (pres. 1987-88), So. Coll. Placement Assn. (chair. local arrangements 1989, chair orgn. com., 1990-91), Coop. Edn. Assn. (co-chair student affairs com. 1980-82, 90-91, chair 1991-92). Office: Fla Internat U Tamiami Trl Miami FL 33199

MAGNUSON, NANCY, librarian; b. Seattle, Aug. 15, 1944; d. James Leslie and Jeanette (Thomas) M.; 2 sons, Daniel Johnson, Erik Johnson. BA in History, 1977; MLS, U. Wash., 1978. With. King County Libr. System, Seattle, 1973-80; rsch. asst. Free Libr. Phila., 1980-81; asst. libr. Haverford (Pa.) Coll., 1981-87; libr. dir. Goucher Coll., Balt., Md., 1987—. Contbr. to profl. publs. Mem. ALA (com. on status of women in librarianship, various others), Online Computer Libr. Ctr. Users Coun., Md. Libr. Assn., Congress Acad. Libr. Dirs., NOW, Women's Internat. League for Peace and Freedom, Balt. Bibliophiles, Jane Austen Soc. N.Am. Democrat. Office: Goucher Coll Julia Rogers Libr Dulaney Valley Rd Baltimore MD 21204

MAGNUSON, SUSAN MARIE FARR, human resources professional; b. Grand Rapids, Mich., Oct. 15, 1949; d. Norman B. and Faye Deane (Baker) Farr; m. David Scott Magnuson, May 7, 1971; children: Keith, Kari. Student, U. Ala., 1978-79. Clk. Wyoming (Mich.) Police Dept., 1968-76; pers. asst. Western Supermarkets, Birmingham, Ala., 1976-79; coord. employee benefits, pers. asst. S.E. Ala. Med. Ctr., Dothan, 1979-84; mgr. human resources Rexham Laminex Inc., Charlotte, N.C., 1984-93, D&K Laminex, Charlotte, 1993—; condr. workshops on career devel. and team bldg. skills; asst. in devel. mng. career workshop. Mem. Soc. for Human Resources Mgmt., Employers Assn. Carolinas, Charlotte Area Pers. Assn., Charlotte Area Compensation Coun., Arrowood Employers Assn. Republican. Methodist. Office: D&K Laminex Inc 10701 Texland Blvd Charlotte NC 28273-6202

MAGOFFIN, CAROLE JEAN, health care executive; b. Lyons, Kans., Apr. 12, 1942; d. Jack Wilmer and Dorothy Virginia (DeSpain) M. BS, Kans. State U., 1965; MSW, U. Iowa, 1978. Protective svc. worker Depts. of Social Svcs., Okla./N.J., 1964-71; social wk. cons. Med. Coll. Vt., Burlington, 1972-74; sr. rsch. asst. U. Iowa Hosps. and Clinics, Iowa City, 1974-78; sr. rsch. assoc. Nat. Conf. on Social Welfare, Washington, 1978-80; dir. cmty and program devel. Vt. Health Policy Corp., Waterbury, Vt., 1980-82; sr. cons. Mark Battle Assocs., Washington, 1982; dir. pvt. sector programs Am. Health Planning Assn., Washington, 1982-84; tech. cons. William M. Mercer Corp., Washington, 1984; exec. dir. Am. Med. Rev. Rsch. Ctr. (now Ctr. Clin. Quality Evaluation), Washington, 1985—; tech. adv. com. Inst. of Medicine, 1988-90. Contbr. articles to profl. jours.; journalist Washington Newsletter, 1984, Mich. Health News, 1984; author: Physicians DRG Handbook, 1987; editor newsletters Today in Health Planning and Bus., Labor and Planning Newsletter, 1982-83. Peabody scholar, 1960; grantee DOD, 1985-87, 86-88, Nat. Ctr. for Health Svcs. Rsch., 1989, HCFA/HSQB, 1991, HHS/PHS AHCPR, 1991—, others; recipient Career award Healthweek, 1989. Office: Ctr Clin Quality Evaluation Ste 1010 1140 Connecticut Ave NW Washington DC 20036

MAGOON, JUDITH LYNN, artist, jeweler, jewelry designer; b. Oakland, Calif., Oct. 11, 1950; d. Walter Dana Jr. and Margaret Elizabeth (Peck) Vance; m. David Charles Johnson, Jan. 20, 1973 (div. Jan. 1983); 1 child, Stephen Michael; m. Eugene Franklin Magoon, May 23, 1986. Student, Ariz. State U., 1968-69, Armstrong Bus. Coll., 1969-70, Feather River Coll., 1970-71, Yuba Coll., 1984-88. Co-owner, operator Magoon's West-Custom Jewelry/Art Gallery, Lower Lake, Calif., 1986-95; co-founder Lake Art Ctr., Clearlake, 1987-89; co-founder, mem. Upstairs Gallery Co-op, Lakeport, 1990-95; mem. Vines Gallery Co-op, Calistoga, Calif., 1992-95. Judge Sch. Dist. Vocat.-Edn. Fair, Lakeport, 1985; juror art in pub. places program Lake County Art Coun., Lakeport, 1990. Exhibited in solo show Lake County Mus., Lakeport, 1990; group shows include Calif. Mus. Art, Santa Rosa, 1990, 92, Sacramento (Calif.) Fine Art Ctr., 1992, 93. Mem. Pastel Soc. of the West Coast, Wine Country Artists, Konocti Art Soc., Lake County Arts Coun. Republican. Office: PO Box 762 Lower Lake CA 95457-0762

MAGRILL, ROSE MARY, library director; b. Marshall, Tex., June 8, 1939; d. Joe Richard and Mary Belle (Chadwick) M. BS, E. Tex. State U., 1960, MA, 1961; MS, U. Ill., 1964, PhD, 1969. Asst. to dean women E. Tex. State U., Commerce, 1960-61, librarian II, 1961-63; teaching asst. U. Ill., Urbana, 1963-64; instr. to asst. prof. E. Tex. State U., Commerce, 1964-67; asst. prof. Ball State U., Muncie, 1969-70; asst. prof. to prof. U. Mich., Ann Arbor, 1970-81; prof. U. N. Tex., Denton, 1981—; dir. libr. E. Tex. Bapt. U., Marshall, 1987—; accreditation site visitor ALA, Chgo., 1975—; cons. in field. Co-author: Building Library Collections, 4th edit. 1974, Library Technical Services, 1977, Building Library Collections, 5th edit. 1979, Acquisition Management and Collection Development in Libraries, 2d edit. 1989. Trustee Memphis Theol. Sem., 1988—; treas. Mission Synod of Cumberland Presbyn. Ch., 1989—; bd. fin. Trinity Presbytery, 1989—; mem. Harrison County Hist. Commn., 1995—. Mem. ALA (RTSD Resources Sect. pub. award 1978), Tex. Libr. Assn. Home: 804 Caddo St Marshall TX 75670-2414 Office: E Tex Bapt Univ 1209 N Grove St Marshall TX 75670-1498

MAGSIG, JUDITH ANNE, early childhood educator; b. Saginaw, Mich., Nov. 9, 1939; d. Harold Howard and Catherine Louise (Barstow) Gay; m. George Arthur Magsig, June 22, 1963; children: Amy Catherine, Karl Joseph. BA, Alma Coll., 1961. Cert. tchr., early childhood tchr., Mich. 1st grade tchr. Gaylord (Mich.) Schs., 1961-64, spl. edn. tchr., 1965-67, kindergarten tchr., 1968—. instr. Suzuki violin method; second violinist Traverse (Mich.) Symphony Orch., 1985-92. Mem. ASCD, NEA, Mich. Edn. Assn., Gaylord Edn. Assn., Assn. for the Edn. Young Children, Assn. for Childhood Edn. Internat., Suzuki Assn. Am., Am. String Tchrs. Assn., Order Ea. Star, Alpha Delta Kappa (pres. Beta Rho chpt. 1980-82, 84-86). Methodist. Home: 2130 Evergreen Dr Gaylord MI 49735 Office: K Ctr 590 W 5th St Gaylord MI 49735

MAGSINO, VANNA THORMAN, psychotherapist; b. July 12, 1928; m. Thomas S. Magsino; 5 children. BS, U. Ill., 1950; MA, U. Chgo., 1964, PhD, 1971. Lic. psychologist Ill., N.C., S.C.; Nat. Register Health Svc. Providers in Psychology. With Ill. Dept. Mental Health, 1964-65, clin. psychology intern Charles Read Zone Ctr., 1965-66, child psychology intern Charles Read Zone Ctr., 1968-69; with Child and Adolescent Psychiatry Clinic Evanston (Ill.) Hosp., 1971-74, mem. affiliate staff dept. psychiatry, 1974-79; assoc. adj. faculty dept. psychiatry, div. psychology Northwestern U. Med. Sch., 1972-79; pvt. practice psychotherapy Evanston, 1972-79, Tryon, N.C., 1980—; cons. psychologist St. Luke's Hosp., Columbus, N.C., 1980—; pvt. practice psychotherapy Greenville, S.C., 1987—; cons. employee assistance prog. Dept. Mental Health, Rutherford-Polk Area Mental Health, 1982-85; supr. psychol. assocs. Polk County Mental Health Ctr., Tryon, 1987—. Mem. APA, Ill. Psychol. Assn., N.C. Psychol. Assn., S.C. Psychol. Assn. Home: RR 2 Box 290 Tryon NC 28782-9726 Office: Koger Ctr 150 Executive Center Dr Ste 21 Greenville SC 29615-4505

MAGSTADT, MARY ANN, counselor; b. Lesterville, S.D., Nov. 14, 1944; d. Elmer Adolph and Erna Viola (Grosz) Mutschelknaus; m. Roger Don Magstadt, Dec. 16, 1961 (div. May 1988); children: Reed, Kurt. BS, S.D. State U., 1967; MS, U. Nebr., Omaha, 1990. Cert. counselor. Tchr. Estelline (S.D.) Pub. schs., 1967-68, Hanson Pub. Schs., Alexandria, S.D., 1969, Andes Ctrl. Schs., Lake Andes, S.D., 1973-75, Scotland (S.D.) Pub. Schs., 1976-80; police dispatcher Fremont (Nebr.) Police Dept., 1981-89; tchr. Humboldt (Nebr.) Pub. Schs., 1989-90; counselor Genoa (Nebr.) Pub. Schs., 1990-92; elem. counselor Griswold (Iowa) Community Schs., 1992-94, Millard Pub. Schs., Omaha, 1994—. EMT, Griswold Vol. Rescue Squad, 1992-94. Mem. NEA, ACA, Am. Sch. Counselor Assn., Nebr. Counseling Assn., Nebr. Sch. Counselor Assn., Nebr. Soc. Adlerian Psychology, Assn. for Play Therapy. Republican. Lutheran. Home: 9707 Jefferson Plz #1 Omaha NE 68127 Office: Holling Heights Elem Sch 6565 S 136th St Omaha NE 68137

MAGUIRE, DEBORAH A., insurance and securities executive; b. Bronx, N.Y., Apr. 27, 1963; d. Richard and Marie (Odell) Nanfeldt; m. Gregory M. Maguire, Oct. 10, 1987. BA cum laude, Fairfield U., 1985. Lic. ins. and securities broker. Customer svc. rep. Shadow Lawn Savings and Loan Assn., Middletown, N.J., 1984-85; account rep. Hayt, Hayt and Landau, Esqs., Eatontown, N.J., 1985-87; from dist. svc. mgr. to asst. v.p., sr. account mgr. Liberty Securities Corp. (formerly Pamco Securities and Ins), Encino, Calif., 1988-94; now nat. dir. tng. Liberty Securities Corp. (formerly Pamco Securities and Ins), Boston, 1994—. Author: (screenplay) Consent of the Governed, 1983. Asst. to campaign mgr. Howard for Congress, Middletown, 1986, Pallone for Congress, Middletown, 1988; com. person Middletown Dem., 1990, 91; media cons. Jacki Walker for Assembly, Middletown, 1985. Mem. NAFE, Alpha Sigma Nu, Pi Sigma Alpha (v.p. 1984-85). Office: Liberty Securities Corp 600 Atlantic Ave Boston MA 02210-2211

MAGUIRE, MILDRED MAY, chemistry educator, magnetic resonance researcher; b. Leetsdale, Pa., May 7, 1933; d. John and Mildred (Sklarsky) Magura. BS in Chemistry, Carnegie-Mellon U., 1955; MS in Phys. Chemistry, U. Wis., 1960; PhD in Phys. Chemistry, Pa. State U., 1967. Devel. chemist Koppers Co., Monaca, Pa., 1955-58; rsch. chemist Am. Cyanamid Co., Stamford, Conn., 1960-63; asst. prof. chemistry Waynesburg (Pa.) Coll., 1967-70, assoc. prof., 1970-74, prof., 1974—; Leverhulme vis. prof. U. Leicester, Eng., 1980-81, summer 1989; cons. Pitts. Energy Tech. Ctr., summers 1978-86, Oak Ridge Assoc. univs. faculty rsch. participant, summers 1978-80, 82-85. Contbr. articles to sci. jours., chpt. to book. Sec. Waynesburg Women's Club, 1981-82. Recipient Woman of the Yr. award AAUW, Waynesburg, 1983; Cottrell grantee Rsch. Corp. N.Y., 1970-71; Leverhulme vis. fellow U.K., 1980-81; Curie Internat. fellow AAUW, U.K., 1980-81. Mem. AAUP, Am. Chem. Soc. Home: 1550 Crescent Hls Waynesburg PA 15370-1654 Office: Waynesburg Coll College St Waynesburg PA 15370

MAGUIRE-KRUPP, MARJORIE ANNE, corporate executive; b. Stamford, Conn., Apr. 29, 1955; d. Walter Reeves and Jean Elisabeth (Cook) Maguire; m. Joseph Michael Krupp, Jr., Nov. 26, 1983; children: Parnell Joseph Maguire Krupp; stepchildren: Theresa Margaret Krupp, Donna Marie Krupp Jepson, Maura Elizabeth Krupp. BA in Acctg. cum laude, Franklin and Marshall Coll., 1977; MBA in Fin. with honors, NYU, 1983, cert. in real estate, 1986; cert. in French, U. Strasbourg, France, 1971. CPA, Conn., N.J. Supervisory auditor Arthur Young & Co., Stamford, 1976-80; mgr. fin. planning Combustion Engring., Stamford, 1980-84; asst. v.p., mgr. fin. planning and analysis Kidder Peabody & Co., N.Y.C., 1984-87, fin. cons. to brokerage industry, 1988-90; dir. fin. svcs. Mass Mut. Life Ins. Co., 1990-91; pres. Parnell Devel. Corp., 1987—; v.p. fin. Jeremiah Devel. Co., 1987-89; v.p. acctg. Sumitomo Bank Ltd., 1991-92, v.p., dir. internal auditing 1992-94, v.p., dep. chief internal auditor, 1994; v.p./mgr. internal auditing Kidder Peabody & Co., Inc., N.Y.C., 1994—. Advisor Jr. Achievement, Stamford, 1979-80; mem. Inst. Internal Auditors, Met. Opera Guild N.Y.C., 1985-89, Met. Mus. Art, N.Y.C., 1983-90, Mus. Modern Art, N.Y.C., 1983-90; treas., bd. dir. Cliffhouse Condo Assn., Cliffside Park, N.J., 1983-85. Mem. AICPA, N.Y. State Soc. CPAs, Inst. Internal Auditors, Stamford Jaycee Women Club (pres. 1980-81, chmn. bd. 1981-82, Stamford Disting. Svc. award, Outstanding Young Woman of Yr. award, 1980), Phi Beta Kappa (honor soc.), Beta Gamma Sigma (bus. honor soc.). Republican. Presbyterian. Avocations: travel, skiing, sailing, gourmet cooking, golf. Home: 107 Shearwater Ct E Jersey City NJ 07305-5401

MAGUIRE-ZINNI, DEIRDRE, federal community development administrator; b. Bklyn., Oct. 21, 1954; d. James Michael and Dorothy Ursula (Gronske) Maguire; m. Nicholas A. Zinni, Aug. 27, 1977; 1 child, Miles Angelo. BA with honors, SUNY, Stony Brook, 1976; MS, Fla. State U., 1981. Housing specialist Suffolk Community Devel. Corp., Coram, N.Y., 1977-78; planner Palm Beach County Housing and Community Devel., West Palm Beach, Fla., 1980-83, sr. planner, 1983-84, mgr. adminstrn. and ops., 1984-87; fed. community planning and devel. rep. HUD, Jacksonville, Fla., 1987-88; community planning and devel. specialist entitlement cmtys. divsn. HUD, Washington, 1988-91, asst. dir. entitlement communities, 1991-94, dir. entitlement communities divsn., 1994—; staff liaison Affordable Housing Task Force, West Palm Beach, 1985-86, Fla. Community Devel. Assn., 1985-87. Democrat. Roman Catholic.

MAGVAS, LINDA CAROL, critical care nurse; b. Plainfield, N.J., May 18, 1958; d. Wallace Earl and Carol (Hickey) Marhoffer; m. Fred Magvas, Apr. 17, 1982; children: Brian Robert, Eric Wallace. AS, Muhlenberg Hosp., 1981. RN, CCRN, N.J. Staff nurse John F. Kennedy Med. Ctr., Edison, N.J. Home: 31 Brandywine Circle Piscataway NJ 08854

MAGYAWE, WILHELMINA L. G., critical care nurse; b. Manila, Dec. 12, 1948; d. Eler D. and Rosa R. (Legaspi) Guerrero; m. Joselito P. Magyawe, Feb. 23, 1971; children: John-Paul, Johannah. BSN, U. Philippines, 1971, MSN, 1979. Cert. critical care nurse. Staff nurse Royal Alexandra Hosp., Edmonton, Alta., Can.; clin. instr. Philippine Heart Ctr. for Asia, Quezon City, Philippines; staff nurse St. Anthony Hosp., Columbus, Ohio; staff and charge nurse Nyack (N.Y.) Hosp.; vol. lectr. Am. Heart Assn. Recipient Excellence in Clin. Practice award Rockland County Nurse Recognition Day award, 1991, 92. Mem. AACN, ANA, N.Y. State Nurses Assn., Sigma Theta Tau (Epsilon Rho chpt.).

MAHADY, SHEILA MURRAY, mathematics and gifted and talented educator; b. Utica, N.Y.; d. Michael Patrick and Anne Theresa (Devaney) Murray; m. D. Bryan Mahady; children: D. Bryan II, Diane E. BA in Math., Ladycliff Coll., 1962; student, Syracuse U., 1963-64; MS in Edn., Elmira Coll., 1978. Cert math. tchr. secondary level, N.Y. Math. tchr. Troupsburg (N.Y.) Ctrl. Sch., 1979-86; gifted and talented, and computer tech. tchr. Corning (N.Y.) Painted Post Sch. Dist., 1986—; presenter annual confs. Nat. Assn. for Gifted Children, Little Rock, Ark., 1990, L.A., 1992, Atlanta, 1993, World Coun. on Gifted Children, Toronto, Can., 1992. Pres. Immaculate Heart Parish Coun., 1989-92; trustee Elmira-Corning Cmty. Found., Elmira, 1990—. Named Woodrow Wilson Math. Inst. Master Tchr., Woodrow Wilson Fellowship Found., Princeton, N.J., 1985. Mem. AAUW, Corning Tchrs. Assn. (pres. 1993—), Delta Kappa Gamma (pres. Beta Chi chpt. 1992-94). Office: Corning Tchrs Assn 201 Cantigny St Corning NY 14836

MAHADY, SUZANNE JANE, lawyer; b. Latrobe, Pa., May 15, 1950; d. Henry Joseph and Dorothy (Poulin) M. BA, U. Pa., 1972; JD, Duquesne U., 1975. Bar: Pa. 1975, U.D. Dist. Ct. (we. dist.) Pa. 1975; lic. real estate broker. Assoc. Mahady & Mahady, Latrobe and Greensburg, Pa., 1975-89, ptnr., 1989—; instr. continuing edn. Westmoreland C.C., Youngwood, Pa., 1977—; bd. dirs. Westmoreland Fed. Savs. and Loan Assn., Latrobe, 1989—. Pres. YWCA, 1982-84, treas., 1984-86; vol. Am. Cancer Soc., 1987—; active Westmoreland Hosp. Aux. Unit # 10, 1987—. Mem. Pa. Bar Assn., Westmoreland Bar Assn., Loyalhanna Watershed Assn., Latrobe Bus. and Profl. Women's Club (v.p. 1993—). Office: Mahady & Mahady 1308 Ligonier St Latrobe PA 15650

MAHADY-SMITH, CATHERINE MICHELE, lawyer, nurse; b. Syracuse, N.Y., Nov. 25, 1952; d. Martin Francis and Gwendolyn W. (Darling) Mahady; m. Donald H. Smith. BS in Nursing cum laude, Georgetown U., 1974; JD cum laude, Dickinson Sch. Law, 1986. Bar: Pa. 1986, N.J. 1986, U.S. Dist. Ct. (mid. dist.) Pa. 1987. RN Georgetown U. Hosp., Washington, 1974-77; nursing coordinator Atlantic City Med. Ctr., Pomona, N.J., 1979-81; dir. nursing Community Gen. Hosp., Harrisburg, Pa., 1981-83; law clk. Angino & Rovner, Harrisburg, 1985-86, assoc., 1986—. Assoc. editor: Dickinson Law Review, 1984-86. Recipient Murry S. Love Trial Advocacy award Pa. Trial Lawyers, 1986, Corpus Juris Secundum award, 1985, I. Emmanuel Myers Appellate Advocacy award, 1985; Nat. Trial Team Regional winner, 1986. Mem. ABA, ATLA, Pa. Bar Assn., Dauphin County Bar Assn., Pa. Trial Lawyers Assn., Am. Assn. Nurse Attys. Inc., Woolsack Legal Honor Soc., Order of Barristers Trial Advocacy Honor Soc., Sigma Theta Tau, Alpha Sigma Nu. Democrat. Roman Catholic. Office: Angino & Rovner 4503 N Front St Harrisburg PA 17110-1799

MAHAFFEY, MARCIA JEANNE HIXSON, secondary school administrator; b. Scobey, Mont.; d. Edward Goodell and Olga Marie (Frederickson) Hixson; m. Donald Harry Mahaffey (div. Aug. 1976); 1 child, Marcia Anne. BA in English, U. Wash.; MA in Secondary Edn., U. Hawaii, 1967. Cert. secondary and elem. tchr. and adminstr. Tchr. San Lorenzo (Calif.) Sch. Dist., 1958-59; tchr. Castro Valley (Calif.) Sch. Dist., 1959-63, vice prin., 1963-67; vice prin. Sequoia Union High Sch. Dist., Redwood City, Calif., 1967-77, asst. prin., 1977-91, ret., 1991; tchr. trainer Project Impact Sequoia Union Sch. Dist., Redwood City, 1986-91; mem. supr.'s task force for dropout prevention, 1987-91, Sequoia Dist. Goals Commn. (chair sub-com. staff devel. 1988); mentor tchr. selection com., 1987-91; mem. Stanford Program Devel. Ctr. Com., 1987-91; chairperson gifted and talented Castro Valley Sch. Dist.; mem. family svcs. bd., San Leandro, Calif. Vol. Am. Cancer Soc., San Mateo, Calif., 1967, Castro Valley, 1965; Sunday sch. tchr. Hope Luth. Ch., San Mateo, 1970-76; chair Carlmont High Sch. Site Council, Belmont, Calif., 1977-91. Recipient Life Mem. award Parent, Tchr., Student Assn., Belmont, 1984, Svc. award, 1989, Exemplary Svc award Carlmont High Sch., 1989; named Woman of the Week, Castro Valley, 1967, Outstanding Task Force Chair Adopt A Sch. Program San Mateo (Calif.) County, 1990. Mem. AAUW, DAR, Assn. Calif. Sch. Adminstrs. (Project Leadership plaque 1985), Sequoia Dist. Mgmt. Assn. (pres. 1975, treas. 1984, 85), Assn. for Supervision and Curriculum Devel., Met. Mus. Art, Smithsonian Inst., Internat. Platform Assn., Animal Welfare Advocacy, Commonwealth Club of Calif., Delta Kappa Gamma, Alpha Xi Delta.

MAHAJAN, JAYASHREE, business educator; b. Pune, India, Jan. 2, 1958; came to U.S., 1981; d. Captain Y.V. and Shailaja Mahajan; m. Asoo J. Vakharia, Sept. 12, 1981; children: Rohan, Ajit. BA with honors, Bombay U., India, 1977, MA, 1979; MBA, U. Windsor, Ont., can., 1981; PhD in Bus., U. Wis., 1986. Asst. prof. bus. U. Ariz., Tucson, 1986-94, U. Fla., Gainesville, 1994—. Contbr. articles to profl. jours. Grantee NSF, Washington, 1992-93. Mem. Am. Mktg. Inst., Assn. Consumer Rsch., Inst. Mgmt. Scis., Soc. for Judgement and Decision Making. Office: U Fla Coll Bus Adminstrn Gainesville FL 32611

MAHAR, FRACESCA MARCINIAK, air transportation executive, lawyer; b. 1957. BA, Loyola U., 1978, JD, 1981. Ptnr. Mayer, Brown & Platt, Chgo., 1981-93; v.p., sec. UAL Corp., Arlington Heights, Ill., 1993—. Office: UAL Corp 1200 E Algonquin Rd Arlington Heights IL 60005*

MAHER, CHRISTINE RITA, emergency room nurse, sexual assault specialist; b. Great Lakes, Ill., Jan. 21, 1952; d. Medard and Rita (Kobus) Schronski; m. William J. Maher, Aug. 23, 1986. BS, U. Ill., Chgo., 1973; AS, Los Medanos Coll., Pittsburg, Calif., 1980. RN, Calif.; cert. BLS, ACLS, MICN; cert. emergency nurse, trauma nurse care, sexual assault nurse examiner, Calif. Nursing asst. Contra Costa County Hosp., Martinez, Calif., 1974-78, surg. technician, 1978-80, RN, 1980-84; emergency room nurse, educator, com. mem. North Bay Med. Ctr., Fairfield, Calif., 1984-91; co-founder ind. nursing group practice, co-dir. William J. Maher RN, Fairfield, Calif., 1991—. Day camp dir. Benicia (Calif.) Recreation Dept., 1980. Mem. AACN, Emergency Nurses Assn. (cert. TNCC), Nat. Nurses in Bus. Assn. Office: William J Maher RN 906 Hidden Cove Way Suisun City CA 94585

MAHER, FRAN, advertising agency executive; b. Chgo., June 22, 1938; d. Edward Stephan and Virginia Rose (Harrington) M.; m. Anthony Peter Petrella, Sept. 17, 1957; children: Roland, Louis, Marcus. Student (univ. scholar) U. Minn., 1956-57; student Spectrum Inst., 1968-71; BA summa cum laude, Kean Coll. N.J., 1979. Office mgr. Lead Supplies, Inc., Mpls., 1957-59; freelance artist and writer, Warren, N.J., 1968-72; prin. Visuals, Warren, N.J., 1974-79; pres. Fran Maher, Inc., Bound Brook, N.J., 1980—; dir. Parent Edn. Advocacy Tng. Center, Alexandria, Va., 1979-85. Officer Friends of Weigand Farm, Milton, N.J., 1977-80, Somerset County Assn. for Retarded Citizens, 1982—, pres., bd. dirs. 1987-89; officer, bd. dirs. Assn. Retarded Citizens N.J., 1989—, chair residential quality life com., 1991-94; trustee Peoplecare Ctr., Inc., 1990-93; bd. dirs. Somerset County Coalition on Affordable Housing, 1991-92; rep. Congress of States, The Arc of USA, 1993—; founding mem. Flintlock Boys' Club. Recipient N.J. Art Dirs. Show award, 1978, 1st place award in graphics Watchung Art Center, 1980. Mem. Art Dirs. Club N.J., Am. Women's Econ. Devel. Corp., Advt. Agy. Network

Internat., Internat. Platform Assn., Somerset County C. of C. (bd. dirs. 1989-94, chair affordable housing 1990-93). Office: 200 E Union Ave Bound Brook NJ 08805-1762

MAHER, JANET LYNN, artist, educator; b. Waterbury, Conn., Apr. 21, 1954; d. Edward James and Joan Arlene (Murphy) M.; m. Manuel Rettinger, July 7, 1988. BS in Art Edn., So. Conn. State U., 1976; MA in Studio Art, U. N.Mex., 1981. Instr. art, dept. chair Holy Cross H.S., Waterbury, 1976-79; coord. edn. Tamarind Inst., Albuquerque, 1990-93; free-lance instr. art Albuquerque, 1988—; juror State Fair Grounds, Albuquerque, 1992, 94, Kimo Gallery, Albuquerque, 1993. One-woman shows include Bradley U., Peoria, Ill., 1975, Davidson Galleries, Seattle, 1978, Gallery One-Forty-Eight, New Haven, Conn., 1978, John Slade Ely House, New Haven, 1979, Va. Commonwealth U., Richmond, 1984, Photogenesis Gallery, Albuquerque, 1984, Ruth Ramberg Gallery, Albuquerque, 1984, 87, Ctr. for Contemporary Art, Santa Fe, 1986, U. N.Mex., Los Alamos, 1991; group shows include John Slade Ely House, New Haven, 1978 (1st prize 49th Ann. Conn. Women Artists Exhbn. 1978), 80, Downtown Ctr. for Arts, Albuquerque, 1979, Univ. Art Mus., U. N.Mex., 1981, Art Inst. Chgo., 1981, Mus. Fine Arts, Santa Fe, 1984, 87 (Merit award 1987), 93, Jonson Gallery, Albuquerque, 1984, 94, Andrew Smith Gallery, Santa Fe, 1986, Wieghardt Gallery, Evanston, Ill., 1988, Raw Space, Albuquerque, 1988, 90, 94, Kimo Gallery, Albuquerque, 1988, 89, 92, 93, Linda Durham Gallery, Albuquerque, Coll. Santa Fe, 1988, 94 (Award of Merit), Centennial Gallery, Albuquerque, 1989, Graham Gallery, Albuquerque, 1989, 93, Smithsonian Regional Ctr., Detroit, 1989, Mus. Fine Arts, Sante Fe (Award of Merit 1993, Cone 10 Gallery, Albuquerque, 1992, Fine Arts Gallery, Albuquerque, 1992, 94, San Diego Art Inst., Braithwaite Fine Arts Gallery, Cedar City, Utah, 1994, Creative Arts Workshop, New Have, Conn., 1994, Mpls. Coll. Art and Design, 1994, Comm. Arts Gallery, Kenosha, Wis., 1995, others; permanent collections include U. N.Mex. Mus. Fine Arts, U. N.Mex.-Los Alamos, N.Y. Pub. Libr., N.Y.C., Oliver LaFarge Libr., Santa Fe, Mus. Fine Arts, Santa Fe, Brigham Young U., Provo, Utah, Ariz. State U., Tempe, others; author artist's books: Drawing Shelter, 1993, The Anatomy of Solitude Vol. I, 1993, Vol. II, 1994, Vol. III, 1995. Active Albuquerque Larger Met. Area Comm. Garden Task Force. Recipient Art in Pub. Places Commn. N.Mex. Arts Divsn., 1989, 90, Award of Merit Mus. Fine Arts, Sante Fe, 1987, 93, 1st Prize Conn. Women Artists Exhbn., 1978. Mem. Ctr. Book Arts, Franklin Furnace, Nat. Mus. Women in Arts, Albuquerque United Artists Coll. Art Assn., Am. Comm. Garden Assn.

MAHER, TERRY MARINA, religious organization administrator; b. Phila., Oct. 13, 1955; d. Thomas Michael and Marion Teresa (Corbett) M. BA in History and Religious Studies, U. San Diego, 1977; M in Theol. Studies, Cath. Theol. U., Chgo., 1989. Dir. religious edn. Diocese of San Diego, 1977-80; dir. religious edn. Archdiocese of Cin., 1982-84, assoc. dir. youth ministry, 1984-87; pastoral assoc. Diocese of Toledo, 1989—; state chancellor Internat. Educators for Peace Edn. Sec. social concerns bd. Met. Chs. United, Dayton; mem. justice com. Sisters of the Precious Blood; active tour to explore conditions in Nicaragua, New Orleans, 1983, 10-day tour of Guatemala, 1991; founder, v.p. bd. dirs. Care and Share Ctr. City of Sandusky; Ohio state chancellor Internat. Educators for World Peace; v.p. Care & Share, Inc. of Erie County, 1993—. Mem. Sanctuary, Pledge of Resistance, Internat. Assn. Educators for Peace (state chancellor). Democrat. Home: 1219 E Perkins Ave Apt 5J Sandusky OH 44870-5057 Office: Saints Peter & Paul Ch 510 Columbus Ave Sandusky OH 44870-2780

MAHLER, STEPHANIE IRENE, marketing executive; b. Bennington, Vt., Jan. 29, 1952; d. Guenther Alexander and Barbara Irene (Overlock) M. BA, Allegheny Coll., 1973. Customer service rep. Albany (N.Y.) Felt Co., 1974-77; order systems analyst Miller Brewing Co., Milw., 1977-78, area mgr., 1978-80, regional adminstr., 1980-83, price promotions mgr., 1983-85, asst. brand mgr., 1985-88, mgr. mktg. projects, 1988-90; market mgr. Johnson Controls, Inc., Milw., 1990-92; sr. agt. AMEX Life Assurance Co., Milw., 1992-93; asst. to the pres. Performance Enhancement Psychol. and Phys. Therapy Svcs., Brookfield, Wis., 1994, mktg. dir., 1994—. Mem. pres.'s club Albany Area C. of C., Albany, 1975-76; mgmt. advisor Jr. Achievment, 1973-74. Named One of Outstanding Young Women of Am., Montgomery, Ala., 1983; Presdl. scholar, 1969, Alden scholar Allegheny Coll., Meadville, Pa., 1970-73. Mem. NOW (at-large), Phi Beta Kappa. Home: 8325 N Links Way Milwaukee WI 53217-2821

MAHNK, KAREN, law librarian, legal assistant; b. Bklyn., July 13, 1956; d. James V. and Mary M. (Jones) Mascari; 1 child, Adam Eugene. Student, Baruch Coll., 1974-75, Miami-Dade Community Coll., 1986-89, St. Thomas U., 1994. Asst. libr. Mershon, Sawyer et al, Miami, Fla., 1976-79; libr., legal asst. Steel Hecton & Davis, Miami, 1980-84; libr. Valdes-Fauli, et al, Miami, 1984-94, Pub. Defender's Office, 11th Jud. Cir., Miami, 1994—; asst. coord. Broward County Multi-Family Devel. Recycling Program, 1990-91. Chair ways and means com. Palm Cove Elem. PTO, 1993—; active vol. Broward County Guardian Ad Litum Program, 1989-92. Mem. ABA (assoc. stat., family law sect., law libr. affiliate), Am. Assn. Law Librs., Southeastern Assn. Law Librs., South Fla. Assn. Law Librs. (bd. dirs. 1988-89, chair constn. and bylaws commn. 1988-91, sec. 1983-84, v.p.-elect 1986-88, nominating com. 1992, sec. 1993—), Spl. Librs. Assn., Internat. Platform Assn. Democrat. Baptist. Office: 1320 NW 14th St Ste 550 Miami FL 33125

MAHON, PAMELA YOUNG, nursing educator; b. Bklyn.; d. John Patrick and Ruth (Riley) Young; m. Kevin Walter Mahon, Oct. 22, 1983; 1 child, Meaghan Claire. BS, SUNY, Bklyn., 1975; MA, NYU, 1980, postgrad., 1991—. Staff nurse gen. med. VA, Bklyn., 1975-77, staff and charge nurse surg. ICU, 1977-79, community health coord., 1979-83, asst. chief nurse community health, 1983-86; asst. dir. ambulatory care N.Y.C. Health and Hosps. Corp., 1986-89, DON spl. projects, 1989-91; asst. prof. nursing Kingsborough Community Coll.-CUNY, Bklyn., 1991—; panel mem. N.Y. State Legislature's Nurse of Distinction Program, Albany, 1989—; participant and presenter in field. Fellow Coro Found., N.Y.C., 1982; mem. St. Patrick's Home Sch. Assn., Bklyn., 1990—. Mem. ANA (cert.), N.Y. State Nurses Assn., Dist. 13 N.Y. Counties Nurses Assn. (Lavinia Dock Disting. Svc. award 1991), Dist. 14 Nurses Assn., Am. Nurses Found., Nurses Orgn. of the VA, Sigma Theta Tau (Upsilon Chi chpt.). Democrat. Roman Catholic. Home: 215 93rd St Brooklyn NY 11209-6805 Office: Kingsborough Community Coll M401 2001 Oriental Blvd # M401 Brooklyn NY 11235-2398

MAHONE, BARBARA JEAN, automotive company executive; b. Notasulga, Ala., Apr. 19, 1946; d. Freddie Douglas M. and Sarah Lou (Simpson). B.S., Ohio State U., 1968; M.B.A., U. Mich., 1972; P.M.D., Harvard U. Bus. Sch., 1981. Systems analyst GM, Detroit, 1968-71, sr. staff asst., 1972-74, mgr. career planning, 1975-78; dir. personnel adminstrn. GM, Rochester, N.Y., 1979-81; mgr. indsl. relations GM, Warren, Ohio, 1982-83; dir. human resources mgmt. Chevrolet-Pontiac-Can. group GM, 1984-86; dir. gen. pers. and pub. affairs Inland div. GM, Dayton, Ohio, 1986-88; gen. dir. pers. Inland Fisher Guide div. GM, Detroit, 1989-91, gen. dir. employee benefits, 1991-93; chmn. Fed. Labor Rels. Authority, Washington, 1983-84; group dir. pers. North Am. Truck Platforms, 1994—; chmn. Spl. Panel on Appeals; dir. Metro Youth; mem. bd. govs. U. Mich. Alumni. Bd. dirs. ARC, Rochester, 1979-82; bd. dirs. Urban League of Rochester, 1979-82; mem. human resorces com YMCA, Rochester, 1980-82; mem. exec. bd. Nat. Council Negro Women; mem. allocations com. United Way of Greater Rochester; bd. dirs. Rochester Area Multiple Sclerosis. Recipient public relations award Nat. Assn. Bus. and Profl. Women, 1976; recipient award for excellence Gen. Motors. Corp., 1978, Mary McLeod Bethune award Nat. Council Negro Women, 1977, Senate Resolution Mich. State Legislature, 1980; named Outstanding Woman Mich. Chronicle, 1975, Woman of Yr. Nat. Assn. Bus. and Profl. Women, 1978, Disting. Bus. Person U. Mich., 1978, 1 of 11 Mich. Women Redbook Mag., 1978. Mem. Nat. Black M.B.A. Assn. (bd. dirs., nat. pres. Disting. Service award, bd. dirs., nat. pres. Outstanding M.B.A.), Women Econ. Club. (bd. dirs.), Indsl. Relations Research Assn., Internat. Assn. for Personnel Women, Engring. Soc. Detroit. Republican. Home: 175 Kirkwood Ct Bloomfield Hills MI 48304-2927 Office: NATP Mail Code 3108-16 31 E Judson St Pontiac MI 48342-2206

MAHONEY, LINDA KAY, mathematics educator; b. Bay Shore, N.Y., June 8, 1951; d. James Nathaniel and Katherine Pauline (Booth) Palmer Jr.; m. Peter Allan Mahoney, Jr., June 5, 1976; children: Matthew J., Michael J., Patrick A. BS, U. Md., 1972; MEd, 1979; postgrad., R.I. Coll., 1988-89, Providence Coll., 1989-90. Tchr. math. Prince George's County Pub. Schs., Benjamin Tasker Jr. High, Bowie, Md., 1973-76; tchr. substitute Warwick (R.I.) Pub. Schs., 1987-90, tchr. math., 1990-91; tchr. math. Ctrl. Tex. Coll., P.R., 1992—. Vol. Sherman Elem. Sch., Warwick, 1989-90, Rohr Elem. Sch., Chula Vista, Calif., 1985-87. Mem. Nat. Coun. Tchrs. Math., ASCD. Republican. Lutheran.

MAHONEY, MARGARET ELLERBE, foundation executive; b. Nashville, Oct. 24, 1924; d. Charles Hallam and Leslie Nelson (Savage) M.; BA magna cum laude, Vanderbilt U., 1946; LHD (hon.), Meharry Med. Coll., 1977, U. Fla., 1980, Med. Coll. Pa., 1982, Williams Coll., 1983, Smith Coll., 1985, Beaver Coll., 1985, Brandeis U., 1989, Marymount Coll., 1990, Rush U., 1993. Fgn. affairs officer State Dept., Washington, 1946-53; exec. assoc., assoc. sec. Carnegie Corp., N.Y.C., 1953-72; v.p. Robert Wood Johnson Found., Princeton, N.J., 1972-80; pres. Commonwealth Fund, N.Y.C., 1980-94; pres. MEM Assocs., Inc., N.Y.C., 1995—. Contbr. articles to profl. jours. Trustee John D. and Catherine T. Mac Arthur Found., 1985—, Dole Found., 1984—, Smith Coll., 1988-93, Columbia U., 1991—; vis. fellow Sch. Architecture and Urban Planning, Princeton U., 1973-80; bd. dirs. Council on Found., 1982-88; mem. N.Y.C. Commn. on the Yr. 2000, 1985-87, MIT Corp., 1984-89; bd. govs. Am. Stock Exchange, 1987-92; adv. bd. Office of the Chief Med. Examiner, N.Y.C., 1987—, Barnard Coll, Inst. Med. Research, 1986-92; vice chmn. N.Y.C. Mayor's Com. for Pub./Pvt. Partnerships, 1990-93; bd. dirs. Alliance for Aging Rsch., 1987—, Overseas Devel. Coun., 1988—, Nat. Found. Center for Disease Control and Prevention, Inc., 1994—; mem. vestry Parish of Trinity Ch., 1982-89, 91—; chmn. Atlantic Fellowships Selection Com., 1994—. Recipient Frank H. Lahey Meml. award, 1984, Women's Forum award, 1989, Walsh McDermott award, 1992, Disting. Grantmaker award Coun. Founds., 1993, Edward R. Loveland award Am. Coll. Physicians, 1994, Special Recognition award AAMC, 1994, Merit medal Lotos Club, 1994. Mem. AAAS, Inst. Medicine of NAS, Am. Acad. Arts and Scis., Am. Philos. Soc., Coun. Fgn. Rels., Fin. Women's Assn. N.Y., N.Y. Acad. Medicine (vice chmn. bd. govs.), N.Y. Acad. Scis., Alpha Omega Alpha. Office: MEM Assocs Inc 521 5th Ave Ste 2010 New York NY 10175

MAHONEY, MARGARET ELLIS, executive assistant; b. Detroit, Mar. 17, 1929; d. Seth Wiley and Mildred Elizabeth (Hill) Ellis; m. Stephen Bedell Smith, Mar. 15, 1956 (div. Oct. 1962); 1 child, Laura Elizabeth; m. Patrick John Mahoney, Sept. 1, 1972 (dec.). BA, Butler U., 1953. Copywriter Hook Drugs Inc., Indpls., 1953; continuity dir. Sta. WXLW, Indpls., 1954-57; ptnr. Steve Smith and Assocs. Advt., Indpls., 1956-62; account mgr. Sive Advt., Cin., 1963-64, Associated Advt., Cin., 1964-65; copywriter SupeRX Drugs Inc., Cin., 1965-72; promotion writer U.S. News and World Report, Washington, 1974; asst. mgr. advt. Drug Fair, Alexandria, Va., 1975-82; dir. advt. Cosmetic and Fragrance Concepts Inc., Beltsville, Md., 1982-89; cons. Woodbridge, Va., 1989-94; asst. to real estate agt. Carmel, Ind., 1994—. vestrywoman St. Matthews Episcopal Ch., Cin., 1969-71; hosp. chmn. Sleepy Hollow Citizens Assn., Falls Church, Va., 1973; vol. resident assoc. program Smithsonian Instn., Washington, 1989-94; chmn. membership and pub. rels. Friends Chinn Park Regional Libr., Woodbridge, Va., 1991-94. Mem. Potomac Valley Aquarium Soc. (past treas., past sec., editor jour.), Am. Cichlid Assn. (nat. pub. rels. chair 1985-90), Delta Delta Delta. Republican. Home: 9850 Greentree Dr Carmel IN 46032

MAHONEY, MARY DZURKO, educator; b. McKeesport, Pa., Apr. 5, 1946; d. William Thomas and Anne Cecelia (Basarab) Dzurko; m. Thomas Francis Mahoney; 1 child, David. BA in Eng. Lit., U. Pitts., 1968; MA in Teaching in Elem. Edn., George Washington U., 1969; MS in Applied Behavioral Counseling, Johns Hopkins U., 1993. Tchr. Seven Locks Elem. Sch., Bethesda, Md., 1970-73, Tuckerman Elem. Sch., Potomac, Md., 1973-78, Stedwick Elem. Sch., Gaithersburg, Md., 1976-78; sub. tchr. Barnesville (Md.) Sch., 1985-86; home instr. Montgomery County Pub. Schs., Rockville, Md., 1984—; instr. writing Montgomery Coll., 1990—. Active PTA, Poolesville, Md., 1990—; vol. counselor Women's Commn.; guide Youth Svcs. Mem. Woman's Club Upper Montgomery County (sec. 1986, scholarship com. 1988), Phi Delta Gamma (historian 1974-75, newsletter editor 1975-76). Democrat. Roman Catholic.

MAHONEY, REBECCA SUE, counselor; b. Cin., Nov. 2, 1954; d. Harrison Lucius and Hazel Evlynn (Dillon) Underwood; m. David Paul Mahoney Jr., Apr. 29, 1978; children: David Paul III, Adam Christopher. BS in Christian Edn., Cin. Bible Coll., 1977; MA in Counseling, Liberty U., 1993. Coord. children's svcs. Jay County Pub. Libr., Portland, Ind., 1981-84; writer Standard Publ., Cin., 1986—; counselor emergency svcs. Fairfield Med. Ctr., Lancaster, Ohio, 1993—; dir. Pregnancy Distress Ctr. of Fairfield County, 1993—; speaker and writer in field. Bd. dirs. Youth Adv. Coun., Columbus, Ind., 1987, 88; sec. bd. Crisis Pregnancy Ctr., Columbus, 1988. Named Outstanding Young Woman of Am., 1977, 88, Outstanding Libr. Assn., Ind. Libr. Assn., 1985. Mem. ACA, Am. Assn. Christian Counselors, Assn. for Spiritual, Ethical and Religious Values in Counseling. Republican. Mem. Ch. of Christ. Office: Fairfield Med Ctr 401 E Ewing St Lancaster OH 43130

MAHONEY, SHEILA IRENE, middle school educator; b. Dallas, Apr. 6, 1945; d. Raymond Francis and June Mary (Hoffman) M. BS in Edn., Ohio State U., 1970; MS in Adminstrn. Supervision, Nova U., Ft. Lauderdale, Fla., 1974-78. Tchr. 4th, 5th grades Avalon Elem. Sch. Collier County Schs., Naples, Fla., 1974-78; tchr. lang. arts, 11th grade Lely High Sch. Collier County Schs., Naples, 1978-80; tchr. lang. arts Gulfview Middle Sch. Collier County Schs., Naples, 1980—; mem. adv. bd. Collier County Reading Coun., Naples, 1975-78. Mem. ASCD, Collier County Reading Coun., Ohio State Alumni Assn., Phi Delta Kappa (adv. bd., historian Naples, 1988-91). Republican. Roman Catholic. Home: 255 2nd Ave S Naples FL 33940-5957

MAI, ELIZABETH HARDY, lawyer; b. Ithaca, N.Y., Nov. 7, 1948; d. William Frederick and Barbara Lee (Morrell) M.; m. Edward John Gobrecht III, May 19, 1990. BA in Am. Studies, Cornell U., 1970; JD, Dickinson Sch. Law, 1975. Bar: Pa. 1975, U.S. Dist. Ct. (mid. dist.) Pa. 1976. Atty. Keystone Legal Svcs., Inc., State Coll., Pa., 1975-76; asst. atty. gen. Pa. Dept. Commerce, Harrisburg, Pa., 1976-77; chief counsel Pa. Dept. Commerce, Harrisburg, 1978; assoc. Wolf, Block, Schorr and Solis-Cohen, Phila., 1979-83, ptnr., 1986—; v.p., gen. counsel EQK Ptnrs., Bala Cynwyd, Pa., 1983-86; chair environ. dept. Wolf, Block, Schorr and Solis-Cohen; mem. long range planning and mktg. com. Loan Workout Group; co-chair Pa. state govt. affairs Internat. Coun. Shopping Ctrs.; founding dir., mem. Comml. Real Estate Women, Phila.; bd. dels. Nat. Network Comml. Real Estate Women; adj. prof. Villanova (Pa.) U. Sch. Law, 1986—. Active Cornell U. Real Estate Coun., 1990—. Mem. ABA, Am. Coll. Real Estate Lawyers, Pa. Bar Assn., Phila. Bar Assn. Office: Wolf Block Schorr and Solis-Cohen 15th & Chestnut Sts 12th fl Philadelphia PA 19102

MAIBENCO, HELEN CRAIG, anatomist, educator; b. New Deer, Aberdeenshire, Scotland, June 9, 1917; came to U.S., 1917; d. Benjamin C. and Mary (Brown) Craig; children: Thomas Allen, Douglas Craig. BS, Wheaton (Ill.) Coll., 1948; MS, DePaul U., 1950; PhD, U. Ill., Chgo., 1956. Asst. prof., assoc. prof., then prof. U. Ill., Chgo., 1956-73; prof. Rush U., Chgo., 1973-86, prof. emeritus, 1993—; anatomist dept. rehab. medicine Rush-Presbyn.-St. Luke's Med. Ctr., Chgo., 1986—, rsch. cons., 1973—; prof. emeritus Rush-U. Chgo., 1986—; cons. on grant application NIH, Bethesda, Md. Contbr. articles to profl. jours. Mem. AAAS, Endocrine Soc., Am. Assn. Anatomists, Sigma Xi. Republican. Presbyterian. Home: 1324 S Main St Wheaton IL 60187-6480

MAICKI, G. CAROL, former state senator, consultant; b. Holden, Mass., July 16, 1936; d. John Arne and Mary Emily (Bumpus) Mannisto; m. Henry F. Maicki, May 4, 1957; children: Henry III, Matthew, Scott, Julia, Mary. BA, U. Mich., 1978. Exec. dir. Sweetwater County Task Force/Sexual Assault, Rocksprings, Wyo., 1978-81; program mgr. Family Violence/Sexual Assault, Cheyenne, Wyo., 1981-85; coord. S.D. Coalition Against Domestic Violence and Sexual Assault, Black Hawk, 1985-90; state senator S.D. Legislature, Pierre, 1990-92; cons. Black Hawk, 1990-94, Nat. Coalition Against Domestic Violence, 1987; speaker Nat. Coalition Against Sexual Assault, Portland, Oreg., 1987, Rutger Ctr. for Women in Politics, San Diego, 1991; mem. planning com. Office for Victims of Crime, U.S. Justice, Phoenix, 1989. Author: (manuels) Operating Standards, 1984, Rules and Regulations, 1986, Shelter Procedures, 1987. Com. mem. Health and Human Svc. State Legislature, Pierre, 1990-92, local govt., 1990-92; commn. mem. local govt. study commn., Pierre, 1990-92; bd. dirs. Crisis Intervention Svcs., 1991—; apptd. def. adv. com. on women in svcs. Sec. of Def., 1995—. Recipient award Gov. Wyo., 1985, Spirit of Peace award Women Against Violence, Rapid City, 1993, U.S. Dept. of Justice award, 1994. Mem. S.D. Alliance for Mentally Ill, Rapid City Womens Network, S.C. Advocacy Network for Women, Lions (Black Hawk), Women Against Violence. Democrat. Home: PO Box 375 Black Hawk SD 57718-0375

MAIDES-KEANE, SHIRLEY ALLEN, psychologist; b. Roanoke Rapids, N.C., Sept. 16, 1951; d. John Thomas and Mary Shirley (Allen) Maides; m. John Thomas Keane, Nov. 8, 1980; children: Josephine Claire Keane, Michael Allen Keane. BA, U. N.C., 1973; MA, Vanderbilt U., 1975, PhD, 1979. Intern U. Calif., Davis, 1977-78; fellow U. Chgo. and Michael Reese Hosp Med. Ctr., Chgo., 1978-79; psychologist Chgo., 1980-81, pvt. practice, 1981—; mem. allied profl. staff Linden Oaks Hosp.; adj. faculty Ill. Sch. Profl. Psychology, 1980-82; mgmt. cons. Mgmt. Sci. Assocs., 1982-86. Contbr. chpt. to book, articles to profl. jours. Mem. APA, Ill. Psychol. Assn., Assn. DuPage County Psychologists in Profl. Practice (past pres.). Methodist. Office: 1100 Jorie Blvd Ste 255 Oak Brook IL 60521

MAIER, DIANA ELIZABETH, epidemiologist, photographer; b. Irvington, N.J., Nov. 11, 1957; d. Erich Joseph and Hildegard (Hennemann) M.; divorced. BS, Rutgers U., 1979; M in Pub. Health, UCLA, 1981. Registered med. technologist; cert. in infection control and healthcare quality. Immunohematology North Jersey Blood Ctr., East Orange, 1979-80; hematology technologist Santa Monica (Calif.) Med. Ctr., 1980-81; community liaison team coord. immunization program N.Y.C. Dept. Health, 1981; epidemiologist St. Joseph's Hosp. and Med. Ctr., Paterson, N.J., 1982-88, supr. epidemiology and infection control, 1988-91; project coord. Mountain Plains Regional AIDS Edn. Tng. Ctr., Denver, 1991-93; dir. epidemiology and quality improvement The Health Care Initiative, Inc., Denver, 1993-95; dir. rsch. and epidemiology Primera Healthcare, LLC, Denver, 1995—; mem. AIDS adv. com. licensure reform project N.J. State Dept. Health, Trenton, 1986-88; developer, speaker AIDS roving symposia, Lawrenceville, N.J., 1989-91; expert cons. Community Health Care, Daycare and Emergency Svcs., 1985-91; speaker, writer, presenter sci. paper on measles First Internat. Conf. Hosp. Infection Soc., London, 1987. Guest commentator on AIDS and HIV Infection Paterson Teen Scene, 1990. Authored legislation regarding Allied Health Edn., N.J., 1988-91; team walker, vol. Walkathon, March of Dimes, Sussex County/Bergen County, N.J., 1988-91, fundraiser, Fairfield, N.J., 1990; expert cons. assembly and senate N.J. State Pub. Health Coun., Trenton, 1988-91. Mem. APHA, Nat. Assn. Quality Assurance Profls., Assn. Health Svc. Rsch., Assn. Practitioners in Infection Control, Colo. Healthcare Outcomes and Utilization Rsch. Coalition (founder 1993), Phi Beta Kappa, Beta Beta Beta. Home: 14330 W 5th Ave Golden CO 80401-5226 Office: The Healthcare Initiative Inc 600 Grant St Ste 700 Denver CO 80203

MAIER, DONNA JANE-ELLEN, history educator; b. St. Louis, Feb. 20, 1948; d. A. Russell and Mary Virginia Maier; m. Stephen J. Rapp, Jan. 3, 1981; children: Alexander John, Stephanie Jane-Ellen. BA, Coll. of Wooster, 1969; MA, Northwestern U., 1972, PhD, 1975. Asst. prof. U. Tex. at Dallas, Richardson, 1975-78; asst. prof. history U. No. Iowa, Cedar Falls, 1978-81, assoc. prof., 1981-86, prof., 1986—; cons. Scott, Foresman Pub., Glenview, Ill., 1975-94; editl. cons. Children's Press, 1975-76, Macmillan Pubs., 1989-90, Haper-Collins Pubs., 1994. Co-author: History and Life, 1976, 4th edit., 1990; author: Priests and Power, 1983; co-editor African Economic History, 1992—; contbr. articles to profl. jours., essays to books. Mem. Iowa Dem. Cen. Com., 1982-90, chmn. budget com., 1986-90; chmn. 3d Congl. Dist. Cen. Com., 1986-88. Fulbright-Hays fellow, Ghana, 1972, Arab Republic Egypt, 1987; fellow Am. Philos. Soc., London, 1978. Mem. Am. Hist. Assn., African Studies Assn., AAUW (fellow Ghana 1973), Quota Club. Home: 219 Highland Blvd Waterloo IA 50703-4229 Office: U No Iowa Dept History Cedar Falls IA 50614

MAIL, PATRICIA DAVISON, public health specialist; b. Kamloops, B.C., Can., Dec. 10, 1940; d. George Allen and Constance (Davison) M.; BS, U. Ariz., 1963, MA, 1970; MS, Smith Coll., 1965; M.P.H., Yale U., 1967; postgrad. Seattle U., 1974, U. Md., 1988—. Commd. officer USPHS, 1970—, chief health edn. br. Portland Indian Health Svc., 1979-86, dep. chief field ops. Nat. Health Svc. Corps., 1986-87, dep. chief clin., prof. activities bd., 1987-88; chief HRSA HIV/AIDS Svcs. Br., 1988; dep. dir. Office PHS Surgeon Gen., 1989; officer pers. specialist, chief profl. edn. ADAMHA, 1990, chief evaluation sect., 1991—; analyst Nat. Inst. Alcohol Abuse and Alcoholism; mem. faculty Seattle U., 1974-78; commr. Nat. Commn. Health Edn. Credentialing, chair, 1993-94; evaluation liaison Nat. Inst. Alcohol Abuse and Alcoholism. Recipient Early Career award Public Health Edn. sect. Am. Public Health Assn., 1979, USPHS Service Plaque, 1979, 86, Exemplary Svc. medal Surgeon Gen., 1990, USPHS Commendation medal, 1981, 86, 90, Outstanding Service medal, 1986, Merit Svc. award USUHS, 1991, Surgeon Gen.'s Medallion, 1993; USPHS trainee Yale U., 1965-67; NDEA grantee, 1968-70. Fellow Soc. Applied Anthropology; mem. AAAS, APHA, AAHPERD, Soc. Public Health Edn., Med. Anthropology Soc., Am. Sch. Health Assn., Assn. Mil. Surgeons U.S., Res. Officers Assn., Commd. Officers Assn. USPHS, Smith Coll. Alumnae Assn., Delta Kappa, Eta Sigma Gamma. Episcopalian. Author: (with D.R. McDonald) Tulapai to Tokay, 1980; editor SOPHE Sounds, 1976-86; contbr. articles to profl. jours. Home: 142 Monroe St Rockville MD 20850-2502 Office: Nat Inst Alcohol Abuse and Alcoholism 6000 Executive Blvd Ste 505 Bethesda MD 20892-7003

MAILHOT, LOUISE, judge; b. Montreal, Que., Can., July 23, 1940; d.Gerard and Jeanne (Bousquet) M.; m. Michael Oliver Lloyd, 1974; 2 children. BA, U. Montreal, LLL. Atty. pvt. practice, 1966-80, Justice Superior Ct., 1980-87, Justice Ct. Appeals, 1987—. Office: Ct Appeals, 1 rue Notre Dame Est # 1786, Montreal, PQ Canada H2Y 1B6

MAILLET, ANTONINE, author, educator; b. Bouctouche, N.B., Can., May 10, 1929; d. Leonine Maillet and Virginie Cormier. BA, Coll. Notre-Dame D'Acadie, 1950; MA, Moncton U., N.B., 1959, D es L (hon.), 1972; LLD, Montreal U., Que., Can., 1962; PhD, Laval U., Que., 1970, DLitt (hon.), 1988; D es L (hon.), Acadia U., 1980, St. Mary's U., 1980, Laurentian U., 1981, McGill U., 1982; DLitt (hon.), Carleton U., 1978, Mount Allison U., 1979, St. Thomas U., 1986, Mt. St-Vincent U., 1987, U. Ste-Anne, 1987, Bowling Green U., 1988, Simon Fraser U., 1989. U. Maine, 1990, Concordia U., 1990; LLD (hon.), U. Alta., 1979, Dalhousie U., 1981, U. Toronto, 1982, Queen's U., 1982, St. Francis Xavier U., 1984, Lyon U., 1989, B.C. U., 1991, Royal Mil. Coll. Can., 1992; LittD (hon.), U. New Eng., 1994. Prof. Coll. Notre-Dame D'Acadie, Moncton, 1954-60, Moncton U., 1965-67, Coll. des Jesuites, Que., 1968-69, Laval U., Que., 1971-74, Montreal U., 1974-75, Nat. Drama Sch., Montreal, 1989-91; writer N.B. Hist. Resources Adminstrn., Central Registry, Fredericton, N.B.; assoc. prof. French studies Moncton U., chancelor, 1989; guest Michener Found., Queen's U., 1991. Author: (novels) Pointe-aux-coques, 1958 (Prix Champlain, 1960), On a mangé la dune, 1962, Don l'orignal, 1972 (Prix du Gouverneur General du Can. 1972), Par derrière chez mon père, 1972, Mariàggélas, 1973 (Prix des Volcans (France) 1975, Grand Prix Litteraire de la ville de Montreal, 1973, Prix France Can. 1975, Prix litteraire La Presse 1976), Emmanuel a Joseph a Davit, 1975, Les Cordes-de-Bois, 1977 (Prix des 4 jures 1978), Pélagie-la-charrette, 1979 (Prix Goncourt 1979); Cent ans dans les bois, 1981, La Gribouille, 1982, Crache-à-Pic, 1984; Le Huitième Jour, 1986, L'Oursiade, 1990, Les Confessions de Jeanne de Valois, 1992; (plays): Poire-Acre, 1960 (Best Can. Play Vancouver Theatre Festival, 1960), Les Jeux d'Enfants sont faits, 1960 (Prix du Conseil des Arts 1960), Les Crasseux, 1968, Gapi et Sullivan, 1973, Evangéline Deusse, 1975, Gapi, 1976, La Veuve Enragée, 1977, Le Bourgeois Gentleman, 1978, La Contrebandière, 1981, Les drolatiques, horrifiques et épouvantables aventures de Panurge, ami de Pantagruel, 1983, Garrochés en Paradis, 1986, Margot la Folle, 1987, William S, 1991; (translations) Richard III (Shakespeare), 1989, La Nuit des Rois (Shakespeare), 1993 (Prix de la traduction l'Association québécoise de critiques de théâtre saison 1992-93), La Foire de la Saint-Barthélemy (Ben Johnson), 1994; (other) L'Acadie pour quasiment rien, 1973; author short stories, and children's literature. V.p. Conseil d'administration du Théâtre du Rideau Vert; mem. Conseil Littéraire Fondation Prince Pierre de Monaco, Haut Conseil Francophonie, 1987, Queen's Privy Coun. Can.; chancellor Noncton U., 1989; Conseil des gouverneurs associés de l'Université de Montréal. Decorated officer, comdr. Order of Can., officier des Palmes académiques françaises, chevalier l'Ordre de la Pléiade (Fredericton), officier l'Ordre Nat. du Québec, officier des Arts et des Lettres (France), comdr. l'Ordre du mérite culturel (Monaco); recipient Prix de la meilleure piece canadienne presented at Festival de Theatre, 1958, Prix Litéraire de la Presse, 1976. Mem. Assn. des Ecrivains de Langue Francaise, l'Ordre des francophones d'Amérique, l'Académie des Grandes Montréalais, Des Auteurs Et Compositeurs Dramatiques de France (sec.), Soc. Des Gens de Lettres de France, Soc. Royale du Canada, Academie Canadienne-Francaise, Pen Club.

MAIN, BETTY JO, management analyst; b. Hatch, N.Mex., May 22, 1939; d. Truman Oliver and Madeline Kate (Bennett) Hickerson; m. Andrew Allan Burich, June 21, 1958 (div. Sept. 1977); children: Cari Lynn, Andrew Allan Jr.; m. Ralph Monroe Main, Apr. 21, 1979; stepchildren: Michael, Randall, Kelly. AA in Liberal Arts, Marymount Coll., 1988; BS in Bus. & Mgmt., U. Redlands, 1993. Escrow officer Palos Verdes Escrow, San Pedro, Calif., 1975-80; sec. City of L.A., San Pedro, 1980-85, wharfinger, 1985-87, mgmt. aide, 1987-89, mgmt. analyst II, 1989—. Mem. City of L.A. Tutoring Program, City of L.A. Spkrs. Bur. Mem. AAUW, Marymount Coll. Alumni, U. Redland Alumni, Alfred North Whitehead Leadership Soc., Emblem Club (L.A.). Episcopalian. Home: 2238 Paseo Del Mar San Pedro CA 90732 Office: City of LA 425 S Palos Verdes St San Pedro CA 90731

MAIN, EDNA DEWEY, education educator; b. Hyannis, Mass., Sept. 1, 1940; d. Seth Bradford and Edna Wilhelmina (Wright) Dewey; m. Donald John Main, Sept. 9, 1961 (div. Dec., 1989); children: Alison Teresa Main Ronzon, Susan Christine Main Leddy, Steven Donald Main. Degree in Merchandising, Tobe-Coburn Sch., 1960; BA in Edn., U. North Fla., 1974, MA in Edn., 1979, M. Adminstrn. and Supervision, 1983; PhD in Curriculum and Instrn.,U. Fla., 1990. Asst. buyer Abraham & Straus, Bklyn., 1960-61; asst. mdse. mgr. Interstate Dept. Stores, N.Y.C., 1962-63; tchr. Holiday Hill Elem. Sch., Jacksonville, Fla., 1974-86; mem. adv. coun. Coll. Edn., U. North Fla., 1982—, instr. summer sci. inst., 1984-92—, prof., 1990-92; asst. prof. Jacksonville U., 1992—, also coord. masters program in integrated learning and ednl. tech.; instr. U. Fla., 1987-90. Co-author: Developing Critical Thinking Through Science, 1990. Rep. United Way, 1981-86; tchr. rep., chpt. leader White House Young Astronaut Program, 1984-85; team leader NSF Shells Elem. Sci. Project. Mem. ASCD, Nat. Sci. Tchrs. Assn. (sci. tchrs. achievement recognition award 1983), Coun. Elem. Sci. Internat., Fla. Assn. Sci. Tchrs., Phi Kappa Phi, Phi Delta Kappa, Delta Kappa Gamma, Kappa Delta Pi. Republican. Episcopalian. Office: Jacksonville U 2800 University Blvd N Jacksonville FL 32211

MAIN, MYRNA JOAN, mathematics educator; b. Kirksville, Mo., Oct. 31, 1947; d. Stanford H. and Jennie Vee (Nuhn) Morris; m. Carl Donet Main, Feb. 22, 1968; children: D. Christopher, Laura S. BSE, Northeast Mo. State U., 1968, MA, 1970. Instr. math. Callao (Mo.) Sch., 1968-73; tchr., chair dept. math. Macon (Mo.) R-I Schs., 1973—; ext. staff Moberly (Mo.) Area C.C., 1983—, Cen. Meth. Coll., 1994; adj. faculty N.E. Mo. State U., Kirksville, 1987-93; mentor Mo. Math. Mentoring Project, Moberly, 1989—. Organist, UBS tchr. Crossroads Christian Ch., Macon, 1981—; troop #503 leader Becky Thatcher coun. Girl Scouts U.S.; team leader 4-H Series, 1993—. Recipient Presdl. award for excellence in math., 1989; semi-finalist The Disney Co. Presents the Am. Tchr., 1991. Mem. AAUW (chpt. pres. 1980-81), Nat. Coun. Tchrs. Math., Mo. Coun. Tchrs. Math. (treas. 1978-79, v.p. 1976), Mo. Alliance for Sci., Math. and Tech. Edn. (bd. dirs. 1988—, mem. Mo. Math. Frameworks), Mo. Math. Coalition (bd. dirs. 1988-93), Math. Assn. Am., Phi Delta Kappa, Delta Kappa Gamma. Democrat.

MAINARDI, CAROL MARGREITHER, artist, framer, bookbinder; b. Hackensack, N.J., Apr. 19, 1967; d. Alan René and Arlene Carol (Clark) Margreither; m. Christopher Louis Mainardi, Apr. 21, 1990; 1 child, Samantha Rose. BFA, William Paterson Coll., Wayne, N.J., 1990. Owner Prints and Books, Wayne, 1987-90, Pompton Plains, N.J., 1987—; gen. ptnr. Expert Framers of North Jersey; conservation libr. intern N.Y. Bot. Garden, Bronx, 1992-93. Bd. dirs. Salute to Women in the Arts, 1991—, pres., 1994—. Recipient Excellence in Mixed Media award Salute to Women in the Arts, Old Church Cultural Ctr., 1993. Presbyterian. Home and Office: 14 White Birch Ave Pompton Plains NJ 07444-1659

MAINE, CATHY LOVING, nurse, educator; b. Bristol, Va., Mar. 2, 1952; d. Howard Payne and Jean Francais (Branson) Loving; m. Wilton M. Hilt, Nov. 14, 1969 (div. Dec. 1992); children: Susan, Amanda; m. Roy C. Maine, Dec. 17, 1994. ADN, East Tenn. State U., 1983. Cert. critical care RN; cert. instr. BCLS, ACLS, PALS. RN pediatrics neonatal ICU Johnston Meml. Hosp., Abingdon, Va., 1983-85; adminstr. Home Nursing Svc. of S.W. Va., Inc., Abingdon, 1985-88; RN surg. ICU, critical care unit Johnston Meml. Hosp., Abingdon, 1988-90; RN educator Bristol (Tenn.) Regional Med. Ctr., 1990—; com. mem. nursing, allied health and human svcs. curriculum adv. com. Va. Highlands C.C., Abingdon, 1986—. Bd. dirs. Am. Heart Assn., Washington County, Va., 1989-92, Am. Cancer Soc., Bristol, 1993; sec., bd. dirs. Regional Healthcare Fed. Credit Union, Bristol, 1993—. Mem. AACN. Home: 19557 Pleasant View Dr Abingdon VA 24210 Office: Bristol Regional Med Ctr 1 Medical Park Blvd Bristol TN 37620

MAINES, CHERYL ANN, accountant; b. Queens, N.Y., Aug. 4, 1969; d. Gilbert Douglas and Carol Ann (Jaroszewski) M. BSBA in Acctg., Rider U., 1992. Staff acct. World Phone Inc., Cranbury, N.J., 1992-94; sr. acct. St. Elizabeth Hosp., Elizabeth, N.J., 1994—. Mem. Inst. Mgmt. Accts., Sierra Club, Appalachian Mountain Club. Home: 15 McFadden Dr Spotswood NJ 08884

MAIOCCHI, CHRISTINE, lawyer; b. N.Y.C., Dec. 24, 1949; d. George and Andreina (Toneatto) M.; m. John Charles Kerecz, Aug. 16, 1980; children: Charles George, Joan Christine. BA in Polit. Sci., Fordham U., 1971, MA in Polit. Sci., 1971, JD, 1974; postgrad., NYU, 1977—. Bar: N.Y. 1975, U.S. Dist. Ct. (so. and ea. dists.), N.Y. 1975, U.S. Ct. Appeals (2nd cir) 1975. Law clk. to magistrate U.S. Dist. Ct. (so. dist.) N.Y., N.Y.C., 1973-74; atty. corp. legal dept. The Home Ins. Co., N.Y.C., 1974-76; asst. house counsel corp. legal dept. Allied Maintenance Corp., N.Y.C., 1976; atty. corp. legal dept. Getty Oil Co., N.Y.C., 1976-77; v.p., mgr. real estate Paine, Webber, Jackson & Curtis, Inc., N.Y.C., 1977-81; real estate mgr. GK Techs., Inc., Greenwich, Conn., 1981-85; real estate mgr., sr. atty. MCI Telecom. Corp., Rye Brook, N.Y., 1985-93; real estate and legal cons. Wallace Law Registry, 1993—. Bd. dirs. League Women Voters, Dobbs Ferry, N.Y., 1988; co-pres. The Home/Sch. Assn., Immaculate Conception Sch., Irvington, N.Y. Mem. ABA, Nat. Assn. Corp. Real Estate Execs. (pres. 1983-84, treas. 1985-86, bd. dirs. 1986), Indsl. Devel. Rsch. Coun. (program v.p. 1985, Profl. award 1987), N.Y. Bar Assn., Women's Bar Assn. Manhattan, The Corp. Bar (sec. real estate divsn. 1987-89, chmn. 1990-92), Home Sch. Assn. Immaculate Conception Sch. (co-pres.), Jr. League Club, Dobbs Ferry Women's Club (program dir. 1981-92, 94—, publicity dir. 1992-94). Home and Office: 84 Clinton Ave Dobbs Ferry NY 10522-3004

MAIORANO, ISABELLE J., former librarian; b. N.Y.C., June 26, 1922; d. Peter and Mary (Balsamo) M. BA summa cum laude, Wagner Coll., 1944, MS in Edn., 1956; MLS, Pratt Inst., 1961. From sr. br. libr. to asst. coord. N.Y. Pub. Lib., 1963-89; ret., 1989. Scholar N.Y. Pub. Lib. Sch. 1958-61. Mem. AAUW, ALA, N.Y. Lib Club, N.Y. Librn. Assn., Beta Phi Mu (Theta chpt.). Republican. Roman Catholic. Home: 86 Kirshon Ave Staten Island New York NY 10314

MAISEL, MARGARET L. (PEGGY MAISEL), lawyer; b. Oakland, Calif., May 10, 1950; d. Sherman Joseph and Lucy Frances (Cowdin) M.; m. Keith Paul Rasey, June 13, 1970 (div. Apr. 1986); m. Ira Horowitz, Oct. 13, 1991; 1 child, Elena Maisel Horowitz; 1 stepchild, Amanda Horowitz. BA, Pomona Coll., 1971; MA in Urban Studies, Occidental Coll., 1972; JD, Boston U., 1975; MA in Clin. Legal Edn., Antioch Sch. Law, 1978. Bar: Calif. 1975, D.C. 1976, Mass. 1987. Trial atty. U.S. Consumer Product Safety Commn., Washington, 1975-76; clin. fellow Antioch Sch. Law, Washington, 1976-78; asst. prof. Sch. Law U. Md., Balt., 1978-79; regional tng. coord. Legal Svcs. Corp., Rosslyn, Va., 1979-81; clin. supr. Harvard Legal Aid Bur., Cambridge, Mass., 1983-85; cons. Mass., 1981-94; dean Sch. Law New Coll. of Calif., San Francisco, 1985-86; atty., clin. dir. Ctr. Pub. Representation, Northampton, Mass., 1986-89; exec. dir. Housing Discrimination Project, Holyoke, Mass., 1990—; cons. Mass. Law Reform Inst., Boston, 1981-85, Mass. Trial Cts., Boston, 1990, Clin. Legal Edn. Assn., 1992-94, various law schs., legal orgns., 1981—. Co-author manual Learning Legal Tactics, 1984. Coro Found. fellow, 1971-72, Nat. Inst. Trial Advocacy fellow, 1980. Mem. Hampshire County Bar Assn., Nat. Lawyers Guild (chair Pioneer Valley 1987-89). Home: 45 Revell Ave Northampton MA 01060-4219 Office: Housing Discrimination Project 57 Suffolk St Holyoke MA 01040-5015

MAISONNEUVE, VICTORIA LYNN, rehabilitation nurse; b. Ft. Wayne, Ind., Dec. 9, 1962; d. William Dennie and Ruth Ann (Dinkel) Fitzgerald; m. Martin Lee Maisonneuve, Nov. 18, 1989. Diploma, Parkview Meth. Sch. Nursing, Ft. Wayne, 1984; student, Ball State U. RN, Ind. Staff nurse Parkview Rehab. Ctr., Ft. Wayne, Ind., 1984-85, case mgr. spinal cord injuries, 1985-86, clin. educator, 1986-88, admission-community liaison, 1988—. Mem. Am. Rehab. Nurses (cert.), Am. Bus. Womens Assn. Office: Parkview Meml Hosp 2200 Randalia Dr Fort Wayne IN 46805-4638

MAJERUS, JANIS MAE, nursing administrator, consultant; b. Great Falls, Mont., Feb. 22, 1954; d. Francis W. and Lorna M. (Burns) M.; divorced; children: Matthew L. Mesaros, Michael S. Mesaros. BSN, Mont. State U., 1976, MSN, 1994. Staff nurse Columbus Hosp., Great Falls, 1976-82, home health nurse, 1982-93, dir. quality improvement, 1993—; bd. dirs. Mont. Fed. Credit Union, Great Falls; instr. Mont. Deaconess Med. Ctr., Great Falls; grad. tchg. instr. Mont. State U., clin. instr., 1989; project dir. Robert Wood Johnson & PEW Charitable Trust, Great Falls, 1991—. Instr. ARC, Great Falls, 1978—; mem. Great Falls Ski Patrol, Neihart, Mont., 1986—. Recipient ARC Nursing Pin, 1985; named Mont.'s Outstanding Young Woman, 1987. Mem. AAUW, Am. Bus. Women's Assn., Mont. Quality Assurance Assn., Sigma Theta Tau. Roman Catholic. Home: 3605 7th Ave N Great Falls MT 59401 Office: Columbus Hosp 500 15th St S Great Falls MT 59401

MAJESKI, GINGER BARNHART, investment/human resource company official; b. Chambersburg, Pa., Aug. 31, 1959; d. Leroy Grant and Helen Mildred (Ward) Barnhart; m. Philip Alexander Majeski, June 12, 1993. BS in Music, Indiana U. Pa., 1981; postgrad., U. N.C., 1981. Asst. music dir. Civic Light Opera, Pitts., 1981; prodn. mgr. Pitts. Opera, 1981-83, co. mgr., 1983-86; conf. planner Federated Investors, Pitts., 1986-87, mgr. conf. planning, 1987-90, employment specialist, 1990—. Vice pres. Vectors/Pitts., 1983, exec. v.p. 1984, pres. Found., 1984; chmn. bd. dirs. Western Pa. Yough Leadership, 1986-89; active Make A Wish Found., Pitts., 1989-90; arrangements chair Pitts. Men and Women of Yr.; mem. fundraising com., arrangements chair Parent and Child Guidance Ctr., 1994. Recipient Outstanding Young Woman of Yr. award, 1989, Woman of Yr., 1993, award Nat. Leadership Coun., 1992, World Leadership Congress, 1992; fellow U. N.C., 1981. Mem. Meeting Planners Internat. (program chmn. 1986-90). Home: 700 Scrubgrass Rd Pittsburgh PA 15243-1124

MAJEWSKI, SANDRA KATHRYN, social scientist, information system geographic specialist; b. Balt., Nov. 15, 1951; d. Carl Matthew and Arrah (Bell) Schultz; m. Michael John Majewski, June 25, 1977 (div. Mar. 1991); children: Natasha Kristine, Alexander Michael. AA in Tchr. Edn., Essex (Md.) C.C., 1971; BS in Geography magna cum laude, Towson (Md.) State Coll., 1974; MA in Geography, U. Ariz., 1979. Rsch. asst. III Md. Dept. State Planning, Balt., 1973; cartographic tchg. asst. dept. geography U. Ariz., Tucson, 1974-76; land use interpreter Tucson Planning Dept., 1976-77; prin. transp. planner Springfield (Ill.)-Sangamon County Regional Planning Commn., 1979-82; planning, graphics specialist Cmty. Devel. Dept. Provo (Utah) City Corp., 1983-86; social scientist Sci. Applications Internat. Corp., Las Vegas, Nev., 1989—; participant ESRI User Conf., 1992, 93, URISA Conf., 1991—, jr. chair integrated sys. SIG, 1994. Troop leader, co-leader Girl Scouts U.S.A., Las Vegas, 1988-90. Mem. Gamma Theta Upsilon. Office: Sci Applications Internat Corp 101 Convention Center Dr Las Vegas NV 89109-2005

MAJOR, MARY JO, dance school artistic director; b. Joliet, Ill., Dec. 5, 1955; d. George Francis and Lucille Mae (Ballun) Schmidberger; m. Perry Rex Major, June 9, 1979. AA, Joliet Jr. Coll., 1976; BA, Lewis U., 1978; MS, Ill. State U., 1983; postgrad., No. Ill. U., Nat. Lewis U. and Gov.'s State U. Cert. tchr., Ill. Tchr., softball coach St. Rose Grade Sch., Wilmington, Ill., 1977-78; tchr., coach volleyball, basketball, softball Reed Custer High Sch., Braidwood, Ill., 1978-79; pvt. tutor, 1979; tchr. Coal City (Ill.) Middle Sc, 1980—, basketball coach, 1980-84; owner, dir., choreographer Major Sch. Dance, Inc., Coal City, 1984—; owner Technique Boutique, 1991; aerobics instr. Wilmington Park Dist.,1977-82, Coal City Shape Shoppe, 1980-82; cheerleading sponsor Joliet Jr. Coll., 1976-77, aerobics instr., 1980-81; pvt. dance instr., Coal City, 1981; dancer, choreographer Coal City Bi-Centennial Celebration, 1981, Coal City Community Celebration, 1982; founder Major Motion Dancers, 1984-95; tchr., Russia, 1990; dancer, choreographer various performances for ch. and civic orgns.; televised half-time performance and tour Citrus Bowl. Dancer Walt Disney World and Universal Studios, Fla., 1992, Mex., 1992-93, Hawaiian Rainbow Classic, 1993, Hula Bowl, 1995; choreographer (video prodn.) Jacinta, Not An Ordinary Love, 1994-95. Recipient Proclamation of Achievement award Dance Olympus, Chgo., 1986, 87, 88, 89, 90, 91, 92, 93, 94, Best Choreographer award, 1990, Best Actress award, 1988, Best Dancer award, 1989, Best Musician award, 1990, Merit award Tremaine Dance Competition, 1991-92. Mem. NEA, IEA, CCCUEA. Office: Major Sch Dance Inc 545 E 1st St Coal City IL 60416-1635

MAJORS, NELDA FAYE, physical therapist; b. Houston, Aug. 3, 1938; d. Columbus Edward and Mary (Mills) M. Cert. in Phys. Therapy, Hermann Sch. Phys. Therapy, Houston, 1960; BS, U. Houston, 1963. Lic. phys. therapist, Tex. Staff therapist Tex. Med. Ctr. Hermann Hosp., Houston, 1960-61; phys. therapist Chelsea Orthopedic Clinic, Houston, 1961-63; dir. phys. therapy Meml. Hosp. Southwest, Houston, 1963-75; owner, pres. Nelda Majors, Inc., Houston, 1975—; mem. profl. adv. bd. Logos Home Health Agy., Houston, 1985-86; adv. dir. 1st Northwestern Bank, Houston. Active with Meml. Dr. Meth. Ch., Houston, 1963—; ptnr. Houston Proud Ptnr., 1986—; founder, pres. Instnl. Safety Advocates Inc., 1994—. Named All Am. Softball Pitcher, Amateur Softball Assn., 1964, All-Regional and All-State Pitcher, Tex. Amateur Softball Assn., 1954-70; named to Houston Amateur Softball Assn. Softball Hall of Fame, 1994. Mem. Am. Phys. Therapy Assn. (pvt. practice sect.), Tex. Phys. Therapy Assn., U. Houston Alumni Assn., E. Cullen Soc. (U. Houston), N.W. Crossing Optimist Club (Houston, charter mem., bd. dirs.), River Oaks Rotary (Houston), Phi Kappa Phi. Republican. Club: U. Houston Cougar.

MAJORS, SARA JANE CLARKSON, nurse anesthetist; b. Springfield, Mo., Apr. 9, 1946; d. Arnold Paul and Lena Mable (Hyde) Clarkson; m. William Durant Wesson, May 22, 1970 (div. Sept. 1983); children: Christopher, Catherine; m. Michael Bruce Majors, Apr. 25, 1987. AS in Nursing, Ga. State U., 1978; BS in Anesthesia, U. Ala., 1982, MPH, 1992; PhD in Health Adminstrn., LaSalle U., 1994. Cert. registered nurse, cert. registered nurse anesthetist, cert. registered nurse practitioner. Youth dir. South Dekalb YMCA, Decatur, Ga., 1972-76; neonatal nurse St. Vincent's Hosp., Birmingham, Ala., 1977-78; nurse practitioner Ala. Neonatology Assn. P.A., Birmingham, Ala., 1978-91; nurse anesthetist Anesthesia Svcs. Birmingham, 1982-94; with Anesthesia Svcs. of Mobile, 1994—. Team leader in anesthesia Operation Smile Internat., Norfolk, Va., 1983—; vol. Birmingham Homeless Shelters, 1993-94, Exch. Club, Birmingham, 1993-94. Mem. ANA, Nat. Assn. Neonatal Nurses, Am. Assn. Nurse Anesthetists. Democrat. Roman Catholic. Home: 20680 Lowry Dr Fairhope AL 36532 Office: Anesthesia Svcs Mobile PC 201 Cox St Mobile AL 36604-3393

MAJUMDAR, SHARMILA, research scientist, educator; b. Calcutta, W. Bengal, India, Nov. 23, 1961; d. Anil Kumar and Sipra (Roy) M. BSc., U. Delhi, India, 1979-82; MS, Yale U., 1984, MPhil, 1985, PhD, 1987. Assoc. rsch. scientist Yale U., New Haven, Conn., 1987-88, asst. prof., 1988-89; asst. prof. U. Calif., San Francisco, 1989—; mem. alumni sch. com. Yale U., 1988—. Contbg. author; contbr. papers in field. Recipient Engrng. award Whittaker Found., 1990—, NIH Career Devel. award, 1993; NIH-RO1 rsch. grantee, 1992. Mem. AAPM, Am. Phys. Soc., Soc. Magnetic Resonance in Medicine, Sigma Xi. Home: 244 Diapian Bay Alameda CA 94502-7911 Office: U Calif Dept Radiology 533 Parnassus Ave San Francisco CA 94143-6533

MAJZOUB, MONA KATHRYNE, lawyer; b. Memphis, June 19, 1949; d. A. Joseph and Mary Majzoub. BA, U. Mich., 1970, MA, 1972; JD, U. Detroit, 1976. Bar: Mich. 1977, U.S. Dist. Ct. (ea. dist.) Mich. 1977. Sr. prin. Kitch, Drutchas, Wagner & Kenney, P.C., Detroit, 1977—. Bd. dirs. Saratoga Community Hosp., Detroit, 1986—, Family Svcs. Detroit and Wayne County, 1988—. Mem. ABA, State Bar Mich. (tort law review com.), Detroit Bar Assn., Women Lawyers Assn. of Mich., Am. Arab Bar Assn. (treas. 1982-86, pres. 1986-94), Am. Hosp. Assn., Mich. Soc. of Hosp. Attys., Nat. Assn. of Women Lawyers, Assn. of Def. Trial Counsel, Inc., Assn. Trial Lawyers of Am., Mich. Def. Trial Counsel, Leadership Detroit XVI. Office: Kitch Drutchas Wagner et al One Woodward Ave 10th Flr Detroit MI 48226-3422

MAKA, ANDREA, microbiologist, research scientist; b. Chgo., Jan. 20, 1957; d. Andrew and Helen (Adamek) M. BS in Biology, Loyola U., Chgo., 1979; MS in Biology, Ill. Inst. Tech., 1982, PhD in Microbiology, 1986. Microbiologist, researcher Inst. Gas Tech., Chgo., 1986-93; microbiologist Met. Water Reclamation Dist. Greater Chgo., Cicero, Ill., 1993—. Author: Encyclopedia of Microbiology, 1992; contbr. articles to profl. jours. Mem. Am. Soc. Microbiology, Soc. Indsl. Microbiology. Home: 5252 S Newland Chicago IL 60638

MAKAR, LINDY CHARLOTTE, model, speaker, professional association executive; b. Ft. Worth, Oct. 18, 1949; d. Charles Kimbrough Jr. and Lydia Joe (Sachse) Cates; m. James Makar, Jr., June 30, 1986; children: Jennifer, Tony, Mike. AA, Okaloosa-Walton Jr. Coll., Niceville, Fla., 1970; student, U. West Fla., 1970; MBA, California U., L.A. Corp. sec. Atlas Utility Supply Co., Ft. Worth, 1977-86; founder, pres. Profl. Models Am., Dallas-Ft. Worth Internat. Airport, 1986—; speaker Motivation in Motion, 1968-91; cover model Noxema, 1970; judge various model and talent competitions and pageants. Author: (with others) Dallas Models Guide, 1991; contbg. editor Ft. Worth Star-Telegram; one-person shows include paintings, Leavenworth, Kans., 1976-77. Amb. Dwight D. Eisenhower Found., Spokane, Wash., 1990; fellow Habitat for Humanity, Americus, Ga., 1991; mem. USA Film Festival, 1991—; bd. rep. Film Commn. No. Tex., Dallas, 1991; mem. event bd. Harris Meth. Hosp. Hurst, Euless and Bedford, Tex., 1987-91, com. chmn., 1990, chmn. 1991; mem. Models Against Drug Abuse, 1987—. Named Miss. N.W. Fla., 1968-69, Miss. Ft. Walton Beach, 1968-70, Maid of Cotton Rep., Fla., 1969-70, Mrs. Dallas-Ft. Worth, Mrs. Tex. Pageant, 1985, Woman of Yr., Ft. Worth Star-Telegram, 1989-90; winner nat. award Profl. Photographers Am., 1988-91. Mem. Internat. Photographers Orgn. (life), Am. Med. Assn. Aux., Nat. Audubon Soc., Ft. Worth Symphony, Tarrant County Med. Soc., Sundance Inst.

MAKARA, CAROL PATTIE, education educator, consultant; b. Norwich, Conn., Feb. 27, 1943; d. Howard G. and Ruth R. Robinson; m. Benjamin Makara, Feb. 19, 1966; children: Cheryl A., John J. AS, Three Rivers Community-Tech. Coll., 1988; BS, Cen. Conn. State U., 1965; MA, U. Conn., 1967. Cert. tchr., Conn. Tchr. Ledyard (Conn.) Bd. of Edn., 1965-66, Preston (Conn.) Bd. of Edn., 1974—; computer analyst Stanley Bostitch Clinton (Conn.) Plant, summers, 1987-92; evening instr. Three Rivers Cmty. Tech. Coll., 1989—; evening mgr. AutoCad Tng. Ctr., 1990—; coop. mentor tchr. Dept. Edn., Conn., 1988—; advisor Conn. Educators' Computer Assn., 1992—. Author: (with others) Pedagogical Guide: Strategies for Improving Instruction, 1992. Active Fellowship Program for Disting. Tchrs., 1987—. Fellow Conn. Bus. and Industry Assn.; mem. NEA, Conn. Edn. Assn. Home: 89 Mathewson Mill Rd Ledyard CT 06339-1114 Office: Preston Plains Sch 1 Route 164 Preston CT 06365-8818

MAKER, JANET ANNE, author, lecturer; b. Woburn, Mass., Feb. 13, 1942; d. George Walter and Margaret Anna (Kopasz) M.; children: Thomas Walter, Jane McKinley. BA, UCLA, 1963; MS, Columbia U., 1967; PhD, U. So. Calif., 1978. lectr. in devlopmental edn., 1979—. Author: Get It All Together, 1979, Interpretive Reading Comprehension, 1984, Keys to a Powerful Vocabulary, Level I, 1981, 88, 94, Level II, 1983, 90, 94, Keys to College Success, 1980, 85, 90, College Reading, Book 1, 1984, 88, 91, Book 2, 1982, 86, 89, 92, Book 3, 1985, Academic Reading with Active Critical Thinking, 1995. Home and Office: 925 Malcolm Ave Los Angeles CA 90024

MAKIN, BARBARA IRENE, financial services executive, consultant; b. Akron, Ohio, May 12, 1965; d. Gretchen E. (Suter) M. Cert., Acad. Pacific, Hollywood, Calif., 1983-84; D (hon.), St. Stephen's Bible Coll., L.A., 1993. Mgr., clk. Smeads, Cuyahoga Falls, Ohio, 1978-83; sec. City of Akron, 1980-83; adminstrv. asst. John Martin & Assocs., L.A., 1983-84, Gruen Assoc., L.A., 1984-85; owner West Coast Adminstrv. Cons., Hollywood, 1985-91, Primerica Fin. Svcs., Glendale, Calif., 1991—; mem., cons. St. Stephen's Bible Coll., L.A., 1993—. Mem. NAFE. Home and Office: 1021 Western Ave Glendale CA 91201-1714

MAKKAY, MAUREEN ANN, broadcast executive; b. Chgo.; d. John Paul and Bernice Ann (Williams) Monaghan; m. Albert Makkay, Oct. 20, 1962; children: Allison, Albert Jr., Colleen. BA, U. R.I., 1974. Cert. secondary sch. tchr., Mass. Adminstr. Ednl. Records Bur., Wellesley, Mass., 1979-81; local sales mgr. Sta. WKZE, Orleans, Mass., 1981-83; nat. sales mgr. Sta. WKFM, Syracuse, N.Y., 1983-85; pres. Sta. WPXC-FM, Hyannis, Mass., 1987—; v.p. Sta. WRZE, Nantucket, Mass., Sta. WCIB-FM, Falmouth, Mass. Pres. Cape and Islands unit Am. Cancer Soc., 1988-91, bd. dirs., 1989—; mem. pers. bd. Town of Barnstable, Mass., 1989-94, chmn., 1990-91; bd. dirs. Cape Cod Alcoholism Intervention and Rehab., Inc., 1995—. Mem. Bus. and Profl. Women Cape Cod (bd. dirs. 1989—), Am. Women in Radio and TV, Nat. Assn. Broadcasters. Office: Sta WPXC-FM Radio 154 Barnstable Rd Hyannis MA 02601-1862

MAKRI, NANCY, chemistry educator; b. Athens, Greece, Sept. 5, 1962; came to the U.S., 1985; d. John and Vallie (Tsakona) M.; m. Martin Gruebele, July 9, 1992; 1 child, Alexander Makris Gruebele. BS, U. Athens, 1985; PhD, U. Calif., Berkeley, 1989. Teaching asst. U. Calif., Berkeley, 1985-87; rsch. asst. U. Calif., 1986-89; jr. fellow Harvard U., Cambridge, Mass., 1989-91; asst. prof. U. Ill., Urbana, 1991—. Recipient Beckman Young Investigator award Arnold & Mabel Beckman Found., 1993; named NSF Young Investigator, 1993; Packard fellow for Sci. and Engring., David and Lucille Packard Found., 1993, Sloan Rsch. fellow Alfred Sloan Found., 1994, Cottrell scholar Rsch. Corp., 1994. Home: 2208 Wyld Dr Urbana IL 61801-6753 Office: U Ill at Urbana Dept Chem 505 S Mathews Ave Urbana IL 61801-3617

MAKUPSON, AMYRE PORTER, television station executive; b. River Rouge, Mich., Sept. 30, 1947; d. Rudolph Hannibal and Amyre Ann (Porche) Porter; m. Walter H. Makupson, Nov. 1, 1975; children: Rudolph Porter, Amyre Nisi. BA, Fisk U., 1970; MA, Am. U., Washington, 1972. Asst. dir. news Sta. WGPR-TV, Detroit, 1975-76; dir. pub. rels. Mich. Health Maintenance Orgn., Detroit, 1974-76, Kirwood Gen. Hosp., Detroit, 1976-77; mgr. pub. affairs, news anchor Sta. WKBD-TV, Southfield, Mich., 1977—, Children's Miracle Network Telethon, 1989—. Mem. adv. com. Mich. Arthritis Found., Co-Ette Club, Inc., Met. Detroit Teen Conf. Coalition, Cystic Fibrosis Soc.; mem. adv. com., bd. dirs. Alzheimers Assn.; mem. exec. com. March of Dimes; pres. bd. dirs. Detroit Wheelchair Athletic Assn.; bd. dirs. Providence Hosp. Found., Sickle Cell Assn., Kids In Need of Direction, Drop-out Prevention Collaborative, Merrill Palmer Inst. Recipient Emmy award for best commentary NATAS, 1993, 10 Emmy nominations NATAS, Editorial Best Feature award AP, Media award UPI, Oakland County Bar Assn., TV Documentary award, Detroit Press Club, numerous svc. awards including Arthritis Found. Mich., Mich. Mchts. Assn., DAV, Jr. Achievement, City of Detroit, Salvation Army, Spirit award City of Detroit, Spirit award City of Pontiac, Golden Heritage award Little Rock Bapt. Ch., 1993; named Media Person of the Yr. Southern Christian Leadership Conf., 1994. Mem. Pub. Rels. Soc. Am., Am. Women in Radio and TV (Outstanding Achievement award 1981, Outstanding Woman in TV Top Mgmt. 1993, Mentor award 1993), Women in Communications, Nat. Acad. TV Arts and Scis., Detroit Press Club, Ad-Craft. Roman Catholic. Office: 26955 W 11 Mile Rd Southfield MI 48034-2292

MALASKY, ILENE POST, stockbroker; b. Columbus, Ohio, July 4, 1938; d. Harry S. and Jeanne (Stone) Post; student Harcum Jr. Coll., 1958; B.S., Youngstown State U., 1961; children—Bruce A., Stephen P. With Murch & Co., Youngstown, Ohio, 1969-70; with Kemper Securities Inc., Youngstown, 1970—, v.p. investments, 1981—; pres. The 759 Corp. Trustee Rodef Sholom Temple, 1982-86; mem. Jr. Guild of St. Elizabeth Hosp., 1970-86; mem. faculty awards com. Youngstown State U., 1984-87. Jewish. Clubs: Youngstown, Squaw Creek Country. Home: 3507A Somerset Dr Youngstown OH 44505-1779 Office: 201 E Commerce St Ste 100 Youngstown OH 44503-1637

MALATESTA, ROSALIE ELINOR, accountant, owner bookkeeping company; b. San Francisco, Feb. 10, 1938; d. Albert Angelo and Alba (Botto) M.; m. Otto Henry Saltenberger, May 16, 1959 (div. Sept. 26, 1977). AA in Acctg., Am. River Coll., 1974; postgrad., Sacramento State U., 1974-76. Staff acct. D.E. Pomerantz & Co., CPA, San Francisco, 1956-63, 66-67; cost acct. Roberts Constrn. Co., San Mateo, Calif., 1963-67; staff acct. Goldsmith, Exline & Seidman, CPAs, San Mateo, Calif., 1968-72; tax examiner Franchise Tax Bd. State of Calif., Sacramento, 1976; staff acct. Phil A. Baender, Acctg. Corp., Danville, Calif., 1976-80; owner Profl. Bookkeeping Systems, Alamo, Calif., 1980—. Pres. Pacifica (Calif.) Police Wives Assn., 1969-71, Vallemar Women's Club, Pacifica, 1966-68; treas. San Ramon Valley Congl. Ch., Danville, 1978-80. Mem. Profl. Bookkeepers Asns. (sec. 1993—), Inst. Mgmt. Accts. (manuscript chmn. 1984-86), Am. Inst. Profl. Bookkeepers (treas.), Diablo Network, Diablo Valley C. of C. Republican. Roman Catholic. Office: Profl Bookkeeping Systems 3237 Danville Blvd Alamo CA 94507-1913

MALCOLM, DAWN GRACE, family physician; b. L.A., Nov. 3, 1936; d. Thomas N. and Grace S. (Salisian) M. BA, UCLA, 1959; MD, Med. Coll. Pa., 1973. Diplomate Am. Bd. Family Practice. Tchr. elem. music Fullerton (Calif.) Sch. Dist., 1960-61; tchr. Ahlman Acad., Kabul, Afghanistan, 1961-65; intern and resident in family practice Kaiser Found. Hosp., L.A., 1973-76; family physician So. Calif. Permanente Med. Group, L.A., 1976—; mem. faculty family practice residency program Kaiser Found. Hosp., L.A., 1976—. Fellow Am. Acad. Family Physicians. Office: So Calif Permanente Med Group 4747 Sunset Blvd Los Angeles CA 90027

MALDONADO-BEAR, RITA MARINITA, economist, educator; b. Vega Alta, P.R., June 14, 1938; d. Victor and Marina (Davila) Maldonado; m. Larry Alan Bear, Mar. 29, 1975. BA, Auburn U., 1960; PhD, NYU, 1969. With Min. Wage Bd. & Econ. Devel. Adminstrn., Govt. of P.R., 1960-64; assoc. prof. fin. U. P.R., 1969-70; asst. prof. econs. Manhattan Coll., 1970-72; assoc. prof. econs. Bklyn. Coll., 1972-75; vis. assoc. prof. fin. Stanford (Calif.) Grad. Bus. Sch., 1973-74; assoc. prof. fin. and econs. Grad. div. Stern Sch. Bus. NYU, 1975-81, prof., 1981—, acting dir. markets, ethics and law, 1993-94; cons. Morgan Guaranty Trust Co., N.Y.C., 1972-77, Bank of Am., N.Y.C., 1982-84, Res. City Bankers, N.Y.C., 1978-87, Swedish Inst. Mgmt., Stockholm, 1982-91, Empresas Master of P.R., 1985-90; bd. dirs. Medallion Funding Corp., 1985-87; apptd. adv. bd. dirs. equity and diversity in ednl. environs. Mid. States Commn. on Higher Edn., 1991—; trustee Securities Industry Assn., N.Y. Dist. Econ. Edn. Found., 1994—. Author: Role of the Financial Sector in the Economic Development of Puerto Rico, 1970; Co-Author: Free Markets, Finance, Ethics, And Law, 1994; contbr. articles to profl. jours. Trustee Bd. Edn., Twp. of Mahwah, N.J., 1991-92. P.R. Econ. Devel. Adminstrn. fellow, 1960-65; Marcus Nadler fellow, NYU, 1966-67, Phillip Lods Dissertation fellow, 1967-68. Mem. Am. Econs. Assn., Am. Fin. Assn., Metro. Econ. Assn. N.Y., Assn. for Social Econs. (trustee exec. coun. 1994—). Home: 95 Tam O Shanter Dr Mahwah NJ 07430-1526 Office: Mgmt Edn Ctr 44 W 4th St Ste 9-190 New York NY 10012-1126

MALEC, RUTH ELLEN, special services director; b. Auburn, N.Y., Aug. 1, 1944; d. Robert James and Edna Louise (Lawrence) Stebbins; m. Edward L. Malec, Sept. 2, 1967 (div. Oct. 1977); children: Edward L., Amy Beth. B, Houghton (N.Y.) Coll., 1966; student, Ohio U., 1966-67; M, Montclair State Coll., 1970. Tchr. Newark Pub. Schs., N.J., 1967-69; social worker Passaic County Bd. Soc. Svcs., Paterson, N.J., 1970-72, Boonton Pub. Schs., N.J., 1979-88; dir. spl. edn. Sch. Union 44, Sabattus, Maine, 1988-90; dir. spl. svcs. Kinnelon Pub. Schs., N.J., 1990-93, Linden (N.J.) Pub. Schs., N.J., 1993—. Women's ministry Jacksonville Chapel, Lincoln Park, N.J. Mem. ASCD, N.J. Dept. Edn. Prof. Svcs. Coun., N.J. Assn. Sch. Social Workers (v.p. 1985-87, pres. 1987-88), N.J. Assn. for Pupil Svcs. Adminstrs., N.J. Prins. and Suprs. Assn., N.E. Coalition of Ednl. Leaders, Union County Assn. of Dirs. of Spl. Svcs., Morris County Assn. Dirs. Spl. Edn., Kinnelon Women's Svc. Orgn. Home: 35 Cliff Trl Kinnelon NJ 07405-3107 Office: Linden Pub Schs 19 E Morris Ave Linden NJ 07036

MALECKI, ELIZABETH ANN, radiology nurse coordinator; b. Troy, Ohio, Nov. 19, 1934; d. Ira G. and Hazel (Fisher) Hartley; m. Ronald J. Malecki, Oct. 4, 1980; children: Douglas, Bruce, Barry, Dalrymple, Hedy, Ronnie, Margaret. AA, Catonsville Community Coll., 1968. Staff nurse med.-surg. St. Agnes Hosp., Balt., 1968-70; staff nurse recovery rm. U. Md. Hosp., Balt., 1970-81, head nurse cardiac catheter lab., 1981-86, nurse coord. radiology, 1986—. Mem. Md. Health Claims Arbitration Com. Mem. ANA, AACN, Am. Radiology Nurses Assn. (nat. nominating com.), Md. Radiology Nurses Assn. (v.p.). Home: 8005 Windsor Mill Rd Baltimore MD 21244-1306

MALEK, MARLENE ANNE, advocate, cultural organization, foundation executive; b. Oakland, Calif., June 22, 1939; d. William Alexander and Yolanda Katherine (Stella) McArthur; m. Frederic Vincent Malek, Aug. 5, 1961; children: Frederic William, Michelle Anne. Student, Armstrong U., 1959; Student, Marymount U., 1979. Women's bd. Am. Heart Assn., 1973—. Bd. dirs. Fed. Rep. Women, Washington, 1972-74; bd. dirs., mem. exec. com. Marymount U., Arlington, Va., 1974—; mem. community bd. J.F. Kennedy Ctr. for the performing Arts, 1991—; chmn. Eisenhower Meml. Found., Washington, 1972-74; mem. adv. bd. Second Genesis Drug Rehab. Program, Bethesda, Md., 1983—; mem. nat. adv. bd. Susan G. Komen Breast Cancer Found., Dallas, 1992—; founding mem. Arena Stage Guild, Washington; bd. dirs. Nat. Mus. Women in Arts, 1987; presdl. appointment to Nat. Cancer Adv. Bd., 1991—. Mem. Nat. Symphony Orch. Assn. (bd. dirs.). Episcopalian. Avocations: cross country skiing, mountain and cross country biking.

MALESKI, CYNTHIA MARIA, lawyer; b. Natrona Heights, Pa., July 4, 1951; d. Richard Anthony and Helen Elizabeth (Palovcak) M.; m. Andrzej Gabriel Groch, Aug. 7, 1982; 1 child, Elizabeth Maria. BA summa cum laude, U. Pitts., 1973; student U. Rouen (France), 1970; JD, Duquesne U., 1976. Bar: Pa. 1976, U.S. dist. ct. (we. dist.) Pa. 1976, U.S. Supreme Ct. 1980, U.S. Ct. Appeals (3d cir.) 1984. Indsl. rels. adminstr. Allegheny Ludlum Industries, Inc., Brackenridge, Pa., 1972-74; law clk. Conte, Courtney, Tarasi & Price, Pitts., 1974, Paul Hammer, Pitts., 1974-76; sole practice Natrona Heights, Pa., 1978-92; ins. commnr. Penna, 1992—; mem. Gov.'s cabinet, 1992—; assoc. dir. pers. Mercy Hosp., Pitts., 1976-77, dir. legal affairs, 1977-81, gen. counsel, 1981-92; spl. master Allegheny County Ct. Common Pleas, 1989; candidate for judge Pa. Ct. Common Pleas; bd. dirs. legal adv. bd. Cath. Health Assn., 1980-82; gen. counsel, vice chmn. nat. assembly of reps. Nat. Confedn. Am. Ethnic Groups, 1980—; health law cons. and lectr. Co-author: The Legal Dimensions of Nursing Practice (Nurses' Book of Month Club award 1982), 1982; contbr. articles to publs. Corp. sec., pres. Duquesne U. Tamburitzans, Pitts.; vice chmn. Czechoslovak room com. Nationality Rooms Program, U. Pitts., 1983; elected mem. Allegheny County Dem. Com., 1986-89; candidate for del. Dem. Nat. Conv. 20th Pa. Congl. Dist., 1984; chmn. Com. to Re-elect U.S. Congressman Doug Walgren, 1982; Ethnic Com. for Pa. Atty. Gen., 1980, Ethnic Com. for Judge Peter Paul Olszewski, 1983; U.S. del 4th Slovak World Congress, 1981; mem. adv. bd. Children's and Youth Services, Allegheny County, 1984—; soloist, speaker various groups, Pitts. Slovakians. Scholar U. Rouen, 1970; Allegheny Ludlum Industries scholar, 1969-73; Andrew Mellon scholar, 1969; tuition scholar U. Pitts., 1969-73; tuition remission grantee Duquesne U., 1975, 76; recipient acad. excellence award Duquesne U., 1976, Disting. Alumnus, 1993; Mem. ABA, Am. Soc. Hosp. Attys., Nat. Health Lawyers Assn., Women Execs. in State Govt. (mem. nat. bd. 1994), Soc. Hosp. Attys. of Hosp. Assn. Pa. (v.p.), Soc. Hosp. Attys. Western Pa., Pa. Bar Assn., Allegheny County Bar Assn., Slavic Edn. Assn. (nat. treas. 1981-86), St. Thomas More Soc. (bd. govs. 1980—), First Cath. Slovak Union, 1st Cath. Slovak Women's Assn., Phi Beta Kappa. Roman Catholic. Home: 137 Oak Manor Dr Natrona Heights PA 15065-1949 Office: Ins Dept 1326 Strawberry Sq Harrisburg PA 17120

MALES-MADRID, SANDRA KAY, medical facility administrator; b. South Gate, Calif., Aug. 1, 1942; d. Albert Odus and Evelyn Louise (Corbett) Males; m. James O. Spurbeck, Apr. 15, 1963 (div. Nov. 1967); m. Miguel Madrid Jr., Feb. 9, 1980; stepchildren: Priscilla, Betty, Dru, Rachel. BA, U. Redlands, Calif., 1987; MHA, Chapman U., 1993. Payroll clk. Lever Bros. Co., Los Angeles, 1961-69; med. asst. William Stafford, M.D., Fullerton, Calif., 1969-71; mgr. office David H. Armstrong, M.D., Inc., Fullerton, 1971-79; mgr. office Med. Ctr. for Women, Fullerton, 1977-79, adminstr., 1986—; owner Sandy's Discount Boutique, Hemet, Sun City, Calif., 1979-83; asst. adminstr. Fullerton Cardiovascular Med. Group, 1983-86; cons., tchr. Riverside (Calif.) Community Coll., 1984-86; bd. dirs. No. Orange County Regional Occupational Ctr., Anaheim, Calif., 1985—. Vol. Riverside Rape Crisis Ctr., 1984-87. Mem. DAR. Republican. Club: Fullerton. Lodge: Soroptimist (Sun City) (sec. 1982-83, Women Helping Women award 1985). Office: Fullerton Cardiovascular Med Group 2720 N Harbor Blvd Ste 210 Fullerton CA 92635-2694

MALEY, PATRICIA ANN, preservation planner; b. Wilmington, Del., Dec. 25, 1955; d. James Alfred and Frances Louise (Fenimore) M.; m. Scott A. Stone, Dec. 7, 1991. AA, Cecil C.C., 1973; BA, U. Del., 1975, MA, 1981. Cert. planner: cert. secondary tchr., Del. Analyst econ. devel. City of Wilmington, 1977-78, evaluation specialist, 1978-80, planner II mayor's office, 1980-86, cons. preservation, 1986-87; dir. Belle Meade Mansion, Nashville, 1987-88; dir. planning, devel. Children's Bur. of Del., Wilmington, 1988; prin. preservation planner Environ. Mgmt. Ctr., Brandywine Conservancy, Chadds Ford, Pa., 1988-92; planning cons., 1992—; cons. cultural resources M.A.A.R. Inc., Newark, Del., 1987, ITC Cons., Wilmington, 1985-86. Contbg. photographer America's City Halls, 1984; author numerous Nat. Register nominations, 1980-86; 88—. Pres., founder Haynes Park Civic Assn., Wilmington, 1977-80; photographer Biden U.S. Senate Campaign, New Castle County, Del., 1984; sec. parish coun. Our Lady Fatima Roman Cath. Ch., 1985-86, choir dir., 1983-87; mem. com. on design & renovation of worship spaces Diocese of Wilmington, also mem. com. on music; bd. dirs. Del. Children's Theatre; music dir. St. Elizabeth Ann Seton parish, Bear, Del., 1988—. U. Del. fellow, 1976-77. Mem. Nat. Trust Hist. Preservation, Am. Inst. Cert. Planners, Am. Planning Assn., Nat. Pastoral Musicians Assn., Del. Soc. Architects, Del. Archeol. Soc., Del. Hist. Soc., Chester County (Pa.) Hist. Soc., Am. Inst. Cert. Planners, Pi Sigma Alpha. Democrat. Office: 122 Compass Dr Claymont DE 19703

MALIHA-NEBUS, JEANETTE ELIZABETH, school nurse; b. Warwick, N.Y., Aug. 15, 1935; d. Charles George Yopp and Charlotte Kathleen (Donley) Keyser; children: Roxane E. Turner, Nadine C. Collard. RN, Middletown (N.Y.) Psychiat. Ctr. Sch. Nursing, 1956; AA, Orange County Community Coll., Middletown, 1970; BS in Psychology, SUNY, New Paltz, 1972; BSN, Mount St. Mary Coll., Newburgh, N.Y., 1977; MS in Counselor Edn., L.I. U., 1979. RN, N.Y., N.J.; cert. tchr., sch. nurse. Staff nurse Middletown (N.Y.) Psychiat. Ctr., 1958-59, from staff nurse to head nurse to nurse instr. dept. staff devel. and Sch. Nursing to nurse supr., 1967-80; pvt. duty nurse Horton Hosp., Middletown, 1957-58, 59-60; staff nurse Valley Hosp., Ridgewood, N.J., 1964-67; coord. clin. care Community Gen. Hosp., Harris, N.Y., 1982-84; sch. nurse Middletown Enlarged City Sch. Dist., 1988—. Mem. ANA (coun. psychiat.-mental health nursing 1991—), AAUW, Nat. Assn. Sch. Nurses, Soc. Edn. and Rsch. Psychiat.-Mental Health Nursing, N.Y. State Nurses Assn. (dist. 18), N.Y. State Assn. of Sch. Nurses, RN Club Middletown, Women's Univ. Club Middletown, Warwick Hist. Soc., Sigma Theta Tau (Mu Epsilon chpt.).

MALINA, ILENE ANN, publishing professional; b. Tarrytown, N.Y., June 28, 1962; d. Meyer and Reva (Arshinoff) M. BA in English and Am. Lit. cum laude, Brandeis U., 1984. Promotion asst. Archon Books, Hamden, Conn., 1984-85; editorial asst. Penny Press, Inc., Norwalk, Conn., 1985, traffic mgr., assoc. editor, illustrator, 1986-87; outside advt. coord. Mag. Group, N.Y. Times Co., Trumbull, Conn., 1988, new bus. coord., 1989-90, promotion mgr., 1991-94, sr. promotion mgr., 1995—; overseas cons. Golf World and Golf Weekly U.K. publs. of Mag. Group, N.Y. Times Co., London, 1993. Editor quar. mag. Original Logic Problems, 1987. Vol. Kewalo Basin Marine Mammal Lab., Earthwatch, Honolulu, 1992, Literacy Vols. Am., Norwalk, 1987; host Fresh Air Fund, Bridgeport, Conn., 1992. Office: NY Times Co 5520 Park Ave Trumbull CT 06611-3426

MALINA, JUDITH, actress, director, producer, writer; b. Kiel, Germany, June 4, 1926; came to U.S., 1945; d. Max and Rosel (Zamora) M.; m. Julian Beck, Oct. 30, 1948 (dec.); m. Hanon Reznikov, May 6, 1988; children—Garrick Maxwell, Isha Manna. Graduate, Dramatic Workshop, New Sch. Social Research, 1945-47. adj. prof. Columbia U. Founder, producer, actress, dir. The Living Theatre, 1947—; dir., actress: The Thirteenth God, Childish Jokes, Ladies Voices, He Who Says Yes and He Who Says No, The Dialogue of the Mannequin and the Young Man, 1951, Man Is Man, 1962, Mysteries and Smaller Pieces, 1964, Antigone, 1965, Paradise Now, 1968, The Legacy of Cain (including Seven Meditations on Political Sadomasochism), 1970-77, Strike Support Oratorium, 1974, Six Public Acts, The Money Tower, 1975, Prometheus, 1978, Masse Mensch, 1980, The Living Theatre Retrospectacle, 1986, The Zero Method, 1991; dir.: Doctor Faustus Lights the Lights, 1951, Desire Trapped by the Tail, Faustina, Sweeney Agonistes, The Heroes, Ubu the King, 1952, The Age of Anxiety, The Spook Sonata, Orpheus, 1954, The Connection, 1959, In the Jungle of Cities, 1960, The Apple, 1961, The Mountain Giants 1962, The Brig, 1963, The Maids, Frankenstein, 1965, The Archeology of Sleep, 1983, Kassandra, 1987, Us, 1987, VKTMS, 1988, I and I, 1989, German Requiem, 1990, Not in My Name, 1994; actress: The Idiot King, 1954, Tonight We Improvise, Phedre, The Young Disciple, 1955, Many Loves, The Cave at Machpelah, 1959, Women of Trachis, 1960, The Yellow Methuselah, 1982, Poland/1931, 1988, Anarchia, 1993; appeared in films: Flaming Creatures, 1962, Amore, Amore, 1966, Wheel of Ashes, 1967, Le Compromise, 1968, Etre Libre, 1968, Paradise Now, 1969, Dog Day Afternoon, 1974, Signals Through the Flames, 1983, Radio Days, 1986, China Girl, 1987, Lost Paradise, 1988, Enemies, A Love Story, 1989, Awakenings, 1990, The Addams Family, 1991, Household Saints, 1993; author: Paradise Now, 1971, The Enormous Despair, 1972, The Legacy of Cain (3 pilot projects), 1973, Seven Meditations on Political Sadomasochism, 1977, Living Means Theater, 1978, Theatre Diaries: Brazil and Bologna, 1978, Poems of a Wandering Jewess, 1983, The Diaries of Judith Malina 1947-57, 1984; translator: Antigone (B. Brecht), 1990. Vice chmn. U.S. Com. for Justice to Latin Am. Polit. Prisoners, 1973-74; sponsor Am. Friends of Brazil, 1973; mem. exec. coun. War Resisters League. Recipient Lola D'Annunzio award, 1959, Page One award Newspaper Guild, 1960, Obie awards, 1960, 1964, 1969, 1975, 87, 89, Grand Prix de Theatre des Nations, 1961, Paris Critics Circle medallion, 1961, Prix de l'Universite Paris, 1961, New Eng. Theatre Conf. award, 1962, Olympio prize Italy, 1967, 9th Centennial medal U. Bologna, Italy, 1988; named Humanist of the Yr., 1984; Guggenheim fellow, 1985. Address: 800 West End Ave New York NY 10025

MALKIEL, NANCY WEISS, college dean, history educator; b. Newark, Feb. 14, 1944; d. William and Ruth Sylvia (Puder) W.; m. Burton G. Malkiel, July 31, 1988. BA summa cum laude, Smith Coll., 1965; MA, Harvard U., 1966, PhD, 1970. Asst. prof. history Princeton (N.J.) U., 1969-75, assoc. prof., 1975-82, prof., 1982—, master Dean Mathey Coll., 1982-86, dean of coll., 1987—. Author (as Nancy J. Weiss): Charles Francis Murphy, 1858-1924: Respectability and Responsibility in Tammany Politics, 1968, (with others) Blacks in America: Bibliographical Essays, 1971, The National Urban League, 1910-1940, 1974, Farewell to the Party of Lincoln: Black Politics in the Age of FDR, 1983 (Berkshire Conf. of Women Historians prize 1984), Whitney M. Young Jr., and the Struggle for Civil Rights, 1989. Trustee Smith Coll., Northampton, Mass., 1984-94, Woodrow Wilson Nat. Fellowship Found., 1975—. Fellow Woodrow Wilson Found., 1965, Charles Warren Ctr. for Studies in Am. History, 1976-77, Radcliffe Inst., 1976-77, Ctr. for Advanced Study in Behavioral Scis., 1986-87. Mem. Am. Hist. Assn., Orgn. Am. Historians (chmn. status women hist. profession 1972-75), So. Hist. Assn., Phi Beta Kappa. Democrat. Jewish. Office: Princeton U Office Dean Of College Princeton NJ 08544

MALL, IDA, church administrator. Pres. Intl. Lutheran Women's Missionary League of the Lutheran Church MO Synod International Ctr., St. Louis. Office: Internat Luth Women's Missionary League 3558 S Jefferson Ave Saint Louis MO 63118-3910

MALLARD, RUTH FRANCES, telecommunications company administrator; b. West Berlin, Germany, Apr. 21, 1963; came to U.S., 1971; d. Paul Bortner and Helen Joy (Higgins-Carter) Rohrbaugh; divorced. BSBA, U. Ctrl. Fla., 1985; postgrad., Rollins Coll., 1993—. Account exec. Metromedia, Orlando, Fla., 1985-87; account exec. MCI Telecomm., Orlando, 1987-91, mktg. mgr., 1991-94; area mgr. Alcoa, 1994—. Vol. WeCare, Orlando, 1992; asst. Dale Carnegie, Orlando, 1992. Mem. Orlando C. of C., So. Bell Large Users Group, Economie Devel. Commn., Toastmasters (Spl. award 1992). Lutheran. Home: 1435 Sunnyside Dr Winter Park FL 32789 Office: MCI Telecomm 201 S Orange Ave Ste 600 Orlando FL 32801

MALLARY, GERTRUDE ROBINSON, civic worker; b. Springfield, Mass., Aug. 19, 1902; d. George Edward and Jennie (Slater) Robinson; student, Bennett Coll., 1921-22, U. Conn., 1941-42; m. R. DeWitt Mallary, Sept. 15, 1923; children: R. DeWitt, Richard Walker. Co-owner, ptnr. Mallary Farm, Bradford, Vt., 1936-93; mem. Vt. Ho. of Reps., 1953-56, sec. agr. com., 1953, mem. appropriations com., 1955; mem. Vt. Senate, 1957-58, mem. appropriations com., clk. pub. health com., vice chmn. edn. com. Pres., Jr. League, Springfield, 1931-33; trustee Wesson Meml. Hosp., Springfield, 1937-42, chmn. nursing services, 1939-42; chmn. Springfield Council Social Agys., 1938-40; mem. Mass. Commn. Pub. Safety, 1941-42; pres. Vt. Holstein Club, 1951-53; mem. Vt. Bd. Recreation, 1959-65; trustee Fairlee (Vt.) Public Library, 1953-84, Asa Bloomer Found., 1963-71, Justin Smith Morrill Found., 1964-71, pres., 1968-71; chmn. Fairlee Bicentennial Com., 1974-77; mem. Com. for New Eng. Bibliography, 1971-84, vice chmn. for Vt., 1977; Orange County chmn. Vt. Achievement Ctr., 1985-89. Recipient Theresa R. Brungardt award, 1979, Co- recipient with Husband Master Breeders award Vt. Holstein Assn., 1979, Master Breeders award New Eng. Holstein Assn., 1969, Disting. Svc. award, 1989. Mem. Vt. Hist. Soc. (hon.), Bradford Hist. Soc. (pres. 1965-69), Fairlee Hist. Socs., Am. Antiquarian Soc. Editor New Eng. Holstein Bull., 1947-50. Address: Mallary Farm RR1 Box 620 Bradford VT 05033

MALLERY, ANNE LOUISE, elementary educator, consultant; b. Myersdale, Pa., June 14, 1934; d. Samuel Addison and Ruth Elizabeth (Meehan) M.; m. Richard Gwen Jones, Mar. 9, 1953 (div. 1974); children: Valerie Anne, Joseph Samuel, Richard Alan (dec.). BS in Edn., Calif. U. Pa., 1970, MEd, 1972; EdD, Pa. State U., 1980. From proficiency coord. to prof. elem. edn. Millersville (Pa.) U., 1980—; asst. to pres. for planning MobileVision Tech., Inc., Key Biscayne, Fla., 1990—; editorial bd. Innovative Learning Strategy, Nat. Publ., 1989—; cons. Pequea Valley High Sch., Lancaster, Pa., 1985, Cambridge Adult Edn. Co., 1987, Conawago Elem. Sch., York, Pa., 1991; co-dir. NEH grant, 1993-94. Co-author The Secret Cave Multimodal Reading Program; contbr. numerous articles to profl. jours. Judge Intelligencer Reg. Spelling Bee, Lancaster, 1990,91. Mem. Assn. Pa. State Coll. and U. Faculty, Internat. Reading Assn., Lancaster Lebanon Reading Assn., Assn. Tchr. Educators, Am. Assn. Colls. Tchr. Edn., Am. Reading Forum. Republican. Presbyterian. Home: 24 Strawberry Ln Lancaster PA 17602-1639 Office: Millersville Univ Stayer Education Ctr Millersville PA 17551

MALLERY, SALLY SELESNICK, psychotherapist; b. Boston, Apr. 28, 1941; d. Sydney and Alice Vesta (McKinney) Selesnick; m. Dave Mallery, Apr. 1, 1970 (div. Apr., 1981); children: Sydra, Sam. BS, Boston U., 1963; MS, Villanova U., 1980. Recreation specialist ARC, Seoul, Korea, 1963-64; dir. adult edn. N.Y. Assn. For Blind, N.Y.C., 1965-67; recreation dir. Sephardic Home for Aged, Bklyn., 1967-70; psychotherapist Bucks County Inst., Longhorne, Pa., 1979-81, Ctr. for Clin. Svcs., Hudson, Fla., 1986—; social worker Gulf Coast Kidney Ctr., New Port Richey, Fla., 1986—; psychotherapist, owner Marriage & Family Counseling Ctr., New Port Richey, Fla., 1982—. Named Bd. Mem. of Yr., Fla. Counseling Assn., 1994. Mem. ACA, Fla. Mental Health Counselors Assn. (pres. elect 1992-93, pres. 1994—), Suncoast Mental Health Counselors Assn. (pres. 1981-83). Jewish. Home: Unit F5 1500 Sunset Rd Tarpon Springs FL 34689-2767 Office: Marriage & Family Counseling Ctr 6014 US Highway 19 Ste 101 New Port Richey FL 34652-2535

MALLETT, HELENE GETTLER, elementary education educator; b. Goshen, N.Y., Aug. 20, 1937; d. John and Anna Gettler; m. Richard David Mallett, July 29, 1967; 1 child, Anna Alma. BS in Fgn. Svc., Georgetown U., 1959; MA, SUNY, Stonybrook, 1989. Supr. Fulbright Program/Europe Inst. Internat. Edn., N.Y.C., 1961-65; editor Am. Assn. Fund Raising Coun., N.Y.C., 1965-67; coord. adult GED/ESL programs BOCES 3, Deer Park, N.Y., 1973-85; tchr. UFSD #3 and UFSD #4, Huntington, N.Y., 1967—; trustee Eastwood Sch., Oyster Bay, N.Y., 1977-83; alumni interviewer, Georgetown U., Washington, 1989—. Mem. ASCD, Nat. Coun. for the Social Studies, N.Y. State United Tchrs. (com. 100). Home: 79 Little Neck Rd Centerport NY 11721-1615

MALLETTE, PHYLLIS EILEEN SPENCER, medical/surgical nurse; b. Chestertown, Md., Nov. 18, 1944; d. Charles P. and Elma (Brown) Spencer; children: Winsor A. Cooper, III and Elma Cooper Henderson; m. Arthur E. Mallette, June 5, 1982. ASN, Rutgers U., 1965; BSN cum laude, Trenton State Coll., 1978. Cert. critical care, IV therapy, acute respiratory care, OSHA regulations employee tng. program, advanced coronary care, med. office mgmt., case mgmt., utilization review; RN, Md., N.J., Pa. Nurse delivery room St. Francis Med. Ctr., Trenton, N.J., 1971-73; nurse ICU Delaware Valley Med. Ctr., Langhorne, Pa., 1973-74; coord. nights Robert Wood Johnson U. Hosp., New Brunswick, N.J., 1974-75; occupational health RN Warner-Lambert/Parke-Davis Co., Morris Plains, N.J., 1977-79; sr. profl. rep. hosp., coord. sales tng. Merck Human Health Svcs. Divsn., Phila., 1979-89; co-coord. 400 trainee field force expansion Merck Sharp & Dohme, Denver, 1989; clin. nurse Johns Hopkins Hosp., Balt., 1989-90; office mgr. Arthur E. Mallette, M.D., Pikesville, Md., 1990-94; quality mgmt. specialist Healthwise of Am., Chesapeake Health Plan, Balt., 1994—; med. cons. N.J. Pub. TV, Trenton, 1974. Mem. Sigma Theta Tau. Democrat. Methodist. Home: 1 Pomona E Apt 102 Pikesville MD 21208-2853 Office: Chesapeake Health Plan 814 Light St Baltimore MD 21230

MALLISHAM, IVY JOETTA, psychologist; b. Tuscaloosa, Ala., Apr. 28, 1956; d. Joseph W. and Sadie B. (Townsend) M. BS, U. Ala., 1978; D. Psychology, Hahnemann U., 1983. Psychologist, counselor, 1983-88; dir. counseling ctr. Columbus (Ga.) Coll., 1988—. Mem. APA, Am. Counseling Assn., Ga. Psychol. Assn. Democrat. Lutheran. Office: Columbus Coll 4225 University Ave Columbus GA 31907-5645

MALLORY, BARBARA ZOMMER, psychologist; b. New Haven, May 25, 1936; d. Peter and Estelle Ann (Serba) Zommer; m. George Boudreau, Apr. 11, 1955 (div. 1969); children: Deborah Boudreau, George Boudreau III, Scott Boudreau; m. Hunter Mallory, May 26, 1972 (div. 1978). BA, So. Conn. State U., 1968; MA, U. Conn., 1971; postgrad., Harvard U., 1973. Lic. capt. Coast Guard. Dir. rsch. study Mass. Gen. Hosp., Boston, 1972-74; dir. edn. Beacon Sch., Brookline, Mass., 1974-76; diagnostician Eagle Hill Clinic, Greenwich, Conn., 1976-78; dir. New Eng. office Edn. Records Bur., Wellesley, Mass., 1977-86; pvt. internat. cons., 1986-92; cons., rsch. analyst Social Cons. Internat., Inc., Alexandria, Va., 1992—. Mem. APA, Newport Yacht Club, Phi Delta Kappa. Address: 8409 Bound Brook Ln Alexandria VA 22309

MALLORY, DORIS ANN, social worker, counselor; b. Jeanerette, La., Aug. 12, 1946; d. Leroy (dec.) and Earlean (Bradley) Bourgeois; m. Booker Tony Mallory, Oct. 25, 1975; children: Vincent, Lieta Lynette, Kimberly Denise. BA, Grambling U., 1968; MSW, SUNY, Albany, 1971; MS in Counseling, L.I. U., 1983. Cert. social worker, N.Y.; nat. cert. counselor; diplomate Am. Register Clin. Social Workers. Substitute tchr. St. Mary Parish Sch. Bd., Franklin, La., 1968-69; chief social worker St. John's Day Care Ctr., Albany, 1971; coord. family care O.D. Heck Devel. Ctr., Valatie, N.Y., 1971-80; consent decree specialist Office Mental Retardation and

Devel. Disabilities, Albany, 1980-85, coord. consent decree, 1985-86, statewide family care coord., 1986—; family therapist D.A.M. Counseling, Albany, 1982-87, Project Hope Albany, 1988-90; mem. adj. faculty SUNY Sch. Social Welfare, 1978-87, Empire State Coll., Albany, 1987-88. Trustee, treas. choir, chmn. renovation com. Morning Star Missionary Bapt. Ch., Albany, 1969—, chmn. bd. trustees, 1994, 95. Recipient plaque Black Women's Assn. Albany, 1977, Family Care Providers Assn., 1977, 80, 94, Hope House, 1990, cert. for outstanding svc. YWCA, Albany, 1982. Mem. NASW, AACD, Assn. Black Social Workers, Assn. Multicultural Devel., Nat. Coun. Negro Women, N.Y. State Assn. Counseling Devel., Order Ea. Star (past mastron Albany 1983), Delta Sigma Theta (rec. sec. 1982, pres. Albany alumnae chpt. 1991-94, 91-95). Home: 44 Berkshire Dr Albany NY 12205-1216

MALLOY, KATHLEEN SHARON, lawyer; b. Evergreen Park, Ill., Apr. 7, 1948, d. Clarence Edmund and Ruth Elizabeth (Petrini) M.; m. Randall Kleinman, Aug. 5, 1978; children: Brighid, Ellena, Grant. BA in Psychology, St. Louis U., 1970; JD, Loyola U., Chgo., 1976. Bar: Ill. 1976, Calif. 1977. CPCU; assoc. in reinsurance. Account exec. Complete Equity Mkts., Wheeling, Ill., 1970-76, corp. counsel, 1976-80, v.p., gen. counsel, 1980-83, exec. v.p., gen. counsel, 1983, chief oper. officer, gen. counsel, 1984-85, vice chmn. bd., gen. counsel, 1986-90; founding ptnr. firm Malloy & Kleinman, P.C., Des Plaines, Ill., 1985—. Vol. atty. legal aid orgns., Calif., 1976-79; dir. Keep Des Plaines Beautiful, Inc., 1990-92. Mem. ABA, Calif. State Bar Assn., Mensa, Women's Bar Assn., Nat. Legal Aid and Defender Assn. (ex-officio mem. ins. com. 1986-94), Am. Soc. Chartered Property Casualty Underwriters. Office: Malloy & Kleinman PC 640 Pearson St Ste 206 Des Plaines IL 60016-4624

MALM, RITA P., securities executive; d. George Peter and Helen Marie (Woodward) Pellegrini; student Packard Jr. Coll., 1950-52, N.Y. Inst. Fin., 1954, Wagner Coll., 1955; m. Robert J. Malm, Apr. 19, 1970. Sales asst. Dean Witter & Co., N.Y.C., 1959-63, asst. v.p., compliance dir., 1969-74; v.p., dir. Securities Ind. Assocs., N.Y.C., 1969-72; chief exec. officer Muriel Siebert & Co., Inc., N.Y.C., 1981-83; pres., founder Madison-Chapin Assocs., N.Y.C., 1984-89; pres. Hayward Malm Securities, Ltd., 1989-93; pres., founder Concord Stuart, Inc., 1993—; art mktg. cons. Mem. NAFE (bd. dirs), Am. Cancer Soc. (bd. dirs. Jupiter/Tequesta chpt. 1992—), Profl. Women's Network (founder Palm Beach and Martin Counties 1991), Women's Bond Club N.Y. (dir., v.p., program chmn., pres. 1980-82), Cornell U. Club Ea. Fla. (bd. dirs. 1992—). Home: 1300 So A1A and Ocean Way Jupiter FL 33477-8458 Office: 900 S US Hwy 1 Ste 105 Jupiter FL 33477

MALME, JANE HAMLETT, lawyer, education researcher; b. N.Y.C., Dec. 2, 1934; d. Robert T. and Minnie (Means) Hamlett; m. Charles I. Malme, June 17, 1961; children: Robert H., Karen I. AB, Brown U., 1956; cert., U. Kobenhavn, Copenhagen, Denmark, 1959; JD, Northeastern U., 1977. Bar: Mass., 1977. Counsel Mass. Tax Commn., Boston, 1978-79; chief bur. local assessment Mass. Dept. Revenue, Boston, 1978-90; owner Mcpl. Mgmt. and Taxation Cons. Svcs., Hingham, Mass., 1990—; fellow Lincoln Inst. Land Policy, Inc., Cambridge, Mass., 1993—; faculty Lincoln Inst. of Land Policy, Inc., Cambridge, 1989—; cons., state, provincial coun. Internat. Assn. Assessing Officers Chgo., 1990—; advisor property tax OECD, Paris, 1993—. Co-author: (with Joan Youngman) Internat. Survey of Taxes on Land and Buildings, 1994; contbr. articles to tax jours., papers for Lincoln Inst. of Land Policy, Inc., 1991—. Mem. Dem. Town Com., Hingham, 1990-93; trustee Old Ship Ch., Hingham, 1992—; treas. Betty Taymor Scholarship Fund, Boston, 1992—; pres. Network for Women in Politics and Govt., McCormick Inst., Boston, 1992-94. Mem. Internat Assn. Assessing Officers (founder, state and prov. adminstrv. sec., Presidential citation 1983), Mass. Assn. Assessing Officers (hon. lifetime), Mass. Bar Assn., Womens Bar Assn., Nat. Assn. Tax Adminstrs. (chair property tax sect. 1988). Unitarian Universalist. Office: Lincoln Inst Land Policy 113 Brattle St Cambridge MA 02138-3400

MALMONT, VALERIE SKUSE, business owner, author; b. Cambridge, Mass., Dec. 20, 1937; d. Paul Howard and Margaret Spalding (Hall) Skuse; m. Bruce S. Malmont, Dec. 19, 1959; children: Paul Howard, Andrea Glynis, Jason Bruce. BA, U. N.Mex., 1961; MLS, U. Wash., 1964. Cert. tchr. in instructional media, Ohio, Pa. Libr. Arlington (Va.) County Libr. System, 1964-65; head libr. USAF Spl. Svcs. Libr., Taipei Air Sta., 1971-72, USN Spl. Svcs. Libr., Taipei, 1972-74; libr. Chambersburg (Pa.) Area Sch. Dist., 1978-83; owner Valerie Malmont Antiques and Collectibles, 1980—; spkr. various orgns. Author: Death Pays the Rose Rent, 1994; contbr. articles to profl. publs. Bd. dirs., treas. Cumberland Valley LINKS, Mont Alto, Pa., 1992—. Mem. AAUW (legis. chair, br. pres., Outstanding Woman 1987), DAR, Mystery Writers of Am., Sisters in Crime, Am. Crime Writers League, Romance Writers of Am., Beta Phi Mu. Democrat. Home: 33 Woodland Way Chambersburg PA 17201-3167

MALONE, DOROTHY ANN, underwriter, marketing executive, consultant, lecturer; b. Logansport, Ind., June 19, 1931; d. Harry and Lena Estella Malone. BBA, McKendree Coll., Radcliff, Ky., 1981; postgrad. in humanities Webster Coll., 1981-84; M. Pub. Service Adminstrn., Western Ky. U., 1984, M. Pub. Counseling, 1985. Lic. life and health agt. Joined U.S. Army, 1952, advanced through grades to master sgt., 1972, ret., 1975; ind. life underwriter, Elizabethtown, Ky., 1977—; dir. mktg. and sales Dixie Rabbit, Inc., Ekron, Ky., 1981—; sr. counselor, tchr. Southeastern Tng. Corp., Elizabethtown, 1987—; sr. instr., counselor AJS Enterprises, Inc., Tng. Corp. Am.; v.p. System, Tng., Employment Mgmt. Concepts, Inc.; cons., lectr. minority and women's subjects; edn. faciliator Advanced Systems in Measurement, Inc.; area mgr. Advanced Systems and Measurement Edn.; pvt. contracter Ky. Edn. Reform Act. First v.p. Hardin County (Ky.) chpt. NAACP, 1975; mem. Hardin County Human Relations Com., 1977-78; chairperson Hardin County Blue Ribbon Com., 1977; mem. Ky. Textbook Review Com.; trustee Embry Chapel AME Ch., Elizabethtown, 1983—; mem. Ky. Gov.'s Council on Volunteerism, 1992—; mem. strategic planning com. Hardin County Pub. Sch. System; commr. apptd. by Ky. Gov.'s Commn. on Human Rights, 1994. Decorated Army Commendation medal with 5 oak leaf clusters; recipient numerous letters of commendation and appreciation and awards, including cert. of appreciation NAACP, 1976, Key to City of Bowling Green, Ky., 1991, Friends of Edn. award Lottie O. Robinson Scholarship Com., 1994; named Honorable Ky. Col., 1986, others. Mem. Federally Employed Women (chairperson program Ft. Knox Area chpt. 1978-79, v.p. Ft. Knox Area chpt. 1978-79), Ky. Assn. Ret. Mil., Nat. Assn. Exec. Women, Ky. Cen. Assn. Life Underwriters, Life Investors' Pacer Club, Am. Defender Life Ins. Co., NAACP (life, chairperson status conf. of brs. for edn., vets. affairs, v.p., edn. chair Ky. conf. brs., edn. chair Hardin county br., Pres.'s award Ky. conf. brs. 1991, Award of Merit 1993), Am. Soc. Profl. and Exec. Women. Lodge: Order Eastern Star.

MALONE, ISABEL-LEE, drama therapist; b. Chgo., Apr. 28, 1940; d. James Eugene Jr. and Isabel Jean (Miller) M. BA in English Lit., Wheeling Jesuit Coll., 1962; MA in Drama Therapy, NYU, 1993; student, West Chester U., 1994—, Phila. Inst. Psychodrama, 1994—. Registered drama therapist. Editor, writer Am. Coun. on Edn., Washington, 1967-68; asst. prodn. mgr. Libr. Congress Press, Washington, 1968-78; property mgmt. asst. Begg Inc. Realtors, Washington, 1979-82; adminstrv. asst., bd. dirs. Claridge House Coop., Washington, 1982-84; asst. to exec. dir. House of Ruth, Washington, 1985-86; program mgr. ednl. theatre co. Creative Arts Team, NYU, 1987-90; drama therapy intern The Inst. Pa. Hosp., Phila., 1990-91; drama therapist, psychiatry Girard Med. Ctr., Phila., 1991—; exec. dir., co-founder Open Studio for the Performer, Washington, 1981-86; workshop producer Phila. Dream Alliance, 1994—. Organizer Fed. Employees for Peace, Washington, 1969-71; co-editor newsletter, mem. exec. com., del. city coun. Am. Fedn. State, County and Mcpl. Employees, AFL-CIO, Libr. Congress, Washington, 1971-75. Recipient First Caviar Club award Drama Soc., Wheeling Jesuit Coll., 1962; storytelling and performance grantee D.C. Cmty. Humanities Coun. and D.C. Com. in Arts and Humanities; honoraria from Washington Project for the Arts and Dance Exch., Jewelweed Mag., Wheeling, W.Va. Mem. Nat. Assn. for Drama Therapy, Am. Soc. for Group Psychotherapy and Psychodrama, Am. Soc. for Study of Dreams, Gamma Pi Epsilon. Democrat. Home: 351 Clearbrook Ave Lansdowne PA 19050-1001

MALONE, LINDA SUE, nurse; b. Shelby, N.C., Sept. 19, 1944; d. Garther Albert and Lucille (Smith) Whisnant; m. Gary P. Malone, Jan. 7, 1965; children: Mark Patrick, Gary Michael, Christopher Matthew. Diploma in nursing Charlotte Presbyn., N.C., 1965; BS, St. Joseph's Coll., 1986. RN, N.C., N.J., Hawaii; cert. profl. in health care quality. Nurse Heilbronn Elem. Sch., Germany, 1967-68; nurse pvt. duty Long Branch Nurses Registry, N.J., 1972-73; staff nurse Cape Fear Valley Med. Ctr., Fayetteville, N.C., 1975-78, coordinator quality assurance, 1978-85, dir. quality assurance, 1985-88, pres., N.C. Quality Assurance Profls., 1988-89; dir. quality assessment and risk mgmt. Highsmith-Rainey Meml. Hosp., Fayetteville, 1992—; cons., lectr. quality assurance. Vol. nurse Westover Jr. High Sch., Fayetteville, 1979; pres. Paramed. Service, Fayetteville, 1982-92. Mem. Presbyn. Hosp. Sch. Nursing Alumni Assn. (pres. 1990-91). Republican. Methodist. Avocations: crafts, gourmet cooking, water sports. Home: 426 Dunmore Rd Fayetteville NC 28303-2614 Office: Lithotripters Inc Dir Quality Mgmt Fayetteville NC 28301

MALONE, PERRILLAH ATKINSON (PAT MALONE), retired state official; b. Montgomery, Ala., Mar. 17, 1922; d. Odolph Edgar and Myrtle (Fondren) Atkinson. BS, Oglethorpe U., 1956; MAT, Emory U., 1962. Asst. editor, then acting editor Emory U., 1958-64; asst. project officer Ga. Dept. Pub. Health, Atlanta, 1965-68; asst. project dir. Ga. Ednl. Improvement Coun., 1968-69, assoc. dir., 1970-71; dir. career svcs. State Scholarship Commn., Atlanta, 1971-74; rev. coord. Div. Phys. Health, Ga. Dept. Human Resources, Atlanta, 1974-79; project dir. So. Regional Edn. Bd., 1979-81; specialist Div. Family and Children Svcs., Atlanta, 1982-91, ret., 1991; mem. Gov.'s Commn. on Nursing Edn. and Nursing Practice, 1972-75, Aging Svcs. Task Force, Atlanta Regional Commn., 1985—; book reviewer Atlanta Jour.-Constn., 1962-79. Recipient Recognition award Ga. Nursing Assn., 1976, Korsell award Ga. League for Nursing, 1974, Alumni Honor award Emory U., 1964. Mem. Am. Pub. Health Assn., Am. Pub. Welfare Assn., Ga. Gerontology Soc. (editor GGS Newsletter 1988-92, Lewis Newmark award 1991). Methodist. Home: 1146 Oxford Rd NE Atlanta GA 30306-2608

MALONEY, CAROLYN BOSHER, congresswoman; b. Feb. 19, 1948; d. R.G. and Christine (Clegg) Bosher; m. C.H.W. Maloney, 1976; children: Christina, Virginia. Student, Greensboro Coll., New Sch. for Social Rsch., N.Y., U. Dijon, Paris. Former mem. N.Y. State Assembly Housing Com., N.Y.C Council dist. 8; mem. 103rd Congress from 14th N.Y. dist., Washington, D.C., 1993—. Past chmn. Common Cause; active Assn. for a Better N.Y., Manahattan Women's Polit. Caucus. Mem. NAACP, Nat. Orgn. Women, Hadassah. Address: 49 E 92nd St Apt 1A New York NY 10128-1326 Office: US Ho of Reps Washington DC 20515

MALONEY, DIANE MARIE, legal nurse consultant; b. Aug. 15, 1951; d. John J. and Ruthe E. (Fournier) Perron; m. Patrick J. Maloney, Apr. 26, 1975; children: Melissa, Sheamus. Grad., Miller Hosp. Sch. Nursing, St. Paul, 1970; degree, Inver Hills Community Coll., Inver Grove Heights, Minn., 1988, cert. in paralegal/medical studies, 1989. Orthopedic specialist St. Luke's Hosp., St. Paul; head nurse Otolaryngology Profl. Assocs., St. Paul; charge nurse Southview Health Ctr., West St. Paul, Minn.; legal nurse cons. Milavetz and Assocs., Bloomington, Minn.; with Milavetz, Gallop & Milavetz, Edina, Minn. Mem. NAACOG, Am. Assn. Legal Nurse Cons., Minn. Assn. Legal Nurse Cons. (steering com.), Interstitial Cystitis Assn.

MALONEY, ERIN LOUISE BROCK, health educator, athletic trainer; b. Duxbury, Mass., May 23, 1959; d. John Anson and Nancy Geraldine (Hazelhurst) Brock; m. Patrick Reid Maloney, Oct. 27, 1984. BS, East Carolina U., 1982; MS in Edn., N.W. Mo. State U., 1984. Registered athletic trainer, Mo. Athletic trainer, educator Tarkio (Mo.) Coll., 1985-86, McCluer High Sch., Florissant, Mo., 1986—. Mem. Nat. Athletic Trainer's Assn. (cert., presenter nat. conv. 1993, test site coord. bd. certification 1989—), Mid Am. Athletic Trainers's Assn. (bd. dirs. 1992-93), Mo. Athletic Trainer's Assn. (pres.-elect 1989-91, pres. 1992-93, Mo. Athletic Trainer of Yr. 1993). Office: McCluer High Sch 1896 S Florissant Rd Florissant MO 63031

MALONEY, LUCILLE TINKER, civic worker; b. Twin Falls, Idaho, Mar. 13, 1920; d. Edward Milo and Lillian (Schaefer) Tinker; Frank E. Maloney, Feb. 20, 1943 (dec.); children: Frank E., JoAnn Maloney Smallwood, Elizabeth Maloney Hurst. Tchr's cert., Idaho State U.; student Wash. State U., 1941. Pres., U. Fla. Women's Club, 1960-61, Gainesville Women's Club, 1974-75, Friends of Five Sta. WUFT-TV, Public Broadcasting, 1976-77; chmn., organizer Gainesville Spring Pilgrimage, 1976; founder, pres. Thomas Center Assocs., 1978-80; v.p. U. Fla. Art Gallery Guild, 1981, pres., 1982-84; mem. Fla. Gov.'s Challenge Program Com., 1981; trustee Fla. House, Washington, 1975-80; chmn. Santa Fe Regional Library Bd., 1980-81; pres. Gainesville Women's Forum, 1984-85; mem. Exec. Commn. Fla. for Statue of Liberty-Ellis Island Centennial; bd. dirs. Classic 89, Nat. Pub. Radio, 1987—; trustee Displaced Homemakers, Santa Fe Community Coll.; adv. bd. Gainesville for Thomas Ctr. Gardens, 1985—; bd. dir. Fla. Performing Arts Affiliates, 1990—. Recipient Fla. Leadership pin Gov. LeRoy Collins, 1961, Disting. Svc. award Women in Communication, Inc., 1975, Appreciation plaque Sta. WUFT-TV, 1977, Community Svc. award Gainesville Sun, 1979, Appreciation cert. Rotary Club Gainesville, 1980, Paul Harris fellow Rotary Club, 1986, Svc. Above Self award, 1991, Gainesville Area Woman of Distinction award Sante Fe Community Coll., 1987, Outstanding Svc. award Jr. League, 1980, Bicentennial plaque Alachua County Bicentennial Com., 1976, plaque Gainesville City Beautification Bd., 1990, Coll. Law U. Fla., 1993, 1st Lifetime Achievement award Channel 5, PBS, Classic 89 Radio and coll. journalism U. Fla., 1994; honoree Alachua County Girls' Club Bd. Roast and Toast, 1990, Lucille T. Maloney Conf. Rm. named in her honor Thomas Ctr. Mem. Friends of Libr., Fla. State Mus. Assocs. (pres. 1985-87), Friends of Music, Hist. Gainesville, Inc., Found. for Promotion Music, Civic Chorus, Fla. Trust for Hist. Preservation, Fla. League Conservation Voters (bd. dirs. 1983—), Gainesville C. of C. (pub. affairs com. 1983-84), Altrusa Internat., Internat. Platform Assn., Fla. Women's Network, Howe Soc. for Rare Books (bd. dirs.), U. Fla. Club, Gainesville Garden Club, Heritage Club (bd. govs.). Home: 1823 NW 10th Ave Gainesville FL 32605-5311

MALONEY, PATSY LORETTA, nursing educator; b. Murfreesboro, Tenn., Feb. 19, 1952; d. Buford Leon Browning and Ina (Bush) Dubose; m. Richard J. Maloney, July 26, 1975; children: Katherine Nalani, Nathaniel Allen, Elizabeth Maureen. BS in Nursing, U. Md., 1974; MA, Cath. U., 1984, MS in Nursing, 1984; EdD, U. So. Calif., 1994. Commd. 1st lt. U.S. Army, 1974, advanced through grades to lt. col., 1989; asst. chief nurse evenings and nights DeWitt Army Hosp., Fort Belvoir, Va.; chief nurse, tng. officer 85th EVAC Hosp., Ft. Lee, Va.; clin. head nurse emergency rm./PCU Tripler Army Med. Ctr., Honolulu, chief nursing edn.; chief surg. nursing sect. Madigan Army Med. Ctr., Tacoma; ret. U.S. Army, 1994; chief acute care nursing sect. Madigan Army Med. Ctr. Mem. Emergency Nurses Assn., Nat. Nursing Staff Devel. Orgn., Assn. Mil. Surgeons, Acad. Med. Surg. Nurses, Sigma Theta Tau, Phi Kappa Phi. Home: 7002 53rd St W Tacoma WA 98467-2214

MALONEY, THERESE ADELE, insurance company executive; b. Quincy, Mass., Sept. 15, 1929; d. James Henry and F. Adele (Powers) M. BA in Econs., Coll. St. Elizabeth, Convent Station, N.J., 1951; AMP, Harvard U. Bus. Sch., 1981. CPCU. With Liberty Mut. Ins. Co., Boston, 1951-94, asst. v.p., asst. mgr. nat. risks, 1974-77, v.p., asst. mgr. nat. risks, 1977-79, v.p., mgr. nat. risks, 1979-86, sr. v.p. underwriting mktg. and adminstrn. 1986-87, exec. v.p. underwriting, policy decision, 1987-94, also bd. dirs.; pres. and bd. dirs. subs. Liberty Mut. (Bermuda) Ltd., 1981-94, LEXCO Ltd.; bd. dirs., dep. chmn. Liberty Mut. (U.K.) Ltd., London; bd. dirs. Liberty Mut. Ins. Co., Liberty Mut. Fire Ins. Co., Liberty Mut. Life Assurance Co., Liberty Fin. Cos.; mem. faculty Inst. Inst., Northeastern U., Boston, 1969-74; mem. adv. bd., risk mgmt. studies Ins. Inst. Am., 1977-83; mem. adv. coun. Suffolk U. Sch. Mgmt., 1984—; mem. adv. coun. to program in internat. bus. rels. Fletcher Sch. Law and Diplomacy, 1985-94. Mem. Soc. CPCUs (past pres. Boston chpt.), Univ. Club, Algonquin Club (Boston), Boston Club, Mass. Women's Forum.

MALOUF-CUNDY, PAMELA BONNIE, visual arts editor; b. Reseda, Calif., July 9, 1956; d. Jubert George and Marguerite I. (Llido) Malouf. AA in Cinema with honors, Valley Community Coll., 1976. Asst. film editor various film studios including Paramount, 20th Fox, CBS MTM, and others, 1976-80; post prodn. coordinator, supr. David Gerber Co., Culver City, Calif., 1981-82; post prodn. coordinator Paramount TV, Los Angeles, 1982-84; sole proprietor Trailers, Etc., North Hollywood, Calif., 1984-85; film and video editor Paramount Pictures, L.A., 1985-86; film editor Universal Studios, Universal City, Calif., 1987-89; film, video editor New World TV, L.A., 1991-92; associate dir. Tri-Star TV, Studio City, Calif., 1992-93; film and video editor various studios, Studio City, 1993—; owner, mgr. Choice Editing Systems, Northridge, Calif., 1993—. Film and video editor: (TV shows) A Year in the Life, MacGyver, Call to Glory, The Making of Shogun, Nightingales, Mission Impossible, Murder C.O.D., I'll Take Romance, Get a Life, A Fire in the Dark, The Fifth Corner, The Edge, others (movies) Search for Grace, Eyes of Terrror, Then There Was One, Sweet Bird of Youth, Without You I'm Nothing, All in the Family, Rockford Files, Is There Life Out There?; asst. film editor: (movies) King of Gypsies, Star Wars, others. Mem. Internat. Alliance of Theatrical Stage Employees and Moving Picture Machine Operators of U.S. and Can., Tri-Network (pres. 1979-80), Acad. Magical Arts, Inc., Am. Cinema Editors, Acad. TV Arts and Scis., Dir.'s Guild of Am. Democrat. Roman Catholic.

MALOY, MARY MONAHAN, school nurse; b. Glenolden, Pa., Feb. 16, 1959; d. John Timothy and Jane Theresa (Murphy) Monahan; m. Joseph A. Maloy, Nov. 19, 1983; children: Joseph III, John. BS cum laude, U. Del., 1981. RN, N.J. Staff nurse Children's Hosp. of Phila., 1981-83, Cape May County Schs. for Spl. Svcs., N.J., 1983-92, Wildwood Crest (N.J.) Schs., 1992—; pvt. duty nurse, Wildwood Crest; drug and alcohol consortium rep. Drug-Free Schs. Consortium, C.M.C.H., N.J., 1992—, peer leader advisor. Emergency mgmt. team Wildwood Crest Polit. Appointment, 1993. Roman Catholic. Office: Wildwood Crest Sch Dist 9100 Pacific Ave Wildwood NJ 08260-3433

MALSON, VERNA LEE, educator; b. Buffalo, Wyo., Mar. 29, 1937; d. Guy James and Vera Pearl (Curtis) Mayer; m. Jack Lee Malson, Apr. 20, 1955; children: Daniel Lee, Thomas James, Mark David, Scott Allen. BA in Elem. Edn. and Spl. Edn. magna cum laude, Met. State Coll., Denver, 1975; MA in Learning Disabilities, U. No. Colo., 1977. Cert. tchr., Colo. Tchr.-aide Wyo. State Tng. Sch., Lander, 1967-69; spl. edn. tchr. Bennett Sch. 29J, Colo., 1975-79, chmn. health, sci., social studies, 1977-79; spl. edn. tchr. Deer Trail Sch., Colo., 1979—, chmn. careers, gifted and talented, 1979-87, spl. edn./preschool tchr. 1992—; course cons. Regis Coll., Denver, 1990; mem. spl. edn. parent adv. com. East Central Bd. Coop. Ednl. Services, Limon, Colo. Colo. scholar Met. State Coll., 1974; Colo. Dept. Edn. grantee, 1979, 81; recipient Cert. of Achievement, Met. State Coll., 1993. Mem. Council Exceptional Children, Bennett Tchrs. Club (treas. 1977-79), Kappa Delta Pi. Republican. Presbyterian. Avocations: coin collecting; reading; sports. Home: PO Box 403 Deer Trail CO 80105-0403 Office: Deer Trail Pub Schs PO Box 26J Deer Trail CO 80105-0026

MALTBY, SUE ELLEN, special education educator; b. Waterford, Ohio, Apr. 30, 1950; d. James Lawrence and Agatha Macel (Crosby) Starcher; m. Marshall Martin Maltby, Nov. 25, 1978; stepchildren: Laura Leigh Maltby Karanthasis, Lisa Michelle Maltby Atkinson. BA, Marietta Coll., 1972; MA, Ga. Coll., 1976. Cert. tchr., adminstr., W.Va. Psychology technician Cen. State Hosp., Milledgeville, Ga., 1972-74, psychologist, 1976-77; psychologist Ga. War Vets. Home, Milledgeville, 1974-76; mental retardation specialist Albany (Ga.) Mental Health/Mental Retardation Ctr., 1977-81; dir. residential program Colin Anderson Ctr., St. Marys, W.Va., 1981-84; tchr. spl. edn. W.Va. Dept. Edn., St. Marys, 1984-91; lead tchr. W.Va. Dept. Edn., Waverly, 1991—; tech. asst. cons. County Bds. Edn., W.Va., 1985—, insvc. presenter, 1985—. Recipient Outstanding Svc. award Ga. Assn. Retarded Citizens, 1978. Mem. Assn. Retarded Citizens, Assn. Severely Handicapped, Coun. Exceptional Children/Persons, Nat. Down Syndrome Assn. Republican. Methodist. Home: Rte 1 Box 21C Waterford OH 45786

MALTIN, FREDA, retired university administrator; b. Calgary, Alta., Can., June 4, 1923; came to the U.S., 1958; d. Meyers Wolfe and Ida (Kohn) Rosen; m. Manny Maltin, Aug. 25, 1950; 1 child, Richard Allan. Diploma Garbutt's Bus. Coll., Calgary, 1942. Various secretarial and bookkeeping positions, 1951; mem. adminstrv. staff U. So. Calif., 1960-92, asst. to exec. dir. Davidson Conf. Ctr., 1987-92, Grad. Sch. Bus. Adminstrn., 1981-92. Recipient staff achievement award U. So. Calif., 1991. Mem. Exec. Women Internat., U. So. Calif. Staff Club (charter), U. So. Calif. Skull and Dagger (hon.), U. So. Calif. Town and Gown.

MAMARCHEV, HELEN LORRAINE, college administrator; b. Houston, Oct. 28, 1949; d. James Dimitri and Marion Helen (Prewett) M. B.A., So. Meth. U., 1971; M.S. in Edn., Ind. U., 1973; Ph.D., U. Mich., 1981. Resident asst. So. Meth. U., Dallas, 1969-71; asst. coord. Ind. U., Bloomington, 1971-73; asst. dean of women U. Kans., Lawrence, 1973-76; asst. dir. and sr. info. specialist Ednl. Resources Info. Ctr., Ann Arbor, Mich., 1976-83; assoc. v.p. for student affairs U. Fla., Gainesville, 1983—. Newsletter editor LWV, Gainesville, 1984-85; bd. dirs. Coordinated Transp. System, Inc., Gainesville, 1985. Mem. AAUW, Nat. Assn. for Women Deans Adminstrs. Counselors (chair adminstrv. div. 1987—, cert. of merit 1980, pres. 1990-91), Am. Coll. Pers. Assn., Pi Lambda Theta, Phi Delta Kappa. Methodist. Club: Altrusa. Avocations: walking; reading. Home: 4507 NW 32d Ave Gainesville FL 32606 Office: U Fla 129 Tigert Hall Gainesville FL 32611

MAMLOK, URSULA, composer, educator; b. Berlin, Feb. 1, 1928; d. John and Dorothy Lewis; m. Dwight G. Mamlok, Nov. 27, 1947. Student, Mannes Coll. Music, 1942-45; MusB, Manhattan Sch. Music, 1955, MusM, 1958. Mem. faculty dept. music NYU, 1967-74, CUNY, 1971-74; prof. composition Manhattan Sch. Music, N.Y.C., 1974—. Composer: numerous works including Variations and Interludes for 4 percussionists, 1973, Sextet, 1977, Festive Sounds, 1978, When Summer Sang, 1980, piano trio Panta rhei, 1981, 5 recital pieces for young pianists, 1983, From My Garden for solo viola or solo violin, 1983, Concertino for wind quintet, Strings and percussion, 1984, Der Andreas Garten for voice, flute and harp, 1986, Alariana for recorder, clarinet, bassoon, violin and cello, 1986, 3 Bagatelles for harpsichord, 1987, 5 Bagatelles for clarinet, violin, cello, 1988, Rhapsody for clarinet, viola, piano Inward Journey for Piano, 1989, Sonata for violin and piano, 1989, Music for flute, violin, cello, 1990, Girasol, a sextet for flute, violin, viola, cello and piano, 1991, Constellations for orch., 1993. Recipient Serge Koussevitzky Found. commn., 1988, Walter Hinrichsen award Acad. Inst. Arts and Letters, 1989, commn. San Francisco Symphony, 1990; Nat. Endowment Arts grantee, 1974, Am. Inst. Acad. Arts and Letters grantee, 1981, 89, Martha Baird Rockefeller grantee, 1982. Mem. Am. Composers Alliance (dir., Opus One Recording award 1987), Am. Soc. Univ. Composers, Am. Women Composers, N.Y. Women Composers, Internat. League Women Composers, Music Theory Soc. N.Y., Am. Music Center, Internat. Soc. Contemporary Music (bd. dirs.). Address: 315 E 86th St New York NY 10028-4714

MAMPRE, VIRGINIA ELIZABETH, communications executive; b. Chgo., Sept. 12, 1949; d. Albert Leon and Virginia S. (Joboul) M. BA with honors, U. Iowa, 1971; Masters degree, Ind. U., 1972; spl. cert., Harvard U., 1981. Cert. tchr. Harris Intern WTTW-TV Sta., Chgo., 1972, asst. dir., 1972-73; prod. and dir. WSIU/WUSI-TV Sta., Carbondale, Ill., 1973-74; instr. So. Ill. U., Carbondale, 1972-77; prog. and prod. mgr. WSIU/WUSI-TV, Carbondale, 1974-77; prog. dir. KUHT-TV Sta., Houston, 1977-83; pres. Victory Media, Inc., Houston, 1984-89, Mampre Media Internat., Houston, 1984—; pres. A.I.C.B.; cons. Corp. for Pub. Broadcasting, Washington, 1981-83; chmn. AWRT/YCOC Houston Metro Area, 1983-85, pres., 1983—, nat. v.p., 1985-90; adv. coun. PBS, Washington, 1981-83; bd. and programming chmn. So. Edn. Comms., Columbia, S.C., 1978-83; bd. dirs. TVPC. Contbg. author/editor to mags. including Focus, 1989, News & Views, 1987-88, In the Black, 1984-93; creator: (report card campaign) Multi-media, U.S., 1985—; exec. prodr. TV spls., pub. affairs and info., 1977-83 (awards 1978-91). Pres. bd. dirs. Houston Fin. Coun., 1983—; pres. Child Abuse Prevention Coun., Houston, 1984—; bd. dirs. Child Abuse Prevention Network, 1990—; officer bd. dirs. Crime Stoppers Houston, 1984—; chmn. exhbns. Mayor's 1st Hearing, Children and Youth, Houston, 1985-88; founder, bd. dirs. Friends of WSIU-TV, 1974-77; chmn. Evening Guild St. John the Divine, St. Kevork/ACYO Nat. sports fair, 1990; rep. for Houston 2d World Conf. on Mayors, Japan, 1989. Fellow W.K. Kellogg Found., Battle Creek, Mich., 1987-90; recipient award for Excellence Pres. Pvt. Sector, White House, Washington, 1987, Ohio State U., Columbus, 1983, Feddersen award for excellence in Pub. TV Ind. U., Bloomington,

1981, Heritage award Child Abuse Prevention Coun., 1990, Dona J. Stone Founders award Nat. Assn. for Prevention of Child Abuse, 1990; named among Outstanding Women Vols. for community, civic and profl. contbns., Fedn. Houston Profl. Women, 1989; finalist Woman on the Move, 1987, Rising Star, 1987. Mem. Am. Women in Radio and TV (nat. v.p. 1986-90, award 1987, pres. Houston chpt. 1990, bd. dirs. 1985—), Houston Fed. Profl. Women (pres., del. 1986-93, chmn. 1994), Nat. Assn. Ednl. Broadcasters (presenter nat. conv. 1975-76), Tex. Lyceum (v.p., bd. dirs. 1990—), Dephians, Nat. Assn. for Programming TV Execs., Fedn. Houston Profl. Women Ednl. Found. (bd. dirs. 1994—), Ctr. for Bus. Women's Deve. (bd. dirs. 1993-94). Republican. Episcopalian. Office: Mampre Media Internat 5123 Del Monte Dr Houston TX 77056-4302

MAMULA, NANCY ANN, sales executive; b. Buffalo, Sept. 29, 1945; d. George and Lucille Mary (Lorenzo) Miserantino; m. Joseph Daniel Gnozzo, May 28, 1966 (div.); children: Jamie, Steven; m. Ronald S. Mamula, Jan. 2, 1994. BS, SUNY, Buffalo, 1967. Tchr. Bd. Coop. Ednl. Services, Umsville, N.Y., 1971-72; dir. Barbizon Sch. Modeling Services, Buffalo, 1978-80; account exec. Sta. WPhD, Buffalo, 1980-82; account exec., regional mgr. Sta. WHTT, Buffalo, 1982—; voice talent coordinator free lance, Buffalo, 1978-88. Mem. Am. Women in Radio and TV, Nat. Assn. Female Execs. Office: Sta WHTT Buffalo Hilton Hotel Church and Terrace Sts Buffalo NY 14202

MAMUT, MARY CATHERINE, retired entrepreneur; b. Calabria, Italy, Oct. 17, 1923; came to U.S., 1928; d. Carmelo Charles and Caterina (Tripodi) Cogliandro; m. Michael Matthew Mamut, May 15, 1954; children: Anthony Carl, Charles Terrance. Student, Stenotype Comml. Coll., 1946-54. Sec. to pres. Thomas Goodfellow, Inc., Detroit, 1942-50; asst. to v.p. R.G. Moeller Co., Detroit, 1951-52; sec. to pres. United Steel Supply Co., Detroit, 1952-54; sec. to libr. Farmington (Mich.) Schs., 1962-68; real estate agt., 1969; owner, mgr. Crystal Fair, Birmingham, Mich., 1969-88; ret. Crystal Fair, Mich.; tchr. Stenotype Comml. Coll., Detroit, 1952-54. Vol. Henry Ford Mus., Dearborn, Mich., 1989-90, Greenfield Village, 1989-90, West Bloomfield Libr., 1993—. Recipient World Lifetime Achievement award ABI U.S.A., 1993. Mem. Am. Bus. Women's Assn., Birmingham-Bloomfield C. of C., Profl. Secs. Internat, NAFE. Roman Catholic. Home: 7423 Coach Ln West Bloomfield MI 48322-4022

MAN, MARY ANN, medical technologist; b. Durham, N.C., Apr. 14, 1945; d. Robert Martin and Edna Lee (Henley) M. BS, Ctrl. Mich. U., 1968. Med. technologist Branch County Community Health Ctr., Coldwater, Mich., 1967-68, Good Samaritan Hosp., Cin., 1968-77, Lykes Meml. Hosp., Brooksville, Fla., 1977, South Fla. Bapt. Hosp., Plant City, 1977-78; med. technologist James A. Haley Vets. Hosp., Tampa, Fla., 1978—, social chmn. lab. svc., 1990. Mem. disability com. Vets. Hosp., 1990-92; mem. abilities guild Abilities of Fla., 1993, Ams. with Disabilities Act Ctr., 1993—. Named Outstanding Handicapped Fed. Employee of Yr., Vets. Adminstrn., 1981. Democrat. Episcopalian. Office: James A Haley Vets Hosp 13000 Bruce B Downs Blvd Tampa FL 33612

MANASC, VIVIAN, architect, consultant; b. Bucharest, Romania, May 19, 1956; d. Bercu and Bianca (Smetterling) M.; m. William A. Dushenski, Feb. 25, 1984; children: Peter Gabriel, Lawrence Alexander. BS in Architecture, McGill U., Montreal, Que., Can., 1977, BArch, 1979; MBA, U. Alta., Edmonton, 1982. Architectural insp. Transport Can., Edmonton, 1977-79; project architect Bell Spotowski Architects, Edmonton, 1980-82; asst. dir. design constrn. Edmonton Pub. Schs., 1982-84; mgr., prin. Ferguson, Simek, Clark Architects Ltd., Edmonton, 1985-88; mng. dir. FSC Groves Hodgson Manasc Architects Ltd., Edmonton, 1988—. Contbr. articles to profl. jours. Advisor YWCA, Edmonton, 1980-82; mentor RAIC Syllabus Program, Edmonton, 1982-88; bd. dirs. Design Workshop, Edmonton, 1983. Scholar McGill U., 1974. Mem. Royal Archtl. Inst. Can. (chmn. architecture for healthcare com.), Alta. Assn. Architects, Coun. Edn. Facility Planners, Nat. Coun. Jewish Women (past pres. Edmonton sect.), Jewish Fedn. Edmonton (v.p. planning). Office: FSC Groves Hodgson Manasc, 10417 Saskatchewan Dr, Edmonton, AB Canada T6E 4R8

MANCALL, JACQUELINE COOPER, library science educator, information science educator; b. Phila., Mar. 31, 1932; d. Morris and Bertha Cooper; 1953; m. Elliott Lee Mancall, Dec. 27, 1953; children: Andrew Cooper, Peter Cooper. B.A., U. Pa., 1954; M.S., Drexel U. Sch. Libr. and Info. Sci., 1970, Ph.D., 1979. Adminstr., Miquon (Pa.) Sch., 1966-67, libr., 1967-76; teaching asst. Drexel U., Phila., 1976-78, rsch. assoc., 1979, asst. prof., 1979-85, assoc. prof., 1985-89, prof., 1989; chair Phila. Children's Reading Round Table, 1982-84, mem. steering com., 1979-89; mem. faculty coun. Drexel U., 1984-89, chair, 1987-89; mem. sch. libr. survey com. State Libr. Pa., 1983; cons. Author: (with M. Carl Drott) Measuring Student Information Use: A Guide for Sch. Library Media Specialists 1983, (with Elizabeth S. Aversa) Management of Online Search Services in Schools, 1989; rsch. editor Sch. Libr. Media quar., 1982-88; editorial bd. Jour. Libr. and Info. Sci. Edn., 1981-86; contbg. editor Catholic Libr. World, 1981-85; contbr. chpts. to books, articles to profl. jours. Bd. dirs. Friends of William Jeannes Meml. Libr., Plymouth Meeting, Pa., 1976-79; pres. bd. dirs. Miquon Sch., 1964-66. Mem. ALA (chair Am. Assn. Sch. Librs. rsch. com. 1983-85, chmn. continuing edn. com. 1985-87, v.p./pres.elect, 1993, pres. 1994), Pa. Sch. Librs. Assn. (bd. dirs. 1984-87, chmn. profl. standard com. 1980-82, 91—, tech. com. 1982-84), Assn. Am. Libr. Schs., Pi Gamma Mu, Beta Phi Mu, Phi Delta Kappa. Democrat. Jewish. Home: Harts Ln Miquon PA 19452 Office: Drexel U Coll Info Studies Philadelphia PA 19104

MANCHER, RHODA ROSS, federal agency administrator, strategic planner; b. N.Y.C., Sept. 28, 1935; d. Joseph and Hannah (Karpf) Ross; m. Melvin Mancher, May 27, 1962 (dec.); children: Amy Meg, James Marc. B.S. in Physics, Columbia U., 1960; M.S. in Ops. Research, George Washington U., 1978. Cons. pvt. practice, Bethesda, Md., 1994—; staff FEA, Washington, 1974-77; dir. info. systems devel. div. The White House, Washington, 1977-79; dir. office systems devel. Social Security Adminstrn., Balt., 1979-80; dep. asst. atty. gen. Office Info. Tech., Dept. Justice, Washington, 1980-84; assoc. dir. info. resources mgmt. Dept. Navy, Washington, 1985-87; dir. Office Info. Tech. VA, Washington, 1987-94; mem. ad hoc com. on recommendations to merge chem. and biol. info. systems Nat. Cancer Inst., Washington; chmn. permanent com. on info. tech. Iternat. Criminal Police Orgn. (INTERPOL); mem. curriculum com. USDA, adv. bd. computer system security and privacy U.S. Govt.; internat. tech. com. AFCEA. Contbr. articles to profl. pubs. Recipient Assoc. Commr.'s citation Social Security Adminstrn., 1980, managerial excellence award Interagy. Com. on ADP, 1983; Meritorious award Sr. Exec. Svc., 1982, 83, 85, 87, 88, 91-93, Presdl. Rank of Meritorious Exec., 1990. Mem. Am. Fedn. Info. Processing Socs. (nat. info. issues panel).

MANCHESTER, CAROL ANN FRESHWATER, psychologist; b. Coshocton, Ohio, Sept. 30, 1942; d. James M. and Kathleen C. (Call) Freshwater; m. Crosby Manchester, Mar. 16, 1963 (dec. 1973). BS, Ohio State U., 1963, MS, 1973, PhD, 1977. Diplomate Internat. Soc. Psychotherapy and Behavioral Medicine. Elem. counselor Columbus (Ohio) Pub. Schs., 1973-79; counselor Regional Alcoholism & Tng. Ctr., Columbus, 1977-79; therapist Beechwold Clinic, Columbus, 1977-80; counselor Gifted and Talented Program, Columbus, 1979-81; dir. Freshwater Mental Health Clinic, Columbus, 1982—; asst. clin. prof. Coll. Medicine Ohio State U., 1990-92; instr. psychology Urbana Coll., Columbus, 1977-79; dir. Freshwater Clinic, Columbus, 1983—; bd. dirs. Ecole Francaise, Columbus, 1985—; cons. Columbus Cmty. Hosp., 1988—, Mt. Carmel Med. Ctr., Park Med. Ctr., Columbus, 1990—; presenter in field. Author: Affective Model The Gifted and Talented Handbook for Columbus Public Schools, 1981. Active Gov.'s Task Force on Child Abuse, Columbus. Recipient Disting. Svc. award Ohio Counselor's Assn., Valley Forge Freedom award. Mem. ACLU, AOA, Am. Acad. Cert. Neurotherapists (v.p. 1993, 94, diplomate, exec. bd. dirs.), Am. Acad. Neurobrainwave Therapists (v.p.), Soc. of Neuronal Regulation (v.p.), Nat. Soc. Clin. Hypnosis, Meninger Soc., Internat. Soc. Post Traumatic Stress, Internat. Soc. Multiple Personality Disorder, Assn. Applied Psychophysiology and Biofeedback, Ohio Psychol. Assn., Delta Omicron, Tau Beta Sigma. Office: Freshwater Clinic 6065 Glick Rd Ste C Powell OH 43065-9604

MANCINI, MARY CATHERINE, cardiothoracic surgeon, researcher; b. Scranton, Pa., Dec. 15, 1953; d. Peter Louis and Ferminia Teresa (Massi) M. BS in Chemistry, U. Pitts., 1974, MD, 1978; postgrad. in Anatomy and Cellular Biolog, La. State U. Med. Ctr., 1994—. Diplomate Am. Bd. Surgery (speciality cert. critical care medicine), Am. Bd. Thoracic Surgery. Intern in surgery U. Pitts., 1978-79, resident in surgery, 1979-87; fellow pediatric cardiac surgery Mayo Clinic, 1987-88; asst. prof. surgery, dir. cardiothoracic transplantation Med. Coll. Ohio, Toledo, 1988-91; assoc. prof. surgery, dir. cardiothoracic transplantation La. State U. Med. Ctr., Shreveport, 1991—. Author: Operative Techniques for Medical Students, 1983; contbr. articles to profl. jours. Recipient Pres.'s award Internat. Soc. Heart Transplantation, 1983, Charles C. Moore Teaching award U. Pitts., 1985, Internat. Woman of Yr. award, 1992-93; rsch. grantee Am. Heart Assn., 1988. Fellow ACS, Am. Coll. Chest Physicians, Internat. Coll. Surgeons (councillor 1991—); mem. Assn. Women Surgeons, Rotary (gift of life program 1991). Roman Catholic. Office: La State U Med Ctr 1501 Kings Hwy Shreveport LA 71103-4228

MANCINI, MARY ELIZABETH, nursing executive; b. Providence, Nov. 7, 1953; d. Thomas Anthony and Letitia (Gentile) Rando; m. David Lee Mancini, Feb. 10, 1974; children: Laura Letitia, Carla Elizabeth. Student, Providence Coll., 1971-73; ADN, R.I. Jr. Coll., 1975; BSN, R.I. Coll., 1976; MS in Nursing in Adminstrn., U. R.I., 1982. RN, R.I., Tex., FAAN, 1994; cert. ACLS instr. Staff nurse Roger Williams Gen. Hosp., Providence, 1976-77; charge nurse Good Samaritan Hosp., Cin., 1977-78; staff nurse ICU and CCU, Miriam Hosp., Providence, 1978-79, asst. head nurse, 1979-81, head nurse, 1981-83; asst. dir. nursing R.I. Hosp., Providence, 1983-84; dir. emergency svcs. Parkland Meml. Hosp., Dallas, 1984-86, v.p. nursing adminstrn., 1986-93, sr. v.p. nursing adminstr., 1993—; mem. affiliate nursing staff U. R.I., Kingston, 1981-83; mem. clin. faculty U. Tex. Southwestern Med. Ctr., Dallas, 1986—; adj. clin. prof. U. Tex., Arlington, 1986—, mem. adv. bd. for grad. edn. in nursing adminstrn. Sch. Nursing, 1990—; adj. assoc. prof. U. N.D., Grand Forks, 1987—; mem. select com. on doctoral nursing programs U. Tex. System, 1989—; asst. clin. prof. Tex. Woman's U. Coll. of Nursing, 1993; adj. prof. Sch. Law Baylor U., 1993; mem. healthcare manpower shortage com. Dallas-Ft. Worth Hosp. Coun., 1989—; mem. assoc. degree nursing adv. com. El Centro Coll., 1991—; mem., chairperson membership com. Am. Hosp. Assn. Inst. for Clin. Nursing Edn., 1992. Contbr. articles to profl. jours. Founder, chairperson Dallas, Ft. Worth Great 100 Nurses Celebration, 1991-93. Grantee Laerdal Found. for Acute Medicine, 1984-87; Wharton nurse fellow Johnson & Johnson, 1987. Fellow ANA (cert. in nursing adminstrn.), Am. Acad. Nursing; mem. AACCN, Nat. Assoc. Pub. Hosp. Tex. Nurses Assn. (Nurse of Yr. award dist. 4, 1991), Am. Heart Assn. (nat. working group for ACLS 1983-85), Nat. League for Nursing (nominations com. 1993), Emergency Dept. Nurses Assn. (profl. practice com. Greater Dallas chpt., sec. 1985-86, editor Tex. Newsletter 1986-87), Dallas-Ft. Worth Hosp. Coun. Nurse Adminstrs. Forum (pres. 1991), Tex. Soc. for Nursing Svc. Adminstrs., Am. Orgn. Nurse Execs., Soc. Trauma Nurses (editorial bd. 1991—), Phi Theta Kappa, Sigma Theta Tau. Home: 4413 Arlen Ct Plano TX 75093-6701 Office: Parkland Meml Hosp 5201 Harry Hines Blvd Dallas TX 75235

MANCINI, WENDY MAE, critical care nurse; b. Neptune, N.J., May 13, 1950; d. John Robert and Shirley Mae (Slater) Morris; m. Wayne A. Mancini, June 15, 1984; children: Heather Lee, Sarah Ashley. ASN, SUNY, Albany, 1985, BSN, 1987; MSN, Seton Hall U., 1993. Cert. clin. nurse specialist; CCRN, CNA, BLS instr., ABLS, ACLS. Staff nurse Jersey Shore Med. Ctr., Neptune, N.J.; asst. nurse mgr. ICU Jersey Shore Med. Ctr., Neptune, critical care nurse clinician intensive care/coronary care, 1991-93; critical care CNS Jersey Shore Med. Ctr., 1993—; clin. instr. Coll. of Nursing Rutgers/State U. of N.J., 1993—; adj. faculty Seton Hall U., N.J. Coll. of Nursing, 1994—; presenter 6th Ann. Reinkemyer Rsch. Day, 1992. Sr. Agnes Reinkemyer scholar, 1992. Mem. AACN (publs. chair Jersey Shoreline chpt. 1989-95, pres. 1993-94), AAUW, NOW, N.J. State Nurses Assn., Soc. Crit. Care Medicine, Soc. Rogerian Scholars, U. of State of N.Y. Regents Alumni Assn., Sigma Theta Tau (presenter, chair fin. com. 1992-93, pres.-elect 1994-95, pres. 1995-96). Office: Jersey Shore Med Ctr Brennan 4 ICU 1945 State Route 33 Neptune NJ 07753

MANDEL, ALICE TEICHLER, psychotherapist; b. Bklyn., Oct. 8, 1936; d. Isidor Teichler and Mildred (Schwartz) Shapiro; m. Steven Mandel, Sept. 15, 1962; children: Ellen, Paul. BSW, Kean Coll., 1978; MSW, Fordham U., 1979; cert. family therapy, N.J. Ctr. Family Therapy, Springfield, 1984. Cert. social worker. Med. social worker West Essex Cmty. Health, West Caldwell, N.J., 1980-82; project dir. mental health players Mental Health Assocs. N.J., Montclair, 1982-84; sch. social worker Elizabeth (N.J.) Bd. Edn., 1984-86; psychotherapist, cmty. educator Jewish Family Svc., Clifton, N.J., 1984-87; psychotherapist Womens Counseling & Psychotherapy Svc., Livingston, N.J., 1984—; sec. Livingston Youth & Family Svc., 1987-88; facilitator Robert Wood Johnson Med. Sch. Human Sexuality Program, Piscataway, N.J., 1988, 92. Mem. Am. Assn. Family Therapists. Home: 35 Fieldstone Dr Livingston NJ 07039-3308 Office: Womens Counseling & Psychother 201 S Livingston Ave Livingston NJ 07039-4040

MANDEL, CAROLA PANERAI (MRS. LEON MANDEL), foundation trustee; b. Havana, Cuba; d. Camilo and Elvira (Bertini) Panerai; ed. pvt. schs., Havana and Europe; m. Leon Mandel, Apr. 9, 1938. Mem. women's bd. Northwestern Meml. Hosp., Chgo. Trustee Carola and Leon Mandel Fund Loyola U., Chgo. Life mem. Chgo. Hist. Soc., Guild of Chgo. Hist. Soc., Smithsonian Assos., Nat. Skeet Shooting Assn. Frequently named among Ten Best Dressed Women in U.S.; chevalier Confrerie des Chevaliers du Tastevin. Capt. All-Am. Women's Skeet Team, 1952, 53, 54, 55, 56; only woman to win a men's nat. championship, 20 gauge, 1954, also high average in world over men, 1956, in 12 gauge with 99.4 per cent; European women's live bird shooting championship, Venice, Italy, 1957, Porto, Portugal, 1961; European woman's target championship, Torino, Italy, 1958; woman's world champion live-bird shooting, Sevilla, Spain, 1959, Am. Contract Bridge League Life Master, 1987. Named to Nat. Skeet Shooting Assn. Hall of Fame, 1970; inducted in U.S. Pigeon shooting Fedn. Hall of Fame, 1992. Mem. Soc. Four Arts. Club: Everglades (Palm Beach, Fla.), The Beach. Home: 324 Barton Ave Palm Beach FL 33480-6116

MANDEL, FRANCINE SHARON, statistician, educator; b. N.Y.C.; d. Benedict and Judith (Abbey) Phillips; m. Alan Ira Mandel, Dec. 3, 1978; 1 child, Judith Elysse. BA, SUNY, Oswego, 1976; MA, MEd, MPhil, Columbia U., 1980, PhD, 1986. Asst. prof. bus. Southampton (N.Y.) Coll., 1981-83; asst. prof. quantitative analysis St. John's U., Queens, N.Y., 1983-90; asst. prof. pub. health Cornell U. Med. Coll., N.Y.C., 1989—; rsch. biostatistician North Shore U. Hosp., Manhasset, N.Y., 1989—; cons., Commack, N.Y., 1978—. Statis. editor: Jour. Pediat. and Behavioral Medicine, 1990-93; reviewer: Decision Line, 1986-90, Fertility Sterility, 1994—, Jour. Am. Coll. Nutrition, 1994; author: Supplements to Computers: An Introduction, 1989; contbr. articles to profl. jours. Ethel Rollison scholar Tchrs. Coll., 1978. Mem. APA, Am. Statis. Assn. Home: 18 Ruth Blvd Commack NY 11725-2105 Office: North Shore U Hosp Div Biostatistics 300 Community Dr Manhasset NY 11030

MANDEL, KARYL LYNN, accountant; b. Chgo., Dec. 14, 1935; d. Isador J. and Eve (Gellar) Karzen; m. Fredric H. Mandel, Sept. 29, 1956; children: David Scott, Douglas Jay, Jennifer Ann. Student, U. Mich., 1954-56, Roosevelt U., 1956-57; AA summa cum laude, Oakton Community Coll., 1979. CPA, Ill. Pres. Excel Transp. Service Co., Elk Grove, Ill., 1958-78; tax mgr. Chunowitz, Teitelbaum & Baerson, CPA's, Northbrook, Ill., 1981-83, tax ptnr., 1984—; sec-treas. Lednam, Inc., Coffee Break, Inc.; mem. acctg. curriculum adv. bd. Oakton Community Coll., Des Plaines, Ill., 1987—. Contbg. author: Ill. CPA's News Jour. Recipient State of Israel Solidarity award, 1976. Mem. AICPA, Am. Soc. Women CPA, Women's Am. ORT (pres. Chgo. region 1972-74, v.p. midwest dist. 1975-76, nat. endowment com., nat investment adv. com.), Ill. CPA Soc. (chmn. estate and gift tax com. 1987-89, legis. contact com. 1981-82, pres. North Shore chpt., award for Excellence in Acctg. Edn., Bd. dirs. 1989-91), Chgo. Soc. Women CPA, Chgo. Estate Planning Coun., Nat. Assn. Women Bus. Owners, Lake County Estate Planning, Coun., Greater North Shore Estate Planning Coun. Office: 401 Huehl Rd Northbrook IL 60062-2300

MANDEL, LESLIE ANN, investment advisor, fundraiser, business owner, author; b. Washington, July 29, 1945; d. Seymour and Majorie Syble (Perlman) M. BA in Art History, U. Minn., 1967; cert., N.Y. Sch. Interior Design, 1969. Pres. Leslie Mandel Enterprises, Inc., N.Y.C., 1972—; sr. v.p. Maximum Entertainment Network, L.A. and N.Y.C., 1988-90; pres. Rich List Co., 1989—; pres., CEO Mandel Airplane Funding and Leasing Corp., N.Y.C., Hong Kong, China and Mongolia, 1990—; CEO Mandel-Khon Inc., Ulaanbaatar, Mongolia, 1994—; fin. advisor Osmed, Inc., Mpls., 1986—, Devine Communication/Allen & Co., N.Y., Del., Utah, N.Mex., 1984—, Am. Kefir Corp., N.Y., 1983—, Shore Group (Internat., Guyana), Flight Internat., 1991—; owner The Rich List Co., 71 internat. catalogues, mags. and fundraising lists; joint venture Mongolian Ind. Broadcasting Channel, Ulaanbaatar, 1995; pres., owner Mandel Airplane Funding and Leasing Corp.; rep. Israeli govt. IAI Satellite, China Romania, Costa Rica Mongolia, Amos Satellite Network, China, 1992—; advisor rep. Great Wall Corp., Long March Corp, China, 1992—, Chinese Silk , 1993—, Am. Oil Refinery, 1993—; purchasing agt. Peoples Republic of China-Aircraft; advisor Aeropostalis, Mex., 1994-95; photographer. Photographer: Vogue, 1978, Fortune mag.; braille transcriber: The Prophet (Kaili Gibran), 1967, Getting Ready for Battle (R. Prawe Jhabuala), 1967; exec. prodr. film: Hospital Audiences, 1975 (Cannes award 1976); author: Hungry at the Watering Hole, Gardiners Island, 1636-1990, 1989, Expedition: In the Steps of Ghengis Kahan, 1994; advisor Port Liberté Ptnrs. 1988-94. Fin. advisor Correctional Assn., Osborn Soc., 1977—; founder, treas. Prisoners Family Transportation and Assistance Fund, N.Y., 1972-77; judge Emmy awards of Acad. TV Arts and Scis., N.Y.C., 1970; bd. dirs. Prisoners Assn., 1990; chmn. U.S.A. com. Violeta B. de Chamarro for Pres. of Nicaragua Campaign. Recipient Inst. for the Creative and Performing Arts fellowship, N.Y.C., 1966, Appreciation cert. Presdl. Inaugural Com., Washington, 1981. Fellow N.Y. Women in Real Estate, Explorers Club; mem. Com. on Am. and Internat. Fgn. Affairs, Lawyers Com. on Internat. Human Rels., Bus. Exec. Nat. Security, Venture Capital Breakfast Club, The Coffee Club House, Sigma Delta Tau, Sigma Epsilon Sigma. Democrat. Home: 4 E 81st St New York NY 10028-0235 also: Mandel-Khan Inc c/o Boldbaatar Mandel Khan, PO Box 97, Ulaanbaatar 210648, Mongolia

MANDELBAUM, DOROTHY ROSENTHAL, psychologist, educator; b. N.Y.C., May 18, 1935; d. Benjamin Daniel and Rachael (Osofsky) Rosenthal; m. Seymour Jacob Mandelbaum, Aug. 19, 1956; children: David Gideon, Judah Michael, Betsy Daniella. AB cum laude, Hunter Coll., 1956; PhD, Bryn Mawr Coll., 1975. Tchr., Valley Road Sch., Princeton, N.J., 1956-59; instr. ednl. psychology dept. Temple U., Phila., 1970; asst. prof. dept. edn. Rutgers U., Camden, N.J., 1974-80, assoc. prof., 1980—, dir. women's studies, 1981-86, chair edn. dept., 1986-91, pres. faculty senate, 1990-91. Author: Work, Marriage and Motherhood: The Career Persistence of Female Physicians, 1981; contbr. articles on psychology of women and med. edn. to profl. publs. Dir. Am. Liver Found., 1991-93. AAUW predoctoral fellow, 1973-74. Mem. AAUP, APA. Home: 2290 N 53d St Philadelphia PA 19131 Office: Rutgers U Camden NJ 08102

MANDELL, ARLENE LINDA, writing and communications educator; b. Bklyn., Feb. 19, 1941; d. George and Esther Kostick; m. Lawrence W. Mandell, May 23, 1982; children by previous marriage: Bruce R. Rosenblum, Tracey B. Grimaldi. BA magna cum laude, William Paterson Coll., 1973; MA Columbia U., 1989. Newspaper reporter Suburban Trends, Riverdale, N.J., 1972-73; writer Good Housekeeping mag., N.Y.C., 1976-78; account exec. Carl Byoir & Assocs., N.Y.C., 1978-86; v.p. Porter/Novelli, N.Y.C., 1986-88; adj. prof. composition, lit., poetry, women's studies William Paterson Coll., Wayne, N.J., 1989—. Contbr. articles to profl. jours. and newspapers, poetry to N.Y. Times and poetry jours. Recipient 1st place women's interest writing N.J. Press Assn., 1973; named John W. Stahr Writer of Yr., Carl Byoir & Assocs., N.Y.C., 1981. Mem. N.J. Coll. English Assn.

MANDELL, JUDITH FRANCIES, systems engineer, consultant; b. Balt., Oct. 5, 1955; d. William Loker and Louanna (Petersen) Francies. Computer programming diploma, Computer Learning Ctr., Fairfax, Va., 1975; BS in Profl. Mgmt., Nova U., 1991, MS in Computer Based Learning, 1993. Programmer Bata Shoe Co., Belcamp, Md., 1975-76, Monumental Life Ins., Balt., 1976-78; programmer analyst Display Data Corp., Hunt Valley, Md., 1978, Citicorp Fin. Inc., Towson, Md., 1978-79; sr. programmer analyst Balt. Life. Ins., 1979-81; tech. cons. computers Compuware Corp., Towson, 1981-84, Computer Dynamics Inc., Ft. Lauderdale, Fla., 1984-85; sr. systems engr., project leader GTE Data Svcs., Temple Terrace, Fla., 1985—.

MANDERS, SUSAN KAY, artist; b. Burbank, Calif., Dec. 29, 1948; d. Gus H. and Erika (Stadelbauer) M.; m. Allan D. Yasnyi, Dec. 18, 1992; children: Brian Mallut, Judith Yasnyi. Attended, U. Guadalajara, 1969; BA, Calif. State U., 1971; postgrad., Otis Parsons, L.A., 1985, Royal Coll. of the Arts, London, 1987. Owner, dir., tchr. The Art Experience Sch. and Gallery, Studio City, Calif., 1978—; cons. in field. One-woman shows include La Logia, Studio City, Calif., 1991, Il Mito, Studio City, 1991, Bamboo, Sherman Oaks, Calif., 1991—, L.A. Art Installations, 1990, 92, Fed. Bldg., L.A., 1993, Art Experience, Studio City, 1993, Emerson's Gallery, Sherman Oaks, 1994, Raphael's, Beverly Hills, Calif., 1994; group shows include Beverly Hills Affair in the Gardens, 1984, 94, Otis Parsons, L.A., 1987, Hilderbrand Galleries, New Orleans, 1993, Studio City Art Festival, 1994, Parents Found., New Haven, Conn., 1994, Project Studio 8, San Francisco, 1994, Bistango Studio-Gallery, Irvine, Calif., 1994—, Montserrat Gallery, N.Y.C., 1995; creator, publ. prints Iron Jane Collections, 1994. Docent UCLA; active Tuesday's Child. Mem. L.A. Art Assn., Beverley Hills Art Assn., Nat. Mus. Women in the Arts, L.A. County Mus. of Art. Office: The Art Experience 11830 Ventura Blvd Studio City CA 91604-2617

MANDLER, SUSAN RUTH, dance company administrator; b. Kew Gardens, N.Y., Feb. 11, 1949; d. Ernest and Clea (Reisner) M.; m. Robert Morgan Barnett, July 30, 1982. B.S., Boston U., 1971. Mgr. Pilobolus, Inc., Washington, Conn., mgr., 1977—. Address: PO Box 388 Washington Depot CT 06794

MANDRAVELIS, PATRICIA JEAN, healthcare administrator; b. Hanover, N.H., May 7, 1938; d. William J. and Ruth E. (Darling) Bartis; m. Anthony M. Mandravelis, Nov. 8, 1959; children: Michael A., Tracy J. Diploma in nursing, Nashua (N.H.) Meml. Hosp. Sch. Nursing; BS in Psychology, Sociology, New Eng. Coll.; MBA, N.H. Coll., 1989. Cert. nursing adminstr., advanced nursing adminstr. Staff nurse Nashua Meml. Hosp. (name now So. N.H. Regional Med. Ctr.), 1959-60, obstet. nurse, 1962-65, charge nurse, 1969-71, supr., 1971-76, assoc. dir. nursing, 1976-81, dir. nursing, 1981-83, asst. exec. dir. nursing, 1983-87, v.p. nursing, 1987-91; v.p. ops., chief operating officer Nashua Meml. Hosp., 1991—. Contbr. articles to profl. jours. Bd. dirs. deNicola Women's Ctr., Nashua, 1987—, Nashua Vis. Nurse Program, 1986-88; v.p. Nashua chpt. ARC, 1985-87; bd. dirs. Home Health Hosp., 1988-94, chmn. bd., 1991-93, vice chmn. bd., 1993-94; mem. citizens adv. bd. W.R. Grace, 1989—. Mem. Am. Coll. Healthcare Execs., Nat. League of Nursing, Am. Nurses Assn., Am. Orgn. Nurse Execs., N.H. Nurses Assn., N.H. Orgn. Nurse Execs., Sigma Theta Tau. Office: So NH Regional Med Ctr 8 Prospect St Nashua NH 03061-2014

MANDRELL, BARBARA ANN, singer, entertainer; b. Houston, Dec. 25, 1948; d. Irby Matthew and Mary Ellen (McGill) M.; m. Kenneth Lee Dudney, May 28, 1967; children: Kenneth Matthew, Jaime Nicole, Nathaniel. Grad. high sch. Country music singer and entertainer, 1959—, performed throughout U.S. and in various fgn. countries; mem., Grand Ole Opry, Nashville, 1972—; star TV series Barbara Mandrell and the Mandrell Sisters, 1980-82, Barbara Mandrell: Get to the Heart, 1987; albums include Midnight Oil, Treat Him Right, This Time I Almost Made It, This is Barbara Mandrell, Midnight Angel, Barbara Mandrell's Greatest Hits, Christmas at Our House, 1987, Morning Sun, 1990, Standing Room Only, 1993. Author (with George Vecsey): Get To the Heart: My Story, 1990. Named Miss Oceanside, Calif., 1965; Named Most Promising Female Singer, Acad. Country and Western Music, 1971; Female Vocalist of Yr., 1978; Female Vocalist of Yr., Music City News Cover Awards, 1979; Female Vocalist of Yr., Country Music Assn., 1979; Entertainer of Yr., 1980, 81; People's Choice awards (6), 1982-84. Mem. Musicians Union, Screen Actors Guild, AFTRA, Country Music Assn. (v.p.). Mem. Order Eastern Star. Home: PO Box 620 Hendersonville TN 37077-0332 Office: Creative Artists Agy 3310 West End Ave 5th Fl Nashville TN 37203

MANEA-MANOLIU, MARIA, linguist; b. Galatz, Romania, Mar. 12, 1934; came to U.S., 1978, naturalized, 1987; d. Ion T. and Ana S. (Codescu) Manoliu; m. Ion S. Manea, Nov. 26, 1968. BA, French Coll., Galatz, 1951; MA, U. Bucharest, Romania, 1955, PhD, 1966. Asst. prof. Romance linguistics U. Bucharest, 1957-61, assoc. prof., 1961-68, prof., 1968-77; prof. linguistics U. Calif., Davis, 1978—; vis. prof. U. Chgo., 1972-74, H. Heine Universitat, Dusseldorf, 1994; cons. NEH, 1980—; mem. adv. bd. Revue Romane, Copenhagen, 1972, Roman Philology, Berkeley, Calif., 1984—, Philologica Canariensia, Spain, 1992—. Author: Sistematica Substitutelor, 1968 (Ministry of Edn. award 1968), Gramatica Comparata a limbilor romanice, 1971, El Estructuralismo Linguistico, 1979, Tipologia e Historia, 1985, Gramatica, Pragmasemantica si Discurs, 1993, Discourse and Pragmatic Constraints on Grammatical Choices. A Grammar of Surprises, 1994; editor-in-chief Bull. de la S.R.L.R., Bucharest, 1975-78; contbr. articles to profl. jours. Recipient Evenimentul award for Outstanding Contbn. to Romanian Culture, 1991; grantee Internat. Com., Linguists, 1972, Fulbright Found., 1972-74, 91-92, IREX, 1993, U. Calif., 1970-90. Mem. MLA, Am. Romanian Acad. (pres. 1992-94), Academia Română (hon.), Soc. de Linguistique Romane, Soc. Roumaine de Linguistique Romane (v.p. 1974-78), Internat. Assn. Hist. Linguistics, Linguistics Soc. Am., Internat. Assn. Pragmatics, Romanian Studies Assn. Am. (pres. 1986-88). Office: U Calif Dept French and Italian 509 Sproul Hall Davis CA 95616

MANEGOLD, CATHERINE SEACAMP, journalist; b. Boston, Oct. 22, 1955; d. Richard F. and Mary Helen (Ruedebush) M. BA in English magna cum laude, Carleton Coll., 1977. Gen. assignment Talbot County Banner, Easton, Md., 1980, Bucks County Courier Times, Levittown, Pa., 1981; SE asian bur. chief The Phila. Inquirer, Manila, 1986-89; corr. Newsweek Mag., Tokyo, 1991; gen. assignment The N.Y. Times, N.Y., 1992-93; Washington correspondent The N.Y. Times, Washington, 1994—; judge Overseas Press Club awards. Recipient Pulitzer prize for team reporting on bombing of World Trade Ctr., 1993. Mem. Phi Beta Kappa.

MANFORD, BARBARA ANN, contralto; b. St. Augustine, Fla., Nov. 13, 1929; d. William Floyd and Margaret (Kemper) Manford; Mus.B. in Voice, Fla. State U., 1951, Mus.M., 1970; studied with L. Palazzini, A. Strano, Japelli, E. Nikolaidi, E. Joseph. Appearances in Europe, performing major roles in 12 leading opera houses, 1951-68, with condrs. including Alfredo Strano, Felice Cilario, Robert Shaw, Arnold Gamson, Giuseppe Patané, Ottavio Ziino, also numerous concerts and recitals in Paris and throughout Italy and Belgium; performed in world premiere Fugitives (C. Floyd), Fla. State U., Tallahassee, 1950; chosen by Gian Carlo Menotti for leading role in world premiere The Leper, Fla. State U., 1970; numerous radio, TV, and concert appearances, U.S., 1968—; artist-in-residence, assoc. prof. voice Ball State U., Muncie, Ind., 1970-90; numerous recs. Semi-finalist vocal contest, Parma, Italy, 1964; winner contest, Lonigo, Italy, 1965. Mem. Nat. Assn. Tchrs. Singing, Chgo. Artists Assn., Am. Tchrs. Nat. Assn., Sigma Alpha Iota, Pi Kappa Lambda. Christian Scientist. Home: 405 S Morrison Rd Apt 106 Muncie IN 47304-4015

MANFRA, YVONNE CARLA, county official; b. Somerville, N.J., June 16, 1959; d. Carmine and Josephine (Duckworth) Manfra; m. Stephen Wayne Sherer, Aug. 23, 1986. BS, Cook Coll., New Brunswick, N.J., 1981; MS, SUNY, Syracuse, 1985; M in City and Regional Planning, Rutgers U., 1988. Lic. profl. planner, N.J. Sr. planner transp. County of Morris, Morristown, N.J., 1985-87; sr. planner land use County of Warren, Belvidere, N.J., 1987-88; planning dir. Pequannock Twp., Pompton Plains, N.J., 1988-90; planning cons. Long Valley, N.J., 1990-93; transp. planner County of Somerset, Somerville, 1990-92, transp. dir., 1992—. Vice chmn. Zoning Bd. Adjustment, Long Valley, 1985-86; active Habitat for Humanity, Somerville, 1993. Mem. Am. Planning Assn. Home: 335 Fairmount Rd Long Valley NJ 07853-3012 Office: County of Somerset Dept Transp PO Box 3000 Somerville NJ 08876-1262

MANGAN, PATRICIA ANN PRITCHETT, research statistician; b. Hammond, Ind., Feb. 4, 1953; d. Edward Clayton and Helen Josephine (Mills) Pritchett; m. William Paul Mangan, Aug. 30, 1980; 1 child, Ryan Christopher. BS in Maths. and Stats., Purdue U., 1975, MS in Applied Stats., 1977. Tobacco devel. statistician R.J. Reynolds Tobacco Co., Winston-Salem, N.C., 1978-82, R&D statistician, 1982-86, sr. R&D statistician, 1986-90, sr. staff R&D statistician, 1990-93; dir. software devel. ARJAY Equipment Corp., Winston-Salem, N.C., 1993—; cons. Lab. for Application of Remote Sensing, West Lafayette, Ind., 1976-77; statis. engr. Corning Glass Works, Harrodsburg, Ky., 1977. Editor Jour. of Sensory Studies, 1992—; contbr. articles to sci. jours. Rep. United Way, Winston-Salem, 1985. Recipient G.R. DiMarco award, 1990, Excaliber award for Outstanding Performance, 1991, 93. Mem. Am. Statis. Assn., Wash. Statis. Assn., Purdue Alumni Assn. Office: RJ Reynolds PO Box 1487 Winston Salem NC 27102-1487

MANGANIELLO, JANICE MARIE, perioperative nurse; b. Pittston, Pa., July 29, 1966; d. Ludwig Sr. and Dorothy Manganiello. AAS, Luzerne County Community Coll., Nanticoke, Pa., 1989; student, Coll. Misericordia, Dallas, Pa., 1989—; cert., Luzerne County Community Coll., 1992. Cert. RN first asst. CNOR, perioperative nurse Nat. Certification. Bd Perioperative Nursing, Inc. Emergency svcs. nurse Pittston Med. Emergency Ctr., 1989; obstetrics nurse Wilkes Barre (Pa.) Gen. Hosp., 1989, surg. svcs. nurse, 1989-91; RN first asst. Office of Sam C. DePasquale, 1992—; perioperative nurse, charge nurse urology and renal transplant surgery Temple U. Hosp., Phila., 1993—; clin. specialist Laser Surgery, 1993—, clin. coord. for students, 1993—; instr. continuing edn. planning, Luzerne County C.C., 1993. Vol. Big Bros./Big Sisters, Am. Cancer Soc., Valley Santa; religious edn. tchr. St. Rocco's Ch., Pittston; mem. Long Range Planning Comm. Pittston Area Sch. District, 1992. Recipient St. John Neumann award, St. Pius X award religious edn. Mem. ANA, NAFE, Assn. Operating Rm. Nurses (chairperson project Alpha 1990-91, chair rsch. 1993—, RN first asst. interest group), Pa. Nurses Assn., Orgn. for Advancement Assoc. Degree Nurses, Nat. League for Nursing, Soc. Peripheral Vascular Nursing, Nat. Assn. Orthopaedic Nurses, Couns. Cardiovascular Nursing and Circulation, Am. Heart Assn. Home: 204 Johnson St Pittston PA 18640-1049

MANGANO, NORA L., media specialist, publishing executive; b. Newark, N.J., May 29, 1948; d. Edwin and Ann Ritger; m. Anthony Mangano, Aug. 26, 1974; children: Terrence, Evan, Guido. BA in Journalism, NYU, 1969, MA, 1975. Editorial asst. Gourmet Mag., N.Y.C., 1975-77; assoc. editor Field and Stream Mag., N.Y.C., 1978-81, sr. editor, 1982-88; mng. editor Modern Bride Mag., N.Y.C., 1988-91; media specialist Whittle Commn., Fairfax, Va., 1991—; instr. The New Sch., N.Y.C., 1989-91. Author: Spinners, 1979, The Lost Russian Samovar, 1984, Fish, Fish, Fish, 1988, A Field of Sky, 1992. Vol. The Pink Ladies of Historic Fairfax, Va., 1993—, Fairfax County Libr., 1994—. Mem. AAUW, NOW, Am. Assn. Female Execs. Office: Werik Towers 10720 Main St Ste 303 Fairfax VA 22030-3794

MANGELSDORF, MARTHA ELIZABETH, journalist; b. Bryn Mawr, Pa., Mar. 23, 1963; d. Paul Christoph Jr. and Mary (Burnside) M. BA in Econs. magna cum laude, Yale U., 1986. Bus. editor Waterbury (Conn.) Republican-American, 1986-87; reporter Inc. Mag., Boston, 1987-88, staff writer, 1988-91, assoc. editor, 1991-94, sr. writer, 1994—. Named one of Top 30 bus. reporters under 30 Jour. Fin. Reporting. Mem. Soc. of Friends. Office: Inc Mag 38 Commercial Wharf Boston MA 02110

MANGERS, CYNTHIA MARIE, elementary education educator; b. Louisville, Feb. 27, 1956; d. Alvin John and Kay Marie (Kohl) M. BS in Elem. Edn., U. Nebr., 1978; M in Curriculum and Instrl. Improvement, Doane U., 1993. Cert. tchr., Nebr. Tchr. Grand Island (Nebr.) Pub. Schs., 1978—; Prairie Visions state adv. bd. Nebr. Dept. Edn., Lincoln, 1989—; presenter in field. Actress, dir., producer Grand Island Little Theatre, 1981—; mem. Crosier Lay Apostolate, Hastings, Nebr. Mem. NEA, Nebr. Art Tchrs. Assn., Nat. Math. Tchrs. Assn., Grand Island Edn. Assn., PTA, Alpha Delta Kappa. Roman Catholic. Office: Newell Elem Sch 2700 W 13th St Grand Island NE 68803

MANGES, MAXINE KRINSKY, art dealer, artist, educator, consultant; b. Johannesburg, South Africa, Aug. 25, 1951; came to U.S., 1977; d. Hillary and Sylvia Gertrude (Davis) Goldberg; m. Julian Krinsky, Apr. 1, 1973 (div. 1981); m. Lewis Clarence Manges III, June 13, 1992; children: Anthony, Jason, Simon, Matthew. BFA with honors, Witwatersrand U., Johannesburg, 1972. Art tchr. Johannesburg Art Found., 1973-77, Main Line Art Ctrs., Pa., 1977-83; founding dir. Art in Progress, Bryn Mawr, Pa., 1981—; ptnr. Axis Fine Art Svcs., Wilmington, Del., 1986, Axis Gallery/Fine Art Svcs., Phila., 1990—. Painter, 1972—. Office: Axis Gallery 718 N 3rd St Philadelphia PA 19123-2904

MANGO-HURDMAN, CHRISTINA ROSE, psychiatric art therapist; b. Garden City, N.Y., May 13, 1962; d. Camillo Andrew and Dorothy Mae (Harrison) Mango; Keith Hurdman, Sept. 11, 1993. BFA summa cum laude, Coll. of New Rochelle, 1984; MA, NYU, 1987. Registered art therapist; cert. structural family therapy tng.; cert. psycho-edn. multi family therapy tng. Art therapist Bronx Mcpl. Hosp. Ctr., 1984-88; art therapist, clin. supr. Fordham-Tremont Cmty. Mental Health Ctr., Bronx, 1988—; art therapy fieldworker Bronx State Hosp., 1984, art therapy intern Bronx Children's Hosp., 1985, Saint Lukes Hosp., N.Y.C., 1986. Contbr. articles to profl. jours. Mem. N.Y. Art Therapy Assn., No. N.J. Art Therapists Assn., Am. Art Therapy Assn. Home: 11 Turnure St Bergenfield NJ 07621-2035

MANGOL, LEONA ALVINA, public broadcasting administrator; b. Fairview, Pa., Dec. 3, 1942; d. Ferdinand Oscar and Julia Catherine (Bausch) Niebauer; m. James L. Mangol, June 26, 1971; children: James Christian, Michael Stephen, (dec.), Matthew Stephen. Student, Erie Bus. Coll., Erie, Pa., 1964, Gannon Coll., 1964-66; postgrad., Ins. Inst. Am., 1965-69. Lic. ins. agt., Commonwealth of Pa. Exec. sec. to exec. v.p. Erie Ins. Exchange, 1960-69; exec. asst., office mgr. Morrow Ins. Agy., Erie, Albion, Pa., 1964-69; exec. sec. to exec. v.p. mktg., corp. sec., office mgr. Systems Capital Corp., Phila., 1969-70; adminstrv. sec., asst. to v.p., sec. bd. Nat. Bd. Med. Examiners, Phila., 1970-77; asst. for info. svcs. Nat. Bd. Med. Examiners, 1977-84, mgr. publs. and the info. office, 1985-88, asst. mgr. publs., 1988-90; asst. sec. bd. dirs., asst. to pres. WHYY, Inc., 1990—. Bd. dirs. Erie Ins. Exchange Activities Assn., 1964-68, sec. bd. dirs., 1964-66, pres. bd. dirs., 1967; bd. dirs. Erie Ins. Credit Union, 1965-69, sec. bd. dirs., 1965-69; chmn. regional heart fund Am. Heart Assn., 1960-69; cert. instr. basic & advanced first-aid ARC, 1966-69; mem. Fairview Centennial Com., 1968, Fairview Vol. Firemen's Aux., 1965-69, St. Vincent Hosp. Aux., 1965-69, Graylady vol. St. Vincent Hosp. Aux., 1966-69. Mem. Internat. Assn. Bus. Communicators. Home: 619 Meadowbrook Ave Ambler PA 19002-4919 Office: WHYY Inc 150 N 6th St Philadelphia PA 19106-1589

MANGOS, RAE CAROL, counselor; b. Milw., Feb. 12, 1940; d. Lester Raymond and June Bernadine (Holdmann) Mathewson; m. John A. Mangos, Dec. 17, 1964; children: June Maria, Marianna Joy, Elena Rae, Yanna Lisa. BSN, U. Wis., 1962; MA in Counseling, St. Mary's U., San Antonio, Tex., 1986. Lic. profl. counselor; lic. marriage and family therapist; cert. chem. dependency specialist; RN, Tex.; diplomate Am. Bd. Med. Psychotherapists. Pub. health nurse City of Madison, Wis., 1962-64; substance abuse nurse Charter Real Hosp., San Antonio, 1985-87, outpatient counselor, 1987, inpatient counselor, 1987-90, coord. of adult chem. dependency outpatients, 1988; counselor, pvt. practice San Antonio, 1990—; counselor and clin. asst. prof. U. Tex. Health and Sci. Ctr., San Antonio, 1992—; adv. bd. St. Mary's U., 1987-91; reviewer of peers Laurel Ridge Hosp., San Antonio, 1993—. Author: Profl. Exam. Review, 1991—. Bd. dirs. St. Sophia Greek Orthodox Ch., San Antonio, 1984-85. Recipient Appreciation award USAF, San Antonio, 1991, Cibolo Valley Alcohol & Drug Abuse Coun., San Antonio, 1992, 93. Democrat. Home: 3402 Hunters Dusk St San Antonio TX 78230-2020 Office: Rae Mangos Counseling 4438 Centerview Ste 303 San Antonio TX 78228-1408

MANGUM-DANIEL, ELMIRA, academic administrator; b. Durham, N.C., Apr. 10, 1953; d. Ernest and Alice Blanche Mangum; divorced; children: Gregory, Gabrielle, Joshua. BS in Geography, Edn., N.C. Cen. U., 1974; MS in Urban and Regional Planning, U. Wis., Madison, 1977; MA in Pub. Policy and Pub. Adminstrn., U. Wis., 1977; postgrad., SUNY, Buffalo. Asst. to dir. Budget and Program Planning Geol. and Natural History Survey U. Wis., Madison, 1978-82; sr. budget and mgmt. analyst Budget and Mgmt. Analysis Div., DeKalb County, Ga., 1982-84; asst. to dir. for univ. fin. analysis Office Student Finances and Records, SUNY, Buffalo, 1984-86, asst. dean for acad. affairs and fin. mgmt., 1986-94; asst. to provost SUNY, Buffalo, 1994—; mem. rsch. bd. advisors Internat. Biog. Ctr., UB-pres. panel. Mem. Erie County Commn. on the Status of Women-Teen Pregnancy Task Force, Refuge Temple; treas. and mem. Buffalo chpt. of the Auxilary to Nat. Med. Assn. Mem. AAUW, AERA, Assn. Black Women in Higher Edn., N.Y. State Soc. Bursars and Bus. Adminstrs., Am. Soc. Profl. and Exec. Women, Coll. Student Personnel Assn., Am. Assn. Individual Investors. Home: 6379 Cloverleaf Circle East Amherst NY 14051

MANHART, MARCIA Y(OCKEY), art museum director; b. Wichita, Kans., Jan. 14, 1943; d. Everett W. and Ruth C. (Correll) Yockey; children: Caroline Manhart Sanderson, Emily Alexandrea Morrison. BA in Art, U. Tulsa, 1965, MA in Ceramics, 1971. Dir. edn. Philbrook Art Ctr., Tulsa, 1972-77, exec. v.p., asst. dir., 1977-83, acting dir., 1983-84; exec. dir. Philbrook Mus. Art (formerly Philbrook Art Ctr.), Tulsa, 1984—; instr. Philbrook Art Ctr. Mus. Sch., Tulsa, 1963-72; gallery dir. Alexandre Hogue Gallery, Tulsa U., 1967-69; NEH Challenge Grant panelist, 1991, presenter to AAM Conv., 1991; MAAA Craft Fellowship panelist, 1988, 93, NEA Craft Fellowship panelist, 1990; curator nat. touring exhibit Nature's Forms/Nature's Forces: The Art of Alexandre Hogue, 1984-85; co-curator internat. exhbn.: The Eloquent Object, 1987-90; curator Sanford and Diane Besser Collection exhbn., 1992. Vis. com. Smithsonian Instn./Renwick Gallery, Washington, 1986; cultural negotiator Gov. George Nigh's World Trade Mission (Okla.), China., 1985; com. mem. State Art Coll. of Okla., 1985—; mem. Assocs. of Hillcrest Med. Ctr., 1983-88, exec. com., 1985-88; com. mem. Neighborhood Housing Services, 1985-87; mem. Mapleridge Hist. Dist. Assn., 1982—; steering com. Harwelden Isnt. for Aesthetic Edn., 1983; com. mem. River Parks Authority, 1976; mem. Jr. League of Tulsa Inc., 1974-78; adv. panel mem. Nat. Craft Planning Project, NEA, Washington, 1978-81; craft adv. panel mem. Okla. Arts and Humanities Council, 1974-76; juror numerous art festivals, competitions, programs; reviewer Inst. Mus. Services, Washington, 1985, 88, 92; auditor Symposium on Language & Scholarship of Modern Crafts, NEA and NEH, Washington, 1981; nominator MacArthur Fellows Program, 1988. Recipient Harwelden award for Individual Contbrn. in the Arts, 1989, Gov.'s award State of Okla., 1992. Mem. Assn. Am. Mus., Assn. Art Mus. Dirs., Art Mus. Assn. Am., Mountain Plains Assn. Mus., Am. Craft Coun., Okla. Mus. Assn., Rotary. Office: Philbrook Mus Art PO Box 52510 Tulsa OK 74152-0510

MANION, BARBARA ANNE, sales representative; b. Phila., Nov. 7, 1954; d. Joseph L. and Helen R. (McKeown) M. Diploma, Laukenau Hosp., 1975; BSN, Villanova U., 1982, cert. in mgmt., 1990. RN, Pa. Staff nurse Laukenau Hosp., Phila., Haverford Dialysis Ctr., Bryn Mawr, Pa.; nurse adminstr. Chestnut Hill Dialysis Ctr., Phila.; pres. Med.-RN, Ltd., Phila.; sales rep. Minntech Corp., Mpls. Mem. Am. Nephrology Nurses Assn. (past pres. local chpt.), Nat. Kidney Found., Coun. Nephrology Nurses and Technicians. Home: 8 Shetland Cir Horsham PA 19044-1146

MANKILLER, WILMA PEARL, tribal leader; b. Stilwell, Okla., Nov. 18, 1945; d. Charley and Clara Irene (Sitton) M.; m. Hector N. Olaya, Nov. 13, 1963 (div. 1975); children—Felicia Marie Olaya, Gina Irene Olaya. Student Skyline Coll., San Bruno College, Calif., 1973, San Francisco State Coll., 1973-75; B.A. in Social Sci., Flaming Rainbow Coll., Okla., 1977; postgrad. U. Ark., 1979. Community devel. dir. Cherokee Nation, Tahlequah, Okla., 1977-83, dep. chief, 1983-85, prin. chief, 1985-87; pres. Inter-Tribal Council Okla.; mem. exec. bd. Council Energy Resource Tribes; bd. dirs. Okla. Indsl. Devel. Commn. Bd. dirs. Okla. Acad. for State Goals, 1985—. Recipient Donna Nigh First Lady award Okla. Commn. for Status of Women, 1985, Am. Leadership award, Harvard U., 1986; inducted Okla. Women's Hall of Fame, 1986. Mem. Cherokee County Democratic Women's Club, Nat. Tribal Chairmen's Assn., Nat. Congress Am. Indians. Avocations: reading; writing. Office: Cherokee Prin Chief PO Box 948 Tahlequah OK 74465-0948*

MANKLE, M. ELAINE, transportation executive; b. Mishawaka, Ind., July 10, 1965; d. Thomas Guy and Kathryn Elaine (McNamara) Pote; m. Christopher Alan Mankle, May 25, 1991. BA, Ind. U., 1987. Sales rep. CF Airfreight, Austin, Tex., 1987-89; account mgr. CF Airfreight/Emery, Austin, 1989-90; internat. account mgr. United Parcel Svc., San Antonio, 1990-93; internat. mgr. Emery Worldwide, Dallas, 1993—. Basketball coach Town and Country Optimists Club, Austin, 1988-90. Mem. Am. Soc. Transp. and Logistics (Outstanding Young Woman award 1987).

MANKOSKI, F. ANDREA, graphic designer; b. Grand Rapids, Mich., Jan. 9, 1967; d. Charles Edward McCallum and Lenda (Bates) Du Bose; m. Joseph Jay Mankoski, Aug. 16, 1993. Student, Rensselaer Polytech. Inst., 1985-86; BA with honors and distinction, U. Mich., 1988. Artist, animator Show & Tell Systems, Palo Alto, Calif., 1989-90; sr. project mgr. Show & Tell Systems, Mountain View, Calif., 1990-93; sr. graphic designer, user interface designer Lotus Devel. Corp., Mountain View, 1993—. Bd. dirs. Menlo Players Guild, Menlo Park, Calif., 1989-91, pres., 1991-92. Mem. Assn. for Software Design (founding mem. Mountain View chpt.), Assn. For Computing Machinery (Bay Area computer-human interactions spl. interest group), Soc. Tech. Communicators,. Office: Lotus Devel Corp 800 W El Camino Real Mountain View CA 94040-2567

MANLEY, AUDREY FORBES, physician; b. Jackson, Miss., Mar. 25, 1934; d. Jesse Lee and Ora Lee (Buckhalter) Forbes; m. Albert Edward Manley, Apr. 3, 1970. A.B. with honors (tuition scholar), Spelman Coll., Atlanta, 1955; M.D. (Jesse Smith Noyes Found. scholar), Meharry Med. Coll., 1959; MPH, Johns Hopkins U.-USPHS traineeship, 1987; LHD (hon.), Tougaloo (Miss.) Coll., 1990, Meharry Med. Coll., Nashville, 1991; LLD (hon.), Spelman Coll., 1991. Diplomate: Am. Bd. Pediatrics. Intern St. Mary Mercy Hosp., Gary, Ind., 1960; from jr. to chief resident in pediatrics Cook County Children's Hosp., Chgo., 1960-62; NIH fellow neonatology U. Ill. Rsch. and Ednl. Hosp., Chgo., 1963-65; staff pediatrician Chgo. Bd. Health, 1963-66; practice medicine specializing in pediatrics Chgo., 1963-66; assoc. Lawndale Neighborhood Health Ctr. North, 1966-67; asst. med. dir., 1967-69; asst. prof. Chgo. Med. Coll., 1966-67; instr. Pritzker Sch. Medicine, U. Chgo., 1967-69; asst. dir. ambulatory pediatrics, asst. dir. pediatrics Mt. Zion Hosp. and Med. Center, San Francisco, 1969-70; med. cons. Spelman Coll., 1970-71, med. dir. family planning program, chmn. health careers adv. com., 1972-76; med. dir. Grady Meml. Hosp. Family Planning Clinic, 1972-76; with Health Services Adminstrs., Dept. Health and Human Services, 1976—; commd. officer USPHS, 1976—; chief genetic diseases services br. Office Maternal and Child Health, Bur. Community Health Services, Rockville, Md., 1976-81; acting assoc. adminstr. clin. affairs Office of Adminstr. Health Resources and Services Adminstrn., 1981-83, chief med. officer, dep. assoc. adminstr. planning, evaluation and legis., 1983-85; sabbatical leave USPHS Johns Hopkins Sch. Hygiene and Pub. Health, 1986-87; dir. Nat. Health Service Corps.; asst. surgeon gen., 1988; dep. asst. Sec. for Health USPHS/HHS, 1989-93, acting asst. Sec. Health, 1993, dep. asst. Sec. Health/intergovtl. affairs, 1993-94; dep. surgeon gen., acting dep. asst. sec. for minority health USPHS, 1994-95; acting surgeon gen., 1995—; mem. U.S. del. UNICEF, 1990-94. Author numerous articles, reports in field. Trustee Spelman Coll., 1966-70. Recipient Meritorious Svc. award USPHS, 1981, Mary McLeod Bethune award Nat Coun. Negro Women, 1979, Dr. John P. McGovern Ann. Lectureship award Am. Sch. Health Assn., Disting. Alumni award Meharry Med. Coll., 1989, Spelman Coll. 108 Founder's Day Convocation, 1989, Disting. Svc. medal USPHS, 1992, Hildrus A. Poindexter award OSG/PHS, 1993, numerous other svc. and achievement awards. Fellow Am. Acad. Pediatrics; mem. Nat. Inst. Medicine of Nat. Acad. Sci., Nat. Med. Assn., APHA, AAUW, AAAS, Spelman Coll. Alumnae Assn., Meharry Alumni Assn., Operation Crossroads Africa Alumni Assn., Delta Sigma Theta (hon.). Home: 2807 18th St NW Washington DC 20009-2205 Office: 200 Independence Ave SW Washington DC 20201-0004

MANLEY, BARBARA LEE DEAN, occupational health nurse, hospital administrator, safety and health consultant; b. Washington, Nov. 5, 1946; d. Robert L. Dean and Mary L. (Jenkins) Smallwood. B.S., St. Mary-of-the-Woods, Terre Haute, Ind., 1973; M.A., Central Mich. U., 1981. Indsl. nurse Ford Motor Co., Indpls., 1973-80; employee health nurse Starplex, Inc., Washington, 1981-84, Doctor's Hosp., Lanham, Md., 1984-85; regional occupational health nurse coordinator Naval Hosp., Long Beach, Calif., 1985-88; project mgr. Health Care Network, Inc., Washington, 1980-84; cons. Health and Human Services, Washington, 1980-84; occupational health and safety cons., mgr. FPE Group, Torrence, Calif., 1988-91; safety and loss control mgr. Assn. Calif. Hosp. Dists., Sacramento, 1991-93, v.p. loss control svcs., 1993—; pvt. practice contract nurse specialist, Washington, 1980-84; part-time lectr. Compton (Calif.) Coll., 1986. Vol. ARC, Ft. Lewis, Wash., 1974-76, Ft. Harrison, Ind., 1978-80; counselor Crisis Hot-Line, Laurel, Md., 1981-83, Laurel Boy's and Girls Club, 1981-84. Recipient Navy's Meritorious Civilian Svc. Medal, 1989, Women of Excellence award Long Beach Press-Telegram Newspaper Guild, 1990. Fellow Acad. Ambulatory Nursing Adminstrs. (Honor plaque 1981); mem. Assn. Exec. Females, Am. Pub. Health Assn., Am. Nurses Assn., Nat. Safety Mgmt. Soc., Am. Assn. Occupational Health Nurses, Assn. Hosp. Employee Health Profls. (sec. 1986-88, conf. chairperson 1988, Outstanding Nurse of Yr. 1987), Fed. Occupational Safety and Health Council, Cen. Mich. U. Alumni Assn. (sec. 1985-88), Chi Eta Phi (regional bd. dirs. 1978-81). Presbyterian. Avocations: reading; crocheting; traveling; roller skating. Office: Assn Calif Hosp Dists 2260 Park Towne Cl Sacramento CA 95865-5668

MANLEY, GERTRUDE ELLA, librarian, media specialist; b. Phila., Dec. 29, 1930; d. William Eugene and Anna G. (Price) Lomas; m. Harley E. Manley, Jr., July 20, 1957; children: Marc Alan, Karen Sue Manley Thornton, Gail Ann Manley Rivera. BRE, Shelton Coll., 1955; MSEd, Queens Coll., 1958, MS in Libr. Edn., 1958; postgrad., various. Libr. tchr. Plainedge (N.Y.) Sch. Dist., 1955-60; libr. dir. Huntington (N.Y.) Christian Sch., 1968-70; libr./media specialist Connetquot Ctrl. Sch. Dist. of Islip, Bohemia, N.Y., 1970—. Editor: Manley Family Newsletter, 1983—; contbr. articles to profl. jours. Mem. nursery sch. bd. New Life Community Ch. Nursery Sch., Sayville, N.Y., 1985-89; adminstr. pre-sch. story time program, E.J. Bosti Sch., Bohemia, 1972—, sign lang. instr., 1988—, Huffine award chairperson, 1985—, spell bee judge, 1984—, arranger speakers program, 1988—, kindergarten screening participant, 1988—, numerous in-house site-base planning and mgmt. coms., 1990-93. Mem. N.Y. State Ret. Tchrs. Assn. (life), Western Suffolk Ret. Tchrs. Assn. (life), Connetquot Tchrs. Assn. (chmn. scholarship com. 1978-93), Connetquot Ret. Tchrs. Assn. (sec. 1993—). Baptist/Reformed Ch. of Am. Home: 171 Nathan Dr Bohemia NY 11716-1319 Office: Connetquot Ctrl Sch Dist Islip 780 Ocean Ave Bohemia NY 11716-3631

MANLEY, NANCY JANE, environmental engineer; b. Ft. Smith, Ark., Sept. 13, 1951; d. Eugene Hailey and Mary Adele (Chave) M. BSE, Purdue U., 1974; MSE, U. Wash., 1976; postgrad., U. Minn., 1976-77; grad., Air Command and Staff Coll., 1984, Exec. Leadership Devel. Program Dept. Def., 1988. Lic. profl. engr., Ga. Sanitary engr. Minn. Dept. Health, Mpls., 1976-77; sanitary engr. water supply EPA, Chgo., 1977; leader primacy unit water supply EPA, Atlanta, 1977-79, leader tech. assistance team, 1979-82; chief environ. and contract planning, project mgr. Grand Bay Range design USAF, Moody AFB, Ga., 1982-84; dep. base civil engr. USAF, Carswell AFB, Tex., 1984-86, Scott AFB, Ill., 1986-89; mem. tech. adv. com. Scott AFB master plan study USAF, Belleville, Ill., 1986-89; dep. base civil engr. USAF, Robins AFB, Ga., 1989-91, acting chief engr., 1990-91, chief pollution prevention divsn., dir. environ. mgmt., 1991-93; chief engr. divsn. 78 Civil Engr. Group, Robins AFB, Ga., 1993—; mem. Fla. Tech. Adv. Com. for Injection Wells, Tallahassee, 1980-82, Nat. Implementation Team for Underground Injection Control Program, Washington, 1979-82, tech. panel Nat. Groundwater Protection Strategy Hearings, 1981; judge Internat. Sci. and Engring. Fair, 1986. Active various ch. support activities, 1969-74; sec. Perry Area Hist. Soc., 1991-93; vol. Meals-on-Wheels, Girl Scouts U.S., others, various locations, 1982—; founder, crisis intervention counselor Midwest Alliance, West Lafayette, Ind., 1970-74; active St. Louis Math. and Sci. Network Day, 1989, Adopt-a-Sch. Program, Lebanon, Ill., 1987-89; scientist by mail Boston Mus. Sci., 1989—. Recipient Presdl. Point of Light award USAF, 1991, Disting. Govt. Svc. award Dallas/Ft. Worth Fed. Exec. Bd., 1986, Lady of the Black Knights award 19th Air Refueling Wing, 1991. Mem. NSPE (v.p. local chpt. 1994—), ASCE, Soc. Women Engrs. (regional mem.-at-large rep. 1990-93, sr. mem. local officers 1979-82, 84-86), Am. Women in Sci., Soc. Am. Mil. Engrs. (local membership and contingency coms.), Internat. Platform Assn. Office: 653 CEG/CEC 78 CEG/CEC Robins AFB GA 31098-1864

MANLEY, NORLEE K., nurse, chemical dependence program administrator; b. Middleport, Ohio; d. James Norwood Van Cooney and Esther Marie Searles; m. Virgil James Manley; children: Michael James, Sandra René. ADN, Cuyahoga Community Coll., 1975; BSN, Kent State U., 1986; MNS in Adminstrn., U. Akron, 1991. Cert. in nursing adminstrn.; cert. chem. dependence counselor. Head nurse Vets. Addiction Recovery Ctr. VA Med. Ctr., Cleve., coord. Drug Depencence Treatment prog., dep. dir. Vets. Addiction Recovery Ctr., dir. Vets. Addiction Recovery Ctr. Contbr. to profl. jours. Chairperson 24th Ann. Nurses Conf. Recipient award for outstanding supr. Fed. Exec. Bd., 1991. Mem. ANA, Ohio Nurses Assn., Greater Cleve. Nurses Assn., Nat. Consortium of Chem. Dependence Nurses, Nurses Orgn. of VA (bd. dirs., Excellence in Nursing award 1986, Regional Adminstrs. award for Excellence in Nursing 1990), Sigma Theta Tau. Home: 4820 Sentinel Dr Cleveland OH 44141-3149

MANN, DOROTHY HOLLAND, health services administrator; b. Annandale, Va.; d. John Sidney and Susie (Crummy) Holland; divorced; 1 child, Keith Robert. BA in Sociology and Psychology, Howard U., 1972; MPH in Health Svcs. Mgmt./Health Policy, U. Mich., 1974; PhD in Health Svcs. Mgmt./Health Policy, Union Inst., 1993. Supervisory pub. health advisor Office Health Affairs OEO, Washington, 1968-73; supervisory pub. health advisor region IX Pub. Health Svc., San Francisco, 1973-75, dep. chief health systems br. divsn. health svcs., 1975-76, dep. dir. divsn. resources devel., 1976-77; exec. asst. to dep. dir. U.S. Action Agy., Washington, 1977-79; regional health adminstr. region X Pub. Health Svc., Seattle, 1979-93; dir. anti-violence project Office of Mayor, City of Seattle, 1993—; trustee Group Health Coop. of Puget Sound, Seattle, 1987—, chair bd. trustees, 1990-93; clin. assoc. prof. dept. health svcs. Sch. Pub. Health and Community Medicine, U. Wash.; advisor nat. fellowship program W.K. Kellogg Found., 1990-93; co-convener Wash. Child Health Rsch. Group, 1992; organizer, tour dir. cross-cultural study tours, 1985, 86. Founder, pres. Seattle chpt. Africare, 1980-86; bd. dirs. Community Home Health Care, 1983-88, Women Plus Bus., 1985-87; bd. dirs. World Affairs Coun., Seattle, 1982-92, v.p., 1985-88; bd. dirs. Seattle Commons, 1992—, mem. exec. com., 1993—; mem. Seattle Art Mus. Devel. Authority, 1992-94; trustee Intiman Theatre, 1993—. Recipient 1st Place Communicator award Wash. Press Assn., 1992, 1st Place award for Mags. and Editorials, Soc. Profl. Journalists, 1992, Leadership in Community Svc. award Big Sisters in King County, 1993, Leadership in Women's Health award Region X Family Planning Program, 1993, Exemplary Svc. award Surgeon Gen., 1993, Am.'s Best and Brightest Profl. and Bus. Women award Dollar and Sense Mag., 1993. Mem. APHA, Wash. State Pub. Health Assn. Office: City of Seattle Office of Mayor 700 3d Ave # 710 Seattle WA 98104

MANN, EMILY BETSY, writer, artistic director, theater and film director; b. Boston, Apr. 12, 1952; d. Arthur and Sylvia (Blut) M.; 1 child, Nicholas Isaac Bamman. BA, Harvard U., 1974; MFA, U. Minn., 1976. Resident dir. Guthrie Theater, Mpls., 1976-79; dir. BAM Theater Co., Bklyn., 1980-81; freelance writer, dir. N.Y.C., 1981-90; artistic dir. McCarter Theater Ctr. for the Performing Arts, Princeton, N.J., 1990—; cons. N.Y. Theatre Workshop, 1987. Author: (plays) Annulla, an Autobiography, Still Life (6 Obie awards 1981, Fringe First award, 1985), Execution of Justice (Helen Hayes award, Bay Area Theatre Critics Circle award, HBO/USA award, Playwriting award Women's Com. Dramatists Guild for Dramatizing Issues of Conscience 1986), To Know a Monster: The Story of the Greensboro Massacre (stage adaptation) Having Our Say; co-author: (with Ntozake Shange) (musical) Betsey Brown; (screenplays) Naked, Fanny Kelly, The Winnie Mandela Story, The Greensboro Massacre; dir. Hedda Gabbler, A Doll House, Annulla, Still Life (Obie award), Execution of Justice (Guthrie and Broadway), Betsey Brown, The Glass Menagerie, Three Sisters, Cat On A Hot Tin Roof, Twilight: L.A., 1992, The Perfectionist, The Matchmaker; adaptor, dir. Miss Julie, Having Our Say; translator: Nights and Days (Pierre Laville), 1985; pub. in New Plays USA 1, New Plays, 3, American Plays and the Vietnam War, The Ten Best Plays of 1986, Out Front. Recipient BUSH fellowship, 1975-76, Rosamond Gilder award New Drama Forum Assn., 1983, NEA Assocs. grant, 1984, Guggenheim fellowship, 1985, McKnight fellowship, 1985, CAPS award, 1985, NEA Playwrights fellowship, 1986. Mem. Soc. Stage Dirs. and Choreographers (bd. dirs.), Theatre Communications Group (v.p.), New Dramatists, PEN, Writers' Guild, Dramatists' Guild, Phi Betta Kappa.

MANN, JONNIE YVONNE, management consultant; b. Ft. Worth, Dec. 7, 1939; d. Delbert W. and Florence Evalynne (Fuller) McAmis; children: Robert, Terry, Shawn. BBA in Acctg., Cleary Coll., 1986. Lic. securities, real estate broker, Tex. Contr., office mgr. J.L. Scott Enterprises, Irving, Tex., 1980-82, Ivan Brown, Inc., Houston, 1982-83; due diligence officer Mut. Svc. Corp., Detroit, 1983-88; v.p. Realty Income Corp., Escondido, Calif., 1988-90; v.p. ops. 1st Pacific Capital Corp., Vancouver, Calif., 1990-91; ind. mgmt. cons. Vancouver, 1991-93; office adminstr. Horenstein & Duggan, P.S., Vancouver, 1993-94; mgmt. cons. pvt. practice, Vancouver, 1994—; instr. bus. and industries div. Clark Coll.; mem. adv. bd. Clark Coll. Bus. Adminstrn. Mem. Columbia River Econ. Devel. Coun. Mem. Women in Action, Rotary Internat. (bd. dirs.), Vancouver C. of C. Home: 7824 NE Loowit Loop #68 Vancouver WA 98662

MANN, KAREN, consultant, educator; b. Kansas City, Mo., Oct. 9, 1942; d. Charles and Letha (Anderson) M. BA, U. Calif.-Santa Barbara, 1964; MPA, Golden Gate U., 1975, PhD, 1994. Cert. lay minister Order of Buddhist Contemplatives. Tchr. Sisters of Immaculate Heart, Los Angeles, 1964-68; group counselor San Francisco and Marin County Probation Depts., parole agt. Calif. Dept. Corrections, Sacramento and San Francisco, 1970-86; researcher and cons. Non-profit Orgnl. Devel., 1986—, Computer Applications for Persons with Disabilities, 1986—; adj. faculty Grad. Theol. Union, Berkeley, 1984—; Compuserve Disabilities Forum, 1988—; asst. forum adminstr.; mem. faculty Golden Gate U., 1990. Co-author: Prison Overcrowding, 1979; Community Corrections: A Plan for California, 1980; sec., bd. dirs. Spirit Rock Meditation Ctr. Active Fellowship of Reconciliation, N.Y., 1970—; co-founder Network Ctr. for Study of Ministry, San Francisco, 1982; pres. San Francisco Network Ministries, 1980-82; mem. Disabled Children's Computer Resource Group, 1988—, Springwater Ctr. for Meditative Inquiry and Retreats, 1986—. Office: PO Box 377 Lagunitas CA 94938-0377

MANN, LAURA SUSAN, editor; b. Houston, Sept. 20, 1958; d. Manfred Walter and Sally Mae (Hennels) Schaefer; m. Richard Drew Mann, Aug. 1, 1987; 1 child, W. Cole. BS in Physics cum laude, U. Houston, 1986. Mktg. sec. Vector Cable/Schlumberger, Sugar Land, Tex., 1981-83; admisntrv. asst. Bekaert Internat. Trade, Inc., Houston, 1983-84; polit. pollster, rsch. and teaching asst. U. Houston, 1984-86; flight contr. Johnson Space Ctr., NASA, Houston, 1986-91, mgr. grapple fixture subsystem, 1991-92, mgr. space sta. engrng. configuration, 1992-93; part time beauty cons. Mary Kay cosmetics, 1992; contract editor R.G. Landes Co., Georgetown, Tex.; mem. tech. adv. com. flight telerobotic servicer Goddard Space Flight Ctr., NASA, Greenbelt, Md., 1989; mission ops. directorate rep. hand contr. commonality study, leader space shuttle payload and deployment system tech. team/space sta. flight compatability rev. Johnson Space Ctr., NASA, 1990; rsch. asst. medium energy physics expt. U. Houston at Brookhaven Nat. Lab., Upton, N.Y., 1985, 86; mem. configuration mgmt. process improvement team for Space Sta. Freedom Program, 1992-93. Pres. Durham Pk. Homeowners Assn., Houston, 1990-92; vol. Tex. Water Commn. Testing Program, 1994—. Mem. Am. Horse Shows Assn., U.S. Combined Tng. Assn., Greater Houston Hunter Jumper Assn. (bd. dirs. 1991-92, contbg. newsletter columnist 1991-92, Jr./Adult Jumper Champion 1990, 4th in open jumper ann. awards 1992), U. Houston Alumni Orgn.., Nat. Arbor Day Found., MENSA, Phi Theta Kappa.

MANN, MARCIA L., state agency administrator; b. Pitts., May 20, 1944; d. Walter W. and Helen Mann. BA, Thiel Coll., 1965; MEd, U. Pitts., 1966; PhD, U. Nebr., 1970. Elem. tchr. Montgomery County Schs., Rockville, Md., 1966, Lincoln (Nebr.) City Schs., 1966-69; grad. asst. U. Nebr., Lincoln, 1969-70; asst. prof. edn. U. South Fla., Tampa, 1970-75, assoc. prof. edn., 1976-85, prof. edn., 1986—, assoc. dean clin. edn. and spl. projects, 1984-91; sec. Fla. Lottery, Tallahassee, 1991—; evaluator dept. edn. Pinellas County Inservice Evaluation, 1978, Fla. Tech. U., 1978; vice chairperson Nat. Forum of Field Dirs., 1977, chairperson, 1978; del. dept. edn. State Conv., 1979; mem. Fla. State program Am. Coun. on Edn., 1978; coord. Hillsborough County for Gov. Graham, 1979-83; chair State Adv. Com. on Tchr. Edn., 1987; vis. scholar N.C. Disting. Vis. Scholars Program, Chapel Hill, 1989; mem. edn. stds. commn. State of Fla., 1990-93; active Nat. Coun. for Accreditation Tchr. Edn. Rev. Team Banks, 1977—, Thirteenth Cir. Jud. Nominating Commn., 1979-83, Gov. Commn. on Status of Women, 1981-85, Gov. Adv. Com. on Edn. Block Grants, 1981-85, Joint Exec. and Legis. Task Force for Tchr. Edn. Quality Improvement, 1982-84, Human Resource Devel. Adv. Com., 1987, Gov.-Elect Lawton Chiles' Edn. Core Task Force, 1990-91; cons., presenter in field. Contbr. articles to profl. jours. Vol. dir. comm. network for Graham Campaign, Tampa, 1976-78; vol. coord. rsch. and adminstrv. transition staff Gov. Graham, Tallahassee, 1978-79; vol. mgr. Hillsborough Campaign for Graham, 1978, Hillsborough County Campaign for Commr. Edn. Ralph Turlington, Tampa, 1982, Hillsborough Campaign for U.S. Senate Bob Graham, Tampa, 1986; bd. dirs. March of Dimes, 1986; active Pres. Adv. Com. for Women, 1980, Mil. Acad. Nominating Bd., 1987—. Recipient Gov. award for outstanding Fla. woman, 1981, Profl. Accomplishment award Thiel Coll., 1989. Mem. ASCD, Am. Assn. Colls. for Tchr. Edn. (Showcase of Excellence award for outstanding accomplishments with talented students 1985), Am. Edn1. Rsch. Assn., Assn. Tchr. Educators (del. 1978-82, mem. exec. bd. 1978-82, chairperson nat. ad hoc com. to establish coun. state pres. 1979-80, mem. '90 com. 1984-86), Fla. Assn. Tchr. Educators (chairperson pub. rels. and publicity com. 1975-76, v.p. 1977, chairperson com. for pub. rels. 1977, program chmn. 1977-78, pres. 1978-79, legis. liaison 1979-80), Greater Tampa C. of C. (mem. edn. coun. 1982—, chair state task force on govt. 1984-85), Phi Delta Kappa (chair scholarship fund 1988-89, 90-91). Democrat. Lutheran. Office: Fla Lottery Capitol Complex Tallahassee FL 32399-4002

MANN, MARYLEN, adult services institute director; b. St. Louis, Mar. 13, 1937; d. Morris and Ruth (Sobel) Lipkind; (widowed); children: Robert Gordon, John Douglas. BA in Philosophy, Washington U., St. Louis, 1957; MA in Edn., Washington U., 1959. Tchr. St. Louis Pub. Schs., 1961-62; supr. student tchrs. dept. edn. Washington U., 1969, rsch. instr. Med. Sch., 1984—; instr. edn. U. Mo., St. Louis, 1972-74, dir. Older Adult Service and Info. System, fellow Ctr. Metro Studies, lctr. Dept. Edn., 1983-84; instr. curriculum devel. Webster U., St. Louis, 1977-78; dir. various programs CEMREL Inc., St. Louis, 1974-82; exec. dir. OASIS Inst. Jewish Hosp., St. Louis, 1984—; bd. dirs. Gerontology Concentration Adv. Com., Washington U., 1987-90; mem. nat. coun. George Warren Brown Sch. Social Work, Washington U., 1987—; trustee Fontbonne Coll., 1989-93. Contbr. articles to profl. jours. Bd. dirs. Jewish Ctr. Aged, 1984-87, 94—, St. Louis Psychoanalytic Inst., 1983-91, Arts and Edn. Council St. Louis, 1981-87, 88—, mem. exec. com., 1986, v.p. bd. dirs., 1986, chair program com., 1986, chmn. membership com., 1989-92, v.p., 1991, co-chair awards com., 1993-94, mem. alllocations and membership coms., 1993-94; mem. Gov.'s Adv. Council Aging, Mo. exec. com., 1984-86, Gov.'s Task Force Alternative Care Elderly, 1982, Clayton (Mo.) Sch. Bd., 1970-84, pres., 1979-81, v.p., 1976, sec., 1975; mem. pres.'s coun. The Repertory Theatre St. Louis, 1988—, bd. dirs., 1989—; mem. community adv. bd. Jr. League St. Louis, 1990—; bd. dirs. St. Louis Regional Commerce and Growth Assn., 1990-94, St. Louis Connection, Internat. Women's Forum, 1992—, Square One Found., 1992-94; bd. govs., v.p. Fair Found., 1991—; mem. adv. bd. St. Louis chpt. Alzheimer's Assn., 1992—; mem. chancellor's adv. panel St. Louis C.C., 1992—; mem. Vision for Children at Risk, Child and Family Task Group, 1992—; mem. adv. bd. nonprofit mgmt. and leadership program U. Mo.-St. Louis, 1994—; bd. dirs. Parents as Tchrs. Nat. Ctr., 1994—. Recipient numerous grants on care of the elderly, Creativity award Adult Edn. Coun., 1979, Spl. Leadership award YWCA, 1985, Bronze medal award U.S. Surgeon Gen., 1988, Community award of merit Jewish Ctr. for Aged of Greater St. Louis, 1991, Cmty. Svc. award St. Louis chpt. Am. Jewish Com., 1992, Woman That Makes A Difference award Internat. Women's Forum, 1992; named Woman of Yr. City of Clayton, 1981, Woman of Achievement St. Louis Globe Democrat, 1980. Mem. Nat. Council Aging Inc., Am. Soc. Aging, Sigma Phi Omega. Home: 900 Audubon Dr Saint Louis MO 63105-2932 Office: OASIS Inst 7710 Carondelet Ave Ste 125 Saint Louis MO 63105-3319

MANN, NANCY LOUISE (NANCY LOUISE ROBBINS), entrepreneur; b. Chillicothe, Ohio, May 6, 1925; d. Everett Chaney and Pauline Elizabeth R.; m. Kenneth Douglas Mann, June 19, 1949 (div. June 1979); children: Bryan Wilkinson, Laura Elizabeth. BA in Math., UCLA, 1948, MA in Math., 1949, PhD in Biostatistics, 1965. Sr. scientist Rocketdyne Div. of Rockwell Internat., Canoga Park, Calif., 1962-75; mem. tech. staff Rockwell Sci. Ctr., Thousand Oaks, Calif., 1975-78; rsch. prof. UCLA Biomath., L.A., 1978-87; pres., CEO, owner Quality Enhancement Seminars, Inc., L.A., 1982—; pres., CEO Quality and Productivity, Inc., L.A., 1987—; curriculum adv. UCLA Ext. Dept. of Bus. and Mgmt., L.A., 1991—; mem. com. on Nat. Statistics, Nat. Acad. Scis., Washington, 1978-82; mem adv. bd. to supt. U.S. Naval Posgrad. Sch., Monterey, Calif., 1979-82. Co-author: Methods for Analysis of Reliability and Life Data, 1974; author: Keys to Excellence, 1985, The Story of the Deming Philosophy, 2d edit., 1987, 3d edit., 1989; contbr. articles to profl. jours. Recipient award IEEE Reliability Soc., 1982, ASQC Reliability Divsn., 1986. Fellow Am. Statis. Assn. (v.p. 1982-84); mem. Internat. Statis. Inst. Office: Quality and Productivity Inc 1081 Westwood Blvd # 217 Los Angeles CA 90024-2911

MANN, SUSAN, university president; b. Ottawa, Ont., Can., Feb. 10, 1941; d. Walter and Marjorie Mann; m. Nicholas Trofimenkoff; 1 child, Britt. BA in Modern History, U. Toronto, 1963; MA in History, U. Western Ont., 1965; PhD, U. Laval, Que., Can., 1970; LLD (hon.), Concordia U., Montreal, Que, Can., 1989, U. Ottawa, 1994. Lectr. English Toyo Eiwa Jogakuin, Tokyo, 1963-64; lectr. in history U. Montreal, 1966-70; asst. prof. history U. Calgary, Alta., Can., 1970-72; from asst. to assoc. prof. U. Ottawa, Ont., Can., 1972-83, prof. history, 1983—, chmn. dept. history, 1977-80, vice rector acad., 1984-90; pres. York U., Toronto, Ont., 1992—; mem. stamp adv. com. Can. Post Corp., Ottawa, 1988-92; chmn. adv. bd. Nat. Archives Can., 1989-91. Author: (as Susan Mann Trofimenkoff) Action Française: French Canadian Nationalism in the 1920s, 1975, Stanley Knowles: The Man From Winnipeg North Centre, 1982, Dream of Nation: A Social and Intellectual History of Quebec, 1983 (Sec. of State Canadian Studies prize 1984), Visions nationales: Une histoire du Québec, 1986; editor: The Twenties in Western Canada, 1972, Abbé Groulx: Variations on a Nationalist Theme, 1973, (with Alison Prentice) The Neglected Majority: Essays in Canadian Women's History, vol. I, 1977, vol II, 1985; acad. editor Social Scis. in Can., 1974-76; assoc. editor Social History, 1982-84; contbr. articles to profl. jours. Assessor of projects SSHRCC, 1972—; chmn., aid to scholarly publs. com. Social Sci. Fedn. Can., 1976-79; mem. appraisals com. Ont. Coun. Grad. Studies, 1983-84; pres. Can. Hist. Assn., 1984-85; chair status of women com. Coun. Ont. Univs., 1985-88; mem. Summer Inst. Women in Higher Edn. Adminstrn. Bryn Mawr (Pa.) Coll., 1986; co-founder Sr. Women Acad. Adminstrs. Can. Publ. Publ. grantee SSHRCC, 1975, Leave fellow, 1980-81, Doctoral fellow Can. Coun., 1968-70; U. Toronto scholar, 1959-61, U. Western Ont. scholar, 1964. Fellow Royal Soc. Can., Canadian Rsch. Inst. Advancement Women (hon., life, founder, bd. dirs. 1976-78). Office: York Univ Office of Pres, 4700 Keele St, North York, ON Canada M3J 1P3

MANN, TRUE SANDLIN, psychologist, consultant; b. Longview, Tex., Aug. 4, 1934; d. Bob Murphy and Stella True (Williams) Sandlin; m. Jack Matthewson Mann, Sept. 4, 1954 (div. Dec. 1989); children: Jack Matthewson Jr., Bob Sandlin, Daniel Williams, Nathaniel Currier. BS, Stephen F. Austin State U., Nacogdoches, Tex., 1973, MA, 1977; PhD, East Tex. State U., 1982. Lic. psychologist, Tex., Ark. Instr. Stephen F. Austin State U., 1975-76, vis. asst. prof. psychology, 1986-87; instr. East Tex. State U., Commerce, 1980-81; postdoctoral fellow Southwestern Med. Sch., Dallas, 1982-83; pvt. practice, Longview, Tex., 1983-92; psychologist dept. family practice U. Tex. Health Sci. Ctr., Tyler, 1990-92; dir. psychol. svcs. St. Michael's Hosp., Texarkana, Tex., 1992-93; cons. psychologist, Longview, 1993—; weekly newspaper columnist HARBUS, Cambridge Mass., 1959-60; cons. Made-Rite Co., Longview, 1989—. Mem. candidate com. Assoc. Reps. Tex., Austin, 1990—; bd. dirs. Mental Health Assn. Tex., 1977-82, 84-92; mem. Leadership Tex., 1988—. Mem. APA, Tex. Psychol. Assn. Episcopalian. Home: 1309 Inverness St Longview TX 75601-3548 Office: 1203 Montclair Dr Longview TX 75601

MANNERS, NANCY, mayor; b. Catania, Sicily, Italy; d. Gioacchino Jack and Maria Providenza (Virzi) Marasa; m. George Manners, Dec. 20, 1941; children: Gene David, Nancy Ellen Manners Sieh, Joan Alice. BA in Pub. Adminstrn., U. La Verne, 1979. Asst. city mgr. City of Covina, 1963-74; mcpl. mgmt. cons., 1975-85; mem. city coun. City of West Covina, Calif., 1984—; pres. Ind. Cities Risk Mgmt. Authority, West Covina, 1988; mayor City of West Covina, 1988-89, 92-93; pres. Ind. Cities Assn., 1989-90. Pres. Covina Coord. Coun., 1970-71, Altrusa Club of Covina-West, 1971-72, Ea. San Gabriel Valley Regional Occupation Program, 1974-76, San Gabriel Valley Planning Com., 1986, Mid-Valley Mental Health Coun., 1988; regional chmn. San Gabriel Valley Lung Assn., 1971-73; trustee Covina-Valley Unified Sch. Dist., 1973-77; foreman pro tem L.A. County Grand Jury, 1980-81; chmn. L.A. County Solid Waste Mgmt. Com., 1986-89; treas., bd. dirs. San Gabriel Valley Commerce and Cities Consortium, 1991, policy and steering com. Nat. League Cities, 1991, 93; chmn. employee rels. policy com. League Calif. Cities; bd. dirs. L.A. County Sanitation Dist., 1992-94, San Gabriel Valley Coun. of Govts., San Gabriel Valley Mosquito Abatement Dist., 1994—. Named Covina Citizen Yr., 1977, West Covina Citizen Yr., 1983, Woman Yr., Calif. State Legislature, 1990; recipient Woman of Distinction award Today's Woman Forum, 1988, Woman of Achievement award YWCA, 1987, 88, Community Svc. award West Covina C. of C., 1989, and others. Mem. LWV (pres. Asn Gabriel Valley 1978), Queen of the Valley Hosp. 2100 Club (bd. dirs. 1991—), Ind. Cities Assn. (v.p. 1988, pres. 1989), West Covina Rotary Club (bd. dirs.). Home: 734 N Eileen Ave West Covina CA 91791-1042

MANNES, ELENA SABIN, film and television producer, director; b. N.Y.C., Dec. 3, 1943; d. Leopold Damrosch and Evelyn (Sabin) M. BA, Smith Coll., 1965; MA, Johns Hopkins U., 1967. Researcher Pub. Broadcast Lab. Nat. Ednl. TV, N.Y.C., 1968-70; writer Sta. WPIX-TV, N.Y.C., 1970-73; assignment editor Sta. ABC-TV, N.Y.C., 1973-76; producer, writer Sta. WCBS-TV, N.Y.C., 1976-80; producer CBS News, N.Y.C., 1980-87, Pub. Affairs TV/Bill Moyers PBS Documentaries, N.Y.C., 1987—; ind. documentary dir. and producer, 1987—. Recipient Emmy awards NATAS, 1984, 85, 87, 90, Peabody award, 1985, Cine Golden Eagle award, 1988, 90, 93, 94, Robert F. Kennedy Journalism award, 1989, DGA awards, 1987, 90. Mem. Writers Guild Am., Dirs. Guild Am., Am. Film Inst. (dir. Workshop for Women).

MANNEY, SHERRITA GLYNN, women's health nurse; b. El Paso, Tex., Aug. 28, 1954; d. Robert DeWitt Jr. and Margaret (Durrill) Garland; m. Michael Wayne Manney, Aug. 5, 1978 (div. Aug. 1986). BA, U. Tex., 1975; BSN, U. Tex., El Paso, 1992. Mgr. Swenson's, El Paso, 1977-81; pers. trainer Iron Tender, El Paso, 1981-83; mgr., bookkeeper Gasoline Alley, El Paso, 1984-91; nurse tech., grad. nurse Thomason Gen. Hosp., El Paso, 1992—, nurse preceptor, 1994; dir. tel med health bd. Tel Med Teen Health Bd., El Paso, 1979-85; instr. English S.W. Inst., El Paso, 1985; rsch. asst. human papalliomavius study Tex. Tech.-The U. Tex., El Paso, 1992. Cost accounts YWCA Day Care Ctrs., El Paso, 1978-79; chmn. El Paso St. Festival, 1983-86; vol. El Paso Pub. Schs., 1986-87; health speaker Girl Scouts-Rio Grande Troop 348, El Paso, 1991; mem. Goodtime Singers: Music Therapy for the Elderly, 1993-95. Recipient scholarship Thomason Gen. Hosp., El Paso, 1991-92. Mem. Assn. Women's Health Obstet. and Neonatal Nurses, Tex. Nursing Student Assn. (project chmn. 1990-91), The Jr. League El Paso (vol.), Sigma Theta Tau. Home: 6632 Fiesta El Paso TX 79912 Office: Thomason Gen Hosp 4815 Alameda El Paso TX 79905

MANNING, BLANCHE M., federal judge; b. 1934. BEd, Chgo. Tchrs. Coll., 1961; JD, John Marshall Law Sch., 1967; MA, Roosevelt Univ., 1972; LLM, Univ. of Va. Law Sch., 1992. Asst. states atty. State's Atty.'s Office (no. dist.), Ill., 1968-73; supervisory trial atty. U.S. EEOC, Chgo., 1973-77; gen. atty. United Airlines, Chgo., 1977-78; asst. U.S. atty. U.S. Dist. Ct. (no. dist.) Ill., 1978-79; assoc. judge Cir. Ct. of Cook County, 1979-86, circuit judge, 1986-87; appellate court judge Ct. of Review Ill. Appellate Ct., 1987-94; district judge U.S. Dist. Ct. (no. dist.) Ill., Chgo., 1994—; tchr. A. O. Sexton Elem. Sch. James Wadsworth Elem. Sch., Wendell Phillips H.S. Adult Program, Morgan Park H.S. Summer Sch. Program, South Shore H.S. Summer Sch. Program, Carver H.S. Adult Edn. Program; lectr. Malcolm X C.C., 1970-71; adj. prof. NCBL C.C. of Law, 1978-79, DePaul Univ. Law Sch., 1992-94; tchg. team mem. Trial Advocacy Workshop, Harvard Law Sch., 1991-94; chmn. Com. on Recent Devels. in Evidence, Ill. Judicial Conf., 1991; faculty mem. New Judges Seminar, Ill. Judicial Conf.; past faculty mem. Profl. Devel. Seminar for New Assoc. Judges, Cook County Cir. Ct.; mem. bd. dirs., trained intervenor Lawyers' Assistance Program, Inc. Mem. Cook County Bar Assn. (second v-p 1974), Nat. Bar Assn., Nat. Judicial Coun., Ill. Judicial Coun. (treas. 1982-85, chmn. 1988, chmn. judiciary com. 1992), Ill. Judges Assn., Women's Bar Assn. of Ill., Nat. Assn. of Women Lawyers, Ill. State Bar Assn., Am. Bar Assn. (fellow 1991), Chgo. Bar Assn., Nat. Assn. of Women Judges, Appellate Lawyers Assn. (hon.); John Marshall Law Sch. Alumni Assn. (bd. dirs.), Chgo. State Univ. Alumni Assn. (bd. dirs.). Office: Everett McKinley Dirksen Bldg 219 S Dearborn St Rm 1756 Chicago IL 60604*

MANNING, CATHERINE MARIE, health care administrator; b. Bradford, Pa., Nov. 10, 1938; d. James Joseph and Mary Magdalen (Chohrach) M. BS in Elem. Edn., Villa Maria Coll., Erie, Pa., 1966; MEd, Gannon U., Erie, 1971; MA in Theology, Boston Coll., 1981. Joined Sisters of St. Joseph, Roman Cath. Ch., 1956. Tchr. Erie Diocesan Sch. Sys., Erie, 1956-66; piano instr. Villa Maria Conservatory, Erie, 1957-58; prin. Erie Diocesan Sch. Sys., 1966-73; dir. admissions Villa Maria Coll., Erie, 1973-76; med. social svc. caseworker St. Vincent Health Ctr., Erie, 1976-79; sociology and psychology instr. Marian Ct. Bus. Coll., Swampscott, Mass., 1981-82; acad. dean Marymount Internat. Sch., Rome, Italy, 1982-85; v.p. St. Vincent Health Ctr., Erie, 1985-91, pres., 1991—; trustee St. Mary's Home of Erie, 1985-95; bd. dirs. Cath. Charities of Erie Diocese, 1991, St. Vincent Health Ctr.; mem. bd. visitors Behrend Sch. Bus., Pa. State U. Bd. dirs. United Way of Erie County, 1994—. Mem. AAUW, Am. Coll. Healthcare Execs., Erie Art Mus., Pax Christi USA. Democrat. Roman Catholic. Home: 2816 Burgundy Dr Erie PA 16506

MANNING, CATHY LORAINE, human resources professional; b. St. Petersburg, Fla., Feb. 21, 1951; d. Bobbie Earl Brandon and Dorothy Loraine (Stean) Key; m. Ralph Wiley English, Aug. 15, 1970 (div. Feb. 1977); m. James A. Manning, Dec. 3, 1983. BBA, Tex. Wesleyan U., 1992. Sec., adminstrv. staff Bell Helicopter Textron Inc., Ft. Worth, 1975-90, staffing adminstr., 1990-92, career devel. specialist, 1992-94, labor rels. rep., 1994—; mem. steering com. United Way at Bell Helicoptor, 1994. Mem. Leadership Club Bell Helicopter Textron (chair awards com. 1993-94). Home: PO Box 1002 Hurst TX 76053-1002

MANNING, DEBORAH A., physician, health facility administrator; b. Clinton, N.C., Dec. 21, 1952; d. George A. and Virginia M. (McLaurin) M. BS, George Washington U., 1974; MD, Howard U., 1977. Diplomate Am. Bd. Internal Medicine. Intern Harbor Gen. Hosp., Torrance, Calif., 1977-78; resident Martinez (Calif.) VA Hosp., 1978-79, Providence Hosp., Washington, 1979-80; physician United Neighborhood Health Svcs., Nashville, 1980-82; pvt. practice Nashville, 1982-93; physician State of Tenn. Corrections, Nashville, 1993-94; med. dir. Matthew Walker Comp. Health Ctr., Nashville, 1994—. Mem. task force Meharry-Gen. merger Nashville C. of C., 1991; chair nat. trends Music City Links, Nashville, 1992—. Mem. ACP, Tenn. Women Medicine (mem. exec. com. 1992-94). Office: Matthew Walker Comp Health Ctr 1501 Herman St Nashville TN 37208

MANNING, JOAN ELIZABETH, chief operations officer; b. Davenport, Iowa, July 7, 1953; d. George John and Eugenie Joan (Thomas) Stolze; m. Michael Anthony Manning, July 30, 1977. BA, U. No. Iowa, 1975; MPH, U. Minn., 1990. Traveling collegiate sec. Alpha Delta Pi Nat. Sorority, Atlanta, 1975-76; recreational therapist Americana Healthcare Ctr., Mason City, Iowa, 1976-81; communication coord. Area Agy. on Aging, Mason City, 1981-83; exec. dir. United Way Cerro Gordo County, Mason City, 1983-85, Health Fair of the Midlands, Omaha, 1985-87; dir. health services ARC, Omaha, 1987-90, chief ops. officer, 1990—. Bd. dirs. YMCA of U.S.A., Chgo., 1981-83, Mason City YMCA, 1980-84, Mason City Parks and Recreation Bd., 1983-85, Camp Fire Coun., 1989—, Potters Therapy House, 1989—; mem. spl. adv. bd. Cerro Gordo County Human Svcs. Bd., 1983-85; mem. spl. activities com. Omaha Wellness Coun. of Midlands, 1986-89; chmn. wider opportunity task force Great Plains (Nebr.) Girl Scouts U.S., 1986-89; bd. dirs. Omaha South YMCA; mem. Jr. League of Omaha.

Mem. U. Minn. Alumnae Assn., Alpha Delta Pi. Republican. Roman Catholic. Office: ARC 3838 Dewey Ave Omaha NE 68105-1148

MANNING, JOSEPHINE ASARO, librarian; b. N.Y.C., July 24, 1940; d. Calogero and Benedetta (Conigliaro) A.; m. Robert Nickerson Manning, Mar. 23, 1962; children—Matthew Nickerson, Tracy Jane. B.A. in English Lit., Queens Coll., 1963; M.S. in L.S., Syracuse U., 1965. Circulation librarian St. Lawrence U. Library, Canton, N.Y., 1966-69; library tchr. Park Hill Sch., East Syracuse, N.Y., 1965-66; indexer/archivist Wash. State U. Library, Pullman, 1969-70; asst. prof. library sci. Central Mich. U., Mt. Pleasant, 1972; sr. reference librarian Citibank Fin. Library, N.Y.C., 1973-75; sr. librarian, head Reader's Digest Gen. Books Library, N.Y.C., 1975—; cons. Am. Studies Research Center, Hyderabad, India, 1979. Author: (audio book) The Prairie Princess, 1994, The Sanskritologist, 1994; contbr. short stories to various publicaltion. Mem. St. George Civic Assn., S.I., 1979—; mem. adv. com. N.Y. Pub. Library Fund, 1988-93. Mem. Spl. Libraries Assn. (editor publishing div. bull. 1981-83, N.Y. chpt. newsletter 1985-87, chmn. pub. div. 1984-85, Roll of Honor award 1987), Archons of Colophon, Romance Writers of Am. Office: Readers Digest Gen Books 260 Madison Ave New York NY 10016-2401

MANNING, MELANIE MARY, veterinarian; b. Edina, Minn., Aug. 13, 1959; d. John Patrick and Mary Margaret (Zambori) M. BS, Ft. Lewis Coll., Durango, Colo., 1980; DVM, Colo. State U., 1985. Relief veterinarian Nairobi, Kenya, 1985-86; veterinarian Alpine Animal Hosp., Laramie, Wyo., 1986-90; veterinarian, owner Gem City Vet. Svcs., P.C., Nairobi, 1990-91; resident in vet. anesthesiology U. Wis., Madison, 1991-93; facility veterinarian W.L. Gore & Assocs., Flagstaff, Ariz., 1993—. Mem. AVMA, Am. Endurance Ride. Home: 12385 Daniel Way Flagstaff AZ 86004-5397 Office: WL Gore & Assocs 4100 Kiltie Ln Flagstaff AZ 86001

MANNING, PATRICIA ANNE, small business owner; b. East Liverpool, Ohio, Jan. 22, 1939; d. Theodore James and Irene Ivy (Adamson) Lessel; m. Richard Edwin Manning, Mar. 30, 1957; children: Lisa Ann, Richard James. BS in Edn. magna cum laude, Kent State U., 1973, postgrad., 1973-79. Cert. elem. sch. educator, N.J. Tchr. math. Daw Jr. High Sch., Wellsville, Ohio, 1974-81; substitute tchr. East Liverpool, Ohio, 1982-83; tchr. supplemental math., reading Middletown (N.J.) High Sch., 1984-85; tchr. basic skills Highlands (N.J.) Elem. Sch., 1985-86; pvt. tutor Atlantic Highlands, N.J., 1986-91; owner, operator Tutors Unltd., Atlantic Highlands, N.J., 1990—. Mem., lector King of Kings Luth. Ch., Middletown, 1984—. Named Woman of Yr., Bus. & Profl. Women, 1986. Mem. AAUW, NEA, N.J. Women Bus. Owners Assn., Bus. and Profl. women (v.p. 1984-85, pres. 1985-86, program chmn. 1989-90), Middletown Newcomers Club, Middletown C. of C. Lutheran. Home: 60 Pape Dr Atlantic Highlands NJ 07716-2549

MANNING, SUE W., selectman; b. Cinn., Sept. 27, 1941; d. Harold Hugh and Ruth Ellen (Volk) Wegman; m. Michael James Manning, Feb. 16, 1963; children: Michael James, Betsy Ruth, David Bradley. BA, DePauw U., 1963. Planning and zoning commr. Town of Ridgefield, Conn., 1976-81, mem. bd. selectman, 1983-87, first selectman, 1987—; pres. League of Women Voters, Ridgefield, 1973-76; vice chmn., chmn. Housatonic Valley Coun. Elected Officials, Brookfield, Conn., 1989-90; vice chmn. Housatonic Resource Recovery Authority, 1989—; mem. Housatonic Valley Economic Devel. Partnership, Danbury, Conn., 1993—. pres. women's fellowship First Congl. Ch., 1978-80; pres., Family Y, 1977-81; mem. instnl. review bd. Danbury Hosp., 1986-89; mem. bd. dirs. A Better Chance, 1985-92; mem. bd. incorporators Ridgefield Bank, 1991—. Named Citizen of the Yr. Ridgefield Jaycees, 1976. Mem. Rotary (com. chair 1991—). Republican. Home: 56 East Ridge Ridgefield CT 06877 Office: Town of Ridgefield 400 Main St Ridgefield CT 06877

MANNING, SYLVIA, English studies educator; b. Montreal, Que., Can., Dec. 2, 1943; came to U.S., 1967; d. Bruno and Lea Bank; m. Peter J. Manning, Aug. 20, 1967; children—Bruce David, Jason Maurice. B.A., McGill U., 1963; M.A., Yale U., 1964, Ph.D. in English, 1967. Asst. prof. English Calif. State U.-Hayward, 1967-71, assoc. prof., 1971-75, assoc. dean, 1972-75; assoc. prof. U. So. Calif., 1975-94, prof., assoc. dir. Ctr. for Humanities, 1975-77, assoc. dir. Ctr. for Humanities, 1975-77, chmn. freshman writing, 1977-80, chmn. dept. English, 1980-83, vice provost, exec. v.p., 1984-94; prof. English U. Ill., 1994—, v.p. for acad. affairs, prof. English, 1994—. Author: Dickens as Satirist, 1971; Hard Times: An Annotated Bibliography, 1984. Contbr. essays to mags. Woodrow Wilson fellow, 1963-64, 66-67. Mem. MLA, Dickens Soc. Office: U of Ill 377 Henry Adm Bldg 506 S Wright St Urbana IL 61801

MANNS, BRIGITTE KARIN, elementary educator; b. Portland, Oreg., Apr. 27, 1961; d. Norbert Oskar and Rosemarie (Widmer) M. BA, U. Wash., 1983, student, 1986. 1st grade tchr. Lake Washington Sch. Dist., Kirkland, Wash., 1983-89, 3rd grade tchr., 1989-91, curriculum and staff devel., 1992—; mem. Dist. Assessment Adv. Bd., Kirkland, 1993-94. Active Leadership Redmond, C. of C., 1993-94; steering com. mem. Educators for Social Responsibility, Seattle, 1990-91. Mem. ASCD, Nat. Coun. Tchrs. of Math., Wash. Edn. Rsch. Assn., Puget Math. Leaders, Alpha Delta Kappa. Office: Lake Washington Sch Dist Adminstrn Ctr PO Box 2909 Kirkland WA 98083

MANNS, LINDA GREENE, community health nurse coordinator; b. Bklyn., May 21, 1951; d. Gaston A. and Cleopatra (Frier) Greene; m. Nov. 25, 1978 (div. 1984); 1 child, Temeca E. AAS, Bronx Community Coll., 1971; BSN, Hunter Coll., 1973; MSN, U. Va., 1988. Staff nurse Kings County Hosp., Bklyn., 1971-73; charge nurse St. John's Episcopal Hosp., Bklyn., 1974-78; pub. health nurse Dept. Health, Bklyn., 1973-78; staff nurse Roanoke (Va.) Meml. Hosp., 1979; staff nurse VA Med. Ctr., Salem, Va., 1979-83, primary nurse oncology clinic, 1983-84, weekend nurse supr., 1986-87, community health nurse, 1984-90, community health nurse coord., 1990—. Coord. Community Awareness Health Fair, High St. Bapt. Ch., 1987; vol. coord. Roanoke City Health Dept. Cardiovascular Risk Reduction Program. Mem. Va. Pub. Health Assn., Roanoke Valley Black Nurses' Assn. (treas.), Sigma Theta Tau. Home: 3103 Northside Rd Roanoke VA 24019

MANRY, MARY LUCILLE, real estate broker; b. St. Cloud, Minn., Nov. 30, 1938; d. Herbert Peter and Leona Elizabeth (Lang) Virnig; m. John Phillip Manry, June 11, 1960 (div. May 1988); children: Lisa Paige, Shannon Lee. BA, Marquette U., 1960. Sales assoc. Brants Realtors, Inc., Ft. Worth, 1977-79, broker assoc., 1979-86, v.p., 1988-84, mng. broker, 1986—. Mem. Jr. Womens Club, Westport, Conn., 1964-67, Arts Coun., 1978—, Sister Cities Internat., 1990—; co-chmn. Marquette U. North Tex. Alumni, 1993—. Mem. Ft. Worth Assn. Realtors (dir. 1988—, chmn. mem. svcs. 1988-90, multiple listing svc. 1989-92, pub. rels. 1991-92), Real Estate Brokerage Coun., Women's Coun. Realtors, Zeta Phi Eta. Office: Brants Realtors Inc 4936 Collinwood Fort Worth TX 76107

MANSEAU, MELISSA MARIE, infosystems specialist; b. Exeter, N.H., Mar. 24, 1962; d. Stuart Wayne and Dorothy Edith (Follis) Cady; m. Gerald Vincent Manseau; children; Lindsay Marie, Megan Elise. AS in Electronic Engrng. Tech., N.H. Tech. Inst., Concord, 1982; BS in Computer Sci., U. So. Maine, 1988. Assoc. system technician Nat. Semiconductor Corp., Inc. (formerly Fairchild Semiconductor), South Portland, Maine, 1982-83, system technician, 1983-85, sr. system technician, 1985, assoc. computer system engr., 1985-88, software engr., 1988—; sr. software engr., 1993; sr. analyst Konica Quality Photo East, Scarborough, Maine, 1994; engr. Systems Consulting Co., Portland, Maine, 1994—. Mem. IEEE, IEEE Computer Soc. (chmn. 1987-91). Congregationalist. Home: 10 Pinecrest Dr Hollis Center ME 04042-9763

MANSELL, LAURIE RUTH, paralegal; b. Homestead, Pa., Apr. 21, 1957; d. Robert Hull and Virginia Ruth (Dougherty) M. BA, Mary Wash. Coll., 1979; MA, U. Pitts., 1982; cert. in mus. studies, Duquesne U., 1983, cert. in paralegal studies, 1987. From asst. curator to curator Pitts. Children's Mus., 1983-87; asst. dir. preservation studies Tom Mistick & Sons Inc., Pitts., 1987-88; paralegal Kirkpatrick & Lockhart, Pitts., 1988-89, Fed. Investors, Pitts., 1989-92, Doepken Keevican Weiss & Medved, Pitts., 1990-91, Alcoa, Pitts., 1991—. Contbr. articles to profl. publs. Mem. Wash. County Humane Soc., Eighty Four, Pa., Marine Corps Hist. Found., Washington. Mem. NOW, Pitts. Paralegal Assn. (co-chair corp. specialty sect. 1994, bd. dirs. 1995), Mensa, Phi Alpha Theta, Pi Gamma Mu, Alpha Pi Sigma. Presbyterian. Home: 430 Saratoga Dr Pittsburgh PA 15236-4457

MANSFIELD, KAREN LEE, lawyer; b. Chgo., Mar. 17, 1942; d. Ralph and Hilda (Blum) Mansfield; children: Nicole Rafaela, Lori Michele. BA in Polit. Sci., Roosevelt U., 1963; JD, DePaul U., 1971; student U. Chgo., 1959-60. Bar: Ill. 1972, U.S. Dist. Ct. (no. dist.) Ill. 1972. Legis. intern Ill. State Senate, Springfield, 1966-67; tchr. Chgo. Pub. Schs., 1967-70; atty. CNA Ins., Chgo., 1971-73; law clk. Ill. Apellate Ct., Chgo., 1973-75; sr. trial atty. U.S. Dept. Labor, Chgo., 1975—, mentor Adopt-a-Sch. Program, 1992—. Contbr. articles to profl. jours. Vol. Big Sister, 1975-81; bd. dirs. Altgeld Nursery Sch., 1963-66, Ill. div. UN Assn., 1966-72, Hull House Jane Addams Ctr., 1977-82, Broadway Children's Ctr., 1986-90, Acorn Family Entertainment, 1993—; rsch. asst. Citizens for Gov. Otto Kerner, Chgo., 1964; com. mem. Ill. Commn. on Status of Women, Chgo., 1964-70; del. Nat. Conf. on Status of Women, 1968; candidate for del. Ill. Constl. Conv., 1969. Mem. Chgo. Council Lawyers, Women's Bar Assn. Ill., Lawyer Pilots Bar Assn., Fed. Bar Assn. Unitarian. Clubs: Friends of Gamelan (performer), 99's Internat. Orgn. Women Pilots (legis. chmn. Chgo. area chpt. 1983-86, legis. chmn. North Cen. sect. 1986-88, legis. award 1983, 85). Home: 204 S Taylor Ave Oak Park IL 60302-3307 Office: US Dept Labor Office Solicitor 230 S Dearborn St Fl 8 Chicago IL 60604-1505

MANSFIELD, KARLA JEAN, financial executive; b. Elmhurst, Ill., Aug. 4, 1950; d. Alfred B. and Marian V. (Caniff) M. B in Bus., Western Ill. U., 1971; M in Mgmt., Northwestern U., 1984. CPA, Ill. Sr. auditor Price Waterhouse, Chgo., 1971-74; mgr. acctg. Admiral group Rockwell Internat., Schaumburg, Ill., 1974-78; program mgr. Automatic Electric div. GTE, Northlake, Ill., 1978-81; dir. planning McGraw-Edison Co., Rolling Meadows, Ill., 1981-82; v.p. fin. and planning Rollins Burdick Hunter, Chgo., 1983-90, v.p., regional contr., 1990—. Mem. AICPAs, N.C. Assn. CPAs, Planning Forum, Ill. Soc. CPAs, Sigma Iota Epsilon, Beta Gamma Sigma. Office: Rollins Hudig Hall 3334 Healy Dr PO Box 25327 Winston Salem NC 27114-5327

MANSFIELD, LOIS EDNA, mathematics educator, researcher; b. Portland, Maine, Jan. 2, 1941; d. R. Carleton and Mary (Bowdish) M. BS, U. Mich., 1962; MS, U. Utah, 1966, PhD, 1969. Vis. asst. prof. computer sci. Purdue U., 1969-70; asst. prof. computer Sci. U. Kans., Lawrence, 1970-74, assoc. prof., 1974-78; assoc. prof. math. N.C. State U., Raleigh, 1978-79; assoc. prof. applied math. U. Va., Charlottesville, 1979-83, prof., 1983—; mem. adv. panel computer sci. NSF, 1975-78; cons., vis. scientist Inst. Computer Applications in Sci. and Engring., Hampton, Va., 1976-78. Contbr. articles to profl. jours. Grantee NSF and DOE. Mem. Am. Math. Soc., Soc. Indsl. and Applied Math. (mem. editorial bd. Jour. Sci. Statis. Computing, 1979-88), Assn. Computing Machinery (bd. dirs. SIGNUM 1980-83). Office: U Va Dept Applied Math Thornton Hall Charlottesville VA 22903

MANSFIELD, SYLVIA ANN, typeface designer, home inspector; b. Lincoln, Ill., Dec. 19, 1957; d. Rogers David and Nina Loetta (Walters) M.; m. Charles Richard Dobson, Feb. 9, 1984; children: Jason, Janssen, Cierra. AA, Brevard C.C., Cocoa, Fla., 1982. Cert. property insp. Sales mgr. United Agys., Inc., Cocoa, 1981-82; font designer Fla. Data Corp., Melbourne, 1982-85; sr. font designer Genicom Corp., Waynesboro, Va., 1985-93, design cons., 1993—; pres. Blue Ridge Home Inspections, Inc., Crimora, Va., 1993—; adj. instr. Blue Ridge C.C., Weyers Cave, Va., 1994. Contbr. poetry to jours. Bd. dirs. Genicom Employees Community Svc. Fund, 1989-93. Recipient art awards Brevard C.C., 1981, Titusville Art League, 1972, 73, 76. Mem. Bus. and Profl. Women, Nat. Assn. Counselors, Nat. Assn. Property Insps., Waynesboro Bd. Realtors (affiliate), Staunton-Augusta County Bd. Realtors (affiliate), Charlottesville Area Assn. Realtors (affiliate). Office: BRHI Inc RR 1 Box 154 Crimora VA 24431-9716

MANSMANN, CAROL LOS, federal judge, law educator; b. Pittsburgh, Pa., Aug. 7, 1942; d. Walter Joseph and Regina Mary (Pilarski) Los; m. J. Jerome Mansmann, June 27, 1970; children: Casey, Megan, Patrick. B.A., J.D., Duquesne U., 1964, 67; LL.D., Seton Hill Coll., Greensburg, Pa., 1985; PhD, La Roche Coll., 1990. Asst. dist. atty. Allegheny County, Pitts., 1968-72; assoc. McVerry Baxter & Mansmann, Pitts., 1973-79; assoc. prof. law Duquesne U., Pitts., 1973-82; judge west dist. U.S. Dist. Ct. Pa., Pitts., 1982-85; judge U.S. Ct. Appeals (3rd cir.), Phila., 1985—; Mem. Pa. Criminal Procedural Rules Com., Pitts., 1972-77; spl. asst. atty. gen. Commonwealth of Pa., 1974-79; bd. dirs. Pa. Bar Inst., Harrisburg, 1984-90; adj. prof. law U. Pitts., 1987—. Mem. adv. bd. Villanova U. Law Sch., 1985-91; bd. dirs. Duquesne U., 1987—, Sewickley Acad., 1988-91. Recipient St. Thomas More award, Pitts., 1983, Phila., 1984. Mem. ABA, Nat. Assn. Women Judges, Pa. Bar Assn., Fed. Judges Assn., Am. Judicature Soc., Allegheny County Bar Assn., Phi Alpha Delta. Republican. Roman Catholic. Office: US Ct Appeals US PO & Courthouse 7th and Grant Sts Pittsburgh PA 15219*

MANSON, CONNIE JEANE, librarian; b. Seattle, Mar. 28, 1950; d. Richard A. and E. Elaine (Hereth) M. BA in English Lit. cum laude, U. Wash., 1972, M in Librarianship with distinction, 1974. Reference libr. Mont. State Libr., Helena, 1974-75; libr. mgr. Wyo. Dept. Econ. Planning, Cheyenne, 1975-77; sr. librarian Wash. Div. Geology and Earth, Olympia, 1978—. Contbr. articles to profl. publs. Recipient Outstanding Contbns. N.W. Geol. Soc., 1993. Mem. Geosci. Info. Soc. (newsletter co-editor 1986—, chair, dir. com. 1990-96, Meritorious Svc. 1993), Assn. of Engring. Geologists, Western Assn. of Map Librs. Office: Wash Div Geology Earth Rsources PO Box 47007 Olympia WA 98504-7007

MANSOUR, FATEN SPIRONIOUS, interior designer, realtor; b. Amman, Jordan, May 8, 1958; came to U.S., 1981; d. Spironous Mansour and Margret Mousa Nijmeh; 1 child, Lara. AS in Bus. Adminstrn., Wasifia Coll., Amman, 1977; AS in Computer Sci., Sec. Bus. Adminstrn., West Valley Coll., 1988; BS in Interior Design, Art, San Jose State U., 1992. Tchr. French Rawdat Al-Sa'adeh, Amman, 1976-78; office mgr. of Min. of Transp. Queen Alia Internat. Airport, Amman, 1977-88; coord. banquets and weddings Marquee Club and Café, San Jose, Calif., 1988-93; interior designer, realtor Esquisite, San Jose, 1992—. Prodr. Arab Am. TV, L.A., 1990—. Active Arab Am. Anti-Discrimination Com. Home: 1274 Spaich Dr San Jose CA 95117 Office: Esquisite PO Box 10355 San Jose CA 95157

MANSPEIZER, SUSAN R., artist, educator; b. N.Y.C., Oct. 17, 1940. BA cum laude, CCNY, 1962, MA in Art Edn., 1966; postgrad., Corcoran Gallery, 1966-68, Art Students League, 1976-81. Art tchr. N.Y.C. Pub. Schs., Coll. of New Rochelle, N.Y., 1974, Kipp St. Art Ctr., Chappaqua, N.Y., 1983, Arts Ctr. of No. N.J., 1990—; tchr. collage workshop Acad. Orthopaedic Surgeons, 1983; tchr. Art Students League, summer 1993; represented by Viridian Gallery, N.Y.C., Nat. Assn. Women Artists, N.Y.C., Hudson River Contemporary Artists, Yonkers, N.Y., Westchester Coun. for the Arts, N.Y., Mamaroneck Artist Guild. One woman shows include Greenburgh Pub. Libr., 1974, 85, Westchester C.C., Valhalla, N.Y., 1975, Chappaqua Libr. Gallery, 1980, The Gallery, Tarrytown, N.Y., 1987, Viridian Gallery, N.Y.C., 1987, 90, 93, Mus. of the Hudson Highlands, Cornwall, N.Y., 1987, Lever Ho., N.Y.C., 1988, Concordia Coll., Bronxville, 1989, Concordia Coll., Bronxville, N.Y., 1989, Kirkland Art Ctr., Clinton, N.Y., 1991, S.W. State U., Marshall, Minn., 1991; group exhbns. include Silvermine Guild of Artists, New Canaan, Conn., 1992, Berkshire Artisans, Pittsfield, Mass., 1994, Onward Gallery, Tokyo, 1994, numerous others; juried exhibitions include Silvermine New Mems. Exhbn., 1990, Hastings-on-Hudson Sculpture Invitational, 1990, No. Westchester Ctr. for the Arts, 1990, Bergen Mus. Art & Sci., 1991, Silvermine-Charlotta Kotik, Juror, 1991, Tweed Gallery, N.Y., 1991, Nabisco Brands, Hanover, N.J., 1992, Hammond Mus., North Salem, N.Y., 1992, Photography and Small Sculptures, Silvermine, 1993, City Coll. Art Alumni, 1993, Arts Ctr. No. N.J., 1993, Katonah Library, N.Y., 1993, Middlesex County Coll., Edison, N.J., 1993, Westbeth Gallery, N.Y.C., 1993, Nexus Gallery, Phila., 1994. Recipient Honorable Mention award Nat. Arts Club, 1985, 1st Place Sculpture award Greenwich Art Soc., 1985, Best in Show award Gallery 54 Soho, 1988, 2d Prize Sculpture award Katonah Libr., 1993. Mem. Nat. Assn. Women Artists, Mamaroneck Artists Guild, Silvermine Artist Guild.

MANTHE, CORA DE MUNCK, real estate and investment company executive; b. Alton, Iowa, Oct. 10, 1928; d. Cornelius John and Bessie Bell (Miller) De Munck; m. Carl Robert Manthe, Apr. 5, 1952 (dec. Dec. 1987); children: Barry Paul, David Glenn. BA in Econs., U. Iowa, 1950; posgrad., U. Wis., Madison and Oshkosh; grad., Realtors Inst., 1972, 73, 74,75. Cert. residential appraiser. Rsch. analyst Dept. Def., Washington, 1951-52; social work investigator Dane County, Madison, 1960-62; civic hostess Welcome Wagon, Beaver Dam, Wis., 1963-70; real estate broker "C" Manthe Realty, Ltd., Beaver Dam, 1979—, property mgr., investment mgr., pres., treas., 1982—. Deacon Grace Presbyn. Ch., 1974-77, elder, 1979-82, ruling elder, 1989-92. Mem. AAUW (life), Internat. Platform Assn., Beaver Dam C. of C., U. Iowa Alumni Assn. (life), Optimist Internat. (life). Home and Office: 404 Declark St Beaver Dam WI 53916-1714

MANTHEI, ROBIN DICKEY, research technician; b. Tucson, May 16, 1956; d. Wilbur Dunbar French and Barbara Dickey; m. Joel Robert Manthei, Sept. 4, 1976; children: Nicholas Robert, Charles Dickey. AS, Augsburg Coll., 1976; cert. med. lab. technician, Med. Inst. Minn., 1978; BA, U. Minn., 1994. Med. lab. technician Lufkin Med. Lab., Mpls., 1978-82; jr. scientist U. Minn., Mpls., 1982-86; rsch. tech. Mayo Found., Rochester, Minn., 1986-89; chpt. leader Young Astronaut Program, 1987—; jr. scientist Inst. Human Genetics U. Minn., 1989-90; rsch. asst. Mpls. Med. Rsch. Found., 1990-93; lab. instr. North Hennepin C.C., Brooklyn Park, Minn., 1994—. Contbr. articles in field. Mem. DAR. Episcopalian. Home: 7630 Lanewood Ln N Maple Grove MN 55311-2670

MANTOOTH, MARGARET LARAH, retired educator; b. Springer, Okla., Mar. 17, 1909; d. Robert Oliver and Nora Belle (Hobson) Beam; m. Laurence Mantooth, Oct. 26, 1929. BS, U. Sci. and Arts of Okla., 1959. Cert. tchr., Okla. Tchr. Okla. Edn., Sulphur, 1930-33, Purcell, 1942-44; buyer, bookkeeper Purcell, 1938-48; acct. U.S. Govt., Beaumont, Calif., 1944-45. Adult tchr. 1st Bapt. Ch.; pres. Bapt. Women of Bapt. Ch., 1990-92; mem. cemetery bd. City of Purcell, 1990-92; coord. style shows Purcell C. of C., 1977-85. Recipient Svc. award Okla. Gardens, 1985, ARC Svc. award for Cols. Mcpl. Hosp., 1977, award for Best Red, White and Blue Flower Bed Okla. State Gardens, 1977; named to Waynes High Sch. Hall of Fame, 1993. Mem. Gladiolus Garden Club (charter), Univ. Sci. and Arts Alumni (bd. dirs. 1990-92), AARP (asst. state dir. 1977-79). Democrat. Home: 528 W Brule St Purcell OK 73080-5215

MANTOR-CLARYSSE, JUSTINE CLAIRE, fine arts educator; b. Neenah, Wis., Aug. 12, 1943; d. Jack Allen and Ann Elizabeth (Suchy) Mantor; m. John Allan Wantz, June 18, 1968 (div. 1982); m. Omer T. Clarysse, July 28, 1983. BFA, Sch. Art Inst. Chgo., 1967; MA, No. Ill. U., 1969, MFA, 1971. Assoc. prof. fine arts Loyola U., Chgo., 1971-93, dir. women's studies, 1982-83; represented by Artisimo Gallery, Scottsdale, Ariz.; instr. Coll. of DuPage, Glen Ellyn, Ill., 1971-72, North Shore Art League, Winnetka, Ill., 1972-73, DuPage Art League, Wheaton, Ill., 1972; gallery dir. Water Tower Gallery, Chgo., 1973-81; lectr. Ill. Conf. L.Am. Studies, U. Ill., 1990, Chantanqua Conf. Fgn. Lang. Tchrs., Pheasant Run, Ill., 1991, Mid-Am. Coll. Art Assn., Madison, Wis., 1991, 92, Nat. Coll. Art Assn., Seattle, 1993, 94. Solo exhbns. include U. Ill. Med. Ctr., Chgo., 1979, Springfield (Ill.) Art Assn., 1979, John Nelson Bergstrom Art Ctr. and Mus., Neenah, Wis., 1980, Aurora (Ill.) Coll., 1980, Arc Gallery, Chgo., 1981, 83, Illini Union Gallery, Champaign, Ill., 1982, Fountain Hills Cmty. Ctr., Ariz., 1990, Downtown Gallery, Phoenix, 1994, others; permanent collections include Ill. State Mus., Rockford Mus., Kemper Ins. Co., Gillman Gallery, Chgo., Byer Mus., others. Grantee Ill. Arts Coun., 1978, Ill. Art Coun./Mellon Found., 1979, Nat. Humanities Assn., 1980, Ill. Humanities Coun., 1980-81; named Best of Show, Fountain Hills Art Fair, Ariz., 1993. Mem. AAUP, Nat. Coll. Art Assn. (lectr. 1993), Mid-Am. Coll. Art Assn. (lectr. 1991, 92), Internat. Friends of Transformative Art (co-editor The Transformer newsletter) Fountain Hills Art League, Ariz. Artists' Guild, Chgo. Artists' Coalition, Sch. Art Inst. Chgo. Alumni Assn., Ariz. Women's Caucus for Art (pres. 1994). Democrat. Presbyterian. Office: Loyola U Chgo Crown Ctr Humanities 6525 N Sheridan Rd Chicago IL 60626-5311

MANTY, NORMA RAE, digital designer; b. Anchorage, Alaska, Apr. 28, 1959; d. Reino John and Jean M.; m. Thomas George Molitor, Oct. 1, 1988. AA in Apparel Design, Diablo Valley Coll., 1979; BA in Studio Art, Art History, U. Calif., Santa Cruz, 1981. Prodn. artist Grey Advt., L.A., 1983; prodn. artist, design asst. Young & Rubicam (Dentsu), L.A., 1984; free-lance cons., graphic designer, prodn. asst. San Francisco, 1985-87, 88-90; graphic designer Morla Design, San Francisco, 1988; free-lance cons., digital designer Chgo., 1991; digital designer Nestlé Beverage Co., San Francisco, 1992-93; cons., digital designer, prodn. project mgr. San Francisco, 1994, Bend, Oreg., 1994—. Designer Levi's Sport Jeans Point of Purchase, 1989 (Merit award), software package Electronic Arts, Instant Synthesizer, 1990 (Award of Distinction from Art Direction Mag., Comm. Arts Mag., Design Annual). Home: 120 SW 17th Bend OR 97702

MANTYLA, KAREN, sales executive; b. Bronx, N.Y., Dec. 31, 1944; d. Milton and Sylvia (Diamond) Fischer; m. John A Mantyla, May 30, 1970 (div. 1980); 1 child, Michael Alan. Student, Rockland Community Coll., Suffern, N.Y., 1962, NYU, 1967, Mercer U., 1981. Mktg. coordinator Credit Bur., Inc., Miami, Fla., 1973-79; dist. mgr. The Research Inst. Am., N.Y.C., 1979-80, regional dir., 1980-85, field sales mgr., 1985-86, nat. sales mgr., 1986-87; dir. mktg. TempsAmerica, N.Y.C., 1987-88; nat. accounts mgr. The Rsch. Inst. Am., N.Y.C., 1989; v.p. sales Bur. Bus. Practice/ Paramount Comm., Inc., Waterford, Conn., 1989-93; pres. Quiet Power, Inc., Washington, 1993—. Mem. ASTD, Sales and Mktg. Execs. (past bd. dirs. N.Y. chpt., v.p. Ft. Lauderdale chpt. 1979), U.S. C. of C., Women Entrepreneurs. Home: 5449 Grove Ridge Way Rockville MD 20852 Office: Quiet Power Inc Ste 300 655 15th St NW Washington DC 20005

MANTZELL, BETTY LOU, school health administrator; b. Brookville, Pa., Oct. 16, 1938; d. Elmer William and Wilda Mae (Enterline) M. Diploma, Ind. (Pa.) Hosp. Sch. Nursing, 1959; BSN, Case Western Res. U., 1969, MA, 1978; cert. supr. ednl. adminstrn., Cleve. State U., 1983; cert. supr., John Carroll U., 1989. RN, Ohio, Pa. Oper. rm. nurse Univ. Hosps. of Cleve., 1963-69; sch. nurse various locations Cleve. Pub. Schs., 1969-85, coord. sch. nurses, 1976-85, acting asst. supr. health svcs., 1985-86, supr. health svcs., 1986—; mem. adv. com. to baccalaureate nursing program Cleve. State U.; prevention of blindness adv. com. Cleve. Sight Ctr.; active All Kids County Consortium Cleve. Dept. Pub. Health, AIDS Commn. Greater Cleve., Children's Lung Health Com. Am. Lung Assn. No. Ohio; mem. sch. health com. Acad. Medicine Cleve.; clin. instr. cmty. health nursing Frances Payne Bolton Sch. Nursing, Case Western Res. U., Cleve., 1988-90. Mem. ANA, Ohio Nurses Assn., Greater Cleve. Nurses Assn., Am. Sch. Health Assn., Nat. Assn. Sch. Nurses, Ohio Assn. Sch. Nurses, Northeastern Ohio Assn. Sch. Nurses, Ohio Assn. Secondary Sch. Adminstrs., Cleve. Coun. Adminstrs. and Suprs., Cleve. Med. Libr. Assn. Office: Lakeside Adminstrv Ctr 1440 Lakeside Ave Cleveland OH 44144

MANUEL, VIVIAN, public relations company executive; b. Queens County, N.Y., May 6, 1941; d. George Thomas and Vivian (Anderson) M. BA, Wells Coll., Aurora, N.Y., 1963; MA, U. Wyo.-Laramie, 1965. Mgmt. analyst Dept. Navy, 1966-68; account supr. Gen. Electric Co., N.Y.C., 1968-72, corp. rep. bus. and fin., 1972-76; dir. corp. comm. Standard Brands Co., N.Y.C., 1976-78; pvt. cons., N.Y.C., 1978-80; pres. V M Comm. Inc., N.Y.C., 1980—. Mem. com. Girls Club N.Y., 1983-84; trustee Wells Coll., 1983-90; mem. adv. bd. Glenholme Sch., 1991-92. Mem. AAUW, N.Y. Women in Comm. (bd. v.p. 1983-85, chair Matrix awards 1985), Women Execs. in Pub. Rels. (bd. dirs. 1985-88), Women's Econ. Roundtable, N.Y.C. Commn. on Status of Women. Office: V M Comm Inc 501 E 79th St New York NY 10021

MANUTI, ANNABELLE THERESA, advertising agency financial executive; b. Bklyn., Sept. 11, 1928; d. Decio Dan and Anna Michelle (Vanacore) Assorto; m. John Thomas Manuti, Dec. 31, 1958. Student, Hunter Coll., 1950, postgrad. in real estate sch. Continuing Edn., 1980-82. Lic. real estate broker, N.Y. Statis. auditor Am. Fore Ins. Group, N.Y.C., 1950-55; bookkeeper Picard Advt., N.Y.C., 1955-60; supr. dept. acctg. Moquel Williams &

Saylor Advt., N.Y.C., 1960-65; comptroller's asst. Frolich Advt., N.Y.C., 1965-70; supr. accounts payable Miller Advt., N.Y.C., 1970-80; v.p. fin. Jaffe Communications, N.Y.C., 1980-90; free-lance, 1990—. Roman Catholic. Home and Office: 5530 80th St Apt D306 Saint Petersburg FL 33709

MANZ, BETTY ANN, nurse administrator; b. Paterson, N.J., Nov. 30, 1935; d. James Albert and Elsie (Basse) Brown; diploma Newark Beth Israel Hosp. Sch. Nursing, 1955; BSN, Seton Hall U., 1964; m. Roger A. Johnson, Feb. 1988; children: Laura, Richard, Garry. Staff nurse oper. room Newark Beth Israel Hosp., 1955-56, recovery room head nurse, 1956-57, oper. room head nurse, 1957-58, supr. oper. room, 1958-60; substitute tchr. pub. schs. Harding Twp., 1966-70; charge nurse St. Barnabas Med. Ctr., Livingston, N.J., 1965-70, head nurse emergency room, 1970-72; oper. room supr. St. Clares Hosp., Denville, N.J., 1972-77; asst. dir. for oper. rooms and post anesthesia rooms Newark Beth Israel Med. Ctr., 1977-82; asst. dir. nursing oper. room care program Thomas Jefferson U. Hosp., Phila., 1982-84; asst. dir./assoc. nursing dir. oper. room, anesthesia ICU, ambulatory surgery Univ. Hosp., SUNY-Stony Brook, 1984-87 dir. oper. room/post anestesia care ambulatory surgery Med. Ctr. Del., Wilmington and Christiana, Del., 1987-88; practice mgr. Del. Orthopaedic Ctr., Wilmington, 1989—; faculty mem. postgrad. course in microsurgy for Am. Coll. Obstetricians and Gynecologists, Newark, 1982; profl. cons. oper. room products, also health cons. Henry E. Wessel Assocs., Moraga, Calif.; profl. tech. cons., lectr. Surgicot, Inc., Smithtown, N.Y. Dep. dir. Harding Twp. CD, 1967-75. Recipient Service award Essex County Med. Soc., 1979. Mem. AAMI, Nat. Assn. Orthopaedic Nurses, Assn. Oper. Room Nurses, Am. Soc. Post Anesthesia Nurses, Del. Med. Group Mgmt. Assn. (sec.), Bones Soc. Orthopedic Mgrs., Newark Beth Israel Hosp. Nursing Alumnae Assn., Seton Hall U. Alumnae Assn., Harding Twp. Civic Assn., Am. Field Svc., Colonial States Knitters Guild (pres.). Republican. Club: Mt. Kemble Lake Community. Editor operating room sect. SCORE mag. Home: 2620 Lamper Ln Wilmington DE 19808-3808 Office: 2501 Silverside Rd Wilmington DE 19810-3726

MANZELLA, KATHLEEN HUGHES, educator; b. West Reading, Pa., Oct. 22, 1947; d. Carl Edward and Dorothy Elizabeth (Kline) Hughes; m. Joseph John Manzella, Jr.; children: Zachary Tey Hughes, Abigail Genee Hughes. AB, Albright Coll., 1969; MA, Lehigh U., 1970; ABD in Polit. Sci., U. Pa. Recreation planner Reading (Pa.) Model Cities Program, 1970, criminal justice planner, 1970-71; state ct. planner Gov.'s Justice Commn., Harrisburg, Pa., 1972-74; instr. Albright Coll., Reading, 1974-89; vis. prof. Ursinus Coll., Collegeville, Pa., 1990, Lafayette Coll., Easton, Pa., 1991-92. Dem. nominee for Pa. Senate, 48th Dist., 1994; bd. dirs. Montessori Children's House, Reading, 1976-80, World Affair Coun., Reading, 1970-75, Lehigh Valley coun. Girl Scouts U.S., 1993—; mem. sch. Bd. Wyomissing (Pa.) Area Sch. Dist., 1981-93. Mem. AAUW, Am. Polit. Sci. Assn., Berks Women's Network. Democrat. Lutheran. Office: PO Box 5963 Wyomissing PA 19610

MANZELMANN, DONNA SMITH, nurse educator and administrator; b. Tulsa, July 18, 1949; d. Grover Hayward and Betty Jane (Just) Smith; m. James Manzelmann Jr., Aug. 22, 1970 (div. May 1992); children: Cara Michelle, Marcia Anne. BSN, U. Okla., 1971; MA, U. Tulsa, 1976; MS, U. Okla., Oklahoma City, 1985; EdD, Okla. State U., 1988. RN, Okla. Staff and charge nurse Hillcrest Med. Ctr., Tulsa, 1971-72; staff and head nurse Paramount (Calif.) Gen. Hosp., 1972-73; head nurse Presbyn. Intercommunity Hosp., Whittier, Calif., 1973-74; instr. nursing U. Tulsa, 1974-75, Tulsa Jr. Coll., 1975-76; cons., dir. nursing edn. Creative Specialists Inc., Tulsa, 1976-85; mgr. patient intervention svcs., stroke team coord. St. Francis Hosp., Tulsa, 1985-87; asst. prof. nursing, coord. advanced practice programs Grand Canyon U., Phoenix, 1987-91; dir. staff devel. John C. Lincoln Hosp. and Health Ctr., Phoenix, 1991-92; dir. nursing edn. and rsch. Tulsa Regional Med. Ctr., 1992—. program dir., dir., editor more than 350 audiovisual programs, 1976-85. Program chmn. Tulsa Ballet Theater and Arts and Humanities Coun., 1983-85; v.p., chmn. com. jr. women's div. Tulsa Philharm., Tulsa, 1983-85; mem. Jr. League of Tulsa, 1983—; bd. dirs. health care sect. Nat. Safety Coun., sec., 1981-86. W.K. Kellogg fellow, 1985. Mem. ANA, Ariz. and Okla. Nurses Assn., Nat. League for Nursing, PEO (pres. Chpt. X 1978-79), Sigma Theta Tau. Mem. Christian Ch. (Disciples of Christ). Home: 5349 E 95th St Tulsa OK 74137-4423 Office: Tulsa Regional Med Ctr 744 W 9th St Tulsa OK 74127-9096

MANZI, ALICE M., artist, educator; b. Bklyn., June 16, 1951; d. Frank J. and Anna M. (Reeves) M. BA, Bklyn. Coll., 1973; MA, NYU, 1976. Dir. art programs Hamilton Hill Art Ctr., Schenectady, N.Y., 1980-82; scenic designer N.E. Ballet Co., Schenectady, 1987-93; cons., artist, owner Manzi Studios, Porter Corners, N.Y., 1994—; adj. prof. Russell Sage/Jr. Coll. Albany, N.Y., 1986-94, Skidmore Coll., Saratoga, N.Y., 1988—. Exhibited in one-woman and group shows at Albany Inst. of History and Art, 1985, N.Y. State Women Artists, Schenectady, N.Y., 1986, Cooperstown (N.Y.) Ann. Nat. Show, 1987-91, Nat. Mus. of Dance, Saratoga Springs, N.Y., 1991, Sculpture '91 Internat. Exhibit, Rochester, N.Y., 1991, Ellen Harris Gallery, Provincetown, Mass., 1988-94, Design Toscano, Arlington Hts., Ill., 1992, Brittany Lore Galleries, Sarasota, Fla., 1992, Skidmore Coll., Saratoga Springs, 1994. CETA grantee Schenectady Employment and Tng. Act, 1978, Spl. Opportunity Stipends grantee N.Y. Found. for the Arts, N.Y., 1991. Mem. Internat. Sculpture Ctr., Albany League Arts, Saratoga Arts Coun. Home and Office: Manzi Studios 1112 North Creek Rd Porter Corners NY 12859

MANZO, MARIE GRACE, psychologist; b. Phila., Feb. 19, 1957; d. James and Connie Rose (Fazio) Giannone; m. Conrad Yaeger (dir. 1992). BA in Psychology with honors, Stockton Coll., Pomona, N.J., 1979; MA in Clin. Psychology with honors, West Chester (Pa.) U., 1983. Lic. psychologist, Pa. Asst. box office mgr. Smithville (N.J.) Theatre, 1976-78; project dir. rsch. unit Atlantic County, Atlantic City, 1979-80; grad. asst. West Chester U., 1980-81; counselor Community Homes, Exton, Pa., 1981-83; psychologist Creative Health Svcs., Pottstown, Pa., 1983—, M. Manzo Psychol. Svcs., Boyertown, Pa., 1984—; mem. bd. dirs. Pottstown YWCA, 1985-89; workshop facilitator, lectr. on empowerment. Bd. dirs. women's support group Potts Town YWCA, 1985-89; bd. dirs., chair adv. bd. Stop Abuse Foster/Empowerment Treatment Program for Male Batterers, 1990—; co-founder and cmty edn. dir. Potts Town SAFE Project-Domestic Violence Project; co-founder Stop Abuse Foster Empowerment Treatment Program Malebatterers; co-chair adv. bd. Domestic Violence Project, 1990—. Recipient Excellence award in assisting domestic violence victims Women's Ctr. Montgomery County and Laurel House, 1992. Mem. APA (women's div.), NOW. Office: Dr Shah Med Ctr 9 Rowell Rd Boyertown PA 19512-8933

MAPEL, PATRICIA JOLENE, farmer, consultant; b. Lake City, Iowa, June 24, 1933; d. John Gilbert and Blanche Evelyn (Taylor) Sharkey; m. J.R. Mapel, Sept. 1, 1952 (dec. 1992); children: Pati Jo, Mark L., Grant L., Penelope R., Kay Collene. Student, Wesley Meml. Hosp. Sch. of Nursing, 1951-52. Ptnr. farming Lake City, Iowa, 1953-92; ptnr., pres. Mapel Farms Ethanol, Inc., Lake City, Iowa, 1984-92; house dir. Delta Delta Delta Simpson Coll., Indianola, Iowa, 1993—; cons. Dept. of Energy, Kansas City, 1981; demonstrator, educator Iowa Cen. Community Coll., Ft. Dodge, Iowa. Contbr. articles to profl. jours. Bd. dirs. Cen. Sch. Preservation, Inc., Lake City, 1984-90. Mem. Entre Nous Music Club, Eastern Star. Democrat. Mem. Ch. of Christ. Home: 705 N C St Indianola IA 50125-1202

MAPLE, MARILYN JEAN, educational media coordinator; b. Turtle Creek, Pa., Jan. 16, 1931; d. Harry Chester and Agnes (Dobbie) Kelley; B.A., U. Fla., 1972, M.A., 1975, Ph.D., 1985; 1 dau., Sandra Maple. Journalist various newspapers, including Mountain Eagle, Jasper, Ala., Boise (Idaho) Statesman, Daytona Beach (Fla.) Jour., Lorain (Ohio) Jour.; account exec. Fredericks & Co., N.Y.C.; producer hist. films Fla. State Mus., Gainesville, 1967-69; writer, dir., producer med. and sci. films and TV prodns. for six medically related colls. U. Fla., Gainesville, 1969—; pres. Media Modes, Inc., Gainesville. Recipient Blakslee award, 1969, spl. award, 1979, Monsour Lectureship award, 1979. Mem. Health Edn. Media Assn. (dir., awards, 1977, 79), Phi Delta Kappa, Kappa Tau Alpha. Author: On the Wings of a Butterfly; columnist: Health Care Edn. mag.; contbr. Fla. Hist. Quar. Home: 1927 NW 7th Ln Gainesville FL 32603-1103 Office: U Fla PO Box 16J Gainesville FL 32602-0016

MAPLE, OPAL LUCILLE, school psychologist; b. Canton, Ill., Nov. 15, 1935; d. Dwight Willard and Eileen Beatrice (Cadwalader) Beaty; m. Gilbert Roy Maple, June 30, 1967 (dec. 1985). BA, Wheaton (Ill.) Coll., 1958; MS, We. Ill. U., 1962. Cert. sch. psychologist, Ill. Tchr. Community Dist. #5, Cuba, Ill., 1958-60, Community Dist. #66, Canton, Ill., 1960-61; asst. dean women Moody Bible Inst., Chgo., 1961-64; sch. psychologist intern Chgo. Pub. Schs., 1964-65; sch. psychologist Peoria (Ill.) pub. schs., 1965-69, Waukegan (Ill.) pub. schs., 1969-81, Knox-Warren Spl. Edn., Galesburg, Ill., 1986—. Co-author pre-sch. test, 1975. Deaconess, treas. Antioch Evang. Free Ch., 1971-81; deaconess, fin. sec. Bethel Bapt. Ch., Galesburg, 1982—. Mem. Cen. Ill. Sch. Psychologists Assn. (pres. 1967-68), Ill. Psychol. Assn. (sec. 1977-79), DAR, Knox County Genealogical Soc., Nat. Assn. Sch. Psychologists, Ill. Sch. Psychologists Assn. Republican. Baptist.

MAPLES, MONICA L., legislative staff member; m. Noel Gould. Student, U. S.D., 1983-86. Legis. asst. to Senator Thomas A. Daschle, 1987-89, rsch. dir. to Senator John D. Rockefeller IV, 1989-90; rsch. dir. Dem. Nat. Campaign Com., 1991-93, polit. dir., 1993; chief of staff to Rep. Vic Fazio, 1993—. Office: Rep Vic Fazio D-Calif 2113 Rayburn House Office Bldg Washington DC 20515*

MARABLE, JUDY VIRGINIA GORDON, insurance company supervisor; b. Roberta, Ga., Jan. 1, 1947; d. Barney Wesley and Bessie Pauline (Averett) Gordon; m. Clifton Ronnie Marable, June 1, 1971; 1 child, Clifton Ronnie II. Cert. assoc. in automation mgmt., assoc. in ins. svcs., underwriting Ins. Inst. Am., profl. ins. woman;cert. gen. ins. Asst. supr. Cigna P&C Ins., Macon, Ga., 1965-76, supr., 1976-80, personal lines underwriter, 1980-90; supr. Cigna Info. Svcs., Macon, 1990-94. Vol. United Way, 1991; pres. Crawford City Hist. Soc., Roberta, Ga., 1988-89; cubmaster Cub Scouts Pack 264, Roberta, 1984-87. Recipient Edn. award Profl. Ins. Agents, 1992. Mem. Nat. Assn. Ins. Women (treas. 1993-94, Ga. state dir. 1991-93, chmn. Ga. membership 1990-91, rep. regional nominating com. 1991, 94, Region III Ins. Profl. of Yr. 1994, Region III Individual Edn. Achievement Award 1993, Region III T.J. Mims Award of Excellence 1992, Nat. Ins. Profl. Yr. 1994), Ins. Women of Macon (Pres. award 1988, 90, 91, Ins. Woman of Yr. 1990, 91, pres.-pres.-elect 1987-89, bd. dirs. 1989-95, 10 various offices, chair 23 coms. 1987-95), Postal Customer Coun. (sec. 1991-92), United Daus. of Confederacy (pres. 1991—), Ctrl. Ga. Geneal. Soc. (pres. 1991-92). Home: RR 1 Box 2460 Roberta GA 31078 Office: # 620 Bass Rd Macon GA 31298

MARALDO, PAMELA JEAN, nursing association executive, lecturer, consultant; b. Wilmington, Del., Oct. 27, 1947; d. Ernest and Helen Cecelia (Antonini) M. B.S., Adelphi U., 1970; M.A., NYU, 1976, Ph.D., 1985; LHD (hon.), Worcester State U., 1989. Registered nurse, N.Y. Cardiovascular nurse NYU Med. Ctr., N.Y.C., 1970-74; research assoc. Nat. Health Council, N.Y.C., 1975-78; dir. pub. policy Nat. League for Nursing, N.Y.C., 1978-83, chief exec. officer, 1983-92; pres. Planned Parenthood Fed. of Am., N.Y.C., 1992—; mem. health care faculty Am. Express, N.Y.C., 1982—, N.Y.C. Bd. Health, 1988—. Contbr. articles to profl. jours., chpts. to books. Mem. legis. com. Village Reform Democrats, N.Y.C., 1985; bd. dirs. Nurses for Polit. Action, N.Y.C., 1978—, Nurses Ednl. Fund, Nurses Houses. Recipient Disting. Alumna award Adelphi U., 1985, Disting. Recent Alumna award NYU, 1989; named one of 12 top execs. of non-profit orgns. Saavy Mag., 1985. Fellow Am. Acad. Nursing; mem. Am. Nurses Assn., Women's Econ. Roundtable, Am. Soc. Assn. Execs., Nat. Health Coun. (v.p. 1989—, bd. dirs. 1987—), Epsilon Phi Tau, Sigma Theta Tau. Democrat. Home: 61 Jane St New York NY 10014-5107 Office: Planned Parenthood Fed of Am 810 7th Ave New York NY 10019*

MARASCO, ROSE C., artist, educator; b. Utica, N.Y., Dec. 25, 1948; d. Ernest Salvatore Marasco and Concetta Regina (Faga) Massa. BFA, Syracuse U., 1971; MA, Goddard Coll., 1981; MFA, Visual Studies Workshop, 1991. Instr. photography Munson-Williams-Proctor-Inst. Sch. of Art, Utica, 1974-79; assoc. prof. dept. art U. So. Maine, Portland, 1979—, chair dept. art, 1992-94; instr. photography Maine Coll. of Art, Portland, 1981-87; mem. adv. roster Maine Arts Commn., Augusta, 1993—. Shows include Photokina, 1988, Portland Mus. Art, 1989, Farnsworth Mus., Rockland, Maine, 1992-93, Davis Mus. and Cultural Ctr., Wellesley, Mass., 1995. Residency fellow MacDowell Colony, 1985, Artists fellow Maine Arts Commn., Women's Studio Workshop, 1994; Percent for Art grantee Maine Arts Commn., 1983, Major grantee Maine Humanities Coun., 1990-92. Mem. Soc. Photographic Edn. Office: U So Maine Dept of Art 37 College Ave Gorham ME 04038

MARAVICH, MARY LOUISE, realtor; b. Fort Knox, Ky., Jan. 4, 1951; d. John and Bonnie (Balandzic) M. AA in Office Adminstrn., U. Nev., Las Vegas, 1970; BA in Sociology and Psychology, U. So. Calif., 1972; grad. Realtors Inst. Cert. residential specialist. Adminstrv. asst. dept. history U. So. Calif., L.A., 1972-73; asst. pers. supr. Corral Coin Co., Las Vegas, 1973-80; realtor, Americana Group div. Better Homes and Gardens, Las Vegas, 1980-85, Jack Matthews and Co., 1985-93, Realty Execs., Las Vegas, 1993—. Mem. Nev. Assn. Realtors (cert. realtors inst.), Las Vegas Bd. Realtors, Nat. Assn. Realtors, Women's Council of Realtors, Am. Bus. Women's Assn., NAFE, Million Dollar Club, Pres.'s Club. Office: Realty Execs 1903 S Jones Blvd # 100 Las Vegas NV 89102-1260

MARAZITA, ELEANOR MARIE HARMON, secondary education educator; b. Madison County, Ind., Oct. 25, 1933; d. William Houston Harmon and Martha Belle (Savage) Hinds; m. Philip Marazita; children: Mary Louise, Frank, Dominic, Vincent, Elizabeth Faye, Candice Marie, Daniel William. BS in Home Econs., Cen. Mich. U., 1955; MA in Human Ecology, Mich. State U., 1971. Cert. vocat. home econs. tchr., K-Jr. Coll., cert. speech correction tchr. Tchr. adult edn. Mt. Pleasant, Mich., 1956; substitute tchr. North Branch (Mich.) Schs., 1961-64; tchr., coordinator Pied Piper Cooperative Nursery Sch., Lansing, Mich., 1964-69; tchr. Lansing Community Coll., 1971-81, Grand Ledge (Mich.) High Sch., 1969—; Mich. tchr. del. World Conf. Teaching Profls., 1985; adv. mem. Mich. Tchr. Competency Testing Program, 1992; mem. bd. dirs. Greater Lansing U.N. chpt., 1995—. Vol. St. Lawrence Mental Health Hosp., 1972-73, Listening Ear Crisis Intervention Ctr., 1973-77, Capital City Convalescent Home, 1969-73; chmn. study com. Delta Twp. Libr., 1969-73, Jr. League, 1969—; interviewer Youth for Understanding, 1978-83; active exchange student orientation program Mich. State U., 1977, exchange trips, 1979-82; mem. adv. bd. Mich. League Human Svcs., 1988-91, Eaton County Extension Svcs., 1988-91, Mich. Women's Assembly, 1986-91; 3rd Cong. Educators Caucus, 1986-92. Recipient State Tchr. Multicultural award, 1989, UN Global Educator award, 1991. Mem. NEA, Mich. Edn. Assn. (mem. political action exec. bd. 1986—, v.p. women's caucus 1986-93,Liz Siddell State Internat. Cultures award 1992), Internat. Platform Assn., Friends Waverly Libr., Circumnavigators Club (travel around the world in one trip 1993), Century Club (travel in 100 countries outside U.S. 1994), Delta Kappa Gamma (co-chair State World Fellowship 1993—, State Woman of Distinction 1993), Phi Delta Kappa (Tchr. of Yr. Mich. State U. 1992). Home: 214 Farmstead Ln Lansing MI 48917-3015

MARBACH, DIANE, food service executive; b. N.Y.C., Mar. 7, 1932; d. Charles Saul and Anne Helen (Leighter) Nusbaum; widowed; children: Barbara Dorset, Edward. BFA, New Sch. for Social Rsch.; student, Pratt Inst. Chmn., owner JAMAC Frozen Food Corp., Jersey City, N.J., 1959—. Contbr. articles to profl. jours. Named Woman of Yr. Food and Beverage Am., 1993; recipient Moderator-Spkr. award for Food Svc. Industry. Mem. Food Svc. Execs. (pres. 1962-64), Soc. Food Mgmt., Hosp. Food Mgmt. Assn. Republican.

MARBLESTONE, BONNIE MELISSA, nurse; b. San Diego, Feb. 7, 1956; d. Alan Freimuth and Naomi Lois (Alpert) M. BA in Psychology, Calif. State U., San Diego, 1978; BSN, Mt. St. Mary's, 1981; MSN, U. San Diego, 1988. Cert. nursing specialist. RN Scripps Meml. Hosp., La Jolla, Calif., 1981-89; cardiac nurse practitioner Specialty Med. Clinic, La Jolla, Calif., 1988-91; family nurse practitioner Sharp Mission Pk. clinic, Vista, Calif., 1991—; guest lectr. U. San Diego, 1993—; guest speaker Critical Care Conf., San Diego, 1991. Vol. Proposition 180 Calif. Pks. and Wildlife Initiative, San Diego, 1993-94. Fellow Calif. Coalition of Nurse Practitioners (region # 16 sec. 1991-93). Democrat. Jewish.

MARCALI, JEAN GREGORY, chemist; b. Jermyn, Pa., May 29, 1926; d. John Robert and Anna Marie Gregory; student U. Pa., 1948-52, U. Del., 1971-72; m. Kalman Marcali, Oct. 6, 1956; children: Coleman, Frederick. Microanalyst E. I. du Pont de Nemours & Co., Deepwater, N.J., 1943-60, tech. info. analyst, Jackson Lab., Deepwater, N.J. also Wilmington, Del., 1960-67, sr. adviser tech. info., Wilmington, 1967-70, supr. tech. info., 1970-82, 85-89, supr. adminstrv. svcs., 1982-85, cons., 1989-92, ret., 1992. Sec., Alfred I. DuPont Elem. PTA, 1971, pres., 1972; pres. PTA of Brandywine Sch. Dist., 1973; mem. Wilmington Dist. Republican Com., 1976—. Mem. Am. Chem. Soc. (treas. div. chem. info. 1976-81, chmn.-elect 1981, chmn. 1982, 83, div. councilor 1983-90), Am. Chem. Soc. (com. on chem. abstracts svc. 1983-85, 87-93, mem. joint bd.-coun. com. on chem. abstracts svc. 1994—). Lutheran. Clubs: Order Eastern Star, Du Pont Country. Home: 312 Waycross Rd Wilmington DE 19803-2950

MARCANTEL, SILVA COOPER, educational administrator, counselor; b. Portola, Calif., July 16, 1940; d. Clarence Laborn Alton and Vivian (Ratcliff) Cooper; m. Wesley Marcantel, Oct. 19, 1961; children—Dawn, Laura. BA, McNeese State U., Lake Charles, La., 1963, MEd, 1967, EdD, 1981. Cert. in elem. edn., secondary social studies, guidance, sch. psychology, child welfare and attendance, adminstrn., supervision and counseling, La. Tchr. Calcasieu Parish Pub. Schs., Lake Charles, 1963-76; asst. dir. Health Counseling Service, Lake Charles, 1976; counselor Calcasieu Parish Pub. Schs., 1976-81, supr. child welfare and attendance, 1981-85, supr. guidance, 1983-85, dir. child welfare and attendance, 1985—; vis. lectr. McNeese State U., 1982, 92—. Bd. dirs. La. Epilepsy Assn., 1980-83; mem. scholarship com. McNeese State U., 1975-76. Acad. scholar, 1958; T.H. Harris scholar, 1958; Phi Delta Kappa research grantee. Mem. NEA (nat. conv. del. 1980), Calcasieu Counselors Assn. (pres. 1978-79), La. Assn. Suprs. Child Welfare and Attendance (pres. 1989-90), La. Assn. Sch. Execs., Phi Delta Kappa (grantee 1983-84, pres. chpt. 1990-91). Democrat. Baptist. Club: Lake Charles Quota.

MARCASIANO, MARY JANE, fashion designer; b. N.J., Sept. 23, 1955. Grad., Parsons Sch. Design, 1978. Designer under own label, 1979—. Recipient Cartier Stargazer award, 1981, Wool Knit award, 1983, DuPont award for most promising designer, 1984, Cutty Sark award for most promising men's wear designer, 1984. Office: Mary Jane Marcasiano Inc 138 Spring St New York NY 10012-3854 also: Marcasiano Inc 145 Spring St New York NY 10012*

MARCEAU, LISA LYNN See **MOORE, LISA LYNN**

MARCEAU, YVONNE, ballroom dancer. Ballet dancer Ballet West; ptnr. with Pierre Dulaine, 1976; founder Am. Ballroom Theatre, N.Y.C., 1984—; guest tchr. Sch. Am. Ballet, N.Y.C.; tchr. ballroom dancing Alvin Ailey Sch. Dance, Profl. Performing Arts Sch. Appearences include The Smithsonian Inst., Washington, JFK Ctr. for Performing Arts, Washington, The White House, 1992, (created by John Roudis) For You, 1982, (Broadway and London show) Grand Hotel, 1989-92; toured with Pierre and Am. Ballroom Theatre all over the world. Recipient Brit. Theatrical Arts Championships 4 times, Spl. Astaire award, Dance Educator awards, Outstanding Achievement in Dance award Nat. Coun. Dance Am., 1992, Dance Mag. award, 1993. Office: Am Ballroom Theatre 129 W 27th St # 705 New York NY 10001-6206*

MARCH, BERYL ELIZABETH, animal scientist, educator; b. Port Hammond, B.C., Can., Aug. 30, 1920; d. James Roy and Sarah Catherine (Wilson) Warrack; m. John Algot March, Aug. 31, 1946; 1 dau., Laurel Allison. B.A., U. B.C., Vancouver, 1942, M.S.A., 1962; D.Sc., U. B.C., 1988. Mem. indsl. research staff Can. Fishing Co. Ltd., 1942-47; mem. research staff, faculty U. B.C., 1947—, prof. animal sci., 1970—. Recipient Poultry Sci. Assn.-Am. Feed Mfrs. award, 1969, Queen's Jubilee medal, 1977, Earle Willard McHenry award Can. Soc. Nutritional Sci., 1986, 125th Can. Confederation Annv. medal, 1993. Fellow Agrl. Inst. Can., Royal Soc. Can., Poultry Sci. Assn.; mem. Profl. Agrologists, Agr. Inst. Can., Can. Soc. Nutritional Sci., Poultry Sci. Assn., Am. Soc. Exptl. Biology and Medicine, Am. Inst. Nutrition, Can. Soc. Animal Sci., Aquaculture Assn. Can. Office: U BC Dept Animal Sci, Vancouver, BC Canada V6T 2A2

MARCH, JACQUELINE FRONT, retired chemist; b. Wheeling, W.Va.; m. A.W. March (dec.); children: Wayne Front, Gail March Cohen. BS, Case Western Res. U., 1937, MA, 1939; postgrad. U. Chgo., U. Pitts., Ohio State U. Clin. chemist, Mt. Sinai Hosp., Cleve.; med. rsch. chemist U. Chgo.; rsch. analyst Koppers Co., also info. scientist Union Carbide Corp., Mellon Inst., Pitts.; propr. March Med. Rsch. Lab., etiology of diabetes, Dayton, Ohio; guest scientist Kettering Found., Yellow Springs, Ohio; Dayton Found. fellow Miami Valley Hosp. Rsch. Inst.; mem. chemistry faculty U. Dayton, info. scientist Rsch. Inst. U. Dayton; on-base supr. Air Force Info. Ctr. Wright-Patterson AFB, 1969-79; chem. info. specialist Nat. Inst. Occupational Safety and Health, PHS, HHS, CDC, Cin., 1979-90; propr. JFM Cons., Ft. Myers, Fla., 1990-93; ret., 1993; designer info. systems, speaker in field. Contbr. articles to profl. publs. Active Retired & Sr. Vol. Program Lee County Sch. Dist., 1992-93, Lee County Hosp. Med. Libr., Rutenberg County Libr., Friends in Svc. Here, 1994; mem. Telephone and Transp. Coms. 7 Lakes Residential Cmty. Wyeth fellow med. rsch. U. Chgo., 1940-42. Mem. AAUP (exec. bd. 1978-79), Am. Soc. Info. Sci. (treas. South Ohio chpt. 1973-75), Am. Chem. Soc. (emeritus, Fla. chpt., pres. Dayton 1977), Dayton Engring. Soc. (hon.), Soc. Advancement Materials & Process Engring. (Fla. chpt., pres. Midwest chpt. 1977-78), Affiliated Tech. Socs. (Outstanding Scientist and Engr. award 1978), Sigma Xi (emeritus, Fla. chpt.), the Scientific Rsch. Soc. (pres. Cin. fed. environ. chpt. 1986-87). Home and Office: 13201 Oakmont Dr # 5 Fort Myers FL 33907

MARCH, KATHLEEN PATRICIA, federal judge; b. May 18, 1949; married; 2 children. BA, Colo. Coll., 1971; JD, Yale U., 1974. Bar: N.Y. 1975, Calif. 1978. Law clk. to hon. judge Thomas J. Griesa U.S. Dist. Ct. (so. dist.) N.Y., 1974-75; assoc. Cahill, Gordon & Reindel, N.Y.C., 1975-77; asst. U.S. atty. criminal div. Office of U.S. Atty. Cen. Dist. Calif., L.A., 1978-82; assoc. Adams, Duque & Hazeltine, L.A., 1982-85; ptnr. Demetriou, Del Guercio & Lovejoy, L.A., 1985-88; judge U.S. Bankruptcy Ct. Cen. Dist. Calif., L.A., Calif., 1988—. Bd. editors Yale U. Law Jour. Mem. ABA, Fed. Bar Assn., L.A. County Bar Assn., Women Lawyers Assn., , Nat. Assn. Women Judges, Phi Beta Kappa. Office: Roybal Fed Ct Bldg 255 E Temple St Ste 1460 Los Angeles CA 90012*

MARCH, MARION D., writer, astrologer, consultant; b. Nürnberg, Germany, Feb. 10, 1923; came to the U.S., 1941; d. Franz and Grete Dispeker; m. Nico D. March, Sept. 1, 1948; children: Michele, Nico F. Diploma, Ecole de Commerce, Lausanne; attended, Columbia U. Cons. astrologer L.A., 1970—; founder, pres., tchr. Aquarius Workshops, L.A., 1975—; internat. lectr. in field, 1976—; chmn. bd. dirs., convention dir. United Astrology Congress, 1986, 89, 92; co-founder, mem. bd. dirs. Assn. for Astrological Networking; cons. in astrology to psychology profls. Author: (books) (with Joan McEvers) The Only Way To... Learn Astrology, 1981-94 (6 vol. series), Astrology: Old Theme, New Thoughts, 1984; editor (mag.) ASPECTS, 1976-93; contbr. numerous articles to jours. in field. Recipient Regulus award for edn. United Astology Congress, 1989, for community svc., 1992, PAI Annual award Profl. Astrologers, Inc., 1990, Syotisha Ratna award Syotish Samsthan of Bombay, India, 1986. Mem. Nat. Coun. for Geocosmic Rsch. (mem. adv. bd.), Internat. Soc. Astrological Rsch., Profl. Astrologers Inc., Astrological Assn. Great Britain. Office: c/o Publisher ACS PO Box 34487 San Diego CA 92163

MARCHAK, MAUREEN PATRICIA, anthropology and sociology educator; b. Lethbridge, Alta., Can., June 22, 1936; d. Adrian Ebenezer and Wilhelmina Rankin (Hamilton) Russell; m. William Marchak, Dec. 31, 1956; children: Geordon Eric, Lauren Craig. BA, U. B.C., Vancouver, Can., 1958, PhD, 1970. Asst. prof. U. B.C., Vancouver, 1972-75, assoc. prof., 1975-80, prof., 1980—, head dept. anthropology and sociology, 1987-90, dean faculty arts, 1990—. Author: Ideological Perspectives on Canada, 1975, 2d edit., 1981, 3d edit., 1988, In Whose Interests, 1979, Green Gold, 1983 (John Porter award 1985), The Integrated Circus, The New Right and The Restructuring of Global Markets, 1991; author, co-editor: Uncommon Property, 1987; mem. editorial bd. Can. Rev. Sociology and Anthropology, Montreal, Que., 1971-74, Studies in Polit. Economy, Ottawa, Ont., Can., 1980-87, Current Sociology, 1980-86, Can. Jour. Sociology, 1986-90, B.C.

Studies, 1988-90. Bd. dirs. U. B.C. Hosp., 1992-93; chair ethics com. Cedar Lodge Trust Soc., 1989-92; adv. coun. Ecotrust, 1992-93, bd. dirs. 1993—; chmn. bd. dirs. B.C. Bldgs. Corp. Fellow Royal Soc. Can. (v.p. Acad. II 1994—); mem. Can. Sociology and Anthropology Assn. (pres. 1979-80, other offices), Internat. Sociol. Assn., Can. Polit. Sci. Assn., Assn. for Can. Studies, Forest History Soc. (mem. exec. com. 1991-92). Mem. New Dem. Party (Can.). Home: 4455 W 1st Ave, Vancouver, BC Canada V6R 4H9 Office: U BC Faculty Arts Office of Dean, 1866 Main Mall, Vancouver, BC Canada V6T 121

MARCHAND, NANCY, actress; b. Buffalo, June 19, 1928; d. Raymond L. and Marjorie F. M.; m. Paul Sparer, July 7, 1951; children: David, Kathryn, Rachel. BFA, Carnegie Inst. Tech., 1949. Vol. actress Am. Theater Wing studio, N.Y.C.; TV appearances include A Touch of the Poet, Marty, Of Famous Memory, Cheers, Coach, Night Court; series regular on TV show Lou Grant, 1977-82 (Emmy award 1978, 1980, 1981, 1982); theater: performed at Circle in the Sq., N.Y.C., Los Angeles Music Center, Lincoln Center, N.Y.C., Am. Shakespeare Festival, Goodman Theater, Chgo., Ahmanson Theatre, Los Angeles; appeared on Broadway in And Miss Reardon Drinks a Little, After the Rain, Miss Isobel, Three Bags Full, Mornings at Seven, 40 Carats, Octette Bridge Club; off-Broadway plays: Children, Sister Mary Ignatius, The Balcony (Obie award 1959), Cocktail Hour (Obie Award 1989), The End of the Day, 1992, White Liars and Black Comedy, 1993; films include Bachelor Party, 1957, Ladybug, Ladybug, 1963, Me, Natalie, 1969, Tell Me That You Love Me Junie Moon, 1969, The Hospital, 1971, The Bostonians, 1984, From the Hip, 1987, Naked Gun, 1988, Brain Doners, 1991, Jefferson in Paris, 1994, Sabrina, 1995; TV films include Some Kind of Miracle, North and South Book II. Recipient Drama Desk award, Outstanding Ensemble Performances, 1979.

MARCHAND, PHYLLIS LINDA, book indexer, municipal official; b. N.Y.C., Jan. 3, 1940; d. Moe Steinberg and Charlotte (Oill) Steinberg Lippman; m. Lucien Simon Marchand, Apr. 5, 1964; children: Michael, Deborah Lynne, Sarah Morrissa. BA, Skidmore Coll., 1961. Indexer Crowell Coll. Pub. Co., N.Y.C., 1961-63, Cowles Comms., N.Y.C., 1963-66; indexer freelance projects Columbia U. Oral History Project-N.Y. Times, N.Y.C., 1973-75; indexer Woodrow Wilson papers Princeton (N.J.) U. Press, 1977-93, indexer Samuel Johnson letters, 1989-93; pres. N.J. State League Municipalities, 1992-93. Trustee McCarter Theater, Princeton, Princeton Montessori Sch., 1972-75; mayor, dep. mayor, committeewoman Princeton Twp., 1987-95; mem. adv. bd. Mercer County Community Found. of N.J., Morristown, 1989-94; alumni bd. trustees Skidmore Coll., Saratoga Springs, N.Y., 1992-95; active Princton YWCA, Coalition for Nuclear Disarmament, LWV; exec. bd. Princeton chpt. Hadassah, 1970-72. Recipient Humanitarian award NCCJ, 1989, Community Svc. award B'nai B'rith Women, 1989, Disting. Alumni award Birch Wathen Sch., 1990, Citation for Significant Contbn., Princeton Montessori Sch., 1993, Pres.'s Disting. Svc. award N.J. League Municipalities, 1994, Elected Ofcl. of Yr. award N.J. Mcpl. Mgmt. Assn., 1994. Mem. N.J. Assn. Elected Women Ofcls. (pres. 1992-93, 93-94). Democrat. Home: 29 Montadale Dr Princeton NJ 08540 Office: Twp of Princeton 369 Witherspoon St Princeton NJ 08540

MARCHIONE, SHARYN LEE, computer scientist; b. Schenectady, Oct. 1, 1947; d. Albert Jr. and Estelle Mabelle (Christiansen) O'Brien; m. Joseph Michael Marchione, May 4, 1972; 1 child, Heather E. AS in Engring., Hudson Valley Community Coll., Troy, N.Y., 1967; BS in Computer Sci., Skidmore Coll., 1987; MBA, Coll. of St. Rose, Albany, N.Y., 1993. Computer programmer info. systems GE, Schenectady, 1967-72, 78-81, shift leader CAD-CAM systems, 1981-84, advanced techniques specialist, 1984-88, mgr. end. user computing decision support ops., 1988—, chmn. windows spl. interest group, 1990—; mem. adv. coun. Software Pub. Co., 1991. Vol. Rep. Town Supr. Campaign, Halfmoon, N.Y., 1987-91, Concerned for Hungry, Schenectady, 1988—; cons. Schenectady Econ. Devel. Coun., 1991—, Cobleskill Coll., SUNY, 1991—. Home: 1361 Helderberg Ave Schenectady NY 12306 Office: GE Decision Support Ops #41-211 1 River Rd Schenectady NY 12345-6001

MARCI-MARIANI, ANITA, designer, illustrator; b. Carbondale, Pa., Feb. 11, 1960; d. William Frank and Anita Mae (Sachele) Marci; m. Robert Joseph Mariani, Dec. 31, 1988. BFA summa cum laude, Kutztown (Pa.) U., 1982. Designer, illustrator Lukasiewicz Design, N.Y.C., 1982-84, Art and Design Assocs., N.Y.C., 1984-85; prin., designer, illustrator Anita Marci Studios, N.Y.C., 1985-91, White Plains, N.Y., 1992—; lect. ednl. orgns., Pa., 1989—. One person shows 1988, 93, 94; exhibited in group shows at Mamaroneck (N.Y.) Artist's Guild Gallery, 1991—, Soc. Illustrators, 1990—; illustrator: A Book of Wildflowers, 1984, Everlastings, 1985, The Whole Christmas Catalogue, 1985, Babyworks, 1985. Mem. Soc. Illustrators (student scholarship award 1982), Graphic Artists Guild, Art Dirs. Club, Mamaroneck Artist's Guild.

MARCINEK, MARGARET ANN, nursing educator; b. Uniontown, Pa., Sept. 29, 1948; d. Joseph Hugh and Evelyn (Bailey) Boyle; m. Bernard Francis Marcinek, Aug. 11, 1973; 1 dau., Cara Ann. R.N., Uniontown Hosp., 1969; B.S. in Nursing, Pa. State U., 1970; M.S.N., U. Md., 1973; Ed.D., W.Va. U., 1983. Staff nurse Presbyn. U., Pitts., 1970-71; instr. nursing W.Va. U., Morgantown, 1973-77, asst. prof., 1977-80, assoc. prof., 1980-83; assoc. prof. California U. of Pa., 1983-87, prof., 1987—, dept. chmn., 1985—. Contbg. author: Critical Care Nursing. Contbr. articles to profl. jours. Mem. adv. coun. In Home Health, Inc.; mem. adv. coun. Albert Gallatin VNA. Mem. Am. Nurses Assn., Am. Assn. Critical Care Nurses, Nat. League for Nurses, Sigma Theta Tau, Phi Kappa Phi.

MARCKMANN, CYDNE JOY, women's health nurse; b. Kansas City, Mo., Sept. 5, 1963; d. C. Scott and Wilma J. (Kirkpatrick) McDaniel; m. Scott R. Marckmann, Jan. 8, 1983; 1 child, Trevor S. BSN, George Mason U., 1991. RN, Va.; cert. BLS instr.-trainer Am. Heart Assn., in-patient obstetric nurse. Nursing extern Bethesda (Md.) Naval Hosp., 1989-91, staff nurse, 1991-92; staff nurse The Arlington (Va.) Hosp., 1992—; CPR instr.-trainer Am. Heart Assn., 1992—. Contbr. articles on nursing and politics to profl. jours. Congl. intern Congressman James P. Moran, Washington, 1991; vice chair Nurses for Mary Sue Terry, 1993. Served USAF, 1981-85, res. 1985-90. Mem. ANA (congl. dist. coord. 1990—), Assn. Women's Health, Obstetric and Neonatal Nurses, Va. Nurses Assn. (chmn. polit. action com. 1991—), Sigma Theta Tau. Democrat.

MARCOUX, JULIA A., midwife; b. St. Helens, England, Aug. 7, 1928; d. Robert Patrick and Margaret Mary Theresa (White) Ashall; m. Albert Marcoux, Apr. 23, 1955; children: Stephen, Ann Marie, Richard, Michael, Maureen, Patrick, Margaret, Julie. Diploma, Withington Hosp., Manchester, England, 1950; grad., Cowley Hill Hosp., St. Helens, England, 1952; BS in Pub. Adminstrn., St. Joseph's Coll. RN, Conn.; lic. midwife, Conn. Nurse, labor, delivery rm. and nursery Day Kimbal Hosp., Putnam, Conn.; sch. nurse Marianapolis Prep. Sch., Thompson, Conn.; occupational nurse U.S. Post Office, Hartford, Conn.; pvt. duty and gerontology nurse Conn. Contbr. articles to profl. jours. Named Internat. Cath. Family of Yr., 1982.

MARCUCCIO, PHYLLIS ROSE, association executive, editor; b. Hackensack, N.J., Aug. 25, 1933; d. Filippo and Rose (Henry) M. AB, Bucknell U., 1955; MA, George Washington U., 1976. Trainee Time, Inc., 1956-57; art prodn. for mags. of Med. Econs., Inc., 1958-60; mem. staff Nat. Sci. Tchrs. Assn., Washington, 1961—; assoc. editor Sci. and Children, 1963-65, editor, 1965—, dir. div. elem. edn., 1974-78, dir. div. program devel. and continuing edn., 1978-83; dir. publs. Nat. Sci. Tchrs. Assn., 1983—, assoc. exec. dir., 1990—; lectr., cons. in field. Author, photographer, illustrator numerous articles; co-author: Investigation in Ecology, 1972; editor: Science Fun, 1977, 2d edit., 94; illustrator: Selected Readings for Students of English as a Second Language, 1966; compiler: Opportunities for Summer Studies in Elementary Science, 1968, 2d edit., 1969. Apptd. commr. Rockville (Md.) Housing Authority, 1981-91, chairperson, 1984-86; bd. dirs. Nat. Sci Resource Ctr., Nat. Acad. Sci., 1986—, Hands on Sci. Outreach, Inc., 1988—. Recipient Citizenship medal DAR, 1951; hon. life mem. Ohio Council Elem. Sch. Sci., 1974. Life mem. Nat. Sci. Tchrs. Assn.; mem. Council Elem. Sci. Internat. (Internat. award outstanding contbns. sci. edn. 1971, 72, 86, 94), Am. Nature Study Soc., Soil Conservation Soc. Am., Nat. Free Lance Photographers Assn., Photog. Soc. Am., Nat. Wildlife Fedn., Nat. Audubon Soc., Nat. Geog. Soc., Wilderness Soc., AAAS, Washington Edn. Press Assn. (treas. 1966-67, pres. 1975-76), Ednl. Press Assn. Am. (regional dir. 1969-71, sec. 1979—, Disting. Achievement award 1969, 71-74, 76, 77, 80, 88, 93, Eleanor Fishburn award 1978), Sci. Teaching Assn. N.Y. (Outstanding Service to Sci. Edn. award 1987), Nat. Assn. Industry Edn. Coop. (bd. dirs. 1980-86), Pocono Environ. Edn. Ctr. (bd. dirs. 1989—), Nat. Press Club, Theta Alpha Phi, Phi Delta Gamma, Phi Delta Kappa., Sigma Delta Chi. Home: 406 S Horners Ln Rockville MD 20850-1556 Office: Nat Sci Tchrs Assn 1840 Wilson Blvd Arlington VA 22201-3000

MARCUM, DEANNA BOWLING, library administrator; b. Salem, Ind., Aug. 5, 1946; d. Anderson and Ruby (Mobley) Bowling; m. Thomas P. Marcum, June 13, 1974; 1 child, Ursula. BA, U. Ill., 1964; MA, So. Ill. U., 1969; MLS, U. Ky., 1971; PhD, U. Md., 1991. Tchr. Deland-Weldon (Ill.) High Sch., 1967-68; instr. English U. Ky., Lexington, 1969-70, cataloging librarian, 1970-73, asst. to dir., 1973-74; asst. dir. pub. svcs. Joint U. Librs., Nashville, 1974-77; mgmt. tng. specialist Assn. Rsch. Librs., Washington, 1977-80; sr. cons. Info. Systems Cons., Inc., Washington, 1980-81; v.p. Coun. on Libr. Resources, Washington, 1981-89; dean Sch. Libr. and Info. Sch. Cath. U., Washington, 1989-92; dir. pub. svcs. and collections mgmt. Libr. of Congress, Washington, 1993-95; pres. Coun. on Libr. Resources, Washington, 1995—; adv. bd. So. Edn. Found., Atlanta, 1986-91; chmn. grants com. Coun. on Libr. resources, Washington, 1990-94. Author: Good Books in a Country Home, 1993; co-author: (with Richard Boss) The Library Catalog, 1980, On-Line Acquisitions Systems, 1981; contbr. articles to profl. jours. Mem. ALA, Am. Studies Assn., Orgn. Am. Historians, Am. Antiquarian Soc. (adv. bd. 1989—), Beta Phi Mu, Phi Kappa Phi. Home: 911 Malta Ln Silver Spring MD 20901-1136 Office: Coun on Libr Resources 1400 16th St NW # 510 Washington DC 20036

MARCUM, DEBRA L., speech pathologist. BA, Western Ky. U., 1975, MA, 1976, teaching cert., 1979. Cert. tchr., Ky. Dir. speech/lang. pathology Lake Cumberland Home Health, Ky., 1980-87; dir. speech/lang. pathology svcs. Lifeline Home Health, Ky., 1987-88; speech/lang. profl. Larue County Sch. System, Greensburg, Ky., 1988—; pvt. practice Hodgenville, Ky., 1988—; founder Lake Cumberland Laryngectomy Club, 1984; founder, incorporator Ctrl. Ky. Horseback Riding for the Handicapped, 1980; founder Pet Therapy, Pulaski Animal Shelter, 1984; founder, incorporator Barren River Horseback Riding for the Handicapped, 1990; founder Larue County Safari Club, 1988; bd. dirs. Project Excell. Contbr. articles to profl. jours.; co-author: Research Manual of Speech/Language Pathology and Audiology for Teachers and Students, 1973-74; inventor infant mobile, 1982, reinforcement box, 1983. Founder Ch. Camp for the Handicapped, 1985; v.p. Meth. Student Ctr., Western Ky. U., 1974-76. Recipient I Dare You award; named one of 2,000 Outstanding Women Am. Mem. Am. Speech/Lang. and Hearing Assn. (mem. com. on manpower, Pres.'s Coun. Excellence cert. 1992), Ky. Speech/Lang. and Hearing Assn., N.Am. Riding for the Handicapped Assn., Coun. for Exceptional Children. Methodist. Home: 468 Stiles Ford Rd Hodgenville KY 42748 Office: 304 Industrial Rd Greensburg KY 42743-1130

MARCUM, VIVIAN VICKERS, director curriculum and instruction; b. Gary Hawk, Ky., Jan. 2, 1939; d. Clifton Henry and Etta Mae (Cook) Vickers; m. Billy Gene Marcum, Jan. 8, 1956 (dec. June 1991); children: Jeffrey Alan, Jennifer Gayle. BA in Elem. Edn., Eastern Ky. U., 1971, MA in Elem. Guidance & Counseling, 1977, postgrad. in adminstrn., 1978-83. Tchr. 4th grade San Gap (Ky.) Sch., 1971-73; tchr. remedial math. San Gapels (Ky.) Sch., 1973-77, McKee (Ky.) Elem. Sch., 1977-81; guidance counselor elem. sch. Jackson County Pub. Schs., McKee, 1981-82, Sand Gap Elem. Sch., 1982-85; program coord. Jackson County Pub. Schs., 1985-87, instructional supr., 1987—; tchr. migrant home instruction Jackson County Pub. Schs., 1979. Mem. exec. com. Growing in the Fifth Together, McKee, 1987—; dist. coord. Ky. Ednl. Television, Lexington, Ky., 1982—. Recipient cert. of Excellence for Teaching Flint (Mich.) Resource Ctr. Satellite Site Sem., 1988. Mem. NEA, Ky. Assn. Sch. Adminstrs., Ky. Assn. Ednl. Supervision, Ky. Edn. Assn., Ky. Assn. Sch. Educators, Ky. Assn. Gifted Educators, Ctrl. Ky. Ednl. Assn. (bd. dirs. 1992-94). Republican. Baptist. Home: 927 US 421 N McKee KY 40447 Office: Jackson County Pub Schs PO Box 217 Hwy 421 S McKee KY 40447

MARCUS, CONSTANCE WASHBURN, nurse, healthcare consultant; b. Saugerties, N.Y., May 10, 1951; d. John George and Fay (Zibella) Washburn; m. Lawrence Irwin Marcus, Aug. 18, 1974; children: Brett Jordan, Alexandra Jillian. Assoc. in Applied Sci., Ulster County Community Coll., 1974. Registered nurse. Staff nurse Greene County Meml. Hosp., Catskill, N.Y., 1974-78; occupational coordinator Gateway Community Industries, Kingston, N.Y., 1978-80; immunization nurse Am. Inst. in Taiwan, Taipei, Republic of China, 1980-81; utilization review specialist Meml. Hosp. and Nursing Home, Catskill, 1982-83; designed-care coordinator Empire Blue Cross & Blue Shield, Albany, N.Y., 1984-85, adminstr. design care program, edn./mktg. coordinator, 1985-89; healthcare cons., 1989-92; quality assurance utilization review coord. Empire Blue Cross & Blue Shield, 1992—; guest lectr. Chung Gung Meml. Hosp., Taipei, 1980. Capt. Am. Heart Assn., Kingston, 1986—; bd. dirs. Ct. Appointed Spl. Advs. Mem. League of Women Voters. Roman Catholic. Club: Community (Saugerties) (pres. 1983-84, v.p.). Home: 47 Clinton Ave Kingston NY 12401-5436

MARCUS, DEVRA JOY COHEN, internist; b. Bronx, N.Y., Sept. 5, 1940; d. Benjamin and Gertrude (Siegel) Cohen; m. Robert A. Marcus, Apr. 1963 (div. 1974); children: Rachel, Adam; m. Michael J. Horowitz, Mar. 2, 1975; 1 child, Naomi. BA, Brandeis U., 1961; MD, Stanford U., 1966. Diplomate Am. Bd. Internal Medicine. Intern in internal medicine Stanford U., 1966-67, resident, 1967-68; gen. internist D.C. Dept. Pub. Health, 1968-69, Cardozo Neighborhood Health Ctr., Washington, 1969-73; med. dir. East of the River Health Assn., Washington, 1973-75; fellow in infectious disease Washington Hosp. Ctr., 1975-77; gen. internist Police and Fire Clinic, Washington, 1977-78; gen. internist, pvt. practice Washington, 1977—; assoc. clin. prof. medicine George Washington U. Med Ctr., Washington, 1978—; gen. internist World Bank, Washington, 1978-81; ptnr. Traveller's Med. Svc. D.C., 1980-82; gen. internist Community of Good Hope Med. Clinic, Washington, 1984-85; assoc. clin. prof. medicine Georgetown U. Med. Ctr., Washington, 1987—; preceptor Georgetown U. Hosp., 1986—. Contbr. articles to profl. jours. Exec. com. Woodley Park Citizen's Assn., 1979-80; chair mayor's adv. com. on prevention, 1982-83; bd. dirs. Exodus Youth Svcs., 1987-89. Fellow ACP; mem. AMA (Physicians Recognition award, 1981, 84, 87, 90, 93), Med. Soc. D.C. (credentials com., communicable disease com., founder com. on women 1983, pres. 1985-87, med. ethics and judiciary com. 1987-91, judiciary coun. 1992—). Home: 1205 Crest Ln Mc Lean VA 22101 Office: 1145 15th St NW Washington DC 20036

MARCUS, EILEEN, public relations and advertising executive; b. Naples, Italy, June 11, 1946; came to U.S., 1947; d. Isaac and Mina (Cyplowicz) Einik; m. Zvi Marcus, May 24, 1974; children: Neely, Kerren. BS in Journalism, U. Fla., 1967. Acct. exec. EV Clay Assocs., Miami, Fla., 1972-74; account exec., pub. relations dir. Hume Smith Mickleberry Advt. Co., Miami, 1974-77; dir. publs. Fla. Internat. U., Miami, 1977-81; dir. mktg. Northshore Hosp., Miami, 1981-85; ptnr. Mktg. Mix, Inc., Miami, 1985-88; sr. v.p., gen. mgr. Burson-Marsteller, Miami, 1988—. Mem. South Fla. Hosp. Assn. (pres. 1985-86), South Fla. Advt. Fedn. (Gold, Silver and Bronze Addy awards 1988). Office: Burson-Marsteller/Miami 601 Brickell Key Dr Ste 900 Miami FL 33131

MARCUS, JOY JOHN, pharmacist, educator, consultant; b. Charleston, S.C., Aug. 13, 1951; d. John Basil and Penelope (Polizos) M. AS, Anderson (S.C.) Jr. Coll., 1971; BS in Health and Phys. Edn., U. S.C., 1976; MS in Sports Adminstrn., St. Thomas U., Miami, 1987; BS in Pharmacy, Southeastern U., Miami, 1992. Assoc. prof. Miami Dade C.C. N, 1987—; pharmacy technician/intern Bay Rexall Drug Store, Miami, 1974-91; intern Eckerd's Pharmacy, Miami, 1991-92, extern and intern, 1991-92; pharmacist Eckerd's Pharmacy, 1992—; lab. instr. Southeastern Coll. of Pharmacy, 1991, asst. prof. pharm. sci., pharmacy practice, 1992-94; cons. pharmacist, 1992—; adj. prof. St. Thomas U., 1988. Treas., Miami Shore Bus. Assn., 1985. Recipient award for Campuses Addressing Substance Abuse, 1991, Women in Pharmacy Leadership, 1993; recipient several grants. Mem. Am. Pharm. Assn. (state del. for nat. conv. ho. of dels. 1994, liaison info. networking and knowledge 1994-95), Nat. Assn. Retail Druggists, Fla. Pharmacy Assn. (mem. exec. com. 1991-92, mem. futuristic com. 1992-94, mem. orgnl. affairs com. 1994—), Dade County Pharmacy Assn. (mem. resolution com. 1992-94, mem. exec. com. 1992-95, chairperson membership com. 1992-94, del. Fla. Pharmacy Assn. conv. 1993—, pres. elect 1993-94, pres. 1994-95, chmn. bd. dirs. 1995-96), Kiwanis Club, Phi Lambda Sigma (sec., treas. 1991-92), Alpha Zeta Omega (v.p. 1989-90, sec. 1990-91). Republican. Greek Orthodox. Home: 13105 Ixora Ct Apt 317 Miami FL 33181-2322

MARCUS, MARIE ELEANOR, pianist; b. Roxbury, Mass., May 25, 1914; d. Frank John and Mary Veronica (McDonough) Doherty; (widowed 1965); children: Jack Brown, Mary Liles, Billy Marcus, Barbara Marcus. Grad. high sch., Roxbury. Freelance jazz pianist various clubs including Venetian Palace, 52d Swing Club, 1933—; freelance jazz pianist for depression era entrepreneurs Dutch Schultz, Frank Costello, 1933—. Performer piano jazz series with Mario McPartland, 1982 (George Foster Peabody medal 1982); features in book: Alec Wilder and His Friends (Whitney Balliet), 1972, also features in video about her life, family and career, 1989. Pres. emeritus Cape Cod Jazz Soc., Dennisport, Mass., 1983—. Recipient 50th Anniversary in Show Bus. tribute Am. Heart Assn., 1982. Democrat. Roman Catholic. Home and Office: 62 Center St Dennis Port MA 02639-1561

MARCUS, PAMELA ELLEN, nurse psychotherapist; b. Binghamton, N.Y., Oct. 8, 1951; d. David and Harriet (Kator) Ribler. Student, Russell Sage Coll., 1970-71; BSN, D'Youville Coll., 1973; MS, U. Md., Balt., 1978. RN, Md., Washington. Clin. nurse Johns Hopkins Hosp., Balt.; nursing supr. asst. staff devel. coord. Capital Hill Hosp., Washington; dept. head, Psychiatry Greater Southeast Community Hosp., Washington; pvt. practice nurse psychotherapist Washington and Upper Marlboro, Md.; presenter Resource Applications Annual Confs., 1989-94, conf. planner, 1994; one-day seminars in several cities on personality disorders, surviving incest, and borderline personality disorder. Mem. ANA (cert. clin. specialist in adult psychiat. nursing), Md. Nurses Assn., Sigma Theta Tau, Phi Kappa Phi. Office: 14460 Old Mill Rd Ste 201 Upper Marlboro MD 20772-3086

MARCUS, ROSE, art association administrator; b. Phila., Mar. 10, 1925; d. Isaac Leib and Sylvia (Deitsch) Slifkin; m. Albert Marcus, Oct. 12, 1958 (dec. 1983); companion Arthur Wishnetz. BFA, Temple U., 1951; cert. occupational therapy, U. Pa., 1955. Registered occupational therapist. Occupational therapist Phila. Gen. Hosp., 1955-56, Phila. State Hosp., 1956-59; artist Phila., 1960-70, 76—; supr. Sheltered Employment Svcs., Phila., 1970-76; v.p. Nuvisions for Disabled Artists, Phila., 1989-91, pres., 1991-93, adminstr., 1993—. Bd. dirs. Regional Comprehensive Health Planning Coun., 1970-76, Health Systems Agy., Phila., 1976, Sheltered Employment Svcs., Phila., 1976-90. Home: 1319 Magee Ave Philadelphia PA 19111

MARCUS, RUTH BARCAN, philosopher, educator, writer, lecturer; b. N.Y.C.; d. Samuel and Rose (Post) Barcan; divorced; children: James Spencer, Peter Webb, Katherine Hollister, Elizabeth Post. BA, NYU, 1941; MA, Yale U., 1942, PhD, 1946. Rsch. assoc. in anthropology Inst. for Human Relations, Yale U., New Haven, Conn., 1945-47; AAUW fellow, 1947-48; vis. prof. (intermittently) Northwestern U., 1950-57, Guggenheim fellow, 1953-54; asst. prof., assoc. prof. Roosevelt U., Chgo., 1957-63; NSF fellow, 1963-64; prof. philosophy U. Ill. at Chgo., 1964-70, head philosophy dept., 1963-69; fellow U. Ill. Center for Advanced Study, 1968-69; prof. philosophy Northwestern U., 1970-73; Reuben Post Halleck prof. philosophy Yale U., 1973—; fellow Ctr. Advanced Study in Behavioral Sci., Stanford, Calif., 1979; vis. fellow Inst. Advanced Study, U. Edinburgh, 1983, Wolfson Coll., Oxford U., 1985, 86; vis. fellow Clare Hall, Cambridge U., 1988, lifetime mem. common room, 1989—; past or present mem. adv. coms. Princeton U., MIT, Calif. Inst. Tech., Cornell U. Humanities Ctr., Columbia U., UCLA, others. Author: Modalities, 1993; editor: The Logical Enterprise, 1975, Logic Methodology and Philosophy of Science VII, 1986; mem. editorial bd. Past or Present Metaphilosophy, Monist, Philos. Studies, Signs, Jour. Symbolic Logic, The Philosophers Annual; editor, contbr. to profl. jours. and books. Recipient Machette prize for contbn. to profession; Medal, College de France, 1986; Mellon sr. fellow Nat. Humanities Ctr., 1992-93; vis. disting. prof. U. Calif., Irvine, 1994; fellow Conn. Acad. Arts & Scis. Fellow Am. Acad. Arts and Scis.; mem. Coun. on Philos. Studies (pres. 1988—), Assn. for Symbolic Logic (past exec. coun., exec. com. 1973-83, v.p. 1980-82, res. 1981-83, coun. 1983-85, pres. 1982-85), Am. Philos. Assn. (past sect., treas., nat. bd. dirs. 1967-83, pres. cen. div. 1975-76, chmn. nat. bd. officers 1977-83), Philosophy of Sci. Assn., Institut Internat. de Philosophie (past exec. com., v.p. 1983-86, pres. 1990-93, pres. hon. 1994—), Fedn. Internat. de Philosophie (exec. com., steering com. 1985—), Elizabethan Club (v.p. 1989, pres. 1989-90), Phi Beta Kappa (professorial lectr. 1993). Office: Yale U Dept Philosophy PO Box 3650 New Haven CT 06525-0650

MARCUSE, TANYA LYNNE, artist; b. N.Y.C., Dec. 22, 1964; d. Donald James and Brigid (Ways) M. AA in Gen. Studies, Simon's Rock of Bard Coll., 1983; BA in Art History and Studio Art, Oberlin Coll., 1985; MFA in Photography, Yale U., 1990. Instr. photography Dutchess C.C., Poughkeepsie, N.Y., 1991—; represented by Yoshii Gallery, N.Y.C.; vis. instr. Pratt Inst., Bklyn., 1990-91; lectr. Vassar Coll., Poughkeepsie, 1993. Exhibited at Yale Art and Architecture Gallery, New Haven, 1990, Washington Ctr. for Photography, 1991, The Berkshire Mus., Pittsfield, Mass., 1992, Alternative Mus., N.Y.C., 1992, Trial Balloon Gallery, N.Y.C., 1993, Michael H. Lord Gallery, Milw., 1994, Yoshii Gallery, N.Y.C., 1994. Recipient Young Artist award Nat. Found. for Advancement in Arts, 1984, George Sakier Meml. prize for excellence in photography Yale U., 1990; Thomas J. Watson fellow, 1986-87. Home: PO Box 364 Tivoli NY 12583 Office: Dutchess C C 53 Pendell Rd Poughkeepsie NY 12601

MARCY, DOROTHY ANN, elementary school and private practice counselor; b. Ft. Smith, Ark., Mar. 16, 1941; d. Theodore Amos Travis and Alpha Elizabeth (Smith) Dodson; m. Norben Tucker, May, 1963 (div. 1965); 1 child, Vincent Travis; m. John E. Marcy, Sept. 14, 1979. BA, Northwestern State Coll., Alva, Okla., 1963; MEd, U. Ark., 1991. Cert. sch. counselor, parent effectiveness trainer; lic. profl. counselor. Tchr. of French Fort Smith (Ark.) Pub. Schs., 1964; early childhood educator Claver Day Care Ctr., Wichita, Kans., 1967-68; tchr. of English Wichita Pub. Schs., 1968-74, 77-82; substance abuse counselor Parallax Treatment Ctr., Wichita, 1974-75; case worker Big Brothers, Big Sisters, Wichita, 1982-83; owner, dir. St. Paul Child Devel. Ctr., Wichita, 1983-87; sch. counselor Jefferson Elem. Sch., Fayetteville, Ark., 1991—; pvt. practice counselor Fayetteville, 1992—; cons., trainer Effectiveness Programs, Wichita, 1974-75; facilitator Developing Capable People classes for parents and teachers. Mem. ACA, Chi Sigma Iota. Democrat. Home: 14211 Sugar Mountain Rd West Fork AR 72774

MARCY, JEANNINE KOONCE, educational administrator; b. Lake City, S.C., Dec. 22, 1935; d. Alton Earle Sr. and Bernice Eva (Gerrald) K.; m. Shawn Jeannine Marcy Suarez, Vanessa Anne Marcy Berrios. BA, Winthrop Coll., 1957; MS, Barry Coll., 1976. Tchr. Florence (S.C.) County Schs., 1957-59, Kershaw County Schs., Camden, S.C., 1959-61; tchr., dept. chmn. Dade County Pub. Schs., Miami, Fla., 1961-82, asst. prin., 1982-86, coord. personnel staffing, 1986-89, dir. cert., 1989-92, pers. adminstr., 1993—; mem. collective bargaining team Dade County Pub. Schs., 1983-84, trainer tchr. assessment devel. systems, 1983-85, trainer master tchr. program, 1984-85; panelist nat. conv. Assn. Supervision and Curriculum Devel., Altanta, 1980; presenter in field. Campaign worker Bob Graham for Gov., Miami, 1980's, Janet Reno for State Dist. Atty., Miami, 1980's. Mem. Dade County Sch. Adminstrn. Assn., Kappa Delta Pi (pres. 1978-80), Alpha Delta Kappa (hist. 1989—), Phi Delta Kappa. Democrat. Episcopalian. Home: 4740 NW 102nd Ave # 208 Miami FL 33178-2231 Office: Dade County Pub Schs 1444 Biscayne Blvd Ste 150 Miami FL 33132-1421

MARDEN, ANNE ELLIOTT ROBERTS, estates and trust specialist; b. N.Y.C., Dec. 17, 1935; d. James Ragan and Jane Ziegler (Elliott) Roberts; m. George Linn Davis, May 29, 1955 (div. Aug. 1967); children: James Roberts, Elliott Britton, George Linn Jr., William Vaughn (dec.); m. Robert Gray Peck III, Oct. 24, 1969 (div. April 1993); children: Andrew Adams, Matthew Canfield Roberts; m. John Newcomb Marden, June 26, 1993. BA in English with honors, Wellesley Coll., 1957; MA in English and Comparative Lit. with honors, Columbia U., 1966; postgrad. Villanova U., 1978-80, U. Bridgeport, 1988; Bus. Law and Corp. Fin. diploma, The Phila. Inst., 1988. Contbg. editor Newsfront mag., 1960-63; English tchr. The Masters

Sch., Dobbs Ferry, N.Y., 1963-65; sports feature writer Westchester-Rockland newspapers, Gannett chain, White Plains, N.Y., 1969-70; corr., weekly column Knickerbocker News-Union Star, Capital Newspapers, Hearst chain, Albany and Schenectady, N.Y., 1971-73; on-screen TV panel moderator "Access", Channel 17, Albany, 1971-73; pub. and exec. tax preparer H & R Block, Inc., Wayne, Pa., 1976-79; sr. estate planning trust officer Provident Nat. Bank-Trust div. PNC Bank, Phila., 1981-86; asst. v.p. estate planning dept., trusts and investments div. Mellon Bank (East) N.A., 1986-87; asst v.p., trust officer People's Bank, Stamford, Conn., 1987-88; estates and trusts paralegal estates dept. Pepper, Hamilton and Scheetz, Berwyn, Pa., 1988-89; pres., ptnr. ChoirMaster, Inc., 1988—; estate and trusts paralegal adminstr. Blank, Rome, Comisky and McCauley, Phila., 1989—. Mem. Mus. Art and Sci., Schenectady, N.Y., 1960-68; asst. producer "Poetry", Channel 25-TV, N.Y.C.; bd. dirs., legis. chmn. Greenacres Sch. PTA, 1967-69; pub. rels. chmn. Planned Parenthood League, Schenectady; sec., parliamentarian N.Y. State Legis. Forum, 1971-73; pres., founder TheCareer Group, Phila., 1983-85; editorcongregation directory St. David's Episcopal Ch., 1976, mem. exec. com. every-member canvass, 1977; ann. fair gates-keeper, Episcopal Diocese Phila., 1974-80, rep. Merion Deanery; maj. gift solicitor Planned Parenthood Southeastern Pa., 1975-76; mem. plant sale exec. com. and Merry Mart com. Haverford Sch., 1976, 77; Rep. pollchecker Tredyffrin Twp., 1978, 79; majority insp. of elections Tredyffrin Twp. E-2, 1980—; mem. ARC; vol. Armed Svcs. to Mil. Families and Vets. and Emergency Svcs., Phila., Major Gifts Campaign, White Plains, N.Y., 1994-95, Hospice of Westchester, Inc., 1994. Recipient prize Coll. Bd. Contest Mademoiselle mag., 1954, Prix de Paris, Vogue mag., 1957. Mem. DAR (bd. mgrs.-pub. rels. Phila. chpt., treas. 1983) Phila. Bicentennial Celebration com. 1987), AAUW (bd. dir. Schenectady 1971-73, legis. chmn. Valley Forge br., Albany-Schenectady br.), Schenectady County Mus. of Arts and Sci., N.Y. State Women's Press Club (Capital dist. br.), Jr. League Phila. (sustainer, pub. affairs com., art com., edn. com., child abuse ctr. com., Bicentennial Cookbook com., Waterworks Restoration com., 1984, bd. dirs. 1960-61), Schenectady Curling Club, Valley Forge Coun. Rep. Women, Mohawk Golf Club (Schenectady), Shenorock Shore Club (Rye, N.Y.), The Merion Cricket Club (Haverford, Pa.), Acorn Club (Phila.), Little Acorns Investment Club, Career Group W. in P. (founder, chair 1983-85), Nat. Soc. Daus. Am. Revolution, Jeptha Abbott Chap (Bryn Mawr), Wellesley Alumnae (Phila.), Phila. Assn. Paralegals, Phila. Bar Assn. (probate and trust law sect., assoc.), Phila. Estate Planning Coun., Chester County Estate Planning Coun., Little Egg Harbor Yacht Club (Beach Haven, N.J.), Jr. League of Phila. (sustainer, waterworks restoration com., pub. affairs com.). Republican. Episcopalian.

MARDER, CAROL, advertising specialist and premium firm executive; b. Bklyn., Sept. 20, 1941; d. Simon and Sylvia (Rothstein) Cohen; m. Edwin Marder, Apr. 15, 1961; children: Elisa, Steven Alan, Susan. Prin. owner Boys Ego Retail Clothing, Englishtown, N.J., 1974-76; pres. Motivators, Inc., Old Bridge, N.J., 1976-83, Inkwell Promotions Corp., Morganville, N.J., 1983—; cons. Specialty Advt. of N.Y., 1988—. Recipient citation Monmouth County Bd. Recreation Commrs., Lincroft, N.J., 1987. Mem. East Flatbush League Retarded Children (bd. dirs. 1965-69), Marlboro Chpt. Retarded Children (founder, pres. 1969-71, 73-74, bd. dirs. 1971-76), Marlboro Jewish Ctr. Sisterhood (bd. dirs. 1971-73), N.J. Women in Bus., Middlesex County C. of C., Western Monmouth C. of C. Democrat. Jewish. Office: Inkwell Promotions 1210 Campus Dr Morganville NJ 07751-1252

MARDER, EVE ESTHER, neuroscientist, educator; b. N.Y.C., May 30, 1948; d. Eric Marder and Dorothy Silverman. AB, Brandeis U., 1969; PhD, U. Calif., San Diego, 1974. Postdoctoral fellow U. Oreg., Eugene, 1975, Ecole Normale Superieure, Paris, 1976-78; from asst. prof. to assoc. prof. Brandeis U., Waltham, Mass., 1978-90, prof., 1990—. Founding editor: Jour. Computational Neurosci.; mem. editorial bd. Jour. Neurosci., Jour. Neurophysiology, Jour. Exptl. Biology; contbr. papers and chpts. to sci. jours. Recipient Javits award in neurosci. NIH, 1987, Investigators award McKnight Found., 1994; Alfred P. Sloan Found. fellow, 1978; McKnight scholar, 1978. Fellow AAAS; mem. Soc. for Neuroscis. Office: Brandeis U Volen Ctr Waltham MA 02254

MARDIS, LINDA KEISER, music educator, consultant, author; b. New Haven, Jan. 9, 1937; d. Donald Eskil and Elizabeth Marie (Horwath) Hallsten; m. Gordon Delbert Craig, June 29, 1957 (dec. Jan. 1963); m. Harry Robert Keiser, June 11, 1964 (div.); children: Harry Rudolph, Robert Hungerford; m. Arthur Lowell Mardis, Dec. 29, 1990. BA, Mount Holyoke Coll., 1957; MA, Yale U., 1958. Chmn. Dept. Foreign Langs. Walter Johnson High Sch., Bethesda, Md., 1960-65; music dir. Geneva United Presbyn. Ch., Rockville, Md., 1966-79; assoc. dir. ICM Tng. Seminars, Balt., 1979-85; Reiki master Archedigm, Inc., Olney, Md., 1982—, pres., 1985—; founder, dir. The Archedigm Collection, 1990—; workshop, retreat leader, 1959—; bd. dirs. Well-Springs Found., Madison, Wis., 1980-88; cons. Lind Inst., San Francisco, 1988—. Author: Conscious Listening, 1986, Light Search, 1987, Teaching Guided Imagery & Music, 1989, (taped music series) Creativity I, II and III: Grieving, Expanded Awareness, Changing Patterns, 1984-88, Mythic Experience, 1984—; contbr. articles to profl. publs. Deacon Christ Congregational Ch, Silver Spring, Md., 1981-84. Fellow Inst. Music and Imagery (bd. dirs. 1981-88, assoc. exec. dir. 1986-89); mem. Soc. Noetic Scis., Assn. Music and Imagery, The Reiki Alliance (coun. elders 1992—), Mt. Holyoke Coll. Alumnae Assn. (bd. dirs. 1978-83). Republican. Home: 17247 Sandy Knoll Dr Olney MD 20832-2036 Office: Archedigm Inc PO Box 1109 Olney MD 20830-1109

MARDIS, YVETTE S., social worker, psychotherapist; b. N.Y.C., Aug. 6, 1953; d. Rudolph E. and Joan E. (Jackson) Samuels; divorced; 1 child. BA in Psychology cum laude, CUNY, 1975; MSW, Columbia U., 1979; postgrad., NYU, 1994—. Cert. social worker. Psychiat. social worker Kingsboro Psychiat. Ctr., Bklyn., 1979-80; foster care worker Children's Aid Soc., N.Y.C., 1980-81; sr. social worker Queens (N.Y.) Child Guidance Ctr., 1980—; therapist pvt. practice Flushing, N.Y., 1987—; assoc. prof. NYU Sch. Social Work, 1982—. Mem. NASW (diplomate), Assn. Black Social Workers. Office: Queens Child Guidance Ctr 41-25 Kissena Blvd Flushing NY 11355

MARECEK, JEANNE ANN, psychologist, educator; b. Berwyn, Ill., May 28, 1946; d. Frank J. and Josephine (Serio) M. BS, Loyola U., Chgo., 1968; MS, Yale U., 1971, PhD, 1973. From asst. prof. to prof. psychology Swarthmore (Pa.) Coll., 1972—, chmn. dept., 1986-91, 94-95; Fulbright sr. lectr., Sri Lanka, 1988. Co-author: Making a Difference: Psychology and the Construction of Gender; contbr. numerous articles to profl. jours. and chpts. to books. Bd. dirs. Women in Transition, Phila., 1980-86. Various fed. research grants. Mem. APA, Ea. Psychol. Assn., Assn. for Asian Studies. Office: Swarthmore Coll Dept Psychology 500 College Ave Swarthmore PA 19081

MAREE, ELIZABETH GOODWIN, psychiatric mental health nurse; b. Winston-Salem, N.C., June 3, 1954; d. Russell McClyde and Mary Watkins (Baird) Goodwin; m. Franklin Kenyon Maree, June 18, 1977; children: Kenyon Russell, Ryon Baird. BSN magna cum laude, U. N.C., Greensboro, 1977; MSN, Med. U. S.C., Charleston, 1993. RN, S.C., N.C., La. Supr. West Jefferson Gen. Hosp., Marrero, La., 1979-81; clin. instr. Touro Sch. Nursing, New Orleans, 1982; team leader Charter Hills Hosp., 1982-83; clin. mgr. psychiatry West Jefferson Gen. Hosp., 1983-84; mental health nurse II Guilford County Mental Health Ctr., 1986; Baylor nurse Charter Hosp. of Greensboro, N.C., 1987-90; team leader Charter Hills Hosp., 1982-83; clin. mgr. psychiatry West Jefferson Gen. Hosp., 1983-84; mental health nurse II Guilford County Mental Health Ctr., 1986; clin. specialist II High Point (N.C.) Mental Health Ctr., 1988-89; shift coord. Med. U. S.C. Inst. Psychiatry, Charleston, 1990-94; outcome mgr. adult gen. svcs. MUSC Inst. of Psychiatry, Charleston, S.C., 1994—; facilitator patient/family support groups Hollings Cancer Ctr., Med. U. S.C. Mem. Low Country Coalition for Cancer Survivorship; mem. admissions and recruitment com. S.C. Govs. Sch. for Sci. and Math. Mem. ANA (cert. specialist in adult psychiat.-mental health nursing, polit. action com.), S.C. Nurses Assn., U. N.C. at Greensboro Sch. Nursing Alumni Assn., The Great 100, Charleston Scottish Soc., Charleston Running Club, Sigma Theta Tau. Democrat. Presbyterian. Home: 55 Fort Royal Ave Charleston SC 29407 Office: Med U SC Inst Psychiatry 3N-#339A 171 Ashley Ave Charleston SC 29425

MAREE, WENDY, painter, sculptor; b. Windsor, Eng., Feb. 10, 1938. Student, Windsor & Maidenhead Coll., 1959; studied with Vasco Lazzlo, London, 1959-62. Exhibited at Windsor Arts Festival, San Bernardino (Calif.) Mus.; exhibited in one woman show Lake Arrowhead (Calif.) Libr., 1989, Amnesty Internat., Washington, 1990, Phyllis Morris Gallery, Many Horses Gallery, L.A., 1990, Nelson Rockefeller, Palm Springs, Calif., 1992, Stewart Gallery, Rancho Palos Verdes, Calif., Petropavlovsk (Russia) Cultural Mus., Kamchatka, Russia, 1993, Nelson Rockefeller Gallery, Palm Springs, Calif., 1994, numerous others; represented in pvt. collections His Royal Highness Prince Faisal, Saudi Arabia, Gena Rowlands, L.A., John Cassavetes, L.A., Nicky Blairs, L.A., Guilford Glazer, Beverly Hills, Calif., June Allyson, Ojai, Calif., Amnesty Internat., Washington. Recipient award San Bernardino County Mus., 1988, Gov. Kamchatka of Russia, 1993. Mem. Artist Guild of Lake Arrowhead. Address: 246 Saturmino Dr Palm Springs CA 92262

MAREMA, LENORE SUE, lawyer; b. Oak Park, Ill., June 5, 1954; d. Clarence Edward and Lena (Stob) M. BA in Econs./Polit. Sci. magna cum laude, Wheaton Coll., 1976; JD, U. Ill., 1979. CPCU. Law clk. welfare litigation divsn. Office of the Ill. Atty. Gen., 1978; atty. law dept. Alliance of Am. Insurers, Schaumburg, Ill., 1979-81, asst. counsel, 1981-82, assoc. counsel, 1982-83, counsel, 1983-85, asst. gen. counsel, 1985-86, asst. v.p., assoc. gen. counsel, 1986-88, v.p. legal affairs, 1988-89, v.p. legal and regulatory affairs, 1989—; spkr. in field. Contbr. articles to profl. jours. Mem. ABA (mem. tort and ins. practice sect. 1979—, mem. coun. tort and ins. practice sect. 1994—, long range planning com., membership involvement com., women in TIPS task force, chair pub. regulation of ins. law com., 1989-90), Chgo. Bar Assn. (ins. law com. 1979—, chair ins. law com. 1988-89, vice chair ins. law com. 1987-88, chair legis. subcom. 1981-86), Nat. Soc. CPCU (bd. dirs. N.W. suburban chpt., governing bd., steering com. legis. and regulatory com.). Home: 4878 Prestwick Pl Barrington IL 60010

MARES, LISA VIOLA, administrative assistant, accountant; b. Ft. Collins, Colo., May 11, 1961; d. Viola Marie (Kelley) M. Student, U. North Colo., 1980-83, Colo. State U., 1983-84, Front Range C.C., Ft. Collins, Colo., 1994. Asst. mgr. Silk Screen Shop, Ft. Collins, Colo., 1979-81; dispatcher, receptionist Columbine Cablevision, Ft. Collins, 1983-85; fabrication operator NCR/AT&T GIS, Ft. Collins, 1985-89, quality control auditor, 1989-94, adminstrv. asst. II, 1994—; acct. J&H Carpentry, Ft. Collins, 1994—. Author, editor: Troubleshooting Guide of Testers/Handlers, 1992. Fund raiser Ptnrs., Ft. Collins, 1993; vol. World Youth Day, 1994; vol. mentor Jr. Achievement; mem. activities team NCR. Democrat. Roman Catholic. Home: 1025 Cunningham Dr Unit C-3 Fort Collins CO 80526 Office: NCR Microelectronics 2001 Danfield Ct Fort Collins CO 80525

MARESCA-SMITH, LUISA ANNAMARIA, computer specialist, art director; b. Salerno, Italy, May 19, 1960; d. Giuseppe and Maria Felice (Amodeo) Maresca; m. Timothy Smith, Nov. 27, 1981; 1 child, Timothy Joseph Gerard. BA, BS, SUNY, Old Westbury, 1982; postgrad., SUNY, Stony Brook, 1991-92. Pres. SCMS Inc., Holtsville, N.Y., 1983—; art dir. Forum Pub., Centerport, N.Y., 1985—; reporter Chanry Comm., Farmingdale, N.Y., 1987-89. Reporter for article series on mental health, 1989. Mem. NAFE. Roman Catholic. Office: SCMS 5 Valley Ct Holtsville NY 11742-1066

MARGED, JUDITH MICHELE, middle school educator; b. Phila., Nov. 27, 1954; d. Bernard A. and Norma Marged. Student, Drexel U., 1972-73; AA in Biology, Broward Community Coll., Ft. Lauderdale, Fla., 1975; BA in Biology, Fla. Atlantic U., 1977, BA in Exceptional Edn., 1980, MEd in Counseling, 1984; EdD in Early and Middle Childhood, Nova U., 1991. Cert. tchr., Fla. Tchr. Coral Springs (Fla.) Mid. Sch., 1979-80, Am. Acad., Wilton Manors, Fla., 1980-83, Ramblewood Mid. Sch., Coral Springs, 1984—; creator programs for mid. sch. students. Author: A Program to Increase the Knowledge of Middle School Students in Sexual Education and Substance Abuse Prevention, An Alternative Education Program to Create Successful Learning for the Middle School Child At-Risk. Mem. NSTA, AACD, ASCD, Am. Sch. Counselors Assn., Nat. Assn. Sch. Psychologists, Fla. Assn. Sch. Psychologists, Fla. Assn. Sci. Tchrs., Fla. Assn. Counseling and Devel., Phi Delta Kappa. Democrat. Jewish. Home: 9107 NW 83rd St Tamarac FL 33321-1509 Office: Ramblewood Mid Sch 8505 W Atlantic Blvd Pompano Beach FL 33071-7456

MARGER, MARY ANN, art critic; b. N.Y.C., Oct. 27, 1934; d. Herman and Theresa (Teiser) Baum; m. Bruce Marger, Feb. 5, 1956; children: William Gary, David Scott, Susan Teiser. AB in English, U. N.C., Greensboro, 1956. Pub. rels. asst. Pan Am. World Airways, Cocoa Beach, Fla., 1956; tchr. Patrick AFB, Cocoa Beach, 1956-57, Malden (Mass.) Sch. System, 1957-59, Pinellas County Schs., St. Petersburg, Fla., 1966-70; freelance writer, 1970-76; columnist Evening Ind., St. Petersburg, 1972-76; corr. St. Petersburg Times, 1976-87, art critic, staff writer, 1987—. Author: Winner at the Dub-Dub Club, 1979, Justice at Peachtree, 1980; contbr. articles to various periodicals. Trustee Bayfront Ctr. Found., St. Petersburg, 1985—; chmn. Arts Adv. Com., City of St. Petersburg, 1980's. Recipient award of Excellence for Print Commentary, Soc. Profl. Journalists, 1992. Mem. LWV (v.p. 1963). Office: St Petersburg Times PO Box 1121 Saint Petersburg FL 33731

MARGESSON, MAXINE EDGE, professor; b. Cordele, Ga., Aug. 29, 1933; d. Bryant Peak and Maxie (Grantham) Edge; m. Burland Drake Margesson, June 24, 1956; children: Anda Margesson Foxwell, Risa Margesson Carpenter. BS, Bob Jones U., 1958; MEd, SUNY, Buffalo, 1971; EdD, Western Mich. U., 1983. Elem. tchr. Cheektowaga (N.Y.) Cen. Sch. Dist., 1965-72; elem. prin. Grand Rapids (Mich.) Bapt. Acad., 1972-85; reading rsch. Wake Forest U., Winston-Salem, N.C., 1987-90; prof. Piedmont Bible Coll., Winston-Salem, 1985-90; reading specialist Randolph (N.Y.) Ctrl. Sch. Dist., 1990—; bd. dirs. Salem Day Sch., Winston-Salem. Mem. Forsyth County Coalition for Literacy Com. Mem. Assn. for Supervision and Curriculum Devel., Assn. Christian Schs. Internat. Republican. Baptist. Office: Randolph Ctrl Sch Randolph NY 14772

MARGIOTTA, MARY-LOU ANN, software engineer; b. Waterbury, Conn., June 14, 1956; d. Rocco Donato and Louise Antoinette (Carosella) M. AS in Gen. Edn., Mattatuck Community Coll., Waterbury, 1982; BS in Bus. Mgmt., Teikyo Post U., 1983; MS in Computer Sci., Rensselaer Polytech. Inst., 1989. Programmer analyst Travelers Ins. Co., Hartford, Conn., 1985-87; sr. programmer analyst Conn. Bank and Trust Co., East Hartford, Conn., 1987-88; programmer analyst Ingersoll-Rand Corp., Torrington, Conn., 1990-91; sr. programmer analyst Orion Capital Cos. Inc., Farmington, Conn., 1991-92; pres., prin. A.M. Consultants, New Britain, Conn., 1992—. Mem. social action com. St. Helena's Parish, West Hartford, Conn., 1988-95; advisor Jr. Achievement, Waterbury, 1981-83; tutor Traveler's Ins. Co. Tutorial Program, West Hartford, 1986-87; trainer CPR, ARC, Hartford, 1986-87. Clayborn Pell grantee Post Coll., 1982-83, State of Conn. grantee, 1982-83; recipient Citation, Jr. Achievement, 1982; Bd. Trustees scholar Post Coll., 1982-83. Mem. IEEE, Assn. for Systems Mgmt., Am. Mktg. Assn., Women in Am. Bus., Assn. Computing Machinery, Toastmasters Internat., Tau Alpha, Beta Gamma. Roman Catholic. Home: 210 Brittany Farms Rd Ste E New Britain CT 06053-1161

MARGO, KATHERINE LANE, physician; b. Buffalo, June 3, 1952; d. Warren Wilson and Virginia (Penney) Lane; m. Geoffrey Myles Margo, Apr. 20, 1980; 1 child, Benjamin; stepchildren: Jenny, Judy. BA, Swarthmore Coll., 1974; MD, SUNY, Syracuse, 1978. Resident physician St. Joseph's Hosp., Syracuse, 1979-82; attending physician Health Svcs. Assn., Syracuse, 1982-90, asst. med. dir. for quality assurance, 1985-90; asst. prof. family medicine SUNY-HSC at Syracuse, 1990-94; residency faculty Harrisburg (Pa.) Hosp., 1994—. Contbr. articles to profl. jours. Bd. of trustees Pt. Choice, Syracuse, 1993-94, Planned Parenthood, Syracuse, 1984-94, Friends of Chamber Music, Syracuse, 1985-94. Mem. Soc. Tchrs. of Family Medicine, Am. Acad. of Family Practitioners (v.p.), Am. Acad. Ortho. Medicine. Home: 4705 Maple Shade Dr Harrisburg PA 17110

MARGOLIES, CYNTHIA ELLIOTT, clinical psychologist, psychoanalyst; b. Palm Springs, Calif., Apr. 8, 1947; d. William Henry and Ruth Elizabeth (Schureman) Elliott; m. Richard Margolies, June 11, 1977; children: Amy, Nicholas. BA in Anthropology, Stanford U., 1969; PhD in Clin. Psychology, Union Grad. Sch., Cin., 1979. Lic. psychologist. Psychotherapist Fifth Ave. Ctr. for Counseling and Psychotherapy, N.Y.C., 1978-79; postdoctoral intern, psychology staff St. Luke's Hosp. Ctr./Columbia U. Student Mental Health Svc., N.Y.C., 1979-80; cons. psychologist ACORN Employee Assistance Program, 1985; associated staff Washington Sch. of Psychiatry Meyer Treatment Ctr., 1980-85; pvt. practice psychotherapy Washington, 1982—; pvt. practice psychoanalysis, 1991—; faculty dynamics of psychotherapy tng. program Washington Sch. of Psychiatry, 1990—; cons. Swedish Coun. for Mgmt. and Work Life Issues, Stockholm, Sweden, 1982-86; rsch. fellow Project on Tech., Work and Character, Washington, 1981-86, rsch. assoc., 1977-79; faculty seminar, 1982-83; faculty Inst. Labor-Mgmt. Rels., Howard Univ., Washington, 1982-83, U.S. Dept. of Agriculture Grad. Sch., 1981-83; asst. prof. psychology George Mason Univ., Fairfax, Va., 1980-81; rsch. asst. Harvard Project on Tech., Work and Character, 1972-76; asst. to dir. Met. Ecumenical Tng. Ctr., 1971-72; med. cons. Peace Corps, 1989—. Chair community svc. com. Parents Assn., Georgetown Day Sch., 1990—. Mem. Am. Psychoanalytic Assn. (affiliate), Am. Psychol. Assn. (divsn. 39), Washington Psychologists for the Study of Psychoanalysis. Democrat. Home and Office: 1724 S St NW Washington DC 20009-6145

MARGOLIES, LYNN SUSAN, clinical psychologist; b. L.I., N.Y., Dec. 10, 1958; d. Robert and Sonya Linda (Schachter) M. BA, Brandeis U., 1980; MA, Boston Coll., 1983, L.I. U., 1987; PhD, L.I. U., 1989. Lic. health care profider, Mass. Psychology intern McLean Hosp., Belmont, Mass., 1988-89, postdoctoral clin. fellow, 1989-90, asst. attending psychologist, 1990—; clin. fellow Harvard Med. Sch., Cambridge, Mass., 1988-89, postdoctoral clin. fellow, 1989-90, instr. in psychology, 1990—; cons. Fenway Health Ctr., Boston, 1990-91; inpatient therapist women's unit Charles River Hosp., Wellesley, Mass., 1990-91; cons., presenter in field. Mem. Internat. Soc. Traumatic Stress Studies, Interant. Soc. for Study of Dissociation, New Eng. Soc. for Study of Dissociation, Harvard Trauma Study Group. Office: 53 Langley Rd Ste 210 Newton MA 02159

MARGOLIN, APRIL SANDRA, secondary education educator, travel consultant; b. Bklyn., Jan. 1, 1940; d. Benjamin and Lena (Blacker) Solot; m. Richard J. Margolin; children: Elissa, Dina. BS in Edn., Adelphi U., 1961; MA in Theatre, Bklyn. Coll., 1964. Cert. tchr., N.Y. Kindergarten tchr. Pub. Sch. 24, Bklyn., 1961-62; English tchr. Jr. High Sch. 57, Bklyn., 1962-64, Tottenville High Sch., S.I., N.Y., 1973—; speech arts tchr. John Jay High Sch., Bklyn., 1964-68; pub. speaking adult edn. tchr. Keyport (N.J.) High Sch., 1969-71; travel cons. Shrewsbury (N.J.) Travel, 1989—; gymnastics judge U.S. Gymnastics Fedn., 1984-88. Bd. dirs. PTO, Hazlet, N.J., 1980-82; pres. Gymnastics Parent Assn., Plainfield, N.J., 1984-85. Nat. Def. fellow, 1966-68. Mem. Am. Coun. Travel, N.Y. State Tchr. Cert. Commn., Internat. Assn. Travel Agts., United Fedn. Tchrs. (rep. 1966, Woodrow Wilson scholar 1992). Democrat. Jewish. Office: Tottenville High Sch 100 Luten Ave Staten Island NY 10312

MARGOLIS, ANITA JOY, lawyer; b. Mpls., May 29, 1959; d. Herbert A. and Ursula (Ries) M. BA, U. Wis., 1981; JD, Calif. Western Sch. of Law, 1985. Bar: Calif. 1985, U.S. Dist. Ct. (so. dist.) Calif. 1985, U.S. Dist. Ct. (ctrl. dist.) Calif. 1993. Assoc. Phillips, Campbell, Haskett, Noone & Ingwalson, San Diego, 1986-93; pvt. practice The Law Offices of Anita J. Margolis, San Diego, 1993—. Mem. task force Women's Resource Fair San Diego Vol. Lawyers Program, 1989—, vol. lawyer, 1993—; mem. gender equity adv. bd. San Diego C.C. Dist., single parent/displaced homemakers adv. bd., 1990—, chair, 1994; judge mock trial Calif. St. Law, 1991-93. Mem. San Diego County Bar Assn., San Diego Trial Lawyers Assn., Lawyers Club of San Diego (bd. dirs. 1989-93, sec. 1991-92, asst. sec. 1992-93, chmn. cmty. rels. com. 1989-91, chmn. continuing edn. com. 1992-93). Office: Law Office Anita J Margolis 185 W F St 7th Fl San Diego CA 92101

MARGOLIS, NANCY KROLL, marketing and advertising executive; b. N.Y.C., Sept. 12, 1947; d. Herman and Florence (Yondorf) Kroll; m. Paul D. Margolis, Nov. 12, 1972; children: Kara, Seth. Student, Parsons Sch. Design, 1964-65; BA, Ohio State U., 1969. Traffic coord. Wells, Rich, Greene, N.Y.C., 1970-72; asst. producer Nadler & Larimer, N.Y.C., 1972-73; pres. Nancy Britton Agy., Greenwich, Conn., 1973-75; v.p. Joseph Jacobs Orgn., N.Y.C., 1976-84; assoc. pub. advt. dir. Hadassah Mag., N.Y.C., 1984-86; prin. Margolis & Kroll Mktg. Pub., 1986—: The Jewish Traveler, 1987; founder Zero In Promotions, 1989; editor in chief Newlywed mag., 1989-92. Recipient 4 advt. awards The Advt. Club of Westchester, 1987. Bd. dirs. N.Y. Jewish Week. Office: 36 Devonshire Dr White Plains NY 10605-5444

MARGOLIS, RUTH LYS, marketing manager; b. Pitts., Dec. 4, 1962; d. Herbert M. and Esther (Luterman) M. BA in English Lit., San Francisco State U., 1987; MBA, Nova-Southeastern U., 1994. Nat. account support mgr. MCI Telecomm., San Jose, Calif., 1983-90; mktg. mgr. BellSouth Bus. Sys., Ft. Lauderdale, Fla., 1992—. Contbr. articles to profl. jours. Organizer blood drive Broward Cmty. Blood Ctr., Coral Springs, Fla., 1993—. Lucky-Gemco Stores scholar, 1980. Mem. Comm. Workers of Am. (steward 1992-94). Democrat.

MARGULIES, BETH ZELDES, lawyer; b. Hartford, Conn., Apr. 24, 1954; d. Benjamin and Edith Rose (Herrmann) Zeldes; m. Martin B. Margulies, July 26, 1981; children: Max, Adam. BA in Anthropology, McGill U., Montreal, 1976; JD summa cum laude, U. Bridgeport, 1983; LLM, Yale U., 1985. Bar: Conn. 1983, U.S. Dist. Ct. Conn. 1983, U.S. Ct. Appeals (D.C. dir.) 1988, U.S. Supreme Ct., U.S. Ct. Appeals (2d cir.) 1993. Asst. atty. gen. Atty. Gen.'s Office State of Conn., Hartford, 1985—. Contbr. articles to profl. jours. Home: 79 High Rock Rd Sandy Hook CT 06482-1623 Office: Atty Gen's Office State of Conn 55 Elm St Hartford CT 06106-1773

MARGULIS, LYNN (LYNN ALEXANDER), biologist; b. Chgo., Mar. 5, 1938; d. Morris and Leone (Wise) Alexander; m. Carl Sagan, June 16, 1957; m. Thomas N. Margulis, Jan. 18, 1967; children: Dorion Sagan, Jeremy Sagan, Zachary Margulis, Jennifer Margulis. A.B., U. Chgo., 1957; A.M., U. Wis., 1960; Ph.D., U. Calif., Berkeley, 1965. Mem. faculty Boston U., 1966-88, asst. prof. biology, 1967-71, assoc. prof., 1971-77, prof., 1977-88, Univ. prof., 1986-88; Disting. Univ. prof. U. Mass., Amherst, 1988—; Sherman Fairchild Disting. scholar Calif. Inst. Tech., 1976-77; vis. prof. dept. microbiology U. Autónoma de Barcelona, Spain, 1986, 88; Disting. univ. prof. U. Mass. Author: Origin of Eukaryotic Cells, 1970, Symbiosis in Cell Evolution, 1981, 2d edit., 1993, Early Life, 1982, (with K.V. Schwartz) Five Kingdoms, 1982, 2nd edit., 1988, (with Dorion Sagan) Microcosmos, 1986, (with Dorion Sagan) Origins of Sex, 1986, (with Dorion Sagan), Garden of Microbial Delights, 1988, 2d edit. 1993, (with Dorion Sagan) Biospheres From Earth To Space, 1988, (with Dorion Sagan) Mystery Dance: On the Evolution of Human Sexuality, 1991, (with René Fester) Symbiosis as a Source of Evolutionary Innovation, 1991, (with Lorraine Olendzenski) Environmental Evolution: The effect of the origin and evolution of life on planet Earth, 1992, (with L. Olendzeski and H. McKhann) Glossary of Protoctista, 1993; editor:(with René Fester), Global Ecology, 1989, (with others) Handbook of Protoctista, 1990, (with René Fester) Symbiosis as a Source of Evolutionary Innovation: Speciation and Morphogenesis, 1991, What Happens to Trash and Garbage: An Introduction to the Carbon Cycle, 1993, (with Dorion Sagan) What is Life?, 1995; contbr. articles to profl. jours. Guggenheim fellow, 1979. Fellow AAAS; mem. NAS, Soc. Evolutionary Protistology (co-founder). Office: U Mass Biology Dept Morrill Science Ctr Amherst MA 01003

MARHOFFER, CAROL, obstetric/gynecology nurse; b. Cambridge, Mass.; d. George T. and Constance (Ritchie) Hickey; m. Wallace Marhoffer; children: Linda Magvas, Terri, Kathleen. Diploma, Muhlenberg Hosp. Sch. Nursing, Plainfield, N.J.; grad. degree mgmt. svcs., Middlesex Coll., Edison, N.J. RN, Fla., N.J. Staff nurse labor and delivery Muhlenberg Hosp., 1956-75; nursing care coord. labor and delivery J.F. Kennedy Med. Ctr., Edison, 1975-86; ob-gyn staff nurse Comprehensive Womens Health Ctr, West Palm Beach, Fla., 1986—. Home: 5600 Poinsettia Ave # 1801 West Palm Beach FL 33407-2651

MARIANI, CHANTAL SANDRA, makeup designer, actress; b. N.Y.C., Feb. 2, 1960; d. Jean Mariani and Renee Setton; m. Robert Bialek, Apr. 1, 1984 (div. Sept. 1991). AAS in Fashion Buying and Merchandising, FIT, N.Y.C., 1980. Makeup designer CNN-TV, N.Y.C., 1989, Fox TV, N.Y.C., 1990—; freelance cons. The Guiding Light, 1991, As the World Turns, 1992;

makeup designer She's Back, Vestron Films, 1988; spl. effects makeup artist for film The Gifted, 1987; commls. makeup artist Dean Witter, J.P. Morgan, Peat Marwick, Ticketron, Nutri-System, 1986; theater makeup designer South Pacific, Guys and Dolls, N.Y.C. Regional Theater, 1985; instr. profl. makeup Parsons Sch. Design, N.Y.C., 1985, Christine Valmy Beauty and Theatrical Seminars, N.Y.C., 1986, James Cola Course, N.Y.C., 1987—. Mem. IATSE. Home: 347 E 65th St Apt 3re New York NY 10021-6895 Office: Fox TV 205 E 67th St New York NY 10021-6048

MARICICH, SUZANNE A., advertising, marketing executive; b. New Haven, Sept. 11, 1941; d. Harold Paul and Edwina Ayotte; m. Tom J. Maricich; chldren: Mark, Janet, David. BA, Albertus Magnus Coll., 1963; MA, Moorhead State U., 1971. Mgr. pub. rels. Children's Village Family Svc., Fargo, N.D., 1971-73; dir. pub. rels. Southeast Mental Health and Retardation Ctr., Moorhead, Minn., 1973-75, St. Mary Med. Ctr., Long Beach, Calif., 1976-79, Hoag Meml. Presbyn. Hosp., Newport Beach, Calif., 1979-86; pres. Suzanne Maricich & Assocs., Seal Beach, Calif., 1986—. Account exec. mag. and direct mail campaign, Arthro-Ease, 1987 (Helios award 1988). Recipient Gold Quill award, Internat. Assn. Bus. Communicators, 1986. Mem. Healthcare Pub. Rels. and Mktg. Assn. (bd. dirs. 1987—), Pub. Rels. Soc. Am. (bd.dirs. hosp. sect. 1987—), Orange County Advt. Fedn. (numerous awards). Office: Suzanne Maricich & Assocs 610 Pacific Coast Hwy Ste 209 Seal Beach CA 90740-5708

MARIDO, ANN DOZIER, real estate agent; b. Durham, N.C., Apr. 22, 1944; d. Walter Joseph and Ellen G. (Cheek) Dozier; m. John Harrison Marino, Oct. 15, 1966 (div. Jan. 1981); children: John Harrison Jr., Ann Southerlyn. BA, Salem Coll., 1966. Sales assoc. Rector Assocs. Realtors, Alexandria, Va., 1984—. Vol. Jr. League, Chgo., 1970-74; bd. dirs. Jr. League, Washington, 1979-95, Vol. Clearing House, Washington, Project Open Rd., Chgo., Fire and Burn Inst., Washington; mem. parents coun. Burgundy Farm Sch., 1983; mem. parish coun. St. Mary's, Oldtown, 1977-80. Recipient Rookie of Yr. award No. Va. Bd. Realtors, 1985, Lifetime Top Producer award, Million Dollar Club, No. Va. Bd. Realtors, 1985-94. Mem. Salem Coll. Alumnae Club (pres. Chgo. chpt. 1970-73), Million Dollar Club (life). Republican. Roman Catholic. Office: Rector Assocs 211 N Union St Ste 250 Alexandria VA 22314

MARIE, EVETTE, fashion designer; b. N.Y.C., Oct. 31, 1958; d. Benjamin and Luella Carswell. AA, Fashion Inst. Tech., 1978. Owner, creative dir. Evette Marie Enterprise, Bklyn., 1980—. Editor: Recipes for Healthy Eating, 1994; prodr. (feature film) Country Rock, 1988; exec. prodr. (feature film) Matriarch, 1991. Active Community Watch, Ft. Green-Bklyn., 1980; bd. dirs. Bklyn. Plz. Med. Ctr. Inc., 1994—. Mem. Black Fashion Collective. Office: Evette Marie Enterprise 123 Dekalb Ave Brooklyn NY 11217

MARIE, LINDA, artist, photographer; b. Cheverly, Md., Nov. 8, 1960; d. Thomas Grason Jr. and Rosalinda (Wepf) McWilliams; 1 child, Ann Marie. AA with honors, Cecil C.C., North East, Md., 1991. Solo exhbns. include Franklin Hall Arts Ctr., Chesapeake City, Md., 1993, Humanities and Arts Gallery-Essex C.C., Essex, Md., 1993; group exhbns. include Del. Ctr. Contemporary Art, Wilmington, 1991, Md. Fedn. Art, Annapolis, Md., 1991, 92, 93, Acad. of Arts, Easton, Md., 1992, Elkton (Md.) Arts Ctr., 1990, 91, 92, Md. Gallery East, Havre de Grace, Md., 1992, Chautaqua (N.Y.) Inst., 1992, Washington Project for Arts, 1992, Ward-Nasse Gallery, N.Y.C., 1994, Sinclair C.C., Dayton, Ohio, 1994, AAAS, Washington, 1994, ACP, College Park, Md., 1994; permanent collections include AAAS, Cecil C.C. Mem. Del. Ctr. Contemporary Arts, Md. Fedn. Art, Cecil County Arts Coun., Alpha Alpha Theta. Home: 6 Walnut St North East MD 21901

MARIE, SYLVIA, psychotherapist; b. Iowa City, Apr. 1, 1945; d. Wendell Jay and Bertelle (Budman) Hansen; 1 child, Leif Larson. M in Social Welfare, UCLA, 1969. Lic. clin. social worker and marriage, family, child counselor. Pvt. practice Sebastopol, Calif., 1972—; co-founder, dir. Centerfield Aikido, Sebastopol, 1985—; founder, dir. Soulful Creations, Sebastopol, 1994. Home and Office: PO Box 1019 Sebastopol CA 95473

MARIENTHAL, ELAINE WITTERT, sculptor, interior designer; b. Chgo., July 12, 1924; d. Alfred and Dorothy (Goldfarb) Wittert; m. Harold Marienthal, 1945 (div. 1972); children: Penny, Paul, Kim, Tony, Alisa. Student, U. Wis., 1941-42, U. Chgo., 1942-44, Maholy-Nagy Inst. Design, Chgo., 1946-47. Artist Chgo. and L.A., 1942—; children's book illustrator Wilcox & Follett, Chgo., 1942-44; artist-in-residence UCLA, 1960-66; design cons. Law and Devel. Corps., Century City, Calif., 1966-72; pres. EMI and Assocs., L.A., 1972-88; creative dir. interior design FHP Healthcare, Inc., Fountain Valley, Calif., 1989—; personal decorator Robert G. Gumbiner, pres., chmn. bd. FHP Healthcare, Inc., Long Beach, Calif., 1975—, Armand Hammer, pres. Occidental Oil, L.A., 1980-82. Tile mural executed Marian Davies Clinic, UCLA, 1963, sculptured ceramic mural UCLA Dental Sch., 1966, Plaza Med. Ctr., Long Beach, 1975. Watson art scholar Art Inst. Chgo., 1938-39; apprentice Taller de Grafica Popular, Mexico City, 1944-45. Fellow Mus. Contemporary Art, L.A.; mem. ACLU. Democrat. Home: 1230 E Ocean Blvd Unit 705 Long Beach CA 90802-6909 Office: FHP Inc Corp Hdqrs 9000 Talbert Ave Fountain Vly CA 92708-4439

MARINELLI, ADA SANTI, retired government official, real estate broker; b. Borgo a Mozzano, Italy, July 27, 1942; came to U.S., 1953; d. Attilio and Maria Josephine (Biondi) Santi; m. Rudolph Marinelli, July 12, 1964; children: Gina Marie Basile, Marisa Bianca Marinelli Harper. Student, Rivier Coll., 1962-63, George Washington U., 1963; AA with high honors, Prince Georges Community Coll., 1980. Sec. U.S. Post Office, Washington, 1963-70; administrv. sec. U.S. Postal Service, Washington, 1970-80, real estate specialist trainee, 1980-82, realty mgmt. and acquisition analyst, 1982-84; real estate specialist Washington, 1984—; realty mgmt. specialist U.S. Postal Service, Washington, 1989-92; ret., 1992; assoc. broker Century 21 Advantage, Camp Springs, Md., 1992—; assoc. broker Larry Eul Realty, Inc., Camp Springs, 1977-83, Alvin Turner Real Estate Upper Marlboro, Md., 1988-92. Recipient spl. achievement award U.S. Postal Svc., 1987, meritorious award U.S. Postal Svc., 1991. Mem. Fed. Real Property Assn., Alumnae Assn. Rivier Coll., Orsogna Club (pres. Washington, 1975-76). Democrat. Roman Catholic. Home: 7006 Sheffield Dr Temple Hills MD 20748-4149 Office: 6320 Allentown Rd Camp Springs MD 20748

MARINELLI, LYNN M., county official; b. Akron, Ohio, Aug. 4, 1962; d. Michael and Christine (Golonka) Madden; divorced; 1 child, Jessica. BA in English, Daemen Coll., 1985. Pub. rels. coord. Bison Baseball Inc., Buffalo, 1985-86; exec. asst. to Assemblyman William B. Hoyt N.Y. State Assembly, Buffalo, 1986-92; exec. dir. Erie County Commn. on Women, Buffalo, 1992—; chair Erie County Coalition Against Family Violence, 1992-95; co-chair domestic violence com. Multidisciplinary Coordinating Coun., 1992—; mem. adv. bd. Dept. Social Svcs., Erie County, 1992—. Sec. dem. com. Town of Tonawanda, 1991—; active Jud. Adv. Com. Erie County, 1990—, Reapportionment Com., Erie County, 1991, Court Care Project, 1992—, Compass House, Erie County, 1993—, Women for Downtown, 1993—, Citizens Com. on Rape and Sex Assault, 1993—, Leadership Buffalo, 1994, United Way Family Support and Safety, 1994—. Recipient Disting. Svc. award Coalition Against Family Violence, 1992; named Young Careerist, Bus. and Profl. Women, 1991; named to 40 Under Forty list, Bus. First, 1993. Roman Catholic. Office: Erie County Commission on Women 95 Franklin St # 1655 Buffalo NY 14202

MARING, NORMA ANN, military academy administrator; b. Humboldt, Kans., Oct. 1, 1933; d. Edward Simon and Anna Agnes (Frederich) Breiner; m. L. Keith Maring, Dec. 27, 1951 (dec. July 1988); children: Stan, Steve, Scot, Ron. Grad. high sch., Chanute, Kans. Cert. swimming pool operator. Instr. dance, water safety courses Wentworth Mil. Acad., Lexington, Mo., 1968-91, alumni dir., 1979—; operator Chanute Mcpl. Swimming Pool, 1956—; water safety trainer ARC, Kans., Mo., 1969—. Bd. dirs., chmn. water safety Neosho County unit ARC, Chanute, 1965-85; pres. Lexington PTA, 1960-64, Lafayette County PTA, 1965-70. Recipient Disting. Svc. award Nat. ARC, 1982, Employee of the Month, Outstanding Pub. Rels., City of Chanute, 1993, Pub. Cmty. Svc. award, 1993; named 1st hon. alumnus Wentworth Mil. Acad. Alumni Assn., 1992; coll. scholarship in her name given by PTA Coun., Chanute, 1982. Mem. Kans. Swimming Pool Assn., Kans. PTA (hon. life), Wentworth Mil. Acad. Alumni Assn. (named 1st hon. mem. 1992), Gen. Fed. Women's Clubs (pres. Lexington 1970-72), Lexington Garden Club (v.p. 1969-70), Am. Contract Bridge League. Roman Catholic. Home: 1622 South St Lexington MO 64067-1432 Office: Wentworth Mil Acad 18 And Washington Sts Lexington MO 64067

MARINHO, RITA DUARTE, political science educator, association executive; b. New Bedford, Mass, Oct. 11, 1942; d. Roger and Hilda (Daniels) M.; m. Robert Moniz, Oct. 21, 1961 (div. Apr. 1990); children: Robert John Moniz, Michael Joseph Moniz, Marc Andrew Moniz; m. Kenneth S. Duarte, Sept. 7, 1990. BA summa cum laude, U. Mass., North Dartmouth, 1974; MA, Brown U., 1975, PhD, 1979. Asst. prof. polit. sci. U. Mass., Dartmouth, 1978-82; assoc. prof. U. Mass., North Dartmouth, 1982-88, prof., 1988—, dir. women's studies, 1981-84, spl. asst. to pres., 1982-83, prof., 1988—; lectr. Nathan Mayhew Seminars, Martha's Vineyard, Mass., 1976-88; cons., exec. dir. Fall River (Mass.) Regional Task Force, Inc., 1984—, Coalition for Excellence in Edn.: FR2000, Atlantis Charter Sch. Corp., 1994—; polit. analyst WSMU-TV, New Bedford, 1980; owner Elegance of Martha's Vineyard, Edgartown, Mass., 1989-94. Author: APSA News, 1984; co-author: (book) Politics of Portuguese, 1991; moderator Feminine Forum, Sta. WBSM, New Bedford, Mass., 1980-84; contbr. polit. sci. articles to publs. Councillor New Bedford City Coun., 1978-80, Dem. com., 1976-84; membership chair Women's Caucus for Polit. Sci., 1978-83; 1st v.p. nat. bd. YWCA of U.S.A., N.Y.C., 1984-90, bd. dirs., 1982-94. Mellon scholar Wellesley Ctr. Rsch. for Women, 1983-84. Mem. Portuguese-Am. Women's Assn. (bd. dirs. 1994—, membership chair 1994—). Home: 500 Rivet St New Bedford MA 02740 Office: U Mass 235 Old Westport Rd North Dartmouth MA 02747-2512

MARINO, ELIZABETH R., pediatrician; b. Bronx, N.Y., Aug. 28, 1961; d. Elias Robert and Daisy (Halegua) M. BA, NYU, 1983, MD, 1987. Intern in pediatrics North Shore U. Hosp., Manhasset, N.Y., 1987-88; resident in pediatrics Mt. Sinai Med. Ctr., N.Y.C., 1988-90; attending physician in charge of pediatrics St. Francis Hosp., Jersey City, 1991; fellow in adolescent medicine UMDNJ, Newark, 1991-93; assoc. dir. adolescent and young adult med. inpatient svcs. Children's Hosp. of N.J., Newark, 1993—; faculty Newark Sexually Transmitted Disease Tng. Ctr., 1994—. Mem. Fieri, Hoboken, N.J., 1993—. Fellow Am. Acad. Pediatrics; mem. AMA, Soc. Adolescent Medicine, N.J. Soc. Adolescent Medicine. Office: Children's Hosp N.J. 15 S 9th St Newark NJ 07107-2147

MARINO, JOANNE MARIE, psychotherapist, consultant; b. Greenwich, Conn., Feb. 15, 1951; d. Frank Dominic and Matilda (Salvatore) M. B.A., U. Conn., 1973, M.A. in Ednl. Psychology/Rehab. Counseling, 1975. Cert. profl. counselor, Conn.; nat. cert. counselor, cert. clin. mental health counselor. Counselor Ea. Ct. Drug Action Program, Inc., Willimantic Conn., 1974-77; sr. counselor Liberation Programs, Inc., Stamford, Conn., 1977-79, program dir. 1980-83, quality assurance coordinator, 1982-83; gen. practice psychotherapy, cons. counseling and vocat. assessment, 1983-92; clin. coord. Guideline Info. & Referral Phone Line, 1992—. Mem. Am. Counseling Assn., Conn. Counseling, Assn., Ct. Mental Health Counseling Assn., Am. Mental Health Counselors Assn., Assn. Gay, Lesbian and Bisexual Issues in Counseling. Avocations: films, traveling, sports, gardening, reading. Office: The Learning Exch 21 Strickland Rd Cos Cob CT 06807-2727

MARINO, SHEILA BURRIS, education educator; b. Knoxville, Nov. 24, 1947; d. David Paul and Lucille Cora (Maupin) Burris; m. Louis John Marino, Dec. 19, 1969; children: Sheila Noelle, Heather Michelle. BS, U. Tenn., 1969, MS, 1971, EdD, 1976; postgrad., W.Va. U. Elem./early childhood tchr. Knoxville City Schs., 1969-71; cooperating tchr. U. Tenn., Knoxville, 1969-71; dir. early childhood edn./tchr. Glenville (W.Va.) State Coll., 1971-72, Colo. Women's Coll., Denver, 1972-73; asst. prof. edn. Lander U., Greenwood, S.C., 1973-75; instr., spl. asst. coordinator of elem./early childhood edn. U. Tenn., 1975-76; prof. edn., dir. clin. experiences, asst. dean Sch. Edn. Lander U., 1976-95, dean sch. edn., 1993-94; cons. in field; dir. Creative Activities Prog. for Children, Lander U., 1979—; mem. W.Va. Gov.'s Early Childhood Adv. Bd., 1971-72, Gov.'s Team of Higher Edn. Profls. on Comprehensive Plan for S.C. Early Childhood Edn., 1982. Contbr. articles to profl. jours.; author: International Children's Literature, 1989. Bd. dirs. Greenwood Lit. Coun., v.p., 1990, pres., 1991; bd. dirs. St. Nicholas Speech and Hearing Ctr., Greenwood, pres., 1992; bd. dirs. Old Ninety-Six coun. Girl Scouts U.S.A., 1987-92; vol. March of Dimes Program, Greenwood, 1987. Mem. AAUW (pres. 1990—), AAUP, SNEA (state advisor 1981-88), S.C. Student Edn. Assn., Piedmont Assn. Children and Adults with Learning Disabilities (pres. 1986—, exec. bd.), Learning Disabilities Assn. S.C. (pres. 1990-94), S.C. Edn. Assn., S.C. Assn. for Children Under Six, So. Assn. for Children under Six, S.C. Assn. Tchr. Educators, Piedmont Reading Coun. (v.p. 1985-86, 90-91, pres. 1986-88, 91-92), S.C. Coun. Internat. Reading Assn. (exec. bd. 1986-88, 91—), Delta Kappa Gamma (pres. Epsilon chpt. 1984-88, 92-94, mem. exec. bd.), Pi Lambda Theta, Kappa Delta Pi (pres. U. Tenn. chpt. 1974-75), Phi Delta Kappa (v.p. 1988-90, pres. Lander U. chpt. 1990-91, 94—). Democrat. Presbyterian. Home: 103 Essex Ct Greenwood SC 29649-9561 Office: Lander U Stanley Avenue Greenwood SC 29649

MARINO ANGSTADT, MARLENE, fine artist, artist agent; b. N.Y.C., Jan. 1, 1947; d. Michael John and Anne (Bisogno) Marino; m. Robert David Angstadt, Dec. 29, 1972. Student, Caldwell Coll., 1965-66; BA, So. Ill. U., 1966-69, Teaching Cert., 1970. Free-lance art dir. J. Walter Thompson; Foote, Cone & Belding; Michael Marino & Assocs., N.Y.C., 1970-72; art dir. Sun Printing Corp., Naperville, Ill., 1973-79; art dir./prodn. mgr. New World Pub. Co., Chgo., 1980-86; pres., owner FDM Prdons., Inc./Marlene Marino Mktng. and Creative Svcs., Chgo., 1986—; lectr. career seminar North Cen. Coll., Naperville, 1978; pvt. tutor art creativity, Chgo. area, 1985—; tchr. Columbia Coll., Chgo., 1992. Mem. The Art Inst. of Chgo., Nat. Mus. of Women in the Arts, Am. Craft Coun.

MARION, GAIL ELAINE, reference librarian; b. Bloomington, Ill., May 31, 1952; d. Ralph Herbert and Norma Mae (Crump) Nyberg; m. David Louis Marion, May 13, 1972 (div. Apr. 1983). AA in Liberal Arts, Fla. Jr. Coll., 1976; BA in U.S. History, U. North Fla., 1978; MS in Libr. and Info. Sci., Fla. State U., 1985. Law libr., legal rschr. Mathews Osborne et al, Jacksonville, Fla., 1979-82; reference libr. City of Jacksonville-Pub. Librs., 1982—. With U.S. Army, 1970-72, maj. U.S. Army Res., 1978—, with Fla. Army N.G., 1974-78. Named to Outstanding Young Women of Am., 1985; N.G. Officers Assn. scholar, 1980. Mem. ALA, WAC Vets. Assn., Adj. Gen. Regimental Corps, Res. Officers Assn., Fla. Libr. Assn., Fla. Paleontol. Soc., Jacksonville Gem and Mineral Soc. Republican. Methodist. Home: 3200 Hartley Rd Apt 70 Jacksonville FL 32257-6719 Office: Jacksonville Pub Librs 122 N Ocean St Jacksonville FL 32202-3314

MARION, GEORGETTE A. (GIGI MARION), freelance writer; b. Hollywood, Calif., Nov. 17, 1927; d. George Francis and Dorothy Whelan (Maldeis) M.; m. Robert P. Collier, Mar. 20, 1952 (div. 1974); children: Robert P. Collier Jr., Marion C. Collier. BA in History, Stanford U., 1949. Reporter, editor Mademoiselle Mag., N.Y.C., 1950-57; editor, writer Daily News, N.Y.C., 1959-61; news dir. Vogue, N.Y.C., 1962; columnist Caracas (Venezuela) Daily Jour., 1962-68; editor Glamour Mag., N.Y.C., 1971; Am. Cancer Soc., 1973-92; v.p. creative svcs. Am. Cancer Soc., Atlanta, 1988-92; freelance speechwriter, Carmel, Calif., 1992—; freelance writer Seventeen Mag., Metro News, Leavitt Advt., 1971-73. V.p. bd. dirs. Older Women's League, N.Y.C., 1983-88; bd. dirs. Caracas Circulating Libr., 1962-68. Mem. Women in Comm.

MARION, MARJORIE ANNE, English educator; b. Winterset, Iowa, May 6, 1935; d. Virgil Arthur and Marilyn Ruth (Sandy) Hammon; m. Robert H. Marion, Dec. 20, 1964; 1 dau., Kathryn Ruth. BA, Colo. Coll., 1958; MA, Purdue U., 1969; postgrad., Inst. Mgmt. Lifelong Edn. Harvard U., 1981. Chairperson English dept. Lincoln-Way High Sch., New Lenox, Ill., 1964-68; dir. pub. rels. Coll. St. Francis, Joliet, Ill., 1968-70, chairperson English dept., 1971-75, chairperson div. humanities and fine arts, 1975-79, coord. instructional devel., 1979-80, dir. continuing edn., 1980-84, acting v.p. for acad. affairs, 1984-85, dean of faculty, 1985-89, assoc. prof. English, 1989—; dir. Freshman Core Program, 1993—; mem. vis. team North Cen. Assn., Joliet & Lockport, Ill, 1975-79; lectr. at ednl. workshops and insts.; TV and radio appearances regarding lifelong edn., Chgo., St. Louis, Albuquerque, Pheonix, 1982-85. Drama critic Joliet Herald News, 1970-82. Recipient Pres.'s award Coll. St. Francis, 1975. Mem. Am. Assn. Higher Edn., Nat. Coun. Tchrs. of English. Roman Catholic. Office: Coll St Francis 500 Wilcox St Joliet IL 60435-6169

MARIS, BARBARA ENGLISH, music educator, pianist; b. Granite City, Ill., Oct. 13, 1937; d. Robert William and Margaret Catherine (Smith) English; m. Ronald W. Maris, Sept. 6, 1959 (div. Aug. 1973); children: Elizabeth Anne, Catherine Lynn; m. David WIlloughby, Dec. 30, 1989; stepchildren: Sharon, Sylvia, Cindy, Suzy. MusB, U. Ill., 1958, MusM, 1961; degree, Ecole de Musique, Paris, 1959; DMA, Peabody Conservatory, 1976. Mem. piano faculty Peabody Inst., Balt., 1969-78; asst. prof. music U. Wis.-Parkside, Kenosha, 1978-81; prof. music Cath. U. Am., Washington, 1981—; vis. asst. prof. Fed. City Coll., Washington, 1973, 74; vis. artist Smith Coll., Northampton, Mass., 1976-77; adj. faculty Peabody Conservtory, Balt., 1984-85; panelist Coun. Internat. Exch. of Scholars, 1984-86; lectr., instr. master classes, U.S., Europe, Australia. Solo piano recitals, performances worldwide; contbr. articles to profl. jours. Fulbright fellow, 1958-59, NEH fellow, 1976-77, 85. Mem. Music Tchrs. Nat. Assn. (program com., cert. master tchr.), Coll. Music Soc. (pres. 1981-82), Am. Liszt Soc. (bd. dirs. 1982-91), Nat. Conf. Piano Pedagogy, Nat. Piano Found. (edn. adv. bd. 1977-85). Home: 172 W View Dr Elizabethtown PA 17022 Office: Cath Univ Am Michigan Ave Washington DC 20064

MARISOL (MARISOL ESCOBAR), sculptor; b. Paris. Ed., Ecole des Beaux-Arts, Paris, 1949, Art Students League, N.Y.C., 1950, New Sch. for Social Research, 1951-54, Hans Hofmann Sch., N.Y.C., 1951-54; DFA (hon.), Moore Coll. Arts, Phila., 1969, R.I. Sch. Design, 1986, SUNY, Buffalo, 1992. One-woman shows include Leo Castelli Gallery, 1958, Stable Gallery, 1962, 64, Sidney Janis Gallery, N.Y.C., 1966, 67, 73, 75, 81, 84, 89, Hanover Gallery, London, 1967, Moore Coll. Art, Phila., 1970, Worcester (Mass.) Art Mus., 1971, N.Y. Cultural Center, 1973, Columbus (Ohio) Gallery of Fine Arts, 1974, Makler Gallery, Phila., 1982, Boca Raton Mus. Art, Fla., 1988, Galerie Tokoro, Tokyo, 1989, Hasagawa Gallery, Tokyo, 1989, Nat. Portrait Gallery, Washington, 1991, numerous others; exhibited in group shows including Painting of a Decade, Tate Gallery, London, 1964, New Realism, Municipal Mus., The Hague, 1964, Carnegie Internat., Pitts., 1964, Art of the U.S.A, 1670-1966, Whitney Mus. Am. Art, N.Y.C., 1966, American Sculpture of the Sixties, Mus. of Art, Los Angeles, 1967, Biennale, Venice, 1968, Art Inst. Chgo., 1968, Boymans-van Beuningen Mus., Rotterdam, The Netherlands, 1968, Inst. Contemporary Art, London, 1968, Fondation Maeght, Paris, 1970, Hirshhorn Mus. and Sculpture Garden, 1984, Nat. Portrait Gallery, Washington, 1987, Heckscher Mus., Huntington, N.Y., 1987, Whitney Mus. at Philip Morris, N.Y.C., 1988, Rose Art Mus., Waltham, Mass., 1990, Nat. Portrait Gallery, London, 1993; represented in permanent collections at Mus. Modern Art, N.Y.C., Whitney Mus. Am. Art, Albright-Knox Gallery, Buffalo, Hakone Open Air Mus., Tokyo, Nat. Portrait Gallery, Washington, Harry N. Abrams Collection, N.Y.C., Yale U. Art Gallery, Art Inst. Chgo., Met. Mus., N.Y.C., numerous others; pub. installation Am. Mcht. Mariner's Meml., Promenade Battery Pk. Pier A., Port of N.Y., N.Y.C. Mem. Am. Acad. and Inst. Arts and Letters (v.p. art 1984-87). Address: Marlborough Gallery 40 W 57th St New York NY 10019

MARK, DARA, artist, educator; b. Stamford, Conn., Jan. 26, 1950; d. Mayo and Eleanor Sorgman. BA, Yale U., 1971; MFA, U. Calif., Santa Barbara, 1981. Artist-in-residence Calif. Arts Coun., Los Olivos, 1986-89, Arts Outreach, Los Olivos, 1989-93; assoc. faculty mem. Allan Hancock Coll., Santa Maria, Calif., 1990—; workshop leader, dir. Drawing the Blues Workshops, Los Olivos, 1989—. Group shows include Artspace Gallery, Woodland Hills, Calif., 1990, Security Pacific Gallery, Costa Mesa, Calif., 1990, Colored Pencil Soc. Am., Mich., 1993. Coord., fund raiser Sedgwick Solution Coalition, Santa Barbara, Calif., 1993—; active Sedgwick Preservation Com., Santa Ynez, Calif., 1993—, Women's Environ. Watch, Santa Ynez, 1993—. Nat. Endowment for Arts grantee, 1977, U. Calif.-Santa Barbara Patent Funds grantee, 1980, Calif. Arts Coun. Artist-in-Residence grantee, 1986-87, 87-88, 88-89; U. Calif.-Santa Barbara grad. teaching assistantship, 1979-80. Mem. Colored Pencil Soc. Am. Home: PO Box 465 Los Olivos CA 93441-0465

MARK, LILLIAN GEE, school administrator; b. Berkeley, Calif., Mar. 18, 1932; d. Pon Gordon and Sun Kum (Wong) Gee; m. Richard Muin Mark, June 20, 1954; children: Dean, Kim, Faye, Glenn, Lynne. AB in Psychology, U. Calif., Berkeley, 1954; MS in Christian Sch. Adminstrn., Pensacola Coll., 1987. Sec., Western Life Ins. Co., San Francisco, 1944-54; child care tchr. San Diego Child Care Ctr., 1954-55; dir. pre-sch. ABC Nursery, San Mateo, Calif., 1969—; founder, supt. Alpha Beacon Christian Sch., San Carlos, Calif., 1976—; chief exec. officer Alpha Beacon Christian Ministries. Author: Handbook for Parents and Students, 1983, How to Encourage Your Staff. Mem. Christian Ministries, Assn. Christian Schs. Internat., Internat. Fellowship Christian Sch. Adminstrs. Republican. Avocations: tennis, swimming, piano, Bible study. Home: 182 Exbourne Ave San Carlos CA 94070-1828 Office: Alpha Beacon Christian Ministries 750 Dartmouth Ave San Carlos CA 94070-1709

MARK, MARSHA YVONNE ISMAILOFF, artistic director; b. Bridgeport, Conn., Mar. 15, 1938; d. Nicholas and Louba (Foullon) Ismailoff; m. Robert Louis Mark, June 25, 1960; children: Robert, William, Staci. Ballet tng. with, George Balanchine, 1946-50, George Volodine, 1945-60, 65-69; student, Skidmore Coll., 1978-80, Vaganova Method Sch., Minsk, USSR, 1983, U. of the Arts, 1990. Founder Marsha Imailoff Mark Sch. of Ballet, Newtown, Conn., 1969—; artistic dir. Com. for Ballet Miniatures, Newtown, Conn., 1974—, Malenkee Ballet Repertoire Co., Newtown, Conn., 1979—; v.p. Cmty. Arts Project Ext., Newtown, 1987-91; artistic dir. Danbury (Conn.) Music Ctr., 1989; instr. for neurologically impaired Ripton Sch., Shelton, Conn., 1992; choreographed section of Nutcracker Ballet for Special Children; toured Russia with Malenkee Ballet Repertoire Co. Choreographer including original works: Mademoiselle Angot, 1974, Circus, 1975, Haydn Concerto, 1976, Evening at the Zoo, 1977, Match Girl, 1978, The Four Seasons, 1979, Malenkee Waltz, 1980, Magic Key, 1981, Midsummer Night's Dream, 1982, Macbeth A Witches Haunt, 1983, Etudes, 1984, Toy Boutique, Etudes, 1985, Under the Sea, 1986, Nutcracker, 1987, 88, 89, 90, 91, 92, 93, 94, Mere, Mere, Mere, 1988, Ellis Island Memoirs, 1991, Moonlight Etudes, 1992; premiered in Baku USSR. Hostess for artists from Russia, translator UN Hostess Com., N.Y.C., 1988; Russian translator Friends of Music, Newtown, 1990, Sacred Heart U., Fairfield, Conn., 1994. Home: 57 Mount Pleasant Rd Newtown CT 06470-1530

MARK, PHYLLIS BLAUFARB, sculptor; b. N.Y.C., Jan. 20, 1921; d. Jacob and Bessye (Klein) Blaufarb; m. Alan Mark; children: Pamela Mark-Whitley, Ira Stuart. Student, Ohio State U., NYU; studied with Seymour Lipton, New Sch., N.Y.C. Co-pres. SOHO 20 Gallery, N.Y.C., 1993-94, also bd. dirs.; bd. dirs. Artists Representing Environ. Art, N.Y.C., 1977—. One-woman shows include Carl Schurz Park, N.Y.C., 1973, Images Gallery, Toledo, 1974, DuBose Gallery, Houston, 1974, Gallery 99, Fla., 1975, Guild Hall, East Hampton, N.Y., 1977, John Edwards Hughes, Inc., Dallas, 1978, Art Fiero, Bologna, Italy, 1978, Elaine Benson Gallery, Bridgehampton, N.Y., 1980, 91, 93, Fontana Gallery, Bala Cynwyd, Pa., 1981, Friedberg Gallery, Long Boat, Fla., 1981, Sculpture Ctr., N.Y.C., 1983, Houston-Bowery Outdoor Exhbn. Space, 1987, Soho 20 Gallery, 1987, 89, 92, Bi-Coastal Sculpture Exhibit, San Francisco, 1989, Shidoni Outdoor Gallery, Tesque, N.Mex., 1989, Manhattan C.C., 1992, Cast Iron Gallery, 1992; exhibited in group shows including the Morris Mus., Morristown, N.J., 1972, Hudson River Mus., Westchester, N.Y., 1972, N.Y.C. Cultural Ctr., 1973, Bklyn. Mus. Art, 1975, 77, Guggenheim Mus., N.Y.C., 1976, Huntsville (Ala.) Mus., 1978, L.A. Mus., 1978, Albright-Knox Mus., Buffalo, 1980, Barbara Gilman Gallery Miami, Fla., 1980, Theo Portnoy Gallery, N.Y.C., 1980, Payson Weisberg Gallery, N.Y.C., 1982, Mus. Graphic Arts, Bilbao, Spain, 1982, Muscarelle Mus., Williamsburg, Va., 1982, 84, Desert Botanical Garden, Phoenix, Ariz., 1983, Phila. Art Alliance, 1987, Kulturforum, Monchengaldbach, Germany, 1989, South Vt. Art Ctr., 1991, Fed. Reserve Bank, Phila., 1992, Guild Hall, East Hampton, N.Y., 1983 (hon. mention 1983), 92, 93; represented in permanent collections including Corcoran Gallery of Art, Washington, Fort Wayne (Ind.) Mus. Art, Syracuse U. Permanent Collection, Allentown (Pa.) Mus. Art, Lowe Mus., Fla., Cornell Univ., Ithaca, N.Y., Merryman Collection, Stanford U., Calif., Am. Collection, Galveston, Tex., RCA Collection, Fla., and N.Y.C., Tupperware Collection, Fla., Southampton (N.Y.) Hosp., Dancer, Fitzgerald & Sample Agy.,

N.Y.C., Orlando (Fla.) Conv. Ctr. and Civic Ctr., AT&T, Gulf and Western Inc., CIGNA Corp., Phila., Golden Nugget Hotel, N.J., Royal Palace Collection, Brunei Sultanate, Borneo, Fujiya Co. Ltd., Japan. Recipient sculpture installation Assn. Better N.Y., 1973, N.Y.C. Dept. Cultural Affairs, 1973, Montgomery Coll., Rockville, Md., 1984; grantee Nat. Endowment of Arts/Ind. Arts Coun., 1979. Mem. Sculptors Guild (v.p. pubs., editor 1986—, exec. v.p. 1993-94). Home: 803 Greenwich St New York NY 10014 Gallery: SOHO 20 Gallery 469 Broome St New York NY 10013

MARKEE, KATHERINE MADIGAN, librarian, educator; b. Cleve., Feb. 24, 1931; d. Arthur Alexis and Margaret Elizabeth (Madigan) M. AB, Trinity Coll., Washington, 1953; MA, Columbia U., 1962; MLS, Case Western Res. U., 1968. Employment mgr., br. store tng. supr. The May Co., Cleve., 1965-67; assoc. prof. libr. sci., data bases libr. Purdue U. Libr., West Lafayette, Ind., 1968—. Contbr. articles to profl. jours. Mem. ALA, AAUP, Spl. Librs. Assn., Med. Libr. Assn., Ind. Online Users Group, Sigma Xi (Rsch. Support award 1986). Office: Purdue U Libr West Lafayette IN 47907-1530

MARKER, RHONDA JOYCE, librarian; b. Ft. Meade, Md., Sept. 25, 1956; d. James W. and Virginia Mae (Conaway) M.; m. William F. Pittock, Oct. 1, 1983; 1 child, Alexandra Mae Marker. BA, Greenville (Ill.) Coll., 1978; MS in Libr. and Info. Sci., Pratt Inst., Bklyn., 1985. Catalog libr. Port Authority of N.Y. and N.J., N.Y.C., 1981-85, assoc. chief libr., cataloging svcs., 1985-89; head, original monographic cataloging Rutgers U. Librs., New Brunswick, N.J., 1989—. Contbr. articles to profl. jours. Recipient Wilson R. King Sr. Religion award Greenville Coll., 1978. Mem. ALA, NOW, Assn. for Libr. Collections and Tech. Svcs. (cataloging com. for description and access cataloging and classification sect.), Govt. Documents Round Table (cataloging com. 1991-95, chair 1992-93), Documents Assn. N.J. (chmn. state documents task force 1990—, pres. 1992, travel grantee 1991), N.J. Libr. Assn. (sec. tech. svcs. sect. 1992, pres. tech. svcs. sect. 1993-94, edn. com. 1991-93), Spl. Librs. Assn., Coalition N.J. Cyclists (v.p. 1993), Alpha Kappa Sigma, Beta Phi Mu. Office: Rutgers U Librs PO Box 1350 Piscataway NJ 08855-1350

MARKFERDING, GAIL MAUREEN, educator; b. Windber, Pa., July 20, 1947; d. William and Elaine June (Holsopple) Maggs; m. Dennis Robert Markferding, June 7, 1969 (div. 1986); children: Jennifer Nicole, Damian Russell. BS, U. Pitts., 1968, cert. reading specialist, 1977; postgrad., We. Md. U., 1970, Frostburg U., 1993; MEd, U. Md., 1973. Cert. tchr., reading specialist, Pa. Tchr. Greater Johnstown (Pa.) Sch. Dist., 1969, Prince George's County Sch. Dist., Upper Marlboro, Md., 1969-73; tchr. North Star Sch. Dist., Boswell, Pa., 1973—, fed. project coord., 1976—; reading specialist Conemaugh Twp. Sch. Dist., Davidsville, Pa., 1985-86; tchr. Project Kids, Lewisburg, Pa., 1989; cons. Macmillan Pub. Co., Riverside, N.J., 1990. Fin. com. St. David's Luth. Ch., Davidsville. Grantee NSF, 1971. Mem. NEA, AAUW, Pa. State Edn. Assn., North Star Edn. Assn., Internat. Reading Assn., Somerset Reading Assn., Keystone State Reading Assn., Pa. Assn. Fed. Program Coords. Republican. Home: 35 Hilltop Ave Davidsville PA 15928 Office: North Star Sch Dist 1200 Morris Ave Boswell PA 15531-1297

MARKGRAF, ROSEMARIE, real estate broker; b. Grantsburg, Wis., Oct. 31, 1934; d. Helen Elizabeth Pribil. BS, U. Wis., 1957, MS, 1958. Cert. educator;. Tchr. High Schs., Wis., Conn, 1958-61; office mgr. Robert S. Palmer, Middletown, Conn., 1962-64; edn. adv. Girl Scouts U.S.A., N.Y.C., 1964-66; community relation assoc. Motion Picture Assn. Am., N.Y., 1967-69; mgr. The Chateau Inn, Stamford, N.Y., 1970-78; real estate salesman Atkins Realty, Ltd., Bklyn., 1979-80; real estate broker, prin. The Markgraf Group, Ltd., Bklyn., 1980–; cons. Real Estate Counseling Group Conn., Storrs, 1963-91; pres. Tuff Transport, Inc. 1977—. Mem. NOW, Real Estate Bd. N.Y., Steuben Soc., C. of C. Roman Catholic. Home: 60 Remsen St Brooklyn NY 11201-3453 Office: The Markgraf Group Ltd 144 Montague St Brooklyn NY 11201

MARKLE, CHERI VIRGINIA CUMMINS, nurse; b. N.Y.C., Nov. 22, 1936; d. Brainard Lyle and Mildred (Schwab) Cummins; m. John Markle, Aug. 26, 1961 (dec. 1962); 1 child, Kellianne. RN, Ind. State U. and Union Hosp., 1959; BS in Rehab. Edn., Wright State U., 1975; BSN, Capital U., 1987; postgrad. in nursing adminstrn., Wright State U., 1987-89; postgrad., Calif. Coll. Health Sci. Administration, 1994, Columbia Pacific U., 1995—. Cert. clin. hypnotherapist Nat. Guild Hypnotherapists. Coordinator Dayton (Ohio) Children's Psychiat. Hosp., 1962-75; dir. nursing Stillwater Health Ctr., Dayton, 1975-76; rehab. cons. Fairborn, Ohio, 1976-91; sr. supr. VA, Dayton, 1977-85, nurse coord. alcohol rehab., 1985-86; DON Odd Fellows, Springfield, Ohio, 1987-88, Miami Christel Manor, Miamisburg, Ohio, 1988—; DON, rehab. cons. NMS Tng. Sys., Dayton, 1989-91; rehab. cons., N.Y.C., 1991—; psychiat. rsch. unit nurse VA Med. Ctr., N.Y. Rehab., 1991, mem. com. women vets., 1991-93. Newspaper columnist Golden Times, Clark County. Bd. dirs. Temple Universal Judaism. 1st lt. USAF, 1959-61. Mem. ANA (cert. adminstrn. 1983, cert. gerontology 1984), NAFE, AAUW, Nat. Rehab. Nursing Soc., Nurse Mgrs. Assembly, Gerontol. Nurse Assembly, Rehab. Soc., Nat. Guild Hypnotherapists, Wright State U. Alumni Assn., Am. Legion, Womens' City Club N.Y., Gilbert & Sullivan Soc., Alpha Sigma Alpha, Sigma Theta Tau. Democrat. Jewish. Office: VA Med Ctr 423 E 23rd St New York NY 10010

MARKLE, MARY RUTH, accountant; b. Chambersburg, Pa., Nov. 7, 1967; d. Richard James and Marian Elizabeth (Grim) Mummert; m. Bradley D. Markle, May 21, 1988. BS summa cum laude, York Coll. of Pa., 1989. CPA, Pa. Sr. acct. Schultz Snyder Mutzel & Plesic, Harrisburg, Pa., 1989-93; acct. York Wallcoverings, Inc., 1993—. Republican. Lutheran. Office: 750 Linden Ave York PA 17404

MARKOVICH-TREECE, PATRICIA, economist; b. Oakland, Calif.; d. Patrick Joseph and Helen Emily (Prydz) Markovich; BA in Econs., MS in Econs., U. Calif.-Berkeley; postgrad. (Lilly Found. grantee) Stanford U., (NSF grantee) Oreg. Grad. Rsch. Ctr.; children: Michael Sean, Bryan Jeffry, Tiffany Helene. With pub. rels. dept. Pettler Advt., Inc.; pvt. practice polit. and econs. cons.; aide to majority whip Oreg. Ho. of Reps.; lectr., instr., various Calif. instns., Chemeketa (Oreg.) Coll., Portland (Oreg.) State U.; commr. City of Oakland (Calif.), 1970-74; chairperson, bd. dirs. Cable Sta. KCOM, Piedmont; coord. City of Piedmont, Calif. Gen. Planning Commn.; mem. Piedmont Civic Assn., Oakland Mus. Archives of Calif. Artists.; commr. Core Adv. Com. City of Oakland, Calif. Mem. Internat. Soc. Philos. Enquiry, Mensa (officer San Francisco region), Bay Area Artists Assn. (coord., founding mem.), Berkeley Art Ctr. Assn., San Francisco Arts Commn. File, Calif. Index for Contemporary Arts, Pro Arts, No. Calif. Pub. Ednl. and Govt. Access Cable TV Com. (founding), Triple Nine Soc., Nat. Coord. Coun. Emergency Mgmt.

MARKOWITZ, PHYLLIS FRANCES, mental health services administrator, psychologist; b. Malden, Mass., Sept. 2, 1931; d. Abraham and Rose (Kaplan) Kalishman: children: Gary Keith, Carol Diane Donnelly. AB, Harvard U., 1972, EdM, 1974; EdD, Boston U., 1987. Lic. psychologist, social worker, Mass.; cert. sch. psychologist, secondary English and social studies tchr., Mass. Rsch. asst. Boston Coll., Newton, Mass., 1971-73; social worker Combined Jewish Philanthropies, Boston, 1973-74; instr. Harvard U., Cambridge, Mass., 1974-75, counselor, 1974-79; supr. Dept. Social Svcs., Newton and Marlborough, Mass., 1979-88; area dir. case mgmt. and tng., chair empowerment project Dept. Mental Health, Boston, 1988—; instr. human devel. U. Mass., Boston, 1990-94; dir. Svcs. Integration Met. Boston Area; chair com. case mgmt., Dept. Mental Health, Boston, 1988-94; area coord. medically-mentally ill, 1988, chair multi-cultural consumer/family employment project. Grantee Radcliffe Inst., 1972; recipient Rsch. scholar award Boston U., 1981-82. Mem. APA, Mass. Psychol. Assn. Office: Dept Mental Health 20 Vining St Boston MA 02115-6194

MARKOWSKA, ALICJA LIDIA, neuroscientist, researcher; b. Warsaw, Poland, Aug. 22, 1948; came to U.S., 1986; d. Marian Boleslaw and Eugenia Krystyna (Wodzynska) Pawlak; m. Janusz Jozef Markowski, Oct. 23, 1971; children: Marta Agnieszka, Michal Jacek. BA, MSc, Warsaw U., 1971; PhD, Nencki Inst., Warsaw, 1979. Postdoctoral fellow Nencki Inst., 1979-81, asst. prof., 1981-86; assoc. rschr. Johns Hopkins U., Balt., 1987-91, rsch. scientist, 1991-92, prin. rsch. sci., prof., 1992—; vis. fellow Czechoslovak Acad. Sci., Prague, 1981; rschr., lectr. U. Bergen, Norway, 1983; vis. faculty Johns Hopkins U., 1986-87; cons. Sigma Tau & Otsuka Co., Italy, Japan, 1990-92. Reviewer Neurobiology of Aging, 1992—, Behavioral Brain Rsch., 1992—' contbr. chpts. to Preoperative Events, 1989, Prospective on Cognitive Neuroscience, 1990, Encyclopedia of Memory, 1992, Neuropsychology of Memory, 1992, Methods in Behavioral Pharmacology, 1993. Grantee Nat. Inst. Age, 1989—, NSF, 1990-93, NIH, 1992—. Mem. AAAS, Soc. for Neuroscience, Internat. Brain Rsch., N.Y. Acad. Sci. Home: 1301 Kingsbury Rd Owings Mills MD 21117-1343 Office: Johns Hopkins U 34th Charles St Baltimore MD 21218

MARKS, FLORENCE C. ELLIOTT, nursing informaticist; b. Louisville, Ky., Oct. 15, 1928; d. David Carlin and Anna Marie (Lance) Elliott; m. George Edward Marks, Mar. 18, 1961; children: Mary Ellen Marks Fox, Ruth Ann, Charles Douglas. BS in Chemistry, Zoology, U. Cin., 1949; BSN, U. Minn., 1953, M of Nursing Adminstrn., 1956. RN, Minn. From staff nurse to asst. head nurse U. Minn. Hosps., Mpls., 1953-54; staff nurse Marseilisbog Hosp., Aarhaus, Denmark, 1954-55; nursing supr. U. Minn. Hosps., Mpls., 1956-61, spl. asst. to dir. of nursing svc., 1962; rsch. asst. Hill Family Found. Nursing Rsch. Project, Mpls., 1966-69; writer U. Minn. Sch. of Nursing, Mpls., 1976; cons. U. Minn. Sch. of Nursing, 1976, 1978; nursing program specialist Hennepin County Med. Ctr., Mpls., 1978-84, nursing info. systems dir., cons., 1987—; nursing utilization system coord. U. Minn. Hosps., Mpls., 1984-87; cons. Creative Nursing Mgmt., 1992—; speaker, lectr. various nursing confs. in U.S. Contbr. articles to profl. publs., chpts. to profl. books, posters, abstracts; co-author: (with Joan Williams) (TV series) TLC, 1953 (McCall's award 1954); editor: Tomorrow's Nurse, 1960-62; Minn. Nursing Accent (commemorative issue 60th anniversary) May, 1965. Prin. flutist St. Anthony Civic Orch., 1975—, bd. dirs., 1988-92, adminstrv. bd. Hennepin Ave. United Meth. Ch., 1974-77, tchr. 1966-83 intermittently, cmty. outreach ministry, chair adv. com. 1992—; troop leader Mpls. Coun. Girl Scouts of U.S., 1971-85, bd. dirs. 1977-79, svc. unit mgr. 1973-77, Cub Scout Webelo den leader Viking Coun. Boy Scouts Am., 1977-79; v.p. Wilshire Park PTSA, 1975-76, pres. 1976-77. Recipient Thanks Badge Greater Mpls. Girl Scout Coun. Mem. Minn. Nurses Assn. (various coms., bd. dirs. 1959-61), Minn. League for Nursing, Minn. Heart Assn. (profl. edn. com. 1959-61), Nursing Info. Discussion Group (chmn. Twin City program com. 1985-91), U. Minn. Sch. Nursing Alumni Assn. (bd. dirs. 1963-67, pres. 1965-66), Mortar Bd., Zeta Tau Alpha, Tau Beta Sigma, Sigma Theta Tau (bd. dirs. Zeta chpt. 1969-73, 89-91, pres. 1972-73, heritage com. 1990). Home: 3424 Silver Lake Rd NE Minneapolis MN 55418-1605

MARKS, IDA RENAE, psychological counselor; b. Merced, Calif., Aug. 13, 1954; d. Samuel Joseph and Laudine Francess (Carter) Marks; divorced; children: Isaiah, Charity, Angela. BAS, Stephen F. Austin State U., 1980; MA, Chapman U., 1986; AA, U. S.D., 1989. Edn. counselor Civil Svc., Offutt AFB, Nebr., 1985-86; coord. job placement program ARC, Omaha, 1987-88; vocat. rehab. counselor Dept. Edn. State of Nebr., Omaha, 1989-91; vocat. rehab. specialist Heartland Rehab., Omaha, 1991-92; cons. Am. Ins. Health and Reahb. Svcs., Omaha, 1992; psychol. counselor U. Tex., Tyler, 1993—. With USAF, 1973, Res. Decorated Mil. Commendation medal. Mem. Am. Counseling Assn. Office: U Tex 3900 University Blvd Tyler TX 75799

MARKS, LILLIAN SHAPIRO, secretarial studies educator, author; b. Bklyn., Mar. 16, 1907; d. Hayman and Celia (Merowitz) Shapiro; m. Joseph Marks, Feb. 21, 1932; children: Daniel, Sheila Blake, Jonathan. BS, NYU, 1928. High sch. tchr., N.Y.C., 1929-30; tchr. Evalina de Rothschild Sch., Jerusalem, Palestine, 1930-31; social worker United Jewish Aid, Bklyn., 1931-32; tchr. Richmond Hill High Sch., 1932-40, Andrew Jackson High Sch., Cambria Heights, N.Y., 1940-71; mem. faculty New Sch. Social Rsch., N.Y.C., 1977-87; staff Vassar Summer Inst., 1946. Am. editor: Teeline, A System of Fast Writing, 1970; author: College Teeline, 1977, College Teeline Self-Taught, 1983, Touch Typing Made Simple, 1985; contbr. articles to profl jours. Mem. Am. Fedn. Tchrs., English-Speaking Union. Democrat. Home and Office: 11716 Park Ln S Kew Gardens NY 11418-1021

MARKS, MARTHA ALFORD, author; b. Oxford, Miss., July 27, 1946; d. Truman and Margaret (Parnell) Alford; m. Bernard L. Marks, Jan. 27, 1968. BA, Centenary Coll., 1968; MA, Northwestern U., 1972, PhD, 1978. Tchr. Notre Dame High Sch. for Boys, Niles, Ill., 1969-74; teaching asst. Northwestern U., Evanston, Ill., 1974-78, lectr., lang. coord., 1978-83; asst. prof. Kalamazoo (Mich.) Coll., 1983-85; writer Riverwoods, Ill., 1985—; cons. WGBH Edn. Found., Boston, 1988-91, Am. Coun. on the Teaching of Fgn. Langs., 1981-92, Ednl. Testing Svcs., 1988—, Peace Corps., 1993—. Co-author: Destinos: An Introduction to Spanish, 1991, Al corriente, 1989, 93, Que tal?, 1986, 90; author: (workbook) Al corriente, 1989, 93; contbr. articles to profl. jours. Mem. Forest Preserve Commn., Lake County (Ill.) Bd., 1992—, Lake County Conservation Alliance. Home: 2940 Cherokee Ln Riverwoods IL 60015 Office: County Bd Office County Bldg Rm 1001 18 N County St Waukegan IL 60085

MARKS, MARY ANN, adult educator; b. Milw., Aug. 26, 1951; d. Robert James and Marion Elizabeth (Bischel) Hackett; m. Thomas John Marks, Oct. 26, 1973; children: Emily Laura, David Robert. BEd in Spl. Edn. summa cum laude, U. Wis., Whitewater, 1972; MEd in Counseling, U. Wis., Osh Kosh, 1993. Cert. counselor; cert. vocat. edn. instr. Spl. edn. instr. Boscobel (Wis.) Pub. Schs., 1973-76; substitute tchr. Rosholt (Wis.) Pub. Schs., 1981-86; GOAL instr. Mid-State Tech. Coll., Stevens Point, Wis., 1984—; cons. Community Indsl. Corp., Stevens Point, 1991—. Mem. Extension Homemakers, 1980—, various offices; group leader 4-H, Rosholt, 1985-88; vol. Hospice, Portage County, 1994—. Mem. Wis. Vocat. Assn., Nat. State Career Devel. Assn. Office: Mid State Tech Coll 933 Michigan Ave Stevens Point WI 54481-3141

MARKS, MARY RUTH, human resources administrator; b. Jackson, Miss., Sept. 14, 1948; d. Charles Miller and Lillian (Russell) Burke; m. Randall Thomas Marks, Aug. 15, 1970 (div. Oct. 1982); children: Thomas Marshall, Russell Scott. BS, U. Miss., 1970; student, Am. Inst. Paralegal Studies, Chgo., 1987. Cert. profl. in human resources, paralegal, health ins. assoc. Paralegal, mgr. Harvey & Hough, Madison, Wis., 1982-84; paralegal Ross & Stevens, S.C., Madison, 1984-88; dir. human resources N.Am. Ins. Co., Madison, 1988—. Author, cons. video series Harnessing the Single Horse, 1991. Coord. United Way Campaign, Madison, 1990-93. Team champion World Equestrian Cup, Tampa, 1989; Gladstone preliminary team championship Gladstone Equestrian Assn., 1989, others. Mem. Wis. Arabian Horse Assn. (dir.), Dairyland Driving Club (pres. 1982-92), Soc. Human Resource Mgmt. (coord. programs Greater Madison Area 1982-92). Presbyterian. Office: N Am Ins Co 150 E Gilman St Madison WI 53703

MARKS, ROBERTA BARBARA, artist, educator; b. Savannah, Ga.; d. Philip W. and Eleanore (Margolis) Dilner; children: Jeffery Allen, Steven Craig. BFA, U. Miami, Coral Gables, Fla., 1980; MFA, U. S. Fla., 1981. Instr., lectr. multi-media, lectr., vis. artist to numerous art schs., including U. S. Fla., Tampa, Chgo. Art Inst., Valparaiso U., Ind., Rochester Inst. Tech. Am. Sch. of Crafts, N.Y., Galerie de Koull, Murten, Switzerland, Santa Fe Community Coll., Gainesville, Brookfield Craft Ctr., Conn., Fla. Keys Community Coll., U. Wis.-Milw., Parson Sch. Design, Key West (Fla.) C.C., 1991, Am. Embassy, Bern, Switzerland, 1993; juror Riverside Avondale Preservation Art Festival, Jacksonville, Fla., 1981, Ybor Square Art Festival, Tampa, 1980, Miami Lakes Art Festival, Fla., 1975. One woman shows include Brevard Community Coll., Melbourne, Fla., 1982, Cocoa, Fla., 1982, Coventry Galleries, Ltd., Tampa, 1983, Barbara Gillman Gallery, Miami, 1984, 87, Tennessee Williams Fine Arts Ctr., Key West, 1985, Garth Clark Gallery, N.Y.C., 1985, Fred Gros Gallery, Key West, 1985, Key West Art and Historical Soc. East Martello Mus. and Gallery, 1985, U. Miami New Gallery, Fla., 1987, Katie Gingrass Gallery, Milw., 1987, Zimmerman Saturn Gallery, Nashville, 1987, Bern, Zurich Switzerland, 1988, Galerie Alte Krone, Altstadt, Biel, Switzerland, 1990, Helander Gallery, N.Y.C., 1990, Gump's Gallery, San Francisco, 1990, Helander Gallery, N.Y.C., 1991, LeMieux Gallery, New Orleans, 1991, Helander Gallery, Palm Beach, 1992, Galerie Etc., Bern, 1992, Galerie Bel Arte, Lengnau, Switzerland, 1992, Lucky Street Gallery, Key West, 1994, Barbara Gillman Gallery, Miami Beach, Fla., 1994, Galerie Vinelz, Switzerland, 1994, Galerie Quattro, Zurich, 1994, many others; exhibited in group shows at Netsky Gallery, Miami, 1982, The Craftsman's Gallery, Scarsdale, N.Y., 1982, Garth Clark Gallery, Los Angeles, 1983, Nelson-Atkins Mus. Art, Kansas City, Mo., 1983, Am. Craft Mus., N.Y.C., 1984, N. Miami Mus. and Art Ctr., 1985, Joanne Lyon Gallery, Aspen, Colo., 1984, Key West Art and Hist. Soc. East Martello Mus. and Gallery, 1985, Garth Clark Gallery, N.Y.C. and Los Angeles, 1985, 24X24, Ruth Siegel Ltd., N.Y.C., 1987, Artforms Gallery, Louisville, 1986, The Pvt. Collection Women Artists, Ohio, 1987, East Martello Mus., Key West, Fla., 1990, East Martello Mus., Key West, Fla., 1990, Philharmonic Ctr. for Arts, Naples, Fla., 1993, Ctr. for Arts, Vero Beach, Fla., 1993, Helander Gallery, Palm Beach, 1993, Gingrass Gallery, Milw., 1993, many others; represented in permanent collections Smithsonian Instn., Renwick Gallery, Rochester Inst. Tech. Fine Arts Dept., U. Utah Mus., U. South Fla. Fine Arts Dept., Galerie du Manoir, La Chaux-de-Fonds, Switzerland, Valencia Community Coll., Okum Gallery, Victoria and Albert Mus., London, IBM, Jacksonville, Fla., AT&T, N.Y.C. , others. Recipient Regional Visual Artist fellow, Miami, Fla., 1990, also numerous awards. Mem. World Craft Council, Artists Equity Assn., Internat. Sculpture Ctr.

MARKS, SHARON LEA, nurse, primary school educator; b. Arroyo Grande, Calif., June 12, 1942; d. Donald Elmore and Gertrude (Grieb) Shaffer; m. George Conrad Schmidt, June 23, 1963 (div. 1975); children: Kerrilynn, Robert, Marianne; m. Keith Dalton Marks, June 4, 1978; children: Joseph, Erik, Alice. Diploma, Sch. Nursing Samuel Merritt Hosp., 1963; BS in Nursing, Lewis and Clark State Coll., 1984, BS in Mgmt., 1986. RN, Calif., Wash. Staff nurse Vesper Meml. Hosp., San Leandro, Calif., 1968-74; night nurse supr. Tuolumne Gen. Hosp., Sonora, Calif., 1975; nurse Orleans (Calif.) Search and Rescue Team, 1975-78; instr. nursing Pasadena (Calif.) City Coll., 1978-79; resource coord. learning ctr. div. health sci. Spokane (Wash.) Community Coll., 1979-84; staff nurse Kootenai Med. Ctr., 1979-85; instr. North Idaho Coll., Coeur d'Alene, 1984-85; staff nurse North Idaho Home Health, Coeur d'Alene, 1985-86; coord. br. office Family Home Care, Spokane, 1986-87; devel., dir. Good Samaritan Home Health Plummer, Idaho and Fairfield, Washington, 1987-88; mgr. patient svcs. VNS Seattle-King County, Tukwila, Wash., 1988-89; co-owner, v.p. The Wooden Boat Shop, Seattle, 1989—; primary sch. tchr. Marisposa Sch., 1994—; owner Marks and Assocs., 1994—; instr. in emergency med. tech. Orleans campus Coll. Redwoods, Eureka, Calif., 1977-78; book reviewer Brady Co., Besterfield and Assocs., 1994; film reviewer Olympia Media Info. Mem. Nat. Head Injury Found., Wash. State Head Injury Found. Office: 8023 Park Lawn Ct Fontana CA 92336

MARKUSON, CIRA PROFIT, college administrator; b. Jersey City, Apr. 15, 1947; d. Joseph Francis and Aldona Frances (Novak) P.; m. Roger Alcide Masse, Aug. 23, 1976 (div. Mar. 1989); children: Jeanine Elizabeth, Crissa Marie, Paul Joseph; m. Stephen Harvey Markuson, Oct. 12, 1991. BA, Rosary Coll., River Forest, Ill., 1969; MS, Rutgers U., 1971. Cert. clin. competence Am. Speech & Hearing Assn.; cert. in health care mgmt. Rutgers U. Dir. speech and hearing ctr. Mercer Med. Ctr., Trenton, N.J., 1970-73, dir. vol. svcs., 1973-75; dir. vol. svcs. Friends Hosp., Phila., 1975-76; asst. dir. devel. Hartwick Coll., Oneonta, N.Y., 1986-88, dir. ann. fund, 1988—. Pres. bd. dirs. Catskill Symphony Orch., Oneonta, 1992-94. Mem. AAUW (pres. 1982-86, co-pres. 1988-90, corporate rep. for Hartwick Coll.), Coun. for Advancement and Support of Edn. Home: PO Box 719 Oneonta NY 13820 Office: Hartwick Coll Oneonta NY 13820

MARKWOOD, SANDRA REINSEL, program and policy development analyst; b. Washington, Aug. 27, 1955; d. Francis Eugene and Delores Jean (Horning) Reinsel-Kahn; m. James Scott Markwood, Aug. 4, 1984; children: Christopher Scott, Anne Meredith. BA with distinction, U. Va., 1977, M in Urban and Environ. Planning, 1979. Sr. rsch. asst. Nat. League of Cities, Washington, 1979-80; rsch. assoc./ project dir. Nat. Assn. Counties, Washington, 1980-84; asst. to county exec. Albemarle County, Charlottesville, Va., 1984-86; sr. rsch. assoc./ project dir. Nat. Assn. Counties, Washington, 1986—; exec. sec. Nat. Assn. County Aging Programs, Washington, 1986—; com. co-chair Generations United, Washington, 1988-90, intergovtl. liaison Nat. Hwy. Traffic Safety Adminstrn., Washington, 1989-91; chair Aging Needs Assessment Com., Charlottesville, 1985-86. Author: (handbook) Local Officials Guide to Urban Recreation, 1980, (guide) Building Support for Traffic Safety Programs, 1991; co-author (guide) Graying of Suburbia, 1988; editor: Counties and Volunteers, Partners in Svc., 1992-93; contbr. articles to profl. jours. Vol. tchr. St. Louis Cath. Sch., Alexandria, Va., 1980-83, St. Rita's Cath. Sch., Alexandria, 1987-89; coord. Sister Cities Exch. Program, Charlottesville, 1985. Recipient Cert. of Appreciation, Nat. Hwy. Traffic Safety Adminstrn., 1991. Mem. Women's Transp. Seminar, Smithsonian Assocs., Generations United. Roman. Catholic. Home: 3106 Lot A Russell Rd Alexandria VA 22305-1742

MARLAND, MELISSA KAYE, judge; b. Beckley, W.Va., Feb. 16, 1955; d. James Robert and Fannie Evelyn (Cook) M. BA in Polit. Sci., W.Va U., 1976, JD, 1979. Bar: W.Va. 1979, U.S. Dist. Ct. (so. dist.) W.Va. 1979, U.S. Supreme Ct. 1983. Law clk. Pub. Svc. Commn. W.Va., Charleston, 1979-82, hearing examiner, 1982-87, dep. chief adminstrv. law judge, 1987-89, chief adminstrv. law judge, 1989—; faculty mem. ann. regulatory studies program Nat. Assn. Regulatory Commrs./Inst. Pub. Utilities, Mich. State U., 1994—. Assoc. editor: West Virginia Digest of Public Utility Decisions, vols. 1-7, 1986-91; contbr. articles to profl. jours. Mem. ABA, NAFE, W.Va. State Bar (com. on corp., banking and bus. law 1987—), Nat. Assn. Regulatory Commrs. (chmn. subcom. on adminstrv. law judges 1991—), Phi Beta Kappa, Phi Alpha Delta, Pi Sigma Alpha. Democrat. Office: Pub Svc Commn WVa 201 Brooks St Charleston WV 25301-1827

MARLAR, JANET CUMMINGS, public relations officer; b. Burnsville, Miss., Dec. 22, 1942; d. James E. and Juanita (Hale) Cummings; m. David C. Linton, May 21, 1961 (div. 1984); 1 child, Jeffory Mark; m. Thomas Gilbert Cupples, Mar. 5, 1984 (div. 1990); m. Fredrick Marlar, Nov. 19, 1994. Student, NE Miss. Jr. Coll., 1960-61, Memphis State U., 1975-76, Sheffield Tech. Ctr., Memphis, 1984-85. Property owner, Burnsville, 1974—; mem. bus. adv. com. Sheffield Tech. Ctr., 1987—; with community svcs. St. Francis Hosp., 1989—; exec. bd. Internat. Heritage Commn., Memphis, 1987-92; pub. rels. officer Internat. Heritage Ethnic Festival, Memphis. Co-editor Internat. Heritage Bull./Newsletter. Vol. Memphis Brooks Mus. Art, 1980—; mem. exec. com., pub. info. officer Bldg. Bridges for A Better Memphis, 1985—; pres. Eagle Watch Assn.; founder Janet C. Cupples Citizenship awards, Memphis City Inter-City Sch., Student Leadership award, Memphis City Schs.; founder, chair women's com. on crime, City of Memphis, 1985—, chair Heritage-City of Memphis, chair internat. heritage program, 1987, 88—, Ethnic Outreach Neighborfest, 1988; hon. mem. city council, 1987; donor, exec. com. Women of Achievement, Inc., Memphis, 1986; mem. speakers bur. United Way of Greater Memphis, Friends of Shelby County Library, 1986—, YWCA; chair ethnic outreach com. Neighborfest, Memphis, 1987, chairperson exec. com. 1988; amb. Memphis Internat. Heritage Commn., 1988; youth mentor Memphis Youth Leadership Devel. Inst.; internat. coord. Neighborfest '88; chairperson Internat. Heritage City of Memphis, 1987, Ethnic Outreach Neighborfest, 1988. Contbr. articles to newspapers. Mem. community coun. Memphis City Schs., Memphis Cablevision Edn. Task Force; appointed col. aide de camp to staff of Gov. Ned McWherter of Tenn., 1988; sec. Shelby County Dem. Women, 1991; sec. safety com. St. Francis Hosp., 1992. Recipient 10 certs. of recognition Memphis City Council, 1986-89, Outstanding Service to Pub. Edn. award, 1986, merit award City of Memphis, 1987; named Outstanding Female Participant, Neighborhood, Inc., 1987; named Woman of Achievement 1988; honored by Pres. George Bush as Outstanding Vol., 1989; featured one of top 1000 Vols. in Mid-South, 1989; Svc. award Cummings Sch., 1993. Mem. NAFE, NOW (2d v.p. Memphis chpt. 1987, del. nat. conf. 1987, 2d v.p.), Network Profl. Women's Orgn., NCCJ, Rep. Career Women, Memphis Peace and Justice Ctr., Women's Polit. Caucus Tenn. Methodist. Avocations: community service, writing, teaching. Office: St Francis Hosp 5959 Park Ave Memphis TN 38119-5198

MARLEAU, DIANE, Canadian government official; b. Kirkland Lake, Ont., Can., June 21, 1943; d. Jean-Paul and Yvonne (Desjardins) LeBel; m. Paul C. Marleau, Aug. 3, 1963; children: Brigitte, Donald, Stéphane. Student, U. Ottawa, Ont., 1960-63; BA in Econs., Laurentian U., Sudbury, Ont., 1976. With Donald Jean Acctg. Svcs., Sudbury, 1971-75; receiver mgr. Thorne Riddell, Sudbury, 1975-76; treas. No. Regional Residential Treatment Program for Women, Sudbury, 1976-80, Com. for the Industry and Labour Adjustment Program, Sudbury, 1983; chmn. Can.

Games for the Physically Disabled, Sudbury, 1983; rep. Ont. Adv. Coun. on Women's Issues, Toronto, 1984-85; mem. transition team Ont. Premier's Office, Toronto, 1985; firm adminstr. Collins Barrow-Maheu Noiseux, Sudbury, 1985-88; M.P. from Sudbury House of Commons, Ottawa, 1988—; minister of health for Can., 1993—; councilor Regional Municipality of Sudbury, 1980-85; alderman City of Sudbury, 1980-85; mem. No. Devel. Coun., Sudbury, 1986-88; vice chair Nat. Liberal Standing Com. on Policy, 1989; chair Ont. Liberal Caucus, 1990; apptd. nat. exec. Liberal Party Can., 1990, assoc. critic Govt. Ops., 1990, Dep. Opposition Whip, 1991, assoc. critic Fin., 1992; vice chair standing com. finance, 1992. Chmn. fund-raising Canadian Cancer Soc., Sudbury, 1987-88; co-chmn. Laurentian Hosp. Cancer Care Svcs. fund-raising campaign, Sudbury, 1988; chair bd. govs. Cambrian Coll., 1987-88, bd. govs., 1983-88; mem. Sudbury and Dist. Health Unit Bd., 1981-82; mem. fin. com., bd. dirs. Laurentian Hosp., 1981-85; chair Can. Games for the Physically Disabled, 1983; apptd. Ont. Adv. Coun. Women's Issues, 1984. Mem. Sudbury Bus. and Profl. Women Club. (named Woman of the Day 1989). Office: House of Commons, Confederation Bldg Rm 613, Ottawa, ON Canada K1A 0A6 also: 36 Elgin St, Sudbury, ON Canada P3C 5B4

MARLER, SUSAN ANN, cardiology nurse, educator; b. Henryetta, Okla., Aug. 23, 1946; d. Grover E. and LouCille M. (Whippo) M. Nursing diploma, Hillcrest Med. Ctr., Tulsa, 1967. Staff nurse ICU Hillcrest Med. Ctr., Tulsa, 1967-71, head nurse ICU, 1971-80, critical care clinician, 1980-86, critical care edn. specialist, 1986-92; patient svcs. mgr. Okla. Heart, Inc., Tulsa, 1992-93; cons., lectr. owner Cardiovasc. Ednl. Svc., Tulsa, 1993—; BLS instr. Am. Heart Assn., Okla., 1986—, BLS instr. trainer, 1991-92, 93—, ACLS instr., 1989—. Author, cons.: (film strip series) Critical Care Skills, 1982; cons.: (video series) Neurological Critical Care, 1985; revising author: (ind. learning packet) Basic Electrocardiography, 1991. Mem. AACN (CCRN 1976-89, bd. mem. Greater Tulsa Area Chpt. 1974-81). Republican. Baptist. Home and Office: 1809 S 91st East Ave Tulsa OK 74112-8422

MARLETT, JUDITH ANN, nutritional sciences educator, researcher; b. Toledo. BS, Miami U., Oxford, Ohio, 1965; PhD, U. Minn., 1972; post-grad., Harvard U., 1973-74. Registered dietitian. Therapeutic and metabolic unit dietitian VA Hosp., Mpls., 1966-67; spl. instr. in nutrition Simmons Coll., Boston, 1973-74; asst. prof. U. Wis., Madison, 1975-80, assoc. prof. dept. nutritional scis., 1981-84, prof. dept. nutritional scis., 1984—; cons. U.S. AID, Leyte, Philippines, 1983; acting dir. dietetic program dept. Nutritional Scis. U. Wis., 1977-78, dir., 1985-89; cons. grain, drug and food cos., 1985—, adv. bd. U. Ariz. Clin. Cancer Ctr., 1987—; sci. bd. advisors Am. Health Found., 1988—; reviewer NIH, 1982—. Mem. editorial bd. Jour. of Sci. of Food and Agrl., 1989—, Jour. Food Composition and Analysis; contbr. articles to profl. jours. Mem. AAAS, NIH (Diabetes and Digestive and Kidney Disease spl. grant rev. com. 1992—), Am. Inst. Nutrition, Am. Dietetic Assn., Am. Soc. for Clin. Nutrition, Inst. of Food Technologists, Am. Assn. Cereal Chemists. Office: U Wis Dept Nutritional Sci 1415 Linden Dr Madison WI 53706-1571

MARLEY, MARY LOUISE, psychologist; b. Columbia, Pa., Apr. 18, 1923; d. William Edward and Carrie Cook (Lockard) M. BS in Edn., Millersville (Pa.) State U., 1944; MEd in Psychology and Audiology, Franklin and Marshall Coll., 1952. Lic. psychologist, speech pathologist, audiologist, Pa. Cons. remedial reading Dearborn (Mich.) Elem. Schs., 1944-49; tchr. spl. edn. Hershey (Pa.) Elem. Sch., 1949-52; speech pathologist York (Pa.) County Schs. Office, 1952-55, asst. psychologist, 1955-68; clin. psychologist stroke unit York Hosp., 1968-74; pvt. practice clin. psychology York, 1974—; cons. to police depts. of Gettysburg, Glen Rock Boro, Hanover Boro, Hazleton, Jackson Twp., Manheim Twp., Eastern Adams Regional, North Codorus Twp., Northeastern, No. Regional, Penn Twp., Red. Lion, Spring Garden Twp., Springettsbury Twp., West Manchester Twp., West Manheim Twp., West York, Windsor Twp., Wrightsville, York City, York Twp.; cons. to fire depts. of Spring Garden, Emigsville, Hanover; cons. York County Parks and Recreation. Author: Organic Brain Pathology and the Bender Gestalt Test, 1982. Mem. Pa. Psychol. Assn., Nat. Assn. Neuropsychology, Nat. Register Clin. Psychology, York County Psychol. Assn. Republican. Methodist. Home: 926 Mckenzie St York PA 17403-3712

MARLING-BUSSARD, ROSE MARIE, geriatrics nurse; b. Lowell, Mass., July 18, 1934; d. Edward Mark and Alice (Godsell) Culleton; m. William J. Bussard, June 4, 1988(dec. Sept. 1991); children: Kathleen Marling Persinger, James M. Marling, Dianne Marling Good, David P. Marling. LPN, B.M. Spurr Sch. Practical Nursing, 1980; ADN, Hocking Tech. Coll., 1987. RN, Del. Soc. editor The Times Leader, Martins Ferry, Ohio; nurse Ohio Valley Med. Ctr., Wheeling, W.Va.; staff nurse telemetry, med.-surg. Beebe Med. Ctr., Lewes, Del.; charge nurse, dir. nursing Lewes Convalescent Ctr.; camp nurse 4-H. Parish Coun. pres. St. Mary's Cath. Ch., Shadyside, Ohio; mem. Upper Ohio Valley Girl Scout coun. Recipient Writing award Writer's Digest, Journalism award Shadyside Woman's Club; Bus. and Profl. Women Nursing grantee. Mem. ANA (cert. gen. nurse), Nat. League Nursing, Del. Nurses Assn., Del. Dir. Nursing Assn., Nat. Writers Club, Bus. and Profl. Women. Home: 28 Gunpowder Ln Rehoboth Beach DE 19971-9758

MARLOW, JEANNETTE, pediatrician; b. N.Y.C., Oct. 30, 1922; d. Charles William and Dorothy Edna (Clarke) M.; m. John Shami, June 14, 1947 (div. 1978); children: Susan Evans, Dorothy Shami, John Shami, Wendy Shami. BA, Denison U., 1943; MD, Womans Med. Coll. of Pa., 1947. Diplomat Am. Bd. Pediatrics. Pvt. practice Bedford Hills, N.Y., 1953-60; sch. physician Chappaqua (N.Y.) Pub. Schs., 1960-67; pediatric unit chief Letchworth Devel. Ctr., Thiells, N.Y., 1967-74; dir. med. svcs. Wassaic (N.Y.) Devel. Ctr., 1974-90. Vol. clin. physician pediatrician Collier County Pub. Health, Naples, Fla., 1993—. Recipient Alumnae Citation Alumnae Assn. Denison U., 1993. Fellow Am. Acad. Pediatrics; mem. AMA, AAUW (pres. 1964-65), Am. Med. Women's Assn., Women's Emergency Svcs. (bd. dirs. 1980-82). Congregationalist. Home: 320 Seaview Ct Marco Island FL 33937

MARLOWE, ANN RACHEL, legal recruitment company executive, writer; b. Suffern, N.Y., June 28, 1958; d. Bernard and Bernice (Nachman) M. BA, Harvard U., 1979; MBA, Columbia U., 1984. Fin. analyst Paine Webber Group, N.Y.C., 1980-82; mgmt. cons. Booz Allen & Hamilton, N.Y.C., 1984-85; pres. Ann Marlowe Inc., N.Y.C., 1985-87; legal recruiter A-L Assocs., N.Y.C., 1987-90; pres. Legal Matches, N.Y.C., 1990—; pub. Pretty Decorating, 1994—. Contbr. articles to Village Voice, L.A. Weekly, Artforum.

MARMER, ELLEN LUCILLE, pediatrician; b. Bronx, N.Y., June 29, 1939; d. Benjamin and Diane (Goldstein) M.; m. Harold O. Shapiro, June 5, 1960; children: Cheri, Brenda. BS in Chemistry, U. Ala., 1960; MD, U. Ala., Birmingham, 1964. Cert. Nat. Bd. Med. Examiners; diplomate Am. Bd. Sports Medicine, Bd. Pediatrics, Bd. Qualified and Eligible Pediatric Cardiology, Bd. cert. sports medicine. Intern Upstate Med. Ctr., Syracuse, N.Y., 1964-65, resident, 1965-66; fellow in pediatric cardiology Columbia Presbyn. Med. Ctr.-Babies Hosp., N.Y.C., 1967-69; pvt. practice Hartford, Vernon, Conn., 1969—; examining pediatrician child devel. program Columbia Presbyn. Med. Ctr.-Babies Hosp., N.Y.C., 1967, instr. pediatrics, 1967-69; dir. pediatric cardiology clinic St. Francis Hosp., Hartford, 1970-80; asst. state med. examiner, Tolland County, Conn., 1974-79; sports physician Rockville (Conn.) High Sch., 1976—; advisor Cardiac Rehab. com., Rockville, 1984-90; mem. bd. examiners Am. Bd. Sports Medicine, 1991—, chmn. credentials com., 1991—. Mem. Vernon Town Coun., 1985-89; bd. dirs. Child Guidance Clinic, Manchester, Conn., 1970—; life mem. Tolland County chpt. Hadassah, v.p., 1969-70, pres., 1970-72, bd. dirs., 1973-74; mem. B'nai Israel Congregation and Sisterhood, Vernon, 1969—, chmn. youth commn., 1970-72. Recipient Outstanding Svc. award Indian Valley YMCA, 1985. Fellow Am. Acad. Pediatrics, Am. Coll. Cardiology, Am. Coll. Sports Medicine (bd. examiners 1991—, chmn. credentials com. 1991—); mem. Conn. Med. Soc., Am. Heart Assn. (mem. coun. cardiovascular disease in young 1969—, chmn. elect New Eng. regional heart com. 1990-91), Conn. Heart Assn. (bd. dirs. 1974-75, 83-84, pres. 1986-88), Heart Assn. Greater Hartford (bd. dirs. 1970-89, mem. exec. com. 1972-73, 79-84, pres. 1982-84), Tolland County Med. Assn. (sec. 1971-72), Vis. Nurse and Community Care Tolland County, LWV (state program chairperson Vernon chpt. 1971-73). Democrat. Jewish. Office: 520 Hartford Tpke Vernon CT 06066-5037

MARMON, BETTY LEWIS, real estate executive; b. N.Y.C., Feb. 27, 1927; d. Samuel and Ida (Cohen) Lewis; m. Bradley S. Marmon, June 15, 1947; children: Stephen, Nan Marmon Sabel, Elise Marmon Raymond. BA, Bklyn. Coll., 1948. Ptnr. White's Pharmacy, East Hampton, N.Y., 1954—; pres., broker Nanstel Corp. Real Estate Mgmt., East Hampton, N.Y., 1961—. Fin. chmn. Ladies Village Improvement Soc., East Hampton, 1984—, v.p., 1989-92; mem. Design Rev. Bd. East Hampton, 1984-92; v.p. Jewish Ctr. of the Hamptons, 1988-94, pres., 1994—. Mem. AAUW, Am. Arbitration Assn. Home: 68 Mill Hill Ln East Hampton NY 11937 Office: Nanstel Corp 68 Mill Hill Ln East Hampton NY 11937

MAROHN, ANN ELIZABETH, health information professional; b. Grand Rapids, Mich., Feb. 26, 1946; d. Luther Alfonse and Mary Inez (Pinkstaff) M. BS, Ind. U., 1968; MS, SUNY, Buffalo, 1978. Asst. med. record dir. Highland Park (Mich.) Gen. Hosp., 1968-70; asst. dir. med. record svcs. Meml. Hosp., Elmhurst, Ill., 1970-73; dir. med. record tech. program Alfred (N.Y.) State Coll., 1974-76; mem. faculty med. record adminstrn. dept. Lincoln Coll., Melbourne, Australia, 1977-78, Kean Coll., Union, N.J., 1984-85, Med. U. S.C., Charleston, 1985-87; mem. faculty health record dept. Ferris State Coll., Big Rapids, Mich., 1979-80; dir. health info. mgmt. Armstrong State Coll., Savannah, Ga., 1980-84; dir. med. record dept. Tucson Gen. Hosp., 1988-89, N.D. State Hosp., Jamestown, 1990-92; cons. Prospective Payment Specialists, Tucson, 1992-93; health info. mgr. Sierra Med. Ctr., El Paso, Tex., 1993-94; dir. health info. mgmt. program Southern U., Shreveport, La., 1994—; cons. Oglethorpe Ctr., Savannah, 1983-84. Columnist Australian Med. Record Jour., 1981-87, Communique, 1981-84, Palmetto Breeze, 1985-87, Progress Notes, 1984-85. Recipient disting. mem. award Ga. Med. Record Assn., 1984. Mem. NAFE, Am. Hosp. Assn., Ariz. Health Info. Mgmt. Assn. (program chmn. 1988-89, sec. 1989—), Am. Health Info. Mgmt. Assn., Clin. Coding Soc., Tex. Health Info. Mgmt. Assn. (dist. III v.p.), La. Health Info. Mgmt. Assn., New Orleans Info. Mgmt. Assn. Episcopalian. Home: 1846 Fairfield Ave Shreveport LA 71101

MARONE, REGINA KENNY, medical librarian; b. Manchester, Conn., Nov. 27, 1943; children: Lisa, Christine. BA magna cum laude, Albertus Maynus Coll., 1975; MLS, So. Conn. State U., 1978. Pub. svc. asst. Yale U. Med. Libr., New Haven, 1976-78, sr. reference libr., 1979-81; pub. svcs. libr. Boehringer Ingelheim Ltd., R & D Libr., Ridgefield, Conn., 1981-82; head reference svcs. Yale U. Harvey Cushing-John Hay Whitney Med. Libr., New Haven, 1982-90, 92-93, acting dir., 1990-92, assoc. dir., 1991—; mem. user adv. bd. BRS Info. Techs., 1982-85, tech. subcom., 1982-84, election subcom., 1986; presenter in field. Contbr. articles to profl. jours. Sr. warden St. Thomas Ch., New Haven, 1988-90; chmn. bd. mgrs. St. Thomas Day Sch., New Haven, 1989-91, treas., 1991—. Mem. Med. Libr. Assn. (chairperson nat. chpt. coun. elections com. 1989-91, chpt. coun. 1987-92, pharmacy and drug info. sect. membership com. 1986-87, sec./treas. 1987-88, program chair/chair elect 1988-89, chairperson 1989-90, chairperson nominating com. 1990-91), North Atlantic Health Sci. Librs. (program chairperson 1990-91, and various others), Conn. Assn. Health Sci. Librs. (chair by laws com. 1981-84, chair continuing edn. com. 1985-87, v.p. 1987-89, exec. bd. 1981-84, 85-89, 93—, rep. Nat. Assn. Health Sci. Librs. 1993—), Acad. Health Info. Profls. (disting. 1991—). Home: 96 Lakeview Ave Hamden CT 06514-3010 Office: Yale U Cushing-Whitney Med Libr 333 Cedar St New Haven CT 06510

MARONEY, JANE P., state legislator; b. Boston, July 29, 1923; d. John Henry and Mary (Boland) Perkins; m. John Walker Maroney, July 7, 1956; children: Jane Maroney El Dahr, John Walker Jr. Student, Radcliffe Coll., 1940-41; studnet, Katharine Gibbs Sch., 1941-42. Elected official Del. Gen. Assembly, Dover, 1978—. Chmn. Del. Family Law Commn., 1990—, Human Needs and Devel. Com., 1984—; moderator, panelist Pub. Policy Conf., annually; bd. dirs. YWCA, New Castle County, (J.Thompson Brown award 1992), Child Care Connection, Coord. Coun. Children with Disabilities, chmn. 1990-91; mem. adv. bd. Rockwood Mus., Del. Hospice, Girl Scouts Del., Del. Internat. Yr. of Family, March of Dimes, Coalition for Literacy, Inst. Human Behavior; past mem. Jr. League Wilmington. Named 1 of 10 Best Rep. Legislators of Yr. Pres. Reagan, 1985; recipient Outstanding Svc. to Children award Acad. Pediatrics, Disting. Svc. award Del. Bar Assn., Alfred R. Shands Disting. Svc. award, 1992, Order of Merit award U. Del., 1993. Roman Catholic. Home: 4605 Concord Pike Wilmington DE 19803 Office: Del House of Reps PO Box 1901 Dover DE 19901

MARONEY, LENORE ELLEN, guidance counselor, photographer; b. Bronx, Feb. 13, 1951; d. William Robert and Eleanor Rose (Mucci) M. BS in Art Edn., Coll. Mt. St. Vincent, 1972; MA in Counseling Psychology, Manhattan Coll., 1976, profl. diploma in Acad. Counseling, 1979; postgrad., Pace U., 1993—. Cert. art tchr., N.Y.; cert. counselor, N.Y. Art tchr. Red Hook (N.Y.) Jr. High Sch., 1972-78, guidance counselor, 1978—; owner, videographer, photographer Video Prose, Rhinebeck, N.Y., 1976-86; advisor equestrian club Red Hook Ctrl. Sch., 1972-74, advisor drama club, 1972-75, advisor sr. play, 1978-84, advisor Students Against Drunk Driving, 1984-93; riding instr., Dutchess County, 1982-85. Exhibited at various art galleries, banks, law offices, restaurants. Active Barrett House, Poughkeepsie, N.Y., 1991—. Recipient Advisor award Students Against Drunk Driving, 1993. Mem. Dutchess County Counselor's Assn. (Achievement award 1993-94), Dutchess County Arts Assn., Dutchess Arts Coun., Appalachian Mountain Club. Democrat. Home: 889 Fiddlers Bridge Rd Rhinebeck NY 12572-3207 Office: Red Hook Ctrl Sch 6373 W Market St Red Hook NY 12571

MARONI, ALICE C., federal official; b. Washington, D.C., Oct. 8, 1953; d. Yves and Francis (Tower) M. BA magna cum laude, Mount Holyoke Coll., 1975; MA, Williams Coll., 1974, Tufts U., 1978; attended, Nat. War Coll., 1988-89. Internat. risk analyst Rockwell Internat., 1979-80; specialist in nat. defense Congl. Rsch. Svc., Libr. of Congress, 1980-90; prof. staff mem. House com. on armed svcs., 1990-93; prin. dep. comptroller Dept. of Defense, Washington, 1993—. Contbr. article to profl. publs. Office: Dept of Defense 1100 Defense Pentagon Washington DC 20301-1100*

MARONI, DONNA FAROLINO, retired science administrator; b. Buffalo, Feb. 27, 1938; d. Enrico Victor and Eleanor (Redlinska) Farolino; m. Gustavo Primo Maroni, Dec. 16, 1974. BS, U. Wis., 1960, PhD, 1969. Project assoc. U. Wis., Madison, 1960-63, 68-74; Alexander von Humboldt fellow Inst. Genetics U. Cologne, Fed. Republic Germany, 1974-75; Hargitt fellow Duke U., Durham, N.C., 1975-76, rsch. assoc., 1976-83, rsch. assoc. prof., 1983-87; sr. program specialist N.C. Biotech. Ctr., Research Triangle Park, 1987-88, dir. sci. programs div., 1988-92, v.p. for sci. programs, 1992-94; ret., 1995—; mem. adv. com. MICROMED at Bowman Gray Sch. Medicine, Winston-Salem, N.C., 1988—, Minority Sci. Improvement Alliance for Instrn. and Rsch. in Biotech. Ala. A & M U., Normal, 1990-91. Contbr. over 20 articles and revs. to profl. jours. Grantee NSF, 1977-79, NIH, 1979-82, 79-83, 82-87. Mem. Am. Soc. Cell Biology, Genetics Soc. Am., N.C. Acad. Sci., Inc. (bd. dirs. 1983-86), Sigma Xi (mem. exec. com. Duke U. chpt. 1989-90).

MAROON, MICKEY, clinical social worker; b. Flint, Mich., July 20, 1948; d. Harold Clifford and Dorothy Ruth (Fuller) McDaniel; m. Michael Martin Maroon, Aug. 22, 1970. BA, Bradley U., 1970; MSW, Denver U., 1975. Lic. clin. social worker, Colo.; bd. cert. diplomate. Social worker Ill. Dept. Children and Family Svcs., Peoria, Ill., 1970-73; clin. social worker Adams County Social Svcs., Westminster, Colo., 1975-77, Bethesda Hosp., Denver, 1977-84; pvt. practice Denver, 1979—; clin. cons. Human Svcs., Inc., Denver, 1988-91; vol. faculty Health Sci. Ctr. U. Colo., Denver, 1987—; chair attending social work staff West Pines Hosp., Wheat Ridge, Colo., 1988-89. Mem. NASW (pres. Colo. chpt. 1994—), Colo. Soc. Clin. Social Work (Denver chpt. pres. 1992, state pres. 1993).

MAROOTIAN, DOROTHY, artist; b. New Haven. BFA, Cooper Union, N.Y.C., 1978. Asst. art dir. Neiman-Marcus, Dallas; art dir. Bullock's, L.A.; freelance designer, art dir. L.A.; artist KCET, Channel 28, L.A.; tchr. Chouinard Art Sch., L.A.; art dir. Max Factor, L.A.; painter. Illustrator: A Taste of Texas; designer Christmas wrap; painter 3 ch. altar pieces; painter 4 paintings for USAF. Recipient painting awards Pasadena Art Soc., Irvine Creative Art Guild, Costa Mesa Art League; award for paper design Portfolio Mag. Mem. Soc. Illustrators (treas.). Home: 69 Claret Irvine CA 92714-7942

MAROT, LOLA, accountant; b. Providence, Oct. 6; d. Frank and Iola (Lombardi) Ansuini; m. Joseph Marot (div. 1973); 1 child, David Joseph. B.A. with distinction, U. R.I., 1973; postgrad. Bryant Coll. Bookkeeper, Diamond Paper Box Co., Providence, 1958-69; export sales adminstr. Brite Industries, Providence, 1973-77; property services asst. Met. Property and Liability Ins. Co., Warwick, R.I., 1977-79, buyer, 1979-83, sr. buyer, 1983-86, supr. printing adminstrn., 1986-87, expense control adminstr., 1987-88; accountant Dept of Adminstrn. State of R.I. Divsn. Ctrl. Svcs., 1992—. Mem. Univ. Soc. Providence (pres. 1978). Office: 1 Capitol Hl Providence RI 02908-5803

MARPLE, MARY LYNN, software engineer, environmental scientist; b. Norristown, Pa., July 4, 1951; d. M. Robert and Elsie Alice (Lawton) M.; m. Cyrus Duncan Cantrell, Nov. 18, 1972; children: Katherine Anne and Sarah Montgomery Marple Cantrell. BA in Math., Swarthmore Coll., 1973; MS in Biology, U. N.Mex., 1975, PhD, 1979. Environ. scientist N.Mex. Environ. Improvement Agy., Santa Fe, 1974-75, Los Alamos (N.Mex.) Nat. Lab., 1975-79, French AEC, Paris, 1980; environ. quality specialist Tex. Dept. Health, Austin, 1981-83; software engr. Tele-Drill Inc., Richardson, Tex., 1983-86, Merit Tech., Dallas, 1986-89, Halliburton Reservoir Svcs., Carrollton, Tex., 1989-92, Superconducting Super Collider, Dallas, 1992-93, SBS Sensor Sys., Farmers Branch, Tex., 1994—. Contbr. articles to profl. jours. Mem. IEEE, Soc. Petroleum Engrs., Computer Soc., Dallas Accueil, Health Physics Soc., Canyon Creek Country Club, Sigma Xi (treas. 1986-87). Home: 2409 Lawnmeadow Dr Richardson TX 75080-2342 Office: SBS Sensor Sys 4885 Alpha Rd Ste 110 Farmers Branch TX 75244

MARQUARDT, ALICE MARGARET, retired elementary education educator; b. Coleridge, Nebr., Apr. 18, 1927; d. Will John and Hilda Hattie (Ebmeier) Griesel; m. Elwood Raymond Marquardt, June 20, 1959; children: Janet Arden, Jody Jones. BA in Edn., Wayne State Tchrs. Coll., 1951. Tchr. Waterbury (Nebr.) Sch. Dist., 1945-46, Norfolk (Nebr.) Sch. Dist., 1946-48, Sioux City (Iowa) Sch. Dist., 1948-94; ret., 1994; credit union bldg. rep. Sioux City Tchrs. Mem. Sioux City PTA, 1948-94; past Sunday Sch. tchr., Luth. Ch. Mem. AAUW, Sioux City Woman's Club, Alpha Delta Kappa. Home: 2212 Helmer St Sioux City IA 51103-1742

MARQUARDT, ANN MARIE, small business administrator; b. Plainview, N.Y., Oct. 28, 1964; d. Steven Peter Paul and Virginia Ann (Gallo) M. Grad., Harry B. Ward Occupational Ctr, Riverhead, N.Y., 1982; student, Dowling Coll., 1982-84; Assoc. Acctg., Suffolk Community Coll., 1990; BS in Bus. Mgmt., St. John's U., 1993. Sec. Dowling Coll., Oakdale, N.Y., 1982-84; sec., office mgr. Pudge, Peteco & Peanuts Corp., Southold, N.Y., 1984-86, Era Albo Agy., Mattituck, N.Y., 1986-87; legal sec. Wickham, Wickham & Bressler, P.C., Mattituck, 1987-89, 93—; bus., gen. mgr. Mattituck Laundromat, 1987-89, Gaslight Cafe, Ltd., Mattituck, 1989; office/bus. mgr., bookkeeper accounts payable/receivable Minerva's Tree Svcs. Ltd., Cutchogue, N.Y., 1990—; office/bookkeeping cons. Dickerson's Marine, Mattituck, 1990, Hobby's Plus, Southold. Author poetry and short stories. Mem. NAFE, AAUW, Mattituck C. of C., Am. Mgmt. Assn., Nat. Arborist Assn., Nat. Assn. for Self-Employed. Office: Minervas Tree Svcs Ltd Stillwater Ave Cutchogue NY 11935-2208

MARQUARDT, CHRISTEL ELISABETH, lawyer; b. Chgo., Aug. 26, 1935; d. Herman Albert and Christine Marie (Geringer) Trolenberg; children: Eric, Philip, Andrew, Joel. BS in Edn., Mo. Western Coll., 1970; JD with honors, Washburn U., 1974. Bar: Kans. 1974, Mo. 1992, U.S. Dist. Ct. Kans. 1974, U.S. Dist. Ct. (we. dist.) Mo. 1992. Tchr. St. John's Ch., Tigerton, Wis., 1955-56; pers. asst. Columbia Records, L.A., 1958-59; ptnr. Cosgrove, Webb & Oman, Topeka, 1974-86, Palmer & Marquardt, Topeka, 1986-91, Levy and Craig P.C., Overland Park, Kans., 1991-94; sr. ptnr. Marquardt and Assocs., L.L.C., Fairway, Kans., 1994—; mem. atty. bd. discipline Kans. Supreme Ct., 1984-86. Mem. editorial adv. bd. Kans. Lawyers Weekly, 1992—; contbr. articles to legal jours. Bd. dirs. Topeka Symphony, 1983-92, Arts and Humanities Assn. Johnson County, 1992—, Brown Found., 1988-90; hearing examiner Human Rels. Com., Topeka, 1974-76; local advisor Boy Scouts Am., 1973-74; bd. dirs., mem. nominating com. YWCA, Topeka, 1979-81; bd. govs. Washburn U. Law Sch., 1987—, v.p., 1994-95; mem. dist. bd. adjudication Mo. Synod Luth. Ch., Kans., 1982-88. Names Woman of Yr., Mayor, City of Topeka, 1982; Obee scholar Washburn U., 1972-74. Fellow Am. Bar Found., Kans. Bar Found. (trustee 1987-89); mem. ABA (labor law, family and litigation sects., mem. ho. dels. 1988—, mem. specialization com. 1987-93, chmn. 1989-93, lawyers referral com. 1993—, constrn. law), Kans. Bar Assn. (sec., treas. 1981-82, 83-85, v.p. 1985-86, pres. 1987-88, bd. dirs. 1981—, lectr. 1974—, Disting. Svc. award 1980), Kans. Trial Lawyers Assn. (mem. bd. govs. 1982-86, lectr.), Topeka Bar Assn., Am. Bus. Women's Assn. (lectr., corr. sec. 1983-84, pres. career chpt. 1986-87, named one of Top 10 Bus. Women of the Yr., 1985. Home: 8572 Hauser Ct Lenexa KS 66215 Office: 4330 Shawnee Mision Pky Ste 107 Fairway KS 66205

MARQUARDT, KATHLEEN PATRICIA, association executive; b. Kalispell, Mont., June 6, 1944; d. Dean King and Lorraine Camille (Buckmaster) Marquardt; m. William Wewer, Dec. 6, 1987; children: Shane Elizabeth, Montana Quinn. Purser, Pan Am. World Airways, Washington, 1968-75; info. specialist Capital Systems Group, Kensington, Md., 1979-81; dir. pub. affairs Subscription TV Assn., Washington, 1981-83, exec. dir., 1983-86; pres. Internat. Policy Studies Orgn., 1983-90; pres., designer Elizabeth Quinn Couture; lectr. in field. Chmn. bd. Friends of Freedom, 1982-90, Putting People First, 1990—; bd. dirs. Tex. Sportsman's Legal Fund, 1992—; treas. Yes on Caps, 1994—. Author: Animal Scam-The Beastly Abuse of Human Rights, 1993, (national newpaper column) From the Trenches; contbr. articles to syndicated newspapers and mags.; host Grass Roots radio. Recipient Citizen Achievement award Ctr. fo Def. Free Enterprise, 1992, Gold Medal award Pa. State Fish and Game Protective Assn., 1993. Mem. Outdoor Writers Assn. Am. Home: 533 5th Ave Helena MT 59601 Office: 21 N Last Chance Gulch Helena MT 59601

MARQUEZ, HOPE, school system worker, educator; b. Winters, Tex., Sept. 12, 1948; d. Richard Ruiz and Candelaria (Medrano) Palomo; m. Arthur G. Marquez Jr.; children: Beverly Ruth Gonzales, Lytha Maria Mendoza, Hope. Bus driver, office asst., safety officer Ft. Worth Ind. Sch. Dist., 1977-90; ops.mgr., in charge bus driver tng. and cert. Ednl. Svc. Ctr., Ft. Worth, 1990—, coord., 1994. Vol. Ft. Worth Fire Dept. Relief, 1987, sec., 1991. Mem. Tex. Assn. for Pupil Transp. (reporter). Office: Edn Svc Ctr Region XI 3001 North Freeway Fort Worth TX 76106-6526

MARQUEZ, MARTINA ZENAIDA, elementary education educator; b. Santa Rosa, N.Mex., Nov. 5, 1935; d. José Zenon and Adelina (Romero) Sanchez; m. George J. Marquez, June 17, 1972. Student, Mt. St. Scholastica Coll., 1954-56, Regis Coll., 1956-59; BA, Coll. Santa Fe, 1963; MA, U. N.Mex., 1968. Cert. tchr., N.Mex. Elem. tchr. St. Rose Lima Sch., Santa Rosa, 1959-67, Cristo Rey Sch., Santa Fe, 1967-68, Los Lunas (N.Mex.) Consol. Schs., 1975-78, head tchr. adults operation; SER Manpower Devel. Tng. Act, Albuquerque, 1968-71, 73-75; tchr., cons. Regional Resource Ctr., N.Mex. State U., Las Cruces, 1971-72; counselor, coord. Taos (N.Mex.) Career Edn. Program, 1972-73; chpt. I reading tchr. Grants (N.Mex.) & Cibola County Schs., 1978—; chmn. ethics com. Profl. Standards Commn., N.Mex. Dept. Edn., 1986-88. Dir. choir St. Vivian's Ch., Milan, N.Mex., 1978—; del. Dem. Women's Club, Grants, N.Mex., 1981—; v.p. Literacy Vols. Am. of Cibola County. Selected as 1991 Cibola County Woman of Achievement 3rd Ann. Women's Resource Conf. Mem. AAUW (bylaws chmn. 1984, Grants Woman of Yr. award 1988), Internat. Reading Assn. (1st v.p. Malpais coun. 1988-89, pres. 1989-90, state pres. 1992-93, dist. 3 facilitator, Local Literacy award 1986, State Literacy award 1987, state pres. N.Mex. 1992-93), Delta Kappa Gamma (pres. Psi chpt. 1986-88). Democrat. Roman Catholic. Home: PO Box 11 Bluewater NM 87005-0011 Office: Grants-Cibola County Schs Jemez And Del Norte St Grants NM 87020

MARR, DIANE DEMPSEY, counselor, school psychologist, educator; b. San Francisco, Oct. 31, 1954; d. Robert Harold and Emma Delia (Bianchi) Dempsey; m. Dargan Howell Marr, July 26, 1985; children: Dina Marie, Jacob Reese. BA, San Jose State U., 1976; MA, EdS in Sch. Psychology, U.

Idaho, 1982, PhD, 1991. Lic. profl. counselor; nat. cert. sch. psychologist. Pvt. practice counseling and sch. psychology various cities, Idaho, 1981-85, Naphtali Psychol. Svcs., Cape Girardeau, Mo., 1993—; sch. psychologist Tri-Dist. Spl. Svcs., St. Anthony, Idaho, 1984-85, Coos Edn. Svc. Dist., Coos Bay, Oreg., 1985-89; instr./grad. asst. U. Idaho, Moscow, 1989-91; sch. psychologist Moscow Sch. Dist., 1991-92; asst. prof. counseling S.E. Mo. Stte U., Cape Girardeau, 1992—; cons. in field. Author: Gender Specific Treatment: A Program for Chemically Dependent Women in Recovery, 1994. Mem. Children's Caring Coun., Cape Girardeau, 1992—. Mem. Am. Counseling Assn., Am. Counselor Educators, Mo. Counseling Assn., Nat. Assn. Sch. Psychologists, S.E. Mo. Sch. Counselors Assn. Office: SE Missouri State Univ One University Pla Cape Girardeau MO 63701

MARR, PHEBE ANN, historian, educator; b. Mt. Vernon, N.Y., Sept. 21, 1931; d. John Joseph and Lillian Victoria (Henningsen) Marr. B.A., Barnard Coll., 1953; Ph.D., Harvard U., 1967. Research assoc. ARAMCO, Dhahran, Saudi Arabia, 1960-62; dir. middle east program Fgn. Service Inst., 1963-66; research fellow Middle East Ctr., Harvard U., Cambridge, Mass., 1968-70; asst. prof. Stanislaus State Coll., Turlock, Calif., 1970-71, assoc. prof., 1971-74; assoc. prof. history U. Tenn., Knoxville, 1974-85, chmn. Asian Studies Program, 1977-79; sr. fellow Nat. Def. U., Washington, 1985—; cons. ARAMCO, 1979-83. Harvard U. traveling fellow, 1956; mem. Coun. Fgn. Rels. Author: The Modern History of Iraq, 1985; co-editor: Riding the Tiger: Middle East Challenge After the Cold War, 1993; contbr. articles to profl. jours. Mem. Middle East Inst. (bd. govs.), Middle East Studies Assn., Am. Hist. Assn. Home: 2902 18th St NW Washington DC 20009 Office: Nat Def U 4th & P Sts SW Fort McNair DC 20319

MARRIOT, SALIMA SILER, state legislator, social work educator; b. Batl., Dec. 5, 1940; d. Jesse James and Cordie Susie (Ayers) Silver; m. David Small Mariott, Sept. 24, 1964 (div. 1972); children: Terrex Siler, Patrice Kenyatta. BS, Morgan State Coll., 1964; M in Social Work, U. Md., 1972; D in Social Work, Howard U., 1988. Tchr. Balt. City Pub. Sch., 1964-65; social worker N.Y.C. Social Svcs., 1965-67, Balt. City Social Svcs., 1968-72; instr., asst. prof. Morgan State U., Balt., 1972—; now also mem. Md. Ho. of Dels.; chair Park Heights Devel. Corp., Balt., 1976-92, Nat. Black Women's Health Project, 1993-94. Co-editor: U.S. Policy Toward Southern Africa, 1984. Cons. Balt. City Head Start, 1985-94; del. Dem. Conv., Altanta, 1988; active Md. Dem. Ctrl. Com., 1988-90; bd. dirs. Nat. Black Women's Health Project, Atlanta, 1991-94. Mem. Nat. Polit. Cong. Black Women, Nat. Coun. Negro Women, Delta Sigma Theta. Office: Md House of Dels 4515 Homer Ave Baltimore MD 21215-6302

MARRIOTT, MARCIA ANN, human resources administrator, educator, consultant; b. Rochester, N.Y., Mar. 21, 1947; d. Coyne and Alice (Schleper) M.; children: Brian, Jonathan. AA, Monroe Community Coll., Rochester, 1967; BS, SUNY, Brockport, 1970, MA, 1975; PhD, S.W. U. La., 1985. Program adminstr. N.Y. Dept. of Labor, N.Y.C., 1970-75; employment mgr. Rochester Gen. Hosp., 1975-77, salary adminstr., 1982—; dir. wage and salary dept. Gannett Newspapers, Rochester, 1977-80; compensation and benefits adminstr. Sybron Corp., Rochester, 1980-82; instr. N.Y. State Sch. Indsl. Rels., Cornell U., N.Y.C., 1976-79; assoc. prof. Rochester Inst. Tech., 1978—, Monroe Community Coll., 1981—, dir. career adv. coun., 1989—; cons. in field; dir. Rochester Presbyn. Home, 1987-91; dir. area hosp. coun. Kidney Svc. Ctrs., Rochester, 1988-91. Author: (pamphlet) Guideline for Writing Job Descriptions, 1983, (manual) Career Planning Manual, 1985, (booklet) Guideline for Writing Criteria-Based Job Descriptions, 1988, Skill-based Job Descriptions, A Quality Approach, 1994. Campaign mgr. Carter Campaign Commn., Rochester, 1975; mem. coun. Messiah Luth. Ch., Rochester, 1991-94. Davenport-Hatch Found. grantee, 1973, Wegman Found. grantee, 1975. Mem. Am. Compensation Assn., Single Adopted Parents Group (pres. 1988-93). Office: Rochester Gen Hosp 1425 Portland Ave Rochester NY 14621-3001

MARRON, DARLENE LORRAINE, real estate development executive, financial and marketing consultant; b. Auburn, N.Y., July 20, 1946; d. William Chester and Elizabeth Barbara (Gervaise) Kulakowski; m. Edward W. Marron, Jr., Apr. 28, 1973. BS cum laude, Rider Coll., 1968; MBA, NYU, 1970. Lic. securities broker. Dir. mktg. Am. Airlines, N.Y.C., 1970-79; asst. v.p. Merrill Lynch, N.Y.C., 1979-83; v.p. Kidder, Peabody & Co., N.Y.C., 1983-86; owner, principal, Marron Cos., Upper Saddle River, N.J., 1986—, Marron Bros. Realty Corp., 1990—; fin. and mktg. cons. to real estate devel. industry. Avocations: pianist, flutist, skiing, fly fishing. Home: 9 Normandy Ct Ho Ho Kus NJ 07423-1217 Office: Marron Cos 118 Rte 17 N Upper Saddle River NJ 07458

MARROW, MARVA JAN, photographer, writer, video and multimedia producer; b. Denver, Apr. 22, 1948; d. Sydney and Helen Berniece (Garber) M. Student, Carnegie-Mellon U., 1965-67. Singer, songwriter RCA Records, Italy, 1972-77; pvt. practice photography Italy and U.S., 1976—; dir. acquisitions RAI TV, L.A., 1990-91; mng. agt. Thomas Angel Prodns., L.A., 1991-94; represented by Shooting Star Photo Agy., Agenzia Marka, Agenzia Masi, Italy, Uniphoto Press Internat., Japan; corr., photographer Italian TV Guide, Milan, 1979—; collaborator, photographer for other U.S. and European publs., radio and TV; TV news and documentary prodr. RAI TV, 1990—. Author numerous songs for Italian pop artists including Lucio Battisti, Battiato, Premiata Forneria Marconi (PFM), Patty Pravo, 1972—; author: (photobook) Inside the L.A. Artist, 1988; project dir. Digital Art Mus. (CD-Rom), 1994—; prodr. (CD-Rom) The Kat's Meow, 1995; contbr. photographs for covers and articles to nat. and internat. mags. Mem. Motion Picture Assn. of Am., Fgn. Press Assn. Democrat. Home and Studio: 2080 N Garfield Ave Altadena CA 91001 Office: Shooting Star Agy PO Box 93368 Los Angeles CA 90093-0368

MARRS, SHARON CARTER, librarian; b. Andover, Va., May 7, 1943; d. Wallace Ralph and Dorothy (Stout) Carter; m. Glenn Robert Marrs, July 3, 1965. BS, East Tenn. State U., 1965; MLS, U. Pitts., 1974, postgrad., 1983—. Cert. libr. sci. and English libr., Pa. Tchr. English grades 8 and 10 Powell Valley H.S., Big Stone Gap, Va., 1964-65; libr. Coeburn (Va.) Elem., 1967-68, tchr. grade 2, 1968; libr. Wise (Va.) Elem., 1968-69; tchr. English grade 7 Christiansburg (Va.) Elem. Sch., 1969-70, libr., 1970-71; libr. Myrtle, Vernridge and Kelton Schs., Pitts., 1972—. Mem. ALA, Pa. Libr. Assn., Internat. Assn. Sch. Librarianship, Beta Phi Mu. Home: 620 Broughton Rd Bethel Park PA 15102-3775

MARS, VIRGINIA CRETELLA, volunteer; b. New Haven; d. Albert William and Josephine Vera (Nutile) Cretella; m. Forrest E. Mars Jr., Oct. 20, 1955 (div. Jan. 1990); children: Victoria B., Valerie A., Pamela D., Marijke E. BA, Vassar Coll., 1951. Cert. tchr. Mem. Nat. Symphony Orch. Bd., Washington, chair exec. com., 1980-83, pres., 1983-87; mem. Smithsonian Women's Com., Washington, 1988—; trustee The Potomac Sch. Bd., McLean, Va., The Langley Sch., McLean, Vassar Coll. Bd., Poughkeepsie, N.Y., 1987—; bd. dirs. Wildlife Preservation Trust Internat., 1990—; chair Campaign for Vassar; mem. Cathedral Chpt. bd. dirs. Washington Nat. Cathedral, 1994—. Mem. Vassar Club Washington, Cosmos Club, Chevy Chase Club, Sulgrave Club. Republican. Episcopalian. Home: 702 Belgrove Rd Mc Lean VA 22101-1836

MARSDEN, HERCI IVANA, classical ballet artistic director; b. Omis-Split, Croatia, Dec. 2, 1937; came to U.S., 1958; d. Ante and Magda (Smith) Munitic; m. Myles Marsden, Aug. 10, 1957 (div. 1976); children—Ana, Richard, Mark; m. Dujko Radovnikovic, Aug. 27, 1977; 1 child, Dujko. Student, Internat. Ballet Sch., 1955. Mem. corps de ballet Nat. Theatre, Split, 1954-58; founder Braecrest Sch. Ballet, Lincoln, R.I., 1958—; founder State Ballet of R.I., Lincoln, 1960—, artistic dir., 1976—; artistic dir. U. R.I. Classical Ballet, Kingston, 1966—, lectr., 1966—.

MARSDEN, MARILYN WEBER, airline executive, consultant; b. N.Y.C., Oct. 27, 1944; d. Martin Jack and Naomi Ruth (Sternberg) Weber; m. Charles Joseph Marsden, Nov. 12, 1988; stepchildren: Anne, George. BA, American U., 1966; MA, New Sch. Social Rsch., 1981. Cert. tchr., N.Y. Elem. sch. tchr. N.Y.C. and Chevy Chase, Md., 1966-70; flight attendant, purser Pan Am. World Airways, Inc., N.Y.C., 1970-72, coord. community action programs, 1972-75, mgr. crew staffing, 1975-76, mgr. mgmt. devel., 1976-78, dir. mgmt. resources, 1978-81, mgr. charter mktg., planning and analysis, 1981-84, dir. contract adminstrn., 1984-91; cons. N.Y.C., 1992—. Aux. police officer, Mounted Div., N.Y.C. Police Dept., 1973-75; organizer Viet Nam Orphan Escort Program, Pearl S. Buck Found., 1974. Recipient Citation of Merit, Nat. Multiple Sclerosis Soc., 1973, Outstanding Achievement award N.Y. Interline Club, 1973. Mem. Nat. Bus. Aircraft Assn. Jewish. Home: 880 5th Ave New York NY 10021-4951

MARSEE, SUSANNE IRENE, lyric mezzo-soprano; b. San Diego, Nov. 26, 1941; d. Warren Jefferson and Irene Rose (Willis) Dowell; m. Mark J. Weinstein, May 1987; 1 child, Zachary. Student, Santa Monica City Coll., 1961; BA in History, UCLA, 1964. Mem. voice faculty Am. Mus. and Dramatic Acad., N.Y.C.; voice faculty The Am. Musical & Dramatic Acad., 1994; assoc. prof. La. State U. Appeared with numerous U.S. opera cos., 1970—, including N.Y.C. Opera, San Francisco Opera, Boston Opera; appeared with fgn. cos., festivals, Mexico City Bellas Artes, 1973, 78, Canary Islands co., 1976, Opera Metropolitana, Caracas, Venezuela, 1977, Spoleto (Italy) Festival, 1977, Aix en Provence (France) Festival, 1977, Calgary, Alta., Can., Montreal, Que., Can., 1986; recorded Tales of Hoffman, ABC/Dunhill Records; TV appearances include Live from Lincoln Ctr., Turk in Italy, Cenerentola, 1980, Live from Wolftrap, Roberto Devereux's, Rigoletto, 1988, A Little Night Music, 1990, Marriage of Figaro, 1991, (PBS TV) Rachel, La Cubana; recs. and CD's Anna Bolena with Ramy, Scotto, Roberto Devereux with Beverly Sills, Roberto Devereux with Monserat Caballé, Tales of Hoffman with Beverly Sills, Rigoletto with Quilico and Carreras; video tape Roberto Devereux with Beverly Sills. Recipient 2d place award Met. Opera Regional Auditions, 1968, San Francisco Opera Regional Auditions 1968; named winner Liederkranz Club Contest, 1970; Gladys Turk Found. grantee, 1968-69; Corbett Found. grantee, 1969-73; Martha Baird Rockefeller grantee, 1969-70, 71-72. Mem. AFTRA, Am. Guild Artists, Nat. Assn. Tchrs. Singing (bd. dirs.). Democrat.

MARSH, CAROLE, author, photographer, publisher; b. Marietta, Ga., Dec. 22, 1946. Pres. Carole Marsh Books, Atlanta, Ga., 1979—; pres. Carole Marsh Interactive Media, Books-on-Disk, CD-ROM for the Home, School and Library, Decatur, 1992—. Author over 2500 books and software including: (children's ednl. series) Carole Marsh State Books, Our Black Heritage Series, Smart Sex Stuff for Kids 7-17, Quantum Leap Books, The Naked Gourmet, Lifewrite and Propub Books, History Mystery Books, Lost Colony Collection; (single titles) The Teddy Bear's Annual Report, A Kid's Book of Smarts, Meet in the Middle, and others. Author various corp. annual reports and econs. communications. Named Communicator of Yr., Assn. Bus. Communicators; recipient Top Honors, Nat. C. of C. Office: Gallopade Publishing Group 359 Milledge Ave Ste 100 Atlanta GA 30312

MARSH, CLARE TEITGEN, school psychologist; b. Manitowoc, Wis., July 7, 1934; d. Clarence Emil and Dorothy (Napiezinski) Teitgen; m. Robert Irving Marsh, Jan. 30, 1955; children: David, Wendy Marsh Tootle, Julie Marsh Domino, Laura Marsh Beltrame. MS in Ednl. Psychology, U. Wis., Milw., 1968. Sch. psychologist Milw. Pub. Schs., 1975-76; lead psychologist West Allis (Wis.)-West Milw. Pub. Schs., 1968—; sch. psychologist Wauwatosa (Wis.) Pub. Schs., 1987; instr. Milw. Sch. Engring., 1989-90, Alverno Coll., 1990—. NDEA fellow, 1966-68. Mem. AAUW, Internat. Sch. Psychologists Assn., Nat. Assn. Sch. Psychologists (del.), Suburban Assn. Sch. Psychologists (pres. 1976-77, 86-87), Wis. Assn. Sch. Psychologists (pres. 1990-91, chmn. membership com. 1980-84, sec. 1985-89, chmn. conv. 1987), Wis. Fedn. Pupil Svcs., Phi Kappa Phi, Pi Lambda Theta (pres.), Kappa Delta Pi, Phi Delta Kappa, Sigma Tau Delta, Alpha Chi Omega. Home: 14140 W Honey Ln New Berlin WI 53151-2442 Office: West Allis Sch System 10230 W Grant St Milwaukee WI 53227-1310

MARSH, FREDDIE, artist, educator; b. Beaver, Pa., Mar. 19, 1927; d. William and Martha Caroline (Chambers) Erzinger; children: Analie Perko, Sylvia Simpson, Don Cartwright, Dorian Cartwright, Jill Cartwright. BFA in Art, Calif. Coll. of Arts & Crafts, Oakland, 1972; MA in Painting, Calif. State U., Chico, 1991. art instr. Calif. State U., Chico, 1991-92; drawing instr. Chico Art Ctr., 1991—, Chico Recreation Dept., 1991—; asst. to chair Arts Task Force, Chico, 1993—. Exhibitions include Chico Art Ctr., 1989, 91, 93, Calif. State U., Chico, 1989, 91, Mendocino Art Ctr., 1989, Third Fl. Gallery, Chico, 1990, Stansbury House, Chico, 1990, Wall St. Ctr., Chico, 1990, 1078 Gallery 10th Anniversary Show, Chico, 1991, 92, Cafe Sandino, Chico, 1992, Zephyr's, Chico, 1992, Audubon Celebration, Chico, 1992, Yuba Sutter Regional Arts Coun., 1992, 93, ARTSCHICO, 1993, Cory's, Chico, 1993, Women's Health Ctr., Paradise, 1993, Red Oak Gallery, Berkeley, 1994. Mem. Calif. State U. Alumni Assn., Calif. Coll. of Arts and Crafts Alumni Assn. Home: 1183 Bille Rd Paradise CA 95969

MARSH, HELEN UNGER, retired educational administrator; b. Grenada, Miss., May 4, 1925; d. John Waugh and Hortense (Baker) Unger; m. Loren C. Marsh, Sept. 4, 1950 (div. Dec. 1981); children: Keith S., Douglas L., Charlene M., Margaret Marsh Woods. AB, Bob Jones U., 1947; MA, Northwestern U., 1950; EdD, Ball State U., 1975. Cert. profl. adminstr., supr., secondary tchr., supt., Ind. Intermittent instr. speech and English Ball State U., Muncie, Ind., 1961-83, mem. adv. bd. for lab. expts., 1987-93; tchr. lang. arts Southside High Sch., Muncie, 1963-74, dept. chmn., 1974-76, dir. guidance, 1976-83; supr. lang. arts and guidance Muncie Community Schs., 1983-87, dir. rsch. and univ. rels., 1987-93; ret., 1993, 1994; judge nat. writing contest Nat. Coun. Tchrs. English, 1974-80; proposal writer Eli Lilly Found.; student placement coord., rschr. coord. Ball State U. and Muncie Community Schs.; community projects coord. Muncie Community Schs.; cons. Brainbow Learning Ctr. Writer, editor, coord. Muncie Community Schs. publs. Bd. dirs. univ. div. Ind. U., Bloomington, 1984-87; bd. dirs. East Ctrl. Ind. Area Libr. Svc., 1987—; chmn. edn. div. Shakespeare Festival, Ind. Com. for Humanities, Muncie, 1987; chair Mayor's Steering Com. for Muncie/Delaware County History, 1994—; cons. Brainbow, Inc., 1993-94; assoc. Minn. Cultural Ctr.. Mem. AAUW, Am. Econ. Rsch. Assn., Assn. for Lifelong Learning, Muncie Bus. and Profl. Women's Club (treas. 1980-82, pres. 1982-84), Delaware County Ret. Tchrs. Assn. (sec. 1993-94). Republican. Methodist. Home: 606 N Alden Rd Muncie IN 47304-3827

MARSH, HELENA ANN, language arts educator; b. Columbus, Ohio, Oct. 26, 1956; d. Arthur L. Steele and Betty Jane (Haken) Brill; m. James E. Marsh, Jan. 18, 1992; children: Danielle, Andrea. BA in English, Lindenwood Coll., 1990, MA in Sch. Counseling with honors, 1994. Asst. dir. admitting St. Louis U. Hosp., 1979-83; lang. arts educator Ft. Zuwalt Sch. Dist., O'Fallon, Mo., 1990—. Author: (poetry) My Children, My Love, 1989. Sponsor Save-A-Student, 1993; organizer, counselor World's of Awareness, St. Peters, Mo., 1992-94; TESOL Lindenwood Coll., St. Charles, Mo., 1989-90. Mem. Nat. Coun. Tchrs. English, Phi Delta Kappa (newspaper editor 1994-95). Republican. Roman Catholic. Office: Ft Zuwalt Sch Dist 300 Knaust Rd Saint Peters MO 63376

MARSH, JOAN KNIGHT, educational film, video and computer software company executive, publisher children's books; b. Butler, Mo., Apr. 8, 1934; d. E. Lyle and Ruth (Hopkins) Knight; m. Alan Reid Marsh, Sept. 27, 1958; children: Alan Reid, Clayton Knight. BA, Tex. Tech. U., 1956. Owner, pres. MarshMedia, Kansas City, Mo., 1969—. Bd. dirs., Crittenton Ctr., Kansas City, 1983-88, Mark Twain Pla. Bank, 1981-89; mem. council Family Study Ctr., U. Mo., Kansas City, 1983-89, Children's Relief Assn. Mercy Hosp., Kansas City, 1984—, pres. 1989-91. Gamma Phi Beta. Republican. Presbyterian. Club: Jr. League (sustaining chmn. 1982-84). Avocation: Egyptology, filmology.

MARSH, ROBERTA REYNOLDS, educator, consultant; b. Kokomo, Ind., June 2, 1939; d. Elwood Bert and Mildred Bell (Wolford) Reynolds; m. Ronald Dean Marsh Sr., Apr. 5, 1958; children: Ronald Jr., Bryan William, Joel Allen. BEd, Ind. U., Kokomo, 1970; MEd, Ind. U., Bloomington, 1971. Cert. tchr., spl. edn. tchr., Ind., Ariz. Tchr. spl. edn. Kokomo Ctr. Schs., 1970-77; tchr. spl. edn. Tempe (Ariz.) Elem. Dist. #3, 1978-86, tchr. civics, geography, English/lit., 1986—. Local dir. Spl. Olympics, Kokomo, 1974-77, Tempe Assn. Retarded Citizens, 1978-88; den mother Boy Scouts Am., Kokomo, 1967-73; leader 4-H Club, Kokomo, 1974-77. Recipient Excellence in Edn. award Tempe Diablo, 1991. Mem. Coun. for Exceptional Children (state pres. 1986-87, Tempe chpt. pres. 1994-95, Outstanding Leader 1985), Internat. Reading Assn., Assn. for Children with Learning Disabilities, Ind. U. Alumni Assn., Alpha Delta Kappa (corr. sec. 1986-88, Theta pres. 1990-92). Democrat. Home: 4113 E Emelita Circle Mesa AZ 85206 Office: Hudson Sch 1325 E Malibu Dr Tempe AZ 85282

MARSHAK, HILARY WALLACH, psychotherapist, owner; b. N.Y.C., May 27, 1950; d. Irving Isaac and Suni (Fox) Wallach; m. Harvey Marshak, Jan. 1, 1981; children: Emily Fox, Jacob Randall. BA, U. Conn., Storrs, 1973; MSW, N.Y.U., 1992; cert., Inst. for Study of Culture, and Ethnicity, N.Y.C., 1994. Cert. social worker, N.Y. Tchr. English Glastonbury (Conn.) High Sch., 1973, U. Autonoma de Guerrero, Acapulco, Mexico, 1974; adminstrv. asst. 4M Pub. Svcs. Corp., N.Y.C., 1975, bus. mgr.; exec. v.p. Vitalmedia Enterprises Inc., N.Y.C., 1977-87, pres., chief exec. officer, 1987—; psychotherapist Fifth Ave. Ctr. Counseling and Psychotherapy, N.Y.C., 1992-95; pvt. practice N.Y.C., 1992—; mktg. cons. Frana Ltd., London, 1988-89. Editor: Before the Bar, 1978-80, Guide to Higher Edn., 1980. Founder Women's Radical Caucus, U. Conn., 1970; broadcaster Sta. WHUS; bd. dirs. N.Y. Theater Ballet, 1990—, Am. Aids Assn., 1992—. Recipient 2nd Place Flowers Ulster County Agrl. Fair, New Paltz, N.Y., 1987, 1st Place Herbs, 1988. Mem. NASW, Am. AIDS Assn. (bd. dirs. 1992—), Soc. for Sci. Study of Sex, Sex Edn. and Info. Coun. of U.S., Nat. Coun. Family Rels. Jewish. Home and Office: 95 Horatio St 629 New York NY 10014-1520

MARSHALL, CAK (CATHERINE ELAINE MARSHALL), music educator, composer; b. Nashville, Nov. 24, 1943; d. Dean Byron and Petula Iris (Bodie) M. BS in Music Edn., Ind. U. Pa., 1965; cert., Hamline U., 1981, 82, 83, Memphis State U., 1985; MME, Duquesne U., 1992. Nat. registered music educator, 1993; vocal music tchr., Pa. Tchr. music Mars (Pa.) Area Sch. Dist., 1965-66; music specialist Fox Chapel (Pa.) Area Sch. Dist., 1966—; Orff specialist Chatham Coll. Fine Arts Camp, Pitts., 1977-91; instr. rep. elem. curriculum Dist. I, Pitts., 1986-92; arts curriculum project Pa. Dept. Edn., 1988. Author: (plays) The Rainbow Recorder, 1988, The Gift Disk Dilemma, 1989; composer, author: (play) Pittsburgh-The City with a Smile on Her Face, 1986, (holiday musical) The Dove That Could Not Fly, 1986, (book) Seasons in Song, 1987, (play) The Search for Happiness, 1990; composer: What Color Was the Baby, 1990, Kaia, 1990, Sing Praises To His Name, 1990, Go In Peace, 1990, Sing Unto The Lord, 1990, I Love America, 1992. Actor North Star Players, Pitts., 1975-80; soloist Landmark Bapt. Ch., Penn Hills, Pa., 1981-86, Bible Bapt. Ch., 1987; performer Pitts. Camerata, 1977-89; group leader Pitts Reocrder Soc., 1985-86; soloist Grace Bapt. Ch., Monroeville, 1991—. Mem. NEA, Am. ORFF-Schulwerk Assn., Pitts. Golden Triangle Chpt. (pres. 1985—), Music Educators Nat. Confl., Pa. Music Educators Assn. (elem. jour. 1986—), Am. Recorder Assn., Pi Kappa Lambda. Baptist. Home: 1707 Kirk Dr Verona PA 15147-3917 Office: O'Hara Elem Sch 115 Cabin Ln Pittsburgh PA 15238-2500

MARSHALL, CAROL JOYCE, clinical research data coordinator; b. Mt. Holly, N.J., July 29, 1967; d. Oliver Jr. and Ruby Jean (Bennefield-Smith) M. BA in Biol. Scis., Rutgers U., 1985-89. Transplant-procurement coord. Nat. Disease Rsch. Interchange, Phila., 1989-90, supr. procurement dept., 1990-91, rsch. mgr., 1991-92; clin. rsch. data coord. U.S. Biosci., West Conshohocken, Pa., 1992-93, G.H. Besselaar Assocs., Princeton, N.J., 1993—. Home: 2211 Durham Ct Mount Laurel NJ 08054 Office: GH Besselaar Assocs 210 Carnegie Ctr Princeton NJ 08540-6233

MARSHALL, CAROLYN ANN M., church official, consultant; b. Springfield, Ill., July 18, 1935; d. Hayward Thomas and Isabelle Bernice (Hayer) McMurray; m. John Alan Marshall, July 14, 1956 (dec. Sept. 1990); children: Margaret Marshall Bushman, Cynthia Marshall Kyrouac, Clinton, Carol. Student, De Pauw U., 1952-54; BSBA, Drake U., 1956; D of Pub. Svc. (hon.), De Pauw U., 1983; LHD (hon.), U. Indpls., 1990. Corp. sec. Marshall Studios, Inc., Veedersburg, Ind., 1956-89, exec. cons., 1989-93; sec. Gen. Conf., lay leader South Ind. conf. United Meth. Ch., 1988—; Carolyn M. Marshall chair in women studies Bennett Coll., Greensboro, N.C., 1988; fin. cons. Lucille Raines Residence, Inpls., 1977—. Pres. Fountain Ctrl. Band Boosters, Veedersburg, 1975-77; del. Gen. Conf., United Meth. Ch., 1980, 84, 88, 92, pres. women's divsn. Gen. Bd. Global Ministries, 1984-88; bd. dirs. Franklin (Ind.) United Meth. Home. Home: 204 N Newlin St Veedersburg IN 47987-1358

MARSHALL, CONSUELO BLAND, federal judge; b. Knoxville, Tenn., Sept. 28, 1936; d. Clyde Theodore and Annie (Brown) Arnold; m. George Edward Marshall, Aug. 30, 1959; children: Michael Edward, Laurie Ann. A.A., Los Angeles City Coll., 1956; B.A., Howard U., 1958, LL.B., 1961. Bar: Calif. 1962. Dep. atty. City of L.A., 1962-67; assoc. Cochran & Atkins, L.A., 1968-70; commr. L.A. Superior Ct., 1971-76; judge Inglewood Mcpl. Ct., 1976-77, L.A. Superior Ct., 1977-80, U.S. Dist. Ct. Central Dist. Calif., L.A., 1980—; lectr. U.S. Information Agy. in Yugoslavia, Greece and Italy, 1984, in Nigera and Ghana, 1991, in Ghana, 1992. Contbr. articles to profl. jours.; notes editor Law Jour. Howard U. Mem. adv. bd. Richstone Child Abuse Center. Recipient Judicial Excellence award Criminal Cts. Bar Assn., 1992; research fellow Howard U. Law Sch., 1959-60;. Mem. State Bar Calif., Calif. Women Lawyers Assn., Calif. Assn. Black Lawyers, Calif. Judges Assn., Black Women Lawyers Assn., Los Angeles County Bar Assn., Nat. Assn. Women Judges, NAACP, Urban League, Beta Phi Sigma. Office: US Dist Ct 312 N Spring St Los Angeles CA 90012-4701*

MARSHALL, ELLEN RUTH, lawyer; b. N.Y.C., Apr. 23, 1949; d. Louis and Faith (Gladstone) M. AB, Yale U., 1971; JD, Harvard U., 1974. Bar: Calif. 1975, D.C. 1981, N.Y. 1989. Assoc. McKenna & Fitting, Los Angeles, 1975-80; ptnr. McKenna, Conner & Cuneo, Los Angeles and Orange County, Calif., 1980-88, Morrison & Foerster, Orange County, Calif., 1988—. Mem. ABA (bus. law sect., savs. inst. com., asset securitization com., tax sect., employee benefits com.), Orange County Bar Assn. Club: Center (Costa Mesa, Calif.). Office: Morrison & Foerster 19900 Macarthur Blvd Irvine CA 92715-2445

MARSHALL, JANE PRETZER, newspaper editor; b. Chase County, Kans.; married; 2 children. BS in Home Econs. and Journalism, Kans. State U., 1967; student, Tex. A&M, U. Mo., Tex. Christian U., Brite Divinity Sch. Asst. editor dept. agr. info. Tex. Agrl. Ext. Sta. Tex. A&M U., College Station, 1967-70; staff writer Gazette-Telegraph, Colorado Springs, Colo., 1970-72; editor corporate publ. Colorado Interstate, Colorado Springs, 1972-75; co-editor The Pampa (Tex.) News, 1975-78; exec. features editor Ft. Worth Star-Telegram, 1978-84; features editor Denver Post, 1984-88, Houston Chronicle, 1988—. Recipient 1st place for feature writing Tex. AP Mng. Editors Assn., 1978. Mem. Am. Assn. Sunday and Features Editors (bd. dirs., founding chairperson Features First), Women's Found. Health Edn. and Rsch. (bd. dirs.), Journalism and Women Symposium (1st pres.). Office: Houston Chronicle 801 Texas St Houston TX 77002-2907

MARSHALL, JOSEPHINE PRINCE, retired educator, councilwoman; b. Bellwood, W.Va., May 8, 1931; d. Robert Lee and Mattie Marie (Clinton) Prince; m. Lewis Randolph Marshall, Apr. 20, 1950; children: Timothy LeRoy, Lewis Anthony, Teresa Ellen. BS, Bluefield State Coll., 1950; MEd, U. Va., 1968; cert. in advance grad. studies, Va. Tech., Balcksburg, 1984. Tchr. Mecklenburg Pub. Schs., Clarksville, Va., 1952-68, Halifax County Pub. Schs., South Boston, Va., 1968-71; instr. fgn. langs. Ctrl. Va. C.C., Lynchburg, Va., 1971-75; assoc. prof. Danville (Va.) C.C., 1975-93, ret., 1993; mem. South Boston City Coun., 1984—, chmn. policy com., 1991—; bd. dirs. Halifax Regional Hosp., South Boston, 1988—. Bd. dirs. Halifax/South Boston C. of C., 1986-88; chmn. Dem. Com., South Boston, 1990—; pres. Habitat for Humanity, South Boston, 1991—; pres. South Boston Devel. Corp., 1991—; mem. Va. Adv. Com. on Intergovernmental Rels., vice chmn., 1992—. Mem. Va. Mcpl. League (exec. com. 1988—, pres.), Delta Sigma Theta. Democrat. Methodist. Office: South Boston City Coun Main St South Boston VA 24592

MARSHALL, JULIE W. GREGOVICH, engineering executive; b. Pasadena, Calif., Mar. 3, 1953; d. Gibson Marr and Anna Grace (Peterson) Wolfe; m. Michael Roy Gregovich Dec. 18, 1976 (div. June 1994); children: Christianna, Kerry Leigh; m. Robert Brandon Marshall, Aug. 6, 1994. BA magna cum laude, Randolph-Macon Woman's Coll., 1975; MBA, Pepperdine U., 1983. cert. tchr. K-12, Calif. Test engr. Westinghouse Hanford, Richland, Wash., 1975-76; startup engr. Bechtel Power Corp., Norwalk, Calif., 1976-77; test engr. Wash. Pub. Power, Richland, 1978-80; from mgr. to v.p. Sun Tech. Svcs., Mission Viejo, Calif., 1983-93; cons. Mission Energy Co., Irvine, Calif., 1993-94; owner, CEO, pres. Key Employee Svcs., Inc., Key Largo, Fla., 1994—. contbr. article to jour. Named Young Career

Woman of the Yr. Wash. Pub. Power Supply System, 1979. Mem. Am. Nuc. Soc. (mem. bd. trustees pub. edn. program 1992—), Phi Beta Kappa.

MARSHALL, LINDA LOUISE, radiological nurse; b. Kansas City, Mo., Sept. 19, 1952; d. Earl Franklin and Glen Louise (Brooks) M.; m. Archibald Wallace Templeton, Nov. 10, 1984. BSN with distinction, U. Kans., 1974. RN, Kans.; cert. CPR, BCLS. Staff, charge nurse, pediatric inpatient unit Univ. Kans. Med. Ctr., Kansas City, Kans., 1974-79; ambulatory care nurse Univ. Kans. Med. Ctr., Kansas City, 1979, radiology nurse mgr., dept. diagnostic radiology, 1979—; lectr. and presenter in field. Contbr. articles to profl. jours. Vol. Kansas City Metro-wide Nat. Nurses' Day Celebration, 1989. Mem. ANA (rep. joint meeting com. nursing practice standards & guidelines 1989—, intersociety liaison, rep. ho. dels.), Am. Radiol. Nurses Assn. (liaison Nursing Orgn. Liaison Forum 1987—, bd. dirs. 1987—, mem. com. nominations 1988-89, chair com. strategic planning 1988—, co-chair resource com. patient edn. 1985-87, chair com. standards and credentials 1989-90, pres.-elect 1990-91, pres. 1992—), U. Kans. Med. Ctr. Aux., Nurses' Alumni Assn. U. Kans., Sigma Theta Tau (Delta chpt.). Home: 33 Rhetts Bluff Rd Johns Island SC 29455-5200 Office: U Kans Med Ctr Rainbow Blvd At 39th St Kansas City KS 66103

MARSHALL, LINDA RAE, cosmetic company executive; b. Provo, Utah, Aug. 1, 1940; d. Arvid O. and Tola V. (Broderick) Newman; children: James, John. Student Brigham Young U., 1958-59, U. Utah, 1960-61. Buyer, Boston Store, 1961-62; sec. Milw. Gas & Light Co., 1962-64; mktg. rep. Elysee Cosmetics, Madison, Wis., 1971-75, pres., 1975—; v.p., Dionne, Inc., 1987—, ptnr. Pres. Falk Sch. PTA, Madison. Author: Discover the Other Woman in You, 1980; monthly beauty columnist Beauty Fashion mag.; contbg. author Cosmetic Industry Sci. and Regulatory Found., 1984. Mem. Aestheticians Internat. Assn. (adv. bd.), Cosmetic, Toiletry and Fragrance Assn. (exec. com., bd dirs., chmn. voluntary program, chmn. small cosmetic com., membership com. task force), Cosmetic Exec. Women. Address: PO Box 4084 Madison WI 53711

MARSHALL, LYNETTE LOUISE, development director; b. Peoria, Ill., Apr. 29, 1961; d. Rodger Dean and Janet Louise (Bateman) M.; m. Jeffery L. Ford, Oct. 27, 1991; stepchild, Michael Douglas; child, Katharine Marie. BS in Agr., U. Ill., 1983. Dir. resource devel. Coll. Agr., U. Ill., Urbana, 1983—. Author: (brochure) Family Farm, 1989 (Bronze award Coun. for the Advancement and Support of Edn.). Chair Ministry with Women, The Wesley Found., Urbana, 1989-92; pres. The Wesley Found. Bd. Trustees, Urbana, 1991. Mem. NOW, Nat. Agr. Alumni and Devel. Assn. (pres. 1992-94), Nat. Soc. Fund Raising Execs., Religious Coalition for Abortion Rights, Rotary of Savoy (internat. com. chair 1991-93).

MARSHALL, MARGARET DELORES, securities trader, marketing professional; b. Kingston, Jamaica, West Indies, Mar. 20, 1935; came to U.S., 1959; d. Vincent and Jeslyn Ianthy (Nunez) Brown; m. Frances Ustace Marshall, Oct. 30, 1957 (dec. Feb. 1988); children: Christopher, Stephen, Kimberly. BS, NYU, 1963. Registered securities-ins. broker, Okla. Mktg. assoc. Hudson Pulp & Paper, N.Y.C., 1963-65; regional sales mgr. Celebrity Gems, N.Y.C., 1975-83; regional v.p. A.L. Williams Ins. Co., Atlanta, 1983-84; tng. dir. Pre-Paid Legal Svcs., Inc., Ada, Okla., 1985-88, dir., 1991—; regional v.p. U.S. Legal Protection Co., Clearwater, Fla., 1989-91. Vol. coord. Miracle Children's Network, Atlanta, 1989, Atlanta Womens Polit. Caucus, Atlanta, 1990. Fellow: Leads & Contact (asst. dir. 1987-90), Ind. Order Foresters (dep. 1989-90), Ga. Crime Prevention Assn. Office: Direct Marketing Cons 6065 Roswell Rd NE Ste 1172 Atlanta GA 30328-4019

MARSHALL, MARGARET HILARY, lawyer; b. Newcastle, Natal, South Africa, Sept. 1, 1944; came to U.S., 1968; d. Bernard Charles and Hilary A.D. (Anderton) M; m. Samuel Shapiro, Dec. 14, 1968 (div. Apr. 1982); m. Anthony Lewis, Sept. 23, 1984. BA, Witwatersrand U., Johannesburg, 1966; MEd, Harvard U., 1969; JD, Yale U., 1976; LHD (hon.), Regis Coll., 1993. Bar: Mass. 1977, U.S. Dist. Ct. Mass., U.S. Dist. Ct. N.H., U.S. Dist. Ct. D.C., U.S. Dist. Ct. (ea. dist.) Mich., U.S. Tax Ct., U.S. Ct. Appeals (1st, 11th and D.C. cirs.), U.S. Supreme Ct. Assoc. Csaplar & Bok, Boston, 1976-83, ptnr., 1983-89; ptnr. Choate, Hall & Stewart, Boston, 1989-92; v.p., gen. counsel Harvard U., Cambridge, Mass., 1992—; mem. jud. nominating coun., 1987-90, 92; chairperson ct. rules subcom. Alternative Dispute Resolution Working Group, 1985-87; mem. fed. appts. commn., 1993; mem. adv. com. Supreme Judicial Ct., 1989-92, mem. gender equality com., 1989-94; mem. civil justice adv. group U.S. Dist. Ct. Mass., 1991-93; spl. counsel Jud. Conduct Commn., 1988-92; trustee Mass. Continuing Legal Edn., Inc., 1990-92. Trustee Africa News, Crittenton Hastings House, Africa Fund, Regis Coll., 1993—; mem. lawyer's fund com. Sch. Vols. for Boston (Star); bd. dirs. Internat. Design Conf. Aspen, 1986-92, Boston Mcpl. Res. Bur., 1990—, Supreme Judicial Ct. Hist. Soc., 1990-94, sec., 1990-94. Fellow Am. Bar Found. (Mass. state chair); mem. Boston Bar Assn. (treas. 1988-89, v.p. 1989-90, pres.-elect 1990-91, pres. 1991-92), Internat. Women's Forum, Mass. Women's Forum, Boston Club, Phi Beta Kappa (hon.). Home: 8 Lowell St Cambridge MA 02138-4726 Office: Harvard U Massachusetts Hall Cambridge MA 02138

MARSHALL, MARGO, artistic director; b. Louisville, Nov. 3, 1934; d. Irving Robert and Elizabeth (Greenleaf) Lisbony; m. Jay C. Marshall, 1952 (div. 1971); 1 child, Dennis. BA, U. Houston, 1953. Pvt. tchr. dance Houston, 1950-58, owner, operator pvt. dance sch., 1958—; guest tchr. Joffrey Sch., N.Y., Internat. Acad. Dance, Portugal, Louisville Ballet, Boston Ballet's Summer Workshops, 1981-85, The Place, London, and others; part-time faculty mem. High Sch. for the Performing and Visual Arts, Houston; tchr. dance U. Houston, Sam Houston State U. Artistic dir. City Ballet Houston, 1967—; mem. dance panel Cultural Arts Coun. Houston; advisor Tex. Commn. on the Arts. Recipient Adjudicator award Mid-States Regional Ballet Assn., 1986. Mem. Southwestern Regional Ballet Assn. (officer 1965—). Office: City Ballet 9902 Long Point Rd Houston TX 77055-4199

MARSHALL, MARILYN JOSEPHINE, lawyer; b. Dayton, Ohio, May 31, 1945; d. Foy Wylie and Inez Virginia (Smith) Gard; m. Alan George Marshall, June 13, 1965; children: Gwendolyn Scott, Brian George. Student, Northwestern U., 1963-65; BA, Stanford U., 1967; cert. in teaching, U. B.C., Vancouver, 1977; JD, Capital Law Sch., Columbus, Ohio, 1985. Bar: Ohio 1985, Fla. 1993, U.S. Dist. Ct. (so. dist.) Ohio, U.S. Dist. Ct. (no. dist., mid. dist., and so. dist.) Fla., U.S. Ct. Appeals (6th cir.), U.S. Ct. Appeals (11th cir.). Tchr. Sutherland Secondary Sch., North Vancouver, B.C., 1977-79; instr. Brit. Coll. Inst. Tech., Burnaby, B.C., 1979-80; assoc. Crabbe, Brown, Jones, Potts & Schmidt, Columbus, Ohio, 1985-86; clk. to judge U.S. Dist. Ct. (so. dist.) Ohio, Columbus, 1986-88; clk. to justice Ohio Supreme Ct., 1988-89; assoc. Squire, Sanders & Dempsey, 1989-92; with Columbus City Atty.'s Office, Columbus, Ohio, 1992-93; asst. atty. gen. civil divsn. State of Fla., Tallahassee, 1994—. Mem. ABA, Am. Judicature Soc., Ohio Bar Assn., Fla. Bar Assn., Tallahassee Bar Assn., Capital U. Law Sch. Alumni Assn., Northwestern U. Alumni Assn. Republican. Office: care of Office HRS Gen Counsel 1323 Winewood Blvd Bldg E Rm 200 Tallahassee FL 32301

MARSHALL, MARY JONES, civic worker; b. Billings, Mont.; d. Leroy Nathaniel and Janet (Currie) Dailey; m. Harvey Bradley Jones, Nov. 15, 1952 (dec. 1989); children: Dailey, Janet Currie, Ellis Bradley; m. Boyd T. Marshall, June 27, 1990. Student, Carleton Coll., 1943-44, U. Mont., 1944-46, UCLA, 1959. Owner Mary Jones Interiors. Founder, treas. Jr. Art Council, L.A. County Mus., 1953-55, v.p., 1955-56; mem. costume council Pasadena (Calif.) Philharm.; co-founder Art Rental Gallery, 1953, chmn. art and architecture tour, 1955; founding mem., sec. Art Alliance, Pasadena Art Mus., 1955-56; benefit chmn. Pasadena Girls Club, 1959, bd. dirs., 1958-60; chmn. L.A. Tennis Patron's Assn. Benefit, 1965; sustaining Jr. League Pasadena; mem. docent council L.A. County Mus.; mem. costume council L.A. County Mus. Art., program chmn. 20th Century Greatest Designers; mem. blue ribbon com. L.A. Music Ctr.; benefit chmn. Venice com. Internat. Fund for Monuments, 1971; bd. dirs. Art Ctr. 100, Pasadena, 1988—; pres. The Pres.'s L.A. Children's Bur., 1989; co-chmn. benefit Harvard Coll. Scholarship Fund, 1974, steering com. benefit, 1987, Otis Art Inst., 1975, 90th Anniversary of Children's Bureau of L.A., 1994; mem. Harvard-Radcliffe scholarship dinner com., 1985; mem. adv. bd. Estelle Doheny Eye Found., 1976, chmn. benefit, 1980; adv. bd. Loyola U. Sch. Fine Arts, L.A., Art Ctr. Sch. Design, Pasadena, Calif., 1987—; patron chmn. Benefit Achievement Rewards for Coll. Scientists, 1988; chmn. com. Sch. Am. Ballet Benefit, 1988, N.Y.C.; bd. dirs. Founders Music Ctr., L.A., 1977-81; mem. nat. adv. council Sch. Am. Ballet, N.Y.C., nat. co-chmn. gala, 1980; adv. council on fine arts Loyola-Marymount U.; mem. L.A. Olympic Com., 1984, The Colleagues; founding mem. Mus. Contemporary Art, 1986; chmn. The Pres.'s Benefit L.A. Children's Bur., 1990; exec. com. L.A. Alive for L.A. Music Ctr., 1992; mem. exec. com. Children's Bur. of L.A. Found., 1992; chmn. award dinner Phoenix House, 1994. Mem. Am. Parkinson Disease Assn. (steering com. 1991), Valley Hunt Club (Pasadena), Calif. Club (L.A.), Kappa Alpha Theta. Home: 10375 Wilshire Blvd Apt 8B Los Angeles CA 90024-4727

MARSHALL, MARYANN CHORBA, office administrator; b. Scranton, Pa., Apr. 18, 1952; d. Edward M. and Mildred (Polc) Chorba; m. Daniel V. Marshall III. BA, Emmanuel Coll., 1974. Personal, social sec. Jordan Embassy Mil. Office, Washington, 1974-76; exec. asst, office mgr. Jordan Embassy Info. Bur., Washington, 1976-81; asst. to pres. Nat. Press Club, Washington, 1982-91. Mem. League Rep. Women. Republican. Roman Catholic. Home: 1140 23rd St NW Washington DC 20037-1437 Office: 1010 Vermont Ave NW #301 Washington DC 20005

MARSHALL, NANCY HAIG, library administrator; b. Stamford, Conn., Nov. 3, 1932; d. Harry Percival and Dorothy Charlotte (Price) Haig; m. William Hubert Marshall, Dec. 28, 1953; children—Bruce Davis, Gregg Price, Lisa Reynolds, Jeanine Haig. B.A., Ohio Wesleyan U., 1953; M.A.L.S., U. Wis., 1972. Dir. Wis. Inter Libr. Svcs., Madison, 1972-79; Reference librarian U. Wis., Madison, 1972, assoc. dir. univ. libraries, 1979-86; dean univ. librs. Coll. William and Mary, Williamsburg, Va., 1986—; mem. adv. com. Copyright Office, Washington, 1978-82; dir. USBE, Inc., Washington, 1983-86; trustee OCLC, Inc., Dublin, Ohio, 1982-88. Contbr. articles to profl. jours. Mem. ALA (coun. 1980-88, 90-93), Wis. Libr. Assn. (Libr. of the Yr. award 1982), Va. Libr. Assn., Beta Phi Mu. Office: Coll William and Mary E G Swem Libr Williamsburg VA 23185

MARSHALL, NAVARRE, retired secondary educator; b. Stockton, Calif., Oct. 31, 1916; d. Winfield Scott and Elizabeth (Brophy) Baggett; m. Robert Frank Marshall, Aug. 10, 1947; 1 child, Roberta Navarre Marshall. BA, San Francisco State U., 1937; postgrad., U. Calif., Berkeley, 1945-47, U. Calif., Santa Cruz, 1970-72. Cert. elem.-jr. high tchr. Tchr. Pittsburg (Calif.) Sch. Dist., 1937-40, Martinez (Calif.) Sch. Dist., 1941-49, Pajaro Valley Sch. Dist., Watsonville, Calif., 1958-76; ret., 1976. Sec., sponsor Watsonville Friends of the Libr. Mem. AAUW (sec. 1963-64, pres. Watsonville br. 1992-93, sec. 1994-95), Calif. Tchrs. Assn., Order Ea. Star, Delta Kappa Gamma (charter pres. 1961-62), Internat. Zeta Epsilon (charter pres. 1961-62, chpt. pres. 1986-88, scholarship chair 1984-86, 88-90, Woman Making History award 1994). Democrat.

MARSHALL, (C.) PENNY, actress, director; b. N.Y.C., Oct. 15, 1943; d. Anthony W. and Marjorie Irene (Ward) M.; m. Michael Henry (div.); 1 child, Tracy Lee; m. Robert Reiner, Apr. 10, 1971 (div. 1979). Student, U. N.Mex., 1961-64. Appeared on numerous television shows, including The Odd Couple, 1972-74, Friends and Lovers (co-star), 1974, Let's Switch, 1974, Wives (pilot), 1975, Chico and the Man, 1975, Mary Tyler Moore, 1975, Heaven Help Us, 1975, Saturday Night Live, 1975-77, Happy Days, 1975, Battle of Network Stars (ABC special), 1976, Barry Manilow special, 1976, The Tonight Show, 1976-77, Dinah, 1976-77, Mike Douglas Show, 1975-77, Merv Griffin Show, 1976-77, Blansky's Beauties, 1977, Network Battle of the Sexes, 1977, Laverne and Shirley (co-star), 1976-83; TV films More Than Friends, 1978, Love Thy Neighbor, 1984; appeared in motion pictures How Sweet It Is, 1967, The Savage Seven, 1968, The Grasshopper, 1970, 1941, 1979, Movers and Shakers, 1985, The Hard Way, 1991, Hocus Pocus, 1993; dir. films: Jumpin' Jack Flash, 1986, Big, 1988, Awakenings, 1990, A League of Their Own, 1992, Renaissance Man, 1994; co-exec. prodr. TV series A League of Their Own, 1993 (also dir. pilot). Office: care CAA/Todd Smith 9830 Wilshire Blvd Beverly Hills CA 90212-1825

MARSHALL, SHARON BOWERS, nursing educator, director clinical trials; b. Alameda, Calif.; d. Stanley Jay and Rosalie Kathryn (Soldati) Bowers; m. Lawrence F. Marshall; children: Derek, Kathryn, Samantha. BS in Nursing, San Francisco State U., 1970. RN. Charge nurse med./surg. unit Mt. Zion Hosp., San Francisco, 1970-73, charge nurse med./surg. ICU, 1973-75; clin. nurse U. Calif. San Diego Med. Ctr., 1975-78, coordinator neurotrauma study, 1978-79, project coordinator Nat. Traumatic Coma Data Bank, 1979-88, project mgr. Comprehensive Cen. Nervous System Injury Ctr., 1979-86, mgr. neurotrauma research, 1984-91; asst. clin. prof. neurol. surg. U. Calif. San Diego Sch. Medicine, 1992—; dir. study Internat. Tirilazad Study, 1991—; prin. investigator Internat. Selfotel Trial, 1994—. Author: Head Injury, 1981; Neuroscience Critical Care: Pathophysiology and Patient Management, 1990; mem. editorial rev. bd. Jour. Neuroscience Nursing, 1984-86, Brain Injury, 1985-91; contbr. articles to profl. jours. Mem. Internat. Soc. Study of Traumatic Brain Injury, Am. Assn. Neurosci. Nursing. Office: 1899 McKee St Ste 200 San Diego CA 92110

MARSHALL, SHEILA HERMES, lawyer; b. N.Y.C., Jan. 17, 1934; d. Paul Milton and Julia Angela (Meagher) Hermes; m. James Josiah Marshall, Sept. 30, 1967; 1 child, James J.H. BA, St. John's U., N.Y.C., 1959; JD, NYU, 1963. Bar: N.Y. 1964, U.S. Ct. Appeals (2d, 3d, 5th and D.C. cirs.), U.S. Supreme Ct. 1970. Assoc. LeBoeuf, Lamb, Greene & MacRae, N.Y.C., 1963-72, ptnr., 1973—; specialist in field. Mem. ABA, N.Y. State Bar Assn., Assn. of Bar of City of N.Y. Republican. Home: 1035 Park Ave New York NY 10028-0912 Office: LeBoeuf Lamb Greene & MacRae 125 W 55th St New York NY 10019-4513

MARSHALL, SUSAN LOCKWOOD, civic worker; b. Orange, N.J., Dec. 2, 1939; d. Richard Douglas and Helen Lockwood (Stratford) Nelson; B.E., Wheelock Coll., 1961; m. William Pendleton Marshall, Aug. 20, 1960; children: Jill, James. Vol., Newton-Wellesley (Mass.) Hosp., 1962-63, New Eyes for the Needy, Inc., 1963-64, amblyopia screening program, Short Hills, N.J., 1969-71; bd. dirs. Jr. League of Oranges and Short Hills, Inc., 1967-69, 70-72, corr. sec., 1970-72; fund raising vol. Children's Aid and Adoption Soc. N.J., 1969-73, dir., 1970-73, asst. sec., 1970-72, 1st v.p., 1972-73; bd. dirs. Jr. League Stamford-Norwalk (Conn.), 1974-78, asst. treas., 1976-77, treas., 1977-78; bd. dirs. Program One to One, Inc., 1975-76, also treas.; vol. Voluntary Action Center 1975-76; bd. dirs. Episcopal Churchwomen of St. Luke's Parish, 1974-75, 76-81, 2d v.p., 1976-77, asst. treas., 1977-78, treas., 1978-80, pres., 1980-81; bd. dirs. Lockwood Mathews Mansion Mus., 1979-88, 89—, vol., 1979, treas., 1979-88, 89—, v.p., 1983-88; mem. council Darien Sch. Parent Bd., 1978-83, recording sec. 1981-83; bd. dirs. Middlesex Jr. High Parents Assn., 1979-83, treas., 1982-83; mem. The Vol. Ctr., 1984—; mem. vol. mgmt. assistance program adv. comm. Darien Chpt. Am. Field Service, 1984-87; Darien High Sch. Parents Assn., 1982-85, chmn., 1984-85; bd. dirs. Darien United Way, 1984-95, asst. treas., 1988—, treas. 1995—. Address: 358 Hollow Tree Ridge Rd Darien CT 06820-3218

MARSHALL, TRAUTE M., publishing executive; b. Vienna, Austria, Jan. 7, 1942; came to U.S., 1966; d. Albrecht and Gertrud (Tittelbach) Maass; m. Robert L. Marshall, Sept. 9, 1966; children: Eric, Brenda. MA, State Conservatory, Hamburg, Germany, 1966, U. Chgo., 1968; PhD, U. Chgo., 1974. Accredited translator. Prodn. dir. Ligature, Inc., Boston, 1989-91, mng. dir., 1991-93; dir. prodn. and project mgmt. Silver, Burdett, Ginn, Needham, Mass., 1993—. Republican. Home: 100 Chestnut St Newton MA 02165 Office: Silver Burdett Ginn 160 Gould St Needham MA 02194

MARSHALL, WENDY J., surgeon, educator; b. London, July 16, 1946; d. Frederick and Alice (Robinson) M. BS in Physical Therapy, London U., Eng., 1968; MD, U. Vt., U.S.A., 1978. Diplomate Am. Bd. Surgery; cert. ATLS. Physical therapist Guy's Hosp., London, 1968-70, S.W.M. Hosp., Galt, Ont., Can., 1970; asst. dir. physical therapy Med. Ctr. Hosp. of Vt., Burlington, Vt., 1971-74; resident in gen. surgery U. Hosp. Vt., Burlington, Vt., 1978-83; fellow traumatology and critical care Md. Inst. of Emergency Med. Svcs. Systems, Balt., 1983-84; asst. prof. surgery Eastern Va. Med. Sch., 1984-87; asst. prof. surgery Stritch Sch. Medicine, Loyola U. of Chgo., 1987-91, assoc. prof. surgery, 1991—; traumatologist Norfolk Gen. Hosp., 1984, med. dir. of trauma, 1984-87; chief sect. trauma and critical care, dir. trauma svcs. Loyola U. Med. Ctr., 1987, med. dir. aeromedical program, 1988-92; asst. dir. clin. affairs Shock Trama Inst., Loyola U. Med. Ctr., 1992—; med. dir. Tidewater Emergency Med. Svcs. Coun., 1984-87, Tissue Bank Com. Eastern Va. Transplant Program, 1984-87, Norfolk EMS, 1987; dir. burn unit com. Norfolk Gen. Hosp., 1984-87, trauma and disaster com., 1984-87; predsl. physician trauma State Va., 1985-87, State Ill., 1988-92; bd. mem. Ill. Trauma Adv. Bd. Ill. Dept Health, 1994—; facualty coun. Loyola U. Chgo., 1994—; lectr. in the field. Author: (with others) Minimally Invasive Surgery, 1994, Chemical Paralysis in the Emergency and I.C.U. Settings, 1995; author (with Maull) Missed Injuries, 1995; movies: Insights in Surgery, Laparoscopy in the Evaluation of the Septic Intensive Care Unit Patient, Laparoscopy in the Evaluation of the Trauma Patient; editor: H.L.S. and SAGE's, 1993. Fellow Am. Bd. Surgery; mem. AMA, Internat. Soc. Burn Injuries, Norfolk Acad. Medicine, Va. Surgical Soc., Va. Trauma Soc., Am. Trauma Soc., Am. Coll. Surgeons (Chgo. com. on trauma), Eastern Assn. Surgery of Trauma, Air Medal Physician Assn., Am. Assn. Surgery of Trauma, Chgo. Surgical Soc., Am. Soc. Gen. Surgeons, Air Medal Physicians Assn. (exec. bd. 1992, steering com. 1992, rsch. com. chairperson), Alpha Omega Alpha. Editorial adv. bd. Journal of Neurological Injuries, 1993—. Office: Loyola U Dept Surgery 2160 S First Ave Maywood IL 60153

MARSHALL-NADEL, NATHALIE, artist, writer, educator; b. Pitts., Nov. 10, 1932; d. Clifford Benjamin and Clarice (Stille) Marshall; m. Robert Alfred Van Buren, May 1, 1952 (div. June 1965); children: Christine Van Buren Popovic, Clifford Marshall Van Buren, Jennifer Van Buren Lake; m. David Arthur Nadel, Dec. 30, 1976. AFA, Silvermine Coll. Art, New Canaan, Conn., 1967; BFA, U. Miami, Coral Gables, 1977, MA, 1982, PhD in English and Fine Art, 1982. Instr. humanities Miami Ednl. Consortium, Miami Shores, Fla., 1977-79, Barry U., Miami Shores, 1979-81, U. Miami, Coral Gables, 1977-81; sr. lectr. Nova U., Ft. Lauderdale, Fla., 1981-84, assoc. prof. humanities, 1985-86; prof. art, chair dept. art. Old Coll., Reno, Nev., 1986-88; chief artist Rockefeller U., N.Y.C., 1973-75; asst. registrar Lowe Art Mus., Coral Gables, 1976-78; co-founder, dir. The Bakehouse Art Complex, Miami, 1984-86; advisor, bd. mem. NAH YAH EE (Indian children's art exhibits), Weimar, Calif., 1984—; mem. adv. bd. New World Sch. Arts, Miami, 1985-86. One-woman shows include Silvermine Coll. Art, New Canaan, Conn., 1968, Ingber Gallery, Greenwich, 1969, Capricorn Gallery, N.Y.C., 1969, Pierson Coll. at Yale U., New Haven, 1970, The Art Barn, Greenwich, 1972, Art Unltd., N.Y.C., 1973, Benevy Gallery, N.Y.C., 1974, Richter Libr., U. Miami, 1985, Nova U., Ft. Lauderdale, 1985, Ward Nasse Gallery, N.Y.C., 1985, Old Coll., Reno, 1986, Washoe County Libr., Reno, 1987, Sabal Palms Gallery, Gulfport, Fla., 1992, Ambiance Gallery, St. Petersburg, 1995; group shows include: Capricorn Gallery, N.Y.C., 1968, Ingber Gallery, Greenwich, 1968, Compass Gallery, N.Y.C., 1970, Optimums Gallery, Westport, Conn., 1970, Finch Coll. Mus., N.Y.C., 1971, Town Hall Art Gallery, Stamford, Conn., 1973, 74, Jewish Community Ctr., Miami Beach, 1981, Continuum Gallery, Miami Beach, 1982, South Fla. Art Inst., Hollywood, Fla., 1984, Met. Mus., Coral Gables, Fla., 1985, Ward Nasse Gallery, N.Y.C., 1985, Brunnier Mus., Iowa State U., Ames, 1986, Nat. Mus. of Women in The Arts Libr., Washington, 1987, 89, U.S. Art in Embassies Program, 1987-88, UN World Conf. Women, Nairobi, 1987, Raymond James Invitational, St. Petersburg, Fla., 1989-92, Arts Ctr., St. Petersburg, 1990, 91, 92, Global Gallery, Tampa, Fla., 1990, 91, Sabal Palms Gallery, Gulfport, Fla., 1992, No. Nat. Nicolet Coll., Rhineland, Wis., 1992, Internat. Biennale, Bordeaux, France, 1993, Salon de Vieux Colombier, Paris, 1993, Synchronicity Space, N.Y.C., 1993, Women's Internat. Biennal, Stockholm, 1994, Tampa Arts Forum, Fla., 1995; author, artist: Vibrations on Revelations, 1973, The Firebird, 1982, Homage to John Donne's Holy Sonnets 10 & 13, 1987, Tidepool, 1995; numerous artist books, 1968—; author: Be Organized for College, 1980; artist: (children's book) The Desert: What Lives There?, 1972; editor, designer: Court Theaters of Europe, 1982; writer, dir. T.V. programs Moutain Mandala: Autumn, Mountain Mandala: Winter, The Unexpected, 1992; contbr. poems to poetry mags., articles to profl. jours. Recipient Sponsor's award for Painting Greenwich Art Soc., 1967; Steven Buffton Meml. award Am. Bus. Women's Assn., 1980; grantee Poets & Writers, 1993; one of 300 global artists in Internat. Hope and Optimism Portfolio, Oxford. Mem. MLA, Coll. Art Assn., Nat. Women's Studies Assn., Women's Caucus for Art (nat. adv. bd. 1983-88, pres. Miami chpt. 1984-86, southeast regional v.p. 1986). Address: 2914 Clinton St South Gulfport FL 33707

MARSHALL-NOLT, SYLVIA JANE, rehabilitation nurse; b. Greensboro, N.C., Nov. 21, 1953; d. Troy and Audrey (Southard) Marshall; m. Glenn Nolt, Dec. 19, 1992. BSBA, High Point U., 1976; ASN, Valencia C.C., 1987. RN, Fla.; cert. rehab. nurse. Apparel mgr. K-Mart Corp., Orlando, Fla., 1976-82; sales rep. EGP, Orlando, Fla., 1982-83; acctg. SJM Bus. Svcs., Orlando, Fla., 1983-87; rehab. clin. evaluator Fla. Hosp. Rehab. Ctr., Orlando, 1987—. Mem. Nat. Assn. Rehab. Nurses, Fla. State Assn. Rehab. Nurses (bd. dirs. 1994), Ctrl. Fla. Assn. Rehab. Nurses (nominating com. 1991, scholar com. 1992, treas. 1992, pres. elect 1993, pres. 1994), Heart Fla. Civitan Club (bd. dirs. 1992, sec. 1992), Valencia C.C. Alumni Assn. (bd. dirs. 1990-94, sec. 1992), Phi Beta Kappa, Delta Mu Delta. Republican. Methodist. Home: 349 Silver Pine Dr Lake Mary FL 32746-4831 Office: Fla Hosp Rehab Ctr 601 E Rollins St Orlando FL 32803-1248

MARSTELLER, HELEN SUE, financial analyst; b. Middletown, Ohio, June 24, 1960; d. Fred. and Eva Annabelle Dalton; m. Michael Newman, May 31, 1980 (div. Dec. 1982); m. Todd Jeffrey Marsteller, Aug. 25, 1984; children: Daniel K., Kevin C. Student, Miami U., 1978-83; B in Acctg., York Coll. Pa., 1985, MBA, 1993. CPA, Pa. Accounts receivable clk. Armco, Inc., Middletown, 1977-83; jr. acct. Hanover (Pa.) House Industries, 1983-84; cost acct. Honeywell, Inc., York, Pa., 1984-86; fin. analyst York (Pa.) Internat., 1986-88, supr. acctg., 1988-92, mgr. investor rels., 1992—. Bd. dirs. Atkins House, York, 1988-90, Access York, 1993—. Mem. Inst. Mgmt. Accts. Republican. Lutheran. Home: 760 Spring Ln York PA 17403-3416 Office: York Internat 760 Spring Ln York PA 17403-3416

MARSTON, JULIE KIM, executive; b. White Plains, N.Y., Nov. 20, 1956; d. Albert Oliver and Margrit Julie (Neubaner) M; 1 child, Noah Ivory Carr. AB, Smith Coll., 1978; MPH, Boston U., 1986. With UN Fund for Population Activities, N.Y.C., 1979; fin. mgr. Vol. Lawyers Project, Boston, 1983-86; assoc. dir. divsn. pub. health Dept. Health & Hosps., Boston, 1986-88, adminstrv. dir. pub. health AIDS program, 1988-90; exec. dir. Community Rsch. Initiative of New England, Boston, 1990—; bd. dirs. GLAD, Boston; mem. steering com. Boston AIDS Consortium, 1988—; mem. planning coun. Ryan White Care Act Com., Boston, 1990—; mem. local organizing com. 8th Internat. Conf. on AIDS, Amsterdam, 1991. Mem. Am. Pub. Health Assn., Nat. Soc. Fundraising Execs., Mass. Pun. Health Assn.

MARTEAU, KIMBERLY K., federal agency administrator; b. L.A., Feb. 22, 1959; d. Donald S. and Roberta (Launspach) Mart; m. John B. Emerson, Sept. 15, 1990. BA magna cum laude, U. Calif., 1981, JD, 1984. Practicing atty. Tuttle & Taylor, 1986-88; mem. nat. adv. staff Dukakis for Pres. Com., 1988; dir. internat. devel. and distbn. Patchett-Kaufman Entertainment, 1989-90; mgmt. assoc. Sont Pictures Entertainment, 1990-92; v.p. Motion Pictures, Savoy Pictures, Entertainment, 1992-93; dir. office of pub. liaison U.S. Info. Agy., 1993—. Editor Hastings Law Review, 1984-85. Grantee Edn. Abroad Program, 1979; fellow Rotary Club, 1984-85. Office: Public Liaison US Info Agy 301 4th St SW Rm 602 Washington DC 20547-0009*

MARTEL, EVA LEONA, accountant; b. Bristol, Conn., Feb. 14, 1945; d. Samuel L. and Irene A. (Beaulieu) Martel. BS in Acctg., N.H. Coll., 1986; MBA, Plymouth State Coll., 1990. Cert. continuing edn. educator. Accounts payable clk. Elliot Hosp., Manchester, N.H., 1971-79; bookkeeper Elliot Hosp., Manchester, 1979-84, dir. acctg., 1984-94; portfolio mgr. Elliot Hosp., Manchester, N.H., 1994—; adj. faculty N.H. Coll., 1991—; speaker Daniel Webster coun. Boy Scouts Am., Manchester, 1988; panel mem. ednl. seminar, 1993. Treas. N.H. Indian Cun., 1980-84; vol. United Way, Manchester, 1988—, accountexec., 1990, 91; mem. adv. coun. health care adminstrn. N.H. Coll., 1990, faculty advisor weekend program, 1990-91; vol. N.H. Heart Assn., 1990-92; bd. dirs. N.H. chpt. Am. Cancer Soc., 1991—; road race com. Elliot Hosp. Mem. NAFE, Hosp. Fin. Mgmt. Assn., Speaker's Bur. (smoke free com., recycling com. 1991), IMA, Healthcare Fin. Mgmt. Assn. Roman Catholic. Home: RR 4 11 Medford Farms Goffstown NH 03045-9804

MARTELL, ANGIE IGLESIA, lawyer; b. Bronx, N.Y., Nov. 7, 1959; d. Iris (Iglesia) Bleck. BA in Spanish Lit., NYU, 1982; MA in Media Studies,

New Sch. Social Rsch., 1986; JD, CUNY, 1989; LLM in Constl. Law, Harvard U., 1990. Bar: N.Y. 1990, Mass. 1990. Law clk. Allan H. Wernick, Esquire, N.Y.C., 1987, U.S. Dept. Justice, Bklyn., 1987, Levinson Mogulescu & Kaplan, N.Y.C., 1987-88, Ctr. for Constl. Rights, N.Y.C., 1988; rsch. asst. CUNY, Flushing, N.Y., 1987-88; staff atty. criminal def. divsn. Legal Aid Soc., N.Y.C., 1990-94; asst. atty. gen. civil rights bur. N.Y. State Dept. Law, N.Y.C., 1994—. Coun. mem. Mayor's Police Coun. for Gay and Lesbian Cmty., N.Y.C., 1994; adv. com. mem. N.Y.C. Contr. Gay and Lesbian Com., 1994, N.Y. State Atty. Gen. Lesbian and Gay Com., 1994; bd. dir. Gay and Lesbian Cmty. Ctr., 1992-94; cooperating atty LAMBDA Legal Defense and Edn. Fund, 1990-92. Nat. Hispanic scholar Nat. Hispanic Scholarship Fund, 1987-90. Mem. Lesbian and Gay Law Assn. of Greater N.Y. (bd. dir. 1995, sec. 1995). Office: NY State Dept Law Civil Rights Bur 120 Broadway 23d Flr New York NY 10271

MARTELL, DENISE MILLS, lay worker; b. Newberry, S.C., Apr. 8, 1965; d. Wyman Harman and Evangeline (Berry) Mills; m. Marty Martell, FEb. 29, 1992. Grad., Newberry High Sch., 1983. Tchr. Vacation Bible Sch., Newberry, 1984—, Sun. Sch., Newberry, 1989-92; dir. Bapt. Young Women, Newberry, 1989-92; sec. Sunday Sch. Bapt. Ch., Newberry, S.C., 1993—; tchr. mission trips, various locations, 1987-89; tchr. Mission Friends, Newberry, 1987—, mem. choir, 1986—, mem. Newberry Cmty. choir, 1992—, tchr. children's choir, 1993—; leader Weekday Bible Club, 1990-92. Active March of Dimes Walk Am., Am. Diabetes Assn. Bike-a-thon. Home: 2237 Fire Tower Rd Prosperity SC 29127-9616 Office: Shakespeare E and F Newberry SC 29108

MARTELL, MAXINE A., artist; b. Muskogee, Okla., Aug. 23, 1937; d. Carroll Max and Anna Mae (Corr) M.; m. Richard DiBene, Feb. 4, 1955 (div. Feb. 1970); 1 child, Deanna; m. James Douglas Burns, Nov. 25, 1971. BA, Holy Names Coll., 1960; MFA, U. Wash., 1962. Curator of art Cheney Cowles Meml. Mus., Spokane, Wash., 1970-73; dir. Spokane Art Sch., 1970-74; mem. staff and/or, Seattle, 1978-79; resident Western Wash. U., Bellingham, 1973, Centrum, Port Townsend, Wash., 1984, Pilchuck Glass Ctr., Stanwood, Wash., 1987; represented by Grover/Thurston Gallery, Seattle. Prin. works include glass installations at St. Joseph Children's Home, Spokane, Temple Beth Shalom, Spokane, Clover Park H.S., Tacoma, U.S. Customs Sta., Lynden, Wash., paintings at Sea-Tac Internat. Airport, 1992; creator film Elle, 1978 (1st prize Women's Film Festival, Seattle); curator Suspended Animation exhbn., 1979. Trustee Pratt Fine Art Ctr., Seattle, 1988-92, v.p., 1989-91; mem. art adv. com. Expo '74, 1973-74; trustee Western Assn. Art Mus., 1971-72. Home: PO Box 927 Coupeville WA 98239-0927

MARTELLI, JENNIFER A., social welfare administrator; b. Pawtucket, R.I., Jan. 24, 1970; d. Frank Paul III and Valerie Ann (Vecchio) M. BA in Polit. Sci., U. Mass., North Dartmouth, 1992. Mem. R.I. Ho. of Reps., Providence, 1992-94; cmty. edn. coord. R.I. Coalition Against Domestic Violence, Warwick, 1994—; bd. dirs. Reform Watch; mem. health, edn. and welfare com., 1992-94, mem. waste reutilization commn., 1992-94, mem. welfare reform commn., 1992-94. Mem. Sons of Italy (trustee). Home: 19 Warren Ave Johnston RI 02919

MARTENS, PATRICIA FRANCES, adult education educator; b. St. Louis, Nov. 27, 1943; d. John William and Mary Ruth (Bolds) Martens; m. George Joseph Miller, Aug. 7, 1965; children: Nicolette, George Jr., Jeffrey. BS in Psychology, So. Ill. U., 1975; MA in Counseling, St. Louis U., 1990. Cert. sexuality educator. Primary, intermediate tchr. St. Hedwig Sch., St. Louis, 1961-66; jr. high tchr. Assumption Sch., St. Louis, 1976-81; tchr. trainer grad. students Paul VI Cathechetical Inst., St. Louis, 1986-88; nat. tchr. trainer St. Louis, 1989—; cons. Archdiocese L.A., Archdiocese St. Louis; frequent speaker and presenter at schs., parishes ednl. confs., nat. and internat. religious edn. mtgs.; TV appearances on ABC and CTNA. Author: (videos) In God's Image: Make and Female, 1989, God Doesn't Make Junk, 1989 (Cath. Audio Visual Educators award 1991), (books) Parent to Parent, 1989, Sex Is Not A Four-Letter Word!, 1994. Mem. AACD, Nat. Cath. Educators Assn., Am. Assn. Sex Educators, Counselors, Therapists, Assn. for Religious Values in Counseling, Am. Sch. Counselor Assn., Am. Coll. Personnel Assn., Soc. for Sci. Study of Sex, Pi Lambda Theta. Home and Office: 8061 Daytona Dr # 1E Clayton MO 63105

MARTER, JOAN, art historian; b. Phila., Aug. 13, 1946. BA magna cum laude, Temple U., 1968; MA, U. Del., 1970, PhD, 1974. Instr. Pa. State U., 1970-73; asst. prof. Sweet Briar (Va.) Coll., 1974-77; assoc. prof. Rutgers U., New Brunswick, N.J., 1977-89; prof., 1989—. Author: Alexander Calder, 1991, also other books on various artists including Dorothy Dehner, Jose de Rivera, Theodore Roszak; contbr. articles to profl. jours. including Art Jour., Arts Mag., Am. Art Jour., Sculpture Mag., Archives of Am. Art Jour.; essayist and guest curator for exhbns. at major mus. including Met. Mus. Art. John Sloan Found. grantee, 1989; recipient Chester Dale Fellowship award Nat. Gallery of Art, 1973, Charles F. Montgomery prize Decorative Arts Soc., 1983, George Wittenborn award, Art Libr. Soc. of N.Am. award, 1984, Diamond Achievement Humanities award Temple U., 1993. Mem. Coll. Art Assn. of Am., Internat. Assn. of Art Critics (Am. Sect. exec. bd. 1986-89), Women's Caucus for Art (adv. bd. 1984-87), Am. Assn. Mus. Office: Rutgers U Dept Art History Voorhees Hall New Brunswick NJ 08903

MARTICH, DAWNA, nurse; b. McKeesport, Pa., June 14, 1958; d. Daniel and Julia (Medich) Martich; m. John W. Thomas, Apr. 17, 1988. BSN, U. Pitts., 1980, MSN, 1984. RN, Pa. Staff nurse Presbyn. Univ. Hosp., Pitts., 1980-84; tchr. sch. of nursing Shadyside Hosp., Pitts., 1984-86; nursing edn. specialist Mercy Hosp., Pitts., 1986-90, patient care delivery specialist, 1990-92, mgr. adminstrv. svcs., 1992-94; freelance health care cons., Pitts., 1994—; v.p. Idea Exch., new product devel. co., Pitts., 1994-95, 1995—; pres. pub. Mislim Pub., Pitts., 1994—. Author: Home Business Medical, 1990, Multi-Level Marketing, 1992; editor: Clinical Excellence, 1991-94; reviewer HRD Rev., 1988—. Mem. Sigma Theta Tau. Serbian Orthodox. Home: 4001 Greenridge Rd # 201 Pittsburgh PA 15234 Office: Mislim Pub Ste 2210 200 Mt Lebanon Blvd Pittsburgh PA 15234

MARTICHUSKI, DIANE KAY, psychology educator; b. Dallas, Oct. 27, 1964; d. Bill and Helena (Clements) M. BS, Lamar U., 1986; MS, Colo. State U., 1989, PhD in Social Psychology, 1992. Instr. Colo. State U., Ft. Collins, 1989-91, teaching fellow, 1991-92; asst. prof. Weber State U., Ogden, Utah, 1992-93, adj. prof., 1993; adj. prof. Columbia Coll., Salt Lake City, 1993; asst. prof. Wayne (Nebr.) State Coll., 1993—. Contbr. articles to profl. jours. Mem. Am. Psychol. Assn., Rocky Mountain Psychol. Assn., AAUW (v.p. programming 1994-95). Democrat. Home: PO Box 285 Winside NE 68790 Office: Wayne State Coll Divsn Social Scis 130 Connell Hall Wayne NE 68787

MARTIKAINEN, A(UNE) HELEN, retired health education specialist; b. Harrison, Maine, May 11, 1916; d. Sylvester and Emma (Heikkinen) M.; AB, Bates Coll., 1939, DSc (hon.), 1957, Smith Coll., 1969; MPH, Yale, 1941; DSc, Harvard U., 1964. Health edn. sec. Hartford Tb and Public Health Assn., 1941-42; cons. USPHS, 1942-49; chief health edn. WHO, Geneva, 1949-74; chair internat. affairs N.C. div. AAUW, 1986-94. Trustee Bridgton Acad., North Bridgton, Maine; mem. N.C. Women's Forum, 1984—; bd. dirs. N.C. Ctr. of Laws Affecting Women, Inc.; mem. Orange and Durham Counties chpt. UN Assn., chair cmty. outreach, bd. dirs. N.C. divsn. Recipient Delta Omega award Yale U.; Nat. Adminstrv. award Am. Acad. Phys. Edn.; Bates Key award; Internat. Service award, France, 1953; Prentiss medal, 1956; spl. medal, certificate for internat. health edn. service Nat. Acad. Medicine for France, 1959; Profl. award Soc. Pub. Health Educators, 1963, Benjamin Elijah Mays award Bates Coll. Alumni Assn., 1989. Fellow APHA (chmn. health edn. sect., Excellence award 1969); mem. AAUW, LWV (Chapel Hill, N.C. br. 1987—), Women's Internat. League for Peace and Freedom, U.S. Soc. Pub. Health Educators, Internat. Union Health Edn. (Parisot medal, tech. adviser), Acad. Phys. Edn. (assoc.), N.C. Coun. Women's Orgns. (mem. coun. assembly 1988-92, Women of Distinction award 1989), Phi Beta Kappa. Home: PO Box 2315 Chapel Hill NC 27515-2315

MARTIN, ANGELA CARTER, nursing educator; b. Reidsville, N.C., June 24, 1957; d. R. Philip and Carol (Walker) Carter; m. Dale Martin, Apr. 3, 1976; children: Melissa, Christopher. BSN, U. N.C., Greensboro, 1979; MS in Nursing, U. N.C., Chapel Hill, 1983. Cert. family nurse practitioner, N.C. Dir. Children's Med. Clinic Person-Chatman-Caswell County Health Dept., Yanceyville, N.C., 1983; family nurse practitioner Nat. Health Svc. Corps, Atlanta, 1983-86; asst. prof. dept. family and community medicine Med. Coll. Hampton Rds., Norfolk, Va., 1986—; asst. prof., coord. family nurse practitioner program Sch. Nursing, Old Dominion U., Norfolk, 1987-92, 94—; asst. prof., coord. distance family nurse practitioner program Suffolk Family Physicians, PC, 1992-94; pvt. practice family nurse practitioner; cons. in field. Contbr. articles to profl. publs. Mem. ANA, Va. Nurses Assn., Nat. Orgn. Nurse Practitioners Faculties (bd. dirs. 1992-93), Am. Acad. Nurse Practitioners (state award for excellence 1992), Sigma Theta Tau (Rsch. award 1988, award for excellence Epsilon Chi chpt.). Home: 3228 Pineridge Dr Chesapeake VA 23321-5404

MARTIN, ANGELA SUSAN, physician; b. Ft. Lauderdale, Fla., Nov. 17, 1961; d. Eugene Jr. and Vivian Carol (King) M. BS in Microbiology, U. Fla., 1983; MD, U. South Fla., 1987. Intern Sacred Heart Hosp., Pensacola, Fla., 1987-88; resident physician N.W. Fla. Ob/Gyn. Found., Pensacola, 1987-91; attending physician Meml. Med. Ctr., Jacksonville, Fla., 1991—. Jr. fellow Am. Bd. Ob/Gyn.; mem. Fla. Med. Assn., Duval County Med. Soc., Coun. Cath. Women. Republican. Catholic. Office: Womens Med Group 3550 U Blvd S Ste 301 Jacksonville FL 32216

MARTIN, ANN MATTHEWS, writer, juvenile; b. Princeton, N.J., Aug. 12, 1955; d. Henry R. and Edith Aiken (Matthews) M. BA cum laude, Smith Coll., 1977. Elem. sch. tchr. Plumfield Sch., Noroton, Conn., 1977-78; editorial asst. Simon & Schuster, N.Y.C., 1978-80; copywriter Teenage Book Club, Scholastic Books, Inc., N.Y.C., 1980-81; assoc. editor Scholastic Books, Inc., N.Y.C., 1981-83, editor, 1983; sr. editor Bantam Books, N.Y.C., 1983-85; free lance writer, editor N.Y.C., 1985—. Author: (novels) Bummer Summer, 1983, Just You and Me, 1983, Inside Out, 1984, Stage Fright, 1984, Me and Katie (the Pest), 1985, With You and Without You, 1986, Missing Since Monday, 1986, Just a Summer Romance, 1987, Slam Book, 1987, Yours Turly, Shirley, 1988, Ten Kids, No Pets, 1988, Fancy Dance in Feather Town, 1988, Ma and Pa Dracula, 1989, Moving Day in Feather Town, 1989, Eleven Kids, One Summer, 1991, Rachel Parker, Kindergarten Show-off, (novels in series) Baby-sitters Club, Baby-sitters Little Sister, Baby-sitters Club Mystery Series. Mem. PEN, Authors Guild, Soc. Children's Book Writers. Democrat. Office: Scholastic Inc Bethany Buck 555 Broadway New York NY 10012-3999

MARTIN, BARBARA JEAN, elementary school principal; b. Mt. Vernon, Tex., May 17, 1940; d. Billy Earl and Wilene (Dawson) Dade; m. J.B. Martin III, Aug. 29, 1959; children: J.B. IV, Mark Anthony. BA, Fisk U., Nashville, 1961; MEd, U. Ill., Chgo., 1979, PhD, 1992. Cert. tchr. kindergarten to 3rd grade, type 75 adminstr., Ill. Tchr. Chgo. Pub. Schs., 1969-93, prin., 1993—. Mem. Nat. Alliance Black Sch. Educators, Delta Kappa Gamma (sec. 1992—), Pi Lambda Theta, Alpha Kappa Alpha. Home: 825 E Drexel Sq Chicago IL 60615-3705 Office: O W Holmes Sch 955 W Garfield Blvd Chicago IL 60621-2240

MARTIN, BARBARA JEAN, dance educator; b. New London, Conn., Oct. 13, 1951; d. Arthur D. and Suzanne Mary (Babigian) M.; m. Keith Justin Martin, Jan. 6, 1973; 1 child, Jason. Grad., Morse High Sch., 1969. Soloist dancer San Francisco Ballet, 1969-71, Pa. Ballet, Phila., 1971-74, Pitts. Ballet, 1979-83; prin. dancer San Diego Ballet, 1976-79, Phoenix Ballet, 1983-86; dancer, instr. Vanderbilt U., Nashville, 1986-90; prin. dancer, instr. Ballet Calif., Santa Rosa, 1990—. Home: 2106 Northwood Dr Santa Rosa CA 95404 Office: Ballet Calif 569 Summerfield Rd Ste B Santa Rosa CA 95405

MARTIN, BETSY, magazine publishing executive. Sales rep. Money mag., N.Y.C., 1981; then mgr. New Eng. sales group Money mag., Boston, until 1986; head sales dept. Women's Sports and Fitness mag., 1986-87; nat. advt. sales dir. Working Woman mag., 1987-88; advt. sales dir. Money mag., N.Y.C., 1988-94, assoc. pub., 1993-94, pub., 1994—. Office: Money Time Inc Rockefeller Ctr. New York NY 10020-1393*

MARTIN, BETTY CAROLYN, library director; b. Louisville, Nov. 2, 1933; d. Earl Francis and Marie Dorothy (Baertich) Snyder; m. Charles Frank Martin, Aug. 18, 1956. BS, Ind. U., 1956, MLS, 1982. Sch. libr. Decatur Twp. Schs., Indpls., 1955-57; tchr. Indpls. Schs., 1957-58; libr., libr. dir. Vigo County Pub. Libr., Terre Haute, Ind., 1958—; exec. bd. Ind. State Libr. Adv. Coun., Indpls., 1989—. Contbr. articles to profl. jours. Bd. dirs. State Student Assistance Commn., Indpls., 1991—, United Way Wabash County, Terre Haute, 1989—, Alliance for Growth and Progress, Sec., 1989; bd. dirs. LWC, pres., 1980; bd. dirs. Pres. Adv. Bd. St. Mary of Woods Coll., Salvation Army, pres., 1990-92; sec. bd. dirs. Work Force Devel. Commn. Western Ind., Terre Haute, 1990—. Recipient Louise Maxwell award SLIS-IU Alumni Assn., Bloomington, Ind., 1991; named Outstanding Woman of COmmunity, Bus. & Profl. Womens Club, Terre Haute, 1990. Mem. ALA, Ind. Libr. Fedn. (bd. dirs., pres. 1989-90, Assn. Leadership award 1990), Ind. U. Libr. Sch. Alumni Assn. (pres.-elect 1992-94), C. of C. (terre award 1989). Democrat. Roman Catholic. Home: 5351 N 13th St Terre Haute IN 47805-1613 Office: Vigo County Public Lib 1 Library Sq Terre Haute IN 47807-3609

MARTIN, CAROL JACQUELYN, art educator, artist; b. Ft. Worth, Tex., Oct. 6, 1943; d. John Warren and Dorothy Lorene (Coffman) Edwards; m. Boe Willis Martin, Oct. 6, 1940; children: Stephanie Diane, Scott Andrew. BA summa cum laude, U. N. Tex., 1965; MA, U. Tex., El Paso, 1967. Tchr. Edgemere Elem. Sch., El Paso, Tex., 1965-66, Fulmore Jr. H.S., Austin, 1966-67, Monnig Jr. H.S., Ft. Worth, 1967-68, Paschal H.S., Ft. Worth, 1968-69; instr. Tarrant County Jr. Coll., Ft. Worth, 1968-69, 71-72; press sec. U.S. Sen. Gaylord Nelson, Washington, 1969-71; instr. Eastfield C.C., Dallas, 1981, Richland C.C. Dist., 1982. Editor The Avesta Mag., 1964-65; exhibited in group shows at City of Richardson's Cottonwood Park, 1970-86, Students of Ann Cushing Gantz, 1973-85, Art About Town, 1979, 80, shows by Tarrant County and Dallas County art assns. Active Dallas Symphony Orch. League, Easter Seal Soc., Dallas Hist. Soc., Women's Bd. of the Dallas Opera, Dallas Arboretum and Garden Club. Mem. Internat. Platform Assn., Mortar Bd., Alpha Chi, Sigma Tau Delta, Kappa Delta Pi, Delta Gamma. Democrat. Methodist. Address: 4435 Arcady Dallas TX 75205

MARTIN, CAROLYN FRANCES, elementary education educator; b. Mt. Vernon, Ohio, Feb. 4, 1948; d. Charles Wayne and Blanche Evelyn (Rine) Mills; m. Terry E. Martin, Dec. 19, 1970. BS in Edn., Muskingum, 1970. Cert. tchr., Ohio. Tchr. Mt. Vernon (Ohio) City Schs., 1970—. Home: 344 Maple Ave Utica OH 43080-9702 Office: East Sch 714 E Vine St Mount Vernon OH 43050-3651

MARTIN, CHERI CHRISTIAN, health services administrator; b. Nashville, Mar. 9, 1956; d. Jesse Thomas and Eloise (McClain) Christian; m. George A. Martin, June 25, 1977; children: Matthew Alexander, Kristin Leigh. BS in Family Resources and Consumer Scis., U. Wis., 1977; cert. healthcare mgmt., U. St. Thomas, 1991. Asst. buyer Dayton Hudson, Mpls., 1978-79, assoc. buyer, 1979-81; instr. Nat. Coll., Mpls., 1981-82; mgr. store Connco Shoes, Inc., Mpls, 1982-83; patient svcs. rep. Group Health, Inc., Mpls., 1984-89, dental mgr., 1989-94, regional mgr., 1994—. Facilitator seminar Non-Verbal Communication, 1986. Mem. Minn./Dakota Assn. Patient Reps. (v.p. 1989-90), U. Wis. Alumni Assn., Group Health Social Club Mpls. (pres. 1987-89). Home: 4640 Nevada Ave N Minneapolis MN 55428-5042

MARTIN, CHRISTINA MARIE, public relations executive; b. Shawnee Mission, Kans., June 28, 1966; d. Rafael Luis and Rebecca Barbara (Bunck) M. BA in Econs., U. Kans., 1988. Dep. asst. to chief speechwriter, rschr., dep. asst. to the asst. to the president The White House, Washington, 1989-93; chief of staff, press sec. Rep. Michael Huffington, Washington, 1993-94; press sec. Gov. Branstad, Des Moines, 1994—; spl. asst. Office Pres. Elect., Washington, 1988-89. Staff asst. Bush-Quayle 88, Washington, 1988. Republican. Roman Catholic. Home: 300 Walnut St # 87 Des Moines IA 50309 Office: Office of the Gov State Capitol Bldg Des Moines IA 50319

MARTIN, CLARA RITA, elementary educator; b. Steubenville, Ohio, Oct. 14, 1953; d. Robert Emmett and Mary Agnes (Flynn) Joyce; m. Gary Dean Martin, July 8, 1978; children: Bradley A., Douglas A. BS in Elem. Edn., Coll. Steubenville, 1975; MS in Interdisciplinary Skills, U. Dayton, 1984. Cert. tchr., Ohio. Reading specialist Steubenville City Sch. Dist., 1975; tchr. elem. schs. Harrison Hills City Sch. Dist., Jewett and Hopedale, Ohio, 1975—; coord. spelling bee Harrison News Herald Spelling Bee, Cadiz, Ohio, 1984—. Jump Rope for Heart coord., asst. coord. Meml. Day Program, 1992. Mem. Harrison Hills Tchrs.' Assn. (grievance chair, chief negotiator 1980—, bldg. rep. 1985—, del. Ohio Edn. Assn. Conv., 1981—), Ladies Ancient Order Hibernians (sec. 1991-92). Roman Catholic. Home: PO Box 184 Bloomingdale OH 43910-0184

MARTIN, DALE, vocational rehabilitation executive; b. N.Y.C., May 10, 1935; d. Byron Pink Molter and Ruth (Nobel) Gestram; m. Robert A. Wishart, Dec. 13, 1985; children by previous marriage: Elizabeth, Devon. BS, U. Conn., 1957. RN, cert. case mgr., ins. rehab. specialist, lic. rehab. counsellor, Mass. Dental asst. Hempstead, N.Y., 1951; with Wesson Maternity Hosp., Springfield, Mass., 1957-58, Huntington Hartford Meml. Hosp., Pasadena, Calif., 1958-59; office mgr. Indsl. By Products Inc., Kalamazoo, Mich., 1969-72; controller Indsl. By Products Inc., Chgo., 1970-74; cons. Mgmt. Resources Inc., Broomall, Pa., 1978-81; cons., owner Martin-Collard Assocs., Inc., Monmouth Beach, N.J., 1980-84; cons., owner, chmn. bd. dirs. MCA, Inc., Boston, 1984—; bd. dirs. MCA Inc., Boston, Consortium Advantage, Inc.; cons. Viewfinder, Old Chatham, N.Y., 1987—, Phoenix Inc., Global Explorations, Inc. Contbr. articles to profl. jours.; painter, sculptor. Bd. govs. Rumson-Fair Haven H.S., 1976-78. Mem. Nat. Assn. Rehab. Profls. in Pvt. Sector (mem. forensic sect., past rep. region I to bd. dirs.), Nat. Rehab. Assn. (pvt. sector group), Mass. Nurses Assn. (mem. image com. 1984-85), Internat. Assn., Psychosocial Rehab. Specialists, New Eng. Claims Assn., Individual Case Mgmt. Assn., Town Club (v.p., Mountain Lakes Ski Club (founder), Jr. Women's Club, Jr. League, Sigma Theta Tau, Alpha Delta Pi. Office: MCA Inc PO Box 5438 Boston MA 02102-5438 also: MCA Inc PO Box 789 Port Salerno FL 34992-0789

MARTIN, DAWN ADAMS, gifted/talented education educator; b. Wilmington, Ohio, Feb. 4, 1960; d. Robert Lee and Wanda Jean (Waits) Adams; m. Wyman Bradley Martin, Apr. 16, 1990. BS, U. Cin., 1982; MEd, Kennesaw State U., 1991. Tchr. Fayetteville (Ohio) Elem. Sch., 1982-84; salesperson IBM Corp., Cin., 1984-88; tchr. sci. Daniell Mid. Sch., Marietta, Ga., 1988-92; tchr. gifted Dodgen Mid. Sch., Marietta, 1992—. Mem. Audubon Soc., Ga. Conservancy of Nature, So. Order of Storytellers. Home: 35 W Blackland Ct Marietta GA 30067

MARTIN, DEBRA MICHELE, registered nurse; b. Hagerstown, Md., Sept. 19, 1950; d. James Kingsley and Mary Madalan (Bultman) Noel; m. David Richard Rawls, June 9, 1973 (div. June 1981); children: Derek Joseph, Dayna Noel; m. Sydney Lee Martin, June 25, 1982 (div. Oct. 1988). RN, Sinai Hosp., Balt., 1971. RN, Pa., Md.; cert. ACLS, CPR, CEN, Basic Trauma Life Support, emergency vehicle operator, health profl., vehicle rescue tng., rappeling and hazardous materials tng. Asst. head RN Sinai Hosp., Balt., 1971-73, postpartum charge RN, 1975-77; ob-gyn. office RN Scher, Muher & Lowen, PA, Balt., 1973-74; emergency dept. RN Meml. Hosp., York, Pa., 1978-80, advance life charge RN, 1980—; teaching EMT's and paramedics Harrisburg (Pa.) Area C.C., 1984—, St. Joseph's Hosp., Lancaster, Pa., 1984—. Health profl. Pa. Dept. of Health, Harrisburg, 1988—. Named ALS Provider of Yr., Emergency Med. Svcs. Assn. of York County, 1990. Mem. Emergency Health Sys. Fedn. (RN adv. bd. 1986—), Emergency Nurses Assn. Democrat. Roman Catholic. Home: 123 S Main St Shrewsbury PA 17361-1528

MARTIN, FRANCES LOUISE, medical/surgical nurse; b. Johnstown, Pa., June 6, 1940; d. Percy Embrose and Norma (Ream) M. Diploma, Conemaugh Valley Meml. Hosp., Johnstown, 1961; BS in Nursing, U. Pitts., 1966. Cert. nurse adminstr. Staff nurse Conemaugh Valley Meml. Hosp., 1961-63, nurse mgr., 1966—; del. Project Assist Health Care, Latvia. Mem. Am. Trauma Soc., Am. Nurses Assn., Oncology Nursing Soc., United Ostomy Assn., West Va. Head Injury Found., Nat. Spinal Cord Injury Found., Sino Am. Oncology Sci. Exchange, Affiliated Orgn. Nurse Mgrs., Pa. Orgn. Nurse Execs. Republican. Lutheran. Home: 608 Fronheiser St Johnstown PA 15902-2106 Office: Conemaugh Valley Meml Hosp Rose 8 1086 Franklin St Johnstown PA 15905-4398

MARTIN, HELEN ELIZABETH, secondary mathematics and science educator; b. West Chester, Pa., Feb. 19, 1945; d. Thomas Edwin and Elizabeth Temple (Walker) M.; BA, The King's Coll., Briarcliff Manor, N.Y., 1967; MEd, West Chester U., 1970; postgrad. Goethe Inst., Freiberg, Fed. Republic Germany, 1979, Oxford U., 1979. Tchr. math. and sci. Unionville (Pa.) High Sch., 1967—; adj. prof. W. Chester (Pa.) U., 1989—; mem. Carnegie Forum on Edn. and the Economy. Mem. Pa. Rep. State Com., 1982-90, Rep. Com. of Chester County, 1984-94. Named Alumna of the Yr. The King's Coll., 1987; recipient State Presdl. award, 1989, Frank G. Brewer Civil Air Patrol Meml. Aerospace award, 1989, Outstanding Achievement award U.S. Dept. Commerce, 1993; Bus. Week/Challenger Seven fellow, 1991. Fellow Am. Sci. Affiliation; mem. AAAS (founding dir.), Nat. Bd. Profl. Teaching Standards (founding dir.), Satellite Educators Assn. (pres. 1987-94), Nat. Sci. Tchrs. Assn., Nat. Council Tchrs. Math., History Sci. Soc., So. Chester County Rep. Women's Council. Clubs: Delaware Camera, Women's Rep. of Chester County, Nat. Sci. Tchrs. Assn. (internat. lectr. 1987), Assn. for Sci. Edn. in U.K. (internat. lectr. 1987). Home: PO Box 605 Unionville PA 19375-0605 Office: Unionville High Sch Unionville PA 19375

MARTIN, HELEN R., executive secretary; b. Marion County, Miss., Jan. 7, 1959; d. L.W. and Emmie M. (Quinn) Lampton; m. Herman Martin, Jan. 12, 1974; children: Pamela D., Timmy W., Kelly, Angela T. Secretarial grad., Moore Career Coll., 1993. Operator sewing machine Pioneer Aerospace MFC, Columbia, Miss., 1982-92; teachers' aid Moore Career Coll., Hattiesburg, Miss., 1993; gen. sec. New Jerusalem C.O.G.I.C., Foxworth, Miss., 1985—; exec. sec. Jesus People Against Pollution, Columbia, 1992—. Mem. NAFE. Mem. Holiness Ch. Home: PO Box 719 Foxworth MS 39483-3102 Office: Jesus People Against Pollution PO Box 765 Columbia MS 39429

MARTIN, HELENE GETTER, university administrator; b. Boston, May 24, 1940; d. Seymour Samuel and Doris Viola (Taylor) Getter; children: Lauren Renee, Susannah Taylor. AB in English Lit. with distinction, Wheaton Coll., 1962; MS, Columbia U., 1964; postgrad., U. Calif., Berkeley, 1981. Caseworker, cons. Mass. Dept. Mental Health, Milton, 1965-78; program analyst dept. nursing Ambulatory Care Ctr., U. Calif., San Francisco, 1980-81; cons. mental health, mem. faculty Boston Coll. Legal Assistance Bur., Waltham, Mass., 1978-80; mktg. assoc. Vesper Hosps., San Leandro, Calif., 1981-83; dir. resource devel. Am. Acad. Ophthalmology, San Francisco, 1983-85; mgr. membership devel. The Mus. Soc., San Francisco, 1986-89; dir. devel. and alumni rels. Sch. Social Work Columbia U., N.Y.C., 1989-93; sr. devel. officer, dir. campaign L.I. U., Bklyn., 1993—; case worker Mass. Dept. of Mental Health, 1965-78; programs dir. Mass. Mental Health Assn., 1978-80. Co-founder Marin Parents and Community Together, Marin County, Calif., 1987; bd. dirs., mem. exec. com. Oxfam-Am., Boston, 1973-79; mem. Com. to Aid East Pakistan, Cambridge, Mass., 1970; chairperson Emergency Relief Fund-Bangladesh, Newton, Mass., 1972, Ad-Hoc Com. to Remove Asbestos, Newton, 1978; mem. Dem. City Com., Newton, 1978; chairperson welfare com. LWV, Newton, 1970. Mem. Nat. Soc. Fund Raising Execs. (Golden Gate chpt., bd. dirs 1989, chairperson Nat. Philanthrophy Day awards com. 1989). Home: 263 W End Ave Apt 3G New York NY 10023-2621 Office: Long Island University Brooklyn NY 11201-5372

MARTIN, JANET MARIE, government educator; b. Milw., Aug. 23, 1955; d. John and Mary Jane (Marks) M. BA summa cum laude, Marquette U., 1977; MA, Ohio State U., 1980, PhD, 1985. Grad. tchg., rsch. assoc. Ohio State U., Columbus, 1978-83; polit. sci. instr. Gettysburg (Pa.) Coll., 1983-85, asst. prof. polit. sci., 1985-86; fellow, legis. asst. Senators Herb Kohl and George Mitchell U.S. Senate, Washington, 1989-90; asst. prof. govt. Bowdoin Coll., Brunswick, Maine, 1986-92, assoc. prof. govt., 1992—; Maine state mgr. News Election Svc., 1990-92. Author: Lessons from the Hill: The Legislative Journey of an Education Program, 1994; contbr. articles to profl.

jours. Recipient Dorothy Shaw Leadership award Alpha Delta Pi, 1977. Mem. Am. Polit. Sci. Assn., Midwest Polit. Sci. Assn., Phi Beta Kappa, Phi Kappa Phi. Democrat. Office: Bowdoin Coll Dept Govt Brunswick ME 04011

MARTIN, JEAN ANN, youth services administrator, diagnostician; b. Omaha, June 27, 1942; d. Clarid Fee and Frances Catherine (Dugan) McNeil; m. Robert William Martin, Dec. 28, 1968. BS, Pa. State U., 1963; MEd, U. Del., 1968. Cert. English tchr., Pa., N.Y., Del., reading specialist, Va., N.Y., Del., secondary prin., reading supr., dir. of instrn., Del. Tchr. English Neshaminy Sch. Dist., Langhorn, Pa., 1963-65; tchr. English and reading Unionville (Pa.) Sch. Dist., 1965-68; tchr. reading Jamesville-DeWitt (N.Y.) Sch. Dist., 1968-69, South Colonie Sch. Dist., Albany, N.Y., 1969-70; tchr. English Bethlehem Cen. Sch. Dist., Delmar, N.Y., 1970-71, Smyrna (Del.) Sch. Dist., 1971-73; reading specialist, tchr. English Delmar Sch. Dist., 1973-88; reading specialist Accomack (Va.) County Schs., 1988-93; adminstr., diagnostician Del. Dept. Svcs. for Children, Youth and Their Families, Wilmington, 1994—. Past pres. Lioness, Delmar. Mem. ASCD, Del. ASCD, Va. Reading Assn. (bd. dirs. 1989-93, editorial adv. bd. Reading in Va. 1990-92), Ea. Shore Reading Coun. Va. (pres. 1989-91), Sussex County Orgn. for Reading Excellence (pres. 1980-81), Diamond State Reading Assn. (pres. 1985-86), Del. Assn. Sch. Adminstrs., Internat. Reading Assn., Cedar Shores Condominium Assn. (sec.), Alpha Delta Kappa (past pres. Theta chpt. and Del.). Home: 33 E Sixth St New Castle DE 19720 Office: Del Dept Svcs Children Youth and Their Families 1825 Faulkland Rd Wilmington DE 19805

MARTIN, JENNIFER KAYE, artist, educator; b. Pearisburg, Va., Dec. 13, 1947; d. Arthur Paul and Lorraine (Porterfield) M.; m. Danny L. Evans, Sept. 6, 1967 (div. Jan. 1985); 1 child, Paul Edward Evans. BA cum laude, Va. Polytech. Inst., 1991, MFA, 1994. Prototype electronic tech. model shop Electro-Tec Corp. KDI, Blacksburg, Va., 1971-83; supr., coord. electronic prodn. Internat. Sci. Industries, Christiansburg, Va., 1983-85; electronic tech., supr., coord. tech. staff Va. Polytech. Inst., Blacksburg, 1985-88, electronic tech., physics cons., 1988-92; artist, cons. Blacksburg, 1992—; physics cons. AMY rsch. detector in supercollider, Ibaraki, Japan. Group shows include Artlink Contemporary Art Space, Fort Wayne, Ind., 1986 (purchase award 1986), Ariel Gallery, N.Y.C., 1988, Art Gallery Fells Point, Balt., 1988 (Best in show award 1988), Davidson County Art Guild, Lexington, N.C., 1988 (Best in Graphics Category 1988). Mem. Golden Key Nat. Honor Soc., Phi Kappa Phi, Tau Sigma Delta (life). Home and Studio: 411 W Main St Christiansburg VA 24073

MARTIN, JUDITH LEE, English language educator; b. Roswell, N.Mex.; d. Noble G. and Mary F. (Unfried) Ellison; children: Kevin, Angela. BA, U. Evansville, 1971, MA, 1978; PhD, Southern Ill. U., 1991. Tchr. English Mt. Vernon (Ind.) Sr. High Sch., 1971-76; prof. English, dept. chair Lockyear Coll., Evansville & Indpls., 1984-87; asst. prof. English Mo. Western State Coll., St. Joseph, 1991—; adj. instr. English U. Evansville, U. Southern Ind., 1987-88. Contbr. articles to profl. jours. Grad. Dean's fellow Southern Ill. U., 1989-90. Mem. MLA, Nat. Coun. Tchrs. English (com. on pub. Doublespeak), Conf. Coll. Composition and Comm., Phi Kappa Phi. Office: Mo Western State Coll Saint Joseph MO 64507

MARTIN, JUDY BRACKIN HEREFORD, foundation administrator; b. York, Ala., May 25, 1943; d. Julian Byron and Willie Lee (Aiken) B.; m. Roy Nichols Hereford, Jr., Apr. 1, 1962 (dec. Mar. 1988); children: Leanne, Roy Nichols III, Rachel, Samantha; m. John Lawrence Martin Sr., Nov. 23, 1988. BA, Judson Coll., 1964. Lic. apprentice auctioneer, Ala. Co-owner, ptnr. Hereford Haven Farms, Faunsdale, Ala., 1962-93; ptnr. The Mustard Seed, Demopolis, Ala., 1974-76; ptnr., sales mgr. Hereford & Assocs. Auction Co., Faunsdale, Ala., 1967-91; alumnae dir., dir. admissions Judson Coll., Marion, Ala., 1988-90, asst. to pres., 1990-94; exec. sec.-treas. Ala. Women's Hall of Fame, Judson Coll., Marion, 1991—; exec. dir. Ala. Rural Heritage Found., Thomaston, 1991—. Officer Marengo County Red. Cross, 1987-88; mem. Marengo County Hist. Soc., Econ. Devel. Assn. Ala., 1991—; com. mem. Marengo Dem. Exec. Com.; bd. dirs. Dept. Human Resources, Marengo County, 1987-91, Marengo County Farmers Fedn. Bd., 1985-91; mem. So. Arts Fedn. Adv. Coun., 1994—; mem. steering com. Leadership Marengo, 1994; chmn. bd. Faunsdale United Meth. Ch., 1989-91. Mem. Blackbelt Tourism Coun. (bd. dirs. 1991), Judson Coll. Alumnae Assn. (treas. 1992—). Methodist.

MARTIN, JUNE JOHNSON CALDWELL, journalist; b. Toledo, Oct. 6; d. John Franklin and Eunice Imogene (Fish) Johnson; m. Erskine Caldwell, Dec. 21, 1942 (div. Dec. 1955); 1 child, Jay Erskine; m. Keith Martin, May 5, 1966. AA, Phoenix Jr. Coll., 1939-41; BA, U. Ariz., 1941-43, 53-59; student Ariz. State U., 1939, 40. Free-lance writer, 1944—; columnist Ariz. Daily Star, 1956-59; editor Ariz. Alumnus mag., Tucson, 1959-70; book reviewer, columnist Ariz. Daily Star, Tucson, 1970-94; ind. book reviewer and audio tape columnist, Tuscon, 1994—; panelist, co-producer TV news show Tucson Press Club, 1954-55, pres., 1958; co-founder Ariz. Daily Star Ann. Book & Author Event. Contbg. author: Rocky Mountain Cities, 1949; contbr. articles to World Book Ency., and various mags. Mem. Tucson CD Com., 1961; vol. campaigns of Samuel Goddard, U.S. Rep. Morris Udall, U.S. ambassador and Ariz. gov. Raul Castro. Recipient award Nat. Headliners Club, 1959, Ariz. Press Club award, 1957-59, Am. Alumni Council, 1966, 70. Mem. Nat. Book Critics Circle, Jr. League of Tucson, Tucson Urban League, PEN U.S.A. West, Pi Beta Phi. Democrat. Methodist. Club: Tucson Press. Home: Desert Foothills Sta PO Box 65388 Tucson AZ 85728

MARTIN, KATHLEEN ANNE, information management consultant; b. Rochester, N.Y., Aug. 19, 1942; d. Edwin Wilkins and Hilda Ellen (Hartell) Martin; BA, Marygrove Coll., Detroit, 1964; MA in Libr. Sci. (Josenhans scholar 1965), U. Mich., 1965; advanced online tng. cert. Nat. Libr. Medicine, 1979; m. Oliver Kalman Peterdy, Oct. 15, 1971 (div. 1981); children: Elizabeth, Matthew. Libr. Detroit Pub. Libr., 1964-66; bibliographer, then asst. tech. svcs. libr. Edward G. Miner Med. Libr., U. Rochester, 1969-72; libr. lab. indsl. medicine Eastman Kodak Co., Rochester, 1966-69, libr. health, safety and human factors lab., 1972-78, tech. info. analyst, 1978-84, health and environment lab., 1978-86, Info Edge, 1987—; libr. Monroe Devel. Ctr., 1987-90, Park Ridge Hosp., 1990—. Mem. AAUW (treas. Rochester br. 1979-80), Spl. Librs. Assn., Med. Libr. Assn., N.Y. Libr. Assn. Home: 332 Gnage Ln Rochester NY 14612-3200

MARTIN, KATHLEEN DEARY, art educator; b. Boston, Feb. 22, 1948; children: Joshua, Christopher. BA, Emmanuel Coll., 1969; MAT, Manhattanville Coll., 1984; cert., Sotheby's, N.Y.C., 1989. Tchr. spl. edn. Greenwich (Conn.) Schs., 1983-84; dir. fine arts Litchfield (Conn.) Auction Gallery, 1989-90; asst. v.p. Sotheby's, N.Y.C., 1990—. Editor: The Great Estates: Greenwich 1880-1930. Office: Sotheby's Ednl Studies 411 E 76th St New York NY 10021

MARTIN, LAURA BELLE, real estate and farm land manager, retired educator; b. Jackson County, Minn., Nov. 3, 1915; d. Eugene Wellington and Mary Christina (Hanson) M. BS, Mankato State U., 1968. Tchr. rural schs., Renville County, Minn., 1937-41, 45-50, Wabasso (Minn.) Pub. Sch., 1963-81; pres. Renville Farms and Feed Lots, 1982—. Pres. Wabasso (Minn.) Edn. Assn., 1974-75, publicity chmn., 1968-74; sec. Hist. Renville Preservation Com., 1978—; publicity chmn. Town and Country Boosters, Renville, 1982-83. Mem. Genealogy Soc. Renville County, Am. Legion Aux. Democrat. Lutheran. Home and Office: 334 NW 1201 Rt 3 Holden MO 64040-9804

MARTIN, LAURA JEAN, accountant; b. Muskegon, Mich., July 2, 1952; d. Eldred L. and Ella (Yokubonus) M. A in Applied Sci. Acctg., Muskegon C.C., 1980; BS in Bus., Aquinas Coll., 1983. Payroll clk. Anaconda Wire & Cable, Muskegon, 1971-73; payroll clk. Dresser Industries, Muskegon, 1973-74, accts. payable clk., 1974-78, managerial sec., 1978, credit corr., 1978-81, jr. staff acct., 1981-83, cost acct., 1984-85; instr. English YBU English Ctr., Kyoto, Japan, 1983-84; cost analyst Lorin Industries, Muskegon, 1985—. Assoc. Friends of Hackley Pub. Libr., 1993-94; mem. choir St. Jean's Ch., Muskegon, 1989-94; loan exec. United Way, Muskegon, 1992; bd. dirs. Shaw Box Credit Union, Muskegon, 1992-94. Mem. Inst. Mgmt. Accts. (sec. 1992-94, sec./treas. 1994—), Nat. Assn. Accts. (dir. pub. rels. 1991-93), West Shore Tennis Club, Omni Fitness Club, Fraternal Order of Eagles, Pulaski Lodge P.N.A. Republican. Roman Catholic. Home: 5049 Valentine Ln Muskegon MI 49442 Office: Lorin Industries 1960 S Roberts Muskegon MI 49442

MARTIN, LINDA SUE, minister of pastoral care; b. Fort Wayne, Ind., Oct. 3, 1953; d. Myron Lee and Helen Louetta (Hughes) M. BS, Manchester Coll., 1976; MS, Saint Francis Coll., Fort Wayne, Ind., 1984; Cert. of Gerontology, Ind. U., 1988. Cert. art educator. Art instr. Met. Sch. Dist., Wabash County, Ind., 1977-78; arts and crafts coord. Sr. Citizens Ctr., Fort Wayne, Ind., 1978-90; minister of pastoral care Saint Joseph United Meth. Ch., Fort Wayne, Ind., 1990—; owner Down Home Designs, Ft. Wayne, 1978—; tchr., cons. Very Spl. Arts Ind., Ft. Wayne, 1989—. Freelance artist including logo design for Am. Lawyers Aux., 1986; contbg. author: (poetry) At The Crossroads, 1988. Sec. bd. dirs. Arthritis Found., Allen County, Ind., 1984-94, bd. dirs. Ind. chpt., 1990-94; mem. St. Joseph United Meth. Ch., Ft. Wayne, 1984—; sr. PAC chair, bd. dirs. Jr. League Ft. Wayne, 1991-93. Recipient "Food Hero" award Community Harvest Foodbank, 1992, Artist Recognition award Johnny Appleseed Festival, 1988. Mem. Am. Bus. Women's Assn. (mem. ways and means chair 1989-91). Methodist. Office: Saint Joseph United Meth Ch 6004 Reed Rd Fort Wayne IN 46835-2215

MARTIN, LORA LEE, university administrator; b. Woodland, Calif., Jan. 13, 1954; d. William Leland and Elizabeth Louise (Stadtfeld) M. BS Zoology, U. Calif., Davis, 1976; MBA, U. Calif., Berkeley, 1979. Fundraising officer Carter-Mondale Campaign, Washington, 1979-81; advance person White House, Washington, 1980; Washington rep. Nat. Environ. Controls, Washington, 1981; nat. fundraiser Friends of Robert C. Byrd Ctr., Washington, 1982; regl. devel. office Natural Resources Def. Coun., Washington, 1983-85; exec. dir. Aerobics and Fitness Found., Sherman Oaks, Calif., 1985-87; bus. mgr. Organizing Inst., Pacific Grove, Calif., 1987-90; dir. regl. econ. devel. U. Calif., Santa Cruz, 1990—; cons. Nat. Fitness Found., El Segundo, Calif., 1987. Bd. mem. Monterey (Calif.) Bay Regl Futures, 1994, Santa Cruz City Mus., 1990-93, Friends of Sea Otters, Carmel, Calif., 1991-93; witness congrl. testimony U.S. Ho. Reps., Washington, 1993. Mem. AAAS (presenter), Rotary Internat. (bd. dirs. 1991-93). Office: Univ Calif Carriage House Santa Cruz CA 95064

MARTIN, LORRAINE B., humanities educator; b. Utica, N.Y., Aug. 18, 1940; d. Walter G. and Laura (Bochenek) Bolanowski; m. Charles A. Martin; children: Denise, Tracy. Student, SUNY, Albany, 1958-60, postgrad.; BA in English and Edn. magna cum laude, Utica Coll. of Syracuse U., 1977; MS in Edn. and Reading, SUNY, Cortland, 1979, CAS in Edn. Adminstrn., 1984; postgrad., Syracuse U., 1990—, SUNY, Albany, 1992—. Cert. elem. tchr., secondary tchr., sch. adminstr. and supr., sch. dist. adminstr., reading specialist, N.Y. Tchr. Poland (N.Y.) Cen. Sch., 1972-80, reading specialist, 1980-84; instr. reading Utica Coll. of Syracuse U., summer 1982-84; adminstr. spl. edn. and chpt. 1 remedial program Little Falls (N.Y.) City Sch. Dist., 1984-85; adminstr. adult and continuing edn. Madison-Oneida Bd. Coop. Ednl. Svcs., Verona, N.Y., 1985-86; dir. gen. programs Herkimer (N.Y.) Bd. Coop. Ednl. Svcs., 1986-88; asst. prof. English, children's lit., reading, and freshman seminar Herkimer County Community Coll., Herkimer, 1988—; ednl. cons., 1979—; pvt. cons. for reading and writing, 1980; participant SUNY brainstorming session on underprepared students, 1993; trainer tchr. performance evaluation program N.Y. State Dept. Edn., Herkimer, 1984, facilitator effective schs. program, 1986-88; cons. Two-Yr. Coll. Devel. Ctr. SUNY, 1985-89, tchr. trainer for the Writing Process; developer summer reading, writing and study skills course for Bridge program. Author: The Bridge Program—Easing the Transition from High School to College, 1990; editorial bd. Research and Teaching in Developmental Education; contbr. to Teaching Writing to Adults Tips for Teachers: An Idea Swap, 1989; textbook reviewer for pubs., 1993—. Vol. arts and crafts fair HCCC Found.; active Myasthenia Gravis Found., 1988-95, Muscular Dystrophy Assn., 1989-95, Thyroid Found. of Am., 1988-95; advisor Network for Coll. Re-Entry Adults; mem. Profl. Devel. Com., Acad. Computer Com. Recipient Leader Silver award for volunteerism 4-H Coop. Extension, Utica, 1980; HCCC Found. grantee, Writing grantee Reader's Digest. Mem. Internat. Reading Assn., N.Y. State Reading Assn., Assn. Supervision and Curriculum Devel., Nat. Coun. Tchrs. English, Conf. on Coll. Composition and Communication, N.Y. Coll. Learning Skills Assn., N.Y. State Assn. Two-Yr. Colls., Inc., Phi Kappa Phi, Alpha Lambda Sigma. Home: 7099 Crooked Brook Rd Utica NY 13502 Office: Herkimer County Comm Coll Reservoir Rd Herkimer NY 13350-1545

MARTIN, LUCY Z., public relations executive; b. Alton, Ill., July 8, 1941; d. Fred and Lucille J. M. BA, Northwestern U., 1963. Adminstrv. asst., copywriter Batz-Hodgson-Neuwoehner, Inc., St. Louis, 1963-64; news reporter, Midwest fashion editor Fairchild Publs., St. Louis, 1964-66; account exec. Milici Advt. Agy., Honolulu, 1967; publs. dir. Barnes Med. Ctr., St. Louis, 1968-69; communications cons. Fleishman-Hillard, St. Louis, 1970-74; communications cons., chief exec. officer, pres. Lucy Z. Martin & Assocs., Portland, Oreg., 1974—; chmn. Good Samaritan Hosp. Assocs., 1991—; speaker Healthcare Assn. Hawaii, 1993, Oreg. Assn. Healthcare, 1992, Healthcare Fin. Mgmt. Assn., 1993, Healthcare Communicators Oreg., 1994; alumni coun. Northwestern U., 1992—; bd. Inst. Managerial and Profl. Women, 1992—, Am. Mktg. Assn. Oreg. chpt. 1992-93, Oreg. Sch. Arts and Crafts, 1989—; bd., chair Good Samaritan Hosp. Assocs. 1991-96; adv. bd. Jr. League, 1994—. Featured in Entrepreneurial Woman mag.; contbr. articles to profl. jours. Chmn. women's adv. com. Reed Coll., Portland, 1977-79; mem. Oreg. Commn. for Women, 1984-87; bd. dirs. Ronald McDonald House Oreg., 1986, Oreg. Sch. Arts & Crafts, 1989—, Inst. Managerial and Profl. Women, 1992—, Northwestern U. Alumni Coun., 1992—; chmn. bd. Good Samaritan Hosp. Assocs., 1991—; mem. alumni coun. Northwestern U., 1992—; mem. pub. policy com. YMCA, 1993—; mem. adv. bd. Jr. League, 1994—. Recipient MacEachern Citation Acad. Hosp. Pub. Relations, 1978, Rosey awards Portland Advt. Fedn., 1979, Achievement award Soc. Tech. Communications, 1982, Disting. Tech. Communication award, 1982, Exceptional Achievement award Council for Advancement and Support Edn., 1983, Monsoon award Internat. Graphics, Inc., 1984; named Woman of Achievement Daily Jour. Commerce, 1980. Mem. Pub. Rels. Soc. Am. (pres. Columbia River chpt. 1984, chmn. bd. 1980-84, Oreg. del. 1984-86, judicial panel N. Pacific dist 1985-86, exec. bd. health care sect. 1986-87, mem. Counselors Acad., Spotlight awards 1985, 86, 87, 88, nat. exec. com. 1987-91), Portland Pub. Rels. Roundtable (chmn. 1985, bd. dirs. 1983-85), Assn. Western Hosps. (editorial adv. bd. 1984-85), Best of West awards 1978, 80, 83, 87), Oreg. Hosp. Pub. Relations Orgn. (pres. 1981, chmn. bd. 1982, bd. dirs. 1992-93), Acad. Health Service Mktg., Am. Hosp. Assn., Am. Mktg. Assn. (Oreg. chpt. bd. dirs. 1992-93), Am. Soc. Hosp. Mktg. & Pub. Relations, Healthcare Communicators Oreg. (conf. keynote speaker 1994), Internat. Assn. Bus. Communicators (18 awards 1981-87), Oreg. Assn. Hosps. (keynote speaker for trustee, 1991, speaker, 1993, bd. dirs. 1992-93), Oreg. Press Women, Nat. and Oreg. Soc. Healthcare Planning and Mktg., Women in Communications (Matrix award 1977), Inst. Managerial and Profl. Women (bd. dirs. 1992—), City Club Portland. Office: 1881 SW Edgewood Rd Portland OR 97201-2235

MARTIN, MARGARET GATELY, elementary education educator; b. Teaneck, N.J., July 24, 1928; d. Martin F. and Grace (Hammell) Gately; m. Phillips H. Martin, June 27, 1953 (div. 1977); children: Paul H., Patrick W., Thomas P. BA, Hunter Coll., 1950, MA, 1953. Cert. elem. tchr., N.Y. Tchr. Pub. Sch. # 5, Queens, N.Y., 1950-53, Wappingers Cen. Sch., Wappingers Falls, N.Y., 1953-55, Jamestown (N.Y.) Pub. Schs., 1968—; tchr. S.S. Peter and Paul Sunday Sch., Jamestown, 1977—. Mem. NEA, AAUW (pres. 1980-82, 92-94, Edn. Found. Program award 1985), Jamestown Tchrs. Assn. (membership chair 1976-78, sec. 1982-84), Jamestown Inter Club Coun. (pres. 1984-86, Woman of Yr. 1991), Green Thumb Garden Club (pres. 1986-88, v.p. 1991-93, 95—), Delta Kappa Gamma (membership chair 1991-94, corr. sec. 1988-90, v.p. 1994—). Republican. Roman Catholic. Home: 130 Ellis Ave Jamestown NY 14701-6218 Office: Lincoln Sch 301 Front St Jamestown NY 14701-6242

MARTIN, MARILYN JOAN, library director; b. Golden Meadow, La., Jan. 17, 1940; d. Marion Francis Mobley and Audrey Virna (Goza) Sapaugh; m. James Reginald Martin, Dec. 16, 1958; children: James Michael, Linda Jill Michaels. BA in History, U. Wash., 1975, MLS, 1976; MA in Pub. History, U. Ark., 1992; PhD in Libr. Sci., Tex. Woman's U., 1993. Cataloger, reference libr. St. Martin's Coll., Lacey, Wash., 1976-78; asst. reference libr. Pacific Luth. U., Tacoma, 1978-85; serials libr. Henderson State U., Arkadelphia, Ark., 1985-86, collection devel. libr., 1987-88, dir. learning resources, 1989—. Contbr. articles to profl. jours. Pres. Ark. United Meth. Hist. Soc., 1994—, also bd. dirs.; chmn. Little Rock Conf., Commn. on Archives and History, United Meth. Ch., 1993—, sec., mem. exec. bd. Gen. Commn. on Archives and History, 1984-92. Mem. ALA (rsch. com. 1993-94, stds. com. 1994-95), Assn. Coll. and Rsch. Librs., Ark. Libr. Assn. (chmn. future conf. site com. 1993-94), Ark. Hist. Assn. (awards com. 1992-940. Republican. Office: Henderson State U Huie Libr Box 7540 Arkadelphia AR 71999-0001

MARTIN, MARSHA ANN, federal agency administrator, social work educator; b. Iowa City, May 22, 1952; d. Fred Jr. and Helen (Paige) M. BA in Psychology, U. Iowa, 1974, MSW, 1975; DSW, Columbia U., 1982. Program specialist Willkie House Inc., Des Moines, 1976-77; cons. research Clark, Phipps, Clark and Harris Inc., N.Y.C., 1979-81; dir. Midtown Outreach Program, Manhattan Bowery Corp., N.Y.C., 1980-85; assoc. prof. Hunter Coll. Sch. Social Work, N.Y.C., 1985-91; dir. Office on Homelessness and SRO Housing, Office of the Mayor, N.Y.C., 1991-93; exec. dir. Interagency Coun. on the Homeless, Dept. of Housing and Urban Dev., Washington, 1993—; cons. Port Authority N.Y. and N.J., 1982-90, NIMH, 1985—. Contbr. articles to profl. jours. Cons. U.S. Conf. Mayors, Five City Project, 1986; sec. The Riverside Ch. Coun., 1987—; co-chair, bd. dirs. Women Need Inc., 1984-90, vice-chair, bd. dirs. N.Y. Coalition Homeless, 1982-90; advisor Office Mayor Homeless Svcs., N.Y.C., 1987-90; com. chair, bd. dirs. N.Y.C. Coalition Mental Health, 1986-92. Nat. Assn. Social Workers, Internat. Conf. Social Welfare, Council Social Work Edn. Democrat. Mem. United Ch. Christ. Office: Interagency Coun on Homeless Dept of Housing and Urban Dev 451 Seventh St SW Rm 7274 Washington DC 20410*

MARTIN, MARY, educator; b. Detroit, Mich., May 17, 1954; d. Enos and Sara (Evans) M. AS, Highland Park C.C., 1975; BA, Wayne State U., 1975, MA in Teaching, 1981; postgrad., So. Calif. Sch. Ministry, Detroit, 1992—. Dietary aide Allan Dee Nursing Home, Detroit, 1972; dietary aide Harper Hosp., Detroit, 1973, 74, nurse aide, 1974-75, respiratory technician, 1975-80; respiratory technician Dr.'s Hosp., Detroit, 1980; head cook, supr. Focus Hope, Detroit, 1981; substitute tchr. Detroit Bd. Edn., 1984-90, tchr. adult edn., 1990-93, tchr., 1993—; interim advisor student coun. Wayne State U., Detroit, 1985. Sunday sch. teaching trainer People's Missionary Bapt. Ch., Detroit, 1986, del., 1984-87, mem. All Aid, 1984-87, mem. choir, 1984, usher, 1984; precinct del. 13th Congl. Dist., 1986-88, 90-92, model, 1985. Recipient Spirit of Detroit award Detroit City Coun., 1993, Spl. Congl. cert. Hon. Barbara Rose Collins, 1994, Proclamation, Wayne County Commr. George Cushingberry, 1994. Mem. Nat. Sociol. Honor Soc. Democrat.

MARTIN, MARY COATES, genealogist, writer; b. Gloucester County, N.J.; d. Raymond and Emily (Johnson) Coates; m. Lawrence O. Kupillas (dec.); m. Clyde Davis Martin (dec.); 1 child, William Raymond. Contbg. editor Md. & Del. Genealogist, St. Michaels, Md., 1985—. Author: The House of John Johnson (1731-1802) Salem County, N.J. and His Descendants, 1979, Fifty Year History of Daughters of Colonial Wars in the State of New York, 1980, 350 Years of American Ancestors: 38 Families: 1630-1989, 1989, Colonial Families: Martin and Bell Families and Their Kin: 1657-1992, 1992. Pres. Washington Hdqrs. Assn., 1970-73, bd. dirs., 1962—; Centennial pres. Sorosis, Inc., 1966-68; bd. dirs. Soldiers Sailors Airmen's Club, N.Y.C., 1976-81, Yorkville Youth Coun., N.Y.C., 1954-60; co-chmn. Colonial Ball, N.Y.C., 1965-67; rec. sec. Parents League of N.Y., Inc., 1954-57; mem. com. Internat. Debutante Ball, N.Y.C., 1977-81; mem. Am. Flag Inst., N.Y.C., 1963-72. Mem. Hereditary Order of Descendants of Colonial Govs. (gov. gen. 1981-83), Nat. Soc. Colonial Dames of Seventeenth Century (N.Y. State pres. 1977-79, parlimentarian 1979-81), Nat. Soc. Daus. of Colonial Wars (N.Y. State pres. 1977-80), Nat. Soc. DAR (regent 1962-65, pres. roundtable 1964-65, N.Y. State chaplain 1968-71, parliamentarian 1980-83, nat. platform com. 1970-76, certificate of award 1971, nat. vice chmn. lineage rsch. com. 1977-80, geneal. com. 1980-83), Nat. Soc. New Eng. Women (dir. gen. 1972-77, nat. vice chmn. helping hand disbursing fund 1968-71), Order of Crown of Charlemagne U.S.A. (corr. sec. gen. 1985-88, 3rd v.p. 1988-89, 2nd v.p. 1989-91), Nat. Soc. Children Am. Revolution, Nicasius de Sille Soc. (pres. 1960-62), Order Ams. of Armorial Ancestry (1st v.p. gen. 1985-88, councillor gen. 1988—), Nat. Gavel Soc., Nat. Soc. Magna Carta Dames, Descendants of Soc. of Colonial Clergy, Huguenot Soc. Am., Descendants of a Knight of Most Noble Order Garter, Nat. Soc. Daus. Am. Colonists, Nat. Soc. U.S. Daus. 1812, Order of Descendants of Colonial Physicians and Chirurgiens, Plantagenet Soc., Vt. Soc. Colonial Dames, Del. Geneal. Soc., Huguenot Hist. Soc., DuBois Family Assn. (1st v.p.), Cumberland County N.J. Hist. Soc., Gloucester County N.J. Hist. Soc., Md. Hist. Soc., Hist. Soc. Del., Salem County N.J. Hist. Soc., Woodstown-Pilesgrove N.J. Hist. Soc., Hereditary Order First Families of Mass., Inc. Home: Hague Towers # 1815 330 W Brambleton Ave Norfolk VA 23510-1307

MARTIN, MARY EVELYN, advertising, marketing and business writing consultant; b. Lexington, Ky.; d. George Clarke and Georgann Elizabeth (Bovis) M. BA magna cum laude, Lindenwood Coll., 1980; MA with honors, U. Ky., 1991. Asst. to pres. The Hamlets, Ltd/Park Place Country Homes, Louisville, 1984-85; advt. designer, copywriter Park Place Country Homes, Anchorage, Ky., 1985-86; creative dir. of advt., mktg., v.p., treas. Park Place Country Homes/Park Place Properties, Anchorage, Ky., 1986—; founder, pres. Good Help Cons. Svc., Louisville and Lexington, Maison Marche Advt. & Promotions, Louisville, 1989; instr. dept. English U. Ky., 1989-91; adj. prof. composition U. Louisville, 1991-95; vis. lectr. lit. Bellarmine Coll., Louisville, 1992; adj. prof. humanities Ind. U. S.E., 1991-94; prof. arts and humanities McKendree Coll., Louisville, 1993-95. Editor: (poetry mag.) The Griffin, 1979-80. Mem. People for the Am. Way, Greenpeace. Recipient Spahmer Creative Writing award, 1979; Haggin fellow U. Ky., 1987; grantee U. Louisville, 1992-94. Mem. Am. Film Inst., Nat. Assn. Home Builders (affiliate), Internat. Platform Assn., Ky. Film Artists Coalition. Democrat. Home: PO Box 23282 Anchorage KY 40223-0282 Office: Park Place Country Homes PO Box 23226 Anchorage KY 40223-0226

MARTIN, MARY WOLF, newspaper editor; b. Corwith, Iowa, Nov. 6, 1930; d. Henry Herbert and Mabel M. (Keeney) Wolf; m. Charles William Martin, Oct. 16, 1950; children: Stephen C., Neal J., Sally Martin Kindell. Grad. high sch., Weyauwega, Wis. Corr. Britt (Iowa) News Tribune, 1946-47; staff writer Wheaton (Ill.) Daily Jour., 1963-65; reporter, photographer Rhinelander (Wis.) Daily News, 1967-69, news editor, 1969-74, mng. editor, 1974-76; mng. editor Neenah-Menasha Northwestern, Neenah, 1976-80; editor Oshkosh Northwestern, 1980-94. Pres. Fox Valley Press Club, Oshkosh, 1982; bd. dirs. Goodwill Industries N.E. Wis., Menasha, 1978-86, Rape Crisis Ctr., Oshkosh, 1981-85, Fox Valley Arts Alliance, Appleton, Wis., 1980-85, Fox Valley Cmty. Tech. Coll., Oshkosh, 1986-92; trustee Paine Art Ctr. Arboretum, Oshkosh, 1990-93. Named Woman of Yr., Bus. and Profl. Women, Rhinelander, 1975, Vol. of Yr., Sexual Abuse Svcs., Oshkosh, 1989. Mem. Wis. Assoc. Press Mng. Editors (pres. Milw. 1985-86), Nat. Assoc. Press Mng. Editors, Am. Soc. Newspaper Editors, Media-Law Com. Wis. Bar Assn. Roman Catholic. Home: 898 County Rd Q Pelican Lake WI 54463

MARTIN, MARY-ANNE, art gallery owner; b. Hoboken, N.J., Apr. 26, 1943; d. Thomas Philipp and Ruth (Kelley) M.; m. Henry S. Berman, June 9, 1963 (div. 1976); 1 child, Julia Berman. Student, Smith Coll., 1961-63; BA, Barnard Coll., 1965; MA, NYU, 1967. Head dept. painting Sotheby Parke Bernet, N.Y.C., 1971-78; sr. v.p. Sotheby's, N.Y.C., 1978-82; pres. Mary-Anne Martin, Fine Art, N.Y.C., 1982—; founder Latin Am. dept. Sotheby's, 1977. Mem. Art Dealers Assn. Am. (v.p., bd. dirs.). Office: 23 E 73rd St New York NY 10021-3522

MARTIN, MELISSA CAROL, radiological physicist; b. Muskogee, Okla., Feb. 7, 1951; d. Carl Leroy and Helen Shirley (Hicks) Paden; m. Donald Ray Martin, Feb. 14, 1970; 1 child, Christina Gail. BS, Okla. State U., 1971; MS, UCLA, 1975. Cert. radiol. physicist, Am. Bd. Radiology, radiation oncology, Am. Bd. Med. Physics. Asst. radiation physicist Hosp. of the Good Samaritan, L.A., 1975-80; radiol. physicist Meml. Med. Ctr., Long Beach, Calif., 1980-83, St. Joseph Hosp., Orange, Calif., 1983-92, Therapy Physics, Inc., Bellflower, Calif., 1993—; cons. in field. Editor: (book) Current Regulatory Issues in Medical Physics, 1992. Fund raising campaign div. mgr. YMCA, Torrance, Calif., 1988-92; dir. AWANA Youth Club-Guards Group, Manhattan Beach, Calif., 1984—. Named Dir. of Symposium, Am. Coll. Med. Physics, 1992. Fellow Am. Coll. Med. Physics (chancellor western region 1992-95); mem. Am. Assn. Physicists in Medicine (profl. coun. 1990-95), Am. Coll. Radiology (econs. com. 1992-95), Calif. Med. Physics Soc. (treas. 1991-95), Am. Soc. for Therapeutic Radiology and Oncology, Health Physics Soc. (pres. So. Calif. chpt. 1992-93), Am. Brachytherapy Soc. Baptist. Home: 507 Susana Ave Redondo Beach CA 90277 Office: Therapy Physics Inc 9156 Rose St Bellflower CA 90706-6420

MARTIN, PATRICIA ANN, music educator; b. Salinas, Calif., Mar. 11, 1939; d. Kenneth Duane and Hazel Gertrude (Setser) Lowe; m. Raymond Dalton Martin, Aug. 22, 1959; children: William Dalton, Brian David. BA, Calif. State U., 1965. Choir accompanist Salinas Christian Ch., 1954-57; choir accompanist North Fresno Christian Ch., Fresno, Calif., 1957-93, organist, 1965—, choir dir., 1968-70; tchr. music pvt. lessons Fresno, 1962—; tchr. music Mountain View Christian Sch., Fresno, 1992-93; organist for weddings, various chs., Fresno, 1962—; dir. bell choir North Fresno Christian Ch., 1985-86, dir. ministry, 1989-90. Composer songs, piano teaching pieces, 1974—; contbr. poetry to anthologies, 1981—. Mem. AAUW, Am. Guild Organists (sec. 1978-79), Calif. Fedn. Music Clubs (pres. 1988-91), Music Tchrs. Assn. Calif. (state chmn. Cal-Plan 1981-83, pres. 1983-85, condr. workshops 1978—, dir. pianorama 1976-88), Jr. Music Festival (pres. 1987-91). Republican.

MARTIN, REBECCA REIST, librarian; b. Princeton, N.J., Mar. 2, 1952; d. Benjamin A. and Harriet (Nold) Reist; m. Joseph M. Lubow; 1 child, Benjamin R. Martin. BA, U. Calif., Santa Cruz, 1973; MA, San Jose State U., 1975; DPA, U. So. Calif., 1992. Med. libr. VA Med. Ctr., San Francisco, 1975-77, chief libr. svc., 1977-81; head biology libr. U. Calif., Berkeley, 1981-85; assoc. libr. dir. San Jose (Calif.) State U., 1985-90; dir. librs. and media svcs. U. Vt., Burlington, 1990—. Author: Libraries and the Changing Face of Academia, 1994; contbr. articles to profl. jours., chpts. in books. Mem. Libr. Commn. San Jose, 1989-90. Mem. ALA, New England Libr. Assn., Am. Soc. Pub. Adminstrn., Am. Assn. Coll. and Rsch. Librs., Libr. Adminstrn. and Mgmt. Assn. (bd. dirs. 1987-89). Office: U Vt Bailey/Howe Libr Burlington VT 05405

MARTIN, RETHA JANE, lawyer; b. Bloomington, Ind., Mar. 8, 1955; d. Delbert Eugene and Beverly June (Carr) M.; m. Robert Ralph Van Alstine, Dec. 26, 1986. BS, Taylor U., 1977; JD, Ind. U., 1980. Assoc. Alexander & Zaleva, Chgo., 1980-83; legal counsel Kimberly Clark Corp., Neenah, Wis., 1983-86; sr. counsel Kimberly Clark Corp., Roswell, Ga., 1986-88; v.p., sr. counsel Whirlpool Corp., Benton Harbor, Mich., 1988-94. Sponsor, advisor Project Together, Benton Harbor, Mich., 1993-94. Mem. Internat. Trademark Assn. (bd. dirs. 1993—). Home: 4232 Ridge Rd Stevensville MI 49127 Office: Whirlpool Properties Inc 400 Riverview Dr Ste 420 Benton Harbor MI 49022

MARTIN, ROSE KOCSIS, law librarian; b. Kiralyrev, Hungary, Aug. 25, 1928; came to U.S., 1949, naturalized, 1954; d. Ferenc and Zsuzsanna (Nehai Szabo) Kocsis; m. Donald L. Martin, Aug. 23, 1961; 1 child, Virginia Kim. Student Seton Hall U., 1960-61; BBA, Kensington U., Glendale, Calif., 1968-69; cert. Cath. U. Am. 1981, George Washington U., 1982. Documents libr. Seton Hall U., South Orange, N.J., 1958-61; mem. office staff Dept. Def., Washington, 1962-63, Dept. Agr., Washington, 1963-67; info. specialist law Office Adminstrv. Law Judges, Dept. Labor, Washington, 1976—. Active Rep. Club, Great Falls, Va., 1986—. Recipient Meritorious award Dept. Agr., 1966, Outstanding award Dept. Labor, 1977, Honorable Svc. to the Nation award Dept. Labor, 1988, Spl. Achievement award, 1990. Mem. Am. Assn. Law Libraries, NAFE, Nat. Mus. Women in Arts, Internat. Platform Assn., Great Falls Woman's Club, River Bend Golf and Country Club. Roman Catholic. Avocations: travel, tennis, reading, swimming, cooking. Home: PO Box 651 Middleburg VA 22117-0651

MARTIN, SARA HINES, counselor, writer; b. Clarkton, Va., Apr. 7, 1933; d. William Bryan and Ruth (Oliver) Hines; separated; children: Carolyn, Rebekah, Martha. BA, Carson-Newman Coll., 1954; MRE, Southwestern Sem., 1957; MS, Ga. State U., 1985. Tchr. Pub. Sch., Warwick, Va., 1954-55, Silver Spring, Md., 1958-59; youth dir. Ch., Atlanta, 1957-58; pvt. practice Marietta and Acworth, Ga., 1986—; free-lance writer, 1957—. Author: Frente al Cancer, 1984, Healing for Adult Children of Alcoholics, 1988, Shame on You!, 1990, Meeting Needs Through Support Groups, 1992. Fgn. missionary, Trinidad and Santo Domingo, Dominican Republic, 1967-81. Mem. Am. Assn. Christian Counselors, Ga. Mental Health Counselors Assn. United Methodist. Home: 4946 Holborn Way Acworth GA 30101-4883

MARTIN, SHIRLEY BOGARD, maternal/women's health nurse administrator; b. Samuels, Ky., Sept. 30, 1941; d. Vernie D. and Eliza (Snawder) Bogard; m. Weldon Martin, Aug. 24, 1962; children: Jospeh Kevin, Jeffery Scott. Grad., Louisville Gen. Hosp., 1962; BSN, Bellarmine Coll., 1980; postgrad., U. Louisville. Cert. perinatal nurse. Charge nurse obstetrics Meth. Evang. Hosp., Louisville; continuing edn. coord. Louisville Gen. Hosp.; dir. CareTenders Children's Clinic, Louisville; transformational leadership team Teenage Parent Program Jefferson County Bd. Edn., Louisville, 1980—; lectr. in field. Adv. bd. Link Project-Drug and Alcohol Program for Pregnant Women, Fairdale Edn. Complex Youth Svc. Ctr.; health adv. com. Jefferson County Pub. Schs. Mem. AWHONN, ANA, Ky. Nurses Assn., Dist. Nurses Assn., Internat. Childbirth Educators Assn., Nat. Orgn. Adolescent Pregency/Parenting, Coun. Early Childhood Edn., Alexander Graham Bell Assn. for the Deaf, Sigma Theta Tau. Home: 3125 Pomeroy Dr Louisville KY 40220-3001 Office: 8800 Westport Rd Louisville KY 40242

MARTIN, STACEY, accountant; b. Dallas, Dec. 5, 1951; d. Orval Calvin and Adella Aloise (Morgan) M.; m. Bryan Keith Ellis, Jan. 31, 1987; 1 child, Martin Harrison. BA in Bus. Adminstrn., Austin Coll., 1973; MBA in Acctg., So. Meth. U., 1974. CPA, 1982. Jr. acct. MacIver & Bell, CPA's, Dallas, 1974-76; staff acct. Steak & Ale Restaurants, Inc., Dallas, 1975-76; internal auditor Columbia Gen. Corp., Dallas, 1976-80; tax specialist MARC, Inc., Dallas, 1981—; owner Sallie's Baby, Infant & Toddler Knitwear, 1988—. Mem. Greenland Hills Neighborhood Assn., Dallas, 1983-94, Dallas Heritage Soc., 1987, Dallas Arboretum Soc., 1987. Mem. AICPA, Tex. Soc. CPA's, DAR (treas. White Oak chpt. 1990—), Daus. Republic of Tex. (treas. Peter James Bailey chpt. 1993—). Presbyterian. Office: MARC Inc 7850 N Belt Line Rd Irving TX 75063-6098

MARTIN, SUSAN ABBOTT, artist, educator; b. Oakland, Calif., June 21, 1948; d. John Chandler and Vae (Hogan) M. BA, Holy Names Coll., 1970; postgrad., U. Calif., Berkeley, 1976; MFA, Calif. Coll. Arts and Crafts, 1981. Grad. coord. Calif. Coll. Arts and Crafts, Oakland, 1981-83; asst. to the dir. Berkeley (Calif.) Art Ctr., 1983; instr. Coll. Marin, Kentfield, Calif., 1983; asst. dir. AICA N.Y. Studio Program, N.Y.C., 1985-86, 88-91; co-dir. internships Pratt Inst., Bklyn., 1991-94, dir. Saturday art sch., 1993—; instr. Jr. Ctr. of Art and Sci., Oakland, 1987, Oakland (Calif.) Mus., 1987; panelist N.Y. State Coun. for the Arts Decentralization Program, S.I., 1992; vis. artist Queens (N.Y.) Coll., 1992, Cleve. (Ohio) Inst. Art, 1993, Chrysler Mus., Norfolk, Va., 1993; artist-in-residence Bemis Found., Omaha, 1990, Lila Wallace Readers Digest, Giverny, France, 1992, Yaddo, Saratoga Springs, N.Y., 1993. Works have appeared at Fiberworks, Berkeley, 1987, Stephen Wirtz Gallery, San Francisco, 1991, Sybaris Gallery, Royal Oak, Mich., 1992, 94. Mem. artist adv. bd. Bemis Found., Omaha. Grantee Pollock-Krasner Found., N.Y.C., 1987. Mem. Nat. Art Edn. Assn., Coll. Art Assn.

MARTIN, SUSAN KATHERINE, librarian; b. Cambridge, Eng., Nov. 14, 1942; came to U.S., 1950, naturalized, 1961; d. Egon and Jolan (Schonfeld) Orowan; m. David S. Martin, June 30, 1962. BA with honors, Tufts U., 1963; MS, Simmons Coll., 1965; PhD, U. Calif., Berkeley, 1983. Intern libr. Harvard U., Cambridge, Mass., 1963-65, systems libr., 1965-73; head systems office gen. libr. U. Calif., Berkeley, 1973-79; dir. Milton S. Eisenhower Libr. Johns Hopkins U., Balt., 1979-88, exec. dir. Nat. Commn. on Libraries and Info. Sci., 1988-90; univ. libr. Georgetown U., Washington, 1990—; mem. libr. adv. com. Princeton (N.J.) U., 1987—; mem. vis. com. Harvard U. Libr., 1987-93, 94—; bd. overseers for univ. libr. Tufts U., 1986—; mem. libr. adv. com. Hong Kong U. Sci. Tech., 1988—; mem. acad. libr. adv. group U. Md. sch. of Librs. and Info. Sci., 1994—; cons. to various librs. and info. cos., 1975—; mem. adv. bd. ERIC, 1990-92, History Assocs., Inc., 1990-92. Author: Library Networks: Libraries in Partnership, 1986-87; editor: Jour. Libr. Automation, 1973-77; mem. editorial bd. Advanced Tech./Librs., 1973-94, Jour. Libr. Adminstrn., 1986-92, Libr. Hi-Tech, 1989—; contbr. articles to profl. jours. Trustee Phila. Area Libr. Network, 1980-81; bd. dirs. Universal Serials and Book Exch., 1981-92, v.p., 1983, pres., 1984; trustee Capital Consortium, 1992-95. Recipient Simmons Coll. Disting. Alumni award, 1977; Council on Library Resources fellow, 1973. Mem. ALA (coun. 1988-92), Rsch. Librs. Group (gov., exec. com. 1985-87), Libr. and Info. Tech. Assn. (pres. 1978-79), Assn. Rsch. Librs., Libr. of Congress (optical disk pilot project adv. com. 1985-89), Coalition for Networked Info. (leader working group 1990-92), Assn. Coll. and Rsch. Librs. (pres. 1994-95), Cosmos Club, Grolier Club, Phi Beta Kappa. Home: 4709 Blagden Ter NW Washington DC 20011-3719 Office: Georgetown U Lauinger Libr Washington DC 20057

MARTIN, WILLIE PAULINE, elementary school educator, illustrator; b. Pendleton, Tex., May 27, 1920; d. Lester B. and Stella (Smith) M.; m. Charles M., June 23, 1946; 1 child, Charles Jr. BS, Middle Tenn. State U., Murfreesboro, 1944; MS, U. Tenn., 1965; postgrad., U. Ga., 1980. Cert. tchr., Tenn., Tex., Ga. Elem. tchr. Bd. Edn., Sparta, Tenn., 1940-44; home econs. tchr. Bd. Edn., Salado, Tex., 1944-46; rsch. technician Oak Ridge (Tenn.) Nat. Lab., 1946-50; art, gen. sci. tchr. Bd. Edn., State of Tenn., 1965-69; art, reading, elem. tchr. Bd. Edn., State of Ga., 1970-83; elem. tchr. Bd. Edn., Augusta, Ga., 1984-86; tchr. aerospace edn. workshop Middle Tenn. State U., 1969; spkr. in field. Contbr. articles in field to profl. jours. Exhibitor Oak Ridge (Tenn.) Festival. Mem. Nat. Art Edn. Assn. (del. conv. Washington 1989, Balt. 1994), Ga. Art Edn. Assn. (del. state conv., dist. pres. 1974, del. conv. Savannah 1986, Augusta 1993, del. state conv. Athens 1994), Tenn. Edn. Assn. Methodist. Home: 1406 Flowing Wells Augusta GA 30909

MARTIN-BOWEN, (CAROLE) LINDSEY, freelance writer; b. Kansas City, Kans., Aug. 4, 1949; d. Lawrence Richard and V. Marie (Schaffer) Pickett; m. Frederick E. Nicholson, July 3, 1971 (div. 1977); 1 child, Aaron Frederick; m. Edwin L. Martin, June 18, 1980 (div. 1987); 1 child, Ki Elise; m. Michael L. Bowen, Dec. 23, 1988. BA in English Lit., U. Mo., Kansas City, 1972, MA in English and Creative Writing, 1988, postgrad., 1991—. Tech. editor Office Hearings and Appeals, U.S. Dept. Interior, Washington, 1976-77; reporter, photographer Louisville Times, 1982-83; reporter, features editor Sun Newspapers, Overland Park, Kans., 1983-84; assoc. editor Modern Jeweler, Overland Park and N.Y.C., 1984-85; writer Coll. Blvd. News, Overland Park, 1985-89, KC View, Kansas City, Mo., 1988-89; editor Number One, Kansas City, Mo., 1986-88, cons., 1988-89; copywriter Sta KXEO/KWWR Radio, Mexico, Mo., 1989; editorial asst. New Letters, 1985—; features writer, columnist The Squire, Prairie Village, Kans., 1990—; instr. English U. Mo., Kansas City, 1986-88, Johnson County C.C., 1988—; tchr. English and fiction Longview C.C., 1988—; instr. writing and mass comm. Webster U., 1990—; instr. women in lit. and creative writing Penn Valley C.C., 1993—; faculty sponsor The Penn (Penn Valley C.C. lit. mag.); owner, writer Paladin Freelance Writing Svc., Kansas City, 1988—; production editor, staff writer Nat. Paralegal Reporter, 1992—; judge New Letters lit. mag. writing contest, 1987—. Author: (novel) The Dark Horse Waits in Boulder, 1985, (poetry) Waiting for the Wake-Up Call, 1990, (fiction) Second Touch, 1990, Cicada Grove and Other Stories, 1992; contbr. poems, book revs., features, cartoon, artwork and photographs to numerous publs. including New Letters, Lip Service and Contemporary Lit. Criticism. Campaigner McGovern for Pres. Campaign, Kansas City, 1971-72. Regents scholar, 1967; GAF fellow, 1986. Mem. U. Mo.-Kansas City Alumni Assn. (media com. 1983-84), Phi Kappa Phi. Roman Catholic. Home: 7109 Pennsylvania Ave Kansas City MO 64114-1316 Office: Penn Valley CC 3201 Southwest Trafficway Kansas City MO 64111-2764

MARTINDALE, JEANIE ARLENE, nursing administrator and educator; b. Valentine, Nebr., Aug. 12, 1956; d. Dale George and Viola Louise (Nollett) Coleman; m. Shelby Ray Martindale, Mar. 2, 1985 (div. July 1994); children: Katherine, William, Margaret. Diploma in Nursing, Bishop Clarkson, Omaha, 1977; BSN, U. Nebr. Med. Ctr. Coll. of Nursing, 1989; postgrad., U. Wyo., 1990—. RN, Wyo., Nebr.; cert. gen. nursing practice. Staff nurse West Nebr. Gen. Hosp., Scottsbluff, Nebr., 1977-79, staff nurse CICU, 1979-82; community clinic supr. Nebr. State Health Dept., Scottsbluff, 1982-89; nursing instr. Laramie County C.C., Cheyenne, Wyo., 1989-93; dir. home care Cmty. Hosp., Torrington, Wyo., 1993—. Mem. ANA, Wyo. Nurses Assn., Sigma Theta Tau. Home: 2535 Main St Torrington WY 82240-1923 Office: Cmty Hosp Home Care Dept 2000 Campbell Dr Torrington WY 82240

MARTINEZ, DIANA LYNN, real estate salesperson, marketing consultant; b. Long Beach, Calif., Oct. 20, 1949; d. Robert Fleming and Mary Caroline (Todd) Hostutler; m. Marty M. Martinez, Aug. 12, 1983; stepchildren: Michael, Denise. BA in Polit. Sci. and Journalism, U. N.Mex., 1971. Various positions including head teller, loan supr. Albuquerque U.S. Employees Fed. Credit Union, 1971-78; realtor, salesperson Bellamah Realty and Picard Realty, Albuquerque, 1978-81; mktg. coord. salesperson Real Estate Co. Am. Better Homes and Gardens, Albuquerque, 1981—. Pres. Park at Peppertree Homeowners Assn., 1991-93; active N.Mex. Ballet Co., Albuquerque, 1991—, Civic Light Opera Guild, Albuquerque, 1991—. Mem. Nat. Assn. Realtors (cert. residential specialist residential sales coun. br. 1991), Albuquerque Bd. Realtors (bd. dirs. 1988-91, Salesperson of Yr. 1991). Roman Catholic. Home: 5745 Peppertree Pl NE Albuquerque NM 87111-6256 Office: RECA Better Homes Gardens 10400 Academy Rd NE Ste 110 Albuquerque NM 87111-1229

MARTINEZ, HERMINIA S., banker, economist; b. Havana, Cuba; came to U.S., 1960, naturalized, 1972; d. Carlos and Amelia (Santana) Martinez Sanchez; B.A. in Econs. cum laude, Am. U., 1965; M.S. in Fgn. Service (Univ. fellow), M.S. in Econs., Georgetown U., 1967; postgrad. Nat. U. Mex. Instr. econs. George Mason Coll., U. Va., Fairfax, 1967-68; researcher World Bank, 1967-69, indsl. economist, industrialization div., 1969-71, loan officer, Central Am., 1971-79, loan officer, economist, Mex., 1973-74, Venezuela and Ecuador, 1973-77, sr. loan officer in charge of Panama and Dominican Republic, Washington, 1977-81, sr. loan officer for Middle East and North Africa, 1981-84, sr. loan officer for Western Africa region, 1985-87, sr. economist Africa Region, 1988-91, prin. ops. officer Africa region, 1991—. Mid-Career fellow Princeton U., 1988-89. Mem. Am. Econ. Assn., Soc. Internat. Devel., Brookings Inst. Latin Am. Study Group. Roman Catholic. Contbg. author: The Economic Growth of Colombia: Problems and Prospects, 1973. Home and Office: 5145 Yuma St NW Washington DC 20016-4336

MARTINEZ, JANE ALICE, library media specialist, consultant; b. Salem, Mass., July 26, 1936; d. Francis S. and Mary E. (Smith) Fennessy; m. Max G. Martinez, Aug. 29, 1959; children: Francis, Rita, Mary, Catherine. BA, Merrimack Coll., North Andover, Mass., 1957; MLS, Rutgers U., 1973. Cert. ednl. media specialist, N.J. Med. technologist West Essex Gen. Hosp., Livingston, N.J., 1963-73; elem. sch. libr. Essex Fells (N.J.) Schs., 1973-77; libr. Parsippany (N.J.)-Troy Hills Schs., 1977-88; libr. media coord. Summit (N.J.) Pub. Schs., 1988—; cons. Fennessy Assocs., East, Roseland, N.J., 1984-91, Prolibra, Maplewood, N.J., 1991-92. Mem. ALA, Am. Assn. Sch. Librs., Libr. and Info. Tech. Assn., Ednl. Media Assn. N.J., N.J. Libr. Assn., N.J. Edn. Assn. Office: Summit Pub Schs 507 Morris Ave Summit NJ 07901-1544

MARTINEZ, MARIA DOLORES, pediatrician; b. Cifuentes, Cuba, Mar. 16, 1959; d. Demetrio and Alba Silvia (Perez) M.; m. James David Marple, Apr. 25, 1992. MD, U. Navarra, Pamplona, Spain, 1984. Med. diplomate. Resident in pediatrics Moses Cone Hosp., Greensboro, N.C., 1986-89; pvt. practice Charlotte, N.C., 1989-93, Mooresville, N.C., 1993—. Mem. AMA, Am. Acad. Pediatrics, N.C. Med. Soc., Mecklenburg County Med. Soc. Republican. Roman Catholic. Office: Mooresville Pediatric Assoc 656 Carpenter Ave Mooresville NC 28215

MARTINEZ, PATRICIA ANN, middle school educator, administrator; b. Phoenix, Oct. 12, 1963; d. Jack Leon and Eleanor Jean (Gripman) McMullen; m. Gerald Marc Martinez, Aug. 11, 1984. BA, Calif. State U., 1986, MA magna cum laude, 1994. Cert. tchr. Calif. Tchr. St. Athanasius Elem. Sch., Long Beach, Calif., 1987-93; vice prin. St. Athanasius Elem. Sch., Long Beach, 1990-93; lang. arts specialist Washington Mid. Schs., Long Beach, 1993—; mentor tchr. St. Athanasius Elem. Sch., Long Beach, 1988-90. Mem. ACLU, Greenpeace, 1988—. Mem. ASCD, NEA, Nat. Cath. Edn. Assn., Internat. Reading Assn., Tchrs. Assn. Long Beach, Calif. Tchrs. Assn., Kappa Delta Pi, Phi Kappa Phi. Democrat. Lutheran. Home: 3601 Gardenia Ave Long Beach CA 90807-4303 Office: Washington Mid Sch 1450 Cedar Ave Long Beach CA 90813-1705

MARTINEZ, RITA RHOADS, women's health nurse, nurse midwife; b. Lancaster, Pa., Oct. 21, 1953; d. Ervin C. and Jeannette M. (Whetstone) Rhoads; m. Juan Carlos Martinez, Aug. 28, 1982; children: Juan G., Carlos, J. Ervin, Rosa, Manuel. Diploma, St. Joseph Hosp., Lancaster, 1974; BSN, Millersville (Pa.) U., 1987. Cert. family nurse practitioner, cert. nurse-midwife. Staff nurse Community Hosp. of Lancaster; dist. nurse Frontier Nursing Svc., Hyden, Ky.; dir. midwifery Birth Care and Family Health Svcs., Quarryville, Pa., 1978—; also bd. dirs., pres. Birth Care and Family Health Svcs., 1993-94; founder 1st out-of-hosp. birth ctr. in Pa., 1978; participant rsch. study on safety of out-of-hosp. birth ctr. Nat. Assn. Childbearing Ctrs., 1989. Named Woman of Distinction, Soroptimists, 1992; recipient March of Dimes award for excellence in maternal-child health, 1993. Mem. Am. Coll. Nurse Midwives, Nat. Assn. Childbearing Ctrs., Millersville U. Nursing Honor Soc., Phi Kappa Phi. Office: 1180 Dry Wells Rd Quarryville PA 17566-9514

MARTINEZ SMITH, ELIZABETH, librarian. BS in Latin Am. Studies, UCLA, 1965; MS in Libr. Sci., U. So. Calif., 1966. County libr. Orange County Pub. Libr., Orange, Calif.; dir. L.A. Pub. Libr. Systems, 1990—; exec. dir. ALA, 1994—. Contbr. articles to profl. jours. Named Woman of Achievement Orange County, 1988, Hispanic Libr. of Yr., Hispanic Book Distributers, 1990; recipient Woman's Alert Award Orange County, 1990. Office: LA Pub Libr System Office of Dir 630 W 5th St Los Angeles CA 90071-2002

MARTING, JANET, English language educator; b. Burlington, Vt., Apr. 3, 1951; m. William F. Marting, May 25, 1986. BA, U. Vt., 1973; MA, Colo. State U., 1975; PhD, Mich. State U., 1982. Instr. English Tex. Tech. U., Lubbock, 1975-78; asst. prof. English Ohio State U., Marion, 1982-84; assoc. prof. English U. Akron, Ohio, 1984—. Editor: Making a Living: A Real World Reader, 1993, The Voice of Reflection: A Writer's Reader, 1995. Mem. Nat. Coun. Tchrs. English, Coll. English Assn., Writing Program Adminstrs. Office: Univ Akron E Buchtel Ave Akron OH 44325

MARTINSON, CONSTANCE FRYE, television program hostess, producer; b. Boston, Apr. 11, 1932; d. Edward and Rosalind Helen (Sperber) Frye; m. Leslie Herbert Martinson, Sept. 24, 1955; 1 child, Julianna Martinson Carner. BA in English Lit., Wellesley Coll., 1953. Dir. pub. relations Coro Found., Los Angeles, 1974-79; producer/host KHJ Dimensions, Los Angeles, 1979-81, Connie Martinson Talks Books, Los Angeles, 1981—; instr. dept. humanities UCLA, 1981—; moderator, instr. Univ. Judaism; celebrity advisor Book Fair-Music Ctr., L.A., 1986; bd. dirs. Friends of English UCLA. Author Dramatization of Wellesley After Images, 1974; book editor, columnist Calif. Press Bur. Syndicate, 1986—. Pres. Mayor's adv. council on volunteerism, Los Angeles, 1981-82; chmn. community affairs dept. Town Hall of Calif., Los Angeles, 1981-85; bd. dirs. legal def. fund NAACP, Los Angeles, 1981-84. Mem. Women in Cable, Am. Film Inst., Jewish TV Network (bd. dirs. 1985-87), PEN, Nat. Book Critics Assn., Wellesley Coll. Club (pres. 1979-81), Mulholland Tennis Club. Democrat. Jewish. Home and Office: 2288 Coldwater Canyon Dr Beverly Hills CA 90210-1756

MARTINSON, IDA MARIE, nurse, physiologist, educator; b. Mentor, Minn., Nov. 8, 1936; d. Oscar and Marvel (Nelson) Sather; m. Paul Varo Martinson, Mar. 31, 1962; children—Anna Marie, Peter. Diploma, St. Luke's Hosp. Sch. Nursing, 1957; B.S., U. Minn., 1960, M.N.A., 1962; Ph.D., U. Ill., Chgo., 1972. Instr. Coll. St. Scholastica and St. Luke's Sch. Nursing, 1957-58, Thornton Jr. Coll., 1967-69; lab. asst. U. Ill. at Med. Ctr., 1970-72; lectr. dept. physiology U. Minn., St. Paul, 1972-82; asst. prof. Sch. Nursing U. Minn., 1972-74, assoc. prof. rsch., 1974-77, prof., dir. rsch., 1977-82; prof. dept. family health care U. Calif., San Francisco, 1982—, chmn. dept., 1982-90; vis. rsch. prof. Nat. Taiwan U., Def. Med. Ctr., 1981; vis. prof. nursing Sun Yat-Sen U. Med. Scis., Guang Zhou, Republic of China, Ewha Women's U., Seoul, Korea, vis. prof. nursing Frances Payne Bolton Sch. of Nursing, Case Western U., Cleve., 1994—. Author: Mathematics for the Health Science Student, 1977; editor: Home Care for the Dying Child, 1976, Women in Stress, 1979, Women in Health and Illness, 1986, The Child and Family Facing Life Threatening Illness, 1987, Family Nursing, 1989, Home Health Care Nursing, 1989; contbr. chpts. to books, articles to profl. jours. Active Am. Cancer Soc. Recipient Book of Yr. award Am. Jour. Nursing, 1977, 80, 87, 90, Children's Hospice Internat. award, 1988, Humanitarian award for pediatric nursing, 1993; Fulbright fellow, 1991. Mem. Council Nurse Researchers, Nat. League for Nursing, Am. Acad. Nursing, Am. Nurses Assn., Inst. Medicine, Sigma Xi, Sigma Theta Tau. Lutheran. Office: U Calif Family Health Care Nursing San Francisco CA 94143-0606

MARTINSON, RITA R., state legislator; b. Gloster, Miss., Sept. 11, 1937; d. D.M. and Beulah (LeDoux) Randall; m. William K. Martinson Sr., Aug. 2, 1958; children: Ginny Martinson Vampran, Karen Martinson McKie, W.K. Jr., Allen. BA in Polit. Sci., Millsaps Coll., 1991. Mem. Miss. Ho. of Reps., 1992—. Mem. Madison County Rep. Exec. Com., 1988-91; active Madison Arboretum, 1992—. Mem. Madison County C. of C. (Outstanding Citizen 1992), City of Madison C. of C., South Madison Rep. Women's Club, Ridgeland/Northpark Lions Club (past v.p. 1990-91). Roman Catholic. Home: 1472 Hwy 51 Madison MS 39110 Office: Miss State Ho of Reps PO Box 1018 Jackson MS 39215-1018

MARTONE, JEANETTE RACHELE, artist; b. Mineola, N.Y., June 5, 1956; d. John and Mildred Cecilia (Loehr) M. BFA, SUNY, Purchase, 1978. One woman shows include Ariel Gallery, N.Y.C., 1990, La Mantia Gallery, Northport, N.Y., 1994; exhibited in group shows from 1980 to 1995 including Harbor Gallery, Cold Spring Harbor, 1980, Huntington coun. Arts, 1986, Pindar Gallery, N.Y.C., 1987, Mills Pond House, Smithtown, N.Y., 1987, Suffolk County Exec. Offices, Hauppage, N.Y., 1988, La Mantia Gallery, Northport, N.Y., 1990, Nassau County Office Cultural Affairs, 1991, Ward-Nasse. Gallery, N.Y.C., 1991, Monsterrat Gallery, N.Y.C., 1991, Priscilla Redfield Roe Gallery, Bellport, N.Y., 1991, L.I. U., Brookville, 1992 Northport B.J. Spoke Gallery, Huntington, N.Y., 1992, Fischetti Gallery, N.Y., 1992, Artists Space, N.Y.C., 1992, N.Y. Botanical Gardens, Bronx, N.Y., 1993, L.I. U., Brookville, N.Y., 1994, Goodman Gallery, Southampton, N.Y., 1994, B.J. Spoke Gallery, Huntington, N.Y., 1994, Islip Art Mus., East Islip, N.Y., 1994. Recipient Award of Excellence Gold medal Art League of Nassau County, 1993, Best in Show award Nat. League Am. PEN Women Artists, 1990, 92, Windsor and Newton award for oil Arts Coun. East Islip, N.Y., 1989, award of excellence Art League of Nassau County, 1987, 88, many best in shows. Mem. Catherine Lorillard Wolfe Art Club (Frank B. and Mary Anderson Cassidy Meml. award 1992, Award for Oil 1987), Allied Artists of Am. (John Young Hunter Meml. award 1993, Antonio Cerino Meml. award 1990), Hudson valley Art Assn., Knickerbock Artists of Am., Nat. Art League. Home: 47 Summerfield Ct Deer Park NY 11729

MARTONE, LINDA ANN, real estate salesperson; b. Troy, N.Y., Sept. 13, 1957; d. Robert Francis and Phyllis Rita (Ciarlone) M. Student, Hudson Valley C.C., Troy, 1980-82. Real estate salesperson Roberts Real Estate, Troy, 1986-90; site coord. Date Constrn., Clifton Park, N.Y., 1988-90; site rep. Nags Head (N.C.) Constrn., 1991-92; real estate salesperson Beach Realty, Kill Devil Hills, N.C., 1992—. Mem. Dane County Bd. Realtors, Nat. Assn. Realtors, N.C. Assn. Realtors. Republican. Roman Catholic. Office: Beach Realty & Constrn PO Box 69 Kill Devil Hills NC 27948-0069

MARTYNICK, KAREN L., county commissioner; b. Ridley Park, Pa., Sept. 2, 1952; d. Edward Svend and Margaret Regina (McLaughlin) Holst; m. George Martynick; children: George, Daniel Edward. BA in Polit. Sci.,

West Chester U., 1976, MS in Health Adminstrn., 1984. Adminstrv. asst. Chester County Commrs., West Chester, 1984-86; exec. dir. Rep. Com. Pa., Harrisburg, 1986-89, Rep. Com. Chester County, 1989-91; dir. intergovtl. affairs com. Senate of Pa., Harrisburg, 1991; commr. County of Chester, 1991—, chmn., 1993—. Pres. Friends Hist. Goshenville, East Goshen, Pa., 1990—; pub. svc. chair United Way Chester County, 1992—; del. Rep. Nat. Conv., Houston, 1992; mem. Southeastern Pa. Transp. Authority, Greater Phila. Econ. Devel. Coalition; chmn. Chester County Prison Bd., 1992—. Recipient Ballade de Lourdes award Chester County Ballet Co., 1992, West Chester YWCA Leadership award, 1993; named Woman of Achievement, Delaware Valley March of Dimes, 1992, Women of Yr. Chester County Women's Coalition, 1994. Mem. Nat. Assn. Counties (steering com. 1993—), Pa State Assn. County Commrs. (vice chair 1992—, legis. com.). Epsicopalian. Office: County of Chester 2 N High St West Chester PA 19380-3023

MARUMOTO, BARBARA CHIZUKO, state legislator; b. San Francisco, July 21, 1939; d. Takeo and Kathleen (Tsuchiya) Okamoto; B.A., U. Hawaii, 1971; student U. Calif., 1957-60, UCLA, 1957; children—Marshall, Jay, Wendy, Megan. Legis. aide, researcher, Honolulu, 1972-78; mem. Hawaii Ho. of Reps., 1978—, minority floor leader, 1981; elected del. to Constl. Conv., 1978; real estate agt., 1979—. Mem. exec. bd. Hist. Hawaii Found.; bd. dirs. Pacific council Girl Scouts U.S.A.; active Rep. Party, Common Cause, LWV, PTA, Ripon Soc. Clubs: Honolulu, Jr. League Honolulu. Contbr. various news columns to publs. Office: State Office Tower 235 S Beretania St Rm 1305 Honolulu HI 96813-2437*

MARUOKA, JO ANN ELIZABETH, information systems manager; b. Monrovia, Calif., Jan. 1, 1945; d. John Constantine and Pearl (Macovei) Gotsinas; m. Lester Hideo Maruoka, Nov. 8, 1973 (div. Aug. 1992); stepchildren: Les Scott Kaleohano, Lee Stuart Keola. BA, UCLA, 1966; MBA, U. Hawaii, 1971. Office mgr. and asst. R. Wenkam, Photographer, Honolulu, 1966-69; computer mgmt. intern and sys. analyst Army Computer Sys. Command, Honolulu, 1969-78; reservations mgr. Hale Koa Hotel, Honolulu, 1978-79; equal employment opportunity specialist U.S. Army Pacific Hdqs., Honolulu, 1979-80, computer specialist, 1980-87, supervisory info. sys. mgr., chief plans & resource mgmt. divsn., 1987—; bd. dirs. High Performance Computing and Comm. Coun., Tiverton, R.I.; Pacific v.p. Fedn. Govt. Info. Processing Couns., Washington, 1992—. Mem. Nat. and Hawaii Women's Polit. Caucus, Honolulu, 1987—; advisor Fed. Women's Coun. Hawaii, Honolulu, 1977—. Mem. AAUW, LWV, Armed Forces Comm.-Electronics Assn. (Hawaii chpt.), Assn. U.S. Army (Mgr. award 1990), Federally Employed Women (advisor Aloha and Rainbow chpts. 1977—), Army Signal Corps Regimental Assn., Hawaii Intergovt. Info. Processing Coun. (pres. 1988-89, Svc. award 1989). Democrat. Office: APIM-PR US Army Pacific Hdqs Fort Shafter HI 96858

MARVEL, WANDA FAYE, home health administrator; b. Price, Utah, Nov. 10, 1951; d. Albert Jr. and Hazel A. Marvel; m. John M. Robinsin Jr. ADN, Westark Community Coll., 1978; BSN, U. Mo., 1986, MSN, 1993. Cardiac nurse Bapt. Med. Ctr., Little Rock, 1978-79; ICU staff nurse Ellis Fischel Cancer Ctr., Columbia, Mo., 1982-84; staff nurse emergency svc., med. ICU U. Mo., Columbia, 1984-87; head nurse surgery dept. Ellis Fischel Cancer Ctr., Columbia, 1988-89; rsch. asst. U. Mo., Columbia, 1988-89; asst. dir. Columbia Regional Hosp. Home Health, 1990-92; area v.p. HealthCor, Inc., Dallas, 1993-94, clin. cons., 1995—; guest lectr. Columbia Coll. RN Completion, 1989; clin. instr. Cen. Meth. Coll., Fayette, Mo., 1987; bd. dirs. Carpe Diem Hospice, Inc. Vol. Hospice Cen. Mo., Columbia, 1990; bd. dirs. Hospice Found., Columbia, 1990-91. Recipient Grad. Nurse Assn. scholarship U. Mo., 1989, Nursing Fund scholarship, 1989, Superior Grad. Achievement award, 1990. Mem. AAUW, ANA, Grad. Nurses Assn. (pres. 1988-89), Oncology Nurses Soc., Emergency Nurses Assn. (chmn. govtl. 1988), Sigma Theta Tau.

MARVIN, NIKI, film producer. films include: Flight of the Spruce Goose, 1986, A Nightmare on Elm Street Part III: Dream Warriors, 1987, The Hidden, 1987, Midnight Cabaret, 1991, The Shawshank Redemption, 1994 (Acad. Awd. nom., Best Picture); TV films include: Buried Alive, 1990, Strays, 1991. Office: c/o William Morris Agency 151 El Camino Beverly Hills CA 90212*

MARVIN, URSULA BAILEY, geologist; b. Bradford, Vt., Aug. 20, 1921; d. Harold Leslie and Alice Miranda (Bartlett) Bailey; m. Lloyd Burton Chaisson, June 28, 1944 (div. 1951); m. Thomas Crockett Marvin, Apr. 1, 1952. BA, Tufts Coll., 1943; MA, Harvard/Radcliffe Coll., 1946; PhD, Harvard U., 1969. Rsch. asst. dept. geology U. Chgo., 1947-50; mineralogist Union Carbide Corp., N.Y.C., 1952-58; instr. dept. geology Tufts U., Medford, Mass., 1958-61; geologist, sr. staff Smithsonian Astrophys. Obs., Cambridge, Mass., 1961—, fed. womens program coord., 1974-77; vis. prof. dept. geology Ariz. State U., Tempe, 1978; lectr. geology Harvard U., 1974-92; trustee Tufts U., 1975—, U. Space Rsch. Assn., Columbia Md., 1979-84. Author: Continental Drift, 1973; contbr. chpt.: Astronomy from Space, 1983, The Planets, 1985; assoc. editor Earth in Space, Am. Geophys. Union, 1988-90; contbr. articles to profl. jours. Mem. Lunar and Planetary Sci. Coun., Houston, 1987-91; chair antarctic meteorite working group Lunar and Planetary Inst., Houston, 1993—. Recipient Antarctic Svc. medal NSF, 1983, Group Achievement award NASA, 1984; Asteroid Marvin named in her honor, Minor Planet Bur. of Internat. Astron. Union, 1991, Marvin Nunatak (mountain peak rising through the Antarctic ice sheet) named in her honor, 1992. Fellow AAAS, Meteoritical Soc. (pres. 1975-76), Geol. Soc. Am. (History of Geology award 1986); mem. Assn. Women in Sci., Am. Geophys. Union, History of Earth Scis. Soc. (pres. 1991), Internat. Commn. on History Geol. Scis. (sec.-gen. 1989—). Office: Harvard-Smithsonian Ctr for Astrophysics 60 Garden St Cambridge MA 02138-1516

MARX, KATHRYN, photographer, author; b. N.Y.C., June 4, 1950; d. Arthur and Emilie (Hyman) M. Freelance journalist, photographer N.Y. Newsday, N.Y. Daily News, Village Voice, Soho News, 1974-82; with Infinito Mag., Italy, 1986; photographer Photo-Reporter, Paris, 1986, Editions Paris-Musées, 1992. Photography exhbns. include Le Grand Palais, Paris, 1991, U.S. Embassy, Brussels, 1990, Carnavalet Mus., Paris, 1992, N.Y. Pub. Libr., 1992, Mus. Modern Art, Paris, 1994; author: Photography for the Art Market, 1988, Right Brain/Left Brain Photography, 1994; collaborator (with author Michael S. Lasky) The Complete Junkfood Book, 1974-76; contbr. articles to profl. jours. Rape crisis counselor St. Vincents Hosp., N.Y.C., 1981-83; active ACLU, N.Y.C., 1974-76; mem. Plan Internat. Foster Program, R.I., 1992—. Grantee Acad. Am. Poets, 1982, Eastman Kodak Co., Paris, N.Y., 1992—, Fuji Film France, Paris, 1991-94, Sernam Corp., Paris, 1992—. Mem. Author's Guild, Author's League of Am. Democrat. Home: 61 Jane St New York NY 10014 Office: 77 rue Notre Dame Des Champs, 75006 Paris France

MARZETTI, LORETTA A., government agency executive, policy analyst; b. N.Y., Mar. 13, 1943; d. Lawrence Arthur and Josephine (Palazzo) M.; m. Gerald Oren Miller, July 12, 1986. AB in Sociology, Cath. U. Am., 1965. Chief info. svcs. br., OARM EPA, Washington, 1985-88, dir. comm., analysis and budget divsn., office of solid waste, 1988—. Home: 3088 S Woodrow St Arlington VA 22206 Office: Environmental Protection Agency Solid Waste 5305 401 M St SW Washington DC 20460

MARZOCCHI, JUDITH ANN, librarian; b. Lexington, Ky., Oct. 4, 1948; d. Charles B. and Jean Bennett (Hensley) Chidester; 1 child, Annette. BS, U. R.I., 1976; MS, Purdue U., Hammond, Ind., 1980; EdS, Purdue U., W. Lafayette, 1987. Libr. media specialist Sch. City of Hammond, 1978—. Co-author: Gifted/Talented Guidelines for Middle/High School and Computer Curriculum for K-5; contbr. articles to profl. jours. Recipient PTA Svc. award; Hammond Edn. Found. grantee; grantee Ind. Dept. Edn. Mem. ASCD, Nat. Coun. Tchrs. English, Assn. of Media Educators, Hammond Area Reading Coun., Ind. Assn. for Gifted and Talented, Kappa Delta Pi, Delta Kappa Gamma. Home: 6642 Monroe Ave Hammond IN 46324-1547

MASCETTI, LINDA F., psychologist; b. Washington, Jan. 11, 1947; d. Romano and Elvira (Capponi) M.; m. Joseph B. Romesser, Feb. 1, 1976; 1 child, Lisa Romesser. BA in Psychology, Wellesley Coll., 1968; PhD in Clin. Psychology, Cath. U. Am., 1973. Lic. psychologist, Pa. Staff psychologist Community Counseling Svcs., Wilkes-Barre, Pa., 1973-75; regional ctr. dir. Community Counseling Svcs., Pittston, Pa., 1975-77; pvt. practice psychology Drums, Pa., 1977—; psychiat. reviewer Bur. Disability Determination, Wilkes-Barre, 1985-89, 92—; mental health cons. Keystone Job Corp Ctr., Drums, 1977-88. Bd. dirs. Hazleton (Pa.) Gen. Hosp., 1986-91, Hazleton Health Care Found., 1988—, Planned Parenthood of N.E. Pa., Trexlertown, 1978-94; chair of bd. Health Care Plus, Hazleton, 1988—; alumnae admissions rep. Wellesley (Mass.) Coll., 1979—. Recipient Margaret Sanger Cir. award Planned Parenthood of N.E. Pa., 1992. Mem. APA, NOW, Pa. Psychol. Assn., Northeastern Pa. Psychol. Assn., Women's Coalition of Greater Hazleton. Home and Office: RR 3 Box 714 Drums PA 18222

MASCHERONI, ELEANOR EARLE, investment company executive; b. Boston, June 6, 1955; d. Ralph II and Eleanor Forbes (Owens) Earle; m. Mark Mascheroni, May 30, 1981; children: Olivia Forbes, Isabella Starbuck, Rex Owens. AB, Brown U., 1977. Dept. adminstr. Sotheby Parke Benet, N.Y.C., 1978-79; asst. dir. devel. Inst. Architecture and Urban Studies, N.Y.C., 1979-81; assoc. in pub. rels. Prudential Securities Inc., N.Y.C., 1981-84, asst. v.p. pub. rels., 1984-86, assoc. v.p. pub. rels., 1986-87, v.p., mgr. pub. rels., 1987-89, 1st v.p., dir. pub. rels., 1989-91; v.p. pub. rels. Scudder, Stevens & Clark, N.Y.C., 1991—. Advisory com. Duke Comprehensive Cancer Ctr., Durham, N.C., 1986—; devel. and communications com., Cancer Care, Inc., N.Y.C., 1985—; bd. govs. St. Timothy's Sch., Stevenson, Md., 1987-94. Democrat. Episcopalian.

MASHIN, JACQUELINE ANN COOK, medical sciences consultant; b. Chgo., May 11, 1941; d. William Hermann and Ann (Smidt) Cook; m. Fredric John Mashin, June 7, 1970; children: Joseph Glenn, Alison Robin. BS, U. Md., 1984. Cert. realtor. Adminstrv. asst. CIA, Washington, 1963-66; asst. to mng. dir. Aerospace Edn. Found., Washington, 1966-74; exec. asst. to asst exec. dir. Air Force Assn., Washington, 1974-79; v.p., ptnrship. owner Discount Linen Store, Silver Spring, Md., 1979-81; asst. regional polit. dir. Office of Pres.-elect, Washington, 1980-81; confidential asst. to dir. Office of Personnel Mgmt. (US), Washington, 1981-83; spl. asst. to dep. dir. Office of Mgmt. and Budget, Washington, 1983-86; dir. internat. communications and spl. asst. to commr. Dept. of the Interior, Washington, 1986-89, cons., 1989—. Pres. Layhill Civic Assn., Silver Spring, Md., 1980; state chmn. Md.'s Reagan Youth Delegation, Annapolis, Md., 1980; state treas., office mgr. Reagan-Bush State Hdqrs. of Md., Silver Spring, 1980; mem. Women's Com. Nat. Symphony Orch. Mem. Air Force Assn. (life), Aux. Salvation Army (life), Am. League Lobbyists, Am. Soc. Pers. Adminstrn., Am. Soc. Pub. Adminstrn., Internat. Platform Assn., Chevy Chase Women's Club, U.S. Capital Hist. Soc., Women's Nat. Rep. Club (N.Y.C.), Indian Springs Country Club. Republican. Home and Office: 2429 White Horse Ln Silver Spring MD 20906-2243

MASHKIN, KAREN BETH, family therapist, educator, psychologist; b. Hartford, Conn., Nov. 12, 1949; d. Jacob and Frances Mashkin. BA, George Washington U., 1971; MA, U. Ariz., 1974, PhD, 1976. Lic. psychologist, Calif., marriage, family and child counselor, Calif. Psychology extern Palo Verde Hosp., Tuscon, 1972-73; psychology extern dept. psychology Coll. Medicine Univ. Hosp.-U. Ariz., Tuscon, 1973-74; tchr. dept. psychology U. Ariz., Tuscon, 1974; intern clin. psychology Langley Porter Neuropsychiat. Inst. U. Calif. Coll. Medicine, San Francisco, 1975-76, postdoctoral fellow Langley Porter Neuropsychiat. Inst., 1976-77; co-dir. family therapy program U. Calif. Med. Sch., San Francisco, 1977; mem. faculty John F. Kennedy U., Orinda, Calif., 1976-80; assoc. clin. prof. family therapy tng. program Langley Neuropsychiatric Inst. U. Calif. Med. Sch., San Francisco, 1976—; mem. core faculty Calif. Grad. Sch., San Rafael, 1975—; pvt. practice Mill Valley, Calif., 1977—; adj. faculty Calif. Sch. Profl. Psychology, San Francisco and Berkeley, 1976-78, Calif. Inst. Integral Studies, 1985—; mem. evaluation cons. team dept. psychology U. Ariz., 1974, mem. human sexuality program dept., 1974; presenter U. Hawaii, Manoa, Mt. Zion Hosp., San Francisco, Woodside Sch. Dist., Community Mental Health Agys., World of Family Therapy Symposium, U. Calif. Sch. Medicine, Tavistock Clinic, London, co-presenter internat. family therapy conf. Contbr. articles to profl. jours. NIMH scholar, 1971, 72. Mem. AAUW, APA, Calif. Psychol. Assn., Marin County Psychol. Assn., Alpha Lambda, Phi Beta Kappa, Psi Chi. Office: 45 Camino Alto Ste 203 Mill Valley CA 94941-2935

MASINI, DONNA, poet, educator; b. Bklyn., Dec. 13, 1954; d. Bruno Francis and Betty (La Morte) M.; m. Judd Tully, June 28, 1986. BA summa cum laude, Hunter Coll., 1985; MA in English Lit., NYU, 1988. Tchr. The Writer's Voice-West Side YMCA, N.Y.C., 1992—, Hunter Coll., N.Y.C., 1995—. Author: (poetry) That Kind of Danger, 1994 (Barnard Women Poet's prize 1994 Beacon Press). Recipient Poetry fellowship/grant N.Y. Found. for Arts, 1985, Yaddo fellowship, summer 1988, 89, 90, Poetry fellowship/grant Nat. Endowment for Arts, 1991, Poetry prize Madison Rev., 1991, New Letters Poetry prize New Letters Mag., 1992. Mem. Phi Beta Kappa. Home: PO Box 5 New York NY 10012-0001

MASKALL, MARTHA JOSEPHINE, executive recruiter, publisher; b. Kearny, N.J., Mar. 30, 1945; d. Charles Edgar and Mathilda (Comba) M. BA in Biology, Stanford U., 1966; MA, Duke U., 1969. Cert. data processor, 1979. Data base adminstr. Armco Steel, Ashland, Ky., 1972-74; project mgr. Rand Info. Systems, San Francisco, 1974-78; sales rep. Datacom ADR, San Francisco, 1980-81; systems engr. Four-Phase Systems, Sacramento, Calif., 1981-83; exec. recruiter Sacramento, 1983—; owner Attitude Works Pub., Fair Oaks, Calif., 1990—. Author: The Attitude Treasury: 101 Inspiring Quotations, 1990, The Athena Treasury: 101 Inspiring Quotations by Women, 1993. NDEA fellow, 1966-68. Mem. Data Processing Mgmt. Assn. (program dir. 1980, 82, sec. 1983), Sierra Club, Nat. Assn. Profl. Saleswomen (pres. 1992), Bus. and Profl. Women, Optimists, Toastmasters (v.p. 1985, pres. 1986, div. gov. 1987, speakers bur. 1988, Disting. Toastmaster award 1989). Democrat. Home: 8456 Hidden Valley Cir Fair Oaks CA 95628-6121 Office: Marty Maskall & Assoc PO Box 1765 Fair Oaks CA 95628-1765

MASLAND, LYNNE S., university official; b. Boston, Nov. 18, 1940; d. Keith Arnold and Camilla (Puleston) Shangraw; m. Edwin Grant Masland, Sept. 19, 1960 (div. 1975); children: Mary Conklin, Molly Allison. Student, Mt. Holyoke Coll., South Hadley, Mass., 1958-60; BA, U. Calif., Riverside, 1970; MA, U. Calif., 1971; PhD, U. B.C., Vancouver, Can., 1994. Asst. pub. rels. dir. Inter-Am. U., San German, P.R., 1963-64; asst. to dir. elem. edn. Govt. of Am. Samoa, Pago Pago, 1966-68; project dir., cons. Wash. Commn. for Humanities, Seattle, 1976-80; exec. editor N.W. Happenings Mag., Greenbank, Wash., 1980-84; media specialist Western Wash. U., Bellingham, 1984-88; dir. pub. info. Western Wash. U., 1988—; cons. William O. Douglas Inst., Seattle, 1984, Whatcom Mus. History and Art, Bellingham, 1977; instr. U. Nebr., Omaha, 1972-86, Western Wash. U., 1972-86. Editor: The Human Touch: Folklore of the Northwest Corner, 1979, Proceedings: The Art in Living, 1980, Reports to the Mayor on the State of the Arts in Bellingham, 1980-81; contbr. numerous articles to profl. jours. Pres. LWV, Whatcom County, Bellingham, 1977-79; bd. dirs. N.W. Concert Assn., 1981-83, Wash. State Folklife Coun., 1985-90; docent Nat. Gallery, Washington, 1969; bd. dirs. Sta. KZAZ, nat. pub. radio, Bellingham, 1992-93. Univ. grad. fellow U. B.C., 1990-94. Mem. Am. Comparative Lit. Assn., Nat. Assn. Presswomen, Wash. Press Assn. (pres. 4th Corner chpt. 1987-88, Superior Performance award 1986), Can. Comparative Lit. Assn., Internat. Comparative Lit. Assn., Philological Assn. of Pacific Coast, Coun. for Advancement and Support Edn. (Case Dist. VIII Gold award for Media Rels.), Rotary (bd. dirs. 1992-94). Episcopalian. Office: Western Wash U High St Bellingham WA 98225

MASLANSKY, CAROL JEANNE, toxicologist; b. N.Y.C., Mar. 3, 1949; d. Paul Jeremiah and Jeanne Marie (Filiatrault) Lane; m. Steven Paul Maslansky, May 28, 1973. BA, SUNY, 1971; PhD, N.Y. Med. Coll., 1983. Diplomate Am. Bd. Toxicology; cert. gen. toxicology. Asst. entomologist N.Y. State Dept. Health, White Plains, 1973-74; sr. biologist Am. Health Found., Valhalla, N.Y., 1974-76; rsch. fellow N.Y. Med. Coll., Valhalla, 1977-83, Albert Einstein Coll. Medicine, Bronx, N.Y., 1983; copr. toxicologist Texaco, Inc., Beacon, N.Y., 1984-85; prin. GeoEnviron. Cons., Inc., White Plains, N.Y., 1982—; lectr. in entomology Westchester County Parks and Preserves, 1973—, lectr. toxicology and hazardous materials, 1985—. Author: Air Monitoring Instrumentation, 1993, (with others) Training for Hazardous Materials Team Members, 1991 (manual, video) The Poison Control Response to Chemical Emergencies, 1993. Mem. Harrison (N.Y.) Vol. Ambulance Corps., 1986-91, Westchester County (N.Y.) Hazardous Materials Response Team, 1987—. Monsanto Fund Fellowship in Toxicology, 1988-90; grad. fellowship N.Y. Med. Coll., 1977-83. Mem. AAAS, N.Y. Acad. Sci., Am. Coll. Toxicology, Am. Indsl. Hygiene Assn. (NYCON chpt.). Home: 122 Saxon Woods Rd White Plains NY 10605

MASLIN, JANET, film critic; b. N.Y.C., Aug. 12, 1949; d. Paul and Lucille (Becker) M.; m. Benjamin Cheever; children: John, Andrew. BA in Math., U. Rochester, 1970. Film and music critic The Boston Phoenix, 1972-76; film critic Newsweek, N.Y.C., 1976-77; dep. film critic The N.Y. Times, N.Y.C., 1977-93, chief film critic, 1993—. Office: The NY Times 229 W 43rd St New York NY 10036-3913

MASLOW, MELANIE JANE, physician; b. N.Y.C., Mar. 11, 1952; d. Morris and Rosalie (Kaufman) Schwartz; m. James Edward Maslow, June 17, 1973 (div. 1977); m. David Tice, Sept. 12, 1985. B.A., Barnard Coll., 1973; M.D., NYU, 1977. Diplomate Am. Bd. Internal Medicine. Intern NYU Med. Ctr.-Manhattan VA Hosp., N.Y.C., 1977-78, resident, chief resident, 1978-81, fellow, 1981-83; co-physician-in-charge infectious disease L.I. Coll. Hosp., Bklyn., 1983-87, co-chief infectious diseases, 1987-92; asst. chief infectious diseases VA Med Ctr, N.Y.C., 1992—; clin. asst. prof. medicine NYU Med. Sch., 1992—. Fellow ACP; mem. Am. Soc. for Microbiology, Infectious Diseases Soc. Am., N.Y. Acad. Sci. Democrat. Jewish. Office: VA Med Ctr 423 E 23rd St New York NY 10010

MASON, AIMEE HUNNICUTT ROMBERGER, retired philosophy and humanities educator; b. Atlanta, Nov. 3, 1918; d. Edwin William and Aimee Greenleaf (Hunnicutt) Romberger; m. Samuel Venable Mason, Aug. 16, 1941 (dec. 1988); children: Olivia Elizabeth (Mrs. Mason Butcher), Christopher Leeds. BA, Conn. Coll., 1940; postgrad. Emory U., 1946-48; MA, U. Fla., 1979, PhD, 1980, MA, Stetson U., 1968. Jr. exec. merchandising G. Fox & Co., Hartford, Conn., 1940-41; air traffic contr. CAA, Atlanta, 1942; ptnr. Coronado Concrete Products, New Smyrna Beach, Fla., 1953-81; adj. faculty Valencia Jr. Coll., Orlando, Fla., 1969; instr. philosophy and humanities Seminole Community Coll., Sanford, 1969, ret. Area cons. ARC, 1947-50; del. Nat. Red Cross, Washington, 1949; founding mem. St. Joseph Hosp. Aux., Atlanta, 1950-53; v.p., treas. New Smyrna Beach PTA 1955-60; bd. dirs. Atlanta Symphony Orch., Fla. Symphony Orch., 1954-59; mem. Code Enforcement Bd., Edgewater, Fla., 1992-94. Lt. USCGR, 1943-46. Recipient award in graphics Nat. Assn. Women Artists, 1939, 41. Mem. AAUP, AAUW (founding mem. New Smyrna Beach, exec. bd. 1984-85, chmn. scholarship com. 1984-87, coll./univ. liaison 1987-91, citizen's code enforcement bd. Edgewater 1992-94), DAV, Am. Philos. Assn., Fla. Philos. Assn. (exec. coun. 1978-79), Collegium Phenomenologicum, Soc. Existential and Phenomenological Philosophy, Soc. Phenomenology in Human Scis., Merleau-Ponty Circle, Fla. Assn. Community Colls. Home: 511 N Riverside Dr Edgewater FL 32132-1631

MASON, BOBBIE ANN, novelist, short story writer; b. Mayfield, Ky., May 1, 1940; d. Wilburn A. and Christianna (Lee) M.; m. Roger B. Rawlings, April 12, 1969. BA, U. Ky., 1962; MA, SUNY, Binghamton, 1966; PhD, U. Conn., 1972. Asst. prof. English Mansfield (Pa.) State Coll., 1972-79. Author: Nabokov's Garden, 1974, The Girl Sleuth: A Feminist Guide to the Bobbsey Twins, Nancy Drew and Their Sisters, 1976, 2nd edit., 1995, Shiloh and Other Stories, 1982 (Ernest Hemingway award, Nat. Book Critic's Circle award nominee, Am. Book award nominee, PEN Faulkner award nominee), In Country, 1985, Spence + Lila, 1988, Love Life, 1989, Feather Crowns, 1993 (Nat. Book Critic's Circle award nominee, So. Book award); contbr. regularly to The New Yorker, 1980—; contbr. fiction to The Atlantic, Redbook, Paris Rev., Mother Jones, Harpers, N.Am. Rev., Va. Quar. Rev.; contbr. works Best American Short Stories, 1981, The Pushcart Prize: Best of the Small Presses, 1983, Best American Short Stories, 1983. Recipient O. Henry Anthology awards, 1986, 88; grantee Pa. Arts Coun., 1983, 89, Nat. Endowment Arts, 1983, Am. Acad. and Inst. Arts and Letters, 1984; Guggenheim fellow, 1984. Address: care Amanda Urban Internat Creative Mgmt 40 W 57th St New York NY 10019

MASON, DORIS ANN, county official; b. Storm Lake, Iowa, Sept. 30, 1943; d. Joseph and Agnes (Zelenka) Vodicka; m. Gary Lee Smith, Mar. 21, 1962 (div. 1980); children: Barry Dee Smith, Brenda Lee Esquitin; m. Donald Ray Mason, Aug. 25, 1990. Grad. high sch., Fairmont, Nebr. Typist, clk. Hall County Treas.'s Office, Grand Island, Nebr., 1962-76; dep. treas. Hall County Treas.'s Office, Grand Island, 1976-90, treas., 1990—. Active Hall County Rep. Party, Hall County Rep. Women, Grand Island. Mem. Internat. Tng. Comm. (LaGrande chpt.), Nat. Assn. County Treas. and Fin. Officers, Nebr. Assn. County Ofcls., Grand Island C. of C., Nebr. Rep. Party Booster Club, Grand Island Luncheon Bus. and Profl. Women's Club (corr. sec. 1992), Eagles Aux., Grand Island Women's Bowling Assn. Office: Hall County Treasurer 121 S Pine Grand Island NE 68801

MASON, ELIZABETH ABRUZESE, marketing consultant; b. Richmond, Va., Oct. 20, 1960; d. Thomas Joseph and Judith Ann (Toler) Abruzese; m. Richard Gary Mason, May 22, 1983. BS in Mass Communications, Va. Commonwealth U., 1984. Account exec. Pezzano and Co., N.Y.C., 1985-86; account supr. Levine Huntley Schmidt & Beaver, N.Y.C., 1986-87, assoc. dir. strategic svcs., 1989, v.p., assoc. dir. new bus., 1989-90, v.p., dir. new bus., 1990-91; sr. v.p., dir. bus. devel. Levine, Huntley, Vick and Beaver, N.Y.C., 1991; advt. mgr. Trans World Airlines, N.Y.C., 1987-88; pres. Friedman & Benjamin Advt., N.Y.C., 1992-93; prin. Newton, Lao, Leonard & Locke, Inc., N.Y.C., 1993—. Recipient Va. Commonwealth U. Leadership and Svc. award, 1984, Va. Commonwealth U. Alumni award, 1991. Mem. Am. Mktg. Assn. (Gold Effie award 1987, Effie judge 1991, 92, 95, chair Effie award 1992, 93, 94), Advt. Club. N.Y., Advt. Women N.Y. (chair Addy award 1991-92, judging com. chair Addy awards 1990-91, co-chair career issues 1992-93), Turnaround Mgmt. Assn. Home: 921 Hudson St Hoboken NJ 07030-5101 Office: Newton Lao Leonard & Locke 921 Hudson St Hoboken NJ 07030-5101

MASON, JOANN BURCHETT, counselor, consultant; b. Fleming County, Ky., Sept. 16, 1940; d. Herbert Cloyd and Minnie Jewell (Saunders) Burchett; m. Lowell Thomas Mason, Jan. 11, 1958 (dec.); children: Timothy James, Lowell Mason II, Toni Shea Riales. Cert. tchg., Clear Creek Bapt. Coll., Pineville, Ky., 1978; BS in Psychology, Liberty U., 1992, MA in Counseling, 1993. Social svcs. dir. Sr. Citizens Nursing Home, Madisonville, Ky., 1982-89; case mgr. Green River Area Devel. Dist., Owensboro, Ky., 1991-93; coord. family resource/youth svcs. Breckenridge County Bd. Edn., Hardinsburg, Ky., 1993—; cons. Mary Kay Cosmetics, Hardinsburg, 1994—; counselor Trauma Assistance Team, Hardinsburg, 1993—; dir. Ben Johnson Consortium, Hardinsburg, 1993—. Mem. Breckenridge County Social Svc. Working Group, Hardinsburg, 1993—. Named to Honorable Order of Ky. Colonels. Mem. Ky. Edn. Assn., Ky. Assn. Counseling and Devel., Am. Assn. Christian Counseling, Assn. for Adult Devel. and Aging. Republican. Baptist. Home: 107 W 6th St Hardinsburg KY 40143 Office: Breckenridge County Bd Edn # 1 Airport Rd Hardinsburg KY 40143

MASON, JUDITH ANN, freelance writer; b. Newark, Dec. 27, 1945; d. Richard Algie and Mary Ann (Beneck) M. Diploma in legal sci., Spencerian Bus. Coll., 1965; BA, Northeastern Ill. U., 1984. Legal sec. Harney B. Stover, Atty., Milw., 1967-69, Robert P. O'Meara, Atty., Waukegan, Ill., 1969-70; sec. to pres. First Midwest Bank, Waukegan, 1970-72, asst. cashier, 1972-76; legal sec. Eugene M. Snarski, Atty., Waukegan, 1976-81; adminstrv. aide Lake County Forest Preserve Dist., Libertyville, Ill., 1981-89; freelance writer Tucson, 1989—; legal sec., asst. Jeffrey H. Greenberg, Atty.; travel rep. Antioch (Ill.) Travel Agy., 1980-89, Advance Travel Agy., Zion, Ill., 1980-89; pub. speaker for various orgns., Lake County, Ill., 1984-89. Author: Why I Remember Yesterday, 1979, Haggadah (play), 1982; editor poetry column: Bank Man Magazine, 1972-75; contbg. article writer Compendum Mag. Tchr. Confraternity Christian Doctrine St. Patrick's Ch., Wadsworth, Ill., 1980-85; lector, eucharistic min. Prince of Peace Ch., Lake Villa, Ill., 1980-89; hospice vol. St. Therese Hosp., Waukegan, 1984; speech writer Grace Mary Stern lt. gubernatorial campaign, Lake County, 1984; voter registrar County of Lake Ill., 1986-89; cons. pub. rels. Lake County Cir. Ct. Judge campaign, 1988, Presdl. Campaign Paul Simon; co-chmn., organizer Women's Exhibit, Evergreen Air Show, 1993. Recipient Brian F.

Shehanhan Creative Writing award Am. Inst. Banking, 1972, 1st Place pub. speaking, 1974. Mem. AAUW (pub. rels. chair 1986, pres. Chain O'Lakes br. 1988-89, Ill. Pub. Info. award 1987, pub. rels. chair Tucson br. 1991-92), NAFE, Northeastern Ill. U. Alumni Assn., Soc. Southwestern Authors, Pi Rho Zeta (pres. 1964-65). Democrat. Roman Catholic. Home and Office: 2195 E River Rd Tucson AZ 85718-6586

MASON, LINDA, softball and basketball coach; b. Indpls., Jan. 29, 1946; d. Harrison Linn and Hazel Marie (Bledsoe) Crouch; divorced; children: Cassandra, Andrew. B.S., Ind. U., 1968, M.S., 1977. Cert. phys. edn. tchr., K-12, Ind. Tchr. phys. edn. Woodview Jr. High Sch., Indpls., 1968-71; tchr. phys. edn., coach Ind. U.-Purdue U. of Indpls., 1972-76; basketball coach Butler U., Indpls., 1976-84; head softball coach, asst. basketball coach Westfield Washington High Sch., Westfield, Ind., 1985; tch. phys. edn., basketball coach Orchard Park Elementary Sch., Carmel, Ind., 1985—; asst. coach softball Carmel High Sch., 1993—; elem. physical edn. tchr., Carmel-Clay Schs., Carmel, 1985—; asst. varsity coach softball, Carmel High Sch., 1993—; head coach Ind. Girls' High Sch. All-Stars, Indpls., 1980. Named Coach of Yr. Dist. 4, Nat. Collegiate Athletic Assn., 1983. Mem. Delta Psi Kappa.

MASON, LUCILE GERTRUDE, fundraiser, consultant; b. Montclair, N.J., Aug. 1, 1925; d. Mayne Seguine and Rachel (Entorf) M. AB, Smith Coll., 1947; MA, NYU, 1968, 76. Editor ABC, N.Y.C., 1947-51; asst. casting dir. Compton Advt., Inc., N.Y.C., 1951-55, dir. and head casting, 1955-65; conf. mgr. Camp Fire Girls, Inc., N.Y.C., 1965-66; exec. dir. Assn. of Jr. Leagues of Am. Inc., N.Y.C., 1966-68; dir. div. pub. affairs Girl Scouts U.S.A., N.Y.C., 1969-71; dir. pub. rels. YWCA of City of N.Y., 1971-73; dir. community rels. and devel. Girl Scout Coun. of Greater N.Y., N.Y.C., 1973-76; dir. devel. Montclair Kimberley Acad., Montclair, N.J., 1976-78, Ethical Culture Schs., N.Y.C. and Riverdale, N.Y., 1978-80; pres. Lucile Mason & Assocs., Montclair, 1980-83; devel. officer founds. Fairleigh Dickinson U., Rutherford, N.J., 1983-85; dir. devel. Whole Theatre, Inc., Montclair, 1985-86, YMWCA of Newark & Vicinity, 1986-88; v.p. adminstrn. and fin. devel. Inst. Religion and Health, N.Y.C., 1988-90; dir. corp. and found. rels. Upsala Coll., East Orange, N.J., 1990-91; pres. Lucile Mason & Assocs., Montclair, 1991—. Vol. bd. counselors Smith Coll., 1964-74, chmn. theatre com., mem. exec. com., 1969-74; trustee Citizens Com. Presby Meml. Iris Gardens of Montclair, 1992—; trustee Friends of Barnet, 1994—; v.p. Neighborhood Ctr., Inc., Montclair, 1987—; mem. fund devel. com. Girl Scout Coun. Greater Essex County, 1986-92. Mem. Am. Women in Radio and TV (pres. N.Y.C. chpt. 1955-56), Community Agys. Pub. Rels. Assn. (membership chmn. 1973-76), Nat. Soc. Fund Raising Execs. (bd. dirs. N.J. chpt 1983-86, mem. awards com. 1994), Pub. Rels. Soc. Am., Smith Coll. Club of Montclair (bd. dirs. 1986-90). Home and Office: 142 N Mountain Ave Montclair NJ 07042-2350

MASON, MARCIA ELISABETH, lawyer; b. Chariton, Iowa, Aug. 24, 1954; d. Ray Elijah and Marlene Lucile (Shore) M.; m. John Charles Lufkin, July 24, 1982; children: Jessica Rose Lufkin, Kevin Mason Lufkin. BS, Iowa State U., 1976; JD, U. Iowa, 1982. Bar: Iowa 1982, U.S. Dist. Ct. (so. dist.) Iowa 1984, U.S. Supreme Ct. 1985, U.S. Dist. Ct. (no. dist.) Iowa 1990. High sch. tchr. Festus, Mo., 1976-77; high sch. math. tchr. Farragut, Iowa, 1977-79; legal intern Johnson County Atty., Iowa City, 1981-82; asst. Iowa Atty. Gen. Criminal Appeals Divsn., 1982-85, Revenue Divsn., 1985—. Mem. Polk County Women Attys. Democrat. United Methodist. Office: Iowa Atty Gen Hoover State Office Bldg Des Moines IA 50319

MASON, MARILYN GELL, library administrator, writer, consultant; b. Chickasha, Okla., Aug. 23, 1944; d. Emmett D. and Dorothy (O'Bar) Killebrew; m. Carl L. Gell, Dec. 29 1965 (div. Oct. 1978); 1 son, Charles E.; m. Robert M. Mason, July 17, 1981. B.A., U. Dallas, 1966; M.L.S., N. Tex. State U., Denton, 1968; M.P.A., Harvard U., 1978. Libr. N.J. State Libr., Trenton, 1968-69; head dept. Arlington County Pub. Libr., Va., 1969-73; chief libr. program Metro Washington Coun. Govts., 1973-77; dir. White House Conf. on Librs. and Info. Svcs., Washington, 1979-80; exec. v.p. Metrics Rsch. Corp., Atlanta, 1981-82; dir. Atlanta-Fulton Pub. Libr., Atlanta, 1982-86, Cleve. Pub. Libr., 1986—; trustee Online Computer Library Ctr., 1984—; Evalene Parsons Jackson lectr. div. librarianship Emory U., 1981. Author: The Federal Role in Library and Information Services, 1983; editor: Survey of Library Automation in the Washington Area, 1977; project dir.: book Information for the 1980's, 1980. Bd. visitors Sch. Info. Studies, Syracuse U., 1981-85, Sch. of Libr. and Info. Sci. , U. Tenn..-Knoxville, 1983-85; trustee Coun. on Libr. Resources, Atlant, 1992—. Recipient Disting. Alumna award N. Tex. State U., 1979. Mem. ALA (mem. council 1986—), Am. Assn. Info. Sci., Ohio Library Assn., D.C. Library Assn. (pres. 1976-77). Home: 12427 Fairhill Rd Cleveland OH 44120 Office: Cleve Pub Libr 325 Superior Ave E Cleveland OH 44114-1271

MASON, MARSHA, actress, director, writer; b. St. Louis; d. James and Jacqueline M.; m. Gary Campbell, 1965 (div.); m. Neil Simon, Oct. 25, 1973 (div.). Grad., Webster (Mo.) Coll. Performances include cast Broadway and nat. tour Cactus Flower, 1968; other stage appearances include The Deer Park, 1967, The Indian Wants the Bronx, 1968, Happy Birthday, Wanda June, 1970, Private Lives, 1971, You Can't Take It With You, 1972, Cyrano de Bergerac, 1972, A Doll's House, 1972, The Crucible, 1972, The Good Doctor, 1973, King Richard III, 1974, The Heiress, 1975, Mary Stuart, 1982; one-woman show off-Broadway, The Big Love, Perry St. Theatre, 1988, Lake No Bottom, Second Stage, 1990, Escape From Happiness, With the Naked Angels, 1994; film appearances include Blume in Love, 1973, Cinderella Liberty, 1973 (recipient Golden Globe award 1974, Acad. award nominee), Audrey Rose, 1977, The Goodbye Girl, 1977 (recipient Golden Globe award 1978, Acad. award nominee), The Cheap Detective, 1978, Promises in the Dark, 1979, Chapter Two, 1979 (Acad. award nominee), Only When I Laugh, 1981 (Acad. award nominee), Max Dugan Returns, 1982, Heartbreak Ridge, 1986, Stella, 1988, Drop Dead Fred, 1990, I Love Trouble, 1994; TV appearances include PBS series Cyrano de Bergerac, 1974, The Good Doctor, 1978, Lois Gibbs and the Love Canal, 1981, Surviving, 1985, Trapped in Silence, 1986, The Clinic, 1987, Dinner At Eight, 1989, The Image, 1990, Broken Trust, 1994, series Sibs, 1991; dir. (plays) Juno's Swans, 1987, Heaven Can Wait; dir. ABC Afternoon Spl. Little Miss Perfect, 1988. Office: care Internat Creative Mgmt 8942 Wilshire Blvd Beverly Hills CA 90211

MASON, NANCY TOLMAN, state agency director; b. Buxton, Maine, Mar. 14, 1933; d. Ansel Robert and Kate Douglas (Libby) M. Grad., Bryant Coll., Providence, R.I., 1952; BA, U. Mass., Boston, 1977; postgrad., Inst. Governmental Services, Boston, 1985, The Auditor's Inst., 1988. Asst. to chief justice Mass. Superior Ct., Boston, 1964-68; community liaison Action for Boston Community Devel., Boston, 1968-73; mgmt. cons. East Boston Community Devel. Assn., Boston, 1973-78; asst. dir. Mass. Office of Deafness, Boston, 1978-86; dir. of contracts Mass. Rehab. Commn., Boston, 1986—; cons. Jos. A Ryan Assocs., Boston and Orleans, Mass., 1981-86, Radio Sta. WFCC, Chatham, Mass., 1987-91. Author: Bromley-Heath Security Patrols, 1974, Reorganization of East Boston Community Development Corporation, 1976, How to Start Your Own Small Business, 1981. Bd. dirs. Deaf-Blind Contact Ctr., Boston, 1988-91; vol. Am. Cancer Soc., Winchester, Mass., 1986-93, Tax Equity Alliance Mass., 1994. Recipient Good Citizen award DAR, 1950, Community Svc. award Northeastern U., 1986, Gov.'s citation for outstanding performance, 1993; named to Outstanding Young Women of Am., 1965. Mem. NOW, NAFE, Mass. State Assn. Deaf, MRC Statewide Cen. Office Dirs. Democrat. Episcopalian. Office: Mass Rehab Commn 27-43 Wormwood St Boston MA 02210

MASON, ROSE F., nurse administrator; b. Chinle, Ariz., Nov. 7, 1940; d. Edward and Ida (Hosgan) Francis; m. Richard Mason, June 1, 1963; children: Ralph, Cindy, Cheryl. Diploma, St. Anthony's Sch. Nursing, 1962; BSN, U. N.Mex., 1983. Clin. nurse specialist in adminstrv. nursing svcs. Clin. nurse Albuquerque Indian Hosp., 1971-73; supr. clin. nurse Albuquerque PHS Indian Hosp., 1973-81; clin. nurse Nursing Edn. Ctr., Albuquerque, 1981-83; supr. clin. nurse PHS Indian Health Svcs., Shiprock, N.Mex., 1983-84; clin. nurse Albuquerque PHS Indian Hosp., 1984-85; supr. clin. nurse Chinle (Ariz.) PHS Indian Hosp., 1983-84, Ft. Defiance (Ariz.) Indian Hosp., 1983-84; supr. clin. nurse Albuquerque PHS Indian Hosp., 1985-88, nurse specialist, 1988-91, acting dir. nurses, 1991, nurse specialist, 1992—. Contbr. ednl. video taping Oncology Nursing: Making a Difference, 1993. Bd. dirs. adult day care program Share Your Care Inc., 1993-94; mem. Tb Task Force Com. N.Mex., 1993—; mem. steering com. N.Mex. Cancer Pain Initiative, 1993—. Mem. Assn. Practitioners in Infection Control, Inc. (treas. 1992-93, Edn. Advancement award 1991), N.Mex. Indian Nurses Assn. (bd. dirs.), N.Mex. Assn. Continuity of Care (hon. mention award of excellence 1992). Home: 1325 Sasebo St NE Albuquerque NM 87112-6329

MASON, SARA SMITH, managed care consultant; b. Rochester, N.Y., May 30, 1948; d. Harry F. and Louise S. (Sullivan) Smith; m. Larry S. Mason, Oct. 14, 1972. BA, Lewis and Clark Coll., Portland, Oreg., 1970, MA in Teaching, 1972; MBA, U. Oreg., 1987. Dir. N.W. area Intracorp., Portland, 1979-90; dir. ops. Western region Ptnrs. In Exec. Solutions, Irvine, Calif., 1990-91; asst. v.p. group and casualty svcs. ETHIX Nat., Portland, Oreg., 1992; managed care product mgr. Fireman's Fund Ins. Cos., Portland. Mem. med. subcom. Worker's Compensation, Salem, Oreg., 1987. Mem. Oreg. Exec. MBA Alumni Bd. (bd. dirs.), Nat. Assn. Rehab. Profl. in Pvt. Sector, Portland City Club (bus. labor com. 1990-91). Office: Firemans Fund Ins Cos 101 SW Main # 710 Portland OR 97204-9999

MASOTTI, JANET, school psychologist; b. Sept. 13, 1962; d. Arthur and Esther (DeSiena) M. BA, Coll. Mt. St. Vincent, 1984; MS, Coll. New Rochelle, 1987; postgrad., Pace U., 1987—. Cert. sch. psychologist, N.Y. Sch. psychologist Assn. Help of Retarded Children, Bronx, N.Y., 1988—; staff trainer Blue Feather Early Childhood Program, Bronx, 1992—, seminar leader, N.Y.C., 1993—. Assoc. mem. APA.

MASSEY, BARBARA LYNN, advertising manager; b. Mannaset, N.Y., May 14, 1958; d. Hall W. and Margaret R. (Carr) M.; divorced; 1 child, Matthew. Classified supr./coord. Gold Coast Shopper, Boca Raton, Fla., 1984-88; classified advt. mgr. Boca Raton/Del Ray Beach/Boynton Beach News, Boca Raton, 1988-90, Times-Tribune, Scranton, Pa., 1990—. Bd. dirs. Lackawanna Homebuilders Assn., Scranton, 1992—; co-chair community svc. Greater Scranton Bd. Realtors, 1992—. Mem. Pa. Newspaper Pub. Assn. (mem. classified exec. com., chair 1994 classified conf., instr. classified advt. sales, 1st pl. award 1990). Office: Times-Tribune 149 Penn Ave Scranton PA 18503-2022

MASSEY, ELEANOR NELSON, school librarian, media specialist; b. Providence, Apr. 1, 1930; d. Walter K. and Jeanette (Perlman) Nelson; m. Marvin Donald Massey, June 29, 1952; children—Henry, David, Michael, Jonathan. BA, Douglass Coll., New Brunswick, N.J., 1952; postgrad. Rutgers U. Cert. ednl. media specialist. Children's librarian Westfield (N.J.) Pub. Library, 1952-55; librarian Franklin Jr. High Sch., Metuchen, N.J., 1959-61; media specialist Campbell Sch., Metuchen, 1962—; coordinator libraries Metuchen Pub. Schs., 1982—; dir. Woodbridge-East Brunswick Area Coordination Council, 1982-85; mem. interim planning com. N.J. Library Network, 1984-85; cooperating tchr. Kean Coll. and Rutgers U., 1975—; speaker; bibliographer. Author. Vice pres. Sisterhood Neve Shalom, Metuchen, 1960; dir. Neve Shalom, 1959-60; bd. dirs. Union-Middlesex Regional Library Cooperative, Region IV, Inc., 1985-89; active Metuchen Cable TV Adv. Commn., 1994—. Title II Demonstration Library grantee State of N.J., 1974-76, Sch.-Pub. Libr. Coop. grantee 1986. Recipient N.J. Gov.'s Tchr. Recognition award, 1991. Mem. Ednl. Media Assn. N.J. (exec. bd. 1976-78), ALA, N.J., Library Assn., Ednl. Media Assn. Middlesex County (treas. 1982-83). Office: Campbell Sch Talmadge Ave Metuchen NJ 08840

MASSEY, LUANNE ELAINE, firefighter, paramedic, therapist; b. Iowa City, July 30, 1955; d. Orie Ernest and Anna Margaret (Kimball) Grim; m. Gary N. Massey, June 2, 1973 (div. Dec. 1983). BS, East Tex. State U., 1988, MS, 1993. Driver engr. paramedic Dallas Fire Dept., 1979—; therapist Lancaster, Tex., 1993—; cons. Uniformed Women's Network for the Dallas Fire Svc., 1993—, v.p., 1994—. Mem. NOW, Am. Counseling Assn., Assn. for Humanistic Edn. and Devel., Nat. Abortion Rights Action League, Greenpeace, Old West Newfoundland Club, Chi Sigma Iota. Democrat.

MASSIE, ANN MACLEAN, law educator; b. South Bend, Ind., Sept. 17, 1943; d. John Allan and Gladys Sherill (Wilkie) MacLean; m. Kent Belmore Massie, Aug. 25, 1973; children: Allan Barksdale, Laura Sherrill. BA, Duke U., 1966; MA in English, U. Mich., 1967; JD, U. Va., 1971. Bar: Ga. 1971. Assoc. Alston, Miller & Gaines, Atlanta, 1971-73, Long and Aldridge, Atlanta, 1974-76; staff atty. regional office FTC, Atlanta, 1973-74; law clk. to Hon. J. Harvie Wilkinson III U.S. Ct. Appeals (4th cir.), Charlottesville, Va., 1984-85; adj. prof. law Washington & Lee U., Lexington, Va., 1985-88, asst. prof. law, 1988-93; assoc. prof. law Washington & Lee U., Lexington, 1993—. Contbr. articles to law jours. Deacon Waynesboro (Va.) Presbyn. Ch., 1986-88; bd. dirs., v.p. Hosp. Aux., Waynesboro, 1986-88. Named Prof. of Yr., Women Law Students Orgn., 1993. Mem. Am. Soc. Law, Medicine and Ethics, Hastings Ctr., Choice in Dying. Home: PO Box 1076 Lexington VA 24450 Office: Washington and Lee U Sch of Law Lexington VA 24450

MASSIE, ANNE ADAMS ROBERTSON, artist; b. Lynchburg, Va., May 30, 1931; d. Douglas Alexander and Annie Scott (Harris) Robertson; m. William McKinnon Massie, Apr. 30, 1960; children: Anne Harris, William McKinnon, Jr. Grad., St. Mary's Coll., Raleigh, N.C., 1950; BA in English, Randolph Macon Woman's Coll., 1952. Tchr. English E.C. Glass High Sch., Lynchburg, 1955-60. Bd. dirs. Lynchburg Hist. Found., 1968-81, 91—, pres., 1978-81; bd. dirs. Lynchburg Fine Arts Ctr., 1992—; trustee Va. Episcopal Sch., Lynchburg, 1983-89. Mem. Am. Watercolor Soc. (signature, Dolphin fellow 1993, Gold medal Honor 1993), Nat. Watercolor Soc., (signature, Artist's Mag. award), Nat. League Am. Pen Women, (pres. 1987, Best in Show 1994), Knickerbocker Artists (signature, Silver medal Watercolor 1993), Watercolor West (signature), Va. Watercolor Soc. (artist mem., Best in Show 1992, chmn. exhbns. 1986), Colonial Dames Am. (chmn. 1987-90), Hillside Garden Club (pres. 1974-76), Jr. League (editor 1953-72), Lynchburg Art Club (bd. dirs., chmn. 1981-84), Antiquarian Club. Episcopalian. Home: 3204 Rivermont Ave Lynchburg VA 24503

MASSIE, JUDITH KAY, administrative assistant; b. Allegan, Mich., Nov. 8, 1946; d. Clayton George and Marion (Esseltine) Oisten; m. Larry B. Massie, 1968 (div. 1977); children: Adam C., Wallace G., Larry B. II. Student, Parsons Bus. Sch., 1970, Western Mich. U., 1971, 92—. Sec. to capt. of detectives Kalamazoo City Police Dept., 1968-73; adminstrv. asst. Western Mich. U., Kalamazoo, 1975—; corr. Allegan County News and Union Enterprise, 1993—; mem. student bd. Western Herald Bd. Dirs., Kalamazoo, 1993-94. Trustee, chair Otsego (Mich.) Pub. Schs. Found., 1986—; chair 3-on-3 tournament Otsego Pub. Schs. Found. and Otsego C. of C., 1990—, March Madness 3-on-3, 1992—. Named Citizen of Yr., Otsego Bd. of Edn., 1995. Mem. Soc. Profl. Journalists, Theta Alpha Phi (hon.). Home: 229 W Allegan Otsego MI 49078 Office: Western Mich U Dept Elec and Computer Engring Kalamazoo MI 49008

MASSIE, LEOTA EARLINE, medical technologist; b. Seattle, Jan. 7, 1918; d. Lundy Earl Smith and Olive Alice Kerschner; m. Elbert Halvor Ahlstrom, July 3, 1939 (div. 1951); m. Mark Massie, Dec. 1, 1962. BA, UCLA, 1939; postgrad., San Jose State U., 1950s, Calif. State U., Fresno, 1970s, 80s, Fresno City Coll., 1960s, 70s. Registered med. technologist Am. Soc. Clin. Pathologists; lic. bioanalyst and m ed. technologist, Calif. Clerical/libr. rsch. worker N.Y.A., L.A., 1935-39; clerical worker war dept. Presidio of San Francisco, 1939-42; clerical worker U.S. Air Force Liason Office, Moffett Field, Calif., 1942-49; med. technologist Santa Clara County Hosp., San Jose, Calif., 1949-59; supr., med. tech. VA Med. Ctr., Menlo Park, Palo Alto, Calif., 1959-63, Fresno, Calif., 1963-84; docent Fresno Met. Mus., 1984—, Chaffee Zool. Gardens, Fresno, 1985—; riverguide San Joaquin River Pkwy. and Trust, Fresno, 1992—; tutor St. Agnes Med. Ctr. Club 55 Plus, Fresno, 1993—. Instrumental in AABB accreditation for Fresno VA Hosp. Vis. Am. Cancer Soc., Fresno.

MASSIMO, DIANE CATHERINE, counseling administrator; b. Yonkers, N.Y., Oct. 11, 1951; d. Carmen and Sophie (Poleshuk) M. BA, Syracuse U., 1973, MS, 1974; CAS, SUNY, New Paltz, 1984; postgrad., Fordham U., 1994—. Cert. sch. dist. adminstr., sch. counselor, N.Y.; nat. cert. counselor, career counselor. High sch. counselor Ellenville (N.Y.) Ctrl. Sch., 1974-81; dir. guidance Highland (N.Y.) Ctrl. Sch., 1981-85, Byram Hills Ctrl. Sch., Armonk, N.Y., 1985-89; dir. counseling City Sch. Dist. of New Rochelle, N.Y., 1989—; lectr. Long Island U., 1990—. Mem. N.Y. State Assn. for Counseling and Devel. (pres. 1990-91, Disting. Profl. Svc. award 1991-92, Outstanding Program award 1992, 94), N.Y. State Sch. Counselors Assn. (pres. 1986-87, Counselor Adminstr. of Yr. 1988-89), Am. Counseling Assn. (professionalizaton com. 1993), Phi Delta Kappa (pres. 1980-82, Educator of Yr. 1987). Home: 208 Harris Rd # FA3 Bedford Hills NY 10507-2125 Office: City Sch Dist New Rochelle 265 Clove Rd New Rochelle NY 10801-1200

MASSON, GAYL ANGELA, airline pilot; b. L.A., Feb. 5, 1951; d. Jack Watson and Margaret Jean (Evans) M.; 1 child, Athena. BFA, U. So. Calif., 1970, MA, 1972, MPA, 1975, PhD, 1976. Lic. airline transport, seaplane, glider pilot, flight instr., flight engr. Pilot Antelope Valley Land Investment Co., Century City, Calif., 1972; ROTC flight instr. Claire Walters Flight Acad., Santa Monica, Calif., 1973; flight instr. Golden West Airways, Santa Monica, 1974; co-pilot Express Airways, LaMoore Naval Air Sta., Calif., 1975-76; charter pilot, instr. Shaw Airmotive, Orange County Airport, Calif., 1976; flight engr. Am. Airlines, Dallas, 1976-79, co-pilot, 1979-86, capt., 1986—; accident prevention counselor FAA, 1993—. Contbr. articles to profl. publs. Participant Powder Puff Derby, Angel Derby, Pacific Air Race and others. First woman type-rated on Boeing 747, also type-rated on DC-10, DC-9, Boeing 767, Boeing 757, Airbus-310. Mem. Airline Pilots Assn., Internat. Soc. Women Airline Pilots (charter), Ninety-Nines (past v.p. Smo Bay chpt.), Aerospace Med. Assn., Aerospace Human Factors Assn.

MASSURA, EILEEN KATHLEEN, family therapist; b. Chgo., July 25, 1925; d. John William and Loretta (Feil) Stratemeier; m. Edmund Karamanski, July 24, 1948 (dec.); children: John, Kathleen; m. Alfred Massura, Aug. 30, 1963; children: Michael, Kathryn, Mark. BS in Nursing, DePaul U., 1963; MS in Nursing, St. Xavier Coll., 1971. RN; cert. family therapist. Dir. nurses Franklin Blvd. Hosp., Chgo., 1958-62; adminstr. Mich. Ave Hosp., Chgo., 1962-64; instr. St. Xavier Coll., Chgo., 1972-74, Joliet (Ill.) Jr. Coll., 1972-81; family therapist Oak Lawn (Ill.) Family Svc., 1978-88; prof. nursing Govs. State U., University Park, Ill., 1981-89; family therapist McCarthy & Assocs., Oak Lawn, 1982-93, Massura & Assocs., Oak Lawn, 1994—; preceptor to grads. St. Xavier Coll., 1980-90, Govs. State U., 1980-89; co-leader Clin. Study Med./Surg. Nursing, Moscow, 1984; presenter Am. Nursing Rev., Ala., Fla., Va., Pa., Tex., Md., 1985-86. Leader Campfire Girls, Oak Lawn, 1964-74; co-leader Orient/Am. Med./ Surg. Nursing, 1987; mem. Marist Women's Bd., Chgo., 1978-82, Bro. Rice Women's Bd., Chgo., 1969-72; Luth. Family Svc. Bd. Day Care for Srs., 1988-89. Grantee HEW, 1969-71; named Disting. Nurse Alumnae, St. Xavier Coll., 1985; named Nursing Prof. of Yr., Govs. State U., 1983. Mem. Am. Nurses Assn. (nominating com. 1982-87), Ill. Nurses Assn. (program com. 1980-84), Am. Assn. Marital and Family Therapists, Cath. Order Foresters, Sigma Theta Tau (v.p. 1971-75). Roman Catholic. Office: 5660 W 95th St Oak Lawn IL 60453-2380

MASSY, PATRICIA GRAHAM BIBBS (MRS. RICHARD OUTRAM MASSY), social worker, author; b. Newbury, Eng., Mar. 21, 1918; came to U.S., 1963, naturalized, 1969; d. Oswald Graham and Dorothy (French) Bibbs; m. Richard Outram Massy, July 22, 1944 (dec. Aug. 1986); children: Patricia Lynn Massy Holmes, Julie Suzanne, Shaun Adele Massy Brink. BA, U. B.C., 1941, MSW, 1962. With B.C. Welfare Field Svc., Vancouver, Kamloops, Abbottsford, 1942-44; social worker Brandon Welfare Dept., Man., Can., 1945; with Children's Aid Soc., Vancouver, 1948-62; supr. Dept. Pub. Social Svc., L.A., 1963-70, staff devel. specialist-mgmt., 1970-77; lectr. colls. and seminars; lectr. Rogue Coll., Grants Pass, 1990; author, publisher: A Study Guide for a Course in Miracles, 1984; One, 1985. Mem. AAUW (treas. 1970), Nat. Assn. Social Workers, Alpha Phi. Mem. Unity Ch. Home: 18936 Upper Cow Creek Rd Azalea OR 97410-9730

MASTEN, ANN STRINGFELLOW, child development educator; b. Augusta, Ga., Jan. 27, 1951; d. Charles Chester and Ruth (Graham) Stringfellow; m. Stephen Bruce Masten, Dec. 30, 1971; children: Carrie Lowe, Madeline Russell. AB cum laude, Smith Coll., Northampton, Mass., 1973; PhD, U. Minn., Mpls., 1982. Lic. psychologist, Minn. Rsch. asst. NIMH, Bethesda, Md., 1973-76; intern Neuropsychiat. Inst. UCLA, 1981-82; rsch. assoc. U. Minn., Mpls., 1983-86, asst. prof. Inst. Child Devel., 1986-91, assoc. prof. Inst. Child Devel., 1991—, assoc. dir. Inst. Child Devel., 1991—, adj. asst. prof. dept. psychology, 1983-91; adj. assoc. prof. dept. psychology Inst. Child Devel., 1991—; McKnight-Land Grant prof. U. Minn., Mpls., 1988-91; prin. investigator, dir. Project Competence, U. Minn., 1988—; cons. Wilder Child Guidance Clinic, 1989-93, clin. child psychologist, 1983-93. Co-editor Risk and Protective Factors in the Development of Psychopathology, 1990; contbr. articles to profl. jours., chpts. to books. NIMH tng. fellow, 1976-79, Eva O. Miller fellow U. Minn., 1979-80, Salzburg Seminar Presdl. fellow, 1994; grantee W.T. Grant Found., 1983-89, 91-95, NIMH, 1983-92. Mem. APA, Soc. Rsch. in Child Devel., Soc. Rsch. on Adolescence, Internat. Soc. Traumatic Stress Studies, Am. Psychol. Soc., Soc. for Rsch. in Child and Adolescent Psychopathology. Office: Inst Child Devel U Minn 51 E River Rd Minneapolis MN 55455-0345

MASTEN, W. YONDELL, nursing educator; b. Alexandria, La., Sept. 7, 1940; d. Kelly and Alyne (Shankles) Bingham; m. Larry Burce Masten, May 27, 1960; children: Gordon, Larry Bryan, John, Lari. BS in Math., West Tex. State U., 1973, BSN, 1977; MS in Nursing, U. Tex., 1981; MS, Tex. Tech. U., 1978, PhD, 1985. Prof. Tex. Tech. U. Health Scis. Ctr. Sch. Nursing; women's health nurse practitioner, instr. Meth. Hosp. Sch. Nursing, Lubbock; head nurse Meth. Hosp., Lubbock; faculty Tex. Tech. U., Lubbock. Contbr. articles to profl. jours. Mem. ANA, Assn. Women's Health Obstet. and Neonatal Nurses, Nat. League for Nursing, Human Factors Soc., Inst. Indsl. Engrs., Internat. Childbirth Edn. Assn., Sigma Theta Tau, Iota Mu.

MASTERS, BARBARA J., lawyer; b. Denver, July 17, 1933; d. Richard P. and Ruth Ann (Savage) Johnson; children: Eliot, Joan. BA, Middlebury Coll., 1955; JD, U. Conn., 1976. Bar: Conn. 1976, U.S. Dist. Ct. Conn. 1976. Assoc. Maruzo & Lucas, Norwich, Conn., 1976-80; pvt. practice Norwich, 1980—. Bd. dirs. United Comty. Svcs., Norwich, 1980-87, Women's Ctr. Southeastern Conn., New London, 1983-89, Madonna Pl., Norwich, 1989-93; vice-chmn. Lebanon (Conn.) Bd. Fin., 1984-88; mem. People to People del. women lawyers to China, 1986, Norwich Arts Coun., 1989-93; alt. Old Lyme Zoning Bd. Appeals, 1993—, Old Lyme Dem. Town Com., 1994—. Mem. Conn. Bar Assn., New London County Bar Assn. (bd. dirs.), Assn. Trial Lawyers Am., Conn. Trial Lawyers Assn. Unitarian. Home: 9 Stonewood Rd Old Lyme CT 06371-1846 Office: 199 W Town St Norwich CT 06360-2106

MASTERS, BEDA DORIS, elementary educator; b. McComb, Miss., Feb. 14, 1942; d. Robert C. and Selma Doris (Barksdale) Moak; m. Terry Labe Masters Sr., Oct. 12, 1940; children: Terry Labe Jr., Karen Denise Masters Ishee. AS, S.W. Miss. Jr. Coll., 1971; BS, U. So. Miss., 1975; M in Edn., William Carey Coll., 1981. Cert. elem. educator, Miss. Teller 1st Nat. Bank, McComb, 1971-72, Laurel, Miss., 1972-73; tchr. Jones County Schs., Laurel, 1975—; presenter Miss. Reading Assn. Conf., 1986, 94. Mem. Internat. Reading Coun., Miss. Reading Coun., Laurel-Jones County Reading Coun. (pres. 1980-81, membership dir. 1988-89), Assn. for Excellence in Edn., PhiTheta Kappa, Phi Kappa Phi, Kappa Delta Pi, Delta Kappa Gamma (corr. sec. state Zeta Mu chpt. 1986-88, chmn. world fellowship 1990-92). Baptist. Home: RR 12 Box 590 Laurel MS 39440-8401

MASTERS, NORA JEANNE ESTERON, auditor; b. Bethesda, Md., Sept. 6, 1960; d. Isabelo B. and Mary Catherine (Riggleman) Esteron; m. Charles Craig Williams; 1 child, Isabel Sondrie. BBA in Acctg., U. Tex., Arlington, 1983; MBA, U. Tex., 1989. CPA, Wash. Acct., auditor Arthur Young & Co., Dallas, 1984-86; tax acct. Arthur Andersen & Co., Austin, 1986-87; teaching asst. U. Tex., Austin, 1987-88; sr. auditor City of Austin, Tex., 1989-91; fin. analyst City of Bellevue, Wash., 1991-92; legis./policy analyst City of Seattle, Wash., 1992-93, city auditor, 1993—. Recipient High scholarship U. Wash., 1981, Endowed Presdl. scholarship U. Tex., Austin, 1987, 88. Mem. Inst. Internal Auditors (bd. mem. 1993—), Wash. Soc. CPA. Home: 7805 S 112th St Seattle WA 98178-3229 Office: City of Seattle 1100 Municipal Bldg Seattle WA 98104

MASTERSON, LINDA HISTEN, medical company executive; b. N.Y.C., May 21, 1951; d. George and Dorothy (Postler) Riddell; m. Robert P. Masterson, March 6, 1982; m. William J. Histen, May 24, 1971 (div. 1979). BS in med. tech., U. R.I., 1973; MS in microbiology, U. Md., 1977; student, Wharton U. Pa., Phila., 1988. Med. technologist various hosps., 1972-78; microbiology specialist Gen. Diagnostics, Warner-Lambert, Morris Plains, N.J., 1978-80; from tech. sales rep. to dir. internat. mktg. Micro-Scan, Baxter Internat., Sacramento, 1980-87; dir. mktg. Ortho Diagnostics, Johnson & Johnson, Raritan, N.J., 1987-89; sr. v.p. mktg/sales GenProbe, San Diego, 1989-92; v.p. mktg./sales Bio Star, Boulder, Colo., 1992-93; exec. v.p. Cholestech Inc., Hayward, Calif., 1994—; bd. dirs. Ethicon Employee Fed. Credit Union, Sommerville, N.J., 1988-89. Tribute to women in industry Young Women's Christian Assn., N.J., 1989. Mem. Biomedical Mktg. Assn., Med. Mktg. Assn., Phi Kappa Phi. Office: Cholestech Inc 5347 Investment Blvd Hayward CA 94541-9999

MASTERSON, MARY STUART, actress; b. N.Y.C., June 29, 1966; d. Peter and Carlin Glynn Masterson. Theatre appearances include Alice in Wonderland, 1982, Been Taken, 1985, The Lucky Spot, 1987, Lily Dale, 1987; TV movies include Love Lives On, 1985, City in Fear; films: The Stepford Wives, 1975, Heaven Help Us, 1984, At Close Range, 1985, My Little Girl, 1986, Gardens of Stone, 1987, Some Kind of Wonderful, 1987, Mr. North, 1988, Chances Are, 1989, Immediate Family, 1989, Funny About Love, 1990, Fried Green Tomatoes, 1991, Married To It, 1993, Benny and Joon, 1993, Bad Girls, 1994, Radioland Murders, 1994, Heaven's Prisoners, 1994. Office: David Lewis Paul Matins Internat Creative Mgmt 8942 Wilshire Blvd Beverly Hills CA 90211*

MASTERSON, PATRICIA O'MALLEY, publications editor, writer; b. Worcester, Mass., May 15, 1952; d. Paul Francis and Dorothy M. (O'Malley) M. BFA, Emerson Coll., 1974; MA, Goddard Coll., 1980. Reporter, photographer Patriot Newspaper, Webster, Mass., 1975-78; pub. relations dir. Mt. Pleasant Hosp., Lynn, Mass., 1980-84; pubs. editor Ocean Spray Cranberries, Inc., Plymouth, Mass., 1984-89; mktg. comms. coord. Groundwater Tech., Norwood, Mass., 1989-93; pres. O'Malley Masterson Comm., Belmont, Mass., 1993—; freelance writer newspaper and mag. articles, 1974—. Mem. adv. bd. Ad. Com. mag.; contbr. numerous articles to newspapers, mags.; stringer Hanover (Mass.) Mariner Newspaper, 1987-91. Bd. dirs. YWCA, Cambridge, Mass., 1982-86; elected Nat. Alumni Assn., Emerson Coll.; judge Coop. Info. Fair, 1992; publicity com. mem. Healthworks, United Way, 1987; pres. Softball Leagues, Abington, Mass., 1991-92; vol. Rosie's Homeless Shelter, Boston, 1987-93. Recipient Amy England award YWCA, 1986, Green Eyeshade award Internat. Assn. Bus. Communicators, 1987, Yankee Ingenuity award Internat. Assn. Bus. Communicators, 1991, Employee Pub. 2d Place award Cooperative Info. Fair, 1987, 88, Membership Mag. award Cooperative Info. Fair, 1988; named One of Outstanding Young Women in Am. Jaycees, 1983. Mem. Internat. Assn. Bus. Communicators (ann. internat. conf. planning bd. 1993-94, accredited 1993—), South Shore Ad Club (publicity com., newsletter com., 9th Wave award 1987, 89, 92, judge 9th Wave Awards 1994), Coop. Communicators Assn. (1st pl. employee publ. award 1987, 3d, pl. mag. award 1989). Home: 5 Henshaw Ter West Roxbury MA 02132-2305

MASTERSON, ROANN DEE, librarian; b. Fargo, N.D., Dec. 28, 1953; d. Edward Glenn and Anna Delia (Boyd) M. BS, Valley City (N.D.) State Coll., 1975; MA, U. Wis., 1980. Media specialist Maurice-Orange City (Iowa) Pub. Schs., 1975-79; asst. periodicals U. Wis. Law Libr., Madison, 1979-80; audiovisual coord., librarian Univ. of Mary, Bismarck, N.D., 1981—. Mem. ALA, N.D. Libr. Assn. (treas. 1987-89), Assn. for Edn. and Tech., Mountain Plains Libr. Assn., Bismarck-Mandan Libr. Assn. (pres. 1992—), Libr. and Info. Tech. Assn., Assn. Coll. and Rsch. Librs., Consortium of Coll. and Univ. Media Ctrs. Republican. Lutheran. Home: 1917 E Capital Ave # 1 Bismarck ND 58501

MASTNY-FOX, CATHERINE LOUISE, administrator, consultant; b. New Rochelle, N.Y., June 4, 1939; d. Louis Francis and Catherine Marie (Haage) Kacmarynski; m. Vojtech Mastny, July 25, 1964 (div. Oct. 1987); m. Richard K. Fox, Oct. 10, 1993; children: Catherine Paula (dec.), John Adalbert (dec.), Elizabeth Louise. BA magna cum laude, Coll. New Rochelle, 1961; MA, Columbia U., 1963, PhD, 1968. Lectr. in history various colls., N.Y. and Calif., 1968-71; researcher, writer H. W. Wilson Co., N.Y.C., 1971-81; contbg. editor Columbia U. Press, N.Y.C., 1972-74; v.p., exec. dir. Internat. Mgmt. and Devel. Inst., Washington, 1978-84, exec. dir., spl. asst. to chmn., 1986-91; v.p. Meridian House Internat., Washington, 1984-85; dir. corp. devel. Washington Music Ensemble, 1991—, also bd. dirs.; cons. in field; panelist NEH, Washington, 1983; internat. advisor Global Nomads, Washington, 1990—. Contbg. author: The American Book of Days, 1978, World Authors, 1970-1971, 1980; contbg. editor: Columbia Ency., 3d edit., 1975. Fulbright Found. grantee, 1961-62; fellow Woodrow Wilson Found., 1962-63, Walter L. Dorn, 1963-64, Konrad Adenauer fellow, 1965-66. Democrat. Roman Catholic. Home: 5102 Wyoming Rd Bethesda MD 20816-2267

MASTRANTONIO, MARY ELIZABETH, actress; b. Lombard, Ill., Nov. 17, 1958; d. Frank A. and Mary D. (Pagone) M. Student, U. Ill., 1976-78. Actress: (stage prodns.) Copperfield, 1981, Oh, Brother, 1981, Amadeus, 1982, Sunday in the Park with George, 1983, The Human Comedy, 1984, Henry V, 1984, Measure for Measure, 1985, The Knife, 1987, Twelfth Night, (feature films) Scarface, 1983, The Color of Money, 1986 (Acad. award nomination 1986), The January Man, 1989, The Abyss, 1989, Fools of Fortune, 1990, Class Action, 1991, Robin Hood: Prince of Thieves, 1991, Consenting Adults, 1992; (TV movie) Mussolini: The Untold Story, 1985. Office: Internat Creative Mgmt 8942 Wilshire Blvd Beverly Hills CA 90211*

MASTRINI, JANE REED, social worker, consultant; b. Lincoln, Nebr., July 23, 1948; d. William Scott and Ellen (Daly) Cromwell; m. Charles James Mastrini, July 19, 1969. BA, Western State Coll., Gunnison, Colo., 1970; MSW, U. Denver, 1980. Lic. social worker Colo.; cert. alcohol counselor Colo. and nat. Tchr. Flandreau (S.D.) Indian Sch., 1970; social worker S.D. Dept. Welfare, Pierre, 1970-75; child care worker Sacred Heart Home, Pueblo, Colo., 1975-76; counselor Fisher Peak Alcohol Treatment Ctr., Trinidad, Colo., 1976-77; family therapist West Nebr. Gen. Hosp., Scottsbluff, 1980-81; adolescent coord. St. Luke's Hosp., Denver, 1981-86; exec. dir. New Beginnings At Denver, Lakewood, Colo., 1986-90; pres. Counseling Dimensions of Colo., Denver, 1990-92; trainer Mile High Inst., 1987-93; outpatient mgr. Arapahoe House, 1992-94; therapist Kaiser Permanente, Denver, 1994—; cons. Colo. Counseling Consortium, Denver, 1984-90; field work supr. U. Denver, 1983—. Lectr., group leader Colo. Teen Inst., Denver, 1984-85. Mem. NASW (cert.), P.E.O. (pres. 1984-87, 94—), Colo. Counseling Consortium, Colo. Assn. Addiction Treatment Programs (v.p. 1991-92). Democrat. Episcopalian. Home: 11785 W 66th Pl # D Arvada CO 80004-2473 Office: Kaiser Permanente CDTP 360 S Garfield Ste 4000 Denver CO 80209

MATA, ZOILA, chemist; b. Galveston, Tex., Aug. 8, 1937; d. Francisco Zuniga and Leonarda (Sustaita) M. BS in Biology, Chemistry, Tex. A&I U., 1975. Office asst. Galveston Pub. Health Nursing Service, 1959-63; draftswoman Wilson Real Estate Index and Pub, Houston, 1964-65; bookkeeper City Products Corp, Galveston, 1966-67; research asst. U. Tex. Med. Br., Galveston, 1967-70; clk. State Dept. Pub. Welfare, Houston, 1971-72, Quinby Temporary, Houston, 1972-76; research technician Baylor Coll. Medicine, Houston, 1976; sr. chemist Nalco Chem. Co., Sugarland, Tex., 1976-94, Nalco/Exxon Energy Chemicals, LP, Sugarland, 1994—. Active Rep. Nat. Hispanic Assembly of Tex. (chair membership credentials 1986—), Rep. Nat. Hispanic Assembly of Harris (vice chair 1986, treas. 1991—), Iota Sigma Pi. Named one of Notable Woman of Tex., 1984-85. Mem. Am. Chem. Soc. (rubber div.), Amigas de las Americas, Nat. Chicano Health Orgn. Home: 7733 Dixie Dr Houston TX 77087-5507 Office: Nalco/Exxon Energy Chemicals LP PO Box 87 Sugar Land TX 77487-0087

MATALIN, MARY, political consultant; d. Steven and Eileen Matalin; m. Artie Arnold (div.); m. James Carville, Nov. 25, 1993. Grad., Western Ill. Univ.; student, Hofstra Univ. With the Rep. Nat. Com., since the early 80's; polit. dir. George Bush's 1992 re-election campaign. Co-host, CNBC talk show Equal Time, 1993—; author: (with James Carville) All's Fair, 1994. Office: Equal Time w/ M Mtln & J Wallace 1825 K St NW Ste 917 Washington DC 20006-1202*

MATARAZA, DIANE LOUISE, arts administrator; b. Poughkeepsie, N.Y., May 12, 1952; d. Michael Morano and Rita (Abbruzzese) M. MusB, Ithaca Coll., 1974; MA, NYU, 1978; Grantsmanship Tng. Cert., U. Del., 1992; cert. in assn. mgmt., U.S. C. of C. Inst., 1992. Music dir. Chester (N.Y.) Union Schs., 1974-78; asst. dir. music Minisink Schs., Slate Hill, N.Y., 1978-79; acting dir. Dutchess County Arts Council, Poughkeepsie, N.Y., 1980; exec. dir. Dutchess County Arts Council, Poughkeepsie, 1981-84, Alliance of N.Y. State Arts Councils, New Windsor, N.Y., 1985-91; program dir. Nat. Endowment for the Arts, Washington, 1992—; panelist Nat. Endowment for the Arts, Washington, 1988-90, N.J. State Arts Coun., 1990, N.Y. State Gov.'s Arts Awards, N.Y.C., 1987-91; mem. N.Y. State Bu. Coun. Tourism Com., Albany, 1987-91; vice chmn. N.Y. State Coun. on the Arts adv. Com., 1983-84; mem. Greater Hudson Valley Coord. Coun., 1991, Art Table, 1990—. Com. mem. N.Y. State Senate Sub-Com. on Culture, Albany, 1983-85; bd. dirs. State Arts Adv. League of Am., 1988-91; com. mem. Commr.'s Adv. Com., N.Y. State Edn. Dept., 1986-91; assembly steering com. Nat. Assembly of Local Arts Agys., Washington, 1986—. Mem. NYU Alumni Assn., Ithaca Coll. Alumni Assn., Mu Phi Epsilon, Ptnrs. of Ams. Roman Catholic. Office: The Dupont East #913 1545 18th St NW Washington DC 20036

MATARESE, ELIZABETH ANN, federal aviation official; b. Framingham, Mass., Jan. 9, 1941; d. Antonio Andrew and Dorothy (Houston) M.; children: Joseph Richard, James Antonio. AB in English, Rutgers U., 1963; MA in English, U. N.H., 1971. FAA cert. as instrument flight instr SEL/MEL. Secondary sch. educator Thornton Acad., Saco, Maine, 1963-68; rsch. assoc. Booz, Allen, Hamilton TCD, Bethesda, Md., 1978-81; dir. gen. aviation Md. Aviation Admnstrn., BWI Airport, Md., 1981-87; airport certification inspector FAA, AEA, JFK Airport, N.Y.C., 1987-88; airport certification specialist FAA, Washington, 1988-91, tech. program analyst, 1991—. Mem. pres. adv. bd., U. Md., Princess Anne, 1984—. Mem. Maine Pilots Assn. (charter), Mid-Atlantic Helicopter Assn. (charter), Nat. Aviation Club (bd. govs.), Internat. Orgn. Women Pilots (many offices 1972—), Aircraft Owners and Pilots Assn., Exptl. Aircraft Assn., Internat. Aerobatic Club. Home: 1486 Velmeade Ln Davidsonville MD 21035 also: PO Box 23737 L'Enfant Plaza Station Washington DC 20026-3737 Office: FAA Nat Hdqrs Office Aviation Safety Flight Safety Divsn ASA-100 800 Independence Ave SW Washington DC 20591

MATARESE, LAURA ELLEN, nutritionist; b. New Haven, Mar. 27, 1956; d. Benjamin Michael and Rosina (Conte) M. AS, Ohio Dominican Coll., 1978, BA, 1978; MS, Case Western Res. U., 1980. Lic. dietitian, Ohio;. Nutrition support dietitian U. Cin. Med. Ctr., 1980-83, cons. nutrition adv. com., 1982-83; nutritional assessment dietitian Cleve. Clinic Found., 1983-85, clin. nutrition specialist, 1985-89, nutrition support coord., 1989—; cons. Nutritional Support Svcs., 1983—, Clinicare Health Resources, Cleve. 1985. Contbr. articles to profl. jours., various photographic publs. Named One of Outstanding Young Women of Am., 1981 and 1984; David Allen Hamilton Christopher scholar, Kraft Inc. Grad. scholar, 1979, Conn. State scholar, 1974. Mem. AAUW, Am. Dietetic Assn., Am. Soc. Parenteral and Enteral Nutrition, N.Y. Acad. Scis., Am. Dietetic Assn., Nat. Nutritional Time (co.comn. 1984-85), Cleve. Dietetic Assn. (bd. dirs. 1985-87), Clin. Dietetics and Rsch. (chmn. 1984-85), Dietitians in Nutrition Support Practice Group, Kappa Gamma Pi, Delta Epsilon Sigma. Home: 6842 Bellflower Ct Mentor OH 44060-3989 Office: Cleve Clin Found 9500 Euclid Ave Cleveland OH 44195-0001

MATAS, MYRA DOROTHEA, interior architect and designer, kitchen and bath designer; b. San Francisco, Mar. 21, 1938; d. Arthur Joseph and Marjorie Dorothy (Johnson) Anderson; m. Michael Richard Matas Jr., Mar. 15, 1958; children: Michael Richard III, Kenneth Scott. Cert. interior design, Canada Coll.; cert. interior design, Calif. Owner, operator Miquel's Antiques Co., Millbrae, Calif., 1969-70, Miguel's Antiques & Interiors Co., Burlingame, Calif., 1970-79, Country Elegance Antiques & Interiors Co., Menlo Park, Calif., 1979-84, La France Boutique Co., 1979-84, Myra D. Matas Interior Design, San Francisco, 1984—, Lafayette, La., 1994—; mgr. La France Imports, Inc., 1982-92; pres., gen. contractor Artisans 3 Inc., Burlingame, 1988-92; gen. contractor Matas Constr., Millbrae, 1993—; instr. interior design dept. Canada Coll. Mem. Calif. Coun. Interior Design. Contbr. articles in field to profl. jours. Office: 921 Harding St Lafayette LA 70503

MATASAR, ANN B., former dean, business and political science educator; b. N.Y.C., June 27, 1940; d. Harry and Tillie (Stein) Bergman; m. Robert Matasar, June 9, 1962; children—Seth Gideon, Toby Rachel. AB, Vassar Coll., 1962; MA, Columbia U., 1964, PhD, 1968; M of Mgmt. in Fin., Northwestern U., 1977. Assoc. prof. Mundelein Coll., Chgo., 1965-78; prof., dir. Ctr. for Bus. and Econ. Elmhurst Coll., Elmhurst, Ill., 1978-84; dean Roosevelt U., Chgo., 1984-92; prof. Internat. Bus. and Fin. Walter E. Heller Coll. Bus. Adminstrn. Roosevelt U., 1992—; dir. Corp. Responsibility Group, Chgo., 1978-84; chmn. long range planning Ill. Bar Assn., 1982-83; mem. edn. com. Ill. Commn. on the Status of Women, 1978-81. Author: Corporate PACS and Federal Campaign Financing Laws: Use or Abuse of Power?, 1986; (with others) Research Guide to Women's Studies, 1974. Contbr. articles to profl. jours. Dem. candidate 1st legis. dist. Ill. State Senate, no. suburbs Chgo., 1972; mem. Dem. exec. com. New Trier Twp., Ill., 1972-76; rsch. dir., acad. advisor Congressman Abner Mikva, Ill., 1974-76; bd. dirs. Ctr. Ethics and Corp. Policy, 1985-90. Named Chgo. Woman of Achievement Mayor of Chgo., 1978. Fellow AAUW (trustee ednl. found. 1992—, v.p. fin.); mem. Am. Polit. Sci. Assn., Midwest Bus. Adminstrn. Assn., Acad. Mgmt., Women's Caucus for Polit. Sci. (pres. 1980-81), John Howard Assn. (bd. dirs. 1986-90), Am. Assembly of Coll. Schs. of Bus. (bd. dirs. 1989-92, chair com. on diversity in mgmt. edn. 1991-92), North Ctrl. Assn. (commr. 1994—), Beta Gamma Sigma. Democrat. Jewish. Office: Roosevelt U Coll Bus Adminstrn Dept Fin 430 S Michigan Ave Chicago IL 60605-1301

MATASOVIC, MARILYN ESTELLE, business executive; b. Chgo., Jan. 7, 1946; d. John Lewis and Stella (Butkauskas) M. Student, U. Colo. Sch. Bus., 1963-69. Owner, pres. UTE Trail Ranch, Ridgway, Colo., 1967—; pres. MEM Equipment Co., Mokena, Ill., 1979—; sec./treas. Marlin Corp., Ridgway, 1991—, v.p., sec.-treas., 1991—; sec.-treas. Linmar Corp., Mokena, 1991—; ptnr. Universal Welding Supply Co., New Lenox, Ill., 1964-90; v.p. OXO Welding Equipment Co, Inc., New Lenox, 1964-90; ptnr. Universal Internat., Mokena, Ill., 1990—; ind. travel agt. Ideal Travel Concepts, Mokena, Ill., 1994—. Co-editor newsletters. U.S. rep. World Hereford Conf., 1964, 68, 76, 80, 84. Mem. Am. Hereford Aux. (charter, bd. dirs. 1989-94, historian 1990-92, v.p. 1992, pres.-elect 1993, pres. 1994), Am. Hereford Assn., Am. Hereford Women (charter, pres. 1994, bd. dirs. 1994—), Am. Agri-Women, Colo. Hereford Aux., Ill. Hereford Aux. (v.p. 1969-70), U. Colo. Alumni Assn., Ill. Agri-Women.

MATCHETT, JANET REEDY, psychologist; b. Chgo., Sept. 2, 1926; d. Joseph Franklin and Minnie Mae (Burr) Reedy; m. Russell W. Kemerer, Jan. 20, 1949 (div. Aug. 1974); children: Brian Lee, Pamela Ann, Patricia Lynn, Bruce Reed, Bryce Jason; m. Charles Ernest Matchett, Nov. 17, 1984. BS summa cum laude, U. Pitts., 1974; MEd, Indiana U. of Pa., 1977, Ednl. Specialist, 1978; postgrad., U. Akron, U. Pitts., Pa. State U. Lic. psychologist; cert. sch. psychologist, Pa., Ohio, W.Va. Tchr. adult edn. Greensburg (Pa.)-Salem Sch., 1963-70; teaching cons. Peterson Systems, Inc., Greensburg, 1967-75, Ednl. Self-Devel., Inc., Greensburg, 1975-78; sch. psychologist Columbiana Bd. Edn., Lisbon, Ohio, 1979, Struthers (Ohio) City Schs., 1979-80; instr. Monroeville (Pa.) Sch. Bus., 1983; sch. psychologist Community Mental Health Ctr. of Beaver County, Rochester, Pa., 1983-84, South Side Area Sch. Dist., Hookstown, Pa., 1984-87, Blackhawk Sch. Dist., Beaver Falls, Pa., 1984—; instr. Pa. State U., New Kensington, 1984-86; substitute tchr. Greensburg (Pa.)-Salem Sch. Dist., 1975-83, long range planning com. 1981-82; cons. Allegheny East Mental Health/Mental Retardation Ctr., Monroeville, Pa., 1981-83, Westmoreland County Community Coll, Youngwood, Pa., 1981-83; sch. psychologist Wetzel County Schs., New Martinsville, W.Va., 1981; com. action team, strategic planning com. Blackhawk Sch. Dist., Beaver Falls, 1991—. Vol. Adelphi House, 1978; chmn. drug/alcohol abuse prevention program, City of Greensburg, 1981; troop leader Girl Scouts Am.; asst. den mother Boy Scouts Am.; ch. sch. tchr. United Meth. Ch., Greensburg; Bible sch. program vol. United Ch. of Christ, Greensburg; chmn. PTO, Greensburg. Mem. NEA, Nat. Assn. Sch. Psychologists, We. Pa. Assn. Sch. Psychologists, Assn. Sch. Psychologists Pa., Beaver County Sch. Psychologists Assn., Blackhawk Edn. Assn., Alpha Sigma Lambda. Republican. Home: 48 W Manilla Ave Pittsburgh PA 15220-2838 Office: Blackhawk Sch Dist 635 Shenango Rd Beaver Falls PA 15010-1498

MATE, MARY CONSTANCE, accountant; b. Bayonne, N.J., Aug. 15, 1964; d. Julius and Helen (Murtha) De Martino; m. Laszlo Mate, Mar. 9, 1990. BA, Rutgers U., 1986. Staff acct. Murdoch Mags., N.Y.C, 1986-89; sr. acct. Phoenix Motor Express, Elizabeth, N.J., 1989—. Mem. Nat. Assn. Exec. Women, Inst. Mgmt. Accts. (dir. acad. rels. 1992—). Home: PO Box 3070 Bayonne NJ 07002-0297

MATER, MAUD E., federal agency administrator, lawyer. BA in English, Case Western Reserve U., 1969, JD, 1972. Asst. gen. counsel Fed. Home Loan Mortgage Corp., 1976-78, assoc. gen. counsel, 1978-79, dep. gen. counsel, 1979-81, v.p., dep. gen. counsel, 1981-84, sr. v.p., gen. counsel, sec., 1984—. Mem. ABA, Fed. Bar Assn., Ohio Bar Assn., D.C. Bar Assn., Washington Met. Corp. Counsels Assn. (dir., sec.). Office: Fed Home Loan Mortgage Corp 8200 Jones Branch Dr Mc Lean VA 22102*

MATER, PAT RAE, human resource consultant; b. Manitowoc, Wis., Apr. 17, 1957; d. Vernon Robert and Dorothy Jean (Kreienkamp) Poertner; m. Dwight Albert Mater III, July 26, 1980; children: Stephanie and Daniel (twins). BBA, U. Wis., Eau Claire, 1979; MS in Indsl. Rels., Purdue U., 1981. Compensation analyst Purdue U., West Lafayette, Ind., 1979-81; specialist human resources Owens-Corning Fiberglas, Toledo, Ohio, 1981-82, corp. human resources, 1983-84; supr. human resources mfg. Owens-Corning Fiberglas, Newark, Ohio, 1984-85; mgr. area human resources Am. Hosp. Supply, Dallas, 1985-88; mgr. human resourcees Baxter Internat., Northbrook, Ill., 1988-89; dir. human resources Baxter Internat., Deerfield, Ill., 1989-92; dir. human resources planning and devel. Caremark Internat., Lincolnshire, Ill., 1992-93; human resources cons. PM Cons., Buffalo Grove, Ill., 1993—. Editor The Express, 1993-94. Dir. endowment fund Hope Luth. Ch., Long Grove, Ill., 1993—; founder Act 1, Long Grove, 1993—; dir. Ill. Orgn. Mothers of Twins Clubs, Inc., Libertyville (Ill.) chpt., 1993-94. Mem. ASTD, Human Resources Planning Assn. Home and Office: 248 Stanton Ct E Buffalo Grove IL 60089

MATERIA, KATHLEEN PATRICIA AYLING, nurse; b. Jersey City, Nov. 7, 1954; d. Donald Anthony and Muriel Cecilia (Joyce) Ayling; m. Francis Peter Materia, June 5, 1983; children: Christopher Michael, Donna Nicole. BS in Nursing, Fairleigh Dickinson U., 1976. RN. Critical care nurse Palisades Gen. Hosp., North Bergen, N.J., 1976-87, grad. nurse, 1976-77; nurse CCU, North Hudson Hosp., Weehawken, N.J., 1977-78. Mem. Alpha Sigma Tau. Democrat. Roman Catholic. Avocations: bowling, dancing.

MATHAI-DAVIS, PREMA ANNA, association executive; b. Thiruvalla, Kerala, India, Oct. 28, 1950; came to U.S., 1974; d. Stephen and Susy (Kovoor) Mathai; m. Wallace Mathai-Davis, Oct. 15, 1978; children: Stephen, Lisa, Tara. BS, Delhi U., 1970, MS, 1972; EdD, Harvard U., 1979. Family and child care specialist Grail Internat., New Delhi, 1972-73; instr. Samoa Coll., Western Samoa, 1973-74; project dir., rsch. assoc. Grad. Sch. Edn. Harvard U., Cambridge, Mass., 1978-79; dir. Gerontology Ctr. Mt. Sinai-Hunter Coll., N.Y.C., 1979-81; dir. S.I. social svc. programs Cmty. Svc. Soc., N.Y.C., 1981-85; pres., CEO Cmty. Agy. for Sr. Citizens, Inc., S.I., 1985-90; commr. City of N.Y. Dept. Aging, 1990-94; nat. exec. dir. YWCA of U.S., N.Y.C., 1994—; bd. dirs. Health Sys. Agy. of N.Y.C., 1990-94; vis. lectr. Sch. Social Sci. Bhopal U., India, 1972-73; mem. adv. coun. N.Y. State Assembly Com. on Aging; chair policy com. N.Y. State Assn. of Area Agencies on Aging; vis. fellow New Sch. Social Rsch.. Bd. dirs. Met. Transp. Authority State of N.Y., N.Y.C., 1991—. Recipient Staten Island Borough medallion, numerous other awards. Fellow N.Y. Acad. Medicine; mem. Asian Am. Fedn. of N.Y. (bd. dirs.), Women's Club of N.Y. Episcopalian. Office: YWCA of the USA 726 Broadway New York NY 10003-9511

MATHAY, MARY FRANCES, marketing executive; b. Youngstown, Ohio, July 26, 1944; d. Howard E. and Mary C. (Siple) M.; m. Thomas Stone Withgott, Dec. 20, 1969 (div. June 1973). BA in English Lit. and Composition, Queens Coll., 1967; grad. in bus., Katharine Gibbs Sch., 1968. Corp. mktg. mgr., assoc. Odell Assocs., Inc., Charlotte, N.C., 1973-90; dir. pub. rels. and spl. events Charlotte (N.C.)-Mecklenburg Arts and Sci. Coun., 1990-92; pres. Mathay Comm., Inc., Charlotte, 1992—; speakers bur. chmn. Hospice at Charlotte, Inc., 1980-83; pub. rels. and advt. dir. "Chemical People" program PBS, Charlotte, 1983-84. Author: Legacy of Architecture, 1988; editor: Mint Mus. Antiques Show Mag., 1980, editorial advisor Crier, 1987-92; producer Charlotte's Web, 1977. Bd. dirs. Jr. League of Charlotte, Inc., 1978-79, mem. 1968—; bd. dirs. ECO, Inc., Charlotte, 1979-86, Queens Coll. Alumni, Charlotte, 1984-87, Learning How, Inc., Charlotte, 1988-91; bd. dirs. on adolescent pregnancy Mecklenburg County Coun., 1986-88; vol. tchr. ABLE Cen. Piedmont C.C., 1987-90; comm. com. vol. Am. Cancer Soc., 1994—, Charlotte-Mecklenburg Edn. Found., 1992-94, Charlotte-Mecklenburg Sr. Ctrs., 1994—. Mem. Pub. Rels. Soc. Am. (bd. dirs. 1989—, pres. 1995), Charlotte Pub. Rels. Soc. (bd. dirs. 1986-89, 92-93), Olde Providence Racquet Club, Tower Club. Republican. Presbyterian.

MATHENY, RUTH ANN, editor; b. Fargo, N.D., Jan. 17, 1918; d. Jasper Gordon and Mary Elizabeth (Carey) Wheelock; m. Charles Edward Matheny, Oct. 24, 1960. B.E., Mankato State Coll., 1938; M.A., U. Minn., 1955; postgrad., Universidad Autonoma de Guadalajara, Mex., summer 1956, Georgetown U., summer, 1960. Tchr. in U.S. and S.Am., 1938-61; asso. editor Charles E. Merrill Pub. Co., Columbus, Ohio, 1963-66; tchr. Confraternity Christian Doctrine, Washington Court House, Ohio, 1969-70; assoc. editor Jr. Cath. Messenger, Dayton, Ohio, 1966-68; editor Witness Intermediate, Dayton, 1968-70; editor in chief, assoc. pub. Today's Cath. Tchr., Dayton, 1970—; editor in chief Catechist, Dayton, 1976-89, Ednl. Dealer, Dayton, 1976-80; v.p. Peter Li, Inc., Dayton, 1980—. Editorial collaborator: Dimensions of Personality series, 1969—; co-author: At Ease in the Classroom; author: Why a Catholic School?, Scripture Stories for Today: Why Religious Education?. Mem. Bd. Friends Ormond Beach Library. Mem. Nat. League Am. Pen Women, Nat. Coun. Cath. Women, Cath. Press Assn., Nat. Cath. Ednl. Assn., 3d Order St. Francis (eucharistic minister 1990—). Home: 26 Reynolds Ave Ormond Beach FL 32174-7043 Office: Peter Li Inc 330 Progress Rd Dayton OH 45449-2322

MATHENY-WHITE, PATRICIA LYNN, librarian, researcher; b. Bemidji, Minn., July 28, 1945; d. Keith Alton and Elvie Inez (Alsop) Matheny; m. Sidney D. White, Jan. 14, 1972. BA, Macalester Coll., 1967; MA in Libr. Sci., U. Denver, 1968. Catalog libr. S.W. Minn. State Coll., Marshall, 1968-70; assoc. libr. Evergreen State Coll., Olympia, Wash., 1970-71, head of tech. svcs., 1971-73, coord. of tech. svcs., 1973-77, coord. user svcs., 1978-81; faculty libr. The Evergreen State Coll., Olympia, Wash., 1981—; Evergreen State Coll.; rsch. coord. Evergreen State Coll., Olympia, Wash., 1982, 1987-90, also lectr., media producer; cons. Exhibit Touring Svcs. for Wash. State, 1980-90; mem. rev. panel Seattle Arts Commn., 1986-87. Author: Bibliography of Chicano/Latino Art and Culture in the Pacific Northwest, 1982, Chicano and Latino Artists in the Pacific Northwest, 1984, Peoples of Washington, 1990. Mem. Hispanic Arts Com., Olympia, Wash., 1982-86, Friends of Wash. State Commn. for the Humanities, Seattle, 1984—. Mem. Art Librs. Soc. of North Am. Democrat. Home: 835 Phelps Ln NW Olympia WA 98502-1770 Office: Evergreen State Coll Olympia WA 98505

MATHER, ELIZABETH VIVIAN, health care executive; b. Richmond, Ind., Sept. 19, 1941; d. Willie Samuel and Lillie Mae (Harper) Fuqua; m. Roland Donald Mather, Dec. 26, 1966. BS, Maryville (Tenn.) Coll., 1963; postgrad., Columbia U., 1965-66. Tchr. Richmond Community Schs., 1963-67, Indpls. Pub. Schs., 1967-68; systems analyst Ind. Blue Cross Blue Shield, Indpls., 1968-71, Ind. Nat. Bank, Indpls., 1971; med. cons. Ind. State Dept. Pub. Welfare, Indpls., 1971-78, cons. supr., 1978-86; systems analyst Ky. Blue Cross Blue Shield, Louisville, 1988-89; contracts specialist Humana Corp., Louisville, 1989—. Active Rep. Cen. Com. Montgomery County,

Crawfordsville, 1976-86, Centenary Meth. Ch., adminstrv. bd., 1990. Mem. DAR (treas. 1963-66, sec. 1978-86). Home: 6106 Partridge Pl Floyds Knobs IN 47119-9427 Office: Humana Corp 500 W Main St Louisville KY 40201-1438

MATHER, STEPHANIE J., lawyer; b. Kansas City, Mo., Dec. 5, 1952; d. Edward Wayne and H. June (Kunkel) M.; m. James B. Croy, Aug. 8, 1980 (div. April 1985); m. Miles Christopher Zimmerman, Sept. 23, 1988. BA magna cum laude, Okla. City U., 1975, JD with honors, 1980. Lawyer Pierce, Couch, Hendrickson, Johnston & Baysinger, Okla. City, Okla., 1980-88, Manchester, Hiltgen & Healy, P.C., Okla. City, 1989-90; sr. staff counsel Nat. Am. Ins. Co., Chandler, Okla., 1990—; asst. v.p. Lagere & Walkingstick Ins. Agy., Inc., Chandler, Okla., 1993—. Co-chair Lincoln County Dem. Party, 1991-92; v.p. Lincoln Co. Dem. Women, 1992—; dir. Lincoln County Partnership for Children, 1994—. Mem. Okla. Bar Assn.(editor bd. of editors, 1992—), Lincoln County Bar Assn. (mem. library bd. 1990—), Lincoln County Profl. Women. Democrat. Home: PO Box 246 Chandler OK 74834 Office: Nat Am Ins Co PO Drawer 9 Chandler OK 74834

MATHERS, MARGARET, charitable agency administrator, consultant, political activist; b. Ada, Okla., Feb. 16, 1929; d. Robert Lee and Josephine Margaret (Reed) Erwin; m. Coleman F. Moss, Sept. 1956 (div. 1966); children: Carol Lee Doria, Marilyn Frances; m. Boyd Leroy Mathers, Apr. 10, 1967. BS in Music, Tex. U., 1950. Svc. rep. Gen. Tel. Co., Santa Monica, Calif., 1955-58; tchr. pvt. sch., Santa Monica, 1958-60; computer program and data analyst System Devel. Corp., Santa Monica, 1961-66; computer programmer Inst. Def. Analyses, Arlington, Va., 1966-70; typist, transcriber, Edgewater, Md., 1971-80; sec. People Assisting the Homeless, 1992-94, bd. dirs., 1985—; asst. dir. San Juan Cath. Charities, Farmington, N.Mex., 1993—; sec. Cmty. Network Coun., 1992-94; pres. San Juan Coun. Community Agys., 1986-87, treas., 1987-89, 92—, sec., 1989-90; pres. Davidsonville-Mayo Health Assn., Edgewater, 1973-76, 77-80; cons. in field, 1983—. Chmn. county Libertarian Party of N.Mex., San Juan County, 1985, sec. ctrl. com., 1988-92, mem. ctrl. com., 1988—; asst. sec. Our Lady of Perpetual Health, Parish Coun., Edgewater, 1979-82, Parish Coun. Sacred Heart, Farmington, 1987, sec., 1988-90, mem. social justice com., 1992; mem. adv. bd. San Juan County DNA Legal Aid, 1992, sec., 1993; sec. River Club Community Assn., Edgewater, 1975-82; mem. selection com. Habitat for Humanity, 1990; mem. San Juan County Task Force on Housing, 1991, Task Force on Transp., 1991; sec. Com. Preserve 2d Amendment Rights, 1994. Mem. Informed Citizens Alliance, Secular Franciscan Order. Roman Catholic. Avocations: nature study, birdwatching, reading, music, Indian studies. Office: San Juan Cath Charities 119 W Broadway Farmington NM 87401-6419

MATHES, DOROTHY JEAN HOLDEN, occupational therapist; b. Paterson, N.J., Mar. 13, 1953; d. Cornelius Fred and Dorothy Johanna (Ferguson) Holden; m. Clayton Derald Mathes, May 26, 1973 (div. Dec. 1984); children: Christy, Carl, Chuck, Chad; m. Elie Youssef Hajjar, Oct. 4, 1989. BS in Occupational Therapy, Tex. Woman's U., Denton, Tex., 1988. Lic. occupational therapist, Tex.; cert. pediatric occupational therapist. Occupational therapy cons. Denton State Sch.-Outreach, 1988—. Mem. Am. Occupational Therapy Assn., Tex. Occupational Therapy Assn. Home: 2608 Woodhaven St Denton TX 76201-1340 Office: Denton State Sch Outreach PO Box 368 Denton TX 76202-0368

MATHESON, LINDA, retired clinical social worker; b. Martna, Estonia, Dec. 29, 1918; came to U.S., 1962, naturalized, 1969; d. Endrek and Leena Endrekson; m. Charles McLaren Matheson, Feb. 5, 1955. Diploma, Inst. for Social Scis., Tallinn, Estonia, 1944; MS, Columbia U., 1966; D in Social Work, Columbia U., 1974. Diplomate clin. social work. Social work officer UN Rehab. and Resettlement Assn., Germany, 1946-48; social worker Victorian Mental Hygiene, Australia, 1955-62; rsch. assoc., social work project dir. Arthritis Midway Ho., N.Y.C., 1966-68; rschr. Columbia Presbyn. Med. Center, N.Y.C., 1971-75; field instr. Columbia U. Sch. Social Work, 1977-79, Columbia Presbyn. Med. Ctr., NYU Sch. Social Work, 1989-90; ret., 1992. Family Found. fellow, 1966, 89-90; NIMH grantee, 1969-72. Mem. Nat. Assn. Social Workers, Am. Security Council, Nat. Wildlife Fedn., Center for Study of Presidency, Smithsonian Assn., English Speaking Union, Alliance Francaise, Columbia U. Alumni Assn., Internat. Platform Assn., Met. Mus. of N.Y. Lutheran. Home: 30-95 29th St Astoria NY 11102

MATHEWS, ANNE JONES, international consultant, library director; b. Phila., Feb. 5, 1928; d. Edmond Fulton and Anne Ruth (Reichner) Jones; m. Frank Samuel Mathews, June 16, 1951; children: Lisa Anne Bingham, David Morgan, Lynne Elizabeth Beitenhader, Alison Fulton Sawyer. AB, Wheaton Coll., 1949; MA, U. Denver, 1965, PhD, 1977. Mem. field staff Intervarsity Christian Fellowship, Chgo., 1949-51; Interviewer supr. Colo. Market Rsch. Svcs., Denver, 1952-64; reference libr. Oreg. State U., Corvallis, 1965-67; program dir. Ctrl. Colo. Libr. System, Denver, 1969-70; inst. dir. U.S. Office of Edn., Inst. Grant, 1979; dir. pub. rels. U. Denver Grad. Sch. Librarianship & Info. Mgmt., 1970-76, dir. continuing edn., 1977-80, asst. prof., 1970-77, assoc. prof., 1977-79, prof., 1979-85; dir. Office Libr. Programs U.S. Dept. Edn., Washington, 1986-91; dir. Nat. Libr. Edn., Washington, 1992-94; cons. Acad. Ednl. Devel., Washington, 1994—; vis. lectr. Simmons Coll. Sch. Libr. Sci., Boston, 1977; cons. USIA, 1984-85, mem. book and libr. adv. com., 1981-91; faculty assoc. Danforth Found., 1974-84; speaker in field; mem. secondary sch. curriculum com. Jefferson County Pub. Schs., Colo., 1976-78; mem. adv. com. Golden H.S., 1973-77; mem. adv. coun. White House Conf. on Librs. and Info. Svs., 1991; del. Internat. Fedn. Libr. Assns. Author, editor 3 books; contbr. articles to profl. jours., numerous chpts. to books. Mem. rural librs. and humanities program Colo. planning and resource bd. NEH, 1982-83; bd. mgrs. Friends of Denver Pub. Libr., 1976-82; pres. Faculty Women's Club, Colo. Sch. Mines, 1963-64. Mem. ALA (visionary leaders com. 1987-89, coun. mem. 1979-83, com on accreditation 1984-85, orientation com. 1974-77, 83-84, pub. rels. com.), Am. Soc. Info. Sci. (pub. rels. chmn. 1971), Mountain Plains Libr. Assn. (profl. devel. com. 1979-80, pub. rels. and publs. com. 1973-75, continuing edn. com. 1973-76), Colo. Libr. Assn. (pres. 1974, bd. dirs. 1973-75, continuing edn. com. 1976-80), Assn. Libr. & Info. Sci. Edn. (communication com. 1978-80, program com. 1977-78), Cosmos Club (Washington). Home: 492 Mount Evans Rd Golden CO 80401

MATHEWS, BARBARA BAILEY, special education educator; b. Cambridge, Mass., Apr. 20, 1943; d. Herbert Sternbergh and Inez (Wells) Bailey; m. J.D. Mathews, Aug. 20, 1966 (div. 1987); children: David Herbert, Diana Grace. AB, Syracuse U., 1965, MS, 1992; postgrad., SUNY, Brockport, 1965-66, SUNY, Oswego, 1968-70. Cert. spl. edn. tchr., German tchr., sci. tchr., N.Y. Jr. high sch. German tchr. Phoenix, N.Y., 1965-68; high sch. German tchr. Parish, N.Y., 1968-71; sci. and German tchr. North Syracuse, N.Y., 1984-91; spl. educator resource room North Syracuse Cen. Schs., 1992-94; spl. educator Westmoreland Ctrl. Schs., N.Y., 1994—; steering com. ann. sci. fair North Syracuse Schs., 1985-87. Bd. mgrs. North Area YMCA, Liverpool, N.Y., 1982-84. Mem. Delta Phi Alpha, Chi Omega (past pres. alumnae, treas. 1966—). Home: 8100 Maple Rd Clay NY 13041-8908

MATHEWS, BARBARA EDITH, gynecologist; b. Santa Barbara, Calif., Oct. 5, 1946; d. Joseph Chesley and Pearl (Cieri) Mathews; AB, U. Calif., 1969; MD, Tufts U., 1972. Diplomate Am. Bd. Ob-Gyn. Intern, Cottage Hosp., Santa Barbara, 1972-73, Santa Barbara Gen. Hosp., 1972-73; resident in ob-gyn Beth Israel Hosp., Boston, 1973-77; clin. fellow in ob-gyn Harvard U., 1973-76, instr., 1976-77; gynecologist Sansum Med. Clinic, Santa Barbara, 1977—; faculty mem. ann. postgrad. course Harvard Med. Sch.; bd. dirs. Sansum Med. Clinic; dir. ann. postgrad course UCLA Med. Sch. Bd. dirs. Meml. Rehab. Found., Santa Barbara, Channel City Club, Santa Barbara, Music Acad. of the West, Santa Barbara; mem. citizen's continuing edn. adv. council Santa Barbara C.C.; moderator Santa Barbara Cottage Hosp. Cmty. Health Forum. Fellow ACS, Am. Coll. Ob-gyn.; mem. AMA, Am. Soc. Colposcopy and Cervical Pathology (dir. 1982-84), Harvard U. Alumni Assn., Tri-counties Obstet. and Gynecol. Soc. (pres. 1981-82), Phi Beta Kappa. Clubs: Birnam Wood Golf (Santa Barbara). Author: (with L. Burke) Colposcopy in Clinical Practice, 1977; contbg. author Manual of Ambulatory Surgery, 1982. Home: 2105 Anacapa St Santa Barbara CA 93105-3503 Office: 317 W Pueblo St Santa Barbara CA 93105-4365

MATHEWS, CARMEN SYLVA, actress; b. Phila., May 8, 1918; d. Albert Barnes and Matilde (Keller) M. Student, Bennett Jr. Coll., 1936-38, Royal Acad. Dramatic Art, Eng., 1938, 39. Appeared numerous stage plays; roles include Ophelia in Hamlet, Queen in Richard II, Lady Mortimer in Henry IV, Varya in Cherry Orchard, 1943, Violet in Man and Superman, 1945, Mrs. Sullen in Beaux Strategem, 1945, Miss Ronberry in The Corn is Green, 1946, Miss Neville in She Stoops to Conquer, 1946, Madame Ducotel in My Three Angels, 1952, Mary in Holiday for Lovers, 1957, Candida in Shaw's Candida, 1958, Eileen in Man in Dogsuit, 1958, Lady Utterword in Heartbreak House, 1959-60, Contessa in mus. adapted from Candide, Voltaire, 1956, Ceil in Night Life, 1962, Maria in Lorenzo, 1963, Louise in Zenda, 1963, Queen in Hamlet, 1964, Grandma Hutto in mus. adaptation The Yearling, 1965, Edna in A Delicate Balance, 1966, Bathsheeba in mus. adaptation I'm Solomon, 1967-68, Constance in mus. adaptation Dear World, 1968, Rabbit Run, 1969, Fraulein Schneider in mus. adaptation Cabaret, 1970, Wife in All Over, 1970, Grandma in Ring around the Bathtub, 1971, Gloriani in mus. Ambassador, 1972, Mrs. Aigreville in mus. In Fashion, 1973, Mamita in mus. Gigi, 1974, Arietta in Mornings at Seven, 1974, Mrs. Higgins in Pygmalion, 1975, Mother in Children, 1976, Mrs. Ellis in The Autumn Garden, 1976, Madame Arcati in Blithe Spirit, 1977, Mrs. Tilford in The Children's Hour, Catherine in Arms and the Man, 1979, Fanny Farrelly in Watch on the Rhine, 1980, Cornelia in The Bat, 1980, Betsy Trotwood in mus. David Copperfield, 1981, Cora in Mornings at Seven, 1981, Sarah Delano Roosevelt in Sunrise at Campobello, 1982, Old Lady in Sunday in the Park with George, 1983, Helen in The Road to Mecca, 1984, Mother in Night, Mother, 1985, Grandmother in A Grand Romance, 1985, Mrs. Hardcastle in She Stoops to Conquer, 1986, Cecelia in Autumn Elegy, 1989, Dowager Empress in The Anastasia Game, 1989, Mme. Armfeldt in A Little Night Music, 1990; movie appearances include Butterfield 8, A Rage To Live, Mrs. Boatwright in Sounder, 1971, Fanny Ascher in Daniel, 1983; also in various dramatic TV shows, and other TV show including Judge in TV after sch. spl. To Take A Stand, 1988, role of Lil in MASH, HBO spl. The Last Day in the Life of Brian Darling, 1990, The Best Year of My Life, 1990; recording books for Am. Found. for Blind. Named one of Conn. Outstanding Women United Nations, 1987. Mem. Actors Equity, Screen Actors Guild, AFTRA. Home: New Pond Farm West Redding CT 06896

MATHEWS, JESSICA TUCHMAN, policy researcher, former government official; b. N.Y.C., July 4, 1946; d. Lester Reginald and Barbara (Wertheim) Tuchman; m. Colin D. Mathews, Feb. 25, 1978; children: Oliver Max Tuchman, Jordan Henry Morgenthau; stepchildren: Zachary Chase, Hilary Dustin. AB magna cum laude, Radcliffe Coll., 1967; PhD, Calif. Inst. Tech., 1973. Congrl. sci. fellow AAAS, 1973-74; profl. staff mem. Ho. Interior Com. on Energy and Environment, Washington, 1974-75; dir. issues and rsch. Udall Presdl. campaign, 1975-76; dir. Office of Global Issues NSC staff, Washington, 1977-79; mem. editorial bd. The Washington Post, 1980-82; v.p., dir. rsch. The World Resources Inst., Washington, 1982-92; dep. to undersec. for global affairs U.S. Dept. State, Washington, 1993; sr. fellow Coun. on Fgn. Rels., Washington, 1993—; mem. trade and environ. com. of nat. adv. coun. for environ. policy and tech. EPA, 1991-92; mem. numerous adv. panels Office Tech. Assessment, NAS, AAAS; bd. dirs. Population Ref. Bur., Washington, 1988-93. Columnist Washington Post, 1991-92, 93—. Bd. dirs. Joyce Found., Chgo., 1984-91, Radcliffe Coll., 1992—, Carnegie Endowment for Internat. Peace, Washington, 1992—, Rockefeller Bros. Fund, N.Y.C., 1992—, Inter-Am. Dialogue, 1991—. Disting. fellow Aspen Inst. Mem. Coun. Fgn. Rels., Fedn. Am. Scientists (bd. dirs. 1985-87, 88-92), Inst. for Internat. Econs. (adv. com.). Democrat. Jewish. Office: Council on Fgn Relations 2400 N St NW Washington DC 20037

MATHEWS, JOAN HELENE, pediatrician; b. Manchester, N.H., Feb. 3, 1940; d. John Barnaby and Helen A. Wlodkoski; m. Ernest Stephen Mathews, June 1, 1965; 3 children. BS, U. N.H., 1961; MD, Columbia U., 1965. Diplomate Am. Bd. Pediatrics. Med. intern Roosevelt Hosp., N.Y.C., 1965-66; pediatric resident Babies Hops. Columbia Presbyn. Med. Ctr., N.Y.C., 1966-68, pediatric endocrine fellow Babies Hosp., 1968-70; instr. clin. pediat. Columbia U. Coll. Physicians and Surgeons, N.Y.C., 1973-77; asst. prof. pediat. Cornell U. Med. Coll., N.Y.C., 1977-81; clin. instr. pediat. Harvard Med. Sch., Boston, 1985—; clin. assoc. children's svc. Mass. Gen. Hosp., Boston, 1985—. Fellow Am. Acad. Pediat.; mem. Phi Beta Kappa. Office: 777 Concord Ave Cambridge MA 02138-1053

MATHEWS, LINDA MCVEIGH, newspaper editor; b. Redlands, Calif., Mar. 14, 1946; d. Glenard Ralph and Edith Lorene (Humphrey) McVeigh; m. Thomas Jay Mathews, June 15, 1967; children—Joseph, Peter, Katherine. B.A., Radcliffe Coll., 1967; J.D., Harvard U., 1972. Gen. assignment reporter Los Angeles Times, 1967-69, Supreme Ct. corr., 1972-76, corr., Hong Kong, 1977-79, China corr., Peking, 1979-80, op-ed page editor, 1980-81, dep. nat. editor, 1981-84, dep. fgn. editor, 1985-88, editorial writer, 1988-89, editor L.A. Times mag., 1989-92; sr. producer ABC News, 1992-93; nat. editor N.Y. Times, 1993—; corr. Wall St. Jour., Hong Kong, 1976-77; lectr.; freelance writer. Author: (with others) Journey Into China, 1982; One Billion: A China Chronicle, 1983. Mem. Women's Legal Def. Fund, 1972-76; co-founder, pres. Hong Kong Montessori Sch., 1977-79; bd. dirs. Ctr. for Childhood. Mem. Fgn. Corrs. Club Hong Kong. Office: NY Times 229 W 43rd St New York NY 10036-3913

MATHEWS, MARY KATHRYN, government official; b. Washington, Apr. 20, 1948; d. T. Odon (dec.) and Kathryn (Augustine) M. Student, Pa. State U., 1966-68; BBA, Am. U., 1970, MBA, 1975. Personnel mgmt. specialist, coordinator coll. recruitment program, GSA, Washington, 1971-75, adminstrv. officer, 1975-78; personnel mgmt. specialist Office of Personnel Mgmt., Washington, 1978; employee devel. specialist Office Sec. Transp., Washington, 1978-80, dep. chief departmental services and spl. programs div., 1980-81; asst. dir. adminstrv. div. Farm Credit Adminstrn., Washington, 1981-84; dir. adminstrv. div. Farm Credit Adminstrn., McLean, Va., 1984-86; chief adminstrv. services div. Farm Credit Adminstrn., McLean, 1987-88; dep. staff dir. for mgmt. U.S. Commn. Civil Rights, Washington, 1988-90, asst. staff dir. for mgmt., 1990-91, asst. staff dir. for congl. affairs, 1991-94, staff dir., 1994—; chief spl. programs staff and homebound handicapped employment program GSA, Washington, 1973-74; mem. task force Presdl. mgmt. intern program U.S. Office Pers. Mgmt., Washington, 1977-78; coord. mgmt. devel. program for women Office Sec. Transp., Washington, 1979-81. Vol. mentor, speaker Alexandria Commn. on Women. Mem. Exec. Women in Govt. (treas. 1993-94, v.p. 1994—, bd. dirs.), Small Agy. Coun. (exec. com. 1990-91, 94, chmn. micro agy. group 1990-91), Nat. Trust Hist. Preservation, Nat. Assn. Mus. Women in Arts (charter), Delta Gamma (rush advisor 1971-73, pres. bd. dirs. local chpt. house corp. 1972-73). Home: 405 S Royal St Alexandria VA 22314-3717 Office: U S Commn on Civil Rights 624 9th St NW Washington DC 20425-0002

MATHEWS, MARY PAINTER, acquisitions librarian; b. Balt., Feb. 1, 1932; d. Sidney and Nivea Elizabeth (Forbes) Painter; m. John Hopper Mathews, July 27, 1951; children: Sara Forbes, Laura Inslee, Christine Winslow. BA, U. Mich., 1955, MA, 1957; MLS, U. Md., 1968. Editorial sec. U. Mich./Smithsonian, Ann Arbor, 1957-59; registrar Marjorie Webster Jr. Coll., Washington, 1962; sch. libr. Prince Georges County Pub. Schs., Upper Marlboro, Md., 1968-89; acquisitions libr. ERIC Faculty, Rockville, Md., 1989—. Mem. AAUW, Internat. Assn. Sch. Librarianship, Md. Libr. Assn., Md. Edn. Media Assn. (pres. 1988-89). Office: ERIC Processing Facility 1301 Piccard Dr Rockville MD 20850

MATHEWS, SUSAN MCKIERNAN, health care executive; b. N.Y.C., May 28, 1946; d. Thomas Joseph and Eileen Ann (Looschen) McK.; m. Robert Emmett Mathews, June 17, 1967; children: Colin Robert, Brendan Robert, Devin Robert, Kiernan Robert. Diploma in nursing, St. Francis Sch. Nursing, 1966; BS in Health Adminstrn., St. Joseph's Coll., 1979; MS in Pub. Svc. Adminstrn., Russell Sage Coll., 1983; PhD in Health Adminstrn., Columbia Pacific U., 1985. RN, N.Y. Utilization rev. analyst N.Y. State Office Mental Retardation & Devel. Disabilities, Albany, 1980-83; with Empire Blue Cross & Blue Shield, Albany, 1983-86, dir. instl. utilization rev., cons. in field, 1986-88; COO, pres. Corp. Health Dimensions, Troy, N.Y., 1988-92, pres., 1992—; spkr. in field. Mem. bus. adv. bd. SUNY Coll., New Paltz; grad. Capital Leadership, 1990; mem. pres. coun. Sage Colls., 1994. Recipient Excellence in Mgmt. Pvt. Sector award, 1992. Mem. Med. Group Mgmt. Assn., Albany Colonie Regional C. of C. (bd. dirs., exec. com.), Rensselaer County C. of C. (Woman of Achievement award 1994). Roman Catholic. Home: 20 Viewpoint Dr Troy NY 12812 Office: Corp Health Dimensions 500 Federal St Ste 601 Troy NY 12180-3340

MATHEWS, WILMA KENDRICK, public relations executive; b. Danville, Va., Dec. 23, 1945; d. Clarence Blanchard and Tina Collins (Powell) Kendrick; AA, Stratford Coll., 1966, BA, 1970; student East Carolina U., 1966-67, U. Md., European div., 1967-68, Guilford Coll., 1978-80. Asst. editor The Commonwealth Mag., Richmond, Va., 1970-72; news editor The Comml. Appeal, Danville, Va., 1972-73; pub. rels. mgr. Danville C. of C., 1973-74; publs. officer Bowman Gray Bapt. Hosp. Med. Ctr., Winston-Salem, N.C., 1974-78; sr. pub. rels. specialist Western Electric, 1978-82; mgr. pub. rels. AT&T Internat., Basking Ridge, N.J., 1982-84; media rels. mgr. AT&T Network Systems, 1985-87, mgr. pub. rels. field support, 1987-90, pub. rels. adv. dir., 1990-93, comm. cons. and trainer, 1993—; sr. pub. rels. adv. N.C. Epilepsy Info. Svc., 1979-80. Co-author: On Deadline: Managing Media Relations, 1985, 94; Inside Organizational Communications, 2d edit., 1985, Marketing Communications, 1987; Mem. Danville Bicentennial Commn., 1972-74; bd. dirs. Nat. Tobacco-Textile Mus., 1973-74; mem. Danville City Beautiful Com., 1973-74, Maplewood Cultural Commn., 1986-87. Fellow Internat. Assn. Bus. Communicators (dir. 1978-81, pres. N.C. chpt. 1977, 78, dir. Found. 1984-87, chmn. Found. 1987-90, accreditation bd. 1983-89, 94—, bd. chmn. 1990-91), Pub. Rels. Soc. Am.; mem. Danville Hist. Soc. (dir. 1973-74), N.C. Zool. Soc., Smithsonian Instn., Internat. TV Assn. (sec. N.C. chpt. 1979-80), Internat. Pub. Rels. Assn., Coun. for Communications Mgmt. (bd. dirs. 1987-89), Friends of Maplewood Libr. (pres. 1985-86), Ahwatukee Foothills C. of C. (bd. dirs. 1994—), Stratford Coll. Alumni Assn., Internat. Order Job's Daus. Republican. Baptist. Home and Office: 14836 S Foxtail Ln Phoenix AZ 85044-4335

MATHEWSON, DORIS MAY, nurse; b. Providence; d. Hugh Edward and Nellie May (Smith) Massey; m. Donald Walter Mathewson, May 25, 1946; 1 child, Susan Elaine. Diploma, R.I. Hosp. Sch. Nursing, 1944; BS in Nurse-Tchr. Edn., R.I. Coll., 1974; MS in Health Svcs. Adminstrs., Salve Regina Coll., 1986. From staff nurse to head nurse R.I. Hosp., Providence, 1961-67, coord., supr., 1967-69, nurse leader orthopedics, 1969-71, nurse leader med., 1971-81, asst. dir. nursing, 1981-86; primary nurse, chmn. edn. Hospice Care R.I., Providence, 1986-91; parish nurse Beneficent Congl. Ch., Providence, 1992—; mem. human and health svcs. task force R.I. Conf. U.C.C., Providence, 1990—; bd. dirs. Lucy Ayres Residence for Nurses, Providence; mem. Interfaith Counseling Ctr. Bd., Providence, 1991—. Del. Religious Adminstrs. Exch. U.S.-USSR, Moscow, 1991; v.p., bd. dirs. Beneficent Congl. Ch., 1990—; mem. R.I. State Coun. Chs.; mem. adv. bd. Cranston (R.I.) Adult Sr. Svcs., 1989—. Mem. ANA, R.I. State Nurses Assn. (govt. affairs com.), Western Cranston Garden Club (pres. 1994—), R.I. Hosp. Nurses Alumni Assn. (bd. dirs. 1987—), R.I. Coll. Alumni, Salve Regina Coll. Alumni. Home: 44 Forsythia Ln Cranston RI 02921-2315

MATHIAS, ALICE IRENE, health plan company executive; b. N.Y.C., Mar 2, 1949; d. Murray and Charlotte (Kottle) M. B.S. in Math., Western New Eng. Coll., 1972. Programmer, Carnation Co., Los Angeles, 1973-78; programmer/analyst Cedars-Sinai Med. Ctr., Los Angeles, 1978-79, Union Bank, Los Angeles, 1979-81; group leader Kaiser Found. Health Plan, Pasadena, Calif., 1981—. Mem. Nat. Assn. Female Execs., Am. Mgmt. Assn., Kaiser Mgmt. Assn., Kaiser Women in Mgmt., Los Angeles County Mus. Art (sponsor), Smithsonian Inst., KCET Pub. TV, Choice In Dying, U.S. Holocaust Meml. Mus. (charter mem.), Caithness Collectors Club, Statue of Liberty Ellis Island Found. Home: 4210 Via Arbolada Apt 311 Los Angeles CA 90042-5124 Office: Kaiser Found Health Plan Info Svcs Dept 393 E Walnut St Pasadena CA 91188-0001

MATHIAS, BETTY JANE, communications and community affairs consultant, writer, editor, lecturer; b. East Ely, Nev., Oct. 22, 1923; d. Royal F. and Dollie B. (Bowman) M.; student Merritt Bus. Sch., 1941, 42, San Francisco State U., 1941-42; 1 child, Dena. Asst. publicity dir. Oakland (Calif.) Area War Chest and Community Chest, 1943-46; pub. rels. Am. Legion, Oakland, 1946-47; asst. to pub. rels. dir. Cen. Bank of Oakland, 1947-49; pub. rels. dir. East Bay chpt. of Nat. Safety Council, 1949-51; propr., mgr. Mathias Pub. Rels. Agy., Oakland, 1951-60; gen. assignment reporter and teen news editor Daily Rev., Hayward, Calif., 1960-62; freelance pub. rels. and writing, Oakland, 1962-66, 67-69; dir. corp. communications Systech Fin. Corp., Walnut Creek, Calif., 1969-71; v.p. corp. communications Consol. Capital companies, Oakland, 1972-79, v.p. community affairs, Emeryville, Calif., 1981-84, v.p. spl. projects, 1984-85; v.p., dir. Consol. Capital Realty Svcs., Inc., Oakland, 1973-77; v.p., dir. Centennial Adv. Corp., Oakland, 1976-77; communications cons., 1979—; cons. Mountainair Realty, Cameron Park, Calif., 1986-87; pub. rels. coord. Tuolumne County Visitors Bur., 1989-90; lectr. in field; bd. dirs. Oakland YWCA, 1944-45, ARC, Oakland, So. Alameda County chpt., 1967-69, Family Ctr., Children's Hosp. Med. Ctr. No. Calif., 1982-85, March of Dimes, 1983-85, Equestrian Ctr. of Walnut Creek, Calif., 1983-84, also sec.; adult and publs. adv. Internat. Order of the Rainbow for Girls, 1953-78; communications arts adv. com. Ohlone (Calif.) Coll., 1979-85, chmn., 1982-84; mem. adv. bd. dept. mass communications Calif. State U.-Hayward, 1985; pres. San Francisco Bay Area chpt. Nat. Reyes Syndrome Found., 1981-86; vol. staff Columbia Actors' Repertory, Columbia, Calif., 1986-87, 89; mem. exec. bd., editor newsletter Tuolumne County Dem. Club, 1987; publicity chmn. 4th of July celebration Tuolumne County C. of C., 1988; vol. children's dept. Tuolumne County Pub. Libr., 1993—. Recipient Grand Cross of Color award Internat. Order of Rainbow for Girls, 1955. Order Eastern Star (publicity chmn. Calif. state 1955). Editor East Bay Mag., 1966-67, TIA Traveler, 1969, Concepts, 1979-83. Home: 20575 Gopher Dr Sonora CA 95370-9034

MATHIAS, MARGARET GROSSMAN, manufacturing company executive, leasing company executive; b. Detroit, June 26, 1928; d. D. Ray and Lila May (Skinner) Grossman; children: Deborah, Robert, Lesley, Jennifer, Mary. BA, Mt. Holyoke Coll., 1949; cert., Am. Acad. Art, 1951. Artist and co-mgr. Mary Chase Marionettes, N.Y.C., 1951-54; exec. v.p. Star Five Corp., Elkhart, 1975-88, pres., treas., chmn. bd., 1985-90; sec., chmn. bd. L & J Press Corp., Elkhart, Ind., 1985-91, also chmn. bd. dirs.; chmn. MAGCo Inc., Elkhart, 1986—; pres. Tech Products, Inc., Elkhart, 1992—. Mem. fin. com. United Fund, Elkhart, 1960-64, parents adv. bd. Furman U., Greenville, S.C., 1978-83, art adv. bd. Mount Holyoke Coll., South Hadley, Mass., 1982—; pres. Tri Kappa Service Orgn., Elkhart, 1965-66; trustee Stanley Clark Sch., South Bend, Ind., 1977-87. Recipient Lawson Top Sculpture Purchase award Midwest Mus. Am. Art, 1990. Mem. Elkhart C. of C. Republican. Clubs: Elcona Country (Elkhart), Woman's Athletic (Chgo.), Thursday (Elkhart) (pres. 1976). Home and Office: 1077 Greenleaf Blvd Apt 209 Elkhart IN 46514-3563

MATHIEU, HELEN M., state legislator; b. Newport, R.I., May 8, 1940; m. Roger E. Mathieu, 1964. Student, Salve Regina Coll. Mem. R.I. State Senate, dist. 46. Mem. Kappa Gamma Pi. Democrat. Roman Catholic. Home: 160 Lawrence Dr Portsmouth RI 02871-4063 Office: R I State Senate State Capital Providence RI 02903*

MATHIEU, MARY MARTHA, accountant, consultant; b. Shreveport, La., Oct. 2, 1952; d. Clyde Benjamin and Mary Frances (Cornelius) Phillips; m. Reese Alfred Mathieu III, Dec. 28, 1974; children: Mary Charlotte, Sarah Elizabeth, Reese Alfred IV. BBA in Acctg. summa cum laude, Tex. Christian U., 1975. CPA, Tex.; cert. mgmt. acct. Budget mgr. Arco Exploration Co., Dallas, 1984, mgr. internal control, 1985; various acctg. positions Arco Oil and Gas Co., Dallas, 1975-78, coord. acctg. devel., 1979, supr. cost acctg., 1980-81, cons. planning, 1985, cons. property sales, 1986, mgr. land and mktg. systems, 1987-91, transition mgr., 1992—; Arco Oil and Gas Co. recruiter Tex. Christian U., 1981-88; presenter oil industry conf. IBM, Monterey, Calif., 1990; mem. steering com. Arco-Haliburton Strategic Alliance, Houston, 1992. Editor: (tng. manual) Natural Gas Marketing System, 1990; author, editor publs. in field for Arco Oil and Gas Co. Chmn. Arco United Way campaign, Dallas and Plano, Tex., 1988; mem. Arco Civic Action Program, 1978—. Recipient recognition for mgmt. support El Centro Coll., Dallas, 1991. Mem. Tex. Soc. CPAs, Dallas chpt. Tex. Soc. CPAs, Inst. Mgmt. Accts., Am. Petroleum Inst., Tex. Christian U. Alumnae Assn. (student body treas. 1974-75, scholar 1975), Dallas County Med. Soc. Alliance, Assn. Baby Boomers, Delta Delta Delta. Presbyterian.

MATHIEU-HARRIS, MICHELE SUZANNE, association executive; b. Chgo., Mar. 24, 1950; d. Joseph Edward Mathieu and Mary Ellen (Knapp) Fisher; m. Robert Steven Harris, May 1, 1988. Student DePaul U., 1971, 74-76, Regents Coll., Albany, N.Y., 1987—. Broadcast coord. Grey-North Advt., Chgo., 1967-71; head drama dept. Patricia Stevens Coll., Chgo., 1972; instr. beginning acting Ted Liss Sch. of Performing Arts, Chgo., 1973-75; project coord. grants and contracts Am. Dietetic Assn., Chgo., 1974-81, adminstr. govt. affairs, 1981-86, mgr. licensure communications, 1986-90, adminstr. nutrition svcs. payment systems, 1990-94, team leader, health care fin. team, 1994—; grant proposal cons. various performance arts, Chgo., 1978—. Editor Legis. Newsletter, 1981-86; contbg. editor Nutrition Forum, 1986, Courier, 1987—; contbr. articles to profl. jours., mags., newspapers. Treas. Am. Dietetic Assn. polit. action com., Washington, 1981-86. Ill. Arts Coun. grantee, 1981; recipient award Excellence in Govt. Rels. Am. Soc. Assn. Execs., 1989, gen. mgnt. certificate program, 1992. Mem. Am. Soc. Assn. Execs.. Roman Catholic. Avocations: reading, fitness walking. Office: Am Dietetic Assn 216 W Jackson Blvd Chicago IL 60606-6909

MATHIS, JUNE GREEN, business office manager; b. Louise, Miss., June 12, 1941; d. Thomas Leo and Louella (Sanders) Green; m. P. Michael Mathis, Mar. 27, 1960; children: Jon Michael, Gregory D., Thomas Vincent. Student, Holmes Jr. Coll., Goodman, Miss., 1977-78. Operator South Cen. Bell. Telephone Co., Yazoo City, Miss., 1959-63; with King's Daughters Hosp., Yazoo City, 1963—, personnel adminstr., 1971-78, mgr. bus. office, 1978—; chmn. Health Fair, King's Daughters Hosp., 1986, 88. Chmn. Nat. Hosp. Week, Yazoo City, 1983—; v.p. Merry Gardeners Garden Club, Yazoo City, 1981. Mem. Miss. Hosp. Assn., Soc. Personnel Adminstrn., Ord. Ea. Star. Baptist. Home: PO Box 1677 Yazoo City MS 39194-1677 Office: Kings Daughters Hosp 823 Grand Ave Yazoo City MS 39194-3233

MATHIS, LOIS RENO, retired educator; b. Vinson, Okla., June 10, 1915; d. William Dodson and Trudie Frances (Brady) Reno; m. Harold Fletcher Mathis, June 6, 1942 (dec.); children: Robert F., Betty Mathis Sproule. BS, Southwestern Okla. U., 1939; MA, U. Pitts., 1945; PhD, Ohio State U., 1965. Cert. elem. tchr.; cert. elem. supr. Tchr. Okla. Pub. Schs., Tea Cross, 1936-39, Tipton, 1939-42; tchr. Ohio County Schs., Wheeling, W.Va., 1944-45, Norman (Okla.) Pub. Schs., 1951-52, Kent (Ohio) State U., 1954-60, Ohio State U., Columbus, 1961-62, Columbus (Ohio) Pub. Schs., 1967-80; ret., 1980; ednl. cons. in field, 1965—. Mem. Women's Round Table, Columbus, 1986-88; mem. data collection com. 100 Good Schs., Columbus, 1982-84. Mem. AAUW (pres. 1986-88), Ohio State Univ. Women's Club, Phi Delta Gamma (pres. 1980-82), Pi Lambda Theta, Alpha Delta Kappa, Kappa Delta Pi (counselor 1976—, alumni counselor exec. coun. internat. 1990-92, Honor Key 1991). Democrat. Baptist. Home: 2905 Halstead Rd Columbus OH 43221-2917

MATHIS, MARSHA DEBRA, software company executive; b. Detroit, Dec. 22, 1953; d. Marshall Junior and Anita Willene (Biggers) M. BS, Fla. State U., 1978; MBA, Miss. Coll., 1982. With telecommunications dept. Fla. State Dept. Safety, Tallahassee, 1973-76; asst. to chmn. Tallahassee Savs. and Loan Assn., 1976-78; sales engr. Prehler, Inc., Jackson, Miss., 1978-82; mktg. mgr. Norand Corp., Arlington, Tex., 1982-87; v.p. mktg. and sales Profl. Datasolutions, Inc., Irving, Tex., 1987-88; v.p. mktg. and sales, ptnr. Target Systems, Inc., Irving, 1988-89, also bd. dirs.; v.p. mktg. Profl. Datasolutions, Inc., Temple, Tex., 1990—. Contbr. articles to industry trade jours. Advisor Am. Diabetes Assn., Jackson, 1983—. Mem. Internat. Platform Assn., Nat. Adv. Group, Nat. Assn. Convenience Stores (Industry Task Force 1987-88). Republican. Roman Catholic. Home: 325 Old York Rd Irving TX 75063-4247 Office: Profl Datasolutions Inc 3407 S 31st St Temple TX 76502-1902

MATHIS, SHARON BELL, author, elementary educator, librarian; b. Atlantic City, Feb. 26, 1937; d. John Willie and Alice Mary (Frazier) Bell; m. Leroy F. Mathis, July 11, 1957 (div. Jan. 1979); children: Sherie, Stacy, Stephanie. B.A., Morgan State Coll., 1958; M.L.S., Catholic U. Am., 1975. Interviewer Children's Hosp. of D.C., Washington, 1958-59; tchr. Holy Redeemer Elementary Sch., Washington, 1959-65, Charles Hart Jr. High Sch., Washington, 1965-72; spl. edn. tchr. Stuart Jr. High Sch., Washington, 1972-74; librarian Benning Elementary Sch., Washington, 1975-76, Friendship Ednl. Center, 1976—; writer-in-charge children's lit. div. D.C. Black Writers Workshop; writer-in-residence Howard U., 1972-73. Author: Brooklyn Story, 1970, Sidewalk Story, 1971 (Council on Interracial Books for Children award 1970), Teacup Full of Roses, 1972 (Outstanding Book of Yr. award New York Times 1972), Ray Charles, 1973 (Coretta Scott King award 1974), Listen for the Fig Tree, 1974, The Hundred Penny Box, 1975 (Boston Globe-Horn Book Honor book 1975, Newbery Honor Book 1976), Cartwheels, 1977, Red Dog Blue Fly: Football Poems, 1991 (Children's Book of Yr. award Bank St. Coll. 1992). Mem. bd. advisers lawyers com. D.C. Commn. on Arts, 1972. Nominated Books for Brotherhood list NCCJ, 1970; recipient D.C. Assn. Sch. Librs. award 1976, Arts and Humanities award Archdiocese of Washington Black Secretariat, 1978; Weekly Reader Book Club fellow Bread Loaf Writers Conf., 1970, MacDowell Colony fellow, 1978. Roman Catholic.

MATHISEN-REID, RHODA SHARON, international communications consultant; b. Portland, Oreg., June 25, 1942; d. Daniel and Mildred Elizabeth Annette (Peterson) Hager; m. James Albert Mathisen, July 17, 1964 (div. 1977); m. James A. Reid Sr., Jan. 1, 1991. BA in Edn., Music, Bible Coll., Mich., 1964. Community Rels. officer Gary-Wheaton Bank, Wheaton, Ill., 1971-75; br. mgr. Stivers Temporary Personnel, Chgo., 1975-79; v.p. sales Exec. Technique, Chgo., 1980-83; prin. Mathisen Assocs., Clarendon Hills, Ill., 1983—; presenter seminars; featured speaker Women in Mgmt. Oak Brook Chpt., 1988.; cons. Haggai Inst., Atlanta; adv. mem. Nat. Bd. Success Group, 1986. Pres. chancel choir Christ Ch. of Oak Brook, 1985-87; mem., 1992—, bd. dirs. Career Devel. Inst., Oak Brook, 1992; judge Mrs. Ill., USI Pageant, 1994. Mem. NAFE, Bus. and Profl. Women (charter mem. Woodfield chpt.), Execs. Club Oak Brook, Assn. Commerce and Industry (named Ambassador of Month N.W. suburban chpt. 1979), Oak Brook Assn. Commerce and Industry (mem. membership com.), Women Entrepreneurs of DuPage County (membership chmn., featured speaker Jan. 1988), Art Inst. Chgo. Republican. Office: Mathisen Assocs 17 Lake Shore Dr Clarendon Hills IL 60514-2221

MATISOFF, SUSAN, cultural research organization administrator. Dir. Ctr. East-Asian Studies, Stanford U., Calif. Office: Stanford University Ctr E-Asian Studies 300 Lasuen St Stanford CA 94305-5013

MATLIN, MARLEE, actress; b. Morton Grove, Ill., Aug. 24, 1965; m. Kevin Grandalski, Aug. 29, 1993. Attended William Rainey Harper Coll. Appeared in films Children of a Lesser God (Acad. award for best actress), 1986, Walker, 1987, Linguini Incident, 1990, The Player, 1992, Hear No Evli, 1993; TV film: Bridge to Silence, 1989, Against Her Will: The Carrie Buck Sotry, 1994; TV series: Reasonable Doubts, 1991-93; guest of Picket Fences, 1993 (Emmy nomination, Guest Actress-Drama Series, 1994), Seinfeld, 1993 (Emmy nomination Guest Actress-Comedy Series, 1994). Recipient Golden Globe award Hollywood Fgn. Press Assn., 1987, named Best Actress. Office: care ICM 8942 Wilshire Blvd Beverly Hills CA 90211

MATLOF, DEBORAH ANN, clinical pharmacist, consultant; b. St. Louis, Aug. 2, 1950; d. Aaron Nathan and Elizabeth Ann (Huber) Singer; m. Gary Matlof, Aug. 4, 1974. AB in biology, St. Louis U., 1973, BS in pharmacy, 1976, MBA in fin., 1984. Registered pharmacist, Mo. Staff pharmacist St. Louis County Hosp., 1976-81; clinical pharmacist St. Louis State Hosp., 1982-91, Malcolm Bliss Mental Health Ctr., St. Louis, 1992—; clinical pharmacist cons. Hawthorn Children's Psychiatric Hosp., St. Louis, 1986—. Mem. St. Louis Soc. Hosp. Pharmacists, Mo. Soc. Hosp. Pharamcist, Delta Zeta, Beta Beta Beta, Rho Chi. Office: Malcolm Bliss Mental Health 5400 Arsenal St Saint Louis MO 63139-1403

MATLOW, LINDA MONIQUE, photographic agency executive, publishing executive; b. Chgo., July 24, 1955; d. Charles and Milly Matlow. Grad. high sch., Chgo.; student, Sch. Modern Photography, N.Y.C., 1977-79. Promotions and pub. relations staff Jaydee Enterprises, Chgo., 1971-73; mgr. First Venture, Inc., Chgo., 1973-77; photographer, pub. relations staff Bands & Mags., Chgo., 1977—; photographer, writer, editor Pix Internat., Chgo., 1982—; photo-editor Beat. Chgo. Sounds; bur. chief. Prairie Sun. Contbr. photographs to pubs. including N.Y. Times, Chgo. Tribune, Boston Globe. Vol. telethon Variety Club of Chgo., 1986, Spl. Childrens' Charities, Little City Found., Chgo. Acad. for the Arts. Named Rock Photographer Night Rock newspaper, Chgo., 1980, 81, one of Chgo.'s Most Successful and Eligible Bachelorettes Today's Chgo. Woman mag., 1989; recipient Hon. mention Internat. Photographer Mag., 1990, winner B&W Print of Ray Charles, 1991; finalist Photographers Forum B&W Print, 1991. Mem. Nat. Press Protographers Assn., NARAS, Internat. Freelance Photographers Orgn., Chgo. Women in Pub. Roman Catholic.

MATON, ANTHEA, education consultant; b. Burnley, Lancashire, England, Feb. 1, 1944; d. William Douglas Newton-Dawson and Beatrice Joan (Simpson) Bateman; m. K.F. Edward Asprey, Nov. 13, 1965 (div. 1978); children: George William Edward, Mariana Alexandra Beatrice; m. Paul Nicholas Maton, Mar. 23, 1978; 1 child, Petra Beatrice Suzanne. MSR in Radiotherapy, Soc. Radiographers, 1965; FETC, Chiswick Poly., U.K., 1976; HDCR, Coll. Radiographers, 1976, TDCR, 1977; postgrad., U. Okla. Clin. instr. radiotherapy Hammersmith Hosp., London, 1970-75; prin. sch. radiotherapy Royal Free Hosp., London, 1977-80, acting supt., 1979-80; head of careers Putney High Sch. for Girls, London, 1981-83; head of physics St. Andrews Episc. High Sch., Bethesda, Md., 1984-88; vis. fellow Am. Assn. Physics Tchrs., 1988-89; nat. coord. project scope, sequence, and coordination Nat. Sci. Tchrs. Assn., 1989-91; exec. dir. Edn. Commections, Oklahoma City, 1991—, dir. exhbn. on art and physics, 1994—; organizer U.S.-Soviet High Sch. Physics Student Exch. and Visit, 1989; conducted numerous workshops on sci. curriculum reform and assessment reform, 1987—; faculty USA Physics Olympiad Team, 1986, 89; physics tchr. St. Andrews Episc. High Sch., 1984-88, Putney High Sch. for Girls, 1980-83, tchr. med. ethics, 1982-83; tchr. physics, anatomy and physiology, radiobiology Royal Free Hosp., 1977-80, contemporary physics edn. project, 1989—. Lead author Prentice Hall Sci., 1993; contbr. articles to profl. jours. Mem. Nat. Mus. Women Arts (charter), Women's Philharm. (charter); apptd. to scientific adv. bd. OMNIPLEX Sci. Mus., Okla. City; cons. Sta. WGBH, Boston, Smithsonian, Am. Mus. of Moving Image, UCLA, Del. Edn. Dept., Ark. Project Advise, Newcastle (Del.) Sch. Dist. Named one of Today's Leaders Okla. Edn. Equity Roundtable, 1992. Mem. NAFE, ASCD, AAUW, NOW (coord. metro chpt. 1992—, treas. Okla. state chpt. 1993—), Assn. for Women in Sci., Nat. Sci. Tchrs. Assn., Am. Assn. Physics Tchrs., N.Y. Acad. Scis., Assn. for Sci. Edn., Soc. Radiographers U.K. Home and Office: 1804 Dorchester Dr Oklahoma City OK 73120

MATOWIK, DEENA, accountant; b. Anchorage, Dec. 8, 1952; d. James Joseph and Charlotte (Page) M. BA in Music, U. Calif., L.A., 1975; MBA in Fin., UCLA, 1986. Corp. acctg. supr. R.L. Kautz & Co., L.A., 1976-79; payroll mgr. Nat. Med. Enterprises, L.A., 1979-84; asst. dir. fiscal svcs. Century City Hosp., L.A., 1984; controller, interim pres. New Market Mgmt. Svc., Long Beach, Calif., 1985-88; pvt. practice L.A., 1988—.

MATSA, LOULA ZACHAROULA, social services administrator; b. Piraeus, Greece, Apr. 16, 1935; came to U.S., 1952, naturalized 1962; d. Eleftherios Georgiou and Ourania E. (Fraguiskopoulou) Papoulias; student Pierce Coll., Athens, Greece, 1948-52; BA, Rockford Coll., 1953; MA, U. Chgo., 1955; m. Ilco S. Matsa, Nov. 27, 1953; 1 child, Aristotle Rick-y. Diplomate clin. social worker. Marital counselor Family Soc. Cambridge, Mass., 1955-56; chief unit II, social service Queen's (N.Y.) Children's Psychiat. Ctr., 1961-74; dir. social services, supr.-coord. family care program Hudson River Psychiat. Ctr., Poughkeepsie, N.Y., 1974-91; supr. social work Harlem Valley Psychiat. Ctr., Wingdale, N.Y., 1991-93; supr. social work Hudson River Psychiat. Ctr., 1993—; field instr. Adelphi, Albany and Fordham univs., 1969—. Fulbright Exch. student, 1952-53; Talcott scholar, 1953-55. Mem. NASW, Internat. Platform Assn., Internat. Coun. on Social Welfare, Acad. Cert. Social Workers, Assn. Cert. Social Workers (bd. cert.), Pub. Employees Fedn., Pierce Coll. Alumni Assn. Democrat. Greek Orthodox. Contbr. articles to profl. jours.; instrumental in state policy changes in treatment and court representation of emotionally disturbed and mentally ill. Home: 81-11 45th Ave Elmhurst NY 11373 Office: Hudson River Psychiat Ctr Branch B Poughkeepsie NY 12601

MATSON, VIRGINIA MAE FREEBERG (MRS. EDWARD J. MATSON), retired educator, author; b. Chgo., Aug. 25, 1914; d. Axel George and Mae (Dalrymple) Freeberg; m. Edward John Matson, Oct. 18, 1941; children: Karin (Mrs. Donald E. Skadden), Sara M. Drake, Edward Robert, Laurence D., David O. BA, U. Ky., 1934; MA, Northwestern U., 1941. Tchr. high schs. Chgo., 1934-42, Ridge Farm, 1944-45, Lake County (Ill.) Pub. Schs., 1956-59; founder Grove Sch., Lake Forest, Ill., 1958-87, ret., 1987. Author: Shadow on the Lost Rock, 1958, Saul, the King, 1968, Abba Father, 1970 (Friends Lit. Fiction award 1972), Buried Alive, 1970, A School for Peter, 1974, A Home for Peter, 1983, Letters to Lauren, A History of the Methodist Campgrounds, Des Plaines. Mem. Friends of Lit. Dem. Recipient Humanitarian award Ill. Med. Soc. Aux. Home: 4133 Mockingbird Ln Suffolk VA 23434

MATSUI, DOROTHY NOBUKO, educator; b. Honolulu, Jan. 9, 1954; d. Katsura and Tamiko (Sakai) M. Student, U. Hawaii, Honolulu, 1972-76, postgrad., 1982; BEd, U. Alaska, Anchorage, 1979, MEd in Spl. Edn., 1986. Clerical asst. U. Hawaii Manoa Disbursing Office, Anchorage, 1974-76; passenger service agt. Japan Air Lines, Anchorage, 1980; bilingual tutor Anchorage Sch. Dist., 1980, elem. sch. tchr., 1980—; facilitator for juvenile justice courses Anchorage Sch. Dist., Anchorage Police Dept., Alaska Pacific U., 1992-93; mem. adv. bd. Anchorage Law-Related Edn. Advancement Project. Vol. Providence Hosp., Anchorage, 1986, Humana Hosp., Anchorage, 1984, Spl. Olympics, Anchorage, 1981, Municipality Anchorage, 1978, Easter Seal Soc. Hawaii, 1975. Mem. NAFE, NEA, Alaska Edn. Assn., Smithsonian Nat. Assoc. Program, Nat. Space Soc., Smithsonian Air and Space Assn., World Aerospace Edn. Orgn., Internat. Platform Assn., Nat. Trust for Hist. Preservation, Nat. Audubon Soc., Planetary Soc., Cousteau Soc., Alaska Coun. for the Social Studies, Alaska Coun. Tchrs. Math., World Inst. Achievment, U.S. Olympic Soc., Women's Inner Circle Achievement, U. Alaska Alumni Assn., Alpha Delta Kappa (treas. Alpha chpt. 1988-92). Office: Anchorage Sch Dist 7001 Cranberry St Anchorage AK 99502-3199

MATTERSON, JOAN MCDEVITT, physical therapist; b. Bryn Mawr, Pa., Feb. 24, 1949; d. William J. and Wanda Jean (Edwards) McD.; children: Brian, Jennie, Kira. BS in Biology, St. Joseph's U., Phila., 1973; cert. in phys. therapy, U. Pa., 1974. Assoc. pharmacologist, researcher immunology and arthritis Progressive Phys. Therapy, P.A., Wilmington, Del., 1968-73, pediatric phys. therapist, 1974-81, pres., 1976—; rehab. svc. dir. Achievement Rehab.; lectr. in field of low level laser therapy. Dep. gov. Am. Biog. Rsch. Inst. Mem. Am. Soc. Laser Medicine and Surgery, Internat. Platform Assn., Am. Phys. Therapy Assn., Am. Acad. Pain (assoc.), Inst. of Noetic Sci.

MATTES, JANE, psychotherapist, human services administrator; b. N.Y.C., May 30, 1943; d. Robert and Hilda (Goldstein) Mattes; 1 child, Eric. BA, CCNY, 1965; MSW, Boston U., 1967. Pvt. practice N.Y.C., 1969—; founder, dir. Single Mothers by Choice, N.Y.C., 1981—. Author: Single Mothers By Choice, 1994. Fellow N.Y. State Soc. Clin. Social Workers; mem. NASW (cert.), Am. Bd. Cert. Social Workers.

MATTESON, CLARICE CHRIS, artist, educator; b. Winnipeg, Man., Can., Sept. 2, 1918; came to U.S., 1922; d. Sergis and Nina (Balter) Alberts; m. D.C. Matteson, 1956 (dec. 1976); children: Kemmer, Gretchen. BA, Met. State U., 1976; MA in Liberal Studies, Hamline U., 1986; postgrad., LaSalle U. Mem. Orson Welles staff Hollywood, Calif., 1945-46; owner Hilde-Gardes Co., L.A., 1947-56; instr. art North Hennepin C.C., Brooklyn Park, Minn., 1975-81; prodr., host Accent on Art TV Program, St. Paul, 1979—; instr. art Lakewood C.C., U. Minn., Normandale C.C., Bloomington (Minn.) Sch. Dist., Mpls. Sch. Dist., St. Paul Sch. Dist., 1981—. Exhibited works at Mpls. Inst. Art, 1994, Gov.'s 1006 Com., 1994; represented in permanent collections Peterson Gallery, Mpls., Premier Gallery, Mpls.,; corr. Schaumburg (Ill.) Newspapers, 1962; patentee plastic products. Active Minn. Orch. (WAMSO), Mpls., 1972—, vol. Recipient award for creative leadership Minn. Assn. for Continuing Adult Edn., 1977, Gold Cup award Bloomington Cable, 1989; Park Cable TV grantee, 1982, Minn. Humanities Commn. grantee, 1985. Mem. ASCAP, AAUW (dir. arts com. 1989-90, bd. dirs. 1990-92), Am. Pen Women (v.p. 1994), Minn. Artists Assn., Minn. Composers Forum, Cable Access St. Paul, Minn. Territorial Pioneers (prodr.- host TV series "Kids Art" Channel 6 Mpls.-St. Paul 1995, mem. Gov.'s 1006 Com.). Home and Office: 2119 Sargent Ave Saint Paul MN 55105

MATTHAEUS, RENATE G., high school principal; b. Dresden, Saxony, Germany, Aug. 18, 1942; d. Gerhard R. and Gerda (Kemter) M. BA, DePaul U., 1964; MS, No. Ill. U., 1974, CAS, 1977; doctoral studies, Loyola U., 1991. Cert. adminstr., supt. Statistician Jewel Cos., Melrose Pk., Ill., 1964-66; tchr. German Larsen & Ellis Jr. & Elgin (Ills.) Sr. High Sch., 1966-74; asst. prin. Abbott Jr. High Sch., Elgin, 1974-82; prin. Canton Mid. Sch., Elgin, 1982-88, Larkin High Sch., Elgin, 1988—. Team mem. Jayne Shover Easter Seal Ctr. Telethon, Elgin, 1991, team capt. Telethon, 1992-95; team leader Elgin Symphony Sustaining Fund Drive, Elgin, 1991. Recipient Women of Achievement award Women in Mgmt., 1988, YWCA Harriett Gifford award in Edn., 1993. Mem. Ill. Prins. Assn. (Region VIII legis. chair 1991—, program chair 1989-91, mem. chair 1986-89), Assn. Elgin Sch. Adminstrs. (sec., v.p., pres. 1975-77), Rotary Club (bd. dirs. Elgin chpt. 1991—, community svc. chair 1991-92, new project com. chair 1990-91, vocat. svc. chair 1992-93, sec. 1993-94, pres.-elect 1994, pres. 1995—). Lutheran. Office: Larkin High Sch 1475 Larkin Ave Elgin IL 60123-5198

MATTHEIS, DOLORES IRENE, librarian, educator; b. Graceton, Minn., Nov. 10, 1929; m. Robert E. Mattheis, May 7, 1950 (dec. June 1989); 1 child, Patricia Ann Haviland. Student, Valley City State Coll., 1958, Mary Coll., 1970, Ellendale State U., 1964, Washburn U., 1969. Tchr. German Dist., Streeter, N.D., 1948-50, Germania Dist., Streeter, 1950-51, Broadview Dist., Karnak, N.D., 1954-58, Burnstad (N.D.) Dist., 1958-64; tchr., libr. Linton (N.D.) Dist., 1964-70, St. Regis (Mont.) Sch. Dist., 1970—; bookkeeper Farmer's Elevator, Hazelton, N.D., 1965-69, N.W. Lumber/Cedar, St. Regis, 1978-80; owner St. Regis Motel, 1971-80. Mem. Mont. Libr. Assn., Delta Kappa Gamma (sec.). Republican. Lutheran. Home: 24 Four Mile Rd Saint Regis MT 59866-9722 Office: St Regis Sch Saint Regis MT 59866

MATTHEW, LYN, art marketing consultant, educator; b. Long Beach, Calif., Dec. 15, 1936; d. Harold G. and Beatrice (Hunt) M.; m. Wayne Thomas Castleberry, Aug. 12, 1961 (div. Jan. 1976); children: Melanie, Cheryl, Nicole, Matthew. BS, U. Calif.-Davis, 1958; MA, Ariz. State U., 1979. Cert. hotel sales exec., 1988, meeting profl. Pres., Davlyn Cons. Found., Scottsdale, Ariz., 1979-82; cons., vis. prof. The Art Bus., Scottsdale, 1982—; pres., dir. sales and mktg. Embassy Stes., Scottsdale, 1987—, bd. trustees Hotel Sales and Mktg. Assn. Internat. Found., 1988—, chmn., 1991-93, mem. exec. com., 1993—; vis. prof. Maricopa C.C., Phoenix, 1979—, Ariz. State U., Tempe, 1980-83; cons. Women's Caucus for Art, Phoenix, 1983-88. Bd. dirs. Rossom House and Heritage Square Found., Phoenix, 1987-88. Author: The Business Aspects of Art, Book I, 1979, Book II, 1979; Marketing Strategies for the Creative Artist, 1985. Mem. Women Image Now (Achievement and Contbn. in Visual Arts award 1983), Women in Higher Edn., Nat. Women's Caucus for Art (v.p. 1981-83), Ariz. Women's Caucus for Art (pres. 1980-82, hon. advisor 1986-87), Ariz. Vocat. Edn. Assn. (sec. 1978-80), Ariz. Visionary Artists (treas. 1987-89), Hotel Sales and Mktg. Assn. Internat. (pres. Great Phoenix chpt. 1988-89, regional dir. 1989-90, bd. dirs. 1985-90), Meeting Planners Internat. (v.p. Ariz. Sunbelt chpt. 1989-91, pres. 1991-92, Supplier of Yr. award 1988), Soc. Govt. Meeting Planners (charter bd. dirs. 1987, Sam Gilmer award 1992, nat. conf. co-chmn. 1993-94), Ariz. Visionary Artists (treas. 1987-88), Ariz. Acad. Performing Arts (v.p. bd. dirs. 1987-88, pres. 1988-89).

MATTHEWS, BETTY PARKER, special education educator; b. Port Arthur, Tex., Dec. 9, 1929; d. Clarence G. and Florence (Sudduth) Parker; m. Paul A. Matthews, Mar. 25, 1955; children: Michael A., Scott P., Lisa M. Alexander. BS, La. Coll., 1975; MEd, Northwestern U., 1981. Specialist in edn. La., 1984; cert. elem. tchr., mentally retarded, learning disabled, ednl. cons., generic mild/moderate, assessment tchr., ednl. diagnostician, La. 3d grade tchr. Rapides Parish Sch. Bd., Alexandria, La., 1975-76, tchr. spl. edn., 1976-81, assessment tchr., ednl. diagnostician, 1981—; ednl. diagnostician, 1993—; ednl. cons. Briarwood Psychiatric Hosp., Alexandria, La., 1986-93, Crossroads Psychiat. Hosp., Alexandria, 1993—; adj. prof. La. State U., Alexandria, 1990—. Dir. children's Bible study 1st Bapt. Ch., Pineville, La., 1985—. Mem. La. Edn. Assessment Tchrs. Assn. (regional rep. 1987-88, exec. coun. 1987-94, treas. 1988-90, Pres.'s Svc. award 1990-91, La. Assessment Tchr. of Yr. 1993), Coun. Exceptional Children, Reading Coun., Alpha Delta Kappa, Phi Delta Kappa, Epsilon Sigma Alpha (state pres., regional sec.). Home: 3050 Rigolette Rd Pineville LA 71360

MATTHEWS, CARI PINEIRO, lawyer, author; b. Nov. 16, 1942; d. Calixto R. and Dionisia G. Pineiro; m. Frederic Lawrence Matthews III, Mar. 20, 1964 (dec. Apr. 1981); children: Barbara C., Christopher James. BA, Hunter Coll., 1964; JD, U. Miami, 1975. Bar: Fla. 1975. Assoc. Cramer & Matthews, Miami, 1975-77; asst. U.S. atty. U.S. Justice Dept., So. Dist. Fla., 1977-79; mem. Civil Rights Reviewing Authority, U.S. Dept. Edn., Washington, 1983-84; assoc. dep. atty. gen. U.S. Justice Dept., Washington, 1984-86; asst. gen. counsel fed. litigation U.S. Def. Dept. Navy, Washington, 1986-88; gen. counsel, v.p. ICN Pharms., Costa Mesa, Calif., 1988-89. Author: Federal Civil Trialbook, 1991; co-author: West's Federal Practice Manual, rev. 2d edit., vol. 8, 1993. Mem. women's com. Nat. Symphony Orch., Washington, 1985—. Mem. Fed. Bar Assn. (mem. continuing legal edn. bd. 1994, Outstanding Legal Edn. Programs award 1987), Fla. Bar Assn.

MATTHEWS, CATHERINE LEE, psychologist; b. Tulsa, Okla., Mar. 5, 1954; d. John B. and Lois Carol (Neilson) Henson; m. James Marc Matthews, Dec. 28, 1985. BA, North Tex. State, 1976, MA, 1983, PhD in Psychology, 1986. Lic. psychologist, Tex. Pvt. practice Psychol. Svcs., Lubbock, Tex., 1988—; adj. prof. Tex. Tech. Univ., Lubbock. Mem. Am. Psychol. Assn., Tex. Psychol. Assn. (chair children's div.). Office: # 15 Briercroft Lubbock TX 79412

MATTHEWS, CHARYLENE ANN, executive secretary; b. Trenton, N.J., May 14, 1955; d. Frank Wilson and Grace Elizabeth (Fink) M. Diploma, Allentown (N.J.) H.S., 1973. Sec. Trenton (N.J.) State Coll., 1973-74; CRT operator McGraw-Hill Pub. Co., Hightstown, N.J., 1974; sr. clk. typist Trenton Psychiat. Hosp., 1975-77; sr. sec. Congoleum Corp., Trenton, 1977-88; sec., typesetter Area Auto Racing News, Trenton, 1988—. Sec. CARS for Matheny Sch. & Hosp., 1991—, also bd. dirs. Named Reporter of Yr., Flemington Speedway, 1985. Mem. Ea. Motorsport Press Assn. (bd. dirs. 1993—, 1st place in weekly news 1990, Writer of Yr. 1991, Bill Simmons Meml. award for outstanding efforts during year 1991). Republican. Office: Area Auto Racing News 2829 S Broad St Trenton NJ 08610

MATTHEWS, DIANNE FERNE, mathematics educator; b. New Hyde Park, N.Y., Nov. 30, 1966; d. Robert and Gloria (Hall) M.; m. Michael Leibowitz, Feb. 14, 1992. BS, SUNY, Stonybrook, 1987, MA in Math., 1989. Cert. tchr. math. Tchr. math., sci. Three Village Sch. Dist., Setauket, N.Y., 1989-91, advisor, coord. cheerleading and pep squad, 1989-92; coord., tchr. remedial math. Mid. County Sch. Dist., Centereach, N.Y., 1992—, advisor, coord. cheerleading and pep squad, 1992—; adj. instr. coll. math. Suffolk C.C., Selden, N.Y., 1991—; judge L.I. Math. Fair., Selden, 1989—. Home: 59 Celeste Ave Holbrook NY 11741

MATTHEWS, EILEEN MARIE, critical care nurse; b. Phila., Mar. 25, 1953; d. Thomas Joseph and Evelyn E. (Besch) M.; children: Anthony, Tanya. ADN, Bucks County Community Coll., Newtown, Pa., 1981; student, U. Del. RNN, Pa.; CCRN, ACLS, BLS. Staff nurse med./surg. Pa. Hosp., Phila., 1981-83; staff nurse ICU Lower Bucks Hosp., Phila., 1983, Thomas Jefferson U. Hosp., Phila., 1983-88; agy. nurse PRN Nursing Agy., Langhorne, Pa., 1981-90; Protemps ICU agy. nurse Presbyn. Hosp., Phila., 1988-89; staff nurse ICU Fox Chase Cancer, Am. Oncologic Hosp., Phila., 1989—. Me. com. YMCA, Fairless Hills, Pa., 1992-93. Mem. AACN, Southeastern Pa. Nurses Assn., Golden Key Soc. Office: Am Oncologic Hosp 7701 Burholme Ave Philadelphia PA 19111

MATTHEWS, ELIZABETH WOODFIN, law librarian, law educator; b. Ashland, Va., July 30, 1927; d. Edwin Clifton and Elizabeth Frances (Luck) Woodfin; m. Sidney E. Matthews, Dec. 20, 1947; 1 child, Sarah Elizabeth Matthews Wiley. BA, Randolph-Macon Coll., 1948, LLD (hon.), 1989; MS in Libr. Sci., U. Ill., 1952; PhD, So. Ill. U., 1972; LLD, Randolph-Macon Coll., 1989. Cert. law libr., med. libr., med. libr. III. Libr. Ohio State U., Columbus, 1952-59; libr., instr. U. Ill., Urbana, 1962-63, lectr. Grad. Sch. Libr. Sci., 1964; libr., instr. Morris Libr. So. Ill. U., Carbondale, 1964-67, classroom instr. Coll. Edn., 1967-70, med. libr., asst. prof. Morris Libr., 1972-74, law libr., asst. prof., 1974-79, law libr., assoc. prof., 1979-85, law libr., prof., 1985-93; prof. emeritus, 1993—. Author: Access Points to Law Libraries, 1984, 17th Century English Law Reports, 1986, Law Library Reference Shelf, 1988, 2d edit., 1992, Pages and Missing Pages, 1983, 2d edit., 1989, Lincoln as a Lawyer: An Annotated Bibliography, 1991. Mem. AAUW (pres. 1976-78, corp. rep. 1978-88), Am. Assn. Law Librs., Mid Am. Assn. Law Librs., Beta Phi Mu, Phi Kappa Phi. Methodist. Home: 811 S Skyline Dr Carbondale IL 62901-2405 Office: So Ill U Law Libr Carbondale IL 62901

MATTHEWS, ESTHER ELIZABETH, education educator, consultant; b. Princeton, Mass., June 20, 1918; d. Ralph Edgar and Julia Ellen (Cronin) M. BS in Edn., Worcester State Coll., 1940; EdM, Harvard U., 1943, EdD, 1960. Tchr. various Mass. schs., 1942-47; guidance dir. Holden (Mass.) Pub. Schs., 1947-53, Wareham (Mass.) Pub. Schs., 1954-57; counselor Newton (Mass.) High Sch., 1957-60, head counselor, 1960-66; assoc. prof. edn. U. Oreg., 1966-70, prof. edn., 1970-80, prof. emerita, 1980—; vis. prof. U. Toronto, Ont., Can., summer 1971; lectr. on edn. Harvard U., 1963-66; cons. in field; lectr. various colls. and univs. Author book chpts.; contbr. numerous articles to profl. jours. and papers to conf. proc. Mem. ACD (Recognition for Contbn. to Promote Human Rights 1987), World Future Soc., Nat. Vocat. Guidance Assn. (pres. 1974-75, chair nat. com. 1966-67, sec. 1967-68, bd. trustees 1968-71, editl. bd. Vocat. Guidance Quar. 1966-68), Oreg. Pers. and Guidance Assn. (Leona Tyler award 1973, Disting. Svc. award 1979), Oreg. Career Devel. Assn. (Disting. Svc. award 1987, Esther E. Matthews Ann. award for outstanding contbn. to career devel. in Oreg. established in her honor 1993). Home: 832 Lariat Dr Eugene OR 97401-6438

MATTHEWS, GAIL THUNBERG, marketing executive; b. Hartford, Conn., July 29, 1938; d. Harold Einar and Mildred (Wentland) Thunberg; m. Glenn Holbrook Matthews, Aug. 9, 1959; children: Scott Holbrook, Brett Holbrook. Student Boston U., 1958-59. Hostess show, copywriter Sta. WJDA, Boston, 1956-58; fashion coord. Jordan Marsh, Boston, 1958-59, Miller & Rhoades, Richmond, Va., 1959-60, Sage Allen, Hartford, 1960-61; columnist Boston Globe, 1962-63, Hartford Times, 1961-63; freelance writer, contbr. articles to New Englander mag., Christian Sci. Monitor, Yankee, 1961-65; v.p., treas. Coll. Mktg. Group, Inc., Winchester, Mass., 1968-86; corporator Reading Savs. Bank; mem. adv. coun. Baybank Middlesex; writer, co-host TV show Kearsarge Valley Magazine; coord. Harrods London, New London, 1992, Brit. Isles Festival for Scotland-England, Wales, No. Ireland by Brit. Dept. Trade & Industry for New London, 1994—. Chmn. Love Lights a Tree, Am. Cancer Soc., New London, 1988. Author: Hors'd'oeuvre Cooking, 1966, Gourmet Cooking, 1966, Birthday Fortune Book, 1967, (children's series) The Adventures of a Shih Tzu, The Good Luck Puppy, 1980; co-host TV show Kearsarge Valley Magazine. Choral dir. Barrows Sch., Reading; pres. local PTA; chmn. Heart Fund Reading; founder, chmn. Reading chpt. Am. Cancer Soc., Love Lights A Tree chpt. New London Am. Cancer Soc., named Citizen of Yr., 1983-84; pres. Kimpton Brook Gardens Restorations; coord. London, Eng.-New London N.H. Twinning, 1992; coord. anniversary oldest theatre N.H., 1993. Recipient Svc. to Youth award Reader's Digest, 1962; CAP award 1965; Spl. award Am. Cancer Soc., 1981-82; Citizenship award Reading Tchrs. Assn., 1980. Mem. Antiquarian Soc., Dartmouth Coll. Women's (bd. dirs., founder mammography fund for women in need).

MATTHEWS, JANA B., foundation administrator; b. Chgo., Oct. 23, 1940; d. L. Emmet and Helen J. (Severson) Beauchamp; m. Samuel R. Matthews, June 1, 1963 (div. 1971); 1 child, Carolyn E.; m. Charles C. Halbower, May 13, 1975. BA, Earlham Coll., 1962; MA, U. R.I., 1970; EdD, Harvard U., 1979. Tchr. Portsmouth (N.H.) and Coventry (R.I.) Pub. Schs., 1963-68; asst. provost Mass. State Coll. System, Boston, 1970-73; sr. staff Arthur D. Little, Inc., Cambridge, Mass., 1973-76; div. dir. NCHEMS, Boulder, Colo., 1980-83; pres. NCHEMS Mgmt. Svcs., Inc., Boulder, Colo., 1983-85; pres. M & H Group Inc., Boulder, 1985-92, chmn. bd. dirs., 1993—; sr. fellow, program dir. ctr. entrepreneurial leadership Kauffman Found., Kansas City, Mo., 1993—. Co-author: Managing the Partnership between Higher Education and Industry, 1984, Winning Combinations: The Coming Wave of Entrepreneurial Partnerships between Large and Small Companies, 1992; author: Effective Use of Management Consultants in Higher Education, 1983; also articles. Apptd. commr. Colo. Adv. Tech. Inst., 1988-90. Mem. Assn. Univ. Related Rsch. Parks (dir. 1987-91), Soc. Coll. & Univ. Planning (v.p. 1973-75), Assn. Instl. Researchers, Harvard Club. Home: 6520 Indian Ln Shawnee Mission KS 66208-1744 Office: Kauffman Found Ctr Entrepreneurial Leadership 4900 Oak St Kansas City MO 64112-2753

MATTHEWS, MARGARET ELLEN, physician; b. Quincy, Mass., Sept. 30, 1951; d. C. Dixon and Marion Louise (Strader) M.; children: Cora Lee, Tessa Ellice, Alicia Gale. BSN, Boston U., 1975, MSN, 1979; MD, Med. Coll. Pa., Phila., 1984. Diplomate Am. Bd. Family Practice. Staff nurse various hosps., Boston, 1975-80; Phila., 1980-84; staff nurse Med. Coll. Pa. Hosp., Phila., 1982-83; resident physician Cen. Maine Med. Ctr., Lewiston, 1984-87; physician The Health Ctr., Auburn, Maine, 1987—. Office: The Health Center 59 East Ave Lewiston ME 04240-5622

MATTHEWS, PATRICIA ANNE, writer; b. San Fernando, Calif., July 1, 1927; d. Roy Oliver and Gladys (Gable) Ernst; m. Marvin Owen Brisco, Dec. 3, 1946 (div. 1961); children: Michael A. Brisco, David R. Brisco; m. Clayton Hartley Matthews, Nov. 3, 1971. Student, Pasadena Jr. Coll., 1943-44, Calif. State U., L.A., 1960. With Calif. State U., 1959-77. Author: Love's Avenging Heart, 1977, Love's Wildest Promise, 1977, Love, Forever More, 1977, Love's Daring Dream, 1978, Love's Pagan Heart, 1978, Love's Magic Moment, 1979, Love's Golden Destiny, 1979, Love's Raging Tide, 1980, Love's Sweet Agony, 1980, Love's Bold Journey, 1980, Tides of Love, 1981, Embers of Dawn, 1982, Flames of Glory, 1983 (Bronze medal West Coast Rev. Books 1983), Dancer of Dreams, 1984, Gambler in Love, 1985, Tame The Restless Heart, 1986, Destruction at Dawn, 1986, Twister, 1986, Enchanted, 1987 (Best Hist. Gothic award Romantic Times 1986-87), Thursday and The Lady, 1987, Mirrors, 1988, Oasis, 1988, The Night Visitor, 1988, The Dreaming Tree, 1989, Sapphire, 1989, The Death of Love, 1990, The Unquiet, 1991, (poetry) Love's Many Faces, 1979, (with Clayton Matthews) Midnight Whispers, 1981, Empire, 1982 (Silver medal West Coast Rev. Books 1983), Midnight Lavender, 1985, The Scent of Fear, 1992, Vision of Death, 1993, Taste of Evil, 1993, The Sound of Murder, 1994, The Touch of Terror, 1995, (play) Honky Tonk, 1993, (under pseudonym Patty Brisco) Merry's Treasure, 1969, Horror at Gull House, 1973, House of Candles, 1973, The Crystal Window, 1973, The Carnival Mystery, 1974, Mist of Evil, 1976, The Campus Mystery, 1977, Raging Rapids, 1978, Too Much in Love, 1979, (under pseudonym P.A. Brisco) The Other People, 1970, (under pseudonym Laura Wylie) The Night Visitor, 1979 (Silver medal West Coast Rev. Books 1979); contbg. author: Your First Romance, My First Romance, Love's Leading Ladies, Writing the Romance, Writer's Digest, Candlelight, Romance and You, various anthologies; author numerous short stories; contbr. poetry to profl. jours. Recipient (with Clayton Matthews) Team Writing award Romantic Times, 1983. Mem. Mystery Writers Am., Romance Writers Am., Sisters in Crime, Novelists Ink.

MATTHEWS, ROSALIND M., systems manager; b. Reading, Pa., Mar. 6, 1943; d. William Wilson and Jessye Long; m. Jackie L. Matthews, Aug. 9, 1965 (div. 1977); children: Kym, Derek, Darryl. BS, Kutztown U., 1966; MS, Pratt Inst., 1970. Asst. v.p. ABN/AMRO Svcs. Corp., Uniondale, N.Y., 1974—; systems analyst Savs. Banks Trust, N.Y.C., 1970-74, Anchor Savs. Bank, Bay Ridge, N.Y., 1969-70; systems engr. IBM, N.Y.C., 1966-69; programmer Berks County Trust, Reading, Pa., 1963-66; adj. prof. LaGuardia C.C., L.I. City, N.Y., 1983—, Adelphie U., Garden City, N.Y., 1990—. Mentor N.Y. State Mentoring Program, Uniondale, N.Y., 1993. Named Balck Achiever in Industry, Harlem YMCA, N.Y.C., 1983. Mem. Delta Sigma Theta. Democrat. Methodist. Office: EAB Plaza Uniondale NY 11555

MATTHEWS, ROWENA GREEN, biological chemistry educator; b. Cambridge, Eng., Aug. 20, 1938 (father Am. citizen); d. David E. and Doris (Cribb) Green; m. Larry Stanford Matthews, June 18, 1960; children: Brian Stanford, Keith David. BA, Harvard U., 1960; PhD, U. Mich., 1969. Instr. U. S.C., Columbia, 1964-65; postdoctoral fellow U. Mich., Ann Arbor, 1970-75, asst. prof., 1975-81, assoc. prof. biol. chemistry, 1981-86, prof. 1986—, assoc. chmn., 1988-92; mem. phys. biochemistry study sect. NIH, 1982-86; mem. adv. coun. Nat. Inst. Gen. Med. Scis., NIH, 1991-94; adv. bd. NATO, 1994—. mem. editorial adv. bd. Biochem. Jour., 1984-92, Biochemistry, 1993—, Jour. Bacteriology, 1993—. Contbr. articles to profl. jours. Recipient Faculty Recognition award U. Mich., 1984, Merit award Nat. Inst. Gen. Med. Scis., 1991; NIH grantee, 1978—; NSF grantee, 1992—. Mem. AAAS, Am. Soc. Biochemical & Molecular Biol. (program chair 1995), Am. Chem. Soc. (program chmn. biochemistry div. 1985, sec. biochemistry div. 1990-92, chair elect 1992-94, chair 1994—), Phi Beta Kappa, Sigma Xi. Avocations: bicycling, snorkeling, cross country skiing, cooking. Home: 1609 S University Ave Ann Arbor MI 48104-2620 Office: U Mich Biophysics Rsch Divsn 1055 Chem Bldg 930 N University Ann Arbor MI 48109-1055

MATTHEWS, SHARRON DEBRA, social welfare administrator; b. Chgo., Oct. 5, 1950; d. John Hunter M. and Princella Marie (Hudson) Gilliam. BA, Nat. Louis U., 1981; MPA, Harvard U., 1993. Community organizer Black Strategy Ctr., Chgo., 1968-70; programs field coord. Vol. Action Ctr., United Way, Chgo., 1970-72; dir. Met. Planning Coun., Tenant Edn. Project, Chgo., 1972-73; cons., trainer U.S. Census Bur., Chgo., 1974-76; regional sr. mgt. action trainer Fed. Agy. Vols., Ill., Ind., Mich., Minn., Ohio and Wis., 1976-81; program coord. Lawndale Peoples Planning and Action Com., Chgo., 1982-83; cons., trainer State Bd. Edn., Chgo., 1983-84; dir., advocacy dept. Chgo. Urban League, 1984-89; bur. chief Minority and Female Bus. Enterprise, Dept. Mgmt. Svcs., Chgo., 1989-94; exec. dir. Pub. Welfare Coalition of Ill., Chgo., 1994—; instr., Roosevelt Coll., Chgo., 1988-90. Author: Love Poems, 1986. Founder, mem. Lit. Exch., Chgo., 1e985—; mem. Chgo. Urban League, 1984—, People United to Save Humanity, Chgo., 1989—; mem. adv. bd. Chgo. Found. Women, 1989—; v.p. Kennedy Sch. Harvard Alumni Midwest Assn., 1994—. Mem. Nat. Assn. Women Execs. Home: 4800 S Chgo Beach Dr Ste 1810 N Chicago IL 60615

MATTHEWS, SUSAN DIANE, student housing assistant director; b. Palo Alto, Calif., Aug. 18, 1964; d. Garry C. and Betty J. (Nelson) M. BSBA, San Diego State U., 1989; MA in Social Sci., Azusa (Calif.) Pacific U., 1991. Resident adv. San Diego State U., 1986-87, hall adv., 1987-89; adminstrv. asst. Azusa Pacific U., 1989-90, academic counselor, 1990-91; resident dir. U. Calif., Santa Barbara, 1991-92; asst. dir. student housing Calif. State U., Dominguis Hills, 1992—. Recipient Nat. Residence Hall Honorary award Nat. Assn. Coll. and U. Residence Halls., 1986, named Resident Adv. of Month pacific affiliate, 1987. Mem. Am. Coll. Pers. Assn. (recipient Roberta Christie Essay award Atlanta, 1991), Nat. Assn. Student Pers. Adminstrs. (continuing edn. com. mem. 1991, 92), Nat. Assn. Women in Higher Edn., Calif. Assn. Coll. and U. Residence Halls (So. Rap presenter 1990, 92, chairperson So. Rap programming com. 1990, So. Rap com. mem. 1989-90). Home & Office: PO Box 6228 Carson CA 90749

MATTHEWS, VALERIE JO, development company executive; b. Omaha, June 6, 1947; d. Blaine Leroy and Betty Rae (Peterson) Rish; m. L. D. Matthews (div. 1975); children: Amy Lynne, Timothy Bryan. Grad. high sch., Omaha, 1965. Acct. various firms, Fremont, Nebr., 1967-78; sales assoc. Sunrise Home, Lincoln, Nebr., 1979-81, Lamb Realty, Thousand Oaks, Calif., 1981-82; rep. and mgr. sales Centex Homes, Oklahoma City, 1982-85; div. pres. Oklahoma City and Denver, 1985-87; with Lamb Realty, Thousand Oaks, Calif., 1988; dir. constrn. and land C.R. Wood Devel. Inc., Thousand Oaks, 1987-91; pres. C.R. Wood Devel., Inc., Thousand Oaks, 1991-92, Rish Homes, Inc., Meridian, Idaho, 1992—; pvt. practice tax and fin. cons. Vol. YMCA, Fremont, 1972, Vols. in Arts, Oklahoma City, 1985, Make-A-Wish-Found.; active Boys Scouts Am., F.O.P. Mem. Calif. Assn. Realtors, Nat. Assn. Home Builders, Bldg. Industry Assn.

MATTIE, JEANNE M., public relations and communications consultant; b. Sendai, Japan, Aug. 4, 1950; d. John D. and Edna H. M.; m. Donald J. Patrican, June 14, 1986; 1 child, Julian M. Patrican. BA, U. Del., 1970. Co-founder Cyrk, Inc., Gloucester, Mass., 1975-80; pres. Mattie Assocs., Inc., Boston and Rockport, Mass., 1980—. Office: Mattie Assocs Inc 178 South St Rockport MA 01966

MATTINGLY, MARY CONSTANCE, accountant; b. Chgo., Feb. 4, 1957; d. Hilary Bell and Mona Jane (Shuttleworth) M. BS in Acctg., U. Conn., 1979. CPA, Conn.; CMA. Auditor Price Waterhouse & Co., Stamford, Conn., 1979-82, sr. auditor, 1982; acctg. mgr. Combe, Inc., White Plains, N.Y., 1982-83, asst. controller mfg., 1983-85, controller mfg., 1985-90; fin. mgr. The Reader's Digest Assn., Inc., Pleasantville, N.Y., 1990-91, mgr. global fin. systems, 1991—. Treas. Chappaqua (N.Y.) Drama Group, 1991-93. Mem. Conn. State Soc. CPAs, Inst. Mgmt. Accts. Office: The Reader's Digest Assn Reader's Digest Rd Pleasantville NY 10570

MATTINGLY, THERESE SHANDLE, psychotherapist; b. Painesville, Ohio, Aug. 11, 1959; d. Philip George Shandle and Barbara Ann (Brown) Stiles; m. William David Riemer, Oct. 15, 1983 (div. Mar. 1987); 1 child, Daniel James; m. Kelly James Mattingly, Sept. 3, 1988; 1 child, Caitlin Mae. BA with honors, U. Wis., Whitewater, 1981, M in Guidance and Counseling with honors, 1988. Lic. marriage and family therapist, lic. profl. counselor, lic. ind. clin. social worker, Wis. Ednl. coord. Harmony Group Home/Pathways Group Home, Janesville, Wis., 1981-82, Beginnings Group Home, Janesville, Wis., 1983-85; juvenile probation agt. Rock County Juvenile Probation, Janesville, Wis., 1985-88; family therapist Rock County Adolescent Day Svcs., Janesville, Wis., 1988-91; psychotherapist Crossroads Counseling Ctr., Inc., Janesville, Wis., 1991—. Mem. YWCA, 1990, Wis. Now, 1992, YMCA, 1982—. Mem. NOW, Am. Mental Health Counselors Assn., Wis. Mental Health Counselors Assn., Janesville Women's Mcpl. Golf Assn. (sec. 1993—), Am. Assn. for Marriage and Family Therapists, Alpha Delta Mu. Democrat. Office: Crossroads Counseling Ctr 301 E Milwaukee St Janesville WI 53545

MATTISON, ELISA SHERI, organizational psychologist; b. Grand Rapids, Mich., Apr. 24, 1952; d. Andrew and Loraine R. Wierenga. BS cum laude, Western Mich. U., 1974, MA, 1979; postgrad., Fielding Inst., 1990. Trainer No. Inst., Anchorage, 1980; mgmt. cons., trainer Alaska Assocs. Human Devel. Inc., Anchorage, 1980-82; job devel. specialist Collins, Weed and Assocs., Anchorage, 1982-83; owner, pres. Mattison Assocs. Inc., Anchorage, 1993—; mem. adj. faculty Anchorage Community Coll., 1981-82; work environment and design coord. ARCO Alaska Inc., 1983-86; cons. Employee Assts. Cons. Alaska, Anchorage, 1982; v.p. Human Resource Mgmt. and Mktg. Alaskan Fed. Credit Union, 1986-90; asst. dir. degree completeion program, adult and continuing edn., Alaska Pacific U., 1990-92, adj. faculty, 1990—. Mem. Am. Soc. Tng. and Devel., Soc. Human Resource Mgmt. Contbr. articles to profl. publs. Office: 3910 Iona Circle Anchorage AK 99507-3340

MATTMILLER, CHARLOTTE FREDA, librarian; b. DeWitt, Ark., 1949; d. Charles Frederick and Mattie Louise (Black) M. BA, Centenary Coll., 1977; MLS, La. State U., 1984, MA, 1987. Clk. Wolfensen Electric, Inc., Houston, 1978-80; restaurant mgr. Snow Enterprises, Ltd., Newman, Ga., 1980-81; from clerk to libr. La. State U., Baton Rouge, 1982-87; libr. Capital City Press, Baton Rouge, 1987-89, computer operator, 1989—. Editor (news bulletin) Conf. Update, 1984-88; (jour.) Instructional Resources, 1987-92; contbr. articles to profl. jours. Pres. Friends of Pub. Edn., Baton Rouge, 1986—, Family Life Edn. Coalition, E. Baton Rouge Parish, 1989-90; mem. AIDS coalition Capital Area United Way, Baton Rouge, 1991—, Coalition for Maternal and Infant Health, 1990—. Invitee Girl's State of Ark., 1966; recipient Citizenship award Am. Legion Aux., Gillett, Ark., 1967, Betty Crocker award, 1967; Golden Apple, Vols. in Pub. Schs., East Baton Rouge Parish, 1990. Mem. AAUW (chmn. pub. policy La., v.p. membership com. Baton Rouge, treas., chmn. campus study group), La. Assn. for Ednl. Tech. (pres. 1991-92), Patrons of Pub. Libr. (bd. dirs. 1990—), La. Libr. Assn. (bull. bus. editor 1988—). Home: PO Box 21801 Baton Rouge LA 70802

MATTOCKS-WHISMAN, FRANCES, nursing administrator, educator; b. Cedar Vale, Kans., Dec. 20, 1945; d. Thomas Emerson and Lavonna Laura (Myers) McKinney; m. Jim L. Whisman, Nov. 6, 1981; stepchildren: Toni Zweigart, Gay Asbell, Jenny Watts, Beth Whisman. Diploma, William Newton Sch. Nursing, Winfield, Kans., 1966; student, Tulsa Jr. Coll., Cen. State U., Edmond, Okla., Graceland Coll., Lamoni, Iowa, 1989—. RN; cert. operating room nurse. Operating room nurse Hillcrest Med. Ctr., Tulsa, 1968-72, 74-76; office mgr. Myra A. Peters, M.D., 1972-76; pvt. duty nurse Homemakers Upjohn, Inc., Tulsa, 1976-77; staff nurse, head nurse, insvc. instr. Doctors Med. Ctr., Inc., Tulsa; co-dir. Sch. Surg. Tech. Tulsa County Area Vo-Tech. Sch., 1981-89; asst. dir. transplantation/retrievals Tulsa chpt. ARC, 1989; staff nurse, infection control coord. Wetumka (Okla.) Gen. Hosp., 1989-91; dir. nurses Bristow (Okla.) Meml. Hosp., 1991-93, Doctors Homecare, Sapulpa, Okla., 1993—; br. supr. Sapulpa br. Doctors Homecare, 1994—; instr. Wes Watkins Area Vo-Tech. Sch., Wetumka, 1989-90; cons. ARC, Tulsa chpt. Transplantation, 1990. Contbr. articles to profl. jours. Active ARC. Mem. NEA, Nat. Assn. Orthopedic Nurses, Nat. League for Nursing, Am. Vocat. Assn., Okla. Vocat. Assn., Okla. Edn. Assn., Concerned Oklahomans for Nurse Edn., Assn. Operating Rm. Nurses, Infections Control. Nurses. Home: RR 1 Box 154 Okemah OK 74859-9801 Office: Doctors Homecare 1030 E Taft Ste 123 Sapulpa OK 74066

MATTSON, CAROL LINNETTE, social services administrator; b. Frederic, Wis., Oct. 3, 1946; d. Clarence Waldemar and Lucille Anna Mathilda (Bengtson) Hedlund; m. Wesley Harlan Mattson, June 24, 1967; 1 child, Aaron Ray. BS, U. Wis., Menomonie, 1968. Home econs. tchr. Luck (Wis.) High Sch., 1968-72; clk. Daniels Twp., Siren, Wis., 1973-75; family living instr. Wis. Indianhead Tech. Inst., New Richmond, 1974-77; aging program dir. Polk County, Balsam Lake, Wis., 1977—; sec., bd. dirs. Polk County Transp. for the Disabled and Elderly, Inc., Balsam Lake, 1978—; sec., mem. com. Long Term Support Com., Balsam Lake, 1985-90. Mem. Wis. Assn. Nutrition Dirs., Wis. Assn. Aging Unit Dirs. Lutheran. Office: Polk County Aging Programs PO Box 605 Bldg Balsam Lake WI 54810-0605

MATTSON, JOY LOUISE, oncological nurse; b. Moline, Ill., Feb. 1, 1956; d. Norman O. and Jeannette (Squier) M.; m. Duncan F. Crannell, Sept. 9, 1988. BA magna cum laude, Bates Coll., 1977; MTS, Harvard U., 1982; BSN magna cum laude, Rutgers U., Newark, 1988; MLS, Rutgers U., 1993. RN, N.J. Staff nurse oncology Muhlenberg Reg. Med. Ctr., Plainfield, N.J., 1987-88; staff nurse St. Lawrence Rehab. Ctr., Lawrenceville, N.J., 1988-89; clin. rsch. asst. G.H. Besselaar Assocs., Princeton, N.J., 1990-91; med. writer Convatec, Skillman, N.J., 1991-92, G.H. Besselaar Assocs., Princeton, N.J., 1992-94; clin. safety assoc. Pfizer Inc., N.Y.C., 1994—. Mem. Phi Beta Kappa. Home: 145 W High St Bound Brook NJ 08805

MATTSON, LISA GAIL, automotive engineer; b. Millington, Tenn., Oct. 27, 1960; d. Russell Byrum and Barbara Lee (Martin) Lyle; m. Douglas Bryan Mattson, Aug. 2, 1986; children: Bryan, Stephen. BS in Mech. Engring., U. Okla., 1984. Grad. tng. Truck Engring. divsn. GM, Pontiac, Mich., 1984-86, lab. test engr., 1986-87, program controller, 1992-94, design engr., 1994—; test engr. proving grounds Truck Engring. divsn. GM, Milford, Mich., 1987-89; engring. analysis engr. Truck Engring. divsn. GM, Troy, Mich., 1989-92. Mem. ASME, Engring. Soc. Detroit. Republican.

MATTY, RUTH ESTHER, controller; b. Akron, Ohio, Aug. 27, 1950; d. Chester Wandow and Esther Julia (Failor) M. BS in Acctg., U. Akron, 1979, MBA, 1986. Cert. mgmt. acct., Ohio; CPA, Ohio. Account clk. La. Pacific Corp., Barberton, Ohio, 1968-76, cost acct., 1979-80; gen. ledger acct. U. Akron, 1980-87, asst. controller, 1987—. Mem. Inst. Mgmt. Accts. Lutheran. Office: U Akron 302 Buchtel Mall Akron OH 44325-6205

MATULEF, GIZELLE TERESE, secondary education educator; b. Budapest, Jan. 17, 1945; came to the U.S., 1948; d. Louis and Gizelle Beke; m. Gary Matulef, Mar. 21, 1975; 1 child, Margaret. AA in Bus., Phoenix (Ariz.) Coll., 1964; BS in Edn., No. Ariz. U., 1966; MA, Ind. U., 1970, PhD in Comparative Lit., 1983. Cert. secondary teaching credential, Calif., C.C. instr. credential, Calif. Bus. instr. Drake Bus. Coll., N.Y.C., 1973, Cerro Coso Coll., Ridgecrest, Calif., 1973-74; English and bus. instr. Sawyer Bus. Coll., Westwood, Calif., 1974-75; bus. instr. Sierra Sands Adult Sch., Ridgecrest, 1975-82; Indian edn. dir. Sierra Sands Unifed Sch. Dist., Ridgecrest, 1980-82; sch. improvement program dir. Murray Jr. High Sch., Ridgecrest, 1982-89; English and econs. instr. Trona (Calif.) High Sch., 1989-92; tng. dir. High Desert Experience Unlimited Career Counseling, Ridgecrest, 1991-92; substitute tchr. Sierra Sands Unified Sch. Dist., Ridgecrest, 1993; archives asst. Albert Michelson Mus., Naval Weapons Ctr., China Lake, Calif., 1976-77, editorial asst. Tech. Info. Dept., 1977-78. Contbr. articles to profl. jours. Active PTA, Ridgecrest Schs., 1983-93, Music Parents Assn., Ridgecrest, 1985-93. Recipient fellowship Ind. U., Bloomington, 1966-69. Mem. AAUW (pres. China Lake/Ridgecrest br. 1992—), NEA. Home: PO Box 1041 Ridgecrest CA 93556

MATULICH, ERIKA, marketing educator; b. Sacramento, Sept. 14, 1963; d. Serge and Margarete (Manderscheid) M. BBA, Tex. Christian U., 1984, MBA, 1986; PhD, U. Wis., 1994. Ops. officer M Bank Dallas, 1986-87; ops. analyst Bell Helicopter, Textron, Ft. Worth, 1987-89; teaching asst. U. Wis., Madison, 1989-92; instr. Tex. Christian U., Ft. Worth, 1986-89, asst. prof. mktg., 1993—; market researcher All Saints Epis. Hosp., Ft. Worth, 1984, Shakespeare in the Park, Ft. Worth, 1985, Informart, Dallas, 1985; strategic planner Williamson-Dickie, Ft. Worth, 1985; presenter at confs. Mem. Am. Mktg. Assn. (conf. presenter 1991), Am. Assn. Advances in Health Care Rsch., Assn. for Consumer Rsch., Acad. Mktg. Sci. (conf. presenter 1992), Beta Gamma Sigma. Office: Tex Christian U PO Box 32868 Fort Worth TX 76129

MATUSOW, NAOMI C., state legislator; b. Nashville, Oct. 31, 1938; m. Gene R. Matusow; children: Gary, Jason. BA cum laude, Vanderbilt U.; MA in Counseling and Guidance, NYU; JD, Pace U. Bar: N.Y. 1981. Editl. asst. Golden Press; tchr. math. N.Y.C. pub. schs., guidance counselor; pvt. practice as lawyer Armonk, 1981-90, White Plains, 1990—; mem. N.Y. State Assembly, 1992—, mem. various coms. Past mem. Dem. State Com., Westchester County Dem. Exec. Com., North Castle Dem. Com.; assoc. Westchester Land Trust; bd. dirs. Family Svc. Westchester. Mem. NOW, Am. Jewish Com. (Westchester chpt.), N.Y. State Women's Bar Assn., Westchester County Bar Assn., White Plains Bar Assn., Westchester Civil Liberties Union, Westchester Assn. Woman Bus. Owners. Office: NY State Assembly State Capitol Albany NY 12224*

MATUSZAK, ALICE JEAN BOYER, pharmacy educator; b. Newark, Ohio, June 22, 1935; d. James Emery and Elizabeth Hawthorn (Irvine) Boyer; m. Charles Alan Matuszak, Aug. 27, 1955; children: Matthew, James. BS summa cum laude, Ohio State U., 1958, MS, 1959; postgrad., U. Wis., 1959-60; PhD, U. Kans., 1963. Registered pharmacist, Ohio, Calif. Apprentice pharmacist Arensberg Pharmacy, Newark, 1953-58; rsch. asst. Ohio State U., Columbus, 1958, lab. asst., 1958-59; rsch. asst. U. Wis., Madison, 1959-60, U. Kans., Lawrence, 1960-63; asst. prof. U. of the Pacific, Stockton, Calif., 1963-67, assoc. prof., 1971-78, prof., 1978—; vis. fgn. prof. Kobe-Gakuin U., Japan, 1992. Contbr. articles to profl. jours. Recipient Disting. Alumna award Ohio State U. Coll. Pharmacy, 1995; NIH grantee, 1965-66. Mem. Am. Assn. Colls. of Pharmacy (chmn. chemistry sect. 1979-80, bd. dirs. 1993-95), Am. Pharm. Assn. (chmn. basic scis. 1990), Am. Inst. History of Pharmacy (exec. coun. 1984-88, 90-92, 92-95, chmn. contributed papers 1990-92, pres.-elect 1995—, Cert. of Commendation 1990), Am. Chem. Soc., Internat. Fedn. Pharmacy, Acad. Pharm. Rsch. Sci. (pres. 1993-94), Sigma Xi, Rho Chi, Phi Kappa Phi, Kappa Epsilon (Unicorn award), Lambda Kappa Sigma, Delta Zeta. Democrat. Episcopalian. Home: 1130 W Mariposa Ave Stockton CA 95204-3021 Office: U of the Pacific Sch of Pharmacy Stockton CA 95211

MATZ, KAY ELAINE, savings and loan executive; b. Warren, Ohio, Apr. 18, 1946; d. Nick M. and Julia H. (Petrulak) Kovic. grad. bus. mgmt. Hiram Coll., 1987. Staff acct. R.M. Robbins & Assocs., Warren, 1964-73; with 1st

Fed. Savs. & Loan Assn. Warren, 1973—, asst. treas., 1980-81, contr., 1982-90, reporting officer, 1991-92, asst. treas., 1992—; ann. fin. auditor Children's Rehab. Ctr., Warren, 1970-74; bd. dirs. Someplace Safe, Inc. Mem. Am. Soc. Women Accts. (pres. Youngstown chpt. 1975-76), Fin. Mgrs. Soc. (pres. Pa.-Ohio chpt. 1983-84), Warren Area C. of C., Exec. Link of Warren, Emblem Club, Lions (Warren). Democrat. Avocations: travel, golf. Home: 2940 Reeves Rd NE Warren OH 44483-3614 Office: 1st Fed Savs & Loan Assn Warren PO Box 551 185 E Market St Warren OH 44481-1135

MATZKE, SUSAN MARIE, psychotherapist; b. Milw., Sept. 4, 1946; d. Harold T. and Fern M. (Bergman) Wardius; m. Robert F. Matzke, Feb. 10, 1973; children: Thad, Andrea, Kirstin, Ronald, Rob. AA, U. Wis., Janesville, 1980; BA in Psychology summa cum laude, U. Wis., Whitewater, 1982, MS in Guidance and Counseling, 1984. Cert. profl. counselor, Wis. Pres., clin. dir. Genesis Counseling Svcs., Ltd., Janesville, Wis., 1988—; cons. Dist. Com. on Ordained Ministry, Salem, Wis., 1993—. staff mem. Cargill United Meth. Ch., Janesville, 1990—. Mem. ACA, Rock County Mental Health Assn., Phi Kappa Phi, Psi Chi. Methodist. Office: Genesis Counseling Svcs 2020 E Milwaukee St Janesville WI 53545-2600

MAU, BEVERLY KWAI SIM, real estate manager; b. Honolulu, Nov. 6, 1950; d. James On and Dorothy Mew Kai (Chun) M.; m. Richard D. S. Ho Jr., Aug. 21, 1981 (div. Oct. 1986); 1 stepchild, Richard III. B of Edn., U. Hawaii-Manoa Campus, 1972; cert., Gypsy Norton Modeling Sch., Honolulu, 1977, Am. Inst. Banking, 1978; grad., saleman, Stapleton Sch. Real Estate, Honolulu, 1978, grad., broker, 1980; grad., Graduate Realtors Inst., 1979. Cert. residential specialist; cert. mortgage broker; cert. internat. property specialist. Broker salesman Herbert K. Horita Realty, Honolulu, 1979-86; broker salesman/projects Conley Dew, Ltd., Honolulu, 1986-91; broker-in-charge RE/MAX Profls., Honolulu, 1991-92, prin. broker, 1992-93, relocation specialist, 1992—; pres., owner, property mgr. Real Estate Magic, Honolulu, 1993—; mortgage solicitor United Mortgage, Inc., Honolulu, 1993—, ins. solicitor, 1994—; comml. cons. RE/MAX, Conley Dew, Real Estate Magic, Honolulu, 1988—; vice chairperson city affairs com., mem. program com. Honolulu Bd. Realtors, 1991, mem. election com., 1992. Editor: (newsletters) Information is Power, 1991, Information is Magic, 1993; contbg. editor Downtown Planet, 1992, Pacific Bus. News, 1994; author (with others) Pioneering Chinese Women, 1994; columnist Hawaii Realtor Jour., 1993. Advisor Jr. Achievement, 1976; club advisor H.S. students YWCA, 1970; del. to nat. conv. Young Women's Christian Assn., Houston, 1969; registration asst. Adult Friends for Youth, 1991; vol. Chamber Music Hawaii, 1989; mem. Honolulu Symphony Assocs.; active Employee Relocation Coun., 1992—; make-up cons. Hawaii Opera Theatre, 1991; spotter co-chairperson Hawaii Youth at Risk, 1991, fundraiser auction coord., 1992, 93; cadet leader Girl Scouts U.S., 1961; mem. Smithsonian Inst. Mem. Am. Bus. Women's Assn. (sec. 1988-89, pres. 1989—, Woman of Yr. 1990), Nat. Assn. Realtors (cert., polit. action com., polit. participation com. 1992), Hawaii Assn. Realtors (vice-chair pub. rels. 1992, chair state registration 1992, govt. affairs com. 1991—), Assn. Apt. Owners-Crosspointe (bd. dirs. 1993), Associated Chinese Univ. Women's Assn. (chair Christmas banquet 1990, nominating com. 1991), Real Estate Educators Assn. (sec. 1993—), Internat. Order Eastern Star, Soroptimist Internat., Mau Club Hawaii (sec. 1993),. Home: 625 Mananai Pl Apt D Honolulu HI 96818-5325 Office: Real Estate Magic 1210 Auahi St Ste 105 Honolulu HI 96814-4922

MAUER, ELIZABETH BANGEL, stockbroker; b. N.Y.C.; d. Arthur Benjamin and Millicent Sara (Hancles) Bangel; m. David Mauer, May 21, 1972 (div. 1991); children: Beth, Carolyn, Amanda. BA, SUNY, Stony Brook, 1970; MEd, U. Cin., 1974; postgrad., U. Bridgeport, Conn., 1978-79, U. Cin., 1991—. Trainee Lehman Bros., N.Y.C., 1971-72; head reading dept. Cin. Country Day Sch., 1973-77; cons. GTITC Corp., Cin., 1984-85, Little People Workshop, Cin., 1991; stockbroker Gradison & Co., Cin., 1992—. Bd. dirs. Cin. Ballet, 1990—, Coll. Conservatory of Music, Cin., 1989—, Children's Psychiat. Ctr., Cin., 1989-91, AHRC; bd. dirs. govt. rels. com. Cin. Inst. Fine Arts, 1992; v.p. exec. bd. dirs. Nat. Coun. Jewish Women, Cin., 1984-91. Mem. Town Club (chmn. events 1990—), Losantivilla Country Club (chmn. events 1989), Met. Club (charter mem.). Home: 2861 Fair Acres Dr Cincinnati OH 45213-1015 Office: Gradison & Co 580 Walnut St Cincinnati OH 45202-3198

MAUER, MARY EDSON, secondary education educator; b. Ross, Calif., Nov. 26, 1949; d. Leo Bartholomew and Jeanne Elizabeth (Eachus) Edson; m. Thomas Alfred Mauer, Sept. 6, 1969 (div. June 1988); children: Katie, John. Student, U. Calif., Davis, 1967-69; BA in Biol. Scis. cum laude, Calif. State U., Chico, 1971, MA in Biol. Scis. with distinction, 1973. Secondary teaching credential in biol. scis. Tchr. biology Morse High Sch. San Diego Unified Sch. Dist., 1979—, chair sci. dept., 1988—; developer advanced placement biology program Morse High Sch., San Diego Unified Sch. Dist., 1986, developer, coord. sci. lecture series, 1993-94; lead tchr. NSF recombinant DNA workshop San Diego State U., 1991; lab. instr. sci. tchr. enhancement program U. Calif., San Diego, 1993. Grantee Mellon Found., 1988; Howard Hughes fellow Scripps Rsch. Inst., 1991, Am. Soc. Cell Biology fellow Scripps Rsch. Inst., 1992, Am. Physiol. Soc. fellow U. Calif. San Diego Med. Ctr., 1993, Industry fellow Advanced Tissue Scis., 1994. Mem. Nat. Sci. Tchrs. Assn., Nat. Assn. Biology Tchrs., Calif. Tchrs. Assn., San Diego Tchrs. Assn., San Diego Sci. Educators Assn. (Secondary Sci. Tchr. of Yr. 1994), San Diego Regional Forum Biotechnology Edn., Scripps Charter Soc. Home: 3203 Chelsea Park Cir Spring Valley CA 91978 Office: Morse High Sch 6905 Skyline Dr San Diego CA 92114

MAUGHAN, DONNA See ALLISON, DONNA M.

MAUKE, LEAH RACHEL, counselor; b. Newport, R.I., Aug. 29, 1924; d. Louis and Annie (Price) Louison; m. Otto Russell Mauke, June 18, 1950. BSBA, Boston U., 1946, MBA, 1948. Teaching fellow Boston U., 1946-48; head advt. dept. Endicott Coll., Beverly, Mass., 1948-66; guidance counselor Vineland (N.J.) Sr. High Sch., 1966-69; guidance counselor Black Horse Pike Regional Sch. Dist., Blackwood, N.J., 1969-86, ret., 1986. Vol. ARC, Vero Beach, Fla., 1988—. Boston U. fellow 1946. Mem. AAUW (life, pres. North Shore br. 1955-59, state fellowship chmn. 1957-58), NEA, N.J. Edn. Assn., Camden County Pers. and Guidance Assn. (sec. 1972). Home: 2119 E Lakeview Dr Sebastian FL 32958-8519

MAULDIN, JEAN ANN, controller; b. Ft. Chaffee, Ark., Oct. 12, 1957; d. Lawrence Ray and Antoinette Marie (Tusa) Mitchell; 1 child, Michele L. Carter. BBA in Acctg., U. Ctrl. Ark., 1979, MBA, 1985. Cost acct. FMC Automotive Svc. Divsn., Conway, Ark., 1979-82, mgr. cost acctg., 1982-85, divsnl. fin. analyst, 1985, plant contr., 1985-86, divsn. contr., 1986-88; mgr. cost acctg. Columbian Chems. Co., Atlanta, 1988-90, dir. field acctg., 1990-92, No. Am. contr., 1992-93, corporate controller, 1993-94; v.p., CFO Accuride Corp., Henderson, Ky., 1995—. Recipient Young Career Woman award Bus. and Profl. Women, 1986. Mem. Inst. Mgmt. Accts. (cert., v.p. adminstrn. 1993-94). Republican. Roman Catholic.

MAULDIN, JEAN HUMPHRIES, aviation company executive; b. Gordonville, Tex., Aug. 16, 1923; d. James Wiley and Lena Leota (Noel-Crain) Humphries; B.S., Hardin Simmons U., 1943; M.S., U. So. Calif., 1961; postgrad. Westfield Coll., U. London, 1977-78, Warnborough Coll., Oxford, Eng., 1977-78; m. William Henry Mauldin, Feb. 28, 1942; children—Bruce Patrick, William Timothy III. Psychol. counselor social services 1st Baptist Ch., 1953-57; pres. Mauldin and Staff, public relations, Los Angeles, 1957-78; pres. Stardust Aviation, Inc., Santa Ana, Calif., 1962—. Mem. Calif. Democratic Council, 1953-83; rep. 69th Assembly Dist. Caucus to Calif. Dem. State Central com. exec. bd., 1957—, Orange County Dem. Central Com., 1960—; mem. U.S. Congl. Peace Adv. Bd., 1981—; del. Dem. Nat. Conv., 1974, 78, Dem. Mid-Term Conv., 1976, 78, 82, 86, Dem. Nat. Issues Conf.; mem. nat. advisor U.S. Congl. Adv. Bd. Am. Security Council; pres. Santa Ana Friends of Public Library, 1973-76, McFadden Friends of Library, Santa Ana, 1976-80; chmn. cancer crusade Am. Cancer Soc., Orange County, 1974; mem. exec. bd. Lisa Hist. Preservation Soc., 1970—; lay leader Protestant Episcopal Ch. Am., Trinity Ch., Tustin, Calif. Named Woman of Yr., Key Woman in Politics, Calif. Dem. Party, 1960-80. Am. Mgmt. Assn. (pres.'s club), Bus. and Profl. Women Am., Exptl. Aircraft and Pilots Assn., Nat. Women's Polit. Caucus, Dem. Coalition Central Coms., Calif. Friends of Library (life), Women's Missionary Soc. (chmn.), LWV, Nat. Fedn. Dem. Women, Calif. Fedn. County Central Com. Mems., Internat. Platform Assn., Peace Through Strength, Oceanic Soc., Nat. Audubon Soc., Sierra Club, Nat. Wildlife Fedn., Internat. Amnesty Assn., Am. Security Council, Nat. Women's Pilot. Club: U. So. Calif. Ski, Town Hall of Calif. Author: Cliff Winters, The Pilot, The Man, 1961; The consummate Barnstormer, 1962; The Daredevil Clown, 1965. Home: 1013 S Elliott Pl Santa Ana CA 92704-2224 also: 102 E 45th St Savannah GA 31405-2115 Office: 16542 Mount Kibby St Fountain Valley CA 92708-2437

MAUN, MARY ELLEN, communications company analyst; b. N.Y.C., Dec. 18, 1951; d. Emmet Joseph and Mary Alice (McMahon) M. BA, CUNY, 1977, MBA, 1988. Sales rep. N.Y. Telephone Co., N.Y.C., 1970-76, comml. rep., 1977-83, programmer, 1984-86; systems analyst Telesector Resources Group, N.Y.C., 1987-89, sr. systems analyst, 1990—. Corp. chmn. United Way of Tri-State Area, N.Y.C., 1985; recreation activities vol. Pioneers Am., N.Y.C., 1982—; active Sleepy Hollow Hist. Soc. Recipient Outstanding Community Service award, Calvary Hosp., Bronx, N.Y., 1984. Mem. N.Y. Health and Racquet Club, Road Runners. Democrat. Home: 3 Farrington Ave N Tarrytown NY 10591-1302 Office: Telesector Resources Group 1166 Avenue Of The Americas New York NY 10036-2708

MAUPIN, ELIZABETH THATCHER, theater critic; b. Cleve., Oct. 21, 1951; d. Addison and Margaret (Thatcher) M. BA in English, Wellesley (Mass.) Coll., 1973; M in Journalism, U. Calif., Berkeley, 1976. Editorial asst. Houghton-Mifflin Co., Boston, 1973-74; intern Washington bureau McClatchy Newspapers, 1975; reporter, movie critic Times-Standard, Eureka, Calif., 1976-78; theater and movie critic Chronicle-Telegram, Elyria, Ohio, 1978-79; movie and restaurant critic Ledger-Star, Norfolk, Va., 1979-82; feature writer Va.-Pilot and Ledger-Star, Norfolk, 1982-83; sr. theater critic Orlando (Fla.) Sentinel, 1983—. Fellow Nat. Critics Inst.; mem. Am. Theatre Critics Assn. (exec. com. 1993—). Office: Orlando Sentinel 633 N Orange Ave Orlando FL 32801

MAURER, ADAH ELECTRA, psychologist; b. Chgo., Oct. 26, 1905; d. Frank Ulysses and Mary Louise (Meng) Bass; m. Harry Andrew Maurer, June 14, 1937 (div. 1947); children: Douglas, Helen. BS, U. Wis., 1927; MA, U. Chgo., 1957; PhD, Union Inst., 1976. Lic. sch. psychologist, Calif. Tchr. pub. schs. Chgo., 1927-61; psychologist pub. schs. Calif., 1962-71; pvt. practice marriage, family and child counselor Berkeley, Calif., 1965-75; organizer, chief exec. officer End Violence Against the Next Generation, Inc., Berkeley, 1972—; lectr. U. Calif., Davis, 1965-68; bd. dirs. Nat. Ctr. for Study Cpl. Punishment & Alternatives in Schs. Temple U., Phila.; liaison People Opposed to Paddling Students, Houston, 1981—; v.p. Nat. Coalition to Abolish Cpl. Punishment in Schs., Columbus, Ohio, 1987—; cons. Calif. State Dept. Social Svcs., 1988. Author: Paddles Away, 1981, 1001 Alternatives, 1984, (with others) The Bible and the Rod, 1983, Think Twice, 1985; editor: (newsletter) The Last? Resort, 1972—; contbr. numerous articles to profl. jours. Sponsor End Phys. Punishment of Children Worldwide. Recipient Disting. Humanitarian award Calif. State Psychol. Assn., Presdl. award Nat. Assn. Sch. Psychologists, 1988, Donna Stone award Nat. Commn. for Prevention of Child Abuse, 1988, commendation Giraffe Project, 1988, award in recognition of pioneering efforts in banning corporal punishment in nation's schs. Nat. Coalition to Abolish Corporal Punishment in Schs., Achievement award Child, Youth and Family Svcs. Am. Psychol. Assn., 1994. Mem. Am. Psychol. Assn. (Lifetime Career Achievement award 1995), Hemlock Soc. Home and Office: 977 Keeler Ave Berkeley CA 94708-1498

MAURER, BEVERLY BENNETT, school administrator; b. Bklyn., Aug. 23, 1940; d. David and Minnie (Dolen) Bennett; m. Harold M. Maurer, June 12, 1960; children: Ann Maurer Rosenbach, Wendy Maurer Rausch. BA, Bklyn. Coll., 1960, postgrad., 1961; postgrad., U. Richmond, 1980-90, Va. Commonwealth U., 1980-90. Cert. tchr., N.Y., Va. Math. tchr. Col. David Marcus Jr. High Sch., Bklyn., 1960-61, Pomona (N.Y.) Jr. High Sch., 1967-68; math. tchr. Hebrew day sch. Rudlin Torah Acad., Richmond, Va., 1969-80, asst. prin., 1980-86, prin., 1986-89; dir. edn. Jewish Community Day Sch. Ctrl. Va., Richmond, 1990-93. Developed talented and gifted program, preadmission program for children at Med. Coll. Va., 1982. Bd. dirs. Jewish Comty. Ctr., Richmond, 1980s; bd. dirs. Aux. to Med. Coll. Va., Richmond, 1980s, Aux. to U. Nebr. Med. Ctr., 1994—, Uta Hallee, 1994—. Recipient Master Tchr. award Rudlin Torah Acad., 1983. Mem. Jewish Community Day Sch. Network, Anti-Defamation League, Jewish Women's Club. Republican.

MAURER, ELEANOR JOHNSON, oil company executive; b. Milan, Mo., Jan. 23, 1914; d. Harvey Clifton and Bertha Delaney (Wilkerson) M.; m. Darwin T. Maurer, Aug. 5, 1968 (dec. 1978); 1 child, Jacqueline Eleanor. Student, Stephens Coll., Columbia, Mo., 1930-31, Southwestern State U., Weatherford, Okla., 1932, Draughons Bus. Coll., Oklahoma City, 1933. Sec. Kirkpatrick Oil Co., Oklahoma City, 1951-66, asst. to pres., 1966-80, chief exec. officer, 1980-93, cons., 1993—. Treasl. Oklahoma City Community Found., Okla. Ctr. for Sci. and Arts; treas., bd. dirs. Kirkpatrick Found.; bd. dirs. Okla. Sch. Sic. and Math. Found. Named Corp. Woman of Yr. Jour. Record Newspaper/Okla. City Woman's Forum, 1984, one of Ladies in the News Okla. Hospitality Club, 1992; recipient Trustees' award Omniplex Sci. Mus., Oklahoma City, 1988. Mem. Exec. Women Internat. (pres. 1964), Com. of 200 (S.W. regional chmn. bd. 1989-90), English Speaking Union U.S. (Oklahoma City chpt.), Rotary. Republican. Mem. Christian Ch. Home: 7900 Lakehurst Dr Oklahoma City OK 73120-4324 Office: Kirkpatrick Oil Co 1300 N Broadway Dr Oklahoma City OK 73103-4894

MAURER, GERALDINE MARIE, obstetrics nurse; b. Greenville, Ohio, Aug. 15, 1952; d. Ronald Keith and Marie Anne (Supak) Reck; m. Bradley Floyd Maurer, June 21, 1975; children: Dane, Jared, Joshua. Student, Ohio U., 1970-72; BSN, Wright State U., 1976; M Pub. Mgmt., Carnegie Mellon U., 1989. RN, Pa., Ohio; cert. NAACOG. Nurses aide geriatric patient care The Brethren's Home, Greenville, Ohio, 1974-75; nursing asst. II pool staff St. Elizabeth Med. Ctr., Dayton, Ohio, 1975-76; staff nurse rooming-in unit Magee-Women's Hosp., Pitts., 1976-77, charge nurse, 1977-79, head nurse, 1979-82, head nurse 2700/Family Centered Care obstet. unit, 1982-85, nurse mgr. 2700/high risk antepartum/Family Centered Care, 1985-87, nurse mgr. 2700/high risk antepartum unit and 3700, 1987-90, nurse mgr. 2700/High Risk Antepartum Unit, 1990-94, dir. patient care svcs., 1994—; adj. faculty Sch. Nursing U. Pitts., 1991—; mem. Wyeth Pediat. Nat. Perinatal Adv. Bd., 1990-93; mem. trauma liaison/cons. com. Presbyn. U. Med. Ctr., U. Pitts. Med. Ctr., 1990-92; item writer Nat. Cert. Corp. cert. exam, 1992-93. Bd. dirs., funding com. Sojourner House for Drug Rehab., Pitts.; CPR/first aid instr. Cub Scouts/Boy Scouts Am., Allegheny coun. Pitts.; CPR/first aid instr., leader troop 1189 Jr. Scouts/Girl Scouts Am., Allegheny Coun.; mem. parent-tchr. group St. John the Bapt. Sch., Unity, Pa. Office: Magee Womens Hosp 300 Halket St Pittsburgh PA 15213-3180

MAURER, LAURA SHANNON, fitness product manufacturing executive; b. N.Y.C., May 28, 1942; d. Harold H. and Bertha (Feldmann) Braverman; m. J. Bonnar Shannon, Jr., Feb. 27, 1965 (div. June 1974); m. A. Donald Maurer, Sept. 28, 1974; children: Gregory D., Amanda C., Heather Shannon. BA, Vassar Coll., 1963. Systems engr. IBM, N.Y.C., 1963-69; industry mktg. specialist IBM, Washington, 1970-74; various tech. mgmt. positions IBM, Phila., 1975-81, br. mgr., 1982-84, regional mgr. market support, 1984-86, area bus. devel. mgr., 1986-89, area dir. internat. ops., 1990-92; exec. dir. A.S.I., Phila., 1992-93; gen. mgr. Tng. Camp Internat., Merion, Pa., 1993—. Mem. NAFE. Republican. Office: Tng Camp Internat 601 Upland Ave Upland PA 19015

MAURER, LUCILLE DARVIN, state treasurer; b. N.Y.C., Nov. 21, 1922; d. Joseph Jay and Evelyn (Levine) Darvin; m. Ely Maurer, Apr. 29, 1945; children: Stephen Bennett, Russell Alexander, Edward Nestor. Student, U. N.C., Greensboro, 1938-40; BA, U. N.C., Chapel Hill, 1942; MA, Yale U., 1945; DH (hon.), Hood Coll., 1984; HLD (hon.), U. Coll., U. Md., 1990. Economist U.S. Tariff Commn., 1942-43; econ. and market research for pvt. firms, 1957-60; cons. Nat. Center for Ednl. Stats., 1969-70; mem. Md. House of Dels., 1969-87, mem. ways and means com., 1971-87, chmn. joint com. on fed. relations, 1983-87; state treas. State of Md., 1987—; mem. intergovtl. adv. coun. U.S. Dept. Edn., 1980-82. Del., Md. Constl. Conv., 1967-68; mem. Montgomery County Bd. Edn., 1960-68; trustee Montgomery Community Coll., 1960-68; vice chmn. nat. planning com., advanced leadership program of seminars on edn. and ednl. policy for state legislators Edn. Commn. of States, 1979-81; mem. exec. com. of edn. com. Nat. Conf. of State Legislatures, 1975-84, chmn., 1978-79, chmn. com. on taxes, trade and econ. devel., 1985-86; mem. adv. com. Servicemems. Opportunity Colls., 1978-82; mem. nat. adv. bd. Inst. for Ednl. Leadership, 1979-81; mem. Nat. Com. on Postsecondary Accreditation, 1974-1979; bd. dirs. Montgomery United Way, 1971-76, 84-94; mem. Commn. Higher Edn. of Middle States Assn., 1982-85; mem. Gov.'s Employment and Tng. Coun., 1983-91. Recipient Legislator of Yr. award Md. Assn. for Retarded Children, 1972, John Dewey award Montgomery County Fedn. Tchrs., 1972, Hornbook award Montgomery County Edn. Assn., 1972, Legislator of Yr. award Md. Assn. Counties, 1984, Willis award for outstanding service Md. Assn. Bds. Edn., 1984, Louis B. Brandeis Justice in Govt. award Am. Jewish Congress, 1988, Judge Sarah T. Hughes award for disting. pub. svc. Goucher Coll., 1989, Disting. Pub. Svc. award Md. C. of C., 1989, Nat. Identification Program award Am. Coun. Edn., 1993; named Energy Warrior of Yr., Md. Energy Adminstrn., 1994; inductee Md. Women's Hall of Fame, 1990. Mem. LWV (past dir. Montgomery County, past dir. Md.), AAUW (Internat. Women's Yr. award Silver Spring 1975), NOW (Legis. Excellence award 1981), Bus. and Profl. Women's Club (Woman of Yr. 1984), Nat. Assn. State Treas. (v.p. 1989-90, chmn. legis. com. 1989-91, sr. v.p. 1991-92, pres. 1992-93, Jesse M. Unruh award 1994), Nat. Assn. State Auditors, Comptrs. and Treas. (exec. com. 1988-91, fed./state cash mgmt. reform task force 1988-92), Women Execs. State Govt. (bd. dirs. 1988-92), Women's Equity Action League, Women's Polit. Caucus, Montgomery County Hist. Soc., Order Women Legislators, Delta Kappa Gamma. Jewish. Office: State Treas Office Goldstein Treasury Bldg Annapolis MD 21401

MAURER, VIRGINIA GALLAHER, lawyer, educator; b. Shawnee, Okla., Nov. 7, 1946; d. Paul Clark Gallaher and Virginia Ruth (Watson) Abernathy; m. Ralph Gerald Maurer, July 31, 1971; children: Ralph Emmett, William Edward. BA, Northwestern U., 1968; MA, Stanford U., 1969, JD, 1975. Bar: Iowa 1976. Tchr. social studies San Mateo (Calif.) High Sch. Dist., 1969-71; spl. asst. to pres. U. Iowa, Iowa City, 1976-80, adj. asst. prof. law, 1979-80; affiliate asst. prof. law U. Fla., Gainesville, 1981, asst. prof. bus. law, 1980-85, assoc. prof., 1985-93, prof., 1993—, dir. MBA Program, 1987, chair dept. mgmt., 1994—; vis. prof. Wolfson Coll., Cambridge, 1994, SDA Bocconi U., Milan, 1994; cons. Gov.'s Com. on Iowa 2000, Iowa City, 1976-77, Fla. Banker's Assn., Gainesville, 1982. Contbr. articles to profl. jours.; jr. editor Am. Bus. law Jour., 1989-90, mng. editor, 1990-91, editor-in-chief, 1992-94. Bd. dirs. Gainesville Chamber Orch., 1990-93; mem. fundraising com. Pro Arte Musica, Gainesville, 1980-84; sr. warden, mem. vestry, Holy Trinity Episc. Ch., 1991-93; bd. dirs. Holy Trinity Found., Gainesville, 1991-93; mem. com. charter and canon law Episc. Diocese Fla., 1994—. Mem. ABA, Acad. Legal Studies in Bus. (ho. of dels., 1989-90, exec. com. 1992), Southeastern Bus. Law Assn. (Proc. editor 1984-87, treas. 1985-86, v.p. 1986-87, pres.-elect 1987-88, pres. 1988-89), Iowa Bar Assn., LWV, U. Fla. Athletic Assn. (bd. dirs. 1982-88; v.p., chmn. fin. com.), Gainesville Womens' Forum (bd. dirs. 1988-91), Fla. Women' Network, Beta Gamma Sigma, Kappa Alpha Theta, Delta Sigma Pi, Univ. Women's Club (Gainesville, Fla.), Rotary (bd. dirs. 1989-91). Home: 2210 NW 6th Pl Gainesville FL 32603-1409 Office: U Fla Grad Sch Bus Gainesville FL 32611

MAURO, GINGER LOURDES BAERJE, bank officer, consultant; b. Guayaquil, Ecuador, July 7. Student, 28 de Mayo U., Guayaquil, Columbia U. Loan officer Bank of Am., North Hollywood, Calif., 1979—. Home: 11251 Elkwood St Sun Valley CA 91352-4438

MAUS, CONNIE, nurse administrator, transcultural health educator; b. Nampa, Idaho, Apr. 10, 1945; d. Raymond Vera and Connie (Acevez) Serratos; m. James McMurtrey, Aug. 12, 1967 (div. 1974); 1 child, James Jason; m. Errol R. Maus, Dec. 28, 1976; 1 child, Martha. Diploma in nursing, St. Alphonsus Sch. Nursing, 1966; BS, Boise State U., 1976; MS, Idaho State U., 1993. RN, Idaho. Staff nurse Mercy Med. Ctr., Nampa, 1964-67, head nurse, 1967-68, dir. insvc., 1968-72; instr. staff devel. St. Alphonsus Med. Ctr., Boise, Idaho, 1972-73, asst. dir., 1973-76, nurse mgr., 1976-81, oncology cons./supportive care, 1981-83, mgr. home health, 1983-86, coord. utilization/discharge mgmt., 1986-94; mgr. med. oncology St. Alphonsus Med. Ctr., Boise, 1994—; mem. quality improvement coun. St. Alphonsus Med. Ctr., Boise; bd. dirs. Ronald McDonald House, Idaho; presenter, participant ednl. programs on ethics. Mem. Mujeres Unidos De Idaho, Image. Contbr. poems to profl. publs. (Golden award 1987, 89, Silver award 1990). Mem. Asns. Christian Therapists, Am. Soc. Quality Control (chmn. transcultural com., past. chmn. hosp. ethics com.), Sigma Theta Tau (provider continuing edn. in transcultural issues). Roman Catholic. Home: 2066 Varian Pl Boise ID 83709-2459 Office: St Alphonsus Med Ctr 1055 N Curtis Rd Boise ID 83706-1309

MAVROGORDATO, ALICE BLUM, artist; b. Vienna, Austria, Mar. 14, 1916; came to U.S., 1951; d. Ludwig and Friederike (Grossmann) B.; m. Ralph S. Mavrogordato, July 23, 1948. Knitwear designer W&A Glaser, Vienna, 1932-38; postal censor U.S. Army, Esslingen, Germany, 1945-47; translator, editor Nuremberg War Crimes Trials, Germany, 1947-48; artist, 1954—. Exhibited in many group and three-person shows at mus. and various comml. and coop. art galleries. Mus. shows include the Corcoran Gallery of Art, Washington, Nat. Collection of Fine ARts, Smithsonian, Washington, Smithsonian 22d Met. Art Exhbn., Washington, Athenaeum, Alexandria, Va., Washington Project for the Arts, Women's Caucus for Art, Wash. Art '79; solo shows include Collectors' Corner, Origo Gallery, Emerson Gallery, McLean, Va., Cramer Gallery, Plum Gallery, O St. Studio, Inc., Marymount U., Arlington, Va.; and numerous pvt. collections in U.S. and abroad. Mem. Washington Project for the Arts, McLean Project for the Arts. Home: 5730 Herbert St Burke VA 22015-3630

MAX, CLAIRE ELLEN, physicist; b. Boston, Sept. 29, 1946; d. Louis William and Pearl (Bernstein) M.; m. Jonathan Arons, Dec. 22, 1974; 1 child, Samuel. AB, Harvard U., 1968; PhD, Princeton U., 1972. Postdoctoral researcher U. Calif., Berkeley, 1972-74; physicist Lawrence Livermore (Calif.) Nat. Lab., 1974—; dir. Livermore br. Inst. Geophysics and Planetary Physics, 1984-93, dir. of insts., phys. sci. dept., 1993—; mem. Math.-Sci. Network Mills Coll., Oakland, Calif.; mem. com. on fusion hybrid reactors NRC, 1986, mem. com. on internat. security and arms control, 1986-89, mem. com. on phys. sci., math. and applications, 1991-94, mem. policy and computational astgrophys. panels, astron. and astgrophys. survey, 1989-91. Editor: Particle Acceleration Mechanisms in Astrophysics, 1979; contbr. numerous articles to sci. jours. Fellow Am. Phys. Soc. (exec. com. div. plasma physics 1977, 81-82); mem. AAAS, Am. Astron. Soc. (exec. com. div. high energy astrophysics 1975-76), Am. Geophys. Union, Internat. Astron. Union, Phi Beta Kappa, Sigma Xi. Office: Lawrence Livermore Nat Lab PO Box 808 7000 East Ave L-413 Livermore CA 94550-9900

MAX, JENNIFER PAUL, financial controller; b. Fairfax, Va., Dec. 7, 1962; d. R. Shale Paul and Carolyn (Canham) Dain; m. Scott Allen Max, July 12, 1986 (div. July 1992). BS in Bus., U. Colo., 1983; MBA, U. Va., 1988. Internal auditor Coughlin & Co., Denver, Colo., 1984-86; analyst Chemical Bank, N.Y.C., 1987; financial controller Oracle Corp., Redwood Shores, Calif., 1988—; cons. Moose Racing, Littleton, Colo., 1993-94. Vol. Bay Area Model Mugging, San Carlos, Calif., 1991-93. Mem. Mensa, Commonwealth Club, Beta Gamma Sigma.

MAXFIELD, ANNE M., sales executive; b. Cin., Apr. 18, 1961; d. Howard B. and Nancy C. (O'Connell) M.; m. William Eugene Lege. BA, No. Ky. U., 1994; cert., Inst. Orgn. Mgmt., 1990, Salesability, 1991. Supr. St. Elizabeth Med. Ctr., Covington, Ky., 1979-86; v.p. No. Ky. C. of C., Covington, 1986-90; account rep. Olsten STaffing Svcs., Florence, Ky., 1990—; bd. dirs. New Perceptions, Inc., Edgewood, Ky., 1990— (chairwoman nominating com., 1992). Advocacy mgr. Wood Hudson Cancer Rsch., Newport, Ky., 1988-90; chmn. small bus. sect. Cin. United Way, 1990. Mem. Nat. Assn. Temp. Svcs., Ky. Assn. Temp. Svcs., No. Ky. C. of C. (chmn. bus. svcs. com.). Democrat. Office: Olsten Staffing Svcs 5 Spiral Dr Florence KY 41042-1395

MAXFIELD, CAROL TUNICK, neuropsychologist; b. N.Y.C., Oct. 27, 1942; d. Irve E. and Adele (Lehnstul) Tunick; m. Guy B. Maxfield, Dec. 27, 1970; children: Susan Ann, Guy Stephen, Karen Isabelle. BS, N.Y.U., 1969, MA, 1975, PhD, 1989. Intern, fellow N.Y.U. Med. Ctr., 1985-88, from cons.

in neuropsychology to neuropsychologist, 1988—; adj. asst. prof. N.Y.U., 1989—, CUNY, 1992—. Mem. APA, N.Y. State Psychol. Assn. Office: NYU Med Ctr 560 1st Ave New York NY 10016-6497

MAXFIELD, LORI ROCHELLE, educational consultant; b. Denver, Jan. 16, 1959; d. Lawrence Wesley and Caroline Kay (Gideon) M. BS, U. Nebr., 1983, MEd, 1991. Cert. elem. tchr., Nebr., S.D. Recreation aide Lincoln (Nebr.) Parks and Recreation, 1976-84; tchr. Harding County Pub. Schs., Reva, Buffalo, S.D., 1984-89; rsch. assoc. U. Nebr., Lincoln, 1990-91, asst. project coord., 1991-92; sch. enrichment coord. Sch. Dist. 145, Waverly/Eagle, Nebr., 1992-94, also future problem solving coach, Invent America! coord., 1992-94; adv., coach Nat. History Day Harding County Pub. Schs., Reva, 1987-89; coach Odyssey of the Mind, 1986, 93; head coach Jr. High Sch. girls basketball, 1988; asst. coach varsity track, 1989. Youth advisor Slim Buttes Luther League, Reva, 1988-89; ptnr. Spl. Olympics, 1992—. Recipient Outstanding Youth award Nebr. Coun. for Youth and Children, 1977, Outstanding Leadership award Elks, 1977, Golden Apple award Harding County Tchrs., Buffalo, S.D., 1988, Nebr. Ednl. Tech. Assn. grant, 1993. Mem. Am. Ednl. Rsch. Assn., Nat. Coun. Measurement in Edn., Nat. Coun. Tchrs. Math., Nat. Geography Soc., World Coun. for Gifted and Talented, Coun. for Exceptional Children (Assn. of the Gifted), Nebr. Assn. for Gifted (adv. bd. 1991-93, bd. dirs. 1993-94, mem. editl. bd. 1992-94, Disting. Svc. award 1994), Nebr. State Edn. Assn., Nebr. U. Alumni Assn. (life), Smithsonian Instn., Wilson Ctr. Assocs., Nat. Assn. for Gifted Children, Friends of U. Nebr. State Mus., Phi Delta Kappa. Democrat. Lutheran. Home: 5231 W Superior St Lincoln NE 68524-1040 also: PO Box 829 Storrs CT 06268-9998 Office: U Conn Ctr Talent Devel 362 Fairfield U-7 Storrs CT 06269-2007

MAXFIELD, MARY CONSTANCE, management consultant; b. Washington, Mar. 16, 1949; d. Orville Eldred and Rose Mary (Stiarwalt) Maxfield; m. Robert Charles Kneip, III, Aug. 21, 1971 (div. Apr. 1981); 1 child, Stephanie Alexandra; m. Richard Howard Cowles, May 16, 1981 (dec.); m. Phillip Walker, July 25, 1985 (div. June 1991). Clk.-typist HEW, Social Security Adminstrn., New Orleans, 1971-72, service rep., 1972-73; mgmt. analyst Office Comptroller of Currency, Treasury Dept., Washington, 1974-77; dir. mgmt. analysis div. U.S. Customs, New Orleans, 1978-80, mgmt. analyst, Houston, 1980-81, program analyst, 1981-82, chief data processing br., 1982-83, chief mgmt. analysis br., 1983-85; pres. Constance Walker Assocs., Inc., 1985-91, Maxfield Productivity Cons.,Inc., 1991—. Author: MBO Handbook, 1979, Professional Problem Solving, 1985, The Productivity Ascent, 1987, Participative Problem Solving: A Guide for Work Teams, 1988; (with others) Program Management Handbook, 1983, Introduction to Employee Involvement, 1985, Team Approach to Problem Solving, 1991, Quality School Facilitator Training, 1992, Gender Awareness Training, 1992, Interpersonal Communications Skills, 1992, Introduction to Total Quality Schools, 1992, Tex. Leadership Ctr. DuPont LDP Tng., TQM Module, 1993, Intro. to ISO 9000, 1993, Total Quality Mgmt., 1993; contbr. numerous articles to profl. jours. Mem. Friends of Stehlin Found., 1982-88, Friends of the Cabildo, 1978-80. Named Customs Woman of Yr., U.S. Customs, 1979, recipient Outstanding Performance award, 1979, 80, 81, 82, 83, 84, 85; named Fed. Exec. Bd. Woman of Yr., 1979; recipient Outstanding Service award Office of Sec. of Treasury, 1976, Key to City, New Orleans, 1990; Cora Bell Wesley scholar, UDC, 1969. Mem. DAR, Am. Soc. for Quality Control, Assn. for Quality and Participation, Treasury Hist. Assn., Daus. Rep. of Tex., Daus. 1812. UDC, Va. Tech. Alumni Assn., Delta Zeta. Episcopalian. Home and Office: Maxfield Productivity Cons Inc 8007 Liberty Elm Ct Spring TX 77379-6125

MAXON, MARTHA ANNE, biologist, consultant, researcher; b. Reed City, Mich., Aug. 2, 1941; d. Byron Martin and Olive Ione (Bullard) White; m. Lawrence Emil Maxon, Oct. 16, 1982. BA in Psychology magna cum laude, Baylor U., 1963; PhD in Animal Ecology, U. Okla., 1971. Curator of birds Oklahoma City Zoo, 1969-70; rsch. assoc. internat. biol. program N.Mex. State U., Las Cruces, 1972-73, rsch. coord. N.Mex. Environ. Inst., 1973-75; asst. prof. biology U. No. Iowa, Cedar Falls, 1976-78; ecol. cons. RUST Environ. and Infrastructure (formerly Brice Petrides-Donohue Co.), Waterloo, Iowa, 1977—; mem. roadside vegetation commn. Iowa Dept. Transp., Ames, Iowa, 1991—; chair state preserves adv. bd. Iowa Dept. Natural Resources, Des Moines, 1992-94; chair Waterloo Hist. Commn., 1994. Contbr. articles to profl. jours. Mem. citizen's adv. com. wetland issues Black Hawk County, Iowa, 1983-84. Grad. fellow NSF, 1964-66; rsch. grantee Nat. Park Svc., 1968. Mem. Iowa Acad. Sci., Cornell Lab. of Ornithology, Soc. Ecol. Restoration, Natural Areas Assn., Nature Conservancy.

MAXSON, HELEN FLEMING, English language educator; b. Norwich, Conn., May 29, 1949; d. William Edgar and Donna Louise (Curtis) M.; 1 child, William Maxson Doolittle. BA, Middlebury Coll., 1971, MA, 1977; MA in English, Cornell Univ., 1983, PhD in English, 1987. English tchr., dorm parent Cushing Acad., Ashburnham, Mass., 1972-75, Northfield (Mass.) Mount Hermon Sch., 1975-77; English tchr. Fayetteville-Manlius (N.Y.) High Sch., 1977-79; grad. teaching asst. Cornell Univ., 1979-87; asst. prof. div. lang. arts Southwestern Okla. State Univ., 1989-94, assoc. prof., 1994—; vis. asst. prof dept. English lang. and lit. U. Mich., 1987-89. Editorial adv. bd. Collegiate Press Handbook, 1992-93; contbr. articles to profl. jours. Leader, tchr. Teen-Age and Women's Orgn., LDS Ch., Ithaca, N.Y., 1986-87, Ann Arbor, Mich., 1987-89, Clinton, Okla., 1989—. Mem. South Cen. Modern Lang. Assn. (chair spl. session on autobiography and biography for conv. 1995, sec. 1994), Okla. coun. of Tchrs. of English, Virginia Woolf Soc., Sigma Tau Delta. Office: Div of Lang Arts Southwestern Okla State U Weatherford OK 73096

MAXSON, LINDA ELLEN, biologist, educator; b. N.Y.C., Apr. 24, 1943; d. Albert and Ruth (Rosenfeld) Resnick; m. Richard Dey Maxson, June 13, 1964; 1 child, Kevin. BS in Zoology, San Diego State U., 1964, MA in Biology, 1966; PhD in Genetics, U. Calif. and San Diego State U., 1973. Instr. biology San Diego State U., 1966-68; tchr. gen. sci. San Diego Unified Sch. Dist., 1968-69; instr. biochemistry U. Calif., Berkeley, 1974; asst. prof. zoology, dept. genetics and devel. U. Ill., Urbana-Champaign, 1974-76, asst. prof. dept. genetics, devel. and ecology, ethology & evolution, 1976-79, assoc. prof., 1979-84, prof., 1984-87, prof. ecology, ethology and evolution, 1987-88; prof., head dept. biology Pa. State U., State College, 1988-94; assoc. vice-chmn. acad. affairs/dean undergrad. affairs U. Tenn., Knoxville, 1995—; exec. officer biology programs Sch. Life Scis., U. Ill., 1981-86, assoc. dir. acad. affairs, 1984-86, dir. campus honors program, 1985-88; vis. prof. ecology and evolutionary biology U. Calif., Irvine, 1988; mem. adv. panel rsch. tng. groups Behavioral Biol. Scis., NSF, 1990—. Author: Genetics: A Human Perspective, 3d edit., 1992; edtl. bd. Molecular Biology Evolution, Amphibia/Reptilia; exec. editor Biochem. Sys. & Ecology, 1993—; contbr. numerous articles to scientific jours. Recipient Disting. Alumna award San Diego State U., 1989. Fellow AAAS (Disting. Herpetologist award 1993); mem. Am. Men and Women in Sci., Am. Genetics Assn. (mem. coun., 1994—), Soc. for Study of Amphibians and Reptiles (pres. 1991), Internat. Herpetol. Com., Soc. Study Evolution, Soc. Systematic Biology, Soc. Molecular Biology and Evolution (sec. 1992—, treas. 1992-94), Am. Soc. Ichthyologists and Herpetologists, Am. Soc. Zoologists, Herpetologists League, Soc. Euroeaea Herpetologica, European Soc. Evolutionary Biology. Home: 5201 Western Ave Apt 522 Knoxville TN 37921 Office: U Tenn 505 Andy Holt Twr Knoxville TN 37996-0154

MAXWELL, AUDREY L., academic administrator; b. Wilmington, Del., Sept. 2, 1957; d. Richard Lee and Dorothy Jean (Bass) M.; children: Curtis Maxwell Frey, Emily Rose Frey. BS in Edn. with honors, U. Del., 1979; postgrad., Del. Tech. and Community Coll., 1984-85; MBA, Widener U., 1991. Cert. tchr., Del., 1980. Tchr. New Castle County Sch. Dist., Wilmington, Del., 1979-81; pvt. practice as editor New Castle, Del., 1981-83; asst. office mgr. VVM, Inc., Claymont, Del., 1983-86; mktg. coord. Enterprise Pub., Inc., Wilmington, 1986-88; supr. of edn. Alfred I. duPont Inst., Wilmington, 1988-90, asst. to rsch. dir., 1990-91, asst. dir. rsch., 1991—; cons. Enterprise Pub., Inc., Wilmington, Del., 1988-89. Editor: The Golden Mailbox, 1988; prodn. editor: Capitalism for Kids, 1987 (Phila. Book Show award 1987); asst. editor First State Woman, 1988-91; tech. reviewer Pediatric References, 1990—; contbr. articles to profl. jours. Vol. Girl Scouts Am., Claymont, Del., 1990—; tchr. St. Paul's United Meth. Ch., Wilmington, Del., 1981—. Mem. NAFE, Nat. Fedn. Bus. and Profl. Women (pres. 1991-92, sec. 1987-89, Young Careerist award 1989), Del. Assn. Quality Mgmt. Profls., Am. Coll. Healthcare Execs., Kappa Delta Pi. Republican. Methodist. Office: Alfred I duPont Inst PO Box 269 Wilmington DE 19899

MAXWELL, BARBARA SUE, consultant, educator; b. Bklyn., Feb. 22, 1950; d. Vincent and Esther Alice (Hansen) M. BA in Math Edn., Rider Coll., 1972; postgrad., Montclair State U., 1973. Cert. secondary tchr., N.J. Math tchr. Westwood (N.J.) High Sch., 1973-80; programmer Prudential Ins. Co., Roseland, N.J., 1980-81; programmer, analyst Grand Union, Paramus, N.J., 1981-82; project mgr. Info. Sci., Montvale, N.J., 1982-84; cons. Five Techs., Montvale, N.J., 1985-87; cons., project mgr. Info. Sci., Inc., Montvale, N.J., 1987-90; pres. B. Maxwell Assoc., Inc., Westwood, N.J., 1990—; guest spkr. Info. Sci., Best of Am., Computer Assocs. B.A.C. Contbr. articles to profl. jours. Mem. Westwood Heritage Soc. Mem. NAFE, Human Resource Systems Profls., N.J. Info., Am. Payroll Assn. Republican. Lutheran. Office: PO Box 291 Westwood NJ 07675-0291

MAXWELL, CARLA LENA, dancer, choreographer, educator; b. Glendale, Calif., Oct. 25, 1945; d. Robert and Victoria (Carbone) M. Student, Bennington Coll., 1963-64; B.S., Juilliard Sch. Music, 1967. Mem. José Limón Dance Co., N.Y.C., 1965; prin. dancer Jose Limón Dance Co., 1969—, acting artistic dir., 1977-78, artistic dir., 1978—; lectr., tchr. in field. Soloist, Louis Falco Dance Co., 1967-71, Harkness Festival at N.Y.C. Delacorte Theater, from 1964, artist-in-residence, Gettysburg Coll., 1970, Luther Coll., Decorah, Iowa, 1971, U. Idaho, 1973, guest tchr., performer, Centre Internat. de la Danse, Vichy, France, 1976; choreographer: Function, 1970, Improvisations on a Dream, 1970, A Suite of Psalms, 1973, Homage to José Linón, Place Spirit, 1975, Aadvark Brothers; Schwartz and Columbo Present Please Don't Stone The Clowns, 1975, Blue Warrier, 1975, Sonata, 1980, Keeping Stil, Mountain, 1987; featured in Carlota, Dances For Isadora, La Malinche, Comedy, The Moor's Pavane, The Winged, There Is A Time, The Shakers, Brandenburg Concerto No. 4, Trnaslucence, Caviar, Missa Brevis, Day on Earth, Two Ecstatic Themes, A Choreographic Offering, The Exiles, Sacred Conversations; toured East and West Africa, 1969. N.Y. State Cultural Council grantee, 1971. Home: 7 Great Jones St New York NY 10012-1135 Office: Jose Limon Dance Ctr 622 Broadway Fl 5 New York NY 10012-2617

MAXWELL, CHRISTINE, publishing executive; b. Maisons Laffitte, France, Aug. 16, 1950; came to U.S., 1979; d. Robert and Elisabeth (Meynard) Maxwell; m. Roger Frank Malina; children: Xavier Jan, Yuri. BA in Latin Am. Studies and Sociology, Pitzer Coll., Claremont, Calif., 1972. Current awareness editor World Devel. Jour., Pergamon Press, Oxford, Eng., 1972-73; tchr. Shephards Hill Middle Sch., Oxford, 1974-76; editor sch. book div. A. Wheaton & Co., Exeter, Eng., 1976-78; pres. Sci./Tech. Pub. Svcs., Inc., Berkeley, Calif., 1979—; chief exec. officer Info. on Demand, Inc., Berkeley, 1982-88, pres., 1985-88; dir. mktg. Pergamon Press, Inc., N.Y.C., 1983-85; v.p., dir. internat. mktg. SRA, Chgo., 1988-89; pres. Rsch. on Demand, Inc., Berkeley, 1989—. Author: Pergamon Dictionary of Perfect Spelling, 1977, Practice Your Spelling, 1977; editor ednl. programs. Bd. dirs. Marimed Found., Honolulu, 1984—, San Francisco Vols., 1989—. Mem. LEONARDO, Internat. Soc. Arts, Sci. and Tech. (dir. mktg.), Spl. Libr. Assn. Democrat. Office: Rsch on Demand Inc 2421 4th St Ste C Berkeley CA 94710-2430*

MAXWELL, DIANA KATHLEEN, early childhood educator; b. Seminole, Okla., Dec. 16, 1949; d. William Hunter and ImoJean (Mahurin) Rivers; m. Clarence Estel Maxwell, Jly 3, 1969; children: Amanda Hunter, Alexandra Jane. BS, U. Md., 1972; M of Secondary Edn., Boston U., 1974; PhD, U. Md., 1980. Cert. tchr., counselor, Tex., Va. Tchr. Child Garden Presch., Adelphi, Md., 1969-71; tchr., dir. PREP Edn. Ctr., Heidelberg, Germany, 1972-74; tchr. N.E. Ind. Schs. Larkspur, San Antonio, 1974-77, Headstart, Boyds, Md., 1978; dir., founder First Bapt. Child Devel. Ctr., Bryan, Tex., 1982-84; asst. prof. Incarnate Word Coll., San Antonio, 1987-89; tchr. N.E. Ind. Schs. Larkspur, San Antonio, 1989-90; tchr. kindergarten Fairfax County Pub. Schs., Kings Park, Va., 1990-94; tchr. Encino Park, San Antonio, Tex., 1994—; cons. Sugar N'Spice Child Devel. Ctr., Kilgore, Tex., 1980-90; bd. dirs. Metro Area Assn. for Childhood Edn. Internat., 1992-93. Author: (book revs.) Childhood Education, 1979, 80, 92. Block chair Am. Heart Assn., Fairfax, Va., 1991, 92, Am. Diabetes Assn., Fairfax, 1992; judge speaking com. Burke Optimists, 1992, 93; Bible tchr. First Bapt. Ch., Alexandra, Va., 1992—. Named Tchr. of Yr., Larkspur Elem. Sch., 1976, 77, One of Outstanding Young Women, 1983, Md. fellow State of Md., 1978, 79; grantee San Antonio, 1990, Springfield, 1991. Mem. NEA, ASCD, Va. Edn. Assn., Internat. Reading Assn., Metro Area Assn. for Chilhood, Edn. Internat., Assn. for Childhood Edn. Internat. Home: 2027 Oak Vista San Antonio TX 78232 Office: Encino Park Elem Sch 2550 Encino Rio San Antonio TX 78259

MAXWELL, DOROTHEA BOST ANDREWS, civic worker; b. Greenville, Ill., Apr. 20, 1911; d. Samuel Washington and Viola Maud (Bost) Andrews; m. Richard Wesley Maxwell, June 1, 1935; children: Andrea Judith Maxwell Platz, Anne Dorothea Maxwell Walsh. BA with honors, diploma in piano, Greenville Coll., 1933; MusM, Northwestern U., 1937. Cert. prinary and secondary tchr., music tchr., Mo. Dir. sch. music Spring Arbor (Mich.) Jr. Coll., 1933-34; tutor orthopedic handicapped children St. Louis Pub. Schs., 1950-56. Pres. Women's Assn., 2d Presbyn. Ch., St. Louis, 1956-58; tour guide Mo. Bot. Garden, St. Louis, 1975-87; pres. The Wednesday Club St. Louis, 1983-85, archivist, 1985-92; guide tours of distinction St. Louis Symphony Soc., 1980-85. Mem. Clan Maxwell Soc. U.S.A., Mo. Hist. Soc., St. Louis Genealogy Soc., Nat. Soc. DAR (Jefferson chpt. St. Louis), Piano Club St. Louis, Washington U. Faculty women's Club, Mu Phi Epsilon. Republican. Presbyterian. Home: 901 S Skinker Blvd Saint Louis MO 63105-3242

MAXWELL, FLORENCE HINSHAW, civic worker; b. Nora, Ind., July 14, 1914; d. Asa Benton and Gertrude (Randall) Hinshaw; BA cum laude, Butler U., 1935; m. John Williamson Maxwell, June 5, 1936; children: Marilyn Maxwell Grissom, William Douglas. Coord., bd. dirs. Sight Conservation and Aid to Blind, 1962-73, nat. chmn., 1969-73; active various fund drives; chmn. jamboree, hostess coms. North Cen. High Sch., 1959, 64; Girl Scouts U.S., 1937-38, 54-56; mus. chmn. Sr. Girl Scout Regional Coun., 1956-57; scorekeeper Little League, 1955-57; bd. dirs. Nora Sch. Parents' Club, 1958-59, Eastwood Jr. High Sch. Triangle Club, 1959-62, Ind. State Symphony Soc. Women's Com., 1965-67, 76-79, Symphoguide chmn., 1976-79; vision screening Indpls. innercity pub. sch. kindergartens, pre-schs., 1962-69, also Headstart, 1967—; asst. Glaucoma screening clinics Gen. Hosp., Glendale Shopping Ctr., City County Bldg., Am. Legion Nat. Hdqrs., Ind. Health Assn. Conf., 1962-73; chmn. sight conservation and aid to blind Nat. Delta Gamma Found., Indpls., Columbus, Ohio, 1969-73; mem. telethon team Butler U. Fund, 1964; symphoguide hostess Internat. Conf. on Cities, 1971, Nat. League of Cities, 1972; mem. health adv. com. Headstart, 1976—, sec., 1980—, mem. social svcs. com., 1987—, assessment team of compliance steering com., 1978-79, 84, 86, 87, 88, 91, 92 (appreciation award 1983); founder People of Vision Aux., 1981, bd. dirs., 1981—, v.p., 1990-92, mem. coordinate vision and glaucoma screenings and office svcs.; initiated vision screening and eye safety education at Jameson Camp for Children:, 1987; trainer vision screening, 1988—. Recipient Key to City of Indpls., 1972, Those Spl. People award Women in Communication, 1980, Jefferson award for disting. pub. svc. Indpls. Star, 1991. Mem. Nat. Soc. to Prevent Blindness (now Prevent Blindness Am.), Ind. Audubon Soc., Ind. Hist. Soc., Ind. Soc. to Prevent Blindness (now Prevent Blindness Ind., dir. 1962—, exec. com. 1971—, v.p. 1983-86, sec., 1971-83, asst. sec.-treas., 1987-92), Ind. del. to nat. 3-yr. program planning conf. 1985, internal analysis task force for svcs. 1987, Sight Saving award 1974, life hon. v.p. 1983—), Jameson Camp Auxiliary, Ind. State Symphony Soc. Women's Com. (vol. Indpls. symphony orch.'s discovery concerts, vol. Indpls. noontime concerts, vol. Yuletide concerts), People of Vision, Delta Gamma (chpt. golden anniversary celebration decade and communication chmn. 1975, treas. Alpha Tau house corp. 1975-78, nat. chmn. Parent Club Study Com. 1976-77, instr. province leadership seminar workshop 1989, Cable award 1969, Outstanding Alumna award 1973, Svc. Recognition award 1977, Shield award 1981, scholarship honoree 1981, Stellar award 1986, Oxford award, 1992). Republican. Address: 1502 E 80th St Indianapolis IN 46240-2706

MAXWELL, GINGER SUE, high school counselor; b. Pearsall, Tex., May 22, 1945; m. Darrell Dee Maxwell, Aug. 1, 1969; children: David Lane, Douglas Wayne. BS in Home Econs., S.W. Tex. State U., 1968; MS in Edn., Our Lady of the Lake U., 1988. Cert. counselor. Tchr. home econs. Krueger Jr. High Sch., San Antonio, 1967-68, D'Hanis (Tex.) H.S., 1968-69; spl. edn. tchr. Westside Elem. Sch., Pearsall, Tex., 1969-70; home econs. tchr. Pearsall H.S., 1970-74, 1979-89, counselor, 1989—. Mem. ACA, Nat. Career Devel. Assn., Tex. Counseling Assn., Tex. Career Devel. Assn.

MAXWELL, JANE DENISE, paralegal; b. Astoria, N.Y., Sept. 4, 1950; d. Edward Francis and Leontime Frances (Costenoble) O'Rourke; divorced. Student, Middlesex C.C., Conn., Southampton Coll., N.Y., 1969; AA, Nassau C.C., N.Y., 1970; student, Hartford Coll. for Women, 1987-88, U. Conn., 1994. Mem. acctg. dept. car loans L.I. Trust Co., 1970; office mgr., corp. sec. SKO Inc., L.I., 1970-85; real estate agent Century 21 Real Estate, L.I., 1984; paralegal Law Office of Scott W. Jezek, 1985—. Mem. E. Haddam Land Trust, Lions Club. (sec. pres. 1994, mem. bd. dirs. 1995). Republican. Home: 156 Falls Rd Moodus CT 06469

MAXWELL, MARGARET WITMER, musician, editor; b. Irwin, Pa., Jan. 9, 1918; d. Charles Kendrick and Winona (Harrison) W.; m. Paul Russell Maxwell, Jan. 8, 1954 (dec. Oct. 1973); 1 child, James Witmer. MusB, U. Rochester, 1939; MEd, Lehigh U., 1969. cert. music tchr., Pa., Mass., N.Y. Feature writer Gannett Newspapers, Rochester, N.Y., 1945-52; staff mem. Fred Waring Enterprises, Delaware Water Gap, Pa., 1952-55; editor Mus. Jour., N.Y.C., 1953-56; tchr. music, English various pub. schs., Stroudsburg, Pa., Cape Cod, Mass. and Rochester, N.Y., 1956-76, ret., 1976; organist, choir dir. various chs., Pa., N.Y., Mass., N.J. and Fla., 1940—. Contbr. numerous articles to mags., newspapers. Mem. Am. Guild Organists, Sigma Alpha Iota (nat. editor, nat. exec. bd. 1979—). Republican. Presbyterian. Home: 1809 Beneva Ct Apt 602 Sarasota FL 34232-2142

MAXWELL, MARILYN CARTER PACE, human services director; b. Sheffield, Ala., Apr. 18, 1946; d. John Albert and Martha Wilson (Carter) Pace; m. William French Maxwell, Jan. 6, 1986. BS, U. Ala., 1968; MSW, U. N.C., 1972. ACSW; cert. specialist in aging U. Mich. Gerontology Inst. Social worker Tenn. Dept. Pub. Welfare, Memphis, 1968-70; asst. prof. Clinch Valley Coll. of U. Va., Wise, 1972-74; gerontology planner Dilenowisco Ednl. Coop., Norton, Va., 1974-75; exec. dir. Mountain Empire Older Citizens, Inc., Area Agy. on Aging, Big Stone Gap, Va., 1975—; mem. Govs. Alzheimers Commn., Va., 1987-93; mem. exec. com. S.W. Va. Health Systems Agy., Roanoke, 1988-94; vice chair Oxbow Human Svcs. Consortium, St. Paul, Va., 1989—; mem. Va. Health Planning Bd., Va., 1992-94; mem. Lenowisco Health Dist. Adv. Bd., 1988—; v.p. Va. Assn. Area Agencies on Aging; mem. Svc. Delivery Area-One, Inc. pvt. industry coun., 1995—. Vol. coach for high sch. girls basketball; chair Lenowisco Long-Term Care Coordinating Coun., 1982—; mem. bd., public policy chair Alzheimer's Assn. Local Chpt., pres. 1986-90; mem. Blue Ridge Inst. for So. Community Svc. Execs., Black Mountain, N.C., 1988—, Wisc/Norton Friends of the Libr., Ctrl. Highlands Appalachian Leadership Initiative on Cancer; del. White House Conf. Aging, 1995. Named to Honorable Order of Ky. Cols., 1994. Mem. AAUW, LWV, NASW, Poor Farm Soc., U. N.C. Alumni Assn., Knights of Okra (bd. 1978—). Methodist. Home: 900 Ridge Ave Box 796 Norton VA 24273 Office: Mountain Empire Older Citizens PO Box 888 Big Stone Gap VA 24219

MAXWELL, MELISSA FAYE, business owner; b. Pensacola, Fla., Sept. 19, 1939; d. James Crawford and Zadie Magdalene (Wise) Maxwell. Grad. high sch. Founder, owner Carburetor World, Inc., Miami, Fla., 1973—. Author: Gas Mileage for the Serious Tinkerer, 1982; patents and blueprints twenty known carburetors claiming 50-200 MPGs; inventor in field of carburetors. Benefactor various youth orgns., 1976—; mem. coun. Carburetor World Rehab. for Troubled Youths, Miami, 1976-80. Home and Office: PO Box 13482 Las Vegas NV 89112-1482

MAXWELL, PATRICIA ANNE, writer; b. Winn Parish, La., Mar. 9, 1942; d. John Henry and Daisy Annette (Durbin) Ponder; m. Jerry Ronald Maxwell, Aug. 1, 1957; children: Jerry Ronald Jr., Richard Dale, Delinda Anne, Katherine Leigh. GED, 1960. Author (as Patricia Maxwell): Secret of Mirror House, 1970, Stranger At Plantation Inn, 1971, The Bewitching Grace, 1974, Notorious Angel, 1977, Night of the Candles, 1978, numerous others; (as Elizabeth Trehearne): Storm At Midnight, 1973; (as Patricia Ponder); Haven of Fear, 1977, Murder For Charity, 1977; (as Maxine Patrick): The Abducted Heart, 1979, numerous others; (as Jennifer Blake): Love's Wild Desire, 1977, Golden Fancy, 1980, Embrace and Conquer, 1981, Royal Seduction, 1983, others. Recipient Hist. Romance Author of Yr. award Romantic Times Mag., 1985. Mem. Nat. League Am. Penwomen, Romance Writers of Am. (charter) (Golden Treasure award 1987). Home: PO Box 9218 Quitman LA 71268-9218

MAXWELL, RUTH ELAINE, artist, interior designer, decorative painter; b. Cleve., Oct. 7, 1934; d. Norman Lee and Katherine Ellen (Hamilton) Brown; m. Clarence LeRoy Maxwell, June 25, 1955; children: Lisa Maxwell Callahan, Lynne Maxwell Quinn, Laura Maxwell Jochem, James. BFA, Ohio State U., 1956, teaching cert., 1956. Cert. elem. sch. tchr., Ohio. Tchr. Hilliard (Ohio) Elem. Sch., 1956-58; comptr. Callahan Family Golf Ctr., Hilliard, 1989—. Pres. Capa Colleagues, Ohio Theatre, Columbus, 1986; pres., governing bd. Theatre Shop, 1988; vol. Columbus Assn. Performing Arts Colleagues, 1981—; mem. Hilliard Arts Coun., 1989-91; vocalist Damenchor of Columbus Maennerchor, 1975—, treas., 1979-81, fin. sec., 1991-94; sec. Canterbury Unit Columbus Symphony Orch. Women's Assn., 1993—; mem. Women's Guild of Opera, Columbus, 1994—. Mem. Gamma Alpha Chi (hon., sec. Ohio State U. chpt. 1954), Gamma Phi Beta. Republican.

MAXWELL, SARA ELIZABETH, psychology educator, speech & language pathologist; b. DuQuoin, Ill., Jan. 23; d. Jean A. (Patterson) Green; m. David Lowell Maxwell, Dec. 27, 1960 (div. Mar. 1990); children: Lisa Marina, David Scott. BS, So. Ill. U., 1963, MS, 1964, MSEd, 1965; MEd, Boston Coll., 1982, PhD, 1992. Cert. and lic. speech./lang. pathologist, early childhood specialist, guidance counselor, sch. adjustment counselor, EMT. Clin. supr. Clin. Ctr. So. Ill. U., Carbondale, 1964-65, grad. instr. Campus Sch., 1965-66; speech/lang. pathologist Westwood (Mass.) Pub. Schs., 1967-93; grad. faculty Emerson Coll., Boston, 1979-81; cons. Mass. Dept. Mental Health, Boston, 1979-82; grad. clin. supr. Robbins Speech/Hearing Ctr., Emerson Coll., Boston, 1979-82; cons. Westwood Nursery Preschs., 1986-93; devel. and clin. psychologist S. Shore Mental Health Ctr., Hingham and Quincy, Mass., 1989-93; emergency svcs. S. Shore Mental Health Ctr., Quincy, Mass., 1990-93; pvt. practice Twin Oaks Clin. Assocs., Westwood, Mass, 1986-88, S. Coast Counseling Assocs., Quincy, 1990-93; cons. local collaboratives and preschs., Westwood, 1980-93; profl. worshops presenter Head Start, 1980—; predoctoral intern in clin psycology S. Shore Mental Heatlh Ctr., Quincy, 1985-86; program specialist Broward County (Fla.) Schs., 1993—; adj. faculty sch. of psychology Nova Southeastern U., 1995—; presenter Head Start, ASHA, CEC, APSC, and other profl., nat. and state confs., 1980-93. Contbr. articles to profl. jours., chpts. to textbooks. Mem. adv. coun. Westwood Bd. Health, 1977-80; emergency med. technician Westwood Pub. Schs. Athletic Dept., 1981. Vocat. Rehab. fellow So. Ill. U., 1964; scholar Perry County, Ill., 1959-64, Gloria Credi Meml. scholar So. Ill. U., 1964. Mem. Am. Speech & Hearing Assn. (nat. schs. com., nat. chairperson pub. sch. caucus 1985-87), Am. Psychol. Assn., Assn. Psychiat. Svcs. for Children, Coun. Exceptional Children, Internat. Assn. of Logopedics, Boston Coll. Alumni Assn., Harvard Club. Episcopalian. Office: Nova Southeastern U 3301 College Ave Fort Lauderdale FL 33314-7721

MAXWELL-BROGDON, FLORENCE MORENCY, school administrator, educational adviser; b. Spring Park, Minn., Nov. 11, 1929; d. William Frederick and Florence Ruth (LaBrie) Maxwell; m. John Carl Brogdon, Mar. 13, 1957; children: Carole Alexandra, Cecily Ann, Daphne Diana. B.A., Calif. State U., L.A., 1955; MS, U. So. Calif., 1957; postgrad. Columbia Pacific U., San Rafael, Calif., 1982-86. Cert. tchr., Calif. Dir. Rodeo Sch., L.A., 1961-64; lectr. Media Features, Culver City, Calif., 1964—; dir. La Playa Sch., Culver City, 1968-75; founding dir. Venture Sch., Culver City, 1974—, also chmn. bd.; bd. dirs., v.p. Parent Coop. Preschools, Baie d'Urfe Que., Can., 1964—; del. to Ednl. Symposium, Moscow-St. Petersburg, 1992,

U.S./China Joint Conf. on Edn., Beijing, 1992, Internat. Confedn. of Prins., Geneva, 1993, Internat. Conf., Berlin, 1994. Author: Let Me Tell You, 1973; Wet'n Squishy, 1973; Balancing Act, 1977; (as Morency Maxwell) Framed in Silver, 1985; (column) What Parents Want to Know, 1961—; editor: Calif. Preschooler, 1961-74; contbr. articles to profl. jours. Treas. Democrat Congl. Primary, Culver City, 1972. Mem. Calif. Council Parent Schs. (bd. dirs. 1961-74), Parent Coop. Preschools Internat. (advisor 1975—), Pen Ctr. USA West, Mystery Writers of Am. (affiliate), Internat. Platform Assn., Nat. Assn. Secondary Sch. Prins., Libertarian. Home: 10814 Molony Rd Culver City CA 90230-5451 Office: Venture Sch 5333 Sepulveda Blvd Culver City CA 90230-5215

MAY, ANNE MARIE, accountant; b. N.Y.C., Nov. 22, 1955; d. Edward James and Elizabeth Rose (McGrory) Logue; m. John Paul May, Aug. 2, 1980; 1 child, Jacob Paul. BS in Acctg., West Chester (Pa.) U., 1983. CPA, Pa. Inventory control Lonza, Inc., Fair Lawn, N.J., 1975-79; budget analyst Givaudan Corp., Clifton, N.J., 1979-80; acct. Gen. Rehab. Svcs., Villanova, Pa., 1980-82; audit and acctg. mgr. Stiteler, Douglas & Clarke Ltd., West Chester, 1984-90; assoc. Douglas & Assocs., West Chester, 1991-92; owner Anne Marie May, CPA, Gettysburg, Pa., 1993—. Mem. AICPA, Pa. Inst. CPAs, Inst. Mgmt. Accts. (pres. 1990-91), Exch. Club of Exton, Pa. (pres. 1992-93), Exch. Club of Gettysburg, Pa. Roman Catholic. Home: 766 Goldenville Rd Gettysburg PA 17325-0051

MAY, AVIVA RABINOWITZ, music educator, linguist, musician; b. Tel Aviv; naturalized, 1958; d. Samuel and Paula Pessia (Gordon) Rabinowitz; (divorced); children: Chelley Mosoff, Alan May, Risa McPherson, Ellanna May/Gassman. AA Oakton Community Coll., 1977; BA in Piano Pedagogy, Northeastern Ill. U., 1978. Folksinger, educator, musician Aviva May Studio/Piano and Guitar, 1948—; Sunday sch. dir. Canton (Ohio) Synagogue, 1952-54; nursery sch. tchr. Allentown (Pa.) Jewish Community Ctr., 1954-56; Hebrew, music tchr. Brith Shalom Community Ctr., Bethlehem, Pa., 1954-62; Hebrew tchr. Beth Hillel Congregation, Wilmette, Ill., 1964-83, Beth Emet Congregation, Evanston, Ill., 1964-83; tchr. B'nai Mitzva, 1973; tchr., music dir. McCormick Health Ctrs., Chgo., 1978-79, Cove Sch. Perceptually Handicapped Children, Chgo., 1978-79; prof. Hebrew and Yiddish, Spertus Coll. Judaica, Chgo., 1980-89; Hebrew tchr. Anshe Emet Day Sch, 1989—, West Suburban Temple Har Zion, Oak Park, Ill, 1993—; music studio tchr. Cosmopolitan Sch., Chgo., 1992—; tchr. continuing edn. Northeastern Ill. U., 1978-80, Niles Twp. Jewish Congregation, 1993—, also Jewish Community Ctrs.; with Office Spl. Investigations, Dept. Justice, Washington; music dir. Temple Emanuel Rosenwald Sch. Composer classical music for piano, choral work, folk songs; developer 8-hour system for learning piano or guitar; contbr. articles to profl. jours. Recipient Magen David Adom Pub. Service award, 1973; grantee Ill. State, 1975-79, Ill. Congressman Woody Bowman, 1978-79. Mem. Music Tchrs. Nat. Assn. (cofounder), North Shore Music Tchrs. Assn. (charter mem., sec.), Ill. Music Tchrs. Assn., Organ and Piano Tchrs. Assn., Am. Coll. Musicians, Ill. Assn. Learning Disabilities, Sherwood Sch. Music, Friends of Holocaust Survivers, Nat. Yiddish Book Exchange, Nat. Ctr. for Jewish Films, Chgo. Jewish Hist. Soc., Oakton Community Coll. Alumni Assn., Northeastern Ill. U. Alumni Assn. Democrat. Office: Aviva May Studio 410 S Michigan Ave Ste 527 Chicago IL 60605-1401

MAY, ELEANOR GODDARD, retired business administration educator; b. Groton, Mass., Sept. 26, 1925; d. Robert Morse and Virginia Ames (Woods) M. BS in Math. magna cum laude, Tufts Coll., 1947; postgrad., Am. U., 1966-68; MBA in Mktg., George Wash. U., 1971. Actuarial trainee group annuity dept. John Hancock Mut. Life Ins. Co., Boston, 1947-48; mem. staff Bur. Bus. Rsch. Harvard U. Grad. Sch. Bus. Adminstrn., Boston, 1948-51, asst. exec. sec., 1951-55, asst. and assoc. staff rschr., 1955-62; asst. dir., then dir. rsch. Woodward & Lothrop, Inc., Washington, 1962-70; lectr., then asst. prof. bus. adminstrn. U. Va. Darden Grad. Sch. Bus. Adminstrn., Charlottesville, 1970-74, assoc. prof., 1974-78, prof., 1978-90, prof. emerita, 1990—, dir. Bus. Studies Ctr., Tayloe Murphy Inst., 1970-86; staff cons. Menswear Retailers Am., 1970-72; faculty assoc. Mgmt. Analysis Ctr., Inc., 1979-86; cons. Main Street Project, Nat. Trust for Hist. Preservation, 1985-90; rschr. Mktg. Sci. Inst., 1970-85; presenter in field, 1972—; mem. adv. com. Retail Rsch. Inst., 1964-65, dir., 1966-70; mem. retail store stats. subcom. Retail Bur., Met. Washington Bd. Trade, 1964-66; expert witness various law firms; cons. to various retail cos. Mem. editorial bd. Jour. Retailing, 1979—, Jour. Mktg. Channels, 1989—; contbr. articles to profl. jours. Founding mem. bd. dirs. Cmty. Meals on Wheels, Charlottesville, 1978-88; bd. dirs. Adventure Bound Sch., Charlottesville, 1986-93, pres., 1990-93; bd. dirs. Elk Hill Farm, Goochland, Va., 1992—. Mem. Am. Collegiate Retailing Assn., Acad. Mktg. Sci., Ret. Faculty Assn. (bd. dirs., v.p. 1992—), Colonial Dames Am. (bd. dirs., treas. 1993—), Contemporary Club (bd. dirs. 1994—), Sigma Pi Sigma. Unitarian. Home: Mayfield North Garden VA 22959

MAY, GITA, French language and literature educator; b. Brussels, Sept. 16, 1929; came to U.S., 1947, naturalized, 1950; d. Albert and Blima (Sieradska) Jochimek; m. Irving May, Dec. 21, 1947. BA magna cum laude, CUNY-Hunter Coll., 1953; MA, Columbia U., 1954, PhD, 1957. Lectr. French CUNY-Hunter Coll., 1953-56; instr. Columbia U., 1956-58, asst. prof., 1958-61, assoc. prof., 1961-68, prof., 1968—, chmn., 1983-93, mem. senate, 1979-83, 86-88, chmn. Seminar on 18th Century Culture, 1986-89; lecture tour English univs., 1965. Author: Diderot et Baudelaire, critiques d'art, 1957, De Jean-Jacques Rousseau à Madame Roland: essai sur la sensibilité préromantique et révolutionnaire, 1964, Madame Roland and the Age of Revolution, 1970 (Van Amringe Disting. Book award), Stendhal and the Age of Napoleon, 1977; co-editor: Diderot Studies III, 1961; mem. editorial bd. 18th Century Studies, 1975-78, French Rev., 1975-86, Romanic Rev., 1959—; contbg. editor: Oeuvres complètes de Diderot, 1984; gen. editor: The Age of Revolution and Romanticism: Interdisciplinary Studies, 1990—; contbr. articles and revs. to profl. jours. Decorated chevalier and officier Ordre des Palmes Acad.; recipient award Am. Coun. Learned Socs., 1961, award for outstanding achievement CUNY-Hunter Coll., 1963; Fulbright rsch. grantee, 1964-65; Guggenheim fellow, 1964-65, NEH fellow, 1971-72. Mem. AAUP, MLA (del. assembly 1973-75, mem. com. rsch. activities 1975-78, mem. exec. coun. 1980-83), Am. Assn. Tchrs. of French, Am. Soc. 18th Century Studies (pres. 1985-86, 2nd v.p. 1983-84, 1st v.p. 1984-85), Soc. Française d'Etude du Dix-Huitième Siècle, Am. Soc. French Acad. Palms, Phi Beta Kappa. Home: 404 W 116th St New York NY 10027-7202

MAY, JAYNE E., hydrologist; b. Connersville, Ind., Dec. 10, 1954; d. Carl Eldon and Ruth Virginia (Werking) M. BA in Zoology, Ind. U., 1977; postgrad., U. Minn., St. Paul, 1977-79. Hydrologist water resources divsn. U.S. Geol. Survey, Nashville, 1979-83; hydrologist U.S. Geol. Survey, Trenton, N.J., 1983-88; hydrologist, database adminstr. U.S. Geol. Survey, Oklahoma City, 1988-95; chief hydrologic surveilance sect. U.S. Geol. Survey, Iowa City, 1995—; mem. ctrl. region groundwater data base policy com. U.S. Geol. Survey, Reston, Va., 1992-93, Nat. Water Info. Sys.-II tester, instr., 1993—. Author: Feasibility of Artificial Recharge...Atlantic City, 1985. Big sister Buddies Nashville, 1980-83; mem. chorus bd. Oklahoma City Chorus, Sweet Adelines, 1990-94; mem. regional bd. region 25 Sweet Adelines, Inc., Tulsa, 1993—; pres. bd. So. Hills Christian Ch., Edmond, Okla., 1993. Mem. Am. Water Resources Assn., Nat. Ground Water Assn. Office: US Geol Survey WRD 400 S Clinton St Rm 269 Iowa City IA 52240

MAY, JUDITH ANN, anesthesiologist; b. Milw., Oct. 28, 1958; d. Patrick and Patricia (Roets) May; m. Paul S. Pagel, Sept. 14, 1987. BS in Biology magna cum laude, Carroll Coll., 1981; MD, Med. Coll. Wis., 1985. Diplomate Am. Bd. Anesthesiology. Intern Med. Coll. Wis., Milw., 1985-86, resident, 1986-89, asst. prof. dept. anesthesiology, 1989-91; staff anesthesiologist Columbia Hosp., Milw., 1991—. Mem. AMA, Am. Soc. Anesthesiologists, Internat. Anesthesia Rsch. Soc., Soc. Cardiovascular Anesthesiologists, Am. Med. Women's Assn., State Med. Soc. Wis. Roman Catholic. Home: 13365 Nicolet Ave Elmgrove WI 53122

MAY, LINDA KAREN CARDIFF, safety engineer, nurse; b. San Mateo, Calif., Oct. 26, 1948; d. Leon Davis and Jane Vivian (Gallow) Cardiff; m. Donald William May, Dec. 7, 1969 (div. Feb. 1988); children: Charles David, Andrew William. Student in nursing So. Ill. U., 1969, Ill Wesleyan U., 1989; AAS, Parkland Coll., 1977; BS in Pub. Health and Safety Engring. with honors, U. Ill., Urbana, 1987; RN, BSN, Lakeview Coll., 1990. RN, Ill., Ind., Mo., N.Mex., Tex., Wis.; registered profl. nurse; nat. registered EMT, Ill.; accredited instr. constrn. safety and health, OSHA. Indsl. nurse C.S. Johnson Co., Champaign, Ill., 1978-79; safety dir. Solo Cup Co., Urbana, Ill., 1979-84; safety engr. Clinton Nuclear Power Plant, Ill. Power Co., 1984-86, occupational safety and health specialist Danville Vet.'s Med. Ctr., 1986—; with LKM Health and Safety Cons., Inc., Champaign, Ill. Mem. Champaign County Crime Prevention Coun., 1978-83, bd. dirs., 1980-82; active Champaign County Task Force on Arson, 1981—, Mercy Hosp. Aux., Covenant Hosp Auxiliary, 1977—. Ill. State Gen. Assembly scholar, 1967. Mem. AACN, APHA (mem. occupational health and safety sect.), Am. Soc. Safety Engrs. (vice chair Ctrl. Ill. sect. 1985-86), Am. Nuclear Soc. (mem. biology and medicine divsn., mem. radiopharm. and isotope product stds. com.), Am. Assn. Occupational Health Nurses, Nat. Registery EMT, Ill. Environ. Health Assn., Ill. Soc. Pub. Health Educators, Associated Ill. Milk, Food and Environ. Sanitarians, Pre-Hosp. Care Providers Ill., Ill. EMTs Assn., N.Y. Acad. Sci, U. Ill. Alumni Assn. (life), Parkland Coll. Almuni Assn. (life, bd. dirs. 1987—, v.p. 1992—), Parkland Coll. Found. Bd. (alumni assn. liason bd. dirs. 1993), Ill. Wesleyan U. Alumni Assn., Lakeview Coll. Nursing Alumni Assn., Eta Sigma Gamma. Methodist. Home: PO Box 3954 Champaign IL 61826-3954

MAY, MARGRETHE, allied health educator; b. Tucson, Ariz., Oct. 6, 1943; d. Robert A. and Margrethe (Holm) M. BS in Human Biology, U. Mich., 1970, MS in Anatomy, 1986. Cert. surg. technologist. Surg. technologist Hartford (Conn.) Hosp., 1965-68, U. Mich. Hosps., Ann Arbor, 1968-70; asst. operating room supr. U. Ariz. Med. Ctr., Tucson, 1971-72; coord. operating room tech. program Pima Coll., Tucson, 1971-76; prof., coord. surg. tech. and surg. first asst. programs Delta Coll., University Center, Mich., 1978—; commr. Commn. on Accreditation of Allied Health Ednl. Programs, Chgo., 1994—, Coun. Accreditation and Unit Recognition, 1994—. Editor: Core Curriculum for Surgical Technology, 3d edit., 1990, Core Curriculum for Surgical First Assisting, 1993; contbr. articles to profl. jours. Mem. Assn. Surg. Technologists (bd. dirs. 1987-89, pres.-elect 1989-90, pres. 1990-91, on-site visitor program accreditation 1974—, chmn. exam writing com. 1981, liaison coun. on cert. co-chmn. 1977, chmn. 1978, sec.-treas. 1979, chmn. accreditation review com for edn. in surg. tech. 1994—), Am. Soc. Law, Medicine and Ethics, Mich. Assn. Allied Health Professions (sec. 1994—), Nat. Network Health Career Programs in Two-Year Colls. Home: 2506 Abbott Rd Apt P-2 Midland MI 48642 Office: Delta Coll University Center MI 48710

MAY, MAUREEN SEXTON, search consultant, chemistry educator, drug development researcher; b. London, Feb. 15, 1938; came to U.S., 1959; d. Daniel Christopher and Elsie Jane (Watson) Sexton; m. John Walter May, July 11, 1964; children: Vivian Margot, Beverly Wynne. BA with honors, Trinity Coll., Dublin, Ireland, 1959; MS, Cornell U., 1961, PhD, 1969. Sci. libr. Oxford (Eng.) U., 1961-63; pharmacology fellow U. Rochester, N.Y., 1979-82; adj. prof. chemistry Rochester Inst. Tech., 1986-92, St. John Fisher Coll., Rochester, 1990. Contbr. articles to Jour. Molecular Biology, Jour. Bacteriology, Jour. Clin. Pharmacology and Therapeutics. Recipient postgrad. travel award Trinity Coll., Dublin, 1960; named Ednl. Found. honoree AAUW, 1983. Mem. AAAS, AAUW (pres. Rochester 1985-87), Am. Chem. Soc. Home: 44 Southwood Ln Rochester NY 14618-4020

MAY, MONIKA MARIA, artist, entrepreneur; b. Hillesheim, Germany, Jan. 27, 1964; arrived in U.S., 1964; d. Franz and Katharina May. BA in English, BA in Edn., U. Colo., 1987; postgrad., Santa Rosa Jr. Coll., 1990-92, U. Hawaii, 1993. Tchr. Boulder (Colo.) Valley Pub. Schs., 1987-88; store mgr. Heartwood Inst., Garberville, Calif., 1988-89; co-owner Infinitee Designs, Middletown, Calif., 1989-92; catalog prodn. dir. Garden of Gods Trading Post, Colorado Springs, Colo., 1994; owner, mgr. Vertu eARTh, Colorado Springs, 1994—. Photographer various musicians including The Grateful Dead, Gregg Allman, Steve Miller, members of Moby Grape, Santana, Journey, Huey Lewis & The News, Bunny Wailer; prodr. Telluride Daily Planet. Active Artists Helping Artists, Middletown, 1989-92. Recipient young people's artist award Colorado Springs Fine Arts Ctr., 1976, Kodak Prof. Network award, 1994. Mem. NAFE, Calif. Lawyers for the Artist (working artist mem.). Home: PO Box 1121 Telluride CO 81435

MAY, PHYLLIS JEAN, financial executive; b. Flint, Mich., May 31, 1932; d. Bert A. and Alice C. (Rushton) Irvine; m. John May, Apr. 24, 1971. Grad. Dorsey Sch. Bus., 1957; cert. Internat. Corr. Schs., 1959, Nat. Tax Inst., 1978; MBA, Mich. U., 1970. Registered real estate agt; lic. life, auto and home ins. agent. Office mgr. Comml. Constrn. Co., Flint, 1962-68; bus. mgr. new and used car dealership, Flint, 1968-70; contr. various corps., Flint, 1970-75; fiscal dir. Rubicon Odyssey Inc., Detroit, 1976-87, Wayne County Treas.'s Office, 1987-93; exec. fin. officer Grosse Pointe Meml. Ch., 1993—; acad. cons. acctg. Detroit Inst. Commerce, 1980-81; pres. small bus. specializing in adminstrv. cons. and acctg., 1982—; supr. mobile svc. sta., upholstery and home improvement businesses; owner retail bus. Pieces and Things. Pres. PTA Westwood Heights Schs., 1972; vol. Fedn. of Blind, 1974-76, Probate Ct., 1974-76; mem. citizens adv. bd. Northville Regional Psychiat. Hosp., 1988, sec. 1989-90. Recipient Meritorious Svc. award Genesee County for Youth, 1976, Excellent Performance and High Achievement award Odyssey Inc., 1981. Mem. NAFE (bd. dirs.), Am. Bus. Women's Assn. (treas. 1981, rec. sec. 1982, v.p. 1982-83, Woman of Yr. 1982), Womens Assn. Dearborn Orch. Soc., Dearborn Community Art Ctr., Mich. Mental Health Assn., Internat. Platform Assn., Pi Omicron (officer 1984-85). Baptist.

MAY, VICKI ANN WEBB, county treasurer; b. Springfield, Mo., Dec. 24, 1959; d. John Cargile and Doris Janell (Hickman) Webb; m. Terry Lynn May, Nov. 4, 1977; 1 child, Taressa Lynne. BS in Fin., So. Mo. State U., 1990. Clk. ext. svc. County of Stone, Galena, Mo., 1978-82, treas., 1983—. Mem. Stone County Steering Com., Galena, 1993. Mem. Mo. County Treas. Assn. (pres. 1985-87), Cystic Fibrosis Mo., Bus. and Profl. Women (historian 1988-94, v.p. 1988-90, pres. 1992-94, Young Careerists award 1985), Stone County Rep. Women. Presbyterian. Office: County of Stone Courthouse PO Box 207 Galena MO 65656-0207

MAYDEN, BARBARA MENDEL, lawyer; b. Chattanooga, Sept. 18, 1951; d. Eugene Lester Mendel and Blanche (Krugman) Rosenberg; m. Martin Ted Mayden, Sept. 14, 1986. AB, Ind. U., 1973; JD, U. Ga., 1976. Bar: Ga. 1976, N.Y. 1980. Assoc. King & Spalding, Atlanta, 1976-79, Willkie Farr & Gallagher, N.Y.C., 1980, Morgan Lewis & Bockius, N.Y.C., 1980-82, White & Case, N.Y.C., 1982-89; spl. counsel Skadden, Arps, Slate, Meagher & Flom, N.Y.C., 1989—. Mem. U. Ga. Bd. Visitors, Athens, 1986-89. Fellow Am. Bar Found. (life); mem. ABA (chairperson young lawyers div. 1985-86, house of dels. 1986—, commr. commn. on women 1987-91, commr. commn. opportunities for minorities in profession 1986-87, chmn. assembly resolutions com. 1990-91, select com. of the house 1989-91, membership com of the house 1991-92, bd. govs. 1991-94, chair bd. govs. ops. com., exec. com. 1993-94, mem. task force long range fin. planning 1993—), Nat. Assn. Bond Lawyers (bd. dirs. 1985-86), Bond Attys.' Workshop (chmn. 1986), N.Y. State Bar Assn. (mem. ho. of dels. 1993—), Assn. of Bar of City of N.Y. (internat. human rights com. 1986-89, 2d century com. 1986-90, com. women in the profession, 1989-92), N.Y. County Lawyers Assn. (com. spl. projects, chair com. rels with other bars). Democrat. Jewish. Home: 465 West End Ave New York NY 10024-4926 Office: Skadden Arps Slate Meagher & Flom 919 3d Ave 43d Fl New York NY 10022*

MAYEKAWA, MARY MARGARET, education counselor; b. Neptune, N.J., Nov. 13, 1941; d. Willis Gilbert and Thelma Anita Virginia (Anderson) Bills; m. Jackie Toshio Mayekawa, Nov. 28, 1970; 1 child, Leland Willis Magokichi. BA, Western Ky. U., 1965; postgrad., U. Va., 1966-68; MEd in Counseling, Coll. of William and Mary, 1971. Educator Fairfax County Schs., Annandale, Va., 1965-68; project transition counselor U.S. Army, Ft. Hood, Tex., 1971-73; student officer wives liason U.S. Army Transp. Sch., Ft. Eustis, Va., 1980-83; guidance counselor U.S. Army Japan IX Corp, Japan, 1983-87, 2nd Infantry Divsn., Korea, 1987-89, USAF, Reese AFB, Tex., 1989—. Vol. Edn. Divsn. Tex. Tech. Mus., Lubbock, 1990—, mem. women's coun., 1990—; vestry Episcopal Ch., Okinawa and Sagamihara City, Japan, 1974, 76, 84-86; counselor Camp Blue Yonder, Reese AFB, Tex., 1989—. Capt. U.S. Army, 1968-71. Mem. Am. Counselor Assn., Mil. Educator Counselor Assn., Tex. Assn. for Counseling and Devel., Tex. Career Guidance Assn. Home: PO Box 434 Reese AFB TX 79489-0001

MAYER, ELIZABETH BILLMIRE, educational administrator; B.Ed., Nat. Coll. Edn., Evanston, Ill., 1953; M.A. in Liberal Studies, Wesleyan U., 1979. Teaching asst. Hull House, Chgo., 1950-51; teaching scholar Nat. Coll. Edn. Demonstration Sch., 1952-53; pre-sch. tchr. St. Matthew's Sch., Pacific Palisades, Calif., 1959-63, tchr. 2d grade, 1963-67; librarian Chandler Sch., Pasadena, Calif., 1971-72, tchr. 4th grade, 1972-80, curriculum coordinator 1st-8th grades, 1979-80; tchr. 4th-6th grades Inst. for Experimentation in Tchr. Edn., SUNY-Cortland, 1980; asst. prof. edn. SUNY-Cortland, 1980-82; founder, headmistress The Mayer Sch., Ithaca, N.Y., 1982-92, Ariz. State U., Tempe, 1992—, Coll. Edn., 1992-94, faculty liaison Acad. Affairs, 1994—. Mem. Nat. Council Tchrs. Math., Nat. Council Tchrs. English, Nat. Sci. Tchrs. Assn., Rotary Internat. (mem. bd. dirs. 1994—), Phi Delta Kappa (officer 1980-81, 92—). Office: Ariz State U MS 3N21 Box 870101 Tempe AZ 85287

MAYER, KAY MAGNOR, writer; b. Chgo.; d. Frank J. and Harriet (Schnell) Magnor; m. Kenneth W. Mayer, May 2, 1943; children: Michael J., Patricia A., Mark T. Student Northwestern U., 1938-43. News reporter Tampa Times, 1943; advt. copywriter Marshall Field & Co., Chgo., Earle Ludgin & Co., Chgo., Henri, Hurst & McDonald, Chgo., 1944-58; spl. editor, writer Scott, Foresman & Co., Glenview, Ill., 1966-71; freelance writer Ariz. Hwys., Southwest Art, Am. Artist, Am. Way, Columbia, 1971—. Recipient Press Women's awards, 1983, 84, 85, 89, 92, 93. Mem. Nat. Fedn. Press Women, Ariz. Press Women, Nat. Council Social Studies, Western History Assn., Soc. Southwestern Authors (dir. 1981-83), The Writers. Home: 1855 Tanglewood Dr Apt C Glenview IL 60025-1629

MAYER, MARGERY WEIL, publishing executive; b. Beaufort, S.C., Feb. 11, 1952; d. Warren Burke Weil and Elise Jean (Schiff) Rubel; m. Theodore Van Huysen Mayer, Dec. 28, 1975; children: Lily, Henry. BA, Middlebury Coll., 1974; MS, MIT, 1976. Planning analyst Digital Equipment Corp., Maynard, Mass., 1976-77; editor-in-chief sch. pub. sect. Holt, Rinehart & Winston, N.Y.C., 1977-87; pres. Ginn div. Silver, Burdett & Ginn, Needham, Mass., 1987-90; exec. v.p. Scholastic Inc., N.Y.C., 1990—. Editor Sloan Mgmt. Rev., 1975-76. Trustee program Read With Me, Dedham, Mass., 1989; mem. rev. panel U.S. Dept. Edn. Sch. Recognition Program. Mem. Phi Beta Kappa. Office: Scholastic Inc 555 Broadway New York NY 10012-9511*

MAYER, MARILYN GOODER, steel company executive; b. Chgo.; d. Seth MacDonald and Jean (McMullen) Gooder; m. William Anthony Mayer, Nov. 14, 1959; children—William Anthony Jr., Robert MacDonald. grad. Career Inst. Chgo., 1941; student Lake Forest Coll., Ill., 1942. Adminstrv. asst. Needham, Louis & Brorby, Chgo., 1949-53; v.p. RMB Corp., Chgo., 1963-71, Mayer Motors, Ft. Lauderdale, Fla., 1965-74, Gooder-Henrichsen, Chicago Heights, Ill., 1975—; dir. Barnett Bank, West Palm Beach, Fla. Trustee Gulf Stream (Fla.) Sch., St. Andrew's Sch., Boca Raton, Fla.; bd. dirs. Bethesda Hosp. Assn., Boynton Beach, Fla., pres. 1981-82; bd. dirs. Gulf Stream Civic Assn. Mem. Soc. Four Arts. Republican. Episcopalian. Clubs: Little, Gulf Stream Bath and Tennis. Avocation: travel. Home: 2925 Polo Dr Delray Beach FL 33483-7331

MAYER, PATRICIA JAYNE, financial officer, management accountant; b. Chgo., Apr. 27, 1950; d. Arthur and Ruth (Greenberger) Hersh; m. William A. Mayer Jr., Apr. 30, 1971. AA, Diablo Valley Coll., 1970; BSBA, Calif. State U., Hayward, 1975. Cert. mgmt. acct. Staff acct., auditor Elmer Fox Westheimer and Co., Oakland, Calif., 1976; supervising auditor Auditor's Office County of Alameda, Oakland, 1976-78; asst. acctg. mgr. CBS Retail Stores doing bus. as Pacific Stereo, Emeryville, Calif., 1978-79; contr. Oakland Unified Sch. Dist., 1979-84; v.p. fin., chief fin. officer YMCA, San Francisco, 1984—; instr. acctg. to staff YMCA, San Francisco, 1984—, CBS Retail Stores, 1978-79. Draft counselor Mt. Diablo Peace Ctr., Walnut Creek, Calif., 1970-72; dep. registrar of voters Contra Costa County Registrar's Office, Martinez, Calif., 1972-77. Mem. Fin. Execs. Inst. (San Francisco chpt.), Inst. Mgmt. Accts., Dalmatian Club No. Calif., Dalmatian Club Am. Democrat. Jewish. Home: 2395 Lake Meadow Cir Martinez CA 94553-5475 Office: YMCA of San Francisco 44 Montgomery St Ste 770 San Francisco CA 94104

MAYER, PATRICIA LYNN SORCI, mental health nurse, educator; b. Chgo., July 22, 1942; d. Ben and Adonia (Grenier) Sorci; 1 child, Christopher David Mayer. AGS with high honors, Pima Community Coll., Tucson, 1983; BSN with honors, U. Ariz., 1986, MS in Nursing, 1987. RN, Ariz.; cert. addictions counselor, chem. dependency therapist; lic. pvt. pilot. Nurse educator Tucson. Contbr. articles to profl. jours. Mem. Nat. Nurses Soc. on Addictions, Phi Kappa Phi, Sigma Theta Tau, Pi Lambda Theta, Golden Key.

MAYER, VERA, information services executive; b. Budapest, July 5, 1927; d. Joseph and Marguerite (Guttman) Strasser; m. Klaus Mayer, May 6, 1950; children: Rulon R., Carla Mayer Glasser. Student, U. Geneva, 1947, U. Zurich, Switzerland, 1948, U. Budapest Pazamany Peter Law, 1946; MS in Libr. Sci. Journalism, Columbia U., 1965. Reporter gen. assignment "Kis Ujsag" Hungarian Daily, Budapest, 1945-46; reporter N.Y. Times, Geneva, 1947-50; rsch. project leader Brought Up Children Meml. Sloan-Kettering, N.Y.C., 1951-65; rsch. asst. N.Y. Hosp., N.Y.C., 1965-68; mgr. records admissions, archivist, dir. inf. and archives, v.p. info. svcs. NBC, N.Y.C., 1968—; advisor Soros Found., N.Y.C.; judge Internat. Festival, Montreux, Switzerland, South Africa. Editor (newspaper) Fieldston Bulletin. Advisor Sutton Community Bd., N.Y.C.; chmn. Forum Com., Riverdale, N.Y.; assoc. chmn. Hungarian Peasant Youth Orgn. Scholar U. Geneva, 1947, U. Zurich, 1948, Pazamany Peter Law U. Budapest, Hungary. Mem. Am. Women Radio and TV Soc., Spl. Libr. Assn., Am. Records Mgmt. Assn., Hungarian-Am. Studies Assn. Office: Nat Broadcasting Co 30 Rockefeller Plz New York NY 10112-0001*

MAYER, WENDY WIVIOTT, special education educator; b. Madison, Wis., Aug. 25, 1962; dd. Wilbert W. and Matilda (Silbar) W. BS in Edn., Drake U., 1984; MS in Spl. Edn., U. Wis., Milw., 1990. Tchr. exceptional ednl. needs-emotionally disturbed and learning disabilities Mequon (Wis.)-Thiensville Sch. Dist., 1985—. Mem. Coun. for Exceptional Children, Orton Dyslexia Soc.

MAYERNICK, GLENDA GAY, nurse; b. Pensacola, Fla., July 1, 1943; d. Buren Winford and Alice Estelle (Folsom) Burgess; m. Arthur Michael Mayernick, Apr. 10, 1938; children: Ruth Marie, Arthur Michael II, Amanda Gay. RN, Bapt. Hosp. Sch. Nursing, Nashville, 1964; postgrad., U. Tenn., Nashville, 1988-91. RN, Tenn., cert. infection control nurse. Surg. nurse Bapt. Hosp., Nashville, 1964-65; surg. nurse, ICU nurse Nashville Meml. Hosp., Madison, Tenn., 1965, 69-70; surg. nurse Bapt. Hosp., Pensacola, Fla., 1970; emergency rm. nurse Nashville Meml. Hosp., Madison, 1973-76, infection control nurse, 1976—. Choir mem., substitute tchr. First Bapt. Ch., Hendersonville, Tenn., 1987—. Mem. Assn. Practitioners Infection Control and Epidemiology. Republican. Office: Nashville Meml Hosp 612 W Due West Ave Madison TN 37115-4402

MAYERSOHN, NETTIE, state legislator; m. Ronald Mayersohn; children: Jeffrey, Lee. BA, Queens Coll., 1978. Exec. dir. N.Y. State Crime Victims Bd.; mem. N.Y. State Assembly, 1982—, chairperson assembly ho. ops. com. and subcom. elderly crime victims, vice chair legis. women's caucus, mem. various coms.; dist. leader 27th N.Y. State Assembly Dist.-Part A, 1972—. Past mem. Cmty. Bd. # 8, former chairperson youth com.; past chairperson Pomonok Cmty. Ctr.; founder, organizer Pomonok Neighborhood Ctr., Inc.; active Electchester Jewish Ctr., Israel Ctr. of Hillcrest Manor; N.Y. state del. Internat. Women's Conf., 1977; bd. dirs. Harry Van Arsdale, Jr. Meml. Assn. Recipient Builders of Brotherhood award Nat. Conf. Christians and Jews, 1977, Legislator of Yr. award N.Y. State chpt. NOW, 1989. Mem. Stevenson Regular Dem. Club, Inc. (exec. mem.), Alpha Sigma Lambda. Home: 67-11 Parsons Blvd Queens NY 11365 Office: NY State Assembly State Capitol Albany NY 12224*

MAYERSON, SANDRA ELAINE, lawyer; b. Dayton, Ohio, Feb. 8, 1952; d. Manuel David and Florence Louise (Tepper) M.; m. Scott Burns, May 29, 1977 (div. Oct. 1978). BA cum laude, Yale U., 1973; JD, Northwestern U., 1976. Bar: Ill. 1976, U.S. Ct. Appeals (7th cir.) 1976, U.S. Dist. Ct. (no.

dist.) Ill. 1977, U.S. Dist. Ct. Md. 1989. Assoc. gen. counsel JMB Realty Corp., Chgo., 1979-80; assoc. Chatz, Sugarman, Abrams et al, Chgo., 1980-81; ptnr. Pollack, Mayerson & Berman, Chgo., 1981-83; dep. gen. counsel AM Internat., Inc., Chgo., 1983-85; ptnr. Kirkland & Ellis, Chgo., 1985-87; ptnr., chmn. bankruptcy group Kelley Drye & Warren, N.Y.C., 1987-93; ptnr., chmn. N.Y. bankruptcy group McDermott, Will & Emery, N.Y.C., 1993—. Bd. dirs. Jr. Med. Rsch. Inst. coun. Michael Reese Hosp., Chgo., 1981-86; mem. met. div. Jewish Guild for Blind, 1990-92; mem. nat. legal afffairs com. Anti-Defamation League, 1990—. Fellow Branford Coll., Yale U., 1993—. Mem. ABA (bus. bankruptcy com. 1976—, sec. 1990—), Ill. State Bar Assn. (governing council corp. and securities sect. 1983-86), Chgo. Bar Assn. (current events chmn. corp. sect. 1980-81), 7th Cir. Bar Assn. Democrat. Jewish. Clubs: Yale (N.Y.C.), Metropolitan (Chgo.). Office: McDermott Will & Emery 1211 Ave of the Americas New York NY 10036*

MAYES, ILA LAVERNE, minister; b. Eldorado, Okla., Dec. 23, 1934; d. Thomas Floyd and Irene Elizabeth (Buchanan) Jordan; m. Forrest Clay Mayes, July 2, 1954; children: Barbara, Marian, Cynthia, Janice. BA, U. Tex., 1973; MSW, U. Mich., 1976; MDiv, Austin Presbyn. Sem., 1986. Ordained to ministry Presbyn. Ch. (U.S.A.), 1986; cert. social worker. Pastor First Presbyn. Ch., Childress, Tex., 1986—; med./social worker Tex. Dept. Health, Childress, 1994—; mem. Austin Sem. Alumni Bd., 1991-94, Synod of the Sun Evangelism Com., Denton, 1990-93, Transition Coordinating Agy., 1991—. Chmn. ARC, Childress, 1990; bd. dirs. Am. Cancer Soc., Childress, 1988-89. Mem. AAUW, Mortarboard, Rotary Internat., Alpha Chi, Alpha Lambda Delta. Home: 309 Avenue B SE Childress TX 79201 Office: First Presbyn Ch 311 Commerce St Childress TX 79201-4525 also: Tex Dept Health 811 Commerce Childress TX 79201

MAYES, MAUREEN DAVIDICA, physician, educator; b. Phila., Oct. 16, 1945; d. David M. and Marguerite Cecilia (Fineran) M.; m. Charles William Houser, Dec. 18, 1976; children: David Steven, Edward Charles. BA, Coll. Notre Dame, 1967; MD, Ea. Va. Med. Sch., 1976; MA in Pub. Health, U. Mich., Ann Arbor, 1994. Resident in internal medicine Cleve. Clinic Found., 1977-79, fellow in rheumatology, 1979-81; asst. prof. medicine W.Va. U., Morgantown, 1981-85; asst. prof. medicine Wayne State U., Detroit, 1985-90, assoc. prof. medicine, 1990—; bd. dirs. United Scleroderma Found., Watsonville, Calif., 1986—; dir. scleroderma unit Wayne State U., Detroit, 1991—. Contbr. articles to profl. jours. Pres. bd. United Scleroderma Found., 1988-89. NIH fellow, 1993-94. Fellow Am. Coll. Rheumatology, Am. Coll. Physicians; mem. Am. Fedn. Clin. Rsch., Mich. Rheumatism Soc. Office: Wayne State U Hutzel Hsp 4707 St Antoine St Detroit MI 48201-1498

MAYFIELD, PATRICIA DIANNE, former community college program director; b. West Palm Beach, Fla., Jan. 22, 1945; d. Ralph Lewis and Bessie Evon (Miller) Maxwell; m. E.N. Mayfield Jr., May 17, 1968; children: Earl N. III, Galen M. Student, La. State U., 1963-65; AS, Yuba Coll., 1981. Registered radiol. tech. X-ray tech. Pearl City, Hawaii, 1982-84, Wainae (Hawaii) Med. Ctr., 1983-85, Midlands Community Hosp., Papillion, Nebr., 1985-89, Bergan Mercy Hosp., Omaha, 1985-87, Primus, Papillion, 1988-89; program dir. Indian Hills C.C., Ottumwa, Iowa, 1989-94. Den mother, com. mem. Cub Scouts, Boy Scouts Am., Milanli, Hawaii, Omaha, 1983-88; active Mothers Against Drunk Driving, Omaha, 1986-89. Home: 813 Queen Anne Ottumwa IA 52501-4821

MAYFIELD-KOCH, LORI JAYNE, insurance processor; b. Newport Beach, Calif., Sept. 11, 1955; d. John Vincent and Marilyn Jane (Huish) M. Student Linn-Benton Community Coll., 1973-75, N.W. Coll., 1975-76; AA in Gen. Edn. Saddleback Community Coll., 1993. Gen. ins. cert. Ins. Inst. Am. Cashier Auto Club So. Calif., Anaheim, 1977-80, ins. clk., sec., Fullerton, 1980-81, ins. rep., 1981, field coord., Costa Mesa, Calif., 1981-86; auto. club sales rep., 1986-88; pres. LJM Enterprises; customer svc. rep. Roadway Express, Irvine, Calif., 1989-93; ins. processor Prudential Ins., Laguna Hills, Calif., 1993—. Recipient Outstanding Citizenship award YMCA, Santa Ana, Calif., 1984. Mem. NAFE. Office: Prudential Fin Svcs 24036 Ave De La Carlotta 570 Laguna Hills CA 92653

MAYGINNES, BARBARA ANN, chemicals executive; b. Portland, Oreg., Mar. 20, 1945; d. John Wesley and Marion Josephine (Hill) Clausen; children: Shamaz, Hukam, Mardana. Bachelor's, Underwood Coll. for Women, 1968; MA, Portland State U., 1972. Owner Shamaz Trading Co., Ukiah, Calif., 1974-77; mgr. small bus. dept. Ernst & Ernst, Portland, 1977-78; CFO All Heart Lumber Co., Ukiah, 1978-83; CEO, CFO Performance Coatings, Inc., Ukiah, 1983-84. Active Leadership Mendocino. Mem. Nat. Paint & Coatings Assn., Golden State Paint & Coatings Assn., Ukiah C. of C. (mem. econ. devel. com.), Women in Coatings (Leadership award 1994). Office: Performance Coatings Inc 360 Lake Mendocino Dr Ukiah CA 95482

MAYHAND, EDNA LEWIS, health facility administrator; b. Darlington, S.C., Oct. 11, 1938; d. Edward Hires and Ellen (Dargan) Lewis; m. Ernest A. Mayhand, June 6, 1968 (div. Oct. 1994); 1 child, E. Kambarage. Student, Barnard Coll., 1956-59; BA, Simmons Coll., 1966; MSW, Calif. State U., Fresno, 1968; MPH, UCLA, 1971. Cons. Office of the Prime Min.-UN/FAO, Dar es Salaam, Tanzania, 1971-76; dep. dir. YWCA of San Francisco, 1976-78, Calif. Dept. Consumer Affairs, Sacramento, 1978-83; dir., coord. U. Calif., San Francisco, 1986-90; mgr. Med. Ctr. U. Calif. Davis, Sacramento, 1990—; pres., CEO Mayhand and Assocs., San Francisco, 1979-86. Author: Where I've Been and Where You're Going, 1994; contbr. articles to profl. jours. Bd. dirs. Local Artists for Charity Events, chair, 1989—; pres. North Area Improvement Coalition, 1990—, bd. dirs.; chair, pub. mem. Calif. Bd. Barber Examiners, 1984-92; pub. mem. state licensing Calif. Bd. Registered Nurses, 1976-78. Recipient numerous awards Rotary, Elks, and Literacy orgns., scholarship Delta Sigma Theta, 1956; fellow Children's Welfare Fund, 1966. Mem. Nat. Forum for Black Pub. Adminstrs. Office: U Calif Davis 2315 Stockton Blvd Sacramento CA 95817-2201

MAYHEW, JOSEPHINE, state legislator; b. Italy, Aug. 17, 1924. Student, NYU. Mem. N.H. Ho. Reps., mem. children, youth and juvenile justice com., mem. legis. adminstrn. com. Bd. dir. Upper Conn. Valley Mental Health Svc.; leader Girl Scouts; leader Brownies. Democrat. Roman Catholic. Home: 3 State St Groveton NH 03582-1409 Office: NH Ho Reps State Capitol Concord NH 03301*

MAYNARD, BARBARA HAHN, educator; b. North Tonawanda, N.Y., June 8, 1939; d. Norman John and Mary Margaret (Miller) Hahn; divorced; 1 child, Wendy Gray Maynard. AB, U. Miami, 1967; MEd, Temple U., 1978. English tchr. Parkway Program, Phila., 1972-73; dean of students Franklin Learning Ctr., Phila., 1979-82, English tchr., 1973-82; dir. writing lab. Manatee Com. Coll., Bradenton, Fla., 1983-86; English tchr. Miami Northwestern High, 1986—. Author: Poetry Anthology, 1990, 93. Active NOW, 1990-93. Named Most Valuable Tchr., MNW Valedictorians, Dade County Sch. Sys., 1989, 93. Mem. Nat. Coun. Tchrs. Eng., Dade County Coun. Tchrs. of Eng. Democrat. Home: Royal Oaks Apt 212 447 NE 195 St Miami FL 33179

MAYNARD, GLADYS WILCOCK, artist; b. Norwich, Conn., Aug. 2, 1926; d. Roland and Dorothy M. (Heibel) Wilcock; m. William Maynard, Sept. 16, 1950. Grad., Norwich Art Sch., 1944, Sch. of Mus. of Fine Arts, Boston, 1948. 1st asst. tchr. graphic arts Sch. of Mus. of Fine Arts, Boston, 1948-50; tchr. art Cambridge (Mass.) Ctr. for Adult Edn., 1949-59; tchr. art New Eng. Sch. of Art and Design, Boston, 1955-70, chairperson, coord. fine arts, 1967-70; tchr. art Boston Mus. Fine Arts, 1970-71; mem. faculty art Chamberlayne Jr. Coll., Boston, 1970-80, chairperson fine arts dept., 1977-80; originator, dir. Cronin Gallery, Casa Del Sol tutoring program; pvt. tutor Maynard Studio. Exhbns. include Boston Mus. Fine Arts, Lib. of Congress, Washington, Chgo. Art Inst., Phila. Art Mus., Whitney Mus., N.Y.C., Shore Studio Galleries, Boston and Provincetown, Provincetown Art Assn., many others; works in permanent collections at U. Miami, Oxford, Ohio, Bibliotheque Nationale, Paris, and many pvt. collections; designer Boston Printmakers seal. Mem. Nat. Fedn. Women's Clubs, Provincetown Art Assn., Boston Printmakers (charter). Home: 72A Commercial St Provincetown MA 02657-1924

MAYNARD, JOAN, education educator; b. Louisa, Ky., Oct. 18, 1932; d. Macon Scott and Jeanette (Thompson) Chambers; m. Frank Maynard Jr., June 15, 1951 (dec. Oct. 1988); children: Mark Steven, Julia Beth Maynard McFann, Robert Blake. BA, Wittenberg U., 1977; MEd, Wright State U., 1980, Wright State U., 1984. Tchr., reading specialist Mechanicsburg (Ohio) Exempted Village Schs., 1976—; pres. TOTT Publs. Inc., Bellbrook, Ohio, 1988—; rep. Career Edn., Mechanicsburg, 1981-88, mem. Thompson Grant Com., Mechanicsburg, 1987-88. Author: Mud Puddles, 1988, Mud Pies, 1989. Vol. Mechanicsburg Schs. Levy, 1980, 82, 88, Congl. Race, Campaign County, Ohio, 1982, 84, 86; cons. Urbana U., Ohio, 1988-90, 91, 92, 93; tutor Laubach Lit. Action, Urbana, 1989-90, 91-93, 94. Recipient Thompson grant, 1982, 88, 92. Mem. AAUW (edn. chmn. Champaign County chpt. 1988-89, treas. 1989-90), Internat. Reading Assn., Champaign County Reading Coun. (treas. 1990-91), Midwestern Assembly Lit. Young People (treas. 1989-93), Kappa Delta Pi. Home: 1546 Parkview Rd Mechanicsburg OH 43044-9779 Office: Exempted Village Schs 60 High St Mechanicsburg OH 43044-1098

MAYNARD, KATHERINE KEARNEY, English language educator; b. Kittanning, Pa., July 16, 1953; d. Robert Ewing and Vera Isobel (Edwards) Kearney; m. Michael Scott Maynard, May 27, 1984; children: Heather Dawn, Jarod Paul Kearney. BS in English, SUNY, Brockport, 1977; MA, U. Rochester, 1979, PhD, 1984. Asst. prof. I Rider U., Lawrenceville, N.J., 1988-89, asst. prof. II, 1989-92, assoc. prof. English, 1992—. Author: Thomas Hardy's Tragic Poetry: The Lyrics and the Dynasts, 1991, Men and Women at Work, 1994, (libretto) The Band of Five in the Cave of Testing, 1994; contbr. articles to scholarly jours. Recipient Award for Disting. Teaching Lindback Found., 1992. Mem. MLA, Nat. Coun. Tchrs. English, Internat. Soc. for Study of European Ideas. Office: Rider U 2083 Lawrenceville Rd Lawrenceville NJ 08648

MAYNARD, MICHELINE ANN, journalist, writer; b. Ann Arbor, Mich., Aug. 5, 1957; d. Frank Henry and Bernice Genevieve Maynard. BA in Humanities, Mich. State U., 1979; MA in Journalism, Columbia U., 1990. Assoc. editor U.S. News & World Report, Washington, 1984-86; sr. bus. writer Newsday, N.Y.C., 1986-88; bur. chief Reuters News Svc., Detroit, 1988-90; bus. journalist USA Today, Arlington, Va., 1990—. Knight-Bagehot fellow Columbia U., 1990. Mem. Washington Automotive Press Assn. (1st v.p. 1991-93), Habitat for Humanity, Washington Performing Arts Soc., Folger Shakespeare Theater Guild, Jr. League. Office: USA Today 1000 Wilson Blvd Arlington VA 22209-3991

MAYNARD, NANCY GRAY, biological oceanographer; b. Middleboro, Mass., Apr. 18, 1941; d. Thomas LaSalle and Clara (Gray) M.; m. Conrad Dennis Gebelein, Jan., 1969 (div. 1977); 1 child, Jennifer Lynn. BS, Mary Washington Coll., 1963; MS, U. Miami (Fla.), 1968, PhD, 1974. Rsch. assoc. Bermuda Biol. Sta., Ferry Reach, 1972-75; rsch. fellow Lamont-Doherty Geol. Obs. Columbia U. (CLIMAP), 1972-75; post-doctoral fellow Div. Engring., Applied Physics Harvard U., Cambridge, Mass., 1975-76; field coord. environ. studies Alaska Outer Continental Shelf Office U.S. Dept. Interior, Anchorage, 1976-78; with oil spills sci. support Nat. Oceanic and Atmospheric Adminstrn., Alaska and S.E. U.S., 1978-81; policy analyst Exec. Office Pres. U.S. Office Sci. and Technology Policy, Washington, 1982-83; fellow Dept. of Commerce Sci. and Tech., 1982-83; staff dir. Bd. Ocean Sci. and Policy NAS, Washington, 1983-85; resident rsch. assoc. Nat. Rsch. Coun. Scripps Instn. Oceanography and Jet Propulsion Lab NASA, 1985-87; br. head Oceans and Ice Br. Goddard Space Flight Ctr. NASA, Greenbelt, Md., 1987-88, assoc. chief rsch. Lab. for Oceans, 1988-89; asst. dir. for environment Exec. Office of Pres. Office Sci. and Tech. Policy, Washington, 1989-93; dep. dir. sci. div. NASA Mission to Planet Earth HQ, Washington, 1993—. Contbr. numerous articles profl. jours. Recipient Pub. Svc. Commendation USCG, 1979. Mem. AAAS, Assn. Women in Sci., The Oceanography Soc., Am. Geophys. Union, Women's Aquatic Network (bd. dirs.), Corp. Bermuda Biol. Sta. Rsch. Office: NASA Mission Planet Earth Sci Divsn 300 E St SW/Code YS Washington DC 20546

MAYNARD, REBECCA, economics educator; b. Dover-Foxcroft, Maine, Sept. 1, 1949. BA in Econs., U. Conn., 1971; PhD in Econs., U. Wis., 1975. Inst. for Rsch. on Poverty, U. Wis., Madison, 1973-74; V.p., sr. economist Mathematica Policy Rsch., Inc., Princeton, N.J., 1974-86, sr. v.p., dir. Princeton Rsch., 1986-92, sr. fellow, 1993—, also bd. dirs.; trustee prof. edn. U. Pa., Phila., 1993—; cons. GAO, 1987—, Rockefeller Found., 1984-89; strategic advisor Quality 2000 Initiative, 1993—; panel on Econs. of Ednl. Reform and Teaching, 1990—; adv. bd. Job Opportunities and Basic Skills Tng. (JOBS) Program Implementation Study, 1990—; adv. panel Nat. Household Edn. Survey, Adult Edn. Component; adv. team Inter-generational Literacy Rsch. Action Project, 1989-90; mem. Panel on Econs. of Ednl. Reform, 1992-94. Contbr. articles to profl. jours. Mem. NAS (mem. panel on quality control of student fin. aid programs 1991-93, mem. panel on child care policy 1987-89), Com. on Econ. Devel. (mem. adv. panel on child care policy 1991-92, mem. rsch. adv. panel 1994—), Bus. Tomorrow (leader policy conf. 1989), Phi Beta Kappa. Office: U Pa Grad Sch of Edn 3700 Walnut St Philadelphia PA 19104-6216

MAYNARD, VIRGINIA MADDEN, charitable organization executive; b. New London, Conn., Jan. 29, 1924; d. Raymond and Edna Sarah (Madden) Maynard; B.S., U. Conn., 1945; postgrad. Am. Inst. Banking, 1964-66, Cornell U., 1975. With Nat. City Bank (now Citibank), N.Y.C., 1954-79, asst. cashier, 1965-69, asst. v.p., 1969-74, v.p. internat. banking group, 1974-76, comptroller's div., 1976-79; v.p. First Women's Bank, N.Y.C., 1979-80; Internat. Fedn. Univ. Women rep. UN, 1982—; cons. in field. Trustee fellowships endowment fund AAUW Ednl. Found., Washington, 1977-80, Va. Gildersleeve Internat. Fund Univ. Women, Inc. (pres., 1987-93, dir. 1994—). Mem. AAUW (fin. chmn. N.Y.C. br. 1976-79, bylaws chmn. 1979-83, adminstr. Meml. Fund 1983-92, dir., 1992-94, Woman of Achievement 1976). Republican. Congregationalist. Home: 601 E 20th St New York NY 10010-7622

MAYNE, DIANE See MUELLER, DIANE MAYNE

MAYO, JOAN BRADLEY, microbiologist, epidemiologist; b. Ada, Okla., Oct. 24, 1942; d. Samuel S. and Norene (Parker) Bradley; m. Harry D. Mayo III, Sept. 30, 1967. BA, Drake U., 1964; MS in Microbiology, NYU, 1978; MBA in Mgmt., Fairleigh Dickinson U., 1989. Technologist clin. labs. St. John's Episc. Hosp., Bklyn., 1964-66; supr. Med. Tech. Sch. Bklyn.-Cumberland Med. Ctr., 1966-71; clin. instr., technologist SUNY Downstate Med. Ctr., Bklyn., 1970-73; supr. bacteriology lab. Meml. Sloan-Kettering Cancer Ctr., N.Y.C., 1973-82, mgr. microbiology labs., 1982-87; dir. infection control svc. N.Y.C. Health and Hosp. Corp./Harlem Hosp. Ctr., 1987—; mem. com. for prevention of bloodborne diseases N.Y.C. Health and Hosp. Corp., 1990—. Contbr. articles to profl. publs. Active Friends of Harlem Hosp., 1988—, North Bergen (N.J.) Action Group, 1987—. Mem. Am. Soc. Microbiology, Am. Pub. Health Assn., Assn. Practitioners in Infection Control, Delta Mu Delta, Alpha Kappa Alpha. Home: 7855 Boulevard E North Bergen NJ 07047-5938 Office: NYC Health/Hosp Corp Harlem Hosp Ctr 506 Lenox Ave New York NY 10037-1802

MAYO, KELLY ZALEWSKI, community health nursing educator; b. Raleigh, N.C., Sept. 29, 1946; d. Edward and Louise (Upchurch) Zalewski; m. Thomas Malon Mayo, Dec. 23, 1966 (div. 1981); children: Thomas Clayton, Jonathan Edward; m. Phil Hugh Dunn, July 8, 1989. BS, Boston Coll., 1977; MS, Boston U., 1979; PhD, U. Tex., 1990. RN, S.C. Staff nurse Rex Hosp., Raleigh, 1967-70; family planning nurse North Shore Regional Family Planning, Danvers, Mass., 1971-73; dir. counseling Planned Parenthood League Mass., Newton, 1973-75; instr. Northeastern U., Boston, 1979-85; rsch. and teaching asst. U. Tex., Austin, 1986-89; asst. prof. Med. U. of S.C., Charleston, 1990—; cons. Project Rap, Beverly, Mass., 1978, Laboure Ctr. Vis. Nurses Assn., South Boston, Mass., 1980; vis. nurse Boston Vis. Nurses Assn., 1982-85, Vis. Nurses Assn. of North Shore, Danvers, 1983-85. Manuscript reviewer: Qualitative Health Rsch. Jour., State College, Pa., 1992—; reviewer: Am. Nurses Found., Washington, 1993; contbr. articles to profl. jours. Mem. Mayor's Coun. on Homelessness, Charleston, 1990-93, Sea Island Health Care Corp. Planning Com., Johns Island, S.C., 1992—. Program dir./grantee for nurse clinic for homeless Divsn. Nursing, Health Resources Adminstrn., Pub. Health Svcs., HHS, 1990-93. Mem. APHA, Soc. for Applied Anthropology, So. Nursing Rsch. Soc. (reviewer 1992, 94), Sigma Theta Tau (com. chair 1991-93). Democrat. Home: 1442 N Edgewater Dr Charleston SC 29407-7613 Office: Med Univ SC College Nursing 171 Ashley Ave Charleston SC 29425-0001

MAYO, PAMELA ELIZABETH, fine arts appraiser; b. Richmond, Va., June 18, 1959; d. Robert Bowers and Margaret (Thomas) M. BFA, Longwood Coll., Farmville, Va., 1981. V.p. Gallery Mayo, Inc., Richmond, Va., 1981—. Author: Lue Osborne and Cordray Simmons, 1980, Doris Spiegel, 1992, Oscar D. Soellner, 1994; editor: America: The Sporting View, 1985. Mem. Internat. Soc. Appraisers (chmn. fine arts com., pres. Old Dominion chpt., bd. councillors). United Methodist.

MAYO HOBBS, ANN THERESA, environmental specialist; b. San Francisco, Mar. 25, 1961; d. James Joseph and Alice Theresa (Watterson) Mayo; m. Douglas Harland Hobbs, Sept. 6, 1986. AA, City Coll., San Francisco, 1982; BS, U. Calif., Berkeley, 1984. Air pollution specialist Sacramento County, Sacramento, 1987, No. Sierra Air Quality Mgmt. Dist., Grass Valley, Calif., 1987-92; air pollution specialist/planner Placer County, Auburn, Calif., 1992—. Mem. AAUW (pres. Auburn br. 1993-95), Bus. and Profl. Women (sec. No. Mines orgn. 1992-93, Young Careerist award 1993). Home: 12453 Willow Valley Rd Nevada City CA 95959-9484

MAYR, LINDA HART, internal medicine nurse; b. Orange, Tex., July 15, 1951; d. Richard Gail and Gwendolyn (Condrey) Hart; m. Julius Charles Mayr, Nov. 20, 1987; children: Christopher Feazel, Keith Feazel, Kimberly Feazel, Christina Duke, Thomas Mayr. Diploma, North Harris County Coll., Houston, 1980. Newborn nursery and neonatal ICU nurse Houston N.W. Med. Ctr., 1980-81, 1982-84; pvt. nurse Frederick Hill, D.O., Houston, 1981-82; nurse FM 1960 Pediatric Ctr., Houston, 1984-85; nurse ob-gyn. Steven Zarzour, M.D., Houston, 1985-86; office mgr. Bert Williams, D.C., Houston, 1986-87; office nurse Ronald E. Sims, M.D., Houston, 1987—; allied health profl. Meth. Hosp., Houston, 1987—. Mem. Am. Assn. Office Nurses, Assn. Nurses AIDS Care, The Care Group, Inc. (profl. adv. com.). Home: 206 E Oak St Deer Park TX 77536-4104

MAYROSE, MONA PEARL, critical care nurse, educator; b. Levittown, N.J., Nov. 3, 1961; d. William Joseph and Sarah (Tanne) Tillis; m. Alan Gary Mayrose, Nov. 1, 1987; 1 child, Kattey; stepchildren: Dale, Brian. BA, NYU, 1982; MSN, Pace U., 1986. Cert. critical care nurse, trauma nurse, staff devel. nurse; instr. ACLS. Nursery nurse No. Westchester Hosp. Ctr., Mt. Kisco, N.Y., 1987-88; ICU nurse Meth. Hosp., Houston, 1988-89; dir. nursing Golden Age and Winslow Nursing Homes, Houston, 1989; hospice case mgr. Vis. Nurse Assn., Houston, 1989-91; critical care charge nurse Woodlands (Tex.) Meml. Hosp., 1990-92; commd. 1st lt. USAF, 1992, advanced through grades to capt., 1992; charge nurse surg. ICU 59th Med. Wing USAF, Lackland AFB, Tex., 1992-94, critical care educator, 1994—. Mem. AACN, NNSDO, AFA, Sigma Theta Tau. Jewish. Home: 6115 Ridgebrook St San Antonio TX 78250-4022

MAYS, CAROL JEAN, state legislator; b. Independence, Mo., July 16, 1933; m. Ronald H. Mays; children: Terri, Melanie, Hugh. Student, Baker U. State rep., chmn. consumer protection edn. appropriations com., mem. transp., ways & means & comm. coms. Mo. Ho. of Reps., Jefferson City; restaurant owner. Mem. Mo. Restaurant Assn., Independence C. of C., Fairmount Comml. Club, Alpha Chi Omega. Democrat. Methodist. Home: 3603 S Hedges Ave Independence MO 64052-1167 Office: Mo Ho of Reps State Capital Jefferson City MO 65101*

MAYS, JANICE ANN, lawyer; b. Waycross, Ga., Nov. 21, 1951; d. William H. and Jean (Bagley) M. AB (hon.), Wesleyan Coll., Macon, Ga., 1973; JD, U. Ga., 1975; LLM in Taxation, U. Georgetown, 1980. Bar: Ga. 1976. Tax counsel com. on ways and means U.S. Ho. Reps., Washington, 1975-88, chief tax counsel com. on ways and means, staff dir. subcom. select revenue measures, 1988-93, chief counsel, staff dir. com. on ways and means, 1993-95, minority chief counsel, staff dir. com. on ways and means, 1995—. Mem. Tax Coalition (past chair). Office: Ways and Means Com 1102 Longworth Ofc Bldg Washington DC 20515

MAYSILLES, ELIZABETH, speech professional, educator; b. Sleepy Creek, W.Va.; d. Evers and Rose (Scott) M. AB, W.Va. U.; MA, Hunter Coll., 1963; PhD, NYU, 1980. Announcer Radio Sta. WAJR, Morgantown, W.Va.; broadcaster Radio Sta. WGHF-FM, Rural Radio Network, N.Y.C.; group leader GMAC, N.Y.C.; instr. NYU, N.Y.C.; adj. prof. speech communication Pace U., N.Y.C.; exec. adminstr. Am.-Scottish Found., N.Y.C.; adminstrv. asst. Brit. Schs. and Univs. Found., Inc.; cons. to hosps. and acctg., 1971—; lectr. seminars in field, travel Eng. and Scotland. Counselor Help Line, N.Y.C., 1971-75. Recipient Disting. Svc. award NYU Grad. Orgn., 1970, 71. Mem. Internat. Platform Assn. (bd. govs. 1980—), N.Y. Acad. Scis., Speech Comm. Assn., Ctr. for Study of Presidency, English-Speaking Union, Caledonian Club N.Y. Home: 155 E 77th St Apt 6-F New York NY 10021 Office: Pace U 41 Pace Plz New York NY 10038-1508

MAZUR, MARJORIE AKERS, retired librarian; b. Glasgow, Ky., Jan. 5, 1927; d. George Homer and Mamie Alice (Goff) Akers; m. John Henry Mazur, Oct. 28, 1954 (dec.); children: John Daniel, Frances Susan, Mary Alice Mazur Juarez. BA, U. Ky., 1948; BS in Libr. Sci., U. N.C., 1951. Cert. libr., Ky., S.C. Cataloger U. Ky., Lexington, 1951-54; asst. head tech. processes W. Va. U., Morgantown, 1955-58; head tech. svcs. Cleveland Heights (Ohio)-University Heights Pub. Libr., 1958-59; cataloger Cleve. Pub. Libr., 1960-66, asst head catalog dept., 1966-70, head catalog dept., 1970-78; dir. tech. svcs. S.C. State Libr., Columbia, 1978-92; instr. cataloging Case-Western Res. U., Cleve., 1963, 65; advisor for libr. sci. curriculum Cuyahoga Community Coll., Cleve., 1971-75. Mem. ALA, S.C. Libr. Assn., S.C. State Employees Assn. Baptist. Home: 6651 Formosa Dr Columbia SC 29206-1150

MAZUR, STELLA MARY, former organization administrator; b. Lowell, Mass.; d. Stanley and Katherine (Cichowicz) M.; BS in Edn., U. Mass., Lowell; student ARC Mgmt. Tng. Sch., 1962, Nat. Tng. Lab. for Applied Behavioral Sci., 1963. USO club dir., Windsor Locks, Conn., 1942; gen. field rep. ARC, 1944, mgr., Waltham, Mass., 1944-79. Spl. assignment State Dept. USIA Graphic Arts Cultural Exchange Program, Eastern Europe, Poland, 1965. Mem. pres. cir. U. Mass., Lowell, also mem. centennial planning com. Recipient Waltham Rotary Club spl. citation, 1952; Waltham Community 25 Year Service award, 1969; Recognition award Waltham chpt. ARC, 1971; Outstanding Woman, Waltham News Tribune, 1974; Woman of Today, Waltham Bus. and Profl. Women's Club, 1976; Outstanding Service award ARC New Eng., 1979; Disting. Alumni award U. Mass., Lowell, 1979. Mem. Internat. Platform Assn., ARC Retiree Assn., Am. Assn. Ret. Persons, Smithsonian Assos., Lowell U. Alumni Assn. (hon. life). Seton Guild Lowell, Lowell Hist. Soc., Lowell Mus. Corp. Clubs: Vesper Country (Tyngsboro, Mass.); Longmeadow Golf, Country. Author, pub.: Roots and Heritage of Polish People in Lowell, 1976. Home: 170 Andover St Lowell MA 01852-2360

MAZZA, BARBARA BOLAND, elementary school guidance counselor; b. Newberry, S.C., Sept. 19, 1955; d. James Andrew and Ivey Lee (Reynolds) Boland; m. Michael Joseph Mazza, Apr. 11, 1987. BA, Winthrop U., 1976; MBA, The Citadel, 1980, MEd, 1991. Cert. tchr. middle and secondary social studies, guidance counselor elem. and secondary schs., Lion's Quest Internat. educator. Tchr. Berkeley County schs., Moncks Corner, S.C., 1977-90, summer sch. tchr., 1980, 91; elementary sch. guidance counselor Charleston County Schs., Charleston Heights, S.C., 1991—; mem. student recognition com. PTA, Mary Ford Elem. Sch., 1991—, mem. staff morale com., mem. cultural diversity com., mem. emphasis com. Mem. PTA, Sedgefield Mid. Sch., Goose Creek, S.C., 1977-90, "Just Say No" Club, Goose Creek, 1983-90. Grantee for drug edn. club, 1991—, grantee for drug edn. magic show, 1993. Mem. AACD, Tri-County Assn. Counseling and Devel., Internat. Fitness Ctr. Baptist. Home: 196 Bridgecreek Dr Goose Creek SC 29445-5214

MAZZA, LINDA MARIE, international flight attendant, purser; b. N.Y.C., Dec. 12, 1962; d. John and Marylin Ann (Eger) M. BS, Niagara U., 1984. Customer svc. rep. Capitol Air, N.Y.C., 1982, Command Airways, Poughkeepsie, N.Y., 1984-85; internatl sales rep. N.Y.-Tokyo Tours, N.Y.C.,

1985; corp. travel counselor Thomas Cook Travel, N.Y.C., 1985-86; internat. flight attendant, pures. Tower Air, N.Y.C., 1986—. Author: (booklet) Hairstyles for You, 1993. Mem. Hudson River Sloop: Clearwater, Newburgh, N.Y., 1992-93. Recipient Civilians of Desert Shield/Desert Storm award USAF, 1993, Cert. of Achievement for Contbn. to Desert Storm/Desert Shield, U.S. Army, 1993. Mem. NOW, Internat. Assn. Travel Agts. Presbyterian. Home: 13 Overlook Bluff Marlboro NY 12542

MAZZAFERRI, KATHERINE AQUINO, lawyer, bar association executive; b. Phila., May 14, 1947; d. Joseph William and Rose (Aquino) M.; m. William Fox Bryan, May 5, 1984; 1 child, Josefa Mazzaferri Bryan; 1 stepchild, Patricia M. Bryan. BA, NYU, 1969; JD, George Washington U., 1972. Bar: D.C., 1972. Trial atty. EEOC, Washington, 1972-75; dir. litigation LWV Edn. Fund, Washington, 1975-78; dep. asst. dir. for advt. practices FTC, Washington, 1978-80, asst. dir. for product liability, 1980-82, asst. dir. for advt. practices, 1982; exec. dir., v.p. pub. svcs. activities corp. D.C. Bar, Washington, 1982—; bd. dir. regulatory analysis project U.S. Regulatory Coun.; mediator D.C. Mediation Svc., 1982; vis. instr. Antioch Law Sch., Washington, 1985; mem. Bd. of Women's Bar Assn. Found., 1990-93. Recipient Superior Service award FTC, 1979. Mem. ABA (rep. of the homeless project steering com. 1988-90), D.C. Bar , Womens Legal Def. (pres. 1972-73, bd. dirs. 1971-75, 76-79). Home: 5832 Lenox Rd Bethesda MD 20817-6070 Office: DC Bar 1250 H St NW Fl 6 Washington DC 20005-3952*

MAZZATENTA, ROSEMARY DOROTHY, school administrator; b. Phila., Sept. 17, 1932; d. John and Mary Aida (Perrucci) M. BS in Edn., U. Pa., 1953, MS in Edn., 1956. Cert. tchr., prin., Pa. Tchr. Haverford Twp. (Pa.) Sch. Dist., 1953-54; tchr. Sch. Dist. Phila., 1954-63, cons., 1963-65, elem. sch. prin., 1965-72, asst. dir. pre-kindergarten Head Start, 1965-80, dir. child care, 1980-86, dir. pre-kindergarten Head Start, parent coop. nurseries, 1986—, dir. Even Start program, 1986—; dir. Head Start Learning Ctr., 1993—. dir. Southeastern Pa. unit ARC, 1969—; mem. Phila. Fellowship Commn., 1957—; bd. dirs. Delaware Valley Child Care Coun., 1982—. Decorated Legion of Honor Chapel of 4 Chaplains, 1975. Mem. Nat. Assn. Edn. Young Children, Alumnae Club Phila. (past pres.), Edn. Alumni Assn. (past pres., award of distinction 1970), Sons of Italy (charter mem. Columbus forum, Pres.'s award 1985), Soroptomists (Woman of Distinction 1993), Kappa Delta Epsilon, Pi Lambda Theta, Phi Delta Kappa. Office: Prekindergarten Head Start 13th at Spring Garden St Philadelphia PA 19123

MAZZEI, LINDA FAZIO, lawyer; b. Pitts., Aug. 17, 1963; d. James William and Anna Marie (Miller) Fazio; m. Mark Eugene Mazzei, Nov. 19, 1988; 1 child, Kathryn Anne. BS, Pa. State U., 1985; JD, U. Pitts., 1988. Bar: Pa. 1988. Law clk. Evashavik, Capone & Dellavecchia, Pitts., 1985-87; staff atty. Arthur Young-Ernst & Young, Pitts., 1987-90; atty. Horovitz, Rudoy & Roteman, Pitts., 1990—. Instr. Allegheny County Jail/United Way, Pitts., 1991-92. Mem. Pa. Bar Assn., Allegheny County Bar Assn., Allegheny County Tax Soc.

MAZZEO-MERKLE, LINDA L., legal administrator; b. Washington, Apr. 6, 1947; d. Robert Clifton Shreeves II and Esther A. (Harrison) Shreeves; m. John T. Mazzeo; children: Christina L., Regina L. Hodges. Lic. real estate, Prince Georges C.C., Largo, Md., 1972. Various secretarial positions, 1964-65, 67-72; real estate saleswoman, 1973-74; div. sec. Prince Georges C.C., 1974-75; real estate saleswoman Harvest Realty Inc., Clinton, Md., 1974-75; legal adminstr., property mgr., investment mgr. firm Tucker, Flyer, Sanger, Reider & Lewis P.C., Washington, 1975-84; legal adminstr. Anderson, Heibey, Nauheim & Blair, Washington, 1984-85; v.p. fin. and adminstrn. Barnes, Morris, Pardoe & Foster, Inc., Washington, 1985-93; former CFO, chief adminstrv. officer Barnes, Morris & Pardoe, Inc.; legal adminstr. Payne, Negroni & Winston, Washington, 1994—; with Md. Corp.; pres. Lawtabs Inc. Del. Corp.; cons., speaker. Mem. Assn. Legal Adminstrs. (chmn. new adminstrs. and gen. adminstrn. sect. 1984-85), ABA (assoc.). Home: 4100 N River St Mc Lean VA 22101-5814 Office: 22101 Office 1250 24th St NW Washington DC 20008

MAZZIE, SANDRA ANNE, health care consultant; b. Buffalo, Oct. 12, 1951; d. Laverne Edward and Carol Ann (Matthews) Myers; m. A. Vincent, May 19, 1973. BS in Nursing, SUNY, Brockport, 1973; MA, NYU, 1978; postgrad., Columbia U., 1986—. Staff nurse VA Hosp. Castle Point, Beacon, N.Y., 1973-74, rehab. nurse, 1974-78; rehab. program dir., clin. nurse specialist St. Francis Hosp., Poughkeepsie, N.Y., 1978-82, dir. patient care services, 1982-86, div. dir., 1986-88, dir. bus. planning and devel., 1988; dir. nursing St. Luke's Hosp., Newburgh, N.Y., 1988-91, v.p. patient care svcs., 1991-92; cons. Sandra A. Mazzie Assocs., 1992—; sr. patient care exec. A.P.M., Inc., 1993—; nursing expert witness H.U.M. Ins. Co., White Plains, N.Y., 1978—; clin. assoc. Sch. Allied Health Profls., Ithaca, N.Y., 1986—; preceptor Pace U., White Plains, N.Y., 1986-91, W. Conn. U., 1990-92; community adv. com. Mount St. Mary's Coll., 1992—. Mem. program coun. Am. Heart Assn., 1982-86; bd. dirs. Holden Home of Newburgh. Mem. ANA (cert. advanced nursing adminstr.), Mid-Atlantic Regional Nursing Assn., N.Y. State Nurses Assn. (v.p. 1986, chmn. coun. on legis. 1980-82, dist. v.p. 1985), Am. Orgn. Nurse Execs., Ea. Orange C. of C. (bd. dirs. 1991—), Nat. League for Nursing, Sigma Theta Tau (v.p. 1992—). Roman Catholic. Office: Sandra A Mazzie Assocs 77 Balmville Rd Newburgh NY 12550

MAZZONI, BARBARA JEAN, advice nurse; b. Cumberland, Md., July 23, 1949; d. Robert Taylor and Loretta (Miller) McLaughlin; m. Robert A. Mazzoni, Feb. 17, 1979; 1 child, Michael. Diploma, Ch. Home/Hosp. Sch. Nursing, 1971; BS in Nursing, U. Md., 1976. Advice nurse Kaiser Permanente, Lutherville, Md.; clin. mgr. Greater Balt. Med. Ctr., Towson, Md.; nurse clinician U. Md. Hosp. Mem. Emergency Nurses Assn. (past pres. Met. Balt. chpt.), Md. State ENA (founder). Home: 670 Post Ln Rock Hill SC 29730

MAZZUCELLI, COLETTE GRACE, educator, researcher; b. Bklyn., Nov. 26, 1962; d. Silvio Anthony and Adeline Marie (De Ponte) M. BA, U. Scranton, 1983; MALD, Fletcher Sch. Law & Diplomacy, 1987; postgrad., Georgetown U., 1991—. Instr. European Integration Sch. Summer & Continuing Edn. Georgetown U., Washington, 1990—; rsch. fellow Inst. fuer Europaeische Politik, Deutsche Gesellschaft fuer Auswaertige Politik, Bonn, Deutsch-Franzoesisches Inst., Ludwigsburg; cons. Jean Monnet Coun., Washington, 1994—; lectr. U.S. Info. Svc. Speakers Program in Europe, 1994—; active IPSA rsch. com. on European unification. Author: Pew Case Studies in International Affairs, 1995; asst. editor: The Evolution of an International Actor: Western Europe's New Assertiveness, 1990; contbr. Dimensions of German Unification, 1994. Swiss Univ. grantee, 1984-85; Pi Gamma Mu scholar, 1985, Rotary grad. scholar, 1987-88, Fulbright scholar, 1991; Jean Monnet Coun. dissertation fellow, 1991, European Commn. fellow, 1992, Robert Bosch Found. fellow, 1992—. Fellow Internat. Biog. Assn.; mem. Atlantic Coun. U.S., Am. Polit. Sci. Assn., European Cmty. Studies Assn., Internat. Platform Assn., Acad. Polit. Sci., Robert Bosch Found. Alumni Assn. (exec. com.), Alpha Sigma Nu (student pres. 1984), Pi Gamma Mu (chpt. sec. 1982-84, Frank C. Brown scholarship medal 1984), Phi Sigma Tau (founder), Phi Alpha Theta, Pi Sigma Alpha, Alpha Mu Gamma, Delta Tau Kappa. Home: 1864 74th St Brooklyn NY 11204-5752 Office: Georgetown U 37th And O St Washington DC 20057

MC AFEE, MARILYN, ambassador; b. Portsmouth, N.H., Jan. 23, 1940; m. Joel William Febel. BA in History with honors, U. Pa., 1961; MA, Johns Hopkins U., 1962. Joined Fgn. Svc., Dept. State, Washington, 1968; served with U.S. Embassy, Guatemala, 1969-70, Nicaragua, 1970-72, Iran, 1972-77; served with Fgn. Svc., Dept. State, Washington, 1977-80; served with U.S. Embassy, Costa Rica, 1980-83, Venezuela, 1983-86, Chile, 1986-89; dep. chief of mission U.S. Embassy, Bolivia, 1989-92; amb. U.S. Embassy, Guatemala City, Guatemala, 1993—. Ford Found. fellow; recipient 4 Meritorious Honor awards, 1 Superior Honor award, 1 Presdl. Meritorious Svc. award. Office: Am Embassy Guatamala APO AA 34024-5000

MCALINDON, MARY NAOMI, nursing administrator; b. Ebensburg, Pa., Oct. 16, 1935; d. S. David and Genevieve (Little) Solomon; m. James Daniel McAlindon, Nov. 25, 1961; children: Robert, Donald, James, Peter, M. Catherine. BS in Nursing, Georgetown U., 1957; MA, U. Mich., 1979; EdD, Wayne State U., 1992. RN, Mich.; cert. advanced nurse adminstr. Staff nurse Georgetown U. Hosp., Washington, 1957-59; instr. St. Joseph Hosp., Flint, 1959-62; clin. instr. Mott Community Coll., Flint, 1980-81; asst. dir. nursing McLaren Hosp., Flint, 1980-89, adminstrv. asst., 1989-92, asst. v.p., 1992—; cons. Nat. Leauge Nursing, N.Y., 1986-89, mem. exec. com., 1988, 1993-95. Bd. trustees United Way of Genesee County, Flint, 1988—. Mem. ANA (exec. com. 1991-93), Am. Med. Informatics Assn. (chair nursing group 1993-94), Vis. Nurses Assn. (pres., bd. dirs. 1986-89), Dist. Nurses Assn. (pres. 1993-96), Nursing Honor Soc. U. Mich. (pres. elect 1994-96). Office: McLaren Gen Hosp 401 S Ballenger Hwy Flint MI 48532-3685

MCALLISTER, NANCY HARDACRE, music academy administrator; b. Highland Park, Ill., Feb. 24, 1940; d. Milton Joseph Jr. and Virginia Letitia (Engels) Hardacre; m. Claude Huntley McAllister, Sept. 5, 1970. MusB, B Music Edn., Denison U., 1962; MA, U. N.C., 1967, M Music Edn., 1968. Cert. in music edn., violin performance, composition. Organist, choir dir. St. Mark's Episcopal Ch., Barrington, Ill., 1957-58; orch. dir. Adrian (Mich.) Pub. Schs., 1964-66, Luther Coll., Decorah, Iowa, 1966-67; orch. dir., tchr. New Hanover Pub. Schs., Wilmington, N.C., 1964-87; dir., owner Wilmington Acad. Music, 1987—; grad. asst. U. N.C., Chapel Hill, 1962-66; violinist Columbus (Ohio) Symphony Orch., 1961-62, Acad. Music Chamber Trio, Wilmington, 1987—; concertmaster Wilmington Symphony Orch., 1987-92; condr. Acad. Music Orch., 1987—. Composer: Sonata in A Major for violin and piano, 1961, Suite for Horn and Strings, 1961 (2d place Priz de Rome 1965). Mem. Am. String Tchrs. Assn. (sec. 1987-91), Music Educators Nat. Conv., Nat. Sch. Orch. Assn., Wilmington C. of C., P.E.O. Episcopalian. Office: Wilmington Acad Music 1635 Wellington Ave Wilmington NC 28401-7758

MCANDREWS, MIMI K., state legislator; b. St. Joseph, Mo., Oct. 28, 1956; divorced; children: Summer R. Cooper, Chase C. Cooper. BA, Fla. Atlantic U., 1988; JD, Georgetown U., 1992. Former aide Rep. Lois Frankel; now state rep. Fla. House of Reps., Tallahassee, 1992—; past restaurant owner; now law clk. Democrat. Office: Fla House of Reps State Capitol Tallahassee FL 32301*

MCANIFF, NORA P., publishing executive. BA, CUNY. Pub. People Weekly, N.Y.C., 1994—. Office: People Magazine Time Inc Rockfeller Ctr New York NY 10020-1393*

MC ANULTY, MARY CATHERINE CRAMER (MRS. CHARLES GILBERT MC ANULTY), retired principal, educator; b. Braddock, Pa., June 26, 1908; d. Albert R. and Sara (Kelly) Cramer; AB, Fla. So. Coll., 1929; MA, Tchrs. Coll. Columbia, 1937; postgrad. Fla. State U., 1946-50; m. Charles Gilbert McAnulty, Dec. 25, 1937. Elem. tchr. Lake Ann Sch., Lake Garfield, Fla., 1930-31, elem. prin., 1932-34; prin. South Winter Haven Elem. Sch., Winter Haven, Fla., 1935-55; adminstrv. asst. to supervising prin. Winter Haven Area Schs., 1956-60; prin. Fred Garner Elem. Sch., Winter Haven, 1961-68, Lake Alfred Elem. Sch., 1969-70. Asst. chmn. vols., asst. tng. chmn., local chpt. ARC, 1967-68, 2d v.p., also chmn. vols., 1969-70, bd. mem. 12 yrs., chmn. service to mil. families, 1970-71, chmn. coll. youth, 1971-72; treas. Imperial Harbours Condominium, 1980-82, pres., 1984; v.p. Beymer United Methodist Women, 1973-75, pres., 1976-77; lay del. ann. conf. Meth. Ch., 1978, 79, 89-91; pres. Lake Region Extension Homemaker's Club, 1974, 75; bd. dirs. Winter Haven Hosp. Aux., rec. sec., 1985-86, corr. sec., 1986-88; co-chmn. Residents Coun., 1992, 93, 94, Lake Howard Heights. Mem. Am. Assn. Supervision and Curriculum Devel., Internat. Reading Assn. (pres., Polk County chpts.), NEA, Nat. Ret. Tchrs. Assn., Fla. Edn. Assn. (dir. dept. elem. sch. prins. 1965-67), Polk County Elem. Prins. Assn. (sec.), LWV (local dir. 1962), AAUW (local br. chmn. status women com. 1963), DAR (chpt. treas. 1967-68, historian 1969-70, regent 1970-72, state chmn. jr. Am. citizens 1972—, dir. dist. VI 1973-74, parliamentarian 1986-94), Fla. So. Coll. Alumni Assn. (sec.), Internat. Platform Assn., P.E.O. (chpt. treas. 1970-74, 80-89, chaplain 1976, 77, chpt. pres. 1978-79), Ch. Women United (v.p. 1977-93, chmn. adminstrn. bd. 1980-81), Pi Gamma Mu, Delta Kappa Gamma (State Achievement award 1964, Fla. pres. 1962-63, chpt. parliamentarian 1968-73, 87-94, pres., state v.p., treas., expansion chmn.). Methodist (choir mem., chmn. commn. edn. 1959-60, supt. study program 1969-70, organist 1970-77, pres. Wesley fellowship class 1972-73, chmn. adminstrv. bd. 1980, 81, 83-85 trustee 1983-88, hon. trustee 1989—, pres. bd. trustees 1987-88, lay leader 1985, 86, fin. com., worship com., staff Parish com, 1989-91, organ com., 1987-93). Clubs: Pilot (charter, pres. 1954-55, 61-62), Poinsettia Garden (pres. 1984-85). Lodge: Order Eastern Star (fin. chair 1987-89), Winter Haven Woman's (edn. chmn. 1967-68, v.p. 1983-84, pres. 1984-85, parliamentarian 1986-94, dist. 9 parliamentarian 1988-90). Home: 650 N Lake Howard Dr Apt 4B Winter Haven FL 33881-3133

MCATEE, PATRICIA ANNE ROONEY, medical educator; b. Denver, Apr. 20, 1931; d. Jerry F. and Edna E. (Hansen) Rooney; m. Darrell McAtee, Sept. 4, 1954; 1 son, Kevin Paul. BS, Loretto Heights Coll., 1953; MS, U. Colo., 1961; PhD, Union of Univs., 1976. Supr. St. Anthony Hosp., Denver, 1952-55; pub. health nurse, edn. dir. Tri-County Health Dept., Colo., 1956-58; adminstr. sch. health program Littleton (Colo.) Pub. Schs., 1958-60; asst. prof. community health, acad. adminstr. continuing edn. U. Colo., 1968-70; project dir. Western Interstate Commn. for Higher Edn., 1972-74; asst. prof. pediatrics, project co-dir. Sch. Medicine U. Colo., 1975—; mem. profl. svcs. staff Mead Johnson & Co., 1981—; cons. Colo. Safety Coun.; treas. Vista Nueva Assocs. Editor: Pediatric Nursing, 1975-77. Chmn. bd. dirs. Found. for Urban and Neighborhood Devel.; mem. Arapahoe Health Planning Coun. Mem. NAS, APHA, Inst. Medicine, Nat. Bd. Pediatric Nurse Practitioners and Assocs. (pres.), Nat. Assn. Pediatric Nurse Practitioners (v.p.), Am. Acad. Polit. and Social Scientist, Nat. League Nursing, Western Soc. Rsch., Am. Sch. Health Assn., Sigma Theta Tau. Home: 877 E Panama Dr Littleton CO 80121-2531 Office: 4200 E 9th Ave Box C-219 Denver CO 80262

MCATEER, DEBORAH GRACE, travel executive; b. N.Y.C., Nov. 3, 1950; d. Edward John and Ann Marie (Cassidy) McAteer; m. William A. Helms, Feb. 5, 1948 (div. 1993); children: Elizabeth Grace, Kathleen Marie, Margaret Ann. Student, Montgomery Coll., 1969, Am. U., 1972. Sec. Polinger Co., Chevy Chase, Md., 1969-72, Loews Hotels, Washington, 1972-73; adminstr. asst. Am. Gas Assn., Arlington, Va., 1973-75; mgr. Birch Jermain Horton Bittner, Washington, 1975-77; asst. mgr. Travel Services, McLean, Va., 1977-79; founder, pres. Travel Temps, Washington, Atlanta, Phila., Miami and Ft. Lauderdale, Fla., 1979-90; pres. Diversified Communications, Atlanta, 1990—; tchr. Montgomery Coll., Rockville, Md., 1980-84. Mem. Christ Child Soc., Washington, 1975—. Mem. Internat. Travel Soc. (pres. 1983-84), Am. Soc. Travel Agts., Pacific Area Travel Assn., Inst. Cert. Travel Cons. (cert., life mem.), Nat. Assn. Women Bus. Owners (chair membership com. 1983-84), Women Bus. Owners Atlanta (bd. dirs. 1991—, pres. 1994), Women's Commerce Club, PROST (v.p. 1991). Republican. Roman Catholic. Home: 7390 Twin Branch Rd NE Atlanta GA 30328-1771 Office: Travel Temps 7390 Twin Branch Rd NE Atlanta GA 30328-1771

MCAVOY, ROSEMARY THOMPSON, administrative assistant; b. Harrisburg, Pa., Apr. 17, 1952; d. Franklin Sylvester and Georgette Mary (Long) Thompson; m. Jerome J. McAvoy, Jr., Sept. 13, 1975; children: Mary Catherine, Jerome Joseph III. Student, Harrisburg Area C. C., 1970-73; cert. paralegal, Pa. State U., 1994. Chief accounts receivable student loans Pa. Higher Edn. Assistance Agy., Harrisburg, 1974-76; writer Lancaster (Pa.) New ERA newspaper, 1977-78; purchasing agt. ESI/ISC Internat., Lancaster, 1977-78; corp. treas. Bankers Trust of N.Y., Lancaster, 1976-79; gen. mgr., proprietor Safari Sun/Georgettes, Harrisburg, 1979-88; legis. asst. Pa. Ho. of Reps., Harrisburg, 1988-95; adminstrv. asst. Pa. Commn. for Women, Harrisburg, 1995—; pres. Capitol Area Coun. of Women in Govt., Harrisburg, 1991—. Producer/dir. (film documentary) Mock Trial on Domestic Violence, 1992. Candidate Pa. Ho. of Reps., 1990; co-chmn. Pa. Coun. Rep. Women, Harrisburg, 1992—; mem. exec. com. More Women's Candidates, 1990-93; bd. dirs. YWCA Pub. Policy, Harrisburg, 1990-93; exec. bd. dirs. Pa. Women's Campaign Fund, 1990—; co-chair Women's Network for Ridge, 1993-94. Mem. Nat. Fedn. Rep. Women, Navy Enlisted Reserve Assn., Chambers Hill Civic Assn. (devel. chair 1990—), Women's Polit. Network of Pa. (exec. com. 1990—). Roman Catholic. Home: 7775 Chambers Hill Rd Harrisburg PA 17111-5425

MCBEAN, SHARON ELIZABETH, church administrator; b. Chgo., July 15, 1937; d. Archibald Lewis Jr. and Mary Elizabeth (Rees) McBean; children: Debra Sue Sanders, Catherine Leigh Sanders Ferguson. BA cum laude, La Roche Coll., 1977; MS in Edn., Duquesne U., 1978. Cert. ch. bus. adminstr. Adminstrv. asst. 1st Presbyn. Ch., Santa Barbara, Calif., 1988-89, bus. mgr., 1989—; deacon 1st Presbyn. Ch., Santa Barbara, 1987-89. Mem. bd. mgrs. Valle Verde Retirement community. Mem. Presbyn. Ch. Bus. Adminstrn. Assn., Nat. Assn. Ch. Bus. Adminstrs.

MCBEE, MARY LOUISE, state legislator, former academic administrator; b. Strawberry Plains, Tenn., June 15, 1924; d. John Wallace and Nina Aileen (Umbarger) McB. BS, East Tenn. State U., 1946; MA, Columbia U., 1951; PhD, Ohio State U., 1961. Tchr. East Tenn. State U., Johnson City, 1947-51; asst. dean of women, 1952-56, 57-60, dean of women, 1961-63; dean of women U. Ga., Athens, 1963-67; world campus afloat adminstr., 1966-67, assoc. dean of students, 1967-72, dean of students, 1972-74, asst. v.p. acad. affairs, 1974-76, assoc. v.p. acad. affairs, 1976-86, v.p. acad. affairs, 1986-88; now mem. Ga. Gen. Assembly; bd. dirs. Ga. Nat. Bank, Athens, 1989—. Author: College Responsibility for Values, 1980; co-author: The American Woman: Who Will She Be?, 1974, Essays, 1979,, 2d edit. 1981. Bd. dirs. Salvation Army, Athens, 1978—, United Way, Athens. Fulbright scholar, The Netherlands, 1956-57. Mem. Athens C. of C. (bd. dirs.). Democrat. Methodist. Home: 145 Pine Valley Pl Athens GA 30606-4031 Office: GA House of Reps State Capitol Atlanta GA 30334

MCBEE, SUSANNA BARNES, journalist; b. Santa Fe, Mar. 28, 1935; d. Jess Stephen and Sybil Elizabeth (Barnes) McBee; m. Paul H. Recer, July 2, 1983. AB, U. So. Calif., 1956; MA, U. Chgo., 1962. Staff writer Washington Post, 1957-65, 73-74, 77-79, asst. nat. editor, 1974-77; asst. sec. for public affairs HEW, 1979; articles editor Washingtonian mag., 1980-81; assoc. editor U.S. News & World Report, 1981-86; news editor Washington Bur. of Hearst Newspapers, 1987-89, asst. bur. chief, 1990—; Washington corr. Life mag., 1965-69; Washington editor McCall's mag., 1970-72. Recipient Penney-Missouri mag. award, 1969; Sigma Delta Chi Pub. Svc. award, 1969. Mem. Nat. Press Club, Washington Press Club Found., Cosmos Club. Home: 5190 Watson St NW Washington DC 20016-5329 Office: 1701 Pennsylvania Ave NW Washington DC 20006-5801

MCBRIDE, ANGELA BARRON, nursing educator; b. Balt., Jan. 16, 1941; d. John Stanley and Mary C. (Szczepanska) Barron; m. William Leon McBride, June 12, 1965; children: Catherine, Kara. BS in Nursing, Georgetown U., 1962; LHD (hon.), 1993; MS in Nursing, Yale U., 1964; PhD, Purdue U., 1978; D of Pub. Svc. (hon.), U. Cin., 1983; LLD (hon.), Ea. Ky. U., 1991. Asst. prof., rsch. asst. inst. Yale U., New Haven, 1964-73; assoc. prof., chairperson Ind. U. Sch. Nursing, Indpls., 1978-81, 80-84, prof., 1981-92, disting. prof., 1992—; assoc. dean rsch. Ind. U. Sch. Nursing, 1985-91, interim dean, 1991-92, univ. dean, 1992—. Author: The Growth and Development of Mothers, 1973, Living with Contradictions. A Married Feminist, 1976, How to Enjoy A Good Life With Your Teenager, 1987; editor: Psychiatric-Mental Health Nursing: Integrating the Behavioral and Biological Sciences, 1995. Recipient Disting. Alumna award Yale U., Disting. Alumna award Purdue U., Univ. Medallion, U. San Francisco, 1993; Kellog nat. fellow; Am. Nurses Found. scholar. Fellow Am. Acad. Nursing (pres.), Am. Psychol. Assn., Nat. Acads. Practice; mem. Midwest Nursing Rsch. Soc., Soc. for Rsch. in Child Devel., Sigma Theta Tau Internat. (past pres.). Office: Ind U Sch Nursing 1111 Middle Dr Indianapolis IN 46202-5107

MCBRIDE, BEVERLY JEAN, lawyer; b. Greenville, Ohio, Apr. 5, 1941; d. Kenneth Birt and Glenna Louise (Ashman) Whited; m. Benjamin Gary McBride, Nov. 28, 1964; children: John David, Elizabeth Ann. BA magna cum laude, Wittenberg U., 1963; JD cum laude, U. Toledo, 1966. Bar: Ohio 1966. Intern Ohio Gov.'s Office, Columbus, 1962; asst. dean of women U. Toledo, 1963-65; assoc. Title Guarantee and Trust Co., Toledo, 1966-69; spl. counsel Ohio Atty. Gen.'s Office, Toledo, 1975; assoc. Cobourn, Smith, Rohrbacher and Gibson, Toledo, 1969-76; gen. counsel The Andersons, Maumee, Ohio, 1976—. Exec. trustee, bd. dirs. Wittenberg U., Springfield, Ohio, 1980—; trustee Anderson Found., Maumee, 1981—; mem. Ohio Supreme Ct. Task Force on Gender Fairness, 1991—; chmn. Sylvania Twp. Zoning Commn., Ohio, 1970-80; candidate for judge, Sylvania Mcpl. Ct., 1975; trustee Goodwill Industries, Toledo, 1976-82, Sylvania Community Svcs. Ctr., 1976-78, Toledo-Lucas County Port Authority, 1992—; vice chair St. Vincent Med. Ctr., 1992—, trustee; founder Sylvania YWCA Program, 1973; active membership drives Toledo Mus. Art, 1977—. Recipient Toledo Women in Industry award YWCA, 1979, Outstanding Alumnus award Wittenberg U., 1981. Fellow Am. Bar Found.; mem. ABA, AAUW, Ohio Bar Assn. Toledo Bar Assn. (pres., treas., chmn., sec. various coms.), Toledo Women Attys. Forum (exec. com. 1978-82), Pres. Club (U. Toledo, exec. com.). Home: 5274 Cambrian Rd Toledo OH 43623-2626 Office: The Andersons 480 W Dussel Dr Maumee OH 43537-1639

MCBRIDE, CATHY HAND, communications executive; b. Anderson County, S.C., Nov. 23, 1957; d. Harmon L. and Margaret D. (Duncan) Hand; m. Steven M. McBride, Feb. 8, 1986; children: Ryan, Kevin. BA, Furman U., 1980. Systems mgr. MC, Inc., Greenville, S.C., 1980-82; customer svc. coord. IBM, Atlanta, 1982-84; program support rep. IBM, Jacksonville, Fla., 1985-86, ops. support specialist, 1986-89, systems engr., 1990-93, svcs. specialist, 1994—. Loaned exec. United Way N.E. Fla., Jacksonville, 1991. Methodist. Office: IBM 10407 Centurion Pkwy N Jacksonville FL 32256

MCBRIDE, JOYCE BROWNING, accountant; b. Ga., May 28, 1927; d. Eph and Zula (Harden) Browning; grad. So. Bus. U., 1947; children: Jan Burge, Gary McBride, Kandie Van Affelen. Asst. controller Hampton Court Knits, Los Angeles, 1967-78; owner, mgr. McBride & Assocs. Bookkeeping Service, 1978—. Address: 2925 Tyler Ct Simi Valley CA 93063

MCBRIDE, LINDA GERTRUDE ROBACK, beauty consultant; b. Phila., Jan. 18, 1956; d. John George and Elaine Audrey (Brandt) Roback; m. William H. McBride, Oct. 28, 1990; 1 child, Mark William. BA in Polit. Sci., Pa. State U., 1977; JD, U. Bridgeport, 1980. Bar: Pa., U.S. Dist. Ct. (ea. dist.) Pa. Formerly lawyer in pvt. practice Oreland, Pa.; sr. cons. Mary Kay Cosmetics, Oreland, 1993—. Bd. dirs., mem. nominating com. Girl Scouts U.S., Valley Forge, Pa., 1992-93; vol. Oreland Town Watch, 1993—. Office: PO Box 168 Flourtown PA 19031-0168

MCBRIDE, SANDRA TEAGUE, critical care nurse; b. Corinth, Miss., Sept. 13, 1958; d. Clarence R. and Alice (Ingram) T. AAS, Shelby State Community Coll., 1983; BSN, U. North Ala., 1987. RN, Miss., Tenn. Nurse supr. Alcorn County Care, Inc., Corinth, Miss., 1985-87; staff nurse Bolivar (Tenn.) Community Hosp., 1988-90; staff nurse West Tenn. High Security Facility Tenn. Dept. of Corrections, Ripley, Tenn., 1990-91; staff nurse for fed. prisoners U.S. Med. Ctr., 1991-92; staff nurse Western Mental Health Inst., Bolivar, 1992—.

MCBRIDE, VICKIE DARLENE, geriatrics nurse; b. Tampa, Fla., Jan. 17, 1944; d. Harold Victor Burch and Dorothy June (Higley) Keen; m. Dennis McBride, July 12, 1969 (div. June 1980); m. John Lawrence Petonic Jr., Mar. 20, 1982 (div. Dec. 1993); children: Elizabeth, Christopher. BSN, Marycrest Coll., Davenport, Iowa, 1966; MBA, Baldwin-Wallace Coll., Berea, Ohio, 1986. Cert. rehab. nurse, dir. nursing. Charge nurse Mercy Hosp., Davenport, 1966; staff devel. for critical care Cleve. Clinic, 1969-73; dir., med. svcs. coord. Free Clinic West, Cleve., 1973-74; DON Cuyahoga Falls (Ohio) Gen. Hosp., 1974-76; DON Kaiser Found. Hosp., Cleve., 1976-79, regional coord. staff devel., 1979-83; DON Forest Hills Nursing Home, Cleve., 1983-86; sr. cons. Clemens Nelson & Assocs., Worthington, Ohio, 1986-88; corp. cons. Altercare Inc., Navarre, Ohio, 1988—; course coord. critical care Cleve. State U., 1973-75; trustee Free Med. Clinics of Cleve., 1972-73; affiliate faculty Capital U., 1976-79. Lt. USN, 1966-69. Mem. AACN, Nat. Dirs. Nursing Long Term Care, Ohio Dirs. Nursing Long Term Care, Am. Healthcare Assn., Nat. League for Nursing, Am. Rehab. Nurses. Roman Catholic. Home: PO Box 1053 Medina OH 44258-1053 Office: Altercare 7222 Day Ave SW Navarre OH 44662-9449

MCBRIDE-HOUTZ, PATRICIA ANN, psychologist; b. Oklahoma City, Aug. 11, 1959; d. Earl Richard and Buena June (Ramsey) McB.; m. Andrew William Houtz, May 22, 1987; 1 child, Keverly Lauren. BS in Psychology, Southwest Tex. State U., 1982; MS in Counseling Psychology, U. North Tex., 1987, PhD in Counseling Psychology, 1993. Lic. psychologist, Tex. Rsch. asst. Southwest Tex. State U., San Marcos, 1981-83, Ctr. for Studies in Aging, Denton, Tex., 1984-87; therapist Family Svc., Inc., Bedford, Tex., 1988-91; psychology intern Dallas VA Med. Ctr., 1991-92; psychologist Dallas County Schs., 1993-94, St. Joseph Hosp., Ft. Worth, Tex., 1994—. Contbr. articles to profl. jours. Teaching fellow U. North Tex., 1987-90. Mem. APA, Golden Key Nat. Honor Soc. (life), Psi Chi. Office: 1401 S Main St Fort Worth TX 76104

MCBRIDE-JONES, JACQUELINE RAE, city official; b. Bridgeton, N.J., Oct. 3, 1950; d. J. Elwood and Lucy May (Coursey) McBride; m. Norman P. Jones; children: D'Andre, Pheon, Coyuca, Matoya. BS, Howard U., 1972; MA, Fairleigh Dickinson U., 1976; PhD, Union Inst., 1991. Asst. dir. social svcs. N.A.R.C.O. Inc., Atlantic City, 1972-75; therapist, counselor Seabrook (N.J.) House, 1976-77, Alternatives, Atlantic City, 1978; corrd. project tng. and tech. asst. HEW, N.Y.C., 1978-79; legis. aide N.J. Gen. Assembly, Trenton, 1980-81; supr. pension fund Office of Compt., City of Atlantic City, 1980-83, adminstrv. analyst Office Emergency Mgmt., 1983-85, dep. coord., 1985—; pres. McBride-Jones & Assocs., Inc., 1980—; project dir. Atlantic County (N.J.) Mental Health Assn., 1977-78; div. dir. Judge Jacobs Youth Programs, Atlantic City, 1978-79; mem. Local Fed. Emergency Mgmt. Bd., 1986—; co-founder Atlanta County Adv. Commn. on Women, 1994—. Editor newsletter Hallway, 1982-85. Pres. Santuary Assn. Atlantic County, 1979—; vol. NCCJ, Atlantic City, 1980—; bd. dirs. Boys and Girls Club Atlantic City, 1981—; co-founder Altantic City Adv. Commn. on Women, 1994—. Recipient award Chapel of Four Chaplains, 1974, Golden Deed award Exch. Club Atlantic City, 1982, Outstanding Black During 50s, 60s, and 70s award Assn. Afro-Am. Life and History, 1982, Role Model of South Jersey award Assn. Negro Bus. and Profl. Women, 1985. Mem. NAACP, ASPA (cert. pub. mgr.), Nat. Forum Black Pub. Adminstrs., Cert. Pub. Mgrs. Soc. N.J., Nat. Coordinating Coun. on Emergency Mgmt., N.J. Emergency Mgmt. Assn., N.J. Women's Summit, Inc., Zonta. Home: 2 Surrey Dr Pleasantville NJ 08232-9575 Office: City of Atlantic City 1301 Bacharach Blvd Atlantic City NJ 08401-4603

MCBROOM, NANCY LEE, insurance executive; b. Tulsa, Nov. 7, 1925; d. Lee Webster and Dora Irene (Londigan) Adams; m. Robert B. McBroom, Jan. 22, 1945 (dec. Aug. 1969); children: Dacia Adams, Rene McBroom, Robert McBroom. Student, John Brown U., 1941-42, Little Rock Bus. Coll., 1941-42. Profl. horse trainer, judge, breeder N.C., Va. and Calif., 1955-75; owner Stombock's West, Inc., Del Mar, Calif., 1968-74; agt. Mut. Omaha Ins. Co., San Diego, 1978-84; owner, broker McBroom Ins. Svcs., San Diego, 1984—; dir. Dependent's Riding Program, USMC, Camp LeJeune, N.C., 1963-66. Author: Handbook for Riding Instructors, 1963. Mem. com. Civitan Fund Raiser for Spl. Olympics, 1986. Mem. Nat. Assn. Securities Dealers, Rancho Bernardo C. of C. (com. 1986). Republican. Lodge: Soroptomist Internat. (mem. com. Women Helping Women 1985-86). Home: 12093 Caminito Campana San Diego CA 92128-2061 Office: McBroom Ins Svcs Ste 114 16776 Bernardo Center Dr San Diego CA 92128-2559

MCBURNEY, ELIZABETH INNES, physician, educator; b. Lake Charles, La., Dec. 24, 1944; d. Theodore John and Martha (Caldwell) Innes; divorced, 1980; children: Leanne Marie, Susan Eleanor. BS, U. Southwestern La., 1965; MD, La. State U., 1969. Diplomate Am. Bd. Internal Medicine, Am. Bd. Dermatology. Intern Pensacola (Fla.) Edn. Program, 1969-70; resident in internal medicine Boston U. and Carney Hosps., 1970-72; resident in dermatology Charity Hosp., New Orleans, 1972-74; staff physician Ochsner Hosp., New Orleans, 1974-80; assoc. head of dermatology Ochsner Clinic, New Orleans, 1974-80; clin. asst. prof. Sch. Medicine La. State U., New Orleans, 1976-79, clin. assoc. prof., 1979-90, clin. prof., 1990—; clin. asst. prof. Sch. Medicine Tulane U., New Orleans, 1976-88, clin. assoc. prof., 1988-91, clin. prof., 1991—; mem. staff Northshore Regional Med. Ctr., Slidell, La., 1985—, Slidell Meml. Hosp., 1980—; chair libr. com. Slidell Meml. Hosp., 1988—, chmn. CME courses, 1988—; regional dir. Mycosis Fungoides Study Group, Balt., 1974—. Author: (with others) Dermatologic Laser Surgery, 1990; contbr. articles to profl. jours. Bd. dirs. Slidell Art Coun., 1988—, Camp Fire, New Orleans, 1979-83, Cancer Assn. New Orleans, 1978-83; juror Art in Pub. Places, Slidell, 1989. Fellow ACP; mem. Am. Soc. Dermatologic Surgery (treas. 1991-94, bd. dirs. 1988-91), Am. Acad. Dermatology (bd. dirs. 1994—), Am. Bd. Laser Surgery (bd. dirs. 1986—), Women's Dermatology Soc. (bd. dirs. 1991—), La. Dermatologic Soc. (pres. 1989-90), St. Tammary Med. Soc. (pres. 1988), Phi Kappa Phi, Alpha Omega Alpha. Office: 1051 Gause Blvd Ste 460 Slidell LA 70458-9999

MCBURNEY, MARGOT B., librarian; b. Lethbridge, Alta., Can.; d. Ronald Laurence Maness and R. Blanche (Lott) Hart; children: Margot Elisabeth McBurney Lane, James Ronald Gordon. B.A. with honours, Principia Coll., 1953; M.Sc. in L.S, U. Ill., 1969. Sec. Marshall Brooks Library, Principia Coll., Elsah, Ill., 1966-69; reference librarian Marshall Brooks Library, Principia Coll., 1969-70; systems analyst trainee in library systems U. Alta. Library, Edmonton, 1970-71; undergrad. reference librarian U. Alta. Library, 1971-72, editor periodicals holdings list, 1972-73, serials cataloguer, 1973-74, head acquisitions div., 1974-77; chief librarian Queen's U. Library, Kingston, Ont., Can., 1977-90. Editor: Am. Soc. Info. Sci. Western Can. chpt. Proceedings, 1975, 76. Mem. ALA, Am. Soc. Info. Sci. (councilor-at-large 1976-79, past chmn. chpt.), Assn. Research Libraries (dir. 1978-81, chmn. task force on library edn. 1980-83), Can. Assn. Info. Sci., Can. Assn. Research Libraries, Can. Library Assn., Council on Library Resources (PETREL com. 1981-84), Phi Alpha Eta, Beta Phi Mu.

MCCABE, CONNIE LEE, elementary counselor; b. Bloomington, Ill., Aug. 14, 1948; d. Dwight D. and Madelynne (Lee) Carmichael; m. Ed N. McCabe, Aug. 13, 1967; children: Brian Edward, Amy Lee. BS in Bus. Edn., Ill. State U., 1971; MS, Purdue U., 1985. Cert. middle and elem. sch. counselor, Ind. Instr. Ivy Tech., Lafayette, Ind., 1983; instr. Purdue U., West Lafayette, Ind., 1983, 86, grad. instr., 1984, rsch. assoc., 1987-90, program specialist, 1990-91; elem. sch. counselor Rensselaer (Ind.) Sch. Corp., 1991—. Contbr. articles to profl. jours. Recipient Award of Merit, Ind. Vocat. Assn., 1988. Mem. Am. Counseling Assn., Ind. Counselor Assn. (v.p. Northwest chpt.), Am. Sch. Counselors Assn. Republican. Methodist. Home: 3786 S 1100 E Otterbein IN 47970-8516 Office: Van Rensselaer Elem Sch 309 W Washington St Rensselaer IN 47978-2823

MCCABE, MARY WILLIAMSON, computer systems analyst; b. Memphis, Aug. 8, 1934; d. Edwin Lacey and Mary Maxine (Maners) Williamson; m. Henry Arthur McCabe, Sept. 22, 1973; stepchildren: Patrick, Anne, Kevin, Cathleen, John. BA, Rhodes Coll., 1956. Math. tchr. Bolton (Tenn.) High Sch., 1956-57; programmer/analyst Mallory AF Sta., Memphis, 1957-61; sr. systems specialist computer dept. GE, Huntsville, Ala., 1961-66; sr. systems specialist Honeywell Info. Systems, Phoenix, 1966-78, Honeywell Bull, Mpls., 1979-88; pres. McCabe & Assocs., Inc., Minnetonka, Minn., 1990-91, v.p. 1992. Vol. Am. Cancer Soc., Minnetonka, 1980-91. Mem. Alpha Omicron Pi (v.p. Kappa Omicron chpt. 1955-56). Republican. Episcopalian. Home: 7967 E Via Costa Scottsdale AZ 85258-2821

MCCABE, MONICA PETRAGLIA, lawyer; b. Bronx, N.Y., Jan. 11, 1959; d. John Francis and Eleanor Angela (Gengaro) Petraglia; m. Edward D. McCabe, May 27, 1984. BA summa cum laude, Fordham U., 1981; MA in Polit. Sci., U. of Chgo., 1984; JD cum laude, Georgetown U., 1985. Bar: N.Y. 1986, D.C. 1987, U.S. Dist. Ct. (so. dist.) N.Y. 1987, U.S. Dist. Ct. (ea. dist.) N.Y. 1988, U.S. Supreme Ct. 1991. Law clk. U.S. Dept. of State, Washington, 1984-85; jud. clk. to judge U.S. Dist. Ct. U.S. Dist. Ct., Washington, 1985-86; assoc. Simpson, Thacher & Bartlett, N.Y.C., 1986-89, Reid and Priest, N.Y.C., 1989—; assoc. counsel gov.'s judicial screening com. First Judicial Dept., 1991—. Exec. editor Internat. Law Rev., 1988-91, editor-in-chief, 1991-94, mem. adv. bd., 1994—; editor Law Policy in Internat. Bus., 1985. Bd. dirs. Bay Street Landing Homeowners Corp. Mem. ABA, Internat. Bar Assn., N.Y. State Bar Assn., Assn. Bar City N.Y. (mem. fgn. and comparative law com. 1990-93, mem. internat. human rights com. 1993—), Women in Music, Women's Inner Cir. of Achievement (N.Am.), Phi Beta Kappa. Democrat. Roman Catholic. Home: 20 Bay Street Lndg #BIJ Staten Island NY 10301-2534 Office: Reid & Priest 40 W 57th St New York NY 10019-4001

MCCAFFERTY, BARBARA JEAN (BJ MCCAFFERTY), sales executive; b. Lincoln, Nebr., Dec. 6, 1940; d. Russell Rowley and Ruth Alice (Williams) Wightman; m. Eriks Zeltins, Dec. 29, 1962 (div. Oct. 1976); 1 child, Brian K. Zeltins; m. Charles F. McCafferty Jr., Oct. 3, 1981 (div. July 1986). BS magna cum laude, Del. Valley Coll. Sci. and Agri., Doylestown, Pa., 1984; student, Drexel U., 1958-61. Dept. mgr. Strawbridge & Clothier, Neshaminy, Pa., 1968-73; asst. buyer Strawbridge & Clothier, Phila., 1973-76; office adminstr. Am. Protein Products, Croydon, Pa., 1976-78; tech. librarian Honeywell Power Sources Ctr., Horsham, Pa., 1978-85; sales dir. Colonial Life and Accident Ins., Wayne, Pa., 1985-86; adminstrn. mgr. Mobi Systems, Inc., Ft. Washington, Pa., 1986-88; spl. rep. Universal Mktg. Corp., Southampton, Pa., 1988-89; ind. contractor McCafferty Ins. Svcs., Doylestown, Pa., 1989—. Mem. alumni recruitment connection Delaware Valley Coll. Sci. and Agr. Mem. NAFE, Nat. Assn. Profl. Saleswomen, Options, Inc., Franklin Mint Collectors Soc., Optomists, Shawnee-at-Highpoint Racquet Club (Chalfont, Pa.). Republican. Presbyterian. Home: 224 Hastings Ct Doylestown PA 18901-2506

MCCAFFREY, CARLYN SUNDBERG, lawyer; b. N.Y.C., Jan. 7, 1942; d. Carl Andrew Lawrence and Evelyn (Back) Sundberg; m. John P. McCaffrey, May 24, 1967; children: John C., Patrick, Jennifer, Kathleen. Student, Barnard Coll., 196.; AB in Econs., George Washington U., 1963; LLB cum laude, NYU, 1967, LLM in Taxation, 1970. Bar: N.Y. 1974. Law clk. to presiding justice Calif. Supreme Ct., 1967-68; teaching fellow law NYU, N.Y.C., 1968-70, asst. prof. law, 1970-74; assoc. Weil, Gotshal & Manges, N.Y.C., 1974-80, ptnr., 1980—; prof. in residence Rubin Hall NYU, 1971-75; adj. prof. law NYU, 1975—, U. Miami, 1979-81, 83—; lectr. in field. Contbr. articles to profl. jours. Mem. ABA (chmn. generationskipping trusts 1979-81, 93—, real property probate and trust law sect.), N.Y. State Bar Assn. (exec. com. tax sect. 1979-80, chmn. estate and gift tax com. 1976-78, life ins. com. 1983-85, trusts and estates sect.), Assn. of Bar of City of N.Y. (matrimonial law com., chmn. tax subcom. 1984-86). Home: 38 Sidney Pl Brooklyn NY 11201-4607 Office: Weil Gotshal & Manges 767 Fifth Ave New York NY 10153-0002

MCCAFFREY, JANE CUSHING, pediatrician; b. Camden, N.J., Apr. 8, 1940; d. Henry Stanley and Francis Anita (Laurie) Cushing; m. Patrick Joseph McCaffrey, May 15, 1965 (div. Jan. 1980); children: Laurie Margaret, Kevin Patrick. BA, Cornell U., 1962; MD, U. Md., 1966. Cert. Bd. Am. Acad. Pediatrics. Pediat. intern U. Md. Hosp., Balt., 1966-67, pediat. resident, 1967-69; clin. instr. dept. pediatrics U. Md. Sch. Medicine, Balt., 1969-73; pediatrician Geneva (N.Y.) Pediatric Assocs. P.C., 1973—; preceptor Pediatric Clinic and Rochester (N.Y.) Gen. Hosp., 1992—; assoc. attending pediatrician Rochester Gen. Hosp. Freedom writer Amnesty Internat., N.Y., 1987—. Fellow Am. Acad. Pediatrics. Office: Geneva Pediatric Assocs 116 Lewis St Geneva NY 14456

MCCAFFREY, JUDITH ELIZABETH, lawyer; b. Providence, Apr. 26, 1944; d. Charles V. and Isadore Frances (Langford) McC.; m. Martin D. Minsker, Dec. 31, 1969 (div. May 1981); children: Ethan Hart Minsker, Natasha Langford Minsker. BA, Tufts U., 1966; JD, Boston U., 1970. Bar: Mass. 1970, D.C. 1972, Fla. 1991. Assoc. Sullivan & Worcester, Washington, 1970-76; atty. FDIC, Washington, 1976-78; assoc. Dechert, Price & Rhoads, Washington, 1978-82, McKenna, Conner & Cuneo, Washington, 1982-83; gen. counsel, corp. sec. Perpetual Savs. Bank, FSB, Alexandria, Va., 1983-91; ptnr. Powell, Goldstein, Frazer & Murphy, Washington, 1991-92, McCaffrey & Raimi, P.A., 1992—. Contbr. articles to profl. jours. Mem. edn. com. Bd. Trade, Washington, 1986-92. Mem. ABA (chairperson subcom. thrift instns. 1985-90), Fed. Bar Assn. (exec. com., banking law com. 1985-91), D.C. Bar Assn. (bd. govs. 1981-85), Women's Bar Assn. (pres. 1980-81). Episcopalian. Office: McCaffrey & Raimi, PA Ste 202 4501 Tamiami Trl N Naples FL 33940

MCCAHON, NAOMI ROSE, retired elementary educator; b. Deport, Tex., Nov. 22, 1937; d. Russell Lee and Bessie Lee (Tucker) York; m. Royal W. Jones, Sept. 4, 1951 (div. Aug. 11, 1981); children: Royal, Suzan, Rachel, Nanette, Jason; m. James Hildreth McCahon, Jan. 12, 1984. B.Music Edn., U. Tex., El Paso, 1973, postgrad., 1976, 85-90. Elem. music tchr. El Paso Ind. Sch. Dist., 1973-83, chpt. I reading and bilingual transfer tchr., 1983-93; clothing designer/dressmaker Anthony, Tex., 1993—. Choral dir. La Tuna Fed. Prison, Anthony, 1978-84, Anthony Bapt. Ch., 1973-78, Anthony Meth. Ch., 1978-82; handbell choir dir. various schs., chs., 1976-84; v.p. Valley Cmty. Libr., Anthony, 1993-94, PTA, Anthony, 1965, Dist. PTA 6, El Paso County, 1968-69; pres. bd. trustees Anthony Ind. Sch. Dist., 1981-84, 89—; trustee Tex. Grass Roots Com., 1992-93; mem. Region XIX Edn. Svc. Ctr. nominating com., 1993. Named Tchr. of the Yr., Wainwright Sch., El Paso, 1976. Mem. AAUW, Tex. Sch. Bd. Leadership Group, Parent Tchrs. Wainwright Sch. (life), Alpha Delta Kappa (chaplain, courtesy chair), Order Ea. Star. Republican. Presbyterian. Home: PO Box 936 601 Celeste Anthony TX 79821

MCCAIN, BETTY LANDON RAY (MRS. JOHN LEWIS MCCAIN), political party official, civic leader; b. Faison, N.C., Feb. 23, 1931; d. Horace Truman and Mary Howell (Perrett) Ray; student St. Marys Jr. Coll., 1948-50; AB in Music, U. N.C., Chapel Hill, 1952; MA, in Edn. Columbia U., 1953; m. John Lewis McCain, Nov. 19, 1955; children: Paul Pressly III, Mary Eloise. Courier, European tour guide Ednl. Travel Assocs., Plainfield, N.J., 1952-54; asst. dir. YWCA, U. N.C., Chapel Hill, 1953-55; chmn. N.C. Democratic Exec. Com., 1976-79 (1st woman); mem. Dem. Nat. Com., 1971-72, 76-79, 80-85, chmn. sustaining fund, N.C., 1981, 88-91, mem. com. on Presdl. nominations (Hunt Commn.), 1981-82, mem. rules com., 1982-85, mem. cabinet Gov. James B. Hunt, Jr., sec. dept. cultural resources 1993—; mem. Winograd Commn., 1977-78; pres. Dem. Women of N.C., 1971-72, dist. dir., 1969-72; pres. Wilson County Dem. Women, 1966-67; precinct chmn., 1972-76; del. Dem. Nat. Conv., 1972, 88; mem. Dem. Mid-term Confs., 1974, 78, mem. judicial council Dem. Nat. Com., 1985-89; dir. Carolina Tel. & Tel. Co., 1981— (1st woman). Sunday sch. tchr. First Presbyn. Ch., Wilson, 1970-71, 86-88, 90-92, mem. chancel choir, 1985—, deacon, 1986-92, elder, 1992—, chmn. fin. com., 1990-91; treas. Wilson on the Move, 1990-92; mem. Council on State Goals and Policy, 1970-72, Gov.'s Task Force on Child Advocacy, 1969-71, Wilson Human Relations Commn., 1975-78, chmn. Wilson-Greene Morehead scholarship com., 1986-89; mem. career and personal counseling service adv. bd. St. Andrews Coll.; charter mem. Wilson Edn. Devel. Council; active Arts Council of Wilson, Inc., N.C. Art Soc., N.C. Lit. and Hist. Assn.; regional v.p., bd. dirs. N.C. Mental Health Assn.; pres., bd. dirs., legis. chmn. Wilson County Mental Health Assn.; bd. dirs. U. N.C. Ctr. Pub. TV, 1993—, Country Doctor Mus., 1968-93, Wilson United Fund; bd. govs., sec. personnel and tenure com. U. N.C., chmn. budgets and fin. com. 1991-93; bd. regents Barium Springs Home for Children; bd. dirs., pres. N.C. Mus. History Assocs., 1982-83, membership chair, 1987-88; co-chmn. Com. to Elect Jim Hunt Gov., 1976, 80, co-chmn. senatorial campaign, 1984; mem. N.C. Adv. Budget Com., 1981-85 (1st woman); chmn. State Employees Combined Campaign N.C., 1993; bd. visitors Peace Coll., Wake Forest U. Sch. Law, U. N.C., Chapel Hill; co-chmn. fund drive Wilson Community Theatre; state bd. dirs. N.C., Am. Lung Assn., 1985-88; bd. dirs. Roanoke Island Commn. 1994—, USS/NC Battleship Commn. Recipient state awards N.C. Heart Assn., 1967, Easter Seal Soc., 1967, Community Service award Downtown Bus. Assocs., 1977, award N.C. Jaycees, 1979, 85, Women in Govt. award N.C. and U.S. Jaycettes, 1985; named to Order of Old Well and Valkyries, U. N.C., 1952; named Dem. Woman of Yr., N.C., 1976, Disting. Alumna U. N.C., Chapel Hill, 1993. Mem. U. N.C. Chapel Hill Alumni Assn. (dir.), St. Marys Alumni Assn. (regional v.p.), AMA Aux. (dir., nat. vol. health services chmn., aux. liaison rep. Council on Mental Health, aux. rep. Council on Vol. Health Orgns.), N.C. (pres., dir., parliamentarian) med. auxs., UDC (historian John W. Dunham chpt.), DAR, N.C. Found. for Nursing (bd. dirs. 1989-92), N.C. Agency Pub. Telecoms.(bd. dirs. 1993—), Info. Resources Mgmt. Commn. N.C. (bd. dirs. 1993—), N.C. Symphony (bd. dirs. 1993—), N.C. Soc. Internal Medicine Aux. (pres., bd. dirs. N.C. Equity), N.C. Sch. Arts (bd. trustees), Pi Beta Phi. The Book Club (pres.), Little Book Club , Wilson Country Club. Contbg. editor History of N.C. Med. Soc. Home: 1134 Woodland Dr NW Wilson NC 27893-2122

MCCAIN, CAROLYN, librarian; b. Winnsboro, Tex., Aug. 30, 1948; d. Pete and Ruth (Turner) Bacon; m. Gary Olan McCain, Aug. 23, 1969; children: Gregory O'Brian McCain, Kurt Allen McCain. BS in Home Econs., Stephen F. Austin U., 1970; MS in Libr. Sci., East Tex. State U., 1979. Cert. tchr., Tex. Libr. aide Mt. Pleasant (Tex.) Ind. Sch. Dist., 1971-72; elem. tchr. Clarksville (Tex.) Ind. Sch. Dist., 1972-82; libr. Holliday (Tex.) Ind. Sch. Dist., 1982-83, Como (Tex.)-Pickton Ind. Sch. Dist., 1983-91, Chisum Ind. Sch. Dist., Paris, Tex., 1991—. Asst. youth dir. McKenzie United Meth. Ch., Clarksville, 1972-82. Mem. Tex. Libr. Assn., Delta Kappa Gamma (v.p. 1991-93, scholarship 1978). Home: 103 Greenhill Ln Cooper TX 75432-1001 Office: Chisum Ind Sch Dist 3250 S Church St Paris TX 75462-8909

MCCAIN, LYNNE ANNETTE, counselor; b. St. Augustine, Fla., July 13, 1961; d. Robert George and Mildred (Cone) McC. BSN, Duke U., 1983. Cert. BCLS, RN, Ga. Nurse hemotology/oncology to nurse plastic surgery Emory Clinic, Atlanta, 1985-91, patient counselor, educator, 1991—; founder, coord. Image Reborn, 1988—. Contbr. articles to profl. jours. Founder, coord. Image Reborn Nat. Support Group, 1988—. Mem. Am. Soc. Plastic and Reconstructive Surgery Nurses (co-chmn. southeastern dist. 1990, exec. bd. seat east 1995, Nurse of Yr. 1994). Office: Emory Clinic 1327 Clifton Rd NE Atlanta GA 30307-1013

MCCAIRNS, REGINA CARFAGNO, pharmaceutical executive; b. Phila., Dec. 23, 1951; d. Carmen Augustus and Regina Mary (Yost) Carfagno; m. Robert Gray McCairns Jr., Nov. 6, 1982. BS, Marymount Manhattan Coll., 1973; MS, Villanova U., 1976; cert. bus., U. Pa., 1982. Rsch. asst. Temple U. Med. Coll., Phila., 1975-77; mfg. supr. William H. Rorer, Ft. Washington, Pa., 1977-79; mgmt. trainee, tech. asst. SmithKline & French Labs., Phila., 1979-80, shift leader antibiotics, 1980-81, validation team mem., 1984-87, validation coord., 1987; mgr. validation svcs. SmithKline Beecham, Phila., 1987—. Trustee Country Day Sch. of the Sacred Heart, 1993—. Mem. Parenteral Drug Assn. (bd. dirs. 1985-92, chmn. spring program 1988, 90, chmn. tng. com. 1986-88, chmn. nat. program com. 1990-93), Jefferson Med. Coll. Faculty Wives Club (v.p. 1988-90, program chmn., 1988-90, pres.-elect 1990-92, pres. 1992-94). Democrat. Roman Catholic. Office: 801 River Rd # L-97 Conshohocken PA 19428-2648

MCCALE, KARLA MARIE, secondary school educator; b. Philipsburg, Mont., Feb. 9, 1960; d. David Miller and Loretta (Walkup) Mazza; m. Matthew R. McCale, Aug. 8, 1981; children: Levi, Sarah. BS in Edn., U. Mont., 1981. Bus. and computer instr. Centerville Pub. Sch., Sand Coulee, Mont., 1981—; exec. distbr. Nuskin Internat., Provo, Utah, 1990—; adult computer tchr. Centerville Sch. Dist., 1987—; camp basketball coach Carroll Coll., Helena, Mont., 1983-85. Meadow gold basketball coach YWCA, Great Falls, Mont., 1983-86; cheerleader advisor, 1985-90. Recipient Outstanding Educator award Dufrense Found., 1989, 94. Mem. Centerville Edn. Assn. (sec. 1981-94), Centerville PTA, Centerville Booster Club. Home: 2221 6th Ave S Great Falls MT 59405 Office: Centerville Pub Schs 693 Hwy 227 Sand Coulee MT 59472

MCCALL, DOROTHY KAY, social worker, psychotherapist; b. Houston, July 18, 1948; d. Sherwood Pelton Jr. and Kathryn Rose (Gassen) McC. BA, Calif. State U., Fullerton, 1973; MS in Edn., U. Kans., 1978; PhD, U. Pitts., 1989. Cert. alcoholism counselor, N.Y.; lic. social worker. Counselor/intern Ctr. for Behavioral Devel., Overland Park, Kans., 1976-77; rehab. counselor Niagra Frontier Voc. Rehab. Ctr., Buffalo, 1978-79; counselor/instr. dept. motor vehicles Driving While Impaired Program N.Y. State, 1979-80; alcoholism counselor Bry Lin Hosp., Buffalo, 1979-81; instr. sch. social work U. Pitts., 1984, 91; alcohol drug counselor The Whale's Tale, Pitts., 1984-86; sole practice drug and alcohol therapy Pitts., 1986—; faculty Chem. People Inst., Pitts., 1987-89; guest lectr. sch. social work U. Pitts., 1982-87, 89; educator, trainer Community Mental Health Ctr., W.Va., 1986-87, Tenn., 1986; tchr. Tri-Community Sch. System, Western Pa., 1984-87; cons. Battered Women's Shelter, Buffalo, 1980, Buffalo Youth and Alcoholism Abuse program, 1980; lectr. in field. Mem. Spl. Adv. Com. on Addiction, 1981-83; bd. dirs. Chem. People, Task Force Adv. Com., 1984-86; bd. dirs. Drug Connection Hot Line, 1984-86; mem. Coalition of Addictive Diseases, 1984—; co-founder Greater Pitts. Adult Children of Alcoholics Network, 1984; mem. adv. bd. Chem. Awareness Referral and Evaluation System Duquesne U., 1988-93. Recipient Outstanding Achievement award Greater Pitts. Adult Children of Alcoholics Network, 1987, Disting. Svc. award Pa. Assn. for Children of Alcoholics, 1993; Nat. Inst. Alcohol Abuse tng. grantee, 1981; U. Pitts. fellow, 1983. Mem. NASW, Pa. Assn. for Children of Alcoholics (bd. dirs. 1987—, v.p. 1990-94, Disting. Svc. award 1993), Employee Assistance Profls. Assn., Inc, Assn. Labor Mgmt. Adminstrs. and Cons. on Alcoholism, Nat. Assn. for Children of Alcoholics. Democrat. Office: 673 Washington Rd Pittsburgh PA 15228-1917

MCCALL, LOUISE HARRUP, artist; b. Oklahoma City, July 8, 1925; d. Paul Louis and Lucile (Martin) Harrup; m. Robert Theodore McCall, July 20, 1945; children: Linda Louise, Catherine Anne. Student, Okla. State U., 1943-44, U. N.Mex., 1944-45, Art Inst., 1946; pvt. study, N.Y., 1955-65. Freelance artist Chgo., 1946-48, Tarrytown, N.Y., 1949-53, Chappaqua, N.Y., 1953-67, 68-71, London, 1967, Paradise Valley, Ariz., 1971—; owner McCall Studios, Inc., Paradise Valley, 1986—. Murals executed (with husband) Air and Space Mus., Washington, 1975-76, Johnson Space Ctr., Houston, 1978, Disney Epcot Ctr., L.A., 1983. Designed, with husband, windows of Valley Presbyn. Chapel, Scottsdale; paintings in private collection of H.R.H. Prince Fahd Bin Salman and H.R.H. Prince Sultan Bin Salman of Saudi Arabia. Fundraiser Crisis Nursery, Phoenix, 1984, Ariz. Hist. Soc., Phoenix, 1986, Scottsdale Cultural Ctr. 1990-92; ann. fund raiser Hospice Phoenix, 1983-92. Winner 1st Prize, State of Tex., 1943, 1st Prize, Jr. League Artists No. Westchester and N.Y., 1961. Mem. NASA Permanent Art Collection, Nat. Mus. Women in the Arts, Jr. League of Phoenix. Republican. Presbyterian. Home and Office: 4816 E Moonlight Way Paradise Valley AZ 85253-2926

MCCALLA, SANDRA ANN, principal; b. Shreveport, La., Nov. 6, 1939; d. Earl Gray and Dorothy Edna (Adams) McC. BS, Northwestern La. State U., 1960; MA, U. No. Colo., 1968; EdD, Tex. A&M U., 1987. With Caddo Parish Sch. Bd., Shreveport, 1960-88; asst. prin. Capt. Shreve High Sch., 1977-79, prin., 1979-88, 94—; dir., dean div. edn. Northwestern State U., Natchitoches, La., 1988-94; instr. math. La. State U., 1979-81. Named Educator of Yr. Shreveport Times-Caddo Tchrs. Assn., 1966, La. High Sch. Prin. of Yr., 1985, 87; recipient Excellence in Edn. award Capt. Shreve High Sch., 1982-83; Danforth fellow, 1982-83. Mem. adv. bd. Sta. KDAQ Pub. Radio, 1985-89. Active Shreveport Women's Commn., 1983-89. Mem. Nat. Assn. Secondary Sch. Prins., Am. Assn. Sch. Adminstr., Am. Assn. Coll. of Tchr. Edn., La. Assn. Prins. (Prin. of Yr. 1985), La. Assn. Sch. Execs. (Disting. Svc. award 1983), La. Assn. Colls. of Tchr. Edn. (sec., treas.), Times-Caddo Educators Assn. (Educator of Yr. 1984), Rotary Internat., Phi Delta Kappa, Kappa Delta Pi. Democrat.

MCCALLEY, HEATHER BARNHILL, bank executive; b. Tuscaloosa, Ala., Nov. 1, 1966; d. Charles William B. and Doris Carolyn (Bell) Hatch. AB, Duke U., 1988. Comml. officer Phila. Nat. Bank, 1988-92; asst. v.p. comml. loans 1st Comml. Bank, Birmingham, Ala., 1992-95; sch. coord. Ala. Young Bankers Assn., Birmingham, 1993-94. Active Jr. League, Birmingham, 1992—, Phila., 1990-92; mem. bldg. team Habitat for Humanity, 1993-94, Bethel Ensley Action Task, 1994; advisor, founder Cahaba Girl Scouts Career Interest Group, Birmingham, 1993—; mem. Duke Ann. Fund Gifts Com., 1993-95. Named to Dean's List Duke U., 1987. Mem. Nat. Park Conservation Assn., Exec. Women's Golf League. Mem. LDS Ch. Home: 102 Ridge Rd Homewood AL 35209

MCCALLISTER, CORLISS JEAN, psychologist, neuroscientist; b. New Orleans, Nov. 23, 1951; d. Edward Albert and Olga Mary (Denenea) Crabtree; m. Joe Michael McCallister, Apr. 28, 1973; children: Gillian, Grady. BA, La. Tech. U., 1973; MA, U. North Tex., 1978, Northwestern U., Natchitoches, La., 1984; PhD, Tex. A&M U., 1992. Sec. various temp. agys., U.S. Corps Engrs., New Orleans, 1969-73; elem. tchr. Caddo and Bienville Parishes, La., 1973-76, 83-85; costume designer Lagniappe, New Orleans, 1976-82; ednl. cons. various cities, 1988-93; adj. coll. faculty Northwestern State U., Natchitoches, La., Blinn Coll., College Station, Tex., S.E. Mo. State U., Cape Girardeau, 1981—; spl. edn. speaker at nat. and internat. confs. Contbr. articles to profl. jours. Regents fellow Tex. A&M U., 1988-92. Mem. APA, Am. Creativity Assn., Nat. Assn. Gifted Children, Tex. Assn. Gifted and Talented, Mo. Psychol. Assn., Soc. Neuroscience, Assn. Gifted and Talented Students.

MCCALLUM-HAUSSER, GLORIA JEAN, bank executive, educator; b. Indpls., Feb. 1, 1947; d. Jack Craig and Ann (Zablo) McCallum; children: Ginger Lee Hausser, Carrie Marie Hausser. BS, U. Tenn., Chattanooga, 1982; MBA, Brenau U., 1990. Mktg. rep. Xerox Corp., Chattanooga, 1982-84; econ. developer N. Ga. Regional Devel. Ctr., Dalton, 1984-91; asst. v.p. Am. Nat. Bank, Chattanooga, 1991-94; mgr. bus. banking ctr. First Am. Nat. Bank, Chattanooga, 1994—; instr. Chattanooga State Coll. Mem. Nat. Assn. Women Bus. Owners (sponsor), Small Bus. Coun. (small bus. person of yr. com. 1992), Civitan, Chattanooga C. of C. (econ. devel. com.). Democrat. Unitarian-Universalist. Home: 1775 Pine Needles Trl Chattanooga TN 37421-3366

MCCAMMON, HELEN MARY, government administrator; b. Winnipeg, Man., Can., Aug. 16, 1933; came to U.S., 1956; d. Joseph Zaborniak and Mary Choman; m. Richard B. McCammon, Sept. 5, 1956; children—Catherine Ann, Ian David. B.S. with honors, U. Man., 1955; M.S., U. Mich., 1956; Ph.D., Ind. U., 1959. Research geologist Man. Mines Br., Winnipeg, 1952-59; lectr. U. N.D., Grand Forks, 1960-61; from lectr. to assoc. prof. U. Pitts., 1963-68; vis. assoc. prof. U. Ill.-Chgo., 1968-70; research assoc. Field Mus. Natural History, Chgo., 1970-72; from research rep. to research dir. U.S. EPA, Boston, 1972-76; from sr. oceanographer to dir. ecol. research div. U.S. Dept. Energy, Washington, 1976-91. Contbr. articles to profl. jours. Ind. U. fellow, 1957-59, Orgn. Am. States fellow, 1969-70, Commerce Science and Tech. fellow, 1991-92; NSF grantee, 1967-72. Fellow AAAS (council 1981-84, sect. sec. 1985-89); mem. Am. Geol. Inst. (chmn. edn. com. 1978-82), Am. Soc. Limnologists and Oceanographers, Am. Women in Sci., Am. Soc. Zoologists, Marine Tech. Assn., Sigma Xi. Home: 8430 Bradley Blvd Bethesda MD 20817-1914 Office: Dept Energy ER-74 Washington DC 20585

MC CANDLESS, ANNA LOOMIS, university official; b. Aspinwall, Pa., July 21, 1897; d. George Wilberforce and Estella (Loomis) McC.; BS, Carnegie-Mellon U., 1919. Pres. Vis. Nurses Assn. of Allegheny County, 1955-57; mem. vis. com. Margaret Morrison Carnegie Coll., 1962-66; v.p. Alumni Fedn. Carnegie Inst. Tech., 1963-66. Trustee Carnegie-Mellon U., 1966—. Mem. AAUW. Clubs: Coll., Univ., Twentieth Century (pres. 1956-58) (Pitts.); Appalachian Mountain. Home: Park Plaza Apts Craig St Pittsburgh PA 15213

MCCANDLESS, BARBARA J., auditor; b. Cottonwood Falls, Kans., Oct. 25, 1931; d. Arch G. and Grace (Kittle) McCandless; m. Allyn O. Lockner, 1969. BS, Kans. State U., 1953; MS, Cornell U., 1959; postgrad. U. Minn., 1962-66, U. Calif., Berkeley, 1971-72; Cert. home economist; enrolled agt. IRS. Home demonstration agt. Kans. State U., 1953-57; teaching asst. Cornell U., 1957-58, asst. extension home economist in marketing, 1958-59; consumer mktg. specialist, asst. prof. Oreg. State U., 1959-62; instr. home econs. U. Minn., 1962-63, research asst. agrl. econs., 1963-66; asst. prof. U. R.I., 1966-67; assoc. prof. family econs., mgmt., housing, equipment dept. head S.D. State U., 1967-73; asst. to sec. Dept. Commerce and Consumer Affairs, S.D., 1973-79; tax cons., 1980-91. Mem. Nat. Council Occupational Licensing, dir., 1973-75, v.p., 1975-79. Mem. Am. Agrl. Econs. Assn., Am. Assn. Family and Consumer Scis., Am. Coun. Consumer Interests, Assn. Govt. Accts., Nat. Council on Family Relations, LWV, Kans. State U. Alumni Assn., Pi Gamma Mu. Research on profl. and occupational licensing bds. Address: 2114 Potomac Dr Topeka KS 66611

MCCANDLESS, CAROLYN KELLER, entertainment, media company executive; b. Patuxent River, Md., June 6, 1945; d. Stevens Henry and Betty Jane (Bethune) Keller; m. Stephen Porter McCandless, Apr. 22, 1972; children: Peter Keller, Deborah Marion. BA, Stanford U., 1967; MBA, Harvard U., 1969. Fin. analyst Time Inc., N.Y.C., 1969-72, mgr. budgets and fin. analysis, 1972-78, asst. sec., dir. internal adminstrn., 1978-85, v.p., dir. employee benefits, 1985-90; v.p human resources and adminstrn. Time Warner, Inc., N.Y.C., 1990—; bd. dirs. LifeRe Corp. Republican. Mem. Unitarian Ch. Office: Time Warner Inc 1271 Ave Of The Americas New York NY 10020-1300

MCCANDLESS, J(ANE) BARDARAH, emeritus religion educator; b. Dayton, Ohio, Apr. 16, 1925; d. J(ohn) Bard and Sarah Catharine (Shuey) McC. BA, Oberlin Coll., 1951; MRE, Bibl. Sem., N.Y.C., 1953; PhD, U. Pitts., 1968. Dir. Christian edn. Wallace Meml. United Presbyn. Ch., Pitts., 1953-54, Beverly Heights United Presbyn. Ch., Mt. Lebanon, Pa., 1956-61; instr. religion Westminster Coll., New Wilmington, Pa., 1961-65, asst. prof., 1965-71, assoc. prof., 1971-83, prof. religion, 1983-94, prof. emeritus, 1994—, chair dept. religion and philosophy, 1988-92; leader Christian edn. workshops Presbytery of Shenango, Presbyn. Ch. (U.S.A.), 1961—, Synod of Trinity, 1972, 76. Author: An Untainted Saint...Ain't, 1978; contbr. articles to profl. jours., Harper's Ency. Religious Edn. Mem. session New Wilmington Presbyn. Ch., 1977-79. Mack grantee Westminster Coll., 1962-63, Faculty rsch. grantee, 1972, 78, 90. Mem. Religious Edn. Assn., Assn. Profs. and Researchers in Religious Edn. (mem. exec. com. 1978-80), Soc. for Sci. Study Religion, Phi Beta Kappa, Pi Lambda Theta.

MCCANDLESS, SANDRA RAVICH, lawyer; b. Revere, Mass., Sept. 5, 1948; d. Merrill Earl and Goldie (Clayman) Ravich; m. Ross Erwin McCandless; 1 child, Phyra. BA, Radcliffe Coll., 1970; JD, Georgetown U., Washington, 1973. Bar: Calif. 1973, U.S. Ct. Appeals (1st and 7th cirs.) 1974, U.S. Ct. Appeals (6th and 9th cirs.) 1975, U.S. Dist. Ct. (no. dist.) Calif. 1976, U.S. Dist. Ct. (ea. dist.) Calif. 1978. Law clk. NLRB, Washington, 1971-73, atty. appellate ct. br., 1973-75; assoc. Pillsbury, Madison & Sutro, San Francisco, 1975-79; from assoc. to ptnr. Graham & James, San Francisco, 1979-93; atty. Sonnenschein, Nath & Rosenthal, San Francisco, 1993—; mem. faculty Nat. Inst. Appellate Advocacy, San Francisco. Mem. ABA, Bar Assn. San Francisco, San Francisco Barrister Club (co-chair com. on labor law 1979-82). Office: Sonnenschein Nath & Rosenthal 685 Market St 10th fl San Francisco CA 94105*

MCCANN, BARBARA ANN, educator; b. Pendleton, Oreg., Sept. 27, 1951; d. John Gordon Bensel and D. Lois (Carey) Bohlender; m. James Noel McCann, Aug. 6, 1982 (div. 1987); children: Sage, David. Cert., Fla. Inst. Tech., 1969; BA, Western Wash. U., 1974; cert. in manual interpretation, Blue Mountain Coll., 1987; MS in Edn., Lewis and Clark Coll., 1988. Cert. tchr., Wyo.; cert. interpretor, domestic violence counselor, Oreg.; cert. fed. contract specialist, Wash. Housing and employment commr. City of Bellingham, Wash., 1970-74; contract specialist U.S. Forest Svc., Seattle, 1974-76; ind. contract cons. Seattle and Tacoma, 1976-78; loan specialist Island Savs. and Loan, Mt. Vernon, Wash., 1978-80; materials specialist Umatilla County Edn. Svc. Dist., Pendleton, Oreg., 1980-87; specialist for hearing impaired Fremont County Sch. Dist. 1, Lander, Wyo., 1988-91; instr. sign lang. and edn. Cen. Wyo. Coll., Riverton, 1988—; dir. Title VII and V programs and curriculum Wyo. Indian Schs., Ethete, 1991—; mem. north ctrl. accreditation team Wyo. Indian Schs., 1991—; English instr. Blue Mountain C.C.; drama dir. Lander Dist. 1. Author, illustrator sign lang. edn. materials. Mem. Fairhaven com. Fairhaven Coll., Bellingham, 1970-71, advocate, 1970-72; mem. Bellingham Landlords' Assn., 1970-74; rep. Pioneer Sq. Assn., Seattle, 1976-78; vol. counselor Domestic Violence Svcs., Pendleton, Oreg., 1982-87; vol. sign lang. interpreter various orgns., Wyo., 1988—. Named Outstanding Vol., Domestic Violence Svcs., Pendleton, 1986; recipient Exceptional Svc. award United Way Umatilla County, 1986, Outstanding Instr. award Ctrl. Wyo. Coll., 1990. Mem. ASCD, NEA, Nat. Indian Edn. Assn., Nat. Assn. Bilingual Edn., Wyo. Speech and Hearing Assn., Conv. Am. Instrs. of Deaf, Ethete Ednl. Assn., Wyo. Edn. Assn. Home: 609 S 7th St Lander WY 82520-3219 Office: Wyo Indian Sch Box 340 Lander Rte Ethete WY 82520

MCCANN, BARBARA JEANNE, manufacturing executive; b. Shelton, Wash., Aug. 13, 1953; d. William Willert and Barbara Ann (Shortsleeves) McC. B in Edn., U. Wash., 1981, M in Edn., 1981, EdD, 1985. Tchr. Lk. Wash. Spl. Edn. Ctr., Kirkland, 1973-75; teaching asst. U. Wash., Seattle, 1975-76; tchr. Perpetual Help Sch., Seattle, 1977-83; merchandiser Mallory & Ch., Seattle, 1983-88; purchasing agt. Baxter Healthcare, Seattle, 1988-90; purchasing mgr. Luxar Corp., Seattle, 1990-92; ops. mgr. Babcock & Wilcox, Seattle, 1992—; cons. APICS, Seattle, 1985—, Biotech., Seattle, 1988—. Democrat. Roman Catholic.

MC CANN, CECILE NELKEN, writer; b. New Orleans; d. Abraham and Leona (Reiman) Nelken; children: Dorothy Collins, Cecile Isaacs, Annette Arnold, Denise Bachman, Albert Hews III. Student, Vassar Coll., Tulane U.; BA, San Jose State Coll., 1963, MA, 1964; postgrad., U. Calif.-Berkeley, 1966-67; hon. doctorate, San Francisco Art Inst., 1989. Tool designer Convair Corp., New Orleans, 1942-45; archtl. draftsman, various companies New Orleans and Clinton, Iowa, 1945-47, 51-53; owner, operator ceramics studio Clinton, 1953-58; instr. San Jose State Coll., 1964-65, Calif. State U., Hayward, 1964-65, Chabot Coll., Hayward, 1966-69, Laney Coll., 1967-70, San Francisco State U., 1977-78; founder, editor, pub. Artweek mag., Oakland, Calif., 1970-89; freelance writer, art advisor Kensington, Calif., 1989—; cons. Nat. Endowment Arts, 1974-78, fellow in art criticism, 1976; panelist numerous confs. and workshops. Contbr. to profl. publs.; one-woman shows at, Davenport Mus. Art, Robert North Galleries, Chgo., Crocker Art Mus., Sacramento, Calif., Calif. Coll. Arts and Crafts, Oakland, others; exhibited in group shows at, DeYoung Mus., San Francisco, Everson Mus. Art, Syracuse, N.Y., Oakland Mus., Pasadena Mus., Los Angeles County Mus. Art, others; represented in permanent collections, San Jose State Coll., Mills Coll., Coll. Holy Names, City of San Francisco, State of Calif., others. Recipient Vesta award Woman's Bldg. mag., L.A., 1988, Honor award Art Table, 1988, Media award Bay Area Visual Arts Coalition, 1989, Achievement award Art Table, 1992. Mem. Art Table, Internat. Assn. Art Critics, Coll. Art Assn., Soc. Encouragement Contemporary Art. Office: 244 Colgate Ave Kensington CA 94708-1122

MCCANN, COLLEEN MARY, governmental affairs specialist, lobbyist; b. Phila., June 28, 1964; d. John Francis and Agnetta Marie (McLaughlin) McC. BA, Rutgers U., 1986. Staff asst. subcom. on commerce, transp. and tourism U.S. Congress, Washington, 1986; staff asst., legis. coord. U.S. Rep. Jim Florio, Washington, 1986-88; legis. asst. U.S. Rep. Jim Florio, 1988-89; policy analyst Gov.-elect Jim Florio's Transition Team, 1989-91; legis. liaison Dept. of State, Trenton, N.J., 1990-93; dir. state govtl. affairs MWW/ Strategic Comms., Trenton, 1993—. Active N.J. Women's Polit. Caucus, 1990—; mem. govt. affairs com. Rutgers U., trustee, 1994—; literacy vol., Trenton, 1990—. Democrat. Roman Catholic. Home: 45 Quarry St Lambertville NJ 08530 Office: 46 W Lafayette St Trenton NJ 08608

MCCANN, CYNTHIA LYNNE, financial specialist; b. Bridgeport, Conn., Nov. 24, 1959; d. Albert Charles Gilmore and Renee Sylvia (Benoit) Jalbert; m. John Michael McCann, Oct. 10, 1992. BS, Sacred Heart U., 1989; MBA, U. Maine, 1994. Fin. asst. Instrument Cases Corp., Bridgeport, Conn., 1982-90; fin. specialist U. Maine, Orono, 1990—; staff devel. coord. Coll. of Scis., Orono, 1990—. Vol. Literacy Vols. of Am., Bangor, Maine, 1993—. Mem. Soc. Human Resource Mgmt. Roman Catholic. Office: U Maine 251B Aubert Hall Orono ME 04469-5706

MC CANN, FRANCES VERONICA, physiologist, educator; b. Manchester, Conn., Jan. 15, 1927; d. John Joseph and Grace E. (Tuttle) Mc C.; m. Elden J. Murray, Sept. 20, 1962 (dec. Nov. 1975). AB with distinction and honors, U. Conn., 1952, PhD, 1959; MS, U. Ill., 1954; MA (hon.), Dartmouth Coll., 1973. Investigator Marine Biol. Lab., Woods Hole, Mass., 1952-62; instr. physiology Dartmouth Med. Sch., Hanover, N.H., 1959-61, asst. prof., 1961-67, assoc. prof., 1967-73, prof., 1973—; adj. prof. biol. scis. Dartmouth Coll., 1974—; mem., cons. physiology study sect. NIH, 1973-77, mem. biomed. rsch. devel. com., 1978-82, chmn, 1979; cons. Hayer Inst., 1979—; cons. staff Hitchcock Hosp., Hanover, 1980—, sr. staff rsch. Norris Catton Cancer Ctr., 1980—; mem. NRC, 1982-86; chmn. Symposium on Comparative Physiology of the Heart, 1968. Editor: Comparative Physiology of the Heart: Current Trends, 1965; contbr. numerous articles to profl. jours. Trustee Lebanon Coll., 1970-73, Montshire Mus. Sic., Hanover, 1975—, Hanover Health Coun., 1976, Lebanon Coll., 1978—; incorporator Howe Libr., 1975—; active LWV, 1980—, Conservation Coun., 1983—, Hist. Soc., 1975—, N.H. Lakes Assn., 1992—; pres. Armington Lake Assn., 1991—. Nat. Heart Inst. fellow, 1959; NIH rsch. grantee, 1959—, Nat. Heart Inst., 1960, N.H. Heart Assn., 1964-65, Vt. Heart Assn., 1966—. Mem. AAAS, Am. Assn. Advancement of Lab. Animal Care, Am. Physiol. Soc., Soc. Gen. Physiologists, Biophys. Soc., Am. Heart Assn. (coun. basic sci., exec. coun. Dallas chpt. 1982-86), Soc. Neurosci. Marine Biol. Lab., LWV, Sigma Xi, Phi Kappa Phi. Office: Dartmouth Med Sch Lebanon NH 03756

MCCANN, JEAN FRIEDRICHS, artist, educator; b. N.Y.C., Dec. 6, 1937; d. Herbert Joseph and Catherine Brady (Ward) Friedrichs; m. William Joseph McCann, May 14, 1960; children: Kevin, Brian, Maureen, William, James, Denis Gerard, Kathleen. Student, Caton-Rose Inst. Fine Arts, 1955-57; AAS, SUNY, Farmingdale, 1959; BS, SUNY-Empire State Coll., Binghamton, 1986; MA summa cum laude, Marywood Coll., 1987, MFA in Art summa cum laude, 1989; grad. Kellog Leadership Program-Sch. Mgmt., SUNY, Binghamton, 1992. Dir. ArtSpace Gallery, Owego, N.Y., 1992-94; substitute art tchr. Owego-Apalachin Sch. Dist., Owego, 1968-88; tutor, evaluator SUNY-Empire State Coll., 1987-95; v.p. bd. dirs. Tioga County Coun. on Arts, 1990-91, pres., 1992-95; demonstrator for various schs., ednl. TV and county mus. One woman shows include IBM, Owego, 1972, Tioga County Hist. Soc. Mus., Owego, 1975, Nat. Hist. Ct. House, 1982, Visual Arts Ctr., Scranton, Pa., 1989-90, ArtSpace Gallery, 1991, MacDonald Art Gallery of Coll. Misericordia, Dallas, Pa., 1992, Plaza Gallery, Binghamton, 1992, Artist Guild Gallery, Binghamton, 1993, Wilson Gallery, Johnson City, N.Y., 1994; exhibited in numerous group shows, including IBM, Owego, 1970, Roberson Ctr., Binghamton, 1972, Arnot Art Mus., Elmira, 1974, 89, 92, Nat. Exhibits at Arena, Binghamton, 1974-76, Riise Gallery, St. Thomas, 1975-78, Pennino's Gallery, Burlington Vt., 1975-77, Visual Arts Ctr., Scranton, Pa., 1987, Grand Concourse Gallery, Albany, N.Y., 1989, Tioga County Hist. Soc. Mus., 1990, ArtSpace Gallery, 1990, Contemporary Gallery, Scranton, 1992; art represented in numerous pvt. and pub. collections. Bd. dirs. Birthright of Owego. Recipient Nat. Strathmore Silver award, 1989, 1st Place in Graphic Arts award Jericho Arts Coun., 1994. Mem. Nat. mus. Women in Arts (charter), Kappa Pi (pres. Zeta Omicron chpt. 1987-89, life). Home: 23 Paige St Owego NY 13827-1617

MCCANN, LOUISE MARY, paralegal; b. Bklyn., Apr. 12, 1949; d. James Joseph and Edith Dorothea (Wubbe) McC. AAS, Elizabeth Seton Coll., 1967; BS, N.Y. Inst. Tech., 1981; paralegal cert., Adelphi U., 1987. Cert. ind. adjustor, motor vehicle and casualty, N.Y. Adminstrv. asst. J.P. Stevens & Co., Inc., N.Y.C., 1969-86; legal asst. Congdon, Flaherty, O'Callaghan, Reid, Donlon, Travis & Fishlinger, Garden City, N.Y., 1986—. Capt. tng. div. Aux. Police Force, N.Y.C. Police Dept., 1975-92; sustaining mem. Roslyn (N.Y.) Landmark Soc., 1990; contbg. sponsor U.S. Equestrian Team, Gladstone, N.J., 1980. Master Sgt. USAR. Decorated Nat. Def. Svc. medal, Army Achievement medal, Army Commendation medal. Mem. Nassau Suffolk (L.I.) Horseman's Assn. Republican. Roman Catholic. Home: 305 Main St Roslyn NY 11576-2114

MCCANN, MARY CHERI, medical technologist, horse breeder and trainer; b. Pensacola, Fla., July 29, 1956; d. Joseph Maxwell and Cora Marie (Underwood) McC.; m. Robert Lee Spencer, July 20, 1977 (div. Nov. 1983). AA, Pensacola Jr. Coll., 1975; student, U. Md., 1977-78; BS in Biology, Troy State U., 1979; postgrad., U. Fla., 1979. Med. technologist Cape Fear Valley Med. Ctr., Fayetteville, N.C., 1981-85, Doctors Diagnostic Ctr., Fayetteville, 1985-86; sales rep. Waddell & Reed, Fayetteville, 1985-86; med. technologist Roche Biomed. Lab., Burlington, N.C., 1986-87; lab. mgr. Cumberland Hosp., Fayetteville, 1987-89, Naval Hosp., Pensacola, 1989-90, chemistry supr., 1990—. With U.S. Army, 1976-77. Mem. NAFE, Am. Soc. Clin. Pathologists (registrant), Am. Quarter Horse Assn., Japan Karate Assn., Pinto Horse Assn. Am. Republican. Avocations: horses, karate, guns, oil painting. Home: 300 Dogwood Dr Pensacola FL 32505-4129 Office: Naval Hosp Pensacola Lab Us Hwy 98 Pensacola FL 32512

MCCANSE-ADKINS, ANNE (MARIE) ADAMS, management consultant, graphic design firm owner; b. San Antonio, Apr. 4, 1954; d. Harry Stiles and Inger Johanne (Dahlgren) Adams; m. Howard Henry Adkins, Mar., 1992. BA in Polit. Sci. magna cum laude, U. Tex., 1975. Rsch. asst. Sci. Methods, Inc., Austin, Tex., 1975-78, with rsch. and materials devel. dept., 1978-87, dir. rsch., wrting and devel., sr. cons., sr. editor, 1987-91, assoc. dir. product devel., sr. cons., v.p., 1991-93, also bd. dirs.; co-owner, v.p. Howard Adkins Comm., Austin, 1993—; condr. Grid Seminars and Grid Orgn. Devel. Seminars, Turkey, Korea, Hong Kong, The Philippines, USSR, Venezuela, U.S., Mex., Brazil; presenter and cons. in field. Author: (with Robert R. Blake) Results-Oriented Goal Setting, 1988, Change by Design, 1989, Spanish edit., 1991, Leadership Dilemmas, Grid Solutions, 1991, Swedish edit., 1991, German edit., 1992, Spanish edit., 1992, Japanese edit., 1992, also articles. Sec. Austin Campaign for John Anderson, Austin, 1980; vol. alcohol and drug rehab., 1985-90. Mem. Assn. for Moral Edn., Ctr. for Bus. Ethics, Phi Beta Kappa. Methodist. Home: 4812 Twin Valley Dr Austin TX 78731-3539 Office: Howard Adkins Comms Ste 170 4505 Spicewood Springs Rd Austin TX 78759-8540

MCCANTS, RENEE DENISE, state official; b. N.Y.C.; d. Thomas Harold McCants and Florence Roberta (Clarke) Robinson; 1 child, Brian Kelly. BS in Labor Studies, SUNY, N.Y.C., 1986. Purchasing dir., tng. cons. Strategic Learning Systems, Queens, N.Y., 1979-86; various positions N.Y. State Dept. Labor, N.Y.C. and Albany, 1970-88; pers. adminstr. N.Y. State Dept. Labor, Albany, 1988—. Vol. Cath. Charity's Farano House Hospice. Mem. Internat. Pers. Mgmt. Assn., Internat. Assn. Persons in Employment Svc., NAACP (regional v.p. N.Y. State Dept. Labor br. 1989—), Blacks in Govt. (pub. rels. officer, parliamentarian 1988-89). Office: NY State Dept Labor Campus View Dr # 12 Albany NY 12240-1404

MCCANTS, ZAUDITU ESTHER, social worker; b. Chgo., Feb. 29, 1944; d. Lester and Dorothy D. Solobilings (McCants); 1 child, Zia P. Hill. BA, Calif. State U., 1966; MSW, Atlanta U., 1970; postgrad., Ill. Inst. Tech., Chgo., 1979, U. So. Miss., 1989. Lic. ind. clin. social worker, Washington; cert. social worker, Md., Miss. Counselor, dist. supr. Miss. Office of Youth Svcs., Jackson; psychiatric and med. social work therapist VA Med. Ctr., Washington, L.A., Chgo.; psychiatric social work therapist St. Elizabeth's Hosp., Washington; social work therapist Family and Children's Svcs., Nashville; social worker, child and family svcs. divsn. D.C. Dept. Human Svcs. Mem. NASW (foster care review bd. 1986, headstart policy coun. 1983-86), Acad. Cert. Social Workers, So. States Correctional Assn. Home: 121 Crestline Dr Apt 203 Clarksdale MS 38614-1916

MCCARROLL, KATHLEEN ANN, radiologist, educator; b. Lincoln, Nebr., July 7, 1948; d. James Richard and Ruth B. (Wagenknecht) McC.; m. Steven Mark Beerbohm, July 10, 1977 (div. 1991); 1 child, Palmer Brooke. BS, Wayne State U., 1974; MD, Mich. State U., 1978. Diplomate Am. Bd. Radiology. Intern/resident in diagnostic radiology William Beaumont Hosp., Royal Oak, Mich., 1978-82, fellow in computed tomography and ultrasound, 1983; radiologist, dir. radiologic edn. Detroit Receiving Hosp., 1984—, vice-chief dept. radiology, 1988—; pres.-elect med. staff Detroit Receiving Hosp., 1992-94, pres. 1994-96; mem. admissions com. Wayne State U. Coll. Medicine, Detroit, 1991—; officer bd. dirs. Dr. L. Reynolds, Assoc., P.C., Detroit; presenter at profl. confs. Editor: Critical Care Clinics, 1992; mem. editorial bd. Emergency Radiology; contbr. articles to profl. publs. Mem. AMA, Radiol. Soc. N.Am., Assn. Univ. Radiologists, Am. Roentgen Ray Soc., Am. Soc. Emergency Radiologists, Mich. State Med. Soc., Wayne/Oakland County Med. Soc., Phi Beta Kappa. Office: Detroit Receiving Hosp 3L-8 4201 Saint Antoine St Detroit MI 48201

MCCARTAN, LUCY, geologist; b. Miami Beach, Fla., Oct. 4, 1942; d. Arthur Austin and Edith (Newby) McC.; m. J.P. Owens, 1981. BA, Occidental Coll., 1965; MS, Lehigh U., 1967, PhD, 1972. Rsch. geologist U.S. Geol. Survey, Reston, Va., 1973—. Author maps, books and articles on geology of U.S. Atlantic seaboard, the Fla. peninsula, New Zealand, and Antarctica. Fulbright-Hays grantee, New Zealand, 1967-68; scholar AAUW, New Zealand, 1968-69; NSF Summer Teaching fellow, Fla., 1966; recipient NSF medal for Antarctic Rsch., 1980. Fellow Geol. Soc. Am.; mem. Soc. Econ. Pateontologists and Mineralogists, Clay Minerals Soc., Assn. for Women Geoscientists (v.p. Found. 1991-93). Office: US Geol Survey 928 Nat Ctr Reston VA 22092

MCCARTHY, BETTIE S., public relations executive; b. Washington, June 26, 1948. BA in History, Duke U., 1970; MBA in Fin., George Washington U., 1986. Sr. assoc. pub. affairs Borden, 1974-76; mgr. govt. rels. Borden Inc., 1976-79; mgr. pub. rels. Rexnord, Inc., 1980-87; pres. Bettie McCarthy & Assocs., Washington, 1987—; legis. analyst Grocery Mfrs. of Am. Mem. Women in Govt. Rels. (founder 1975, v.p. 1977, pres. 1978), Pub. Affairs Coun. Office: 733 15th St NW Ste 700 Washington DC 20005*

MCCARTHY, BEVERLY FITCH, retired civic leader, educator; b. St. Louis, Aug. 10, 1933; d. Clyde and Elsie (Graf) Fitch; children: Charles, Elizabeth; m. John Linley McCarthy, Mar. 17, 1973. AA, L.A. City Coll., 1953; BA in Social Scis., U. Calif., Berkeley, 1955; MA in Edn., Stanford U., 1957; adminstrv. credential, U. Pacific, 1980. Mem. faculty Monterey (Calif.) Peninsula Coll., 1957-58, Santa Barbara (Calif.) City Coll., 1958-59, San Jose (Calif.) City Coll., 1959-60; tchr. Bret Harte High Sch., Angels Camp, Calif., 1960-62; instr. psychology San Joaquin Delta Coll., Stockton, Calif., 1962-85, dir. reentry program for women and men, 1974-85; mem. Stockton City Coun., Calif., 1990-92; ret., 1992; pres. Sunflower Presents, Inc., 1990-95; with The Stockton Record Found., 1994-95. Pres. Assistance League Stockton, 1969-71, Dem. Women's Club San Joaquin County, 1987, San Joaquin chpt. Nat. Women's Polit. Caucus, 1982, Stockton Symphony Assn., 1973-77, Stockton Opera Guild, 1977-78, 87-89, 94-95, Stockton Civic Theatre League, 1981-82, San Joaquin County Child Abuse Prevention Coun. Aux., 1989-90; chmn. Stockton Redevel. Commn., 1986, San Joaquin County Commn. on Status Women, 1974-82, 93-95, San Joaquin Family Resource and Referral Employer-Assisted Child Care Coalition, 1986-89; elected Jr. Aid Stockton, 1993; dir.-treas. Children's Mus. Stockton, 1994-95. Recipient Woman of Yr. award Soroptimist Club, Stockton, 1970, 74, arts recognition award Stockton Arts Commn., 1978, Women of Achievement award San Joaquin County Commn. on Status Women, 1983; Rosalie M. Stern award U. Calif.-Berkeley Alumni Assn., 1976, Alumni citation, 1985. Mem. AAUW (named gift Ednl. Found. 1977-78), Women Execs. Stockton (founder), Cal Club San Joaquin County (founder, pres. 1981-82), Stanford Women's Club San Joaquin County (founder, pres. 1974-76), Mortar Bd., Prytanean Soc., Gavel and Quill, North Stockton Rotary Club, Nu Sigma Psi, Delta Psi Omega, Pi Lambda Theta, Phi Delta Kappa. Democrat. Home: 215 W Stadium Dr Stockton CA 95204-3115

MCCARTHY, DENISE EILEEN, clinical psychologist; b. Syracuse, N.Y., Jan. 25, 1941; d. Raymond Dennis McCarthy and Elizabeth Dorne MacBrearty. BS, Cornell U., 1962; MA, Syracuse U., 1969; postgrad., SUNY, Albany, 1977-83; D in Clin. Psychology, Antioch/New Eng. Grad. Sch., Keene, N.H., 1988. Lic. psychologist, N.Y. Home econ. Monroe County Extension Svc., Rochester, N.Y., 1962-65; team leader, sr. counselor N.Y. State Dept. Labor, Albany, Syracuse, 1966-73; rehab. counselor N.Y. State Office Vocat. Rehab., Albany, 1973-80; dir. community support systems Schenectady Shared Svs., 1981-82; masters level psychologist O.D. Heck Devel. Ctr., Schenectady, 1982-83, A.I.M., Saratoga Springs, N.Y., 1983-84; staff counselor Siena Coll., Loudonville, N.Y., 1985; asst. psychologist Capital Dist. Psychiat. Ctr., Cairo, N.Y., 1985-88, assoc. psychologist, 1988-93; pvt. practice Albany, 1990—; co-founder Ctr. for Cognitive Therapy of the Capital Dist. Bd. dirs. Dominion House, Schenectady, 1981-82. Mem. Am. Psychol. Assn., N.Y. State Psychol. Assn., Psychologists of Northeastern N.Y., Nat. Registry Health Svc. Providers. Office: Ctr Cognitive Therapy of Capital Dist 1414 Western Ave Albany NY 12203

MCCARTHY, HELEN H., civic worker, retired educator; b. Fresno, Calif.; d. Frederick Henry and Louise A. (Scharenberg) Hacke; m. J. Thornton McCarthy, Mar. 2, 1946; children: Thornton Randall, Deborah McCarthy Edwards. BA with honors, U. Calif., Berkeley, 1943. Cert. tchr., Calif. Pres. Pasadena (Calif.) chpt. Nat. Assistance League, 1963-64, mem. admissions and inspection com.; active Nat. Charity League, 1966-72; mem. Pasadena philharm. com. Hollywood Bowl Assn., 1965-68; active Children's Hosp. Inc., Oakland, Calif., 1989-90, br. chmn., bd. dirs., 1993—; pres. Cascade Guild, John Muir Hosp., Walnut Creek, Calif., 1990-91; mem. Assistance League Diablo Valley. Mem. AAUW. Republican. Presbyterian. Home: 5545 Terra Granada Dr Walnut Creek CA 94595-4058

MCCARTHY, JOANN JESSICA, secondary school educator; b. Detroit, Sept. 30, 1951; d. Frank Joseph Weier and Helen Joann (Elliott) Weir; m. David Norman Fluegge, Aug. 19, 1972 (div. May 1981); m. Gerald Blair McCarthy, July 17, 1993. AA in Liberal Arts, Macomb C.C., 1971; B in Bus. Edn., Wayne State U., 1977; M in Bus. Edn., Mich. State U., 1982. Cert. secondary tchr., Mich. Sec. Mfrs. Bank, Detroit, 1971-72, Van Dyke Sch. Dist., Warren, Mich., 1972-76; rsch. asst. Wayne State U., Detroit, 1977; tchr., coord. Troy (Mich.) Sch. Dist., 1977—. Editor curriculum program, 1977. Vol. Cystic Fibrosis Found., Southfield, Mich., 1988-92. Mem. Mich. Bus. Edn. Assn., Macomb-Oakland Coords. Assn., Delta Pi Epsilon. Office: Troy Sch Dist Athens High 4333 John R Troy MI 48098-4799

MCCARTHY, JOANNE MARY, reading specialist. AB in Hist., Emmanuel Coll., 1967; MEd in Elem. Edn., Boston State Coll., 1969; EdD in Reading, Boston U., 1990. Cert. elem. tchr., sch. psychologist, hist. tchr., guidance counsleor, cons. tchr. reading, supr. reading, elem. prin., social studies tchr., English tchr., supt., dir., Mass. With dept. of def. Nat. Security Agy., 1967-68; tchr. St. Gregory's Sch., Dorchester, Mass., 1969-74; ednl. coord., tchr. Boston Children's Svcs., 1974-75; testing diagnostician Duxbury (Mass.) Pub. Schs., 1975-76; reading tchr. Duxbury High Sch., 1975-81; reading specialist Chandler Sch. and Duxbury Elem. Sch., 1981—; adult literacy program vol. Odwin Learning Ctr., Dorchester, 1990-92. Presenter in field. Exec. bd. mem. Boston U. Sch. Edn. Alumni Assn. Mem. ASCD, Nat. Coun. Tchrs. of English, Internat. Reading Assn., Assn. Childhood Edn. Internat., Duxbury Tchrs. Assn., Greater Boston Reading Coun., Mass. Tchrs. Assn., New England Assn. Tchrs. of English, Pi Lambda Theta.

MCCARTHY, JULIANA MARIE, book and magazine editor; b. Sacramento, May 12, 1958; d. Robert Earl and Ottilie (Brand) McC. BA in Anthropology, U. Calif. at San Diego, La Jolla, 1979; MA, U. Chgo., 1984. Bus. mgr. lit. mag. Chgo. Rev., 1985-87; editorial asst. Books divsn. U. Chgo. Press, 1984-87, mng. editor Nat. Bur. Econ. Rsch. series, 1987-92, acquiring editor Econ. History, 1990-92; mng. editor ABA Press, Chgo., 1992-94, editor, 1994—; freelance manuscript editor, Chgo., 1988—. Bd. dirs., officer 54th St. Coop. Assn., Chgo., 1986-92. Deutscher Akademischer Austauschdienst summer fellow, 1983, Univ. fellow U. Chgo., 1981-82, 82-83. Mem. Women in Scholarly Pub. Home: 1170 E 54th St # 1 Chicago IL 60615-5124

MCCARTHY, KAREN P., congresswoman, former state representative; b. Mass., Mar. 18, 1947. BS in English, Biology, U. Kans., 1969, MBA, 1985; MEd in English, U. Mo., Kansas City, 1976. Tchr. Shawnee Mission (Kans.) South High Sch., 1969-75, The Sunset Hill (Kans.) Sch., , 1975-76; mem. Mo. House of Reps., Jefferson City, Mo., 1977-95; cons. govt. affairs Marion Labs., Kansas City, Mo., 1986-93; congresswoman, Mo. 5th Dist. U.S. Congress, Washington, D.C., 1995—; rsch. analyst pub. fin. dept. Stearn Bros. & Co., 1984-85, Kansas City, Mo.; rsch. analyst Midwest Rsch. Inst., econs. and mgmt. scis. dept., Kansas City, 1985-86. Del. Dem. Nat. Conv., 1992, Dem. Nat. Party Conf., 1982, Dem. Nat. Policy Com. Policy Commn., 1985-86; community advisor The Jr. League of Kansas City, 1980-88; spl. adviser Genesis Sch. Recipient Outstanding Young Woman Am. award, 1977, Outstanding Woman Mo. award Phi Chi Theta, Civil Liberties award ACLU of Western Mo., 1983, Woman of Achievement award mid-continent coun. Girl Scouts U.S., 1983, 87, MOVA award, Mo. Victiom Assistance Network, 1988, Annie Baxter award, 1993; named Conservation Legislator of Yr., Conservation Fed. Mo., 1987. Fellow Inst. of Politics; mem. Nat. Conf. on State Legis. (del. on trade and econ. devel. to Fed. Republic of Germany, Bulgaria, Japan, France and Italy, mem. energy com. 1978-84, fed. taxation, trade and econ. devel. com. 1986, chmn. fed. budget and taxation com. 1987, vice chmn. state fed. assembly 1988, pres.-elect 1993), Nat. Dem. Inst. for Internat. Affairs (instr. No. Ireland 1988, Baltic Republics 1992, Hungary 1993). Office: US House Reps 2334 Rayburn House Office Bldg Washington DC 20515-2505*

MC CARTHY, KATHRYN A., physicist; b. Lawrence, Mass., Aug. 7, 1924; d. Joseph Augustine and Catherine (Barrett) McCarthy. A.B., Tufts U., 1945, M.S., 1946; Ph.D., Radcliffe Coll., 1957; D.Sc. (hon.), Coll. Holy Cross, 1978; D.H.L. (hon.), Merrimack Coll., 1981. Instr. physics Tufts U., 1946-53, asst. prof., 1953-59, assoc. prof., 1959-62, prof., 1962—; dean Tufts U. (Grad. Sch.), 1969-74, provost, sr. v.p., 1973-79; research fellow in metallurgy Harvard, 1957-59, vis. scholar, 1979-80; research assoc. Baird Assocs., 1947-49, 51, Boston U. Optical Research Lab., summer 1952; assoc. research engr. U. Mich., summer 1957-58; dir. Mass. Electric Co., State Mut. Assurance Co. Trustee Southeastern Mass. U., 1972-74, Merrimack Coll., 1974-83, Coll. Holy Cross, 1980—; corporator Lawrence Meml. Hosp., 1975—, dir., 1978—, chmn., 1991. Fellow Optical Soc. Am., Am. Phys. Soc.; mem. Soc. Women Engrs. (sr.), Phi Beta Kappa, Sigma Xi. Roman Catholic. Home: 1580 Massachusetts Ave Apt 5D Cambridge MA 02138-2926 Office: Tufts U Dept Physics 4 Colby St Medford MA 02155-6013

MCCARTHY, MARY ELIZABETH, psychologist; b. N.Y.C., Feb. 22, 1937; d. Timothy and Bridget (Hester) McC. BA in Polit. Sci./Psychology, Hunter Coll., 1964; MS in Guidance and Counseling, Fordham U., 1965; PhD in Clin. Psychology, U. Santo Tomas, 1970, MA in Philosophy, 1971; MBA in Mgmt./Mktg., Golden Gate U., 1990. Tchr., dir. guidance Notre Dame Acad., N.Y.C., 1965-66; career guidance counselor Bklyn. Coll., 1966-68; asst. prof. Ateneo de Manila U., Quezon City, Philippines, 1968-71; dir. Epoch House Friends Med. Sci. Rsch. Ctr., Inc., Balt., 1971-72; lectr. U. ILE-IFE, Nigeria, 1972-73; assoc. prof. psychology U. V.I., St. Thomas, 1973-80; program dir. Santa Rosa Geriat. Residential Ctr., Milton, Fla., 1981; dir. Regional Alcohol Rehab. Program West Tidewater Community Svcs. Bd., Suffolk, Va., 1982-83; from clin. svcs. mgr. to cmty. rels. coord. Chesapeake (Va.) Cmty. Svcs. Bd., 1983—; adj. prof. Troy State U., Norfolk, Va., 1992—, Old Dominion U., Norfolk, 1991—, Golden Gate U., Va. and N.C., 1984-91, St. Leo Coll., Va., 1983-87, Norfolk State U., 1983-86; cons. Peninsula Alcohol Svcs., Newport News, Va., 1982-83. Author: An Assessment of the Unique Needs of the Elderly Offender, 1980, When Someone You Love Goes to Prison, 1992, (with Jerome McElroy) An Assessment of the Needs of the Older Adult in the U.S. Virgin Islands, 1979; editor: Gerontology in the Virgin Islands: Readings and Research, 1978; Procs. of the First Gerontology Institute, 1979; contbr. articles to profl. jours., chpts. to books. Bd. dirs. V.I. coun. Alcoholism, 1975-79, v.p., 1976-78; bd. dirs. St. Dunstan's Episc. Ch., St. Croix, V.I., 1977, Antilles Sch., St. Thomas, 1979; sr. Companion Program Adv. Coun., 1985-89; advisor gerontology curriculum Tidewater C.C., 1985-87; mem. task force refugee resettlement, Tidewater, 1985-87; bd. dirs. Alzheimer's Disease and Related Disorders Assn., Hampton Rds., Va., 1983-90, pres. 1987-90; corr. sec. Headstart Policy Coun., 1984-85, vice chair, 1987-88, bd. dirs., 1984-89; mem. long term care coun. City of Chesapeake, 1983-89; bd. dirs. Am. Cancer Soc., 1986—, chairperson svcs. and rehab. com., 1988-89, 2d v.p., 1990-91, pres. 1992-94. Fellow U.S.P.H.S., 1979-80; grantee U.S. Dept. Edn., 1976, V.I. Commn. of Aging, 1978-79, Va. Dept. Corrections, 1984, 85, Commonwealth of Va., 1985-86, State of Va. and City of Chesapeake, 1985, Alzheimer's Disease and Related Disorders Bd., 1985; recipient Cert. Appreciation Philippine Guidance and Pers. Assn., 1968, Philippine Mental Health Assn., 1971, Am. Cancer Soc. for Patient Svcs., 1987, 88, 89, 90-91, 91-92, Alzheimer's Assn., 1984, 90, Peer Recognition award Chesapeake Cmty. Svcs. Bd., 1990, award Nat. Assn. Mental Health Officers 1990, 91, 92, 94, Vol. Yr. award Am. Cancer Soc., 1993, Star Performer award City of Chesapeake, 1993, Jefferson award Outstanding Community Svc., 1994. Mem. APA, Am. Marriage and Family Therapy, Pub. Rels. Soc. Am., Nat. Assn. Mental Health Info. Officers (Pub. Rels./Writing awards 1990, 91, 92, 94), Bio ethics Network of Southwestern Va. Roman Catholic. Home: 5639 Picadilly Ln Portsmouth VA 23703-1649 Office: Chesapeake Cmty Svcs Bd 1417 Battlefield Blvd N Chesapeake VA 23320-4516

MCCARTHY, PATRICE ANN, lawyer; b. New Haven, Jan. 23, 1957; d. Robert Edmund and Faith Arline (Augur) McC.; m. Donald Allen Kirshbaum, Oct. 25, 1986; children: Lynn Anne, Sara. BA, Mt. Holyoke Coll., 1978; JD, U. Conn., 1981. Bar: Conn. 1981, U.S. Dist. Ct. Conn. 1981. Staff assoc. Conn. Conf. Municipalities, New Haven, 1981-83; legal counsel Conn. Assn. Bds. Edn., Hartford, 1983-88, gen. counsel, assoc. exec. dir. for govt. rels., 1988-91; dep. dir., gen. counsel, 1991—. Editor: Conn. Manual Bd. Policy Regulations and By-laws, 1987; contbr. articles to profl. jours. Mem. ABA, Nat. Sch. Bds. Assn. Coun. Sch. Attys. (bd. dirs. 1990-94), Am. Soc. Pub. Adminstrn. (coun. 1988—), Nat. Orgn. for Legal Problems in Edn., Conn. Bar Assn., Conn. Sch. Attys. Coun. (pres. 1988-89), Conn. Pub. Employers Labor Rels. Assn. (bd. dirs. 1985-88), Mt. Holyoke Club (v.p. 1986-88, pres. 1990-94). Office: Conn Assn Bds Edn 309 Franklin Ave Hartford CT 06114-1851

MC CARTHY, PATRICIA MARGARET, retreat house administrator, social worker; b. L.A., Mar. 2, 1943; d. Alphonsus Martin and Margaret (Kroutil) Mc C. BA, Dominican Coll., San Rafael, Calif., 1964; MSW, U. So. Calif., 1967. Lic. clin. social worker, Calif. Community organizer Holy Name Parish Archdiocese L.A., 1980-82; social worker St. Anne's Maternity Home, L.A., 1967-73, Holy Family Adoption Svc., L.A., 1973-78, Stanford Home, Sacramento, 1982-84; info. specialist Info. & Referral Svc. L.A. County, El Monte, Calif., 1984-87; exec. dir. Holy Spirit Retreat Ctr., Encino, Calif., 1987—. Mem. Jericho, L.A., 1988; inc. mem. Sisters of Social Svc. L.A., 1978—. Named Outstanding Citizen L.A. City Coun., 1982. Mem. NASW, Retreats Internat. (so. Calif. area rep. 1990-93). Democrat. Roman Catholic. Office: Holy Spirit Retreat Ctr 4316 Lanai Rd Encino CA 91436-3698

MCCARTNEY, RHODA HUXSOL, farm manager; b. Floyd County, Iowa, June 30, 1928; d. Julius Franklin and Ruth Ada (Carney) Huxsol; m. Ralph Farnham McCartney, June 25, 1950; children: Ralph, Julia, David. AA, Frances Shimer, 1948; BA, U. Iowa, 1950. Mng. dir. McCartney-Huxsol Farms, Charles City, Iowa, 1969—; prin. trustee J.F. Huxsol Trusts, Charles City, Iowa, 1984—. Pres. Nat. 19th Amendment Soc., Charles City, 1991—; mem. Terace Hill Commn., Des Moines, 1988-94, bd. dirs. Iowa Children and Family Svcs., Des Moines, 1963-68; mem. Iowa Arts Coun., Des Moines, 1975-78. Mem. AAUW, Iowa LWV, PEO. Mem. Congregational Ch. Home: 1828 Cedarview Dr Charles City IA 50616 Office: McCartney-Huxsol Farms 117 N Jackson St Charles City IA 50616

MCCARTY, LORRAINE CHAMBERS, painter, educator; b. Detroit, Aug. 17. Student, Detroit Art Acad., 1938, Stephens Coll., 1940, Wayne State U., 1942; studied with, Glen Michaels, Emil Weddidge, Robert Wilbert. Mem. faculty Flint (Mich.) Inst. Arts, 1970—, Grosse Point (Mich.) War Meml., 1972—; pvt. tchr. art Royal Oak, Mich.; mem. faculty Muskegon (Mich.) Inst. Arts, 1978—, Flint Inst. Arts, 1978—; artist in residence Stephens Coll., Columbia, Mo., 1981; advisor, designer Internat. Women's Air & Space Mus., Ohio, 1986, Okla., juror, critic in field, lectr.in field; ofcl. artist USAF, 1981; instr. Birmingham Bloomfield (Mich.) Art Assn., Islanders of St. Loud-Workshop Retreats in No. Mich., Paint Creek Ctr. for Arts, Rochester, Mich., Mt. Clemens Ctr. for Arts, Mich., Flint Inst. Arts,, Muskegon Mus. of Art, Jessee Besser Mus., Alpena, Ella Sharpe Mus., Jackson, Mich, Ctr. for Creative Studies, Detroit, others; cons. Greenfield Village Mus., 1991; mentor U. Mich., 1992. Numerous one woman shows including Midland Arts Coun., 1978, Dayton Art Inst., 1978, Flint Inst. Arts, 1980, Nat. Acad. Arts and Letters, 1980, Stephens Coll., 1981; numerous group shows including Women '71, DeKalb, Ill., Butler Mus. Am. Art, Youngstown, Ohio, Detroit Inst. Arts, 1980, Smithsonian, Washington, 1981, Ohio Arts Coun. Nat. Traveling Show, 1982; represented in permanent collections including Smithsonian Nat. Air and Space Mus., Muskegon Mus. Art, Butler Mus. Am. Art, Dow Chem. Co., Midland, Mich., No. Ill. U., DeKalb, K Mart Internat. Hdqrs., Troy, Mich., Capital City Airport, Lansing, R.L. Polk Co., Detroit, Bohn Cooper and Brass, Southfield, Mich., Jug Pilots P047s, N.Y.C.; commns. include murals for Gen. Dynamics Landsystems 1 Mich., Alpena Light & Power Co., art works for Lear Siegler Seating Co., Mich., 4 H Hdqrs., Washington, Trusswall Internat., Mich., R.L Polk Co., Mich., Capitol City Airport, Mich., Gerald Behaylo, Mich.; producer TV series The Artist in You; inventor, designer Artist's Eye: Visual Aid for Artists. Mem. exec. com. Oakland County Cultural Coun. Recipient numerous awards including Purchase prize Butler Mus. Am. Art, 1969, Grand Jury award 16th Ann. Mid-Mich., Best Painting by a Woman award Detroit Inst. Arts, 1971, Disting. Alumnae award Stephens Coll., 1982, 1st place award Nat. Fedn. Local Cable Programmers, 1984; recipient grant Lester Hereward Cooke Found., 1984, creative artist, Mich. Coun. Arts, 1983, master to apprentice, Mich. Coun. Arts, 1983, artists consultancy, Mich. Coun. Arts, 1983, OIP Project, Savannah, Ga., 1965, 67, 72. Mem. Detroit Soc. Women Painters and Sculptors, All Women Transcontinental Air Race Assn., Mich. Watercolor Soc., Artists Equity Assn., Mich. Acad. Arts Sci. Letters. Home: 1112 Pinehurst Ave Royal Oak MI 48073-3370

MCCARTY-POWELL, DEBRA LYNN, social services administrator; b. Chgo., June 8, 1955; d. Thomas Arthur and Carrie Sue (Workman) Foley; m. Ronald Claude Powell, Dec. 7, 1991; children: Anthony, Ronald Jr., John, Jeromy. BS in Criminal Justice with honors, U. Tenn., Martin, 1989, MS in Ednl. Psychology and Guidance, 1991. Libr. asst. Paul Meek Libr., U. Tenn., Martin, 1986-90; state case mgr., clinician NW Counseling Ctr., Martin, 1990—; cons. in field, 1991—. Mem. NAFE, Nat. Honor Soc. Psychology, Weakley County Literacy Assn. (tutor), Criminal Justice Soc. (sec. 1980's, treas. 1988-89, Outstanding Criminal Justice Student 1989). Baptist. Home: 1588 Old Troy Rd Union City TN 38261-5514 Office: NW Counseling Ctr 930 Mount Zion Rd Union City TN 38261-7655

MCCARY, ANNE MARGARET, trauma nurse, medical case management service professional; b. Anniston, Ala., Sept. 26, 1967; d. Elvin Columbus and Margaret Pauline (Waters) McC. BSN, Birmingham So. Coll., 1989; MSN, U. Ala., Birmingham, 1991. RN, Ala.; cert. emergency nurse Bd. Certification Emergency Nursing; cert. case mgr.; cert. ins. rehab. specialist commn. Staff nurse AMI Brookwood Med. Ctr., Birmingham, 1989-90, preceptor, 1990-91, clin. nurse specialist, 1992-94; clin. nurse specialist U. Ala. Hosp., Birmingham, 1992-94; case mgr. Directions Mgmt. Svcs. Inc., 1994—. Mem. ANA, Emergency Nurses Assn., Am. Assn. Spinal Cord Injury Nurses, Sigma Theta Tau. Episcopalian. Home: 411 Skyview Dr Apt A Birmingham AL 35209-3037 Office: Directions Mgmt Svcs Inc 200 Cahaba Park S Ste 217 Birmingham AL 35242

MCCASLIN, F. CATHERINE, consulting sociologist; b. Chattanooga, Feb. 21, 1947; d. John Jacob and Elizabeth Dorothy (Johnson) McC. AB, Hollins Coll., Roanoke, Va., 1969; MA, Ga. State U., 1972; PhD, UCLA, 1979. Assoc. dir. Ga. Narcotics Treatment Program, Atlanta, 1972-73; research assoc., dir. research Health Care Delivery Services, Inc., Los Angeles, 1974-76; sr. survey analyst Kaiser Found. Health Plan, Los Angeles, 1978-80; program officer The Robert Wood Johnson Found., Princeton, 1980-84; faculty U. Pa. Sch. Medicine, Phila., 1984-86; ptnr. Schuhmacher & McCaslin Assocs., Phila., 1986—; exec. dir. The H.F. Lenfest Found., Pottstown, Pa., 1988-89; dir. rsch. Beaufort (S.C.) County Sch. Dist., 1992—; adj. faculty sociology U. S.C., Beaufort, 1992-93; mem. adv. bd. Nat. Childhood Asthma Project, NHBLI, Washington, 1982-84; adv. com. mem. Statewide Adolescent Pregnancy, New Brunswick, 1981-84; trainee NIH, 1973-79; cons. in field. Mem. editorial bd. Jour. Health & Social Behavior, 1988—; editor Med. Sociology newsletter, 1984—; contbr. articles to profl. jours. Fellow NIMH, 1975; grantee Spl. Action Office for Drug Abuse Prevention, 1972, Robert Wood Johnson Found., 1984. Mem. Am. Sociol. Assn. (nat. council med. sociology sect. 1984—). Am. Pub. Health Assn., Sociologists for Women in Soc. Democrat. Episcopalian. Home: 2100 Berkeley Circle Port Royal SC 29935 Office: Beaufort County Sch Dist 1300 King St Beaufort SC 29902-4936

MCCASLIN, NANCY SHAFF, continuing education consultant; b. Schenectady, N.Y., May 3, 1941; d. Seneca and Gladys Eva (Crittenden) Shaff; m. David Earl Dean, Mar. 23, 1963 (div. Dec. 1971); 1 child, Andrew; m. Darryl William McCaslin, Mar. 24, 1973 (div. Sept. 1992); 1 child Meredith. BSN, Syracuse U., 1963; MS, Johns Hopkins U., 1982; postgrad., Cath. U. Am., 1983-84. RN, Md., N.Y., Va., Pa., Maine, Nebr. Charge nurse Syracuse (N.Y.) Meml. Hosp., 1963-65; staff nurse Johns Hopkins Hosp., Balt., 1965; med.-surg. nurse Anniston (Ala.) Meml. Hosp., 1968-69, Bryan Meml. Hosp., Lincoln, Nebr., 1969-70; charge nurse Ea. Maine Med. Ctr., Bangor, 1972; staff nurse Staff Builders, Balt., 1979-83; mem. faculty Harford Community Coll., Bel Air, Md., 1979-85; dir. nursing program Health and Edn. Coun., Balt., 1985-90; pres. Healthcare Edn. Resources, Joppa, Md., 1990—; CEO Publ. Resources for Nurses, 1991—. Editorial reviewer Kramer Publs., 1989, Health Leadership Assocs., 1990, 92. Mem. Md. Nurses' Assn. (pres. 1991-93, Rosalie S. Abrams award 1986, interim exec. dir. 1993-94, editor Md. Nurse 1993—, conv. mgr. 1994—), Assn. Nurses in AIDS Care (founding mem., bd. dirs. 1988-91, ANACdotes editor 1989-92). Home: 516 Shore Dr Joppa MD 21085-4542 Office: Healthcare Edn Resources PO Box 476 Joppa MD 21085-0476

MCCASLIN, TERESA EVE, management executive; b. Jersey City, Nov. 22, 1949; d. Felix F. and Ann E. (Golaszewski) Hrynkiewicz; m. Thomas W. McCaslin, Jan. 22, 1972 (div.). BA, Marymount Coll., 1971; MBA, L.I. U., 1981. Adminstrv. officer Civil Service Commn., Fed. Republic Germany, 1972-76; personnel dir. Oceanroutes, Inc., Palo Alto, Calif., 1976-78; mgr., coll. relations Continental Grain Co., N.Y.C., 1978-79, corp. personnel mgr., 1979-81, dir. productivity, internal cons., 1981-84; dir., human resources Grow Group, Inc., N.Y.C., 1984-85, v.p. human resources, 1985-86, v.p. adminstrn., 1986-89; corporate v.p. human resources Avery Dennison Corp., Pasadena, Calif., 1989-94, Monsanto Co., St. Louis, 1994—. Career counselor Marymount Coll. Career Ctr., Tarrytown. Recipient Sustained Superior Performance award U.S. Civil Service Commn., Fed. Republic Germany. Mem. Conf. Bd., Am. Mgmt. Assn., Human Resources Coun. Roman Catholic. Office: Monsanto Co 800 N Lindbergh Blvd Saint Louis MO 63167

MCCASLIN-SMITH, CHERYL ANN, librarian; b. Carroll, Iowa, Dec. 27, 1947; d. Claude L. and Nema E. (Hook) Finley; m. Bill J. McCaslin, Mar. 8, 1985 (dec. Mar. 1987). BA in Elem. Edn., Buena Vena Vista Coll., 1970; MEd, North Tex. State U., 1986. Libr. Clarion (Iowa) Sch. Systems, 1972-83; media specialist vision program Dallas Ind. Sch. Dist., 1986—. Author: Sharrian the Librarian is Blind - A True Story, 1982. Mem. AAUW (grantee 1982), Dallas Assn. Sch. Librs. Democrat. Methodist. Home: # B 7717 Eastern Ave Dallas TX 75209

MCCAUGHEY, ELIZABETH P., state official; b. Oct. 20, 1948; d. Albert Peterkin; m. Thomas McCaughey, 1972 (div. 1994); children: Amanda, Caroline, Diana. BA, Vassar Coll., 1970; MA, Columbia Univ., 1972, PhD, 1976. Public policy expert Manhattan Inst., N.Y.C.; lt. gov. State of N.Y., 1995—; instr. Vassar Coll., 1979, Columbia Univ., 1980-84; chmn. Governor's Medicaid Task Force, 1994. Author: From Loyalist to Founding Father, 1980, Government By Choice, 1987; also articles. Recipient Bancroft Dissertation award, Richard B. Morris prize; Woodrow Wilson fellow, Herbert H. Lehman fellow, Honorary Vassar fellow, John Jay fellow, Post Doctoral Rsch. fellow NEH, 1984, John Molin fellow Manhattan Inst., 1993. Republican. Office: Office of Lt Governor Executive Chamber State Capitol Rm 326 Albany NY 12224

MCCAULEY, FLOYCE REID, psychiatrist; b. Braddock, Pa., Dec. 30, 1933; d. John Mitchel and Irene (Garner) Reid; m. James Calvin McCauley, July 15, 1955; children: James Stanley, Lori Ellen. BS in Nursing, U. Pitts., 1956; D.O., Coll. Osteopathic Medicine, Phila., 1972. Bd. eligible in child and adult psychiatry. Intern Suburban Gen. Hosp., Norristown, Pa., 1972-73; resident in adult psychiatry Phila. State Hosp. and Phila. Mental Health Clinic, 1973-75; fellow Med. Coll. of Pa. and Ea. Pa. Psychiat. Inst., Phila., 1975-78; Chief child psychiatry inpatient unit Med. Coll. Pa., Phila., 1978-80; med. dir. Carson ValleySch., Flourtown, Pa., 1980-82; dir. outpatient psychiat. clinic Osteopathic Med. Ctr. Phila., 1980-86; staff psychiatrist Kent Gen. Hosp., Dover, Del., 1986-89; psychiat. cons. Del. Guidance Svcs. for Children, Dover, 1986-91; clin. dir. children's unit HCA Rockford Ctr., Newark, 1991-93; with Kid's Peace Nat. Hosp. for Kids in Crisis, 1993—; mem. Mental Health Code Rev. Com. for Del., 1991; inducted into the Chapel of Four Chaplains, Phila., 1983; psychiat. cons. Seaford (Del.) Br. of New Eng. Fellowship for Rehab., 1991-93, Cath. Charities Day Treatment Program for 3-6 Yr. Olds, Dover, Del., 1990—; cons. Del. Guidance Day Treatment Program, 1990—; staff psychiatrist Kids Peace Nat. Hosp. for Kids in Crisis, 1993—. Mem. Mayor's Com. for Mental Health, Phila., 1983. Mem. Am. Osteopathic Assn., Am. Coll. Neuropsychiatrists, Am. Psychiat. Assn., Am. Acad. Child Psychiatrists (Del. br.). Democrat. Methodist.

MCCAULEY, MARY ANN, public relations executive; b. Moline, Ill., Feb. 20, 1947. BS in Journalism, U. Columbia, 1969. Reporter Mason City Globe Gazette, 1969-71; editor Hallmark Cards, 1971-72; assoc. editor ANA, 1972-76; owner Galena Sentinel Times, 1976-78; pub. rels. supr. Centerre Bancorp., 1978-81; pub. rels. dir. United Technologies Comms. Co., 1981-83; acct. supr. Brum & Anderson Pub. Rels., 1983-84, v.p., 1984-86; pres. McCauley & Assocs., 1987-93; prin. Ketchum Metz McCauley, Inc., 1993—. Mem. Internat. Assn. Bus. Communicators (dir. mkt. rsch. 1990-91, pres. Northstar 1989, dir. U.S. dist. 4 1984-85, program devel. dir. 1981, 83, 86). Office: Ketchum Metz McCauley Inc 333 Washington Ave N Minneapolis MN 55401*

MCCHESNEY, S. ELAINE, lawyer; b. Bowling Green, Ky., Sept. 14, 1954; d. Kelsey H. McChesney and Lorraine (Carter) Durey; m. Paul Boylan; children: Michael, Jessica, Andrew. AB summa cum laude, Western Ky. U., 1975; JD, Harvard U., 1978. With Bingham Dana & Gould, Boston, 1978—, ptnr., 1985—; chair joint MBA/BBA bar com. on jud. appts., 1988-89, 90-91; trial practice advisor moot ct. exercises Harvard Law Sch.; moot ct. judge Harvard Law Sch., Boston U., Suffolk U. Bd. editors Mass. Lawyer's Weekly, 1987-88; panelist, speaker in field; contbr. articles to profl. jours. Treas., bd. dirs. St. Paul's Nursery Sch., Dedham, Mass., 1990—; parent rep. Charles River Sch., Dover, Mass., vol. numerous coms.; vol. Am. Heart Found., March of Dimes; vol. street canvassing on zoning issues. Mem. ABA (labor law sect. subcom. individual rights in the workplace 1982—, comml. banking or fin. transactions litigation 1982), Mass. Bar Assn., Boston Bar Assn. (coun. 1994—, law sch. liaison com. 1984-85, IOLTA com., co-chair ann. mtg.), Women's Bar Assn. (editor calendar 1988-92). Office: Bingham Dana & Gould 150 Federal St Boston MA 02110

MCCLANAHAN, CONNIE DEA, pastoral minister; b. Detroit, Mar. 1, 1948; d. Manford Bryce and Dorothy Maxine (Keely) McC. BA, Marygrove Coll., 1969; MRE, Seattle U., 1978; D Ministry, St. Mary Sem. and U., Balt., 1988. Cert. in spiritual direction, youth ministry, advanced catechist. Campus minister Flint (Mich.) Newman Ctr., 1970-80; coord. religious edn. Blessed Sacrament Ch., Burton, Mich., 1981-84; pastoral assoc. Good Shepherd Cath. Ch., Montrose, Mich., 1984-90; pastor Sacred Heart Ch., Flint, 1990—; music minister New Light Prayer Cmty., Flint, 1979—; co-chair Flint Cath. Urban Ministry, 1992-94; co-chaplain Dukette Cath. Sch., Flint, 1991—; ind. spiritual dir., 1988—; rep. Diocesan Regional Adult Edn., 1993—. Mem. Assn. Cath. Lay Ministers (co-chair Region III 1986-87), Profl. Pastoral Ministers Assn. (co-chair 1988-90). Office: Sacred Heart Ch 719 E Moore St Flint MI 48505-3997

MC CLANAHAN, RUE (EDDI-RUE MC CLANAHAN), actress; b. Healdton, Okla.; d. William Edwin and Dreda Rheua-Nell (Medaris) McC.; m. 1st, Tom Bish, 1958; 1 child, Mark Thomas Bish; m. 2nd, Norman Hartweg; m. 3rd, Peter DeMaio; m. 4th, Gus Fisher, 1976; m. 5th, Tom Keel, 1984 (div. 1985). B.A. cum laude, U. Tulsa, 1956. Appearences include (theatre) Erie (Pa.) Playhouse, 1957-58; (Broadway) Jimmy Shine, 1968-69, Sticks and Bones, 1972, California Suite, 1977, After-Play, 1995; (TV appearances) L.A., 1959-64, N.Y.C., 1964-73; (TV series) Maude, 1973-78, Apple Pie, 1978, Mama's Family, 1982-84, Golden Girls, 1985-92, Golden Palace, 1992-93; (TV movies) Having Babies III, 1978, Sgt. Matlowch vs the U.S. Air Force, 1978, Rainbow, 1978, Topper, 1979, The Great American Traffic Jam, 1980, Word of Honor, 1981, The Day the Bubble Burst, 1982, The Little Match Girl, 1987, Liberace, 1988, Take My Daughters Please, 1988, Let Me Hear You Whisper, 1988, To the Heroes, 1989, After the Shock, 1990, Children of the Bride, 1990, To My Daughter, 1990, The Dreamer of Oz, 1990, Baby of the Bride, 1991, Mother of the Bride, 1993, Danielle Steele's Message from Nam, 1993, Burning Passion: The Margaret Mitchell Story, 1994; (films) The People Next Door, 1970, They Might Be Giants, 1971, The Pursuit of Happiness, 1971, Modern Love, 1990. Recipient Obie award for leading off-Broadway role in Who's Happy Now, 1970; Emmy award Best Actress in a comedy, 1987; named Woman of Yr., Pasadena Playhouse, 1986; Spl. scholar Pasadena (Calif.) Playhouse, 1959, Phi Beta Gamma scholar, 1955. Mem. Actors Studio, Actors Equity Assn., AFTRA, Screen Actors Guild. Office: Agy for Performing Arts 9000 Sunset Blvd Ste 1200 Los Angeles CA 90069*

MCCLANAHAN, TERESA MARIE, artist; b. South Bend, Ind., Nov. 7, 1961; d. Thomas O. and Carolyn Marie (Kidd) McCl.; m. David M.

Sovinksi, Aug. 23, 1980 (div.); children: Christine Marie, Ryan Mary. Degree magna cum laude, Herron Sch. Art, 1993. Childrens photographer Photo Corp. Am., Houston, 1984-85, Chgo., 1986-87; personnel officer Ind. Dept. Labor, Indpls., 1987-88; program coord. Masonry Inst. Ind., Indpls., 1988-92. Artist Buick Mural Food Finders Food Bank, Lafayette, Ind., 1993; vol. art smart program Walt Disney Elem. Sch. Recipient George Spencer Scholarship Internat. Masonary Inst., 1993. Mem. No. Ind. Artist, Inc., Golden Key Hon. Soc. Office: PO Box 19 Mishawaka IN 46546

MC CLARIN, MICHELE MARIE, chemist; b. Bellfonte, Pa., May 3, 1965; d. Bernard Earl and Janet Marie (Karr) Droney; m. Richard Lee McClarin, Jr., June 9, 1990 (div. Feb. 1995). BA in Chemistry, East Stroudsburg (Pa.) U., 1987. Assoc. chemist Lancaster (Pa.) Labs., Inc., 1987-88, chemist I, 1988-89, chemist II, coord., 1989-91, group leader, 1991—. State dir. Mountville (Pa.) Jaycees, 1993-94, pres., 1992-93. Recipient Winfield Cook award Pa. Jaycees, 1993; named Jaycee Mountville of Yr., 1993. Mem. NAFE, Am. Chem. Soc., Alpha Omicron Pi. Office: Lancaster Labs Inc 2425 New Holland Pike PO Box 12425 Lancaster PA 17605-2425

MCCLEAF, SANDRA WOOD, computer programmer; b. Newport News, Va., Nov. 21, 1960; d. Robert Stuart and Mona Lee (Gillikin) Wood; m. Alan Stewart McCleaf, Sept. 30, 1989. BS in Computer Sci., U. Va., 1983; MBA, James Madison U., 1992. Programmer, analyst Commonwealth Clin. Systems, Charlottesville, Va., 1983-85, project dir., 1986-87, dir. programming, 1988—. Methodist. Office: Commonwealth Clin Systems 1650 State Farm Blvd Charlottesville VA 22901-8609

MCCLEARY, BERYL NOWLIN, civic worker, travel agency executive; b. Ft. Worth, Feb. 22, 1929; d. Henry Bryant and Phyllis (Tenney) Nowlin; m. Henry Glenn McCleary, May 29, 1950; children: Laura Gail, Glenn Nowlin, Neil Ray, Paul Tenney. BS in Zoology, Tex. Tech U., 1950. Owner, mgr. Beryl McCleary Travels, Chicago, 1975-81, Denver, 1981-84. Treas. Kappa Alpha Theta Ednl. Found., Tex. Christian U., Ft. Worth, 1958-61; pres. study club Jr. Woman's Club, Ft. Worth, 1959-60; pres. Symphony League, Ft. Worth, 1961-62; v.p., dir. Ft. Worth Symphony Orch. Assn. Inc., 1961; treas. Jr. Pro-Am Tarrant County, 1961-62; corr. sec. Ft. Worth Children's Mus. Guild, 1961; sec. Tarrant County (Tex.) Democratic Exec. Com., 1956-62; pres. guild, bd. dirs. Maadi Community Ch., Cairo, 1964-66; mem. women's bd. Lincoln Park Zool. Soc., Chgo, 1976-81; mem. Episcopal Ch. Women's Diocesan Bd., Chgo., 1976-79; pres., charter mem. Rainbow Investment Club, London, 1970-71, travel dir. Over the Hill Gang Ski Team Internat., Denver, 1982-84. Mem. AAAS, DAR, Geol. Geophys. Aux., Service Club Chgo., Jr. League Denver, Denver Symphony Guild, Central City Opera Guild, Houston Symphony League, Alpha Epsilon Delta, Kappa Alpha Theta (charter mem. Gamma Phi chpt. 1953). Home: 232 Warrenton Dr Houston TX 77024-6226

MCCLELLAN, ANNE STARR, environmentalist; b. Detroit, Sept. 27, 1960; d. John Drew and Barbara Ann (Kaumneimer) McC.; m. John Alan Rosett, Aug. 15, 1987. BA in Urban Planning, SUNY. With Neighborhood Open Space Coalition, N.Y.C., 1986-87, program dir., 1987-93, exec. dir., 1993—; program dir. Friends of Gateway, N.Y.C., 1992-93, exec. dir., 1993—; cons. South Bronx Greenway System/Consumer Farmer Found., N.Y.C., 1989-93, Pratt Inst., Bklyn., 1989-93, Village of Lansing, N.Y. Greenway Study/Tompkins County Dept. of Planning, 1992—; mem. environ. com. Atlantic Terminal Urban Renewal Area Coalition, 1986-87, exec. com., 1986-93, chairperson alternative plan, 1988-89; mem. Bronx Borough Pres.'s Office Greenway Steering Com., 1990—, East Coast Greenway Alliance, 1991—, chair N.Y. State com., 1994; mem. Flushing Meadows-Corona Park Redevel. Corp. Environ. Com., 1988-90; chairperson environ. impact statement com., mem. design com. Hudson River Park Conservancy Adv. Bd., 1993—; apptd. N.Y. State Intermodal Surface Transportation Efficiency Act Adv. Bd./Enhancement Funding, 1993—; writer, photographer Met. Coun. on Housing, 1985-89; co-chairperson Met. Greenways Coun., 1987—; mem. urban park and natural resources task force Nat. Recreation and Park Assn., Nat. Soc. Park Resources, 1993—; mem. greenways and blueways com. Pub. Space for Pub. Life, 1991-93; co-chair Rockaway/Gateway Greenway Adv. Bd., 1993—; bd. dirs. Transp. Alternatives, 1988-90, mem. adv. bd., 1990—. Author: The Brooklyn/Queens Greenway: A Feasibility Study, 1987, The Brooklyn/Queens Greenway: A Design Study, 1988, Toward a Regional Greenway System--An Urban Greenways Inventory for Metro NY, 1992. Active N.Y.C. Bicycle Adv. Com., 1987—, N.Y. State Bicycle Adv. Coun., 1989—, N.Y.C. Bikeway/Walkway Working Group, 1991—. Recipient Nat. Merit award Am. Soc. Landscape Architects, 1990, Rudy Bruner award for Excellence in the Urban Environment, Rudy Bruner Found., 1991; NEA grantee, 1988. Mem. Am. Planning Assn. (chair N.Y.C. chpt. open space com. 1988—, exec. com. 1992—). Office: Neighborhood Open Space Coalition 72 Reade St New York NY 10007-1822

MCCLELLAN, KARI TURNER, minister; b. Wheeling, W.Va., Apr. 17, 1951; d. William John and Flora Bella (McQuiston) Turner; m. Ralph L. McClellan Jr., Apr. 1988; 1 child, Mardi Lyn. BA in Religion and Philosophy, Westminster Coll., 1973; MDiv, Princeton Theol. Sem., 1976; DMin., Evangel. Theol. Sem., 1992. Ordained to ministry Presbyn. Ch. (U.S.A.), 1976. Asst. to pastor Lenape Valley Ch., New Britain, Pa., 1973-74, St. Mark's Luth. Ch., Trenton, N.J., 1974-76; chaplain Yardville (N.J.) Prison, 1974-76; asst. pastor, then assoc. pastor 1st Presbyn. Ch., Levittown, Pa., 1976-79, sr. pastor, 1979—; chaplain Lower Bucks Hosp., 1993—. Pres. Local Ministerium, Levittown/Fairless Hills, 1980-81; trustee Princeton Theol. Sem., 1983—; mem. chaplains bd. Lower Bucks Hosp. Named Citizen of Yr. Levittown/Fairless Hills, 1982. mem. Evangelical Coalition, Network Presbyn. Women in Leadership, Presbyns. for Faith, Family and Ministry (pres.), Princeton Regional Alumni Assn. (v.p. Pa. and Del. chpts. 1979-81). Home: 28 Fruitree Rd Levittown PA 19056-1904 Office: 1st Presbyn Ch 5918 Emilie Rd Levittown PA 19057-2606

MCCLELLAN, REBEKAH JUDITH, accountant; b. Buffalo, Apr. 17, 1968; d. Robert Allen and Judith Mildred (Driver) McC. BS in Bus. Adminstrn., SUNY, Buffalo, 1991. Staff acct. HSC Controls, Inc., Buffalo, 1989-92, ops. cons., 1992-93; contr. Monoflo Internat., Inc. & TMC of Am., Inc., Winchester, Va., 1993-94; sr. staff acct. Three Rivers Aluminum Co., Cranberry, Pa., 1994—. Mem. Worldwide Ch. of God. Home: 661 Galway Dr Bethel Park PA 15102 Office: Three Rivers Aluminum Co 71 Progress Ave Cranberry PA 16319

MCCLELLAND, CAROL L., transition consulting company executive; b. Ithaca, N.Y., Aug. 9, 1960; d. Wilson Melville and Margaret Gordon Mahy (Lloyd) M. BA in Gen. Psychology, U. Calif., Santa Barbara, 1982; MA in Indsl./Orgnl. Psychology, Purdue U., 1984, PhD in Indsl./Orgnl. Psychology, 1986. Rsch. intern State Farm Ins., Bloomington, Ill., 1985; rsch. analyst in human resources Allstate Ins., Menlo Park, Calif., 1986-91; cons., owner Transition Dynamics, Palo Alto, Calif., 1991—; vis. instr. indsl./orgn. psychology San Jose State U., 1993—; co-founder Insight Inst. Cons. Group, Palo Alto, 1993—. Alt. bd. mem. Creative Health Network, 1993—; group facilitator Women Entrepreneurs Program, 1992—. Mem. Phi Beta Kappa. Office: Transition Dynamics 3790 El Camino Real Ste 2021 Palo Alto CA 94306

MCCLELLAND, EMMA L., state legislator; b. Springfield, Mo., Feb. 26, 1940; m. Alan McClelland; children: Mike, Karen. BA, U. Mo., 1962. Dir. field office, corp. divsn. Mo. Sec. of State, St. Louis; committeewoman Gravis Township; mem. St. Louis County Rep. Cent. Com., Mo. Rep. State Com.; mem. Mo. State Ho. Rep., 1991—, mem. appropriations com., edn. and state parks com., rec. and natural resources com. Bd. Dirs. Epworth Children's Home, St. Louis Child Abuse Network; elder Webster Groves Presbyn. Ch. Recipient Silver Svc. award Nat. Soc. Autistic Children, Outstanding Svc. award Am. Assn. Mental Deficiency. Mem. Webster Groves C. of C., Pi Lambda Theta. Republican. Presbyterian. Home: 455 Pasadena Webster Grove MO 63119 Office: Mo Ho of Reps State Capitol Jefferson City MO 65101*

MCCLELLAN-HOLT, JEAN ELIZABETH, physical education educator, administrator; b. Pine Bluff, Ark., June 25, 1960; d. James Fennimore and Lois Jean (DeDeaux) McClellan; m. William Howard Holt, Dec. 15, 1990. BS, James Madison U., 1981; cert., N.C. State U., 1986; MS, Va. Commonwealth U., 1990. Cert. leisure profl., Va., recreational sports specialist. Jr. athletic specialist, then sr. athletic specialist Chesterfield (Va.) Parks and Recreation, 1981-83; athletic supr. Chesapeake (Va.) Parks and Recreation, 1983-88; program supr., then grad. asst. Va. Commonwealth U., Richmond, 1988-90; dir. recreation Mary Washington Coll., Fredericksburg, Va., 1990-92; dir. intramurals Fla. State U., Tallahassee, 1992-93; sr. program dir. student activities U. Ctrl. Fla., Orlando, 1993-94, dir. student activities, 1994—; rsch. cons. Richmond Conv. and Visitors Bur., 1990; bd. regents Sch. Sports Mgmt., Raleigh, N.C., 1992—; bd. dirs. Leadership Tng. Inst., Richmond, 199-92. Recipient Robert F. Kennedy Merit award Fla. Jaycees, 1993; named to Outstanding Young Women of Am., 1991. Mem. AAHPERD, Nat. Assn. Campus Activities, Va. Alliance Health, Phys. Edn., Recreation and Dance, Aquatic Exercise Assn., U.S. Water Fitness Assn., Am. Assn. Cheerleading Coaches and Advisors, Va. Recreation and Park Soc., Va. Recreational Sports Assn. (exec. bd. 1990-92), Nat. Intramural-Recreational Sports Assn., Nat. Recreation and Parks Assn., Jaycees Am., Delta Sigma Theta. Democrat. Episcopalian. Home: 700 MacGlenross Dr Ovideo FL 32765-8772 Office: U Cen Fla SC Rm 203 PO Box 163240 Orlando FL 32816-3240

MCCLEMENT-WORN, JOY JEAN, budget analyst; b. Independence, Mo., Jan. 4, 1946; d. Roy Gene and Mary Lee (Brooks) Webster; m. Eugene Emil Worn, Apr. 24, 1992; children: Margaret, Joy Elizabeth, Eugenia. BS, Lincoln Univ., 1985; MPA, U. Mo., 1991. Warranty adminstr. L.P. Steuart, Inc., Silver Spring, Md., 1971-74, Heritage Chrysler-Plymouth, Alexandria, Va., 1974-76; sec., libr. George Washington Univ., Coll. Gen. Studies, Washington, 1978-80; exec. sec. Mo. Automobile Dealers' Assn., Jefferson City, Mo., 1981-83; sec. State of Mo., Mo. Ho. of Reps., Jefferson City, 1983-87, acct. II, 1987-91, budget analyst, 1991—; exec. sec. Lake of the Ozarks Yachting Assn., Camdenton, Mo., 1986-87. Bd. dirs. Mo. Inst. of Pub. Adminstrs.; adminstrv. bd. First Ch., Jefferson City, Mo.; CPR instr. ARC, 1986-87; mem. Cole County Dems., Jefferson City. Mem. Assn. of Govtl. Accts., Mo. Inst. of Pub. Adminstrs., Am. Legion Aux., Mo. Univ. Alumni Assn. Home: 1605 Beverly St Jefferson City MO 65109-1206 Office: Mo Ho of Reps B-20 Capitol Bldg Jefferson City MO 65101

MCCLENDON, MAXINE, artist; b. Leesville, La., Oct. 21, 1931; d. Alfred Harry and Clara (Jackson) McMillan; student Tex. U., 1948-50, Tex. Woman's U., 1950-51, Pan Am. U., 1963-64; m. Edward Edson Nichols, Mar. 28, 1967; children—Patricia Ann, Joan Terri, Christopher, Jennifer. One-woman shows include: Art Mus. S. Tex., Corpus Christi, 1971, McAllen (Tex.) Internat. Mus., 1976, Amarillo (Tex.) Art Center, 1982, U. Tex., Pan American; group shows in Wichita, Kans., 1972, Marietta, Ohio, 1975, Dallas, 1977; represented in permanent collections: Mus. Internat. Folk Art, Santa Fe, Ark. Mus. Fine Art, Little Rock, McAllen Internat. Mus., Lauren Rogers Mus., Laurel, Miss.; commns. include: Caterpillar Corp., Peoria, Ill., Union Bank Switzerland, N.Y.C., Crocker Bank, Los Angeles, Tarleton U., Tex., Hyatt Regency, Ft. Worth Forbes Inc., San Francisco, First Savs. & Loan, Shreveport, La., Continental Plaza, Ft. Worth. curator Mexican folk art McAllen Internat. s., 1974-80. Recipient judges award 4th Nat. Marietta, 1975, numerous others. Mem. World Crafts Council, Am. Crafts Council (Tex. rep. 1976-80), Tex. Designer/Craftsmen (pres. 1973-74). Christian Scientist. Home and Studio: 2018 Sharyland St Mission TX 78572

MCCLENDON, SARAH NEWCOMB, news service executive, writer; b. Tyler, Tex., July 8, 1910; d. Sidney Smith and Annie Rebecca (Bonner) McClendon; 1 child, Sally Newcomb Mac Donald. Grad., Tyler Jr. Coll., U. Mo. Mem. staff Tyler Courier-Times and Tyler Morning Telegraph, 1931-39; reporter Beaumont (Tex.) Enterprise; Washington corr. Phila. Daily News, 1944; founder McClendon News Svc., Washington, 1946—; talk show host Ind. Broadcasters Network; lectr. Faneuil Hall, Boston, Poor Richard's Club, Phila., Cobo Hall, Detroit, Chautauqua Instn., N.Y., Comstock Club, Sacremento; adv. to Senior Beacon; v.p. Nat. Press Club. Author: My Eight Presidents, 1978 (1st prize); contbr. articles to mags. including Esquire, Penthouse, Diplomat; TV appearances include Merv Griffin Show, Tomorrow, Inside the White House, PBS, NBC Meet the Press, KUP Show, NBC Today Show, C-Span, CNN, Fox Morning News, Late Night with David Letterman, Michael Jackson Show (L.A. radio). Mem. VA Adv. Bd. on Women Vets, def. adv. com. Women in the Svcs.; army advisor, mem. task force Women in the Army Policy Rev.; bd. dir. Sam Rayburn Libr., In Our Own Way, So. Poverty Relief Orgn. Served with WAC. Recipient Woman of Achievement award Tex. Press Women, 1978, 2d prize Nat. Fedn. Press Women, 1979, Headliner award Women in Comm., 1st Pres. award for Journalism in Washington, Nat. Fedn. Press Women, Pub. Rels. award Am. Legion, Bob Considine award, 1990, Am. Woman award Women's Rsch. Edn. Inst., 1991. Mem. DAR (Nat. Constn. award 1990), U. Mo. Alumni Assn. (chpt. pres.), Women in Comm. (Margaret Caskey award), Am. Legion (post comdr.), Nat. Woman's Party (v.p.), Nat. Coun., Soc. Profl. Journalists (Hall of Fame Washington chpt.), Nat. Press Club (v.p.), Am. Newspaper Women's Club (pres.), Capitol Hill First Friday Club (pres.). Club: Capitol Hill First Friday (pres.).

MCCLENNEN, MIRIAM J., former state official; b. Seattle, Sept. 16, 1923; d. Phillip and Frieda (Golub) Jacobs; m. Louis McClennen, Apr. 25, 1969; stepchildren: Peter Adams, James C.A., Helen, Persis, Crane, Emery. BA, U. Wash., 1945; MBA, Northwestern U., 1947. Exec. trainee Marshall Field & Co., Chgo., 1945-47; asst. buyer Frederick & Nelson (subs. of Marshall Field), Seattle, 1947-49; buyer Frederick & Nelson (subs. of Marshall Field), 1949-57; fashion coordinator, buyer Levy Bros., Burlingame/San Mateo, Calif., 1957-63; buyer Goldwaters, Phoenix, 1963-67; adminstrv. asst. to pres. Ariz. State Senate, Phoenix, 1973-76; dir. publs. Office of Sec. of State, Phoenix, 1976-87; chairwoman legis. subcom. adminstrv. procedure Ariz. State Legislature, Phoenix, 1984-85. Original compiler, codifier, editor publ. Ariz. Adminstrv. Code, 1973-87, Ariz. Adminstrv. Register, 1976-87. Bd. dirs., mem. Phoenix Art Mus. League, 1972-90, Phoenix Symphony Guild, 1970-88; bd. dirs., sec. Combined Metro. Phoenix Arts and Scis., 1974-90, mem. adv. bd., 1990—; bd. dirs. Phoenix Arts Coun., Master Apprentice Programs, 1980-83; bd. dirs., mem. exec. com. Heard Mus., 1982-88, 90—, chmn. publs. com., 1982-88, chmn. exhibit and edn. com., 1990-93; mem. Ariz. State Hist. Records Adv. Bd., 1987-90, Ariz. Commn. on Arts, 1989—, Phoenix Art Mus., 1972—. Recipient Disting. Svc. award Atty. Gen. Ariz., 1987, Outstanding Svc. to People, Ariz. State Senate, 1987, Nat. Assn. Secs. of State award, 1987. Mem. English Speaking Union, Nat. Soc. Arts and Letters, Charter 100 (bd. dirs. 1981-85), Phoenix County Club, Ariz. Club. Home: 5311 N La Plaza Cir Phoenix AZ 85012-1415

MCCLINTIC, DENISE ARCAND, lawyer; b. Waterbury, Conn., Sept. 17, 1958; d. Robert Eugene and Irene Roberta (Pauloski) Arcand; m. David Wallick McClintic, Sept. 10, 1983. BA, Tufts U., 1980; JD cum laude, Suffolk U., 1983; LLM in Taxation, Boston U., 1986. Bar: Mass. 1984, N.H. 1988, U.S. Dist. Ct. Mass. 1984, U.S. Dist. Ct. N.H. 1988. Tax acct. State St. Bank & Trust, Boston, 1986-87, sr. estate adminstr., 1987; asst. v.p. Lake Sunapee Fin. Svcs., Newport, N.H., 1987-88, v.p., gen. counsel, 1988-91; v.p., trust officer Charter Trust Co., Concord, N.H., 1993—; mem. bd. advisors Lake Sunapee Savs. Bank, Newport, N.H., 1991—; lectr. in field. Trustee Spaulding Youth Ctr., Tilton, N.H., 1992—. Mem. New London Bar Assn., Rolling Rock Club, Pitts. Golf Club, Phi Delta Phi. Republican. Episcopalian. Home: 27 Stoney Brook Rd New London NH 03257-0432 Office: Charter Trust Co PO Box 776 24 Newport Rd New London NH 03257-0776

MCCLINTOCK, JESSICA, fashion designer; b. Frenchville, Maine, June 19, 1930; d. Rene Gagnon and Verna Hedrich; m. Frank Staples (dec. 1964); 1 child Scott. BA, San Jose State U., 1963. Elem. sch. tchr. Marblehead, Mass., 1966-68, Long Island, N.Y., 1968, Sunnyvale, Calif., 1964-65, 68-69; fashion designer Jessica McClintock, Inc., San Francisco, 1969—. Active donor, AIDS and Homeless programs; scholarship sponsor Fashion Inst. Design and Merchandising. Recipient Merit award Design, 1989, Dallas Fashion award, 1988, Tommy award, 1986, Pres. Appreciation award, 1986, Best Interior Store Design, 1986, Calif. Designer award, 1985, Earnie award, 1981, numerous others. Mem. Coun. Fashion Designers of Am., Fashion Inst. Design & Merchandising (adv. bd. 1979—), San Francisco Fashion Industry (pres. 1976-78, bd. dirs. 1989). Office: Jessica McClintock Inc 1400 16th St San Francisco CA 94103-5181*

MCCLINTOCK, SANDRA JANISE, writer, editor; b. Connersville, Ind., July 28, 1938; d. Owen Dale and Mary Janis (Tierney) M.; m. Harvey Miles Garrison, Jr., Aug. 1, 1959 (div. 1967); children: Heidi, Katherine, H. Miles III; m. Joseph Lloyd Fagen, May 15, 1969; 1 child, Adam Joseph. BA, Drake U., 1960; postgrad., Calif. State U., Fullerton, 1966-67; cert., Am. Grad. U., 1987. Lic. gen. contractor. Coord. copy desk Time Mag., N.Y.C., 1960-62; mem. graphics prodn. staff Times-Mirror Co., L.A., 1962-64; mgr. prodn. Miller Freeman Publs., Long Beach, Calif., 1964-68; supr. Design Svc., Anaheim, Calif., 1968-73; prin. Fagen Graphics, Long Beach, 1973-77, Palomar Publs., Ranchita, Calif., 1977-84; cons. Cons. & Designers, Anaheim, 1984-87; mgr. publs. Tracor Flight Systems, Inc., Santa Ana, Calif., 1987-88; coord. publs. Rockwell Internat. Corp., Anaheim, 1988-92; dir. comms. Terra Christa Comms., Tucson, 1992-93; tech. writer CH2M Hill, Santa Ana, Calif., 1993—; cons. Aerotest, Inc., Mojave, Calif., 1986, Voice Telecom Corp., Laguna Beach, Calif., 1986. Editor: Psychopharmacology, 1984, Joseph of Aramathea, 1982, Who is Who at the Earth Summit, 1992; guest editor Interface Age mag., 1976; contbg. editor Rockwell News in U.S. and Can., 1988. Bd. dirs. Vol. Fire Dept., Ranchita, 1979; fund raiser Dem. candidate Calif. Assembly, Orange county, 1964. Mem. NAFE, Nat. Mgmt. Assn., So. Calif. Astrological Network, Amnesty Internat. Mem. Religious Sci. Ch. Home: 2442 S Coast Hwy Laguna Beach CA 92651

MCCLINTON, EDNA GRACE, real estate broker; b. Windom, Kans., Jan. 2, 1925; d. Ira Francis and Ella Nancy (Joslin) Hites; m. Arthur LeRoy Copeland, Feb. 20, 1943 (div. 1948); children: Clair Arthur, Richard Wade; m. Raymond Arthur McClinton, May 26, 1952 (div.); children: Roxane Dora, Renee Ella, Tamara Yvonne, James Ray, Phillip Lee. Grad. high sch., Albion, Pa. Owner, broker McClinton Real Estate, Meadville, Pa., 1967-70; real estate saleswoman, Meadville, 1967; broker, owner McClinton Co., Meadville, 1971—; beauty tchr. Wel Mar, Meadville, 1983—; owner rooming house, Meadville, 1975—, sr. citizen home, Hickernell, Pa. Mem. Bus. and Profl. Women, Grange. Methodist. Avocations: rebuilding older homes, fishing, travel. Home: 1010 Market St Meadville PA 16335-3356 Office: Meadville-McClinton Real Estate and Notary Svc 1010 Market St Meadville PA 16335-3356

MCCLINTON, JOANN, state legislator; m. Emory McClinton; 3 children. Grad., Washington High Sch. State rep., mem. children & youth, human rels., aging, state planning, cmty. affairs coms. Ga. House of Reps., Atlanta, 1992—. Democrat. Office: Ga House of Reps State Capitol SE Atlanta GA 30334*

MCCLOSKEY, MARY M., state government administrator, writer; b. Jersey City, Oct. 23, 1948; d. James Ellwood and Mary Elizabeth (Daly) McC.; divorced; 1 child, J. Mack Lennon. AAS in Comms., SUNY-F.I.T., N.Y.C., 1969; BA in Journalism, Edison State Coll., Trenton, N.J., 1994. Cert. pub. mgr. News writer WINS Radio, N.Y.C., 1970-71; asst. articles editor Argosy Mag., N.Y.C., 1971-72; assoc. editor and writer Woman's World Mag., N.Y.C., 1970-72; sr. editor, writer Coronet Mag., N.Y.C., 1973-74; editor, writer Daily Intelligencer, Doylestown, Pa., 1978-82; exec. dir. South Hunterdon C. of C., Lamberton, N.J., 1982-84; with State of N.J., 1984—, dep. pub. edn. officer Bur. of Fire Safety, 1988-91, sr. mgr. asst. Div. Consumer Affairs, 1991—; founder Citizens Alliance for Fire Safety in N.J., Trenton, 1989. Author numerous articles and features. Founder, pres. Irish Am. G.O.P. Club of N.J., Trenton, 1989; Rep. committeewoman, Lawrence, N.J., 1989; mem. Mercer County Disabilities Adv. Coun., Trenton, 1991—, Mercer County Human Svcs. Adv. Coun., Trenton, 1992—. Recipient various awards. Republican. Roman Catholic.

MCCLUNG, CHRISTINA J., training company executive; b. Newark, N.J., Jan. 19, 1948; d. Fred and Maria (Dallinger) Palensar; m. Kenneth A. McClung, Mar. 21, 1975. BA, Kean Coll., 1970; MA, Seton Hall U., 1973; EdD, U. So. Calif., 1976. Tchr. Chatham Twp. (N.J.) pub. schs., 1970-74; instructional designer Tratec Co., L.A., 1976-79; asst. prof. Lehman Coll., N.Y., 1977-79; ind. cons., 1978-80; v.p., bd. dirs. Instrnl. Design Group, Morristown N.J., 1980—; gen. ptnr. MGM Investments, 1985—. Author: (5 books series) Computers for Profls., 1983. Mem. ASTD, Nat. Soc. Performance Instrn. (pres. N.J. chpt.), Phi Delta Kappa. Office: Instrnl Design Group 144 Speedwell Ave Morristown NJ 07960-3850

MCCLURE, CHARLOTTE SWAIN, English language educator; b. Newark, Ohio, July 30, 1921; d. Ursel Kenneth and Jeannette Frances (Ayers) Swain; m. John C. McClure, Aug. 1, 1945; children: John Thomas, James Allen, Barbara McClure Schroeder. AB with honors, Denison U., 1944; MA, U. N.Mex., 1966, PhD, 1973. Feature and staff writer Internat. News Svc., Columbus, Ohio, 1944-45, Dayton (Ohio) Jour., 1946-47; programmer Gen. Programmed Teaching Corp., Albuquerque, 1962-63; tchr. English, Sandia High Sch., Albuquerque, 1964-65, Sandia Sch., Albuquerque, 1966-68; asst. prof. English, Ga. State U., Atlanta, 1969, assoc. prof., acad. dir. honors program, 1982-92, assoc. prof. emerita, acad. dir. honors program emerita, 1992—; sec.-treas. bd. trustees Nat. Found. for Honors Edn., Atlanta, 1988-91; program chmn. Publ. Svcs. Guild, Atlanta, 1989; assoc. instr. U. Greater Atlanta. Author: (monograph) Gertrude Atherton, 1976, (book) Gertrude Atherton, 1979; co--author: (biography) David C. Schilling, 1995; co-editor: Feminist Visions, 1984; contbr. articles to profl. jours. U.S. Dept. Edn. Women's Ednl. Equity Act Program grantee, 1979-82. Mem. MLA, South Atlantic MLA (program chmn. women's studies 1977, 80), Western Lit. Assn. (exec. com. 1980-83, 89-92), Nat. Collegiate Honors Coun. (exec. com. 1982-85, 87-90), So. Regional Honors Coun. (v.p. 1982, pres. 1983), Nat. Women's Studies Assn., AAUW, LWV, Mortar Bd., Phi Beta Kappa, Omicron Delta Kappa. Home: 2674 Leslie Dr NE Atlanta GA 30345-1562

MCCLURE, JULIA M., personal property appraiser, state legislator; b. Atlanta, Nov. 24, 1944; d. John Herman and Josephine Valentine (Bryant) Geffken; children: Elizabeth, Jack. BA in History, So. Meth. U., 1966. Owner Appraisals and Sales by Julie McClure, Inc., Bradenton, Fla., 1970—; mem. Fla. Ho. of Reps., Tallahassee, 1992—. Bd. dirs. So. Fla. Mus. and Bishop Planetarium, Bradenton, 1990—, Girls Club of Manatee County, Bradenton, 1989—. Recipient Friend of Agriculture award Manatee County Farm Bur., 1993, Conservation award Fla. Conservation Assn., 1993, 94, Legis. Support award Fla. Assn. Cmty. Colls., 1994, Fla. C. of C., 1993, 94. Mem. AAUW, Am. Soc. Appraisers (cert., sr.), Appraisers Assn. Am., Sarasota-Manatee Antique Dealers Assn., Manatee County C. of C., Kiwanis. Democrat. Episcopalian. Home: 202 N 35th St W Bradenton FL 34205 Office: Appraisals & Sales by Julie McClure 1101 6th Ave W Ste 111 Bradenton FL 34205 also: Fla House of Reps State Capitol Tallahassee FL 32301

MCCLURE, SANDRA LEE, writer; b. Detroit, July 8, 1941; d. Charles Marvin and Estelle Gertrude (Golladay) Grisham; m. Michael Glenn McClure, June 29, 1963 (div. Sept. 1967). BA, Wayne State U., 1963. Reporter East Side Newspapers, Detroit, 1963, United Press Internat., Detroit, 1964-66; asst. press. sec. G. Mennen Williams for Senate Campaign, Mich., 1966; adminstrv. asst. to exec. dir. War on Poverty, Detroit, 1967; adminstrv. asst., speechwriter City of Detroit Mayor Jerome P. Cavanagh, 1967-69; press sec. New Detroit, Inc., 1970; dep. dir. City of Detroit Charter Revision Commn., 1971; Mich. press sec. McGovern for Pres. campaign, 1972; pub. rels. account exec. Yaffe Stone August, Inc., 1973-74; producer Sta. WXYZ-TV, 1974-78; reporter The Detroit Free Press, 1978-92; host, Sandy McClure's Newstalk Sta. WXYT-AM, 1992-93; owner Song Dog Prodns., 1993; communications dir. Wolpe for Gov. Campaign, Mich., 1994. Office: Song Dog Prodns PO Box 240101 Orchard Lake MI 48324-0101

MCCLURE, VIMALA, writer; b. L.A., June 7, 1952; d. Peter Edwin Miller and Dorothy Jane (Thurman) Prather; m. Ronald D. Schneider, June 20, 1970 (div. 1988); children: Narayana, Sadhana; m. Michael B. McClure, Aug. 14, 1988; 1 child, Adam. Textile artist, 1988—. Author: Infant Massage: A Handbook for Loving Parents, 1978, 82, 88, The Infant Massage Instructor Manual, 1980, Super Bengali: Teach Yourself!, 1986, Bangladesh: Rivers in a Crowded Land, 1988, Some Still Want the Moon: A Woman's Introduction to Tantra Yoga, 1989, The Tao of Motherhood, 1990, The Ethics of Love: Using Yoga's Timeless Wisdom to Heal Yourself, Your Family and the Earth, 1992; contbr. numerous articles to mags. Founding mem. Cesarean Birth Edn. Group, Boulder, Colo., 1976-78; co-owner, mng.

editor Nucleus Publs., Willow Springs, Mo., 1987—. Recipient 1st prize art category Ozarks Quilt Show, 1992, 94, 1st prize art category Western Heritage Ctr. for the Arts Textile Art Show, 1993; named Best of Show, Nat. Quilting Chpt. Show, 1994. Mem. Progressive Women's Spiritual Assn., Am. Quilters Soc., Nat. Quilting Assn. (Best of Show award 1994), Renaissance Artists and Writers Assn., Internat. Assn. of Infant Massage Instrs. (adv. bd. 1987—, founder, pres., head trainer 1976-86). Home: RR 2 Box 48 Willow Springs MO 65793-9500

MCCLURE-BIBBY, MARY ANNE, former state legislator; b. Milbank, S.D., Apr. 21, 1939; d. Charles Cornelius and Mary Lucille (Whittom) Burges; m. D.J. McClure, Nov. 17, 1963 (dec. Apr. 1990); 1 child, Kelly Joanne; m. John E. Bibby, May 1, 1993. BA magna cum laude, U. S.D., 1961; postgrad., U. Manchester, Eng., 1961-62; M of Pub. Adminstrn., Syracuse (N.Y.) U., 1980. Staff asst. U.S. Senator Francis Case, Washington, 1959-61; sec. to lt. gov. State of S.D., Pierre, 1963, with budget office, 1964; exec. sec. to pres. Frontier Airlines, Denver, 1963-64; tchr. Pub. High Schs., Pierre and Redfield, S.D., 1965-66, 68-70; mem. S.D. State Senate, Pierre, 1975-89, pres. pro tem, 1979-89, vice chmn. coun. of state govts., 1987, chmn. coun. of state govts., 1988; spl. asst. to Pres. Bush for intergovernmental affairs, 1989-92; exec. dir. S.D. Bush-Quayle Campaign, 1992. Vice chmn. sch. bd. Redfield Ind. Sch. Dist., 1970-74. Fulbright scholar, 1961-62, Bush Leadership fellow, 1977-80. Mem. Phi Beta Kappa. Republican. Congregationalist. Home: 817 8th Ave Brookings SD 57006-1315

MCCLURE-MONHOLLEN, KRISTINE LOIS, nurse, addictions therapist; b. San Francisco, Dec. 7, 1949; d. James Everett McClure and Lois Lorraine (Cowan) Robson; m. Paul Edward Erhard, Jan. 17, 1969 (div. June 1975); 1 child, James Everett; m. Maurice Monhollen, Aug. 30, 1985. Lic. practical nurse, Cen. Piedmont Community Coll., 1978. Lic. practical nurse, N.C. LPN Mercy Hosp., Charlotte, N.C., 1978-80; alcoholism worker Mecklenburg County Govt., Charlotte, 1980-87; substance abuse counselor Vets. Affairs Med. Ctr., Salisbury, N.C., 1987-1991, nurse, addictions therapist, 1991—. Vol. United Way, Charlotte, 1990—. Mem. N.C. Assn. Alcoholic Residential Facilities, N.C. Assn. Children of Alcoholics, Addiction Profls. N.C., Menninger Found. Roman Catholic. Home: 10709 Brief Rd Charlotte NC 28227-8477 Office: VA Med Ctr Substance Abuse Treatment Program 1601 Brenner Ave Salisbury NC 28144-2515

MCCLURG, PATRICIA A., minister; b. Bay City, Tex., Mar. 14, 1939; d. T.H. and Margaret (Smith) McC. BA, Austin Coll., 1961; M in Christian Edn., Presbyn. Sch. of Christian Edn., 1963; BD, Austin Presbyn. Theol. Sem., 1967; postgrad., So. Meth. U., 1971-73; DD (hon.), Austin Coll., 1978. Dir. Christian edn. 2d Presbyn. Ch., Newport News, Va., 1963-65; asst. pastor Westminster Presbyn. Ch., Beaumont, Tex., 1967-71; assoc. pastor 1st Presbyn. Ch., Pasadena, Tex., 1969-71; assoc. exec. Synod of Red River, Denton, Tex., 1973-75; dir. gen. assembly mission bd. Presbyn. Ch., Atlanta, 1975-86; assoc. exec. for mission The Presbytery of Elizabeth, Plainfield, N.J., 1986-91; exec. Presbytery of New Castle, Newark, Del., 1992—; pres. Nat. Coun. Chs. of Christ in the U.S.A., N.Y.C., 1988-89, v.p., 1985-87; del., budget com. chmn. World Coun. Chs. Assembly, Vancouver, Can., 1985; sect. leader World Coun. Chs. Mission and Evang. Confs., Melbourne, Australia, 1980. Contbr. articles to prof. jours. Mem. chs. spl. commn. on South Africa, N.Y.C., 1985—, Anti-Pollution Campaign, Pasadena, 1970. Recipient Disting. Alumni award Austin Coll., 1979. Democrat. Presbyterian. Lodge: Rotary.

MCCLUSKEY, GAYLA JACQUE, health, safety and environmental executive; b. Enid, Okla., Apr. 5, 1955; d. Jack and S. Andrea (Matthiesen) McC.; m. David McClure Humphrey. BS in Engring. Tech., Okla. State U., 1977; MBA in Engring. Mgmt., U. Dallas, 1984. Diplomate Am. Acad. of Indsl. Hygiene; cert. safety profl.; registered occupational hygienist. Indsl. hygienist Exxon Nuclear Co., Richland, Wash., 1978-79, OSHA, Dept. Lab., Irving, Tex., 1979-81, United Techs.-Mostek, Carrollton, Tex., 1981-82; cons. risk mgmt. Sun Exploration and Prodn. Co., Dallas, 1982-88; mgr. health, safety & security Interchem Inc., Louisville, 1988-91; dir. health safety and environ. affairs Rhone-Poulenc Rorer, Phila, 1991-94; mng. cons. Sun Co., 1994—. Mem. editorial bd. Indsl. Safety and Hygiene News, 1993. Chmn., Responsible Citizenship Program, 1984-86, Dallas Women's Coalition, Dallas, 1984-88, Leadership Dallas, 1987-88; active Leadership Louisville, 1988-91, Leadership Phila., 1991—; co-chair auction Louisville Jaycees, 1989-90; mem. priority programs com. Metro United Way, Louisville, 1990—; founding mem. Louisville Network, 1990—; pres., bd. dirs. Women's Ctr. of Dallas, charter supporter fund for women; dir. Women in Search of Exec. Responsibilities, 1988; mem. Ctr. for Women and Families, 1990—; trustee, pres. elect Am. Indsl. Hygiene Found., 1991—; mem. bd. health Radnor Township, 1994—, bd. dirs. Women's Resource Ctr., 1994—, chair search com., 1995. Named to Hon. Order of Ky. Cols., 1990. Mem. LWV, Am. Mgmt. Assn., Am. Soc. Safety Engrs., Am. Acad. Indsl. Hygiene (profl. conf. com. 1994—), Chm. Mfrs. Assn. (responsible care com. 1990—), Pharm. Mfrs. Assn. (water com. 1993—), Dallas C. of C. (natural resources adv. council), Am. Indsl. Hygiene Assn. (chair mgmt. com. 1990-92, nat. conf. com. 1989—, pub. rels. com. 1990—, internat. task force 1992, internat. com. 1992—, nat. bd. dirs. 1994—, NAFTA task force 1993—, health care reform task force 1994—), Am. Assn. Univ. Women, Network of Career Women (officer Irving chpt. 1980-88), Leadership Louisville Alumni, Third Century (bus. & econ. devel. com. 1990-92), Soc. of St. Patrick, Thorobreds (Ky. Derby festival com. 1991-92), Main Line Women's Caucus, Tau Iota Epsilon, Omicron Delta Kappa, Sigma Iota Epsilon (officer U. Dallas chpt. 1984-88), Alpha Chi Omega (officer Louisville chpt 1990-91). Methodist. Home: 6 Harford Ln Radnor PA 19087-4529 Office: Sun Co 10 Penn Ctr 1801 Market St Philadelphia PA 19103-1699

MCCLUSKEY, LOIS THORNHILL, photographer; b. Boston, Apr. 7, 1945; d. Fred S. and Mary (Evans) T.; BA, Middlebury Coll., 1966; postgrad. U. St. Thomas, Houston, 1967-69; MA, NYU, 1971; cert. in graphic design U. Calif.-Santa Cruz, 1983; m. Edward J. McCluskey, Feb. 14, 1981. Research technician dept. virology Baylor Sch. Medicine, Houston, 1966-68; with Kelly Girls, Palo Alto, 1971-72; slide curator dept. art Stanford (Calif.) U., 1972-80; founder, pres. Stanford Design Assocs., Palo Alto, 1981—; cons. copy and museum photography; designer, producer custom lecture slides. Mem. Smithsonian Assos. Home: 895 Northampton Dr Palo Alto CA 94303-3434 Office: PO Box 60451 Palo Alto CA 94306-0451

MCCLUSKEY, SUSAN D., lawyer; b. Osmond, Nebr.; d. Earle R. and Deloris C. (Olson) M.; m. Charles D. Gray, Feb. 17, 1980; children: Charles W., Johanna M. BA, U. Denver, 1973; JD, Cornell U., 1977; cert. sr. mgrs. in govt., Harvard U., 1992. Bar: D.C., 1977, U.S. Supreme Ct., 1993. Asst. counsel Nat. Treasury Employees Union and Panel Assoc., 1984-86, Fed. Svc. Impasses Panel, 1984-86; spl. asst. to exec. dir. Fed. Labor Rels. Authority, 1984-86, exec. asst. to chmn., 1986-89, chief counsel to chmn., 1989—. Methodist. Office: Fed Labor Relations Authority 607 14th St NW Rm 410 Washington DC 20424-0001*

MCCLYMONDS, JEAN ELLEN, marketing professional; b. Richmond, Calif.; d. Rollin John Lepley and Doris Ellen Baughman; m. Gareth Lynn McClymonds, Sept. 18, 1981. BS in Edn., U. Calif., Berkeley, 1970; M Bus. Communications, San Jose State U., 1987. Adminstr. sales Dohrmann Div. Envirotech, Santa Clara, Calif., 1970-74; supr. order processing Molectron Corp., Sunnyvale, Calif., 1974-79; mgr. mktg. svcs. Gould-Biomation, Santa Clara, 1979-84; dir. corp. communications Madic Corp., Santa Clara, 1984-86; dir. mktg. nat. accounts Skyway Freight Systems, Inc., Watsonville, Calif., 1986-89; pres. Just Mktg., Scotts Valley, Calif., 1989—; pub. speaker various local orgns., 1984—. Contbr. articles industry jours., 1986—. Mem. Am. Trucking Assn. (allied dir. 1995, outstanding achievement award 1992), Bus. Profl. Advt. Assn., Nat. Assn. Quality Control, Peninsula Mktg. Assn., Coun. Logistics Mgmt., San Jose Women in Bus. Republican. Office: Ste 21 5524 Scotts Valley Dr Scotts Valley CA 95066-4518

MCCLYMONDS, PAULINE RUTH, brokerage house executive; b. Grove City, Pa., Apr. 14, 1948; d. Paul Russel and Dorothy G. (Gamble) Snyder; m. Kenneth I. McClymonds, Aug. 30, 1968; 1 child, Matthew. EdB, Slippery Rock (Pa.) Coll., 1969. CFP. Tchr. sci. Ellwood City (Pa.) High Sch., 1969-70; coord. congregate dining Luth. Soc. Svcs., Waynesboro, Pa., 1973-75; tchr. sci. Waynesboro High Sch., 1974-76; supr. savs. First Fed. Savs. and Loan, Davenport, Iowa, 1978-83; fin. planner Fin. Planning Group, Bettendort, Iowa, 1983-84; fin. planner, trust officer N.W. Bank & Trust, Davenport, 1984-86; pres. Cuyahoga Fin. Svcs. Agy., Cleve., 1987—. Contbr. articles to newspapers. Mem. Internat. Assn. Fin. Planning, Inst. Cert. Fin. Planners, Kappa Delta Pi. Republican. Presbyterian. Office: Cuyahoga Fin Svcs Agy 1 Erieview Plz Cleveland OH 44114-1706

MCCLYMONT, ELEANOR JEAN, educational administrator, pathologist; b. Newark, July 5, 1938; d. Michael Joseph and Selena (Gilchrist) Gargan; m. William James McClymont, June 20, 1959; children: Scott William, Lisa Eleanor McClymont Chowansky. BA, Montclair State Coll., 1960, MA, 1975; prin.-supr. cert., Kean Coll., 1982. Speech and lang. pathologist Saddle Brook (N.J.) Bd. Edn., 1960-61, Vis. Nurse Assn., Plainfield, N.J., 1963-65; speech and lang. pathologist Scotch Plains (N.J.) Fanwood Bd. Edn., 1969-83, chair dept. speech and lang., 1983-86, supr. spl. edn., 1986-90; dir. spl. edn., 1990—. Mem. Jaycetts, Scotch Plains, 1968-72; v.p. Fanwood Jr. Women's Club, 1964-65; mem. bd. deacons 1st Bapt. Ch., Somerville, N.J., 1988-89, chair presch. com., 1980-90, choir mem., 1975—, sec. bd. trustees, 1993—. N.J. State Dept. Edn. grantee, 1986, 87-88, 88. Mem. Assn. for Supervision and Curriculum Devel., N.J. Prins. and Suprs. Assn., N.J. Speech and Hearing Assn., Coun. for Exceptional Children. Republican. Home: 292 Goldfinch Dr Bridgewater NJ 08807-1190 Office: Office of Pupil Svcs 721 Westfield Rd Scotch Plains NJ 07076-2156

MCCOLLOUGH, CAROL KEENEY, academic administrator; b. Dallas, Aug. 4, 1937; d. D. L. Keeney and H. Adelle (Fogle) Bowsher; m. Charles Randolph McCollough, June 2, 1959; children: Colin, Wendy, Timothy. BA, So. Meth. U., 1959, MA, 1960; postgrad., Princeton Theol. Sem., 1979-81. Tchr. English Mountain Lakes (N.J.) High Sch., 1960-64, Barrington (R.I.) Coll., 1966-70; instr. English Ea. Coll., Villanova U., St. David's, Pa., 1968-73; dir. Resource Ctr. Ctrl. Atlantic Conf., Montclair, N.J., 1975-81; from asst. to dir. planning to mgr. dept. history Princeton (N.J.) U., 1981-91; asst. to pres. Mercer County Community College, West Windsor, N.J., 1991—. Author: (ch. curriculum) Always Growing Up!, 1983; co-author: Lifestyles of Faithfulness, 1983. Founder, chairperson Network of Dirs. of Resource Ctrs. in the United Ch. of Christ, 1977-79; singer Singing City Choir, Phila., 1978—, Princeton Pro Musica; bd. dirs. Princeton Coun. Community Svcs., 1985-90, Ctrl. Atlantic Conf. United Ch. of Christ, Catonsville, Md.; trainer Assn. for Couples in Marriage Enrichment, Winston-Salem, N.C., 1980—. Grad. scholar So. Meth. U., 1960. Mem. Am. Fedn. Tchrs., N.J. Am. Coun. on Edn.-Nat. Identification Program. Democrat. Home: 165 Hopewell Wertsville Rd Hopewell NJ 08525-1106 Office: Mercer County CC PO Box B Trenton NJ 08690-0182

MCCOLLUM, BETTY, state legislator; b. July 12, 1954; m. Douglas McCollum; 2 children. BS in Edn., Coll. St. Catherine. Retail store mgr. Minn.; mem. Minn. Ho. Reps., 1992—, mem. edn. com., environ. and natural resources com., mem. gen. legis. com., vet. affairs and elections com., mem. transportation and transit com. Mem. St. Croix Valley Coun. Girl Scouts, Greater East Side Boy Scouts. Democrat. Home: 2668 4th Ave E North Saint Paul MN 55109-3116 Office: Minn Ho of Reps State Capitol Saint Paul MN 55155*

MCCOLLUM, JEAN HUBBLE, medical assistant; b. Peoria, Ill., Oct. 21, 1934; d. Claude Ambrose and Josephine Mildred (Beiter) Hubble; m. Everett Monroe Patton, Sept. 4, 1960 (div. Jan. 1969); 1 child, Linda Joanne; m. James Ward McCollum, Jan. 2, 1971; 1 child, Steven Ward. Grad. high sch., Peoria; student, Bradley U., Ill. Cen. Coll. Stenographer Caterpillar Tractor Co., Peoria, 1952-53, supr. stenographer pool, 1953-55, adminstrv. sec., treas., 1955-60, sec., asst. dept. mgr., 1970-71; med. staff sec. Proctor Community Hosp., Peoria, 1978-82; med. asst. Drs. Taylor, Fox and Morgan, Peoria, 1982-84; freelance med. asst. Meth. Hosp. and numerous physicians, Peoria, 1984-93; office mgr. Dr. Danehower, McLelland and Stone, Peoria, 1994-95. Vol. tutor Northmoor Sch., Peoria, 1974-78; bd. dirs., mem. exec. com., com. chmn. Planned Parenthood, Peoria, 1990-92. Recipient Outstanding Performance award Proctor Hosp., 1981, also various awards for svc. to schs., ch. and hosps. for mentally ill. Mem. Nat. Wildlife Fedn., Mensa Internat. (publs. officer, editor 1987-89), Mothers League (treas. 1977), Willow Knolls Country Club (social com. 1989-90), Nature Conservancy, World Wildlife Fund, Forest Park Found., Jacques Cousteau Soc., Wilderness Soc. Methodist. Home: 2822 W Pine Hill Ln Peoria IL 61614-3256

MCCONNELL, BARBARA ANN ROGERS, accounting manager; b. Pelzer, S.C., July 27, 1939; d. Walter Herbert and Genav (Garrett) Rogers; 1 child, William D. Jr.; m. William Dendy McDonnell, Aug. 24, 1957. AAS, Greenville Tech. Coll., 1973; B of Gen. Studies magna cum laude, U. S.C., 1975, MBA, 1986. CPA, N.C. Gen. acct. J. P. Stevens & Co., Greenville, S.C., 1975-77; acctg. mgr. Reliance Electric Co., Greenville, S.C., 1977-81; fin. analyst Digital Equip. Corp., Greenville, S.C., 1981-83, cost acct., 1983-86, planning analyst, 1986-88, planning mgr., 1988-92; dir. cost acctg. London Internat. U.S. Holdings, Inc., 1993-94; fin. mgr. Motorola, Inc., Lawrenceville, Ga., 1994—. Mem. AAUW (coalition bds. and commns. 1981), Nat. Assn. Accts., Order of Ea. Star (worthy matron 1978), Am. Legion (pres. 1977). Home: 161 New Hope Rd Pelzer SC 29669-9076

MCCONNELL, PATRICIA ANN, health facility administrator; b. Bklyn., Feb. 28, 1935; d. Philip P. and Dagney C. (Petersen) Powers; m. Alexander McConnell, Jan . 15, 1955; children: Francis X., Robert M., Bonnie J., Douglas P. AAS in Nursing, Milw. Area Tech. Coll., Milw., 1978; student, U. Wis., 1980; BA, Nat. Lewis U., 1989. RN, Ill., Ind., Wis., Inc.; registered profl. nurse; cert. case mgr.; cert. pain mgr.; cert. ins. rehab. specialist; cert. occupational hearing conservationalist. Nursing asst., RN oncology dept. St. Luke's Hosp., Milw., 1976-79; supr. employee health dept. Harnisfeger P&H, Cudahy, Wis., 1979-82; staff nurse employee health dept. 1st Wis. Nat. Bank, Milw., 1982-83; med. svcs. cons. Crawford Risk Mgmt. Svcs., Schaumburg, Ill., 1983-86; case mgmt. specialist Nat. Rehab. Cons., Westmont, Ill., 1986-87; pres., dir. Mid-State Health and Rehab., Westmont, 1987—; bd. dirs. Women in Workers Compnsation of Ill., vice chmn. 1993-94, sponsor chair 1994-95. Founding mem. Rape Recovery Project Hot Line, vol. support group, Chgo., 1989—, bd. dirs. 1990—; active Ill. Coalition Against Sexual Assault, 1990; vol. literacy tutor World Relief Orgn. and Literacy Vols. Am., 1990—; den mother Cubs, Boy Scouts of Am., 1966-68; health and safety svcs. instr. ARC, 1993-94; religion instr. St. Helena Cath. Ch., Greendale, Wis. 1973-75. Mem. LWV, Am. Assn. Occupational Health Nurses (local treas. 1986-87), Rehab. Inst. Nurses Group (treas. 1990-91, pres. 1992-93), Assn. Rehab. Nurses., Am. Acad. Pain Mgmt. (clin. assoc. 1991—), Assn. Vocat. Rehabilitationists in Ill., Oak Brook Assn. Commerce and Industry (small bus. com. 1989-90), Dolton Regional Hosp. Aux. (charter, nominating com., publicity chair 1965), Women in Mgmt. (hospitality chair). Roman Catholic. Home: 821 Oakwood Dr Westmont IL 60559-1035 Office: 504A E Ogden Ave Ste 249 Westmont IL 60559-1277

MCCONNELL, PATRICIA LYNN, vocational consultant; b. Denver, Feb. 20, 1956; d. James Donald and Joyce Clemence (Wortman) McC.; m. Roger Tribble, 1989. BS, U. No. Colo., 1979. Mental health worker Arapahoe Mental Health Ctr., Littleton, Colo., 1977-79; work adjustment cons. recycling ctr. City of El Cerrito (Calif.), 1980-83; job developer, ind. contractor with Dept. of Rehab., Pleasant Hill, Calif., San Pablo, Vallejo, Calif., 1983-87; vocat. rehab. cons. Guitterez & Co., Oakland, Calif., 1987-89; owner, vocat. cons. JobPerfect, Berkeley, Calif., 1989—; owner, fundraiser Community Svcs. Mktg., Oakland; workshop leader Calif. Dept. of Rehab., Pleasant Hill, 1983-87, San Pablo, 1989. Author: (workbook) Job Search for the disabled, 1985, Job Perfect Job Search Manual Datebook and Organizer, 1995; dir., producer (video) JobPerfect, 1992, How To Improve Your Communication and Interview Skills, 1994. Mem., fundraiser No. Calif. Recyclers Assn., Berkeley, 1982-87, Calif. Marine Mammal Ctr., Marine Headlands, Calif., 1987-90, Bay Area Cmty. Svcs., 1993—. Recipient Dance award Englewood High Sch., Colo., 1974, Appreciation award Regional Occupational Program, San Pablo, 1989. Mem. Calif. Assn. for Rehab. Profls., Nat. Rehab. Assn. (bd. dirs. 1983-85). Office: JobPerfect at BFTI 2236 Derby St Berkeley CA 94705-1018

MCCONNELL, VIOLA CARLBERG, author, editor; b. Albia, Iowa, Jan. 1, 1903; d. John Sven and Anna-Marie (Anderson) Carlberg; m. Harold Graham McConnell, Jan. 8, 1927 (dec. Feb. 1974); 1 child, Anderson Graham (dec. May 1991). BA, U. Minn., 1930, postgrad., 1957-59, 1970. Diocesan pres. Girls' Friendly (Episcopal) Soc., Minn., 1944-57; Bishop's pub. relations dir. Episcopal Diocese of Minn., 1964-79; Diocesan correspondent Living Ch. and Episc., U.S.A., Minn., 1954-86; v.p. St. Paul's Ch. Women, Mpls., 1960-64; with State Bd. Church Women United, Minn., 1944-73; numerous positions with Episc. Ch.; State chmn. 50th anniversary State Bd. Ch. Women United, Minn., 1984-86; Episc. rep. Minn. Coun. of Chs., Mpls., Radio-TV com., 1964-74; nat. missions chmn. Girl's Friendly Soc., N.Y.C., 1951-54, nat. pub. rels. chmn., 1954-57; pub. rels. dir. Internat. Ctr. of U. Minn., 1958-71; non-govt. rep. for Episc. Exec. Bd. UN Planning Session 10th Anniversary, N.Y.C., 1954; comm. cons. Minn. Episc. Diocese, 1989-90. Author: The Virgin Islands, 1952, Haiti, 1953, Focus on Liberia, 1954; editor mag. Communique, Internat. Ctr. U. Minn., 1957-71; producer (TV program) Citizens For Eisenhower in East Rm. White House, Washington, 1956; editor newsletter Episcopal Ch. Women, Diocese of Minn., commun. chmn., 1976-86; writer video St. Paul's Episc. Parish House; contbr. articles to mags. Pub. rels. chmn. YWCA Bd., Mplw., 1946-47, 53-54, Rep. Com.; rep. Police Adv. Coun., Mpls., 1976-81; state radio/TV chmn. Citizens for Eisenhower, Mpls., 1956; rschr. for hist. com. Friends of Inst. Mpls. Inst. Art, 1990-92, also vol.; rschr. St. Paul's Parish Hall, Minn., 1980—; active Minn. Hist. Soc., 1989—. Recipient 6 yr. svc. award ARC, Mpls., 1945, merit award Ch. Women United, 1973, Nat. Ch. Women United, N.Y.C., 1986, Valiant Woman award, 1986, WCCO Good Neighbor of N.W., 1973, Civic and Cultural Vol. award Mayor of Mpls., 1985. Mem. Religious Pub. Rels. Coun. (life, nat. bd. dirs. 1964-66, various offices Twin Cities chpt. 1955-86), Ch. Periodical Club Episcopal (life), Minn. Press Club, Episcopal Communicators, Mpls. Inst. Art (sustaining), Women's Club Mpls., Mpls. Club, Alpha Chi Omega (50 Yr. Golden Girl award Mpls. 1976, Best of Best Alumnae award Indpls. 1987, Lowry Hill hist. com. 1993-94), Nat. Rep. Com. (sustaining). Republican. Home: 3434 Heritage Dr Apt 410 Edina MN 55435-2226

MCCONNON, ELIZABETH KING, clinical counselor; b. Ft. Leavenworth, Kans., Oct. 22, 1953; d. John Joseph Jr. and Geraldine Louise (Wyman) King; m. James C. McConnon, Jr., Sept. 15, 1979; 1 child, Christopher M. BA, Wheeling Coll., 1975; MEd, U. Va., 1976; student, Iowa State U., 1981-87. Lic. clin. profl. counselor, substance abuse counselor. Intern, counselor rehab. Devereux Found., Devon, Pa., 1976-77, vocat. counselor, 1977-78; counselor, adj. instr. Montgomery County C.C., Bluebell, Pa., 1978-79; sr. counselor Ctr. Personal Devel., Ames, Iowa, 1980-84; clin. coord. Ctr. for Addictions Recovery, Ames, 1984-89; counselor II Penobscot Nation Health Dept., Old Town, Maine, 1989—; sec. Substance Abuse Assn. Iowa, Des Moines, 1985-88, contbr. newsletter, 1987. Clin. fellow Devereux Inst. Clin. Tng.; mem. Nat. Assn. Alcohol and Drug Abuse Conselors, Am. Counseling Assn., Assn. Group Work Specialists, Maine Assn. Alcohol and Drug Abuse Counselors.

MCCOOK, KATHLEEN DE LA PEÑA, university educator; b. Chgo.; d. Frank Eugene and Margaret L. (de la Peña) McEntee; m. Philip G. Heim, Mar. 20, 1972 (div.); 1 child, Margaret Marie; m. William Woodrow Lee McCook, Oct. 12, 1991; stepchildren: Cecilia, Billie Jean, Nicole. B.A., U. Ill.; M.A., Marquette U.; U. Chgo.; Ph.D., U. Wis.-Madison. Reference librarian Elmhurst Coll. Library, Ill., 1971-72; dir. pub. services Rosary Coll. Library, River Forest, Ill., 1972-76; lectr. U. Wis., Madison, 1976-78; asst. prof. library sci. U. Ill., Urbana, 1978-83; dean, prof. La. State U. Sch. Library and Info. Sci., Baton Rouge, 1983-90; dean grad. sch. La. State U., 1990-92; dir. Sch. Libr. and Info. Sci. U. South Fla., 1993—. Author: (with L. Estabrook) Career Profiles, 1983, (with William E. Moen) Occupational Entry, 1989, Adult Services, 1990, (with Gary O. Rolstad) Developing Readers' Advisory Services, 1993, Toward a Just and Productive Soc., 1994; contbr. essays to books, articles to profl. jours. Chmn. Equal Rights Amendment Task Force, Ill., 1977-79; mem. Eugene McCarthy campaign, U. Ill., Chgo., 1968; mem. La. Gov.'s Commn. for Women, 1985-88; bd. dirs. La. Endowment for Humanities, 1991-92. Recipient Disting. Alumnus award U. Wis., 1991; Bradshaw scholar Tex. Woman's Univ., 1994. Mem. ALA (com. chmn. 1980—, editor RQ jour., 1982-88, Pub. Librs. jour. 1989-90, Equality award 1987, Adult Svc. award 1991), Assn. for Libr. and Info. Sci. Edn. (com. chmn. 1981—, pres. 1987-88), Southeastern Libr. Assn., Fla. Libr. Assn. (treas. 1995—), Tampa Bay Libr. Consortium (bd. dirs. 1994—), Women Libr. Workers, Ill. Libr. Assn. (treas. 1981-83), Beta Phi Mu. Democrat. Roman Catholic. Office: U South Fla Sch Libr and Info Sci 4202 Fowler Ave E CIS 1040 Tampa FL 33620-8300

MCCORKINDALE, CAROLYN CHRISTINE, dietitian; b. Berkeley, Calif., Oct. 18, 1962; d. John McCorkindale and Joan (Roth) Finnie. BS, Calif. Poly., 1984; MPH, San Jose State U., 1989. Registered dietitian, Calif.; cert. diabetes educator. Nutritionist San Francisco Gen. Hosp., 1989-91; clin. dietitian Laguna Honda Hosp., San Francisco, 1991—. Mem. Am. Diabetes Assn., Am. Dietetic Assn. (author jour. 1990, Huddleson award 1991), Am. Assn. Diabetic Educators, Calif. Dietetic Assn. Democrat. Home: 555 Corbett Ave # 4 San Francisco CA 94114-2240 Office: Laguna Honda Hosp 375 Laguna Honda Blvd San Francisco CA 94116

MCCORMACK, GRACE LYNETTE, civil engineering technician; b. Dallas, Nov. 2; d. Audley and Janice Meredith (Metcalf) McC. Tech. degree, Durham's Coll., 1958; grad. in civil engring., El Centro Coll., 1972; grad. in advanced surveying, Eastfield, 1975. Cert. sr. engr. technician. Contract design technician various engring firms, Dallas, 1958-70; sr. design engr. technician City of Dallas Survey Div., 1970-80, street light div., 1980-95, ret. 1995. Mem. Unity Ch. Avocations: numerology, astrology, metaphysics, Egyptian-Arabian horses, lighting and designing black and white portrait photography. Home: 1428 Meadowbrook Ln Irving TX 75061-4435

MCCORMACK, KATHERINE MCGRATH, nursing administrator; b. Waterbury, Conn., Sept. 6, 1949; d. Francis John and Katherine (Kelly) McGrath; m. Robert James McCormack, Sept. 30, 1972; 1 child, Patrick Ryan. B.S. in Nursing, Russell Sage Coll., 1971; M.P.H., Yale U., 1981. R.N., Conn. Staff nurse New Eng. Deaconess Hosp., Boston, 1971-72; pub. health nurse Health Dept., Waterbury, 1972-77, supr. nursing, 1977-80, dir. nursing, 1980-94; clin. mgr. ambulatory svcs. St. Francis Hosp. and Med. Ctr./Mt. Sinai Hosp., Hartford, Conn., 1994—; profl. adv. com. Med. Pers. Pool (name changed to Interim Health Care), New Haven, 1985—. Bd. dirs. Am. Cancer Soc., Waterbury, 1981-89, Collaboration for Prevention Child Abuse and Neglect, Waterbury, 1981-83, Alcohol and Drug Council, Waterbury, 1984-90; sec. 1987-90; class agt. Russell Sage Coll., 1986—; shelter mgr. City of Waterbury Disaster Planning, 1986-94; Maternal Child Health adv. com., 1987-94; v.p. Waterbury Adminstrs. Assn., 1988-89, exec. bd., 1989-94; active Teenage Pregnancy Prevention, 1989-94; CSAP adv. bd., 1990-94; Healthy Conn. Coalition, 1991—; United Way allocations com., 1991. Recipient Soroptimist Tng. award, 1980; Recognition award Child Guidance, Inc., 1994. Mem. ANA, APHA, Conn. Pub. Health Assn., Ct. Assn. Sch. Health, Conn. Nurses Assn. Democrat. Roman Catholic. Avocations: reading, knitting, sports. Office: Waterbury Health Dept 402 E Main St Waterbury CT 06702-1701

MCCORMACK, MARJORIE GUTH, psychology educator, career counselor, communications educator, public relations consultant; b. Jersey City, Dec. 27, 1934; d. Joseph Leo and Vera Marie (Clossey) Guth; m. Kevin T. McCormack, Nov. 11, 1961. BA, St. Peter's Coll., 1974; MA, Jersey City State Coll., 1990. Editor, AT&T, N.Y.C., 1952-60, libr., 1960-67; libr. St. Peter's Coll., Jersey City, 1967-71; pub. rels. mgr. Blue Cross of N.J., Newark, 1971-81; instr. history, econs. St. Aloysius High Sch., Jersey City, 1981-82; pub. rels. cons. Creative Pub. Rels. Assocs., Jersey City, 1981—; prof. psychology Hudson County Cmty. Coll., 1995—. adj. instr. comm. St. Peter's Coll., 1982-88; copy editor Glens Falls, (N.Y.) Post-Star, 1986; dir. career placement Hudson County C.C., 1988-91. Bd. mgrs. Am. Cancer Soc., Jersey City, 1978-79; mem., sec. parish coun. St. Aloysius Ch., 1981-85; mem. Jersey City Tenants Orgn., 1981—, Rent Leveling Bd. Jersey City, 1983-86, St. Peter's Coll. Community Chorus, 1988—; 2nd v.p. and pub. rels. chair Sodality of The Children of Mary of St. Teresa, 1993—. Mem. AAUP, Mid. Atlantic Career Counselors Assn., N.J. Assn. Counseling & Devel., N.J. Edn. Assn., NAFE (pub. rels. chmn. 1980-82), Jersey City Bus. and Profl. Women's Assn. (legis. chmn. 1975-77, Nat. Program award 1976, State Press award 1982), Hudson County Women's Network. Avocations: music, theater, gourmet cooking.

MCCORMACK, MARY BEATRICE (BEE MCCORMACK), retired food manufacturing executive; b. Albany, Ga., Aug. 21, 1925; d. Robert Emmet and Anna Louise (Keller) McC. BA, Ga. Coll., 1946. Dir. personnel Bobs Candies, Inc., Albany, 1946-61; v.p. Bob's Candies, Inc., Albany, 1961-94; ret., 1994. Pres. Albany Symphony, 1972-74; co-chmn. capital funds campaign Albany Mus., 1981-82, sec. 1990-93; chmn. arts devel. dir. Albany Arts Coun., 1984; mem. Ga. Bus. Com. for the Arts, 1989-93, Albany Local Devel. Commn., 1986-93. Recipient Pro Deum et Juventatum medal Roman Cath. Diocese of Savannah, Ga., 1970, Alumni Achievement award Ga. Coll., Milledgeville, 1983; co-recipient Albany Woman of Yr. award, 1978. Mem. Nat. Confectioners Assn. (dir., v.p. 1979-84, Candy Mfr. Yr. 1981), Profit-sharing Council Am. (dir. 1975-81), Profit Sharing Research Fedn. (dir. 1978-81), Albany C. of C. (dir. 1982-85). Roman Catholic. Office: Bobs Candies Inc PO Box 3170 1505 W Oakridge Dr Albany GA 31707-5308

MCCORMICK, ALMA HEFLIN, writer, retired educator, psychologist; b. Winona, Mo., Sept. 2, 1910; d. Irvin Elgin and Nora Edith (Kelley) Heflin; m. Archie Thomas Edward McCormick, July 14, 1942 (dec.); children: Thomas James, Kelly Jean. BA, Ea. Wash. Coll., 1936, EdM, 1949; PhD, Clayton U., 1977. Originator dept. severely mentally retarded Tri-City Public Schs., Richland, Wash., 1953, Parkland, Wash., 1955; co-founder, dir. Adastra Sch. for Gifted Children, Seattle, 1957-64; author profl. publs., novels; contbr. articles to various publs., 1937—. Mem. Am. Psychol. Assn., OX 5 Aviation Pioneers, Kappa Delta Pi. Republican. Roman Catholic. Editor: Cub Flyer, Western Story Mag., Wild West Weekly; assoc. editor: Mexico City Daily News (English sect. of Novedades). One of the first Am. woman test pilot's, 1942.

MCCORMICK, BETTY LEONORA, accountant; b. Missoula, Mont., July 18, 1961; d. George Oliver and Betty June (Dolton) W. BBA, U. Mont., 1983. CPA, Mont. Staff acct. Ellis & Assocs., Boise, Idaho, 1984; acct. Glacier Electric Coop., Cut Bank, Mont., 1984-86, office mgr., 1986—; income tax cons. Mem. AICPA, Beta Gamma Sigma. Democrat. Roman Catholic. Avocations: skiing, sewing, reading, hunting. Office: Glacier Electric Coop Inc 410 E Main St Cut Bank MT 59427-3012

MCCORMICK, CAROL BROWN, executive; b. Williamsport, Pa., Nov. 14, 1942; d. Lee Confair and Clair Elda (Winters) Brown; m. Robert Leroy Masorti Sr., Dec. 2, 1962 (div. Apr. 1975); children: Barbara Lee, Robert Leroy Jr., Angela; m. George Hess McCormick, Dec. 22, 1984; stepchildren: Gregory, Stephen, Nina. Coord. domestic violence Clinton County Women's Ctr., Lock Haven, Pa., 1984-91; exec. dir. Tioga County Woman's Coalition, Wellsboro, Pa., 1991—; bd. dirs. Pa. Coalition Against Domestic Violence, Harrisburg. Mem. domestic violence task force Tioga County Chpt., 1984—. Republican. Methodist. Home: RR #1 Box 502 Jersey Shore PA 17740 Office: Tioga County Women's Coalition PO Box 933 Wellsboro PA 16901

MCCORMICK, DALE, state legislator; b. Jan. 17, 1947. BA, U. Iowa, 1970. Mem. Maine State Senate from 18th dist, 1991—. Home: Box 697 RR 1 Box 697 Monmouth ME 04259-9801 Address: 1250 Turner St Auburn ME 04210-6436*

MCCORMICK, ELAINE ALICE, former nurse, fundraising executive; b. Jersey City, Nov. 19, 1943; d. Johannes and Anni (Gantenberg) Kratz; m. Thomas A. McCormick, Oct. 1, 1966; 1 child, Thomas John. Diploma in nursing, Mt. Sinai Sch. Nursing, 1964; BA summa cum laude, Georgian Ct. Coll., 1982. RN, N.Y., N.J., Fla. Staff nurse Holy Name Hosp., Teaneck, N.J., 1964-65, 69-70; office nurse Drs. Higdon, Beaugard and Fox, Teaneck, 1965-67; indsl. nurse Dun & Bradstreet, Inc., N.Y.C., 1967-69; camp nurse, ski area dir. Camp Arrowhead, Community YMCA, Marlboro, N.J., 1974-78; adminstrv. asst. DeJesse Advt., Woodbrige, N.J., 1982-83; staff writer Georgian Ct. Coll., Lakewood, N.J., 1983-84, dir. pub. rels., 1984-92, asst. v.p. for coll. advancement, 1992-94; v.p. for coll. advancement Georgian Ct. Coll., Lakewood, 1994—; cons. in field. Mem. adv. bd. Ret. Sr. Vol. Program Ocean County, Toms River, N.J., 1987-94, mem. bd. advisors, 1994—; mem. adv. coun. Eldermed Scan Ocean City; mem. Sr. Citizen Action Network Monmouth County, chairwoman, bd. advisors, mem. exec. bd.; mem. Mercy Higher Edn. Colloquim, Monmouth Ocean Devel. Coun. Mem. Am. Mgmt. Assn., Nat. Soc. Fundraising Execs., West Monmouth C. of C., Sigma Tau Delta. Republican. Roman Catholic. Home: 9 Pamela St Marlboro NJ 07746-1621 Office: Georgian Ct Coll 900 Lakewood Ave Lakewood NJ 08701-2600 also: 4452 NE Ocean Blvd Jensen Beach FL 34957-4373

MCCORMICK, KATHLEEN MARIE, medical/surgical nurse; b. McKeesport, Pa., Sept. 20, 1962; d. Raymond P. Jr. and Eileen M. (Roper) Kerrigan; m. Dennis J. McCormick, May 23, 1992; 1 child, Mallory Elizabeth. BSN, Coll. of Mt. St. Joseph, Cin., 1984; postgrad., Ohio Dominican Coll., Columbus, Ohio. RN, Ohio; cert. med.-surg. nurse, BLS instr. Asst. mgr. and educator peripheral vascular/gen. surgery unit Park Med. Ctr., Columbus, Ohio. Mem. Soc. Peripheral Vascular Nursing, Sigma Theta Tau.

MCCORMICK, MARY BETH, lawyer; b. Syracuse, N.Y., Sept. 19, 1953; d. Paul Vincent and Elizabeth Frances (Moore) McC.; m. James Oliver McCutcheon, Oct. 17, 1986. Student, Frostburg State Coll., 1975; JD, U. Balt., 1980. Bar: Md. 1980, D.C. 1982. Aide Pub. Defenders Office, Rockville, Md., 1975-79; law clk. McInerney, Layne, McCormick, Sullivan & Rice, Rockville, 1979-80; law clk. The Hon. Richard B. Latham, Rockville, 1980-81, assoc. law clk., 1980-81; asst. pub. defender Pub. Defender's Office Montgomery County, Rockville, 1981-82; assoc. Robert Ades & Assocs., Landover, Md., 1982-85, Gleason & Flynn, Chartered, Rockville, 1985-93; ptnr. Gleason, Flynn, McCormick & Emig, Rockville, 1993—. Mem. Gaithersburg Bus. and Profl. Women (1st v.p. 1992-93). Democrat. Home: 10828 Game Preserve Rd Gaithersburg MD 20879-3104 Office: Gleason Flynn McCormick & Emig 2275 Research Blvd # 200 Rockville MD 20850-3268

MCCORMICK, MAUREEN OLIVEA, computer systems programmer; b. Toledo, Mar. 24, 1956; d. Richard Ernest and Rita Maureen (Pratt) McC. BS in Elem. Edn., Kent State U., 1978, MA Reading Specialization, 1980. Reading instr. Elyria City Schs., Elyria, Ohio, 1978-79; tchr. Wellington Village Schs., Wellington, Ohio, 1979-80; devel. edn. instr. Lorain County Community Coll., Elyria, 1980-83; computer programmer analyst Navy Fin. Ctr., Cleve., 1981-86, Naval Mil. Personnel Command, Arlington, Va., 1986; computer systems analyst Marine Corps Cen. Design & Programming Activity/MCDEC, Quantico, Va., 1986-87; computer systems programmer Navy Fin. Ctr., Cleve., 1987-91, Def. Fin. and Acctg Svc.-Cleve. Ctr., 1991-92, Def. Info. Tech. Svc. Orgn.-Cleve. Ctr., Cleve., 1992-93; supervisory computer specialist Def. Fin. & Acctg. Svc.-Fin. Sys. Activity, Cleve., 1993—. Mem. AAUW, Am. Soc. Mil. Compts., TransAtlantic Brides & Parents Assn., Daus. Brit. Empire. Home: 153 Burns Rd Elyria OH 44035-1510 Office: DFAS-FSA-CL 1240 E 9th St Cleveland OH 44199-2075

MCCORMICK, PAMELA ANN, artist, sculptor; b. Grand Rapids, Mich., Jan. 7, 1948; d. William Albert McCormick and June (Wente) Schuster; m. William K. Scarvie, Mar. 19, 1965 (div. Jan. 1972); children: Will, Jeffrey. BA in Art, San Jose (Calif.) State U., 1972, MA in Art Sculpture, 1974; postgrad., Stanford U., 1975-76. Instr. art Am. River Coll., Sacramento, 1976; dir. Children's Art Studio, N.Y.C., 1981-84; prodn. mgr. Precision Imaging Corp., N.Y.C., 1986-88; cons. desktop pub. various pub. cos., N.Y.C., 1988-90; set design Color Story Chaparral, N.Y., 1992, Living Theatre prodn. Sixth Book, N.Y., 1991; solo exhbn. sculpture and photography Mus., N.Y., 1991. Prin. works include Quatrain sculpture Cen. Park, N.Y.C., 1986-89, Flying Light Flushing Park, Queens, N.Y., 1986, Channeling, Erie Barge Canal, Lockport, N.Y., 1988, numerous floating sculptures for Cen. Park, N.Y.C., 1989, set design for Ice Theatre of N.Y., 1989, set and costume design Carmen Beuchat Dance Co., N.Y., 1990, Sixth Book, Living Theater, 1991, Ice Theater of N.Y., 1991, Living Theater, 1991, Color Story, Chaparral, N.Y., 1992; one-person exhbn. of sculpture & photography N.Y.C. Mus. 1991, D&H Canal Rail Trail, Accord, N.Y., 1994. Recipient Distinction award Audubon Naturalist Soc., 1986; NEA fellow, 1974; grantee Pollock Krasner Found., Inc., 1990, N.Y. State Coun. for Arts, 1994, Lila Wallace Reader's Digest Arts Internat. grantee, 1994. Mem. Artists Representing Environ. Art, Internat. Sculpture Orgn. Democrat. Studio: 97 Wooster St New York NY 10012

MCCORMICK, VANDA CHANDLER, art educator, artist; b. Gulfport, Miss., June 21, 1955; d. Artis Pennington and Jimmaleen (Davidson) Chandler; m. Frank David McCormick. BFA, William Carey Coll., 1985, MEd in Art, 1994. Cert. art edn. tchr., Miss., K-8 elem. edn. tchr., Miss. Freelance artist Gulfport, Miss., 1985-89; graphic artist Gayfers, Biloxi, Miss., 1989-90; elem. art tchr. Biloxi Pub. Schs., 1990—; sub. tchr. Biloxi Pub. Schs., 1985-89. Recipient 3d award for painting Wiregrass Mus. of Art, 1992, Purchase award So. Miss. Art Assn., 1991, 3d place for sculpture So. Miss. Art Assn., 1992. Mem. Artwave (charter, chmn. 1985-94, Merit award 1992), Ocean Springs Art Assn. (Merit award 1985). Southern Baptist. Home: 13170 John Rd Gulfport MS 39503-5205

MCCOY, CAROL P., psychologist, training executive; b. Bronxville, N.Y., June 14, 1948; d. Rawley Deering and Jane (Wiske) McC.; m. Lanny Gordon Foster, Nov. 29, 1975 (div. 1985). BA, Conn. Coll., 1970; MS in Psychology, Rutgers U., 1974, PhD in Psychology, 1980. Adj. instr. psychology Rutgers U., New Brunswick, N.J., 1974-75; faculty chair dept. social sci. Misericordia Hosp. Sch. Nursing, Bronx, N.Y., 1976-79; tng. and devel. cons. Chase Manhattan Bank N.A., N.Y.C., 1980-85, tng. mgr. internat. consumer banking div., 1985-88, tng. mgr. individual banking, 1988-91; dir. corp. tng. UNUM Life Ins. Co. Am., Portland, Maine, 1991—. Author: Managing a Small HRD Department, 1993. Mem. Am. Soc. Tng. and Devel., Am. Psychol. Assn. Home: 11 Johnson Rd Falmouth ME 04105-1408 Office: UNUM Life Ins Co Am 2211 Congress St Portland ME 04122-0002

MCCOY, CAROLYN SMITH, middle school educator; b. DeWitt, Ark., Sept. 7, 1952; d. Cleo and Willie B. (Mosby) Smith; m. A.C. McCoy, Dec. 24, 1977; 1 child, Carla ShaNai. BS, U. Ark., 1974; MS in Edn., So. Ark. U., 1978. Cert. sci. tchr., Ark. Tchr. sci. DeWitt Pub. Schs., 1974—, tchr. sci. to gifted and talented, 1986-87; tchr. adult edn. sci. Rice Belt Vocat.-Tech. Sch., DeWitt, 1975-77; mem. Project ADVISE (Alliance for Devel. Vision and Initiative for Sci. Edn. in Ark., 1991-92; chmn. textbook adoption com. for elem. schs. Ark. Dept. Edn., Little Rock, 1991-92; mem. NASA-Newest Honor Tchrs. Program, 1989-92, expert review team Southwest Edn. Devel. Labs, 1993, trainer to trainer program tech. coun. Ark. River Ednl. Svc. Coop.; mem. New Standards Project, 1993, U. Ark. Med. Scis. Sci. Enrichment Program. 1993; mem. steering com. dept. higher edn. Ark. Science Crusade 93-94, curriculum devel. team, 1993-94; mem. pilot project DeWitt Pub. Schs., State of Ark. Science Frameworks Devel., 1993-94; mem. frameworks team Hendrix Coll., 1993-94; regional coord. math and sci. Ark. Systematic Initiative. Author: Jammer's Right about Drug Abuse, 1988, A Family Raps about Drug Abuse, 1989. Bd. dirs. Literacy Coun. for Ark. County, Stuttgart, 1990-93; del. Ark. Dem. Conv., 1992; troop leader Girl Scouts U.S.A., Almyra, Ark., 1992; leader 4-H, Almyra, 1992. Named Tchr. of Yr., Oldsmobile Dealers Assn., 1989, Ark. Power & Light, 1990; recipient Young Alumni award So. Ark. U., 1992, Vol. of Yr. award Girl Scouts Am., 1993. Mem. NEA, NSTA, Ark. Sci. Tchrs. Assn., (Elem. Sci. Tchr. Spl. award 1989), Ark. Edn. Assn. (alt. bd. dirs. for bd. dirs.-at-large position 3, bd. dirs. 1985-86, task force on ednl. excellence 1990-92), Delta Sigma Theta. Democrat. Baptist. Office: DeWitt Mid Sch 301 N Jackson St DeWitt AR 72003

MCCOY, DOROTHY ELOISE, writer, educator; b. Houston, Sept. 4, 1916; d. Robert Major and Evie Letha (Grimes) Morgan; m. Roy McCoy, May 22, 1942; children: Roy Jr., Robert Nicholas (dec.). B., Rice U., 1938; M., Tex. A&I U., 1968; postgrad., Ind. U., 1971, U. Calif., Berkeley, 1972, U. Calif., Santa Cruz, 1977. Cert. secondary tchr. BA Corpus Christi (Tex.) Independent Schs., 1958-84, MA, 1985; freelance writer Corpus Christi, 1987—; co-owner United Iron and Machine Works, Corpus Christi, 1946-82; freelance lectr.; master tchr. Nat. Coun. Tchrs. English, 1971, Nat. Humanities Faculty, Concord Mass., 1977-78; mem. steering com. Edn. Summit, Corpus Christi, 1990-91, mem. summit update, 1991. Author: A Teacher Talks Back, 1990, Let's Restructure the Schools, 1992; contbr. articles and columns to profl. jours. Sr. advisor to U.S. Congress, Washington, 1982-85; trustee Corpus Christi Librs., 1987-90; mem. Corpus Christi Mus., Corpus Christi Arts Coun.; mem. Friends Corpus Christi Librs., chmn. publicity com., 1988; participant Walk to Emmaus Group, 1990, UPDATE, U. Tex., 1978-92; cons. Libr. Bd. Democracy competition Am. 2000; sec. adminstrv. bd. First United Meth. Ch., 1992-93. Recipient Teacher of Yr. Paul Caplan Humanitarian award, 1981, Advanced Senior Option Program award, 1968. Mem. AAUW, LWV, U.S. Press Club, Corpus Christi C. of C., Phi Beta Kappa. Home and Office: 612 Chamberlain St Corpus Christi TX 78404-2605

MCCOY, JOENNE RAE, psychiatric clinic administrator; b. Detroit, Jan. 26, 1941; d. Harlan and Dorothy (Simpson) Heinmiller; children: Harlan Craig, Cathi-Jo. BA, Mich. State U., 1966; MSW, U. Mich., 1983. Tchr. pub. schs., Owosso and Garden City, Mich., 1962-73; psychotherapist, group leader Wayne County Hosp., Mich., 1981-82; psychotherapist East Point, Westland, Mich., 1982-83, Midwest, Dearborn, Mich., 1982-83; owner, dir. Personal Devel. Ctrs., Inc., Plymouth, Mich., 1981—, Co-Dependency Specialists S.E. Mich. Ltd., Livonia, Mich., 1988—, Intergrated Health, 1994—; bd. dirs. Hospice Suport Svcs., Inc., Livonia; cons. Westland (Mich.) Convalescent Ctr., 1983-89; supr. grad. students U. Mich., 1986—; cons., facilitator Women-the Emerging Entrepreneurs, Wayne State U. and Small Bus. Assn., 1985—; chmn. Substance Abuse Com., Plymouth Schs., 1982; cons. Salvation Army, Plymouth. Mem. bd. advisors (newsletter) Personal Performance, Balt., 1986—. Mem. steering com. for neighborhood programs YWCA. Soroptimist scholar, 1982. Mem. NAFE, Internat. Assn. Pediatric Social Workers, Internat. Platform Assn., Mich. Assn. Bereavement Counselors, Families in Crisis: Domestic Violence Inc., Nat. Assn. Social Workers (cert.), Am. Entrepreneurs Assn., Women's Network (pres.), Acad. Cert. Soc. Workers, Agora Club, Passport Club, Agora Club. Avocation: international business and finance. Home: 37644 N Laurel Park Dr Livonia MI 48152-2662 Office: Co-Dependency Specialist SE Mich Ltd Pc 37677 Professional Dr Livonia MI 48154

MC COY, LEE BERARD, paint company executive; b. Ipswich, Mass., July 27, 1925; d. Damase Joseph and Robena Myrtle (Bruce) B.; student U. Ala., Mobile, 1958-60; m. Walter Vincent de Paul McCoy, Sept. 27, 1943; children: Bernadette, Raymond, Joan, Richard. Owner, Lee's Letter Shop, Hicksville, L.I., N.Y., 1950-56; mgr. sales adminstrn. Basila Mfg. Co., Mobile, Ala., 1957-61; promotion mgr., buyer Mobile Paint Co., Inc., Theodore, Ala., 1961—. Curator, Shepard Meml. Libr., 1972—; bd. dirs. Monterey Tour House, Mobile, 1972-78, Old Dauphin Way Assn., 1977-79, Friends of Mus., Mobile, 1978—, Miss Wheelchair Ala., 1980—; del. Civic Roundtable, 1977-78, bd. dirs., 1980-81, 1st v.p., 1980-81, pres., 1981-82; pres.'s Com. Employment of Handicapped, 1981—; chmn. Mobile, Nat. Yr. Disabled Persons, 1982; chmn. Mobile, Internat. Decade Disabled Persons, 1983—; mem. Nat. Project Adv. Bd., 1983—, Nat. Community Adv. Bd., 1983—, World Com. for Decade of Disabled Persons, 1983—; v.p. Bristol Sister City Soc.; active Mobile Area Retarded Citizens, Am. Heart Assn.; mem. City of Mobile Cultural Enrichment Task Force, 1985—, Mobile United Recreation and Culture Com.; dir. Culture Mobile, 1986—; v.p., bd. dirs. Joe Jefferson Players, 1986; co-chmn. Brit. Faire, 1983; chmn. Mobile Expo, 1990, Culture & Recreation Com. Mobile United, 1989, steering com., 1990. Recipient Honor award Civic Roundtable, 1979, 80; Service award Women's Com. of Spain Rehab. Center, State of Ala., 1980; award Nat. Orgn. on Disability, 1983, Gayfer's Outstanding Career Woman award, 1988; Golden Rule award, 1991. Mem. Spectromatic Assos., Nat. Paint Distbrs., Hist. Preservation Soc., Color Mktg. Group, English Speaking Union (v.p., pres. 1992, 94, 95), U.S. C. of C. (local cultural enrichment task force 1986), Toastmasters. Methodist. Republican. Clubs: Quota (charter mem. Mobile chpt., dir. 1977—, pres. 1978-80, chmn. numerous coms., recipient Service award Dist. 8, 1979, Internat. award for serving club objectives, 1980, editor Care-Gram, Weekly newsletter for nursing homes 1980—), Bienville; writer 10 books. Home: 1553 Monterey Pl Mobile AL 36604-1227 Office: 4775 Hamilton Blvd Theodore AL 36582-8523

MCCOY, LINDA KORTEWEG, media specialist; b. Passaic, N.J., Oct. 12, 1948; d. Christian Adrian and Irene (Morse) Korteweg; m. Rudolph William, Aug. 1, 1970; children: Jill Ann, Lori Lynn. BA in Math. Edn., William Paterson, 1970, BA in Acctg., 1987, MA in Ednl. Media, 1993. Cert. math. tchr. grades 7-12, media specialist grades K-12, N.J. Math. tchr. Woodrow Wilson Middle Sch., Clifton, N.J., 1970-71; media specialist Schs. 5, 11, 13, Clifton, 1971-78, Schs. 2 & 5, Clifton, 1984-93, Clifton High Sch., 1993—; adj. math. tchr. Tombrock Coll., West Patterson, N.J., 1970-72; adv. bd. Grove Hill Nursery Sch., Clifton, 1984-86; tchr's adv. bd. Clifton (N.J.) Bd. Edn., 1992-93. Treas. Advs. for Quality Edn., Clifton, 1990-93; exec. bd. Clifton (N.J.) Concert Choir Parents, 1992—. Recipient grant computer study NSF, St. Peter's Coll., 1970-71, N.J. Gov.'s Tchr. Recognition, N.J. State Bd. Edn., Trenton, 1992. Mem. ALA, NEA, N.J. Libr. Assn., N.J. Edn. Assn., Clifton Tchrs. Assn., Ednl. Media Assn. N.J., Passaic County Ednl. Media Assn., Assn. for Ednl. Comm. and Tech., Pi Lambda Theta, Kappa Delta Pi. Home: 82 Mountainside Terr Clifton NJ 07013-1177 Office: Clifton High Sch 333 Colfax Ave Clifton NJ 07013

MC COY, LOIS CLARK, emergency services professional, retired county official, magazine editor; b. New Haven, Oct. 1, 1920; d. William Patrick and Lois Rosilla (Dailey) Clark; m. Herbert Irving McCoy, Oct. 17, 1943; children: Whitney, Kevin, Marianne, Tori, Debra, Sally, Daniel. BS, Skidmore Coll., 1942; student Nat. Search and Rescue Sch., 1974. Asst. buyer R.H. Macy & Co., N.Y.C., 1942-44, assoc. buyer, 1944-48; instr. Mountain Medicine & Survival, U. Calif. at San Diego, 1973-74; cons. editor Search & Rescue Mag., 1975; cons. editor, Rescue Mag., 1988—; editor Press On Newsletter, 1992—. coord. San Diego Mountain Rescue Team, La Jolla, Calif., 1973-75; exec. sec. Nat. Assn. for Search and Rescue, Inc., Nashville and La Jolla, 1975-80, comptr., 1980-82; disaster officer San Diego County, 1980-86, Santa Barbara County, 1986-91, ret. Contbr. editor Rescue Mag., 1989—, editor-in-chief Response! mag., 1982-86; editor Press On! Electronic mag., 1994—; mem. adv. bd. Hazard Montly, 1991—; cons. law enforcement div.; Calif. Office Emergency Svcs., 1976-77; pres. San Diego Com. for Los Angeles Philharmonic Orch., 1957-58. Bd. dirs. Search and Rescue of the Californias, 1976-77, Nat. Assn. for Search and Rescue, Inc., 1980-87, pres., 1985-87, trustee, 1987-90, mem. Calif. OES strategic com., 1992—; pres., CEO Nat. Inst. For Urban Search & Rescue, 1989—; mem. Gov.'s Task Force on Earthquakes, 1981-82, Earthquake Preparedness Task Force, Seismic Safety Commn., 1982-85. Recipient Hal Foss award for outstanding service to search and rescue, 1982. Mem. AIAA, IEEE, Armed Forces Comm. and Electronics Assoc., Nat. Assn. for Search & Rescue (life, Svc. award 1985), San Diego Mountain Rescue Team (hon. life), Santa Barbara Amateur Radio Club. Episcopalian. Author: Search and Rescue Glossary, 1974; contbr. to profl. jours. Office: PO Box 91648 Santa Barbara CA 93190

MCCOY, MARILYN, university official; b. Providence, Mar. 18, 1948; d. James Francis and Eleanor (Regan) McC.; m. Charles R. Thomas, Jan. 28, 1983. BA in Econs., Smith Coll., 1970; M in Pub. Policy, U. Mich., 1972. Dir. Nat. Assn. for Higher Edn. Mgmt. Systems, Boulder, Colo., 1972-80; dir. planning and policy devel. U. Colo., Boulder, 1981-85; v.p. adminstrn. and planning Northwestern U., Evanston, Ill., 1985—; bd. dirs. First Prairie Mutual Funds; mem. nat. adv. panel Nat. Ctr. for Postsecondary Governance and Fin. Co-author: Financing Higher Education in the Fifty States, 1976, 3d edit., 1982. Bd. dirs. Evanston Hosp., 1988—, United Charities, Chgo., 1988—, Chgo. Met. YMCA, 1989—, Mather Found., 1995—. Mem. Am. Assn. for Higher Edn., Soc. for Coll. and Univ. Planning (pres., v.p., sec., bd. dirs. 1980—), Assn. for Instnl. Rsch. (pres., v.p., exec. com., publs. bd. 1978-87), Chgo. Network (chmn. 1992-93), Chgo. Econ. Club. Home: 1100 N Lake Shore Dr Chicago IL 60611-1053 Office: Northwestern U 633 Clark St Evanston IL 60208-0001

MCCOY, PHYLLIS STEVENS, elementary education educator; b. Kinston, N.C., July 14, 1959; d. Johnie and LeVaughn (Cobb) Stevens; m. Jeffrey Jerome McCoy, June 27, 1987. BA, U. N.C., 1981. Cert. tchr., N.C. Devel. technician Caswell Ctr., Kinston, N.C.; tchr. Lenoir County Pub. Schs., Kinston; textbook evaluator N.C. Textbook Commn., Raleigh; participant 1st tchr. academy N.C. Dept. Pub. Instrn., Raleigh. VISIONS fellow Semiconductor Rsch. Corp., 1991. Mem. NEA, Am. Bus. Women's Assn., N.C. Assn. Educators, N.C. Coun. Math., N.C. Sci. Tchrs. Assn., East Carolina Reading Coun., Alpha Kappa Alpha (sec.). Home: 2315 Corey Ct Kinston NC 28501 Office: Savannah Mid Sch Rte 2 Box 275 Grifton NC 28530

MCCOY, SANDRA JO, pharmacist; b. Burkesville, Ky., July 30, 1953; d. Jesse Martin and Wanda Lee (Biggerstaff) McC. BS in Pharmacy, Samford U., 1977; D Pharmacy, 1983. Lic. pharmacist Ala., Ky., Tenn. Staff pharmacist St. Vincent's Hosp., Birmingham, Ala., 1977-83; staff pharmacist St. Thomas Hosp., Nashville, 1983—, ptnrs. in excellence quality leadership process trainer, pharmacy dept. coord., 1992—, drug interaction specialist pharmacy, 1992—, profl. achievement system participant, 1994-95; pres. S.J. McCoy Timber, S.J. McCoy Properties; mem. Consumer Mail Panel, Chgo., 1989—; adv. bd. Town and Country Mag. Mem. Opera Guild, Nashville, 1989, membership com., standing bd. mem., com. event chair, 1994-95; mem. Symphony Guild, Nashville, 1992—, Ballet Guild, 1992—, com. chair, 1993-94; mem. Friends of Cheekwood, Nashville, 1994—, Tenn. Performing Arts Ctr. Friends, 1994—; stewardship Ky. Dept. Forestry, Ky. Dept. Fish & Wildlife, 1994. Mem. Am. Soc. Hosp. Pharmacists (midyear presentation 1993, 94, alt. del. state of Tenn. 1994), Mid. Tenn. Soc. Hosp. Pharmacists (bd. dirs. 1987-91, sec. 1987-88, pres. elect 1988-89, pres. 1989-90, scholarship com. 1992, poster presentation 1995), Tenn. Soc. Hosp. Pharmacists (membership com. 1989-90), Nashville Area Pharmacists Assn., Lambda Kappa Sigma (Women in Pharm. Leadership in Am. award 1993). Republican. Home: 3415 West End Ave # 608 Nashville TN 37203 Office: St Thomas Hosp Dept Pharmacy 4220 Harding Rd Nashville TN 37205

MCCRACKEN, ALINE CANTRELL, secondary education educator; b. Stuttgart, Ark., Mar. 10, 1939; d. Russell Amos and Christine Irene (Settle) Cantrell; m. Richard Allen McCracken, July 20, 1974; children: Amos Byron, Richard Love. BFA, Memphis Coll. of Art, 1961; MFA, U. Miss., 1963; postgrad., U. Bridgeport, 1969. Instr. Woman's Coll., Milledgeville, Ga., 1963-65; tchr. Darien (Conn.) Pub. Schs., 1965-74, Batesville (Ark.) Pub. Schs., 1979—; part-time instr. Gateway Tech. Coll., Batesville, 1990—. Lay speaker Batesville dist. United Meth. Ch., 1980; founding mem. Batesville Area Arts Coun., 1986. Named one of Outstanding Young Women of Am., 1967; exch. scholar Can.-Am. Women's Assn., Queen's U., 1966. Mem. AAUW, NEA, Ark. Edn. Assn., Batesville Edn. Assn. (bd. dirs.), Order Ea. Star (pres. 1993, Worthy Matron 1981). Democrat. Home: 4 Big Pine Rd Batesville AR 72501

MCCRACKEN, CARON FRANCIS, data processing consultant; b. Detroit, Jan. 12, 1951; d. William Joseph and Constance Irene (Kramer) McC. AS, Mott Community Coll., 1971; BS, Cen. Mich U., 1973; MA, U. Mich., 1978; Post Bachelor in Computer Sci., Wayne State U., 1993. Tchr. Elkton, Pigeon, Bayport (Mich.) High Sch., 1973-74, Davison (Mich.) Jr. High Sch., 1974-75; instr. Mott Community Coll., Flint, Mich., 1974-78; planning and research specialist Flint Police Dept., 1977-79; campus coord., programmer Systems & Computer Tech. Corp., Detroit, 1981-82, acad. specialist, 1982-83, mgr. acad. computing systems, 1983-84, mgr. adminstrv. computing systems, 1984-85; communications analyst Fruehauf Corp., Detroit, 1985-86, sr. communications analyst, 1986-87; account cons. US Sprint Communications Co., Detroit, 1987-89; account mgr. US Sprint Communications Corp., Detroit, 1989-90; sr. mgr. Technology Specialists, Inc., Phila., 1990-91; tech. cons. Digital Mgmt. Group, Detroit, 1991-92; sr. assoc. info. tech. practice, tech. delivery svcs. Coopers & Lybrand, Detroit, 1992—; adv. bd. CONTEL Bus. Networks, Atlanta, 1987. Vol. charitable, homeless orgns. including COTS, Core Cities, Paint the Town; vol. computer project Wayne State U., Detroit, 1993—; vol. tech. adv. Detroit cmty. project. Mem. NAFE, Data Processing Mgmt. Assn., Assn. Computing Machinery, Detroit Inst. Arts, Alumni Assn. U. Mich., Bikecentennial Club (Missoula, Mont.). Home: 100 W Hickory Grove H4 Bloomfield Hills MI 48304 Office: Coopers & Lybrand 400 Renaissance Ctr Detroit MI 48276

MCCRACKEN, LINDA, librarian, commercial artist; b. Rochester, N.Y., Apr. 13, 1948; d. Frederick Hugh Craig and Shirley Betty (Shacter) Bickford; m. Alan Cheah, June 13, 1972 (div. 1978); m. Bruce E. McCracken, Sept. 23, 1978 (div. 1985); 1 child, Karen Elizabeth. BA in History, SUNY-Geneseo, 1970, MLS, 1970. Reference libr. Northeastern U., Boston, 1971-72; asst. libr. Burlington Pub. Libr., Mass., 1972-74; rsch. asst. Data Resources, Inc.,

Lexington, Mass., 1974-76; comml. artist McCracken's, Wolfeboro, N.H., 1973-91; asst. libr. N.H. Vocat.-Tech. Coll., Manchester, 1985-87; libr. N.H. Hosp., Concord, 1987-91. Participant paintings Horseheads Mall Art Show (3rd place award 1968); graphic artist Rare Coin Rev. mag., 1983; layout artist: Market Media Guide, 1979; market rschr. Delahaye Group, Newington, N.H., 1993—; author Burlington Times-Union, 1973, Pleasant News, 1987-88. Treas. Village Players, Wolfeboro, 1982-83; pub. rels. com. Gov.'s Arts Coun., Wolfeboro, 1982. Mem. State Employees Assn. N.H. Avocations: skiing, gardening, singing, acting, hiking, reading, computers. Home: 44 Pine Hill Rd Wolfeboro NH 03894-9778 Office: NH Hosp Dorothy M Breene Meml Libr 105 Pleasant St Concord NH 03301-3861

MCCRARY, EUGENIA LESTER (MRS. DENNIS DAUGHTRY MCCRARY), civic worker, writer; b. Annapolis, Md., Mar. 23, 1929; d. John Campbell and Eugenia (Potts) Lester; m. John Campbell Howard, July 15, 1955 (dec. Sept. 1965); m. Dennis Daughtry McCrary, June 28, 1969; 1 child, Dennis Campbell. AB cum laude, Radcliffe Coll.-Harvard U., 1950; MA, Johns Hopkins U., 1952; postgrad., Harvard U., 1953, Pa. State U., 1953-54, Drew U., 1957-58, Inst. Study of USSR, Munich, 1964. Grad. asst. dept. Romance langs. Pa. State U., 1953-54; tchr. dept. math. The Brearley Sch., N.Y.C., 1954-57; dir. Sch. Langs., Inc., Summit, N.J., 1958-69; trustee Sch. Langs., Inc., Summit, 1960-69. Co-author: Nom de Plume: Eugenia Campbell Lester, (with Allegra Branson) Frontiers Aflame, 1987. Dist. dir. Eastern Pa. and N.J. auditions Met. Opera Nat. Coun., N.Y.C., 1960-66, dist. dir. publicity, 1966-67, nat. vice chmn. publicity, 1967-71, nat. chmn. public rels., 1972-75, hon. nat. chmn. pub. rels., 1976—; bd. govs., chmn. Van Cortlandt House Mus., 1985-90. Mem. Nat. Soc. Colonial Dames Am. (bd. mgrs. N.Y. 1985-90), Met. Opera Nat. Coun., Soc. Mayflower Desc. (former bd. dirs. N.Y. soc., chmn. house com. 1986-89), Soc. Daus. of Holland Dames (bd. dirs. 1982-87, 3d directress gen. 1987-92, directress gen. 1992—), L'Eglise du Saint-Esprit (vestry 1985-88, sr. warden 1988-90), Huguenot Soc. Am. (governing coun. 1984-90, asst. treas. 1990-91, sec. 1991-95, 2d v.p. 1995—), Colonial Dames Am., Colony Club (bd. govs. 1988—). Republican. Episcopalian. Home: 24 Central Park S New York NY 10019-1632

MCCRAVEN, EVA STEWART MAPES, health service administrator; b. L.A., Sept. 26, 1936; d. Paul Melvin and Wilma Zech (Ziegler) Stewart; m. Carl Clarke McCraven, Mar. 18, 1978; children: David Anthony, Lawrence James, Maria Lynn Mapes. ABS magna cum laude, Calif. State U., Northridge, 1974, MS, Cambridge Grad. Sch. Psychology, 1987; PhD, 1991. Dir. spl. projects Pacoima Meml. Hosp., 1969-71, dir. health edn., 1971-74; asst. exec. dir. Hillview Community Mental Health Center, Lakeview Terrace, Calif., 1974—; past dir. dept. consultation and edn. Hillview Ctr., developer, mgr. long-term residential program, 1986-90; former program mgr. Crisis Residential Program, Transitional Residential Program and Day Treatment Program for mentally ill offenders, dir. mentally ill offenders svcs.; former program dir. Valley Homeless Shelter Mental Health Counseling Program; dir. Integrated Services Agy., Hillview Mental Health Ctr., Inc., 1993—; Former pres. San Fernando Valley Coordinating Coun. Area Assn., Sunland-Jujunga Coordinating Coun.; bd. dirs. N.E. Valley Health Corp., 1970-73, Golden State Community Mental Health Ctr., 1970-73. Recipient Resolution of Commendation award State of Calif., 1988, Commendation award, 1988, Spl. Mayor's plaque, 1988, Commendation awards for community svcs. City of L.A., 1989, County of L.A., 1989, Calif. State Assembly, 1989, Calif. State Senate, 1989, award Sunland-Tujunga Police Support Coun., 1989, Woman of Achievement award Sunland-Tujunga BPW, 1990. Mem. Assn. Mental Health Adminstrs., Am. Pub. Health Assn., Valley Univ. Women, Health Services Adminstrn. Alumni Assn. (former v.p.), Sunland-Jujunga Bus. and Profl. Women, LWV. Office: Hillview Community Mental Health Ctr 11500 Eldridge Ave San Fernando CA 91342-6523

MCCRAY, DOROTHY MAY, artist and educator; b. Madison, S.D., Oct. 13, 1915; d. Robert Spencer and Annie Mary (Otter) Westaby; m. Francis F. McCray, Aug. 6, 1938 (dec. Jan. 1960); 1 child, Peter Michael. BA, State U. of Iowa, 1937, MA in Painting, 1939; MFA in Printmaking, Calif. Coll. Arts and Crafts, Oakland, 1955. Prof. art Western N.Mex. U., Silver City, 1948-81, prof. emeritus, 1981—; profl. painter/printmaker McCray Studios, Silver City. Solo exhbns. include Mezzanine Gallery, Oakland, Calif., Art Directions Gallery, N.Y.C., Lebanon Valley Coll., Pa., Coralles Art Assn., N.Mex., Richard Levy Gallery, Albuquerque, numerous others; group exhbns. include Art Inst. Chgo., 1940-41, Phila. Acad., 1941, Kansas City Art Inst., 1941, 42, Smithsonian Inst., Washington, 1941, 58, Am. Fine Arts Gallery, N.Y.C., 1943, Joslyn Meml. Art Mus., Omaha, 1947, Mus. Fine Arts, Santa Fe, 1950, 51, 52, 53, 54, 56, 57, 58, 59, 63, 66, Oakland (Calif.) Art Mus., 1955, Cin. Art Mus., 1956, 58, NAD, Newton, Kans., 1956, Dallas Mus. Fine Arts, 1956, 58, Roswell (N.Mex.) Art Mus., 1958, Bradley U., Peoria, Ill., 1960, Highlands U., Las Vegas, 1960, Bklyn. Mus., 1961, Pa. Acad. Art, Phila., 1965, Museo de Arte Historia, Juarez, Mexico, 1978, The Shellfish Collection, Silver City, N.Mex., 1990, 91, Deming (N.Mex.) Ctr. for Arts, 1991, Grant County Art Guild, Pinos Altos, N.Mex., 1991, 92, Carlsbad (N.Mex.) Mus. and Art Ctr., 1992, Richard Levy Gallery, Albuquerque, 1992, numerous others;

MC CRAY, EVELINA WILLIAMS, librarian, researcher; b. Plaquemine, La., Sept. 1, 1932; d. Turner and Beatrice (Gordon) Williams II; m. John Samuel McCray, Apr. 7, 1955; 1 child, Johnetta McCray Russ. BA, So. U., Baton Rouge, 1954; MS in Library Sci., La. State U., 1962. Librarian, Iberville High Sch., Plaquemine, 1954-70, Plaquemine Jr. High, 1970-75; proofreader short stories, poems Associated Writers Guild, Atlanta, 1982-86; library cons. Evaluation Capitol High Sch., 1964, Iberville Parish Educators Workshop, 1980, Tchrs. Core/Iberville Parish, 1980-81. Contbr. poetry New Am. Poetry Anthology, 1988, The Golden Treasury of Great Poems, 1988, Acres of Diamonds A Collection of Poetry; annual contbr. Nat. Libr. of Poetry, 1991—. Vol. service Allen J. Nadler Library, Plaquemine, 1980-82; librarian Local Day Care Ctr., Plaquemine, 1978-79; mem. adv. bd. Iberville parish Project Independence, 1992—. Recipient Golden Poet award World Poetry, 1988, 89. Mem. ALA, La. Library Assn., Nat. Ret. Tchrs. Assn., La. Ret. Tchrs. Assn. (cons. ann. workshops 1986—, state appointee to informative and protective svcs. com. 1988-92), Iberville Ret. Tchrs. Assn. (info. and protective services dir. 1981—), So. Poetry Assn. (asst. coll. State Arts Mus. Miss., Blue Ribbon award 1989, SPA's Finest award 1992), Internat. Soc. Poets. Democrat. Baptist. Home: PO Box Q Plaquemine LA 70765-0220

MCCREA, ERLINDA MA SEGURA, radiologist; b. Cebu, The Philippines, Oct. 12, 1943; came to U.S., 1963; d. Manuel F. and Josefina Roa Segura; m. Jay T. McCrea, June 8, 1963; children: John-Jay, Leslie. Medical degree, Cebu Inst. Medicine, 1965. Intern Clark USAF Hosp., Angeles, The Philippines, 1966; assoc. prof. U. Md. Med. Ctr., Balt., 1983-87; cons. Howard County Gen. Hosp., Columbia, Md., 1987-90, Prince George's Med. Ctr., Chiverly, Md., 1987-90; mem. staff Franklin Sq. Hosp., Balt., 1994—, Kernan Hosp., Balt., 1994—. Com. chair, divsn. dir. Am. Cancer Soc., Balt., 1993—. Recipient Vol. of Yr. award Am. Cancer Soc., 1992. Mem. AMA, Am. Coll. Radiology, Am. Assn. Women Radiologists, Md. Radiol. Soc., Med. and Surg. Soc. Md., Radiol. Soc. N.Am. Independent. Home: 11365 Heathertoe Ln Columbia MD 21044

MCCREADY, KAREN MARIE, art dealer, writer, curator; b. Beaver Falls, Pa., May 2, 1946; d. Robert Richard and Ellen (Hausrath) McC.; m. Jean-Yves Noblet, Aug. 26, 1989. BA, Austin Coll., 1968. Dir. Pace Edits., Inc., N.Y.C., 1972-82, Crown Point Press, N.Y.C., 1982-94; founded Karen McCready Fine Arts, 1994—; program chair ArtTable, Inc., N.Y.C., 1990-93, v.p., bd. dirs., 1991-93. Author: Porcelain: Traditions and New Visions, 1982. Mem. Internat. Fine Print Dealers Assn. (program com.). Office: 39 Bond St New York NY 10012

MCCREADY, SHEILA CLARKE, legislative staff member; b. Greenwood, Miss., Nov. 16, 1959; d. James F. Boja and Love (Carter) Clarke. BS, Miss. U. for Women, 1980. Staff asst. to Rep. David Bowen, 1980; staff asst. House Com. on Small Bus., 1981; legis. asst. to Rep. Tom Luken, 1981-84; legis. asst. to Rep. Solomon P. Ortiz, staff dir. subcom. on oceanography Gulf of Mexico and Outer Continental Shelf House Com. on Merchant Marine and Fisheries, 1985—. Mem. Miss. State Soc., Tex. State Soc., Tex. Breakfast Club, House Legis. Assts. Assn., Gamma Beta Phi, Sigma Tau Delta, Phi Beta Phi. Episcopalian. Office: Subcom Oceanog Gulf Mex & Outer Cont Shelf 575 Ford House Office Bldg Washington DC 20515*

MCCRIMMON, BARBARA SMITH, writer, librarian; b. Anoka, Minn., May 3, 1918; d. Webster Roy and Jessie (Sargeant) Smith; m. James McNab McCrimmon, June 10, 1939; children—Kevin Mor, John Marshall. B.A., U. Minn., 1939; M.S.L.S., U. Ill., 1961; Ph.D., Fla. State U., 1973. Asst. librarian Ill. State Nat. Hist. Survey, Champaign, Ill., 1961-62; research assoc. Bur. Community Planning, U. Ill., Champaign, 1962-63; librarian Ill. Water Survey, Champaign, 1964-65; librarian Am. Meteorol. Soc., Boston, 1965-67; editorial asst. Jour. Library History, Tallahassee, 1967-69, 73-74; adj. asst. prof. Sch. Library Sci., Fla. State U., Tallahassee, 1976-77. Author: Power, Politics and Print, 1981, Richard Garnett: The Scholar as Librarian, 1989; editor: American Library Philosophy, 1975; contbr. articles to profl. jours. Mem. ALA, Pvt. Libraries Assn., Beta Phi Mu, Manuscript Soc. Democrat.

MCCUBBIN, SUSAN BRUBECK, real estate executive, lawyer; b. Decatur, Ill., Mar. 16, 1948; d. Rodney Earl Brubeck and Marilyn Jean (McMahon) Hopkins; 1 child, Martin Charles Jr.; m. William James McCubbin, May 30, 1987. LLB, Western State U., Fullerton, Calif., 1977. Bar: CAlif. 1977; lic. real estate broker, Calif. Ptnr. Blue Chip Constrn. Co., Santa Ana, Calif., 1969-73; pres. Brubeck Co., San Francisco and Newport Beach, Calif., 1973-78; sole practice San Francisco, 1978-79; sr. mktg. cons., broker Grubb & Ellis Co., San Francisco, 1979-87; pres. Greenwich Corp., San Rafael, Calif., 1987—; broker assoc. Fox & Carskadon, Mill Valley, Calif. Columnist Automotive Age Mag., 1974-75. Chmn. U.S. Senate Primary Campaign, Orange County, Calif., 1976. Republican.

MCCUE, JUDITH W., lawyer; b. Phila., Apr. 7, 1948; d. Emanuel Leo and Rebecca (Raffel) Weiss; m. Howard M. McCue III, Apr. 3, 1971; children: Howard, Leigh. BA cum laude, U. Pa., 1969; JD, Harvard U., 1972. Bar: Ill. 1972, U.S. Tax Ct. 1984. From assoc. to ptnr. Keck, Mahin & Cate, Chgo., 1972—; dir. Schawk, Inc., Des Plaines, Ill., Chgo. Estate Planning Coun. Governing mem. The Orchestral Assn., 1979—. Fellow Am. Coll. Trust and Estate Counsel (com. chair 1991-94, regent 1993—); mem. Chgo. Bar Assn. (chmn. probate practice com. 1984-85, chmn. fed. estate and gift tax divsn. fed. tax com. 1988-89). Office: Keck Mahin & Cate 77 W Wacker Dr Fl 49 Chicago IL 60601-1629

MCCUE, MARY MADELINE, public relations executive; b. Long Branch, N.J., Aug. 25, 1947; d. Alfred Raymond and Margaret Ann (Egan) McC. BS, Boston U., 1969. Copywriter, co-dir. pub. info. Foster Parents Plan (now PLAN Internat.), N.Y.C., 1969-72; dir. pub. info. Office Neighborhood Govt., City of N.Y., 1972-73; account exec. Burson Marstellar, N.Y.C., 1973-75; v.p., sr. v.p. Burson Marstellar, Washington, 1991—; with editl. svcs. dept. Hill and Knowlton, N.Y.C., 1975-78; from dir. corporate info. to v.p. First Boston (now CS First Boston), N.Y.C., 1978-84; dir. Office Pub. Affairs, SEC, Washington, 1984-91. Mem. Nat. Investor Rels. Inst., D.C. Bar (sect. corporate and securities law), Women in Housing and Fin. Republican. Home: 305 11th St SE Washington DC 20003 Office: Burson Marsteller 1850 M St NW Ste 900 Washington DC 20036

MCCUE, SARAH S., program manager; b. Port Huron, Mich., May 19, 1967; d. William Douglas and Carol Sue (Strang) McC. BA, U. Mich., 1988; MPA, George Washington U., 1991; postgrad., Wayne State U. Internat. bus. rschr. U.S. Customs Svc., Washington, 1989-91; internat. bus. dir. Lake Michigan Coll., Benton Harbor, Mich., 1991-92; program mgr. Mich. Small Bus. Devel. Ctr., Detroit, 1992—. Author: Trade Secrets: The Export Answer Book. Commr. Pres. Commn. on Status of Women, Wayne State U., 1994—; vol. The Vol. Project, Detroit, 1992. Mem. Nat. Assn. Small Bus. Internat. Trade Educators (bd. govs. 1994—). Republican. Home: 1512 Elk St Port Huron MI 48060 Office: Mich Small Bus Devel Ctr 2727 Second Ave Detroit MI 48201

MCCULLERS, GAIL HAYNES, academic administrator; b. Cullman, Ala., Feb. 15, 1939; d. James Euel and Vileta Anise (Yeager) Haynes; m. Richard E. McCullers, Sept. 10, 1960; children: Richard Mark, Collie Anne. BS, Auburn U., 1961, MEd, 1966. Testing clk. Auburn (Ala.) U., 1957-61, psychometrist, 1962-65, counselor, 1966-69, coord. testing, 1970, counseling specialist, 1971-72, coord. counseling, 1973-74, acting dir., 1975-76, dir. student devel., 1977-79, dir. housing, 1980—. Mem. prodn. team (ednl. video) It Still Hurts, 1984, Decisions, 1989; editor (handbook) Policies, 1989. Sec., bd. dirs. Student Ministeries, Auburn, 1980—; bd. trustees Crisis Ctr., Auburn, 1980—. Mem. Am. Counseling Assn., Ala. Counseling Assn. (Disting. Svc. award 1976, Pres. award 1976-92, Disting. Profl. Devel. award 1983, Humanitarian/Caring Person award 1992), Southeastern Housing Officers, Coll. Personnel Assn., Assn. Psychol. Type, Student Personnel Adminstrs., Univ. Housing Officers. Democrat. Baptist. Home: 656 Forestdale Auburn AL 36830 Office: Housing/Residence Life Burton Hall Auburn AL 36849

MCCULLOCH, KATHRYN VALERIE, lawyer; b. N.Y., Apr. 30, 1953; d. John Kenneth and Muriel Anne M.; m. Paul William Feeney, Jan. 14, 1984; children: Brian, Megan. BA, Vassar Coll., 1973; JD, Fordham Law Sch., 1976. Bar: N.Y., 1977. Atty. Mfrs. Hanover Trust Co., N.Y., 1976-82, v.p., 1982-92; v.p., asst. gen. counsel Chemical Bank, N.Y., 1982—. Office: Chemical Bank 270 Park Ave 9th Fl New York NY 10017

MCCULLOCH, RACHEL, economics researcher, educator; b. Bklyn., June 26, 1942; d. Henry and Rose (Offen) Preiss; m. Gary Edward Chamberlain; children: Laura Meressa, Neil Dudley. BA, U. Pa., 1962; MA in Teaching, U. Chgo., 1965, MA, 1971, PhD, 1973; student, MIT, 1966-67. Economist Cabinet Task Force on Oil Import Control, Washington, 1969; instr., then asst. prof. Grad. Sch. Bus. U. Chgo., 1971-73; asst. prof., then assoc. prof. econs. Harvard U., Cambridge, Mass., 1973-79; assoc. prof., then prof. econs. U. Wis., Madison, 1979-87; prof. Brandeis U., Waltham, Mass., 1987—, Rosen Family prof., 1989—, dir. Lemberg Program in Internat. Econs. and Fin., 1990-91, dir. PhD program Grad. Sch. Internat. Econs. and Fin., 1994—; mem. Pres.'s Commn. on Indsl. Competitiveness, 1983-84; mem. adv. coun. Office Tech. Assessment U.S. Congress, 1979-88; cons. World Bank, Washington, 1984-86; mem. com. on internat. rels. studies with People's Republic of China, 1984-91; rsch. assoc. Nat. Bur. Econ. Rsch., Cambridge, 1985-93; mem. adv. com. Inst. for Internat. Econs., Washington, 1987—; faculty Advanced Mgmt. Network, La Jolla, Calif., 1985-92; mem. com. examiners econs. test Grad. Record Exam. Ednl. Testing Svc., 1990—, chair, 1992—; mem. discipline adv. com. for Fulbright scholar awards in econs. Coun. Internat. Exch. Scholars, 1991-93, chair, 1992-93; cons. Global Economy Project, Edn. Film Ctr., 1993-94. Author: Research and Development as a Determinant of U.S. International Competitiveness, 1978; contbr. articles to profl. jours. and books. Grantee NSF, 1975-79, Hoover Inst., 1984-85, German Marshall Fund of U.S., 1985, Ford Found., 1985-88, U.S. Dept. Edn., 1990-91. Mem. Am. Econ. Assn. (dir. summer program for minority students 1983-84), Internat. Trade and Fin. Assn. (bd. dirs. 1993—), New England Women Economists Assn. Home: 10 Frost Rd Lexington MA 02173-1904 Office: Brandeis U Dept Econs Waltham MA 02254

MCCULLOCH, TERRI, secondary school educator; b. Salt Lake City, Sept. 18, 1957; d. Hilton Clair and Ranae (Brown) McCulloch; m. John Carl Stoughton, July 28, 1989. BS, Weber State U., Ogden, Utah, 1979; MBA, Utah State U., 1987, adminstr. and supervisory endorsement, 1993. Night mgr. Dee's, Ogden, 1973-78; with Smith's Food King, Clearfield, Utah, 1978-89; smoking cessation instr. Humana Hosp., Layton, Utah, 1987-91; tchr. Ogden Sch. Dist., 1979—, secondary math. specialist, 1992—; tutor Ogden, 1990-92; workshop presenter Utah Bd. Edn., Ogden, 1979—. Bd. dirs. Cath. Cmty. Svcs., 1987-89, Utah Election Law Task Force, 1989-92; mem. Atty. Gen.'s Cmty. AGREE Team. Named Tchr. of the Yr., Ogden Sch. Dist., 1988-89, Woman of the Yr., YWCA, Ogden, 1986, Focus on Excellence award, Ogden Sch. Dist., 1988, Golden Apple award, 1988. Mem. ASCD, Tchr. Acad. for Math., AAUW, Utah LWV (state pres. 1989-92, dir. resource devel. 1992—), Weber County LWV (local pres. 1985-89, treas. 1993—), Delta Kappa Gamma, Phi Delta Kappa. Democrat. Mem. LDS Ch. Home: 1369 Orchard Ave Ogden UT 84404-5853 Office: Mt Ogden Middle Sch 3260 Harrison Blvd Ogden UT 84403-1227

MCCULLOH, KAREN INDALL, county commissioner; b. Iowa City, Iowa, Dec. 29, 1943; d. Floyd J. Indall and Ruth (Schmidt) Machin; m. John M. McCulloh, Dec. 26, 1965; children: Andrew, Katherine. BA, Kans. U., 1965; MA, Kans. State U., 1989. Commr. Riley County, 1993—; treas. Riley County Health Dept., Manhattan, Kans., 1993-95. Bd. dirs. Manhattan Arts Coun., 1993; sec. Friends of the Librs., Manhattan, 1993. Office: Riley County 110 Court House Plaza Manhattan KS 66502

MCCULLOUGH, KATHRYN T. BAKER, social worker; b. Trenton, Tenn., Jan. 5, 1925; d. John Andrew and Alma Lou (Wharey) Taylor; m. John R. Baker, Sept. 30, 1972 (dec. Oct. 1981); m. T.C. McCullough, May 14, 1988. BS, U. Tenn., 1945, MSW, 1954; postgrad., U. Chgo., 1950, Vanderbilt U., 1950-51. Lic. social worker, Tenn.; emeritus diplomate in clin. social work Am. Bd. Examiners. Home demonstration agt., agrl. extension svc. U. Tenn., Hardeman County, 1946-49; Dyer County, 1949-50; dir. med. social work dept. Le Bonheur Children's Hosp., Memphis, 1954-57; chief clin. social worker clinic mentally retarded children U. Tenn. Dept. Pediatrics, Memphis, 1957-59; clin. social worker Children's Med. Ctr., Tulsa, 1959-60; dir. med. social work dept. Coll. of Medicine U. Tenn., Memphis, 1960-69; dir. community svcs. regional med. program Coll. of Medicine, 1969-76; dir. regional clinic program Child Devel. Ctr. Coll. of Medicine, 1976-85; mem. faculty Coll. of Medicine, Coll. of Social Work U. Tenn., Memphis, 1960-85; social worker admissions rev. bd. Arlington Devel. Ctr., Memphis, 1976—. Author 14 books. Active Gibson County Fedn. Dem. Women, 1987—; commr. Gibson Utility Dist., 1990—. Fellow Am. Assn. Mental Retardation (life); mem. NASW, AAUP, Acad. Cert. Social Workers, Tenn. Conf. on Social Welfare, Trenton Music Club. Mem. Ch. of Christ. Home: 627 Riverside Yorkville Rd Trenton TN 38382-9513

MCCULLOUGH, SANDY DANIEL, psychometrist; b. Memphis, Dec. 7, 1956; d. Harold Lee and Lois Levern (Arnold) Daniel; m. Edward H. McCullough, Aug. 10, 1980; children: Mandy, Danny. BS in Home Econs. Edn., Memphis State U., 1979; MEd in Ednl. Psychology, U. Miss., 1993, EdS in Ednl. Psychology, 1994. Lic. counselor, psychometrist, Miss. Interim vocat. child care tchr. Memphis City Schs., 1979-80; tchr. vocat. preparation Tate County Schs., Independence, Miss., 1985-87; psychometrist Marshall County Schs., Holly Springs, Miss., 1993—. Mem. New Beginnings Civic Club, Olive Branch, Miss., 1991-92. Mem. APA, ACA, Miss. Counseling Assn., Miss. Assn. for Psychology in the Schs. Baptist. Home: 1003 County Road 62 New Albany MS 38652-8929 Office: Marshall County Schs 158 E College Ave Holly Springs MS 38635-3003

MCCULLY, EMILY ARNOLD, illustrator, writer; b. Galesburg, Ill., 1939; d. Wade E. and Kathryn (Maher) Arnold; m. George E. McCully, 1961 (div. 1975); children: Nathaniel, Tad. BA, Brown U., 1961; MA, Columbia U., 1964. Author: How's Your Vacuum Cleaner Working? O'Henry Collection, 1977, A Craving, 1982, Picnic, 1984 (Christopher award), First Snow, 1985, Life Drawing, 1986, The Show Must Go On, 1987, School, 1987, You Lucky Duck!, 1988, New Baby, 1988, The Grandma Mix-up, 1988, The Christmas Gift, 1988, Zaza's Big Break, 1989, Grandma's at the Lake, 1990, The Evil Spell, 1990, Speak Up, Blanche!, 1991, Mirette on the Highwire, 1992 (Caldecott medal 1992), Grandma's at Bat, 1993, The Amazing Felix, 1993, My Real Family, 1994, Crossing The New Bridge, 1994, Little Kit, or: The Industrious Flea Circus Girl, 1995; illustrator: Sea Beach Express, 1966, The Seventeenth Street Gang, 1966, Rex, 1967, Luigi of the Streets, 1967, That Mean Man, 1968, Gooney, 1968, Journey From Peppermint Street, 1968 (Nat. Book award 1969), The Mouse and the Elephant, 1969, The Fisherman, 1969, Tales from the Rue Brocca, 1969, Here I Am, 1969, Twin Spell, 1969, Hobo Toad and the Motorcycle Gang, 1970, Slip! Slop! Gobble!, 1970, Friday Night is Papa Night, 1970, Maxie, 1970, Steffie and Me, 1970, The Cat and the Parrot, 1970, Gertrude's Pocket, 1970, Go and Hush the Baby, 1971, Finders Keepers, 1971, Ma n Da La, 1971 (Bklyn. Mus. award 1976, N.Y. Pub. Libr. award 1976), Hurray for Captain Jane!, 1971, Michael Is Brave, 1971, Finding Out With Your Senses, 1971, Henry's Pennies, 1972, Jane's Blanket, 1972, Grandpa's Long Red Underwear, 1972, Girls Can Too!, 1972, The Boyhood of Grace Jones, 1972, Black Is Brown Is Tan, 1973, Isabelle the Itch, 1973, When Violet Died, 1973, That New Boy, 1973, How To Eat Fried Worms, 1973, Jenny's Revenge, 1974, Her Majesty, Grace Jones, 1974, Tree House Town, 1974, I Want Mama, 1974, Amanda, the Panda and the Redhead, 1975, The Bed Book, 1976, My Street's A Morning Cool Street, 1976, Professor Coconut and the Thief, 1977, Martha's Mad Dog, 1977, That's Mine, 1977, Where Wild Willie, 1978, No Help At All, 1978, Partners, 1978, The Twenty-Elephant Restaurant, 1978, What I Did Last Summer, 1978, The Highest Hit, 1978, I and Spraggy, 1978, Edward Troy and the Witch Cat, 1978, My Island Grandma, 1979, Whatever Happened to Beverly Bigler's Birthday?, 1979, Last Look, 1979, Ookie-Spooky, 1979, The Black Dog Who Went Into the Woods, 1980, How I Found Myself at the Fair, 1980, How We Got Our First Cat, 1980, Oliver and Allison's Week, 1980, Pajama Walking, 1981, The April Fool, 1981, I Dance in My Red Pajamas, 1982, The Halloween Candy Mystery, 1982, Go and Mush the Baby, 1982, Mitzi and the Terrible Tyrannosaurus Rex, 1983, Best Friend Insurance, 1983, Mail-Order Wings, 1984, Gertrude's Pocket, 1984, Fifth Grade Magic, 1984, The Ghastly Glasses, 1985, Fourth of July, 1985, The Explorer of Barkham Street, 1985, Wheels, 1986, Lulu and the Witch Baby, 1986, Richard and the Vratch, 1987, Molly, 1987, Molly Goes Hiking, 1987, Jam Day, 1987, The Boston Coffee Party, 1988, The Take-Along Dog, 1989, Selene Goes Home, 1989, The Magic Mean Machine, 1989, It Always Happens to Leona, 1989, The Grandpa Days, 1989, Dinah's Mad, Bad Wishes, 1989, Stepbrother Sabotage, 1990, Lulu Goes to Witch School, 1990, The Evil Spell, 1990, The Day Chubby Became Charles, 1990, The Christmas Present Mystery, 1990, Sky Guys to White Cat, 1991, Meatball, 1991, Leona and Ike, 1991, The Butterfly Birthday, 1991, Yankee Doodle Drumsticks, 1992, One Very Best Valentine's Day, 1992, Meet the Lincoln Lions Band, 1992, Jingle Bells Jam, 1992, In My Tent, 1992, Anne Flies the Birthday Bike, 1993, Amzat and His Brothers, 1993. Office: c/o Putnam Pub Group 200 Madison Ave New York NY 10016-3901

MCCULLY, RUTH ALIDA, elementary education educator; b. Port Huron, Mich., Feb. 13, 1933; d. Leon Eugene Lounsberry and Rachel Elizabeth (DeSerano) Lounsberry-Maser; m. Donald Cecil McCully, Feb. 8, 1952; children: Stephen Donald, Robert Leon, Julie Ann. BS, Ea. Mich. U., 1976, MA, 1980. Asst. children's librarian Monroe County Library, Mich., 1962-64; dir. Weekday Nursery Sch., Youngstown, Ohio, 1964-71; dir. children's programs Lake-in-the-Woods, Ypsilanti, Mich., 1974-76; tchr. 1st grade Dundee Community Schs., Mich., 1976-88; tchr. young fives Dundee Community Schs., 1988-90; tchr. 1st grade, 1990—. Lay speaker Ann Arbor Dist., United Meth. Ch., 1979—, dir., 1990-92; chmn. Dundee Community Caring and Sharing, 1982—; active Monroe County Food Bank, 1983—, Dundee Interfaith Coun., 1984—, Dundee Area Against Substance Abuse, 1984-88. Named Woman of Yr., United Meth. Women, Dundee United Meth. Ch., 1983, United Meth. Ann Arbor Dist. Coun. on Ministries; recipient cert. of Commendation Village of Dundee, 1993, State of Mich., 1994. Mem. NEA, Nat. Assn. Edn. Young Children, The Whole Lang. Umbrella, Mich. Edn. Assn., Mich. Reading Assn., Mich. Assn. Edn. Young Children, Monroe County Edn. Assn., Monroe County Tchrs. Elem. Lit. and Lang., Dundee Sch. Employees Club (sec. 1985-86), Phi Delta Kappa. Avocations: playing piano/guitar, needlework, sketching/painting, gardening, reading. Home: 510 E Monroe St Dundee MI 48131-1310

MCCUNE, MARY JOAN HUXLEY, microbiology educator; b. Lewistown, Mont., Jan. 14, 1932; d. Thomas Leonard and Anna Dorothy (Hardie) Huxley; m. Ronald William McCune, June 7, 1965; children: Anna Orpha, Heather Jean. BS, Mont. State Coll., 1953; MS, Wash. State U., 1955; PhD, Purdue U., 1965. Rsch. technician VA Hosp., Oakland, Calif., 1956-59; bacteriologist U.S. Naval Radiol. Def. Lab., San Francisco, 1959-61; teaching assoc. Purdue U., West Lafayette, Ind., 1961-65, vis. asst. prof., 1965-66; asst. prof. Occidental Coll., L.A., 1966-69; asst. rsch. bacteriologist II U. Calif., L.A., 1969-70; affiliate asst. prof. Idaho State U., Pocatello, Idaho, 1970-80, from asst. prof. to prof. microbiology, 1980—; instr. U. Calif., Davis, 1964. Contbr. articles to profl. jours. Pres. AK chpt. PEO, Pocatello, 1988-89; chair faculty senate Idaho State U., 1994-95. David Ross fellow Purdue U., 1964. Mem. AAAS, N.Y. Acad. Sci., Idaho Acad. Sci. (trustee 1989—, v.p. 1992-93, pres. 1993-94), Am. Soc. for Microbiology (v.p. Intermountain br. 1988-89, pres. 1989-90), Idaho Edn. Alliance for Sci. (bd. dirs.), Sigma Xi, Sigma Delta Epsilon. Presbyterian. Home: 30 Colgate St Pocatello ID 83201-3459 Office: Idaho State U Dept Biol Scis Pocatello ID 83209

MCCURDY, MARY JACQUELINE, lawyer; b. Balt., Dec. 1, 1933; d. Robert Davis and Lillian J. (Schmidt) McC. BA, Hood Coll., 1955; JD, U. Md., 1958. Bar: Md. 1958. Asst. state's atty. County of Baltimore, 1962-63, asst. county solicitor, 1967-68; mem. Md. Ho. of Dels., 1963-66; assoc. gen. counsel Distilled Spirits Coun. U.S., 1969-76, Seagram, 1976-79; v.p. Joseph E. Seagram & Sons, Inc., N.Y.C., 1979-94; cons. govt. rels. Washington, 1994—. Trustee Hood Coll., Social Security Fund Distillery Wine and Allied Workers Internat. Union AFL-CIO; bd. visitors Towson State U. Mem. Md. State Bar Assn., N.Y. Bar Assn., Balt. County Bar Assn., Nat. Assn. Alcoholic Beverage Importers (bd. dirs.), Women's Assn. Allied Beverage Industries, Com. of 200. Democrat. Episcopalian. Office: 4140 Bayhead Dr # 206 Bonita Springs FL 33923

MCCUSKER, MARY LAURETTA, library science educator; b. Sillery, Que., Can., Jan. 18, 1919; came to U.S., 1938, naturalized, 1942; d. Albert James and Laura (Cleary) McC. B.A., Western Md. Coll., 1942; M.S.L.S., Columbia U., 1952, D.L.S., 1963. Joined Order of Preachers, Roman Catholic Ch., 1961; librarian Annapolis (Md.) High Sch., 1942-44, McDonogh Mil. Sch., 1944-47; asst. prof. Iowa State Tchrs. Coll. (now No. Iowa U.), Cedar Falls, 1948-59; vis. prof. library sci. U. Minn., Mpls., summers, 1958-59; assoc. prof. Sch. Library Sci. Rosary Coll., 1963-67, dir., prof. Grad. Sch., 1967-81, prof. emeritus, rsch. assoc., 1981-94, dean grad. sch., 1969-81, dean emeritus, 1994—. Contbr. articles to profl. jours. Continuing Edn. grantee World Book Ency., 1994. Mem. ALA, Assn. Lib. and Info. Sci. Edn., Nat. Cath. Libr. Assn. (pres. No. Ill. chpt. 1987-89, chair acad. sect. No. Ill. chpt. 1992—, sec./treas. acad. session, v.p., pres.-elect), Ill. Libr. Assn., Ill. Sch. Libr. Media Assn. (chair awards com. 1990-91, 94—), Chgo. Libr. Club, Sch. Libr. Assn. Office: Rosary Coll Grad Sch Library and Info Sci 7900 Division St River Forest IL 60305-1099

MCCUTCHEON, HOLLY MARIE, accountant; b. Pitts., Aug. 14, 1950; d. George and Ruth (Bradburn) Rudawski. Student, Ohio Dominican Coll., 1968-69, Wittenburg U., 1979-81; BS in Acctg. and Fin. magna cum laude, Wright State U., 1983. Cert. mgmt. acct. Acct. Morris Bean & Co., Yellow Springs, Ohio, 1983-86; contr. Speco Aerospace Corp., Springfield, Ohio, 1986—; cons. Glenwood Tng. Ctr., Yellow Springs, 1983-86. Coach City Recreation Youth Soccer, Springfield, 1982-85; mem. st. Raphael Adult Choir, Springfield, 1986-89. Mem. Inst. Mgmt. Accts. (pres. Dayton chpt. 1994-95). Office: SPECO Corp PO Box 1288 Springfield OH 45501-1288

MCDADE, LINNA SPRINGER, retired academic program administrator; b. Lincoln, Ill., May 18, 1932; d. Clifford Harry and Lois Mae (Lovett) S.; m. Wesley Dale McDade, June 13, 1951; children: Kimberly Rachel, Chance Linnea, Wesley Dale Jr., Bryan Anthony, Darby Erin. Student, Northwestern U., 1950; AB with honors, U. Ill., 1971. Cert. tchr., Ill. Substitute tchr. Sch. Dist. 116, Urbana, Ill., 1972-74; mng. editor Am. Sociol. Rev., Am. Sociol. Assn., Urbana, 1977-80; asst. to head dept. sociology U. Ill., Urbana, 1980-90; ret., 1990. Chorus mem. Ill. Opera Theatre, 1979-82; pres. Evening Etude Music Club, 1958-60; dir. children's choir 1st Presbyn. Ch., Urbana, 1977, deacon, 1985—, elder, 1989—; co-pres. Washington Sch. PTA, Urbana, 1963-64; bd. dirs. Frances Nelson Health Ctr., Champaign, Ill., 1989-93; vol. fundraising coord. New Hope Jobs, Champaign, 1994—; bd. dirs. Adoption Studies Inst., Washington, 1995—. Recipient " So Proudly We Hail" Community Svc. award The Exch. Club Urbana, 1990. Mem. Phi Alpha Theta. Home: 2433 County Road 1225 N Saint Joseph IL 61873-9727

MCDANIEL, CYNTHIA TINGLE, counselor; b. Atlanta, Feb. 8, 1953; d. Robert Francis Tingle and Ruby (Williams) O'Conor; 1 child, Jeremy. BS in Edn., Ga. State U., 1975; MEd, La. State U., 1984. Lic. profl. counselor, La. Tchr. Silliman Inst., Clinton, La., 1976-78, 79-80; tchr., counselor Redemptionist High Sch., Baton Rouge, 1980-87; counselor I Care program East Baton Rouge Parish Sch. Bd., 1987-93; pvt. practice counseling, Baton Rouge, 1993—; *ounselor Most Blessed Sacrement Sch., Baton Rouge, 1993—; aftercare counselor Tau Ctr., Our Lady of Lake Hosp., Baton Rouge, 1989-93, workshop speaker, 1993; speaker Drug-Free Sch. Conf., Alexandria, La., 1991. Mem. ACA, La. Counselors Assn. (speaker 1992, 93), Internat. Assn. Marriage and Family Counseling, La. Marriage and Family Counseling Assn., Orton Dsylexia Soc. Methodist. Office: 7341 Jefferson Hwy Ste D Baton Rouge LA 70806-8203

MCDANIEL, MYRA ATWELL, lawyer, former state official; b. Phila., Dec. 13, 1932; d. Eva Lucinda (Yores) Atwell; m. Reuben Roosevelt McDaniel Jr., Feb. 20, 1955; children: Diane Lorraine, Reuben Roosevelt III. BA, U. Pa., 1954; JD, U. Tex., 1975; LLD, Huston-Tillotson Coll., 1984, Jarvis Christian Coll., 1986. Bar: Tex. 1975, U.S. Dist. Ct. (we. dist.) Tex. 1977, U.S. Dist. Ct. (so. and no. dists.) Tex. 1978, U.S. Ct. Appeals (5th cir.) 1978, U.S. Supreme Ct. 1978, U.S. Dist. Ct. (ea. dist.) Tex. 1979. Asst atty. gen. State of Tex., Austin, 1975-81, chief taxation div., 1979-81, gen. counsel to gov., 1983-84, sec. of state, 1984-87; asst. gen. counsel Tex. R.R. Commn., Austin, 1981-82; gen. counsel Wilson Cos., San Antonio and Midland, Tex., 1982; assoc. Bickerstaff, Heath & Smiley, Austin, 1984, ptnr., 1987—; mem. asset mgmt. adv. com. State Treasury, Austin, 1984-86; mem. legal affairs com. Criminal Justice Policy Council, Austin, 1984-86; mem. legal affairs com. Inter-State Oil Compact, Oklahoma City, 1984-86; bd. dirs. Austin Cons. Group, 1983-86; lectr. in field. Contbr. articles to profl. jours., chpts. to books. Del. Tex. Conf. on Libraries and Info. Scis., Austin, 1978, White House Conf. on Libraries and Info. Scis., Washington, 1979; mem. Library Services and Constrn. Act Adv. Council, 1980-84, chmn., 1983-84; mem. long range plan task force Brackenridge Hosp., Austin, 1981; clk. vestry bd. St. James Episcopal Ch., Austin, 1981-83, 88-90; bd. visitors U. Tex. Law Sch., 1983—, vice chmn., 1983-85; bd. dirs. Friends of Ronald McDonald House of Cen. Tex., Women's Advocacy, Inc., Capital Area Rehab. Ctr.; trustee Episcopal Found. Tex., 1986-89, St. Edward's U., Austin, 1986—, chmn. acad. com. 1988—; chmn. div. United Way/Capital area campaign, 1986; active nat. adv. bd. Leadership Am.; trustee Episcopal Sem. of SW, 1990—, Assn. Governing Bds. Univs. and Colls. Recipient Tribute to 28 Black Women award Concepts Unltd., 1983; Focus on women honoree Serwa Yetu chpt. Mt. Olive grand chpt. Order of Eastern Star, 1979, Woman of Yr. Longview Metro C. of C., 1985, Woman of Yr. Austin chpt. Internat. Tng. in Communication, 1985, Citizen of Yr. Epsilon Iona chpt. Omega Psi Phi. Master Inns of Ct.; mem. ABA, Am. Bar Found., Tex. Bar Found. (trustee 1986-89), Travis County Bar Assn., Travis County Women Lawyers' Assn., Austin Black Lawyers Assn., State Bar Tex. (chmn. Profl. Efficiency & Econ. Rsch. subcom. 1976-84), Golden Key Nat. Honor Soc., Longhorn Assocs. for Excellence in Women's Athletes (adv. coun. 1988—), Order of Coif (hon. mem.), Omicron Delta Kappa, Delta Phi Alpha. Democrat. Home: 3910 Knollwood Dr Austin TX 78731-2915 Office: San Jacinto Ctr 98 San Jacinto Blvd Ste 1800 Austin TX 78701-4039

MCDANIEL, SARA A., public relations executive; b. Borger, Tex., Mar. 11, 1949. BA in English and Fine Arts, Rice U., 1971. Pub. rels. asst. Hermann Hosp., 1973-75; pub. rels. specialist Neurosensory Ctr. Baylor Coll. & Methodist Hosp., 1975-78; asst. to pres. A.R. Busse, 1978, acct. exec., 1978-80; sr. acct. exec. A.R. Busse & Assocs., 1980; pres. McDaniel & Tate, 1981-86, v.p., 1986-89; pres. McDaniel & Co., 1989—. Mem. Pub. Rels. Soc. Am. Office: PO Box 49 Schulenburg TX 78956*

MCDANIEL, SARA SHERWOOD (SALLY MCDANIEL), trainer, consultant; b. St. Louis, Apr. 24, 1943; d. Edward Leighton and Dolores Edic (Pitts) Sherwood; m. Allen Polk McDaniel, Dec. 29, 1967; children: James Polk, Fontaine Maury. AA, Mt. Vernon Coll., 1963; BS, Vanderbilt U., 1965. Tchr. Kanawha Valley Schools, Charleston, W.Va., 1965-66, Fulton County Schools, Atlanta, 1966-68; tournament dir. Atlanta Classic, 1972-77; dir. alumni affairs Leadership Atlanta, 1988-89; pvt. practice cons., trainer Atlanta, 1988—. Bd. dirs. Girl Scouts U.S., Ga., High Mus. Art, Atlanta Opera, UNICEF Atlanta, Aid Atlanta, Fine Art Collectors; active Com. on Women and Minorities for 1996 Olympics; mem. exec. com. Leadership Atlanta, Jr. League; mem. Friends of Spelman; trustee Mt. Vernon Coll.; bd. chair Atlanta Women's Fund. Mem. Am. Soc. Trainers and Dirs., Atlanta Women's Network (bd. dirs., pres.), Vanderbilt U. Alumni Assn., Alumni Assn. Peabody Coll. Presbyterian. Home and Office: 3777 Paces Ferry Rd NW Atlanta GA 30327-3003

MCDANIEL, SUE POWELL, cultural organization administrator; b. Jefferson City, Mo., Mar. 13, 1946; d. Ernest Gayle and Ruth Angeline (Raithel) Powell; m. Walter Lee Zimmerman, Aug. 14, 1966 (div. 1980); m. Olin Cleve McDaniel, June 23, 1985. BS in Edn., U. Mo., 1968, MEd in Edn., 1977, EdS, 1980, PhD, 1985. Cert. tchr., Mo. Tchr. Jefferson City Pub. Schs., 1968-80; fiscal assoc. Mo. Coordinating Bd. for Higher Edn., Jefferson City, 1980-90; exec. dir. Mo. Women's Coun., Jefferson City, 1990—. Co-author: Missouri Women Today, 1993, Status of the Women, 1994. Mem. Zonta Internat., Lincoln Women in Devel. (pres. 1993—). Office: Mo Women's Coun PO Box 1684 Jefferson City MO 65102

MCDANIEL, SUSAN HOLMES, psychologist; b. Jersey City, Oct. 31, 1951; d. Grover Cleveland and Anna Lou (Toms) McD.; m. David Morton Siegel, July 22, 1984; children: Hanna, Marisa. BA, Duke U., 1973; PhD, U. N.C., 1979. Fellow in family therapy Tex. Rsch. Inst. Mental Scis., Houston, 1980; Supr., staff psychologist W. Monroe Mental Health Ctr., Rochester, N.Y., 1980-82; pvt. practice psychologist Rochester, 1980-88; assoc. prof. psychiatry and family medicine U. Rochester Sch. Medicine, 1987—, co-dir. psychosocial edn. dept. family medicine, dir. family therapy tng. program dept. psychiatry, 1988-94, assoc. dir. div. family programs, 1994—. Co-author: Systems Consultation, 1986, Family-oriented Primary Care, 1990, Medical Family Therapy, 1992, Counseling Families with Chronic Illness, 1995, Integrating Family Therapy, 1995; co-editor Families, Systems & Health, 1995—; contbr. articles to profl. jours. Recipient Nat. Patient Care award for innovation in family med. edn. Patient Care, Soc. for Tchrs. Family Medicine, 1988. Mem. APA (bd. family div.), Am. Family Therapy Acad., Soc. for Tchrs. Family Medicine. Democrat. Office: Dept Family Medicine 885 South Ave Rochester NY 14620-2318

MCDANIELS, PEGGY ELLEN, special education educator; b. Pulaski, Va., Jan. 4, 1945; d. James H. and Gladys M. (Hurd) Fisher; m. Robert A. McDaniels, Feb. 17, 1973; children: Dawn Marie, Robert C. A Gen. Studies, Schoolcraft Coll., 1976; BA, Ea. Mich. U., 1980, MA, 1985. Payroll sec. Otto's Painting and Drywall, West Bloomfield, Mich., 1964-75; office mgr., closing sec. Bing Constrn. Co., West Bloomfield, 1964-75; substitute tchr. Wayne-Westland Schs., Westland, Mich., 1980-83, Farmington (Mich.) Schs., 1980-83; tchr. spl. edn. Romulus (Mich.) Community Schs., 1983-85, Cros-Lex Schs., Croswell, Mich., 1985-87, Pointe Tremble Elem. Sch., Algonac, Mich., 1987—; organizer, recorder Tchr. Assistance Team, Algonac, 1991—. Mem. Coun. Exceptional Children, Learning Disability Assn. (treas. 1988-90), Mich. Assn. Learning Disability Edn., ASCD. Home: 2406 Military St # 1 Port Huron MI 48060-6665

MCDARRAH, GLORIA SCHOFFEL, editor, author; b. Bronx, N.Y., June 22, 1932; d. Louis and Rose Schoffel; m. Fred W. McDarrah, Nov. 5, 1960; children: Timothy, Patrick. BA in French, Pa. State U., 1953; MA in French, NYU, 1966. Editorial asst. Crowell-Collier, N.Y.C., 1957-59; exec. asst. to pub. Time Inc., N.Y.C., 1959-61; libr., tchr. N.Y.C. Pub. Schs. and St. Luke's Sch., 1972-76; exec. asst. to pres. Capital Cities Communications Inc., N.Y.C., 1972-76; analyst N.Y.C. Landmarks Preservation Commn., 1976-79; project editor Grosset & Dunlap Inc., N.Y.C., 1979-80; sr. editor Prentice Hall trade div. Simon & Schuster Inc., N.Y.C., 1980-88; pres. McDarrah Media Assocs., N.Y.C., 1988—. Author: Frommer's Guide to Virginia, 1992, 2d edit., 1994-95, Frommer's Atlantic City and Cape May, 1985, 4th edit., 1991, 5th edit., 1993-94, The Artist's World, 2d edit., 1988; co-author: Museums in New York, 5th edit., 1990, Photography Marketplace, 1975 (book rev. sect.); co-editor Exec. Desk Diary Saturday Rev., 1962-64; contbg. editor quar. Dollarwise Traveler; editor book rev. The Picture Profl., 1990—; book columnist Manhattan Spirit, 1989—; book reviewer Pub.'s Weekley, 1994—.

MCDAVID, SARA JUNE, librarian; b. Atlanta, Dec. 21, 1945; d. William Harvey and June (Threadgill) McRae; m. Michael Wright McDavid, Mar. 23, 1971. BA, Mercer U., 1967; MLS, Emory U., 1969. Head librarian Fernbank Sci. Ctr., Atlanta, 1969-77; dir. rsch. libr. Fed. Res. Bank of Atlanta, 1977-81; mgr. mem. services SOLINET, Atlanta, 1981-82; media specialist Parkview High Sch., Atlanta, 1982-84; ptnr. Interncontinental Travel, Atlanta, 1984-85; librarian Wesleyan Day Sch., Atlanta, 1985-86; mgr. info. svcs. Internat. Assn. Fin. Planning, Atlanta, 1986-90; dir. rsch. Korn Ferry Internat., Atlanta, 1990—; bd. dirs. Southeastern Library Network, Atlanta, 1977-80, vice chmn. bd., 1979-80. Contbr. articles to profl. jours. Pres., mem. exec. com. Atlanta Humane Soc., 1985-86, bd. dirs. aux., 1978-90. Mem. Ga. Library Assn. (v.p. 1981-83), Spl. Libraries Assn. Home: 1535 Knob Hill Dr NE Atlanta GA 30329-3206 Office: Korn Ferry Internat 303 Peachtree St Ste 1600 Atlanta GA 30308

MCDERMOTT, CAROLE SNIDER, banker, international trade specialist; b. Newburgh, N.Y., Aug. 15, 1941; d. Cushing Bosworth and Elsa Marjorie (Bold) Snider; m. David Douglass McDermott, Nov. 14, 1964; children: David Russ, Stacie McDermott DeSalvo. AAS in Acctg., Orange County C.C., Middletown, N.Y., 1976. Cert. credit exec. Gen. mgr. Credit Bur. Orange County, Inc., Newburgh, 1973-82; comml. lending officer Bank of N.Y., Newburgh, 1982-86; credit officer First Nat. Bank of Highland, N.Y., 1986-90; asst. v.p. internat. trade Marine Midland Bank, Newburgh, 1990—; exec. officer Assoc. Credit Burs. N.Y. State, Syracuse, 1977-82. Bd. dirs. United Way of Orange County, Goshen, N.Y., 1985—; pres. bd. trustees Calvary Presbyn. Ch., Newburgh, 1993—. Fellow Soc. Credit Execs., Orange County C. of C. (bd. dirs. 1994—), Hudson Valley Internat. Trade Assn. (bd. dirs. 1994—), Fort Orange Club. Republican. Home: 2 Carriage Dr Newburgh NY 12550-2914 Office: Marine Midland Bank 100 Auto Park Plz Newburgh NY 12550-6700

MCDERMOTT, DONA M., superintendent. Supt. Valley Forge Nat. Hist. Park, Valley Forge, Pa. Office: Valley Forge Nat Hist Park PO Box 953 Valley Forge PA 19482-0953

MCDERMOTT, LUCINDA MARY, minister, teacher, philosopher, poet, author; b. Lynwood, Calif., June 3, 1947; d. R. Harry and Cathrine Jaynne (Redmond) Boand. BA, U. So. Calif., L.A., 1969; MS, Calif. State U., Long Beach, 1975; PhD, Saybrook Inst., 1978. Pres. Environ. Health Systems, Newport Beach, Calif., 1976-90, Forerunner Publs., Newport Beach, 1985—; founder, pres. Life-Skills Learning Ctr., Newport Beach, 1985—; founder, dir. Newport Beach Ecumenical Ctr., 1993—; bd. dirs. Key Mgmt., The Board Family Found.; founder, dir. Newport Beach (Calif.) Ecumenical Ctr., 1993—. Author: Bridges to Another Place, 1972, Honor Thy Self Vol. I and II, 1973, Hello-My-Love-Good Bye, 1973, Life-Skills for Children, 1984, Myrika-An Autobiographical Novel, 1989, White Knights and Shining Halos: Beyond Pair Bonding, 1995. Mem. APA, Alpha Kappa Delta, Kappa Kappa Gamma.

MCDERMOTT, MOLLY, lay minister; b. Cloquet, Minn., Aug. 19, 1932; d. Harry W. McD.; children: Elizabeth Sanders Hellenbrand, Sarah Sanders, Mary Sanders Day, Margaret Kathleen Sanders Lorfeld. Student, Oreg. State Coll., 1951, U. Minn., Duluth, 1953. Claims specialist Cuna Mut. Ins. Soc., Madison, Wis., 1975—; propr. Molly's Garden. Storyteller, ventriloquist St. Bernard's Parish, mem. faith cmty. commn., liturgical environ. com.; mem. Friends of Aboretum. Mem. Pevennail Soc., Toastmasters, The Rose Soc. (storyetller, ventriloquist). Roman Catholic. Home: 1724 Parmenter St Middleton WI 53562-3153

MCDERMOTT, PATRICIA ANN, nursing administrator; b. Bklyn., July 10, 1943; d. John J. and Lillian E. (Sweeney) Skelly; m. Joseph Kevin McDermott, Oct. 5, 1963; children: Colleen Mary, John Joseph. Diploma, Kings County Hosp. Ctr. Sch. Nursing, Bklyn., 1963; BS in Health Care Adminstrn., St. Francis Coll., Bklyn., 1979. Staff nurse Kings County Hosp., Bklyn., 1963-66, head nurse outpatient dept., 1966-74; evening supr. Park Nursing Home, Rockaway Park, N.Y., 1974-83; day supr. Hyde Park Nursing Home, Staatsburg, N.Y., 1984-85, DON, 1985—; nurse aide evaluator PRI assessor, MDS, coord. N.Y. State. Active local Girl Scouts U.S.A., 1971-78, Boy Scouts Am., 1978-82, Stella Maris Parents Club, 1978-82, St. Francis de Sales Altar and Rosary Soc., 1970-83, St. Francis de Sales Little League, 1978-80, also softball coach, 1974-77. Republican. Roman Catholic. Avocations: knitting; crocheting; roller skating; bowling; oil painting. Home: 286A Shadblow Ln Clinton Corners NY 12514 Office: Hyde Park Nursing Home RR 9 Staatsburg NY 12580

MCDERMOTT, PATRICIA LOUISE, lawyer; d. Peter A. and Emily W. McDermott;. Student, Creighton U., 1955-56; BA in Polit. Sci., Idaho State U., 1958; JD, George Washington U., 1961, LLM in Labor Law, 1964. Bar: U.S. Dist. Ct. D.C. 1961, U.S. Ct. Appeals (D.C. cir.) 1961, U.S. Supreme Ct. 1965, Idaho 1966, U.S. Dist. Ct. (ea. dist.) Idaho 1966, U.S. Ct. Appeals (9th cir.) 1966. Mem. staff U.S. senator Frank Church, 1958-61; house counsel United Planning Orgn., Washington, 1964-65; cons. office of manpower U.S. Labor Dept., 1966; ptnr. McDermott & McDermott, 1965-76; sr. ptnr. McDermott, Zollinger, Olley & Webber, Pocatello, Idaho, 1976—; instr. communications law Idaho State U., 1974-77, Rocky Mountain Labor Sch., 1975, 79; speaker various schs. and orgns. Regional v.p. Idaho Young Dems., 1966-68; mem. legis. council Idaho State Legislature, 1973—, Ho. of Reps., 1968-90, house minority leader, 1975-80, mem. Idaho State Senate, 1990-92; mem. Idaho Bicentennial Commn., 1969-77, Idaho State Commn. on Women, 1969-72, Employment Security Adv. Council, 1983-88, NAACP; mem. adv. bd. Idaho Alcohol Safety Commn., 1968-76; bd. dirs. State Legislature Leaders Found., 1978-80; bd. dirs. Idaho Spl. Olympics Inc., 1985-87; mem. Idaho Commn. on the Bicentennial of U.S. Constitution, 1985-90. Recipient Cert. of Appreciation Assn. of Idaho Cities, 1974, Assoc. Students Idaho State U., 1975, Martin Luther King award NAACP, 1970, Pres.'s award Idaho TV Assn., 1986; named Statesman of Yr. Idaho State U., 1982, one of 10 Outstanding Women March of Dimes, 1985. Mem. ABA, Idaho Bar Assn. (criminal law seminar 1971, corrections com. grading team 1975, 76, 78, 80, 82, 87, svc. award 1989), 6th Jud. Dist. Bar Assn. (sec.-treas. 1968), Assn. Trial Lawyers Am., Idaho Libr. Assn. (Legislator of Yr. award 1991), Idaho State U. Alumni Assn. (bd. dirs. 1972-77, pres. 1976), Idaho Fedn. Bus. and Profl. Women (Woman of Yr. award 1976), Pocatello C. of C. (govtl. affairs com.), Zonta, Pi Sigma Alpha, Alpha Omicron Pi. Office: PO Box 3 Pocatello ID 83204-0003

MCDERMOTT, RENÉE R(ASSLER), lawyer; b. Danville, Pa., Sept. 26, 1950; d. Carl A. and Rose (Gaupp) Rassler; m. James A. McDermott, Jan. 1, 1986. BA, U. So. Fla., 1970, MA, 1972; JD, Ind. U., 1978. Bar: Ind. 1978, U.S. Dist. Ct. (so. and no. dists.) Ind. 1978, U.S. Dist. Ct. Ariz. 1984, U.S. Ct. Appeals (7th cir.) 1979, U.S. Ct. Appeals (9th cir.) 1985. Law clk. to presiding judge U.S. Dist. Ct. (no. dist.) Ind., Ft. Wayne, 1978-80; assoc. Barnes & Thornburg, Indpls., 1980-84, ptnr., 1985-93; pvt. practice Nashville, Ind., 1994—; county atty. County of Brown, Ind., 1994—. Editor in chief Ind. U. Law Jour., 1977-78. Bd. visitors Ind. U. Law Sch., Bloomington, 1979—; bd. dirs. Environ. Quality Control Inc., Indpls. Named one of Outstanding Young Women Am., 1986. Fellow Ind. Bar Found., Am. Bar Found. (life); mem. ABA (chmn. environ. controls com. 1991—, liaison to standing com. on environ. law bus. law sect.), Ind. State Bar Assn. (chmn. young lawyers sect. 1985-86, chmn. environ. law sect. 1989-91), Bar Assn. 7th Fed. Cir., Ind. Mfrs. Assn. (environ. affairs com), Order of Coif. Home and Office: 1008 W McLary Rd Nashville IN 47448-9702 Address: 1008 W McLary Rd Nashville IN 47448

MCDERMOTT, SUSAN JEAN CASSI, fundraising and development consultant; b. Astoria, N.Y., Mar. 1, 1953; d. Walter George and Jean Louise (Krivicich) Cassi; m. Michael I. McDermott, Apr. 13, 1980; 1 child, Ian Walter. AA in Liberal Arts and Spanish, Nassau Community Coll., Garden City, N.Y., 1973; BA in Speech and Communications, SUNY, Oneonta, 1975; postgrad. bus. law and stats., SUNY. With advt. sales dept. N.Y. Daily News, N.Y.C., 1975-78, mgr. circulation dept., 1978-82; sales rep. Radio Relay, Hicksville, N.Y., 1983; with circulation ops. dept. USA Today, Bayside, N.Y., 1983-85; exec. dir. AHHS Neighborhood Press Coalition, Rockaway, N.Y., 1985-86; dir. devel. Threshold Svcs. Inc., Kensington, Md., 1989-94; founder, pres. S&M Devel. Resources, Silver Spring, Md., 1994—. Contbg. editor Newspix mag., 1982. Adv. com. Montgomery County Pub. TV Network; mem. cmty. adv. com. Visions, Montgomery County, Md., 1993-94, bd. dirs., 1995. Mem. Silver Spring C. of C. (bd. dirs.). Democrat. Roman Catholic. Home: 9009 2nd Ave Silver Spring MD 20910-2158 Office: S&M Devel Resources 9009 2d Ave Silver Spring MD 20910

MCDERMOTT, SUZANNE ELIZABETH, foreign language educator; b. Rocky River, Ohio, Jan. 2, 1942; d. Frederick William and Angelin Elizabeth (Kofoed) Taylor; m. Gordon L. McDermott, July 25, 1964 (dec. Mar. 1969); 1 child, Ginger Lee. BA, Wittenberg U., 1964; MEd, Rollins Coll., 1975. Cert. French tchr. French tchr. Vandalia (Ohio) City Schs., 1964-73; English tchr. Teague Middle Sch., Altamonte Springs, Fla., 1974-75; compensatory English Sanford (Fla.) Grammar, 1975-77, Seminole High Sch., Sanford, 1977-80, Teague Middle Sch., Almonte Springs, 1980-83; French tchr. Seminole High Sch., Sanford, 1983—. Mem. Friends of the Wekiva River, Longwood, Fla., 1993. Named Educator of Year, Greater Seminole County C. of C., 1987-88. Mem. NEA, Am. Assn. Tchrs. of French, Fla. Fgn. Lang. Assn., Delta Kappa Gamma (literacy chmn. 1991—), Alpha Delta Kappa (recording sec. 1991—). Republican. Lutheran. Home: 130 Tindale Cir Longwood FL 32779-4614 Office: Seminole High Sch 2701 Ridgewood Ave Sanford FL 32773-4999

MCDEVITT, SHEILA MARIE, lawyer, energy company executive; b. St. Petersburg, Fla., Jan. 15, 1947; d. Frank Davis and Marie (Barfield) McD. AA, St. Petersburg Jr. Coll., 1966; BA in Govt., Fla. State U., 1968, JD, 1978. Bar: Fla. 1978. Research asst. Fla. Legis. Reference Bur., Tallahassee, 1968-69; adminstr., research assoc. Constitution Revision Commn. Ga. Gen. Assembly, Atlanta, 1969-70; adminstrv. asst., analyst Fla. State Sen., Tallahassee, Tampa, 1970-79; assoc. McClain, Walkley & Stuart, P.A., Tampa, Seminole, Fla., 1979-81; govtl. affairs counsel Tampa Electric Co., 1981-82, corp. counsel, 1982-86; sr. corp. counsel Teco Energy, Inc., Tampa, 1986-89, asst. v.p., 1989-92; v.p., asst. gen. counsel, 1992—; mem. Worker's Compensation Adv. Council Fla. Dept. Labor, Tallahassee, 1984-86. Bd. dirs. Vol. Ctr. Hillsborough County, Tampa, 1984-85; chmn., trustee Tampa Lowry Park Zoo Soc., 1986-94, also legal advisor; bd. dirs. Hillsborough County Easter Seal Soc., 1994—; mem. Fla. State Rep. Exec. Com., Tallahassee, 1974-75, Hillsborough County Reps. Exec. Com., 1974-75; transition team Fla. Gov. Bob Martinez, 1986-87; apptd. by Sen. Connie Mack to Fed. Jud. Adv. Commn., 1989—. Mem. ABA, Fed. Energy Bar Assn., Fla. Bar (vice-chmn. then chmn. energy law com. 1984-87, jud. nominating procedures com. 1986-91, jud. adminstrn. selection and tenure com. 1991-93), Hillsborough County Bar Assn. (chmn. law week com. 1990, chmn. corp. counsel com. 1986-87, chmn. internat. law com. 1994—), Am. Corp. Counsel Assn. (bd. dirs. Ctrl. Fla. chpt. 1986-87), Tampa Club, Tiger Bay Club, Tampa Yacht and Country Club. Republican. Roman Catholic. Home: 3211 W Swann Ave Apt 201 Tampa FL 33609-4651 Office: TECO Energy Inc PO Box 111 702 N Franklin St Tampa FL 33601

MCDONAGH, JAN, pathology educator; b. Wilmington, N.C., Nov. 9, 1942; d. James B. and Mary Katherine (Elkins) McQuere; m. Richard P. McDonagh (dec. 1979); 1 child, Jonathan McDonagh; m. Eric T. Fossel, Jan. 7, 1983. BS, Wake Forest U., 1964; PhD, U. N.C., 1968. From asst. prof. to assoc. prof. pathology and biochemistry U. N.C., Chapel Hill, 1971-82; assoc. prof. pathology Harvard U. Med. Sch., Boston, 1982—; established investigator Am. heart Assn., 1977. Author 14 monographs, 1 book; contbr. articles to profl. jours.; patentee in field. NIH grantee, 1968—. Mem. Am. Heart Assn., Internat. Soc. on Thrombosis and Haemostasis (chair factor XIII), Am. Soc. Biol. Chemistry and Molecular Biology, Japan Haematological Soc., Am. Fed. Clin. Rsch., Phi Beta Kappa, Sigma Xi. Episcopalian. Office: Beth Israel Hosp HMS Dept Pathology Boston MA 02150

MCDONALD, ALICE COIG, state education official; b. Chalmette, La., Sept. 26, 1940; d. Olas Casimere and Genevieve Louise (Heck) Coig; m. Glenn McDonald, July 16, 1967; 1 child, Michel. B.S., Loyola U., New Orleans, 1962; M.Ed., Loyola U., 1966; cert. rank I sch. adminstrn., Spalding Coll., 1975. Tchr. St. Bernard Pub. Schs., Chalmette, La., 1962-67; counselor, instructional coordinator Jefferson County Schs., Louisville, 1967-77; ednl. adviser Jefferson County Govt., Louisville, 1977-78; chief exec. asst. Office of Mayor, Louisville, 1978-80; dep. supt. pub. instrn. Ky. Dept. Edn., Frankfort, 1980-83, supt. pub. instrn., 1984—; bd. dirs., com. mem. Ky. Council on Higher Edn., 1984—, Ky. Juvenile Justice Com., 1984—, Ky. Ednl. TV Authority, 1984—, So. Regional Council Ednl. Improvement, 1984—. Mem. Pres.'s Adv. Com. on Women, 1978-80; active Democratic Nat. Convs., 1972, 76, 80, 84; pres. Dem. Woman's Club Ky., 1974-76 Ky. mem. Nat. Dem. Com., 1976-79, mem. exec. com. 1977—. Mem. Council Chief State Sch. Officers, Women in Sch. Adminstrn., NEA, Ky. Edn. Assn.,

River City Bus. and Profl. Women. Home: 6501 Gunpowder Ln Prospect KY 40059-9334 Office: Ky Dept Edn Capital Plaza Towers Fl 1 Frankfort KY 40601

MCDONALD, ANNE B., state legislator; b. Syracuse, N.Y.. BS, LeMoyne Coll.; MS, Syracuse U. Mem. Commn. on Aging, Stamford, Conn., 1969-76, chair, 1972-76; mem. State Adv. Coun. on Aging, 1977-80; mem. Bd. of Edn., Stamford, 1980-87, pres., 1984-85; chmn. Housing Authority, Stamford, 1988-90; state rep. Conn. House of Reps., Hartford, 1991—. Democrat. Home: 53 Courtland Hill Ave Stamford CT 06906 Office: Conn House Reps State Capitol Hartford CT 06106*

MC DONALD, BARBARA ANN, psychotherapist; b. Mpls., July 15, 1932; d. John and Georgia Elizabeth (Baker) Rubenzer; B.A., U. Minn., 1954; M.S.W., U. Denver, 1977; m. Lawrence R. McDonald, July 27, 1957 (dec. Sept. 1993); children—John, Mary Elizabeth. Diplomate Am. Bd. Social Work; lic. psychotherapist. Day care cons. Minn. Dept. Public Welfare, St. Paul, 1954-59; social worker Community Info. Center, Mpls., 1959-60; exec. dir. Social Synergistics Co., Littleton, Colo., 1970—; cons. to community orgns., Indian tribes. Family therapist , 1979—. Bd. dirs. Vol. Bur. Sun Cities, Ariz., 1988, 89, 90. Named 1 of 8 Women of Yr. and featured on TV spl. Ladies Home Jour., 1974; Clairol scholar, 1974; Am. Bus. Women's Assn. scholar, 1974; Alpha Gamma Delta scholar, 1974. Mem. Minn. Pre-Sch. Edn. Assn. (hon. life), AAUW, Nat. Assn. Social Workers, Ariz. Assn. Social Workers, Assn. Clin. Social Workers, Am. Bus. Women's Assn., U. Minn. Alumni Club, Alpha Gamma Delta (Disting. Citizen award 1975). Club: Altrusa (hon.). Author: Selected References on the Group Day Care of Pre-School Children, 1956; Helping Families Grow: Specialized Psychotherapy with Hearing Impaired Children and Their Families, 1984. Office: 13720 W Franciscan Dr Sun City West AZ 85375-5219

MCDONALD, CAROLYN ANN, dance educator, choreographer; b. Blytheville, Ark., Aug. 27, 1963; d. Travis Eugene and Barbara Jean (Myers) McD. BA in Dance, U. Calif., Irvine, 1987; postgrad., U. Iowa, 1995—. Instr. dance Kirkwood C.C., Cedar Rapids, Iowa, 1987-90; choreographer Kirkwood C.C., Cedar Rapids, 1987—, coord. performing arts camp, 1990—; instr. dance Coe Coll., Cedar Rapids, 1989—; owner, pres. McDonald Arts Ctr., Marion, Iowa, 1988—; cons. Jane Boyd Cmty. House, Cedar Rapids, 1993-94. Office: 105 Southview Dr Marion IA 52302

MCDONALD, DEBORAH HALCOMB, state educational consultant; b. Ky., July 11, 1949; d. Thurston Clay and Berniece (Cole) Halcomb; m. Richard Curtis McDonald (dec.); 1 child, Ty. Student, Sue Bennett Coll., London, Ky., 1967-69; BA, Ea. Ky. U., 1972, MA, 1973, postgrad., 1982. Cert. tchr., ednl. adminstrn., Ky. Tchr. McKee (Ky.) Mid. Sch., 1973; tchr. math., chmn. dept. Clark-Moores Mid. Sch., Richmond, Ky., 1974-92, Madison Mid. Sch., Richmond, 1992-93; ednl. cons. in sch. improvement Ky. Dept. Edn., Frankfort, 1993—; curriculum and assessment cons. Region 6 Svc. Ctr., Corbin, Ky., 1993; trainer Ky. Effective Schs. Network, Frankfort, 1990—; mem. Ky. Gov.'s Adv. Bd. dor Title II Funding; rep. curriculum com. Madison County (Ky.) Bd. Edn.; mgmt. dir. Nat. Cheerleader's Assn., Dallas, summers; conf. presenter on effective schs. and practical arts. Mem. Ky. Task Force for Missing and Exploited Children; former treas., v.p., pres., exec. advisor, edn. chmn., del. to state conv. Richmond Younger Woman's Club; treas., mem. coms. charity ball Pattie A. Clay Hosp. Aux.; chmn. mother's march Kidney Found.; chmn., treas. Madison County Jr. Miss Program. Named Ky. Disting. Educator, Ky. Dept. Edn., 1993. Mem. ASCD, Nat. Coun. Tchrs. Math., Ky. Coun. Tchrs. Math., Ky. Mid. Sch. Assn., Ky. Edn. Assn., Madison County Edn. Assn., Richmond Women's Investment Group (treas.), Beta Sigma Phi, Alpha Kappa Delta, Phi Delta Kappa. Baptist. Home: 215 Martin Dr Richmond KY 40475-3509

MCDONALD, GABRIELLE ANNE KIRK, lawyer, former federal judge; b. St. Paul, Apr. 12, 1942; d. James G. and Frances R. Kirk; m. Mark T. McDonald; children: Michael, Stacy. LLB, Howard U., 1966. Bar: Tex. 1966. Staff atty. NAACP Legal Def. and Ednl. Fund, N.Y.C., 1966-69; ptnr. McDonald & McDonald, Houston, 1969-79; judge U.S. Dist. Ct., Houston, 1979-88; now ptnr. Matthews Branscomb, Austin, Tex.; asst. prof. Tex. So. U., Houston, 1970, adj. prof., 1975-77; lectr. U. Tex., Houston, 1977-78; active UN Gen. Assembly War Crime Tribunal, 1993. Bd. dirs. Community Service Option Program; bd. dirs. Alley Theatre, Houston, Nat. Coalition of 100 Black Women, ARC; trustee Howard U., from 1983; bd. vistors Thurgood Marshall Sch. Law, Houston. Mem. ABA, Nat. Bar Assn., Houston Bar Assn., Houston Lawyers Assn., Black Women Lawyers Assn. Democrat. Congregationalist. Office: Matthews & Branscomb PC 301 Congress Ave Ste 2050 Austin TX 78701-4082*

MCDONALD, GAIL CLEMENTS, government official; b. Ft. Worth, Tex., Mar. 9, 1944; d. Eugene and Cornelia (Nagle) Clements; m. William C. Scott, Aug. 26, 1967 (div. 1976); 1 child, Jill Miriah Scott; m. Danny Lee McDonald, Aug. 6, 1982. BA, Tex. Christian U., Ft. Worth, 1966, MA, 1967. Instr. social sci. Cooke County Jr. Coll., Gainesville, Tex., 1967-69, Langston (Okla.) U., 1969, Tulsa Jr. Coll., 1977-79; instr. humanities Okla. State U., Stillwater, 1971-74; adminstrv. asst. edn. and cultural affairs Gov. David L. Boren, Oklahoma City, 1975-78; legis. aide Sen. David L. Boren, Tulsa, 1979; state assoc. Inst. for Ednl. Leadership, George Washington U., Washington, 1979-81; exec. asst. Commr. Norma H. Eagleton, Okla. Corp. Commr., Oklahoma City, 1979-81; commr. ICC, Washington, 1990—, vice chmn., 1993, chmn, 1993—. Bd. dirs. Okla. Sci. & Arts Found., 1975-83; exec. com. Frontiers of Sci. Found., 1976-80; fundraiser Washington chpt. Spl. Olympics. Named Woman of Yr., Women's Transp. Seminar, 1991. Mem. Nat. Assn. Regulatory Commrs. (transp. com.), Ind. Agy. Women, Exec. Women in Govt., Conservation Round Table (chmn. 1990), Transp. Table Washington, Toastmasters (pres. 1988), Phi Alpha Theta. Democrat. Episcopalian. Office: ICC Rm 4211 12th and Constitution Ave NW Washington DC 20423-0001

MCDONALD, JACQUELYN MILLIGAN, parent and family studies educator; b. New Brunswick, N.J., July 28, 1935; d. John P. and Emma (Mark) Milligan; m. Neil Vanden Dorpel; five children. BA, Cornell U., 1957; MA, NYU, 1971; MEd, Columbia U., 1992, EdD, 1993. Cert. behavior modification, N.J.; cert. tchr. grades K-8, N.J. Instr. Montclair (N.J.) State Coll., 1982-93, Edison C.C., Naples, Fla., 1994—; mem. steering com. Fla. Gulf Coast U. Family Ctr.; parent vol. tng. project coord. Montclair (N.J.) Pub. Schs., 1984-86; coord. Collier and Charlotte Counties IDEAS for Parenting, Inc., Naples, 1993—. Chairperson Interfaith Neighbors Juvenile Delinquency Prevention, N.Y.C., 1960-68; support family Healing the Children, 1970-90; founder The Parent Ctr., Montclair, 1983, Essex County N.J. Fair Housing Coun., 1990. Mem. Children's Action Network, Pre-Sch. Interagy. Couns., Family Svc. Planning Team, Needs Assessment Children Collier and Charlotte Counties, Raven and Serpent Hon. Soc. (pres. 1956), Psi Chi, Kappa Delta Pi. Home: 27075 Kindlewood Ln Bonita Springs FL 33923

MCDONALD, JEANNE GRAY (MRS. JOHN B. MCDONALD), television producer; b. Seattle, Sept. 10, 1917; d. George Patrick and Mary Edna (Gray) Murphy; m. John B. Mc Donald, June 30, 1951; children: Gregory Roland Stoner, Jeanne Eve. Student, Columbia U., 1940, Art Students League, 1940-43, Nat. Acad. Dramatic Art, 1945. Radio producer, commentator The Woman's Voice Sta. KMPC, L.A., 1947-50; TV producer, commentator, writer The Woman's Voice Sta. KTTV-CBS, L.A., 1950-51; TV producer, commentator The Jeanne Gray Show Sta. KNXT-TV CBS, L.A., 1951-53; West Coast editor Home Show NBC, L.A., 1955-56; TV film producer documentaries and travelogues Virgonian Prodns., L.A., 1953—. Author: The Power of Belonging, 1978. Women's chmn. Los Angeles Beautiful, 1971; mem. Women's Aux. St. John's Hosp.; trustee Freedoms Found. at Valley Forge, 1966—, founder, pres. women's chpt., Los Angeles County chpt., 1965-66, Western dir. women's chpt., 1967-68, nat. chmn. 1968-71, nat. chmn. women vols., 1973-75, hon life mem. Recipient Francis Holmes Outstanding Achievement award, 1949, Silver Mike award, 1948, Emmy award Acad. TV Arts and Scis., 1951, Lulu award Los Angeles Advt. Women, 1952, Genii award Radio and TV Women, 1956, George Washington Honor award Freedoms Found. Valley Forge, 1967, honor cert., 1972, Morale award Christians and Jews for Law and Morality, 1968, Exceptional Service award Freedoms Found., 1975, Liberty Belle award Rep. Women's Club, 1975, Leadership award Los Angeles City Schs., 1976, Theodore Roosevelt award USN League, 1986. Mem. Am. Women in Radio and TV, Radio and TV Women So. Calif. (hon., life, founder, 1st pres. 1952), Footlighters (v.p. 1958-59), Los Angeles C. of C. (bd. dirs. women's div. 1948-54, exec. bd., women's div. 1954-66, pres. women's div. 1963-64, hon. past pres. women's div. 1979), L.A. Orphanage Guild, DAR, Les Dames de Champagne, Bel Air Garden Club, Calif. Yacht Club. Home: 910 Stradella Rd Bel Aire CA 90077

MCDONALD, JOANNE, human resources company executive; b. San Diego, June 10, 1947; d. Paul and Dolores (Paganucci) McD. BA, U. Md., 1970. High tech. exec. ENSCO Inc., Springfield, Va., 1981—, v.p. adminstrn. and human resources, 1992—. Bd. dirs. Yorktowne Sq., Falls Church, Va., 1981; trustee Elizabeth Seton High Sch., Bladensburg, Md., 1988, High Tech. Coun. No. Va., Fairfax, 1992. Mem. ASTD, Am. Mgmt. Assn., Soc. for Human Resource Mgmt. Office: ENSCO Inc 5400 Port Royal Rd Springfield VA 22151-2301

MCDONALD, LISA DAWN, payroll and personnel administrator; b. Topeka, June 1, 1965; d. David Merle and Anna Lou (Jennings) Schlaegel; m. Larry McDonald, Apr. 16, 1983; children: Michael, T.J. Grad. high sch., Mulvane, Kans. Bill clk. TNT Dugan, Inc., Wichita, Kans., 1987, acctg. asst., 1987-91, mgr. payroll and pers., 1991—; group leader health ins. plan TNT Dugan, Inc., 1991—, coord. 401K and stock purchase plan, 1993—. Active PTO, Mulvane, 1989—, Curriculum Improvement Commn., Mulvane, 1993. Republican. Office: TNT Dugan Inc 2020 W Harry Wichita KS 67213

MCDONALD, MARIANNE, classicist; b. Chgo., Jan. 2, 1937; d. Eugene Francis and Inez (Riddle) McD.; children: Eugene, Conrad, Bryan, Bridget, Kirstie (dec.), Hiroshi. BA magna cum laude, Bryn Mawr Coll., 1958; MA, U. Chgo., 1960; PhD, U. Calif., Irvine, 1975, doctorate (hon.) Am. Coll. Greece, 1988, hon. diploma Am. Archaeological Assn. Teaching asst. classics U. Calif., Irvine, 1974, D Litt (hon.) U. Athens, Greece, 1994, U. Dublin, 1994. instr. Greek, Latin and English, mythology, modern cinema, 1975-79, founder, rsch. fellow Thesaurus Linguae Graecae Project, 1975—; bd. dir. Centrum. Bd. dirs. Am. Coll. of Greece, 1981—, Scripps Hosp., 1981; Am. Sch. Classical Studies, 1986—; mem. bd. overseers U. Calif. San Diego, 1985—; nat. bd. advisors Am. Biog. Inst., 1982—; founder Hajime Mori Chair for Japanese Studies, U. Calif., San Diego, 1985, McDonald Ctr. for Alcohol and Substance Abuse, 1984, Thesaurus Linguarum Hiberniae, 1991—; vis. prof. U. Dublin, 1990—; adj. prof. theatre U. Calif., San Diego, 1990, prof. theatre and classics, 1994; prof. U. Dublin, 1990—, U. Calif., San Diego, 1994. Recipient Ellen Browning Scripps Humanitarian award, 1975; Disting. Svc. award U. Calif.-Irvine, 1982, Irvine medal, 1987, 3rd Prize Midwest Poetry Ctr. Contest, 1987; named one of the Community Leaders Am., 1979-80, Philanthropist of Yr., 1985, Headliner San Diego Press Club, 1985, Philanthropist of Yr. Honorary Nat. Conf. Christians and Jews, 1986, Woman of Distinction Salvation Army, 1986, Eleventh Woman Living Legacy, 1986, Woman of Yr. AHEPA, 1988, San Diego Woman of Distinction, 1990, Woman of Yr. AXIOS, 1991; recipient Bravissimo gold medal San Diego Opera, 1990, Gold Medal Soc. Internationalization of Greek Lang, 1990, Athens medal, 1991, Piraeus medal, 1991, award Desmoi, 1992, award Hellenic Assn of Univ. Women, 1992, Academy of Achievement award AHEPA, 1992, Woman of Delphi award European Cultural Ctr. Delphi, 1992, Civis Universitatis award U. Calif. San Diego, 1993, Hypatia award Hellenic U. Women, 1993, Am.-Ireland Fund Heritage award, 1994, Contribution to Greek Letters award Aristotle U. Thessaloniki, 1994, Order of the Phoenix, Greece, 1994. Vol. Decade Women's International Ctr., 1994. Mem. MLA, AAUP, Am. Philol. Assn., Soc. for the Preservation of the Greek Heritage (pres.), Libr. of Am., Am. Classical League, Philol. Assn. Pacific Coast, Am. Comparative Lit. Assn., Modern and Classical Lang. Assn. So. Calif., Hellenic Soc., Calif. Fgn. Lang. Tchrs. Assn., Internat. Platform Assn., Greek Language Found. (pres.), Royal Irish Acad., Greece's Order of the Phoenix (commdr. 1994), Olbos Enterprises (pres.), KPBS Producers Club, Hellenic Univ. Club (bd. dir.). Author: Terms for Happiness in Euripides, 1978, Semilemmatized Concordances to Euripides' Alcestis, 1977, Cyclops, Andromache, Medea, 1978, Heraclidae, Hippolytus, 1979, Hecuba, 1984, Hercules Furens, 1984, Electra, 1984, Ion, 1985, Trojan Women, 1988, Iphigenia in Taurus, 1988, Euripides in Cinema: The Heart Made Visible, 1983; translator: The Cost of Kindness and Other Fabulous Tales (Shinichi Hoshi), 1986, (chpt.) Views of Clytemnestra, Ancient and Modern, 1990, Classics and Cinema, 1990, Modern Critical Theory and Classical Literature, 1994, A Challenge to Democracy, 1994; writer: Ancient Sun/Modern Light: Greek Drama on the Modern Stage, 1990; contbr. numerous articles to profl. jours. Avocations: karate, harp (medieval), skiing, diving. Home: PO Box 929 Rancho Santa Fe CA 92067-0929 Office: U Calif at San Diego Dept Theatre La Jolla CA 92093

MCDONALD, MARY M., lawyer; b. 1944. BA, D'Youville Coll., 1966; JD, Fordham U., 1969. Bar: N.Y. 1969. Counsel corp. staff Merck & Co., v.p., gen. counsel, 1991—. Office: Merck & Co PO Box 2000 126 E Lincoln Ave Rahway NJ 07065*

MCDONALD, MEG, public relations executive; b. Santa Monica, Calif., Oct. 11, 1948. Dir. radio & TV svcs. Fran Hynds Pub. Rels., 1969-75; owner, CEO McDonald Media Svcs., 1975—. Recipient Buccaneer award PIRATES, 1980, 82, Prisms award Pub. Rels. Soc. Am., 1981, Pro awards Publicity Clubs. of L.A. Mem. Pub. Rels. Soc. Am. (sec. 1985), Radio & TV News Assn. of So. Calif. (mem. bd. dirs. 1973-88), Publicity Club of L.A. (pres. 1979-80), L.A. Advtg. Women (v.p. 1984-85), Pub. Interest Radio & TV Ednl. Soc. (PIRATES) (mem. bd. dirs.), Radio & TV News Assn. Office: Media Services 11076 Fruitland Dr Studio City CA 91604*

MCDONALD, MICHELLE RENEE, financial analyst; b. Roanoke, Va., May 16, 1970; d. Virgil Olin and Kathy Sue (Doyle) McD. BS, Va. Tech., 1992. CPA, Va. Staff acct. Coastal Corp., Roanoke, Va., 1992-93; fin. analyst Hoechst Celanese, Narrows, Va., 1993—. Mem. Inst. Mgmt. Accts., Beta Alpha Psi (alumni mem., v.p. pledging 1991-92). Democrat. Baptist. Home: 750 Hethwood Blvd # 400K Blacksburg VA 24060 Office: Hoechst Celanese Corp PO Box 1000 Rt 460 Narrows VA 24124

MCDONALD, NANCY EVANS, research scientist; b. Quitman, Ga., June 21, 1948; d. Fred F. and Elizabeth H. (Harrell) Evans; children: Burton F. III, Brian C. AS, Port Huron C.C., 1981; BS, U. Ctrl. Fla., 1991. Quality assurance supr. Gold Kist Soy, Valdosta, Ga., 1969-71; lab. technician Port Huron (Mich.) Hosp., 1980-81; lab. technician, nutrition counselor Nutri-Systems, Orlando, Fla., 1982-83; lab. technician III R & D divsn. Coca-Cola Foods, Plymouth, Fla., 1984-90, rsch. chemist, 1991—. Mem. Am. Assn. Cereal Chemists, Inst. Food Technologists (chairperson hospitality com. 1993-94, sec.-elect 1994-95), Phi Theta Kappa, Phi Kappa Phi. Methodist. Office: Coca-Cola Foods R & D Divsn 2651 Orange Ave Plymouth FL 32768

MCDONALD, PATRICIA ANNE, professional society executive; b. Detroit, Mar. 16, 1947; d. William and Esther Carpenter (Rodger) McD. Student, Eastern Mich. U., 1965-68, Wayne State U., 1970-71, U. Mich., 1983. Cert. social worker, Mich. Caseworker State Mich., Detroit, 1968-69; counselor City Detroit Health Dept., 1970-75; psychotherapist The Life Ctr., Ferndale, Mich., 1975-79; field rep. Nat. Multiple Sclerosis Soc., Southfield, Mich., 1979-80, dir. svcs., 1980-83, exec. dir., 1983—; bd. dirs. Mariners Inn, Detroit, Housing Alternatives Inc., Lansing, Mich., 1984-89; svc. cons. Nat. Multiple Sclerosis Soc., N.Y.C., 1981-82, others. Coun. mem. Judson Ctr., Royal Oak, Mich., 1991—. Recipient The Americans with Disabilities Act award, Washington, 1990. Mem. Coun. Exec. Officers (sec. 1988-89). Roman Catholic. Office: Nat Multiple Sclerosis Soc 26111 Evergreen Rd Ste 100 Southfield MI 48076-4481

MCDONALD, PATRICIA HAMILTON, insurance agency administrator, real estate broker; b. Raleigh, N.C., Sept. 15, 1952; d. Marvin Stancil Hamilton and Josephine (Blake) Rummage; m. Thomas Wayne McDonald, Jan. 22,1972; children: Wendi Dannette, Thomas Wayne. Diploma, Inst. of Ins., Phila., 1987. Cert. in gen. ins., agy. mgmt.; cert. profl. ins. woman; real estate broker. Sr. comml. lines account rep. Tomlinson Insurors, Fayetteville, N.C., 1970-76, Wachovia Ins. Agy., Fayetteville, 1976--78; agy. mgr., sec.-treas. Ins. Svc. Ctr., Fayetteville, 1978-91, Assoc. Ins. Agy. of Fayetteville, Inc., 1991—; instr. continuing edn. N.C. Dept. Ins., Raleigh, 1990-91; agts. adv. coun. Seibels Bruce Ins. Co., 1991-92, 94—; ins. agts. pre-licensing instr., CPCU instr. Fayetteville Tech. C.C., 1993, 94. Bd. dirs. Fayetteville Tech. Community Coll., 1990—. Recipient State award Cystic Fibrosis Found., 1988. Mem. Ind. Ins. Agts. (assoc., bd. dirs. 1989—), Fayetteville Assn. Ins. Profls. (pres. 1989—, chmn. edn. 1987-89, chmn. pub. rels. 1988, Ins. Woman of Yr. 1989), N.C. Assn. Ins. Women (chmn. edn. 1990, Edn. award 1989, Gen. Excellence award 1991, 92, state treas. 1992-93), Nat. Assn. Ins. Women (dec. 1985—), Ind. Ins. Agts. N.C. (trainer 1986—), Home Builders Assn. Fayetteville (Life Spike award), N.C. Foresters Assn., N.C. Grange, Hope Mills Kiwanis Club (treas. 1994—, bd. dirs. 1994—), Kiwanis Internat., Hope Mills Assn. Ins. Profls. (edn. chmn. 1992-93, long-range planning chmn. 1992-93), Fayetteville Area C. of C. Republican. Baptist. Office: Assoc Ins Agy Fayetteville 2547 Ravenhill Dr Ste 101 Fayetteville NC 28303-5461

MCDONALD, PEGGY ANN STIMMEL, retired automobile company official; b. Darbyville, Ohio, Aug. 25, 1931; d. Wilbur Smith and Bernice Edna (Hott) Stimmel; missionary diploma with honor Moody Bible Inst., 1952; B.A. cum laude in Econs. (scholar), Ohio Wesleyan U., 1965; M.B.A. with distinction, Xavier U., 1977; m. George R. Stich, Mar. 7, 1953 (dec.); 1 son, Mark Stephen (dec.); m. Joseph F. McDonald, Jr., Feb. 1, 1986. . Missionary in S. Am., Evang. Alliance Mission, 1956-61; cost acct. Western Electric Co., 1965-66; acctg. mgr. Ohio Wesleyan U., 1966-73; fin. specialist NCR Corp., 1973-74, systems analyst, 1974-75, supr. inventory planning, 1975, mgr. material planning and purchasing control, 1976-78; materials mgr. U.S. Elec. Motors Co., 1978; with Gen. Motors Corp., 1978-92, shift supt. materials, Lakewood, Ga., 1979-80, gen. ops. supr. material data base mgmt. Central Office, Warren, Mich., 1980, dir. material mgmt. GM Truck and Bus div., Balt., 1980-91; dir. edn. & tng. GM Truck and Bus, Linden, N.J., 1991-92; ret., 1992. vis. lectr. Inst. Internat. Trade, Jiao Tong U., Shanghai, China, 1985, Inst. Econs. and Fgn. Trade, Tianjin, China, 1986-87; part time instr. Towson (Md.) State U., 1986-87. Capt. USCG. Mem. Am. Prodn. and Inventory Control Soc., Am. Soc. Women Accts., AAUW, Balt. Exec. Women's Network, Balt. Council on Fgn. Relations, Presbyterian. Avocation: sailing. Home: 455 S Alt 19 # 182 Palm Harbor FL 34683

MCDONALD, PENNY S(UE), educational administrator; b. Portland, Oreg., May 1, 1946; d. Norman James and Edna (Kaufmann) McD. BA, Oreg. State U., 1968, MEd, 1974; EdD, Portland State U./U. Oreg., 1981, Harvard U., summer 1987. Tchr. English, Fleming Jr. High Sch., Los Angeles, 1968-69; tchr. lang. arts and social studies Highland View Jr. High Sch., Corvallis, Oreg., 1970-72; tchr. English, dir. student activities Crescent Valley High Sch., Corvallis, 1973-78; grad. asst. Portland State U., Oreg., 1978-80; evaluation intern N.W. Regional Edn. Lab., Portland, 1980; Nat. Inst. Edn. assoc., edn. policy fellow Nat. Commn. on Excellence in Edn., Washington, 1981-83; prin. Inza R. Wood Middle Sch., West Linn Sch. Dist., Wilsonville, Oreg., 1983-88; adminstr. in residence for ednl. adminstrn. Lewis & Clark Coll., Portland, 1988-91; prin. Adams Traditional Alternative Elem., Eugene (Oreg.) Sch. Dist., 1991—; cons. Oreg. Dept. Edn., 1980-81; sr. counselor Oreg. Assn. Student Councils Camps, 1976-78, 80; adj. prof. ednl. adminstrn. Lewis & Clark Coll., 1987-88. Coord., com., adminstr. Oreg. Mentorship Program, 1986-87. Named to Outstanding Young Woman Am., U.S. Jaycees; AFL-CIO scholar Oreg. State U., Corvallis, 1964; Univ. scholar Oreg. State U., 1965-68; nat. Alpha Delta Pi scholar Oreg. State U., 1967-68; Delta Kappa Gamma scholar Portland State U./U. Oreg. 1979-81. Mem. Nat. Assn. Student Councils, Oreg. Assn. Activities Advisors (chmn. 1976-77, bd. dirs. 1977-78), Oreg. Assn. Student Councils, Confedn. Oreg. Sch. Adminstrs. (curriculum commn. 1985-86, asst. chmn., sec. 1986-87, chmn. 1987-88, ex-officio mem. exec. bd. 1987-88), Nat. Assn. Secondary Sch. Prins., N.W. Women in Ednl. Adminstrn. (Oreg. bd. dirs., pres. elect), Delta Kappa Gamma (chpt. rec. sec.), Phi Delta Kappa. Democrat. Office: Adams Trad Alternative Elem Sch 950 W 22nd Ave Eugene OR 97405-2119

MCDONALD, ROSA NELL, federal research and budgets manager; b. Boley, Okla., Feb. 12, 1953; d. James and Beatrice Irene (Hayes) McD. BS, Calif. State U., Long Beach, 1975; MBA, Calif. State U., Dominquez Hills, 1980 also postgrad; BS computer information systems, Chapman Coll, 1988. Acct., The Aerospace Corp., El Segundo, Calif., 1976-77; analytical accountant, 1977-79, budget analyst, 1979-81, sr. budget analyst, 1981-84, budget adminstr., 1984-86, mgr. indirect budgets, 1986-91, head budgets and pricing dept., 1991—. Vol., Youth Motivation Task Force, El Segundo, 1980—, Holiday Project, El Segundo, 1984, 85. Recipient Adminstrn. Group Achievement award The Aerospace Corp., 1985, Robert Herndon Image award, 1988; named Woman of Yr, Aerospace Corp., 1987, NAACP Legal Def. Fund Woman of Achievement, 1988. Mem. Am. Bus. Woman's Assn., Nat. Assn. Female Execs., Beta Gamma Sigma. Democrat. Avocations: dancing; aerobics; reading; contests. Office: 2350 E El Segundo Blvd M1/400 El Segundo CA 90245

MCDONALD, SUSAN ANN, performance consultant; b. Tulsa, Okla., Nov. 2, 1950; d. Marvin Neil and Rosemary (Ramsey) M.; m. Robert Wilson Brown, Aug. 17, 1974 (div. Sept. 1986); children: William Ramsey, David Wilson. BA in English, Wake Forest U., 1973; MEd in Counseling, U. N.C., 1978. Tchr. English, guidance counselor Forsyth Country Day Sch., Winston-Salem, N.C., 1973-76; case mgr. Richland County Dept. Social Svcs., Columbia, 1976-77; grad. asst. U. N.C., Charlotte, 1977-78; dir. placement Queens Coll., Charlotte, 1978-81; employment mgr., tng. mgr. Barclays American, Charlotte, 1981-83; sales trainer, tng. mgr., sales mgr., cons. NCNB-NOW Nations Bank, Charlotte, 1983-92; account mgr. Omega Performance, Charlotte, 1992-94, mgr. cons., 1994—. Democrat. Baptist. Home: 2923 Polo Ridge Ct Charlotte NC 28210 Office: Omega Performance Charlotte NC 28210

MCDONALD, SUSAN F., business executive, city official; b. Rockford, Ill., Jan. 18, 1961; d. John Augustus and Jeanne (Reitsch) Floberg; m. Robert Arthur McDonald, June 19, 1981; children: Molly Jeanne, Amanda Elizabeth. AAS in Bus. Mgmt., Colo. Mountain Coll., Glenwood Springs, 1981. Teller, bookkeeper Alpine Bank, Glenwood Springs, 1981-82; teller Macktown State Bank, Rockford, 1982-83; treas., mgr., owner Roscoe (Ill.) Movie House, 1984-94; sales cons. Lou Bachroot, Inc., Rockford, 1992-93; mem. bd. suprs. Winnebago County Bd., Rockford, 1992—; exec. v.p., owner Corp. Svc. Alliance, Machesney Park, Ill., 1993—; leasing and fleet mgr. Budweiser Motors, Inc., Beloit, Wis., 1994—. Pres. Roscoe Bus. Assn., 1990, 91, v.p., 189; chair, founder Roscoe Beautification Assn., 1991; mem. county bd. dirs. Winnebago County, 1992—, vice chmn. econ. devel. com., 1993—; chmn. econ. devel. environ. com. Winnebago County Bd., 1994—; commr. Winnebago County Forest Preserve, Rockford, 1992—; co-founder, bd. dirs. Very Important Pregnancy, Rockford Meml. Hosp.; bd. dirs. Family Advocate Aux., Rockford, 1987-88; bd. dirs. U. Ill. Extension Svc./Winnebago County, 1994—. Nominated Video Retailer of Yr., Am. Video Assn., 1989, Leadership award, Stateline YWCA, 1989. Republican. Methodist. Office: Corp Svc Alliance Ltd 6702 Yale Bridge Rd Rockton IL 61072

MCDONALD, THERESA BEATRICE (PIERCE) (MRS. OLLIE MCDONALD), church official; b. Vicksburg, Miss., Apr. 11, 1929; d. Leonard C. Pierce and Ernestine Morris Templeton; m. Ollie McDonald, Apr. 23, 1966. Student, Tougaloo Coll., 1946-47, Roosevelt U., 1954-56, 59-62, 64, U. Chgo. Indsl. Rels. Ctr., 1963-64. Vol. rep. Liberty Bapt. Ch., Am. Legion Aux., VA West Side Hosp., Chgo., 1971-73; nat. instr. ushers dept. Prog. Nat. Bapt. Conv. Inc., Washington, 1973-75, nat. sec. ushers dept., 1975-76, v.p. at large, 1980-82, chmn. pers. com., 1982-84; mem. faculty Congress of Christian Edn., 1978-85; mem. pub. rels. staff Liberty Bapt. Ch., Chgo., 1973-79, trustee, 1987-91; cons., lectr. in field; guest speaker TV and radio programs. Participant White House Regional Confs., 1961. Recipient Christian Svc. award Prog. Nat. Bapt. Conv. Inc., 1986, 92. Mem. Bethlehem Bapt. Dist. Assn. Chgo. (asst. sec. 1982-84), Ch. Women United in Greater Chgo. (Ecumenical Actions com. 1981-83), Am. Legion (Outstanding Svc. award 1972, 73), Order Ea. Star. Address: 9810 S Calumet Ave Chicago IL 60628-1432

MCDONALD, WYLENE BOOTH, former nurse, pharmaceutical sales professional; b. Kinston, N.C., Sept. 29, 1956; d. Wiley Truett and Hilda Grey (Brinson) Booth; m. Robert H. McDonald; stepchildren: Stephanie Lynn, Robin Leigh. BSN, Barton Coll., 1979; MSN, East Carolina U., 1984. Pub. health nurse Sampson Co. Health Dept., Clinton, N.C., 1979-81;

pub. health coord. New Hanover Co. Health Dept., Wilmington, N.C., 1981-83; med. ctr. liaison Cape Fear Valley Med. Ctr., Fayetteville, N.C., 1984-85; profl. sales rep. Merck, Human Health Div., West Point, Pa., 1985-88; hosp. specialist sales rep. Human Health divsn. Merck, West Point, Pa., 1988-90, sr. prostate health specialist rep., 1990-94; exec. cardiovascular specialist Human Health divsn. Merck, West Point, Pa., ž, 1995—; speaker Coastal Area Perinatal Assn., 1983, Career Week, U. N.C. Sch. Bus., Wilmington, 1987, 88, 89, 93. Fundraiser March of DImes, Fayetteville, 1987, Wilmington, 1991, Am. Heart Assn., Wilmington, 1991-93. Named one of Outstanding Young Women of Am., 1981. Mem. ANA, AAUW, N.C. Nurses Assn., N.C. Pub. Health Assn., Sigma Theta Tau. Home and Office: 108 Seapath Est Wrightsville Beach NC 28480-1964

MCDONELL, WILMA ELLEN DANIEL, technical information center manager; b. Jackson, Miss., Nov. 18, 1952; d. Charles Lewis and Wilma (Yarborough) Daniel; m. Kevin A. McDonell, May 20, 1978; children: Robert Frasier, Daniel Coppedge Douglass. BAE, U. Miss., 1973; MSLS, U. Tenn., 1975; postgrad., Nova U., 1985—. Cert. Acad. Health Info. Profls. Head serials Rowland Med. Libr., U. Miss. Med. Ctr., Jackson, 1976-78; head serials dept. instr. U. Tenn. Ctr. for the Health Scis., Memphis, 1978-82, asst. prof. reference, 1982-85; mgr. tech. info. ctr. Buckman Labs. Internat., Inc., Memphis, 1985—; coord. West Tenn. Region Libr. Legis. Network, 1979-82; cons. Oxford (Miss.)-Lafayette County Hosp., 1981-85; presenter in field. Author: Mini Manual for End User Searching Medlars, 1983; contbr. chpts. to books and articles to profl. jours. Mem. Am. Mgmt. Assn., Spl. Libr. Assn. (pres. midsouth chpt. 1981-82), Med. Libr. Assn., Nat. Assn. Corrosion Engrs., Am. Soc. Info. Sci., Kappa Delta Pi, Beta Phi Mu. Presbyterian. Office: Buckman Labs Internat Inc 1256 N Mclean Blvd Memphis TN 38108-1241

MCDONNELL, JEANNE FARR, museum director; b. Akron, Ohio, Mar. 26, 1931; d. Ernest and Marie (Koerber) Farr; m. Eugene Edward McDonnell, Oct. 18, 1926; children: Julia, Luke, Peter, Albert, James. AA, Stephens Coll., 1950; BA, Ohio State U., 1952; MA, Columbia U., 1956. Adminstrv. asst. Houghton Mifflin Publs., Palo Alto, Calif., 1981-83; exec. dir. Nature Explorations, Palo Alto, Calif., 1979-84, Womens Heritage Mus., Palo Alto, Calif., 1985—. Editor: (newsletter) Women's Heritage Mus., 1985—. Bd. dirs. Youth Advocates, Media, Pa., 1972-74, LWV, Yorktown Heights, N.Y., 1969-70, Assn. Performing Arts, Yorktown Heights, 1965-70. Fulbright scholar, U. Brussels, 1952-53; Rsch. grantee Sourisseau Acad., San Jose, Calif., 1981, Inst. Hist. Study, San Francisco, 1982. Mem. Western Assn. Women Historians, Orgn. Am. Historians, Women's Club Palo Alto (1st v.p. 1983-84).

MC DONNELL, LORETTA WADE, lawyer; b. San Francisco, May 31, 1940; d. John H. and Helen M. (Tinney) Wade; m. John L. McDonnell, Jr., Apr. 27, 1963 (div.); children: Elizabeth, John L. III, Thomas. BA, San Francisco Coll. for Women, 1962; MA, Stanford U., 1963; grad. Coro Pub. Affairs Tng. Program for Women, 1976; JD Golden Gate U., 1989. Bar: Calif. 1990. High sch. tchr. East Side Union High Sch. Dist., San Jose, Calif., 1962-63; project coordinator Inter Agency Collaboration Effort, Oakland, Calif., 1977; legal asst. Pacific Gas and Electric Co., 1980-89, coord., 1989—. Bd. dirs. Carden Redwood Sch., 1975-77, St. Paul's Sch., 1974-75; budget panelist United Way of Bay Area, 1975-77; community v.p. Jr. League, 1976-77, nat. conv. del., 1976; bd. dirs. Alameda County Vol. Bur., 1973-74; chmn. speakers panel Focus on Am. Women, 1973-74. Mem. Jr. League of Oakland-East Bay, Inc., Stanford Alumni. Democrat. Roman Catholic. Clubs: Stanford San Francisco Luncheon, Commonwealth. Assoc. editor The Antiphon, 1971-74.

MCDONNELL, MARY THERESA, travel service executive; b. N.Y.C., Nov. 9, 1949; d. John J. and Mary B. (Lunney) McD.; m. Robert T. Barber, Oct. 7, 1989. Mgr. Kramer Travel Agy., White Plains, N.Y., 1967-79; owner, mgr. New Trends Travel, Rye, N.Y., 1979-90; mgr. Honey Travel Inc., Rye, N.Y., 1990—. Office: Honey Travel Inc 11 Elm Pl Rye NY 10580-2918

MCDONNELL, MARYANN MARGARET, medical marketing executive; b. Detroit, Aug. 26, 1947; d. Patrick J. and Margaret Ann (Novallo) McD.; children: Anais Kathryn Alexander, Colin Michael McDonnell. BS, Wayne State U., 1970. Consumer protection specialist FTC, Washington, 1970-73; fin. analyst Price Commn., Washington, 1972-73; co-founder Full Circle Process & Xenium, Los Gatos, Calif., 1973-77; asst. adminstr. Arts In the Image of Man, Fair Oaks, Calif., 1981-83; adminstr. Mariposa Waldorf Sch., Cedar Ridge, Calif., 1983-84; pres. Counseling Endevors, Grass Valley, Calif., 1984-86; v.p. Sr. Vision Inst., Carmichael, Calif., 1986-88; pres. Empire Health Mktg., Grass Valley, 1988—, Elder Sight Inst., Grass Valley, 1988—; exec. Cell Tech, Klammath Falls, Oreg., 1994—. Founder, chairperson Los Gatos (Calif.) Waldorf Sch. Assn., 1977; mem. Mariposa Waldorf Sch. Bd. Trustees, Cedar Ridge, 1984; founding mem. Gia Sophia, Nevada City, Calif., 1987. Mem. Orthopedic Edn. Alliance (pres. 1992—). Democrat. Home: 16611 Alexandra Way Grass Valley CA 95949-7353

MCDONNELL, PATRICIA JOAN, art museum curator; b. Mpls., Mar. 30, 1956; d. Robert Frances and Joan Ruth (Fortune) McD.; m. Gregory Joseph Pluth, Nov. 1977; 1 child, Kate Marie. BA in German Studies cum laude, Mills Coll., 1978; MA in Art History, Brown U., 1985, PhD in Art History, 1991. Profl. tng. coord. Art Mus. Assn. Am., San Francisco, 1978-83; asst. to dir. Mus. of Art, R.I. Sch. Design, Providence, 1984; curator Frederick R. Weisman Art Mus., U. Minn., Mpls., 1991—; grant reviewer NEH, Washington, 1993; bd. dirs. Nash Art Gallery, Mpls., 1993—, adv. com. Marsden Hartley Catalogue Raisonné, N.Y.C., 1993—. Contbr. articles to profl. jours. Teaching fellow Brown U., 1984-87, Dissertation fellow Deutscher Akademischer Austauschdienst Freie U. Berlin, 1987, Smithsonian Inst., Hirshhorn Mus., 1988-90, Samuel H. Kress Found., 1990. Mem. Coll. Art Assn. Office: Frederick R Weisman Art Mus U Minn 333 E River Rd Minneapolis MN 55455

MCDONNELL, ROSEMARY CYNTHIA, special populations programmer; b. Washington, July 31, 1969; d. Joseph Patrick and Judith Ann (Bruscino) McD. BS, Bradley U., Peoria, Ill., 1991; postgrad., Ill. Ctrl. Coll., 1993. Qualified mental retardation profl. Team leader Community Workshop and Tng. Ctr., Peoria, 1989-92; polit. sci. intern City of Peoria, 1991; undergrad. teaching asst. Bradley U., Peoria, 1991; family support coord. Tazewell County Resource Ctr., Pekin, Ill., 1992-93, early intervention asst., 1993-94; spl. populations programmer Pekin Pk. Dist. Recreation Office, 1994—. Asst. coach Spl. Olympics, Peoria, 1992. Olive B. White scholar Bradley U., 1990. Mem. NOW, Pi Gamma Mu, Phi Alpha Theta. Roman Catholic. Home: PO Box 363 Pekin IL 61555-0363

MCDONNELL, SUE KARTIN, lawyer; b. Phila., Mar. 15, 1948; d. William and Ruth F. (Swyer) Kartin; m. John Joseph McDonnell III, June 14, 1970; 1 child, Liam Kartin. BA, Barnard Coll., 1970; JD, Columbia U., 1973. Bar: N.Y. 1974, Calif. 1979, Ohio, 1988, U.S. Dist. Ct. (so. dist.) N.Y., U.S. Dist. Ct. (cen. dist.) Calif., U.S. Dist. Ct. (so. dist.) Ohio, U.S. Ct. Appeals (2d, 4th and 9th cirs.), U.S. Supreme Ct. Assoc. Donovan Leisure Newton & Irvine, N.Y.C. and L.A., 1973-82; ptnr. Donovan Leisure Newton & Irvine, L.A., 1982-87; shareholder Smith & Schnacke, Dayton, Ohio, 1988-89; ptnr. Thompson, Hine and Flory, Dayton, Ohio, 1989—. Bd. dirs. Legal Aid Soc. Dayton, Inc. Mem. ABA (antitrust, litigation, patent, trademark and copyright sects.), Calif. State Bar Assn., Dayton Bar Assn., Am. Inns of Ct. (Master of the Bench, Carl Kessler Inn), Phi Beta Kappa. Office: Thompson Hine and Flory 2000 Courthouse Pla NE Dayton OH 45401

MCDONOUGH, KATHERINE ANN, public relations executive; b. Lawrence, Mass., June 4, 1950; d. William F. and Olga A. (Andruchow) McD.; m. Mark F. Dichter, Nov. 6, 1988. BS, Boston U., 1972; M in City and Regional Planning, Harvard U., 1977. Producer Sta. WCVB-TV, Boston, 1972-75; pub. affairs spl. asst. New Eng. Regional Commn., Boston, 1976-78; v.p. New Eng. Council, Inc., Boston, 1978-81, Citibank, N.Y.C., 1981-85; mng. dir. Adams & Rinehart, Inc., N.Y.C., 1985—. bd. dirs. Broque Opera Co., N.Y.C., 1983-86; vol. cons. Arts & Bus. Council, N.Y.C., 1982-85; mem. mktg. devel. com. N.Y. Botanical Garden, 1987—. Office: Adams & Rinehart 708 3rd Ave New York NY 10017

MCDONOUGH, MAMIE, public relations executive; b. Plainfield, N.J., Mar. 24, 1952; d. Peter J. and Elizabeth (Driscoll) McD. BA, Elmira Coll., 1974; DFA (hon.), Pratt Inst., 1990. Protocol asst. U.S. Dept. State, Washington, 1974-75; staff asst. Office of U.S. V.P., Washington, 1975-77; dir. info. service Rep. Nat. Com., Washington, 1977-79; pres. Festive Occasions, Inc., Washington, 1979-81; staff asst. Office of Dep. Chief of Staff The White House, Washington, 1981-82; sr. ptnr. Britt-McDonough Assocs., Washington, 1982-86; owner The McDonough Group, Washington and N.Y.C., 1986—; Co-author, developer Student/Corp. Jr. Bd. Dirs. Program, 1984. Admissions rep. Washington area Elmira Coll., 1975-76; bd. dirs. Jr. League Washington, 1977—, Camp Fire Boys and Girls, Washington area, 1985-90; mem. fin. com. various Rep. congl. campaigns, 1979—; corp. bd. Vanderbilt Mus., 1985—. Recipient Outstanding Service award Camp Fire Council, 1986. Roman Catholic. Office: 157 E 75th St Apt 1W New York NY 10021-3279

MCDONOUGH, PEGGY, healthcare administrator, nurse; b. Winthrop, Mass., Dec. 22, 1949; d. William Joseph and Marguerite Mary (Flinn) McD. BSN, Northeastern U., 1972. RN, Mass., N.Y., N.H.; cert. operating rm. nurse. Staff nurse operating and recovery rm. Beth Israel Hosp., Boston, 1972-73; staff nurse recovery rm. NYU Hosp., 1973; various positions Brockton (Mass.) Hosp., 1974-76; charge nurse observation unit New England Deaconess Hosp., Boston, 1976; nurse mgr. critical care The Faulkner Hosp., Boston, 1976-79; supr. operating rm., recovery rm. ctrl. supply Brooks Hosp., Lahey Clinic Found., Boston, 1979-80; dept. head operating rm. Anna Jaques Hosp., Newburyport, Mass., 1981-83; cons. McFaul & Lyons, Inc., Trenton, N.J., 1984-87, InterQual, Inc., North Hampton, N.H., 1987-88; staff nurse New England Nursing Svcs., Inc., Dover, N.H., 1988-89; adminstrv. dir. quality mgmt. Providence Hosp., Holyoke, Mass., 1990-94; dir. quality mgmt. Melrose-Wakefield Hosp., Melrose, Mass., 1994—; presenter in field. Mem. Mass. Assn. for Healthcare Quality (state pres.-elect 1995, chairperson region I, 1992-94), Western Mass. Q.M. Consortium (chairperson 1991-92), Nat. Assn. Healthcare Quality, Mass. Soc. for Healthcare Risk mgmt., Nurse Cons. Assn., Assn. Operating Rm. Nurses (chpt. pres. 1982-84). Home: 110 Burton Ave Whitman MA 02382 Office: Melrose-Wakefield Hosp 585 Lebanon St Melrose MA 02176

MCDOUGAL, MARIE PATRICIA, English and psychology educator; b. Mt. Clemens, Mich., Apr. 10, 1946; d. Allan Charles and Dorothy Nadine (Berger) Ling; m. Douglas Stevens McDougal, Aug. 23, 1969. BA, Cen. Mich. U., 1968. Lic. tchr., Mich. Tchr. L'Anse Creuse High Sch., Harrison Twp., Mich., 1969—; mem. L'Anse Creuse High Crisis Team, 1988-93, S.A.F.E. Task Force, Harrison Twp., 1986—. Columnist The Jour. Newspaper, Mt. Clemens, 1983-90; speaker in field. Mem. L'Anse Creuse Athletic Boosters; chair Harrison Twp. Hist. Commn. Recipient Appreciation award Macomb County Hist. Soc., 1989, Pres. award for lit. excellence The Nat. Authors Registry, 1994. Mem. NEA, Soc. Children's Book Writers, Romance Writers Am., Venice Shores Property Owners (bd. dirs. 1990—, corr. sec. 1994), Detroit Women Writers, Bay Area Writers' Guild. Lutheran.

MCDOUGALD, VICKY LYNN GRIDER, gifted/talented education educator; b. Warren, Ark., June 24, 1957; d. Howard Gorman and Anna Louise (Carter) Grider; m. Robert Michael McDougald, Dec. 20, 1975; children: Selena Hope, Joshua Seth. BA in Kindergarten and Elem. Edn., U. Ark., Monticello, 1980. Cert. tchr. K-6, gifted edn., Ark. Elem. tchr. Hermitage (Ark.) Pub. Schs., 1981-88, gifted/talented tchr., coord., 1988—. Mem. S.E. Ark. Gifted Educators Adv. Com., Monticello, 1989-94; Sun. sch. tchr. Landmark Mission Bapt. Ch., Hermitage, 1982-91; mem. Hermitage PTO, 1983-94. Mem. ASCD, Ark. Gifted/Talented Educators. Home: 417 Old Ingalls Rd Hermitage AR 71647 Office: Hermitage Pub Schs PO Box 38 Hermitage AR 71647

MCDOUGALL, JACQUELYN MARIE HORAN, therapist; b. Wenatchee, Wash., Sept. 24, 1924; d. John Rankin and Helen Frampton (Vandivort) Horan; m. Robert Duncan McDougall, Jan. 24, 1947 (div. July 1976); children: Douglas, Stuart, Scott. BA, Wash. State U., 1946. Lic. therapist, Wash.; cert. nat. addiction counselor II. Pres. oper. bd. Ctr. for Alcohol/Drug Treatment, Wenatchee, 1983-85; sec. Wash. State Coun. on Alcoholism, 1988-89, supr. out-patient svcs., 1989-90; case mgmt. counselor Lakeside Treatment Ctr., East Wenatchee, Wash., 1991-92. Treas. Allied Arts, Wenatchee, 1984; pres. Rep. Women, Wash., 1969-70.

MCDOUGALL, SUSAN, professional financial services executive; b. Pitts., Dec. 21, 1961; d. Robert James and Barbara (Hicks) McD.; m. Kirk Thomas Dackow, Sept. 24, 1988; 1 child, Christopher Thomas. Student, Am. Univ., 1982; BS, Carnegie Mellon U., 1983; MBA, U. Pitts., 1986. Lobbying asst. Bayh, Tabbert and Capehart, Washington, 1982; legal asst. Agent Orange plaintiffs' mgmt. com. Henderson and Goldberg, N.Y.C., Pitts., 1983-85; bus. analyst. corp. staff Mobay Corp., Pitts., 1986-88, market devel. rep. Specialities dept., 1988-89; asst. product dir. mktg. planning The Nat. Assn. Securities Dealers, Inc., Washington, 1990; product dir. trading and market svcs. The NASDAQ Stock Mkt., Inc., Washington, 1991, dir. trading and market svcs., 1992—. Office: Nat Assn of Securities Dealers 1735 K St NW Washington DC 20006-1506

MCDOWELL, ELIZABETH MARY, pathology educator; b. Kew Gardens, Surrey, Eng., Mar. 30, 1940; came to U.S., 1971; d. Arthur and Peggy (Bryant) McD. B Vet. Medicine, Royal Vet. Coll., London, 1963; BA, Cambridge U., 1968, PhD, 1971. Gen. practice vet. medicine, 1964-66; Nuffield Found. tng. scholar Cambridge (Eng.) U., 1966-71; instr. dept. pathology U. Md., Balt., 1971-73, asst. prof., 1973-76, assoc. prof., 1976-80, prof., 1980—. Co-author: Biopsy Pathology of the Bronchi, 1987; editor: Lung Carcinomas, 1987; contbr. over 120 articles to sci. jours., chpts. to books. Rsch. grantee NIH, 1979-92. Fellow Royal Coll. Vet. Surgeons Gt. Britain and Ireland. Home: 606 W 37th St Baltimore MD 21211-2230 Office: U Md 10 S Pine St Baltimore MD 21201-1192

MCDOWELL, JENNIFER, sociologist, composer, playwright, publisher; b. Albuquerque; d. Willard A. and Margaret Frances (Garrison) McD.; m. Milton Loventhal, July 2, 1973. BA, U. Calif., 1957; MA, San Diego State U., 1958; postgrad., Sorbonne, Paris, 1959; MLS, U. Calif., 1963; PhD, U. Oreg., 1973. Tchr. English Abraham Lincoln High Sch., San Jose, Calif., 1960-61; free-lance editor Soviet field, Berkeley, Calif., 1961-63; rsch. asst. sociology U. Oreg., Eugene, 1964-66; editor, pub. Merlin Papers, San Jose, 1969—, Merlin Press, San Jose, 1973—; rsch. cons. sociology San Jose, 1973—; music pub. Lipstick and Toy Balloons Pub. Co., San Jose, 1978—; composer Paramount Pictures, 1982-88; tchr. writing workshops; poetry readings, 1969-73; co-producer radio show lit. and culture Sta. KALX, Berkeley, 1971-72. Author: (with Milton Loventhal) Black Politics: A Study and Annotated Bibliography of the Mississippi Freedom Democratic Party, 1971 (featured at Smithsonian Instn. spl. event 1992), Contemporary Women Poets: An Anthology of California Poets, 1977, Ronnie Goose Rhymes for Grown-ups, 1984; co-author: (plays off-off Broadway) Betsy and Phyllis, 1986, Mack the Knife Your Friendly Dentist, 1986, The Estrogen Party to End War, 1986, The Oatmeal Party Comes to Order, 1986, (plays) Betsy Meets the Wacky Iraqi, 1991, Bella and Phyllis, 1994; contbr. poems, plays, essays, articles, short stories, book revs. to lit. mags., news mags. and anthologies; researcher women's autobiog. writings, contemporary writing in poetry, Soviet studies, civil rights movement and George Orwell, 1962—; writer: (songs) Money Makes a Woman Free, 1976, 3 songs featured in Parade of Am. Music; co-creator: (mus. comedy) Russia's Secret Plot to Take Back Alaska, 1988. Recipient 8 awards Am. Song Festival, 1976-79, Bill Casey award in Letters, 1980; AAUW doctoral fellow, 1971-73; grantee Calif. Arts Council, 1976-77. Mem. Am. Sociol. Assn., Soc. Sci. Study of Religion, Poetry Orgn. for Women, Dramatists Guild, Phi Beta Kappa, Sigma Alpha Iota, Beta Phi Mu, Kappa Kappa Gamma. Democrat. Office: care Merlin Press PO Box 5602 San Jose CA 95150-5602

MCDOWELL, KAREN ANN, lawyer; b. Ruston, La., Oct. 4, 1945; d. Paul and Opal Elizabeth (Davis) Bauer; m. Gary Lee McDowell, Dec. 22, 1979. BA, N.E. La. U., 1967; JD, U. Mich., 1971; diploma, John Robert Powers Sch., Chgo., 1976, Nat. Inst. Trial Advocacy, 1990. Bar: Ill. 1973, Colo. 1977, U.S. Dist. Ct. (so. dist.) Ill. 1973, U.S. Dist. Ct. Colo. 1977. Reference libr. assoc. Ill. State Library, Springfield, 1972-73; asst. atty. gen. State of Ill., Springfield, 1973-75; pvt. practice Boulder, Colo., 1978-79, Denver, 1979—. Mem. So. Poverty Law Ctr., Jewish Community Ctr., Amnesty Internat. Mem. ABA, DAR, Colo. Bar Assn. (com. alcohol and related problems), Denver Bar Assn., Colo. Women's Bar Assn. (editor newsletter 1982-84), Colo. Soc. Study Multiple Personality and Dissociation, Survivors United NEtwork (legal coord. 1992-93), Survivors United Network profls. (exec. com. 1992), Internat. Platform Assn., Mensa (local sec. Ann Arbor, Mich. 1968), Colonial Dames, Nat. Soc. Magna Carta Dames, Phi Alpha Theta, Sigma Tau Delta, Alpha Lambda Delta. Office: 428 E 11th Ave Ste 100 Denver CO 80203-3264

MCDOWELL, NAN HAZEL, occupational therapist, rehabilitation services professional; b. Quincy, Mass., June 23, 1940; d. Arthur Pierce and Hazel Florence (Foley) Thomas; m. Billy M.L. McDowell, Dec. 16, 1966; 1 child, Tara Brooke. BS in Occupational Therapy, Edn., Tufts U., 1964; Cert. in Rehab. Facilities Adminstrn., U. Mo., 1991. Registered occupational therapist, Mo. Spl. edn. tchr. Anchorage Borough Sch. Dist., 1965-70; dir. occupational therapy Mid Maine Med. Ctr., Waterville, 1978-80, Hillcrest Med. Ctr., Tulsa, 1980-84; dir. adjuctive therapy St. Vincent Hosp., Santa Fe, 1985-86; rehab. coord., analyst Muskogee (Okla.) Regional Med. Ctr., 1986-87; mgr. rehab. svcs. and in-patient clinics U. Mo. Hosps. and Clinics, Columbia, 1988-89; mgr. rehab. svcs. Still Regional Med. Ctr., Jefferson City, Mo., 1990-91, Claremore (Okla.) Regional Hosp., 1992-93; mgr. outpatient rehab. Sisters of St. Mary's Rehab. Inst., Jefferson City, 1994; dir. rehab. therapies Rehab Visions at Lake of the Ozarks Gen. Hosp., Osage Beach, Mo., 1994—; cons. occupational therapy svcs. EPIC-Cornerstone Geriatic Psychology, Miami, Okla., 1989-90; cons. program devel. Coffyville (Kans.) Meml. Hosp., 1984; chmn. hosp. safety com. Claremore Regional Hosp., 1992; mem. mgmt. coun. U. Mo. Hosp. and Clinics, Columbia, 1987-88. Active Spl. Olympics, Alamosa, Colo., 1977. Mem. Am. Occupational Therapy Assn. Democrat. Methodist. Home: HCR 3 Box 1137 Rocky Mount MO 65072

MCDOWELL, RUTH BECKLEY, artist; b. Washington, June 8, 1945; d. Lawrence Edward and Ruth Wilma (Manuel) Beckley; m. George Q. McDowell, June 18, 1966 (div. Nov. 1982); children: Emily Jane, Leah Elizabeth. BS in Art and Design, MIT, 1967. Author: Pattern on Pattern, 1991, Symmetry: A Design System for Quiltmakers, 1994; quilt commd. for New Eng. Quilt Mus., 1987. Mem. Quilter's Connection, Studio Art Quilt Assn., New Eng. Quilters Guild. Home and Office: 993 Main St Winchester MA 01890-1928

MCDOWELL, SUZANNE ROSS, publishing executive; b. Raleigh, N.C., Feb. 8, 1949; d. George R. Romulus Jr. and Suzanne (Perkins) Ross; m. Robert L. McDowell Jr., Aug. 27, 1971; children: Ashley Ross, Andrew Perkins. BA in Am. Studies, Smith Coll., 1971; JD with high honors, George Washington U., 1977. Bar: D.C. 1977. Law clk. to Judge Theodore Tannenwald Jr. U.S. Tax Ct., Washington, 1977-79; assoc. Steptoe & Johnson, Washington, 1979-83; assoc. tax. legis. counsel Office of Tax Policy, U.S. Dept. Treasury, Washington, 1983-87; counsel Ropes & Gray, Washington, 1987-90; assoc. counsel Nat. Geog. Soc., Washington, 1990-92, asst. v.p., dir. bus. affairs publs. and mktg., 1992—; speaker numerous seminars in field of exempt orgns. Fundraiser Smith Coll. and Beauvoir Sch., Washington; bd. dirs. Nat. Capital Poison Ctr., Washington. Mem. ABA (cochair subcom. unrelated bus. income taxes, exempt orgns. com. sect. taxation), D.C. Bar (div. taxation steering com., tax policy com., chair exempt orgn. com., Best Com. award 1992). Office: Nat Geog Soc 1145 17th St NW Washington DC 20036-4701

MCEACHERN-CORBETT, SUSAN MARY, financial analyst; b. Royal Oak, Mich., May 3, 1960; d. Donald Keith and Lois Jean (Robison) McE.; m. James Paul Corbett, Jan. 8, 1983. BS, Mich. State U., 1982; MBA, New Mex. State U., 1985. From acct. adminstr. trainee to acct. adminstr. IBM, El Paso, Tex., 1985-89; customer support rep. IBM, Southfield, Mich., 1989-90; sr. adminstrv. specialist IBM, Southfield, 1991-92, adv. customer support rep., 1992-93; fin. analyst IBM, Boulder, Colo., 1993—; cons. Integrated Sys. Solutions Co., Dallas, 1990-93. Author: Treasury of Poetry, 1992. Vol. supr. Easter Seals, Southfield Mich., El Paso, Tex., 1978-88, Crisis Pregnancy, Las Cruces, New Mex., 1982-86, Multiple Sclerosis, Mich., 1983, Longmont (Colo.) Vol. Assn., 1994. Recipient Photography award Mich. State Fair, 1991, 92. Mem. IBM PC Club, Creative Designs (pres. 1994—, Nat. Sci. and Engring. vol. rep. 1994). Home: 1736 Collyer St Longmont CO 80501-2008

MCELHINNEY, SUSAN KAY (KATE MCELHINNEY), legal assistant; b. Greeley, Colo., May 20, 1947; d. Glenn Eugene and Maxine (Filkins) McE. Student, U. N.C., 1965-67, U. Kans., 1969, U. Colo., 1971-72, 80. Adminstrv. sec. Colo. Pub. Defender, Denver, 1970-74; clk. Colo. Dist. Ct., Boulder, 1974-80; legal asst., office mgr. Law Office Ben Echeverria, San Marcos, Calif., 1986—. Mem. black tie fund raising com. Palomar Community Coll., 1991-92. Democrat. Office: Law Offices Ben Echeverria 1350 Grand Ave # 200 San Marcos CA 92069-2640

MCELHINNY, TARA LYNN ISBAN, nurse; b. McConnellsburg, Pa., Aug. 11, 1970; d. Henry P. and Linda (Walters) I. ADN, Harrisburg Area C.C., 1991; BS in Edn., California U. Pa., 1992, MEd, 1993. RN, Pa.; cert. ACLS Am. Heart Assn. Staff nurse Fulton County Med. Ctr., McConnellsburg, 1991—, Uniontown (Pa.) Hosp., 1992—; sch. nurse Tuscarora Sch. Dist., 1993; coord. health svcs. Westmoreland Intermediate Unit, 1994; instr. lifeguarding ARC, McConnellsburg, 1988—; instr., trainer BLS Am. Heart Assn., McConnellsburg, 1989—; instr. karate. Inst. first aid ARC, 1993; instr. Pride Parent to Parent Program, 1993, Early Childhood STEP Program, 1993. Home: 124 River View Dr White Oak PA 15131

MCELROY, ABBY LUCILLE WOLMAN, financial consultant; b. Washington, Oct. 16, 1957; d. M. Gordon and Elaine (Mielke) Wolman; m. Peter J. McElroy, Mar. 15, 1986; 1 child, Abel Hurst. BA, St. Lawrence U., 1979; MS, Ind. U., 1981. Account mgr. U.S. Lines, Norwalk, Conn., 1984-86; fin. cons. Smith Barney, Westport, Conn., 1986—. Lacrosse coach Wilton High Sch., Wilton, Conn., 1988-89. Recipient Tom & Ruth Rivers Scholarship award World Leisure & Recreation Assn., Can., 1981; London Group Study Exch. grantee Rotary Internat., 1989. Mem. Fairfield Network Exec. Women (treas. 1989—), Bridgeport Bus. Coun., Women's Lacrosse Assn. (treas. 1983-84), Am. Assn. for Fitness in Bus. and Industry (state rep. 1982-83). Office: Smith Barney 1 Village Sq Westport CT 06880-3211

MCELROY, CHARLOTTE ANN, principal; b. Dimmitt, Tex., Oct. 24, 1939; d. William Robert and Mary Ilene (Cooper) McE. BA, West Tex. State U., 1962, MEd, 1964; postgrad., Calif. State U., Santa Barbara, 1966-68. Tchr. Amarillo (Tex.) Schs., 1962-65; 1st and 2d grade tchr. Ventura (Calif.) Schs., 1965-66, 4th, 5th and 6th grade tchr., 1966-74, elem. counselor, 1974-76, spl. edn. tchr., 1976-77, counselor, phys. edn. tchr., 1977-78; asst. prin. Cabrillo Jr. High Sch., Ventura Unified Schs., 1978-80; prin. E. P. Foster Elem. Sch., Ventura Unified Schs., 1980-84, Anacapa Middle Sch., Ventura Unified Schs., 1984—; presenter in field. Recipient Nat. Blue Ribbon Sch. award Nat. Edn. Dept., 1990-91, Calif. Disting. Sch. award, 1989-90; named one of Outstanding Principals, State Calif., 1992-93. Mem. Ventura Adminstrs. Assn., Calif. League Middle Schs., Assn. Calif. Sch. Adminstrs., Kappa Kappa Gamma. Democrat. Home: 2250 Los Encinos Rd Ojai CA 93023-9709 Office: Anacapa Middle Sch 100 S Mills Rd Ventura CA 93003-3487

MCELROY, JANICE HELEN, government agency executive; b. Topeka, Kans., Dec. 12, 1937; d. Rudolph Ralph and Josephine Elizabeth (Kern) Jilka; m. James Douglas McElroy, June 25, 1967; children: Helen Elizabeth, Bryan Douglas. BS cum laude, Colo. Coll., Colorado Springs, 1960; MAT, Johns Hopkins U., 1964; PhD, U.S. Internat. U., San Diego, 1970. Biology tchr. Roland Park Country Day Sch., Balt., 1962-63, Edmundston High Sch., Balt., 1964; chmn. dept. sci. Bishop's Sch., La Jolla, Calif., 1964-69; instr. Somerset County Community Coll., Somerville, N.J., 1973-75, Cedar Crest Coll., Allentown, Pa., 1976-82; dir. re-entry program Cedar Crest Coll., 1979-82; exec. dir. Resource Devel. Svcs., Allentown, 1982-86; dir. planning and devel. Montgomery County Community Coll., Blue, Pa., 1986-88; exec. dir. Pa. Commn. for Women, Harrisburg, 1988—. Research dir./editor: Our Hidden Heritage: Pennsylvania Women in History, 1983; contbr. articles to profl. jours. Mem. Women's Adv. Bd. Task Force, Lehigh County, Pa., 1981-82, Nat. Child Care Adv. Coun.; chair Gov.'s Conf. on Responses to

Workforce 2000, 1990; lay corp. mem. Pa. Blueshield, 1992; alt. del. Dem. Nat. Conv., 1992; elder, trustee, commr. Presbyn. Ch.; mem. bd. dirs. Women's Pol. Network Pa., 1988—, Pa. Coalition Adult Literacy, 1989—. Fulbright scholar, 1960; Ford Found. fellow, 1963; NSF fellow, 1965. Mem. AAUW (pres. Pa. divsn. 1984-88, nat. bd. dirs. 1989-93), Nat. Assn. Commns. for Women (nat. bd. dirs. 1991-93), LWV, Delta Epsilon, Phi Beta Kappa, Alpha Lambda Delta, Kappa Kappa Gamma. Home: 2826 Crest Ave N Allentown PA 18104-6106 Office: Pa Commn for Women 209 Finance Bldg Harrisburg PA 17120

MCELROY, JUNE PATRICIA, sales consultant; b. Atlantic City, Sept. 26, 1929; d. Edmund N. and Dorothy R. (McDowell) Ricchezza; m. David Waycott Carson, Apr. 8, 1947 (div. 1954); m. Ottavio Gelmi, Dec. 16, 1954 (div. 1964); 1 child, Alessandra; m. Robert Joseph McElroy, Oct. 16, 1970 (dec. May 1974). Student Temple U., 1947-48, Inst. linguistics, Georgetown U., 1951-53. Mem. staff Am. consulate gen., Milan, Italy, 1954; legis. asst. U.S. Senate, Washington, 1956; social sec. to ambassador of Finland, Washington, 1958; legis. asst. to congressman, Washington, 1960-65; sr. assoc. Gillmore M. Perry Co., Washington, 1965-76; sales exec./cons. furniture industry, Hilton Head, S.C., 1985-87; ptnr. Mfrs. Representatives Internat., 1987—. Mem. Georgetown U. Alumni Assn., John Carroll Soc. Republican. Roman Catholic. Club: Army Navy (Washington). Home: 4000 Cathedral Ave NW Washington DC 20016

MCELROY, MARY KAYE, art educator; b. Oklahoma City, July 5, 1945; d. George Hamilton McElroy and Lelah Beatruce (Clow) Sparks. BA in Humanities, Okla. State U., 1968; MEd in Art, U. Ctrl. Okla., 1973; MFA, Sch. of Art Inst. of Chgo., 1986. Artist in residence Okla. State Arts Coun., Oklahoma City, 1978; teaching asst. Sch. of Art Inst. of Chgo., 1986; art instr. City Arts, Oklahoma City, 1989-91, 92-93, Rose State Coll., Midwest City, Okla., 1988-94, U. Ctrl. Okla., Edmond, 1988-94; bd. dirs. Individual Artists of Okla., Oklahoma City, FlyCatcher Coop., Oklahoma City; judge Okla. Jr. Art Exhibit, Oklahoma City, Okla. Summer Art Inst., various art festivals in Okla.; tchr. Sch. of Art Inst. of Chgo. Mem. com. Festival of the Women, First Unitarian Ch., Oklahoma City, 1993; vol. stage hand Carpenter Sq. Theater, Oklahoma City, 1991; block capt. Cancer Dr., Oklahoma City, 1993. Mem. AAUW, Okla. Art Edn. Assn., Oklahoma City Art Mus., Okla. Visual Arts Coalition, U. Ctrl. Okla. Women's Club.

MCENTIRE, REBA N., country singer; b. McAlester, Okla., Mar. 28, 1955; d. Clark Vincent and Jacqueline (Smith) McE.; m. Narvel Blackstock, 1989; 1 child, Shelby Steven McEntire Blackstock. Student elem. edn., music, Southeastern State U., Durant, Okla., 1976. Rec. artist Mercury Records, 1978-83, MCA Records, 1984—. Albums include Whoever's in New England (Gold award), 1986, What Am I Gonna Do About You (Gold award), 1987, Greatest Hits (Gold award, Platinum award, U.S., Can.), 1987, Merry Christmas To You, 1987, The Last One To Know (Gold award), 1988, Reba (Gold award 1988), Sweet 16 (Gold award 1989, U.S.), Rumor Has It (Gold award 1991, Platinum award 1992, Double Platinum 1992), Reba Live (Gold award 1990, Gold award 1991, Platinum award 1991), For My Broken Heart, 1991, Forever in Your Eyes, 1992, It's Your Call, 1992, Read My Mind, 1994, Reba compilation video (Gold award, Platinum award 1992); author: (with Tom Carter) Reba: My Story, 1994. Spokesperson Middle Tenn. United Way, 1988, Nat. and State 4-H Alumni, Bob Hope's Hope for a Drug Free Am.; Nat. spokesperson Am. Lung Assn., 1990-91. Recipient numerous awards in Country music including Disting. Alumni award Southeastern State U., Female vocalist award Country Music Assn., 1984, 85, 86, 87, Grammy award for Best Country Vocal Performance, 1987, 2 Grammy nominations, 1994, Grammy award, Best Country Vocal Collaboration for "Does He Love You" with Linda Davis, 1994, Entertainer of Yr. award Country Radio Awards, 1994, Female Vocalist award, 1994; named Entertainer of Yr., Country Music Assn., 1986, Female Vocalist of Yr. Acad. Country Music, 1984, 85, 86, 87, 92, Top Female Vocalist, 1991, Am. Music award favorite female country singer, 1988, 90, 91, 92, 93, Am. Music award, 1989, 90, 91, 92, Best Album, 1991, Favorite Female Vocalist, 1994, Favorite Female Vocalist, Peoples Choice Award, 1992, Favorite Female Country Vocalist, 1992, 93, Favorite Female Vocalist, TNN Viewer's Choice Awards, 1993, Favorite Female Country Artist, Billboard, 1994. Mem. Country Music Assn., Acad. County Music, Nat. Acad. Rec. Arts and Scis., Grand Ol' Opry, AFTRA, Nashville Songwriters Assn. Inc. *

MCEVOY, NAN TUCKER, publishing company executive; b. San Mateo, Calif., July 15, 1919; d. Nion R. and Phyllis (de Young) Tucker; m. Dennis McEvoy, 1948 (div.); 1 child, Nion Tucker. Student, Georgetown U., 1975. Reporter San Francisco Chronicle, 1944-46, N.Y. Herald-Tribune, N.Y.C., 1946-47, Washington Post, 1947-48; pub. rels. rep. John Homes, Inc., Washington, 1959-60; spl. asst. to dir. Peace Corps, Washington, 1961-64; mem. U.S. del. UNESCO, Washington, 1964-65; dir. Population Coun., Washington, 1965-70; co-founder, dep. dir. Preterm, Inc., Washington, 1970-74; chmn. bd. The Chronicle Pub. Co., San Francisco, 1975—. Bd. overseers U. Calif., San Francisco, 1990-93; mem. U. Calif.-San Francisco Found., 1993—; mem. Am. Art Forum, Washington; commr. Nat. Mus. Am. Art, Washington; mem. nat. bd. Smithsonian Instn., Washington, 1994—; mem. Brookings Coun., Brookings Instn., Washington, 1994—. Named Woman of Yr., Washingtonian mag., 1973. Mem. World Affairs Coun., Villa Taverna, Burlingame Country Club (Calif.), River Club, Commonwealth Club Calif. Office: The Chronicle Pub Co 901 Mission St San Francisco CA 94103

MCEVOY, SHARLENE ANN, business law educator; b. Derby, Conn., July 6, 1950; d. Peter Henry Jr. and Madaline Elizabeth (McCabe) McE. BA magna cum laude, Albertus Magnus Coll., 1972; JD, U. Conn., West Hartford, 1975; MA, Trinity Coll., Hartford, 1980, UCLA, 1982; PhD, UCLA, 1985. Bar: Conn., 1975. Pvt. practice Derby, 1984—; asst. prof. bus. law Fairfield (Conn.) U. Sch. Bus., 1986—; adj. prof. bus. law, polit. sci. Albertus Magnus Coll., New Haven, Conn., 1978-80, U. Conn., Stamford, 1984-86; acting chmn. polit. sci. dept. Albertus Magnus Coll., 1980; assoc. prof. law Fairfield U., 1992—; Chmn. Women's Resource Ctr., Fairfield U., 1989-91. Staff editor Jour. Legal Studies Edn., 1989—; reviewer Am. Bus. Law Assn. jour., 1988—; contbr. articles to profl. jours. Mem. Derby Tercentennial Commn., Derby, 1973-74; bd. dirs. Valley Transit Dist., Derby, 1975-77, Justice of Peace, City of Derby, 1975-83; alt. mem. Parks and Recreation Commn., Woodbury, 1995—. Recipient rsch. grant Fairfield U., 1989, 91, 92, Best Paper award N.E. Regional Bus. Law Assn., 1990, Best Paper award Tri-State Regional Bus. Law Assn., 1991. Mem. ABA, Conn. Bar Assn., Am. Bus. Law Assn., Assn. of Trial Lawyers of Am., Acad. Legal Studies in Bus. (coord. SINISTRAL spl. interest group 1977—). Democrat. Roman Catholic. Office: Sharlene A McEvoy Atty at Law 198 Emmett Ave Derby CT 06418-1258

MCFADDEN, BRENDA MAXINE, field services supervisor; b. Owensboro, Ky., July 24, 1957; d. James Herbert and Emily Maxine (Whitaker) McF. BA in Govt. and History, Western Ky. U., 1979. Pers. clk. Owensboro (Ky.) Davies County Hosp., 1979; casework specialist Ky. Cabinet Human Resources, Dept. Social Ins., Owensboro, 1979-90, casework prin., 1990, field svcs. supr., 1990—. Democrat. Baptist. Home: 783 Berwyn Ave Owensboro KY 42301-8321 Office: Ky Cabinet Human Resources Dept Social Ins 311 W 2nd St Owensboro KY 42301

MCFADDEN, LUCY-ANN ADAMS, planetary scientist; b. N.Y.C., May 23, 1952; d. Louis Ettlinger and Ruth Enright Neilson; m. Gregory Smith McFadden, Dec. 15, 1982; children: Whitney Carroll, Katherine Smith. BA, Hampshire Coll., 1974; MS, MIT, 1977; PhD, U. Hawaii, 1983. Research asst. dept. geography U. Md./NASA Goddard Space Flight Ctr., Greenbelt, 1983-84; research assoc. astronomy prog. U. Md., College Park, 1984-86; asst. research scientist U. Md., 1986-87, Calif. Space Inst., UCSD, LaJolla, 1987—. Contbr. articles to profl. jours. Mem. AAAS, Am. Astron. Soc. (nominating com. 1986-88), Am. Geophys. Union, Meteoritical Soc. Office: U Calif San Diego Calif Space Inst A016 2274 Sverdrup Hall La Jolla CA 92093-0216

MCFADDEN, MARY JOSEPHINE, fashion industry executive; b. N.Y.C., Oct. 1, 1938; d. Alexander Bloomfield and Mary Josephine (Cutting) McF.; m. Philip Harari; 1 child, Justine. Ed., Sorbonne, Paris, France, Traphagen Sch. Design, 1957, Columbia, 1959-62; DFA, Internat. Fine Arts Coll., 1984. Pub. relations dir. Christian Dior, N.Y.C., 1962-64; merchandising editor Vogue South Africa, 1964-65, editor, 1965-69; polit. and travel columnist Rand (South Africa) Daily Mail, 1965-68; founder sculptural workshop Vukutu, Rhodesia, 1968-70; spl. projects editor Vogue U.S.A., 1973; pres. Mary McFadden, Inc., N.Y.C., 1976—; ptnr. MMcF Collection by Mary McFadden, 1991—; bd. dirs., advisor Sch. Design and Merchandising Kent State U., Eugene O'Neill Meml. Theatre Ctr.; mem. profl. com. Cooper-Hewitt Mus., Smithsonian Inst., Nat. Mus. of Design. Fashion and jewelry designer, 1973—. Advisor Nat. Endowment for Arts. Recipient Am. Fashion Critics award-Coty award, 1976, 78, 79, Audemars Piguet Fashion award, 1976, Rex award, 1977, award More Coll. Art, 1977, Pa. Gov.'s award, 1977, Roscoe award, 1978, Pres.'s Fellows award RISD, 1979, Neiman-Marcus award of excellence, 1979, Design Excellence award Pratt Inst., 1993, award N.Y. Landmarks Conservancy, 1994; named to Fashion Hall of Fame, 1979; fellow RISD. Mem. Fashion Group, Coun. Fashion Designers Am. (pres., past bd. dirs.). Office: Mary McFadden Inc 240 W 35th St Fl 17 New York NY 10001-2506

MCFADDEN, MILLIDENE KATHLEEN, nurse educator; b. Alburtis, Pa., Mar. 3, 1925; d. Fred A. and Helen Daisy (Heintzelman) Grim; m. Robert John McFadden, June 19, 1948; children: Robert William, James Patrick. RN with honors, St. Lukes Hosp. Sch. Nursing, 1948; BS, Kutztown (Pa.) State Coll., 1963; MS, East Stroudsburg (Pa.) U., 1984; NP, U. Pa., 1987. NP, Pa. Project assoc. Pa. Dept. Health, Reading; exec. dir. Am. Cancer Soc., Lansford, Pa.; sch. NP Pleasant Valley Sch. Dist., Brodheadsville, Pa. Recipient Citation, Pa. Dept. Health. Mem. Monroe County Sch. Nurse Practitioners of Pa. (rep.), Lioness (bd. dirs. western Pocono chpt. 1990-92).

MCFARLAND, JANE ELIZABETH, librarian; b. Athens, Tenn., June 22, 1937; d. John Homer and Martha Virginia (Large) McFarland. AB, Smith Coll., 1959; M in Divinity, Yale U., 1963; MS in LS, U. N.C., 1971. Tchr. hist. and religion Northfield Schs., Mass., 1961-62; head librarian reference and circulation Yale Divinity Library, New Haven, Conn., 1963-71; head librarian Bradford (Mass.) Coll., 1972-77; reference librarian U. Tenn., Chattanooga, Tenn., 1977-80; head librarian reference dept Chattanooga-Hamilton County Bicentennial Library, Tenn., 1980-86, acting dir., 1986, dir., 1986—. Mem. Chattanooga Library Assn., Tenn. Library Assn., Southeastern Library Assn., Am. Library Assn., Phi Beta Kappa (treas. 1987, 88). Democrat. Roman Catholic. Home: 1701 Estrellita Cir Chattanooga TN 37421-5754 Office: Chattanooga-Hamilton County Libr 1001 Broad St Chattanooga TN 37402-2620

MCFARLAND, JANET CHAPIN, consulting company executive; b. New Castle, Pa., Jan. 5, 1962; d. Robert Chapin McFarland and Dorothy Jean (Heade) Jost. BS in Imaging Sci. and Engring., Rochester Inst. Tech., 1985; MBA in Innovation Mgmt. and Mktg., Syracuse U., 1990. Rsch. engr. Shipley Co., Inc., Newton, Mass., 1985-88; mktg. cons. Syracuse (N.Y.) U. Sch. Mgmt., 1988-90; market rsch. coop. AT&T Consumer Comms. Svcs., Basking Ridge, N.J., summer 1989; tech. analyst DynCorp Meridian, Alexandria, Va., 1991-93; dir. studies and analysis Tech. Strategies & Alliances, Burke, Va., 1993-94; pres. ArBar, Inc., Alexandria, Va., 1994—; presenter in field. Mem. Internat. Soc. Optical Engrs., Soc. Mfg. Engrs. (chpt. chair 1995), Beta Gamma Sigma, Alpha Mu Alpha. Office: ArBar Inc 824 S Pitt St Alexandria VA 22314

MCFARLAND, JENNIFER LIGHT, accountant; b. Okla. City, Feb. 21, 1958; d. John Wesley and Grace Elise (Harkins) Light; m. Jay Jon McFarland, Aug. 9, 1980; children: Jessica Elise, Jacqueline Jayne, Jacob Jay, Joanna Grace. BSBA, Okla. State U., 1980. CPA, Mont., Okla. Acct. Anadarko Prodn. Co., Houston, 1982-84; prin. Jennifer L. McFarland, CPA, Spring, Tex., 1984-86; supr. internat. acctg. Kerr-McGee Corp., Oklahoma City, 1986-91; dir. fin. svcs. Starkey Inc., Wichita, 1991—. Mem. AICPA, Okla. Soc. CPA's, Kans. Soc. CPA's, Okla. Heritage Assn., Okla. 1989er's Soc., P.E.O. Republican. Presbyterian. Home: 925 Honeybrook Ln Derby KS 67037-3621

MCFARLAND, KAY ELEANOR, state supreme court justice; b. Coffeyville, Kans., July 20, 1935; d. Kenneth W. and Margaret E. (Thrall) McF. BA magna cum laude, Washburn U., Topeka, 1957, JD, 1964. Bar: Kans. 1964. Sole practice Topeka, 1964-71; probate and juvenile judge Shawnee County, Topeka, 1971-73; dist. judge Topeka, 1973-77; assoc. justice Kans. Supreme Ct., 1977—. Mem. Kans. Bar Assn., Irish Wolfhound Clubs of Eng., Ireland and Am. Office: Kans Supreme Ct Kans Jud Ctr 301 W 10th St Topeka KS 66612*

MCFARLAND, KAY FLOWERS, medical educator; b. Daytona Beach, Fla., Jan. 27, 1942; d. Ernest Clyde and Sarah Elizabeth (Holder) Flowers; m. Dee Edward McFarland, Aug. 18, 1963; children: Grace, Joy, Eric, Sarah. BS, Wake Forest Coll., 1963; MD, Bowman Gray Sch. Medicine, 1966. Diplomate Am. Bd. Internal Medicine, Am. Bd. Endocrinology. Intern N.C. Bapt. Hosp., Winston-Salem; resident medicine Cleve. Clinic; fellow endocrinology Med. Coll. Ga., Augusta, from instr. to asst. prof. medicine, 1971-77; assoc. prof. to prof. ob-gyn. Sch. Medicine U. S.C., Columbia, 1977-86, prof. medicine Sch. Medicine, 1986—, assoc. dean continuing edn. Sch. Medicine, 1986-91. contbr. chpts. to books and articles to profl. jours. Fellow ACP; mem. Am. Diabetes Assn. (past pres. Augusta chpt., Profl. award 1975). Office: Univ S C Sch Medicine 2 Richland Medical Park Ste 506 Columbia SC 29203

MCFARLAND, LESLIE KING, special education educator; b. Canton, Ohio, July 13, 1954; d. John Edward and Nadine Mae (Phillips) King; m. James David McFarland, July 16, 1977. BS in Edn., Bowling Green State U., 1976. Cert. specific learning disabilities, spl. edn. tchr. K-12, developmentally handicapped spl. edn. tchr. K-12, elem. tchr. 1-8, Ohio. Tchr. developmentally handicapped Warren (Ohio) City Schs., 1976—; bd. dirs. McFarland and Son Funeral Svcs., Inc., v.p., 1992—. Mem. Fine Arts Coun. Trumbull County, 1988—; bd. dirs. Warren Dance Ctr., sec., 1988-90; bd. dirs. Warren Chamber Orch., 1986-92; mem. Trumbull County Women's History Com., 1993—; deacon 1st Presbyn. Ch., 1994. Mem. NEA, Ohio Edn. Assn., Warren Edn. Assn., AAUW (past sec.), Embroiderers' Guild Am. (Western Res. chpt., rep. to Fine Arts Coun. Trumbull County). Home: 197 Washington St NW Warren OH 44483

MCFARLAND, LYNNE VERNICE, pharmaceutical executive; b. San Antonio, Tex., June 3, 1953; d. Earle Clifford and Avis Marie (Jones) Olson; m. Marcus Joseph McFarland, July 27, 1975. BS in Microbiology, Portland State U., 1975, MS, 1980; PhD in Epidemiology, U. Wash., 1988. Pub. Health Cert. Rsch. asst. U. Oreg. Health Sci. Ctr., Portland, 1977-79, lab. supr., 1980-82; intern Wash. State Pub. Health Labs, Seattle, 1983; teaching asst. Dept. Epidemiology U. Wash., Seattle, 1984, rsch. asst., 1984-88, postdoctoral researcher Dept. Med. Chemistry, 1988, lectr. Dept. Med. Chemistry, 1988, rsch. asst. prof., 1991—; dir. scientific affairs Biocodex, Inc., Seattle, 1988—; reviewer McGraw-Hill Book Co., N.Y.C., 1982; editorial reviewer Ob-Gyn, L.A., 1989—, Jour. of Infect Diseases, 1991, Vet. Adminstrn., 1991; also review for gastroenterology and infectious diseases. Reviewer Gastroenterology; contbr. articles to profl. jours. Lobbyist environ. issues Wash. State Biotech. Assn., Seattle, 1990; vol. Literacy Plus, Seattle, 1990. Recipient Poncin scholarshp, Seafirst Bank, Seattle, 1985-88. Mem. Am. Soc. Microbiology, Soc. for Epidemiol. Rsch., Soc. Microbiol. Ecology and Diseases, Wash. Assn. of Epidemiology. Office: Biocodex Inc 1910 Fairview Ave E Ste 208 Seattle WA 98102-3697

MCFARLAND, MARY A., elementary/secondary school educator/administrator; b. St. Louis, Nov. 12, 1937; d. Allen and Maryann (Crawford) Mabry; m. Gerald McFarland, May 30, 1959. BS in Elem. Edn., S.E. Mo. State U., 1959; MA in Secondary Edn., Washington U., St. Louis, 1965; PhD in Curriculum and Instrn., St. Louis U., 1977. Cert. tchr. elem., secondary, supt., Mo. Elem. tchr. Berkeley Sch. Dist., St. Louis, 1959-64; secondary tchr. Parkway Sch. Dist., St. Louis, 1965-75, social studies coord. K-12, 1975—, dir. staff devel., 1984—; adj. prof. Maryville U., St. Louis, 1990—; cons. pvt. practice, Chesterfield, Mo. Co-author: (text series) The World Around Us, 1990, 3d rev. edit., 1995; contbr. articles to profl. jours. Nat. faculty Nat. Issues Forum, Dayton, Ohio; mem. ABA Spl. Com. on Youth Edn., Chgo. Mem. ASCD, Social Sci. Edn. Consortium, Nat. Coun. for Social Studies (pres. 1989-90), Mo. Coun. for Social Studies (pres. 1980-81). Democrat. Methodist. Office: Parkway Schs Dist Instrnl Svcs 12657 Fee Fee Rd Saint Louis MO 63146

MCFARLAND, NAOMI LOUISE, school system administrator; b. Chillicothe, Ohio, Feb. 19, 1947; d. William Harrison and Vera Marie (Hott) Smith; m. John Alfred Immell, Aug. 29, 1970 (div. 1974); 1 child, Jon; m. John Allen McFarland, July 10, 1976; children: Jamie, Lisa. Student, Ohio U., Chillicothe, 1965-66, Mata Coll., Columbus, Ohio, 1967. Supr. Reynolds Aluminum Co., Ashville, Ohio, 1970-77; bus driver Westfall Local Schs., Williamsport, Ohio, 1983-92, dir. transp., 1992—, tchr., 1985-93. Orgn. advisor 4-H Club, Circleville, Ohio, 1988-93. Recipient cert. of achievement Ohio Dept. Edn., 1991, safe driving award Franklin County Bd. Edn., 1992, 93. Mem. Ohio Assn. for Pupil Transp., Ohio Assn. Sch. Bus Ofcls. (chairperson Ohio Sch. Bus ROAD-E-O, ctrl. region). Methodist. Office: Westfall Local Schs 19463 Pherson Pike Williamsport OH 43164-9745

MCFARLAND-ESPOSITO, CARLA RAE, nursing executive; b. Cin., July 20, 1957; d. Jay Crawford McFarland and Stella (Herndon) O'Donnell; m. S. Esposito; 1 child, Jayson Vicenso Esposito. BSN, Ea. Ky. U., 1979. RN, Calif.; cert. pub. health nurse. Charge nurse St. Elizabeth Med. Ctr., Covington, Ky., 1980-82; traveling nurse various cities, 1983-86; nurse recruiter Med. Recruiters of Am., Culver City, Calif., 1987; nurse recruiter, liaison nurse, br. mgr. traveling nurse program NSI Svcs., Inc., Beverly Hills, Calif., 1987-90; dir. traveling nurse network, dir. nursing acute care Associated Health Profls. Inc., Culver City, 1990-91; dir. traveling profls., dir. bus. devel. NSI Svcs., Inc., Beverly Hills, 1991-92; clin. dir. ultra care and med. surg. units Westside Hosp., L.A., 1992-94, dir. admitting, dir. utilization rev., 1994—, mem. case mgmt. team, 1992—; mem. utilization rev. com. Associated Physicians of St. John's, 1994. Vol. pediatric assessments, immunizations Oscar Romera Clinic., L.A., 1991—. Mem. NAFE, AACN, Assn. Nurse Execs., Networking Orgn. Democrat. Home: 2567 Lee St Simi Valley CA 93065-3751 Office: Westside Hosp 910 S Fairfax Ave Los Angeles CA 90036-4499

MCFARLANE, BETH LUCETTA TROESTER, former mayor; b. Osterdock, Iowa, Mar. 9, 1918; d. Francis Charles and Ella Carrie (Moser) Troester; M. George Evert McFarlane, June 20, 1943 (dec. May 1972); children: Douglas, Steven (dec.), Susan, George. BA in Edn., U. No. Iowa, 1962, MA in Edn., 1971. Cert. tchr. Tchr. rural and elem. schs., Iowa, 1936-50, 55-56; elem. tchr. Oelwein Community Schs., Iowa, 1956-64, jr. high reading tchr., 1964-71, reading specialist, 1971-83; mayor of Oelwein, 1982-89; evaluator North Cen. Accreditation Assn. for Ednl. Programs; mem. planning team for confs. for Iowa Cities, N.E. Iowa, 1985; v.p. N.E. Iowa Regional Council for Econ. Devel., 1986-89; mem. Area Econ. Devel. Com. N.E. Iowa, 1985, Legis. Interim Study Com. on Rural Econ. Devel., 1987-88; mem. policy com. Iowa League Municipalities, 1987-88; bd. dirs. Oelwein Indsl. Devel. Corp., 1982-91, Oelwein Betterment Corp., 1982-94. V.p. Fayette County Tourism Council, 1987-88; Iowa State Steering Com. on Road Use Tax Financing, 1988-89; chmn. bd. govs. Oelwein Community Ctr, 1990-94; chmn. Reorganized LDS Ch. Bldg. and Fin. Com., 1980—, Dist. Ch. Fin. Com., 1992—, Dist. Ch. Revolving Loan Com., 1982—. Named Iowa Reading Tchr. of Yr., Internat. Reading Assn. Iowa, 1978; recipient Outstanding Contbrn. to Reading Council Activities award Internat. Reading Assn. N.E. Iowa, 1978, State of Iowa's Gov.s' Leadership award, 1988. Mem. N.E. Iowa Reading Council (pres. 1975-77), MacDowell Music and Arts Orgn. (pres. 1978-80), Oelwein Bus. and Profl. Women (Woman of Yr. 1983), Oelwein Area Ret. Sch. Pers. (pres. 1994—), Oelwein Area C. of C. (bd. dirs. 1986-89, Humanitarian award 1987), Delta Kappa Gamma (pres. 1980-82). Republican. Mem. Reorganized Ch. of Jesus Christ of Latter Day Saints. Avocations: hiking, refinishing antiques, gardening, jogging, creative sewing. Home: 512 7th Ave NE Oelwein IA 50662-1326

MC FARLANE, KAREN ELIZABETH, concert artists manager; b. St. Louis, Jan. 2, 1942; d. Nicholas and Bonita Margaret (Fults) Walz; m. Ralph Leo McFarlane, Nov. 30, 1968 (div.); children: Sarah Louise.; m. Walter Holtkamp, June 19, 1982. B.Mus.Ed. (Presser Music Found. scholar), Lindenwood Coll., 1964. Public sch. music tchr. St. Louis County, 1964-66; music asst. Riverside Ch., N.Y.C., 1966-70; dir. music St. Mark's Episc. Ch., San Marcos, Tex., 1971-73, Park Ave. Christian Ch., N.Y.C., 1974-81; also pres. Murtagh/McFarlane Artists, Inc., Cleve., 1976-88; pres. Karen McFarlane Artists, Cleve., 1989—. Mem. Am. Guild Organists, Nat. Assn. Performing Arts Mgrs. and Agts., Inc., Internat. Soc. Performing Arts Adminstrn. Republican. Presbyterian. Office: 12429 Cedar Rd Cleveland OH 44106-3172

MCFARLIN, DIANE H., newspaper editor; b. Lake Wales, Fla., July 10, 1954; d. Ruffie Denton Hooten and Anna Loraine (Peeples) Huff; m. Henry Briggs McFarlin, Aug. 28, 1976 (div. 1993). BS, U. Fla., 1976. Reporter Sarasota (Fla.) Jour., 1976-77, asst. news editor, 1977-78, city editor, 1978-82; asst. mng. editor Sarasota (Fla.) Herald Tribune, 1983-84, mng. editor, 1985-87; exec. editor Gainesville (Fla.) Sun, 1987-90, Sarasota Herald-Tribune, 1990—; mem. adv. bd. U. Fla. Coll. Journalism and Comm., 1987—. Mem. accrediting coun. Edn. in Journalism and Mass Comms., 1994—. Mem. Am. Soc. Newspaper Editors (com. chair 1992, 94, bd. dirs. 1994—), Fla. Soc. Newspaper Editors (sec.-treas. 1993, v.p. 1994, pres. 1995). Office: Sarasota Herald-Tribune 801 S Tamiami Trail Sarasota FL 34236

MC FATE, PATRICIA ANN, scientist, educator, foundation executive; b. Detroit, Mar. 19, 1936; d. John Earle and Mary Louise (Bliss) McF.; m. Sidney Norman Graybeal, Sept. 10, 1988. B.A. (Alumni scholar), Mich. State U., 1954; M.A., Northwestern U., 1956, Ph.D., 1965; M.A. (hon.), U. Pa., 1977. Assoc. prof. English, asst. dean liberal arts and scis. U. Ill., Chgo., 1967-74; assoc. prof. English, assoc. vice chancellor acad. affairs U. Ill., 1974-75; assoc. prof. folklore Faculty Arts and Scis., U. Pa., Phila., 1975-81; prof. tech. and soc. Coll. Engring. and Applied Sci., 1975-81, vice provost, 1975-78; dep. chmn. Nat. Endowment for Humanities, Washington, 1978-81; exec. v.p. Am.-Scandinavian Found., N.Y.C., 1981-82, pres., 1982-88; sr. scientist Sci. Applications Internat. Corp., Mc Lean, Va., 1988—, program dir. Ctr. for Nat. Security Negotiations, 1988—; cons. UN, 1994—; vis. assoc. prof. dept. medicine Rush U., Chgo., 1970-85; bd. dirs. CoreStates Bank, N.A., CoreStates Fin. Corp., Raoul Wallenberg Com. of U.S. Author: The Writings of James Stephens, 1979, Uncollected Prose of James Stephens, 1983; exec. producer Northern Stars, 1985, Diego Rivera: I Paint What I See, 1989; contbr. articles in fields of sci. policy and lit. to various jours. Bd. dirs. Inst. Cancer Rsch., Swedish Coun. Am. Decorated officer Order of Leopold II Belgium, comdr. Order Icelandic Falcon, comdr. Royal Order of Polar Star (Sweden), comdr. Order of Lion (Finland), comdr. Royal Norwegian Order Merit, Knight 1st class Royal Order Dannebrog (Denmark); U. Ill. Grad. Coll. faculty fellow, 1968; Swedish Bicentennial Fund grantee, 1981. Fellow N.Y. Acad. Scis.; mem. AAAS (chmn. com. on sci., engring. and pub. policy 1984-87, com. on sci. and internat. security 1976-79, 88-93), Coun. on Fgn. Rels., Acad. Scis. Phila. (founding mem., corr. sec. 1977-79), N.Y. Sci. Policy Assn., Am. Women for Internat. Understanding, Cosmpolitan Club (Phila.), Theta Alpha Phi, Omega Beta Pi, Delta Delta Delta. Office: Sci Applications Internat Corp 1710 Goodridge Dr Mc Lean VA 22102-3701

MCFAUL, PATRICIA LOUISE, editor; b. Jersey City, June 28, 1947; d. James Leo and Ethel Louise (Shea) McF.; 1 child, Jennifer Jeanne. Student Nassau Community Coll., 1969-70. Pub. info. officer L.I. Cath. Newspaper, Hempstead, N.Y., 1967-68, researcher, 1968-70, staff writer, 1970-73, copy editor, 1973-78, layout and copy editor, 1978—, advt. layout editor, 1989—; readership surveyor, Rockville Centre, N.Y., 1971, 75; mem., com. chmn. Diocesan Family Life Bd., Rockville Centre, 1978-82. Researcher: Mission to Latin America, 1976. Pres. Florence A. Smith Sch. PTA, Oceanside, N.Y., 1982-84, Oceanside High Sch. Marching Band Parents Assn., 1987-89; chmn. talented and gifted com. Oceanside Council PTAs, 1984-85; elem. tchr. aide, 1985—; mem., sec.-treas. L.I. Interfaith Council, Rockville Centre, 1977-80; band dir. search com. Oceanside Sch. Dist., 1988, art and music dir. search com., 1989. Recipient Citation, Diocese of Rockville Centre, 1984, 88. Mem. Cath. Press Assn. (U.S. and Can. citations 1985; mem. research com. 1975-80, mem., chmn. credentials and inspectors of elections com. 1976—, 1st place award design 1978, 86, citations 1980-85). Democrat. Roman Catholic. Avocations: flying, classical music. Home: 37 Rodney Pl Rockville Centre NY 11570-5823 Office: The LI Catholic 99 N Village Ave Rockville Centre NY 11570

MCGANN, BARBARA ELIZABETH, military officer; b. Newport, R.I., Sept. 27, 1946; d. John Henry and Rose Elizabeth (Hein) McG. BA in English, Coll. of Our Lady of Elms, 1969; MS in Mgmt., Salve Regina U., 1983; MA in Nat. Security Affairs, Georgetown U., 1987. Commd. officer USN, 1970, advanced through grades to rear admiral select, 1993; pub. affairs officer Tng. Air Wing ONE, Meridian, Miss., 1970-72; manpower anlayst Navy Recruiting Dist., Navy Recruiting Command, L.A., 1972-1974; surface warfare assignment officer Naval Mil. Pers. Command, Washington; manpower analyst Plans and Policy Directorate Joint Chiefs of Staff, Washington; exec. officer Navy Recruiting Dist. N.J.; manpower analyst Sec. of the Navy, Washington, 1983-85; staff of the comdr., sr. gen. unrestricted line officer Mil. Pers. Command, 1985-87; comdr. Naval Support Activity, Holy Loch, Scotland, 1987-89; staff, watch capt. Middle East crisis Office of Dep. Chief Naval Ops., 1989-90; exec. asst. to the commdr. Navey Recruiting Command, 1990-91; assumed command Navey Recruiting Area Eight, 1991-93; with strategic studies group Chief of Naval Ops., Naval War Coll., Newport, R.I., 1993—. Roman Catholic. Office: Naval War Coll SSG Naval Base Newport RI 02841

MCGAREY MADKOUR, MARY ELAINE BLISS, state legislator; b. Swanton, Vt., Apr. 12, 1927; d. Robert Porter Sr. and Edith Louise (Tuscany) Bliss; m. Walter Allen McGarey, Aug. 26, 1950 (dec. Aug. 1964); children: Pamela McGarey Murphy, Patricia McGarey Berard, Michael James; m. Joseph Louis Madkour, Dec. 29, 1966; 1 child, Carrie Madkour Major. Clk. typist Ctrl. Vt. Ry., St. Albans, Vt., 1945-46, 48-50; psychiat. aide Inst. Living, Hartford, Conn., 1946-47, 50—; asst. mgr. Jesse Welden Inn, St. Albans, 1947-48; real estate agt. Hoisington Realty, Bennington, Vt., 1985-92; mem. Vt. Ho. of Reps., Montpelier, 1992—. Bd. dirs. Vt. affiliate Am. Diabetes Assn., Burlington, 1982-88; town chmn. Vt. Green Up Day, Bennington, 1989; trustee Bennington Mus., 1975—; chmn. Bloodmobile canteen ARC, Bennington, 1980-86; mem. Southwestern Vt. Hosp. Aux., 1980—. Named Red Oak Homemaker, Red Oak (Iowa) C. of C., 1961. Mem. Southwestern Vt. Realtors Assn., Plain Dirt Gardeners (past pres.), Women's Fellowship (past pres.), Park McCullough Assn., Garden Club Am. (trustee, Pres. award 1992). Republican. Congregationalist. Home: 401 Jefferson Heights Bennington VT 05201 Office: Vt State Legislature State House State St Montpelier VT 05602

MCGARITY, MARGARET DEE, federal judge; b. 1948. BA, Emory U., 1969; JD, U. Wis., 1974. Bar: Wis. 1974. Pvt. practice, 1974-87; bankruptcy judge U.S. Dist. Ct. (ea. dist.) Wis., 1987—; lectr. on marital property, bankruptcy and family law Fed. Judicial Ctr., Nat. Conf. Bankruptcy Judges, State Bar Wis., Nat. Child Support Enforcement Assn., others. Co-author: Marital Property Law in Wisconsin, 2d edit. 1986, Collier Family Law and the Bankruptcy Code, 1991. Mem. Nat. Conf. Bankruptcy Judges, State Bar Wis. Office: 160 US Courthouse 517 E Wisconsin Ave Milwaukee WI 53202-4506

MCGARRY, MARCIA LANGSTON, community service coordinator; b. Washington, Dec. 9, 1941; d. Emil Sylvester and Bernice B. (Bland) Busey. BS, Morgan State U., 1964. Cert. tchr., law enforecment officer, Fla. Payroll clk., jr. acct. U.S. Dept. Labor, Washington, 1964-65; English tchr., Taiwan, 1968-70; tchr. Monroe County Sch. Bd., Key West, Fla., 1971-81; exec. dir. Monroe Assn. Retarded Citizens, Key West, 1977-79; dep. sheriff Monroe County Sheriff's Dept., Key West, 1979-83, 1986-90; probation/parole officer Fla. State Dept. Corrections, Key West, 1983-91; law enforcement instr. Fla. Keys C.C., 1983-91; cmty. svc. coord. City of Bradenton, 1991—. Active local polit. campaigns; co-founder day schs. for under-privileged children; former mem. Big Bros./Big Sisters Am., mem. com. 1985-86, former bd. dir., Spouse Abuse, former bd. dirs.; bd. dirs. Adv. Coun. Orange Elem., 1991-93; bd. dirs. mayor's com., chmn. task force Drug Free Communities, 1991-94; bd. dirs. Human Rels. Commn., 1991-93, Drug Free Schs. and Cmty. Adv. Coun., 1991—; former mem. adv. coun. Byrd Edn. Found., Sweet Adelines Internat., 1992-94, commr. 12th Jud. Nominating Commn. 1992-94, cons., facilitator Cultural Diversity Conflict Resolution Workshops, Manatee County High Schs. and Bradenton Police Dept.; attendance avd. com. Bayshore High, 1993, multicultural com., 1994, former rep. Women's Forum; former dir. Choir, Lutheran Ch.; founding mem. Comprehensive Neighborhood Support Network; mem. adv. bd. Manatee County Sheriff's Dept., 1994—. Recipient Appreciation cert. Lions Club, 1978, 79, Career Week award Harris Elem. Sch., 1981, Glynn Archer Elem. Sch., 1989. Mem. NAFE, Fla. Police Benevolent Assn., Fla. Women in Govt. (mem. Manatee County chpt.), Ecumanical Luth. Ch. of Am. (elected consultation con. Fla. Synod 1989), Key West Profls., Luth. Ch. Women, Delta Sigma Theta. Office: City of Bradenton Caller Svc 25015 Bradenton FL 34206

MCGARVEY, VIRGINIA CLAIRE LANCASTER, volunteer; b. Erie, Pa., Feb. 10, 1934; d. Walter Joseph and Clara Marguerite (Johannesen) Lancaster; m. Raymond Leroy McGarvey, Sept. 3, 1955; children: Keith Thomas, Emy Sue, Stephen Bruce. Cert., Thiel Coll., 1954; BS in Bus. Edn., U. Ill., 1957. Sec. P.A. Meyer & Sons, Erie, 1952, Thiel Coll., Greenville, 1953-55; sec. coord. placement office U. Ill., Champaign, 1955-59; tchr. adult edn. Champaign Sch. Dist., 1957-58; dir. Sarah A. Reed Retirement Ctr., Erie, 1972—, chmn., 1980-83, endowment treas., 1984—; dir. Meadow Brook Dairy Co., Erie, 1975-91; dir., treas. Erie County Hist. Soc., 1989-94; dir. Country Fair, Inc., Erie, 1975—. Mem. Harborcreek (Pa.) Zoning Bd.; chmn., supt. Wesley United Meth. Ch. Christian Edn., 1960-84, chmn. adminstrv. bd., 1987-93. Recipient Edward C. Doll Cmty. Svc. award, 1994. Mem. AAUW (pres. 1970-72, Woman of Yr. 1981), Greater Erie Young Men's Christian Assn. (dir. 1981—, pres. elect 1991-93, chmn. 1993—, bicentennial commr. 1994—, Woman of Yr. 1987). Republican. Home and Office: 5191 Jordan Rd Erie PA 16510-4617

MCGARY, BETTY WINSTEAD, minister, counselor, individual, marriage, and family therapist; b. Louisville, June 21, 1936; d. Philip Miller and Mary Jo (Winstead) McG.; married, 1960 (div. 1979); children: Thomas Edward, Mary Alyson, Andrew Philip Pearce. BS, Samford U., 1958; MA, So. Bapt. Theol. Sem., 1961; EdD, U. Louisville, 1988. Ordained to ministry Bapt. Ch., 1986; cert. secondary tchr., Ky., Ga.; lic. profl. counselor, marriage and family therapist, Tex. Min. to youth Broadway Bapt. Ch., Louisville, 1958-60; learning disability and behavior disorders specialist Jefferson County Schs., Muscogee Schs., Cobb County Schs., Louisville, Columbus, Ga., Atlanta, 1964-88; min. to adults South Main Bapt. Ch., Houston, 1986-90; assoc. pastor Calder Bapt. Ch., Beaumont, Tex., 1991—; marriage enrichment cons. Pastoral Inst., Columbus, 1973-76; co-founder and coord. Ctr. for Women in Ministry, Louisville, 1983-86, exec. bd. dirs., 1983-90; cons. Tex. Christian Life Commn., Ft. Worth, 1989-93; co-therapist pvt. practice, Houston, 1989—. Author: (with others) The New Has Come, 1988, A Costly Obedience: Sermons by Women of Steadfast Spirit, 1994; co-editor nat. newsletter Folio: A Newsletter for Southern Bapt. Women in Ministry, 1983-86. Vice-chairperson exec. bd. dirs. handicapped Boy Scouts Am., Houston, 1986-90. Recipient citation for Disting. Svc. So. Bapt. Theol. Sem., 1984, Dean's citation Outstanding Achievement U. Louisville, 1988. Mem. The Alliance of Bapts. (exec. bd. dirs. 1988-90, v.p. 1990-91), So. Bapt. Women in Ministry (pres. 1988-90), Bapt. Gen. Congress of Tex. (exec. bd. dirs.), Leadership Beaumont. Home: 2107 Bartlett St Houston TX 77098-5305 Office: Calder Bapt Ch 1005 N 11th St Beaumont TX 77702-1204

MCGAVIC, JUDY L., coal company official; b. Evansville, Ind., June 29, 1944; d. M. Galen and Helen L. (Sims) Barclay; m. Ronald R. McGavic, Aug. 22, 1962; 1 child, Michael D. Student, Ky. Wesleyan Coll., 1965-66, Murray (Ky.) State U., 1968, U. Ky., 1969; B of Liberal Arts, U. Evansville, 1994. Mine clk. Peabody Coal Co., Centertown, Ky., 1973-78, chief mine clk., 1978-81, sr. mine clk., 1981-86, panel technician, 1986, sr. coord. employee rels., 1987-88, employee rels. rep., 1988-92; sr. employee rels. rep. Peabody Coal Co., Lynnville, Ky., 1993—. Peabody Coal Co. campaign chmn. United Way, 1992, 93, also chmn. blood drive. Home: 7600 Edgedale Dr Newburgh IN 47630-3062 Office: Peabody Coal Co Lynnville Bus Unit PO Box 7 Lynnville IN 47619

MCGEADY, KATHLEEN BIRMINGHAM, grant administrator; b. Oceanside, N.Y., Aug. 27, 1949; d. James Joseph and Doris Martha (Fraser) Birmingham; m. Dennis J. McGeady, June 14, 1970; children: Kelly, Lauren. Student, Mercer County Community Coll., Mercer County Vocat. Tech. Sch, 1976-77. Office asst. Madison Square Garden, N.Y.C., 1967-69, PICA, N.Y.C., 1969-70; exec. sec. Pubs. Distbg. Corp., N.Y.C., 1970-74; program mgr. Princeton U.; mem. animal care com. Princeton U., 1974-90; grant adminstr. Law Sch. Admission Svcs., Newtown, Pa., 1990—. Vol. libr. Plainsboro Free Pub. Libr., 1982-86; co-dir. Plainsboro Founders Day, 1982-87; co-coord. Bicycling Portion Liberty to Liberty Triathlan, Plainsboro, 1983-86; founder, dir. Bookworm Five Mile Race, Plainsboro, 1984-85; elected councilman Plainsboro Town Coun., 1986-89, acting chmn., 1987-88, vice chmn., 1986-89, chmn., 1988-89; mem. Plainsboro-Cranbury Juvenile Conf. Com., 1988—, chmn. 1992—; vice chmn. Plainsboro Dem. Mcpl. Com., 1990-92; v.p. Plainsboro Dem. Club, 1991-92. Home: 50 Linden Ln Plainsboro NJ 08536-2521

MCGEADY, SISTER MARY ROSE, religious organization administrator, psychologist; b. Hazelton, Pa., June 28, 1928; d. Joseph James and Catherine Cecilia (Mundie) McG. BA in Sociology, Emmanuel Coll., 1955; MA in Clin. Psychology, Fordham U., 1961; DHL (hon.), St. John's U., Queens, N.Y., 1982, Coll. New Rochelle, N.Y., 1991, Fordham U., 1991, Niagara U., 1991, Coll. St. Rose, Albany, N.Y., 1991, DePaul U., 1991. Joined Daus. of Charity St. Vincent De Paul, Roman Cath. Ch., 1946. Dir. Astor Home Clinics, Rhinebeck, N.Y., 1961-66; exec. dir. Nazareth Child Care Ctr., Boston, 1966-71; dir. mental health Cath. Charities Bklyn., 1971-79, assoc. exec. dir., 1987-90; dir. Kennedy Child Study Ctr., N.Y.C., 1979-81; provincial supr. Daus. of Charity St. Vincent DePaul, Albany, 1981-87; pres., chief exec. officer Covenant House, N.Y.C., 1990—; bd. dirs. Cardinal Cooke Health Care Ctr., N.Y.C., Meninger Found., Kans., St. Michael's Coll., Vt., Ctr. for Human Devel., Washington. Author: Catholic Special Education, 1979. Mem. N.Y. State Mental Health Svcs. Coun., Albany, 1983-90, N.Y. State Mental Health Planning Coun., Albany, 1986-91, Cath. Charities USA, 1966—. Recipient svc. award N.Y.C. Dept. Mental Health, 1988, Encouragement award Cath. U. Am., 1991. Home: 75 Lewis Ave Brooklyn NY 11206-7097 Office: Covenant House 346 W 17th St New York NY 10011-5002

MCGEE, BARBARA, publishing executive; b. N.Y.C., Feb. 24, 1949; d. Adolph and Lena (Bicocchi) Marzoli; m. John McGee, June 6, 1970; 1 child, Brian. BS, Douglass Coll., New Brunswick, N.J., 1971; postgrad., Chubb Inst., Summit, N.J., 1983, Montclair (N.J.) State Coll.; cert., Small Bus. Assn., 1983. Subscription acctg. mgr. Newsweek, Inc., Livingston, N.J., 1979-81; mgr. order processing Newsweek, Inc., Mountain Lakes, N.J., 1981-90, dir. order processing svcs., 1991—. Mem. NAFE, Assn. for Work Process Improvement, Fulfillment Mgrs. Assn., Data Entry Mgrs. Assn., Computer Entry Sys. Users Assn., Recognition Equipment Inc., User Assn., Douglass Coll. Alumni Assn. Office: 333 Route 46 Mountain Lakes NJ 07046

MCGEE, BETSY CARR, career development consultant; b. Dallas, Feb. 17, 1927; d. Thomas Alaine and Nancy Kathryn (Colgin) Carr; children: Timothy Carr McGee, Nancy Ann McGee. BA in Speech Comm., Tex. Christian U., 1961, BFA in Theater History, 1961. Asst. dir. conferencing U. Denver, 1976-79, dir. continuing edn., 1979-82, dir. corp. rels., 1982—, dir. alumni career devel., 1989—; pres. The McGee Group, Littleton, Colo., 1985—; staff mem. Dick Bolles' What Color is Your Parachute? Workshop, 1994; career cons. to alumni U. Denver, 1982—; career cons. specializing in mid-life career changes and srs. in career transition. Author: Resource Guide for Successful Job Development, 1992. Vol. career cons. Forty Plus, State of Colo., various chs., others. Mem. Am. Assn. for Counseling and Devel., Western Coll. Placement Assn. Episcopalian. Office: The McGee Group 5866 S Lupine Dr Littleton CO 80123

MCGEE, DOROTHY DIANNE, nursing administrator; b. Baton Rouge, Nov. 13, 1951; d. Douglas S. Nurdin and Dorothy (Clyde) Lambeth; m. Jay W. McGee, July 7, 1987; children: Rachel, Matthew, Maxx, Sean. BSN, Northwestern State U., Natchitoches, La., 1973; postgrad., Tex. Women's U., 1977. RN, Tex.; cert. in obstet. ultrasound. Case mgr. infusion therapy Home Care Plus, Houston; mgr. home care infusion therapy Inst. Immunological Diseases, Houston; infusion therapy specialist Med. Innovations, Houston; dir. nurses CarePlus, Inc., Houston; DON Critical Care Am.; adminstr. Vanguard Healthcare, Vanguard Healthcare of Tex.; clin. cons. Menlow Care, 1990. Mem. ASPEN, INS, ANAC, Oncology Nursing Soc. Home: 3723 Linkview Dr Houston TX 77025-3515

MCGEE, DOROTHY HORTON, writer, historian; b. West Point, N.Y., Nov. 30, 1913; d. Hugh Henry and Dorothy (Brown) McG.; ed. Sch. of St. Mary, 1920-21, Green Vale Sch., 1921-28, Brearley Sch., 1928-29, Fermata Sch., 1929-31. Asst. historian Inc. Village of Roslyn (N.Y.), 1950-58; historian Inc. Village of Matinecock, 1966—. Author: Skipper Sandra, 1950; Sally Townsend, Patriot, 1952; The Boarding School Mystery, 1953; Famous Signers of the Declaration, 1955; Alexander Hamilton-New Yorker, 1957; Herbert Hoover: Engineer, Humanitarian, Statesman, 1959, rev. edit., 1965; The Pearl Pendant Mystery, 1960; Framers of the Constitution, 1968; author booklets, articles hist. and sailing subjects. Chmn., Oyster Bay Am. Bicentennial Revolution Commn., 1971—; historian Town of Oyster Bay, 1982—; mem. Nassau County Am. Revolution Bicentennial Commn.; hon. dir. The Friends of Raynham Hall, Inc.; treas. Family Welfare Assn. Nassau County, Inc., 1956-58; dir. Family Service Assn. Nassau County, 1958-69. Recipient Cert. of award for outstanding contbn. children's lit. N.Y. State Assn. Elem. Sch. Prins., 1959; award Nat. Soc. Children of Am. Revolution, 1960; award N.Y. Assn. Supervision and Curriculum Devel., 1961; hist. award Town of Oyster Bay, 1963; Cert. Theodore Roosevelt Assn., 1976. Fellow Soc. Am. Historians; mem. Soc. Preservation L.I. Antiquities (hon. dir.), Nat. Trust Hist. Preservation, N.Y. Geneal. and Biol. Soc. (dir., trustee), Oyster Bay Hist. Soc. (pres. 1971-75, chmn. 1975-79, trustee), Theodore Roosevelt Assn. (trustee), Townsend Soc. Am. (trustee). Republican. Address: Box 142 Locust Valley NY 11560

MCGEE, JACQUELINE T., state legislator; b. Hayti, Mo., Nov. 5, 1952; d. Augustus and Robbie (Williams) Townes; 1 child, Kevin Roshawn. BA, U. Mo., St. Louis; JD, U. Mo., Kansas City. With Mo. House of Reps., Jefferson City, 1986—; atty. pvt. practice, Kansas City, Mo., 1989-91, Wirken & King, Kansas City, Mo., 1991—; speaker in field. Bd. dirs. Children's Trust Fund; mem. Mo. Child Support Adv. Com., Assn. Coun. Children, United Way Met. Child Abuse Prevention Coalition, Assn. Children Enforcement Support, Heart Am. Family Svcs. (family tree), Jr. League Kansas City, NAACP (subscribing life mem.), Vineyard Neighborhood Assn., East Area Community Coalition. Recipient Avila Coll. Women's Leadership Inst. Excel award, 1988. Mem. ABA, Mo. Bar Assn., Kansas City Bar Assn., Jackson County Bar Assn., Assn. Women Lawyers, Mo. Assn. Trial Lawyers, Nat. Order Women Legislators, Nat. Conf. State Legislators, Nat. Black Caucus State Legislators, Mo. Legis. Black Caucus, Women's Polit. Caucus, Delta Theta Phi, U. Mo. Kansas City Law Found., U. Mo. Alumni Assn. Democrat. Baptist. Home: 4740 Grand Ave Kansas City MO 64112-2204 Office: Mo House of Reps State Capital # 403A Jefferson City MO 65101*

MCGEE, JANE MARIE, retired educator; b. Paducah, Ky., Nov. 3, 1926; d. William Penn and Mary Virginia (Martin) Roberts; m. Hugh Donald McGee, Oct. 11, 1946; children: Catherine Jane McGee Bouchard, Nancy Ann McGee McManus. BS in Elem. Edn., Murray State U., 1948; cert. in gifted edn., Nat. Coll. Edn., 1976. Tchr. Hazel (Ky.) Pub. Schs., 1948-49, Pittsford (Mich.) Pub. Schs., 1949-50, Leal Elem. Sch., Urbana, Ill., 1950-53, Cleveland Elem. Sch., Skokie, Ill., 1953-57; pvt. tutor, pre-sch. tchr., 1953-61; tchr. Woodland Park Elem. Sch., Deerfield, Ill., 1968-83; ret., 1983; beauty and skin care cons. Mary Kay Cosmetics, Gunnison, Colo., 1984—. Soprano Western State Coll. and Cmty. Chorus, Gunnison, 1986—, European concert tour, 1990. Mem. AAUW, Top o' the World Garden Club (sec. 1984—, winner first place at numerous garden club shows). Republican. Baptist. Home: 206 N Colorado St Gunnison CO 81230-2104

MCGEE, JULIA ANN, publishing company executive; b. Dallas, Nov. 2, 1942; d. C. Stanley and Josephine Elizabeth (Arledge) Clifton; m. G. William McGee, July 12, 1975 (div. 1979); children: Shelly Smith, Matthew Clemmer. BA with highest honors, U. Okla., 1964, MA, 1968. Tchr. Midland (Tex.) Pub. Schs., 1964-68, Lebanon (N.H.) Pub. Schs., 1969-71; tchr., dean women Detroit County Day Sch., Birmingham, Mich., 1971-75; tchr. Lyons Township High Sch., LaGrange, Ill., 1975-82; dir. ednl. tech. and product devel. World Book, Inc., Chgo., 1982-83; dir. product devel. and mktg. Tandy Corp., Oak Brook, Ill., 1983-86; account dir. Ligature, Inc., Chgo., 1986-88; editorial dir. McDougal, Littell & Co., Evanston, Ill., 1988-89, editor-in-chief, 1990-94, pres., 1991-94; v.p. Houghton Mifflin Co., 1994—, sr. exec. v.p., 1995—; pres. McDougal, Littell/Houghton Mifflin, 1994—; bd. dirs. DeVry Inc. Mem. vestry, chair budget com. St. Luke's Episc. Ch., 1992-95, warden, 1995—; diocesan del. Episc. Diocese Chgo., 1994—. Mem. Phi Beta Kappa, Alpha Phi. Democrat. Office: McDougal Littell/Houghton Mifflin 1560 Sherman Ave Evanston IL 60201

MCGEE, LYNNE KALAVSKY, principal; b. Jersey City, N.J., July 25, 1949; d. Michael V. and Ann (Fedowitz) K.; m. Thomas Robert, Aug. 12, 1972; children: Todd Michael, Ryan Thomas. BS, St. Francis Coll., Loretto, Pa., 1971; MEd, Seton Hall U., 1972; EDS, Fla. Atlantic U., 1978, EdD, 1986. Cert. tchr., Fla., Ill., prin., Fla. Asst. prin. for curriculum, math instr. Palm Beach County (Fla.) Bd. Edn., 1980-82, asst. prin. for student svcs., 1982-86, asst. prin. for adminstrn., 1986-91; prin. Belle Glade (Fla.) Elem. Sch., 1991-94, New Horizons Elem. Sch., West Palm Beach, Fla., 1994—; adj. prof. grad. Nova U., 1991—. Mem. Assn. Supervision and Curriculum Devel., Phi Kappa Phi. Office: New Horizons Elem Sch 13900 Greenbriar Blvd West Palm Beach FL 33414

MCGEE, MARY ALICE, health science research administrator; b. Winston-Salem, N.C., Oct. 14, 1950; d. C.L. Jr. and Mary Hilda (Shelton) McG. AB, Meredith Coll., 1972. Tchr. Augusta (Ga.) Schs., 1972-73; specialist grants Med. Sch. Brown U., Providence, R.I., 1974-76; profl. basketball player, 1975-76; dir. research adminstn. Med. Sch. Brown U., Providence, 1976—. Bd. dirs. Sojourner House, Providence, 1983—, v.p., 1986, 91, treas. 1987-89. Mem. Soc. Rsch. Adminstrs., Nat. Coun. U. Rsch. Adminstrs., R.I. Assn. Women in Edn. Home: 121 Plain St Rehoboth MA 02769-2513 Office: Brown U Med Sch Box G A322 Providence RI 02912

MCGEE, PATRICIA K., state legislator; m. Mike McGee, 1960; forster children: Ann, Carol, Norma. BA with honors, Alfred State Coll. Asst. to the dean Jamestown C.C., Cattaraugus, N.Y.; mem. N.Y. State Assembly, vice chmn. minority joint conf. com., ranking minority mem. assembly higher edn. com., assembly intern com., ranking minority mem. assembly transportation com., mem. assembly standing com. on environ. conservation and higher edn. com., appointed asst. minority wip.; mem. legis. commn. on Hazardous and Toxic Waste and Rural Resources Commn.; rep. task force mem. on Econ. Devel. and the Future of SUNY; guest speaker Chautauqua Inst. Mem. 219 Liaison Com., Farm Bur., Portville Parent Tchr Assn., Cattaraugus County Tourist Bur. Mem. Am. Legis. Exchange Coun., Nat. Conf. State of State Legis., Nat. Order of Women Legis., N.Y. State Fire Safety Consortium, VFW, Am. Legion, Disabled Am. Vets. Home: 20 Green St Franklinville NY 14737-1045 Office: NY State Assembly State Capitol Albany NY 12224*

MCGEHEE, JACKIE SUE SEAY, concert pianist, educator; b. Winters, Tex., Dec. 26, 1931; d. Andrew Jackson and Denzil Nadine (Barnhill) Seay; m. Cleo Everett McGehee, Jr., July 29, 1949; children: C.L. (dec.), Meredith. BMus summa cum laude, U. Albuquerque, 1977; MMus, N.Mex. State U., 1979. Cert. profl. master. Profl. concert pianist; owner/tchr. pvt. music studio various locations, 1957—; music instr. Midland (Tex.) Pub. Schs., 1964-66, El Paso (Tex.) Pub. Schs., 1967-69; assoc. prof. music U. Albuquerque, 1975-77; adj. prof. Mesa Coll., Grand Junction, Colo., 1979-81; edn./arts liaison N.Mex. Music Tchrs., Albuquerque, 1984-93; presenter piano workshops Billings, Mont., Music Tchrs. Assn., 1981, Cheyene, Mont., 1981, Grand Junction, Mont., 1982, Albuqurque, N.Mex., 1983, 1985, 92, Santa Fe, N.Mex., 1985, Roswell, N.Mex., 1988; performer numerous recitals; lectr. in field. Performer Internat. Music Workshop, Hawaii, 1981, Exeter, Eng., 1987; piano debut N.Mex. state U., Las Cruces, 1978; author (newsletter) Symphony Guild, 1991-93; contbr. to profl. jours. Young people's dir. Santa Fe (N.Mex.) Opera, 1972-73, vol. Opera Gala Com., 1991-93; pres. Southwest Opera, 1975-76; chair summer concerts El Paso Symphony, 1980. Recipient Women of the Yr. award El Paso, Tex., 1970. Mem. N.Mex. Symphony Guild (young artists chair 1992-95, edn. v.p. 1982-93, sec. 1974), El Paso Opera Assn., Am. Coll. Musicians, Nat. Guild Pianist. Home and Office: 1503 Plaza Encantada NW Albuquerque NM 87107-3256

MCGERVEY, TERESA ANN, technology information specialist; b. Pitts., Sept. 27, 1964; d. Walter James and Janet Sarah (Donehue) McG. BS in Geology, Calif. U. Pa., 1986, MS in Earth Sci., 1988. Phys. sci. technician U.S. Geol. Survey, Reston, Va., 1989-90; editor, indexer Am. Geol. Inst., Alexandria, Va., 1990-91; cartographer Def. Mapping Agy., Reston, 1991-93; tech. info. specialist Nat. Tech. Info. Svc., Springfield, Va., 1993—; intern Dept. Mineral Scis., Smithsonian Instn., summers 1985, 1986.

MCGHEE, LORI JEAN VOTE, medical/surgical nurse; b. Sac City, Iowa, Nov. 22, 1958; d. Bud Lee and Joanne Kay (Brouchous) V.; m. Wayne McGhee, June 30, 1990; 1 child, James. Diploma, Allen Meml. Hosp. Sch. Nursing, Waterloo, Iowa, 1980; student, U. No. Iowa, 1978. Staff nurse in orthopedics Allen Meml. Hosp., 1980-85; charge nurse in orthopedics/renal nursing Humana Hosp. Med. City, Dallas, 1985-88; med. reviewer Blue Cross and Blue Shield of Tex., Inc., Richardson, 1988-89, unit coord., trainer, 1989-90, supr. dept. precert., 1990-93; dir. nursing Integrated Health Svcs. Richardson (Tex.) Manor, 1994—.

MCGILL, GRACE ANITA, health services administrator, nurse; b. Lawrence, Mass., Mar. 8, 1943; d. Joseph John and Tina Mary (Sicurella) Tabacco; m. Howard L. McGill, Jr., Feb. 28, 1965; children: Cynthia, Deborah, David. RN, Mass. Gen. Hosp., 1963; BS, Lesley Coll., 1987; MS in Mgmt., Lesley Grad. Sch., 1990. Cert. occupational health nurse, 1992. Nurse Phillips Acad., Andover, Mass., 1963-65, 97th Gen. Hosp., Frankfurt, Germany, 1966, Highsmith-Rainey Hosp., Fayetteville, N.C., 1968, Lawrence (Mass.) Gen. Hosp., 1969-78, Baldpate Psychiat. Hosp., Georgetown, Mass., 1978-79; nursing staff St. Joseph's Hosp., Lowell, Mass., 1980-81; head nurse St. Joseph's Hosp., Lowell, 1981-83; occupational health nurse Wang Labs., Inc., Lowell, 1983-87, corp. safety specialist, 1987-90; health services adminstr. Loral Infrared and Imaging Systems, Inc., Lexington, Mass., 1990-93; supr. health svcs. Osram Sylvania, Inc., Danvers, Mass., 1993—; contract instr. Harvard U. Sch. Pub. Health. Mem. Mass. Gen. Hosp. Nurses Alumnae Assn., Am. Soc. Safety Engrs., NAFE, Lesley Coll. Allumnae, Am. Assn. Occupational Health Nurses, Am. Bd. Occupational Health Nurses. Episcopalian. Home: 81 Lancaster Dr Tewksbury MA 01876-1322

MCGILL, JENNIFER HOUSER, non-profit association administrator; b. Abingdon, Va., Mar. 3, 1957; d. Mason L. and Margaret Jane (Powers) H.; m. James B. McGill, July 15, 1978; children: Melissa Diane, Mark James. AA, Va. Highlands Community Coll., Abingdon, 1978; BA, U. S.C., 1980. Reporter, editor Sumter (S.C.) Daily ITEM, 1980-81; assoc. editor Sandlapper Mag., Columbia, S.C., 1981-82; membership editor Assn. for Edn. in Journalism/Mass Comm., Columbia, 1982-83, adminstrv. asst., 1984-85, exec. dir., 1985—; mem. nat. steering com. Journalist-in-Space Project, Columbia, 1985-86. Mem. Lioness Club (3d v.p. 1990-91, 2d v.p. 1991-92). Office: Assn Schs Journalism & Mass Comm 1621 College St Columbia SC 29208

MCGILL, JUDY ANNELL MCGEE, elementary school educator; b. Kosciusko, Miss., Oct. 16, 1949; d. Reeves and Martha Lee (Thompson) McGee; m. Ronald Eugene McGill, June 5, 1971; 1 child, Thomas Eugene. Student, U. Colo., 1979, James Madison U., 1974; BS, Miss. State U., 1971; MEd, Northeast La. U., 1984. 4th grade tchr. Harrison County Schs., Gulfport, Miss., 1971; 1st and 2d grade tchr. Oktibbeha County Schs., Starkville, Miss., 1971-72; 4th grade tchr. Natchez-Adams (Miss.) County Schs., 1972-74; 2d and 3d grade tchr. Shenandoah County Schs., Woodstock, Va., 1974-78; elem. sch. tchr. Jefferson County Schs., Lakewood, Colo., 1980-81; 7th and 8th grade tchr. Ouachita Parish Schs., Monroe, La., 1982; elem. sch. tchr. Union Parish Schs., Farmerville, La., 1982-85, Ouachita Parish Schs., Monroe, La., 1985—; master tchr., intern assessor Ouachita Parish Schs., Monroe, La., 1993—; in-svc. instr. Natchez-Adams County Schs., 1972-74, Shenandoah County Schs., 1974-78; trainer Sci. Rsch. Assocs., Woodstock, 1978; chairperson curriculum revision Ouachita Parish Schs., 1986-92, staff devel. trainer, 1990-92. Den leader Boy Scouts Am., West Monroe, La., 1986-88. Qaulity in Sci. amd Maths. grantee, 1994-95. Mem. ASCD, NEA,

La. Assn. Educators, Ouachita Parish Assn. Educators, So. Early Childhood Assn., La. Assn. on Children Under Six (Jane Herrin grantee 1987), N.E. La. Reading Coun. (chairperson grants 1987-88, Reading Tchr. of Yr. 1987-88), Internat. Reading Assn., La. Reading Assn., La. Assn. on Children Under Six (v.p., program chair 1988-94). Methodist. Home: 424 Tull Rd West Monroe LA 71292-2239 Office: Ouachita Parish Schs 100 Bry St Monroe LA 71201-8406

MCGILL, KATHLEEN A., lawyer; b. Pensacola, Fla., Sept. 14, 1957; d. L.H.R. and Frances Patterson (Landell) McG.; m. Ronald Ahlert, Apr. 5, 1989; 1 child, John Richard Ahlert. BA, U. Colo., 1978; JD, MS in Fgn. Svc., Georgetown U., 1985. Bar: N.Y., D.C. Assoc. Cadwalader, Whickershaun & Taft, Washington, 1984-86, Skadden, Arps, Slate, Meagher & Flom, N.Y.C., 1986-92; v.p., legal counsel Westdeutsche Landesbank, N.Y.C., 1992—. Mem. N.Y. County Lawyers Assn. (banking com.). Republican. Episcopalian. Office: Westdeutsche Landesbank 1211 Ave of the Americas New York NY 10036

MCGILLEY, SISTER MARY JANET, nun, educator, writer, academic administrator; b. Kansas City, Mo., Dec. 4, 1924; d. James P. and Peg (Ryan) McG. B.A., St. Mary Coll., 1945; M.A., Boston Coll., 1951; Ph.D., Fordham U., 1956; postgrad., U. Notre Dame, 1960, Columbia U., 1964. Social worker Kansas City, 1945-46; joined Sisters of Charity of Leavenworth, 1946; tchr. English Hayden High Sch., Topeka, 1948-50, Billings (Mont.) Central High Sch., 1951-53; faculty dept. English St. Mary Coll., Leavenworth, Kans., 1956-64; pres. St. Mary Coll., 1964-89, Disting. prof. English and Liberal Studies, 1990—. Contbr. articles, fiction and poetry to various jours. Bd. dirs. United Way of Leavenworth, 1966-85; mem. Mayor's Adv. Coun., 1967-72; bd. dirs. Kans. Ind. Coll. Fund, 1964-89, exec. com., 1985-86, vice chmn., 1984-85, chmn., 1985-86. Recipient Alumnae award St. Mary Coll., 1969; Disting. Service award Baker U., 1981, Leavenworth Bus. Woman of Yr. Athena award, 1986. Mem. Nat. Coun. Tchrs. of English, Nat. Assn. Ind. Colls. and Univs. (bd. dirs. 1982-85), Kans. Ind. Coll. Assn. (bd. dirs. 1964-89, treas. 1982-84, v.p. 1984-85, chmn. exec. com. 1985-86), Am. Coun. Edn. (com. on women in higher edn. 1980-85), Am. Assn. Higher Edn., Kansas City Regional Coun. for Higher Edn. (bd. dirs. 1965-89, treas. 1984-85, v.p. 1986-88), Ind. Coll. Funds Am. (exec. com. 1974-77, trustee-at-large 1975-76), North Cen. Assn. Colls. and Schs. (exec. commr. Com. on Insts. Higher Edn. 1980-88, vice chair 1985-86, chair 1987-88), Leavenworth C. of C. (bd. dirs. 1964-89), Assn. Am. Colls. (commn. liberal learning 1970-73, com. on curriculum and faculty devel. 1979-82) St. Mary Alumni Assn. (hon. pres. 1964-89), Delta Epsilon Sigma. Democrat. Office: St Mary Coll 4100 S 4th St Leavenworth KS 66048-5082

MCGILLIS, KELLY, actress; b. Newport, Calif., July 9, 1957; m. Fred Tillman, Dec. 31, 1988; 3 children. Student, Pacific Conservatory of Performing Arts, Juilliard Sch. Music. Actress: (feature films) Reuben, Reuben, 1983, Witness, 1985, Top Gun, 1986, Made in Heaven, 1987, Promised Land, 1988, The House on Carroll Street, 1988, The Accused, 1988, Winter People, 1989, The Babe, 1992, North, 1994; (TV films) Sweet Revenge, 1984, Private Sessions, 1985, Grand Isle (also prod.), 1991, Bonds of Love, 1993, In the Best of Families: Marriage, Pride and Madness, 1994; (stage) Hedda Gabler, Roundabout Theatre Company, 1994. *

MCGILLIVRAY, KAREN, elementary school educator; b. Richland, Oreg., Aug. 24, 1936; d. Kenneth Melton and Catharina (Sass) McG. BS in Edn. cum laude, Ea. Oreg. State Coll., 1958; MRE, Pacific Sch. Religion, 1963. Cert. tchr., Oreg. 4th grade tchr. Salem (Oreg.)-Keizer Pub. Schs. Contbr. articles, stories to ednl. mags. U.S. Govt. grantee. Mem. NEA (rep. assembly), NEAR, Oreg. Edn. Assn. (rep. assembly), Oreg. Retired Educators Assn., Salem Edn. Assn. (officer), Oreg. Ret. Tchrs. Assn., Phi Delta Kappa (officer), Delta Kappa Gamma (officer). Methodist. Home: 325 Cedarwood Ave McMinnville OR 97128

MCGILL-MEMBRINO, DEBORAH LYNN, lawyer; b. Waterbury, Conn., May 23, 1955; d. Hugh John and Helen (Alishauskas) McGill; m. Ralph G. Membrino, July 22, 1977; 1 child, Hugh John. BA in Econs./Sociology summa cum laude, Marymount Coll., 1977; JD, Western New Eng. Sch. of Law, 1980. Bar: Conn. 1981, D.C. 1983. Pvt. practice Waterbury, Conn., 1982—. Mem. Wolcott (Conn.) Town Coun., 1980-82; magistrate Waterbury Ct. System, 1994; mem. alumni bd. Cheshire (Conn.) Acad., 1993. Mem. ABA, ATLA, Waterbury Bar Assn. (med.-legal com. 1993, 94, co-chair women in law sect. 1993, 94, scholarship 1979), Conn. Trial Lawyers. Office: 571 Wolcott St Waterbury CT 06705

MCGINN, EILEEN, public health advisor, researcher; b. Phila., Mar. 29, 1947. BA cum laude, CUNY, 1968; MPH, U. Pitts., 1974. Tchr. English Peace Corps, Dogondoutchi, Niger, 1968-70; tchr. sci. Diocese of Bklyn., 1971-72; clinic dir. Monsour Med. Ctr., Jeannette, Pa., 1974-76; grants officer Assn. for Voluntary Surg. Contraception, N.Y.C., 1976-79; program officer Planned Parenthood Fedn., N.Y.C., 1979-81; chief of party USAID/Zaire, Kinshasa, 1983-85; dep. chief of party John Snow, Inc., Nepal, Kathmandu, 1986-89; program mgr. Asia Assn. Voluntary Surg. Contraception, N.Y.C., 1989-92; cons., 1992—; cons. CEDPA, Washington, 1985, Population Svcs. Internat., Washington, 1985, USAID, Togo, 1993, John Snow/SEATS, Papua New Guinea, 1994. Author: Field Worker's Manual, 1989, Nurse's Manual, 1989; contbr. articles to profl. jours. N.Y.S. State Regents scholar, 1964-68, NYU scholar, 1982; USPHS grantee, 1972-73. Mem. Am. Pub. Health Assn., Nat. Coun. for Internat. Health. Office: 210 East 15th St New York NY 10003

MCGINN, MARY JOVITA, lawyer, insurance company executive; b. St. Louis, Apr. 9, 1947; d. Martin J. and Janet (Hogan) McG.; m. Bernard H. Shapiro, Sept. 6, 1971; children: Sara, Colleen, Molly, Daniel. BA, Rosary Coll., River Forest, Ill., 1967; JD, St. Louis U., 1970. Bar: Mo. 1970, Ill. 1971. Atty. tax div. U.S. Dept. Justice, Washington, 1970-73; atty. Allstate Ins. Co., Northbrook, Ill., 1973—; v.p., asst. gen. counsel Allstate Ins. Co., 1980—. Mem. ABA, Am. Coll. Investment Counsel, Chgo. Bar Assn., Assn. Life Ins. Counsel. Roman Catholic. Home: 155 N Buckley Rd Barrington IL 60010-2607 Office: Allstate Ins Co Allstate Plz West-M2A Northbrook IL 60062

MCGINN, MARY LYN, real estate company executive; b. New Orleans, Aug. 12, 1949; d. Dan Creedon and Millicent Virginia (White) Midgett; m. Walter Lee McGinn, Mar. 14, 1985. BA, La. State U., 1970, MA, 1972; PhD, U. So. Miss., 1976; MBA, Loyola Coll., 1990. Cert. comml.-investment mem., cert. property mgr., master appraiser. Dir., prof. Dillard U., New Orleans, 1972-76, Loyola U., New Orleans, 1976-80; sr. v.p. Equity Investment Svcs., Inc., New Orleans, 1980-84; pres. Mgmt. Svcs. Group, Inc., New Orleans, 1984-85, Assoc. Investment Svcs. Inc., New Orleans, 1985-87, Northshore Property Mgmt., Inc., New Orleans, 1985-87; asst. v.p. USF&G Realty, Balt., 1987-89, v.p., 1989-90; exec. mng. dir. Galbreath Co., 1990—; cons. colls. and univs., 1976—. Bd. dirs. Pitts. Zoo, Salvation Army, Jr. Achievement. Mem. Nat. Assn. Corporate Real Estate Execs., Bldg. Owners and Mgrs. Assn., Comml.-Investment Council, Nat. Assn. Master Appraisers. Office: Galbreath Co 600 Grant St Pittsburgh PA 15219-2756

MCGINN, SUSAN FRANCES, musician; b. Detroit, May 26, 1961; d. Michael Thomas and Bernice Frances (DePollo) McG. MusB, U. Mich., 1983; MusM, U. Ill., 1985; postgrad., Ind. U., 1985-89. Co-prin. flute L.A. Philharm. Inst., 1985, Nat. Repertory Orch., Keystone, Colo., 1987, Nat. Orchestral Inst., College Park, Md., 1989, Schleswig-Holstein Musik Festival, Salzau, Germany, 1988, 89; prin. flute, flutist wind quintet Canton (Ohio) Symphony Orch., 1989-90, Honolulu Symphony Orch., 1990—; grad. teaching asst. U. Ill., Urbana, 1983-85; assoc. instr. Ind. U., Bloomington, 1986-89; flutist spring wind quinted Chamber Music Hawaii, Honolulu, 1990-92. Scholar U. Ill., 1983-85; fellow Ind. U., 1985-86, scholar, 1986-89. Office: Hawaii Symphony Orch Ste V-IB 444 Hobron Ln Honolulu HI 96815

MCGINN, THERESE JOAN, international health researcher; b. Bklyn., Oct. 3, 1956; d. Shawn Patrick and Agnes Rosaire (Finnen) McG. BA, Cornell U., 1978; MPH, U. Mich., 1983. Sr. staff assoc. Ctr. Population and Family Health Columbia U., N.Y.C. and Abidjan, Ivory Coast, 1983-91; dep. dir. population unit CARE, N.Y.C., 1991-93; ind. cons. N.Y.C., 1993—; bd. dirs. population-environment fellows program U. Mich., Ann Arbor; mem. Working Groups for Internat. Health U. N.C., Chapel Hill and evaluation project Tulane U., New Orleans, 1992-94; co-instr. Columbia U., N.Y.C., 1990—; presenter in field. Contbr. articles to profl. jours. Scholar Women's Fedn. Cornell Clubs, 1976-77, Mabel Estey Rose Found., 1976-77, N.Y. State Bd. Regents, 1974-78, Cornell U., 1974-78; Jessie Smith Noyes Found. fellow, 1981-83. Mem. Am. Pub. Health Assn., Nat. Coun. Internat. Health. Democrat. Home: 201 E 17th St Apt 26F New York NY 10003-3641

MCGINNIS, DONNA MAY, artist; b. Spokane, Wash., Dec. 17, 1940; d. Burton Oliver Belknap and Dora Mary (Clausen) Herrman; m. John Warren McGinnis, Dec. 11, 1965; children: Jody Ann, Scott Warren. BA in Fine Arts, Wash. State U., 1963. Color cons. Fiberboard Co., San Francisco, 1963-64; lectr. drawing Indian Valley Coll., Novato, Calif., 1981, Sonoma State U., Cotati, Calif., 1981; gallery lectr. Merced (Calif.) Coll., 1993. One-woman shows include Anna Gardner Gallery, Stinson Beach, Calif., 1980, Allport Assocs. Gallery, Larkspur, Calif., 1981, 82, 84, Dominican Coll., San Rafael, Calif., 1982, Seipp Gallery, Palo Alto, Calif., 1983, Dubins Gallery, L.A., 1984, 85, 86, 88, Montalvo Ctr. Arts, Saratoga, Calif., 1984, The Gallery, Burlingame, Calif., 1987, 89, 91, 93, Marin Theater Co., Mill Valley, Calif., 1987, Eva Cohon Galleries, Chgo., 1989, Harleen and Allen Gallery, San Francisco, 1990, Grants Pass (Oreg.) Mus. Art, 1991, St. Francis Found., San Francisco, 1991, Stanford U., Palo Alto, 1992, Olga Dollar Gallery, San Francisco, 1992, Merced (Calif.) Coll. Art Gallery, 1993, Patricia Stewart Gallery, Napa, Calif., 1993; exhibited in numerous group shows, including Marin County Exhbn., San Rafael, Calif., 1980, 81, San Francisco Mus. Modern Art Gallery, 1980, Fine Arts Mus. San Francisco, 1981, 82, 83, 85, Triton Mus. Art, Santa Clara, Calif., 1981, Coll. of Mainland Nat., Texas City, Texas, 1981, Crocker Art Mus., Sacramento, 1981, 82, Fairfield-Suisum Arts Coun., Calif., 1982, 7th Falkirk Ann., San Rafael, 1982, Richmond Art Ctr., Calif., 1982, San Mateo County Arts, Belmont, Calif., 1982, Quadrum Gallery, Boston, 1983, Coll. Marin, Kentfield, Calif., 1984, Marin Arts Coun., Larkspur, Calif., 1985, Oakland Mus. Collectors Gallery, 1985, 91, Susan Cummins Gallery, Mill Valley, 1986, VanStraaten Gallery, Chgo., 1987, 88, Artisans, Mill Valley, 1989, SOMAR Gallery, San Francisco, 1990, Jessel Gallery, Napa, Calif., 1990, Calif. Mus. Art, Santa Rosa, 1991, 94, Gail Severn Gallery, Ketchum, Idaho, 1991, Art in Embassies, Abu Dhabi, United Arab Emirates, 1992, So. Exposure Gallery, San Francisco, 1993, Edith Caldwell Gallery, San Francisco, 1993, Gallery Rte. One, Pt. Reyes Station, Calif., 1993, I. Wolk Gallery, St. Helena, Calif., 1994, Cabrillo Coll., Aptos, Calif., 1994, Freeport (Ill.) Art Mus., 1995; represented in permanent collections, including San Francisco Fine Arts Mus., Coll. of Mainland, Texas City, also numerous corp. collections. Recipient cash award Falkirk 2d Ann., San Rafael, Calif., 1977, Best in Show award Marin Soc. Artists, 1979, Artisans Competition, San Rafael, 1981, Bay Arts '82, Belmont, Calif., 1982, Fairfield Art Shows, 1982, Grumbacher Art award, 1982, Best in Class award Marin County Expn., 1981. Home: 351 Devon Dr San Rafael CA 94903-3709 Studio: 124 Belvedere St Ste 8 San Rafael CA 94901-4707

MCGINNIS, JOÁN ADELL, secondary school educator; b. Erie, Pa., Jan. 20, 1932; d. Roy Hamilton and Sara Zelma (Gorman) Sjöberg; m. Richard H. Edwards, Aug. 6, 1954 (div. 1965); m. George William McGinnis, Dec. 29, 1966 (dec. Apr. 1994). BA, St. Lawrence U., Canton, N.Y., 1953. Cert. tchr., Calif. Spl. proxies Sun Life Assurance Co., Montreal, 1952-53; pvt. sec. Detroit Trust, 1953-54; sec. Meth. Ch., Lancaster, Calif., 1964—; tchr. Sunny Hills High Sch., Fullerton, Calif., 1966—; contr. Mission Viejo (Calif.) Sheet Metal, 1980-81; dept. sec. Fgn. Lang. Dept. Sunny Hills High Sch., 1966-80, dept. chair, 1987-89; internat. baccalaureate examiner in Spanish, 1991—, French, 1992—; advanced placement examiner in Spanish, 1990—. Mem. Am. Assn. Tchrs. Spanish and Portuguese, Modern Classical Lang. Assn. Calif., Fgn. Lang. Assn. Orange County (Exptl. Tchr. of Orange County award 1994), Am. Women's Orgn. Republican. Home: 26382 Estanciero Dr Mission Viejo CA 92691 Office: Sunny Hills High Sch 1801 W Warburton Way Fullerton CA 92633-2299

MCGINNIS, JUDITH B., marketing executive; b. Tallahassee, Fla., Mar. 10, 1938; d. Charles William Benedict and Catherine (Wilson) Granger; m. Casimir Michael Szpak, June 30, 1989; children: Kevin, Lance, Scott. Student, Florida State U., 1956-60. Dir. mcpl. ctr. City of Tallahassee, Fla., 1970-74; asst. to the advt. dir. Tallahassee Democrat, Fla., 1974-77; coord., dir. Tallahassee Open PGA Tour, Fla., 1977-84; acct. rep. Microtel Inc., Fla., 1983-84; mktg. and sales dir. Benedict Engring Co., Tallahassee, 1984—; bd. dirs. Tall Open-PGA Tour, 1984-92; bd. dirs., com. chmn. FIA, Tallahassee, 1980-92. Mem. Tallahassee C. of C., Altrusa Internat. Republician. Episcopalian. Office: Benedict Engring Co PO Box 4229 Tallahassee FL 32315-4229

MCGINNIS, MARCY ANN, television news executive producer; b. Long Branch, N.J., Apr. 9, 1950; d. Joseph Arthur and Ruth (Thomas) McG. AAS, Marymount U., 1970. Exec. sec. news Sta. CBS News, N.Y.C., 1970-71; adminstrv. asst. Sta. CBS TV, N.Y.C., 1971-73, asst. producer, 1973-76, assoc. producer, 1976-82, producer, 1982-85, sr. producer, 1985-89, exec. producer, 1989-92; dep. bur. chief London, dir. CBS NEWSNET Europe, 1992—. Mem. NATAS, NAFE, TV and Radio Working Press Assn. Roman Catholic. Home: 14 Southwell Gardens # 6, London SW7 4RL, England Office: CBS News, 68 Knightsbridge, London SW1X 7LL, England

MCGINNIS, PAULA KATHLEEN, nutritionist, dietitian; b. Ft. Dodge, Iowa, July 27, 1960; d. Dale Eugene and Ella Mae (Coleman) McG. BS in Bus. Adminstrn./Mktg., Fontbonne Coll., 1986, BS in Gen. Dietetics, 1990; postgrad., Washington U., St. Louis, 1990-91. Registered dietitian. Lab tech. DCA Golden Dipt Inc, St. Louis, 1988-90; nutrition specialist Ralston Purina Co., St. Louis, 1991-92, Pet Inc., St. Louis, 1992—; mem. pub. rels. com. Combined Health Appeal of Greater St. Louis, 1994—. Mem. Am. Dietetic Assn. (mem. bus./comm. practice group), Mo. Dietetic Assn. (industry panel mem. 1993), St. Louis Dietetic Assn. (student rep. 1989-90, mem. nutrition update com. 1991, chair-elect pub. rels. com. 1993-94). Republican. Home: 1204 Francis Pl Saint Louis MO 63117 Office: Pet Inc 400 S 4th St Saint Louis MO 63102

MCGINNITY, MAUREEN ANNELL, lawyer; b. Monroe, Wis., Apr. 6, 1956; d. James Arthur and Marie Beatrice (Novak) McG.; m. Richard W. Ziervogel, July 17, 1982; 1 child, Brigitte Kathleen. BS, U. Wis., Milw., 1977; JD, U. Wis., 1982. Bar: Wis. 1982, U.S. Dist. Ct. (ea. and we. dists.) Wis. 1982, U.S. Ct. Appeals (7th cir.) 1989, U.S. Supreme Ct. 1991, U.S. Ct. Appeals (1st cir.) 1991. Assoc. Foley & Lardner, Milw., 1982-91, ptnr., 1991—; mem. Wis. Supreme Ct. Planning and Policy Adv. Com., Madison, 1991-94; adv. bd. Domestic Violence Legal Clinic, Milw., 1991—. Treas. Waukesha (Wis.) County Emergency Food Pantry, 1988-94; trustee Boys & Girls Club Greater Milw., 1991—; bd. dirs. Task Force on Battered Women & Children, Inc., 1994—. Recipient Outstanding Svc. award Legal Action Wis., Milw., 1984, 93 Outstanding Fundraising awards Boys & Girls Club Grater Milw., 1987-92, Cert. Recognition, Common Coun. Task Force on Sexual Assault & Domestic Violence, Milw., 1991, Cert. Appreciation, Wis. Equal Justice Task Force, Madison, 1991. Mem. ABA, State Bar Wis. (bd. govs. 1992—, Pro Bono award 1990, chair 1993-94), Assn. for Women Lawyers (various offices, pres. 1992-93), Milw. Young Lawyers Assn. (bd. dirs. 1987-92, pres. 1990-91, Pres.' award 1991), Profl. Dimensions. Office: Foley & Lardner 777 E Wisconsin Ave Milwaukee WI 53202-5302

MCGINTY, SUSAN MAE YOUNG, physical therapist; b. Red Bluff, Calif., Aug. 22, 1944; d. Raleigh Garvey and Juanita May (Walton) Young; m. Denis Michael McGinty, June 15, 1968; children: Michael Brian, Patrick Martin. Student, Linfield Coll., 1962-65; BS in Phys. Therapy, U. Calif., San Francisco, 1966; MS in Phys. Therapy, U. So. Calif., 1980. Registered phys. therapist, Calif. Phys. therapist Vis. Nurse Assn. of San Francisco, 1966-69, U. So. Calif. Med. Ctr., L.A., 1969-70, Red Cross/121st Evacuation Hosp., Seoul, Korea, 1970-71, Marin Gen. Hosp., San Rafael, Calif., 1972-73, Vis. Nurse Assn. of E. San Gabriel Valley, Pasadena, Calif., 1973-78; rehab. supr. Sutter Vis. Nurse Assn., Sacramento, Calif., 1981—. Co-editor newsletter Am. Cancer Soc. Interdisciplinary Newsletter, 1991, 92, 93 (Best New Publ. award 1991). Chair, sec., mem. area V parent advisory Sacramento City Sch. Dist., 1980-85, chair, mem. GATE parent Advisory, 1982-86, mem. dist. desegregation com., 1984; vol. Sacramento Habitat for Humanity, Sacramento, 1992—. Mem. Am. Phys. Therapy Assn. (QA com. mem. Calif. chpt. N.E. dist. 1986—, mem. geriatric and community health sects. 1966—). Democrat. Roman Catholic. Office: Sutter Vis Nurse Assn 1455 Response Rd Ste 200 Sacramento CA 95815

MCGLASSON, CHRISTINA ADAMS, psychology educator; b. Springfield, Ill., Sept. 19, 1963; d. Edward K. and Lois J. Adams; m. William E. McGlasson Jr., Aug. 19, 1989. BA, So. Ill. U., Carbondale, 1985, MA, 1988, PhD, 1991. Asst. prof. psychology St. Cloud (Minn.) State U., 1989—. Author: (with others) Handbook of Dichotic Listening, 1988. Fellow So. Ill. U., Carbondale, 1985-86. Mem. APS, APA, MPA, Minn. Psychol. Assn., Cen. Minn. Psychol. Assn., Sigma Xi. Office: St Cloud State U Dept Psychology Wh # 102 Saint Cloud MN 56301

MCGLONE, DENISE MARIE, financial company executive; b. Bklyn., Feb. 2, 1952; d. Joseph Najib and Elizabeth (Ara) B.; m. Vincent John McGlone, Sept. 28, 1991; 1 child, Elizabeth Ara. BA, Dunbarton Coll., Washington, 1973; MBA, Am. U., 1977. Various positions fed. govt., Washington, 1973-77; dir. corp. fin. Student Loan Mktg. Assn., Washington, 1977-84; v.p. 1st Nat. Bank Chgo., 1984-85; sr. v.p. Security Pacific Nat. Bank, N.Y.C., 1985-91; exec. v.p. dKB Fin. Products, N.Y.C., 1991-94; exec. v.p., CFO Sallie Mae, 1994—. Mem. Internat. Swap Dealers Assn. (sec. 1985-91, bd. dirs.). Roman Cathaolic. Office: Student Loan Mktg Assn 1050 Thomas Jefferson St NW Washington DC 20007*

MCGLYNN, BARBARA JEAN, radiation oncology nurse; b. Randolph Field Army Base, Tex., May 27, 1943; d. Earl A. and Gertrude E. (Krempin) Slaughter; m. Frank S. McGlynn, Dec. 26, 1964 (div. 1993); children: Sean Patrick, Erin Marie. ADN, Coatesville Hosp. Sch. Nursing, 1964; BA in Anthropology with honors, U. Pitts., 1992. Cert. oncology nurse. Staff nurse, asst. head nurse Meml. Hosp., West Chester, Pa., 1964-66; staff nurse nursery MaGee Womens Hosp., Pitts., 1966-67; nurse coord. Pitts. (Pa.) Free Clinic, 1971-73; staff nurse radiation oncology, ednl. material coord. St. Francis Med. Ctr., Pitts., 1974—; guest lectr. Speakers Bur. St. Francis Med. Ctr., Pitts., 1990-93; presenter in field. Mem., plaintiff Pitts. (Pa.) Sch. Desegregation Project and Suit, 1978-79; mem. Election David Engel Sch. Bd., Pitts., 1979. Co-recipient New Person award Thomas Merton Ctr., Pitts., 1979; named Univ. scholar U. Pitts., 1988-92, Chancellors Undergrad. Tchg. fellow U. Pitts., 1989. Mem. Oncology Nursing Soc., Pa. Pain Initative, Radiation Nurse-Oncology Nursing Soc., Patient Edn. Nursing Networking Group. Democrat. Home: 42 Harwood St Pittsburgh PA 15211-2130 Office: St Francis Med Ctr 45 And Penn Ave Pittsburgh PA 15201

MCGLYNN, BETTY HOAG, art historian; b. Deer Lodge, Mont., Apr. 28, 1914; d. Arthur James and Elizabeth Tangey (Davey) Lochrie; m. Paul Sterling Hoag, Dec. 28, 1936 (div. 1967); children: Peter Lochrie Hoag, Jane Hoag Brown, Robert Doane Hoag; m. Thomas Arnold McGlynn, July 28, 1973. BA, Stanford U., 1936; MA, U. So. Calif., 1967. Cert. secondary tchr., Calif. Rsch. dir. So. Calif. Archives of Am. Art, L.A., 1964-67, Carmel (Calif.) Mus. Art, 1967-69; dir. Triton Mus. Art, Santa Clara, Calif., 1970; archivist, libr. San Mateo County (Calif.) Hist. Soc. Mus., 1971-74; cons. Monterey Peninsula Mus. Art, Calif., 1964—; tchr. art extension Monterey Peninsula Coll., Calif., 1970, San Jose City Coll., 1971; lectr. in field. Author: The World of Mary DeNeale Morgan, 1970, Carmel Art Association: A History, 1987; contbg. author: Plein Air Painters of California, The North, 1986, Orchid Art and the Orchid Isle, 1982, Hawaiian Island Artists and Friends of the Arts, 1989; editor, author of jours. La. Peninsula, 1971-75, Noticias, 1983-88; author of booklets; contbr. articles to profl. jours. Appraiser art work City of Carmel, 1967, City of Monterey, 1981. Mem. Butte (Mont.) Arts Chateau, Carmel Art Assn. (hon.), Carmel Heritage Soc., Carmel Found., Carmel Residents Assn., Chinese Hist. Soc., Monterey History and Art Assn. (art cons.), Monterey Peninsula Mus. Art (acquisitions bd.), Stanford Alumni Assn., Robinson Jeffers Tor House Found. (art cons.), Hawaiian Hist. Soc., Nat. Mus. of Women in the Arts, The Westerners, P.E.O., Book Club of Calif. Republican. Home and Office: PO Box 7189 Carmel-by-the-Sea CA 93921-7189

MCGLYNN, KATHERINE MARIE, academic counselor; b. Detroit, July 21, 1959; d. Victor Josepha and Eleanor Louis (McNamara) Cervini; m. Kenneth Craig McGlynn, dec. 23, 1984; 1 child, Jessica Marie. Student, Macomb C.C., Mt. Clemens, Mich.; BS in Edn., Ctrl. Mich. U.; student, Calif. Poly., Pomona; MS in Counseling, Calif. State U., San Bernardino. Tchr. spl. edn. L.A. County Schs., Downey, Calif., 1984-87; tchr. learning disabled Emot Disturbed Advocate Schs., Riverside, Calif., 1987-90; substitute counselor Corona-Norco Sch. Dist., 1990; vocat. counselor Cosona (Calif.)-Nosco Sch. Dist., 1991—. Vol. Right to Life, Riverside, Calif., Habitat for Humanity, Riverside. Mem. Am. Counselign Devel., Counsel for Excpetional Children. Republican. Roman Catholic. Home: 11329 N Silver Pheasant Loop Tucson AZ 85737

MCGONIGAL, SHIRLEY JOAN O'HEY, secondary education educator; b. Phila., Aug. 13, 1920; d. Joseph Matthew and Alice Agnes (Smith) O'Hey; m. Edward Stephen McGonigal, Oct. 30, 1948; children: Alice, Stephen, Richard, Nancy Lynn, Michelle, Barry Joseph. BA, Coll. of Chestnut Hill, 1942, postgrad., 1943-44; postgrad., Community Coll. Mays Landing, N.J., 1955-56, Community Coll. Mays Landing, N.J., 1983-84. Libr. Pa. Dept. of Agr., Wynnemore, 1943-45; tchr. grade sch. Barren Hill, Pa., 1945-46, Mays Landing, 1962-83; tchr. English Oakcrest High Sch., Mays Landing, 1984—; tchr. Literacy Vols. of Am., Atlantic County, N.J., 1983—. Mem. exec. com. Betty Bacharach Rehab. Ctr., Ventnor, N.J.; sec. adv. bd. Children's Seashore Hosp., Ventnor, N.J.; chairperson Atlantic Cultural and Hist. Com., Northfield, N.J. Recipient Cert. of Appreciation, Family Svc. Assn., Svc. award Oakcrest High Bd. of Edn., 1967-82, Cert. of Appreciation, Rutgers U., Svc. Plaque, County Cultural and Hist. Com., 1988-90. Mem. AAUW, Nat. Edn. Soc. (life), Navy League of U.S., Delta Kappa Gamma (fellow, scholarship com. 1979). Republican. Roman Catholic. Home and Office: Box 539 221 Lenape Ave Mays Landing NJ 08330-1843

MCGOVERN, CYNTHIA ANN, state legislator; b. Methuen, Mass., Apr. 17, 1948. BA, U. N.H., 1970; JD, Franklin Pierce Law Ctr., Concord, N.H., 1984. Cons. N.H.; mem. N.H. State Ho. Reps., mem. exec. depts. and adminstrn. com., legis. adminstrn. com.; del. Dem. State Com., 1984; asst. Dem. Leader, 1993—. Bd. Dir. N.H. Women's Lobby, 1981-86. Mem. NOW (asst. state coord., 1980-83), Civil Liberties Union (bd.dir. 1975-80, 1987—), N.H. Ptnrs. of Am. Democrat. Home: 41 Salter St Portsmouth NH 03801-5229*

MCGOVERN, KAREN MARIE, special education educator; b. Lynn, Mass., Mar. 31, 1959; d. Francis Thomas and Constance (Ceranna) McG. BS, Fitchburg State Coll., 1981; MEd in Spl. Edn., Boston Coll., 1986; MEd in Computers, Lesley Coll., 1992. Spl. needs tchr. Lakeside Sch., Peabody, Mass., 1981-83, diagnostic-prescriptive tchr., 1983-84; job devel. tchr. Peabody Pub. Schs., 1984-87, spl. needs tchr., 1987—; dir. spl. needs program Danvers (Mass.) Recreation, 1987-89; chairperson Mass. Transition Initiative, Peabody, 1994. Coach Spl. Olympics, Peabody, 1986—. Mem. North Shore Assn. Retarded Citizens, Coun. Exceptional Children, Kiwanis (Key Club advisor 1994—). Home: 4 Jefferson Rd Peabody MA 01960 Office: Peabody High Sch 485 Lowell St Rm B107 Peabody MA 01960

MC GOVERN, MAUREEN THERESE, entertainer; b. Youngstown, Ohio, July 27, 1949; d. James Terrence and Mary Rita (Welsh) McG. Student pub. schs., Youngstown. Exec. sec. Youngstown Cartage Co., 1968-69; sec. Assocs. in Anesthesiology, Youngstown, 1970-71. Entertainer, 1972—; stage appearances include: The Sound of Music, 1981, The Pirates of Penzance, 1981, South Pacific, 1982, Nine, 1984, Brownstone, 1984, Guys and Dolls, 1984, Three Penny Opera, 1989; cameo appearance in movie The Towering Inferno, 1975; appeared in film Ky. Fried Theater's Airplane, 1979; albums recorded include: The Morning After, 1973 (Gold Record award), Nice To Be Around, 1974, Academy Award Performance, 1975, Maureen McGovern, 1979, Another Woman In Love, 1987, Naughty Baby, 1989, Baby I'm Yours, 1992; composer: Midnight Storm, 1973, If I Wrote You a Song, 1973, All I Want, 1974, Memory, 1974, Little Boys and Men, 1974, Love Knots, 1974, You Love Me Too Late, 1979, Thief in the Night, 1979, Don't Stop Now, 1979, Hello Again, 1979, Halfway Home, 1980, others. Recipient

Gold Record for single The Morning After, Record Industry Assn. Am., 1973; Can. RPM Gold Leaf award, 1973; Australian gold award, 1975; resolution for bringing fame and recognition to Ohio, Ohio Senate, 1974; Grand prize Tokyo Music Festival, 1975. Mem. ASCAP, Am. Fedn. Musicians, AFTRA, Screen Actors Guild. Office: care Warner Bros Records 3300 W Warner Blvd Burbank CA 91505-4694*

MCGOWAN, BRENDA JOY, executive secretary; b. Washington, Pa., Nov. 30, 1956; d. Frank Arthur Sr. and Wilma Waneta (Cook) Morris; m. David Lynn McGowan, Feb. 18, 1978; children: Brea Suzanne, Misti Lynn. Grad. high sch., Washington, Pa. Sr. mktg. sec. Cerdec Corp., Drakenfeld Products, Washington, Pa., 1974—. Presbyterian. Home: 459 Palm St Washington PA 15301 Office: Cerdec Corp Drakenfeld Products W Wylie Ave PO Box 519 Washington PA 15301

MCGOWAN, PATRICIA ANN, marketing professional; b. Uniontown, Pa., Sept. 29, 1965; d. Robert Francis and Marion Nelle (Ford) McG. BS, U. Tenn., 1987. Mktg. intern Carnation Co., Knoxville, 1987; territory sales rep. Bristol Myers Products, Nashville, 1988-91; key acct. mgr. PIA Merchandising Co., Nashville, 1992—. Mem. Hands on Nashville, Hendersonville High Sch. Alumni (chmn. bd. dirs.), Phi Mu Alumni Assn. (bd. dirs. 1988—). Home: 3733 Meadowbrook Ave # A Nashville TN 37205-2351 Office: PIA Merchandising Co Ste 1000 3220 Peachtree Pointe Pky Norcross GA 30092

MCGOWAN, RUTHANN LOUISE, information systems manager; b. Seward, Nebr., Feb. 2, 1954; d. Glenn Walter and Gertrude Ann (Roeder) Wiechmann; m. Robert Carl Hedin, July 5, 1974 (div. May 12, 1993); children: Robert George Hedin, Chadwick Glenn Hedin, Richard Louis Hedin. AS in Acctg., Hutchinson Tech. Coll., 1974. Cert. in prodn. and inventory mgmt. Catalog sales J.C. Penney Co., Hutchinson, Minn., 1973-74; bookkeeper Bonniwell Inc., Hutchinson, Minn., 1974-76; office mgr. Standard Printing, Hutchinson, Minn., 1976-77; acctg. asst. Goebel Fixture Co., Hutchinson, Minn., 1983-85, info. systems mgr., 1985-94; with McGowan Mfg., Hutchinson, Minn., 1994—; cons. Systems Consulting, Hutchinson, 1993—. Held various offices Our Saviors Luth. Ch., Hutchinson, 1978—. Mem. Assn. Sys. Mgmt., Assn. Prodn. Inventory, Am. Prodn. and Inventory Control Soc. Republican. Lutheran. Office: McGowan Mfg 25 Michigan St Hutchinson MN 55350

MCGOWIN, JANET DEAN, actuary; b. Charleston, W.Va., Apr. 6, 1962; d. John Elbon and Barbara Lee (Sutton) Dean; m. Steven Edward McGowin, June 28, 1986. BS in Stats., U. Ala., Tuscaloosa, 1985. Staff actuarial analyst Blue Cross-Blue Shield Ala., Birmingham, 1986-88, advanced staff actuarial analyst, 1988-91, assoc. actuary, 1991-93, mgr. actuarial dept., 1993—. Patron Birmingham Humane Soc., 1988—; mem. vis. allocations team United Way Ctrl. Ala., Birmingham, 1992—; advisor Explorers' post Boy Scouts Am., Birmingham, 1994. Mem. Am. Acad. Actuaries, Soc. Actuaries (assoc.), Nat. Mgmt. Assn., Leadership Devel. Assn., Southeastern Actuaries Club, Ala. HMO Guaranty Assn. (bd. dirs. 1991—), Cahaba River Soc. Office: Blue Cross-Blue Shield Ala 450 Riverchase Pky E Birmingham AL 35298

MCGRADY, CORINNE YOUNG, design company executive; b. N.Y.C., May 6, 1938; d. Albert I. and Reda (Bromberg) Young; m. Michael Robinson McGrady; children: Sean, Siobhan, Liam. Student, Bard Coll., Annandale-on-Hudson, N.Y., 1960, Harvard U., 1968-69. Founder, pres. Corinne McGrady Designs; designer Corinneware (joint venture of Corinne McGrady Designs and Boston Warehouse Trading Corp. 1990), East Northport, N.Y., 1970—. Acrylic works exhibited in group shows at Mus. Contemporary Crafts, N.Y.C., 1969-70, Smithsonian Instn., 1970-71, Pompidou Ctr., Paris, 1971, Mus. Sci. and Industry, 1970; sculpture exhibited at Guild Hall Show, Southampton, N.Y., 1968, Hecksher Mus., 1968. Vice pres. Woman's Internat. League for Peace and Freedom, Huntington, N.Y., 1971. Recipient Design Rev. award Indsl. Design, 1969, 70; Instant Supergraphic Indsl. Design Rev. award, 1971. Patentee cookbook stand. Home and Office: PO Box 27 Lilliwaup WA 98555-0027

MCGRADY, SHARON ALYSE, university administrator; b. Madison, Tenn., July 27, 1955; d. George Elmer Webster and Helen Ruth (Martin) DeLong; m. Glenn McGrady III, Oct. 9, 1977 (div. 1991); children: Glenn IV, Justin Scott. BA, So. Coll., 1977. Recorder So. Coll., Collegedale, Tenn., 1977-93, asst. dir. records and advisement, 1993—. So. union dir. Adventist Singles Ministries, 1993—. Republican. Home: PO Box 395 5691 Sherry Ln Collegedale TN 37315 Office: So Coll PO Box 370 Collegedale TN 37315

MCGRAIL, SUSAN KING, travel agency executive, accountant; b. Richmond, Va., Mar. 7, 1952; d. William Jr. and Anne Winn (Gibson) King; m. John Patrick McGrail, Jr., June 2, 1979; children: Katharine Anne, Patricia Lynn, John Patrick III. BBA, Coll. William and Mary, 1974. CPA, Va., Ohio. Employment counselor Avante Gard of Richmond, Inc., 1970-73; staff acct. Touche Ross & Co., Washington, 1974-75, Richmond, 1975-78; contr. Continental Cablevision, Richmond, 1978-81; v.p. fin. Warner Amex Cable Communications, Cin., 1981-85; prin. Travel Agts. Internat., Cin., 1985-92; sec., treas. Warner Amex Minority Loan Fund, Cin., 1981-85. Alumni career advisor Coll. William and Mary, Williamsburg, Va., 1982—, fund raiser, 1984—. Fellow Am. Inst. CPA's, Va. Soc. CPA's; mem. Am. Soc. Travel Agts., Cruise Lines Internat. Assn., Greater Cin. C. of C. (chief exec. officer roundtable), Pi Beta Phi, Blue Ash-Montgomery Exchange Club (pres. 1989-90). Republican. Episcopalian. Avocations: scuba diving, snorkeling, reading. Home: 2207 Spinningwheel Ln Cincinnati OH 45244-4114

MCGRANE, MARY MARGARET, legislative counsel; b. N.Y.C., Apr. 18, 1953. BA, Muhlenberg Coll., 1975; MA, Drew U., 1977; JD, Cath. U., 1987. Legal asst. Baker & Hostetler, Washington, 1977-79; legis. analyst Assn. Am. Med. Colls., Washington, 1979-83; dir. govt. rels. Am. Coll. Cardiology, Bethesda, Md., 1983-84; profl. minority staff mem., 1984-88; minority counsel Ho. Com. Energy & Commerce, 1988-92, 93—; dep. asst. sec. mktg. and inspection svcs. USDA, 1992. Office: Energy & Commerce B-333 Rayburn House Office Bldg Washington DC 20515*

MCGRATH, ANNA FIELDS, library director; b. Westfield, Maine, July 4, 1932; d. Fred Elber and Nancy Phyllis (Tarbell) Fields; m. Bernard McGrath (div.); children: Timothy, Maureen, Patricia, Colleen, Rebecca. BA, U. Maine, Presque Isle, 1976; MEd, U. So. Maine, 1979; MLS, U. R.I., 1982. Libr. U. Maine, 1976-86, assoc. libr. dir., 1986-89, interim libr. dir., 1989-92; dir., 1992—. Editor: County: Land of Promise, 1989. Mem. Friends of Aroostook County Hist. Ctr. at Libr., U. Maine-Presque Isle. Mem. ASCD, ALA, Maine Libr. Assn., Friends of Aroostook County Hist. Ctr. at Libr. U. Maine-Presque Isle, Inst. Noetic Scis. Office: U Maine Libr 181 Main St Presque Isle ME 04769-2888

MCGRATH, ERIKA WEIS, economics educator, management consultant; b. Laufenselden, Hessen, Federal Republic of Germany, Nov. 17, 1937; d. Wilhelm A. and Auguste Louise (Vogt) Weis; m. Thomas J. McGrath, Oct. 1, 1963 (dec. Sept. 1984). BA, U. Calif., Santa Cruz, 1982; MA, Calif. State U., San Jose, 1984; PhD, U. Calif., Santa Barbara, 1989. Adj. asst. prof. Golden Gate U., Monterey, Calif., 1990—, Monterey Inst. Internat. Studies, 1992—; mgmt. cons. Weis Consulting, Monterey, 1992—. Mem., 1st chair Monterey County Commn. on Status of Women, Monterey, 1990-93; mem. LWV, Monterey, 1994—, Dem. Women's Club, Monterey, 1994—, Profl. Women's Network, Monterey, 1991—. Mem. ASTD, Profl. Orgn. Women in Edn., Kappa Delta Pi. Democrat. Home: 625 Filmore St Monterey CA 93940

MCGRATH, JUDITH, broadcast executive; b. Scranton, PA, 1952. Former fashion copywriter Mademoiselle; now pres. MTV Networks, Inc., New York, NY. Office: MTV Networks 1515 Broadway New York NY 10036-1903*

MCGRATH, KATHRYN BRADLEY, lawyer; b. Norfolk, Va., Sept. 2, 1944; d. James Pierce and Kathryn (Hoyle) Bradley; m. John J. McGrath Jr., June 8, 1968; children: Ian M., James D. AB, Mt. Holyoke Coll., 1966; JD, Georgetown U., 1969. Ptnr. Gardner, Carton & Douglas, Washington, 1979-83; dir. div. investment mgmt. SEC, Washington, 1983-90; ptnr. Morgan, Lewis & Bockius, Washington, 1990—. Named Disting. Exec. Pres. Reagan, 1987. Mem. Fed. Bar Assn. (exec. council securities law com.). Office: Morgan Lewis & Bockius 1800 M St NW Washington DC 20036-5869

MCGRATH, MARY HELENA, plastic surgeon, educator; b. N.Y.C., Apr. 12, 1945; d. Vincent J. and Mary M. (Manning) McG.; m. Richard H. Simon, Apr. 11, 1970; children: Margaret E. Simon, Richard M. Simon. BA, Coll. New Rochelle, 1966; MD, St. Louis U., 1970; MPH, George Washington U., 1994. Lic. surgeon, D.C. Resident in surg. pathology U. Colo. Med. Ctr., Denver, 1970-71, intern in gen. surgery, 1971-72, resident in gen. surgery, 1971-75, chief resident in gen. surgery, 1975-76; resident in plastic and reconstructive surgery Yale U. Sch. Medicine, New Haven, Conn., 1976-77; chief resident plastic and reconstructive surgery Yale U. Sch. Medicine, New Haven, 1977-78; fellow in hand surgery U. Conn.-Yale U., New Haven, 1978; instr. in surgery divsn. plastic and reconstructive surgery Yale U. Sch. Medicine, New Haven, 1977-78, asst. prof. plastic surgery, 1978-80; attending in plastic and reconstructive surgery Yale-New Haven Hosp., 1978-80, Columbia-Presbyn. Hosp., N.Y.C., 1980-84, George Washington U. Med. Ctr., Washington, 1984—, Children's Nat. Med. Ctr., Washington, 1985—; asst. prof. plastic surgery Columbia U., N.Y.C., 1980-84; assoc. prof. plastic surgery Sch. Medicine, George Washington U., Washington, 1984-87, prof. plastic surgery, 1987—; attending physician VA Hosp., West Haven, Conn., 1978-80; attending in surgery Hopital Albert Schweitzer, Deschapelles, Haiti, 1980; co-investigator Charles W. Ohse Fund, Yale U. Sch. Medicine, 1979; prin. investigator various rsch. grants, 1979-89; historian, bd. dirs. Am. Bd. Plastic Surgery, 1991-95; guest examiner certifying exam., 1986-88; specialist site visitor Residency Rev. Com. for Plastic Surgery, 1985, 87, 91, 94; presenter in field; cons. in field. Co-editor: (with M.L. Turner) Dermatology for Plastic Surgeons, 1993; assoc. editor: The Jour. of Hand Surgery, 1984-89, Plastic and Reconstructive Surgery, 1989-95, chmn. nominating com., 1994—; contbr. book chpts.: Problems in General Surgery, 1985, Human and Ethical Issues in the Surgical Care of Patients with Life-Threatening Disease, 1986, Problems in Aesthetic Surgery, Biological Causes and Clinical Solutions, 1986; guest reviewer numerous jours.; contbr. articles, abstracts to profl. jours. Fellow ACS (1st prize resident papers Conn. chpt. 1977); mem. AAAS, AMA, Am. Assn. Hand Surgery (exec. sec. 1988-90, rsch. grants com. 1983-86, chmn. edn. com. 1983-88, 1st prize ann. resident contest 1978, and numerous other coms.; D.C. chpt. program ann. meeting chmn. 1992, v.p. 1993-94, pres. 1994—), Am. Assn. Plastic Surgeons (pub. info. com. 1988-89, James Barrett Brown com. 1990-92, rsch. and edn. com. 1992-95), Am. Burn Assn., Am. Soc. for Aesthetic Plastic Surgery (FDA implant task force 1990—, pub. edn. com. 1991-92, sci. rsch. com. 1990—), Am. Soc. Maxillofacial Surgeons, Am. Soc. Plastic and Reconstructive Surgery (chmn. ethics com. 1985-87, chmn. device/tech. evaluation com. 1993-94, bd. dirs. 1994—; mem. ednl. found. bd. dirs. 1985-88, treas. 1989-92, v.p. 1992-93, pres.-elect 1993-94, pres. 1994-95, numerous other coms.), Am. Soc. Reconstructive Microsurgery (mem. edn. com. 1992-94), Am. Soc. Surgery of Hand (chmn. 1987 ann. residents' and fellows conf. 1986-87, mem. rsch. com. 1988-90, and others), Assn. Acad. Chmn. Plastic Surgery (mem. prerequisite tng. com. 1990-92, mem. com. aesthetic surgery tng. 1992—), Assn. Acad. Surgery, D.C. Met. Area Soc. Plastic and Reconstructive Surgeons, Internat. Soc. Reconstructive Surgery, Met. D.C. Soc. Surgery Hand, N.Y. Surg. Soc., Northeastern Soc. Plastic Surgeons (chmn. sci. program com. 1991, chmn. fin. com. 1992-93, treas. 1993—, others), Plastic Surgery Rsch. Coun. (chmn.-elect 1989, chmn. 1990), Soc. Ancient Medicine, Surg. Biology Club III, The Wound Healing Soc., Washington Acad. Surgery, Washington Med. and Surg. Soc. Office: George Washington U # 6B-422 2150 Penn Ave NW Washington DC 20037

MCGRATTAN, MARY K., state legislator; b. N.Y.C.. RN, St. Catherine's Hosp. Sch. of Nursing. Mem. town coun. City of Ledyard, Conn., 1977-83, mayor, 1983-90; pres. Conn. Conf. of Municipalities, 1990-91; mem. Ledyard Dem. Town Com.; state rep. Conn. Ho. of Reps., 1993—. Address: 8 Eagle Ridge Dr Gales Ferry CT 06335-1904 Office: Conn Ho of Reps State Capitol Hartford CT 06106*

MCGRAW, JANET GOLLER, executive secretary; b. Tulsa, Sept. 23, 1936; d. Walter Henry and Caroline Wilhelmina (Pedersen) Goller; m. Russell McGraw, Oct. 11, 1958; children: Theresa A. McGraw-French, Jeanne M. McGraw Garalis, Mary K., Alice E. McGraw Lively. Cert. in acctg., DeKalb Community Coll., 1983, cert. profl. sec., 1986; cert. of mgmt., U. Ga., 1988. Cert. profl. sec. Sec. to mgr. Merrill, Lynch, Pierce, Fenner & Smith, Miami Beach, Fla., 1954-59; sec. to v.p. Am. Bonded Mortgage Co., Miami, Fla., 1960-62; sec. John Nicholas, Miami, 1962-72; exec. sec. to fire chief DeKalb County Fire Services, Decatur, Ga., 1973—. Mem. adv. coun. Goodwill Industries, Inc., DeKalb Tech. Inst. Recipient Disting. Leadership award, 1988. Mem. NAFE, Profl. Sec. Internat. (membership com. 1985-86, ways and means com. 1985-86, publicity com. 1986-87, Statewide Sec. of Yr. award 1989, 1991, DeKalb chpt. sec. 1989-90, pres. 1991-92, 92-93, sec. bd. Ga. divsn. 1994-95, Mem. of Yr. award 1994),. Office: DeKalb County Dept Pub Safety 4400 Memorial Dr Decatur GA 30032-1300

MCGRAW, LAVINIA MORGAN, former retail company executive; b. Detroit, Feb. 26, 1924; d. Will Curtis and Margaret Coulter (Oliphant) McG. AB, Radcliffe Coll., 1945. Mem. Phi Beta Kappa. Home: 2501 Calvert St NW Washington DC 20008-2620

MCGREEVY, MARY, retired psychology educator; b. Kansas City, Kans., Nov. 10, 1935; d. Donald and Emmy Lou (Neubert) McG.; m. Phillip Rosenbaum (dec.); children: David, Steve, Mariya, Chay, Allyn, Jacob, Dora. BA in English with honors, Vassar Coll., 1957; postgrad., New Sch. for Social Rsch., NYU, 1958-59, Columbia U., 1959-60, U. P.R., 1963-65, U. Mo., 1965-68, U. Kans.; PhD, U. Calif., Berkeley, 1969. Formerly exec. Doubleday & Co., N.Y.C., 1957-60; chief libr. San Juan Sch., P.R., 1962-63; NIMH drug researcher Russell Sage Found., Clinico de los Addictos, Rio Piedras, P.R., 1963-65; psychiat. researcher U. P.R. Med. Sch., 1963-65, U. Kans., Lawrence, 1966-68; rsch. assoc. Ednl. Rsch., 1966-68; prof. U. Calif., Berkeley, 1968-69, disting. prof., ret., 1969; yacht owner Encore; lectr. in field. Author: (poetry) To a Sailor, 1989, Dreams & Illusions, 1993, also articles, poems. Founder, exec. dir. Dora Achenbach McGreevy Poetry Found., Inc.; active Fla. Atlantic U. Found., 1993—; vol. Broward County Hist. Commn.; chair subcom. Jeanne Farkis Meml. Scholarship Fund, chair cultural events, 1995—. Recipient Cert. for Svc. Broward County Hist. Commn., 1994; Sproul fellow; fellow Bancroft Libr., Russell Sage Found.; postdoctoral grantee U. Calif. Mem. AAUW (corr. sec. 1991—, bd. dirs. 1991—, honoree Ednl. Found. Fund 1993, scholarship com. 1992—, Women of History awards), Pres.'s Coun., Broward Women's History Coalition (bd. dirs. 1991—, archivist), Am. Phil. Assn. (bd. dirs. 1991—), Am. Philos. Assn., Women in Psych., Union of Concerned Scientists, South Fla. Poetry Inst. (yearly poetry anthology 1991—), Fla. Philos. Assn. (spkr. 1991, 93, chair self in philosophy 1994), Poets of the Palm Beaches, Ft. Lauderdale Philharm. Soc., Vassar Alumni Assn. (class historian), Oxfam Am., Pem-Hill Alumni Assn., Naval Base Hist. Soc. Ft. Lauderdale, St. Anthony's Cath. Women's Club, Sierra Club (newspaper reporter, environ. com., archivist 1993—, co-chair beach clean-up 1993), Secular Humanists, Poets of the Palm Beaches (yearly poetry anthology 1992—), Fla. Women's Consortium. Home: PO Box 900 Fort Lauderdale FL 33302-0900

MCGREGOR, CONSTANCE LEONARD, state official, nurse; b. Hartford, Conn., May 31, 1931; d. Harry Peter and Helen (Psinakis) Leonard; m. Bruce McGregor, May 29, 1959; children: Elena, Bruce III. BSN, Union U., 1958; postgrad., Russell Sage Coll., Sienna Coll. Pub. health nurse, epidemiologist N.Y. State Dept. Health, Albany, N.Y., 1954-62, spl. cons. nurse Bur. Long Term Care, 1983-85; jr. rsch. asst. N.Y. State Assembly, Albany, 1978, project coord. Office Minority Leader, 1981-83; cons. case mix nurse reviewer Office Health Sys. Mgmt. N.Y. State Senate, Albany, 1985—; chmn. Otsego County Health Planning Coun., 1987-89, active, 1986—, Otsego County Pub. Health Com., 1974, active, 1965-80; screening nurse cons. Utilization Rev. Com., 1978—; mem. adv. coun. on nursing edn. Dept. Health & Human Svcs., Washington, 1990-94, mem. needs assessment adv. panel, 1988-90; active Otsego County Mental Health Bd., 1965-66, Maternal and Fertility Drug Adv. Com., 1984, Needs Assessment Instrument Adv. Panel, 1988. N.Y. State dir., hostess and bus. telephone program Com. to Re-elect the President, 1972; dir. 6th jud. dist. N.Y. State Fedn. Rep. Women, 1973-75, 2nd v.p., 1975-77, 1st v.p., 1977-79, pres., 1979-81; vice chmn. for women N.Y. State Com., 1979-81, mem. platform com., 1982; mem.-at-large, bd. dirs. Nat. Fedn Rep. Women, 1981-83, bd. dirs., 1979-88, 4th v.p., 1983-85, mem. faculty campaign mgmt. sch., 1983-88; co-chmn. N.Y. State Fedn. Ford-Dole Telephone Program, 1976, N.Y. State Commitment - '80 Reagan Bush Campaign, 1980; del. and co-chmn. N.Y. State Delegation to Rep. Nat. Nominating Conv., 1980; chmn. N.Y. Rep. Women's Polit. Action Com., 1985—; surrogate spkr. prominent women Bush-Quayle Campaign, 1988; mem. external adv. com. Hartwick Coll., Oneonta, N.Y., 1991—; active 6th Jud. Dist. Supreme Ct. Campaign, 1978, N.Y. State Heritage Adv. Coun., 1980, Rep. Women's Leadership Forum-Reagan Bush Spkrs. Bur., 1984, Glimmerglass Opera Guild. Mem. AAUW, Am. Hellenic Inst. (mem. pub. affairs com.), Fortnightly Club of Worcester, Women's Nat. Rep. Club (bd. govs. 1982—, 3d v.p. 1985-86, 2nd v.p. 1986-88). Greek Orthodox. Home: 43 Decatur Rd Worcester NY 12197 Office: NY State Senate 41 S Main St Oneonta NY 13820

MCGREGOR, MICHELE LYNN, civil designer, agricultural engineer; b. Pitts., May 3, 1963; d. Marlin Ford and Andrea Mae (Hollier) McG. BS in Landscape Architecture, Pa. State U., 1986; postgrad., Rutgers U., 1993—. Project designer Abbington-Ney Assocs., Kendall Pk., N.J., 1986-87, Lippincott Engrng. Assocs., Delanco, N.J., 1987-88, John F. Kennedy & Assocs., Lambertville, N.J., 1988-90; project engr. Elam & Popoff Profl. Assn., Fairlawn, N.J., 1990-93, Thomas L. Yager & Assocs., Doylestown, Pa., 1994—. Fellow mem. Names Project, N.J., 1987—, People for the Ethical Treatment of Animals, 1989—, Nat. Pks. and Conservation Assn., 1987—. Named Most Improved Sr. student Pa. State U., 1986. Mem. NOW, Nat. Womens Martial Arts Fedn., Big Bros./Big Sisters, Gamma Phi Beta Sorority. Home: 102 Spring St Easton PA 18042-6155 Office: Thomas L Yager & Assocs Grayrock Rd Clinton NJ 08809

MCGRIFF, DENYSE CYD, land use planner; b. Ft. Lenordwood, Mo., July 24, 1951; d. Asberry D.; m. R.E. Guttridge, Aug. 24, 1985; 1 child, Stephen. BA in History and Polit. Sci., Coll. of Notre Dame, 1973; MS in Polit. Sci., U. Oreg., 1978, M in Urban & Regional Planning, 1979. Planner Columbia County, St. Helens, Oreg., 1978; city planner City of Tillamook City, Oreg., 1981-79; assoc. planner-land use Port of Portland, Oreg., 1981-82; sr. planner Deschutes County, Bend, Oreg., 1982-88; prin. planner City of Oreg. City, 1988—. Regional rep. Hist. Preservation League of Oreg., Portland, 1989—; v.p. Old Home Forum, Oreg. City, 1993-94, McLoughlin Meml. Assn., Oreg. City, 1993-94. Mem. Am. Planning Assn. Democrat. Office: City of Oreg City PO Box 351 Oregon City OR 97045

MC GRORY, MARY, columnist; b. Boston, 1918; d. Edward Patrick and Mary (Jacobs) McGrory. A.B., Emmanuel Coll. Reporter Boston Herald Traveler, 1942-47; book reviewer Washington Star, 1947-54, feature writer for nat. staff, 1954-81; now syndicated columnist The Washington Post, Universal Press Syndicate. Recipient George Polk Meml. award; Pulitzer prize for commentary, 1975. Office: Washington Post 1150 15th St NW Washington DC 20071*

MCGRORY, MARY KATHLEEN, university official; b. N.Y.C., Mar. 22, 1933; d. Patrick Joseph and Mary Kate (Gilvary) McG. BA, Pace U., 1957; MA, U. Notre Dame, 1962; PhD, Columbia U., 1969; DHL, Albertus Magnus Coll., 1984; LLD, Briarwood Coll., 1990; DHL, Trinity Coll., 1991. Prof. English Western Conn. State U., Danbury, 1969-78; dean of arts and scis. Eastern Conn. State U., Willimantic, 1978-80, v.p. for acad. affairs, 1981-85; pres. Hartford Coll. for Women, Conn., 1985-91; sr. fellow U. Va. Commonwealth Ctr., Charlottesville, 1991-92; exec. dir. society values in higher edn. Georgetown U., Washington, 1992—; pres. MKM Assocs., Holland, Ma., 1983—. Author: Yeats, Joyce & Beckett, 1975. Bd. dirs. Hartford Hosp., 1985-93; chmn. bd. govs. Greater Hartford Consortium Higher Edn., 1989-90. Fels Found. fellow, 1966-67, NEH summer fellow, 1975; Ludwig Vogelstein Found. travel grantee, 1973. Mem. New Eng. Jr. Community and Tech. Coll. Coun. (v.p. 1988-91), Am. Assn. Higher Edn., Med. Acad. of Am., Greater Hartford C. of C. (bd. dirs. 1989-91), Hartford Club (bd. dirs. 1988-91). Home: 1727 Massachusetts Ave NW Washington DC 20036 Office: Georgetown U Soc For Values Higher Washington DC 20057

MCGUCKIN, WENDY MICHELLE BLASSINGAME, accounting specialist; b. Guymon, Okla., June 11, 1966; d. Ronald Clifford Blassingame and Evelyn Marie (Maddox) Martin; m. Randall Mack McGuckin, Sept. 11, 1993. BS, U. Okla., 1989. Cert. tchr. Okla. Sales assoc. Sound Warehouse, Dallas, 1985-86; tchr. Norman (Okla.) Pub. Schs., 1989-90; pub. rels. coord. Hatfield and Bell, Inc., Norman, 1990-91; fin. cons. Sun Fin. Group, Oklahoma City, 1991; acctg. specialist U. Okla., Norman, 1991—; co-owner Wildfire Horse Ranch. Environ. activist, Oklahoma City, 1990; vol. Okla. Equine Hosp., 1994. Mem. NAFE, NRA, Little Timbers Riding Assn., Okla. Equestrian Trail Riders Assn., Ducks Unltd. Republican. Methodist. Office: Univ Okla 620 Elm Ave Norman OK 73069-8801

MCGUE, CHRISTIE, federal official; b. Columbus, Ohio, Feb. 1, 1949; m. Robert Calt, Nov. 13, 1992. Sr. mgmt. analyst Nuclear Regulatory Comm., Washington, 1973-76; asst. sec., asst. dir. Office of Elec. Power Regulations, asst. dir. Office of Hydropower Licensing Fed. Energy Regulatory Comm., Washington, 1977-85; with Dept. Interior, Washington, 1986-88; dep. exec. dir. Fed. Energy Regulatory Commn., Washington, 1990-93, exec. dir., CFO, 1994—. Office: Fed Energy Regulatory Commn 825 N Capitol St NE Rm 9106 Washington DC 20426

MCGUFFEY, TERRI ANN, guidance counselor; b. Paris, Mar. 5, 1964; came to U.S., 1968; d. Robert Aaron and Mabel Itaska (Steph) McG. BA in Phys. Edn., Calif. State U., Fresno, 1987, MA in Edn. Counseling, 1990. Cert. sch. counselor, N.Y. Career counselor Fresno City Coll., 1989-90; coord. acad. resources SUNY, Syracuse, 1993-94; personal trainer Utica, N.Y., 1992—; guidance counselor USAF, Griffiss AFB, N.Y., 1994—; tutor, evaluator SUNY, Syracuse, 1993—; leader civil svc. workshops USAF, 1994—. Vol. Steven-Swan Humane Soc., Utica, 1994; activities coord., participant 416 Mission Support Squadron, Griffiss AFB, 1994—; mem. ASPCA, 1994; mem. VA, 1994. With USAF, 1990-92. Decorated Nat. Def. Svc. medal, 1992. Mem. Nat. Assn. Female Execs., Nat. Acad. Advising Assn. Democrat. Home: PO Box 1771 Utica NY 13503-1771 Office: 416 MSS/DPE 333 Wright Dr Griffiss A F B NY 13441-4625

MCGUINNESS, BARBARA SUE, food products executive; b. Lansing, Mich., Feb. 8, 1947; d. William Harrison and Gertrude Esther (Parker) Coleman; m. Michael L. Mueller, Aug. 12, 1965 (div. June 1973); children: Meredith Sue, Matthew Parker; m. John McGuinness, Dec. 8, 1978. Student, Meramec Community Coll., 1975-77, Florissant Valley Community Coll., 1984-87. Instr. Lindbergh Sch. Dist., St. Louis, 1975-77; surp. Velvet Freeze Ice Cream Co., St. Louis, 1977-81, v.p., 1981—. Chmn. Fin. Com. Chesterfield (Mo.) Transition Com., 1988—, campaign chmn. Chesterfield Inc. Com., 1988—, chmn. Chesterfield Planning & Zoning Commn., 1988—, chmn. Chesterfield Inaugural Commn., 1988; rep. State Mo. Electoral Coll. U.S., 1988; apptd. vice-chmn. Selective Svc. System Draft Bd. #20, 1981-91, chmn., 1991-92; state parliamentarian Mo. Fedn. Women's Dem. Clubs, 1989-91, 93—; del. Dem. Nat. Conv., 1972, 80, 92; mem. Leadership St. Louis, 1991—, St. Louis County Pvt. Industry Coun., 1991—, St. Louis County DARES Bd., 1991-94, Mayor's Chester Valley Flood Recovery Task Force, 1993-94, Chesterfield Valley Rebuilding Task Force, 1993-94, Chesterfield Intergovernmental Rels. Com., 1993-94; campaign mgr. Robert McCulloch for county prosecuting atty., St. Louis, 1990-94, Howard Wagner Mo. Sec. of State, 1992; active Chesterfield Econ. Devel. Coun., 1990-91; chmn. St. Louis County Inagural Commn., 1991. Recipient Key to City award City Govt. Crestwood, Mo., 1974, Key to City Chesterfield, 1988, Distinguished Service award, 1988, St. Louis County Dem. of Yr. award, 1986, Planning Comsnr. or Yr. award Dwight Davis Am. Planning Assn., 1993, Excellence in Community Devel. award Chesterfield Civ. Progress, 1993, Humanitarian award 1993, End Hunger award U.S. Mayors, 1993, Disting. Svc. awad Mid-East Area Agy. on Aging, 1994; named Chesterfield Citizen of Yr., 1989. Mem. Am. Planning Assn., Area Ice Cream Retailers Assn. (pres. 1979-84), Chesterfield C. of C. (Civic award 1988). Democrat. Baptist. Home: 95 Riverbend Dr Chesterfield MO

63017-2645 Office: Velvet Freeze Ice Cream Co 7355 W Florissant Ave Saint Louis MO 63136-1348

MCGUINNESS, EVELYNN R., clinical psychologist; b. Orange, N.J., July 29, 1946; d. Peter Francis and Evelyn M.; m. John Morgan Allman, June 26, 1976 (April 1991). BS, Shimer Coll., 1968; MS, Rutgers U., 1974; PhD, Vanderbilt U., 1979. lic. psychol. Calif. Rsch. asst. Rutgers U., New Brunswick, N.J., 1971-72; teaching asst. Rutgers U., New Brunswick, 1972-73; rsch. asst. Vanderbilt U., Nashville, 1974-76; postdoctoral fellow UCLA, 1979-80; rsch. fellow Calif. Inst. Tech., Pasadena, 1980-84, mem. profl. staff, 1984-90; primary therapist Foothill Mental Health, Sylmar, Calif., 1991—; clin. psychol. Deacon, Parent and Assocs., Glendale, Calif., 1992—; cons. Commn. Ednl. Opportunity for Economically Disenfranchised, 1973. Contbr. articles to profl. jours. and chpts. to books. pres. La Tuna Cyn Community Awareness Assn., 1988-89; rep. 2d dist. L.A. City Solid Waste Citizens Adv. Com., 1989-94. Named Ethel Mae Wilson Fellow Vanderbilt U., 1976. mem. APA, Am. Primatological Soc., L.A. County Psychol. Assn., Glendale Mental Health Providers, Internat. Soc. Primatologists. Office: Deacon Parent & Assocs 3245 Verdugo Rd Glendale CA 91208

MCGUINNESS-MUKERJEE, JOANNE HELENE, nursing administrator, consultant; b. Providence, Aug. 22, 1942; d. John William and Helen Louise (McCormack) McGuinness; m. Dilip K. Mukerjee, Feb. 6, 1975 (div. 1979). BS in Nursing, Simmons Coll., 1979; MEd, Cambridge Coll., 1982. Clin. specialist Lawrence (Mass.) Gen. Hosp., 1980-81; asst. dir. nursing Essex Hall, Beverly, Mass., 1981-82, Greenery Rehab. Ctr., Brighton, Mass., 1982-83; dir. nursing Elder Care Services, Tewksbury, Mass., 1983-84; asst. adminstr. Webster Manor, Mass., 1984-85, adminstr., exec. dir., 1985-89; adminstr. ADS Mgmt., Boston, 1989-93; CEO Univ. Commons Nursing Care Ctr., Worcester, Mass., 1993—; lectr. Regis Coll., Weston, Mass., 1990—, Assn. Mass. Homes for the Aging, 1993; presenter in field. Author: An Understanding of Policy Analysis, 1982. Mem. ANA (cert. adminstr., mem. gerontol. council), Am. Coll. Health Care Execs., Mass. Nurses Assn. (mem. nominating com. dist. IV 1987-88, mem. long term care task force, conveyor for nurse practice act legis.), Mass. Fedn. Nursing Homes (program chair 1984-85), Am. Nurses Found. Roman Catholic. Avocations: private and comml. pilot multiengine rating, golf, collecting 17th and 18th century French antiques. Home: 378 Plantation St Worcester MA 01650 Office: 120 Fisher Ave Boston MA 02120-3320

MCGUIRE, CAROLE BAKER, legislative staff member; b. Seattle, Dec. 26, 1951. BA, Western Wash. U., 1974. Budget aide Sen. Warren Magnuson, 1974-76; legis. analyst, 1976-81, legis. and budget analyst, 1981-85; dir. appropriations activities Budget Com., 1985—. Office: Com Budget 635 Senate Dirksen Office Bldg Washington DC 20510*

MC GUIRE, DOROTHY HACKETT, actress; b. Omaha, June 14, 1916; d. Thomas Johnston and Isabel (Flaherty) McG.; m. John Swope, July 18, 1943 (dec.); children: Topo Swope, Mark Swope. Student, Pine Manor Jr. Coll., 1936-38. Stage debut in A Kiss for Cinderella, Omaha, 1933; played stock in Deertrees, Maine; N.Y.C. debut as understudy in Stop-Over, 1938; played role of Emily in Our town, on Broadway, 1938; toured with My Dear Children, 1939; starred in Claudia, 1941; toured in USO prodn. Dear Ruth, Europe, 1945, USO prodn. Tonight at 8:30, 1947, Summer and Smoke, 1950; appeared in Broadway prodn. Legend of Lovers, 1951, Joan at the Stake, 1954, Winesburg, Ohio, 1958, The Night of the Iguana, 1976, Cause Celebre, 1979; film appearances include: Claudia, 1943, A Tree Grows in Brooklyn, 1945, The Enchanted Cottage, 1945, Claudia and David, 1946, The Spiral Staircase, 1946, Gentlemen's Agreement, 1947, Mr. 880, Invitation, 1952, Make Haste to Live, 1954, Three Coins in the Fountain, 1954, Trial, 1955, Friendly Persuasion, 1956, Old Yeller, 1957, This Earth is Mine, 1959, A Summer Place, 1959, The Remarkable Mr. Penny Pincher, The Swiss Family Robinson, 1960, The Dark at the Top of the Stairs, 1960, Susan Slade, 1961, Summer Magic, 1962, The Greatest Story Ever Told, 1965, Flight of the Doves, 1971; film appearances include (voice only) Jonathan Livingston Seagull, 1973; appeared in: TV movie She Waits, 1971, TV prodn Am. Playhouse: I Never Sang For My Father, 1988; radio serial Big Sister, 1937; Juliette in: Romeo and Juliette; Ophelia in Hamlet, 1951; TV appearances include U.S. Steel Hour, 1954, Lux Video Theatre, 1954, Climax, 1954, 56, Play House 90, Another Part of the Forest, 1972, The Runaways, 1975, The Philadelphia Story, 1954, Rich Man Poor Man, 1970, Little Women, 1978, The Incredible Journey of Doctor Meg Laurel, Ghost Dancing, 1983, Love Boat, 1984. Recipient N.Y. Drama Critics Circle award, 1941; named Best Actress by Nat. Bd. Rev., 1955. Mem. Screen Actors Guild, Actors Equity Assn., AFTRA. Office: Raymond J Gertz Acctg Corp 10351 Santa Monica Blvd Los Angeles CA 90025-6912

MCGUIRE, MARY JO, state legislator; b. 1956. BA in Bus. Adminstrn., Coll. of St. Catherine; JD, Hamline U. Mem. Minn. State Senate, 1988, 90, 92—, mem. environ. and natural resources fin., vice chair, judiciary com., judiciary fin. divsn., mem. rules and legis. adminstrn. Democrat. Home: 1529 Iowa Ave W Saint Paul MN 55108-2128 Office: Minn State Senate State Capital Saint Paul MN 55155*

MCGUIRE, MICHELE, film and televison producer. prodn. auditor asst.: Teen Wolf Too, 1987, Barfly, 1987, Doin' Time on Planet Earth, 1988; prodn. coord.: (films) Rich Girl, 1991, A Climate for Killing, 1991, Shadowhunter, 1993, (TV films) A Place to Be Loved, 1993, Fatherland, 1994; prodn. auditor: (films) Dice Rules, 1991, (TV spls.) Missing Parents, 1991, Without a Pass, 1992, The Washing Machine Man, 1992, Session Man, 1992, Under the Car, 1993, Traveler's Rest, 1993; prodr.: (TV spls.) The Witness, 1993, Love Matters, 1993, The Last Shot, 1993, Texan, 1994, On Hope, 1994 (Acad. award nom., Best Live Action Short Film), Leslie's Folly, 1994, A Hard Rain, 1994. *

MCGUIRE, PAMELA COTTAM, lawyer; b. Boston, Aug. 25, 1947; d. Robert D., and Marion E. (Swift) Cottam; m. Eugene G. McCuire, Sept. 14, 1969; children—Lauren Lambert, Christopher Cottam. B.A., Vassar Coll., 1969; M.S. in Urban Planning, Columbia U., 1973, J.D., 1973. Bar: N.Y. 1974, U.S. Dist. Ct. (ea. dist.) N.Y. 1974, U.S. Dist. Ct. (so. dist.) N.Y. 1974, U.S. Ct. Appeals (2d cir.) 1974. Law clk. to presiding judge U.S. Dist. Ct. (ea. dist.) N.Y., Bklyn., 1973-74; asst. U.S. atty., U.S. Atty.'s Office, Blkyn., 1974-75; staff counsel Moreland Commn., N.Y.C., 1975-76; assoc. Hughes, Hubbard & Reed, N.Y.C., 1976-77; staff counsel PepsiCo, Inc., Purchase, N.Y., 1977-82, div. counsel, 1982-84, food law counsel, 1984—, now v.p., div. counsel. Woodrow Wilson Found. fellow, 1973. Office: Pepsi Cola Co Anderson Hill Rd Purchase NY 10577-2002*

MCGUIRE, PATRICIA A., lawyer, academic administrator; b. Phila., Nov. 13, 1952; d. Edward J. and Mary R. McGuire. BA cum laude, Trinity Coll., 1974; JD, Georgetown U., 1977. Bar: Pa. 1977, D.C. Ct. Appeals 1979. Program dir. Georgetown U. St. Law Clinic, Washington, 1977-82; asst. dean for devel. and external affairs Georgetown U. Law Ctr., Washington, 1982-89; pres. Trinity Coll., Washington, 1989—; adj. prof. law Georgetown U., 1977-82, Georgetown Law Ctr., 1987—; commr. Middle States Commn. on Higher Edn., 1991—. Editor: Street Law Mock Trial Manual, 1984; contbr. articles to profl. jours. Trustee Trintiy Coll., Washington, 1986—, mem. presdl. search com., 1987; bd. dirs. Assn. Cath. Colls. and Univs., 1991—; mem. adv. bd. Merion Mercy Acad. and Sisters of Mercy, 1990—; bd. dirs. Nat. Assn. Ind. Colls. and Univs.; mem. commn. govt. rels. Am. Coun. Edn. Recipient Daytime Emmy, TV Acad., N.Y.C., 1979-80. Mem. ABA, Assn. Am. Law Schs. (instl. advancement 1985—), Coun. for the Advancement and Support of Edn., Trinity Coll. Alumnae Assn. (pres. 1986-89). Democrat. Roman Catholic. Office: Trinity Coll Office of the President 125 Michigan Ave NE Washington DC 20017-1094

MCGUIRE, SANDRA LYNN, nursing educator; b. Flint, Mich., Jan. 28, 1947; d. Donald Armstrong and Mary Lue (Harvey) Johnson; m. Joseph L. McGuire, Mar. 6, 1976; children: Matthew, Kelly, Kerry. BS in Nursing, U. Mich., 1969, MPH, 1973, EdD, 1988. Staff nurse Univ. Hosp., Ann Arbor, Mich., 1969; pub. health nurse Wayne County Health Dept., Eloise, Mich., 1969-72; instr. Madonna Coll., Livonia, Mich., 1973; pub. health coordinator Plymouth Ctr. for Human Devel., Northville, Mich., 1974-75; asst. prof. community health nursing U. Mich., Ann Arbor, 1975-83; asst. prof. U. Tenn., Knoxville, 1983-88, assoc. prof., 1990—; dir. Kids Are Tomorrow's Srs. Program, 1988—; resource person Gov.'s Com. Unification of Mental Health Services in Mich.; speaker profl. assns. and workshops; bd. dirs. Ctr. Understanding Aging, 1987-93, v.p. 1995—. Author: (with S. Clemen-Stone and D. Eigsti) Comprehensive Family and Community Health Nursing, 1981, 3d edit., 1991, 4th edit. 1995. Bd. dirs. Mich. chpt. ARC, 1980-83, Knoxville chpt., 1984-85; founder Knoxville Intergenerational Network, 1989. USPHS fellow, 1972-73. Mem. APHA, ANA, Tenn. Nurses Assn., Nat. League Nursing, Tenn. League Nursing, Tenn. Pub. Health Assn. (chmn. mental health sect. 1976) Mich. Pub. Health Assn. (dir., co-chmn. residential services com. 1976-79, chmn. health services 1979-82), Plymouth (chmn. residential services com. 1975-77) Tenn. Assn. Retarded Citizens, So. Nursing Rsch. Soc., Sigma Theta Tau, Pi Lambda Theta, Phi Kappa Phi. Home: 11008 Crosswind Dr Knoxville TN 37922-4011 Office: 1200 Volunteer Blvd Knoxville TN 37916-3806

MCGUIRL, MARLENE DANA CALLIS, law librarian, educator; b. Hammond, Ind., Mar. 22, 1938; d. Daniel David and Helen Elizabeth (Baludis) Callis; m. James Franklin McGuirl, Apr. 24, 1965. A.B., Ind. U., 1959; J.D., DePaul U., 1963; M.A.L.S., Rosary Coll., 1965; LL.M., George Washington U., 1978, postgrad. Harvard U., 1985. Bar: Ill. 1963, Ind. 1964, D.C. 1972. Asst., DePaul Coll. of Law Library, 1961-62, asst. law librarian, 1962-65; ref. law librarian Boston Coll. Sch. Law, 1965-66; library dir. D.C. Bar Library, 1966-70; asst. chief Am.-Brit. Law Div. Libr. of Congress, Washington, 1970, chief, 1970-90, environ. cons., 1990—; counsel Cooter & Gell, 1992-93; libr. cons. Nat. Clearinghouse on Poverty Law, OEO, Washington, 1967-69, Northwestern U. Nat. Inst. Edn. in Law and Poverty, 1969, D.C. Office of Corp. Counsel, 1969-70; instr. law librarianship Grad. Sch. of U.S. Dept. of Agr., 1968-72; lectr. legal lit. Cath. U., 1972; adj. asst. prof., 1973-91; lectr. environ. law George Washington U., 1979—; judge Nat. and Internat. Law Moot Ct. Competition, 1976-78, 90—; pres. Hamburger Heaven, Inc., Palm Beach, Fla., 1981-91, L'Image de Marlene Ltd., 1986-92, Clinique de Beauté Inc., 1987-92, Heads & Hands Inc., 1987-92, Horizon Design & Mfg. Co., Inc., 1987—; dir. Stoneridge Farm Inc., Gt. Falls, Va., 1984—. Contbr. articles to profl. jours. Mem. Georgetown Citizens Assn.; trustee D.C. Law Students in Ct.; del. Ind. Democratic Conv., 1964. Recipient Meritorious Service award Library of Congress, 1974, letter of commendation Dir. of Personnel, 1976, cert. of appreciation, 1981-84. Mem. ABA (facilities law library Congress com. 1976-89), Fed. Bar Assn. (chpt. council 1972-76), Ill. Bar Assn., Women's Bar Assn. (pres. 1972-73, exec. bd. 1973-77, Outstanding Contbn. to Human Rights award 1975), D.C. Bar Assn., Am. Bar Found., Nat. Assn. Women Lawyers, Am. Assn. Law Libraries, (exec. bd. 1973-77), Law Librarians Soc. of Washington (pres. 1971-73), Exec. Women in Govt. Home: 3416 P St NW Washington DC 20007-2705

MCGUIRL, SUSAN ELIZABETH, lawyer; b. Providence, Sept. 10, 1952; d. John Raymond and Rita Mary (Ryan) McG. BA, R.I. Coll., 1974; JD, Suffolk U., 1977. Bar: R.I. 1977, U.S. Dist. Ct. R.I. 1977, U.S. Ct. Appeals (1st cir.) 1983, U.S. Supreme Ct. 1983. Spl. asst. atty. gen. State of R.I., Providence, 1977-80, dep. atty. gen., 1980-84; assoc. Lipsey & Skolnik, Providence, 1985-87; chief justice Providence Housing Ct., 1987-93; ptnr. Cerilli, McGuirl & Bicki, Providence. Pres. R.I. Young Dems., 1974-76; mem. R.I. Coll. Found., 1984—, Providence 350 Jubilee Commn., 1986—; chmn. R.I. Coll. Ann. Drive, 1986—. Recipient Woman's Achievement award Gov.'s Adv. Com. on Women, 1980; Named Hon. Capt. R.I. State Police, 1982, Woman of Yr., R.I. Jaycees, 1983. Mem. ABA, R.I. Bar Assn., R.I. Women's Bar Assn., Assn. Trial Lawyers Am., R.I. Trial Lawyers Assn. Democrat. Roman Catholic. Office: Cerilli McGuirl & Bicki 56 Pine St Providence RI 02903-2819

MCGULPIN, ELIZABETH JANE, nurse; b. Toledo, Oct. 18, 1932; d. James Orville and Leah Fayne (Helton) Welden; m. David Nelson Buster, Apr. 9, 1956 (div. Nov. 1960); children: David Hugh, James Ray, Mark Stephen; m. Fredrick Gordon McGulpin, Oct. 7, 1973. AA in Nursing, Pasadena City Coll., 1968. RN, Wash. Lic. nurse Las Encinas Hosp., Pasadena, Calif.; nurse Hopi Indian Reservation HEW, Keams Canyon, Ariz., 1969-70; nurse, enterostomal therapist Pasadena Vis. Nurse Assn., 1972-74; nurse Seattle King County Pub. Health, 1977-81; home care nurse Victorville, Calif., 1983-85; nurse Adult Family Home, Woodinville, Wash., 1986—; vol. nurse, counselor Child Protective Svcs., Victorville, 1984; realtor Century 21, Lynden, Wash., 1993—. Vol. nurse Am. Cancer Soc., Pasadena, 1973-75, United Ostomy Assn., Los Angeles, Victorville, 1973-84. Am. Cancer Soc. grantee. Mem. Nat. Assn. Realtors, Wash. Assn. Realtors, Whatcom County Assn. Realtors, Vis. Nurse Assn. (Enterostomal Therpay grantee 1973). Home: 106 Kale St Everson WA 98247-9660

MCGURK-KREMKOW, HEATHER, sales executive; b. Allentown, Pa., Apr. 5, 1966; d. James H. and Lavern M. (Kraynek) McGurk; m. Robert Kremkow, Aug. 20, 1989; children: Matthew Craig and Ryan Jeffrey (twins). Degree in interior design, Mich. State U., 1987. V.p. Western/Pegasus Inc., Holland, Mich. Treas. Aramis Square Condo Assn., Holland. Mem. Delta Gamma Beta Xi Housing Corp. (pres.). Home: 1323 Steaders Pass Zeeland MI 49464-1451 Office: 728 E 8th St Holland MI 49423-3080

MCILROY, KATHRYN RUTH, engineer; b. La Rochelle, France, Mar. 12, 1953; came to U.S., 1953; d. Richard James McIlroy and Mary Jane (Gillard) Sprong. Assoc in Computer Tech., Wake Tech. Coll., 1982; degree in elec. engring., Nat. Edn. Tng. Corp., 1986. Registered profl. engr., N.C. Relay design technician Carolina Power & Light, Raleigh, N.C., 1982-86, divsn. engr., 1986-93; relay stds. engr. Carolina Power & Light, Raleigh, 1993—. Mentor Women and Math. Program, 1995. Sgt. U.S. Army, 1976-80. Mem. Now (treas. Raleigh chpt. 1990), ASPCA, Humane Soc., Nature Conservancy, Sierra Club. Democrat. Office: Carolina Power & Light Co CPB-6C3 411 Fayetteville St Mall Raleigh NC 27602

MCILWAIN, CLARA EVANS, agricultural economist, consultant; b. Jacksonville, Fla., Apr. 5, 1919; d. Waymon and Jerusha Lee (Dickson) Evans; m. Ivy McIlwain, May 15, 1942 (dec. 1987); children: Ronald E., Carol A. McIlwain Edwards, Marilyn E. McIlwain Ross, Ivy J. McIlwain Lindsay. BS, U. D.C., 1939; M Agrl. Econs., U. Fla., 1972. Notary pub., Va.; lic. life and health ins. agt., Md., Va., D.C. Statis. asst. Hist. and Statis. Analysis Div., Washington, 1962-67; statistician Econ Devel. Div. USDA, Washington, 1967-70, 72, agrl. economist, 1972-74; program analyst Office Equal Opportunity, USDA, Washington, 1974-79; staff writer Sci. Weekly, Chevy Chase, Md., 1988-89; ins. agt. A.L. Williams, Primerica, Camp Springs, Md., 1990—; workshop coord. Author: Steps to Eloquence, 1989; contbr. to profl. publs. Coord., instr. Youth Leadership and Speechcraft, Toastmasters Internat., Washington area, 1972-78; tchr., bd. dirs. Sat. Tutorial Enrichment Program, Arlington, Va., 1988-89; mem. network Christian women, mem. women's fellowship com. Christ Fellowship Ministries. Rockefeller Found. scholar, 1970-72. Mem. Toastmasters Internat. (past pres. Potomac Club, Gavel award 1976, Able Toastmaster award 1978), Am. Assn. Notaries, So. Assn. Agrl. Economists, Nat. Assn. Agrl. Econs., Internat. Platform Assn. Office: Evans Unlimited 8350 Greensboro Dr Mc Lean VA 22102-3533

MCILWAINE, DEBORAH, state legislator; b. Bronxville, N.Y., Nov. 26, 1923; m. John C. McIlwaine; 4 children. BA, Smith Coll., 1944; MA, Middlebury Coll., Vt., 1973; MEd, U. Bridgeport, 1978; MSW, Fordham U., 1982. Ret. social worker, 1986; mem. N.H. Ho. Reps, mem. children, youth and juvenile justice com.; mediator Youth and Family Mediation; bd. dirs. Burch House. Del. No. County Coun. Mem. Nat. Assn. Social. Workers, Soc. Am. Friends (facilitator alternatives to violence workshops). Democrat. Home: PO Box 603 Lisbon NH 03585-6000 Office: NH Ho of Reps State Capitol Concord NH 03301*

MCINERNEY, SUZANNE DOVE, association executive; b. Seattle, Calif., Feb. 2, 1945; d. William Eldred and Julia Louise (DeLorme) Townsend; m. Russell Arthur McInerney, Oct. 14, 1967 (div. Jan. 1981); 1 child, Maureen Dove. BA in Sociology, U. Tampa, 1967. Asst. dir. donor resources ARC, L.A., 1984-85; dir. vols. St. Luke Hosp., Pasadena, Calif., 1985-86; dir. cmty. rels. St. Jude Hosp., Yorba Linda, Calif., 1986-89; program dir. Teleflora, L.A., 1989-93; exec. dir. YWCA, Riverside, Calif., 1993—. Chmn. Riverside (Calif.) County Perinatal Substance Abuse Coalition, 1994—. Mem. AAUW, Am. Soc. Assn. Execs., Leadership Riverside. Office: YWCA of Riverside 8172 Magnolia Ave Riverside CA 92504-3441

MCINNIS, HELEN LOUISE, publishing company executive; b. Fall River, Mass.; d. Hugh Michael and Louise Patricia (Waldron) McI. B.A., Merrimack Coll., 1967; M.A., Duquesne U., 1969. Asst. editor Holt, Rinehart & Winston, N.Y.C., 1971-73; editor D. Van Nostrand Co., N.Y.C., 1972-75; sr. v.p., dir. coll. dept. Scribner Book Cos., Inc., N.Y.C., 1976-91; asst. v.p., exec. editor Macmillan Pub. Co., 1985-91; v.p., exec. editor Humanities and Social Scis., Oxford U. Press, N.Y.C., 1991—. Editor, author: Viewpoints: American Cities, 1972. Mem. Assn. Am. Pubs. (chmn. com. higher edn. div. 1980-82, exec. bd. 1982-84). Democrat. Roman Catholic. Home: 253 W 72d St Apt 1505 New York NY 10023 Office: Oxford U Press 200 Madison Ave New York NY 10016

MCINNIS, SUSAN MUSÉ, corporate communications specialist; b. Seattle, July 22, 1955; d. Emmett Emory Jr. and Florence Howardine (McAteer) McI. BSBA, U. Denver, 1977; cert. in environ. design, UCLA, 1985; MA in Journalism, Calif. State U., Fullerton, 1992. Researcher Denver Gen. Hosp., summer 1973; mktg. coord. 3M Bus. Products, Emeryville, Calif., 1978-79; spl. libr. Reel Grobman & Assocs., L.A., 1981-83; tchr. Mayfield Sr. Sch., Pasadena, Calif., 1985-87; advt. coord. Reynolds Advt., 1987; cmty. and employee rels. mgr. Calif.-Am. Water Co. (oper. co. Am. Water Works), San Marino, Calif., 1988—. Mem. Am. Water Works Assn. (cert. water distbn.), Pub. Rels. Soc. Am., Kiwanis (pres. Duarte, Calif. chpt. 1994-95).

MCINTIRE, MELINDA I., public relations executive; b. Seattle. BA in Psychology, Duke U. Rsch. asst. Bus. Rsch. Assocs.; paralegal Burns & Fox Attys. at Law; news asst. WTVD-TV; mgr., writer Dunwoody Crier; news prodn. asst., assoc prodr. CNN, TBS, 1987-88; awards coord. TBS, 1988-89; unit publicist TNT, Turner Broadcasting, 1989-90; mgr. pub. rels., nat. assignment desk CNN, 1990—. Office: Turner Broadcasting System Inc 1 CNN Ctr PO Box 105366 Atlanta GA 30348*

MCINTOSH, CAROLYN MEADE, retired educational administrator; b. Waynesburg, Ky., Oct. 21, 1928; d. Clarence Hobert and Sarah Letitia (Bentley) Meade; m. Edgar G. McIntosh, Aug. 21, 1948; children: Wayne, Jeanne, Penny, Jimmi, Carol. BS, Miami U., Oxford, Ohio, 1962; MEd, Xavier U., Cin., 1966. Elem. tchr. Ohio, 1961-79; prin. New Richmond (Ohio) Sch. Dist., 1980-91; ret., 1991; tchr. Clermont County Adult Edn. Program, 1970-95, Clermont County dir.of Headstrart 1971-72, Clearmont County Rep. to Ohio elem. adminstr., 1985-87, Pres. Clermont and Brown County adminstr., 1988-89. Editor Ret. Tchrs. Newsletter. Pres. New Richmond Bd. Edn.; v.p. U.S. Grante Vocat. Sch. Bd. Edn.; mem. Clermont County Excellence in Edn. Com.; mem. edn. adv. com. clermont coll.; mem. adv. bd. Bethany Chidlren's Home; mem. Clermont 2001 Com.; mem. Rep. Ctrl. Com. of Clermont County. Recipient New Richmond Adminstr. of the Yr. award City of New Richmond, 1989. Mem. AAUW, ASCD, NAESP, Nat. Sch. Bd. Assn., Ohio Sch. Bd. Assn., Ohio Assn. Elem. Sch. Adminstrs. (all county legis. liaison), Ohio County Ret. Tchrs. Assn., Clermont County Ret. Tchrs. Assn. (v.p.), Order Eastern Star, Phi Delta Kappa, Delta Kappa Gamma (pres. chpt.). Baptist.

MCINTOSH, ELAINE VIRGINIA, nutrition educator; b. Webster, S.D., Jan. 30, 1924; d. Louis James and Cora Boletta (Bakke) Nelson; m. Thomas Henry McIntosh, Aug. 28, 1955; children: James George, Ronald Thomas, Charles Nelson. BA magna cum laude, Augustana Coll., Sioux Falls, S.D., 1945; MA, U. S.D., 1949; PhD, Iowa State U., 1954. Registered dietitian. Instr., asst. prof. Sioux Falls Coll., 1945-48; instr. Iowa State U., Ames, 1949-53, rsch. assoc., 1955-62; postdoctoral rsch. assoc. U. Ill., Urbana, 1954-55; asst. prof. human biology U. Wis., Green Bay, 1968-72, assoc. prof., 1972-85, prof., 1985-90, emeritus prof., 1990—, writer, cons., 1990—, chmn. human biology dept., 1975-80, asst. to vice chancellor, asst. to chancellor, 1974-76. Contbr. numerous articles on bacterial metabolism, meat biochemistry and nutrition edn. to profl. jours. Fellow USPHS, 1948-49; grantee U. Wis. System, 1972. Mem. Am. Dietetic Assn., Inst. Food Technologists, Wis. Dietetics Assn., Wis. Nutrition Coun. (pres. 1974-75), Sigma Xi. Republican. Office: U Wis 2420 Nicolet Dr Green Bay WI 54311-7001

MCINTOSH, ROBERTA EADS, social worker; b. Milw., Oct. 1, 1936; d. Robert Howard and Carlene (Rosboro) Eads; m. James Stuart Cameron McIntosh, Sept. 19, 1959; children: Ronald Stuart, Ian Robert, Peter Cameron. BA, Bucknell U., 1958; MS in Social Adminstrn., Case Western Reserve U., 1977. Lic. social worker, Ohio, Fla. Foster care caseworker Monroe County Child Welfare, Rochester, N.Y., 1958-63; group home counselor Betterway, Inc., Elyria, Ohio, 1974-75; group program coord. Elyria YWCA, 1975; caseworker, group home supr. Lorain County Children's Svcs., Elyria, 1977-83; treatment counselor Glenbeigh Adolescent Hosp., Cleve., 1984-86; youth dir. Washington Ave. Christian Ch., Elyria, 1984-85; outreach counselor Spouse Abuse Shelter Religious Community Svcs., Clearwater, Fla., 1986-93; pvt. practice Dunedin, Fla., 1993—; presenter in field. Bd. pres. Elyria YWCA, 1972-75; sec., pres. Community Coordinated Child Care, Lorain County, 1970-72. Named Friend of Guidance Guidance Counselors Assn., 1982, Woman of Interest Elyria YWCA & City of Elyria, 1985. Mem. NASW, Fla. Coalition Against Domestic Violence (v.p. bd. 1993-94), Nat. Coalition Against Domestic Violence, Leadership Pinellas, Pinellas Assn. Marriage and Family Therapy, Deaf Svc. Ctr. (bd. dirs. 1991-94), Victim Rights Coalition Pinellas County (v.p. bd. 1992-93), Fla. Network Victim Witness Svcs., Ctrl. Christian Ch. Christian Women's Fellowship (pres. 1988-90), Delta Zeta Alumna. Democrat. Home: 1501 Pleasant Grove Dr Dunedin FL 34698-2341 Office: PO Box 32 Dunedin FL 34697

MCINTOSH, TERRIE TUCKETT, lawyer; b. Ft. Lewis, Wash., July 20, 1944; d. Robert LeRoy and Elda (Perry) Tuckett; m. Clifton Dennis McIntosh, Oct. 13, 1969; children: Alison, John. BA, U. Utah, 1967; MA, U. Ill., 1970; JD, Harvard U., 1978. Bar: N.Y. 1979, Utah 1980. Assoc. Hughes, Hubbard & Reed, N.Y.C., 1978-79; assoc. Fabian & Clendenin, Salt Lake City, 1984-86, shareholder, 1979-84; staff atty. Questar Corp., Salt Lake City, 1986-88, sr. atty., 1988-92, sr. corp. counsel, 1992—; instr. philosophy Douglass Coll. Rutgers U., New Brunswick, N.J., 1971-72; mem. adv. com. civil procedure Utah Supreme Ct., Salt Lake City, 1987—; mem. jud. nominating com. 5th Cir. Ct., Salt Lake City, 1986-88. Mem. Utah State Bar (ethics and discipline screening panel 1989—, co-chair law related edn. com. 1985-86), Women Lawyers of Utah (chair exec. com. 1986-87), Harvard Alumni Assn. Utah (bd. dirs. 1987—), Phi Beta Kappa, Phi Kappa Phi. Office: Questar Corp PO Box 45433 180 E 1st South St Salt Lake City UT 84147

MC INTURF, FAITH MARY, engineering company executive, thoroughbred harness racing executive; b. Grand Ridge, Ill., Aug. 22, 1917; d. Lynne E. and Margaret (Garver) McInturf; grad. high sch. With The J.E. Porter Corp., Chgo., 1939-65, v.p., 1951-65, sec., 1951-65, also dir.; with Potomac Engring. Corp., 1941—, now pres., treas., bd. dirs.; dir. Chgo. Harness Racing Inc., also Balmoral Jockey Club, Inc., 1967-72, sec., dir., 1974-78; sec., treas., dir. Balmoral Park Trot, Inc., 1969-72; sec., dir. Horse Racing Promotions, Inc., 1974-77. Roman Catholic. Home: 1360 N Lake Shore Dr Chicago IL 60610-2181 Office: 919 N Michigan Ave Chicago IL 60611

MCINTYRE, BARBARA LYNN, elementary school counselor; b. Lincoln, Nebr., May 6, 1955; d. Keith Eugene and Marian Jean (Nelson) Ivey; m. Randall Lee McIntyre, Oct. 28, 1978; children: Zachary John, Colby Jacob. BS, U. Nebr., 1977; MS, Wayne State Coll., 1993. Cert. elem. tchr., guidance counselor, Nebr. Elem. tchr. East Butler Pub. Schs., Brainard, Nebr., 1977-79, 85-87, Murdock (Nebr.) Pub. Schs., 1979-85, Fremont (Nebr.) Pub. Schs., 1987-92; phys. edn. tchr. Morse Bluff (Nebr.) Pub. Schs., 1992-93; elem. counselor David City (Nebr.) Pub. Schs., 1993—, head of student assistance team, 1993—. Bd. dirs. North Bend (Nebr.) Elem. Sch., 1994—; recreation coord. United Presbyn. Ch., North Bend, 1991-93. Named Outstanding Young Educator Fremont Jaycees, 1989. Mem. Nat. Sch. Edn. Assn., Nebr. Counseling Assn., Nebr. Edn. Assn., Kappa Delta Pi. Democrat. Presbyterian. Home: 406 S 10th David City NE 68632 Office: David City Pub Schs 826 E St David City NE 68632-1733

MCINTYRE, COLLEEN ALISON, special education educator; b. Seattle, Sept. 20, 1963; d. David Joseph and Lois Ann McIntyre. BA in Spl. Edn., Seattle Pacific U., 1985, MA in Curriculum and Instrn., 1993. Tchr. spl. edn. Seattle Pub. Schs., 1985-86, substitute tchr. spl. edn., 1986-87; tchr. spl.

edn. Sumner (Wash.) Sch. Dist., 1987-89, Lower Yukon Sch. Dist., Alakanuk, Alaska, 1989—. Recipient Exemplary Tchr. of Yr. award Edmark Corp., 1994. Mem. NEA, Nat. Assn. Edn. Young Children, Coun. for Exceptional Children (v.p. 1985, sec. 1990-91, pres. 1991-93). Home: PO Box 69 Alakanuk AK 99554

MCINTYRE, ELIZABETH GEARY, Olympic athlete; b. Hanover, N.H., 1965. AB, Dartmouth Coll., 1988. Silver medalist, women's moguls final freestyle skiing Olympic Games, Lillehammer, Norway, 1994. Office: US Olympic Com 1750 E Boulder St Colorado Springs CO 80909

MCINTYRE, LOUISE S., income tax consultant; b. Cin., Jan. 29, 1924; d. George Washington and Bertha (McDaniels) Sullivan; m. Harry McIntyre Jr., Jan. 18, 1947; children: Carol L., Patricia A., Harriet L., Harry J., Brenda R. AA, Mira Costa Coll., Oceanside, Calif., 1972; grad. in auditing, Nat. Tax Practice Inst., 1989. Hydraulic testor Paterson Field, Fairfield, Ohio, 1942-45; control clk. Hickam Field, Honolulu, 1945-47; clk.-typist Patterson Field, Fairfield, 1947-49, Camp LeJeune, Jacksonville, N.C., 1951-56; sec., bookkeeper Mission Bowl, Oceanside, 1973-79; income tax cons. Oceanside, 1974—. Mem. Oceanside Human Rels. Commn., 1970; bd. dirs. Armed Forces YMCA, Oceanside, 1969-71, Oceanside Christian Women's Club, 1988-91. Mem. Inland Soc. Tax Cons. (bd. dirs. 1988—), Am. Soc. Women Accts. (v.p. 1989-90), Enrolled Agts. Palomar, Nat. Assn. Enrolled Agts., Nat. Soc. Pub. Accts., Calif. Assn. Ind. Accts., Palmquist PTA (hon. life). Home: 328 Camelot Dr Oceanside CA 92054-4515

MCINTYRE, MILDRED JEAN, clinical neuroscientist, psychologist, writer; b. Boston; d. William James and Theodora Grace (McCullough) McI. BA, Swarthmore Coll., 1965; MA, Clark U., 1972, PhD, 1975. Lic. psychologist, Mass., Alaska, Hawaii. Pvt. practice Mass., 1977—, Alaska, 1984—, Hawaii, 1992—. Ford Found. fellow, 1972, 73. Mem. APA, Internat. Neuropsychol. Soc., Cognitive Neurosci. Soc. Office: PO Box 990124 Boston MA 02199-0124

MCINTYRE, VALENE SMITH, anthropology educator; b. Spokane, Wash., Feb. 14, 1926; d. Ernst Frank and Lucy (Blachly) S.; m. Edwin Chesteen Golay, June 7, 1970 (dec. June 1980; m. Stanley George McIntyre, Nov. 26, 1983. BA in Geography, U. Calif., 1946, MA in Geography, 1950; PhD in Anthropology, U. Utah, 1966. Prof. earth sci. L.A. City Coll., 1947-67; prof. anthropology Calif. State U., Chico, 1967—; cons. World Tourism Orgn., Madrid, 1987. Editor: Hosts and Guests: The Anthrop, 1989, Tourism Alternatives: Potentials and Problems in the Development of Tourism, 1992. Mem. Internat. Acad. for Study Tourism, Anthrop. Soc. Wash., Cert. Travel Counselors, Am. Anthrop. Assn., AAUW, Butte Creek Country Club, Soroptimists. Republican. Office: U Calif Dept Anthropology Chico CA 95929

MCINTYRE-IVY, JOAN CAROL, data processing executive; b. Portchester, N.Y., Mar. 1, 1939; d. John Henry and Molly Elizabeth (Gates) Daugherty; m. Stanley Donald McIntyre, Aug. 24, 1957 (div. Jan. 1986); children: Michael Stanley, David John, Sharon Lynne; m. James Morrow Ivy IV, June 1, 1988. Student, Northwestern U., 1956-57, U. Ill., 1957-58. Assoc. editor Writer's Digest, Cin., 1966-68; instr. creative writing U. Ala.-Huntsville, 1975; editor Strode Pubs., Huntsville, 1974-75; paralegal Smith, Huckaby & Graves (now Bradley, Arant, Rose & White), Huntsville, 1976-82; exec. v.p. Micro Craft, Inc., Huntsville, 1982-85, pres., 1985-89, chief exec. officer, chmn. bd., 1989—, also dir. and co-owner. Author numerous computer-operating mans. for law office software, 1978-88; co-author: Alabama and Federal Complaint Forms, 1979; Alabama and Federal Motion and Order Forms, 1980; also numerous articles, short stories, poems, 1955-88. Editor: Alabama Law for the Layman, 1975. Bd. dirs. Huntsville Lit. Soc., 1976-77. Hon. scholar Medill Sch. Journalism, Northwestern U., 1956. Republican. Methodist. Office: Micro Craft Inc 6703 Odyssey Dr NW Ste 102 Huntsville AL 35806-3301

MCKAY, ALICE VITALICH, school system administrator; b. Seattle, Sept. 6, 1947; d. Jack S. and Phyllis (Bourne) Vitalich; m. Larry W. McKay, Aug. 14, 1973 (div. Jan. 1983). BA, Wash. State U., 1969; MEd, U. Nev., Las Vegas, 1975; EdD, U. Nev., Reno, 1986. High sch. tchr. Clark County Sch. Dist., Las Vegas, 1972-77, specialist women's sports, 1977-80, high sch. counselor, 1980-84, high sch. asst. prin., 1984—; pres. Lotus Profit, Inc., Las Vegas, 1985-86. Mem. Am. Assn. Counseling and Devel. (committee on women 1985—), Nev. State Counseling and Devel. (pres. 1985-86), Nat. Assn. Female Execs., AAUW, Phi Delta Kappa (exec. bd. 1980-82). Office: Washoe County Sch Dist 425 E 9th St Reno NV 89520-0106

MCKAY, CONSTANCE GADOW, retired hotel executive; b. Aurora, Ill., Mar. 7, 1928; d. William H. and Esther E. (Olson) Gadow. Student U. Ill., U. Wis.-Madison, U. Wis.-Milw.; widow; children: Richard A., Scott A., Mark G. Dir. catering Arlington Park (Ill.) Race Track, 1966-68, Arlington Park Hilton Hotel, Arlington Heights, Ill., 1969-85, O'Hare Kennedy Holiday Inn, 1985-89, ret.; eagles nest pavillion gen. mgr., dir. oper. Eagle Casino Cruiser, 1992-94. Commr. Arlington Heights Bd. Local Improvements, 1979—, Arlington Heights Relocation of Post Office Com., 1958-59, Arlington Heights Zoning Bd., 1959-60; commr. Youth Commn., 1981—. Named Outstanding Bus. Woman, Paddock Publs., Arlington Heights, 1977. Mem. Catering Execs. Club Am. Republican. Home: 1030 S Gunlock Lake Ln Minocqua WI 54548-9615 also (summer): 604 S Waterman Ave Arlington Heights IL 60004-6930

MCKAY, DIANNE ADELE MILLS, humanities educator; b. New Brunswick, N.J., Mar. 23, 1947; d. George M. and Dorothy Allen Mills; m. Thomas McKay III; children: Robert Allen, Heather Anne. BA in Am. Studies, Douglass Coll., 1969; MA, U. Pa., 1970, postgrad. Cert. substitute tchr., N.J. Mgr., trainer Fidelity Mut. Life Ins. Co., 1977-80; instr. humanities U. So. Colo., 1991—, Burlington County Coll., 1990—. Trustee New Covenant Presbyn. Ch., 1988—; mem. Hainesport Twp. Bd. Edn., 1983-90, 92—, v.p., 1985-90; mem. Hainesport Twp. Zoning Bd. Adjustment, 1983—, chair, 1985-89; bd. dirs. Burlington County Girl Scout Coun., 1993—, Burlington County Red Cross, 1994—; Burlington County Com. on Women, 1993-96, chair, 1994; adv. com. mem. N.J. Coalition for Battered Women, 1993-95; gender equity task force N.J. State Employment and Tng. Commn., 1993-95; equity adv. com. N.J. Dept. Edn., 1993-94. Mem. AAUW (pres. 1994—, bd. dirs., exec. com, v.p. N.J. membership 1989—, br. pres. 1985-87), Assoc. Alumnae of Douglass Coll. (bd. dirs. 1989—, alumnae class pres. 1985-89, 94—), N.J. Women's Political Caucus, LWV. Home: 12 Whittier Dr Mount Holly NJ 08060

MCKAY, JANET HOLMGREN, college president; b. Chgo., Dec. 1, 1948; d. Kenneth William and Virginia Ann (Rensink) H.; m. Gordon A. McKay, Sept. 7, 1968 (div. 1990); children: Elizabeth Jane, Ellen Katherine. BA in English summa cum laude, Oakland U., Rochester, Mich., 1968; MA in Linguistics, Princeton U., 1971, PhD in Linguistics, 1974. Asst. prof. English studies Federal City Coll. (now U. D.C.), Washington, 1972-76; asst. prof. English U. Md., College Park, 1976-82, asst. to chancellor, 1982-88; assoc. provost Princeton (N.J.) U., 1988-90, vice-provost, 1990-91; pres. Mills Coll., Oakland, Calif., 1991—; mem. external adv. bd. English dept. Princeton U. Bay Area Biosci. Ctr. Author: (with Spencer Cosmos) The Story of English: Study Guide and Reader, 1986, Narration and Discourse in American Realistic Fiction, 1982; contbr. articles to profl. jours. Faculty rsch. grantee U. Md., 1978; fellow NEH, 1978, Princeton U., 1968-69, 70-72, NSF, 1969-70; recipient summer study aid Linguistic Soc. Am., Ohio State U., 1970. Mem. Assn. Ind. Caif. Colls. and Univs. (exec. com.), Nat. Assn. Ind. Colls. and Univs., Am. Coun. on Education (chair office of women in higher edn.), Calif. Acad. Sci. (coun.). Democrat. Episcopal. Office: Mills Coll Office Pres 5000 Macarthur Blvd Oakland CA 94613-1301

MCKAY, LAURA L., banker, consultant; b. Watonga, Okla., Mar. 3, 1947; d. Frank Bradford and Elizabeth Jane (Smith) Drew; m. Cecil O. McKay, Sept. 20, 1969; 1 child, Leslie. BSBA, Oreg. State U., 1969. New br. research U.S. Bank, Portland, Oreg., 1969-80; cash mgmt. officer U.S. Bank, Portland, 1980-82, asst. v.p., 1982-87, v.p., 1987-94; founder, cons. LLM Cons., Milw., 1994—. Chmn. Budget Com., North Clackamas Sch. Dist., 1982-84. Mem. Nat. Corp. Cash Mgrs. Assn., Nat. Assn. Bank Women (chmn. Oreg. group 1979-80), Portland Cash Mgrs. Assn., Portland C. of C. Republican. Office: LLM Cons 5686 SE Viewcrest Milwaukie OR 97267

MCKAY, LAURIE MARIE, special education educator; b. Cadillac, Mich., Sept. 10, 1960; d. Leonard Max and Mary Ann (Pierzina) Tykwinski; m. John William McKay, June 27, 1992; 1 child, Abbe Rose; stepchildren: David John, Chad Richard. BA in Psychology, Mich. State U., 1983; cert., Ctrl. Mich. U., 1990; postgrad., Grand Valley State U., 1992—. Cert. tchr. elem. edn., emotionally impaired, Mich. Tchr. spl. edn. Reed City (Mich.) Pub. Schs., 1990-91; instrl. aide Wexford-Missaukee Intermediate Sch., Cadillac, Mich., 1983-89, tchr. spl. edn., 1991—; rep., student assistance program com. mem., CCD instr. grade 4 Wexford-Missaukee Profl. Assn. Cookie mgr. Crooked Tree Girl Scout Coun., Cadillac, 1989. Mem. Mich. Assn. of Tchrs. of Emotionally Disturbed Children, Coun. for Exceptional Children, Wexaucola Reading Coun. Democrat. Roman Catholic. Home: 121 Henderson Pl Cadillac MI 49601 Office: Wexford Missaukee Sch Dist 9905 E 13th St Cadillac MI 49601

MCKAY, MEGAN ELIZABETH, librarian; b. Elma, Wash., Oct. 9, 1953; d. William Peabody and Janet (Karshner) Rutter; m. Dwight Spencer McKay, May 27, 1983; children: Marisa Iris, Brianna Katlyn, Taylor Morgan Kolbe. Student, South Puget Sound C.C., 1972-73, 85-87. Cert. dental asst., Wash. Indsl. forklift operator Simpson Timber Co., Shelton, Wash., 1974-85, corp. libr., 1990—; payroll coord. Simpson Door Co., McCleary, Wash., 1987-90. Republican. Office: Simpson Timber Co 215 N 3rd PO Box 460 Shelton WA 98584

MCKAY, MIMI, pediatric nurse, psychiatric nurse; b. Louisville, June 7, 1954; d. Charles Henry and Helen Dorothy (Palla) McK. BSN, Ind. U., New Albany, 1986; MSN, IUPUI, Indpls., 1992. RN, Ky.; cert. RNC-mental health, psychiat. nursing. Charge nurse Kosair Children's Hosp., Louisville, 1988-94; clin. nurse specialist child/adolescent psychiat. Alliant Health System/Kosair Children's Hosp., Louisville, 1994—; adolescent group psychotherapist Bingham Child Guidance Ctr., Louisville, 1994—.

MCKAY, RENEE, artist; b. Montreal, Que., Can.; came to U.S., 1946, naturalized, 1954; d. Frederick Garvin and Mildred Gladys (Higgins) Smith; m. Kenneth Gardiner McKay, July 25, 1942; children: Margaret Craig, Kenneth Gardiner. BA, McGill U., 1941. Tchr. art Peck Sch., Morristown, N.J., 1955-56; one woman shows: Pen and Brush Club, N.Y.C., 1957, Cosmopolitan Club, N.Y.C., 1958; group shows include: Weyhe Gallery, N.Y.C., 1978, Newark Mus., 1955, 59, Montclair (N.J.) Mus., 1955-58, Nat. Assn. Women Artists, Nat. Acad. Galleries, 1954-78, N.Y. World's Fair, 1964-65, Audubon Artists, N.Y.C., 1955-62, 74-79, N.Y. Soc. Women Artists, 1979-80, Provincetown (Mass.) Art Assn. and Mus., 1975-79; traveling shows in France, Belgium, Italy, Scotland, Can., Japan; represented in permanent collections: Slater Meml. Mus., Norwich, Conn., Norfolk (Va.) Mus., Butler Inst. Am. Art, Youngstown, Ohio, Lydia Drake Library, Pembroke, Mass., many pvt. collections. Recipient Jane Peterson prize in oils Nat. Assn. Women Artists, 1954, Famous Artists Sch. prize in watercolor, 1959, Grumbacher Artists Watercolor award, 1970; Solo award Pen and Brush, 1957; Sadie-Max Tesser award in watercolor Audubon Artists, 1975, Peterson prize in oils, 1980; Michael Engel prize Nat. Soc. Painters in Casein and Acrylic, 1983. Mem. Nat. Assn. Women Artists (2d v.p. 1969-70, adv. bd. 1974-76), Audubon Artists (pres. 1979, dir. oils 1986-88), Artist Equity (dir. 1977-79, v.p. 1979-81), N.Y. Soc. Women Artists, Pen and Brush, Nat. Soc. Painters in Casein and Acrylic M.J. Kaplan prize 1984, Nat. Arts Club, Provincetown Art Assn. and Mus., Key West Art Assn. Club: Cosmopolitan. Address: 200 E 66th St New York NY 10021-6728 also: 100 Carolina Meadows #5-206 Chapel Hill NC 27514

MCKEAG, JANE DICKSON, judge. Bankruptcy judge U.S. Bankruptcy Ct. (Calif. ea. dist.), 9th circuit, Sacramento, 1994—. Office: US Courthouse 650 Capitol Mall Rm 8308 Sacramento CA 95814*

MCKECHNIE, MARGARET A., public relations professional; b. Niagara Falls, N.Y., Jan. 7, 1944; d. Donald and Margaret Frances (Hayes) McK. BS in Journalism cum laude, Ohio U., 1966. Pub. rels. asst. The 1st Nat. Bank Cin., 1966-69; assoc. dir. prodn. Computer Image Corp., Denver, 1969-75; comm. mgr. United Bank Denver, 1976-85; dir. corp. comm. Norwest Colo., Inc. (formerly United Banks Colo., Inc.), Denver, 1986—. Mem. Pub. Rels. Soc. Am. (Accredited Pub. Rels., bd. dirs. Colo. chpt. 1980-92, pres. 1991, assembly del. 1994—), Women Comm. (bd. dirs. 1976-80, v.p. fin.). Office: Norwest Colorado Inc 1740 Broadway Denver CO 80274-8705

MCKEE, ADELE DIECKMANN, retired church music director, educator; b. Atlanta, Oct. 29, 1928; d. Christian William and Emma Pope (Moss) D.; m. Dean Greer McKee, Nov. 14, 1972 (dec. July 1987). BA summa cum laude, Agnes Scott Coll., 1948; MA, Wellesley Coll., 1949; M in Sacred Music magna cum laude, Union Theol. Sem., N.Y.C., 1955. Tchr. Latin and music theory, chapel organist The Northfield Schs., East Northfield, Mass., 1949-53; tchr. Latin and English Westminster Schs., Atlanta, 1955-58; dir. music, organist Trinity Presbyn. Ch., Atlanta, 1955-83; asst. organist Cathedral St. Philip, Atlanta, 1984-85; organist, choir master St. Luke's Presbyn. Ch., Atlanta, 1985-89; ret., 1989; dir. Montreat Conf. on Worship and Music, 1968; chmn. new music commns. Am. Guild of Organists Nat. Convention, Atlanta, 1992—. Choral reviewer The Am. Organist, 1967-71; contbr. articles to Reformed Liturgy mag., 1970—. Mem. City of Decatur Hist. Preservation Task Force, 1989-90. Fellow Am. Guild Organists (nat. councillor 1967-70, dean 1964-66, 76-78, program chmn. nat. conv. 1966); mem. Choristers Guild (nat. bd. dirs. 1976-79), Decatur Book Lovers' Club (pres. 1991), Young Singers Callanwolde (pres. bd. 1993—).

MCKEE, BARBARA JEFFCOTT, consultant; b. Madison, Wis., Jan. 21, 1948; d. William Francis and Florence Ann (Jeffcott) McK.; m. Richard Arthur Rocha, Oct. 1, 1988. BBA, U. Wis., 1968; M in Mgmt., Northwestern U., 1981. CPA, Ill.; cert. internal auditor. Auditor Peat, Marwick, Mitchell & Co., Chgo., 1968-78; cons. Esmark, Inc., Chgo., 1978-79; audit mgr. Deloitte Haskins & Sells, Chgo., 1979-84, controller, 1984-85; v.p. Safeway Stores, Inc., Oakland, Calif., 1985-90; co-founder Achievers Internat., Oakland, Calif., 1990—. Mem. AICPA, Am. Womens Soc. CPA's, Inst. Internal Auditors. Office: Achievers Internat 5255 Pinecrest Dr Oakland CA 94605-3812

MCKEE, KATHRYN DIAN GRANT, banker; b. L.A., Sept. 12, 1937; d. Clifford William and Amelia Rosalia (Shacher) G.; m. Paul Eugene McKee, June 17, 1961; children: Scott Alexander, Grant Christopher. BA, U. Calif., Santa Barbara, 1959; grad. Sch. Mgmt. Exec. Program, UCLA, 1979. Cert. compensation and benefits. Mgr. Mattel, Inc., Hawthorne, Calif., 1963-74; dir. Twentieth Century Fox Film Corp., L.A., 1975-80; sr. v.p. 1st Interstate Bank, Ltd., L.A., 1980-93; sr. v.p. and human resources dir. Am.'s Standard Chartered Bank, 1993—; dir. Accordia benefits of Southern Calif., 1991—, mem. exec. com. H.R. div. of Am. Bankers Assn., 1991-93; bd. dirs. Bank Certification Inst. Am. Bankers Assn., 1992-94; treas. Pers. Accreditation Inst., 1983-86, pres., 1986. Contbr. articles to profl. jours. Pres. GEM Theatre Guild, Garden Grove, Calif., 1984-86; bd. dirs. Vis. Nurses Assn., L.A., 1984-88; bd. dirs. SHRM, 1986-92, treas., 1989, vice-chmn., 1990, chmn., 1991, pres. SHRM Found., 1994, 95. Recipient Sr. Honor Key award U. Calif., Santa Barbara, 1959, named Outstanding Sr. Woman, 1959; recipient William Winter award Am. Compensation Assn., 1986, Excellence award L.A. Pers. Indsl. Rels. Assn., 1990, Profl. Excellence award SHRM, 1994. Mem. Internat. Assn. Pers. Women (various offices, past nat. pres., Mem. of Yr. 1986), Orgn. Women Execs., L.A. Athletic Club. Office: Standard Chartered Bank 707 Wilshire Blvd Los Angeles CA 90017-3501

MCKEE, LAURIS ANNETTE, anthropology educator; b. Crosbyton, Tex., Feb. 21, 1931; d. Robert McBride and Rebecca Virginia (Williams) McK.; m. Joseph Beyda, Sept. 15, 1950 (div. 1972); children: Kent, David, Katherine, Adam; m. Robert Laurence Moore, July 26, 1987. BA with honors, George Washington U., 1972; MA, Cornell U., 1975, PhD, 1980. Lectr. Cornell U., Ithaca, N.Y., 1980-81, rsch. assoc., 1982-85; asst. prof. Franklin & Marshall Coll., Lancaster, Pa., 1985-89, assoc. prof., 1990—, dept. chair, 1991-94; adj. asst. prof. SUNY Cortland, Ithaca, 1982-85. Contbg. editor: Nuevas Investigaciones Antropologicas, Ecuatorianas, 1988; guest editor Jour. Med. Anthropology; direction and script five video documentaries, 1984-86. Recipient pre-doctoral fellowship NIMH, Ecuador, 1975-78, postdoctoral rsch. grantee NSF, 1982-85, Fulbright Found., 1982-83, film-making grant Nat. Archeol. Mus. of Ecuador, Quito, 1984. Fellow Am. Anthrop. Assn.; mem. Soc. for Cross-Cultural Rsch. (rep. for anthropology 1988-92), Soc. for Psychol. Anthropology, Soc. for Visual Anthropology (Film award for Excellence 1988), Soc. Med. Anthropology, Soc. for Latin am. Anthropology, Nat. Coun. on Family Rels. Democrat. Home: 633 W Chestnut St Lancaster PA 17603-3410 Office: Dept Anthropology Franklin & Marshall Coll PO Box 3003 Lancaster PA 17604-3003

MCKEE, LINDA KAREN, secondary education educator; b. Cambridge, Mass., Sept. 13, 1946; d. Davis Bell Jr. and Frances Gwendolyn (Martin) McK. BA in Biology, St. Anselm's Coll., Manchester, N.H., 1967; MS, West Ga. Coll., Carrollton, 1989. Sci. tchr. Manchester Ctrl. High Sch., 1967-68; sci. instr. Lawrence (Mass.) Gen. Hosp. Sch. Nursing, 1968-72; lab. instr. Met. Coll. Atlanta, 1981-84; sci. tchr. Stockbridge (Ga.) Jr. High Sch., 1984-85, Fayetteville County High Sch., Fayetteville, Ga., 1985-93, Morrow (Ga.) Sr. High Sch., 1993—. Author lab. manuals. Mem. Nat. Sci. Tchrs. Assn., Ga. Sci. Tchrs. Assn., Ga. Acad. Scis. Home: 7605 Old South Ln Jonesboro GA 30236-2849 Office: Morrow Sr High Sch 2299 Old Rex Morrow Rd Morrow GA 30260-1361

MCKEE, MARGARET CRILE, pulmonary medicine and critical care physician; b. Cleve., Jan. 12, 1945; d. Richard List and Florence Mae (Johnson) McK. BA, Coll. Wooster, 1967; MRP, Cornell U., 1971; MD, SUNY, Stony Brook, 1976. Diplomate Am. Bd. Internal Medicine, Pulmonary Medicine and Critical Care. Social planner Model Cities, Binghamton, N.Y., 1970-71; resident internal medicine Harlem Hosp., N.Y.C., 1976-79; physician Health Ins. Plan, Bedford-Williamsburg, N.Y., 1979-80; pulmonary fellow Columbia Presbyn. Med. Ctr., N.Y.C., 1980-82; chief of medicine Phoenix Indian Med. Ctr., 1983-92; pvt. practice Ariz. Med. Clinic, Sun City, Ariz., 1992—. Mem. Am. Coll. Chest Physicians, Am. Thoracic Soc., Soc. of Critical Care Medicine, Union of Concerned Scientists, Sierra Club. Methodist. Office: Ariz Med Clinic 13640 N Plaza del Rio Blvd Peoria AZ 85381

MCKEE, MARGARET JEAN, federal agency executive; b. New Haven, June 20, 1929; d. Waldo McCutcheon and Elizabeth (Thayer) McKee; A.B., Vassar Coll., 1951. Staff asst. United Rep. Fin. Com., N.Y.C., 1952; staff asst. N.Y. Rep. State Com., N.Y.C., 1953-55; staff asst. Crusade for Freedom (name later changed to Radio Free Europe Fund), N.Y.C., 1955-57; researcher Stricker & Henning Research Assocs., Inc., N.Y.C., 1957-59; exec. sec. New Yorkers for Nixon (name later changed to N.Y. State Ind. Citizens for Nixon Lodge), N.Y.C., 1959-60; asst. to Raymond Moley, polit. columnist, N.Y.C., 1961; asst. campaign com. Louis J. Lefkowitz for Mayor, N.Y.C., 1961; research programmer, treas. Consensus, Inc., N.Y.C., 1962-67; spl. asst. to U.S. Senator Jacob K. Javits, N.Y., 1967-73, adminstrv. asst., 1973-75; dep. adminstr. Am. Revolution Bicentennial Adminstrn., 1976, acting adminstr., 1976-77; chief of staff Perry B. Duryea (minority leader) N.Y. State Assembly, 1978; public affairs cons., 1979-80; dir. govt. relations Gen. Mills Restaurant Group, Inc., 1980-83; exec. dir. Fed. Mediation and Conciliation Service, 1983-86; mem. Fed. Labor Rels. Authority, 1986-89, chmn., 1989-94; mem. Nat. Partnership Coun., 1993-94; bd. dirs. Interam. Life Ins. Co., 1979-86. Mem. N.Y. State Bingo Control Commn., 1965-72, U.S. Adv. Commn. on Public Diplomacy, 1979-82; mem. Nat. Partnership Coun., 1993—; pres. Bklyn. Heights Slope Young Rep. Club, 1955-56; co-chmn. Bklyn. Citizens for Eisenhower-Nixon, 1956; chmn. 2d Jud. Dist. Assn. N.Y. State Young Rep. Clubs, Inc., 1957-58, vice-chmn., mem. bd. govs., 1958-60, v.p., 1960-62; pres., 1962-64; mem. exec. com. Fedn. Women's Rep. Clubs N.Y. State, Inc., 1960-64, mem. council, 1964-70; mem. exec. com. N.Y. Rep. State Com. 1962-64; co-chmn. spl. assts. Rockefeller for Pres. Nat. Campaign com., N.Y.C., 1964; co-dir. N.Y. Rep. State Campaign Com., 1964; asst. campaign mgr. Kenneth B. Keating for Judge Ct. Appeals, N.Y., 1965; dir. scheduling Gov. Rockefeller campaign, 1966, Sen. Charles E. Goodell campaign, 1970; dir. scheduling and speakers' bur. N.Y. Com. to Re-elect the Pres., 1972; dir. planning and strategy, Conn. Reagan-Bush campaign, Hartford, 1980; mem. annual fund adv. com. Vassar Coll., 1992—. Mem. bd. govs. Women's Nat. Rep. Club, N.Y.C., 1963-66. Mem. Jr. League of Bklyn. (past dir.), Exec. Women in Govt. (chmn. 1986), Nat. Women's Edn. Fund (mem. bd.), Am. Newspaper Women's Club, Nat. Soc. Colonial Dames Am. Episcopalian. Club: Vassar (past dir., Bklyn.). Home: 3001 Veazey Ter NW Washington DC 20008-5407

MCKEE, MARY ELIZABETH, producer; b. Syracuse, N.Y., Feb. 14, 1949; d. Anthony Henry and Mary (Robards) Krystosik; m. Peter S. Fama, June 27, 1970 (div. Mar. 1973); 1 child, Kiralie Fama; m. Michael R. McKee, Feb. 15, 1975 (Oct. 1978); 1 child, Quinn. BFA, Fla. Internat. U., Miami, 1974; MFA, Memphis State U., 1977. Copywriter announcer Sta. WREC/WZXR Radio, Memphis, 1978-79; creative dir. Cit Neifert & Assoc. Advt., Memphis, 1979-82; promotion dir. Sta. WGNX-TV, Atlanta, 1982-86; program mgr. Sta. WVEU-TV, Atlanta, 1986-90; v.p., sta. mgr. Sta. WHSP-TV, Vineland, N.J., 1990—; adj. prof. Glassboro State U., 1990—. Actor in field (Top 10 Memphis Mag. 1979). Vol. Com. to Feed the Hungry, Atlanta, 1988, Tenn. Talking Libr., Memphis, 1982; mem. Greenpeace, 1987—; mem. adv. coun. SES, Easter Seal Soc. N.J. Recipient Merit award Tenn. Talking Libr., 1982; named Best TV Comml. Memphis Advt. Club, 1982; Hair scholar Fla. Internat. U., 1973. Mem. AFTRA, Nat. Assn. Broadcasters, Am. Women in Radio and TV (publicity chmn. 1985-86), Nat. Assn. TV Program Execs., Internat. Platform Soc., Rotary. Democrat. Roman Catholic. Home: 55 S Dover Ave Atlantic City NJ 08401-5912 Office: Sta WHSP-TV 4449 Delsea Dr Newfield NJ 08344-9609

MCKEE, PENELOPE MELNA, library director; b. New Liskeard, Ont., Can., Dec. 31, 1938; d. Melvin Hugh and Violet Mary (Hooton) Olimer; m. Arthur Donald McKee, Mar. 5, 1960 (div. 1985); children: Suzanne, Carolyn, Stephen. BA with honors, U. Toronto, Can., 1960, BLS, 1961, MLS, 1980; diploma, Coll. Applied Arts and Tech., 1976. Cert. mcpl. mgr., Ont. Mcpl. Mgmt. Devel. Bd. Fine arts libr. North York Pub. Libr., Ont., Can., 1961-63, reference libr., 1969-74; reference libr. Toronto Montessori Schs., Thornhill, Ont., 1974-76; cons. Grolier Pub., Toronto, 1976; libr. supr. Toronto Pub. Libr., 1977-80; dir. Aurora Pub. Libr., Ont., Can., 1980-86, Peterborough Pub. Libr., Ont., Can., 1986-90, Edmonton Pub. Libr., Alta., Can., 1990—; adj. assoc. prof. U. Alta., Edmonton, 1992—; cons. Edmonton Cath. Sch. Bd., 1992. Contbr. articles to profl. jours. Vice chmn. Project Hostel, Aurora, 1986-89; bd. dirs. Friends of Trent Severn Waterway, Peterborough, 1990; active Edmonton Centennial Celebrations Com., 1992. Russell scholar U. Toronto, 1956. Mem. Canadian Libr. Assn., Ontario Libr. Assn. (pres.), Libr. Assn. Alta., Alta. Pub. Libr. Dirs. Coun. (chair), Rotary Club of Downtown Edmonton (pub. rels. chmn.). Office: Edmonton Public Libr, 7 Sir Winston Churchill Sq, Edmonton, AB Canada T5J 2V4

MCKEE, TONI LYNN, nurse; b. Crawfordsville, Ind., Dec. 26, 1957; d. Loren C. and Thelma Lucille (Nichols) McKee. AA, Springfield Coll., Ill., 1979; diploma in Nursing, Saint John's Hosp., Ill., 1979; BS in Nursing, Southern Ill. U., 1981; MBA, Sangamon State U., 1992. Cert. registered profl. nurse Ill., Mo., 1979; orthopaedic nurse, 1992. Mgmt. asst., skills instr. Pla-Mor Skate, Pana, Ill., 1970-87; student nurse, hall supr. Pana Health Care Ctr., Pana, Ill., 1977; nursing asst. Pana Community Hosp., Pana, Ill., 1978-79, registered nurse, 1979-81; registered nurse, charge nurse, orthopedic nurse, educator St. John's Hosp., Springfield, Ill., 1981—; mktg. bus. cons. Pla-Mor Danceland, Pana, Ill., 1988—; pain resource nurse St. John's Hosp., Springfield, Ill., 1994—. Mem. Am. Soc. Pain Mgmt. Nurses, Nat. Orthopaedic Nurse Assn., Nat. Red Cross Nurses, Sigma Theata Tau, Women's Internat. Bowling Congress (v.p. local league 1994—). Methodist. Home: 1913 Scarbrough Rd Springfield IL 62702 Office: St John's Hosp 800 E Carpentar St Springfield IL 62769

MCKEEL, LILLIAN PHILLIPS, education educator; b. Rocky Mount, N.C., Aug. 23, 1932; d. Ellis Elma and Lillian Bonner (Archbell) Philipps; m. James Thomas McKeel Jr., July 23, 1955; children: Sarah Lillian McKeel Youngblood, Mary Kathleen McKeel Welch. BA, U. N.C., 1954; MEd, Pa. State U., 1977, DEd, 1993. Tchr. State Coll. (Pa.) Area Schs., 1964-90; instr. Pa. State U., University Park, 1990-93; asst. prof. Shippensburg (Pa.) U., 1993-94; mem. of panel NSTA Book Rev. Panel/Outstanding Sci. Tradebooks for Children, Washington, 1992; faculty sponsor Shippensburg

U. Sch. Study Coun., 1993-94. Contbr. articles to profl. jours. Recipient Presdl. award for Excellence in Sci. and Math. Tchng., NSF, Washington, 1990; finalist Tchr. of Yr. program Pa. Dept. Edn., Harrisburg, 1992, cert. Recognition, Hon. Robert Casey/Gov., Harrisburg, Pa., 1991; named Achieving Women of Penn State, Pa. State U., 1993. Mem. Nat. Sci. Tchrs. Assn., Soc. Presdl. Awardees, Assn. Edn. Tchrs. in Sci., Coun. Elem. Sci. Internat., Phi Delta Kappa (Disting. Svc. award 1992), Pi Lambda Theta. Office: Shippensburg U 1871 Old Main Dr Shippensburg PA 17257

MCKEITHAN, DONNA BOYCE, maternal/child health nurse, nursing educator; b. Suffolk, Va., Apr. 17, 1959; d. Floy Glenn and Hilda Gray (Johnson) Boyce; children: Caren Denise, Kimberly Lynn, Tracy Dawn; m. Jinks Wilson McKeithan Jr., March 6, 1993. ADN, Coll. of Albemarle, 1980; BSN, East Carolina U., 1986, postgrad., 1988—. RN, N.C. Staff nurse Chowan Hosp., Inc., Edenton, N.C., 1979-87; charge nurse Britthaven of Edenton, 1984-85; staff nurse Albemarle Hosp., Elizabeth City, N.C., 1986-87; supr. obs. unit Washington County Hosp., Plymouth, N.C., 1987-89; staff nurse Pitt County Meml. Hosp., Greenville, N.C., 1988—; clin. nursing instr. Pitt Cmty. Coll., Greenville, N.C.; presenter workshops. Mem. N.C. Nurses Assn. (dist. v.p. 1986-89, conv. del. 1986-89, continuing edn. provider 1988-91, coun. nursing mgmt. 1990-93, coun. on cont. edn. 1994—, coun. on maternal child health, 1993—). Baptist. Home: RR 2 Box 208A Robersonville NC 27871-9802 Office: Pitt CC PO Drawer 7007 Greenville NC 27835

MCKENNA, FAY ANN, electrical manufacturing company executive; b. Bennington, Vt., Jan. 7, 1944; d. George Francis and Barbara Mae (Youngangel) Hoag; m. James Dennis McKenna, Sept. 3, 1963 (div. 1983); children: Russell (dec.), Laura, James, Sean, Michael. Student, Mercy Coll. Key punch operator N.Y. State Taxation and Fin. Dept., Albany, 1960-61; receptionist Trine Mfg./Square D Co., Bronx, 1972-76; clk. Square D Co., Bronx, 1976-78, exec. sec., 1978-79, personnel mgr., 1979-86; mgr. mktg. adminstrn. Trine Products Corp., 1986-89, adminstrv. mgr., 1989-92; prin. Bookkeeping & Tax Preparation Svc., 1976—; full charge bookkeeper Absolute Coatings Inc., New Rochelle, N.Y., 1994—. Mfg. Fund raiser YMCA, Bronx, 1979—; mem. Community Bd. #9, Bronx, 1984—. Recipient Svc. to Youth award YMCA, 1985. Mem. Adminstrv. Mgmt. Soc. Republican. Roman Catholic. Avocations: physical fitness, reading, interior decorating. Home and Office: 4100-20 Hutchinson River Pky E Bronx NY 10475

MCKENNA, KATHLEEN KWASNIK, visual artist; b. Detroit, Nov. 6, 1946; d. John J. and Eleanor H. (Ciosek) K.; m. Frank J. McKenna, Jr., Mar. 16, 1968. Cert., Cooper Sch. Art, Cleve., 1973; student, Art Students' League, N.Y.C., 1972, 74. Instr. portrait painting Baycrafters, Bay Village, Ohio, 1976-79; self-employed painter, 1972—. One-person exhbns. include Ctrl. Nat. Bank, Cleve., 1975, Women's City Club Gallery, Cleve., 1979, Kennedy Ctr. Art Gallery, Hiram, Ohio, 1980, Chime Art Gallery, Summit, N.J., 1985, Bolton Art Gallery, Cleve., 1986, 91; exhibited in group shows at Butler Inst. Am. Art, 1981, 89, 91, 93, Mansfield (Ohio) Art Ctr., 1990, Circle Gallery, N.Y.C., 1978, Canton (Ohio) Art Inst., 1990, others. Recipient Pres.'s award Am. Artists Profl. League, 1993, other awards. Mem. New Orgn. for the Visual Arts, Catharine Lorillard Wolfe Art Club (Pastel Soc. plaque 1989, Mae Berlind Bach award 1983, Cert. of Merit 1981), Allied Artists Am. (assoc.; Gold medal of Honor 1989). Roman Catholic. Studio: 15914 Chadbourne Rd Shaker Heights OH 44120

MCKENNA, MARGARET ANNE, college president; b. R.I., June 3, 1945; d. Joseph John and Mary (Burns) McK.; children: Michael Aaron McKenna Miller, David Christopher McKenna Miller. BA in Sociology, Emmanuel Coll., 1967; postgrad., Boston Coll. Law Sch., 1968; JD, So. Meth. U., 1971; LLD (hon.), U. Upsala, N.J., 1978, Fitchburg (Mass.) State Coll., 1979, Regis Coll., 1982; D Community Affairs, U. R.I., 1979. Bar: Tex. 1971, D.C. 1973. Atty. Dept. Justice, Washington, 1971-73; exec. dir. Internat. Assn. Ofcl. Human Rights Agys., Washington, 1973-74; mgmt. cons. Dept. Treasury, Washington, 1975-76; dep. council to Pres. White House, Washington, 1976-79; dep. undersec. Dept. Edn., Washington, 1979-81; dir. Mary Ingraham Bunting Inst., Radcliffe Coll., Cambridge, Mass., 1981-85; v.p. program planning Radcliffe Coll., Cambridge, 1982-85; pres. Lesley Coll., Cambridge, 1985—; bd. dirs. Stride Rite Corp., Cambridge, Best Products Co., Inc., Richmond, Va., Consolidated Natural Gas Co., Pitts., Coun. of Ind. Colls., Washington. Chair higher edn. task force Clinton Transition, 1992-93; chair edn. task force Mayor Thomas Marino Transition Com., 1994. Recipient Outstanding Contribution award Civil Rights Leadership Conf., 1978; named Woman of Yr. Women's Equity Action League, 1979, Outstanding Woman of Yr. Big Sister Assn., 1986. Democrat. Office: Lesley Coll Office of the President 29 Everett St Cambridge MA 02138-2790

MCKENNA, MICHELE LEE, sales and marketing executive, consultant; b. Teaneck, N.J., June 22, 1959; d. Vincent Thomas and Yvonne Lee (Terango) McK. BS, Marquette U., 1981; degree in Italian, Università per Stranieri, Italy, 1994. Acct. exec. Times Computer Svcs., London, 1981, Dun & Bradstreet, N.Y.C., 1982-85; nat. tng. mgr. Dun & Bradstreet, Parsippany, N.J., 1985-86, regional sales mgr., 1987-88; sr. tng. officer Dun & Bradstreet, London, 1989, U.K. sales and mktg. mgr., 1990-91; nat. sales mgr. Dun & Bradstreet, Parsippany, 1991-92, asst. v.p., 1993-94; quality assurance cons. Western Union Fin. Svcs. Internat., Paramus, N.J., 1994—; spkr. confs. in field. Mem. Ctr. Italian and Italian-Am. Culture. Roman Catholic. Home: 5J Foxwood Dr Morris Plains NJ 07950

MCKENNEY, KATHERINE ELIZABETH, small business owner, biofeedback specialist; b. Houston, Nov. 13, 1957; d. Robert Lee Jr. and Joyce Elaine (Russell) McK. Student, Okaloosa-Walton C.C., Niceville, Fla., 1975-78; BA in Psychology and Biology, Carleton U., Ottawa, Ont., Can., 1982. Cert. biofeedback specialist. Exec. sec., contr., sales and banquet sec., sales coord. Sheraton Coronado Beach Resort, Ft. Walton Beach, Fla., 1976-86, sales mgr., 1986, dir. sales and mktg., 1986-87; sales rep. Holiday Inn, Ft. Walton Beach, 1987, Blue Horizon Resort, Ft. Walton Beach, 1987; dir. sales Holiday Ind-Destin, Fla., 1987-89; biofeedback specialist Rivendell Cinic, Ft. Walton Beach, 1983-94; dist. sales mgr. Davis and Assocs., Navarre, Fla., 1989-91; owner, mgr. KEM Publs., hotel-condominium in-room directories, Mary Esther, Fla., 1992—. Mem. Am. Bus. Women's Assn. (chmn. hospitality com. 1987-88), Biofeedback Soc. Fla. Home: 300 Miracle Strip Pky SW Fort Walton Beach FL 32548-5201 Office: KEM Publs 429 Page Bacon Rd Ste 146 Mary Esther FL 32569-1633

MCKENNY, COLLIN GRAD, banker; b. Seattle, July 29, 1944; d. Edward Paul and Betty B. (Collins) Grad; m. Jon W. McKenny, June 15, 1975 (div. June 1982); m. Spencer Frank Ison, Dec. 31, 1985. BA, U. Wash., Seattle, 1966; MBA, Seattle U., 1969; grad., Pacific Coast Banking Sch., 1979. From mgmt. trainee to v.p. Peoples Nat. Bank, Seattle, 1966-85; sr. v.p. Barclays Bank of Calif., San Francisco, 1985-88, Star Banc Corp., Cin., 1988—. Treas. Salvation Army, Federal Way, Wash., 1981-83; bd. dirs. Boys & Girls Clubs, Seattle, 1982-85. Mem. Am. Bankers Assn. (bd. dirs. bancard exec. com., chmn. ann. conf. 1989—, chmn. bankcard schools 1990-94), Cin. Bus. Incubator (chmn.), Bankers Club, Chi Omega. Office: Star Banc Corp 425 Walnut St Cincinnati OH 45202-3912

MCKENZIE, BARBARA KAY, elementary education educator; b. Mattoon, Ill., Apr. 26, 1946; d. Gail C. and Emily May (Sims) Foster; m. Joseph Arnold McKenzie, Mar. 18, 1972; children: Jonathan, James, Timothy. BS in Edn., Ea. Ill. U., 1968, MS in Edn., 1972. Cert. elem., art, spl. reading and libr. sci. tchr., Ill. 1st grade tchr. Elem. Sch., Morrisonville, Ill., 1968-69; 5th and 6th grades tchr. Elem. Sch., Gays, Ill., 1969-74; 1st grade tchr. Elem. Sch., Windsor, Ill., 1975-77; 2nd grade tchr. Elem. Sch., Mattoon, Ill., 1983-84; 3d grade tchr. Elem. Sch., Mattoon, 1984—. Mem. NEA, Ill. Edn. Assn., Mattoon Edn. Assn., EIU Reading Coun., Coles County Home Ext. (pres., v.p.), Ladies of the Moose. Republican. Presbyterian. Home: 2821 Oak Ave Mattoon IL 61938

MCKENZIE, CINDY LYNN, research biologist; b. Dallas, July 27, 1961; d. Billy Eugene and Cherry Sue (Cooper) McK. BS in Agrl. Bus., SulRoss State U., 1983, MS in Range Animal Sci., 1987, MS in Biology, 1987; PhD in Biology and Entomology, N.Mex. State U., 1991. Grad. rsch. asst. SulRoss State U., Alpine, Tex., 1985-87, N.Mex. State U., Las Cruces, 1987-91; postdoctorate rsch. assoc. Okla. State U., Lane, 1991-94; rsch. biologist FMC Corp., Yuma, Ariz., 1994—. Contbr. articles to profl. jours. Mem. Entomol. Soc. Am., Southwestern Entomol. Soc., Beta Beta Beta, Delta Tau Alpha. Republican. Home and Office: 10609 Calle Raquel Yuma AZ 85367

MCKENZIE, GWENDOLYN VERON, marketing, business development and public relations executive; b. Durham, N.C., Aug. 10; d. Lionel Wilfred and Blanche (Veron) McK. BS, U. Rochester, 1977; MEd, Harvard U., 1982. Adminstrv. asst. Kennedy Sch. Govt., Cambridge, Mass., 1981; mktg. coord. Payette Assocs., Boston, 1983-86; mktg. mgr. Profl. Designs Inc., Boston, 1986, Staats Internat., Boston, 1987-89; dir. pub. rels., mgr. bus. devel. Arrowstreet Inc., Somerville, Mass., 1990—. Vol. John Kerry for Senator, Boston, 1989; adv. bd. City/Build. Mem. Urban Land Inst., Internat. Assn. Corp. Real Estate Execs. (pres. New Eng. chpt. 1993-94), Instnl. and Mcpl. Parking Congress, New Eng. Soc. for Assn. Execs., Am. Soc. Assn. Execs., Soc. for Mktg. Profl. Svcs., Nat. Alliance for the Mentally Ill, Boston Soc. Architects, Harvard Faculty Club. Democrat. Office: Arrowstreet Inc 212 Elm St Somerville MA 02144-2946

MCKENZIE, KAY BRANCH, public relations executive; b. Atlanta, Feb. 12, 1936; d. William Harllee and Katherine (Hunter) Branch; m. Harold Cantrell McKenzie, Jr., Apr. 11, 1958; children: Ansley, Katherine, Harold Cantrell III. Student, Sweet Briar Coll., 1955, Emory U., 1956-57. Account exec. Hill and Knowlton Inc., Atlanta, 1979-80, account supr./dir. southeast govt. relations, 1981-83; ptnr. McKenzie, Gordon & Potter, Atlanta, 1983-85; pres. McKenzie & Assocs. Inc., Atlanta, 1986-89; sr. v.p. Manning Selvage & Lee, Atlanta, 1989-93; v.p. comm. and creative svcs. 1996 Atlanta Paralympic Games, 1993—. Mem. Commn. on Future of South, 1974; co-chmn. John Lewis for Congress, Atlanta, 1986; bd. dirs. Bedford Pines Day Care Ctrs., Atlanta, 1987-92, Ga. Clean and Beautiful, 1987-88, Ga. Fund for Edn., 1987-92; regional bd. dirs. Inst. Internat. Edn., 1987-93. Fellow Internat. Bus. Fellows (bd. dirs. 1983-85, 92-93, v.p. 1986-88); mem. Pub. Rels. Soc. Am., Ga. C. of C. (bd. dirs. 1983—), Leadership Atlanta. Democrat. Episcopalian. Home: 172 Huntington Rd NE Atlanta GA 30309 Office: 1201 W Peachtree St NW Ste 2500 Atlanta GA 30309

MCKENZIE, LORENE LANDS, marriage and family counselor, educator; b. Arab, Ala., Mar. 3, 1932; d. Alver Lee and Maggie Jane (Nixon) Lands; m. Jesse E. McKenzie, Nov. 22, 1947; children: Barbara Hemrick, Dennis, Rayford J., Debbie Argo, Dianne Morgan. BA in Psychology, West Ga. Coll., 1977, MEd, 1980, postgrad., 1982. Clergy counselor Mt. Pleasant Bapt. Ch., Carrollton, Ga., 1964-84; tchr. Bremen (Ga.) High Sch., 1980-81, Spemedial-Bowdon H.S., 1981-82, Heritage Pvt. Sch., Newman, Ga., 1982-83; pvt. practice counselor in field; indsl. supr. Sewell Mfg. Co., Bremen, Ga., 1970-72, mental health counselor, Carrrollton, 1978. Chaperoned tour group pen-pals to Eng.; mem. Rep. campaign, Carrollton, 1980; speaker, Bible lectr. to women's groups. Home and Office: 218 Perry St Carrollton GA 30117-2423

MCKENZIE, MARY BETH, artist; b. Cleve.; d. William Jennings and Mary Elizabeth (McCray) McK.; m. Tony Mysak, May 8, 1974; children: Zsuzsa McKenzie, Maria McKenzie. Student, Mus. Fine Arts, Boston, 1964-65, Cooper Sch. Art, Cleve., 1965-67; diploma, Nat. Acad. Design, N.Y.C., 1974. Painting instr. Nat. Acad. Design, N.Y.C., 1981—. Author: A Painterly Approach, 1987; contbr. articles to profl. jours.; one-woman shows include Nat. Arts Club, N.Y.C., 1976, FAR Gallery, N.Y.C., 1980, Perin and Sharpe Gallery, New Canaan, Conn., 1981, Frank Caro Gallery, N.Y.C., 1988-89, Joseph Keiffer Gallery, N.Y.C., 1991; exhibited in group shows at Sindin Gallery, N.Y.C., 1985-86; permanent collections include Met. Mus. Art, N.Y.C., The Butler Mus. Am. Art, Mus. City of N.Y., NAD, Art Student's League of N.Y., Great Modern Pictures. Recipient Nat. Scholastic award Mus. Fine Arts, Boston, numerous awards including Thomas B. Clark prize and the Isaac N. Maynard prize Nat. Acad. Design, Greenshields Found. grantee, Stacey Found. grantee. Mem. Nat. Acad. Design, Pastel Soc. Am. (Best In Show, Award of Exceptional Merit, Exhbn. Com. award), Allied Artists Am. (Gold medal, The Jane Peterson award, Grumbacher Cash award, Silver medal), Audubon Artists (Pastel Soc. Am. award). Home: 525 W 45th St New York NY 10036-3405

MCKENZIE, NOREEN ANN, secondary school educator; b. Eureka, Calif., Feb. 14, 1948; d. Salvatore and Ruth Naomi (Ryer) Mylie; m. Daniel Owen McKenzie, June 28, 1969. BA in English, Humboldt State U., Arcata, Calif., 1970, teaching credential English, 1971. Cert. tchr. English, Math., Calif. English and math. tchr. Jacobs Jr. High Sch., Eureka, Calif., 1972-81; college prep. math. instr. Eureka High Sch., 1981—, computer and math. mentor tchr., 1985—. Editor, pub. (newsletter) The Eureka Tchr., 1992—. Grantee State of Calif., 1984, 85. Mem. AAUW (organizer, presenter Expanding Your Horizons, Arcata. 1985-87), NEA, Calif. Tchrs. Assn., Eureka Tchrs. Assn. (mentor tchr. selector 1986—, contract negotiating team 1988—, v.p. 1988-91). Office: Eureka High Sch 1915 J St Eureka CA 95501-3098

MCKENZIE, SUSAN SMITH, business writer; b. N.Y.C., Dec. 30, 1964; d. John Brewster and Ida (Hawa) Smith. BA in English, Tex. A&M U., 1986; MA in Journalism, Ind. U., 1988. Parachutist and broadcast journalist 1st Special Ops. Command, Ft. Bragg, N.C., 1989-91; media rels. journalist U.S. Army Parachute Team - Golden Knights, Ft. Bragg, N.C., 1991-92; TV reporter Sta. WLTX-TV, Columbia, S.C., 1992; bus. writer The Herald, Rock Hill, S.C., 1992-94; plant comms. specialist Brunswick Nuclear Plant Carolina Power & Light, Southport, 1994—. With U.S. Army, 1988-92, Panama, Persian Gulf. Recipient South Korean Jump Wings Republic of Korea Spl. Warfare Ctr., 1989. Mem. Women in Communications, Inc., Soc. Profl. Journalists, Nat. Press Photographers Assn. Presbyterian. Home: 3917 Mayfield Ct Wilmington NC 28412 Office: Carolina Power & Light PO Box 10429 Southport NC 28461-0429

MCKENZIE-ANDERSON, RITA LYNN, psychologist; b. Boston, Nov. 25, 1952; d. Wallace Andrew and Angelina Rita (Bagnoli) McK. BA, Framingham State Coll., 1974; MEd, Northeastern U., 1975; PhD, Temple U., 1983. Lic. psychologist, Mass. Pvt. practice Fairfield, Conn., 1984-86; psychologist Johnson Life Ctr., Springfield, Mass., 1986-87, dir. outpatient therapy, 1987-88; pvt. practice Springfield, 1988—; investigator Springfield Juvenile Ct., 1989—; adj. faculty Holyoke (Mass.) Community Coll., 1989-90, Springfield Tech. Community Coll., 1989-90; dir. day treatment DuBois Day Treatment Ctr., Stamford, Conn., 1982-86; cons. psychologist Community Care Mental Health Ctr., Springfield, 1989—, Spofford Hall Treatment Ctr., Ludlow, Mass., 1991-92. Trustee Northampton (Mass.) State Hosp.; mem. organizing com. Week of Young Child, Springfield; bd. dirs. Stop Abuse Against Kids. Mem. Women Bus. Owners Alliance, Zonta Internat. Office: 380 Union St Ste 14 West Springfield MA 01089

MCKEOWN, MARY ELIZABETH, educational administrator; d. Raymond Edmund and Alice (Fitzgerald) McNamara; BS, U. Chgo., 1946; MS, DePaul U., 1953; m. James Edward McKeown, Aug. 6, 1955. Supr. high sch. dept. Am. Sch., 1948-68, prin., 1968—, trustee, 1975—, v.p., 1979, exec. v.p., 1992—. Mem. ASCD, LWV, Nat. Assn. Secondary Sch. Prins., North Cen. Assn. Colls. and Schs. (exec. bd. 1990-93). Assn., Nat. Home Study Coun. (chairperson rsch. and edn. com. 1988-93). Author study guides for algebra, geometry and calculus. Home: 1469 Sheridan Rd Kenosha WI 53140-4444 Office: 850 E 58th St Chicago IL 60637-1459

MCKEOWN, MARY MARGARET, lawyer; b. Casper, Wyo., May 11, 1951; d. Robert Mark and Evelyn Margaret (Lipsack) McK.; m. Peter Francis Cowhey, June 29, 1985; 1 child, Megan Margaret. BA in Internat. Affairs, U. Wyo., 1972; JD, Georgetown U., 1975. Bar: Wash. 1975, D.C. 1982. Assoc. Perkins Coie, Seattle, 1975-79, Washington, 1979-80; White House fellow U.S. Dept. Interior and White House, Washington, 1980-81; ptnr., mem. exec. com. Perkins Coie, Seattle, 1981—, mng. dir. strategic planning and client rels., 1990—; trustee The Pub. Defender, Seattle, 1982-85; rep. 9th Cir. Judicial Conf., San Francisco, 1985-89, mem. gender bias task force, 1992-93. Author: Girl Scout's Guide to New York, 1990; contbr. chpt. to book and articles to profl. jours. Nat. bd. dirs. Girl Scouts Am., N.Y.C., 1976-87; bd. dirs. Family Svcs., Seattle, 1982-84, Corp. coun. for the Arts, Seattle, 1988—; bd. gen. counsel Downtown Seattle Assn., 1986-89; mem. exec. com. Wash. Coun. Internat. Trade, 1994—. Recipient Rising Stars of the 80's award Legal Times Washington, 1983, 100 Young Women of Promise, Good Housekeeping, 1985; named Washington's Winningest Trial Lawyers Washington Journal, 1992; Japan leadership fellow, 1992-93. Fellow ABA (ho. of dels. 1990—); mem. ACLU (chmn. legal com. 1982-85), Fed. Bar Assn. (trustee western dist. Wash. 1980-90), Wash. Bar Assn. (chmn. jud. recommendations 1989-90), Seattle-King County Bar Assn. (trustee, sec. 1984-85, Outstanding Lawyer award 1992), Legal Found. Wash. (trustee, pres. 1989-90), Washington Women Lawyers (bd. dirs., pres. 1978-79), Nat. Assn. Iolta Programs (bd. dirs. 1989-91), Fed. Ct. Pro Bono Civil Rights Panel. Home: 1522 40th Ave Seattle WA 98122-3510 Office: Perkins Coie 1201 3rd Ave Seattle WA 98101-3099

MCKERROW, AMANDA, ballet dancer; b. Albuquerque; d. Alan and Constance McKerrow; m. John Gardner. Student, Met. Acad. Ballet, Bethesda, Md., Washington Sch. Ballet. With Washington Ballet Co., 1980-82; with Am. Ballet Theatre, N.Y.C., 1982—, soloist, from 1983, prin. dancer, 1987—. Toured Europe with Washington Ballet; danced in Margot Fonteyn Gala at Metropolitan Opera House; featured in Pavlova Tribute film, also many guest appearances; leading roles in Ballet Imperial, La Bayadere, Manon, Birthday Offering, Dim Lustre, Donizetti Variations, Giselle, Graduation Ball, The Leaves Are Fading, Nine Sinatra Songs, The Nutcracker, Pillar of Fire, Requiem, Romeo and Juliet, The Sleeping Beauty, Les Sylphides, Push Comes to Shove, Symphony Concertante, Symphonic Variations, Theme and Variations, Stravinsky Violin Concerto, Swan Lake, Triad, Duets, Etudes, Coppelia, Voluntaries and Rodeo; created leading role in Bruch Violin Concerto No. 1, Some Assembly Required and Agnus De Mille's The Other. Recipient N.Y. Woman award for dance, 1991; co-winner gold prize for women Moscow Internat. Ballet Competition, 1981. Office: Am Ballet Theatre 890 Broadway New York NY 10003-1211

MCKEW, BRIGID ANNE, producer; b. Balt., June 25, 1965; d. John Fahey and Catherine Lucille (Murphy) McK. BA, Coll. Notre Dame of Md., Balt., 1987. Office mgr. Telemessage, Inc., Balt., 1986-87; traffic coord., prodn. mgr. advt. Blue Cross/Blue Shield, 1987-88; desk assignment editor Sta. WMAR-TV, Balt., 1988-89, assoc. producer, 1989-93; sales and svc. MCI Telecomm., Hunt Valley, Md., 1993—. Producer prodns. Turn It Up, Balt., 1991—. Campaign vol. Dan McKew for Ho. of Dels., Md., 1990-91. Home: 7320 Tred Avon Rd Baltimore MD 21220 Office: MCI Telecomm 230 Schilling Cir Hunt Valley MD 21031

MCKIBBON-TURNER, BAMBI, management firm executive; b. Columbus, Ohio, Apr. 12, 1947; d. Alfonso Jackson and Myra Josephine (Kelley) McKibbon; (div. 1971); children: John M. III, Linda Marie, Lisaj Denise Turner Chappelle. BS in Human Svcs., N.H. Coll., 1989, MS in Community Econ. Devel., 1989. Caseworker Office of Congressman Don J. Pease, Washington, 1977-79, fed. grant specialist, 1979-89, econ. devel. and fed. grant specialist, 1989-90, legis. asst. and econ. devel. specialist, 1990-91, econ. devel. dir., 1991-93; pres., CEO McKibbon Mgmt., Inc., Washington, 1987-90, Arlington, Va., 1993—. Mem. No. Va. Dem. Club, Arlington, 1991. Named Outstanding Young Woman of Am., 1983; recipient Outstanding Congl. Black Assocs. Worker award, 1984. Mem. Coalition of 100 Black Women (charter mem. Nat. City chpt. 1983), Nat. Assn. Women Bus. Owners, Orgn. Caribbean Bus. Persons. Home: 1600 S Eads St Arlington VA 22202-2930 Office: 2101 Crystal Plz Arcade Ste 140 Arlington VA 22202

MCKILLIP, PATRICIA CLAIRE, operatic soloist; b. Milw., Apr. 28; d. Lester J. and Ruth J. (Lohneis) McK.; m. Mark Richard McKillip, June 16, 1990. BA in English-Drama, Creative Writing, Lit., Alverno Coll., 1980; MusB in Applied Music, Alverno Coll., Milw., 1981; postgrad., Wis. Conservatory of Mus., 1981-82, U. Wis., Milw., 1982, The Juilliard Sch., 1982-84, Am. Acad. Dramatic Arts, 1983-84, Adelphi U., 1984. Soloist Amadeus Opera Co.; instr. vocal music seminars various high schs., N.Y.; co-founder, co-dir. The Masque Consort, N.Y.C., 1990-91, exec. v.p., 1991; v.p., co-founder Creative Learning Assocs.; instr. Cardinal Stritch Coll., Milw., 1994—. Performed with numerous opera cos. including The Florentine Opera Co., Music Under the Stars Prodns., Milw. Opera Co., Westchester Lyric Opera Co., Profl. Opera Workshop at Lincoln Ctr., Met. Opera Co., N.Y. Grand Opera Co., Monteverdi Opera Guild Prodns., Republic Opera Co., La Puma Opera Co., and other chamber, theater and folk groups; puppeteer, costumer, designer Puppet Art Troupe; performed in over 50 mus. shows and prodns., 6 solo recitals, also medieval concerts, choruses, orchestras, oratorio; 42 other recitals. Exec. v.p. Masque Consort, a multi-media theatrical orgn. Music dept. scholar Alverno U. Mem. AFTRA, SAG, Nat. Assn. Music Tchrs., Music Educators Nat. Conf. (treas.), Internat. Platform Assn., Wis. Fedn. Music Clubs, Music Clubs Am., Am. Guild Mus. Artists, Q'ahal-Liturgical Music Soc., Delta Omicron (v.p., chaplain, warden Gamma Gamma chpt., WMA State and Regional Vocal award 1978, Star of Delta Omicron award 1980, 40 music medals from state and dist. WSMA), Alpha Sigma Tau. Democrat. Roman Catholic. Home: 4860 S 69th St Greenfield WI 53220

MCKIM, HARRIET MEGCHELSEN, education educator; b. Keokuk, Iowa, Oct. 17, 1919; d. Herbert John and Florence Josephine (Ottowa) Megchelsen; m. Lanier McClure, Nov. 1, 1944 (div. 1948); 1 child, Janet Gray; m. L.A. McKim, July 28, 1950 (div. 1968). BA, Calif. State U., Sacramento, 1952; MA, U. So. Calif., 1963, EdD, 1979. Tchr., prin. Cumberland County Schs., Crossville, Tenn., 1939-42; sec. Tenn. Valley Authority, Oak Ridge Def. Plant, Mare Island Naval Shipyard and Cal-West Ins., 1942-52; tchr., vice-prin., reading specialist, dir. ESEA I various pub. schs., Oxnard, Orcutt, Sacramento, Edwards AFB, Calif. and Spokane, Wash., 1950-64; coord. Yuba City and Yuba County Schs., 1964-70; cons. Calif. Dept. Edn., 1970-83; part-time instr. Alan Hancock Community Coll., Santa Maria, Calif., Polytech. U., San Luis Obispo, Calif., U. Calif., Davis, Santa Barbara, 1960-70; supr. student tchrs. Calif. State U., Sacramento, 1984; adj. prof. edn. Nat. U., Sacramento, 1986-88. Vol. tchr. ARC parenting classes, Sacramento, 1984-85; docent, spkr. Crocker Art Mus.; vol. Loaves and Fishes; bd. dirs. Sacramento Internat. Students' coun., Friends of Libr. Calif. State U., Elderhostel Calif. State U.; docent Sacramento History Ctr.; deacon Fremont Presbyn. Ch.; v.p. Sacramento World Affairs Coun. Mem. AAUW, Nat. Assn. Edn. Young Children, Calif. Ret. Tchrs., Am. Assn. Ret. Persons, Profs. of Early Childhood Edn., Sacramento Affiliates, Amnesty Internat., World Affairs Coun. (adminstrv. v.p.), Sierra Club, Delta Kappa Gamma, Phi Delta Kappa. Address: 5332 State Ave Sacramento CA 95819

MCKIM, JOANNA, lawyer; b. El Centro, Calif., July 12, 1964; d. Joseph Paul and Mary (Legakes) McK. BA in Govt., Pomona Coll., 1986; JD, U. Santa Clara, 1989; postgrad. in Edn., Nat. U., 1994—. Bar: Calif. 1989. Assoc. Graham & James, Palo Alto, Calif., 1989-90, Farrow, Bramson, Baskin & Plutzik, Walnut Creek, Calif., 1990-92. Comments editor Santa Clara U. Law Review. Musician violin I East County Jewish Community Ctr. Symphony Orch., 1994. Mem. ABA. Republican. Episcopalian. Home: 1353B Caminito Gabaldon San Diego CA 92108

MCKINLESS, KATHY JEAN, accountant; b. Augusta, Ga., June 15, 1954; d. Jack M. and Jean K. (Norby) VanderWood; m. Darryl P. Calderon, Mar. 17, 1979 (dec. June 1988); children: Christopher, Jackie; m. Richard T. McKinless, July 1, 1989; children: Ashley, Thomas. BS in Acctg., U. S.C., 1975, MBA, 1978. CPA, D.C. Acct. Clarkson, Harden & Gantt, Columbia, 1975-79; sr. acct. KPMG Peat Marwick, Washington, 1979-80, mgr., 1980-86, ptnr., 1986—; spkr. Mortgage Bankers Assn., Fin. Mgrs. Soc., Nat. Assn. Coll. and Univ. Bus. Officers, Fed. Fin. Insts. Exam. Coun. Mem. Governance com., treas., bd. dirs. Coun. of Nation's Capital Girl Scouts U.S., 1985—. Office: KPMG Peat Marwick 2001 M St NW Washington DC 20036-3310

MCKINLEY, CAMILLE DOMBROWSKI, psychologist; b. Buffalo, May 6, 1922; d. Eugene Anthony and Anne Victoria (Sliwinska) Dombrowski; m. Thomas Leroy Smith, Dec. 30, 1944 (div. 1977); children: Thomas Dan, Cynthia Camille (dec.), Pamela Susan; m. William Frank McKinley, Oct. 7, 1984 (dec. Mar. 1985). BA, Syracuse U., 1943; MA, Boston U., 1947; edn. specialist, Mich. State U., 1970, PhD, 1978. Acad. advisor Mich. State U., East Lansing, 1966-70, dir. Career Ctr., 1970-81, counseling psychologist Counseling Ctr., 1981-91; pres. Priam Pubs., 1978—; mem. Career Planning and Placement Coun. Mich. State U., 1970-91. Editor: The Mich. State Univ. Referral Directory, 1970-91, The Gracious Reader, 1970-80; editor, publisher The CAM Report, 1978—. Founding pres. Greater Lansing chpt. Planned Parenthood, Mich., 1967; v.p. Opera Co. of Mid-Mich., 1983-85; bd. dirs. Wharton Ctr. for Performing Arts and Dean's Community Coun.,

Mich. State U., mem. Platinum Cir. Mem. Mich. State U. Pres.'s Club, Pontiac Yacht Club, Mackinac Island Yacht Club, Zonta Internat., Zeta Tau Alpha. Home: PO Box 1862 East Lansing MI 48826-1862 Office: 611 Cowley Ave East Lansing MI 48823-3007

MCKINLEY, ELLEN BACON, priest; b. Milw., June 9, 1929; d. Edward Alsted and Lorraine Goodrich (Graham) Bacon; m. Richard Smallbrook McKinley, III, June 16, 1951 (div. Oct. 1977); children: Richard IV, Ellen Graham, David Todd, Edward Bacon. BA cum laude, Bryn Mawr Coll., 1951; MDiv Yale U., 1976; STM, Gen. Theol. Sem., N.Y.C., 1979; PhD, Union Theol. Sem., N.Y.C., 1988. Ordained to ministry Episcopal Ch. as deacon, 1980, as priest, 1981. Intern St. Francis Ch., Stamford, Conn., 1976-77; pastoral asst. St. Paul's Ch., Riverside, Conn., 1979-80, curate, 1980-81; priest assoc. St. Saviour's Ch., Old Greenwich, Conn., 1982-90; asst. St. Christopher's Ch., Chatham, Mass., 1987-88, interim asst., Trinity Ch., Princeton, N.J., 1990-91; priest assoc. All Saints Ch., Princeton, 1992—, interim rector, 1993; mem. major chpt. Trinity Cathedral, Trenton, 1992—. Mem. Episcopal Election Com., Diocese of Conn., 1986-87, Com. on Human Sexuality, 1987-90; Com. on Donations and Bequests Diocese of Conn., 1987-90; sec., Greewich Com. on Drugs, 1970-71; bd. dirs. Greenwich YWCA, 1971-72. Mem. Episcopal Women's Caucus, Colonial Dames Am., Jr. League. Clubs: Sulgrave, Rocky Point. Avocations: theatre, concerts, swimming, art, iconography, reading, building and remodeling houses.

MCKINLEY, MARGARET ANN, advertising executive; b. Cin., Oct. 29, 1956; d. Peter Michael and Enriqueta (Liaño) McK. BA in Sociology and Anthropology, Oberlin Coll., 1978. Account coordinator Young and Rubicam, N.Y.C., 1978-81, staff asst., 1981-82, asst. account exec., 1982-83, account exec., 1983-87, account supr., 1987—; promotional video cons., N.Y.C., 1981-83; officer Now & Then Prodns., N.Y.C., 1983—. Prodn. mgr. short subject film Mirage, 1981. Episcopalian. Home: 1465 E Putnam Ave Apt 211 Old Greenwich CT 06870-1331 Office: Young and Rubicam 285 Madison Ave New York NY 10017-6401

MCKINLEY, (JENNIFER CAROLYN) ROBIN, writer; b. Warren, Ohio, Nov. 16, 1952; d. William and Jeanne Carolyn (Turrell) McK; m. Peter Dickinson, Jan. 3, 1992. Student, Dickinson Coll., 1970-72; BA, Bowdoin Coll., 1975, PhD (hon.), 1986. Editor, transcriber Ward and Paul, Washington, 1972-73; rsch. asst. Rsch. Assocs., Brunswick, Maine, 1976-77; tchr., counselor pvt. secondary sch., Natick, Maine, 1978-79; edit. asst. Little, Brown & Co., Boston, 1979-81; barn mgr. horse farm Holliston, Mass., 1981-82; clerk Books of Wonder, N.Y.C., 1983—; freelance reader, copy and line editor, 1983—. Author: Beauty: A Retelling of the Story of Beauty and the Beast, 1978 (Horn book Honor list citation 1978), The Door in the Hedge, 1981, The Blue Sword, 1982 (Best Young adult books citation ALA 1982, Newbery Honor citation 1983), The Hero and the Crown, 1984 (Horn book honor list citation 1985, Newbery medal 1985), The Outlaws of Sherwood, 1988, Rowan, 1992, My Father is in the Navy, 1992, Deerskin, 1993 (Best Young Adult Books citation ALA 1993, Best Adult Books for Young Adults citation ALA 1993), A Knot in the Grain and Other Stories, 1994; contbr.: Elsewhere Vol. II, 1982, Vol. III, 1984, Faery, 1985, Writers for Children, 1988; editor, contbr.: Imaginary Lands, 1985 (World Fantasy award Best Anthology 1986); adapter: Jungle Book Tales, 1985, Black Beauty, 1986, The Light Princess, 1988. Office: Merrilee Heifetz Writers House 21 W 26th St New York NY 10010-1003*

MCKINLEY BALFOUR, STEPHANIE ANN, learning resources director, librarian; b. Galesburg, Ill., Mar. 27, 1948; d. William Chester and Virginia Ann (Clugsten) McKinley; m. James Robert Miller, Mar. 2, 1968 (div. Mar. 1978); 1 child, Christopher Antonin Miller; m. David Alan Balfour, Nov. 23, 1991. BA in Speech, Drama, Western Ill. U., 1970; MLS, Drexel U., 1974. Cert. tchr., Ill., media specialist, Ill. Libr. William McKinley Elem. Sch., Phila., 1971-76, Regional Jr. H.S., Amherst, Mass., 1976-77, Garfield Elem. Sch., Monmouth, Ill., 1977-79; dir. learning resources Spoon River Valley Sch. Dist., London Mills, Ill., 1979—; dir. summer reading program Avon (Ill.) Pub. Libr., 1980—. Leader 4-H, Avon, 1983-92; vol. EMT Galesburg Hosp. Ambulance Svc., Galesburg/Avon, 1978—; dir. religious edn. Avon Federated Ch., 1984—. Named Outstanding Young Educator by Monmouth Jaycees, 1979. Mem. Ill. Optometric Assn. (auxiliary 1st v.p.), Nat. Edn. Assn., Ill. Edn. Assn., Ill. Sch. Libr. Media Assn., Phi Delta Kappa, Gamma Lambda-Delta Kappa Gamma Soc. Internat. (pres. 1992-94, 1st v.p. 1990-92, recording sec. 1988-92). Republican. Mem. United Ch. of Christ. Home: RR2 274 Funcheon Ct Avon IL 61415 Office: Spoon River Valley Sch Dist RR1 London Mills IL 61544

MCKINLEY-HAAS, MARY, artist; b. St. Louis; d. Lee Carrington and Florence (Dowden) McK.; m. Saul Haas; children: Christopher, Matthew. BA, Smith Coll.; student, Art Students League, 1973-74, Nat. Acad. Design, 1965-66, Studio and Forum Stage Design. Head costume design dept. ABC-TV, NYC, 1968-73. One women shows include Tarlowe Gallery, Westhampton Beach, N.Y., 1974, Fontbonne Gallery, St. Louis, 1977, Gallery Yssa, N.Y.C., 1979, Vered Gallery, East Hampton, N.Y., 1981, Netherlands Bank & Ludlow-Hyland Gallery, N.Y.C., 1981, U. Tex., Austin, 1988, RVS Fine Art, Southampton, N.Y., 1990, TSS Gallery, N.Y.C., 1992, U. Tex., Austin, 1992; exhibited in group shows at Vered Gallery, 1985, Works II Gallery, 1986, RVS Fine Art, 1987, Marymount Manhattan Gallery, 1988, Nabisco Brands Gallery, 1989, Lincoln Ctr., 1990, Queens Coll., 1991, Water Mill Mus., 1992, Dorothy Chandler Pavillion, 1993, Stony Brook U., 1994, others; costume designer for Broadway and TV shows. Mem. United Scenic Artists, Women in the Arts.

MCKINNEY, BETSY, state legislator; b. Bangor, Maine, Mar. 24, 1939. BS, Bentley Coll., 1972. Accountant N.H.; mem. N.H. Ho. Rep., mem. budget com., 1977-81, 87-88, mem. computer study com., 1983-84, mem. regulated revenues com.; del. N.H. Constl. Conv., 1984. Treas. Friends of the Libr. 1988—; chmn. Old Home Day, 1990, treas. 1978—; chmn. Rockingham County Exec. Com., 1991-92. Recipient Citizen of the Yr. award City of Londonderry, 1987. Mem. Londonderry C. of C. (treas. 1980-88). Republican. Roman Catholic. Home: 120 Litchfield Rd Londonderry NH 03053-7407 Office: 120 Litchfield Rd Londonderry NH 03053-7407*

MCKINNEY, CAROLYN JEAN, lawyer; b. Holly Springs, Miss., Sept. 28, 1956; d. Walter H. and Elizabeth (Lawrence) McK. BA in History and Polit. Sci., Rust Coll., Holly Springs, 1977; JD, Harvard U., 1980. Bar: Tex. 1980, U.S. Dist. Ct. (no., ea., so., and we. dists.) Tex. Atty. Gulf Oil Corp., Houston, 1980-84; sr. atty. ARCO, Dallas, 1984-90; atty. Amoco Corp., Houston, 1990-94, Chgo, 1994—; vis. prof., mentor black exec. exch. program Nat. Urban League, 1985—; mem. adv. bd. Nat. Soc. Black Engrs., 1987—. Vol. Meals on Wheels program Vis. Nurse's Assn., 1985, Kid Care, 1992; participant Miss. Gov.'s Leadership Conf. on Youth, 1988. Recipient Outstanding Alumni award Nat. Assn. for Equal Opportunity in Higher Edn., 1989. Mem. ABA. Office: Amoco Corp 200 E Randolph Chicago IL 60601

MCKINNEY, CAROLYN MARIE, librarian; b. Cleve., Feb. 6, 1939; d. Morris E. and Margaret L. (Keller) Nall; m. Allyn C. McKinney, June 13, 1964 (div. 1987); children: Paul W., Scott A., Eileyn M. Sobeck. BA, Bethany Coll., 1961; MSLS, Case Western Res., 1962. Reference libr. Cleve. (Ohio) Pub. Libr., 1962-67; adult svcs. libr. Mentor (Ohio) Pub. Libr., 1977-82; libr. I Lee County Libr. System, Cape Coral, Fla., 1983-84; br. libr. Lee County Libr. System, Cape Coral, 1984-94, acquisitions coord., 1994—. Dir. Lake County Mental Health Ctr., Mentor, 1977. Mem. ALA, Fla. Libr. Assn., Nat. Audubon Soc.

MCKINNEY, CYNTHIA ANN, congresswoman; b. Mar. 17, 1955; d. Billy and Leola McKinney; 1 child, Coy Grandison, Jr. B, U. So. Calif.; post-grad., Ga. State U., U. Wis.; Tufts U. Former instr. Clark Atlanta U., Atlanta Met. Coll.; former mem. Ga. Ho. of Reps.; mem. 103rd Congress from 11th Ga. dist., 1993—; instr. Agnes Scott Coll. Diplomatic fellow Spellman Coll. Home: 765 Shorter Ter NW Atlanta GA 30318-7140 Office: US Ho of Reps Office Of House Mems Washington DC 20515

MCKINNEY, JANET KAY, law librarian; b. Kansas City, Mo., Feb. 15, 1959; d. Charles Durward and Helen Jean (Bost) Freeman; m. Larry Emmett McKinney, July 11, 1981. BA, Avila Coll., 1981; MA in Libr. Sci., U. Mo., 1989. Circulation libr. Midwestern Bapt. Theol. Sem., Kansas City, 1981-84, acquisitions libr., 1984-85, reference libr., 1985-90; environ. divsn. libr. Black & Veatch, Kansas City, 1990-91; acquisitions/serials libr. U. Mo. Leon E. Bloch Law Libr., Kansas City, 1991—. Mem. ALA, Am. Assn. Law Libr. (com. on rels. with info. vendors 1994—, editorial bd. Tech. Svcs. Law Libr., 1994—), Mid-Am. Assn. Law Librs. (newsletter adv. mgr. 1993-94), Southwestern Assn. Law Librs., N.Am. Serials Interest Group, Spl. Librs. Assn. (employment com. chmn. 1990-91, chpt. treas. 1991-94, chpt. pres.-elect 1994-95). Office: U Mo Kansas City Leon E Bloch Law Libr 5100 Rockhill Rd Kansas City MO 64110-2499

MCKINNEY, JOAN DIANE, licensed practical nurse, gastroenterology clinician; b. Evanston, Ill., May 20, 1949; d. Robert Albert and Irene Alma (Thuerk) Miller; m. Bryan Lee McKinney, June 6, 1981. LPN, Oakton C.C., 1970. cert. gastroenterology clinician. LPN Lutheran General Hosp., Park Ridge, Ill., 1972-80, Suburban Med. Ctr., Hoffman Estates, Ill., 1980-81; opthalmic asst. Eye Inst. Med. Coll. of Wis., Milw., 1982; anesthesia asst. Community Meml. Hosp., Menomonee Falls, Wis., 1982-83; rsch. coord. Gastroenterology Cons., Racine, Wis., 1983-85; LPN GI clinician Falls Med. Group, Menomonee Falls, Wis., 1986—; v.p. edn. & vis. program Chgo. chpt. CCFA, Park Ridge, Ill., 1977-81. Mem. Soc. Gastroenterology Nurses and Assocs., Inc. Home: 7424 W Willowbrook Ct Mequon WI 53092

MCKINNEY, JOAN HEIDAL, artist; b. Elizabeth, N.J., Mar. 27, 1934; d. Jack and Claire (Smith) Heidal; m. Norman McKinney, Nov. 5, 1955; children: Sam, Jill, Karen, Merry. Grad. high sch. Works in permanent collections at Shering-Plough, Madison, N.J., Middlesex County Libr., AT&T, Basking Ridge, N.J., Carrier Clinic, Belle Meade, N.J., Chubb Ins., Bridgewater, N.J., Douglas Kelly Assocs., Pub. Svc. and Gas Co., Newark. Recipient Best in Show awards Westfield Art, Raritan Valley Art, Somerset Art, others, Judges Choice awards Westfield, Carrier Clinic, Raritan Valley Art, Summit Art, others. Mem. N.J. Watercolor Soc. (newsletter editor), Am. Artists Profl. League, Assoc. Am. Watercolor Soc., Phila. Watercolor Assn., Westfield Art Assn., Raritan Valley Art Assn. (program chmn.), Garden State Watercolor Soc., Somerset Art Assn. (v.p.). Presbyterian (deacon). Home: 1095 Westbrook Rd Bridgewater NJ 08807-1419

MCKINNEY, VENORA WARE, librarian; b. Meridian, Okla., June 16, 1937. BA, Langston U., 1959; MLS, U. Ill., 1965. Librarian Milw. Pub. Library, 1962-68, br. librarian, 1979-83, dep. city librarian, 1983—; librarian Peoria Pub. Schs., Ill., 1969, Milw. Pub. Schs., 1972-79; adj. faculty U. Wis., Milw.; mem. Wis. Govs. Coun. on Libr. Devel., 1983-92; bd. dirs. V.E. Carter Child Devel. Group. Bd. dirs. Milw. Repertory Theatre; coun. adv. Sch. Libr. and Info. Sci., U. Wis., Madison, 1992—. Nat. Forum for Black Pub. Adminstrs. fellow Exec. Leadership Inst., George Mason U. Mem. ALA Black Caucus, Wis. Libr. Assn. (v.p. 1994, pres. 1995—), Wis. Black Librs. Network, Pub. Libr. Assn., Links Inc., Delta Sigma Theta. Baptist. Office: Milw Pub Libr 814 W Wisconsin Ave Milwaukee WI 53233-2309

MCKINNEY-KELLER, MARGARET FRANCES, retired special education educator; b. Houston, Mo., Nov. 25, 1929; d. George Weimer and Thelma May (Davis) Van Pelt; m. Roy Calvin McKinney Sr., Nov. 11, 1947 (dec. Feb. 1990); children: Deanna Kay Little, Roy Calvin Jr.; m. Clarence Elmore Keller, June 8, 1991; 1 child, Dennis Lee Keller. BS with honors, Bradley U., 1963, MA in Counselor Edn., 1968, postgrad., 1992; postgrad., U. Ill., 1993—, Aurora Coll., Ill. Ctrl. Coll. In real estate Peoria, Ill., 1951-57; tchr. Oak Ridge Sch., Willow Springs, Mo., 1947-48, pvt. kindergarten, Washington, Ill., 1957-59, Dist. 50 Schs., Washington, Ill., 1959-67; tchr. socially maladjusted Washington Twp. Spl. Edn. Coop., 1967-70; tchr. behavior disordered Tazewell-Mason Counties Spl. Edn., Washington, Ill., 1970-78; resource tchr. Dist. 50 Schs., Washington, 1978-94; ret., 1994; cons. moderator Active Parenting Group, Washington, 1972—. Vol. Proctor Hosp., 1994—; com. mem. to establish Tazewell County Health Dept., 1960s; pres. gov. bd. Faith Luth. Day Care Ctr., Washington, 1970—, Washington Sr. Citizens, 1982-91; coach Spl. Olympics, Washington, 1979—; pres. Faith Luth. Ch. Coun., Washington, 1985-86; laity v.p. No. Conf. Evang. Luth. Ch. Am., Ctrl. Ill., 1986-92. Mem. AAUW, Washington Bus. and Profl. Women (pres. 1979-80, 88-89), Am. Legion Aux., German-Am. Soc., Alpha Delta Kappa (state office). Home: 603 Sherwood Park Rd Washington IL 61571

MCKINNON, CHRISTINE A., biologist; b. Stoughton, Mass., Feb. 20, 1964; d. Kenneth John and Natalie McK. B, Clark U., Worcester, Mass., 1986. Sr. rsch. asst. Worcester Found. Expl. Biology, Shrewsbury, Mass., 1986—; cons. Sensor Techs., Shrewsbury, 1990—; teaching asst. Marine Biol. Lab., Woods Hole, Mass., 1991—. Contbr. articles to profl. jours. Resident dir. Becker Coll., Leicester, Mass., 1988-94. Home: 133 Howard St Northboro MA 01532 Office: Worcester Found Exptl Biology 222 Maple Ave Shrewsbury MA 01545

MCKISSACK, PATRICIA CARWELL, children's book author; b. Nashville, Sept. 9, 1944; d. Robert and Erma Carwell; m. Frederick L. McKissack, Dec. 12, 1965; children: Fredrick L. Jr., Robert, John. BA, Tenn. State U., 1964; MA, Webster U., 1975. Jr. high sch. tchr. Kirkland, Mo., 1968-75; children's book editor Concordia Pub. House, 1976-81, Inst. Children's Lit., 1984—; part-time English instr. Forest Park Coll., St. Louis, 1975—; instr. U. Mo., St. Louis, 1978—. Author: Good Shepard Prayer, 1978, God Gives New Life, 1979, Ask the Kids, 1979, Who is Who?, 1983, Martin Luther King, Jr.: A Man to Remember, 1984, Paul Laurence Dunbar: A Poet to Remember, 1984, Michael Jackson, Superstar, 1984, Lights Out, Christopher, 1984, It's the Truth, Christopher, 1984 (C.S. Lewis Silver Medal award Christian Sch. Mag., 1984), The Apache, 1984, Mary McLeod Bethune: A Great American Educator, 1985, Aztec Indians, 1985, The Inca, 1985, The Maya, 1985, Flossie and the Fox, 1986, Our Martin Luther King Book, 1986, Who is Coming?, 1986, Give It with Love, Christopher: Christopher Learns about Gifts and Giving, 1988, Speak Up, Christopher: Christopher Learns the Difference Between Right and Wrong, 1988, A Troll in a Hole, 1988, Nettie Jo's Friends, 1988 (Parent's Choice award 1990), Mirandy and Brother Wind, 1988, Monkey-Monkey's Trick: Based on an African Folk-Tale, 1989, Jesse Jackson: A Biography, 1989, (with Ruthilde Kronberg) A Piece of Wind and Other Stories to Tell, 1990, No Need for Alarm, 1990, A Million Fish-More or Less, 1992, The Dark Thirty: Southern Tales of the Supernatural, 1992, Christmas in the Big House-Christmas in the Quarters, 1992, Sojourner Truth: "Ain't I a Woman?", 1992 (Boston Globe/Horn Book award 1993); (with Frederick L. McKissack) Look What You've Done Now, Moses, 1984, Abram, Abram, Where Are We Going?, 1984 (C.S. Lewis Silver Medal award Christian Sch. Mag. 1984), Cinderella, 1985, Country Mouse and City Mouse, 1985, The Little Red Hen, 1985, The Three Bears, 1985, The Ugly Little Duck, 1986, When Do You Talk to God? Prayers for Small Children, 1986, King Midas and His Gold, 1986, Frederick Douglass: The Black Lion, 1987, A Real Winner, 1987, The King's New Clothes, 1987, Tall Phil and Small Bill, 1987, Three Billy Goats Gruff, 1987, My Bible ABC Book, 1987, The Civil Rights Movement in America from 1865 to the Present, 1987, All Paths Lead to Bethlehem, 1987, Messy Bessey, 1987, The Big Bug Book of Counting, 1987, The Big Bug Book of Opposites, 1987, The Big Bug Book of Places to Go, 1987, The Big Bug Book of the Alphabet, 1987, The Big Bug Book of Things to Do, 1987, Bugs!, 1988, The Children's ABC Christmas, 1988, Constance Stumbles, 1988, Oh, Happy, Happy Day! A Child's Easter in Story, Song and Prayer, 1989, God Made Something Wonderful, 1989, Messy Bessey's Closet, 1989, James Weldon Johnson: "Lift Every Voice and Sing", 1990, A Long Hard Journey: The Story of the Pullman Porter, 1990 (Coretta Scott King award 1990, Jane Addams Peace award 1990), Taking a Stand Against Racism and Racial Discrimination, 1990, W.E.B. DuBois, 1990, The Story of Booker T. Washington, 1991, Messy Bessey's Garden, 1991, African Americans, 1991, From Heaven Above: The Story of Christmas Proclaimed by the Angels, 1992, Tennessee Trailblazers, 1993, Black Diamond: The Story of the Negro Baseball League, 1994, African-American Scientists, 1994, African American Inventors, 1994, The Royal Kingdoms of Ghana, Mali, and Songhay: Life in Medieval Africa, 1994; (Great African American series with Frederick McKissack) Carter G. Woodson: The Father of Black History, 1991, Frederick Douglass: Leader Against Slavery, 1991, George Washington Carver: The Peanut Scientist, 1991, Ida B. Wells-Barnett: A Voice Against Violence, 1991, Louis Armstrong: Jazz Musician, 1991, Marian Anderson: A Great Singer, 1991, Martin Luther King, Jr.: Man of Peace, 1991, Mary Church Terrell: Leader for Equality, 1991, Mary McLeod Bethune: A Great Teacher, 1991, Ralph J. Bunche: Peacemaker, 1991esse Owens: Olympic Star, 1992, Langston Hughes: Great American Poet, 1992, Soujourner Truth: A Voice for Freedom, 1992, Zora Neale Hurston: Writer and Storyteller, 1992, Satchel Page: The Best Arm in Baseball, 1992, Paul Robeson: A Voice to Remember, 1992, Madam C.J. Walker: Self-Made Millionare, 1992, Booker T. Washington: Leader and Educator, 1992, Lorraine Hansberry: Dramatist and Activist, 1994; (with others) The World in 1492, 1992; (with Ron Berry and Bartholomew) Scrappy the Squabbler, 1993, Moogie the Messy Beastie, 1993, Hogger the Hoarding Beastie, 1993, Glumby the Grumbler, 1993, Fritter the Wasteful Beastie, 1993, Crassy the Crude Beastie, 1993. Recipient Helen Keating Ott award Nat. Ch. and Synagogue Librs. Assn., 1980. Office: 5900 Pershing Ave Saint Louis MO 63112-1514*

MC KNIGHT, BERNARDINA, administrative assistant; b. Jersey City, N.J., Feb. 27, 1949; d. John Thomas and Marie Antoinette (Rozzi) Cogelia; m. John Mc Knight Dec. 12, 1971; 1 child, David J. Mc Knight. A, Drake Sch. of Bus., 1969. Notary Pub., N.J. Spl. exec. asst. Sperry and Hutchinson Co., N.Y.C., 1969-80; exec. asst. Mary C. Rockefeller, N.Y.C., 1980-83; fin. asst. to chmn. AMEX, N.Y.C., 1989-91; fin. exec. asst. Joseph T Maloney Assocs., Inc., N.Y.C., 1989—; v.p., treas. Failla-McKnight Funeral Home, Inc., Hoboken, N.J., 1995—. Author: (cookbook) Angel Food, 1993. Vol. St. Mary Hosp.; fund raiser Franciscan Health System of N.J.; co-chmn. 1984 Charity Ball Plaza Hotel, N.Y.C.; arrangement chmn. St. Mary Hosp. Charity Balls; pres. St. Mary Hosp. Auxiliary, 1988-90; treas. St. Mary Hosp. Auxiliary, 1983-85; chmn. St. Mary Hosp. Luncheons, 1987, 88; mem. FAITH Svcs., 1988—; fund raiser Immaculate Conception Roman Catholic Ch., arrangements chmn., 1991—, gala jour. com. mem., 1991—. Roman Catholic. Home: 657 Chestnut Pl Secaucus NJ 07094

MCKNIGHT, ELIZABETH CONWAY, conservation organization executive; b. Proctor, Vt., May 27, 1945; d. John Thomas and Phyllis Irene (Creaser) Conway; m. James Brian McKnight, June 6, 1964 (div. 1983). BS with honors, Northeastern U., 1975; cert., Doscher Sch. Photography, Woodstock, Vt., 1976; MA in Environ. Affairs, Clark U., 1978. Reporter AP, Boston, 1974-75; tchr. journalism and environ. sci. Lawrence Acad., Groton, Mass., 1975-78; publs. mgr. Zellars-Williams, Inc., Lakeland, Fla., 1978-79; photographer, writer E.C. McKnight, Burlington, Vt., 1979-81; communications and mktg. mgr. Dufresne-Henry, Inc., North Springfield, Vt., 1981-82; gen. mgr. Assoc. Cons., Inc., Londonderry, Vt., 1982-85; dir. ops. Group Design Architects, Rutland, Vt., 1986-90; co-leader Rio Roosevelt Expedition, 1991-92, Livingstone's Last Journeys Expedition, 1993; pres., founder New Century Conservation Trust Inc., 1991—; freelance photographer, writer. Co-prodr. (documentaries for PBS' New Explorers): The River of Doubt, 1992, In the Footsteps of Dr. Livingstone, 1993. Chairwoman citizens adv. com. Rutland County (Vt.) Solid Waste Dist., 1989-90; mem. Rutland Mayor's Com. on Volvo Site Selection, 1989; cons. Rutland Partnership, 1988-90, interim dir., mem. exec. com., 1989-90; bd. dirs. Merrymeeting AIDS Support Svcs., 1991—. Recipient Theodore Roosevelt Disting. Svc. medal Theodore Roosevelt Assn., 1992. Fellow Explorers Club, Royal Geog. Soc.; mem. Soc. Profl. Journalists, Soc. Woman Geographers, Women's Environment and Devel. Orgn., Worldwide Network. Home: PO Box 748 Boothbay Harbor ME 04538-0748

MCKNIGHT, JOYCE SHELDON, college administrator; b. Meadville, Pa., Oct. 12, 1949; d. Seth Carlyle and Juanita Bessie (Sheets) Sheldon; m. Hugh Frank McKnight, Aug. 22, 1970; children: Frank Nathan, Joanna Michelle. BA in Psychology and Sociology, Allegheny Coll., 1971; MEd in Counseling, Gannon Coll., 1977; postgrad., Pa. State U., 1987—. Cert. nat. counselor. Asst. met. dir. Ecumenical Inst., Chgo. and Tulsa, 1970-73; health planner East Okla. Devel. Dist., Muskogee, 1973; juvenile counselor Tulsa County Aftercare Program, 1973; program specialist psycho-social rehab. Counseling Svcs. Ctr., Corry, Pa., 1975-77; counselor Adult Diploma Program, Corry, Pa., 1974-79; dir. Anchor House Agy., Corry, Pa., 1977-78; community programs dir. Warren-Forest Counties Econ. Opportunity Coun., Warren, Pa., 1979-80; dir. Corry Ctr. Mercyhurst Coll., Corry, Pa., 1981-87; cons. Pulaski, Pa., 1987-89; adj. faculty, 1981-87, program devel. cons., 1987—; adj. faculty Allegheny Coll., 1984, Jamestown C.C., 1991—; mentor Empire Coll. SUNY, 1989-93; coord. adult svcs. Alfred State Coll., 1992—, adj. faculty, 1994—, distance edn. team, 1994—. Contbr. rsch., papers in field. Pres., Corry Concerned for Youth, Inc., 1975-77; pres. Community Care Coun. of Agys., Corry, 1976-79, sec., 1975; mem. steering com. Vol. Action Ctr., Corry, 1977; bd. dirs. Erie County Citizens Coalition for Human Svcs., Erie, 1979-80. Horizon House for Women, 1981-87; mem. coordinating bd. Corry Reindustrialization Coun., 1983-87; mem. Allegany County N.Y. Gateway Project. Mem. AACD, Pa. Assn. Pub. Continuing Adult Edn. (dir. 1977-78), Pa. Assn. for Adult Continuing Edn. (bd. dirs. 1985-90), Pa. Community Edn. Assn., Rural Mental Health Assn., Corry C. of C., Corry Bus. and Profl. Women. Methodist. Home: 22 Pine St Port Allegany PA 16743-1344 Office: Alfred State Coll 250 Student Devel Ctr Alfred NY 14708

MCKNIGHT, LENORE RAVIN, child psychiatrist; b. Denver, May 15, 1943; d. Abe and Rose (Steed) Ravin; m. Robert Lee McKnight, July 22, 1967; children: Richard Rex, Janet Rose. Student, Occidental Coll., 1961-63; BA, U. Colo., 1965, postgrad. in medicine, 1965-67; MD, U. Calif., San Francisco, 1969. Diplomate Am. Bd. Psychiatry and Neurology. Cert. adult and child psychiatrist Am. Bd. Psychiatry. Intern pediatrics Children's Hosp., San Francisco, 1969-70; resident in gen. psychiatry Langley Porter Neuropsychiat. Inst., 1970-73, fellow child psychiatry, 1972-74; child psychiatrist Youth Guidance Center, San Francisco, 1974-74; pvt. practice medicine specializing in child psychiatry, Walnut Creek, Calif., 1974-93; asst. clin. prof. Langley Porter Neuropsychiat. Inst., 1974—; clin. assoc. in psychiatry, U. Calif. at Davis Med. Sch; asst. clin. prof. psychiatry U. Calif. San Francisco Med. Ctr. Internat.; med. dir. CPC Walnut Creek (Calif.) Hosp., 1990-93. Insts. Edn. fellow U. Edinburgh, 1964; NIH grantee to study childhood nutrition, 1966. Mem. Am. Acad. Child Psychiatry, Am. Psychiat. Assn., Am. Coll. Physician Execs., Psychiat. Assn. No. Calif., Am. Med. Women's Assn., Internat. Arabian Horse Assn., Diablo Arabian Horse Assn. Avocation: breeding Arabian Horses. Office: Kaiser Martinez Inpat Psych 200 Muir Rd Martinez CA 94553

MCKOWEN, DOROTHY KEETON, librarian; b. Bonne Terre, Mo., Oct. 5, 1948; d. John Richard and Dorothy (Spoonhour) Keeton; m. Paul Edwin McKowen, Dec. 19, 1970; children: Richard James, Mark David. BS, Pacific Christian Coll., 1970; MLS, U. So. Calif., 1973; MA in English, Purdue U., 1985, postgrad., 1991—. Libr.-specialist Doheny Libr., U. So. Calif., L.A., 1973-74; asst. libr. Pacific Christian Coll., 1974-78; serials cataloger Purdue Univ. Librs., 1978-88; head children's and young adult svcs. Kokomo-Howard County Pub. Libr. (Ind.), 1988-89, coord. children's and tech. svcs., 1989-91; cataloger, network libr. Ind. Coop. Libr. Svcs. Authority, 1991—; vice chairperson Christian Edn. Com., Brady Lane Ch. of Christ, 1986-87, chairperson, 1987-88, pianist, 1978—, adult Sunday Sch. tchr., 1989—, choir dir., 1990—, organist, 1992—; bd. dirs. Good Shepherd Learning Ctr., 1990—, vice-chairperson, 1991-92, chairperson, 1992-94; bd. dirs. Purdue Christian Campus House, 1985-90, v.p., 1986-88, pres., 1988-90. Mem. ALA, Modern Lang. Assn., Soc. Early Americanists, Assn. for Libr. Collections and Tech. Svcs. (bd. dirs. 1986-90, vice chairperson, chairperson elect coun. of regional groups 1986-88, chairperson 1988-90, conf. program com. 1986-88, internat. rels. com. 1986-88, micropub. com., 1986-87, subject analysis com., subcom. to rev. Dewey 621.38, 1987, membership com. 1988-90, libr. resources and tech. svcs. editorial bd. 1988-90, planning and rsch. com. 1988-90, planning com. 1990-91, program initiatives com. 1991-93, chairperson 1991-93, orgn. and bylaws com. 1991-92), Ind. Libr. Fedn. (vice chmn. tech. svcs. div. 1983-84, chmn. 1984-85), Ohio Valley Group Tech. Svcs. Librs. (vice chmn. 1984-85, chmn. 1985-86). Republican. Home: 7625 Summit Ln Lafayette IN 47905-9729 Office: INCOLSA 5929 Lakeside Blvd Indianapolis IN 46278-1996

MCKOWN, JANE ANN, medical/surgical nurse, educator; b. Greenfield, Ohio, Dec. 18, 1924; d. Ralph Worley and Hazel Mae (Smith) Hull; m. James Williams McKown, May 1, 1948; children: James Thomas, Janet Ann. Diploma, Christ Hosp. Sch. Nursing, Cin., 1945; BSN cum laude, Ohio U., 1978. Cert. by Dept. Aging, Am. Heart Assn. Office nurse, lab trainee Cin.; staff devel. Greenfield (Ohio) Area Med. Ctr.; nursing educator Area Agy. on Aging Dist. 7, Rio Grande, Ohio; instr. So. State Community

Coll., Hillsboro, Ohio. With Army Cadet Nurse Corps, 1945. Mem. ANA, Ohio Nurses Assn., Highland County Heart Assn. Home: 10935 State Route 138 SW Greenfield OH 45123-9281

MCLACHLIN, BEVERLEY, supreme court judge; b. Pincher Creek, Alta., Can., Sept. 7, 1943; m. Roderick McLachlin (dec. 1988); 1 child, Angus; m. Frank E. McArdle, 1992. B.A., U. Alta., MA in Philosophy, LLB, LLD, 1990; LLD, U. B.C., 1990. Bar: Alta. 1969, B.C. 1971. Assoc. Wood, Moir, Hyde and Ross, Edmonton, Alta., Can., 1969-71, Thomas, Herdy, Mitchell & Co., Fort St. John, B.C., Can., 1971-72, Bull, Housser and Tupper, Vancouver, B.C., 1972-75; lectr., assoc. prof., prof. with tenure U. B.C., 1974-81; appointed to County Ct., Vancouver, 1981; justice Supreme Ct. of B.C., 1981-85, B.C. Ct. of Appeal, 1985-88; chief justice Supreme Ct. of B.C., 1988; justice Supreme Ct. Can., Ottawa, Ont., 1989—. Co-author: B.C. Supreme Court Practice, B.C. Court Forums, Canadian Law of Arch. and Engring.; mem. editorial adv. bd. Family Law Restatement Project, 1987-88, Civil Jury Instruction, 1988; contbr. numerous articles to profl. jours. Office: Supreme Ct Bldg, Wellington St, Ottawa, ON Canada K1A 0J1

MCLAIN, ELIZABETH ANN, state agency administrator; b. Balt., Dec. 18, 1942; d. Joseph Howard and Ann (Hollingsworth) McLain; m. John Clyde Deppman, Aug. 29, 1964 (div. April 1980); children: Ann, Jed, Benj; m. John Hardy Fitzhugh, Sept. 4, 1993; stepchildren: Nicholas, Eliza. BA, Middlebury Coll., 1964; MEd, St. Michael's Coll., Colchester, Vt., 1989. Rep. Vt. Legislature, Montpelier, Vt., 1980-86; spl. edn. tchr. Weybridge Sch., Beeman Acad., Weybridge, New Haven, Vt., 1986-91; legis. liaison, chief of Staff for Gov. Snelling State Vt., Montpelier, Vt., 1991; commr. Dept. Environ. Conservation, State of Vt., Waterbury, Vt., 1991-93; dep. sec. Agency for Natural Resources, State of Vt., Waterbury, Vt., 1993—. Office: Agy of Natural Resources 103 S Main St Waterbury VT 05671

MCLAIN, JANICE DARLENE, magazine general manager; b. Ottumwa, Iowa, Dec. 20, 1943; d. Arthur George and Daisy (Thompson) Sells; m. Richard L. McLain, July 4, 1964; 1 child, Christopher. BS in Journalism, Iowa State U., 1967. Asst. women's editor La Crosse (Wis.) Tribune, 1967-69, feature editor, 1969-74; with rsch. and pub. rels. depts. La Crosse Econ. Devel., 1975; pres., pub. Gazette Newspapers, La Crosse, 1976-79; with sales and pub. rels. depts. Wilson Learning, Sydney, Australia, 1980-81; news editor Minn. Suburban Newspapers, Mpls., 1986-87; rsch. asst. Custom Rsch., Mpls., 1988-89; gen. mgr., editor Format mag., Mpls., 1989—. Named Outstanding Young Alumnus, Iowa State U., 1975, Woman of Achievement, Wis. Press Woman, 1979, numerous journalism awards. Mem. Women in Communications, Minn. Newspaper Found. Home: 4125 Upland Ln N Minneapolis MN 55446-2636 Office: Format 275 Market St Ste 19C Minneapolis MN 55405-1620

MCLAIN, KATHY HART, marketing exexutive; b. Norwalk, Conn., June 5, 1960; d. R. Kenneth and V. Jean (Beck) H.; m. Jeffrey Baird McLain, June 29, 1985. BS, Rollins Coll., 1982. With guest svcs. dept. Sheraton-Lakeside Inn, Kissimmee, Fla., 1982-83; acct. exec. Ad Inns, Inc., Orlando, Fla., 1983-86; free-lance media asst. Walt Disney World Mktg., Lake Buena Vista, Fla., 1986; advt. sales rep. World Publs., Winter Park, Fla., 1986-90; sales promotion, pub. rels. dir. Worth Internat. Communications, Miami Lakes, Fla., 1991-92; account exec. Taglairino Advt. Group, Miami, Fla., 1992-92; v.p. account svcs. Gilbert & Manjura Mktg., Altamonte Springs, Fla., 1993—. Treas. College Park Women's Civic Club; active Jr. League Greater Orlando, First Presbyn. Ch. of Maitland. Mem. Ad 2 (charter, co-chmn. membership Greater Orlando chpt. 1984-85, 88-89, sec. 1985-86, v.p. 1986-87, pres. 1987-88, AAF Ad 2 Liaison 4th Dist. 1988-89, nat. chmn. pub. svc. 1989-90, 4th dist. ann. conv. chmn. 1991, 4th dist. AAF conf. co-chair 1992), Orlando Advt. Fedn., Rollins Coll. Ctrl. Fla Alumni Club (pres. 1994-95), Chi Omega Alumni. Home: 1240 Norwood Pl Orlando FL 32804-6726

MCLANAHAN, EDITH LORRAINE, educator; b. Erie, Pa., May 19, 1937; d. Edwin August and Delpha Louise (Gates) Winter; m. George Everett McLanahan, July 27, 1963; children: Michael G., Judy Lynn McLanahan King, Joan Lynnette McLanahan Henry. BA in Biology magna cum laude, Mercyhurst Coll., 1960; grad., St. Vincent's Sch. MEd. Tech., 1960; postgrad., SUNY, Buffalo, 1961-62; MS in Environ. Edn., Gannon U., 1982. Registered med. technologist. Med. technologist St. Vincent's Hosp., Erie, 1960-61; tech. cancer rsch. Roswell Park Cancer Hosp., Buffalo, 1962-63; educator biology Villa Maria Coll., Erie, 1964-65; instr., med. asst. J.H. Thompson Allied Health Acad., Erie, 1983-84; cancer rsch. asst. Mercyhurst Coll. Biology Dept., Erie, 1989-91; receptionist Mercyhurst Coll. Health Dept., Erie, 1991-94. Fellow grantee Immunology Study, U. Buffalo, 1961-62. Mem. Am. Soc. Clin. Pathologists, Alpha Xi. Home: 1274 E 41st St Erie PA 16504-2468

MCLANE, BOBBIE JONES, retired government official, genealogist, publisher; b. Hot Springs, Ark., Feb. 19, 1927; d. Julian Everette and Eula (Deaton) Jones; m. Gerald Bert McLane, Aug. 14, 1954 (dec. 1994). Chief clk. Army and Navy Hosp., Hot Springs, 1950-52; adminstrv. asst. Wis. Mil. Dist., Milw., 1952-54; exec. sec. to postmaster U.S. Postal Svc., Hot Springs, 1954-70, supr. employment svcs., 1970-74, dir. employee and labor rels., 1974-80; acting postmaster U.S. Postal Svc., Arkadelphia, Ark., 1978; dir. employee and labor rels. U.S. Postal Svc., Ft. Smith, Ark., 1980-86; ret., 1986. Compiler, author pub. Ark. Ancestors, 72 titles, 1962; editor The Record, 1966—. Organizer, charter mem. Garland County Hist. Soc., Hot Springs, 1960—; bd. dirs., chmn. Ark. History Commn., 1966-80, 90—; charter mem., bd. dirs. Community Players Hot Springs, 1949-55. Recipient award for contbns. to hist. and geneal. rsch. Am. Assn. State and Local History, 1967, Bicentennial award Postmaster Gen. U.S. Postal Svc., 1976; named One of 100 Ark. Women of Achievement, Ark. Press Women, 1980; Am. Assn. State and Local History fellow Vanderbilt U., 1967. Mem. Profl. Genealogists Ark. (bd. dirs. 1988—), Ark. Geneal. Soc. (charter, bd. dirs. 1960—, past pres.). Democrat. Episcopalian. Home and Office: 222 Mcmahan St Hot Springs National Park AR 71913-6243

MCLANE, SUSAN NEIDLINGER, state legislator; b. Boston, Sept. 28, 1929; d. Lloyd Kellock and Marion (Walker) Neidlinger; m. Malcolm McLane, 1948; children: Susan B., Donald W., Deborah, Alan, Ann Lloyd. Ed., Mt. Holyoke Coll.; LLD (hon.), New England Coll., 1983, Franklin Pierce Coll., 1988. Mem. N.H. Ho. of Reps., Concord, 1969-80; chmn. ways and means com. N.H. Ho. of Reps., 1976-80; mem. N.H. State Senate, Concord, 1980—, chmn. ways and means, 1990—; del. Rep. Nat. Conv., 1976; pres. N.H. Coun. Affairs, 1976-80. Office: NH State Senate State Capitol Concord NH 03301 also: 205 Mountain Rd Concord NH 03301-6934

MCLAREN, KAREN LYNN, advertising executive; b. Flint, Mich., Feb. 14, 1955; d. Max W. and Barbara J. (Cole) Hoeffgen; m. Michael L. McLaren, June 18, 1974. AA, Mott Community Coll., Flint, 1976; BA, Mich. State U., 1978. Writer Sta. WGMZ-FM, Flint, 1979-84; writer, producer Tracy-Stephens Advt., Flint, 1984-87; pres. McLaren Advt., Troy, Mich., 1987—. Contbr. articles to profl. jours. Mem. centennial com. Wolverine region ARC, 1981, pub. rels. com., 1981-84; vol. coord., pub. rels. tour guide Whaley Hist. Ho., Flint, 1980-91; home designer, tour guide Romeo (Mich.) Hist. Home Tour, 1992; mem. Nat. Trust for Hist. Preservation, 1991-95; com. chair Crim Festival of Races, Flint, 1992, 93, 94; active Sta. WFUM-Pub. TV, Flint, 1980-91; panelist career fair Modona U., Livonia, Mich., 1994. Recipient 3 awards, 2 Nat. Health Care Mktg. Competition awards, Women's Adv. Club Detroit Pres.'s award, 1994. Mem. NAFE, Women's Advt. Club Detroit (scholar chair 1987, 88, bd. dirs. 1989, 92, 93, chair scholarship fundraiser 1991, co-chair career fair 1989, 90, 92, career fair panelist 1993, v.p. 1990, pres. 1991,. ambassador 1992, co-chair Woman of Yr. awards 1994, by laws chair 1994).

MCLARNEY, MARY JANE, finance officer; b. Oakland, Calif., June 3; m. John Henry (div.); 1 child, Christina; m. Patrick McLarney. BS, Calif. State U., 1982. CPA, Calif. Pvt. practice in acctg. Costa Mesa, Calif., 1982-83; sr. acct. Deloitte, Haskins & Sells, Costa Mesa, 1983-85; asst. contr. Birtcher Devel. Corp., Laguna Hills, Calif., 1985-87; pvt. practice Mission Viejo, Calif., 1987-89; mgr. Moreland & Assocs., Newport Beach, Calif., 1989-90; fin. officer City of Temecula, Calif., 1990—. Mem. Calif. Soc. CPA, Calif. Mpcl. Treas. Assn., Govt. Fin. Officers Assn., Calif. Soc. Mcpl. Fin. Officer (inter-governmental affairs com. 1993-94). Republican. Mem. Ch. LDS. Office: City of Temecula 43174 Business Park Dr Temecula CA 92590

MCLARNON, MARY FRANCES, neurologist; b. Montreal, Que., Canada, May 13, 1944; came to U.S., 1969; d. John Francis and Patricia Jessica (Dore) McL.; m. Malcolm Weiner, Dec. 21, 1975; m. Lawrence Zingesser, Oct. 12, 1982; children: Andrea, Eliza. BS, McGill U., 1965, MD, 1969. Intern St. Vincent's Hosp., N.Y.C., 1969-70; fellow seizure unit Boston Children's Hosp., 1970-71; resident in neurology Albert Einstein Coll. Medicine, Bronx, N.Y., 1971-73; resident in radiology N.Y. Hosp.-Cornell Med. Ctr., N.Y.C., 1973-76; pvt. practice.

MCLAUGHLIN, ANN, educational administrator, former federal official, lecturer, advisor; b. Newark, Nov. 16, 1941; d. Edward Joseph and Marie (Koellhoffer) Lauenstein. B.A., Marymount Coll. Supr. network comml. schedule ABC, N.Y.C., 1963-66; dir. alumnae relations Marymount Coll., Tarrytown, N.Y., 1966-69; account exec. Myers-Infoplan Internat. Inc., N.Y.C., 1969-71; dir. communications Presdl. Election Com., Washington, 1971-72; asst. to chmn. and press sec. Presdl. Inaugural Com., Washington, 1972-73; dir. Office of Pub. Affairs, EPA, Washington, 1973-74; govt. relations and communications exec. Union Carbide Corp., N.Y.C. and Washington, 1974-77; pub. affairs, issues mgmt. counseling McLaughlin & Co., 1977-81; asst. sec. for pub. affairs Dept. Treasury, Washington, 1981-84; under sec. Dept. of Interior, Washington, 1984-87; cons. Ctr. Strategic and Internat. Studies, Washington, 1987; sec. of labor Dept. of Labor, Washington, 1987-89; vis. fellow The Urban Inst., 1989-92; pres., CEO New Am. Schs. Devel. Corp., 1992-93; vis. fellow The Urban Inst., 1989-92; chmn. Pres.'s Commn. Aviation Security and Terrorism, 1989-90; mem. Am. Coun. on Capital Formation, 1976-78; mem. environ. edn. task force HEW, 1976-77; mem. Def. Adv. Com. of Women in the Svcs., 1973-74; bd. dirs. GM, Union Camp Corp., Kellogg Co., Nordstrom Co., Host Marriott Corp., Vulcan Materials Co., AMR Corp., Fannie Mae, Potomac Electric Power Co., Pub. Agenda Found.; vice chmn., trustee Aspen Inst.; pres. Fed. City Coun., 1990—. Mem. bd. overseers Wharton Sch. U. Pa.; bd. dirs. Ctr. Strategic and Internat. Studies, The Conservation Fund; trustee Urban Inst., 1989—. Mem. Cosmos Club, Met. Club, Econ. Club, F St. Club. Republican. Roman Catholic.

MCLAUGHLIN, CONSTANCE NETHKEN, science educator; b. Elkins, W.Va., Feb. 3, 1949; d. Ralph David and Helen Irene (Shreve) Nethken; m. Terry Walthall McLaughlin, May 23, 1970; 1 child, Veronica McLaughlin Mercure. BS in Chemistry, W.Va. U., 1971; MA in Sci. Edn., U. No. Colo., 1980; cert. in Ednl. Adminstrn., U. Denver, 1988. Cert. tchr., Colo. Tchr. Jefferson County Schs., Golden, Colo., 1982—; participant Process Consultation Cadre Jefferson County Schs., Jefferson County Life Sci. Cadre. Recipient Outstanding Tchr. award Colo. Awards Com. Mem. Colo. Biology Tchrs. Assn., NEA, Colo. Assn. Sch. Execs., Alpha Delta Kappa. Methodist.

MCLAUGHLIN, DEBORAH ANN, public relations and marketing executive; b. Hoisington, Kans., Nov. 12, 1952; d. Kenneth Theodore and Mildred Marie (Steiner) Siebert; m. Donald Raymond McLaughlin, July 17, 1976; 1 child, Kalla Dawn. AS, Barton County Coll., Great Bend, Kans., 1972; BS, Kans. State U., 1975. News editor Great Bend Tribune, 1975-76; deposition indexer Turner & Boisseau, Great Bend, 1976-77; feature editor Mid-Kans. Ruralist, Hoisington, 1977-78; copywriter, audio-editor Advt. Assocs., Great Bend, 1978-79; photographer, sales mgr. Clay Ward Color Portraits, Great Bend, 1979-80; news editor, photographer St. John (Kans.) News, 1980-83; freelance writer, photographer Great Bend, 1984-85; pres., owner McLaughlin Pub. Rels. Agy., Great Bend, 1985-87; owner Cen. Kans. Sunrise mag., Great Bend, 1987-88, Creative Mktg. Svcs., Great Bend, 1988—; dir. pub. info. Unified Sch. Dist. 428, Great Bend, 1991-93. Contbr. articles and photographs to various publs. Mem. Coalition for Prevention Child Abuse, Great Bend, 1986-87; mem. 75th anniversary com. Kansas State U. Coll. Journalism and Mass Communications, Manhattan, 1986. Mem. Kans. State U. Alumni Assn. Roman Catholic. Home and Office: 381 Grove Ter Great Bend KS 67530-9710

MCLAUGHLIN, JEANNE MARIE, bank examiner; b. Salina, Kans., Jan. 16, 1964; d. William Leo and Peggy Sue (Haynes) McL. BS, Marymount Coll. Kans., 1986; grad., U. Wis., 1992. Bank examiner FDIC, Wichita, Kans., 1986-88, Detroit, 1988—.

MCLAUGHLIN, LINDA LEE HODGE, federal judge; b. 1942. BA, Stanford U., 1963; LLB, U. Calif., Berkeley, 1966. With Keatinge & Sterling, L.A., 1966-70, Richards, Martin & McLaughlin, Beverly Hills and Newport Beach, Calif., 1970-73, Bergland, Martin & McLaughlin, Newport Beach, 1973-76, Bergland & McLaughlin, Costa Mesa, Calif., 1976-80; judge North Orange County Mcpl. Ct., Fullerton, Calif., 1980-82, Orange County Superior Ct., Santa Ana, Calif., 1982-92, U.S. Dist. Ct. (ctrl. dist.) Calif., Santa Ana, 1992—; mem. adv. com. jud. forms Jud. Coun., 1978—, mem. adv. com. gender bias in cts., 1987-90. Active Edgewood Sch. Parents Assn., Cate Sch. Parents Aux.; mem. governing bd. Victim-Witness Assistance Program Orange County. Mem. Nat. Assn. Women Judges, Calif. State Bar Assn. (mem. com. profl. ethics 1976-80, disciplinary referee dist. 8 1978-80), Calif. Women Lawyers (gov. dist. 8 1978-80), Calif. Judges Assn. (chair civil law and procedure com. 1985-86), Orange County Bar Assn. (mem. com. adminstrn. justice 1975-78, client rels. com. 1978-80, com. jud. appointments 1979-80), Orange County Women Lawyers, Boalt Hall Alumni Assn., Stanford U. Alumni Assn., Cap and Gown Hon. Soc. Office: US District Court Rm 101 751 W Santa Ana Blvd Alta Loma CA 91701-4599*

MCLAUGHLIN, LISA MARIE, educational administrator; b. Sioux City, Iowa, Dec. 27, 1957; d. Donald James and Shirley Jean (Bartlett) Warden; m. Steven A. McLaughlin, Apr. 22, 1978; children: Mark Alan, Catherine Lynn. BS, Cen. State U., Edmond, Okla., 1978, MEd, 1982. Cert. tchr., Okla. Tchr. learning disabilities Putnam City Schs., Oklahoma City, 1979-80, tchr. visually impaired, 1980-81; devel. therapist Child Study Ctr., Okla. Teaching Hosps., Oklahoma City, 1981-83; ednl. cons. Oklahoma City, 1983-85; regional program specialist Okla. State Dept. Edn., Oklahoma City, 1985-87, spl. edn. data cons., 1987-90, tech. assistance officer, 1990-91, asst. state dir. spl. edn., 1991-92; ednl. cons., vision specialist, special edn. adminstr. Edmond, Okla., 1992—. Co-author: (chpt.) Assessing and Screening Preschoolers: Psychological, Social and Educational Dimensions, 1991. Mem. coun. on adminstrn. YWCA, Ione br., Oklahoma City, 1985-88, 92-94; mem. at large bd. dirs. YWCA, Met. br., Oklahoma City, 1989-91; mem. adv. com. Okla. Sch. for Blind, 1992—; pres. Parkview Sch. for Blind Ednl. Found., 1994—; bd. dirs. Prevent Blindness Okla., 1993—. Mem. Coun. Exceptional Children (v.p. Oklahoma City chpt. 1988-89, Spl. Educator of Yr. 1991), Learning Disabilities Assn., Assn. for Edn. and Rehab. of Blind and Visually Impaired (state pres. Okla. chpt. 1989-90), Advocates and Parents of Okla. Sight Impaired (treas. 1984-87), Okla. Women in Edn. Adminstrn., Delta Kappa Gamma (2d v.p. 1990-92), Kappa Delta Pi. Home and Office: 6813 NW 130th St Oklahoma City OK 73142-6011 also: RR 1 Box 137 Edmond OK 73003-9801 also: 215 N Boulevard St Edmond OK 73034-3768

MCLAUGHLIN, MARGARET BROWN, educator, writer; b. Miami Beach, Fla., Aug. 24, 1926; d. J. Clifford and Grace Lindsey (DuPre) Brown; m. Francis Edward McLaughlin, Oct. 30, 1982 (dec.). BA cum laude, U. Miami, 1946; MA, Duke U., 1949; PhD, Tulane U., 1976. Instr., lectr. in English, U. Miami, Coral Gables, Fla., 1946-47, 56-61, 73-91; English tchr. Narimasu Am. Sch., Tokyo, 1963-65; asst. prof. Manchester Coll., North Manchester, Ind., 1965-67; instr. Miami-Dade Community Coll., 1977, 81; prodr. Dade County Cable TV series Caribbean Writers and Their Art, 1991; prodr., host cable tv series Haiti Cherie, 1993-94; dir. writing workshop for fgn. students U. Miami Sch. Medicine, 1991, 92. Contbr. articles to popular mags. and newspapers. Trustee Mus. Sci., Miami, 1977-78. Mem. MLA (Am. lit. sect.), Egyptology and Asian Civilizations Soc. Miami (bd. dirs., pres. 1976-78, 83-85). Home and Office: 1621 S Bayshore Dr Miami FL 33133-4201

MCLAUGHLIN, MARGUERITE P., state senator, logging company executive; b. Matchwood, Mich., Oct. 15, 1928; d. Harvey Martin and Luella Margaret (Livingston) Miller; m. George Bruce McLaughlin, 1947; children: Pamela, Bruce Jr., Cynthia. Owner, operator contract logging firm, Orofino, Idaho; mem. Idaho Ho. of Reps., 1978-80; mem. Idaho Senate, 6th term., asst. Dem. leader, 1990, 91, 92, 93; chair Democrat Caucus, 1995—. mem. Senate Fin. Com., 1987—, Gov.'s Adv. Coun. Workers Compensation, 1990—, State of Idaho Endowment Fund Investment Bd., 1991—, legis. coun., 1989-94, State of Idaho Job Tng. Coun., 1989—. Trustee Joint Sch. Dist. 171, 1976-80; pres. Orofino Celebration, Inc. Democrat. Roman Catholic. Office: Idaho State Senate State Capital Boise ID 83702*

MCLAUGHLIN, MARY RITTLING, magazine editor; b. Buffalo; d. Joseph and Irene (Meyer) Rittling; m. Charles Edward McLaughlin, June 21, 1962 (div. June 1981) children—Daniel (dec.), Maud Rosie. BA, Manhattanville Coll., 1956. Reporter Buffalo Evening News, 1956-58; copywriter Harper's Bazaar, N.Y.C., 1959-61; editor McCall's Mag., N.Y.C., 1973-79; mng. editor Working Mother Mag., N.Y.C., 1979-85; exec. editor Working Mother Mag., 1985—. Mem. Am. Soc. Mag. Editors, Women's Media Group. Office: Working Mother Mag 230 Park Ave New York NY 10169-0005

MCLAUGHLIN, MAUREEN A., federal agency administrator. BA in Econs., Boston Coll., 1977; MA in Pub. Policy, U. Pa., 1979. Asst. assoc. and prin. analyst U.S. Congressional Budget Office, 1979-88; dir. post secondary edn. divsn., Planning and Evaluation Svc. U.S. Dept. Edn., 1988—, acting asst. sec. for postsecondary edn., 1993, acting dep. asst. sec. for higher edn. programs, student fin. assistance programs, 1993-94, sr. policy advisor to the asst. sec. for post secondary edn., 1994—. Chair adv. com. mem. Fiscal Affairs 1990-92; mem. bd. dirs. Arlington Symphony, 1990-93, sec. 1992-93, v. chair Arlington Adv. Com. on Arts and Humanities, 1987-88, mem. Commn. on Arlington's Future, 1986, chair task force on housing and neighborhoods. Office: Post Secondary Edn Office US Dept Edn 7th & D St SW Washington DC 20202

MCLAUGHLIN, PATRICIA, columnist; b. Boston, Aug. 11, 1945; d. William Philip Jr. and Mary Margaret (Harrington) McL. Student, Rosemont (Pa.) Coll., 1963-65; BA in English Lit., Boston U., 1967; postgrad. Annenberg Sch., U. Pa., 1969-70. Jr. editor Vogue Mag., N.Y.C., 1967-68; asst. to fashion editor Phila. Bull., 1969-70; assoc. editor Pa. Gazette, Phila., 1971-76; dir. publ. Reliance Ins. Co., Phila., 1979-84; freelance writer Phila., 1970—; style columnist Phila. Inquirer Mag., 1983—; weekly style columnist syndicated to 250 newspapers Universal Press Syndicate, 1988—; commentator Fresh Air program Sta. WHYY FM, Phila., 1989-93; contbr. Collier's Yearbook, 1989—. Mem. Phila. Green Adv. bd.; active St. Francis Xavier Ch. Choir, 1985—. Mem. Pa. Hort. Soc., Ea. State Penitentiary Gardeners. Democrat. Roman Catholic. Office: Phila Inquirer Mag 400 N Broad St Philadelphia PA 19101

MCLAUGHLIN, SHARON GAIL, principal, small business owner; b. Little Rock, Jan. 2, 1946; d. William Harry and Marion Virginia (Johnson) Fowler; m. Elbert Leroy Anderson, Apr. 3, 1969 (div. 1975); 1 child, William Eric; m. James Jerry McLaughlin, Nov. 22, 1986. BA, Baker U., Baldwin City, Kans., 1968; MA, U. Mo., Kansas City, 1976; EdS, U. Cen. Ark., 1987. Tchr. Kansas City (Mo.) Sch. Dist., 1968-77; dir. recruiting Lincoln U., Jefferson City, Mo., 1977-78; tchr., dept. chmn. Magnet Sch., Kansas City, 1978-79; asst. prin. Pulaski County Sch. Dist., Little Rock, 1979-87; prin. Little Rock Sch. Dist., 1987-91; owner L Image Ltd, Little Rock, 1989—; tchr. broadcast journalism, tv prodn., theatre arts Dallas Ind. Sch. Dist., 1991—; speaker Clinto-Gore Campaign; cons. in field. Producer/dir.: Take: Teen, Bridging the Gap, 1980—; author prog. for women, Prisms, 1980, prog. for youth, Kaleidescope III, 1980. Mem. nat. bd. ethics Mrs. Am. Pageant Sys., 1991; Tex. state chair rsch. and status women of African descent AME Ch., 1992—. Named Outstanding Black Arkansan, Women in Motion, 1988, Outstanding Educator, Ark. PTA, 1988, Mrs. Ark. Am., 1990-91. Mem. NAACP, Nat. Assn. Black Sch. Educators, Student Adminstrs. Assn. (prog. chmn. 1986-87), Nat. Assn. Sec. Sch. Prins., Internat. Platform Assn., Smithsonian Assocs., Urban League of Mo.-Ark., Top Ladies of Distinction (Dallas chpt.), Alpha Kappa Alpha, Phi Delta Kappa. Democrat. Home: PO Box 754699 Dallas TX 75205

MCLAUGHLIN-TRAVIS, DONNA CAROL, graphic designer; b. Chgo., Oct. 13, 1965; d. Thomas Arnold and Carol Ann (Jensen) McLaughlin; m. Michael Allen Travis, Mar. 23, 1991. BFA, Art Inst. Chgo., 1987; MA, Loyola U. Chgo., 1994. Designer Bonus Books, Chgo., 1986-88, Holt, Rinehart, Winston, Libertyville, Ill., 1988; assoc. prodn. design mgr. Loyola U. Press, Chgo., 1988-90; pub. design mgr. Loyola U. Chgo., 1990—, orgnl. devel. cons., 1992-93; art dir. book: Legend of the Golden Straw, 1990. Mem. Univ. Coll. Designer Assn. Lutheran. Office: Loyola Univ of Chicago 6525 N Sheridan Rd Chicago IL 60626-5311

MCLAURIN, MARTHA REGINA, parking service company executive; b. Raleigh, N.C., Feb. 17, 1948; d. William Lentis and Martha Catherine (Hester) McL. BA, Meth. Coll., 1970. Pres., chief fin. officer McLaurin Parking Co., Inc., Raleigh, 1970—; dir. So. Nat. Bank, Cary, N.C., 1980—. Pres. bd. dirs. Raleigh Mchts. Bur., 1988-89; mem. Cary Town Coun., 1987—; chmn. Wake County Planning Bd., 1983-86. Named Outstanding Bus. Alumnus Meth. Coll., 1985, Cary's Outstanding Woman Cary Jaycettes, 1984. Mem. Nat. Parking Assn. (bd. dirs. 1979—, pres. 1989-90, chmn. 1990-92), Parking Industry Inst. (bd. dirs. 1987-89, 92-94), Zonta (bd. dirs. 1987-89). Office: McLaurin Parking Co Inc PO Box 781 Raleigh NC 27602-0781

MCLAURIN, SUSAN CAROLYN, educational administrator; b. Honolulu, Aug. 20, 1948; d. William J. and Mary R. (Williams) Cheek; m. Robert P. McLaurin; children: Kate Elizabeth, Mary Virginia. BS in Elem. Edn., Troy (Ala.) State U., 1973; MEd in Elem. Edn., U. So. Miss., 1979, doctoral candidate, 1990—. Elem. tchr. Kreole Elem. Sch., Moss Point, Miss., 1969-70, Houston County Schs., Ashford, Ala., 1970-73, St. Tammany Parish Schs., Lacombe, La., 1973-74, Pecan Park Elem. Sch., Ocean Springs, Miss., 1975-80, Singing River Elem. Sch., Pascagoula (Miss.) Schs., 1980-81; elem. tchr. Coll. Park Elem. Sch., Gautier, Miss., 1981-83, asst. prin., 1983-85, prin., 1985-91; dir. fed. programs Pascagoula Schs., 1991—; cert. trainer MegaSkills Parent Edn. Program, 1992—. Named Outstanding Educator of Miss., Miss. Parent Tchr. Assn., 1991. Mem. ASCD, Internat. Reading Assn., Miss. PTA, Phi Delta Kappa, Bet Lambda Epsilon Sigma Alpha (v.p. 1992-94). Office: Pascagoula Sch Dist 1006 Communy Ave PO Box 250 Pascagoula MS 39568-0250

MCLAY, MARTHA, educational administrator; b. Portland, Maine, Sept. 18, 1939; d. Doric Preston and Annabelle Violet (Clark) C.; m. Daniel Allan McLay, Oct. 16, 1965; 1 child, Jason Allan. Student Bouve-Boston Coll., 1962; B.S. in Edn., Tufts U., 1962; M.S. in Edn., Nova U., 1982. Cert. tchr., adminstr. Instr. Harpur Coll., N.Y. State U., Binghamton, 1962-65; tchr. Burlington High Sch., Vt., 1965-66, Ganesha High Sch., Pomona, Calif., 1966-67, Enterprise High Sch., Redding, Calif., 1968-76, chmn. implementation of Title IX, 1973; tchr. Adirondack-Southern Sch., St. Petersburg, Fla., 1977-84, dean (headmistress), 1980-85; dir. academics Cedu Sch., Running Springs, Calif., 1985—; lectr. in field. Contbr. articles to profl. jours., poetry to mags. Debator LWV, Redding, 1968; active PTA, various locations. Recipient Service award Mid-Day Bus. and Profl. Women, St. Petersburg, 1984, Dedication awards Adirondack-Southern Sch. Yearbook, 1978, 85. Mem. AAHPER Fla. Council Ind. Schs., Bus. and Profl. Women (1st v.p. 1982-83, 84-85, pres. 1983-84). Republican. Club: WISP (Women Investors of St. Petersburg) (sec. 1982-83). Avocations: tennis; snow skiing; archery; fly-fishing; hiking. Office: Dir Academics Cedu Sch PO Box 1176 Running Springs CA 92382-1176

MCLEAN, HELEN CANDIS, writer, publisher, professional speaker; b. Yorkton, Sask., Feb. 27, 1949; m. J. Ross McLean; children: Stuart, Steven. BA in English Lit., U. Sask., 1970, MA in English Lit., 1977. Psychiat. social worker Sask. Dept. Social Svcs., 1970-71; free-lancer CBC Radio, 1975-76, weekly theatre reviewer Calgary Eye Opener program, 1976-77, news reporter, 1979; writer, prodr. Creative Assocs., 1976-77; tchr. journalism U. Calgary, Alta., 1976-77; news reporter Sta. CHQR Radio, 1977-79, The Albertan, 1979-80; free-lance writer, 1980-90; pres., CEO Hummingbird Press, Calgary, 1987—. Author: Mother Love is Solar Powered...That Would Account for What Happens to Me at Night and on Rainy Days, 1987, Surviving a Nuclear Powered Family, 1992; contbr. articles to Calgary Mag., Alta. Report, Western Prodr., Parent's Mag., Great Expectations, The Compleat Mother. Recipient Nat. Dan McArthur award for Outstanding Work in Documentary Field; various scholarships. Office: 324 Silver Crest Dr NW, Calgary, AB Canada T3B 2Y2

MCLEAN-WAINWRIGHT, PAMELA LYNNE, educational consultant, college educator, counselor, program developer, clinical therapist; b. Rockville Centre, N.Y., Oct. 25, 1948; d. George Clifford Sr. and Violet Maude (Jones) McLean; m. Joseph Charles Everest Wainwright Jr., Jan. 20, 1982; children: Joseph Charles Everest III, Evan Clifford Jerome. BS, NYU, 1973; MEd, Fordham U., 1974; MSW, Adelphi U., 1986. Qualified clin. social worker. Tchr. Martin Deporres Day Care Ctr., Bklyn., 1973-77; dir. student personnel services Ujamaa Acad., Hempstead, N.Y., 1977-78; coordinator Youth Employment and Tng. Program Hempstead, 1978; ednl. opportunity counselor SUNY, Farmingdale, 1978-79; assoc. prof. student pers. svcs. Nassau Community Coll., Garden City, N.Y., 1979-93; founder, program dir. Adult Individualized Multi-Service Program, Garden City, 1985—; with counseling and advisement for health occupations program Cen. Fla. Community Coll., Ocala, 1991—. Mem. L.I. Coalition for Full Employment; mem. citizens adv. coun. Nassau Tech. Ctr., Women-on-Job Task Force, Port Washington, N.Y.; mem. adv. bd. Region 2 Displaced Homemakers Network; bd. dirs. Children's Greenhouse Inc., 1987-89, mem. founding com., 1980-81; civil rights adv., 1963—; mem. adv. bd. L.I. Cares, Hempstead, 1986-90. Recipient Women's History Month citation Nassau County, N.Y., 1988, honoree in edn. Women-on-Job Task Force, 1989, Alumni Achievement award Fordham U. Grad. Sch. Edn., 1994. Mem. Assn. Black Psychologists, Assn. Black Women in Higher Edn. (bd. dirs.), Nat. Assn. Black Coll. Alumni, Nat. Assn. Female Execs., Women's Faculty Assn. Nassau Community Coll. (pres. 1986-88), L.I. Women's Council for Equal Edn. Employment and Tng. Office: Ctrl Fla CC Citrus County Campus 3820 W Educational Path Lecanto FL 34461-9488 also: Heritage Psychiat Hosp of Beverly Hills 2804 W Marc Knighton Ct Beverly Hills FL 34465

MCLEER, LAUREEN DOROTHY, marketing professional; b. N.Y.C., Feb. 5, 1955; d. William Myers and Una Lee (Massey) McL. BS, Columbia U., 1977; MBA, U. London, 1981. RN, N.Y.; state registered nurse Eng., Wales. Staff nurse NYU Med. Ctr., N.Y.C., 1977-78; charge nurse Scripps Clinic and Rsch. Found., La Jolla, Calif., 1979-80; clin. researcher Ayerst Labs., N.Y.C., 1982-83; sales rep. Pfizer, Inc., N.Y.C., 1983-87, Cahners Pub. Co., N.Y.C., 1988-89; dir. bus. devel. Pro Clinica, N.Y.C., 1990-91; account supr. Salthouse Torre Norton, Inc., Rutherford, N.J., 1992-93; dir. bus. devel. Med. & Tech. Rsch. Assocs., Inc., Wellesley, Mass., 1993-94; account exec. Biometric Rsch. Inst., Inc., Arlington, Va., 1994—; mem. com. for helathcare issues and legislation United Hosp. Fund., N.Y.C., 1992-94. Chmn. Help Our Neighbors Eat Yr. 'Round, N.Y.C., 1987-89; trustee Murray Hill Com., N.Y.C., 1988-90; bd. dirs. East Midtown Svcs. for Older People, 1987-94. Mem. Pharm. Advt. Coun., Healthcare Bus. Women's Assn. Home: Apt 1210 1301 N Courthouse Rd Arlington VA 22201 also: Mansion Farm Courthouse Point Rd Chesapeake City MD 21915 Office: Biometric Rsch Inst Inc 1300 N 17th St Ste 300 Arlington VA 22209-3801

MCLEES, AINSLIE ARMSTRONG, French language educator; b. Phila., Feb. 17, 1947; d. Maurice Whitman and Irene (Macdonald) Armstrong; m. John Hill McLees Jr., June 5, 1969; children: Angus Armstrong, Ainslie Heather Armstrong. Diplomas, McGill U. Fr. S.S., Montreal, Quebec, 1966, 67, 68; BA, Ursinus Coll., Collegeville, Pa., 1968; MA, Bryn Mawr Coll. (Pa.), 1969; PhD, U. Va., 1980. Instr. French Mary Washington Coll., Fredericksburg, Va., 1969-70, Kapiolani C.C., Honolulu, 1970-73, No. Va. C.C., Sterling, 1979-85; teaching asst., instr. U. Va., Charlottesville, 1973-77; lang. cons. Fairfax, Va., 1977-79; vis. assoc. prof. romance langs. Randolph-Macon Coll., Ashland, Va., 1985-93; coord. Bryn Mawr Coll. Career Network, Washington, 1979; bd. dirs., editor bull. Fgn. Lang. Assn. Va., 1986—, editor; project dir. Acad. Alliance in Fgn. Lang. and Lit., Richmond, 1990—. Author: Baudelaire's Argot Plastique, 1989. Sec. Guilford Coll. Parents Assn., Greensboro, N.C., 1989-91. U. Va. and Am. Coun. on Teaching of Fgn. Langs. grantee, 1988. Mem. Am. Pen Women (sec. 1987-88), Fgn. Lang. Assn. Va. (bd. dirs. 1986—), Am. Assn. Tchrs. of French, MLA, South Atlantic MLA (chair women's caucus disc group II 1992-93, bd. dirs. 1993—), Va. Writers Club (treas. 1991-92). Home: 1628 Park Ave Richmond VA 23220-2909 Office: Regional Gov Sch 4100 W Grace St Richmond VA 23230

MCLENDON, DEBORAH DAY, educational program coordinator; b. Blakely, Ga., Sept. 21, 1951; d. A. Marshal and Betty (Wise) Day; m. Hoyle McLendon Jr., Dec. 19, 1970; children: Jennifer Kristen, Tre, Alexandria Day McLendon. A of Home Econs., Abraham Baldwin U., 1971; BS in Elem. Edn., Ga. Southwestern U., 1973, MEd in Early Childhood Edn., 1976. Tchr. kindergarten Early County Elem. Sch., Blakely, Ga., 1974-76, tchr. 2d grade, 1976, instrnl. supr. K-5, 1977-83; cons. lang. arts S.W. Ga. Regional Ednl. Svc. Agy., Leary, 1983-88, coord. drug-free schs. and communities program, 1988—; presenter Ga.'s Student Assistance Conf., 1991, Edn. Nat. Employee Assistance Program Conf., Atlanta, 1992, Fla.'s Student Assistance Conf., 1992, Nat. Student Assistance Conf., New Orleans, 1994; state chmn. Smoke Free 2000, 1993—; co-chair State Sch. Comprehensive Health Edn. Coalition, 1992—; mem. S.E. Regional Drug-Free Sch. Adv. Coun., 1992—. Co-author: (mag.) Student Assistance Jour., 1993, (manual) Twelve Steps for Teacher Support Group, 1992, Twelve Steps for Administrator Support Group. Tchr. Sunday sch. 1st Bapt. Ch. Mem. DAR. Office: SW Ga Regional Ednl Svc Agy 183 Merce Ave Leary GA 31762

MCLENDON-MCCULLOUGH, BEVERLY J., city official; b. Daytona Beach, Fla., July 28, 1949; d. George McLendon Jr. and Bernice Lillian (Wiley-McLendon) Thompson; m. Tyrone L. McCullough, June 28, 1980 (div.); 1 child, Kendle Joi. B.Sc., Ky. State U., 1971; M.Sc., Howard U., 1973. Adult edn. tchr. Washington Sch. Dist., 1972-73; curriculum specialist Howard U., Washington, 1971-73; price stabilization analyst Cost of Living Council, Washington, 1973-75; housing mgr. Community Devel. Div., City of Houston, 1975-79, housing adminstr., 1979-82; community liaison, aid to police chief Police Dept., Houston, 1982-90; owner, chief exec. TBM Enterprises Mgmt. Cons., 1990—; cons. Social Systems Intervention, Washington, 1972-74. Co-author: (tng. manual), Training of Community Personnel in Health Maintenance Organizations, 1972; creator: E-Z Reminder Grocery Shopping List pads, 1988. Mem. Am. Assn. Pub. Adminstrs., Omicron Nu. Democrat. Office: TBM Enterprises 368 Denbigh Village Ctr # 150 Newport News VA 23602

MCLENNAN, BERNICE CLAIRE, human resources professional; b. Malden, Mass., Dec. 26, 1936; d. Ralph Cyril Worth and Alice Seaman (Hunter) Worth Barrett; m. Hubert Earle McLennan, Oct. 28, 1961; 1 child, Cynthia Alice. Student, Moody Bible Inst., 1958, Salem State Coll., 1988, Bentley Coll., 1989. Youth dir. Faith Evangelical Ch., Melrose, Mass., 1971-77; adminstrv. asst. Boston (Mass.) Redevel. Authority, 1977-85, adminstr. coord., 1985-87, asst. sec. to the authority, 1981—, dir. human resources, 1988—; moderator Faith Evangelical Ch., Melrose, 1985-88, Christian edn. chair, 1973-76. Sec. Melrose (Mass.) Sch. Com., 1983-85; vol. Boston (Mass.) Youth Campaign, 1989, 90. Mem. Internat. Pers. Mgmt. Assn., Assn. Affirmative Action Profls. Home: 31 Botolph St Melrose MA 02176-1126 Office: Boston Redevel Authority 33 3rd Ave Boston MA 02129

MCLENNAN, MYRA ANN, technical information specialist; b. Albany, Ky., Sept. 17, 1936; d. Logan Cyrus Frost and Mabel Delane (Bertram) Williams; m. Lawrence William McLennan, Aug. 25, 1962 (div. Sept. 1972); children: Mary Jana Sagastegui, William Lane, Laura Michelle. BA, Union Coll., 1960; BSCE, U. Louisville, 1989. Civil engring. tech. U.S. Army Corps of Engrs., Louisville, 1989-90; tech. info. specialist Def. Tech. Info. Ctr., Alexandria, Va., 1990—. Publicity chmn. Christian County Reps., Hopkinsville, Ky., 1983; coord. Christian County Rep. Com., Hopkinsville, 1980; del. Dist. Rep. Conv., Hopkinsville, 1980, 83. Mem. ASCE, Chi Epsilon (sec. 1988—). LDS Ch. Office: Def Tech Info Ctr DTIC-OCS Bldg 5 Rm 5A 317 Duke St Cameron Station Alexandria VA 22304-6145

MCLIN, ELVA BELL, archivist; b. Norcatur, Kans., June 5, 1917; d. James Shirley and Ruth Inez (Diefendorf) Bell; m. Paul Edward McLin Sr., Oct. 18, 1940; children: Jan Ellen Bexhoeft, Paul Jr., Carl Whitfield, Sheila roberts. BA, BS in Edn., Emporia (Kans.) State U., 1940; MA, U. Ala., 1962; PhD, Peabody of Vanderbilt, 1971. Tchr. U.S. Army Dependent Schs.; historian, pub. info. officer U.S. Army Ordnance; tchr. Brooke Hill Sch. for Girls, Birmingham, Ala., 1962-64; prof. English Athens (Ala.) State Coll., 1965-87, archivist, 1987—. Author plays including Woman Grown, 1940, Zelda, 1974; author: History of Athens College 1921-1991, 1991, revised edition, 1994, (biographies) Mollie!, 1992, Madame Childs, 1993. Named Disting. Alumnus, Emporia State U., 1991; named Outstanding Tchr., Athens State Alumni Assn., 1987, Tchr. of the Yr., Phi Mu, 1972, 80. Mem. AAUW, Coll. English Assn. (officer) Shakespeare Assn., Sigma Tau Delta, Phi Mu. Democrat. Episcopalian. Home: 210 S Beaty St Athens AL 35611-2606 Office: Archives Athens State Coll Athens AL 35611

MCLIN, RHINE LANA, state legislator, funeral service executive, educator; b. Dayton, Ohio, Oct. 3, 1948; d. C. Josef, Jr., and Bernice (Cottman) McL. B.A. in Sociology, Parsons Coll., 1969; M.Ed., Xavier U., Cin., 1972; postgrad. in law U. Dayton, 1974-76, AA in Mortuary Sci., Cin. Coll., 1988. Lic. funeral dir.; cert. tchr., Ohio. Tchr. Dayton Bd. Edn., 1970-72; divorce counselor Domestic Relations Ct., Dayton, 1972-73; law clk. Montgomery Common Pleas Ct., Dayton, 1973-74; v.p., dir., embalmer McLin Funeral Homes, Dayton, 1972—; instr. Central State U., Wilberforce, Ohio, 1982—; mem. Ohio Ho. of Reps., 1988-94; state senator Ohio State Senate, 1994—. com. mem. Human Svcs. and Aging Com., Agrl. Com., Edn. and Ret. Com., Energy, Natural Resources and Environ. Com. Mem. Democratic Voters League, Dayton. Mem. Nat. Funeral Dirs. Assn., Ohio Funeral Dirs. Assn., Montgomery County Funeral Dirs. Assn., NAACP (life), Nat. Council Negro Women (life), Delta Sigma Theta. Home: 1130 Germantown St Dayton OH 45408-1465 Office: Ohio State Senate State House Columbus OH 43215

MCMACHEN, MARY JOY, clinical psychologist; b. Mattawan, Mich., Nov. 28, 1955; d. Walter Adelbert and Anastasia Julia McMachen. BA, Ea. Mich. U., 1986, MS, 1988; PhD, U. Detroit-Mercy, 1992. Lic. psychologist. Psychologist Arbor Clinic, Ann Arbor, Mich., 1988-89, North Point Mental Health, Farmington Hills, Mich., 1989—; pvt. practice, 1988—. Mem. APA, Mich. Psychol. Assn., Mensa, Psi Chi. Office: North Point Mental Health 28595 Orchard Lake Rd Farmington Hills MI 48334

MCMAHAN, GALE ANN SCIVALLY, school system administrator; b. Anna, Ill., Oct. 19, 1946; d. George Oliver and Jessie Lee (Johnson) Scivally; m. Joe Henry McMahan, Dec. 14, 1963; children: Randy Scott, Joseph Paul. BS, So. Ill. U., 1971, MS, 1974, PhD, 1994. Cert. tchr., supr., adminstr., Ill. Resource tchr. Jonesboro (Ill.) Sch. Dist. 43, 1971-73, dir. early intervention, 1991-94; resource tchr. Anna Sch. Dist. 37, 1973-94; supt. Lick Creek Sch. Dist. 16, Buncombe, Ill., 1994—; lectr. Shawnee C.C., Ullin, Ill., 1986-88, So. Ill. U., Carbondale, 1990, 92, 93; reader Ill. Bd. Edn., Springfield, 1989, 92; mem. adv. bd. for early intervention Anna Interagy. Coun., 1991—, Ill. Interagy. Coun., Springfield, 1991—; mem. team North Cen. Evaluation, Vienna, Ill., 1991. Co-author: (video) Jenny...Our Child of Today!, 1991; editor: Churches in Clear Creek Association, 1988. Recipient Those Who Excel in Edn. award of recognition Ill. Bd. Edn., 1992, grantee, 1990—. Mem. Coun. for Exceptional Children (presenter 1991), Ill. Women Adminstrs., Ill Supt. Assn., Ill. Prin. Assn., DAR, Delta Kappa Gamma (scholar 1989-90, co-contbr. articles to Delta Kappa Gamma Bull. 1993), Phi Kappa Phi, Kappa Delta Phi, Phi Delta Kappa. Baptist. Home: Rt 1 Box 84 Anna IL 62906

MCMAHAN, SUSAN EVON, travel agency executive; b. McMinnville, Oreg., Apr. 9, 1962; d. James Donald and Delores Ann (Miller) McM. BA, Linfield Coll., 1984. Jr. acct. J. Ormiston, Beaverton, Oreg., 1985; analyst, mgr. ops. Rosenbluth Travel Agy Inc, Portland, Oreg., 1988-93; Rosenbluth Internat. account leader IVI/Bus. Travel Internat. at Nike, Beaverton, Oreg., 1993—; cons. Evergreen Internat. Aviation, McMinnville, Oreg., 1989. Fellow DAR; mem. Internat. Air Transport Assn., Airline Reporting Corp., Nat. Assn. Female Execs., Bus. Oreg. Women in Travel, Linfield Coll. Alumni Assn., Phi Sigma Sigma (scholarship chmn. 1983-84). Republican. Roman Catholic. Office: Nike One Bowerman Dr AS-1 Beaverton OR 97005

MCMAHON, ANITA SUE, women's health nurse; b. Elgin, Ill., Dec. 11, 1940; d. Herman Henry and Neva Imogene (Lusted) Mass; m. Daniel D. McMahon, Aug. 20, 1960; children: Daniel, Patrick, Christine, Joseph, Susanne. AAS with high honors, Elgin Community Coll., 1983; BS, St. Francis Coll., Joliet, Ill., 1992; student, Alverno Coll., Milw. Nurse preceptor, staff nurse med.-surg. Sherman Hosp., Elgin, 1983-90, ob-gyn. nurse, 1990—, childbirth instr., 1991—, charge nurse, 1992—. Creator, editor quar. Nurse's Notes. Home: 617 Hawthorne Ct Carpentersville IL 60110-1970

MCMAHON, CATHERINE DRISCOLL, lawyer; b. Mineola, N.Y., Apr. 28, 1950; d. Matthew Joseph and Elizabeth (Driscoll) McM.; m. Gregory Arthur McGrath, Sept. 10, 1977 (div. 1991); children: Elizabeth Driscoll, Kerry Margaret, Michael Riley. BA, Simmons Coll., 1972; JD, Boston Coll., 1975; postgrad., Suffolk U., 1972-73; LL.M., NYU, 1980. Bar: N.Y. 1976, D.C. 1979, U.S. Supreme Ct. 1980, U.S. Tax Ct., 1991. Tax atty. asst. Exxon Corp., N.Y.C., 1975-76, asst. tax atty., 1976-77, sr. tax atty., 1979-81; tax atty. Exxon Internat. Co., N.Y.C., 1977-79, sr. tax counsel, Florham Park, N.J., 1990-92; sr. tax counsel Exxon Co., U.S.A., Houston, 1992—; tax mgr. Exxon Rsch. & Engring. Co., Florham Park, 1981-90. Bd. dirs. S.E. Morris chpt. ARC, Madison, N.J., 1983. Recipient TWIN award YMCA, Plainfield/Westfield, N.J., 1983. Mem. ABA, N.Y. State Bar Assn., D.C. Bar Assn. Roman Catholic. Office: Exxon Co USA 800 Bell Houston TX 77001

MCMAHON, COLLEEN, lawyer; b. Columbus, Ohio, July 18, 1951; d. John Patrick and Patricia Paterson (McDanel) McM.; m. Frank V. Sica, May 16, 1981; children: Moira Catherine, Patrick McMahon, Brian Vincent. BA summa cum laude, Ohio State U., 1973; JD cum laude, Harvard U., 1976. Bar: N.Y. 1977, U.S. Dist. Ct. (so. and ea. dists.) N.Y. 1977, U.S. Ct. Appeals (2d cir.) 1978, U.S. Supreme Ct. 1980, U.S. Ct. Appeals (5th cir.) 1985, D.C. 1985. Spl. asst. U.S. mission to the UN, N.Y.C., 1979-80; assoc. Paul, Weiss, Rifkind, Wharton & Garrison, N.Y.C., 1976-79, 80-84, ptnr., 1984—; bd. dirs., gen. counsel Danceworks, Inc., N.Y.C., 1977-83; mem. Coun. N.Y. Law Assocs., 1977-81; chair The Jury Project, N.Y. Office Ct. Adminstrn., 1993—. Bd. dirs. Vol. Lawyers for the Arts, N.Y.C., 1979-83, Dance Theater Workshop, 1978-83; vice chancellor Episcopal Diocese of N.Y. Mem. ABA, Assn. of Bar of City of N.Y. (mem. coun. on jud. adminstrn. 1983-89, chmn. com. on state cts. of superior jurisdiction 1983-86, com. on women profession 1989—, chmn. 1992—), Am. Law Inst., Am. Judicature Soc., Westchester County Bar Assn., N.Y. State Bar Assn. (mem. ho. of dels. 1986-89), Fed. Bar Coun. Republican. Episcopalian. Office: Paul Weiss Rifkind Wharton & Garrison 1285 Avenue Of The Americas New York NY 10019-6028

MCMAHON, EILEEN MARIE, artist's agent; b. Jersey City, July 15, 1953; d. William John and Marie Rita (Stringer) M. BA in Art, Jersey City State Coll., 1974; postgrad., Rutgers U., 1974-76, New Sch. for Social Research, 1976-77, Sch. of Visual Arts, 1976. Asst. curator Jersey City Mus., 1975-77; curator Ian Woodner Family Collection, N.Y.C., 1977-78; assoc. rep. Artist's Assocs., Inc., N.Y.C., 1978-81; sr. rep. Gerald and Cullen Rapp, Inc., N.Y.C., 1981-86; mktg. dir. Corey Chaloner Millen, N.Y.C., 1986-88; assoc. rep. John Locke Studios Inc., N.Y.C., 1988—. Co-author, designer: mus. catalog, August Will: Scenes of Old Jersey City, 1976. Office: John Locke Studios Inc 15 E 76th St New York NY 10021-1719

MCMAHON, LILLIAN ELIZABETH, hematologist; b. Bklyn., Sept. 17, 1937; d. Manuel Dos Santos and Eufemia (Diaz) Caldeira; m. Leonard George McMahon, June 25, 1966; 1 child, David Leonard Caldeira McMahon. MD, U. Pará, Belém, Brazil, 1963. Intern Carney Hosp., Dorchester, Mass., 1964-65, med. resident, 1965-66; pediatric resident Boston City Hosp., 1966-68, hematology/oncology fellow, 1968-69, dir. Boston Sickle Cell Ctr., 1978—, chief clin. pediatric hematology, 1989—; ped. hematology/oncology fellow N.Y. Hosp.-Cornell Med. Ctr., N.Y.C., 1969-70; assoc. clin. prof. pediatrics Boston U. Sch. Medicine, 1989—. Author, presenter abstracts in field. Comprehensive sickle cell ctr. grantee Nat. Heart, Blood & Lung Insts., NIH, 1978—. Home: 35 Ridgecrest Terr West Roxbury MA 02132 Office: Boston City Hosp Boston Sickle Cell Ctr 818 Harrison Ave FGH 2 Boston MA 02118

MCMAHON, MARY PATRICIA, business analyst; b. N.Y.C., Nov. 16, 1948; d. Matthew Joseph and Catherine Teresa McMahon; m. George E. Krayem. BS in Math., CCNY, 1970; MS in Math., NYU, 1973; MBA, Marist Coll., 1981. Chmn. bus. dept. Lavelle Sch. for Blind, Bronx, N.Y., 1970-74; program mgr. IBM, Kingston, N.Y., 1974—; mgr. devel., bus. analyst IBM, Poughkeepsie, N.Y., 1974%. Pres. Friends of Kingston Area Libr., 1980-91; sec. HVF Credit Union Supr. Com., Poughkeepsie, 1993—. Mem. Zonta Club (pres. Poughkeepsie chpt. 1994-96). Home: 7 Wayne Dr Poughkeepsie NY 12601-5818

MCMAKEN, LYNDA HAMILTON, lawyer; b. Chgo.; m. James A. Lagdon, Nov. 12, 1988. BS, Ind. U.; JD, Ind. U., Indpls., 1987. Bar: Wash. 1988, U.S. Dist. Ct. Wash. 1991. Project specialist City of Indpls., 1980-81; chief adminstr. officer sch. plan Saturday Evening Post, Indpls., 1981-82; brokerage mgr. Golden Rule Ins. Co., Indpls., 1982; pres. The Mgmt. Co., Indpls., 1983-87; lectr. Ind. U., Bloomington, 1984, Mich. Arts Sci. Coun. Inc., South Bend, Ind., 1987, Ind. Assn. Women Bus. Owners, Indpls., 1987. Vol. Big Sisters Greater Indpls., 1982-87; organizing chair, bd. dirs. Big Bros. Big Sisters Kitsap County, 1990-91, pres. bd. dirs., 1992—; chair corp. sponsorships Bainbridge Classic, 1990-91; bd. dirs. United Way, 1993—; chair Needs Assessment Com., 1994. Recipient cert. appreciation United Way, 1984, recognition for support svc., Big Sister. 1984. Mem. ABA, Network Women in Bus., Women Leader Round Table. Office: Atty at Law 16710 Agate Pass Rd NE Bainbridge Is WA 98110-1041

MCMAKIN, MIMI MADDOCK, interior designer; b. Palm Beach, Fla., Sept. 25, 1947; d. Paul Lacoste and Ruth (Quigley) Maddock Fleitas; m. William Tyson Kemble, Jr., Apr. 10, 1971 (div.); children: Cecilia Lacoste, Phoebe Powers; m. Leigh Ashley McMakin, Dec. 31, 1989. AA, Briar Cliff Coll., 1969. Designer Smith Knudson, Palm Beach, 1975-77, Jessup Inc., Palm Beach, 1977-87; pres., owner Kemble Interiors, Inc., Palm Beach, 1987—. Contbr. articles to profl. jours. Featured on cover of Town and Country mag., 1988; awarded Garden Club of Am. Conservation Com. Cert. for Hist. Preservation, 1994. Mem. Garden Club (chmn. 1988), Bath and Tennis Club (bd. dirs. 1985—), Everglades Club. Republican. Episcopalian. Office: Kemble Interiors 294 Hibiscus Ave Palm Beach FL 33480-4301

MCMANAMA, TRUDY E., psychologist; b. Pitts., Mar. 30, 1945; d. Francis J. and Mary Margaret (McDonough) Figura; m. Patick J. McManama, Nov. 25, 1967 (div. 1977); 1 child, Steven Patrick. B.S., Mansfield U., 1967; M.S., So. Conn. U., 1973, postgrad., 1974; postgrad., Harvard U., 1988. Cert. sch. psychologist. Tchr. New Milford Schs., Conn., 1967-69, Shepaug Valley High Sch., Washington Depot, Conn., 1969-72; tng. cons. Danbury Area Unified Social Svcs., Conn., 1971-72; psychologist Bd. Coop. Svcs., Poughkeepsie, N.Y., 1974-75; psychologist Berrien County Ind. Sch. Dist., Berrien Springs, Mich., 1975—; cons. Stanley Clark Sch., South Bend, Ind., 1981-88; adj. prof. Ind. U., South Bend, 1979—; instr. St. Joseph Hosp., South Bend, 1985-87; elected trustee South Bend Sch. Corp., 1987-90, pres. 1989. Vol. Internat. Spl. Olympics, 1987; pres., Neighborhood Watch Program, South Bend, 1982-83; hospice vol., South Bend; bd. dirs. Child Abuse and Neglect Coordination Orgn., South Bend, 1986-92; mem. Selective Svc. Bd., 1989—; mem. Handicapped Camping Bd., 1986-89; mem. Dem. Precinct Com., South Bend, 1980-82; del. Ind. Dem. State Conv., 1984; co-chair Carnival for The Arts, 1991-92; chair polit. action Mich. Edn. Assn. Berrien County, 1993—, SNAP negotiator, 1994. Berrien County Task Force grantee, 1979. Mem. Assn. Supervision and Curriculum Devel., NASP, Panhillenic Assn. Democrat. Roman Catholic. Avocations: jogging, reading, cross country skiing, international travel. Home: 2725 Erskine Blvd South Bend IN 46614-1201 Office: Berrien County Intermediate Sch Dist 711 St Joseph Ave Berrien Springs MI 49103-1648

MCMANIGAL, SHIRLEY ANN, university dean; b. Deering, Mo., May 4, 1938; d. Jadie C. and Willie B. (Groves) Naile. BS, Ark. State U., 1971; MS, U. Okla., 1976, PhD, 1979. Lic. med. technologist, clin. lab. dir. Med. technologist, 1958-75; chair dept. med. tech. U. So. Miss., Hattiesburg, 1979-83; chair dept. med. tech. Tex. Tech U. Health Scis. Ctr., Lubbock, 1983-87, dean Sch. Allied Health, 1987—; gov.'s appointee to statewide health coord. coun., 1994—. Leadership Tex., 1992; Lt. Alumnae Regl. dir., 1994—. Recipient Citation, State of Tex., 1988; named Woman of Yr., AAUW, Tex. div., 1990, Woman of Excellence in Edn. YWCA, Lubbock, 1990. Mem. AAUW (bd. dirs. Tex. 1990-94), Am. Coun. on Edn./Nat. Identification Program (steering com. for Tex.), Clin. Lab. Mgmt. Assn. (chair edn. com. 1989, 91), Am. Soc. Med. Tech., Nat. Assn. Women in Edn., So. Assn. Allied Health Deans at Acad. Health Ctrs., S.W. Assn. Clin. Microbiology, Tex. Soc. Allied Health Professions (pres. 1990-91), Tex. Soc. Med. Tech. (Educator of Yr. 1990), Alpha Eta, Phi Beta Delta (gov. appointee to statewide health coord. coun. 1994—). Home: 5003 94th St Lubbock TX 79424-4813 Office: Tex Tech U Health Scis Ctr Sch Allied Health Lubbock TX 79430

MCMANN, PATRICIA ANN, nurse, small business owner; b. Phila., July 19, 1946; d. Ray Hilton and Lucille Gertrude (Lehnerd) McM. Diploma, Holy Cross Sch. of Nursing, South Bend, Ind., 1967; BS in Health Arts, Coll. St. Francis, 1983. RN, Tex. Nurse hosp. staff, home health pvt. practice South Bend, Elkhart, Ind., 1968-75; from insvc. dir. to dir. nursing Turtle Creek (SNF-ICF), Elkhart, 1975-80; dir. med./surg. nursing Elkhart Gen. Hosp., 1980-85; medicare nurse Kimberly Home Health, Fort Worth, 1985; network developer Amicare (preferred provider orgn.), Irving, Tex., 1985-86; dir. med. svcs. Alliance Health (health maintenance orgn.), Fort Worth, 1986-89; pres. Med. Industry Cons., Arlington, Tex., 1989—; pres., CEO The Automated Advantage, Inc., Arlington, 1993-94; guest speaker Goshen (Ind.) Coll., 1979-80. Bd. dirs. Salvation Army, Goshen, Ind., 1976; children's group facilitator The Women's Shelter, Arlington, Tex., 1993. Mem. Am. Coll. of Med. Quality (affiliate). Roman Catholic. Office: Med Industry Cons PO Box 170401 Arlington TX 76003

MCMANUS, LANA RAE, court reporter; b. New Orleans, Mar. 8, 1965; d. Calvin Claiborne and Betty Jane (Reed) McM. AAS, Alvin (Tex.) C.C., 1992. Court reporter A. William Roberts Jr. & Assocs., Charleston, S.C., 1992—. Glassell Sch. Art scholar, 1982-83. Mem. Nat. Ct. Reporters Assn., Tex. Ct. Reporters Assn., S.C. Shorthand Reporters Assn. Roman Catholic. Office: A. William Roberts Jr & Assocs 46-A State St Charleston SC 29401

MCMANUS, MICHELLE ANN, state legislator, cherry farmer; b. Traverse City, Mich., Oct. 5, 1966; d. Michael and Janet (Courtad) McM.; m. Keith Nelson. BS in Polit. Sci., Cen. Mich. U., 1989. Senate aide Mich. Senate, Lansing, 1990-91; legis. aide Mich. Ho. Rep., Lansing, 1991-92; state rep. State of Mich., Lansing, 1992—; cherry farmer Leland, Mich. Republican. Roman Catholic. Office: Mich House Rep PO Box 30014 Lansing MI 48909-7514

MCMASTER, JULIET SYLVIA, English language educator; b. Kisumu, Kenya, Aug. 2, 1937; emigrated to Can., 1961, naturalized, 1976; d. Sydney Herbert and Sylvia (Hook) Fazan; m. Rowland McMaster, May 10, 1968; children: Rawdon, Lindsey. B.A. with honors, Oxford U., 1959; M.A., U. Alta., 1963, Ph.D., 1965. Asst. prof. English U. Alta., Edmonton, Can., 1965-70; assoc. prof. U. Alta., 1970-76, prof. English, 1976-86, Univ. prof., 1986—. Author: Thackeray: The Major Novels, 1971, Jane Austen on Love, 1978, Trollope's Palliser Novels, 1978, (with R.D. McMaster) The Novel from Sterne to James, 1981, Dickens the Designer, 1987; illustrator/editor children's picture book: (by Jane Austen) The Beautifull Cassandra, 1993; contbr. articles to prof. jours. Fellow Can. Coun., 1969-70, Guggenheim Found., 1976-77, Killam Found., 1987-89; recipient Molson prize in Humanities for Outstanding Contbn. to Canadian Culture, 1994. Fellow Royal Soc. Can.; mem. Victorian Studies Assn. Western Can. (founding pres. 1972), Assn. Can. Univ. Tchrs. English (pres. 1976-78), MLA, Jane Austen Soc. N.Am. (dir. 1980-91). Office: U Alta, Dept English, Edmonton, AB Canada T6G 2E5

MCMASTER, KATHERINE COX, surgical nurse; b. Rock Hill, S.C., Oct. 24, 1954; d. Fleet Henson and Judy (Lines) Cox; m. Harry A. Mullis, Apr. 20, 1974 (div. 1980); 1 child, Eric Christoper. BSN, Med. U. S.C., 1983; MS in Health Sci. Adminstrn., Fla. Inst. Tech., 1991. RN, N.C., S.C., Fla.; cert. nurse adminstr., oper. rm. nurse. Charge nurse York Gen. Hosp., Rock Hill, S.C., 1975-79; head nurse Divine Savior Hosp., York, S.C., 1979-83; edn. coord. surg. svcs. Halifax Med. Ctr., Daytona Beach, Fla., 1983-91; dir. surg.

svcs. AMI Palm Beach Gardens (Fla.) Med. Ctr., 1991—; affiliate faculty Daytona Beach Community Coll., 1985-86; organ donor liaison HMC-East Cen. Fla. transplant, Daytona Beach, 1984-90, trauma seminar coord., 1984-90. Mem. ARC, AORN (cert., bd. dirs.), Am. Heart Assn., South Fla. Orgn. Nurses Execcs., Sigma Theta Tau. Democrat. Seventh-day Adventist. Home: 4104 Water Oak Ct Palm Beach Gardens FL 33410 Office: AMI Palm Beach Gardens Med Ctr 3360 Burns Rd Palm Bch Gdns FL 33410-4323

MCMATH, ELIZABETH MOORE, graphic artist; b. Iredell, Tex., Feb. 20, 1930; d. Fred William and Elizabeth Carol (Smith) Moore; m. Charles Wallis McMath, Jan. 16, 1978 (dec. Dec. 1990); children: Charles Wallis, John Seals. BA, BS in Advt. Design, Tex. Woman's U., Denton, 1951; grad. gemologist, Gemol. Inst. Am., L.A., 1977. Layout artist Leonard's Dept. Store, Ft. Worth, Tex., 1951-52; artist/bookkeeper Bud Biggs Studio, Dallas, 1953; sec./artist Squire Haskins Studio, Dallas, 1953-54; artist/art dir. Dowdell-Merrill, Inc., Dallas, 1954-58; owner/artist Moore Co., Dallas, 1958-90. Mem. Stemmons Corridor Bus. Assn., Dallas, 1988-89. Mem. Dallas/Ft. Worth Soc. Visual Comm. (founder), Tex. Woman's U. Nat. Alumnae Assn., Greater North Tex. Orchid Soc. (treas. 1987), Daylily Growers of Dallas (sec. 1989-90, 1st v.p. and program chmn. 1992), Internat. Bulb Soc., Native Plant Soc. Tex. Presbyterian. Home: PO Box 1068 Denton TX 76202-1068

MCMATH, VIRGINIA KATHERINE See ROGERS, GINGER

MCMEANS, MARY ANN, rehabilitation nurse, case manager; b. Cullman, Ala., May 26, 1950; d. Jack J. and Theresa Lena (Graveman) Moore; m. Charles Royce McMeans Jr., June 16, 1972 (div. 1988); children: Charles, Teresa. Diploma in nursing, St. Vincent Sch. Nursing, 1971; BS, Coll. St. Francis, 1982. Cert. rehab. RN; cert. case mgr. Charge nurse Cullman Hosp., 1971-74; house supr. evening shift Dr.'s Hosp., Cullman, 1974-79; head nurse emergency room, infection control Woodland Community Hosp., Cullman, 1979-82, infection control-insvc. supr., 1982-84; med. rev. specialist Intracorp, Birmingham, Ala., 1984-85, rehab. specialist med. case mgmt., 1985-88; case mgr. Lakeshore System Svcs., Huntsville, Ala., 1988-89; rehab. coord. Lakeshore Rehab. Ctr., Huntsville, 1989-91, TBI day treatment program mgr., 1991-94; clinic nurse, case mgr. Ala. Pain Clinic, Huntsville, 1994; med. case coord. Profl. Med. Mgmt., Inc., Birmingham, 1994—. V.p. adult activities Parents Without Ptnrs., Huntsville, 1991, v.p. edn., 1990; CPR instr. Am. Heart Assn., Ala., 1982-84. Mem. Ala. Head Injury Found., Assn. Rehab. Nurses, Ala. Assn. Rehab. Profls. Pvt. Sector (north Ala. rep. 1991-92). Roman Catholic. Home: 12423 Chicamauga Tr Huntsville AL 35803 Office: Profl Med Mgmt Inc PO Box 380155 Birmingham AL 35238

MCMEEKIN, DOROTHY, botany, plant pathology educator; b. Boston, Feb. 24, 1932; d. Thomas LeRoy and Vera (Crockatt) McM. BA, Wilson Coll., 1953; MA, Wellesley Coll., 1955; PhD, Cornell U., 1959. Asst. prof. Upsala Coll., East Orange, N.J., 1959-64, Bowling Green State U., Ohio, 1964-66; prof. natural sci. Mich. State U., East Lansing, 1966-89, prof. botany, plant pathology, 1989—. Author: Diego Rivera: Science and Creativity, 1985; contbr. articles to profl. jours. Mem. Am. Phytopath. Soc., Mycol. Soc. Am., Soc. Econ. Bot., Mich. Bot. Soc. (bd. dirs. 1985—), Mich. Women's Studies Assn., Sigma Xi, Phi Kappa Phi. Home: 1055 Marigold Ave East Lansing MI 48823-5128 Office: Mich State U Dept Botany-Plant Pathology 335 N Kedzie East Lansing MI 48824-0001

MCMEEKIN, GAIL ELIZABETH, career consultant; b. Tulsa, Okla., Mar. 24, 1951; m. Russell Street, Oct. 10, 1987. BA, Conn. Coll., 1973; MSW, Boston U., 1976; cert. human resources, Bentley Coll., 1985. Lic. ind. clin. social worker. Owner Guided Growth, Brookline, Mass., 1982—. Mem. NASW, Boston Human Resource Assn. (placement com.). Home and Office: Guided Growth PO Box 686 Brookline MA 02146

MCMICHAEL, JEANE CASEY, real estate corporation executive; b. Clarksville, Ind., May 7, 1938; d. Emmett Ward and Carrie Evelyn (Leonard) Casey; m. Norman Kenneth Wenzler, Sept. 12, 1956 (div. 1968); m. Wilburn Arnold McMichael, June 20, 1978. Student Ind. U. Extension Ctr., Bellermine Coll., 1972-73, Ind. U. S.E., 1973—, Kentuckiana Metroversity, 1981—; Grad. Realtors Inst., Ind. U., 1982; grad. Leadership Tng., Clark County, Ind.; lic. real estate broker, Ind., Ky.; master Grad. Realtors Inst., Cert. Residential Specialist, Cert. Real Estate Broker, Leadership Tng. Grad. Owner, pres. McMichael Real Estate, Inc., Jeffersonville, 1979-88, 90-95; mgr., owner Buzz Bauer Realtors, Clark County, 1989-91; mng. broker Parks & Weisberg Realtors, Jeffersonville, Ind., 1989-91; instr. real estate Tng. Concepts, Inc. Pres.-elect of congregation St. Mark's United Ch. of Christ, 1995, pres., Mr. and Mrs. Class, chmn., fin. trustee and bus. adv., chmn. devel. com., 1993, 94; chmn. bd. trustees, Brooklawn Youth Svcs., 1988-94, chmn. 1994—; chmn. social com. Rep. party Clark County (Ind.); v.p. Floyd County Habitat for Humanity, 1991, 94/95. Recipient cert. of appreciation Nat. Ctr. Citizen Involvement, 1983; award Contact Kentuckiana Teleministries, 1978. Mem. Nat. Assn. Realtors (nat. dir. 1989—), Ind. Assn. Realtors (state dir. 1987—, quick start speaker 1989-91), Nat. Women's Council Realtors (state pres., chmn. c)ms., state rec. sec., 1984, state pres. 1985-86, Nat. Achievement award 1982, 83, 84, 85, 86, 87, 88, 89, 90, nat. gov. Ind. 1987, v.p. region III 1988, Ind. Honor Realtor award 1982—), Women's Council of Realtors (speaker 1990-94, Mem. of Yr. 1988), Ky. Real Estate Exchange, So. Ind. Bd. Realtors (program chmn. 1986-87, bd. dirs., pres., 1988—, Realtor of Yr. 1985, instr. success series, 1989-92, Snyder Svc. award 1987, Omega Tau Rho award 1988, Excellence in Edn. award 1989), Ind. Assn. Realtors (state dir. 1985—, bd. govs., instr./trainer, speaker 1989-94, chair bd. govs. 1991), Toastmasters (pres. Steamboat chpt.), Psi Iota Xi. Office: McMichael Real Estate Inc 615 Redwood Dr Clarksville IN 47129-1227

MCMILLAN, ADELL, educational administrator, retired; b. Portland, Oreg., June 22, 1933; d. John and Eunice A. (Hoyt) McM. AB in Social Sci., Whitman Coll., 1955; MS in Recreation Mgmt., U. Oreg., 1963. Program dir. Erb Meml. Union, U. Oreg., Eugen, 1955-68; program cons. Willard Straight Hall, Cornell U., Ithaca, N.Y., 1966-67; assoc. dir. Erb Meml. Union, U. Oreg., Eugene, 1968-75; dir. Erb Meml. Union, U. Oreg., 1975-91, dir. emeritus, 1992—. Editor, co-author: College Unions: Seventy-Five Years, 1989; interviewer, editor oral history interviews, 1978, 92, 93, 94. Bd. dirs. United Way, Lane County, Oreg., 1976-83, 87—, pres., 1982-83, 88-90; commr. Eugene City Planning Commn., 1992—; mem. Hist. Rev. Bd., 1992—; mem. Tree Commn., 1992-93; bd. dirs., treas. Eugene Opera Co., 1992—. Named Woman of Yr. Lane County Coun. Orgns., Eugene, Oreg., 1985. Mem. Assn. Coll. Unions-Internat. (v.p. 1977-80, pres. 1981-82, Butts-Whiting award 1987, hon. 1992), Zonta Club of Eugene, Zonta Internat. (pres. 1984-86, dist. treas. 1990-92, 92-94, v.p. 1994-95, pres. 95-96), Emerald Valley Women's Golf Club. Democrat. Episcopalian. Office: 55 W 39th Ave Eugene OR 97405

MCMILLAN, JOANETTE HART, elementary educator; b. Mayo, Fla., Apr. 28, 1932; m. William R. McMillan, June 19, 1959; 1 child, Leenette. BS, Fla. State U., 1954; MS, Valdosta State U., 1973. Cert. elem. tchr., early childhood tchr., reading tchr., Fla. Tchr. various sch. dists. Gadsden, Brevard Counties, Fla., 1955-68, Suwannee County, Fla., 1968-78; tchr., chpt. I coord. Lafayette County, Fla., 1978—. Active Dem. Ctrl. Com., Mayo, 1982—; chairperson Mayo Family Med. Svcs., 1986—; mem. Seminole Boosters, 1987—, Builders Guild Advent Christian Village, 1974—, United Meth. Ch., 1942—, PTA. Mem. Fla. Edn. Assn., Order Eastern Star (assoc. matron, sec. 1989—), Fla. State U. Alumni Assn., Alpha Delta Kappa (pres., v.p., sec., historian, altruistic chmn. 1967—). Office: Lafayette Elem Sch Rt 2 Box 260 Mayo FL 32066-9642

MCMILLAN, TERRY L., writer, educator; b. Pt. Huron, Mich., Oct. 18, 1951; d. Edward McMillan and Madeline Washington Tillman; 1 child, Solomon Welch. B.S. in Journalism, U. Calif., Berkeley, 1979; M.F.A., Columbia Univ., N.Y.C., 1979. Instr. U. Wyoming, Laramie, 1987-90; prof. U. Ariz., Tucson, 1990-92. Author: Mama, 1987, Disappearing Acts, 1989, Waiting to Exhale, 1992; (with Nawal El Saadawi) Ergo! the Bumbershoot Literary Magazine (vol. 8 no. 1), 1993; editor: Breaking Ice: An Anthology of Contemporary African-American Fiction, 1990. Recipient National Endowment for the Arts fellowship, 1988. Office: care Free at Last PO Box 2408 Danville CA 94526 also: care Molly Friedrich Aaron Priest Literary Agency 122 East 42nd St Ste 3902 New York NY 10168*

MCMILLEN, ABBIE, environmental manager; b. N.Y.C., Oct. 10, 1942; d. Albert Edward and Beatrice Cuthbert (Collingwood) Miller; B.S. in Chemistry, Brown U., 1964; M.S., Purdue U., 1969; m. David S. Page, Sept. 30, 1964; children—David C., Vivian W.; m. Michael A. McMillen, Feb. 14, 1980. mem. Maine gov.'s cabinet, dir. Maine Office Energy Resources, Augusta, 1975-77; project dir. Roy F. Weston, Inc., Burlington, Mass., 1981-92; pres. McMillen Environ. Inc., 1992-93; exec. dir. Island Heritage Trust, 1993—. founder, organizer Lafayette (Ind.) Environ. Action Fedn., 1969; mem., chmn. Poland (Maine) Planning Bd., 1971-73; mem. exec. com., chmn. solid waste com., Poland rep. Androscoggin Valley Regional Planning Commn., 1971-73; chmn. New Eng. steering com. for ERDA pub. meeting, 1975; mem. New Eng. Congl. Caucus Energy Congress, 1979, New Eng. Power Plant siting task force, 1980; treas. Concord Art Assn., 1987-89; through-hiker Long Trail, 1989; bd. dirs. Solid Waste Composing Coun., 1991-93; trustee Castine Conservation Trust, 1994—. David Ross fellow Purdue U., 1965. Mem. ASME (tech. papers chmn. solid waste div. 1991-93), Maine Organic Farmers and Gardeners Assn. (organizer, v.p. 1970-72). Contbr. articles to profl. jours.

MCMILLEN, ELIZABETH CASHIN, artist; b. Chgo., 1944; d. James Blaine and Hortense (Fears) Cashin; m. Michael Albert McMillen (div. 1980); 1 child, Michael Nereus; m. John Stephen Jerabek. Student, Western Coll. for Women, 1961-63; BA, Bard Coll., 1965. coord. & juror Spectra I, sponsor state exhbn. women artists Westbrook Coll., Portland, Maine, 1979; dir. Hancock County Auditorium Art Gallery, Ellsworth, Maine, 1984, 85. Prin. works include sculpture Ahimsa Gallery, Maine, 1976; exhibited at Frick Gallery, Belfast, Maine, 1993, 94, Maine Coast Artists, Rockport, 1994; one-person shows incl. Area Gallery, Portland, Maine, 1994. Dem. chair Town of Lamoine, Maine, 1984-85, 86-87, 88-89; legislation coord. Amnesty Internat., Ellsworth, 1991—. Democrat. Episcopalian.

MCMILLER, ANITA WILLIAMS, army officer, transportation professional, educator; b. Chgo., Dec. 23, 1946; d. Chester Leon and Marion Claudette (Martin) Williams; m. Robert Melvin McMiller, July 29, 1967 (div. 1980). BS in Edn., No. Ill. U., 1968; MBA, Fla. Inst. Tech., 1979; M of Mil. Arts and Sci., U.S. Army Command & Gen. Staff Coll., 1990; postgrad., US Army War Coll., Carlisle, Pa., 1993-94. Social worker County of Cook, Chgo., 1968-69; recruiter analyst, dir. personnel State of Ill., Chgo., 1969-75; commd. 1st lt. U.S. Army, 1975, advanced through grades to lt. col., 1991; platoon leader, motor officer, exec. officer 155th Transp. Co., Ft. Eustis, Va. and Okinawa, Japan, 1976-78; S-1 pers. and adminstrn. officer 38th Transp. Bn., Ft. Eustis, 1978-79; installation transp. officer, fin. mgr. 3d Armor Div., Hanau, Germany, 1979-82, transp. co. comdr., 1982-83; transp. plans officer Mil. Traffic Mgmt. Command, Falls Church, Va., 1983-85; tour with Sea Land Corp., Menlo Park, N.J., 1985-86; dep. comdr., ops. officer Bremerhaven (Germany) Terminal, 1986-89; logistics staff officer The Pentagon, Washington, 1990-91; comdr. 1320th Port Battalion Mil. Traffic Mgmt. Command, U.K. Terminal, Felixstowe, Great Britain, 1991-93; Washington, $D; staff officer Office Joint Chiefs of Staff, The Pentagon, Arlington, Va., 1994—; instr. Cen. Tex. Coll., Hanau, Fed. Republic Germany, 1981-83, Phillips Bus. Coll., Alexandria, Va., 1983-84, City Colls. Chgo., 1987-89. Contbr. articles to profl. jours. Child advocate, foster mother Army Community Service, Hanau, 1980-83; tutor Parent-Tchr. Club Hanau Schs., 1981-83; vol. Vis. Nurses Assn. No. Va., 1983-85; coordinator, English tutor Adopt-a-Sch. Project, Washington, 1983-85; treas. Bremerhaven Girl Scouts Coun., 1987-89, mem. Red Cross. Mem. Nat. Def. Transp. Assn., Assn. U.S. Army, Fedn. Bus. Profl. Women, Am. Legion, British Legion, Alpha Kappa Alpha. Home: PO Box 46344 Washington DC 20050-6344 Office: The Joint Staff J7/EAD 7000 The Pentagon Washington DC 20318-7000

MCMINN, VIRGINIA ANN, human resources consulting company executive; b. Champaign, Ill., Apr. 7, 1948; d. Richard Henry and Esther Lucille (Ellis) Taylor; m. Michael Lee McMinn, Dec. 29, 1973. BA in Teaching of English, U. Ill., 1969; MS in Indsl. Rels., Loyola U., Chgo., 1985. Pers. sec. Solo Cup Co., Urbana, Ill., 1972-74; pers. asst. Rust-Oleum Corp., Evanston, Ill., 1974-75, asst. pers. mgr., 1974-80; mgr. employee rels. Rust-Oleum Corp., Vernon Hills, Ill., 1980-81, mgr. human resources, 1981-84; dir. human resources Field Container Corp., Elk Grove Village, Ill., 1984-87; regional mgr. human resources Hartford Ins. Corp., Chgo., 1987-90; owner, pres. McMinn & Assocs., Ltd., Palatine, Ill., 1988—; instr. bus. and mgmt. divsn. Trinity Coll., Deerfield, Ill., 1984-85; instr. bus. and social scis. Harper Coll., Palatine, Ill., 1990-93; bd. dirs. Nierman's Hard-To-Find Sizes Shoes, Chgo.; spkr. on legal issues, terminations, employment at will, career planning, job search, and human resources function to area colls., industry and profl. and women's groups. Bd. dirs. Ill. Crossroads coun. Girls Scouts USA, Elk Grove, 1988-92; mem. Ill. Com. to Implement Clean Indoor Air Act, Chgo., 1990-91; past mem. adv. bd. Coll. of Lake County, 1982-84. Mem. Soc. for Human Resource Mgmt., Nat. Network Sales Profls. (program chmn. 1990-93), North Suburban Network Women Enterpreneurs (v.p. programs 1992-94), Women in Mgmt. (Chpt. Leadership award corp. category, past pres.), Palatine C. of C., Mt. Prospect C. of C. Office: 1423 Michele Dr Palatine IL 60067

MCMORRIES, MELISSA ELIOT, lawyer; b. Bethesda, Md., Nov. 18, 1952; d. Edwin Eliot and Cynthia Lowe (Read) McM.; m. Jonathan Daniel Simmons, June 23, 1990. AB cum laude, Duke U., 1973; JD cum laude, Wake Forest U., 1982. Bar: N.C. 1982, Ga. 1990. Data svcs. officer Wachovia Svcs., Inc., Winston-Salem, N.C., 1975-79; atty. R.J. Reynolds Industries, Winston-Salem, N.C., 1982-85; asst. counsel RJR Nabisco, Inc., Winston-Salem, N.C., 1985-87; assoc. counsel RJR Nabisco, Inc., Atlanta, 1987-89, counsel, 1989; v.p., gen. counsel, sec. The Regina Co., Atlanta, 1989—. Exec. editor Wake Forest Law Rev., 1981-82. Bd. dirs. Winston-Salem Coun. on Status of Women, 1983-87, pres. 1987; bd. dirs. law alumni coun. Wake Forest U., 1988-93, Metro. Atlanta Coun. on Alcohol and Drugs, 1993—. Mem. ABA, Ga. Bar Assn., Atlanta Bar Assn., Am. Corp. Counsel Assn., Phi Alpha Delta. Democrat. Episcopalian. Office: The Regina Company 1955 Lake Park Dr Smyrna GA 30080

MCMORROW, MARGARET MARY (PEG MCMORROW), retired educator; b. N.Y.C., Dec. 18, 1924; d. Patrick Joseph and Ellen Veronica (Quinn) McIntyre; m. Joseph Patrick McMorrow, Oct. 12, 1948; children: Linda Karen, Robert Michael, Patrice Ann, Jane Ellen. BS, Queens Coll., 1946; MS in Edn., Hofstra U., 1959. Space controller Am. Airlines Co., N.Y.C., 1946-48; bus. rep. N.Y. Telephone Co., N.Y.C., 1948-52; tchr. Elwood Sch. Dist, Huntington, N.Y., 1965-89, ret., 1989. Fellow Elwood Tchrs. Assn., L.I. Scribes, N.Y. State United Tchrs., Mensa; mem. Elwood Ret. Tchrs. Assn., Alpha Lambda Omicron. Roman Catholic.

MCMORROW, MARY ANN G., judge; b. Chgo., Jan. 16, 1930; m. Emmett J. McMorrow, May 5, 1962; 1 dau., Mary Ann. Student Rosary Coll., 1948-50; J.D., Loyola U., 1953. Bar: Ill. 1953, U.S. Dist. Ct. (no. dist.) Ill. 1960, U.S. Supreme Ct. 1976. Atty. Riordan & Linklater Law Offices, Chgo., 1954-56; asst. state's atty. Cook County, Chgo., 1956-63; sole practice, Chgo., 1963-76; judge of Cir. Ct. Cook County, 1976-85, Ill. Appellate Ct., 1985-92, Supreme Ct. Ill., 1992—. Contbr. articles to profl. jours. Faculty adv. Nat. Jud. Coll., U. Nev., 1984. Mem. Chgo. Bar Assn., Ill. State Bar Assn., Women's Bar Assn. of Ill. (pres. 1975-76, bd. dirs. 1970-78), Ill. Judges Assn., Nat. Assn. Women Judges, Advocates Soc., Cath. Lawyers Guild (bd. dirs. 1980—), Northwest Suburban Bar Assn., West Suburban Bar Assn., Loyola Law Alumni Assn. (bd. govs. 1985—), Ill. Judges Assn. (bd. dirs.), Cath. Lawyers Guild (v.p.). Office: Supreme Ct of Ill 160 N LaSalle St Chicago IL 60601

MCMULLEN, KAREN, human resource consultant; b. Johnstown, Pa., Jan. 19, 1950; d. James L. McMullen and Violet (Schultz) Bottger; m. Robert J. Marsenich, Oct. 20, 1980; stepchildren: Eric, Shawn. BS, W. Va. U., 1971; MEd, Ga. State U., 1976. Adolescent counselor, health educator Maternal/Infant Proj. Grady Meml. Hosp., Atlanta, 1971-77; human resource cons., counselor Metamorphosis, Polson, Mont., 1978—. Bd. dirs., pres. Planned Parenthood of Missoula, Mont., 1984-87, edn. chair, 1978-86. Office: Metamorphosis 205 3rd Ave E Polson MT 59860-2344

MCMULLEN, RITA GAMBLE, insurance sales manager; b. Chambersburg, Pa., Mar. 25, 1962; d. Randall William and Glenna (Fogal) Gamble; m. Clyde Philip McMullen, Sept. 7, 1985; 1 child, Jessica Marie. Student, Ins. Ins., 1984, 94, Nat. Assn. Ins. Women, 1986. Lic. ins. agt. Pa., Md., CPCU, AAI, CPIW. Sec. Strickler Agy., Inc., Chambersburg, Pa., 1979-82, farm ins. underwriter, 1982-85; ins. agt. Rita McMullen Ins., Dry Run, Pa., 1985-87; merger sales mgr. Stine Davis & Peck Ins., Chambersburg, 1987—. V.p. Fannett Metal Vol. Fire Dept., Dry Run, 1992-93; bd. dirs. Spring Run (Pa.) Cable TV Co., 1991—. Mem. Nat. Assn. Ins. Women (state dir. 1988-89, Nat. Rookie of Yr. 1984), Pa. Ind. Agts. Assn. (edn. bd. 1992—), Pa. Ind. Agts. Assn. (mem. edn. bd. 1992—), South Ctrl. Ind. Agts. (v.p. 1992—), South Ctrl. Ins. Assn. (pres. 1983-85, chmn., Ins. Woman of Yr. 1985, 92), South Ctrl. C. of C. Republican. Roman Catholic. Home: PO Box 115 18157 Dry Run Rd W Dry Run PA 17220 Office: Stine Davis & Peck Ins 4050 Lincoln Way W Chambersburg PA 17201

MCMULLIN, JOYCE ANNE, general contractor; b. Tulsa, Jan. 6, 1952; d. Junior Lawrence Patrick and Carol Anne (Morris) McM.; m. David Lawrence Tupper, Jan. 1, 1980 (div. May 1982). BFA, Calif. Coll. Arts and Crafts, 1973. Interior designer Design Assocs., Oakland, Calif., 1974; interior designer, sales rep. Sullivan's Interiors, Berkeley, Calif., 1975; supr. bldg. maintenance Clausen House, Inc., Oakland, 1975-82; owner New Life Renovation, Lafayette, Calif., 1981—. Contbr. articles to mags., newspapers. Mem. Contra Costa Coun., Nat. Trust Historic Preservation. Mem. AAUW, NAFE, Bus. and Profl. Women, Contra Costa County Women's Network, Self-Employed Tradeswomen (sec. 1984), Contra Costa Coun., Leads Club.

MCMULLIN, RUTH RONEY, publishing company executive, management fellow; b. N.Y.C., Feb. 9, 1942; d. Richard Thomas and Virginia (Goodwin) Roney; m. Thomas Ryan McMullin, Apr. 27, 1968; 1 child, David Patrick. BA, Conn. Coll., 1963; MS in Pub. and Pvt. Mgmt., Yale U., 1979. Market researcher Aviation Week Mag. McGraw- Hill Co., N.Y.C., 1962-64; assoc. editor, bus. mgr. Doubleday & Co., N.Y.C., 1964-66; mgr. Natural History Press, 1967-70; v.p., treas. Weston (Conn.) Woods, Inc., 1970-71; staff assoc. Gen. Electric, Fairfield, Conn., 1979-82; mng. fin. analyst GECC Transp., Stamford, Conn., 1982-84; credit analyst corp. fin. dept. GECC, Stamford, 1984-85; sr. v.p. GECC Capital Markets Group, Inc., N.Y.C., 1985-87; exec. v.p., chief operating officer John Wiley & Sons, N.Y.C., 1987-89, pres., CEO, 1989-90; pres., CEO Harvard Bus. Sch. Pub. Corp., Boston, 1991-94; mgmt. fellow Yale Sch. of Mgmt., 1994—; mem. chmn.'s com., acting CEO UNR Industries Inc., Chgo., 1991-92; mgmt. fellow Sch. Mgmt. Yale U., New Haven, Conn., 1994—; bd. dirs. Bausch & Lomb, Rochester, N.Y., UNR Industries Inc., Chgo., Middlesex (Conn.) Mut. Assurance, Fleet Fin., Providence; vis. prof. Sch. Mgmt., Yale U., New Haven, Conn., 1994—. Mem. dean's adv. bd. Sch. Mgmt. Yale U.; bd. dirs. Yale U. Alumni Fund, Yale U. Press, Math. Scis. Edn. Bd. Mem. N.Y. Yacht Club, Stamford Yacht Club. Home: 274 Beacon St Boston MA 02116 Office: Yale U Sch Mgmt Box 208200 New Haven CT 06520-8200

MCMURRAY, CAROL DOLBER, human services administrator; b. Marilla, N.Y., July 31, 1948; d. Clinton Charles and Frances Ann (Gilmore) Dolber; m. James Michael McMurray, Oct. 21, 1972; children: Christian, Stefan. BA, SUNY, Binghamton, 1970; MSW, Va. Commonwealth U., 1977. Caseworker Warren County Children Svcs., Lake George, N.Y., 1973-75; social worker Chesterfield (Va.) County Mental Health/MR Svcs., 1977-79; dir. Vol. Emergency Foster Care of Va., 1979-80; regional tng. coord. Va. Bapt. Children's Home and Family Svcs., 1980-82; Va. area program coord. Welcome House Adoption Svcs., Inc., Richmond, Va., 1982-90; child and family trainer, cons., 1988—; adj. faculty Divsn. of Continuing Edn., U. Va.; program tng. coord. Prevent Child Abuse; pres. Va. Assn. Lic. Child Placing Agys., 1988-90, v.p., 1986-88; mem. trainer Conflict Resolution Team Tng., Richmond Peace Edn. Ctr., Va. Contbr. articles to profl. jours. and mags. Organizer, past pres. Richmond Domestic Violence Project, Richmond, Va., 1977-79; chairperson Bd. of Child Care Ctr., Richmond, 1985-88, Job Study Review Com. of Chs. Profl. Ministerial Staff, Richmond, 1989-90. Mem. ASTD, Acad. Cert. Social Workers, Nat. Assn. Social Workers, Adoption Devel. Outreach Planning Team. Home and Office: 1915 Floyd Ave Richmond VA 23220-4515

MCMURRAY, CLAUDIA A., lawyer; d. Raymond D. and Sally Kathryn (Martin) McM.; m. Donald V. Moorehead, June 6, 1987. AB with honors, Smith Coll., 1980; JD, Georgetown U., 1984. Bar: D.C. 1985. Legis. asst. to Rep. Bill Emerson, 1980-81; law clk. Office of Counsel to the Pres. The White House, 1983-84; atty. Patton, Boggs & Blow, 1984-87, Kirkland & Ellis, 1987-89; legis. counsel to Senator John W. Warner, 1989-90; minority counsel Senate Com. on Environment and Pub. Works, 1990—. Editor The Tax Lawyer. Office: Environ & Pub Works 410 Senate Dirksen Office Bldg Washington DC 20510*

MCMURRAY, LOLLA JEAN, corporate professional; b. Sulphur, Ok., June 27, 1939; d. Clifford Orvil and Jean Francis (Webb) Kirby; m. Donald Lee King, May 1958 (div. 1959); m. Kenneth Edward McMurray, Dec. 17, 1960; children: Marlene, Julie. Student, West Valley Coll., 1983. Adminstrv. sec., office mgr. Mt. Pleasant Sch. Dist., San Jose, Calif., 1976-80; exec. sec. Micro Metallics Corp., San Jose, 1980-84; office mgr., sec. bd. dirs. G.E. Stephens & Assoc., San Jose, 1984-87; bus. office mgr. A. Hirsh & Son, San Jose, 1987-93; corp. ops. mgr. Dietz Assocs., Inc., San Jose, 1993—. Sec. Fred Maiten Home and Sch., San Jose, 1973. Mem. NAFE, Calif. Assn. Residential Lenders, Assn. Profl. Mortgage Women. Democrat. Lutheran. Office: Dietz Assocs Inc 1155 N 1st St # 111 San Jose CA 95112

MCMURTRY, FLORENCE JEAN, educator; b. Schenectady, N.Y., Feb. 1, 1947; d. Louis Frederick Jr. and Eleanore Jean (Noyes) McM. BA in Edn. with honors, Simmons Coll., 1969; MEd, U. Vt., 1975; grad. cert. advanced studies in mgmt., Radcliffe Coll., 1993. Elem. tchr. Pittsford, N.Y., 1969-70; reading specialist Lincoln, Vt., 1971-73, Pembroke, Mass., 1976; grad. teaching asst U. Vt., 1975; elem tchr. Chatham, Mass., 1977-80; with Arthur D. Little, Cambridge, Mass., 1981-82; exec. sec. Merdith & Grew, Inc., Boston, 1982—; v.p. alumnae fund Simmons Coll., Boston, 1994-96. Mem. edit. bd. The Beacon jour., 1985-92, (book) Boston Cooks, 1991. Corp. mem. Ch. of the Advent, Boston, 1990—, adminstr. ch. sch. program, 1988-93; bd. mgrs. Jr. League Boston, 1990-92, v.p. pres., 1992, 93, chair endowments, 1993-94; chair Boston Pub. Libr. com., 1987-90; pres., v.p., rec. sec., ednl. loan fund chmn. Boston chpt. Philanthropic Ednl. Orgn., Des Moines, 1983—. Recipient Vol. Recognition award Jr. League Boston, 1989. Mem. Women's Ednl. and Indsl. Union, Women in Devel. (pres. 1994—), The Coll. Club (pres. 1994—), PEO. Episcopalian.

MCNABB, DARCY LAFOUNTAIN, medical management company executive; b. Middletown, N.J., Aug. 27, 1955; d. Donald Mark LaFountain and Suzanne (Gilman) LaFountain Westergard; m. Leland Monte McNabb, July 4, 1981 (div. Feb. 1989); 1 child, Leland Monte Jr. BBA in Internat. Fin. cum laude, U. Miami, 1977. Real estate agent, Grad. Realtor's Inst. Market rsch. asst. Burger King Corp., Miami, Fla., 1975-77; regional mktg. supr. Burger King Corp., Huntington Beach, Calif., 1977-78; mgr., restaurant planning Holiday Inns, Inc., Memphis, 1978-79, mgr., nat. promotions, 1979-83; dir., lodging and travel planning Holiday Corp., Memphis, 1983-86; affiliate broker The Hobson Co., Realtors, Memphis, 1986-88, Crye Leike, Memphis, 1988-92; v.p. comm. and planning Medshares Mgmt. Group, Inc., Memphis, 1991—. Mem. Friends Pink Palace Mus., Memphis, 1987-91, Family Link/Runaway, Memphis, 1980-88; chmn. Foster Care Rev. Bd., Memphis, 1988—; bd. dirs. Bethany House, Memphis, 1989—, pres.; bd. dirs. Am. Cancer Soc., 1994—; mem. mktg. com. Health Industry Coun., 1994-95. Named Profl. Vol. of Yr., Friends of Pink Palace Mus., Memphis, 1989, 93, U.S. Masters Swimming All-Am., 1993, 94; grad. Leadership Memphis, 1995. Mem. Le Bonheur Club, Memphis Runners Track Club. Republican. Episcopalian. Home: 1948 Harbert Ave Memphis TN 38104-5216 Office: Medshares Mgmt Group Inc 2714 Union Avenue Ext Memphis TN 38112-4402

MCNABB, DIANNE LEIGH, investment banker, accountant; b. Huntsville, Ala., Sept. 7, 1956; d. Walter David and Mary Josephine (Hawkins) McN.; m. William Roland Lantz, July 1, 1983. BS in Acctg., U. Ala., Tuscaloosa, 1976. CPA. Acct. Lilly Flagg Assocs. & Subsidiaries, Huntsville, 1977-78; mgr. Johnston, Joyce & Wigginton, CPA's, Huntsville, 1978-84; sr. mgr.

KPMG Peat Marwick, CPA's, Atlanta, 1984-91; v.p. A.G. Edwards & Sons, Inc., Atlanta, 1991—. Mem. ways and means com. Atlanta Jr. League, 1991—; instr., advisor Jr. Achievement, Atlanta, 1985-88; mem. hospitality com. Dem. Nat. Conv., Atlanta, 1988; vol. Ga. Spl. Olympics, Atlanta, 1989-91. Mem. AICPA, Govt. Fin. Officers Assn. (spl. rev. com. 1991—), Ga. Soc. CPA (govtl. acctg. and auditing com. 1992), Assn. of Govt. Accts. (bd. dirs. Atlanta chpt. 1990-92), Ala. Soc. CPA (sec.-treas. 1984), Am. Soc. Women Accts. (pres. Huntsville chpt. 1983-84), U. Ala. Alumni Assn. (treas. 1983-84), Zeta Tau Alpha (advisor 1988-93, v.p. 1983, treas. 1987-89, pres. 1984, 89-91, panhellenic del. 1988-91, dist. pres. 1993—, Cert. of Merit 1992, Zeta Lady award 1991, Alum Chum award 1991). Home: 2530 Alpine Way Duluth GA 30136-4440 Office: A G Edwards 3399 Peachtree Rd NE Ste 1270 Atlanta GA 30326-1150

MCNAIR, CLAUDIA JARDINE, human resource manager; b. Ogden, Utah, Sept. 14, 1947; d. Claude Barton and Lucile Broadhead Jardine; m. Robert J. McNair, Apr. 6, 1967; 1 child, Kristen Manon. BA summa cum laude, U. Mass., 1976. Dir. adminstrn. BioTech. Internat., Inc., Cambridge, Mass., 1982-88, dir. human resources, 1988-89; mng. human resources Summit Tech., Inc., Waltham, Mass., 1990—. Mem. Soc. Human Resource Mgmt., New Eng. Employee Benefits Coun., N.E. Human Resource Assn., Assoc. Industries of Mass., Phi Beta Kappa. Office: Summit Tech Inc 21 Hickory Dr Waltham MA 02154

MCNAIR, TERESA IRENE, human resources executive, consultant; b. Conway, S.C., Oct. 3, 1966; d. Archie Mack and Betty Jo (Bratcher) McN. BSBA, U. S.C., Conway, 1987; MA in Human Resources & Mgmt., Webster U., 1989. V.p. ops. Cabinet World, Inc., Myrtle Beach, S.C., 1986-89; data processing operator Coastal Carolina Hosp., Conway, 1989, human resources asst., 1989-90, human resources dir., 1990—; cons. Ramsay Health Care, New Orleans, 1993—. Coastal Carolina Hosp. chair United Way Horry County, Conway, 1990—, Mar. Dimes Walk Am., 1990—. Named Dist. III Young Careerist, Conway Bus. and Profl. Women's Orgn., 1992. Mem. Soc. Human Resource Mgmt., Coastal Area Pers. Assn. (treas. 1990, membership chair 1991). Republican. Baptist. Office: Coastal Carolina Hosp 152 Waccamaw Medical Park Dr Conway SC 29526-8922

MCNAIRN, PEGGI JEAN, speech pathologist, educator; b. Dallas, Sept. 22, 1954; d. Glenn Alton Harmon and Anna Eugenia (McVay) Hicks; m. Kerry Glen McNairn, Jan. 27, 1979; children: Micah Jay, Nathan Corey. BS in Speech Pathology, Tex. Christian U., 1977, MS in Communications Pathology, 1978; PhD in Ednl. Adminstrn., Kennedy Western U., 1991. Cert. speech pathologist, mid mgmt. Staff speech pathologist, asst. dir. infant program Easter Seal Soc. for Crippled Children and Adults Tarrant County, Ft. Worth, 1978-80; staff speech pathologist, spl. edn. lead tchr. Sherrod Elem. Sch. Arlington (Tex.) Ind. Sch. Dist., 1981-84, secondary speech/lang. specialist, early childhood assessment staff Spl. Services dept., 1984-89; owner, dir. Speech Assocs., 1989-92; mem. state forms com. Arlington (Tex.) Ind. Sch. Dist., 1985-86, chairperson assessment com., 1986-87; cons. augmentative communication Prentke Romich Co., 1992—; adj. prof., clin. supr. Tex. Christian U., Ft. Worth, 1978-79; clin. speech pathologist North Tex. Home Health Assn., Ft. Worth, 1980-92. Author: Quick Tech Activities for Literacy, 1993, Readable, Repeatable Stories and Activities, 1994. Chairperson United Cerebral Palsy Toy Lending Libr., 1989-90; sunday sch. tchr. 1st United Meth. Ch., Arlington, 1982-87; mem. South Arlington Homeowners Assn., Arlington, 1985-87; 3rd v.p. Bebensee Elem. PTA. Recipient Outstanding Svc. to Handicapped Am. Biog. Inst., 1989; Cert. of Achievement John Hopkins U. for computing to assist persons with disabilities, 1991. Mem. Internat. U.S. Tex. Socs. for Augmentative and Alternate Comm. (sec. Tex. branch), Neurodevelopmental Assn., Assn. for Curriculum and Supervision, Am. Speech and Hearing Assn., Tex. Speech-Lang.-Hearing Assn., Tex. Speech and Hearing Assn. (task force mem for augmentative comm.) Teaching Tex. Tots Consortium, Tex. Christian U. Speech and Hearing Alumni Assn., Kappa Delta Pi, Alpha Lambda Delta. Democrat. Home and Office: 215 Spanish Moss Dr Arlington TX 76018-1540

MCNALLY, AMY, insurance company executive; b. Pittsfield, Mass., June 24, 1964; d. Richard D. and Juliane M. (Mongeon) H.; m. Charles Edward McNally, May 30, 1987. AA in Bus. with honors, Berkshire/County C. C., 1984; BS in Bus. cum laude, North Adams State Coll., 1988. Shipping and receiving clk. Nelson's Inc., Pittsfield, Mass., 1981-84; spl. processing analyst Berkshire Life Ins. Co., Pittsfield, 1984-86, corr. typist, 1986-87, supr. underwriting support, 1987-89, pers. analyst, 1989-91, mgr. compensation and tng., 1991-94, mgr. benefits and compensation, 1994—; mem. compensation com. Life Office Mgmt. Assn., Atlanta, 1991—. Bd. mem., pers. chair, 2nd v.p. Girls Inc. Pittsfield, 1989—; small bus. solicitor Berkshire United Way, Pittsfield, 1991, allocations vol., 1991-92. Office: Berkshire Life Ins Co 700 South St Pittsfield MA 01201-8212

MCNAMARA, ANN DOWD, medical technologist; b. Detroit, Oct. 17, 1924; d. Frank Raymond and Frances Mae (Ayling) Sullivan; m. Thomas Stephen Dowd, Apr. 23, 1949 (dec. 1980); children: Cynthia Dowd Restuccia, Kevin Thomas Dowd; m. Robert Abbott McNamara, June 15, 1985. BS Wayne State U., 1947. Med. technologist Woman's Hosp. (now Hutzel Hosp.), Detroit, 1946-52, St. James Clin. Lab., Detroit, 1960-62; supr. histo-pathology lab. Hutzel Hosp., Detroit, 1962-72, Mt. Carmel Mercy Hosp., 1972-87, ret., 1987; docent Domino's Ctr. for Architecture & Design, Ann Arbor, Mich., 1988. Mem. Am. Soc. Clin. Pathologists, Am. Soc. Med. Technology, Mich. Soc. Med. Tech., Nat. Soc. Histotechnology, Mich. Soc. Histotechnologists, Wayne State U. Alumni Assn., Smithsonian Assocs., Detroit Inst. Arts Founders Soc. Home: 29231 Oak Point Dr Farmington Hl MI 48331-2774

MCNAMARA, ANNE H., lawyer, corporate executive; b. Shanghai, Republic of China, Oct. 18, 1947; came to U.S. 1949; d. John M. and Marion P. (Murphy) H.; m. Martin B. McNamara, Jan. 15, 1977. AB, Vassar Coll., 1969; JD, Cornell U., 1973. Bar: N.Y. 1973, Tex. 1981. Assoc. Shea, Gould, Climenko & Casey, N.Y.C., 1972-76; from asst. corp. sec. to corp. sec. Am. Airlines, Inc., Dallas, 1976-88, v.p. pers. resources, 1988; sr. v.p. adminstrn., gen. counsel American Airlines (AMR Corp.), Dallas, 1988—; bd. dirs. Louisville Gas & Electric Co., LG&E Energy Corp. Office: Am Airlines Inc Mail Drop 5675 PO Box 619616 Dallas TX 75261-9616*

MCNAMARA, BRENDA NORMA, secondary education educator; b. Blackpool, Lancashire, Eng., Aug. 8, 1945; came to U.S., 1946; d. Milford Hampson and Nola (Welsby) J.; m. Michael James McNamara, July 19, 1969. BA in History, Calif. State U., Long Beach, 1967; postgrad., Calif. State U., various campuses, 1967—. Cert. secondary tchr. and lang. devel. specialist, Calif. Tchr. history West High Sch., Torrance, Calif., 1968—, dept. chair, 1989—; cons. in field. Co-author: World History, 1988. Western Internat. Studies Consortium grantee, 1988. Mem. Calif. Tchrs. Assn., Calif. Coun. for Social Studies, Torrance Tchrs. Assn. (bd. dirs. 1992—), South Bay Coun. for Social Studies, Nat. Tchrs. Assn., Nat. Coun. for Social Studies. Office: West High Sch 20401 Victor St Torrance CA 90503-2297

MCNAMARA, EILEEN MARIE, human resources professional; b. Garfield Heights, Ohio, May 7, 1967. BGS, Ohio U., 1989. Dir. ops. Security Mgmt. Profls., Westlake, Ohio, 1989-91; human resources specialist LDI, Inc., Solon, Ohio, 1991-93; commr. human resources City of Brook Park, Ohio, 1993—. Campaign asst. Citizens for Coyne, Brook Park, 1993. Mem. Am. Mgmt. Assn., Soc. Human Resource Mgmt. Roman Catholic. Office: City of Brook Park 6161 Engle Rd Brook Park OH 44142

MCNAMARA, PATRICIA RAE, religious organization administrator; b. Lima, Ohio, Oct. 24, 1936; d. Raymond Joseph and Hildreth Josephine (Kuhn) McN. AA, St. Catharine Coll., Springfield, Ky., 1959; BA, Siena Coll., 1966; MA, Morehead State U., 1973; postgrad. in religious edn. Loyola U., Chgo.; cert. devel. edn. specialist Appalachian State U., 1983, cert. English lang. arts tchrs/instr., life-time tchr. cert., Ky. Dominican Sisters of St. Catharine of Siena, Roman Cath. Ch., 1955. Tchr. elem. and jr. high Cath. schs., Springfield, Ky., Memphis, 1956-63; mid. and jr. high tchr. Cath. schs., Forrest City, Ark., McMechen, W.Va., 1963-67; tchr. Cath. high schs., Springfield, Louisville, 1968-79; instr. English St. Catharine Coll., Springfield, 1979-86, chair humanities divsn., 1982-84, part-time instr., 1986-89, dir. community rels., alumni, editor 10 yr. self-study for So. Assn. Accreditation, 1986-89, dir. of parish religious edn. and catechist formation, co-chair Parish Coun. Comm. Commn. St. Jerome Ch., Fancy Farm, Ky., 1989-91; dir. parish religious edn. St. Martin Tours Ch., Vine Grove, Ky., 1991—; pres. Greater Louisville High Sch. Press Assn., 1973-75, mem. exec. bd., 1973-79. Ga. State Coll. Newspaper Fund grantee, 1970; Eastern Coll. Am. Studies grantee, 1977. Mem. Ky. Council Internat. Reading Assn. (chmn. coll. reading com. 1983-86, regional leader 1984-85), Nat. Council Tchrs. of English (regional judge, ann. awards in writing 1978-88, 89-90, cons. to Coll. English Edn. Commn. 1984-90), Nat. Cath. Catechists Soc., Greater Louisville English Council (v.p. 1977-79), Ky. Council Tchrs. of English (v.p. 1981-82, pres. 1982-83, exec. bd. 1983-84, Faithful Service plaque, 1984). Democrat. Avocations: creative and newsletter writing, singing in ch. choir and cantoring for liturgies, reading, visiting hist. and literary landmarks. Home: 467 Saint Martin Rd Vine Grove KY 40175-8617 Office: Religious Edn Office 440 Saint Martin Rd Vine Grove KY 40175-8617

MCNAMARA, PAULA RUTH WAGNER, therapeutic recreation programs director; b. St. Louis, Feb. 23, 1925; d. Paul Brooks and Leah Ruth (Dick) Wagner; m. Raymond Edmund McNamara, May 28, 1949; children: Carol Rae, Marla Ann, Cynthia Ruth, Erin Marie, Brian Francis. BFA, Sch. of Art Inst., 1948; MA, W. Va. Grad. Coll., 1988. Cert. therapeutic recreation specialist. Supr. leisure edn. W. Va. Rehabilitaion Ctr., Institute, 1970-91; exec. dir. W. Va. Therapeutic Recreation Assn., Institute, 1992—; rep. Nat. Therapeutic Recreation Assn., Arlington, Va., 1984—. Amb. Friendship Force, 1993—; conf. del. Partners of the Americas, Washington, 1991. Mem. Nat. Therapeutic Recreation Assn., Am. Therapeutic Recreation Assn., W.Va. Therapeutic Recreation Assn. (sec. 1991). Office: WVa Therapeutic Recreation Assn PO Box 554 Institute WV 25112-0554

MCNAMARA, WANDA G., state legislator; b. Bristol, S.D., Sept. 4, 1944; widowed; 4 children. Student, No. State Coll., Aberdeen, S.D., 1962-65. Bus. cons. N.H.; mem. N.H. State Ho. Reps., mem. children, youth and juvenile justice com. Mem. Chesterfield Sch. Bd., 1985-88, chair, 1987-88. Republican. Protestant. Office: NH Ho of Reps State Capitol Concord NH 03301*

MCNAMEE, SISTER CATHERINE, educational association executive; b. Troy, N.Y., Nov. 13, 1931; d. Thomas Ignatius McNamee and Kathryn McNamee Marois. B.A., Coll. of St. Rose, 1953, D.H.L. (hon.), 1975; M.Ed., Boston Coll., 1955, M.A., 1958; Ph.D., U. Madrid, 1967. Grad. asst. Boston Coll., 1954-55; asst. registrar Boston Coll. (Grad. Sch.), 1955-57; acad. v.p. Coll. St. Rose, Albany, N.Y., 1968-75; dir. liberal arts Thomas Edison Coll., Trenton, 1975-76; pres. Trinity Coll., Burlington, Vt., 1976-79, Coll. St. Catherine, St. Paul, 1979-84; dean Dexter Hanley Coll., U. Scranton, Pa., 1984-86; pres. Nat. Cath. Ednl. Assn., Washington, 1986—. Bd. dirs. Am. Forum, Kotz Grad. Sch. Mgmt., Minn., Boston Coll. Spanish Govt. grantee, 1965-67; OAS grantee, 1967-68; Fulbright grantee, 1972-73. Mem. Am. Assn. Execs., Assn. Cath. Colls. and Univs., Internat. Fedn. Cath. Univs., Delta Epsilon Sigma, Delta Kappa Gamma. Roman Catholic. Club: Zonta. Office: Nat Cath Ednl Assn 1077 30th St NW Ste 100 Washington DC 20007-3829*

MCNAMEE, EVELYN HAYNES, civilian military employee; b. Monticello, Miss., Dec. 10, 1947; d. Leroy and Leslie (Hammond) Haynes; m. George Allen McNamee Jr., Aug. 23, 1970; children: Leonard, George Allen, Paula Elizabeth, Candace Renee. BS, Alcorn State U., Lorman, Miss., 1969; MS, Tuskegee Inst., 1971. Indsl. hygienist U.S. Army, White Sands Missile Range, N.Mex., 1985-88; sr. indsl. hygienist USN Naval Hosp., San Diego, 1988-90; indsl. hygienist, command staff Naval Aviation Depot Naval Air Sta. North Island, San Diego, 1990-91; sr. indsl. hygienist David Taylor Model Basin Carderock Divsn. Naval Surface Warfare Ctr., Bethesda, Md., 1991—. Mem. Sidwell Friends' Parent Group, Washington, Sidwell Friends' Resource Bank, 1991-95. Mem. NAFE, Am. Conf. Govt. Indsl. Hygienists, Am. Indsl. Hygiene Assn., Navy Indsl. Hygiene Assn., Internat. Platform Assn., Toastmasters (past pres. local chpt.). Democrat. Roman Catholic. Home: 13009 Flack St Silver Spring MD 20906-4068 Office: Nat Navy Med Ctr Bldg 22 Br Med Clinic Carderock DTMB CDNSWC Code 3061 IH Bethesda MD 20084

MCNAUGHT, JUDITH, author; b. San Luis Obispo, Calif., May 10, 1944; d. Clifford Harris and Rosetta (Prince) Spath; m. J. Michael McNaught, June 1, 1974 (dec. 1983); children: Whitney, Clayton. BS, Northwestern U., 1966. Pres. Pro-Temps, Inc., St. Louis, 1983-84, Eagle Syndication, Inc., Dallas, 1987—. Author Tender Triumph, 1983 (Critics Choice award 1983); Double Standards, 1984; Whitney, My Love (Best Hist. Novelist 1985), Once and Always, 1987 (Best Hist. Novel 1987), Something Wonderful 1988 (N.Y. Times Best seller, Critics Choice award Best Hist. Novel 1988), A Kingdom of Dreams, 1989 (N.Y. Times Bestseller, Award for Best Hist. Novel 1989), Almost Heaven, 1990 (N.Y. Times #1 Bestseller, Persie award, Romantic Times award), Paradise, 1991 (N.Y. Times Bestseller award for best hardcover contemporary romance, Romantic Times award), Perfect , 1993 (N.Y. Times Bestseller), Until You, 1994. Mem. Novelists, Inc. Roman Catholic. Avocations: racquetball, skiing.

MCNEAL, ANN P. WOODHULL, physiology professor; b. Orange, N.J., Oct. 20, 1942; d. James D. W. and Hazel V. Mc.; m. Albert S. Woodhull, May 1, 1965 (div. 1986); 1 child, Gordon. BA, Swarthmore Coll., 1964; PhD, U. Wash., Seattle, 1972. From asst. prof. to prof. Hampshire Coll., Amherst, Mass., 1972—; program dir. divsn. undergrad. edn. NSF, 1993-94. Contbr. articles to profl. jours. Mem. Peace Activists East West (sec. 1985-89), Amherst, Mass., Pelham Athletic Club (pres. 1986-89), Pelham, Mass. Mem. Am. Coll. Sports Medicine. Office: Hampshire Coll Natural Sci Amherst MA 01002

MCNEAL, KAREN LYNN, management consultant; b. Chgo., Sept. 25, 1947; d. Joseph S. and Camille Marie (Podlesak) Erazmus; m. David G. McNeal, Aug. 1, 1970; 1 child, Karleen Marie. BA, St. Mary of the Woods (Ind.) Coll., 1969; MS, Ind. St. U., 1972; MBA, U. Chgo., 1980. Programmer Aldens Inc., Chgo., 1970, systems analyst, 1971-74, mgmt. sci. sect. mgr., 1975-78; sr. applications specialist Gen. Electric Info. Svcs., Oak Brook, Ill., 1978-79, project mgr., 1980-81, tech. mgr., 1982-84, sr. cons., 1985—; advisor Am. Nat. Standards Electronic Data Interchange Com., N.Y.C., 1985—; developer Nat. Health Care Stas.; cons. truck Adv. Group, Detroit, 1987—. Contbr. articles to profl. jours. Bd. dirs. Palos Hts. Recreation Bd., 1979-89. Recipient Automotive Industry Action Group Outstanding Achievement award, 1990. Mem. Automotive Industry Action Group, Marriage Encounter-Dialogue Group (sec. 1978—). Roman Catholic. Home: 66 Country Squire Rd Palos Heights IL 60463-1227 Office: Gen Electric Info Svcs Ste 295 2015 Spring Rd Oak Brook IL 60521-1892

MCNEAL, SHAY, advertising executive; b. Sturgis, Ky., Nov. 5, 1946; d. John H'Earl Evans and Mary Ellen Baird; 1 child, Richard McNeal (dec. 1972); 1 child, Hethur; m. Gordon K. Smith, Oct. 24, 1975 (div. 1982); 1 child, Paris. Student, DeKalb Coll. Asst. dir. Savannah St. Mission, Atlanta, 1968-70; spl. project asst. Lovable Co., Atlanta, 1970-71; assoc. buyer Montgomery Ward/Knit Div., N.Y., 1971-73; nat. fashion dir. Dan River Mills, N.Y.; mktg. dir. Macy's SE div., Atlanta, 1974-78; pres. Smith McNeal Advt., 1978-86; sr. v.p., gen. mgr. William Cook Advt., Atlanta, 1986-89; pres. Preemptive Ltd., Beverly Hills, Calif., 1989-91, Georgetown Prodns., Washington, 1991—; key cons. Jack Watson for Gov., Atlanta and Savannah; mem. faculty, jurist Portfolio Ctr., Atlanta, 1988-89; media cons. anti David Duke campaign Dem. Party, Washington. Bd. dirs. Travelers Aid, Atlanta, 1982-84; vol. ARC, Atlanta, 1978—, various advt. clubs nationwide; appointed by the gov. to Ga. Film Commn., 1989; media cons. Anti-David Duke Campaign for Dem. Party, Washington. Named one of the Top Advt. Women in the S.E. AdWeek, Atlanta, 1987. Mem. Am. Assn. Advt. Agys., Exec. Womens Assn., Atlanta Advt. Club, Ansley Golf Club Atlanta. Democrat.

MCNEAR, BARBARA BAXTER, financial communications executive, consultant; b. Chgo., Oct. 9, 1939; d. Carl Henden and Alice Gertrude (Parrish) Baxter; m. Robert Erskine McNear, Apr. 13, 1968 (div. 1981); 1 child, Amanda Baxter; m. Glenn Philip Eisen, June 7, 1987. B.S. in Journalism, Northwestern U., 1961. Editorial asst. Scott Foresman & Co., Chgo., 1961; pub. rels. dir. Market Facts Inc., Chgo., 1961-63; account supr. Philip Lesly Co., Chgo., 1963-68, 69; account exec. Burson-Marsteller, Chgo., 1968; dir. communications CNA Fin. Corp., Chgo., 1969-74; dir. pub. rels. Gould Inc., Chgo., 1974; v.p. Harris Bank, Chgo., 1974-80, Fireman's Fund Ins. Co., San Francisco, 1980-83; sr. v.p. First Chgo. Corp., 1983-86; v.p. communications Xerox Fin. Svcs., Inc., Stamford, Conn., 1987-93; mgr. shareholder comm. Xerox Corp., Stamford, 1993—. Bd. dirs. Seneca, Inc., Basking Ridge, N.J., Fairfield County Pub. Rels. Assn. Mem. Pub. Relations Soc. Am., Nat. Investor Rels. Inst. (pres. Chgo. chpt. 1974-75, bd. dirs. Chgo. chpt.). Episcopalian. Club: Cliffdwellers, Princeton. Home: 23 Telva Rd Wilton CT 06897-3733 Office: Xerox Corp 800 Long Ridge Rd Stamford CT 06904

MCNEESE, BRENDA LUNNON, community health nurse, researcher; b. Houston; d. George and Mattie (Prescott) Lunnon; 1 child, Marcel Wade McNeese. BSN, Prairie View A&M U., Prairie, Tex., 1973; MS in Nursing, Tex. Woman's U., Houston, 1978; DrPH, U. Tex., Houston, 1994. Cert. gerontol. nurse. Admissions coord. Vis. Nurse Assn., Houston; coord. post hosp. planning VA, Houston. Contbr. articles to profl. jours. 2d lt. USAF, 1971-76. Recipient Diamond Anniversary award Prairie View A&M U. Coll. Nursing, 1993. Mem. Am. Assn. Spinal Cord Injury, Tex. Nurses Assn. (Dist. 9 Nursing Celebration award 1993), Sigma Theta Tau. Home: 4502 University Oaks Houston TX 77004

MC NEESE, WILMA WALLACE, social worker; b. Chgo., Apr. 30, 1946; d. Nettie Fletcher Wallace; student Wilson City Coll., 1964-66; B.A., So. Ill. U., 1969; M.S.W., Loyola U., Chgo., 1976; m. Mose D. McNeese, Dec. 27, 1969; children—Derrick, Christina. Program coordinator Intensive Tng. and Employment Program, East St. Louis, Ill., 1970-71; methods and procedures adviser Ill. Dept. Pub. Aid, Chgo., 1972-73; social work intern Robbins (Ill.) Presch. Center, 1974; with U.S. Probation Office, Chgo., 1975; officer U.S. Pretrial Services Agy., Chgo., 1976-87; chief U.S. pretrial services officer for western dist. Pa., 1987—; fieldwork instr. Aurora Coll., 1981, Chgo. State U., 1981-82; grad. fieldwork instr. U. Ill. Sch. of Social Work, 1986; mem. bd. trustees The Wesley Inst. Inc., 1993—. Recipient Community Service award Village of Robbins, 1975; advanced tng. cert. Fed. Jud. Ctr. Mem. Nat. Assn. Social Workers, Acad. Cert. Social Workers, Nat. Assn. Pretrial Svcs. Agencies, Greater Pitts. Commn. for Women. Baptist. Home: 833 Chalmers Pl Pittsburgh PA 15243-1967 Office: 1000 Liberty Ave Rm 822 Pittsburgh PA 15222

MCNEIL, MARY ELIZABETH, school system administrator; b. Boston, Oct. 15, 1946; d. Joseph C. and Margaret A. (Murray) McN.; 1 child, Ryan McNeil Pierce. BS in Social Scis. and Elem. Edn., U. Vt., 1968, MEd in Spl. Edn., 1972; EdD in Systems Devel. and Adaptation, Boston U., 1979. Tchr. remedial reading Burlington (Vt.) Sch. Dist., 1968, tchr. elem. sch., 1968-70; instr. intensive reading program Chittenden South Supervisory Sch. Dist., Hinesburg, Vt., 1972; cons. tchr. Chittenden South Supervisory Sch. Dist., Shelburne, Vt., 1972-76, co-dir. Title VI G Model Demonstration Ctr., 1974-76; lectr. spl. edn. Coll. Edn. and Social Svcs. U. Vt., 1976-79, lectr., coord. responsive teacher program dept. profl. edn., 1979-81, facilitator workshop on effective schs. Vt. Sch. Improvement Inst., 1981, coord. Woodstock/UVM collaborative project Coll. Edn. and Social Svcs., 1981-84, mem. faculty grad. coll., 1980—, asst. prof. responsive tchr. program dept. profl. edn. and cirriculum devel., 1980-83, assoc. prof., 1983-91, coord. respnsive tchr. program, 1980-85, adminstr. Ednl. Devel. Ctr., 1985-86, interim chair dept. profl. edn. and cirriculum devel. Coll. Edn. and Social Svcs., 1988-89; dir. spl. edn. and evaluation, coord. responsive tchr. program. Merced (Calif.) Union High Sch. Dist., 1992—; mem. steering com. Vt. Outcomes-Based Instrn. Network; vis. prof. U. Moncton, N.B., Can., 1983; mem. Calif. Statewide Spl. Edn. Task Force. Author: Partner Learning, 1984; assoc. editor Edn. and Treatment Children, 1982-89, mem. editorial rev. bd., 1982—; co-editor Jour. Tchr. Edn. and Spl. Edn., 1987-90; guest editor Pro Ed Publ., 1981; reviewer Jour. Applied Behavioral Analysis, 1983-86; contbr. articles to profl. jours. Pres. Vt. Coun. for Exceptional Children. Mem. Ptnrs. of Ams. (pres.). Office: Merced Union High Sch Dist Merced CA 95344

MCNEIL, MONA MARGARET, clinical psychologist; b. Bklyn., Sept. 12, 1947; d. William A. and Margaret M. (Kenny) McLoughlin; m. Donald R. Takush, July 7, 1966 (div. 1981); 1 child, Melissa Takush; m. Randall Ring Kleinhesselink, Aug. 5, 1983. Student, Manhattanville Coll., 1965-66; BS in Zoology, U. Wash., 1976; MS in Clin. Psychology, Calif. State, Bakersfield, 1979; PhD in Clin. Psychology, Wash. State U., 1987. Lic. psychologist, Oreg., Wash. Psychology cons. Pioneer Community Hosp., Bakersfield, 1978-79; instr. Wash. State U., Pullman, Wash., 1983; lectr. U. Idaho, Moscow, 1984-85; psychol. asst. Lewiston, Idaho, 1981-85; intern Seattle VA Med. Ctr., 1985-86; lectr., supr. U. Idaho, Moscow, 1986-87; acting dir. alcohol studies Wash. State U., Pullman, 1988; clin. psychologist Affiliated Psychol. Assocs., Inc., Portland, Oreg., 1988—; adj. faculty Wash. State U., Pullman, 1984—. Vol. therapist Cascade AIDS Project; active NOW, Nat. Abortion Rights Action League, Planned Parenthood. Mem. APA, Oreg. Psychol. Assn., Portland Psychol. Assn., N.W. Woman's Therapy Project, Nat. Register Health Svc. Providers in Psychology. Office: Affiliated Psychol Assocs 5319 SW Westgate Dr Ste 147 Portland OR 97221-2411

MC NEILL, CARMEN MARY, business broker; b. Charles City, Iowa, July 16; d. Benjamin T. and Mary (Orvis) McN. M.B.A., U. Chgo., 1957. Sec.-treas., Old Rep. Life Ins. Co., 1943-62; cons., officer life cos., 1962-70; broker-finder, owner Am. Cons., Chgo., 1970—. Methodist. Home: 918 Argyle Ave Flossmoor IL 60422-1257 Office: 18118 Martin Ave Ste 1ee Homewood IL 60430-2120

MCNEILL, JOAN REAGIN, volunteer consultant; b. Atlanta, July 8, 1936; d. Arthur Edward and Annie May (Busby) Reagin; m. Thomas Pinckney McNeill, Sr., Aug. 3, 1957; childen: Thomas Pinckney, Clyde Reagin. Student, U. Louisville, 1955-57; BA, U. Tenn., Chattanooga, 1976. Founding pres. Family and Children's Svcs. Assocs., Chattanooga, 1987-88; bd. dirs. Chattanooga Symphony and Opera Assn., 1984-88, pres., 1984-87; pres. Chattanooga Ballet Assn., 1986-88; bd. dirs. U. Chattanooga Found., 1986-89; mem. vol. coun. bd. dirs. Am. Symphony Orch. League, Washington, 1986—, pres.-elect., 1992-93, pres., 1993—. Recipient Outstanding Svc. award U. Tenn., Chattanooga, 1988. Mem. U. Tenn. Chattanooga Alumni Assn. (pres. 1985-86), Golden Key, Sigma Kappa Found. (trustee 1992—, sec. 1993-94, pres. 1994—, Colby award for volunteerism 1990). Republican. Episcopalian. Home and Office: 7457 Preston Cir Chattanooga TN 37421-1839

MCNEILL, MAXINE CURRIE, county official; b. Rockingham, N.C., Oct. 17, 1934; d. Daniel Franklin and Lollie Mae (Davis) Currie; m. James Albert McNeill, May 5, 1956; children: James C., David A., Jon S., Ellen F. BSN, Wingate Coll., 1986; MPH, U. N.C., 1991. Lic. nurse practitioner; cert. in ambulatory health care NCC. Dir. nursing svc. Hamlet, N.C., 1967-69; sch. nurse Rockingham, N.C., 1970-72; dir. Richmond County Home Health Agy., Rockingham, 1972-74; pub. health nurse Scotland County Health Dept., Laurinburg, N.C., 1974-75, nurse practitioner, 1975-79; nurse practitioner Laurinburg Surg. Clinic, 1979-80; nursing supr. Scotland Count Health Dept., Laurinburg, 1980-82, Richmond County Health Dept., Rockingham, N.C., 1982-88; local health dir. Montgomery County Health Dept., Troy, N.C., 1988-92; nurse practitioner Richmond OBGYN, Rockingham, N.C., 1992-93, Bladen County Health Dept., 1993—; staff nurse, relief supr. Richmond Meml. Hosp., Rockingham, N.C., 1955-67; mem. Maternal-Health Liason Com., 1990-91, N.C. State Pers. Liason Com., 1990-91. Mem. ANA, N.C. Nurses Assn. (disting. achievement award dist. V 1986), N.C. Pub. Health Assn. (dist. 12), N.C. Assn. Local Health Dirs., N.C. Dist. V Perinatal Assn., Kiwanis, Sigma Theta Tau. Democrat. Presbyterian. Home: 471 Newport Dr Woodrun Mount Gilead NC 27306

MCNEILLY, JEAN CRAIG See **CRAIG, JEAN**

MCNICHOLAS, KATHLEEN WINIFRED, cardiac surgeon; b. Phila., May 5, 1948; d. Edward M. and Josephine (Nelezek) McN. BS with honors, Chestnut Hill Coll., 1969; MD magna cum laude, Thomas Jefferson U., 1973. Diplomate Am. Bd. Surgery, Am. Bd. Thoracic Surgery. Intern Presbyn. Hosp., N.Y.C., 1973-74, resident in gen. surgery, 1974-78, resident and chief resident thoracic and cardiovascular surgery, 1978-80; surg. ho. officer Hosp. for Sick Children, London, 1976, sr. registrar thoracic unit, 1980; attending physician United Hosp. Med. Ctr., 1981; attending physician

Deborah Heart and Lung Ctr., Brown Mills, N.J., 1981-85, dir. dept. pediats. thoracic and cardiovascular surgery, 1983-85, dir. pediat. ICU, 1983-85; attending physician dept. surgery sect. cardiovascular surgery Christiana Hosp., Newark, Del., 1986—, dir. pediat. cardiac surgery, 1987—; clin. asst. prof. Rutgers Med. Sch., Piscataway, N.J., 1984—; clin. assoc. prof. Med. Coll. Pa., Phila., 1987—; attending physician dept. surgery sect. cardiovascular surgery Grad. Hosp., Phila., 1985—, A.I. duPont Inst., Wilmington, Del., 1986—; presenter in field. Contbr. articles to profl. jours. Montgomery County Med. Soc. scholar, 1969-73. Fellow ACS, Am. Coll. Cardiology, Am. Coll. Chest Physicians, Am. Coll. Angiology (mem. sci. coun.); mem. AMA, Am. Heart Assn. (mem. coun. cardiovascular surgery), Pa. Assn. Thoracic Surgery, Pa. Acad. Cardiology, Pa. Acad. Cardiovascular Perfusion, Pa. Med. Soc., Del. Acad. Pediats., Del. Med. Soc., N.J. Soc. Thoracic Surgeons, Burlington Med. Soc., Assn. Women Surgeons, Acad. Medicine N.J., Colls. Phila. County Med. Soc., Hobart A. Hare Honor Med. Soc., John H. Gibbon Jr. Surg. Soc., Soc. Heart Transplantation, Soc. Thoracic Surgery. Roman Catholic. Home: 4 Rockland Mills Rockland DE 19732 Office: Med Arts Pavilion 4745 Stanton-Ogletown Rd Ste 2 Newark DE 19713-2070

MCNICOL, LOIS ELAINE, librarian; b. Wichita, Kans., Oct. 19, 1947; d. John L. and Elizabeth H. (Hall) Hager; m. Bruce W. Kilander, July 10, 1971 (dec. May 1975); 1 child, Melinda; m. Douglas K. McNicol, Apr. 11, 1979. BSE, Emporia State U., 1969, MLS, 1970. Cert. tchr., Pa. Libr. Lake County Pub. Libr., Merriville, Ind., 1969-74; sec., libr. asst. Wichita (Kans.) Pub. Schs., 1980-83, tchr., 1983-85; with Interboro Sch. Dist., Prospect Park, Pa., 1985-89, libr., 1989-93; libr. Garnet Valley Sch. Dist., Glen Mills, Pa., 1993—. Mem. ALA, Pa. Sch. Libr. Assn. (conf. com. 1985—), Delaware County Sch. Librs. Assn. (treas. 1989—). Republican. Congregationalist. Office: Garnet Valley High Sch 552 Smithbridge Rd Glen Mills PA 19342

MCNULTY, CYNTHIA DEIRDRE, environmental scientist; b. Bisbee, Ariz., Sept. 10, 1953; d. James Francis and Jacqueline Charlotte (Boevers) McN. BA, Scripps Coll., 1975; MS, U. Ariz., 1978; M in Internat. Mgmt., Thunderbird Coll., 1980. Tech. editor Du Pont Chemical Co., Aiken, S.C., 1980-82; long range planner Du Pont Chemical Co., Aiken, 1982-83; internal auditor Du Pont Chemical Co., Wilmington, Del., 1983-85, City of Phoenix, 1986-90; environ. cons. PRC Environ. Mgmt., Phoenix, 1991-93, Earth Tech., Tempe, Ariz., 1993—; mem. strategic planning team for Ariz. environ. cluster Govs. Strategic Plan for Econ. Devel., Phoenix, 1994. Mem. Ariz. Women in Internat. Trade (bd. dirs.). Home: 2700 N Hayden Apt 2071 Scottsdale AZ 85257 Office: Earth Tech 1501 W Fountainhead Tempe AZ 85282

MCNULTY, NANCY G(ILLESPIE), business writer, editor, management consultant; b. Greenville, Pa., May 1, 1919; d. Stanley A. and Bess (Anthony) Gillespie; m. Arthur P. McNulty, July 16, 1942 (dec. 1961); 1 child, Terence. BA, Thiel Coll., 1940; MA, NYU, 1948. Industry analyst Equity Corp., 1940-42; writer, researcher Time Inc., N.Y.C., 1942-45; internal cons., 1957-68; founder, dir. Internat. Survey of Mgmt. Edn., N.Y.C., 1968—; cons. Chase Bank World Info. Svc., Japan Soc., Am. Mgmt. Assn., Inst. for Advancement of Economy, Austria, The Conf. Bd., UN Dept. of Tech. Coop. for Devel., N.Y. State Commn. on Edn., Time Inc.; editor, writer, cons. mgmt. edn., 1968—; lectr. St. Thomas U. Editor: Training Managers-The International Guide, 1969, Management Education Programs-The World's Best, 1980, The International Directory of Executive Education, 1985; contbr. numerous articles to profl. jours. Ford Found. scholar, 1968, 78. Fellow Internat. Acad. Mgmt. (hon.); mem. N.Am. Mgmt. Coun. (v.p., editor newsletter 1990—), Internat. Cons. Found., European Found. Mgmt. Devel., Internat. Found. Action Learning (U.S. rep.), Acad. Internat. Bus., Acad. Mgt., Yale Club of N.Y.C. Episcopalian. Home and Office: K-104 Pennswood Village Newtown PA 18940

MCNULTY, ROBERTA JO, educational administrator; b. Cin., July 17, 1945; d. Edward Norman and Ruth Marcella (Glass) Stuebing; children: Meredith Corinne, Brian Edward, Stephen Barrett. BS in Edn., U. Cin., 1967; MA in Edn., Coll. of Mount St. Joseph, 1989; PhD in Ednl. Adminstrn. and Supervision, Bowling Green State U., 1993. Elem. tchr. St. Mary Sch., Urbana, Ohio, 1968; elem. tchr. Urbana (Ohio) City Schs., 1968-70, middle sch. tchr., 1970-71; off-campus liaison Mt. St. Joseph Coll., 1987-89; adj. faculty Bowling Green State U., 1990—; gen. edn. supr., testing coord. curriculum devel. and implementation Fulton County Office of Edn., Wauseon, Ohio, 1992—; Lamaze instr. Scioto Meml. Illustrated Lamaze Edn., Portsmouth, Ohio, 1983-84, Tiffin (Ohio) Childbirth Edn. Assn., 1984-87; mem. Project Discovery. Grad. editor Am. Secondary Edn., 1989-92. Sch. bd. mem. St. Mary Sch., Urbana, Ohio, 1971-75; parent adv. com. Wheelersburg (Ohio) Local Schs., 1978-84; parents coun. U. Evansville, 1990-93; exec. dir. Am. Cancer Soc., Tiffin, Ohio, 1985; treas. Parents' Boosters Club, Portsmouth YMCA, 1979-84; Y-Wives com. chairperson Tiffin-Cmty. YMCA, 1984-87. Recipient Doctoral fellowship Bowling Green State U., 1989-92, Svc. Appreciation award Cub Scouts, 1990-92. Mem. ASCD, Ednl. Leadership Assn., N.W. Ohio Assn. for Supervision and Curriculum Devel., Ohio Sch. Suprs. Assn., Ohio Coun. Tchrs. English Language Arts, Assn. Tchr. Educators, Ohio Assn. Tchr. Educators (nat. del.), Phi Delta Kappa. Office: Fulton County Office of Edn 602 S Shoop Ave Wauseon OH 43567-0338

MCNUTT, KRISTEN WALLWORK, consumer affairs executive; b. Nashville, Nov. 17, 1941; d. Gerald M. and Lee Wallwork; m. David McNutt, Sept. 13, 1969. BA in Chemistry, Duke U., 1963; MS in Nutrition, Columbia U., 1965; PhD in Biochemistry, Vanderbilt U., 1970; JD, DePaul U., 1984. Bar: N.Y. 1984, D.C. 1984. Exec. dir. Nat. Nutrition Consortium, Washington, 1979-81; asst. prof. pub. health U. Ill., Chgo., 1981-83; assoc. dir. Good Housekeeping Inst., N.Y.C., 1982-85; v.p. consumer affairs Kraft Inc., Glenview, Ill., 1985-87; pres. Consumer Choices Unltd. Inc., Evanston, 1988—. Author: Nutrition and Food Choices, 1979; editor: Sugars in Nutrition, 1975, Consumer Mags. Digest, 1989—. Bd. dirs. Better Bus. Bur. Chgo. and No. Ill., 1986-88; FDA Food Adv. Com., 1992-94. Mem. N.Y. Bar Assn., D.C. Bar Assn., Fedn. Am. Socs. Exptl. Biology (Congl. Sci. fellow), Soc. for Nutrition Edn. (pres. 1983-84), Am. Inst. Nutrition, Am. Dietetics Assn., Am. Coun. on Consumer Interests. Home and Office: Consumer Choices Inc 2272 Woodview Dr Ste 401 Ypsilanti MI 48198-6818

MCNUTT, MARCIA KEMPER, geophysicist; b. Mpls., Minn., Feb. 19, 1952; married, 1978; 3 children. BA, Colorado Coll., 1973; PhD, Scripps Inst. Oceanography, 1978. Geophysicist US Geol. Survey, 1979-82; asst. prof. geophysics MIT, 1982-86, assoc. prof., 1986—; vis. asst. prof. Univ. of Minn., 1978-79; mem. Sci. Steering Group Geopotential Rsch. Mission, NASA, 1978—, Geodesy Nat. Rsch. Coun. 1982-84, Tectonics Edit. Search Com. 1983, Geodynamics Com. 1984-87; assoc. editor Jour. Geophys. Rsch., 1980-83, guest editor, 1983; editl. bd. Tectonophysics, 1982—; mem. earth sci. com. Nat. Rsch. Coun., 1987—. Mem. Am. Geophys. Union (Macelevane award 1988), John Muir Geophys. Soc. (sec. 1979-83). Office: MIT Dept of Earth & Planetary Sci 77 Massachusetts Ave Cambridge MA 02139-3594*

MCPHEE, ESTHER RUTH, medical, surgical, geriatrics and oncology nurse; b. Kansas City, Mo., Mar. 20, 1951; d. Fred Bicknell and Mary Elizabeth (Williams) Crigler; 1 child, Scott Lee McPhee. ADN, Eastern N.Mex. U., Roswell, 1989. Cert. chemotherapy nurse. Staff nurse med. floor St. Mary's Hosp., Roswell, Eastern N.Mex. Med. Ctr., Roswell; night nurse Sunset Villa Care Ctr., Roswell; nurse supr. Turtle Creek Health Care Ctr., Jacksonville, Fla.; oncology staff nurse, active with dept. corrections unit Meml. Med. Ctr., Jacksonville. Mem. Merrill Rd. Bapt. Ch. Nursing Found. scholar. Mem. N.Mex. Nurses Assn. (publicity chmn. Dist. 5), Oncology Nurses Soc., Phi Theta Kappa (v.p.).

MCPHEE, SISTER JOHN GABRIEL, nurse; b. Woodrow, Colo., Feb. 24, 1917; d. Jess John and Agnes Ellen (Fitzgerald) McP. RN, St. Joseph (Mo.) Sch. Nursing, 1939; BS in Nursing Edn., La. State U., 1952. Operating rm. supr. Hotel Dieu Hosp., New Orleans, 1944-53; CEO Providence Hosp., Waco, Tex., 1953-58; exec. dir. St. Elizabeth's Infant Hosp., San Francisco, 1958-65; CEO St. Thomas Hosp., Nashville, 1965-69; regional health councillor Daus. of Charity, Evansville, Ind., 1969-81; pres. Daus. of Charity Nat. Health System, St. Louis, 1981-86; regional treas. Daus. of Charity-East Cen., Evansville, 1987-92; bd. chmn. Providence Hosp., Southfield, Mass., 1986-87; devel. asst. St. Mary's Hosp. Found., Milw., 1992—, also bd. dirs. Contbr. articles to profl. jours. Pres. Tex. Conf. of Cath. Hosps., Waco, 1956-57; com. mem. San Francisco Conf. of White House on Children and Youth, San Francisco, 1963; mem. gov.'s adv. com. on children and youth, San Francisco, 1960. Recipient Svcs. to Mankind award Gov. of Tenn., Nashville, 1969; named to Outstanding Woman of Yr., Nashville Jaycees, 1969. Mem. Am. Coll. Health Execs. (life). Roman Catholic. Office: Saint Marys Hosp PO Box 484 Milwaukee WI 53211

MCPHERSON, GAIL, advertising and real estate sales executive; b. Fort Worth; d. Garland and Daphne McP. Student U. Tex.-Austin; BA, MS, CUNY. Advt. sales exec. Harper's Bazaar mag., N.Y.C., 1974-76; sr. v.p., fashion mktg. dir. L'Officiel/USA mag., N.Y.C., 1976-80; fashion mgr. Town and Country mag., N.Y.C., 1980-82; v.p. advt. and mktg. Ultra mag., Tex. and N.Y.C., 1982-84; fragrance, jewelry and automotive mgr. M. Mag., N.Y.C., 1984-85; sr. real estate sales exec. Fredric M. Reed & Co., Inc., N.Y.C., 1985-88; AT&T security system rep. Home-Watch Inc., Amarillo, Tex.,1989-92; sales rep. Universal Comm., Dallas, 1992—. Sponsor Southampton Hosp. Benefit Com., N.Y.; mem. jr. com. Mannes Sch. Music, N.Y.C., Henry St. Settlement, N.Y.C. Mem. Fashion Group N.Y., Advt. Women N.Y., Real Estate Bd. N.Y., U. Tex. Alumni Assn. of N.Y. (v.p.), Amarillo C. of C. (Comm. com.). Republican. Presbyterian. Clubs: Corviglia (St. Moritz, Switzerland), Doubles, El Morocco (mem. jr. com. 1976-77), Le Club (N.Y.C.). Home: 10812 Stone Canyon Rd Apt 3143 Dallas TX 75230

MCPHERSON, VANZETTA PENN, federal judge; b. Montgomery, Ala., May 26, 1947; d. Luther Lincoln and Sadie Lee (Gardner) P.; m. Winston D. Durant, Aug. 17, 1968 (div. Apr. 1979); 1 child, Raegan Winston; m. Thomas McPherson Jr., Nov. 16, 1985. BS in Speech Pathology, Howard U., Washington, 1969; MA in Speech Pathology, Columbia U., 1971, JD, 1974. Bar: N.Y. 1975, Ala. 1976, U.S. Dist. Ct. (so. dist.) N.Y. 1975, U.S. Dist. Ct. (mid. dist.) Ala. 1980, U.S. Ct. Appeals (2d cir.) 1975, U.S. Ct. Appeals (11th cir.) 1981, U.S. Supreme Ct. Assoc. Hughes, Hubbard & Reed, N.Y.C., 1974-75; asst. atty. gen. Ala. Atty. Gen. Office, Montgomery, 1975-78; pvt. practice Montgomery, 1978-92; magistrate judge U.S. Dist. Ct. (mid. dist.) Ala., Montgomery, 1992—; co-owner Roots & Wings, A Cultural Bookplace, Montgomery, 1989—. Dir. Ala. Shakespeare Festival, Montgomery, 1987—; chmn. trustees Dexter Ave. King Meml. Bapt. Ch., Montgomery, 1988; chmn. Leadership Montgomery; bd. mem. Lighthouse Counseling Ctr., Montgomery, 1981-84, Montgomery County Pub. Libr., 1989-90; v.p. Lanier High Sch. Parent Tchr. Student Assn., Montgomery, 1990-91. Recipient cert. Ala. Jud. Coll.; named Woman of Achievement Montgomery Advertiser, 1989, Boss of Yr. Montgomery Assn. Legal Secs., 1992, Woman of Yr. Gamma Phi Delta, Montgomery, 1992, Citizen of Yr. Delta Sigma Theta, Montgomery, 1992. Mem. ABA (law office design award 1985), Nat. Bar Assn., Ala. State Bar Assn. (chmn. family law sect. 1989-90), N.Y. State Bar Assn., Montgomery Inn of Cts. (master bencher 1992—), Ala. Black Lawyers Assn. (pres. 1979-80). Office: US Dist Ct Mid Dist Ala PO Box 1629 15 Lee St Montgomery AL 36102*

MCQUAGE, CLARETTA DIANNE, surgical care administrator; b. Laurinburg, N.C., July 16, 1951; d. Horace Franklin and Clara M. (Walters) McQ. ADN, Florence-Darlington Tech. Coll. Charge nurse Security Forces Hosp., Riyadh, Saudi Arabia; head nurse King Fahad Hosp., Riyadh, charge nurse; same day surg. coord. Chesterfield Gen. Hosp., Cheraw, S.C. Recipient Cert. of Appreciation Am. Internat. Div.

MCQUAID, LUCILLE, brokerage firm account executive; b. Cleve., Sept. 24, 1928; d. Peter and Beatrice (Coughlin) McQuaid. BA, Case Western Reserve U., 1950; MBA, U. Calif., 1957. Personnel adminstr. Greyhound Corp., Cleve., 1950-55; acct. exec. Dean Witter Reynolds, San Francisco, 1957—. Sec.-treas. San Francisco Young Republicans, 1974-75. Mem. Bay Area Women in Finance (chmn. 1962-68, dir. 1968-75).

MCQUEEN, DINAH MARIE, accountant; b. Alto, Tex., July 9, 1962; d. Ernest Eugene and Marie (Dunsmore) McQ. BBA, Stephen F. Austin State U., 1984; MBA, U. Tex., Dallas, 1994. CPA, Tex. Acct. I, II, III Mobil Oil Corp., Dallas, 1984-90, corp. acct., 1991-92, supr., 1992-93; ABS staff Price Waterhouse, 1995—. Mem. adv. bd. New Horizons Theatre Co., Dallas, 1993—; chair fin. com. St. Stephen United Meth. Ch., Mesquite, Tex., 1992-94; mem. Campus Hispanic Assn., Richardson, Tex., 1994. Mem. Fin. Mgmt. Assn. (pres. 1993-94), Am. Woman's Soc. of CPAs (membership chair 1992-94), Eagles Toastmasters. Home: 325 Firecrest #2 Pacifica CA 94044

MCQUEEN, REBECCA HODGES, health care executive, consultant; b. Dothan, Ala., July 20, 1954; d. Edward Grey and Shirley Louise (Varner) Hodges; m. David Raymond McQueen, Mar. 5, 1982; children: Matthew David, Owen Grey. BS, Emory U., 1976, MPH, 1979. Research assoc. North Cen. Ga. Health Systems Agy., Inc., Atlanta, 1979-80; assoc. dir. Health Services Analysis, Inc., Atlanta, 1980-82; med. group adminstr. Southeastern Health Services, Inc./Prucare, Atlanta, 1982-84; sr. v.p., COO SouthCare Med. Alliance, Atlanta, 1985-93; pres., CEO PROMINA N.W. Health Network, Atlanta, 1993—; cons. North Cen. Ga. Health Systems Agy., 1980-81, Region 4 HHS, Atlanta, 1980-82, instr. Applied Stats., Washington, 1980-82; mem. Health Data com. and Health Cost subcom. Atlanta Healthcare Alliance, 1985—; cons. Atlanta Com. for the Olympic Games, 1992. Contbr. articles to profl. jours. Adviser to med. support panel Atlanta Com. for Olympic Games; mem. Morningside/Lenox Park Civic Assn., Friends of Atlanta-Fulton Pub. Libr., Atlanta Bot. Garden, Planned Parenthood-Atlanta, Ga. Coun. on Child Abuse, Atlanta Wellness Coun. Recipient rsch. award Nat. Conf. on High Blood Pressure Control, 1981; nominee Woman of Achievement award YWCA. Mem. APHA (women's caucus com., presenter 1980, 81), ACLU, NOW, Am. Coll. Healthcare Execs. (diplomate), Women Healthcare Execs., Am. Managed Care and Rev. Orgn. (presenter nat. conf. 1989), Am. Assn. Preferred Provider Orgns., Delta Omega, Delta Delta Delta. Democrat. Baptist. Office: PROMINA NW Health Network 1791 Mulkey Rd Ste 103 Austell GA 30001-1124

MCQUERN, MARCIA ALICE, newspaper publishing executive; b. Riverside, Calif., Sept. 3, 1942; d. Arthur Carlyle and Dorothy Louise (Krupke) Knopf; m. Lynn Morris McQuern, June 7, 1969. BA in Polit. Sci., U. Calif., Santa Barbara, 1964; MS in Journalism, Northwestern U., 1966. Reporter The Press-Enterprise, Riverside, 1966-72, city editor, 1972-74, capitol corrs., 1975-78, dep. mng. editor news, 1984-85, mng. editor news, 1985-87, exec. editor, 1988-94; pres., 1992—; asst. metro editor The Sacramento Bee, 1974-75; editor state and polit. news The San Diego Union, 1978-79, city editor, 1979-84; juror Pulitzer Prize in Journalism, 1982, 83, 92, 93. Mem. editorial bd. Calif. Lawyer mag., San Francisco, 1983-88. Bd. advisors U. Calif.-Berkeley Grad. Sch. Journalism, 1991—, U. Calif.-Riverside Grad. Sch. Mgmt., 1994—. Recipient Journalism award Calif. State Bar Assn., 1967, Sweepstakes award Twin Counties Press Club, Riverside and San Bernardino, 1972. Mem. Am. Soc. Newspaper Editors (bd. dirs. 1992—), Calif. Soc. Newspaper Editors (bd. dirs. 1988—), Calif. Newspaper Pubs. Assn. (bd. dirs. 1992—), Soc. Profl. Journalists, U. Calif.-Santa Barbara Alumni Assn. (bd. dirs. 1983-89). Home: 5717 Bedford Dr Riverside CA 92506-3404 Office: Press-Enterprise Co 3512 14th St Riverside CA 92501-3878

MCQUIE, SALLY ANN, mental health counselor, educator; b. St. Louis, Feb. 5, 1954; d. James Langdon and Suzanne (Mccawley) M.; m. Albert Ray Turner Jr., Feb. 28, 1976. BA in Bus. Mgmt., U. Md., Okinawa, Japan, 1981; MS in Mental Health Counseling, Troy State U., 1991. Russian linguist USAF, Monterey, Calif., 1975-76; ins. claims adjuster United Svcs. Auto Assocs., San Antonio, 1982-86; substitute tchr. Dept. Defense Schs., Stuttgart, Germany, 1986-87; instr. Big Bend C.C., Stuttgart, Germany, 1987-89; comp. lab. asst. Troy State U., Ft. Walton Beach, Fla., 1990-91; psychology instr. Phillips Jr. Coll., Huntsville, Ala., 1993—; vol. counselor Hope Place, Huntsville, Ala., 1992—. Airman USAF, 1975-76. Mem. NOW, AAUW.

MCQUINN, LINDA MARIE, waste management consultant; b. Malone, N.Y., Dec. 10, 1952; d. Douglas William and Beatrice Mary (Oakes) McQ.; children from previous marriage: Shawn P. Mix, Matthew J. Mix, Kelly M. Mix; m. Thomas Aaron Smith, Feb. 14, 1990. AA, Mater Dei Coll., Ogdensburg, N.Y., 1973; BA, Postdam (N.Y.) Coll., 1982; postgrad., Russell Sage Coll., 1989-93. Drafter City of Ogdensburg, N.Y., 1982; rsch. asst. Dept. of Engring., Ogdensburg, 1983; pres., bd. dirs. Cava Rape Crisis Ctr., Canton, N.Y., 1982-85, adminstrv. asst., 1988; constrn. specialist St. Lawrence Housing Coun., Canton, N.Y., 1986; planning cons. Sear-Brown Assocs., Canton, N.Y., 1987; recycling coord. St. Law County Solid Waste, Ogdensburg, 1988-91; adminstr. Glow Solid Waste Mgmt., Batavia, N.Y., 1991-93; pres., founder Tasmith Assocs., Inc., Ogdensburg, 1992—, cons., 1993—. Cub master Heuvelton (N.Y.) coun. Boy Scouts Am., 1985. Mem. N.Y. Assn. for Recycling, Am. Planning Assn., St. Lawrence County C. of C. Office: Tasmith Assocs Inc PO Box 544 Ogdensburg NY 13669-0544

MCRAE, CAROL ANNE, nurse, nursing administrator; b. Orillia, Ont., Can., Dec. 29, 1949; d. Ross Elliott and Mary Theresa (Leonard) McR.; m. Steve Alan Blanchette, Oct. 10, 1981 (div. 1989). Diploma in nursing, Wellesley Hosp. Sch. Nursing, Toronto, 1972; BSN with honors, U. Tex., El Paso, 1990, MSN, 1991. RN, Victoria, Australia, Ont., Can., La., Tex.; cert. CCRN, ACLS. Nursing office float Wellesley Hosp., Toronto, 1972-75; charge nurse Trillium Home for Aged, Orillia, Ont., Can., 1976-78; staff nurse, team leader, charge nurse Sunnybrook Med. Ctr., Toronto, 1978-81; staff nurse emergency rm. Humber Meml. Hosp., Toronto, 1982-88; anesthetic asst. Orsurg Mgmt. Ltd., Toronto, 1983-88; staff nurse critical care Providence Meml. Hosp., El Paso, Tex., 1988-92, adminstr. on duty, 1992-93, project coord. nursing resources, 1993-94; clin. case mgr. Mother Frances Hosp., Tyler, Tex., 1994; asst. adminstrv. officer patient svcs. South Muskoka Meml. Hosp., Bracebridge, Ont., Can., 1994—; clin. nurse specialist adult health Bd. Nurse Examiners, State of Tex., 1992; instr. basic cardiac life support Am. Heart Assn., Tex., 1994. Mem. AAUW, Am. Assn. Critical Care Nurses, Tex. Nurses Assn., Ont. Nurses Assn., Registered Nurses Assn. Ont., Tex. Orgn. Nurse Execs., Sigma Theta Tau, Alpha Chi, Golden Key, Wellesley Hosp. Sch. Nursing Alumni Assn., U. Tex. at El Paso Alumni Assn. Home: 27 Birch Dr, Washago, ON Canada L0K 2B0 Office: South Muskoka Meml Hosp, PO Box 1570, 75 Ann St, Bracebridge, ON Canada P1L1R6

MCRAE, KAREN K., state legislator; b. Detroit, Feb. 19, 1944; m. Gossett W. McRae; 2 children. BSL, Georgetown U., 1965. Mem. N.H. Ho. of Reps.; vice chmn. sci., tech. and energy com. Active Goffstown Conservation Com., 1972—, chmn., 1975-79. Mem. Georgetown U. Alumni Assn. (class rep. 1975—). Home: 469 Black Brook Rd Goffstown NH 03045 Office: NH Ho of Reps State Capitol Concord NH 03301*

MCREE, CELIA, composer; b. Memphis; d. John Louis and Leta Gwendolyn (Phillips) McR. Student, Phila. Coll. Art, 1976-77, Herbert Berghof Studio, 1989, Playwrights Horizon Theater, 1989; cert. with distinction, Nat. Acad. Paralegal Studies, Christian Bros. U., 1992. Pres. Mother Records, Memphis, 1984—, You Should Meet My Mother (Publishing), Memphis, 1984—, Wild Thing Music, Memphis, 1987—, Mother Prodns., Memphis, 1986—; producer, host Indian Talk, WEVL-FM90, Memphis, 1992—. Artist, group and solo exhbns. including Eads Gallery, Grover Cleveland Arts Inst., Phila. Mus. Natural History; screenwriter, film scoring; singer, writer (nat. album) including Celia McRee/Back From Under, 1985 (ASCAP Spl. Pop award 1985-86, 86-87), Celia McRee/Passion, 1994; composer, arranger, producer, pub. background and feature music ABC Network, Cable TV and Radio. Entertainer Vets. Bedside Network, N.Y.C., 1981. Recipient cert. of scholarly distinction Nat. Acad. for Paralegal Studies, 1992, cert. of appreciation United Music Heritage, 1990, spl. pop award ASCAP, 1982-84m, 87-93, Henrietta Hickman Morgan writing award DAR; named Female Pop Songwriter and Female Pop Vocalist, Entertainment-Indie Assn., 1994. Mem. AFTRA, ASCAP, Broadcast Music Inc. (pub. mem.), N.Y. Acad. Sci., Assn. Am. Indian Affairs, Nat. Mus. of the Am. Indian (charter), Environ. Def. Fund, Animal Legal Def. Fund, Greenpeace, Humane Soc. U.S., Mensa, Memphis Kennel Club. Office: Mother Prodns 5159 Wheelis Dr # 110 Memphis TN 38117-4519

MCREYNOLDS, BARBARA, artist; b. Omaha, May 5, 1956; d. Zachariah Aycock and Mary Barbara (McCulloh) McR.; m. Stephen Dale Dent, Mar. 12, 1983 (div. Dec. 30, 1992); children: Madeleine Barbara, Matthew Stephen; m. Ross Coleman, Oct. 16, 1993. Student, U. N.Mex., 1979, MA in Community and Regional Planning, 1984. Artist, 1986-92; lectr. U. N.Mex. Sch. of Architecture, Albuquerque, 1979-82, 91—; assoc. planner, urban designer City of Albuquerque Planning Div., 1982-84; city planner, urban designer City of Albuquerque, N.Mex. Redevel. Div., 1984-88; cons. City of Albuquerque Redevel. Dept., 1987-88; urban design cons. Southwest Land Rsch., Albuquerque, 1991. Columnist for "Kids and Art", 1990-92; author: Coors Corridor Plan (The Albuquerque Conservation Assn. urban design award 1984), Electric Facilities Plan, Downtown Core Revitalization Strategy and Sector Development Plan; contbg. author: Anasazi Architecture and American Design, 1994; contbr. articles to profl. publs.; exhibited in shows at Dartmouth St. Gallery, Brandywine Galleries, Albuquerque, Laurel Seth Gallery, Santa Fe, Chimayo (N.Mex.) Trade and Mercantile, Ruby Blakeney Gallery. Vol. art tchr. Chaparral Elem. Sch., Albuquerque, 1989-92. Recipient First Pl. for Pastels, 20th Ann. Nat. Small Painting Exhibition, N.Mex. Art League, 1991, Best of Show awards Pastel Soc. of N.Mex., 1990, Award of Merit, Pastel Soc. of S.W., 1989, TACA award for Urban Design, 1984. Mem. Pastel Soc. of Am., Pastel Soc. N.Mex. (pres. 1991-92). Democrat. Episcopalian. Office: U NMex Sch Architecture Univ Of New Mexico NM 87131

MCREYNOLDS, MARY ARMILDA, lawyer; b. Carthage, Mo., Sept. 2, 1946; d. Allen and Virginia Madeleine (Hensley) McR. BA, Mt. Holyoke Coll., 1968; JD, Georgetown U., 1971; LL.M., Harvard U., 1973. Bar: D.C. 1971, U.S. Ct. Appeals (D.C. cir.) 1971, U.S. Ct. Appeals (2d cir.) 1975, U.S. Ct. Appeals. (4th cir.) 1979, U.S. Ct. Appeals. (1st, 5th, 6th, 9th, 10th cirs.) 1980, U.S. Supreme Ct. 1980, U.S. Ct. Appeals. (11th cir.) 1981, U.S. Ct. Appeals (3d, 7th, 8th cirs.) 1983, U.S. Ct. Appeals (Fed. cir.) 1988. Law clk. U.S. Ct. Appeals for D.C. cir., 1971-72; assoc. Wilmer, Cutler & Pickering, Washington, 1973-77; sr. trial atty. civil div. fed. program br. U.S. Dept. Justice, 1977-79, mem. appellate staff, 1979-81; ptnr. McReynolds & Mutterperl, Washington, 1981-83, Wilner & Scheiner, 1983-89, Haley, Bader & Potts, 1989-92; prin. Law Offices of Mary A. McReynolds, P.C. 1992—. Bd. dirs., gen. counsel Washington Bach Consort, 1977-81, 1985-92, pres. 1981-82, 89-90; pres. Calla, 1993—. Mem. ABA, Fed. Communications Bar Assn., Am. Soc. Legal History, Kenwood Club, City Tavern Club. Episcopalian. Contbr. articles to profl. jours. Home: 2101 Connecticut Ave NW Apt 26 Washington DC 20008-1754 Office: 888 16th St NW Ste 400 Washington DC 20006-4103

MC REYNOLDS, MARY BARBARA, secondary school educator; b. Los Angeles, Feb. 18, 1930; d. Clyde C. and Dorothy (Slaten) McCulloh; m. Zachariah A. McReynolds, Feb. 9, 1952 (dec.); children: Gregg Clyde, Barbara, Zachariah A.; m. John Richard Street, May 7, 1994. BA, U. N.Mex., 1951, MA, 1972, Edn. Specialist, 1975, postgrad., 1981—. Dept. sec. USAF Intelligence, Wiesbaden, W. Ger., 1953-54; tchr. Annandale (Va.) Elem. Sch., 1962-65, supr. adult edn., 1965-66; tchr. Albuquerque High Sch., 1968-77, 79-91, social studies curriculum dir., 1973-75; instr. U. N.Mex., Albuquerque, 1975-76, acad. decathlon coach Albuquerque High Sch., 1986-91; evaluator N. Central Assn., 1970-81, dir. Cultural Awareness Workshop, 1976, 79; coord. Sex Equality, 1979, 80. Bd. dirs. Greater U. N.Mex. Fund, 1978-79, 79-80, fund raiser, 1976-81, pres. club, 1977-80; campaign mgr. state senatorial campaign, 1976; exec. sec. Civic Assn., 1958-60; sponsor Black Student Union, 1978-80; sponsor Boys and Girls State, 1968-75; rep. Am. Fedn. Tchrs., 1982-91; sponsor Close-Up, 1987—; precinct chmn. Democratic Party, Albuquerque, 1985-86; mem. exec. bd. Albuquerque Rehab. Ctr., 1993-95. Indian research and tuition edn. grantee, 1971; grantee U. N.Mex., 1975-76, others. Mem. Assn. Supervision and Curriculum Devel., Nat. Social Studies Council, N.Mex. Social Studies Council, Phi Kappa Phi, Phi Delta Kappa, Pi Alpha Theta, Kappa Kappa Gamma. Democrat. Episcopalian. Clubs: N.Mex. Democratic Women, Air Force Officers Wives, Kappa Kappa Gamma Alumni (pres. 1991-93, chmn. ways and means com. 1994, Outstanding Alumna award 1994). Condr. research in field. Home: 749 Tramway Ln NE Albuquerque NM 87122-1601

MCREYNOLDS, MARY MAUREEN, municipal environmental administrator, consultant; b. Tacoma, July 15, 1940; d. Andrew Harley and Mary

Leone (McGuire) Sims; m. Gerald Aaron McReynolds, Dec. 10, 1964. Student Coll. Puget Sound, 1957-59; BA, U. Oreg., 1961; PhD, U. Chgo., 1966; postgrad. San Diego State U., 1973-75. NIH postdoctoral fellow U. Tex., Austin, 1966-68, mem. adj. faculty, 1980-82, mem. biohazards com., 1981—; research assoc. Stanford U., Calif., 1968-71; chemist assoc. Syva Co., Palo Alto, Calif., 1972; environ. specialist County of San Diego, Calif., 1973-75; dept. head City of Austin, 1976-84, chief environ. officer, 1984-85, utility environ. mgr., 1985-92, mgr. environ. and regulatory support, 1992—; dir. Ctr. for Environ. Rsch., 1992—; part-time mem. faculty Austin Community Coll., 1993—; cons. ecologist Mirassou Vineyards, San Jose, Calif., 1969-72; lectr. Wright Inst., Berkeley, Calif., 1971-72; instr. San Diego State U., 1974-75. Editor Dist. 56 newsletter, 1989-90; contbr. articles to profl. publs. Mem. Austin-Satillo Sister City Assn., 1980—; U.S.-Mexico Sister Cities del., 1983-85; sponsor, chaperone Tex.-South Australia Youth Exchange, 1986; active Leadership Austin, 1987-88; mem. Austin-Adelaide Sister City Com., 1986—, chmn., 1989-91, sec., 1992—; bd. dirs. Internat. Hospitality Com., 1989—. USPHS tng. grantee U. Chgo., 1961-64; univ. fellow U. Chgo., 1961-66. Mem. NAFE, AAAS, Water Environment Fedn. (v.p. local chpt. 1988-89, pres.-elect 1989-90, pres. 1990-91, sect. rep. 1991-94), Am. Planning Assn., Am. Inst. Cert. Planners (cert.), Assn. Environ. Profls., Am. Water Resources Assn., Tex. Assn. Met. Sewage Agys. (sec. 1994, v.p. 1995), Austin Soc. Pub. Adminstrn., Zeta Tau Alpha. Lodges: Soroptimists (dir. Soroptimist Manor 1978-80, 83-85, v.p. chpt. 1983-85, pres. chpt. 1985-87, chpt. dir. 1987-88, rep. youth citizenship award com. 1986-88, chmn. South Cen. region UN com. 1988-90, rep. youth forum com. 1990-92), Toastmasters (club pres. 1981, 88, area gov. 1981-82, div. lt. gov. 1982-83, Able Toastmaster award 1983, Dist. 56 Table Topics award 1986, Disting. Toastmaster award 1987, Outstanding Toastmaster Dist. 56 no. divsn. 1987, Able Toastmaster Bronze award 1993). Avocations: gourmet food and wine. Office: City of Austin PO Box 1088 Austin TX 78767-8801

MCREYNOLDS, PAMELA KAY, controller; b. Knoxville, Tenn., July 19, 1953; d. Harold Edward and Betty Jane (Badgett) McR. BS, U. Tenn., 1975; MBA, Berry Coll., 1979. Acct. Ala. Kraft Co., Mahrt, 1975; corp. acct. Ga. Kraft Co., Rome, 1979-81, ops. acctg. supr., 1981-86, fin. acctg. mgr., 1987-88; mgr. MIS Holliston Mills, Inc., Kingsport, Tenn., 1988-90, controller, 1991-92; controller Elo TouchSys., Inc., Oak Ridge, Tenn., 1992—; mem. adv. bd. S.I. Users Group, Boston, 1983-88; seminar leader. Republican. Baptist. Office: Elo TouchSys Inc 105 Randolph Rd Oak Ridge TN 37830-5028

MCROBBIE, BONNIE JEAN, lawyer; b. Pitts., Nov. 19, 1949; d. Henry William and Betty Louise (Wilson) McR.; 1 child, Heather Victoria. Diploma Deestudios Hispanicos, U. De Madrid, 1970; BA magna cum laude, Randolph-Macon Womans Coll., 1971; JD, Cornell U., 1975. Bar: Pa. 1976, U.S. Dist. Ct. (we. dist.) Pa. 1976, U.S. Dist. Ct. (mid. dist.) Pa. 1979, Calif. 1980, U.S. Dist. Ct. (cen. dist.) Calif. 1980, U.S. Ct. Appeals (3d and D.C. cirs.) 1980, U.S. Supreme Ct. 1980. Jud. clk. Commonwealth Ct. of Pa., Pitts., 1976; asst. atty. gen. counsel Pa. Dept. of Banking, Harrisburg, Pa., 1976-80; sr. assoc. Mon & Ota, L.A., 1980-83; assoc. gen. counsel Coast Svgs. and Loan, L.A., 1983-85; sr. counsel Meri Bank, Phoenix, 1985-86; v.p., sr. counsel Wells Fargo & Co., San Francisco, 1986—. Past chmn. Whittier (Calif.) Babysitting Coop., 1986—. Mem. Calif. Bar Assn. (chmn. subcom. on subsidiaries 1984—), Pa. Bar Assn. (legal edn. com., bar admission com. 1977-80). Episcopalian. Office: Wells Fargo & Co Legal Dept # 6702 111 Sutter St 20th fl San Francisco CA 94163*

MCROBERTS, JOYCE, state legislator; b. Salmon, Idaho, July 31, 1941; m. Darrel S. McRoberts; children: Walter, Angela, Douglas. Ed., Twin Falls Bus. Coll. Senate maj. leader Idaho State Senate. Republican. Home: PO Box 2016 Twin Falls ID 83303-3855

MCSHIRLEY, SUSAN RUTH, gift industry executive, consultant; b. Glendale, Calif., July 31, 1945; d. Robert Claude and Lillian Dora (Mable) McS. BS, U. Calif.-Berkeley, 1967. Nat. sales dir. McShirley Products, Glendale, Calif., 1967-71, Viade Products, Camarillo, Calif., 1972-80; pres. SRM Press, Inc., L.A., 1980—; nat. sales cons. Warner Bros. Records, Burbank, Calif., 1985. Author: Racquetball: Where to Play, USA, 1978; patentee picture pen; creator novelty trademarks including The Pig Pen, The Road Hog, DFZ/Drug Free Zone, Tobacco Free Zone, Protect Our Planet. Mem. Calif. Alumni Assn., Alpha Omicron Pi. Avocations: travel, photography, tennis, foreign languages. Home: 15947 Temecula St Pacific Palisades CA 90272-4239 Office: SRM Press Inc 4216 Glencoe Ave Marina Del Rey CA 90292-5612

MCSTEEN, MARTHA ABERNATHY, organization executive; b. Iowa Park, Tex., May 25, 1923; d. King Peyton and Iva Mae (Dawson) Abernathy; m. George Steven McSteen, Oct. 13, 1943 (dec. Jan. 1945); m. Marshall Parks, Apr. 6, 1991. BA, Rice U., 1944; MA, U. Okla., 1972; JD (hon.), Austin Coll., 1985. Claims rep., supr. and dist. mgr. Social Security Adminstrn., Dallas, 1947-65, regional commr., 1976-83; acting commr. Social Security Adminstrn., Washington, 1983-86; regional adminstr. Medicare, Denver and Dallas, 1965-76; cons. Nat. Com. To Preserve Social Security and Medicare, Dallas, 1987-89, pres., 1989—; U.S. rep. to Internat. Social Security Assn., 1985, 86. Bd. dirs. Buck Found., San Francisco, 1991—, Setting Priorities for Retirement Yrs. Found., Washington, 1991—, Prevention of Blindness Found., Washington, 1993—. Recipient Commr.'s citation Social Security Adminstrn., 1961, 66, 71, Disting. Svc. award HEW, 1979, Presdl. Meritorious Exec. award, 1980, Nat. Pub. Svc. award Am. Soc. for Pub. Adminstrn., 1986, Presdl. Disting. Exec. award, 1987; fellow Social Security Adminstrn., 1968-69. Office: Nat Com Preserve Social Security & Medicare 2000 K St NW # 800 Washington DC 20006-1873

MCSWEENEY, FRANCES KAYE, psychology educator; b. Rochester, N.Y., Feb. 6, 1948; d. Edward William and Elsie Winifred (Kingston) McS. BA, Smith Coll., 1969; MA, Harvard U., 1972, PhD, 1974. Lectr. McMaster U., Hamilton, Ont., Can., 1973-74; asst. prof. Wash. State U., Pullman, 1974-79, assoc. prof., 1979-83, prof. psychology, 1983—, chmn. dept. psychology, 1986-94; cons. in field. Contbr. articles to profl. jours. Woodrow Wilson fellow, Sloan Fellow, 1968-69; NSF fellow, 1970-72; NIMH fellow, 1973. Fellow Am. Psychol. Assn., Am. Psychol. Soc.; mem. Western Psychol. Assn., Psychonomic Soc., Assn. Behavior Analysis, Phi Kappa Phi, Phi Beta Kappa, Sigma Xi. Home: SW 860 Alcora Pullman WA 99163 Office: Wash State U Dept Psychology Pullman WA 99164-4820

MCTERNAN, ANN CIBUZAR, adult nurse practitioner; b. Brainerd, Minn., Nov. 26, 1950. BS in Family Social Sci., U. Minn., 1973; BSN, U. N.C., Greensboro, 1976; MSN, George Mason U., Fairfax, Va., 1990. RN, Va., Md., Calif., Minn., Washington; cert. adult nurse practitioner. Mem. nursing staff U.S. Naval Hosp., Beaufort, S.C., 1976-77, Eskaton Monterey Hosp., Monterey, Calif., 1977-78; staff Drug Enforcement Adminstrn., Bangkok, 1978-80; mem. nursing staff US Naval Hosp., Okinawa, Japan, 1981-82; mem. nursing staff. St. Joseph's Med. Ctr., Brainerd, 1986-87, Potomac Hosp., Woodbridge, Va., 1987-90, Marymount U., Arlington, Va., 1989-90; low impact/expectant mothers aerobic instr. Saratoga Dance Ctr., Springfield, Va., 1990-94; adult nurse practitioner Prime Care, Annandale, Va., 1991—; master mem. IDEA Found., San Diego, 1990—; aerobic fitness instr. Am. Coun. on Exercise, San Diego, 1990—. Mem. AAUW, Am. Coll. Sports Medicine, Am. Coun. on Exercise, Exer-Safety Assn., Am. Acad. Nurse Practitioners. Home: c/o Cibuzar #202 727 SW 4th St Brainerd MN 56401

MCTIGUE, TERESA ANN, biologist, researcher, educator; b. Washington, July 9, 1962; d. William Edward and Bernice Ann (Bakajza) McT. BS in Zoology, U. Md., 1984; MS in Marine Sci., U. S.C., 1986; PhD in Wildlife and Fisheries Scis., Tex. A&M U., 1993. Lab. asst. U. Md., College Park, 1981-83; rsch. asst. U. S.C., Columbia, 1984-86; staff biologist Sea Camp, Galveston, Tex., 1988-93; fisheries biologist Nat. Marine Fisheries Svc., Galveston, 1987-93, Lafayette, La., 1993—. Contbr. articles to profl. jours. Recipient Grad. Rsch. award Sea Grant, 1986. Mem. Estuarine Rsch. Fedn., Am. Fisheries Soc., Sigma Xi. Democrat. Roman Catholic. Office: NMFS Lafayette Office PO Box 42451 Lafayette LA 70504-2451

MCVAY, ELLEN M., nursing administrator; b. Kenmare, N.D., Sept. 26, 1946; d. Harry M. and Catherine E. (Ennis) Enget; m. John McVay, Aug. 13, 1966; children: Scott, Andrew, Allison. Diploma, Trinity Hosp. Sch. Nursing, Minot, N.D., 1967; BSN, U. Minn., 1981, MS in Nursing Adminstrn., 1983. RN, Minn. Staff nursing supr. various hosps., Calif., Oreg., Minn., 1967-81; asst. dir. nursing Met. Mt. Sinai Med. Ctr., Mpls., 1981-84; exec. dir. 3d Dist. Minn. Nurses Assn., Monticello, 1984-92; writer, auditor Found. for Health Care Evaluation, Minn.; condr. nursing edn. seminars, summer 1983; sexual health counselor; presenter in field; clin. adminstr. Salvation Army Harbor Lights Shelter. Contbr. articles to Press Agt. Bd. dirs. Met. Mpls. YWCA, 1985-89; program dir. Detox-Receiving and Referral Crisis Mental Health Unit, St. Cloud, Minn.; active Boy Scouts Am. Recipient Valued Vol. award Salvation Army, 1987. Mem. Minn. Nurses Assn. (Creative Nursing award 1987), 3d Dist. Minn. Nurses Assn., Minn. Soc. Assn. Execs., Minn. Assn. Resources for Recovery and Mental Health (bd. dirs. 1994), U. Minn. Nurses Alumni Assn. (bd. dirs. 1990—), Lioness (pres. Monticello 1987), Sigma Theta Tau (chpt. program chmn. 1989). Methodist. Home: PO Box 425 Monticello MN 55362-0425

MCVAY, MARY FRANCES, portfolio manager; b. Washington, Sept. 17, 1955; d. Joseph J. and Stella F. (Walejko) McVay; m. Theodore R. Rosenberg, Sept. 21, 1991. BS in Acctg., Va. Tech., 1978, MBA, 1981. CPA; CFA. Auditor CIA, Washington, 1975-83; sr. cons. Booz, Allen & Hami ton, Arlington, Va., 1983-85; portfolio mgr. Burney Mgmt. Co., Danbury, Conn., 1985—. Mem. Inst. Mgmt. Accts. (dir. newsletter 1992-93, dir. mem. acquisition 1993-94, Svc. award 1993, Perfect Attendance award 1993), Assn. Investment, Mgmt. and Rsch. Office: Burney Mgmt Co 123 Rowell Ct Falls Church VA 22046

MCVEETY, CATHERINE SMITH, academic administrator, fundraiser; b. Great Falls, Mont., Apr. 29, 1963; d. Thomas Charles Sr. and Grace Barbara (Hopkins) S.; m. John Allen McVeety, Jr., Apr. 23, 1994. BA in Polit Sci., U. Oreg., 1987. Coord. telefund U. Oreg., Eugene, 1982-85; spl. events coord. Eastside Cath. High Sch., Bellevue, Wash., 1985-86, dir. ann. giving, 1986-87, assoc. dir. devel., 1987-88; dir. ann. giving U. Portland, 1988—, bd. dirs. vol. svcs. com., 1991—; dir. regional devel. Wash. State U. at Vancouver, 1992—. Vol. Christmas in April, Portland, 1991—; bd. dirs. Grant House Folk Art Ctr., 1993—. Recipient Design Merit award Internat. Assn. Bus. Communicators, 1990. Mem. Coun. for Advancement and Support of Edn. (chair dist. VIII conf. 1991—, bd. dirs. 1988—, chair recognition and awards program 1989-92, Grand gold award, Bronze award fund raising publs. 1990, Silver award fundraising direct mail 1989, Bronze award pub. rels. projects 1995), Wilamette Valley Devel. Officer, U. Oreg. Alumni Assn. (pres. Puget Sound chpt. 1987-88), City Club. Democrat. Roman Catholic. Office: Wash State U at Vancouver 1812 E Mcloughlin Blvd Vancouver WA 98663-3509

MCVEIGH-PETTIGREW, SHARON CHRISTINE, communications consultant; b. San Francisco, Feb. 6, 1949; d. Martin Allen and Frances (Roddy) McVeigh; m. John Wallace Pettigrew, Mar. 27, 1971; children: Benjamin Thomas, Margaret Mary. B.A. with honors, U. Calif.-Berkeley, 1971; diploma of edn. Monash U., Australia, 1975; M.B.A., Golden Gate U., 1985. Tchr., adminstr. Victorian Edn. Dept., Victoria, Australia, 1972-79; supr. Network Control Ctr., GTE Sprint Communications, Burlingame, Calif., 1979-81, mgr. customer assistance, 1981-84, mgr. state legis. ops., 1984-85, dir. revenue programs, 1986-87; communications cons. Flores, Pettigrew & Co., San Mateo, Calif., 1987-89; mgr. telemarketing Apple Computer, Inc., Cupertino, Calif., 1989—; telecommunications speaker Dept. Consumer Affairs, Sacramento, 1984. Panelist Wash. Gov.'s Citizens Council, 1984; founding mem. Maroondah Women's Shelter, Victoria, 1978; organizer nat. conf. Bus. Women and the Polit. Process, New Orleans, 1986; mem. sch. bd. Boronia Tech. Sch., Victoria, 1979. Recipient Tchr. Spl. Responsibilities award Victoria Edn. Dept., 1979. Mem. Women in Telecommunications (panel moderator San Francisco 1984), Am. Mgmt. Assn., Peninsula Profl. Women's Network, Am. Telemktg. Assn. (bd. dirs. 1992), Women's Econ. Action League. Democrat. Roman Catholic. Office: 445 Georgetown Ave San Jose CA 94402-2251

MCVEY, DIANE ELAINE, accountant; b. Wilmington, Del., Apr. 20, 1953; d. C. Granville and Margaret M. (Lindell) McV. AA in Acctg., Goldey Beacom Coll. (Del.), 1973, BS in Acctg., 1980; MBA in Mgmt., Fairleigh Dickinson U., 1985. Acct. Audio Visual Arts, Wilmington, 1973; cost acct. FMC Corp., Kennett Sq., Pa., 1973-75; asst. acct. NVF Corp., Kennett Sq., 1978-80; staff analyst GPU Nuclear, Parsippany, N.J., 1980-93; staff acct., 1993—; owner, Demac Cons., Dover, N.J., 1988—. Elder First Presbyn. Ch., Rockaway, N.J., 1986—, session mem., 1988-91; commr. to bd. adjustment, Dover, N.J., 1994—. With U.S. Army, 1975-78. Mem. Assn. MBA Execs. Republican. Presbyterian.

MCVICAR, SHERRY FISHER, human resources executive; b. N.Y.C., Sept. 17, 1952; d. William Sidney and Beverly (Harris) Miller; m. Allan A McVicar III, July 28, 1986. BA, Hofstra U., 1973; MS, Queens Coll., 1976. With Cox & Co., Inc., N.Y.C., 1973-76; mgr. tng. and labor rels. Quantor Corp., Mountain View, Calif., 1976-78; v.p. human resources Qume Corp., San Jose, Calif., 1978-87, Convergent, Inc., San Jose, 1987-91; group v.p. human resources Unisys Network Computing Group, San Jose, 1989-90; v.p. human resources Unisys Computer Systems Product Group, San Jose, 1990-91, Read-Rite Corp., Milpitas, Calif., 1991—; cons. in field; speaker on labor rels. Recipient of 1992 YWCA Twin award. Mem. Am. Arbitration Assn. Office: READ-RITE Corp PO Box 6685 345 Los Coches St Milpitas CA 95035-5428

MCVICKER, MARY ELLEN HARSHBARGER, museum director, art history educator; b. Mexico, Mo., May 5, 1951; d. Don Milton and Harriet Pauline (Mossholder) Harshbarger; m. Wiley Ray McVicker, June 2, 1973; children: Laura Elizabeth, Todd Michael. BA with honors, U. Mo., 1973, MA, 1975, PhD, Columbia, Mo., 1989. Instr. Columbia U., Mo., 1977-78, Cen. Meth. Coll., Fayette, Mo., 1978-85, mus. dir., 1980-85; project dir. Mo. Com. for Humanities, Fayette, 1981-85, Mo. Dept. Natural Resources Office Hist. Preservation, 1978-85; owner, Memories of Mo. & Tour Tyme, Inc., 1986—; prof. history Kemper Mil. Coll., 1993—. Author: History Book, 1984. V.p. Friends Hist. Boonville, Mo., 1982-87, pres., 1989-90; bd. dirs. Mus. Assocs. Mo. U., Columbia, 1981-83, Mo. Meth. Hist. Soc., Fayette, 1981-84; chmn. Bicentennial Celebration Methodism, Boonville, Mo., 1984; pres. Arts & Sci. Alumni, U. Mo., 1992—; bd. dirs. Mo. Humanities Coun., 1993—. Mem. Mo. Alliance for Hist. Preservation (charter), AAUW (treas. 1977-79), Am. Assn. Museums, Centralia Hist. Soc. (project dir. 1978), Mus. Assocs. United Meth. Ch. (charter, bd. dir. 1981-83), Phi Beta Kappa, Mortar Bd. Democrat. Clubs: Women's (treas. 1977-79), United Meth. Women's Group (charter mem.). Avocations: collecting antiques, gardening, family farming, singing, travelling. Home: 22151 Highway 98 Boonville MO 65233-9802 Office: Memories of Mo Inc PO Box 228 Boonville MO 65233-0228

MCWETHY, PATRICIA JOAN, educational executive; b. Chgo., Feb. 27, 1946; d. Frank E. and Emma (Kuehne) McW.; m. H. Frank Eden; children: Kristin Beth, Justin Nicholas. BA, Northwestern U., 1968; MA, U. Minn., 1970; MBA, George Washington U., 1981. Geog. analyst CIA, McLean, Va., 1970-71; research asst. NSF, Washington, 1972-74, spl. asst. to dir., 1975; assoc. program dir. human geography and regional sci. program NSF, 1976-79; exec. dir. Assn. Am. Geographers, Washington, 1979-84, Nat. Assn. Biology Tchrs., Reston, Va., 1984-95; pres., CEO Eden Ednl. Enterprises, 1995—; prin. investigator NSF grant on biotechnology equip. ednl. resource partnership, 1989-93, NSF funded internat. symposium on "Basic Biol. Concepts: What Should the World's Children Know?", 1992-94; chmn. adv. com. Nat. Com. Sci. Standards & Assessment, 1992—; mem. Commn. for Biology Edn., Internt. Union Biol. Sci., 1988—; mem. exec. com. Alliance for Environ. Edn., 1987-90, chmn. program com. 1990; conductor seminars in field; lectr. in field. Author monograph and papers in field; editor handbook. Recipient Outstanding Performance award, NSF, 1973; NSF fellow, 1968-69. Mem. Am. Soc. Assn. Execs., Phi Beta Kappa.

MCWHIRTER, GLENNA SUZANNE (NICKIE MCWHIRTER), newspaper columnist; b. Peoria, Ill., June 28, 1929; d. Alfred Leon and Garnet Lorene (Short) Sotier; m. Edward Ford McWhirter (div.); children: Suzanne McWhirter Orlicki, Charles Edward, James Richard. BS in English Lang. and Lit., U. Mich., postgrad., 1960-63. Editl. asst. McGraw-Hill Pub. Co., Detroit, 1951-54; staff writer Detroit Free Press, Inc., Detroit, 1963-88; columnist Detroit News Inc., Detroit, 1988—; advt. copy writer Campbell-Ewald Co., Detroit, 1967-68. Author: Pea Soup, 1984. Winner 1st Place Commentary award UPI, Mich., 1979; 1st Place Columns AP, Mich., 1978, 81; 1st Place Columns Detroit Press Club Found., Mich., 1978; Disting. Service award State of Mich., 1985. Mem. Women in Comm. (Headliner award 1978), Detroit Press Club, Alpha Gamma Delta. Home: 88 Meadow Ln Grosse Pointe MI 48236-3803

MCWHORTER, KATHLEEN, orthodontist; b. Houston, May 29, 1953; d. Archer and Lucile (Taft) McW. BA summa cum laude, U. Houston, 1986; DDS with honors, Baylor Coll., 1990. Mgr. Am. Internat. Rent-A-Car, Houston, 1974-79; mktg. researcher Concoco Oil Co., Houston, 1979-83; orthodontist Baylor Coll. Dentistry, Dallas, 1990—; presenter Am. Assn. Dental Rsch., Montreal, Que., Can., 1988, Cin., 1990; rsch. fellow Baylor Coll. Dentistry, Dallas, 1987, 88, 89. Contbr. articles to profl. jours. Mem. ADA, Am. Assn. Orthodontists, Am. Assn. Women Dentists, Am. Assn. Dentistry for Children, Internat. Assn. Dental Rsch., Am. Assn. Dental Rsch., Tex. Dental Assn., Dallas County Dental Soc., The Crescent Club. Office: Baylor U Coll Dentistry Dept Orthodontics 3302 Gaston Ave Dallas TX 75246-2013

MCWHORTER, RUTH ALICE, counselor, marriage and family therapist; b. Norfolk, Va., May 14, 1946; d. Lester Arthur and Mabel Winifred (Hopwood) Gorman; m. R. Dale Lawhorn, Jan. 6, 1972 (div. Nov. 1979); m. Brent Wilson McWhorter, Aug. 16, 1986; stepchildren: Daniel Chastin, Kenley Reid, Scott Jason. BA in Edn., Ariz. State U., 1970, M of Counseling Psychology, 1979. Cert. profl. counselor, Ariz., cert. marriage and family therapist, Ariz. Tchr. lang. arts Globe (Ariz.) Mid. Sch., 1969-72; tchr. English Isaac Jr. High Sch., Phoenix, Ariz., 1973-74; real estate salesperson Ben Brooks & Assocs., Phoenix, 1975-76, Century 21 Metro, Phoenix, 1976-77; overnight counselor The New Found., Phoenix, 1978-80; family therapist Youth Svc. Bur., Phoenix, 1980-81; owner, corp. officer, psychotherapist Family Devel. Resources, P.C., Phoenix, 1981—; cons., vol. counselor Deseret Industries, Phoenix, 1992—. Bd. dirs. Westside Mental Health Svcs., Phoenix, 1982-87; vol. facilitator Ariz. Multiple Sclerosis Soc., Phoenix, 1988. Mem. ACA, Internat. Assn. Marriage and Family Therapists, Am. Assn. Marriage and Family Therapists, Am. Mental Health Counselors Assn., Ariz. Counselors Assn., Ariz. Mental Health Counselors Assn. (sec.-treas. ctrl. chpt. 1982, sec. ctrl. chpt. 1995), Am. Assn. Christian Counselors, Assn. Mormon Counselors and Psychotherapists. Office: Family Devel Resources PC PO Box 55291 Phoenix AZ 85078-5291

MCWHORTER, SHARON LOUISE, business executive, inventor, consultant; b. Detroit, Feb. 22, 1951; d. Leroy Byron Harris Jr. and Josiebell (Richards) Harris Aaron; m. Abner McWhorter II, Mar. 15, 1969 (div. Aug. 1974); 1 child, Abner III. BA, Wayne State U., 1988; cert., SBA, Detroit, 1978; cert. in sound engring. Detroit Rec. Inst., Warren, Mich., 1982. Directory asst. Mich. Bell Telephone Co., Detroit, 1969; quality control clk. Chevrolet Gear & Axle, Detroit, 1971-74; circulation clk. Wayne County Community Coll., Detroit, 1977-85, mem. library standing com. and open house com., 1983-84; pres. Galactic Concepts & Designs, Detroit, 1977-88, cons., 1983—; gen. ptnr., mgr. S.M.J. Corridor Devel., Detroit, 1982—, hist. researcher, 1982; del. Small Bus. Conf., 1981; ad-hoc mem. Minority Tech. Council, 1981-82; elected alt. Mich. del. White House Conf. on Small Bus., Washington, 1985-86. Author, editor Creative Dilemma newsletter, 1985—. Co-patentee cup holding apparatus. Vol. counselor Barat House/March of Dimes, Detroit, 1977; active Concerned Citizens Cass Corridor, Detroit, 1982-87, Cass Corridor Citizen's Patrol, Detroit, 1983-84; pres. Wayne County chpt. Mothers Against Drunk Driving, Mich., 1987-88; apptd. citizen review com., 1988—; mem. adv. bd. Neighborhood Family Initiative, Southeastern Community Found.; pres. Am. Res. Tng. Sys., Inc., 1990—; lectr., cons. Recipient Hist. Landmark award Dept. Interior, 1983, cert. appreciation Tri-County Substance Abuse Awareness Com., 1984. Mem. Inventors Council Mich. (bd. dirs. 1985-88), Black Women in Bus. (sec. 1984-85), Greater Detroit C. of C., South Cass Bus. Assn. (v.p. 1987-88, pres. 1988-89), Detroit Econ. Club. Democrat. Methodist. Avocations: inventing; writing, re-adaptive furniture design, photography, video production. Office: SMJ Corridor Devel Co 453 Myrtle St Ste 102 Detroit MI 48201

MCWILLIAMS, CHRIS PATER ELISSA, elementary school educator; b. Cin., Oct. 23, 1937; d. Ray C. and Mary Loretta (Collins) Pater; m. Nabeel David Elissa, Aug. 15, 1964 (dec. Aug. 1975); children: Sue Renee, Ramsey Nabeel; m. Jim Bill McWilliams, Apr. 14, 1977 (dec. Sept. 1993). BA, Our Lady of Cin. Coll., 1959; MEd, Xavier U., 1965. Cert. tchr. elem., social studies, Tex. Elem. tchr. Cin. Parochial Schs., 1960-64, Champaign County Schs., Urbana, Ohio, 1968; tchr. social studies St. Mary's Elem. Sch., Urbana, 1968-73; tchr. Granbury (Tex.) Ind. Sch. Dist., 1981—; instr. Tarleton State U., Stephenville, Tex., 1989-90. Contbr. (text) Texas: Yesterday, Today and Tomorrow, 1988; music editor (newspaper) Jerusalem Star, 1966. Me. Hood Gen. Hosp. Aux., 1978—; chmn. Hood County Blood Drive, Granbury, 1978-82. Recipient scholarship Our Lady of Cin. Coll., 1955, Betty Crocker Homemaker award, Gen. Mills, 1955. Mem. Nat. Coun. Social Studies, Tex. Alliance for Geog. Edn., Phi Delta Kappa, Delta Kappa Gamma (pres. Lambda Pi chpt. 1988-90). Roman Catholic. Home: 249 Northwood Ter Granbury TX 76049

MCWILLIAMS, MARGARET ANN, home economics educator, author; b. Osage, Iowa, May 26, 1929; d. Alvin Randall and Mildred Irene (Lane) Edgar; children: Roger, Kathleen. BS, Iowa State U., 1951, MS, 1953; PhD, Oreg. State U., 1968. Registered dietitian. Asst. prof. home econs. Calif. State U., L.A., 1961-66, assoc. prof., 1966-68, prof., 1968-92, prof. emeritus, 1992—, chmn. dept., 1968-76; pres. Plycon Press, 1978—. Author: Food Fundamentals, 1966, 6th edit., 1995, Nutrition for the Growing Years, 1967, 5th edit., 1993, Experimental Foods Laboratory Manual, 1977, 4th edit., 1994, (with L. Kotschevar) Understanding Food, 1969, Illustrated Guide to Food Preparation, 1970, 7th edit., 1995, (with L. Davis) Food for You, 1971, 2d edit., 1976, The Meatless Cookbook, 1973, (with F. Stare) Living Nutrition, 1973, 4th edit., 1984, Nutrition for Good Health, 1974, 2d edit., 1982 (with H. Paine), Modern Food Preservation, Fundamentals of Meal Management, 1978, 2d edit., 1993, Foods: Experimental Perspectives, 1989, 2d edit., 1993. Chmn. bd. Beach Cities Symphony, 1991-94. Recipient Alumni Centennial award Iowa State U., 1971, Profl. Achievement award, 1977; Phi Upsilon Omicron Nat. Founders fellow, 1964; Home Economist in Bus. Nat. Found. fellow, 1967; Outstanding Prof. award Calif. State U., 1976. Mem. Am. Dietetic Assn., Inst. Food Technologists, Phi Kappa Phi, Phi Upsilon Omicron, Omicron Nu, Iota Sigma Pi, Sigma Delta Epsilon, Sigma Alpha Iota. Home: PO Box 220 Redondo Beach CA 90277-0220

MEACHAM, ANNABELLE, artist; b. Portsmouth, Va., Dec. 9, 1942; d. Kenneth Mortimer and Ana Maria (Borrero) Erskine; m. Robert Rhodes Meacham Jr., Dec. 11, 1965; children: Robert Rhodes III. Student, Tex. Christian U., 1960-62; BS, Fla. State U., 1963; postgrad., M.W. Miss. C.C., 1974-75, Memphis Coll. of Art, 1975-78. Pvt. art tchr., 1972—; One-woman shows include Mus. of U. Miss., Oxford, 1980, Lauren Rogers Mus. Art, Laurel, Miss., 1981, Turner Clark Gallery, Memphis, 1981, Meridian (Miss.) Mus. Art, 1981, F. Wright Art Ctr., Delta State U., Cleveland, 1982, Sycamore Gallery, Memphis, 1982, Lok Exhbn. Ctr., U. So. Miss., 1983, Ft. Smith (Ark.) Art Ctr., 1984, Clough Hanson Gallery, Memphis, 1985, Bell-Ross Gallery, Memphis, 1989, 91, 94, Duke U. Libr. Gallery, 1990, Katz Gallery, Memphis, 1994, others. Group shows include Miss. Mus. Art, Jackson, 1981, Rare Discoveries Gallery, Dallas, 1982, Sch. of Art Inst. Chgo., 1982, Gallery K, Washington, 1983, Marie Pellicone Gallery, N.Y.C., 1983, 85, Alberts Fine Art Gallery, Memphis, 1986, 87, Bell Gallery, Memphis, 1992, Taproot Sch. Arts, St. Louis, 1993; works in permanent collections of Former Gov. and Mrs. William F. Winter, Jackson, Miss., Ray Bradbury, L.A., Holiday Inns Hotel Group, Embassy Suites, Dallas, Ingram Group, Nashville, others. Recipient Memphis Acad. Arts award, 1977, Exhbn. South award Tenn. Valley Art Ctr., Tuscumbia, Ala., 1979, Purchase award Beaumont Art League, 1993. Mem. Senatobia Home and Garden Club (v.p., pres. 1991-92), Senatobia Young Homemakers Club (v.p., pres. 1992-93), Artist Link (historian 1990-93). Home: 211 Brookside Dr Senatobia MS 38668

MEAD, BEVERLY MIRIUM ANDERSON, writer, educator; b. St. Paul, May 29, 1925; d. Martin and Anna Mae (Oshanyk) Anderson; m. Jerome Morton Nemiro, Feb. 10, 1951 (div. May 1975); children: Guy Samuel, Lee

Anna, Dee Martin; m. William Isaac Mead, Aug. 8, 1992. Student Reed Coll., 1943-44; BA, U. Colo., 1947; postgrad., U. Denver. Tchr., Seattle Pub. Schs., 1945-46; fashion coordinator, dir. Denver Dry Goods Co., 1948-51; fashion model, Denver, 1951-58, 78—; fashion dir. Denver Market Week Assn., 1952-53; free-lance writer, Denver, 1958—; moderator TV program Your Preschool Child, Denver, 1955-56; instr. writing and communications U. Colo. Denver Ctr., 1970—, U. Calif., San Diego, 1976-78, Met. State Coll., 1985; dir. pub. relations Fairmont Hotel, Denver, 1979-80; free lance fashion and TV model; author, co-author: The Complete Book of High Altitude Baking, 1961, Colorado a la Carte, 1963, Colorado a la Carte, Series II, 1966, (with Donna Hamilton) The High Altitude Cookbook, 1969, The Busy People's Cookbook, 1971 (Better Homes and Gardens Book Club selection 1971), Where to Eat in Colorado, 1967, Lunch Box Cookbook, 1965, Complete Book of High Altitude Baking, 1961, (under name Beverly Anderson) Single After 50, 1978, The New High Altitude Cookbook, 1980. Co-founder, pres. Jr. Symphony Guild, Denver, 1959-60; active Friends of Denver Libr., Opera Colo. Recipient Top Hand award Colo. Authors' League, 1969, 72, 79-82, 100 Best Best Books of Yr. award N.Y. Times, 1969, 71; named one of Colo.'s Women of Yr., Denver Post, 1964. Mem. Am. Soc. Journalists and Authors, Colo. Authors League (dir. 1969-79), Authors Guild, Authors League Am., Friends Denver Library, Rotary, Sigma Delta Chi, Kappa Alpha Theta. Address: 23 Polo Club Dr Denver CO 80209

MEAD, HARRIET COUNCIL, librarian, author; b. Franklin, Va., Jan. 11; d. Hutson and Ollie (Whitley) Council; m. Berne Matthews Mead, Jr., Dec. 2, 1940; children—William Whitley, Charles Council. BA, Coll. William and Mary, 1935; postgrad. Fla. State U., 1958-62, Rollins Coll., 1966, 70, 84. County libr. Carroll County, Hillsville, Va., 1935-36; city libr. Suffolk City Schs., Va., 1936-41; libr., media specialist Orange County Schs., Orlando, Fla., 1961-80. Author: The Irrepressible Saint, 1983, A Family Legacy, 1987, Stained Glass in Cathedral Churches of St. Luke, 1994. Contbr. article to mag. Mem. LWV (Orlando), DAR, Fla. Hist. Soc., Friends of Libr., Fla. Coun. Librs., Orange County Media Specialists (pres. 1968-69), Colonial Dames, Jr. League, Orange County Ret. Educators. Democrat. Episcopalian. Avocation: watercolor painting. Home: 500 E Marks St Orlando FL 32803-3922

MEAD, LISA LOUISE, mayor; b. Wooster, Ohio, Jan. 22, 1962; d. William V and Joanne (Thorley) M. BA, U. Mass., 1984; JD, New Eng. Sch. Law, 1987. Bar: Mass., 1988, U.S. Dist. Ct. Mass., 1988, U.S. Ct. Appeals (1st cir.), 1988. Asst. gen. counsel Mass. Dept. Pub. Welfare, Boston, 1987-90; assoc. Finneran & Nicholson, P.C., Newburyport, Mass., 1990-93; mayor City of Newburyport, 1993—. Mem. city councilor-at-large, Newburyport City Coun., 1990-93; bd. dirs. Newburyport Women's Crisis Ctr., 1991-93, Newburyport Five Cents Savs. Bank, 1994. Democrat. Lutheran. Office: City of Newburyport 60 Pleasant St Newburyport MA 01950-2606

MEAD, MARY, artist, educator; b. N.Y.C., Apr. 6, 1957; d. Edgar Thorn Jr. and Emily Prouty (McMurray) M.; m. James Mark Lennon, Aug. 2, 1980 (div. May 1988); children: Emerson Drake Mead, Edgar James; m. James Mark Lennon, June 15, 1990. BS in Fine Arts with honors, U. Wis., 1984; MFA, Tufts U., 1989. Assoc. instr. drawing Boston Mus. Sch., 1985-86; asst. to the curator of collections, dir. Gallery Eleven Tufts U., Medford, Mass., 1986-88; instr. drawing Lebanon (N.H.) Coll., 1988; instr. sculpture Ava Art Ctr., Lebanon, 1990—; asst. to pediatric play therapist Mary Hitchcock Meml. Hosp., Hanover, N.H., 1976-79; exhibiting artist mem. Ava Gallery and Art Ctr., 1988—, selections com. curated exhbn., 1989-90; program officer USIA, Hanover, 1987-89. Exhibited in solo shows at Bromfield Gallery, Boston, Pleasant Grove, McLean, Va., other; group shows include Keene (N.H.) State Coll., Manchester (N.H.) Inst. Arts and Scis., AVA Gallery and Art Ctr., Lebanon, N.H., Vt. Coun. on Arts, Woodstock, Nashua (N.H.) Ctr. for the Arts, Bromfield Gallery, Internat. Place, Boston, Attleboro (Mass.) Mus.; featured in articles. promoter, organizer Triathalon Fund Raising Event, Upper Valley Youth Svcs., Lebanon, 1988; worker suicide prevention hotline, alcohol/drug abuse advisor Headrest, Inc., Lebanon, 1988-90; former sec., advisor Josiah Bartlett Ctr. for Pub. Policy, Concord, N.H., 1993—. Recipient Boit Competition award Boston Mus. Sch., 1986; Cary Jones Cady Fine Arts fellow U. Wis., Madison, 1983. Mem. Internat. Sculpture Ctr., New Eng. Sculptors Assn. Episcopalian. Home: Pumpkin Hill Rd Warner NH 03278

MEAD, PHILOMENA, mental health nurse; b. Yonkers, N.Y., June 23, 1934; d. Alfonso F. and Jennie (Saltarelli) D'Amato; m. Kenneth Mead, Nov. 10, 1956; children: Scott Kenneth, Jeanne Bette. RN, St. Vincents Hosp., Bridgeport, Conn., 1955; BS in Psychology, Sacred Heart U., 1980; cert. in nursing mgmt., Fairfield U., 1988. Cert. psychiat. mental health nurse, nat. chem. dependency nurse, CPR. Day supr.-relief, night supr. Hall Brooke Hosp., Westport, Conn., 1956-58, day supr., asst. dir. nurses, 1958-66, evening supr.-relief, 1967-68, team nurse, 1974-83, coord. nursing care, 1983-86, adminstrv. coord., 1986-87, nursing care coord. substance abuse treatment unit, 1987-91; charge evening nurse Carolton Hosp., Fairfield, Conn., 1971-73; nurse psychiat. emergency rm. and brief treatment unit West Haven (Conn.) VA, 1991—. Roman Catholic. Home: 67 Adams Rd Fairfield CT 06430

MEAD, PRISCILLA, state legislator; m. John L. Mead; children: John, Willian, Neel, Sarah. Student, Ohio State U. Councilwoman Upper Arlington, Ohio, 1982-90, mayor, 1986-90; mem. Ohio Ho. of Reps. Mem. Franklin County Child Abuse and Neglect Found., Coun. for Ethics and Econs. Recipient Svc. award Northwest Kiwanis, Woman of Yr award Upper Arlington Rotary, Citizen of Yr. award U.S. C. of C. Mem. LWV, Upper Arlington Edn. Found., Jr. League Columbus, Upper Arlington C. of C., Delta Gamma. Republican. Home: 2281 Brixton Rd Columbus OH 43221-3117 Office: Ohio Ho of Reps State House Columbus OH 43215*

MEAD, TERRY EILEEN, hospital and clinic administrator, consultant; b. Portland, Oreg., Mar. 14, 1950; d. Everett L. and Jean (Nonken) Richardson; divorced; 1 child, Sean Wade Adcock. AA, Seattle U., 1972; postgrad., U. Wash., 1971, USAF Acad., Colorado Springs. Project mgr. Assoc. Univ. Physician, Seattle, 1971-74; pathology supr. Swedish Hosp., Seattle, 1974-77; svcs. supr. Transamerica, Seattle, 1977-78; various mgmt. positions Providence Hosp., Seattle, 1978-83; adminstr. Evergreen Surg. Ctr., Kirkland, Wash., 1983-86; bus. mgr. Ketchikan (Alaska) Gen. Hosp., 1986—; instr. U. Alaska, Ketchikan, 1990; adminstr. Bethel (Alaska) Family Clinic, 1994—; sec. S.E. adv. bd. U. Alaska, Ketchikan, 1987—; cons. to hosps. and physicians, Wash., Alaska, 1980-89; mgr. Practice Mgmt. Cons., Seattle, 1982-83. Mem. City Charter Rev. Com., Ketchikan, 1990, High Sch. Facilities Com, Ketchikan, 1990; S.E. dir. search com U. Alaska, Ketchikan, 1990; treas. Calvary Bible Ch., Ketchikan, 1989-91; bd. dirs. S.E. Alaska Symphony, 1992—, Jr. Achievement, 1992-93; mem. fin. com. City of Bethel; chmn. Alaska dist. 39 Republican Party. Mem. Rotary Internat. Home: PO Box 2221 Bethel AK 99559-2221 Office: PO Box 1796 Bethel AK 99559-1796

MEADE, DOROTHY WINIFRED, retired educational administrator; b. N.Y.C., Jan. 26, 1935; d. Percival and Fraulien Franklin; m. Gerald H. Meade (div. 1987); 1 child, Myrla E. BA in Am. History, Queens Coll., Flushing, N.Y., 1970; MA in Corrective Reading, Bklyn. Coll., 1975; BA in Religious Edn., United Christian Coll., Bklyn., 1980; postgrad., Bklyn. Coll., 1984. Tchr. social studies cluster Pub. Sch. 137, Bklyn., 1979-83, curriculum coord. Follow Through Program, 1984-88, adminstrv. intern, 1983-84; staff developer social studies Cen. Sch. Dist. 23, Bklyn., 1988-89, dist. coord. Project Child, 1989-91; mem. faculty Coll. of New Rochelle, Bklyn., 1994; mem. coop. bd. dirs. 1053 E 13th St., Bklyn. Former mem. Ch. of the Master; participant in Crossroads Africa, 1958; nursery worker Bklyn. Tabernacle, 1986—, mem. sr. choir, 1992. Mem. African Christian Tchrs., N.Y. Pub. Sch. Early Childhood Edn., N.Y. Geography Inst. Pentecostal. Home: 1053 E 13th St Brooklyn NY 11230-4252

MEADE, KATHRYNE ANN, librarian; b. L.A., Mar. 7, 1953; d. William Wood and Marguerite (King) M. BA in English and Classics, San Diego State U., 1976; MA in Classics, Ohio State U., 1978; MLS, Syracuse (N.Y.) U., 1988. Teaching assoc. Ohio State U., Columbus, Ohio, 1976-78; proofreader, editor Arthur Andersen & Co., L.A., 1978-80; proofreader Raychem Corp., Menlo Park, Calif., 1981-86; indexer, abstractor Eric Clearinghouse for Info. Resources, Syracuse, 1986-87; tech. info. analyst AT&T Bell Labs., Murray Hill, N.J., 1988—. ESL tutor Literacy Vols. of Am., Union County, N.J., 1988—. Mem. ALA, Phi Kappa Phi, Phi Beta Kappa, Beta Phi Mu. Office: AT&T Bell Labs 600 Mountain Ave # 6301A Murray Hill NJ 07974-2010

MEADE, NANCY LOWMAN, accounting educator; b. Biloxi, Miss.; d. Theodore B. and Margaret Lowman; children: Ted, Lisa. BA, Marshall U., Huntington, W.Va., 1966; M.Accountancy, Va. Poly. Inst. and State U., 1986, PhD, 1990. CPA, Va. Quality control engr. E.I. duPont Co., Martinsville, Va., 1966-67; office mgr. E.B. Lowman Co., Ashland, Ky., 1967-85; pres. and tchr. The Dance Studio Inc., Flatwoods, Ky., 1972-85; asst. prof. acctg. Northeastern U., Boston, 1990, Radford (Va.) U., 1990-92, U. Louisville, 1992—. Contbr. articles to profl. jours. Mem. Third Century, Louisville; vol. Nat. Kidney Found. of Ky. Mem. AICPAs, AAUW, Am. Acctg. Assn., Inst. Mgmt. Accts., Fin. Women Internat., C. of C. of Louisville, Beta Gamma Sigma, Beta Alpha Psi. Office: U Louisville Dept Accountancy Coll Bus and Pub Adminstrn Louisville KY 40292

MEADERS, NOBUKO YOSHIZAWA, therapist, psychoanalyst; b. Kobe, Hyogo-ken, Japan, Mar. 2, 1942; d. Shigenobu and Ayako (Takahashi) Tsuchiya; m. Wilson E. Meaders, Apr. 2, 1976 (div. Apr. 1985); m. Takeshi Yoshizawa, June 15, 1989. AA, Seiwa Coll., Nishinomiya, Japan, 1965, Warren Wilson Coll., Swannanoa, N.C., 1967; BA, So. Meth. U., Dallas, 1969; MS in Social Work, U. Tex., Arlington, 1971; cert. psychotherapy-psychoanalysis, Postgrad. Ctr. Mental Health, N.Y.C., 1977, cert. in supervision psychotherapeutic process, 1979. Cert. social worker, N.Y.; diplomate Am. Bd. Examiners in Clin. Social Work. Psychiat. social worker Killgore Children's Psychiat. Hosp., Amarillo, Tex., 1971-73, Jewish Child Care Assn., Childville div., N.Y.C., 1973-74; supr. social work, social work dept. Bellevue Hosp., N.Y.C., 1974-76; asst. dir. tng. Postgrad. Ctr. Mental Health, N.Y.C., 1979-82, assoc. supr., 1979-82, supr., 1982-85, sr. supr., 1985—, tng. analyst, 1989—; pvt. practice psychotherapy and psychoanalysis N.Y.C., 1976—; clin. cons. Pace U. Personal Devel. Ctr., N.Y.C., 1987—; mem. adv. bd. Japanese-Am. Cons. Ctr., N.Y.C., 1983—. Fellow N.Y. Soc. Clin. Social Work Psychotherapists; mem. NASW, Acad. Cert. Social Workers.

MEADOW, CYNTHIA W., legislative counsel; b. Ft. Smith, Ark., July 27, 1941. BA, Baylor U., 1964; JD, Cath. U., 1978. Staff asst. Senator Ralph Yarborough, 1964-70; staff adminstr. Joint Com. Congl. Ops., Ho. Commn. Info. and Facilities, Select Com. Congl. Ops., 1971-79; profl. staff mem., counsel Subcom. Legislation and Nat. Security Ho. Govt. Ops. Com., 1979-89; counsel Ho. Judiciary Com., 1989-91, chief counsel Subcom. Econ. and Comml. Law, 1991—. Office: Subcom Econ & Comml Law B-353 Rayburn House Office Bldg Washington DC 20515*

MEADOW, LYNNE (CAROLYN MEADOW), theatrical producer and director; b. New Haven, Nov. 12, 1946; d. Frank and Virginia R. Meadow. BA cum laude, Bryn Mawr Coll., 1968; postgrad., Yale U., 1968-70. Dir. Theatre Communications Group, 1978-80; adj. prof. SUNY, Stony Brook, 1975-76, Yale U., Circle in the Sq., 1977-78, 89-91, NYU, 1977-80; theatre and music/theatre panelist Nat. Endowment for Arts, 1977-88; artistic advisor Fund for New Am. Plays, 1988-90. Artistic dir. Manhattan Theatre Club, N.Y.C., 1972—; guest dir. Nat. Playwrights Conf., Eugene O'Neill Theatre Ctr., 1975-77, Phoenix Theatre, 1976; dir. Ashes for Manhattan Theatre Club and N.Y. Shakespeare Festival, 1977; prodr. off-Broadway shows Ain't Misbehavin', 1978, Crimes of the Heart, 1981, Miss Firecracker Contest, 1984, Frankie and Johnny, 1987, Eastern Standard, 1988, Lisbon Traviata, 1989, Lips Together, Teeth Apart, 1991, Four Dogs and a Bone, 1993, Love! Valour! Compassion!, 1994; dir. Principia Scritoriae, 1986, Woman in Mind, 1988 (Drama Desk award), Eleemosynary, 1989, Absent Friends, 1991; dir. Broadway prodn. A Small Family Business, 1992, The Loman Family Picnic, 1993; co-prodr. off-Broadway and Broadway show Mass Appeal, 1981. Recipient Citation of Merit Nat. Coun. Women, 1976, Outer Circle Critics award 1977, Drama Desk award, 1977, Obie award for Ashes, 1977, Margo Jones award for Continued Encouragement New Playwrights, 1981, Critics Circle award Outstanding Revival on or off Broadway for Loot, 1986, Lucille Lortel award for Outstanding Achievement, 1987, Spl. Drama Desk award, 1989, N.Y. Drama Critics Circle award Best Fgn. Play for Aristocrats, 1989, Torch of Hope award, 1989, Manhattan Mag. award, 1994, Lee Reynolds award League Profl. Theatre Women, 1994; named Northwood Inst. Disting. Woman of Yr., 1990, Person of Yr., Nat. Theatre Conf., 1992. Office: Manhattan Theatre Club 453 W 16th St 2nd Fl New York NY 10011-5896

MEADOWS, JENNIFER ELIZABETH, retired editor, tattoo artist; b. Texarkana, Tex., Jan. 20, 1947; d. Walter Edward and Martha Elizabeth (McCoy) Willis; m. Joe R. Matthews (div.); 1 child, Chris; m. Rich Meadows. AA, Cottey Coll., 1965; BS, U. Tex., Arlington, 1978. Actuarial asst. S.W. Life Ins. Co., Dallas; proofreader Royal Bus. Forms, Arlington, Tex.; substitute tchr. Arlington (Tex.) Ind. Sch. Dist.; reporter The Dallas Morning News, 1980-83, asst. editor, 1983-86, editor, 1986-94; columnist The Dallas Morning News, 1980-94. Vol. The Dallas Opera; tng. coord. Kairos Found., 1990—. Office: 904 W Pioneer Pky Arlington TX 76013-6330

MEADOWS, PATRICIA BLACHLY, art curator, civic worker; b. Amarillo, Tex., Nov. 12, 1938; d. William Douglas and Irene Bond Blachly; m. Curtis Washington Meadows, Jr., June 10, 1961; children: Michael Lee, John Morgan. BA in English and History, U. Tex., 1960. Program dir. Ex-Students Assn., Austin, Tex., 1960-61; dir. Dallas Visual Art Ctr., 1981-86, curator, 1987—, founder The Collectors, 1988—; exhbn. dir. Tex. bd. Nat. Mus. Women in Arts, Washington, 1986-91; mem. acquisition com. Dallas Mus. Art, 1988-92; chmn. adv. bd. Oaks Bank and Trust, 1993—; juror numerous exhibits, Dallas and Tex.; speaker on arts subjects; cons. city, state and nat. projects concerning arts; bd. dirs., mem. exec. com. Uptown Pub. Improvement Dist., 1993—; chmn. bd. dirs. State-Thomas Tax Increment Financing Zone # 1. Author: (art catalogues) Critic's Choice, 1983—, Texas Women, 1989-90, Texas: reflections, rituals, 1991; organizer exhbns. Presenting Nine, D-Art Visual Art Ctr., 1984, Mosaics, 1991—, Senses Beyond Sight, 1992-93. Bd. dirs. Mid-Am. Arts Alliance, Kansas City, Mo., 1989-93, Tex. Bd. Commerce, Austin, 1991-93, Women's Issues Network, Dallas, 1994—; bd. dirs. Dallas Summit, 1989—, pres., 1993-94; mem. Charter 100, 1993—, Dallas Assembly, 1993—, Leadership Tex., 1987; co-founder, mem. steering com. Emergency Artists Support League, Dallas, 1992—; mem. originating task force Dallas Coalition for Arts, 1984; also others. Recipient Dedication to Arts award Tex. Fine Arts Assn., 1984, Assn. Artists and Craftsmen, 1984, Southwestern Watercolor Soc., 1985, Flora award Dallas Civic Garden Ctr., 1987, James K. Wilson award TACA, 1988, Maura award Women's Ctr. Dallas, 1991, Disting. Woman award Northwood U., 1993, Excellence in the Arts award Dallas Hist. Soc., 1993. Mem. Tex. Assn. Mus., Tex. Sculpture Assn. (originating task force), Arts Dist. Mgmt. Assn. (bd. dirs., exec. com. 1984-92, Artists Square design com. 1988-90), Artists and Craftsmen Assn. (pres. bd. dirs. 1982-83), Dallas Woman's Club. Presbyterian. Office: 2707 State St Dallas TX 75204

MEADOWS, SHARON MARIE, investment banker; b. Cin., Aug. 10, 1950; d. Norbert J. and Dorothy J. (Ruth) Strahler; m. Randall S. Meadows, June 26, 1971; children: Scott, Peter. BA, Wayne State U., 1974; MBA, U. Mich., 1976. V.p. Citibank, N.A., N.Y.C., 1976-83; mng. dir., group head The First Boston Corp., N.Y.C., 1983—. Mem. Phi Beta Kappa, Psi Chi. Office: First Boston Corp Park Ave Plz 55 E 52nd St New York NY 10055

MEAL, LARIE, chemistry educator, consultant; b. Cin., June 15, 1939; d. George Lawrence Meal and Dorothy Louise (Heileman) Fitzpatrick. BS in Chemistry, U. Cin., 1961, PhD in Chemistry, 1966. Rsch. chemist U.S. Indsl. Chems., Cin., 1966-67; instr. chemistry U. Cin., 1968-69, asst. prof., 1969-75, assoc. prof., 1975-90, prof., 1990—, researcher, 1980—; cons. in field. Contbr. articles to sci. jours. Mem. AAAS, N.Y. Acad. Scis., Am. Chem. Soc., Internat. Assn. Arson Investigators, NOW, Planned Parenthood, Iota Sigma Pi. Democrat. Home: 2231 Slane Ave Norwood OH 45212-3615 Office: U Cin 2220 Victory Pky Cincinnati OH 45206-2822

MEALING, ESTHER MORRISON (MOLLIE MEALING), artist; b. Corinth, Miss., Aug. 8, 1916; d. Errett Arthur and Marguerite (Adams) Morrison; m. John Pace Mealing, July 20, 1940 (dec. Nov. 1979); children: John Pace IV (dec.), Robert Adams, Esther Lee Mealing Lehew, Marguerite Anna Mealing Ozley; stepchildren: Thorpe, Margaret Mae. Grad., Draughons Bus. Coll., 1935; student, Columbus Coll., 1966. Cashier, sec. Ace Power Assn., Corinth, 1935-36; clk. typist TVA, Chattanooga and Tupelo, Miss., 1936-41; civil def. warden, 1957; art tchr. Wynnton Meth. Ch., Columbus, Ga., 1970—; tchr. crafts Camp Joy, summers, 1983-94. dir. art dept. Chattahoochee Valley Fair, 1973-76, 80-83, 84, 85, 86, 87, 88, 93, 94; paintings exhibited Hamilton Art Gallery, That Place, Derium's Antiques, Curio Creations, George De Ville, Muter Book Store, New Orleans, Kirvens, Talent Tree, others; author: Grandmother's Poem; author, pub.: sketch books Century Old Houses of Columbus and Vicinity, vol. 1, 1971, vol. 2, 1975, Century Old Houses of N ew Orleans and Lousianna Plantations, Vol. 1, 1984—; (Haiku verse) Memories of Sudio 10, 1975. Asst. den mother Ozark coun. Boy Scouts Am., 1953-54; leader or co-leader Concharty coun. Girls Scouts U.S.A., 1952-57, 62-67; sec.-treas. Muscogee County Citizens assn., 1955-59; bd. dirs. Muscogee County Welfare Dept., 1957-72, chmn. adv. bd., 1971-72, rep. dist. 3, 1971-72; mem. adv. bd. State of Ga., 1971-72; former Sunday sch. tchr., substitute organist, choir mem. Christian Ch.; substitute organist Seven Day Adventist Ch.; tchr. Bible class Deerfield Nursing Home, 1990-95. Recipient various prizes in art for water colors, oils, sculptures, 1990-94. Mem. Nat. League Am. Pen Women (past pres. Columbus br., pres. Colbrach br., pres. Ga. 1976-78, nat. chaplain 1983-84), Columbus Artists Guild (past pres.), Columbus Mus. Arts and Crafts, Hist. Columbus Found. and Hist. Trust for Preservation, DAR, Colonial Soc. Daughters of Indian Wars (former chaplain), Benning Hills Woman's Club (charter), Columbus Woman's. Republican. Home: 809 Cooper Ave Columbus GA 31906-3501

MEANS, CATHERINE ELIZABETH, nurse; b. Logansport, Ind., Dec. 4, 1954; d. Elmer Clyde and Margaret (Stewart) M. BS, Tuskegee U., 1977. Staff nurse Meml. Hosp., Logansport, Ind., 1977; staff nurse neonatal unit Home Hosp., Lafayette, Ind., 1978-80; charge nurse Americana Health Care, Lafayette, 1980; asst. head nurse St. Elizabeth Med. Ctr., Lafayette, 1980—. Mem. Apostolic Ch. Office: St Elizabeth Med Ctr PO Box 7501 Lafayette IN 47903-7501

MEANS, ELIZABETH ROSE THAYER, financial consultant, lawyer; b. N.Y.C., Aug. 29, 1960; d. Cyril Chesnut and Rosaline (Limtiuco) M. BS, Chatham Coll., 1983; JD, Samford U., 1989; LLM, Boston U., 1990; Cert. in Comparative Law, Heidelberg U., 1988. Bar: Mass. 1991, Pa. 1991; cert. for piloting, seamanship and small boat handling USCG Aux. Dancer The N.Y.C. Ballet Co., 1971, Balanchine Cast for PBS "The Nutcracker Suite", N.Y.C., 1971; docent The Hammond Castle Mus., Gloucester, Mass., 1982-85; asst. mgr. The Gallery, Rockport, Mass., 1977-83; cons. The Galleries, Ltd., Wellesley, Mass., 1988; legal intern U. Ala. Health Svcs. Found., Birmingham, 1988-89; loan officer UN/UNFCU, N.Y.C., 1984-86; contracts mgr. for Eastern Region Unisys Corp., Berkeley Heights, N.J., 1990-92; fin. cons. Innovatech, Lexington, Mass., 1992-93; chairwoman Cordell Hull Speakers' Forum, Birmingham, 1988-89; alumnae class sec. Chatham Coll. Class of 1980s, Pitts., 1983-88. Clk. of the vestry The Ch. of the Resurrection, N.Y.C., 1993—. Recipient Cert. of Appreciation 1990 Alumni award Cumberland Sch. Law, 1990; named to Nat. Dean's List, 1989-90. Mem. DAR (Cape Ann chpt. chairwoman Const. Week 1993—), The Federalist Soc. (Cumberland chpt. treas. 1988-89, adv. bd. 1988, sec. 1987-88), The Clan Menzies Soc. NA, The Clan Menzies Soc. Scotland, Princeton Club. Republican. Episcopalian. Office: Innovatech 6 Abbott Rd Lexington MA 02173-3612

MEANS, MARIANNE, political columnist; b. Sioux City, Iowa, June 13, 1934; d. Ernest Maynard and Else Marie Johanne (Andersen) Hansen; m. Warren Weaver, Jr. B.A., U. Nebr., 1956; J.D., George Washington U., 1977. Copy editor Lincoln (Nebr.) Jour., 1955-57; woman's editor No. Va. Sun, Arlington, 1957-59; Washington bur. corr. Hearst Newspapers, 1959-61, White House corr., 1961-65; polit. columnist King Features Syndicate, 1965—, N.Y. Times News, 1994—; commentator Spectrum CBS radio, Mut. Broadcasting Network, Voice of Am., U.S.I.A. World Network, Post Newsweek Stas., Nat. Pub. Radio. Author: The Woman in the White House, 1963. Recipient Front Page award N.Y. Newspaper Women, 1962; Tex. Headliners award, 1976, Hall of Fame-Sigma Delta Chi, 1988. Mem. White House Corrs. Assn., Nat. Press Found. (chmn.), Internat. Women's Media Found. (bd. dirs.), Gridiron Club, Cosmos Club, Nat. Press Club, Phi Beta Kappa, Delta Delta Delta, Sigma Delta Chi (Hall of Fame). Home: 1521 31st St NW Washington DC 20007-3075 Office: 1701 Pennsylvania Ave NW Washington DC 20006-5801*

MEARA, ANNE, actress, writer; b. Bklyn., Sept. 20; d. Edward Joseph and Mary (Dempsey) M.; m. Gerald Stiller, Sept. 14, 1954; children: Amy, Benjamin. Student, Herbert Berghoff Studio, 1953-54. Apprentice in summer stock, Southold, L.I. and Woodstock, N.Y., 1950-53; off-Broadway appearances include A Month in the Country, 1954, Maedchen in Uniform, 1955 (Show Bus. off-Broadway award), Ulysses in Nightown, 1958, The House of Blue Leaves, 1970, Spookhouse, 1983, Bosoms and Neglect, 1986, also with Shakespeare Co., Two Gentlemen of Verona, Cen. Park, N.Y.C., 1957, Romeo and Juliet, 1988, Eastern Standard, 1989, Anna Christie, 1993 (Tony nomination Best Supporting Actress); film appearances include The Out-of-Towners, 1968, Lovers and Other Strangers, 1969, The Boys From Brazil, 1978, Fame, 1979, Nasty Habits (with husband Jerry Stiller), 1976, An Open Window, 1990, Mia, 1990, Awakenings, 1991, Reality Bites, 1994; comedy act, 1963—; appearances Happy Medium and Medium Rare, Chgo., 1960-61, Village Gate, Phase Two and Blue Angel, N.Y.C., 1963, The Establishment, London, 1963; syndicated TV series Take Five With Stiller and Meara, 1977-78; numerous appearances on TV game and talk shows, also spls. and variety shows; rec. numerous commls. for TV and radio (co-recipient Vocie of Imagery award Advt. Bur. N.Y.); star TV series Kate McShane, 1975; other TV appearances Archie Bunker's Place, 1979, The Sunset Gang, The Detective, 1990, Avenue Z Afternoon, 1991, Alf, 1986; writer, actress TV movie The Other Woman, 1983 (co-recipient Writer's Guild Outstanding Achievement award 1983), Alf, To Make Up to Break Up, The Stiller and Meara Pilot; author: (play) After-Play, 1994.

MEARS, JOYCE LUND, educational counselor; b. Davenport, Iowa, Aug. 20, 1937; d. Hilding Eugene and Thelma (Peitscher) Lund; m. Walter R. Mears, Aug. 4, 1963 (div. Dec. 1983); children: Stephanie Joy, Susan Marie. BFA, Drake U., 1960; postgrad., U. Va., 1984; MS in Edn., Va. Poly. Inst. and State U., 1992. Cert. tchr., Iowa. Travel coordinator Kennedy Summer White House, Hyannis, Mass., 1961; sec. Bank Am., Los Angeles, 1962; quality control Census Bur., Dept. Commerce, L.A., No. Va., 1980; owner, mgr. cons. firm J.L. Mears, Inc., McLean, Va., 1981-86; ednl. counselor Fairfax County Adult and Cmty. Edn., Fairfax, Va., 1992—. Patentee tech cart. Bd. dirs. Deborah's Pl., Washington, 1982, Fairfax County (Va.) PTA, 1978, 84. Grantee Ctr. for Innovative Tech., 1988. Mem. MIT Enterprise Forum Washington/Balt., Met. Area Career/Life Planning Network (steering com.), Mortar Bd., Kappa Kappa Gamma. Lutheran. Home: 1338 Potomac School Rd Mc Lean VA 22101-2331

MEARS, RONA ROBBINS, lawyer; b. Stillwater, Minn., Oct. 3, 1938; d. Glaydon Donaldson and Lois Lorane (Hoehne) Robbins; m. John Ashley Mears, Aug. 20, 1960; children: John LaMonte, Matthew Von. BS, U. Minn., 1960; MBA, JD, So. Meth. U., 1982. Bar: Tex. 1992. Bus. adminstr. 1st Unitarian Ch., Dallas, 1973-77; assoc. atty. Haynes and Boone, Dallas, 1982-89, ptnr., internat. sect., 1989—; exec. bd. dirs. Sch. Law, So. Meth. U., Dallas, 1991—; mem. adv. bd. S.W. Inst. Dispute Resolution, Dallas, 1990—. Co-editor: International Loan Workouts and Bankruptcies, 1989; contbr. articles to profl. jours. Mem. U.S. Delegation, NAFTA Adv. Com. on Pvt. Comml. Disputes, 1994—. Rsch. fellow Southwestern Legal Found., Dallas, 1986; recipient 1st prize INSOL Internat. Article Competition, 1989. Mem. ABA (sec. internat. sect. 1994—), Tex. Bar Found., State Bar Tex. (chmn. internat. sect. 1993-94), Tex.-Mex. Bar Assn. (co-vice chair 1994—), Dallas Bar Assn. (chmn. internat. sect. 1984-86), Internat. Bar Assn. (mem. com. on creditors rights, coord. internat. insolvency coop. project 1988-91), U.S.-Mex. C. of C. (bd. dirs. S.W. chpt. 1987—). Democrat. Office: Haynes and Boone 3100 Nations Bank Plaza 901 Main St Dallas TX 75202-3707

MEASON, ALISON GAY, lawyer; b. Cambridge, Eng., June 25, 1962; came to U.S., 1962; d. Curtis Griffin and Bess Elaine (Thompson) Smith; m.

James Edward Meason, Aug. 24, 1991. BA, Mount Holyoke Coll., 1984; JD, Georgetown U., 1991. Bar: Ill. 1992, D.C. 1992. Coord. info. resources Competitive Telecomm. Assn., Washington, 1985-88; law clk. Baker & Hostetler, Washington, 1988-90; honors legal intern Office of Gen. Counsel, Dept. of Def., Washington, 1990; legis. coun. Councilmem. Linda W. Cropp, Washington, 1991—. Vol. Mount Carmel Ho. shelter for homeless women; founder Georgetown Law Students for Dukakis/Bentsen; v.p. Mount Holyoke Club of Washington; pro bono advocate D.C. Emergency Domestic Rels. Project. Mem. ABA, Ill. Bar Assn., Chgo. Bar Assn., D.C. Bar Assn. Democrat. Episcopalian. Office: Coun of the DC 1350 Pennsylvania Ave NW Washington DC 20004

MEBANE, BARBARA MARGOT, service company executive, studio owner; b. Sylacauga, Ala., July 21, 1947; d. Audrey Dixon and Mary Ellen (Yaikow) Baxley; m. James Lewis Mebane, Dec. 31, 1971; 1 child, Cieson Brooke. Grad. high sch., Albany, Ga. Line performer J. Taylor Dance Co., Miami, Fla., 1964-65; sales mgr. Dixie Readers Svc., Jackson, Miss., 1965-67; regional sales mgr. Robertson Products Co., Texarkana, Tex., 1967-75; owner, pres. Telco Sales, Svc. and Supply, Dallas, 1976—; owner The Dance Factory, ATS Svcs., Lewisville, Tex.; mem. Dance Masters, Miami, 1975—; mgmt. specialist SBA; choreographer music videos for pay/cable TV, 1985; founder, dir. The Dance Factory, Lewisville, Tes.; owner, tchr. Dancers Workshop; contract cons. for self-employed women; pub. speaker in field. Author: Paper on Positive Thinking, 1983. Sponsor St. Jude's Rsch. Hosp., Memphis, Cancer Rsch. Ctr., Dallas; active Cancer Rsch. Found.; sponsor Nat. Kidney Found., Dallas, Lewisville Cultural Arts; part time tchr. for children with motor skill problems. Mem. Nat. Fedn. Ind. Businesses, Internat. Register of Profiles Cambridge, Eng., Female and Minority Owned Bus. League, Assoc. Gen. Contractors (assoc.), Female Exec. Club N.Y.C. Avocations: working with children, teaching dance, writing. Home: 3701 Twin Oaks Ct Lewisville TX 75028-1244 Office: Telco Sales Svc & Supply PO Box 29763 Dallas TX 75229-0763

MECHIGIAN, NANCY LEE, word processing company executive; b. Highland Park, Mich., Feb. 8, 1941; d. John Peniamin and Arpie (Abajian) M. Student secretarial sci., Highland Park Jr. Coll., 1959-6l; legal sec. studies, Florence Rose Study Course, Southfield, Mich., 1969. Sec. Mich. Employment Security Commn., Detroit, 196l-68; legal sec. Law Offices Stephen A. Crane, Southfield, Mich., 1969-71, Sheldon M. Lutz, Southfield, 1971-73, Clarence G. Carlson, Bloomfield Hills, Mich., 1975-76, Rubenstein, Allen & Isaacs, Southfield, 1976; owner, mgr. Typing By Nan, Southfield, l977-85; account exec. 55Plus/Golden Yrs. newspaper, Southfield, 1985; sr. mcht. cons. Mich. Credit Card Svcs., Southfield, 1985; adminstrv. asst. Cliff Adams, CLU, ChFC, Troy, Mich., 1987; owner, mgr. Efficient Word Processing Svcs., Southfield, 1987—; owner Scholarships for Students, Southfield, 1989-92. Data entry cons. St. John's Armenian Ch., Southfield, l988-90, computer operator Armenia Earthquake Fund, 1988-90; nominated sec. of the day St. John's Armenian Ch. Parish Coun. Meeting, 1985. Home and Office: 19965 Butternut Ln Southfield MI 48076-1796

MECHLEM, DAPHNE JO, educator; b. Cin., Oct. 20, 1946; d. Louis Edward Griffith and Esther Eileen (Calvert) Griffith-Schultz; m. James T. Mechlem, Nov. 18, 1967 (div. June 1983); 1 chld, Louis Henry. BS summa cum laude, U. Cin., 1982, MS, 1983, MEd, 1984. Cert. vocat. and adult dir., supr., cosmetology instr., real estate agt. Stylist, mgr. Fashion Flair Styling, Cin., 1965-70, Ann Wolfe Coiffures, Cin., 1970-71; salon owner Curls by Daphne, Cin., 1971-77; tchr. Great Oaks Joint Vocat. Sch. Dist., Cin., 1976-83, adminstrv. intern, 1983; probation officer Hamilton County Juvenile Ct., Cin., 1983—; tchr. Great Oaks Joint Vocat. Sch. Dist., Cin., 1983—; spkr., presenter workshops in field. Author: Critical Issues in Campus Policing, 1983. Mem. ASCD, Nat. Cosmetology Assn., Criminal Justice Assn., Am. Vocat. Assn., Ohio Vocat. Assn., Ohio Vocat. Cosmetology Tchrs. Assn. Home: 5776 Pleasant Hill Rd Milford OH 45150-2301

MEDALIE, MARJORIE LYNN, educational administrator, consultant; b. Bklyn., June 25, 1947; d. Charles and Bette P. (Feldman) Drucker; m. Randolph Medalie, Mar. 26, 1970; children: Jeremy Chad, Daniel Bradley. BA, Ithaca Coll., 1969; MA, Adelphi U., 1973, spl. edn. cert., 1985; profl. diploma, C. W. Post Coll., 1991. Cert. spl. educator, sch. dist. adminstr. Tchr. English, Island Trees (N.Y.) Sch. Dist., 1970-73, West Hempstead (N.Y.) Sch. Dist., 1973-76; tchr. spl. edn. Summit Sch., Forrest Hills, N.Y., 1976-77; coord. alternative class program Huntington (N.Y.) U.F.S.D. # 3, 1982-86; tchr. spl. edn. self-contained classroom Center Moriches (N.Y.) Sch. Dist., Riverhead, N.Y., 1986-88; lead tchr. for alternative high schs. Bd. Coop. Scnl. Svcs. 1, Riverhead, N.Y., 1988—; presenter in field. v.p. Am. Cancer Soc., Melville, N.Y., 1974-81; mgr. Tri-Village Little League, Greenlawn, N.Y., 1986-90; active edn. com. Temple Chaverim. Mem. ASCD, Nat. Coun. Tchrs. English, United Fedn. Tchrs., East End Counselors Assn., Western Suffolk Counselors, Kappa Delta Pi, Epsilon Nu Gamma. Jewish.

MEDEROS, CAROLINA LUISA, transportation policy consultant; b. Rochester, Minn., July 1, 1947; d. Luis O. and Carolina (del Valle) M. BA, Vanderbilt U., 1969; MA, U. Chgo., 1971. Adminstrv. asst. Lt. Gov. of Ill., Chgo., 1972; sr. research assoc. U. Chgo., 1972; project mgr., cons. Urban Dynamics, Inner City Fund and Community Programs Inc., Chgo., 1972-73; legis. asst. to Senate pres. Ill. State Senate, Chgo. and Springfield, 1973-76; program analyst Dept. Transp., Washington, 1976-79, chief, trans. assistance programs div., 1979-81, dir. programs and evaluation, 1981-88, chairwoman, sec.'s safety rev. task force, 1985-88; deputy asst. sec. for safety Dept. Transp., 1988-89; cons. Patton Boggs LLP, Washington, 1990—. Recipient award for Meritorious Achievement, Sec. Transp. 1980, Superior Achievement award U.S. Dept. Transp., 1981, Sec.'s Gold Medal Award for Outstanding Achievement, 1986, Presdl. Rank award, 1987. Mem. Womens Transp. Seminar, Coun. for Excellence in Govt. Home: 2723 O St NW Washington DC 20007-3128 Office: Patton Boggs LLP 2550 M St NW Washington DC 20037-1301

MEDICUS, HILDEGARD JULIE, retired dentist, orthodontist, educator; b. Frankfurt, Germany, July 25, 1928; came to U.S., 1961; d. Gustav and Elizabeth Berta (Neunhoeffer) Schmelz; m. Heinrich Adolf Medicus, June 15, 1961. DMD, U. Marburg, W. Germany, 1953; orthodontics diploma, U. Düsseldorf, W. Germany, 1957. lic. dentist, N.Y. Postdoctoral fellow dental sch. U. Zürich, Zürich, Switzerland, 1957; postdoctoral fellow U. Liège, Belgium, 1958; postdoctoral fellow Forsyth Dental Ctr., Boston, 1959, orthodontics rsch. affiliate, 1963-74; sch. dentist Pub. Sch. System, Zürich, 1975-76; dental hygiene instructor Hudson Valley Community Coll., Troy, N.Y., 1976-77; pvt. practice Troy, N.Y., 1977-89. Active Hudson Mohawk Swiss Soc. Mem. AAUW, ADA, European Orthodontic Soc., German Orthodontic Soc. Presbyterian. Home: 1 The Knoll Troy NY 12180

MEDIN, ALICE LOUISE, librarian; b. Eau Claire, Wis., July 17, 1935; d. Ongle Ever and Esther Bianca (Rasmussen) Moholt; m. Myron James Medin, May 14, 1955; children: John, Kären, Anne. BA in Edn., Ea. Wash. U., 1957; MA in Libr. Sci., U. Wis., 1977. Libr. asst. U. Wis. Fond du Lac Ctr., 1979; reference libr. Plaza br. Kansas City (Mo.) Pub. Libr., 1984-86, describer old and rare books main libr., 1985; dir. Rogers (Ark.) Pub. Libr., 1987—; mem. N.W. Ark. C.C. Found. Bd., Rogers, 1987—. Mem. AAUW (pres. Fond du Lac br. 1973-75), Ark. Libr. Assn. (mem. intellectual freedom com. 1993—), N.W. Ark. Libr. Assn. (v.p. 1988-89), Round Table Lectr. Club (v.p. 1979). Lutheran. Home: 1 Audley Cir Bella Vista AR 72714 Office: Rogers Pub Libr 711 S Dixieland Rd Rogers AR 72758

MEDIN, JULIA ADELE, mathematics educator, researcher; b. Dayton, Ohio, Jan. 16, 1929; d. Caroline (Feinberg) Levitt; m. A. Louis Medin, Dec. 24, 1950; children: Douglas, David, Thomas, Linda. BS in Maths. Edn., Ohio State U., 1951; MA in Higher Edn., George Washington U., 1977; PhD in Counseling and Edn., Am. U., 1985. Cert. tchr., Fla., Md. Rsch. engr. Sun Oil Co., Marcus Hook, Pa., 1951-53; tchr. maths. Montgomery County Pub. Schs., Rockville, Md., 1973-88; asst. prof. maths. U. Ctrl. Fla., Orlando, 1988-90, sr. ednl. technologist Inst. for Simulation and Tng., 1990—; mem. adv. steering com. U.S. Dept. Edn. Title II, Washington, 1985-89; sr. math. educator, rschr. Inst. for Simulation & Tng., Orlando, 1988—. Author: Loc. of Cont. & Test Anxiety of Mar. Math. Studies, 1985; contbg. author: Math for 14 & 17 Yr. Olds, 1987; contbr. articles to profl. jours. Dem. committeewoman Town of Monroeville, Pa., 1962; religious sch. dir. Beth Tikva Religious Sch., Rockville, 1971; cons. Monroeville Mental Health, 1960. Mem. Nat. Coun. Tchrs. of Math., Maths. Assn. Am. (task force on minorities in math.), Women and Maths. in Edn., Sch. Sci. and Maths. Assn., Assn. Tchr. Educators. Home: 714 Bear Creek Cir Casselberry FL 32708-3857 Office: U Ctrl Fla Inst for Simulation and Tng 3280 Progress Dr Orlando FL 32826-0544

MEDINA, KATHRYN BACH, book editor; b. Plainfield, N.J.; d. F. Earl and Elizabeth E. Bach; m. Standish F. Medina Jr.; 1 child, Nathaniel Forde. B.A., Smith Coll. Various editorial positions Doubleday Pub. Co., Inc., N.Y.C., 1965-85; exec. editor, v.p. Random House, N.Y.C., 1985—; assoc. fellow Jonathan Edwards Coll., Yale U., New Haven, 1982—. Editor books by James Atlas, Peter Benchley, Anita Brookner, Ethan Canin, Agnes deMille, Mary Gordon, James A. Michener, Anna Quindlen, Nancy Reagan, James Reston, William Safire, Maggie Scarf, Hedrick Smith, Daniel Yergin, others.

MEDINA, MONICA P., lawyer; b. Montgomery, Ala., Feb. 7, 1962; d. Angel and Jeanne (Plessis) M.; m. Ronald A. Klain, June 22, 1986; 1 child, Hannah Leosa. BA cum laude, Georgetown U., 1983; vis. student Law Sch., Harvard U.; JD, Columbia U., 1986. Bar: Ga. 1986, D.C. 1990. Assoc. Hunton & Williams, 1990-92; regional counsel Oames & More, 1992-93; sr. counsel for air and environment Senate Com. on Environment and Pub. Works, 1993—. Capt. U.S. Army, 1986. Decorated Disting. Svc. medal, Army Commendation medal; Stone scholar, 1983-86; named One of Am.'s Top Ten Coll. Women, Glamour Mag., 1983. Mem. ABA, D.C. Bar Assn. Roman Catholic. Office: Environ & Pub Works 415 Senate Hart Office Bldg Washington DC 20510*

MEDINA-DIAZ, MARIA DEL ROSARIO, education educator; b. Oct. 22, 1959. BA in Edn., U. P.R., Rio Piedras, 1980, MS in Edn., 1986; PhD in Ednl. Psychology, U. Wis., 1991. Lic. secondary sch. math. tchr. Math. tchr. Dept. Pub. Instrn., San Juan, P.R., 1981-86; project asst. U. Wis., Madison, 1989-91; asst. prof. U. P.R., Rio Piedras, 1992—. Advance opportunity fellow U. Wis., Madison, 1986-89; Nat. Hispanis Scholarship Fund scholar, 1988. Mem. APA, Assn. Math. Tchrs. P.R. (v.p. 1993-94), Psychometric Soc., Am. Ednl. Rsch. Assn., Nat. Coun. Ednl. Measurement, Nat. Coun. Tchrs. Math., Am. Evaluation Assn. Office: U PR Faculty Edn Rio Piedras PR 00931

MEDLEY, SHERRILYN, auditor; b. Oneida, Ky., Sept. 7, 1946; d. Ora E. and Rheba (Allen) Rice; m. James F. Laughlin, Sept. 20, 1966 (div. Apr. 1969); m. James Silas Medley, Jan. 25, 1980. BS in Acctg., U. Ky., 1975; MBA, Xavier U., 1986. Cert. internal auditor, cert. fraud examiner; CPA. Tchr. Ky. Bus. Coll., Lexington, 1976-78; claims approver Met. Life Ins. Co., Lexington, 1967-73; staff acct. Jerrico, Inc., Lexington, 1976-77, acctg. supr., 1977-80, sr. auditor, 1980-82, internal audit supr., 1982-86; internal audit mgr., 1986-87; sr. internal. audit mgr., 1988-92; gen. mgr. U.S. Achievement Acad., Lexington, 1994—. Vol. Cen. Bapt. Aux., Lexington, 1984. Mem. AICPA, NRA (internal audit group), Nat. Assn. Cert. Fraud Examiners, Inst. Internal Auditors (chpt. pres. 1985-86), Nat. Assn. Accts., Bluegrass Soc. MBA's, Am. Assn. Female Execs. Beta Alpha Psi. Republican. Home: 2436 Brookshire Cir Lexington KY 40515-1226

MEDLOCK, ANGELA ROSEANN, business educator; b. Rockford, Ill., June 2, 1954; m. Michael Joe Medlock, Aug. 14, 1976; children: Michael Jered, Jillian Roseann, Jessica Layne. AAS, Westlark C.C., 1976; BSBA, Coll. of the Ozarks, 1983, BSBE, 1983. Telephone operator Contel, Alma, Ark., 1972-76; asst. planning adminstr. City of Fayetteville, Ark., 1977-78; city clk. City of Fayetteville, 1979-80; bus. instr. Alma High Sch., 1983-87, Mulberry (Ark.) High Sch., 1988—. Alderman City of Mulberry, 1990—, recycling com., 1991—. Democrat. Methodist. Office: Mulberry High Sch Drawer D Mulberry AR 72947

MEDVED, SANDRA LOUISE, elementary education educator; b. Moscow, Idaho, May 26, 1953; d. Donald James and Pearl Helen (Brown) Jensen; m. Jeffrey Alan Medved, Aug. 6, 1977. BS in Edn., U. Idaho, 1975; postgrad., Boise State U., 1976, U. Idaho, 1977—. Tchr. St. Mary's Elem. Sch., Boise, Idaho, 1975-78, Coeur d'Alene (Idaho) Sch. Dist., 1978—; tchr. edn. instr. Coeur d'Alene Sch. Dist., 1986-88, 92—, U. Idaho, 1987-88; lang. arts com. Coeur d'Alene (Idaho) Sch. Dist., 1988—, staff devel. curriculum adv. com., 1990—, mentor tchr., 1990-93, dist. coord. handicap awareness program, 1989-91, puppeteer, 1985-91; instr. Lewis & Clark State Coll., 1994; active Idaho State Sch. Reform Com., 1994—. Vol. Kootenai County Diversion Program, Coeur d'Alene, 1980's. Recipient grants EXCEL, Coeur d'Alene, 1991, 92. Mem. ASCD, NEA, Idaho Edn. Assn., Coeur d'Alene Edn. Assn., Internat. Reading Assn., Panhandle Reading Assn., Phi Delta Kappa. Office: Sorensen Elem Coeur d Alene Sch Dist 9th and Coeur d Alene Ave Coeur D Alene ID 83814

MEDVEDOW, PHYLLIS KRONICK, service executive; b. New Haven, Feb. 18, 1931; d. Louis Barnard and Anna Helen (Skolnick) Kronick; m. Leon A. Medvedow, June 29, 1952; children: Jill Susan, Elisabeth Jane. BS, U. Conn., 1952; cert. advanced mgmt., Yale U., 1988. Exec. v.p. Congress Printers, Inc., New Haven, 1977-81; adminstrv. aide Conn. Gen. Assembly, Hartford, 1979-80; cons. community affairs Yale New Haven Hosp., 1982-83, pub. affairs specialist, 1983-85; asst. dir. community and govt. rels. Yale U., New Haven, 1985-87, assoc. dir. community and govt. rels., 1987-88, dir. community and govt. rels., 1988—; hosp. rep. Conn. Organ and Tissue Donor Coalition, New Haven, 1985—, Coalition on Financing Health Care for the Poor, New Haven, 1987—. Bd. dirs. Anti-Defamation League, New Haven, 1972-81, Shubert Performing Arts Ctr., New Haven, 1994—, trustee, sec., chmn. metro unit Am. Cancer Soc., Woodbridge, Conn., 1955-74, active door-to-door drive, 1955-58; v.p. New Haven Bd. Edn., 1970-74; mem. distbn. com. New Haven Found., 1973-79, United Way, Greater New Haven, 1988—; mem. cmty. rels. com. Greater New Haven Jewish Fedn., 1972—. Mem. Jewish Fedn. Bus. and Profl. Womens Group (bd. dirs. New Haven chpt. 1986-88), Nat. Coun. Jewish Women (publicity chair 1984), Urban League of Greater New Haven (bd. dirs. and 2nd vice chair), C. of C. of Greater New Haven (govtl. affairs com.), New Haven Lions (1st Woman, 1988—). Democrat.

MEED, RITA GOLDWASSER, clinical psychologist; b. Lodz, Poland, Jan. 27, 1951; d. Israel and Tauba (Zylberman) Goldwasser; m. Steven David Meed, Aug. 19, 1973; children: Jessica Tsesha, Chava Leah, Jonathan Lev. BA, U. Chgo., 1973; MA, L.I. U., 1977, PhD, 1988; cert., Tng. Inst. Psychotherapies, N.Y.C., 1992. Lic. psychologist, N.Y. Researcher U. Chgo., 1969-73; microbiologist N.Y.C. Pub. Health Lab., 1973-75; psychology intern Wash. U. and Malcolm Bliss Mental Health Ctr., St. Louis, 1977-78; psychologist West End Psychoneurol. Svcs., N.Y.C., 1987—; pvt. practice N.Y.C. Columnist: Can This Marriage Be Saved?, 1990, Ladies Home Jour., 1993. Chair, liaison Heschel Sch., N.Y.C., 1989-91, calendar chair, 1989-91; bd. dirs. Roosevelt Jewish Congregation, 1988-91. Mem. APA, Internat. Network of Children of Holocaust Survivors (chair kinship group St. Louis and N.Y.C. 1975-89). Democrat. Jewish. Home: 531 Main St New York NY 10044-0105 Office: 270 W End Ave New York NY 10023-2624

MEEHAN, ANN MICHELLE, museum curator; b. Poughkeepsie, N.Y., Sept. 5, 1966; d. Brian B. Moore and Kathleen (Meehan) Soults. BA, Newcomb Coll., 1988; MA, Tulane U., 1992; postgrad., Cambridge U., Eng., 1989, Am. Inst. Fgn. Study, Florence, Italy, 1986. Asst. to exec. v.p. SPECTRA Comm. Assocs., New Orleans, 1987-91; mgr. sales and mktg. SPECTRA Inc., pubs., New Orleans, 1988-91; curator edn. and lectr. New Orleans Mus. Art, 1991—; rsch. assoc. Stone + Press Gallery, New Orleans, 1993—, Tulane U. Art Collection, New Orleans, 1991; lectr. Tulane U. Contbr. articles to profl. publs. Mem. cmty. svc. young alumni mentor program Tulane U., New Orleans, 1991—; coord. art activities My House, Inc., New Orleans, 1992-94; founding mem., treas. Young at Art of New Orleans, 1994—. Home: 1601 Broadway St Apt B New Orleans LA 70118-5301 Office: New Orleans Mus Art PO Box 19123 New Orleans LA 70179-0123

MEEHAN, PAULA KENT, cosmetic company executive; b. West Los Angeles, Calif., Aug. 9, 1931; d. Richard Moorehead and Lois Evelyn (Martin) Bear; m. John Edwin Meehan, Apr. 20, 1973; children: Michael D. Miller, Chris Meehan, Matthew Meehan. Extension student, UCLA. Founder, chmn., chief exec. officer Redken Labs. Inc., Canoga Park, Calif., 1960—. Republican. Address: Redken Labs Inc 6625 Variel Ave Canoga Park CA 91303-2809*

MEEHAN, SANDRA GOTHAM, advertising executive, communications consultant; b. Tokyo, June 9, 1948; d. Fred C. and Evelyn (Dirr) Gotham; m. James P. Jenkins, June 15, 1970 (div. 1989); m. Dayton T. Carr, Dec. 27, 1986 (div. 1989); m. Michael J. Meehan, Jan. 16, 1992. Student, Stanford-in-France, Tours, 1968-69; BA, Stanford U., 1970, MA, 1971. Account exec. Young & Rubicam Inc., N.Y.C., 1972-78, account supr., 1978-80; pres., Gotham Prodns., N.Y.C., 1980-82; v.p., mgmt. supr. Ogilvy & Mather, 1982-85; v.p. Steuben Glass, N.Y.C., 1985-88; sr. v.p. Siegel & Gale, N.Y.C., 1988-92; prin. Gotham Meehan Ptnrs., N.Y.C., 1992—; cons. Congl. coms., FDA, FTC for exec. program Am. Assn. Advt. Agys., Washington, 1978-80; cons. Ctr. Arctic Studies Sorbonne, Paris, in U.S. and Can., 1980-82; seminar dir. N.Y. chpt. Women in Bus., N.Y.C., 1983-84. Writer and editor 4-part TV documentary script Invit! The Universal Cry of the Eskimo People, 1981. Writer speeches for Georgetown Ctr. Strategic and Internat. Studies, also newsletter for Am. Assn. Advt. Agys. Bd. dirs. Rensselaerville (N.Y.) Inst., trustee; fund raiser Stanford U., N.Y.C., promotion coord. of benefits and advt. Medic Alert, N.Y.C., 1983-84; mem. exec. com. Youth Counseling League, N.Y.C., 1984. Mem. Writers Guild Am., Young Profls. Group of Fgn. Policy Assn. (organizing chmn. 1980-81), N.Y. Women in Communications, Stanford Club. Home: 220 E 73d St New York NY 10021 Office: Gotham Meehan Ptnrs 220 E 73d St Ste 5G New York NY 10021

MEEK, AMY GERTRUDE, retired elementary education educator; b. Frostburg, Md., Jan. 3, 1928; d. Arthur Stewart and Amy Laura (Brain) M. BS, Frostburg State U., 1950; MEd, U. Md., 1956; postgrad., Columbia U., 1964, Am. U., 1968-70. Cert. tchr., Md. Tchr. elem. sch. Prince Georges County Schs., Bradbury Heights, Md., 1950-51; tchr. elem. sch. Allegany County Schs., Cumberland, Md., 1951-60, Frostburg, 1960-84; now ret. Author: (with others) Stir Into Flame, 1991; contbr. articles to hist. publs. Mem. Frostburg Hosp. Aux., 1987-91; bd. dirs. Frostburg Hist. Mus., 1988, Coun. of Alleghenies, 1991; sec. Braddock Estates Civic Assn., Frostburg, 1988; mem. com. Frostburg Libr., 1989; tchr. Ch. Conf. Schs. Missions, 1970; vol. tutor, 1986—; pres. Ch. Women United, Frostburg, 1989—; trustee Frostburg United Meth. Ch.; mem. endowment fund com. Balt Conf. United Meth. Ch., 1992—; pres. Cumberland-Hagerstown dist. United Meth. Women, 1985-89, chmn. fin. interpretation Balt. Conf., 1990-94. Mem. AAUW (pres. 1993, treas. Md. divsn. 1974, Woman of Yr. award Frostburg br. 1980, New Frostburg Libr. Bldg. com. 1994). Republican.

MEEK, CARRIE P., congresswoman; 3 children. BS, Fla. A&M U., 1946, MS, U. Mich., 1948. Mem. Fla. Senate from Dist. 36, 1982-1992. Mem. 103rd-104th Congress from 17th Fla. dist., 1993—. Democrat. Office: US Ho of Reps 404 Cannon House Office Bldg Washington DC 20515

MEEK, VIOLET IMHOF, dean; b. Geneva, Ill., June 12, 1939; d. John and Violet (Krepel) Imhof; m. Devon W. Meek, Aug. 21, 1965 (dec. 1988); children: Brian, Karen; m. Don M. Dell, Jan. 4, 1992. BA summa cum laude, St. Olaf Coll., 1960; MS, U. Ill., 1962, PhD in Chemistry, 1964. Instr. chemistry Mount Holyoke Coll., South Hadley, Mass., 1964-65; asst. prof. to prof. Ohio Wesleyan U., Delaware, Ohio, 1965-84, dean for ednl. svcs., 1980-84; dir. annual programs Coun. Ind. Colls., Washington, 1984-86; assoc. dir. sponsored programs devel. Rsch. Found. Ohio State U., Columbus, 1986-91; dean, dir. Ohio State U., Lima, 1992—; vis. dean U. Calif., Berkeley, 1982, Stanford U., Palo Alto, Calif., 1982; reviewer GTE Sci. and Tech. Program, Princeton, N.J., 1986-92, Goldwater Nat. Fellowships, Princeton, 1990-92. Co-author: Experimental General Chemistry, 1984; contbr. articles to profl. jours. Bd. dirs. Lutheran Campus Minsitries, Columbia, 1988-91, Lutheran Social Svcs., 1988-91, Americom Bank, Lima, 1992—, Lima Symphony Orch., 1992—, Art Space, Lima, 1993—, Allen Lima Leadership, 1993—, Am. House, 1992—, Lima Veterans Meml. Civic Ctr. Found., 1992—; chmn. synodical coms. Evangelical Luth. Ch. in Am., Columbus, 1982. Recipient Woodrow Wilson Fellowship, 1960. Mem. Nat. Coun. Rsch. Adminstrs. (named Outstanding New Profl. midwest region 1990), Am. Assn. Higher Edn., Phi Beta Kappa. Home: 209 W Beechwold Blvd Columbus OH 43214-2012 Office: Ohio State U 4240 Campus Dr Lima OH 45804

MEEKER, ARLENE DOROTHY HALLIN (MRS. WILLIAM MAURICE MEEKER), manufacturing company executive; b. Glendale, Calif., June 13, 1935; d. Haddon Eric and Martha (Randow) Hallin. Grad. John Muir Jr. Coll., 1953; Student, L.A. Valley Coll., 1956-58, BA, Whittier Coll., 1973, MBA, 1980; m. William Maurice Meeker, Aug. 19, 66; 1 child, William Michael. Statewide sec. pub. rels. United Reps. Calif., L.A., 1964; pers. specialist Sanford Mgmt. Svcs., Inc., L.A., 1964-66; v.p. pers. Grover Mfg. Corp., Montebello, Calif., 1966-75, pres., 1975—, bd. dir., 1969—, chmn. of bd. 1975—; bd. dir. Brit. Marine Industries, Montebello, 1969-86, chmn. bd. 1986—, Grover Ltd., Clonakilty, County Cork, Ireland, 1986—, Grover Internat., 1969—. Author: Stress Differences Between Male and Female Executives, 1980. Mem. City of Whittier Transp. and Parking Commn., 1976-84, chmn. commn., 1977-79, vice-chmn., 1982-84; coun. mem. L.A. County Art Mus., 1969-80; chmn. fine arts bd. Hillcrest Congl. Ch., mem. ch. coun., 1977-79; trustee Oxford Prep. Sch., Whittier, Calif., 1981-86; visitors bd. Whittier Coll., 1983-89; press chmn. Whittier Rep. Women Federated, 1977-78, 1st v.p., 1981-83; Rep. precinct capt., 1964; active L.A. World Affairs Coun.; pres. Friendly Hills Property Owners Assn, 1982-84. Mem. Docian Soc. (pub. rels. chmn. 1967-68), AAUW, Conglist., Newport Harbor Yacht Club (Newport Beach, Calif.), Friendly Hills Country Club (Whittier, Calif.), Whittier Lincoln Club (pres. 1982-84). Home: 9710 Portada Dr Whittier CA 90603-1326 Office: 620 S Vail Ave Montebello CA 90640-4952

MEEKS, CAROL JEAN, educator; b. Columbus, Ohio, Mar. 9, 1946; d. Clarence Eugene and Clara Johanna (Schwartz) B.; m. Joseph Meeks, Aug. 17, 1968 (div. 1981); 1 child, Catherine Rachael. BS, Ohio State U., Mex., 1968; MS, Ohio State U., 1969, PhD, 1972. Rsch. asst., assoc. Ohio State U., Columbus, 1968-71; internship Columbus Area C. of C., Ohio, 1970; lectr. Ohio State U., Columbus, 1970, 72; asst. prof. U. Mass., Amherst, 1972-74; asst. prof. Cornell U., Ithaca, N.Y., 1974-78, assoc. prof., 1978-80; legis. fellow Senate Com. Banking, 1984; supr. economist, head housing section USDA, Washington, 1980-85; assoc. prof. housing and consumer econs. U. Ga., Athens, 1985-90, prof., 1990—, head housing and consumer econs., 1992—; rsch. fellow Nat. Inst. for Consumer Rsch., Oslo, Norway, 1982; cons. Calif. Dept. Real Estate, 1976, Yale U., 1976-77, HUD, Cambridge, Mass., 1978, MIT Ctr. for Real Estate Devel. Ford Found. Project on Housing Policy; del. N.E. Ctr. for Rural Devel. Housing Policy Conf. Reviewer Home Econ. Rsch. Jour., 1987—, ACCI conf., 1987—; contbr. articles to profl. mags. Mem. panel Town of Amherst Landlord Tenant Bd.; bd. dirs. Am. Coun. Consumer Interests; mem. adv. coun. HUD Nat. Mobile Home, 1978-80, 91-93; chair Housing Mfg. Inst. Consensus Commn. on Fed. Standards. Recipient Young Profl. award Ohio State U., 1979; named one of Outstanding Young Women of Am., 1979; Columbus Womens Chpt. Nat. Assn. Real Estate Bds. scholar, Gen. Foods fellow 1971-72, HEW grantee, 1978, travel grantee NSF bldg. rsch. bd. , AID grantee. Mem. Soc. Govt. Economists (bd. dirs. 1984-85, co-chmn. 1985), Am. Assn. Housing Educators (newsletter editor 1976-79, pres. 1983-84), Nat. Inst. Bldg. Sci. (bd. sec. 1984, 85, 89—, bd. dirs. 1981-83, 85, 87-93, futures commn.), Am. Real Estae and Urban Econs. Assn., Internat. Assn. Housing Sci., Com. on Status of Women in Econs., Nat. Assn. Home Builders (Smart House contract 1989), Epsilon Sigma Phi, Omicron Nu, others. Office: U Ga 215 Dawson Hall Athens GA 30602-3622

MEEKS, MARY JANICE, librarian; b. Newberry, S.C., Sept. 25, 1949; d. Oscar Hugh and Mary Ada (Derrick) Boozer; m. James Thomas Meeks, June 14, 1969; children: Shelley Marie, Stephanie Ann. AA, North Greenville Coll., 1969; BA, Newberry Coll., 1971; MEd in Pers. Svcs., Clemson U., 1979; M in Librarianship, U. S.C., 1982. Cert. secondary social studies and gen. sci. tchr., media specialist. Tchr. Gallman Jr. High Sch., Newberry, 1971-72; tchr. Newberry (S.C.) High Sch., 1972-80, 82-84, asst. libr., 1980-82; elem. libr. M.S. Bailey Elem. Sch., Clinton, S.C., 1984—; co-sponsor Literary Club, M.S. Bailey Elem. Sch., Clinton, 1991—; child support leader Sistercare, Newberry, 1992-93. Mem. NEA, S.C. Edn. Assn. (membership chmn. 1979-80), S.C. Assn. Sch. Librs., Palmetto State Tchrs. Assn. Baptist. Home: 1229 Hillcrest Rd Newberry SC 29108-2019 Office: M S Bailey Elem Sch 625 Elizabeth St Clinton SC 29325-1921

MEELHEIM, HELEN DIANE, nursing administrator; b. Charleston, W.Va., Mar. 25, 1952; d. Richard Young and Dolores (Frick) M. BS in Nursing, U. N.C., 1974; MS in Nursing, East Carolina U., 1982; JD, U. N.C., 1992. Charge nurse Pitt County Health Dept., Greenville, N.C., 1974-77; nursing adminstr. East Carolina U. Sch. of Med., Greenville, N.C., 1978-89, clin. instr., 1986-92; cons. Eastern Area Health Edn. Ctr., Greenville and Fayetteville, 1989-92; staff emergency room U. N.C. Hosps., Chapel Hill, 1989-92; asst. exec. sec. N.C. Bd. Med. Examiners, 1992—. Maj. Army Nurse Corps, USAR, Oper. Desert Storm/Shield, 1990-91. Mem. ANA (cert. family nurse practitioner), Nat. Health Lawyers Assn., N.C. Soc. Health Care Attys, The Assn. Nurse Attys., N.C. Assn of Women Attys., Sigma Theta Tau. Democrat. Episcopalian. Avocation: painting. Home: 4622 Pine Trace Dr Raleigh NC 27613 Office: NC Bd Med Examiners PO Box 26007 Raleigh NC 27619

MEESE, CELIA EDWARDS, pharmaceutical company executive; b. San Diego, May 10; d. Roy Clifford Edwards and Bessie Lucille (Lang) Hill; m. Jed D. Meese; 1 child, Scott Edwards. BA, U. Wis., 1964; BA (hon.), U. Taiwan, 1965. Pres. Vitaline Corp., Ashland, Oreg., 1972—; v.p. RenalChem, Inc., San Jose, Calif., 1982-90, Formulations Tech., Inc., Oakdale, Calif., 1982—; dir. Spectra Diagnostics, San Jose. pres. So. Oreg. State Coll. Found., Oreg. Shakespeare Festival. Mem. Pharm. Mfrs. Assn., Mensa. Home: 88 Granite St Ashland OR 97520-2711 Office: Vitaline Corp 385 Williamson Way Ashland OR 97520-3702

MEFFORD, NAOMI DOLBEARE, secondary education and elementary education educator; b. Pittsfield, Ill., Feb. 10, 1944; d. Donald Pryor and Ruth Allyne (Utter) Dolbeare; m. Clark L. Mefford, Feb. 8, 1964; children: Joseph Clark, Christopher Lee. BA, William Penn Coll., 1977; MA, N.E. Mo. State U., 1986, EdS, 1991. Cert. profl. tchr., adminstr., Iowa. Undergrad. instr. Buena Vista, Ottumwa, Iowa, 1984-87; grad. instr. So. Prairie AEA and Marycrest Coll., Ottumwa, 1988-92; tchr. Ottumwa Schs., 1985—; dir. summer sch. Ottumwa. Chmn. Hosp. Major Fund Raiser, Ottumwa, 1995—. Mem. AAUW (Iowa pub. rels. dir.), Delta Kappa Gamma. Home: 8 Country Club Pl Ottumwa IA 52501 Office: Horace Mann Sch 1523 N Court Ottumwa IA 52501

MEGARGEE, KATHLEEN ANNE, state public information officer; b. Somers Point, N.J., Oct. 12, 1954; d. Irwin Ferdinand and Althea Myrtle (Evans) M. BA in English, Montclair State Coll., 1976. News anchor, reporter Sta. WMID Radio, Atlantic City, 1977-78, Sta. WIIN Radio, Atlantic City, 1979-81, Sta. WHAG-TV, Hagerstown, Md., 1982-84, Sta. WHP-TV, Harrisburg, Pa., 1984-86; news writer The Sun newspaper, Atlantic City, 1978; news reporter, anchor Sta. WRBV-TV, Vineland, N.J., 1981; news anchor Sta. WCAU Radio, Phila., 1981-82; news anchor, reporter, prodr. Sta. WQED-TV, Pitts., 1986-89, Sta. WITF-TV, Harrisburg, 1989-91; press sec. Pa. Dept. Aging, Harrisburg, 1991—. Vol., fund raiser Mothers Against Drunk Driving, 1985, Alzheimer's Assn., Harrisburg, 1994; vol., reader Harrisburg Area Radio Reading Svc. for the Blind, Harrisburg, 1991—. Recipient N.J. AP Broadcasters Assn. award, 1979, N.J. State Bar Assn. award, 1979, Golden Microphone award Atlantic City Press Club, 1980, Reporter/Prodr. award Chesapeake AP Broadcasters Assn., 1982, Nat. Mature Media Market award, 1993, 94, Corp. Pub. Broadcasting award, 1994. Roman Catholic. Home: 1228 Capital St Harrisburg PA 17102 Office: Pa Dept Aging 400 Market St Harrisburg PA 17101-2301

MEGEE, GERALDINE HESS, social worker; b. Newark, Ohio, June 9, 1924; d. A.P. Hess and Ethel Stoyle Luther; children: John Megee, Sarah Martens, Thomas Megee. BS, Northwestern U., 1944; MSEd, Ind. U., 1976, MSW, 1978; PhD candidate, Fielding Inst. Cert. social worker, Ill., Fla.; cert. addictions profl., Fla.; diplomate social work. Dir. Foster Care Prog., Webster-Cantrel Hall, Decatur, Ill., 1978-81; owner, dir. Family Systems Ctr., Decatur, 1981—; pvt. practice clinic and employee assistance Decatur, 1981—; dir. Charter Counseling Ctr., Charter Glade Hosp., Naples, Fla., 1985-87; co-owner FamilyWorks, Naples, 1991—. Mem. Nat. Assn. Social Workers, Am. Assn. Marriage and Family Therapists, Sigma Pi Lambda. Home: 9856 Tonya Ct Bonita Springs FL 33923-4717 Office: 5051 Castello Dr Naples FL 33940

MEGGINSON, ELIZABETH R., legislative director, federal and state government lawyer; b. Clarksdale, Miss., Oct. 27, 1947; d. Mitford Ray and Cleo Ruth (Faggard) M.; m. Mark W. Menezes; children: Paige Jennings, Marisa Menezes. BM, La. State U., 1969, MM, 1970, JD, 1977. Pvt. practice, 1977-78; counsel natural resources com. La. Ho. Reps., 1978-81, legis. svc. coord. comml. regulation divsn., 1981-84; asst. atty. gen. environ. enforcement divsn. La. Dept. Justice, 1984-88; asst. sec. for office legal affairs and enforcement La. Dept. Environ. Quality, 1988-89; adminstrv. asst. to Rep. W.J. Billy Tauzin, Washington, 1989-90; staff dir. counsel sub-com. om coast guard and navigation Ho. Com. on Merchant Marine and Fisheries, Washington, 1990—. Mem. Phi Kappa Phi. Office: Ho Com Mcht Marines & Fisheries Ford House Office Bldg Rm 541 Washington DC 20515*

MEGHERBI, DALILA, electrical and computer engineer, researcher; b. Algiers, Algeria, May 29, 1957; came to U.S., 1983; d. Mohamed and Salima (Astite) M. Diploma in Elec. Engring. with distinction, Ecole Nationale Polytechnique, Algeria, 1983; MSc in Elec. Engring., Brown U., 1986, MSc in Applied Math., 1987, PhD in Elec. Engring., 1993. Rschr. Nat. Ctr. New Energies, Algiers, 1982-83; sr. rsch. engr. Nat. Railway Co., Algiers, 1983; rschr. LEMS lab. divsn. engring. Brown U., Providence, 1986-92, postdoctoral rsch. assoc. LEMS lab. divsn. engring., 1993-94; sr. mgr. Loral Aerospace LADS, Cambridge, Mass., 1994—; tech. cons. IDS Co., East Arlington, Mass., 1993; guest lectr. Northeastern U., 1988-91. Reviewer tech. articles; contbr. articles to profl. jours. Recipient award for excellence and disting. rsch. work IEEE Control Systems Soc., 1993. Mem. IEEE (Control Systems Soc. award for demonstrated rsch. excellence 1993), Computer Soc. of IEEE, Robotics Soc. of IEEE, Sigma Xi. Home: 1427 Commonwealth Ave Apt 401 Brighton MA 02135-6251

MEGLINO, JOSEPHINE, home improvement products company executive; b. Bklyn., Dec. 28, 1928; d. Donato and Olimpia Buglione; m. Nicholas Meglino, May 13, 1951; children: Patricia, James, Don. BA, Hunter Coll., 1949, MA, 1951. Cert. tchr., N.Y. Engring. aide Bell Labs., N.Y.C., 1951-52, tchr. N.Y.C. Pub. Schs., 1950-53; v.p. Jodee Plastics, Inc., Westbury, N.Y., 1953—; pres. Patrician Products, Inc., Westbury, 1965-88, Jodee Plastics, Inc., L.I., N.Y., 1988—; bd. dirs. CLFMI. Mem. AAUW (bd. dirs. local chpt.). Roman Catholic. Avocation: duplicate bridge. Home: 37 Fox Run Roslyn Heights NY 11577-1982 Office: Jodee Plastic Inc PO Box 770 Hicksville NY 11802-0770

MEHRMANN, CRAIGANN, nurse practitioner; b. Hershey, Pa., Jan. 6, 1953; d. Charles Craig and Martha Arlene (Shepler) M.; B.S., Bloomsburg State Coll., 1974; A.A. in Nursing, Harrisburg Area Community Coll., 1979; B.S. in Nursing, Pa. State U., 1985, MSN in Nursing, U. Pa., 1986. R.N., Pa. Substitute tchr., Derry Twp., Central Dauphin, and Middletown Area sch. dists., 1974-77; nursing asst. Milton Hershey Med. Center, 1978; staff nurse Holy Spirit Hosp., Camp Hill, Pa., 1979, Milton Hershey Med. Center, Hershey, Pa., 1979-80; clin. coordinator Hillcrest Women's Med. Ctr., Harrisburg, Pa., 1980-85; nurse practitioner Tri County Planned Parenthood, 1986-89; nurse practitioner Orndorf, Raschid and Assocs., 1989—; nurse lectr. Pa. State U., 1986, Messiah Coll., 1987-89, U. Pa., 1990—. Vol., Am. Cancer Soc., ARC. Mem. Assn. Women's Health, Obstetric and Neonatal Nurses, Am. Acad. Nurse Practitioners, Messiah Coll. Nursing Honor Soc., AAUW, Harrisburg Area Community Coll. Alumni Assn., U. Pa. Sch. of Nursing Alumni Assn., Bloomsburg State Coll. Alumni Assn., Sigma Theta Tau. Methodist. Office: Ste A 761 5th Ave Chambersburg PA 17201

MEHRTENS, SUSAN EMILY, research company executive; b. Elmhurst, N.Y., Sept. 27, 1945; d. William Frederic, and Pauline (Kaufmann) M.; m. Edwin M. Davis, May 31, 1981 (div. Apr. 1984). BA, Queens Coll, 1967; MPhil, Yale U., 1969, PhD, 1973. Asst. prof. Queens Coll., Flushing, N.Y., 1971-77; assoc. prof. Coll. of Atlantic, Bar Harbor, Maine, 1977-87; pres., chief exec. officer Potlatch Group Inc., Mineola, N.Y., 1987—; cons. Family Care Am., Phoenix, 1991, F.C. Nahser Advt. Inc.; instr. Mt. Desert (Maine) Island Adult Edn., 1977-87, U.S Power Squadron-Sewanaka, Freeport, N.Y., 1975-77. Author: Earthkeeping, 1974, Being Human in the West, 1991, Ecoguide, 1991, Revisioning Science, 1991; co-author: The Fourth Wave; contbr. articles to profl. jours. Grantee Am. Philos. Soc., 1974, 86, Am. Coun. Learned Socs., 1974; Yale U. fellow, 1967-69. Mem. Phi Beta Kappa. Home and Office: 239 Barwick Blvd Mineola NY 11501-3234

MEI, DOLORES MARIE, research administrator; b. Ludlow, Mass., Sept. 3, 1955; d. Paul John and Pauline Lavoie M.; m. Jack Irwin, June 28, 1981 (div. Feb. 1988); 1 child, Robert Aaron. AB in Psychology cum laude with honors, Smith Coll., 1977; MA, Columbia U., 1979, M of Philosophy, 1980, PhD, 1981. Rsch. assoc. Columbia U., Henry Krumb Sch. Mines, N.Y.C., 1981-82; mem. staff Office Ednl. Rsch., Bklyn., 1982-83, evaluation mgr., 1983—; ind. cons. N.Y. Zool. Soc., Bronx, 1980-82, 86—. Recipient Nat. Rsch. Svc. award Nat. Inst. Mental Health, 1979-80. Democrat. Roman Catholic. Home: 138 71st St Apt 1F Brooklyn NY 11209-1141 Office: Office Ednl Rsch 110 Livingston St Rm 740 Brooklyn NY 11201-5065

MEIER, ENGE, preschool educator; b. N.Y.C., Jan. 17; d. Rudolf and Kate (Furstenow) Pietschyck; children: Kenneth Randolph, Philip Alan. BBA, Western States U., 1987, MBA, 1989. Tchr. nursery sch. Neu Ulm, Fed. Republic Germany, 1963-64; sec. Brewster (N.Y.) Mid. Sch., 1969-72; teaching asst. Brewster Elem. Sch., 1972-73; office asst. Bd. Coop. Edn., Yorktown Heights, N.Y., 1973-76; sec. Am. Can. Co., Greenwich, Conn., 1976-77, adminstrv. sec., 1977-79, exec. sec., 1979-84; adminstrv. asst. U. Tex., Austin, 1984-85, 88-90, adminstrv. assoc., 1985-86, sr. adminstrv. assoc., 1986-88; exec. asst. DTM Corp., Austin, 1990; funds asst. mgr. Tex. Assn. Sch. Bds., Austin, 1991-92; nursery sch. tchr. Westlake Presbyn. Sch., Austin, 1992—. Docent LBJ Libr. and Mus., Austin, 1984—; mem. Women's Polit. Caucus, 1988—; bd. dirs. Leadership, Edn. and Devel., 1991. Mem. Women in Mgmt., Bus. and Profl. Women (pres. 1989, bd. dirs. Austin chpt. 1987—), Women's C. of C. Presbyterian. Office: Westlake Hills Presbyn Presch 7127 Bee Caves Rd Austin TX 78746-4102

MEIER, JEANNETTE PATRICIA, lawyer; b. Chgo., May 15, 1947; d. Edward Daniel and Darlene Phyllis (White) M. BA, Northwestern U., 1969, JD, 1972. Bar: Colo. 1972, Calif. 1974, Tex. 1987. Assoc. Holland & Hart, Denver, 1972-73; asst. gen. counsel Boothe Computer Corp., San Francisco, 1974-76; asst. gen. counsel Pertec Computer, L.A., 1976-81, v.p., gen. counsel, 1981-82; assoc. counsel Wickes Cos., Santa Monica, Calif., 1982-84; v.p., gen. counsel Informatics Gen., Woodland Hills, Calif., 1984-85; sr. v.p., gen. counsel Sterling Software (acquired Informatics Gen.), Dallas, 1985-93, exec. v.p., gen. counsel, 1993—. Office: Sterling Software Inc 8080 N Central Expy Ste 1100 Dallas TX 75206-1807

MEIER, NANCY JO, nursing consultant; b. Sidney, Nebr., Dec. 15, 1951; d. Donald William and Clara Jo (Miller) M. BA, Midland Luth. Coll., 1974; diploma in Nursing, Immanual Hosp. Sch. Nursing, Omaha, 1974; MS in Nursing Edn., Tex. Women's U., 1978. RN, Tex. Staff nurse St. Lukes Episcopal Hosp./Tex. Heart Inst., Houston, 1974-75, Park Plaza Hosp., Houston, 1976; clin. nursing specialist Houston Thoracic and Cardiovascular Assn., 1977-78; instr. clin. nursing Cedar Sinai Med. Ctr., Los Angeles, 1978-79; dir. dept. nursing edn. Los Angeles New Hosp., 1979-80; ind. cons. nursing edn. Los Angeles, 1980-81; systems support specialist IVAC Corp., San Diego, 1981-83; med. specialist, advt. account exec. Kenneth C. Smith & Assocs., La Jolla, Calif., 1983-87; ind. nursing cons. San Diego, 1987—; cons. nursing edn. Nat. Med. Enterprises, Saudi Arabia, 1980-81, Nursing Services Internat., Los Angeles, 1980, Grossmont Hosp., San Diego, 1985; instr. cardiac life support Los Angeles chpt. Am. Heart Assn., 1978-84; lectr. in field. Organist United Meth. Ch., Sidney, 1967-69, Immanual Sch. Nursing, 1971-74, Meml. Luth. Ch., Houston, 1977-78; bd. dirs. Bluffs of Fox Run Homeowners Assn., San Diego, 1984-85, pres., 1985-86. Mem. Am. Nurses Assn., Am. Assn. Operating Room Nurses, Med. Mktg. Assn., Sigma Theta Tau. Republican. Lutheran. Home and Office: 2963 Old Bridgeport Way San Diego CA 92111-7724

MEIKLEJOHN, (LORRAINE) MINDY JUNE, political organizer, realtor; b. Staunton, Colo., June 9, 1929; d. Edward H. and Erna E. (Schwabe) Mindrup; m. Alvin J. Meiklejohn, Apr. 25, 1953; children: Pamela, Shelley, Bruce, Scott. Student Ill. Bus. Coll., 1948, Red Rocks C.C., 1980-81. Pvt. sec. Ill. Liquor Commn., 1948-51, David M. Wilson, Ill. Sec. of State's Office, 1951-52; flight attendant Continental Airlines, 1952-53, pvt. sec. to mgr. flight svcs. office, 1953-54; organizational dir. Colo. Rep. Party, Denver, 1981-85, mem. Cen. Com., 1987—; campaign coord. Hank Brown's Exploratory Campaign for Gov., 1985, mgr. Hank Brown for Congress, 1985-86; dep. campaign dir. Steve Schuck for Gov., 1985-86; vice chmn. 2d Congl. Cen. Com. Colo.; active campaigns; del., alt. to various, county, state, dist. and nat. assemblies and convs.; Colo. chmn. Citizens for Am., 1987—; realtor, sales assoc. Metro Brokers, Inc.; mem. polit. action com. Jefferson County Bd. Realtors. Apptd. trustee Harry S. Truman Scholarship Found., 1991; mem. Jefferson County Hist. Commn., Colo., 1974-82, pres., 1979; vol. Jefferson County Legal Aid Soc., 1970-74; vice chmn. Jefferson County Rep. Party, 1977-81, exec. com., 1987; vice chmn. Colo. State Rep. Party, 1981-85; chmn. Rep. Nat. Pilot Project on Volunteerism, 1981; mem. adv. coun. U.S. Peace Corps, 1982-84; sect. chmn. Jefferson County United Way Fund Drive; mem. exec. bd. Colo. Fedn. Rep. Women; pres. Operation Shelter, Inc., 1983—; state chair Citizens for Am., 1987—; bd. dirs. Scientific and Cultural Facilities dist. 1989—, Jefferson County chpt. Am. Cancer Soc., 1987-94, Jefferson Found., 1991—. Mem. Jefferson County Women's Rep. (edn. chmn. 1987-91). Lutheran. Home: 7540 Kline Dr Arvada CO 80005-3732

MEIKLEJOHN-WILSON, SHIRRA, religious studies educator; b. Port Chester, N.Y., Aug. 10, 1946; d. David Shirra and Mary Jean (Faulkner) Meiklejohn; m. Paul Neil Wilson; children: Jennifer, Laura, David, Adam. M in Arts and Religion, Yale Divinity Sch., 1987. Founder Spiritual Devel. Guild, Guilford, Conn., 1983; founder so. divsn. Spiritual Devel. Guild, Tryon, N.C., 1990; founder Sojourner Inst., Guilford, 1987; founder so. divsn. Sojourner Inst., Tryon, 1990; abuse counselor Steps to Hope, Polk County, N.C., 1991-94. Author: Conscience & Incarnation, 1992, Daddy Near, Father Away, 1993. Mem. AACD, Assn. Humanistic Studies, Assn. for Humanistic Edn. and Devel., Assn. for Specialists in Group Work, Am. Mental Health Counselors Assn. Episcopalian. Home and Office: 1143 Hwy 176N Tryon NC 28782

MEIL, KATE, sculptor; b. N.Y.C., June 15, 1925; d. Jacob and Becky (Lichtman) Meil; 1 child, Maria Rebecca Black. BBA in Acctg., CCNY, 1949. Acct. chem., printing, garment, machine and tool, film and car industries, 1943-91. Sculptor: Mein Kind, 1976, Determined to Be, 1977, Inner Mirror, 1979, Zeyda, 1980, Meydele, 1985, Remembering, 1987, Single Parent, 1988, Survivors, 1989, Einstein, 1991, We Too Have Dreams, 1992. Leader Hudson Ave Area Residents Assn., Edgewater, 1973; participant Can. Nat. Exhibit, 1989, Cork Gallery, N.Y.C., 1994. Recipient Red and Blue ribbons 3d Ann. N.J. Woodcarving and Wildlife Art Show, 1987, 3d Pl. ribbon Bergen County Dept. Parks, 1991, 92, 2nd Place Bergan County Dept. Parks, 1994, 3d place Ringwood State Manor Exhibit of Salute to Women in the Arts, 1992. Mem. Salute to Women in Arts, Whittle Ones, Ethical Culture Soc., Palisades Nature Assn. Avocations: chess; theater; folk dancing.

MEILAN, CELIA, food products executive; b. Bklyn., Jan. 21, 1920; d. Ventura Lorenzo and Susana (Prego) M. Student, CCNY, 1943-46. Codes and ciphers translator security divsn. U.S. Censorship Office, N.Y.C., 1942-46; sec., treas. Albumina Supply Co., N.Y.C., 1946-55; co-founder, co-owner, sec., treas., fin. officer Internat. Proteins Corp., Fairfield, N.J., 1955-86, exec. v.p., 1986-93; pres. Internat. Proteins Corp., Fairfield, 1993; also bd. dirs. Internat. Proteins Corp., Fairfield, N.J.; bd. dirs. Pesquera Taboquilla, Panama City, Republic of Panama, 1969—, Inversiones Pesqueras S.A., Brit. V.I.; v.p., bd. dirs. Atlantic Shippers of Tex. Inc., Port Arthur, 1989, Atlantic Shippers Inc., Morehead City, N.C., Empacadora Nacional S.A., Panama City, Republic of Panama; exec. v.p., bd. dirs. Fairfield Fishing Co., Liberia, Internat. Proteins Chile S.A., Santiago. Named One of Top 50 Women Bus. Owners, Working Woman mag. and Nat. Found. Women Bus. Owners, 1994. Mem. Nat. Found. Women Bus. Owners, Spanish Benevolent Soc. (bd. dirs. 1955-62). Avocations: travel, hand crafts, backgammon, puzzles. Office: 204 Passaic Ave Fairfield NJ 07004-3407

MEINELT, ELLEN MARIE, immunologist; b. Kew Gardens, N.Y., Oct. 12, 1956; d. Kenneth Harold and Lorraine Marie (Rousseau) M. BS, U. Utah, 1978; MS, U. Minn., 1984. Clin. lab asst. I U. of Utah Med. Ctr., Salt Lake City, 1976, clin. lab asst. II, 1977-78; med. technologist Mountain Head and Neck, Layton, Ut., 1978-82; rsch. assoc. Coulter Immunology, Hialeah, Fla., 1984-88; supr. Immunopath Labs., Hialeah, 1988-93; flow cytometry rsch. technologist Krug Life Scis., Houston, 1993—; cons. Davis North Internal Medicine, Layton, Utah, 1980-82. Mem. Am. Soc. for Med. Tech., Utah Soc. for Med. Tech. (student rep. 1977-88, editor-newsletter 1980-81, Spl. award 1981). Democrat. Lutheran. Office: Krug Life Scis Ste 120 1290 Hercules Dr Houston TX 77058

MEINER, SUE ELLEN THOMPSON, gerontologist, nursing educator and administrator; b. Ironton, Mo., Oct. 24, 1943; d. Louis Raymond and Verna Mae (Goggin) Thompson; m. Robert Edward Meiner, Mar. 5, 1971; children: Diane Thompson Bubb, Suzanne Elaine. AAS, Meramec Community Coll., 1970; BS in Nursing, St. Louis U., 1978, MS in Nursing, 1983; EdD, So. Ill. U., Edwardsville, 1991; cert. in gerontology, So. Ill. U., 1990; Clin. Specialist in Gerontol. Nursing, 1992. RN, Med. Surg. Clinician, Mo.; clin. practitioner in life span nursing. Staff RN St. Joseph's Hosp., St. Charles, Mo., 1976-78; nursing supr. Bethesda Gen. Hosp., St. Louis, 1975-76, 71-74; adult med. dir. Family Care Ctr.-Carondelet, St. Louis, 1978-79; program dir., lectr. Webster Coll./Bethesda Hosp., Webster Groves, Mo., 1979-82; diabetes clin. specialist Washington U. Sch. Medicine, St. Louis, 1982; chmn. dept. nursing, asst. prof. St. Louis Community Coll., 1983-88, Barnes Hosp. Sch. Nursing, 1988-89; instr. U. Mo., St. Louis, 1989; assoc. prof. St. Charles County Community Coll., St. Peters, Mo., 1990-92, Deaconess Coll. of Nursing, 1991-93; patient care mgr. Deaconess Hosp., St. Louis, 1993-94; assoc. prof. Jewish Hosp. Coll. of Nursing and Allied Health, 1994—; nat. dir. edn. Nat. Assn. Practical Nurse Edn. and Svc., Inc., St. Louis, 1984-86; mem. task force St. Louis Met. Hosp. Assn., 1987-88; mem. adv. com. Bd. Edn. Sch. Nursing, St. Louis, 1986-90. Contbr. articles to profl. jours. and books. Chmn. bd. dirs. Creve Coeur Fire Protection Dist. Mo., 1984-89; vice chmn. Bd. Cen. St. Louis County Emergency Dispatch Svc., 1985-87; asst. leader Girl Scouts U.S., St. Louis, 1975; treas. Older Women's League, St. Louis, 1992-93. Recipient Woman of Worth award Gateway chpt. Older Women's League, 1993. Mem. ANA, Am. Nurses Found., Nat. League for Nursing, Am. Soc. of Aging, Mid-Am. Congress on Aging, Creve Coeur C. of C., Order Ea. Star (chaplain 1970), Jobs Daus. (guardian 1979-80), Sigma Theta Tau (fin. chmn. 1984, archivist 1985-87), Sigma Phi Omega (pres. 1990-91), Kappa Delta Pi. Home and Office: 700 Wren Path Ct Ballwin MO 63021-4794

MEINERS, PHYLLIS HENRI, fund development consultant; b. Boston, Nov. 8, 1940; d. Samuel Henry and Edith (Salvin) Bloom; m. William F. Meiners Jr.; 1 child, Hilary Henri Tun-Atz. BA, U. Calif., Berkeley, 1962; postgrad., MIT, 1971-72, Rockhurst Coll., 1980-83. Cert. fund raising exec. Dir. rsch. Harbridge House, Boston, 1964-70; rsch. assoc. MIT, Cambridge, 1970-71; advocate planner Urban Planning Aid, Cambridge, 1972-73; program adminstr. U. Hawaii, Honolulu, 1974-79, Mo. div. Community Devel., Kansas City, 1980-82; pres. Corp. Resource Cons., Kansas City, Mo., 1982—; founder libr. corp. philanthropy Corp. Resource Ctr., 1988; founder, pres. CRC Pub. Co., 1993. Mem. Nat. Com. of Responsive Philanthropy, 49/63 Neighborhood Coalition, South Town Coun., Kansas City, Friends of Art, Kansas City; staff coord. Mayor Charles B. Wheeler campaign, Kansas City, 1979. Mem. NAFE, Nat. Soc. Fundraising Execs. (bd. dirs.), Brush Creek Trolley Bar Assn., Greater Kansas City C. of C. (entrepreneurs coun.), Greater Kansas City Coun. Philanthropy, Native Ams. in Philanthropy, Brookside Neighborhood Assn., Kansas City Consensus, Nat. Coun. Jewish Women, Nat. Assn. Individual Investors. Democrat. Jewish. Home: 5800 Grand Ave Kansas City MO 64113-2128 Office: 6233 Harrison St Kansas City MO 64110-3411

MEINERT, PATRICIA ANN, compensation planning executive; b. Chgo., Feb. 9, 1949; d. Clarence Fredrick and Evelyn Mae (Nicklas) M.; m. Joseph Vito Di Palma, Aug. 24, 1974 (div.); m. David Mark Van De Voort, Apr. 23, 1988; 1 child, Michael David Van De Voort. BS in Acctg., Ball State U., 1971; M in Labor and Human Resources, Ohio State U., 1980. Asst. contr. Ziesel Bros. Co., Inc., Elkhart, Ind., 1971-73; internal auditor Singer Co., Syosset, N.Y., 1973-75, sr. acct., 1975-77; sr. acct. Anchor Hocking Co., Inc., Lancaster, Ohio, 1977-78; compensation specialist Nationwide Ins. Co., Columbus, Ohio, 1980-87, asst. pers. mgr., 1987-89, compensation planning mgr., 1989—; adj. prof. Franklin U., Columbus, 1986-88. Participant Columbus Area Leadership Program, 1988-89; fin. dir. Women's Conf. 1988; mem. steering com. Columbus Woman's Round Table, 1989—; bus. advisor Assn. Retarded Citizens' Industries ARC; mediator Small Claims Ct., 1988-90; mem. human resources com. Franklin County United Way, 1991—. Mem. Am. Compensation Assn., Cen. Ohio Pers. Assn., Bus. and Profl. Women's Assn. (bd. dirs. dist. 12 1985-87, chair state long range planning com. 1988, chair state fin. com. 1990-91, pres. Worthington chpt. 1983-85). Home: 1129 Sleeping Meadow Dr New Albany OH 43054 Office: Nationwide Ins Co 1 Nationwide Pla Columbus OH 43216

MEINHARDT, CAROLYN LORIS, computer company executive; b. Yankton, S.D., Dec. 23, 1949; m. Jerome F. Foecke, Nov. 11, 1982. BS, St. Cloud State U., 1974. From tchr. to bus. mgr. Pine City (Minn.) Pub. Schs., 1974-79; mgr. computer svcs. ESV Region III, St. Cloud, Minn., 1979-81; computer specialist S.D. City Schs., 1981-83; pres. Wordware, Inc., Dassel, Minn., 1983—; guest speaker several ednl. computing assn., 1982—; tech. cons. Dept of Def. Dependent Schs., Washington, 1987-88; instr. Hutchinson Tech. Coll., 1988-92. Author: (textbook) Business Applications for the IBM-PC, 1987; (software) Lunch Cashier System, 1989—, Food Inventory System, 1989—, others. Mem. Internat. Assn. Computing Edn. (pres. 1984-85), Am. Fedn. Info. Processing Socs. (bd. dirs. 1985), Internat. Soc. for Tech. in Edn. Home and Office: 26616 Csah 24 Dassel MN 55325-3107

MEIS, NANCY RUTH, marketing and development executive; b. Iowa City, Aug. 6, 1952; d. Donald J. and Theresa (Dee) M.; m. Paul L. Wenske, Oct. 14, 1978; children: Alexis Meis Wenske, Christopher Meis Wenske. BA, Clarke Coll., 1974; MBA, U. Okla., 1981. Cultural program supr. City of Dubuque, Iowa., 1974-76; community services dir. State Arts Council of Okla., Oklahoma City, 1976-78, program dir., 1978-79; mgr. Cimarron Circuit Opera Co., Norman, Okla., 1979-82, bd. dirs., 1982-86; account exec. Bell System, Kansas City, Mo., 1982; mgr. spl. svcs. Children Internat., Kansas City, 1983-86; dir. mktg. and fund raising, 1986-87, dir. devel., 1987-88, v.p. devel., 1988-90; dir. mktg. and consulting svcs, Unimedia div. Universal Press Syndicate, Kansas City; cons., copywriter; speaker in field; co-founder Sage Enterprises, Inc. Chair satisfaction com. Cen. Exch.; co-founder Girls to Women; founder The Garnet Ring; program com. Ho. Menuda. Mem. Direct Mktg. Assn. Roman Catholic.

MEISCH, JANENE KAY, women's health nurse; b. Caledonia, Minn., Aug. 10, 1950; d. Charles Arvid and Alma Leota (Kannenberg) Rollins; m. Arnold Leo Meisch, Nov. 2, 1968; children: Kelly, Abigail. ADN, Western Wis. Tech. Coll., LaCrosse, 1979. Cert. reproductive endocrinology/infertility NAACOG. Staff nurse ob/gyn. Luth. Hosp. LaCrosse, 1979-86; staff nurse ob/gyn. Gundersen Clinic, LaCrosse, 1986-87, staff nurse infertility, 1987-91, nurse clinician, 1991—; cons. Infertility Support Group, 1988—. Mem. Nurses Spl. Interest Group, Am. Fertility Soc. Office: Gundersen Clinic Ltd 1836 South Ave La Crosse WI 54601

MEISKEY, SHIRLEY SUZANNE, health information administrator; b. Lancaster, Pa., Mar. 5, 1945; d. Norman Burnell and Nevo Nannette (West) Snader; m. Thomas Eugene Meiskey, Aug. 24, 1968. AAS, No. Va. Community Coll., 1974; BACC in Health Info. Mgmt., Stephens Coll., 1983; MS in Health Care Adminstrn., Cen. Mich. U., 1987. Corr. sec. Greater S.E. Community Hosp., Washington, 1974-76, patient care evaluation asst., 1976-77, asst. to dir., 1977-80, assoc., mgr. record svcs., 1980-87; assoc. prof., coord. health info. technician Montgomery Coll., Takoma Park, Md., 1987—; cons. in field; mem. adv. com. med. record adminstrn. program George Washington U., Washington, 1988-89. Mem. Am. Health Info. Mgmt. Assn. (program com. 1992 assemble on edn.), D.C. Health Info. Mgmt. Assn. (pres. 1985-86, editor D.C. Current 1989, 92-93), chair tri-state spl. events 1987-88). Democrat. Lutheran. Home: 3107 Collard St Alexandria VA 22306-1419

MEISNER, JUDITH ANNE, clinical social worker, marital and sex therapist, psychotherapist; b. Dayton, Ohio, Mar. 20, 1931; d. Lowell DeWight and Mary Elizabeth (Anderson) Richardson; m. S. Clair Varner, 1953 (div. 1964); m. Carl E. Meisner, Dec. 31, 1970; children: Christopher, Cynthia, Deborah, Catherine; stepchildren: Janet, Elizabeth, Barbara. BA, Oberlin Coll., 1952; MSW, Fla. State U., 1970; PhD, Inst. Advanced Study Human Sexuality, 1987. Cert. Acad. Cert. Social Workers; bd. cert. diplomate; lic. clin. social worker; lic. marriage and family therapist; diplomate Am. Bd. Sexology, Am. Coll. Sexologists, clin. supr. Am. Bd. Sexology. Psychiat. aide Inst. Living, Hartford, Conn., 1952-53; caseworker, supr. Div. Family Svcs., Dept. Health and Rehabilitative Svcs., St. Petersburg, Fla., 1964-66, 66-68; dir. standing com. on health and rehabilitative svcs. Fla. Ho. Reps. , Fla. State Legis., Tallahassee, 1970-72; adj. prof. grad. sch. social work Fla. State U., Tallahassee, 1972-73; family life cons. Family Counseling Ctr., St. Petersburg, 1973-75; coord. Teenage Info. Program for Students Pinellas County Sch. Bd., St. Petersburg, 1975-78, coord. Citizen's Task Force on Edn. for Family Living, 1978-80; psychotherapist Counseling & Cons. Svcs., St. Petersburg, 1975—; profl. adv. bd. Nat. Found. March of Dimes Pinellas chpt., Clearwater, Fla., 1976-85, Parents Without Ptnrs. chpt. 186, St. Petersburg, 1973—; mem. Family Life Edn. Coun. Pinellas County Sch. Bd., Clearwater, 1980-85. Bd. dirs. Neighborly Sr. Svcs., Clearwater, 1974-85, pres., bd. dirs., 1982, 83; bd. dirs. Marriage and Family Counseling of Pinellas County, Inc., 1993—. Fellow Am. Acad. Clin. Sexologists (life); mem. NASW, Am. Assn. for Marriage and Family Therapists (clin.), Pinellas Assn. for Marriage and Family Therapists (clin.), Am. Assn. Sex. Educators, Counselors and Therapists (life, cert. sex educator, sex therapist), Soc. for the Sci. Study of Sex, Fla. Soc. Clin. Social Workers, Soc. of Neuro-Linguistic Programming (cert. master practitioner), Harry Benjamin Internat. Gender Dysphoria Assn., Fla. Soc. of Clin. Hypnosis. Home: 7 Marina Ter Treasure Island FL 33706-1203

MEISNER, MARY JO, editor; b. Chgo., Dec. 24, 1951; d. Robert Joseph and Mary Elizabeth (Casey) M.; 1 child, Thomas Joseph Gradel. BS in Journalism, U. Ill., 1974, MS in Journalism, 1976. Copy editor Wilmington (Del.) News Jour., 1975-76, labor and bus. reporter, 1975-79; labor and gen. assignment reporter Phila. Daily News, 1979, city editor, 1979-83, met. editor, 1983-85; PM city editor San Jose (Calif.) Mercury News, 1985-86, met. editor, 1986-87; city editor The Washington Post, 1987-90; mng. editor The Ft. Worth Star-Telegram, 1991-93; editor and v.p. The Milw. Jour., 1993—. Mem. AP Mng. Editors (bd. dirs. 1992—), Am. Soc. Newspaper Editors, Internat. Press Inst. (bd. dirs. 1994—), Pulitzer prize juror 1994). Office: The Milw Jour 333 W State St Milwaukee WI 53203-1305

MEISSNER, ALICE MARTHA, real estate broker; b. Bklyn., June 30, 1926; d. Karl Frederick and Marta Alexandria (Kaipiainen) Nilsson; m. Charles Joseph Meissner, Mar. 31, 1952; children: Gregory, Christopher, Melissa. Diploma, Adelphi Coll., 1946; BS cum laude, Adelphi U., 1949; postgrad., NYU, 1950-51. RN, N.Y.; registered real estate broker, Fla. V.p. North Manor Constrn., Great Neck, N.Y., 1955-58; vol. ARC, Bradenton, Fla., 1960-66; owner, founder Meissner Real Estate, Bradenton, 1969—. Mem. AAUW, Nat. Assn. Realtors, Fla. Assn. Realtors, Manatee County Bd. Realtors, Manatee County Art League, Epsilon Sigma Alpha (v.p. 1970, pres. 1979). Presbyterian. Home: 500 Palma Sola Blvd Bradenton FL 34209-3226 Office: Meissner Real Estate 4411 60th St West Bradenton FL 34210

MEISSNER, DORIS MARIE, federal commissioner; b. Nov. 3, 1941; d. Fred and Hertha H. (Tromp) Borst; m. Charles F. Meissner, June 8, 1963; children: Christine M., Andrew D. BA, U. Wis., 1963, MA, 1969. Asst. dir. student fin. aid U. Wis., 1964-68; exec. dir. Nat. Women's Polit. Caucus, 1971-73; asst. dir. office policy and planning U.S. Dept. Justice, 1975, exec. dir. cabinet com. illegal aliens, 1976, dep. assoc. atty. gen., 1977-80, acting commr. immigration and naturalization svc., 1981, exec. assoc. commr. immigration and naturalization svc., 1982-86, commr. immigration and naturalization svc., 1993—; sr. assoc., dir. immigration policy project The Carnegie Endowment for Internat. Peace, 1986-93; adv. coun. U.S./Mex. project Overseas Devel. Coun., 1981-86; trustee Refugee Policy Group, 1987-93; adv. bd. Program for Rsch. on Immigration Policy Rand Corp./Urban inst., 1988-92; cons. panel to comptroller gen. GAO, 1989-93; with Coun. Fgn. Rels., 1990—, Washington Office Latin Am., 1989-93. White Ho. fellow, 1973-74. Mem. Nat. Women's Polit. Caucus (nat. adv. bd. 1976—), White House Fellows Alumni Assn. and Found. (sec., exec. com. 1979-82, Assn. Governing Bds. Colls. and Univs. (panel higher edn. issues 1990-92), Phi Kappa Phi, Mortar Board, Alpha Chi Omega. Office: Dept Justice Immigration & Naturalization Svc 425 Eye St NW Rm 7100 Washington DC 20536

MEISTAS, MARY THERESE, endocrinologist, diabetes researcher; b. Grand Rapids, Mich., July 22, 1949; d. Frank Peter and Anne Therese (Karsokas) M. MD, U. Mich., 1975. Diplomate Am. Bd. Internal Medicine, Am. Bd. Endocrinology. Intern, then resident in internal medicine Cleve. Clinic Hosp., 1975-78, endocrinology fellow, 1978-79; fellow in pediatric endocrinology Johns Hopkins Hosp., Balt., 1979-81; diabetes researcher Joslin Diabetes Ctr., Boston, 1981-86; assoc. in medicine Brigham and Women's Hosp., Boston, 1981-86; asst. in medicine, diabetes researcher Mass. Gen. Hosp., Boston, 1986—. Contbr. articles to profl. jours. Mem. ACP, Am. Diabetes Assn., Am. Fedn. Clin. Research, Endocrine Soc. Office: Emerson Hosp 747 Main St Ste 111 Concord MA 01742

MEISTER, DORIS POWERS, investment management executive; b. Ames, Iowa, Sept. 12, 1954; d. James Phillip and Doris (Goess) P.; m. Gilbert Meister Jr., Oct. 18, 1980. AB, Smith Coll., 1976; MBA, U. Chgo., 1979. Mgr. currency Harris Trust & Savs. Bank, Chgo., 1976-78; sr. engagement mgr. McKinsey & Co. Inc., N.Y.C., London, 1979-84; dir., dept. head portfolio strategies dept., adminstrv. mgr. fixed income rsch. group C S First Boston, N.Y.C., 1984-90; exec. v.p., COO Christie, Manson & Woods Internat. Inc., N.Y.C., 1990-94; mng. dir. Copley Real Estate Advisors, Boston, 1994—. Bd. dirs. Women's Econ. Roundtable, ArtsConnection, 1990, Am. Women's Econ. Devel. Corp., 1994. Named one of "Top 40 under 40" Execs., Crain's N.Y., 1992. Mem. Fin. Women's Assn., Women's Bond Club, ArtTable, Com. of 200, Women's Forum. Episcopalian. Office: Copley Real Estate Advisors 399 Boylston St Boston MA 02116

MEITIN, DEBORAH DORSKY, health care executive; b. Cleve., July 25, 1951; d. Irving and Rosalind (Lewis) D.; m. Samuel R. Meitin, Dec. 6, 1987. BS, Mich. State U., 1973; M Health Adminstrn., Ohio State U., 1981. Cert. med. technologist. Med. technologist U. Hosps., Cleve., 1974-79; adminstrv. dir. surgery and anesthesiology Cleve. Met. Gen. Hosp., 1981-86; sr. cons. Ernst & Whinney, Chgo., 1986-87; sr. v.p. Diversified Health Search, Maitland, Fla., 1988-89; pres. Health Search Cons., Altamonte Springs, Fla., 1989-91; pres. Greater Fla. Devel. Co., Altamonte Springs, 1988—; sr. cons. Ernst & Young, Orlando, 1991-92, mgr., 1992-94; TQM analyst Fla. hosp., Orlando, 1995—. Mem. bd. profl. women's group Jewish Fedn., Chgo., 1986-87; mem. coms. Jewish Cmty. Ctr., Chgo., 1986-87, Orlando, Fla., 1990—, v.p., 1991-94; bd. dirs. Michael Reese Hosp.-Jr. Med. Rsch. Coun., Chgo., 1986-87, Temple Israel, Orlando, 1989—. Fellow Am. Coll. Healthcare Execs.; mem. NOW, Ohio State U. Grad. Program in Health Adminstrn. Alumni Assn. (bd. dirs. 1982-84), Phi Kappa Phi, Beta Beta Beta. Democrat. Home: 268 Buttercup Cir Altamonte Springs FL 32714-5844 Office: 601 East Rollins St Orlando FL 32803

MEITNER, PAMELA, lawyer, educator; b. Phila., Aug. 23, 1950; d. Alfred Victor Meitner and Claire Jane (Carroll) Harmer; m. William Bruce Larson, Sept. 13, 1980; 1 child, William Bruce, Jr. BS in chem. engring., Drexel U., 1973; JD, Del. Law Sch., 1977. Bar: Del. 1977, U.S. Dist. Ct. Del. 1977. Engr. DuPont Co., Deepwater, N.J., 1973-77; lawyer DuPont Co., Wilmington, Del., 1977; prof. Del. Law Sch., Wilmington, 1985—. Commr. State Emergency Response Com., Dover, Del., 1986-90. Mem. Del. Bar Assn. Club: DuPont Country (Wilmington) (bd. govs. 1984-85). Home: 211 Welwyn Rd Wilmington DE 19803-2951 Office: DuPont Co Legal Dept 1007 Market St Wilmington DE 19898

MEIWES, JOYCE ELIZABETH, accountant, auditor; b. Eugene, Oreg., Jan. 15, 1964; d. William Henry and Elizabeth Jean (Van Dyke) M. BSBA, U. Oreg., 1986. Cost acct. EL-Jay Mfg., Eugene, Oreg., 1982-87; acctg. supr. State Farm Ins. Cos., Salem, Oreg., 1987-91; internal staff auditor State Farm Ins. Cos., Bloomington, Ill., 1991—. Mem. Nat. Assn. Ins. Women, Am. Bus. Womens Assn., Inst. Mgmt. Accts., Inst. Internal Auditors. Office: State Farm Ins Cos One State Farm Plz LDB Bloomington IL 61710

MEIXNER, NANCY SUE, psychotherapist; b. Phila., Feb. 16, 1955; d. David and Gretchen (Mertens) M. BS in Behavioral Psychology, Lynchburg Coll., 1977; MS in Counseling Psychology and Family Therapy, Loyola Coll., 1984. Cert. profl. counselor, Md. Residential treatment counselor, supr. Villa Maria Residential Treatment Ctr., Timonium, Md., 1978-85, asst. dir. residential svcs., 1985-86, psychotherapist, 1986—; pvt. practice, 1985—; owner Concept Application Seminars, Balt., 1989—. Office: Villa Maria 2300 Dulaney Valley Rd Timonium MD 21093

MELAMED, CAROL DRESCHER, lawyer; b. N.Y.C., July 12, 1946; d. Raymond A. and Ruth W. (Schwartz) Drescher; children: Stephanie Weisman, Deborah Weisman; m. Arthur Douglas Melamed, May 26, 1983; children: Kathryn, Elizabeth. AB, Brown U., 1967; MAT, Harvard U., 1969; JD, Catholic U. Am., 1974. Bar: Md. 1974, D.C. 1975, U.S. Ct. Appeals, (D.C. cir.) 1975, U.S. Dist. Ct. D.C. 1981, U.S. Supreme Ct. 1982. Tchr. English, Wellesley High Sch., Mass., 1968-69; law clk. U.S. Ct. Appeals, (D.C. cir.), Washington, 1974-75; assoc. Wilmer, Cutler & Pickering, Washington, 1975-79; dir. govt. affairs, assoc. counsel, The Washington Post, 1979-95, v.p. govt. affairs, 1995— . Mem. Phi Beta Kappa. Office: The Washington Post 1150 15th St NW Washington DC 20071-0002

MELAMEDE, ADA KARMI, architectural firm executive. Prin. Karmi Assocs., Tel Aviv, Israel. Prin. work (with Ram Karmi) Supreme Ct. of Israel. Office: Karmi Assocs, Tel Aviv Israel

MELANSON, ANNE M., advertising agency executive. Former sr. v.p. Ted Bates Advt., N.Y.C.; sr. v.p., dir. human resources Backer Spielvogel Bates Worldwide, Inc., N.Y.C.; now exec. v.p., dir. human resources and ops. Bates Worldwide, Inc., N.Y.C. Office: Bates Worldwide 405 Lexington Ave New York NY 10174-0002

MELCHER, CHARLOTTE RAE, psychologist; b. Lindsborg, Kans., Dec. 5, 1944; d. Clarence Paul and Beth Elaine (Myers) Almquist; m. Charles Paul Melcher, Aug. 29, 1965; children: Deborah Marie, David Paul, Daniel Joshua. BS in Lang. Arts, U. Kans., 1966; MS in Counseling Psychology, U. Ky., 1984, PhD in Counseling Psychology, 1989. Lic. psychologist. Mem. campus staff Campus Crusade for Christ, San Bernadino, Calif., 1966-85; clin. dir. Focus on Relationships, Inc., Lexington, Ky., 1985—; presenter in field. Mem. Am. Assn. Marriage and Family Therapists. Republican. Home: 4748 Scenicview Rd Lexington KY 40514

MELCHER, TRINI URTUZUASTEGUI, accounting educator; b. Somerton, Ariz., Dec. 1, 1931; d. Francisco Juan and Dolores (Barraza) Urtuzuastegui; m. Arlyn Melcher, Aug. 3, 1957 (div. Feb. 1972); children: Teresa Dolores, Michael Francis, Jocelyn Marie. BS, Ariz. State U., 1954; MBA, Kent State U., 1964; PhD, Ariz. State U., 1977. Acct. CPA firm, L.A., 1954-56; instr. L.A. Sch. Dist., 1956-58, Dolton (Ill.) Sch. Dist., 1958-61; asst. prof. Kent (Ohio) State U., 1962-72; prof. Calif. State U., Fullerton, 1976-89; founding faculty mem. Calif. State U., San Marcos, 1990—. Author: Intermediate Accounting Study Guide, 1984. Treas. Community Devel. Coun., Santa Ana, 1985-88, chmn. bd., 1989; mem. com. U.S. Dept. Labor, 1989—. Named Outstanding Educator, League of United Latin Am. Citizens, Stanton, Calif., 1987, Mex. Am. Women's Nat. Assn., Irvine, Calif., 1987; recipient Outstanding Faculty award Calif. State U. Sch. Bus., 1983, Pub. Svc. award Am. Soc. Women CPAs, San Antonio, 1989; Affirmative Action grantee, 1990. Mem. AICPA (editorial bd. The Woman CPA), Am. Acctg. Assn., Calif. Soc. CPAs (Merit award 1991), Hispanic CPAs. Home: 2c24 Sequoia St San Marcos CA 92069 Office: Calif State U San Marcos CA 92069

MELCONIAN, LINDA JEAN, state senator, lawyer; b. Springfield, Mass.; d. George and Virginia Elaine (Noble) Melconian. B.A., Mt. Holyoke Coll., 1970; M.A., George Washington U., 1976, J.D., 1978. Bar: Mass. Chief legis. asst. to Ho. of Reps. Speaker Thomas P. O'Neill, Jr., U.S. Congress, Washington, 1971-80; pros. atty. Hampden County Dist. Atty., Springfield, Mass., 1981-82; state senator Mass. Gen. Ct., Boston, 1983—; instr. Western New Eng. Coll., Springfield, 1978-82; Our Lady of the Elms Coll., Springfield, 1982-83. Chmn., Heart Fund Ball, Western Mass., 1983; incorporator Springfield Coll., 1982—; ex officio trustee Ella T. Grasso Found., Conn., 1982—; active Democratic State Com., Mass., 1983, Hampden County Dems. Recipient Appreciation award Vietnam Vets. of Greater Springfield, 1983; Equal Edn. for All Children award Bilingual Parents of Springfield, 1983; Appreciation award Vets.-Hampden County Council, 1984. Mem. Hampden County Bar Assn. Home: 257 Ft Pleasant Ave Springfield MA 01108-1521 Office: Mass State Senate Rm 213-b Boston MA 02133

MELE, JOANNE THERESA, dentist; b. Chgo., Dec. 5, 1943; d. Andrew and Josephine Jeanette (Calabrese) M. Diploma, St. Elizabeth's Sch. Nursing, Chgo., 1964; diploma in Dental Hygiene, Northwestern U., 1977; A.S., Triton Coll., 1979; D.D.S., Loyola U., 1983. Registered nurse, dental hygienist. Staff nurse in medicine/surgery St. Elizabeth's Hosp., Chgo., 1964-66, operating room nurse, 1966-67; head nurse operating room Cook County Hosp., Chgo., 1967-76, head nurse ICU, 1976-77; dental hygienist Mele Dental Assocs., Ltd., Oakbrook, Ill., 1977-79, practice dentistry, 1983—; clinical asst. prof. Loyola U., Chgo., 1988. Recipient Northwestern U. Dental Hygiene Clinic award, 1977; Dr. Duxler Humanitarian award scholar Loyola U., 1982. Mem. Chgo. Dental Soc., Ill. State Dental Soc., Acad. Gen. Dentistry, Am. Assn. Women Dentists, Acad. Operative Dentistry, Am. Prosthodontic Soc., Psi Omega (Kappa chpt.). Roman Catholic. Avocations: reading; music; golfing; jogging; skiing.. Office: Mele Dental Assocs Ltd 120 Center St Ste 610 Hinsdale IL 60521

MELÉNDEZ, ZULMA CECILIA, bilingual/bicultural education evaluator; b. Santurce, P.R.; d. Miguel Antonio and Consuelo (Torres) Carrio. AA in Psychology, Bronx C.C., 1976; BA in Psychology, Columbia U., 1981; MS in Edn., CUNY, 1990. Lic. tchr., N.Y.C., bilingual spl. edn. tchr. (Spanish), N.Y. Project coord., tchr. The Ednl. Alliance, N.Y.C., 1975-79; cons. to pres. Strategic Learning Systems Inst., Bayside, N.Y., 1982-92; asst. dir. Ednl. and Vocat. Rehab. Svcs., Samaritan Village Inc., Forest Hills, N.Y., 1983-84; rsch. assoc. Columbia U. Sch. Social Work, N.Y.C., 1985-86; tchr./trainer, asst. to Bronx coord. The Inst. of Tng. for Future Careers, N.Y., 1985-86; bilingual spl. edn. tchr. The Bilingual Sch. P25, N.Y.C., 1987-89, P17 at 89, N.Y., 1989-90, Multi-lingual/Multi-cultural Sch. P53, N.Y.C., 1990-91, N.Y.C. Dist. 3 Com. on Spl. Edn., 1991—; bilingual/bicultural edn. evaluator, diagnostician, cons. PS 165, N.Y.C., 1991—; cons. in field for numerous orgns. Mem. Nat. Assn. for Bilingual Edn., N.Y. State Assn. for Bilingual Edn., Coun. for Exceptional Children, Coun. for Ednl. Diagnostic Svcs., Puerto Rican Educators Assn. Office: Pub Sch 165 Rm 217 Sch Based Support Team 234 W 109th St New York NY 10025

MELICH, DORIS S., public service worker; b. Salt Lake City, Apr. 8, 1913; d. Edward Harrison and Marie Cushing Snyder; m. Mitchell Melich, June 3, 1935; children: Tanya Marie Melich Silverman, Michael E., Nancy Lynne, Robert Allen. BA in Western History, U. Utah, 1934. Mem. Nat. Commn. Arthritis and Related Musculoskeltal Diseases, 1974-76, Nat. Arthritis Adv. Bd., 1977-84, 86-90; Utah del. Nat. Ho. of Dels. Arthritis Found., 1982-87; pres. Utah Arthritis Found. Bd., 1975-78, v.p., 1968-69, 73-74; Utah rep. Arthritis Found. Govt. Affairs, 1983—. Leader, founder 1st Girl Scouts Lone Troop U.S., Moab, Utah, 1947, regional selections com., 1958-67; active Utah Ballet Guild, Salt Lake Art Ctr., Utah Arts Coun., 1988—, Utah State Rep. Women, YWCA; trustee emeritus Arthritus Found. Recipient Pyramid award Nat. Arthritis Found., 1986, Utah Coun. Girl Scouts award, 1987, Thanks Badge, 1963, Merit Honor award U. Utah Emeritus Club, 1978, Minute Man award Utah N.G., 1985; named to Nat. Women's Wall of Fame, Seneca Falls, N.Y., 1993. Mem. AAUW, Nat. Assistance League of Salt Lake City (charter mem.), Utah Women's Forum, Order Ea. Star, Alpha Delta Pi, Beta Sigma Phi (sponsor). Home: 900 Donner Way Apt 708 Salt Lake City UT 84108-2112

MELLEN, ANNE PIDA, software developer; b. Washington, July 11, 1952; d. George and Josephine (Drinkwine) Pida; m. Donald Berry Mellen, July 12, 1980; children: Barbara, Pamela, Dawn, Sheila. BS in Math. and Computer Sci., Va. Tech. U., 1974; MS in Mgmt. Sci., Stevens Inst. Tech., 1978. From systems engr. to software devel. Murray Hill, Warren etc., N.J., 1974—; chairperson fundraising AT&T Pioneer (F.B. Jewett chpt. 54), Whippany, N.J., 1982—. Editor (newsletter) Working Parent Newsletter, 1982—. Chairperson Whippany Working Parents Group, 1982—, planning adv. com. Warren (N.J.) Sch. Bd., 1991, 93; leader Girl Scouts of U.S., Warren Twp., 1987—. Mem. AAUW (program v.p. 1987-89, edn. com. head 1990— Watching Hills Br., Warren), AT&T Pioneers (Chpt. award 1992, Coun. award 1993). Office: AT&T Bell Labs 184 Liberty Corner Rd Warren NJ 07059

MELLI, MARYGOLD SHIRE, law educator; b. Rhinelander, Wis., Feb. 8, 1926; d. Osborne and May (Bonnie) Shire; m. Joseph Alexander Melli, Apr. 8, 1950; children: Joseph, Sarah Bonnie, Sylvia Anne, James Alexander. BA, U. Wis., 1947, LLB, 1950. Bar: Wis. 1950. Dir. children's code revision Wis. Legis. Coun., Madison, 1950-53; exec. dir. Wis. Jud. Coun., Madison, 1955-59; asst. prof. law U. Wis., Madison, 1961-66, assoc. prof., 1966-67, prof., 1967-84; Voss-Bascom prof. U. Wis., 1985-93, emerita, 1993—; assoc. dean U. Wis., 1970-72, rsch. affiliate Inst. for Rsch. on Poverty, 1980; mem. spl. rev. bd. State of Wis. Dept. Health and Social Svcs., Madison, 1973—. Author: (pamphlet) The Legal Status of Women in Wisconsin, 1977, (book) Wisconsin Juvenile Court Practice, 1978, rev. edit., 1983, (with others) Child Support & Alimony, 1988, The Case for Transracial Adoption, 1994; contbr. articles to profl. jours. Bd. dirs. Am. Humane Assn., 1985—. Named one of five Outstanding Young Women in Wis., Jaycees, 1961; rsch. grantee NSF, 1983; recipient award for Outstanding Contbn. to Advancement of Women in State Bar of Wis., award for Lifelong Contbn. to Advancement of Women in the Legal Prof., 1994. Fellow Am. Acad. Matrimonial Lawyers (exec. editor jour. 1985-90); mem. Am. Law Inst. (reporter project on law of family dissolution), Internat. Soc. Family Law (v.p.), Wis. State Bar Assn. (reporter family law sect.), Nat. Conf. Bar Examiners (chmn. bd. mgrs. 1989). Democrat. Roman Catholic. Home: 2904 Waunona Way Madison WI 53713-2238 Office: U Wis Law Sch Madison WI 53706

MELLIS, MARIE E., account executive; b. Fairlawn, N.J., Jan. 4, 1964; d. John George and Helen Christine (Giovanakis) M. BS in Journalism and Advt., U. Md., 1986. Account rep. Young & Rubicam, N.Y.C., 1986-88; account exec., comms. cons. AT&T, Balt., 1988—. Recipient Achievement award Dale Carnegie, 1992. Mem. Md. C. of C.

MELLO, LINDA LOUISE, dental hygienist; b. Nashua, N.H., May 5, 1963; d. Robert Norman and Jeanne Mable (Pelletier) Daigle; m. Allen James Mello, Oct. 2, 1992. Assocs., N.H. Tech. Inst., 1983. Registered Dental Hygieniest. Dental hygienist Reginald Danboise DMD, Nashua, 1983-85, Charles T. Arnold DMD, Nashua, 1985-87, John C. Machell DMD, Nashua, 1987-92; dental cons. in pvt. practice Nashua, 1992—. Author (pamphlet) Practice Enhancement, 1993; interviewed for audio cassette series: ProSynergy Listening for Excellence, 1991. Vol. Children's Wellness Clinic, Nashua, 1993. Mem. NAFE, Am. Dental Hygiene Assn. Home and Office: 10-605 Mountain Laurels Dr Nashua NH 03062

MELLON, JOAN ANN, educator; b. Massena, N.Y., Nov. 29, 1932; d. Leo Herbert and Irene (Tyo) French; m. Donald Emmett Mellon, Aug. 24, 1963. B.A., Coll. St. Rose, 1954; M.Ed., St. Lawrence U., 1956; M.Ed., Tchrs. Coll. Columbia U. 1972, Ed.D., 1985. Tchr. math. Copenhagen Sch. Dist., N.Y., 1954-57, Massena Sch. Dist., N.Y., 1957-62; supr. student tchrs. SUNY-Albany, 1962-63; asst. prof. math SUNY-Potsdam, 1963-67; tchr. math. Long Beach Sch. Dist. (N.Y.), 1967-70; chmn. math. dept. Edgemont Sch. Dist., Scarsdale, N.Y., 1971—; instr. inservice course for elem. tchrs. SUNY-Potsdam, 1965; instr. Inst. for Jr. High Sch. Tchrs., 1966; vis. com. Middle States Assn., 1973, 76, 79. Vice grand regent Cath. Daus. Am., Norwood, N.Y., 1959, grand regent, 1960; treas. St. Lawrence Deanery of Council Cath. Women, Ogdensburg, N.Y., 1958; chmn. Jr. Cath. Daus., Norwood, 1964. Mem. Assn. Math. Tchrs. N.Y. State (exec. council 1977-78), N.Y. Assn. Math. suprs. (v.p. 1978-79), Nat. Council Tchrs. Math., Math. Assn. Am., Edgemont Tchrs. Assn. (pres.), Delta Kappa Gamma. Republican. Roman Catholic. Home: 8 Woodhaven Dr New City NY 10956-4417 Office: Edgemont High Sch White Oak Ln Scarsdale NY 10583-1712

MELMAN, JOY, civic volunteer; b. St. Louis, Jan. 15, 1927; d. Simon Monroe and Esther Marion (Friedman) Werner; m. Albert Morris Melman, June 5, 1949; children: Robin Melman Feder, Kenneth, Mark. Student, Washington U., St. Louis, 1943; BS in Speech and Hearing, Emerson Coll., 1948. Cert. tchr., Mo. Tchr. Cen. Inst. for Deaf, St. Louis, 1948-50; bd. dirs. Temple Israel, St. Louis, 1974-80, Dance St. Louis, 1976—, Arts and Edn. Coun., St. Louis, 1977-90, Nat. Coun. Jewish Women, St. Louis, 1980-91, Gifted Resource Coun., St. Louis, 1983-88, KWMU Pub. Radio, St. Louis, 1980-84, bd. dirs. Jewish Community Ctrs. Assn., St. Louis, 1980-90, treas., 1986-88; v.p. St. Louis Symphony Women's Assn., 1975; adv. coun. KETC-TV pub. broadcasting, St. Louis, 1978—. Chmn. Camelot fund raiser Arts and Edn. Coun., St. Louis, 1972, 77; dir. fund raising auction PBS, 1978; adminstrv. chmn. St. Louis Bicentennial, 1974-76; Mo. chmn. Nat. Advs. for Arts, Washington, 1975-77; dir. fund raising auction PBS, 1978; chmn. Jewish Book Festival, Jewish Community Ctrs. Assn., St. Louis, 1980; couturier sale chmn. Nat. Coun. Jewish Women, St. Louis, 1982, v.p. fund raising, 1984-86; chmn. 3,000 vols. Nat. Sr. Olympics, 1987, 89; vol. chmn. vols. Jewish Hosp. Assocs., 1991; chmn. Phantom of Opera fund raiser Nat. Coun. Jewish Women, 1993; chmn. fundraiser featuring Thomas Keneally, Nat. Coun. Jewish Women, 1994. Named Woman of Achievement for Cumminuty Svcs., St. Louis Globe-Democrat, 1984. Home: 10933 Rondelay Dr Saint Louis MO 63141-7757

MELNIKOFF, SARAH ANN, gem importer, jewelry designer; b. Chgo., Feb. 12, 1936; d. Harry E. and Marie Louise (Straub) Caylor; m. Casimir Adam Jestadt, Feb. 27, 1959 (div. Sept. 1972); 1 child, Christina Marie Jestadt-Russo; m. Sol Melnikoff, July 31, 1981. Student Gemol. Inst. Am., 1968-69, Am. Acad. Art, Chgo., 1952-56, Art Inst. Chgo., 1953, Mundelein Coll., Chgo., 1953-54. Pres., Casmira Gem, Inc., Chgo., 1963—; comml. artist, Chgo., 1957-78; owner Acorn Antiques and Uniques, Chgo. U.S. del. Internat. Colored Gemstone Dealers Assn., W.Ger., 1985; lectr., cons. in field. Mem. Chgo. Salesman's Alliance, MINK Inc., Women's Jewelry Assn., Am. Gem Trade Assn. (nat. sec. 1982-86, 88—, dir. 1988-92), Chgo. Jewelers Assn. (bd. dirs. 1994—), Women's Jewelry Assn., Inc., Am. Horse Show Assn., Am. Saddlebred Horse Show Assn., Mid-Am. Horse Show Assn. (dir. 1980-83). Republican. Roman Catholic. Avocation: horses, antiques.

MELNIKOVA, SONIA, fine art curator; b. Moscow, Mar. 17, 1947; came to U.S., 1987; d. Mikhail A. Melnikov-Eichenwald and Maya F. Israilevich; 1 step-child, Sam Levigne. MA in archtl. design, fine arts, art history, Moscow State Archtl. Inst., 1971. Lic. art dealer, specializing in Russian 20th century art. Artist, architect, interior designer Moscow, 1971-85; art curator San Francisco, 1987-95; art and story cons. for Am. film Prisoner of Time, 1992. Curated exhibits for galleries and museums; contbr. articles to profl. jours.; translated into English prose by renowned Russian writers. Pub. speaker Bay Area Coun. Soviet Jews, San Francisco, 1986-94; polit. actionist Nat. Conf. and Union of Couns. for Soviet Jewry, Washington, 1986-88; polit. dissident, Moscow, 1979-86. Sonia Melnikova Day, City of Pitts. created in her honor; remembered at Am. Immigrant Wall of Honor, Statue of Liberty Found. Mem. Bay Area Coun. Soviet Jewry, San Francisco Mus. Modern Art, Mycological Soc. of San Francisco. Home: 82 Parker Ave # 1 San Francisco CA 94118

MELOY, SYBIL PISKUR, lawyer; b. Chgo., Dec. 1, 1939; d. Michael M. and Laura (Stevenson) Piskur; m. Paul W. Meloy, June 29, 1963 (div.); children: William S., Bradley M. B.S. in Chemistry with honors, U. Ill., 1961; J.D., Chgo. Kent Coll. Law, 1965. Bar: Ill. 1965, Fla. 1985, U.S. Dist. Ct. (no. dist.) Ill. 1965, U.S. Supreme Ct. 1972, U.S. Ct. Appeals (fed. cir.) 1983, U.S. Dist. Ct. (so. dist.) Fla. 1985. Patent chemist, patent atty., sr. atty., internat. counsel G.D. Searle & Co., Skokie, Ill., 1961-72; regional counsel Abbott Labs., North Chicago, Ill., 1972-78; pvt.practice, Arlington Heights,

Ill., 1978-79; asst. gen. counsel Alberto Culver Co., Melrose Park, Ill., 1979-83; corp. counsel Key Pharms., Inc., Miami, Fla., 1983-86; assoc. Ruden, Barnett McCloskey, Smith, Schuster and Russell, Pa., 1987-89, ptnr., 1990-91; ptnr. Foley & Lardner, Miami, Washington 1991—; adj. prof. Univ. of Miami Sch. of Law, 1986—. Recipient Abbott Presdl. award, 1977; Bur. Nat. Affairs prize, 1965; Law Rev. prize for best article. Mem. ABA, Chgo. Bar Assn. (chmn. and vice chmn. internat. and fgn. law com.), Am. Patent Law Assn., Am. Chem. Soc., Licencing Execs. Soc., Phi Beta Kappa, Phi Kappa Phi. Patentee oral contraceptive, 1965; contbr. article on fertility control and abortion laws, book rev. on arbitration to law revs. Home: 1915 Brickell Ave Apt 1108C Miami FL 33129-1736 also: 1676 32nd St NW Washington DC 20007-5109 Office: Foley & Lardner 3000 K St NW Washington DC 20007-5109*

MELSON, RENÉ HARBER, elementary school educator; b. Atlanta, Dec. 4, 1954; d. Talmon Eugene and June (Slaton) Harber; children: Presley, Cameron. BS in Elem. Edn., Ga. State U., 1977. Cert. tchr., Ga. Tchr. Greater Atlanta Christian Schs., Norcross, Ga., 1977-82, 88—. Republican. Ch. of Christ. Home: 445 Cambria Ln Lilburn GA 30247 Office: Greater Atlanta Christian PO Box 277 Norcross GA 30091-0277

MELSTED, MARCELLA H., retired administrative assistant, civic worker; b. Mayville, N.D., Mar. 3, 1922; d. Hans Morris and Betsey (Stenerson) Hanson; m. Alvin K. Melsted, June 6, 1965 (dec. June 1994). BS in Commerce, U. N.D., 1946, postgrad. Sec. Off. Sci. R&D, Washington, 1943-45; adminstrv. asst. Am. Embassy (Marshall Plan), Oslo, 1948-50, Paris, 1950-52; adminstrv. asst. N.D. Geol. Soc., Grand Forks, 1953-65. Co-editor: Memories of Homemakers, 1988. Pres. Borg Home Auxiliary, 1984—; apptd. cons. rep. State Plumbing Bd.; chmn. needlepointing dining room chairs N.D. Gov.'s mansion; parliamentarian N.D. Extension Homemakers, Women of Evang. Luth. Ch. Am., v.p., bd. dirs., 1985-91; mem. N.D. Humanities Coun., 1985-91; bd. dirs. Friends of N.D. Mus. Mem. AAUW (parliamentarian N.D. State divsn., 2 fellowships, author branch history, state pres. 1962-64, nat. membership com. 1964-66), N.D. State Fedn. Garden Clubs (state pres., life, tree chmn. nat. bd., state treas. 1991—), Four Seasons Garden Club (sec.-treas. 1987—), Homemakers Clubs (various coms.), China Painters Guild (various coms.). Home: RR 1 Box 57 Edinburg ND 58227

MELTEBEKE, RENETTE, career counselor; b. Portland, Oreg., Apr. 20, 1948; d. Rene and Gretchen (Hartwig) M. BS in Sociology, Portland State U., 1970; MA in Counseling Psychology, Lewis and Clark Coll., 1985. Lic. profl. counselor, Oreg.; nat. cert. counselor. Secondary tchr. Portland Pub. Schs., 1970-80; project coord. Multi-Wash CETA, Hillsboro, Oreg., 1980-81; coop. edn. specialist Portland C.C., 1981-91; pvt. practice career counseling, owner Career Guidance Specialists, Lake Oswego, Oreg., 1988—; mem. adj. faculty Marylhurst (Oreg.) Coll., 1989-93, Portland State U., 1994—; assoc. Drake Beam Morin Inc., Portland, 1993—; career cons. Occupational Health Svcs. Corp., 1994—, Career Devel. Svcs., 1990—, Life Dimensions, Inc., 1994—. Author video Work in America, 1981. Pres. Citizens for Quality Living, Sherwood, Oreg., 1989; mem. Leadership Roundtable on Sustainability for Sherwood, 1994—. Mem. ASTD, Assn. for Psychol. Type, Nat. Career Devel. Assn., Oreg. Career Devel. Assn. (pres. 1990), Assn. for Quality Participation, Assn. for Humanistic Psychology, Willamette Writers. Home: 890 SE Merryman St Sherwood OR 97140-9746 Office: Career Guidance Specialists 15800 Boones Ferry Rd # C104 Lake Oswego OR 97035-3456

MELTON, BARBARA MCDONALD, psychotherapist, mediator; b. Rockville, N.Y., Sept. 23, 1952; d. William Edward and Catherine Bridget (Morrissey) McDonald; m. Robert Howard, Dec. 5, 1971 (div. May 1981); m. Mitchell Don Melton, May 26, 1983. BS, Charleston So. U., 1988; MEd, The Citadel, 1991. Cert. family mediation practitioner, Acad. Family Mediators. Pers. mgr. Law Offices of G.J. Morris, Charleston, S.C., 1976-91; mental health counselor S.C. Dept. Mental Health, Charleston, 1992—; pvt. practice Charleston, 1991—. Sec.-treas. Grimke Ctr. for Mediation, 1992-94; bd. dirs. Low Country Mediation Network, 1992-94, pres., 1992-94; coord. Helping Profls. Network, 1992-94; mem. Trauma Recovery Network, 1992-94. Mem. S.C. Coun. for Mediation (bd. dirs. 1991-94), Am. Counseling Assn., Chi Sigma Iota. Home: 1225 Wildgame Rd Summerville SC 29483-7038 Office: 217 Calhoun St Ste 1 Charleston SC 29401-1313

MELTON, CHERYL ANN, educator, small business owner; b. Bklyn., Jan. 5, 1949; d. Raymond Franklin and Irene Louise (Cotton) Blair; m. Gilbert Edmund Melton, Aug. 26, 1972; children: Byron Adrian, Brandie Alicia. BS in Edn., Ohio State U., 1971; MS in Edn., Nazareth Coll., Rochester, N.Y., 1976. Prof. clear multiple subject teaching credential, Calif. Elem. tchr. N.Y.C. Bd. Edn., Bklyn., 1971-72, Rochester City Sch. Dist., 1973-84; elem. tchr. Long Beach (Calif.) Unified Sch. Dist., 1984-90, lang. arts specialist, 1990—, reading recovery tchr., 1992—; v.p. sales and mktg., orange county M2 Solutions, L.A., 1992—; mem. Sch. Program Improvement Leadership Team, Long Beach, 1990—; adv. bd. Scholastic, Inc.-Literacy Place, 1994-95. Chmn. membership devel. Jr. League Long Beach, 1991-92, mem. by-laws task force, 1992-93, adv. future planning, 1989—, selected mentor, 1991—, sustaining advisor placement com. 1994-94; chosen delegate Jr. League Dallas. Scholar Calif. literature project Calif. State U., Dominguez Hills, 1992. Mem. Nat. Coun. Tchs. English, English Coun. Long Beach, Calif. Tchrs. Assn., Nat. Coun. Negro Women, Links (Orange County chpt. Inc., co-chair 1st model initiative youth project, Rochester chpt., charter), Jack and Jill of Am. (charter Long Beach chpt.), Internat. Reading Assn., Reading Recovery Council of N. Am., Delta Sigma Theta (charter, Long Beach alumnae). Democrat. Baptist. Home: 4508 Hazelnut Ave Seal Beach CA 90740-2918

MELTON, ELAINE WALLACE, small business owner; b. Rock Hill, S.C., June 14, 1948; d. David Dewitt Wallace and Myrtle Mae (Johnson) Threatt; m. John H. Melton, July 21, 1966 (div. 1979); children: John David, Rodney Dwayne. BS in Bus. Mgmt., Wingate Coll., 1987. Sec. Monroe (N.C.) City Schs., 1969-73; supr. Comar Mfg., Monroe, 1974-78; with Mut. Industries, Monroe, 1978—; owner, operator Melton's Acctg., Secretarial and Tax Svc., Monroe, 1978—. Walk coord. March of Dimes, Monroe, 1988—. Recipient Spl. Svcs. award March of Dimes, 1988—. Mem. Am. Inst. Profl. Bookkeepers, Federated Tax Svc., NAFE, Am. Soc. for Notary Pub., Monroe Bus. Assn. Home: PO Box 1272 Monroe NC 28111-1272

MELTON, FLORETTE JEANNE, realtor, marketing consultant; b. Newton, Iowa, Oct. 30, 1945; d. Floyd Leroy and Donna Jean (Engle) Mulbrook; m. James Francis Rittenmeyer (div.); 1 child, Matthew David Rittenmeyer; m. Charles Wade Melton; 1 child, Jennifer. Student, U. Iowa, 1964-66; BA, U. N.C., 1977, MA, 1983. Comm. cons. Booke & Co., Winston-Salem, N.C., 1977-78; pres. RCC, Winston-Salem, 1980-85; real estate agent Merrill Lynch, Winston-Salem, 1986-88, ReMax, Winston-Salem, 1988-92; broker, pres. Unique Properties of the Triad, Winston-Salem, 1992—; mktg. cons. Creative Advt. Active Triad Health Orgn., Greensboro, 1994—. Mem. Bd. Realtors. Office: Unique Properties of the Triad 112 Cambridge Park Winston Salem NC 27104

MELTON, LYNDA GAYLE, reading specialist, educational diagnostician; b. Gatesville, Tex., Mar. 11, 1943; d. Dee and Myrtle (Dunlap) White; divorced; children: Melanie Gayle, William Matthew. BS, U. Tex., 1964; MA, U. North Tex., 1979, PhD, 1983, postgrad., 1993, 94; postgrad., Tex. Womans U., 1983. Cert. elem. tchr., spl. edn. tchr., supervision, spl. edn. supr., learning disabilities tchr., orthpedically handicapped tchr., reading specialist, Tex., adminstrs., ednl. diagnostician. Tchr. 2d and 4th grades, spl. edn. tchr. Irving (Tex.) Ind. Sch. Dist., 1964-79, tchr., 1982-83; 4th grade tchr. Northwest Ind. Sch. Dist., Justin, Tex., 1980-81; asst. prin. Grapevine-Colleyville Ind. Sch. Dist., Tex., 1983-87; tchr. reading improvement Carrollton (Tex.)-Farmers Branch Ind. Sch. Dist., 1988-89; cons. lang. arts Edn. Svc. Ctr. Region 10, Richardson, Tex., 1989-91; pvt. practice diagnostic reading and ednl. diagnostician Grapevine, Tex., 1991—; reading clinician N.Tex. State U., Denton, 1980; instr. spl. edn. U. Tex., Dallas, 1983, U Tex., Arlington, 1988; vis. prof. Tex. Women's U., Denton, 1983, 84, 87-88. Contbr. Reading Rsch. Revisited, also revs. to Case Mgmt. Monthly Confs., Scottish Rite Hosp. and profl. jours. Mem. ASCD, Internat. Reading Assn. (North Tex. coun.), Learning Disabilities, Orton Disability Soc., Coun. for Exceptional Children, Phi Delta Kappa. Home and Office: 30 Sonora Dr Trophy Club TX 76262

MELTON, MARIE FRANCES, university dean; b. Bayshore, N.Y.; d. Edward Kilgallon and Anne (Mohan) M. BS in Edn., St. John's U., Jamaica, N.Y., 1960, MS in Edn., 1975; MLS, Pratt Inst., Bklyn., 1961; EDD, St. John's U., Jamaica, N.Y., 1981. Dir. media ctr. Mater Christi High Sch., Astoria, N.Y., 1961-72; libr. sci. libr. St. John's U., Jamaica, N.Y., 1972-76, asst. dir., 1976-83, dir. Univ. Libr., 1983-89, dean Univ. Libr., 1989—. Mem., officer St. John's Prep Bd. of Trustees, Astoria, N.Y., 1980—, Holy Cross High Sch., Flushing, N.Y., 1979-89; chair Sunnyside Hist. Com., Sunnyside, N.Y., 1988-91. Mem. Am. Libr. Assn., Cath. Libr. Assn., N.Y. Libr. Assn., Council Nat. Libr. & Info. Assns. Roman Catholic. Office: St Johns University Utopia Pkwy Jamaica NY 11439

MELTZ, DEBORA, artist, writer, photographer; b. N.Y.C., Sept. 8, 1945; d. Leonard and Roslyn (Fox) Friedland; m. David J. Meltz, Dec. 26, 1965; children: Daniel, Elizabeth. BFA, Cooper Union, 1966; MA, William Paterson Coll., 1980. Graphic artist various advt. orgns., N.Y.C., 1966-69; art tchr. Susan E. Wagner High Sch., S.I., N.Y., 1969-71; photographer, photo stylist, 1986-89, freelance writer, 1991—. Solo exhbns. include Douglass Coll., New Brunswick, N.J., Ltd. Edits. Gallery, Lafayette, N.J., Urban Art Retreat/Liz Long Gallery, Chgo., Gallery at Traveller, Sparta, N.J.; group exhbns. at Printmaking Coun. N.J., Somerville, Newark Mus., N.J. Ctr. for Visual Arts, Summit, N.J., WomanKraft Gallery, Tucson, Light Solutions East, N.Y.C., Gallery at Marsh Comms., Mt. Kisco, N.Y., others; representer in collections Terrance Gallery, Palenville, N.Y., Artists Book Archives, Mus. Modern Art, N.Y.C. Bd. trustees Domestic Abuse Svcs., Newton, N.J., 1992—. Democrat. Home and Office: 4 Briar Patch Rd Newton NJ 07860

MELTZER, E. ALYNE, educator, social worker, volunteer; b. Jersey City, May 16, 1934; d. Abraham Samuel and Fannie Ruth (Nydick) M. BA, Mich. State U., 1956. Acctg. clerk Louis Marx Co. Inc., N.Y.C., 1957-60; social studies tchr. Haverstraw High Sch., N.Y., 1960-61; tchr. Sachem Cen. Sch. Dist., Farmingville, N.Y., 1961-63, East Paterson Sch. Dist., N.J., 1964-65; case worker Human Resource Adm. Social Service Dept., N.Y.C., 1966-89. Policy advisor Senator Roy Goodman Adv. Com., Albany, N.Y., 1987-90; social action facilitator Katherine Engel Ctr. for Sr. Adults, 1995—; active Yorkville Civic Coun., 1988-93, Temple Shaaray Tefila. Recipient Sabra Soc. Plaque award State of Israel New Leadership Div., N.Y.C., 1979, Prime Minister Club Plaque award State of Israel Bonds, 1986-87. Mem. AAUW, Nat. Coun. Jewish Women (life N.Y. and Rockland County sects., N.Y. sect. bd. dirs. 1991—, state & sect. sec. 1990-93, pub. affairs com. 1990—, co-chairperson Hunger Program Sunday Family Soup Kitchen, 1991-93, chairperson Roosevelt Island Svcs. 1993—, Outstanding Vol. award 1973-74, 90-91, nat. sect. Israel affairs com. 1991—, nat. conv. 1987, 93, N.E. dist. conv. 1988, Albany Inst. 1987, 88, 91, 93, Washington Inst. 1987, 89, 92, Israel Summit V 1988, Washington Mission 1991, Donor awards 1987-93), Internat. Coun. Jewish Women (Jerusalem seminar 1991), Mich. State U. Alumni Orgn. (life, sec. N.Y. chpt. 1959-60), Am. Jewish Com., Assn. Ref. Zioninists Am., Jewish Geneol. Soc., Hadassah (life), Womens League for Israel (life).

MELTZER, MIRIAM SCHLESINGER, social worker, administrator; b. Pitts., Oct. 3, 1938; d. Hymen and Ida Rose (Mirowitz) Schlesinger; m. Donald Meltzer, Apr. 15, 1961; children—Deborah, Alan. B.A., U. Mich., 1960; M.S.W., U. Md., 1966. Counselor, Counseling and Testing, So. Ill. U., Carbondale, 1966-67, dir. social service Meml. Hosp., 1973-75; social worker Sch. Dist. No. 95, Carbondale, 1975-76; field ops. asst. U.S. Census Bur., Belleville, Ill., 1980; dir. truancy alternate program Regional Supt. Schs., Murphysboro, Ill., 1983—; mem. panel specialists Ill. Dept. Rehab., 1985-87. Advisor Welfare Rights Orgn., Carbondale, 1973; pres. Beth Jacob Sisterhood, Carbondale, 1979, 80, 81, Lincoln Jr. High Sch. PTA, Carbondale, 1981-82; bd. dirs. Temple Beth Jacob, 1979, 80, 81; area chmn. United Jewish Appeal Women's Drive, 1987-89. Home: 3007 W Kent Dr Carbondale IL 62901-1920 Office: Regional Supt Schs Courthouse Murphysboro IL 62966

MELVIN, MARGARET, nurse, consultant; b. Thomasville, Ga., July 13, 1927; d. Robert and Lorene Elizabeth (Barrett) M. BS in Nursing Edn., Duke U., 1953. Cert. Occupational Health Cons. Head nurse Duke U. Med. Ctr., Durham, N.C., 1947-54; charge nurse med. clinic U. Mich. Med. Ctr., Ann Arbor, 1955-59; occupational health nurse State Farm Ins. Co., Jacksonville, Fl., 1960-65; dir. ins. edn. Baptist Hosp. Med. Ctr., Jacksonville, 1965-68; various positions Wausau Ins. Co., Orlando, Fla., 1968-80; sr. cert. occupational health cons. Wausau Ins. Co., Orlando, 1980—; lectr. various hosps. and orgns. Developed, created nat. teaching program for back problems, 1976, program for emergency care industry, 1974. Am. Cancer Soc. grantee, 1968. Mem. ANA, Am. Assn. Occupational Health Nurses, Fla. State Assn. Occupational Health Nurses (chmn. 1982, conf. sec. 1980-84), Am. Bd Occupational Health Nurses. Republican. Home: 610 Cranes Way # 301 Altamonte Springs FL 32701-7781

MELVIN, MAXINE MARIE, teacher; b. Parsons, Kans., Oct. 9, 1905; d. John Patrick and Flora May (Cribbett) M. BS, U. Tex., 1940; MA, Tex. Western Coll., 1952. Tchr. El Paso (Tex.) Ind. Sch. Dist., 1932-75, Father Yermo Parochial Sch., El Paso, Tex., 1976-82; mem. adv. com. tchrs. home econ. edn. Tex. 1956; participant workshops tchrs. home econ. Tex. 1940-75;. Jr. Red Cross sponsor El Paso, Tex., 1940-42, instr. summer Red Cross courses, 1950-76, Girl Scouts Am., 1943; bd. dirs. Austin H.S. PTA, El Paso, 1965-57. Recipient Dorothy Brownlow award El Paso chpt. Red Cross, 1975, Mable Erwin award Tex. Home Econ. Assn. 1985. Mem. AAUW (hon. life, treas. 1943), Am. Home Econ. Assn. (life), NEA, Tex. State Tchrs. Assn., El Paso Tchrs. Assn. (outstanding svc. cert. 1976), Delta Kappa Gamma. Home: 1800 N Stanton Apt 505 El Paso TX 79902

MELZER-LANGE, MARLENE DOLORES, physician, educator; b. Milw., Nov. 14, 1949; d. John R. and Dolores Norma Melzer; m. George Lange, May 18, 1974; children: James, Karen. BS in Chemistry and Math., Marquette U., 1971; MD, Med. Coll. Wis., 1975. Diplomate Am. Bd. Pediatrics, Am. Bd. Pediatric Emergency Medicine. Pediatric intern and resident Milw. Children's Hosp., 1975-78; attending physician Children's Hosp. Wis., Milw., 1978—; pediatrician Teen Pregnancy Svc. Milw., 1981-94; from asst. clin. prof. to asst. prof. Med. Coll. Wis., Milw., 1979-94, assoc. prof., 1994—. Fellow Am. Acad. Pediatrics; mem. Midwest Soc. Podiatric Rsch., Milw. Pediatric Soc., Ambulatory Pediatric Assn., Phi Beta Kappa. Roman Catholic. Office: Children's Hosp Wis Dept Pediatrics 9000 WWI Ave Milwaukee WI 53201

MENAKER, SHIRLEY ANN LASCH, psychology educator, academic administrator; b. Jersey City, July 22, 1935; d. Frederick Carl and Mary Elizabeth (Thrall) Lasch; m. Michael Menaker, June 4, 1955; children: Ellen Margaret, Nicholas. BA in English Lit., Swarthmore Coll., 1956; MA, Boston U., 1961, PhD in Clin. Psychology, 1965. Adminstrv. asst. N.J. State Fedn. Dist. Bds. Edn., Trenton, 1956-59; trainee clin. psychology Mass. Mental Health Ctr., Boston, 1960-61; intern clin. psychology Thom Guidance Clinic for Children, Boston, 1961-62; research assoc. ednl. psychology U. Tex.-Austin, 1964-67, asst. prof. ednl. psychology, 1967-70. assoc. prof., 1970-79, assoc. dean grad. sch., 1975-77, psychology cons. Research and Devel. Ctr. for Tchr. Edn., 1965-67, faculty investigator, 1967-74; assoc. prof. counseling psychology U. Oreg., Eugene, 1979-85, prof., 1985-87 , assoc. dean grad. sch., 1979-84, acting dean grad. sch., 1980-81, 82-83, dean grad sch., 1984-87; assoc. provost for acad. support, prof. gen. faculty, U. Va., Charlottesville, 1987—. Bd. dirs. Nat. Grad. Record Exam. Bd. and Policy Council-Test of English as Fgn. Lang., Ednl. Testing Services, 1984-88. Contbr. articles to profl. jours. NIMH fellow, 1963-64. Office: U Va Adminstrn Madison Hall Charlottesville VA 22906-9014

MENARD, EDITH, English language educator, artist, poet, actress; b. Washington, Dec. 5, 1919; d. Willis Monroe and Edith Berncenia (Gill) M. BS summa cum laude, Miner Tchrs. Coll., Washington, 1940; MA in English, Howard U., 1942; postgrad., NYU, 1944-46; MA in Teaching English, Columbia U., 1952; postgrad. in edn., George Washington U., 1966-79, 89-92, doctoral candidate, 1992—. Instr. English and speech Howard U., Washington, 1946-53; high sch. tchr. English D.C. Pub. Schs., Washington, 1953-73; chmn. dept. English Woodrow Wilson High Sch., Washington, 1972-73; adj. asst. prof. English fundamentals U. D.C., 1988-90; founder, dir. Miss Menard's Exclusive English Tutorial Svc., 1991—; substitute tchr. D.C. and Montgomery County (Md.) pub. schs. Contbr. articles and poetry to various publs., including At Day's End, 1994. Reader poetry to civic orgns.; vol. Washington Nat. Cathedral Assn., 1993—. Recipient Golden Poet award World of Poetry, 1988, Silver Poet award, 1989, Editor's Choice award The Nat. Libr. of Poetry, 1994; Julius Rosenwald fellow Yale U., 1943-44. Mem. Smithsonian Assocs. Episcopalian. Home: Rittenhouse Apts 6101 16th St NW # 916 Washington DC 20011

MENARD, JAYNE BUSH, management and computer system consultant; b. Dover, N.J., Dec. 21, 1946; d. Peter Thomas and Emily Marie (Suk) Bush; m. Michael Paul Menard, Feb. 3, 1979. AB in History, Coll. William and Mary, 1969; postgrad., Fairleigh Dickinson U., 1970-71. With Exxon Corp., Florham Park, N.J., 1970-89, mktg. systems coord., 1985-86, planning controls coord., 1986-87, audit systems advisor, 1987-89; pres. Changewise, Inc., Portland, Oreg., 1989—. Republican. Methodist. Home and Office: 2757 SW English Ct Portland OR 97201-1690

MENCEY, HELEN V. L., educator; b. Anahuac, Tex., Oct. 19, 1960; d. Milton M. and Narvis C. (Malone) M. BFA, Sam Houston State U., 1983; tchr. cert., Lamar U., 1985; MEd, Prairie View Coll., 1989; postgrad., Tex. Woman's U., 1990, U. Houston, 1990. tutor in field. Mem. NEA, ACLD, Tex. State Tchrs. Assn., NAFE, Tex. Reading Assn., Internat. Reading Assn., Platform Soc., Pi Lambda Theta.

MENCONI, SUSAN EWEN, art dealer; b. Bronxville, N.Y., May 26, 1952; d. Ralph Joseph and Marjorie Livingston (Ewen) M.; m. Bruce Anthony Hoheb, Sept. 24, 1983. Student, Nat. Acad. Design, N.Y., 1971, Pa. Acad. Fine Arts, Phila., 1973; BA, U. Pa., 1974. Sales and info. asst. The Frick Collection, N.Y.C., 1974-77; from asst. to ptnr. to dir. dept. Am. sculpture Hirschl & Adler Galleries, N.Y.C., 1977-93; exec. v.p. Richard York Gallery, N.Y.C., 1993—; exhibitions curated include William Stanley Haseltine and Herbert Haseltine, N.Y.C., 1992, Six American Modernists, N.Y.C., 1991, Primary Models: American Plasters 1880-1945, N.Y.C., 1990, Uncommon Spirit: Sculpture in America 1800-1940, N.Y.C., 1989, Herman Trunk: Paintings and Watercolors, N.Y.C., 1989, Edward Hopper: Light Years, N.Y.C., 1988, Edward Hopper, Early and Late, N.Y.C., 1987, From the Studio: Selections of American Sculpture 1811-1941, N.Y.C., 1986. Publs. accompanying curated exhibitions. Mem. Masterworks Found. (bd. dirs. Bermuda Artworks Found.). Office: Richard York Gallery 21 E 65th St New York NY 10021

MENDELL, PHYLLIS, psychologist, health facility administrator, researcher, educator; b. N.Y.C., July 25, 1949; d. Morris and Esther (Spielman) Goldstein; m. André Wilson Mendell, July 4, 1979; children: D'vorah, Aliza, Mikel. BA magna cum laude, Queens Coll., 1972, MA in Physiol. Psychology, 1976; PhD in Psychology, Hofstra U., 1987. Lic. psychologist N.Y. Rsch. asst. Albert Einstein Coll. of Medicine, Bronx, 1972-74; acad. cons. Latham Pub. Co., N.Y.C., 1976-77; coord. of sci. Coll. of Discovery & Devel., N.Y.C., 1980-81; dir. rsch. NCTRH, Washington, 1983-84; therapist psychology svcs. SUNY, Farmingdale, 1986; pvt. practice clin. psychologist Huntington, N.Y., 1988—; asst. prof. psychology Adelphi U., Garden City, N.Y., 1989—; dir. psychol. svcs. Nassau Ctr. for the Developmentally Disabled, Woodbury, N.Y., 1980—; adj. prof. psychology, Nassau Community Coll., 1974-89; lectr., guest speaker Bronx Bot. Gardens, Bronx, 1983-86; guest speaker NCTRH, Ind., Phila., Washington, 1983-85, Rusk Inst., N.Y.C., 1989. Contbr. articles to profl. jours. Mem. Huntington Hist. Soc., 1989-90, Women's Sports Found., 1984—. Mem. Am. Psychol. Assn., Nassau County Regional Planning Group, ITES Spl. Edn. Task Force (chairperson behavior rev. com., 1989—, mem. rsch. rev. com. 1984—), Phi Beta Kappa. Jewish. Home: 232 Park Ave Huntington NY 11743-2703 Office: Nassau Ctr Devel Disabled 72 S Woods Rd Woodbury NY 11797-1099

MENDELSOHN, NAOMI, biopharmaceutial and medical pharmaceutical consultant. BA, NYU; MA, Boston U.; PhD, CUNY, 1975. Fellow Meml. Sloan-Kettering Cancer Ctr., N.Y.C., 1975-78; asst. prof. Mt. Sinai Med. Ctr., N.Y.C., 1978-82; assoc. sci. dir. Sterling Drug, Inc. Internat., N.Y.C., 1982-91; adjunct asst. prof. Mt. Sinai Med. Ctr., 1982—. NSF fellow, 1969, NIH fellow 1975-78. Mem. Am. Assn. Advancement Sci., Am. Chem. Soc., Am. Soc. Hematology, Fedn. Am. Socs. Exptl. Biology (ednl. affairs com. 1989—), Am. Heart Assn., N.Y. Acad. Scis. (Women Sci. com., Planning com. 1983-85), Drug Info. Assn., Fgn. Policy Assn. Office: 322 W 57th St Apt 37C New York NY 10019-3723

MENDELSOHN, ZEHAVAH WHITNEY, data processing executive; b. Houston, Nov. 22, 1956; d. Alfred Peter and Sarah (Carsey) Whitney; m. Avrum Joseph Mendelsohn, June 27, 1982. AA, College of DuPage, 1988; BA, Nat. Louis U., 1989. Cert. quality analyst. Mgmt. analyst U. Ill., Abraham Lincoln Sch. Medicine, Chgo., 1976-83; sr. analyst quality assurance Ofcl. Airline Guides, Oak Brook, Ill., 1983—; cons. Police Cons., Westmont, Ill., 1983—. Mem. Quality Assurance Inst., Am. Soc. for Quality Control, Quality and Productivity Mgmt. Assn., Chgo. Quality Assurance Assn. (dir. cert.), Chicagoland Handicapped Skiers (pres. 1986-87, 89-91), Profl. Ski Instrs. Am. Office: Official Airline Guides 2000 Clearwater Dr Oak Brook IL 60521

MENDENHALL, JANICE S., nursing administrator; b. Morgantown, W.Va., Oct. 24, 1952; d. Vincent Peter and Catherine Rita (Sindik) Schiavoni; m. Hiram Wayne Mendenhall, Feb. 6, 1988. BSN, U. South Ala., 1993, postgrad. Staff nurse Providence Hosp., Mobile, Ala., 1974, Bapt. Hosp., Pensacola, Fla., 1974-76; staff nurse U. South Ala. Med. Ctr., Mobile, 1976-77, nurse mgr., 1977—. Roman Catholic. Home: 3966 Wimbledon Park Mobile AL 36608 Office: Univ S Ala Med Ctr 2451 Fillingim St Mobile AL 36617

MENDER, MONA SIEGLER, writer, music educator; b. Jersey City, May 24, 1926; d. George and Freda (Steierman) Siegler; m. Irving M. Mender, Aug. 25, 1946; children: Donald Matthew, Judith J. Mender. BA, Mt. Holyoke Coll., 1947. Instr. piano and music theory, Fair Lawn, N.J., 1947-75; state edn. chmn. N.J. Symphony Orch., Newark, 1980-82, state chmn. bd. regents, 1983-84, bd. dirs., 1983-91. Author: Music Manuscript Preparation: A Concise Guide, 1991. Recipient Women's Network commendation Sen. Bill Bradley, 1984. Mem. Mountain Ridge Country Club (West Caldwell, N.J.), Williams Coll. Faculty Club (Williamstown, Mass.), Taconic Golf Club (Williamstown), Plantation Golf and Country Club (Venice, Fla.).

MENDEZ, C. BEATRIZ, obstetrician/gynecologist; b. Guatemala, Apr. 21, 1952; d. Jose and Olga (Sobalvarro) M.; m. Mark Parshall, Dec. 12, 1986. BS in Biology and Psychology, Pa. State U., 1974; MD, Milton Hershey Coll. Medicine, 1979. Diplomate Am. Bd. Ob-gyn. Resident in ob-gyn. George Washington U., Washington, 1979-83; pvt. practice Santa Fe, 1985—; chair perinatal com. St. Vincent's Hosp., Santa Fe, 1986-89, quality assurance mem., 1986—, chief ob-gyn, 1992-94; bd. dirs. Milton S. Hershey Coll. Medicine, Hershey, Pa., 1977-82. With USPHS, 1983-85. Mosby scholar Mosby-Hersey Med. Sch., Hershey, 1979. Fellow Am. Coll. Ob-Gyn. (Continuing Med. Edn. award 1986—); mem. AMA (Physician Recognition award 1986—), Am. Assn. Gynecol. Laparascopists, Internat. Soc. Gynecol. Endoscopy, Am. Fertility Soc., Am. Soc. Colposcopy and Cervical Pathology, N.Mex. Med. Soc., Santa Fe Med. Soc., Residents Assn. George Washington U. (co-founder 1981-83). Democrat. Office: Gallisteo Ob-gyn 539 Harkle Rd Santa Fe NM 87501

MENDEZ, JANA WELLS, state senator; b. Moscow, Idaho, Jan. 18, 1944; d. Earl Dean and Alverta (Dalberg) Hall; m. Richard Albert Mendez, Sept. 16, 1965; children: Amy, Jennifer, Christopher. BS in Journalism, U. Colo., 1981. Community and issue activist Boulder County Housing Authority and Citizens for the Right To Vote, Longmont, Colo., 1975-83; legis. asst. Senate Minority Leader, Denver, 1982-84; Colo. state senator, 1985—; asst. whip minority leader, 1986, caucus chair, 1990—. Author: (with others) Chile From The Ground Up, 1982. Dem. precinct leader, area coordinator, senate dist. chmn. Boulder County, Colo., 1975-84; chair, commr. Boulder County Housing Authority, 1974-83. Regents scholar, 1963, Cervi scholar, 1980; U. Colo. Women's Ctr. grantee, 1980; named Outstanding Freshman Senator Colo. Social Legis. Com., 1985; recipient tax fairness award, 1988, 89, various awards Common Clause, Audibon Soc., Am. Cancer Soc., 1992,

Children's Advocacy Network, 1992. Mem. Kappa Tau Alpha. Avocations: gardening, reading, photography, cooking. Office: State Senate Capitol Bldg Denver CO 80203*

MENDEZ, OLGA A., state legislator; b. Mayaguez, P.R.. BA, U. P.R.; MEd, Columbia U., 1960; PhD in Ednl. Psychology, Yeshiva U., N.Y.C., 1975. Previously assoc. prof. SUNY-Stony Brook, research psychologist Albert Einstein Coll. Med., N.Y.C., dep. commr. N.Y.C. Agy. for Child Devel., N.Y. state senator, 1978—; del. Dem. Nat. Conv., 1980, leadership position, 1984—, sec. minority conf., 1992—, chairperson conf. Home: 1215 Fifth Ave Apt 15D New York NY 10029-5209 Office: N Y State Senate State Capitol Albany NY 12224

MENDIOLA, ANNA MARIA G., mathematics educator; b. Laredo, Tex., Dec. 21, 1948; d. Alberto and Aurora (Benavides) Gonzalez; m. Alfonso Mendiola Jr., Aug. 11, 1973; children: Alfonso, Alberto. AA, Laredo C.C., Tex., 1967; BA, Tex. Woman's U., 1969, MS, 1974. Tchr. math. Laredo Ind. Sch. Dist., 1969-81; math instr. Laredo C.C., 1981—, organizer Jaime Escalante program, 1991-92; tech. prep. com. mem., 1991-92; ednl. coun., sec. Christen Mid. Campus, 1992-94; mem. site based campus com. Martin H.S., 1994—; vis. instr. St. Augustine Sch., Laredo, 1987-88; evaluator So. Assn., Corpus Christi, 1981, So. Assn. Colls. and Schs., United H.S., 1991; juror Higher Edn. Coord. Bd. Report, San Antonio, 1989; mem. quality improvement coun. Laredo C.C., 1993-94. Producer slide promo, Mathematics at LCC, 1983. V.p., bd. dirs. Our Lady of Guadalupe Sch., Laredo, 1988-91; sec. Laredo C.C. Faculty Senate, 1986-87; active Boy Scouts Am., 1985-86. Recipient Teaching Excellence award NISOD, 1993. Mem. AAUW (pres. 1979-81, v.p. 1987-89, scholarship chair 1993-94, membership chair 1994—), Am. Math. Assn. Two-Yr. Colls., Math. Assn. Am., Tex. State Tchrs. Assn., Tex. Jr. Coll. Tchrs. Assn., Tex. Woman's U. Alumnae Assn., Blessed Sacrament Altar Soc., Tex. Assn. Ch. Higher Edn., Delta Kappa Gamma (membership chair 1993—). Democrat. Roman Catholic. Office: Laredo CC West End Washington St Laredo TX 78040

MENDIUS, PATRICIA DODD WINTER, editor, educator, writer; b. Davenport, Iowa, July 9, 1924; d. Otho Edward and Helen Rose (Dodd) Winter; m. John Richard Mendius, June 19, 1947; children: Richard, Catherine M. Graber, Louise, Karen M. Chooljian. BA cum laude, UCLA, 1946; MA cum laude, U. N.Mex., 1966. Cert. secondary edn. tchr., Calif., N.Mex. English teaching asst. UCLA, 1946-47; English tchr. Marlborough Sch. for Girls, L.A., 1947-50, Aztec (N.Mex.) High Sch., 1953-55, Farmington (N.Mex.) High Sch., 1955-63; chair English dept. Los Alamos (N.Mex.) High Sch., 1963-86; sr. technical writer, editor Los Alamos Nat. Lab., 1987—; adj. prof. English, U. N.Mex., Los Alamos, 1970-72, Albuquerque, 1982-85; English cons. S.W. Regional Coll. Bd., Austin, Tex., 1975—; writer, editor, cons. advanced placement English test devel. com. Nat. Coll. Bd., 1982-86, reader, 1982-86, project equality cons., 1985-88; book selection cons. Scholastic mag., 1980-82. Author: Preparing for the Advanced Placement English Exams, 1975; editor Los Alamos Arts Coun. bull., 1986-91. Chair Los Alamos Art in Pub. Pls. Bd., 1987-92; chair adv. bd. trustees U. N.Mex., Los Alamos, 1987-93; pres. Los Alamos Concert Assn., 1972-73; chair Los Alamos Mesa Pub. Libr. Bd., 1990-94. Mem. Soc. Tech. Communicators, AAUW (pres. 1961-63, state bd. dirs. 1959-63, Los Alamos Coordinating Com. 1992-93, pres. Los Alamos br. 1993-94), DAR, Order of Ea. Star, Mortar Bd., Phi Beta Kappa (pres. Los Alamos chpt. 1969-72), Phi Kappa Phi, Delta Kappa Gamma, Gamma Phi Beta. Home: 124 Rover Blvd Los Alamos NM 87544-3634 Office: Los Alamos Nat Lab Diamond Dr Los Alamos NM 87544

MENDOZA, CORAZON CABRERA, anesthesiologist; b. Bay, Laguna, The Philippines, Aug. 26, 1941; came to U.S., 1966; m. Martin M. Mendoza, June 9, 1966; children: Mark, Maria, Michael. MD, Far Ea. U., Manila, 1964. Diplomate Am. Bd. Anesthesiology. Intern Pitts. Hosp., 1966-67; resident in anesthesiology Allegheny Gen. Hosp., Pitts., 1967-68, St. Francis Hosp., Pitts., 1968-69; resident in gen. practice Perth Amboy (N.J.) Hosp., 1969-70; clin. instr. N.J. Coll. Med. & Dentistry, Newark, 1972-79; attending anesthesiologist VA Hosp., East Orange, N.J., 1972-79; staff anesthesiologist St. Clares Riverside Med. Ctr., Denville, N.J., 1979—. Mem. Am. Soc. Anesthesiologists, Assn. Filipino Physicians in Am., N.J. Soc. Anesthesiologists, Asian Am. Soc. N.J. (performer, prodr. cultural shows), Philippine Am. Assn. N.J. (past pres.), Far Ea. Univ. Alumni Found. (past pres.), Bereen Lions Club. Home: 3 Culver Rd Livingston NJ 07039

MENDOZA, JOANN AUDILET, nurse; b. Beaumont, Tex., Sept. 15, 1943; d. Jack Ernest and Ottie (Craig) Audilet; m. M.A. Mendoza, June 2, 1971; children: Danny Russell Myers, Shawna Laurene Rosco. BSN magna cum laude, Lamar U., Beaumont, 1989. RN, Tex.; CEN; cert. ACLS, advanced burn life support, basic trauma life support, instr. trauma nurses core course, basic trauma life support, ACLS instr.; provider pediatric advanced life support, emergency nurse pediatric course. Vocat. nurse Stat Care Inc., Beaumont; lic. vocat. nurse Jefferson County Jail Infirmary, Beaumont, Bapt. Hosp., Beaumont; emergency rm. relief charge nurse Beaumont Regional Med. Ctr., Beaumont; Mem. Coun. Workplace Issues Dist. and State. Mem. ANA, Tex. Nurses Assn. (pres. Dist. 12), Lamar U. Student Nurse Assn. (sec.), Internat. Honor Soc. Nurses, Emergency Nurses Assn., Sigma Theta Tau, Phi Kappa Phi. Baptist. Home: RR 5 Box 23 Beaumont TX 77713-9673 Office: Beaumont Regional Med Ctr 3680 College Beaumont TX 77726

MENES, PAULINE H., state legislator; b. N.Y.C., July 16, 1924; d. Arthur B. and Hannah H. Herskowitz; m. Melvin Menes, Sept. 1, 1946; children: Sandra Jill Menes Ashe, Robin Joy Menes Elvord, Bambi Lynn Menes Gavin. BA in Bus. Econs. and Geography, Hunter Coll., N.Y.C., 1945. Economist Quartermaster Gen. Office, Washington, 1945-47; geographer Army Map Service, Washington, 1949-50; chief clk. Prince George's County Election Bd., Upper Marlboro, Md., 1963; substitute tchr. Prince George's County High Schs., Md., 1965-66; mem. Md. Ho. of Dels., Annapolis, 1966—, mem. judiciary com., 1979—; mem. com. on rules and exec. nominations Mo. Ho. of Dels., Annapolis, 1979-94, chmn. spl. com. on drug and alcohol abuse, 1986—, chmn. Prince George's County del., 1993—. Mem. Md. Arts Coun., Balt., 1968—, Md. Commn. on Aging, Balt., 1975—; bd. dirs. Prisoner's Aid Assn., Balt., 1971—. Recipient Internat. Task Force award Women's Yr., 1977; named to Hall of Fame Hunter Coll. Alumni Assn., 1986, Women's Hall of Fame Prince George County, 1989. Mem. NOW, Nat. Conf. State Legislators (com. on drugs and alcohol 1987), Md. NOW (Ann London Scott Meml. award for Legis. Excellence 1976), Nat. Order Women Legislators (pres. 1979-80), Women's Polit. Caucus, Bus. and Profl. Women, B'nai B'rith. Home: 3517 Marlborough Way College Park MD 20740-3925 Office: Md Ho of Reps Rm 201 Lowe State Office Bldg Annapolis MD 21401

MENGES, PAMELA ANN, aerospace engineer, consultant; b. Northport, Mich., May 10, 1962; d. Raymond Alfred and Margaret Carolyn (St. Amand) M. BS in Biomathematics, Thomas More Coll., 1985; postgrad. in Aerospace Engring., Union Inst., Cin. Teaching asst. in physics Am. U. Paris, 1982-83; intern sci. writing Behringer-Crawford, Covington, Ky., 1984; specialist overseas prodn. GE, Evendale, Ohio, 1984; dir. project svcs., rsch. engineer, mgr. intern ops. Ray A. Menges and Assocs. (formerly RAM Assocs. Inc.), Cin., 1984-92; pres., CEO Menges Consulting, Inc., Cin., 1992—. Mem. AIAA (assoc. flight testing tech. com.), Am. Def. Preparedness Assn., Am. Soc. Tesing and Materials, Am. Phys. Soc., Am. Nuclear Soc. (student). Unitarian. Office: Menges Consulting Inc 2196 W North Bend Rd Cincinnati OH 45239

MENKE, SALLY, film editor. films include: Tom Goes to the Bar, 1986, Teenage Mutant Ninja Turtles, 1990, The Search for Signs of Intelliegent Life in the Universe, 1991, Reservoir Dogs, 1992, Heaven and Earth, 1993, Pulp Fiction, 1994 (Acad. award nom., Best Film Editing). Office: care IATSE Local 776 7715 Sunset Blvd #220 Los Angeles CA 90046*

MENKEN, JANE AVA, demographer, educator; b. Phila., Nov. 29, 1939; d. Isaac Nathan and Rose Ida (Sarvetnick) Golubitsky; m. Matthew Menken, 1960 (div. 1985); children: Kenneth Lloyd, Kathryn Lee; m. Richard Jessor, Nov. 13, 1992. A.B., U. Pa., 1960; M.S., Harvard U., 1962; Ph.D., Princeton U., 1975. Asst. in biostats. Harvard U. Sch. Pub. Health, Boston, 1962-64; math. statistician NIMH, Bethesda, Md., 1964-66; research assoc. dept. biostats., Columbia U., N.Y.C., 1966-69; mem. research staff Office of Population Research Princeton U., N.J., 1969-71, 75-87, asst. dir., 1978-86, assoc. dir., 1986-87, prof. sociology, 1980-82, prof. sociology and pub. affairs, 1982-87; prof. sociology and demography U. Pa., Phila., 1987—, UPS Found. prof. social scis., 1987—, dir. Population Studies Ctr., 1989—; mem. social scis. and population study sect., NIH, Bethesda, Md., 1978-82, chmn., 1980-82, population adv. com. Rockefeller Found., N.Y.C., 1981-93, com. on population and demography, NAS, Washington, 1978-83, com. on population, 1983-85, com. nat. stats., 1983-89, com. on AIDS research, 1987-94, co-chair panel data and rsch. priorities for arresting AIDS in sub-Saharan Africa, 1994—, Commn. on Behavioral and Social Scis. and Edn., 1991—, sci. adv. com., Demographic and Health Surveys, Columbia, Md., 1985-90, Nat. Adv. Child Health and Human Devel. Council, 1988-91; cons. Internat. Centre for Diarrhoeal Disease Research, Bangladesh, Dhaka, 1984—. Author: (with Mindel C. Sheps) Mathematical Models of Conception and Birth, 1973; editor: (with Henri Leridon) Natural Fertility, 1979, (with Frank Furstenberg, Jr. and Richard Lincoln) Teenage Sexuality, Pregnancy and Childbearing, 1981, World Population and U.S. Policy: The Choices Ahead, 1986; contbr. articles to profl. jours. Bd. dirs. Alan Guttmacher Inst., N.Y.C., 1981-90, 93—. Nat. Merit scholar, 1957; John Simon Guggenheim Found. fellow, 1992-93, Ctr. for Advanced Study in Behavioral Scis. Fellow, 1995—. Fellow AAAS, Am. Statis. Assn.; mem. NAS, Am. Acad. Arts and Scis., Population Assn. Am. (Mindel Sheps award 1982, pres. 1985), Am. Pub. Health Assn. (Mortimer Spiegelman award 1975, program devel. bd. 1984-87), Am. Sociol. Assn., Soc. for Study of Social Biology, Internat. Union for Sci. Study of Population (coun. 1989—), Sociol. Research Assn. (exec. com. 1991—). Office: U Pa Population Studies Ctr 3718 Locust Walk Philadelphia PA 19104-6298

MENNA, CHRISTINE ANN, public relations executive; b. Johnstown, Pa., Dec. 4, 1955; d. Joseph and Cecilia (Wojnaroski) Pisczek; m. Thomas Menna, Oct. 20, 1984; 1 child, Elizabeth. BA in Journalism, U. Pitts., 1977. Copywriter, account exec. Accent-Midstate Advt., Johnstown, Pa., 1977-85; mgr. corporate comm. Crown Am. Realty Trust, Johnstown, 1985—; pub. rels. cons. Johnstown Chiefs, 1990—. Mem. adv. bd. Salvation Army, Johnstown, 1989—; bd. dirs. United Way, Johnstown, 1993—. Mem. Nat. Orgn. Underwater Instrs. (open water I diver), Internat. Coun. Shopping Ctrs. Office: Crown Am Realty Trust Pasquerilla Plz Johnstown PA 15901

MENSINGER, PEGGY BOOTHE, retired mayor; b. Modesto, Calif., Feb. 18, 1923; d. Dyas Power and Margaret (Stewart) Boothe; m. John Logan Mensinger, May 25, 1952; children: John B., Stewart I., Susan B. AB in Polit. Sci, Stanford U., 1944. Reporter San Francisco Red Cross Chpt. News Bur., 1944; acting mgr. Boothe Fruit Co., Modesto, Calif., 1945; asst. dir. Stanford (Calif.) Alumni Assn., 1947; exec. sec. pub. exercises com. Stanford U., 1949-51; mem. Modesto City Council, 1973-79, mayor, 1979-87; ret., 1987; Mem. adv. bd. Agrl. Issues Ctr. U. Calif., 1988-94. Bd. dirs. Nat. coun. Girl Scouts U.S.A., 1978-87, Calif. PLanning and Conservation League, 1990—, Friends Outside Nat. Bd., 1991—; chmn. Citizens Com. for Internat. Students, 1965-70; pres. Modesto PTA Council, 1967-69, Modesto chpt. Am. Field Svc., 1969-70, Stanislaus County Hist. Soc., 1970-71; mem. state bd. Common Cause, 1973-75; chmn. Modesto City Cultural Commn., 1968-73; del. White House Conf. on Families, L.A., 1980; chmn. Stanislaus Area Assn. Govts., 1976-77; chmn. air quality subcom. U.S. Conf. Mayors, 1985-87. Recipient Woman of Year award VFW Aux., 1980 , Man of Yr. award Am. Legion, 1987. Mem. Nat. League Am. Pen Women (assoc.), Stanford Assocs. (pres. 1985-87), Soroptimist (hon., Women Achievement award 1980), Phi Beta Kappa, Gamma Phi Beta. Unitarian. Home: 1320 Magnolia Ave Modesto CA 95350-5250

MENTZER, MERLEEN MAE, adult education educator; b. Kingsley, Iowa, July 25, 1920; d. John David and Maggie Marie (Simonsen) Moritz; m. Lee Arnold Mentzer, June 1, 1944. Student Westman Coll., 1939, Wayne State U., Nebr., 1942, Bemidji State U., 1950, Mankato Coll., 1978, U. Minn.-St. Paul, 1979. Lic. health and life ins., Minn. Tchr., Kingsley, Iowa, 1938-41; owner, mgr. Mentzer's Sundries, Hackensack, Minn., 1946-76, House of Mentzers, Pine River, Minn., 1974-77; instr. Hennepin Tech., Eden Prairie, Minn., 1978—; owner, mgr. Cass Co. Minn. Real Estate, 1993—; mem. score evaluation bd. Small Bus. Assn. Loans, 1993—; sales rep. in annuity and insurance investment; counselor Sr. Citizen Orgn. Ret. Execs.-Via of Mpls. C. of C. Coord. motivational program (with others) Five Steps to the Best Years of Your Life, 1991, Five Steps to Success, Attitudes Are Everything. Mem. Mpls. C. of C., Hackensack C. of C., (v.p. 1970-76), Northern Lights Federated Woman's Club (pres. 1958-59). Republican. Lutheran. Avocations: dancing, bowling, reading, theatre, seminars. Home and Office: 6781 Tartan Curve Eden Prairie MN 55346-3355

MENZEL, DIANA ANNA, small business owner; b. Trenton, N.J., Mar. 29, 1958; d. Rena (Paterra) M. Grad. high sch., West Trenton, N.J. Transit operator Ewing Bank & Trust, West Trenton, 1975-80; comms. operator N.J. State Police, Trenton, 1981-84; owner, mgr. Muscle Magic Fitness Ctr., Lambertville, N.J., 1984-86; carpenter Paul Raywood, Contractor, New Hope, Pa., 1987-90; head chef Marcella's Restaurant, Lambertville, 1984-87; chef, owner DeAnna's Restaurant, Lambertville, 1990—. Named N.J.'s Top 5 New Restaurants, N.J. Monthly mag., 1991, 3 1/2 Stars, Princeton Packet Restaurant Rev., 1991, My 50 Favorite Restaurants, Suzanne Goldenson, 1991, Top Restaurants in New Hope and Lambertville, N.J. Monthly mag., 1993. Mem. N.J. Police Acad., Lambertville C. of C. Office: DeAnna s Restaurant 18 S Main St Lambertville NJ 08530-1827

MEO, ROXANNE MARIE, critical care nurse; b. Saginaw, Mich., Oct. 10, 1959; d. Joseph S. and Margaret V. (Gillam) M. BSN, Saginaw Valley State U., University Center, Mich., 1982; student, Delta Coll., 1987-90; overseas studies, Mich. State U., 1983; postgrad., U. Mich., 1993. Nurse extern St. Luke's Hosp., Saginaw, 1982, staff nurse, 1983-88; Nurse in Washington intern Nat. Fedn. Specialty Nursing Orngs., 1987; resource nurse Ask-A-Nurse, Saginaw, 1988-91, Seton Health Care Corp. East Cen. Mich.; staff nurse St. Mary's Med. Ctr., Saginaw, 1983, 91—. Mem. ANA, Am. Assn. Neurosci. Nurses, Mich. Nurses Assn., Saginaw Nurses Assn., Soc. Gastrointestinal Assts., Emergency Nurses Cancel Alcohol Related Emergencies, Sigma Theta Tau.

MERCER, ELIZABETH JANE, administrator; b. Detroit, July 30, 1950. BS, Eastern Mich. U., 1972; JD, Thomas Cooley Law Sch., 1983. Bar: Mich. 1983. Labeling specialist Food Divsn. Agr., Lansing, Mich., 1973-83, compliance officer, 1983-87; dep. dir. Charitable Gaming Lottery, Lansing, Mich., 1987-92; exec. dir. Office Hwy. Safety Planning, Lansing, Mich., 1993—. Bd. dirs. St. Vincent Home for Children, Lansing, 1993. Mem. Mich. State Bar Assn. Office: 300 S Washington Ste 300 Lansing MI 48913

MERCER, JOANNE ELLEN, state agency administrator; b. Harrisburg, Pa., Dec. 25, 1954; d. Dominick and Joan Marie (Wesner) Sgrignoli; divorced; 1 child, Jessica Ellen; m. James Brock Mercer, June 9, 1990. Clerical support state real estate commn. Commonwealth of Pa., Harrisburg, 1973-76, adminstr. state bd. accountancy, 1976-83, adminstrv. asst. to chief of law enforcement, 1984-85, adminstr. exam. and contract mgmt., 1985—. Founder, former chair Paxtang Manor Crime Watch, 1991; mem. adminstrv. coun. Trinity United Meth. Ch., 1994. Democrat. United Methodist. Office: Pa State Bur Profl Occupl Affairs Exam Contract Mgmt Unit PO Box 2649 Harrisburg PA 17105

MERCER, LAURA A., public relations executive; b. St. Petersburg, Fla., July 8, 1959. BA in Journalism, U. N.C., 1980. Reporter Wilmington (N.C.) Star News, 1980-84; staff writer Barclays American, Charlotte, N.C., 1984-88; acct. exec. Price/McNabb, Charlotte, 1988-89, sr. acct. exec., 1989-92, account supr., v.p., 1990-92, sr. v.p., dir. pub. rels., 1992—. Mem. Pub. Rels. Soc. Am., U. N.C. Journalism Sch. Found. Office: Price/McNabb Pub Rels 2800 NationsBank Group Ctr Charlotte NC 28211

MERCER, MARGARET TEELE, medical and software marketing executive; b. Bronxville, N.Y., Sept. 10, 1962; d. William Earl Jr. and Judith (Forster) M.; m. Robert Mitchell Fromcheck, May 23, 1993. BS, U. Colo., 1985. With 1986-88, Prescription Products divsn. Fisons Pharms., Denver, 1988-92; pharm. sales rep. HealthScan Products, Cedar Grove, N.J., 1992-93; with Sandler Comm., N.Y.C., 1993-94, Spectrum Human Resource Systems, Denver, 1994—. Youth leader Calvary Ch., Denver, 1988-91. Mem. NAFE, Healthcare Bus. Assn. Home: 2 Rose Clover Littleton CO 80127

MERCHANT, ANITA KATALIN, psychologist, educator; b. Rapid City, S.D., Sept. 13, 1965; d. Alexander Steven and Carol Jean (Luckert) Finta. BA, U. Nebr., Lincoln, 1987, MA, 1990, PhD in Clin. Psychology, 1992. Lic. practicing psychologist, N.C. Acad. advisor Dean's Office, Coll. Arts and Scis. U. Nebr., Lincoln, 1985-87; pre-doctoral intern Iowa State U., Ames, 1990-91; asst. prof. dept. psychology Appalachian State U., Boone, N.C., 1991—, outreach coord. Counseling and Psychol. Svcs., 1991-92, clin. svcs. dir., 1992—; program evaluator Lincoln-Lancaster Drug Projects, Inc., 1990-91. Contbr. chpt. to book, articles to profl. jours. Vol. Hospice of Watauga County, Boone, 1993; mem. AIDS task force Appalachian State U., 1993; mem. campus ministry com. Grace Luth. Ch., Boone, 1993. Regents scholar U. Nebr., Lincoln, 1983-87. Mem. APA, Am. Counseling Assn., Am. Coll. Pers. Assn., N.C. Assn. for Women in Edn., Phi Beta Kappa, Psi Chi. Office: Appalachian State U Counseling and Psychol Svcs Student Svcs Bldg Boone NC 28608

MERCHANT, JUDITH MIRIAM, state agency administrator, educator, counselor; b. Burlington, Iowa, Aug. 27, 1940; d. Arnold Walter and Dorothy Lulu (Kretzschmar) Schmidt; m. Richard Ival Merchant, Dec. 19, 1961; children—Michael Brian, David Bradley. B.A. Summa cum laude, U. Iowa, 1962; M.A., Ball State U., 1974; cert. advanced grad. study Boston U., 1976. Adminstr. alcohol program Wash. Dept. Social and Health Services, Olympia, 1977-79, mgr. day care services, 1978-80, dir. bur. alcohol and substance abuse, 1980-81, exec. asst. to dept. sec. and chief intergovtl. relations, 1981-82, dir. div. income assistance, 1982-86; dep. dir. Mich. Dept. Social Services, 1986; dep. dir. Wash. Dept. of Fisheries, 1986-93; dir. Wash. State Energy Office Gov. Cabinet, 1993—; adminstr. alcohol and drug services, also educator secondary edn. Dept. Def., Fed. Republic of Germany, 1971-76; dep. dir. Wash. State Dept. Fisheries, 1986—. Ch. council Lutheran Ch. of Good Shepherd, Olympia, 1979-82; adv. com. Community Vol. Med. Program for Low-Income Families, Olympia, 1982—; bd. dirs. Wash. State Employees Credit Union, Olympia, 1983—. Recipient Service award VIIth Corps Hdqrs. U.S. Army, Fed. Republic of Germany, 1975. Mem. Nat. Assn. State Alcohol and Drug Dirs. (exec. bd. 1980-81), Am. Pub. Welfare Assn. (exec. bd.), Pacific Fisheries Mgmt. Coun., N. Pacific Mgmt. Coun., 1987-93, Nat. Assn. State Energy Officials (vice chair), We. Interstate Energy Bd. (mem. exec. com. 1994), European Congress Am. Parents and Tchrs. (v.p. 1972-74), Exec. Women in State Govt., Phi Beta Kappa. Home: 3724 Pifer Ct SE Olympia WA 98501-4160 Office: Energy Office PO Box 43165 Olympia WA 98504-3165

MERCHANT, NILOUFER MOIZ, education educator; b. Sept. 22, 1959. BA, U. Pune, India, 1979, MA, 1981; MS, U. Wis., 1985; EdD, U. Cin., 1991. Psychology asst. Stuart Bassman, Inc., Cin., 1986-89; coord. racial awareness program U. Cin., 1989-91; asst. prof. St. Cloud (Minn.) State U., 1991—; conductor cultural diversity workshops for various orgns. Contbr. articles to profl. jours. Mem. affirmative action com. Land O'Lakes Girl Scouts, St. Cloud, 1993—; bd. dirs. Sexual Assault Ctr., St. Cloud; mem. pluralism com. Girl Scouts U.S., Cin., 1990-91. Mem. Am. Counseling Assn., Multicultural Counseling and Devel. Assn., Minn. Counseling Assn. Office: St Cloud State Univ Dept Applied Psychology 720 6th Ave S Saint Cloud MN 56301-4308

MERCHEY, RUTH ANN, artist, designer; b. Bell, Calif., Feb. 26, 1947; d. Charles Wesley and Esther (Rogers) Lester; m. Morton Donald Merchey, Aug. 19, 1971 (div. Sept. 1991); children: Jason Aaron, Kelly Leigh. BA, Woodbury U., L.A., 1971; postgrad., UCLA, 1972-73. Designer Regal Rugs, Inc., Beverly Hills, Calif., 1968-75; designer, artist Ruth Merchey Designs, Downey, Calif., 1975-90; artist, builder Ruth Merchey Designs, Big Bear City, Calif., 1990—; owner R&S Designs, Downey, 1980-91. Author: (play) 12 Steps for 12 and Under, 1988 (spl. recognition award 1989); exhibited in group shows L.A. County Fair, 1978 (Best of Show), Valley Art Guild, Encino, Calif., 1989, 90 (1st place 1989, Best of Show award 1990), Costa Mesa Art Guild, 1991, San Bernardino County Art Mus., Redlands, Calif., 1991. Fundraiser L.A. County Med. Assn. Aux., Downey, 1975-80, City of Hope, Downey; officer Downey Elem. Sch., Downey Mid. Sch., Downey High Sch., 1979—; chmn. election campaign Downey Unified Sch. Bd., 196-88; cons., vol. S.E. Coun. on Alcohol Abuse, Downey, 1986-89, Polonaise Ball, Beverly Hills, Calif., 1985—. Recipient hon. award City of Hope, 1976, 80, 84. Mem. Redlands Art Assn., Taos Art Assn., Fine Arts Inst., Bear Valley Art Assn. Republican.

MERCIER, EILEEN ANN, forest products executive; b. Toronto, Ont., Can., July 7, 1947; d. Thomas Sidley and Frances Katherine (Boone) Falconer; m. Ernest Cochrane Mercier, Jan. 29, 1980; children: Jenny, Sheelagh, Peter, Michael, Stuart. BA with honors, Waterloo Luth. U., 1968; MA, U. Alberta, 1969; fellow, Instn. Can. Bankers, 1975; MBA, York U., 1977. Mgr. corp. fin. Toronto-Dominion Bank, 1972-78, portfolio mgr. TD capital; dir., U.S. comm. ops. Canwest Capital Corp., Toronto, 1978-81; mgr. fin. strategy & planning Gulf Can. Ltd., Toronto, 1981-86, mgr. corp. fin.; v.p. The Pagurian Corp., Toronto, 1986-87; v.p., treas. Abitibi-Price, Inc., Toronto, 1987-88, v.p. corp. devel., 1989-90, sr. v.p., CFO, 1990—; leader fin. and investment working group; participant prosperity initiative, bd. dirs. John Labbatt Ltd.; bd. dirs. C.I.C.P.A. Bus. Ventures Fund Inc. Bd. dirs. Toronto Hosp. Found., Metro Toronto YMCA; past chmn., mem. bd. govs. Wilfrid Laurier U., Waterloo, Ont. Recipient Outstanding Bus. Leader award Sch. Bus. & Econs., Wilfrid Laurier U., 1991. Office: Abitibi-Price Inc, PO Box 120, 207 Queen's Quay W Ste 6800, Toronto, ON Canada M5J 2P5 also: Abitibi Price Sales Corp 45 Rockefeller Plz New York NY 10111-0001

MERCOUN, DAWN DENISE, manufacturing company executive; b. Passaic, N.J., June 1, 1950; d. William S. and Irene F. (Micci) M. BS in Bus. Mgmt., Fairleigh Dickinson U., 1978. Personnel payroll coordinator Bentex Mills, Inc., East Rutherford, N.J., 1969-72; employment mgr. Inwood Knitting Mills, Clifton, N.J., 1972-75; gen. mgr. Consol. Advance, Inc., Passaic, 1975-76; v.p. human resources Gemini Industries, Inc., Clifton, 1976—; v.p., bd. dirs. Contact Morris-Passaic. Mem. Soc. for Human Resource Mgmt., Am. Compensation Assn., Internat. Found. Employee Benefits, Earthwatch Rsch. Team, Daus. of the Nile (Maalas Temple No. 20, elective officer 1993—). Republican. Office: 179 Entin Rd Clifton NJ 07014

MEREDITH, LYNNETTE ANN LOGAN, accountant; b. Carthage, Ill., Sept. 23, 1966; d. Ralph Kenneth and Eileen May (Redenius) Logan; m. Richard LaMont Meredith, Dec. 18, 1993. BA, Augustana Coll., Rock Island, Ill., 1988. Internal auditor Deere & Co., Moline, Ill., 1988-89, acct., 1989-93, internal auditor, 1993-94; acct. John Deere Harvester Works, Moline, 1994—. Mem. panel United Way, Moline/Rock Island, 1990-93; advisor Jr. Achievement, Moline, 1990-94; treas. Cedars at Woodfield Condo Assn., 1992-94, pres., 1995, John Deere Mixed Softball League, 1992—, John Deere Mixed Volleyball League, 1992—. Named Advisor of Yr. Jr. Achievement, 1993. Lutheran. Office: John Deere Harvester Works 1300 River Dr Moline IL 61265

MEREE, AUDRIE VALVO, food service executive; b. Pitts., Mar. 16, 1959; d. Ross Angelo and Dorothy Louise (Voytell) Valvo. Student, Indiana U. of Pa., 1977-82. Franchise devel. mgr. Arby's Roast Beef, Ft. Lauderdale, Fla., 1989-92; v.p. ops. Mamma Ilardo's, Balt., 1992-94; internat. devel. mgr. Manchu Wok, Toronto, Ont., Can., 1994—. Mem. Roundtable for Women in Food Svc., Alpha Phi (pres. 1988-89). Republican. Roman Catholic. Home: 5345 A Columbia Rd Columbia MD 21044

MERHIGE, NANCY RUTH MOORE, environmental protection specialist; b. Richmond, Va., Nov. 14, 1949; d. James Thomas Jr. and Martha Elizabeth (Riis) Moore; m. Robert R. Merhige, III, Mar. 5, 1969 (div. Mar. 1993); 1 child, Christopher Allan. BS in Geography magna cum laude, Old Dominion U., Norfolk, Va., 1991. Adminstrv. asst. Robinson, Piitchard & Boyer, Alexandria, Va., 1987-89; real estate agt. Albergotti & Co., Norfolk, 1989-91; environ. protection specialist, base civil engr. Environ. div. Naval Amphigious Base, Little Creek, Norfolk, 1992—. Mem. Old Dominion U. Area Alumni Orgn. (v.p. 1992-93), Old Dominion Crew Alumni, Hampton Roads Rowing Club (membership chmn. 1992—), Phi Kappa Phi, Gamma Theta Upsilon (pres. 1990—). Methodist. Home: 1106 Westmoreland Ave

2 Norfolk VA 23508-1422 Office: NAB Little Creek BCE Code N462 Environ Div 1450 Gator Blvd Norfolk VA 23521-2614

MERILAN, JEAN ELIZABETH, statistics educator; b. Columbia, Mo., Sept. 18, 1962; d. Charles Preston and Phyllis Pauline (Laughlin) M. AB summa cum laude, U. Mo., 1985, MA in Math., MA in Stats., 1987; post-grad., U. Ariz., 1987—. Grad. teaching asst. U. Mo., Columbia, 1985-87; grad. rsch. asst. U. Ariz., Tucson, 1988-89, grad. teaching asst., 1989—. Nat. Merit scholar, Univ. Curators scholar U. Mo., 1981-85, Grad. Acad. scholar U. Ariz., 1990—, Arts and Sci. Grad. scholar U. Mo., 1985-87; Gregory fellow U. Mo., 1985-87, Faculty of Sci. fellow U. Ariz., 1987-88. Mem. Am. Statis. Assn., Inst. Math. Stats., Soc. for Indsl. and Applied Math., Biometric Soc., Am. Math. Soc., Math. Assn. Am., Golden Key Nat. Honor Soc., Sigma Xi, Phi Beta Kappa, Phi Kappa Phi, Phi Eta Sigma, Pi Mu Epsilon. Office: U Ariz Dept Stats Tucson AZ 85721

MERINO, BARBARA DUBIS, accounting educator; b. Westfield, Mass., Oct. 6, 1939; d. Stephen Edward and Josephine Mary (Gorney) Dubis; m. James Anthony Merino, Sept., 1962; children: Catherine Merino Reisman, Anthony Dubis Merino, Dominic John Merino. BA, U. Mass., 1962; MBA, Murray State U., 1972; PhD, U. Ala., 1975. Faculty resident Arthur Andersen, N.Y.C., 1978; asst. prof. NYU, 1975-80, assoc prof., 1980-83; vis. assoc. prof. CUNY, 1981; prof. U. North Tex., Denton, 1983-88; O.J. Curry and Regents prof. Acctg. U. North Tex., 1988—. Author: History of Accounting in America, 1979 (Outstanding Book award 1980); contbr. articles to profl. jours. Fulbright prof., Poland, 1992-93. Fellow Beta Gamma Sigma; mem. NAFE;, Am. Acctg. Assn. (doctoral consortium faculty 1985, chair pub. interest sect. 1985), Acad. Acctg. Historians (pres. 1990, editor Acctg. Historians jour. 1994)., Beta Alpha Psi. Democrat. Roman Catholic. Home: 1913 Willowcrest Loop Denton TX 76205-6981 Office: Dept Acctg U North Tex Denton TX 76203

MERKEL, BEVERLY DUANNE ATTEBERY, counselor; b. Dallas, Aug. 19, 1955; d. James Alvin and Velma Estelle (Fenton) Attebery; 1 child, Lauren Michelle. AA, Hill Coll., 1975; BA, Sam Houston State U., 1977; MS in Edn., U. Houston, 1982; postgrad., Tarleton U., 1991. Cert. elem. tchr., kindergarten, early childhood lang./learning disabilities, edn. diagnostician, English K-8, mid-mgmt., counseling. Tchr. kindergarten, LLD K-4 Columbia-Brazoria Ind. Sch. Dist., Brazoria, Tex., 1979-80; LLD tchr. Angleton (Tex.) Ind. Sch. Dist., 1981-82; ednl. diagnostician Grand Prairie (Tex.) Ind. Sch. Dist., 1982-86; edn. diagnostician Hill County Co-op Spl. Edn., Hillsboro, Tex., 1986-88; jr. high counselor Hillsboro Ind. Sch. dist., 1988—; coord. Ptnrs. in Edn., Hillsboro Jr. High, 1988—; tchr. Peer Assistance and Leadership (PALS), Hillsboro Jr. High, 1990—; past coord., judge Univ. Interscholastic League, 1988—; others; presenter cultural diversity seminars; cons. multicultural curriculum, 1994—. Docent/vol. Bond's Alley Arts and Crafts Show, Hillsboro, 1966—; docent BBQ judge Cotton Pickin Fair, Hillsboro, 1993—; counselor, facilitator singles' support group, Cen. Bapt. Ch., Hillsboro, 1994—. Named Vol. of Yr., Heart of Tex. Coun. Drug and Alcohol Abuse, Waco, 1992. Mem. Assn. of Tex. Profl. Educators, Tex. Counseling Assn., Heart of Tex. Counseling Assn., Tex. Mid. Sch. Assn., Am. Counseling Assn., Am. Sch. Counselors Assn. Home: 76 Delmore St Hillsboro TX 76645 Office: Hillsboro Jr High Sch 310 E Walnut PO Box 977 Hillsboro TX 76645

MERKEL, PATRICIA MAE, school system administrator; b. Spokane, Wash., June 18, 1935; d. Hugo Oscar and Mary Jane (Blackwelder) Koenig; m. Gordon Henry, Nov. 10, 1956 (div. 1973); children: Katherine Marie Merkel Fisk, Karol Ann Merkel Korte, John Henry. BA cum laude, Ea. Washington U., 1989. Cert. ednl. office employee. Acctg. clk. Pacific N.W. Bell, Spokane, 1954-56; book-keeper Edwall (Wash.) Sch. Dist., 1969-75; book-keeper Reardan (Wash.)-Edwall Sch. Dist., 1975-78, bus. mgr., 1978-82; asst. to supr. fin. Dayton (Wash.) Sch. Dist., 1982—. Mem. Town of Reardan Planning Commn., 1977-82, sec., 1978-82; treas. Citizens for Edn. Com., Dayton, 1983-91, Columbia County Courthouse Restoration Project, Dayton, 1988—; mem. fin. adv. com. Dayton Gen. Hosp., 1986-90, Dayton City Coun., 1986-87; mem. vocat. bus. adv. com. Dayton High Sch., 1990—. Recipient Mary Shields Wilson Medallion award. Mem. AAUW, Wash. Assn. Ednl. Office Profls. (treas. 1984-86, pres.-elect 1986-87, pres. 1987-88, Ednl. Office Profl. of Yr. award 1990), Nat. Assn. Ednl. Office Profls. (Ednl. Office Profl. of Yr. award 1990), Assn. Assn. Sch. Bus. Ofcls. (chmn. com. 1978-81), S.C. Assn. Ednl. Office Profls. (pres. 1991-92), Blue Mountain Assn. Ednl. Office Profls., Assn. Sch. Bus. Ofcls. Internat. (com. 1984-86, scholar 1987), Order Ea. Star, Order of Eagles, Kiwanis (sec. 1991—, Kiwaniain of Yr. award 1993). *. Democrat. Presbyterian. Home: 218 S 4th St Dayton WA 99328-1412 Office: Dayton Sch Dist # 2 609 S 2nd St Dayton WA 99328-1598

MERKEL-HESS, MARY LYNNE, artist; b. Waterloo, Iowa, Apr. 6, 1949; d. Lee John and Margaret (Delagardelle) Hess; m. Stephen Paul Merkel, May 5, 1973; children: Kathryn, Matthias. BA, Marquette U., 1971; BFA, U. Wis., Milw., 1976; MA, U. Iowa, 1981, MFA, 1983. instr. Cornell Coll., Mt. Vernon, Iowa, 1986; guest curator Waterloo Mus. Art, 1993. Contbr. essays to book: Basketmaker's Art, 1986, photos to book: Papermaking for Basketry, 1988; represented in permanent collections at Met. Mus., Am. Craft Mus. Mem. Am. Craft Coun., Iowa City Arts Coun. (bd. dirs. 1988), Iowa Designer Crafts Assn. (v.p. 1987). Home: 2609 Friendship St Iowa City IA 52245-5006

MERKLE, HELEN LOUISE, chef; b. Carrington, N.D., May 23, 1950; d. Orville F. and Lillian M. (Argue) M. BS, N.D. State U., 1972. Asst. dir. food mgmt. Stouffer's Atlanta Inn, Atlanta, 1972-74; dir. food mgmt. Stouffer's Indpls. Inn, 1974-78; adminstrv. dir. food mgmt. Stouffer's Riverfront Towers, St. Louis, 1978-80; food mgmt. cons. Fraser Mgmt., Westlake, Ohio, 1980-83; exec. chef Marriott Hotel, Cleve., 1983-89; exec. chef Snavely Mgmt. Svcs, 1989—. Recipient First Place award for soups Taste of Indpls., 1976. Mem. NAFE, Am. Culinary Fedn., Am. Culinary Fedn. (cert. exec. chef, sec. Cleve. chpt. 1989-92, Pres.'s award 1992, treas. 1993, 94, first v.p. 1995, named Chpt. Chef of the Yr., 1993). Democrat. Lutheran. Home: 4137 W 160th St Cleveland OH 44135-4349 Office: Snavely Mgmt Svcs 1100 Crocker Rd Cleveland OH 44145-1033

MERMELSTEIN, ISABEL MAE ROSENBERG, senior citizen consultant; b. Houston, Aug. 20, 1934; d. Joe Hyman and Sylvia (Lincove) Rosenberg; m. Robert Jay Mermelstein, Sept. 6, 1953 (div. July 1975); children: William, Linda, Jody. Student U. Ariz., 1952, Mich. State U., 1974, Lansing (Mich.) Community Coll., 1975. Exec. dir. Shiawassee County YWCA, Owosso, Mich., 1975-78; real estate developer F&S Devel. Corp., Lansing, Mich., 1978-79, Corum Devel. Corp., Houston, 1979-81; adminstrv. fin. planner, sr. citizen cons. Investec Asset Mgmt. Group, Inc.; owner Ins. Filing Svcs. Sr. Citizens, 1985—; guardian VA, 1990—. Author: For You! I Killed the Chicken, 1972. Mem. Older Women's League, Houston, 1st Ecumenical Council of Lansing, Nat. Mus. Women in Arts, Judaica Mus., Houston, Mus. Fine Arts, Houston, Mus. Natural Sci., Houston. Recipient State of Mich. Flag, 1972, Key to City, City of Lansing, 1972-73. Mem. Nat. Assn. Claims Assistance Profls., Internat. Women's Pilot Orgn. (The 99's), Jewish Geneal. Soc., Internat. Directorate Disting. Leadership. Republican. Jewish. Lodges: Zonta, Licoma, B'nai B'rith, Hadassah, Nat. Fedn. Temple Sisterhoods. Flew All Women's Transcontinental Air Race (Powder Puff Derby), 1972, 73. Avocations: flying, gourmet cooking, needlepoint, knitting, snow skiing. Home: 4030 Newshire Dr Houston TX 77025-3921

MERNALYN, actress, writer, producer; b. Detroit, July 23; d. Irwin and Myldred (Kolb) Hamburger. GPA with highest honors, Northwood of Mich. Profl. internat. model, freelance fashion cons.; creator, producer for pvt. Clubs Art Deco Fashion Shows; former fashion commentator Radio Luxembourg; nat. spokesperson GM; internat. spokesperson Jaguar; concierge L'Ermitage Hotel Group; customer cons. Tiffany & Co., Beverly Hills; pub. rels. Bunny Playboy Club Internat.; radio personality various USA stas.; creator, pres. PillowTalk Ltd., U.K. and U.S. Producer, writer, narrator nationally syndicated radio shows In a Word Mood, BabyTalk, The Children's Corner, FlashBack, The Veneration Generation, Today's Woman, Movie Moments; recurring role ABC-TV primetime sitcom New World Television, others; frequent guest nat. TV and radio talkshows; author: My Book, two volumes Philosophy/Humanity, contbg. author poetry anthology to profl. journals; dir. creator, instr. of Improving Quality of Humanity and Personal Certitude Classes; Shakespearean lead actress The Globe Theatre, American debut, A Yorkshire Tragedy, Much Ado About Nothing, Twelfth Night, Taming of the Shrew, Man of La Mancha, and many others. Active Am. Lung Assn., Friends of Animals. Named the Most Perfect Girl, Miss Budweiser Anheuser-Busch, Miss Internat. MG Brit. Leyland Eng.-USA. Mem. Screen Actors Guild, Am. Film Inst., Museum of the City of New York, Los Angeles County Museum of Art, Northwood of Mich. Alumni Assn., Art Deco Soc. N.Y. and L.A., Smithsonian.

MERO, MARJORIE ANNE, compensation specialist; b. Oregon City, Jan. 17, 1940; d. Richard Nyquist and Julia Annetta (Loy) Schopp; m. Gordon Duane Mero, Feb. 4, 1958; children: Sheryl Ann Mero Burns, Duane Morris. Student, Kinman Bus. U., 1972, Spokane Falls Community Coll., 1974-79. Cert. compensation profl. Dir. M. Smith Childcare Ctr., Kalispell, Mont., 1966-70; clk. Power Co., Spokane, Wash., 1970-71, engr. technician, 1972-75, job analyst, 1975-80; compensation supr. Wash. Water Power Co., Spokane, 1980-89, compensation administr., 1989-91, compensation mgr., 1991—; mem. survey steering com. N.W. Electric and Light, 1984—; mem. ops. com. Consumer Credit Counseling Svc., 1993—, bd. dirs., 1994—. Artist watercolor paintings, 1967—. Panel chmn. United Way, Spokane, 1975-79. Mem. Am. Compensation Assn. (western regional rep. for Wash., Oreg. and Alaska compensation groups 1991-94), Pacific Coast Gas Assn., N.W. Compensation Forum, Spokane Calligraphic Art Soc., Write On Calligraphers, Extension Homemakers Club, Rabbit Breeders Club, Scripts and Scribes. Republican. Methodist.

MERRIAM, CHRISTINE ELIZABETH, elementary art educator; b. Ladysmith, Wis., Oct. 21, 1952; d. Daniel Bruhey and Frances Elaine (Doland) M.; m. Thom Dougherty (div. Sept. 1979); children: Jessica Tachii'ni-i. BS, U. Wis., 1975; MA in Art Edn., U. Colo., 1990. Cert. art edn. and elem. edn. Staff photographer Navajo C.C., Tsaile, Ariz., 1973-74; mus. educator U. Wis., Madison, 1975; GED tchr. Kayenta (Ariz.) Unified Schs., 1976, first grade tchr., 1976-81, art tchr., 1981—; freelance jewelry designer, Kayenta, 1968—; grad. asst. U. Colo., Boulder, 1988-90; presenter, panelist Ariz. Commn. on the Arts, Phoenix, 1988—; art tchr. cadre Ariz. State Dept. Edn., Phoenix, 1989—; presenter in field. Artist: (mag.) Ornament, 1990, (book) Art Talk, 1994. Co-chairperson Laguna Creek Arts Assn., Kayenta, 1987—; bd. mem. Kayenta (Ariz.) Vendor Village, 1993-94. Grantee NEH, 1994. Mem. NEA, Nat. Art Edn. Assn. (Ariz. Art Educator award 1994), Ariz. Art Edn. Assn. (Pacific Region Elem. Art Educator award 1989, Pacific Region Ariz. Art Educator award 1993, regional coun. 1994—), Internat. Soc. for Edn. in the Arts, U.S. Soc. for Edn. in the Arts Assn. (presenter 1993), Alpha Delta Kappa. Mem. Baha'i Faith. Home: Box 1301 Kayenta AZ 86033 Office: Kayenta Unified Sch Dist #27 Box 337 Kayenta AZ 86033

MERRICK, BEVERLY CHILDERS, journalism, communications educator; b. Troy, Kans., Nov. 20, 1944; d. Horace Buchanan Merrick and Vola Yolantha (Clausen) Maul; m. John Douglas Childers, July 10, 1963; children: John Kevin, Pamela Christine, Jessica Faye. BA in Journalism with honors, Marshall U., 1980, BA in English with honors, 1980, M Journalism, 1982; M Creative Writing, Ohio U., 1986, cert. in Women's Studies, 1984, PhD in Comm. with honors, 1989. Reporter, photographer Ashland (Ky.) Daily Ind., 1981; tchr., instr. Albuquerque Pub. Schs., 1986-89; gen. assignment reporter, photographer Rio Rancho (N.Mex.) Observer, 1986; editor, rsch. cons. Ins. Pub. Law, Sch. of Law U. N.Mex., Albuquerque, 1990; asst. prof. Ga. So. U., Statesboro, 1991-94; assoc. prof. dept. mass comm. U. S.D., Vermillion, 1994—; part-time tchr., teaching assoc. Ohio U., Athens, 1981-84; part-time copy editor Albuquerque Tribune, 1991; vis. prof. East Carolina U., Greenville, N.C., 1989-90; adj. prof. Embry-Riddle U., Kirtland AFB, N.Mex., 1989, 91; organizer diversity conf., 1st amendment conf. Ga. So. U.; mem. session MIT, 1989. Author: (poetry) Navigating the Platte, 1986, Pearls for the Casting, 1987, Closing the Gate, 1993; contbr. poems to profl. publs., chpts. to books. Pub. rels. liaison Nat. Convention Bus. and Profl. Women, Albuquerque, 1988; pres. Albuquerque Bus. and Profl. Women, 1986-87, Rio Rancho Civic Assn., 1987-89, So. Ohio Improvement League, 1973-76; pres. bd. dirs. Pine Creek Conservancy Dist., 1976-83. Named Outstanding Citizen, N.Mex. Legislature, Truly Fine Citizen of Ohio, Ohio Gen. Assembly, 1973, Outstanding Homemaker of Ohio, Gov. of Ohio, 1974; grantee Reader's Digest, 1980, 83; John Houk Meml. grantee W.Va. Women's Conf., 1982; fellow Nat. Women's Studies Inst., Lilly Found., 1983; E.W. Scripps scholar, 1984; recipient Silver Clover award 4-H, Writing award Aviation/Space Writers Assn., 1981. Mem. Soc. Profl. Journalists, Assn. for Edn. in Journalism and Mass Comm. (mem. nat. convention com. 1993-94), N.Mex. State Poetry Soc. (pres. 1987-89), Sigma Tau Delta. Office: U SD Dept Mass Comm 414 E Clark St Vermillion SD 57069

MERRICK, PATRICIA RILEY, merger and acquisitions executive; b. N.Y.C., Mar. 19, 1942; d. John Francis and Mary Dibble Riley. BA in Polit. Sci., Hunter Coll., 1978; postgrad., Harvard U., 1984. Sec., treas. Charterhouse Group Internat., Inc., N.Y.C., 1973-77, v.p. new bus. devel., 1977-84, sr. v.p., 1984—; bd. dirs. Wundies, Inc., N.Y.C., Charter Power Systems, Inc., Plymouth Meeting, Pa., Charterhouse Automotive Group, Fenton, Mich., Everfresh Beverages, Inc., Chgo. Bd. dirs. The Jericho Project. Mem. Harvard Club. Office: Charterhouse Group Internat 535 Madison Ave New York NY 10022-4212

MERRILL, AMANDA A., state legislator; b. Amesbury, Mass., May 9, 1951; m. Kenneth Fuld; 2 children. BA, U. N.H., 1974; PhD, Dartmouth Coll., 1978. Mem. N.H. Ho. of Reps.; mem. environment and agriculture com.; fund raiser. Bd. dirs. Strafford Hospice, 1990—; mem. exec. com. Friends of U. N.H. Libr., 1990—. Mem. U. N.H. Alumni Assn. (bd. dirs. 1990—). Office: NH House of Reps State Capitol Concord NH 03301*

MERRILL, LORRAINE STUART, journalist; b. Ayer, Mass., Sept. 5, 1951; d. James Allen and Lorraine Alma (Pote) Stuart; m. John Charles Merrill, June 2, 1970; children: Nathan Charles Stuart Merrill, Justin James Stuart Merrill. BS magna cum laude, U. N.H., 1973. Tchr. Montessori Sch., Exeter, N.H., 1983-86; ptnr. Stuart Farm, Stratham, N.H., 1975—; freelance agrl. journalist, columnist Stratham, 1983—; cons. writer Office of Econ. Devel., Canton of Fribourg, Switzerland, 1987; mem. nat. sustainable agrl. adv. coun. USDA, 1993—, chair N.H. state com. USDA Agrl. Stabilization and Conservation Svc., 1994—, external rev. team Leopold Ctr. for Sustainable Agrl., Iowa State U., Ames, 1993; bd. dir. New England Dairy and Food Council. columnist/feature writer: Hoard's Dairyman mag., Ft. Atkinson, Wis.; contbr. Turf mag., St. Johnsbury, Vt., numerous others. Mem. sch. bd. Stratham Sch. Dist., 1980-87; chmn. N.H. Sch. Adminstrv. Unit 16 Joint Sch. Bd., Exeter, N.H., 1983-84; adv. coun. to the dean Coll. of Life Scis. and Agr., U. N.H., Durham, 1991—. Recipient Fred E. Beane Meml. award for agrl. journalism, N.H. Farm and Forest Expo, Manchester, 1989, Excellence in Agrl. Journalism award Ea. Cooperative Milk Producers Assn., Syracuse, N.Y., 1988. Mem. N.E. Farm Communicators Assn., N.H. Farm Bur. (state info. com.), Agri-Mark, Inc., Audubon Soc. N.H., N.H. Timberland Owners Assn. (county dir.) Phi Kappa Phi, Phi Upsilon Omicron. Office: PO Box 176 Stratham NH 03885-0176

MERRILL, MARTHA, instructional media educator; b. Anniston, Ala., Apr. 21, 1946; d. Walter James and Polly (McCarty) M. BA, Birmingham-So. Coll., 1968; MS, Jacksonville (Ala.) State U., 1974; PhD, U. Pitts., 1979. Social worker Tuscaloosa (Ala.) County Dept. Human Resources, 1968-71, Calhoun County Dept. Human Resources, Anniston, Ala., 1971-73; social scis./bus. libr. Jacksonville State U., 1974-86, prof. instrnl. media, 1987—. Mem. Friends of Libr. bd. Anniston-Calhoun County Pub. Libr., 1984—. Recipient Ala./SIRS Intellectual Freedom award, Intellectual Freedom Com., Ala. Libr. Assn., 1992. Mem. ALA (exec. bd., Intellectual Freedom Round Table 1987-93), Ala. Libr. Assn. (pres. 1990-91, Disting. Svc. award 1995), Ala. Assn. Coll. and Rsch. Librs. (pres. 1989-90), Southeastern Libr. Assn. (chair intellectual freedom com. 1986-88, chair resolutions com. 1990-92). Office: Jacksonville State U Dept Ednl Resources Coll Edn Jacksonville AL 36265

MERRILL, MARY ANN, preschool education educator; b. Chillicothe, Ohio, Aug. 25, 1950; d. Lawrence Dale and Mary Hisle (Gowin) Pyle; m. Gregory John Merrill, Dec. 30, 1976; children: Griffin Jennings, Hannah Winfield. AA, Miami-Jacobs Coll., Dayton, Ohio, 1970; BS in Sociology with honors, Wright State U., Dayton, 1980; MS in Edn., Ind. U., Ft. Wayne, 1984. Contract negotiator Wright-Patterson AFB, Dayton, 1976-78; adminstrv. asst. Coll. Bus. Wright State U., 1978-80; dir. sponsored rsch. Ind. U.-Purdue U., Ft. Wayne, 1980-85; presch. tchr. First Sch., Centerville, Ohio, 1989—; tutor math. Wilbur Wright Mid. Sch., Dayton, 1990; mem. faculty Be Wise Math. Sci. Camp Wooster, Ohio, 1990, adminstrv. staff Be Wise Math. Sci. Camp Muskingum Coll., summers, 1991, 92, Denison U., summer 1993, 94. Mem.-at-large exec. com. Miami Valley Tenn Pregnancy-Parenting-Prevention Coalition, Dayton, 1987-90; vol. Philharm. Women's Assn., Dayton, 1987, 89, 91, 93; bd. dirs. Friends of Ballet, Dayton, 1989-91, vol. young audience program, 1994, Natural History Mus., Dayton, chmn. spl. events, by-laws com., sunwatch com, 1991—, chair, 1994, chmn. by-laws, 1993, active, 1994; asst. chmn. adv. planning Jr. League Dayton, 1986-87, chmn. coun. implementation, 1987-88, project coord., 1988-89, chmn. membership devel., 1989-90, community v.p., bd. dirs., 1990-91; fundraising chmn., bd. dirs. New Friends Club, Dayton, 1987-88. Named Outstanding Tchr., First Sch., 1989. Mem. AAUW (bd. dirs., v.p. membership Dayton 1987-89, chmn. bylaws 1990-92), Ind. U. Alumni Assn., Wright State U. Alumni Assn., Pi Lambda Theta, Alpha Kappa Delta. Roman Catholic. Home: 5610 Harlamert Dr Dayton OH 45449-2828

MERRILL, MARY PETERMANN, financial consultant; b. Laurium, Mich., Aug. 15, 1937; d. Albert Edward Jr. and Dorothy (Cox) Petermann; m. Alan W. Merrill, June 4, 1960 (div. Jan. 1987); children: Peter, Philip. AB, Cornell U., 1959; MBA, U. Wis., 1982. Cert. fin. planner. Owner, mgr. Mary Merrill Fin. Adv. Svc., Madison, Wis., 1981—; asst. v.p. 1st Wis. Nat. Bank, Madison, 1986-90. Mem. Inst. Cert. Fin. Planners, Nat. Assn. Personal Fin. Advisors. Home and Office: 306 N Pinckney St Madison WI 53703-2134

MERRIMAN, ILAH COFFEE, financial executive; b. Amarillo, Tex., Mar. 22, 1935; d. Oran and Frances Elizabeth (Rocque) Coffee; children: Pamela, Michael. BS in Math., Tex. Tech. U. Cert. secondary tchr., Tex. Pres., chief exec. officer H&R Block Inc. of Houston; pres. H&R Block Inc., Tex.; exec. bd. Tex. Tech U. ex students assn., pres., 1989, past trustee; mem. steering com. Pres.'s Council, bd. dirs. Tex. Tech Double T Connection, Tex. Tech Found., Women's Basketball Tournament, Southwest Athletic Coun., past; mem. Tex. Tech U. enterprise fund Dallas Chpt.; dir. Cotton Bowl Assn. representing Tex. Tech U. Named Disting. Alumni, Texas Tech U., 1992; recipient Ernest T. Steward award Coun. Advancement and Support Edn., 1993. Mem. Dallas Mus. Fine Art, Dallas Shakespeare Festival, Dallas Symphony Assn., Dallas Hist. Soc., Cotton Bowl Assn. (exec. com.), Women's Basketball Coaches Assn. dir. nat. corp. bd.), Red Raider Club of Tex. Tech U. (past mem. exec. com.). Methodist. Office: PO Box 743275 Dallas TX 75374-3275

MERRITT, DEBORAH FOOTE, state legislator, marketing professional; b. Peterborough, N.H., June 19, 1961; d. William Lewis and Mary Elizabeth (Moore) Foote. BA in Sociology, Bowdoin Coll., 1983; MPA, U. N.H., 1994. Tchr. math. Buckley Sch., Sherman Oaks, Calif., 1983-84, Chaminade Coll. Prep. Sch., Canoga Park, Calif., 1984-85; saleswoman Smith Barney, L.A., 1985-87, B.R. Stickle & Co., Chgo., 1987; trader Harris Trust, Chgo., 1988-90; bus. mgr. Merritt Chiropractic, Durham, N.H., 1990-94; state rep. N.H. Gen. Ct., Concord, 1993—; marketer Devel. Svcs. of Stafford County, Dover, 1994—. Bd. dirs. Our House, 1993—. Mem. NOW, N.H. Women's Lobby, Gt. Dover C. of C., Planned Parenthood Northern New Eng., Women's Legis. Lobby. Democrat. Home: 20 Cedar Point Rd Durham NH 03824 Office: Devel Svcs Strafford County 1 Forum Ct 113 Crosby Rd Dover NH 03820

MERRITT, NANCY-JO, lawyer; b. Phoenix, Sept. 24, 1942; d. Robert Nelson Meeker and Violet Adele Gibson; children: Sidney Kathryn, Kurt, Douglas. BA, Ariz. State U., 1964, MA, 1974, JD, 1978. Bar: Ariz. 1978, U.S. Dist. Ct. Ariz. 1978, U.S. Ct. Appeals (9th cir.) 1984. Assoc. Erlichman, Fagerberg & Margrave, Phoenix, 1978-79, Pearlstein & Margrave, Phoenix, 1979-81, Corwin & Merritt, P.C., Phoenix, 1982-87; with Nancy-Jo Merritt & Assocs., P.C., Phoenix, 1987-88; shareholder Bryan Cave, Phoenix, 1988—. Author: Understanding Immigration Law, 1993; contbr. articles to profl. jours. Active Ariz. Coalition for Immigration Representation, Phoenix, 1988—. Fellow Ariz. Bar Found.; mem. ABA, Am. Immigration Lawyers Assn. (chairperson Ariz. chpt. 1985-87, several coms., Pro Bono award), Am. Immigration Law Found. (trustee), Ariz. Bar Assn. (immigration sect.), Nucleus Club. Democrat. Office: Bryan Cave 2800 N Central Ave Fl 21 Phoenix AZ 85004-1007

MERRITT, SALLY HODGSON, retired librarian, association executive; b. Gloversville, N.Y., Dec. 11, 1906; d. Joseph Ernest and Katharine (Hurd) Hodgson; m. Charles Hart Merritt, May 28, 1932; children: Edwin Thomas, Katharine Merritt Brown. BA, Vassar Coll., 1927; MA, Columbia U., 1928. Br. children's libr. N.Y. Pub. Libr., N.Y.C., 1928-32; lectr. children's libr. work Columbia U., N.Y.C., 1930-33; lectr. children's lit. and storytelling Fannie A. Smith Sch., Bridgeport, Conn., 1933-35. Bd. dirs. Bridgeport YWCA, 1944-64, pres.; mem., Easton (Conn.) Pub. Libr., 1961-80, chmn.; nat. bd. dirs. YWCA, N.Y.C., 1960-72; bd. dirs. Thirty Thirty Park, 1974-86. Recipient Salute to Women Bridgeport YWCA, 1980. Mem. AAUW (pres. 1935), Delta Kappa Gamma. Congregationalist. Home: 3030 Park Ave Apt 8E4 Bridgeport CT 06604-1150

MERRITT, SUSAN MARY, computer science educator, university dean; b. New London, Conn., July 28, 1946; d. Nelson Alfred and Mary (Cory) M. BA summa cum laude, Cath. U. Am., 1968; MS, NYU, 1969, PhD, 1982; Cert., Inst. for Edn. Mgmt., Harvard U., 1985. Joined Sisters of Divine Compassion, 1975; permanent cert. tchr., N.Y. Systems programmer Digital Equipment Corp., Maynard, Mass., 1969-70; tchr. Good Counsel Acad. High Sch., White Plains, N.Y., 1970-75; adj. instr. computer sci. Pace U., White Plains, 1972-78, asst. prof., 1978-82, assoc. prof., 1982-85, prof., 1985—, chmn. dept., 1981-83, dean Sch. Computer Sci., 1983—; mem. gen. coun. Sisters Divine Compassion, 1988-92. Contbr. articles to profl. jours. Fellow Soc. for Values in Higher Edn.; mem. ACM (edn. bd. 1988—), Assn. Computer Sci. and Computer Engring. Chair (pres. 1989-90), Phi Beta Kappa, Sigma Xi. Roman Catholic. Office: Pace U 1 Martine Ave White Plains NY 10606

MERSEREAU, LORI MICHELLE, lawyer; b. Cin., Aug. 12, 1963; d. Leo and Sonya Ingrid (Rosenfeld) Roos; m. Richard Charles Mersereau, Nov. 20, 1988. BS, U. Calif., Davis, 1985; JD, U. So. Calif., 1989; LLM, Univ. of Pacific, 1992. Bar: Calif. 1989, U.S. Dist. Ct. (ea. dist.) Calif., U.S. Ct. Appeals (9th cir.), U.S. Tax Ct. Assoc. tax and corp. div. Weintraub, Genshlea, Hardy, Erich and Brown, Sacramento, 1989-90; pvt. practice Fair Oaks, Calif., 1990-91; atty. office of dist. counsel U.S. Dept. Treasury, Sacramento, 1991—; spl. asst. to U.S. atty. East and North Dists. Calif., Sacramento, 1994—; lectr. in bus., corp., tax law Lincoln Sch. Law U. Calif. Davis Law Sch. Sr. assoc. U. So. Calif. Law Rev., 1988-89; sr. editor Harvard Jour. Law and Pub. Policy, 1988. Bd. dirs. Protection and Advocacy, Inc., Sacramento, 1987-93; vol. atty. Vol. Legal Svcs., Sacramento, 1989—; chair fundraising Hadassah, Sacramento, 1990-91. Mem. Order of Coif, Phi Kappa Phi, Phi Alpha Delta. Republican. Jewish.

MERSEREAU, SUSAN, information systems company executive; b. Portland, Oreg., Sept. 5, 1946; d. Roland William Mersereau and Barbara Munro; m. Robert Stier, June 19, 1968; 1 child, Arran Elizabeth; m. Philip White, Nov. 17, 1989; children: Richard, Brandon. BA in History, Scripps, 1968; MAT in Edn. History, U. Chgo., 1971; MA in Whole Systems Design, Antioch, 1990. Tchr. South Shore High Sch., Chgo., 1969-70; adminstrv. asst. U. Ill., Chgo., 1970; rsch. analyst U. Wash., Seattle, 1971-72; dir. planning rsch. and evaluation Seattle Sch. Dist., 1972-80; program mgr. Weyerhauser Co., Tacoma, 1980-81, mgr. advanced tech., 1981-83, dir. telecom., 1983-88; gen. mgr., v.p. Weyerhauser Info. Systems, Tacoma, 1988-92, v.p. total quality region adminstrv. svcs. and aviation, 1992—. Mem. Wash. Gov.'s Adv. Com. on Info. Systems, Olympia, 1986-90; bd. dirs. On the Bds., Seattle, 1987-90; mem. adb. bd. Ctr. for Spiritual Devel., Seattle, 1988-90; bd. dirs. King County Jr. Achievement, 1994—, King County United Way, 1994—. Mem. Soc. Info. Systems (communication group 1990—). Office: Weyerhaeuser Company CH1B25 Tacoma WA 98477

MERSEREAU, SUSAN S., clinical psychologist; d. John Andy Jr. and Dorothy Grace (Smith) Smith; m. Peter Roland Mersereau, May 30, 1970; children: Barrett, Travis, Courtney. AB, Vassar Coll., 1969; MSEd, Elmira

Coll., 1973; D in Psychology, Pacific U., 1989. Lic. psychologist, Oreg. Psychology intern Pacific Gateway Hosp., Portland, Oreg., 1987-88, Psychol. Svcs. Ctr., Hillsboro, Oreg., 1988-89; psychology resident Lee Doppelt, Beaverton, Oreg., 1990-91; pvt. practice psychologist Beaverton, 1991-93; dir. Pacific Ctr. for Attention and Learning, Beaverton, 1993—. Tchr. Incentive grantee Guam Dept. Edn., 1979. Mem. APA, Oreg. Psychol. Assn., Vassar Club Oreg. (admissions com. 1984—, pres. 1984-88). Office: Pacific Ctr Attention & Learning Westgate Plz Ste 266 3800 SW Cedar Hills Blvd Beaverton OR 97005

MERSKEY-ZEGER, MARIE GERTRUDE FINE, retired librarian; b. Kimberley, South Africa, Oct. 10, 1914; came to U.S., 1960, naturalized, 1965; d. Herman and Annie Myra (Wigoder) Fine; m. Clarence Merskey, Oct. 8, 1939 (dec. 1982); children: Hilary Pamela Merskey Nathe, Susan Heather Merskey Sinistore, Joan Margaret Merskey Schneiderman; m. Jack I. Zeger, July 15, 1984. Grad. Underwood Bus. Sch., Cape Town, South Africa, 1934; BA, U. Cape Town, 1958, diploma librarianship, 1960. Sec. to Chief Rabbi Israel Abrahams, South Africa, 1945-49, Jewish Sheltered Employment Council, 1954-56; reference librarian New Rochelle Pub. Library, 1960-63; research librarian Consumers Union, Mt. Vernon, 1963-66; asst. readers services, head union catalog Westchester Library System, 1966-69, trustee, 1989-93, v.p., 1991; dir. Harrison (N.Y.) Pub. Library and West Harrison Br., 1969-84; acting dir. Mamaroneck (N.Y.) Free Library, 1987-88, also trustee, 1988-93. Pub. edn. officer USCG Aux. Flotilla 63. Author: History of the Harrison Libraries, 1980; editor: (cookbook) On Harrison's Table, 1976; Harrison Highlights and Anecdotes, 1989. Bd. dirs. Shore Acres Point Corp., Mamaroneck, 1985-89, Friends of the Mamaroneck Libr., N.Y., 1993—. Recipient Brotherhood award B'nai B'rith, 1974; named Woman of Yr., Harrison, 1984. Mem. ALA, Westchester Library Assn., N.Y. Library Assn. (adult edn. com. for continuing edn. 1971-75, adult services com. 1973-75, vice chmn., 1975, exec. bd. 1981-82), Pub. Library Dirs. Assn. (tech. services com. chmn. Westchester County 1971, exec. bd. 1974-75, vice chmn. 1975), Clubs: YMCA, Charles Dawson History Ctr. (bd. dirs., founder), Rye Womans Club. Contbr. articles to local newspapers. Home: 316 S Barry Ave Mamaroneck NY 10543-4201

MERTEN, LYNNANNE, career officer, pilot; b. Bklyn., Nov. 30, 1956; d. Joseph Francis and Patricia Ann (McCaul) M. BA in Econs., Holy Cross Coll., 1979; MS in Gen. Adminstrn., Cen. Mich. U., 1994. C-141 pilot, tng. officer Military Airlift Squadron, McGuire AFB, N.J., 1982-85; T-37 instr., evaluator pilot Air Tng. Command, Williams AFB, Ariz., 1985-88; program mgr. HQ Air Tng. Command, Randolph AFB, Tex., 1988-91; C-12 instr., evaluator pilot 89th Airlift Wing, Andrews AFB, Md., 1991-93, chief C-12 Cen. Tng. Facility, 1993-94; attending Air Command and Staff Coll., Maxwell AFB, Ala., 1994—. active Sierra Club, 1990—. Mem. NAFE, Women Military Aviators Assn., Air Force Assn. Home: 7713 Copperfield Dr Montgomery AL 36117 Office: Air Command and Staff Coll Maxwell AFB AL 36112-5000

MERVES, PEGGY TUTELMAN, artist; b. Phila., Apr. 28, 1951; d. Sol Tutelman and Louise Grossman Kleinman; m. Edward Hofkin Merves, June 3, 1979; 1 child, Hannah Solomon. Student, U. Rochester, 1969-71; BA in English cum laude, U. Pa., 1973; student, Hebrew U. of Jerusalem, 1972; Cert., Pa. Acad. Fine Arts, Phila., 1988. Real estate legal asst. Morgan, Lewis & Bockius, Phila., 1974-83; founder Protean Gallery, Phila., 1989; lectr. on workshop discussion series: Searching for the Muse, 1990. One-woman shows include Episcopal Acad., Merion, Pa., 1991, Pa. Acad. Fine Arts, Phila., 1986; exhibited in group shows at Cheltenham Art Ctr., 1984, The Print Club, Phila., 1986, Ocean City and Rittenhouse Sq. Fine Arts Anns., 1987, Phila. Sketch Club, 1989, Art Sales and Rental Gallery Phila. Mus. Art, 1993, 94, Borders Book Shop, 1994, numerous Protean Group Shows, 1989-94, The Small Painting, Abington Art Ctr. (Best of Show), 1990, The Baum Sch. Art, 1991, Woodmere Art Mus. Art Auction, 1991, PAFA Fellowship Show, 1991; color photographs exhibited at Paragon Gallery, 1994. Recipient Monoprint Purchase prize (honorable mention) Pa. Acad. Fine Arts, 1986, Morris Blackburn Watercolor prize (honorable mention), 1987. Mem. Fellowship of the Pa. Acad. of Fine Arts. Home: 339 Winding Way Merion PA 19066-1521

MERWIN, MARY KAYE, educational association administrator; b. Elkhorn, Wis., Feb. 27, 1942; d. George Reek and Gladys Lucille (Schnitcke) M. BS in Home Econ. Edn., U. Wis. Stout, 1964; MS in Extension Edn. Youth Devel., U. Wis., 1971. 4-H home economist U. Wis. Waukesha County Extension, 1964-67; 4-H youth agt. U. Wis. (Rock County) Extension, 1967-73; area 4-H specialist Tex. A & M U. Systems, Tex. Agr. Extension Svc., College Sta., 1973-75, dist. extension agt. home econ., 1975-78; assoc. dir., edn. program Nat. 4-H Coun., Chevy Chase, Md., 1978-79, dir., program svcs., 1979-81, assoc. adminstr. programs, 1981-84, dir., program div., 1984-86; exec. dir. Cornell Coop. Extension Assn. of Nassau County, Plainview, N.Y., 1987—; coun. for Advancement of Citizenship, Washington; cons. Consortium for Internat. Curriculum in Higher Edn., Washington, 1986-87; intern nat. ext. leadership devel. Kellogg Found., 1993-95. Bd. dirs. Wis. 4-H Found., Madison; elder, clk. of session Gaithersburg (Md.) Presbyn. Ch., 1981-83; elder Presbyn. Community Ch., Massapequa, N.Y., 1989-91, clk. of session, 1993-95. Mem. Am. Home Econ. Assn., N.Y. Home Econs. Assn. (bd. dirs. 1988-90, 92-95, state conf. co-chair 1990, state pres. 1993-94, L.I. bd. 1988-95, L.I. pres. 1990-91), Am. Soc. Assn. Execs., Nat. Ext. 4-H Agts. Assn. (Wis chpt. pres. 1971-72), Order Ea. Star, Epsilon Sigma Phi (nat. award chmn. 1985), Phi Upsilon Omicron, Alpha Phi. Republican. Home: 26 Camp Rd Massapequa NY 11758-3742 Office: Cornell Coop Extension of Nassau County 1425 Old County Rd Bldg J Plainview NY 11803

MESCH, JOAN ANNE, nurse; b. Summit, N.J., May 29, 1955; d. Andrew Owar and Anne Marie (Cullen) M.; m. Denis J. Heather, July 4, 1987; 1 child, Brian A. BSN, U. Bridgeport, 1979; MS, Oreg. Health Scis., 1992. Staff nurse Dover (N.J.) Gen. Hosp., 1979-80; patient care supr. Vale (Colo.) Valley Med. Ctr., 1981; critical care nurse Hosp. Shared Svcs. of Colo., Denver, 1982-83; staff nurse, charge nurse Portland (Oreg.) VA Med. Ctr., 1983-87, clin. mgr. surg. ICU, 1987—; regional instr. Kontron Inst., Portland, 1989; guest lectr. Portland (Oreg.) VA Med. Ctr., 1990-93. Co-author: (patient/family handbook) Survival Guide, 1991; contbg. author: (textbook) Clinical Nursing, 3d edit., 1993; contbr. chpt. to book. Mem. NOW, ANA (nurse adminstr. cert. 1990), AACN (CCRN), N.Am. Nursing Diagnosis Assn., Oreg. League Conservation Voters, Greenpeace. Office: Portland VA Med Ctr 3710 SW Us Veterans Rd Portland OR 97201

MESCHKE, DEBRA JOANN, polymer chemist; b. Elyria, Ohio, Oct. 22, 1952; d. Loren Willis and JoAnne Elizabeth (Meyer) M. BS, U. Cin., 1974; MS, Case Western Res. U., 1976, PhD, 1979. Sr. chemist Union Carbide Corp., South Charleston, W.Va., 1979-82, project scientist, 1982-85, chair research and devel. Exempt Women's Group, 1980-81, chair research and devel. Ctr. Safety Team, 1981-82, coordinator Polymer Methods Course, 1982-83; project scientist Union Carbide Corp., Tarrytown, N.Y., 1985-86; sr. prin. research chemist Air Products and Chems. Inc., Allentown, Pa., 1986-88, chmn. waste disposal com., 1986-88; rsch. scientist Union Carbide Corp., South Charleston, 1988—. Author chpts. in textbooks; patentee in field. Bd. dirs. Overbrook Home Owners Assn., Macungie, Pa., 1987. Case Western Res. U. grad. fellow, 1974-79. Mem. AAAS, Am. Chem. Soc. (Polymer div.), Iota Sigma Pi. Home: 2022 Parkwood Rd Charleston WV 25314-2244

MESCH-SPINELLO, JOYCE CARREL, psychologist, administrator, educator, consultant; b. Buffalo, Sept. 16, 1942; d. Meyer and Goldyne (Carrel) Mesch; m. Anthony Gerald Spinello, Sept. 5, 1976; children: Daniel, Andrew, Jennifer. Student, U. Mich., 1959-60; BA, U. Buffalo, 1963; MS, SUNY, Buffalo, 1964; PhD, NYU, 1974. Temp. tchr. Buffalo Bd. Edn., 1962-64; rehab. and placement counselor NYU Med. Ctr., N.Y.C., 1964-66, sr. rehab. counselor, 1966-74, sr. psychologist, 1974-77, clin. supr., 1977-80; dir. vocat. svcs. Rusk Inst. Rehab. Medicine, N.Y.C., 1980—; assoc. clin. prof. NYU Sch. Medicine, N.Y.C., 1976—; pvt. practice N.Y.C., 1980—; cons. State of N.Y., Albany, 1976-79; conf. speaker, 1974—. Contbr. to books, articles to profl. jours. Advisor N.Y.C. Bd. Edn., Bklyn., 1981—. counselor Assn. Help of Retarded Children, N.Y.C., 1964. N.Y.C. Dept. Employment grantee, 1991-94; recipient Transitional Program for Youth award Private Industry Coun., 1988-91, Outstanding Program for Handicapped Employment award N.Y. State Bd. Regents, 1993. Mem. APA. Office: NYU Med Ctr 550 1st Ave New York NY 10016-6497

MESIC, HARRIET LEE BEY, medical support group administrator; b. Norfolk, Va., Aug. 4, 1937; d. Daniel Douglas and Bessie Lee (Wrenn) Bey; m. Harry Randolph Mesic, Mar. 18, 1956; children: Catherine Denise Mesic Stringer, Daniel Douglas Mesic. AA, Trident Tech. Coll., Charleston, S.C., 1981, 1984. Editor L.E. Beacon, Lupus Erythematosus Support Group, Charleston, S.C., 1984-88, exec. dir., 1988—. Contbr. articles to profl. jours. Leader Girl Scouts Am., Isle of Palms, S.C., 1968-79; svc. unit chmn. Carolina Low Country Girl Scouts, E. Cooper, S.C., 1972-79. Recipient Friendship award, Carolina Low Country Girl Scouts, 1978. Lutheran. Office: LE Support Group 8039 Nova Ct North Charleston SC 29420-8934

MESKIN, ESTELLE ROSE, college/vocational counselor, educational consultant; b. Detroit, Apr. 16, 1939; d. Julius and Helen (Krolik) R.; m. Larry Meskin, Aug. 23, 1959; children: Scott, Sarah. BS, U. Minn., 1974; MA, U. Colo., 1986. Nat. cert. counselor; registered dental hygienist. Pvt. practice dental hygiene Detroit, 1960-75; instr. dental hygiene NormanDale C.C., Mpls., 1970-74; instr. health occupations Mpls. Area Vo/Tec-Mpls. Pub. Schs., 1975-79; health educator Pilot City Health Ctr./Mpls. Pub. Schs., 1979-81; career resource specialist Arapahoe-Douglas Area Vocat., Littleton, Colo., 1981-90; edn. cons. Santa Fe C.C., 1990-91; vocat. counselor Arapahoe-Douglas Area Vocat. Sch., Littleton, 1989-92; health educator Denver Sch.-Based Health Ctrs., 1992—; ednl. cons. U.S. West Pathways Program, Denver, 1987-90; health edn. adv. bd. Denver Pub. Schs., 1992-94; scholarship com. Pres.'s Leadership Class, U. Colo., Boulder, 1990—. Bd. dirs. Jewish Family and Childrens Svc., Denver, 1994—. Recipient Health Edn. grant March of Dimes, 1992-94; recipient Award of Excellence for Spl. Programs, Colo. C.C.s and Occupational Edn., 1986, Vocat. Edn. Policy fellow, 1989, 90, Women's Leadership Inst. fellow, 1990-91. Mem. Colo. Career Devel. Assn. (pres.-elect 1991-92, pres. 1992-93), Colo. Counseling Assn., Am. Counseling Assn., Nat. Career Devel. Assn., Colo. Vocat. Assn., Am. Vocat. Assn., Nat. Assn. Coll. Admissions Counselors. Jewish. Home: 282 Monroe St Denver CO 80206

MESNEY, DOROTHY TAYLOR (HEDI MUNRO), mezzo-soprano, pianist, composer, comedienne, educator; b. Bklyn., Sept. 15, 1916; d. Franklin and Kathryn Munro Taylor; diploma Berkeley Inst., 1934; m. Peter Michael Mesney, Oct. 15, 1942; children: Douglas, Kathryn, Barbara. BA, Sarah Lawrence Coll., 1938; MA in Journalism, Columbia U., 1939; postgrad. Juilliard Sch. of Music, 1963-71, Manhattan Sch. Music, 1971-73. Mezzo-soprano, operetta, mus. comedy, concert and oratorio; ch. soloist, N.Y.C., 1956—; debuts include: N.Y. Cultural Center, 1971, Carnegie Recital Hall, 1974; leading roles with local opera and Gilbert and Sullivan groups, (as Hedi Munro singing comedienne), various nightclubs and cabarets including Trocadero, Don't Tell Mama, Dangerfield's Adams Apple, Sullivan Street Theatre, Broadway Baby, Danny's Skylight Rm., 55 Grove St.; appeared on Joe Franklin TV Show, Joey Adams Radio Show; dir. a capella vocal quintet The Notebles; rec. artist Folkways Records, Musicanza Records; dir. American Experience ensemble, also An Elizabethan Encounter, Renaissance Revels; tchr. piano and singing, Douglaston, N.Y., 1958—, also tchr. "Introduction to Music Classes" for pre-schoolers, tchr. of condr. James Conlon and clarinetist Jon Manasse and singer, songwriter Steve Stavola; founder, dir. children's series Concerts for Children, Community Ch. Concert Series; soloist Community Ch. Douglaston, N.Y.; founder Introduction to Music for Preschoolers; performer early Am. music for mus., hist. socs., schs., colls.; performer Renaissance music N.Y. State Renaissance Festival, 15 yrs.; 2c authority on Am. and Renaissance music; composer hymns, songs, instrumental quartets and trios, ballads, also songs for children; recordings for Folkways-Smithsonian, Musicanza Records. Com. chmn. PTA, Douglaston, 1952-55; den mother Greater N.Y. council Cub Scouts Am., 1953-56; Brownie leader Greater N.Y. council Girl Scouts U.S.A.; bd. dirs. Community Concerts Assn. of Great Neck, N.Y. Mem. ASCAP (songwriter), AFTRA, Nat. Piano Tchrs. Guild, Nat. Fedn. Music Clubs (N.Y. chpt.), Met. Opera Guild, Tuesday Morning Music Club (pres. 1979-81), Manhattan Assn. Cabaret Artists. Democrat. Congregationalist.

MESROBIAN, ARPENA SACHAKLIAN, publisher, editor, consultant; b. Boston; d. Aaron Harry and Eliza (Der Melkonian) Sachaklian; m. William John Mesrobian, June 22, 1940; children: William Stephen, Marian Elizabeth (Mrs. Bruce MacCurdy). Student, Armenian Coll. of Beirut, Lebanon, 1937-38; A.A., Univ. Coll., Syracuse (N.Y.) U., 1959, B.A. magna cum laude, 1971; MSsc, Syracuse U., 1993. Editor Syracuse U. Press, 1955-58, exec. editor, 1958-61, asst. dir., 1961-65, acting dir., 1965-66, editor, 1968-85, assoc. dir., 1968-75, dir., 1975-85, 87-88, dir. emeritus, 1985; dir. workshop on univ. press. pub. U. Malaysia, Kuala Lumpur, 1985; cons. Empire State Coll. Book rev. editor: Armenian Rev., 1967-75; mem. publs. bd. Courier, 1970-94; mem. adv. bd. Armenian Rev., 1981-83; contbr. numerous articles, revs. to profl. jours. Pres. Syracuse chpt. Armenian Relief Soc., 1972-74; sponsor Armenian Assembly, Washington, 1975; mem. mktg. task force Office of Spl. Edn., Dept. Edn., 1979-84, Adminstrn. of Developmental Disabilities, HHS; mem. publs. panel Nat. Endowment for Humanities, Washington; bd. dirs. Syracuse Girls Club, 1982-87; pres. trustees St. John the Bapt. Armenian Apostolic Ch. and Community Ctr., 1991—. Named Post-Standard Woman of Achievement, 1980; recipient Chancellor's award for disting. service Syracuse U., 1985; Nat. award U.S. sect. World Edn. Fellowship, 1986; N.Y. State Humanities scholar. Mem. Women in Communications, Soc. Armenian Studies (adminstrv. council 1976-78, 85-87, sec. 1978, 85-87), Syracuse U. Library Assocs. (v.p. 1983-88), Am. Univ. Press Services (dir. 1976-77), Armenian Lit. Soc., Armenian Community Center, Assn. Am. Univ. Presses (v.p. 1976-77), UN Assn. (bd. dirs. 1983-88, v.p. 1985), Phi Kappa Phi, Alpha Sigma Lambda. Mem. Armenian Apostolic Ch. (trustee). Club: Zonta of Syracuse (pres. 1979-80, 1st v.p. 1985-86, dist. historian Dist. 2 Zonta Internat. 1993). Home: 4851 Pembridge Cir Syracuse NY 13215-1023

MESSÉ, MADELYN RENEE, clinical psychologist, consultant; b. N.Y.C., Sept. 13, 1957; d. Abba Alan Messé and Carolyn Joy Fielding. BA in Psychology, Biology, Vassar Coll., 1978; MA in Clin. Psychology, SUNY Stony Brook, 1981; PhD in Clin. Psychology, SUNY, Stony Brook, 1983. Diplomate Am. Bd. Med. Psychotherapy. Instr. Mt. Sinai Sch. Medicine, N.Y.C., 1984-86; clin. rsch. psychologist Nat. Cancer Inst., N.Y.C., 1984-86; pvt. practice N.Y.C., 1986—; cons. to industry, 1986—. Author: (chpt.) Behavioral Medicine and Clinical Psychology: Overlapping Disciplines, 1982; contbr. articles to profl. jours. including Oncology Digest, Cancer, Psychosomatic Medicine, Proceedings of APA, and others. Fellow Internat. Soc. Philos. Enquiry; mem. APA, Sigma Xi (Sci. Rsch. award 1982).

MESSER, CAROLYN KERR, food technologist; b. Kansas City, Mo., Jan. 15, 1955; d. Ralph Leonard and Mary Josephine (Kerr) M. BA in Geography, U. Kans., 1983, BA in Latin Am. Area Studies, 1983; BS in Bakery Sci. & Mgmt. cum laude, Kans. State U., 1984; Minister of Theology, Impact Internat. Sch. Ministry, Huntsville, Ala., 1990. Asst. coord. Henry Simon, Inc., Kansas City, Kans., 1982-83; pastry chef cookies The French Bakery, Overland Park, Kans., 1984; asst. instr. Am. Inst. of Baking, Manhattan, Kans., 1985; dir. product devel., quality assurance Specialty Bakers, Marysville, Pa., 1985; new product devel. bakery technologist Freihofer Baking Co., Albany, N.Y., 1986-89; project leader R & D Tasty Baking Co., Phila., 1991-94. Creator, simulator new bakery products for supermarket shelf and snack food market Freihofer Baking Co., 1991-92, Tasty Baking Co., 1991-94. Mem. Zonta Club of Albany, N.Y., 1988-89, Phila. Leadership Found. Women's Com., Phila., 1992—. Recipient Continental Baking Co. scholarship Kans. State U., 1984, Universal Baking Co., Am. Inst. Baking, 1984. Mem. Am. Soc. Baking Engrs., Inst. Food Technologists, Am. Inst. Baking Alumni Assn., Gamma Sigma Delta, Golden Key. Republican. Home: PO Box 49 Layfayette Hill PA 19444

MESSERLE, JUDITH ROSE, medical librarian, public relations director; b. Litchfield, Ill., Jan. 16, 1943; d. Richard Douglas and Nelrose B. (Davis) Wilcox; m. Darrell Wayne Messerle, Apr. 26, 1968; children: Kurt Norman, Katherine Lynn. BA in Zoology, So. Ill. U., 1966; MLS, U. Ill., 1967. Cert. med. libr., St. Joseph's Sch. Nursing, Alton, Ill., 1967-71, dir. med. info. ctr., 1971-76, dir. info. services, 1976-79, dir. ednl. resources and community relations, St. Joseph's Hosp., Alton, Ill., 1979-84; dir. Med. Ctr. Libr., St. Louis U., 1985-88; libr. Francis A. Countway Libr. for the Harvard Med. Sch. and Boston Med. Libr., 1989—; instr. Lewis and Clark Coll., 1975; cons. 1973—; instr. Med. Library Assn. Bd. dirs. Family Services and Vis. Nurses Assn., Alton, 1976-79. Mem. Med. Library Assn. (dir. 1981-84, pres. 1986-87, task force for knowledge and skills, 1988-92, Legis. task force 1986-90, search com. for exec. dir. 1979), Ill. State Libr. Adv. Com., Midwest Health Sci. Libr. Network (dir. health sci. council), St. Louis Med. Librs., Hosp. Pub. Relations Soc. of St. Louis, Nat. Libr. Medicine (biomed. libr. rev. com. 1988-92), AMA (com. on allied health edn. and accreditation 1991-94), Assn. Acad. Health Sci. Libr. Dirs. (pres. 1993, joint legis. task force 1992—, editorial bd. for ann. stats. 1989-94, Region 8 Adv. Bd. 1992-93), Am. Med. Informatics Assn. (planning com. 1990, publications com. 1994—). Office: Countway Libr of Medicine 10 Shattuck St Boston MA 02115

MESSIMER, JUDITH RIDDELL, communications professional; b. Herkimer, N.Y., Sept. 12, 1961; d. Harold Howard and Eleanor Marie (Smith) R.; m. Richard Ward Messimer, May 29, 1990 (div.). BA magna cum laude, Wells Coll., 1983. Photographer, editor Schiffer Pub., Exton, Pa., 1983-85; prodn. editor J.B. Lippincott, Phila., 1985-87, sr. editor, 1987-89, assoc. mng. editor, 1989-90, mng. editor, 1990-93; mgr. jours. editing Mosby-Yearbook, Inc., St. Louis, 1993—. Vol. Pet Search, Glencoe, Mo., 1993, PAWS St. Louis, 1993—, Habitat for Humanity, Phila., 1992, 93. Named Outstanding Teenage Young Person, Jaycees, 1979, Outstanding Young Woman of Am., 1984. Mem. Mensa, AAUW (recording sec. 1991-93), Nat. Assn. Investor's Clubs, River City Pedallers, Tandem Club of Am., Am. Med. Writers Assn. Democrat. Presbyterian. Home: 1128 Town and Four Pkwy Dr Creve Coeur MO 63141 Office: Mosby-Yearbook Inc 11830 Westline Industrial Saint Louis MO 63146

MESSING, CAROL SUE, communications educator; b. Bronx, N.Y.; d. Isidore and Esther Florence (Burtoff) Weinberg; m. Sheldon H. Messing; children: Lauren, Robyn. BA, Bklyn. Coll., 1967, MA, 1970. Tchr. N.Y.C. Bd. Edn., 1967-72; prof. lang. arts Northwood U., Midland, Mich., 1973-93, prof., 1993—; owner Job Match, Midland, 1983-85; cons. Mich. Credit Union League, Saginaw, 1984-87, Nat. Hotel & Restaurant, Midland, 1985-89, External Degree program, Continuing Edn. program, Northwood U., 1986—, Dow Chem. Employee's Credit Union, 1988—. Author: (anthology) Symbiosis, 1985, rev. edit. 1987, Controlling Communication, 1987, rev. edit. 1993; co-author: PRIMIS, 1993. Mem. LWV, Nat Coun. Tchrs. English, Kappa Delta Pi, Delta Mu Delta (advisor). Office: Northwood U 3225 Cook Rd Midland MI 48640-2311

MESSING, JANET AGNES KAPELSOHN, economist, educator; b. Bklyn., Oct. 12, 1918; d. Louis and Kate (Cohen) Kapelsohn; m. Joseph Messing, Feb. 1, 1948 (dec. July 1987); children—Robert, Alice. A.B., Hunter Coll., 1939; M.S., Columbia U., 1940; Ph.D., NYU, 1959. C.P.A., N.Y. Acct. Seidman and Seidman, CPAs, N.Y.C., 1943-46; mem. faculty dept. econs. Hunter Coll., 1943-69, prof., 1969; prof. Herbert H. Lehman Coll. CUNY, Bronx, 1975-89, chmn. dept. econs., 1982-85, prof. emeritus, 1989—; tax cons. N.Y.C., 1960; mem. core faculty Walden U., summers 1980-82; mem. women's study council Lehman Coll., 1981—; treas. PSC/CUNY Welfare Fund, 1974-83, del., 1960-83, del. to NEA/Am. Fedn. Tchrs., 1972-75, trustee, 1966—, del. to N.Y. State United Tchrs., Am. Fedn. Tchrs.-CIO, 1976—. Author: (with Joshua Wachtel) Tax Considerations in Non-Profit Organizations-The Treatment of Exempt Organizations under the Income Tax Laws, 1978, rev. edit., 1979, 80, 81, 82, 83; contbr. articles and book revs. to profl. jours. V.p. Queensborough Library Council, 1960-68. Mem. Am. Econ. Assn., Am. Acctg. Assn., Eastern Econ. Assn., Am. Inst. C.P.A.s, Am. Soc. Women Accts., Met. Econ. Assn., Lehman Coll. Retirees Assn. (pres. 1989-91). Home: 35-23 171st St Flushing NY 11358 Office: CUNY HH Lehman Coll Bedford Park Blvd W Bronx NY 10468-1539

MESSINGER, RUTH W., borough president; b. N.Y.C., Nov. 6, 1940; d. Wilfred and Marjorie (Goldwasser) Wyler; m. Eli C. Messinger, June 13, 1961 (div.); children: Daniel Solomon, Miriam Sara, Adam Carp; m. Andrew J. Lachman, Dec. 31, 1989. BA, Radcliffe Coll., 1962; MSW, U. Okla., 1964. Cert. social worker. Sch. adminstr. Children's Cmty. Workshop Sch., N.Y.C., 1968-74; coll. adminstr. Coll. for Human Svcs., N.Y.C., 1974-78; mem. coun. N.Y.C. Coun., 1978-90; borough pres. N.Y.C. Govt., 1990—. Bd. dirs. Women in Mcpl. Govt., Washington, 1981—; past mem., bd. dirs. Nat. League of Cities, Washington, mem. adv. coun., 1979—; mem. adv. bd. Jewish Fund for Justice, 1988—. Democrat. Jewish. Home: 91 Central Park W New York NY 10023 Office: Office Borough President Municipal Bldg 19th Fl South One Centre St New York NY 10007

MESSMORE, ROSEMARY EDELENE, real estate agent; b. Ft. Lauderdale, Fla., Mar. 12, 1949; d. Leland Lester Sr. and Rosanna Dane (Rowland) Loach; m. Peter Burl Messmore, Nov. 17, 1990. Student, U. Tenn., 1967-68. Stockbroker Bache & Co., Ft. Lauderdale, 1969-76, E. F. Hutton, N.Y.C. and Naples, Fla., 1982-83, Merrill Lynch, Naples, 1983-86; musician, pianist, vocalist various hotels, 1977-78; owner Computers R Here!, Boca Raton, Fla., 1988-93; real estate sales assoc. Coldwell Banker, Boca Raton, 1993-94; sales rep. Computer Den, Boca Raton, 1994—. Office: Computer Den 820 SW 21st St Boca Raton FL 33486

MESSNER, KATHRYN HERTZOG, civic worker; b. Glendale, Calif., May 27, 1915; d. Walter Sylvester and Sadie (Dinger) Hertzog; m. Ernest Lincoln, Jan. 1, 1942; children: Ernest Lincoln, Martha Allison Messner Cloran. BA, UCLA, 1936, MA, 1951. Tchr. social studies L.A. schs., 1937-46; mem. L.A. County Grand Jury, 1961. Mem. exec. bd. L.A. Family Svc., 1959-62; dist. atty.'s adv. com., 1965-71, dist. atty.'s adv. coun., 1971-82; mem. San Marino Community Coun.; chmn. San Marino chpt. Am. Cancer Soc.; bd. dirs. Pasadena Rep. Women's Club, 1960-62, San Marino dist. coun. Girl Scouts U.S.A., 1959-68, Am. Field Svc., San Marino, 1983—; pres. San Marino High Sch. PTA, 1964-65; bd. mem. Pasadena Vol. Placement Bur., 1962-68; mem. adv. bd. Univ. YWCA, 1956—; co-chmn. Dist. Atty.'s Adv. Bd. Young Citizens Coun., 1968-72; mem. San Marino Red Cross Coun., 1966—, chmn., 1969-71, vice chmn., 1971-74; mem. San Marino bd. Am. Field Svc.; mem. atty. gen.'s vol. adv. com., 1971-80; bd. dirs. L.A. Women's Philharm. Com., 1974-89, Beverly Hills-West L.A. YWCA, 1974-85, L.A. YWCA, 1975-84, L.A. Law Affiliates, 1974-89, Pacificulture Art Mus., 1976-80, Reachout Com., Music Center, Vol. Action Center, West L.A., Calif., 1980-85, Stevens House, 1980—, Pasadena Philharm. Com., 1980-85, Friends Outside, 1983—, Internat. Christian Scholarship Found., 1984—; hon. bd. dirs. Pasadena chpt. ARC, 1978-82. Recipient spl. commendation Am. Cancer Soc., 1961; Community Svc. award UCLA, 1981. Contbr. articles to profl. jours. Mem. Pasadena Philharmonic, Las Floristas, Huntington Meml. Clinic Aux., Nat. Charity League, Gold Shield (co-founder), Pi Lambda Theta (sec. 1983-89), Pi Gamma Mu, Mortar Bd., Prytanean Soc. Home: 1786 Kelton Ave Los Angeles CA 90024-5508

MESTER, CATHY SARGENT, speech educator; b. Bellefonte, Pa., Jan. 20, 1947; d. Lowrie Barnett and Phyllis Elizabeth (Pollock) Sargent; m. Richard Arnold Mester, Aug. 31, 1974; children: Cari Ann, Clark Andrew. BA in Speech, Westminster Coll., 1969; MA in Speech, Pa. State U., 1970. Teaching asst. Pa. State U., University Park, 1969-70; instr. Concordia Coll., Morehead, Minn., 1970-71; instr. Pa. State U.-Behrend Coll., Erie, 1971—, chair faculty coun., 1991-92, dir. forensics tournaments, 1990-92; ind. comms. cons. for chs. and bus., Erie, 1975—. Author: Oral Communications for Vocational-Technical Students, 1991, Acting Lessons for Teachers, 1994; contbr. articles to profl. jours. Reader Radio Talking Libr., Erie; sch. bd. pres. St. Boniface Sch., Erie, 1991-93, v.p., 1994; mem. sch. choice com. Diocese of Erie, 1990—; parents coun. rep. Westminster Coll., New Wilmington, Pa., 1993—; coll. chairperson United Way, Erie, 1976-80. Grantee Pa. State U., 1993. Mem. Speech Comm. Assn., Speech Comm. Assn. Pa., Ea. Comm. Assn., Religious Speech Comm. Assn., Nat. Wildlife Fedn.

METCALF, LAURIE, actress; b. Edwardsville, Ill., June 15, 1955; 1 child, Zoe. Student, Ill. State U. Off-Broadway appearances: Balm in Gilead (debut, Theatre World award), 1984; stage appearances: Who's Afraid of Virginia Woolf?, 1982, Coyote Ugly, 1985, Bodies Rest, and Motion, 1986, Educating Rita (Joseph Jefferson award best performance by principal actress in a play), 1987, Little Egypt, 1987, Killers, 1988; films: Desperately Seeking Susan, 1984, Making Mr. Right, 1987, Stars and Bars, 1988, Candy Mountain, 1988, Miles from Home, 1988, Uncle Buck, 1989, Internal Affairs,

1989, Pacific Heights, 1990, JFK, 1991, Mistress, 1992, A Dangerous Woman, 1993, Blink, 1994; TV series: Saturday Night Live, 1981, Roseanne, 1988— (Emmy award, Outstanding Supporting Actress in a Comedy Series, 1993, 94); TV appearances: The Equalizer, 1986, The Execution of Raymond Graham, 1985. Address: care Carsey-Werner/CBS-MTM Roseanne 4024 Radford Ave Studio City CA 91604*

METCALF, LYNNETTE CAROL, naval officer, journalist, educator, gemologist; b. Van Nuys, Calif., June 22, 1955; d. William Edward and Carol Annette (Keith) M.; m. Scott Edward Hruska, May 16, 1987. BA in Communications and Media, Our Lady of Lake, 1978; MA in Human Rels., U. Okla., 1980; MA in Mktg. Webster U., 1986; cert. diamond grading, gem identification and colored stone grading Gemology Inst. Am., 1991, diploma, grad. gemologist, 1992. Enlisted USAF, 1973, advanced through grades to sgt., 1975; intelligence analyst, Taiwan, Italy and Tex., 1973-76; historian, journalist, San Antonio, 1976-78; commd. officer USN, 1978, advanced through ranks to lt. comdr., 1988; pub. rels. officer, Rep. of Panama, 1979-81; mgr. system program, London, 1981-82; ops. plans/tng., McMurdo Sta., Antarctica, 1982-84; exec. officer transient pers. unit Naval Tng. Ctr., Great Lakes, Ill., 1984-86, comdg. officer transient pers. unit, 1986-87; asst. prof. naval sci. U. Notre Dame NROTC, 1987-89; nat. curriculum, 1987-89; staff communications plans U.S. Naval Forces Japan, 1989-91, network transp. officer pers. support activity Japan, 1991-92, Far East, 1992-93, adminstrv. mgr., automated Data processing and management review dir. pers. support activity, 1992-93; ret., 1993; anchorwoman USN-TV CONTACT, 1986-87; adj. prof. Far East divsn. Chapman U., 1990-93; founder Profl. Gemological Cons., Japan, 1992, Far East Fed. Sales Group, Inc., 1993; founder. Profl. Gemol. Svc., Japan 1992, Far East Trading Co., Desk Top Publishing, 1993. Author: Winter's Summer, 1983; editor Naval Station Anchorline, 1979-81, WOPN Caryatides, 1985-86; contbr. articles to profl. jours. Sec. San Vito Dei Normanni theatre group, Italy, 1975-76; coord. Magic Box Theater, Zion, Ill., 1984-86; dir. Too Bashful for Broadway variety show, Naval Tng. Ctr., 1986-87; treas. Yokosuka Little Theatre Group, 1990-91. Mem. Women Officers' Prof. Network (communications chair 1985-86, programs chair 1986-87), Am. Legion, Nat. Press Photographers Assn., Internat. Soc. Appraisers, Corp. Sponsor Tokyo Internat. Players, JHF Theater Soc. (co-founder 1990-93), McMurdo Club, Soc. of South Pole, Gemological Inst. Am. Alumni. Avocations: golf, mineralogy, gemology, scuba diving, travel, theatre. Home: 38060 12th St East Palmdale CA 93550

METHVIN, MILDRED E., judge; b. Alexandria, La., Oct. 24, 1952; d. DeWitt T. Jr. and Lallah Hill (Cunningham) M.; m. James T. McManus, Jan. 2, 1988; children: Michael James, Connor Hill; stepchildren: Christine Lynn, Matthew Robert, John Thomas. BA in Philosophy, Newcomb Coll., Tulane Univ., 1973; student, Tulane Univ. Law Sch., 1973-74; JD, Georgetown Univ. Law Ctr., 1976. Bar: La. 1977, D.C. 1977. Staff asst. to U.S. Rep. Gillis Long La., 1974-77; assoc. Gist, Methvin & Trimble, Alexandria, La., 1977-78; asst. U.S. atty. U.S. Dist. Ct. (we. dist.) La., Shreveport, 1979-81; staff atty. Dept. of Interior, Charleston, W. Va., 1981-83; magistrate judge U.S. Dist. Ct. (we. dist.) La., Lafayette, 1983—. Mem. D.C. Bar Assn., La. Bar Assn., Nat. Assn. of Women Judges, Fed. Magistrate Judges Assn., Am. Inn of Ct. Acadiana (pres.-elect 1994-95). Office: Federal Bldg 705 Jefferson St Rm 107 Lafayette LA 70501-6909*

METOYER, ADRIENNE ROSE, finanicial analyst; b. Jersey City, N.J., Oct. 22, 1963; d. Victor and Marie Susan (Madison) M. AB, Brown U., 1981; MBA, U. Calif., 1989. Bond mgr. Inland Underwriters, Boston, 1985-87; fin. analyst Hewlett-Packard, Mountain View, Calif., 1989—. Mem. AAUW (chair contempos group), Jr. League of Palo Alto.

METROS, MARY TERESA, librarian; b. Denver, Nov. 10, 1951; d. James and Wilma Frances (Hanson) M. BA in English, Colo. Women's Coll., 1973; MA in Librarianship, U. Denver, 1974. Adult svcs. libr. Englewood (Colo.) Pub. Libr., 1975-81, adult svcs. mgr., 1983-84; libr. systems cons. Dataphase Systems, Kansas City, Mo., 1981-82; circulation libra. Westminster (Colo.) Pub. Libr. 1983; pub. svcs. supr. Tempe (Ariz.) Pub. Libr., 1984-90, libr. adminstr., 1990—. Mem. ALA, Pub. Libr. Assn., Ariz. Libr. Assn, Libr. Adminstrn. and Mgmt. Assn. Democrat. Home: 11860 E Purdue Ave Scottsdale AZ 85259 Office: Tempe Pub Libr 3500 S Rural Rd Tempe AZ 85282-5482

METTEE-MCCUTCHON, ILA, army officer; b. Mobile, May 1, 1945; d. John Martin and Anna Ruth (Cleveland) Mettee; BS, Auburn (Ala.) U., 1967, MS, 1969; grad. various army schs.; m. John Robert McCutchon, Oct. 13, 1974; 1 child, Erin Tempest. Research psychologist VA Hosp., Tuskegee, Ala., 1967-69; clin. psychologist U. Ala. Med. Center, Birmingham, 1969-71; commd. 1st lt. U.S. Army, 1971, advanced through grades to col., 1992; OIC, Alcohol and Drug Abuse Rehab. Center, Presidio, San Francisco, 1971-73; strategic intelligence officer 8th Psychol. Bn., 1973-75; tactical intelligence officer, ops. officer, co. comdr. 525th MI Brigade (Airborne), Ft. Bragg, N.C., 1976-79; project officer Command, Control, Communications and Intelligence Directorate, Combined Arms Combat Devel. Activity, Ft. Leavenworth, Kans., 1979-82; student Command and Gen. Staff Coll., 1982-83; ops. officer Army Spl. Security Group, Washington, 1983-86; Def. Lang. Inst. Presidio of Monterey, 1986-87; chief U.S. So. command Joint Intelligence Ctr., Republic of Panama, 1987-89; comdr. 741st M.I. Bn., Ft. Meade, Md., 1989-91; U.S. Army War Coll., 1991-92; strategic intelligence officer Internat. Military Staff NATO, Brussels, Belgium, 1992-94; comdr. Presidio of Monterey and Ft. Ord, Calif., 1994—. Decorated Army Commendation medal (3), Meritorious Svc. medal (4), Defense Meritorious Svc. medal (1), Army Achievement award (2). Mem. Assn. U.S. Army. Mem. Alumni Assn. U.S. Army War Coll., Women's Army Corps Found., Women in NATO. Home: 7 Bayonet Dr Fort Ord CA 93955 Office: Presidio of Monterey ATZP-GC Monterey CA 93944

METZ, HELEN CHAPIN, Middle East analyst; b. Beijing, China, Apr. 13, 1928; d. Selden and Mary Paul (Noyes) Chapin; m. Ronald Irwin Metz, July 14, 1951; children: Mary Selden Metz Evans, Helen Winchester Metz Ketchum, Grace Chapin Metz. AB, Vassar Coll., 1949; MA, Am. U., Beirut, 1954; postgrad., Berkeley Div. Sch. of Yale U., 1966-69. Hostess to The Honorable Selden Chapin, U.S. Amb. to the Netherlands, The Hague, 1950; instr. Beirut Coll. for Women (now Beirut Univ. Coll.), 1954-55, Madeira Sch., Greenway, Va., 1959-60; rsch. analyst Arabian Am. Oil Co., Dhahran, Saudi Arabia, 1956-58, 63-66; adminstrv. asst. Office Anglican Archbishop, Jerusalem, 1969-75; instr. Mercyhurst Coll., Erie, Pa., 1977-79; exec. dir. Internat. Inst., Erie, 1978-81; dep. head, devel. officer Brent Internat. Sch., Baguio, Philippines, 1981-82; analyst, sr. analyst Fed. Rsch. div. Libr. of Congress, Washington, 1983-87, supr. Middle East, North Africa, 1987-90, supr. Middle East, Africa, Latin Am., 1990—. Editor: Libya: A Country Study, 1989, Iran: A Country Study, 1989, Iraq: A Country Study, 1990, Israel: A Country Study, 1990, Jordan: A Country Study, 1991, Egypt: A Country Study, 1992, Nigeria: A Country Study, 1992, Sudan: A Country Study, 1992, Somalia: A Country Study, 1993, Saudi Arabia: A Country Study, 1993, Persian Gulf States: Country Studies, 1994, Algeria: A Country Study, 1995. Mentor Edn. for Ministry St. Margaret's Ch., Washington, 1984-92; mem. mission devel. adv. com. Diocese Washington, 1987-90, mem. evangelism com., 1990-93. Vassar Coll. fellow, 1954-55. Mem. Middle East Studies Assn., Middle East Inst., Phi Beta Kappa (prize, 1949). Democrat. Episcopalian. Home: 3001 Veazey Ter NW Apt 334 Washington DC 20008-5455 Office: Libr of Congress Fed Rsch div 2d and C Sts SE Washington DC 20540

METZ, MARILYN JOYCE, bank executive; b. Denver, Colo., Nov. 10, 1949; d. James C. and Lois M. (Roach) M.; m. Jack W. Calabrese, Apr. 15, 1977 (div. 1981); m. Frank C. Margowski, Oct. 13, 1986 (div.). Student, Colo. State U., 1968-72; diploma, Colo. Grad. Sch. Banking, 1983. With First Interstate Bank Denver, 1972-83; v.p., mgr. United Banks Colo., Denver, 1983-88; v.p., area mgr. First Interstate Bank Oreg., Portland, 1988-89; v.p., dist. mgr. 5 brs. 1st Interstate Bank Wash., Seattle, 1989-91; v.p., dist. mgr. 11 brs. 1st Interstate Bank, Bellevue, Wash., 1991—. Bd. dirs., Met. Child Dental Care Assn., 1985-87. Mem. Nat. Assn. Bank Women (state pres. Colo. 1986-87), Cherry Creek Commerce Assn., Seattle C. of C., Pres. Club Seattle. Republican. Office: First Interstate Bank Bellevue Fin Ctr 225 108th Ave NE Bellevue WA 98004

METZ, MARY SEAWELL, university dean, retired college president; b. Rockhill, S.C., May 7, 1937; d. Columbus Jackson and Mary (Dunlap) Seawell; m. F. Eugene Metz, Dec. 21, 1957; 1 dau., Mary Eugena. BA summa cum laude in French and English, Furman U., 1958; postgrad., Institut Phonetique, Paris, 1962-63, Sorbonne, Paris, 1962-63; PhD magna cum laude in French, La. State U., 1966; HHD (hon.), Furman U., 1984; LLD (hon.), Chapman Coll., 1985; DLT (hon.), Converse Coll., 1988. Instr. French La. State U., 1965-66, asst. prof., 1966-67, 1968-72, assoc. prof., 1972-76, dir. elem. and intermediate French programs, 1966-74, spl. asst. to chancellor, 1974-75, asst. to chancellor, 1975-76; prof. French Hood Coll., Frederick, Md., 1976-81, provost, dean acad. affairs, 1976-81; pres. Mills Coll., Oakland, Calif., 1981-90; dean of extension U. Calif., Berkeley, 1991—; vis. asst. prof. U. Calif.-Berkeley, 1967-68; mem. commn. on leadership devel. Am. Coun. on Edn., 1981-90, adv. coun. Stanford Rsch. Inst., 1985-90, adv. coun. Grad. Sch. Bus., Stanford U.; assoc. Gannett Ctr. for Media Studies, 1985—; bd. dirs. PG&E, Pacific Telesis, PacTel & PacBell, Union Bank, Longs Drug Stores, S.H. Cowell Found. Author: Reflets du monde francais, 1971, 78, Cahier d'exercices: Reflets du monde francais, 1972, 78, (with Helstrom) Le Francais a decouvrir, 1972, 78, Le Francais a vivre, 1972, 78, Cahier d'exercices: Le Francais a vivre, 1972, 78; standardized tests; mem. editorial bd.: Liberal Edn., 1982—. Trustee Am. Conservatory Theater. NDEA fellow, 1960-62,, 1963-64; Fulbright fellow, 1962-63; Am. Council Edn. fellow, 1974-75. Mem. Western Coll. Assn. (v.p. 1982-84, pres. 1984-86), Assn. Ind. Calif. Colls. and Univs. (exec. com. 1982-90), Nat. Assn. Ind. Colls. and Univs. (govt. rels. adv. coun. 1982-85), So. Conf. Lang. Teaching (chmn. 1976-77), World Affairs Coun. No. Calif. (bd. dirs. 1984-93), Bus.-Higher Edn. Forum, Women's Forum West, Women's Coll. Coalition (exec. com. 1984-88), Phi Kappa Phi, Phi Beta Kappa. Address: PO Box 686 Stinson Beach CA 94970

METZER, PATRICIA ANN, lawyer; b. Phila., Mar. 10, 1941; d. Freeman Weeks and Evelyn (Heap) M.; m. Karl Hormann, June 30, 1980. BA with distinction, U. Pa., 1963, LLB cum laude, 1966. Bar: Mass. 1966, D.C. 1972, U.S. Tax Ct. 1988. Assoc., then ptnr. Mintz, Levin, Cohn, Glovsky and Popeo, Boston, 1966-75; assoc. tax legis. counsel U.S. Treasury Dept., Washington, 1975-78; shareholder, dir. Goulston & Storrs, P.C., Boston, 1978—; lectr. program continuing legal edn. Boston Coll. Law Sch., Chestnut Hill, Mass., spring 1974; mem. adv. com. NYU Inst. Fed. Taxation, N.Y.C., 1981-87; mem. practitioner liaison com. Mass. Dept. of Revenue, Mass., 1985-90; mem. editorial bd. Am. Jour. of Tax Policy, 1995—; speaker in field. Author: Federal Income Taxation of Individuals, 1984; contbr. chpts. to books and articles to profl. jours. Bd. mgrs. Barrington Ct. Condominium, Cambridge, Mass., 1985-86; bd. dirs. University Road Parking Assn., Cambridge, 1988—; trustee Social Law Libr., Boston, 1989-93. Mem. ABA (tax sect., chmn. subcom. allocations and distbns. partnership com. 1978-82, vice chmn. legis. 1991-93, chmn. 1993-95, com. govt. submissions, vice liaison 1993-94, liaison 1994—, North Atlantic regional liaison meetings com.), Mass. Bar Assn., Boston Bar Assn. (coun. 1987-89, chmn. tax sect. 1989-91), Fed. Bar Assn. (coun. on taxation, chmn. corp. taxation com. 1977-81, chmn. com. partnership taxation 1981-87), Boston Estate Planning Coun. (exec. com. 1975, 79-82), Am. Coll. Tax Counsel. Office: Goulston & Storrs PC 400 Atlantic Ave Boston MA 02110-3333

METZGER, CAROLYN DIBBLE, accountant, educator; b. South Bend, Ind., May 27, 1924; d. Harry Hurlburt and Mae Floretta (Parker) Dibble; m. Franklin Dale Metzger, Aug. 17, 1946; children: Lawrence, Bruce, Douglas. BS in Acctg. with honors, Ind. U., South Bend, 1972, MS in Bus. Adminstrn., 1975. CPA, Ind. Ptnr. Metzger and Co. CPAs, South Bend, 1972-84; mng. ptnr. Metzger and Mancini CPAs, South Bend, 1984-93; adj. prof. Ind. U., South Bend, 1975-90. Treas. St. Joseph County Rep. Party, 1973-79, co-auditor candidate, 1973, 77; mem. exec. coun. audit com. Ind. U., Bloomington, 1978-88; mem. alumni bd. dirs. Ind. U., South Bend, 1974-81, orgn. com., 1973, founding pres., 1974, rep. to alumni assn., exec. coun., 1975-81, chancellor's com. on curriculum priorities, 1975; bd. dirs., sec., vice chmn. Michiana Community Hosp., 1977-80, 90-93; vol. speaker Women in Bus., 1975-91; guest tour guide Spl. Olympics, Chgo., 1987, numerous others. Recipient Athena award South Bend C. of C., 1992, Alumni award Ind. U., 1993. Mem. AICPA (mem. exam, tax forms and sml. bus. coms., Pub. Svc. award 1989), Ind. CPA Soc. (mem. ethics com., bd. dirs., Pub. Svc. award 1989), Am. Women's Soc. CPAs (nat. bd. dirs. 1979-81, charter pres. local chpt. 1982), Nat. Assn. Accts. (pres. 1978-79, bd. dirs.), Order of the Eastern Star. Presbyterian. Home and Office: Metzger and Mancini CPAs PO Box 4143 South Bend IN 46634-4143

METZGER, DIANE HAMILL, paralegal, poet; b. Phila., July 23, 1949; d. David Alexander Sr. and Eunice (Shelton) Hamill; m. Frank Allen Metzger, Aug. 29, 1969; 1 child, Jason. AA in Bus. Adminstrn. magna cum laude, Northampton Coll., 1980; BA in Polit. Sci. magna cum laude, Bloomsburg U., 1987; paralegal cert., Pa. State U., 1988; postgrad., Calif. State U., Dominguez Hills. Statistician Am. Viscose div. FMC Corp., Phila., 1967-72; research asst. Temple U., Phila., 1972-73; freelance writer, 1964—, paralegal, 1989—. Author: (poems) Coralline Ornaments, 1980; lyricist: Come Now, Shepherds, 1979, Sleep Now, My Baby, 1986; poetry pub. in numerous mags., publs. including Phila. Poets, The Grit, The Long Islander, Inside/Out, Working Parents, South Coast Poetry Jour., Pearl (featured poet 1989), ANIMA: A Jour. of Human Experience, Collages and Bricolages. Recipient numerous awards for poetry including 2d place award Phila. Writers Conf., 1969, 1st prize PEN Writing Awards, 1985, 2d prize Carver Prize Essay Competition, 1986; also Citation for Outstanding Achievement Pa. Ho. of Reps., 1988, Citation for Outstanding Achievement Pa. Senate, 1988, Honorable Mention award Writers Digest Nat. Writing Competition, 1994. Mem. Am. Humanist Assn., Mensa, Am. Atheist Assn., Nat. Wildlife Found. Office: SCIM # 005634 PO Box 180 Rt 405 Muncy PA 17756

METZGER, KATHERINE H., state legislator; b. Middletown, Ohio, Nov. 5, 1923; m. J. Hayes Metzger; 5 children. BS, Ohio State U., 1945; MA, St. Bonaventure, 1974. Mem. N.H. Ho. of Reps.; mem. corrections and criminal justice coms. Chmn. exec. com. Southwest Regional Planning Com.; chmn. Conservation Commn. Home: Lower Troy Rd Fitzwilliam NH 03447 Office: NH Ho of Reps State Capitol Concord NH 03301*

METZGER, KATHLEEN ANN, computer systems specialist; b. Orchard Park, N.Y., Aug. 4, 1949; d. Charles Milton and Anna Irene (Matwijow) Wetherby; m. Robert George Metzger, Aug. 29, 1970 (div. June 1988). BS in Edn. cum laude, SUNY Coll., Buffalo, 1970; postgrad., SUNY, Fredonia, 1975. Cert. secondary tchr. Math. tchr. Crestwood High Sch., Mantua, Ohio, 1970-71; sec., bookkeeper Maple Bay Marina, Lakewood, N.Y., 1972; math., bus. tchr. Falconer (N.Y.) High Sch., 1972-76; bookkeeper Darling Jewelers, Lakewood, 1977-78; computer operator Ethan Allen Inc., Jamestown, N.Y., 1978-79, So. Tier Bldg. Trades, Jamestown, 1979; program analyst TRW Bearings Div., Inc., Jamestown, 1980-82, Fla. Power Corp., St. Petersburg, 1982—. Campaign advisor United Way, St. Petersburg, 1985; Beachfest vol. Suncoast Children's Dream Fund, 1988-92; vol. Christmas Toy Shop. Mem. Data Processing Mgmt. Assn. (sec.), St. Petersburg Second Time Arounders Marching Band Color Guard, Kappa Delta Pi. Republican. Roman Catholic. Home: 8701 Blind Pass Rd Apt 110 Saint Petersburg FL 33706-1463 Office: Fla Power Corp 3201 34th St S Saint Petersburg FL 33711-3897

METZL, MARILYN NEWMAN, clinical psychologist, educator; b. N.Y.C., Apr. 12, 1938; d. George and Rose (Shanen) Newman; m. Kurt Metzl, June 25, 1961; children: Jonathan, Jordan, Jamie, Joshua. BA, Queens (N.Y.) Coll., 1959; MA, Hunter Coll., 1968; PhD, U. Kans., 1978; postgrad., Nat. Inst. Psychotherapies, 1992-95. Cert. in healing arts, Mo. Dir. clin. services Psychol. Ednl. Assocs., Kansas City, Mo., 1971—; assoc. prof. Avila Coll., Kansas City, 1976-84; assoc. clin. prof. U. Kans., 1989—. State of Mo. grantee, 1978, Menorah Med. Ctr. grantee, 1980. Mem. APA, Mo. Psychol. Assn. (pres.), Greater Kansas City Psychol. Assn. (pres. 1992-93), Jackson County Med. Soc., Soc. for Rsch. in Child Devel. Democrat. Jewish. Office: Psychol Ednl Assocs 8080 Ward Pky Ste 115 Kansas City MO 64114-2020

METZLER, YVONNE LEETE, realtor; b. Bishop, Calif., Jan. 25, 1930; d. Ben Ford and Gladys Edna (Johnson) Leete; m. Richard Harvey Metzler, June 2, 1950; children: David Grant, Regan M., Erin E. Student, U. Calif., Berkeley, 1949, JD, Empire Coll., 1992. Lic. realtor, Calif. Vocat. instr. Ukiah (Calif.) Jr. Acad., 1962-63; bookkeeper Sid Beamer Volkswagen, Ukiah, 1963-64; acct. Ukiah Convalescent Hosp., 1964, Walter Woodard P.A., Ukiah, 1964-66; assoc. dir. Fashion Two Twenty, Ukiah, 1966-67, dir., Santa Rosa, Calif., 1967-71; acct. P.K. Marsh, M.D., Ukiah, 1971-72, Walter Woodard P.A. and Clarence White CPA, Ukiah, 1972-74; ptnr., travel agt. Redwood Travel Agy., Ukiah, 1973-76; owner, mgr. A-1 Travel Planners, Ukiah, 1976-90; owner A-1 Travel Planners of Willits, Calif., 1979-88; realtor Mendo Realty, Ukiah, 1989-92; law clk. Family Support div. Sonoma County Dist. Atty., 1990-91; freelance legal asst., 1991—; loan officer, Allied Bank, Ukiah, 1994; realtor Maudlin Realty, Ukiah, 1994—. Commr., Ukiah City Planning Commn., 1979-84, chmn., 1981-83; bd. dirs., rep. Mendocino County Visitors and Conv. Bur., 1988, Pvt. Industry Coun., 1988-90; mem. Rep. County Cen. Com., 1978-80. Mem. Am. Soc. Bus. and Profl. Women, Sonoma County Bar Assn., Sonoma County Young Lawyers Assn., Ukiah C. of C. (1st v.p. 1980, pres. 1981, 82), Mendocino County C. of C. (dir. 1981), Soroptimist (pres. 1977-78, v.p. 1993-94, pres. 1994—), Ukiah Soc. Bus. and Profl. Women (treas. 1977-78, named Woman of the 80's).

METZNER, BARBARA STONE, university counselor; b. St. Louis, June 9, 1940; d. Wendell Phillips and Lois Custer (Rake) Metzner. AB, Ind. U., 1962, MS, 1964, EdD, 1983; BA, Purdue U., 1979. Asst. dean students U. Ill., Urbana, 1964-68; undergrad. advisor UCLA, 1968-69; asst. dean students Ohio State U., 1969-72; student affairs officer San Diego State U., 1972-76; sr. counselor Ind. U. - Purdue U., Indpls., 1976—; supr. Ednl. Testing Svc., Indpls., 1980-90; cons. editorial bd. Nat. Acad. Advising Assn., Manhattan, Kans., 1987-93; adj. prof. Ind. U., 1987—; mgr. Info. Svcs., Ind. U.-Purdue U., 1989-91. Contbr. articles to profl. jours. Mem. Marion County Precinct Election Bd., 1980—; exec. com. Ind. Allied Health Assn., 1983-84; VIP escort Pan Am. Games, 1987. Spencer Found. grantee, 1985. Mem. APA, Am. Edn. Rsch. Assn., Nat. Acad. Advising Assn., Assn. Instl. Rsch., Assn. Study Higher Edn., Internat. Platform Assn., Kappa Alpha Theta, Alpha Theta (vol. charity benefits 1980—). Office: IUPUI 620 Union Dr UN 242 Indianapolis IN 46202-5167

MEULI, JUDITH K., communications executive, real estate developer, small business owner; b. Chippewa Falls, Wis., Jan. 15, 1938; d. Earle Joseph and Isabel M. (Dresel) M. B.S., U. Minn., 1963. Sr. designer Women's Graphic Comm., L.A., 1970—; real estate broker, 1990. Editor Nat. NOW Times, 1977-85, Financing the Revolution, 1973, NOW Acts, 1970-71; designer Women's Equality symbol, Human Liberation symbol, Woman Thinker in cloisonne, Women's Peace symbol; author: (with Toni Carabillo) The Feminization of Power, 1988, (with Toni Carabillo and June Bundy Csida) The Feminist Chronicles 1953-1993, 1993. Vice pres. L.A. chpt. NOW, 1969, chpt. coord., 1970, nat. bd. dirs., 1972, 75-77; sec. Fund for the Feminist Majority, 1987—; sec. Feminist Majority Found., 1987—, bd. dirs., 1987—. Recipient Los Angeles Feminist Achievement and Womens Rights Advocacy award, 1981, Women's Rights award NOW, 1982. Democrat. Home: 1126 Hi Point St Los Angeles CA 90035-2610

MEUSBURGER, PATRICIA ANN, television news anchor; b. Lake City, Iowa, Sept. 16, 1963; d. Kenneth Everett and June Frances (Myers) M. BS, Kans. State U., 1986. TV news intern KCTV-5, Kansas City, Mo., 1986; TV news anchor KSNF-TV, Joplin, Mo., 1987-91, KCEN-TV, Waco, Tex., 1991—. Co-host Children's Miracle Network Telethon. Bd. dirs. Am. Heart Assn., March of Dimes; aux. bd. Peaceable Kingdom Retreat of Chronically Ill Children. Named one of Outstanding Young Women Am., 1988, 1991, Career Woman Yr., Bus. Profl. Women, Joplin, Mo., 1989; named Miss Mo., Miss Am. Pageant, 1989. Mem. Radio-TV News Dirs. Assn., Soc. Profl. Journalists, Alpha Chi Omega. Office: Sta KCEN-TV PO Box 314 S I-35 Eddy TX 76524

MEUTER, MARIA COOLMAN, lawyer; b. New Albany, Ind., July 17, 1915; d. William Edmund and Hundley Love (Wells) Coolman; m. Walter Frederick Meuter, Jan. 9, 1942; children: Stephen, Craig Frederick. Student, New Albany Bus. Coll., 1933; LLB, Jefferson Sch. Law, 1939; JD, U. Louisville, 1971. Bar: Ky. 1939, U.S. Ct. Internat. Trade, 1980. Clk. Fed. Land Bank of Louisville, 1933-41; exec. dir. Louisville Bar Assn., 1952-70; trial judge County Ct., Jefferson County, Louisville, 1962-70; assoc. dir. Law Alumni Affairs, U. Louisville, 1970—; exec. dir. Continuing Legal Edn., U. Louisville, 1978-83; pvt. practice, Louisville, 1970—; life trustee Law Alumni Found. Vice pres. Beechmont Civic Club, Louisville, 1987-91. Named Disting. Alumnae, U. Louisville Sch. Law, 1976, Ky. col., 1968, Master of Steamboat Flotilla of Jefferson County, 1968. Mem. Ky. Bar Assn. (rec. sec. ho. of dels. 1964-68), Louisville Bar Assn., Jefferson County Women Lawyers (pres.), Nat. Assn. Bar Execs. (rec. sec. 1969-70), AAUW, DAR (com. chmn. John Marshall chpt. 1991), Daus. Am. Colonists, Colonial Dames, Law Alumni Assn. U. Louisville (treas., sec. 1970-75), South Park Country Club. Republican. Episcopalian. Home: 1313 Marret Pl Louisville KY 40215-2368 also: 2855 Gulf Shore Blvd N Naples FL 33940-4339

MEYER, ALICE VIRGINIA, state official; b. N.Y.C., Mar. 15, 1921; d. Martin G. and Marguerite Helene (Houzé) Kliemand; m. Theodore Harry Meyer, June 28, 1947; children: Robert Charles, John Edward. BA, Barnard Coll., 1941; MA, Columbia U., 1942. Tchr. pub. schs. Elmont, N.Y., 1942-43; tchr. Fairlawn (N.J.) High Sch., 1943-47; office mgr., sales rep. N.Y.C., 1948-55; substitute tchr. Pub. Schs., Easton, Conn., 1965-72; state rep., asst. minority leader Conn. State Legislature, Hartford, 1976-93; mem. Ct. Bd. of Govs. for Higher Edn. Mem. bd. trustees Discovery Mus., 1882—, United Way Regional Youth Substance Abuse Project, Bridgeport, 1983-93; bd. dirs. Fairfield County Lit. Coalition, Bridgeport, 1988—, 3030 Park, 1993—; vice chmn. Easton Rep. Town Com., 1970-78; mem. strategic planning com. Town of Easton, 1993—; vice-chmn. adv. coun. on intergovtl. rels., 1988—; mem. Conn. Commn. on Quality Edn., 1992-93; supporter of Conn. small towns, 1988; mem. lt. gov's. commn. on mandate reduction, 1995. Named Legislator of Yr. Conn. Libr. Assn. 1985; Guardian Small bus. grantee Nat. Fedn. Ind. Bus., 1987. Mem. AAUW (past local pres. 1976, bd. dirs. 1982), LWV, Bus. and Profl. Women, Nat. Order Women Legislators (regional dir. 1987—, past pres. Conn. chpt.). Congregationalist. Home: 18 Lantern Hill Rd Easton CT 06612-2218

MEYER, ANDREA PEROUTKA, small business owner; b. Prague, Czechoslovakia, Nov. 29, 1963; came to U.S. 1970; d. George and Alena Peroutka; m. Dana Charles Meyer, Oct. 16, 1983. BA in Liberal Arts, U. Tex., 1985, M in Libr. of Info. Sci., 1986. Libr. IBM, Austin, Tex., 1985-86; rsch. specialist Career Track Seminars, Boulder, Colo., 1986-88; founder, pres. Working Knowledge, Boulder, 1988—; cons. The Tom Peters Group, Palo Alto, Calif., 1989—. Author: (workbooks) Stress Management Strategies, 1987, How to Give Presentations, 1988, (bimonthly newsletter) Working Knowledge, 1994—; co-author: (audio tape) How to Set Up a Corporate Library, 1989; contbr. chpt. to book. Recipient Ray C. Janeway scholarship, Tex. Libr. Assn., 1985, Philip Morris scholarship, 1981-85. Mem. Planning Forum (v.p. comm., bd. dirs. Denver chpt.), Product Devel. and Mgmt. Assn. (newsletter editor), Toastmasters, Mensa (chmn. scholarship com.), Pres.'s Assn., European Consortium of Info. Cons., Phi Beta Kappa. Home and Office: 515 Forest Ave Boulder CO 80304-2550

MEYER, ANN JANE, human development educator; b. N.Y.C., Mar 11, 1942; s. Louis John and Theresa M. B.A., U. Mich., 1964; M.A., U. Calif.-Berkeley, 1967, Ph.D., 1971. Asst. prof. dept. human devel. Calif. State U.-Hayward, 1972-77, assoc. prof., 1977-84, prof., chmn. dept., 1984—. Mem. Am. Psychol. Assn., Western Psychol. Assn., Western Gerontol. Soc. Office: Dept Human Devel Calif State U Hayward CA 94542

MEYER, BETTY JANE, former librarian; b. Indpls., July 20, 1918; d. Herbert and Gertrude (Sanders) M.; B.A., Ball State Tchrs. Coll., 1940; B.S. in L.S., Western Res. U., 1945. Student asst. Muncie Public Library (Ind.), 1936-40; library asst. Ohio State U. Library, Columbus, 1940-42, cataloger, 1945-46, asst. circulation librarian, 1946-51, acting circulation librarian, 1951-52, adminstrv. asst. to dir. libraries, 1952-57, acting asso. reference librarian, 1957-58, cataloger in charge serials, 1958-65, head serial div. catalog dept., 1965-68, head acquisition dept., 1968-71, asst. dir. libraries, tech. services, 1971-76, acting dir. libraries, 1976-77, asst. dir. libraries, tech. services, 1977-83, instr. library adminstrn., 1958-63, asst. prof., 1963-67, asso. prof., 1967-75, prof., 1975-83, prof. emeritus, 1983—; library asst. Grandview Heights Public Library, Columbus, 1942-44; student asst. Case

Inst. Tech., Cleve., 1944-45; mem. Ohio Coll. Library Center Adv. Com. on Cataloging, 1971-76, mem. adv. com. on serials, 1971-76, mem. adv. com. on tech. processes, 1971-76; mem. Inter-Univ. Library Council, Tech. Services Group, 1971-83; mem. bd. trustees Columbus Area Library and Info. Council Ohio, 1980-83. Ohio State U. grantee, 1975-76. Mem. ALA, Assn. Coll. and Research Libraries, AAUP, Ohio Library Assn. (nominating com. 1978-81), Ohioana Library Assn., Ohio Valley Group Tech. Services Librarians, No. Ohio Tech. Services Librarians, Franklin County Library Assn., Acad. Library Assn. Ohio, PEO, Beta Phi Mu, Delta Kappa Gamma. Club: Assn. Faculty and Profl. Women Ohio State U. Home: 970 High St Apt H2 Worthington OH 43085-4061

MEYER, MRS. C. M. See DANNER, PATSY ANN

MEYER, CAROL FRANCES, pediatrician and allergist; b. Berea, Ky., June 2, 1936; d. Harvey Kessler and Jessie Irene (Hamm) Meyer; m. Daniel Baker Cox, June 5, 1955 (div. Apr. 1962). AA, U. Fla., 1955; BA, Duke U., 1957; MD, Med. Coll. Ga., 1967. Diplomate Am. bd. Pediatrics, Am. Bd. Allergy and Immunology. Intern in pediatrics Med. Coll. Ga., Augusta, 1967-68; resident in pediatrics Gorgas Hosp., Canal Zone, 1968-69; fellow in pediatric respiratory disease Med. Coll. Ga., 1969-71; med. officer pediatrics Canal Zone Govt., 1972-79; med. officer pediatrics Dept. of Army, Panama, 1979-82, med. officer allergy, 1982-89, physician in charge allergy clinic, 1984-89; asst. prof. pediatrics and medicine Med. Coll. Ga., Augusta, 1990—; mem. Bd. of Canal Zone Merit System Examiners, 1976-79. Contbr. articles to profl. jours. Mem. First Bapt. Ch. Orch., 1992—; founding mem., violoncello Curundu Chamber Ensemble, 1979-89. Recipient U.S. Army Exceptional Performance awards, 1985, 86, 89, Merck award Med. Coll. Ga., 1967; U. Fla. J. Hillis Miller scholar, 1954. Mem. AAAS, Am. Coll. Rheumatology, Allergy and Immunology Soc. Ga., Hispanic-Am. Allergy and Immunology Assn., Ga. Pediatric Soc., Pan Am. Med. Assn., Soc. Leukocyte Biology, Am. Coll. Allergy and Immunology, Am. Acad. Allergy and Immunology, Am. Acad. Pediat., Am. Med. Women's Assn., Panama Canal Soc. Fla., Ga. Ornithol. Soc., Ga. Thoracic Soc., Am. Lung Assn. (Ga. East Ctrl. br. exec. bd.), Am. Assn. Ret. Persons, Nature Conservancy, Royal Soc. for Preservation Birds, Nat. Assn. Ret. Fed. Employees, Nat. Audubon Soc., Panama Audubon Soc., Willow Run Homeowner's Soc. (pres.), Alpha Omega Alpha. Office: Med Coll Ga CJ-141 1120 15th St Augusta GA 30912

MEYER, DIANE CRIMMINS, psychotherapist, consultant; b. N.Y.C., Feb. 3, 1945; d. Charles J. and Mary (Margadonna) Crimmins; m. Charles R. Meyer, Nov. 15, 1973; 1 child, Tara. MS, U. Hartford, 1985. Clin. instr. out patient psychiatry U. Conn. Health Ctr., Farmington, Conn., 1985-86; cons. Luth. Child and Family Svcs., Hartford, Conn., 1987-90; psychiat. clinician Kaiser Permanente, East Hartford, Conn., 1990—; pvt. practice psychotherapy, Farmington, 1985—. Mem. AACD, New Eng. Assn. for Specialists in Group Work. Home: 62 Stoner Dr West Hartford CT 06107-1308 Office: Kaiser Permanente 99 Ash St East Hartford CT 06108-3273

MEYER, DONNA MARIA, aerospace company executive; b. Washington, Mar. 14, 1950; d. Gratian Jerome and Kathryn (Sullivan) Meyer; m. James Thomas Giganti, Nov. 17, 1988; 1 child, Julia Claire Giganti. BS, U. Md., 1974. Dir. internat. fundraising Gratian Meyer & Assocs., Washington, 1970-76; legal exec. Am. Internat. Law Offices, Arlington, Va., 1976-81; exec. sales rep. Concord (N.H.) Litho Co., 1981-86; chmn., co-founder Save Sexually Abused Children, Silver Spring, Md., 1988—; pres. Youngstar Space Acad., Silver Spring, 1986—; founder The Daisy Program for the Chesapeake Inst., Nat. Resource Ctr. for Child Abuse, 1990. Author: Angela Duke Story, 1989; author, editor Children's Dictionary of Space, 1989; contbg. author Factor Ten, 1979; contbg. author: Parents Resource Book, 1990. Recipient Key to City of Guatemala, 1980. Mem. Nat. Assn. of Women Execs., Young Astronaut Coun. (chpt. leader), Jr. Engrng. Tech. Soc. (chpt. leader), Ninety-Nines (Potomac). Republican. Roman Catholic. Office: 11301 Georgia Ave Ste 3 Silver Spring MD 20902-4667

MEYER, GAIL BARRY, real estate broker; b. Athens, Ga., Oct. 13, 1940; d. John Carlton and Addie Lorene (Harris) Barry; m. Leo Marcus Meyer Jr., July 2, 1960; Rand Marcus, Brian Kevin, Kelli Paige. Cert., Grad. Realtors Inst., 1979. Cert. residential specialist, cert. rape counselor. Assoc. broker, owner So. Realty, Statesboro, Ga., 1977-80; assoc. broker Zetterower-Olliff Realty, Statesboro, 1980-84, Century 21, Johnny Cobb Realty, Statesboro, 1984—. Pres., v.p., treas. Citizens Against Crime, Statesboro, 1990—; pres. Victim Witness Assistance Program, Statesboro, 1990—; mem. Georgians for Victims Justice, Parents and Childrens Counsel. Recipient Deen Day Smith award C. of C. and Statesboro Herald News, 1989. Mem. NOW (pres. 1980—, v.p., treas.), MADD. Roman Catholic. Home: 105 W Mockingbird Ln Statesboro GA 30458 Office: Century 21 Johnny Cobb Real 433 Fair Rd Statesboro GA 30458

MEYER, HELEN (MRS. ABRAHAM J. MEYER), retired editorial consultant; b. Bklyn., Dec. 4, 1907; d. Bertolen and Esther (Greenfield) Honig; m. Abraham J. Meyer, Sept. 1, 1929; children—Adele Meyer Brodkin, Robert L. Grad. pub. schs. With Popular Sci., McCall's mag., 1921-22; pres., dir. Dell Pub. Co., Inc., N.Y.C., 1923-57, Dell Distbg., Inc., from 1957, Dell Internat., Inc., from 1957; pres. Dell Pub. Co., Inc., Montville Warehousing Co., Inc.; chmn. bd. Noble & Noble Pubs., Inc.; v.p. Dellprint, Inc., Dunellen, N.J.; pres. Dial Press.; later editorial cons. Doubleday & Co., N.Y.C.; cons. Fgn. Rights, N.Y.C. Bd. dirs. United Cerebral Palsy. Named to Pub.'s Hall of Fame, 1986. Mem. Assn. Am. Pubs. (dir.). Home: 1 Claridge House Apt 608 Verona NJ 07044

MEYER, IVAH GENE, social worker; b. Decatur, Ill., Nov. 18, 1935; d. Anthony and Nona Alice (Gamble) Viccone; AA with distinction, Phoenix Coll., 1964; BS with distinction, Ariz. State U., 1966, MSW, 1969; postgrad. U.S. Internat. U.; m. Richard Anthony Meyer, Feb. 7, 1954; children—Steven Anthony, Stuart Allen, Scott Arthur. Social worker Florence Crittendon Home, Phoenix, 1969-70; social worker Family Service of Phoenix, 1970-73; faculty asso. Ariz. State U., 1973; field supr. Pitzer Coll., Claremont, Calif., 1977—; social worker Family Service of Pomona Valley, Pomona, Calif., 1975—; field supr. Grad. Sch. Social Services, U. So. Calif., 1978—; pvt. practice Chino (Calif.) Counseling Center. Lic. clin. social worker, Calif. Mem. Nat. Assn. Social Workers, Acad. Cert. Social Workers. Republican. Roman Catholic. Deceased. Office: 12632 Central Ave Chino CA 91710

MEYER, JANET FAYE, law librarian; b. Rockford, Ill., Mar. 22, 1955; d. William F. and Alma Faye (Crawford) Price; m. Charles Daniel Meyer, July 23, 1977. BA, Carson-Newman Coll., 1977; MLS, U. S.C., 1986. Library tech. asst. III Thomas Cooper Library, U. S.C., Columbia, 1982-85; asst. librarian McNair Law Firm, Columbia, 1985-88, librarian, 1988-89; librarian S.C. Supreme Ct., Columbia, 1989—. Mem. Am. Assn. Law Libraries (Lucille Elliot scholar Southeastern chpt. 1987), S.C. Libary Assn. (pres. spl. libraries sect. 1988-89). Office: SC Supreme Ct Libr 1231 Gervais St Columbia SC 29201-3206

MEYER, JEAN, fashion consultant; b. N.Y.C., Mar. 18, 1934; d. George and Grace (Lieberman) Weingart; m. Harold Walton Meyer, Apr. 6, 1971; 1 child, Steven Michael. Student, Mayer Sch. Design, 1970. Asst. account exec. Theodore R. Sills and Co., N.Y.C., 1963-64; advt. asst. Bond Stores, Inc., N.Y.C., 1964-66; adminstrv. asst. Revlon, Inc., N.Y.C., 1966-68; asst. to pres. The Villager, N.Y.C., 1970-71; freelance fashion cons. Charlotte, N.C., 1984—; sewing tchr. Mecklenburg County Home Econs., Charlotte, 1980-82, Queens Coll., Charlotte, 1988—; image seminar instr. Woman Reach, Charlotte, 1986; antique textile and clothing restorer, Costume Com. Mint Mus., Charlotte, 1984—. Mem. Nat. Assn. Female Execs. Home and Office: 5805J Sharon Rd Charlotte NC 28210-6367

MEYER, JOAN ALICE, civic worker; b. Mt. Vernon, N.Y., July 19, 1936; d. Robert and Martha Ruth (Mayberger) Gelin; m. Jerome Meyer, Mar. 6, 1960; children: Dana Stack, Edward Meyer, Barbara Meyer. AAS, Bklyn. C.C.; student, NYU, 1955-56, Brown Bus. Sch., 1957. Asst. buyer Interstate Dept. Stores, N.Y.C., 1955-56, I Magnin, N.Y.C., 1956-57; sec., conv. mgr. U.S. Vitamin and Pharm., N.Y.C., 1957-62. active women's aux. Franklin Gen. Hosp., Franklin Square, N.Y., 1982-94; chmn. asst. to raise funds Woodmere Hadassah, Hewlett-East Rockaway, 1984-94. Republican. Jewish. Home: 140 Jeffrey Ln Oceanside NY 11572-5936

MEYER, KAREN LYNNE, theatre educator, theatre artist; b. Buffalo, July 3, 1957; d. Ion LeRoy and Joan Betty (Strasburg) M.; m. Ronald Jay Palmer, Sept. 3, 1977 (div. Aug. 1981). Student, SUNY, Buffalo, 1975-76; AA, Leeward C.C., Pearl City, Hawaii, 1982; postgrad., U. Hawaii at Manoa, Honolulu. Artist, educator Alliance for Drama Edn., Kaneohe, Hawaii, 1982—, administr., 1990—. Actress (musical) Oklahoma! (Po'okela award 1986); costume designer Anything Goes (Po'okela award 1989), Joseph and the Amazing Technicolor Dreamcoat (Po'okela award 1986), The Diary of Anne Frank (U.S. Army FORSCOM Theater award 1979). Counselor Hale Kipa Emergency Shelter, Honolulu, 1990; v.p., bd. dirs. Na Hulu Makua Honor Soc., Honolulu, 1993—; active Planned Parenthood, Honolulu. McInerny Found. scholar U. Hawaii, 1993, Hemenway Found. scholar, 1992-93, Hawaii Vets. Meml. scholar Hawaii Cmty. Found., 1992-93. Mem. Alliance for Drama Edn., Hawaii State Theatre Coun. (pres., bd. dirs. 1989-92), Hawaii Alliance for Arts Edn., Ka Hui Heluhelu, Golden Key Honor Soc. Office: Alliance for Drama Edn 45-382 Kanaka St Kaneohe HI 96744

MEYER, KAREN MCCUE, office manager; b. Pitts., Dec. 9, 1954; d. William Laverne and Charlotte Elizabeth (Wyman) McCue; m. Ronald Wesley Franklin Meyer, Aug. 1, 1982; children: Derek Rogue William, Kendra Rose Whitney. AA in Liberal Arts, Santa Monica Coll., 1977. Coord. Riviera Tennis Club, Pacific Palisades, Calif., 1976-78, head coord., 1980-88, asst. to mgr., 1988-89, activities dir., 1989-90, asst. mgr., 1990-91, membership mgr., 1991-92; office mgr. Lake Arrowhead (Calif.) Tennis Club, 1978-79; mgr. Malibu (Calif.) Riding and Tennis Club, 1979-80; office mgr. P.A.C.T., Venice, Calif., 1992—. Democrat. Roman Catholic. Home: 1268 Hendrix Ave Thousand Oaks CA 91360 Office: PACT 811 Victoria Ave Venice CA 90291-3931

MEYER, KATHLEEN ANNE, school psychologist; b. Houston, Nov. 4, 1951; d. William Harry Delany and Clara Louise (Soland) Peltier; m. Michael Wayne Meyer; 1 child, Kristopher Rex. Student, Tex. Chiropractic Coll., 1968-70; AA in Elem. Edn., San Jacinto Jr. Coll., Pasadena, Tex., 1975; BS in Elem. Edn., U. Houston, 1980, MA in Psychology, 1985, postgrad., 1988, 94—. Cert. tchr., Tex.; lic. assoc. psychologist, Tex.; nat. cert. sch. psychologist, Tex. Instr. Pasadena I.S.D., Tex., 1980-84; tchr., and part time sch. psychologist St. Maur's Internat. Sch., Yokohama, Japan, 1985-87; assoc. sch. psychologist Santa Fe I.S.D., Tex., 1990-92; owner K & M Affiliates, Pasadena, Tex., 1993—. V.p. PTA, Pasadena, 1978, community rels., 1978-79; counselor Boy Scouts Am., Yokohama, Japan, 1986-87. Mem. APA, S.E. Psychol. Assn., Nat. Assn. Sch. Psychologists, Tex. Psychol. Assn. Home: 4211 Los Verdes Dr Pasadena TX 77504-2415

MEYER, KATHLEEN MARIE, college educator; b. St. Louis, Oct. 29, 1944; d. Richard Henry and Leonora (Moser) Bailey; m. Thomas A. Meyer, Dec. 26, 1966; children: Richard, Amy, Mindy, Heidi. BA, Webster Coll., Webster Groves, Mo., 1966; MA, Fla. Atlantic U., 1981; postgrad., No. Ill. U., 1982—. Cert. secondary tchr., Mo., Ill. Tchr. English Notre Dame High Sch., St. Louis, 1966-67; tchr. English, chmn. dept. Rosary High Sch., Aurora, Ill., 1981-1991; instr. English DeKalb Coll., Decatur, Ga., 1992—; mem. adv. bd. Univ. High Sch.; mem. joint enrollment coun. DeKalb Coll. Mem. ASCD, Nat. Coun. Tchrs. English, Joint Enrollment Coun.

MEYER, LYNN NIX, lawyer; b. Vinita, Okla., Aug. 10, 1948; d. William Armour and Joan Ross Nix; m. Lee Gordon Meyer; children: Veronica, Victoria, David. BA, Baldwin Wallace Coll., 1978; JD, Case Western Res. U., 1981. Bar: Ky. 1982, Colo. 1984. Paralegal Texaco Devel., Austin, Tex., 1976-77; legal asst. Alcan Aluminum, Cleve., 1977-79; assoc. Wyatt, Tarrant & Combs, Lexington, Ky., 1982-83; ptnr. Meyer, Meyer & Assocs., P.C., Denver, 1984—; pres. Cherokee Fuel Systems, Inc.; v.p., gen. counsel Carbon Fuels Corp., Denver. Mem. ABA, Am. Trial Lawyers Assn., Colo. Bar Assn., Ky. Bar Assn., Arapahoe County Bar Assn. Republican. Home: 10487 E Ida Ave Englewood CO 80111-3746 Office: Carbon Fuels Corp 5105 Dtc Pky # 317 Englewood CO 80111-2600

MEYER, MARION M., editorial consultant; b. Sheboygan, Wis., July 14, 1923; d. Herman O. and Viola A. (Hoch) M. BA, Lakeland Coll., 1950; MA, NYU, 1957. Payroll clk. Am. Chair Co., Sheboygan, 1941-46; tchr. English and religion, dir. athletics Am. Sch. for Girls, Baghdad, Iraq, 1950-56; mem. edn. and publ. staff United Ch. Bd. for Homeland Ministries, United Ch. Press/Pilgrim Press, 1958-64, sr. editor, 1965-88, ret., 1988; cons. to individuals and orgns. on editorial matters and copyrights. Editor Penney Retirement Community Newsletter, 1990—; writer (hymns) Look to God, Be Radiant, 1989, Be Still, 1990, Come, God, Creator, 1992, Something New! (extended work), 1993; contbr. articles to various publs. Incorporating mem. Contact Phila., Inc., 1972, bd. dirs., 1972-75, v.p., chmn. com. to organize community adv. bd., chmn. auditing com., editor newsletter, 1972-74, pres., 1974-75, assoc. mem., 1977—; mem. ofcl. bd. Old First Reformed Ch., Phila., 1984-89; deacon United Ch. Christ, 1984—, Mid.-East Com. of Pa. SE Conf. United Ch. Christ, 1986-88. Honored as role model United Ch. of Christ, 1982, 85. Mem. AAUW, NOW, Nat. Mus. Women in the Arts (charter mem.), Nat. Trust for Hist. Preservation. Home: PO Box 656 Penney Farms FL 32079

MEYER, MARY-LOUISE, art gallery executive; b. Boston, Feb. 21, 1922; d. Alonzo Jay and Louise (Whitledge) Shadman; m. Norman Meyer, Aug. 9, 1941; children: Wendy C., Bruce R., Harold Alton, Marilee, Laurel. BA, Wellesley Coll., 1943; MS, Wheelock Coll., 1965. Head tchr. Page Sch., Wellesley Coll., Mass., 1955-60; instr. early childhood edn. Pine Manor Coll., Brookline, Mass., 1960-65; chaplain/counselor Charles St. Jail, Boston, 1974-79; Christian Sci. practitioner, Wellesley, Mass., 1974—; owner Alpha Gallery, Boston, 1972-87; cons. Living & Learning Centers, Boston, 1966-69; 2d reader Christian Sci. Ch., 1979-82. Contbr. articles to profl. jours. Overseer Sturbridge Village, 1981—, trustee, 1986; visitor Am. Decorative Arts dept. Mus. Fine Arts, Boston, 1973—; chmn. Wellesley Voters Rights Com., 1983-84; state organizer Ednl. Channel 2 Group, Boston, 1960; co-founder Boston Assn. for Childbirth Edn., 1950; overseer Strawberry Banke Living Mus., 1987; trustee Maine Coast Artists, Rockport, Maine, 1991, v.p. Friends of Montpelier (Knox Mansion-Thomaston), 1994—; trustee Bay Chamber Concerts, Rockport, 1990. Mem. Mus. Trustees Assn., Farnsworth Mus., Waldoboro Hist. Soc., Soc. for Pres. New Eng. Antiquities, Wellesley Coll. Club.

MEYER, PATRICIA ANN, veterinarian; b. Greenwich, Conn., Jan. 13, 1945; d. William Charles and Dorothy Ann (Natter) M. BS, Mich. State U., 1967, DVM, 1967. Assoc. veterinarian Belmont (Mass.) Animal Hosp., 1968-69, Pieper Vet. Hosp., Middletown, Conn., 1969-70, Greenwich (Conn.) Animal Hosp., 1970-71, East Longmeadow (Mass.) Vet. Hosp., 1971-72, Clinton (Conn.) Vet. Hosp., 1972-74, MacDonald Vet. Hosp., Bloomfield, Conn., 1974-78, Manchester (Conn.) Vet. Clinic, 1978-83, Whitney Vet. Clinic, Orange, Conn., 1983-93; pvt. practice New Haven, 1993—. Fellow AVMA, Am. Animal Hosp. Assn., Conn. Vet. Med. Assn. (chmn. Acad. Vet. Medicine 1977—); mem. Baldwin Yacht Club, Hartford Ski Club, Hartford County Vet. Med. Assn. (sec.-treas. 1978—). Republican. Roman Catholic. Home and Office: House Calls for Pets 146 Springside Ave New Haven CT 06515-1076

MEYER, PAULINE MARIE, retired special education educator; b. Gilead, Nebr., Dec. 15, 1928; d. Bernhard Martin and Helena Sophia (Vorderstrasse) Hellbusch; m. Calvin John, June 8, 1951 (dec. Nov. 1973); 1 child, Phyllis; m. Tim Gaspar. BA, U. Nebr., 1968, MA, 1972. Tchr. rural schs. Thayer County, Nebr., 1946-66; tchr. rural schs. Fairbury (Nebr.) Pub. Sch., 1966-91, ret., 1991. Mem. Bus. and Profl. Women's Club (pres. 1987-90), Delta Kappa Gamma (pres.). Democrat. Lutheran.

MEYER, PEARL, executive compensation consultant; b. N.Y.C.; d. Allen Charles and Rose (Goldberg) Weissman; m. Ira A. Meyer. BA cum laude, NYU, postgrad. Statis. specialist, exec. comp. div. Gen. Foods Corp., White Plains, N.Y.; exec. v.p. and cons. Handy Assocs., Inc., N.Y.C.; founder, pres. Pearl Meyer & Ptnrs., N.Y.C., 1989—; lectr. on exec. compenstation at confs. and seminars. Contbr. numerous articles to profl. jours. Recipient Entrepreneurial Woman award Women Bus. Owners N.Y., 1983. Mem. Am. Mgmt. Assn., Am. Compensation Assn., Soc. for Human Resources Mgmt. (cert. accredited pers. diplomate), Women's Econ. Roundtable, Pers. Accreditation Inst., Women's Forum, Sedgewood Club, Atrium Club, Sky Club, Phi Beta Kappa, Pi Mu Epsilon, Kappa Pi Sigma. Clubs: Sedgewood, Bd. Rm., Atrium, Sky. Office: Pearl Meyer & Partners Inc 300 Park Ave 21st Fl New York NY 10022-7402

MEYER, PUCCI, newspaper editor; b. N.Y.C., Sept. 1, 1944; d. Charles Albert and Lollo (Offer) M.; m. Thomas M. Arma, Sept. 16, 1979. BA, U. Wis., 1966. Asst. editor Look mag., N.Y.C., 1970-71; editorial asst. Look mag., Paris, 1967-69; reporter Newsday, Garden City, L.I., N.Y., 1971-73; style editor N.Y. Daily News Sunday Mag., N.Y.C., 1974-76, assoc. editor, 1977-82, editor, 1983-86; sr. editor Prodigy, White Plains, N.Y., 1987; spl. projects editor N.Y. Post, N.Y.C., 1988-89, style editor, 1990-92, food editor, 1992-93, assoc. features editor, 1993—, travel editor, 1994—. Contbr. articles to various nat. mags. Recipient Pulitzer prize as mem. Newsday investigative team that wrote articles and book The Heroin Trail, 1973. Office: NY Post 210 South St New York NY 10002-7807

MEYER, RACHEL ABIJAH, foundation director; b. Job's Corners, Pa., Aug. 18, 1963; d. Jacob Owen and Velma Ruth (Foreman) M.; children: Andrew Carson, Peter Franklin. Student, Lebanon Valley Coll., 1982-84. Restaurant owner Purcy's Place, Ono, Pa., 1985-87; restaurant mgr. King's Table Buffet, Citrus Heights, Calif., 1987-89; product finalizer TransWorld Enterprises, Blaine, Wash., 1989-91; dir. Tacticar Found., Rocklin, Calif., 1991—. Author: Year of the Unicorn, 1994. Office: Tacticar Found PO Box 961 Rocklin CA 95677-0961

MEYER, RUTH KRUEGER, museum administrator, art historian; b. Chicago Heights, Ill., Aug. 20, 1940; d. Harold Rohe and Ruth Halbert (Bateman) Krueger; m. Kenneth R. Meyer, June 15, 1963 (div. 1978); 1 child, Karl Augustus. B.F.A., U. Cin., 1963; M.A., Brown U., 1968; Ph.D., U. Minn., 1980. Lectr. Walker Art Ctr., Mpls., 1970-72; instr. U. Cin., 1973-75; curator Contemporary Arts Ctr., Cin., 1976-80; dir. Ohio Found. Arts, Columbus, 1980-83, Taft Mus., Cin., 1983-93; prof. Miyazaki (Japan) Internat. Coll., 1994—; adj. prof. The Union Inst., Cin., 1994. Pub. Dialogue Mag., Columbus, 1980-83; author: (exhbn. catalogues) Sandy Rosen Vestal Vases, 1986, Oblique Illusion: An Installation by Rick Paul, 1986, David Black an American Sculptor, 1985, Brad Davis: The Pines, 1984, The American Weigh, 1983, New Epiphanies, 1982, (with others) The Tafts Collection: The First Ten Years of Its Development, 1988, The Tafts of Pike St., 1988, (exhbn. catalogue) The History of Travel: Paintings by William Wegman, 1985-90, 1990, The Artist Face to Face: Two Centuries of Self-Portraits from the Paris Collection of Gerald Shurr, 1989, Tributes to the Tafts, 1991, The Taft Museum: Its Collection and Its History, 1995; contbr. articles to profl. jours. Recipient rsch. award Kress Found., 1967, 76; named Chevalier in the Order of Arts and Letters, Govt. of France, 1989. Mem. Internat. Assn. Art Critics, Coll. Art Assn. Democrat. Office: Miyazaki Internat College, 1405 Kano Kiyotake-Cho, Miyazaki 88916, Japan

MEYER, SHERRY DEE, educator; b. Oak Park, Ill., Dec. 29, 1947; d. Odd Jr. and Ida Mae (Richmond) M.; 1 child, Lina Graciela. AB in English, U. Mich., 1973, AM in Edn., 1975. ESL tchr. U.S. Peace Corps, Mango, Togo, 1969-72; resident dir. U. Mich., Ann Arbor, 1973-75, tchg. asst., 1975-76; ESL tchr., tchr. trainer Instituto de Estudios Sociales, Santo Domingo, Domincan Republic, 1977-80; elem. tchr. Carol Morgan Sch., Santo Domingo, 1979-80; migrant/bilingual tchr. Van Buren Intermediate Sch. Dist., Lawrence, Mich., 1980—; coord. Migrant Even Start, Lawrence, 1993-94. Co-author (ESL songs) Singing Time, 1984-85. Sec. Creative Arts Acad. PTO, Benton Harbor, Mich., 1990-93, pres., 1993-94; treas. Van Buren Intermediate Sch. Dist. Edn. Assn., Lawrence, 1984-88, pres., 1988-89; mem. Bd. Youth Edn.-U.C.C., Coloma, Mich., 1992—. Recipient Irma Ramos Bilingual Educator award Mich. Edn. Assn., Lansing, 1988. Mem. Tchrs. English to Speakers of Other Langs., Friends of Togo. Office: Van Buren Intermediate Sch Dist 701 S Paw Paw St Lawrence MI 49064

MEYER, SUSAN THERESA, business and training industry consultant; b. Ames, Iowa, Mar. 29, 1950; d. Robert William Keirs and Jeanne Marion (Thomas) Kaufer; m. John Allen Meyer, Dec. 18, 1972; children: Katherine Jeanne, Robert John. BS cum laude, U. Wis., 1972; MBA, Ea. Mich. U., 1982. Cert. spl. edn. tchr., Wis., Va. Spl. edn. tchr. Prince George (Va.) Pub. Schs., 1972-73; acct. DEMPUBCO Printing Co., Colorado Springs, Colo., 1973-74; adminstr., dir. EEO Dept. of Army, Frankfurt, Fed. Rep. of Germany, 1974-77; program coordinator Wake Up La., New Orleans, 1977-78; buyer Ford Motor Co., Dearborn, Mich., 1978-81; fgn. procurement specialist Ford Motor Co., Dearborn, 1981-85; pres. Mgmt. Recruiters of No. Del., Wilmington, 1985-91, The Obermeyer Group Ltd., Fort Collins, Colo., 1991—; dir. Small Bus. and Internat. Devel. Ctr., Ft. Collins, Colo., 1993-94; adj. prof. mktg. U. No. Colo., 1991—, Colo. State U., 1992—; cons. Fed. Women's Program, Frankfurt, 1974-77. Adv. bd. Women's Devel. Coun./Women Bus. Owners, Ft. Collins, 1993—, Ft. Collins Chamber Bus. Assistance Ctr., Ft. Collins, 1992—; mem. adv. bd. Comty. Involvement for Bank One, Ft. Collins, 1993—. Mem. Wilmington Women in Bus., Nat. Assn. Female Execs. Republican. Roman Catholic. Home: 6465 Hidden Springs Rd Fort Collins CO 80526 Office: The Obermeyer Group Ltd PO Box 270711 Fort Collins CO 80527-0711

MEYER-BORDERS, JANET LOUISE, artist; b. Shreveport, La., June 20, 1955; d. Russell Barton Meyer and Shirley Ann (Emerson) Rydberg; m. Steven Fredric Cogliano, Apr. 21, 1975 (div. Apr. 1981); 1 child, Jeremy Steven Borders; m. Douglas Harold Borders, June 26, 1982; 1 child, Heather Nicole Borders. AA, Coll. of the Desert, 1983; student, Saddleback Coll., 1990; BA in Art and Art History, U. Calif., Santa Cruz, 1993. docent, artist Long Marine Lab., Santa Cruz, 1992—. Tchr. Lawndale (Calif.) Unified Schs., 1976-77; with Employment Devel. Dept., Mammoth Lakes, Calif., 1978-79, Standard Mortgage Co., Palm Desert, Calif., 1980-82, IBM, Gilroy, Calif., 1983-84, Holidy Host RV Ctr., Scotts Valley, Calif., 1985-86; sec. Classic Framing Constrn. Co., Irvine, Calif., 1988-89; co-owner Santa Cruz Constrn., 1993—. One woman shows include Bridge Gallery, 1992, St. George Expresso, S.C., 1994; Group shows include Saddleback Coll., Calif., 1990, Rt. 66 Gallup, N.Mex., 1990, UCSC Student Ctr., Calif., 1991, 92, 93, Squid Festival, Santa Cruz, Calif., 1991. Mem. Western Arts Assn. Conservators. Democrat. Roman Catholic. Home: 213 Continental St Santa Cruz CA 95060 Office: Wildflowers Studio PO Box 463 Santa Cruz CA 95061

MEYERROSE, SARAH LOUISE, bank holding company executive; b. Jefferson City, Mo., Nov. 26, 1955; d. William J. and Mary L. (Fricke) Wollenburg; m. Michael J. Meyerrose, Aug. 18, 1978. BA, Vanderbilt U., 1978, MBA, 1987. Chartered fin. analyst. Corp. fin. asst. Commerce Union Corp., Nashville, 1978-80, money market sales rep., 1980-82; asst. treas. First Tenn. Nat. Corp., Memphis, 1982-84, v.p., treas., 1984-88, v.p. sr. fin. officer, 1988-90; sr. v.p. fin. & adminstrn. First Tenn. Nat. Corp., 1990-93; exec. v.p. retail, mortgage, trust First Tenn. Bank, N.A., Johnson City, 1994—; guest lectr. Vanderbilt U., 1987; instr. Am. Inst. Banking, Memphis, 1985, Tenn. Bankers Assn., Nashville, 1987, 88, 89. Chair-elect Johnson City Symphony Orch., 1994, chair, 1995—. Mem. Fin. Analysts Fedn., Econs. Club Memphis. Office: First Tenn Bank NA 2112 N Roan Johnson City TN 37601

MEYERS, ANN ELIZABETH, sports broadcaster; b. San Diego, Mar. 26, 1955; d. Robert Eugene and Patricia Ann (Burke); m. Donald Scott Drysdale, Nov. 1, 1986; children: Donald Scott Jr., Darren John, Drew Ann. Grad., UCLA, 1978. Profl. basketball player N.J. Gems, 1979-80; profl. basketball player Ind. Pacers NBA, 1979; sports broadcaster Ind. Pacers, 1979-80; sportscaster men's basketball U. Hawaii, Honolulu, 1981-82; sportscaster men's and women's basketball UCLA, 1982-84, 89—; sportscaster volleyball, basketball, softball, tennis ESPN, 1981-94; sportscaster Olympic Games ABC, L.A., 1984; sportscaster volleyball, softball, tennis, basketball, soccer Sportsvision, 1985-87; sportscaster volleyball, basketball, softball Prime Ticket, 1985-95; sportscaster CBS-TV, 1991—; sportscaster Goodwill Games, WTBS, 1986, 90. Winner Silver medal Montreal Olympics, 1976, Gold medal Pan Am. Games, 1975, Silver medal, 1979; All-Am. UCLA, 1975, 76, 77, 78; 1st woman named to Hall of Fame UCLA, 1987; named to

Women's Sports Hall of Fame, 1987, Orange County Sports Hall of Fame, 1985, Calif. High Sch. Hall of Fame, 1990, Basketball Hall of Fame, 1993. Office: c/o Lampros and Roberts 16615 Lark Ave # 101 Los Gatos CA 95030-2439

MEYERS, CAROLE TERWILLIGER, writer; b. San Francisco; married; 2 children. BA in Anthropology, San Francisco State U.; Teaching Credential, Fresno State U. Editor, pubr. Family Travel Guides Catalogue, 1986—; pub. Carousel Press, 1975—; columnist: San Francisco Examiner, 1989-91, San Jose Mercury News, 1978-79, 89-90, Parents' Press, 1980-90, San Francisco Focus, 1988-90, Calif. Mag., 1981-88, Goodlife Mag., 1983, Calif. Travel Report, 1982-83, Oakland Mag., 1980, Adventure West Mag., 1994—; contbr. numerous articles to mags. including Parenting, Family Fun, Diablo, Family Cir., Parents, Motorland. Author: How to Organize a Babysitting Cooperative and Get Some Free Time Away from the Kids, 1976, Getting in the Spirit: Annual Bay Area Christmas Events, 1979, Eating Out with the Kids in San Francisco and the Bay Area, 1976, 3d edit. 1985, Weekend Adventures for City-Weary People: Overnight Trips in Northern Calif., 1977, 5th edit. 1993, San Francisco Family Fun, 1990, Miles of Smiles: 101 Great Car Games and Activities, 1992; editor: The Family Travel Guide: An Inspiring Collection of Family-Friendly Vacations, 1995. Bd. advisors San Francisco Internat. Toy Ctr. and Mus., 1986-91. Recipient 1st place in self-published travel book category (for Weekend Adventures) Travel Pub. News Awards, 1990. Mem. Internat. Food, Wine and Travel Writers Assn., Bay Area Travel Writers, Northern Calif. Book Publicists Assn. Office: PO Box 6061 Albany CA 94706-0061

MEYERS, CHRISTINE LAINE, publishing and media executive, consultant; b. Detroit, Mar. 7, 1949; d. Ernest Robert and Eva Elizabeth (Laine) M.; 1 child, Kathryn Laine; m. Oliver S. Moore III, May 12, 1990. BA, U. Mich., 1968. Editor, indsl. relations Diesel div. Gen. Motors Corp., Detroit, 1968; nat. advt. mgr. J.L. Hudson Co., Detroit, 1969-76, mgr. internal sales promotion, 1972-73, dir. pub., 1973-76; nat. advt. mgr. Pontiac Motor div., Mich., 1976-78; pres., owner Laine Meyers Assocs., Troy, Mich., 1978—; dir. Internat. Inst. Met. Detroit, Inc. Contbr. articles to profl. publs. Mem. bus. adv. council Cen. Mich. U., 1977-79; mem. pub. adv. com. on jud. candidates Oakland County Bar Assn.; mem. adv. bd. Birmingham Community Hosp., bd. dirs. YMCA, Mich., 1992—; Named Mich. Ad Woman of Yr., 1976, one of Top 10 Working Women Glamour mag., 1978, one of 100 Best and Brightest Advt. Age, 1987, one of Mich.'s top 25 female bus. owners Nat. Assn. Women Bus. Owners, One of Top 10 Women Owned Bus., Mich., 1994; recipient Vanguard award Women in Communications, 1986. Mem. Internat. Assn. Bus. Communicators, Adcraft Club, Women's Advt. Club (1st v.p. 1975), Women's Econ. Club (pres. 1976-77), Internat. Women's Forum Mich. (pres. 1986—), Internat. Inst. of Detroit (bd. dirs. 1986-89), Detroit C. of C., Troy C. of C., Mortar Board, Quill and Scroll, Pub. Relations Com. Women for United Found., Founders Soc. Detroit Inst. Arts, Fashion Group, Pub. Relations Soc. Am., First Soc. Detroit (exec. com. 1970-71), Kappa Tau Alpha. Home: 1780 Kensington Rd Bloomfield Hills MI 48304-2428 Office: Laine Meyers Inc 3645 Crooks Rd Troy MI 48084-1642

MEYERS, DOROTHY, educator, writer; b. Chgo., Jan. 9, 1927; d. Gilbert and Harriet (Levitt) King; m. William J. Meyers, Oct. 9, 1947; children: Lynn, Jeanne. BA, U. Chgo., 1945, MA, 1961, postgrad.; postgrad. Columbia U., New Sch. Social Rsch., Northwestern U. Instr. sr. adults, Chgo. Bd. and/City Colls. Chgo., 1961-78; coord. pub. affairs forum and health maintenance program City Colls. Chgo.-Jewish Community Ctrs., Chgo., 1975-78; lectr. adult program City Colls. Chgo., 1984; tchr. Dade County Adult Edn. Program, Miami, Fla., 1983-85; discussion leader Brandeis U. Adult Edn., 1985-86; cons., lectr. in field. Contbr. articles to profl. jours. Chmn. legis. PTA; discussion leader Great Decisions, 1984-86; chmn. civic assembly Citizens Sch. Com.; v.p. community rels. Womens Fedn. and Jewish United Fund; discussion leader LWV, Gt. Decisions, Fgn. Policy Assn.; program chmn. Jewish Community Ctrs., 1966-67, mem. sr. adult com.; bd. dirs. coun. Jewish Elderly, Open U.; mem. art and edn. com. Chgo. Mayor's Com. for Sr. Citizens and Handicapped; mem. com. on media Met. Coun. on Aging; active Bon Secour's Villa Maria Hosp.; founder Mt. Sinai Hosp., Miami Beach; sponsor Miami Heart Inst.; active Royal Notable Alzheimer Care Unit-Douglas Home Miami; com. mem. March of Dimes; ambassador Project Newborn U. Miami Pre Natal Unit. Mem. Am. Sociol. Assn., Gerontol. Assn., Nat. Coun. Aging, Nat. Coun. Jewish Women, Women's Auxiliary Jewish Community Ctr., Chgo. Met. Sr. Forum (media com.), Coun. Women Chgo. Real Estate Bd., Women in Communications, Chgo. Real Estate Bd., Nat. Assn. Real Estate Bds., Cultural Ctr. (Miami, Fla.), Mus. Art Ft. Lauderdale, Miami Internat. Press Club, Gastrointestinal Rsch. Found., Brandeis U., Art Inst. Chgo., Mus. Contemporary Art, Soc. Contemporary Art, Mus. Art Boca Raton, Brandeis Women's Auxiliary, Circumnavigator Club (Chgo. and Fla. chpts.). Office: 77 W Washington St Chicago IL 60602-2801

MEYERS, ELEANOR SCOTT, seminary president; b. Kansas City, Mo., Jan. 3, 1940; d. Walter A. and Dorothy Ann (Davis) M.; m. Brower R. Burchill, 1960 (div. 1978); children: Gaile, Scott B. BA in Edn., Fla. State U., 1961; student, Menninger Found., 1974-75; MA in Religion, Yale U., 1977; MS in Sociology, U. Wis., 1981, PhD in Sociology, 1985. Ordained to ministry Christian Ch. (Disciples of Christ), 1978. Tchr. Tallahassee Pub. Schs., 1961-63, Las Alamos (N.Mex.) Pub. Schs., 1966-68; pvt. practice artist, 1968-74; exec. dir. U. Kans. YWCA, YMCA, Lawrence, 1972-79; nat. program dir. World Student Christian Fedn., Toronto, Can., 1979-82; assoc. min. 1st Congrl. Ch. United Ch. of Christ, Madison, Wis., 1981-84; asst. prof. Union Theol. Sem., N.Y.C., 1985-88; acad. dean St. Paul Sch. Theology, Kansas City, Mo., 1988-91; pres. Pacific Sch. Religion, Berkeley, Calif., 1991—; cons. in field. Editor: Envisioning the New City: A Reader in Urban Ministry, 1992. Founder, bd. dirs. Women's Transitional Care Ctr., Lawrence, Kans., 1977-79; active planning com. Internat. Conf. on Edn. for Justice, 1979-82; chair Wis. conf. Commn. on Lay Life and Leadership, United Ch. Christ, 1984-85; nat. panel evaluators ch. finance coun. Christian Ch. (Disciples of Christ), 1988-89. Mem. Am. Acad. Religion, Soc. Scientific Study of Religion. Office: Pacific Sch of Religion 1798 Scenic Ave Berkeley CA 94709

MEYERS, JAN, congresswoman; b. Lincoln, Nebr., July 20, 1928; m. Louis Meyers; children—Valerie, Philip. A.A. in Fine Arts, William Woods Coll., 1948; B.A. in Communications (hon.), U. Nebr.-Lincoln, 1951; LittD, William Woods Coll., 1986; LLD (hon.), Baker U., 1993. Mem. Overland Park (Kans.) City Coun., 1967-72; pres. Overland (Kans.) Park City Council; mem. Kans. Senate, 1972-84, chmn. pub. health and welfare com., local govt. com.; mem. 99th-103rd Congresses from 3rd Kans. Dist., 1985—, mem. com. internat. rels., sml. bus. com., com. chmn. on econ. and ednl. opportunities. 3rd Dist. co-chmn. Bob Dole for U.S. Senate, 1968; chmn. Johnson County Bob Bennett For Gov., 1974; mem. Johnson County Community Coll. Found.; bd. dirs. Johnson County Mental Health Assn. Recipient Outstanding Elected Ofcl. of Yr. award Assn. Community Mental Health Ctrs. Kans., Woman of Achievement Matrix award Women in Communications, Disting. Service award Bus. and Profl. Women Kansas City, William Woods Alumna award of distinction, Community Service award Jr. League Kansas City, 1st Disting. Legislator award Kans. Assn. Community Colls., Outstanding Service award Kans. Library Assn., United Community Services, Kans. Pub. Health Assn., award Gov.'s Conf. Child Abuse and Neglect, Outstanding Legislator award Kans. Action for Children, Friend award Nat. Assn. County Park and Recreation Ofcls., 1987, Disting. Alumna award, 1991, numerous others. Mem. LWV (past pres. Shawnee Mission). Methodist. Office: US Ho of Reps Rayburn House Office Bldg 2303 Rayburn House Office Washington DC 20515

MEYERS, JUDITH ANN, education educator; b. Scranton, Pa., Aug. 5, 1946; d. Paul Meyers and Elaine Jenkins; m. Stuart M. Olinsky, July 10, 1977; children: Seth, Noah. BA with honors, Rutgers U., 1969; MA in Early Childhood Edn., Kean Coll., 1973. Cert. tchr. early childhood K-8, N.J., Pa. Tchr. Tchr.'s Corp., Newark, 1970-71; head tchr. Arlington Ave. Presch., East Orange, N.J., 1972-75, ednl. dir., 1976-78, exec. dir., 1979-81; program developer for early childhood program, instr. early childhood Williamsport (Pa.) Area C.C./Penn Tech., 1987-89; community mem. curriculum rev. com. Penn Tech. C.C., Williamsport, 1990-91; parent mem. West Branch. Sch., tchr. selection com., 1991-93, tchr. evaluation com., 1991-93, curriculum devel. com., 1993. Author, program developer early childhood edn. courses. Chmn. Victorian Williamsport Preservation Com., 1993-94; bd. dirs. Community Theatre, Williamsport, 1993-94. Home: 150 Selkirk Rd Williamsport PA 17701-1869

MEYERS, KAREN DIANE, lawyer, educator, corporate officer; b. Cin., July 8, 1956; d. Willard Paul and Camille Jeannette (Schutte) M.; m. William J. Jones, Mar. 27, 1982. BA summa cum laude, Thomas More Coll., 1974; MBA, MEd, Xavier U., 1978; JD, U. Ky., Covington, 1978. Bar: Ohio 1978, Ky. 1978; CLU; CPCU. Clk. to mgr. Baldwin Co., Cin., 1970-78; adj. prof. bus. Thomas More Coll., Crestview Hill, Ky., 1978—; asst. sec., asst. v.p., sr. counsel The Ohio Life Ins. Co., Hamilton, 1978-91; prin. KD Meyers & Assocs., 1991; v.p. Benefit Designs, Inc., 1991—. Bd. dirs. ARC, Hamilton, 1978-83, vol., 1978—; bd. dirs. YWCA, Hamilton, 1985-91; v.p. Benefit Designs Inc., 1991—. Gardner Found. fellow, 1968-71; recipient Ind. Progress award Bus. & Profl. Women, 1990. Fellow Life Mgmt. Inst. Atlanta; mem. ABA, Soc. Chartered Property Casualty Underwriters (instr. 1987—), Cin. Bar Assn., Butler County Bar Assn., Ohio Bar Assn., Ky. Bar Assn. Roman Catholic. Home: 7903 Hickory Hill Dr Cincinnati OH 45241-1363

MEYERS, LYNN BETTY, architect; b. Chgo., Dec. 2, 1952; d. William J. and Dorothy (King) M.; m. Dana Terp, May 17, 1975; children: Sophia, Rachel. Student, Royal Acad. Architecture, Copenhagen, Denmark, 1971; BArch, Washington U., St. Louis, 1974, MArch, 1977. Registered architect, Ill., Fla. Architect Holabird & Root Architects, Chgo., 1973, 76, Jay Alpert Architects, Woodbridge, Conn., 1976, City of Chgo. Bur. Architects, 1978-80; sole practice architecture Chgo., 1980-82; prin., architect Terp Meyers Architects, Chgo., 1982—; real estate salesman, Ill., 1991, Fla.; v.p. Paradise Grove Devel. Corp., 1991—. Exhbns. include: Centre George Pompidou, Paris, 1978, Fifth Internat. Congress Union Internat. Des Femmes Architects, Seattle, 1979, Frumkin Struve Gallery, Chgo., 1981, Art. Inst. Chgo., 1983, Inst. Francais d'Architecture, Paris, 1983, Mus. Sci. and Industry, Chgo., 1985, Hyde Park Art Ctr., 1990, 91, Chgo. Architecture and Design Art Inst. 1923-1993, 1993; pub. in profl. jours. including Progressive Architecture, Modo Design, Inland Architect, 1984, Chgo. Archtl. Jour., 1983, L.A. Architect; work featured in various archtl. books; exhibited 150 Yrs. of Chgo. Architecture, Mus. Sci. and Industry, Chgo., 1985, Chgo. Women in Architecture - Progress and Evolution, Chgo. Hist. Soc., 1974-84. Recipient Progressive Architecture mag. award, 1980, citation Archtl. Design, 1980. Mem. AIA (task force com. for 1992 World's Fair, 1st place award L.A. Real Problems Competition 1986, Art By Architects award 1989, Art award 1990), Union Internat. Des Femmes Architects, Chgo. Women in Architecture (v.p. 1980-81, Allied Arts award 1974), Young Chgo. Architects. Office: Terp Meyers Architects 919 N Michigan Ave Chicago IL 60611-1601

MEYERS, MARY ANN, writer, consultant; b. Sodus, N.Y., Sept. 30, 1937; d. Harold Galpin and Clarice Mildred (Daniel) Dye; m. John Matthew Meyers, Aug. 22, 1959; children: Andrew Christopher, Anne Kathryn. BA magna cum laude, Syracuse U., 1959; MA, U. Pa., 1965, PhD, 1976. Editorial asst. Ladies' Home Jour., Phila., 1959-62; editor, asst. dir. news bur. U. Pa., Phila., 1962-65, asst. to pres., 1973-75, univ. sec., lectr. in Am. civilization, 1980-90; contbg. writer The Pennsylvania Gazette, Phila., 1965—; dir. coll. rels., editor Haverford Horizons, lectr. in religion Haverford (Pa.) Coll., 1977-80; pres. The Annenberg Found., St. Davids, Pa., 1990-92. Author: A New World Jerusalem, 1983; contbg. author: Death in America, 1975, Gladly Learn, Gladly Teach, 1978, Coping with Serious Illness, 1980, Religion in American Life, 1987; contbr. articles to profl. jours. Judge recognition program Coun. for Advancement and Support Edn., Washington, 1977-78, chair creative editing and writing workshop, 1978; mem. Picker Found. Program on Human Qualities in Medicine, N.Y.C. and Phila., 1980-83; del. Phila.-Leningrad Sister Cities Project, 1986; trustee U. Pa. Press, 1985—, vice chmn. U. Pa., 250th Anniversary Commn., 1987-90, mem. steering com. of bd. trustees, U. Pa., Annenberg Sch. for Communication, 1990-92, mem. bd. overseers, U. Pa., Sch. Arts and Scis., 1990—; mem. steering com. of bd. trustees Annenberg Ctr. for Communication, U. So. Calif., L.A., 1990-92, The Annenberg Washington Program in Communications Policy Studies of Northwestern U., Washington, 1990-92; trustee Am. Acad. Polit. and Social Sci., 1992—, World Affairs Coun. Phila., 1990—; dir. Diagnostic and Rehab. Ctr., Phila., 1993—. Recipient Excellence award Women in Communications, Inc., 1973-74, award for pub. affairs reporting Newsweek/Coun. for Advancement and Support Edn., 1977, Silver medal Coun. for Advancement and Support Edn., 1986. Mem. Cosmopolitan Club, Sunday Breakfast Club, Phi Beta Kappa. Roman Catholic. Home: 217 Gypsy Ln Wynnewood PA 19096

MEYERS, MELISSA CAROLINE, lawyer, nurse; b. Syracuse, N.Y., Oct. 3, 1954; d. Edwin Clarke and Phyllis (Schiess) M. BSN, U. Rochester, 1976; MA in Nursing, NYU, 1983; JD, Yeshiva U., 1992. Bar: N.Y.; RN; cert. oncology nurse. Staff nurse Montefiore Hosp., Bronx, N.Y., 1976-77; clin. nurse II Meml. Sloan-Kettering Cancer Ctr., N.Y.C., 1977-79, clin. instr., 1979-80; nurse specialist NYU Med. Ctr., 1981-89; adj. prof. Hunter-Bellevue Coll. Nursing, N.Y.C., 1986-89; assoc. atty. Belair & Evans, N.Y.C., 1992—. Author: (with others) Oncology Nursing, Advances, Treatments and Trends, 1990; feature editor Cancer Nursing Jour., 1981. Home: 330 E 33rd St Apt 3E New York NY 10016-9427 Office: Belair & Evans 61 Broadway New York NY 10006

MEYERS, NANCY JANE, screenwriter, producer; b. Phila., Dec. 8, 1949; d. Irving H. and Patricia (Lemisch) M. BA, Am. U., Washington, 1971. Co-writer, prodr.: (films) Private Benjamin (Acad. Award nominee, Writers Guild award 1980), Irreconcilable Differences, 1984, Baby Boom, 1987, Father of the Bride, 1991, I Love Trouble, 1994, Father of the Bride II, 1995. Mem. ASCAP, Acad. Motion Picture Arts and Scis., Writers Guild Am. West. Office: care ICM 8942 Wilshire Blvd Beverly Hills CA 90211-1908

MEYERS, PAMELA SUE, lawyer; b. Lakewood, N.J., June 13, 1951; d. Morris Leon and Isabel (Leibowitz) M.; m. Gerald Stephen Greenberg, Aug. 24, 1975; children: David Stuart, Allison Brooke. AB with distinction, Cornell U., 1973; JD cum laude, Harvard U., 1976. Bar: N.Y. 1977, Ohio 1990. Assoc. Stroock & Stroock & Lavan, N.Y.C., 1976-80; staff v.p., asst. gen. counsel Am. Premier Underwriters, Inc., Cin., 1980—. Mem. Am. Soc. Corp. Secs. (membership chmn. 1990-91), Cin. Bar Assn., Greater Cin. Women's Bar Assn., Harvard Club of Cin. (bd. dirs. 1993—), Phi Beta Kappa. Jewish. Home: 3633 Carpenters Creek Dr Cincinnati OH 45241-3824 Office: Am Premier Underwriters 1 E 4th St Cincinnati OH 45202

MEYERS, THEDA MARIA, textile company executive; b. Bremen, Germany, Feb. 16; came to U.S. 1957; d. Johann-Friedrich and Christophina E.L.J. (Fentrohs) Ficke; m. Laurence Jay Meyers, Oct. 2, 1960 (div. 1970); 1 child, Jayson Bennett. Dipl., U. Bremen, 1956; student, Fashion Inst. Tech., N.Y.C., 1960. Artist-stylist Rosewood Fabrics, N.Y.C., 1960-62; textile stylist Belding Corticelli, N.Y.C., 1962-65; chief designer Jerry Mann of Calif., L.A., 1969-74; fashion designer Sunbow Ltd., Prisma Corp., L.A., 1974-81, Frig & Frag Inc., L.A., 1981-83, Jonathan Martin, L.A., 1983-85; textile stylist, v.p. design E.M.D.A.Y., Inc., L.A., 1985-92; cons. Theda Meyers Consultancy, L.A., 1993—; part-time tchr. Fashion Inst. of Design & Merchandising, L.A., to 1974; part-time judge Trade Tech. Coll., L.A. to 1981; textile designer extensive nat. and internat. experience in womenswear apparel design and textile design. designer Calif. apparel. Mem. NAFE. Office: 600 W 9th St Ste 1003 Los Angeles CA 90015-4328

MEYERSICK, SHARON KAY, insurance administrator, nurse; b. Waynesville, Mo., Mar. 19, 1945; d. James Monroe and Fannie Mae (Williams) Atkinson; m. Bernard William Meyersick Jr., July 27, 1974 (dec. May 1992). AD in Nursing, Mercamec Community Coll., St. Louis, 1970; BS in Nursing, Tarkio Coll., Mo., 1983; postgrad., Webster Coll., St. Louis, 1988. Staff nurse Normandy Osteopathic Hosp., St. Louis, 1970-76, head nurse, 1976-79, instr. nursing edn., 1979-81; quality assurance nurse Barnes Hosp., St. Louis, 1981-84; review analyst Blue Cross-Blue Shield of Mo., St. Louis, 1985-87, supr. program review, 1987-91; patient care coord. Prudential Ins. Co. Am./St. Louis Health Care Mgmt., St Louis, 1991—. Office: Prudential Ins Co Am Saint Louis Health Care Mgmt 12312 Olive Blvd Saint Louis MO 63141-6448

MEYN, SUSAN STIRLING, counselor; b. Pitts., May 6, 1946; d. James Walker and Elizabeth Craig (Young) Stirling; m. James Christopher Meyn, May 6, 1967 (div. Nov. 1977); children: Jennifer Lynn, Jeffrey David. BA, Bucknell U., 1969; M in Counseling, Ariz. State U., 1979; cert. in gestalt therapy, Gestalt Inst. Phoenix, 1981. Cert. prof. counselor, Ariz. Staff therapist Terros, Inc., Phoenix, 1979-81; clinician Tri-City Cmty. Behavioral Health Ctr., Mesa, Ariz., 1981-86; social worker II Desert Samaritan Hosp., Mesa, Ariz., 1986-88, 89-92; pvt. practice Phoenix, 1986—. Vol. counselor, trainer Shanti Group, Phoenix, 1988-90. Mem. ACA. Democrat. Home: 7607 E Minnezona Ave Scottsdale AZ 85251-2101 Office: Counseling Svcs 4545 N 36th St #212 Phoenix AZ 85018

MEYR, SHARI LOUISE, computer consultant, computer company executive; b. San Diego, Dec. 6, 1951; d. Herchell M. and Etta Louise (Bass) Knight; m. William Earl Groom, Oct. 22, 1977 (div. Sept. 1989), Herbert Carl Meyr Jr., Feb. 23, 1990. AS in Fire Scis., San Diego Mesa Coll., 1976. T.O.S.S. specialist Spectrum Scis. & Software, Mountain Home AFB, 1989-94; equestrian instr. Summerwind Ctr., Mountain Home, 1979-91; Chow Chow breeder Meyr Kennels, Mountain Home, 1990—; multimedia P.C. cons., CEO Access to Answers, Mountain Home, 1990—. Mem. NRA, U.S. Ski Assn. (competition lic., alpine ofcl., assoc. coach, master's alpine racer 1991—), Summerwind Riding Club (founder, pres. 1981-89), Mountain Home Ski Club (founder, bd. dirs. 1991—), Bogus Basin Ski Club, Sun Valley Ski Club, Amateur Trapshooting Assn. (life), Mensa. Home: 570 E 16th N Mountain Home ID 83647-1717

MIA, ANDREA, film producer; b. San Francisco, June 30, 1966; d. Martin Gary Groder and Raquel Strauss. BA, Columbia Coll., 1988; MFA, U. So. Calif., 1993. Asst. English tchr. Japan Exch. and Teaching Program, Osaka, 1988-90; creative assoc. Chestnut Hill Prodns., Santa Monica, Calif., 1992—. Producer: (documentaries) Setting Boundaries, 1993 (student Emmy award in documentary), Neighbors (Anti-Defamation League humanitarian award 1993). Office: Chestnut Hill Prodns 1460 4th St # 210 Santa Monica CA 90401

MIASKIEWICZ, THERESA ELIZABETH, secondary educator; b. Salem, Mass., Aug. 29, 1933; d. Chester and Anastasia (Zmijewski) M. BA, Emmanuel Coll., Boston, 1954. Cert. tchr., Mass.; lic. real estate broker, Mass. Tchr. fgn. lang. dept. Salem Sch. Dept., 1954—; head tchr. Salem High Sch., 1954-94;, 1990-94, retired, 1994; vol. Salem Hosp., 1994—; playground instr. City of Salem, summers 1951-54; mem. vis. com. NEASC. Vol. Salem Hosp., 1979-88, House of Seven Gables, Salem, summers 1987-89; active North Shore Med. Ctr. Aux. Mem. Am. Assn. Ret. Persons (NRTA divsn.), Ret. State, County and Mcpl. Employees Assn., Mass. Ret. Tchrs. Assn., Mass. Fedn. Polish Women's Clubs (v.p. 1988-89, regional chmn. scholarship com.), Polish Bus. and Profl. Women's Club Greater Boston (past corr. sec., chmn. scholarship com., pres. 1988-89).

MICH, CONNIE RITA, mental health nurse, educator; b. Nebr., Feb. 5, 1926; d. Henry B. and Anna (Stratman) Redel; m. Richard Mich. BSN, Alverno Coll.; postgrad., Marquette U.; MSN, Cath. U. Am. Asst. clin. dir. in-patient svcs. Fond du Lac (Wis.) County Health Ctr., 1974-78; head nurse, program coord. acute psychiat. unit St. Agnes Hosp., Fond du Lac, 1979-83; mental health clinician Immanuel Med. Ctr., Omaha, 1984-89; instr., clin. supr., asst. prof. psychiat. mental health Coll. St. Mary, Omaha, 1989-93; med. programs dir. Inst. Computer Sci. Ltd., 1989—; program dir. med. programs ICS Career Sch., Omaha; chair Examining Coun. on RNs; writer items State Bd. Test Pool Examination; pres. Milw. Coun. Cath. Nurses; vice chair Wis. Conf. Group Psychiat. Nursing Practice. Mem. Sigma Theta Tau, Pi Gamma Mu.

MICHAEL, DENISE MARIE, communications executive; b. Wyandotte, Mich., Sept. 14, 1960; d. Arthur Thomas and Gloria Jean Francis (Kudron) Sigler; m. Richard James Michael, Oct. 3, 1980 (div. Jan. 1990). B Comm. Arts, Oakland U., Rochester, Mich., 1984. Computer typesetter Entertainment Publs., Troy, Mich., 1981-86; systems cons. Resource Data Systems Corp., Southfield, Mich., 1986-90; applications engr. Info. Decisions, Inc., Indpls., 1990-92; v.p. ConTech, Inc., Carmel, Ind., 1992—, sec.-treas., 1992—. Producer: (film) Detroit News-Scholastic Writing, 1976; author: (poem) World;s Best Poets, 1992. Tutor Greater Indpls. Lit. League, 1991—; camp counselor Muscular Dystrophy Assn., Indpls., 1993—. Mem. Ind. Folk Music and Mountain Dulcimer Soc., Blues Soc. Ind. Office: ConTech Inc 776 Wedgewood Ln Carmel IN 46033-9268

MICHAEL, DOROTHY ANN, nurse, naval officer; b. Lancaster, Pa., Sept. 20, 1950; d. Richard Linus and Mary Ruth (Hahn) Michael. Diploma, R.N., Montgomery Hosp. Sch. Nursing, Norristown, Pa., 1971; BS in Nursing, George Mason U., 1980; MS in Nursing U. Tex. Health Sci. Ctr., 1985. Commd. ensign USN, 1970, advanced through grades to capt. Nurse Corps, 1994; staff nurse Nat. Naval Med. Ctr., Bethesda, Md., 1971-73; charge nurse Naval Hosp., Guantanamo Bay, Cuba, 1973-74, Naval Regional Med. Ctr., Phila., 1974-76, Naval Hosp., Keflavik, Iceland, 1977, Naval Hosp., Bethesda, 1980-84, sr. nurse, asst. officer-in-charge Br. Med. Clinic, Naval Weapons Ctr., China Lake, Calif., 1986-89; coord. quality assurance Naval Hosp., Oakland, Calif., 1989-92, assoc. dir. inpatient nursing, 1992-93; divsn. officer USNS Mercy, Persian Gulf, 1990-91, assoc. dir. surg. nursing, 1993—; splty. advisor to dir. Navy Nurse Corp., Navy Med. Command, Washington, 1983-84. V.p. Deepwood Homeowners Assn., Reston, Va., 1978-82; advisor, com. mem. Reston Found., 1979. Recipient R.W. Bjorklund Mgmt. Innovator award Kern County, Calif., 1988, Comdr.'s Award for Outstanding Professionalism in Pub. Health Support, 1988. Mem. Vietnam Vets Am., Vets. Fgn. Wars, Orgn. Nurse Execs., Am. Nurses Assn. (cert. nursing adminstrn.), Am. Legion, Sigma Theta Tau. Roman Catholic. Home: 2510 Lynn Ave Concord CA 94520-3013

MICHAEL, MARY AMELIA FURTADO, retired headmaster; m. Eugene G. Michael; children: David, Douglas, Gregory. BA, Albertus Magnus Coll.; MS, U. Bridgeport, 1975; CAS, Fairfield U., 1982. Cert. secondary sch. sci. tchr., ednl. adminstr. Housemaster, sci. tchr. Fairfield (Conn.) Pub. Schs., adminstrv. housemaster, sci. tchr., sci. dept. coord., 1992, retired, 1992; freelance fin. rsch. and investment writer and cons., 1994—. Author: The Art and Science of Cooking, 1994; contbr. articles to profl. jours. Mem. AAUW, LWV, Conn. Assn. Suprs. and Curriculum, Fairfield Sch. Adminstrs. Assn., Retired Educators of Fairfield, Fairfield Hist. Soc. Home: 942 Valley Rd Fairfield CT 06432-1630

MICHAEL, MARY ELLEN, instructional designer; b. St. Louis, Sept. 11, 1942; d. James Charles and Mary Agnes (Woodworth) Jennings; m. Gary Raymond Michael, July 14, 1972. BS, U. Mo., 1964; MA, U. Ill., 1968, U. Ill., 1972; postgrad., U. Ill., 1980. Elem. tchr. St. Louis County Schs., St. Louis, 1964-68; rsch. assoc. Libr. Rsch. Ctr., U. Ill., Urbana, 1971-75, Tex. Tech U., Lubbock, 1978-79; courseware developer Courseware Applications, Champaign, Ill., 1979-82, Duosoft Corp., Champaign, 1983-86; assoc. head Office of Instrnl. Resources U. Ill., Urbana, 1986—; cons. McDonnell Douglas Aircraft, St. Louis, 1986-90, World Bank, Washington, 1992-93. Author: (with Comaromi and Bloom) A Survey of the Dewey Decimal Classification in the U.S. and Canada, 1976; Business Planner, 1982, Citizen Advocacy Resources, 1979; editor Instrnl. Microcomputing Newsletter, U. Ill., 1986-94; contbr. articles to profl. jours. Mem. Post-Polio Support Group, Urbana, 1986-93; coord. Well Spouse Support Group, Champaign County, 1994—; mem. edni. techs. bd. U. Ill., 1992-93. Mem. Educom. Democrat. Office: U Ill Office Instrnl Resources 505 E Armory Ave Rm 182 Urbana IL 61000

MICHAEL, PHYLLIS CALLENDER, composer; b. nr. Berwick, Pa., Dec. 24, 1908; d. Bruce Miles and Emma (Harvey) Callender; grad. Bloomsburg Coll., 1928; B. Mus., U. Extension Conservatory, Chgo., 1953; m. Arthur L. Michael, Aug. 21, 1933; children: Robert Bruce, Keith Winton. Elem. tchr. Berwick Schs., 1928-33; substitute tchr. Shickshinny and Northwest Area, Pa., 1954-66; tchr. Northwest Area High Sch., 1966-71; gen. tchr. piano, organ, theory and voice, 1943-89; hymnwriter, poet, author, composer, 1943—. Recipient first place in Nat. Favorite Hymns contest for Take Thou My Hand, 1953, Cert. of Merit for disting. service to composition outstanding hymns, 1967, and others. Adv. mem. MBLS. Mem. Nat. Ret. Tchrs. Assn., Internat. Platform Assn., Nat. Soc. Lit. and the Arts, Hymn Soc. Am. Author: Poems for Mothers, 1963, Poems From My Heart, 1964,

Beside Still Waters, 1970, Fun to Do Showers, 1971, Bridal Shower Ideas, 1972, Is my Head on Straight, 1976, This Is Christmas, 1985, Quotes, 1986, Surely Goodness and Mercy, 1986, Hi, Lord!, 1987, Bright Tomorrows, 1989, Home Sweet Home, 1991, Reach for the Rose, 1992, God Promised, 1992, Why Me Lord, 1993, Golden Gems, 1994; contbr. songs, articles, poems to books, hymn-books, booklets, mags. and other national and international publications. Address: Berwick Retirement Village II 901 E 16th St Rm 725 Berwick PA 18603

MICHAEL, SANDRA DALE, reproductive endocrinology educator, researcher; b. Sacramento, Calif., Jan. 23, 1945; d. Gordon G. and Ruby F. (Johnson) M.; m. Dennis P. Murr, Aug. 12, 1967 (div. 1974). BA, Calif. State Coll., Sonoma, 1967; PhD, U. Calif., Davis, 1970. NIH predoctoral and postdoctoral fellow U. Calif., Davis, 1970-73, asst. rsch. geneticist, 1973-74; asst. prof. SUNY, Binghamton, 1974-81, assoc. prof., 1981-88, prof. reproductive endocrinology, 1988—, dept. chair, 1992—; mem. NIH Reproductive Endocrinology Study Sect., 1991—; cons., presenter in field; grant reviewer NIH, NSF, USDA and others. Contbr. articles to profl. jours. Vice chair Tri Cities Opera Guild, Binghamton, 1987-90, chair, 1990-92; mem. Harpur Forum, Binghamton, 1987—, SUNY Found., Binghamton, 1990—. Fulbright Sr. scholar Czech Republic, 1994; grantee NIMH, 1976-79, Nat. Cancer Inst., 1977-80, 83-87, Nat. Inst. Environ. Health Scis., 1979-80, NSF, 1981-83, NIH, 1987—. Mem. Endocrine Soc., Soc. for the Study of Reprodn., Soc. for Study of Fertility, Am. Soc. for Immunology of Reprodn., Women in Endocrinology (sec.-treas. 1992—), Soc. for Exptl. Biology and Medicine, N.Y. Acad. Sci., Sigma Xi. Office: State Univ of NY Dept Biol Scis Binghamton NY 13902

MICHAEL, SHARON LYNN, public health administrator, nurse; b. Cumberland, Md., Oct. 21, 1949; d. Okey Ellsworth and Dorothy Ellen (Fresh) M. BSN, U. Md., 1971; MSN, U. Colo., 1974. RN, Colo. Staff nurse VA Adminstrn. Hosp., Washington, 1971-73; head nurse med. clinics Denver Gen. Hosp., 1974-76; pub. health nursing cons. Denver Visiting Nurse Svc., 1976-78; svc. dir. Upjohn Healthcare Svcs., Denver, 1978-79; diabetes nurse educator Colo. Dept. Health, Denver, 1979-80, pub. health nursing cons., 1980-88, chief chronic disease sect., 1988—; owner, cert. orthopedic and mastectomy fitter Chalet du Corset, Englewood, Colo., 1983-92. Contbr. articles to profl. jours. Mem. ANA, Am. Diabetes Assn. Coun. on Health Care Delivery and Pub. Health (sec. 1992-93, program chair 1993-94, vice chair 1994—), Assn. of State and Territorial Chronic Disease Program Dirs. (mem. exec. com. 1994—), Colo. Pub. Health Assn., Phi Kappa Phi, Sigma Theta Tau. Republican. Methodist. Home: 1130 S Ogden St Denver CO 80210 Office: Colo Dept Pub Health & Environ 4300 Cherry Creek Dr S Denver CO 80222-1530

MICHAEL, TAMARA, postmaster; b. Allentown, Pa., June 29, 1949; d. Leo Franklin and Gloria Anna (Kuhns) M.; m. Paul Edwin Stauffer Jr., Mar. 7, 1970 (div. Oct. 1981); 1 child, Sean Michael Stauffer. BA in Art History, Moravian Coll., 1973. Postmaster U.S. Postal Svc., Sumneytown, Pa., 1982-85; dist. women's program coord. U.S. Postal Svc., Cherry Hill, N.J., 1985-86; assoc. office coord. U.S. Postal Svc., New Orleans, 1986-87, supr. delivery and vehicle programs, 1987-90; postmaster U.S. Postal Svc., Gulf Shores, Ala., 1990—. Mem. fin. com. Gulf Shores Meth. Ch., 1993-94; vol. Baldwin County Family Violence Project. Mem. Nat. Assn. Postmasters, Emmaus Jr. Woman's Club (pres. 1984-85). Republican. Home: PO Box 747 Gulf Shores AL 36547-0747 Office: US Postal Svc 2149 W 1st St Gulf Shores AL 36542-3057

MICHAELS, CATHERINE ANN, religious studies educator; b. N.Y.C., Apr. 15, 1950; d. Arthur and Ann Johanna (Ilchert) M. BA, SUNY, Stony Brook, 1972; MS, Fordham U., Bronx, 1976; postgrad., John XXIII Inst. Ea. Ch. Stud., Bronx, 1978-81. Cert. spiritual dir. Religion tchr. Mater Christi High Sch., Astoria, N.Y., 1972-75; asst. dir. religious edn. St. Joan of Arc Ch., Jackson Heights, N.Y., 1976-77; religion tchr. Msgr. Scanlan High Sch., Bronx, 1977-85; dir. religious edn. St. Paul the Apostle Ch., N.Y.C., 1985-86; religion tchr. The Mary Louis Acad., Jamaica, N.Y., 1986—; pastoral leader Charismatic Renewal, Bklyn., 1982-85; spiritual dir., Queens, N.Y., 1974—; facilitator for rap groups Program for the Devel. of Human Potential, Jamaica, 1987—. Recipient Award for Outstanding Contbn. to Higher Edn., St. Francis Coll., Bklyn., 1990. Mem. Nat. Cath. Edn. Assn., religious Edn. Assn. Roman Catholic. Office: The Mary Louis Academy 17621 Wexford Ter Jamaica NY 11432-2926

MICHAELS, CINDY WHITFILL (CYNTHIA G. MICHAELS), instructional services consultant; b. Plainview, Tex., Aug. 31, 1951; d. Glenn Tierce and Ruby Jewell (Nichols) Whitfill; m. Terre Joe Michaels, July 16, 1977. BS, W. Tex. State U., 1972; MS, U. Tex., Dallas, 1976; postgrad. cert., E. Tex. State U., 1982. Registered profl. ednl. diagnostician, Tex.; cert. supr. (gen. and spl. edn.), elem. edn. tchr., K-8 English tchr., spl. edn. tchr. (generic and mental retardation), Tex. Gen. and spl. edn. tchr. Plano (Tex.) Ind. Sch. Dist., 1972-76; dependents' sch. tchr. U.S. Dept. Def., Office of Overseas Edn., Schweinfurt, West Germany, 1976-77; asst. dir. edn. dept. spl. edn. Univ. Affiliated Ctr., U. Tex., Dallas, 1977-80; asst. to acting dir. edn., dept. pediatrics, Southwestern Med. Sch. Univ. Affiliated Ctr., U. Tex. Health Sci. Ctr., Dallas, 1980-82; dir. Collin County Spl. Edn. Coop., Wylie, Tex., 1982-89; dir. spl. svcs. Terrell (Tex.) Ind. Sch. Dist., 1989-92; cons. for at-risk svcs. instrnl. svcs. dept. Region 10 Edn. Svc. Ctr., Richardson, Tex., 1992-93, cons. for staff devel., 1993—; regional cons. presenter and speaker Region 10 Adminstrs. Spl. Edn., Dallas, 1982-92; state conf. presenter and speaker Tex. Assn. Bus. Sch. Bds., Houston, 1991, Tex. Edn. Agy., Austin, 1992, grant reveiwer, 1984; cons. S.W. regional tng. program educators U. So. Miss., 1992-93; regional coord. H.S. mock trial competition State Bar Tex., 1993; regional liaison Tex. Elem. Mentor Network, 1993—; state presenter Tex. Vocat. Educators Conf., 1994. Active Dance-A-Thon for United Cerebral Palsy, Dallas, 1986; area marcher March of Dimes, Dallas, 1990, Park Cities Walkathon for Multiple Sclerosis, 1994. Grantee Job Tng. & Partnership Act, 1991, Carl Perkins Vocat. Program, 1991, Tex. Edn. Agy., 1990, 91, 92; named Outstanding Young Woman in Am., Outstanding Young Women in Am., 1981. Mem. Nat. Coun. Adminstrs. Spl. Edn., Coun. Exceptional Children (chpt. pres. 1973-74), Tex. Assn. Supervision & Curriculum Devel. (mem. leadership team Project Pathways 1992-93), Tex. Coun. Adminstrs. Spl. Edn. (region 10 chairperson 1985-87, state conf. presenter 1989, 92), Tex. Ednl. Diagnosticians Assn. (Dal-Metro v.p., state conf. program chair 1982-83, state conf. presenter 1983), Internat. Reading Assn., Nat. Assn. Supervision and Curriculum Devel., AAUW, Alpha Delta Pi (Richardson alumnae, philanthropy chair 1988, v.p. 1989, 90, 91, v.p./sec. 1993-94, v.p. 1994—). Home: 2613 Oak Point Dr Garland TX 75044 also: 232 Broadmoor Alto NM 88312 Office: Region 10 Edn Svc Ctr PO Box 831300 Richardson TX 75083-1300

MICHAELS, ELISE MARIE See GILLEM, ELISE MARIE

MICHAELS, ELIZABETH ANNE, principal; b. Hanover, Pa., Mar. 3, 1943; children: Elaine, John. BA, Ursinus Coll., Collegeville, Pa., 1964; MA, Calif. State U., Northridge, 1977; postgrad., U. Phoenix, Nova U., Pa. State U., Lehigh U. Lic. elem. and secondary prin., reading specialist, Pa., Ariz. ESL tchr. Am. Acad. for Girls, Uskudar, Istanbul, Turkey, 1964-67; tchr. grades 3, 6 Guam Pub. Schs., Agana, 1967-70; tchr. grades 6-8 English/social studies Socorro (N.Mex.) Pub. Schs., 1971-74; tchr. ESL grades 7-9 Sun Valley Jr. High Sch., North Hollywood, Calif., 1974-77; Chapt. I dir./tchr. Apache Junction (Ariz.) Schs., 1978-88; staff devel. coord. Shikellamy Sch. Dist., Sunbury, Pa., 1989-90; prin., dir. reading Solanco Sch. Dist., Quarryville, Pa., 1990-94; presenter Pa. Dept. Edn. Summer Seminars, Regional Chpt. 1 Meetings, Parent Awareness Confs. (Chpt. I and Pa. Assn. Fed. Program Coords.). Mem. NAESP, ASCD, PAESP, Internat. Reading Assn. (state and local couns.), Pa. Assn. Fed. Program Coords.

MICHAELS, GENEVA LANE, lay worker, retired elementary school administrator; b. Dayton, Ohio, June 27, 1929; d. William Bert and Ethel Lee (Jackson) O'Neal; m. James Edward Michaels, Oct. 6, 1951 (dec. Mar. 1989); children: Ethel Adeline, Geneva Lee, Jamie Bert. Student, Cedarville Coll., 1952-54, Zola Levitt Jewish Christian Inst., Dallas, 1990-91, Liberty Bible Home Inst., Lynchburg, Va., 1991. Dir. youth, tchr. Bible, musician Ft. McKinley (Ohio) Bapt. Ch., 1952-56; dir. youth, musician Sidney (Ohio) Bapt. Ch., 1957-59; tchr. Bible, musician Hope Bapt. Ch., Kettering, Ohio, 1959-64; dir. youth Liberty Bapt. Ch., Xenia, Ohio, 1978—, tchr. Bible, head of music, Gospel soloist, musician, 1978—; sec. Huffman Elem. Sch., Dayton, 1966-80, pres., 1965-70. Pres. PTA, 1965-70. Recipient cert. and blue ribbon Ohio State PTA, 1964-65, 67. Mem. Smithsonian Instn. Republican. Home: 417 Huffman Ave Dayton OH 45403-2505 Office: Liberty Bapt Ch PO Box 641 Xenia OH 45385-0641

MICHAELS, JENNIFER ALMAN, lawyer; b. N.Y.C., Mar. 1, 1948; d. David I. and Emily (Arnow) Alman; 1 child, Abigail Elizabeth. BA, Douglas Coll., 1969; JD, Cardozo Sch. of Law, 1990. Ptnr. Alman & Michaels, Highland Park, N.J., 1990—. Author, composer: (record) Music for 2's and 3's, 1981; producer, writer: (film) Critical Decisions in Medicine, 1983. Mem. ABA, Middlesex County Bar Assn., N.J. State Bar Assn., Am. Trial Lawyers Assn., Phi Kappa Phi. Office: Alman and Michaels 611 S Park Ave Highland Park NJ 08904

MICHAELS, MARION CECELIA, writer, editor, news syndicate executive; b. Black River Falls, Wis.; d. Leonard N. and Estelle O. (Payne) Doud; m. Charles Webb (div.); children: Charles, David, Robert; m. Mark J. Michaels (div.); 1 child, Merry A. Student, MIT, 1962-64, U. Wis., 1971-76; BS in Bus. Edn., U. Wis., 1978, MS in Spl. Edn., 1981. Sec. Washington, Chgo.; mgr. bus. program Blackwell Job Corps Ctr.; mgr. Michaels Secretarial Svc., Black River Falls, Wis., 1979-83; columnist, editor Michaels News, Black River Falls, 1983—, pres., 1989—. Contbr. (columns) Single Parenting, 1983-94, Parenting Plus, 1990—; editor, contbr. (column) Surviving Single, 1990—, To Read or Not, Report From Planet Earth, 1989—. Chmn. Brockway Community Orgn., 1969-71; chair, counselor Brockway Youth Group, 1970-72; chmn. labor com. Dem. Platform Com., Wis., 1975-76; candidate State Assembly, 1978-82. Mem. Bus. Edn. Honor Soc., Edn. Hon. Soc. Office: Michaels News Rt 5 Box 367 Black River Falls WI 54615-9160

MICHAELSON, MARSHA, human resources administrator; b. Chgo., July 30, 1943; d. Sol and Ethel (Cooper) Uritz; m. Jeffrey D. Michaelson, Dec. 23, 1961 (div. 1984); children: Alaina Gaye, Gregory Brian; m. Alan S. DeWolfe, Aug. 4, 1991. BS, Northwestern U., 1984, MBA, 1991. Employment counselor Northwestern U., Evanston, Ill., 1979-80, asst. to the assoc. v.p. human resources, 1980-84, mgr. employee rels., 1984-87, mgr. employee rels. and EEO, 1987-88, dir. Chgo. human resources, 1988-91, dir. Chgo. human resources and univ. labor rels., 1991—. Mem. Coll. and Univ. Pers. Assn. (state membership chair 1991-93), Human Resources Mgmt. Assn. Chgo. (employee rels. com. chair 1990), Indsl. Rels. Rsch. Assn. of Chgo. Office: Northwestern Univ Wieboldt Hall 339 E Chicago Ave #119 Chicago IL 60611

MICHAK, HELEN BARBARA, educator, nurse; b. Cleve., July 31; d. Andrew and Mary (Patrick) M. Diploma Cleve. City Hosp. Sch. Nursing, 1947; BA, Miami U., Oxford, Ohio, 1951; MA, Case Western Res. U., 1960. Staff nurse Cleve. City Hosp., 1947-48; pub. health nurse Cleve. Div. Health, 1951-52; instr. Cleve. City Hosp. Sch. Nursing, 1952-56; supr. nursing Cuyahoga County Hosp., Cleve., 1956-58; pub. information dir. N.E. Ohio Am. Heart Assn., Cleve., 1960-64; dir. spl. events Higbee Co., Cleve., 1964-66; exec. dir. Cleve. Area League for Nursing, 1966-72; dir. continuing edn. nurses, adj. assoc. prof. Cleve. State U., 1972-86; asst. regional cons. Ohio Bd. Nursing, 1991—. Trustee N.E. Ohio Regional Med. Program, 1970-73; mem. adv. com. Dept. Nursing Cuyahoga Community Coll., 1967-87; mem. long term care com. Met. Health Planning Corp., 1974-76, plan devel. com. 1977; mem. policy bd. Ctr. Health Data N.E. Ohio, 1972-73; mem. Rep. Assembly and Health Planning and Devel. Commn., Welfare Fedn. Cleve., 1967-72, Cleve. Community Health Network, 1972-73, United Appeal Films and Speakers Bur., 1967-73; mem. adv. com. Ohio Fedn. Lic. Practical Nurses, 1970-73; mem. tech. adv. com. No. Ohio Lung Assn., 1967-74, 90-93. Cuyahoga County, 1967-74, 90-91; mem. Ohio Commn. on Nursing, 1971-74; mem. citizens com. nursing homes Fedn. Community Planning, 1971-73; mem. com. on home health services Met. Health Planning Corp., 1973-75; mem. profl. adv. com. on home care Fairview Gen. Hosp., 1987-91. Mem. Nat. League Nursing (mem. com. 1970-72), Am. Nurses Assn. (accreditation visitor 1977-78, 83-88) Ohio Nurses Assn., (com. continuing edn. 1974-79, 82-87, 89-92, chmn. 1984-86), Greater Cleve. (joint practice com. 1973-74, Greater Cleve. Nurses Assn. (trustee 1975-76) , Cleve. Area Citizens League for Nursing (trustee 1976-79, v.p. 1988-90), Zeta Tau Alpha, Sigma Theta Tau. Home and Office: 4686 Oak Ridge Dr N Royalton OH 44133-2070

MICHALS, LEE MARIE, travel agency executive; b. Chgo., June 6, 1939; d. Harry Joseph and Anna Marie (Monaco) Perzan; children: Debora Ann, Dana Lee, Jami. BA, Wright Coll., 1959. Cert. travel specialist, 1978; Destination Specialist, 1991. Internat. travel sec. E.F. MacDonald Travel, Palo Alto, Calif., 1963-69; pres. Travel Experience, Santa Clara, Calif., 1973-88, ret., 1988; ptnr. Cruise Connection, Mountain View, Calif., 1983-85. Mem. Am. Soc. Travel Agts., Inst. Cert. Travel Agts., Bay Area Travel Assn., Pacific Area Travel Agts., San Jose Women in Travel (organizing pres. 1971, 1st v.p. 1989). Office: Allways Travel 139 S Murphy Ave Sunnyvale CA 94086-5308

MICHALSKI, JEANNE ANN, human resources professional; b. Tampa, Fla., Nov. 7, 1958; d. Enrique and Mary Ellen (Bandi) Escarraz; m. Michael John Michalski, Nov. 24, 1984. BA in Psychology, U. South Fla., 1979, MA in Indsl. Psychology, 1983, PhD in Indsl. Psychology, 1990. Human resource coord. GTE Data Svcs., Tampa, 1984-86, mgmt. cons., 1986-87, mgr. human resource planning, employment office, 1987-88, mgr. human resource, 1988-89; mgr. testing and performance mgmt. GTE Telephone Ops., Irving, Tex., 1989-90, mgr. continuity planning and performance mgmt., 1990-94; human resources asst. v.p. planning Burlington No., Fort Worth, 1994—; cons. Herb Meyer Assocs./TECO, Tampa, 1983-84, Mail Prescriptions, Tampa, 1989-90. Campaign worker Dem. state legislator election, St. Petersburg, Fla., 1980; mem. Polit. Action Com., Irving, 1989-90. Grad. fellowship scholar U. South Fla., 1979. Mem. APA, Soc. for Indsl./Orgnl. Psychologists, Dallas/Ft. Worth Indsl. Orgn. Psychologist Group, Human Resource Planning Soc. Roman Catholic. Home: 505 Woodland Trail Keller TX 76248 Office: Burlington No 3000 Continental Plz Fort Worth TX 75039

MICHALSKI, NANCY ELIZABETH, software manager; b. Mpls., Dec. 10, 1957; d. Howard Malcolm and Mary Elizabeth (Strand) Kirst; m. Chris Alan Michalski, Oct. 25, 1980; children: Evan Michael, Paul Howard. AA, Cottey Coll., 1977; BS in Computer Sci., Purdue U., 1979. Tech. mktg. engr. Intel Corp., Santa Clara, Calif., 1979-81, tech. mktg. mgr., 1981-82, sr. software engr., 1983-86; sr. software engr. Intel Corp., Hillsboro, Oreg., 1986-87, project mgr., 1987-88; 1st levelmgr. Tandem Computers, Cupertino, Calif., 1989-90, 2nd level mgr., 1991-93, quality program mgr., 1993—. Christian Scientist. Home: 1507 Kingsgate Dr Sunnyvale CA 94087-4143 Office: Tandem Computers 10100 N Tantau Ave Loc 251-01 Cupertino CA 95014

MICHAM, NANCY SUE, information systems executive; b. Toledo, May 15, 1956; d. Charles Edward and Dorothy Ruth (Bittner) Linker; m. Donald Thomas Kerner, June 20, 1975 (div. June 1980); children: Brittni Mae, Stephanie Noelle. AS with high honors, U. Toledo, 1980; BSM cum laude, Pepperdine U., 1983. Cert. systems profl.; cert. aerobics instr. Programmer, Owens-Ill., Toledo, 1973-80; programmer analyst Smith Tool Co., Irvine, Calif., 1980-82; systems analyst Denny's, Inc., La Mirada, Calif., 1982-83; sr. corp. systems analyst, mgr. corp. systems group Libbey-Owens-Ford Co., Toledo, 1983-86, pres. Seagate Systems Cons., 1986—. Participant ToledoScape. Mem. NAFE, Nat. Mgmt. Assn., Assn. Systems Mgmt., Inst. for Cert. of Sys. Profls. Republican. Roman Catholic. Avocations: travel, backpacking, bicycling.

MICHAUD, NORMA ALICE PALMER, real estate investor, paralegal; b. Concord, N.H., May 6, 1946; d. Leon Charles and Goldie May (Maxfield) Palmer (both dec.); m. Bob Michaud, July 21, 1973; 1 child, Derrick Charles. AAS in Bus. Mgmt., Mississippi County C.C., 1994; student, State Tech., Memphis, 1994—. With United Life & Accident Ins. Co., Concord, N.H., 1965-68, 71-74; data processor Blue Cross/Blue Shield, Concord, 1968-71; adminstr. fed. agy. U.S. Govt., 1976-92; house renovator, real estate owner Blytheville, Ark., 1988—; dep. cir. clk., 1994; with Daniel Law Firm, 1994—. Mem. NAFE, Nat. Wildlife Assn., Nat. Geog. Soc., Bus. Profls. Am. (chpt. v.p. 1994), Phi Theta Kappa. Methodist.

MICHEL, HARRIET R., association executive; b. Pitts., July 5, 1942; d. John and Vida (Fish) Richardson; m. Yves Michel, Apr. 13, 1968; children: Christopher, Gregory. BA, Juniata Coll., 1965; LHD (hon.), Baruch Coll., 1990. Dir. spl. projects Nat. Scholarship Svcs. & Fund for Negro Students, N.Y.C., 1971; asst. to Mayor Lindsay City of N.Y. for Anti-Drug Efforts, 1971-72; exec. dir. N.Y. Found., 1972-77; dir. Cmty. Youth Employment Program U.S. Dept. Labor, Washington, 1977-79; established Women Against Crime Found. John Jay Coll., N.Y.C., 1980-81; cons. U.S. Dept. Housing & Urban Devel., Washington, 1982; pres., CEO N.Y. Urban League, 1983-88; pres. Nat. Minority Supplier Develop. Coun., N.Y.C., 1988—; bd. dirs. Ctr. for Advance Purchasing Studies, Phoenix, Maxima Corp., Balt., N.Y.C. Parntership; mem. nat. adv. coun. U.S. Small Bus. Adminstrn., Washington, 1993—; lectr. in field; mem. del. Ctrl. Am. Peace and Democracy Watch, 1987; U.S. rep. Ditchley Found. Confs., London; cons. in field. Vice chair N.Y.C. Charter Revision Commn., 1986-91; bd. dirs. African Am. Inst., N.Y.C., 1985—, Citizens Com. of N.Y., 1984—, Juniata Coll., Huntington, Pa., 1989—, Trans Africa Forum, Washington, 1988—. Recipient 1st Non-Profit Leadership award new Sch. Social Rsch., 1988, Women on the Move award Anti-Defamation League of B'nai B'rith, 1990, Appreciation award Pres. Commn. Minority Bus. Devel., 1992, Bus. Advocate award Mayor of N.Y.C., 1993, Black Entrepreneurial award Wall St. Jour., 1994, others; named one of 50 Outstanding Internat. Bus. and Profl. Women by Dollars and Sense Mag., 1987. Mem. Assn. Black Found. Execs. (founder), Coun. on Founds. (bd. dirs.). Office: Nat Minority Supplier Devel Coun 15 W 39th St 9th Fl New York NY 10018

MICHEL, MARILYN LUELLA, dietitian; b. Oakland, Calif., July 27, 1931; d. John Frederick and Esther Mae (Bennett) Beaber; m. Frank Edward Michel, Nov. 25, 1959; children: Cora Ann, Martha Louise, Stephen Walter, Fredrick Edward, Amy Edna. BS, U. Calif., Berkeley, 1953. Registered dietitian, Calif. Clin. dietitian Herrick Meml. Hosp., Berkeley, 1954-55; asst. dir. dietitics Alameda (Calif.) Hosp., 1955-61, Fairmont Hosp., San Leandro, Calif., 1961-63; dir. dietitics Pittsburg (Calif.) Community Hosp., 1963-67, Nat. Health Enterprises, Oakland, Calif., 1967-77; quality assurance program mgr. Beverly Enterprises, Rancho Cordova, Calif., 1979—; product devel. specialist Griffith Labs, Union City, Calif., 1977-79; instr. nursing home food svc. mgmt. Chabot Coll., Hayward, Calif., 1972-75; speaker in field. Leader Girl Scouts U.S.A., Hayward, 1968-70. Mem. Am. Dietitic Assn., Calif. Dietitic Assn., Bay Area Dietitic Assn (sec. 1958), Cons. Dietitians of Calif. (sec. 1988), Bay Area Consultation Dietitians (pres. 1965). Presbyterian. Home: 24962 Papaya St Hayward CA 94545-2415

MICHEL, MARY ANN KEDZUF, nursing educator; b. Evergreen Park, Ill., June 1, 1939; d. John Roman and Mary (Bassar) Kedzuf; m. Jean Paul Michel, 1974. Diploma in nursing, Little Company of Mary Hosp., Evergreen Park, 1960; BS in Nursing, Loyola U., Chgo., 1964; MS, No. Ill. U., 1968, EdD, 1971. Staff nurse Little Co. of Mary Hosp., 1960-64; instr. Little Co. of Mary Hosp. (Sch. Nursing), 1964-67, No. Ill. U., DeKalb, 1968-69; asst. prof. No. Ill. U., 1969-71; chmn. dept. nursing U. Nev., Las Vegas, 1971-73; prof. nursing U. Nev., 1975—, dean Coll. Health Scis., 1973-90; pres. PERC, Inc.; mgmt. cons., 1993—; mgmt. cons. Nev. Donor Network, 1993; mem. So. Nev. Health Manpower Task Force, 1975; mem. manpower com. Plan Devel. Commn., Clark County Health Sys. Agy., 1977-79, mem. governing body, 1981-86; mem. Nev. Health Coordinating Coun., Western Inst. Nursing, 1971-85; mem. coordinating com. assembly instnl. adminstrs. dept. allied health edn. and accreditation AMA, 1985-88; mem. bd. advisors So. Nev. Vocat. Tech. Ctr., 1976-80; sec.-treas. Nev. Donor Network, 1988-89, bd. dirs., 1986-90, chmn. bd., 1988-90. Contbr. articles to profl. jours. Trustee Desert Spring Hosp., Las Vegas, 1976-85; bd. dirs. Nathan Adelson Hospice, 1982-88, Bridge Counseling Assocs., 1982, Everywoman's Ctr., 1984-86; chmn. Nev. Commn. on Nursing Edn., 1972-73, Nursing Articulation Com., 1972-73, Nursing Articulation Com., 1972-73, Yr. of Nurse Com., 1978; moderator Invitational Conf. Continuing Edn., Am. Soc. Allied Health Professions, 1978; active Nev. Donor Network, Donor Organ Recovery, S.W. Eye and Tissue Banks. Named Outstanding Alumnus, Loyola U., 1983; NIMH fellow, 1967-68. Fellow Am. Soc. Allied Health Professions, 1991, (chmn. nat. resolutions com. 1981-84, treas. 1988-90, sec's. award com. 1982-83, 92-93, nat. by-laws com. 1985, conv. chmn. 1987); mem. AAUP, Am. Nurses Assn., Nev. Nurses Assn. (dir. 1975-77, treas. 1977-79, conv. chmn. 1978), So. Nev. Area Health Edn. Coun., Western Health Deans (co-organizer 1985, chair, 1988-90), Nat. League Nursing, Nev. Heart Assn., So. Nev. Mem. Hosps. (mem. nursing recruitment com. 1981-83, mem. nursing practice com. 1983-85), Las Vegas C. of C. (named Woman of Yr. Edn.) 1988, Slovak Catholic Sokols, Phi Kappa Phi (chpt. sec. 1981-83, pres.-elect 1983, pres. 1984, v.p. Western region 1989—, editorial bd. jour. Nat. Forum 1989-93), Alpha Beta Gamma (hon.), Sigma Theta Tau, Zeta Kappa. Office: U Nev Las Vegas 4505 S Maryland Pky Las Vegas NV 89154-3018

MICHELFELDER, ELLEN HADEN, hospital administrative executive; b. Richmond, Va., Dec. 8, 1945; d. William H. III and Dorothy (Fowler) Miller; m. Joerg R. Michelfelder, June 10, 1972. BS, Longwood Coll., 1967; MBA, Pepperdine U., 1982. Tchr. Jefferson High Sch., Alexandria, Va., 1967-69, Stuttgart (Germany) High Sch., 1969-73; adminstrv. asst. Sanwa Bank, San Francisco, 1973-74; asst. v.p. Security Pacific Nat. Bank, San Francisco, 1974-78; dir. human resources Nat. Semiconductor, Santa Clara, Calif., 1978-82; exec. dir. human resources Atari, Inc., Sunnyvale, Calif., 1983-84; dir. human resources Fujitsu Am., Inc., San Jose, Calif., 1985; exec. v.p. Bank of Calif., San Francisco, 1985-92; v.p. Lucile Packard Children's Hosp. at Stanford, Palo Alto, Calif., 1993—; bd. dirs., pres. Alumnae Resources, San Francisco, 1990—. Vol. Am. Cancer Soc., San Francisco, 1991-92. Mem. City Club San Francisco.

MICHELINI, SYLVIA HAMILTON, auditor; b. Decatur, Ala., May 16, 1946; d. George Borum and Dorothy Rose (Swatzell) Hamilton; m. H. Stewart Michelini, June 4, 1964; children: Stewart Anthony, Cynthia Leigh. BSBA summa cum laude, U. Ala., Huntsville, 1987. CPA, Ala.; cert. govt. fin. mgr. Acct. Ray McCay, CPA, Huntsville, 1987-88; auditor Def. Contract Audit Agy., Huntsville, 1989-92; auditor-office of inspector general George C. Marshall Space Flight, Center, Ala., 1992—. Mem. exec. bd. Decatur City PTA, 1976-78; pres., v.p. Elem. Sch. PTA, Decatur, 1977-79; leader Girl Scouts U.S. and Cub Scouts, Decatur, 1972-77; active local ARC, 1973-77. Mem. AAUW (chpt. treas. 1988-90), Nat. Assn. Accts. (dir. community svc. 1987-88, v.p. adminstrn. and fin. 1988-89, pres. 1989-90, nat. com. on ethics 1990-91), Am. Inst. CPAs, Am. Soc. Women Accts. (chpt. treas. 1989-90, dir. chpt. devel. 1989-90), Assn. Govt. Accts. (sec. 1992-93, chmn. pub. rels. 1993-94), Ala. Soc. CPAs (profl. ethics com. 1993-94), Inst. Internal Auditors, Inst. Mgmt. Accts. (v.p. communications, dir. program book 1991—, Dixie coun. dir. newsletters 1992-93, dir. ednl. programs 1992-93, 93-94, nat. com. ethics, 1990—), Ala. Soc. CPAs (govtl. acctg. and auditing com. 1994—), Inst. Mgmt. Accts. (nat. bd. dirs. 1994—), Phi Kappa Phi. Baptist. Home: 2801 Sylvia Dr SE Decatur AL 35603-9381 Office: NASA Office Inspector Gen M-DI Marshall Space Flight Ctr Huntsville AL 35812

MICHELL, KRISTINE MARIE, elementary educator; b. Marinette, Wis., Sept. 4, 1951; d. Adolph Jr. and Ruth Caroline (Swanson) Limberg. BA, U. Wis., Green Bay, 1973; postgrad., Nat. Coll. Edn., 1978; MA, Cardinal Stritch Coll. Edn., 1982. Cert. reading specialist, elem. tchr., English tchr., Wis. Title III reading aide Green Bay Pub. Schs., 1973-77; reading diagnostician Oconto (Wis.) Falls Pub. Schs., 1978; chpt. I reading tchr., reading specialist Howard-Suamico Sch. Dist., Green Bay, 1978—; reviewer Wis. Sch. Evaluation Consortium, Madison, 1991; reviewer goal/ESL/ABE program Northeastern Wis. Tech. Coll., Green Bay. Mem. Brown County Literacy Coun., Green Bay; mem. Northeastern Wis. Literacy Task Force. Mem. Wis. State Reading Assn. (v.p. elect 1993, v.p. 1994, conf. presenter, spkr. 1982, 85, 92, pub. rels. com. 1991-92, sec. 1990, 3 Outstanding Svc. awards), Greater Bayland Reading Coun. (pres., v.p., sec.), Internat. Reading Assn. (Mid. Sch. Spl. Interest Group, bd. dirs., state liaison). Home: 1265 Reed St Green Bay WI 54303-3024

MICHELLE, JOAN CLAIRE, critical care nurse; b. Youngstown, Ohio, Mar. 24, 1938; d. Patrick Joseph and Margaret Catherine (Johnson)

Devanny; divorced; children: Robert Fahlgren (dec.), Susan Fahlgren Rothschild, Tammy Fahlgren, Russell Fahlgren. ADN, Montgomery Coll., Takoma Park, Md., 1974; BSN, U. Tex., Arlington, 1981. RN, Tex. Asst. head nurse All Saints Episcopal Hosp., Ft. Worth; nurse ICU, Med.-Plaza, Ft. Worth; coord. patient care Family Svc., Ft. Worth; pool nurse med.-surg. unit, ICU, CCU and emergency room Osteo. Med. Ctr. Tex., Ft. Worth. Home: 3820 Bendale Rd Fort Worth TX 76116-8525

MICHELSON, LILLIAN, motion picture researcher; b. Manhattan, N.Y., June 21, 1928; d. Louis and Dora (Keller) Farber; m. Harold Michelson, Dec. 14, 1947; children: Alan Bruce, Eric Neil, Dennis Paul. Vol. Goldwyn Libr., Hollywood, Calif., 1961-69; owner Former Goldwyn Rsch. Libr., Hollywood, Calif., 1969—; ind. location scout, 1973—. Bd. dirs Beverlywood After Care Ctr., L.A., 1988—; mem. Friends of L.A. Pub. Libr. Office: care Paramount Pictures Bldg 264 5555 Melrose Ave Los Angeles CA 90038-3149

MICHELZ, DAWN MARIE, fine arts educator; b. Milw., Sept. 2, 1958; d. Simon John and Ruth Mary (Reichertz) M. BFA, U. Wis., Milw., 1989, MFA, 1992. Lectr. in drawing U. Wis., Milw., 1989-92; instr. drawing Milw. Inst. Art and Design, 1992—. Painter figurative oil paintings; exhbns. include N.Y. and Washington galleries, 1990-93. Home: 3429 N 83rd St Milwaukee WI 53222-3864

MICHETTI, SUSAN JANE, media relations director, video producer, communications consultant; b. Kenosha, Wis., Dec. 20, 1948. BA cum laude, U. Wis., 1981; Cert. A, B, C for real estate law, appraisal and mktg., Gateway Tech. Inst., Kenosha, 1979; postgrad., Carthage Coll., Kenosha, 1984. Pub. rels. and media dir. Big Bros./Big Sisters of Kenosha County, Wis., 1978-79; newspaper editor U. Wis., Parkside, 1979-81; news reporter, newscaster Sta. WRJN Radio, Racine, Wis., 1982-84; pub. info. specialist, graphic designer Kenosha Unified Sch. Dist., 1983-84; book editorial and prodn. coord. Scott, Foresman and Co., Glenview, Ill., 1985-88; instr. profl. devel. U. Wis., Parkside, 1988-89; fin. svcs./pub. rels. editor Phillips Pub., 1986—; propr. Michetti Multi-Media Assocs., Kenosha, 1981—; cons. in field. Contbr. articles to profl. jours. Media cons. Friends of Peter Barca for State Legislature, Kenosha, 1985-92; art fair asst. Friends of Kenosha Pub. Mus., 1986-92; mem. program devel. com. Racine Hist. Soc. and Pub. Mus., 1984-85. Scholar, Kenosha Found., 1979-81, Kenneth L. Greenquist, 1980, Vilas, 1968-71, Ida D. Altemus, 1969-70. Mem. NAFE, Am. Soc. Profl. and Exec. Women, Internat. Soc. Unified Sci. Home and Office: Michetti Multi-Media Assocs PO Box 54 Kenosha WI 53141-0054

MICHNA, ANDREA STEPHANIE, real estate agent and developer; b. Chgo., Nov. 4, 1948; d. Andrew Stephen and Ann Barbara (Ciesla) M. Student, Northwestern U., 1984-86. Travel cons. Internat. Sporting Travel, Chgo., 1975-77; office mgr., legal asst. Law Office of J.A. Rosin, Chgo., 1977-83; asst. to pres. Mt. Sinai Hosp., Chgo., 1983-85; exec. v.p. real estate Continental Fin., Ltd., Northbrook, Ill., 1985—. Office: Continental Financial Ltd 555 Skokie Blvd Ste 285 Northbrook IL 60062

MICK, MARGARET ANNE, communications executive; b. Phila., Apr. 24, 1947; d. Charles Philip and Helen Margaret (Amig) Maurer; m. Donald Kenneth Mick, Sept. 8, 1979. BS with honors, Pa. State U., 1969; MA, NYU, 1972. Assoc. producer Visual Edn. Corp., Princeton, N.J., 1972-73; program devel. specialist AEtna Life & Casualty, Hartford, Conn., 1973-78; sr. program devel. specialist AEtna Life & Casualty, Hartford, 1978-81, mgr. audiovisual communications, 1981-82, dir. audiovisual and mktg. communications, 1982-84, dir. mktg. communications, 1984-86, dir. bus. devel., 1986-88, asst. v.p. customized communications, 1988—; juror EFLA Am. Film Festival, Hartford, 1977-79. Writer, dir., producer TV films including (ednl.) PAC-Man in the Money Works. Mem. Info. Film Producers Am. (chmn. 1981, treas. 1982, Conn. Valley Chpt.), Internat. TV Assn. (chmn. 1983), Hartford Women's Network, Mature Market Inst., Bus. and Profl. Advt. Assn. Republican. Home: 185 Turtle Bay Dr Branford CT 06405-4903

MICKIEWICZ, ELLEN PROPPER, political science educator; b. Hartford, Conn., Nov. 6, 1938; d. George K. and Rebecca (Adler) Propper; m. Denis Mickiewicz, June 2, 1963; 1 son, Cyril. B.A., Wellesley Coll., 1960; M.A., Yale U., 1961, Ph.D., 1965. Lectr. dept. polit. sci. Yale U., 1965-67; asst. prof. dept. polit. sci. Mich. State U., East Lansing, 1967-69; assoc. prof. Mich. State U., 1969-73, prof., 1973-80; prof. dept. polit. sci. Emory U., Atlanta, 1980-88; dean Grad. Sch. Arts and Scis. Emory U., 1980-85, Alben W. Barkley prof. polit. sci., 1988-93; James R. Shepley prof. pub. policy, prof. polit. sci. Duke U., Durham, N.C., 1994—, dir. DeWitt Wallace Ctr. for Comm. and Journalism Terry Sanford Inst. Pub. Policy, 1994—; vis. prof. Kathryn W. David Chair Wellesley Coll., 1978; vis. com. dept. Slavic lang. and lit. Harvard U., 1978-85, vice chmn. vis. com. Russian Research Ctr., Harvard U., 1986-92; mem. subcom. on communications and society Am. Council Learned Socs./Soviet Acad. Scis., 1986-90; mem. com. on internat. security studies, Am. Acad. Arts and Scis., 1988-90; fellow The Carter Ctr., 1985—, dir. Internat. Media and Communications Program; mem. area adv. com. for Ea. Europe and USSR, Coun. for Internat. Exchange of Scholars, 1987-90; mem. acad. adv. coun. The Kennan Inst. for Advanced Russsian Studies, 1989-93. Author: Soviet Political Schools, 1967, Media and the Russian Public, 1981, Split Signals: Television and Politics in the Soviet Union, 1988 (Electronic Book of Yr. award Nat. Assn. Broadcasters and Broadcast Edn. Assn. 1988: co-author: Television and Elections, 1992, Television/Radio News and Minorities, 1994; editor: Soviet Union Jour., 1980-90; co-editor: International Security and Arms Control, 1986, The Soviet Calculus of Nuclear War, 1986; editor, contbr.: Handbook of Soviet Social Science Data, 1973; mem. editorial bd. Jour. Politics, 1985-88. Founder, 1st chmn. bd. dirs. Opera Guild of Greater Lansing, Inc., 1972-74. Recipient Outstanding Svc. to Promote Dem. Media in Russia award Journalists Union of Russia, 1994; Ford Found. fgn. area tng. fellow, 1962-65; Guggenheim fellow, 1973-74; Sigma Xi grantee, 1973-74, Ford Found. grantee, 1985-85, 88-91, 92—, Rockefeller Found. grantee, 1985-87, W. Alton Jones Found. grantee, 1987-88, Eurasia Found. grantee, 1993-94; fellow The Carter Ctr. Mem. Am. Assn. for Advancement Slavic Studies (bd. dirs. 1978-81, mem. awards com., mem. endowment com. 1984-86, pres. 1987-88), Am. Polit. Sci. Assn.,Internat. Studies Assn. (v.p. N.Am. 1983-84), Dante Soc. Am., So. Conf. Slavic Studies (exec. com. 1983-84), Counc. Fgn. Rels. Office: Sanford Inst Pub Policy PO Box 90241 Duke U Durham NC 27708-0241

MICKLE, KATHRYN ALMA, security company executive; b. Pittsfield, Mass., May 17, 1946; d. Frederick Louis and Bertha Laura (Webster) Wick; m. William Joseph Mickle III, May 11, 1968; children: William J. IV, Deborah Sharon. Cert. in nursing Cooley Dickinson Hosp., Northampton, Mass., 1967. Charge nurse Berkshire Med. Ctr., Pittsfield, 1967-75; intensive and coronary care nurse, 1975-81; nursing cons. Springside Nursing Home, Pittsfield, 1974-76; owner New Eng. Security, Pittsfield, 1978—. Stage mgr. Doo Wah Days Variety Show, 1989, 90-94. Active Western Mass. coun. Girl Scouts U.S., 1975—, Citizen's Against Child Abuse, 1989-93; dir., tchr. Dalton Vacation Bible Sch., Mass., 1979-83; vice chmn. bd. Berkshire County Christian Sch., 1984-86, bd. chmn., 1986-88, bd. dirs., 1982-88; chmn. pub. rels. exec. com. Billy Graham Crusade, Pittsfield area, 1982; Dalton coord. Silvio O. Conte Re-election Campaign, 1984; deaconess Congregationalist Ch., 1989, 90. 91, 94. Recipient numerous sales awards Dynamark Inc., 1980—, Internat. Franchise award, 1987, Appreciation award Dalton Vacation Bible Sch., 1983, John Walsh award Nat. Ctr. Missing and Exploited Children, Dynamark, 1992, David Shapiro award, 1993. Fellow Cen. Berkshire C. of C. (Outstanding Vol. award 1991, 93, 94, bd. dirs. 1992-94, mem. exec. com. 1993—, vice chair 1993-95, chair edn. coun. 1993-94, chair-elect 1994-95), Cooley Dickinson Alumni Assn., Pittsfield Bus. and Profl. Women, Exch. Club (child abuse prevention chmn., bd. dirs. Pittsfield club 1992-93). Avocations: reading, gardening, camping. Home: 72 Braeburn Rd Dalton MA 01226-1019 Office: New England Dynanark Security 397 North St Pittsfield MA 01201-4603

MICKLITSCH, CHRISTINE NOCCHI, health care administrator; b. Hazleton, Pa., Oct. 23, 1949; d. Nicholas Edmund and Matilda Nocchi; m. Wayne D. Micklitsch, May 20, 1972; children: Sarah N., Emily M. BS, Pa. State U., State College, 1971; MBA, Boston U., 1979. Blood bank med. technologist The Deaconess Hosp., Boston, 1971-73; sr. blood bank med. technologist Tufts New Eng. Med. Ctr., Boston, 1973-76, environ. svcs. coord., 1976-78; adminstrv. resident Joslin Diabetes Found., Boston, 1978-79; sr. analyst Analysis, Mgmt. & Planning, Inc., Cambridge, Mass., 1979-80; adminstrv. dir. Hahnemann Family Health Ctr., Worcester, Mass., 1980-84; exec. dir. Swampscott (Mass.) Treatment & Trauma Ctr., 1984-85; dir. practice mgmt., instr. U. Mass. Med. Ctr., Worcester, 1985-91; dir. adminstrv. svcs. The Fallon Clinic, Worcester, 1991-94; mgr. physician network devel. The Fallon healthcare Sys., Worcester, 1994—. Incorporator, pres. Newton (Mass.) Highlands Community Devel. Corp., 1981-82; treas. Patriot's Trail Girl Scout Troop 3041, Newton, 1993; Christian edn. instr. Newton Highlands Congl. Ch., 1987-94. Kellogg fellow Ctr. for Rsch. in Ambulatory Health Care Adminstrn., Denver, 1979; grantee in grad. tng. in family medicine HHS, U. Mass. Med. Sch., Worcester, 1989. Fellow Am. Coll. Med. Practice Execs. (state coll. forum rep. 1989—, ea. sect. coll. forum rep. 1993—); mem. Mass. Med. Group Mgmt. Assn. (pres. 1987-89, newsletter editor 1984—), Boston U. Health Care Mgmt. Program Alumni Assn., Alpha Omicron Pi (parlimentarian Epsilon Alpha chpt. 1969-70). Home: 320 Lake Ave Newton MA 02161-1212 Office: Fallon Healthcare Sys Chestnut Pl 10 Chestnut St Worcester MA 01608-1220

MICKLOS-MAISEY, JANET M., state agency administrator, human services director; b. Jacksonville, Fla., July 24, 1947; d. Thomas Anthony and Yolanda Mae (Murphy) Micklos; married; children: Shawn E. Satterthwaite, Ryan W. Satterthwaite; m. Terry Mercer Maisey, May 28, 1988. BA, U. No. Colo., 1969; MA disting. grad., Webster U., 1985. Phys. edn. tchr. Terrell Wells Middle Sch., San Antonio, 1969-70; fitness instr./gymnastic coach Victor Valley Community Coll., Apple Valley, Calif., 1977-79; dir. phys. dept. Victor Valley YMCA, Victorville, Calif., 1978-79; secretarial support joint U.S. mil. mission aid to Turkey Ankara, Turkey, 1981-82; secretarial support U.S. Logistics Group, Ankara, 1982-83; pub. edn. dir. Alamo Area Rape Crisis Ctr., San Antonio, 1986-88; admissions coord. Horizon Hosp., San Antonio, 1988; psychiat. counselor Portsmouth Pavilion, Portsmouth, N.H., 1988-89; dir. human svcs. Rockingham County (N.H.) Dept. of Corrections, Brentwood, 1989—. Adv. task force N.H. Coun. of Churches, 1992; mem. gov.'s coun. on volunteerism Seacoast, 1990-93; chmn. outreach commn. 1st United Meth. Ch., Portsmouth, 1990-93; mem. task force on victim restitution Rockingham County, 1992—. Mem. Am. Correctional Assn., Am. Jail Assn., Rockingham County Law Enforcement Officers Assn., AAUW. Independent. Methodist. Office: Rockingham County Dept Corrections 99 North Rd Brentwood NH 03833-6620

MICO, ELVA JEANNE, performing company executive, choreographer; b. Athens, Ohio, Jan. 18, 1940; d. Virgil Ellis Hill and Ruth Beatrice (Maxwell) Perala; m. Richard Mico, Apr. 21, 1961; children: Kimberly Lynn, Karen Daune, Mark Antony. BFA, U. N.Mex., 1984. Dancer various profl. cos., U.S., 1952-68; mgr. Richard's Book Nook, Worthington, Ohio, 1976-78; instr. Gigante Cunningham Sch. Dance, Gahanna, Ohio, 1978-79; choreographer, instr. Fitness Alternatives and Aerobacize, Inc., Albuquerque, 1983-88; teaching asst. dance dept. U. N.Mex., Albuquerque, 1984-85; dir., choreographer Jr. Performing Line, Rio Rancho, N.Mex., 1985-89; owner, artistic dir. Elva's Sch. Ballet and Dance, Rio Rancho, 1985—; pres., chmn. Elva's, Inc. Dance, Rio Ranche; guest instr. various schs., 1975-79; guest speaker on dance and related topics U. N.Mex., 1990—, at career forums, to fine art classes. Creator, choreographer: (dance form) Creative Movement, 1985, (yoga/exercise movement) Tone and Stretch, 1987; dancer various TV performances; founder, artistic dir. Prima Ballet Co., The Tap Co., The Classics, 1989—. Vol., display artist Women's Aux. of Mt. Carmel East, Columbus, Ohio, 1978-79, pres. 1979. Mem. ASCAP, Dance Educators Am., Nat. Exercise Instrs. Tng. Assn. (cert.), Nat. Dance Assn., Rio Rancho C. of C., Italian/Am. Club (Rio Rancho). Roman Catholic. Club: Italian/Am. (Rio Rancho). Office: Elva's Inc 1207 Golf Course Rd SE Rio Rancho NM 87124-1966

MIDDLEBROOK, DIANE WOOD, English language educator; b. Pocatello, Idaho, Apr. 16, 1939; d. Thomas Isaac and Helen Loretta (Downey) Wood; m. Jonathan Middlebrook, June 15, 1963 (div. 1972); 1 child, Leah Wood Middlebrook; m. Carl Djerassi, June 21, 1985. BA, U. Wash., 1961; MA, Yale U., 1962, PhD, 1968. Asst. prof. Stanford (Calif.) U., 1966-73, assoc. prof., 1973-83, Howard H. and Jessie T. Watkins univ. prof., 1983—, Howard H. and Jessie T. Univ. prof., 1985-90, dir. Ctr. for Rsch. on Women, 1977-79. Author: Walt Whitman and Wallace Stevens, 1974, Worlds into Words: Understanding Modern Poems, 1980, Anne Sexton, A Biography, 1991, (poems) Gin Considered as a Demon, 1983; editor: Coming to Light: American Women Poets in the Twentieth Century, 1985. Founding trustee Djerassi Resident Artists Program, Woodside, Calif., 1980-83, chair, 1994; trustee San Francisco Art Inst., 1993. Ind. study fellow NEH, 1982-83, Bunting Inst. fellow Radcliffe Coll., 1982-83, Guggenheim Found. fellow, 1988-89, Rockefeller Study Ctr. fellow, 1990; recipient Yale Prize for Poetry; finalist Nat. Book award, 1991. Mem. MLA. Home: 1101 Green St Apt 1501 San Francisco CA 94109-2006 Office: Stanford U Dept English Stanford CA 94305-2087

MIDDLEBROOKS, DELORIS JEANETTE, nurse, retired; b. Cedar Rapids, Iowa, Apr. 9, 1931; d. Harland R. and Rosa V. (Anderson) Hickey; m. Johnnie L. Middlebrooks, Apr. 25, 1963 (dec.); children: James, Kathleen. Diploma, Evang. Hosp. Sch. Nursing, 1956; BSN, State U. Iowa, 1958; MS in Nursing, U. Calif., San Francisco, 1960; EdD, U. Nev., Las Vegas, 1985. Instr., coord. Nev. State Hosp. Sch. Practical Nursing, Sparks, 1963-66; staff nurse St. Mary's Hosp., Reno, 1968; instr., coord. Reno VA Sch. Practical Nursing, 1968-72; instr,. coord. health occupations Wooster High Sch., 1972-73; nursing faculty Truckee Meadows C.C., 1973-94, retired, 1994; intermittent staff nurse VA Hosp., 1984-86; instr., review course Stanley Kaplan Ednl. Ctr., 1987-89; clin. nursing faculty Western Nev. C.C., Carson City, 1987, Northern Nev. C.C., Elko, 1979-93; guest assoc. prof. nursing Lewis-Clark State Coll., Lewiston, Idaho, 1989; cons. Irish Bd. Nursing, Dublin, Ireland, 1985. Nominated Nev. Voc. Tchr. of Yr., 1975, 79, 88, 89; Recipient March of Dimes Community Leadership award, 1990. Mem. ANA, Am. Voc. Assn., Western Inst. Nursing, Western Soc. Rsch. Nursing, Nev. Nurses Assn., Nev. Voc. Assn., Sigma Theta Tau, Phi Kappa Phi. Home: 1385 Ebbetts Dr Reno NV 89503-1918

MIDDLETON, AMY CATHERINE, psychotherapist; b. Waterloo, Iowa, Dec. 24, 1966; d. Richard Arnold and Shirley Ann (Stief) Walker; m. Patrick L.R. Middleton, Oct. 12, 1991. BS in Psychology, Calif. Luth. U., 1989; MA in Psychol. Counseling, Pepperdine U., 1991; Clin. Hypnotherapist, Hypnosis Motivation Inst., Tarzana, Calif., 1992. Cert. ind. clin. social worker. Asst. to psychologist Camarillo (Calif.) State Hosp., 1988-89; sr. crisis interventionist Interface, Thousand Oaks, Calif., 1988-91, sr. suicide hotline counselor, 1988-91; hypnotherapist Hypnosis Motivation Inst., Tarzana, Calif., 1992; psychotherapist Jane Addams, Inc., Freeport, Ill., 1992-94, Directions Counseling Ctr., Watertown, Wis., 1994—. Mem. Hypnotherapists Assocs., Inc., Med. Hypnoanalysts, CAMFT, Am. Hypnotherapists Assn., Assn. for Play Therapists, Assn. for Prevention Child Sexual Abuse, Psi Chi. Democrat. Methodist. Office: Directions Counseling Ctr 129 Hospital Dr Watertown WI 53098

MIDDLETON, CHARLENE, medical/surgical nurse, educator; b. Ennis, Tex., Sept. 13, 1922; d. Charles Silvester and Harriet Eugenia (Ford) M. Diploma, Scott and White Hosp., Temple, Tex., 1945; AA, Temple Jr. Coll., 1947; BA, U. Tex., Austin, 1956. Nurse coord., ambulatory care svcs. Naval Regional Med. Ctr., Long Beach, Calif.; instr. nursing arts Scott and White Hosp., evening supr. Lt. comdr. U.S. Navy, 1957-77. Mem. Scott and White Alumni Assn. (past pres. Dist. 7).

MIDDLETON, LINDA JEAN GREATHOUSE, lawyer; b. Poplar Bluff, Mo., Sept. 22, 1950; d. Casper Scott and Anna Garnelle (Qualls) Greathouse; m. Roy L. Middleton, Sept. 27, 1969. BS cum laude, Ark. State U., 1972; JD, Baylor U., 1974. Bar: Tex., 1974; CPCU, CLU. Asst. v.p., asst. sec., atty. Equitable Gen. Ins. Co., Ft. Worth, 1977-81; gen. counsel, corp. sec. Chilton Corp., Dallas, 1981-83; asst. corp. sec., sr. atty., mgr. pub. affairs Fina Oil and Chem., Dallas, 1983-85; sec. Parliamentarian, Dallas, 1985—. Sec. Homeowners Assn., Dallas, 1981—. Mem. Tex. Bar Assn., Dallas Bar Assn. Baptist. Office: Fina Inc 8350 N Ctrl Expwy PO Box 2159 Dallas TX 75221

MIDDLETON, MARY, secondary education educator; b. Lackawana, N.Y., Nov. 13, 1942; d. Arthur Jordan and Kathryn (Sternburg) M. BS in Edn., Ohio State U., 1965; postgrad., Akron U., 1970, Cleve. State U., 1981-84. Profl. cert. in edn. Tchr. Columbus (Ohio) Schs., 1966-68, Brooklyn (Ohio) Schs., 1968—; co-dir. C.A.R.E. (Chem. Abuse Reduced through Edn.), Brooklyn (Ohio) City, 1986—; English dept. chair, acad. team advisor Brooklyn (Ohio) Schs., 1987—; mem. dimensions of learning task force Bklyn. Schs. Contbr. articles to profl. jours. Campaign worker North Olmsted (Ohio) Dem. Club, 1988, 92. Recipient N.E. Ohio Writing Project fellowship Martha Holden Jennings, Cleve. State U., 1985. Mem. ASCD, NEA, Ohio Edn. Assn., Brooklyn (Ohio) Edn. Assn. (sec.), Ohio Coun. Tchrs. English and Lang. Arts (sec.). Methodist. Home: 7127 Bayberry Cir North Olmsted OH 44070-4765 Office: Brooklyn City Schs 9200 Biddulph Brooklyn OH 44144

MIDDLETON, PAULETTE BAUER, atmospheric chemist; b. Beeville, Tex., Dec. 8, 1946; d. Paul Wylie and Lillian Grace (Schoppe) Bauer; m. John William Middleton, July 12, 1970; div. 1990; children: Mären Katherine, Erin Ann. BA, U. Tex., 1968, MA, 1971, PhD, 1973. Research asst., then instr. chemistry U. Tex., 1968-73, research assoc. chem. engring., 1973-75; postdoctoral fellow Nat. Ctr. Atmospheric Research, Boulder, Colo., 1975-76, sci. visitor, 1977-79, spl. project scientist, 1979, staff scientist, 1979-87; research assoc. then sr. research assoc. Atmospheric Scis. Research Ctr., SUNY, Albany, 1987—; lectr., seminar leader in field. NSF, DOE, EPA, EPRI grantee, 1982—. Author over 50 papers. Mem. Air Pollution Control Assn., AAAS. Office: Nat Ctr Atmospheric Rsch PO Box 3000 Boulder CO 80307-3000

MIDDLETON, SILVIA GILBERT, dean, engineering educator; b. Florence, S.C., Nov. 3, 1953; d. Silvanus Taco II and Jewell Virginia (Saylor) Gilbert; m. John Richard Middleton II, May 21, 1988; children: Lindsey Grace, John III. BS, Clemson U., 1975, MS, 1976, PhD, 1984. Jr. engr. Union Carbide Corp.-Linde Div., Florence, 1974; grad. rsch. asst. Clemson U., S.C., 1975-76, instr. elec. & computer engring., 1976-81, grad. rsch. asst., 1981-84; asst. prof. U. N.C., Charlotte, 1984-90, asst. dean engring., 1990—; chair N.C. state subcom. for engring. transfer, 1994—. Co-inventor remote control for heliarc welders. Adult Edn. Coord. First Presbyn. Church, Concord, 1989-90. Mem. IEEE (sec. 1987, 2d vice chmn. 1988, 1st vice chmn. 1989, chmn. 1990, awards and nominations com. 1991-93, treas. N.C. coun. chpt. 1992-93, sec. 1994, gen. chmn. ann. southeastern region conf. 1993), Soc. Women Engrs. (pres. Western Carolina chpt. 1981), Am. Soc. for Engring. Edn. Presbyterian. Avocations: reading, needlework, traveling, gardening, investments. Home: PO Box 520 Newell NC 28126-0520 Office: U NC William States Lee Coll Engring Charlotte NC 28223

MIDKIFF, ELEANOR ELIZABETH, psychology educator; b. George Field, Ill., Sept. 11, 1943; d. Morris E. Jr. and Elizabeth C. (Duncan) M.; m. Philip Tolin, Aug. 19, 1966 (div. June 1983); children: David F., Jeffrey J., Elizabeth L. AB, Bryn Mawr Coll., 1965; MA, U. Iowa, 1967; PhD, U. Wash., 1986. Instr. Cen. Wash. U., Ellensburg, 1969-80; lectr., teaching asst., rsch. asst. U. Wash., Seattle, 1981-86; asst. prof. Pacific U., Forest Grove, Oreg., 1986-89; asst. prof. Eastern Ill. U., Charleston, 1989-92, assoc. prof., 1992—; presenter in field. Contbr. articles, abstracts to profl. publs. Ea. Ill. U. grantee, 1990-93, NSF grantee, 1991-95; recipient Nat. Rsch. Svc. award HHS, 1984-85. Mem. Am. Psychol. Assn., Am. Psychol. Soc., Assn. for Chem. Senses, Internat. Soc. for Devel. Psychobiology, Soc. for Study of Ingestive Behavior, Sigma Xi. Episcopalian. Home: 1807 Meadowlake Dr Charleston IL 61920-3242 Office: Eastern Ill U Charleston IL 61920

MIDLARSKY, ELIZABETH RUTH, psychology educator; b. N.Y.C.; d. Abraham Allan and Frances Lucille (Wiener) Steckel; m. Manus Issachar Midlarsky, June 25, 1961; children: Susan Rachel, Miriam Joyce, Michael George. MA, Northwestern U., 1966, PhD, 1968. Lic. psychologist, N.J., Mich., Colo. Asst. prof. U. Denver, 1968-73; dir. rsch. and evaluation Malcolm X Med. Ctr. (now Park East), Denver, 1973-75; assoc. prof., dir. psychol. tng. program Met. State Coll., Denver, 1975-77; assoc. prof. psychology U. Detroit, 1977-83, prof. psychology, 1983-90, chair dept. psychology, 1978-81, dir. Ctr. Study Devel. and Aging, 1977-83; prof. clin. psychology Tchrs. Coll. Columbia U., N.Y.C., 1990—, dir. Ctr. for Lifespan and Aging Studies, 1992—; mem. initial rev. group NIMH, Bethesda, Md., 1976-82; mem. ad hoc rev. groups NHLBI, Bethesda, 1985—; mem. study sect. NIH, Bethesda, 1986-91; mem. reviewers rsch., 1991-94. Author: Altruism in Late Life, 1994; co-editor Humboldt Jour. Social Rels., 1985-86; editor Acad. Psychol. Bull., 1982-86; contbr. chpts. to books and articles to profl. jours. Mem. exec. coun. Mich. Psychol. Assn. Grantee Nat. Inst. Aging, 1982-85, 87-90, AARP, 1982-83, 88-89, 92-95; postdoctoral rsch. fellow AAUW, 1974-75. Fellow APA (publs. com. 1990-92, student award com. 1990), Am. Psychol. Soc., Am. Orthopsychiat. Assn.; mem. Gerontol. Soc. Am. (exec. com. on program com. 1983-84), Soc. Psychol. Study Social Issues. Home: 3 Falcon Rd East Brunswick NJ 08816 Office: Columbia U Dept Clin Psych Box 148 525 W 120th St New York NY 10027-6625

MIDLER, BETTE, singer, entertainer, actress; b. Honolulu, Dec. 1, 1945; m. Martin von Haselberg, 1984; 1 child, Sophie. Student, U. Hawaii, 1 year. Debut as actress film Hawaii, 1965; mem. cast Fiddler on the Roof, N.Y.C., 1966-69, Salvation, N.Y.C., 1970, Tommy, Seattle Opera Co., 1971; nightclub concert performer on tour, U.S., from 1972; appearance Palace Theatre, N.Y.C., 1973, Radio City Music Hall, 1993; TV appearances include The Tonight Show, Bette Midler: Old Red Hair is Back, 1978, Gypsy, 1993 (Golden Globe award best actress in a mini-series or movie made for television 1994, Emmy nomination, Lead Actress - Special, 1994); appeared Clams on The Half-Shell Revue, N.Y.C., 1975; recs. include The Divine Miss M, 1972, Bette Midler, 1973, Broken Blossom, 1977, Live at Last, 1977, The Rose, 1979, Thighs and Whispers, 1979, Songs for the New Depression, 1979, Divine Madness, 1980, No Frills, 1984, Mud Will Be Flung Tonight, 1985, Some People's Lives, 1990; motion picture appearances include Hawaii, 1966, The Rose, 1979 (Academy award nomination best actress 1979), Divine Madness, 1980, Jinxed, 1982, Down and Out in Beverly Hills, 1986, Ruthless People, 1986, Outrageous Fortune, 1987, Oliver and Company (voice), 1988, Big Business, 1988, Beaches, 1988, Stella, 1990, Scenes From a Mall, 1991, For the Boys, 1991 (Academy award nomination best actress 1991), Hocus Pocus, 1993; appeared in cable TV (HBO) prodn. Bette Midler's Mondo Beyondo, 1988; author: A View From A Broad, 1980, The Saga of Baby Divine, 1983. Recipient After Dark Ruby award, 1973; Grammy awards, 1973, 1990; spl. Tony award, 1973; Emmy award for NBC Spl., Ol' Red Hair is Back, 1978; Emmy award The Tonight Show appearance, 1992. Office: care Atlantic Records 75 Rockefeller Plz New York NY 10019-6907*

MIDORI (MIDORI GOTO), classical violinist; b. Osaka, Japan, Oct. 25, 1971. Attended, Juilliard Sch. Music; grad., Profl. Childrens Sch., 1990. Performer worldwide, 1981—. Recordings on Philips, Sony Classical, Columbia Masterworks; performed with N.Y. Philharmonic Orch., Boston Symphony Orch.; worldwide performances include Berlin, Chgo., Cleve., Phila., Montreal, London. Named Best Artist of Yr. by Japanese Govt., 1988; recipient Dorothy B. Chandler Performing Arts award, L.A. Music Ctr., 1989, Crystal award Ashani Shimbun Newspaper contbn. arts, Suntory award, 1994. Office: ICM Artists 40 W 57th St New York NY 10019-4001

MIEHLS, MADELEINE M., electrical engineer; b. Royal Oak, Mich., Nov. 23, 1962; d. Donald George and Lorraine Esther (Landre) M.; m. Gerald Joseph Cormier, Oct. 14, 1989. BSEE, U. Mich., 1985; MSIE, Oakland U., Rochester, Mich., 1988; postgrad., Walsh Coll., Troy, Mich., 1992—. Assoc. project engr. Parker Amchem, Madison Heights, Mich., 1985-88; devel. engr. Ford Motor Co., Dearborn, Mich., 1988-91; sr. design/devel. engr. GM-Powertrain, Warren, Mich., 1991—. Vol. Giving Tree chairperson St. Anastasia Parish, Troy, 1991-93, religious edn. instr., 1991-92, marriage sponsor, 1992-93.

MIEL, VICKY ANN, municipal government executive; b. South Bend, Ind., June 20, 1951; d. Lawrence Paul Miel and Virginia Ann (Yeagley) Hernandez. BS, Ariz. State U., 1985. Word processing coordinator City of Phoenix, 1977-78, word processing adminstr., 1978-83, chief dep. city clk., 1983-88, city clk. dir., 1988—; assoc. prof. Phoenix Community Coll., 1982-83, Mesa (Ariz.) Community Coll., 1983; speaker in field, Boston, Santa Fe, Los Angeles, N.Y.C. and St. Paul, 1980—. Author: Phoenix Document Request Form, 1985, Developing Successful Systems Users, 1986. Judge Future Bus. Leaders Am. at Ariz. State U., Tempe, 1984; bd. dirs. Fire and Life Safety League, Phoenix, 1984. Recipient Gold Plaque, Word Processing Systems Mag., Mpls., 1980, Green Light Productivity award City of Phoenix, 1981, Honor Soc. Achievement award Internat. Word Processing Assn., 1981, 1st Ann. Grand Prize Records Mgmt. Internat. Inst. Mcpl. Clks., 1990, Olsten Award for Excellence in Records Mgmt., 1991. Mem. Assn. Info. Systems Profls. (internat. dir. 1982-84), Internat. Inst. Mcpl. Clks. (cert.), Am. Records Mgrs. Assn., Assn. Image Mgmt., Am. Soc. Pub. Adminstrs., Am. Mgmt. Assn. Office: City of Phoenix 200 W Washington Ste 1500 Phoenix AZ 85003-1611

MIELE, EILEEN CECELIA, financial insurance company executive; b. Paterson, N.J.; d. Carmine and C. Celeste (Ferrazzano) M.; married, two children. BS in Acctg. cum laude, Montclair (N.J.) State Coll., 1975. CPA, N.J. Intern audit staff Arthur Young & Co. (now Ernst & Young), Saddle Brook, N.J., 1974-75, from staff acct. to supervising sr., 1975-80, audit mgr., 1980-82; asst. contr. Continental Ins., Piscataway, N.J., 1982-84; asst. v.p., asst. contr. Continental Ins., Cranbury, N.J., 1984-90; v.p., dir. internal audit Continental Corp., N.Y.C., 1990-93; chief fin. officer Info. Tech. Divsn. Continental Ins., Neptune, N.J., 1993—. Recipient Twin award Princeton YWCA, 1991, Ridgewood YWCA, 1979, Business Advisor of Yr. award Inroads of No. N.J., 1988. Mem. AICPA, N.J. Soc. CPAs, Soc. Ins. Accts., Inst. Internal Auditors, Acctg. Club, Phi Chi Theta (founding, 1st pres. local chpt. 1973).

MIELE, MARCIA LYNN, restaurant owner, operator; b. Williamsport, Pa., May 18, 1954; d. Ernest and Daisy Edna (Lee) M. BA in Composition & Lit., Brown U., 1976. Co-owner Court & Willow Café, Williamsport, Pa., 1972-93, Peter Herdic House, Williamsport, Pa., 1984—; ptnr. Hist. Properties, Williamsport, Pa., 1991—. Bd. dirs. Hist. Archtl. Rev. Bd., Williamsport, 1988—, Main St. Adv. Bd., 1980-86, Lyc. County C. of C., 1983-89; tutor Lyc. County Literacy Assn., Williamsport, 1989—. Named Woman of the Yr., NYU, 1989; recipient Preservation award Hist. Archtl. Rev. Bd., 1993. Mem. NOW, Preservation Williamsport (bd. dirs. 1988-92), Pembroke Ctr. (assoc.). Home: 522 W 4th St Williamsport PA 17701-6072 Office: Peter Herdic House 407 W 4th St Williamsport PA 17701-6001

MIELKE, SUSAN KAY, mental health nurse; b. Saginaw, Mich., Apr. 4, 1963; d. Walter John Jr. and Sally Jane (Spiekerman) Hetzner; m. Gary Alan Mielke, Aug. 16, 1986; children: Caroline, Elizabeth, Trevor. BSN, Mich. State U., 1985. Staff nurse Weight Loss Clinic, Saginaw, 1987, St. Mary's Hosp., Saginaw, 1985-88; RN II supr. psychiat. nursing Caro (Mich.) Regional Mental Health Ctr., 1987—; co-dir., co-owner CM Med.-Legal Cons. Inc, Saginaw, 1990—. Mem. Mich. State U. Nursing Alumni Assn. Lutheran. Home: 2855 Sheridan Rd Caro MI 48723 Office: Caro Regional Mental Health Ctr Lock Box A Caro MI 48723

MIELKE, THELMA JANE, librarian; b. Rochester, N.Y., Dec. 14, 1916; d. Charles Frederick and Sophia Louise (Gottschalk) Mielke; A.B., Elmhurst Coll., 1937; M.A., U. Rochester, 1939; postgrad. Union Theol. Sem., Columbia, 1941-45, N.Y.U., 1954-60; M.S., Columbia, 1961. Asst. dept. philosophy U. Rochester, 1937-39; group worker Baden St. Settlement House, 1939-41; resident Ch. of All Nations, N.Y.C., 1942-43; librarian Harlem Boys Club, 1943-45; UN corr. Revista, P.R., 1945-50; observer UN, 1945-50, OAS, Commn. of Dependent Territories, Havana, Cuba, 1949; pub. relations Hill & Knowlton, N.Y.C., 1952-54; reference asst. to sr. reference librarian, N.Y. U., 1954-63; reference librarian L.I. U., Bklyn., 1963-78, head reference services, 1978—, asst. prof., 1963-65, asso. prof. 1965-76, prof., 1976—, v.p. faculty fedn., 1979—. Exec. sec. Eastern States Hist. Clearing House, 1965-78. Mem. A.L.A., United Fedn. Coll. Tchrs. (sec., exec. bd. 1972-74, v.p. 1976-78), NOW, Nat. Women's Polit. Caucus, Am. Mus. Natural History, Salalm. Editor: Library Leaves, 1964—. Home: 175 W 12th St New York NY 10011-8275 Office: LI U Plaza Brooklyn NY 11201

MIENIK, CATHERINE RENEE, marketing production manager; b. Mineola, N.Y., Aug. 8, 1962; d. John Thomas and Noreen Marie (Rawlins) M. BS in Advt., U. Fla., 1985. Traffic mgr. Direct Mktg. Ent., Westbury, N.Y., 1985-87; asst. prodn. mgr. North Shore Animal League, Port Washington, N.Y., 1987-93, prodn. mgr., 1993—. Vol. PWAC (People with AIDS Coalition), L.I., N.Y., 1993. Office: North Shore Animal League 750 Port Washington Blvd Port Washington NY 11050-3739

MIERSMA, DEBRA LYNN, engineer, research company executive; b. Kalamazoo, Mich., Nov. 5, 1959. BS in Paper Engring., We. Mich. U., 1982. Team mgr. Procter & Gamble, Green Bay, Wis., 1982-86; sr. rsch. engr. Procter & Gamble, Cin., 1987-93; v.p., COO Process Labs. Corp., Cin., 1994—, also bd. dirs. Mem. NAFE, Tech. Assn. Pulp and Paper Industry (former pres., v.p., treas. student chpt.), Paper Industry Mgmt. Assn., Internat. Kiln Assn. Office: Process Labs Corp 10275 Pendery Dr Cincinnati OH 45242

MIESSE, MARY ELIZABETH (BETH MIESSE), special education educator; b. Amarillo, Tex. BA, BS, MEd in Guidance and Counseling, MA, West Tex. State U., Canyon, 1952, MBA, 1960; M in Pers. Svc., U. Colo., Boulder, 1954. Cert. in spl. edn. supr., spl. edn. counselor, ednl. diagnostician, spl. edn. (lang. and/or learning disabled, mentally retarded) tchr., profl. counselor, profl. tchr., supt., prin., Tex. With various bus. firms and radio stas., 1940-47; prof. Amarillo Coll., 1947-63; tchr. pvt. and pub. schs., also TV work, 1963-78; spl. edn. cons., 1978—; freelance writer-prodr. in radio/TV, 1978—. Former editor Tex. Jr. Coll. Tchrs. Assn. Mag. Pioneered in ednl. TV in West Tex.; recipient various lit. awards, awards in ednl. TV. Mem. AAUP, AAUW, APA, ASCAP, NEA, Nat. Fedn. State Poetry Socs., Poetry Soc. Tex., Tex. State Tchrs. Assn., Bus. Profl. Womens Club, Am. Bus. Women's Assn. (named one of Top Ten Women of Yr.), North Plains Assn. for Children with Learning Disabilities, Panhandle Profl. Writers, ASCA Writers, High Plains Poetry Soc., Inspirational Writers, Alive!, Cowboy Poets Assn., Toastmistress Internat. Home and Office: PO Box 3133 Valle De Oro TX 79010-3133

MIGALA, LUCYNA JOZEFA, broadcast journalist, arts administrator, radio station executive; b. Krakow, Poland, May 22, 1944; d. Joseph and Estelle (Suwala) M.; came to U.S., 1947, naturalized, 1955; student Loyola U., Chgo., 1962-63, Chicago Conservatory of Music, 1963-70; BS in Journalism, Northwestern U., 1966. Radio announcer, producer sta. WOPA, Oak Park, Ill., 1963-66; writer, reporter, producer NBC news, Chgo., 1966-69, 1969-71, producer NBC local news, Washington, 1969; producer, coord. NBC network news, Cleve., 1971-78, field producer, Chgo., 1978-79; v.p. Migala Communications Corp., 1979—; program and news dir., on-air personality Sta. WCEV, Cicero, Ill., 1979—; lectr. City Colls. Chgo., 1981, Morton Coll., 1988. Columnist Free Press, Chgo., 1984-87. Founder, artistic dir., gen. mgr. Lira Ensemble (formerly The Lira Singers), Chgo., 1965—; mem., chmn. various cultural coms. Polish Am. Congress, 1970-80; bd. dirs. Nationalities Svcs. Ctr., Cleve., 1973-78; bd. dirs., v.p. Cicero-Berwyn Fine Arts Coun., Cicero, Ill.; mem. City Arts I and II panels Chgo. Office of Fine Arts, 1986-89, 94; v.p. Chgo. chpt. Kosciuszko Found., 1983-86; bd. dirs. Polish Women's Alliance Am., 1983-87, Ill. Humanities Coun., 1983-89, mem. exec. com., 1986-87; bd. dirs. Ill. Arts Alliance, 1989-92; founder, gen. chmn. Midwest Chopin Piano Competition (now Chgo. Chopin Competition), 1984-86; founding mem. ethnic and folk arts panel Ill. Arts Coun., 1984-87, 92—. Recipient AP Broadcasters award, 1973, Emmy award NATAS, 1974, Cultural Achievement award Am. Coun. for Polish Culture, 1990, Award of Merit Advocates Soc. Polish Am. Attys., 1991, Human Rels. Media award City of Chgo., 1992, outstanding achievement in Polish culture award Minister of Rep. of Poland, 1994; Washington Journalism Ctr. fellow, spring 1969. Mem. Soc. Profl. Journalists. Office: Sta WCEV 5356 W Belmont Ave Chicago IL 60641-4103 also: The Lira Ensemble 3750 W Peterson Chicago IL 60659

MIGDEN, CAROLE, county official; b. N.Y.C., Aug. 14, 1948. BA, Adelphi U., 1970; M in Psychology, Sonoma State U., 1976. Exec. dir. Operation Concern, San Francisco, 1981-89; mem. bd. suprs. City of San Francisco, 1991—; former commr. Calif. State Health Commn. Former chair San Francisco Dem. Party; chair Calif. Dem. Party Platform Com.; active Dem. Nat. Com. Recipient Lavendar award Harvey Milk Lesbian/Gay Dem. Club, 1991. Jewish. Office: Bd Suprs City Hall 400 Van Ness Ave Rm 235 San Francisco CA 94102

MIGLIORINO, CAROLINE TERESA, nursing consultant; b. Shaker Heights, Ohio; d. Albino and Albina (Tognaccini) Milano; m. Myron A. Migliorino; children: Paul P., Monica M., Marc J., Laura E. ADN, Prairie State Jr. Coll., Chicago Heights, Ill., 1974; BSN, Gov.'s State U., University Park, Ill., 1977, MSN, 1984. Dir. health svcs. Art Inst. Chgo.; managed care specialist dept. psychiatry Christ Hosp., Oak Lawn, Ill.; nurse, therapist, counselor chem. dependency and addictions Oak Lawn; managed care specialist Christ Hosp., Oak Lawn. Recipient Acad. award Gov.'s State U. Alumni Assn., 1984. Mem. ANA, Ill. Nurses Assn., Nat. Nurses Soc. on Addictions. Home: 37 S Stough St Hinsdale IL 60521-3014

MIGUEL DESOUSA, LINDA J., critical care nurse, nursing educator; b. Honolulu, Dec. 6, 1946; d. Gregory and Irene N. (Calasa) Furtado; children: Joseph H. Miguel Jr., Brett A. Miguel. ADN, Maui Community Coll., Kahului, Hawaii, 1980; BSN, U. Hawaii, 1987, MS, 1990. RN, Hawaii. Charge nurse ICU-CCU Maui Meml. Hosp., Wailuku; nursing instr. Maui Community Coll., Kahului; unit supr.-coronary care Straub Clinic and Hosp., Honolulu; nursing instr. Kapiolani Community Coll., Honolulu; edn. dir. Waianae Health Acad.; researcher in field. Contbr. articles to profl. jours. Outer Island Students Spl. Nursing scholar, 1988-90, Rsch. scholarship, 1989. Mem. AACN, Hawaii Nurses Assn., Hawaii Soc. for Cardiovascular and Pulmonary Rehab., Sigma Theta Tau. Home: 98-402 Loauka Loop #1202 Aiea HI 96701

MIHELICH, JEANETTE AMELIA, retired educator; b. Chgo., June 20, 1921; d. Wesley Leo and Esther Lucille (Maxson) VanOsdol; m. John William Mihelich, Dec. 22, 1946; children: John William Jr., Kathryn Lee, Margaret Lucille. BA with honors, Hanover (Ind.) Coll., 1944; postgrad., U. Ill., 1945-46. Cert. secondary tchr., Ind. Secondary sch. South Bend (Ind.) City Schs., 1966-74; ret., 1981; secondary tchr. Counseling of Girls program YWCA, South Bend, 1971-74; adj. prof. physics Ind. U., South Bend, 1977-81; program dir., interviewer TV program Status of Women, 1978-79. Editor newsletter UN Assn. U.S.A. St. Joseph County, 1984—. Pres. South Bend Mayor's Commn. on Status of Women, 1978-79; precinct committeeman South Bend Rep. Com., 1979-87, 90-92; scholarship chmn. South Bend Area Panhellenic, 1971-72; pres. Presbyn. Women, South Bend, 1975-79, presbyterial pres., 1983-85, chmn. nominations synod bd., 1990-93; chair mgmt. team UN Assn./USA Gift Shop, 1994—; active Women's Assn. South Bend Symphony Orch. Mem. AAUW (pres. South Bend br. 1966-68, pres. state div. 1975-77, state bd. dirs. 1970-79, named fellowship award 1980), Am. Assn. Ret. Persons (tax counselor South Bend 1976—, coord. IRS tax aide program 1983—, asst. dist. coord. tax aide 1990—), Ladies of Notre Dame (pres. 1986-87), DAR, Delta Epsilon, Alpha Delta Pi (pres. 1958-60, 80-82).

MIHRAM, DANIELLE, librarian, educator; b. Alexandria, Egypt, July 23, 1942; came to U.S., 1965; d. Albert and Aimee (Seidman) Redibaum; m. George Arthur Mihram, Dec. 22, 1965. B.A. with honors, U. Sydney (Australia), 1964; diplôme d'études supérieures, Ecole des Hautes Etudes, Paris, 1965; Ph.D., U. Pa., 1970; M.L.S., Rutgers U., 1982. Vis. lectr. Swarthmore (PA.) Coll., 1971; asst. prof. Haverford (Pa.) Coll., 1971; vis. lectr. U. Pa., 1974; bus./research assoc. G. A. Mihram, Cons., Haverford, Pa., 1974-79; library staff Princeton U., 1980-82; reference librarian NYU, N.Y.C., 1982-89; head of reference U. Southern Calif., L.A., 1989—; vis. lectr. Sydney U., Australia, summer 1993; adj. asst. prof. NYU, 1985-89; reviewer rsch. programs NEH, 1989—. Editorial bd. WESS Newsletter, 1986-90; contbr. articles to profl. jours. British Commonwealth scholar Australian Govt., U. Sydney, 1959-65; NATO travel grantee, 1977. Mem. ALA, Assn. Internat. de Cybernétique (Titre Scientifique), Assn. for Computers and the Humanities, Assn. Coll. and Research Libraries, Modern Lang. Assn. Office: U Southern Calif Meml Libr Los Angeles CA 90089-0182

MIICK, MARY ANN, elementary education educator; b. Johnstown, Pa., Oct. 17, 1932; d. Irvin E. and Madelene (McKay) Risser; m. Harold Glenn Heisey, Dec. 14, 1951 (div. 1967); children: Randall George, Robin Glen; m. Robert Edward Miick, Aug. 23, 1981. Student, Goshen (Ind.) Coll., 1950, 51; BS in Edn., Shippensburg (Pa.) Coll., 1971. IBM machine operator Fed. Govt., Olmsted AFB, Pa., 1955-56; tchr. San Diego County, Harrisburg suburbs, Middletown, Pa., 1963-69; parent surrogate Pa. State Hosp., Harrisburg, 1969-71; hostess bed and breakfast Dreamhouse, Annville, Pa., 1990—; tchr. Harrisburg City Sch., 1971—. Mem. Harrisburg Edn. Assn. (union rep. 1985—). Home: RD 2 Box 600A Annville PA 17003 Office: Melrose Elem Sch 2041 Berryhill St Harrisburg PA 17104

MIILLER, SUSAN DIANE, artist; b. N.Y.C., June 10, 1953; d. Elwood Charles and Alyce Mary (Gebhardt) Knapp; m. Denis Miiller, May 22, 1982. MA, Queens Coll., 1980; BFA, SUNY, 1988; MFA, U. North Tex., 1992. Teaching asst. Queens Coll., N.Y.C., 1978-79, Rsch. asst., 1979-80; palynologist Phillips Petroleum Co., Bartleville, Okla., 1980-85; scenic designer Forestburgh (N.Y.) Playhouse, 1989; rsch. asst. Lamont-Doherty Geol. Observatory, Palisades, N.Y., 1990; adj. prof. Tex. Christian U., Ft. Worth, 1992-94; adj. prof. Mountain View Coll., Dallas, 1992-93; treas. mem. 500X Gallery, Dallas, 1991-92; curator Dallas Pub. Libr., 1991, Newburgh Free Libr., 1988; gallery com. Del. Art Ctr., Narrowsburg, N.Y., 1989. One-woman shows include Westen Tex. Coll., 1993, Brazos Gallery, Richland Coll., 1993, Women & Their Work Gallery, 1995 (Gallery Artists Series award 1995). Civic Planner Planning Bd., Deerpark, N.Y., 1989. Tchg. fellow U. North Tex., Denton, 1990-92; recipient Mus. Abilene award, 1992, Lubbock Art Festival Merit award, 1992, 4th Nat. Biennial Exhbns. Grand Purchase award, 1991. Mem. Tex. Fine Arts Assn., Dallas Mus. Art, Coll. Art Assn., D-Art Visual Art Ctr., Art Initiatives. Home: 449 Harris St #J102 Coppell TX 75019 Studio: 3309 Elm St # 3E Dallas TX 75226

MIKA, KAREN, nurse, administrator; b. Jersey City, Jan. 27, 1957; d. Robert and Lois (Fedroff) Sandaal. Grad. in nursing, Middlesex Coll., 1977; BS in Health Care Mgmt., Rutgers U., 1989. Clin. coord. Life Med. Sci., Princeton, N.J. Home: 423 Ridge Rd Dayton NJ 08810 Office: Life Med Sci 214 Carnegie Ctr Ste 100 Princeton NJ 08540-6237

MIKE, DEBORAH DENISE, systems engineer, financial consultant; b. Norfolk, Va., Oct. 19, 1959; d. William A. and Mophecia (Cook) Brickhouse. BA in Math., U. Va., 1981; postgrad., Johns Hopkins U., 1982-88; MS in Computer Systems Mgmt., U. Md., 1994. Primary systems engr. GTE Govt. Systems Corp., Rockville, Md., 1984-85, Vienna, Va., 1985-87; computer analyst Info. Systems and Networks Corp., Arlington, Va., 1987-88; realtor Mount Vernon Realty, Chevy Chase, Md., 1988-89; primary systems engr. Grumman Corp., McLean, Va., 1988-91, J.G. Van Dyke & Assocs., Alexandria, Va., 1991-93; systems engr. Pulse Engring., Inc., Beltsville, Md., 1993-94, Primerica Fin. Svcs., Rockville, Md., 1994—; owner DDM Travel, Designs by Debbie. Active Smithsonian Resident Assoc. Program, 1988; mem. Friends of the Kennedy Ctr. Mem. NAFE (bd. dirs. Reston chpt. 1986), Nat. Assn. Realtors, Md. Assn. Realtors, Montgomery County Bd. Realtors, Nat. soc. Black Engrs., N.Y. Inst. Photography, U. Va. Alumni Assn., U. Va. Club Washington.

MIKEL, SARAH ANN, librarian; b. Bklyn., Aug. 29, 1947; d. Robert H. and Sarah A. (Saver) Whalen; m. John R. Mikel, Oct. 21, 1977; 1 dau., Katherine Ann. B.A., U. Miami, 1969; M.A., U. Fla., 1971; M.A.L.S., Rosary Coll., River Forest, Ill., 1973. Editorial researcher Field Ednl. Enterprises, Chgo., 1971-72; librarian Purdue U., West Lafayette, Ind., 1973-75, U.S. Army Corps of Engrs., Rock Island, Ill., 1975-76, chief librarian, Washington, 1976-87, major command librarian, 1987-91; libr. dir. Nat. Def. Libr., Washington, 1991—; chmn. FEDLINK Users Group, 1980-83; mem. exec. adv. coun. FEDLINK, 1988-90; program chmn. Fed. Interagy. Field Librarians Workshop, 1983-84. Mem. Spl. Library Assn. (chmn. mil. librarians 1978-79), Army Lib. Inst. (chmn. 1988, Army dep. functional chiefs rep. 1992-94). Home: 3343 Reservoir Rd NW Washington DC 20007-2312 Office: Nat Def Univ Ft Leslie J McNair 4th & P St SW Washington DC 20319

MIKE-NARD, BEVERLY JEAN, nurse; b. Youngstown, Ohio, Nov. 3, 1957; d. Michael Ablen and Marion Charlotte (Saba) Mike; children: Stacy Nicole, Kenneth Robert Jr. Nursing diploma, St. Elizabeth Hosp. Med. Ctr., 1978; student, Youngstown State U., 1988-89; BSN, Pa. State U., 1991; MSN, Case Western Res. U., 1993. RN, Ohio; cert. hosp. based neonatal resuscitation program instr., cert. CPR instr., cert. neonatal nurse practitioner. Nurse asst. St. Elizabeth Hosp. Med. Ctr., Youngstown, 1977-78, nurse orthopaedic dept., 1978-81, nurse neonatal ICU, 1982-93, neonatal nurse, CPR instr., asst. apnea home monitor program, 1993—; sec. Color My World Day Care Ctr., 1986-92; one of the first neonatal nurse practitioner's in Mahoning, Trumbull, Columbiana, Mercer and Lawrence County. Active PTA, Austintown, Ohio, 1985-89, Poland, Ohio, 1989—; mem. St. Maron Parish Coun., 1994—. Mem. ANA, NAACOG (cert.), Ohio Nurses Assn., Nat. Assn. Neonatal Nurses, Nat. Apostolate Maronites. Democrat. Maronite Catholic. Home: 3330 Partridge Park Dr Poland OH 44514-2807 Office: St Elizabeth Hosp Med Ctr 1044 Belmont Ave Youngstown OH 44504-1006

MIKHAIL, MARY ATTALLA, computer systems development executive; b. Cairo, Egypt, Apr. 2, 1945; came to U.S., 1980.; d. Attalla Shehata and Soad (Kamel) Abd-El-Malek; m. Ibrahim Fahmy Mikhail, May 1 ,1967; 1 child, Ireny. BS in Math. and Physics, U. Assiut, Egypt, 1965; MS in Math. and Computer Sci., U. Clausthal, Fed. Republic Germany, 1973; PhD in Math., U. Tuebingen, Fed. Republic Germany, 1976. Lectr. Math. Inst., Assiut, Egypt, 1965-67; from instr. to asst. prof. Math. Inst., Tuebingen, Fed. Republic Germany, 1973-78; cons., project mgr. Datel, Fed. Republic Germany, 1978-80; planner, systems analyst C.F. Braun, Alhambra, Calif., 1980-82; optic dept. mgr. Burroughs Corp., City of Industry, Calif., 1982-87; project mgr. continuous transaction processing Unisys Corp., Mission Viejo, Calif., 1987-88, project mgr. systems software devel. Open Systems Interconnectivity, 1988-92, program mgr. Open/OLTP, 1992—. Contbr. articles to profl. jours. Mem. IEEE (standards for software error, faults and failures com., standards for quality metrics com.), Am. Mgmt. Assn. Mem. Coptic Orthodox Ch.

MIKIEWICZ, ANNA DANIELLA, marketing and sales representative; b. Chgo., Dec. 22, 1960; d. Zdislaw and Lucy (Magnusewska) K. BS in Mktg., Elmhurst Coll., 1982; postgrad. Triton Coll. Asst. to Midwestern regional mgr. Meister Pub. Co., Chgo., 1983; sales rep. First Impression, Elk Grove, Ill., 1984; mktg. and customer svcs. rep. Airco Ind. Gases, Broadview and Carol Stream, Ill., 1985, Yamazen USA, Inc., Schaumburg, Ill., 1985-88; nat. sales and mktg. coord. Kitamura Machinery U.S.A, Inc., 1988—. Named Chgo. Polish Queen Polish Am. Culture Club, 1983-84; nominated White House Fellowship Program. Mem. NAFE. Republican. Roman Catholic.

MIKOL, IRENE RITA, banker, artist; b. Bklyn., Oct. 20, 1912; d. Henry and Mary (Adamski) Bruce; m. Stanley J. Mikol, Sept. 9, 1939; 1 child, Vincent. Student, St. John's U., L.I., N.Y., Woodhaven Sch. Art, Y.T. Creative Arts, Farmingdale, L.I., Richmond Hill Artists. Asst. prodn. mgr. Fruit of the Loom, N.Y.C., 1931-45; v.p., mortgage officer Columbia Fed. Savs. Bank, Woodhaven, N.Y., 1960-77. One-person show at Mari Gallery, Mamaroneck, N.Y.; exhibited in group shows at Cork Gallery-Lincoln Ctr. Avery Fisher Hall, George W.V. Smith Art Mus., Springfield, Mass., Bibl. Art Ctr., Dallas, Corner Gallery, World Trade Ctr., Helio Galleries, N.Y.C., Heckscher Mus., Sumner Mus., Washington, Paul VI Inst. for Arts, Washington, Hoyt Fine Arts Inst., Pa., Salon Internat., Jackson, Miss., 1994; represented in permanent collections at Polish Heritage Soc., Phila., Mari Gallery, Mamaroneck; also pvt. collections. Recipient awards Cooperstown (N.Y.) Art Assn., 1979, Chung Cheng Gallery, St. John's U., 1980, Internat. Art Competition, Glendale, Calif., 1984, City of N.Y., Arsenal, 1987, Sea Heritage Found.-Jacob Javits Conv. Ctr., N.Y.C., 1987, Art Investments Internat., divsn. Simonex, Toronto, 1990, Dutch Can. Soc. Internat. Art Festival, 1990, Manhattan Arts Internat., N.Y.C., 1993, Pantechnicon Illustrations, Paradise, Calif., 1993; named winner in Winsor Newton competition. Mem. Nat. League Am. Pen Women (art chmn. N.Y.C. br. 1987-94, rec. sec. 1987-94, biennial award Lever House 1987), Burr Artists (newsletter editor 1988-93), Artist's Equity, Huntington Art League, Women's Caucus for Arts, Am. Artists Profl. Club., Cath. Fine Arts Soc., Cath. Mus. Am. (assoc. mem.), Salmagundi Club (libr. com., awards 1989-92). Roman Catholic. Home and Office: 89-10-91 St Woodhaven NY 11421

MIKULSKI, BARBARA ANN, senator; b. Balt., July 20, 1936. BA, Mt. St. Agnes Coll., 1958; MSW, U. Md., 1965; LLD (hon.), Bowie State U., 1989, Morgan State U., 1990, U. Mass., 1991. Social worker Balt. Dept. Social Services, 1961-63, 66-70; Balt.; mem. Balt. City Council, 1971-76, 95th-99th Congresses from 3d Md. Dist., 1977-87; U.S. senator from Md., 1987—; adj. prof. Loyola Coll., 1972-76.

MIKUS, ELEANORE ANN, artist; b. Detroit, July 25, 1927; d. Joseph and Bertha (Englot) M.; m. Richard Burns, July 6, 1949 (div. 1963); children: Richard, Hillary, Gabrielle. Student, Mich. State U., 1946-49, U. Mex., summer 1948; B.F.A., U. Denver, 1957, M.A., 1967; postgrad., Art Students League, 1958, NYU, 1959-60. Asst. prof. Cornell U., Ithaca, N.Y., 1979-80, assoc. prof., 1980-92, prof. art, 1992-94, prof. emerita, 1994—; asst. prof. art Monmouth Coll., West Long Branch, N.J., 1966-70, prof. Cornell, Rome, 1989; vis. lectr. painting Cooper Union, N.Y.C., 1970-72, Central Sch. Art and Design, London, 1973-77, Harrow (Eng.) Coll. Tech. and Art, 1975-76. Exhibited in 14 one-person shows at, Pace Gallery, N.Y.C. and O.K. Harris Gallery, N.Y.C., Baskett Gallery, Cin., 1982, 84, 85; represented in permanent collections including, Mus. Modern Art, N.Y.C., Whitney Mus., N.Y.C., Los Angeles County Mus., Cin. Mus., Birmingham (Ala.) Mus. Art, Indpls. Mus. Art, Nat. Gallery Art, Washington, Victoria and Albert Mus., London, Library of Congress, Washington; subject of book Eleanore Mikus, Shadows of the Real (by Robert Hobbs and Judith Bernstock), 1991. Guggenheim fellow, 1966-67; Tamarind fellow, summer 1968; MacDowell fellow, summer 1969; grantee Cornell U., 1988. Mem. AAUP. Home: PO Box 6586 Ithaca NY 14851-6586 Office: Cornell U Dept Art Tjaden Hall Ithaca NY 14853

MILAM, JUNE MATTHEWS, life insurance agent; b. Preston, Ga., Mar. 27, 1931; d. Curtis J. and Mary (Doster) Matthews; m. James Cage Lowry, Dec. 20, 1952 (dec.); m. Walker Hinton Milam, Jr., June 15, 1957; children: James L., Melinda K., Lisa W., Matthew W. BA, La. State U., 1952. Agt. N.Y. Life Ins. Co., Metairie, La., 1966—; alderman City of Harahan, La., 1980-86; mayor pro-tem City of Harahan, 1982-84; guest spkr. to industry in 26 states, 1968—; charter leader N.Y. Life Ins. Women's Network, N.Y.C., 1981-83. Contbr. articles to profl. and trade jours. Mem. adv. bd. Battered Women's Program New Orleans, 1978-86; mem. adv. bd. Jefferson Parish Econ. Devel. Coun., 1988-92, sec., 1990; bd. dirs. Abused Children's Advocacy Ctr., 1990—, Extra Mile; co-founder, charter pres. Jefferson 25 Women's Polit. Orgn., 1991-92; chairperson JEDCO Citizen's Adv. Group, 1993. Named Boss of Yr. Am. Bus. Women's Assn., Metairie, 1976, Man of Yr. New Orleans Assn. Life Underwriters, La. State Assn. Life Underwriters, 1976; recipient Natt. Quality award 25 yrs.; Quality of Life grantee, 1990. Mem. Nat. Assn. Life Underwriters, La. Assn. Life Underwriters, New Orleans Assn. Life Underwriters, N.Y. Life Securities Inc., Womens Bus. Owners Assn. (adv. bd. 1984-88), Million Dollar Round Table, New Orleans Top Twenty Study Group. Republican. Presbyterian. Office: NY Life Ins Co 3333 W Napoleon Ave Ste 200 Metairie LA 70001-2882

MILANOVICH, NORMA JOANNE, occupational educator, training company executive; b. Littlefork, Minn., June 4, 1945; d. Lyle Albert and Loretta (Leona) Drake; m. Rudolph William Milanovich, Mar. 18, 1943; 1 child, Rudolph William Jr. BS in Home Econs., U. Wis., Stout, 1968; MA in Curriculum and Instrn., U. Houston, 1973, EdD in Curriculum and Program Devel., 1982. Instr. human svcs. dept. U. Houston, 1971-75; dir. videos project U. N.Mex., Albuquerque, 1976-78, dir. vocat. edn. equity ctr., 1978-88, asst. prof. tech. occupational edn., 1982-88, coord. occupational vocat. edn. programs, 1983-88, dir. consortium rsch. and devel. in occupational edn., 1984-88; pres. The Alpha Connecting Tng. Corp., Albuquerque, 1988—; adj. instr. Cen. Tng. Acad., Dept. Energy, Wackenhut; mem. faculty U. Phoenix; mem. adj. faculty So. Ill. U., Lesley Coll., Boston. Author: Model Equitable Behavior in the Classroom, 1983, Handbook for Vocational-Technical Certification in New Mexico, 1985, We, The Arcturians, 1990, Sacred Journey to Atlantis, 1991, A Vision for Kansas: Systems of Measures and Standards of Performance, 1992, Workplace Skills: The Employability Factor, 1993, The Light Shall Set You Free, 1995; editor: Choosing What's Best for You, 1982, A Handbook for Handling Conflict in the Classroom, 1983, Starting Out...A Job Finding Handbook for Teen Parents, Going to Work...Job Rights for Teens, Modeling Equitable Behavior in the Classroom, 1988. Bd. dirs. Albuquerque Single Parent Occupational Scholarship Program, 1984-86; del. Youth for Understanding Internat. Program, 1985-90; mem. adv. bd. Southwestern Indian Poly. Inst., 1984-88; com. mem. Region VI Consumer Exch. Com., 1982-84; tour dir. internat. study tours to Japan, Austria, Korea, Mex., Eng., Greece, Egypt, Australia, New Zealand, Fed. Republic Germany, Israel, Guatemala, Peru, Bolivia, Chile, Easter Island, Tibet, China, Hong Kong, Turkey, Italy, 1984-95. Grantee N.Mex. Dept. Edn., 1976-78, 78-86, 83-86, HEW, 1979, 80, 81, 83, 84, 85, 86, 87, JTPA Strategic Mktg. Plan. Mem. ASTD, Am. Vocat. Assn., Vocat. Edn. Equity Coun., Nat. Coalition for Sex Equity Edn., Am. Home Econs. Assn., Inst. Noetic Scis., N.Mex. Home Econs. Assn., N.Mex. Vocat. Edn. Assn., N.Mex. Adv. Coun. on Vocat. Edn., Greater Albuquerque C. of C., NAFE, Phi Delta Kappa, Phi Upsilon Omicron, Phi Theta Kappa. Democrat. Roman Catholic.

MILBERG, MELINDA SHARON, lawyer; b. L.A., May 11, 1953; d. Albert Irving and Gloria Joy (Nathanson) M.; m. Philip B. Benjamin, Aug. 8, 1976; children: Jason G.M., Alex N.M. BA magna cum laude, Brandeis U., 1974; JD, Boston U., 1977. Bar: Mass. 1977, U.S. Dist. Ct. Mass. 1980, U.S. Ct. Appeals (1st cir.) 1985. Civil rights compliance atty. Mass. Com. Criminal Justice, Boston, 1978-80; counsel Mass. Dept. Correction, Boston, 1980-83; spl. asst. atty. gen. Exec. Office Human Svcs., Boston, 1983-85; assoc. Glovsky & Assocs., Boston, 1985—; instr. Boston U. Sch. Law, 1983-85, Flaschner Jud. Inst., Boston, 1990-91; pub. mem. Bd. Registration in Medicine, Boston, 1985-88; mem. faculty Mass. Continuing Legal Edn., 1989-90. Co-author: Chapter 93A Rights and Remedies, 1989. Recipient Pub. Svc. award Am. Jewish Congress, Boston, 1988, Svc. award Bd. Registration in Medicine, Boston, 1988. Fellow Mass. Bar Found.; mem. Mass. Bar Assn. (pub. law sect. coun. 1984-87), Women's Bar Assn. Mass. (pres., v.p. 1981-82), Am. Arbitration Assn. (panel mem. 1993—). Office: Glovsky & Assocs Ste 810 31 Milk St Boston MA 02109

MILBERG, SUSAN BODNER, marketing and communications executive; b. N.Y.C., Apr. 20, 1949; d. Milton Meyer and Muriel Ruby (Walash) Swersky; m. Lawrence Bodner, Oct. 25, 1970 (div. June 1975); children: Jennifer Lynn Bodner, Jason Ross Bodner; m. Barry A. Milberg, Apr. 14, 1983. BA in Edn., U. Md., 1970; BA in English, 1971; paralegal cert., Barry Coll., 1980; MBA, Ga. State U., 1980. Tchr. devel. curriculum Solomon Shecter Hillel Community Day Sch., North Miami Beach, Fla., 1974-77; English tchr. Hebrew Acad. Atlanta, 1977-78; life underwriter, estate planner Life Va. Ins., Atlanta, 1978-79; paralegal, probate and estate mgmt. Abrams, Anton Robbins, Resnick, Schneider & Mager, Hollywood, Fla., 1980-81; svc. cons. mktg. dept. Southern Bell, Ft. Lauderdale, Fla., 1981-83; dir. community rels. The Jewish Home, Atlanta, 1984-87; dir. mktg. and comm. svcs. The United Jewish Fedn. Metrowest, Whippany, N.J., 1988—; pubs. rep., adminstr. The Metrowest Jewish News, Whippany, 1988—; cons. pub. rels. for philanthropic orgn. and beneficiary agys., Whippany, 1988—; pub. Metrosource, community resource book, 1990—, Inside Quar., lifestyle mag., 1994. Life mem. Nat. Coun. Jewish Women, Millburn-Shorthills, 1984—. Mem. NAFE, N.J. Press Women (state and nat. comm. award 1990, 91, 92, 93), N.J. Exec. Women, Pub. Rels. Soc. Am., Am. Mktg. Assn. Office: United Jewish Fedn 901 Rte 10 Whippany NJ 07981-1156

MILBRATH, MARY MERRILL LEMKE, quality assurance professional; b. Evanston, Ill., Aug. 13, 1940; d. William Frederick and Martha Merrill (Slagel) Lemke; m. Gene McCoy Milbrath, Aug. 22, 1964; children: Elizabeth Ann, Sarah Toril Jeanne. BA in Biology, Albion Coll., 1962; MS in Plant Pathology, U. Ariz., 1966. Microbiologist Abbott Labs., North Chicago, Ill., 1962; toxicologist U. Ariz., Tucson, 1965-67; toxicologist U. Ill., Urbana, 1976-77, entomologist, 1978; plant pathologist State of Oreg., Salem, 1979, chemist, 1980-82; quality auditor Siltec Corp., Salem, 1983-84, quality control supr., 1985-91, quality auditing mgr., 1992—, implementor ISO 9002, 1994; Active Ill. Emergency Svcs.toxic sub task force U. Ill., Urbana, 1978; mem. Responsible Corp. Citizens Com., Salem, 1989—. Mem. citizens adv. com. Sch. Bd., Urbana, 1976-78; campaigner Oreg. 5th dist. race, Salem, 1984, Oreg. Nat. Abortion Rights Assn. League, Salem, 1986; mem. bd. Tribute to Outstanding Women, YWCA, 1993; vol. Tree Giving, 1991, 92, YWCA Tribute to Women Bd., 1992, 93, 94, Salem Hosp. Aux., 1985—, Women in Math and Sci. Mentor Program, 1993, 94. NDEA fellow U.S. Dept. Def., 1962. Mem. AAUW (chmn. interest group), Am. Soc. for Quality Control (cert. quality auditor exam writing com.), Willamette U. House Corp. (treas. 1982-85, v.p. 1991—), Delta Gamma (treas. Salem Alumnae chpt. 1981-85, pres. Salem Alumnae chpt. 1987-89, scholarship advisor Willamette U. chpt. 1986-90). Office: Siltec Corp 1351 Tandem Ave NE Salem OR 97303-4199

MILCH, PAMELA H., television producer; b. Bronx, N.Y., Feb. 9, 1960; d. Edward and Sylvia (Nessman) M. BS cum laude, Syracuse U., 1982. Prodn. technician Cablevision, Woodbury, N.Y., 1983-85, dir., editor, 1985-86; producer News 12 L.I., Woodbury, 1986-88; sr. producer Fin. News Network, N.Y.C., 1988-91; producer CBS News Up To The Minute, 1992—. Youth dir. United Synagogue Youth, Babylon and Queens, N.Y., 1983-88.

MILDVAN, DONNA, infectious diseases physician; b. Phila., June 20, 1942; d. Carl David and Gertrude M.; m. Rolf Dirk Hamann; 1 child, Gabriella Kay. AB magna cum laude, Bryn Mawr Coll., 1963; MD, Johns Hopkins U., 1967. Diplomate Am. Bd. Internal Medicine and Infectious Diseases. Intern, resident Mt. Sinai Hosp., N.Y.C., 1967-70, fellow, infectious diseases, 1970-72; asst., assoc. prof. clin. medicine Mt. Sinai Sch. Medicine, N.Y.C., 1972-87; prof. clinical medicine Dept. Medicine, Mt. Sinai Sch. Medicine, N.Y.C., 1987-88, prof. medicine, 1988-94; physician-in-charge infectious diseases Beth Israel Med. Ctr., N.Y.C., 1972-79, chief, div. infectious diseases, 1980—; prof. medicine Albert Einstein Coll. of Medicine, N.Y.C., 1994—; mem. AIDS charter rev. com., NIH/Nat. Inst. Allergy and Infectious Diseases, Bethesda, 1987—; cons. FDA, Rockville, 1987—, Ctrs. for Disease Control, Atlanta, 1985-86; among first to describe AIDS, "Pre-AIDS", AIDS Dementia, 1982, among first to study AZT, 1986; Keynote speaker, II Internat. Conf. on AIDS, Paris, 1986 and other achievements in field; Sophie Jones Meml. lectr. in infectious diseases U. Mich. Hosps., 1984. Contbr. numerous articles to profl. jours; co-editor two books, several book chpts. and abstracts on infectious diseases and AIDS. Recipient Woman of Achievement award AAUW, 1987; contract for antiviral therapy in AIDS, Nat. Cancer Inst./Nat. Inst. Allergy and Infectious Diseases, 1985-86, grant N.Y. State AIDS Inst., 1986-87, subcontract Nat. Inst. Allergy and Infectious Diseases, 1987-95; Henry Strong Denison scholar, Johns Hopkins U. Sch. Medicine, 1967. Fellow Infectious Diseases Soc. Am.; mem. Am. Soc. Microbiology, AAAS, Harvey Soc., Internat. AIDS Soc. Democrat. Jewish. Office: Beth Israel Med Ctr 1st Ave New York NY 10003-7903

MILES, CHARLENE, small business owner; b. Pine City, Ark., Dec. 4, 1928; d. Albert and Katherine (Coakes) Banks; m. James Dixon Jr., Jan. 5, 1947 (div. 1955); children: James Walter II, Shirley; m. Joe Miles, Apr. 21, 1955 (dec.); 1child, Donell. AA, Shorter Coll., Little Rock, Ark., 1946; cert., Buffalo (N.Y.) Beauty Coll., 1960. Lic. cosmetologist. Technician Posner Beauty Products, N.Y.C., 1960-63; instr. Peter Piccolo Beauty Sch., Buffalo, 1974-75; founder, pres. Charlene's Unisex Salon of N.Y., Detroit, 1975—; judge Student Cosmetology Assn., Buffalo, 1980—. Pres. Profls. Against Drugs, Detroit, 1988—; corp. dir. Op. Push, Chgo., 1987—. Named Pres. of Yr. CUS Bd. Dirs., 1984. Mem. Nat. Hairdressers Assn., Pacesetters (outstanding service award 1984), Mary B. Tolbert Assn., Beverly Area Planning Assn. Democrat. Home: PO Box 7518 Bloomfield Hills MI 48302-7518 Office: Charlenes Unisex Salon NY 433 Fifth Ave New York NY 10016-2207

MILES, CHRISTINE MARIE, museum director; b. Madison, Ind., Mar. 2, 1951; d. Leland Weber and Mary Virginia (Geyer) M.; B.A., Boston U., 1973; M.A., George Washington U., 1982; postgrad. Mus. Mgmt. Inst., 1985. Curatorial asst. Mus. of the City of N.Y., 1973-75; art gallery dir. South Street Seaport Mus., N.Y.C., 1975-77; researcher The Octagon, AIA Found., Washington, 1978-80; dir. Fraunces Tavern Mus., N.Y.C., 1980-86, Albany (N.Y.) Inst. History and Art, 1986—; bd. dirs. Sta. WMHT-TV, SUNY-Albany Found., Hist. Albany Found., Fedn. Hist. Svcs.; pres. Gallery Assn. N.Y. State, 1991-93; pres. N.Y. State Assn. Museums, Lower Manhattan Cultural Coun.; mus. aid panel N.Y. State Council on Arts, 1985-88;. Author, writer/coordinator, compiler of catalogs in field. Mem. Am. Assn. Mus. Office: Albany Inst History & Art 125 Washington Ave Albany NY 12210-2296

MILES, JANICE ANN, news reporter; b. Abilene, Tex., July 22, 1949; d. Theodore Winston and Clarice (Buie) M.; m. Martin Jerome Wiesenthal, Feb. 24, 1973; children: Alexis Ann Wiesenthal, Alison Claire Wiesenthal. BFA, U. Tex., 1971; postgrad., Trinity U., 1980. Social worker Tex. Dept. Human Svcs., San Antonio, 1971-79; TV news reporter Sta. KENS-TV, San Antonio, 1981—. Bd. dirs. Sunshine Cottage Sch. for Deaf Children, 1982-89, San Antonio Botanical Ctr., 1984-90, Univ. Presbyn. Children's Ctr., San Antonio, 1986-90, San Antonio Day Hosp., 1990, San Antonio AIDS Found., 1995—, Alamo Theatre Arts Coun., 1995—, SIDS, 1994. Recipient Guardian Angel award Boysville, Inc., 1987, Barbara Jordan award Gov.'s Com. for Disabled Persons, 1988, 90, 92, Pat Weaver award Nat. Muscular Dystrophy Assn., 1989, Recognition award Lighthouse for the Blind, 1990, Tex. Child Welfare Bd. Media award, 1991, San Antonio award, 1992; named Media Person of Yr., San Antonio Planning com., 1993. Mem. Women in Communications Inc., San Antonio 100, San Antonio Forum. Presbyterian. Office: KENS-TV Eyewitness News 5400 Fredericksburg Rd San Antonio TX 78229-3504

MILES, JEANNE PATTERSON, artist; b. Balt.; d. Walter and Edna (Webb) M.; m. Frank Curlee, Dec. 31, 1935 (dec.); m. Johannes Schiefer, Feb. 11, 1939 (div.); 1 child, Joanna. BFA, George Washington U.; postgrad., Philips Meml. Gallery Sch., Atelier Gromaire, Grand Chaumiere, Paris. One-woman shows include Betty Parsons Gallery, N.Y.C., 1945, 52, 55, 56, 59, 77, 82, Grand Central Moderns, N.Y.C., 1968, Wesbeth Galleries, N.Y.C., 1972; group shows include N.Y. Rome Found., 1957, Walker Art Gallery, Mpls., 1954, Corcoran Biennial, Yale U. Mus., 1957, Chateau Gagnes, France, 1938, Whitney Mus., 1963, Nat. Fedn. Am. Art, 1963, Mus. Modern Art, 1966, Riverside Mus., N.Y.C., 1964, Guggeheim Mus., 1965-66, Geodok Am. Women Show, Hamburg and Berlin, 1972, Springfield (Mass.) Art Mus., 1975, Hunterton Art Center, Clinton, N.J., 1975, Betty Parsons Gallery, 1977, 82, Sid Deutch, 1978, 79, Marlyn Pearl Gallery, N.Y.C., 1986, 88, Bronx Mus. Art, 1986, George Washington, 1989, 55 Mercer St, N.Y.C., 1989, Marlyn Pearl Gallery, N.Y.C., 1991, Anita Shapalsky Gallery, N.Y.C., 1992, Shapalsky Gallery, 1993; represented in permanent collections NYU, Santa Barbara (Calif.) Mus., Muson Proctor Mus., Utica, N.Y., Rutgers Coll., U. Ariz., Guggenheim Mus., Cin. and Newark museums, White Art Mus., N.Y. State U. at Purchase, Cornell U., Ecumenical Inst., Garrison, N.Y., Graymoor, Garrison, Springfield Art Mus., Weatherspoon Art Mus., U. N.C., Wichita (Kans.) Mus., Mus. of Wichita, Mus. of St. Mary's (Md.) Coll., L.A. County Mus., Alexander Mus., La., also pvt. collections, N.Y.C. and France; traveling exhibits; poster and cover for catalogues, 1987-92; video tape showing of exhibits on cable TV, N.Y.C., 1989. Charles C. Ladd painting scholar Tahiti, 1938, 56, traveling scholar France, 1937-48; grantee Am. Inst. Arts and Letters, 1968, Mark Rothko Found., 1970-73, Pelham von Stoeffler Art Fund, 1974; invited residency (award) to Yaddo Art Colony, Saratoga Springs, N.Y., 50s and 60s, MacDowell Colony, N.H. Mem. Abstract Artists Am., George Washington U. Alumni Assn. (Disting. Achievement award 1987).

MILES, JOANNA, actress, playwright; b. Nice, France, Mar. 6, 1940; came to U.S., 1941, naturalized, 1941; d. Johannes Schiefer and Jeanne Miles; m. William Burns, May 23, 1970 (div. 1977); m. Michael Brandman, Apr. 29, 1978; 1 child, Miles. Grad., Putney (Vt.) Sch., 1958. Mem. Actors Studio, N.Y.C., 1966; co-founder, mem. L.A. Classic Theatre, 1986; founder, artistic dir. Playwrights Group at the Irish Arts Ctr. Appeared in: motion pictures The Way We Live Now, 1969, Bug, 1975, The Ultimate Warrior, 1975, Golden Girl, 1978, Cross Creek, 1983, As Is, 1986, Blackout, 1988, Rosencrants and Guildenstern Are Dead, 1991, The Rhinehart Theory, 1994, Judge Dredd, 1994; numerous television films, including In What America, 1965, My Mothers House, 1963, Glass Menagerie, 1974, Born Innocent, 1974, Aloha Means Goodbye, 1974, The Trial of Chaplain Jensen, 1975, Harvest Home, 1977, Fire in the Sky, 1978, Sophisticated Gents, 1979, Promise of Love, 1982, Sound of Murder, 1983, All My Sons, 87, The Right To Die, 1987, The Habitation of Dragons, 1991, Heart of Justice, 1991, Water Engine, 1991, Cooperstown, 1992, Legionnaires, 1992, Life Lessons, 1992, Willing to Kill, 1992, The American Clock, 1993, Dark Reflections, 1993, Outcry, 1994; episodes in numerous TV series including Barney Miller, Dallas, St. Elsewhere, The Hulk, Trapper John, Kaz, Cagney and Lacey, Studio 5B, 1989, Star Trek: The Next Generation, 1990, 91, Life Stories, 1991, HBO Life Stories, 1993; stage plays Walk-Up, 1962, Once in a Life Time, 1963, Cave Dwellers, 1964, Drums in the Night, 1968, Dracula, 1968, Home Free, 1964, One Night Stands of A Noisy Passenger, 1972, Dylan, 1973, Dancing for the Kaiser, 1976, Debutante Ball, 1985, Kramer, 1977, One Flew Over The Cuckoo's Nest, 1989, Growing Gracefully, 1990, Cut Flowers, 1994; performed in radio shows Sta. KCRW Once in a Lifetime, 1987, Babbit, 1987, Sta. KPFK, Grapes of Wrath, 1989, The White Plague, Sta. KCRW, 1991, Chekhov Short Stories, Sta. KCRW, 1992; playwright, v.p. Brandman Productions. Pres. Children Giving to Children. Recipient 2 Emmy awards, 1974, Women in Radio and TV award, 1974, Actors Studio Achievement award, 1980. Mem. Acad. Motion Picture Arts and Scis., Acad. TV Arts and Scis., Dramatists Guild. Office: c/o Howard Askew 6217 Glenary St Hollywood CA 90068

MILES, LAVEDA ANN, advertising executive; b. Greenville, S.C. Nov. 21, 1945; d. Grady Lewis and Edna Sylvia (Mahaffey) Bruce; m. Charles Thomas Miles, Nov. 10, 1974; 1 child, Joshua Bruce. A in Bus. Adminstrn., North Greenville Jr. Coll. Traffic mgr. WFBC-TV, Greenville, S.C., 1968-74; pub. svc. dir., traffic mgr. WTCG-TV, Atlanta, 1974-75; traffic mgr. Henderson Advt. Co., Greenville, 1975-77, broadcast coord., 1977-79, dir. broadcast bus., 1979-82, dir. broadcast bus., v.p., 1982-89, bus. mgr. creative dept., 1989-91, dir. creative svcs., 1991-93, sr. v.p., 1993—. Named one of 100 Best and Brightest Women for 1988 Ad Age and Advt. Women of N.Y. Mem. Advt. Fedn. of Greenville (sec. 1979-81, Leadership S.C. Class 1994-95). Democrat. Baptist. Office: Henderson Advt Co 60 Pelham Pointe Greenville SC 29615-2142

MILES, LISA LORRAINE, banker; b. Fort Rucker, Ala., Sept. 19, 1966; d. Robert and Margaret (Moore) M. AS in Computer Info. Systems, South Coll., 1988; BBA in Acctg., Savannah State Coll., 1994. Daytime supervisor Bankers First, Savannah, 1988-90; adminstr. ops. Bank South, Savannah, 1990-93; consumer assoc. First Union Nat. Bank, Savannah, 1994—. cochair bd. of trustees First African Baptist of East Savannah, 1993—, chair fin. com., 1994. Mem. Inst. Mgmt. Accts. (v.p. 1993-94). Republican. Baptist. Home: 1901 Vassar St Savannah GA 31405 Office: First Union Nat Bank 2 East Bryan St Savannah GA 31401

MILES, MARGARET, librarian; b. San Francisco, May 6, 1963; d. Robert Donald and Norma Ann (Crawford) Hughes; m. Thomas Alan Miles, May 14, 1988. BA in English, U. Calif., Davis, 1985; M Libr. and Info. Studies, U. Calif., Berkeley, 1987. Children's libr. Tracy (Calif.) br. Stockton-San Joaquin County Pub. Libr., 1987-89; chmn. children's film com. Stockton-San Joaquin County Pub. Libr., Stockton, 1987-89; supervising children's librarian Downtown br. Sacramento Pub. Library, 1990—; mem. Calif. Young Reader Medal Com., 1991-94, chair children's and young adult svcs. sect., 1994—. Amy Wood Nyholm scholar, 1987. Mem. ALA, Calif. Libr. Assn. (children's svcs. chpt. film com. 1989), AAUW, Phi Kappa Phi. Office: Sacramento Pub Library 828 I St Sacramento CA 95814-2508

MILES, MINNIE CADDELL, retired business educator; b. Glen Allen, Ala., Mar. 4, 1910; d. Thomas Elias and Bertha Eveline (Griggs) Caddell; m. Murphie Alton Miles, Mar. 4, 1928 (dec. 1979). BS, Mary Hardin-Baylor, 1936; MBA, Northwestern U., 1941; PhD, Purdue U., 1951; LLD (hon.), Mary Hardin-Baylor, 1965; D Humanities (hon.), U. Ala., 1987. Tchr. rural schs. Ala. Sch. System, 1926-32; collector student loans Mary Hardin-Baylor, Belton, Tex., 1934-41; exec. sec. Northwestern U., Evanston, Ill., 1941-42; bus. tchr. U. Ala., Tuscaloosa, 1942-78; dir. indsl. rels. Olan Mills, Chattanooga, 1945-47; Fulbright prof. Pusan (Republic of Korea) Nat. U., 1969, Victoria U., Wellington, New Zealand, 1977-78; vis. prof. Purdue U., Lafayette, Ind., 1951; cons. Druid City Hosp., Tuscaloosa, 1954-55, TVA, Knoxville, Tenn., 1972, U.S. Civil Svc. Commn., Washington, 1973-77; field assoc. Fry Assocs., Consultants, Chgo., 1957-73. Contbr. articles to profl. jours. Chmn. Ala. Status of Women Commn., Montgomery, 1964-70; mem., chmn. Def. Adv. Com. on Women in Svc., Washington, 1965-67; specialist Latin Am. program U.S. Dept. State, 1963; bd. dirs. U.S. Bus. and Profl. Women's Found., Washington, 1957-64; nat. trainer Widowed Persons Svc. Rsch. grantee U. Ala., Tuscaloosa, 1954; named to Faculty hall of Fame/Coll. of Bus., U. Ala., Tuscaloosa, 1990, Women Committed to Excellence Girl Scouts U.S., 1989, inducted Ala. Women's Acad. of Honor, 1992, Civitan Citizen of Yr., 1993. Mem. U.S. Fedn. Bus. and Profl. Women (pres. 1962-63), Ala. Fedn. Bus. and Profl. Women (pres. 1955-57), Ala. Bus. and Profl. Women's Found. (life mem. bd. dirs., chmn. bd. dirs. 1981-88), ASTD (life), APA, Tuscaloosa Club Altrusa Internat. (pres. 1952-53). Democrat. Methodist. Home: 27 Beech Hls Tuscaloosa AL 35404-4959 Office: U Ala Tuscaloosa AL 35487-0122

MILES, ROSEMARY CLAIRE, marriage and family therapist; b. N.Y.C., July 13, 1953; d. Salvatore Joseph and Josephine Marie (Bocchiere) Di Pietro; m. Donald Bruce Kershaw, Sept. 25, 1982 (dec. Sept. 1986); m. Robert Johnstone Miles, June 11, 1988; 1 child, Martin Jonathan. BA in Behavioral Scis., Psychology, SUNY, Stonybrook, 1975; Ma in Ednl. Psychology, Calif. State U., Northridge, 1979. Lic. marriage, family and child counselor 1984. Psychiat. technician Northridge (Calif.) Found. Hosp., 1977-80; vocat. rehab. counselor DS Assocs., Burbank, Calif., 1980-86, Crawford Rehab. Svcs., L.A., 1980-86, North County Vocat. Cons., Palmsdale, Calif., 1986-90; counselor marriage, family and child Family Svc. Agy., Sacramento, Calif., 1990-93, pvt. practice, Sacramento, Calif., 1991-93, Visions Unltd., Inc., Sacramento, Calif., 1993—. Contbr. articles to profl. jours. Mem. Calif. Assn. Marriage and Family Therapists, Sacramento chpt. Assn. Marriage and Family Therapists, Toastmasters Internat. Democrat. Office: Visions Unltd Inc 7000 Franklin Blvd Ste 200 Sacramento CA 95823-1820

MILES, VERA, actress; b. Boise City, Okla., Aug. 23, 1930; d. Thomas and Burnice (Wyrick) Ralston; divorced; children: Debra, Mrs. Kelley Essoe, Michael, Erik. Film roles include: For Men Only (debut), 1952, Rose Bowl Story, Backstreet, Charge at Feather River, 1954, Pride of the Blue Grass, Wichita, 1955, The Searchers, 1956, 23 Paces to Baker St, 1956, Autumn Leaves, 1956, The Wrong Man, 1957, Beau James, 1957, Web of Evidence, 1959, F.B.I. Story, 1959, Psycho, 1960, The Man Who Shot Liberty Valance, 1962, Gentle Giant, 1967, Kona Coast, 1968, Hellfighters, 1969, Mission Batangos, Wild Country, 1971, Run for the Roses, 1978, Psycho II, 1983, Into the Night, 1985; TV appearances include Rough Necks, 1980, others; TV movies include Judge Horton and the Scottsboro Boys, 1976, McNaughton's Daughter, 1976, State Fair, 1976, Runaway!, 1973, The Underground Man, 1974, The Strange and Deadly Occurrence, 1974, Smash-Up on Interstate 5, 1976, Our Family Business, 1981; Rona Jaffe's Mazes and Monsters, 1982, Travis McGee, 1983, Helen Keller-The Miracle Continues, 1984, The Highjacking of the Achille Lauro, 1989. Address: PO Box 1704 Big Bear Lake CA 92315-1704*

MILES-LAGRANGE, VICKI, federal judge; b. Oklahoma City, Sept. 30, 1953; d. Charles and Mary (Greenard) Miles; m. Jacques Lagrange. BA, Vassar Coll., 1974; LLB, Howard U., 1977. Formerly trial atty. U.S. Dept. Justice; congl. aide Speaker of the Ho., Rep. Carl Albert; mem. Okla. Senate from Dist. 48, 1987-93; U.S. atty. U.S. Dept. of Justice, Oklahoma City, Okla., 1993-94; judge U.S. Dist. Ct. (we. dist.) Okla., Oklahoma City, 1994—. Democrat. Baptist. Home: 4020 N Lincoln Blvd #204 Oklahoma City OK 73105-5219 Office: US Courthouse 200 NW 4th St Oklahoma City OK 73102*

MILEWSKI, BARBARA ANNE, pediatrics nurse, neonatal intensive care nurse; b. Chgo., Sept. 11, 1934; d. Anthony and LaVerne (Sepp) Witt; m. Leonard A. Milewski, Feb. 23, 1952; children: Pamela, Robert, Diane, Timothy. ADN, Harper Coll., Palatine, Ill, 1982; BS, Northern Ill. U., 1992; postgrad., North Park Coll. RN, Ill.; cert. CPR instr. Staff nurse Northwest Community Hosp., Arlington Heights, Ill., Resurrection Hosp., Chgo.; nurse neonatal ICU Children's Meml. Hosp., Chgo.; CPR instr. Stewart Oxygen Svcs., Chgo.; instr., organizer parenting and well baby classes and clinics; vol. Children's Meml. Hosp.; health coord. CEDA Head Start. Vol. first aid instr. Boy Scouts Am.; CPR instr. Harper Coll., Children's Meml. Hosp.; dir. Albany Park Community Ctr. Head Start, Chgo. Mem. Am. Mortar Bd., Sigma Theta Tau.

MILICEVIC, JELENA, health science specialist; b. Skopje, Macedonia, Yugoslavia, Jan. 1, 1939; came to U.S., 1972; d. Miladin and Hedy (Hem) M.; m. Ernst Anzbock, Dec. 14, 1959 (div. 1971); children: Harald, Evelyn; m. Ranko Caric, Nov. 3, 1973 (div. 1980); 1 child, Peter. Student, Molloy Coll., 1979-81, L.I. U., 1981-82, Rockland Community Coll., 1985, Vt. Coll., 1985-86, Orange County Community Coll., 1988, Empire State Coll., 1990—. Ordained to ministry Universal Spiritualist Assn. U.S.A., 1985; lic., real estate agt., N.Y.; registered and cert. reflexologist, N.Y. Owner Walter's Bake Shop, 1973-79; nurse's aide Hillside Manor, 1980; clerical worker Molloy Coll., 1980-81, L.I. U., 1981-82; chiropractor asst. Steven R. Siegel D.C., 1982; owner Linden Motel, 1983; lectr. on Shiatsu and reflexology New Age Ctr., 1985-86; v.p., min. Universal Ctr. New Age Consciousness, Inc., Milford, Pa., 1985—; with Abatelli Realty, 1988; gen. agt. Intern Cons. Exchange, San Diego, Calif., 1986. Mem. Am. Massage Therapy Assn., Alliance of Massage Therapists, Inc., Universal Spiritualist Assn., N.Y. State Soc. Med. Massage Therapists, Internat. Platform Assn., Warwick Art League. Home: 119 Wickham Ave Middletown NY 10940 Office: Universal Ctr New Age 313 Broad St Milford PA 18337-1322

MILKMAN, BEVERLY L., federal agency administrator; b. Ft. Pierce, Fla., Jan. 9, 1945; d. Robert George and Annette (Leatherwood) Lyford; m. Raymond H. Milkman, Feb. 27, 1972; 1 child, Katherine. BA magna cum laude, U. Ariz., 1967; MLA with honors, Johns Hopkins U., 1972; MA valedictorian, George Washington U., 1978. Rsch. analyst Peat, Marwick, Mitchell & Co., 1967-69, program analyst, 1970-72, spl. asst. to dep. sec., 1972-74, spl. asst. to asst. sec., 1974-80, dir. office tech. assistance, 1980-81, dir. office of planning, tech. assistance, rsch. and evaluation, 1981-86, dep. dir. grant programs, econ. devel. adminstrn., 1986-88; exec. dir. Com. for Purchase from People Who are Blind or Severely Disabled, 1988—. Assoc. editor Economic Development Quarterly; contbr. articles to profl. publs. Office: Com Purchase from People Who Are Blind or Severely Disabled 1735 Jefferson Davis Hwy Rm 403 Arlington VA 22202*

MILKMAN, MARIANNE FRIEDENTHAL, city planner; b. Berlin, May 13, 1931; came to U.S., 1957; d. Ernst Leopold and Margarethe (Goldschmidt) Friedenthal; m. Roger Dawson Milkman, Oct. 18, 1958; children: Ruth, Louise, Janet, Paul. BA, Cambridge (Eng.) U., 1952, MA, 1956; teaching diploma, London U., 1953. Tchr. biology Milham Ford High Sch., Oxford, Eng., 1953-57; teaching fellow, rsch. asst. U. Mich., Ann Arbor, 1957-59; sci. dir. Children's Sch. Sci., Woods Hole, Mass., 1971-72; planning technician dept. planning and program devel. City of Iowa City, 1975-76, planner I, 1976-79, assoc. planner, 1979-85, coord. community devel., 1986—. Bikeways chmn. Project Green, Iowa City, 1968-75. State scholar Cambridge U. and London U., 1949-53, Fulbright travelling scholar U. Mich., 1957; fellow English Speaking Union, 1957-58. Mem. Am. Planning Assn. (sec.-treas. Iowa chpt. 1982-84, v.p. 1984-86, pres. 1986-88, chmn. univ. rels. com. 1987-91, President's award 1988), Nat. Assn. Housing and Redevel. Ofcls., Nat. Community Devel. Assn. Jewish. Home: 12 Fairview Knls NE Iowa City IA 52240-9147 Office: Iowa City Dept Planning and Community Devel 410 E Washington St Iowa City IA 52240-1825

MILLAN, ANGELA, television news reporter; b. Bogota, Colombia, Dec. 13, 1962; came to U.S., 1987; d. Alirio Antonio and Lilia (Martinez) M. BA, INPAHU, Bogota, 1984. Parliamentary asst. Nat. Congress Columbia, Bogota, 1982-84; press asst. Camera of Reps., Bogota, 1984-85, press aide, 1986-87; news reporter El Diario La Prensa, N.Y.C., 1987, Sta. WNJV-TV, Teterboro, N.J., 1989-90, Univision Network, N.Y.C., 1991-94; assignment editor Sta. WXTV-TV, Secaucus, N.J., 1988, news reporter, 1990—; cons. Epstein and Assocs., N.Y.C., 1993—. Mem. Nat. Assn. Hispanic Journalists, Ams. Soc.

MILLANE, LYNN, town official; b. Buffalo, N.Y. Oct. 14, 1928; d. Robert P. Schermerhorn and Justine A. (Ross) m. J. Vaughan Millane, Jr.; Aug. 16, 1952 children: Maureen, Michele, John, Mark, Kathleen. EdB, U. Buffalo,

1949, EdM, in Health Education 1951. Mem. Amherst Town Bd., 1982—, dep. town supr., 1990—; pres., E. J. Meyer Hosp. Jr. Bd., 1962-64; pres. Aux. to Erie County Bar Assn., 1966-68; pres. Women's Com. of Buffalo Philharm. Orch., 1976-78, v.p. adminstrn., 1975-76, v.p. pub. affairs, 1974-75, chmn. adv. bd., 1979-82; v.p. Buffalo Philharm. Orch. Soc., Inc., 1976-78, mem. coun., trustee, 1979-87, bd. overseers, 1987-92; dir. 8th judicial dist. N.Y. State Assn. of Large Towns, 1989-90, 90-91; bd. dirs. oper. bd. Millard Fillmore Suburban Hosp., 1992-2001; 1st v.p. Fans for 17, 1980-82; 1st. v.p. Friends of Baird Hall, SUNY-Buffalo, 1980-82; exec. bd. mem. Longview Protestant Home for Children, 1979-85, 2d v.p., 1982-85; bd. dirs. ARC, Town of Amherst br., 1982-91, by-laws com., 1981, 84, chmn. sr. concerns com., 1982-91, liaison code of ethics com., 1987-89; bd. dirs. Amherst Symphony Orch. Assn., 1981-87, roster chmn., 1982-84, nominating chmn., 1985-86, vice-chmn. 50th anniversary com. 1994—; nat. music com. Women's Assn. for Symphony Orchs. in Am. and Can., 1977-79; coun. mem. Am. Symphony Orch. League; sec. Amherst Sr. Citizen's Adv. Bd., 1980-81, liaison from Amherst Town Bd., 1982—; founder, liaison 1st adult day svcs. adv. bd. Town of Amherst, 1988; liaison to ad hoc cable TV com., 1992—, mem. 1st records mgmt. adv. bd., liaison ethics bd. Town of Amherst, 1994—, dep. supr. 1990—; liaison to the Alternate Fuel and Clean Cities Com., 1994-95; dir.-at-large community adv. coun. SUNY-Buffalo, 1981-91; co-assoc. chmn. maj. gift div. capital campaign Daemen Coll., 1983-84; co-chmn. Women United Against Drugs Campaign, 1970-72; founding mem. Lunch and Issues, Amherst, 1981—; mem. edn. com. Network in Aging of Western N.Y., Inc., 1982-89, bd. dirs., 1982-89, housing com., 1987-89; bd. dirs. Amherst Elderly Transp. Corp., 1982—; committeeman dist. Town of Amherst Republican Com.; treas. Town and Country Rep. Club, 1980-81; mem. nominating com. Fedn. Rep. Women's Clubs Erie County, 1980; exec. bd. mem. Women's Exec. Coun. of Erie County Rep. Com., 1969-71; dir. Amherst Rep. Women's Club, 1963-65; delegate White House Conf. on Aging, 1995. Named Homemaker of Yr., Family Circle Mag., 1969; Woman of Substance, 20th Century Rep. Women, 1983; Woman of Yr., Buffalo Philharm. Orch. Soc., Inc., 1982; Outstanding Woman in Community Svc., SUNY-Buffalo, 1985; recipient Good Neighbor award Courier Express, 1978; Merit award Buffalo Philharm. Orch., 1978; award Fedn. Rep. Women's Clubs Erie County, 1982; Disting. Svc. award Town of Amherst Sr. Ctr., 1985; Susan B. Anthony award Interclub Coun. of Western N.Y., 1991, Community Svc. award Amherst Rep. Com., 1991, D.A.R.E. award Town of Amherst Police Dept., 1994, Disting. Svc. award Amherst Adult Day Care and Vis. Nurses Assn., 1994. Mem. Amherst C. of C. (VIP dinner com. 1984), LWV, SUNY-Buffalo Alumni Assn. (life, presdl. advisor 1977-79), Zonta (pres. Amherst chpt. 1986-88, Zontian of Yr. 1992), Pi Lambda Theta (hon.). Office: 5583 Main St Buffalo NY 14221-5409

MILLAR, DORINE MARIE AGNES, real estate agent, artist; b. Pos, Td'ad, West Indies, Apr. 20, 1924; d. Victor and Elsie (Dumoret) Sellier. Lic. real estate agt., Fla. Artist Millar Agencies Inc., Ft. Lauderdale, Fla., 1964—; real estate agt. Ft. Lauderdale, Fla., 1970—. Recipient 1st pl. award Hollywood Art Guild Ann. Mem. Show, 1993, 2d pla. prize Palm Beach Water Color Soc., 1990, 3rd pl. prize Coral Springs Art Guild, 1990. Mem. Gold Coast Watercolor Soc., Palm Beach Watercolor Soc., Fla. Watercolor Soc., Broward Art Guild.

MILLER, ADELE ENGELBRECHT, educational administrator; b. Jersey City, July 31, 1946; d. John Fred and Dorathea Kathryn (Kamm) Engelbrecht; m. William A. Miller, Jr., Dec. 21, 1981. BS in Bus. Edn., Fairleigh Dickinson U., 1968, MBA magna cum laude, 1974; cert. in pub. sch. adminstrn. and supervision, Jersey City State Coll., 1976. Bus. tchr. Jersey City Bd. Edn., 1967—, coord. coop. bus. edn. programs, 1973—, acting v.p., 1985-86, prin. of summer sch., 1986; adj. instr. St. Peter's Coll., 1974-75; curriculum cons. Cittone Bus. Sch., 1981-82; mem. adv. coun. Dickinson High Sch., 1973—, chmn., 1978-80; organizer, bd. dirs. Frances Nadel and Cooke-Connolly-Coffey-Witt Faculty Meml. Scholarships, 1978—; trustee Dickinson High Sch. Parents Coun., 1985—. Co-author: New Jersey Cooperative Business Education Coordinators Resource Manual, 1984; author coop. bus. edn. study course Jersey City Pub. Schs., 1980, 84. Mem. Citizens Adv. Coun. to Mayor of Jersey City, 1968-71; organizer, dir. Jersey City Youth Week, 1970-72; mem. juv. conf. com. Hudson County Juv. Ct., 1978—; v.p., sec., trustee, chmn. dinner-musicale Jersey City Coll. - Community Orch., 1979-88; Explorer Scouting adv. bd. Hudson-Hamilton coun. Boy Scouts Am., 1985-88; trustee YWCA of Hudson County, 1988—. Recipient Dickinson High Sch. Key Club Tchr. of Yr. award 1971; named Educator of Yr. Dickinson High Sch. Parents Coun., 1987, 88. Mem. NEA, N.J. Edn. Assn., Jersey City Edn. Assn. (bldg. dir.), N.J. Coop. Bus. Edn. Coords. Assn. (pres., v.p., sec., treas. 1991-92, Coop. Edn. Coord. of Yr.), N.J. Bus. Edn. Assn., Vocat. Edn. Assn. N.J., N.J. Fedn. Women's Clubs, Jersey City Woman's Club (scholarship chmn., adviser Jr. Women's Club), AAUW (edn. chmn., sec. N.J. div., del. to White House briefing on edn., women's issues, arms control, dist. coord., chmn. nominations, historian), Coll. Club Jersey City (pres., v.p., sec.), Jersey City Rotary Club (Interact club adviser, program chmn.), Phi Delta Kappa. Home: 91 Sherman Pl Jersey City NJ 07307-3729 Office: Dickinson H S 2 Palisade Ave Jersey City NJ 07306-1299

MILLER, ANGELA PEREZ, academic administrator; b. Chgo., Oct. 1, 1936; d. Jesse and Emily (Ibarra) P.; m. John F. Miller, May 6, 1961 (div.); 1 son, Dion. BA, U. Ill., 1958; MA, Northeastern Ill. U., 1975; MEd, De Paul U., 1984; PhD, U. Ill.-Chgo., 1990. Cert. elem. tchr., spl. edn., bilingual edn., adminstrn., Ill. Tchr. Chgo. pub. schs., 1962-70; exchange tchr. Mexico City schs., 1970-71; asst. prin. Burns Elem. Sch., Chgo., 1972-77; asst. prin. Benito Juarez High Sch., Chgo., 1977-85; field adminstr. Chgo. Pub. Schs., 1985-88; prin. Chgo. Pub. Schs, 1988-89; adminstr. Office of Reform Implementation Chgo. Pub. Schs., 1989-91; dir. staff training and devel., Chgo. Pub. Schs. 1991-94; asst. prof. DePaul U., Chgo., 1994—; vis. asst. prof. U. Ill., Chgo., 1992, 93. Pres., bd. dirs. Latino Inst., Alivio Med. Ctr., Prevention Ptnrs.; active Future Tchrs. Chgo. Mem. ASCD, Nat. Staff Devel. Coun., Am. Ednl. Rsch. Assn., Coun. Exceptional Children. Office: 2320 N Kenmore Ave Chicago IL 60614

MILLER, ANNE KATHLEEN, training company executive and technical marketing consultant; b. Denver, Sept. 15, 1942; d. John Henry and Kathryn Elizabeth (Doherty) Meyer; m. Edgar Earle Miller, Aug. 20, 1966 (div. Aug. 1976); children: Sheila Anne, Rebecca Elizabeth; m. Warren Ross Landry, Dec. 11, 1982 (dec. Oct. 1990). BS in Chemistry, St. Mary Coll., Leavenworth, Kans., 1964. Cert. jr. coll., secondary tchr., Calif. Lectr. San Jose (Calif.) State U., 1978-82; product mgr. Jasco Chem., Mountain View, Calif., 1979-82; v.p., gen. mgr. Micropel, Hayward, Calif., 1982-84; product mgr. Cambridge Instruments, Santa Clara, Calif., 1984-86; product mktg. mgr. KLA Instruments, Santa Clara, 1986-87; pres., owner Meyland Enterprises, Redwood City, Calif., 1987—, Semiconductor Svc. Tng. Orgn., Redwood City, Calif., 1988—. Inventor formation of optical film. Mem. Soc. Photo Optical Instrumentation Engrs., Am. Chem. Soc., Semiconductor Industry Equipment Materials Internat., Am. Electronics Assn. Office: Meyland/Semiconductor Svcs 735 Hillcrest Way Redwood City CA 94062-3428

MILLER, ARLINE W., health care products manufacturing executive; b. N.Y.C.; d. Samuel and Clara (Schaeffer) M.; children: Loren Greenberg, Kevin Walpin, Robin Walpin. BA, Queens Coll., Queens, N.Y., 1958. Lic. elem. tchr. Pvt. practice interior design L.A., 1971-77; chief exec. officer, chief operating officer RoLoKe Co., L.A., 1978—. Patentee back support, body positioner. Mem. NAFE, Beverly Hills Women's Network, Healthcare Businesswomen's Assn., Health Industries Rep. Assn. Office: RoLoKe Co 5760 Hannum Ave Culver City CA 90230-6501

MILLER, ARLYN HOCHBERG, psychologist; b. N.Y.C., Dec. 2, 1925; d. Nathaniel and Marie (Weinstein) Hochberg; m. Arthur M. Miller, May 29, 1947 (div. June 1971); children: David, Eve. BS in Edn., CCNY, 1946, MS in Psychology, 1949; EdD in Psychology, Temple U., 1965. Lic. sch. psychologist, N.J., N.Y., Pa., lic. pvt. practice psychologist, N.J., Pa. Faculty Littaur Hosp., Gloversville, N.Y., 1954-58; sch. psychologist Cherry Hill, N.J., 1958-63, Collingswood, Glassboro, Delran, N.J., 1958-65; staff psychologist Children's Hosp., Pa., 1963-64; sr. psychologist Camden County Child Guidance Clinic, 1964-69; psychologist N.J. Divsn. Youth and Family Svcs., 1965-85; pvt. practice N.J., Pa., 1965—; supr. clin. tng. Sch. Psychology Rutgers U., 1968-70; psychologist N.J. Divsn. Vocat. Rehab., 1970-85; prof. Hahnemann Hosp., 1975-85; bd. dirs. N.J. Assn. Children with Learning Disabilities, psychologist, 1968-74; bd. dirs. Camden County Mental Health Assn., mem. profl. adv. bd.; N.Y. state bd. dirs. Assn. for Help of Retarded Children; bd. dirs. Sch. for Retarded Children, Fulton County, N.Y.; adj. prof. Drexel U., 1969-70, Glassboro Coll., 1972-74, Our Lady of Lourdes Hosp., 1974-75, Temple U., 1975-81; cons. to tech. adv. svc. to attys., 1991—; presenter numerous seminars. Author: (booklets) Guidelines for Divorcing Parents, 1986, Guidelines for Step-Parents, 1986; contbr. articles and tapes to profl. jours. Founder, coord. Hemlock Soc. Delaware Valley, 1991-92; bd. dirs. Camden County divsn. Parents without Partners, 1987; mem. profl. adv. bd. Single Parents Soc. Fellow in sex counseling and therapy Internat. Coun. Sex Edn. and Parenthood. Mem. APA, Am. Soc. Sex Educators, Counselors and Therapists (cert. sex therapist), N.J. Psychol. Assn., Phila. Soc. Clin. Psychologists, Camden County Psychol. Assn. (charter, founder), Victorian Soc. Am., Internat. Profl. Exch., Am. Bd. forensic Examiners. Home: 1420 Locust St Philadelphia PA 19102 Office: 8 E Mount Vernon Ave Haddonfield NJ 08033

MILLER, BARBARA L., financial manager; b. Phoenixville, Pa., Jan. 28, 1963; d. Mahlon K. Jr. and Nancy M. (Marshall) M. BS in Acctg., U. Del., 1985; postgrad., Drexel U. CPA, Pa. Internal auditor Pennwalt Corp., Phila., 1985-88; plant acctg. mgr. Pennwalt Corp., King of Prussia, Pa., 1988-91; acctg. supr. Elf Atochem N.Am., Inc., Phila., 1991-92, group fin. mgr., 1992—. Mem. Pa. Inst. CPAs. Office: Elf Atochem NAm 2000 Market St Philadelphia PA 19103

MILLER, BARBARA STALLCUP, medical foundation administrator; b. Montague, Calif., Sept. 4, 1919; d. Joseph Nathaniel and Maybelle (Needham) Stallcup; m. Leland F. Miller, May 16, 1946; children: Paula Kay, Susan Lee, Daniel Joseph, Alison Jean. B.A., U. Oreg., 1942. Women's editor Eugene (Oreg.) Daily News, 1941-43; law clk. to J. Everett Barr, Yreka, Calif., 1943-45; mgr. Yreka C. of C., 1945-46; Northwest supr. Louis Harris and Assocs., Portland, Oreg., 1959-62; dir. pub. relations and fund raising Columbia River council Girl Scouts U.S.A., 1962-67; pvt. practice pub. relations cons., Portland, 1967-72; adviser of student publs., asst. prof. communications U. Portland, 1967-72, dir. pub. relations and info., asst. prof. communications, 1972-78, dir. devel., 1978-79, exec. dir. devel., 1979-83; assoc. dir. St. Vincent Med. Found., 1983-88; dir. planned giving Good Samaritan Found., 1988—. Pres. bd. dirs. Vols. of Am. of Oreg., Inc., 1980-84, pres. regional adv. bd., 1982-84; chmn. bd. dirs. S.E. Mental Health Network, 1984-88; nat. bd. dirs. Vols. of Am., Inc., 1984—; pres., bd. dirs. Vol. Bur. Greater Portland, 1991-93; mem. U. Oreg. Journalism Advancement Coun., 1991—; named Oasis Sr. Role Model, 1992. Recipient Presdl. Citation, Oreg. Communicators Assn., 1973, Matrix award, 1976, 80, Miltner award U. Portland, 1977, Communicator of Achievement award Oreg. Press Women, 1992, Willamette Valley Devel. Officers award, 1992 (Barbara Stallcup Miller Profl. Achievement award, 1992), Mem. Nat. Soc. Fundraising Execs., Nat. Planned Giving Coun, Women in Comm. (NW regional v.p. 1973-75, Offbeat award 1988), Nat. Fedn. Press Women, Oreg. Press Women (dist. dir.), Pub. Rels. Soc. Am. (dir. local chpt., Marsh award 1989), Oreg. Fedn. Womens Clubs (communications chmn. 1978-80), Alpha Xi Delta (found. trustee, editor 1988—). Unitarian. Clubs: Portland Zenith (pres. 1975-76, 81-82). Contbr. articles to profl. jours. Home: 1706 Boca Ratan Dr Lake Oswego OR 97034-1624 Office: 1015 NW 22d Ave Portland OR 97210

MILLER, BARBARA TUTTLE, small business owner; b. Winston Salem, N.C., Apr. 23, 1947; d. Glen E. and Vera E. (Eldridge) Payne; divorced; 2 children. Investment asst. Wachovia Bank & Trust Co., Winston Salem, N.C., 1967-77; academic sec. Cancer Rsch. Ctr., Bowman Gray Sch. Medicine, Winston Salem, N.C., 1978-94; owner D & B Antiques, Winston Salem, N.C., 1995—. Author (with others): (poetry) World of Poetry, 1985, 86 (Golden Poet award 1985, 86), National Library of Poetry, 1993 (Editors Choice award 1993). Home and Office: D & B Antiques 2840 E Waughtown St Winston Salem NC 27107

MILLER, BERNICE DEARING, funeral director, member school board; b. Altavista, Va.; d. Joseph B. and Thelma B. (Younger) Dearing; m. Jack Miller; 1 child, Tscharner Jaenese. BA in Bus. Adminstrn., Howard U., 1965. Tchr. Pittsylvania County Sch. System, Gretna, Va., 1965-78; dir. Miller Funeral Home, Inc., Gretna, 1978—. Treas. Callands-Gretna Voters League, 1985—; mem. coop. office edn. adv. bd. Gretna High Sch., 1980—; vice chmn. Pittsylvania County Sch. Bd., 1989—; mem. president's adv. panel for minority concerns Danville C.C., 1990—. Recipient outstanding svc. to community plaque Callands-Gretna Voters League, 1988. Mem. Va. Morticians Assn., Western Dist. Funeral Dirs. Assn. (Woman Mortician of Yr. 1992), Va. Funeral Dirs. Assn., Gretna Mchts. Assn. (bd. dirs.), NAACP. Home: RR 2 Gretna VA 24557

MILLER, BEVERLY WHITE, college president; b. Willoughby, Ohio; d. Joseph Martin and Marguerite Sarah (Storer) White; m. Lynn Martin Miller, Oct. 11, 1945 (dec. 1986); children: Michaela Ann, Craig Martin, Todd Daniel, Cass Timothy, Simone Agnes. AB, Western Res. U., 1945; MA, Mich. State U., 1957; PhD, U. Toledo, 1967; LHD (hon.), Coll. St. Benedict, St. Joseph, Minn., 1979; LLD (hon.), U. Toledo, 1988. Chem. and biol. researcher, 1945-57; tchr. schs. in Mich., also Mercy Sch. Nursing, St. Lawrence Hosp., Lansing, Mich., 1957-58; mem. chemistry and biology faculty Mary Manse Coll., Toledo, 1958-71; dean grad. div. Mary Manse Coll., 1968-71, exec. v.p., 1968-71; acad. dean Salve Regina Coll., Newport, R.I., 1971-74; pres. Coll. St. Benedict, St. Joseph, Minn., 1974-79, Western New Eng. Coll., Springfield, Mass., 1980—; cons. U.S. Office Edn., 1980; mem. Pvt. Industry Coun./Regional Employment Bd., exec. com., 1984-94; cons. in field. Author papers in field. Corporator Mercy Hosp., Springfield, Mass. Recipient President's citation St. John's U., 1979; also various service awards. Mem. AAAS, Am. Assn. Higher Edn., Assn. Cath. Colls. and Univs. (exec. bd.), Internat. Assn. Sci. Edn., Nat. Assn. Ind. Colls. and Univs. (govt. rels. adv. com., bd. dirs. 1990-93, exec. com. 1991-93, treas. 1992-93), Nat. Assn. Biology Tchrs., Assn. Ind. Colls. and Univs. of Mass. (exec. com. 1981—, vice chmn. 1985-86, chmn. 1986-87), Nat. Assn. Rsch. Sci. Teaching, Springfield C. of C. (bd. dirs.), Am. Assn. Univ. Adminstrs. (bd. dirs. 1989-92), Delta Kappa Gamma, Sigma Delta Epsilon. Office: Western New Eng Coll Office of the President 1215 Wilbraham Rd Springfield MA 01119-2693

MILLER, BONNIE SEWELL, marketing professional; b. Junction City, Ky., July 24, 1932; d. William Andrew and Lillian Irene (McCowan) Sewell; m. William Gustave Tournade Jr., Nov. 5, 1950 (div. 1974); children: Bonnie Sue Tournade Zaner, William Gustave III, Sharon Irene Tournade Leach; m. Bruce George Miller, Nov. 15, 1981. BA, U. South Fla., 1968, MA, 1973. Cert. tchr., Fla. Chair dept. English Tampa (Fla.) Cath. High Sch., 1972-78; tchr. Clearwater (Fla.) High Sch., 1978-80; mgr. prodn. svcs. Paradyne Corp., Largo, Fla., 1980-83; freelance writer, cons. Tampa, 1983-84; mgr. product documentation PPS, Inc., Largo, 1984-86; mgr. mktg. communications PPS, Inc., 1986-87; writer Nixdorf Computer Corp., Tampa, 1988-89; mktg. dir. Suncoast Schs. Fed. Credit Union, Tampa, 1989—; instr. English, Hillsborough C.C., Tampa, 1975-87; adj. instr. profl. writing U. South Fla., 1993; cons. bus. writing Coronet Instrnl. Media Writing Project, Tampa, 1976, Nat. Mgmt. Assn., Tampa, 1981-87. Contbr. tech. articles to various publs. Bd. dirs. SERVE, Tampa, Sing Parent Displaced Homemakers Group; legis. chair Tampa PTA, 1965; judge speech contest Am. Legion, Tampa, 1976; vol. North Tampa Vol. Libr., 1988. NEH fellow, 1975. Mem. NAFE, Internat. Assn. Bus. Communicators, Soc. Tech. Communicators, Am. Assn. Bus. Women, Internat. Platform Assn., Toastmasters Internat., Kappa Delta Pi. Democrat. Baptist. Home: 4014 Hudson Ter Tampa FL 33624-5349 Office: Suncoast Schs Fed Credit Union 6801 E Hillsborough Ave Tampa FL 33610-4110

MILLER, CANDICE S., state official; b. May 7, 1954; m. Donald G. Miller; 1 child, Wendy Nicole. Student, Macomb County C.C., Northwood Inst. Sec., treas. D.B. Snider Inc., 1972-79; trustee Harrison Twp., 1979-80, supr., 1980-92; treas. Macomb County, 1992-95; sec. of state State of Mich., Lansing, 1995—; chair Mich. State Safety Commn., 1995—; mem. M-59 Task Force Strategy Com. Mem. community coun. Selfridge Air Nat. Guard Base. Mem. Govt. Finance Officers Assn., Mich. Assn. County Treas., Macomb County Treas. and Assessors Assn., Boat Town Assn., Ctrl. Macomb C. of C., Harrison Twp. Indsl. Corridor. Office: PO Box 16248 Lansing MI 48901*

MILLER, CAROLE ANN LYONS, editor, publisher, advertising specialist; b. Newton, Mass., Aug. 1; d. Markham Harold and Ursula Patricia (Foley) Lyons; m. David Thomas Miller, July 4, 1978. BA, Boston U., 1964; bus. cert., Hickox Sch., Boston, 1964; cert. advt. and mktg. profl. UCLA, 1973; cert. retail mgmt. profl. Ind. U., 1976. Editor Triangle Topics, Pacific Telephone, L.A.; programmer L.A. Cen. Area Speakers' Bur., 1964-66; mng. editor/mktg. dir. Teen mag., L.A. and N.Y.C., 1966-76; advt. dir. L.S. Ayres & Co., Indpls., 1976-78; v.p. mktg. The Denver, 1978-79; founder, editor, pub. Clockwise mag., Ventura, Calif., 1979-85; mktg. mgr., mgr. pub. rels. and spl. events Robinson's Dept. Stores, L.A., 1985-87, exec. v.p., dir. mktg. Harrison Svcs., 1987-93; pres. divsn. Miller & Miller Carole Ann Lyons Mktg., Camino, Calif., 1993—; instr. retail advt. Ind. U., 1977-78. Recipient Pres.'s award Advt. Women of N.Y., 1974; Seklemian award 1977; Pub. Svc. Addy award, 1978. Mem. Advt. Women N.Y., Fashion Group Internat., Bay Area Integrated Mktg., San Francisco Fashion Group, San Francisco Direct Mktg. Assn. UCLA Alumni Assn. Editor: Sek Says, 1979. Home: 3709 Carson Rd Camino CA 95709-9506

MILLER, CAROLINE, editor-in-chief. Exec. editor Variety mag., N.Y.C., 1989-92; editor-in-chief Lear's mag., N.Y.C., 1992-94, Seventeen mag., N.Y.C., 1994—. Office: Seventeen 850 Third Ave New York NY 10022*

MILLER, CATE, psychologist, educator; b. Baton Rouge, Apr. 1, 1964; d. Benjamin Robertson and Mertie Cate (Barnes) Miller, Jr. BA, Cath. U., 1985; MEd, Harvard U., 1986; MPhil, Columbia U., 1989, PhD, 1991. Lic. psychologist, N.Y.; cert. sec. edn. tchr. Psychology intern NYU Med. Ctr., Rusk Inst., N.Y.C., 1988-89, rsch. scientist, 1990—; pvt. practice specializing in psychotherapy N.Y.C., 1991—; adj. asst. prof. Columbia U., N.Y.C., 1991—. Contbr. (textbook): Geometry, 1985. Vol. St. Francis Xavier Soup Kitchen, N.Y.C., 1991. Columbia U. Merit scholar, 1987-88. Mem. APA, Nat. Trust for Historic Preservation, Jr. League, Phi Beta Kappa, Sigma Xi, Phi Delta Kappa, Kappa Gamma Pi, Psi Chi,. Democrat. Office: NYU Med Ctr Rusk Inst 400 E 34th St New York NY 10016-4901

MILLER, CECELIA SMITH, chemist; b. Tyron, N.C., Apr. 3, 1965; d. Thad Lewis Jr. and Johnnie Lucille (Staley) Smith; m. Ronnie Edward Miller, Apr. 16, 1988; children: Joshua Edward, Jaylin. BA in Chemistry, Converse Coll., 1987. Lab. technician Groce Labs., Greer, S.C., 1988; quality assurance technician Baxter Pharmaseal, Spartanburg, S.C., 1988-89; lab. dir. CAPSCO, Inc., Greenville, S.C., 1989, quality assurance mgr., 1989—. Mem. Am. Soc. Quality Control, S.C. Lab. Mgmt. Soc. Democrat. Baptist. Home: 3017 Southfield Rd Inman SC 29349 Office: CAPSCO Inc 1101 W Blue Ridge Dr Greenville SC 29604

MILLER, CHRISTINE MARIE, education executive; b. Williamsport, Pa., Dec. 7, 1950; d. Frederick James and Mary (Wurster) M.; m. Robert M. Ancell, Mar. 30, 1985. BA, U. Kans., 1972; MA, Northwestern U., 1978, PhD, 1982. Pub. rels. asst. Bedford County Commr., Bedford, Pa., 1972-73; teaching asst. Northwestern U., Evanston, Ill., 1977-80; asst. prof. U. Ala., Tuscaloosa, 1980-82, Loyola U., New Orleans, 1982-85; vis. prof. Ind. U. Sch. Journalism, Bloomington, 1985-86; mktg. dir. Nat. Inst. Fitness & Sport, Indpls., 1986-88; program dir. Nat. Entrepreneurship Acad., Bloomington, 1986-88; mgmt. assoc. community and media rels. Subaru-Isuzu Automotive, Inc., Lafayette, Ind., 1988-91; dir. pub. rels. Giddings & Lewis, Fond Du Lac, Wis., 1991-93; v.p. comm. and enrollment mgmt. Milton Hershey (Pa.) Sch., 1993-94, dir. adminstrn., 1994—. Contbr. articles to profl. jours. Bd. dirs. Indpls. Entrepreneurship Acad., 1988-91, Area IV Agy., Greater Lafayette Mus. Art, 1989-91. With USN, 1973-77, USNR, 1977—. Mem. Am. Mgmt. Assn., Am. Mktg. Assn., Pub. Rels. Soc. Am., U.S. Naval League, Naval Res. Assn., Res. Officers Assn. Presbyterian. Home: 95 Brook Dr PO Box 435 Hershey PA 17033 Office: Milton Hershey Sch Founders Hall PO Box 830 Hershey PA 17033

MILLER, CHRISTINE ODELL COOK, federal judge; b. Oakland, Calif., Aug. 26, 1944; d. Leo Marshall and Carolyn Grant (Odell) Cook; m. Dennis F. Miller, Sept. 10, 1994. BA, Stanford U., 1966; JD, U. Utah, 1969. Bar: Utah 1969, D.C. 1972, Calif. 1982. Clk. to chief judge U.S. Ct. Appeals (10th cir.), 1969-70; trial atty. U.S. Dept. Justice, Washington, 1970-72, Fed. Trade Commn., Washington, 1972-74; litigation Hogan & Hartson, Washington, 1974-76; spl. counsel Pension Benefit Guaranty Corp., Washington, 1976-78; asst. gen. counsel U.S. Ry. Assn., Washington, 1978-80; litigation Shack & Kimball P.C., Washington, 1980-83; judge U.S. Ct. of Fed. Claims, Washington, 1983—. Mem. State Bar Assn. Calif., D.C. Bar Assn., Order of Coif. Republican. Presbyterian. Club: University. Office: US Ct of Fed Claims 717 Madison Pl NW Washington DC 20005-1086

MILLER, CINDY LOU, real estate agent; b. Clarksburg, W.Va., Dec. 18, 1956; d. Ersel R. and Charlene Edna (Austin) M. BS in Recreation, W.Va. U., 1978, BSBA, 1979. Sales trainee Borg Warner, Ithaca, N.Y., 1978; customer svc. rep. Borg Warner, Aurora, Ill., 1979-81; sales rep. Borg Warner, Ft. Wayne, Ind., 1981-83; mfg. cons. Barry & Assocs., Lilburn, Ga., 1983-84; customer svc. rep. Westvaco, Chamblee, Ga., 1984-87, prodn. supv., 1987, customer svc. mgr., 1987-93; realtor ReMax Gwinnett Inc., Snellville, Ga., 1994—; info. specialist Lake Lanier Regional Libr., Lawrenceville, Ga., 1994—. Chair mgmt. supv. devel. Gwinnett Tech. Inst., Lawrenceville, Ga., 1989—; treas. League Women Voters, Duluth, Ga., 1993-94, 1st v.p., 1994—. Mem. Ga. Bd. Realtors, Gwinnett Bd. Realtors, Womens Coun. Realtors. Republican. Lutheran. Home: 5597 Mountainbrooke Ct Stone Mountain GA 30087 Office: ReMax Gwinnett Inc 3732 Stone Mountain Frwy Snellville GA 30278

MILLER, CLARA BURR, education educator; b. Higganum, Conn., July 19, 1912; d. Eugene Orlando and Mabel (Clark) Burr; m. James Golden Miller, Sept. 19, 1942; children: Clara Elizabeth, Eugenia Manelle. BA, Mt. Holyoke Coll., 1933; MA, Columbia U., 1942. Cert. tchr., Conn., N.Y. Tchr. Suffield (Conn.) Jr. High Sch., 1934-36, Rockville (Conn.) High Sch., 1936-41, Buckeley High Sch., Hartford, Conn., 1941-42, Pitts. Schs., 1952-55, Winchester-Thurston Sch., Pitts., 1955-58, Vail-Deane Sch., Elizabeth, N.J., 1959-69, Kingman (Ariz.) High Sch., 1971-76; mem. res. faculty Mohave C.C., Kingman, 1978-94; pres. bd. edn., clk. Mohave Union H.S. Dist. 30, 1983-91, bd. dirs., 1983-94; bd. dirs. Mohave Mental Health Clinic, v.p. bd. dirs., 1988, pres. bd. dirs., 1989-90. Author: Trails, Rails and Tales, 1981, (with others) Short Stories, 1984. Bd. dirs. No. Ariz. Comprehensive Guidance Ctr., Flagstaff, 1985-90, Kingman Aid to Abused People; sec. Good Samaritan Assn., Inc., Kingman, 1979—; pres. Ch. Women United, 1972-74, Presbyn. Women, 1987; elected elder session Kingman Presbyn. Ch., 1986—; mem. Mohave County Cmty. Action Bd., Western Ariz. Coun. Govts.; coord. League Friendship Indians and Ams., 1981—; co-chmn. Women Making History Com., 1992-94. Recipient Nat. Community Svc. award Mohave County Ret. Tchrs. Assn., 1987, Leta Glancy/Cecil Lockhart-Smith award No. Ariz. Comprehensive Guidance Ctr., 1990; named one of Women Making History Kingman Multi-Club Com., 1985. Mem. NEA, AAUW (pres. 1979-81), Ariz. Edn. Assn., Ariz. Sch. Bds. Assn., Soc. Profl. Journalists, Mohave County Ret. Tchrs. Assn. (v.p. 1991-93, pres. 1993—), Footprinters. Democrat. Home: 2629 Mullen Dr Kingman AZ 86401-4264

MILLER, DAWN MARIE, meteorologist, product marketing specialist; b. Hartford, Conn., Sept. 17, 1963; d. Eugene E. Miller and Audrey E. (Flagg) Laurel; m. Dennis James Miller, Sept. 9, 1989; 1 child, Zackarey. BS in Meteorology, SUNY, Oneonta, 1985. Customer support specialist WSI Corp., Bedford, Mass., 1985-87; in media (TV) mktg. WSI Corp., Billerica, Mass., 1987-91, media (TV) and industry mktg. rep., 1991-92, mktg. communications specialist, 1992-93, product mktg. specialist-data svcs., 1993—. Mem. Oneonta Alumni Assn., Nat. Arbor Day Found., Nat. Audubon Soc., The Nature Conservancy. Republican. Episcopalian. Home: 37 Wren St Litchfield NH 03051-2540 Office: WSI Corp 4 Federal St Billerica MA 01821-3569

MILLER, DEBORAH JEAN, computer training and document consultant; b. Elmhurst, Ill., Oct. 2, 1951; d. Thomas Francis and Ruthe Conn (Johnston) M. BFA, Ill. Wesleyan U., 1973; MA, Northwestern U., 1974. Pres.

Miller & Assocs., Evanston, Ill., 1980—. Mem. AAUW, NOW, Internat. Interactive Communications Soc., Soc. Tech. Communication, Ind. Writers Chgo. (bd. dirs. 1985-86), Chgo. Coun. Fgn. Rels., Nat. Soc. Performance and Instrn. (Chgo. chpt.), Northwestern U. Alumni Assn. Office: 814 Mulford St Evanston IL 60202-3331

MILLER, DIANE DORIS, executive search consultant; b. Sacramento, Calif., Jan. 18, 1954; d. George Campbell and Doris Lucille (Benninger) M. BA, U. Pacific, 1976, Golden Gate U., 1985, MBA, 1987. Mgr., A.G. Spanos, Sacramento, 1977-81, Lee Sammis, Sacramento, 1981-83; v.p. Consol. Capital, San Francisco, 1983-86; ptnr. Wilcox, Bertoux and Miller, Sacramento, 1986—. Bd. dirs. Sacramento Symphony En Corps, 1982-84, Sacramento Ballet, 1983-84, 86—, Sacramento Symphony Assn., 1988—, Oakland Ballet, Calif., 1984-85. Named Vol. of Yr., Junior League, 1983, Bus. Vol. in the Arts, Sacramento C. of C., 1989. Mem. U. Pacific Alumni Assn. (bd. dirs. 1978-85). Republican. Avocations: ballet, water sports.

MILLER, DIANE MOON, data processing educator; b. Montgomery, Ala., Feb. 22, 1942; d. Benjamin Alfred and Georgia Elizabeth (Godwin) Moon; m. James Edward Miller, June 6, 1964; Deborah Elaine, Michael Edward. BA, Auburn U., 1964; BS, U. West Fla., 1981, MA, 1970, MBA, 1988; PhD, U. Ala., 1992. Cert. systems profl., data processor. Systems analyst Dept. Navy, Pensacola, Fla., 1980-86; asst. prof. U. So. Miss., 1986—. Named Faculty fellow NASA, Stennis Space Ctr., Miss., 1993—. Mem. Decision Scis. Inst., Inst. for Mgmt. Sci., Data Processing Mgmt. Assn. (bd. dirs. 1992-93, chair edn. com.), Internat. Assn. for Computer Info. Systems, Assn. for Bus. Simulation and Experiential Learning; Phi Kappa Phi, Beta Gamma Sigma, Sigma Iota Epsilon. Democrat. Methodist. Office: U So Miss 730 E Beach Blvd Long Beach MS 39560-6259

MILLER, DIANE WILMARTH, human resources director; b. Clarinda, Iowa, Mar. 12, 1940; d. Donald and Floy Pauline (Madden) W.; m. Robert Nolen Miller, Aug. 21, 1965; children: Robert Wilmarth, Anne Elizabeth. AA, Colo. Women's Coll., 1960; BBA, U. Iowa, 1962; MA, U. No. Colo., 1994. Cert. tchr., Colo.; vocat. credential, Colo.; cert. sr. profl. in human resources. Sec.-counselor U. S.C., Myrtle Beach AFB, 1968-69; instr. U. S.C., Conway, 1967-69; tchr. bus. Poudre Sch. Dist. R-1, Ft. Collins, Colo., 1970-71; travel cons. United Bank Travel Svc., Greeley, Colo., 1972-74; dir. human resources Aims Community Coll., Greeley, 1984—; instr. part-time Aims Community Coll., Greeley, 1972—. Active 1st Congl. Ch., Greeley. Mem. Women's Investment Group Soc., Questers, Coll. Univ. Pers. Assn., Coll. Univ. Pers. Assn. Colo., No. Colo. Human Resources Assn., Soc. Human Resource Mgmt., Philanthropic Ednl. Orgn. (pres. 1988-89), Women's Panhellenic Assn. (pres. 1983-84), Scroll and Fan Club (pres. 1985-86), WTK Club. Home: 3530 Wagon Trail Pl Greeley CO 80634-3405 Office: Aims Community Coll 5401 20th St Greeley CO 80634-3000

MILLER, DORIS HANSON, artist; b. Turlock, Calif., Dec. 15, 1938; d. Howard and Ruth (Arnett) Hanson; m. Alexander Lewis Miller, May 1, 1965; children: William Lewis, John Hanson. BA in English, San Jose State U. vice chair Cultural Arts Bd., San Antonio, 1993—; founder City Art San Antonio, chair. One woman shows include San Francisco Craft and Folk Art Mus., Sol del Rio Gallery, San Antonio, Artenergies, Ft. Worth, Gallery at Shoal Creek, Austin, Wyndy Morhead Gallery Fine Art, New Orleans; exhibited in group shows at Tex. Designer Craftsman, Lil Street Studios, Chgo., Jessel's, Napa, Rockport Ctr for Arts, St. Phillips Coll., San Antonio, Front Room, Dallas; represented in numerous corp. and pvt. collections. Mem. Univ. Roundtable (program chair 1989-90). Democrat. Episcopalian. Home and studio: 204 Fawn Dr San Antonio TX 78231-1517

MILLER, DOROTHY ANNE SMITH, cytogenetics educator; b. N.Y.C., Oct. 20, 1931; d. John Philip and Anna Elizabeth (Hellberg) Smith; m. Orlando Jack Miller, July 10, 1954; children: Richard L., Cynthia K., Karen A. BA in Chemistry magna cum laude, Wilson Coll., Chambersburg, Pa., 1952; PhD in Biochemistry, Yale U., 1957. Rsch. assoc. dept. ob-gyn Columbia U., N.Y.C., 1964-72, from rsch. assoc. to asst. prof. dept. human genetics-devel., 1973-85; prof. depts. molecular biology and genetics and pathology Wayne State U., Detroit, 1985-94, prof. Ctr. for Molecular Medicine, Genetics and Pathology, 1994—; vis. scientist clin. and population cytogenetics unit Med. Rsch. Coun., Edinburgh, Scotland, 1983-84; vis. prof. dept. genetics and molecular biology U. la Sapienza, Rome, 1988; vis. disting. fellow La Trobe U., Melbourne, Australia, 1992. Contbr. numerous articles to sci. jours. Grantee March of Dimes Birth Defects Found., 1974-93, NSF, 1983-84. Mem. Am. Soc. Human Genetics, Genetics Soc. Am., Genetics Soc. Australia, Phi Beta Kappa. Presbyterian. Home: 1915 Stonycroft Ln Bloomfield Hills MI 48304-2339 Office: Wayne State U 540 E Canfield St Detroit MI 48201-1998

MILLER, DOROTHY ELOISE, education educator; b. Ft. Pierce, Fla., Apr. 13, 1944; d. Robert Foy and Aline (Mahon) Wilkes. BS in Edn., Bloomsburg U., 1966, MEd, 1969; MLA, Johns Hopkins U., 1978; EdD, Columbia U., 1991. Tchr. Cen. Dauphin East High Sch., Harrisburg, Pa., 1966-68, Aberdeen (Md.) High Sch., 1968-69; asst. dean of coll., prof. Harford C. C., Bel Air, Md., 1969—. Editor: Renewing the American Community Colleges, 1984; contbr. articles to profl. jours. Pres. Harlan Sq. Condominium Assn., Bel Air, 1982, 90—, Md. internat. divsn. St. Petersburg Sister State Com., 1993—; edn. liaison AAUW, Harford County, Md., 1982-92; cen. com. mem. Rep. Party, Harford County, 1974-78; crusade co-chair Am. Cancer Soc., Harford County, 1976-78; mem. faculty adv. com. Md. Higher Edn. Commn., 1993—. Recipient Nat. Tchg. Excellence award Nat. Inst. for Staff and Orgn. Devel., U. Tex.-Austin, 1992. Mem. NAFE, Nat. Mus. Women in the Arts. Republican. Methodist. Office: Harford Community Coll 401 Thomas Run Rd Bel Air MD 21015

MILLER, ELAINE WILSON, computer consultant; b. Ft. Worth, Sept. 16, 1944; d. Phillip Loren and Artie Inez (Neel) Wilson; m. Robert J. Copeland, Aug. 17, 1963 (div. 1983); children: Karen Kay Prince, Donna Lynn Copeland-Nay; m. Jared N. Miller Jr., Dec. 12, 1993. BS in Bus., Info. Systems, U. Colo., Denver, 1984. Sec. Hartford Life Ins. Co., Dallas, 1964-66, St. George's Episcopal Ch., Dallas, 1976-77; technician data processing Manville Corp., Denver, 1980-81, assoc. analyst, 1984-85, analyst data processing, 1985-94; fin. technician 1st Interstate Bank, Denver, 1982-84; computer cons. Miller Cons., Lakewood, Colo., 1994—; bus. process analyst US West Comm., Inc., Denver, 1994—. Chmn. precinct Rep. Party Tex., Dallas, 1970-76. Recipient Silver Spark award Camp Fire Girls, Denver, 1982. Mem. Home Based Bus. Connection, Data Processing Mgmt. Assn. (v.p. publicity 1986-88, 90-91, sec. 1989-90, asst. editor newsletter 1985-86, v.p. newsletter 1991-94, Individual Performance award 1991, exec. v.p. 1994-95), Jaycee-Ettes (hon. lifetime), Grand Prairie (Tex.) C. of C. (Newcomer of Yr. 1971), St. Paul's Ultreya Club (lay leader 1987-88). Episcopalian. Office: US West Comm 1801 California St Rm 2810 Denver CO 80202-1984

MILLER, ELIZABETH ANN, mathematician, human services manager; b. Alexandria, La., Sept. 11, 1939; d. Brice Turrentine and Thelma Elizabeth (Stalsby) Harrison; m. Tilton Anthony Auenson, Nov. 26, 1957 (div. Oct. 1963); children: Rebecca Ann Auenson Issa, David Brice Auenson; m. Donald Keith Miller, Nov. 17, 1984. BS, La. Coll., 1962; MS, Northwestern State U., Natchitoches, La., 1964. Cert. tchr., La. Tchr. Rapides Parish Schs., Alexandria, La., 1964-65, 67-69; instr. Itawamba Jr. Coll., Fulton, Miss., 1965-66, Jefferson State. Jr. Coll., Birmingham, Ala., 1966-67; human svc. worker II Rapides Parish Office Human Devel., Alexandria, 1969-82; subs. tchr. various Alexandria schs., 1982-87; instr. Comm. Coll. Alexandria, 1987-88; subs. tchr. Rapides Parish Schs., Alexandria, 1989—; adj. instr. St. Leo Coll., England AFB, La., 1990-92, La. Coll., Pineville, 1992; subs. tchr. Holy Savior Menard Ctrl. H.S., Alexandria Country Day Sch., 1993—; grad. teaching asst. Northwestern State U., 1963-64. Mem. AAUW (sec. Alexandria-Pineville br. 1990-92), DAR (Am. History Month chair 1991-94). Democrat. United Methodist. Home: 5821 Starling Cir Alexandria LA 71301

MILLER, ELLEN S., marketing communications executive; b. Indpls., June 28, 1954; d. Harold Edward and Lilian (Gantner) M. BA, DePauw U., 1976; postgrad., Sch. Visula Arts, N.Y.C., 1981-82. Editorial asst. Daisy mag., N.Y.C., 1976-77; asst. dept. mgr., Christmas hiring mgr. Bloomingdale's, N.Y.C., 1978; sales rep. Rosenthal USA Ltd., N.Y.C., 1979, mktg. asst., 1980-81, dir. mktg. comms., 1982-90; mgr. consumer mktg. Creamer Dickson Basford, Providence, 1990, v.p., 1991-94; prin. E.S. Miller Comm., Providence, 1994—. Editor Community Prep. Sch. newsletter, 1993. Mem. Jr. League R.I., Providence, 1993—; trustee Cmty. prep Sch., Providence, 1993—. Recipient Bell Ringer award New Eng. Pub. Club, 1992, 93, Iris award N.J. chpt. Internat. Assn. Bus. Communicators, 1993, Silver Quill award Dist. I, 1993. Mem. Pub. Rels. Soc. Am., Nat. Tabletop Assn. (com. chair 1989), Internat. Tabletop Awards (bd. dirs. 1989). Republican. Presbyterian.

MILLER, EMILIE F., state senator; b. Chgo., Aug. 11, 1936; d. Bruno C. and Etta M. (Senese) Feiza; m. Dean E. Miller; children: Desireé M., Edward C. BS in Bus. Adminstrn., Drake U., 1958. Asst. buyer Jordan Marsh Co., Boston, 1958-60, Carson, Pirie, Scott & Co., Chgo., 1960-62; dept. mgr., asst. buyer Woodward & Lothrop, Washington, 1962-64; polit. cons. various cos., Va., 1980-87; legis. aide Senator Adelard Brandt, Va., 1980-83; legis. cons. Va. Fedn. Bus. Profl. Women, 1986-87; senator Va. Gen. Assembly, Richmond, 1988-92; mem. Edn. and Health com., Gen. Laws com., Local Gov. com., Rehab. and Social Scis. com. Guest editorial writer No. Va. Sun, 1981; host, producer weekly TV program, Channel 61. Mem. State Cen. Com. Dem. Party Va., Richmond, 1974—; chmn. Va. Assoc. Dem. County and City Chmn., 1980, Fairfax County Dem. Com., 1976-80; past v.p. Women's Nat. Dem. Club.; bd. dirs. Mental Health Assn. No. Va., 1980—, State Mental Health and Mental Retardation Bd., 1982-88; fin. dir. Saslaw for Congress, 1984; state labor coord. Robb-Davis-Baliles Joint Campaign; bd. dirs. Stop Child Abuse Now, 1988; chmn. Va. Assn. Community Svcs. Bd., 1980-82; v.p. Fairfax County Coun. of Arts, exec. com., internat. childrens festival; mem. exec. bd. Mantua Citizens' Assn., 1985-87, nat. alumni bd. J.A. Achievement, BRAVO adv. com. for the first Gov.'s Awards for the Arts in Va., 1979-80; lay tchr. St. Ambrose Cath. Ch., 1963-80; del. to White House Conf. on Children, 1970; chmn. Va. Coalition for Mentally Disturbed, 1992—; bd. dirs. Ctr. Innovative Tech., 1992-94, Ct. Appointed Spl. Advocates, 1993—. Recipient Disting. Grad. award Jr. Achievement, 1973, Woman of Achievement award Fairfax (Va.) Bd. Suprs., 1982, Cmty. Svc. award Friends of Victims Assistance Network, 1988, Founders award Fairfax County Coun. of Arts, 1989, Mental Health Assn. award, 1991, Psychology Soc. of Washington Cmty. Svc. award, 1993. Mem. Va. Assn. Female Execs. (v.p. 1992—), Fairfax County Coun. Arts (v.p. 1988—), Fairfax County C. of C., Ctrl. Fairfax C. of C., Bus. and Profl. Women's Fedn. Va. (bd. dirs., pres. 1994-95), Tower Club (Fairfax), Downtown Club (Richmond). Roman Catholic. Home: 8701 Duvall St Fairfax VA 22031-2711

MILLER, ERICA, marriage and family therapist; b. Tsernovitz, Buscovina, Romania, Nov. 10, 1933; came to U.S., 1958; d. Emanuel and Fani (Türkfeld) Gelber; m. Jerry Miller, June 5, 1959; children: Diana, Johnny. PhD, Calif. Sch. Profl. Psychology, L.A., 1978. Staff therapist Forte Found., Encino, Calif., 1978-82; founder, exec. dir. Miller Psychol. Ctrs., Tarzana, Calif., 1982-93; founder, exec. officer Calif. Diversion-Intervention Found., Orange, Calif., 1993—. With Israeli Air Force, 1954-56. Mem. APA, NAFE, CAMFT, Womens Am. Orgn., Emily, U. Woman. Democrat. Jewish. Office: Calif Diversion Invtervention Found. 23055 Sherman Way # 4007 West Hills CA 91307-2000

MILLER, ERIN L., audiologist; b. Greensburg, Pa., Dec. 15, 1962; d. Ronald William and Elizabeth Ann (Ludwig) M. BS, Clarion U., 1983; MA, Kent State U., 1986. Cert. clin. competence in audiology; lic. audiologist, Pa., Ohio. Dir. clin. svcs. Neuro-Comm. Svcs., Boardman, Ohio, 1986—; supr. audiology Hillside Rehab. Hosp., Warren, Ohio, 1992-94; cons. Morley, Auschmer, Engler, et. al., Youngstown, Ohio, 1993—. Vol. Com. to Elect David Engler for Commr., Youngstown, 1992. fellow Am. Acad. Audiologists, Am. Audiology Soc. Republican. Office: Neuro-Comm Svcs Inc Southbridge West Bldg C-1 755 Boardman-Canfield Rd Youngstown OH 44512

MILLER, ESTHER SCOBIE POWERS, real estate appraiser, professional watercolorist; b. Peninsula, Ohio, Apr. 16, 1929; d. John Henry and Hazel Blanche (Appleton) Scobie; m. Elmer Duane Powers, June 13, 1948 (div. 1965); m. Kenneth Ward Miller, Aug. 26, 1980; children: Terrance, Michael, Susan, Jennifer. Student, Kansas City (Mo.) Art Inst., 1948-50, Bethel Coll., 1965-67, Ind. U., South Bend, 1965-67. Designated SRA-real estate appraiser. Owner brokerage Powers Realty, Culver, Ind., 1967-76; pvt. practice fee appraising South Bend, 1978-84, Culver, 1984-88, Plymouth, Ind., 1988-90; profl. watercolorist. Mem. St. Joe Valley Water Color Soc. Methodist.

MILLER, FRANCES ELIZABETH, assistant superintendent; b. Chestertown, Md., May 23, 1939; d. Edward Rood Sr. and Mary Margaret (Durham) Walls; m. Albert Russell Miller, Dec. 17, 1961 (div.); 1 child, Tracey Lynne. BS, West Chester (Pa.) State U., 1961; MEd in Adminstrn., Kent (Ohio) State U., 1970; postgrad., Towson (Md.) Coll., Loyola Coll., 1981—. Cert. phys. edn. tchr., secondary prin., supr., supt. Tchr. Kent County Pub. Schs., Chestertown, 1961-69, coord. fed. programs, 1972-82, supr. bus. affairs, 1982-86, dir. adminstrv. svcs., 1987-89, asst. supt. adminstrv. svcs., 1989—; specialist in health edn. Eastern Shore Md. Consortium, Centreville, 1970-71; tchr. Kent County High Sch., Chestertown, 1971-72; dir. Md. Legal Svcs. Trust, Annapolis, 1991—. Mem. Am. Assn. Sch. Adminstrs., Internat. Assn. Sch. Bus. Ofcls. (rsch. and fin. coms. Reston, Va. chpt. 1989—, chmn. registration St. Michael's, Md./D.C. chpt. 1988—). Democrat. Methodist. Home: 301 Manor Ave Chestertown MD 21620-3318 Office: Kent County Pub Schs 215 Washington Ave Chestertown MD 21620-1617

MILLER, FRANCES SUZANNE, historic site curator; b. Defiance, Ohio, Apr. 17, 1950; d. Francis Bernard Johnson and Nellie Frances (Holder) Culp; m. James A. Batdorf, Aug. 7, 1970 (div. Aug. 1979); 1 child, Jennifer Christine Batdorf; m. Rodney Lyle Miller, Aug. 8, 1982 (div. Apr. 1987). BS in History/Museology, The Defiance Coll., 1990; AS in Bus. Mgmt., N.W. Tech. Coll., 1986. With accts. receivable dept. Ohio Art Co., Bryan, Ohio, 1984-87; leasing agent Williams Met. Housing Authority, Bryan, 1987-91; curator, property mgr. James A. Garfield Nat. Historic Site, Mentor, Ohio, 1991—. Mem. AAUW (pres. 1993-95), Nat. Trust Hist. Preservation Ohio Mus. Assn., Ohio Assn. Host. Socs. and Mus., Cleve. Restoration Soc., Phi Alpha Theta. Office: James A Garfield Nat Historic Site 8095 Mentor Ave Mentor OH 44060

MILLER, FRANCIE LORADITCH, college recruiter; b. Avilton, Md., Apr. 18, 1937; d. John William and Agnes Wilda (Broadwater) Loraditch; m. George Aloys Miller, Feb. 27, 1965; children: Peter Raymond, Sandra Patricia. Student, Kent State U., Dominguez Hills, 1955-57; BA in English, Calif. State U., 1978; Ma in English, Calif. State U., Carson, 1980. Flight attendent Western Airlines, L.A., 1957-65; lectr. English Calif. State U., Carson, 1980-82, asst. coord. learning assistance ctr., 1979-84, asst. dir. univ. outreach svcs., 1984—. Editor Campus Staff Newsletter, 1992—. Mem. edn. com. Palos Verdes (Calif.) C. of C., 1994—; vol. Olympic Games, L.A., 1984; campus rep. Statewide Alumni Coun., Sacramento, 1982-84; participant Civic Chorale, Torrance, Calif., 1993—. Recipient acad. scholarship Kent State U., 1955. Mem. Calif. Intersegmental Articulation Coun. (newsletter editor 1993), Western Assn. Coll. Admission Counselors, South Coast Higher Ednl. Coun., Phi Kappa Phi (chpt. pres. 1992—). Republican. Roman Catholic. Office: Calif State U Dominguez Hills 1000 E Victoria St Carson CA 90747

MILLER, GENEVIEVE, retired medical historian; b. Butler, Pa., Oct. 15, 1914; d. Charles Russell and Genevieve (Wolford) M. AB, Goucher Coll., 1935; MA, Johns Hopkins U., 1939; PhD, Cornell U., 1955. Asst. in history of medicine Johns Hopkins Inst. of History of Medicine, Balt., 1943-44, instr., 1945-48, rsch. assoc., 1979-94; asst. prof. history of medicine Sch. Medicine, Case Western Res. U., Cleve., 1953-67, assoc. prof., 1967-79, assoc. prof. emeritus, 1979—; research assoc. in med. history Cleve. Med. Library Assn., 1953-62, curator Howard Dittrick Mus. of Hist. Medicine, 1962-67, dir. Howard Dittrick Mus. Hist. Medicine, 1967-79. Author: William Beaumont's Formative Years: Two Early Notebooks 1811-1821, 1946; The Adoption of Inoculation for Smallpox in England and France (William H. Welch medal Am. Assn. for History of Medicine 1962), 1957; Bibliography of the History of Medicine of the U.S. and Canada, 1939-1960, 1964; Bibliography of the Writings of Henry E. Sigerist, 1966; Letters of Edward Jenner and Other Documents Concerning the Early History of Vaccination, 1983; assoc. editor Bull. of History of Medicine, 1944-48, acting editor, 1948, mem. adv. editorial bd. 1960-92; mem. bd. editors Jour. of History of Medicine and Allied Scis., 1948-65; editor Bull. of Cleve. Med. Library, 1954-72; editor newsletter Am. Assn. for History of Medicine, 1986—; contbr. articles in field to profl. jours. Am. Council Learned Socs. fellow, 1948-50; Dean Van Meter fellow, 1953-54. Alumna trustee Goucher Coll., Balt., 1966-69. Hon. fellow Cleve. Med. Library Assn.; mem. Am. Assn. for History of Medicine (pres. 1978-80, mem. council 1960-63), Am. Hist. Assn., Internat. Soc. for History of Medicine, Soc. Archtl. Historians, Phi Beta Kappa; corr. mem. fgn. socs. for history of medicine. Democrat. Home and Office: Judson Manor 1890 E 107th St Apt 816 Cleveland OH 44106-2245

MILLER, GEORGIA ELLEN, business owner; b. Seattle; d. George Rynd Sr. and Mary Edith (Martin) M. BE, UCLA, 1934, MEd, 1956. Tchr. Punahou Sch., Honolulu, 1948-74; owner Miller's Bus. Svcs., Honolulu, 1975—. Bd. dirs. Waikiki Improvement Assn., Honolulu, 1980-95, Waikiki Community Ctr., Honolulu, 1992—; pres. Waikiki Resident's Assn., Honolulu, 1978—; sec. Waikiki Neighborhood Bd., 1980-86, v.p., 1990—, acting chair, 1992-93; county chmn. Oahu (Hawaii) Rep. Party, 1976. Mem. Bus. and Profl. Women (pres. 1973, legis. chair 1980, 88, state lobbyist 1988—), AAUW, Alpha Chi Omega, Pi Lambda Theta. Mem. United Ch. of Christ. Home: 2415 Ala Wai Blvd Apt 1603 Honolulu HI 96815-3460 Office: Millers Bus Svcs Ste B4c 1720 Ala Moana Blvd Honolulu HI 96815-1302

MILLER, GERRI, magazine editor, writer; b. Bklyn., Mar. 2, 1954; d. Norman and Isobel (Rand) M. BA, SUNY, Binghamton, 1976. Assoc. editor Sixteen Mag., N.Y.C., 1977-80; editor, then exec. editor Sterling/Macfadden, N.Y.C., 1981—. Office: Metal Edge TV Picture Life Sterling/Macfadden 233 Park Ave S New York NY 10003

MILLER, HARRIET EVELYN, management consultant; b. Council, Idaho, July 4, 1919; d. Colwell and Vera (Crome) M. B.A. magna cum laude, Whitman Coll., 1941, D.H.L., 1979; M.A., U. Pa., 1949. Chemist Atlantic Refining Co., Phila., 1944-50; student personnel adminstr. U. Mont., Missoula, 1950-54; acting asso. dean students U. Mont., 1954-55, asso. dean students, 1955-56; supt. pub. instrn. Mont., 1956-69; pres. Harriet Miller Assocs. (mgmt. cons.), Helena, Mont., 1969-75; assoc. dir. Am. Assn. Ret. Persons/Nat. Ret. Tchrs. Assn., 1975-76, exec. dir., 1976-77; mgmt. cons., 1977—; pres. HMA, Inc., 1984-88; exec. dir. U.S. Occupational Safety and Health Rev. Commn., Washington, 1979-81. Commr. Santa Barbara County (Calif.) Parole Bd., 1981-84; chmn. City Housing Authority, Santa Barbara, 1984-86; bd. overseers Whitman Coll., Walla Walla, Wash., 1983—; mem. city coun. City of Santa Barbara, City Housing Authority, 1982-87; bd. dirs. Ctrl. Coast Congregation Care, Inc., Westside Neighborhood Med. Clinic, Community Action Commn., Santa Barbara County Assn. Govt., Santa Barbara County Air Pollution Control Dist. Mem. P.E.O., Mont. Congress Parents and Tchrs. (life), AAUW, Phi Beta Kappa, Delta Kappa Gamma, Phi Kappa Phi, Psi Chi, Alpha Chi Omega. Unitarian (former trustee). Address: PO Box 1346 Santa Barbara CA 93102-1346

MILLER, HARRIET SANDERS, art center director; b. N.Y.C., Apr. 18, 1926; d. Herman and Dorothy (Silbert) S.; m. Milton H. Miller, June 27, 1948; children—Bruce, Jeffrey, Marcie. B.A., Ind. U., 1947; M.A., Columbia U., 1949; M.S., U. Wis., 1962, M.F.A., 1967. Dir. art sch. Madison Art Ctr., Wis., 1963-72; acting dir. Center for Continuing Edn., Vancouver, B.C., 1975-76; mem. fine arts faculty Douglas Coll., Vancouver, 1972-78; exec. dir. Palos Verdes Arts Center, Calif., 1978-84; dir. Junior Arts Center, Los Angeles, 1984—; one woman exhibits at Gallery 7, Vancouver, 1978, Gallery 1, Toronto, Ont., 1977, Linda Farris Gallery, Seattle, 1975, Galerie Allen, Vancouver, 1973. Mem. Calif. Art Edn. Assn., Museum Educators of So. Calif., Arts and Humanities Symposium. Office: Junior Arts Ctr 4814 Hollywood Blvd Los Angeles CA 90027-5387

MILLER, IRIS ANN, landscape architect, urban designer, educator; b. Pitts., Jan. 6, 1938; d. Bernard and Sadye (Topel) Ress; m. Lawrence Alan Miller, Jan. 24, 1959; children: Bradley Stuart, Richard Lyle, Stefan Ress. BS cum laude, U. Pitts., 1959, MEd in Secondary Edn., 1961; postgrad. in psychology and counseling, U. Md., 1962-68; MArch, Cath. U. Am., 1979. Tchr. various pub. and pvt. schs., Pitts., Monroeville, Pa., Montgomery County, Md., 1959-61, 63-64; free lance landscape design Washington, 1965-81; architecture design and research O'Neil and Manion Architects, Bethesda, Md., 1979, 81; architecture and design drawing Frank Schlesinger Architects/Planners, Washington, 1979-80; prin. Iris Miller Urbanism and Landscape Design, 1982—; cons. architecture design Washington, 1982—; vis. lectr. Cath. U. Am., Washington, 1983-86, vis. asst. prof., 1987-93, adj. asst. prof., 1993—, dir. landscape and architecture studies, 1986-89, dir landscape studies, 1990—; urban design cons. Techworld, Washington, 1984-86; devel. dir. Tech 2000 Mus., 1985-86; dir., presenter lectr. series Resident Assoc. Program Smithsonian Instn., Washington, 1982, 83, 85, 87, 89; dir., founder 7th, 8th, and 9th Sts. Group Streetscape project, Washington, 1986—, others; founder Charrette urban design seminar, Washington, Dallas, Alexandria, Va., St. Louis and Cleve., 1982-89; initiator, participant Sarasota (Fla.) Regional Urban Design Assistance R/UDAT team, 1983, seminar Nat. Gallery Art, Washington, 1984, Nat. Arboretum, 1988, symposia Cath. U. of Am., 1987—; founder dir. symposium Libr. of Congress, 1995; dir., mem. steering com. numerous confs. in field; program speaker, Congrss for New Urbanism, 1994—, U.S. Embassy Amman, Jordan, 1992, U. Va., 1993, Ecole Nationale Superieure du Paysage/Versailles, France, 1993, U. Osaka, Japan, 1993. Tokyo Inst. Tech. U., 1993, SUNY, Buffalo, 1994, U. Colo., Denver, 1994, Mayors Inst. on City Design, St. Louis, 1994; jury critic Cath. U. Am., 1980-94, U. Puerto Rice, U. Va., 1993. Author, co-editor (book): Urban Design: Visions and Reflections, 1991, (map and text) Visions of Washington: Composite Plan of Urban Interventions, 1991; contbr. articles to profl. publs.; curator, author exhbn. and catalogue on Washington Maps Sumner Sch. Mus., 1987, 92, U. Md., 1993, Embassy of France, 1993, SUNY Buffalo, 1994, U. Calif., Berkeley, 1994, U. Toronto, 1995; curator, author map exhbn. ACSA Ann. Meeting, Montreal, 1994; co-curator, author exhbn. and catalogue Octagon Mus., 1987; project dir., curator Paris-Washington Exhbn., 1987—; architecture design and drawing Georgetown H.S., Washington, 1988, W.Va. Wesleyan Coll. Campus plan for religious art ctr., 1992, L'Iris Espace et Animation Cultural Ctr., Francheville, France, 1993, Hebrew Congregation Meml. Park Info. pavilion and landscape renovation, 1993-94; recent landscape projects include Kahn Residence, Arlington, Va., 1993-94, Marks Residence, Silver Spring, Md., 1993, Nesse, Lewis Residence, Silver Spring , Md., 1992, Friedman Residence, Washington, 1992, Drysdale Hershon Residence, Washington, 1991, Miller Residence, Washington, 1990—, Sexton Residence, Kenwood, Chevy Chase, Md., 1990, Romano Residence, Fairfax Station, Va., 1989, Mushinski Residence, Bethesda, Md., 1989, 8th St. Mall Washington, 1987-88, Mishkin, Jennis Residence, Bethesda, 1988, Cramer Residence, Bethesda, 1988; recent home design and renovations include Sexton Residence, Chevy Chase, Md., 1994, Miller Jayapal Residence, San Francisco, 1993, Marks Residence, Silver Spring, Md., 1993, Miller Residence, Washington, 1991, Mishkin Jennis Residence, Bethesda, 1988. Co-chmn. stamp com. Bicentennial Washington, 1987-90; founding mem. Washington Network, 1986-89; mem. adv. panel L'Enfant Forum, Washington, 1987-90, Hist. Georgetown Found., 1989-92; trustee John J. Sexton Fund for Local Govt. Studies, Sch. Pub. Affairs, U. Md., College Park, 1983—; dir., founder Pub.-Pvt. Partnership and Univ. Scholarship Outreach High Sch. Program, Cath. U. Am., Washington Pub. Schs., 1985—; dir., founder Intern Exch. Program Landscape Architecture, France-U.S.A., Cath. U. Am., U. Va., Friends of Vieilles Maisons Francaises, 1991—; mem. historic landscape com. U.S/ Internat. Coun. on Monuments and Sites, 1990—; active Cultural Alliance Greater Washington, Nat. Trust for Historic Preservation, Ikebana Internat., Hist. Soc. Washington, Nat. Bldg. Mus., alumni coun. Sch. Architecture and Planning, Cath. U. Am., 1986—. Travel rsch. grantee Cath. U. Am., 1978, 79, Rsch. grantee Govt. France, 1985; grantee NEA (2), 1982, grantee D.C. Commn. on Arts, 1991, 92; recipient Program Devel. award Cath. U. Am., 1978. Mem. Am. Planning Assn., U.S.-Internat. Coun. on Monuments and Sites (program speaker 1987, 92, 93, hist. landscapes com.), Friends Vieilles Maisons Francaises (program speaker 1987, 92), AIA (assoc., regional and urban design com. 1982—, chmn. edn. subcom 1987—, chmn., founder data base on design edn. and urban design 1993, urban design exhbn. and panel, 1989—, chmn. edn. conf. 1983, chmn. newsletter 1993, edn. com. D.C. chpt. 1981-83, Charrette co-chmn., program devel.

award 1982), Assn. Collegiate Schs. Architecture (speaker N.E. region conf. 1989, speaker ann. meeting 1991-92, chmn. panel on urban design 1989—, chair Collegiate Exhbn. for Excellence in Urban Design, 1990—, author conf. procs. 1991-93 , Citation for Urban Design 1993), Am. Soc. Landscape Architects (Potomac chpt. strategic planning com., 1994—), Inst. Urban Design, Friends of Vieilles Maisons Francaises, Alpha Epsilon Phi (pres. D.C. alumni 1965-67). Home: 3820 52nd St NW Washington DC 20016-1924 Office: 914 11th St NW Washington DC 20001-4408

MILLER, JACQUELINE WINSLOW, library director; b. N.Y.C., Apr. 15, 1935; d. Lynward Roosevelt and Sarah Ellen (Grevious) W.; 1 child, Percy Scott. BA, Morgan State Coll., 1957; MLS, Pratt Inst., 1960; grad. profl. seminar, U. Md., 1973. Cert. profl. librarian. With Bklyn. Pub. Library, 1957-68; head extension services New Rochelle (N.Y.) Pub. Library, 1969-70; br. adminstr. Grinton Will Yonkers (N.Y.) Pub. Libr., 1970-75; dir. Yonkers Pub. Library, 1975—; mem. adj. faculty grad. libr. studies Queens Coll., CUNY, 1989, 90. Mem. commr.'s com. Statewide Libr. Devel., Albany, N.Y., 1980; mem. N.Y. Gov.'s Commn. on Librs., 190, 91; bd. dirs. Community Planning Coun., Yonkers, N.Y., 1987; mem. Yonkers Black Women's Polit. Caucus, 1987; pres. bd. Literacy Vols. of Westchester County, 1991-92. Recipient Yonkers Citizen award Ch. of Our Saviour, 1980, 2d Ann. Mae Morgan Robinson award Yonkers chpt. Westchester Black Women's Polit. Caucus, 1992, 3d Ann. Equality Day award City of Yonkers, 1992, African-Am. Heritage 1st award YWCA, 1994; named Outstanding Profl. Woman Nat. Assn. Negro Bus. and Profl. Women's Clubs Inc., 1981. Mem. ALA (councilor 1987-91), N.Y. State Libr. Assn., Pub. Libr. Dirs. Assn. (exec. bd.), N.Y. State Pub. Libr. Dirs. Assn., Westchester Libr. Assn., Yonkers C. of C. (bd. dirs. 1992-95), Rotary (Yonkers chpt.). Office: Yonkers Pub Libr 7 Main St Yonkers NY 10701-2711

MILLER, JANE ANDREWS, accountant; b. Nashville, Aug. 14, 1952; d. Joseph Raymond Andrews and Allison (Bartlett) Fang; m. Thomas C. Heselton, June 22, 1970 (div. 1978); 1 child, Elizabeth Lyn; m. Keith Evan Miller, Apr. 14, 1984. Degree in Bus. Typing and Computers, Fairfax (Va.) Bus. Sch., 1974. Cert. notary public. Adminstrv. asst. T.J. Fannon & Sons, Alexandria, Va., 1973-79; distbn. clk., adminstrv. asst. U.S. Post Office, Merrifield, Va., 1980-83; acct., sec., treas. Aux. Electric Power Co., Fairfax, 1983—; pvt. practice, investment counselor, Fairfax; sec., treas. AEPCO, Inc., K & J, Inc., 1990—. Mem. Friends of Calypso; assoc. mem. Smithsonian Inst.; v.p. Grand Masters Bowling League, 1994-95. Mem. Hist. Preservation Soc., Grand Masters League (v.p.). Republican.

MILLER, JANEL HOWELL, psychologist; b. Boone, N.C., May 18, 1947; d. John Estle and Grace Louise (Hemberger) Howell; B.A., DePauw U., 1969; postgrad. Rice U., 1969; M.A., U. Houston, 1972; Ph.D., Tex. A&M U., 1979; m. C. Rick Miller, Nov. 24, 1968; children: Kimberly, Brian, Audrey, Rachel. Asso. sch. psychologist Houston Ind. Sch. Dist., 1971-74; research psychologist VA Hosp., Houston, 1972; asso. sch. psychologist Clear Creek Ind. Sch. Dist., Tex., 1974-76; instr. psychology, counseling psychology intern Tex. A. and M. U., 1976-77; clin. psychology intern VA Hosp., Houston, 1977-78; coordinator psychol. services Clear Creek Ind. Sch. Dist., 1978-81, assoc. dir. psychol. services, 1981-82; pvt. practice, Houston, 1982—; faculty U. Houston-Clear Lake, 1984—; adolescent suicide cons., 1984—. DePauw U. Alumni scholar, 1965-69; NIMH fellow U. Houston, 1970-71; lic. clin. psychologist, sch. psychologist, Tex. Mem. Am. Psychol. Assn., Tex. Psychol. Assn., Houston Psychol. Assn. (media rep. 1984-85), Am. Assn. Marriage and Family Therapists, Tex. Assn. Marriage and Family Therapists, Houston Assn. Marriage and Family Therapists, Soc. for Personality Assessment. Home: 806 Walbrook Dr Houston TX 77062-4030 Office: Southpoint Psychol Svcs 11550 Fuqua St Ste 450 Houston TX 77034-4537

MILLER, JANETTE PATRICIA, mental health counselor, marriage and family therapist; b. Pasadena, Calif., Mar. 15, 1949; d. Einar Bernhardt and Jean Patricia (McGougan) Dixen; m. Loren Karl Miller, June 27, 1970; children: Elisa Christine, Karl Gustav. AA, Grand View Coll., 1969; BA, U. No. Iowa, 1971; MS, U. Nebr. Omaha, 1977; postgrad., Iowa State U., 1988-90. Nat. cert. counselor and clin. mental health counselor. Income maintenance technician Douglas County (Nebr.) Social Svcs., Omaha, 1972-74; job devel. for handicapped N. Santa Barbara County (Calif.) Rehab. Ctr., Santa Maria, 1977-78; spl. needs-adult edn. instr. Iowa Ctrl. C.C., Ft. Dodge, 1978-83; in-home family counselor Iowa Children's and Family Svcs., Ft. Dodge, 1983-87; asst. supr. Ft. Dodge br. Iowa Children's and Family Svcs., 1987-89; mental health counselor, marriage and family therapist N. Ctrl. Iowa Mental Health Ctr., Ft. Dodge, 1989—; coord. primary level child abuse prevention program Area V Coun. Child Abuse and Neglect, Ft. Dodge, 1980-83; sec., co-chair, chair, mem. Webster County (Iowa) Coalition Victim Svcs., Ft. Dodge, 1988—; mem. adv. bd. Specialized Child Svc. Ctr., Ft. Dodge, 1988—; mem. Attention Deficit Disorder work group Iowa Dept. Edn.-Bur. Spl. Edn., Des Moines, 1990-91; former bd. dirs. Family Violence Ctr. N. Ctrl. Iowa, Ft. Dodge; former mem. devel. and planning com. Attention Deficit Disorder parents support group, Ft. Dodge. Former mem. League Women Voters, Ft. Dodge. Mem. AAUW, Am. Assn. Marriage and Family Therapy (clin.), Iowa Assn. Marriage and Family Therapy (clin.). Office: N Ctrl Iowa Mental Health Ctr 720 S Kenyon Rd Fort Dodge IA 50501

MILLER, JANICE MICHELLE, physical education educator, coach; b. Washington, Nov. 7, 1954; d. Louise (Mowrey) Miller. BS, Trinity U., 1976; MS of Mid-Mgmt., Tex. A&I U., 1988. Cert. adminstr., tchr. Tchr., coach Judson High Sch. Judson Ind. Sch. Dist., Converse, Tex., 1976-79; tchr., coach Clark High Sch. Northside Ind. Sch. Dist., San Antonio, 1979-90; tchr., coach MacArthur High Sch. N.E. Ind. Sch. Dist., San Antonio, 1990—. Vol. Elf Louise, San Antonio, 1990-93. Named Coach of Yr., San Antonio Light Newspaper, 1989, 91. Mem. Tex. Assn. Basketball Coaches (bd. dirs. 1985-93), Tex. Girls Coaches Assn. (regional dir. 1993—, clinician 1991), Fellowship of Christian Athletes (sponsor 1979-93), Phi Delta Kappa. Roman Catholic. Home: 5823 Lake Champlain St San Antonio TX 78233-5123 Office: MacArthur High School 2923 Bitters San Antonio TX 78217

MILLER, JANISE LUEVENIA MONICA, lawyer; b. Atlanta, Dec. 25, 1956; d. James Thomas and Vera Luevenia (Brown) M.; 1 child, Brandyn Matthew Cooper. BA, Spalding U., 1976; JD, John Marshall Law Sch., 1979. Bar: Ga. 1982, U.S. Ct. Appeals (11th cir.) 1989. Mental health law specialist Ga. Legal Svcs., Atlanta, 1987-88; atty., paralegal Rogers & Sparks, Atlanta, 1980-82; staff counsel Ga. Dept. Med. Assistance, Atlanta, 1982-83; assoc. atty. Cuffie, Mitchell & Assocs., Atlanta, 1983-84, Cuffie & Assocs., Atlanta, 1984-85; pvt. practice Atlanta, 1985-86; of counsel Albert A. Mitchell & Assocs., Atlanta, 1987-92, A.A. Mitchell & Assocs., Atlanta, 1987-92; pvt. practice, 1993—; judge pro hac vice Atlanta Mcpl. Ct. 1989-91. Assoc. editor Nexus, 1980. Chairperson, pres. United Schleroderma Found., Atlanta, 1991-92. Fellow Ga. Bar Found.; mem. State Bar of Ga., Ga. Assn. of Black Women Attys. (Svc. award 1986), Atlanta Bar Assn. (chairperson, seminar com. 1987-88, sec./treas. criminal law sect. 1988-89), Nat. Bar Assn. (chairperson Gertrude Rush Dinner 1992), Gate City Bar Assn. (pres. 1987, editor newsletter 1992). Democrat. Roman Catholic. Office: 230 Peachtree St Ste 675 Atlanta GA 30303

MILLER, JEAN ELLEN, academic development director; b. Brockton, Mass., Mar. 10, 1928; d. John Wright and Dorothy (Dean) M. AB, Brown U., 1949; MA, Middlebury Coll., 1953. Tchr. pub. high schs., Maine, 1949-50; tchr., counselor Mt. Vernon Sem., Washington, 1956-58; asst. head, tchr. Masters Sch., Dobbs Ferry, N.Y., 1958-63; dir. student pers. Bennington (Vt.) Coll., 1963-64; head mistress St. Timothy's Sch., Stevenson, Md., 1964-77; regional dir. AFS Internat., N.Y.C., 1978-84; head mistress Vivian Webb Sch., Claremont, Calif., 1984-87; head Palmer Sch., Miami, Fla., 1988-90; dir. devel. Poly Prep Country Day Sch., Bklyn., 1991—; cons. Md. State Edn. Com., Balt., 1960's. Fund raiser Brown U., Providence, 1992-94; pres. Women of Brown of So. Calif., 1986-88; chmn. Pembroke Ctr. Tchg. and Rsch. on Women, Providence, 1994—. Mem. NOW, Nat. Assn. Ind. Schs. (bd. dirs. 1968-78, chmn. 1976-78), Nat. Mus. for Women in the Arts (charter), Nat. Assn. Prins. Schs. for Girls, Planned Giving Group N.Y., Dorset Field Club, Sierra Club. Home: PO Box 349 Arlington VT 05250 Office: Poly Prep Country Day Sch 9216 7th Ave Brooklyn NY 11228

MILLER, JEAN RUTH, librarian; b. St. Helena, Calif., Aug. 4, 1927; d. William Leonard and Jean (Stanton) M. BA, Occidental Coll., 1950; MLS, U. So. Calif., Los Angeles, 1952. Base librarian USAF, Wethersfield, Eng., 1952-55; post librarian USMC Air Sta., El Toro, Calif., 1955-63; data systems librarian Autonetics (Rockwell), Anaheim, Calif., 1963-65; mgr. library services Beckman Instruments, Inc., Fullerton, Calif., 1966-93; mem. adv. com. Library Technician Program, Fullerton Coll., 1969—. Author: (bibliography) Field Air Traffic Control, 1965, Electrical Shock Hazards, 1974. Chair Fullerton Are U. So. Calif. Scholarship Alumni Interview Program, Fullerton, 1974—. Mem. IEEE, So. Calif. Assn. Law Libraries, Med. Library Group of So. Calif., Spl. Libraries Assn. (pres. So. Calif. chpt. 1975-76, chair Sci./Tech. Div. 1985-86). Republican. Home: 3139 E Chapman Ave Apt 9C Orange CA 92669-3743

MILLER, JEANNE-MARIE ANDERSON (MRS. NATHAN J. MILLER), English language educator, academic administrator; b. Washington, Feb. 18, 1937; d. William and Agnes Catherine (Johns) Anderson m. Nathan John Miller, Oct. 2, 1960. BA, Howard U., 1959, MA, 1963, PhD, 1976. Instr. dept. English Howard U., Washington, 1963-76, asst. prof., 1976-79, assoc. prof., 1979-92, prof., 1992—, also asst. dir. Inst. Arts and Humanities, 1973-75, asst. acad. planning, office v.p. for acad. affairs, 1976-90; cons. Am. Studies Assn., 1972-75, Silver Burdett Pub. Co., Nat. Endowment for Humanities, 1978—; adv. bd. D.C. Libr. for Arts, 1973—, John Oliver Killens Writers Guild, 1975—, Afro-Am. Theatre, Balt., 1975—. Editor, Black Theatre Bull., 1977-86; Realism to Ritual: Form and Style in Black Theatre, 1983; assoc. editor Theatre Jour., 1980-81; contbr. articles to profl. jours. Mem. Washington Performing Arts Soc., 1971—, Friends of Sta. WETA-TV, 1971—, Mus. African Art, 1971—, Arena Stage Assos., 1972—, Washington Opera Guild, 1982—, Wolf Trap Assocs., 1982—. Ford Found. fellow, 1970-72, So. Fellowships Fund fellow, 1972-74; Howard U. Rsch. grantee, 1975-76, 94-95, Am. Coun. Learned Socs. grantee, 1978-79, NEH grantee, 1981-84. Mem. Nat. Coun. Tchrs. of English, Coll. English Assn., Am. Studies Assn., Am. Theatre Assn., AAUP, AAUW, D.C. LWV, Common Cause, ACLU, Am. Acad. Polit. and Social Sci., Coll. Lang. Assn., MLA, Am. Assn. Higher Edn., Nat. Assn. Women Deans, Adminstrs. and Counselors, Friends Kennedy Ctr. for Performing Arts, Pi Lambda Theta. Democrat. Episcopalian. Home: 504 24th St NE Washington DC 20002-4818

MILLER, JERI L. HULL, counselor; b. Quincy, Ill., Mar. 5, 1954; d. Gerald Edward and Ronda Juanita (Nothern) Hull; children: Jennifer Jean, Jaime Terese. BA magna cum laude, Quincy Coll., 1980; MA, Sangamon State U., 1993. Cert. counselor; cert. clin. mental health counselor; nat. bd. cert. counselor; profl. clin. counselor, Ill. Probation officer Adams County Probation Office, Quincy, 1980-81; caseworker Ill. Dept. Pub. Aid, Quincy, 1984-86; truancy officer Adams County Supt. of Schs., Quincy, 1989-91; sch. guidance counselor Quincy Sch. Dist., 1991—; clin. counselor Luth. Child and Family Svcs., Quincy, 1993—. Field worker Am. Cancer Soc., Muscular Dystrophy Assn.; leader Girl Scouts U.S.A. Mem. ACA, Am. Sch. Counselors Assn., Nat. Bd. Cert. Counselors, Chi Sigma Iota. Methodist. Home: 908 Pawn Ave Quincy IL 62301 Office: Berrian Alternative Sch 1327 S 8th Quincy IL 62301 also: Luth Child and Family Svcs 431 Hampshire Quincy IL 62301

MILLER, JO CAROLYN DENDY, family and marriage counselor, educator; b. Gorman, Tex., Sept. 16, 1942; d. Leonard Lee and Vera Vertie (Robison) Dendy; m. Douglas Terry Barnes, June 1, 1963 (div. June 1975); children: Douglas Alan, Bradley Jason; m. Walton Sansom Miller, Sept. 19, 1982. BA, Tarleton State U., 1964; MEd, U. North State, 1977; PhD, Tex. Women's U. Tchr., Mineral Wells (Tex.) High Sch., 1964-65, Weatherford (Tex.) Middle Sch., 1969-74; counselor, instr. psychology Tarrant County Jr. Coll., Hurst, Tex., 1977-82; pvt. practice family and marriage counseling, Dallas, 1982—. Author: (with Velma Walker, Jeannene Ward) Becoming: A Human Relations Workbook, 1981. Mem. ACA, Tex. State Bd. Examiners Profl. Counselors, Tex. State Bd. Marriage and Family Therapists, Tex. Counseling Assn., Am. Mental Health Counselors Assn., North Ctrl. Tex. Counseling Assn., Dallas Symphony Orch. League, Nat. Coun. Family Rels., Tex. Mental Health Counselors Assn., Internat. Assn. for Marriage & Family Counselors. Methodist. Office: Counseling & Consulting of North Dallas 8222 Douglas Ave Ste 777 Dallas TX 75225

MILLER, JOANNE LOUISE, middle school teacher; b. Milton, Mass., Apr. 4, 1944; d. Joseph Louis and Marion Theresa (Saulnier) Fasci; m. William Frederick Miller, Dec. 4, 1962; 1 child, Robert Joseph. BS, U. Oreg., 1972, MS in Curriculum and Instrn., 1973; EdD, Brigham Young U., 1980; postgrad., Oreg. State U., 1995. Lic. counselor, tchr., adminstr., Oreg. Tchr. South Lane Sch. Dist., Cottage Grove, Oreg., 1973—, lang. arts div. chairperson, 1975-78, 89-90, reading coord., 1978-79, 7th grade block chairperson, 1982-92, mid. sch. talented and gifted coord., 1992-93, counselor, 1991-93; mem. Oreg. State Assessment Content Panel Reading, Salem, 1987-88; mem. Oreg. Lang. Arts Curriculum Devel. Com., Salem, 1985-87; del. Citizen Ambassador Program of People to People Internat. First U.S./Russia Joint Conf. on Edn., Moscow, 1994. Vol. Am. Cancer Soc., Am. Diabetes Assn., 1990—. Mem. ACA, NEA, Internat. Reading Assn., Am. Sch. Counselor Assn., Oreg. Counseling Assn., Oreg. Edn. Assn., South Lane Edn. Assn., Oreg. Reading Assn., Delta Kappa Gamma. Democrat. Roman Catholic. Home: 85515 Appletree Dr Eugene OR 97405-9738 Office: Lincoln Mid Sch 1565 S 4th St Cottage Grove OR 97424-2955

MILLER, JUDITH ANN, retired financial executive; b. Chgo., Sept. 8, 1941; d. Frank G. and Kathryn M. (Stocklin) Bell; m. William J. Shrum, Aug. 3, 1958 (div. 1976); children: Steven W., Vickie L. White, Lisa A. Rhodes, Mark A., Brian D.; m. William L. Miller Jr., Nov. 28, 1976. Student, Ind. Cen. Coll., 1959-60, DePaw U., 1964-65. Lic. minister Christian Ch. (Disciples of Christ). Office cashier, mgr. G.C. Murphy Co., Indpls., 1967-70; asst. treas., office mgr. Missions Blvd. Fed. Credit Union, Indpls., 1970-72; treas., office mgr. Bd. Higher Edn., Christian Ch. (Disciples of Christ), Indpls. and St. Louis, 1972-77; dir. fin. Mt. Olive United Meth. Ch., Arlington, Va., 1978-79; exec. dir. Interfaith Forum on Religion, Art and Architecture, Washington, 1979-82; devel. assoc. Nat. Benevolent Assn., Des Moines, Iowa, 1982-85; adminstrv. asst. Davis, Hockenberg, Wine, Brown, Koehn & Shors, Des Moines, 1985-88; fin. officer Episcopal Diocese of Iowa, Des Moines, 1988-93; ret., 1993. Mem. citizen adv. coun. Parkway Schs., St. Louis, 1976-77; county rep., mem. Fairfax County Sch. Bd. adv. coun., Springfield, Va., 1979-81; treas. congl. campaign Des Moines, 1983-85; mem. exec. St. Louis Children's Home, 1976-78; v.p., treas. Emmaus Fellowship Project on Aging, Washington, 1980-82; bd. dirs. Urban Mission Coun., Des Moines, 1983-86, Pre-Trial Release Prog., Des Moines, 1984-87; mem. steering com. Iowa Interfaith Network on AIDS, Des Moines, 1989—; chmn. Cancer Awareness Sunday, Am. Cancer Soc., 1990. Named Vol. of Yr., Iowa Victorian Soc., 1985, Our Community Kitchen, 1986. Mem. Nat. Soc. Fund Raising Execs. (chpt. sec. 1985-87), Nat. Assn. Ch. Bus. Adminstrs., NAFE. Democrat. Mem. Christian Ch. (Disciples of Christ). Home: PO Box 194 Manteo NC 27954

MILLER, JUDITH JUNTURA, artist; b. Ontario, Oreg., Jan. 31, 1939; d. Ben and Hazel Adeline (Richie) Jones; m. Jerry Wayne Miller, Feb. 19, 1956; children: Jeffrey, Andrew. AA with honors, Canada Coll., Redwood City, Calif., 1973, postgrad., Y; BA with honors, San Jose State U., 1976; BFA, San Francisco Art Inst., 1980. guest lectr. Cabrillo Coll. Auditorium, Aptos, Calif., 1991; guest lectr. mixed media work Santa Cruz Mus. Art, Cabrillo Coll. Gallery, 1991. One-woman shows include City Hall Gallery, Sunnyvale, Calif., 1982, So. Exposure Gallery, San Francisco, 1985, Pacific Grad. Sch. Psychology, Palo Alto, Calif., 1989, Stanford (Calif.) U., 1990, Branner Spangenberg Gallery, Palo Alto, 1991, Cabrillo Coll. Gallery, 1991, Art F/X, 1994; group shows include San Francisco Art Inst., 1985, Seipp Gallery, Palo Alto, 1986, 92, San Jose Mus. Art, 1988, 92, Clara Kott Von Storch Gallery, Dexter, Mich., 1994, Gallery 57, Fullerton, Calif., River Gallery, Chattanooga, Tenn., San Diego Art Inst., Triton Mus. of Art, Santa Clara, Calif., One West Contemporary Art Ctr., Ft. Collins, Colo., Gallery 206, St. Joseph, Mo., many others; represented in numerous pvt. and corp. collections; contbr. articles to profl. publs. Recipient Cert. of Excellence, Internat. Art Competition, Metro Art, N.Y., 1986, Best of Show award Aesthetics '89," Friendship Hall Gallery, McPherson, Kans., Patron's award No. Nat. Juried Art Exhibit, LRC Gallery, Nicolet Coll., Rhinelander, Wis., 1989, Cert. of Merit, 87th Open Juried Exhbn., Long Beach (Calif.) Art Assn., 1991, Merit award Calif. Works, Calif. State Fair, Sacramento, 1991, Gold and Silver Discovery awards Art of Calif., 1992. Mem. South Bay Area Women's Caucus for Art (founding, v.p. slide registry 1990), Women's Caucus for Art (v.p. membership 1991-92, coord. Art Reach 1990-91, guest lectr. 1991), Calif. Soc. of Printmakers, L.A. Printmaking Soc., The Print Consortium. Home and Studio: 4141 Old Trace Rd Palo Alto CA 94306-3728

MILLER, KAREN LYNN, clinical social worker; b. Trenton, Mo., Mar. 3, 1956; d. Arthur Leon and JoAnn (Ellis) Sawyer; m. Stuart W. Miller, May 31, 1975; children: Matthew A., and Michael A. AA, Longview C.C., Lees Summit, Mo., 1992; BSW, Ctrl. Mo. State U., 1994; postgrad. in social work, U. Kans., 1994—. Accts. payable clk. Panhandle Ea. Pipeline, Kansas City, Mo., 1975-81; hairdresser The Hairdresser, Independence, Mo., 1984-87; self employed hairdresser Independence, 1987-93; case mgr. intern Hope House, Independence, 1994; clin. social worker, intern Heart Am. Family Svcs., Kansas City, 1994—; vol. hotline Hope House Battered Women's Shelter, Independence, 1989—; mem. adv. bd. home econs. dept. Independence Schs., 1990—. Vol. Juvenile Family Ct., Kansas City; sec. Assn. S.W. Students Ctrl. Mo. State U., 1992-93. Mem. Nat. Assn. S.W., Phi Alpha (sec. 1994—), Phi Theta Kappa. Home: 4815 Kendall Dr Independence MO 64055

MILLER, KATHARINE JANE, insurance executive; b. Zanesville, Ohio, Dec. 6, 1951; d. Albert Nelson and Freda Jane (Anspach) Kishler; m. James Leroy Miller, Aug. 13, 1970 (div. June 1981); 1 child, Jonas Benjamin. Grad., Morgan County H.S., 1970. Asst. underwriter Windsor Ins. Svcs., Inc., St. Petersburg, Fla., 1979-82; brokerage underwriting mgr. Allied Specialty, Inc., St. Petersburg, 1982-85; asst. casualty mgr. Hull & Co., Inc., St. Petersburg, 1985—; assoc. Fla. Farm Bur., St. Petersburg, 1991—. Editor newsletter Ladybugs, 1989; contbr. to periodical Achiever; exhibited in Kissimmee (Fla.) Air Fair/United Way, 1989-91. Mem. Nat. Assn. Ins. Women (mgmt. focus group 1994, Founders Club,. 1994, region III credentials com. 1994), Ins. Women of St. Petersburg (bd. dirs. 1987, 88-91, 92, sec. 1990, pres.-elect 1993, pres. 1994, state del. 1993, regional del. 1994, nat. del. 1994, chair various coms. 1985-94, Communicate with Confidence award 1986, Leadership Devel. award 1987, Individual Edn. award 1987, Ins. Woman of Yr. 1994), Exptl. Aircraft Assn., Fla. Sport Aviation Antique and Classic Assn. Republican. Methodist. Office: Hull & Co Inc 788 Executive Dr W Saint Petersburg FL 33702

MILLER, KATHERINE TOY, writer; b. Taft, Calif., Jan. 9, 1955; d. John Jasper and Betty Irene (Harkleroad) M. BA in English, U. Redlands, 1977; MFA, U. Ariz., 1983. Newspaper reporter Daily Midway Driller, Taft, 1978-80; instr. English and com. Norwich U., Northfield, Vt., 1984-86; instr. English Muskingum Coll., New Concord, Ohio, 1987-88; writing fellow Fine Arts Work Ctr., Provincetown, Mass., 1988-89; part time instr. Calif. State U., Bakersfield, 1989; instr. U. Calif. Santa Barbara, 1990. Contbr. numerous articles to profl. publs. Home: 203 Church St Taft CA 93268

MILLER, KRISTELLE EVELYNE, education educator; b. Marysville, Calif., Aug. 8, 1948; d. Albert Edward II and Alverissa Christina Miller. BS, Ind. State U., 1970; MS, Purdue Calumet, 1974; PhD, Purdue, West Lafayette, Ind., 1987. Cert. tchr., Ind.; nat. cert. counselor. Music tchr. River Forest (Ind.), 1971-74; coll. counselor Valparaiso (Ind.) U., 1977-78; sch. counselor North Judson - San Pierre, 1979-84; teaching asst. Purdue U., West Lafayette, Ind., 1984-86, NIH postdoctoral rsch. fellow, 1985-87; postdoctoral rsch. fellow U. of Ill., Champaign, 1987-89; asst. prof. U. Minn., Duluth, 1989-92, assoc. prof., 1992—. Editorial bd: Jour. of Adolescent Rsch; reviewer NIMH, jours. in field.; contbr. articles to profl. jours. Recipient grant U. Minn., 1992. Mem. Am. Psychol. Assn., Am. Counseling Assn., Soc. Rsch. Adolescence, Soc. for Rsch. in Child Devel. Office: Univ of Minn Dept Of Psychology Duluth MN 55812

MILLER, KUBY SUSIE, dance and modeling school owner; b. Romal, Italy, May 14, 1954; d. Stephen and Josette (Jorma) Kuby; m. Lyle G. Miller, Nov. 14, 1988. Grad. high sch., Madison, Wis. Dancer Royal Ballet, London, 1964-70; model Lynette Berit, Paris, 1967-69; dancer Ballet Repertoire, N.Y.C., 1970-75, Southeast Dancing Co., N.Y.C., 1975-76, Bulter Jazz Co., Salt Lake City, 1976-77, Music Ctr., Salt Lake City, 1977-78, Utah Ballet Co., Salt Lake City, 1979-85; model Channel Runway, Paris, 1986-87; dancer Musical Theater Fine Arts, Salt Lake City, 1988-89, TCG Theatre Group, 1993-94, Accop Arts USA, 1994—; bd. dirs. Musical Theaters, Salt Lake City, 1988-89, Ballet Dept., Salt Lake City, 1989-90, Susie's Dancing Co., Salt Lake City, 1990—, Susie's Modeling Co., Salt Lake City, 1990-92. Mem. Wake Adoption, North Falmouth, 1991, Nat. Abortion Rights Action League, Salt Lake City, 1990, Nat. Wildlife Fedn., Salt Lake City, 1991. Mem. Theatre Critics (honor 1991), N.Y. Theatre. Home and Office: Susies Dance N Modeling 635 E 100 S Ste 3 Salt Lake City UT 84102

MILLER, LAURA ANN, linguistic anthropologist, educator; b. L.A., Dec. 15, 1953; d. Walter Eugene Carlos Valdez-Miller; m. Roland John Erwin, 1988. BA, U. Calif., Santa Barbara, 1977; MA, UCLA, 1983, PhD, 1988. Cert. (life) community coll. instr., Calif. Sr. English instr. Teijin Ednl. Systems Co., Osaka, Japan, 1978-81; teaching asst. UCLA, 1983-84, teaching fellow, 1986-87; asst. prof. Phila. Coll. Textiles and Sci., 1990-93; vis. asst. prof. U. Pa., Phila., 1993—; lectr. Calif. State U., Dominiquez Hills, 1983-85, El Camino Community Coll., Torrance, Calif., 1986, U. Pa., Phila., summers 1989, 90, 91, 92; vis. asst. prof. Temple U., Phila., 1990; project coord. Nat. Fgn. Lang. Ctr., Johns Hopkins U., Washington, 1989-92; Japanese instr. GE Aerospace, Moorestown, N.J., 1989, 91; Japan program cons. West Chester (Pa.) U., 1989; rsch. analyst ZEMI Corp., L.A., 1986; lang. analyst Japan Conv. Svcs., Tokyo, 1985; vis. faculty U. Pa., 1993-94. Editor: Jour. Asian Culture, 1984, assoc. editor, 1987; asst. editor: The American Asian Review, 1992-93, assoc. editor, 1993—; contbr. articles to profl. jours. Chair Act 101 Acad. Achievement Program, Phila., 1990-92; mem. Greater Phila. Internat. Network, 1990. Grantee Dept. Edn., 1972-73, UCLA, 1985; Nat. Resource fellow Dept. Edn., 1982-83, UCLA-Japan Exch. Program fellow, 1986-87. Fellow Am. Anthrop. Assn.; mem. Internat. Pragmatics Assn., Assn. for Asian Studies, Assn. for Japanese Bus. Studies, Soc. for Applied Anthropology, Soc. for Linguistic Anthropology. Home: 39 S Lowrys Ln Bryn Mawr PA 19010-1402 Office: Dept Asian & Mid Ea Studies 847 Williams Hall U Pa Philadelphia PA 19104-6307

MILLER, LENORE, labor union official; b. Union City, N.J., Mar. 10, 1932; d. Louis Shapiro and Lillian (Bergen) Shapiro; m. Louis Miller, Dec. 25, 1952; 1 child, Jessica. BA, Rutgers U., 1952; postgrad., Purdue U., 1952-56, New Sch. Social Research, 1957. Sec., asst. to pres. Panel of Ams.; sec., asst. to pres. Retail, Wholesale & Dept. Store Union, AFL-CIO, CLC, N.Y.C., 1958-78, v.p., 1978-80, sec.-treas., 1980-86, pres., 1986-90; vice chair civil rights com. AFL-CIO, 1990—; exec. bd. AFL-CIO Indsl. Union Dept., Washington, 1980-82, AFL-CIO Food & Beverage Trades Dept., Washington, 1980—, Maritime Trades Dept., 1986; v.p. Transp. Trades Dept. AFL-CIO, 1992—; vice-chmn. Nat. Trade Union Council for Human Rights, N.Y.C., 1980—; mem. Nat. BD. Workers Def. League, N.Y.C., 1980—; mem. com. Am. Trade Union Council for Histadrut & Afro-Asian Inst., N.Y.C., 1980—; bd. dirs. Health Security Action Council, 1986; chmn. RWDSU Welfare and Pension Plan, 1986; vice-chmn. Am. Labor ORT, N.Y.C., 1980—; v.p. Transportation Trades Dept. AFL-CIO, 1992—. Mem. adv. com. AFL-CIO Com. on Polit. Edn., Washington, 1978—, Frontlash, 1978—; bd. dirs. A. Philip Randolph Ednl. Fund, 1988, Cen. Labor Rehab. Coun. N.Y.; charter trustee Rutgers U., 1988-94; pres. Jewish Labor Com., 1989; mem. platform com. Dem. Nat. Conv., 1992; mem. Pres. Commn. on Family and Med. Leave, 1993—. Named to Acad. of Women Achievers YWCA, 1987. Mem. AFL-CIO (v.p. 1987—, mem. exec. coun.), Douglass Soc. Office: Retail Wholesale & Dept Store Union AFL-CIO CLC 30 E 29th St Fl 4 New York NY 10016-7925

MILLER, LILLIE M., nursing educator; b. Atlanta, Nov. 16, 1937; d. George W. and Lillie M. (Reese) McDaniel; m. Harold G. Miller, June 30, 1962; children: Daren K., Lisa K. Diploma in nursing, Jewish Hosp. of Cin., 1959; BSN, U. Cin., 1961; MEd, Temple U., 1970; MSN, Villanova U., 1987. RN, Pa.; cert. sch. nurse, cert. clin. specialist in med.-surg. nursing ANCC. Instr. sch. nursing Jewish Hosp. Cin., 1959-62; instr. Phila. Gen. Hosp. Sch. Nursing, 1962-67; sch. nurse Norristown (Pa.) Area Sch. Dist.,

1967-70; nursing instr. Villanova U., Villanova, Pa., 1988; asst. prof. Montgomery County C.C., Blue Bell, Pa., 1983-93; assoc. prof Montgomery County C.C., Blue Bell, Pa., 1993—; advisor Student Nurses Assn. Pa. Recipient Pi Tau Delta scholarship, Chapel of Four Chaplains. Mem. ANA, Nat. League for Nursing, Pa. League for Nursing, Jewish Hosp. Alumni Assn., Temple U. Alumni Assn., Villanova U. Alumni Assn., Sigma Theta Tau.

MILLER, LINDA LOU, association executive, communications specialist; b. Pottsville, Pa., Feb. 5, 1955; d. Cletus Isaac and Erma Ruth (Brown) M.; m. William Joseph Murray Jr., July 23, 1989; 1 stepchild, Nathan Andrew. BA, Shippensburg (Pa.) U., 1977. Copywriter, media buyer Williams & Assocs., Harrisburg, Pa., 1977-78; dir. communications Pa. Newspaper Pub.'s Assn., Harrisburg, 1978-82; dir. alumni affairs Shippensburg U. Pa., 1982-85; exec. v.p. Pa. Soc. Assn. Execs., Harrisburg, 1985-90; dir. communications The Milton Hershey (Pa.) Sch., 1990—. Sec. Kimberley Meadows Civic Assn., Mechanicsburg, Pa., 1990; adv. coun. Shippensburg U., 1990; pers. chair Chapel Hill United Ch. of Christ, 1992-94, ops. commn., 1992—. Mem. NAFE, Pa. Soc. Assn. Execs., Ctrl. Pa. Assn. Profl. Women, Coun. for Advancement and Support of Edn., Am. Soc. Assn. Execs. (bd. dirs. 1989, cert.), Conf. Assn. Soc. Execs. (pres. 1988-89), Allied Socs. Coun. (chmn. 1988-89), Exec. Club of Ctrl. Pa. (bd. dirs. 1988-90), Rotary Club. Home: 27 Conway Dr Mechanicsburg PA 17055-6136 Office: The Milton Hershey Sch Rt 322 And Homestead Ln Hershey PA 17033

MILLER, LORI LYN, school district administrator; b. Denver, Mar. 13, 1962; d. William and Bonnie Mae (Vander Ark) Van Wyke; m. Randy LaDean Miller, Aug. 6, 1988. BEd, Adams State U., 1986, MEd, 1988. Phys. edn. tchr. Denver Pub. Schs., 1986-87; tchr., coach sci. Arickaree Sch. Dist., Anton, 1987-91; tchr. physics/chemistry Yuma (Colo.) Sch. Dist., 1991-92; supt. Edison Sch. Dist., Yoder, Colo., 1992-93, Holly (Colo.) Sch. Dist., 1992—. Mem. Colo. Assn. Sch. Execs., Phi Delta Kappa, Delta Kappa Gamma. Office: Holly Sch Dist 206 N 3rd Holly CO 81047

MILLER, LORRAINE, business owner. BA in History, U. Utah. Lab. technician U. Utah Med. Ctr., 1972-75; pres. Cactus & Tropicals, Inc., Salt Lake City, 1975—; mem. adv. bd. Utah Securities Commn., 1994; panelist Am. Arbitration Assn., 1991; pres., bd. dirs. Phoenix Inst., 1986-87. Vol. VISTA, 1966-69; mem. Gov.'s Task Force Entrepreneurism, 1988, Gov.'s Task Force Work Force Devel., 1994; mentor Women's Network Entrepreneurial Tng., Small Bus. Adminstrn., 1990; mem. adv. bd. Utah Dem. Health Care Task Force, 1991, Women's Bus. Devel. Office State of Utah, 1990-92; employer Supportive Employment for the Handicapped, 1990-92. Recipient Pathfinder award Salt Lake C. of C., 1986, Women of Achievement award YWCA, 1992; named Nat. Small Bus. Person of Yr. by U.S. Small Bus. Adminstrn., 1994. Mem. Nat. Assn. Women's Bus. Owners (pres. Salt Lake chpt. 1992), Utah Assn. Women's Bus. Owners (pres. 1992, 1st v.p. 1991, bd. dirs. 1985, 89-90, named Woman Bus. Owner of Yr. 1987), Wasatch Cactus & Succulent Soc. (co-founder). Office: Cactus & Tropicals of Utah 2735 S 20th St E Salt Lake City UT 84109

MILLER, LOUISE DEAN, writer, retired journalist; b. Lubbock, Tex., Dec. 10, 1921; d. Arlie David and Ludie Lee (Hart) Dean; m. Mickey Lester Miller, Aug. 30, 1946; children: Mary Linda Miller Kelly, Lee Miller Parks, Lynne Miller Carson. BA in Journalism, Tex. Woman's U., 1943, BS in Journalism, 1943. Gen. reporter Vernon (Tex.) Daily Record, 1943-4; feature gen. reporter Tinker AFB Paper, Oklahoma City, 1944-46; women's editor Albuquerque Tribune, 1946-48; writer Albuquerque Pub. Schs., 1967-68; program dir. Young Women's Christian Assn., Albuquerque, 1970-72; newspaper columnist Albuquerque Jour., 1972-87. Author, editor: The Book of Windows, 1990; co-author, editor: Administration of Secondary Athletics, 1991. Sec./treas. El Vado (N.Mex.) Cabin Owners Assn., 1977—. Mem. AAUW (pres. 1964-66, sec. N.Mex. div. 1989-93), Soc. Profl. Journalists, Women in Communications Inc. (pres. 1968-70). Democrat. Methodist. Home: 1201 Richmond Dr NE Albuquerque NM 87106-2023

MILLER, LYNNE MARIE, environmental company executive; b. N.Y.C., Aug. 4, 1951; d. David Jr. and Evelyn (Gulbransen) M. AB, Wellesley Coll., 1973; MS, Rutgers U., 1976. Analyst Franklin Inst., Phila., 1976-78; dir. hazardous waste div. Clement Assocs., Washington, 1978-81; pres. Risk Sci. Internat., Washington, 1981-86, Environ. Strategies Corp., Vienna, Va., 1986—, Environ. Strategies Ltd., London, 1986—. Editor: Insurance Claims for Environmental Damages, 1989, editor-in-chief Environ. Claims Jour.; contbr. chpts. to books. Named Ins. Woman of Yr. Assn. Profl. Ins. Women, 1983. Mem. AAAS, Am. Cons. Engrs. Coun., N.Y. Acad. Sci., Washington Wellesley Club, Wellesley Bus. Leadership Coun. Office: Environ Strategies Corp 11911 Freedom Dr Ste 900 Reston VA 22090

MILLER, LYNNE MARIE, critical care nurse, administrator; b. Chgo., Apr. 7, 1947; d. Michael John and Helen (Eckardt) Patzek; m. Harry James Miller, Aug. 10, 1968; children: Gretchen Hope, Gary Rutherford. Diploma, Abington (Pa.) Meml. Hosp., 1968; BS, Phila. Coll. Textile and Sci. RN, Pa.; cert. med., surg. nurse, ANA, ACLS practitioner. Pediatric staff nurse Fitzgerald Mercy Hosp., Darby, Pa., 1968-69; vis. nurse Community Nursing Svc., Lansdowne, Pa., 1969-72; staff critical care nurse ICU Doylestown (Pa.) Hosp., 1972-80, night supr., 1980-86, nurse mgr. med./surg., telemetry, ventilator care and cardiac rehab., 1986-90, clin. system mgr., 1990-93, dir. operating rm., 1993—; dir. Surg. Svcs. ICU course 7 yrs. Contbg. editor Springhouse Corp. Mem. AACN, Am. Assn. Oper. Rm. Nurses, Am. Assn. Critical Care, Del. Valley Nursing Computer Assn., Coun. Nurse Mgrs. Assn. Affiliated Organ Nurses Mgrs., Southeastern Affiliated Organ Nurse Mgr. (treas., membership, mem. original steering com.).

MILLER, MADELYN SUE, advertising executive, food and travel writer; b. Chgo., Mar. 4, 1947; d. Seymour and Estelle (Klotwogg) Jensky. Student, NYU, 1966-67; B.A. in Journalism, U. Mich., 1968; m. Howard Brian Miller, May 26, 1968; children: Mallorie Ann, Gregory Scott. Copywriter Young & Rubicam, Detroit, 1968-69, Yaffe Stone August, Huntington Woods, Mich., 1969-70, Dancer Fitzgerald Sample, N.Y.C., 1970-71, Neiman-Marcus, Dallas, 1975-76; sr. copywriter Tracy Locke, Dallas, 1976-81; pres. Madelyn Miller, Inc., Dallas, 1982—. Mem. adv. bd. Dallas Art Inst.; mem. Leadership Dallas; chmn. counselor's program PRSSA. Recipient Clio award, 1981; Matrix award Outstanding Dallas Woman in Advt., 1981, Effie award, 1980, Addy award (2), 1980, Bravo award (4) Detroit Art Dirs. Club, 1981, numerous others. Mem. S.W. Assn. Advt. Agys. (bd. dirs.), Dallas Soc. Visual Communications (Bronze medal, Bronze award 1979, cert. of merit 1979), Women in Communications (student pres. 1968, nat. task force on entrepreneurship, scholarship com.), Dallas Advt. League (cert. of merit 1979), Internat. Assn. Bus. Communicators, Pub. Rels. Soc. Am., Bus. and Profl. Advt. Assn., Am. Inst. Graphic Artists, Northwood Inst. Am. Women in Radio and TV, Dallas C. of C. (pub. rels. chmn., small bus. coun.), Internat. Food, Wine and Travel Writers Assn. (bd. dirs.), Nat. Spkrs. Assn., Mensa (nat. adv. bd. advt. and pub. rels.), CEO Club, Hadassah Nat. Fedn. Jewish Women's Club, Leadership Dallas. Home: 9619 Rocky Branch Dr Dallas TX 75243-7528 Office: PO Box 743242 Dallas TX 75374-3242

MILLER, MARCIA E., legislative counsellor. BA, Miami U., 1977; MA, Johns Hopkins U., 1981. With internat. trade divsn. Am. Textile Mfrs. Inst.; internat. economist Wilmer, Cutler & Pickering, 1985-87; profl. staff mem. Senate Com. on Fin., 1987-93, chief internat. trade counsellor, 1993—. Office: Com on Fin 205 Senate Dirksen Office Bldg Washington DC 20510*

MILLER, MARGARET CATHERINE, artist; b. Columbus, Ohio, Apr. 17, 1918; d. Orin Hamilton and Lena Moore (Good) Craft; m. Leo Henry Miller, Mar. 22, 1942 (dec. 1981). Cert. of completion, Famous Artists Sch., Westport, Conn., 1957; tchg. cert., Ohio State U., 1979. Cert. comml. art tchr. Policy rater Buckete Union Ins. Co., Columbus, 1937-40; asst. underwriter Trinity Universal Ins. Co., Columbus, 1940-43; comml. artist Columbus Citizen Jour., 1943-46; fashion illustrator F.&R. Lazarus Co., Columbus, 1946-52; pvt. practice as artist Columbus, 1952-74, 81—; tchr. advt. and indsl. illustration Columbus Bd. Edn. N.E. Career Ctr., 1974-79; instr. Columbus Coll. Art and Design, 1979-81; cons. curriculum devel. State of Ohio, Columbus, 1977-78; chairperson pride com. N.E. Career Ctr., 1979-80; demonstrated painting Dublin (Ohio) Area Art League, 1989. Co-author: Advertising and Industrial Illustration, 1975; exhibited paintings in numerous one woman shows including Jefferson Gallery, Grandview Libr., Ohio Tuberculosis Soc., Players Theatre, Blue Sky Gallery, On Line Computer Libr., Hilltop Libr., Ohio Dominican Coll.; included in regional show Johnson-Humerickhouse Mus. Soc. Layerists in Multi Media; illustrations appeared in numerous mags. and newspapers. Designer Madison County (Ohio) Hospice, 1982, Lincoln Bapt. Ch., Columbus, 1975; workshop leader Worthington (Ohio) Parks and Recreation, 1993. Mem. Dublin Area Art League, Worthington Area Art League, Am. Watercolor Soc. (assoc.), Nat. Watercolor Soc. (assoc., jury 71st ann. nat. show 1991), Knickerbocker Artists (assoc., jury nat. exhibit 1993), Ohio Watercolor Soc. (assoc., jury ann. exhibit 1991), Ctrl. Ohio Watercolor Soc., Soc. Layerists in Multi-Media (assoc.), Soc. Exptl. Artists, Ky. Watercolor Soc. (assoc.), Assn. Allied Artists, Columbus Mus. Art, Nat. Mus. Women in Arts (charter). Home and Studio: 3879 Inverness Circle Dublin OH 43017

MILLER, MARGARET JOANNE, pediatrics nurse; b. Rolette, N.D., Apr. 12, 1939; d. William J. and Nora (Slaubaugh) Graber; m. Ervin S. Miller, June 16, 1962; children: Charlene, Angela, Lisa. ASN, Vincennes U., 1960; student, St. Mary's-of-the-Woods Coll., Terre Haute, Ind., 1986-87, Ind. U., South Bend, 1989. RN, Ind., Tex. Head nurse St. Joseph Mem. Hosp., Kokomo, Ind.; asst. head nurse Meml. Hosp., South Bend, asst. unit dir.; adminstrv. asst. Mennonite Mut. Aid Assn., Goshen, Ind.; now unit dir. for pediatrics Med. Ctr. Hosp., Odessa, Tex. Mem. Soc Pediatric Nurses. Home: 3411 Rocky Ln Odessa TX 79762

MILLER, MARGERY SILBERMAN, psychologist, speech and language pathologist, higher education adminstrator; b. Roslyn, N.Y., May 7, 1951; d. Bernard and Charlotte (Schatzberg) Silberman; m. Donald F. Moores; children—Kip Lee, Tige Justice. Lic. speech pathologist, N.Y., Md.; cert. tchr. nursery-6th grades, spl. edn., N.Y., advanced profl. tchr. speech and hearing, Md.; cert. sch. psychologist, Md. B.A., Elmira Coll., 1971; M.A., NYU, 1972; Ed.S., M.S., SUNY-Albany, 1975; M.A. Towson State U., 1987, Ph.D Georgetown U., 1991. Speech and lang. pathologist Mental Retardation Inst., Flower and Fifth Ave. Hosp., N.Y.C., 1971-72; community speech/lang. pathologist N.Y. State Dept. Mental Hygiene, Troy, dir. speech and hearing services, 1972-74; instr. communication disorders dept. Coll. of St. Rose, Albany, N.Y., 1975-77; clin. supr. U. Md., College Park, 1978; speech/lang. pathologist Md. Sch. for Deaf, Frederick, 1978-84; auditory devel. specialist Montgomery County Pub. Schs., Rockville, Md., 1984-87; coordinator Family Life program Nat. Acad. Gallaudet U., Washington, 1987-88, interim dir., 1988-89, dir. Counseling & Devel. Ctr. N.W. Campus, 1989-93; adj. assoc. prof. psf. psychology Gallaudet U., 1993—; instr. sign lang. program Frederick Community Coll.; dance instr. for deaf adolescents; diagnostic cons. on speech pathology; mem. editorial rev. com. Gov.'s Devel. Disabilities Council of Md., 1984; presenter at confs. Author: It's O.K. To Be Angry, 1976; contbr. chpt. to Cognition, Education, and Deafness: Directions for Research and Instruction, 1985; contbr. articles to profl. jours. Vol., choreographer Miss Deaf Am. Pageant, 1984. Office of Edn. Children's Bur. fellow, 1971. Mem. Am. Speech, Lang. and Hearing Assn. (cert. clin. competence in speech/lang. pathology), Md. Speech, Lang. and Hearing Assn., D.C. Speech, Lang. and Hearing Assn., Nat. Assn. of Deaf, Nat. Assn. Sch. Psychologists, Am. Psychol. Assn. Jewish. Home: 9807 Meriden Rd Potomac MD 20854-4311 Office: Gallaudet U 800 Florida Ave NE Washington DC 20002

MILLER, MARIA ANN, retail buyer; b. Springfield, Mass., Sept. 25, 1960; d. Charles Frances and Josephine Anne (Catter) M. BS, Western New Eng. Coll., 1994. Buyer Albert Steiger Inc., Springfield, Mass., 1982-94, Filene's Basement, Wellesley, Mass., 1994—. Del. Dem. State Conv., Boston, 1986; mem. bd. agy. funding United Way of Pioneer Valley, Springfield, 1987-93; chmn. ways and means com. Stage West Cmty. Theatre, Springfield, 1987-89; bd. dirs. Western Mass. AIDS Found., Springfield, 1992-94. Maronite Catholic. Home: 2 Euston St Brookline MA 02146-4033

MILLER, MARIAN ESTELLE, financial relations executive; b. Kingston, Ill., July 1, 1936; d. Richard E. and Evelyn I. (Jones) Nottelmann; m. Duane H. Miller, Nov. 29, 1959; children: Robert H., John H., William J. Sec. Horders, Chgo., 1953-55, printing mgr., 1955-62; payroll mgr. Boise Cascade (acquired Horders), Chgo., 1962-67, exec. sec., 1967-70; sec., payroll mgr. Boise Cascade (acquired Horders), Itasca, Ill., 1976-78; exec. sec. Safety-Kleen Corp., Elgin, Ill., 1978-80; fin. relations coordinator Safety-Kleen Corp., Elgin, 1980-88, asst. sec., 1988—, exec. sec., 1986—; treas. Horder Employee Credit Union, Chgo., 1957-67; sec. Safety-Kleen Fed. Credit Union, Elgin, 1980-82. Sec. St. Johns Luth. Sch. Parent Tchr. League, Forest Park, Ill., 1972-74; pres., v.p., sec., treas. Bellwood (Ill.) Youth Baseball, 1972-83; den leader Cub Scout Troop, Forest Park, 1975-82; troop sec. Forest Park Boy Scouts Am., 1976-79. Mem. Nat. Investor Rels. Inst., Nat. Assn. Stock Plan Profls. Republican. Office: Safety-Kleen Corp 1000 N Randall Rd Elgin IL 60123

MILLER, MARIE KAY, accountant; b. Ft. Gordon, Ga., Nov. 16, 1960; d. Victor Buron and Chiyo K. (Kusunoki) LaPaquette; m. Charles Henry, Oct. 1, 1988. BBA, Ga. State U., 1984. CPA. Staff acct. HBO & Co., Atlanta, 1984-86; sr. internat. auditor Premark Internat., Atlanta, 1987-88; plant acct. L.C.P. Chems., Inc., Riegelwood, N.C., 1988-90; sr. cost and inventory acct. Sara Lee Intimates, Winston-Salem, N.C., 1991-94; internat. and tax acct. Champion, Winston-Salem, 1994—. Team leader United Way, Winston-Salem, 1990, Arts Coun., Winston-Salem, 1991; mem. Diversity Task Force, Winston-Salem, 1992-93. Mem. Inst. Mgmt. Accts., N.C. Assn. CPAs, Alpha Kappa Psi. Office: Champion 475 Corporate Square Dr Winston Salem NC 27105-9101

MILLER, MARILYN LEA, library science educator. AA, Graceland Coll., 1950; BS in English, U. Kans., 1952; AMLS, U. Mich., 1959, PhD of Librarianship and Higher Edn., 1976. Bldg.-level sch. libr. Wellsville (Kans.) High Sch., 1952-54; tchr.-libr. Arthur Capper Jr. High Sch., Topeka, Kans., 1954-56; head libr. Topeka High Sch., 1956-62; sch. libr. cons. State of Kans. Dept. of Pub. Instrn., 1962-66; from asst. to assoc. prof. Sch. Librarianship Western Mich. U., Kalamazoo, 1966-73; assoc. prof. libr. sci. U. N.C., Chapel Hill, 1977-87; prof., chair dept. libr. and info. studies U. N.C., Greensboro, 1987—, chair search com., exec. dir., 1994; vis. faculty Kans. State Tchrs., Emporia, 1960, 63, 64, 66, U. Minn., Mpls., 1971, U. Manitoba, Winnipeg, Can., 1971; vis. prof. Appalachian State U., Boone, N.C., 1987; mem. adv. bd. sch. libr. media program Nat. Ctr. for Ednl. Stats., 1989, mem. user rev. panel, 1990; chair assoc. dean search com. Sch. Edn., 1988, coord. Piedmont young writers conf., 1989-94, chair race and gender com., 1990-93, SACS planning and evaluation com., 1990, 91, learning resources ctr. adv. com., 1991-93; hearing panel for honor code U. N.C. Greensboro, 1988-91, assn. women faculty and administrv. staff, 1987—, faculty coun., 1987—, univ. libr. com., 1987-88, com. faculty devel. in race and gender scholarship, 1990-92; lectr. and cons. numerous confs., seminars in field. Mem. editorial bd. The Emergency Librarian, 1981—, Collection Building: Studies in the Development and Effective Use of Library Resources, 1978—; contbr. numerous chpts. to books, and articles to profl. jours., procs. and revs. Selected as one of four children's libr. specialists to visit Russian sch. and pub. librs., book pubs., Moscow, Leningrad, Tashkent, 1979; hon. del. White House Conf. on Libr. and Info. Svcs., Washington, 1991; head del. Romanian Summer Inst. on Librarianship in U.S., 1991; citizen amb. People to People Internat. Program, People's Republic of China, 1992, Russian and Poland, 1992, Russia, 1994. Recipient Freedom Found. medal, 1962, Disting. Svc. to Sch. Librs. award Kans. Assn. Sch. Librs., 1982, Disting. Svc. award Graceland Coll., 1992, Disting. Alumnus award Sch. Libr. and Info. Studies, U. Mich., 1988; Delta Kappa Gamma scholar, 1972. Mem. ALA (pres. 1992-93, adv. com. Nat. Ctr. Ednl. Stats. 1984, standing com. libr. edn. 1987-91 chair 1989-90, chair Chgo. conf. resolutions 1972, awards com. 1971-72, chair 1973-75, resolutions com. 1976-78, yearbook adv. com. 1988-90, Disting. svc. award Am. Assn. Sch. Librs. 1993, other coms.), Am. Assn. Sch. Librs. (nom. com. 1980, pub. com. 1981-82, v.p.- pres.-elect 1985-86, chair search com. exec. dir. 1985, pres. 1986-87), Assn. for Ednl. Comms. and Tech., Assn. for Libr. and Info. Sci. Edn., Assn. of Libr. Svc. to Children (bd. dirs. 1976-81, pres. 1979-80, rsch. com. 1982-85 chair 1984-85, chair nom. com. 1984, other coms.), N.C. Libr. Assn. (edn. libr. com. 1978-80, 82-86, exec. bd.status of women roundtable 1989—), N.C. Assn. Sch. Librs., Southeastern Libr. Assn. (chair libr. educators sect. 1990-92), So. Assn. of Colls. and Schs. (mem. accreditation team 1988). Office: U NC at Greensboro Dept Libr And Studies Greensboro NC 27412

MILLER, MARY HELEN, public administrator; b. Smiths Grove, Ky., June 30, 1936; d. Walter Frank and Lottie Belle (Russell) Huddleston; m. George Ward Wilson, Sept. 12, 1958 (div. Sept. 1973); children: Ward Glenn, Amy Elizabeth Huddleston; m. Francis Guion Miller Jr., June 6, 1981. BA, Western Ky. U., 1958. Tchr. Fayette County Schs., Lexington, Ky., 1958-60, Seneca High Sch., Louisville, 1960-63, Shelby County High Sch., Shelbyville, Ky., 1963-69; rsch. analyst Legis. Rsch. Com., Frankfort, Ky., 1973-79, asst. dir., 1979-83, 90-91; chief exec. asst. Office Gov., Frankfort, 1983-87, 93—, legis. liaison, 1991-93; cabinet sec. Natural Resources and Environ. Protection Cabinet, Frankfort, 1987-88; sales assoc. W. Wagner, Jr. Comml. Real Estate, Louisville, 1989-91. Author: (constl. revision) Citizens Guide To/Perspective, 1978, (booklet) A Look at Kentucky General Assembly, 1979, A Guide to Education Reform, 1990, (handbook) Gubernatorial Transition in Kentucky, 1991. Mem. Leadership Ky. Alumni, Frankfort, 1986, Waterfront Devel. Corp. Bd., Louisville, 1986-87, Greater Louisville Partnership, Econ. Devel., 1988—, Shelbyville 2000 Found. Bd., 1991-92; mem., sec. Regional Airport Authority Bd., Louisville, 1986-89; pres. Shelby County Community Theatre Bd., Shelbyville, 1989-90. Mem. Pendennis Club, Jefferson Club. Democrat. Episcopalian. Home: 1116 W main St Shelbyville KY 40065 Office: State Capitol Frankfort KY 40601

MILLER, MARY RITA, former college educator; b. Williamsburg, Iowa, Mar. 4, 1920; d. James Carl and Bernadette (O'Meara) Rush; m. Clarence Glenn Miller, June 2, 1947 (dec. Aug. 1987); 1 child, Ronald Rush; m. William J. Gibbons, July 14, 1992. BA, U. Iowa, 1941; MA, Denver U., 1959; PhD, Georgetown U., 1969. From instr. to asst. prof. Regis Coll., Denver, 1962-65; from asst. prof. to prof. U. Md., College Park, 1968-91, prof. emeritus, 1991—. Author: Children of the Salt River, 1977, Place—Names of the Northern Neck of Virginia, 1983; contbr. numerous articles and revs. Home: 2825 29th Pl NW Washington DC 20008-3501

MILLER, MAUREEN DENICE, pediatrics nurse; b. Calif., Mar. 16, 1966; d. John Arthur and Betty (Slegers) M. BSN, Point Loma Nazarene Coll., 1988; Master's candidate, UCLA, 1994—. RN, Calif. Pre-registered nurse aide U. Calif. San Diego Med. Ctr., 1987-88; staff RN pediatrics/womans health care Pres. Intercommunity Hosp., Whittier, Calif., 1988-92; pub. health RN Vis. Nurses Assn., Long Beach, Calif., 1991—; RN pediatric ICU Long Beach Meml. Med. Ctr.-Miller Children's Hosp., 1991—; mem. edn. com., transport com. Long Beach Meml. Med. Ctr.-Miller Children's Hosp., 1991—. Mem. Point Loma Nazarene Coll. Nursing Honor Soc., Sigma Theta Tau Internat. Republican. Home: 5453 Twin Lakes Dr Cypress CA 90630-5945 Office: Long Beach Meml Med Ctr 2801 Atlantic Ave Long Beach CA 90806-1737

MILLER, MELISSA COLSON, city official; b. Murray, Ky., Apr. 2, 1959; d. Wallis R. and Anna Brown (Howard) Colson; m. Gary L. Miller, Apr. 2, 1983 (div.); 1 child, Amanda Christine. BSBA in Fin., East Caroline U., 1981. Acct. Edward Weck & Co., Research Triangle Park, N.C., 1983-85; cost acct. Moore Regional Hosp., Pinehurst, N.C., 1986-89; tax collector Town of So. Pines (N.C.), 1985-86, acctg. supr., 1986-92, fin. dir., 1992—; mem. adv. bd. N.C. Capital Mgmt. Trust, bd. dirs., 1993—. Mem. NAFE, Govt. Fin. Officers Assn. (Fin. Reporting Achievement award 1992, 93), N.C. Pub. Fin. Officers Assn., N.C. Local Govt. Investment Assn., Women Profl. Mgrs. (bd. dirs.). Office: Town of So Pines 387 W Pennsylvania Ave Southern Pines NC 28387

MILLER, MICHELE ANN, public relations company executive, consultant; b. Allegan, Mich., Apr. 24, 1961; d. Gary and Anneliese (Metz) M. BS in Music Edn., Western Mich. U., 1983; MusB in Mgmt., Hartt Sch., Hartford, Conn., 1987. Subscription assoc. Hartford Symphony, 1986-87; adminstrv. dir. Internat. Artists Series, Worcester, Mass., 1987-89; adminstr. collection mus. instruments Met. Mus. Art, N.Y.C., 1989-90; mktg. coord. Lincoln Ctr. for Performing Arts, N.Y.C., 1990-91, media cons., 1991—; pres. Miller-Carter Assocs. Pub. Rels., N.Y.C., 1991—; publicity cons. Indpls. Symphony, 1993—. Bd. dirs. Franklin Series, Teaneck, N.J., 1991-93, Le Mont Seminar, Canaan, N.Y., 1993—. Mem. Am. Symphony Orch. League, Chamber Music Am., Pi Kappa Lambda. Democrat. Methodist. Office: 945 W End Ave Apt 1C New York NY 10025-3573

MILLER, MILDRED, opera singer, recitalist; b. Cleve.; d. William and Elsa (Friedhofer) Mueller; m. Wesley W. Posvar, Apr. 30, 1950; children: Wesley, Margot Marina, Lisa Christina. MusB, Cleve. Inst. Music, 1946; hon. doctorate, Cleve. Ins. Music, 1983; artists' diploma, New England Conservatory Music, 1948, hon. doctorate, 1966; MusD (hon.), Bowling Green State U., 1960; hon. doctorate, Washington and Jefferson U., 1988. founder, pres. Opera Theater of Pitts., 1978—. Operatic debut in Peter Grimes, Tanglewood, 1946; appeared N.E. Opera Theater, Stuttgart State Theater, Germany, 1949-50, Glyndebourne Opera, Edinburgh Festival; debut as Cherubino in Figaro, Met. Opera, 1951; 23 consecutive seasons Met. Opera; radio debut Bell Telephone Hour; TV debut Voice of Firestone, 1952; appeared in films including Merry Wives of Windsor (filmed in Vienna), 1964; Vienna State Opera debut, 1963, appearances with San Francisco, Chgo. Lyric, Cin. Zoo, San Antonio, Berlin, Munich, Frankfurt, Pasadena, Ft. Worth, Kansas City, Pitts., Tulsa and St. Paul operas. Bd. dirs. Gateway to Music. Recipient Frank Huntington Beebe award for study abroad, 1949, 50, Grand Prix du Disque, 1965, Outstanding Achievements in Music award Boston C. of C., 1959, Ohioana Career medal, 1985, Outstanding Achievement in Opera award, Slippery Rock U., 1985, YWCA Ann. Tribute to Women award, 1989; named one of outstanding women of Pitts. Pitts. Press-Pitts. Post-Gazette, 1968, Person of Yr. in Music, Pitts. Jaycees, 1980. Mem. Nat. Soc. Arts and Letters (pres. 1989-90, Gold medal 1984), Keystone Salute, Pa. Fedn. Music Clubs (Keystone salute 1994), Disting. Daus. Pa. (pres. 1991-93), Tuesday Mus. Club, Phi Beta Kappa, Phi Delta Gamma, Sigma Alpha Iota. Office: care Robert M Gewald Mgmt 58 W 58th St New York NY 10019-2502 Address: PO Box 110108 Pittsburgh PA 15232-0608

MILLER, MYRA GAIL, clinical dietitian; b. Denver, June 6, 1962; d. David Reese and Helen Louise (Cummins) M.; m. Kenneth John Hulick, Sept. 26, 1992. BA in Dietetics, Benedictine Coll., 1985; MA in Counseling, Adams State Coll., 1995. Registered dietitian; cert. nutrition support dietitian. Dietetic intern VA Med. Ctr., Saginaw, Mich., 1985-86; staff dietitian Bridgeton (N.J.) Hosp., 1987-89; clin. dietitian S.W. Meml. Hosp., Cortez, Colo., 1989-90; clin. dietitian Mercy Med. Ctr., Durango, Colo., 1990—, instr. weight mgmt., 1990—. Bd. dirs., purchaser Durango (Colo.) Soup Kitchen, 1989-93; sec. Sex Offender Treatment Rural Adv. Bd., Durango, 1993—; vol. Rape Intervention Team, Durango, 1993—. Mem. ACA, Am. Dietetic Assn., Am. Soc. Parenteral and Enteral Nutrition, S.W. Dietetic Assn. (treas. 1989-93). Roman Catholic. Office: Mercy Med Ctr 375 E Park Ave Durango CO 81301-5089

MILLER, NANCY ELLEN, computer science educator; b. Maryville, Mo., Jan. 6, 1951; d. Dale LaVerne and Barbara Mae (Gaines) Miller; m. Charles Glenn Petersen, Aug. 12, 1977. BS in Edn. and Math., NW Mo. State U., Maryville, 1973; MS in Computer Sci., Iowa State U., Ames, 1977, PhD in Higher Edn., 1981. Computer programmer NW Mo. State U., 1973-75; lectr. U. Wis., LaCrosse, 1977-80; asst. prof. U. Wis., Oshkosh, 1980-83; asst. prof. computer sci. Miss. State U., Starkville, 1983—. Author: File Structures Using Pascal, 1987; co-author: File Structures with Ada, 1990; contbr. articles to profl. jours. Mem. Assn. Computing Machinery, Computer Sci. Edn., Artificial Intelligence. Republican. Office: Miss State U PO Drawer 5623 Mississippi State MS 39762-5623

MILLER, NANCY JANET, insurance agent; b. Champaign, Ill., Sept. 14, 1954; d. Allan Stephen and Janet Margaret (Worth) M.; m. David M. Sanborn, Nov. 24, 1990; 1 child, Katherine Janet. BA cum laude, U. Mass., 1976. CLU, Chartered Fin. Cons. Spl. agt. Prudential Ins. Co. Am., East Longmeadow, Mass., 1976—; broker various ins. cos., East Longmeadow, 1980—. Recipient Nat. Sales Achievement award for 10 yrs. Nat. Assn. Life Underwriters, 1989; selected one of 125 Univ. of Mass. grads. to watch. Mem. Am. Soc. CLUs, Am. Soc. Chartered Fin. Cons., We. Mass. CLU and ChFC Soc. (v.p. 1994-95), Springfield Assn. Life Underwriters (v.p. 1985-86, pres. 1987-88), Springfield C. of C. (Breakfast Club comm. 1986-89), East

Longmeadow C. of C. (clk. 1989-90, pres. 1991-92). Office: Prudential Ins Co 296 N Main St East Longmeadow MA 01028-1878

MILLER, NAOMI, art historian; b. N.Y.C., Feb. 28, 1928; d. Nathan and Hannah M. B.S., CCNY, 1948; M.A., Columbia U., 1950, NYU, 1960; Ph.D., NYU, 1966. Asst. prof. art history R.I. Sch. Design, 1963-64; asst. prof. U. Calif.-Berkeley, 1969-70; asst. to assoc. prof. Boston U., 1964—, prof. art history, 1981—; vis. prof. U. B.C., Vancouver, 1967, Hebrew U., Jerusalem, 1980, U. Padua, 1990. Author: French Renaissance Fountains, 1977, Heavenly Caves, 1982, Renaissance Bologna, 1989; co-author: Fons Sapientiae: Garden Fountains in Illustrated Books, 16th-18th Centuries, 1977, Boston Architecture 1975-90, 1990; book rev. editor: Jour. Soc. Archtl. Historians, 1975-81, editor, 1981-84; articles, catalogues. Jr. fellow NEH, 1972-73; sr. fellow Dumbarton Oaks, 1976-77, 83-89; vis. sr. fellow Ctr. for Advanced Study in Visual Arts, 1988, 95. Mem. Coll. Art Assn., Soc. Archtl. Historians, Renaissance Soc. Office: 725 Commonwealth Ave Boston MA 02215-1401

MILLER, NICOLE GABRIELLE, clinical psychologist; b. N.Y.C., Apr. 19, 1962; d. Michael David and Merle Judith (Jablin) M. BA in Psychology, U. Pacific, 1984, MA in Psychology, 1988; PhD in Clin. Psychology, Calif. Sch. Profl. Psychology, 1990. Therapist various clinics, Stockton, Calif., 1984-86; psycholog. trainee Calif. Men's Colony State Prison, San Luis Obispo, 1987, Dept. Health, Fresno, Calif., 1987-88; intern VA Med. Ctr., Loma Linda, Calif., 1988-89; psycholog. technician and consultant VA Med. Ctr., Martinez, Calif., 1989-90, researcher, 1990, clin. psychologist, 1990—; clin. instr. psychiatry Sch. Medicine, U. Calif., Davis, 1991—, clin. dir. outpatient substance abuse program, 1990—. Mem. APA. Democrat. Office: VA Med Ctr Psychology Svcs 150 Muir Rd # 116B Martinez CA 94553-4612

MILLER, NICOLE JACQUELINE, fashion designer; b. Ft. Worth, Tex., Mar. 20, 1951; d. Grier Bovey and Jacqueline (Mahieu) M. BFA, RISD, 1973; cert. de coursspeciale, École de la Chambre Syndicale de la Couture Parisienne, Paris, 1971. Asst. designer Clovis Ruffin, N.Y.C., 1974; designer Raincheetahs, N.Y.C., 1974-75, P.J. Walsh, N.Y.C., 1975-82, Nicole Miller, N.Y.C., 1982—. Recipient Dallas Fashion award, 1991; named RISD Alumni of Yr., 1992. Mem. Fashion Group, Fashion Roundtable, CFDA, N.Y. Athletic Club. Office: 525 7th Ave Fl 20 New York NY 10018-4901*

MILLER, PAMELA GUNDERSEN, city official; b. Cambridge, Mass., Sept. 7, 1938; d. Sven M. and Harriet Adams Gundersen; A.B. magna cum laude, Smith Coll., 1960; m. Ralph E. Miller, July 7, 1962; children—Alexander, Erik, Karen. Feature writer Congressional Quar., Washington, 1962-65; dir. cable TV franchizing Storer Broadcasting Co., Louisville, Bowling Green, Lexington, and Covington, Ky., 1978-80, 81-82; mem. 4th Dist. Lexington, Fayette County Urban Council, 1973-77, councilwoman-at-large, 1982— , vice-mayor, 1984-86, 89-93, mayor, 1993—; dep. commr. Ky. Dept. Local Govt., Frankfort, 1980-81; pres. Pam Miller, Inc., 1984—, Community Ventures Corp., 1985—. Mem. Fayette County Bd. Health, 1975-77, Downtown Devel. Commn., 1975-77; alt. del. Dem. Nat. Conv., 1976; bd. dirs. YMCA, Lexington, 1975-77, 85-90, Fund for the Arts, 1984-93, Council of Arts, 1978-80, Sister Cities, 1978-80; treas. Prichard Com. for Acad. Excellence, 1983—. Named Woman of Achievement YWCA, 1984, Outstanding Woman of Blue Grass, AAUW, 1984. Mem. LWV (dir. 1970-73), Profl. Women's Forum, NOW, ACLU, Land and Nature Trust of the Bluegrass. Home: 140 Cherokee Park Lexington KY 40503-1304 Office: 200 E Main St Lexington KY 40507-1315

MILLER, PATRICIA ANN, adult education educator; b. Mich., Dec. 19, 1933; d. Bernard James and Veronica Loretta (Hominga) M.; m. Mar. 2, 1957 (div. 1981); children: Sharon, Paula, Philip Jr., Douglas. BA, Mich. State U., 1955. Tchr. Perry (Mich.) Pub. Schs., 1955-56, Glen Lake (Mich.) Cmty. Schs., 1956-57, various pub. schs., Mich., 1957-61, Traverse City (Mich.) Pub. Schs., 1963; salesperson Theta's Real Estate, Traverse City, 1977-88, 93—, Century 21 Real Estate, Traverse City, 1988-90; tchr. Montessori Children's Ctr., Traverse City, 1984; instr./facilitator adult edn. Enterprise Learning Lab., Kingsley/Traverse City, 1986-94, Traverse Bay area, 1994—; instr./facilitator Pvt. Ind. Coun., summer 1991, 93; pvt. tutor Grand Traverse, 1986-93; bus. ptnr. FitzMiller Learning Ctr., 1992; lectr., conductor workshops in field. Contbr. articles to profl. jours. Mem. League of Women Voters, Traverse City, 1984; vol. Women's Resource Ctr., Traverse, 1983; ambassador Nat. Cherry Festival, Traverse City, 1984. Recipient Cert. of Appreciation, Traverse Bay Intermediate Schs., 1985, award for work in field of improving adult literacy Traverse City Area Pub. Schs. Bd. End., 1991-92; named Region 7 Tchr. of Yr., Mich. Dept. Edn., 1990. Mem. Mich. Reading Assn. (named Mich. Adult Edn. Tchr. of Yr. 1991), Mich. Lit. Coun., Northwestern Mich. Reading Assn. (hon.), Alpha Xi Delta. Office: Enterprise Learning Lab 1707 E Front St Traverse City MI 49684-3016 also: PO Box 4231 Traverse City MI 49685-4231

MILLER, PATRICIA ANN, secondary education educator; b. Champaign, Ill., Apr. 2, 1948; d. William Henry and Harriett Sara (Wagner) Coughlin; m. Glenn Alan Miller, Apr. 7, 1979. BA, U. Ill., 1970, MEd, 1971. English lang. tchr. E.B. Wood Jr. High, Rockville, Md., 1971-82, Martin Luther King Jr. High, Germantown, Md., 1982-84, Damascus (Md.) High Sch., 1984—; honors coord. Montgomery County Pub. Schs., Rockville, 1980-90. Mem. NEA, Md. State Tchrs. Assn., Montgomery County Edn. Assn. Home: 13408 Tilford Ct Germantown MD 20874

MILLER, PATRICIA ELIZABETH CLEARY, American and British literature educator; b. Kansas City, Mo., May 2, 1939; d. John M. and Helen Elizabeth (Kelton) Cleary; m. James Ludlow Miller, July 8, 1961; children: Jo Zach James, Honour Helena, Marika Elizabeth. AB in French, Harvard/Radcliffe, 1961; MA in English, U. Mo., Kansas City, 1970; M. Philosophy, U. Kans., 1977, PhD in English, 1979. Asst. instr. U. Kans., Lawrence, 1974-75; instr. U. Mo., Kansas City, 1979-83; asst. prof. Rockhurst Coll., Kansas City, 1983-92, dir. creative writing program, 1986—, assoc. prof., 1992—, chair English dept., 1993—; chair English dept., 1993—. Author: Westport: Missouri's Port of Many Returns, 1983, Starting A Swan Dive, 1993; contbr. book revs. to profl. jours. Chmn. Vis. Nurse Assn. Corp., 1985-88; bd. dirs. Harvard Alumni Assn., 1982-94; mem. nat. adv. coun. Nat. Conf. Cath. Bishops, 1984-87; mem. bd. mgmt. Radcliffe Coll. Alumnae Assn., 1990-93, mem. leadership coun., 1992-93. Poetry fellow The Bunting Inst. Radcliffe Coll., 1993-94. Mem. DAR, MLA, AAUP, Midwest MLA, Nat. Coun. Tchrs. of English, Mo. Philol. Assn., Mo. Folklore Soc., Westport Hist. Soc., Jackson County Hist. Soc., Soc. Fellow of the Nelson-Atkins Mus., Kansas City Country Club, Rockhill Tennis Club. Home: 708 E 47th St Kansas City MO 64110-1559 Office: Rockhurst Coll Dept English 1100 Rockhurst Rd Kansas City MO 64110-2508

MILLER, PATRICIA G., lawyer; b. Northfield, Vt., Nov. 20, 1933. BS, U. Colo., 1957; JD, U. Pitts., 1976. Bar: Phila. 1976. Ptnr. Reed Smith Shaw & McClay, Pitts. Office: Reed Smith Shaw & McClay James H Reed Bldg 435 6th Ave Pittsburgh PA 15219-1886*

MILLER, PATRICIA LOUISE, state legislator, nurse; b. Bellefontaine, Ohio, July 4, 1936; d. Richard William and Rachel Orpha (Williams) Miller; m. Kenneth Orlan Miller, July 3, 1960; children: Tamara Sue, Matthew Ivan. RN, Meth. Hosp. Sch. Nursing-Indpls., 1957; BS, Ind. U., 1960. Office nurse A.D. Dennison, MD, 1960-61; staff nurse Meth. Hosp., Indpls., 1959, Community Hosp., Indpls., 1958; representative, State of Ind., Dist. 50, Indpls., 1982-83, senator, State of Ind., Dist. 32, Indpls., 1983—, mem. edn., health welfare and aging, labor and pension, legis. apportionment and elections coms., chmn. interim study com. pub. health and mental health Ind. Gen. Assembly, 1986. Mem. Bd. Edn., Met. Sch. Dist. Warren Twp., 1974-82, pres., 1979-80, 80-81; mem. Warren Twp. Citizens Screening Com. for Sch. Bd. Candidates, 1972-74, 84, Met. Zoning Bd. Appeals, Div. I, City-County Council, 1972-76; bd. dirs. Central Ind. Council on Aging, Indpls., 1977-80; mem. State Bd. of Voc. and Tech. Edn., 1978-82, sec., 1980-82; mem. Gov.'s Select Adv. Commn. for Primary and Secondary Edn., 1983; precinct committeeman Republican Party, 1968-74, ward vice chmn., 1975-78, ward chmn., 1978-85, twp. chmn., 1985—; del. Rep. State Conv., 1968, 74, 76, 1980, sgt. at arms, 1982, mem. platform com., 1984; del. Rep. Nat. Conv., 1984; active various polit. campaigns; bd. dirs. PTA, 1967-81; pres. Grassy Creek PTA, 1971-72; state del. Ind. PTA, 1978; mem. child care adv. com. Walker Career Center, 1976-80, others; bd. dirs. Ch. Fedn. Greater Indpls., 1979-82, Christian Justice Center, Inc., 1983-85, Gideon Internat. Aux., 1977—; mem. United Meth. Bd. Missions Aux. of Indpls., 1974-80, v.p., 1974-76; bd. dirs. Lucille Raines Residence, Inc., 1977-80; exec. com. S. Ind. Conf. United Meth. Women, 1977-80, lay del. S. Ind. Conf. United Meth. Ch., 1977—, fin. and adminstrn. com., 1979—, planning and research com., 1980—, co-chmn. law adv. com., chmn. health and welfare, conf. council ministries, also mem. task force, bd. ordained ministry, also panel, chmn. com. on dist. superintendency, dist. council on ministries; sec. Indpls. S.E. Dist. Council on Ministries, 1977-78, pres., 1982; chmn. council on ministries Cumberland United Meth. Ch., 1969-76; chmn. stewardship com. Old Bethel United Meth. Ch., 1982-85, fin. com., 1982-85, adminstrv. bd., mem. council on ministries, 1981-85. Recipient Phi Lambda Theta Honor for outstanding contbr. in field of edn., 1976; Woman of the Year, Cumberland Bus. and Profl. Women, 1979; Ind. Voc. Assn. citation award, 1984, others. Mem. Indpls. Dist. Dental Soc. Women's Aux., Ind. Dental Assn. Women's Aux., Am. Dental Assn. Women's Aux., Council State Govt. (intergovtl. affairs com.), Nat. Conf. State Legislatures (health com.), others. Clubs: Warren Twp. Rep. Franklin Rep., Lawrence Rep., Center Twp. Rep., Fall Creek Valley Rep., Marion County Council Rep. Women, Ind. Women's Rep., Indpls. Women's Rep., Ind. Fedn. Rep. Women, Nat. Fedn. Rep. Women, Beech Grove Rep., Perry Twp. Rep. Home: 1041 Muessing Rd Indianapolis IN 46239-9614

MILLER, PAULA, government employee; b. Warwick, Va., Oct. 31, 1955; d. Alton Roscoe and Verna Mae (Simpson) M. Student, Trident Tech. Coll., N. Charleston, S.C., 1986-87, Park Coll., Arlington, Va., 1988, Coll. of Charleston, 1989, Charleston So. U., 1991—. Purchasing agt. Naval Electronic Systems Engring. Ct., N. Charleston, S.C., 1984-87; logistics mgmt. specialist Navy Logistics Career Intern Program, Washington, 1987-90; logistic support mgr. Naval Command, ISE East Coast divsn., Control and Ocean Surveillance Ctr., North Charleston, S.C., 1990—. Mem. Soc. Logistics Engrs., Am. Def. Preparedness Assn. Republican. Baptist. Office: NISE East 4600 Marriott Dr North Charleston SC 29406-6504

MILLER, PAULA ANN, insurance company executive; b. Syracuse, N.Y., July 27, 1958; d. Donald Paul and Sarah (Harabedian) M. AAS in Bus. Adminstrn., SUNY, Alfred, 1978; BSBA, LeMoyne Coll., Syracuse, 1982. Account clk. Fayette Ins. Agy., Fayetteville, N.Y., 1982-83; comml. lines rater Great Am. Ins. Co., Syracuse, 1983-84; comml. lines rater Excelsior Ins. Co., Syracuse, 1984-86, group leader comml. lines rater, 1986, asst. supr., 1986-88; supr. comml. lines casualty rating Hanover Ins. Cos., Liverpool, N.Y., 1988-89; sr. client rep. Young Ins. Agy., Inc., Syracuse, N.Y., 1989—. Mem. Syracuse Ins. Women's Assn., Ins. Inst. Am., Am. Mktg. Assn. Republican. Roman Catholic. Home: 8146 Scotia Ln Liverpool NY 13090

MILLER, PEGGY MCLAREN, management educator; b. Tomahawk, Wis., Jan. 12, 1931; d. Cecil Glenn and Gladys Lucille (Bame) McLaren; m. Richard Irwin Miller, June 25, 1955; children: Joan Marie, Diane Lee, Janine Louise. BS, Iowa State U., 1953; MA, Am. U., 1959; MBA, Rochester Inst. Tech., 1979; PhD, Ohio U., 1987. Instr. Beirut Coll. for Women, 1953-55, U. Ky., Lexington, 1964-66, S.W. Tex. State U., San Marcos, 1981-84; home economist Borden Co., N.Y.C., 1955-58; cons. Consumer Cons., Chgo., Springfield, Ill., 1972-77; sr. mktg. rep. N.Y. State Dept. Agr., Rochester, 1978-79; asst. prof., coord. bus. and mgmt. Keuka Coll., Keuka Park, N.Y., 1979-81; lectr. mgmt. Ohio U., Athens, 1984—. Co-editor: Fifty States Cookbook, 1977; contbr. articles to profl. jours. Mem. Soc. for Advancement of Mgmt. (advisor campus chpt.), Mortar Bd., Phi Kappa Phi. Home: 17 Briarwood Dr Athens OH 45701-1302 Office: Ohio U Copeland Hall Athens OH 45701

MILLER, PENELOPE ANN, actress; b. Jan. 13, 1964; d. Mark and Beatrice (Ammidown) M. Studies with Herbert Berghof. Appeared in (plays) The People From Work, 1984, Biloxi Blues, 1984-85, Moonchildren, Our Town (Tony Award nom.), (TV shows) The Guiding Light, 1984, As the World Turns, 1984, The Popcorn Kid, (films) Adventures in Babysitting, 1987, Biloxi Blues, 1988, Big Top Pee-Wee, 1988, Miles From Home, 1988, Dead-Bang, 1989, Downtown, 1990, The Freshman, 1990, Kindergarten Cop, 1990, Awakenings, 1990, Other People's Money, 1991, Year of the Comet, 1992, The Gun in Betty Lou's Handbag, 1992, Chaplin, 1992, Carlito's Way, 1993, The Shadow, 1994. Mem. Actors' Equity Assn., AFTRA.

MILLER, PHEBE CONDICT, lawyer, financial executive; b. Columbus, Ohio, Dec. 18, 1949; d. A. Fullerton and Mary Dixon (Sayre) M.; m. O. John Olcay. BA, Princeton U., 1971; JD, Harvard U., 1974. Bar: N.Y. 1975, U.S. Dist. Ct. (so. dist.) N.Y. 1975, U.S. Ct. Appeals (2nd cir.) 1975. Law clk. to judge U.S. Dist. Ct. (so. dist.) N.Y., N.Y.C., 1974-75; spl. asst. to dep. atty. gen. U.S. Dept. Justice, Washington, 1975-76; assoc. Davis Polk & Wardwell, N.Y.C. and London, 1976-83; mng. dir., gen. counsel, sec. Discount Corp. of N.Y., N.Y.C., 1983-94; sr. v.p. Bank of N.Y., N.Y.C., 1994—. mem. ABA. Office: Bank of NY 1 Wall St New York NY 10286-1519

MILLER, PHOEBE AMELIA, marketing professional; b. Jan. 13, 1948; d. William Prescott and Elizabeth Helen (Lucker) M.. BA in Math., U. Wis., 1970; postgrad., Stanford U., 1973, Golden Gate U., 1975-76. Engr. Bechtel, San Francisco, 1972-77; asst. mgr. Rand Info. Systems, San Francisco, 1977-79; sr. mktg. rep. Computer Sci. Corp., San Francisco, 1979-81; mgr. distbr. sales COGNOS Corp., Walnut Creek, Calif., 1981-86; owner, mgr. P.A. Miller & Assocs., San Francisco, 1986—. Office: PA Miller & Assocs 1750 Montgomery St San Francisco CA 94111

MILLER, POLLY U., editor; b. Brattleboro, Vt., July 26, 1937; d. Jay J. and Cornelia Hubbell (Fitzgibbon) U.; m. Kenneth O. Miller, Nov. 29, 1958 (div. Nov. 1983); 1 child, Susan Harriet. AB in Govt., Radcliffe Coll., 1958. Redactor Williams and Wilkins Co., Balt., 1961-66; editor, 1966-78; project editor Med. Econs. Books, Oradell, N.J., 1978-82; devel. editor Med. Econs. Books, Oradell, 1982-85; sr. assoc. editor Med. Econs. Mag., Oradell, 1985-87, sr. editor, 1987, profl. editor, 1987—; freelance editor, N.Y.C. area. Newsletter editor Village Gate at Nyack Homeowners Assn., 1992—; mem. Rockland Peace Dividend Campaign, 1984—. Recipient Jesse H. Neal award Am. Bus. Press, 1988, 93,94. Mem. Am. Soc. of Mag. Editors. Office: Med Econs 5 Paragon Dr Montvale NJ 07645-1725

MILLER, RENEÉ, metallurgical engineer; b. St. Louis, Oct. 19, 1958; d. John Anderson and Wendell Ross (Ballentine) M. BS in Metall. Engring., U. Mo., 1983; MBA, Lindenwood Coll., St. Charles, Mo., 1994. Metallurgist Allison Transmission divsn. GM, Indpls., 1985—. Contbr. articles to profl. jours. Vol. Com. to Elect Freeman Bosley Jr., St. Louis, 1984, Prison fellowship Ministry, Washington, 1990—; Sunday sch. supt. Corinthian Bapt. Ch., St. Louis, 1984-90. Minority Engring. scholar, 1977. Mem. African Am. Singles, Inc. Baptist. Office: GM Allison Transmission Divsn 4700 W 10th St # M13 Indianapolis IN 46222-3277

MILLER, RITA, personnel consultant, diecasting company executive; b. Bklyn., Jan. 15, 1925; d. Joseph and Etta M.; BA, Bklyn. Coll., 1947; MA, Boston U., 1949; children: Erika Greenwald, Roy Barnet Glickman. Personnel officer, sec. to pres. Marine Elec. Corp., Bklyn., 1943-47; script writer Song Debut, Boston, 1949-50; dir. Writers' Workshops, interviewer pub. opinion surveys, New Rochelle, N.Y., 1962-64; mgr. employee relations Dynacast div. Coats & Clark, Inc., Yorktown Heights, 1966-89. Mem. Am. Soc. Personnel Adminstrn., Westchester Personnel Mgmt. Assn. (dir.), Personnel Council New Rochelle, Bus. and Profl. Women U.S.A., Nat. Sociology Hon. Soc. Editor: The Management Consultant (George Kenning), 1965; contbr. articles to profl. jours. Home: 16 Congress St New Rochelle NY 10801

MILLER, RITA GAYLE, respiratory therapist, biofeedback specialist; b. Springfield, Mo., May 27, 1953; d. William Clifford and LaVelle Berniece (Tuttle) Boyd; m. Robert Douglas McKemie, Sept. 10, 1971 (div. 1976); 1 child, Marjorie; m. William F. Miller, Jan. 2, 1980; children: Leslie Herd, Karla Henderson, Chris, Lisa Hearn, Katy Merriman, Mary Frances, Franklin. AS, El Centro Coll., 1975; BA in Psychology, U. Tex., Dallas, 1990; BS in Gerontol. Counseling, U. Tex. S.W. Med. Ctr., 1993. Cert. and registered in respiratory care Nat. Bd. Respiratory Care; cert. biofeedback therapist, respiratory technician; registered respiratory therapist. Supr. respiratory therapy Meth. Hosps. Dallas, 1974-76; instr. respiratory tech. program Tarrant County Jr. Coll., 1976-77; tech. dir. pulmonary rehab., respiratory therapy svcs., biofeedback therapist. Meth. Hosps. Dallas, 1977-80; instr. Tex. Inst. Respiratory Therapy, 1978-80; chief technician, physician's asst. Respiratory Care Ctr., Dallas, 1980-81; researcher pulmonary rsch. div. Meth. Hosps. Dallas, 1981-86; instr. respiratory therapy Dallas County Community Coll., 1981-83; dir. edn. and rehab. pulmonary svcs. Med. City Dallas Hosp., 1983-86; cons. biofeedback program Dallas Rehab. Inst., 1985-86; rsch. asst. to pvt. practice physician Dallas, 1986—. Author: (manuals) Progressive Respiratory Care, 1979, (with William F. Miller) Home Respiratory Care, 1979, Ventilator Dependent Patient Care, 1985; contbr. articles to profl. jours. Bd. adv. El Centro Coll., Respiratory Therapy Program, 1983-86. Mem. Applied Assn. Advancement Behavioral Therapy, Biofeedback Soc. Tex., Assn. Applied Psychophysiology, Am. Assn. Respiratory Care, Tex. Soc. Respiratory Care, North Tex. Region Respiratory Care, Am. Lung Assn. (Dallas area).

MILLER, ROSEMARY MARGARET, accountant; b. Jersey City, Jan. 3, 1935; d. Joseph John and Marguerite (Delatush) Corbin; m. James Noyes Orton, 1956 (div. 1977); m. Julian Allen Miller, Oct. 14, 1978 (dec. 1993); children: Alexandria Lynn Hayes, Jennifer Ann Orton Cole. Student Barnard Coll., 1953-54, Rutgers U., Newark, 1954-56, Howard U., 1962-63, No. Va. Community Coll., 1976-83; AA, Thomas A. Edison State Coll., 1981; BS in Acctg., U. Md., 1987; cert. H & R Block, 1981; cert. tax profl. Am. Inst. Tax Studies. Bookkeeper Gen. Electronics, Inc., Washington, 1970-73; cost acct. Radiation Systems, Inc., Sterling, Va., 1973-80; acct. Bilsom Internat., Inc., Reston, Va., 1980-83; sales mgr. Bay Country Homes, Inc., Fruitland, Md., 1984; sr. staff acct. Snow, Powell & Meade, Salisbury, Md., 1985-86; acct. Meadows Hydraulics, Inc., Fruitland, Md., 1987-88; acct. Porter & Powell CPAs, Salisbury, 1988-93; owner, prin. RCOM Cons., acctg., bookeeping, taxes, Princess Anne, Md. Mem. Accreditation Council for Accountancy (accredited 1981), Nat. Soc. Public Accts., Inst. Mgmt. Accts., Nat. Soc. Tax Profls. (cert. tax profl. 1994). Democrat. Lutheran. Home and Office: 30531 Bardwell Dr Princess Anne MD 21853-2868

MILLER, ROSILAND, retired art history educator, writer; b. N.Y., Oct. 4, 1932; d. John and Gloria Smonian; m. Colemon Miller; 1 child, Susan J. Miller Woods. BA in Art, Balt. Inst. Art, 1954; M in Art History, U. Md., 1975. Assoc. prof. art history, chair fine arts dept. U. Balt., 1969-78; assoc. prof. art history N.Y.C. C.C., 1979-83; rschr. Smithsonian Inst., Washington, 1985-87; ret., 1987; lectr. Met. Mus. Art, N.Y.C., and Balt. Mus., 1979-88, St. Petersburg (Fla.) Jr. Coll., 1987—, Corcoran Gallery, Tampa Mus. Art, St. Petersburg Mus. Fine Arts.; instr. Loyola Coll., Md.; dir. art gallery Johns Hopkins U., Balt., 1984. Author: Magic, Myths and Religions of Primitive Societies, 1985; sculptor bronze works exhibited at N.Y. galleries, Met. Mus., Balt. Art Mus.; contbr. articles to profl. jours. Lectr. Pinellas County Sch. Sys., 1993, 94. Recipient Outstanding Contbn. to Women in Arts award Internat. Women's Yr., 1975, Humanitarian award Md. Humanitarian Affairs Soc., 1985. Mem. AAUW. Home: 4300 39 St S Saint Petersburg FL 33711

MILLER, SALLY DAVIS, sales executive; b. Pitts., Nov. 22, 1957; d. Raymond Anthony and Rita Ann (Marsh) Dobosh; m. Jeffry Gerard Davis, Aug. 12, 1978 (div.); 1 child, Jessica Joann; m. Stuart Miller, Jan. 16, 1993. Pres. Dobosh Svc. Ctr., Pitts., 1975-86, 87—, Lawn Mowers & More, McMurray, Pa., 1986-87. Mem. Nat. Equipment Servicing Dealer's Assn. (v.p. 1987-88, pres. 1992-93), Outdoor Power Equipment Servicing Dealers Assn.(past pres.). Democrat. Roman Catholic. Home: 2871 Old Washington Rd Mc Murray PA 15317 Office: Dobosh Svc Ctr 5167 Brownsville Rd Pittsburgh PA 15236-2644

MILLER, SANDRA PERRY, middle school educator; b. Nashville, Aug. 3, 1951; d. James Ralph and Pauline (Williams) Perry; m. William Kerley Miller, June 22, 1974. BS, David Lipscomb U., 1973; MEd, Tenn. State U., 1983, cert. in spl. edn., reading splty., 1986. Cert. tchr., Tenn. Tchr. Clyde Riggs Elem. Sch., Portland, Tenn., 1973-86; tchr. social studies Portland Mid. Sch., 1986—; adv. bd. tech. and communications in edn. Sumner County Sch. Bd., Gallatin, Tenn., 1990—; co-dir., cons. Tenn. Students-at-Risk, Nashville, 1991—; assoc., edn. cons. Edn. Fgn. Inst. Cultural Exch., 1991-92; fellow World History Inst., Princeton (N.J.) U., 1992—; awards com. Tenn. Dept. Edn., Nashville, 1992; U.S. edn. amb. E.F. Ednl. Tours, Eng., France, Germany, Belgium, Holland, 1991; ednl. cons. Houghton Mifflin Co., Boston, 1992; apptd. Tenn. Mini-Grants award com., Tenn. 21st Century Tech. Com. Author curriculum materials; presenter creative crafts segment local TV sta., 1990-93; producer, dir. documentary on edn. PBS, Corona, Calif., 1990. Performer Nashville Symphony Orch., 1970-73; leader Sumner County 4-H Club, 1976-86; mem. Woodrow Wilson Nat. Fellowship Found. on Am. History, Princeton U., 1994. Recipient Excellence in Teaching award U. Tenn., 1991-92, 92-93, award for outstanding teaching in humanities Tenn. Humanities Coun., 1994; named Tchr. of Yr. Upper Cumberland dist. Tenn. Dept. Edn., 1991-92, 92-93, Mid. Tenn. Educator of Yr. Tenn. Assn. Mid. Schs., 1991, Tenn. Tchr. of Yr. Tenn. Dept. Edn., 1992, Nat. Educator of Yr. Milken Family Found., 1992. Mem. NEA, ASCD, Sumner County Edn. Assn. (sch. rep. 1973—, Disting. Tchr. of Yr. 1992), Tenn. Edn. Assn. (rep. 1973—), Nat. Geographic Tenn. Alliance (rep. 1990—, grantee 1990), Tenn. Humanities Coun. (rep. 1990—), Nat. Coun. Social Studies. Baptist. Office: Portland Mid Sch 922 S Broadway Portland TN 37148-1624

MILLER, SARAH LOUISE, psychiatrist; b. Hartford, Conn., June 30, 1922; d. Michael Joseph and Nora (O'Connor) O'Brien; m. James Charles Miller, May 31, 1969; children: Michael James, Jeffrey Charles. BA, St. Joseph Coll., 1944; MD, Med. Coll. Pa., 1958. Diplomate Am. Bd. Psychiatry and Neurology. Staff psychiatrist Mental Health Dept. Ventura County, Ventura, Calif., 1970-72, dir. local mental health, 1972-76; agy. dir. Health Svcs. Agy. Ventura County, Ventura, 1976-81; dir. pub. health Health Care Svcs. Santa Barbara County, Santa Barbara, Calif., 1987-93; pvt. practice Ventura, 1993—; pres. Calif. Local Health Officers, Sacramento, 1984, Health Sys. Agy., Calif. Health Sys. Agy., Ventura and Santa Barbara, 1985. Office: Ventura Psychiat Med Group 970 S Petit Ave Ventura CA 93004

MILLER, SHANNON, Olympic athlete; b. Rollo, Mo., Mar. 10, 1977. Silver medalist, All-Around Competition Barcelona Olympic Games, 1992, Silver medalist, Balance Beam, 1992, Bronze medalist, Uneven Bars, 1992; Gold medalist all-around competition Birmingham Great World Championships, Britain, 1993, Brisbane Austrlia World Championships, St. Petersburg, Russia, 1994. Bronze medalist in floor exercise, Olympics, 1992; World Champion Gold medalist in all around, 1993, 94, in uneven bars and fl. exercise, 1993, in balance beam, 1994. Christian Scientist. Address: US Olympic Committee 1750 E Boulder St Colorado Springs CO 80909

MILLER, SHERRY ELIZABETH, occupational health nurse; b. Harbor City, Calif., Apr. 9, 1957; d. Richard O. and Kathryn S. (Sorrell) Puckett; 1 child, Mary Kathryn Medina. Lic. Vocat. Nurse, Coll. of the Desert, 1978; student, Chapman Coll., 1992—. LVN, Calif. Pediatric nurse Desert Hosp., Palm Springs, Calif., 1979-81; gerontol. nurse Moyle's Health Care, Yucca Valley, Calif., 1989-91; gerontol. nurse, staff developer Hi-Desert Continuing Care Ctr., Joshua Tree, Calif., 1991—; owner Citrus Nursing Acad., 1993—; owner, founder Eloquence Creative Writing Svcs., Yucca Valley, 1985—; preceptor for Quality Care Health Found. Staff Developer Program, Sacramento, 1992. Creator, facilitator How to Teach Sex Edn. to Your Child, Friendly Hills Elem. Sch., 1990. Mem. Inland County Staff Developers Assn. (sec. 1991—). Republican. Home: 7389 Cibola Trl Yucca Valley CA 92284-3253 Office: Desert Hosp Employee Occup Health 1150 N Indian Canyon Palm Springs CA 92284

MILLER, SUE BARRICK, counseling facility director; b. Pitts., Aug. 26, 1955; d. Eugene Edwin and Shirley Ann (Abbott) B.; m. David John Miller, Mar. 23, 1985; children: Alexander Zachary, Elizabeth Leigh. B Psychology, Edinboro State Coll., 1977, M Profl. Psychology, 1978; PhD in Counselor Edn., U. Pitts., 1988. Staff therapist Harborcreek Sch. for Boys, Erie, Pa., 1975-78; drug and alcohol therapist Myriad Project-D&A Program, Jeannette, Pa., 1979-80; staff psychologist Harmarville Rehab. Ctr., Pitts., 1980-

86, supervising psychologist, 1986-87, program coord., 1987-89, dir. behavioral svcs., 1989-90; exec. dir. Caring Profl. Resources, Inc. (formerly The Caring Pl., Inc.), Monroeville, Pa., 1989-92, exec. co-dir., 1993—; cons. Beulah Christian Presch., Pitts., 1989—. Contbr. articles to profl. jours. Sandoz Pharm. Co. grantee, 1987, Pfizer Pharmaceutic Co. grantee, 1989. Mem. APA, Pa. Psychol. Assn., Greater Pitts. Psychol. Assn. (mem. newsletter com. 1984-85). Office: Caring Profl Resources Inc Parkvale Bldg Ste 504 Monroeville PA 15146

MILLER, SUSAN ANN, school system administrator; b. Cleve., Nov. 24, 1947; d. Earl Wilbur and Marie Coletta (Hendershot) M. BS in Edn., Kent State U., 1969; MEd, Cleve. State U., 1975; PhD, Kent State U., 1993. Cert. supt.; cert. elem. prin., cert. elem. supervisor; cert. Learning Disabled/Behavior Disabled tchr.; cert. tchr. grades 1-8; cert. sch. counselor; lic. counselor. Tchr., guidance counselor, interim prin. North Royalton City Schs., Ohio, 1969-84; dir. elem. and special edn., acting supr. Cuyahoga County Bd. Edn., Valley View, Ohio, 1984—. Contbr. articles to profl. jours. Recipient grant Latchkey Program, State Dept. Edn. Mem. ASCD, Coun. Exceptional Children, N.E. Ohio Sch. Personnel Adminstrs., Phi Delta Kappa. Home: 14508 Cross Creek Ln Cleveland OH 44133-4811 Office: Department Education 5700 W Canal Road Valley View OH 44125

MILLER, SUSAN BLAIR, interior designer; b. Centralia, Ill., July 27, 1946; d. John Dean and Tiona Evelyn (Eagan) Blair; m. Ira Duane Miller, June 11, 1974; children: Robyn Elizabeth, James Wesley. BFA, Washington U., St. Louis, 1968; MS, Fla. State U., 1983. Cert. interior designer Nat. Coun. for Interior Design Qualification. Interior designer The Office Place, Anchorage, 1984-89, 93—, free lance designer, 1990-92; designer Arctic Office Supply, Anchorage, 1992-93; adj. instr. interior design U. Alaska, Anchorage, 1990-92. Mem. Am. Soc. Interior Designers (profl., treas. 1987-89, sec. 1994-95). Home: 13951 Davis St Anchorage AK 99516-3617 Office: The Office Place 4831 Old Seward Hwy Anchorage AK 99503-7449

MILLER, SYLVIA KANWISCHER, editor; b. Fremont, Calif., June 2, 1962. Student, Instituto Internacional, Madrid, 1983; BA in Comparative Lit. summa cum laude, U. Calif., Berkeley, 1984; MA in English and Comparative Lit., Columbia U., 1990. Display ad svc. asst. classified advt. dept. Monterey (Calif.) Peninsula Herald, 1983, 84; adminstrv. asst. ATEL, Inc., San Francisco, 1985; from sr. sec. to project editor Macmillan Profl./Reference books divsn. Macmillan Pub. Co., N.Y.C., 1985-90, from mng. editor to sr. editor Charles Scribner's Sons Reference Books, 1990-95, exec. editor Charles Scribner's Sons Reference Books, 1995—. Mem. Phi Beta Kappa. Office: 866 3d Ave New York NY 10022

MILLER, TAMARA DEDRA, psychologist; b. Cleve., Jan. 13, 1961; d. Taswill Taylor and Ethel (Midgett) M.; stepd. Gwendolyn (Hicks) M. BA in Psychology, Wittenberg U., 1982; D in Psychology, Wright State U., 1987. Lic. clin. psychologist, Ohio. Chief psychol. svc. USAF, Altus, Okla., 1987-89; chief psychol. testing USAF, Dayton, Ohio, 1989-92; dir. PTSD program Dept. VA, Dayton, 1992—; clin. prof. Wright State U., Dayton, 1992—; cons. Jackson County Youth, Altus, 1987-89, Ctr. for Retardation, Altus, 1987-89; adj. prof. Ctrl. State U., Wilberforce, 1991—; mem. panel Women's Fed. Program, Dayton, 1991; clin. advisor Les Femmes Concerned Citizens for Cancer, Dayton, 1992—. Consulting editor: Professional Psychology: Research and Practice, 1994. Capt. USAF, 1986-89. Mem. Nat. Coun. Negro Women Inc., VA Psychologists, Delta Sigma Theta. Home: 5670 Olive Tree Dr Dayton OH 45426 Office: Dept VA Affairs Med Ctr 4100 W 3d St Dayton OH 45428

MILLER, TATIA SLOAN, counselor; b. Bonham, Tex., Nov. 21, 1965; d. Billy L. and Linda J. (Smith) Rogers; m. Barry Glen Miller, Oct. 14, 1989; 1 child, Sydne Sloan. MA in Counseling, La. Tech. U., 1991; BA in Sociology, Hardin-Simmons U., 1988. Discipline coord. Hill Sch., Ft. Worth, Tex., 1989-90; tchr. Highland Bapt. Ch. Sch., Shreveport, La., 1990-91; social svcs. coord. Heritage House Nursing Home, Bossier City, La., 1991-92; mng. editor Commerce (Tex.) News, 1992; social worker Tex. Dept. Human Svcs., Bryan, Tex., 1993-94; drug treatment specialist psychology dept. Dept. of Justice Fed. Prison Camp, Bryan, 1994—; bd. dirs. Brazos Valley Child Care Mgmt. System, Bryan; pub. rels. intern H-SU Pub. Rels. Office, Abilene, Tex., 1987-88; counseling intern Caddo Parrish Employee Assistance Program, Shreveport, 1991. Editor: (newspaper) Commerce News, 1992. Mem. First Bapt. Ch., College Station, Tex.; mem. Com. for Advanced Race Rels., Commerce, 1992. Mem. Am. Counseling Assn., Internat. Assn. Marriage/Family Counselors, Assn. for Spiritual, Ethical, Religious Values in Counseling. Republican. Home: 2810 Jennifer College Station TX 77845

MILLER, TERRIE SUE, librarian; b. Kansas City, Mo., May 29, 1961; d. Bill and Marilyn Janice (Moore) M. BS in Edn., N.W. Mo. State U., 1983, MS in Edn., 1985; postgrad., Cen. Mo. State U., 1986-89. Cert. tchr. libr. sci., reading, learning disabilities, speech-theatre edn., Mo. Tutorial asst. N.W. Mo. State U., Maryville, 1983-85; houseparent Van's Group Home, Maryville, 1983-85; tchr. learning disabilities Lone Jack (Mo.) High Sch., 1985-88; libr. Grain Valley (Mo.) High Sch., 1988-90; libr. clk. Midcontinent Pub. Libr., Independence, Mo., 1986—; libr. Kansas City (Mo.) Sch. Dist., 1990—. Vol. Spl. Olympics. Satellite grantee State of Mo., 1990. Mem. ALA, Am. Fedn. Tchrs., Mo. Assn. Sch. Librs., Greater Kansas City Assn. Sch. Librs. Democrat. Roman Catholic. Home: 2202 Quail Creek Dr Independence MO 64055-6266 Office: Kansas City Sch Dist 1211 Mcgee St Kansas City MO 64106-2416

MILLER, THERESA MORGENSTERN, psychologist; b. N.Y.C., Apr. 24, 1919; d. David and Frances (Brosseau) Morgenstern; m. Marvin Julian Miller, Dec. 24, 1939; children: Peter Daniel, Susan Toni. BA, Bklyn. Coll., 1938; MS, U. Pitts., 1958, PhD, 1961. Psychologist, N.Y. Psychologist Team Teaching Project, Pitts., 1961-64; rsch. scientist NYU, 1966-67; assoc. prof. Kingsborough C.C., Bklyn., 1969-80; pvt. practice N.Y.C., 1980—; lectr. New Sch., Marymount, N.Y.C., 1977-79; vis. prof. Carnegie Mellon U., Pitts., 1964-66. Contbr. articles to profl. jours. Fellow Am. Orthopsychiat. Assn.; mem. APA. Home: 211 E 70th St New York NY 10021

MILLER, VIRGINIA FOOTE, travel agent; b. Cleve., Sept. 14, 1942; d. George Francis and Marion Edith (Fletcher) Foote; m. Ronald Bruce Miller, Sept. 30, 1967; children: Christopher, Victoria. BS in Social Welfare, Fla. State U., 1965; MS in Instrnl. Tech., Towson State U., 1977. Social worker State of Fla., Ft. Lauderdale, 1965-66; travel agent, co-owner Beach Travel Svc., Ft. Lauderdale, 1982—. 1st lt. USAF, 1965-67. Mem. AAUW, Am. Soc. Travel Agts., Fla. State U. Alumni Assn., Fla. State U. Boosters, Coral Springs Philharm. Soc., Seminole Club Broward County (v.p. booster affairs). Republican. Episcopalian. Home: 3601 NW 82d Ave Coral Springs FL 33065 Office: Beach Travel Svc 3280 NE 32d St Fort Lauderdale FL 33308

MILLER, YVONNE BOND, state senator, educator; b. Edenton, N.C.; d. John and Pency Bond. BS, Va. State Coll., Petersburg, 1956; postgrad., Va. State Coll., Norfolk, 1966; MA, Columbia U., 1962; PhD, U. Pitts., 1973; postgrad., CCNY, 1976. Tchr. Norfolk Pub. Schs., 1956-68; asst. prof. Norfolk State U., 1968-71, assoc. prof., 1971-74, prof., 1974-88, head dept. early childhood/elem. edn., 1984-87; mem. Va. Ho. Dels., Richmond, 1984-87, mem. edn. com., health, welfare and instns. com., militia and police com., 1983-87; mem. Va. Senate, Richmond, 1987—; now mem. commerce and labor com., gen. laws com., transp. com., rehab. and social svcs. com. Va. Senate; Va. Dems. vice chair; mem. Nat. Dem. Com.; cons. to chs., parent orgns. and community groups. Commr. Ea. Va. Med. Authority; adv. bd. Va. Div. Children; active C.H. Mason Meml. Ch. of God in Christ. 1st black woman to be elected to Va. Legislature, 1983, 1st black woman to be elected to Va. Senate, 1987. Mem. Nat. Alliance Black Sch. Educators (bd. dirs.), Va. Assn. for Early Childhood Edn., Nat. Assn. Dem. Chairs, Zeta Phi Beta (past officer). Office: 960 Norchester St Norfolk VA 23504-4021 also: Norfolk State U 2401 Corprew Ave Norfolk VA 23504-3907 also: Va Senate Gen Assembly Bldg Rm 365 Richmond VA 23219

MILLER, ZOYA DICKINS (MRS. HILLIARD EVE MILLER, JR.), civic worker; b. Washington, July 15, 1923; d. Randolph and Zoya Pavlovna (Klementinovska) Dickins; m. Hilliard Eve Miller, Jr., Dec. 6, 1943; children: Jeffrey Arnot, Hilliard Eve III. Grad. Stuart Sch. Costume Design, Washington, 1942; student Sophie Newcomb Coll., 1944, New Eng. Conservatory Music, 1946, Colo. Coll., 1965; grad. Internat. Sch. Reading, 1969. Instr. Stuart Summer Sch. Costume Design, Washington, 1942; fashion coord. Julius Garfinckel, Washington, 1942-43; fashion coord., cons. Mademoiselle mag., 1942-44; star TV show Cowbelle Kitchen, 1957-58, Flair for Living, 1958-59; model mags. and comml. films, also nat. comml. recs., 1956—; sr. devel. officer Webb-Waring Lung Inst., Denver, 1973—. Contbr. articles, lectures on health care systems and fund raising. Mem. exec. com., bd. dirs. El Paso County chpt. Am. Lung Assn., Colo., 1954-63; mem. exec. com. Am. Lung Assn. Colo., 1965-84, bd. dirs. 1965-87, chmn. radio and TV coun., 1963-70, mem. med. affairs com., 1965-70, pres., 1965-66, procurer found. funds, 1965-70; developer nat. radio ednl. prodns. for internat. use Am. Lung Assn., 1963-70, coord. statewide pulmonary screening programs Colo., other states, 1965-72; chmn. benefit fund raising El Paso County Cancer Soc., 1963; co-founder, coord. Colorado Springs Debutante Ball, 1967—; coord. Nat. Gov.'s Conf. Ball, 1969; mem. exec. com. Colo. Gov.'s Comprehensive Health Planning Coun., 1967-74, chmn., 1971-72; chmn. Colo. Chronic Care Com., 1969-73, chmn. fund raising, 1970-72, chmn. spl. com. congl. studies on nat. health bills, 1971-73; mem. Colo.-Wyo. Regional Med. Program Adv. Coun., 1969-73; mem. Colo. Med. Found. Consumers Adv. Coun., 1972-78; mem. decorative arts com. Colorado Springs Fine Arts Ctr., 1972-75; founder, state coord. Nov. Noel Pediatrics Benefit Am. Lung Assn., 1973-87; founder, state pres. Newborn Hope, Inc., 1987—; mem. adv. bd. Wagon Wheel Girl Scouts, 1991—. Zoya Dickins Miller Vol. of Yr. award established Am. Lung Assn. of Colo., 1979; recipient James J. Waring award Colo. Conf. on Respiratory Disease Workers, 1963, Nat. Pub. Rels. award Am. Lung Assn., 1979, Gold Double Bar Cross award, 1980, 83, Jefferson award Am. Inst. Pub. Svc., 1991, Recognition award So. Colo. Women's C. of C., 1994, Silver Spur Community award Pikes Peak Range Riders, 1994; named Humanitarian of Yr., Am. Lung Assn. of Colo., 1987, One of 50 Most Influential Women in Colorado Springs by Gazette Telegraph Newspaper, 1990, One of 6 Leading Ladies Colo. Homes & Lifestyles Mag., 1991. Lic. pvt. pilot. Mem. Colo. Assn. Fund Raisers, Denver Round Table for Planned Giving, Nat. Soc. Fund Raising Execs., Nat. Cowbell Assn. (El Paso county pres. 1954, TV chmn., chmn. nat. Father of Yr. contest Colo. 1956-57), Broadmoor Garden Club. Home: 74 W Cheyenne Mountain Blvd Colorado Springs CO 80906-4336

MILLER-BJORNSTAD, DOLORES MARIE, real estate development company executive; b. Pitts., Mar. 3, 1937; d. Joseph Anthony and Irene Clara (Blausen) Miller; m. George Edward Chillcott, July 19, 1968 (dec. Aug. 1981); m. Jack M. Bjornstad, Dec. 19, 1990. Student, San Diego State U., 1975-76, Mesa C.C., 1976-77, Nat. U., 1982-83. Asst. v.p. Trans-State Title Co., L.A., 1967-70; controller Pacific Scene, Inc., San Diego, 1971-73; treas., v.p. subs. Bruce Farley Corp., San Diego, 1973-74; controller Tschantz Devel. Co., San Diego, 1975-76; treas., controller Duluth Sci., Inc., San Diego, 1976-79; controller Patrick Devel. Ltd., San Diego, 1979-93. Pres. bd. Meadow Villas Assn., 1979-80. Mem. Inst. Mgmt. Accts. Republican. Roman Catholic. Home: 425 Hilltop Dr Chula Vista CA 91910-5018

MILLER-CHERMELY, DOROTHY L., sales executive; b. Hof, Bavaria, Germany, Nov. 30, 1947; d. Furman C. and Hilde (Weigold) Alderman; m. Kenneth Eugene Miller, Oct. 8, 1966 (div. 1972); m. Ronald Joseph Chermely, Feb. 14, 1993. AAS in Bus. Adminstrn., Corning Community Coll., 1973; BS in Indsl. and Labor Rels., Cornell U., 1975. Lic. real estate broker, Fla. Exec. sec. Corning (N.Y.) Bldg. Co., 1967-73; personnel adminstr. Xerox Corp., Rochester, N.Y., 1975-77; supt., constrn. mgr. U.S. Home Corp., Port Richey, Fla., 1979-80, sales cons., 1981-82, exec. v.p., 1982-83, v.p., sales mgr., 1990-94, v.p. project mgr., 1995—; constrn. supt. Charles Rutenberg Corp., Clearwater, Fla., 1983-85. Vol., mem. self-sufficiency subcom. Health and Rehab. Svcs., Port Richey, Fla., 1993. Mem. NOW, Fla. Trust for Hist. Preservation, Nat. Trust for Hist. Preservation, Pasco C. of C. (rep. 1990-93), Pasco Builders Assn. (rep. 1990-93), Optimist Club (sec. 1993-94, v.p. 1994—). Home: 8806 Planters Ln New Port Richey FL 34654-4200 Office: US Home Corp 2368 Fairskies Dr Spring Hill FL 34606

MILLERD, KAREN LEE, financial consultant; b. Glendale, Calif., Feb. 28, 1961; d. John Norton and Jane (Mangal) M. BS in BA, U. So. Calif., L.A., 1983; MBA, UCLA, 1988. Cert. mgmt. acct. Fin. analyst TRW Aerospace, Redondo Beach, Calif., 1983-86; staff cons. Arthur Andersen & Co., L.A., 1988, sr. cons., 1989, mgr., 1990-91, experienced mgr., 1992-93; sr. mgr., 1994—. Mem. Inst. Bus. Appraisers, Inst. Mgmt. Accts. (cert.), L.A. Jr. C. of C., Anderson Grad. Sch. Mgmt. Alumni Assn. Home: 12130 Ohio Ave # 103 Los Angeles CA 90025-2583 Office: Arthur Andersen & Co 28 1/2 Myrtle St Apt 3 Boston MA 02114-4545

MILLER DAVIS, MARY-AGNES, social worker; b. Montgomery, Ala., Jan. 21; d. George Joseph and Mollie (Ingersoll) M.; m. Edward Davis, Sept. 20, 1941. BA, Wayne State U., 1944; MSW, U. Mich., 1970. Lic. social worker, Mich. Social caseworker Cath. Family Ctr., Detroit, 1946-48; foster homes worker Juvenile Ct., Detroit, 1953-57; youth svc. bur. League of Cath. Women, Detroit, 1957-59; mayor's community action for youth com. worker City of Detroit, 1963; instr. urban sociology Madonna Coll., Livonia, Mich., 1968; pers. cons. Edward Davis Motor Sales, Detroit, 1963-70; exec. cons. Edward Davis Assocs., Inc., Detroit, 1975—; founder Co-Ette Club, Inc., Detroit, 1941—, Met. Detroit Teen Conf. Coalition, Detroit, 1983—; program chair Wayne State U.-Merrill Palmer Inst., Detroit, 1976—. Editor Girl Friends, Inc. Mag., 1960-62; contbr. numerous articles to profl. publs. Charter mem. Meadowbrook Summer Music Festival, com. of Oakland (Mich.) U.; adv. bd. Women for the Detroit Symphony Orch.; mem./patron Founder's Soc. the Detroit Inst. of Ants; bd. dirs., other offices ARC, Detroit, 1974—; mem. The Detroit Hist. Soc., Heart of Gold Coun., Women for United Found. (named to Heart of Gold coun. 1968), Friends of the Detroit Libr., Mich. Opera Theatre; former bd. dirs. United Community Svcs. Women's Com., Campfire Girls, LWV, Neighborhool Svcs. Orgn., Cath. Interracial Coun. and others. Recipient Nat. Community Leadership award Nat. Coun. Women of U.S., Inc., 1984, Am. Human Resources award Am. Bicentennial Rsch. Inst., 1976, Heart of Gold award United Way, 1968, Nat. Leadership award United Negro Coll. Fund, 1963, Recognition award Westin Hotel, 1991, Top Ladies of Distinction award, 1994; named One of Mich. Outstanding Women City of Detroit, 1976, Heart of Gold 25th Anniversary honoree United Way Southeastern Mich., 1992; Vassar Summer Seminar scholar NCCJ, 1953, Notre Dame Summer Seminar scholar, 1960. Mem. NASW, ARC (bd. dirs. 1973—), Nat. Conf. of Social Work, The Cons. Club of Detroit (adv. bd. edn. com.), Detroit Econ. Club (mem. adv. com.). Home: 2020 Chicago Blvd Detroit MI 48206-1783

MILLER-GIRSON, EILEEN BONNIE, insurance underwriter; b. Chgo., Nov. 22, 1953; d. Sol and Evelyn (Brenner) Miller; m. David Jay Girson, June 12, 1977. AA, Kendall Coll., Evanston, Ill., 1973; BA, MacMurray Coll., Jacksonville, Ill., 1975; MEd, Nat. Coll. Edn., Evanston, 1976. Cert. profl. ins. woman; assoc. in underwriting. Tchr. Evanston Sch. Dist. 65, 1975-76; lawyers profl. liability underwriter Shand Morahan Co., Evanston, 1977-78; personal lines underwriter Farmers Ins. Group, Aurora, Ill., 1978-80; comml. lines underwriter Hanover Ins. Co., Chgo., 1980-81; workers compensation underwriter EBI Cos., Chgo., 1981-83; package underwriter CNA Ins., Chgo., 1983-84, dentists profl. liability underwriter, 1984-86; casualty underwriter Hartford Ins. Co., Chgo., 1986-87; sr. comml. accounts underwriting specialist Home Ins. Co., Chgo., 1987—. Ill. Edn. Assn. scholar, 1975-76. Mem. Ins. Distaff Exec. Assn., The Saints, Cinema Chgo. Home: 511 Leclaire Ave Wilmette IL 60091-2062 Office: Home Ins Co 10 S Riverside Plz Chicago IL 60606-3708

MILLER-GRIFFIE, MAUREEN JO, nurse; b. Hahn, Fed. Republic of Germany, Feb. 1, 1962; came to U.S., 1962; d. Wayne Russell and JoAnne Marie (Crust) Miller; m. Richard Melvin Griffie, Dec. 28, 1991; 1 child, Jacob Thomas. Diploma, Altoona Hosp. Sch. of Nursing, 1982; student, Shippensburg U., 1991—. Cert. emergency nurse, CCRN, basic cardiac life support instr., ACLS instr., EMS instr. Charge nurse med./surg. Lock Haven (Pa.) Hosp., 1982-83, charge nurse emergency dept., 1983-84; charge nurse/staff nurse ICU Lewistown (Pa.) Hosp., 1984-85; prehosp. nurse Carlisle (Pa.) ALS, 1984-86; supr. Sarah Todd Nursing Home, Carlisle, 1986-87; staff, charge nurse, emergency/prehosp. Hanover (Pa.) Gen. Hosp., 1988—. Ambulance capt. Friendship Hose Co., Inc., Newville, 1990, 92, 93. Mem. AACN (critical care RN), Emergency Nurses Assn. Democrat. Home: 20 Heights Rd Newville PA 17241

MILLER-HAVENS, SUSAN ELIZABETH, developmental psychologist, artist; b. Newark, June 20, 1944; d. Charles Eben Jr. and Elizabeth Charlotte (Cluthe) Miller; m. Leston Laycock Havens, 1973; 1 child, Emily; stepchildren: Christopher, Jennifer, Sarah. AS in Nursing Sci., Lasell Coll., 1965; BA in Studio Art, Wellesley Coll., 1978; EdD in Human Devel., Harvard U., 1990. RN, Mass. Staff nurse Mass. Gen. Hosp., Boston, 1965-66, Mass. Mental Health Ctr., Boston, 1966-68; founder psychiat. nursing svc. Cambridge (Mass.) City Hosp., 1968, 1st clin. psychiat. nursing supr., 1969-71; psychotherapist pvt. clinic Boston, 1971-74; pvt. practice devel. psychology Cambridge, 1991—; dir. edn. Am. Adoption Congress, Washington, 1989-94, chair nom. com., 1994—; adoption cons. Cambridge Children and Family Svcs., 1993, mem. corp., 1992—. One woman shows include Wellesley Coll. Mus., 1977, Somerville (Mass.) Mus., 1993; exhibited in group shows at Brenda Taylor Gallery, Boston, 1994, Hofstra U., 1995; contbr. articles to profl. jours.; contbg. author: The Practice of Community Mental Health, 1970. Mem. City of Cambridge Citizen Rev. Com., 1994; past v.p., mem. The Adoption Connection, 1980—. Mem. NOW, Wellesley Coll. Art Assn., Women's Caucus for Art, Cambridge Tennis Club (gov. 1993—). Office: 151 Brattle St Cambridge MA 02138

MILLER-HOUCK, NANCY JOAN, nurse, psychotherapist, consultant, educator; b. Newton, Mass., May 20, 1947; d. Harold Max and Selma Irma (Finkelstein) Gerrish; divorced, 1974; m. Douglas Houck, July 13, 1991. BA in Sociology, C. W. Post Coll. L.I. U., 1968; postgrad., Mich. State U., 1969; RN diploma, Jackson Meml. Hosp., 1977; MS in Mental Health Counseling, Barry U., 1989. Cert. psychiat. RN, specialist in adult mental health nursing, substance abuse counselor, State of Hawaii. Social worker Suffolk (N.Y.) County Social Svcs., 1968-71; social worker, counselor Met. Dade County, Miami, Fla., 1971-74; charge nurse Newton Wellsley Hosp., Newton Upper Falls, Mass., 1977-78; head nurse substance abuse Humana Hosp. Biscayne, Miami, Fla., 1978-80; charge nurse Mt. Zion Hosp., San Francisco, 1980-81; staff nurse mental health unit Marin Gen. Hosp., Greenbrae, Calif., 1981-84; clin. coord. Humana Hosp. Biscayne, Miami, Calif., 1984-86; head nurse, dir. treatment svcs. addiction Victoria Hosp., Miami, 1986-87; per diem nurse Highland Park Hosp., Miami, 1987-89; staff nurse med./surg. Blue Hill (Maine) Meml. Hosp., 1989; pvt. practice Blue Hill, 1989-91, Lahaina, Hawaii, 1992—. HIV/AIDS Teaching grantee State of Maine, 1990, Social Svcs. Program grantee State of Fla., 1974. Mem. AACD, ANA (cert. psychiat. nurse, clin. nurse specialist). Office: Lahaina Shopping Ctr PO Box 11348 Ste 206 Lahaina HI 96761-6348

MILLER-MCMILLEN, KAREN JO, human resources specialist, consultant; b. Allentown, Pa., June 10, 1956; d. Paul Henry and Ruth Ann (Bartholomew) M.; m. Robert Glenn McMillen, Oct. 14, 1978; 1 child, Kelsey Jordan. BS with distinction, Pa. State U., University Park, 1978; MA, Ind. U. of Pa., 1982. Caseworker Indiana (Pa.) County Child Welfare Services, 1978-83; caseworker supr. Ind. (Pa.) County Child Welfare Services, 1983-84; human services coordinator Indiana County Planning Commn., 1984; testing and assessment specialist Susquehanna Employment and Tng. Corp., Lebanon, Pa., 1984-85; personnel dir. Cedar Haven, Lebanon, 1985-87, dir. human resources, 1987-89; tng. officer Gov.'s Exec. Offices, Harrisburg, Pa., 1989-90; dir. personnel Cornwall (Pa.) Manor, 1990—; cons. personnel to various orgns., Indiana, 1979-84, Lebanon, 1987—; bd. dirs. Indiana County Head Start, Inc., 1979-82; corr. Lebanon Daily News, 1986-87; cochmn. Employer Adv. Com., 1987-89. Mem. alumni bd. dirs. Coll. of Health and Human Devel., Pa. State U. Mem. Am. Soc. Pers. Adminstrn. (reviewer 1987—), am. Bus. Women's Assn. (chpt. pres. 1989—, Woman of Yr. 1987), Pa. State U. Alumni Assn. (alumni rep. 1985—), Am. Soc. Tng. and Devel. (cen. Pa. chpt.), Internat. Pers.Mgmt. Assn. (Harrisburg chpt.). Republican. Presbyterian. Home: 1425 E Walnut St Annville PA 17003-2022 Office: Cornwall Manor PO Box 125 222 Finance Bldg Cornwall PA 17016

MILLER-NORMAN, JANET MARIE, computer analyst, programmer; b. High Point, N.C., Oct. 20, 1962; d. James Rayburn and Hannah Marie (Kennedy) Miller; m. Rodney Lewis Norman, Aug. 13, 1981 (div. 1986); children: Cindy Jeanette, Daniel Lee. Student bus. computer programming, Davidson County C.C., Lexington, N.C., 1987-89; student computer info. sys., High Point Coll., 1989-91. Programmer Planters & Lifesavers, Winston-Salem, N.C., 1990-92; programmer analysts Sara Lee, Winston-Salem, 1992-93, sr. programmer analyst, 1993-94; analyst, programmer Wachovia Corp., Winston-Salem, 1994—. Leader 4-H Club, Lexington, N.C., 1985-94. Mem. Data Processing Mgmt. Assn. Home: 3762 Gumtree Rd Winston Salem NC 27107-6426 Office: Wachovia Corp 301 N Main St Winston Salem NC 27107

MILLER-TIEDEMAN, ANNA LOUISE, writer, counselor; b. Huntington, W.Va., Sept. 21, 1934; d. Elmer and Pearl (Todd) Miller; m. David Valentine Tiedeman, Jan. 6, 1973. BBA, Marshall U., 1963, MA, 1967; PhD, Ohio U., 1973. Cert. counselor/nat. bd.; cert. tchr., Ill.; standard designated svcs. cert., Calif. Mgr. sta. merger Chesapeake and Ohio Railroad, Huntington, 1957-66; resident dir. Ohio U., Athens, 1967; human rels. specialist Inst. for Regl. Devel., Athens, 1968; housing specialist Action, Inc., Huntington, 1969; real estate salesperson Massey Reality, Huntington, 1968-71; assoc. edn. devel. specialist Appalachian Edn. Lab., Charleston, W.Va., 1970-71; self-employed writer Palo Alto, Calif., 1971-72; counselor San Mateo (Calif.) City Sch. Dist., 1971-73; vis. lectr. The Johns Hopkins U., Balt., 1984-86, C.W. Post Coll./L.I. U., 1987; spl. issue co-editor Jour. of Career Edn., Columbia, Mo., 1982-84. Author: How Not to Make It . . . And Succeed: Life On Your Own Terms, 1989 (Ben Franklin award finalist 1990), Lifecareer: The Quantam Leap Into a Process Theory of Career, 1988; contbg. author: Developmental Counseling and Teaching, 1980. Prodn. asst. Hollywood (Calif.) Bowl Easter Svcs., 1987; dir. press desk Fourth Ann. Internat. Wilderness Congress, Denver, 1987. Recipient Outstanding Rsch. award Am. Personnel and Guidance Assn., Washington, 1981; co-leader Nat. Assembly to Advance Career, Nat. Inst. for Advancement of Career Edn., L.A., 1983, George E. Hill Disting. Alumnae award Ohio U., Athens, 1986. Mem. Am. Counselor Assn. (Spl. Writing award 1975, 78), Nat. Career Devel. Assn. Home: 1078 La Tortuga Dr Vista CA 92083-6441 Office: Lifecareer Ctr 1078 La Tortuga Dr Vista CA 92083-6441

MILLER WILSON, STACIE, management consultant; b. Eugene, Oreg., Jan. 6, 1964; d. Raymond Clark and Nancy Lou (Taylor) M. BA, Northwestern U., 1986, M of Mgmt., 1990. Acct. asst. R. K. Carvill, Inc., Chgo., 1986-88; acct. mgr. trainee R. K. Carvill & Co., Ltd., London, 1988-89; acct. mgr. Carvill Am., Chgo., 1989-90, asst. v.p., 1990-93, v.p., 1993; exec. cons. Peterson Cons., Chgo., 1993—; mem. Kellogg Adv. Com., Chgo., 1992—. 1st v.p. Am. Cancer Soc., Chgo., 1993-94, mem. jr. bd. exec. com., 1990—. Mem. NAFE, Profl. Assn. Women Within Ins. and Reins. Industry. Republican. Presbyterian. Office: Peterson Cons 310 S Michigan Ave Ste 1900 Chicago IL 60604-4206

MILLETT, KATHERINE MURRAY (KATE MILLETT), political activist, sculptor, artist, writer; b. St. Paul, Sept. 14, 1934; m. Fumio Yoshimura, 1965. BA magna cum laude, U. Minn., 1956; postgrad. with 1st class honors, St. Hilda's Coll. Oxford, Eng., 1956-58; PhD with distinction, Columbia U., 1970. Instr. English U. N.C. at Greensboro, 1958; file clk. N.Y.C., kindergarten tchr., 1960-61; sculptor, Tokyo, 1961-63; tchr. Barnard Coll., 1964-70; tchr. English Bryn Mawr (Pa.) Coll., 1970; disting. vis. prof. Sacramento State Coll., 1972-73; founder Women's Art Colony Farm, Poughkeepsie, N.Y. Author: Sexual Politics, 1970, The Prostitution Papers, 1973, Flying, 1974, Sita, 1977, The Basement, 1979, Going to Iran, 1982, The Loony Bin Trip, 1990, The Politics of Cruelty, 1994; co-prodr., co-dir. film Three Lives, 1970; one-woman shows Minami Gallery, Tokyo, Judson Gallery, N.Y.C., 1967, Noho Gallery, N.Y.C., 1976, 79, 80, 82, 84, 86, 93, Women's Bldg., L.A., 1977; one-woman drawings Andre Wanters Gallery, Berlin, 1980, Courtland Jessup Gallery, Provincetown, Mass., 1991, 92, 93, 94. Mem. Congress of Racial Equality; chmn. edn. com. NOW, 1966, active supporter women's liberation groups. Mem. Phi Beta Kappa. Office: 295 Bowery New York NY 10003

MILLEY, JANE ELIZABETH, academic administrator; b. Everett, Mass., May 20, 1940; d. Walter R. and Florence (Leach) M. MusB, Boston U., 1961; MA in Music, Columbia U., 1966; PhD in Higher/Post Sec. Edn.-

Adminstrn., Syracuse (N.Y.) U., 1977. Coord., founder, pianist Elmira (N.Y.) Coll. Fine Arts Trio, 1967-75; instr. music Elmira Coll., 1967-70, asst. prof. music, 1970-75, dir. arts and scis. program, 1974-75; rsch. assoc. Syracuse U., 1975-76, adminstrv. asst. to dean Coll. Arts and Scis., 1976-77; div. dean humanities and fine arts Sacramento City Coll., 1977-80; assoc. dean sch. fine arts, prof. music Calif. State U., Long Beach, 1980-81, interim dean, sch. fine arts, prof. music, 1981-82, dean, sch. fine arts, prof. music, 1982-84; arts advisor to chancellor Calif. State Univ. System, 1983-84; chancellor N.C. Sch. Arts U. N.C., Winston-Salem, 1984-89; cons. to pres. Sonoma State U., Rhonert Park, Calif., 1989-90; sr. fellow Am. Assn. State Colls. and Univs., Santa Rosa, Calif., 1989-90; provost, v.p. acad. affairs SUNY, Oswego, 1990-94; provost Simmons Coll., Boston, 1994—; speaker, cons. in field. Author: (with J. Sturnick and C. Tisinger) Women at the Helm, 1991; contbr. articles to profl. jours. Ex officio bd. dirs. Regional Arts Found., 1982-84, N.C. Scenic Studios, 1984-89, N.C. Dance Theatre, 1984-89, N.C. Shakespeare Festival, 1984-89; bd. dirs. Sacramento Film Festival, 1979-80, Long Beach Grand Opera, 1980; charter mem., founder Sacramento Exptl. Theatre, 1978-84. Commendation for outstanding svc. Los Rios Community Coll. Bd. Trustees, 1980, Sacramento City Coll., 1980. Mem. AAUW (found. adv. com. 1987-89), Am. Assn. State Colls. and Univs. (chmn. arts com. 1986-89), Nat. Assn. State Univs. and Land Grant Colls. (U. N.C. rep. commn. on arts 1986-89), Internat. Coun. Fine Arts Deans, N.C. Women's Forum, N.Y. Edn. Consortium, N.Y. State Sea Grant Inst. (bd. govs. 1991—), Oswego County Opportunities (bd. dirs. 1991—), Kappa Delta Pi, Pi Kappa Lambda. Office: 300 The Fenway Boston MA 02100

MILLGATE, JANE, language professional; b. Leeds, Eng., June 8, 1937; d. Maurice and Marie (Schofield) Barr; m. Michael Millgate, Feb. 27, 1960. B.A. with honors, Leeds U., Eng., 1959, M.A., 1963; Ph.D., U.Kent, Eng., 1970. Instr. U. Toronto, Ont., 1964-65, lectr., 1965-70, asst. prof., 1970-72, assoc. prof., 1972-77, prof. English, 1977—, vice-dean arts and scis., 1983-87; mem. bd. regents Victoria U., Toronto, 1981-86. Author: Macaulay, 1973, Walter Scott, 1984, 2d edit., 1987, Scott's Last Edition: A Study in Publishing History, 1987. Editor: Editing 19th Century Fiction, 1978. Contbr. articles to profl. jours. Doctoral fellow Can. Council, 1968-70; research fellow Can. Council, 1972, 74-75, Social Scis. and Humanities Research Council Can., 1980-81, 85-87. Fellow Royal Soc. Can., Royal Soc. Edinburgh; mem. Victorian Studies Assn. (pres. 1978-80), Assn. Can. Univ. Tchrs. English (pres. 1980-82), Can. Fedn. for Humanities (exec. 1981-83), Assn. Scottish Studies, Bibliog. Soc. Home: 75 Highland Ave, Toronto, ON Canada M4W 2A4 Office: U Toronto, Victoria Coll, Toronto, ON Canada M5S 1K7

MILLIARD, ALINE, social worker; b. Portage, Maine, Nov. 18, 1937; d. Alderic and Ida (Dionne) M. MSW, Adelphi U., 1976; diploma social work supervision, Hunter Coll., 1986. Nurses' aide Good Samaritan Hosp., West Islip, N.Y., 1964-65, admitting office clk., 1965-70, social svc. asst.; intake worker Maryhaven Diagnostic & Guidance Ctr., Port Jefferson, N.Y., 1972-74; coord. marriage counseling program Diocesan Human Rels. Svcs., Portland, Maine, 1977, family svc. worker, 1977-79; sch. social worker Sanford (Maine) Pub. Sch. Dept., 1979-81; campus social worker Green Chimneys Childrne Svcs., Brewster, N.Y., 1982-85, dir. group homes, 1985-88; social worker Med. Ctr. Hosp. Vt., Burlington, 1989—. Mem. Acad. Cert. Social Workers, NASW. Home: 64 1/2 Howard St Burlington VT 05401-4814 Office: MCHV Colchester Ave Burlington VT 05401

MILLIES, PALMA SUZANNE, school system administrator; b. N.Y.C., Apr. 30, 1943; d. Arpad Geza and Palma Regina (Franko) George; m. Robert John Millies; 1 child, Jennifer. BA in English and French magna cum laude, Elmhurst (Ill.) Coll., 1965; MA with honors, No. Ill. U., 1969; cert. advanced study, U. Ill., 1981; PhD in Curriculum Instrn. and Evaluation, U. Ill., Chgo., 1989. Cert. gen. adminstrn., spl. K-12 teaching and supervising, secondary sch. teaching, Ill. Lang. arts and French instr. Albright Middle Sch., Villa Park, Ill., 1965-70; English instr. Willowbrook High Sch., Villa Park, 1970-87, asst. prin. for instrn., 1988-91; dist. coord. gifted program High Sch. Dist. 88, Villa Park, 1982-86; asst. to dir. Chgo. Area Sch. Effectiveness Coun. Coll. Edn., U. Ill., 1986-87; asst. supt. for instrn. Maine Twsp. High Sch. Dist. # 207, Park Ridge, Ill., 1991—; instr. Nat.-Louis U., 1991, Roosevelt U., 1991; presenter in field; co-founder West Suburban Dirs. Curriculum, 1989; adj. prof. Nat. Coll. Edn., Lombard, Ill., 1988; chairperson AFT Supt.'s Search Com., Villa Park, 1988; mem. task force on gifted edn. State BD. Edn., Springfield, Ill., 1988; adj. prof. U. Ill., Chgo., 1988, 87. Contbr. articles to profl. jours. Mem. Am. Ednl. Rsch. Assn., ASCD, Nat. Coun. Tchrs. English, Ill. Coun. for Gifted (corr. sec.), West Suburban Dirs. Instrn., Villa Park C. of C. (sec.), Phi Delta Kappa. Home: 611 Heritage Ct Naperville IL 60565 Office: 1131 S Dee Rd Park Ridge IL 60068

MILLIGAN, EDITH, financial services executive; b. Evansville, Ind., Oct. 22, 1958; d. William West and Suzanne (Crimm) M.; m. Paul Alan Delphia, Sept. 1, 1984. BA, Tulane U., 1980. CLU Adminstrv. asst. Bryan Wagner, CLU, New Orleans, 1977-80; sec.-treas. Life Mktg. of La., New Orleans, 1980-81; dist. mgr. Creative Fin. Concepts, Columbus, Ohio, 1981-82; pres. Keeping Track, Inc., Columbus, 1982—. Author: Licensing Study Guide, 1982, Track Records, 1983, Addictive Money Misbehavior: Causes, Consequences and Counseling, 1993. Field coordinator Fair and Impartial Redistricting Commn., Columbus, 1981; mem. steering com. Pres. Ford Com., New Orleans, 1976. Mem. LWV, Internat. Assn. Fin. Planning, Employee Assistance Programs Assn., Mensa. Republican. Office: Keeping Track Inc PO Box 14468 Columbus OH 43214-0468

MILLIGAN, SISTER MARY, theology educator, religious consultant; b. Los Angeles, Jan. 23, 1935; d. Bernard Joseph and Carolyn (Krebs) M. BA, Marymount Coll., 1956; Dr. de l'Univ., U. Paris, 1959; MA in Theology, St. Mary's Coll., Notre Dame, Ind., 1966; STD, Gregorian U., 1975; D. honoris causa, Marymount U., 1988. Tchr. Cours Marymount, Neuilly, France, 1956-59; asst. prof. Marymount Coll., Los Angeles, 1959-67; gen. councillor Religious of Sacred Heart of Mary, Rome, 1969-75, gen. superior, 1980-85; asst. prof. Loyola Marymount U., Los Angeles, 1977-78, provost, 1986-90, prof., 1990—, dean liberal arts, 1992—; pres. bd. dirs. St. John's Sem., Camarillo, Calif., 1986-89; mem. exec. com. Internat. Union Superiors Gen., Rome, 1983-85; mem. planning bd. spiritual renewal program Loyola Marymount U., Los Angeles, 1976-78. Author: That They May Have Life, 1975; compiler analytical index Ways of Peace, 1986; contbr. articles to profl. jours. Vis. scholar Grad. Theol. Union, Berkeley, 1986. Mem. Calif. Women in Higher Edn., Coll. Theology Soc., Cath. Biblical Assn. Democrat. Roman Catholic. Office: Loyola Marymount U 7101 W 80th St Los Angeles CA 90045-2699*

MILLIGAN, NONA VERNICE, retired elementary educator, pianist; b. Triadelphia, Ohio, Apr. 13, 1916; d. Harry Milton Nelson and Goldie Edna (Loughman) Nelson-Lipp; m. Dana Clifton Milligan, May 27, 1951. BS in Edn., Ohio U., 1941. Cert. elem., history, English, biology, and music tchr., Ohio. Tchr., prin. Muskingum County, Ohio, 1936-39, tchr. grades 5 and 6, 1939-43; tchr. grade 5 Zanesville (Ohio) Pub. Schs., 1943-51; pvt. tchr. music Zanesville, 1939-53, Takoma Park, Md., 1959-70; ret., 1970; pianist accompanying chorus Lewisdale Sch., Md., 1976-81. Chief judge at voting Prince George's County Bd. Elections, 1968-74; substitute ch. organist, Zanesville and Columbus, Ohio, Silver Spring, Md., 1952-70; vol. Lifeline at Washington Adventist Hosp., Takoma Park, mem. staff, 1984-93; v.p. Christian Women's Fellowship, 1988-92, svc. chmn. Shepherd Park Ch., 1992—, svc. dir., 1992-94, 1994—. Mem. Takoma Park Women's Club (1st v.p. 1974-76, pres. 1976-78, parliamentarian 1992-94, asst. rec. sec. 1994—), D.C. Fedn. Women's Club (2d v.p. 1978-80, 1st v.p. 198-82, pres. 1982-84, parliamentarian 1992-94), Conf. 7 States (chmn. S.E. region 1986, v.p. 1994—), Ky. Col., Sligo Creek Club (program chmn. 1960-64, sec. 1970), Women's City Club of Washington (pres. 1990-92, 92-94, 94—).

MILLIGAN-WELLS, JOYCE ANN, quality assurance consultant, realtor; b. Cleve., Oct. 19, 1955; d. Kenneth L. and Dorothy E. (Broach) Oyler; 1 child, Michael D. Yoha. Cert. med. asst., Mansfield Bus. Coll., 1976. Cert. pharmacy tech., State of Ohio; cert. med. asst. Pharmacy tech., office mgr. Mansfield (Ohio) Gen. Hosp., 1982-93; quality assurance cons. Westhaven Instnl. Pharmacy, Perrysburg, Ohio, 1993—; realtor Haring Realty, INc., Mansfield, 1989—; tech. adv. bd. mem. North Ctrl. Ohio Tech. Coll., 1991-94, bus. adv. bd. mem., 1991-94. Mem. Ohio Soc. Pharmacy Technicians (pres., founder, chmn. 1991-94, editor quar. news 1992), Ohio Soc. Hosp. Pharmacists (com. ednl. affairs 1990-94), North Ctrl. Ohio Soc. Pharmacy Technicians (sec., treas., founder 1985—), North Ctrl. Ohio Soc. Hosp. Pharmacists, Richland County C. of C. Home: 301 Redwood Rd Mansfield OH 44907

MILLIKEN, KAREN MARIE, foreign service officer, economist; b. Denver, Oct. 19, 1955; d. John Gordon and Marie (Machell) M.; m. Valentino Zardi, June 26, 1982. AB, Mt. Holyoke Coll., 1977; MBA, U. Denver, 1979. Fgn. svc. officer Dept. of State, Milan, Italy, 1979-81, Washington, 1981-83, 85-88, Rome, 1983-85, Mogadishu, Somalia, 1985, Lima, Peru, 1988-92, Tegucigalpa, Honduras, 1992—. Office: Dept State 2201 C St NW Washington DC 20520-0001

MILLIN, LAURA JEANNE, museum director; b. Elgin, Ill., June 11, 1954; d. Douglas Joseph and PAtricia Ruth (Feragen) M. BA in Interdisciplinary Studies, The Evergreen State Coll., 1978. Dir. On The Boards, Seattle, 1979; art dir. City Fair Merocenter YMCA, Seattle, 1980; dir. Ctr. on Contemporary Art, Seattle, 1981; co-owner Art in Form Bookstore, Seattle, 1981-89; co-dir. 3d internat festical of films by women dirs. Seattle Art Mus.. & 911 Contemporary Arts, 1988; auction coord. Allied Arts of Seattle, 1989; dir. Missoula (Mont.) Mus. of the Arts, 1990—; dir. Visual AIDS Missoula Missoula Mus. of the Arts, 1989; curator Radio COCA, Ctr. on Contemproary Art, Seattle, 1986, co-curator, 1981, 83; lectr. in field. Co-editor: AnOther (ind. feminist newspaper), Seattle, 1989, editor: (exhibition catalog) James Turrell: Four Light Installations, 1981. Bd. dirs. Internat. Festival of Films by Women Dirs., Seattle, 1987, 89, Nine One One Comtemporary Arts Ctr., Seattle, 1981-87, bd. chmn. 1981-85; bd. advisors REFLEX (art mag.), Seattle, 1988-89, Ctr. on Contemporary Art, Seattle, 1983-86; state vis. Mont. Arts. Coun., Missoula, 1991, NEA, Mpls., 1988, Chgo., 1987; ; panelist Mont. Arts Coun., Helena, 1990; cons. Seattle Arts Commn., 1989, juror, 1985. Home: 1016 Cherry St Missoula MT 59802 Office: Missoula Mus of the Arts 335 N Pattee St Missoula MT 59802-4520

MILLION, KATHY ANN, security company official, consultant; b. New Brunswick, N.J., Feb. 24, 1958; d. August and Felicia Ann (Czarcinski) Pastore; m. Richard Million, Nov. 25, 1994; 1 child, Jessica Lynn. BS in Bus. and Computer Sci., Somerset County Coll., Somerville, N.J., 1986. Sec. Bio/Dynamics,, Somerset, 1978-79, Somerset County Coll., 1980-82, Johnson & Johnson Baby Products Co., Skillman, N.J., 1982-84; microcomputer specialist City Fed. Savs. Bank, Piscataway, N.J., 1985-88; office mgr. Sonitrol Asset Protection, Phoenix, 1990-91; gen. mgr. Affiliated Security Systems, Phoenix, 1991—; computer cons. Benchmark Appraisal, Bridgewater, N.J., 1987-88, Aztec Coffee & Bending, Phoenix, 1991—, Altech Sales & Svc., Phoenix, 1993—. Home: 4133 N 89th Ln Phoenix AZ 85037-2007 Office: Affiliated Security Systems 2701 E Thomas Rd Ste B Phoenix AZ 85016-8218

MILLMAN, JODE SUSAN, lawyer; b. Poughkeepsie, N.Y., Dec. 28, 1954; d. Samuel Keith and Ellin Sadenberg (Bainder) M.; m. Michael James Harris, June 20, 1982; children: Maxwell, Benjamin. BA, Syracuse U., 1976, JD, 1979. Bar: N.Y. 1980, U.S. Dist. Ct. (so. and ea. dists.) N.Y. 1982, U.S. Supreme Ct. 1983. Asst. corp. counsel City of Poughkeepsie, 1979-81; assoc. Law Office of Lou Lewis, Poughkeepsie, 1981-85; pvt. practice Poughkeepsie, 1985—; staff counsel City of Poughkeepsie Office of Property Devel., 1990—; gen. mgr. WCZX-Communicatons Corp. Contbg. author: Kaminstein Legislative History of the Copyright Law, 1979. Pres. Dutchess County (N.Y.) Vis. Bur., 1980-82; bd. dirs. Poughkeepsie Ballet Theater, 1982, Jewish Community Ctr., 1988; mem. assigned counsel program Dutchess County Family Ct., 1985—; trustee Greater Poughkeepsie Libr. Dist., 1991—. Mem. ABA, N.Y. State Bar Assn., Dutchess County Bar Assn. (chmn. pub. rels. 1991—), Mid-Hudson Women's Bar Assn., Poughkeepsie Area C. of C. (econ. devel. com. 1994—). Democrat. Jewish. Office: 97-99 Cannon St Poughkeepsie NY 12601-3140

MILLON, DELECTA GAY, nursing educator; b. Flint, Mich., Aug. 4, 1943; d. Rudolph Albert Spaleny and Odessa Mae (Bergeron) Kelley; divorced; children: Daniel Lawrence, Christopher Matthew. ADN, Flint Community Jr. Coll., 1963; BS in Human Svcs., U. Detroit, 198l; MA in Classroom Teaching, Mich. State U., 1986, cert. in vocat. edn., 1986; post-grad., Mary Grove Coll. RN, Mich.; lic. emergency med. tech.; cert. emergency med. technician instr.-coord., firefighter I. Nurse McLaren Gen. Hosp., Flint, 1963-64, Flint Osteo. Hosp., 1974-76; tchr. Mott Adult High Sch., 1971-75, Flint Comm. Schs., 1974—; occupational nurse GM, 1986—; evaluator emergency med. technician practical exam. State of Mich., nurse's assisting cert. exam; occupl. nursing, summers 1986—. Vol. tchr. Mundy Twp. Fire Dept., Swartz Creek, Mich., 1986—. Mem. Soc. Mich. Emergency Med. Technician Instrs. and Coords. (sec. 1980-87, outstanding contbn. award 1987). Roman Catholic. Office: Genesee Area Skill Ctr G-5081 Torrey Rd Flint MI 48507

MILLOY, MARYROSE, judge; b. Memphis, July 13, 1952. BA, Tex. A & I Univ., 1975; JD, Bates Coll. of Law, Univ. of Houston, 1977. Atty. Leal & Whitworth, 1978; asst. dist. atty. Harris County, Tex., 1979-85; atty. Cook, Davis & McFall, 1985-87; chief, Civil Rights Div. Office of U.S. Atty., 1987-89; ptnr. McFall & Sartwelle, 1989-92; magistrate judge U.S. Dist. Ct. (so. dist.) Tex., Houston, 1992—; assoc. editor Law Review, Univ. of Houston. Houston Bar Found. fellow. Mem. Houston Bar Assn., State Bar of Tex., Am. Bar Assn., Fed. Bar Assn. Office: Fed Bldg 515 Rusk Ave Rm 11144 Houston TX 77002*

MILLS, ANNA M., realtor; b. Toledo, Aug. 27, 1949; d. George William and Ellen Louise (Eckert) Pethe; children: Lori Smotherman Derr, Jerry Donald II; m. Randy Earl Mills, Aug. 4, 1984; 1 stepchild, Rachel. Grad., Electronic Computer Programming Inst. Lic. real estate agt., Ohio, Mich.; lic. notary, Ohio; lic. builder Mich., Ohio. Realtor Century 21 Kasten, Toledo, 1977—; owner Toledo properties; property mgr., Toledo, 1987—. Author: Landlord/Tenant Manual, 1994. Asst. leader Girl Scouts U.S., Toledo, 1979; leader Boy Scouts Am., Toledo, 1980; past pres. Elmhurst Sch. PTA, Toledo; adult advisor cheerleaders DeVeaux Jr. High Sch., Toledo, 1990-91, sec., 1989. Mem. Real Estate Investors Assn. (v.p. 1992-95, dir. bd. trustees Housing Directions 1993-96), Toledo Bd. Realtors, Monroe Bd. Realtors, Ohio Million Dollar Club, Million Dollar Club. Roman Catholic. Home: 4741 Elmhurst Rd Toledo OH 43613-3036 Office: Century 21 Kasten 1421 S Reynolds Rd Toledo OH 43615-7413

MILLS, CAROL MARGARET, business consultant, public relations consultant; b. Salt Lake City, Aug. 31, 1943; d. Samuel Lawrence and Beth (Neilson) M.; BS magna cum laude, U. Utah, 1965. With W.S. Hatch Co., Woods Cross, Utah, 1965-87, corp. sec., 1970-87, traffic mgr., 1969-87, dir. publicity, 1974-87; cons. various orgns., 1988—; dir. Hatch Service Corp., 1972-87, Nat. Tank Truck Carriers, Inc., Washington, 1977-88; bd. dirs. Intermountain Tariff Bur. Inc., 1978-88, chmn., 1981-82, 1986-87; bd. dirs. Mountainwest Venture Group. Fund raiser March of Dimes, Am. Cancer Soc., Am. Heart Assn.; active senatorial campaign, 1976, gubernatorial campaign, 1984, 88, congl. campaign, 1990, 92, 94, vice chair voting dist., 1988-90, chmn. 1990-92, chmn. party caucus legis. dist.; witness transp. com. Utah State Legislature, 1984, 85; apptd. by gov. to bd. trustees Utah Tech. Fin. Corp., 1986—, corp. sec., mem. exec. com., 1988—. Recipient service awards W. S. Hatch Co., 1971, 80; mem. Pioneer Theatre Guild, 1985—; V.I.P. capt. Easter Seal Telethon, 1989, 90, recipient Outstanding Vol. Svc. award Easter Seal Soc. Utah, 1989, 90. Mem. Nat. Tank Truck Carriers, Transp. Club Salt Lake City, Am. Trucking Assn. (public relations council), Utah Motor Transport Assn. (dir. 1982-88), Internat. Platform Assn., Beta Gamma Sigma, Phi Kappa Phi, Phi Chi Theta. Home and Office: 77 Edgecombe Dr Salt Lake City UT 84103-2219

MILLS, CELESTE LOUISE, hypnotherapist, professional magician; b. L.A., May 16, 1952; d. Emery John and Helen Louise (Bradbury) W.; m. Robert Richardson Feigel, Apr. 11, 1971 (div. 1973); m. Peter Alexander Mills, June 12, 1991. (div. 1992). BBA, Western State U., Doniphan, Mo., 1987; PhD in Religion, Universal Life Ch. Univ., 1987; grad., Hypnotism Tng. Inst., Glendale, Calif., 1990. Cert. hypnotherapist. Credit mgr. accounts receivable Gensler-Lee Diamonds, Santa Barbara, Calif., 1973-74, Terry Hinge and Hardware, Van Nuys, Calif., 1975-78; credit mgr., fin. analyst Peanut Butter Fashions, Chatsworth, Calif., 1978-82; personal mgr. Charter Mgmt. Co., Beverly Hills, Calif., 1982-83; co-owner, v.p. Noreen Jenney Communicates, Beverly Hills, 1983-85; corp. credit mgr., fin. analyst Cen. Diagnostic Lab., Tarzana, Calif., 1985-89; credit mgr., fin. analyst Metwest Clin. Lab., Inc., Tarzana, Calif., 1989-90; pvt. practice, 1990—; cons. Results Now, Inc., Tarzana, 1986-87. Prodr., host (TV) Brainstorm, 1993—. Mem. NAFE, Nat. Assn. Credit Mgmt., Credit Mgrs. Assn. So. Calif., Credit Ednl. Found., Nat. Humane Ednl. Found., Credit Mgrs. Assn. Trade Groups (bd. govs. 1988-89), Nat. Clin. Lab. Trade Group (chmn. 1988-89), Med. and Surg. Suppliers Trade Group (vice-chmn. 1988-89, chmn. 1989-90), Soc. Am. Magicians, Acad. Magical Arts, Internat. Brotherhood of Magicians, Assn. Advanced Ethical Hypnosis, Am. Coun. Hypnotist Examiners.

MILLS, DIANE EVANS, development officer; b. Cleve., Sept. 15, 1946; d. Dafydd William and Helen (Tobey) Evans; m. David Kimball Woodbury, June 20, 1970 (div. Sept. 1987); children: Douglas, Dana; m. Roger Marion Mills. Jr., Dec. 19, 1987; children: David, Andrew. BA in History with highest honors, U. Fla., 1993. With Up With People, Inc., Tucson, 1968, United Air Lines, Cleve., 1968-70; with mus. edn. dept. Old Sturbridge Village, Mass., 1970-72; with Sullivan Travel Svc., Worcester, Mass., 1972-74; pvt. practice cons., trainer, facilitator, 1977-85; dir. mgmt. assistance program United Way Ctrl. Mass., Worcester, 1985-88; mktg. dir. Franklin R & D Corp., Boston, 1988-90; dir. devel., coord. major gifts Samuel P. Harn Mus Art U. Fla., U. Fla. Found., Inc., Gainesville, 1990—, dir. mus. devel., 1993—. Bd. dirs., chair regional tng. coun. Assn. Jr. Leagues, Internat., Inc., N.Y.C.; pres. Jr. League Worcester (Mass.) Inc., Samaritan Counseling Ctr. North Ctrl. Fla.; v.p. Ctrl. Mass. Chpt., ARC, WICN Pub. Radio Sta., Worcester; bd. dirs., chair nominating com. Montachusett Girl Scout Coun., Vol. Ctr. Alachua County, Fla.; bd. dirs., chair pers. com. Performing Arts Ctr. Worcester, Foothills Theatre Co. Mem. Am. Mgmt. Assn., Coun. for Advancement and Support Edn., Art Mus. Devel. Assn., Altrusa Internat. Office: Univ Fla Found Box 14425 2012 W University Ave Gainesville FL 32603-1734

MILLS, DONNA, actress; b. Chgo., Dec. 11, 1945. Student, U. Ill. Began career with stage prodns. Chgo. area; appeared on Broadway in Don't Drink the Water; regular in TV series The Secret Storm, Dan August, The Good Life, 1971-72, Knots Landing, 1980-89, Love Is a Many Splendored Thing, 1967; appeared in various TV films including Haunts of the Very Rich, 1972, Rolling Man, 1972, Night of Terror, 1972, The Bait, 1973, Live Again, Die Again, 1974, Who is the Black Dahlia?, 1975, Beyond the Bermuda Triangle, 1975, Look What's Happened to Rosemary's Baby, 1976, Smash-Up on Interstate 5, 1976, Fire!, 1977, Curse of the Black Widow, 1977, The Hunted Lady, 1977, Superdome, 1978, Doctors' Private Lives, 1978, Waikiki, 1980, He's Not Your Son, 1984, Outback Round, 1988, The Lady Regrets, 1989, The World's Oldest Living Bridesmaid, 1990, Runaway Father, 1992, False Arrest, 1991, The President's Child, 1992; actress, co-prodr. In My Daughter's Name, 1992; mini series Hanging By a Thread, 1979, Bare Essence, 1982, Intimate Encounters, 1986; motion pictures (debut) The Incident, 1967, Play Misty for Me, 1971. Address: 822 S Robertson Blvd # 200 Los Angeles CA 90035*

MILLS, DOROTHY ALLEN, investor; b. New Brunswick, N.J., Dec. 14, 1920; d. James R. and Bertha Lovilla (Porter) Allen; m. George M. Mills, Apr. 21, 1945; children: Dianne, Adele, Dorothy L. BA, Douglass Coll., New Brunswick, N.J., 1943. Investment reviewer Cen. Hanover Bank, N.Y.C., 1943-44; asst. to dir. of admissions and sec. undergrad. yrs. Douglass Coll., New Brunswick, 1944-45; sec., regional dir. O.P.A., Ventura, Calif., 1945-46; corp. sec. George M. Mills Inc., Highland Park, N.J., 1946-75; pvt. investor N. Brunswick, N.J., 1975—. Sr. v.p. Children Am. Revolution, N.J., 1965; active alumni com. Douglass Coll., 1990—. Mem. AAUW, New Brunswick Hist. Soc., DAR,,, English Speaking Union, Rutgers Alumni Faculty Club, Princeton-Douglass Alumni Club, N. Brunswick Women's Club. Republican. Mem. Dutch Reformed Ch. Home: 1054 Hoover Dr N Brunswick NJ 08902-3244

MILLS, FRANCES JONES, state official; b. Gray, Ky.; d. William Harrison and Bertie (Steely) Jones. Grad., Cumberland Coll., Williamsburg, Ky. Public sch. tchr.; mem. Ky. Ho. of Reps., 1961-62, asst. to speaker, 1963-65; dir. women's activities Ky. Civil Def., 1965-72; clk. Ky. Ct. Appeals, 1972-76; treas. Commonwealth of Ky., Frankfort, 1976-80, sec. of state, 1979-83, treas., 1984-88, 1992—; bd. dirs. Ky. Lottery Corp.; vice chmn. Ky. Investments Commn.; mem. Ky. Personal Svc. Contract Rev. Commn., 1976—, Ky. Tchrs. Retirement Bd., 1976—; pres. Nat. Conf. Appellate Ct. Clks., 1975-76. Author: Civil Def. booklet What Would You Do?. Del. Dem. Nat. Conv., 1964, 68, 76, alt., 1972; bd. dirs. Ky. Lottery Corp., Ky. Mountain Laurel Festival; vice chmn. Ky. Investments Commn.; mem. devel. com. Cumberland Coll. Named Southeastern Ky. Outstanding Woman, 1973, Bus. and Profl. Women's Club Woman of Achievement, 1978, 88; named to Cumberland 100 Distinguished Grads. Mem. AMA Aux., Whitley County Med. Aux., Nat. Assn. State Treas. (v.p. so. region). Baptist. Clubs: Order Eastern Star, Bus. and Profl. Women's. Office: Treasury Dept New State Capitol Buil Frankfort KY 40601

MILLS, GLORIA ADAMS, environmental service company executive; b. Chgo., Mar. 1, 1940; d. Edward Charles and Olive Margaret (McCarty) Adams; m. Peter Mills, Dec. 29, 1962 (div. July 1986). BA, Rosary Coll., River Forest, Ill., 1962, MALS, 1970; MBA, U. Chgo., 1976. Lit. chemist UOP, Inc., Des Plaines, Ill., 1962-70, supr. patent libr., 1970-77, mktg. engr., 1977-81, mgr. project devel., 1981-83; v.p. mktg. Ogden Projects, Inc., Fairfield, N.J., 1983-87, sr. v.p. mktg., 1987-89, exec. v.p. mktg., 1989-94; exec. v.p. bus. devel., 1994—; mem. indsl. adv. bd. So. Ill. U. Coll. Engring. and Tech., Carbondale, 1985-90. Contbr. articles to profl. jours. Mem. ASME (solid waste processing div.), Am. Chem. Soc., Air and Waste Mgmt. Assn. Office: Ogden Projects Inc 40 Lane Rd Fairfield NJ 07007

MILLS, KATHERINE HELENE, psychologist; b. Detroit, Nov. 15, 1957. BA in Psychology with high honors, Grand Valley State Coll., 1977; PhD in Clin. Psychology, U. S.C., 1983. Lic. psychologist, Mich., Ohio. Rsch. assoc. community companionship program Multi Resource Corp., Southfield, Mich., 1977-78; counselor, supr. operation excellence Ind. U.-Purdue U., Ft. Wayne, 1979; clin. psychology extern Psychol. Svcs. Ctr. U. S.C., Columbia, 1978-82, asst. dir. human sexuality project dept. psychology, 1979-82; clin. psychology intern dept. psychology Lafayette Clinic, Detroit, 1982-83; clin. treatment coord. psychiat. svcs. adult mental health Mich. Osteo. Med. Ctr., Detroit, 1983-85, 86-88; clin. treatment unit supr. Wayne County Clinic Child Study Juvenile divsn. Probate Ct., Detroit, 1986; pvt. practice Birmingham, Mich., 1986-89; supr. psychology svcs. adult mental health Mich. Osteo. Med. Ctr., Detroit, 1988-89; sr. staff psychologist Henry Ford Ctr. for Human Sexuality, Farmington Hills, Mich., 1989—; adj. faculty dept. psychology Wayne State U., Detroit, 1987—; cons. Mich. Osteo. Med. Ctr., Detroit, 1987-89, Psychol. Resources, Inc., Bloomfield Hills, Mich., 1985-86; presenter Human Sexuality Workshop, S.C. Dept. Mental Health, Columbia, 1980, Detroit Psychiat. Inst., 1983, Wayne State U., 1985—, Mich. Osteo. Med. Ctr., Detroit, 1985—, others. Co-author: (with P. R. Kilmann) All About Sex Therapy, 1983; columnist Detroit Free Press, 1991—; contbr. articles to profl. jours. NIMH fellow, U. S.C., 1978-79. Mem. APA, Am. Assn. Sex Educators, Counselors and Therapists (media chair planning com. for dist. IV conf. 1985), Mich. Psychol. Assn. (pub. info. com. 1987), Mich. Interprofl. Assn. on Marriage, Divorce and the Family, Mich. Women Psychologists (charter), Soc. for Sci. Study of Sex. Office: Henry Ford Hosp 6773 W Maple Rd West Bloomfield MI 48322-3013

MILLS, KELLY ANN, marketing professional; b. Valhalla, N.Y., July 31, 1966; d. Benedict and Jane Marie (Belmont) A. Student, Skidmore Coll., Saratoga Springs, N.Y., 1984-86; BS in Polit. Sci., Ariz. State U., 1988. Analyst Concilliation Ct., Ariz., 1987-88; sr. mktg. analyst Walsh Am., Scottsdale, Ariz., 1989-90; client svc. cons., 1991-92; nat. mktg. dir. Nat. Utilization Mgmt. Corp., Phoenix, 1994—; editor jour. PDS Update, 1991. Active Community Action Team, Scottsdale, 1989—, Spl. Olympics Com., 1987—. Office: Nat Utilization Mktg Corp 7301 N 16th St Phoenix AZ 85240

MILLS, LOIS JEAN, legislative aide, former education educator; b. Chgo., Oct. 20, 1939; d. Martin J. and Annabelle M. (Hrabik) Rademacher; m.

Frederick V. Mills, Dec. 1, 1974; children: Todd, Susan, Randal, Merre, Mollie, Michael, Mark. BS in Edn., Ill. State U., Normal, 1962, MS in Edn., 1969. Lectr. elem. curriculum Ill. State U.; in-svc. advisor for elem., gifted, critical thinking and study skills, coop. learning Title I State Bd. Edn., Springfield, Ill.; elem. tchr., supr. Metcalf Lab. Sch. Ill. State U.; legis aide to Asst. Majority Leader Senator John Maitland, Jr., Ill. Gen. Assembly, 1991—. Contbr. articles to profl. jours. Pres. Leadership Ill.; vice chmn. McLean County Regional Planning Commn.; pres. governing bd. Lake Bloomington Assn.; mem. mgmt. com. McLean County 21st Century Com.; bd. govs. Ill. Lincoln Excellence in Pub. Svc. Series; county campaign chair Loleta Didrickson for Ill. State Comptr., 1994, other civic activities. Recipient Exemplary Tchr. awards Ill. State U. Student Elem. Edn. Bd., Women of Distinction award YWCA of McLean County. Mem. NAFE, Nat. Fedn. Rep. Women, Ill. Rep. Committeewoman's Roundtable, Ill. Fedn. Rep. Women, Ill. State U. Alumni Assn. (nat. pres.), McLean County Rep. Women's Club (pres.), McLean County C. of C. (bd. dirs. women's divsn.). Home: K-162 Lake Bloomington RR 2 Box 60A Hudson IL 61748-9414

MILLS, MARSHA LEE, secondary education educator; b. Independence, Kans., Dec. 28, 1948; d. Arthur Robert and Thelma Louise (Esch) M. BS in Edn., N.E. Mo. U., 1970, MA, 1974; real estate cert., Ind. Career Inst., Westport, Mo., 1991. Part time tchr. NMSU Mo. U., Kirksville, 1970-72; jr. high art educator Lincoln County R-3 Schs., Troy, Mo., 1972—; realtor assoc. Century 21 Coose, Troy, 1991—. Exhibitor: (ceramics) Mo. Coll. Art Students, 1969, Mo. Artists and Coll. Educators, 1970 (hon. mention), (multi media) N.E. Mo. U., 1974. Mus. friend St. Louis Art Mus., 1978—; badge cons. Boy Scouts Am., St. Louis Coun., 1978—; trustee Moscow Mills (Mo.) Meth. Ch., 1992—. Recipient I Dare You award Purina, 1966, Regents scholarship NMSU, Kirksville, 1966, Art Guild scholarship NMSU Art Guild, Kirksville, 1969. Mem. Mo. State Tchrs. Assn. (v.p., pres., dist. officer 1987-93), Greater St. Louis Tchrs. Assn. (2nd v.p. 1994, 95), Nat. Art Edn. Assn. (coun. 1978-80), St. Charles Bd. Realtors, Alpha Delta Kappa (Beta Chi chpt. treas., sec., v.p. 1987-93, pres. 1994—), Delta Kappa Gamma. Democrat. Home: 444 Highway MM Moscow Mills MO 63362 Office: Century 21 Coose PO Box 292 Troy MO 63379

MILLS, MIRIAM KOSINER, educator; b. Leipzig, Germany, May 22, 1938; d. Robert and Freida (Leipziger) Kosiner. BA in Philosophy, CUNY, 1964; PA, NYU, 1969, PhD in Pub. Adminstrn., 1978. Asst. prof. N.J. Inst. Tech. Sch. Indsl. Mgmt., Newark, 1975-83, assoc. prof., 1983-88, prof., 1988—; Disting. prof. N.J. Inst. Tech., Newark, 1992; grad. faculty Rutgers U., Newark, 1986—; vis. scholar U. Ill., Urbana, 1984-85; dir. manpower and labor rels. Jersey Med. Ctr., Jersey City, 1972-75; dir. pers. Jewish Home and Hosp. for Aged, N.Y.C., 1965-72; cons. in field; founder Miriam K. Mills Rsch. Ctr. for Super-Optimizing Analysis and Developing Nations, 1992. Author, co-author: Multi-Criteria Methods for Alternative Dispute Resolution: With Microcomputer Software Applications, 1990, The Penny Diary: Countering Illness, 1991, Developing Nations and Super-Optimum Policy Analysis, 1992, Professional Developments in Policy Studies, 1992; editor, co-editor: Conflict Resolution and Public Policy, 1990, Alternative Dispute Resolution in the Public Sector, 1991, Systematic Analysis in Dispute Resolution, 1991, Health Insurance and Public Policy: Risk, Allocation and Equity, 1992, Publica Administration in China, 1993, Public Policy in China, 1993; sponsor Encyclopedia of Policy Studies, 1993, Treatise of Policy Studies and Developing Nations, multi-vol. 1994, Super-Optimizing Methods and Processes, 1994; contbr. articles to jours. Bd. dirs. Am. Cancer Soc., Ill., 1990; mem. exec. bd. Upjohn Home Health Svcs., Newark, 1988-91; bd. govs. Palisades (N.J.) Gen. Hosp., 1983-85; mem. exec. com. Coun. State Govts. Recipient Thomas R. Dye award for policy studies svc., 1992. Mem. Am. Soc. Pub. Adminstrn., Am. Hosp. Assn., Internat. Polit. Sci. Assn., Indsl. Rels. Rsch. Assn., Soc. Profls. in Dispute Resolution, Evaluation Soc. & Evaluation Network, Policy Studies Orgn. (coun. mem. 1991). Democrat. Jewish. Home: 711 Ashton Ln S Champaign IL 61820-7304 Office: NJ Inst Tech Martin Luther King Dr Newark NJ 07102

MILLS, NANCY LOU, industrial engineering educator; b. Burlington, Iowa, Apr. 13, 1951; d. Ivan Glen and Jeanne (Weber) M.; m. David M. Perkins. BS in Engring., Ariz. State U., 1972, MS in Engring., 1975; MBA, Oreg. State U., 1987, PhD in Indsl. Engring., 1988. Facilities planner Gen. Dynamics, San Diego, 1975-76; consulting officer Seattle-First Nat. Bank, 1977-78; sys. engr. Samaritan Health Svcs., Phoenix, 1979-80; ops. analyst Am. Express, Phoenix, 1980-81; ops. supr. Salt River Project, Phoenix, 1981-84; grad. asst. Oreg. State U., Corvallis, 1985-86, instr., 1986-88; asst. prof. U. So. Colo., Pueblo, 1988-93, acting chair, 1992-93, assoc. prof., 1993—, pres. faculty senate, 1991; project mgr. Pueblo Econ. Devel. Corp., 1989-95; prin. investigator NSF, Washington, 1990-92, proposal reviewer NSF, 1991, 95; cons. City of Pueblo, State of Colo., 1991-93; presenter numerous confs. and workshops, 1986—. Author: (with others) Advanced Manufacturing, 1992; contbr. articles to profl. jours. Mem. task force So. Colo. Bus. and Tech. Ctr., Pueblo, 1993, mem. adv. bd., 1994—. Mem. Am. Soc. for Engring. Edn. (treas. 1992-93, editor 1991-92), Inst. Indsl. Engrs. (divsn. dir. 1992-93), Soc. Women Engrs., Sigma Xi (pres. elect 1992-93). Office: U So Colo 2200 Bonforte Blvd Pueblo CO 81001

MILLS, NANCY STEWART, chemistry educator; b. Osceola, Nebr., Mar. 31, 1950; d. Robert Lees and Margaret Eva (Stewart) M.; m. Mark Alan Hurd, Aug. 20, 1977; children: Caroline Margaret Mills Hurd, William Clark Mills Hurd. BA, Grinnell Coll., 1972; PhD, U. Ariz., 1976. Asst. prof. Carleton Coll., Northfield, Minn., 1977-79; asst. prof. Trinity U., San Antonio, 1979-83, assoc. prof., 1983-89, prof., chmn. chemistry dept., 1979—; mem. dept. rev. team Bowdoin Coll., Brunswick, Maine, 1986, Macalester Coll., St. Paul, 1989, Albion Coll., 1991; councilor Coun. on Undergrad. Rsch., 1991—. Contbr. articles to profl. jours. Grantee NSF, Welch Found., Petroleum Rsch. Fund, Rsch. Corp., 1977—; Camille and Henry Dreyfus Found. scholar, 1994; recipient Outstanding Teaching and Campus Leadership award Sears Roebuck Found., 1990, Z.T. Scott Fellowship for outstanding teaching Trinity U., 1992. Mem. AAUP, Sigma Xi. Home: 137 Alta Ave San Antonio TX 78209-4508 Office: Trinity U 715 Stadium Dr San Antonio TX 78212-7200

MILLS, ROBIN KATE, law librarian; b. Chgo., Jan. 10, 1947; d. Dumont Cromwell and Virginia Anne (Nordeng) M.; A.B., Ind. U., 1969, M.L.S., 1970; J.D., U. S.C., 1976. Circulation/reference librarian Ind. U. Sch. Law, Bloomington, 1970-73; asst. law librarian U. S.C. Sch. Law, Columbia, 1973-76, asst. prof. law and law librarian, 1976-81, asso. prof. law and law librarian, 1981-84; assoc. prof. law, law librarian, 1984-87; prof. law, law libr. Emory U. Sch. Law, Atlanta, 1987—. Mem. Am. Assn. Law Libraries (chpt. pres. 1980-82), Am. Bar Assn., S.C. Bar Assn. Office: Emory U Law Libr Gambrell Hall Atlanta GA 30322

MILLS, ROSALIE JANE GREGORY, writer; b. Ottumwa, Iowa, Aug. 24, 1947; d. Robert Todd and Margaret Kathryn (Bentzinger) Gregory; m. Larry Eugene Mills, Mar. 30, 1973 (div.); 1 child, Jason Novell. BS, U. Tex., Austin, 1970; MS Edn., So. Ill. U., 1974; student, Fuller Theol. Sem., Pasadena, 1985-87. Ordained elder, A.M.E. Zion Ch., 1986. Adminstrv. sec. Coldwell Banker, L.A., 1978-84; office mgr. Lincoln Property Co., L.A., 1984-89, Glendale, Calif., 1989—; assoc. pastor 1st A.M.E. Zion Ch., Pasadena, Calif., 1983-90; also dir. Christian edn. 1st A.M.E. Zion Ch.; sec. L.A. dist. Ministerial Alliance, A.M.E. Zion Ch., 1986-89, pres. 1989-90. Author poetry and play. Active children's, teen's and women's ministries Glendale Christian Fellowship, 1991—; leader Moms in Touch Group, Glendale; mem. Purple Cir. Hoover H.S., Glendale; leader Glendale Christian Scribes Writer's Group. Democrat. Home: 628 Alexander St Apt 6 Glendale CA 91203-1679 Office: Lincoln Property Co 800 N Brand Blvd Ste 860 Glendale CA 91203-1244

MILLSAP, BARBARA ANN, clinical social worker; b. Detroit, June 15, 1940; d. John Edward and Irene Julia (Turowski) Wojtylo; m. Claude Millsap, Dec. 14, 1974. BS in Social Work, Mich. State U., 1963; MSW, Wayne State U., 1966. Cert. social worker. Clinician Northeast Guidance Ctr., Detroit, 1966-73, Cabin Fever Clinic, Anchorage, 1975-76; clinician Anchorage Community Mental Health Ctr., 1976-79, supr. adult svcs., 1979-82; social worker Bloomfield (Mich.) Hills Sch. Dist., 1986—. Mem. NASW, Soc. Clin. Social Workers, Mich. Sch. Social Workers Assn. Home: 3284 Schoolhouse Dr Waterford MI 48329-4331 Office: Bloomfield Hills Sch Dist 4200 Andover Rd Bloomfield Hills MI 48302-2000

MILLSAPS, ELLEN MCNUTT, English language educator; b. Sheffield, Ala., Feb. 10, 1947; d. Ershell Jerome and Annie Inez (Quillen) McNutt; m. Douglas Edward Millsaps, Nov. 27, 1971; 1 child, Stephen Edward. BA, Miss. Coll., 1969; MA, U. Tenn., 1972, PhD, 1976. Teaching asst. U. Tenn., Knoxville, 1970-71, 75-76; assoc. prof. English, dept. head Walters State Community Coll., Morristown, Tenn., 1971-79; prof. English, dir. writing across curriculum Carson-Newman Coll., Jefferson City, Tenn., 1979—; cons. on writing Omicron Nu, 1989, Tenn. Network Foxfire Tchrs., 1992. Contbr. essays to profl. jours. NDEA fellow, 1969-72; John C. Hodges fellow U. Tenn., 1975; Appalachian Coll. Found. rsch. grantee, 1993. Mem. MLA, South Atlantic MLA, Nat. Coun. Tchrs. English, Conf. on Coll. Composition and Comm., Soc. for Study So. Lit., Assn. Profl. Writing Cons., Alpha Chi (region v.p. 1992-94, region pres. 1994-96), Sigma Tau Delta, Kappa Delta Pi, Delta Omicron, Alpha Lambda Delta. Baptist. Home: 7604 Sagefield Dr Knoxville TN 37920-9223 Office: Carson-Newman Coll PO Box 71957 Jefferson City TN 37760-7001

MILLS-GOLDSTEIN, BETH HELEN, psychotherapist; b. Phoenix, Feb. 14, 1952; d. William and Marietta (Dawdy) Rumper; 1 child, Sara Elizabeth. BS, Barry U., 1986, MS, 1989. Lic. clin. social worker, Fla. Supr. intake South County Mental Health Ctr., Delray Beach, Fla., 1980-89; psychotherapist Coral Ridge Hosp., Ft. Lauderdale, Fla., 1990-92, Ctr. for Family Svc., Boca Raton, Fla., 1992—; pvt. practice cons., Boca Raton, 1992. Editor: (newspaper) The Voice, 1994. Fellow NOW; mem. NASW (state bd. mem.). Democrat. Jewish. Office: Ctr for Family Svcs 5499 N Federal Hwy Boca Raton FL 33487-4993

MILMAN, DORIS HOPE, pediatrics educator, psychiatrist; b. N.Y.C., Nov. 17, 1917; d. Barnet S. and Rose (Smoleroff) Milman; m. Nathan Kreeger, June 15, 1941; 1 child, Elizabeth Kreeger Goldman. BA, Barnard Coll., 1934; MD, NYU, 1942. Intern Jewish Hosp., Bklyn., 1942-43, resident, 1944-46, fellow in pediatrics, 1946-47; postgrad. extern in psychiatry Bellevue Hosp., N.Y.C., 1947-49; pediatric psychiatry attending Jewish Hosp., Bklyn., 1950-56; asst. prof. pediatrics Health Sci. Ctr. at Bklyn. SUNY, 1956-67, assoc. prof. pediatrics, 1967-73, prof. pediatrics, 1973-93, prof. emeritus, 1993—, acting chmn. dept. pediatrics, 1973-75, 82; pvt. practice child and adolescent psychiatry, Bklyn., 1950-90; vis. prof. Ben Gurion U. of the Negev, Beersheva, Israel, 1977. Mem. adv. bd. N.Y. Assn. for the Learning Disabled, N.Y.C., 1975-80. Recipient Disting. Alumna award Barnard Coll., 1986, Solomon R. Berson Achievement award NYU Sch. Medicine, 1991; Grace Potter Rice fellow Barnard Coll., 1938-39. Fellow Am. Acad. Pediatrics (emeritus), Am. Psychiat. Assn. (life); mem. Am. Orthopsychiat. Assn. (life), Am. Pediatric Soc. (emeritus), N.Y. Pediatric Soc. (emeritus), AAAS. Home: 126 Westminster Rd Brooklyn NY 11218-3444 Office: Health Sci Ctr at Bklyn SUNY Box 49 450 Lenox Rd Brooklyn NY 11203-2020

MILNAR, ROSA-FAY, international human resources management consultant; b. New Orleans, July 16, 1947; d. Grover Cleveland and Agnes (Ehrhardt) Walk; m. Lawrence Milnar, Aug. 12, 1971 (div. Sept. 1975); 1 child, Christopher Ray. BA in English, U. New Orleans, 1969, MA in English, 1971; MS in Human Resource Mgmt., Nova U., 1981. English lang. instr. Nicholls State U., Thibodaux, La., 1971-72; real estate mgr. Bond, Inc., New Orleans, 1972-74; mgr. tng. Ochsner Hosp., New Orleans, 1978-79; tng. mgr. GM, George Engine Co., New Orleans, 1979-81; cons. Orgnl. Mgmt. Assn., New Orleans, 1981-82; supr. Coopers & Lybrand, Houston, 1982-86; prin. candidate Mercer-Meidinger, Houston, 1986; assoc. King, Chapman & Broussard, Inc., Houston, 1986-89; ptnr. Ramsey-Sellers Assocs., Inc., Houston, 1989-91; pres. Milnar & Assocs., Inc., 1991—; chmn. learning resources div. Delgado Coll., New Orleans, 1974-76, mem. adj. faculty, 1974-81; mem. adj. faculty in mgmt. Ind. U., 1978-81; author, presenter seminars in field, 1976—. Contbr. articles on mgmt. to profl. jours., horse tng. to Horse Sheet Mag. Leader Girl Scouts U.S., New Orleans, 1971-73, Boy Scouts Am., New Orleans, Houston, 1981-85; mem. Pres. Council Basic Edn., Washington, 1977-81. Recipient Cert. Appreciation Mayor of Houston, 1985, Mayor of Austin, 1985; named Outstanding Leader Boy Scouts Am., 1983-85. Mem. ASTD (nat. com. 1979-80, bd. dirs. New Orleans 1979-81, Houston 1982-84, Outstanding Trainer award 1980), NAFE, Am. Bus. Women's Assn., U.S. Dressage Found., Houston Dressage Soc. (Houston Livestock Show and Rodeo officer, speakers com. 1986, Big Mouth award 1986-90, Houston Carriage Assn., Nat. Assn. Women Bus. Owners (Internat. Woman of Yr. award 1994). Democrat. Roman Catholic. Club: Appaloosa Horse. Home and Office: 9038 Colleen St Houston TX 77080

MILOY, LEATHA FAYE, university official; b. Marlin, Tex., Mar. 12, 1936; d. J. D. and Leola Hazel (Rhudy) Hill; m. John Miloy, June 20, 1960; children: Tyler Hill, David Reed, Nancy Lee. BA, Sam Houston State U., 1957; MS, Tex. A&M U., 1967, PhD, 1978. Dir. pub. affairs Gulf Univs. Rsch. Corp., College Station, Tex., 1966-69; asst. dir. Ctr. for Marine Resources Tex. A&M U., College Station, 1974-76, dir. edn. svcs., 1974-78; dir. info. and spl. svcs. Tex. Woman's U., Denton, 1978-79; asst. v.p. univ. advancement S.W. Tex. State U., San Marcos, 1979-83, asst. to pres., 1983-84, v.p. student and instl. rels., 1984-90, v.p. univ. advancement, 1990-93, dir. capital campaign, 1993—; vis. lectr. humanities and sea U. Va., 1972-73; cons. Office Tech. Assessment, Washington, 1976-86, Tex. A&M U., Galveston, 1979—, Bemidji State U., Glassboro State Coll., 1984; mem. Task Force on Edn. and Pub. Interest, 1987-88. Editor: The Ocean From Space, 1969; author, editor Sea Grant 70's, 1970-79 (Sea Grant award 1973-74); contbr. articles to profl. jours. Ad hoc mem. Marine Resources Coun. Tex., Austin, 1971-72, Tex. Energy Adv. Coun., 19174-75; chmn. United Way, Bryan, Tex., 1976; com. mem. various local elections, 1974-78. NSF grantee, 1970-78; recipient Marine Resources Info. award NSF, 1969-71, Tex. Energy Info. award Gov.'s Office, 1974-75, Tex. Water Info. award Dept. Interior, 1977-79. Mem. Nat. Soc. Fundraising Execs., Coun. for the Advancement and Support Edn. (bd. dirs. 1979-81), Coun. Student Svcs. (v.p. Tex. 1988-90). Home: PO Box 712 Buchanan Dam TX 78609-0712 Office: SW Tex State U 601 University Dr San Marcos TX 78666

MILROD, MARION BETH, advertising professional; b. Bklyn., July 19, 1950; d. Murray and Helen (Kirsner) M.; 1 child, David Adam Tyler. BA in English, Theater and Edn., SUNY, Buffalo, 1972; MBA, Pace U., 1982. Acctg. clk., mktg. rep. Rochester (N.Y.) Savs. Bank, 1973-76; acct. exec. Giltspur Exhibits, Rochester, 1976-78, L.M. Berry Co., Rochester, N.Y., 1978-79; assoc. product mgr. Am. Tobacco Co., N.Y.C. and Stamford, Conn., 1982-89; mgr. promotions and advt. svcs. Heinz U.S.A., Pitts., 1990—; judge Pinnacle awards Promo Mag., N.Y.C., 1993-94. Mem. Promotion and Mktg. Assn. Am. Office: Heinz USA 1062 Progress St Pittsburgh PA 15212

MILTON, PATRICIA ANN, journalist; b. Rockville Centre, N.Y., Mar. 14, 1948; d. Arthur G. and Marie F. (Landis) Milton; B.A. in History/Polit. Sci., C.W. Post Coll., 1970; M.Pub. Adminstrn., L.I. U., 1973; postgrad. St. John's U., 1971, Sch. of Law 1992—; m. Charles Roy Steinfort, June 28, 1980. Reporter gen. news The AP, N.Y.C., 1971-76, corres., L.I. Bur. chief, 1976—; free-lance reporter CBS Radio News, 1987-88. Democratic leader Village of Westbury, L.I., 1971-73. Recipient Journalism award Am. Acad. Physicians, Reporter of the Yr. award N.Y. Mng. Editors Assn.; James Gordon Bennett scholar, 1967-70; named Reporter of Yr. N.Y. Acad. Physicians, 1993. Mem. Women in Communications, Sigma Delta Chi. Roman Catholic. Clubs: Deadline, Overseas Press., Nat. Press. Author: For Mercy Sake (booklet), 1966; contbr. articles to profl. jours. Home: Carper's Farm Vienna VA 22180 Office: State Supreme Ct Mineola NY 11501

MILZ, PENNY MARIE, learning disabilities educator, consultant; b. Dubuque, Iowa, Apr. 6, 1963; d. Thomas James and Elizabeth Ann (Schadle) Delaney. BA in Spl. Edn. and Elem. Edn. magna cum laude, Loras Coll., 1986; MA in Varying Exceptionalities, U. South Fla., 1994. Cert. learning disabilities tchr., spl. edn., N.J. Spl. edn. tchr. Brevard County Schs., Melbourne, Fla., 1986-89, Hernando County Schs., Brooksville, Fla., 1989-94; learning disabilities tchr., cons. Warren Hills Regional Sch. Dist., Clinton, N.J., 1994—; cons., presenter, instr. Perfect Harmony, Inc., Fla. Dept. Edn., Fla. State U., Hernando County Schs., 1989—, part-time homebound instr., 1992-93; developer programs, presenter state and local workshops, 1993. Author: (arts and crafts program) Perfect Harmony, 1992; contbr. Reaching Out Manual, AAHPERD nat. and state jour.; contbr. brochures. Presenter tng. sessions for Perfect Harmony to numerous civic, parks and sch. orgns., 1990—; bd. dirs. Perfect Harmony Agy. of United Way of Hernando County, 1991-92; radio interviews on Perfect Harmony, 1992. Recipient Creative Concept award Fla. Assn. Health, Phys. Edn., Recreation and Dance, 1992, Best Practice award Fla. Vocat. Assn., Fla. Dept. Edn., 1993, 1st pl. in econs. Hernando County C. of C./Ptnrs. in Edn., 1991. Mem. Coun. for Exceptional Children. Office: Cen High Sch 14075 Ken Austin Pkwy Brooksville FL 34613

MIMS, FRANCES LARKIN FLYNN, English language educator; b. Union, S.C., Sept. 24, 1921; d. Philip Dunne and Edith Kennedy (Smith) Flynn; m. Paul S. Mims Jr., Aug. 25, 1948; children: P. Larkin, P. Linda, Paul S. III. BA, Converse Coll., 1942; MA, Wofford Coll., 1947; PhD, U. S.C., 1972. Lang. tchr. Aiken (S.C.) High Sch., 1943-47; supervisory tchr. dept. edn. U. S.C., Columbia, 1947-50; chmn. dept. sociology Anderson (S.C.) Coll., 1956-67; asst. prof. Erskine Coll., Due West, S.C., 1967-72; freelance writer, researcher Anderson, 1972-75; mem. faculty, dir. writers' confs. Anderson Coll., 1976-84, prof., chmn. dept. English, 1985-92. Author: Buy Hyacinths (poetry), 1971, Jeannie (novel), 1972; contbr. essays, articles to lit. and gen. interest mags. Pres. Anderson County Arts Coun., 1975, Anderson County Writers' Guild, 1976. Mem. S.C. Acad. Authors (life, bd. govs.). Episcopalian. Home and Office: 1212 Rutledge Way Anderson SC 29621-4057

MIMS, PATRICIA S., federal agency administrator; b. Lexington, S.C., May 10, 1959; d. Thomas Calvin and Gladys Rene (Hartley) M. BSBA, S.C. State Coll., 1981. Budget analyst FBI, Washington, 1984—. Active Big Sisters/Little Sisters, Washington, 1986—. African Methodist Episcopal. Home: 9105 Sherwood Forest Way Upper Marlboro MD 20772 Office: FBI 10th and Penn Ave NW Washington DC 20535

MINARD, B. GAIL, speech and language pathologist; b. Grand Rapids, Mich., July 22, 1952; d. Arthur Eduoard and Sylvia Jean (Dorobant) Morris; m. Bradley Alan Minard, July 26, 1980; children: Jacquelynn Michelle, Nicole Ann. BS in Edn., U. Mo., 1974, MA in Speech Pathology, Audiology, 1975, cert. in speech, lang. pathology, 1976. Tchr., supr. Community Nursery Sch., Columbia, Mo., 1974-75; speech-lang. pathologist Columbia Pub. Schs., 1975-78, Cen. Fla. Speech and Hearing Ctr., Lakeland, 1978-79, Spl. Sch. Dist. St. Louis County, St. Louis, 1979-81; specialist in autism and multi-handicapped Columbus (Ohio) Pub. Schs., 1981—; supr. student tchr., U. Mo., Ohio U.; task force rep. Spl. Sch. Dist., St. Louis, 1979-81; diagnostician Speech and Lang. Diagnostic Clinic, Columbus, 1981—. Contbr. to profl. publs. Recipient letter of recognition Columbus Pub. Schs., 1991. Mem. Am. Speech, Lang. and Hearing Assn. (cert. clin. competence), Ohio Speech, Lang. and Hearing Assn., Inst. Lang. and Phonology (cert. trainer), Libr. Speech Pathology Assn. Home: 248 Blue Jay Dr Columbus OH 43235-4606 Office: Columbus Pub Schs Speech Lang Dept 2571 Neil Ave Columbus OH 43202-2522

MINARIK, ELSE HOLMELUND (BIGART MINARIK), author; b. Aarhus, Denmark, Sept. 13, 1920; d. Kaj Marius and Helga Holmelund; m. Walter Minarik, July 14, 1940 (dec.); 1 child, Brooke Ellen; m. Homer Bigart, Oct. 3, 1970 (dec.). BA, Queens Coll., 1942. Tchr. 1st grade, art Commack (N.Y.) Pub. Schs., 1950-54. Author children's books: Little Bear, 1957, Father Bear Comes Home, 1959, Little Bear's Friend, 1960, Little Bear's Visit, 1961, No Fighting, No Biting, 1958, Cat and Dog, 1960, The Winds That Come From Far Away, 1960, The Little Giant Girl and the Elf Boy, 1963, A Kiss for Little Bear, 1968, What If, 1987, Percy and the Five Houses, 1988, It's Spring, 1989, The Little Girl and the Dragon, 1991, Am I Beautiful, 1992. Mem. PEN Club. Home: Rural Delivery Barrington NH 03825

MINCH, ELIZABETH WAUGH, nursing administrator; b. Kokomo, Ind., Mar. 10, 1949; d. Lester L. and Emily P. (Pulling) Waugh; m. Thomas H. Minch, May 9, 1970 (div. Sept. 1984); children: Jeffrey M., Lauren Margaret. Diploma, Mt. Carmel Coll. Nursing, 1970. Staff nurse Mt. Carmel Med. Ctr., Columbus, Ohio, 1970-72; surg. nurse Ctrl. Ohio Surg. Assocs., Columbus, 1972-76; unit supr. Ohio State U. Hosp., Columbus, 1978-81; state supr. Tex. Med. Found., Austin, 1981-84; adminstrv. dir. of utilization mgmt. Nan Travis Hosp., Jacksonville, Tex., 1984-86; dir. provider rels. Health Strategies, Inc., Dallas, 1986-88; regional mgr. Focus Healthcare, Brentwood, Tenn., 1988-92; nat. dir. CorVel Corp., Arlington, Tex., 1992—; RN rep. Tex. Workers' Compensation Commn., Austin, 1992—. Mem. NAFE, Am. Assn. Preferred Provider Orgns., Am. Guild Patient Account Mgrs. Methodist.

MINDES, GAYLE DEAN, education educator; b. Kansas City, Mo., Feb. 11, 1942; d. Elton Burnett and Juanita Maxine (Mangold) Taylor; BS, U. Kans., 1964; MS, U. Wis., 1965; EdD, Loyola U., Chgo., 1979; m. Marvin William Mindes, June 20, 1969 (dec.); 1 son, Jonathan Seth. Tchr. pub. schs., Newburgh, N.Y., 1965-67; spl. educator Ill. Dept. Mental Health, Chgo., 1967-69; spl. edn. supr. Evanston (Ill.) Dist. 65 Schs., 1969-74; lectr. Northeastern Ill. U., Chgo., 1974, Loyola U., Chgo., 1974-76, Coll. St. Francis, Joliet, Ill., 1976-79, North Park Coll., Chgo., 1978; cons. Chgo. Head Start, 1978-79; asst. prof. edn. Oklahoma City U., 1979-80; vis. asst. prof., rsch. assoc. Roosevelt U. Coll. Edn., Chgo., 1983-87, prof., dir. R&D, dir. tchr. edn., dir. early childhood, dir. grad. edn. ctr., Roosevelt U. Coll., Albert A. Robin campus, 1993; prof. sch. edn. De Paul U., 1993—; chair Roosevelt U. Senate, 1986-89; co-chair ILAEYC Bldg. Bridges; cons. Ill. Resource Ctr., Arts Coun. Oklahoma City, Indian Affairs Commn., 1979-80, Lincolnwood (Ill.) Pub. Schs., Chgo. Pub. Schs., Atwood Sch. Dist, Chgo. Assn. Reatrded Citizens, Nat. Assn. Tech. Tng. Schs., Ill. State Bd. Edn., Itasca Pub. Schs., Decatur Pub. Schs., Robin Scholarship Found., 1982—, Rasho Media, Ill. Facilities Fund for Childcare; alt. rep. faculty coun. De Paul U., mem. faculty adv. com. to univ. plan. and info. tech.; mem. tng. sub-com. adv. Ill. Dept. Children & Family Svcs., 1993—; mentor to partnerships project tng. early intervention svcs. U. Ill., Champaign; panelist Ill. Initiative for Articulation between Ill. Bd. Higher Edn. and Ill. Cmty. Coll. Bd., Early Childhood Assessment System. Assoc. editor Ill. Sch. R & D; editor Ill. Div. Early Childhood Edn. Adv. Com. to Ill. Bd. Edn., Depaul U. Sch. Edn. Newsletter. Co-author: Planning a Theme Based Curriculum for 4's or 5's, 1993; contbr. articles to profl. jours. Bd. dirs. North Side Family Day Care, 1981; northside affiliates Mus. Contemporary Art, 1991—; trustee Roosevelt U., 1987-93; mem. edn. adv. com. Okla. Dept. Edn., 1979-80; mem. adv. bd. bilingual early childhood program Oakton Community Coll.; mem. adv. bd. early childhood tech. assistance project Chgo. Pub. Schs., Lake View Mental Health, 1986-90; mem. planning com. Lake View Citizens Coun. Day Care Ctr., 1978-79, local planning coun. Ill. Dept. Child and Family Svcs., childcare block grant tng. sub. com.; co-chair Ill. Assn. for Edn. Young Children Building Bridges Project; chmn. teen com. Florence G. Heller JCC, membership com.; mem. adv. bd. Harold Washington Coll. Child Devel., regional tech. assistance grant LICA; mem. parents com. Francis W. Parker Sch. Cerebral Palsy Assn. scholar, 1965; U. Wis. fellow in mental retardation, 1964-65; U. Kans. scholar, 1960. Fellow Am. Orthopsychiat. Assn.; mem. AAUP, ASCD, AAUW, Assn. Children with Learning Disabilities, Nat. Assn. for Edn. Young Children (tchr. edn. bd. 1990—), Am. Ednl. Rsch. Assn., Coun. for Exceptional Children, Ill. Coun. for Exceptional Children (mem. multicultural affairs com. divsn. early childhood), Ill. Assn. for Edn. Young Children, Coun. for Adminstrs. Spl. Edn., Coun. on Children with Behavioral Disorders, Soc. for Rsch. in Child Devel., Foun. for Excellence in Teaching (selection com. Golden Apple 1989-94), Alpha Sigma Nu, Phi Delta Kappa, Pi Lambda Theta. Office: DePaul Univ Sch Of Edn Chicago IL 60614

MINDLIN, PAULA ROSALIE, educator; b. N.Y.C., Nov. 27, 1944; d. Simon S. and Sylvia (Naroff) Bernstein; m. Alfred Carl Mindlin, Aug. 14, 1965; 1 child, Spencer Douglas. BA in Edn., Bklyn. Coll., 1965; MS in Edn., Queens Coll., 1970, Specialist Sch. Adminstrn, 1973. Tchr. Dist. 16 Pub. Sch., Bklyn., 1965-68; reading tchr. Dist. 29 Pub. Sch. and Dist. 16, Bklyn., 1968-85; instr. insvc. courses Comty. Sch. Dist. 29, Queens Village, N.Y., 1984-93; reading coord. Reading/Comms. Arts Program Comty. Sch. Dist. 29, Queens, N.Y., 1985—; dir. reading Cmty. Sch. Dist. 29, Queens Village, N.Y., 1990-93, reading coord., 1993—; adj. lectr. York Coll., 1989, program dir. Recipient Chpt. I Program Nat. Recognition award U.S. Sec. Edn., 1993, Queensboro Educator of Yr. award, 1994. Mem. ASCD, Internat. Reading Assn., Nassau Reading Coun., Queensboro Reading Coun. (pres. 1994-96), Phi Delta Kappa. Office: Dist 29 Queens 1 Cross Island Plz Rosedale NY 11422

MINEAR, ALANA WILFONG, college administrator; b. Elkins, W.Va., Aug. 25, 1947; d. Dewey Lyle and Gail Ruth (Ours) Wilfong; m. Larry Wayne Minear, May 26, 1973 (dec. Oct. 1993); 1 child, Stacey Elizabeth. BA, Fairmont (W.Va.) State Coll., 1970; postgrad., Davis & Elkins Coll., W.Va., W.Va. U. Lic. social worker, W.Va. Alcoholism and drug abuse counselor Appalachian Mental Health Ctr., Elkins, W.Va., 1970-73; teller Union Fed. Savs. & Loan, Elkins, W.Va., 1973-75; salesperson Fletcher Real Estate, Elkins, W.Va., 1975-79; adminstr., dir. alumni rels. Davis & Elkins Coll., Elkins, 1986—; visual-artist-in-residence Tucker County Visual Artist Program. Pres. Tucker County Planning Commn., Parsons, W.Va., 1982-86; v.p. St. George Med. Clinic Bd., St. George, 1982-86; mem. Randolph County Bi-Centennial Com., Elkins, 1989-90; mem. Elkins state adv. coun. Pub. Transp., Charleston, W.Va., 1984-86; bd. dirs. Am. Heart Assn., 1991—; mem. Woman's Club; campaign chmn. United Way; bd. dirs. Elkins Main St., Adult Christian Edn. Named Pub. Employee of the Yr., C. of C. Tucker County, 1985, Outstanding Leader, Adminstrn. on Aging, 1985. Mem. Nat. Soc. Fund Raising Execs., Coun. for Advancement and Support of Edn., Randolph County C. of C. Republican. Baptist. Home: 115 Westview Dr Elkins WV 26241-3246 Office: Davis & Elkins Coll 100 Campus Dr Elkins WV 26241-3996

MINEHAN, CATHY ELIZABETH, banker; b. Jersey City, Feb. 15, 1947; d. Harry Manford Jones and Rita Jane (Decora) Jones Leary; m. Gerald Paul Minehan, July 18, 1970; children: Melissa Jane, Brian Patrick. BA, U. Rochester, 1968; MBA, NYU, 1977. Various positions to sr. v.p. Fed. Reserve Bank N.Y., N.Y.C., 1968-91; chief operating officer Fed. Reserve Bank Boston, 1991-94, pres., 1994—; cons. IMF, Washington, 1990-91; bd. dirs. Boston Mcpl. Rsch. Bur., Park St. Corp., The New Eng. Coun.; mem. Gov.'s Coun. Econ. Growth and Tech. Mem. Mass. Women's Forum, Boston, 1991—; trustee Bentley Coll., 1992—; trustee coun. U. Rochester, 1993—. Mem. Pub. Securities Assn. (ex officio, govt. ops. com. 1986-91), Beta Gamma Sigma. Democrat. Roman Catholic. Home: 182 Marlboro Rd Sudbury MA 01776-1350 Office: Fed Reserve Bank Boston 600 Atlantic Ave Boston MA 02210-2211

MINEHART, JEAN BESSE, tax preparer, enrolled agent; b. Cleve., Nov. 8, 1937; d. Ralph Moore and Augusta (Mitchell) Besse; m. Ralph Conrad Minehart, Aug. 28, 1959; children: Patricia Minehart Miron, Deborah, Elizabeth, Stephen. BA, Mass. Wellesley Coll., 1959; MEd, U. Va., 1971. Rsch. assoc. Age Ctr. of New Eng., Boston, 1959-61; substitute tchr. Charlottesville (Va.) Sch. System, 1976-81; tax preparer H&R Block, Charlottesville, 1982-94, Huey & Bjorn, Charlottesville, 1994—, 1994—. Past pres. Ephitha Village Housing for the Deaf, Charlottesville, 1984-87; bd. dirs. Tues. Evening Concert Series, Charlottesville, 1990-94; sec., bd. dirs. Family Svc., Inc., Charlottesville, 1987-91; elder Westminster Presbyn. Ch., 1979-81, 94—. Mem. Blue Ridge Wellesley Club (pres. Charlottesville chpt. 1989-91), League of Women Voters (v.p., treas. 1991—). Home: 1714 Yorktown Dr Charlottesville VA 22901-3034 Office: Huey & Bjorn 408 E Market St E 207B Charlottesville VA 22902

MINER, JACQUELINE, political consultant; b. Mt. Vernon, N.Y., Dec. 10, 1936; d. Ralph E. and Agnes (McGee) Mariani; B.A., Coll. St. Rose, 1971, M.A., 1974; m. Roger J. Miner, Aug. 11, 1975; children: Laurence, Ronald Carmichael, Ralph Carmichael, Mark. Ind. polit. cons., Hudson, N.Y.; instr. history and polit. sci. SUNY, Hudson, 1974-79. Rep. county committeewoman, 1958-76; vice chmn. N.Y. State Ronald Reagan campaign, 1980; candidate for Rep. nomination for U.S. Senate, 1982; co-chair N.Y. state steering com. George Bush for Pres. campaign, 1986-88; vice chmn. N.Y. State Rep. Com., 1991-93; del. Rep. Convention, 1992; chmn. Coll. Consortium for Internat. Studies; mem. White House Outreach Working Group on Central Am.; co-chmn. N.Y. State Reagan Roundup Campaign, 1984-86; mem. nat. steering com. Fund for Am.'s Future, 2d cir. Hist. Com. Mem. U.S. Supreme Ct. Hist. Soc., P.E.O. Address: 1 Merlin's Way Camelot Heights Hudson NY 12534

MINGE, JOAN ADELE, information systems professional; b. Knoxville, June 12, 1949; d. James Howard and Helen Regene (Ellenberg) M.; m. Charles Emerson Jones, May 12, 1979 (div. 1981). Student, U. Tenn., 1967-68, 69-78, Xavier U., 1982-85; cert. of data processor, Tenn. Coll. Automation, 1968. Programmer, analyst Pioneer Bank, Chattanooga, Tenn., 1969-72, Ernest Holmes Co., Chattanooga, 1974-76; client cons. Datalogic, Inc., Chattanooga, 1976-81; sys. analyst Nerco Ea. Mining Divsn., Chattanooga, 1981-82; sr. sys. analyst Nerco Coal Co., Cin., 1982-85, Nerco Coal Corp., St. Louis, 1985-87; sr. sys. analyst Mobil Mining and Minerals Co., Richmond, Va., 1987-89, supr. planning tech. ops., 1989-90; sys. mgr. Mobil Chem. Co., Rochester, N.Y., 1990-94; cons. US Xpress, Chattanooga, 1994, Asche Transfer, Inc., Shannon, Ill., 1995. Mem. IBM User Group (spkr. St. Louis 1987, Richmond 1990, sec. 1988-90). Democrat. Baptist. Home: 8820 Ball Camp Pike Knoxville TN 37931

MINGLE, YVONNE MCFOLIN, realtor; b. Chattanooga, Nov. 10, 1931; d. Odis Pierce and Doris Blanche (Williams) McFolin; m. Richard Melvin Mingle, Sept. 4, 1954 (div. Nov. 1978); children: Michael, Sherry, Melanie. BS, Mid. Tenn. U., 1953; grad. realtors inst., U. N.C., 1979. Credit mgr. Nashville Gas Co.; women's dir. Sta. WMTS, Murfreesboro, Tenn.; office mgr. Met. Life Ins., Murfreesboro; substitute tchr. Lenoir (N.C.) City Schs.; co-owner, office mgr. APCO Paint Co., Hickory, N.C.; realtor Century 21, Lenoir; realtor, co-owner Town & Country Realty, Lenoir, Morrison Realty Co., Lenoir, Helton Realty Co., Lenoir, The Prudential Rowland & Wilson, Murfreesboro. Resident mgr. Forest Oaks Condominium; dir. Beautification Com., Hickory; vol. chair Cancer and Heart drives, Lenoir, dir. Sunday sch. Bapt. Ch., Lenoir. Named Miss Murfreesboro, Murfreesboro Jaycees, Mrs. U.T. Dames, U. Tenn. Mem. Nat. Assn. Realtors, N.C. Assn. Realtors (lic.), Tenn. Assn. Realtors, Rutherford County Assn. Realtors, Tenn. Toastmasters, C. of C., Hibriten Garden Club (pres.). Mem. Ch. of Christ. Home: 1107 E Northfield Murfreesboro TN 37130 Office: Prudential Rowland & Wilson Really Co 607 Memorial Blvd Murfreesboro TN 37129

MINI, LOUISE ANN, psychologist; b. Bklyn., Apr. 28, 1949; d. Enrico H. and Anna Marie (Ventrice) M. BA, CUNY, Bklyn., 1971, MS, 1973; MA, Hofstra U., 1977, PhD, 1979. Cert. sch. psychologist N.Y., 1973, psychologist N.Y. 1981. Psychologist in tng. N.Y.C. Bur. Child Guidance, 1973-75, psychologist, 1976; coll. instr. dept. behavioral scis. N.Y. Inst. Tech., N.Y.C., 1976-77; teaching asst. Hofstra U., Hempstead, N.Y., 1977, adj. lectr. psychology dept., 1978-79, field supr., 1982-83; intern S.E. Nassau Guidance Ctr., Wantagh, N.Y., 1977-78; cons. sch. psychologist New Hyde Park (N.Y.) Sch. Dist., 1979-80; psychologist St. Christopher's Residential Treatment Ctr., Sea Cliff, N.Y , 1977-80, cons. psychologist ICF/MR Programs, 1981-83; chief psychologist, childhood unit coordinator The Shield Inst. for the Developmentally Disabled and Mentally Retarded, Queens, N.Y , 1980-81; psychologist; cons. psychologist N.Y. State Dept. Social Services Office of Disability Determination, 1982—, N.Y. State Office Vocat. Rehab., 1983—, Hearing & Speech Ctr. L.I. Jewish Hosp., 1983-85; pvt. practice psychotherapy Hewlett (N.Y.) Con. Ctr., 1981—; cons. Shapiro & Siegel Law Firm, Conn., 1983—. Intern Brookdale Hosp. Comprehensive Child Care Ctr., 1971-72, Coney Island Hosp. Dept. Child Psychiatry, 1973; therapist Nassau Psychol. Services Inst., 1982-86. Mem. APA (assoc. 1974—), Nassau County Psychol. Assn., N.Y. State Psychol. Assn., Bklyn. Psychol. Assn. Office: Hewlett Cons Ctr 255 Broadway Lynbrook NY 11563-3243

MINISTER, KRISTINA, speech communication educator; b. Dayton, Ohio, Aug. 27, 1934; d. Roy J. and Margaret (Cahtterton) Arndt; m. Edward Minister, Mar. 1959 (div. 1972); children: Matthew, Margaret; m. Hal W. Howard, Sept. 10, 1977 (dec. Sept. 1993). BFA, Ohio U., 1958; MA, Columbia U., 1962; PhD, Northwestern U., 1977. Instr. speech St. John's U., Bklyn., 1962-65, Bowdoin Coll., Brunswick, Maine, 1969-71; asst. prof. speech communication U. Ariz., Tucson, 1974-77, Calif. State U., Northridge, 1978-79; vis. asst. prof. communication Ariz. State U., Tempe, 1979-82; oral historian Oral History Ctr., Inc., Phoenix, 1982-89; prof. comm., chair liberal studies Midway (Ky.) Coll., 1989—; cons. oral history to bus., families, mus. and schs., 1982-89. Author: Oral History: The Privilege You Inherit, 1985; contbr. scholarly essays to various publs. Actor Cmty. Profl. Theatre. Mem. NOW, Women in Comm., Inc., Speech Comm. Assn., Oral History Assn., Am. Folklore Soc. Democrat. Unitarian Universalist. Office: Midway Coll 512 E Stephens St Midway KY 40347-1120

MINK, DONNA LOUISE, nurse; b. Portland, Ind., Nov. 3, 1961; d. John D. and Revenna S. (Bird) M.; 1 child, Kellie. BSN, Ball State U., 1984; MSN, Ind. U., 1990. Cert. neonatal intensive care nurse; RN. Staff nurse James Whitcomb Riley Hosp. for Children, Indpls., 1984-89, patient care coordinator, 1989-95, also neonatal transport nurse, 1987—, extracorporeal membrane oxygenation tech. specialist, 1987—, asst. program dir., 1995—; lectr. Ind. U. Sch. Nursing, Indpls.,1 990—. Mem. Nat. Assn. Neonatal Nurses, Cen. Ind. Assn. Neonatal Assn. (pres. 1993, 94), Sigma Theta Tau. Home: 4917 Manning Rd Indianapolis IN 46208-2054 Office: James Whitcomb Riley Hosp 702 Barnhill Dr # 1715 Indianapolis IN 46202-5128

MINK, MAXINE MOCK, real estate executive; b. Lakeland, Fla., Jan. 17, 1938; d. Idus Frank and Elizabeth (Warren) Mock; student Fla. So. Coll.; children: Lance Granger, Justin Chandler. With Union Fin. Co., Lakeland, Fla., 1956-62; ptnr./owner S & S Ent. & Arrow Lake Mobile Home Pk., Lakeland, 1957-66; head bookkeeper Seaboard Fin., Lakeland, 1964-68; ptnr. Custom Chem., Inc., Lakeland, 1968-75, Don Emilio Perfumers, Newport Beach, Calif., 1978-79; owner Maxine Mink Public Relations, Newport Beach, 1978-83; fine homes and relocation specialist Merrill Lynch Realty, Newport Beach, 1985-90, Tarbell Realtors, Newport Beach, 1990-93, Prudential Calif. Realty, Newport Beach, 1993—. Bd. dirs. Guild of Lakeland Symphony Orch., 1972-75; mem. Lakeland Gen. Hosp. Aux., 1974-76, Mus. Modern Art. Mem. NAFE, Newport Beach C. of C., Hoag Hosp. Aux., Orange County Music Center Guild. Republican. Clubs: Balboa Bay, Sherman Library and Gardens, The 552. Office: PO Box 1262 Newport Beach CA 92659-0262

MINK, PATSY TAKEMOTO, congresswoman; b. Paia, Maui, Hawaii, Dec. 6, 1927; d. Suematsu and Mitama (Tateyama) Takemoto; m. John Francis Mink, Jan. 27, 1951; 1 child, Gwendolyn. Student, Wilson Coll., 1946, U. Nebr., 1947; BA, U. Hawaii, 1948; LLD, U. Chgo., 1951; DHL (hon.), Chaminade Coll., 1975, Syracuse U., 1976, Whitman Coll., 1981. Bar: Hawaii. Pvt. practice Honolulu, 1953-65; lectr. U. Hawaii, 1952-56, 59-62, 79-80; atty. Territorial Ho. of Reps., 1955; mem. Ter. Hawaii Ho. of Reps., 1956-58, Ter. Hawaii Senate, 1958-59, State Hawaii Senate, 1962-64, 89-92d Congresses from Hawaii, 93-94th Congresses from 2d dist. Hawaii, 101st-103d Congresses from 2d dist. Hawaii; mem. edn. and labor com., budget com., natural resources com.; mem. U.S. del. to UN Law of Sea, 1975-76, Internat. Woman's Yr., 1975, UN Environ. Program, 1977, Internat. Whaling Commn., 1977; asst. sec. of state U.S. Dept. State, 1977-78. Charter pres. Young Dem. Club Oahu, 1954-56, Ter. Hawaii Young Dems., 1956-58; del. Dem. Nat. Conv., 1960, 72, 80; nat. v.p. Young Dem. Clubs Am., 1957-59; v.p. Ams. for Dem. Action, 1974-76, nat. pres., 1978-81; mem. nat. adv. com. White House Conf. on Families, 1979-80; mem. nat. adv. coun. Federally Employed Women. Recipient Leadership for Freedom award Roosevelt Coll., Chgo., 1968, Alii award 4-H Clubs Hawaii, 1969, Nisei of Biennium award, Freedom award Honolulu chpt. NAACP, 1971, Disting. Humanitarian award YWCA, St. Louis, 1972, Creative Leadership in Women's Rights award NEA, 1977, Human Rights award Am. Fedn. Tchrs., 1975, Feminist of Yr. award Feminist Majority Found., 1991, Margaret Brent award ABA, 1992. Office: US House of Reps 2135 Rayburn House Offices Ofc Washington DC 20515

MINN, PHYLISS MOMI, government special assistant; b. Honolulu, July 12, 1949; d. Philip Pyung ghi Minn and Momii (Ting) Lee. BA in Sociology, Chaminade Coll., Honolulu, 1971; MSW, Cath. U. Am., 1990. Pub. welfare worker Hawaii Dept. Social Svcs., Honolulu, 1973-79; legis. aide to Senator Daniel K. Inouye, U.S. Senate, Washington, 1980-91; policy specialist First Nations Devel. Inst., Washington, 1992-93; spl. asst. to dep. asst. sec. HUD Distressed & Troubled Housing, Washington, 1994—. Mem. Hawaii Dem. Com., 1970—; vol. St. Luke's Home, Bethesda, Md., 1988-89, Neighborhood Cmty. Reinvestment Coalition, 1992-93, Progressive Horizons, Nat. Fish and Wildlife, 1988-89, adv. coun., 1991-92. Mem. NASW. Roman Catholic. Office: HUD 451 7th St SW Washington DC 20410

MINNELLI, LIZA, singer, actress; b. Los Angeles, Mar. 12, 1946; d. Vincente and Judy (Garland) M.; m. Peter Allen, 1967 (div. 1972); m. Jack Haley, Sept. 15, 1974 (div.); m. Mark Gero, Dec. 4, 1979 (div. 1992). Appeared in Off-Broadway revival of Best Foot Forward, 1963; recorded You Are For Loving, 1963, Tropical Nights, 1977, Liza Minelli at Carnegie Hall, 1987; appeared with mother at London Palladium, 1964; appeared in Flora, the Red Menace, 1965 (Tony award), The Act, 1977 (Tony award), The Rink, 1984; nightclub debut at Shoreham Hotel, Washington, 1965; films include Charlie Bubbles, 1967, The Sterile Cuckoo, 1969, Tell Me That You Love Me, Junie Moon, 1970, Cabaret, 1972 (Oscar award), That's Entertainment, 1974, Lucky Lady, 1975, A Matter of Time, 1976, Silent Movie, 1976, New York, New York, 1977, Arthur, 1981, Rent A Cop, Arthur on the Rocks, 1988, Stepping Out, 1991; albums include: Results, 1989; appeared on TV in own spl. Liza With a Z, 1972 (Recipient Emmy award); other TV appearances include Goldie and Liza Together, 1980, Baryshnikov on Broadway, 1980, The Princess and the Pea, Showtime, 1983, A Time to Live, 1985, Sam Found Out, 1988, Liza Minnelli Live from Radio City Music Hall, PBS (Emmy nomination, Music Program Performance, 1993); internat. tour with Frank Sinatra, Sammy Davis Jr., 1988. Awarded the Brit. equivalent of the Oscar for Best Actress, 1972, Italy's David di Donatello award (twice), the Valentino award. Office: care PMK 1776 Broadway, 8th Floor New York NY 10019-2002

MINNER, RUTH ANN, state senator; b. Milford, Del., Jan. 17, 1935; m. Roger Minner. Student Del. Tech. and Community Coll. Office receptionist Gov. of Del., 1972-74; mem. Del. Ho. of Reps., 1974-82; mem. Del. Senate, 1982-92; lt. gov. State of Del., Dover, 1993—; mem. Dem. Nat. Com., 1988. Home: RD 3 Box 694 Milford DE 19963 Office: Office Lt Gov Tatnall Bldg 3rd Fl Dover DE 19901*

MINNICH, DIANE KAY, state bar executive director; b. Iowa City, Feb. 17, 1956; d. Ralph Maynard Minnich and Kathryn Jane (Obye) Tompkins. BA in Behavioral Sci., San Jose State U., 1978. Tutorial program coord./instr. Operation SHARE/La Valley Coll., Van Nuys, Calif., 1979-81; field exec. Silver Sage Girl Scout Coun., Boise, Idaho, 1981-85; continuing legal edn. dir. Idaho State Bar/Idaho Law Found. Inc., Boise, 1985-88, dep. dir., 1988-90, exec. dir., 1990—. Mem. Assn. CLE Adminstrs., Chgo., 1985-90; bd. dirs. Silver Sage Girl Scouts, Boise, 1990-93, nominating com. mem., 1990—, chair nominating com., 1991-92. Named one of Outstanding Young Women in Am., 1991. Mem. Nat. Orgn. Bar Execs. (membership com. 1992), Zonta Club Boise (prs. 1991-92, bd. dirs. 1989-93, chair long range planning com.), Rotary Club Boise. Office: Idaho State Bar/Idaho Law Found PO Box 895 525 W Jefferson St Boise ID 83702-5931

MINNICK, ADRIENNE KAVANAGH, management consultant; b. Evanston, Ill., Dec. 9, 1920; d. Clarence Henry and Elizabeth Victoria (Ashenden) Kavanagh; m. R. Donald Minnick, Mar. 7, 1942 (dec. Mar. 1945); 1 child, Richard Donald. BS, Northwestern U., 1949; MS, U. Mich., 1958, PhD, 1972. Exec. dir. Girl Scouts Bartholomew County, Columbus, Ind., 1945-49, Girl Scouts of Sheboygan, Wis., 1949-51; field supr., dir. research Girl Scouts Met. Detroit, 1951-72; research dir., evaluation analyst Girl Scouts U.S.A., N.Y.C., 1972-85; co-owner Organizational Resource Devel. Cons., Houston, Galveston, Tex., 1986—. Bd. dirs. United Way of Westchester and Putman Counties, N.Y., 1985; tchr. Christian edn. program, St. Helen's Ch., Pearland, Tex., 1988. Mem. Country Place Master Community Assn. (sec. 1986-88, treas. 1988, bd. dirs., chairperson rules and deed restrictions com.), Assn. Girl Scout Professional Workers. Republican. Roman Catholic. Home: 3338 S Country Meadow Ln Pearland TX 77584-2076

MINNOTTE, LINDA DERR, mental health services professional; b. Moline, Ill., Apr. 11, 1955; d. Howard Lyle and Marilyn Elenor (Lundgren) Derr; m. Richard Tilbrook Minnotte, Dec. 22, 1976; 1 child, Kimberly Jayne. BS in Music Edn., Duquesne U., 1977. Supr. therapeutic activities forensic ctr. Mayview State Hosp., Bridgeville, Pa., 1978—; owner LDM Sports, 1992—. Chairperson Mt. Lebanon (Pa.) High Sch. Alumni Band, 1987; dir. adult handbell choir Mt. Lebanon United Meth. Ch., Pitts., 1989—. Mem. Pa. Social Svcs. Union, Mortar Bd. Republican. Home: 115 Abington Dr Pittsburgh PA 15216-1701 Office: Mayview State Hosp 1601 Mayview Rd Bridgeville PA 15017-1599

MINOR, GAIL LINDA, process engineer; b. Mariemont, Ohio, Dec. 7, 1960; d. Cecil John and Beverly June (Sandberg) M. BSChemE, Ga. Inst. Tech., 1984. Sales engr. Mobil Oil, Atlanta, 1984-86; dist. rep. Betz Indsl., Orange Park, Fla., 1986-87; tech. sales rep. Eka Nobel Paper Chems., Atlanta, 1988-91; staff process engr. Ecusta Divsn. of P.H. Glatfelter, Pisgah Forest, N.C., 1991—. Mem. TAPPI (publicity chmn. Pisgah Forest chpt. 1993—, exec. com. 1993—). Home: RR 4 Box 206 Hendersonville NC 28739-9403 Office: Ecusta PO Box 200 Pisgah Forest NC 28768-0200

MINOR, MARIAN THOMAS, educational consultant; b. Richmond, Va., Apr. 16, 1933; d. James Madison and Florence Elwood (Edwards) M. BS, U. Va., 1955; MEd, William and Mary Coll., 1968; postgrad., Va. Commonwealth U., 1987-88. Cert. guidance, health and phys. edn. Educator Richmond (Va.) Pub. Schs., 1955-90, ednl. cons., 1990—; educator Sch. Nursing Med. Coll. Va., Richmond, 1958-68; camp dir. Manakin, Va., 1956-68; nat. basketball ofcl. Richmond (Va.) Bd. Ofcls., 1952-77; mem. faculty adv. com. Albert Hill Middle Sch., Richmond, 1965-90, dept. chmn., 1960-90, Tchr. of Yr., 1980; textbook adoption Richmond (Va.) Pub. Sch., 1975, 85, curriculum planner, 1978-79, 82-83, 84-85; PTA coord. Albert Hill Middle Sch., Richmond, 1985-89, chmn. self-study and accreditation team, 1987-88. Mem. Sherwood Park Civic Assn., Richmond, 1960-75; v.p. alumni weekend Mary Washington Alumni Assn., Fredericksburg, Va., 1965, 66, v.p. annual giving, 1967; chmn. basketball ofcl. examiners Richmond Bd. Women Ofcls., 1966-76; constrn. worker and mem. planning, adminstrv. coms. Habitat for Humanity; mem. Albert Hill PTA (Outstanding Svc. award 1988); mem. exec. com. Northminster Bapt. Ch., 1991-94, deacon, 1989-92, premises chair, 1991-94, mem. by-law revision com., 1986. Mem. AAUW, AAHPERD, Va. Health Phys. Edn. Assn., Va. Ret. Tchrs. Assn., Train Collectors Assn., Va. Hist. Soc., King and Queen Hist. Soc., Mortar Bd., Alpha Phi Sigma, Kappa Delta Pi. Republican. Home: 1507 Brookland Pkwy Richmond VA 23227

MINTER, JIMMIE RUTH, accountant; b. Greenville, S.C., Sept. 28, 1941; d. James C. and Lois (Williams) Jannino; BS Acctg., U. S.C., 1962; m. Charles H. Minter, Nov. 3, 1972; 1 child, Regina M.; stepchildren: Rhonda, Julie, Gregg; adopted child, Michael Minter. Asst. controller Package Supply & Equipment Co., Greenville, 1964-70, Olympia Knitting Mills, Spartanburg, S.C., 1970-72; controller Diacou Knitting Mills, Spartanburg, 1972-74; adminstr. Atlanta Med. Specialists, P.C., Riverdale, Ga., 1974-79; adminstr., corp. sec. David L. Cooper, M.D. P.C., Riverdale, 1979-89; acct. Ted L. Griffin Enterprises, Jonesboro, Ga., 1988-93; chief tax acct. Clayton County Tax Commn., Jonesboro, 1993—. Program chmn. 4th of July Celebration and Beauty Pageant, City of Riverdale; mem. exec. com. Clayton County Dem. Party, 1987—; Ga. State Dem. treas.; active Clinton Campaign Com.; active local and state election campaign fund raising; bd. dirs. Clayton County Human Rels. Coun. Mem. Am. Bus. Women's Assn. (chpt. Bus. Woman of Yr. 1969), Nat. Assn. Female Execs. Am. Cancer Soc. (silent auction com.), Clayton County Alzheimers Assn. (bd. dirs.). Home: 1244 Branchfield Ct Riverdale GA 30296-2148 Office: PO Box 1119 Riverdale GA 30274-1119

MINTON, MARGARET ELIZABETH, management consultant; b. Knoxville, Nov. 22, 1950; d. Troy Blake and Fay (Walker) M.; m. Michael William Lawless, May 24, 1986; 1 child, Blake. BA in Psychology, U. Tenn., 1973; MS in Indsl. Psychology, Calif. State U., 1978; MBA, UCLA, 1982. Sr. human factors analyst System Devel. Corp., Santa Monica, Calif., 1977-81; mktg. asst. Gen. Mills, Inc., Mpls., 1982-83; product mgr. Carnation Co. (Nestle Foods), L.A., 1983-86; mktg. mgr. Gerico Baby Products, Denver, 1986-87; ptnr., sr. cons. Sterling-Rice Group, Boulder, Colo., 1987-90; pres., sr. cons. Minton LAwless Assocs., Ltd., Boulder, Colo., 1990—. Auction chair Bixby Sch., Boulder, 1993, chair fundraising com., 1992-94; dir. Boulder Sch. Massage Therapy, 1990-92; sr. leader Girl Scouts Am., Long Beach, Calif., 1978-80. Lt. U.S. Coast Guard, 1973-77, comdr. U.S. Coast Guard Res., 1977-94, ret. 1994. R.C. Baker Found. scholar, L.A., 1980-81. Mem. NAFE, NOW, ASTD, Nat. Assn. Women Bus. Owners, Am. Mgmt. Assn., Res. Officer Assn., Emily's List. Democrat. Home and Office: Minton Lawless Assocs Ltd 1955 Tincup Ct Boulder CO 80303

MINTON, MELANIE SUE, neuroscience nurse; b. Cin., Apr. 3, 1950; d. Lester L. and Wanda (Harmon) M. Diploma, The Christ Hosp. Sch. Nursing, 1971; BS in Nursing, Prairie View U. A&M, 1982; postgrad., Our Lady of Lake U., Houston, 1993—. RN, Tex.; CNRN, ACLS instr., BCLS instr., bd. cert. neurosci. Staff, charge nurse The Christ Hosp., Cin., 1971-72, Barnes Hosp, St. Louis, 1972; asst. head nurse The Christ Hosp., Cin., 1972-74; relief nurse supr. The Meth. Hosp., Houston, 1975-87, clin. educator, 1989; trauma rehab. nurse Inst. for Rehab. & Rsch., Houston, 1987-89; nurse specialist neurosurg., neurol. and otolaryn. ICUs Meth. Hosp., Houston, 1989—; presenter, speaker in field. Mem. AACN, Am. Assn. Neurosci. Nurses, S.E. Tex. Chpt. Am. Assn. Neurosci. Nurses, World Fedn. Neurosci. Nurses. Home: 2021 Spenwick Dr Apt 210 Houston TX 77055-1546

MINTON, SYLVIA C., information specialist; b. Statesville, N.C., June 3, 1939; d. Vernon Spencer Sr. and Rachel (Nickles) Church. BS, ASU, 1961; MLS, U. South Fla., 1973; postgrad., Assumption U., 1983. Libr. Libr. of Congress, Washington, 1961-69, RL Sikes Libr., Crestview, Fla., 1974-78, Mitchell (S.D.) Libr., 1980-85; info. specialist Memory Bank, Statesville, N.C., 1985—; cons. Genealogy Soc., Mitchell, 1980-85, Crestview, Fla., 1974-78. Cataloger RL Sikes Congressional Papers, Crestview, 1975; mem. Exec. Women, Statesville, 1990; coord. Govs. Vols., Statesville, 1991. Mem. AAUW, C. of C., Kiwanis (sec. 1991—). Episcopalian. Home: 305 Spring St Statesville NC 28677-4242

MINTZ, DALE LEIBSON, health foundation executive; b. Bronx, July 28, 1944; d. Jack and Martha (Tobin) Leibson; m. Stephen Allan Mintz, June 19, 1966; children: Eric Michael, Jaclyn Leibson. BA, SUNY, Purchase, 1982; MPA, Bernard M. Baruch Coll., 1991. Cert. health edn. specialist. Corp. art cons. Merryl Wilson Assoc., N.Y.C., 1982-85; asst. to CEO New Am. Libr., N.Y.C., 1985-86; estates coord. Sotheby's, N.Y.C., 1986-87; program dir. Am. Heart Assn., Purchase, 1987-94; field svcs. exec. Nat. Hemophilia Found., N.Y.C., 1994—; chair task force COMMIT, Yonkers, N.Y., 1988-93. Trustee Cmty. Synagogue, Rye, N.Y., 1975-85, Rye Arts Ctr., 1980-89, Rye Hist. Soc., 1994—. Mem. Nat. Assn. Exec. Women, N.Y. State Profl. Health Educators. Office: Nat Hemophilia Found 110 Greene St New York NY 10012

MINTZ, JANNA SKURA, art gallery office manager, artist; b. Atlanta, May 10, 1963; d. Ezra and Elyse (Levinson) M. BFA, Tufts U., 1986; Diploma, Boston Mus. Sch., 1987. Receptionist Ctr. for Contemporary Arts, Santa Fe, N.Mex., 1992-94; tax preparer H & R Block, Espanola, N.Mex., 1989, 90; asst. to CFO Peters Corp., Santa Fe, 1989-90, asst. to registrar, 1990; adminstrv. sec. Coll. of Santa Fe, 1990-92, asst. registrar, 1992-94; membership coord. Sch. of Am. Rsch., 1994; office mgr. Through the Flower, Santa Fe, 1994-95. One-woman and group shows include Studio Hallway Gallery, The Coll. of Santa Fe, 1992, Monothon, fine Arts Gallery, Coll. of Santa Fe, 1991-94, Gallery at the Rep., Santa Fe, Century Bank, Santa Fe, 1991, Ctr. for Contemporary Arts, 1990. Vol. N.Mex. Right to Choose, Santa Fe, 1989-92, Gallery at the Rep., Santa Fe, 1989-91, Temple Beth Shalom, 1994—. Mem. Bus. and Profl. Women, Assn. of Am. Mus. Democrat. Jewish.

MINTZ, LENORE CHAICE (LEA MINTZ), personnel company executive; b. N.Y.C., Aug. 6, 1925; d. Abraham and Eva (Kornblith) Chaice; m. Lewis R. Mintz, July 4, 1944; children: Richard Lewis, Alan Lee, Douglas Chaice. Student, U. Mich., 1942-44; BA magna cum laude, U. Bridgeport, 1976. Cert. personnel cons. Office mgr., personnel cons. Golden Door, Inc., Norwalk, Conn., 1970-78; v.p. permanent div. Aubrey Thomas, Inc., Stamford and Norwalk, 1978-84; sr. v.p. Aubrey Thomas Temps., N.Y., N.J., Conn., Pa., 1984-88; area v.p. Mid-Atlantic div. Talent Tree Personnel Svcs.,

1988-89; v.p. bus. devel. Human Resources, Inc., Norwalk, Stamford, Statford and North Haven, 1989-90; prin. Lea Mintz & Assocs., Norwalk, 1990—; speaker, panel mem., condr. workshop and seminars in field; justice of peace Fairfield County, Conn., 1954—; bd. corporators Norwalk Savs. Soc. Loaned exec. United Way of Norwalk & Wilton, Conn., 1991-92; mem., chmn. Norwalk Bd. Edn., 1966-72; mem. Norwalk Planning and Zoning Commn., 1971-73, Conn. Edn. Coun., 1979-83, Conn. Small Bus. Adv. Coun., 1984-86; mem. regional adv. coun. Norwalk State Tech. Coll., 1988-90; past pres. Norwalk Community Coll. Found., 1988-90, bd. dirs. 1964-94; del. numerous Dem. state and county convs.; Clinton del. Dem. Nat. Conv., 1992; mem. adv. coun. displaced homemakers Bridgeport YWCA, 1988-90; v.p. Greater Norwalk Community Coun., 1973-75; life mem. Women's Aux. Jewish Home for Aged in Conn.; community rels. cons. Family & Children's Aid Mid-Fairfield County, Conn., 1992—; active numerous other orgns. Recipient numerous awards including Woman of Yr. award Norwalk Bus. and Profl. Womens Club, 1984, Outstanding Woman of Decade award UN Assn. Conn., 1987, Outstanding Svc. award Conn. Community and Tech. Coll. Bd. Trustees, 1991 (1st honoree). Mem. Women in Mgmt. (pres. 1990, Ann. Recognition award Conn. and Met. N.Y. area 1988), Internat. Assn. Personnel Women, Greater Norwalk C. of C. (bd. dirs. 1980-84, Athena award 1986), Nat. Coun. Jewish Women (life), LWV, Midday Club Stamford, B'nai B'rith (life), Alpha Sigma Lambda. Home and Office: Silvermine 4 May Dr Norwalk CT 06850-1033

MINTZ, SUSAN ASHINOFF, menswear manufacturing company executive; b. N.Y.C., Dec. 7, 1949; d. Lawrence Lloyd and Thelma B. (Rubens) A.; m. Robert Beier Mintz, June 18, 1983; children: Geoffrey Harrison, Tyler Edward Richard. BA, Finch Coll., 1971; MPA, NYU, 1977. Menswear advt. asst. New Yorker Mag., N.Y.C., 1971-72; assoc. Staub, Warmbold & Assocs., Inc., exec. search co., N.Y.C., 1972-80; exec. v.p. Muhammad Ali Sportswear, Ltd., N.Y.C., 1980-81; pres. Forum Sportswear, Ltd., N.Y.C. and Portsmouth, Va., 1981—; group v.p. Coronet Casuals, Inc., Portsmouth, 1985—, also bd. dirs. Trustee Dean Jr. Coll. Named to Outstanding Young Women Am., U.S. Jaycees, 1980. Mem. Nat. Assn. Men's Sportswear Buyers, Men's Apparel Guild Calif., Beacon Hill Club. Office: 2615 Elmhurst Ln Portsmouth VA 23701-2736

MINUDRI, REGINA URSULA, librarian, consultant; b. San Francisco, May 9, 1937; d. John C. and Molly (Halter) M. B.A., San Francisco Coll. for Women, 1958; M.L.S., U. Calif.-Berkeley, 1959. Reference librarian Menlo Park (Calif.) Pub. Library, 1959-62; regional librarian Santa Clara County (Calif.) Library, 1962-68; project coordinator Fed. Young Adult Library Services Project, Mountain View, Calif., 1968-71; dir. profl. services Alameda County (Calif.) Library, 1971, asst. county librarian, 1972-77; library dir. Berkeley Pub. Library, 1977-94; lectr. U. San Francisco, 1970-72, U. Calif., Berkeley, 1977-81, 91-93; lectr. San Jose State U., 1994—; cons., 1975—; adv. bd. Miles Cutter Ednl., 1992—. Bd. dirs. Cmty. Memory, 1989-91, Berkeley Cmty. Fund, 1994—, chair youth com., 1994—; mem. bd. mgrs. cen. br. Berkeley YMCA, 1988-93. Recipient proclamation Mayor of Berkeley, 1985, 86, 94, Citation of Merit Calif. State Assembly, 1994; named Woman of Yr. Alameda County North chpt. Nat. Women's Polit. Caucus, 1986, Outstanding Alumna U. Calif. Sch. Library and Info. Scis., Berkeley, 1987. Mem. ALA (pres. 1986-87, exec. bd. 1980-89, council 1979-88, 90—, Grolier award 1974), Calif. Library Assn. (pres. 1981, council 1965-69, 79-82), LWV (dir. Berkeley chpt. 1980-81). Author: Getting It Together, A Young Adult Bibliography, 1970; contbr. articles to publs. including School Library Jour., Wilson Library Bulletin. Office: Reality Mgmt 836 The Alameda Berkeley CA 94707-1916

MIOTA, MARGARET ELIZABETH, psychotherapist; b. Milw., Aug. 14, 1940; d. Raymond Clarence and Elizabeth (Perusick) Frakes; m. John Matthew Miota, Sept. 1, 1962; children: Kevin Gerard, Matthew James, Nicholas John. RN, Milw. County Hosp., 1962; BSN, Alverno Coll., Milw., 1975; MSW, U. Wis., Milw., 1979. Bd. cert. diplomate clin. social work; RN, Wis.; lic. ind. clin. social worker, Wis. Head nurse Milw. County Mental Health Hosp., 1962-64; instr. Childbirth Edn. Assn., Milw., 1964-70; staff nurse West Allis (Wis.) Meml. Hosp., 1968-75; instr. Milw. County Hosp. Nursing Sch., 1975-77; staff nurse Family Hosp., 1977-74, psychotherapist, 1980-85, supr., 1985-87; dir. outpatient svcs. Milw. Psychoat. Hosp., 1987-92; pres. Spa Vesta Ltd., Milw., 1992—. Spl. friend Women's Crisis Line, Milw., 1982-88. Mem. NASW, AAUW, NAFE, NOW, Am. Assn. Marital and Family Therapists (clin.), Nat. Mus. Women in Arts, BPW of West Allis (bd. dirs.), Nat. Women's Health Network, Wis. Women Entrepreneurs (bd. dirs.), Jacobs Inst. for Women's Health, Melpomone Inst., Noetic Scis., Wis. Women's Network Health Care Task Force (co-chmn.), Delta Epsilon Sigma, Alpha Delta Mu. Office: Spa Vesta Ltd 2640 Root River Pky Milwaukee WI 53227-1850

MIR, MARILYN, retired educator; b. Upland, Ind., Dec. 9, 1927; d. Robert Heavin Thompson and Lenora Hults; m. Hashem Robert Mir-Afzali, May 12, 1957 (div. 1976); children: Michael Robert Mir-Afzali, Susan Marie Farrell. BS, Ball State U., 1947; postgrad., U. Colo., 1948; MS, Ind. U., 1950; postgrad., U. Wash., 1951, U. Calif., 1952-53, San Francisco State U., 1984-85. Tchr. bus. Ind., 1947-50, Wenatchee (Wash.) High Sch., 1950-52; exec. sec. Fritzi of Calif., San Francisco, 1958-63; engring. sec. Div. of Westinghouse, San Francisco, 1963-68; tchr. bus. and English San Francisco Unified Schs., 1968-85, attendance coord., 1985-87, cons., 1987-90. Vol. libr. Grossmont High Sch. Dist., El Cajon, Calif., 1990—, San Carlos Pub. Libr., San Diego, 1985; ednl. missionary Utah Presbyn. Schs., 1985, N.Mex. Presbyn. Schs., 1987, N.C. Presbyn. Schs., 1989. Mem. AAUW, San Carlos Women's Club (edn. com.). Democrat. Presbyterian. Home: 7912 June Lake Dr San Diego CA 92119-3120

MIRABELLA, GRACE, magazine publishing executive; b. Maplewood, N.J., June 10, 1930; d. Anthony and Florence (Belfatto) M.; m. William G. Cahan, Nov. 24, 1974. BA, Skidmore Coll., 1950. Mem. exec. tng. program Macy's, N.Y.C., 1950-51; mem. fashion dept. Saks Fifth Ave., N.Y.C., 1951-52; with Vogue mag., N.Y.C., 1952-54, 56-88; assoc. editor Vogue mag., 1965-71, editor-in-chief, 1971-88; founder, publ. dir. Mirabella Mag., 1988—; mem. pub. relations staff Simonetta & Fabiani, Rome, Italy, 1954-56; hon. bd. dirs. Catalyst; lectr. New Sch. Social Research. Adv. bd. Columbia U. Sch. Journalism. Decorated cavalier Order of Merit Republic of Italy; recipient Outstanding Grad. Achievement award Skidmore Coll., 1972; Fashion Critics award Parsons Sch. Design, 1985; Woman of Distinction award Birmingham-So. Coll., 1985, Girl Scouts Am. Leadership award, 1987, Excellence in Media award Susan G. Komen Found., 1987, Equal Opportunity award NOW, 1987; officer Order of Merit, Republic of Italy, 1987; Mary Ann Magnin award, 1988; Achievement award Am. Assn. Plastic and Reconstructive Surgery, 1988; Spl. Merit award Coun. Fashion Designers Am., 1989. Mem. Women's Forum N.Y. Office: Mirabella Mag 200 Madison Ave New York NY 10016-3903*

MIRE, BETTY, writer; b. Abbeville, La., Dec. 8, 1938; d. Edmar Jr. and Lillian (Vallot) Broussard; m. Jerome Mire, Feb. 4, 1956; children: Lillian, Jerome, Jacqueline, Sonnie, Kim. Grad. high sch., Abbeville, La. Author: A Rose Among the Weeds, 1981, It's Funny How Things Change, 1985, T-Pierre Frog and T-Felix Frog Go to School, 1993. Roman Catholic. Home: RR 5 Box 1444 Abbeville LA 70510-9325

MIRIPOL, JERILYN ELISE, poet, writer, writing therapist; b. Chgo., Jan. 22; d. Albert and Janice (Tuchin) M.; m. Richard Palmer Van Duyne, Dec. 30, 1986. BA in English Lit., Northeastern Ill. U., 1974. Writing therapist Northshore Retirement Hotel, Evanston, Ill., 1983; creative writing tchr. Oakton Community Coll., Evanston, 1985—; writing therapist St. Francis Hosp., Evanston, 1989—; artist-writer-in-residence Dawes Sch., Evanston, 1985; artist-in-residence Evanston Twp. High Sch., 1988; writing facilitator for individual students, Chgo., 1987—; tchr. writing therapy to mental health profls. and caregivers U. Wis., Milw., 1989; presenter writing therapy workshop, 1990, Nat. Assn. Poetry-Therapy, Chgo., 1991. Author: Discovering Self-Awareness Through Poetry, 1987, (poetry) The Sounds Were Distilled, 1977; author numerous poems; contbr. articles to profl. jours. Vol. Ridgeview Nursing Home, Evanston, 1982-83; advocate of children of abuse, human and civil rights. Talent scholar in creative writing Northeastern Ill. U., Squaw Valley Community Writers scholar, 1980, Radgale Found. scholar, 1985, Aspen Writer's Workshop Breadloaf Writer's Conf. scholar; Danforth fellow nominee; Dawes Sch. grantee, 1987. Mem. NOW, PEN, UNICEF, ACLU, Nat. Assn. Poetry Therapy, Women's Internat. League for Peace, Humanitas Internat. (human rights com.), Amnesty Internat., Am. Acad. Poets, Ill. Alliance of Arts, 11th Ann. Poetry Therapy Conf. (keynote speaker), Greenpeace, Death Penalty Foes. Home: 1520 Washington Ave Wilmette IL 60091-2417

MIRISOLA, LISA HEINEMANN, air quality engineer; b. Glendale, Calif., Mar. 25, 1963; d. J. Herbert and Betty Jane (Howson) Heinemann; m. Daniel Carl Mirisola, June 27, 1987; 1 child, Ian Cataldo. BSME, UCLA, 1986. Cert. engr.-in-tng., Calif. Air quality engr. South Coast Air Quality Mgmt. Dist., Diamond Bar, Calif., 1988—. Chancellor's scholar UCLA, 1981. Mem. ASME, NSPE, Soc. Women Engrs. Office: South Coast Air Quality Mgmt Dist 21865 Copley Dr Diamond Bar CA 91765-4178

MIROW, SUSAN MARILYN, psychiatry educator; b. Manhattan, N.Y., Feb. 15, 1944. BA in Biology, Temple U., 1964; PhD in Anatomy, N.Y. Med. Coll., 1970; MD, Med. Coll. Pa., 1973. Diplomate Nat. Bd. Med. Examiners, Am. Bd. Psychiatry and Neurology. Intern in medicine and psychiatry Temple U. Hosp., Phila., 1973-74, resident in psychiatry, 1973-75; pvt. practice psychiatry Salt Lake City, 1976—; clin. asst. prof. psychiatry U. Utah Sch. Medicine, Salt Lake City, 1976—; clin. asst. prof. psychiatry Neuropsychiat. Inst. U. Utah; mem. staff Salt Lake Regional Med. Ctr., 1976—, Latter Day Saints Hosp., 1985—; prin. investigator Marine Biol. Lab., Woods Hole, Mass., 1968; research investigator Temple U., Dept. Biology, summer 1971, Hosp. Joint Diseases, N.Y.C., 1969-70; clin. dir. Utah State Hosp., Provo, 1980-82; psychiat. extern Phila. Child Guidance Clin, 1973, neurology clk. Med. Coll. Pa. Dept. Neurology, 1973, cons. psychiatrist Adolescent Residential Treatment Ctr., Salt Lake City, 1976-77; vis. prof. St. George's U., Grenada, 1990—; psychiat. cons. Divsn. Youth Corrections, Salt Lake City, 1992—; lectr. in field. Contbr. articles to profl. jours. NSF fellow 1965-69; grantee John Polachek Research Found., 1969-70; recipient Weisman award Excellence Child Psychiatry, 1973. Fellow Am. Psychiat. Assn.; mem. AAAS, AMA, Utah State Med. Assn. (impaired physician's com. 1983—), Salt Lake County Med. Soc., N.Y. Acad. Scis., Soc. Clin. and Exptl. Hypnosis, Internat. Soc. Clin. Hypnosis, Utah Soc. Clin. Hypnosis (sec. 1982-83), Am. Soc. Clin. Hypnosis. Office: 73 G St Salt Lake City UT 84103-2951

MIRRA, SUZANNE SAMUELS, neuropathologist, researcher; b. N.Y.C., Feb. 16, 1943. BA, Hunter Coll., 1962; MD, SUNY, Bklyn., 1967. Instr. pathology Yale U. Sch. Medicine, New Haven, 1971-73; staff pathologist Atlanta VA Med. Ctr., Decatur, Ga., 1973—; asst. prof. pathology Emory U. Sch. Medicine, Atlanta, 1973-80, assoc. prof. pathology, 1981-93, prof. pathology, 1993—; bd. dir., prin. investor Emory Alzheimer's Disease Ctr., Atlanta, 1991—;. Editorial bd. Arch Pathol Lab Med, 1988—, Jour. Neuropathology Exptl. Neurology, 1991—. Recipient Albert E. Levy Sci. Faculty Rsch. award Emory U., 1987, Presdl. award Coll. Am. Pathologists, 1987, 89, Herbert Lansky award Coll. Am. Pathologists, 1990, Disting. Alumnus Achievement award SUNY, 1992. Fellow Coll. Am. Pathologists (chair neuropathology commn. 1992—); mem. Am. Assn. Neuropathologists (v.p. profl. affairs 1992—), Alzheimer's Assn. (bd. dir. Atlanta chpt. 1987—). Office: VA Med Ctr 113 Emory U 1670 Clairmont Rd Decatur GA 30033-4004

MIRREN, HELEN, actress; b. London, 1946. First appeared with Nat. Youth Theatre; appeared as Cleopatra in Antony and Cleopatra, Old Vic, 1965; joined Royal Shakespeare Co., 1967; appeared as Castiza in The Revenger's Tragedy and Diana in All's Well That Ends Well; other roles include: Cressida in Troilus and Cressida, Royal Shakespeare Co., Stratford, Eng., 1968; Hero in Much Ado About Nothing, Stratford, 1968; Win-the-Fight Littlewit in Bartholomew Fair, Aldwych, 1969; Lady Anne in Richard III, Stratford, Ophelia in Hamlet, Julia in The Two Gentlemen of Verona, Stratford, 1970 (last part also at Aldwych); Tatyana in Enemies, Royal Shakespeare Co., Aldwych, 1971; title role in Miss Julie, Elynae in The Balcony, The Place, 1971; with Peter Brook's Centre Internationale de Recherches Theatrales, Africa and U.S., 1972-73; Lady Macbeth, Royal Shakespeare Co., Stratford, 1974, and Aldwych, 1975; Maggie in Teeth 'n' Smiles, Royal Ct., 1975; Nina in The Seagull and Ella in The Bed Before Yesterday, Lyric for Lyric Theatre Co., 1975, Antony and Cleopatra, The Roaring Girl, Henry VI-Parts 1, 2, 3, 1977-78, Measure for Measure, 1979, The Duchess of Malfi, 1980-81, Faith Healer, 1981, Royal Shakespeare Co., Barbican, 1983, Extremities, 1984, Madame Bovary, 1987, Two Way Mirror, 1988, Sex Please We're Italian, 1991, A Month in the Country, 1994; films include: Age of Consent, 1969, Savage Messiah, O Lucky Man!, 1973, Caligula, 1977, The Long Good Friday, Excalibur, 1981, Cal, 1984 (Best Actress award Cannes Film Festival 1984), 2010, 1984, White Knights, 1984, Heavenly Pursuits, 1985, The Mosquito Coast, 1986, Pascali's Island, 1987, When The Whales Came, 1988, Bethune, Making of a Hero, 1988, The Cook, The Thief, His Wife, and Her Lover, 1989, The Comfort of Strangers, 1990, Where Angels Fear to Tread, 1991, The Gift, 1991, The Hawk, 1991, The Prince of Jutland, 1991, The Madness of King George, 1994 (Acad. award nominee for Best Supporting Actress); TV appearances include: Behind the Scene, Cousin Bette, Coffin for the Bride, Jackanory, The Changeling, Bellamira, The Philanthropist, Mussolini And Claretta Petacci, The Collection, The Country Wife, Blue Remembered Hills, The Serpent Son, Quiz Kids, Midsummer Night's Dream, After the Party, Cymbeline, Coming Through, Cause Celebre, Miss Julie, The Apple Cart, The Little Minister, As You Like It, Mrs. Reinhardt, Soft Targets, 1982, Heavenly Pursuits, 1985, Red King White Knight, 1988, Prime Suspect, 1991 (Best Actress award BAFTA 1991), Prime Suspect 2, 1992, Prime Suspect 3, 1993 (Emmy award, 1994). Mem. PTO. Office: Ken McReddie Ltd, 91 Regent St, London WIR TTB, England*

MIRSKY, SONYA WOHL, librarian, curator; b. N.Y.C., Nov. 12, 1925; d. Louis and Anna (Steiger) Wohl; m. Alfred Ezra Mirsky, Aug. 24, 1967 (dec. June 1974). B.S. in Edn., CCNY, 1948; M.S.L.S., Columbia U., 1950. Asst. libr. Rockefeller U., N.Y.C., 1949-60, assoc. libr., 1960-77, univ. libr., 1977-91, univ. libr. emeritus, 1991—; trustee Med. Libr. Ctr. N.Y., 1965-91, v.p., 1980-88; cons. libr. mgmt. Mem. Bibliog. Soc. Am., Biblog. Soc. Can., Bibliog. Soc. Gt. Britain, Soc. Bibliography of Natural History. Home: Sutton Ter 1161 York Ave Apt 4F New York NY 10021-7945 Office: Rockefeller U Libr 1230 York Ave New York NY 10021-6399

MIRZA, LEONA LOUSIN, educator; b. Chgo., July 1, 1944; d. Max B. and Opal Lousin; m. David B. Mirza; children: Sara Anush, Elizabeth Ann. BA in Math., North Park Coll., Chgo., 1965; MA in Edn., Western Mich. U., Kalamazoo, 1967, EdD in Edn., 1972; cert. in computer studies, North Park Coll., 1983. Tchr. Kalamazoo Pub. Schs., 1965-69; prof. math. edn. North Park Coll., 1969—. Editor The Illinois Mathematics Teacher, 1992—; contbr. articles to profl. jours. Chmn. adv. com. on edn. in Ill., 1975-77. Mem. Nat., Ill. Coun. Tchrs. Math., Ill. Assn. Colls. of Tchr. Edn., Ill. Assn. Tchrs. Edn. in Pvt. Colls. (officer 1974-86). Specialist in elem. curriculum and adminstrn. Home: 795 Lincoln Ave Winnetka IL 60093-1920 Office: 3225 W Foster Ave Chicago IL 60625-4895

MISALE, JUDI MARIE, psychologist; b. Blue Island, Ill., July 30, 1946; d. Richard Arvid and Billie Jean (Frazier) Adams; m. Joseph Misale, Aug. 17, 1979; children: Donna, Michael, Theresa, Melissa. BA in Psychology, Calif. State U., Northridge, 1987; MA in Psychology, U. Calif., Santa Barbara, 1989, PhD in Social Psychology, 1992. Tchng. asst. U. Calif., Santa Barbara, 1987-91, tchng. assoc., 1991-92; asst. prof. Northeast Mo. State U., Kirksville, 1992—. Faculty rsch. grantee Northeast Mo. State U., 1993-94, instructional improvement grantee, 1994, Jepson fellow, 1995. Mem. APA, Am. Psychol. Soc., Midwestern Psychol. Assn., Soc. for Psychol. Study of Social Issues, AAUW, AAUP, Coun. Tchrs. of Undergrad. Psychology, Soc. for Personality and Social Psychology. Home: 301 S Cottage Grove Ave Kirksville MO 63501-3336 Office: NE Mo State U Social Sci Divsn Kirksville MO 63501

MISCHKE, BARBARA SUZANNE, research geneticist; b. Great Bend, Kans., Feb. 1, 1944; d. Charles John and Barbara May (Storer) Hauser; m. Charles Franklin Mischke; children: James Franklin, John Charles. BA, U. Colo., 1966; PhD, U. Ariz., 1973. Secondary teaching cert., Ariz. Rsch. assoc. Mich. Cancer Found., Detroit, 1973-74; assoc. faculty U. Denver, 1977-78; adj. grad. faculty U. Colo., Denver, 1978; fellow inst. Eleanor Roosevelt Inst. Cancer Rsch., Denver, 1978-79; rsch. assoc., assoc. faculty zoology dept. Ohio Wesleyan U., Delaware, 1979-81; rsch. plant pathologist plant pathology dept. U. Calif., Davis, 1981-82; rsch. geneticist USDA, Agrl. Rsch. Svc., Beltsville, Md., 1983—; grant rev. panel mem. AID, Washington, 1985—; rsch. grant reviewer Nat. Rsch. Initiative-CRGO and BARD, Washington, 1986—; judge sci. fair Prince George's County (Md.) Pub. Schs., 1991—; career day vol. AAUW, Md., 1991-93. Manuscript reviewer various profl. jours., 1989—; contbr. articles to profl. jours., chpt. to book. Den mother Cub Scouts, Boy Scouts Am., Leicester, N.Y., 1976-77. NDEA Title IV fellow U.S. Dept. Edn., Tucson, Ariz., 1969, predoctoral fellow U. Ariz., Tucson, 1972. Mem. AAAS, Mycol. Soc. Am., Am. Phytopath. Soc. (biocontrol com. 1988-91), Mid-Atlantic Plant Molecular Biology Soc. (registration chmn. 1984-88), Am. Soc. Plant Physiologists (Washington area), Alpha Chi Omega. Roman Catholic. Office: USDA Agrl Rsch Svc Systematic Botany/Mycol Lab Blgd 011A Rm 304 Beltsville MD 20705

MISENHEIMER, PATRICIA MOBLEY (TRISH MISENHEIMER), lay church worker, church secretary; b. Barstow, Calif., Apr. 22, 1943; d. Jesse Ralph and Elizabeth (Gard) Mobley; m. Jerry D. Smith, 1962 (div. 1978); children: Paul David Smith, Susanne Rachelle Smith; m. Robert Joseph Misenheimer, Mar. 22, 1985 (div. Nov. 1985). Student, Life Bible Coll., L.A., 1960-62. Pianist, leader high sch. youth group Foursquare Ch., Barstow, 1959-61; pianist, coord. jr. ch., Foursquare Ch., Arlington, Calif., 1964-66; pianist, tchr. Grace Bapt. Ch., Newhall, Calif., 1971-75; pianist, jr. high dir. choir 1st Bapt. Ch., Lake Arrowhead, Calif., 1975-78; pianist, mem. cabinet, visitation team, tchr. 1st Bapt. Ch. Singles Ministry, Pomona, Calif., 1978-85, pianist, mem. Regional Single Adult Task Force, leader, 1988-90; pianist, tchr., mem. bd. curriculum devel. 1st Evang. Free Ch., Single Parent Fellowship, Fullerton, Calif., 1985-88; sec. Todd Meml. Chapel, Pomona, 1984—. Mem. Com. to Re-call Clay Bryant, Pomona, 1989; treas. Com. to Elect Bob Jackson, Pomona, 1991. Barstow Bus. and Profl. Women's scholar, 1961. Mem. Nat. Notary Assn. (cert.). Republican.

MISNER, LORRAINE, laboratory technologist; b. Fitchburg, Mass., June 24, 1948; d. Cedric Winfield and Pearl Erma (Hallisey) M. BA in Biology, Fitchburg State Coll., 1971; MS in Med. Technology, Anna Maria Coll., 1983. Lab. technologist Leominster (Mass.) Hosp., 1971-87; research asst. U. Lowell Rsch. Found. (now U. Mass. Lowell Rsch. Found.), 1987—. Piccolo Townsend (Mass.) Mil. Band, 1964-93; mem. choir United Ch. of Christ, 1961—. Mem. Am. Soc. Clin. Pathologists (assoc., registrant), Am. Soc. for Clin. Lab. Sci., Mass. Soc. for Med. Tech.

MISSIMORE, MAUREEN MARGARET, sales professional; b. St. Louis, Apr. 22, 1959; d. Amos Sawyer and Kathleen Blanche (McCotter) M.; m. Terrence R. Fournier, June 22, 1979 (div. 1981). AA in Retailing, St. Louis Community Coll., 1980; BS in Bus., Fontbonne Coll., 1991, MBA, 1995. Sales rep. various retail stores St. Louis, 1975-79; store mgr. Lerner's, St. Louis, 1979-81; sales rep. Eisenhart Brokerage, St. Louis, 1981-83, O'Brien & Assocs., Food Broker, St. Louis, 1983-85, Best Foods-CPC Internat., St. Louis, 1985-87; mktg. asst. Fantasy Coachworks, Ltd., St. Louis, 1990; sales rep. Dillard's, St. Louis, 1991; program rep. Fontbonne Coll. OPTIONS Program, 1992—; cons. Small Bus. Inst., St. Louis, 1988-91. Vol. Humane Soc. Mem. Women's Commerce Assn. (mktg. 1989—), Delta Mu Delta (v.p. 1990—), Kappa Gamma Pi. Democrat. Roman Catholic. Home: 60 Grantwood Ln Saint Louis MO 63123-2055

MITCHAL, KAREN S., food products company executive; b. Massillon, Ohio, Aug. 12, 1964; d. Clyde Richard and Marilyn Francis (Barnes) M. BBA, Tex. Christian U., 1985. Pre-sell rep. retail Pepsi-Cola Co., Dallas, 1985-86, sr. rep. sales on premise, 1986-88; acct. mgr. on premise Pepsi-Cola Co., Atlanta, 1988-90; mgr. franchises Pepsi-Cola Co., Birmingham, Ala., 1990-92; key acct. mgr. retail Pepsi-Cola Co., Atlanta, 1992-94, mgr. bus. devel., 1994—. Bd. dirs. Tuskegee (Ala.) U. Bus. and Industry, 1990—, Hosp. Mgmt., 1994—. Mem. Ch. Christ. Home: 601 Sutton Way SW Marietta GA 30064 Office: Pepsi-Cola Co 180 Interstate N Pky 300 Atlanta GA 30339

MITCHELL, ADA MAE BOYD, legal assistant; b. Nov. 23, 1927; d. Allen T. Boyd and Marjorie (Bigger) Boyd Mills; 1 child, Joseph W. Student, NYU, 1972-73. Supr. Faberge, Inc., Mahwah, N.J.; mgr. Demostration Svcs. and Promotional Monies; mgr. accounts receivables, credit mgr. Faberge, Inc., Mahwah, N.J.; legal asst. Wright Patterson Med. Ctr., Dayton, Ohio, 1990—. Pres. Urban League Guild, Bergen County, N.J., 1982—, bd. dirs., 1982-83; treas. Bethany Presbyn. Ch., Englewood, N.J., 1975, fin. sect., 1966-67, chairperson bldg. and renovation com., 1978-81, choir mem., elder, 1979—; 1st Black woman moderator Presbytery of Palisades-Presbyn. Ch., 1986. Mem. NAFE, NAACP, Order Eastern Star (Queen of Sheba chpt. 4, Worthy Matron 1972-73).

MITCHELL, ALTHEA ALLEN, investment banker; b. L.A., Feb. 12, 1960; d. Jewel Goode. BA in Bus. Adminstrn., Calif. State U., 1988. Cert. instr. bus. mgmt.; registered gen. prin. rep. series 24 and 7. CEO WMBE Resource Ctr., L.A., 1991—; adv. bd. Renaissance Bancorp, L.A., Pine Cobble Ptnrs., L.A. Author, prodr. numerous video documentaries and publs. Bd. dirs. Beyond Shelter, L.A., Cmty. Devel. Ctr., L.A.; chair Exposition Park. Office: WMBE Resource Ctr Calif Mus Sci & Ind # 136 700 State Dr Los Angeles CA 90037-1237

MITCHELL, ANDREA, journalist; b. N.Y.C., Oct. 30, 1946; d. Sydney and Cecile Mitchell. B.A., U. Pa., 1967. Polit. reporter KYW Newsradio, Phila., 1967-76; polit. corr. Sta. KYW-TV, Phila., 1972-76; corr. Sta. WTOP-TV, Washington, 1977-78; gen. assignment and energy corr. NBC News, Washington, 1978-81; White House corr. NBC News, 1981-88, chief congl. corr., 1989-92, chief White House corr., 1993-94; chief fgn. affairs corr. NBC News, Washington, 1995—, 1994—; instr. Gt. Lakes Colls. Assn., 1974-76; co-anchor Summer Sunday, USA, NBC-TV News, 1984, substitute anchor Meet the Press, 1988—. Overseer Coll. Arts and Scis. U. Pa., 1989—, trustee, 1991—; mem. nat. adv. bd. Girl Scouts U.S. Recipient award for pub. affairs reporting Am. Polit. Sci. Assn., 1969, Pub. Affairs Reporting award AP, 1976, AP Broadcast award, 1977; named Communicator of the Yr., Phila. chpt. Women in Comms., 1976, Woman of the Yr., Phila. chpt. Am. Women in Radio and TV, 1989, Lucretia Mott award Woman's Way, 1991. Mem. White House Corrs. Assn. Office: NBC News 4001 Nebraska Ave NW Washington DC 20016-2733*

MITCHELL, BETTIE PHAENON, religious organization administrator; b. Colorado Springs, Colo., June 6, 1934; d. Roy William and Laura Lee (Costin) Roberts; m. Gerald Mitchell, May 3, 1952; children: Michelle Smith, Laura Sweitz, Jennie Grenzer, Mohammad Bader. BS in Edn., Lewis & Clark Coll., 1954; postgrad., Portland State U., 1962-72; MA in Religion summa cum laude, Warner Pacific Coll., 1979. Cert. counselor, Oreg. Elem. tchr. Quincy Sch. Dist., Clatskanie, Oreg., 1955-56; substitute tchr. Beaverton (Oreg.) and Washington County Schs., 1956-77; tchr. of the Bible Portland (Oreg.) C.C., 1974-92; counseling and healing ministry, 1977-79; founder, exec. dir. Good Samaritan Ministries, Beaverton, 1979-88; founder, internat. exec. dir. Good Samaritan Ministries, 1988—; tchr. Christian Renewal Ctr. Workshops, 1977-85; speaker, presenter in field; leader tours in the Mid. East. Author: Who Is My Neighbor? A Parable, 1988, The Power of Conflict and Sacrifice, A Therapy Manual for Christian Marriage, 1988, Good Samaritan Training Handbook, 1989, Be Still and Listen to His Voice, The Story of Prayer and Faith, 1990, A Need for Understanding - International Counselor Training Manual, 1993. Mem. Israel Task Force, Portland, 1974-80; Leader Camp Fire Internat., 1962-73, elem. sch. coord., 1962-68; asst. dir. Washington County Civil Def., 1961-63; precinct committeewoman Rep. Party, 1960; bd. dirs. Beaverton Fish, 1966-74; v.p. NCCJ, Portland, 1983-85; chmn., speaker's bur. Near East Task Force for Israel; chmn. fire bond issue campaign City of Beaverton, mgr. mayoral campaign, 1960; sunday sch. tchr., speaker, organizer Sharing and Caring program Bethel Ch., 1974-79. Mem. ACA, Christian Assn. for Psychol. Studies, Oreg. Counseling Assn. Republican. Home: 6550 SW Imperial Dr Beaverton OR 97005 Office: Good Samaritan Ministries 7929 SW Cirrus Dr # 23 Beaverton OR 97005

MITCHELL, BETTY JO, writer, publisher; b. Coin, Iowa, May 2, 1931; d. Edith Darrah McWilliams; B.A., S.W. Mo. State U., Springfield; M.S.L.S., U. So. Calif. Asst. acquisitions librarian Calif. State U., Northridge, 1967-69, librarian for personnel and fin., 1969-71, acting asso. library dir., 1971-72, asso. dir. univ. libraries, 1972-81; owner Viewpoint Press, Tehachapi, Calif.; cons. Western Interstate Commn. for Higher Edn. USOE Inst. for Tng. in Staff Devel. Problem Solving; participant workshops in field. Bd. dirs. San Fernando Valley council Girl Scouts U.S.A., 1974-77, employed personnel com., 1979-81; bd. dirs. Bear Valley Springs Condominium Owners Assn., 1978, Empyrean Found., 1978-81. Mem. Assn. Women in Computing (bd. dirs. 1987-89), ALA (mem., chmn. various coms.), Nat. Library Assn., Calif. Library Assn., Assn. Calif. State U. Profs. (sec., exec. com., 1971-72), AAUP, Pi Beta Chi, Alpha Mu Gamma. Author: ALMS: A Budget Based Library Management System, 1982, The Secret of Hilhouse: An Adult Book for Teens; co-author: Cost Analysis of Library Functions: A Total System Approach, 1978, How to See the U.S. on $12 a Day; speaker profl. confs.; contbr. writings to profl. publs.; editor Staff Development column in Special Libraries, 1975-76. Home: 29650 Starland Star Route 3 Box 4600-7 Tehachapi CA 93561 Office: PO Box 1090 Tehachapi CA 93581-1090

MITCHELL, BEVERLY ANN BALES, agency owner, women's rights advocate; b. Fremont, Nebr., July 27, 1944; d. Richard Lee Roy Stillwell Bales and Thelma May (Nelson) Lemen (dec.). BA, Midland Luth. Coll., 1967; postgrad., U. Iowa, 1970, 71. Reporter, film columnist, entertainment sect. editor Fremont (Nebr.) Daily Guide and Tribune, 1961-66; tchr. H.S. English Cedar Bluffs (Nebr.) Valley PUb. Schs., 1967-71; dir. quality control, dir. field ops. Frank N. Magid Assocs., Marion, Iowa, 1971-76; employment specialist U.S. Dept. Labor, Cedar Rapids, Iowa, 1976-78; owner, gen. agy. Mitchell Ins., Cedar Rapids, 1978—. Founder, editor: (monthly periodical) Lilith Speaks, 1971-76, 88—; contbr.: Strong Minded Women, 1992. Co-founder, pres. Cedar Rapids (Iowa) Womens Caucus, 1971-76; commr. Cedar Rapids (Iowa) Civil Rights Commn., 1976-80; pres. Linn County (Iowa) Women's Polit. Caucus, 1977-79; mem. Linn County Bd. Condemnation and Compensation, 1994—. Recipient Creighton By-Line award Creighton U., Omaha, 1963, Best Editorial award Nebr. Press Assn., Lincoln, 1963; named Women of the Yr., Cedar Rapids (Iowa) Women's Orgns., 1977. Mem. NAACP, NRA, NOW (coord. Iowa state divsn. 1973-76, pres. Cedar Rapids chpt. 1994—), Bus. and Profl. Women (bd. dirs. 1994—), Dodge County Humane Soc. Lutheran. Unitarian. Office: Mitchell Ins 1000 Maplewood Dr NE Cedar Rapids IA 52402

MITCHELL, BONNIE JEAN, social worker; b. Pawnee, Okla., Apr. 17, 1947; d. William Elmer and Lillie Lee (Dougherty) M.; m. Brian David Alexander (div. Jan. 1980). BA, U. Okla., 1981. Cert. armed security officer, Okla. Ptnr. B&F Club Cleaning, Oklahoma City, 1980-82; security officer IHR Security/Vanguard Security, Oklahoma City, 1983-87, Security One, Valley Brook, Okla., 1987-88; social work asst. Dept. Human Svcs. State of Okla., Oklahoma City, 1988-89, social worker I Dept. Human Svcs., 1989-90, social worker II Dept. Human Svcs., 1990—. With U.S. Army Res., 1968-69. Mem. Okla. Pub. Employees Assn., Sierra Club, Smithsonian Assocs., Nature Conservancy. Democrat.

MITCHELL, CAROL ANN, nursing educator; b. Portsmouth, Va., Aug. 31, 1942; d. William Howell and Eleanor Bertha (Wesarg) M.; m. David Alan Friedman, June 17, 1971 (div. 1988). Diploma, NYU, 1963; BS, Columbia U., 1968, MA, 1971, EdM, 1974, EdD, 1980; MS, SUNY, Stony Brook, 1990. Charge nurse Nassau County Med. Ctr., East Meadow, N.Y., 1963-65; staff nurse Meml. Hosp., N.Y.C., 1965-68; head nurse, supr. Community Hosp. at Glen Cove (N.Y.), 1969-71; assoc. prof. dept. nursing Queensborough Community Coll. CUNY, Bayside, 1971-80; assoc. prof. Marion A. Buckley Sch. Nursing Adelphi U., Garden City, N.Y., 1981-88; ednl. cons. Nat. League for Nursing, N.Y.C., 1980-81; prof. sch. nursing SUNY, Stony Brook, 1988-92, chmn. adult nursing, 1988-92; prof., chair Coll. Nursing East Tenn. State U., 1992—; mem. faculty Regents Coll. degrees in nursing program USNY, Albany, 1978-91, cons., 1978—; faculty cons. geriatrics Montefiore Med. Ctr., 1991-93. Editor Scholarly Inquiry in Nursing Practice jour., 1983—; contbr. articles to profl. jours. Robert Wood Johnson clin. nurse scholar postdoctoral fellow U. Rochester (N.Y.), 1983-85. Mem. Am. Nurses Assn., Nat. League for Nursing, Gerontol. Soc. Am., N.Am. Nursing Diagnosis Assn., Soc. for Research in Nursing Edn.

MITCHELL, CAROL ANN, lawyer; b. New Bedford, Mass., Sept. 2, 1957; d. John E. and Edith A. (Mogensen) M. AB, Vassar Coll., 1979; JD, William and Mary Coll., 1982. Bar: D.C. 1983, U.S. Ct. Appeals (Fed. cir.) 1988, U.S. Ct. Internat. Trade 1986. Atty.-advisor Benefits Rev. Bd., Washington, 1982-83; import compliance specialist Internat. Trade Adminstrn. U.S. Dept. Commerce, Washington, 1983-85; assoc. Collier, Shannon & Scott, Washington, 1985-90, Akin, Gump, Strauss, Hauer & Feld, Washington, 1990-91, Dewey, Ballantine, Washington, 1991-94; Steptoe & Johnson, Washington, 1994—. Mem. ABA, Women in Internat. Trade, Vassar Club. Office: Steptoe and Johnson 1330 Connecticut Ave NW Washington DC 20036

MITCHELL, CAROLYN COCHRAN, academic administrator; b. Atlanta, Dec. 27, 1943; d. Clemern Covell and Agnes Emily (Veal) Cochran; m. W. Alan Mitchell, Aug. 30, 1964; 1 child, Teri Marie. AB magna cum laude, Mercer U., 1965, M in Svc. Mgmt., 1989. Caseworker Ga. Dept. Family & Children Svcs., Macon, 1965-67, Covington, 1967-69; presch. dir. Southwestern Theol. Sem., Ft. Worth, 1969-70; presch. tchr., dir. Noah's Ark Day Care, Bowden, Ga., 1970-72, First Bapt. Ch., Bremen, Ga., 1972-75, Roebuck Park Bapt. Ch., Birmingham, Ala., 1975-79; freelance office mgr. and bookkeeper Macon, 1979-84; asst. to pres. Ga. Wesleyan Coll., Macon, 1984—; exec. dir. Ga. Women of Achievement, 1991-95; dir. Macon Arts Alliance, 1987-91; mem. Cultural Plan Oversight Com., 1989-90. Mem. Get Out the Vote Task Force, Macon, 1981—, Macon Symphony Guild, 1986-91; dep. registrar Bibb County Bd. Elections, Macon, 1981-95. Mem. AAUW (bd. dirs. Ga. chpt., v.p. 1991-93, chair coll.-univ. rels. 1993-94, v.p., treas., historian Macon chpt., Named Gift honoree 1988), NAFE, Am. Mgmt. Assn., Presdl. Assts. in Higher Edn., Sigma Mu. Democrat. Unitarian. Office: Ga Wesleyan Coll 4760 Forsyth Rd Macon GA 31297-4299

MITCHELL, CHERRY ANNE, financial planner; b. Glendale, Calif., Nov. 14, 1950; d. John R. and Mabel B. (Stevenson) M. AA in Nursing, Los Angeles Valley Coll., 1971. Cert. Fin. Planner; RN, Calif. Registered rep. and agt. Prin. Fin. Group, Visalia, Calif., 1984-87, agt., 1984—; registered rep. Foothill Securities, Inc., Visalia, 1987-88, SunAm. Securities, Inc., Visalia, 1988-90, Fin. Network Investment Corp., Visalia, Calif., 1990—; owner Prosperity Planning Svcs., Visalia, 1987—. Vol. Hospice of Tulare County Guild, Visalia, 1986—, pres. 1989-90. Mem. Inst. Cert. Fin. Planners, Networking for Women (bd. dirs. Visalia chpt. 1986-90), treas. 1989), Kaweah Bus. and Profl. Women (pres. 1989-91), Tulare-Kings County Assn. Life Underwriters (sec.-treas. 1985-89, v.p. 1989-90, pres.-elect 1990-01, pres. 1991-92), Estate Planning Coun. Tulare County, Visalia C. of C. Republican. Baptist. Home: 5621 W Elowin Ct Visalia CA 93291-8917 Office: 130 N Kelsey St Ste H-4 Visalia CA 93291-9000

MITCHELL, CHERYL ELAINE, marketing executive; b. Oceanside, N.Y., Dec. 27, 1951; d. Harold Bertram and Doris Meredith (Hose) M. BA in History, Polit. Sci., Hartwick Coll., 1973; postgrad., Syracuse U., 1973-75. Campaign staffer Udall for Pres., N.Y., 1975-76; sr. writer Syracuse (N.Y.) Record, 1976-78; assoc. nat. dir. pub. relations Cushman & Wakefield, Inc., N.Y.C., 1978-81; sr. account exec. JP Lohman Orgn., N.Y.C., 1981-84; v.p. SPGA Group, N.Y.C., 1984-86; pres. Mitchell & Assocs., N.Y.C., 1986—; lectr. in field; press agt. to internat. real estate developers, sports product mfrs., maj. league sports, architects, catering and gourmet foods, and filmmakers. Contbr. articles to profl. jours; prin. works include numerous corp. and product brochures, advt. and publicity. Dep. press sec. N.Y. Area, Tsongas for Pres. Campaign, 1992. Recipient ANDY award Art Dirs. N.Y., 1983, Champion award of excellence Graphic Arts Exhbn., 1985, Award of Merit Design and Mktg. Comm., 1986, Tech. Difficulty award Assn. Graphic Arts, 1992; co-winner 1990 AIGA Best of Show Bus. to Bus. Category. Mem. NAFE, Alliance of Bldg. Community (bd. dirs.), Urban Solutions (bd. dirs.). Democrat. Lutheran. Office: Mitchell & Assocs 36 W 20th St New York NY 10011-4212

MITCHELL, ELIZABETH H., state legislator; b. June 22, 1940. BA, Furnam U.; MA, U. N.C. Mem. Maine Ho. of Reps.; mem. legis. com., chmn. banking and ins. com.; exec. dir. Housing Authority, Augusta, Maine. Recipient Disting. Alumna award Furman U. Democrat. Home: RFD 1 Box 520 Augusta ME 04330 Office: Maine Ho of Reps State Capitol Augusta ME 04330*

MITCHELL, GENEVA BROOKE, hypnotherapist; b. Ringgold, Tex., Feb. 15, 1929; d. Roy Banks and Willie Jewel (Lemons) Shaw; m. Roy David Mitchell, Nov. 30, 1947; children: Ronald, Donald, Joel, Pamela, Annette. Cert. master hypnotist Hypnosis Tng. Inst., L.A., 1980, cert. hypnotherapist, 1983; cert. in advanced investigative and forensic hypnosis Tex. A&M U., 1982; D. Clin. Hypnosis, Am. Inst. Hypnotherapy, Calif., 1989. Chiropractic asst. Alamogordo, N.Mex., 1962-79; hypnotherapist Alamogordo Hypnosis and Counseling Ctr., 1980-92; mgr. Shaw Mobile Home Park, 1986—; mng. ptnr. Shaw, Mitchell & Mallory, Albuquerque, 1986, mgr., 1987-88; hypnotherapist M&M Horses Corp., Tularosa, N.Mex., 1985-92; owner A New Image Hypnosis Ctr., Albuquerque, retired, 1992; pres. N.Mex. Chiropractic Aux., 1984-85; mem. Am. Council Hypnotist Examiners, 1980-85; hypnotist for tape series; instr. New Forever Trim Life Loss Program. Author: Take The Power, 1991. Charter pres. La Sertoma, Alamogordo, 1957; pres. Oregon sch. PTA, Alamogordo, 1958, La Luz Sch. Parents Club, N.Mex., 1962; sec. N.Mex. Jr. Rodeo Assn., 1964; co-founder Pre-Sch. La Luz, 1969; mem. N.Mex. Gov.'s Council on Youth, 1969; bd. dirs. Otero County Jr. Rodeo Assn., N.Mex., 1968; dir. self-hypnosis sch.; speaker Am. Bd. Hypnotherapy Conv., 1991. Recipient Speakers award Life Found., 1984. Mem. Am Assn. Profl. Hypnotherapists, Ladies for Life (Appreciation award 1984, 90), N.Mex. Ladies Life Fellowship (pres. 1983, bd. dirs. 1985), S.W. Hypnotherapy Examining Bd., Internat. Chiropractic Assn. Aux. (pres. 1994—, conv. chmn. 1993), Ladies for Life Chiropractic Orgn. (pres. elect 1993). Avocations: golf, painting, swimming, martial arts, writing.

MITCHELL, JANET ALDRICH, fund raising executive, reference materials publisher; b. Providence, Jan. 12, 1928; d. Norman Ackley and Janet (Gordon) Aldrich; m. Raymond Warren Mitchell, Jan. 9, 1954 (div. 1967); children—Lydia Aldrich, Polly Burbank. A.B., Smith Coll., 1949; M.Ed., Rutgers U., 1975. Engaged in devel. various non-profit orgns., 1954-72; dir. devel. Wilson Fellowship Found., Princeton, N.J., 1972-74; dir. spl. projects N.J. Dept. Higher Edn., Trenton, 1974-76; pub., editor-in-chief Mitchell Guide, 1976-87, 93—; pres., chmn. Mitchell Guide, 1987—; cons. to numerous non-profit orgns., 1976-86; lectr. Adult Sch., Princeton, 1983-84. Editor: Directory of Woodrow Wilson Fellows, 1968; Guide to Federal Aid to Higher Education, 1975; Higher Education Exchange, 1978; A Community of Scholars, 1980. Exec. officer Princeton Community Democratic Orgn., 1984-86; elected mem. Princeton Twp. Com., 1987-89; mem. NAACP Legal Def. Fund, 1980-86; trustee N.J. Hist. Soc., 1984-86. Episcopalian. Clubs: Smith Coll. (pres. 1968-70), Princeton Dog (bd. dirs. 1962-68). Avocation: breeding and showing standard poodles. Home and Office: 430 Federal City Rd Pennington NJ 08534

MITCHELL, JANET BREW, health services researcher; b. N.Y.C., Oct. 20, 1949; d. Robert Moscrip Mitchell and Dorothy Brennan; m. Jerry Lee Cromwell, June 15, 1980; children: Alexander, Genevieve. BA with highest honors, U. Calif., San Diego, 1971; MSW, UCLA, 1973; PhD, Brandeis U., 1976. Rsch. asst. Brandeis U./Worcester Tng. Program in Social Rsch. & Psych., Waltham, Mass., 1973-75; sr. analyst Abt Assocs., Cambridge, Mass., 1975-77; asst. prof. Boston U. Sch. Medicine, 1977-80; pres. Ctr. for Health Econs. Rsch., Waltham, Mass., 1980—; mem. com. on monitoring access to health care svcs. Inst. Medicine, 1989-92; mem. nat. adv. com. Robert Wood Johnson Health Care Fin. Fellows, 1988-93; cons. VA, 1982-85, NIH, 1983-85, Health Care Financing Adminstrn., 1979—; advisor Physician Reimbursement Study, Congl. Budget Office, 1984-85; mem. adv. panel on physicians & med. tech. Office of Tech. Assessment, 1984-85; mem. health care tech. study sect. Nat. Ctr. for Health Svcs. Rsch., 1984-88; psychiat. social worker UCLA Med. Ctr., 1971-72; med. social worker U. So. Calif., 1972-73, Univ. Hosp. San Diego, 1973. Author (with F.A. Sloan & J. Cromwell) Private Physicians and Public Programs, 1978; contbr. chpts. to 8 books; contbr. numerous articles to profl. jours. Thesis grantee VA, 1976-77. Office: Ctr for Hlth Econ Rsch 300 5th Ave Waltham MA 02154

MITCHELL, JO ANN, newspaper feature editor; b. Hale County, Tex., Feb. 16, 1935; d. Phillip Thomas and Lillie Adele (Henderson) Huffine; m. James Clayton Mitchell, Oct. 30, 1954; children: Jerry Michael, James Lawrence, Jana Lynn Mitchell Hill. Student, Tex. Women's U., 1952-54; BS in English, West Tex. State U., 1964, MS in English, 1975. Cert. elem. and secondary tchr., Tex. Tchr. English and journalism White Deer (Tex.) Sch. Dist., 1964-65; tchr. English Pringle Sch. Dist., Stinnett, Tex., 1966-73; radio news dir. Sta. KQTY, Borger, Tex., 1976-84; reporter Borger News-Herald, 1984-85, Lifestyle editor, 1985—; corr. Sta. KAMR-TV, Amarillo, Tex., 1986—. Recipient Mark Twain award AP, Dallas, 1980, 1st Pl. Bus. Column Writing award, 1990, 2d Pl. Feature Writing award, 1990, Tex. Mng. Editors Assn., Dallas, 1983, 88, Sch. Bell award Ret. Tchrs. Assn. Tex., 1988, 91, 92. Mem. Tex. Press Women (writing awards 1988, 89, 90, 91, 92, 93, 94), Panhandle Press Assn. (writing awards 1985, 86, 87, 88, 90, 91, 92, 94), Nat. Fedn. Press Women, Tex. Hosp. Assn. (2d place Silver Star award), Borger C. of C. (editor newsletter 1980-84, publicity com. Women's Divsn. 1980-88). Republican. Methodist. Home: 300 Mesquite St Borger TX 79007-7542 Office: Borger News-Herald 209 N Main St Borger TX 79007-4711

MITCHELL, JO KATHRYN, hospital technical supervisor; b. Clarksville, Ark., Dec. 1, 1934; d. Vintris Franklin and Melissa Lucile (Edwards) Clark; m. James M. Mitchell, June 4, 1955 (dec. Feb. 1973); children: James, Karen Ann, Leslie Kay, Vicki Lynn. Student, U. Ark., Fayetteville, 1952-53; student, Coll. Ozarks, 1953-54, U. Ark., 1954-55, Little Rock U., 1958. Technologist clin. chemistry U. Hosp., Little Rock, 1956-57, asst. supr., 1957-59, rsch. technologist, 1960-62, asst. supr. clin. chemistry, 1979-82, supr. clin. chemistry, 1982—; technologist Conway County Hosp., Morrilton, Ark., 1959; office mgr., co-owner Medic Pharmacy, Little Rock, 1962-71; owner The Cheese Shop, Little Rock, 1977-80. Adult advisor Order Rainbow Girls local, Little Rock, 1970-84, state, Ark., 1977-84. Mem. Pharmacy Aux. (pres. 1967-69), Order Eastern Star. Methodist. Home: 6908 Lucerne Dr Little Rock AR 72205-5029 :

MITCHELL, JOAN LAGRONE, staff nurse; b. Chattanooga, May 22, 1939; d. Vance Allen and Florence Beatrice (Karr) LaGrone; m. George Robert Mitchell, June 2, 1963 (div. Feb. 1989); 1 child, Michelle. BA, Atlantic Union Coll., 1961; AS, Weber State Coll., 1970. Nurses aide St. Benedicts Hosp., Ogden, Utah, 1969, grad. nurse, 1970; charge nurse, staff Riverside (Calif.) Community Hosp., 1970-71; charge nurse med.-surg. Long Island (N.Y.) Jewish Hosp., 1971-72, charge nurse post cardiac intensive care, 1972-73; supr. Mercy Hosp., Davenport, Iowa, 1973-74, assoc. dir., 1974-77; charge nurse, staff Worcester (Mass.) Hahnemann Hosp., 1977-80; asst. dir. nursing Bancroft House Healthcare, Worcester, Mass., 1980-83; office mgr. Main St. Chiropractic Offices, Worcester, 1983-87; charge nurse, staff Clinton (Mass.) Hosp., 1987-89; per diem nurse, 1989-90; asst. nurse mgr. 3-11 shift med.-psychiat. unit Clinton (Mass.) Hosp., 1990-92, staff charge nurse spl. care unit, 1993—; per diem nurse Worcester VNA, 1992—. Seventh-day Adventist. Office: Clinton Hosp 201 Highland St Clinton MA 01510

MITCHELL, JONI (ROBERTA JOAN ANDERSON), singer, songwriter; b. Ft. Macleod, Alta., Can., Nov. 7, 1943; d. William A. and Myrtle M. (McKee) Anderson; m. Chuck Mitchell (div.); m. Larry Klein, Nov. 21, 1982. Student, Alta. Coll. Albums include Song to a Seagull, Clouds, Ladies of the Canyon, Blue, For the Roses, Court and Spark, 1974, Miles of Aisles, The Hissing of Summer Lawns, 1975, Hejira, 1976, Don Juan's Reckless Daughter, Mingus (Jazz Album of Year and Rock-Blues Album of Year, Downbeat mag. 1979), Shadows and Light, 1980, Wild Things Run Fast, 1982, Dog Eat Dog, 1985, Chalk Mark in a Rainstorm, 1988, Night Ride Home, 1991, Turbulent Indigo, 1994. Recipient Grammy award for Best Folk Performance, 1969, Grammy award for Best Arrangement Accompanying Vocalists (with Tom Scott), 1974. Address: care Peter Asher Mgmt 644 N Doheny Dr Los Angeles CA 90069-5526

MITCHELL, KATHLEEN ANN, illustrator, graphic designer; b. Cin., July 27, 1948; d. Gerald Paige and Velma Alice (Bleier) Clary; m. Terence Nigel Mitchell, Feb. 2, 1977; children: Jessica Rose, Alexander Christien. BSc in Design, U. Cin., 1971. Graphic designer Lippincott & Margulies, N.Y.C., 1971, Allied Internat., London, 1972, Moura-George Briggs, London, 1973-75; art dir., photographer Phonograph Record Mag., L.A., 1976-77; ptnr. Walter Morgan Assocs., Santa Monica, Calif., 1977-80; illustrator Artists Internat., L.A. and N.Y.C., 1983—. Illustrator: (book) Beauty and the Beast, 1995. Democrat. Home: 1040 22d St Santa Monica CA 90403-2041

MITCHELL, KATHRYN ELIZABETH, sales executive; b. Norman, Okla., Feb. 13, 1964; d. Jess Clark and Mary Kathryn (Stobaugh) M. BBA in Mktg., U. Okla., 1986. Sales rep. Campbell Soup Co., Dallas, 1986-87, sales specialist, 1987-89, account mgr., 1989-90, account exec., 1990-92; account dir. Campbell Soup Co., San Antonio, Tex., 1992-93; regional mgr. Stanley Hardware, San Antonio, 1993-94; account exec. Brandon Sys., Dallas, 1994—. Republican.

MITCHELL, KIM SARAHJANE, lawyer; b. Geneseo, Ill., Nov. 19, 1954; d. Edward Franklin and Lorraine Marie (Jung) Kittrell; m. Gary Everett Mitchell, May 19, 1979. BA, U. Notre Dame, 1976; JD, U. Mich., 1979. Bar: Ill. 1979, U.S. Dist. Ct. (no. dist.) Ill. 1979, Mich. 1988. Law clk. Ill. Appellate Ct. for 2d Dist., Waukegan, 1979-81; atty. Interstate United Corp., Chgo., 1981-85; asst. gen. counsel Canteen Corp., Chgo., 1985-87; corp. counsel Amway Corp., Grand Rapids, Mich., 1987—. Mem. ABA, Ill. Bar Assn., Mich. Bar Assn. Office: Amway Corp 7575 E Fulton St Ada MI 49355

MITCHELL, LAURA ANNE GILBERT, critical care nurse; b. Anniston, Ala., Oct. 13, 1957; d. Leonard A. and Betty Joyce (Wilkinson) Gilbert; m. Lee H. Mitchell, June 20, 1981; 1 child, Joseph L. ADN, DeKalb Coll., 1987; BSN magna cum laude, Med. Coll. Ga., 1993. CCRN. Staff nurse, preceptor ICU and CCU Gwinnett Med. Ctr., Lawrenceville, Ga., 1987-89, charge nurse cardiac catheterization lab., 1989—. Mem. AACN, Phi Theta Kappa (internat.), Sigma Theta Tau. Home: 435 Clark Lake Estate Dr Grayson GA 30221-1234

MITCHELL, LAURA ELLEN, adult critical care and high-risk/critical care obstetrics nurse; b. Boston, July 5, 1959; d. Milton G. and Bruce (Bowman) Campbell; m. Edward L. Mitchell, Apr. 12, 1987; 1 child, Amy. ADN, Palomar Coll., 1988; BSN, Calif. State U., Dominguez Hills, 1994. CCRN, cert. in med.-surg. perinatal nursing. Staff nurse Nurse Care Plus, Oceanside, Calif., Tri-City Med. Ctr., Oceanside; clin. nurse II U. Calif. Med. Ctr., Irvine; clin. nurse U. Calif. San Diego Med. Ctr. With U.S. Army, 1977-81. Mem. AACN, AAUW, ANA (practice couns. advanced practice and acute care), Assn. Women's Health, Obstetric and Neonatal Nursing, Jacobs Inst. Women's Health. Home: PO Box 4915 Oceanside CA 92052-4915

MITCHELL, LINDA SUE, accountant; b. Louisville, Aug. 28, 1951; d. Lawrence Damon and Evia (Sands) Jaggers; m. John Robert Hodge, June 14, 1969 (div. Mar. 1980); children: John Clinton Hodge, Christa Hodge Graham; m. Anthony Wayne Mitchell, Mar. 26, 1991; 1 child, Robert Taylor. BSBA, U. Louisville, 1981; MBA, Bellarmine Coll., 1986. CPA, Ky. Tchrs. aide Jefferson County Schs., Louisville, 1977-79; instr. Spencerian Coll., Louisville, 1982-87, Jefferson C.C., Louisville, 1988-91; acct. Mark Hottell, CPA, Louisville, 1988-91, Mitchell Bus. Svcs., Louisville, 1991—; tutor Bellarmine Coll., Louisville, 1986—. Home and Office: 5310 Robinwood Rd Louisville KY 40218

MITCHELL, MARGARET JEAN, management consultant; b. Ft. Leavenworth, Kans., Jan. 1, 1968; d. Gene Allen and Judith Ann (Clayman) M. BS in Computer Sci., Coll. William and Mary, 1989. Cons. KPMG Peat Marwick, Washington, 1989-91; sr. cons. KPMG Peat Marwick, San Diego, 1992—; mgr. Radiation Oncology Computer Systems, Carlsbad, Calif., 1991-92. Mem. NAFE, Am. Prodn. and Inventory Control Soc., Kappa Delta Alumnae Assn., William & Mary Alumni. Roman Catholic. Office: KPMG Peat Marwick 750 B St Ste 3000 San Diego CA 92101-8132

MITCHELL, MARILYN SUE, psychologist; b. St. Louis, June 5, 1942; d. Ray M. and Zelda (Adelstein) M.; m. Donn G. Kessler, Oct. 5, 1991; children: Jeffrey Lipschultz, David Lipschultz. BA, U. Ariz., 1963; MEd, U. Colo., 1969; M of Counseling, Ariz. State U., 1978, PhD in Psychology, 1984. Lic. psychologist, Ariz. Faculty assoc. Ariz. State U., Tempe, 1985-87; psychol. svcs. coord. John C. Lincoln Hosp.-Behavioral Health Ctr., Phoenix, 1986-87; staff psychologist Maricopa County Hosp., Phoenix, 1990-92; pvt. practice Phoenix and Tempe, 1985—; lectr., workshop presenter Mesa (Ariz.) Community Coll., 1986—. Mem. social action com. Temple Chai, Paradise Valley, Ariz., 1991—. Mem. Am. Psychol. Assn., Ariz. Psychol. Assn. Office: 333 E Osborn Rd Ste 365 Phoenix AZ 85012-2365

MITCHELL, MARJORIE TAYLOR, executive recruiter, consultant; b. Nashville, Aug. 11, 1946; d. George W. and Millie A. (Jenkins) T.; m. James C. Heath, Dec. 6, 1964 (div. June 1977); children: Lori M., Jennifer K.; m. Carl E. Mitchell, July 6, 1977. Student, El Paso C.C. Cashier Kroger, Nashville, 1967-69, Malone & Hyde, Murfreesboro, Tenn., 1974-77; credit analyst ABC Bank, El Paso, Tex., 1978-81; profl. recruiter Mary Greens Employment, El Paso, 1983-94, Keysource, El Paso, 1994—; cons. in field. Named Woman of Yr., Am. Bus. Women's Assn., 1988. Home: 6044 Sorrento St El Paso TX 79924-4226 Office: Keysource 4120 Rio Bravo St Ste 311 El Paso TX 79902-1051

MITCHELL, MOZELLA GORDON, English language educator, minister; b. Starkville, Miss., Aug. 14, 1936; d. John Thomas and Odena Mae (Graham) Gordon; m. Edrick R. Woodson, Mar. 20, 1951 (div. 1974); children: Cynthia LaVern, Marcia Delores Woodson Miller. AB, LeMoyne Coll., 1959; MA in English, U. Mich., 1963; MA in Religious Studies, Colgate-Rochester Divinity Sch., 1973; PhD, Emory U., 1980. Instr. in English and Speech Alcorn A&M Coll., Lorman, Miss., 1960-61; instr. English, chmn. dept. Owen Jr. Coll., Memphis, 1961-65; asst. prof. English and religion Norfolk State Coll., U. Norfolk, Va., 1965-81; assoc. prof. U. South Fla., Tampa, 1981-93, prof., 1993—; pastor Mount Sinai AME Zion Ch., Tampa, 1982-89; presiding elder Tampa dist. AME Zion Ch., 1988—; vis. assoc. prof. Hood Theol. Sem., Salisbury, N.C., 1979-80, St. Louis U., 1992-93; vis. asst. lectr. U. Rochester, N.Y., 1972-73; co-dir. Ghent VISTA Project, Norfolk, 1969-71; cons. Black Women and Ministry Interdenominational Theol. Ctr.; lectr. tour Fla. Trinity. Author: Spiritual Dynamics of Howard Thurman's Theology, 1985, Howard Thurman and the Quest for Freedom, Proc. 2d Ann. Howard Thurman Convocation (Peter Lang), 1992, African American Religious History in Tampa Bay, 1992;, New Africa in America: The Blending of African and American Religious and Social Traditions Among Black People in Meridian, Mississippi and Surrounding Counties (Peter Lang), 1994, also articles, essays in field; editor: Martin Luther King Meml. Series in Religion, Culture and Social Devel.; editorial bd. Cornucipia Reprint Series. Mem. connectional coun. A.M.E. Zion Ch., Charlotte, 1984—, staff writer Sunday sch. lit., 1981—, mem. jud. coun.; mem. Tampa-Hillsborough County Human Rels. Coun., 1987—; pres. Fla. Coun. Chs., Orlando, 1988-90; del. 7th assembly World Coun. Chs., Canberra, Australia, 1991; founder Women at the Well, Inc. Recipient ecumenical leadership citation Fla. Coun. Chs., 1990, Inaugural lectr. award Geddes Hanson Black Cultural Ctr. Princeton Theol. Sem., 1993; fellow Nat. Doctoral Fund, 1978-80; grantee NEH, 1981, Fla. Endowment for Humanities, 1990—, U. South Fla. Rsch. Coun., 1990—. Mem. Coll. Theology Soc., Am. Acad. Religion, Soc. for the Study of Black Religion (pres. 1992—), Joint Ctr. for Polit. Studies, Black Women in Ch. and Soc., Alpha Kappa Alpha. Phi Kappa Phi. Democrat. Methodist. Office: U South Fla 301 CPR Religious Studies Dept Tampa FL 33620

MITCHELL, PAMELA ANN, airline pilot; b. Otis AFB, Mass., May 6, 1955; d. Gene Thomas and Rose Margaret (Jones) Mitchell; m. Robert Carroll Stephens, May 26, 1984 (div. Dec. 1992). BFA, Colo. State U., 1975; postgrad., Webster Coll., 1981. Lic. pilot Ill., comml. instr., airline transport pilot, jet rating, Boeing 747 and 727, Boeing 747-400. Flight attendent United Airlines, Chgo., 1976-80; charter pilot Air Aurora, Sugar Grove, Ill., 1978-80; owner, operator Deliverance, Unltd. Ferry Co., Aurora, Ill., 1978-81; flight test pilot Cessna Aircraft Co., Wichita, Kans., 1981-82, nat. spokeswoman, 1982-83; airline pilot Rep. Airlines, Mpls., 1983-84, Northwest Airlines, Mpls., 1985—; pres., ptnr., artist Aerographics Jacksonville, Fla., 1986-90. Mem. Safety Coun. Airline Pilots Assn., 99's Internat. Women Pilots Assn., Mooney Aircraft Pilots Assn. (exec. bd.), Internat. Women Airline Pilots Soc. (mem. exec. bd.), Nat. Aviation Club, N.W. Airline Ski Team (capt.), Kappa Kappa Gamma. Republican. Presbyterian. Home: 12502 Mission Hills Cir Jacksonville FL 32225 Office: Northwest Airlines Minn/St Paul Internat Airport Saint Paul MN 55111

MITCHELL, PATSY MALIER, school founder and administrator; b. Greenwood, Miss., Aug. 28, 1948; d. William Lonal and Lillian (Walker) Malier; m. Charles E. Mitchell, Apr. 20, 1970; children: Christopher, Kara, Angela. BS in Edn., Delta State U., 1970, MEd, 1974, Edn. Specialist, 1979; MA in Ch. Ministries, Ch. of God Sch. Theology, 1990; PhD in Psychology and Counseling, La. Bapt. U., 1994; D in Edn. Christian Sch. Adminstrn., Baptist Christian U., 1992. Cert. sch. adminstr. Youth, Christian edn. dir. Ch. of God, Minter City, Miss., 1975—; teen talent dir. Ch. of God, Minter City, 1983—, missions rep., 1975—; dist. Christian edn. dir. Ch. of God, Cleveland, Miss., 1983-85; sch. adminstr. Ch. of God, Cleveland, 1985—; del. Ch. of God Edn. Leadership, Cleveland, Tenn., 1990; del., speaker Christian Schs. Internat., Chattanooga, Tenn., 1991. Contbr. articles to profl. jours. Dir. St. Jude Children's Hosp., Memphis, 1991; vol. 4-H Club, Greenwood, Miss., 1985-91. Named to Outstanding Young Women of Am., 1983; recipient Community Pride award Chevron, 1988, Internat. Woman of Yr. award, 1993. Mem. Christian Sch. Adminstrs., Christian Schs. Internat., Ch. of God Edn. Assn., Delta State Alumni Assn., Ch. of God Sch. of Theology Alumni Assn, Gospel Music Assn. Democrat. Home: RR 1 Box 72A Minter City MS 38944-9801

MITCHELL, PEGGY CARROLL, wellness program coordinator; b. Evergreen Park, Ill., Oct. 28, 1953; d. Robert Joseph and Joan (Templeman) Carroll; m. Dale Eugene Mitchell, May 6, 1977; children: Megan, Joseph, Ryan, Christopher. BS, Western Ill. U., 1975; MS, U. Ill., 1979. Teacher, coach Niles East High Sch., Skokie, Ill., 1975-76, Maine West High Sch., Des Plaines, Ill., 1976-79; instr. Maine-Niles Assn. Spl. Recreation, Skokie, 1978-79, Skokie Valley Hosp., 1978-79; instr., coach SUNY, Brockport, 1979-82; cons. Genesee Hosp., Rochester, N.Y., 1988—; wellness program coord. Hobart & William Smith Colls., Geneva, N.Y., 1990—, dir. recreation and intramurals, 1992—; instr. Honeoye (N.Y.) Cen. Sch. Adult Edn., 1991—. Vol., instr. ARC, 1972—, sec. West Ontario County, Canandaigua, N.Y., 1989—; mem. Geneva Red Cross Health and Safety, 1991—; bd. dirs. Am. Cancer Soc., Canandaigua, 1991—. Mem. Am. Coll. Sports Medicine, Nat. Intramural Recreational Sports Assn., Nat. Dance Exercise and Instr. Tchrs. Assn., Nat. Wellness Assn. Office: Hobart & William Smith Coll Geneva NY 14456

MITCHELL, SALLY SAWYER, artist; b. Leominster, Mass., Aug. 16, 1935; d. Herbert Leroy and Jane (Hyde) Sawyer; m. Charles B. Mitchell; children: Charles S., Glenn H. Grad., Sch. of Worcester Art Mus., 1978; ind. study, China, 1989-92. One-woman shows at Cape Cod Conservatory of Music and Art, Barnstable, Mass., 1990. Named First in Pastel, Creative Art Ctr., Chatham, Mass., 1988, First in Abstract Painting, 1992, First in Watercolor, New Eng. Exhbn., 1994; recipient Most Original Compositions award Worcester Art Mus., 1978. Mem. New Eng. Watercolor Soc., Copley Soc. Boston (Jurors Choice in abstract painting 1992), Cape Cod Art Assn. (Witterveld award of merit 1993, Yarmouth award 1993, first in watercolor), Nauset Painters (pres. 1992-93), Orleans Art Assn. (Best of Show 1986), Falmouth Artist Guild, Creative Art Ctr. Home: 105 Fox Meadow Dr Brewster MA 02631-1937

MITCHELL, SHARON STANLEY, supply analyst; b. Roanoke, Va., July 29, 1953; d. Jack Dempsey and Juanita Jeannette (Reed) Stanley; m. Jack W. Hobbs, July 20, 1980 (div. 1987); 1 child, Sarah Whitney; m. R. Edward Mitchell, Jr., Feb. 12, 1993. Acctg., Va. Western Coll., 1971-73, 80-81. Lic. realtor, Va. Accounts receivable Am. Motor Inns, Inc., Roanoke, Va., 1973-76; cost acct. VA Med. Ctr., Salem, Va., 1976-90, supply analyst, 1990—; mem. Valley Views publ. com., VA Med. Ctr.; v.p. Rose Motors, Ltd., Roanoke, 1982-81; real estate salesperson Peery & Flora, Ltd., 1988—. Contbr. articles to profl. jours. Chmn. edn. Fed. Women's Program, Salem, Va., 1984-87; co-chmn. hist. com. Grandin Ct. Bapt. Ch., Roanoke, Va., 1986—; admission com. North Cross Sch., 1988—; mem. Jr. League of Roanoke, Hist. Mus. Com., Dept. Va. Med. Cntr., Salem; vol. Mill Mountain Theatre, Mus. of Theatre History at Ctr. in the Sq., Roanoke, Va.; loaned exec. Combined Fed. Campaign/United Way, 1994. Recipient Equal Employment Opportunity award Fed. Women's Program Wk., 1984, Star award VA Med. Ctr., 1990. Mem. Va. Assn. Realtors, Nat. Assn. Realtors, Porsche Club Am. (bd. dirs. Blue Ridge region 1992—), Roanoke Symphony Assn. (season ticket com., polo com.). Home: 4938 Mount Holland Dr SW Roanoke VA 24018-1630

MITCHELL, STACY L., sales executive; b. Houston, Jan. 7, 1963; d. Donald Gene and Gloria Ann (Lester) T.; m. Joe Don Mitchell, April 2, 1981 (div. July 1986). Acct. exec. Merisel, San Jose, Calif., 1986-92; dealer, sales rep. Intuit, Palo Alto, Calif., 1992-93; sales rep. Silicon Graphics, Mountain View, Calif., 1994—. Office: Silicon Graphics 1295 Charleston Mountain View CA 94043

MITCHELL, STEPHANIE J., lawyer, government official; b. Lytham St. Annes, Lancashire, Eng., May 20, 1957; came to U.S., 1962; d. Frank and Jeanne Mitchell. Student, Chinese U., Hong Kong, 1976-77; AB with distinction, Cornell U., 1978, JD, 1980. Bar: D.C. 1980, U.S. Ct. Appeals (fed. cir.) 1988, U.S. Ct. Internat. Trade, 1988. Assoc. Akin, Gump, Strauss, Hauer & Feld, Washington, 1980-83; internat. trade specialist Office Peoples Republic of China and Hong Kong, Washington, 1983-84; assoc. Kaye, Scholer, Fierman, Hays & Handler, Washington and Beijing, 1984-87; atty.-advisor office chief counsel for import adminstrn. U.S. Dept. Commerce, Washington, 1987-90, with spl. projects on Cen. and Ea. European Law, Office of Gen. Counsel, 1990-91; asst. prof. Sch. of Law Oklahoma City U., 1991—; Asia-Pacific legal counsel Autodesk, Inc., Wanchai, 1993—; v.p. Bus. Software Alliance, Wanchai, 1993—; instr. Internat. Law Inst., Washington, 1986; adj. prof. Cornell U. Law Sch., 1990; mem. adv. bd. East Asia program Cornell U., Ithaca, N.Y., 1986—; fluent in Chinese, French, Spanish, and Russian langs. Mng. editor China Law Reporter, 1987-93; contbr. articles to legal books and jours. Mem. ABA, D.C. Bar Assn. Jewish. Office: Autodesk Inc, 18 Harbour Rd, Wanchai Hong Kong

MITCHELL, SUSAN BARANOWSKI, military officer, environmental health educator; b. Phoenix, July 3, 1955; d. Joseph John and Patricia Anne (Wolfe) Baranowski; m. Robert Edwin Mitchell, Dec. 17, 1988; children: Robert Edwin Jr., Kathryn Elizabeth. BSN, U. Ariz., 1977; MPH, U. Tex. Health Sci. Ctr., Houston, 1982. Cert. occupational health nurse. Commd. officer USAF, advanced through grades to maj., 1979—; ward/charge nurse St. Luke's Hosp. USAF, Phoenix, 1977-79; asst. charge nurse USAF Hosp. USAF, San Antonio, 1979-81; chief environ. health AFB USAF, Wichita Falls, Tex., 1982-84, Osan, Republic of Korea, 1984-85, Honolulu, 1985-88; instr. public health Sch. Aerospace Medicine USAF, San Antonio, 1988—; cons. Pacific Air Force Surgeon Gen./Occupational Health, Hawaii, 1986-88. Active Habitat for Humanity, San Antonio, 1991. Mem. Soc. Environ. Health Profls. (sec. 1988-89), Kappa Kappa Gamma (various offices 1975—). Republican. Methodist. Home: 12703 Country Crest San Antonio TX 78216-2337

MITCHELL, TAMARA O., judge; b. Mobile, Ala., Apr. 19, 1952; d. Maurice E. and Harriett (Roth) Olen; m. George E. Mitchell, Mar. 17, 1981. BS, U. South Ala., Mobile, 1974; JD, Whittier Coll., L.A., 1980. Bar: Calif. 1980, Ala. 1981. Pvt. practice Mobile, 1981-83; ptnr. Grodsky & Mitchell, Mobile, 1983-91; judge U.S. Bankruptcy Ct., Birmingham, Ala., 1992—. Mem. Nat. Conf. Bankruptcy Judges, Calif. State Bar, Ala. State Bar (exec. bd. bankruptcy sect. 1989-90, vice chairperson, chairperson com. on lawyer pub. rels. 1990-92, com. on bench and bar rels.), Mobile Bar Assn. (treas. 1991), Birmingham Bar Assn. Office: US Bankruptcy Ct 1800 5th Ave N Birmingham AL 35203-2111*

MITCHELL, TONJA KEASHAVEL, nutritional consultant; b. Miami, Fla., Dec. 15, 1963; d. Harold and Barbara-Jean (Underwood) King; m. Vernon Ray Lofton, Mar. 3, 1984 (div. 1991); 1 child, Shatana Mailis Lofton; m. Marco Antonio Mitchell, July 27, 1991. BS in Bus., Fla. Internat. U., 1989; BSN in Nutrition, Am. Coll. Nutrition, Birmingham, Ala., 1993. Mgr. Amoco minimart, Miami, 1983-84; nail technician TKL Nails, Miami, 1988-90; office clk. Inst. Med. Specialties, Miami, 1990-91; nutritional cons. Quick Weight Loss Inc., Houston, 1993—; assoc. Nature's Sunshine Products, Houston, 1993—. Mem. NAFE, Am. Naturopathic Med. Assn. Baptist. Home: 16510 Rainbow Lake Rd Houston TX 77095-4066

MITCHELL, VERNICE VIRGINIA, nurse, poet, author; b. Scott, Miss., Mar. 11, 1921; d. Isaiah and Martha Magdalene (Edwards) Smith; m. Willis Mitchell, Aug. 17, 1940; children: Elaine, Kenneth, Liethia, John, Ransom, Paul. Diploma, Princeton Continuation Coll., 1955. Nurse Cook County Sch. Nursing, Chgo., 1951-59, U. Ill. Hosp., Chgo., 1959-67, Grant Hosp., Chgo., 1967-78, Northwestern Meml. Hosp., Chgo., 1979-84; with U. Ill. Hosp. Aetna Nurse's Registry, Chgo., 1984—. Author: The Book Success Through Spiritual Truths, 1987, (poems) A Women, Chicago, The 12 Months; also numerous poetry and musical lyrics; guest poet on Dial-A-Poem, Chgo., 1988-89. Chmn. cookbook project 1988-89. Recipient merit cert. Am. Poetry Assn., 1982, merit cert. World of Poetry, 1983, 85, Golden Poet award 1986, 87, 88, Silver Poet award, 1989, 90; inducted into the Hall of Fame for Sr. Citizens, Chgo., 1991. Mem. 6700 Emerald Ave. Block Club (pres. 1971-92).

MITCHELL, VIRGINIA BRINKMAN, office manager; b. New Brunswick, NJ, Jan. 20, 1949; d. Douglas Haig and Mary Alice (Cullinane) Brinkman; divorced; 1 child, Michael Joseph Mitchell. Cert., Durham Bus. Coll., Houston; student, Brevard C.C., Cocoa, Fla. Cert. profl. sec. Sec. ITT-Fed. Electric, Houston, 1968, Mullins Investments, Houston, 1968-69; exec. sec. U. Houston, 1969-79; adminstrv. asst. Tex. A&M U., Corpus Christi, 1979-88; sales coord. Hewlett-Packard, Corpus Christi, 1988-89; exec. sec., visitors svc. mgr. Tex. State Aquarium, Corpus Christi, 1989-91; office mgr. Unified Svcs., Inc., Kennedy Space Ctr., Fla., 1992—. Mem. Nat. Mgmt. Assn., Profl. Secs. Internat., Space Coast Pet Therapy Program, Phi Theta Kappa. Episcopalian. Home: 5575 Broad Acres Merritt Island FL 32953 Office: Unified Services Inc PO Box 21082 Kennedy Space Center FL 32815

MITCHELL, WANDA GAYLE, chemist; b. Florence, Ala., Oct. 27, 1949; d. William Marvin and Agnes Jerene (Ferguson) M. BA, U. North Ala., 1973; PhD, Vanderbilt U., 1977. Chemist TVA, Muscle Shoals, Ala., 1969-72, chemistry technician, 1973; chemist New Brunswick Lab. Dept. Energy, Argonne, Ill., 1978-94, mgr. devel. program, 1986-90, mgr. safeguards assistance program, 1990, divsn. dir., 1993—. Contbr. articles to profl. jours., 1976—. Mem. ASTM (task group 1987-94), Inst. Nuclear Materials Mgmt. (membership sec. 1993-94), Am. Chem. Soc. (com. pub. affairs 1982-86), Sigma Xi, Phi Kappa Phi. Office: New Brunswick Lab US Dept Energy 9800 Cass Ave Lemont IL 60439-4802

MITCHELL-CHAVEZ, BETTIANNE (BA MITCHELL-CHAVEZ), franchise consulting company executive; b. Washington, Nov. 27, 1952; d. Noriar and Marylou (Lenk) Pahigian; m. John J. Stabers (div.); 1 child, John Chad; m. Robert Franklin Chavez, Mar. 11, 1991; stepchildren: Andrea, Julia. BS in English cum laude, Suffolk U. Cert. Wilson sales trainer; cert. in Brian Tracy sales and sales mgmt. instrn.; cert. instr. internat. bus., sales mgmt. Sr. account rep. Letter Men Inc., pub., mktg., advt., Burlington, Mass., 1978-82; mgr. Boston sales br. The Boston Herald, 1982-83; telemktg. ter. mgr. Compugraphic Corp. div. AGFA Corp., Wilmington, Mass., 1983-85; pres., mktg. cons. Advance Inc., mktg., recruitment and search co., Marlboro, Mass., 1985-88; dir. sales devel. AlphaGraphics Printshops of Future Inc. affiliate R.R. Donnelly and Sons, Tucson, v.p. tng. and support, 1991-93, v.p. franchise devel., 1993-94; CEO/founder The Consortium, Inc., Tucson, 1994—; adj. bus. instr. Pima C.C.; presenter in field. Mem. ASTD, NAFE, AAUW, Ariz. Franchisor Assn. (bd. dirs., program chairperson 1994—, licensor, liaison to Internat. Franchisor Assn. 1993—). Home: 2967 E Greenlee St Tucson AZ 85716 Office: AlphaGraphics 3760 N Commerce Dr Tucson AZ 85705

MITCHELL-RANKIN, ZINORA MONA, judge; b. Washington, Apr. 16, 1956; d. Walter, Sr. and Mary Lucinda (Sharpe) Mitchell; m. Michael Lee Rankin, May 14, 1988; 1 child, Everett. BA, Spelman Coll., 1976; JD, George Washington U., 1979. Bar: D.C. 1979. Law clk. voting rights divsn. U.S. Civil Rights Commn., Washington, 1977-78; law clk. divsn. of advice Nat. Labor Rels. Bd., Washington, 1978-79; trial atty. U.S. Dept. Justice, Washington, 1979-82; asst. U.S. atty. U.S. Attys.' Office, Washington, 1982-89; assoc. judge Superior Ct., Washington, 1990—; adj. prof. trial practice Nat. Law Ctr., Washington, 1990-92. Vol. Big Sister Program, greater metro. area, Washington, 1992—; mem. task force youth violence D.C. Ct. Appeals, 1994—. Recipient Mentor to Women Lawyers award Law Assn. for Women, 1994. Mem. William B. Bryant Inn of Ct. (master 1988-93). Office: DC Superior Ct 500 Indiana Ave NW Washington DC 20001

MITCHEM, MARY TERESA, publishing executive; b. Atlanta, Aug. 31, 1944; d. John Reese and Sara Letitia (Marable) Mitchem. BA in History, David Lipscomb Coll., 1966. Sch. and library sales mgr. Chilton Book Co., Phila., 1972-79; dir. market devel. Baker & Taylor Co. div. W.R. Grace, N.Y.C., 1979-81; dir. mktg. R.R. Bowker Co. div. Xerox Corp., N.Y.C, 1981-83, dir. mktg. research, 1983-85; mktg. mgr. W.B. Saunders Co. div. Harcourt, Brace & Jovanovich, Phila., 1985-87; mktg. dir. Congl. Quarterly Inc., Washington, 1987-89; dir. mktg. rsch. and devel. Bur. Nat. Affairs, Inc., Washington, 1990—. Mem. Book Industry Study Group, Inc. (chairperson stats. com. 1984-86), Mktg. Research Assn. Home: 4625 Tilden St NW Washington DC 20016-5617 Office: Bur Nat Affairs Inc 1250 23d St NW Washington DC 20037-1156

MITCHUM, MARGARET ELAINE, secondary educator; b. Kingstree, S.C., Apr. 10, 1945; d. Walter Barlow and Lilas Mae (Boyd) M. BA, Limstone Coll., 1967; MEd, U. S.C., 1979. Tchr. Georgetown County Dept.Edn., Hemingway, S.C., 1967—. Contact person United Way, Georgetown, S.C., 1990. Grantee Freedoms Found., 1982; recipient History Tchr. of Yr. award DAR, 1990. Baptist. Office: Pleasant Hill High 7R D Box # 181A Hemingway SC 29554

MITELMAN, BONNIE COSSMAN, public relations executive, writer, lecturer; b. Flint, Mich., Feb. 15, 1941; d. Maurice B. and Frieda H. (Ragir) Cossman; student U. Mich., 1958-61; BA, Northwestern U., 1969; MA, Manhattanville Coll., 1977; m. Stanley D. Lelewer, Mar. 12, 1961 (div. 1969); children: Joanne, Stephen (dec.); m. Alan N. Mitelman, July 23, 1972; 1 son, Geoffrey. Copywriter trainee Dancer-Fitzgerald-Sample, Inc., Chgo., 1956-60; advt. copywriter Spiegel, Inc., Chgo., 1961-63; freelance advt. and public relations writer, Chgo., N.Y., 1963—; co-founder Mitelman & Assocs., Briarcliff Manor, N.Y., 1972-92; with pub. rels. dept. Anti-Defamation League, N.Y.C., 1992—; adj. lectr. dept. history Mercy Coll., Dobbs Ferry, N.Y., 1979—; contbr. articles to N.Y. Times, Reform Judaism, 1977—. Mem. Am. Hist. Assn., Women in Comm., Authors Guild. Author: Mothers Who Work: Strategies for Coping; mem. editorial bd. Reform Judaism, 1977—. Home: 639 Pleasantville Rd Briarcliff Manor NY 10510-1925

MITERA, LAURA L., sales representative; b. Omaha; d. John L. Jr. and Theresa M. (Krupa) M. BSBA in Mktg., U. Nebr., Omaha, 1987. Consumer products sales rep. Boyle-Midway-Reckitt-Colman, Wayne, N.J., 1989-92; pharm. sales rep. Carnrick Labs., Cedar Knolls, N.J., 1992—. Mem. NAFE. Democrat. Roman Catholic. Home: 3317 South 56 St Apt 605 Omaha NE 68106

MITGANG, IRIS FELDMAN, lawyer; b. Chgo., Sept. 2, 1937; d. Harry and Leanore (Nelson) Feldman; m. Robert Newton Mitgang, Sept. 9, 1956 (div. Dec. 1974); children: Alix Susan, Steven Ross, Jennifer Lynn. AB, U. Chgo., 1958; MA, U. Rochester, 1967; JD, U. Calif., Davis, 1976. Bar: Calif. 1976; cert. specialist family law. Ptnr. Dodge, Reyes, Brorby, Randall, Mitgang & Titmus, Walnut Creek, Calif., 1978-90; prin. Law Office Iris F. Mitgang, Walnut Creek, Calif., 1990—; instr. legal writing Sch. Law U. Calif., Davis, 1975-76; adj. prof. law Sch. Law John F. Kennedy U., Walnut Creek, 1977-87, Sch. Law Golden Gate U., San Francisco, 1987; mem. pro tempore panel Contra Costa Superior Ct. Mem. editorial bd. Law Rev. U. Calif., Davis Sch. Law, 1976; contbr. various articles to profl. jours. Bd. dirs. Leadership Conf. Civil Rights, Washington, 1979-81. Recipient Woman of Yr. award Bus. and Profl. Women, 1979, Women's Leadership award State of Calif., 1980. Mem. Nat. Women's Polit. Caucus (nat. chair 1979-81, nat. adv. bd. chair 1981-85, vice chair 1977-79, politic. action chair 1977-79), Contra Costa Bar Assn. (co-chair fam. law mediation sect. 1992—), Alameda Contra Costa Trial Lawyers (bd. dirs. 1992—, chair mentors program). Democrat. Jewish. Office: Law Office Iris F Mitgang 1850 Mount Diablo Blvd Ste 605 Walnut Creek CA 94596-4427

MITRANY, DEVORA, marketing consultant, writer; b. Oak Park, Ill., Mar. 20, 1947; d. John Joseph and Frances Elizabeth (Kirke) Lang; m. Douglas Allen Braun, Sept. 16, 1967 (div. Sept. 1976); m. Stanton Mitrany, Feb. 7, 1988 (div. July 1994). BA cum laude, Beloit Coll., 1969; postgrad., Boston U., 1971-72. Elem. and presch. tchr., Oak Park, Ill. and Boston, 1969-72; regional adminstr. TRW Fin. Systems, Wellesley, Mass., 1972-76; mgr. mktg. communications Computer Sharing Svcs., Denver, 1976-82; dir. corp. communications Corp. Mgmt. Systems, Denver, 1982-85; sr. copywriter On-Line Software Internat., Fort Lee, N.J., 1985-86; mgr. corp. communications Health Mgmt. Systems, N.Y.C., 1986-89; dir. pub. rels. Am. Sephardi Fedn., 1989-92; pres. The Mitrell Group, 1992-94; U.S. mktg. dir. The Best of Israel, 1994—; press release chmn. Nassau Region Hadassah, 1992-94. Warden, vestry mem. Trinity Ch., Wrentham, Mass., 1974-76; mem. vestry St. Philip and St. James Episcopal Ch., Denver, 1983; vol. Hospice of Holy Spirit, Lakewood, Colo., 1980-83; bd. dirs. Talia Hadassah, 1986-94, co-pres., 1990-92; v.p. edn. Long Beach Hadassah, 1992-94; dir. pub. rels. Bus. Roundtable on Nat. Security, Colo., 1983-84. Recipient Nat. Leadership award, Long Beach Hadassah, 1991-92, Nat. Leadership award Talia Hadassah, 1993-94; named Woman of Yr. Talia Hadassah, 1993. Mem. Denver Advt. Fedn. (bd. dirs. 1981-83, Alfie award 1984), Colo. Conf. Communicators (Denver Advt. Fedn. liasion 1981-84), Am. Sephardi Fedn. (edn. com. 1987-89). Jewish. Democrat.

MITRUSHINA, MAURA NICOLAEVNA, psychologist, researcher; b. Lvov, Ukraine, Aug. 4, 1949; came to U.S., 1980; 1 child, Maria. Grad., Conservatory Music, Leningrad, Russia, 1973, U. Leningrad, 1977; PhD, SUNY, Stony Brook, 1985. Lic. psychologist, Calif.; diplomate Am. Bd. Profl. Psychology. Assoc. prof. Calif. State U., Northridge, 1985—; assoc. clin. prof. UCLA, 1989—; pvt. practice Los Angeles, 1988—; adj. prof. Pepperdine U., L.A., 1988—; dir. Olive View Hosp./UCLA predoctoral practicum, Sylmar, Calif., 1990—; commr. Bd. Psychology, Sacramento, 1992—; qualified med. examiner State of Calif., L.A., 1990—. Contbr. chpts. to books, numerous articles to profl. jours. Grantee State of Calif. Dept. Mental Health, Sacramento, 1985-88; recipient Individual Nat. Rsch. Svc. award NIH, Washington, 1988-89. Mem. APA, Internat. Neuropsychol. Soc., Nat. Acad. Neuropsychologists. Office: UCLA Neuropsychiat Inst 760 Westwood Plz Los Angeles CA 90024

MITTLER, DIANA (DIANA MITTLER-BATTIPAGLIA), music educator and administrator, pianist; b. N.Y.C., Oct. 19, 1941; d. Franz and Regina (Schilling) Mittler; m. Victor Battipaglia, Sept. 5, 1965 (div. 1982). BS, Juilliard Sch., 1962, MS, 1963; DMA, Eastman Sch. Music, 1974. Choral dir. William Cowper Jr. High Sch. and Springfield Gardens Jr. High Sch., Queens, N.Y., 1963-68, coordinator of music Flushing High Sch., Queens, 1968-79; asst. prin. music Bayside High Sch., Queens, 1979-86; assoc. prof. music Lehman Col. CUNY, 1986-87, prof., 1987—, choral dir., 1986—; dir. ednl. projects New World Records, 1987—; ednl. cons. Flushing Coun. on Culture and the Arts; cons. Sta. WNET; assoc. condr. Queens Borough-Wide Chorus, 1964-70; pianist, founder Con Brio Chamber Ensemble, 1978; faculty So. Vt. Music Festival, 1979-83; soloist with N.Y. Philharmonic, 1956; solo and chamber music appearances; examiner N.Y.C. Bd. Edn. Bd. Exams., 1985—. Author: 57 Lessons for the High School Music Class, 1983, Franz Mittler: Austro-American Composer, Musician and Humourous Poet, 1993. Choral dir. and accompanist various charitable, religious, mil., civic holiday functions. N.Y. State Regents scholar, 1958-62; scholarships, Juilliard Sch. and Eastman Sch. Music. Contbr. articles to music publs. Mem. Golden Key Soc., Am. Choral Dirs. Assn., Music Edn. Nat. Conf., Sonneck Soc. Democrat. Home: 10857 66th Ave Flushing NY 11375-2247 Office: Lehman Coll Music Dept Bedford Pk Blvd W Bronx NY 10468

MIX, ESTHER, federal judge; b. Warner, Okla., Dec. 21, 1920; d. Burk and Bertie (Hawkins) Markham; children—Sarah, Richard. Student U. Okla., 1937-39; McGeorge Coll. Law, 1948. Bar: Calif. 1951, U.S. Dist. Ct. (ea. dist.) Calif. 1956, U.S. Ct. Appeals (9th cir.) 1956. Practice law, 1951-71; magistrate judge U.S. Dist. (ea. dist.) Calif., Sacramento, 1971—. Mem. Women Lawyers Sacramento, Nat. Council Fed. Magistrates, Sacramento County Bar Assn., Calif. State Bar Assn., Fed. Bar Assn. Office: US Courthouse 650 Capitol Mall Rm 4049 Sacramento CA 95814-4708*

MIYASHIRO, RUTH E., bank executive; b. 1936. With Boysen Paint Co., Honolulu, 1955-56, Occidental Life Ins. Co., L.A., 1956-58; officer Bank of Hawaii, Inc., Honolulu, 1958—; v.p., sec. Bancorp Hawaii, Inc., Honolulu, 1971—. Office: Bancorp Hawaii Inc 130 Merchant St Honolulu HI 96813*

MIZELL, JOY REGISTER, critical care nurse; b. Canal Point, Fla., Dec. 3, 1936; d. Noonan A. and Opal A. (Duncan) Register; children: Sandra, Randa, William Michael. Student, Cook County Coll., Gainesville, Tex., 1977, 81; BS in Nursing, Tex. Womans U., Denton, 1978. Nurse Mariners Hosp., Tavernier, Fla., 1980-81; founder, owner, operator The Silk Leaf, Lewisville, Tex., 1981-83; sales exec. Sea Pines Real Estate, Fernandina Beach, Fla., 1984-85; developer's rep. Excel-Edco Investments, Inc., Palataka, Fla.; pub. rels. officer Bank of Burke County, Waynesboro, Ga., 1987-88; nurse critical care unit/ICU Kennestone Hosp., Marietta, Ga., 1988-90; nurse ICU Nassau Gen. Hosp., Fernandina Beach, Fla., 1990—; contract field RN Vis. Nurse Assn., 1991-93; community educator Assoc. Home Health, West Palm Beach, Fla., 1993—. Mem. Fla. Assisted Living Assn., Pres. Round Table for Women in Bus., Lewisville C. of C., Ambassador's Club (Lewisville), Fernandina Beach Builders Assn. (co-founder), Sardis (pres. 1986-87), Sardis Bus. Assn. (sec. 1987-88), Waynesboro Bus. Assn. (sec., bd. dirs.), Broadway Home Health Bd., Profl. Resource Network. Office: Associated Home Health Ste 110 185 E Indian Town Rd Jupiter FL 33477

MLAY, MARIAN, government official; b. Pitts., Sept. 11, 1935; d. John and Sonia M.; A.B., U. Pitts., 1957; postgrad. (Univ. fellow) Princeton U., 1969-70; J.D., Am. U., 1977. Mgmt. positions HEW, Washington, 1961-70, dep. dir. Chgo. region, 1971-72, dir. div. consol. funding, 1972-73, dep. dir. office policy devel. and planning USPHS, Washington, 1973-77; dir. program evaluation EPA, Washington, 1978-79, dep. dir. Office of Drinking Water, 1979-84, dir. Office of Ground Water Protection, 1984-91, dir. Oceans and Coastal Protection, 1991-95; sr. rschr. Nat. Acad. Pub. Adminstrn. 1995—. Bd. dirs. D.C. United Fund, 1979-80. Recipient Career Edn. award Nat. Inst. Public Affairs, 1969. Mem. ABA, D.C. Bar (steering com. energy, environment and natural resources sect.). Author articles in field. Home: 3747 1/2 Kanawha St NW Washington DC 20015-1838 Office: Nat Acad Pub Adminstrn 1120 G St NW Ste 850 Washington DC 20005

MLOCEK, SISTER FRANCES ANGELINE, financial executive; b. River Rouge, Mich., Aug. 4, 1934; d. Michael and Suzanna (Bloch) M. BBA, U. Detroit, 1958; MBA, U. Mich., 1971. CPA, Mich. Bookkeeper Allen Park (Mich.) Furniture, 1949-52, Gerson's Jewlery, Detroit, 1952-53; jr. acct. Meyer Dickman, CPA, Algaze, Staub & Bowman, CPAs, Detroit, 1953-58; acct., internal auditor Sisters, Servants of Immaculate Heart of Mary Congregation, Monroe, Mich., 1959-66, asst. gen. treas., 1966-73, gen. treas., 1973-76; internal auditor for parishes Archdiocese of Detroit, 1976-78; asst. to exec. dir. Leadership Conf. of Women, Silver Spring, Md., 1978-83; dir. of fin. Nat. Conf. of Cath. Bishops/U.S. Cath. Conf., Washington, 1989-94; CFO Sisters Servants of the Immaculate Heart of Mary, Monroe, Mich., 1994—; trustee Sisters, Servants of Immaculate Heart of Mary Charitable Trust Fund, Monroe, 1988—. Author: (manual) Leadership Conference of Women Religious/Conference of Major Superiors of Men, 1981. Treas. Zonta Club of Washington Found., Washington, 1983-88, pres., 1992-93; bd. dirs. Our Lady of Good Counsel High Sch., Wheaton, Md., 1983-89. Mem. AICPA, D.C. Inst. CPAs (mem. not-for-profit com. 1992-94, CFOs com. 1990-94. Democrat. Roman Catholic. Office: Sisters Servants Immaculate Heart Mary 610 W Elm Ave Monroe MI 48161-2884

MLSNA, KATHRYN KIMURA, lawyer; b. Yonkers, N.Y., Apr. 23, 1952; d. Eugene T. and Grace (Watanabe) Kimura; m. Timothy Martin Mlsna, Oct. 4, 1975; children: Lauren Marie, Matthew Christopher, Michael Timothy. BA, Northwestern U., 1974, JD, 1977. Bar: Ill. 1977, U.S. Dist. Ct. (no. dist.) Ill. 1977. Sr. counsel McDonald's Corp., Oak Brook, Ill.,

1977—; speaker in field. Contbr. chpt. to book. Bd. dirs. Japanese Am. Svc. Com. Mem. ABA, Ill. Bar Assn., Chgo. Bar Assn., Promotion Mktg. Assn. Am. (v.p. 1988-92, chmn., pres. 1992-93, chmn. integrated mktg. com.), Northwestern U. Alumni Assn. (officer). Office: McDonald's Corp 1 McDonald's Plz Oak Brook IL 60521

MMAHAT, ARLENE CECILE, steel company executive, insurance company executive, civic activist; b. New Orleans, Oct. 5, 1943; d. John Alden and Margaret Therese (Nuccio) Montgomery; divorced; children—Arlene, Amy, John Anthony, Jr. B.A., La. State U., 1965. Clk., Shell Oil Co., New Orleans, 1965; claims rep. Social Security, New Orleans, 1966-67; chmn. bd. New Era Tubulars, New Orleans, 1979-84; chief exec. officer Olympia Tubular Corp., New Orleans, 1984-88; ins. broker Frank B. Hall of La., New Orleans, 1988—. Bd. dirs. New Orleans Symphony, 1983-86 , chmn. musicians adv. com., 1984, 85, membership chmn., 1985, oil and gas chmn. devel. com., 1983, devel. chmn. pub. sector, 1984; mem. Houston Bus. Council, 1980—, Dallas Regional Bus. Council, 1987—, New Orleans Mus. Art Odyssey, 1987; Ind. Women's Orgn., 1968—steering com. Internat. Gastroenteroly Research Fellowship Fund, Tulane U. Med. Ctr.; mem. adv. bd. Kennedy Ctr. for Performing Arts, 1980, Loyola U. Sch. Music, 1982—, New Orleans Mus. Art, 1986— ; fin. advisor New Orleans Symphony Soc. Jr. Com., 1977-79, fin. chmn., 1976; bd. dirs. Young Audiences, Inc., 1985—; mem. nat. adv. bd. on tech. and the disabled U.S. Dept. HHS; bd. dirs. Leukemia Soc. Am., Inc., 1978, corp. del., 1979; founder Ladies Leukemia League, Nat. Assn. Women Bus. Owners chpt. 1980; Odyssey Weekend chmn. New Orleans Mus. Art, 1985, fellows, 1983; mem. adv. com. St. Michael's Sch. for Spl. Students, 1978—, fin. chmn., 1977, mem. fin. com., 1973-76; fin. chmn. La. Landmarks Soc., 1973-75; bd. dirs. Preservation Resource Ctr., 1980, ways and means com., 1979, Christmas Benefit advisor, 1975, 76, mem. Women in Bus./ Women in Politics, Acad. Sacred Heart Adv. Study Com. Assoc. producer Film Am., Inc. Gottschalk, A Musical Portrait, 1986. Named One of 10 Outstanding Persons, New Orleans Inst. Human Understanding, 1977; One of 83 People to Watch in 1983, New Orleans Mag.; recipient Vol. Activist award Germain Monteil and D.H. Holmes Co., Ltd., 1977. Democrat. Roman Catholic. Home: 828 Royal St # 236 New Orleans LA 70116-3115

MOAK-MAZUR, CONNIE J., investment consultant, marketing professional; b. Ft. Worth, Feb. 5, 1947; d. David Clark and Dorothy Carol (Jackson) Moak; m. Jay Mazur, May 31, 1987. BBA, N. Tex. State U., 1969. Cert. bus. edn. tchr. V.p. Lionel D. Edie & Co., N.Y.C., 1969-77; mgr. Peat, Marwick, Mitchell & Co., N.Y.C., 1977-80; v.p. Shaw Data, N.Y.C., 1980, Fred Alger Mgmt., N.Y.C., 1980-82; ptnr. Glickenhaus & Co., N.Y.C., 1982-93; mng. dir. Wasserstein Perella Capital, 1993—; speaker in field. Contbr. articles to profl. jours. Mem. Fin. Women's Assn., Am. Pension Conf., Internat. Found. Employee Benefit Plans, Assn. Investment Mgmt. Sales Execs. (bd. dirs., pres.). Home: 150 E 69th St Apt 19C New York NY 10021-5704 Office: Wasserstein Perella 31 W 52d St New York NY 10019

MOAN, MARY CATHERINE, software engineer; b. Houston, June 23, 1962; d. Louis Nicholas and Elizabeth Anne (Williams) Kuehler; m. Michael Raymond Moan, Sept. 1, 1984; children: Adrienne Christine, Ashley Marie. BS in Computer Sci., Baylor U., 1984. Process control programmer SETPOINT, Houston, 1984; software engr. Frontier Engring., Inc., Stillwater, Okla., 1984-89; software lead engr. Frontier Engring., Inc., Stillwater, 1989-92, project engr., 1992-94; prin. software engr. Hughes Tng., Inc., Arlington, Tex., 1994—. Republican. Roman Catholic. Home: 2002 Tarrant Ln Colleyville TX 76034 Office: Hughes Tng Inc 612 Six Flags Dr Arlington TX 76005

MOAZZAMI, SARA, civil engineering educator; b. Tehran, July 24, 1960; d. Morteza Moazzami and Ezzat Akbari. BS, George Washington U., 1981; MS, U. Calif., Berkeley, 1982, PhD, 1987. Rsch. asst. George Washington U., Washington, 1980-81; teaching asst. U. Calif., Berkeley, 1982-83, rsch. asst., 1983-87; prof. Univ. Conn., Stamford, 1987-91, Calif. Polytechnic State U., San Luis Obispo, 1991—; mem. 1989 Santa Cruz Earthquake Reconnaissance Team, Earthquake Engring. Rsch. Inst., Oakland, Calif., 1989; speaker internat. confs. in field. Author: (book) 3-D Inelastic Analysis of Reinforced Concrete Frame-Wall Structures, 1987. Recipient Genevieve McEnerney fellowship U. Calif., Berkeley, 1981-82, Martin Mahler prize in Materials Testing, George Washington U., 1981, Columbian Women Soc. scholarship, Washington, 1979-80. Mem. Am. Soc. Civil Engring. (scholarship 1980), Earthquake Engring. Rsch. Inst., Soc. Women Engrs. Office: Calif Polytechnic State Univ Sch Engring San Luis Obispo CA 93407

MOBERLY, BONNIE LOU, travel services executive; b. Ft. Wayne, Ind., Apr. 10, 1930; d. James Loyd and Rilla Elizabeth (Starner) Boyer; m. William Gregg Moberly, Oct. 26, 1952. Student, St. Francis Coll., 1971. Stock registrar Midwestern United Life Ins. Co., Ft. Wayne, 1956-59, adminstrv. asst., 1959-71; exec. sec. Zimmer, Inc., Warsaw, Ind., 1977-87; adminstrv. asst. Bristol-Myers Squibb, Warsaw, 1988-90, travel mgr., 1990-93; pres. Heritage Travel Svcs., 1994—. Mem. NAFE, Nat. Bus. Travel Assn. Home: 653 Heritage Ln Warsaw IN 46580-1932

MOBLEY, BARBARA JEAN, state legislator; b. Dec. 1, 1947; divorced. BS, Savannah State U.; postgrad., U. Ill., Miss. State U.; JD, So. Meth. U. Atty.; mem. Ga. Ho. of Reps., 1992—; mem. regulated beverages, spl. judiciary and transp. coms. Democrat. Baptist. Home: PO Box 371442 Decatur GA 30037 Office: Ga Ho of Reps State Capitol Atlanta GA 30334 also: 511-C Legis Office Bldg Atlanta GA 30334*

MOBLEY, EMILY RUTH, library dean, educator; b. Valdosta, Ga., Oct. 1, 1942; d. Emmett and Ruth (Johnson) M. AB in Edn., U. Mich., 1964, AM in Libr. Sci., 1967, postgrad. Tchr. Ecorse (Mich.) Pub. Schs., 1964-65; adminstrv. trainee Chrysler Corp., Highland Park, Mich., 1965-66, engring. libr., 1966-69; libr. II Wayne State U., Detroit, 1969-72, libr. III, 1972-75; staff asst. GM Rsch. Labs. Libr., Warren, Mich., 1976-78, supr. reader svcs., 1978-81; libr. dir. GMI Engring. & Mgmt. Inst., Flint, Mich., 1982-86; assoc. dir. for pub. svcs. & collection devel., assoc. prof. libr. sci. Purdue U. Librs., West Lafayette, Ind., 1986-89, acting dir. librs., assoc. prof. libr. sci., 1989, dean librs., prof. libr. sci., 1989—; adj. lectr. U. Mich. Sch. Libr. Sci., Ann Arbor, 1974-75, 83-86; mem. editorial bd. Reference Svcs. Rev., 1989—; grants reader Libr. of Mich., 1980-81; project dir. Mideastern Mich. Region Libr. Cooperation, 1984-86; cons. Libr. Coop. of Macomb, 1985-86, Clark-Atlanta U., 1990, 91; mem. search com. for new dir. of libr. Smithsonian Instn., 1988; mem. GM Pub. Affairs Subcom. on Introducing Minorities to Engring. Author numerous publs.; mem. editl. bd. Infomanage, 1993—; presenter in field. Mem. corp. vis. com. for librs. MIT, 1990—; mem. Ind. Statewide Libr. Automation Task Force, 1989-90; mem. state tech. strategy subcom. on info. tech. & telecommunications Ind. Corp. for Sci. & Tech., 1989; mem. nat. adv. com. Libr. of Congress, 1988; trustee Libr. of Mich., 1983-86, v.p., 1986, long range plan com., 1979-82, task force on document access and delivery, 1977-79; info. project mem. Rep. Nat. Conv., 1980; bd. dirs. Small Farms Assn., Southfield, Mich. Recipient Bausch & Lomb award for Scientific Achievement, 1960, Cert. for Outstanding Performance in Acad. Achievement State of Mich. Ho. of Reps., 1976, Spl. Tribute for Outstanding Contbns. Libr. of Mich. Bd. Trustees, 1986, Disting. Alumnus award U. Mich. Sch. Info. & Libr. Studies, 1989; U. Mich. Regents Alumni scholar, 1960-64; CIC doctoral fellow in libr. sci., 1973-76. Mem. ALA (com. on accreditation, subcom. to rev. 1972, standards for accreditation 1988-89, OLOS minority internship com. 1988-89, nominating com. 1992-93, mem. coun. resolutions com. 1993—), Assn. Coll. & Rsch. Librs. (task force on libr. sch. curriculum 1988-89, com. on profl. edn. 1990-92), Libr. Adminstrn. & Mgmt. Assn., Assn. Rsch. Librs. (bd. dirs. 1990-93), Spl. Librs. Assn. (pres. 1987-88, fellow 1991, numerous coms. and other offices), Alpha Kappa Alpha. Office: Purdue U Librs Stewart Ctr West Lafayette IN 47907

MOCCIA, MARY KATHRYN, social worker; b. Harrisburg, Pa.; d. John Joseph and Winifred Louise Trephan. BEd, U. Hawaii, 1978, MSW with distinction, 1980; postgrad., Fuller Theol. Sem., 1987. Intern Koko Head Mental Health Clinic, Honolulu, 1978-79, Dept. Social Services and Housing, Honolulu, 1979-80; vol. worker, group co-leader Waikiki Mental Health Ctr., Honolulu, 1979, social worker, 1980; workshop facilitator St. Louis-Chaminade Edn. Ctr. Dept. Insts. and Workshops, Honolulu, 1980-83; founding mem. Anorexia and Bulimia Ctr. Hawaii, Honolulu, 1983, pvt. practice psychotherapy and cons., 1983—; personal counselor Chaminade U. Honolulu, 1980-88; clin. social worker Queen's Med. Ctr., 1988—; group leader obesity program Honolulu Med. Group, 1988—; practicum instr. U. Hawaii, 1992—; guest lectr. U. Hawaii Sch. Social Work, Honolulu, 1980-81; vol. telephone specialist Suicide and Crisis Ctr. and Info. and Referral Service, Honolulu, 1981-83; mem. Hawaii Coun. Self Esteem, 1993; condr. various workshops on anorexia and bulimia. Guest appearances on local tv and radio programs. Mem. Manoa Valley Ch. Mem. Nat. Assn. Social Workers, Nat. Assn. Christians in Social Work, Acad. Cert. Social Workers, Mortar Bd. (pres., nat. del. 1978), Phi Kappa Phi, Pi Lambda Theta, Alpha Tau Delta (pres.). Office: Queens Med Ctr Dept Social Work 1301 Punchbowl St Honolulu HI 96813

MOCHARY, MARY VERONICA, lawyer; b. Budapest, Hungary, Sept. 7, 1942; d. Alexander and Elizabeth (Aranyi) Kasser; m. Stephen E. Mochary, Sept. 25, 1965 (div. 1990); children: Alexandra Veronica, Matthew Neal. BA, Wellesley Coll., 1963; JD, U. Chgo., 1967. Bar: Ark. 1968, N.J. 1970. Ptnr. Fayetteville, Ark., 1968-70, Mochary & Mochary, Montclair, N.J., 1970-85, Cerny & Mochary, Montclair, 1980-84, Lane & Mittendorf, Woodbridge, N.J., 1984-85; legal advisor U.S. Dept. State, Washington, 1985-89, spl. negotiator real estate issues, 1989-92; ptnr. Wine & Assocs., Washington, 1990—; cons. Hughes, Hubbard & Read, Washington; pres. Technopulp, Inc., Montclair, 1982—, Iamco, Inc., Montclair, 1982—; ptnr. Kand M Co., Montclair, 1982—, Atlantic Highlands Real Estate, Montclair, 1982-89. Mayor Twp. of Montclair, 1980-84; mgr. Kasser Art Found., Montclair, 1982—; Rep. candidate U.S. Senate, State of N.J., 1984; co-chmn. re-election campaign Tom Kean for Gov., N.J., 1985; treas. Com. N.J. Rep. Women in 1985; mem. regional adv. bd. Anti-Defamation League of B'nai B'rith, Montclair Library Bd., 1980—, Montclair Twp. Council, 1980—; chmn. Rep. Task Force Women's Polit. Caucus N.J., Overseas Neighbors Internat., 1985; bd. dirs. Am. Hungarian Found., 1970—, Found. Ednl. Alternatives, Urban League, 1985—. Raoul Wallenberg Com. of U.S., 1985—, Nat. Mus. for Women in the Arts, Washington, 1994—; mem. Women's Internat. Forum, 1992—; founder, bd. dirs. WISH;. Recipient Disting. Service award Am. Hungarian Found., 1984. Mem. ABA, N.J. Bar Assn., Ark. Bar Assn., N.J. Conf. Mayors, N.J. Elected Women Ofcls., Suburban Essex Bus. and Profl. Women (named Woman of Yr. 1985), Wellesley Club (pres. N.J. chpt. 1983-84), Women's Internat. Forum, Adirondack League Club, Ocean Reef Club, Angler's Club (Key Largo, Fla.), Rappahannock County Garden Club. Office: 26 Park St Montclair NJ 07042-3443 also: 2700 Virginia Ave NW Washington DC 20037-1908

MOCK, MELINDA SMITH, orthopedic nurse specialist, consultant; b. Austell, Ga., Nov. 15, 1947; d. Robert Jehu and Emily Dorris (Smith) Smith; m. David Thomas Mock, Oct. 20, 1969. AS in Nursing, DeKalb Coll., 1972. RN, Ga.; cert. orthopedic nurse specialist, orthopedic nurse. Nursing technician Ga. Baptist Hosp., Atlanta, 1967, staff nurse, 1979; asst. corr. Harcourt, Brace & World Pub. Co., Atlanta, 1968-69; receptionist-sec. Goodbody & Co., Atlanta, 1969-70; nursing asst. DeKalb Gen. Hosp., Decatur, Ga., 1970-71; staff nurse Doctor's Meml. Hosp., Atlanta, 1972-73; staff nurse Shallowford Community Hosp., Atlanta, 1973, relief charge nurse, 1973, charge nurse, 1973-76, head nurse, 1976-79, orthopedic nurse specialist emergency room, 1979; rehab. specialist Internat. Rehab. Assocs., Inc., Norcross, Ga., 1981, sr. rehab. specialist, 1981, rehab. supr., 1981-82; cons., founder, propr. Healthcare Cost Cons., Alpharetta, Ga., 1982-83; cons., founder, pres. Healthcare Cost Cons., Inc., Alpharetta, 1983—; mem. legis. com. of adv. council Ga. Bd. Nursing, Atlanta, 1984-85; mem. adv. council Milton High Sch. Coop. Bus. Edn., 1986-89; mem. Congressman Patrick Swindall Sr. Citizen Adv. Coun., 1988, Congressman Ben Jones Vets. Affairs Adv. Com., 1989-92, Nat. Fedn. Specialty Nursing Orgns. Task Force on Profl. Liability Ins., 1987-89, Dep. voter registrar Fulton County Voter Registration Dept., Atlanta, 1983-87; Rep. treas. 23d house dist., mem. Fulton County Rep. Com., 1989—, nominating com., 1991, 92, 93, chmn. polit action com., 1993—, asst. treas., 1994—; treas. 41st House Dist. Rep. Party, 1993—; 1st vice chairwoman 6th Congl. Dist. Rep. Party, 1993—; mem. State Com. Ga. Rep. Party, 1993—; del. Fulton County Rep. Conv., 1991, 92, 94, delegate Ga. 4th Congrl. Dist., 1991, 92, parliamentarian, 1992, credentials com., 1992, Ga. Rep. Conv., 1991, 92, 93; mem. Chattahoochee Rep. Women, 1989—, chmn. campaign com., 1992-94, rec. sec., 1995—; chmn. nominating com. House Dist. 23, 1990; mem. steering com. to re-elect state rep. Tom Campbell, 1990; mem. campaign staff to re-elect state senator Sallie Newbill, 1990; health advisor campaign to elect Matt Towery for lt. gov., 1990, health adv. compaign to elect Bob Barr U.S. Senate, 1991-92; mem. election com. Mark Burkhalter for State Rep.; vol. campaign com. to re-elect Congressman Newt Gingrich, 1992, 94; active White House Conf. on Small Bus., 1995. Recipient Nat. Disting. Service Registry award, 1987; named one of Outstanding Young Women Am., 1984. Mem. NAFE, Nat. Assn. Orthopedic Nurses (nat. policies com. 1981-82, chmn. govt. rels. com. 1987-90, nat. treas. 1991—, nurse Washington intern 1987, legis. contbr. editor news 1989, chmn. legis. workshop, 1989, co-chmn. legis. workshop, 1990, guest editorial Orthopaedic Nursing Jour. 1988, speaker 1990, 92, 93, 94, Ann. Congress, del. 1982, 91, 92, 93, 94, Pres's. award 1992, chmn. budget and fin. com. 1991—), Orthopedic Nurses Assn. (nat. bd. dirs. 1977-79, nat. treas. 1979-81, Council Splty. Nursing Orgns. Ga. (nominating com. 1976-77), Ga. Med. Auditors Assn., Nat. Nurses in Bus. Assn., Assn. Rehab. Nurses (bd. dirs. Ga. chpt. 1980-81, del. people-to-people program to China 1981), Nat. Fed. Ind. Bus. (guardian 1988—, adv. coun. 1990—, healthcare task force chmn. 1992—), Am. Bd. Nursing Specialities (chmn. nominating com. 1993-94, chmn. com. on specialty bd. rev. 1993—), Ga. Jaycees (dist. 4C rep. Ga. Jaycee Legis. 1984, 85), Ga. seatbelt coalition, Orthopaedic Nurses Cert. Bd. (bd. dir. 1991—, pres. 1992-93, task force on advanced practice certification 1991-92), North Fulton C. of C. (vice chmn. health service effectiveness alliance 1984-85, chmn. 1985-86, co-chmn./editor periodical 1985, 3rd Quarter Workhorse award 1985), Alpharetta Jaycees (adminstrv. v.p. 1984-85, internal v.p. 1985-86), Alpharetta Jaycee Women (bd. dirs. 1983). Baptist. Avocations: reading, boating, cmty. svc. activities. Home: 424 Michael Dr Alpharetta GA 30201-2122 Offiost Cons Inc PO Box 466 St Alpharetta GA 30239-1952

MOCKLER, ESTHER JAYNE, political party administrator, former state legislator; b. Jackson, Wyo., Sept. 21, 1957; d. Franklin and Nancy (Fisher) Mockler. BA in Polit. Sci., Wellesley Coll., 1980. Mem. Wyo. Ho. of Reps., 1992—; exec. dir. Wyo. Dem. Pary, Cheyenne, 1993—. Office: PO Box 2036 Cheyenne WY 82003-2036

MOCKLER, MARY JEAN, financial manager; b. Montague, Mass., Jan. 2, 1958; d. Eugene Edmund and Mary Katherine (Akey) Sokolosky; m. Colman M. Mockler III, Sept. 28, 1984. BA, Wheaton Coll., Norton, Mass., 1980. Sr. legal assoc. The First Nat. Bank Boston, 1986-90, mgr. spl. projects, 1990-92; fin. mgr. Amesbury, Mass., 1992—; trustee Mockler Charitable Trust, Wayland, Mass., 1992—. Roman Catholic.

MODER, LISA MARIE, software engineer, manufacturing process engineer; b. Muchengladbach, Germany, Apr. 18, 1965; came to U.S., 1967; d. John Andrew and Sue Elaine (Anderson) Bondch; m. David Lincoln Moder, May 2, 1987; children: Daniel Lee, Sean Michael, Christopher James. BSEE, Met. State Coll., 1990. Software engr. Erbtec Engring., Boulder, Colo., 1989—. Mem. IEEE. Democrat. Home: 3355 Newland St Wheat Ridge CO 80033-6440 Office: Erbtec Engring 2760 29th St Ste 100 Boulder CO 80301-1230

MODY, JANET ISBELL, English language educator; b. St. Louis, Apr. 1, 1934; d. Hugh Olin and Norma (Wagner) Isbell; m. Cawas M.S. Mody, Aug. 10, 1966; 1 child, Cyrus M.S. BS, U. Mo., 1955; student, So. Meth. U., Dallas, 1955-56; MA, Columbia U., 1963. Cert. secondary English tchr. Kans. Dir. Christian edn. Maynard Meth. Ch., L.A., 1956-57, Mo. Meth. Ch., Columbia, 1957-62; editor audio-visual resource guide Nat. Coun. Chs., N.Y.C., 1962-66; English tchr. Lawrence (Kans.) High Sch., 1966-70, South High Sch., Omaha, 1970-74, Manhattan (Kans.) Jr. High, 1976-79; English tchr., dept. chair Lawrence High Sch., 1979—. Mem. adminstrv. bd. First United Meth. Ch., Lawrence, 1993, Lawrence Civic Choir, 1979—, also past pres. Recipient SPARK award Kans. Arts Coun., Topeka, 1979. Mem. Mortar Bd. Alumnae (past pres.), Sigma Alpha Iota. Home: 2100 Carolina St Lawrence KS 66046-2860 Office: Lawrence High Sch 1901 Louisiana St Lawrence KS 66046-2999

MOE, VIDA DELORES, civic worker; b. Ryder, N.D., Feb. 29, 1928; d. John Nelson and Inga Marie (Lewis) Ahlgran; m. Placido Ferdinand, July 28, 1950 (div.); children: Terrence Paul, Star Marie; m. Edgar Louis Moe, May 24, 1970 (dec. 1983). Student, Minot State U., 1964-66; diploma interior decorating, LaSalle Extension U., 1976. Sec. Raleigh Ins., Tacoma, 1949-50; clk. stenographer Army Transp. Office, San Francisco, 1951-51; clk.-typist Base Supply, Minot AFB, N.D., 1960-61, clk.-stenographer Base Housing, 1961-62, 74, sec. MIADS Direction Ctr., 1962-63, sec. QC Br., 1963-64, sec. dept. acctg. and fin., 1964-65, med. sec. USAF Regional Hosp., 1965-66, sec. Minuteman AFSC, 1966-67, 74-75, sec. 5th Bomb Wing, 1967-70, sec. 1st Missile Wing, 1973-74, sec. dept. mil. personnel, 1975-76, sec. disaster preparedness, 1987-93; sec., salesperson Allen Realty, Minot, 1980-85. Pres. City Art League, 1977-79, 86-87; chmn. Carnegie Restoration and Art Ctr. Project, 1980-87; bd. dirs. Patrons of Libr., Minot, 1978-87, sec., 1979-80, v.p., 1981, pres., 1982-83; v.p. 40/50 Rep. Women Minot, 1982, chair decorations com., 1983; historian Minot Rep. Women, 1984-86. Recipient Superior Performance award 5th Bomb Wing, Minot AFB, 1968, Devotion to Vol. Duty award USAF Regional Hosp., Minot, 1983, 86, Superior Performance Cash award Dept. of Air Force 857 Combat Support Group, 1988-91. Mem. N.D. Bus. and Profl. Women's Club (rec. sec. 1978-79, 81-82), Minot Bus. and Profl. Women's Club (pres. 1981-82), Am. Legion Aux. (judge jr. art posters contest 1980-82, pres. 1982-84), Minot Shrine Hosp. Aux. (v.p. 1984, 85, pres. 1986, 87), Beta Sigma Phi (v.p. Laureate Epsilon chpt. 1981-82, pres. 1983-85, Valentine Queen 1985, Girl of Yr. 1985, preceptor Eta chpt., Girl of Yr., 1980, life), MidState Porcelain Artists Guild (v.p. 1983 89, pres. 1984) Club, Order Eastern Star (North Dakota Grand chpt., grand rep. 1979-81, dist. dep. 1982-83, chair credentials com. 1983-84, Grand Martha 1984-85, Grand Electa 1985-86, chmn. registration com. 1986-87, assoc. Grand Conductress 1987-88, Grand Conductress 1989-90, assoc. Grand Matron 1990-91, Worthy Grand Matron 1991-92, Worthy Matron Minot Venus chpt. 1976, 87, 88-89, sec. 1993-94, chaplain 1994-95), Elketts (2nd. v.p. 1988-89, sec. 1993-94), Sons Norway (social dir. 1993-94, chmn. social dirs. 1994), Eagles Aux. (conductor 1993-94, chaplain 1994-95). Lutheran. Avocations: china painting, oil painting, sewing, tennis, embroidery. Home: 705 25th St NW Minot ND 58703

MOE-FISHBACK, BARBARA ANN, counseling administrator; b. Grand Forks, N.D., June 24, 1955; d. Robert Alan and Ruth Ann (Wang) Moe; m. William Martin Fishback; children: Kristen Ann, William Robert. BS in Psychology, U. N.D., 1977, MA in Counseling and Guidance, 1979, BS in Elem. Edn., 1984. Cert. elem. counselor, Ill. Tchr. United Day Nursery, Grand Forks, 1977-78; social worker Cavalier County Social Services, Langdon, N.D., 1979-83; elem. sch. counselor Douglas Sch. System, Ellsworth AFB, S.D., 1984-87, Jacksonville (Ill.) Sch. System, 1987—. Vol. Big Sister Program, Grand Forks, 1978-84; leader Pine to Prairie Girl Scout council, Langdon, N.D., 1980-82; tchrs. asst. Head Start Program, Grand Forks, 1979. Mem. Am. Assn. Counseling and Devel., NEA, Ill. Assn. Counseling and Devel., Ill. Sch. Counselor Assn., AAUW (local br. newsletter editor 1980-81, br. sec. 1981-83), Ill. Edn. Assn., Am. Sch. Counselor Assn., Kappa Alpha Theta (newsletter, magazine article editor 1976-77). Club: Jaycettes (Langdon) (dir. 1982-83). Avocations: cooking, camping, curling, ceramics, creative writing. Home: 291 Sandusky St Jacksonville IL 62650-1844 Office: Jacksonville Sch Dist Jacksonville IL 62650

MOEHRLE, CAROL MOSER, public health administrator; b. Pullman, Wash., July 24, 1955; d. Peter Leroy and Lois (Druffel) Moser; m. Bruce R. Moehrle, July 22, 1978; children: Benjamin, Kayla. BSN, Idaho State U., 1978. RN, Idaho. Pub. health nurse North Ctrl. Dist. Health Dept., Lewiston, Idaho, 1978-87, coord. health promotion, 1987-89, nursing supr., 1989-90, dir. phys. health, 1990-92, dist. dir., 1992—. Bd. dirs. Home Health-Hospice, 1990—, Inter-Collegiate Nursing Sch., 1990—. Named hon. Shriner, Lewiston, 1991. Mem. APHA, ANA, Idaho Pub. Health Assn., Idaho Nurses Assn. Office: North Ctrl Dist Health Dept 215 10th St Lewiston ID 83501

MOELLER, LAURA LEE, retail executive, library consultant; b. St. Louis, Feb. 20, 1927; d. Edwin Charles and Henrietta Maude (Schelp) Luedde; m. Gerald Herbert Moeller, June 25, 1949; children: Dereck John, Dori Lee, Merry Cay. AB, Harris Tchrs. Coll., St. Louis, 1948; sch. libr. cert., Washington U., St. Louis, 1965. Elem. tchr. Howard Sch., St. Louis, 1948-50, Bay View Sch., Norfolk, Va., 1951; libr. East Ladue Jr. High Sch., St. Louis, 1965-77; mgr., buyer Wornall House Mus. Shop, Kansas City, Mo., 1978-79; owner Crabtree & Evelyn London on Plaza, Kansas City, 1979—. Vice pres. Women's Coun. U. Mo., Kansas City, 1984-85. Mem. Mo. Assn. Sch. Librs. (pres. 1976-77), Plaza Mchts. Assn. (bd. dirs. 1991-94, nominating com. 1981), AAUW, DAR (treas. 1992-93, vice regent 1994—), Wives of Rotarians (v.p. 1983-84), Rockhill Tennis Club. Presbyterian (sec. Ch. Libr. Guild 1990—). Home: 6247 Rosewood Shawnee Mission KS 66205-3010 Office: Crabtree & Evelyn 505 Nichols Rd Kansas City MO 64112-2007

MOELLER, MARY ELLA, retired home economist, educator, radio commentator; b. Southampton, N.Y., Mar. 11, 1938; d. Harry Eugene and Edith Leone (Reester) Parsons; m. James Myron Moeller, Aug. 5, 1961; 1 child, Mary Beth. BS in Home Econs., U. Nebr., 1960; MLS, SUNY, Stony Brook, 1977. Tchr. home econs. Port Jefferson Schs., N.Y., 1960-70; home econs. program asst. Suffolk County Coop. Extension of Cornell U., Riverhead, N.Y., 1972-82; tchr. home econs. Eastport High Sch., Riverhead, 1982-85, South County Schs., Bellport Middle Sch., N.Y., 1985-93; sch. coord. N.Y. state mentoring program Bellport Middle Sch., 1992—; host Ask Your Neighbor, Sta. WRIV, Riverhead, 1982-87; trainer Home Econs. Entrepreneurship N.Y. State Edn. Dept., 1986—; mem. home and career skills regional team N.Y. State Edn. Dept., 1984-86; mem. consumer homemaking adv. bd. Bd. Coop. Edn.; N.Y. state mentoring sch. coord. Bellport Mid. Sch., 1992—. Contbr. monthly articles to consumer publs. Mem. N.Y. State Home Econs. Assn., Am. Home Econs. Assn. (cert. home economist), Suffolk County Home Econs. Assn., DAR (historian 1985), Eastern Star (matron 1970). Home: PO Box 377 Miller Place NY 11764-0377 Office: Bellport Mid Sch Kreamer St Bellport NY 11713

MOELLER, MARY KAY, printed music specialist; b. Marshfield, Wis., June 2, 1953; d. Wilhelm Heinrich and Hildegard Mary (Koehler) M. BA, U. Wis., Eau Claire, 1977. Printed music specialist Schmitt Music Ctr., Eau Claire, Wis., 1978—; tchr. piano pvt. practice, Eau Claire, Wis., 1987—; internat. coord. Aspect Fgn. Student Exch., Eau Claire, Wis., 1990—. Active Friends of the Libr., Eau Claire, 1991—. Mem. Wis. Music Tchrs. Assn., Chippewa Valley Music Tchrs. Assn. Democrat. Office: Schmitt Music Ctr 2952 London Sq Eau Claire WI 54701

MOELY, BARBARA E., psychology researcher, educator; b. Prairie du Sac, Wis., July 17, 1940; d. John Arthur and Loretta Ruth (Giese) M.; children: John Jacob Moely Wiener, David Andrew Moely Wiener. Student Carroll Coll., 1958-60; BA, U. Wis., 1962, MA, 1964; PhD, U. Minn., 1968. Asst. prof. U. Hawaii, Honolulu, 1967-71; research psychologist UCLA, 1971-72; asst. prof. Tulane U., New Orleans, 1972-75, assoc. prof. psychology, 1975-85, prof., 1985—, dept. chmn., 1992—. Contbr. articles to profl. jours. Grantee U.S. Office Edn., Handicapped Pers. Preparation, 1977-80, Tulane U., 1973, 75, 77, 78, 83-84, Inst. for Mental Hygiene, City of New Orleans, 1983-84, Nat. Inst. Edn., 1983-84, La. Edn. Quality Support Fund, 1988, 89, 91, 92. Mem. AAUP (v.p. La. conf. 1992-93, sec. 1993—, pres. Tulane 1992-94), APA, Soc. Rsch. in Child Devel., Am. Ednl. Rsch. Assn., Southwestern Soc. for Rsch. in Human Devel. (pres. 1986-88), Phi Beta Kappa (pres. Alpha chapter La. 1981-82). Office: Tulane Univ Dept Psychology New Orleans LA 70118

MOFFAT, MARYBETH, automotive company executive; b. Pitts., July 25, 1951; d. Herbert Franklin and Florence Grafe (Knerem) M.; m. Brian Francis Soulier, Nov. 30, 1974 (div.). BA, Carroll Coll., 1973. Indsl. engring. technician Wis. Centrifugal Co., Waukesha, Wis., 1976-77; indsl. engr. Utility Products, Inc., Milw., 1977-79; mgr. indsl. engring. Bear Automotive (div. SPX Corp.), Bangor, Pa., 1980-90; program mgr. Toyota Johnson Controls, Inc. Automotive Systems Group, 1990—. Group home house parent Headwaters Regional Achievement Ctr., Lake Tomahawk, Wis., 1974. Mem. Am. Inst. Indsl. Engrs., MTM Assn. for Standards Rsch., Indsl. Mgmt. Soc., Alpha Gamma Delta (standards chmn. 1971-72). Republican. Methodist. Avocations: skiing, horseback riding, swimming, reading. Office:

Johnson Controls Inc Automotive Systems Group One Quality Drive Georgetown KY 40324-2011

MOFFAT, NANCY J., state legislator, municipal administrator; b. Greenville, S.C., Nov. 7, 1951; d. Jack Thomas and Margie Mae (Harder) Jones; m. H. Wayne Moffat, Dec. 9, 1972; children: Tonya Danene, Dedra Dianne. BS in Psychology and Polit. Sci. magna cum laude, U. North Tex., 1988, MPA, 1990. Real estate agt., 1976-87; gen. mgr. residential constrn. Moffat Constrn. Co., Inc., 1979-87; adminstrv. svcs. coord. City of Denton, Tex., 1990-92; mem. Tex. Ho. Reps., 1991—; asst. city mgr. City of Bedford, Tex., 1992—. Active Meals on Wheels, Adopt a Grandparent, First Bapt. Ch., Grapevine, Tex.; former mem. exec. bd. PTO; mem. Rep. Caucus Policy and Steering Com.; mem. N.E. Leadership Forum; adv. bd. Baylor Hosp.; women's adv. bd. HEB Harris Meth. Hosp. Teaching fellow U. North Tex., 1988-90. Mem. Colleyville C. of C., Grapevine C. of C., Southlake C. of C., Keller C. of C., Women's C. of C. Grapevine, Women's C. of C. Southlake. Address: 1414 Whispering Dell Ct Southlake TX 76092-8854

MOFFATT, JOYCE ANNE, performing arts executive; b. Grand Rapids, Mich., Jan. 3, 1936; d. John Barnard and Ruth Lillian (Pellow) M. BA in Lit., U. Mich., 1957, MA in Theatre, 1960; HHD (hon.), Sch. Psychology, San Francisco, 1991. Stage mgr., lighting designer Off-Broadway plays, costume, lighting and set designer, stage mgr. stock cos., 1954-62; nat. subscription mgr. Theatre Guild/Am. Theatre Soc., N.Y.C., 1965-67; subscription mgr. Theatre, Inc.-Phoenix Theatre, N.Y.C., 1963-67; cons. N.Y.C. Ballet and N.Y.C. Opera, 1967-70; asst. house mgr. N.Y. State Theater, 1970-72; dir. ticket sales City Ctr. of Music and Drama, Inc., N.Y.C., 1970-72; prodn. mgr. San Antonio's Symphony/Opera, 1973-75; gen. mgr. San Antonio Symphony/Opera, 1975-76, 55th St. Dance Theater Found., Inc., N.Y.C., 1976-77, Ballet Theatre Found., Inc./Am. Ballet Theatre, N.Y.C., 1977-81; v.p. prodn. Radio City Music Hall Prodns., Inc., N.Y.C., 1981-83; artist-in-residence CCNY, 1981—; propr. mgmt. cons. firm for performing arts N.Y.C., 1983—; exec. dir. San Francisco Ballet Assn., 1987-93; mng. dir. Houston Ballet Assoc., 1993-95; cons. Ford Found., N.Y. State Coun. on Arts, Kennedy Ctr. for Performing Arts.; mem. dance panels N.Y. State Coun. on Arts, 1979-81; mem. panels for Support to Prominent Orgns. and Dance, Calif. Arts Coun., 1988-92. Appointee San Francisco Cultural Affairs Task Force, 1991; chmn. bd. Tex. Inst. for Arts in Edn., 1994—; trustee of I.A.T.S.E. Local 16 Pension and Welfare Fund, 1991-94. Mem. Assn. Theatrical Press Agts. and Mgrs., Actors Equity Assn., United Scenic Artists Local 829, San Francisco Visitors and Conv. Bur. (bd. dirs.). Club: Argyle (San Antonio).

MOFFATT, KATY (KATHERINE LOUELLA MOFFATT), musician, vocalist, songwriter; b. Ft. Worth, Nov. 19, 1950; d. Lester Huger and Sue-Jo (Jarrott) M. Student, Sophie Newcomb Coll., 1968, St. John's Coll., 1969-70. Rec. artist Columbia Records, 1975-79, Permian/MCA Records, 1982-84, Enigma Records, L.A., 1985, Wrestler Records, L.A., 1987-88, Red Moon Records, Switzerland, 1988-93, Philo/Rounder Records, 1989-93, Round Tower Music, U.K., Ireland, Europe, 1993—, Watermelon Records, U.S., 1994—. Folksinger, Ft. Worth, 1967-68; musician, vocalist, songwriter, rec. artist: (films) Billy Jack, 1970, Hard Country, 1981, The Thing Called Love, 1993; prodn. asst. film, Sta. KIII-TV, Corpus Christi, 1970, audio engr., Sta. KRIS-TV, Corpus Christi, 1970; musician, vocalist in blues band, Corpus Christi, 1970; receptionist, bookkeeping asst., copywriter, announcer, Sta. KFWT, Ft. Worth, 1971, musician, vocalist, songwriter, Denver, 1971-72, on tour, 1973, 75—, Denver, 1974, on tour, 1976-79, European tour, 1977, Can. tour, 1984-85, on tour in Europe, U.S., Can. and Asia, 1985—; albums include Katy, 1976, Kissin' In The California Sun, Am. release, 1977, internat. release, 1978, A Town South of Bakersfield, 1985, Walkin' on the Moon, European release, 1988, U.S. release, 1989, Child Bride, 1990, (duet album with brother Hugh) Dance Me Outside, 1992, (Switzerland only) Indoor Fireworks, 1992, The Greatest Show On Earth A.K.A. The Evangeline Hotel, 1994, Hearts Gone Wild, 1994; singles include Take it as it Comes, 1981, Under Loved and Over Lonely, 1983; songs include The Magic Ring, 1971; Gerry's Song, 1973, Kansas City Morning, 1974, Take Me Back To Texas, 1975, (Waitin' For) The Real Thing, 1975, Didn't We Have Love, 1976, Kissin' in the California Sun, 1977, Walkin' on the Moon, 1989. Named one of 4 Top New Female Vocalists, Cashbox Singles Awards, 1976; nominee for Top New Femal Vocalist, Acad. Country Music, 1985; recipient Record World Album award, 1976. Mem. Am. Fedn. Musicians, AFTRA, SAG.

MOFFATT, MINDY ANN, educational training specialist; b. Mpls., Aug. 3, 1951; d. Ralph Theron and La Vone Muriel (Bergstrom) M. Student, UCLA, 1972-73; BA, Calif. State U., Fullerton, 1975, MS in Edn., 1991. Cert. elem. tchr. and adminstr., Calif. Tchr. early childhood edn. program Meadows Elem. Sch., Valencia, Calif., 1977-78; tchr. United Parents Against Forced Busing, Chatsworth, Calif., 1978-80; founding tchr. Gazebo Two Sch. for Young Gifted and Creative Children, Summerville, Calif., 1980-81; tchr. Anaheim Union High Sch. Dist., Anaheim, Calif., 1981-89, mentor, tchr., 1985-88; tchr. Greentree Elem. Sch., Irvine, Calif., 1989-90; with Thurston Mid. Sch., Laguna Beach, Calif., 1990-92; editor Cypress Pub. Group, Laguna Hills, Calif., 1992; tng. specialist Scripps Clinics and Rsch. Found., LaJolla, Calif., 1993-94; tchr. White Hill Mid. Sch., Ross Valley Sch. Dist., San Anselmo, Calif., 1994—; cons. writing project U. Calif., Irvine, 1982—; textbook cons. McDougal, Littell & Co., Evanston, Ill., 1984-86; facilitator Summer Tech. Tng. Inst., Irvine, 1987. Co-author: Practical Ideas for Teaching Writing as a Process, 1986, 87, Thinking/Writing: Fostering Critical Thinking Through Writing, 1991, Reading, Thinking, and Writing About Culturally Diverse Literature, 1995. Mem. Our Ultimate Recreation (Orange County, Calif., chairperson social com. 1983, chairperson backpacking 1983, v.p. 1993-94). Democrat. Mem. Unity Ch. of Truth.

MOFFIT, GISELA R., German language educator; b. Bad Gottleuba, Sachsen, Germany, Sept. 27, 1940; arrived in U.S., 1965; d. Gunter and Brunhilde (de Fries) Kind; m. Harry R. Doby, July 25, 1965 (dec. 1966); m. Tom C. Moffit, Apr. 26, 1968; children: Andrew, Benjamin. BA, Ctrl. Mich. U., 1967; MA, U. Mich., 1968; PhD, Mich. State U., 1991. With Ctrl. Mich. U., Mt. Pleasant, Mich., 1975—, asst. prof. German, 1987—. Author: Bonds and Bondage, 1993; pub. Deutsche Zeitung, 1990—. Recipient Fgn. Lang. Tchr. of Yr., Mich. Fgn. Lang. Assn., 1993. Mem. Am. Assn. Tchrs. German (v.p. Mich. chpt. 1993), Am. Coun. on Tchg. Fgn. Langs., German Studies Assn., Women in German, Phi Delta Kappa. Office: Ctrl Mich U Dept German Pearce 316 Mount Pleasant MI 48859

MOGERMAN, VERONICA LINDA, organizational administrator; b. Vaughn, N.Mex., Jan. 5, 1954; d. Isidro Joseph and Stella Miriam (Gallegos) Romero; m. Michael Scott Mogerman, Sept. 24, 1978. BA, U. Rochester, 1976, St. Joseph Coll., 1985. Physician, nurses asst. Linwood-Bryant Hosp., Buffalo, 1976-77; acctg. coordinator U. N.Mex., Albuquerque, 1977-78; scientific editor, typist The Sackler Sch. of Medicine, Tel Aviv, Israel, 1978-79; adminstrv. asst. Albany Travel Ltd., Tel Aviv, 1979-81; office mgr. Ketchum Distributors, Inc., Newington, Conn., 1981-84; exec. asst. Greater Hartford Bd. Realtors, Inc., West Hartford, Conn., 1984-85, Coopers & Lybrand, Hartford, Conn., 1985-89, Orthopedic Assocs. Hartford, P.C., 1989-93; adminstrv. dir. HMO and PPO accounts mgr. adminstr. OptiCare Eye Health & Vision Ctrs., P.C., Norwalk, Conn., 1993—. Editor (newsletter) The Workpaper, 1986; contbr. articles to synagogue pub. Organizer, fundraiser Hartford Easter Seals Rehab. Ctr., 1986-88, Newington Children's Hosp., 1986-87; active Women's Orgn. for Conservative Judaism, 1981-81, Conn. Opera; bd. dirs. bus. and profl. women's div. Greater Hartford Jewish Fedn. Recipient Congressman's Medal of Merit U.S. Congress, 1972. Fellow John F. Kennedy Meml. Libr. Found.; mem. AAAS, NAFE, Am. Mgmt. Assn., Nat. Audubon Soc., N.Y. Acad. Scis., Mus. Heritage Soc., Aux. AMA, Smithsonian Assocs., Wilderness Soc., Am. Assn. Individual Investors, Conn. Opera Assn., Mystic Seaport Mus. Assn., Wadsworth Atheneum, Math. Assn. Am., Nat. Mus. Women Arts, Bus. and Profl. Women's Orgn., Cousteau Soc., Assn. of U. Rochester Alumni (treas. AURA, Conn. chpt.). Democrat.

MOGGE, HARRIET MORGAN, educational association executive; b. Cleve.; d. Russell VanDyke and Grace (Wells) Morgan; m. Robert Arthur Mogge, Aug. 17, 1948 (div. 1977); 1 child, Linda Jean. BME, Northwestern U., 1959; postgrad., Ill. State U., 1969. Instr. piano, Evanston, Ill., 1954-58; instr. elem. music pub. schs., Evanston, 1959; editorial asst. archivist Summy-Birchard Co., Evanston, 1964-66, asst. to editor-in-chief, 1966-67, cons., 1968-69, ednl. dir., 1969-74, also historian, 1973-74; supr. vocal music jr. high sch., Watseka, Ill., 1967-68; asst. dir. profl. programs Music Educators Nat. Conf., Reston, Va., 1974-84, dir. meetings and convs., 1984-94, mgr. direct mktg. svc., 1981-89; sr. cons. Convention Consulting Svc., 1993—. Mng. editor Am. Suzuki jour., 1972-74, Gen. Music Today, 1987-91; mgr. diplay advt. Model T Times, 1971—; vice chair editorial bd. Exposition Mgmt., 1991-93; Active various community drives. Mem. Music Educators Nat. Conf., Am. Choral Dirs. Assn., In and About Chgo., Music Educators Assn. (bd. dirs.), Suzuki Assn. Ams. (exec. sec. 1972-74), Internat. Assn. Expn. Mgmt. (cert.; mem. edn. com. 1979-88, chmn. edn. com. 1985-87, bd. liaison edn. com. 1987-88, bd. dirs. Washington chpt. 1983-85, nat. bd. dirs. 1986-91, del. to conv. liaison coun. 1989-90, nat. v.p. 1989, nat. pres. 1990, nat. past pres. 1991), Mu Phi Epsilon, Kappa Delta (province pres. 1960-66, 72-76, regional chpts. dir. 1976-78, nat. dir. scholarship 1981-84). Republican. Presbyterian. Clubs: Bus. and Profl. Women's (Watseka) (bd. dirs. 1968-70); Antique Automobile (registrar ann. meeting 1961-86), Model T Ford Internat. (v.p. 1971-72, 76-77, pres. 1981, treas. 1983-87, bd. dirs. 1971-87). Home: 1919A Villa Ridge Dr Reston VA 22091-4824 Office: PO Box 3362 Reston VA 22090-1362

MOGUL, LESLIE ANNE, marketing communications executive; b. Balt., Mar. 9, 1948; d. Harry and Elaine (Blaustein) M.; m. William Kasper. AS, Miami Dade Jr. Coll., 1969; BA, Temple U., 1976. Accredited pub. rels. Account exec. Gray & Rogers, Inc., Phila., 1976-80; pres. Leslie Mogul, Inc., Phila., 1980-84; v.p. McKinney, Inc., Phila., 1984-87; assoc. dir. comm. Scripps Meml. Hosps., San Diego, 1987-93; dir. pub. rels. Scripps Health, San Diego, 1993, dir. customer rels. and mktg., 1994—. Recipient over 25 awards local and nat. pub. rels. and comm. orgns. Mem. Pub. Rels. Soc. Am. (dir.-at-large 1993-94), Alumni Leadership Calif. Office: Scripps Health PO Box 28 La Jolla CA 92038

MOGY, CATHERINE WADDELL, critical care nurse; b. Florence, S.C., Mar. 13, 1964; d. Harold Dean and Sarah Margaret (Windham) Waddell; m. Richard A. Mogy, Sept. 13, 1986. ADN, Florence-Darlington Tech Ctr., 1985; BSN, Med. U. S.C., Florence, 1989; cert., Richland Meml. Sch. Anesthesia, 1991. RN, S.C.; cert. advanced cardiac life supports, nurse anesthetist. Staff nurse McLeod Regional Med. Ctr., Florence, S.C., 1985-86; staff nurse ICU Bruce Hosp., Florence, 1986-89; nurse anesthetist Bruce Hosp., 1991—. Recipient Francis Marion alumni scholarship. Mem. Am. Assn. Nurse Anesthetists, ANA, Sigma Theta Tau.

MOHAMED, DONNA FAHIMAH, counselor; b. Chapel Hill, N.C., Oct. 19, 1959; d. Thomas Lloyd and Helen Eleanor (Helms) Pendergraft; m. Dilip Gandhi, Aug. 19, 1978; 1 child, Sundeep; m. Mustafa Hussein Al-Bar, Apr. 15, 1991; 1 child, Maidah Nasreen. BA in Religious Studies with high honors and distinction, U. N.C., 1994. Rehab. therapist John Umstead Hosp. Continuing Treatment, Butner, N.C., 1985-86; immigration paralegal Law Offices of Douglas Holmes, Durham, N.C., 1986-87; immigration specialist Law Offices of Manlin Chee, Greensboro, N.C., 1987-92; program dir., accredited counselor Immigration & Minority Assistance Network, Durham, 1992—; pro bono project rep. Lawyers Com. for Human Rights, Fredericksburg, Va., 1987-88; minority devel. counselor, Ibad Ar-Rahman Sch., Durham, 1990-91; immigration cons. to bd. dirs. Jamaat Ibad Ar-Rahman, Inc., Durham, 1990—; dir. cmty. counseling IMAN, Durham, 1991—; speaker N.Am. Coun. for Muslim Women, Chgo., 1994; panelist on cultural awareness, Dept. Edn. and Counseling, U. N.C., Chapel Hill, 1994; organizer, presenter ann. workshops Coll. Bound Program for Youth, Chapel Hill, 1992—. Recipient 1st prize ann. cooking contest Triangle Muslim Women's Group, 1992. Mem. Am. Muslim Coun., Am. Immigration Lawyers Assn. (pro bono affiliation), Muslim Women's Orgn. (pres. Chapel Hill, N.C. chpt. 1991-93), Muslim Student's Assn. (exec. dir. Chapel Hill chpt. 1992-93), Islamic Soc. N.Am., Social Scientists Am., Golden Key Nat. Honor Soc. Democrat. Office: Immigration and Minority Assistance Network PO Box 51458 Durham NC 27717-1458

MOHIUDDIN, YASMEEN NIAZ, economics educator; b. Aligarh, India, Feb. 25, 1948; came to U.S., 1974, naturalized, 1994; d. Niaz Ahmed Siddiqui and Bismillah Niaz Ahmed; m. Muhammad Mohiuddin Siddiqi, July 29, 1972; children: Umar Mohiuddin Siddiqi, Nazia Mohiuddin Siddiqi. BA, U. Karachi, Pakistan, 1965, MA, 1967; MA, Vanderbilt U., Nashville, 1978, PhD, 1983. Staff economist Inst. Devel. Econs., Karachi, Pakistan, 1967-69; asst. prof., assoc. prof. U. Karachi, Pakistan, 1969-74, 78-81, 83-85, prof., 1991; teaching asst. Vanderbilt U., Nashville, Tenn., 1977-78; instr., asst. prof. U. of the South, Sewanee, Tenn., 1981-83, 85-90, assoc. prof., 1990—; cons. World Bank, Washington, D.C., 1988—, World Food Program, Rome, Italy, 1989—; vis. prof. Vanderbilt Univ., summer, 1988; cons. Internat. Labor Orgn., Karachi, 1983-85, Internat. Fund for Agrl. Devel., Rome, Italy, 1991—; assoc. exec. editor Jour. Asian Econs., N.J., 1989—; keynote speaker Soc. for Internat. Devel., Bangladesh, 1990; lecturer in the field. Contbr. numerous articles to profl. jours. Adv. bd. mem. Tenn. Network for Cmty. Econ. Devel.; bd. dirs. Appalachian Women's Guild. Internat. Labor Orgn. travel grantee, 1985, Soc. Internat. Devel. travel grantee, 1985, 91, Can. Internat. Devel. Agy. travel grantee, 1985, U. of South Rsch. grantee, 1986-89, 90—, U. Ky. travel grantee, 1987, 90, 95, Ford Found. fellow, 1974-78, 81, Ford Found. travel grantee, 1992, U Wis. Women's Studies fellow, 1983. Mem. LWV, NOW (co-pres. Sewanee chpt. 1988-89), Nat. Social Sci. Assn., Ea. Econ. Assn., Soc. for Internat. Devel., Pakistan Fedn. of U. Women, Am. Com. on Asian Econ. Studies, Toastmasters Internat. Club, Bread for the World, Pakistan Women's Assns. Moslem. Home: Maxon Ln # 114 Sewanee TN 37375 Office: U of the South Dept Econs Sewanee TN 37383-1000

MOHLER, MARY GAIL, magazine editor; b. Milaca, Minn., Dec. 15, 1948; d. Albert and Deane (Vedders) M.; m. Paul Rodes Trautman, June 5, 1976 (div. 1994); children: Elizabeth Deane, David Albert Rodes, Theodore DeForest Lloyd. B.A., U. Calif.-Davis, 1974; M.A. in Lit., SUNY-Stony Brook, 1976. Asst., then editor-reporter Family Circle Mag., N.Y.C., 1979-81; editorial coordinator Ladies' Home Jour., N.Y.C., 1981, assoc. articles editor, 1982, mng. editor, 1982-93, sr. editor, 1994—; editor in chief Ladies' Home Jour. Parent's Digest. Medieval philosophy fellow SUNY-Binghamton, 1978. Mem. MLA, Am. Soc. Mag. Editors, Phi Beta Kappa. Clubs: Medieval; Overseas Press. Office: Ladies' Home Jour 100 Park Ave New York NY 10017-5516

MOHNER LANGHAMER, WILMA MARIA, artist; b. Karlsbad, Germany, Apr. 7, 1942; came to U.S. 1979; d. Hugo and Juliane (Satzer) Langhammer; m. Carl Martin Rudolf Mohner, Dec. 9, 1978. RN, City of Munich, 1975. Pres. Orange Hill Studio, Inc., Mission, Tex., 1986—; pub. agreement with Gray Stone Press Pubr., Nashville, 1981-84, HMK Fine Art, N.Y.C., 1984-85, Unicef, Geneva, Switzerland, 1985; commn. Winter Dreams, Squibb Pharm. Co., world hdqrs., Princeton, N.J. Exhbns. include BMW Gallery, Munich, Reyn Gallery, N.Y.C., Phillips Gallery, Dallas and Palm Beach, Fla.,, Knightsbridge Gallery, Wichita, Kans., McAllen Internat. Mus., Tex., Neiman Marcus, Houston and Dallas, Miniatures '84, Mpls.; comms. incl. BMW, McAllen Internat. Mus, Nat. Christmas Pageant of Peace, White House, 1983, Heye art calendars, 1976—; works in permanent collections in City of Munic, BMW Hdqrs., Smithsonian Instn., Library of Congress, Bibliotheque Nationale, Paris. Invited to paint Easter Egg, White House Easter Egg Roll, Washington, 1984, 85, Honored with letter, Pres.-elect. Ronald Reagan, 1981. Address: RR 1 Box 322 Mission TX 78572-9773

MOHNEY, SHARON EILEEN, strategic planning executive; b. Bremerton, Wash., Dec. 7, 1944; d. Forest N. and Jane Ellen (Patnoe) Erlandsen; m. Gayle Alexander Mohney Jr., Dec. 14, 1968 (div. 1993). BA, U. Wash., 1971. Mktg. rep. BASF, Williamsburg, Va., 1974-84; mktg. specialist Allied Corp., Petersburg, Va., 1984-85; mktg. mgr. AlliedSignal Inc., Petersburg, 1985-90, mgr. bus. planning, 1990—; speaker Nat. Conv. of Assn. Sch. Bus. Ofcls., San Antonio, 1987, ann. conv. Am. Floorcovering Assn., 1989; mem. adj. faculty Va. Commonwealth U., 1995. Author: Economic Outlook; editor employee newsletter FibersFocus; radio commentator Floor RAdio; contbr. articles to profl. jours. Mem. Planning Forum (pres.), Richmond Profl. Women's Network (past sec., editor newsletter), Women's Network (past co-pres.), Internat. Facility Mgmt. Assn. (speaker 1987 conv.). Office: AlliedSignal Inc PO Box 31 Petersburg VA 23804-0031

MOHR, BARBARA JEAN, telephone company customer service executive; b. St. Louis, Feb. 22, 1939; d. Walter Arnold and Doris Louis (Wilder) Uhl; m. William Edward Mohr, Feb. 7, 1957; 1 child, Kelly Linda Otten. Student, St. Louis U., So. Ill. U. From stenographer to engr. clk. Southwestern Bell Telephone, St. Louis, 1957, sales rep., 1967-70, sales supr., 1970-77, art mgr., 1977-79, staff sales mgr., 1979-80, staff customer svc., 1980-82, from mgr. customer svc. to claims mgr., 1982-88, collection mgr., 1988, mgr. customer svc., 1988-91, staff mgr. customer svc., 1991—. Treas., v.p., stewardship committeeperson ch. bd., Troy, Ill., 1979-82; Sunday sch. mgr. ch., St. Louis, 1974-76; v.p. Pioneers, St. Louis, 1991-92, bd. area rep., 1989-91. Mem. Southwestern Bell Profl. Women (fin. com. women 1987—, charter mem.). Office: SWB Pioneer Orgn 13075 Manchester Rd Saint Louis MO 63131-1836

MOHR, BARBARA JEANNE, educator; b. Santa Monica, Calif., Jan. 26, 1953; d. Edgar Kirchner and Beatrice Jeanne (Anderson) M. BA, Calif. State U., Fullerton, 1976; MS, Calif. State U., 1982. Multiple Subject Teaching Credential, 1977, Single Subject Tchr. Credential, 1977. Substitute tchr. Fullerton (Calif.) Sch. Dist., 1977-78, tchr., 1978—, mentor, 1984—; tchr. calligraphy Luguna Rd. Sch., 1985-92, student coun. advisor, 1988-92, advisor Just Say No Club, 1986-94. Named Tchr. of Yr. Fullerton Sch. Dist., 1989; recipient Hon. Svc. awrd Laguna Rd. Sch. PTA, 1989. Mem. NEA, Calif. Tchrs. Assn., Fullerton Elem. Tchrs. Assn., Calif. State U. Alumni Assn., Phi Kappa Phi.

MOHR, SUSAN EVELENA, automotive company administrator; b. Sault St. Marie, Mich., Nov. 30, 1954; d. Jerry Arden and Eva Susanna (Karns) M. BS, Mich. State U., 1976; MBA, Harvard U., 1987. Civil engr., road design dept. Mich. Dept. State Hwys. and Transp., Lansing, 1974-77; test engr. GM, Lansing, 1977-80, sr. project devel. engr., 1980-85, mgr. supplier devel., 1987-88, purchasing agt., 1988-90, mgr. bus. & strategic planning, 1990-92, mgr. vehicle timing and readiness group, 1992—. Mem. Soc. Automotive Engrs., Mich. State U. Alumni Assn. (bd. dirs.), Tau Beta Pi, Chi Epsilon. Lutheran. Office: GM Lansing Automotive Divsn 920 Townsend Ms # 4015 Lansing MI 48921

MOHRMAN, KATHRYN, academic administrator. Pres. The Colo. Coll., Colo. Springs. Office: Colorado College Office of the President 14 E Cache La Poudre St Colorado Springs CO 80903-3243

MOJO, MELISSA ANNE, corporate communications executive; b. N.Y.C., Nov. 27, 1953; d. Arthur Octavius and Diane Ard (Smith) M.; m. Sean Wester Laakso, Sept. 26, 1992. BFA, Parsons Sch. Design, 1976. Editl. copy person N.Y. Daily News, N.Y.C., 1976-78, asst. mgr. pub. rels., 1978-81; promotions mgr. United Media Enterprises, N.Y.C., 1982; account exec. G.S. Schwartz & Co. Pub. Rels., N.Y.C., 1982-84, v.p. group supr., 1984-88; mgr. editl. svcs. MasterCard Internat., N.Y.C., 1988-89, dir. corporate pub. rels., 1989-92, v.p. corp. comm., 1992—. Recipient Bronze award Fin. World, 1985, 90, Merit and Excellence awards Inside Pub. Rels., 1991, 92, 93, Excellence award IABC U.S. Dist. One, 1993. Mem. Internat. Assn. Bus. Communicators (chpt. newsletter editor 1984-85, co-chair prodl. devel. seminars 1985-86, v.p. spl. programs 1986-87, sec. 1987-88, bd. dirs. 1985-88, awards 1984, 85, 90, 91, Excellence award 1993, Merit award 1994), Women in Comm. Office: MasterCard Internat 888 Seventh Ave New York NY 10106

MOLAND-BOOTH, KATHRYN JOHNETTA, systems analyst; b. Tallahassee, Nov. 5, 1961; d. John and Kathryn Vastavia (Gadson) M.; m. Ronald Lynn Booth, May 7, 1994. BS in Sociology, Fla. A&M U., 1982; MS in Computer Sci., Southern U., 1987; postgrad., Nova U., 1992—. Programmer, summer intern IBM, Lexington, 1985; mem. tech. staff Bell Communications Rsch., Piscataway, N.J., 1986; programmer Logos Corp., Mount Arlington, N.J., 1987-88, Telecommunications Inds., Vienna, Va., 1988; systems analyst Advanced Tech., Inc., Reston, Va., 1988; project leader Advanced Tech., Inc., Aiken, S.C., 1989-90; sr. systems analyst, project leader Westinghouse Savannah River Co., Aiken, S.C., 1990-94; project leader SCT Utility Systems, Inc., Columbia, S.C., 1994—; tech. mem. Occurrence Reporting Spl. Interest Group, Oak Ridge, Tenn., 1991-94. Mem. IEEE (treas. 1991-92, vice chair 1992-93, chair 1993-94), NAFE, Nat. Mgmt. Assn., Project Mgmt. Inst., Assn. Computing Machinery. Home: 3315 Camak Dr Augusta GA 30909-9431 Office: SCT Utility Systems Inc 2700 Middleburg Dr Columbia SC 29204

MOLARZ, SUSAN, guidance counselor; b. Newark, Apr. 26, 1934; d. Anthony and Marie (Frances) Marano; m. Robert Molarz, June 12, 1955 (div. Aug. 30, 1990); children: Robert, Stephen, Linda. BA, Kean Coll., Union, N.J., 1974, MA, 1978. Tchr. St. Joseph's Sch., Carteret, N.J., 1968-74; tchr. Nathan Hale Sch., Carteret, 1974-79, guidance counselor, 1979—. Den mother cub scouts Boy Scouts Am., Carteret, 1965-70. Mem. Alpha Sigma Lambda. Home: 43 Patrick St Carteret NJ 07008-1864

MOLDENHAUER, NANCY A., social worker. BSEd, Valparaiso U., 1976; MSW, U. Mich., 1984, cert. specialist in aging, 1984. Lic. social worker, Mo. Instr. Meiji Gakuin and Tokyo Med. and Dental U., 1977-81; corp. communication trainer Saito Internat., Inc., Tokyo, 1981-82; conf. coord. Ctr. for Japanese Studies U. Mich., Ann Arbor, 1982-84; gerontol. social worker Turner Geriatric Clinic U. Mich. Hosps., Ann Arbor, 1983-84; med. social worker Mo. Bapt. Med. Ctr., St Louis, 1985-88; geriatric social work specialist program on aging Jewish Hosp. Wash. U. Med. Ctr., St. Louis, 1988-92; dir. case mgmt. and corp. svcs. Aging Consult, St. Louis, 1993—; adj. prof. Wash. U., St. Louis, 1991—. Named OWL Woman of Worth, 1993. Mem. NASW, Acad. Cert. Social Workers, Gerontol. Soc. Am., Am. Soc. Aging, Nat. Coun. on Aging, Alzheimer's Assn., Older Women's League (local bd. dirs., pres. 1991—, v.p. 1990, nat. bd. dirs. 1993—), Challenge Metro (bd. dirs., pres. 1986-90). Democrat. Unitarian. Office: Aging Consult Ste 7 10425 Old Oliver St Rd Saint Louis MO 63141-5933

MOLE, MARIE L., stock broker, financial company executive; b. N.Y.C., June 9, 1957; d. Anthony M. and Maria L. (Pastor) Noya; m. Richard A. Mole, July 13, 1984; children: Erica, Richard. BA cum laude, Hunter Coll., 1977. Corp. syndicate asst. Lehman Bros., N.Y.C., 1977-79; sr. trader Westinghouse Pension Investment Corp., N.Y.C., 1979-84; options trader Union Bank of Switzerland, N.Y.C., 1984-85; PCS derivative product mgr., prin. Morgan Stanley & Co., N.Y.C., 1985—. Republican. Roman Catholic. Office: Morgan Stanley & Co Inc 1251 Ave of the Am 33d Fl New York NY 10020

MOLER, ELIZABETH ANNE, federal agency administrator, lawyer; b. Salt Lake City, Jan. 24, 1949; d. Murray McClure and Eleanor Lorraine (Barry) M.; m. Thomas Blake Williams, Oct. 19, 1979; children: Blake Martin Williams, Eleanor Bliss Williams. BA, Am. U., 1971; postgrad., Johns Hopkins U., 1972; JD, George Wash. U., 1977. Bar: D.C. 1978. Chief legis. asst. Senator Floyd Haskell, Washington, 1973-75; law clk. Sharon, Pierson, Semmes, Crolius & Finley, Washington, 1975-76; profl. staff mem. com. on energy and natural resources U.S. Senate, Washington, 1976-77, counsel, 1977-86, sr. counsel, 1987-88; commr. FERC, Washington, 1988-93, chair, 1993—. Mem. ABA, D.C. Bar Assn. Democrat. Home: 1537 Forest Ln Mc Lean VA 22101-3317 Office: FERC 825 N Capitol St NE Rm 9000 Washington DC 20426

MOLES, DIANE CAROL, massage therapist, health advisor; b. Libertyville, Ill., Aug. 7, 1955; d. Ervin William and Therese Sylvia (Wrobleski) Krajecki; m. Robert Paul Moles, Oct. 10, 1975 (div. Oct. 1988); children: Jeremiah Justin, Randy Paul. Cert. med. asst., Rice Bus. Coll., 1978. Cert. Med. Asst. Computer typesetter Color Spectrum, Inc., Charleston, S.C., 1979-83, Vogue Printers, Inc., North Chicago, Ill., 1983-86, Johnston Pump Co., Glendora, Calif., 1986-88, Rothstein & Memsic, L.A., 1988-90, Dynatype Design, Glendale, Calif., 1990-92. Home: 2020 Verdugo Blvd #C Glendale CA 91208

MOLINA, VARNESE ANN, state program administrator; b. West Point, N.Y., June 2, 1951; d. Menzo Sr. and Lillie Ruth Mims; 1 child, Laneisha Joy Shannon; m. Gilbert Molina Jr., Dec. 19, 1984; 1 child, Gilbert Mims III. BS in Psychology, L.I. U., 1973. Cert. employee assistance profl. Mental hygiene therapy aid State of N.Y. Letchworth, Thiells, 1975-77; staff development specialist Office of Mental Retardation and Devel. Disabilities, Thiells, 1977-80; habilitation specialist I & II State of N.Y. OMRDD, Letchworth, Thiells, 1980-84, program mgr. I, 1984-85, coord. employee assistance program, 1985—; exec. dir. Community Svcs. Ctr., Highland Falls, N.Y., 1993—. Com. mem. Orange County, N.Y. Dems., Highland Falls, 1984-86; bd. dirs. McQuade's Children Svcs., New Windsor, N.Y., 1988-93, Sarah Wells Girl Scouts U.S., Middletown, N.Y., 1989-91. Named Outstanding Citizen Afro-Am. Mens Club, 1984. Mem. NAACP (3d v.p. 1986-90, Outstanding Contbn. award Newburgh N.Y. br. 1986), Am. Counseling Assn., Employee Assistance Profl. Assn. Mem. AME Zion Ch. Home: 53 Barclay Rd New Windsor NY 12553 Office: Community Svcs Ctr 26 Schneider Ave Highland Falls NY 10928-0197

MOLINARI, SUSAN K., congresswoman; b. Staten Island, N.Y., Mar. 27, 1958; d. Guy V. and Marguerite (Wing) M.; m. Bill Paxon, 1994. BA, SUNY, Albany, 1980, MA, 1982. Former intern for State Senator Christopher Mega; former rsch. analyst N.Y. State Senate Fin. Com.; former fin. asst. Nat. Rep. Gov.'s Assn.; ethnic community liaison Rep. Nat. Com., 1983-84; minority leader N.Y.C. Council, 1986-90; mem. 101st-103rd Congresses from 14th (now 13th) N.Y. dist., Washington, D.C., 1990—. Roman Catholic. Office: 123 Cannon Washington DC 20515-3213

MOLINARO, VALERIE ANN, lawyer; b. N.Y.C, Oct. 21, 1956; d. Albert Anthony and Rosemary Rita (Zito) M.; m. Howard Robert Birnbach; 1 child, Michelle Annalise Birnbach. BA with honors, SUNY, 1978; JD, Syracuse U., 1980, MPA, 1980. Asst. counsel. New York State Housing Finance Agy., N.Y.C., 1980-82; assoc. counsel, asst. secy. N.Y. State Urban Devel. Corp., N.Y.C., 1982-85; assoc. Mudge Rose Guthrie Alexander & Ferdon, N.Y.C., 1985-87, Bower & Gardner, N.Y.C., 1988, Hawkins, Delafield & Wood, N.Y.C., 1988-91; of counsel Barnes, McGhee, Harper & Segue, N.Y.C., 1991—. Author: Am. Bar Assn. Jour., 1981. Mem. N.Y. State Bar Assn. (tax exempt finance com.), Assn. of Bar of City of N.Y., Nat. Assn. Bond Lawyers, Women in Housing and Fin. Office: Barnes McGhee Harper & Segue 16th Fl 1114 Ave of the Americas New York NY 10036

MOLINE, SANDRA LOIS, librarian; b. San Antonio, Dec. 13, 1938; d. Udo F. and Olivia Marie (Link) Reininger; m. Jon Nelson Moline, Aug. 13, 1960; children: Kevin, Eric. BA in Chemistry, Austin Coll., 1960; postgrad., Duke U., 1962-64; MA in History of Sci., U. Wis., 1976, MLS, 1977. Tchr. chemistry and physics Durham (N.C.) High Sch., 1960-64; head physics libr. U. Wis., Madison, 1977-88; head reference svcs. Sci. & Engring. Libr. U. Minn., Mpls., 1988-94; libr. reader's svc. Luth. Coll., 1994—; reader Svcs. Libr., Tex. Luth. Coll., 1994—. Mem. Spl. Librs. Assn. (physics, astronomy, math, sci.-tech. divsns.), Librs. Assembly (sec., treas. 1980, pres. 1983), Madison Acad. Staff Assn. (steering com. 1980-83, pres. 1982). Home: 605 Fleming St Seguin TX 78155

MOLINO-BONAGURA, LORY JEAN, neurobiologist; b. Quezon, The Philippines, Mar. 1, 1964; came to U.S., 1967; d. Lorenzo Daban and Carmelita (Jason) M.; m. Anthony Francis Bonagura, Aug. 10, 1991; 1 child, Alexandra Grace. BS, SUNY, Brockport, 1986; MA, NYU, 1989. Rsch. asst. dept. psychology SUNY, Brockport, 1985-86; rsch. asst. dept. psychology NYU, N.Y.C., 1986-87, rsch. asst. dept. biology, 1987-88; tech. rsch. specialist dept. psychiatry SUNY, Stony Brook, 1988-90; temp. regulatory affairs dept. Smithkline-Beecham, Phila., 1991-92; assoc. scientist cardiovascular biology dept. Rhone-Poulenc Rorer, Collegeville, Pa., 1992-93; sr. rsch. scientist Sterling-Winthrop PRD, Collegeville, 1993-94. Presenter N.Y. Acad. Sci., 1989, Soc. for Neuroscience, 1989; contbr. articles to profl. jours. Mem. AAAS, Assn. for Women in Scis., N.Y. Acad. Scis., Soc. for Neurosci., Internat. Brain Orgn. Republican. Home: 8716 Wissahickon Ave Philadelphia PA 19128

MOLITOR, ANN E., rehabilitation administrator; b. St. Louis, Aug. 14, 1953; d. Earl Franklin and Ruth Ann (Endres) Parker; m. Theodore Stephen, Jan. 15, 1972; children: Aaron Steven, Eric Michael. ADN, Jefferson Coll., Hillsboro, Mo., 1979; BS, Nova U., 1992, MBA, 1994. Cert. rehab. registered nurse, case mgr. Staff nurse, rehab. nurse Incarnate Wod Hosp., St. Louis, 1979-85; nurse rehab. St. Anthonys Med. Ctr. Anthony House, St. Louis, 1982-84; rehab. specialist Woods Rehab., Orlando, Fla., 1985-86; nurse liaison Pinecrest Hosp., DelRay Beach, Fla., 1985-86; rehab. coord. UpReach Pavillion, Gainesville, Fla., 1986-87; referral coord. Meml. Regional Rehab. Ctr., Jacksonville, Fla., 1987-88, dir. program mgmt., 1988—; co-owner Riverfront Landscape Maintenence Co., St. Louis, 1975-85, Crestwood (Mo.) Garden Shop, 1879-80, Rehab. Historic Homes, St. Louis, 1978-82. Mem. Lafayete Sq. Preservation, St. Louis, 1980—, LaSalle Pk. Preservation St. Louis, 1979—. Mem. Assn. Rehab. Nurses, Fla. Assn. Rehab. Nurses, Fla. Assn. Rehab. Providers Private Sector, Fla. Rehab. Assn. Home: 1910 Secluded Woods Ln Jacksonville FL 32266-1500 Office: Meml Rehab Hosp 3599 University Blvd S Jacksonville FL 32216-4245

MOLLER, ELSBETH, librarian; b. Wedel, Fed. Republic of Germany, Nov. 1, 1944; came to U.S., 1970; d. Adolph and Elisabeth (Hatje) Mayer; m. Peter Moller, Oct. 10, 1967; 1 child, Birgit. BA, Queens Coll., 1980, MLS, 1986. Libr. asst. Dillon Read & Co. Inc., N.Y.C., 1980-85; libr. Cravath, Swaine & Moore, N.Y.C., 1986-88, asst. dir. libr. svcs., 1988-93, dir. libr. svcs., 1993—. Mem. Am. Assn. Law Librs., Spl. Librs. Assn., Law Libr. Assn. Greater N.Y.

MOLLITOR, LINDA COBURN, psychologist, nurse; b. Hicksville, Ohio, Sept. 6, 1941; d. Charles Wilson and Eleanor Mae (Click) Coburn; m. Wayne Mitchell Mollitor, July 15, 1961; children: Elisabeth, Stephanie. AA, Jackson (Mich.) C.C., 1962; BS, Western Mich. U., 1978; MA, U. Detroit, 1980. ICU staff nurse Foote Meml. Hosp., 1967-82, Jackson Osteopathic Hosp., 1982-83; psychological counseling and testing Jackson Hillsdale Community Mental Health, 1983-85; pvt. practice psychology Jackson, Mich., 1985—. Chmn. bd. rev. Sandstone Twp., Parma, Mich., 1984—. Wesleyan Ch. Office: 2617 Wildwood Ave Jackson MI 49202

MOLLOFF, FLORENCE JEANINE, speech and language therapist; b. St. Louis, Aug. 28, 1959; d. Lawrence Allan and Rietta Gertrude (Fiegenbaum) M. BS, Fontbonne Coll., St. Louis, 1983; MEd summa cum laude, Nat. Louis U., St. Louis, 1989; student, Project ACCESS Inst., 1992, Judevine Ctr. Autistic Children Tng., 1992. Cert. speech correctionist, Mo. Intern St. Louis State Sch. for Profoundly Retarded, 1983-84; speech therapist St. Louis Pub. Schs., 1984—; Judvine Ctr. for Autistic Children Tng., 1992; speech/lang. therapist St. Louis Pub. Schs./Autism Program, 1992-93; speech/lang. therapist Michael Sch. Medically Fragile and Multiply Handicapped St. Louis Pub. Schs., 1993—; speech, lang. therapist St. Louis Pub. Schs./Michael Sch. for Medically Fragile and Multiply Handicapped, 1993—; ednl. cons. program devel. Mo. Coalition for Environ., St. Louis, Columbia, Kansas City, 1990—; cons., trainer in puppetry Kids. on the Block, St. Louis Pub. Schs., 1988—. Author, creator transition curriculum: Consultative Resource Program, 1989; creator puppet program: Save Our Astonishing Plantet, 1990; ednl. cons. program devel. young St. Louis audiences (adapted program for severe to profoundly handicapped children "Arabian Nights", 1994; contbr. artist St. Louis Internat. Jazz Mus. Educator, lobbyist Coalition for the Environ., St. Louis, 1990; activist, lobbyist Housing Now, St. Louis, 1989; foster parent Christian Children's Fund, 1986—; activist Habitat for Humanity Internat., 1994—. Mem. AAUW, Coun. Exceptional Children (state rep. Mo. divsn. children with communicative disorders 1988-89, presenter nat. conv. 1989), Internat. Platform Assn., Am. Fed. Tchrs. (bldg. rep. 1992), Nat. Arbor Day Found., Nat. Parks and Conservation Assn., Amnesty Internat., Nat. Women's Polit. Caucus, Coalition for Environment, Mo. Assn. Augmentative Comm. Sys., Metro St. Louis Women's Polit. Caucus, Emily's List. Democrat. Home: 9823 Lullaby Ln Saint Louis MO 63114-2510

MOLLOHAN, KATHLEEN, fiber artist; b. Alamosa, Colo., June 23, 1937; d. Floyd Kenneth and Carol Grace (Albright) Baskette; m. James W. Redman, 1958 (div. 1963); 1 child, David Michael; m. Kent L. Mollohan, July 24, 1966. BFA, U. Colo., 1964. Edn. specialist State Dept. Edn., Helena, Mont., 1972—; self-employed fiber artist, 1980—. Commd. tapestries by Great Am. Bank Corp., San Diego, IBM Corp., Mont., First United Meth. Ch., Missoula, Mont.; artist book cover Heinle & Heinle Pub. Co., 1993. Bd. dirs., past pres. Holter Mus. of Art, 1992-93. Mem. Mont. Assn. Weavers and Spinners (bd. dirs. 1983—, exec. dir. 1983-89).

MOLNAR, EDITH BERES, small business owner; b. Movar, Hungary, Nov. 4, 1939; came to U.S., 1971; d. Eugen and Valerie (Beck) M.; m. Laszlo Beres Sr., May 26, 1957 (dec. Mar. 1962); 1 child, Laszlo T. Beres. BA in Edn., Tchrs. Coll., Pécs, Hungary, 1966; MA in Film Making, MAFILM, Budapest, Hungary, 1970. Elem. tchr. Movar and Budapest Schs., 1962-69; script-girl, asst. to regisseur, script-writer MAFILM, Budapest, 1968-71; asst. mgr. Douglas Film Industries, Chgo., 1972-74; owner, operator Budapest Resteraunt and Carriage Svc., San Antonio, 1974-83; sch. dir., operator Alamo Carriage Svc. Driving Acad./Tex. Tourism Found., Inc., San Antonio, 1983—. Contbr. articles and poems to mags. and local newspapers. Recipient Appreciation award VA, 1992, Vol. award Renaissance Festival, 1979. Mem. Modern Pentathlon Assn., Tex. Restaurant Assn. (awards 1975-82). Republican. Roman Catholic. Home and Office: 4119 Bloomdale San Antonio TX 78218-3522

MOLNAU, CAROL, state legislator; b. Sept. 17, 1949; m. Steven F. Molnau; 3 children. Attended, U. Minn. Mem. Minn. Ho. of Reps., 1992—; mem. agr., econ. devel. coms., mem. infrastructure and regulation fin. com., mem. local govt. and met. affairs com. Active Our Saviors Luth. Ch., 4-H, Chaska City Coun. Republican. Home: 495 Pioneer Trl Chaska MN 55318 Office: 201 State Office Bldg Saint Paul MN 55155*

MOLTZAN, NICOLINE G., nurse, administrator; b. Morehead City, N.C., Dec. 7, 1940; d. Nils George Christiansen and Stella Amelia (Smith) Christiansen Martinez; m. William J. Moltzan, Oct. 5, 1963 (dec.). Diploma, Beth El Sch. Nursing, Colorado Springs, Colo., 1963; BS, Coll. St. Francis, Joliet, Ill., 1982, MS in Health Adminstrn., 1988. Head nurse ICU-CCU Penrose Hosp., Colorado Springs, staff nurse ICU-CCU; staff nurse ICU-CCU Evans Army Community Hosp., Ft. Carson, Colo., evening and night supr. Mem. AACN. Office: PO Box 60386 Colorado Springs CO 80960-0386

MOMAH, ETHEL CHUKWUEKWE, women's health nurse; b. Iyi-Enu, Ogidi, Nigeria, May 28, 1934; d. Zaccheus C. and Victoria U. (Orizu) Obi; m. Christian C. Momah, Nov. 21, 1959; children: Chukwudi, Adaora, Azuka. SRN, Harrow Hosp., Middlesex, U.K., 1956; SCM, Mothers Hosp., London, 1957; MTD, Midwife Tchrs. Coll., Surrey, U.K., 1964; BS, Upsala Coll., 1988. Cert. inpatient obstetric nurse Nat. Cert. Corp. Nurse-midwife Guy's Hosp., London, 1959; nursing sister, head nurse labor/delivery Univ. Coll. Hosp., Ibadan, Nigeria, 1960-62; midwife tutor Lagos (Nigeria) Island Maternity Hosp., 1963-66; nurse-midwife Brit. Hosp., Paris, 1966, Hosp. Cantonal, Geneva, Switzerland, 1967-78; patient care coord. St. Peter's Med. Ctr., New Brunswick, N.J., 1985-90, antenatal testing nurse, 1990—. Mem. Assn. of Women's Health, Obstetric and Neonatal Nurses.

MON, LOURDES GAGUI, school principal; b. Bangar, Philippines, Mar. 6, 1944; came to U.S., 1967; d. Crispin Yabut and Josefa Vergara (Agas) Gagui; m. Francis Lopez Mon, July 17, 1968; children: Catherine, Joey. BS in Elem. Edn., U. of East, Manila, 1963; MEd, Loyola U., Chgo., 1976. Tchr. San Sebastian Coll., 1963-64, St. Joseph's Coll., Philippines, 1964-67, Beloit (Wis.) Pub. Schs., 1967-69, Immaculate Conception Sch., Chgo., 1969-83; prin. St. Josaphat Sch., Chgo., 1983—; ex-officio mem. St. Josaphat Sch. Bd., 1983—; coordinator U.S. State Dept. Confs. for Minorities and Women. Contbg. editor: Maynila mag., 1983-85; contbg. writer: T M Herald, 1983-85; assoc. editor: VIA Times mag., 1984-86, columnist, 1984—, sr. editor, 1986—. Pres. Asian Human Services, Chgo., 1986-88; active Am. Profls. Civic Alliance; vol. Immigration and Naturalization Program, 1985—; exec, dir. immigration program Am. Filipino Profls. Civic Alliance; mem. Filipino Am. Council Bd., 1983-85; co-founder, bd. dirs. Sining Kayumanggi Theatre Group. Named Outstanding Asian of Yr., Asian Am. Coalition Chgo., 1986. Mem. Assn. for Supervision and Curriculum Devel., Archdiocesan Prins. Assn., Nat. Cath. Edn. Assn., Filipino Am. Women's Network (chmn. Ill. chpt. 1987—). Republican. Roman Catholic. Lodge: Lions (v.p. Chgo. chpt. 1984—). Office: St Josaphat Sch 2245 N Southport Ave Chicago IL 60614-3192

MONACO, LINDA GOKEY, school system administrator; b. Dickenson Center, N.Y., Apr. 7, 1947; d. Lionel Henry and Eula Grace (Denno) Gokey; m. James Anthony Monaco, Apr. 26, 1969; children: James, Jason. BS in Elem. Edn., SUNY, Cortland, 1969, MS in Edn. Foundations, 1972; PhD, U. North Tex., 1985, postgrad., 1987, 89. Cert. tchr. nursery to grade 6, N.Y., grades 1-8, Tex.; cert. mid-mgmt. adminstr., supt., Tex. Elem. tchr. McGraw, N.Y., 1969-71, Aubrey (Tex.) Ind. Sch. Dist., 1977-82; teaching fellow U. North Tex., 1983, grad. researcher dean's grant project, 1983-84; lead evaluator dept. R&D Fort Worth Ind. Sch. Dist., 1984-86; elem. prin. Ponder Ind. Sch. Dist., 1986-93, interim supt., 1987; asst. supr. Little Elm (Tex.) Ind. Sch. Dist.; presenter in field. Bd. dirs. Communities in Schs., Denton, Tex., 1993. Named Outstanding Alumnus U. North Tex.; Kellogg scholar A&M Prins.' Ctr. Mem. AAUW (newsletter editor), ASCD, Tex. Assn. Supervision and Curriculum Devel., Tex. Elem. Prins. and Suprs. Assn., Nat. Assn. Elem. Sch. Prins., Tex. Sch. Improvement Initiative, Metroplex Coun. Women Sch. Execs. (past pres.), Phi Delta Kappa (pres. U. North Tex. chpt.). Democrat. Roman Catholic. Home: 2412 Bowling Green Denton TX 76201 Office: Little Elm Ind Sch Dist 500 Lobo Ln Little Elm TX 75068

MONAGHAN, EILEEN, artist; b. Holyoke, Mass., Nov. 22, 1911; d. Thomas F. and Mary (Doona) Monaghan; m. Frederic Whitaker. Student, Mass. Coll. Art. Represented in collections NAD, Okla. Mus. Art, Hispanic Soc., High Mus. Art, Atlanta, Norfolk museums, U. Mass., Springfield (Mass.) Mus. Fine Art, Reading (Pa.) Art Mus., Charles and Emma Frye Mus., Seattle, Kans. State U., Wichita, St. Lawrence U., N.Y., NAD, also in numerous pvt. collections, ann. exhbns., nat. and regional watercolor shows; author: Eileen Monaghan Whitaker Paints San Diego, 1991. Recipient Wong award Calif. Watercolor Soc., Ranger Fund purchase Nat. Acad. Design, Allied Artists Am., DeYoung Mus. show award, Soc. Western Artists award, 1st award Springville (Utah) Mus., numerous others. Mem. NAD (academician, Obrig prize, Walter Biggs Meml. award), Am. Watercolor Soc. (Silver medal, Dolphin fellow), Watercolor West Soc. (hon.), San Diego Watercolor Soc. (hon.), Providence Watercolor Club (award), Phila. Watercolor Club. Address: 1579 Alta La Jolla Dr La Jolla CA 92037-7101

MONAHAN, JULIE ANN, theater manager; b. Glen Cove, N.Y., July 12, 1953; d. Stephen Thomas and Sara Patricia (Hanophy) M. BS, So. Conn. State U., 1976. House mgr. Hartman Theatre, Stamford, Conn., 1977-80; producing assoc. StageWest, Springfield, Mass., 1980-83; dir. ops. Theatre League of Westchester, Tarrytown, N.Y., 1984-85; devel./advt. dir. Conn. Theatre Found., Westport, 1985-86, subscription dir., 1986-90, gen. mgr., 1990—; gen. mgr. Stamford Theatre Works, 1989-92; dir. A-Z Prodns., Norwalk, Conn., 1993-94; cons. Candlewood Playhouse, New Fairfield, Conn., 1990. Mem. Theatre Comms. Group. Democrat. Office: Westport Country Playhouse 25 Powers Ct Box 629 Westport CT 06881

MONAHAN, MARIE TERRY, lawyer; b. Milford, Mass., June 26, 1927; d. Francis V. and Marie I. (Casey) Terry; m. John Henry Monahan, Aug. 25, 1951; children: Thomas F., Kathleen J., Patricia M., John Terry, Moira M., Deirdre M. AB, Radcliffe Coll., 1949; JD, New Eng. Sch. Law, 1975. Bar: Mass. 1977, U.S. Dist. Ct. Mass. 1978, U.S. Supreme Ct. 1982. Tchr. French and Spanish Holliston (Mass.) High Sch., 1949-52; pvt. practice Newton, Mass., 1977—. Mem. Mass. Assn. Women Lawyers (pres. 1986). Home and Office: 34 Foster St Newton MA 02160-1511

MONCHARSH, JANE KLINE, rehabilitation counselor, vocational specialist, mediator; b. Boston, Jan. 15, 1943; d. Paul Kline and Helen (Chartoff) Kline-Gray; m. Philip C. Moncharsh, Dec. 12, 1965; children: Peretz, Mariasha, Yona, Shira. Student, U. Mass., 1960-62; BA, Boston U., 1965. Cert. rehab. counselor and cons., vocat. expert, case mgr. Rsch. asst. Mass. Mental Health Ctr., Harvard U., Bostn, 1964-65; vocat. evaluator Opportunity Workshop, Mpls., 1965-66, sr. vocat. evaluator, 1966-67, rehab. counselor, 1967-71; vocat. expert Social Security Adminstrn. and R.R. disability hearings, third party and div. litigation HHS, Mpls., 1971—; rehab. counselor and cons., Mpls., 1971—; instr. Minn. Inst. Legal Edn., Mpls., 1991, 92; interviewer Boston U., 1989—. Bd. dirs. Mpls. Fedn., 1989-90; mem. adv. com., bd. dirs. Mpls. Jewish Family and Children Svcs., 1990-94. Mem. AACD, Nat. Assn. Rehab. Providers, Minn. Assn. for Counseling and Devel., Am. Counseling Assn., Assn. for Assessments in Counseling, Nat. Career Devel. Assn., Nat. Disting. Registry (Libr. Cong.), Med. and Vocat. Rehab., Psi Chi. Office: 4248 Basswood Rd Minneapolis MN 55416-3849

MONCRIEF, MARY KATHRYN, glass company administrator; b. Houston, Aug. 10, 1955; d. Malcolm Joseph and Dorothy Earlene (King) LeGrande; m. Theodore James Moncrief, Dec. 19, 1987; children: Barry Lee, Anthony Theodore, Mark, Patricia Ann. BS, Sam Houston State U., 1977; cert., Inst. Child Lit., 1988; postgrad., San Jacinto Coll., 1993. Cert. elem. tchr., Tex. Med. records Green Acres Convalescent Home, Huntsville, Tex., 1979-80, 81-82; tchr. Magnolia (Tex.) High Sch., 1980-81; sec. Harris Engring., Huntsville, 1982-83; artist M&M Design, Huntsville, 1983-84; fin. sec. First United Meth. Ch., Huntsville, 1984-87, nursery sch. coord., 1986-87; contractor Tex. Rehabilitation Commn., Huntsville, 1986-87, Pasadena, Tex., 1990-92; counselor Houston Substance Abuse Clinic, Pasadena, 1992-93, Lake Charles Substance Abuse Clinic, 1992-93; adminstr. Johnson Glass & Mirror, 1993—, Johnson Glass, Pasadena, 1993—. Author poetry, 1985. Ballot counter Voting Polling places, Huntsville, 1977, 78, 79. Recipient Lady Kentiggerma Soc. Creative Anachronism, 1986, Sable Comet, 1986. Mem. NAFE. Republican.

MONDA, MARILYN, quality improvement consultant; b. Paterson, N.J., Aug. 11, 1956; d. Thomas John and Lydia Mary (Dal Santo) M.; m. Lawrence G. Gifford, Jr., Aug. 25, 1984. BA, San Diego State U., 1980; MA, Baylor U., 1984. Math. statistician Navy Personnel Rsch. and Devel. Ctr., San Diego, 1984-86; quality engr. Info. Magnetics, Inc., San Diego, 1986-87; mgmt. cons. Process Mgmt. Inst., Inc., Mpls., 1987-89; staff assoc. Luftig & Assocs., Inc., Detroit, 1989-92; founder Quality Disciplines, San Diego, 1992—; bd. dirs. Deming Users Group, San Diego, 1985-87; lecturer in the field. Contbr. articles to profl. jours. Mem. San Diego Deming Users Group, Am. Soc. Quality Consultants, Am. Statistical Assn., Phi Beta Kappa.

MONDALE, JOAN ADAMS, wife of former vice president of U.S.; b. Eugene, Oreg., Aug. 8, 1930; d. John Maxwell and Eleanor Jane (Hall) Adams; m. Walter F. Mondale, Dec. 27, 1955; children—Theodore, Eleanor Jane, William Hall. BA, Macalester Coll., 1952. Asst. slide librarian Boston Mus. Fine Arts, 1952-53; asst. in edn. Mpls. Inst. of Arts, 1953-57; weekly tour guide Nat. Gallery of Art, Washington, 1965-74; hostess Washington Whirl-A-Round, 1975-76. Author: Politics in Art, 1972. Mem. bd. govs. Women's Nat. Dem. Club; hon. chmn. Fed. Coun. on Arts and Humanities, 1978-80; bd. dirs. Associated Coun. of Arts, 1973-75, Reading Is Fundamental, Am. Craft Coun., N.Y.C., 1981-88, J.F.K. Center Performing Arts, 1981-90, Walker Art Ctr., Mpls., 1987-93, Minn. Orch., Mpls., 1988-93, St. Paul Chamber Orch., 1988-90, Northern Clay Ctr., 1988-93, St. Paul, 1988-93, Nancy Hauser Dance Co., Mpls., 1989-93, Minn. Landmarks, 1991-93; trustee Macalester Coll., 1986—. Presbyterian. Office: Unit 45004 Box 200 APO AP 96337-5004

MONDLOCH, BERNADETTE MARY, municipal official, freelance reporter and writer; b. Scott, Wis., Nov. 12, 1933; d. Ernst Robert and Cecelia Johanna (Slavik) Backhaus; m. James Frederick Mondloch, Nov. 27, 1954; children: Richard, Linda, Scott, Peggie, Paul, John, Sarah, Julie, Maria. Student, Sheboygan City Tchrs. Coll., 1969-70. Cert. mcpl. clk. Billing clk. Amity Leather Products, West Bend, Wis., 1951-52; music tchr. Gigante Music Ctr., West Bend, 1951; office mgr., bookkeeper A.G. Koch, Inc., Kewaskum, Wis., 1952-54; reporter Sheboygan and Plymouth, Wis., 1963—; receptionist A&P, Plymouth; mcpl. clk. Town of Sherman, Sheboygan, 1983—; mcpl. treas. Town of Sherman, 1987—; staff writer Random Lake Sounder; clk. mentor program Wis. Mcpl. Clks., Wis. Author: Sammy, The Skunk, 1969 (3rd in State 1979). Mem. precinct com. Dem. Party, Town of Sherman, 1968—; pres. St. Patrick's Christian Mothers, 1955—; sec.-treas. St. Patrick's Ch. Coun., 1987—; gen. leader local 4-H Club, 1950—; ch. organist St. Patrick's Ch., 1956—; clk. Village of Adele, 1986—; treas. Local Food Pantry, 1989—. Mem. AARP (tax aide, pay counselor 1983-94). Home: N 2303 Bates Rd Adell WI 53001-0046

MONDLOCH, PATRICIA ANN, chemist; b. Sheboygan, Wis., June 11, 1943; d. Anton T. and Mathilda (Boyance) Bukovic; m. William Carl Mondloch, Sept. 18, 1965; children: Kurt, Anne Marie. BS in Chemistry, U. Wis., 1965. Chemist Bio-Tech. Resources, Manitowoc, Wis., 1965-71; supervising chemist Donohue & Assocs., Sheboygan, 1979-83; staff chemist Kohler (Wis.) Co., 1983—. Mem. Am. Chem. Soc., N.Am. Thermal Analysis Soc., Clay Minerals Soc. Office: Kohler Co 444 Highland Dr Kohler WI 53044

MONEK, DONNA MARIE, pharmacist; b. New Brunswick, N.J., Aug. 9, 1947; d. James Frank and Angeline Eleanor (Marzella) M. BS, Phila. Coll. of Pharmacy, 1970; MBA, Fairleigh Dickinson U., East Rutherford, N.J., 1976. Reg. pharmacist, N.J. Staff pharmacist Freehold (N.J.) Area Hosp., 1971-72, dir. pharmacy, 1972-76; pharmacy administr. Rahway (N.J.) Hosp., 1976—; cons. home health care intravenous therapy, Rahway, N.J., 1985. Rep. committeewoman Middlesex County, 1972-86, 92—; mem. Bd. Health, Metuchen, N.J., 1987—. Mem. Am. Soc. Hosp. Pharmacists, N.J. Soc. Hosp. Pharmacists, N.J. Hosp. Assn. (group purchasing 1980-88, chairperson profl. standards 1989-90, vice chairperson state pharmacy com. 1990-91, chairperson 1992), Am. Pharm. Assn., N.J. Pharm. Assn., Metuchen Rep. Club, Cranford Dramatic Club, Kappa Epsilon. Roman Catholic. Office: Rahway Hosp 865 Stone St Rahway NJ 07065-2797

MONEKE, NGOZI IFEYINWA, nurse; b. Okigwe, Nigeria, Dec. 28, 1958; came to U.S., 1987; d. Edward Norom and Mary Nlewechi Nzeakor) Okpara; m. Victor Chukwuemeka Moneke, June 9, 1984; children: Chinyelu, Uchenna, Jacqueline. Diploma, U. Nigeria Sch. Nursing, 1980; postgrad., York Coll. RN, CCRN; registered midwife; med.-surg. cert., health risk mgmt. cert. Staff nurse Nat. Orthopedic Hosp., Anambra, Nigeria, 1980-81; staff nurse, midwife Mater Hosp. Afikpo, Imo, Nigeria, 1982-83, U. Nigeria Teaching Hosp., Anambra, 1983-87; staff nurse Cabrini Med. Ctr., N.Y.C., 1988, Columbia Presbyn. Hosp., N.Y.C., 1990-91, Astoria Gen. Hosp., N.Y.C., 1988—, Syosset Community Hosp., L.I., N.Y., 1992—. Mem. AACN, N.Y. State Nurses Assn. Home: 253 S Long Beach Ave Freeport NY 11520

MONETT, L. DIANE, artist; b. Bronxville, N.Y.; d. Alfred and Vivian (Hartson) M.; m. Gary Ray Johnson, Jan. 18, 1986 (dec. Jan. 1990). BS, NYU. Asst. to dir. new product devel., rsch. analyst Pepsico, Purchase, N.Y.; asst. product mgr. Bristo Myers, N.Y.C.; product counselor Avon Products, N.Y.C.; gen. mgr. Promotora Artesanal de Julisco, Guadalajara, Mexico; buyer Nouveau Artists, N.Y.C.; artist, 1986—; One-woman shows include Venable-Neslage Galleries, Washington, 1990, Seibu Gallery, Fujisawa, Japan, 1992, Irving Trust Bank, Scarsdale, N.Y.; exhibited in Members' Gallery, Albright-Knox Mus., Buffalo, 1993—, Omell Galleries, London, Gergdorf Goodman, N.Y.C., Bronxville (N.Y.) Pub. Libr., Mitsukoshi Gallery, Japan; represented in numerous permanent collections; greeting cards pub. by Caspari, Inc., Switzerland, posters by Scandecor, Germany, ltd. edit. silkscreens by John Szoke Graphics, Inc., N.Y. One-woman shows include Venable-Neslage Galleries, Washington, 1990, Seibu Gallery, Fujisawa, Japan, 1992, Irving Trust Bank, Scarsdale, N.Y.; exhibited in Members' Gallery, Albright-Knox Mus., Buffalo, 1993—, Omell Galleries, London, Bergdorf Goodman, N.Y.C., Bronxville (N.Y) Pub. Libr.; represented in numerous permanent collections. Episcopalian.

MONFERRATO, ANGELA MARIA, entrepreneur, investor, writer; b. Wissembourg, Alsace-Loraine, France, July 19, 1948; came to U.S., 1950; d. Albert Carmen and Anna Maria (Vieri) M. Diplomate, Pensionnat Florissant, Lausanne, Switzerland, 1966-67; BS in Consumer Related Studies and Math Environ. Rels. and Mktg., Pa. State U., 1971, postgrad., 1971-72. Simultaneous translator fgn. langs. Inst. for Achievement of Human Potential, Phila., 1976-78; art dir. The Artworks, Sumneytown, Pa., 1975-76; asst. productionist Film Space, State College, Pa., 1976; real property mgr. Pla. 15 Condominium, Ft. Lauderdale, Fla., 1979-80; legal asst. Ft. Lauderdale, Fla., 1981-85; owner Rising Sun the Real Estate Corp. South Fla., Ft. Lauderdale, 1986—; pres. Kideos Video Prodns., 1985—; designer Colo. Remodel &

Design, 1988-92; owner, designer Monferrato Designs, 1993-95. Office: Monferrato Designs Telluride 200 Front St Placerville CO 81430

MONFILS-CLARK, MAUD ELLEN, analyst; b. Amstelveen, The Netherlands, June 7, 1955; d. Wouter William Frederic and Jeane Albertina (Verbauwen) Monfils; m. Harry Carl Clark, Nov. 26, 1983 (div. 1993). BSBA, Calif. State U., L.A., 1990. Physicians assocs. mgr. L.A. County Health Dept., L.A., 1990-92, fin. mgr., 1992-93, health planning analyst, 1993—; active Comm. Strategy Group, L.A., 1994—, Workforce Devel., L.A., 1994—; mem. staff Strageic Planning Leadership Team, L.A., 1994—, High Desert Hosp. Strategic Planning Com., L.A., 1994—. Co-recipient Nat. Assn. Counties award, 1994, Pub. Svc. Excellence award, 1994.

MONGAN, AGNES, museum curator, art historian, educator; b. Somerville, Mass., 1905. B.A., Bryn Mawr Coll., 1927; spl. student, Fogg Mus., Harvard U., 1928-29; A.M., Smith Coll., 1929, L.H.D. (hon.), 1941; Litt.D. (hon.), Wheaton Coll., 1954; L.H.D. (hon.), U. Mass., 1970; D.F.A. (hon.), LaSalle Coll., 1973, Colby Coll., 1973, U. Notre Dame, 1980, Boston Coll., 1985. Research asst. Fogg Mus., Harvard U., Cambridge, Mass., 1929-37; keeper of drawings Fogg Mus., Harvard U., 1937-47, curator of drawings, 1974-75, asst. dir., 1951-64, assoc. dir., 1964-68, acting dir., 1968-69, dir., 1969-71, cons., 1972—; Martin A. Ryerson lectr. fine arts Harvard U., 1960-75; vis. dir. Timken Art Gallery, San Diego, 1971-72; Kreeger-Wolf disting. vis. prof. Northwestern U., 1976; Bingham vis. prof. U. Louisville, 1976; Waggoner vis. prof. U. Tex., Austin, 1977, vis. prof. fine arts, 1981; Samuel H. Kress prof.-in-residence Nat. Gallery Art, Washington, 1977-78; vis. prof. fine arts U. Calif.-Santa Barbara, 1979; vis. dir. Met. Mus. and Arts Ctrs., Coral Gables, Fla., 1980; Brazilian Govt. lectr., 1954; Amy Sackler Meml. lectr. Mt. Holyoke Coll., 1966-67; vis. prof. fine arts U. Tex. Austin, 1981; Baldwin lectr. Oberlin Coll., 1966; lectr. throughout U.S., Can., Japan; organized numerous exhbns.; leader, lectr. yearly tours Europe to Friends of the Fogg groups. Former mem. editorial bd. Art Bull.; mem. adv. bd. Arte Veneta, Venice; editor: Heart of Spain (Georgiana Goddard King), 1941; One Hundred Master Drawings, 1949; contbr. to exhbn. and catalogue In Pursuit of Perfection: The Art of J.-A.-D.-Ingres, 1983; contbr. catalogue In Quest of Excellence, 1983; intro. to catalogue The Fine Line, 1985, exhbn. catalogue Ingres and Delacroix, Germany and Belgium, 1986; contbr. Silverpoint Drawings in the Fogg Art Museum, 1987, Some Brief Comments on Left-Handedness for Fogg Old Master Drawings Symposium, 1987; contbr. to books in field. Trustee, mem. corp. Inst. Contemporary Art, Boston, 1940-60; a founder, v.p. Pan-Am. Soc. New Eng., 1940-62; mem. U.S. Nat. Commn. for UNESCO, 1954-57, White House Com. for Edn. in Age of Sci., 1961; trustee Chaplebrook Found.; mem. vis. com. art dept. Wheaton Coll., 1961-68; mem. vis. com. to Art Mus., Smith Coll., to 1970; mem. council for arts MIT; mem. adv. bd. Skowhegan Sch. Painting and Sculpture, 1974—; mem. exec. com. Save Venice, Council for Villa I Tatti; mem. vis. com. dept. textiles Boston Mus. Fine Arts; bd. dirs. Brit. Inst.; mem. exec. com. Somerville Hist. Soc.; vice chmn. Com. for Restoration of Italian Art. Decorated Palms d'Academie (France), cavaliere ufficiale (Italy); recipient Julius Stratton award Friends of Switzerland, 1978, Signet Soc. Medal for Achievement in the Arts Harvard U., 1986, 350th Harvard medal for Extraordinary Service, 1986, Benemerenti medal Vatican, 1987; honored by Women's Caucus for the Arts, 1987; Benjamin Franklin fellow Royal Acad. Art; Inst. Internat. Edn. grantee, 1935; Fulbright scholar, 1950. Fellow Am. Acad. Arts and Scis.; mem. Coll. Art Assn. (bd. dirs. 1949-54), Am. Assn. Art Mus. Dirs. (assoc.), Academie de Montauban, Phi Beta Kappa (hon.). Office: Fogg Museum Harvard U Art Museums Cambridge MA 02138

MONGOLD, SANDRA K., corporate executive; b. Springfield, Ohio, Aug. 14, 1947; d. Robert Harold and Norma Jean (Fennessy) Rine; m. Alan Darrell Mabry, Aug. 18, 1968 (div. 1977); m. Danny Willard Mongold, Nov. 16, 1979; children: Brian Alan Mabry, Krista Marie Mabry. Student, Wright State U., Urbana Coll., So. State Coll., Ohio. Acctg. clk. Irwin Co. (now Am. Tool Cos., Inc.), Wilmington, Ohio, 1968-80, asst. treas., 1980-85, treas., 1985-94, new product com., 1985-93, corporate dir. tng. and devel., 1994—. Mem. adv. bd. So. State Coll.; elected to Wilmington City Coun., 1991—; mem. bus. adv. coun. Wilmington City Schs.; mem. Regional Planning Commn. Mem. NAFE, Nat. Assn. Accts., Am. Mgmt. Assn., Nat. Corp. Cash Mgmt. Assn., Wilmington C. of C. (dir., bd. dirs., treas. 1990, pres. 1991), Wilmington 2001 Com. (bd. dirs. 1992), Clinton County Women's Rep. Club. Republican. Presbyterian. Avocations: golf, bowling. Home: 330 Washington Ave Wilmington OH 45177-1132 Office: Am Tool Cos Inc 92 Grant St Wilmington OH 45177-2363

MONIA, JOAN, management consultant; b. Teaneck, N.J., Mar. 20, 1938; d. James Anthony and Anne Linden (Cairns) McCaffrey; m. Charles Anthony Monia, Dec. 30, 1961; 1 child, Clare Ann Woodman. BA, Ohio Dominican U., 1960. Info. specialist Battelle Meml. Inst., Columbus, Ohio, 1960-62; project leader Douglas Aircraft Corp., Huntington Beach, Calif., 1962-64; programmer analyst McDonnell Aircraft Corp., St. Louis, 1965-66; project mgr. Sanders Assocs., Nashua, N.H., 1968-70; database adminstrn. project leader Mass. Blue Cross, Boston, 1970-74; data strategist Factory Mut. Engrng. Corp., Norwood, Mass., 1974-78; mgr. data resource planning Digital Equipment Corp., Maynard, Mass., 1978-84; sr. mem. tech. staff GTE Govt. Systems Corp., Needham, Mass., 1984-91; prin. DMR Group, Inc., Waltham, Mass., 1991—. Recipient Sci. medal Bausch & Lomb, 1956. Home: 175 Anderson Rd Marlborough MA 01752 Office: DMR Group Inc 404 Wyman St Waltham MA 02154

MONK, DEBRA, actress. Stage and film appearances include (Broadway) Nick & Nora, Prelude to a Kiss, Pump Boys and Dinettes (also co-author), Redwood Curtain (Tony award featured actress in a play 1993), Picnic (Tony nomination featured actress 1994), (off Broadway) 3 Hotels (Helen Hayes award leading actress 1994), Assassins, Man in His Underwear, The Innocent's Crusade, Molieère in Spite of Himself, Oil City Symphony (co-author, Drama Desk award Best Ensemble 1988), Death Defying Acts; TV appearances include Women and Wallace, The Becky Bell Story, Law and Order, Redwood Curtain; film appearances include Prelude to A Kiss, For Love or Money, 1993, Fearless, 1993, Quiz Show, 1993, Jeffry, 1994, The Bridges of Madison County, 1994. Office: Gage Group 315 W 57th St Apt 4H New York NY 10019-3147

MONK, DIANA CHARLA, artist, stable owner; b. Visalia, Calif., Feb. 25, 1927; d. Charles Edward and Viola Genevieve (Shea) Williams; m. James Alfred Monk, Aug. 11, 1951; children: Kiloran, Sydney, Geoffrey, Anne, Eric. Student, U. Pacific, 1946-47, Sacramento Coll., 1947-48, Calif. Coll. Fine Arts, San Francisco, 1948-51, Calif. Coll. Arts & Crafts, Oakland, 1972. Art tchr. Mt. Diablo Sch. Dist., Concord, Calif., 1958-63; pvt. art tchr. Lafayette, Calif., 1963-70; gallery dir. Jason Aver Gallery, San Francisco, 1970-72; owner, mgr. Monk & Lee Assocs., Lafayette, 1973-80; stable owner, mgr. Longacre Tng. Stables, Santa Rosa, Calif., 1989—. One-person shows include John F. Kennedy U., Orinda, Calif., Civic Arts Gallery, Walnut Creek, Calif., Vallery Art Gallery, Walnut Creek, Sea Ranch Gallery, Gualala, Calif., Jason Aver Gallery, San Francisco; exhibited in group shows at Oakland (Calif.) Art Mus., Crocker Nat. Art Gallery, Sacramento, Le Salon des Nations, Paris. Chair bd. dirs. Walnut Creek (Calif.) Civic Arts, 1972-74, advisor to dir., 1968-72; exhibit chmn. Valley Art Gallery, Walnut Creek, 1977-78; juror Women's Art Show, Walnut Creek, 1970, Oakland Calif. Art. Home and Office: Longacre Tng Stables 1702 Willowside Rd Santa Rosa CA 95401

MONK, MEREDITH JANE, artistic director, composer, choreographer, film maker, director; b. N.Y.C., Nov. 20, 1942; d. Theodore G. and Audrey Lois (Zellman) M. BA, Sarah Lawrence Coll., 1964; ArtsD (hon.), Bard Coll., 1988, U. of the Arts, 1989. Artistic dir. House Found. for Arts, N.Y.C., 1968—. Prin. works include Vessel, 1971, Quarry, 1976, Turtle Dreams, 1983, Recent Ruins, 1979, The Games, 1983, Book of Days, 1988, Facing North, 1990, Atlas, 1991, Three Heavens and Hells, 1992, Volcano Songs, 1994, American Archeology, 1994. Recipient Obie award Village Voice, 1972, 76, 85, Creative Arts award Brandeis U., 1974, Deutches Kritiker Preis for best record 1981, 86, Bessie award N.Y. Dance and Performance awards, 1985, Nat. Music Theatre award, 1986, Dance Mag. award, 1992; Guggenheim fellow, 1972, 86, Norton Stevens fellow, 1993-94. Fellow MacDowell Colony (Sigma Phi Omega award 1987); mem. ASCAP. Office: House Found for Arts 131 Varick St New York NY 10013-1410

MONK, SUSAN MARIE, physician, pediatrician; b. York, Pa., May 7, 1945; d. John Spotz and Mary Elizabeth (Shelly) M.; m. Jaime Pacheco, June 5, 1971; children: Benjamin Joaquin, Maria Cristina. AB, Colby Coll., 1967; MD, Jefferson Med. Coll., 1971. Diplomate Am. Bd. Pediatrics. Pediatrician Children's Med. Ctr., Dayton, Ohio, 1975—; assoc. clin. prof. pediatrics Wright State U., Dayton. Mem. bd. dirs. Children's Med. Ctr., Dayton, 1991—, chief-of-staff, 1992-94. Mem. Am. Acad. Pediatrics, We. Ohio Pediatric Soc., Pediatric Ambulatory Care Soc. Office: Childrens Health Clinic 536 Valley St Dayton OH 45404

MONKS, KAREN ELIZABETH, nursing educator; b. Grand Rapids, Mich., Nov. 3, 1936; d. Louis Francis and Evelyn Anne (Hammerschmidt) McGough; m. Patrick Joseph Monks, Nov. 26, 1966; children: Laura Anne, Joseph Patrick. Diploma in nursing Mercy Central Sch. Nursing, Grand Rapids, 1956; BSN, Marquette U., 1965; MSN, U. Tex. Med. Br., Galveston, 1984. RN, Mich., Wis., Ariz. Staff nurse St. Mary's Hosp., Grand Rapids, 1957-58; staff nurse, then head nurse Kent County Hosp., Grand Rapids, 1958-62; staff nurse part-time St. Joseph's Hosp., Milw., 1962-65, head nurse, 1965-66; staff nurse, then house supr. Yuma Regional Med. Ctr. (Ariz.), 1966-72; nursing instr. Ariz. Western Coll., Yuma, 1972—, div. chmn. human services, 1984-92; case mgr. Olsten Kimberly Quality Care, 1991—; bd. dirs. Yuma Regional Med. Ctr., 1980-91, chmn. 1989, sec./treas., 1987, vice-chmn., 1988, chmn. personnel/nominations, 1981-84; chmn. Ariz. Council Assoc. Drgree Nursing Programs, 1985-86; co-chmn. Ariz. Council on Nursing Edn., 1985-86. Mem. Nat. League Nursing (bd. review 1990, accreditation visitor, 1985—), Toastmasters Internat. (able toastmaster). Democrat. Roman Catholic. Home: 1946 S London Dr Yuma AZ 85364-5023 Office: Ariz Western Coll PO Box 929 Yuma AZ 85366-0929

MONKS, REGINA See WATKISS, REGINA

MONROE, HELEN LEOLA, nurse, consultant, educator; b. Alma, Ga., Jan. 30, 1931; d. Silas Leo Monroe and Thelma (Fussell) Smith; 1 child, Reavena M. M. Oliver. BS, Fla. A&M U., 1954; MS, St. John's U., L.I., N.Y., 1959. Staff nurse Vis. Nurse Assn. Duval County, Jacksonville, Fla., 1954-55; instr. sch. nursing Fla. A&M U., Tallahassee, 1955-57, asst. prof., 1959-64; dir. nursing edn. Mississippi Valley State Coll., Itta Bena, Miss., 1964-67; asst. prof. Norfolk State Coll. Va., 1967-68; asst. prof., dir. nursing edn. Lincoln U., Jefferson City, Mo., 1968-80; pvt. practice nursing Jefferson City, 1981-85; pvt. practice achievement cons. Jacksonville, 1987—; cons. nursing William Woods Coll., Fulton, Mo., 1972-73. Sec. Jefferson City chpt. NAACP, 1971-73; chmn. edn. com. Cancer Soc. Cole County, Jefferson City, 1972-74; v.p. Cole County Mental Health Assn., 1973; mem. fin. com. United Way Cole County, 1975. Recipient Outstanding Achievement award Citizens' Com. of Jefferson City, 1970, Woman of Achievement award AAUW, 1974, Permanent Royal Patronage from Principality of the Hutt River Province, 1994. Home: 5436 Mays Dr Jacksonville FL 32209-2926

MONROE, MARCIA LYNN, customer service representative; b. Parkersburg, W.Va., July 11, 1942; d. Albert Leonard and Margie Louise (Polk) Farnsworth; m. William Paul Jonas, Sept. 2, 1960 (dec. Mar. 1981); children: William Paul Jonas II, Richard Alan Jonas, Jeffrey David Jonas; m. Raymond Robert Monroe, Aug. 16, 1985; stepchildren: Raymond Jr., Christopher Wayne. Cert. gen. ins., Ins. Inst. Am., 1991, A in Automation Mgmt., 1993. Lic. P/C agt. Sec. Big Red Markets, Parkersburg, W.Va., 1960-62, Knapp & Co., Parkersburg, 1980, Johns-Manville, Vienna, W.Va., 1979; customer svc. rep. III Erie Ins. Group, Vienna, 1980—. Recipient Cert. Profl. Svc. Rep., Nat. Assn. Profl. Ins. Agts., 1993. Mem. Nat. Assn. Ins. Women (Cert. Profl. Svc. Ins. Woman award 1994), Mid-Ohio Valley Ins. Women (corr. sec. 1993-95), Mid-Ohio Valley Claims Assn., Marietta Beagle Club (sec., bd. dirs. 1985—).

MONROE, MELROSE, retired banker; b. Flowery Branch, Ga., Apr. 13, 1919; d. Willis Jeptha and Leila Adell Cash; m. Lynn Austin, June 14, 1942. AB in Edn., Ga. State U., 1968. Negotiator Trust Co. Bank, Atlanta, 1962-89, ret., 1989. Mem. Nat. Women's C. of C. (pres. 1987-88), Atlanta Women's C. of C. (dir. 1965-66, pres. Fidelis SS class 1962-63), Am. Legion Aux. (pres. 5th dist. 1986-87, Ga. state chaplain 1989-90, state historian 1991-92, state 2d v.p. 1992-93, 1st v.p. 1993-94, pres. 1994-95), Order of Ea. Star (worthy matron 1951-52). Democrat. Home and Office: 4263 Woodland Brook Dr NW Atlanta GA 30339-4722

MONROE, PAULA RUTH, psychologist; b. Worcester, Mass., Dec. 23, 1951; d. Dudley Benson and Gladys Elinor (Norbery) Sherry; m. David Michael Monroe, Feb. 19, 1977; 1 child, Allison. BA, U. North Tex., 1974; MA, U. Tulsa, 1980, PhD, 1990. Lic. psychologist, Okla. Asst. dean Coll. Arts and Scis. U. Tulsa, 1983-85; staff psychologist, mgr. psychol. testing ctr. Children's Med. Ctr., Tulsa, 1990—. Contbr. articles to profl. jours. Mem. APA. Office: Children's Med Ctr 5300 E Skelly Dr Tulsa OK 74135-6599

MONROE, ROSE MARIA MASK, reading specialist, educator; b. Newport News, Va., Nov. 1, 1955; d. Curtis Van and Mary Ella (Pearson) M.; m. Marke A. Monroe, Sept. 6, 1986 (div. May 1993); children: Monteece C., Jamila T. BA, Utica Coll. Syracuse U., 1976; MS, Morgan State U., 1984. Cert. tchr., Md. Asst. Liberty Street Day Care, Newburgh, N.Y., 1969; jr. counselor Neighborhood Youth Corps, Newburgh, 1974; tutor, counselor Higher Edn. Opportunity Program, Utica, N.Y., 1976; tchr. English Balt. Pub. Schs., 1977-79; agt. Balt. Police Dept., 1979-88; instr. Bowie (Md.) State U., 1988-91; assoc. prof. Balt. City C. C., 1991—; tutor reading Utica (N.Y.) Free Acad., 1975; tutor English, Utica Coll., 1976; reading clinician Towson (Md.) State U., 1984; instr. Reading Community Coll. Balt., 1987-91. Counselor Utica YWCA, 1974. Recipient Merit Sonitrol Security Systems award, 1983; grantee Ottawa Found., 1973, Utica Coll. Higher Edn. Opportunity Program, 1973. Mem. Vanguard Justice Soc. (sec. 1980-82), Alpha Kappa Alpha. Democrat. Baptist. Office: 2901 Liberty Heights Ave Baltimore MD 21215-7807

MONROY, GLADYS H., lawyer; b. N.Y., Aug. 29, 1937; d. Henry B. and Leonora E. (Low) Chu; m. Jaime L. G. Monroy (div.); m. C. Lawrence Marks, Nov. 29, 1980. BA, Hunter Coll., N.Y., 1957; MS, NYU, 1968, PhD, 1973; JD, U. San Francisco, 1986. Bar: Calif. Lab. technician Sloan-Kettering Inst., N.Y., 1957-60; lab. technician Pub. Health Rsch. Inst., N.Y., 1960-63, rsch. asst., 1963-68; post doctoral fellow Albert Einstein Coll. Medicine, Bronx, N.Y., 1973-77; asst. prof. N.Y. Med. Coll., Valhalla, 1977-79; acquisitions editor Acad. Press, Inc., 1979-81; reseach assoc. U. Calif., San Francisco, 1981-83; atty. Irell & Manella, Menlo Park, Calif., 1986-90, ptnr., 1990-91; ptnr. Morrison & Foerster, Palo Alto, Calif., 1991—. Contbr. articles to profl. jours. Mem. bd. dirs. Project Hogar De Los Ninos, Menlo Park, Calif., 1987, mem. Profl. Women's Network, San Francisco, 1988--. Mem. ABA, Am. Intellectual Property Law Assn., Am. Soc. Human Genetics, Am. Chem. Soc., Calif. Bar Assn., San Francisco Intellectual Property Law Assn. (chair patent com. 1992-94), Peninsula Patent Law Assn. (program chair 1993-94, treas. 1994-95), Am. Soc. Microbiology, Phi Alpha Delta. Office: Morrison & Foerster 755 Page Mill Rd 545 Middlefield Rd Palo Alto CA 94304-1018

MONSALVE, MARTHA EUGENIA, pharmacist; b. Bogotá, Colombia, Sept. 27, 1968; came to U.S., 1985; d. Oscar and Martha Lucia (Vidal) M.; m. Dale James Morphionios, Dec. 16, 1989. AA, Miami-Dade Community Coll., 1989; BS in Pharmacy, Southeastern U., 1993. Lab. asst. William Harvey Co., Bogotá, 1981-82; purchasing agt. FEPARVI, Ltd., Miami, 1985-93; pharmacy asst. Galloway Pharmacy, Miami, Fla., 1988; pharmacy intern Bapt. Hosp., Miami, 1992; pharmacist Eckerd Drugs, Miami, 1993-94, Walgreen's, Miami, Fla., 1994—. Vol. Bapt. Hosp., Miami, 1988. Mem. Am. Soc. Hosp. Pharmacists, Fla. Soc. Hosp. Pharmacists. Roman Catholic. Home: 8640 SW 84th Ave Miami FL 33143-6912 Office: 29601 S Dixie Hwy Homestead FL 33033

MONSEN, ELAINE RANKER, nutritionist, educator, editor; b. Oakland, Calif., June 6, 1935; d. Emery R. and Irene Stewart (Thorley) Ranker; m. Raymond Joseph Monsen, Jr., Jan. 21, 1959; 1 dau., Maren Ranker. B.A., U. Utah, 1956; M.S. (Mead Johnson grad. scholar), U. Calif., Berkeley, 1959, Ph.D. (NSF fellow), 1961; postgrad. NSF sci. faculty fellow, Harvard U., 1968-69. Dietetic intern Mass. Gen. Hosp., Boston, 1956-57; asst. prof. nutrition, lectr. biochemistry Brigham Young U., Provo, Utah, 1960-63; mem. faculty U. Wash., Seattle, 1963—; prof. nutrition and medicine U. Wash., 1984—, prof. nutrition, adj. prof. medicine, 1976-84, chmn. div. human nutrition, dietetics and foods, 1977-82, mem. Council of Coll. Arts and Scis., 1974-78, mem. U. Wash. Press com., 1981—; chmn. Nutrition Studies Commn., 1969-83; vis. scholar Stanford U., 1971-72; mem. sci. adv. com. food fortification Pan-Am. Health Orgn., São Paulo, Brazil, 1972; tng. grant coordinator NIH, 1976—. Editor Jour. Am. Dietetic Assn., 1983—; mem. editorial bd. Coun. Biology Editors, 1992—; author research papers on lipid metabolism, iron absorption. Bd. dirs. A Contemporary Theatre, Seattle, 1969-72; trustee, bd. dirs. Seattle Found., 1978—, vice chmn., 1987-91, chmn., 1991-93; pres. Seattle bd. Santa Fe Chamber Music Festival, 1984-85. Grantee Nutrition Found., 1965-68, Agrl. Rsch. Svc., 1969—; recipient Disting. Alumnus award U. Utah, F. Fischer Meml. Nutrition Lectr. award, 1988, L.F. Cooper Meml. Lectr. award, 1991, L. Hatch Meml. Lectr. award, 1992. Mem. Am. Inst. Nutrition, Am. Soc. Clin. Nutrition (sec. 1987-90), Am. Dietetic Assn., Soc. Nutrition Edn., Am. Soc. Parenteral and Enteral Nutrition, Wash. Heart Assn. (nutrition council 1973-76), Phi Beta Kappa, Phi Kappa Phi. Office: U Wash Dept Human Nutrition DL-10 Seattle WA 98195

MONSON, ANGELA ZOE, state legislator; b. Oklahoma City, July 31, 1955; d. Epron Provo Monson. BS, Oklahoma City U., 1976; MPA, U. Okla., 1987. Probation and parole officer Okla. Dept. Corrections, 1976-77; cir. riding city mgr. East Ctrl. Rural Munic Area Coun., 1980-81; fiscal analyst Okla. State Legislature, 1981-84; sales rep. The Equitable, Oklahoma City, 1985-86; exec. dir. Okla. Health Care Project, 1986-90; mem. Okla. Ho. of Reps., 1990—; mem. Okla. adv. com. U.S. Commn. on Civil Rights, 1984-89. Mem. editl. bd. Primary Care News. Past pres. Okla. chpt. NAACP; past bd. pres. Mary Mahoney Meml. Health Ctr., Neighborhood Svcs. Orgn., Tolliver Alt. Care Ctr.; nat. bd. dirs. State Alliance for Universal Health Care; mem. policy adv. bd. Ctr. for Health Care Access & Reform. Recipient Svc. to Achievement award Black Liberated Arts Ctr., 1981, Outstanding Achievement award Cmty. Health Ctrs. Inc., 1988. Mem. AAUW. Democrat. Baptist. Home: 1904 Peachtree Oklahoma City OK 73121 Office: Okla Senate State Capitol Oklahoma City OK 73105*

MONSON, DIANNE LYNN, literacy educator; b. Minot, N.D., Nov. 24, 1934; d. Albert Rachie and Iona Cordelia (Kirk) M. B.S., U. Minn., 1956, M.A., 1962, Ph.D., 1966. Tchr., Rochester Pub. Schs. (Minn.), 1966-59, U.S. Dept. Def., Schweinfurt, W.Ger., 1959-61, St. Louis Park Schs. (Minn.), 1961-62; instr. U. Minn., Mpls., 1962-66; prof. U. Wash., Seattle, 1966-82; prof. literacy edn. U. Minn., Mpls., 1982—, chmn. Curriculum and Instrn., 1986-89. Co-author: New Horizons in the Language Arts, 1972; Children and Books, 6th edit., 1981; Experiencing Children's Literature, 1984; (monograph) Research in Children's Literature, 1976; Language Arts: Teaching and Learning Effective Use of Language, 1988; Reading Together: Helping Children Get A Good Start With Reading, 1991. Recipient Outstanding Educator award U. Minn. Alumni Assn., 1983, Alumni Faculty award, 1991. Fellow Nat. Conf. Rsch. in English (pres. 1990-91); mem. Nat. Coun. Tchrs. of English (exec. com. 1979-81), Internat. Reading Assn. (dir. 1980-83, Arbuthnot award 1993), ALA, U.S. Bd. Books for Young People (pres. 1988-90). Lutheran. Home: 740 River Dr Saint Paul MN 55116-1009 Office: U Minn 350 Peik Hall Minneapolis MN 55455

MONSON, NANCY PECKEL, writer, editor; b. N.Y.C., Mar. 11, 1959; m. John C. Monson, June 18, 1988. BS magna cum laude, Boston U., 1979. Actress, 1979-86; adminstrv. asst. MIT, Cambridge, 1981; assoc. editor Profl. Postgrad. Svcs., Secaucus, N.J., 1984-87; writer, contbg. editor Cardiology Product News, East Orange, N.J., 1985-86; assoc. editor, reporter The Convention Reporter Group, Secaucus, 1985-88, editor, 1988-90; freelance health writer and editor Pomona, N.Y., 1984—; freelance entertainment writer Pomona, 1988—. Contbr. articles to mags. including Glamour, First for Women, Fitness, Redbook, Woman's Day and New Woman. Mem. AFTRA, SAG, Am. Assn. Journalists and Authors. Office: 425 Country Club Ln Pomona NY 10970-2561

MONTAGNA, BERNICE DONNA, education educator; b. Bridgeport, Conn., Mar. 31, 1953; d. Philip Romano and Catherine (MacDaniel) Echinger; m. Robert John Montagna, June 9, 1979; children: Cariann, Robert. AA, Broward Community Coll., 1974; BS, Southern Conn. State U., 1977; MAT, Sacred Heart U., 1992. Cert. tchr. Conn. Substitute tchr. East Haven (Conn.) Bd. Edn., 1981-82, instructional aide, 1985-92; tchr. North Haven (Conn.) Bd. Edn., 1992—. Leader Girl Scouts Am., North Haven, 1989-91. Mem. NEA, Conn. Reading Assn., Conn. Edn. Assn., Kindergarten Assn. Conn., North Haven Edn. Assn., Assn. Supervision & Curriculum Devel. Home: 10 Rance Ct North Haven CT 06473-3454

MONTAGUE, MARY ELLEN, secondary school educator; b. Georgetown, Ohio, Aug. 12, 1933; d. Carrol Russel and Martha Gail (Lucas) Martin; m. Patrick E. Montague, Feb. 14, 1958; children: Catherine, Michael. BS, Fla. State U., 1955; MS, West Ga. Coll., 1989. Cert. tchr., Ga., Fla., N.C. Tchr. Duval County Schs., Jacksonville, Fla., 1955-59, InterLangue, Paris, 1971-74, Jackson County Schs., Jylva, N.C., 1976-79, Fulton County Schs., Atlanta, 1959-71, 80—, Creekside High Sch., Fairburn, Ga. Author various curriculum guides, 1980—. Hostess Tour of Homes, Fairburn, Ga., 1989, 90, 91; vestry person St. Andrews Ch., Peachtree City, Ga., 1989-92. Fellow Smithsonian Instn.; mem. Nat. Coun. Social Studies, Delta Kappa Gamma (1st v.p. 1990-91, pres. 1991-94, dist. treas. 1994—). Home: PO Box 738 Fairburn GA 30213

MONTANARO, LINDA, educator; b. Painesville, Ohio, Feb. 15, 1945; d. Lunda and Mary Ann (Tabone) Brafford; children: Melinda, Joseph, Melissa, Jason. BS, Kent State U., 1968; M, Ariz. State U., 1983. Tchr. Phoenix Union High Sch. Dist., Met. Tech. Vocat. Inst. Phoenix, Geneva (Ohio) High Sch.; bookkeeper/credit investigator Sears Roebuck, Ashtabula, Ohio. Named Ariz.'s Secondary Bus. Edn. Tchr. of Yr., 1993, Ariz.'s Vocat. Edn. Tchr. of Yr., 1993, Vocat. Tchr. of Yr., State Coun. on Vocat. Edn., 1994, Vocat. Bus. Dept. of Yr., State Coun. on Vocat. Edn., 1994. Mem. NEA, NAFE, ASCD, NOW, DAV Aux., Nat. Bus. Edn. Assn. (speaker/presenter 1989, 91), Ariz. Bus. Edn. Assn. (state treas. 1989-93, ctrl. rep. 1993—), Western Bus. Edn. Assn., Internat. Soc. Bus. Educators, Ariz. Edn. Assn. (del. Assembly 1991—), Am. Vocat. Edn. Assn. (voting del. 1991-92), Ariz. Vocat. Assn. (state v.p. 1991-93, Vocat. Program of Yr. 1993).

MONTE, BONNIE J., performing company executive; b. Stamford, Ct., Nov. 27, 1954; d. Eugene N. and Ruth M. (Thompson) M. BA, Bethany Coll., 1976; diploma, Hartman Conservatory, Stamford, 1978. Assoc. artistic dir. Williamstown (Mass.) Theatre Festival, 1981-89; casting dir. Manhattan Theatre Club, N.Y.C., 1989-90; artistic dir. N.J. Shakespeare Festival, Madison, 1990—; mem. faculty Drew U., Madison, 1991—. Grantee Lotte Crabtree Found., Boston, 1977. Democrat. Office: NJ Shakespeare Festival c/o Drew U 36 Madison Ave Madison NJ 07940-1434

MONTEFERRANTE, JUDITH CATHERINE, cardiologist; b. N.Y., Jan. 27, 1949; d. Stanley and Monica (Vinckus) Sosaris; m. Ronald J. (div. 1983); 1 child, Jason Paul; m. Roger E. Salisbury, Mar. 3, 1990. BS, Adelphi U., Garden City, 1970; MS, SUNY, Buffalo, 1973; MD, Mt. Sinai, N.Y.C., 1978. Attending N.Y. Med. Coll., Valhalla, N.Y., 1983-84; pvt. practice White Plains, N.Y., 1984--.; pres. Am. Heart Assn., 1984-86, bd. dirs. Westchester, N.Y., 1987—. Contbr. articles to profl. jours. fellow Am. Colls. of Cardiology, Am. Coll. of Physicians. Fellow Council on Clinical Cardiology of AHA, N.Y. Cardiological Soc.; mem. AMA, FACC, FACP, Soc. of Critical Care Medicine. Office: 222 Westchester Ave # 405 White Plains NY 10604-2906

MONTENEGRO, JEAN BAKER, English language educator; b. Syracuse, N.Y.; d. Ernest Monroe and Lucy Maebelle (Atkins) Baker; m. Roberto Carranza Montenegro, June 21, 1991; 1 child, Al H. Johnson Fr. BA, U. Ky., 1955; MA, No. Ariz. U., 1975, Azusa Pacific U., 1982. Cert. adminstr., supr.; cert. tchr. lang. arts, phys. edn., health edn., journalism. Sr. high sch. phys. edn. instr. San Francisco Unified, 1964, Grossmont Unified, San Diego, 1964-66; prof. phys. edn., recreation, health edn. Imperial (Calif.)

Valley Coll., 1966-81, prof. journalism, 1981-88, prof. English, 1981—; staff devel. coord. Imperial Valley Coll., 1988-94, gender equity coord., 1990-91; coord. Am. Assn. Women in Cmty. and Jr. Colls., San Diego and Imperial County, 1988—; elected to serve 3 yr. term on Acad. Senate, Imperial Valley Coll., 1994—. City editor Imperial Valley Press, summer 1989, copy editor, summers 1989, 91; editor Downtown El Centro Assn. newsletter, ARCHES editor Calif. Women for Agriculture Imperial Valley chpt. newsletter Food for Thought; editor Pvt. Industry Coun. newsletter Ptnrs. Pres. Substance Abuse Adv. Bd. Imperial County, 1976-78; v.p. Imperial Valley Methodone Bd. Dirs., 1974-80; v.p. Imperial County Alcohol Adv. Bd., 1978-80; recreation commr. City of Brawley, 1976-78; auditor Rep. Women, 1990—; head judge Literacy Vols. Am. Spelling Bee. Recipient Arab award Imperial Valley Coll. Student Body, 1989; named Vol. of Yr., Imperial Juvenile Justice Commn., 1982; nominated Woman of Yr., Imperial County, 1982; appointed to commn. State of Calif., Community Coll. League Calif., 1990. Mem. Journalism Assn. So. Calif. (sec. 1988), Pvt. Industry Coun.-Imperial Valley Downtown El Centro Assn., Sunrise Optimists Club (dir. pub. rels.). Lutheran. Office: Imperial Valley Coll PO Box 158 Imperial CA 92251-0158

MONTESANO, GAIL JEAN, hairdresser, cosmetologist, consultant; b. Newark, Jan. 29, 1948; d. Constant John and Mary (Di Vincenzo) M. Course in cosmetology, Masters' Beauty Sch., Passaic, N.J., 1967; student, Maria Pole' Inst., Short Hills, N.J., 1975, Montclair State Coll., 1983, European Acad., Union, N.J., 1987. Hairdresser Delores' Hair Fashions, Nutley, N.J., 1966-70, Paul McGregors, N.Y.C., 1970-72; cons. Conair Corp., Edison, N.J., 1977-80; cons., technician Clairol, Inc., N.Y.C., 1977—, mgr. product evaluation Salon Test Ctr., 1987—; esthetician Skin Care Co., Nutley, N.J., 1975—; haircolorist, cosmetologist Hair Co., Nutley, 1972—; platform artist Internat. Beauty Show, N.Y., 1975-76, 81; artist internat. shows Clairol Hosftra U., N,Y , 1977; chief exec. officer Skin Care Co., Inc., Nutley, 1975—; pres. Natural Hair and Skin Care Co., Inc., Nutley, 1975—; founder Skin Care Assn. Am., Ft. Lee, N.J., 1975; hon. mem. Clairol Presdl. Haircolorists Council, 1981. Contbr. articles to profl. jours. Sponsor, participant 32 Hr. Cut-A-Thon for Kidney Found., Nutley, 1972; participant 48 Hr. Marathon for Charity 5, Monmouth College, N.J., 1974; vol. hairdresser Mt. St. Joseph's Children Ctr., Totowa, 1979-85. Recipient Disting. Service award Nutley Jaycees, 1984. Mem. Nat. Hairdressers and Cosmetologists Assn., Bergen County Hairdressers and Cosmetologists Assn. (v.p., bd. dirs. 1980, Merit award 1980). Roman Catholic. Office: Hair Co PO Box 540 Nutley NJ 07110-0540 also: Clairol Inc Salon Test Ctr 345 Park Ave New York NY 10154-0192

MONTGOMERY, BETTY D., state official, former state legislator. BA, Bowling Green State U.; JD, U. Toledo, 1976. Former criminal clk. Lucas County Common Pleas Ct.; asst. pros. atty. County of Wood, Ohio, pros. atty., 1980-88; asst. pros. atty. City of Perrysburg, Ohio; mem. Ohio Senate, 1989-94; attorney general State of Ohio, Columbus, 1995—. Mem. Nat. Dist. Atty. Assn., Ohio Bar Assn., Toledo Bar Assn., Wood County Bar Assn. Address: 11145 Riverbend Ct W Perrysburg OH 43551-3678 also: Attorney Generals Office State Offical Tower 30 E Broad St Columbus OH 43266*

MONTGOMERY, CAROL HANSEN, librarian; b. Davenport, Iowa, Jan. 3, 1935; d. George Harry and Helen Margaret (Wait) Hansen; m. Irwin Robert Fenichel, July 20, 1957 (div. 1969); 1 child, David Alan; m. John Patterson Montgomery, Aug. 6, 1994. BA, Bryn Mawr Coll., 1957; MS, Drexel U., 1969, PhD, 1979. Group mgr. Inst. for Sci. Info., Phila., 1970-71; cons. Auerbach Assocs., Phila., 1971-73; reference libr. Med. Coll. Pa., Phila., 1973-74; assoc. libr. Med. Coll. Pa., 1974-79, prin. investigator, 1976-79; asst. prof. U. Ky., Lexington, 1979-80; libr. dir. Phila. Coll. Pharmacy and Sci., 1980-85; dir. libr. Hahnemann U., Phila., 1985-94; dir. Ctr. for Acad. Informatics, Med. Coll. Pa. and Hahnemann U., 1994—; adj. prof. Drexel U., Phila., 1982—; bd. dirs. Health Scis. Libr. Consortium, Phila.; mem. adv. bd. Elsevier Sci. Pubs., Amsterdam, The Netherlands, 1985-89, Online, Inc., Weston, Conn., 1987-91; mem. biomed. libr. rev. com. Nat. Libr. Medicine, 1989-93; mem. OCLC User's Coun., 1992-95. Author: Microcomputer User's Guide, 1984; co-author: Online Searching: Primer, 1984; editor: Changing Patterns, 1974; co-editor: In Her Own Words, 1982. Mem. Med. Libr. Assn. (chpt. chair 1976-77, com. chair 1979-80, sect. chair 1988-89), Am. Soc. for Info. Sci. (SIG chair 1984-86). Office: Med Coll Pa and Hahnemann U Broad and Vine Sts Philadelphia PA 19102-1122

MONTGOMERY, DENISE KAREN, nurse; b. N.Y.C., Dec. 23, 1951; d. Thomas Cornell and Dorothy Marie (Castine) Simons; m. Timothy Bruce Montgomery, July 19, 1974 (div. Feb. 1981); m. Joseph Samuel Montgomery, Aug. 20, 1983. A in Nursing, San Jacinto Coll., 1971. RN, Tex. Charge nurse Aaron's Women's Clinic, Houston, 1977; rsch. asst. dept. ob-gyn. Baylor Coll. Medicine, Houston, 1977-81, nursing supr., 1979-81, program coord. population control program, 1979-81; nurse Dr. Eric J. Haufrect, Houston, 1982-83; office mgr., supr. Dr. J.S. Montgomery III, 1987—, Dr. Samuel Law, Houston, 1983-84. Contbr. articles to med. jours. Recipient Disting. Pub. Svc. award Am. Heart Assn., 1976; recipient several grants. Mem. Nat. Assn. Coll. Ob-Gyn. Democrat. Roman Catholic. Home: 8202 N Tahoe Dr Houston TX 77040-1256

MONTGOMERY, JANEY LUANN, education educator; b. Ellsworth, Kans., Aug. 19, 1941; d. Woodrow W. and Opal Irene (Francisco) Weinhold; m. John Denton Montgomery, June 13, 1965; children: Jill Ayn Montgomery Acocella, John Blue. BA, Ft. Hays State U., Hays, Kans., 1963, MS, 1968; PhD, Iowa State U., 1990. Lic. tchr., Iowa. Tchr. Goodland (Kans.) High Sch., 1963-68; temp. instr. Ft. Hays State U., 1968-69; tchr. Hays High Sch., 1969-70; cons. Area Edn. Agy. 6, Marshalltown, Iowa, 1974-86; temp. instr. Iowa State U., Ames, 1986-90; asst. prof. edn. U. No. Iowa, Cedar Falls, 1990—; fgn. vis. rschr. Naruto U. of Edn., Naruto City, Japan, 1992-93. Contbr. articles to profl. jours. Recipient 1990 Rsch. award Iowa Gifted and Talented Assn., 1991; Alpha Delta Kappa internat. travel fellow, 1991. Mem. Assn. of Tchr. Educators, Iowa Ednl. Equity Com., Iowa Career Edn. Assn. (pres. 1980-82), Phi Delta Kappa, Alpha Delta Kappa. Republican. Anglican. Home: 1405 Fairway Dr Marshalltown IA 50158-3825 Office: U No Iowa Malcolm Price Lab Sch 116-0613 Cedar Falls IA 50614

MONTGOMERY, KATE A., therapist, human services manager; b. Santa Ana, Calif., Feb. 7, 1951; d. Charles E. and Charlotte L. (Dunton) M.; m. (div. 1979); 1 child, Carissa Ann Benedict-Montgomery. AA, Butte Coll., 1978, AA in Respiratory Therapy, 1979; postgrad., Internat. Profl. Sch. Bodywork, San Diego, 1984-85, Sports Massage Inst., 1985. Cert. sports massage therapist, respiratory therapist; lic. massage therapist, R.I. Pvt. practice San Diego, 1985—; cons. Pan Am. Games, Indpls., 1987-1988 Winter Olympics, Calgary, Alta., Can., World Cup for Racewalkers, 1991, Hawaiian Ironman competition; host Health At Your Fingertips Radio Sta. WALE, Providence; speaker in field. Author: Sports Touch: The Athletic Ritual, 1990, Carpal Tunnel Syndrome/Prevention and Treatment, 1992, 93; mem. editorial bd. Massage Mag. Mem. Assn. Bodywork and Massage Profls., Holistic Health Practitioners Assn., Elite Sports Massage Team Ind., San Diego Sports Massage Team, Touch for Health Assn., COSMEP Pub. Assn.

MONTGOMERY, KATHLEEN RAE, counselor; b. Bloomington, Ind., Aug. 15, 1950; d. Raymond Hershel and Helen Kathleen (Trent) Montgomery; m. Steven Myers, Oct. 2, 1970 (div. Aug. 1993); children: Jason Paul, Lisa Dawn, Stephanie Kathleen. AS in Psychology, Vincennes U., 1970; BS in Social Svcs., Milligan Coll., 1974; MS in Counseling, Ind. U., 1992. Police dispatcher Ind. State Police, Bloomington, Ind., 1974-76; counselor Cookson Hills Christian Ministries, Kansas, Okla., 1976-78; social worker Health Svcs. Bur., Bloomington, 1982-88; tng. asst. The Associated Group, Indpls., 1990-91; ops. mgr. drug abuse prevention workshops Ind. U., Bloomington, 1991-92; outreach coord. Gender Equity Ivy Tech., Bloomington, 1992—; Counselor Upward Bound program, Vincennes, Ind., 1970; crisis counselor Matrix Lifeline, 1978-79; field instr. Ind. U. BSW program, Bloomington, 1983-88; support group leader Sherwood Oaks Christian Ch., 1991-92. Mem. adv. bd. Expectant Mother's Program, Bloomington, 1984-86, Parent's Group, Ellettsville, Ind., 1986-88, adv. bd. IMPACT, 1992—; mem. retention com. Ivy Tech. Coll. (formerly Ind. Vocat. Tech. Coll.), 1993—. Mem. AAUW, Ind. Coll. Counseling Assn., Ind. Counseling Assn. Republican. Home: 3906 Woods Edge Bnd Bloomington IN 47401-8408

MONTGOMERY, LAURA, business management consultant; b. Arlington, Va., Sept. 8, 1954; d. Robert Paul and Ashley Bell (Hannah) M. BSCE, U. Va., 1976; M Environ. Engring., Rensselaer Poly. Inst., 1977; MBA, Harvard U., 1982. Mgmt. cons. Camp Dresser & Mckee, Boston, 1977-80; bus. and fin. analyst Monsanto Agrl. Products Co., St. Louis, 1982-85, product supr., 1985-87; planning mgr. G. D. Searle, Skokie, Ill., 1987-89, dir. strategic planning, 1989-91, dir. bus. devel., 1991-92, dir. product devel., 1992-93; v.p. bus. devel. Aphios Corp., Woburn, Mass., 1993-94; bus. cons., 1994—. Mem. Am. Assn. Blood Banks, Va. Engring. Found. (v.p. bd. dirs. 1992-94, pres. 1994—). Office: Aphios Corp 3 Gill St Woburn MA 01801-1720

MONTGOMERY, ROBIN VERA, realtor; b. Boise, Idaho, July 21, 1928; d. Bruce Cameron and Grace Evangeline (Matthews) M.; m. Lewis Robert Goldberg, June 10, 1956 (div. June 1978); children: Timothy, Holly, Randall. BA in Journalism, U. Mich., 1957; BArch, U. Oreg., 1972. Architect Robin's Roost, Eugene & Florence, Oreg., 1972-82; realtor Exclusive Realtors, L.A., 1989—. Program chair Hadassah, Eugene, 1968; pres. Elec. Wires Underground, Eugene, 1967. With USN, 1949-53. Mem. Calif. Assn. Realtors, Theta Sigma Phi. Democrat. Home: 1334 Carmelina Ave #7 Los Angeles CA 90025

MONTGOMERY, SHELIA KAY, civil engineer; b. Birmingham, Ala., Jan. 13, 1969; d. David L., Sr. and Mary Sue (Battle) M. BSCE, U. Ala., Birmingham, 1992. Civil engr. City of Birmingham, 1990—. Mem. Tau Beta Pi. Office: City of Birmingham Rm 220 City Hall Birmingham AL 35203

MONTGOMERY, VELMANETTE, state senator; b. Tex. M.Ed., NYU; student U. Ghana; LLD (hon.) St. Joseph's Coll., 1991. Mem. N.Y.C. Dist. 13 Sch. Bd., 1977-80, pres., from 1977; former co-dir. advocacy group Child Care Inc.; mem. N.Y. Senate, 1984—, mem. child care, consumer protection, health, fin. and housing, mental hygiene coms. State of N.Y. Fellow Inst. Ednl. Leadership, 1981, Revson Found., 1984. Democrat. Office: 70 Lafayette Ave Brooklyn NY 11217-1520 also: N.Y. State Senate Albany NY 12224

MONTI, LAURA ANNE, psychology researcher, educator; b. Evanston, Ill., Feb. 28, 1959; d. LeRoy John and Mary Alice (Foley) M. BA in Psychology, U. Ariz., 1981; MA in Cognitive Sci., Loyola U., Chgo., 1986, PhD, 1987; postgrad., Menninger Found., 1988. Mem. bd. dirs., co-owner Monti & Assocs. Inc., Arlington Heights, Ill., 1976—; v.p., co-owner MAM Imports and Creative Gifts, Kildeer, Ill., 1986-89; lectr. psychology Loyola U., Chgo., 1986-89; asst. prof. North Park Coll., Chgo., 1989-91; instr. Rush Presbyn. St. Luke's Med. Ctr., Chgo., 1992—; vis. rsch. specialist U. Ill., Ill. Inst. Devel. Disabilities, 1989-90; cons. Walter H. Sobel FAIA & Assocs., Chgo., 1987—, Yate and Auberle, Oakbrook, Ill., 1987-88; postdoctoral fellow Northwestern U., Evanston, Ill., 1990-92. Contbr. articles to profl. jours.; co-author tech. reports to various orgns. Tuition scholar Loyola U., Chgo., 1983-84; NIH fellow, 1992-94; Loyola U. grad. asst., 1986. Mem. APA (divsn. psychology of women 1989-92, gen. psychology, exptl. psychology 1989—), Psi Chi (faculty rep. for North Park Coll. 1989-91), Sigma Alpha Iota. Roman Catholic. Home: 632 Happfield Dr Arlington Heights IL 60004

MONTOOTH, SHEILA CHRISTINE, state agency administrator; b. Pasadena, Calif., Mar. 12, 1952; d. Gerald Frank and Janet Laura (Ebert) M. BS, Calif. State U., L.A., 1974; MPA, Calif. State U., 1985. CPA, Calif. From auditor 1 to tax auditor IV State Bd. Equalization Calif. Bd. Equalization, Pasadena, 1974-81; supr. tax auditor 1 State Bd. of Equalization Calif. Bd. Equalization, West Los Angeles, 1981-83; bus. taxes adminstr. III State Bd. of Equalization Calif. Bd. Equalization, Lakewood, 1984-87; bus. taxes adminstr. IV State Bd. of Equalization Calif. Bd. Equalization, Downey, 1987-92; bus. taxes adminstr. V State Bd. of Equalization, Hollywood, 1992-93, Arcadia, 1994; bus. taxes adminstr. V State Bd. of Equalization, City of Industry, 1994—. Recipient Bronze award United Way, Los Angeles, 1984, Gold award, 1985. Republican. Roman Catholic. Office: State Bd Equalization 12820 Crossroads Pkwy S City of Industry CA 91746

MONTOYA, VELMA, federal agency administrator; b. L.A., Apr. 9, 1938; d. Jose Gutierrez and Consuelo (Cavazos) M.; m. Earl A. Thompson; 1 child, Bret L. Thompson. BA in Diplomacy and World Affairs, Occidental Coll., 1959; MA in Internat. Rels., Fletcher Sch. of Law and Diplomacy, 1960; MS in Econs., Stanford U., 1965; PhD in Econs., U. Calif., L.A., 1977. Asst. prof. Econs. Calif. State U., L.A., 1965-68; vis. assoc. prof. U. So. Calif., 1979; instr. U. Calif., L.A., 1981-82; staff economist The Rand Corp., Santa Monica, Calif., 1973-82; asst. dir. for strategy, White House Office of Policy Devel. Exec. Office of the Pres., 1982-83; expert economist, Office of Regulatory Analysis, Occupational Safety and Health Adminstrn. U.S. Dept. of Labor, 1983-85; dir. of Studies in Pub. Policy and Assoc. Prof. of Political Economy, Sch. of Bus. Mgmt. Chapman Coll., 1985-87; adj. prof., Sch. of Bus. Mgmt. Pepperdine Univ., 1987-88; pres. Hispanic-Am. Pub. Policy Inst., 1984-90; assoc. prof. of Fin., Sch. of Bus. Adminstrn. Calif. State Polytechnic Univ., Pomona, 1988-90; commr. Ocupational Safety and Health Review Commn., 1990—; cons. Urban Inst., 1974, Mexican-Am. Study Project UCLA, 1966, Graduate and Profl. Fellowships to the Office of Post Secondary Education, U.S. Dept. of Edn.; editorial referee Contemporary Policy Issues, Economic Inquiry, Policy Analysis, The Journal of Economic Literature; discussion leader Am. Assembly on Rels. Between the U.S. and Mex.; pres. del. White House Conf. on Aging, 1981; reader of 1988 proposals for the U.S. Dept of Edn. for the Improvement and Reform of Schs. and Teaching; research participant U.S. Dept. of Edn. Delphi Assessment of Drug Policies for Use in Minority Neighborhoods, 1989; mem. hispanic adv. panel Nat. Commn. for Employment Policy, 1981-82; lectr. Brookings Inst. Seminars for U.S. Bus. Leaders; bd. adv. Close-Up Found., 1982-83; discussant Western Economic Assn. Meetings, 1985, 93; bd. adv. Nat. Rehab. Hosp., 1991-94; mem. nat. exec. adv. bd. Harvard Jour. of Hispanic Policy, 1993—. Bd. regents U. Calif., 1994—; mem. adv. com. U.S. Senate Rep. Conf. Task Force on Hispanic Affairs, 1991—. Named One of the 100 U.S. Hispanic Influentials Hispanic Bus. Mag., 1982, 90, Woman of the Yr. Mex.-Am. Oportunity Found., 1983, The East L.A. Com. Union, 1979, Marshall scholar, Fulbright scholar; recipient Freedom Found. at Valley Forge Honor Econ. Edn. Excellence Cert., 1986, Univ. fellow Stanford Univ., Internat. Rels. fellow Calif. PTA, John Hay Whitney Opportunity fellow; Calif. State Univ. Found. Faculty Rsch. grantee. Mem. ASTM (bd. dirs. 1985-87), Am. Econ. Assn. (session chair ann. meetings 1995), Nat. Coun. of Hispanic Women, State Bar of Calif. (disciplinary bd. 1986-87), Calif. State Bar Ct. (exec. com. 1987-89), Western Econ. Assn., Indsl. Rsch. Inst. for Pacific Nations (adv. bd. 1988-89), Salesian Boys and Girls Club (bd. dirs 1989—), Vets. in Com. Svc. (adv. com. 1989-94), Phi Beta Kappa, Omicron Delta Epsilon, Phi Alpha Theta. Home: 6970 Los Tilos Los Angeles CA 90068

MONTS, ELIZABETH ROSE, insurance company executive; b. LaPorte, Ind., June 13, 1955; d. William David and Marguerite Elizabeth (Burge) Miller; m. James Edwin Monts, May 26, 1978 (div. Aug. 1982); 1 child, Katherine Elizabeth. AA with highest honors, Coll. of Mainland, 1984; BS magna cum laude, U. Houston, Clear Lake, 1989. CPA. Credit adjustment asst. Jaymar-Ruby, Inc., Michigan City, Ind., 1974-79; acctg. clk. Am. Indemnity Co., Galveston, Tex., 1979-80, staff acct., 1980-81, adminstrv. acct., 1981-85, asst. treas., 1985-86, asst. treas., asst. dept. mgr., 1986-87, sec., asst. dept. mgr., 1987-91, asst. v.p., asst. dept. mgr., 1991—. V.I.P. escort Rep. Nat. Conv., Houston, 1992. Mem. AICPA, Fedn. Ins. Women Tex. (regional dir. 1992-94), Tex. Soc. CPA's, Ins. Women Galveston County (pres. 1987-88, 90-91), Beta Gamma Sigma, Phi Kappa Phi, Alpha Chi. Republican. Methodist. Office: Am Indemnity Co PO Box 1259 Galveston TX 77553-1259

MONYOK, EILEEN CLAIRE RAKOCHY, engineer; b. Allentown, Pa., Sept. 5, 1960; d. Michael Samuel and Clara Theresa (Krutul) Rakochy; m. Robert Matthew Monyok, Sept. 21, 1991. BS in Chem. Engring. magna cum laude, U. Notre Dame, 1982. Devel. engr. Hercules, Inc., Wilmington, Del., 1982-84; process engr. I Hercules, Inc., Hopewell, Va., 1984-86, sr. process engr., 1986-88; process control engr. Rohm & Haas, Inc., Bristol, Pa., 1988-90, pilot plant supr., 1990; process control engr. Pub. Svc. Co. Colo., Denver, 1990—. Instr. project bus. Jr. Achievement, Levittown, Pa., 1989. Mem. AIChE, Instrument Soc. Am., Soc. Women Engrs., Toastmasters Internat. (pres. 1988, sec. 1994), Colo. Mountain Club, U.S. Tennis Assn., Tau Beta Pi. Democrat. Roman Catholic. Home: 6889 Frying Pan Rd Boulder CO 80301-3604 Office: Pub Svc Co Colo 1225 17th St Ste 2100 Denver CO 80202-5521

MONZINGO, AGNES YVONNE, veterinary technician; b. Mangum, Okla., July 16, 1942; d. Ira Lee and Opal Alice (McAlexander) Mayfield; m. Monty Brent Monzingo, Dec. 19, 1959; children: Tara, Dawn, Michael, Kermit. AS, San Antonio Coll., 1969. Mgr. Tupperware Corp., Wichita Falls, Tex., 1966-69; with La Louisiane, San Antonio, 1974-79; counselor Diet Ctr., Duncanville, Tex., 1984-87; vet. technician DeSoto (Tex.) Animal Hosp., 1985—. Author: (weekly column) Happy Tracks, 1981. Pres. Dallas Stake Primary, 1983-88; commr. Boy Scouts Am., 1988-93. Recipient Wood badge Boy Scouts Am., 1987, Wisdom Trail Dist. award of merit, 1990, Silver Beaver award Boy Scouts Am., 1993. Mem. Tex. Assn. Registered Vet. Technicians (v.p. 1991), Tex. Assn. Animal Technicians (pres. 1988, com. chair 1990-92), Tex. Assn. Registered Technicians (pres. 1992), Am. Boxer Club, Dallas Boxers Club (sec. 1982-92), Metroplex Vet. Hosp. Mgrs. Assn. Mem. LDS Ch.

MOODY, CHERYL ANNE, social services administrator, social worker; b. Winston-Salem, N.C., July 31, 1953; d. Fred Bertram and Mary Edna (Weekley) M. BSW with honors, Va. Commonwealth U., 1975; MSW, U. Mich., 1979. Social worker Family Svcs., Inc., Winston-Salem, 1974-77; sch. social work intern Huron Valley Jr. High Sch., Milford, Mich., 1977-78; children's social work intern Downriver Child Guidance Clinic, Allen Park, Mich., 1978-79; children's svcs. specialist Calhoun County Dept. Social Svcs., Battle Creek, Mich., 1979-81; children's psychiat. social worker Eastern Maine Med. Ctr., Bangor, 1981-82, sr. med. social worker, 1982-85; clin. social worker Ctr. for Family Svcs. in Palm Beach County, Inc., West Palm Beach, Fla., 1988-89, Jupiter, Fla., 1989-91; program dir. Children's Home Soc. of Fla., West Palm Beach, 1985—; adj. prof. social work Fla. Atlantic U., 1993—. Mem. NASW, Acad. Cert. Social Workers. Democrat. Methodist. Home: 6212 62d Way West Palm Beach FL 33409 Office: Children's Home Soc of Fla 3600 Broadway West Palm Beach FL 33407-4889

MOODY, EVELYN WILIE, consulting geologist; b. Waco, Tex.; d. William Braden and Enid Eva (Holt) Wilie; children: John D., Melissa L., Jennifer A. Student, Baylor U., 1934-35; BA with honors in Geology and Edn. U. Tex., 1938, MA with honors in geology, 1940. Cert. profl. geologist; cert. permanent tchr., Tex. Geologist Ark. Fuel Oil Co., Shreveport, La., New Orleans and Houston, 1942-45; teaching asst. Colo. Sch. Mines, Golden, 1946-47; exploration cons. geologist Gen. Crude Oil Co., Houston, 1975-77; ind. cons. geologist, Houston, 1977—; exploration cons. geologist Shell Oil Co., Houston, 1979-81; faculty dept. continuing edn. Rice U., Houston, 1978. Contbr. articles to profl. jours.; editor: The Manual for Independents, 1983, The Business of Being a Petroleum Independent (A Road Map for the Self Employed), 1987; co-author: How (to Try) To Find An Oil Field, 1981. Mem. Am. Assn. Petroleum Geologists (del. Houston chpt. 1986-89, 89-91, 91—), Soc. Ind. Profl. Earth Scientists (hon., sec. 1978-79, vice chmn. 1979-80, chpt. chmn. 1980-81, nat. dir. 1982-85, chpt. award for Outstanding Svc. 1986, editor SIPES Bull., 1983-85, treas. SIPES Found. 1984, pres. 1985, Nat. award for Outstanding Svc. 1988, SIPES Found. award 1994), Geol. Soc. Am., Watercolor Soc. Houston, Art Students League N.Y.C., Art Assn., Am. Inst. Profl. Geologists, Houston Geol. Soc. (chmn. libr. com. 1978—), Soc. Econ. Paleontologists and Mineralogists, Pi Beta Phi (nat. officer 1958-60, 66-68), Pi Lambda Theta. Republican. Presbyterian.

MOODY, GAYLE ANN LAWSON, English language educator; b. Junction City, Kans., Oct. 21, 1951; d. Ellis Lawrence and Carolyn Marie (Beaven) L.; m. Craig Loring, Nov. 15, 1969; 1 child, Charlotte. BA, S.W. Mo. State U., 1983, MA, 1985; PhD, Baylor Univ., 1993. English instr. U. Md., Heidelberg, Germany, 1985-86, El Paso (Tex.) C.C., 1987, Cen. Tex. Coll., Killeen, 1989-91; asst. prof. English Jarvis Christian Coll., Hawkins, Tex., 1991—; adv. com. Baylor Univ., 1989-90; adviser Jarvis Christian Coll., 1991-93, mem. lyceum com., self-study editing com., 1991-92, scholarship com., sec. libr. com., 1992-93, chair curriculum com., faculty devel. com. 1992-93. With U.S. Army, 1975-81. Mem. MLA, Nat. Coun. for Tchrs. of English, Coll. Composition and Comms., South Cen. MLA. Office: Jarvis Christian Coll PO Drawer G Hawkins TX 75765

MOODY, MARILYN DALLAS, librarian; b. Little Rock, Aug. 28; d. Corbin Luther and Marian (Ricks) Dallas; m. W.I. Moody Jr., June 1, 1970 (div. 1987); m. Jeffry Baumann, 1988. Student, Hendrix Coll, Conway, Ark., 1959, U. Ark., 1960, Drexel U., 1964. Librarian Free Library of Phila., 1964-70, cons. librarian, 1971-76, coordinator dist. library ctr. services, 1976-82, chief extension services div., 1982-91; exec. dir. Bucks County Free Lib., Doylestown, Pa., 1991—. Recipient Cert. of Merit, 1981. Mem. ALA (councilor 1983-86), Pa. Library Assn. (legis. com. 1988-90, chair legis. com. 1980-82, coord. Legis. Day 1980-82, 87). Office: Bucks County Free Lib 150 S Pine St Doylestown PA 18901

MOODY, PATRICIA ANN, psychiatric nurse, artist; b. Oceana County, Mich., Dec. 16, 1939; d. Herbert Ernest and Dorothy Marie (Allen) Baesch; m. Robert Edward Murray, Sept. 3, 1960 (div. Jan. 1992); children: Deanna Lee Murray, Adam James Murray, Tara Michelle Murray, Danielle Marie Murray; m. Frank Alan Moody, Sept. 26, 1992. BSN, U. Mich., 1961; MSN, Washington U., St. Louis, 1966; student, Acad. of Art, San Francisco, 1975-78. RN; lic. coast guard, ocean operator. Psychiat. staff nurse U. Mich., Ann Arbor, 1961-62, Langley-Porter Neuro-Psychiat. Inst., San Francisco, 1962-63; instr. nursing Barnes Hosp. Sch. Nursing, St. Louis, 1963, Washington U., St. Louis, 1966-68; psychiat. nurse instr. St. Francis Sch. Nursing, San Francisco, 1970-71; psychiat. staff nurse Calif. Pacific Med. Ctr., San Francisco, 1991—. Oil and watercolors included in various group exhbns., 1982-93. V.p. Belles-Fundraising Orgn., St. Mary's Hosp., San Francisco, 1974; pres. PTO, Commodore Sloat Sch., 1982. Recipient Honor award Danforth Found., 1954, Freshman award Oreon Scott Found., 1958; merit scholar U. Mich., 1957. Mem. San Francisco Women Artists (Merit award for oil painting 1989), Artist's Equity (bd. dirs. No. Calif. chpt. 1987-89, pres. No. Calif. chpt. 1990), Met. Club. Republican. Lutheran. Home: 1270 Monterey Blvd San Francisco CA 94127

MOODY, WILMA LEE, paralegal; b. Quinton, Okla., May 12, 1949; d. Jesse Luke and Grace Pearl (Prater) Moody-Harris; m. Jerry D. Duvall, Jan. 31, 1964 (div.); children: Darren L., Deanna L.; m. Anderson Brown Morris II, Mar. 24, 1990. Student, Eastern Okla. State Coll., 1971; BS, Northeastern Okla. State U., 1975; Paralegal, U. Okla., 1979. CPCU; cert. BLS. Legal sec. A. James Gordon, Atty., McAlester, Okla., 1973; dep., minute clk. Pittsburg County Ct. Clk., McAlester, Okla., 1973-74; sec., bookkeeper Horne & Co., McAlester, Okla., 1974; legal sec. Bill Ervin, Atty., McAlester, Okla., 1975-77; bookkeeper, dep. & minute clk. Payne County Ct. Clk., Stillwater, Okla., 1977-79; instr. legal secs. Indian Meridian Vo Tech, Stillwater, Okla., 1977-79; sr. trial legal asst. Buck, Merritt & Hoyt, Oklahoma City, 1978-79; sec./legal asst., instr./legal sec. Okla. State Senate, Marvin York Vo Tech, Oklahoma City, 1980-82; legal asst. Warren L. Griffin, Atty., Midwest City, Okla., 1982-87, Lampkin, McAffrey & Tawwater and C.L. Frates and Co., Oklahoma City, 1987, 87—. Ch. missions N.W. Bapt. Ch., Oklahoma City, 1989-90, children's Sun. sch. dir., 1988-92; family support leader 1/160 Field Artillery, Pauls Valley, Okla., 1991—; adv. coun. Okla. Mil. Dept., Oklahoma City, 1993—. Mem. ABA, NAFE, State Filers Assn. (edn. com. 1993—, chair 1994—), Nat. Assn. Legal Secs. (dir. pub. rels. 1980), Nat. Assn. Legal Assts., Bus. Women's Assn. (Beta Sigma Phi chpt. pres.). Democrat. Baptist. Home: 3741 NW 62nd St Oklahoma City OK 73112-1419 Office: C L Frates and Co 5005 N Lincoln Blvd Oklahoma City OK 73105-3334

MOON, CATHERINE HYLAND, art therapist, art therapy educator; b. Ashtabula, Ohio, Dec. 10, 1955; d. Eugene Arthur and Marjorie Jeanette (Dippel) Hyland; m. Bruce Lee Moon, Aug. 20, 1977; children: Jesse Logan, Brea Hyland. BFA, Columbus Coll. Art and Design, 1978; MA in Alcohol & Drug Abuse Ministry, Meth. Theol. Sch. Ohio, 1993. Registered art therapist. Art therapist, co-dir., clin. internship in art therapy Harding Psychiat. Hosp., Worthington, Ohio, 1980—; art therapist Parenthesis Foster Care Network, Columbus, Ohio, 1984-85; instr. art therapy Columbus (Ohio) Coll. Art and Design, 1987-89; adj. faculty expressive therapies Lesley Coll.

Grad. Sch., Cambridge, Mass., summers 1992—. Mem. Am. Art Therapy Assn. (program chair 1992-93, conf. chair 1993—), Buckeye Art Therapy Assn., Harding Hosp. Med. Staff (assoc. mem.). Democrat. Home: 1956 Ford Rd Delaware OH 43015 Office: Harding Hosp 445 E Dublin-Granville Rd Worthington OH 43085

MOON, MONA MCTAGGART, speaker, educational consultant; b. Buffalo, N.Y., Oct. 4, 1934; d. William Daniel and Helen Violet (Dubin) McTaggart; m. James McCallum Moon, July 14, 1957; children: Douglas, Melisa, Bruce. BA, UCLA, 1955; MA, San Diego State U., 1985. Lic. tchr., Calif., cert. adminstrn., supervision, Calif. Tchr. high sch. Acalanes High Sch., Lafayette, Calif., 1956-61, San Diego Unified Sch. Dist., 1967-82; pres. Motivation Dynamics, San Diego, 1982—. Contbr. articles to profl. jours. Dir. LWV San Diego, 1967-72. Recipient Outstanding Contbn. award Calif. Assn. Dirs. of Activities; named San Diego County Tchr. of Yr., 1980. Mem. ASCD, ASTD, Nat. Speakers Assn., Phi Beta Kappa. Republican. Presbyterian. Office: 7910 Ivanhoe Ave Ste 29 La Jolla CA 92037-4511

MOONEY, CATHERINE LEE, real estate broker; b. Newark, Mar. 29, 1953; d. Robert Edward Lee and Catherine Mary (Sorrentino) Gosnell; m. Marvin Granville Coleman, May 20, 1972 (div. 1978); m. Jerome Henri Mooney, May 3, 1986; 1 child, Stephen Lloyd Coleman. Student, Strayer Coll., 1972. Cert. residential specialist; lic. real estate agt., broker, Utah, Fla. Legal sec., 1976-82; mktg. asst. BSD Med. Corp., Salt Lake City, 1983; dir. investor rels. Kenman Corp., Salt Lake City, 1983-85; realtor, 1986-88; owner, broker Mooney Real Estate, Salt Lake City, 1988—. Del. Dem. Cen. Com., Salt Lake City, 1989. Mem. Women's Coun. Realtors (edn. chair 1991, Utah state treas. 1994), Residential Sales Coun., Nat. Assn. Realtors, Salt Lake Bd. Realtors (equal opportunity com. 1989, edn. com. 1989, realtor svcs. exec. com. 1992-94), Utah Assn. Realtors. Roman Catholic. Home: 3066 S Plateau Dr Salt Lake City UT 84109 Office: Mooney Real Estate 1617 SE 15 St Fort Lauderdale FL 33316

MOONEY, MARILYN, lawyer; b. Pitts., July 29, 1952; d. James Russell and Mary Elizabeth (Cartwright) M. BA summa cum laude, U. Pa., 1973, JD, 1976. Bar: Mass. 1977, D.C. 1985, Pa. 1990, U.S. Dist. Ct. D.C. 1985, U.S. Ct. Appeals (D.C. cir.) 1985, U.S. Supreme Ct. 1986. Atty. E. I. du Pont de Nemours & Co., Wilmington, Del., 1976-84, Washington, 1985; with Fulbright & Jaworski L.L.P., Washington, 1985-90, ptnr., 1990—. Contbr. articles to profl. jours. Active Greater Washington Bd. Trade, D.C. Pub. Affairs Coun., 1992—. Mem. ABA, Fed. Regulation of Securities Com. (subcom. registration statements-1933 Act 1986—), Internat. Bar Assn. Office: Fulbright & Jaworski LLP 801 Pennsylvania Ave NW Washington DC 20004-2615

MOONEY, PATRICIA ANNE, sales professional; b. Bronx, N.Y., June 6, 1948; d. Peter Joseph and Helen (Houlihan) M.; m. Anthony John Grasso, Nov. 21, 1970 (div. 1977); 1 child, A. Benjamin. BA, Coll. New Rochelle, N.Y., 1970, MS, 1975. Tchr. Archdiocese of N.Y., Harrison, 1970-78; salesperson N.Y. Telephone, N.Y.C., 1978-82; instr. AT&T, Aurora, Colo., 1983; sales mgr. AT&T, N.Y.C., 1984, mgr. sales support dept., 1985; mgr. pricing and contract support dept. AT&T, Morristown, N.J., 1986; mgr. new bus. support dept. AT&T, Bridgewater, N.J., 1987; sales br. mgr. AT&T, Englewood, Colo., 1988-92; change mgmt. orgn. AT&T, Bridgewater, N.J., 1993; data networking customer svc. AT&T, Bedminster, N.J., 1994, customer svc. strategy, 1994—. Mem. Coll. New Rochelle Alumnae (bd. dirs.). Roman Catholic. Home: 27 Woodruff Rd Morristown NJ 07960-4623

MOONEY, PATRICIA JEAN, legal assistant; b. Moline, Ill., Mar. 24, 1959; d. Wayne L. and Ida M. (Gustafson) M. BA in Legal Assistance/Social Behavioral, Marycrest Coll., 1993; student, Drake U., 1994—. Cert. legal asst. Sec. U.S. Army Armament, Munition and Chem. Command, Rock Island, Ill., 1984-94. Bd. dirs. Hersong, Women's Chorus, Davenport, Iowa, 1990-91, 92-94; vol. Domestic Violence and Rape Assault Advocacy, Davenport, 1993-94; steward, negotiating com. Nat. Fedn. Fed. Employees, Local 15, Rock Island, 1992-94.

MOONEYHAN, ESTHER LOUISE, nurse, educator; b. Wabash, Ind., Oct. 2, 1920; d. Edward Lamont and Ina Louretta (Adams) Smithee; children: William Cecil, Mary Kathleen, Stephen Alan. Student (scholar), Ind. Wesleyan U., 1938-40; diploma (scholar), Meth. Hosp. Sch. Nursing, Indpls., 1943; BS in Gen. Nursing, Ind. U., 1964, MS in Nursing Edn., 1965, Ed. D. (fellow), 1973. Staff nurse Putnam County (Ind.) Hosp., 1943-44, Meth. Hosp., Indpls., 1951; pvt. duty nurse Ind. U. Med. Ctr., Indpls., 1953-60; staff nurse, assoc. supr., ednl. dir. Bur. Pub. Health Nursing Health & Hosp. Corp., Indpls. and Marion County, Ind., 1960-67; nurse adviser AID, Haile Selassie I U. Coll. Pub. Health, Ethiopia, 1967-69; asst. prof. nursing Tex. Woman's U., Denton, 1972-73; assoc. prof. nursing Fla. Internat. U. Miami, 1973-79, chmn., 1974-76; prof., adminstr. Ind. U. Sch. Nursing, South Bend, Ind., 1979-88; prof. Ind. U. Sch. Nursing, Indpls., 1989-91; community health nurse Manatee County Pub. Health unit State of Fla. Health and Rehab. Svc., Bradenton, Fla., 1992—; vis. prof. U. South Fla. Coll. Nursing, 1988-89, U. Ctrl. Fla., Orlando, 1991-92; charter mem. Nursing Rsch. Consortium North Ctrl. Ind.; speaker state workshops and nat. convs.; cons. in field. Contbr. articles to profl. jours. Recipient Outstanding Achievement award Ind. Wesleyan U. Alumni Assn., 1992. Mem. Am. Nurses Assn., Coun. Nurse Researchers, Fla. Nurses Assn. Dist. 4, Nat. League Nursing, Am. Pub. Health Assn., Internat. Health Soc. (bd. dirs. 1977-79), Nat. Coun. Internat. Health, Am. Assn. for World Health, Pi Lambda Theta, Sigma Theta Tau. Baptist.

MOORE, ALDERINE BERNICE JENNINGS (MRS. JAMES F. MOORE), association and organization administrator; b. Sacramento, Apr. 17, 1915; d. James Joseph and Elise (Thomas) Jennings; BA, U. Wash., 1941; m. James Francis Moore, Aug. 14, 1945. Sec. to div. Plant supr. Pacific Tel. & Tel. Co., Sacramento, 1937-39; exec. sec. Sacramento Community Chest Fund Raising Dr., 1941; sec. USAAF, Mather Field, Sacramento, 1942; statistician Calif. Western States Life Ins. Co., 1943; treas. Women's Aux. Stranger's Hosp., Rio de Janeiro, Brazil, 1964-65. Vice pres. Douglaston (N.Y.) Women's Club, 1955; mem. Douglaston Garden Club, 1951-55; pres. Nina Opland chpt. Women's Cancer Assn. U. Miami, 1960-61; corr. sec. Coral Gables (Fla.) Garden Club, 1960-62; pres. Miami Alumnae Club of Pi Beta Phi, 1961-62; mem. Putnam Hill chpt. D.A.R., Greenwich Conn., 1967-75, Palm Beach chpt., 1978—; mem. Woman's Club, Greenwich, Conn., 1967-75; mem. Women's Panhellenic Assn., Miami, 1961-62; internat. treas. Ikebana Internat., Tokyo, Japan, 1966-67, parliamentarian Tokyo chpt., 1966-67, N.Y. chpt., 1968-69; mem. Coll. Women Assn. Japan, 1965-66; mem. Tchrs. Assn. Sogetsu Sch. Japanese Flower Arranging, 1966—, Atlantis Golf Club. Served to 1st.lt. WAVES, 1943-45. Mem. Internat. Platform Assn., AAUW, Pi Beta Phi (local v.p. alumnae club 1969-71). Baptist. Club: Steamboat Investment (pres. 1972-73). Home: 316 Fairway Ct Lake Worth FL 33462-1212

MOORE, ALEDA MAJOR, insurance company executive, real estate executive; b. Greenville, S.C., May 18, 1927; d. Carl Shaw and Amelia Marie (Kellett) Major; m. Curtis Odell Moore, Mar. 17, 1951; 1 child, Brian Stanley. Grad., Draughn's Bus. Coll., Greenville, 1950, Ins. Inst. Am., 1975, S.C. Assn. Realtors, 1980. Cert. pub. ins. woman. Sec. J.P. Stevens & Co., Greenville, 1945-55; legal sec. Bailey & Dority, Attys., Greenville, 1961-73; with ins. dept. Curtis Moore Co., Mauldin, S.C., 1973—, with real estate dept., 1980—. Mem. Nat. Assn. Realtors, Greenville Bd. Realtors, S.C. Assn. of Realtors, Nat. Assn. of Ins. Women, S.C. Ind. Ins. Agts., Greenville Assn. Ins. Women, Inc. Mem. Ch. of Christ. Home: 216 Vesper Cir Mauldin SC 29662-2522 Office: 611 N Main St PO Box 675 Mauldin SC 29662-0675

MOORE, ALICE MARIE, elementary education educator; b. Evanston, Ill., July 10, 1933; d. John Clayton and Maria (Brunn) Campbell; m. Donald E. Moore, Aug. 10, 1968 (div. 1975); children: Andrew, Ian. BA, Mundelein Coll., 1955; MEd, Cambridge Coll., 1994. Cert. elem. edn. tchr. Tchr. Our Lady Help of Christians, Chgo., 1955-57; alumnae dir. Mundelein Coll., Chgo., 1957-59; tchr. San Francisco Bd. Edn., 1959-61, Chgo. Bd. Edn., 1961-65; tchr. Dept. of Def., Midway Island, 1965-66, Aschaffenburg, Fed. Republic of Germany, 1966-69; pharmacy apprentice Campbell's Pharmacy, Chgo., 1975-78; clk.-typist S&C Elec., Chgo., 1978-83; tchr. Chgo. Bd. Edn., 1984—; social chmn. Schneider Sch., Chgo., 1986—. Recipient Found. of Learning grant, 1987. Office: Schneider Sch 2957 N Hoyne Ave Chicago IL 60618-8299

MOORE, ALMA C., publishing executive; b. Cin.; d. Henry Paul and Helena Anne (Link) Clausing; m. Roy Moore. Student, Stephens Coll., Parsons Sch. Design, New Sch. Social Rsch., N.Y.C. Women's editor TV Guide mag., N.Y.C., 1962-70; dir. advt., promotion and pub. rels. Yves Saint Laurent Parfums, 1971-72; v.p., promotion and editorial dir. Viva/Omni mags., 1974-80; dir. mktg. communication Redbook mag., 1980-83; editor, pub. Woman Entrepreneur mag., 1983-85; pres. Alma C. Moore & Assocs. Mag. Cons., N.Y.C., 1983—. Mem. ind. jud. screening panel N.Y.C. Civil Ct. Judges Dem. Com., 1985, Women's Campaign Fund; sponsor Children's Aid Soc. Mem. ACLU, NOW, LWV, Nat. Trust Hist. Preservation, Advt. Women N.Y., Women's Econ. Roundtable (N.Y.), Nat. Women's Polit. Caucus, Women's City Club of N.Y. (bd. dirs.). Home and Office: 171 E 62d St New York NY 10021

MOORE, ALMA MERLE, association executive; b. Webster Springs, W.Va., Aug. 8, 1937; d. Thomas Wayne and Edna Jane (Bullion) M. AB, Glenville (W.Va.) State Coll., 1960; MLS, U. Pitts., 1969; MPA, W.Va. U., 1977. Sch. libr. Webster County Bd. Edn., Webster Springs, 1959-65, Columbian County Bd. Edn., Lisbon, Ohio, 1965-66; libr. asst. W.Va. Libr. Commn., Charleston, 1966-68; libr. dir. Clarksburg (W.Va.)-Harrison Pub. Libr., 1969-89; dir. Lewis County C. of C., Weston, W.Va., 1990—; pres. Back Fork Books, Inc., Webster Springs, 1979-90. Mem. W.Va. Italian Heritage Festival, Clarksburg, 1979—; mem. W.Va. Humanities Coun., Charleston, 1980-86, v.p., 1985-86; mem. W.Va. Libr. Commn., Charleston, 1990—; mem. vis. com. W.Va. U. Libr., 1987—. Named Disting. West Virginian Gov. Gaston Caperton, Charleston, 1988, Hon. Italian, W.Va. Italian Heritage Festival, Clarksburg, 1989. Mem. ALA, W.Va. Libr. Assn. (Dora Ruth Parks award 1987), Sierra Club (treas. W.Va. chpt. 1974-75), W.Va. Highlands Conservancy. Democrat. Home: PO Box 752 Webster Springs WV 26288-0752 Office: Lewis County C of C 134 Center Ave Weston WV 26452-1951

MOORE, ANDREA S., state legislator; b. Libertyville, Ill., Sept. 2, 1944. Attended, Drake U. m. William Moore; 3 children. Mem. Ill. Ho. of Reps., 1993—; mem. com. on elections and state govt., mem. com. on aging, mem. cities and villages com., mem. environ. and energy com., mem. labor and commerce com. Republican. Home: 234 W Cook Ave Libertyville IL 60048 Office: Ill Ho of Reps State Capitol Springfield IL 62706 also: 2014-H Stratton Bldg Springfield IL 62706 also: 733 N Milwaukee Libertyville IL 60048*

MOORE, ANN DOMBOURIAN, librarian; b. New Orleans, July 27, 1939; d. Vartan Nevdon and Adele Irene (Armstrong) Dombourian; m. Tom A. Moore, June 18, 1972. BA in Psychology, La. State U., 1961; MLS, SUNY, Albany, 1973. Cert. libr., N.Y. Libr. asst. New Orleans Pub. Libr., 1962-65; freight auditor Shell Oil Co. Data Ctr., New Orleans, 1965-68; welfare worker Fla. State Welfare, Jacksonville, 1968-69; pension benefits technician New Eng. Mut. Life Ins., Boston, 1969-71; reference libr. Kingston (N.Y.) Area Libr., 1973-75, Mid-Continent Pub. Libr., Independence, Mo., 1975-77; br. libr. Mid-Continent Pub. Libr., Blue Springs, Mo., 1977-86; base libr. McConnell AFB Libr., Wichita, Kans., 1986—; instr. Ind. Study Butler County Community Coll., McConnell AFB, 1991-93. Editor: (newsletter) Am. Bus. Women's Assn., 1987-89. Vol. reading tutor New Orleans Pub. Schs., 1964-66; rec. sec. McConnell AFB Cultural Awareness Coun., 1993—. Named 3D Chpt. Woman of the Yr., Am. Bus. Women Am., Wichita, 1989. Mem. ALA, Internat. Rels. Com., Kans. Libr. Assn., Wichita Area Libr. Assn. (exec. bd. 1989, chmn.-elect 1990-91, chmn. 1991-92, editor newsletter 1990-91), Assn. Coll. Rsch. Librs., Libr. Adminstrn. and Mgmt. Assn., Armed Forces Libr. Roundtable, Fed. Librs. Roundtable, Ethnic Materials Info. Exch. Roundtable. Office: Base Libr 22 SVS/SVRL 53295 Kansas St Ste 1 McConnell AFB KS 67221-3610

MOORE, ANN S., magazine publisher; b. McLean, VA, 1950; d. Monty and Bea Sommovigo; m. Donovan Moore; 1 son, Brendan. MBA, Harvard U., 1978. With Time, Inc., New York, NY, 1978—; founding publisher Sports Illustrated For Kids, 1989-91; publisher People Weekly, 1991-94, pres., 1994—. Office: People Magazine Rockefeller Ct Time & Life Building New York NY 10020*

MOORE, ANNE FRANCES, museum director; b. Jan. 6, 1946; d. William Clifton and Frances Woods M.; m. Michael P. Mezzatesta, Mar. 14, 1970 (div. 1987); children: Philip Moore, Alexander Woods, Marya Frances. BA in Art History, Columbia U., 1969, MA, 1971, MEd in Fine Arts, 1971, MA in Art History, 1982. Tchr. Manassas (Va.) High Sch., 1971-72, Poly. Prep. Country Day Sch., Bklyn., 1972-74; edn. instr. Kimbell Art Mus., Ft. Worth, 1980-83, rsch. assoc., lectr., 1983; assoc. mus. educator, outreach dir. Dallas Mus. Art, 1986-88; curator of edn., lectr. dept. art Oberlin (Ohio) Coll., 1988-90, curator acad. programs, lectr. dept. art, 1991-92; acting dir. The Allen Meml. Art Mus. at Oberlin Coll., 1991-92, dir., 1992—. Bd. trustees Intermus. Conservation Assn. Mem. Assn. Art Mus. Dirs., Assn. Coll. and Univ. Mus. and Galleries, Am. Assn. Mus. (edn. com.), Ohio Mus. Assn., Coll. Art Assn. Office: Allen Memorial Art Museum Oberlin College Oberlin OH 44074

MOORE, BEA, religious organization executive. Pres. The Woman's Home and Foreign Mission Society, Loudon, N.H.; nat. pres. The Woman's Home and Foreign Mission Society, Charlotte, N.C. Office: Woman's Home & Foreign Mission 845 Loudon Ridge Rd Loudon NH 03301

MOORE, BENITA ANN, religious studies and English educator; b. Mt. Etna, Iowa, Mar. 25, 1931; d. John Linus and Teresa Ellen (Keefe) M. AA, Ottumwa Heights Coll., Ottumwa, Iowa, 1950; BA, Marycrest Coll., Davenport, Iowa, 1952; MA, U. Iowa, 1959, PhD, 1976. Tchr. music, English Williams (Iowa) Ind. Pub. Sch., 1952-54, Ottumwa Heights Coll. and Acad., 1954-58, St. Mary's-Lenihan High Sch., Marshalltown, Iowa, 1958-66, St. Austin's Sch., Mpls., 1966-67; instr. music and English Marycrest Coll., Davenport, Iowa, 1967-69, asst. prof., 1974-77, assoc. prof., 1977-86, prof. religious studies and English, 1986-90; prof. Teikyo Marycrest U., Davenport, 1991—. Author: Escape Into a Labyrinth: F. Scott Fitzgerald, 1988. Precinct chairperson, conv. del. Dem. Party, Scott County, Iowa, 1972-88. NEH summer fellow, U. N.C., 1979, U. N.Mex., 1984, U. Ariz., 1988, Univ. House fellow Mellon U. Mem. Am. Acad. Religion, Modern Lang. Assn. Roman Catholic. Office: Teikyo Marycrest U 1607 W 12th St Davenport IA 52804-4096

MOORE, BETTY JEAN, retired education educator; b. L.A., Apr. 4, 1927; d. Ralph Gard and Dora Mae (Shinn) Bowman; m. James H. Moore, Nov. 25, 1944 (div. 1968); children: Barbara, Suzanne, Sandra; m. George W. Nichols, Oct. 15, 1983. BA, Pasadena Coll., 1957; MA, U. Nev., 1963; PhD, U. Ill., 1973. Tchr. Calif. pub. schs., 1953-63, sec. tchr., 1963-68; asst. prof. Ea. Ill. U., Charleston, 1968-71; grad. teaching asst. U. Ill., Champaign, 1971-73; asst. prof. to assoc. prof. S.W. Tex. State U., San Marcos, 1973-83; prof. edn. S.W. Tex. State U., 1983-89, ret., 1989; sch. evaluator; cons. in field; reading clinic dir. S.W. Tex. State U., 1974-85; cons. Min. Edn., Rep. of Singapore, 1980. Contbr. articles to profl. jours.; author: Teaching Reading, 1984; producer/dir. 5 ednl. videos. Active fund raising various charitable orgns. Mem. Internat. Reading Assn. (chpt. pres. 1964-65), Nat. Council Tchrs. English, AAUP. Presbyterian. Office: Southwest Tex State U C & I Dept San Marcos TX 78666

MOORE, BETTY JO, escrow training officer; b. Medicine Lodge, Kans., July 10; d. Joseph Christy and Helen Blanche (Hubbell) Sims; m. Harold Frank Moore, June 19, 1941; children: Terrance C., Harold Anthony, Trisha Jo. Cert., U. West L.A., 1978; student, Wichita (Kans.) U., 1940-41. Cert. legal asst./escrow officer. Sec. UCLA, 1949-59; escrow officer Security Pacific Nat. Bank, L.A., 1959-62, Empire Savs. & Loan Assn., Van Nuys, Calif., 1962-64; escrow supr. San Fernando Valley Bank, Van Nuys, 1964; escrow officer Heritage Bank, Westwood, Calif., 1964-66; escrow coord. Land Sys. Corp., Woodland Hills, Calif., 1966-67; escrow officer/asst. mgr., real estate lending officer Security Pacific Nat. Bank, L.A., 1967-80; real estate paralegal Pub. Storage, Pasadena, 1980-81; asst. mgr. escrow dept. First Beverly Bank, Century City, Calif., 1982-84; escrow trainer/officer Moore's Tng. Temps Inc., Canoga Park, Calif., 1984—; participant People to People Ambassador Program/Women in Mgmt. to USSR, 1989; observer Internat. Fedn. Bus. and Profl. Women's Congress, Washington, 1965, 81, Nassau, Bahamas, 1989, Narobi, Kenya, 1991. Adv. bd. escrow edn. Pierce Coll., Woodland Hills, Calif., 1968-80. Recipient Cert. of Appreciation, Pierce Coll., 1979, Calif. Fedn. Bus. and Profl. Women, 1989. Mem. Nat. Fedn. Bus. and Profl. Women's Clubs, Calif. Fedn. Bus. and Profl. Women (pres. dist. 1987-88, Calif. found. chmn. 1988-89), Woodland Hills Bus. and Profl. Women (pres. 1991-92, 94-95), Tri Valley Dist. Bus. and Profl. Women (legis. chair 1992-93, exec./corr. sec. 1993-94, 94-95), Internat. Fedn. Bus. and Profl. Women, Nat. Women's Polit. Caucus (coord., sec. San Fernando Valley caucus 1986-87, legis. co-chair 1991-92, 92-93), Women's Orgn. Coalition San Fernando Valley (sec. 1992), San Fernando Valley Escrow Assn. (bd. dirs. 1962-64), Woodland Hills C. of C. (assoc.), San Fernando Valley Bd. Realtors, L.A. Women's Legis. Coalition, U. West L.A. Alumni Assn. Democrat. Methodist.

MOORE, CARLA SUE WALKER, enforcement officer; b. Brownwood, Tex., Sept. 9, 1958; d. Ralph Carlton and Jackie Nell (Sparks) W. BBA in Acctg., Angelo State U., 1980. CPA, Tex. Auditor Office of Compt. of Pub. Accounts, Austin, Tex., 1980-81, Dallas, 1981-82, Odessa, Tex., 1981-86; audit supr. Office of Compt. of Pub. Accounts, Waco, Tex., 1986, Dallas, 1986-92; enforcement officer Office of Comptroller of Pub. Accts., Tyler, Tex., 1992—. Vol. Lit. Vols. of Am., Dallas, 1988. Mem. Tex. Soc. CPA's, Angelo State U. Ex-Students Assn. Office: Compt of Pub Accounts 3800 Paluxy Dr Ste 300 Tyler TX 75703

MOORE, CAROL, state legislator; b. N.Y.C., Jan. 1, 1945; 1 child. BA, Boston U., 1967, MSW, 1971. Psychotherapist; mem. N.H. Ho. of Reps., 1993—; mem. children, youth and juvenile justice com. Mem. N.H. Assn. Social Workers, N.H. Women's Lobby (treas. 1983-84, chair 1984-89). Democrat. Home: 38 1/2 South Spring St Concord NH 03301 Office: NH Ho of Reps State Capitol Concord NH 03301*

MOORE, CAROLYN LANNIN, video specialist; b. Hammond, Ind., Aug. 14, 1945; d. William Wren and Julia Audrey (Mathews) Lannin; m. F. David Moore, Oct. 21, 1967; children: Jillian Winter, Douglas Mathew, Owen Glen. BA, Ind. U., 1967, MA, Purdue U., 1991. Stockholders corr. Sears Roebuck and Co., Chgo., 1967-68; caseworker Lake County Dept. of Pub. Welfare, Hammond, Ind., 1968-71; field dir. Campfire Girls Inc., Highland, Ind., 1975-77; project dir. Northwest Ind. Pub. Broadcasting, Highland, 1984-85, interim exec. dir., 1985-87; cons. Telecommunications and Grant Writing, Munster, Ind., 1981-85; prin. Carolyn Moore and Assocs.-Laughing Cat Prodns., Munster, Ind., 1987—; bd. dirs. N.W. Ind. Pub. Broadcasting Sta., Merrillville, 1979—; instr. Purdue U.-Calumet, Ind., 1989; instr. Valparaiso (Ind.) U., 1990-91; lectr. in field. Producer tv series Visclosky Viewpoint, 1985-87; video producer A Kid's Eye View of the Symphony, 1987. Mem. Munster Cable TV Commn., 1984—, chmn., 1993—; bd. dirs., pres. N.W. Ind. Literacy Coalition, Inc.; mem. Lake County Master Gardeners. Mem. AAUW, NAFE, Alliance for Community Media, Assn. Ind. Video and Filmmakers Inc., Munster C. of C., Communicators N.W. Ind., Ind. U. Alumni Assn., Scherwood Ladies Golf Leagues, Wicker Park Ladies Golf League. Democrat. Catholic. Home and Office: Carolyn Moore & Assocs Laughing Cat Prodns 9604 Cypress Ave Hammond IN 46321-3418

MOORE, CINDY HAWKINS, accountant; b. Houston, Apr. 2, 1962; d. Harvey Eugene and Mary Desiree (Pinckney) Hawkins; m. Robert Jason Moore III, Sept. 22, 1990. BBA in Acctg., U. Tex., 1984. CPA, Tex. Intern Senator John Tower, U.S. Senate, Washington, 1983; sr. mgr. Ernst & Young, Houston, 1984—. Sec. improvement com. Bellaire Area Schs., 1992-93; v.p. membership Alley Theatre Guild, Houston, 1993-94; corp. ptnrs. steering com. Mus. Fine Arts, Houston, 1993-94. Fellow Life Mgmt. Inst. (pres. Greater Houston chpt. 1993-94); mem. AICPAs, Tex. Soc. CPAs, University Club. Office: Ernst & Young 1221 Mckinney St Ste 2400 Houston TX 77010-2007

MOORE, DEMI (DEMI GUYNES), actress; b. Roswell, N.Mex., Nov. 11, 1962; d. Danny and Virginia Guynes; m. Bruce Willis, Nov. 21, 1987; 2 daughters: Rumer Glenn, Scout LaRue. Studies with Zina Provendie. Actress: (feature films) Choices, 1981, Parasite, 1981, Young Doctors in Love, 1982, Blame it on Rio, 1984, No Small Affair, 1984, St. Elmo's Fire, 1985, About Last Night..., 1986, Wisdom, 1986, One Crazy Summer, 1987, The Seventh Sign, 1988, We're No Angels, 1989, Ghost, 1990, Mortal Thoughts, 1991 (also co-producer), The Butcher's Wife, 1991, Nothing But Trouble, 1991, A Few Good Men, 1992, Indecent Proposal, 1993, Disclosure, 1994; (TV series) General Hospital, 1982-83. Office: Creative Artists Agy Inc 9830 Wilshire Blvd Beverly Hills CA 90212*

MOORE, DIANNE J. HALL, insurance claims administrator; b. Wadsworth, Ohio, June 9, 1936; d. Glenn Mackey and Dorothy Laverne (Broomall) Hall; widowed; children: Christine M. Gardner Fiocca, Jon R. Gardner. BA in Speech, Heidelberg Coll., Tiffin, Ohio, 1958. Receptionist Buckeye Union Ins. Co., Akron, Ohio, 1966-67; adjuster Liberty Mut. Ins. Co., Akron, 1967-69; claims liaison Ostrov Agy., Akron, 1969-70; underwriter Clark Agy., Wadsworth, 1971-72; adjuster Celina Group, Wadsworth, 1972-73, Nationwide, Canton, Ohio, 1973-77; asst. claim mgr. Motorist Mut. Ins. Co., Akron, 1977-87; claim rep. Ohio Casualty Ins. Co., San Diego, 1987-88; claims adminstr. Riser Foods, Inc. Risk Mgmt., Bedford Heights, Ohio, 1989—. Mem. Ohio Hist. Soc., Friends of Gettysburg. Mem. Ohio State Claims Assn., Akron Claims Assn. (pres. 1985), Canton Claims Assn. Office: Riser Foods Inc 5300 Richmond Rd Bedford Hts OH 44146-1335

MOORE, DIANNE LEA, recording studio owner; b. North Tonawanda, N.Y., Jan. 30, 1949; d. Donald Robert and Dorothy (Ghise) Wilke; m. William Lewis Tremont, Aug. 21, 1966 (div. Apr. 1973); children: Eric, Michelle; m. Allen Charles Moore, July 11, 1981. AA, Scottsdale C.C., 1978; student, Ariz. State U., 1978-81. Powder paint troubleshooter McGraw Edison, Phoenix, 1980-81; v.p., mgr. Cereus Recording, Tempe, Ariz., 1981—; adminstrv. asst. McKesson, Phoenix, 1982-83; owner, mgr. Cereus Letter Processing, Tempe, 1983-93. Mem. Nat. Fedn. Ind. Businessmen, Better Bus. Bur., Steinway Soc., Tempe C. of C., Ariz. Rd. Racers (bd. dirs.). Democrat. Office: Cereus Rec 1733 E Mckellips Rd Ste 107 Tempe AZ 85281-1372

MOORE, EILEEN MARIE, dietitian; b. Buffalo, Feb. 27, 1959; d. Norman J. and Dorothy Phyllis (Kasperek) M. AS in Food Svc. Adminstrn., Erie Community Coll., 1979; BS in Clin. Dietetics, SUNY, Oneonta, 1982. Registered and lic. dietician, Ohio; cert. nutrition support dietitian, Ohio. Clin. dietician Cleve. Metrohealth Systems, 1983—; clin. dietitian home health svcs. Home Intensive Care Inc., 1991—; 1983-94; cons. home health care quality assurance Care Plus, Inc., Beachwood, Ohio, 1988-89; mem. med. intensive care quality assurance com. Metrohealth Med. Ctr., Cleve., 1987-91, mem. home health care com., 1990-91. Statler Hilton Found. scholar, 1979. Mem. Am. Dietetic Assn., Dietitians in Critical Care, Am. Soc. Parenteral And Enteral Nutrition (cert.). Roman Catholic. Home: 950 Tollis Pky Apt 608 Cleveland OH 44147-1848

MOORE, (MARGARET) ELEANOR MARCHMAN, retired librarian; b. Pinckard, Ala., Nov. 6, 1913; d. Robert Lee and Eleanor Rowena (Paris) Marchman; A.B., Fla. State Coll. for Women, 1936; B.S. in L.S., George Peabody Coll. for Tchrs., 1947, M.A. in Library Sci., 1962; m. James William Moore, Feb. 22, 1934 (div. 1940); 1 son, John Robert. Tchr. Alva (Fla.) High Sch., 1938-40, Wacissa (Fla.) Jr. High Sch., 1940-43; librarian Bartow (Fla.) Sr. High Sch., 1943-45, 48-67, Bartow Pub. Library, 1945-48; cataloger Roux Library, Fla. So. Coll., Lakeland, 1967-70, reference librarian, 1970-75; co-sponsor Polk County Student Library Assn., 1957-59; intern tchr. Fla. State U.; former mem. evaluating team So. Assn. Secondary Schs. and Colls. Recipient Polk County Career Increment award, 1961. Mem. NEA, Beta Phi Mu, Delta Kappa Gamma. Democrat. Baptist. Address: 251 Marilyn Dr Lafayette LA 70503-3968

MOORE, ELISABETH LUCE, association executive; b. Shantung, China, Apr. 4, 1903; d. Henry Winters and Elizabeth Middleton (Root) Luce; m. Maurice Thompson Moore, Sept. 17, 1926 (dec.); children: Maurice, Michael. BA, Wellesley Coll., 1924; LHD (hon.), Duke U., 1968; LLD (hon.), Princeton U., 1972, Columbia U., 1973. Past chmn. Inst. of Internat. Edn.; past. mem. adv. com. Marshall Plan. Editor TO INFORM. Chmn. women's divsn., United China Relief, 1940-50; nat. chmn. USO, 1942-46; chmn. Nelson Rockefeller Campaign for Gov., elder Brick Presbyterian Ch., N.Y.; active YWCA of the U.S.A , Internat. YWCA; trustee, past pres. United Bd. for Christian Higher Edn.; trustee SUNY, 1968-78, chmn. bd. trustees, 1970-78; trustee China Inst., The Asia Found. Recipient Gold Medal, Nat. Inst. of Soc. Scis., 1955, Blackwell Medal, Hobart Coll. and William Smith Coll., 1959, Reader's Digest award, Ambassador award YWCA of the U.S.A., 1993; decorated Order of the Brilliant Star, Republic of China, 1964. Home: 1000 Park Ave New York NY 10028-0934

MOORE, ELISE LUCILLE, Christian Science practitioner; b. Pitts.; d. Ernest Lowell Price and Elizabeth Nell (Goodman) Burton; m. Frank David Moore, Jan. 28, 1983; stepchildren: Doug, Brian. BA in Econs., Mich. State U., 1974. Mktg. mgr. Indsl. Tube Divsn. Westinghouse, Horseheads, N.Y., 1974-76; mktg. 7-Up of Ind. Westinghouse, Indpls., 1976-77; sales rep. Microfilm Equipment Divsn. Bell & Howell, Indpls., 1977-79; mktg. mgr. Microfilm Equipment Divsn. Bell & Howell, Lincolnwood, Ill., 1979-81; nat. sales mgr. Phoenix, 1981; owner Pitts., 1982; practitioner First Ch. of Christ, Scientist, Nashville, 1983—; regional rep. Christian Sci. Ch. to coll. orgns. in Tenn., N.C., S.C. Contbr. articles to Christian Sci. publs. Sec. Civitan-Gallatin (Tenn.), 1985-86; pres. Sumner County Literacy Coun., Gallatin, 1988, 89, 90; organizer AIM, Inc., Gallatin, 1989; active United Way of Sumner County; chaplain Storefront Ministries, Nashville. Mem. Nashville Assn. Rabbis, Priests and Mins., Nat. Conf. Christians and Jews, Amnesty Internat., Omicron Delta Epsilon. Home: 1145 S Wrights Ln Gallatin TN 37066 Office: 1719 West End Ave Ste 718W Nashville TN 37203

MOORE, ELIZABETH A., state legislator; b. Reading, Pa., Dec. 22, 1938; married; 3 children. RN, Allentown (Pa.) Hosp. Sch. Nursing, 1959. Ret. nurse; mem. N.H. Ho. of Reps.; mem. judiciary com.; mem. legis. adminstrn. com. Mem. exec. com. Hillsborough County Del.; dir. Monadnock Cmty. Vis. Nurse Assn.; elder Cmty. Ch. of New Boston, also choir dir., organist; chmn. Surrogate Motherhood Com., 1988-89; active Circle Singers of New Boston. Mem. Nat. Order of Women Legislators. Republican. Home: 277 Cochran Hill Rd New Boston NH 03070-3910 Office: NH Ho of Reps State Capitol Concord NH 03301*

MOORE, EMMA SIMS, executive secretary; b. Branford, Fla., Oct. 27, 1937; d. Lawton Edward and Annie Ruth (Hewitt) Sims; m. H. Dean Moore, Sr., Sept. 30, 1961; 1 child, H. Dean Jr. Secretarial sci., Jones Coll., 1955; B., Butler U., 1984; M., Ind. Wesleyan U., 1989; postgrad., The Fielding Inst. Cert. profl. sec.; cert. adminstrv. mgr. Sec. to svc. mgr. Buick Motor div. GM, Jacksonville, Fla., 1956-72, Charlotte, N.C., 1972-74; sec. to br. mgr. Motors Holding div. GM, Washington, 1974-78, Phila., 1978-82; exec. sec. to dir. product support Allison Gas Turbine div. GM, Indpls., 1982-92; ret., 1992; mem. faculty Ind.-Wesleyan U. Mem. exec. com. Boy Scouts Am., West Chester, Pa., 1981-82. Mem. NAFE (profl. secs. internat. goodwill people to people del. to People's Republic of China, Singapore, Thailand, Indonesia and Hong Kong), Profl. Secs. Internat. (v.p. 1986-87, pres. 1987-89, 500 chpt., Sec. of Yr. 1986 500 chpt., 1989 Ind. divsn.), Inst. for Certification, CPS Acad., CPS Soc. Indpls., Secretarial Adv. Coun., Internat. Tel. & Tel. Inst., AAUW. Baptist. Home: 107 Catawba Rd Clemson SC 29631

MOORE, FAY LINDA, software quality engineer; b. Houston, Apr. 7, 1942; d. Charlie Louis and Esther Mable (Banks) Moore; m. Noel Patrick Walker, Jan. 5, 1963 (div. 1967); 1 child, Trina Nicole Moore. Student, Prairie View Agrl. and Mech. Coll., 1960-61, Tex. So. U., 1961, Our Lady Lake U., 1993, Thomas Edison State Coll., 1994—. Cert. ISO 9000 Internal Auditor. Instr. Internat. Bus. Coll., Houston, 1965; keypunch operator IBM Corp., Houston, 1965-67, sr. keypunch operator, 1967-70, programmer technician, 1970-72, asst. programmer, 1972-73, assoc. programmer, 1973-84; sr. assoc. programmer, 1984-87, staff programmer, 1987-92; staff systems analyst, 1992-94; sr. software quality engineer Loral Space Info. Systems, Houston, 1994—; owner, pres. AFT Co., Houston, 1993—; mem. space shuttle flight support team IBM, 1985-92; mem. space sta. team IBM, 1992-93. Recipient Apollo Achievement award NASA, 1969, Quality and Productivity award NASA, 1986, 1992. Mem. NAFE, Soc. Software Quality, Booker T. Washington Alumni Assn., Ms. Found. for Women, Inc. Democrat. Roman Catholic. Avocations: personal computing, board games. Office: Loral Space Info Systems Mail Stop F6MIA 1322 Space Park Dr Houston TX 77058

MOORE, FAYE ANNETTE, social services professional; b. Glasgow, Mont., Feb. 21, 1938; d. Chester Oliver and Viola Adelaide (Skalet) Baker; m. Russell Dale Guthrie, July 1, 1961 (div. Nov. 1975); children: Tamia Lee, Owen Bradley; m. William Bateman Moore, Jan. 6, 1979. BA Sociology, Mont. State U., 1959; MA Social Work, U. Chgo., 1961; MBA, N. Mex. State U., 1984, PhD Ednl. Adminstrn., 1989. Social worker Ill. Childrens Home and Aid Soc., Chgo., 1961-63; social worker Divsn. Social Svcs., Fairbanks, Alaska, 1964-72, supr. social worker, 1972-74, staff mgr., 1974-75; regl. mgr. Divsn. Family and Youth Svcs., Anchorage, Alaska, 1976-80, regl. adminstr., 1991—; adminstr. Rsch. Ctr. N.Mex. State U. Coll. Bus., Las Cruces, 1984-86; instr. Golden Gate U., Holloman AFB/Alamogordo, N.Mex., 1989-91, Webster U., Ft. Bliss, El Paso, Tex., 1989-91; presenter confs. in field. Contbr. articles to profl. jours. Mem. NASW, Realtor Assn. N.Mex. (state dir. 1990-91, chmn. state edn. com. 1991), Las Cruces Assn. Realtors (v.p. 1991), Am. Bus. Comm. Assn., Beta Gamma Sigma, Phi Kappa Phi. Home: PO Box 244403 Anchorage AK 99524-4403 Office: Divsn Family and Youth Svcs 550 W 8th Ave Ste 304 Anchorage AK 99501

MOORE, GISELLE JOSEPHINE, nurse practitioner; b. Nassau, Bahamas; d. John Palmer and Valerie Irene (Merrells) M. BSN, Barry Coll., 1981; MSN, U. Fla., 1990. Advanced registered nurse practitioner, Fla. RN Shands Hosp., Gainesville, Fla., 1982-87; advanced registered nurse practitioner U. Fla./Shands, Gainesville, 1987—; . Fla., Gainesville. Editor: Women's Cancer: A Gynecological Oncology Perspective, 1992—; mem. editl. bd. Cancer Nursing Jour., 1993—. Cons. Am. Cancer Soc., Gainesville, 1993—. Mem. Soc. Gyn Nurse (chmn. publs.), Oncology Nurse Soc., Pediatric Oncology Soc., Fla. Nurses Assn., Sigma Theta Tau. Republican. Ch. of England. Home: 2317 NW 69th Ter Gainesville FL 32606-6393

MOORE, GWEN, state legislator; b. Detroit, Oct. 28; d. Willis and Edna (Posey) Osborne; m. Ronald W. Dobson, Sept. 7, 1978; 1 child, Ronald II. BA, Calif. State U., 1962; cert. tchg., UCLA, 1963. Probation officer County of L.A., 1963-69; pers. dir. Poverty Program, L.A., 1969-75; bd. dirs., trustee L.A. C.C. Dist., 1975-78; assemblyperson Calif. State Legis., Sacramento, 1979—; mem. Commn. on Calif. State Govt., 1983—, Assembly Dem. Econ. Prosperity Team, Calif., 1993—; chair Assembly on the Legis., Nat. Conf. of State Legis., 1991, State and Fed. Assembly, 1992; law enactor Moore Universal Telephone Act, 1983, Act prohibiting tax deductions for expenses at discriminatory pvt. clubs, 1987, Moore-Brown-Roberti Family Rights Act, 1991. Recipient Willie L. Brown Jr. award Black Am. Polit. Assn. Calif., 1988, Legislator of Yr. award, Nat. Assn. of Minorities in Cable, 1993, Calif. NOW, 1992, Homecare Advocate of Yr. award Svc. Employees Internat. Union, 1993, Consumer's Friend award Toward Utilizing Rate Normalization, 1993. Mem. Nat. Black Caucus of State Legislators (chair Western region 1984—), Nat. Orgn. Black Elected Women, 100 Black Women, Nat. Women's Polit. Caucus, Women's Legis. Lobby. Democrat. Presbyterian. Office: Ho of Reps State Capital Rm 2117 Sacramento CA 95814*

MOORE, HAZEL STAMPS, retired librarian; b. Learned, Miss., Jan. 10, 1924; d. Andrew Leeander and Seretha (Hicks) Stamps; widowed; children: Wilbur Dexter, Debra Dannette. BA cum laude, Tougaloo Coll., 1947; MLS, Atlanta U., 1955; cert. 30 hours, Washington U., 1961-68; postgrad. studies, U. New Orleans, 1965, Xavier U., 1966, La. State U., 1967, Tulane U., 1968. Tchr.-libr. Oakley (Miss.) Tng. Sch., 1947-49, Tougaloo (Miss.) Prep. Sch., 1949-51; asst. libr. Tougaloo Coll., 1951-57; head libr. B.T. Washington High Sch., New Orleans, 1957-61, 62-66, 67-72; sr. reference libr. St. Louis Pub. Libr., 1961-62; asst. supr. New Orleans Pub. Schs., 1966-67; head libr. Marion Abramson High Sch., New Orleans, 1972-91; ret., 1992; presenter workshops Orleans Parish Sch. Bd.; instr. U. New Orleans, 1976, 78, 84; supervising libr. U. New Orleans, 1965-91, Xavier U., New Orleans, 1958-62. Contbr. articles to profl. publs. Chair bd, Christian edn. Ctrl. Congl. Ch., United Ch. Christ, 1972-91, tchr. ch. sch., diaconate, past pres. women's fellowship, sec. pasoral search com.; pres. bd. dirs. S. Ctrl. Conf. United Ch. of Christ; chair La. League Good Govt. Essay Contest, 1976. Recipient Modisette award secondary sch. librs. 1986, U.S. Dept. Edn.; named Outstanding Lay Person United Ch. of Christ; grantee edn. La. Dept. Edn., 1974, tchr. incentive , 1978; Robinson grant New Orleans Pub. Schs., 1991. Mem. ALA (del. to Am. Assn. Sch. Librs. state assembly 1983, best books for young adults com. young adult svc. div. 1987-88, selection and use of materials com.), La. Libr. Assn. (2d v.p., chari intellectual freedom com. 1973-74, mem. gov.'s conf. on librs. steering com.). Democrat. Home: 5931 Congress Dr New Orleans LA 70126-2409

MOORE, HELEN ELIZABETH, reporter; b. Rush County, Ind., Dec. 19, 1920; d. John Brackenridge and Mary Amelia (Custer) Johnson; m. John William Sheridan, July 6, 1942 (dec. Jan. 1944); m. Harry Evan Moore, May 15, 1954; 1 child, William Randolph. BS, Ind. U., 1972, MS, 1973. Ofcl. ct. reporter 37th Jud. Cir., Brookville, Ind., 1950-60; freelance reporter Rushvile, Ind., 1960—; conv. reporter various assns. With USMC, 1943. Recipient Sagamore of the Wabash award Gov. Ind., 1984. Mem. Women Marines Assn. (charter, nat. pres. 1966-68), Am. Legion Aux. (various offices 1950— including Eight Forty nat. sec.-treas., pres. Ind. dept. 1966-67, conv. reporter), Bus and Profl. Women (dist. dir., various offices 1967—), Nat. Shorthand Reporters Assn. (registered profl. reporter), Ind. Shorthand Reporters Assn. (state treas., editor Hoosier Reporter, chmn. legal directory), German Geneal. Soc. Am., Ind. German Heritage Soc. (state dir. 1984-92, pres. 1990-92), Ind. U. Alumni Assn. Democrat. Methodist. Home and Office: PO Box 206 Rushville IN 46173-0206

MOORE, HELEN HUNTER, public protection director; b. Mobile, Ala.; d. Robert Hunter and Ann (Pennington) M.; children: Nancy Atchison, Joshua Beatty. BS, Auburn U., 1977. Adminstr. of elections State of Ala., 1978-86; exec. asst. Atty. Gen., State of Ala., 1986-87, dir. Office of Pub. Protection, 1987—; workshop leader. Author, editor: Child Abuse Neglect and Prevention Manual. Bd. mem. Regional Coun. on Alcoholism and Drug Dependency, Easter Seals; mem. bd. dirs. Westminster Childcare Ctr., Montgomery, 1984-86; speaker Nat. Elections Conf., Cocoa Beach, Fla., 1986, Nat. Conf. of the Fed. Election Commn., San Diego, 1987; judge Huntsville Civic Clubs Awards Program, 1988; pres. Ala. Drug Edn. Project, Montgomery, 1990; del. Am. Coun. Young Polit. Leaders Internat. Conf., Bonn, Germany, 1990, Nat. Alliance Treaty Orgn. Conf., Paris, 1990. Mem. Dem. Women's Club. Presbyterian. Office: Office of the Atty Gen 11 S Union St Montgomery AL 36111

MOORE, HERBERTA GRISSOM, small food business executive; b. Knoxville, Tenn., Aug. 30, 1944; d. Herbert Gist and Grace (Gass) Grissom; m. Farris F. Moore Jr., Sept. 17, 1976. AA, Nashville, 1994. Office mgr., v.p. Mrs. Grissom's Salads, Inc., Nashville, 1964—. Mem. Beta Sigma Phi. Methodist. Office: Mrs Grissoms Salads Inc 2500 Bransford Ave PO Box 40231 Nashville TN 37204

MOORE, JACQUELINE SHALEEM, behavioral scientist, educator; b. Chgo., June 13, 1937; d. Clyde Charles and Elizabeth (Lynk) Knudson; m. James Harrington Richards, Sept. 3, 1958; children: Jill Louise, Jeffrey James; m. James Harold Moore, Aug. 5, 1978. AA, RN, Hennipin State Coll.; BA in Bus., Human Svcs., Met. State U.; MA in Religion, PhD in Behavioral Sci., Nat. Christian U. Mo., 1983. Ordained min. Light of Christ Sem., 1983. Surgical technician No. Meml. Hosp., Golden Valley, Mn., 1973-74; RN U. Minn., 1974-75, Sacred Heart Med. Ctr., Spokane, Wa., 1975-76, St. Mary's Hosp., Mpls., 1976-78; internat. speaker, pres. Braintree, Mpls., 1977-94; pres. Personal Growth Found., 1978-85; RN Golden Valley (Minn.) Health Ctr., 1980-86; psychotherapist, 1986-94; nurse U. Colo., 1994—, Mental Health Ctr., 1994—, Luth. Med. Ctr., 1995—; apprentice Sioux Medicine Woman, 1989; master practitioner neuro-linguistics, 1991, Level IV transformational kinesiology, 1992. Author: Patterns for Change, 1982, The Pentagonal Brain, 1984, Intuition-How to Develop and Trust It, 1984, Color Sense, 1984, Inner Space, 1986, Wakankana-Kepper of the Sun, 1989, Seasons of the Red Bear, 1991, Onion Peelings, 1992; founder/dir. Peers Optimal Health Program, 1992. Mem. Internat. Assn. Neuro-Linguistics, Amnesty Internat., Noetic Sci. Inst., Spiritual Frontiers Fellowship. Office: 2428 Franklin Ave Louisville CO 80027

MOORE, JAN R., elementary education educator; b. Birmingham, Ala., Sept. 13, 1952; d. Archie D. and Lucille (Bailey) Renfroe; children: Adam Michael, Anna Katherine. BS in Social Work, U. Montevallo, 1974; MA in Edn., U. Ala., Birmingham, 1989. Social worker St. Vincent's Hosp., Birmingham, 1974-79; tchr. Shades Cahaba Elem. Sch., Birmingham, 1990—; mentor tchr. for new tchrs.; condr. seminar connecting art and lit. to lang. arts U. Ala., Birmingham, Homewood City Schs. Mem. Birmingham Mus. Art, Ala. Edn. Assn., Nat. Edn. Assn., Homewood Edn. Assn., Kappa Delta Pi. Mem. United Methodist Ch. Office: Shades Chaba Elem Sch 3001 Montgomery Hwy Homewood AL 35209

MOORE, JANA LYNN, physical therapist; b. Texas City, Tex., Sept. 17, 1959; d. Calvin Edward and Wanda Kathleen (Mayfield) M. BS in Psychology, Tex. A&M U., 1981; BS in Phys. Therapy, Tex. Women's U., 1986. Mental health work spl. trainer Brown Schs., Austin, Tex., 1981-82; phys. therapist St. Joseph Hosp., Houston, 1987-90, Health South, Austin, 1990—. Mem. Am. Phys. Therapy Assn. Home: 1702 Cresthaven Austin TX 78704

MOORE, JANA MELISSA, nurse and marketing executive; b. Miami, Fla., July 1, 1961; d. Kenneth Arthur and Joanna (O'Brien) M. ASN, Broward C.C., Davie, Fla., 1986. RN, Ohio. Nurse team leader Broward Gen. Med. Ctr., Ft. Lauderdale, Fla., 1986; nurse rural nursing project U.S. Peace Corps, Paraguay, 1987-89; surg. asst. Dr. Roger Stewart, Ft. Lauderdale, 1989-90; home health discharge planner Home Health Corp. of Am., Ft. Lauderdale, 1990-92; mktg. rep. Corpwell Corp. Wellness Inc., Boca Raton, Fla., 1992-93; ind. contract nurse Home Health, Dayton, Ohio, 1993—. Vol. educator for HIV sessions Daybreak Homeless Shelter, Dayton, 1994—; triage nurse vol. ARC, Hurricane Andrew Relief Effort, Miami, Fla., 1992; cmty. outreach vol. Covenant House/Fla., Ft. Lauderdale, 1991-93; mem. Nat. Bone Marrow Donation Program, 1989—; mem./donor Cmty. Blood Bank, 1982—; instr. World Wise Program, 1993—. Named Vol. of the Mo., Covenant House/Fla., 1993. Roman Catholic.

MOORE, JANE ROSS, librarian; b. Phila., Apr. 24, 1929; d. John William and Mary (McClure) Ross; m. Cyril Howard Moore, Jr., June 1, 1956 (div. Mar. 1967). A.B., Smith Coll., 1951; M.S. in L.S, Drexel U., 1952; postgrad., Columbia U.; M.B.A. with distinction, NYU, 1965; Ph.D., Case Western Res. U., 1974. Cataloguer, Yale U. Library, 1952-54; chief tech. processes librarian Lederle Labs., Am. Cyanamid Co., Pearl River, N.Y., 1954-58; chief serials catalog librarian Bklyn. Coll. Library, 1958-65, asst. prof., chief catalog div., 1965-70, asso. prof., chief catalog div., 1971-73, asso. prof. asso. librarian adminstrv. services, 1973-76; prof., chief librarian Mina Rees Libr., Grad. Sch. and Univ. Center, CUNY, 1976-91, prof., chief libr. emerita, 1991—; lectr. Syracuse U. Grad. Sch. Libr. Sci., summer 1967, 69, Queens Coll. Grad. Sch. Libr. and Info. Studies, 1967-69; adj. asso. prof., 1974-76, adj. prof., 1977-86; HEW Title IIB fellow Case Western Res. U. Sch. Library Sci., 1970-72; trustee N.Y. Met. Reference and Rsch. Libr. Agy., 1984-93, 2d v.p., 1985-88, v.p., 1988-90, treas. 1991-93. Bd. dirs. Vis. Nurse Assn. of Bklyn., 1984—, mem. exec. com., 1987—; elder, clk. of session, pres. of corp. Presbyn. Ch. Mem. N.Y. Library Assn. (pres. 1979-80, pres. resources and tech. services sect. 1966-67, councilor 1966-67, 75-76, 78-81, sec.-treas. acad. and spl. libraries sect. 1973-75), ALA (membership com. 1967-71, chmn. council regional groups, resources and tech. services div. 1968-69, dir. div. 1968-70, 75-76, chmn. div. cataloging and classification sect. 1975-76), N.Y. Tech. Services Librarians (pres. 1963-64, award 1976), Assn. Coll. and Research Libraries (chmn. univ. libraries sect. 1983-84), N.Y. Library Club (sec. 1964-66, pres. 1980-81, council 1966-70, 73-77, 79-82), OCLC Users Council (SUNY del. 1981-85), AAUP, AAUW, Am. Printing History Assn., Am. Soc. Info. Sci., Archons of Colophon, Library Assn. of Great Brit., Spl. Libraries Assn., The Typophiles, NYU Grad. Sch. Bus. Adminstrn. Alumni Assn. (rec. sec. 1967-69, dir. 1969-70, 75-79), Smith Coll. Club Bklyn. (pres. 1966-67, 67-68, class treas. 1976-81), Smith Coll. Club N.Y., Princeton Club N.Y., Phi Kappa Phi. Home: 35 Schermerhorn St Brooklyn NY 11201-4826 Office: CUNY Mina Rees Libr Grad Sch & U Ctr 33 W 42nd St New York NY 10036-8099

MOORE, JANET MARIE, state official; b. Butler, Pa., Mar. 13, 1947; d. Jesse Robert and Katherine Mae (Pisor) Moore. A in Specialized Bus., New Castle Bus. Coll., 1972. Cost accountant Package Products Inc., Pitts., 1967-68; audit clk. Liberty Mut. Ins. Co., New Castle, Pa., 1968-71; acct. S.R. Snodgrass & Co., CPAs, New Castle, 1971-74; clerical supr. Pa. vital records Pa. Dept. Health, New Castle, 1974—; pvt. practice acctg., Volant, Pa., 1974—. Mem. NRA (life), Owner Handler Assn., Am. Numismatic Assn., Studebaker Family Nat. Assn. (life), New Castle Kennel Club (sec. 1978, dir. 1977-81, v.p. 1979-81). Democrat. Presbyterian. Home: RR 3 Box 101 Volant PA 16156-8815 Office: PO Box 1528 New Castle PA 16103-1528

MOORE, JANET RUTH, nurse, educator; b. Bridgeport, Conn., Sept. 19, 1949; d. Robert Hartland and Florence (Merritt) Bessom; m. William James Moore, Sept. 5, 1971; children: Jeffrey, Gregory. AA, Green Mountain Coll., 1969; diploma, Mass. Gen. Hosp., 1974; BS in Nursing, Am. Internat. Coll., 1980; MS in Nursing, U. Mass., 1993. RN, Mass.; cert. gerontol. nurse ANCC. Nurse's aide Lynn (Mass.) Hosp., 1967-69, staff nurse, 1972-73; nursing asst. U.S. Army Hosp., Ft. Polk, La., 1971-72; staff nurse Ludlow (Mass.) Hosp., 1980-85; staff edn. instr. Springfield (Mass.) Mcpl. Hosp., 1985-88; dir. staff edn. Jewish Nursing Home, Longmeadow, Mass., 1988-93; instr. Baystate Med. Ctr. Sch. Nursing, Springfield, Mass., 1993—; nurse Camp Wilder, Springfield, 1981-84; clin. instr. Holyoke (Mass.) Community Coll., 1990. Mem. Jr. League of Springfield, 1981-88, Community Health Edn. Council for Children and Adolescents; bd. dirs. Mass. Soc. for Prevention of Cruelty to Children, Springfield, 1985-90, Coun. of Chs., chairperson, Div. on Aging, 1989-90. Mem. ANA, Wilbraham Jr. Women's Club, Sigma Theta Tau, Alpha Chi. Home: 104 Burleigh Rd Wilbraham MA 01095-2620 Office: Baystate Med Ctr Sch of Nursing Springfield MA 01199

MOORE, JEANNE MADELINE, writer; b. Marysville, Calif., June 28, 1943; d. Frederick William and Madeline Rose (Cassidy) Weimann; m. Charles T. Moore, May 22, 1982; 1 child, Charles Karl Thomas Jr. BA in English, Skidmore Coll., 1965; MS in Journalism, Northwestern U., 1968; MA in Ednl. Media Libr. Sci., Fairfield U., 1990. Catalog copywriter Montgomery Ward & Co., N.Y.C., 1966-67; dictionary lexicographer R.R. Donnelley & Sons, Evanston, Ill., 1967-68; retail copywriter Carson Pirie Scott & Co., Chgo., 1968-70; corp. copywriter Continental Assurance Co., Chgo., 1970-71; agy. copywriter Foote, Cone & Belding, Chgo., 1971-78; author Academy Press, Chgo., 1978-81; dir. JM Creative Services, Monroe, Conn., 1982—. Author: The Fair Women, 1982; co-author: Equality in Print, 1978; editor HERS Healthy Kit, 1977; co-editor: Chicago Women's Directory, 1974; contbr. editor World's Fair Journal, 1982—, Antique Almanac, 1984-86, Victorian Homes, 1985—; contbr. articles to profl. jours. and pop. mags. including Americana, MS, Newsday, 1982—. Mem. Lockwood-Mathews mansion, Norwalk, Conn., 1985—. Recipient Wayte-Raymond Literary award Am. Numismatic Assn., 1982. Roman Catholic. Home and office: 15 Cheryl Dr Monroe CT 06468-1005

MOORE, JOAN L., radiology educator, physician; b. Belmont, Mass., Oct. 26, 1935; d. Frank Joseph and Maria L. Mazzio; children: James Thomas, Edwin Stuart. BA in Chemistry and Theology, Emmanuel Coll., 1957; MA in Genetics and Physiology, Mass. Wellesley Coll., 1961; PhD in Genetics, Bryn Mawr (Pa.) Coll., 1964; MD, Phila. Coll. of Medicine, 1977, MSc in Radiology, 1981. Instr. in biochemistry Gwynedd Mercy Coll., Springhouse, Pa., 1963-65; instr. in genetics Holy Family Coll., Phila., 1965-66; instr. in anatomy Phila. Coll. of Medicine, 1971-77, tchr., 1973-77, asst. prof., 1977-84; prof. W.Va. Sch. of Medicine, 1984—; rotating intern Phila. Coll. of Medicine Hosp., 1977-78, resident in radiology, 1978-81; lt. col. USAR, 1984—; prof. W.Va. Sch. of Medicine, Lewisburg, 1984—. Author: (with Dr. DiVirgilito) Essentials of Neuropathology, 1974. Lector St. Ann's Cath. Ch., Phoenixville, Pa., 1981-84; treas. Hist. Soc. of Frankford, Phila., 1968-75, Sch. Mother's Assn., Devon (Pa.) Prep., 1980-81. Lt. col. U.S. Army Med. Corps, 1992. Mem. AAUP, Am. Acad. Family Physicians, Am. Assn. Women Radiologists, Am. Med. Women's Assn., Am. Osteo. Coll. of Radiology, Am. Soc. Clin. Oncology, Am. Soc. Therapeutic Readiologists, Hist. Soc. of Lewisburg (life), Pa. Osteo. Med. Assn., Pa. Osteo. Gen. Practitioner's Soc., Radiol. Soc. N.Am., Radiation Rsch. Soc., Res. Officers Assn. (life), W.Va. Soc. Osteo. Medicine, Greenbrier River Hike and Bike Trail. Home: RR 1 Box 123 Frankford WV 24938 Office: WVa Sch of Medicine 400 N Lee St Lewisburg WV 24901-1128

MOORE, JOANNA ELIZABETH, real estate professional; b. Hot Springs, Ark., Dec. 2, 1937; d. Herbert A. and Jewel (Mosier) Casey; m. Merlin Richard Moore, July 13, 1956; children: Melanie Moore Sevcik, Rick Moore, Michelle Moore Folks. Student, Bethany Nazarene Coll., 1956-57, Houston C.C., 1978, U. St. Thomas, 1987-88, 90—. Cert. residential specialist, Residential Sales Coun. of Realtors Nat. Mktg. Inst. Realtor Red Carpet Realtors, Temple, Tex., 1979-80, Century 21, Temple, 1981-85; broker-owner RE/MAX Realtors, Temple, 1986—; speaker Homebuilders Assn. seminars, 1985-88, 92. Fund chairwoman Bluebonnet coun. Girl Scouts U.S., 1987, mem. exec. bd., 1989; fund chairwoman March of Dimes, Temple, 1988; pres. Cen. Tex. chpt. Rep. Women's Club, 1983-84. Named Woman of Distinction, Girl Scouts U.S., 1992. Mem. Nat. Assn. Realtors, Tex. Assn. Realtors (mem. Polit. Action com. 1983-92), Temple-Belton Realtors (social chairwoman 1986, legis. chairwoman 1987, edn. chairwoman 1989), Temple Area Homebuilders (builder-realtor com. 1991, Realtor of Yr. 1993), Temple C. of C. (mem. govt. com. 1988, visitation com. 1989, tourist com. 1990, awards com., govt. affairs com. 1992). Home: 7112 Boutwell Dr Temple TX 76502-4204 Office: RE/MAX Realtors 4016 S 31st St Ste 200 Temple TX 76502-3348

MOORE, JOANNE IWEITA, pharmacologist, educator; b. Greenville, Ohio, July 23, 1928; d. Clarence Jacob and Mary Edna (Klepinger) M. A.B., U. Cin., 1950; Ph.D., U. Mich., 1959. Rsch. asst. Christ Hosp. Inst. Med. Rsch., Cin., 1950-55; rsch. asst. U. Mich., Ann Arbor, 1955-57, teaching fellow, 1957-59; postdoctoral fellow in pharmacology Emory U., Atlanta, 1959-61; asst. prof. pharmacology U. Okla. Coll. Medicine, Oklahoma City, 1961-66, assoc. prof., 1966-71, acting chmn., 1969-71, prof., interim chmn., 1971-73, prof., chmn. dept., 1973—, David Ross Boyd prof., chair, 1993; mem. gen. rsch. support rev. com. NIH, 1975-79, mem. biomed. scis. study sect., 1986-90; mem. adv. bd. Fogarty Internat. Ctr., 1992-94. Contbr. articles to profl. jours. USPHS grantee, 1963-69, 72-74, 79-87. Mem. AAAS, Am. Soc. Pharmacology and Exptl. Therapeutics, Assn. Med. Sch. Pharmacology, Am. Heart Assn. (bd. dirs. Okla. affiliate 1973-88, pres. 1979-80, chmn. bd. 1983-85, bd. dirs. Oklahoma City div. 1988-91, pres. 1989-90), Sigma Xi. Office: U Okla Coll Medicine Dept Pharmacology 753 BMSB OUHSC Oklahoma City OK 73190

MOORE, JULIA HOFLICH, gifted education educator; b. Russell, Ky., June 3, 1949; d. George Irwin and Minnie Mae (Melvin) Hoflich; m. Jay B. Moore II, Aug. 7, 1971; children: Jonathan Jay, Jeffrey Irwin. BS in Elem. Edn., Morehead State U., 1971, MA in English, 1974. Tchr. Circleville (Ohio) City Schs., 1971-75, Ashland (Ky.) C.C., 1981-82; gifted edn. tchr. Russell (Ky.) Ind. Schs., 1983-84, English and reading tchr., 1984-85, gifted coord. tchr., 1992—, adult edn. tchr., 1977-83, chmn. gifted edn. com., mem. tech. com., 1992—, chmn. primary gifted edn. com., bldg. rep. 1993—. Treas. Ashland Jr. Women's Club, 1979-80, Russell Downtown Civic League, 1989-91. Grantee Ashland Oil Found., 1993, 94, Area Edn. Project, 1994; recipient Jr. Bell award, Ashland Jr. Women's Club, 1978-79. Mem. Ky. Edn. Assn., Zeta Tau Alpha (pres. Ashland alumnae chpt. 1977-79). Republican. Home: 220 Ferry St Russell KY 41169 Office: Russell Ind Schs 409 Belfont St Russell KY 41169

MOORE, JULIE LOUISE, bibliographer, librarian; b. Sioux City, Iowa, Sept. 11, 1941; d. Mabel (DeRaad) Rude. BA, U. Denver, 1962, MS, 1963. Indexer Conservation Libr., Denver, 1965-67; head libr. Gerontology Libr., U. So. Calif., L.A., 1968-85; owner, mgr. Wildlife Info. Svc., Las Cruces, N.Mex., 1971—. Compiler: Thesaurus of Sport-Fish and Wildlife, 1968, Bibliography of Wildlife Theses, 1969, Wildlife Literature in Wildlife Techniques Manual, 1980, Bibliography of Reported Biological Phenomena...Attributed to Microwave and Radio-Frequency Radiation, 1984; indexer: Updata Index to U.S. Dept. Agriculture Handbooks, 1980; editor:

Abstracts in Social Gerontology, 1989—; co-prodr. CD-ROM Wildlife Worldwide, 1990—.

MOORE, KAREN CELYN, systems analyst; b. Waco, Tex., Jan. 7, 1964; d. Royce Kirby and Dorothy Ann (Schaefer) M. BBA, S.W. Tex. State U., 1986, MBA, 1993. Computer inventory assurance specialist Vogel Furniture Co., Lockhart, Tex., 1985-87; systems analyst II Tex. Dept. Transp., Austin, 1987—. Mem. Exec. Women in Tex. Govt., Women's Info. Network.

MOORE, KATHLEEN, dancer; b. Chgo.. Student with Sonia Arova, Thor Sutowski, Ala. Sch. Fine Arts; student, Sch. Am. Ballet, Am. Ballet Theatre Sch. Joined ABT II, 1980; mem. corps de ballet Am. Ballet Theatre, N.Y.C., 1982-88, soloist, 1988-91, prin. dancer, 1991—. Repertoire includes Dark Elegies, Don Quixote (Kitri's Wedding), Fall River Legend, Fancy Free, Giselle, Rodeo, Romeo and Juliet, The Leaves Are Fading, Nine Sinatra Songs, Everlast, Enough Said, Gaite Parisienne, The Rite of Spring, Pillare of Fire, The Informer, Brief Fling, Duets, Sinfonietta, Sunset, Les Liasons Dangereuses, Manon, Undertow, others; created roles in Agnes de Mille's The Informer, Mark Morris' Drink to Me Only With Thine Eyes. Office: Am Ballet Theatre 890 Broadway New York NY 10003-1211*

MOORE, LINDA KATHLEEN, personnel agency executive; b. San Antonio, Tex., Feb. 18, 1944; d. Frank Edward and Louise Marie (Powell) Horton; m. Mack B. Taplin, May 25, 1963 (div. Feb. 1967); 1 child, Mack B.; m. William J. Moore, Mar. 8, 1967 (div. Nov. 1973). Student, Tex. A&I Coll., 1962-63. Co-owner S.R.O. Internat., Dallas, 1967-70; mgr. Exec. Girls Pers. & Modeling Svcs., Dallas, 1970-72, Gen. Employment Enterprises, Atlanta, 1972-88; owner, mgr. More Pers. Svcs., Inc., Atlanta, 1988-94, pres., chmn. bd., 1994—; Contbr. short story to Writer's Digest. Mem. NAFE, Nat. Fedn. Bus. and Profl. Women, Am. Soc. Profl. and Exec. Women, Women Bus. Owners, Nat. Assn. Women Cons., Nat. Assn. Personnel Svcs., Ga. Assn. Personnel Svcs., Women's Clubs, C. of C. (speaker's bur.), Better Bus. Bur. Office: More Pers Svcs Inc 230 Peachtree St NW Ste 900 Atlanta GA 30303-1512

MOORE, LINDA MARIE ZAJICEK, travel company owner; b. Binghamton, N.Y., Feb. 2, 1943; d. Louis Paul and Mary (Opryshka) Zajicek; m. Charles Edward Moore, Feb. 2, 1963; children: Kimberly Anne, Robert Charles. BSBA, Bryant Coll., 1963; postgrad., Eastern Coll., St. Davids, Pa., 1970. Cert. cruise counselor. Adminstrn. asst. ALCOA, Hartford, Conn., 1963-65; pers. adminstr. Volkswagen Northeastern, Waltham, Mass., 1965-67; adminstrv. specialist GCA Corp., Burlington, Mass., 1967-69; sales mgr. Avon Products, Inc., Newark, Del., 1973-78; account exec. Encore Travel, Naperville, Ill., 1984-86; owner The Traveler's Connection, Naperville, 1986-87; owner, pres. Travel Mktg. Assocs., Wilmington, N.C., 1987—; speaker community orgns., 1975—. Author leisure travel guidebook and mktg. book. Leader Girl Scouts Am., Wayne, Pa., 1970-72; asst. leader Boy Scouts Am., 1987-88; vol. Am. Heart Assn., Wayne, 1969-79; bd. dirs. YWCA, 1989—; chair fin. devel. Women of Achievement, 1989-90, co-chair mktg. com., 1990—; sec. Rowland PTA, 1973-74; mem. funding com. Mill St. Sch., Naperville, Ill., 1983-84; chairperson door prizes Red Cross Ball, 1989-90; chairperson vacation raffle Hospice Festival of Trees, 1988; v.p. Jr. Saturday Club, 1973-74, Naperville Welcome Wagon, 1983-84; class parent Alderman Sch., 1987, Cape Fear Acad., Wilmington, 1989; pres. Main Line Welcome Wagon, 1972-73, Main Line Newcomers Club, 1972-73; tchr. St. Timothy's Luth. Ch., Naperville. Named Woman of Achievement Town of Wilmington, N.C., 1988. Mem. NAFE (bd. dirs. 1987—, chpt. founder 1989), Nat. Network Women in Sales (local pres. 1986, nat. pres. 1987, bd. dirs. 1987-91, Kievman Leadership award 1986), Women in Mgmt., Am. Soc. Assn. Execs., Assn. Execs. N.C., Am. Soc. Tng. & Devel., Upper Main Line Women's Investment Assn., Bus. and Profl. Women (v.p. 1974-75, conv. del. 1975), Travel Coun. N.C., Wilmington C. of C., Inst. Cert. Travel Agts. (coord. study group 1988-90), Chgo. Women in Travel, Execs. Breakfast Club Oakbrook, Naperville Jr. Women's Club.

MOORE, LINDA PERIGO, writer; b. Evansville, Ind., Nov. 25, 1946; d. John Myrl and Loraine Jeannette (Hudson) Perigo; 1 child, Jackson Stuart Moore. BS, Miami U., Oxford, Ohio, 1968; MS, MEd, U. Louisville, 1973. Instr., St. Joseph Infirmary, Louisville, 1969-71; tng. dir. Park-DuValle Neighborhood Health Ctr., Louisville, 1971-74; counselor Charlestown High Sch. (Ind.), 1974-75; tng. dir. Midtown Mental Health Ctr., Indpls., 1977-79; freelance writer, 1980—; cons. Kelly & Assocs., Indpls., 1977-81; instr. Ind. U., Indpls., 1979-81, instr., U. So. Ind., 1986. Bd. dirs. Jr. League Evansville, 1982-84, Mothers Assn. Evansville Day Sch., 1985-87; bd. dir. Evansville Mus. Arts and Sci. Guild, 1982-88, treas. 1994—; pres. Parent, Tchr., Student Assn., Cen. High Sch., 1989-91; sec. U. Evansville Theatre Soc., 1994—. Author: Does This Mean My Kid's a Genius?, 1981; (with Mary Kay Ash) On People Management, 1984, 2nd. ed., 1986, Mary Kay; You're Smarter Than You Think, 1985, Japanese and Swedish edits., 1986; (with Bart Conner) Winning the Gold, 1985; (with Richard Simmons) Reach for Fitness, 1986; (with Walter M. Bortz) We Live Too Short and Die Too Long, 1991; (with Robert Eliot) From Stress to Strength, 1994; (TV script for PBS) Tootie Tittlemousie and the Lights of Christmas, 1988 (Ohio State award 1989); contbr. articles in mags. and trade jours; tv appearances include: Oprah Winfrey Show, Today, Sonya Live, Larry King.

MOORE, LINDA PICARELLI, insurance executive; b. Bklyn., Jan. 13, 1943; d. Anthony Joseph and Alma Patricia (D'Angio) Picarelli; m. William H. Moore, Nov. 11, 1962 (div. 1974); 1 child, David A.; m. Spiro D. Demetriou, Dec. 9, 1977. Student, Wagner Coll., 1976, Coll. Ins., 1977-80. Licensed ins. broker. Ins. clk. Tchrs. Ins. and Annuity Assn., N.Y.C., 1959-61; claim examiner Aetna Life and Casualty Co., N.Y.C., 1961-63; claim supr. Northeastern Life Ins. Co., N.Y.C., 1963-66; corr. collector Dun and Bradstreet, S.I., N.Y., 1972-73; asst. underwriter Duncanson and Holt, Inc., N.Y.C., 1973-76; underwriting mgr. CNA Ins. Cos., N.Y.C., 1976-85; account mgr. Marsh and McLennan Group Assn., N.Y.C., 1985-87; asst. mgr. Home Ins. Co., N.Y.C., 1987-89; dir. spl. risk underwriting Cigna Ins. Co., Phila., 1989—. Mem. Am. Spl. Risk Assn. Democrat. Roman Catholic.

MOORE, LISA LYNN (LISA LYNN MARCEAU), geriatrics nurse; b. St. Johnsbury, Vt., Aug. 25, 1967; d. Glendon Paul and Ruth Aleta (Whitney) Marceau; m. Donald Moore Jr., May 18, 1991. ADN, U. Vt., 1987, BSN, 1990. RN, Vt. Charge nurse St. Johnsbury Health and Rehab. Ctr., 1987-91; inservice dir. St. Johnsbury Health & Rehab. Ctr., 1991-93, dir. nursing, 1993—. Mem. Sigma Theta Tau (Kappa Tau chpt.). Home: RR 1 Box 62E Barnet VT 05821-9611

MOORE, LOIS JEAN, health science facility administrator; married; 1 child. Grad., Prairie View (Tex.) Sch. Nursing, 1957; BS in Nursing, Tex. Woman's U., 1970; MS in Edn., Tex. So. U., 1974. Nurse Harris County (Tex.) Hosp. Dist., 1957—; pres., chief exec. officer Harris County Hosp.; adminstr. Jefferson Davis Hosp., Houston, 1977-88, exec. v.p., chief ops. officer, 1988—; Mem. adv. bd. Tex. Pub. Hosp. Assn. Contbr. articles to profl. jours. Mem. Mental Health Needs Council Houston and Harris County, Congressman Mickey Leland's Infant Mortality Task Force, Houston Crack-down Com., Gov.'s task force on health care policy, 1991; chairperson Tex. Assn. Pub. and Nonprofit Hosps., 1991, subcom. of Gov.'s task force to identify essential health care svc., 1992; bd. dirs. ARC, 1991—, Greater Houston Hosp. Coun., March of Dimes, United Way. Recipient Pacesetter award North-East C. of C., 1991; named Nurse of Yr. Houston Area League Nursing, 1976-77, Outstanding Black Achiever YMCA Century Club, 1974, Outstanding Women in Medicine YWCA, 1989. Mem. Am. Coll. Hosp. Adminstrs., Tex. Hosp. Assn. (chmn. pub. hosp. com.), Young Hosp. Adminstrs., Nat. Assn. Pub. Hosps. (bd. dirs., mem. exec. com. Tex. assn.), License Vocat. Nurses Assn., sigma Theta Tau. Home: 3837 Wichita St Houston TX 77004-6536 Office: Harris County Hosp Dist PO Box 66769 Houston TX 77266-6769

MOORE, LORETTA WESTBROOK, banker; b. Cameron, Tex., Jan. 2, 1938; d. Merrill Holman and Gladys Evangeline (Strelsky) Westbrook; m. Joe Gregg Moore Jr., Sept. 22, 1956; children: Terri Lynn, Joe Gregg III. Grad. high sch., Hearne, Tex. With Planters & Merchants State Bank, Hearne, Tex., 1956—, v.p., cashier, 1980—, also bd. dirs.; group pres. Nat. Assn. Bank Women (now Fin. Women Internat.), Waco, Tex., 1980-81. Vocat. adv. coun. Hearne Pub. Schs., 1984—. Named Hon. Chpt. Farmer Future Farmers Am., 1984, Notable Women of Tex., 1984. Mem. Bank Adminstrn. Instn. (pres. Brazos Valley chpt. 1983-84), Am. Inst. Banking (bd. dirs. Brazos Valley chpt., charter), Order Eastern Star (past matron). Methodist. Home: RR 1 Box 395 Hearne TX 77859-9617 Office: Planters & Mchts State Bank 122 4th St Hearne TX 77859

MOORE, MARGARET BEAR, American literature educator; b. Zhenjiang, China, Mar. 14, 1925; came to U.S., 1929; d. James Edwin Jr. and Margaret Irvine (White) Bear; m. Rayburn S. Moore, Aug. 30, 1947; children: Margaret Elizabeth Moore Kopcinski, Robert Rayburn. BA, Agnes Scott Coll., 1946; MA, U. Ga., 1973. Book rev. editor East Ark. Record, Helena, Ark., 1948-50; bibliographer Perkins Libr. Duke U., Durham, N.C., 1950-52; instr. in English Hendrix Coll., Conway, Ark., 1955-56, U. Cen. Ark., Conway, 1958-59; editor Inst. Cmty. & Area Devel. U. Ga., Athens, 1974-79; tchr. Latin Athens Acad., 1980-81; ind. scholar Athens, 1981—. Author (book revs.) Am. Lit., 1989, 94, Nathaniel Hawthorne Rev., 1992; contbr. articles to profl. jours. Active Peabody Essex Mus., Va. Hist. Soc., House of the Seven Gables; tchr. Presbyn. Ch., Va., Ark., N.C. and Ga., 1945—; deacon, elder First Presbyn. Ch., Athens, 1974—. Mem. MLA, Am. Lit. Assn., Philol. Assn. Carolinas, Soc. for Study So. Lit., South Atlantic MLA, Nathaniel Hawthorne Soc. (exec. com. 1987-90), William Gilmore Simms Soc., Peabody Essex Mus., House of Seven Gables, Va. Hist. Soc., Mortar Bd., Phi Beta Kappa, Phi Kappa Phi. Home: 106 St James Dr Athens GA 30606-3926

MOORE, MARIANNA GAY, law librarian, consultant; b. La Grange, Ga., Sept. 12, 1939; d. James Henry and Avanelle (Gay) M. AB in French, English, U. Ga., 1961; MLS, Emory U., 1964; postgrad., U. Ga., 1965-66, U. Ill., 1967-68. Asst. law libr. U. Ga., Athens, 1964-66; asst. libr. Yavapai Coll. Libr., Prescott, Ariz., 1969-72; libr. U. Ill. Law Libr., Urbana, 1966-68; law libr. Leva, Hawes, Symington, Washington, 1972-75; libr. project coord. Wash. Occupational Info. Svc., Olympia, 1976-80, Wash. State Health Facilities Assn., Olympia, 1981-82; mgr. Wash. State Ret. Tchrs. Assn., Olympia, 1982-83, exec. dir., 1984-89; exec. dir. Wash. State Retired Tchrs. Found., Olympia, 1986-89; law libr. Solano County Law Libr., Fairfield, Calif., 1989—; libr. LIBRARY/USA N.Y. World's Fair, N.Y.C., 1965; consulting law libr. Dobbins, Weir, Thompson & Stephenson, Vacaville, Calif., 1989—; law libr. cons. Coconino County Law Libr., Flagstaff, Ariz., 1968-70. Author: Guide to Fin. Aid for Wash. State Students, 1979; tng. package to introduce librs. to Wash. State Info. Svc., 1980. Bd. dirs. Thurston County Sr. Ctr., Olympia, 1976-84, Thurston-Mason Nutrition Program, Olympia, 1977-79, Wash. Soc. Assn. Execs., Edmonds, 1987-89. Mem. Am. Assn. Law Librs., No. Calif. Assn. Law Librs., Calif. Coun. of County Law Librs. Office: Solano County Law Libr Hall of Justice 600 Union Ave Fairfield CA 94533-6321

MOORE, MARILYN PATRICIA, community counselor; b. Nashville, Jan. 16, 1950; m. Roy Allen Moore; children: Christopher Manuel, Christina Marilyn, Catrina Marilyn. Merchandising cert., Bauder Coll., 1969; BS, Tenn. Wesleyan Coll., 1975; MEd., Tenn. Tech., 1979, EdS, 1981. Lic. profl. adminstr. and tchr., Tenn. Head resident/counselor Tenn. Wesleyan Coll., Athens, 1974-75; tchr. Rhea County Dept. Edn., Dayton, Tenn., 1975-81; prin. Rhea County Dept. Edn., 1981, 84-86; adj. coll. instr. Tenn. Tech. U., Cookeville, 1981—; coord. off campus program Tenn. Tech. U., 1981-86; tchr. Rhea County Dept. Edn., Dayton, 1982-83; prin. Rhea County Dept. Edn., 1983-86, supt. schs., 1986-90; evaluator, community intervention counselor Behavioral Health Svcs., Kingsport, Tenn., 1992-94, cmty. intervention counselor, 1994—; voting mem. Rhea County Purchase and Fin., Dayton, 1986—; adj. faculty East Tenn. State U., 1991, Holston Svcs., 1991. Chairperson Polit. Action Com. for Edn., Dayton, 1978-81; bd. dirs. Battered Women, Inc., Crossville, Tenn., 1987—; chairperson allocations United Way, Dayton, 1987-88; mem. Tenn. Sheriff's Assn., Nashville, 1988—; aide-de-camp Rep. Shirley Duer, Nashville, 1987; life mem. Presdl. Task Force, 1991—. Recipient Cert. Appreciation, Am. Legion, 1988, Cert. Participation, Very Spl. Arts, 1989, Am. Fedn. of Police Edgar Hoover award, 1991, John Edgar Hoover Meml. Gold medal, 1991; named Hon. Mem. Staff, Senator Anna Belle O'Brien, Nashville, 1987. Mem. NEA (past del.), Tenn. Edn. Assn., Tenn. Orgn. Sch. Supts., Alliance for a Drug Free Tenn. (chairperson 1987-91), Women Hwy. Safety Leaders Tenn. (county leader 1989—), USAF Aux. Aerospace (capt. 1987—), Tenn. Assn. Sch. Bus. Officials, Dayton C. of C., Nat. Police Assn. (Am. Patriotism award 1993). Republican. Methodist. Home: 205 Santa Fe Dr Bristol TN 37620-6441 Office: Behavioral Health Scis 425 E Stone Dr Kingsport TN 37660 also: Project Kind Med Clinic 441 Clay St Kingsport TN 37662

MOORE, MARTHA W., state legislator; widow; 2 children. Attended, Baldwin Bus. Coll. Mem. Ga. Ho. of Reps., 1992—; mem. def. and vet. affairs, mem. pub. safety and state ins. com., mem. property com. Republican. Baptist. Home: 12 Plantation Hills Dr Evans GA 30809 Office: Ga Ho of Reps State Capitol Atlanta GA 30334 also: 504 Legis Office Bldg Atlanta GA 30334*

MOORE, MARY ANN, chiropractor; b. St. Paul, May 29, 1953; d. Lyman Maurice and Louise Elizabeth (Braymen) M.; m. Stephen Michael Batson, June 21, 1981; children: Michael Stephen, Fauna Louise. Degree summa cum laude, Life Chiropractic Coll., Marietta, Ga., 1981. Nurse's aide Highland Park Nursing Home, St. Paul, 1971; phys. therapy asst. U. Minn. Hosp., Mpls., 1973-74; nurse's aide Pleasant Hill Nursing Home, St. Paul, 1975; sales clk. Dayton's Dept. Store, St. Paul, 1976; waitress, gift shop clk. Yellowstone Nat. Park, Wyo., 1976-77; asst. mgr. Shangri-La Health Resort, Bonita Springs, Fla., 1977-78; nurse's aide Marietta Nursing Home, 1979-80; pvt. practice Chesterfield, S.C., 1986—. Contbr. articles to newspapers. Mem. Chesterfield C. of C. Jehovah's Witness. Home: RR 1 Box 245A Ruby SC 29741-9799 Office: Moore Chiropractic Ctr 102 Marshal St Chesterfield SC 29709-1618

MOORE, MARY FRENCH (MUFFY MOORE), potter, community activist; b. N.Y.C., Feb. 25, 1938; d. John and Rhoda (Teagle) Walker French; m. Alan Baird Minier, Oct. 9, 1982; children: Jonathan Corbet, Jennifer Corbet, Michael Corbet. BA cum laude, Colo. U., 1964. Ceramics mfr., Wilson, Wyo., 1969-82, Cheyenne, Wyo., 1982—; commr. County of Teton (Wyo.), 1976-83, chmn. bd. commrs., 1981, 83, mem. dept. pub. assistance and social svc., 1976-82, mem. recreation bd., 1978-81, water quality adv. bd., 1976-82. Bd. dirs. Teton Sci. Sch., 1968-83, vice chmn., 1979-81, chmn., 1982; bd. dirs. Grand Teton Music Festival, 1963-68, Teton Energy Coun., 1978-83, Whitney Gallery of Western Art, Cody, Wyo., 1995—; mem. water quality adv. bd. Wyo. Dept. Environ. Quality, 1979-83; Dem. precinct committeewoman, 1978-81; mem. Wyo. Dem. Cen. Com., 1981-83; vice chmn. Laramie County Dem. Cen. Com., 1983-84, Wyo. Dem. nat. committewoman, 1984-87; chmn. Wyo. Dem. Party, 1987-89; del. Dem. Nat. Conv., 1984, 88, mem. fairness commn. Dem. Nat. Com., 1985, vice-chairwoman western caucus, 1986-89; chmn. platform com. Wyo. Dem. Conv., 1982; mem. Wyo. Dept. Environ. Quality Land Quality Adv. Bd., 1983-86; mem. Gov.'s Steering Com. on Troubled Youth, 1982, dem. nat. com. Compliance Assistance Commn., 1986-87; exec. com. Assn. of State Dem. Chairs, 1989; mem. Wyo. Coun. on the Arts, 1989—, chmn., 1994—, Dem. Nat. Com. Jud. Coun., 1989—; legis. aide for Gov. Wyo., 1985, 86; project coord. Gov.'s Com. on Childrens' Svcs., 1985-86; bd. dirs. Wyo. Outdoor Coun., 1984-85; polit. dir., dep. mgr. Schuster for Congress, 1994—. Recipient Woman of Yr. award Jackson Hole Bus. and Profl. Women, 1981, Dem. of Yr. Nellie Tayloe Ross award, Wyo. Dems., 1990. Mem. Alden Kindred of Am., Jackson Hole Art Assn. (bd. dirs., vice chmn. 1981, chmn. 1982), Assn. State Dem. Chairs, Soc. Mayflower Descendents, Pi Sigma Alpha. Home: 8907 Cowpoke Rd Cheyenne WY 82009-1234

MOORE, MARY JULIA, educator; b. Pitts., Oct. 10, 1949; d. Edward Henry and Julia Ann (Polkabla) Sauer; 1 child, Jason Michael Sauer; m. John Harold Moore, Oct. 27, 1990. BS in Art Edn., Edinboro State Coll., 1971; MS in Spl. Edn., Clarion State Coll., 1980; postgrad. U. Pitts., 1988—. Cert. art tchr., spl. edn. tchr. for mentally retarded. Tchr. Polk (Pa.) State Sch. & Hosp., 1971-72; vol. VISTA, Bath, N.Y., 1972-73; tchr. Polk Ctr., 1973-80, program specialist, 1980-92; residential svc. supr., qualified mental retardation profl. Polk (Pa.) Ctr., 1992—; lectr., speaker, video on local TV on history of Polk Ctr., 1987. Patentee beer bottle shaper cake pan; cakes displayed in TV videos and in various mags.; creator history video Polk Ctr. Mem. Internat. Cake Exhbn. Soc. Democrat. Roman Catholic. Home: RD # 3 Box 232-AI Franklin PA 16323

MOORE, MARY KAYE, city official; b. Louisville, Mar. 26, 1946; d. Charles King and Marcella Frances (Gast) Hahn; m. Dennis Bowne Moore, July 16, 1966; children: Patrick, Brian, Christopher. Student, Ctrl. Mo. State U., 1979-81; BBA, Sam Houston State U., 1983. CPA, Tex.; cert. govt. fin. officer. Acctg. clk. various firms, 1964-70; owner, operator Coral Lanes & Cafe, Springfield, S.D., 1972-78; staff acct. Ingram, Wallis & Co., P.C., Bryan, Tex., 1983-84; divsn. mgr. City of Bryan, 1984-89, dept. dir., 1989—, interim city mgr., 1992; city liaison Animal Shelter Adv. Bd., Bryan, 1993—; bd. dirs. 911 Emergency Comm. Dist. Divsn. chair Arts Coun/Brazos Valley, Bryan, 1991-93, fall festival co-chair, 1993; divsn. chair United Way, Bryan, 1992; bd. dirs. Brazos Valley Surg. Ctr., Bryan, 1992-95. Mem. AICPAs, Am. Bus. Women's Assn., Tex. Soc. CPAs, Brazos Valley CPAs (Pub. Svc. award 1994), Nat. Govt. Fin. Officers Assn., Govt. Fin. Officers Assn. Tex.,. Republican. Roman Catholic. Office: City of Bryan 300 S Texas Ave Bryan TX 77803

MOORE, MARY MELISSA, financial executive, government consultant; b. Flint, Mich., Feb. 6, 1957; d. Maurice Malcolm and Marian Adelaide (Zierold) M. B.A. in Govt., Wells Coll., 1979; student Georgetown U., 1977-78. Legis. corr. Sen. Hayakawa, Calif., 1979-80, legis. asst., 1980-82; asst. dir. fed. govt. relations ASME, Washington, 1982-86, dir. pub. affairs devel., 1984-88; ptnr. The Delta Group, Washington, 1988-90; mng. dir. Am. Assn. of Engrng. Socs. 1990-93; CEO, exec. dir. AACE Internat., 1993—; govt. liaison cons. Am. Nuclear Soc., 1990-92; cons. in field. Copyright SDI Co. Reference Guide. Mem. Am. Soc. Assn. Execs., Chgo. Soc. Assn. Execs., Coun. Engrng. and Sci. Soc. Execs. Republican. Episcopalian. Avocations: horseback riding, sailing, snow & water skiing, swimming. Home: Hazelwood Two 110 Lakeview Dr Morgantown WV 26505-9284 Office: 209 Prairie Ave Ste 100 Morgantown WV 26505-5949

MOORE, MARY TYLER, actress; b. Bklyn., Dec. 29, 1936; d. George and Marjorie Moore; m. Richard Meeker; 1 child, Richard (dec.); m. Grant Tinker, 1963 (div. 1981); m. Robert Levine, 1983. Chmn. bd. MTM Enterprises, Inc., Studio City, Calif. Appeared in TV series Richard Diamond, Private Eye, 1957-59, Dick Van Dyke Show, 1961-66, Mary Tyler Moore Show, 1970-77, Mary, 1978, Mary Tyler Moore Hour, 1979, Mary, 1985, Annie McGuire, 1988, miniseries Gore Vidal's Lincoln, 1988; in TV movies Love American Style, 1969, Run a Crooked Mile, 1969, First You Cry, 1978, Heartsounds, 1984, Finnegan Begin Again, 1984, The Last Best Year, 1990, Thanksgiving Day, 1990, Stolen Babies, 1993 (Emmy award, Outstanding Supporting Actress in a Miniseries or Special, 1993); films: X-15, 1961, Thoroughly Modern Millie, 1967, Don't Just Stand There, 1968, What's So Bad About Feeling Good?, 1968, Change of Habit, 1969, Ordinary People, 1980 (Acad. Award nominee for best actress 1981), Six Weeks, 1982, Just Between Friends, 1986; appeared on Broadway in Whose Life Is It Anyway?, 1980, Sweet Sue, 1987; in TV spl. How to Survive the Seventies, 1978, How To Raise a Drug Free Child. Recipient Emmy award Nat. Acad. TV Arts and Scis. 1964-65, 73-74, 76, Golden Globe award 1965, 81; named to TV Hall of Fame, 1985. Office: MTM Enterprises 4024 Radford Ave Studio City CA 91604*

MOORE, MERRY ANN, freelance writer, environmental issues consultant; b. Daytona Beach, Fla., Dec. 25, 1961; d. Albert Mitchell Moore and Elaine (Thomas) Kershaw; m. Robert W. Corrigan, May 1, 1993. BA, Harvard Coll., 1984; License, Universite de Paul Valery, Montpellier, France, 1985. Account rep. McGuire, Barnes, Inc., San Francisco, 1985-87; sr. mktg. specialist PMI Mortgage Ins. Co., San Francisco, 1987-90; prin. Moore Creative, San Francisco, 1990—. Recipient Elizabeth Carey Agassiz Merit award Harvard U., 1981-82, Nat. Special Achievement award Sierra Club, 1994; John Harvard scholar, 1983. Mem. Media Alliance, Fairness and Accuracy in Reporting, Profl. Environ. Marketers Assn., Internat. Assn. Bus. Communicators (Independents' Roundtable), Sierra Club (exec. com. Mateo), Calif. Econ. Recovery and Environ. Restoration Project. Democrat.

MOORE, NANCY FISCHER, elementary school educator; b. Milw., Nov. 26, 1937; d. Herbert Conrad and Erma Emma (Schroeder) Fischer; m. William Stang Moore (dec.). BS, U. Wis., Milw., 1958; MS, U. So. Calif., 1969; cert. in reading edn., U. Ga., 1973, cert. in gerontology edn., 1983, postgrad., 1982-91. Tchr. Grand Rapids (Mich.) Bd. Edn., 1958-61; tchr. U.S. Dept. Def. Overseas Schs., Nfld., Can., 1961-62, Bermuda, 1962-64, Japan, 1964-66; dir. handicapped day camp, tchr. 1st grade/trainable MR U.S. Dept. Def. Overseas Schs., Fed. Republic of Germany, 1966-70, Japan, 1970-71; classrm. tchr. Richmond County Bd. Edn., Augusta, Ga., 1971—, tchr. remedial reading, 1973-77, 78-79, Title I resource tchr., 1977-78; pres. Cen. Savannah River Area Reading Coun., Augusta, 1977-78; instr. Art in the Elem. Sch. Workshop, Augusta, 1979-80; tchr. conversational English to architecture students, Japan, 1964-66, to co. employees, Japan, 1966; instr. Augusta Coll., 1995—. Active Ft. Gordon Retiree Coun., 1991—; vol. Ombudsman, Augusta, 1982-83, Shelter for Abused Children. Mem. NEA, Ga. Assn. Educators, Richmond County Assn. Educators (pres. 1976-77, membership chairperson 1972-74, bldg. rep.). Home: 2346 New Mcduffie Rd Augusta GA 30906-9026 Office: Richmond County Bd Edn Heckle St Augusta GA 30904

MOORE, NANCY NEWELL, English language educator; b. Deadwood, S.D., Apr. 11, 1939; d. Harold Richard and Laura Mae (Howe) Newell; m. John Howard Moore, Feb. 23, 1962 (div. Oct. 1980). BA, Lake Forest Coll., 1961; MA, Northwestern U., 1963; PhD, U. Ill., 1968. Instr. of English U. Ill., Champaign-Urbana, 1967-68; asst. prof. of English U. Wis., Stevens Point, 1968-72, assoc. prof., 1972-76, prof., 1976—, asst. to chancellor for women, 1972-74, dept. chmn., 1974-77, chmn. faculty senate, 1981-84. Contbr. articles to profl. jours. Recipient grant for Canadian Studies, Can. Govt., 1986. Mem. Midwest MLA, AAUP, Assn. for Can. Studies in U.S., Shakespeare Assn. Am., Women in Higher Edn., NOW, Phi Eta Sigma. Unitarian. Office: Univ Wisconsin Stevens Point WI 54481

MOORE, PATRICIA ANN, medical technology consulting company executive; b. Huntington, N.Y., July 16, 1954; d. Joseph Nicholas and Dorothy Patricia (Olszewski) Mamola; m. William Martin Moore, Feb. 15, 1986; children: William Eric, Kyle Martin. BS, U. Santa Clara, 1976. Ops. mgr. Laguna Fed. Savs. & Loan, Orange, Calif., 1977-79; customer svc. rep. Bentley Labs., Irvine, Calif., 1979-80, mgr. custom products, 1980-82, internat. custom product specialist, 1981-82; dist. sales mgr. Am. Bentley Labs., San Francisco, 1982-83, Nellcor, Inc., San Francisco, 1983-84; product mgr. Nellcor, Inc., Hayward, Calif., 1984-85, nat. accounts mgr., 1986-88, internat. distbn. mgr., 1985-88; dir. internat. mktg. and sales NATUS Med., Inc., Foster City, Calif., 1989-92; mng. ptnr. Alpine Ptnrs., Las Vegas, Nev., 1992—. Mem. Nat. Account Mktg. Assn., Med. Mktg. Assn., NAFE. Home and Office: Alpine Ptnrs 2201 S Tioga Way Las Vegas NV 89117

MOORE, PATRICIA KAY, investment relations director; b. Peoria, Ill., Jan. 20, 1947; d. David Harold and Mary Jane (Gregoryk) Jenkins; m. James Christopher Moore, Jan. 11, 1980. BS in Bus. Adminstrn., U. Mo., 1978, MBA, 1981. Planning analyst Emerson Electric Corp., St. Louis, 1972-79; mgr. mktg. adminstrn. Emerson Electric WED, Houston, 1979; dir. mktg. adminstrn. HBE Corp., St. Louis, 1979-82; mgr. market research Emerson Electric ESD, St. Louis, 1982-92; dir., investor rels. ESCO Electronics, St. Louis, 1992—. Coordinating advisor Jr. Achievement; chmn. ECCU Bd. Supervisory com. Recipient Woman Leader award YWCA. Mem. Am. Mktg. Assn., U. Mo. Alumni Assn. Home: 712 Sherwood Dr Webster Groves MO 63119 Office: ESCO Electric Corp 8100 W Florissant Ave # 3216 Saint Louis MO 63136-1417

MOORE, PATSY SITES, food services director; b. San Marcos, Tex., Mar. 29, 1939; d. Sam W. and Hilda (Wiede) Sites. BS in Home Econs. Edn., S.W. Tex. State U., 1970. Owner, operator Westoner Kindergarten & Nursery Sch., San Marcos, 1965-68; food svc. dir. San Marcos Consol. Ind. Sch. Dist., 1975—. Mem. steering com. Play Scape/Children's Park, San Marcos, 1992. Mem. Am. Sch. Food Svc. Assn., Tex. Sch. Food Svc. Assn., Ctrl. Tex. Sch. Food Svc. Dirs. Assn. (founder, past pres.), Order Eastern Star. Lutheran. Home: 285 Hilliard Rd San Marcos TX 78666 Office: San Marcos Consol Ind Sch Dist PO Box 1087 San Marcos TX 78667-1087

MOORE, PEGGY SUE, corporation financial executive; b. Wichita, Kans., June 16, 1942; d. George Alvin and Marie Aileene (Hoskinson) M. Student, Wichita State U., 1961-63, Wichita Bus. Coll., 1963-64. Contr. Mears Electric Co., Wichita, 1965-69; exec. v.p., sec., treas., chief fin. officer CPI Corp., Wichita, 1969—, also bd. dirs.; Trustee Fringe Benefits Co., Kansas City, Mo., 1984-85. Active Rep. Nat. Com., Washington, 1985-86, task force, 1986—; treas., bd. dirs. Good Shepherd Luth. Ch., Wichita, 1980-85, mem., 1977—; active Wichita Commn. on Status of Women, 1988. Mem. NAFE, DAR, Nat. Assn. of Women Bus. Owners, Wichita C. of C., Women's Nat. Bowling Assn. (bd. dirs., pub. com. 1969-76), Internat. Platform Assn., Kans. Purveyors Assn. (bd. dirs. 1988-89), Women's Speakers Bur. Office: CPI Corp 816 E Funston St Wichita KS 67211-4309

MOORE, SALLY FALK, anthropology educator; b. N.Y.C., Jan. 18, 1924; d. Henry Charles and Mildred (Hymanson) Falk; m. Cresap Moore, July 14, 1951; children: Penelope, Nicola. B.A., Barnard Coll., 1943; LL.B., Columbia U., 1945, Ph.D., 1957. Asst. prof. U. So. Calif., Los Angeles, 1963-65, assoc. prof., 1965-70, prof., 1970-77; prof. UCLA, 1977-81; prof. anthropology Harvard U., Cambridge, Mass., 1981—, Victor Thomas prof. anthropology, 1991—, dean Grad. Sch. Arts and Scis., 1985-89. Author: Power and Property in Inca Peru, (Ansley Prize 1957), 1958, Law as Process, 1978, Social Facts and Fabrications, 1986, Moralizing States, 1993, Anthropology and Africa, 1994. Trustee Barnard Coll., Columbia U., 1991-92; master Dunster House, 1984-89. Rsch. grantee Social Sci. Rsch. Coun., 1968-69, NSF, 1972-75, 79-80, Wenner Gren Found., 1983; Guggenheim fellow, 1995—. Fellow Am. Acad. Arts & Scis., Am. Anthrop. Assn., Royal Anthrop. Inst.; mem. Assn. Polit. and Legal Anthropology (pres. 1983), Am. Ethnological Soc. (pres. 1987-88). Democrat. Office: Harvard U 348 William James Hall Cambridge MA 02138

MOORE, SANDRA BUCHER, mathematics educator; b. Norfolk, Va., Jan. 5, 1946; d. Clayton Merrill and Helen (Wilson) Bucher; m. Robert Curtis Moore, Aug. 1, 1970; children: Kimberley Anne, Tara Elayne. BS, Radford Coll., 1968; MS, Old Dominion U., 1988. Cert. profl. tchr., Va. Elem. tchr. Hampton (Va.) City Schs., 1968-89, Title I math. specialist, 1989—; math. text reviewer McGraw-Hill Pubs., N.Y., 1985; reader of Eisenhower Proposals, U.S. Dept. of Edn., Washington, 1991; curriculum writer CII WHRO-TV, Hampton Rds., 1987-90. Author: (lesson plan) Computer Teacher Contest, 1987 (1st Pl. award 1987). Mem. Hampton Fedn. Tchrs., AFT, 1981-94, Womans Club, 1969-91; officer Poquoson H.S. Band Boosters, 1990-94. Recipient Tech. Educator of Yr. award CII-WHRO-TV, 1989. Mem. AFT (treas. 1988-92, 3d v.p. 1992-94), Va. Ednl. Computer Assn., Va. Coun. Tchrs. Math., Peninsula Coun. Tchrs. of Math. Democrat. Methodist. Home: 9 Far St Poquoson VA 23662-2115

MOORE, SHARON HELEN SCOTT, gerontological nurse; b. L.I., N.Y., Nov. 7, 1947; d. James G. and Bernice Virginia (Conklin) Scott; m. Richard A. Moore Sr., July 5, 1966; children: Brian Keith, Richard A. Jr., Kevin Scott, Shannon Nicole. AAS, Fayetteville (N.C.) Tech. Inst., 1979; BSN, Med. U. S.S., 1993. Cert. gerontol. nursing. DON Elizabethtown (N.C.) Nursing Home; head nurse VA Med. Ctr., Fayetteville; coord. patient care Hospice Charleston, S.C.; DON, dir. human resources Sea Island Health Care Corp., Johns Island, S.C.; bd. dirs. Phoebe Taylor Family Clinic. Active St. James United Meth. Ch.; pres. family support group S.C. Army NG; vol. ARC, Fayetteville; bd. dirs. CYDC Big Brothers/Big Sisters. Indian Nurse scholar Nat. Soc. Colonial Dames Am., 1992. Mem. Nat. League Nursing, N.C. Nurses Assn. Office: Sea Island Comprehensive Health Care Corp PO Box 689 Johns Island SC 29457

MOORE, SHERYL STANSIL, nursing administrator; b. Birmingham, Ala., May 17, 1963; d. Willie Caesar and Irene (Fisher) Stansil; divorced; children: Tyler Christina Lowe, Danladi Moore, William Moore. BSN, Dillard U., 1987; MSN in Trauma Nursing, U. Ala. in Birmingham, 1992. Staff nurse Nursefinders, Colorado Springs, Colo.; mem. clin. faculty Beth-El Coll. Nursing; staff nurse Progressive Care Ctr., Terrace Gardens, Colo. Named one of Outstanding Young Women of Am., 1988. Mem. ANA, AACN, State Nurses Assn., Sigma Theta Tau. Home: 3485 Rebecca Ln Apt D Colorado Springs CO 80917

MOORE, SHIRLEY THROCKMORTON (MRS. ELMER LEE MOORE), accountant; b. Des Moines, July 4, 1918; d. John Carder and Jessie (Wright) Throckmorton; student Iowa State Tchrs. Coll., summers 1937-38, Madison Coll., 1939-41; M.C.S., Benjamin Franklin U., 1944; CPA, Mc.; m. Elmer Lee Moore, Dec. 19, 1946; children: Fay, Lynn Dallas. Asst. bookkeeper Sibley Hosp., Washington, 1941-42, Alvord & Alvord, 1942-46, bookkeeper, 1946-49, chief accountant, 1950-64, fin. adviser to sr. ptnr., 1957-64; dir. Allen Oil Co., 1958-74; pvt. practice acctg., 1964—. Mem. sch. bd. Takoma Acad., Takoma Park, Md., 1970—; mem. hosp. bd. Washington Adventist Hosp., 1974-85; chmn. worthy student fund Takoma Park Seven Day Adventist Ch., 1987—; trustee Benson Found., 1963—; vol. Am. Women's Voluntary Svc., 1942-45. Recipient Disting. Grad. award Benjamin Franklin U., 1961. Mem. Am., D.C. (pub. rels. com. 1976—) insts. CPAs, Am. Women's Soc. CPAs, Am. Soc. Women Accts. (legislation chmn. 1960-62, nat. dir. 1952-53, nat. treas. 1953-54), Bus. and Profl. Women's Club (treas. D.C. 1967-68), Benjamin Franklin U. Alumni Assn. (Disting. Alumni award 1964, charter, past dir.), D.A.R., Md. Assn. CPAs (charter chmn. membership com. Montgomery Prince George County 1963-64, chmn. student rels. com. 1964-67, pres. 1968-69, mem. fed. tax com. 1971-73). Mem. Seventh Day Adventist Ch. Contbr. articles to profl. jours. Home and Office: 1007 Elm Ave Silver Spring MD 20912-5839

MOORE, SONIA, theatre administrator, researcher; b. Gomel, Russia, Dec. 4, 1902; came to U.S., 1940; d. Evser and Sophie (Pashernstik) Shatzov; m. Leon Moore, May 11, 1926 (dec. Mar. 1957); 1 child, Irene Moore Jaglom. Degrees, Reale Conservatorio Di Musica Santa Cecilia, Rome, 1939, Reale Accademia Filarmonica, Rome, 1939; student, U. Kiev, U. Moscow, Studio Moscow Art Theatre. Dir. Sonia Moore Studio of the Theatre (accredited Nat. Assn. Schs. Theatre), N.Y.C., 1961—; founder, pres. Am. Ctr. for Stanislavski Theatre Art Inc., 1964—; artistic dir. Am. Stanislavski Theatre, N.Y.C., 1970—; tchr. Sonia Moore Studio, N.Y.C., 1961—; guest artist lectr.-demonstrator numerous univs. in U.S. and Can., 1978—; vis. prof. U. Mo., Kansas City, 1981; TV and radio interviews, 1961—; convs. presenter, 1982—; keynote speaker Theater USSR, U. S.C.; lectr. Fordham U., 1991, U. N.C., 1989. Dir. numerous off-Broadway plays, 1960-90, Anna Christie, N.Y.C., 1989, A View from a Bridge, 1990; translator, editor: Stanislavski Today, 1973, Logic of Speech on Stage, 1976; author: The Stanislavski Method, 1960, The Stanislavski System, 1965, 1974, 1984, Training an Actor: The Stanislavski system in class, 1968, rev. 1979, Stanislavski Revealed: The Actor's Complete Guide to Spontaneity on Stage, 1991; contbr. articles to Ency. Britannica, Theatre Jour., Drama Rev., Secondary Sch. Jour., Players Mag.; 10 cassette lectures on Stanislavski System; videocassette interview by Julie Harris. Founding mem. Nat. Mus. Women in the Arts; charter mem. Battle of Normandy Mus. Recipient Am. Heritage award JFK Library for Minorities, N.Y.C., 1974. Mem. ALA, Authors Guild, Soc. Stage Dirs. and Choreographers, Am. Theatre Assn., Internat. Biog. Assn., Smithsonian Instn., Assn. for Theatre in Higher Edn. (lectr. convs. N.Y.C. 1989, Chgo., 1990), Seattle, 1991, Atlanta, 1992, Phila., 1993, Chgo., 1994, Nat. Trust for Hist. Preservation. Home and Office: Am Ctr Stanislavski Theatre Art Inc 485 Park Ave New York NY 10022-1228

MOORE, SUSAN LYNN, television producer; b. Victoria, Tex., Aug. 17, 1944; d. Carl William and Marjorie Louise (Roberts) Schoepfle; m. Robert Clark, June 6, 1964 (div. 1975); m. Gregory Moore, Apr. 7, 1977 (div. 1987); children: Cynthia, Wendy, Christina. Student, Marietta (Ohio) Coll., 1962-65, U. Ariz., 1965-67, Houston Mus. Fine Arts, 1972-75, U. Houston, 1975-78, Edmonds Community Coll., 1985-88. Art tchr. Mus. Modern Art, Houston, 1973-76; tech. writer applied physics lab. U. Wash., Seattle, 1978-80; founder, owner Moore Prodns., Lake Stevens, Wash., 1980—, DupliKate, Everett, Wash., 1992—; exec. dir. Casa de Maria Ctr., Everett, 1991—; founder, exec. dir. Onw Life Ctr., Everett, 1994—; reporter, writer Reader's Digest Books, N.Y.C., 1986. Prin. works include Division of Aeronautics, 1991, Evacuation of Elderly and Disabled Passengers from Public Transportation Emergencies, 1990, Cold Expansion of Holes in Metals, for Engineers, 1989, Nisqually Destiny, 1989, Rails to Trails, 1988, Lynnwood, 1988, Edmonds, 1988, Hospice of Snohomish County, 1987, Household Hazardous Waste, 1987, Small Quantity Generators, 1987, Salhus Bridge, 1987, Principles of Eddy Current Testing, 1987, Long Beach Peninsula-Its Future is Now, 1986, others. Founder Snohomish County Visitor Ctr., Everett, Wash., 1984. Mem. N.W. Wash. Tourism Assn. (bd. dirs. 1983—, chmn. 1986, chair mktg. 1990—). Home and Office: 1215 115th Dr SE Lake Stevens WA 98258-9438

MOORE, SUSAN SHRODER, accountant; b. Memphis, May 27, 1965; d. Robert Edward and Jean Terry (Fisher) Shroder; m. Michael Edward Moore, Aug. 22, 1987. BBA in Fin., Memphis State U., 1988; postgrad., U. Memphis, 1995—. Regional acct. Terminix Internat., Memphis, 1989-91; revenue analyst APL Land Transport Svcs., Memphis, 1991-93; small bus. owner House Calls, Collierville, Tenn., 1994—. Bd. dirs. Responsible Animal Owners of Tenn., 1992-93. Mem. Inst. of Mgmt. Accts. Home and Office: 419 Laura Ann Ave Collierville TN 38017-1169

MOORE, SUSANNA, writer; b. Bryn Mawr, Pa., Dec. 9, 1948; d. Richard Dixon and Anne (Shields) M.; 1 child, Lulu Linnane Sylbert. Author: My Old Sweetheart, 1982 (Am. Book award nomination for best first novel 1983, Sue Kaufman prize for first fiction Am. Acad. Inst. Arts and Letters 1983), Whiteness of Bones, 1989, Sleeping Beauties, 1993. Recipient Literary Lion award N.Y. Pub. Libr., 1993. Office: Wallace & Sheil Agy Inc 177 East 70th St New York NY 10021*

MOORE, SYLVIA MARIE JENNINGS, chemistry educator; b. Windsor, Mo., Sept. 24, 1933; d. Robert Wilton and Evalynn Marie (Powell) Jennings; m. Donald Moore, Aug. 31, 1956; children: Donna, Daniel, Margaret. BA, San Diego State U., 1955; postgrad., Mich. State U., 1955-56. Supr. Dept. Commerce, Galveston, Tex., 1970; substitute tchr. Galveston Ind. Sch. Dist., 1969-75; lectr. chemistlectr. chemistry, lab. instr. Tex. A&M U., Galveston, 1975—, dir. chemistry lab., 1990—. Bd. dirs. South Tex. Girl Scout Coun., 1991-94; dep. voter registrar Galveston County LWV, 1965—. Mem. AAUW (pres. 1990-94), Am. Chem. Soc., Galveston Island Aggie Moms, Bay Area A&M Alumni (treas. 1993—). Republican. Episcopalian. Home: 3404 80th St Galveston TX 77551 Office: Tex A&M U PO Box 1675 Galveston TX 77551

MOORE, TANNA LYNN, business development executive; b. Columbus, Ohio, Oct. 19, 1954; d. Richard Owen and Marianne Ruth (Daries) M.; m. Craig Thomas Swaggert, Aug. 31, 1986; stepchildren: Mitchell, Nickolas. BA in Econs., Kenyon Coll., 1976; MBA, Dartmouth Coll., 1978. With product mgmt. Gen. Mills Inc., 1978-82; account exec., v.p., sr. v.p. U.S. Communications Corp., Mpls., 1982-90; sr. v.p. Keewaydin Group, Inc., Mpls., 1990-91; v.p. planning and bus. devel. Ceridian Corp. (formerly Control Data Corp.), Mpls., 1991-93; v.p., gen. mgr. human resource svcs. and mktg., 1993—; lectr. St. Thomas Coll., St. Paul, prof., 1987; lectr. U. Minn., St. Paul; lectr. promotional mktg., client relationships and career planning to ednl. instns.; bd. dirs. Sta. KTCA-TV, Mpls. Bd. dirs. Illusion Theatre, Mpls., 1979-86, chairperson Crystal Ball, 1987; bd. dirs. Downtown YMCA, Mpls.; commr. Minn. Amateur Sports Commn. Home: 1783 Irving Ave S Minneapolis MN 55403-2820 Office: Ceridian Corp 8100 34th Ave S Bloomington MN 55425-1672

MOORE, TRESI LEA, lawyer; b. Brownwood, Tex., Dec. 3, 1961; d. Dean Moore and Patsy Ruth (Evans) Adams. BA in Fgn. Svc., BA in French, Baylor U., 1984, JD, 1987. Bar: Tex. 1987, U.S. Dist. Ct. (no. dist.) Tex. 1988, U.S. Ct. Appeals (5th cir.) 1989. Atty. Richard Jackson & Assocs., Dallas, 1987-91, Amis, Moore & Davis (and predecessor firm Amis, Freemyer & Davis), Arlington, Tex., 1992—. Vol. Legal Svcs. of North Tex., Dallas, 1988—, Dallas Com. for Fgn. Visitors, 1989-92. Recipient Pro Bono Svc. award Legal Svcs. of North Tex., 1989, 90, 91. Mem. AAUW (pub. policy dir. Plano, Tex. br. 1992, 93-94, v.p. 1994-95), ABA, State Bar Tex. (mem. mentor program for lawyers com. 1994-95, mem. local bar svcs. com. 1994-95), Dallas Bar Assn., Tarrant County Bar Assn., Dallas Women Lawyers Assn. (bd. dirs. 1989-90, v.p. 1992, pres. 1993). Office: Amis Moore & Davis 2301 E Lamar Blvd Arlington TX 76006-7416

MOORE, VIRGINIA BRADLEY, librarian, educator; b. Laurens, S.C., May 13, 1932; d. Robert Otis Brown and Queen Esther (Smith) Bradley; m. David Lee Moore, Dec. 27, 1957 (div. 1973). B.S., Winston-Salem State U., 1954; M.L.S., U. Md., 1970. Cert. in libr. sci. edn. Tchr. John R. Hawkins High Sch., Warrenton, N.C., 1954-55, Happy Plains High Sch., Taylorsville, N.C., 1955-58, Young and Carver elem. schs., Washington, 1958-65; libr. Davis and Minor elem. schs., Washington, 1965-72, Ballou Sr. High Sch., Kramer Jr. High Sch., Washington, 1972-75, 78-80, Anacostia Sr. High Sch., Washington, 1975-77, 80—; class and club sponsor, 1975—; chmn. competency-based curriculum D.C. Pub. Sch., 1978-93; mem. faculty first established pub. svc. acad. in nation Anacostia Sr. High Sch., 1990—; speaker, presenter Ch. and Synagogue Libr. Assn., 1975, 80, 83; dir. ch. libr. workshops Asbury United Meth. Ch., Washington, 1972-74, 76; mem. 1st libr. and info. sci. del. to People's Republic China, 1985. Author: (bibliography) The Negro in American History, 1619-1968, 1968, (with Helen E. Williams) Books By African-American Authors and Illustrators for Children and Young Adults, 1991; TV script for vacation reading program, 1971, sound/slide presentation D.C. Church Librs.' Bicentennial Celebration, 1976; video script and tchr.'s guide for Nat. Libr. Week Balloon Launch Day, 1983; bibliography Black Literature/Materials, 1987; contbr. articles to profl. jours. Rec. sec. Washington Pan-Hellenic Coun., 1975; libr. Mt. Carmel Bapt. Ch., Washington, 1984, Sunday sch. Mother's Day coord., 1990—; co-chmn. nat. libr. involvement com. Martin Luther King, Jr. Fed. Holidy Commn., 1989—. Recipient certs. of award D.C. Pub. Libr., 1980, D.C. Pub. Schs., 1983; NDEA scholar Central State Coll., Edmond, Okla., 1969, U. Ky., 1969; scholar Ball State U., 1969; grad. fellow U. Md., 1969. Mem. NEA (life), ALA (councilor-at-large 1983-91), LWV, Internat. Assn. Sch. Librs., Am. Assn. Sch. Librs. (coms. 1973-83, 87—), D.C. Assn. Sch. Librs. (pres. 1971-73, citation 1973, newsletter editor 1971-75, 83, Soc. Sch. Librs. Internat., Internat. Assn. Sch. Librs., Freedom to Read Found., Intellectual Freedom Roundtable (bd. dirs., exec. com. 1989-91), D.C. Libr. Assn., Md. Ednl. Media Orgn., Internat. Platform Assn., Prince Georges County LWV, S.E. Neighbors Club, Am. Assn. Ret. Persons, Am. First Day Cover Soc., Zeta Phi Beta (v.p. chpt. 1972-74), Delta Kappa Gamma Nu (v.p. Alpha chpt. 1990-92, pres. 1992—, state membership chair 1991-92, state recording sec. 1994—). Democrat. Home: 2100 Brooks Dr Apt 721 District Hts MD 20747-1016 Office: Anacostia Sr H S 16th and R Sts SE Washington DC 20020

MOORE, VIRGINIA LEE SMITH, elementary education educator; b. Middletown, N.Y., May 13, 1943; d. James William and Anna Van Alst (Suydam) Smith; m. Thomas J. Moore, Oct. 16, 1965 (div. Apr. 1980); 1 child, Christian Thomas. AA in Liberal Arts, Orange County C.C., 1963; BA in Sociology magna cum laude, SUNY, Buffalo, 1965; MS in Edn., SUNY, New Paltz, 1980; MS in Edn. of Gifted, Coll. New Rochelle, 1990, cert. staff devel., 1994. Cert. in edn. N.Y. Spl. edn. tchr. The Devereux Found., Glen Loch, Pa., 1965-66; elem. tchr. Harris Sch., Coatesville, Pa., 1967; elem. tchr. Pine Bush (N.Y.) Cen. Schs., 1967-70, 78—, substitute tchr., 1970-71; nursery sch. tchr. Olivet Meth. Nursery Sch., Coatesville, Pa., 1976-78; presenter ednl. workshops Pine Bus Sch. Dist., Haldane Sch. Dist., Cold Spring, N.Y., Eldred (N.Y.) Sch. Dist., Middletown (N.Y.) Tchr. Ctr., 1988—; coord. Invent Am. Program, Pine Bush Sch. Dist., 1988—. Pres. Redtown Residents' Assn., Middletown, 1988—. Recipient Dean's Acad. Excellence award Coll. of New Rochelle, 1991, Orange County Conservation Tchr. of Yr., 1993, N.Y.S. Conservation Tchr. of Yr., 1993; Partnership in Edn. grantee Area Fund Orange County, N.Y., 1991, Energy grantee Orange and Rockland Utilities, 1995. Mem. N.Y. State united Tchrs., Sci. Tchrs. Assn. N.Y. State (Outstanding Sci. Tchr. award 1992), Phi Beta Kappa. Baptist. Home: RR 2 Box 358 Middletown NY 10940-9609 Office: Pakanasink Elem Sch PO Box 148 Circleville NY 10919-0148

MOORE, YVONNE LAUGHLIN HOWARD RICHARDSON, retail manager; b. Newark, N.J., July 24, 1943; d. Marion and Ola D. (Johnson) Laughlin; m. Jesse Moore, Sept. 23, 1984; children: Durand, Anthony, Yvette. Student, Essex County Coll., 1978, 91—. Lic. life ins. producer. Store mgr. Lerner Ltd., N.Y.C., N.J., 1961-87, A & E Stores, Ridgefield, N.J., 1987-88; entrepreneur sponsoring social affairs Oldie But Goodies, N.J., 1990—. Mem. NAFE, NAACP, DAV (life aux.).

MOOREFIELD, JENNIFER MARY, legislative staff member; b. Danville, Va., Nov. 10, 1950; d. Folger Lester and Mildred (Cox) M. BA in Psychology, Averett Coll., 1972; A in Applied Sci., Danville C.C., 1986. Social worker Henry County Social Svcs., Collinsville, Va., 1972-75, sr. social worker, 1975-80; clk. inventory control Dan River, Inc., Danville, Va., 1981-83; staff asst. U.S. Congressman Dan Daniel, Danville, 1984-88; staff asst. U.S. Congressman L.F. Payne, Danville, 1988-91, casework supr., 1991—; office mgr. U.S. Congressman L.F. Payne, Danville, 1991—. Bd. recording sec. Danville Speech & Hearing Ctr., 1988; Sunday Sch. tchr. Emmanuel Wesleyan Ch., Danville, 1975—; dir. Wesleyan Kids for Missions, Danville, 1993—, Ch. Vacation Bible Sch., Danville, 1993. Mem. Luncheon Pilot Club of Danville, Inc. (recording sec. 1988-89, pres.- elect 1989-90, pres. 1990-91), Va. Dist.- Pilot Internat. (area fundraising leader 1990-91, dist. chaplain 1993-94). Home: 136 Brookview Rd Danville VA 24540 Office: Office of Congressman LF Payne 700 Main St Ste 301 Danville VA 24541

MOORES, ANITA JEAN YOUNG, computer consultant; b. Poplar Bluff, Mo., Oct. 11, 1944; d. Joseph Samuel and Irene Anita (Sollars) Young; m. James Stephen Moores, June 5, 1965 (div. Jan. 1979); 1 child, Carolyn Terra. BS in Edn., So. Ill. U., 1972, MS in Edn., 1979. Cons. edn. and bus., sales Forsythe Computers, St. Louis, 1979-81; floor sales mgr., bus. cons., sales Computerland of Southwest Houston-Westheimer, 1981-82; bus. cons., sales Bus. Computer Systems and Software, Houston, 1982-83, MicroTask Computers, 1983-84; adminstrv. asst., tech. support Computerland-Techtron, 1984-85; distributer sales Cyber/Source, Houston, 1985; southwest regional sales mgr. Professions Info. Network, Houston, 1987; adminstrv. asst., computer specialist Human Affairs Internat. Inc., Houston; owner Moores' Consulting, Houston, 1986—. Author: (manuals) Choosing a Business Computer, 1983, Career Management, 1984, Training Manual-Computer, 1989; editor: Hounix Newsletter, 1988-89; artist oil paintings. Cons., trainer Meml. Luth. Ch., Houston, 1980-85; adminstr. Olympic Devel.-Soccer, Houston, 1988-89. So. Ill. U. Grad. fellow, 1975-76; named Outstanding Young Women Athlete, So. Ill. U., 1972.

MOORE-SILVER, ROSLYN O., federal judge; b. Feb. 26, 1946; m. Stephen J. Silver. BA, U. Calif., Santa Barbara, 1968; JD cum laude, Ariz. State U., 1971. Law clerk to Hon. Lorna E. Lockwood Supreme Ct. Ariz., 1971-72; atty. Daughton, Feinstein and Wilson, 1972-74; advisor, litigator edn. divsn. and Native Am. Right Fund. Navajo Nation, 1974-76; atty. Greyhound Corp., 1976-78; ptnr. Logan & Aguirre, 1978-79; trial atty. Equal Employment Opportunity Commn., 1979-80; chief criminal divsn., asst. U.S. atty. Office U.S. Atty. Dist. Ariz., 1980-84, 86-94; asst. atty. gen. State of Ariz., 1984-86; judge U.S. Dist. Ct. Ariz., Phoenix, 1994—; mem. Ariz. bar faculty Ariz. Coll. Trial Advocacy, 1986; spl. atty. Ariz. Commn. on Judicial Conduct, 1994—. Comment editor Ariz. State U. Law Rev.; contbr. articles to legal jours. Bd. dirs. New Ariz. Family, 1976-80, Ariz. Women's Commn., 1977-82, Big Sisters Ariz., 1978-84; vol. Phoenix Zoo., 1985. Recipient Commendation award U.S. Dept. Justce/Trial Advocacy Inst., 1981-84, Big Sisters of Ariz. award, 1984, Disring. Svc. and Merit awards U.S. Atty. Dist. Ariz., 1987, award Inspector Gen., U.S. Dept. Def., 1988, Dir.'s award Atty. Gen. U.S., 1991, Disting. Pub. Lawyer of Yr. award State and County Bar Assns., 1992. Mem. ABA (criminal justice and lit. sects., law and media com.), Am. Bar Found. (victim's bill of rights pro bono panel), Am. Paralegal Inst. (adv. bd. 1987—), Fed. Bar Assn., State Judicial Conduct Commn., Ariz. Bar (bd. dirs. pub. lawyers sect., coms. on disciplinary matters, ethics), Ariz. Women Lawyers Assn., Maricpoa County Bar Assn. (pub. lawyers sect.), Lorna E. Lockwood Inns. Ct. (master Maricpoa county). *

MOORHEAD, ROLANDE ANNETTE REVERDY, artist, educator; b. Périgueux, France, Sept. 24, 1937; d. RémyJean and Andrée Marcelle (Lavollée) Reverdy; liberal arts degree Coll. Technique, Nice, France, 1954; m. Elliott Swift Moorhead, III, Sept. 30, 1960; children—Edward Marc, Roland Elliott, Rémy Bruce. Bi-lingual sec., France, 1957-58, French Embassy, 1959-60, 1968-70; chmn. exhibit com. Lauderdale-By-The-Sea Art Guild, Ft. Lauderdale, Fla., 1972-75, v.p., 1972-74; founder group 5 Women Artists; charter mem. Gold Coast Water Color Soc., Ft. Lauderdale, 1976; mem. exhibit com. Broward Art Guild, Ft. Lauderdale, 1976; treas., dir. Alliance Française, Miami, Fla., 1973-75; one-woman shows include: numerous banks Ft. Lauderdale area, 1971—, Ocean Club Art Gallery, Ft. Lauderdale, 1971-74, Pier 66 Gallery, Ft. Lauderdale, 1973, 75, 76, Ft. Lauderdale City Hall, 1974, 77, 78, 81-85, St. Basil Orthodox Ch., North Miami Beach, 1977, Galerie Vallombreuse, Biarritz, France, 1977, Galerie du Palais des Fêtes, Périgueux, 1978, 88, Le Club Internationale, Ft. Lauderdale, 1979, Leonard Gallery, Ft. Lauderdale, 1990-92, Tallahassee (Fla.) Capitol Bldg., 1990, Lighthouse Pt. (Fla.) Gallery, 1990, Hollywood (Fla.) Art and Cultural Ctr., 1990, 91, Ft. Lauderdale Arts Inst., 1991, Dover Gallery, Boca Raton, Fla., 1992; exhibited in group shows: Broward Art Guild, Ft. Lauderdale, 1971, 73, 74, Point of Am. Gallery, Ft. Lauderdale, 1971, 73, Internat. Festival, Miami, 1976, Internat. Salon, Biarritz, 1977, Internat. Summer Salon, Paris, 1977, Fine Art Gallery Show and Competition, Long Galleries, Ft. Lauderdale, 1979, Pembroke Pines (Fla.) City Hall, 1982, Hollywood (Fla.) City Library, 1982, also area banks, chs. and libraries, numerous local art festivals; represented in permanent collections: Ft. Lauderdale City Hall, DAV Hdqrs., Washington, Associated Aircraft Co., March of Dimes Bldg. (both Ft. Lauderdale), Oakland Park Lib., Fla., St. Joseph Convent, St. Augustine, Fla., U.S. Air Force Mus., Ohio, Main Line Fleets, Inc., Palm Beach, Fla., Creditre form, Dusseldorf, W.Ger., St. Front Cathedral, Périgueux, St. Sacerdoce Cathedral, Sarlat, France, also numerous pvt. collections, U.S. and Europe. Recipient Best in Show award Internat. Salon, Biarritz, 1977; named artist in residence Broward County Sch., 1985. Mem. Fla. Watercolor Soc., Miami Watercolor Soc., Palm Beach Watercolor Soc., Wo/Man's Showcase (dir. visual arts div. 1982—, chmn. edn. com. 1983), Am. Bus. Women's Assn., Nat. League Am. Penwomen, Art 24, Périgueux, Internat. Soc. Marine Painters, The Ann White Theatre, Am. Watercolor Soc., Nat. Mus. Women in Arts, Nat. Mus. Am. Indian, Lauderdale-By-The Sea Art Guild, Broward Art Guild, Boca Raton Center for Arts, Gold Coast Water Color Soc. (pres. 1984-86), 2+3 The Artist's Orgn., Çercle Français of Ft. Lauderdale, Alliance Française of Dade County, Internat. Platform Assn., Union des Français de l'Etranger. Office: PO Box 8692 Fort Lauderdale FL 33310-8692

MOORHOUSE, LINDA VIRGINIA, symphony orchestra administrator; b. Lancaster, Pa., June 26, 1945; d. William James and Mary Virginia (Wild) M. BA, Pa. State U., 1967. Sec. San Antonio Symphony, Tex., 1970-71, adminstrv. asst., 1971-75, asst. mgr., 1975-76; exec. dir. Canton (Ohio) Symphony, 1977—. Mem. Ohio Arts Coun. Music Panel, 1980-82, 87-89, Mich. Arts Coun. Music Panel, 1986; bd. dirs. Stark County unit Arthritis Fedn., 1986-92, treas., 1989-91. Bd. dirs. Canton Palace Theatre Assn., treas. 1994—; active Cen. Stark County United Way Allocations Panel, 1991—. Mem. Met. Orch. Mgrs. Assn. (pres. 1983-85), Orgn. Ohio Orchs. (pres. 1985-86), Am. Symphony Orch. League (bd. dirs. 1983-85), Stark County Women's Hall of Fame (charter inductee), Soroptimist (Canton, Ohio, Women of Distinction 1992). Office: Canton Symphony Orch 1001 Market Ave N Canton OH 44702-1024

MOORJANI, MONA U., accountant; b. Bombay, India, Apr. 18, 1951; came to U.S., 1978; d. Udharam G. and Silwanti; divorced. BS, St. Peter's Coll., 1987; postgrad., NYU. CPA, N.J. Sec. Chase Manhattan Bank, N.Y.C., 1979-81; sr. acct. Exxon, Florham Park, N.J., 1981—; part-time cons.; sec. North Jersey chpt. Inst. Internal Auditors, 1994—; mem. supervisory com. Fed. Credit Union, 1993. Treas. ARC, Madison, N.J., 1992—. Home: 1508 Winans Ave Linden NJ 07036

MOORMAN, ROSE DRUNELL, city administrator, systems analyst; b. Miami, Fla., May 13, 1945; d. Willie and Claudia (Fluker) M. BA in Mathematics, Fisk U., 1967; MSE in Computer and Info. Scis., U. Pa., 1976. Computer programmer GE, Valley Forge, Pa., 1967-70; programmer/analyst Price Waterhouse Co., Phila., 1970-72; sr. programmer/analyst Inst. Environ. Medicine U. Pa., Phila., 1972-77; systems analyst Honeywell, Ft. Washington, Pa., 1977-78; dir. tech. svcs. Gill Assocs., Inc., Washington, 1978-83; owner, CEO Computer and Info. Mgmt., Inc., Miami, 1983-88; mgr. tech. support City of Miami, 1988-94, coord. diversity, 1994—; facilitator Women in Info. Processing, Washington, 1979-83; computer edn. adv. panel Dade County Pub. Schs., 1984-88. Editor: (newsletter) Bits and Bytes, 1979-82; co-editor: (newsletter) Ebenezer Speaks, 1992—. Active

Ebenezer United Meth. Ch., Miami, 1954—, chair fin. com., 1992—, Family Christian Assn., 1989-94; troop leader Girl Scouts Am., 1990—; pres. Lorah Park Sch. PTA, Miami, 1991-93; treas., bd. dirs. Overtown Community Health Clinic, Miami, 1992—; mem. Dade Heritage Trust, Miami, 1994, New Miami Group, Inc., 1994. Recipient Leadership award ARC, 1957, 63, Bronze medallion for Community Svc. NCCJ, 1963, Svc. Excellence award Delta Sigma Theta, 1986. Meritorious Svc. award Fisk U., 1992. Mem. NAACP, Nat. Forum Black Pub. Adminstrs. (bd. dirs., treas. 1993—), Nat. Coun. Negro Women. Republican. Home: 820 NW 172 Ter Miami FL 33169 Office: City of Miami 300 Biscayne Blvd Wy # 240 Miami FL 33131

MOOSBRUKER, JANE BARBARA, organization development consultant; b. Jamaica, N.Y., Oct. 29, 1938; d. Raymond Andrew and Evelyne (Ross) M. BA in Psychology, Adelphi U., 1960; MA, Radcliffe Coll., 1962; PhD in Social Psychology, Harvard U., 1965. Asst. prof. Tufts U. Sch. Dental Medicine, Boston, 1964-66, Boston Coll., Chestnut Hill, Mass., 1966-70; cons. orgn. devel. Bolton, Mass., 1970—; mem. Nat. Tng. Labs., 1975—, bd. dirs., 1992—; rsch. assoc. Harvard Sch. Dental Medicine, Boston, 1967-70, lectr., 1970-82; cons. Honeywell, Inc., Mpls. and Lexington, Mass., 1973-89, Harvard Cmty. Health Plan, Cambridge, Mass., 1983-85, Nashua (N.H.) Meml. Hosp., 1980-86, 91-94, Digital Equipment Corp., Maynard, Mass., 1984-92. Author: (with others) Team Building Blueprints for Productivity and Satisfaction, 1987; contbr. articles to profl. jours. and books. Mem. Bolton Conservation Commn., 1987—, chair, 1990-94; mem. Mass. Pub. Health Assn., Boston, 1977—; bd. dirs. Walden Earthnet, 1991-93. Mem. Soc. for Psychol. Study of Social Issues, Orgn. Devel. Network, Acad. Mgmt., Nat. Audubon Soc., Union Concerned Scientists.

MOOSE, ELLEN AMANDALANE JONES, social worker, retired; b. Brunswick, Ga., July 25, 1913; d. Edward David and Maggie (Lane) Jones; m. Robert Edward Moose, Mar. 12, 1941 (div. Nov. 1951); 1 child, George Edward; m. Burnis McCloud, June 2, 1952 (div. 1958); 1 child, Adonica Louise McCloud Walker. Diploma in Social Group Work, Atlanta U., 1942; MSW, Denver U., 1956; postgrad., Inst. Advanced Awareness, Lakewood, Colo., 1993-94. Tchr., counselor War Prodn. Tng. Ctr., Wilberforce, Ohio, 1941-43; clerical Nat. Coun. Negro Women, Washington, 1943; exec. dir. Phyllis Wheatley YWCA, Lynchburg, Va., 1944-48, Denver, 1948-52; social worker Denver Gen. Hosp., 1956-78; prof. social work Defiance (Ohio) Coll., 1969-70; computer tchr. St. John's Acad., Denver, 1982-83; dir. ch. sch. Holy Redeemer Episc. Ch., Denver, 1948, 93. Cmty. vol. YWCA, Denver, 1971-94; mem. com. Women Thinking Globally, Acting Locally: On the Road to Beijing, 1994, mem. fourth World Conf. on Women, others; del. to county and state assemblies, Denver Dems., 1975-94; active Jose Heath Campaigns, Heath for U.S. Senate, Denver, 1990-93. Grantee NIMH, Denver U., 1954-56; recipient cert. Appreciation U. Denver, 1963, Mayor award of honor City and County of Denver, 1978, Dorothea Spellman award YWCA Metro Denver, 1993, Denver U. Institutional Advancement award 1994. Episcopalian. Home: 380 Colorado Blvd Denver CO 80206

MORA, JUDITH STEVENS, financial institution consultant; b. Oakland, Calif., Dec. 5, 1946; d. Russell Norman and Lorraine C. Stevens; m. Gilbert Mora, Feb. 26, 1977. BA, U. Hawaii, 1969; MA in Mgmt., U. Redlands, 1981. Acting editor ofcl. publ. Navy C.E.C. and Seabees, Pearl Harbor, Hawaii, 1967-70; mgr. pub. relations and advt. Bishop Trust Co., Ltd., Honolulu, 1970-73; mgr. mktg. and promotions Ala Moana Ctr. Dillingham Corp., Honolulu, 1973-75; mus. cons., Hilo, Hawaii, 1975-76; cons. Edward Carpenter & Assocs., Los Angeles, 1976-79; pres., cons. J. Mora & Assocs., Orange, Calif. and Stafford, Va., 1979—. Contbr. to Hawaii Ency., 1977. Mem. spl. gifts and pub. relations coms. Am. Cancer Soc., 1973-76. Mem. Women in Communications (past chpt. pres.), Bank Adminstrn. Inst. (assoc.), Am. Heart Assn., Ind. Bankers Assn. (assoc.). Office: 2230 W Chapman Ave Ste 222 Orange CA 92668-2335 Office: 1116 Richmond Dr Stafford VA 22554-1916

MORA, KATHLEEN RITA, state judicial administrator; b. Atlantic City, Sept. 24, 1948; d. Francis Bernard and Catena Rose (Borzellino) Gribbin; m. Ben P. Mora, June 28, 1969; children: Michael, Brian. AS, Atlantic Community Coll., 1977; BS with program distinction, Stockton State Coll., 1984. Sec. The Press of Atlantic City, Pleasantville, N.J., 1966-69, pers. adminstr., 1969-73, adminstrv. asst., 1973-76, fin. asst., 1976-87, acctg. mgr., 1987-89; dir. fin. Atlantic and Cape May counties Superior Ct. N.J., Atlantic City, 1989—; host Healthline, Sta. WOND, 1989-91. Co-hostess ann. radio broadcast Miss Am. Pageant; judge Miss Cape County Pageant, 1979; co-hostess Amb. Program, United Way, bd. dirs. Atlantic County, 1977-78; commentator TV Telethon, March of Dimes, N.J., 1976-85. Named Miss Atlantic City, Women's div. Atlantic City C. of C., 1968-69, Miss United Way, United Way Atlantic County, 1975, Outstanding Chairperson, 1987, Outstanding Young Woman of Atlantic County, Mainland Jayceettes, 1978; recipient Contemporary Woman award McDonalds Corp./Sta. WAYV-AM, 1978, Svc. award 4-H Club Coun., 1985, N.J. Judiciary Aqces award, 1994. Mem. Mid-Atlantic Assn. for Ct. Mgrs. Roman Catholic. Home: 805 N Derby Ave Ventnor City NJ 08406-1121 Office: Superior Ct NJ 1201 Bacharach Blvd Atlantic City NJ 08401-4526

MORACA-SAWICKI, ANNE MARIE, oncology nurse; b. Niagara Falls, N.Y., Sept. 28, 1952; d. Joseph R. and Joan (Forgione) Moraca; m. Richard L. Sawicki, Sept. 15, 1979. BSN, D'Youville Coll., 1974; MS in Nursing, SUNY at Buffalo, 1977. Asst. prof. nursing D'Youville Coll., Buffalo, 1977-81; clin. editor Springhouse (Pa.) Corp., 1981-82; charge nurse Mt. St. Mary's Hosp., Lewiston, N.Y., 1982-84; surg. coord., adminstrv. asst. Dr. Richard L. Sawicki, Niagara Falls, N.Y., 1983—; part-time faculty mem. Niagara County C.C., Sanborn, N.Y.; bd. dirs. adult day care program Health Assn. Niagara County Inc. Contbr. Pharmacotherapeutics: A Nursing Process Approach, 1986, 3rd rev. edit.1994, Nurses Ref. Libr. Series Vols. on Drugs, Definitions, Procedures & Practices; clin. reviewer Manual of Medical/Surgical Nursing, Critical Care Handbook, and IV Drug Handbook, 1995; clin. cons. 16th edit. Taber's Cyclopedic Med. Dictionary, 1989. Recipient Cert. of Appreciation Niagara County Community Coll., 1988, 91, 92, Community Svc. award Am. Cancer Soc., 1978, Miss Hope award, 1977, Am. Cancer Soc. Nursing Fellowship Grant, 1977. Mem. N.Y. State Nurse's Assn., AAUP, Sigma Theta Tau. Home: 4658 Vrooman Dr Lewiston NY 14092-1049

MORADIAN, ANN-LENORE, choreographer, dancer; b. Warrensburg, Mo., Jan. 8, 1962; d. Kenneth Laverne and Martha Olive (Papo) Tharp; m. Khodadad Khushroo Moradian, Feb. 8, 1986. BA in Art magna cum laude, NYU, 1990. Prin. dancer, rehersal asst. Impulse Theatre and Dance, N.Y.C., 1982-86; prin. dancer, coach Andrea Fisher Dance Co., N.Y.C., 1983-85; co. mem., dancer Manuel Alum Dance Co., N.Y.C., 1986, Anna Sokolow's Players' Project, N.Y.C., 1995; founder, artistic dir., exec. dir. Perspectives in Motion, Ltd., N.Y.C., 1988—; guest faculty Colo. State U., Ft. Collins, 1993; pvt. dance instr. in field. Recipient grant F.O. Butler Found., S.D. State U., 1985, residency-fellowship Djerassi Program, Woodside, Calif., 1991, 93, Emerging Artists Challenge Program grant The Field, N.Y.C., 1993-94. Mem. Dance Theater Workshop, Gallatin Arts Coun. (steering com.), Gallatin Dance Collective.

MORAHAN-MARTIN, JANET MAY, psychologist, educator; b. N.Y.C., Jan. 13, 1944; d. William Timothy and May Rosalind (Tarangelo) Morahan; m. Curtis Harmon Martin, June 2, 1979; 1 child, Gwendolyn May. AB, Rosemont (Pa.) Coll., 1965; MEd, Tufts U., 1968; PhD, Boston Coll., 1978. Asst. mkt. rsch. analyst Compton Advt. Co., N.Y.C., 1965-67; mkt. rsch. analyst Ogilvy & Mather Advt., N.Y.C., 1967; ednl. rsch. asst. Tufts U., Medford, Mass., 1968-69; counselor Psychol. Inst. Bentley Coll., Waltham, Mass., 1971-72; dir. counseling svcs. Bryant Coll., Smithfield, R.I., 1972-75, psychology instr., 1972-76, asst. prof. psychology, 1976-81, assoc. prof. psychology, 1981-91, prof. psychology, 1991—; bd. dirs. Multi-Svc. Ctr., Newton, Mass., 1980-82. Contbr. articles to profl. jours., chpts. to books; reviewer APA Conv., 1985—, Teaching of Psychology Jour., 1988—, Collegiate Micro-Computer Jour., 1991, 93, Nat. Soc. Sci. Jour., 1991—. Bd. dirs. Wellesley (Mass.) Community Children's Ctr., 1986-90, Coun. for Children, Newton, Mass., 1984-86. NIMH fellow, 1967-68; NSF grantee, 1974-76, U.S. Office Edn. grantee, 1980. Mem. Am. Psychol. Assn., Mass. Audubon Soc., Nat. Social Sci. Assn., Mass. Hort. Soc., N.E. Soc. for Behavioral Analysis and Therapy. Home: 17 Fuller Brook Rd Wellesley MA 02181-7108 Office: Bryant Coll 1150 Douglas Pike Smithfield RI 02917-1291

MORALES, CARLOTA ELOISA, principal; b. Havana, Cuba, Oct. 18, 1946; came to U.S., 1961; d. Jose Ramon and Rosa (Paradela) M. AA, Miami Dade Jr. Coll., 1964; BEd in Secondary Edn. Adminstrn., U. Miami, 1966, MEd, 1969, EdD in Adminstrn., 1984. Cert. Math. and langs. tchr., Fla. Tchr. Spanish Acad. of the Assumption, Miami, Fla., 1967-68; tchr. 6th grade Sts. Peter and Paul Sch., Miami, 1968-71, tchr. math., 1971-81, asst. prin., 1981-90; lectr. in Spanish Barry U., Miami Shores, Fla., 1981-82; prin. St. Agatha Sch., Miami, 1990—; judge literary contest Patronato de Cultura Pro-Cuba, Miami, 1973; judge Dade County Youth Fair, Miami, 1985-86; curriculum writer Archdiocese of Miami, 1983—; mem. vis. team Fla. Cath. Conf., Tallahassee, 1982—. Chairperson Sts. Peter and Paul Ann. Festival, Miami, 1971—. Mem. Assn. for Supervision and Curriculum Devel., Phi Delta Kappa. Roman Catholic. Home: 1400 SW 14th Ave Miami FL 33145-1541 Office: St Agatha Sch 1111 SW 107th Ave Miami FL 33174-2506

MORALES, CYNTHIA TORRES, clinical psychologist, consultant; b. L.A., Aug. 13, 1952; d. Victor Jose and Lupe (Pacheco) Torres; m. Armando Torres Morales, June 30, 1989. BA, UCLA, 1975, M in Social Welfare, 1978, D in Counseling Psychology, 1986. Lic. psychologist, Calif. Clin. social worker VA, Brentwood, Calif., 1977-78; med. social worker Harbor-UCLA Med. Ctr., Carson, Calif., 1978-79; psychotherapist San Fernando Valley Child Guidance Clinic, Northridge, Calif., 1979-80; psychiat. social worker L.A. County Dept. Mental Health, 1980-81; child welfare worker L.A. County Dept. Children's Svcs., 1981-86; cons. psychologist, organizational devel. mgr. UCLA, 1986—; pvt. practice and consultation, 1992—; cons. Dept. Children Svcs., Health Svcs. Divsn., 1994—; cons. Hispanic Family Inst., L.A., 1989—, U. Calif., Calif. Youth Authority, Project Info.; mem. diversity com. UCLA, 1988—, mem. mental health emergency task force, 1986-89. Mem. Centro de Ninos Bd. Dirs., L.A., 1984-88; lobbyist self devel. people United Presbyn. Ch. Synod, L.A., 1982-88; chair Inner City Games Acad. Contest Hollenbeck Police Bus. Coun., L.A., 1992; co-chair Inner City Games Acad. Essay Contest, 1993; commr. L.A. County Commn. Children and Family Svcs., 2nd Supervisorial Dist. Recipient Cert. of Appreciation, Children's Bapt. Home, 1984, Cert. of Appreciation, Hollenbeck Police Bus. Coun. 1992, Spl. Recognition award Fed. Judge Takasugi, Pro Bono Bar Rev. and L.A. City Atty. 1993, Cert. of Appreciation, Hollenbeck Youth Ctr., 1992. Mem. APA, L.A. County Psychol. Assn. Office: 1100 Glendon Ave Ste 1701 Los Angeles CA 90024-3521

MORALES, VALERIE ALYCE, secondary school educator; b. Toledo, Ohio, Sept. 8, 1957; d. Albert V. and Geraldine A. (Zbyseinski) Niestuchowski; m. Romain Marcus Morales, Dec. 27, 1990; 1 child, Tyler. AA, Michael J. Owens Coll., 1977; BS, U. Toledo, 1984; MS, Siena Heights U., 1993. Cert. counselor; RN, Mich., Ohio. Nurse Toledo and Monroe, Mich., 1977-79; tchr. Monroe High Sch., 1979—, counselor, 1993—; presenter in field. Counselor psychiat. unit Monroe Hosp., 1993. Mem. NEA, APA, ACA, Mich. Edn. Assn. Baptist. Home: 888 Kings Park Rd Monroe MI 48161 Office: Monroe High Sch 901 Herr Rd Monroe MI 48161

MORAN, BARBARA BURNS, librarian, educator; b. Columbus, Miss., July 8, 1944; d. Robert Theron and Joan (Brown) Burns; m. Joseph J. Moran, Sept. 4, 1965; children: Joseph Michael, Brian Matthew. AB, Mount Holyoke Coll., S. Hadley, Mass., 1966; M.Librarianship, Emory U., Atlanta, 1973; PhD, SUNY, Buffalo, 1982. Head libr. The Park Sch. of Buffalo, Snyder, N.Y., 1974-78; prof. Sch. Info. and Libr. Sci. U. N.C., Chapel Hill, 1981—, asst. dean, 1987-90; dean Sch. Info. and Libr. Sci., U. N.C., Chapel Hill, 1990—; participant various seminars; evaluator various edn. progs.; cons. in field. Author: Academic Libraries, 1984; co-author: (with Robert D. Stueart) Library Management, 4th edit., 1993; contbr. articles to profl. jours., chpts. to books; editl. bd. Jour. Acad. Librarianship, 1992-94. Coun. Libr. Resources grantee, 1985, Univ. Rsch. Coun. grantee, 1983, 89, others. Mem. ALA, Assn. for Libr. and Info. Sci. Edn., Popular Culture Assn., N.C. Libr. Assn., Beta Phi Mu. Home: 1307 Leclair St Chapel Hill NC 27514-3034 Office: Univ NC Sch Info & Libr Sci Chapel Hill NC 27599-3360

MORAN, DONNA MARIE, school psychologist, counselor, educator; b. South Bend, Ind., Dec. 11, 1945; d. Raymond P. and Elsie (DeWitte) DeLee; m. Stephen E. Moran, Apr. 10, 1976; 1 child, Kent S. BA in Secondary Edn., St. Francis Coll., 1973, MS in Secondary Edn., 1976, MS in Guidance and Counseling, 1980, MS in Pre-Clin. Psychology, 1984. Jr. high tchr. Immaculate Conception Sch., Union, Mo., 1970-73; tchr. Huntington (Ind.) Cath. H.S., 1973-76; counselor So. Wells Jr. and Sr. H.S., Poneto, Ind., 1976-77; mid. sch. counselor East Allen County Sch., New Haven, Ind., 1977-93, sch. psychologist, 1993—. Bd. dirs. Family and Children's Svc., Ft. Wayne, Ind., 1987-93, A.J. Blaising Social Svc., Ft. Wayne, 1991—. Mem. ACA, Am. Sch. Counselors Assn., Nat. Assn. Sch. Psychologists, Ind. Counseling Assn. (N.E. region sec., treas., pres.-elect, pres.), Ind. Sch. Counselors Assn. (Counselor of Yr. 1994), Ind. Assn. Sch. Psychologists. Roman Catholic. Home: 4665 S 050 E Wolcottville IN 46795-9260 Office: East Allen County Schs 1000 Prospect Ave New Haven IN 46774-1625

MORAN, DORIS ANN, educational consultant, mathematics educator; b. English, W.Va., Oct. 19, 1944; d. William and Margaret (Pruitt) Vinson; m. John L. Moran, Mar. 17, 1973; children: Geoffrey Patrick, Lauren Kathleen. BS in Edn., Southwestern U., Georgetown, Tex., 1986. Cert. Elem. Edn., Math. Social worker W.Va. Dept. Welfare, Beckley, 1963-68; dir. pub. rels. Meml. Med. Ctr., Corpus Christi, Tex., 1969-75; exec. dir. Kidney Found. Tex. Coastal Bend, Corpus Christi, Tex., 1975-76; tchr. math. Killeen (Tex.) Ind. Sch. Dist., 1986-94; ednl. cons. Creative Edn. Inst., Waco, Tex., 1994—; curriculum writer, 1989— Killeen Ind. Sch. Dist., mem. dist. testbook adoption task force, 1990-91, pre-algebra math module trainer, 1991—, mentor, 1991-94, dept. chmn., 1991-94; sponsor Yearbook Smith MS, Fort Hood, Tex., 1987-93; trainer Reaching the Hard to Teach, 1993—. Bd. mem., chmn. pub. rels. United Way Coastal Bend, Corpus Christi, Tex., 1976, Mental Health Assn., Corpus Christi, Tex., 1972-75; pub. rels. chmn. City of Corpus Christi Ambulance Steering Com., 1972; conf. chmn. Tex. Hosp. Pub. Rels. Assn., Corpus Christi, Tex., 1972. Named fellow Tex. Alternative Blueprint for Curriculum Devel., 1992; recipient Outstanding Tchr. award Killeen (Tex.) Jr. League, 1994. Mem. ASCD, Tex. ASCD, Tex. Computer Educators Assn., Nat. Coun. Tchrs. Math., Grace Episcopal Ch., Tex. Coun. Tchrs. Math. Episcopalian. Home: 116 Oaktree Dr Rockport TX 78382 Office: Creative Edn Inst 5000 Lakewood Dr Waco TX 76710

MORAN, JACQUELINE MARIE, lawyer; b. Johnson City, N.Y., May 18, 1964; d. John Paul and Rosemary (Gutkoski) M. BS cum laude, Albright Coll., 1986; JD, Boston U., 1989. Bar: Pa. With Rhoda, Stoudt & Bradley, Reading, Pa., 1989-90, Morgan & Morgan, Harrisburg, Pa., 1990-91; atty. Commonwealth of Pa. Dept. Pub. Welfare, Harrisburg, 1991-94; atty. Office of Insp. Gen. Commonwealth of Pa., 1994—. Mem. ABA, Pa. Bar Assn., Young Lawyers Assn., Jaycees. Roman Catholic. Home: 6111 Springford Dr Harrisburg PA 17111-4816 Office: Office of Insp Gen Harrisburg PA 17111

MORAN, JULIE LUMPKIN, lawyer; b. Madrid, Spain, July 22, 1963; d. Lee R. and Mona Fay (Long) L.; m. Sean Michael Moran, June 11, 1988; children: Katherine Elizabeth, Sean Michael Jr. Student, Scripps Coll., 1981-83; BA magna cum laude, SUNY, Binghamton, 1984; JD, Fordham U., 1988. Bar: Conn. 1989, N.Y. 1989. Summer assoc. Cahill, Gordon & Reindel, N.Y.C., 1987; assoc. Townley & Updike, N.Y.C., 1988-90; freelance writer Yonkers, 1990—, pvt. practice law, 1990—; in-house counsel, bd. dirs. Pelhamdale Ave. Owner's Corp., Pelham, 1990-93; rschr. for book for dean Fordham U. Law Sch., 1986. Articles editor Forham Environ. Law Reporter, 1987-88; contbr. articles to various consumer publs. Pro bono atty. N.Y. County Lawyer's Assn. Programs, 1990-91. Mem. ABA (subcoms. residential real estate and mortgages), Westchester Women's Bar Assn., Bar of City of N.Y., Am. Soc. Journalists and Authors, Fordham Law Rev., Phi Beta Kappa. Episcopalian. Home and Office: 122 Pelhamdale Ave Pelham NY 10803-2259

MORAN, JULIETTE M., management consultant; b. N.Y.C., June 12, 1917; d. James Joseph and Louise M. B.S., Columbia U., 1938; M.S., NYU, 1948. Research asst. Columbia U., 1941; jr. engr. Signal Corps Lab., U.S. Army, 1942-43; with GAF Corp. (formerly Gen. Aniline & Film Corp.), 1943-82; successively jr. chemist process devel. dept., tech. asst. to N.Y. process devel. dept., tech. asst. to dir. Central Research Lab., tech. asst. to dir GAF Corp., 1953-55, supr. tech. service comml. devel. dept., 1955-59, sr. devel. specialist, 1959-60, mgr. planning, 1961, asst. to the pres., 1962-67, v.p., 1967-71, sr. v.p., 1971-74, exec. v.p., 1974-80, dir., 1974-83, vice chmn., 1980-82, cons., 1982—. Bd. dirs. N.Y. State Sci. and Tech. Found. Recipient Greater N.Y. Advt. award for excellence in communications N.Y. chpt. Assn. Indsl. Advertisers, 1972, Alumni Achievement award N.Y. U. Grad. Sch. Arts and Scis., 1977. Fellow AAAS, Am. Inst. Chemists; mem. Am. Chem. Soc., Comml. Devel. Assn. Home: 10 W 66th St New York NY 10023

MORAN, PATRICIA GENEVIEVE, corporate executive; b. Evanston, Ill., July 26, 1945; d. James M.; children: Christine Coyle, Thomas Beddia, Donald Beddia. Attended, Marquette U. Pers. mgr. Sesco, 1983-84, dir. corp. transp., assoc. rels. dir., 1984-85, v.p. assoc. rels., 1985-88; group v.p. sales Southeast Toyota, Deerfield Beach, Fla., 1988-89, pres., 1989-94; v.p. H.R. JM Family Enterprises, Inc., Deerfield Beach, pres., 1989-94. Dir. Beacon Coun., Miami, Fla., 1992—, Broward Econ. Devel., Ft. Lauderdale, Fla., 1991—, Youth Automotive Tng. Ctr., Hollywood, Fla., 1985—. Named Top 50 Working Women by Working Woman's Mag. Mem. Ft. Lauderdale C. of C. (dir. 1991—), Tower Club, The Haven (adv. bd. 1994-95). Office: JM Family Enterprises 100 NW 12th Ave Deerfield Beach FL 33442-1702

MORAN, SARAH JUDSON, independent option speculator; b. Newport, R.I., July 1, 1956; d. Richard E. and Norma K. (Judson) Brown; m. John P. Moran Jr., Oct. 3, 1988. BA in Anthropology/Geology, U. Mass., 1981. Sales analyst Silas Brown Inc., Westport, Mass., 1982-85, buyer, 1985—; speculator equity options Westport, 1982—; d.b.a. Angle Assets, Westport, 1991—. Mem. Assn. to Overcome Multiple Sclerosis, Phi Beta Kappa. Mem. Soc. of Friends. Home: 1145 Main Rd Westport MA 02790-4402 Office: Angle Assets PO Box 3352 Westport MA 02790-0702

MORAN, SHEILA KATHLEEN, theatrical producer; b. Norwalk, Conn.; d. Edmond Joseph and Alice Marie (Laux) M.; m. John Joseph Reynolds, Apr. 2, 1987 (dec. Apr. 1993). BA, Manhattanville Coll., Purchase, N.Y. Sportswriter, reporter AP, N.Y.C., 1969-71, N.Y. Post, N.Y.C., 1972-76, L.A. Times, 1976-80; actress, freelance writer L.A., 1981-90; producer Evensong Assocs., N.Y.C., 1990—. Vol. VA Hosp., L.A., 1987-90, Meml. Sloan Kettering Cancer Ctr., N.Y.C., 1990-93. Mem. AFTRA, Screen Actors Guild, Actors' Equity Assn., Producers Group, N.Y.C., Inner Circle, Coffee House, N.Y.C. Democrat. Roman Catholic.

MORANT, BRENDA WHITE, publishing executive, business developer, inventor; b. Balt., May 5, 1944; d. Willie and Geneva (Douglas) White. BS, U. Md., 1973; MPA, Cen. Mich. U., 1974. Founder, chief exec. officer Women's Econ. Enterprises, 1988—; publisher Networking Mag., 1990—; bus. devel. The BES Co., 1988—; owner Market Rsch. Cons., Atlanta, 1994—; cons. U.S. Air Force, Oscoda, Mich., 1977, Greater Mt. Calvery Bapt. Ch., Jackson Miss., 1991—, Options & Opportunities Career Ctr., Greenville, N.C., 1991—. Inventor electro thermo engineered insulated refrigeration container system for heat sensitive products. Organizer Battered Women's Ctr., 1979, Juneteen Celebration in Miss., 1980, Commn. on Women, 1986, Industrial Energy Soc., 1984. With USMC, 1962-64. Named 1st Businesswoman on the front Cover of Miss. Official State Mag., 1987; recipient Innovation award U.S. Dept of Energy, 1985, Governor Miss., 1985. Mem. NAFE, Assn. Female Vets. (bd.). Office: BES Techs PO Box 162125 Atlanta GA 30321-0125

MORATH, INGE, photographer; b. Graz, Austria, May 27, 1923; d. Edgar Eugen and Mathilde (Wiesler) M.; m. Arthur Miller, Feb. 1962; 1 child, Rebecca Augusta. BA, U. Berlin; DFA (hon.), U. Hartford, 1984. Formerly translator and editor ISB Feature Sect., Salzburg and Vienna, Austria; later editor lit. monthly Der Optmist, Vienna and Austrian editor Heute Mag.; former free-lance writer for mags. and Red White Red Radio Network; with Magnum Photos, Paris and N.Y.C., 1952—; mem. Magnum Photos, 1953—; tchr. photography course Cooper Union, 2 years; lectr. at various univs. including U. Miami, U. Mich. Exhibited photographs one-woman shows Wuehrle Gallery, Vienna, 1956, Leitz Gallery, N.Y.C., 1958, N.Y. Overseas Press Club, 1959, Chgo. Art Inst., 1964, Oliver Woolcott Meml. Library, Litchfield, Conn., 1969, Art Mus., Andover, Mass., 1971, U. Miami, 1972, U. Mich., 1973, Carlton Gallery, N.Y.C., 1976, Neikrug Galleries, N.Y.C., 1976, 79, Grand Rapids (Mich.) Art Mus., 1979, Mus. Modern Art, Vienna, 1980, Kunsthaus, Zurich, Switzerland, 1980, Burden Gallery Aperture Inc., N.Y.C., 1987, Moscow Ctr. Photojournalists, 1988, Sala del Canal, Madrid, 1988, Cathedral, Norwich, Eng., 1989, Am. Cultural Ctr., Brussels, 1989, Kolbe Mus., Berlin, 1991, Mus. Rupertinum, Salzburg, 1991; retrospective Neue Galerie, Linz, Austria, Amerika House, Berlin, 1993, Hradčin, Prague, 1993, Royal Photographic Soc., Bath, Eng., 1994; numerous group shows include Photokina, Cologne, Ger., World's Fair, Montreal, Que., Can.; represented in permanent collections Met. Mus. Art, Boston Mus. Art, Art Inst. Chgo., Bibliothèque Nationale, Paris, Kunsthaus, Zurich, Prague (Czechoslovakia) Art Mus., Rupertinum Mus., Salzburg, Austria; photographer for books Guerreà la Tristesse (Dominique Aubier), 1956, Venice Observed (Mary McCarthy), 1956, (with Yul Brynner) Bring Forth the Children (Yul Brynner), 1960, From Persia to Iran (Edouard Sablier), 1961, Tunisia (Claude Roy, Paul Sebag), 1961, Le Masque (drawings by Saul Steinberg), 1967, In Russia (Arthur Miller), 1969, East West Exercises (Ruth Bluestone Simon), 1973, Boris Pasternak: My Sister Life (O. Carlisle, translator), 1976, In the Country (Arthur Miller), 1977, Chinese Encounters (Arthur Miller), 1979, Salesman in Beijing (Arthur Miller), 1984, Images of Vienna (Barbara Frischmuth, Pavel Kohout, Andre Heller, Arthur Miller), 1981, Inge Morath: Portraits, 1987, In Our Time, 1990, Russian Journal (E. Yevtushenko, A. Voznesensky, O. Andreyev Carlisle), 1991, Inge Morath: Fotografien 1952-92, Inge Morath: Spain in the 50s, 1994; editor, co-photographer books Paris/Magnum, Aperture Inc., biography Grosse Photographen unserer Zeit, 1975; contbr. numerous photographs to European, U.S., S. Am., Japanese mags., and to numerous anthologies including Life series on photography and photographic yearbooks. Recipient Great Austrian State Prize for photography, 1991, various citations for shows. Mem. Am. Soc. Mag. Photographers. Home: Tophet Rd PO Box 232 Roxbury CT 06783 Office: Magnum Photos 151 W 25th St New York NY 10001-7204

MORAVA, CAROL, lawyer; b. Pasadena, Calif., Oct. 5, 1937; d. Dean Howell and Jeanne Elizabeth (Briggs) Sheldon; m. Emmett Morava, May, 1959; children: Michelle, Leslie. BA, Pomona Coll., 1954; JD, Loyola U., L.A., 1981. Data ctr. assoc. IBM, L.A., 1959-62; assoc. sys. engr. IBM, Pitts., 1962-65, L.A., 1966-67; programmer, analyst MIS Thrifty Corp., L.A., 1967-81, corp. counsel, 1981—. Pres., dir. Huntington Palisades Homeowners Assn., L.A., 1984-87; mem. pres. coun. Planned Parenthood, L.A., 1992—; bd. dirs. Angeles Girl Scout Coun., L.A., 1994—. Recipient Cert. Achievement from YWCA of L.A., Mayor's cert. Mayor of L.A., 1987. Mem. Calif. Women Lawyers, Wilshire Bar Assn., L.A. Area C. of C. (pres. coun. 1986-87). Home: 744 Ocampo Dr Pacific Palisades CA 90272 Office: Thrifty Co 3424 Wilshire Blvd Los Angeles CA 90010

MORAWETZ, CATHLEEN SYNGE, mathematician; b. Toronto, May 5, 1923; came to U.S., 1945, naturalized, 1950; d. John Lighton and Elizabeth Eleanor Mabel (Allen) Synge; m. Herbert Morawetz, Oct. 27, 1945; children: Pegeen Morawetz Rubinstein, John Synge, Lida Morawetz Jeck, Nancy. BA, U. Toronto, 1945; SM, MIT, 1946; PhD, NYU, 1951; hon. degree, Eastern Mich. U., 1980, Smith Coll., 1982, Brown U., 1982, Princeton U., 1986, Duke U., 1988, N.J. Inst. Tech., 1988, U. Waterloo, 1993. Research assoc. Courant Inst., NYU, 1952-57, asst. prof. math., 1957-60, assoc. prof., 1960-65, prof., 1965—, assoc. dir., 1978-84, dir., 1984-88. Editor Jour. Math. Analysis and Applications, Comms. in PDE; author articles in applications of partial differential equations, especially transonic flow and scattering theory. Trustee Princeton U., 1973-78, Sloan Found., 1980—. Guggenheim fellow, 1967, 79; Office Naval Rsch. grantee, until 1990. Fellow AAAS; mem. NAS, Am. Math. Soc. (term trustee 1975-85, pres. 1995—), Am. Acad. Arts and Scis., Soc. Indsl. and Applied Math. Office: 251 Mercer St New York NY 10012-1185

MORBY, JACQUELINE, venture capitalist; b. Sacramento, June 19, 1937; d. Junior Jennings and Bertha (Backer) Collins; m. Jeffrey L. Morby, June

21, 1959; children: Andrew Jennings, Michelle Lorraine. BA in Psychology, Stanford U., 1959; M in Mgmt., Simmons Grad. Mgmt. Sch., Boston, 1978. Assoc. TA Assocs., Boston, 1978-81, gen. ptnr., 1982-89, mng. dir., 1989—; bd. dirs. Ontrack Computer Sys., Mpls., Raxco, Inc., Rockville, Md., Software 2000, Hyannis Mass., Q-Star Techs. Inc., Rockville, Ansys, Inc., Houston, Pa., Smith Gardner Assocs., Inc., Delray Beach, Fla. Trustee Chatham Coll.; mem. Mass. Gov.'s Coun. on Growth and Tech. Mem. Nat. Venture Capital Orgn., New England Venture Capital Assn. (bd. dirs.). Office: TA Assocs 125 High St Boston MA 02110

MOREHEAD, ANNETTE MARIE, disabled children's facility administrator, child advocate; b. San Diego; d. Michael Peter and Katherine Helen (Keegan) Russomondo; m. Peter James Morehead; children: Bradley Michael Caloca, Katherine Dana. Student, Southwestern Coll., Grossmont Coll. Dir. Rayito Day Care Ctr., San Diego, 1981-85; instrnl. asst. for children with disabilities San Diego City Schools, 1985-88; owner, operator Scripps Ranch Childcare Ctr. for Disabled Children, San Diego, 1990—; child advocate; speaker San Diego Bd. Edn., 1986, News Eight Local TV News, 1989, Miramar Coll., 1991, Scottish Rite Charities, 1992, Exceptional Parents Found., 1993. vol. Schweitzer Ctr. for Disabled Children, San Diego, 1985, Stein Edn. Ctr. for Autistic Children, San Diego, 1987-88. Mem. Autism Soc. Am. (bd. dirs.), Mensa. Democrat.

MORELLA, CONSTANCE ALBANESE, congresswoman; b. Somerville, Mass., Feb. 12, 1931; d. Salvatore and Mary Christine (Fallette) Albanese; m. Anthony C. Morella, Aug. 21, 1954; children: Paul, Mark, Laura; guardians of: Christine, Catherine, Louise, Rachel, Paul, Ursula. AA, Boston U., 1950, AB, 1954; MA, Am. U., 1967, D of Pub. Svc. (hon.), 1988; D of Pub. Svc. (hon.), Norwich U. and Dickinson Coll., 1989. Tchr. Montgomery County (Md.) Pub. Schs., 1956-60; instr. Am. U., 1968-70; prof. Montgomery Coll., Rockville, Md., 1970-86; mem. Md. Ho. Dels., Annapolis, 1979-86, 100th-103rd Congresses from 8th Md. dist., 1987—; adv. bd. Am. Univ., Washington; trustee Capitol Coll. Laurel, Md. Trustee Capitol Coll, Laurel, Md., 1977—; mem. P.O. and Civil Svc. com. (ranking mem. subcom. on civil svc.), Select Com. on Aging, Sci., Space, and Tech.; coun. mem. Montgomery County United Way; adv. coun. Montgomery County Hospice Soc.; hon. bd. mem. Nat. Kidney Found; active Human Rights Caucus, Congressional Caucus Women's Issues, Black Caucus; chair Arms Control and Fgn. Policy Cacus and others. Office: US Ho of Reps 223 Cannon House Office Bu Washington DC 20515 also: 57 Monroe St Rockville MD 20850-2417

MORENCY, PAULA J., lawyer; b. Oak Park, Ill., Mar. 13, 1955. AB magna cum laude, Princeton U., 1977; JD, U. Va., 1980. Bar: Ill. 1980, U.S. Dist. Ct. (no. dist.) Ill. 1980, U.S. Ct. Appeals (7th cir.) 1981, U.S. Ct. Appeals (5th cir.) 1990. Assoc. Mayer, Brown & Platt, Chgo., 1980-86, ptnr., 1987-94; ptnr. Schiff Hardin & Waite, Chgo., 1994—. Contbr. author: Federal Litigation Guide Vol. 3, 1985. Mem. ABA, Chgo. Coun. of Lawyers (bd. govs. 1989-93). Office: Schiff Hardin & Waite 7200 Sears Tower Chicago IL 60606

MORENO, RITA, actress; b. Humacao, P.R., Dec. 11, 1931; m. Leonard I. Gordon, June 18, 1965; 1 child, Fernanda Luisa. Spanish dancer since childhood, night club entertainer; appeared on Broadway in The Sign in Sidney Brustein's Window, 1964-65, Gantry, 1969-70, The Last of the Red Hot Lovers, 1970-71, The National Health, 1974, The Ritz, 1975, Wally's Cafe, 1981, The Odd Couple, 1985; motion picture debut, 1950; appeared in numerous films including West Side Story, Carnal Knowledge, The King and I, Singing in the Rain, The Four Seasons, I Like it Like That, 1994. Recipient Acad. Award for best supporting actress, 1962; Grammy award for best rec., 1973; Antoinette Perry award for best supporting actress Broadway play, 1975; Emmy award, 1977, 78. Address: care Agency for Performing Arts 9000 W Sunset Blvd Los Angeles CA 90069-1843

MOREY, SHARON LYNN, psychotherapist, mediator; b. Cherokee, Iowa, Apr. 8, 1948; d. Joseph Glenn and Annie (Bush) M.; m. Edward Devere Beck, July 23, 1988; stepchildren: Mark Edward, Bruce David. Cert. in bus., Mpls. Bus. Coll., 1968; BA in Psychology, Adminstrn., Met. State U., 1988; PhD in Clin. Psychology, The Union Inst., 1992. Exec. dir. Iowa Lakes Regional Orgn., Spirit Lake, 1982-86; peer acad. advisor Met. State U., St. Paul, 1986-88; appointed to mktg. task force Minn. State U. System, St. Paul, 1987-88; crisis phone counselor Lovelines Counseling Ctr., Mpls., 1987-88; mediator North Hennepin Mediation Project, Brooklyn Center, Minn., 1988-93; pvt. practice St. Anthony Mental Health Ctr., Mendota Heights, Minn., 1988-93; intern in clin. psychology Richfield (Minn.) High Sch., 1990-91; psychotherapist, mediator St. Anthony Mental Health Clinic, St. Paul, 1990-93; cons. Iowa Lakes Regional Orgn., Spirit Lake, 1986-90; group facilitator Toughlove Orgn., Eagan, Minn., 1987-90. Mem. Okoboji Area After 5 Christian Bus. Women, Spirit Lake, 1978-82, Okoboji Lakes Bible and Missionary Conf., Spirit Lake, 1978—, Grad. Sch. of Union Inst. Exec. Learner Coun., Cin., 1990-92; bd. dirs. N.W. Iowa Singles Weekend Conf., Spirit Lake, 1978. Met. State U. scholar, 1987, Highland Park Bus. and Profl. Women scholar, 1987; grantee Dept. Vocat. Rehab., 1986-87, Alliss Edn. Foun., 1986, Pell, 1986-87. Mem. APA, N.Am. Soc. Adlerian Psychologists, Minn. Coun. Mediators (interim v.p. 1990-91), Minn. Psychol. Assn., Grad. Sch. of Union Inst. Alumni Assn., Met. State U. Alumni Assn., Minority and Women Doctoral Directory, Soc. Profls. in Dispute Resolution, Assn. Family and Conciliation Cts. Mem. Christian Ch.

MORFORD, LYNN ELLEN, state official; b. Peoria, Ill., June 17, 1953; d. Raymond Scott Jr. and Georgiana (Woodhall) M. BA, Millikin U., 1975; MA, Sangamon State U., Springfield, Ill., 1984. News reporter Stas. WJBC-WBNQ, Bloomington, Ill., 1975-76, Sta. WSOY-AM-FM, Decatur, Ill., 1976-78, Stas. WXCL-WZRO-FM, Peoria, 1978, Sta. KACY-AM-FM, Ventura, Calif., 1978, Sta. WKAN, Kankakee, Ill., 1979-82; freelance news reporter Sta. WMAQ, Chgo., 1982; news dir. Stas. WXCL-WKQA-FM, Peoria, 1983; press sec. Ill. Ho. of Reps. Rep. Press Office, Springfield, 1984-85; chief Press Office, Ill. Dept. Commerce and Community Affairs, Springfield, 1986—; mem. adv. bd. Ill. AP, 1983; radio news contest judge Okla. AP, 1983; bd. dirs. Ill. News Broadcasters Assn., 1980-84. Chmn. pub. rels., mem. adv. bd. Leadership Ill., 1992—, spring conf. chair, 1994; chmn. pub. rels. Springfield St. Patrick's Day Parade Com., 1991—; chmn. pub. rels. film fund raiser Vachel Lindsay Assn., Springfield, 1989; mem. Springfield Jr. League, 1990-91; mem. Samaritans St. John's Hosp., Springfield, 1995. Recipient best contbr. award Ill. AP, 1983; Robert Howard scholar Sangamon State U., 1983; named to Hon. Order of Ky. Cols., 1992. Methodist. Home: 2 Willow Hill Dr Sherman IL 62684-9769 Office: Ill Dept Commerce and Community Affairs 620 E Adams St Springfield IL 62701-1615

MORFORD-BURG, JOANN, state senator, investment company executive; b. Miller, S.D., Nov. 26, 1956; d. Darrell Keith Morford and Eleanor May (Fawcett) Morford-Steptoe; m. Quinten Leo Burg, Nov. 12, 1983. BS in Agrl.-Bus., Comml. Econs., S.D. State U., 1979; cert. in personal fin. planning, Am. Coll., 1992. Agrl. loan officer 1st Bank System, Presho, S.D., 1980-82, Wessington Springs, S.D., 1982-86; agrl. loan officer Am. State Bank, Wessington Springs, 1986; registered investment rep. State Bond and Mortgage Co., Wessington Springs, 1986—; mem. S.D. State Senate, Wessington Springs, 1990—, majority whip, 1993-94, minority whip, 1994—; mem. senate appropriations com. 1993—; chair senate ops. and audit com. 1993, 94; mem. ops. and audit com., 1995—. Mem. Midwestern-Can. task force Midwest Conf., 1990—; mem. transp. com., commerce com., taxation com. S.D. State Senate, Pierre, 1990-92; treas. twp. bd. Wessington Springs, 1990-92; mem. Wessington Springs Sch. Improvement Coun. Mem. Future Farmers Am. (adv. bd. Wessington Springs chpt.), S.D. State U. 4-H Alumni Assn., Nat. Life Underwriters Assn. (Huron chpt.), Order Ea. Star (various offices 1980-90). Democrat. Methodist. Home: 38678 SD Hwy 34 Wessington Springs SD 57382-5806

MORGA BELLIZZI, CELESTE, editor; b. N.Y.C., Mar. 8, 1921; d. Louis and Emma (Macari) Morga; m. John J. Bellizzi, Sept. 1, 1942; children: John J., Robert F. Student, Columbia U., 1940-41, SUNY, Albany, 1970. Cert. med. lab. technician. Medical lab. technician USMC Hosp., N.Y.C., 1942, Woman's Hosp., N.Y.C., 1942-52; spl. investigator N.Y. State Atty. Gen.'s Office, Albany, 1958-65; editor Internat. Drug Report publ., The Narc Officer publ. Internat. Narcotic Enforcement Officers Assn., Albany, 1965—. Dir. Albany Inst. History and Art, 1988-90, N.Y. State Press Women, Albany, 1987; advisor UN Non-govtl. Orgns. Drug Com., N.Y.C., 1980-90, White House Conf. Drug Free Am., Washington, 1987; mem. com. Bethlehem Drug Prevention Program, Delmar, N.Y., 1987-90, Action Commn. Narc Edn., Delmar, 1984-90; v.p. Women's Rep. Party Albany, 1972. Recipient Pres.'s award INEOA, 1982, Disting. Svc. award Houston Police Dept., 1981. Mem. Nat. Fedn. Press Women, Nat. Press Club, Univ. Club, Albany Country Club, Aberdeen Country Club. Office: Internat Narcotic Enforcement Officers Assn 112 State St Albany NY 12207-2005

MORGAN, ANNETTE N., state legislator; b. Kennett, Mo., Aug. 31, 1938; m. William P. Morgan, 1961; children: John, Catherine. BA, U. Mo., MA. Tchr. adult edn.; mem. Mo. Ho. of Reps. Mem. Adult Edn. Assn. Democrat. Presbyterian. Home: 639 W 57th Ter Kansas City MO 64113-1168 Office: Mo Ho of Reps State Capitol Jefferson City MO 65101*

MORGAN, ARDYS NORD, university official; b. South Bend, Ind., Nov. 1, 1946; d. Arthur August and Janet Ardis (Eide) Nord; children: Elizabeth Elayne, Matthew Richard. BS in Elem. Edn., Ind. U., Bloomington, 1968; MS in Elem. Edn., Ind. U., Indpls., 1972; reading cert., Ind. U., South Bend, 1982; EDS, Ind. U., Bloomington, 1992; adminstr. lic., Ind. U.-Purdue U., Indpls., 1989; EdD in Curriculum and Sch. Adminstrn., Ind. U., 1994. Tchr. South Bend, 1968-69, 73-87, adminstr. dept. instrn. and curriculum, 1987-90; tchr. Indpls., 1969-70; resident lectr. Ind. U./Purdue U., Indpls., 1970-73, adminstr., 1989; mem. adj. faculty Ind. U., South Bend, 1985-90, acting program dir. elem. and secondary edn., 1990-92; asst. supt. schs. Michigan City (Ind.) Area Schs., 1992-94; supt. Union North United Schs. Corp., 1995—; cons. mid. grades and effective teaching strategies, elem. curriculum, reading, and lang. arts, fed. and state projects. Recipient Disting. Alumni award div. edn. Ind. U., South Bend, 1990. Lilly Endowment fellow, 1987. Home: 65480 Oak Rd North Liberty IN 46554-9473 Office: Union North United Schs 22607 Tyler Rd Lakeville IN 46536

MORGAN, BARBARA JANETTE, retired librarian; b. Lyndon, Ohio, Oct. 10, 1916; d. Oliver McHenry and Blanche Gertrude (Hamm) M. BS, Capital U., 1939; MS in LS, Western Res. U., 1952. Clk., typist Ohio Dept. Hwys., Chillicothe, Ohio, 1940-42; analytical chemist Mead Corp., Chillicothe, Ohio, 1942-51, corp. libr., 1952-79, ret., 1979—. Mem. AAUW, Spl. Librs. Assn., Ohio Hist. Soc., Century Club. Republican. Presbyterian. Home: 3 Shawnee Dr Chillicothe OH 45601-1149

MORGAN, BETTY MITCHELL, artist, educator; b. Raleigh, N.C., Apr. 17, 1948; d. Carlton Turner and Miriam Grace (Sexton) M.; m. Thomas Vance Morgan, June 24, 1972; children: David Vance, Thomas Mitchell. BS, Appalachian State U., 1970; MA in Art Edn., U. Ga., 1972; postgrad., Calif. State U., Northridge, 1983. Cert. tchr., Calif., Ga., N.J., N.C., Mass. Tchr. art Randolph Jr. High Sch., Charlotte, N.C., 1971-72, Oconee County Intermediate Sch., Watkinsville, Ga., 1972-77; tchr. English 1st Bapt. Day Sch., Van Nuys, Calif., 1982-83; freelance artist, tchr. Hillsborough, N.J., 1984-86; instr. Torrance Ctr. Creative Studies U. Ga., Athens, 1987-93; tchr. Benton Elem. Sch., Nicholson, Ga., 1988-89; tchr. art Jackson County Sch. System, Jefferson, Ga., 1989-93; lectr. art and civic assns., Ga., 1987-93; freelance artist, 1976—; exhibiting mem. Loef Gallery, Athens, 1986-93; art editor Appalachian State U. Yearbook, Boone, N.C., 1970; coord. Japanese and Australian Children's Art Exch., 1992-93. Cover illustrator Philanthropic Ednl. Orgn., 1991; exhibitor group and solo shows in N.J., Calif., N.C., Ga., and Mass., 1976—; works displayed in pvt. and pub. collections in U.S., Australia, Europe, corp. collections including AT&T Comm., Thomas Cook Travel Agy., Nat. Utilities, Inc., Trust Co. Bank N.E. Ga. Docent Art Appreciation in Schs., Hillsborough, N.J., 1984-86; cub den leader Athens and Hillsborough area Boy Scouts Am., 1985-88; mem. Am. Cancer Soc., Athens, 1987-89; vol. Am. Lung Assn., 1988. Selected for Tchr. to Japan program Japanese C. of C., 1992; winner 1st pl. award for artwork San Fernando Valley Artist Assn., Northridge, 1983; named Tchr. of Yr. by Benton Elem. Sch., 1992-93. Mem. Profl. Assn. Ga. Educators, Philanthropic Ednl. Orgn., Ga. Art Edn. Assn., Nat. Art Edn. Assn., Athens Art Assn., Mass. Art Edn. Assn. Home: 14 Valley Rd Natick MA 01760-3415

MORGAN, BEVERLY HAMMERSLEY, middle school educator, artist; b. Wichita Falls, Tex.; d. Vernon C. and Melba Marie (Whited) Hammersley; m. Robert Lewis Morgan, Sept. 21, 1957 (div. 1972); children: Janet Claire, Robert David. BA, So. Meth. U.; MA, U. Ala., 1980, AA certification, 1982; postgrad., U. Tex., 1991—. Cert. art tchr., Tex., Ala., elem. tchr., Ala. Art tchr. Ft. Worth Pub. Schs., 1955-60; 6th grade tchr. Huntsville (Ala.) Pub. Schs., 1960-61; English tchr. Lincoln County Schs., Fayetteville, Tenn., 1961-62; 6th grade tchr. Huntsville Pub. Schs., 1962-68, art tchr., 1972—. One man shows include U. Ala., 1980, Huntsville Art League, 1981. Mem. Huntsville-Madison County Art Tchrs., Huntsville Art League, Huntsville Mus. Art, Huntsville Tchrs. Assn. Republican. Home: 12027 Chicamauga Trl Huntsville AL 35803

MORGAN, CAROLYN F., lawyer; b. Gadsden, Ala., Nov. 23, 1945; d. Sephes Jonah and Garnet Sylvia (Watson) M.; m. Galen Kennah, Dec. 16, 1967 (div. Nov. 1979); children: Jason, Jennifer. BS, Jacksonville State U., 1970; JD, Cumberland Sch. of Law, 1983. Bar: Ala., U.S. Dist. Ct. (no. dist.) Ala., U.S. Ct. Appeals (11th cir.), U.S. Supreme Ct. Social worker II State of Ala., Gadsen, Birmingham, 1969-80; asst. city atty. City of Gadsen, 1983-84; asst. dist. atty. State of Ala., Anniston, 1984-90; corp. counsel BE & K, Inc., Birmingham, 1990—. Office: BE&K Inc 2000 Internat Park Dr Birmingham AL 35243

MORGAN, CATHERINE MARIE, psychologist, writer; b. Duluth, Minn., Mar. 27, 1947; d. George Anthony and Charlotte Ruth (Hicken) Nothhelfer; m. Ralph Rexford Morgan, Aug. 28, 1967 (div., 1994); 1 child, Andrew. BS, U. Nebr., 1968; MEd, U. Okla., 1973; PhD Okla. State U., 1987; postgrad., Menninger Found. Psychotherapy Tng. Program, 1987-89. Child devel. specialist Southwest Guidance Ctr., Wheatland, Okla., 1973-74; pvt. practice Family Counseling Assocs., San Antonio, 1974-75; psychol. asst. Edmond Guidance Ctr., Okla., 1975-82; psychol. asst. supr. Southeast Guidance Ctr., Del City, Okla., 1982-86; psychol. intern Cleve. County Health Dept., Moore, Okla., 1986-87; psychologist Cen. State Hosp., Norman, Okla., 1987-89; pvt. practice assocs. in pschology, Edmond, Okla.; v.p. Behavior Mgmt. Specialists, Oklahoma City, 1983—; pres. Assocs. in Psychology, 1988—. Mem. AAUW, APA, Okla. Psychol. Assn., Southwestern Psychol. Assn., Am. Pers. and Guidance Assn., Am. Bus. Women's Assn., P.E.O., Kappa Delta Pi. Avocations: writing, reading, knitting, racquetball.

MORGAN, DONNA JEAN, psychotherapist; b. Edgerton, Wis., Nov. 16, 1955; d. Donald Edward and Pearl Elizabeth (Robinson) Garey. BA, U. Wis., Whitewater, 1983, MS, 1985. Cert. psychotherapist, Wis.; cert. mental health alcohol and drug counselor; cert. alcohol and drug abuse counselor; lic. marriage and family therapist, Wis.; lic. ind. social worker; lic. clin. social worker. Pvt. practice Janesville, Wis.; clin. supr. Stoughton (Wis.) Hosp.; prin. Morgan and Assocs., Janesville, Wis. Mem. underaged drinking violation alternative program Rock County, 1986—; co-chmn. task force on child sexual abuse, 1989-91; mem. Rock County Multi-disciplinary Team on Child Abuse, 1990—; mem. spkrs. bur. Rock County C.A.R.E. House, 1990—. Mem. ACA, APA, Am. Profl. Soc. on the Abuse of Children, Wis. Profl. Soc. on the Abuse Children (bd. mem. 1994—), Rock County Mental Health Providers, Am. Assn. Mental Health Counselors, Wis. Assn. Mental Health Counselors, South Ctrl. Wis. Action Coalition, Am. Assn. Marriage and Family Therapy, Am. Assn. Christian Counselors. Office: One Parker Pl Ste 625 Janesville WI 53545

MORGAN, ELIZABETH, plastic and reconstructive surgeon; b. Washington, July 9, 1947; d. William James and Antonia (Bell) M.; children: 1 dau., Ellen. BA magna cum laude, Harvard U., 1967; postgrad. (fellow), Oxford U., Somerville Coll., 1967, 70; MD, Yale U., 1971; law student, Georgetown U., 1986-87; PhD in Psychology, U. Canterbury, New Zealand, 1995. Diplomate Am. Bd. Surgery, Am. Bd. Plastic Surgery. Intern Yale-New Haven Hosp., 1971-72, resident, 1972-73, 76-77; resident Tufts-New Eng. Med. Center, Boston, 1973-76, Harvard-Cambridge (Mass.) Hosp., 1977-78; columnist Cosmopolitan mag., 1973-80; practice medicine specializing in plastic and reconstructive surgery Washington, 1978-86, McLean, Va., 1978-86. Author: The Making of a Woman Surgeon, 1980, Solo Practice, 1982, Custody, A True Story, 1986, The Complete Book of Cosmetic Surgery for Men, Women and Teens, 1988. Trustee Kent (Conn.) Sch. Fellow ACS, Am. Soc. Plastic and Reconstructive Surgeons; mem. New Zealand Postgrad. Med. Soc., Inrternat. Soc. for Study Multiple Personality and Dissociation. Episcopalian.

MORGAN, EVELYN BUCK, nursing educator; b. Phila., Nov. 3, 1931; d. Kenneth Edward and Evelyn Louise (Rhineberg) Buck; m. John Allen McGeary, Aug. 15, 1958 (div. 1964); children—John Andrew, Jacquelyn Ann McGeary Keplinger; m. Kenneth Dean Morgan, June 26, 1965 (dec. 1975). R.N., Muhlenberg Hosp. Sch. Nursing, 1955; B.S. in Nursing summa cum laude, Ohio State U., 1972, M.S., 1973; Ed.D., Nova. U., 1978. R.N., N.J., Ohio, Fla., Calif.; cert. clin. specialist Am. Nurses Assn. Psychiat.-Mental Health Clin. Specialists; advanced R.N. practitioner Fla. Bd. Nursing. Staff nurse Muhlenberg Hosp., Plainfield, N.J., 1955-57; indsl. nurse Western Electric Co., Columbus, Ohio, 1957-59; supr. Mt. Carmel Hosp., Columbus, 1960-65; instr. Grant Hosp. Sch. Nursing, 1965-72; cons. Ohio Dept. Health, 1972-74; prof. nursing Miami (Fla.)-Dade Community Coll., 1974—; family therapist Hollywood Pavilion Hosp., 1977-82; pvt. practice family therapy, Ft. Lauderdale, Fla., 1982—. Sustaining mem. Democratic Nat. Com., 1975—. Mem. Am. Nurses Assn., Fla. Council Psychiat.-Mental Health Clin. Specialists, Nat. Guild Hypnotists, Am. Nurses Found., Am. Holistic Nurses Assn., Sigma Theta Tau. Democrat. Roman Catholic.

MORGAN, GRETNA FAYE, retired automotive executive; b. Galveston, Ind., Aug. 24, 1927; d. Fred Monroe and Vera Arnetha (Oakley) Goodier; m. Marvin L. Morgan, Mar. 30, 1946; children: Gary Lynn, Vonna Annette, Marvin Richard, Darla Sue, Janice Arnetha. Diploma in cosmetology, Approved U., Indpls., 1946. Sales distributor Kirby Co., Ft. Wayne, Ind., 1955-62; with Dana Corp., Churubusco, Ind., 1962—; plant mgr. Dana Corp., Athens, Ga., 1978-81, Churubusco, Ind., 1981-90; ret., 1990; bd. dirs. Passages, Inc., Whitley County. Chmn. mayor's com. Employment Handicapped, Athens, Ga., 1980-81; mem. interview bd. selection com. Congressman Dan Coats Mil. Acad., Ft. Wayne, 1985-88, bus. adv. bd. Whitley County Opportunity Ctr., Columbia City, Ind., 1986-90, Chem. Dependency Task Force Whitley County, Ind. Gov.'s Task Force on Drunk Driving, budget com. Whitley County United Way; bd. regents Dana U., Toledo, 1978-82; bd. dirs., pres. Whitley County Jr. Achievement, 1977-78; bd. dirs. Passages, Inc., Columbia City, Ind., 1989—, Whitley County Meml. Hosp. Found., Columbia City, 1989—; mem. Noble County Friends of the Libr., 1990—. Mem. Churubusco C. of C. (pres. 1975-76), Dana Retirees of Fla. Club (pres. 1993—), Calvary Temple Worship Ctr. Home: 1981 Carbonata Dr Alva FL 33920-3647 Office: Dana Corp PO Box 245 Churubusco IN 46723-0245

MORGAN, JACQUI, illustrator, painter, educator; b. N.Y.C., Feb. 22, 1939; d. Henry and Emily (Cook) Morganstern; m. Onnig Kalfayan, Apr. 23, 1967 (div. 1972); m. Tomás Gonda, Jan. 1983 (dec. 1988). B.F.A. with honors, Pratt Inst., Bklyn., 1960; M.A., Hunter Coll., CCNY, 1978. Textile designer M. Lowenstein & Sons, N.Y.C., 1961-62, Fruit of the Loom, N.Y.C., 1962; stylist-design dir. Au Courant, Inc., N.Y.C., 1966—; assoc. prof. Pratt Inst., Bklyn., 1977—; guest lectr. U. Que., Syracuse U., Warsaw TV & Radio, Poland, NYU, Parsons Sch. Design, N.Y.C., Sch. Visual Arts, N.Y.C., Va. Commonwealth U., others; mem. profl. juries; condr. workshops. One-person shows include Soc. Illustrators, N.Y.C., 1977, Art Dirs. Club, N.Y.C., 1978, Gallerie Nowe Miasto, Warsaw, 1978, Gallerie Baumeister, Munich, W.Ger., 1978, Hansen-Feuerman Gallery, N.Y.C., 1980; group shows include Mus. Contemporary Crafts, N.Y.C., 1975, Smithsonian Instn., Washington, 1976, Mus. Warsaw, 1976, 78, Mus. Tokyo, 1979, Nat. Watercolor Soc., 1989, Salmagundi Club, 1990, New Eng. Watercolor Soc. Open, 1990, Miss. Watercolor Grand Nat., 1990, Illustration West 29, 1990, Adirondack Nat., 1990, Die Verlassenen Schuhe, 1994; represented in permanent collections: Smithsonian Instn., Mus. Warsaw; author-illustrator: Watercolor for Illustration; produced three of seven instrnl. watercolor videos; series of prints pub., 1995; series of plates pub., 1995; contbr. articles to profl. jours. Recipient more than 150 awards from various orgns. including Soc. Illustrators, Fed. Design Coun., Comm. Arts Mag., Am. Inst. Graphic Arts, N.Y. Art Dirs. Club, Print Design Ann. Mem. Graphic Artists Guild (dir. 1975-79), Soc. Illustrators, Women Artists of the West, Pa. Watercolor Soc. Studio: 692 Greenwich St New York NY 10014-2876

MORGAN, JANE HALE, retired library director; b. Dines, Wyo., May 11, 1926; d. Arthur Hale and Billie (Wood) Hale; m. Joseph Charles Morgan, Aug. 12, 1955; children: Joseph Hale, Jane Frances, Ann Michele. BA, Howard U., 1947; MA, U. Denver, 1954. Mem. staff Detroit Pub. Library, 1954-87, exec. asst. dir., 1973-75, dep. dir., 1975-78, dir., 1978-87; mem. Mich. Libr. Consortium Bd.; exec. bd. Southeastern Mich. Regional Film Libr.; vis. prof. Wayne State U., 1989—. Trustee New Detroit, Inc., Delta Dental Plan of Mich., Delta Dental Plan of Ohio; v.p. United Southwestern Mich.; pres. Univ.-Cultural Center Assn.; bd. dirs. Rehab. Inst., YWCA, Met. Affairs Corp., Literacy Vols. Am., Detroit, Mich. Ctr. for the Book, Interfaith Coun.; bd. dirs., v.p. United Community Svcs. Met. Detroit; chmn. Detroiters for Adult Reading Excellence; chmn. adv. coun. libr. sci. U. Mich., mem. adv. coun. libr. sci. Wayne State U.; dir. Met. Detroit Youth Found.; chmn. Mich. LSCA adv. coun.; mem. UWA Literacy Com., Attys. Grievance Com., Women's Commn., Mich. Civil Svc. Rev. Com.; vice chair Mich. Coun. for Humanities; mem. Commn. for the Greening of Detroit; adv. com. Headstart; mem. Detroit Women's Com., Detroit Women's Forum, Detroit Exec. Svc. Corps. Recipient Anthony Wayne award Wayne State U., 1981, Summit award Greater Detroit C. of C.; named Detroit Howardite of Year, 1983. Mem. ALA, Mich. Library Assn., Women's Nat. Book Assn., Assn. Mcpl. Profl. Women, NAACP, LWV, Women's Economic Club, Alpha Kappa Alpha. Democrat. Episcopalian.

MORGAN, JOAN MARIE, legislative assistant; b. Richland, Wash., Nov. 21, 1966; d. Howard Leslie and Margo Joan (Farrish) M. BA in Internat. Affairs, Lewis and Clark Coll., 1989; postgrad., Am. U., Washington, 1992—. Legis. asst. U.S. Senator Frank H. Murkowski from Alaska, Washington, 1989—. Mem. World Affairs Coun. Unitarian. Office: Senator Frank H. Murkowski Rm 706 Hart Senate Office Bldg Washington DC 20510

MORGAN, KAREN DENICE, policy analyst; b. Chgo., Feb. 12, 1956; d. George Leo and Audrey Yvonne (Miller) M. BA, Ill. Wesleyan U., 1977; JD, U. Wis., 1980. Bar: Wis., 1980. Legal rsch. asst. Wis. Legis. Coun., Madison, 1978-80; staff assoc. Nat. Conf. State Legislatures, Washington, 1980-83; adminstrv. analyst to prin. analyst Dept. Fiscal Svcs., Annapolis, Md., 1983—; state monitor U.S. Adv. Commn. on Intergovtl. Rels., Washington, 1991—. Contbg. author: (ann. multi-volume book) Analysis of the Executive Budget, 1984-89; editor: (ann. mgmt. reports) Sunset Review of Regulatory Boards, 1988-91, (multi-volume book) Report and Catalog of State Mandates, 1993. Named to Outstanding Young Women of Am., 1984. Mem. Nat. Conf. State Legislatures, Coun. State Govts. Office: Dept Fiscal Svcs 90 State Circle Annapolis MD 21401

MORGAN, LAUREEN GAIL, registered nurse; b. Jersey City, N.J., Aug. 15, 1959; d. Lawrence George and Marion Elizabeth (Possiel) M. BS in Chemistry, St. Peter's Coll., 1977-81; AS, Camden County Coll., 1989-92; RN diploma, Helene Fuld Sch. Nursing, 1989-92; postgrad., Thomas Jefferson U., 1992—. RN. Rsch. chemist Colgate Palmolive Co., Piscataway, N.J., 1981-89; chem. supr. Concord Chem. Co., Camden, N.J., 1989-92; RN Thomas Jefferson U. Hosp., Phila., 1993—. Home: 5636 Magnolia Ave Merchantville NJ 08109-1208

MORGAN, LINDA RICE, secondary education educator; b. Troy, Ohio, Feb. 14, 1949; d. George William and Eileen Dolores (Sines) R.; m. Thomas Buford Morgan, Nov. 25, 1978; 1 child, Malory Sue. BA, Marshall U., 1971, MS, 1974. Cert. profl. tchr., W.Va. Tchr. Marshall U. Community Coll., Huntington, W.Va., part-time 1977-79, Fairfield Sch., Cabell County Pub. Schs., Huntington, 1971-80; tchr. bus. edn. Huntington High Sch., 1980—, chmn. dept. bus., 1989—. Bd. dirs. Tri-State Montessori Pre-Sch., 1988-89. Mem. NEA, W.Va. Edn. Assn., Nat. Bus. Edn. Assn., Cabell County Edn. Assn., Phi Delta Kappa. Democrat. Home: 2224 Pleasant Valley Dr Huntington WV 25701-9304

MORGAN, LINDA ROGERS, editor; b. Seattle, Jan. 18, 1950; d. Fred and Frances (Teitelbaum) Rogers; m. Michael Edward Morgan, Aug. 8, 1971, children: Melissa, Todd. BA with great distinction, U. Calif., Berkeley, 1971; M in Journalism, UCLA, 1972. Editorial assoc. Teen mag., L.A., 1972-73; advt. copywriter Big S Sporting Goods, L.A., 1973; instr. journalism and communications Bellevue (Wash.) Community Coll., 1975-93; feature editor Via mag., Seattle, 1983-84; freelance writer, 1980—; humor columnist Mercer Island (Wash.) Reporter, 1989—, reporter, 1990-93, assoc. editor, 1993—; nat. conf. speaker Journalism Edn. Assn., 1990; bd. dirs. Jewish Transcript, Seattle, 1989—. Bd. dirs. Herzl-Ner Tamid, Mercer Island, 1985-87, Mercer Island Youth Theater, 1987-88, Jewish Transcript, Seattle, 1989-90. Recipient writing awards Pacific N.W. Writers Conf., 1984, Washington Newspaper Pubs. Assn., 1987, 89, 91, Washingotn Press Assn. Writing award, 1989, 90, 91, 92, 93, Sigma Delta Chi Writing awards, 1988, 90, 91, 92, Nat. award Nat. Fedn. Press Women, 1993. Mem. Women in Communications Inc., Washington Press Assn. (judge student contest 1989, writing awards 1989, 90), Nat. Edn. Assn., Phi Beta Kappa, Sigma Delta Chi (writing award 1988).

MORGAN, LORRIE (LORETTA LYNN MORGAN), country singer; b. Nashville, May 9, 1959; d. George Morgan; divorced; m. Keith Whitley (dec. 1989); children: Morgan, Jesse. Rec. artist RCA, 1989—. Albums: Leave the Light On, 1989, Something in Red, 1991, Tell Me I'm Dreaming, 1992, Watch Me, 1992, Trainwreck of Emotion, 1993, (with Sammy Kershaw) War Paint, 1994; # 1 gold single Something in Red, 1991; TV movies include: Proudheart, 1993. Office: RCA Records 1 Music Circle Nashville TN 37203*

MORGAN, LUCY W., journalist; b. Memphis, Oct. 11, 1940; d. Thomas Allin and Lucile (Sanders) Keen; m. Alton F. Ware, June 26, 1958 (div. Sept. 1967); children—Mary Kathleen, Andrew Allin; m. Richard Alan Morgan, Aug. 9, 1968; children—Lynn Elwell, Kent Morgan. A.A., Pasco Hernando Community Coll., New Port Richey, Fla., 1975; student, U. South Fla., 1976-80. Reporter Ocala Star Banner, Fla., 1965-68; reporter St. Petersburg Times, Fla., 1967-86, capitol bur. chief, 1986—; assoc. editor and bd. dirs. Times Pub. Co. Recipient Paul Hansel award Fla. Soc. Newspaper Editors, 1981, First in Pub. Service award Fla. Soc. Newspaper Editors, 1982, First Place award in pub. service Fla. Press Club, 1982, Pulitzer award for investigative reporting Columbia U., 1985, First Place award in investigative reporting Sigma Delta Chi, 1985; named to Kappa Tau Alpha Hall of Fame, 1992. Home: 1727 Brookside Blvd Tallahassee FL 32301-6769 Office: St Petersburg Times 336 E College Ave Tallahassee FL 32301-1551

MORGAN, LYNDA M., state legislator; d. Tommy and Grace (Arviso) Murphy; married; children: Kelly, Russell, Jacob. AA in Elem. Edn., U. N.Mex., Gallup, 1985; BS in Pub. Adminstrn., No. Ariz. U., 1987. Adminstrv. asst. Navajo Skill Ctr. Inc., Crownpoint, N.Mex., 1979-81, acting exec. dir., 1981-83, tng. instr., 1983-84; program mgr. Dept. Youth Svcs., Crownpoint Agy., The Navajo Nation, Crownpoint, N.Mex., 1987-89; mem. N.Mex. Ho. of Reps. Chairwoman Health, Phys., Edn. & Recreation Program Adv. Com., Gallup, N.Mex., 1988—. Home: PO Box 705 Crownpoint NM 87313-0705 Office: N Mex Ho of Reps State Capitol New Mexico State Capitol NM 87503*

MORGAN, M. JANE, computer systems consultant; b. Washington, July 21, 1945; d. Edmond John and Roberta (Livingstone) Dolphin; 1 child, Sheena Anne. Student U. Md., 1963-66, Montgomery Coll., 1966-70; BA in Applied Behavioral Sci. with honors, Nat.-Louis Univ., 1987, MS in Mgmt., 1991, postgrad. Am. U. With HUD, Washington, 1965-84, computer specialist, 1978-84; pres., chief exec. officer Systems and Mgmt. Assocs., 1983-91; dir. systems engring. Advanced Technology Systems, Inc., Vienna, Va., 1984-86; chief tech. staff Tech. and Mgmt. Services, Inc., 1986-89; sr. cons. Advanced Tech. Systems Inc., Vienna, 1989; sr. computer scientist Integrated Systems div. Computer Scis. Corp., 1989-90; computer systems analyst gen. svcs. adminstrn. U.S. Govt., 1991—; mgmt. cons. Mem. Federally Employed Women. Episcopalian. Club: Order Eastern Star.

MORGAN, MARABEL, author; b. Crestline, Ohio, June 25, 1937; d. Howard and Delsa (Smith) Hawk; m. Charles O. Morgan, Jr., June 25, 1964; children—Laura Lynn, Michelle Rene. Ed., Ohio State U. Pres. Total Woman, Inc., Miami, Fla., 1970—; pub. speaker. Author: The Total Woman, 1973, Total Joy, 1976, The Total Woman Cookbook, 1980, The Electric Woman, 1985. Office: care Total Woman Inc 1300 NW 167th St Miami FL 33169-5738

MORGAN, MARILYN, federal judge; b. 1947; 1 child, Terrence M. Adamson. BA, Emory U., 1969, JD, 1976. Bar: Ga. 1976, Calif. 1977. Ptnr. Morgan & Towery, San Jose, Calif., 1979-88; bankruptcy judge U.S. Bankruptcy Ct. (no. dist.) Calif., 1988—; mem. bankruptcy adv. com. U.S. Dist. Ct., 1984-88; law rep. 9th Cir. Jud. Conf., 1987-88. Mem. adv. bd. Downtown YMCA, 1984-88; dir. The Women's Fund, 1987-88. Mem. Santa Clara County Bar Assn. (chmn. debtor and creditor and insolvency com. 1979, 81, treas. 1982, pres. 1985-86), Santa Clara County Bar Assn. Law Found. (trustee 1982, 86-88, pres. 1985, law related edn. trustee 1986-88), Nat. Assn. Bankruptcy Trustees (founding mem., v.p., sec. 1981-88), Rotary Club San Jose (bd. dirs. 1992—), Nat. Assn. Bankruptcy Trustees (founder). Office: US Bankruptcy Ct 280 S 1st St Rm 3035 San Jose CA 95113-3010*

MORGAN, MARY LOUISE FITZSIMMONS, fund raising executive, lobbyist; b. N.Y.C., July 22, 1946; d. Robert John and Mary Louise (Gordon) Fitzsimmons; m. David William Morgan, Aug. 7, 1971; children: Mallory Siobhan, David William. BA, Marquette U., 1964; MA, Catholic U., Wash., 1966. Asst. prof. Monmouth Coll., West Long Branch, N.J., 1966-69; campaign dir. United Way, N.Y.C., 1969-80; pres. Morgan Communications, N.Y.C., 1980-82; capital campaign dir. YMCA of Greater N.Y., 1982-85; dir. devel. N.Y. Med. Coll., Valhalla, 1985-88; counsel Challenger Ctr., Va., 1988—; v.p. Ctr. Molecular Medicine & Immunology, Newark, 1989—, Garden State Cancer Ctr., Newark, 1990-93; chief devel. and pub. affairs officer Mental Health Assn., White Plains, N.Y., 1993-95; v.p. Missing Kids Internat., Inc., Mc Lean, Va., 1995—; adj. prof. Iona Coll., New Rochelle, N.Y., 1994—; dir. Meth. Ch. Home for Aged, Riverdale, N.Y., Casita Maria Inc., N.Y.C., 1975—; pres., founding dir. Achievement Rewards for Coll. Scientists Inc., N.Y.C., 1978-80. Sec. Darien (Conn.) Dem. Town Com., 1984—, vice chmn. Darien nominating com. 1986—. Recipient 50th Anniversary award Casita Maria Inc., N.Y.C., 1984, Iris award Bus. Communicators of Am., 1991, Nat. Depression Awareness Campaign award NMHA, 1994. Mem. Nat. Soc. Fund Raising Execs., Nat. Soc. Hosp. Adminstrn., Spring Lake (N.J.) Bath and Tennis Club. Democrat. Roman Catholic. Office: Missing Kids Internat Inc 6707 Old Dominion Dr Ste 200 Mc Lean VA 22101

MORGAN, MELANIE KARYN, lawyer; b. Kans. City, Mo., July 29, 1962; married; 2 children. BA in Philosophy, Coll. of William and Mary, 1984, JD, 1987. Bar: Tex. 1987. Assoc. atty. Geary, Stahl & Spencer, Dallas, 1987-89; atty. PepsiCo, Inc.-Frito-Lay, Inc., Dallas, 1989-91, sr. atty., 1991-94, of counsel, 1994—. Mem. ABA, Dallas Bar Assn., Dallas Assn. Young Lawyers, Collin County Bar Assn., Promotion Mktg. Assn. of Am. (legal com.).

MORGAN, REBECCA QUINN, business executive; b. Hanover, N.H., Dec. 4, 1938; d. Forrest Arthur and Rachel (Lewis) Quinn; m. James C. Morgan, June 10, 1960; children: J. Jeffrey, Mary Frances. BS, Cornell U., 1960; MBA, Stanford U., 1978. Trustee Palo Alto (Calif.) Bd. Edn., 1973-78; asst. v.p. Bank of Am., Sunnyvale, Calif., 1978-80; county supr. Santa Clara County, San Jose, Calif., 1980-84; state senator State of Calif., Sacramento, 1984-93; pres., CEO Joint Venture: Silicon Valley Network, San Jose, Calif., 1993—; bd. trustees Stanford U., 1993—. Mem. adv. bd. YWCA, Palo Alto, 1983—, Palo Alto Adolescent Svcs., 1975—, Stanford Bus. Sch., 1989—. Named Calif. Legislator of Yr, Sch. Bd. Assn. of Sacramento, 1987, Calif. Probation Parole and Correctional Assn., 1987-88, Calif. Sch. Age Consortium, 1989, Calif. NOW, 1990, Woman of Achievement Santa Clara County, 1983; Am. Leadership fellow, 1993-94. Mem. Calif. Elected Women's Assn. Republican. Office: 99 Almaden Blvd Ste 610 San Jose CA 95113

MORGAN, ROBERTA MARIE, artist, writer; b. Balt., Nov. 24, 1953; d. Joseph Peter Morgan and Roberta Otilia (Imhoff) Carpenter. BFA, Md. Inst., 1975. Juror Carroll County Summer Juried Invitational, 1990; mem. selection com. Gaithersburg Coun. for Arts, 1991, 92, 93, Rockville (Md.) Arts Place, 1994; participant critic's residency program Arlington (Va.) Arts Ctr., 1990, Md. Art Place, Balt., 1991; instr. art history Sr. Adult Summer Inst., Howard C.C., Columbia, Md., 1992; reviewer local art exhbns. Gazette Newspapers, Montgomery County, Md., 1990-94. One-woman shows Howard C.C. Gallery, 1989, C. Alden Phelps Gallery, Reisterstown, Md., 1990, City Hall Gallery, Gaithersburg, 1991, Slayton House Gallery, Columbia, Md., 1992, Capital Gallery, Landover, Md., 1992, Glen Echo (Md.) Gallery, 1994; exhibited in group shows, including Rockville Arts Place, 1991, 92, 93, Columbia Art Ctr., 1991, Capital Hill Arts Workshop, Washington, 1992, 93, Gurmukh Gallery, Olney, Md., 1992, Columbia Assn. Art Ctr., 1993, 94, Howard County Ctr. for Arts, 1992, Westbeth Gallery, N.Y.C., 1994, Smith Art Mus., Springfield, Mass., 1994, Fine Arts Gallery and Mus., Fla. State U., Tallahassee, 1994, Valencia C.C., Orlando, Fla., 1995. Mem. Studio Gallery, Md. Arts Alliance (editor newsletter 1989-90, pres. 1990-91), Capitol Hill Art League. Democrat. Roman Catholic. Home and Studio: 12 Little River Rd Laurel MD 20724-1706

MORGAN, ROBIN EVONNE, poet, author, journalist, activist, editor; b. Lake Worth, Fla., Jan. 29, 1941; 1 child, Blake Ariel. Grad. with honors, The Wetter Sch., 1956; student, pvt. tutors, 1956-59, Columbia U.; DHL (hon.), U. Conn., 1992. Free-lance book editor, 1961-69; editor Grove Press, 1967-70; editor, columnist World column Ms. Mag., N.Y.C., 1974-87, editor in chief, 1989-93, internat. cons. editor, 1993—; vis. chair and guest prof. women's studies New Coll., Sarasota, Fla., 1973; disting. vis. scholar, lectr. Ctr. Critical Analysis of Contemporary Culture, Rutgers U., 1987; invited spl. cons. UN com. UN Conv. to End All Forms Discrimination Against Women, Sao Paulo and Brasilia, Brazil, 1987; mem. adv. bd. ISIS (internat. network women's internat. cross-cultural exch.); spl. advisor gen. assembly conf. on Gender UN Internat. Sch., 1985-86; free-lance journalist, lectr. cons., editor, 1969—; invited speaker numerous confs., orgns., acad. meetings, U.S. and abroad. Author, compiler, editor: Sisterhood Is Powerful: An Anthology of Writings from the Women's Liberation Movement, 1970, Swedish edit. 1972, Sisterhood Is Global: The International Women's Movement Anthology, 1984, U.K. edit., 1985, Spanish edit., 1994; author: (nonfiction) Going Too Far: The Personal Chronicle of a Feminist, 1978, German edit. 1978, The Anatomy of Freedom: Feminism, Physics and Global Politics, 1982, 2d edit., 1994, fgn. edits. U.K., 1984, Germany, 1985, Argentina, 1986, The Netherlands, 1988, Portugal, 1991, The Demon Lover: On the Sexuality of Terrorism, 1989, U.K. edit., 1989, Japanese edit., 1992, The Word of a Woman: Feminist Dispatches 1968-91, 1992, 2d edit., 1994, U.K. edit., 1992, Chinese edit., 1995, (fiction) Dry Your Smile: A Novel, 1987, U.K. edit., 1988, The Mer-Child: A New Legend, 1991, German edit., 1995, (poetry) Monster: Poems, 1972, Lady of the Beasts: Poems, 1976, Death Benefits: Poems, 1981, Depth Perception: New Poems and a Masque, 1982, Upstairs in the Garden: Selected and New Poems, 1968-88, 1990, (plays) In Another Country, 1960, The Duel, 1979; co-editor: (with Bunch and Weeks) The New Woman: Anthology, 1969; contbr. numerous articles, essays, book revs., poems to various publs.; presenter poetry readings univs., poetry ctrs., radio, TV, others, 1970—. Mem. 1st women's liberation caucus CORE, 1965, Student Nonviolent Coordinating Com., 1966; organizer 1st feminist demonstration against Miss Am. Pageant, 1968; founder, pres. The Sisterhood Fund, 1970; founder, pres. N.Y. Women's Law Ctr., 1970; founder N.Y. Women's Ctr., 1969; co-founder, bd. dirs. Feminist Women's Health Network, Nat. Battered Women's Refuge Network, Nat. Network Rape Crisis Ctrs.; bd. dirs. Women's Fgn. Policy Coun.; adv. trustee Nat. Women's Inst. for Freedom of Press; founding mem. Nat. Mus. Women in Arts; co-founder Sisterhood is Global Inst. (internat. think-tank), 1984, officer, 1989—, co-organizer, U.S. mem. official visit Coalition of Philippines Women's Movement, 1988; chair N.Y. state com. Hands Across Am. Com. for Justice and Empowerment, 1988; mem. adv. bd. Global Fund for Women. Recipient Front Page award for disting. journalism, Wonder Woman award for internat. peace and understanding, 1982, Feminist of Yr. award Fund for Feminist majority, 1990; writer-in-residence grantee Yaddo, 1980; grantee Nat. Endowment for Arts, 1979-80, Ford Found., 1982, 83, 84. Mem. Feminist Writers' Guild, Media Women, N.Am. Feminist Coalition, Pan Arab Feminist Solidarity Assn. (hon.), Israeli Feminists Against Occupation (hon.). Office: Ms Mag 230 Park Ave New York NY 10169-0005

MORGAN, RUTH PROUSE, academic administrator, educator; b. Berkeley, Calif., Mar. 30, 1934; d. Ervin Joseph and Thelma Ruth (Prcesang) Prouse; m. Vernon Edward Morgan, June 3, 1956; children: Glenn Edward, Renée Ruth. BA summa cum laude, U. Tex., 1956; MA, La. State U., 1961, PhD, 1966. Asst. prof. Am. govt., politics and theory So. Meth. U., Dallas, 1966-70, assoc. prof., 1970-74, prof., 1974—, asst. provost, 1978-82, assoc. provost, 1982-86, provost ad interim, 1986-87, provost, 1987-93, provost emerita, 1993—; pres. RPM Assocs., 1993—; Tex. state polit. analyst ABC, N.Y.C., 1972-84. Author: The President and Civil Rights, 1970; mem. editorial bd. Jour. of Politics, 1975-82, Presdl. Studies Quar., 1980—; contbr. articles to profl. jours. Active Internat. Women's Forum, 1987—; trustee Hockaday Sch., 1988-94; bd. dirs. United Way Met. Dallas, 1993—; mem. adv. com. U.S. Army Command and Gen. Staff Coll., 1994—. Mem. Am. Polit. Sci. Assn., So. Polit. Sci. Assn. (mem. exec. coun. 1979-84), Southwestern Polit. Sci. Assn. (pres. 1982-83, mem. exec. coun. 1981-84), Charter 100 Club (pres. 1991-92), Dallas Summit Club (pres. 1992-93), Phi Beta Kappa, Pi Sigma Alpha, Phi Kappa Phi, Theta Sigma Phi.

MORGAN, SANDRA LYNN, accountant; b. Chattanooga, Feb. 5, 1951; d. William Burton and Betty Jo Sully M. BBA, U. Tenn., 1973. Acctg. dept. profl. Hamilton Bancshares, Chattanooga, 1973-76; aide in tax dept. Arthur Andersen & Co., Chattanooga, 1976-82; acct. Signal Thread Co., Chattanooga, 1982—. Mem. Inst. Mgmt. Accts. (bd. dirs. 1991-93). Methodist.

MORGAN, SHERRI LYNN, lawyer, human services manager; b. Pitts., Aug. 9, 1963; d. Herbert Charles and Ardyce Mae (Hansen) M.; m. Scott Barkley Garrison, Apr. 20, 1991; 1 child, Philip Morgan Garrison. BS, Columbia Union Coll., 1984; MSW, U. Md., 1988, JD, 1989. Bar: Md., D.C.; lic. social worker, Md. Law clk. Legal Aid Bur., Inc., Balt., 1986-89, spl. edn. advocate, 1987; family, child therapist Kennedy-Krieger Inst. for Handicapped Children, Balt., 1987-88; resident mgr. Family & Children's Svcs. of Ctrl. Md., Balt., 1989; program mgr. Women's Housing Coalition, Balt., 1989-90; coord. transitional housing, clin. social worker Family & Children's Svcs. Ctrl. Md., Balt., 1990-94; legal rschr. Md. Gov.'s Adv. Bd. on Shelter, Nutrition & Svcs. for Homeless, Balt., 1986-87; survey cons. ABA, Washington, 1988; pro bono atty. House of Ruth, Domestic Violence Legal Clinic, Balt., 1992-93. Commr. Takoma Pk. (Md.) Commn. on Landlord Tenant Affairs, 1993—. Recipient Mayor's Proclamation and Cert. of award City of Takoma Pk., 1993, Cert. of Appreciation, Md. Dept. Human Resource, 1992, Mayor's citation Mayor Kurt L. Schmake, 1992. Mem. NOW, D.C. Bar Assn., Women's Bar Assn. D.C., Amnesty Internat., Audubon Naturalist Soc. Democrat. Quaker. Home: 10703 Harding Rd Laurel MD 20723

MORGAN, SHIRLEY ANN, information systems executive; b. Farmington, Mich., Mar. 13, 1940; d. Clyde Elmer and Callie Mae (Morgan) Card; children: Cindy Jeanne, Dennis Carl, Vicki Anne. Student, Phillip Crosby Quality Improvement Process Mgmt. Coll., 1991; BBA, Orlando (Fla.) Coll., 1992. Cert. prodn. and inventory mgmt. With Anchor Coupling Co., Plymouth, Mich., 1959-74; data processing supt. Photon Sources, Livonia, Mich., 1976-80; data processing mgr. S&H Fabricating, Sanford, Fla., 1980-85; MIS mgr. ABB Power Distbn., Sanford, 1985-92, Wheeled Coach, Inc., Winter Park, Fla., 1992-94, Crane Cams, Inc., Daytona Beach, Fla., 1994—. Republican. Office: Crane Cams Inc 530 Fentress Blvd Daytona Beach FL 32114

MORGAN, VIRGINIA, magistrate judge; b. 1946. BS, Univ. of Mich., 1968; JD, Univ. of Toledo, 1975. Bar: Mich. 1975, Federal 1975, U.S. Ct. Appeals (6th cir.) 1979. Tchr. Dept. of Interior, Bur. of Indian Affairs, 1968-70, San Diego Unified Schs., 1970-72, Oregon, Ohio, 1972-74; asst. prosecutor Washtenaw County Prosecutor's Office, 1976-79; asst. U.S. atty. Detroit, 1979-85; magistrate judge U.S. Dist. Ct. (Mich. ea. dist.), 6th circuit, Detroit, 1985—. Recipient Spl. Achievement award Dept. of Justice. Mem. Nat. Coun. of U.S. Magistrates, Nat. Assn. of Women Judges, Mich. Bar Assn. Office: US Courthouse 231 W Lafayette Blvd Detroit MI 48226-2719*

MORGAN, VIRGINIA DEAPO, business owner; b. Syracuse, N.Y., Oct. 28, 1934; d. William John and Mary (Sojewicz) Deapo; m. Robert Lee Morgan Jr., Sept. 1, 1962; 1 child, Robert Lee III. BS, SUNY, Cortland, 1956, MS, 1961; EdD, Nova U., 1979. Tchr. math. Camillus (N.Y.) Sch. Dist. # 1, 1956-61, Dept. Def. Dependent Sch., Clark AFB, The Philippines, 1961-63, Charles County Bd. Edn., La Plata, Md., 1966-68; asst. prof. math. Charles Community Coll., La Plata, 1968-72; instr. Anson Tech. Coll., Ansonville, N.C., 1972-74, dean students, 1974-79; prin. Southview Acad., Wadesboro, N.C., 1979-82; funeral dir. Morgan & Son. Funeral Home, Marshville, N.C., 1982—; dept. chair gen. edn., math. instrn. Montgomery Community Coll., Troy, N.C., 1985—; part time instr. Gardner-Webb Coll., Boiling Springs, N.C., 1988—. Chmn. Union County Bd. Edn., Monroe, N.C., 1977-85. Mem. Am. Math. Assn. Two Yr. Colls., N.C. Assn. Tchrs., N.C. Funeral Dirs. Assn., Women Adminstrs. N.C. Higher Edn., N.C. State Sch. Bd. Assn. (bd. dirs. 1981-85). Office: Montgomery C C PO Box 787 Troy NC 27371-0787

MORGAN, WANDA BUSBY, health care executive, educator; b. Cromwell, Okla., Aug. 27, 1930; d. Charles C. and Gladys J. (Beaty) Busby; m. James O. Morgan, Oct. 23, 1954; children: Terri, Kathleen, Martha. BA, Lincoln (Ill.) Christian Coll., 1954; MA, Kans. State U., 1973; postgrad., Cen. State U., Edmond, Okla., 1977-79, U. Okla., 1980-84, Purdue U., 1983. Prof. Manhattan (Kans.) Christian Coll., Manhattan, 1970-74; instr. Seminole (Okla.) Jr. Coll., 1978-80; prof. Bethany (Okla.) Nazarene Coll., 1980-84; instr. Moravian Coll., Bethlehem, Pa., 1984-85, Allentown Coll., Center Valley, Pa., 1985-88; edn. coordinator Sacred Heart HealthCare System, Allentown, Pa., 1985-87; v.p. Sacred Heart Health Care System, Allentown, Pa., 1987-95; cons. Communication Arts, Ltd., Allentown, 1978—; advisor Okla. Dept. Edn., Oklahoma City, 1981; tchr., cons. U. Okla. Dept. Edn., Norman, 1980—, Okla. Writing Project, 1980—. Author: Bridging the English Gap, 1983; co-author: Grammar, Ltd., 1983. Mem. adv. bd. Lehigh County (Pa.) Human Svcs. Dept., 1986-89, chmn., 1988-89; mem. Lehigh Valley Action Com. United Way, 1992—, Children's Coalition Lehigh Valley, 1993—. Fellow U. Okla., 1980. Mem. Am. Soc. Healthcare Mktg. and Pub. Rels., Okla. Coun. Tchrs. English (vice chair coll. sect. 1983-84), Liberty Bell Rotary Club. Democrat. Presbyterian.

MORGAN, WINIFRED ALICE, English language educator; b. Chgo., June 14, 1938; d. Edward Patrick and Winifred Alice (Scott) M. BA, Rosary Coll., River Forest, Ill., 1961; MA, U. Tex., 1971; PhD, U. Iowa, 1982. Tchr. high sch. Edgewood High Sch., Madison, Wis., 1961-65, O'Gorman High Sch., Sioux Falls, S.D., 1965-68, Bishop Lynch High Sch., Dallas, 1968-71, Cathedral High Sch., Milw., 1971-73, Aquin High Sch., Freeport, Ill., 1973-74; intern Edgewood Coll., Madison, 1974-75, lectr., 1981-83, asst. prof., 1983-88, assoc. prof., 1988-91, prof., 1991—; Fulbright lectr. Spain, 1990. Author: An American Icon: Brother Jonathan and American Identity, 1988; contbr. articles to profl. jours. Mem. AAUW, Am. Studies Assn., Coll. English Assn., Mid-Am. Am. Studies Assn., Modern Lang. Assn., Midwest Modern Lang. Assn., Nat. Coun. Tchrs. English, Am. Folklore Soc. Democrat. Roman Catholic. Home: 833 Erin St Madison WI 53715-1809 Office: Edgewood Coll 855 Woodrow St Madison WI 53711-1958

MORGAN-FADNESS, CORRINA MAY, staff charge nurse; b. Longview, Wash., Jan. 12, 1963; d. Arthur Dallas and Dorothy Irene (Ellis) Miller; 1 child, Michael Patrick. AA, Lower Columbia Coll., 1982; BSN, U. Portland, 1987. RN, Wash. Staff nurse Centralia (Wash.) Gen. Hosp., 1987; charge nurse Walker Care Ctr., Centralia, 1987-89, Park Royal Med. Ctr., Longview, Wash., 1987, 89; house supr. WHCC Riverside, Centralia, 1989-92; staff nurse Auburn (Wash.) Gen. Hosp., 1992—, Morton (Wash.) Long Term Care, 1994—; IV cons. on-call Evergreen Pharms., Inc., 1990—; unit mgr. Oakhurst Convalescent Ctr., Elma, Wash., 1992-93; patient care coord. Rehab. Sharon Care Ctr., Centralia, Wash., 1993—. Home: 403 2nd Ave NE Napavine WA 98565

MORGART, MICHELE, psychologist, consultant; b. Phila., July 2, 1947; d. Robert Paul and Elizabeth (Byrne) M.; divorced; 1 child, Michael Paul. BA in Psychology and English, U. Akron, Ohio, 1981, MA in Psychology, 1984. Cert. tchr., Ohio; lic. profl. clin. counselor; cert. employee assistance profl. Counselor and edn. specialist Timken Mercy Med. Ctr., Canton, Ohio, 1984—; dir. concern: Employee Assistance Program Timken Mercy Med. Ctr., Canton, 1992—; cons. Summit County Adolescent Task Force Svcs. Network, Akron, 1988—; cons. C.A.R.E. Community Drug Edn., Cuy Falls, Ohio, 1984, City Ethics Adv. Bd., 1994. Vol. Summit County Drug Bd., Akron, 1978-81. Mem. APA (cert.), Employee Asst. Profl. Assn., Psi Chi, Phi Sigma Alpha. Office: Timken Mercy Med Ctr 1320 Timken Mercy Dr NW Canton OH 44708-2614

MORGENTHAL, BECKY HOLZ, legal association administrator; b. Altadena, Calif., Aug. 5, 1947; d. E. William and Elizabeth (DeLong) Holz; m. Roger Mark Morgenthal, Aug. 12, 1972. AA, Goldey Beacom Coll., 1967; grad., Wilson Coll., 1990. Clk. Hercules, Inc., Wilmington, Del., 1969-71; acct. Beth Products, Lebanon, Pa., 1971-72; adminstrv. asst. Legal Services, Inc., Carlisle, Pa., 1973-76; office mgr. CEMI Corp., Carlisle, 1976-77; acct. Tressler Luth. Services, Camp Hill, Pa., 1978-79, Benatec Assocs., Inc., Camp Hill, 1979-82; fin. analyst Electronic Data Systems, Camp Hill, 1983-87; owner BHM Bus. Svcs., Carlisle, 1982—; exec. dir. Cumberland County Bar Assn., Carlisle; pres. Morgenthal Aviation Corp. Pres. Carlisle Jr. Civic Club, 1979-80; mem. Coun. Cath. Women, Carlisle, 1986—. Mem. AAUW (treas. 1994—, Ctrl. Pa. chpt. 99's sec. 1994). Republican. Home: 1311 Windsor Ct Carlisle PA 17013-3562

MORGENTHALER, ALISA MARIE, lawyer; b. St. Louis, June 3, 1960; d. Gerald Thomas and Mary Louise (Neece) M. BA, S.W. Mo. State U., 1982; JD, Cornell U., 1985. Bar: N.Y. 1986, D.C. 1988, Calif. 1990. Law clk. City of Springfield, Mo., 1981; bd. govs. FRS, Washington, 1984; staff atty. Fed. Res. System, Washington, 1985-86; assoc. Kirkpatrick & Lockhart, Washington, 1986-88, Stroock & Stroock & Lavan, Washington, 1988-89, Christensen, White, Miller, Fink & Jacobs, L.A., 1989—. Mem. ABA, Calif. Bar Assn., D.C. Bar Assn., N.Y. Bar Assn., Los Angeles County Bar Assn., Beverly Hills Bar Assn., Century City Bar Assn., Order of Omega, Phi Alpha Delta, Rho Lambda, Phi Kappa Phi, Pi Sigma Alpha, Gamma Phi Beta. Office: Christensen White Miller Fink & Jacobs 2121 Avenue Of The Stars Fl 18 Los Angeles CA 90067

MORGILLO, ELAINE BRUNELLI, financial executive; b. New Haven, Nov. 25, 1948; d. Edward M. and Emma (Guida) Brunelli; m. Michael L. Morgillo, May 15, 1971; 1 child, Catherine Margaret. BA in Psychology, Albertus Magnus Coll., 1970; postgrad., Ga. State U., 1977-78, Bentley Coll., 1985-86, Coll. for Fin. Planning, 1985-87. CFP. Bus. mgr. AD Mgmt. & Realty, Lawrence, Mass., 1983-85; fin. counselor Fin. Planning & Mgmt., Lexington, Mass., 1985-88; prin. Tinseth & Morgillo, North Andover, Mass., 1988-91; ptnr. Ryan Fin. Advisors, Andover, Mass., 1991—. Mem. planned giving com. Am. Heart Assn., Framingham, Mass., 1991-93; pres., mem. Merrimack Valley Estate Planning Coun., 1992—. Mem. Inst. Cert. Fin. Planners, New Eng. Women's Investment Club (treas. 1989—), Svc. Club of Andover (bd. dirs. 1993—). Office: Ryan Fin Advisors 89 Main St Andover MA 01845

MORI, HANAE, fashion designer; b. Muikaichi, Shimane, Japan, 1926; m. Ken Mori, May 1947; children: Akira, Kei. BA in Lit., Tokyo Women's Christian Coll., 1947. Pres., founder, designer Hanae Mori Group, N.Y.C., 1951—; uniform designer Japan Airlines, Tokyo, 1967, 70, 73; costume designer Monaco Ballet, 1976, Paris Opera Ballet, 1986, (opera) Madame Butterfly at La Scala, Milan, 1985. Author: Designing for Tomorrow, 1978, A Glass Butterfly, 1984, Hanae Mori 1960-1989, 1989. Adviser Ministry of Cultural Affairs, Tokyo; mem. overseas bd. Boston Symphony Orch.; mem. various cultural coms., Tokyo. Recipient Neiman Marcus award, 1973, Purple Ribbon, Govt. of Japan, 1988, La Croix Chevalier des Arts et Lettres, Govt. of France, 1984, Legion of Honor, 1989. Mem. Chambre Syndicale de Haute Couture Parisienne. Office: Hanae Mori New York Inc 27 E 79th St New York NY 10021-0101

MORIARTY, JUDITH KAY SPRY, state official; b. Fairfield, Mo., Feb. 2, 1942; d. Earl Price and Blanche May (McDavitt) Spry; children: Derek David, Michael Price, Timothy John. Student Central Mo. State U., State Fair C.C.; tng. cert. Elections and County Clks. Assn., Mo., 1985. Motor Vehicle agt. Sedalia Motor Vehicle Registration, Mo., 1977-81; county clk. Pettis County, Sedalia, 1982-93; sec. of state State of Mo., 1993—. Vice regent Daus. Isabella, Sedalia, 1985-86; del. Mo. Dem. Conv., 1980, 84; active Women's Dem. Club Pettis County, Sacred Heart Cath. Ch., Mo. Coun. Econ. Edn., Mo. Hist. Recs. Preservation Bd., Friends of Archives, Local Recs. Bd., State Recs. Commn., Literacy Investment for Tomorrow; bd. dirs. Salvation Army, Sedalia, 1978—, Am. Cancer Soc., Sedalia, 1982—, Sedalia Area Council for Arts, 1980-84. Named Outstanding Young Woman Sedalia, Sedalia Jaycees, 1959. Mem. LWV, Bus. and Profl. Women (legis. chmn. 1984-86), Sedalia Area C. of C. (v.p., bd. dirs. 1982-85), Women's Aglow. Avocations: reading; physical fitness; walking; pen and ink sketching; baking. Office: Office Sec of State PO Box 778 Jefferson City MO 65102*

MORIARTY, MAUREEN C., marketing professional; b. Albany, N.Y., Nov. 4, 1946; d. Richard John and Margaret (Egan) Conners; m. James M. Moriarty, Feb. 1, 1969. BA in History, Coll. St. Rose, 1968; MBA in Mktg., U. Pa., 1976. Sch. tchr. Houston and San Francisco, 1969-74; from asst. product mgr. to group mktg. mgr. Gillette Co., Boston, 1977-86; mktg. dir. men's jean div. Levi Strauss & Co., San Francisco, 1986-92; sr. v.p. mktg. Mattel, Inc., 1992; pres. Global Mktg. Group, Pebble Beach, Calif., 1992—; bd. dirs. Bass Rocks Internat., San Francisco; cons., pub. speaker in field; instr. internat. mktg. Golden Gate U., U. Calif. Extension Program. Author: Goal 4 It, 1988. Bd. dirs. San Francisco Sr. Citizen's Ctr., 1986-89; mktg. adv. bd. United Way, San Francisco, 1990-91, Univ. of Calif. at Berkeley Ext. Prog., San Francisco, 1987-90. Home: PO Box 375 Pebble Beach CA 93953-0375

MORICH, SUSAN MOLLY, insurance agent; b. N.Y.C., Oct. 8, 1946; d. Ronan Joseph and Marie (Trapp) Sumperl; m. Jack Donald Morich, May 29, 1971; children: Kristine Barbara, Harold Joseph. Assoc., Nassau C.C., 1971. CPCU, cert. ins. counselor. Clk. auditing dept. Liberty Mut. Ins., Lynbrook, N.Y., 1964-67, tech. underwriting asst., 1967-69; comml. underwriter Commerce & Industry Ins., N.Y.C., 1969-72, Fireman's Fund Ins., Garden City, N.Y., 1972-73; comml. underwriter, agt. various cos., L.I., N.Y., 1979-86; comml. lines mgr. Arcadian Risk Mgrs., Myrtle Beach, S.C., 1986-90; comml. lines agt. Scottish Inns, Myrtle Beach, 1990—; instr. ins. licensing course Hofstra U., Garden City, 1985-87. Mem. Am. Bus. Women, Coastal Assn. Ins. Women (v.p., pres. 1988—, instr. Am. Assn. Ins. course 1991-92, instr. consumer edn. course 1992—), Ins. Woman of Yr. award 1991). Lutheran. Home: 63 Plantation Rd Myrtle Beach SC 29575-7026

MORILLO, VIRGINIA LYNN, hotel executive; b. Silver Spring, Md., Nov. 20, 1967; d. Petronio E. and Wendy A. Morillo. Student, Strayer Coll., 1990-93. Asst. contr. Sheraton Nat. Hotel, Arlington, Va., 1989—. Mem. Nat. Soc. Pub. Accts. Office: Sheraton National Hotel 900 Orme St Arlington VA 22204

MORIN, NANCY RUTH, botanist; b. Albuquerque, N.Mex., Feb. 16, 1948; d. Seale E. Fuller and Nan (Dunford) Rearick; m. Jerome Morin, 1969 (div. 1971). AA, City Coll. of San Francisco, 1973; AB, U. Calif., Berkeley, 1975; PhD, U. Calif., 1980. Research/teaching asst. U. Calif., Berkeley, 1975-80; postdoctoral fellow Smithsonian Instn., Washington, 1980-81; editor Annals of the Mo. Bot. Garden, St. Louis, 1981-86; curator of herbarium Mo. Bot. Garden, St. Louis, 1981-88, head dept. botany, 1981-88; co-founder, editor Herbarium News, St. Louis, 1981—; convening editor Flora of North Am. Project, St. Louis, 1983—, head dept. botanical info. mgmt., 1989-92; asst. dir. Mo. Botanical Garden, St. Louis, 1992—; adj. prof. U. Mo., St. Louis, 1983—, Washington U., St. Louis, 1994—. NSF grantee, 1977-79, 82—. Mem. AAAS, Am. Inst. Biol. Scis., Am. Soc. Plant Taxonomists, Bot. Soc. Am., Internat. Assn. Plant Taxonomy, Mo. Native Plant Soc. (editor Missouriensis 1983-86), Phi Beta Kappa. Democrat. Home: 6035 Eitman Ave Saint Louis MO 63139-2810

MORING, REBECCA OWEN, university official; b. Louisville, Miss., Mar. 17, 1939; d. Boyd Franklin Owen and Lora Jewell (Hancock) Freeman; m. H. Adrian Moring, July 29, 1955; children: Susanne Moring Jeffcoat, Sharyn Moring Kirk. Student, Faulkner Jr. Coll., Fairhope, Ala., 1981-83, Springhill Coll., Mobile, Ala., 1985-88. Acct. Teledyne-Continental Motors, Mobile, 1968-70; exec. sec. U. South Ala., Mobile, 1970-80, dept. mgr., 1980-88, bus. mgr. Coll. Medicine, 1988—; cons. Assn. Pathology Chmn., 1995, program chair, 1994. Bd. dirs. March of Dimes, Mobile, 1975-84; treas. Edn. for Democracy, Inc., USA, Mobile, 1990—. Mem. NAFE, Med. Group Mgmt. Assn. (coun. mem. 1992-95, acad. practice assembly, pres. pathology mgmt. assembly 1993-94), Clin. Lab. Mgmt. Assn., Southeastern Path. Bus. Mgrs. (program chmn. 1989), Med. Group Mgmt. Assn. Ala. (state membership chmn.). Office: U South Ala 241 Fillingim St Mobile AL 36617

MORIN-MILLER, CARMEN ALINE, writer; b. Montreal, Que., Can., Dec. 20, 1929; came to U.S., 1983; d. J. Gabriel Morin and Marie-Jeanne (Guay Morin) Vincent; m. Benoit H. Massicotte, July 28, 1951 (div. 1975); children: Andree, Chantal, Joane Claude, Anne; m. Jack Conway Miller, Sept. 9, 1983. Diploma, U. Laval, Que., 1950, C.I.M., 1974; diploma in art, Charles-Huot Sch., Que., 1978. Freelance writer, 1954—; info. officer Ministere des Communications of Quebec, Quebec City, 1974-83; gallery owner Equity Art Svcs., Collegeville, Pa., 1983—, Morin-Miller Galleries, N.Y.C., 1985-90; dir. Amities Culturelles, Beauport, Quebec City, 1968-75. Author: Lumiere, 1988, Conspiration, 1977; contbr. articles to Perspectives mag., other mags., newspapers. Pres. Assn. des Parents, Beauport, 1964-74. Mem. Am. Rhododendron Soc., Union des Écrivaines et Écrivains Québécois, Club des Journalistes (pres. com. 1967-69).

MORISATO, SUSAN CAY, actuary; b. Chgo., Feb. 11, 1955; d. George and Jessie (Fujita) M.; m. Thomas Michael Remec, Mar. 6, 1981. BS, U. Ill., 1975, MS, 1977. Actuarial student Aetna Life & Casualty, Hartford, Conn., 1977-79; actuarial asst. Bankers Life & Casualty, Chgo., 1979-80, asst. actuary, 1980-83, assoc. actuary, 1983-85, health product actuary, 1985-86, v.p., 1986—; participant individual forum Health Ins. Assn. Am., 1983; spkr. health forum Life Ins. Mgmt. Rsch. Assn., 1992, long-term care conf. Sharing the Burden, 1994. Mem. adv. panel on long term care financing Brookings' Inst. Fellow Soc. Actuaries (conf. speaker 1988, workshop leader 1990, 93, 94, news editor health sect. news 1988-90); mem. Am. Acad. Actuaries, Health Ins. Assn. Am. (long term care task force 1988—, chair 1993—, conf. speaker 1990, tech. adv. com. 1991-93, mem. health care reform strategy com. 1993—), Nat. Assn. Ins. Commrs. (ad hoc actuarial working group for long term care nonforfeiture benefits 1992), Chgo. Actuarial Assn. (sec. 1983-85, program com. 1987-89), Phi Beta Kappa, Kappa Delta Pi, Phi Kappa Phi. Office: Bankers Life & Casualty Co 222 Merchandise Mart Plaza Chicago IL 60654

MORISIE, SANDRA ELIZABETH, bond trader; b. Staten Island, N.Y., July 3, 1958; d. John David and Alice Margaret (Krieger) M.; m. Ralph Alphonse Fisco, Apr. 19, 1980 (div. Mar. 1990). BBA in Acctg., Siena Coll., 1979. Registered securities rep. Sales mgr. Jordan Marsh Co., Warwick, R.I., 1980-81; retail liaison, instnl. liaison, asst. v.p. trading Merrill Lynch Pierce Fenner & Smith, N.Y.C., 1981-87; trading assoc. Chem. Bank, N.Y.C., 1987-89; v.p. fixed income trading Donaldson Lufkin & Jenrette, N.Y.C., 1989-90, Wertheim Schroder, N.Y.C., 1990; v.p. trading Nomura Securities Internat., Inc., N.Y.C., 1990-93, v.p. fixed income sales, 1994—; prin. Morisie's Seaport, 1991-92, Bayview Enterprises, Inc., 1992; v.p., nat. sales mgr. Ridge Pub. Inc., Burr Ridge, Ill., 1991—. Vol. Tomorrow's Children Fund, Hackensack, N.J., 1992, 93, Our Lady of the Rock, Seattle, 1989-91; sponsor Long Beach Island (N.J.) 18 Mile Commemorative Run, 1991, 92; coord. Nomura sect. Toys for Tots, N.Y.C., 1992-93. Republican. Roman Catholic. Home: 222 Dutchess Ave Staten Island NY 10304-2929

MORISSETTE, CAROL LYNNE, healthcare consultant; b. Connellsville, Pa., Apr. 26, 1941; d. Charles Lynn and Iola Grace (Sembower) Sliger; m. George Van Barriger, May 27, 1966 (div. Feb. 1972); m. Richard W. Morissette, Oct. 25, 1991. RN, Montefiore Hosp., 1962; BS, Coll. St. Francis, 1985; MA in Mgmt., Nat. Louis U., 1988. Pub. health nurse Kendall County Health Dept., Yorkville, Ill., 1970-72; team leader Edward Hosp., Naperville, Ill., 1972-73; emergency nurse Cen. Dupage Hosp., Winfield, Ill., 1973-74; staff nurse and head nurse Palos Community Hosp., Palos Heights, Ill., 1974-77, surg. nurse, 1977-82; auditor Med-Charge Analysis, Chgo., 1982-83; mgr. Intracorp CIGNA, Glen Ellyn, Ill., 1983-86, Metlife Healthcare Network, Schaumburg, Ill., 1986; project mgr. Healthcare Intermediaries, Lombard, Ill., 1986-88; dir., provider services Multicare HMO, Chicago, IL, 1988—; ptnr. Greenberg Assocs., 1989—; OWCP-nurse cons. U.S. Dept. Labor, 1993—; Mem. group comparison studies healthcare delivery/costs USSR, 1981, China, 1982, England, 1985, Egypt, 1992; cons. workers' comp. U.S. Dept. Labor, 1993—. V.p. Indian Oak Condominium Assn., Bolingbrook, Ill., 1972-76; treas. Hickory Heights Condominium Assn., Hickory Hills, Ill., 1978-83, bd. dirs., 1983—. Mem. NAFE, Women's Health Exec. Network, Am. Coll. Healthcare Execs., Chgo. Health Exec. Forum, Am. Assn. Occupational Health Nurses, Individual Case Mgmt. Assn. Home: 9450 Greenbriar Dr Hickory Hills IL 60457

MORLAND, JESSIE PARRISH, retired educator; b. Parrish, Fla., Dec. 3, 1924; d. Jonah and May (Lowry) Parrish; B.A., Fla. Southern Coll., 1947; m. Richard B. Morland, Mar. 17, 1949; 1 child, Laura. Dir. publicity Fla. Southern Coll., 1948-50; editor Dun's Bulletin, Dun and Bradstreet, N.Y.C., 1950-52; feature writer Deland Sun News, Daytona Beach (Fla.) News Jour., 1952-65; tchr. English, journalism Deland (Fla.) Jr. High Sch., 1967-83, tchr. gifted students, 1983-86. Bd. dirs. Deland Mus., 1957-62, Democratic Women's Club, 1952-65; pres. DeLand Cultural Com., 1990-92; sec. exec. bd. DeLand Mus. of Art Guild. Mem. AAUW (dir. 1955-62), Nat. League Am. Pen Women, DeLand Country Club, Alpha Delta Pi. Democrat. Methodist. Home: 524 N Mcdonald Ave Deland FL 32724

MORLEN, PATRICIA ANN, special education educator; b. Newark, N.J., July 11, 1956; d. Leonard Joseph and Dorothy Jean (Sefick) Cummiskey; m. Rickey Allen, June 16, 1979; 1 child, Robert Allen. BA, Georgian Ct. Coll., 1979. Tchr. spl. learning disabilities Fort Knox (Ky.) Sch. Dist., 1979-80, 83-84, Chatham County Sch. Dist., Savannah, Ga., 1980-83, Honolulu Hawaii Sch. Dist., 1984-88; tchr. spl. learning disabilities dept. spl. edn. Archdiocess St. Louis., 1989-94; substitute tchr. Ft. Benning (Ga.) Schs., 1994—. Mem. Spanish Lake Rep. Club, Mo., 1988-94, Concerned Women for Am., 1992—, asst. den leader Boy Scouts Am. Mem. Learning Disabilities Assn. (Tchr. of Yr. 1993-94), Army Officers' Wives Club. Methodist. Home: 102 A Running Ave Fort Benning GA 31905

MORLEY, JANE, historian; b. Hammond, Ind., Feb. 7, 1955; d. Clifford Douglass and Lillian Elizabeth (Varady) Morley; m. Dennis Alden Yao, Mar. 23, 1985. AB in History, Duke U., 1976; MS in Libr. Sci., MA in History, U. N.C., 1983; MA in History and Sociology of Sci., U. Pa., 1984, PhD in History and Sociology of Sci., 1995. Editorial asst. ISIS, Jour. of the History of Sci. Soc., Phila., 1982-83, editorial coord., 1983-84; instr. U. Pa., Shanghai, 1984-85; lectr. Tong Ji U., Shanghai, 1986; instr. Jiao Tong U., Shanghei, 1986; exec. adminstr. Internat. Symposium on Lewis Mumford/U. Pa., Phila., 1987; historian ASCE, Washington, 1990; postdoctoral scholar Ctr. History of Elec. Engring., Rutgers U., New Brunswick, N.J., 1995—; series editor Purdue U. Press, West Lafayette, Ind., 1993—; cons. "How Things Work" series, Time-Life Books, 1990-91. Editorial bd. Design Book Rev., 1991-94, assoc. editor, 1994—; contbr. articles to profl. jours. Smithsonian Instn. fellow, 1988-90, Royal Inst. Tech. vis. fellow, Stockholm, 1988, Am. Scandinavian Found. fellow, 1988, ISIS-History of Sci. Soc. fellow, 1982-84. Mem. Bldg. Tech. & Civil Engring. Interest Group/Soc. for the History of Tech. (founding chair 1987-89, sec.-treas. 1991—, newsletter editor 1987-91). Democrat. Soc. of Friends. Home and Office: 511 E St SE Washington DC 20003-4236

MORONEY, LINDA L.S., lawyer, educator; b. Washington, May 27, 1943; d. Robert Emmet and Jessie (Robinson) M.; m. Clarence Renshaw II, Mar. 28, 1967 (div. 1977); children: Robert Milnor, Justin W.R. BA, Randolph-Macon Woman's Coll., 1965; JD cum laude, U. Houston, 1982. Bar: Tex. 1982, U.S. Ct. Appeals (5th cir.) 1982, U.S. Dist. Ct. (so. dist.) Tex. 1982, U.S. Supreme Ct. 1988. Law clk. to assoc. justice 14th Ct. Appeals, Houston, 1982-83; assoc. Pannill and Reynolds, Houston, 1983-85, Gilpin, Pohl & Bennett, Houston, 1985-89, Vinson & Elkins, Houston, 1989-92; adj. prof. law U. Houston, 1989-91, dir. legal rsch. and writing, 1992—. Fellow Houston Bar Found.; mem. ABA, State Bar Tex., Houston Bar Assn., Assn. of Women Attys., Order of the Barons, Phi Delta Phi. Episcopalian. Home: 3730 Overbrook Ln Houston TX 77027-4036 Office: U Houston Law Ctr Houston TX 77204

MORPHEW, DOROTHY RICHARDS-BASSETT, artist, real estate broker; b. Cambridge, Mass., Aug. 4, 1918; d. George and Evangeline Booth (Richards) Richards; grad. Boston Art Inst., 1949; children—Jon Eric, Marc Alan, Dana Kimball. Draftsman, United Shoe Machinery Co., 1937-42; blueprinter, advt. artist A.C. Lawrence Leather Co., Peabody, Mass., 1949-51; propr. Studio Shop and Studio Potters, Beverly, Mass., 1951-53; tchr. ceramics and art, Kingston, N.H., 1953—; real estate broker, pres. 1965-81; two-man exhbn. Topsfield (Mass.) Library, 1960; owner, operator Ceramic Shop, West Stewartstown, N.H. Served with USNR, 1942-44. Recipient Profl. award New Eng. Ceramic Show, 1975; also numerous certificates in ceramics. Home: 557 Palomino Trl Englewood FL 34223-3951 Studio: Algonac Ave York Beach ME 03910

MORREIM, E. HAAVI, medical ethicist, educator; b. Austin, Minn., July 21, 1950; d. Paul Eugene and Florence Adeline (Haavik) M. BA in Philosophy, St. Olaf Coll., 1972; MA in Philosophy, U. Va., 1976, PhD, 1980. Med. philosopher program in human biology and soc. U. Va. Sch. Medicine, Charlottesville, 1980-82, asst. prof. philosophy in medicine, 1982-84; from asst. to assoc. prof. dept. human values and ethics U. Tenn. Coll. Medicine, Memphis, 1984-93, prof. dept. human values and ethics, 1993—; adj. prof. philosophy Va. Commonwealth U., Richmond, 1980; vis. prof. philosophy St. Olaf Coll., Northfield, Minn., 1982; Andrew Mellon vis. asst. prof. humanities and medicine Georgetown U. Sch. Medicine, Washington, 1983; sr. vis. rsch. scholar Kennedy Inst. Ethics, Georgetown U., 1983; manuscript reviewer; presenter and lectr. in field. Author: Balancing Act: The New Medical Ethics of Medicine's New Economics, 1991: mem. editorial bd. Theoretical Medicine, Jour. Medicine and Philosophy, Jour. Law, Medicine and Ethics; author articles. Active Hastings Ctr. Mem. Am. Philos. Assn., Nat. Health Lawyers Assn., Am. Soc. Law, Medicine and Ethics, Soc. for Bioethics Consultation (bd. dirs. 1993—), Soc. for Health and Human Values (exec. coun. mem. 1992—), Phi Beta Kappa. Home: 2032 Harbert Memphis TN 38104 Office: Univ Tenn Coll Medicine 956 Court Ste B328 Memphis TN 38163

MORRILL, NANCY PORTER, management consultant; b. Natick, Mass., Apr. 14, 1939; d. Rupert Felch and Vera (Richardson) Porter; m. William Ashley Morrill, Aug. 26, 1978; 4 stepchildren. AB in Polit. Sci., Bryn Mawr Coll., 1960. Sr. report specialist McKinsey & Co., Inc., San Francisco, 1960-61; pers. sec., confidental asst. Hon. Edward W. Brooke, Mass. State Atty Gen. and U.S. Senator, 1962-69; pers. asst. to chmn. The Diebold Group, N.Y.C., 1969-70; staff asst. Am. Revolution Bicentennial Commn., Washington, 1970-71; Washington rep. Girl Scouts U.S.A., Washington, 1971-73; spl. asst. to sec. HEW, Washington, 1973-77; owner, pres. New Perceptions, New Hope, Pa., 1977—. Commr. Am. Revolution Bicentennial Commn., 1971-73; mem. exec. com., bd. dirs. Girl Scouts U.S.A., N.Y.C., 1974-78; NCO del. UN Conf. IWY, Mexico City, 1975; del.-at-large Women's Nat. Conf., Houston, 1977; pres., bd. dirs. Planned Parenthood Assn. Bucks County, 1981-86; founding pres. Bucks County Women's Fund, Pa., 1989—; chair ann. fund com. Bryn Mawr Coll., 1990-93; co-founder, bd. dirs. Bucks County Wine and Food Festival, 1992—; mem. steering com. Bucks County Ops. and Rev. Evaluation Com., 1992; mem. Bucks County Adv. Coun. Human Svcs., 1992—. Named Woman of Vision, Bucks County Women's Fund, 1994. Democrat. Home and Office: New Perceptions PO Box 38 New Hope PA 18938

MORRIN, VIRGINIA WHITE, educator; b. Escondido, Calif., May 16, 1913; d. Harry Parmalee and Ethel Norine (Nutting) Rising; BS, Oreg. State Coll., 1952; MEd, Oreg. State U., 1957; m. Raymond Bennett White, 1933 (dec. 1953); children: Katherine Anne, Marjorie Virginia, William Raymond; m. 2d, Laurence Morrin, 1959 (dec. 1972). Social caseworker Los Angeles County, Los Angeles, 1934-40, 61-64; acctg. clk. War Dept., Ft. MacArthur, Calif., 1940-42; prin. clk. USAAF, Las Vegas, Nev., 1942-44; high sch. tchr., North Bend-Coos Bay, Oreg., 1952-56, Mojave, Calif., 1957-60; instr. Antelope Valley Coll., Lancaster, Calif., 1961-73; ret., 1974. Treas., Humane Soc. Antelope Valley, Inc., 1968—. Mem. Nat. Aero. Assn., Calif. State Sheriffs' Assn. (charter assoc.), Oreg. State U. Alumni Assn. (life). Address: 3153 Milton Dr Mojave CA 93501-1329

MORRIS, ANN HASELTINE JONES, executive director; b. Springfield, Mo., Feb. 3, 1941; d. Mansur King and Adelaide (Haseltine) Jones; m. Ronald D. Morris, Nov. 29, 1963 (div. 1990); children: David, Christopher. BA in Edn. and Art, Drury Coll., 1963. Art instr. Ash Grove (Mo.)/Bois D'Arc Pub. Sch. Dist., 1963-64; instr. Drury Coll., Springfield, 1966-67; tchr. Springfield R-12 Sch. Dist., 1974-86; exec. dir. S.W. Ctr. for Ind. Living, Springfield, 1986—; adv. com. Springfield R-12 Spl. Edn., 1993—; tech. cons. and alternative dispute resolution mediator Ams. with Disabilities Act EEOC, Dept. of Justice Network, 1993—. Bd. dirs. Ozark Greenways, 1991-93, Springfield Deaf Relay, 1988-90; adv. task force Allied Health Program Devel. S.W. Bapt Univ., 1988; mem. Drury Coll. Women's Aux., 1984—, conservator of the peace, handicap parking enforcement action team, 1991—; bd. treas. Mo. Parent Act, 1989-91, Diversity Network of the Ozarks, 1990—; svc. coord. Youthnet, 1990—; community adv. bd. Rehab. Svcs., St. John's Regional Health Care Ctr., 1988-91; mem. Springfield Homeless Network, 1989—, others. Mem. NOW (sec. 1991), P.E.O., Mo. Assn. of Ctrs. for Ind. Living (v.p. 1990—), Mo. Assn. for Social Welfare (bd. treas. 1989—), Nat. Assn. of Ind. Living Ctrs. (AIDS task force 1993—), Assn. of Programs for Rural Ind. Living, Nat. Soc. of Fund Raising Execs., Mo. Rehab. Assn., C. of C. (healthcare divsn.), Zeta Tau Alpaha. Home: 1748 E Arlington Rd Springfield MO 65804

MORRIS, ANNA ROCHELLE, retail and wholesale executive; b. Lubbock, Tex., Dec. 31, 1957; d. Raphael and JoAnn (Davis) Gillespie; m. Gary Dean Rosselle (div.); m. Randall C. Fraelich (div.); m. Aaron Myles Morris, Nov. 15, 1988. Photographer Miami Seaquarium, Key Biscayne, Fla., 1975-77, Trader Publs., Clearwater, Fla., 1978; salesperson Rex Art Co., Miami, 1979-81, customer svc. rep., 1981-84, asst. purchaser, 1984-87, exec. asst., 1987—. Mem. hospitality com. Miami Film Festival, 1985-86; sec. Freddick Bratcher & Co., South Miami, Fla., 1986—. Democrat. Jewish. Office: Rex Art Co 2263 SW 37th Ave Miami FL 33145-3009

MORRIS, ARLENE MYERS, marketing professional; b. Washington, Pa., Dec. 29, 1951; d. Frank Hayes Myers and Lula Irene (Slusser) Kolcan; m. John L. Sullivan, Feb. 17, 1971 (div. July 1982); m. David Wellons Morris, July 27, 1984. BA, Carlow Coll., 1974; postgrad., Western New England Coll., 1981-82. Sales rep. Syntex Labs., Inc., Palo Alto, Calif., 1974-77; profl. sales rep. McNeil Pharm., Spring House, Pa., 1977-78, mental health rep., 1978-80, asst. product dir., 1981-82, dist. mgr., 1982-85, new product dir., 1985-87, exec. dir. new bus. devel., 1987-89, v.p. bus. devel., 1989-93; v.p. bus. devel. Scios Nova IMC, Mountain View, Calif., 1993—. Mem. Found. of Ind. Colls., Phila., 1989. Mem. Pharm. Advt. Coun., Am. Diabetes Assn., Am. Acad. Sci., Healthcare Bus. Womens Assn., Lic. Execs. Soc. Home: 11701 Winding Way Los Altos CA 94024-6331 Office: Scios Nova IMC 2450 Bayshore Pky Mountain View CA 94043-1107

MORRIS, BETTY JO, library science educator; b. Vernon, Ala., Oct. 23, 1938; d. Robert Garvice and Ola Grace (Holliday) Moore; m. Bobby G. Morris, Aug. 31, 1958 (div. 1989); children: Timothy Craig (dec.), Jon Eric. BA, U. North Ala., 1967; MLS, U. Ala., Tuscaloosa, 1976, EdS, 1980, PhD, 1984. Cert. sch. media specialist, tchr., Ala. Elem. sch. libr. Decatur (Ala.) City Schs., 1966-71; media coord. Decatur High Sch., 1971-84, head libr., 1985-88; assoc. prof. Sch. Libr. and Info. Sci. L.I. U., Brookville, N.Y., 1988—; adj. prof. U. Ala. Libr. and Info. Svcs., Tuscaloosa, 1986, 87, 88; libr. Redstone Sci. Info. Ctr., Redstone Arsenal, Ala., 1988; adv. com. Ala. Libr. Exch., Huntsville, 1984-88. Author: Administering the School Media Center, 3d edit., 1992; editor: School Library Media Program Connections for Learning, 1991. Libr. Bapt. Ch., Hartselle, Ala., 1970-88. Mem. ALA, AAUW (bd. dirs. 1986-88), Ala. Instrnl. Media Assn. Ala. Libr. Assn., Libr. Mgmt. Network (bd. dirs. 1984-88), Alpha Delta Kappa (past pres.), Phi Delta Kappa, Beta Phi Mu. Baptist.

MORRIS, BEVERLY ANN, elementary education educator; b. Oxford, N.C., Apr. 24, 1962; d. Ebbie Ruppert and Barbara Ann (Faulkner) DeMent; m. Charles Richard Morris, July 2, 1983; 1 child, Carson Michelle. B of Univ. Studies, Ea. N.Mex. U., 1984, BS in Edn., 1986; MEd, No. Ariz. U., 1995. Tchr. presch. Cannon AFB Childcare Ctr., Clovis, N.Mex., 1984-86; instr. ABE Ea. N.Mex. U., Clovis, 1985-86; tchr. kindergarten Cloudcroft (N.Mex.) Schs., 1986-87, tchr. 2d grade, 1987-90, tchr. 4th grade, 1990-91; substitute tchr. Phoenix (Ariz.) Area Schs., 1991—. Mem. Internat. Reading Assn. Republican. Baptist.

MORRIS, CAROLYN EASTIN, film producer; b. Washington, Sept. 13, 1961; d. Robert Eastin and Marjorie (Greene) M. BA, Hampshire Coll., 1984. Freelance producer, 1986-94; exec. producer Little Sun Films, L.A., 1994—. Producer Rainha, She-TV, Dolemans, McDonalds. Home: 839 Milwood Ave Venice CA 90291-3830 Office: 1418 Abbottkinney Blvd Venice CA 90291

MORRIS, DIANNE K. PERRY, counselor, educator; b. Saginaw, Mich., Jan. 30, 1946; d. Merritt B. and Wanda Lois (Kimmel) Perry; m. Earl Alexander Morris, Jr., Nov. 2, 1991; one son and three stepchildren. BA, Alma Coll., 1968; MEd, Wayne State U., 1972; PhD, U. Mich., 1981. Lic. profl. counselor, Mich.; cert. tchr., Mich. Tchr. Detroit Pub. Schs., 1968-72, counselor, 1973-77, counselor, supr., 1979-88; counselor, psychotherapist Alternative Counseling, Sunrise, Fla., 1989-91; dir. tng. Nighthawk, Pompano Beach, Fla., 1990-92; counselor Broward County Adult Edn. Dept., Ft. Lauderdale, Fla., 1992-93; exec. dir. Jesus Charity Mission, Pompano Beach, 1993—; ednl. cons. Detroit, 1972—, New Perspectives on Race, Detroit, 1973-76, People Acting for Change, 1973-78; owner Dianne's Designs. Author: (curriculum) New Perspective on Race, 1973; editor/contbr. (newsletter) The Anointing, 1993. Named to Outstanding Young Women of Am., 1980. Mem. Am. Counseling Assn., Am. Psychol. Assn., NAFE, Mich. Personnel and Guidance Assn. (pres.-elect 1985), Guidance Assn. of Metro Detroit (pres. 1982-83, newsletter editor 1981-82, pub. rels. chair 1981-82). Home: 5108 E Lakes Dr Pompano Beach FL 33064

MORRIS, ELIZABETH TREAT, physical therapist; b. Hartford, Conn., Feb. 20, 1936; d. Charles Wells and Marion Louise (Case) Treat; BS in Phys. Therapy, U. Conn., 1960; m. David Breck Morris, July 10, 1961; children: Russell Charles, Jeffrey David. Phys. therapist Crippled Children's Clinic No. Va., Arlington, 1960-62, Shriners Hosp. Crippled Children, Salt Lake City, 1967-69, Holy Cross Hosp., Salt Lake City, 1970-74; pvt. practice phys. therapy, Salt Lake City, 1975—. Mem. nominating com. YWCA, Salt Lake City. Mem. Am. Phys. Therapy Assn., Am. Congress Rehab. Medicine, Nat. Speakers Assn., Utah Speakers Assn., Salt Lake Area C. of C., Friendship Force Utah, U.S. Figure Skating Assn., Toastmasters Internat., Internat. Assn. for the Study Pain, Internat. Platform Assn., World Confederation Phys. Therapy, Medart Internat. Home: 4177 Mathews Way Salt Lake City UT 84124-4021 Office: PO Box 526186 Salt Lake City UT 84152-6186

MORRIS, ELLEN, association executive. Exec. dir. YWCA, Danville, Ill. Mem. Bismarck-Henning Bd. Edn., 1976—, pres., 1986—. Office: YWCA 201 N Hazel St Danville IL 61832-4789

MORRIS, FAITH GRIFFIN, public relations executive; b. Memphis, Feb. 14, 1956; d. Leon Harlan and Norma Jean (Ford) Griffin; m. James Anthony Morris, July 6, 1980; 1 child, Jami Desiree. BA in English, Memphis State U., 1978. News anchor, reporter Scripts Howard Broadcasting, Memphis, 1978-79; news anchor Sta. WHBQ radio divsn. RKO Gen., Memphis, 1979-82, news dir. Sta. WHBQ radio divsn., 1980-82, dir. pub. rels. Sta. WHBQ radio divsn., 1982-84; pres. Morris Allen & Assocs., Memphis, 1984-86; mktg. comm. mgr. Holiday Inns, Inc., Memphis, 1986-90; account group supr. Burrell Comm. Group, Chgo., 1990-91, v.p., 1991, v.p., mng. dir., 1992—. Recipient Distinction award Comm. Excellence in Black Advt. Internat., 1992, Questar award Internat. Acad. Comm. Arts and Sci., 1993, Creativity in Pub. Rels. award Inside PR Mag., 1993. Mem. NAFE, Pub. Rels. Soc. Am., Publicity Club Chgo., Delta Sigma Theta. Office: Burrell Comm Group 20 N Michigan Ave Chicago IL 60602

MORRIS, JACQUELIN KIM, psychiatrist; b. St. Louis, Sept. 12, 1943; d. Donald and Ada Brubaker; m. Philip Beryl Morris, Nov. 26, 1966. BS, U. Calif., Berkeley, 1965; MD, U. Calif., San Francisco, 1969. Diplomate Am. Bd. Psychiatry and Neurology, Am. Bd. Adult Psychiatry, Am. Bd. Child Psychiatry. Intern pediatrics Children's Hosp. No. Calif., Oakland, 1969-70; resident psychiatry Mt. Zion Hosp., San Francisco, 1970-72, resident child and adolescent psychiatry, 1972-74; pvt. practice child and adolescent psychiatry Santa Rosa, Calif., 1975—; med. dir. Children's Day Treatment Ctr., Santa Rosa, 1976-79; cons. Head Start, Santa Rosa, 1988. Cons., com. liaison Health Plan Redwoods, Santa Rosa, 1992—. Mem. Am. Psychiatric Soc., Calif. Psychiatric Soc., Redwood Empire Psychiatric Soc. (pres. 1976—), Regional Orgn. Child and Adolescent Psychiatrists (sec., program chair 1976—). Office: 1111 Sonoma Ave Ste 204 Santa Rosa CA 95405

MORRIS, JUNE ELLEN, publishing executive; b. Louisville, Sept. 26, 1934; d. E. Louis and Evelyn (Gilbert) M. BS, U. Louisville, 1956, MA, 1960. Mkt. rsch. analyst Reynolds Metals Co., Louisville, 1957-58; statistician and unit supr. U.S. Dept. Commerce, Jeffersonville, Ind., 1958-59; rsch. asst./assoc. Am. Printing House for the Blind, Louisville, 1959-70, behavior rsch. assoc./scientist, 1970-76, asst. dir. ednl. rsch., 1976-77, acting dir. ednl. rsch., 1977-78, dir. ednl. rsch., 1978-88, exec. v.p., 1989—. Mem. APA (assoc.), Assn. for Edn. and Rehab. of Blind and Visually Impaired (Ky. chpt. pres. 1986-89), Coun. for Exceptional Children. Republican. Office: Am Printing Ho for Blind 1839 Frankfort Ave Louisville KY 40206-3148

MORRIS, KATHERINE LANG, counseling psychologist; b. Benson, Minn., Jan. 22, 1947; d. Howard James and Barbara Anne (Bennett) L. BA in Art History, Smith Coll., Northampton, Mass., 1969; MA, Bethel Theol. Sem., St. Paul, 1973; MEd, U. Mo.-Columbia, 1978, Ph.D., 1982. Lic. psychologist, Calif. Tchr., Am. Sch., Barcelona, Spain, 1970-71; campus ministry Univ. Reformed Ch., East Lansing, Mich., 1973-76; counselor Univ. Counseling Ctr., U. Mo., Rolla, 1978-79; coordinator Ctr. for Student Vols. Action, 1979-81; counseling psychologist U. Calif., Davis, 1982-94; pvt. practice counseling psychologist, Sacramento, Calif., 1986-92; dir. counseling dept. health svcs. U. Minn., Duluth, 1994—; cons. in field. Mem. APA. Avocations: skiing, tennis, racquetball, writing. Office: U Minn Health Svcs Duluth MN 55811

MORRIS, KATHLEEN MARIE, clinical psychologist, educational consultant; b. Pullman, Wash., June 4, 1962; d. Junius Hugh and Lonora Vera (Campbell) M. BA, Brandeis U., 1983; PhD, Bowling Green State U., 1990. Lic. clin. psychologist, N.Y. Staff psychologist Albany (N.Y.) County Mental Health, 1989-92; psychologist Karner Psychol. Assn., Albany, 1992—. Vol. Robert C. Parker Sch., Wynantskill, N.Y., 1992-94, Free Sch., Albany, 1992-93, Capital Assn. Sch. Devel., Albany, 1993—. Mem. APA. Home: 469 Morris St Albany NY 12208 Office: Karner Psychol Assn 2280 Western Ave Guilderland NY 12084

MORRIS, LOIS LAWSON, education educator; b. Antoine, Ark., Nov. 27, 1914; d. Oscar Moran and Dona Alice (Ward) Lawson; m. William D. Morris, July 2, 1932 (dec.); 1 child, Lavonne Morris Howell. B.A., Henderson U., 1948; M.S., U. Ark., 1951, M.A., 1966; postgrad. U. Colo., 1954, Am. U., 1958, U. N.C., 1968. History tchr. Delight High Sch., Ark., 1942-47; counselor Huntsville Vocat. Sch., 1947-48; guidance dir. Russellville Pub. Sch. System, Ark., 1948-55; asst. prof. edn. U. Ark., Fayetteville, 1955-82, prof. emeritus, 1982—; ednl. cons. Ark. Pub. Schs., 1965-78. Mem. Commn. on Needs for Women, 1976-78, Hist. Preservation Alliance Ark.; pres. Washington County Hist. Soc., 1983-85; pres. Pope County Hist. Assn.; mem. Ark. Symphony Guild; charter mem. Nat. Mus. in Arts; bd. dirs. Potts Inn Mus. Found. Named Ark. Coll. Tchr. of Year, 1972; recipient Plaque for outstanding svcs. to Washington County Hist. Soc., 1984. Contbr. articles to jours. Mem. LWV, AAUW, Ark. Coun. Social Studies (sec.-treas.), Washington County Hist. Soc. (exec. bd. 1977-80), NEA, Nat. Coun. Social Studies, Ark. Edn. Assn., Ark. Hist. Assn., Pope County Hist. Assn. (pres. 1991-92), The So. Hist. Assn., U. Ark. Alumni Assn., Sierra Club, Nature Conservancy, So. Hist. Assn., Ark. River Valley Arts Assn., Phi Delta Kappa, Kappa Delta Pi, Phi Alpha Theta. Democrat. Episcopalian. Address: 1601 W 3d St Russellville AR 72801

MORRIS, LYNNE LOUISE, psychotherapist; b. Youngstown, Ohio, Nov. 5, 1946; d. Richard Davies and Elsie Margaret Raymond) B.A., Westminster Coll., Pa., 1969; MSW, NYU, 1971. Cert. clin. social worker. Social worker Community Service Soc., N.Y.C., 1971-74, Altro Health and Rehab. Services, Inc., N.Y.C., 1974-79; field instr. Hunter Coll. Sch. Social Work, NYU Grad Sch. Social Work, 1974-79; clin. coordinator Montefiore Hosp. and Med. Center, Bronx, N.Y., 1979-81; asst. dir. II, social service dept. Montefiore Hosp., Bronx, 1981-83; pvt. practice psychotherapy, N.Y.C., 1976—; sr. staff therapist Counseling and Human Devel. Center, N.Y.C., 1979—. Contbr. articles of profl. jours. including Jour. Geriatric Psychiatry, 1975; abstractor Abstracts for Social Workers, 1975. Fellow N.Y. State Soc. Clin. Social Work Psychotherapists; mem. Nat. Assn. Social Workers (clin. diplomate), Acad. Cert. Social Workers, Am. Assn. Pastoral Counselors (profl. affiliate). Home and office: 161 W 75th St Apt 2C New York NY 10023-1802

MORRIS, MARY A., real estate executive; b. Wooster, Ark., Sept. 17, 1932; d. Doyle and Cordelia (Matchett) Holloway; m. Charles D. Powers (div. 1973); children—Carla, Steven, Daniel. Student, Ayers Sch. Bus., Shreveport, La., 1970, Tyler Jr. Coll., Tex., 1977. Legal sec. Atty. C.A. Marvin, Minden, La., 1970-73; sec. Webster Parish Sch., Minden, 1973-75, Howard Lumber, Minden, 1975-77; real estate sales ERA Homes, Longview, Tex., 1977-80, broker-owner-pres. ERA-AAA Real Estate Inc., Longview, 1980-87; chairwoman bd. dirs. PowerTech! Mem., YMCA, Longview, 1980—. Recipient numerous awards for excellence in real estate. Mem. Nat. Assn. Female Execs., Nat. Assn. Realtors, Nat. Assn. Women in Boating (chmn., charter mem. Shrevport La.), Nat. Marine Propeller Assn., Nat. Marine Mfrg. Assn., Nat. Assn. Women Bus. Owners, Electronic Realty Assocs., C. of C. (pub. relations com. 1977—), Found. for Women (assoc.), Tex. Assn. Realtors, Longview Bd. Realtors (bd. dirs. 1983—, pres.-elect 1985-86), Shrevport C. of C., YWCA. Episcopalian. Club: Toastmasters (Longview). Avocations: public speaking, boating, fishing.

MORRIS, MARY ANN, bookkeeper; b. Great Falls, Mont., Feb. 16, 1946; d. Francis Leonard and Dorothy Irene (Howe) De Lacey; m. Donald Edward Wermuth, June 29, 1968 (div. Jan. 1974); 1 child, Deborah Ann; m. Larry Dallas Morris, Apr. 23, 1977; stepchildren: Serena Jo, Bradley Dwayne, Brian Dale, Bruce Dean. Student, North Idaho Coll., 1985. Sales clk. Dundas Office Supply, Great Falls, 1964-68, Stationer's Office Supply, Tacoma, 1969-70; bookkeeper Miller's Office Supply, Puyallup, Wash., 1971-72, Judge Moving & Storage (Allied), Great Falls, 1973-74; bookkeeper, credit mgr. Meadow Gold Dairy, Great Falls, 1974; pro-rate clk. Builders Transport, Great Falls, 1975-77; bookkeeper C&S Glass, Coeur d'Alene, Idaho, 1978-81, Morris Trucking, Coeur d'Alene, 1977-82; bookkeeper LDM Transport, Hayden Lake, Idaho, 1982—, profl. truck driver (class A vehicle), 1988—. Mem. Women's Retail Credit Mgrs. Assn. Republican. Home and Office: PO Box 2350 Hayden ID 83835-2350

MORRIS, M(ARY) ROSALIND, cytogeneticist, educator; b. Ruthin, Wales, May 8, 1920; came to U.S., 1942, naturalized, 1954; d. Aneurin Edmund and Celia Charles (Evans) M. BS in Horticulture, Ont. Agrl. Coll., Guelph, Can., 1942; PhD in Plant Breeding and Genetics, Cornell U., 1947. Mem. faculty U. Nebr., Lincoln, 1947—, prof. agronomy, 1958-90, prof. emeritus, 1990—. Contbr. chpts. to textbooks, articles to sci. jours. U. Nebr. Johnson Faculty fellow, Calif. Inst. Tech., Pasadena, 1949-50; John Simon Guggenheim Found. fellow, Sweden and Eng., 1956-57. Fellow AAAS, Am. Soc. Agronomy, Crop Sci. Soc. Am.; mem. AAUW, Genetics Soc. Can., Nebr. Acad. Sci., Nebr. Ornithologists' Union (editor The Nebr. Bird Rev. 1992—), Lincoln Camera Club, Sigma Xi, Gamma Sigma Delta, Sigma Delta Epsilon. Office: U Nebr Dept Agronomy Lincoln NE 68583-0915

MORRIS, MELANIE MARIE, nurse; b. Lima, Ohio, Aug. 3, 1963; d. Andrew J. and Helen (Kaniclides) Menegos. BS in Nursing, U. Akron, 1986, MBA in Mgmt., 1993. RN, Ohio. Home health aid Nurses' Ho. Calls, Akron, Ohio, 1985, Portamedic, Akron, 1985; intravenous technician Akron City Hosp., 1985-86, nurse, 1987-88; nurse Vis. Nurse Svc., Akron, 1988-89; nurse Akron Gen. Med. Ctr., 1989—, clin. mgr. SICU/MICU, 1994—. Mem. Young Adult League, Akron; mem. Annunciation Ch. Choir, Akron, sec., 1989-90, 92—. Mem. Daus. of Penelope (treas. 1988-90). Republican. Greek Orthodox.

MORRIS, NANCY ANNE, psychotherapist; b. Baton Rouge, La., Mar. 16, 1957; d. Gordon Wilkins Sr. and Anne Marie (Mortellaro) M.; m. Mark David Nowakowski, May 20, 1978 (div. Nov. 1988); children: Michael David, Brian Charles, Elaine Gayle. BA, La. State U., 1982; MEd in Mental Health Counseling, U. North Fla., 1989. Lic. mental health counselor. Mental health technician Charter Hosp. of Jacksonville, 1988-89; psychodiagnostician Child Guidance Ctr., Jacksonville, 1989-90; psychotherapist Daniel Meml., Inc., Jacksonville, 1990-93, Devereux & Assocs., Jacksonville, 1992-93, Psychol. Assocs., Jacksonville, 1993—; therapist, intern Child Guidance Ctr., Jacksonville, 1988-89. Mem. ACA. Office: Psychol Assocs 4160 University Blvd S Jacksonville FL 32216-4317

MORRIS, NAOMI CAROLYN MINNER, medical educator, administrator, researcher, consultant; b. Chgo., June 8, 1931; d. Morris George and Carrie Ruth (Auslender) Minner; m. Charles Elliot Morris, June 28, 1951; children: Jonathan Edward, David Carlton. BA magna cum laude, U. Colo., 1952, MD, 1955; MPH magna cum laude, Harvard U., 1959. Diplomate Am. Bd. Preventive Medicine. Rotating intern L.A. County Gen. Hosp., 1955-56; clin. fellow in pediats. Mass. Gen. Hosp., Boston, 1957; pub. health physician Mass. Dept. Health, Boston, 1957-58; clin. pediatrician Norfolk (Va.) King's Daus. Hosp., 1959-61; from asst. prof. to prof. and chair dept. maternal and child health Sch. Pub. Health, U. N.C., Chapel Hill, 1962-77; prof., dir. cmty. pediats. U. Health Scis., Chgo. Med. Sch., 1977-80; prof., dir. cmty. health scis. divsn. Sch. Pub. Health, U. Ill., Chgo., 1980—; mem. liaison com. with Lake County Med. Soc. 1978-80; resource person Ill. 1980 Ho. Conf. on Children, 1979-80; mem. nursing divsn. adv. com. Lake County Health Dept., 1980—; participant Enrich-A-Life series Chgo. Dept. Health, 1984-85, Ill. Health and Hazardous Substance Registry Pregnancy Outcome Task Force, 1984-86; mem. profl. adv. bd. Beethoven Project Ctr. Child Devel., 1986—; mem. planning com. for action to reduce infact mortality Chgo. Inst. Medicine, 1986-89; founding mem. Westside Futures Infant Mortality Network, 1986; mem. Ill. vital stats. supplement Ill. Dept. Pub. Health, 1987; investigator and team leader Rev. Mo. Families Maternal and Child Health State Svcs., 1989; mem. children and youth 2000 task force MacArthur Found., 1992—; active Ill. Caucus on Teenage Pregnancies, 1978—, Chgo. Dept. Health Child Health Task Force, 1982-83, HSC Interprofessional Edn. Com., 1983-84, Med. Task Force Project Life, 1983-88, Women's Studies Curriculum Com., 1985—, Com. Rsch. on Women, 1985—, Mayor's Adv. Com. on Infant Mortality, 1986—, Gov. Adv. Coun. on Infant Mortality, 1988—; cons. pediat. nursing resources group Ill. Dept. Pub. Health, 1983-84; cons. Cook County Hosp. Study of Preventive Childhood Obesity, 1983-84. Author 8 book chpts; contbr. articles to profl. jours. Fellow APHA (mem. task force on adolescence maternal and child health sect. 1977-85, sec. 1979-80, cons. manpower project 1982-83, mem. publ. bd. 1985-87, mem. coun. pediat. rsch. to Am. Acad. Pediats. 1985-92), Am. Coll. Preventive Medicine, Am. Acad. Pediats. (mem. Ill. chpt. com. on sch. health and com. adolescent health 1993—); mem. Ambulatory Pediat. Assn., Assn. Tchrs. Maternal and Child Health (mem. exec. com. 1981-87, mem. com. on tng. and continuing edn. needs of MCH/CCS dirs. 1982-83, mem. liaison com. to fed. DCMH office 1983-87, pres. 1983-85). Office: U Ill Chgo Sch Pub Health 2035 W Taylor St Chicago IL 60612-7257

MORRIS, PHYLLIS SUTTON, philosophy educator; b. Quincy, Ill., Jan. 25, 1931; d. John Guice and Helen Elizabeth (Provis) Sutton; m. John Martin Morris, Feb. 4, 1950; children: William Robert, Katherine Jill. Student, U. Mich., 1948-51; AB, U. Calif., 1953; MA, Colo. Coll., 1963; PhD, U. Mich., 1969. Instr. humanities Mich. State U., East Lansing, 1968-69; from lectr. to assoc. prof. Kirkland Coll., Clinton, N.Y., 1969-78; assoc. prof. Hamilton Coll., Clinton, 1978-83; adj. assoc. prof. LeMoyne Coll., Syracuse, N.Y., 1983-85; vis. prof. philosophy U. Mich., Dearborn, 1985-88; vis. prof. residential coll. U. Mich., Ann Arbor, 1987, 88, vis. scholar, 1991-93; vis. prof. Oberlin (Ohio) Coll., 1989-91, fall 93, 94-95; vis. prof. U. Mich., Dearborn, 1985-88. Author: Sartre's Concept of a Person, 1976; revs. editor Sartre Studies Internat. jour., 1995; contbr. articles to profl. jours. Travel grantee Am. Coun. Learned Socs., 1988, Summer Seminar grantee NEH, 1974, 82. Mem. Am. Philos. Assn., Sartre Cir., Sartre Soc. N.Am. (co-founder 1985, exec. com. 1985-91), Soc. for Phenomenology and Existential Philosophy, Soc. for Women in Philosophy. Democrat. Home: 2116 Runnymede Blvd Ann Arbor MI 48103

MORRIS, REBECCA ROBINSON, lawyer; b. McKinney, Tex., July 27, 1945; d. Leland Howell and Grace Laverne (Stinson) Robinson; m. Jesse Eugene Morris, July 18, 1964; children: Jesse III, Susan, John. BBA in Acctg., So. Meth. U., 1974, JD, 1978. Bar: Tex. 1979, U.S. Dist. Ct. (no. dist.) Tex. Acct. Electronic Data Systems Corp., Dallas, 1975; assoc. atty. Dresser Industries, Inc., Dallas, 1978-81, staff atty., 1981-83, corp. atty., 1983-86, asst. sec., 1984-90, sr. atty. corp. adminstrn., 1986-87, corp. counsel, 1987—, sec., 1990—, v.p., 1994—. Trustee Plano (Tex.) Ind. Sch. Dist., 1979-91, 93-94, pres., 1980-85, sec., 1986-91; bd. dirs. Plano Futures Found., Inc., 1992—, pres., 1992-93. Mem. ABA, AICPA, Tex. State Bar, Dallas Bar Assn., Tex. Soc. CPAs, Am. Soc. Corp. Secs. (mem. securities law com. 1988—, proxy system com. 1990-93, exec. steering com. 1993-94, budget com. 1993—, bd. dirs. 1991-94, chmn. mem. com. Dallas chpt. 1986, treas. 1987, v.p. 1988, pres. 1989), Am. Corp. Counsel Assn. (corp. and securities law com. 1991—). Methodist. Home: 1718 14th Pl Plano TX 75074-6404 Office: Dresser Industries Inc 2001 Ross Ave Box 718 Dallas TX 75221-3610

MORRIS, ROSELYN EVERTS, accountant, educator; b. Dallas, May 9, 1951; d. Frank and Jimmie Etta (Mayfield) Everts Jr.; m. William Walter Morris, Aug. 3, 1973 (div. Mar. 3, 1987); children: Rachel Adelicia, Ruth Marie. BS in Math., Tex. Christian U., 1973; MS in Accountancy, U. Houston, 1975, PhD in Acctg., 1993. CPA, Tex. Programming analyst Singer Simulation, Houston, 1973-74; teaching fellow U. Houston, 1974-75; sr. acct. Arthur Andersen & Co., Houston, 1975-77; v.p., controller Delta Savs., Alvin, Tex., 1977-79; owner, CPA Roselyn E. Morris, CPA, Missouri City, Tex., 1979-93; teaching fellow U. Houston, 1989-93; asst. prof. acctg. S.W. Tex. State U., San Marcos, 1993—; cons. in field. Acct./vol. Operation Rainbow, Sugarland, Tex., 1991-93, Variety Club, Houston, 1990-93; founder Limbs of Love, Houston, 1988—. Arthur Anderson scholar, 1991, Assn. of Govtl. Accts./U. Houston scholar, 1990. Mem. AICPAs, Tex. Soc. CPAs, Am. Acctg. Assn., Beta Gamma Sigma, Beta Alpha Psi, Kappa Delta. Home: 210 E Mimosa Cir San Marcos TX 78666-3708 Office: SW Tex State Univ 601 University Dr San Marcos TX 78666

MORRIS, SHARON LOUISE STEWART, day care provider; b. Washington, Feb. 9, 1956; d. George Arthur Jr. and Shirley Ann (Dickinson) S.; m. Brian Stanley Morris, Feb. 9, 1979; children: Jessica Kristin, Krystle Maria. BS, Atlantic Christian Coll., Wilson, N.C., 1978. Cert. tchr. elem. edn. and math., N.C. Cashier Safeway Fin., Wilson, 1980-81; cashier Provident Fin., Wilson, 1981-85; mktg. svc. mgr. Beneficial of N.C. Inc., Wilson, 1985-91; ind. carrier Wilson Daily Times, 1991-94; care provider Crestview Day Sch., Wilson, 1994—; agt. Cen. Nat. Life Ins., Wilson, 1988-91, Olde Republic, 1990. Notary pub. State of N.C., 1986—. Democrat. Methodist. Home: 1201 Herring Ave NE Wilson NC 27893-3319

MORRIS, SYLVIA MARIE, university official; b. Laurel, Miss., May 6, 1952; d. Earlene Virginia (Cameron) Hopkins Stewart; m. James D. Morris, Jan. 29, 1972; children: Cedric James, Taedra Janae. Student, U. Utah, 1970-71. From adminstrv. sec. to adminstrv. mgr. mech. engring. U. Utah, Salt Lake City, 1972—. Mem. Community Devel. Adv. Bd., Salt Lake City, Utah, 1984—; nom. chmn. and del. to Dem. Mass Meeting, 1988. Recipient Presdl. Staff award, 1994. Mem. NAACP, NAFE, Consortium Utah Women in Higher Edn. Baptist. Home: 1500 N 1500 W Salt Lake City UT 84116-2027 Office: U Utah 3209 MEB Mech Engr Dept Salt Lake City UT 84112

MORRIS ARCHINAL, GRETCHEN SUZANNE, transportation executive, consultant; b. Detroit, May 8, 1963; d. Richard Frederic and Betty Jean (McNaughton) M.; m. Thomas O. Archinal, Nov. 30, 1991; 1 child, Margaret Kelly. BA, U. Mich., 1985; postgrad., Ctr. for Creative Studies, 1987. Account exec. JL Communications, St. Clair Shores, Mich., 1985-87, sr. account exec., 1987-88; pres. Metro Messenger, Grosse Pointe Woods, Mich., 1988—; owner M Graphics, Grosse Pointe Woods, 1988—; real estate agt. R.G. Edgar & Assocs., Grosse Pointe Farms, 1981-88, cons., 1988—; cons. Mack Ave USA, Grosse Pointe, 1988—. Mem. Hill Assn., Grosse Pointe, 1989—; bd. dirs. Mack Ave USA, 1988-89. Mem. Metro E. C. of C., Grosse Pointe Theatre. Republican. Lutheran. Home: 1403 Nottingham Rd Grosse Pointe MI 48230-1028 Office: Metro Messenger Inc 18720 Mack Ave Ste 230 Grosse Pointe MI 48236-2923

MORRISON, ALBA MARIE, social service agency executive; b. Aug. 25, 1926. B.S. with honors, U. Ark., 1953; M.S.W., Tulane U., 1958. Cert. social worker, N.Y.; lic. social worker, Okla. Tchr. high sch. English, Bradford Sch. Bd., Ark., 1953-54; caseworker La. Dept. Pub. Welfare Bur. for Blind and Sight Conservation, Baton Rouge, 1955-57, 58-61; dir. social services Blind Assn. Central Ohio, Inc., Columbus, 1961-66, acting dir., 1966; regional cons. Am. found. for Blind, Inc., N.Y.C., 1966-73; pvt. practice cons. and family counseling, Tulsa, 1975—; organizer, exec. dir. New View, Inc., Tulsa, 1980—; bd. dirs. League for Blind, Oklahoma City, 1974-80; bd. dirs., v.p., treas. Okla. Council of Blind; past del. White House Confs. on Handicapped; past mem. Okla. Coalition Citizens with Disabilities, Am. Coalition Citizens with Disabilities; past mem. adv. bd. Nat. Pub. Radio, Print Handicapped Services; past pres. consumer adv. bd. Dept. Human Services; past mem. Health Systems Agy. Bd.; past del. Affiliated Leadership League Agys. Serving Blind and Orgns. of Blind. Mem. Acad. Cert. Social Workers, Nat. Assn. Social Workers, Nat. Assn. Workers for Blind, U. Ark. Alumni Assn., Tulane U. Alumni Assn. Office: New View Inc 6734 E 51st Pl Tulsa OK 74145-7601

MORRISON, CONSTANCE FAITH, state legislator, realtor; b. Washington; d. Graham Edward and Cora E. (Smith) Wilson; m. George H. Morrison, May 14, 1955; 4 children. AA, Normandale C.C., 1980. Photojournalist Dakota County Tribune, 1970-76; pub. affairs writer, pub. info. coord. Ind. Sch. Dist. 191, 1976-80; ind. realtor, 1980—; mem. I-R caucus Minn. Ho. of Reps., 1981—; sec.-treas. I-R caucus, 1993-94; mem. Minn. Ho. of Reps., 1986-94. co-chairwoman Com. to Elect Rep. Women, St. Paul, 1987-91; mem. Burnsville City Coun., 1977-82; mayor City of Burnsville, 1982-86, chairwoman chem. health com., 1987-92; chair adminstrv. bd. Grace United Meth. Ch., Burnsville, 1986-90; bd. dirs. Minn. League Cities, 1983-86, Mpls. Area United Way, 1988—. Mem. Burnsville C. of C., Rotary. Home: 909 W 155th St Burnsville MN 55306-9999

MORRISON, DEBORAH JEAN, lawyer; b. Johnstown, Pa., Feb. 18, 1955; d. Ralph Wesley and Norma Jean (Kinsey) Morrison; m. Ricardo Daniel Kamenetzky, Sept. 6, 1978 (div. Nov. 1991); children: Elena Raquel, Julia Rebecca. BA in Polit. Sci., Chatham Coll., 1977; postgrad., U. Miami, Fla., 1977-78; JD, U. Pitts., 1981. Bar: Pa. 1981, Ill. 1985. Legal asst. Klein Y Mairal, Buenos Aires, Argentina, 1978-79; legal intern Neighborhood Legal Svcs., Aliquippa, Pa., 1980-81; law clk. Pa. Superior Ct., Pitts., 1981-84; atty. John Deere Credit Co., Moline, Ill., 1985-89; sr. atty. Deere & Co., Moline, Ill., 1989—. Mem. ABA, Pa. Bar Assn., Phi Beta Kappa, Order of the Coif. Democrat. Mem. United Methodist. Office: Deere & Co John Deere Rd Moline IL 61265

MORRISON, DIANE MARIE, social psychologist, researcher; b. N.Y.C., Sept. 23, 1950; d. Charles Cheever and Marie Theresa (Lowe) M.; m. Joel C. Bradbury, Jan. 1, 1981; 1 child, Alexandra Lynn Bradbury. BA, Reed Coll., 1974; MS, U. Wash., 1979, PhD, 1982. Rsch. assoc. dept. psychology U. Wash., Seattle, 1983-87, rsch. asst. prof. Sch. Social Work, 1988-92, rsch. assoc. prof. Sch. Social Work, 1992—. Contbr. book chpt.: Advances in Adolescent Mental Health, 1990; contbr. articles to profl. jours. Rsch. grantee Nat. Inst. Child Health and Human Devel., 1984, Nat. Inst. Allergy and Infectious Diseases, 1989, 91, NIMH, 1990, 93, Nat. Inst. Drug Abuse, 1991. Mem. APA, Population Assn. Am. Office: U Wash Sch Social Work JH-30 Seattle WA 98195

MORRISON, GLADYS MAE, pilot training firm executive; b. Balmorhea, Tex., Jan. 5, 1928; d. James Henry and Alice Vivian (Totter) Walk; m. James Martin Morrison, Nov. 25, 1957 (dec. June 1988). Cert. master aviation instr. Pntr., mgr. Davis Flying Svc., Concord, Calif., 1946-56, Desert Air Oasis, Thermal, Calif., 1957-62; asst. mgr. flight dept. Beechcraft West, Van Nuys, Calif., 1962-64; dir. publs. Fowler Aeronautics, aviation textbook pubs., Burbank, Calif., 1964-65; owner-mgr. Aviation Tng., Prescott, Ariz., 1965—; chief-pilot North-Aire, Inc., Prescott, 1974-86, pres., 1988—, bd. dirs.; instr. FAA approved flight engring. sch. Fowler Aeronautics, Burbank, 1964-65. Author aviation text books; contbr. articles to newspapers and mags. Named Nat. Flight Instr. of Yr. FAA, 1982, FAA Western-Pacific Flight Instr. of Yr., 1982, Ariz. Flight Instr. of Yr. FAA, 1982; recipient Cert. of Recognition, Fedn. Aero Nautique Internat., Paris, 1982. Mem. Aircraft Owner & Pilot Assn. (Master Flight Instr. award 1983), Nat. Assn. Flight Instrs. (Flights Inst. of Yr. 1982), Ninety-Nines, Inc., Silver Wings Fraternity, Alpha Eta Rho (hon.). Republican. Office: North-Aire Inc Prescott Mcpl Airport 6500 MacCurdy Dr Ste 7 Prescott AZ 86301

MORRISON, HARRIET BARBARA, education educator; b. Boston, Feb. 23, 1934; d. Harry and Harriet (Hanrahan) M. BS, Mass. State Coll., Boston, 1956, MEd, 1958; EdD, Boston U., 1967. Elem. tchr. Arlington (Mass.) Pub. Schs., 1956-67, U. Mass., summer 1967; asst. prof. No. Ill. U., De Kalb, 1967-71, assoc. prof. edn., 1971-85, prof. edn., 1985—. Author book The Seven Gifts, 1988; editor Vitae Scholasticae. Mem. ASCD, Am. Ednl. Studies Assn., Philosophy of Edn. Soc., Midwest Philosophy Edn. Soc., Ill. Assn. Supervision and Curriculum Devel., Pi Lambda Theta. Home: 834 S 8th St De Kalb IL 60115-4551 Office: No Ill U Coll Edn De Kalb IL 60115

MORRISON, JENNIFER ANN, lawyer, oil company executive; b. Providence, Feb. 22, 1956; d. John Stepehn McKnight and Mary Morrison. BA in Polit. Sci., Oakland U., 1976; JD, U. Okla., 1980. Bar: Okla. 1980, Tex. 1988, U.S. Ct. Appeals (5th, 10th, 11th and D.C. cirs.) 1981, U.S. Supreme Ct 1983, U.S. Ct. Appeals (8th cir.) 1985, U.S. Dist. Ct. (no. dist.) Okla. 1986, U.S. Dist. Ct. (so. dist.) Tex. 1994. Atty. Phillips Petroleum Co., Bartlesville, Okla., 1980-88; counsel BP Exploration Inc., Houston, 1988-90; v.p., gen. counsel, sec. Tex./Con Oil & Gas Co., Houston, 1990-92, Plains Mktg. and Transp., Inc., Houston, 1992-93; pvt. practice Houston, 1993—; apptd. by gov. to Commn. on Oil and Gas Practices, 1990-91; mem. legal subcom. Offshore Operators, 1983-87. Editor U. Okla. Law Rev., 1978-80. Pres., adv. council Retired Sr. Vol. Program, Bartlesville, 1982-88; bd. dirs. Bluestem Girl Scout Council, Bartlesville, 1982-88, SunFest, Inc., Bartlesville, 1984-88. Mem. ABA (royalty task force 1983), Okla. Bar Assn., Fed. Energy Bar Assn. (commn. on devel. of fed. lands 1989-90, sec. Houston chpt. 1991-92, pres. Houston chpt. 1992-93, vice chair environ. com. 1992-93), Am. Petroleum Inst. (royalty task force 1983-88), Ind. Petroleum Assn. Am. (natural gas com. 1990-93), Tex. Ind. Petroleum Assn., Natural Gas Supply Assn. (legal subcom. 1988-92), Tex. Mid-Continent Oil and Gas Assn. (legal subcom. 1990-92), Am. Corp. Counsel Assn. (chair Houston chpt. oil and gas com. 1992-93, asst. chair litigation com. 1991-92), Pilot Internat. (coord. 1985-88), Phi Alpha Delta. Office: 9801 Westheimer Rd Ste 602 Houston TX 77042

MORRISON, K. JAYDENE, education counseling firm executive; b. Cherokee, Okla., Aug. 22, 1933; d. Jay Frank and Kathryn D. (Johnson) Walker; m. Michael H. Morrison, Aug. 11, 1955; children: Jay, Mac. B.S., Okla. State U., 1955, M.S., 1957; postgrad. U. Colo., 1965, Central State U., Okla., 1968-70, 84, U. Denver, 1981-82. Lic. coun., Okla.; lic. marriage and family therapist; cert. sch. psycologist; cert. counselor. Psychologist, Okla. Tchr., Cushing Pub. Schs., Okla., 1955-57, Indpls. Pub. Schs., 1958-59; counselor, tchr. spl. edn. Helena-Goltry Pub. Schs., Okla., 1965-73; psychometrist Okla. State Title III Program, Alva, 1974-75; sch. psychologist Okla. State Dept. Edn., Enid, 1977-85; pres., dir. Ventures in Learning, Inc., Helena, 1984—, career counselor, Oklahoma City, 1985-86, rural specialist Okla. Conf. Chs. AG LINK, 1986-88, v.p., sec./treas. Okla. Made, Inc., Oklahoma City, 1988-89; sch. psychologist Okla. City Pub. Schs., 1988-93, therapist and pub. sch. liaison Chisholm Trail Counseling Svc., 1993—; coord. Statewide Farm Stress Program, 1994—; therapist Greenleaf Drug/Alcohol Rehab., 1988-89; sec., treas. Okla. Pure; part-time counselor Clayton Clinic, 1987-89; cons.

Okla. Family Inst., 1990—. Author: Coping with ADD/ADHD, 1995; co-author: Coping With a Learning Disability, 1992. Chmn., Alfalfa County Excise and Equalization Bd., Cherokee, 1979-83; asst. state coord. Okla. Am. Agr. Movement, Oklahoma City, 1982-83; counselor, United Meth. Counseling Ctr., 1987-88; co-chmn. Alfalfa County Democratic party, Cherokee, 1976-83, sec.-treas. 6th Dist. Okla. Dem. State Exec. Bd., 1983-87. Recipient Tchr. of Yr. award Helena Masonic Lodge, 1967, Spl. award Okla. Women for Agr., 1979; named Citizen of Yr., Okla. chpt. Nat. Assn. Social Workers, 1988. Mem. Biofeedback Soc. Am., Okla. Soc. for Advancement Biofeedback, Nat. Assn. Sch. Psychologists, Okla. Sch. Psychologists Assn., Garfield County Interagy. Task Force, Okla. Assn. Learning Disabilities, Delta Kappa Gamma, Chi Omega Alumni. Elder Christian Ch. Office: 3905 NE 143d St Edmond OK 73013

MORRISON, LILLIAN, writer, retired librarian; b. Jersey City, Oct. 27, 1917; d. William and Rebecca (Nehamkin) M. BS in Math., Douglass Coll., 1938; BS in Libr. Svc., Columbia U., 1942. Mem. staff N.Y. Pub. Libr., N.Y.C., 1942-47, specialist vocat. h.s., 1947-52, asst. coord. young adult svcs., 1952-68, coord. young adult svcs., 1968-82; lectr. Columbia Grad. Sch. Libr. Sci., 1960-61, Rutgers U., 1961; gen. editor Crowell Poets Series and Poems of the World Series, 1964-74; poetry editor Film Libr. Quar., N.Y.C., 1968-75. Author: (poetry) The Ghosts of Jersey City, 1967, The Sidewalk Racer, 1977, Who Would Marry a Mineral?, 1978, The Break Dance Kids, 1985, Whistling the Morning In, 1992, others, (folk rhyme collections) Yours Till Niagara Falls, 1950, A Diller, A Dollar, 1955, Touch Blue, 1958, Remember Me When This You See, 1961, Best Wishes, Amen, 1974, others; (anthologies) Sprints and Distances, 1965 (Notable Children's Book 1965), Rhythm Road, 1988 (Notable Children's Book 1988), At the Crack of the Bat, 1992. Recipient Grolier award for contbns. to young people's interest in reading ALA, 1987. Mem. PEN, Authors League, Poets House, Phi Beta Kappa.

MORRISON, MARCY, state legislator; b. Watertown, N.Y., Aug. 9, 1935; m. Howard Morrison; children: Liane, Brenda. BA, Queens Coll., 1957; student, Colo. Coll., U. Colo. Mem. Colo. Ho. of Reps., awd, 1992—; mem. judiciary, health, environ., welfare and instns. coms. Mem. Manitou Springs (Colo.) Sch. Bd., 1973-83, pres., 1980-82, County Park Bd., 1976-83, State Bd. Health, 1985-93, pres., 1988-90, Mountain Scar Commn., 1989, Future Pub. Health, 1989-90, Health Policy Commn., 1990-92; commr. El Paso County, 1985-92, chmn., 1987-89; active Citizens Goals, United Way. Named Outstanding Sch. Bd. Mem., Pikes Peak Tchrs. Assn., 1978, Woman of Spirit, Penrose-St. Francis Hosp. Sys., 1991. Mem. LWV, Health Assn. Pikes Peake Area, Women's Edn. Assn., El Paso Mental Health Assn. Republican. Jewish. Home: 302 Sutherland Pl Manitou Springs CO 80829 Office: Colo Ho of Reps State Capitol Denver CO 80203*

MORRISON, MARTHA KAYE, photolithography engineer; b. San Jose, Calif., Oct. 5, 1955; d. Myrle K. and Arthena R. Morrison; 1 child, Katherine A. AA, West Valley Coll., Saratoga, Calif., 1978. Prodn. worker Signetics Co., Sunnyvale, Calif., 1973-75, equipment engr., 1976-78, 79-80, prodn. supr., 1978-79; expediter Monolithic Memories, Sunnyvale, 1975-76; photolithography engr. KTI Chems., 1980-81; founder, chief engr., CEO Optalign, Inc., Livermore, Forest Ranch, Calif., 1981—; instr. tennis Chico Racquet Club, 1994, Butte Creek Country Club, 1995—; participant exhbn. tennis match with Rosie Cosals and Billie Jean King, 1994. Named Champion Chico Open Finalist Woodridge Open, 1994, 1993 #2 NCTA Women's Doubles. Mem. USPTA (cert.). Office: PO Box 718 Forest Ranch CA 95942-0718

MORRISON, MARY JO, physical education educator; b. Bloomington, Ill., May 18, 1949; d. Frances Lundy and Leona Katherine (Arnold) M. BS, Ill. State U., 1972, MS, 1975, cert. advanced study, 1985, EdD, 1987. Cert. educator phys. edn., gen. supervisory, adminstrv., gen. elem. Elem. phys. edn. specialist Bloomington (Ill.) Pub. Sch. Dist. #87, 1972-77, tchr. driver edn., coach, 1977-82, high sch. phys. edn. tchr., coach, 1982-87, asst. elem. phys. edn. specialist, 1988-90, early childhood program coord., 1990-92, asst. prin., 1990-92, elem. adminstrv. aide, 1992-93, elem. phys. edn. specialist, 1992—; presenter confs. IAHPERD, Chgo., Peoria, Ill., 1989-93, Chpt. I, Chgo., 1992; grant writer Bloomington (Ill.) Dist. #87, 1990, co-developer computer programs for fitness data. Contbr. articles to profl. jours. Vol. McLean County Humane Soc., Bloomington, 1993—. Mem. ASCD, NEA, Ill. Edn. Assn., Ill. Assn. Health, Phys. Edn., Recreation & Dance (Ea. Dist. Phys. Educator of Yr. 1993), Ill. Assn. Supervision and Curriculum Devel., Bloomington Edn. Assn., Phi Delta Kappa. Home: 101 S Orr Dr Normal IL 61761-3221 Office: Bloomington Pub Sch Dist 300 E Monroe St # 87 Bloomington IL 61701-4028

MORRISON, MICHELLE WILLIAMS, nursing educator, administrator, author; b. Reno, Nev., Feb. 12, 1947; d. Robert James and Dolores Jane (Barnard) Williams; m. Harrison Russell Morrison, Dec. 29, 1974. BSN, U. Nev., Reno, 1973; M Health Svc., U. Calif., Davis, 1977. RN, Oreg. Staff nurse VA Hosp., Reno, 1973-77; family nurse practitioner Tri-County Indian Health Svc., Bishop, Calif., 1977-78; instr. nursing Roque C.C., Grants Pass, Oreg., 1978-82; psychiat. nurse VA Hosp., Roseburg, Oreg., 1982; dir. edn. Josephine Meml. Hosp., Grants Pass, 1983-84; geriatric nurse practitioner Hearthstone Manor, Medford, Oreg., 1984-86; chmn. nursing dept. Roque Community Coll., Grants Pass, Oreg., 1986-89; prin. Health and Ednl. Cons., Grants Pass, 1989—; dir. nursing Highland House Nursing Ctr., Grants Pass, 1990; bd. dirs. Tri-County Indian Health Svc. Author: Professional Skills for Leadership; contbr. Basic Skills for Nursing. Mem. Josephine County Coalition for AIDS, Grants Pass, 1990. With USN, 1965-69. Mem. NAFE, Nat. League Nursing, Oreg. Ednl. Assn., Oreg. State Bd. Nursing (re-entry nursing com. 1992-93). Office: PO Box 89 Williams OR 97544-0089

MORRISON, PATRICE B., lawyer; b. St. Louis, July 8, 1948; d. Frank J. and Loretta (S.) Burgert; m. William Brian Morrison, Aug. 12, 1969; 1 child, W. Brett. AB, U. Miami, 1971, MA, 1972; JD, Am. U., 1975; LLM in Taxation, Georgetown U., 1978. Bar: Fla. 1975, D.C. 1977, N.Y. 1983. Atty. U.S. Dept. Treas., Washington, 1975-79; atty., ptnr. Nixon Hargrave Devans & Doyle, Palm Beach County, Fla., 1980-89, Rochester, N.Y., 1989—. Author: (jour.) The Practical Lawyer, 1986, 91. Bd. dirs. Linden Knoll, Inc., Rochester, 1991—, Alzheimer's Assn., Rochester, 1990—, Nat. Women's Hall of Fame, 1990-92; mem. Rochester Women's Network; mem. exec. com. Estate Planning Coun. Rochester, 1992—. Mem. Am. Immigration Lawyers Assn. Republican. Office: Nixon Hargrave Devans & Doyle PO Box 1051 Clinton Sq Rochester NY 14603

MORRISON, PORTIA OWEN, lawyer; b. Charlotte, N.C., Apr. 1, 1944; d. Robert Hall Jr. and Josephine Currier (Hutchison) M.; m. Alan Peter Richmond, June 19, 1976; 1 child, Anne Morrison. BA in English, Agnes Scott Coll., 1966; MA, U. Wis., 1967; JD, U. Chgo., 1978. Bar: Ill. 1978. Ptnr. Rudnick & Wolfe, Chgo., 1978—, also chmn. real estate dept., mem. governing policy com.; lectr. in field. Mem. ABA, Am. Coll. Real Estate Lawyers, Chgo. Bar Assn. (real property com., subcom. real property fin., alliance for women), Pension Real Estate Assn., Chgo. Fin. Exch. Office: Rudnick & Wolfe 203 N La Salle St Ste 1800 Chicago IL 60601-1210

MORRISON, SHELLEY, actress; b. N.Y.C., Oct. 26, 1936; d. Maurice Nissim and Hortense (Alcouloumre) Mitrani; m. Walter R. Dominguez, Aug. 11, 1973. Student, L.A. City Coll., 1954-56. Actress: (films) Interns, 1962, The Greatest Story Ever Told, 1964, Castle of Evil, 1965, Divorce, American Style, 1965, How to Save a Marriage, 1966, Funny Girl, 1967, Three Guns for Texas, 1969, Man & Boy, 1971, Blume in Love, 1972, McKenna's Gold, 1967, Breezy, 1973, People Toys, 1973, Rabbit Test, 1975, Max Dugan Returns, 1982, Troop Beverly Hills, 1988, (TV movies) Three's a Crowd, 1969, Once an Eagle, 1974, The Night That Panicked America, 1975, Kids Don't Tell, 1984Cries From the Heart, 1994, (TV series) Laredo, 1965-67, The Flying Nun, 1966-70, First and Ten, 1987, I'm Home, 1990, The Fanelli Boys, 1990, Love, Lies and Murder, 1990, Playhouse 90, Dr. Kildare, The Fugitive, Gunsmoke, Marcus Welby, and many others, 1960-70, Man of the People, Sisters, 1991, 92, Murder She Wrote, 1992, Johnny Bago, 1993, Columbo, 1993, L.A. Law, 1994, numerous others, (stage prodns.) Pal Joey, 1956, Bus Stop, 1956, Only in America, 1960, Orpheus Descending, 1960, Spring's Awakening, 1962, over 65 other prodns., 1956-1970; prodr., writer live shorts, 1975—. Condr. seminars (with husband Walter Dominquez) about Native Americans to keep traditions and ceremonies flourishing. Honored (with husband Walter Dominguez) for work with homeless City of L.A., 1985, for work during L.A. riots, 1992. Mem. SAG, AFTRA, Actors Equity Assn. Democrat.

MORRISON, TONI (CHLOE ANTHONY MORRISON), novelist; b. Lorain, Ohio, Feb. 18, 1931; d. George and Ella Ramah (Willis) Wofford; m. Harold Morrison, 1958 (div. 1964); children: Harold Ford, Slade Kevin. B.A., Howard U., 1953; M.A., Cornell U., 1955. Tchr. English and humanities Tex. So. U., 1955-57, Howard U., 1957-64; editor Random House, N.Y.C., 1965—; assoc. prof. English SUNY, Purchase, NY, 1971-72; Schweitzer Prof. of the Humanities SUNY, Albany, NY, 1984-89; Robert F. Goheen Prof. of the Humanities Princeton Univ., Princeton, NJ, 1989—; Visiting prof., Yale Univ., 1976-77, Bard Coll., 1986-88. Author: The Bluest Eye, 1969, Sula, 1973 (National Book award nomination 1975, Ohioana Book award 1975), Song of Solomon, 1977 (National Book Critics Circle award 1977, American Acad. and Inst. of Arts and Letters award 1977), Tar Baby, 1981, (play) Dreaming Emmett, 1986, Beloved, 1987 (Pulitzer Prize for fiction 1988, Robert F. Kennedy Book award 1988, Melcher Book award Unitarian Universalist Assn. 1988, National Book award nomination 1987, National Book Critics Circle award nomination 1987), Jazz, 1992, Playing in the Dark: Whiteness and the Literary Imagination, 1992, Nobel Prize Speech, 1994; editor: The Black Book, 1974, Race-ing Justice, En-Gendering Power: Essays on Anita Hill, Clarence Thomas, and the Construction of Social Reality, 1992; lyricist: Honey and Rue, 1992. Recipient New York State Governor's Art award, 1986; Washington College Literary award, 1987; Elizabeth Cady Stanton award National Organization for Women; Nobel prize in Literature Nobel Foundation, 1993. Mem. Author's Guild (council). Office: Princeton U Dept Creative Writing 185 Nassau St Princeton NJ 08544-2095 also: care Suzanne Gluck Internat Creative Mgmt 40 W 57th St New York NY 10019*

MORRISS, MARY RACHEL, art educator, painter; b. Memphis; d. William Dale and Lizzie Henrie (Woodward) M. BS, Memphis U., 1927; post-grad., U. Colo., 1931, 34, 37, 40; various art workshops Maxine Masterfield, 1983, 84. Cert. high sch. tchr., Tenn. Tchr., Bellevue Sch., Memphis, 1936-66; ret.; pvt. art classes, Memphis, 1966—; mem. Friends Memphis Brooks Meml. Art Gallery. Represented by Paul Edelstein Gallery, Memphis; one woman shows include Parthenon Galleries, Nashville, Comm. Appeal, Memphis, 1989, Paul Edelstein Gallery, 1991, numerous others; exhibited in group juried shows Cen. South Parthenon, Nashville, Hunter Ann. Show, Delta Annual, Little Rock, Mid-Am., Owensboro, Ky., 1979, Mid-South Memphis Brooks Gallery, So. Watercolor Soc., 1983, 86, 89, 90, Patrons' Watercolor Gala, Oklahoma City, 1983, 84, Tenn. Watercolor Soc. Annual Traveling Show, 1980-82, 84, 88, 90, Ga. Watercolor Soc., 1986, 94, So. Watercolor, 1989 (Merit award), J.J. White Meml. Watercolor, 1989, Juried Exhbn., 1988, 89, 90, 91, 92, 93, 94, So. Exposure, 1990, 91, Experimental Artists Juried Show, Sarasota, Fla., 1992, Ga. Watercolor Soc. Nat. Juried Show, 1994, and many others; represented in numerous pub. and pvt. collections. Recipient Best Cotton Design award Memphis Brooks Mus.; Purchase prize Mid-South Fair, 1971, Best in Show and 1st in watercolors, 1985, 86, 1st in watercolors and other media, 1987, 88, 90, Mid South Fair, 1991, 93, 2nd. in water media, 1994; 2d prize J.J. White 1988, Meml. Watercolor juried exhbn., Doochin of Madison award Central South, 1984, award Germantown Art League, 1991, Juror's Choice award, 1992, Best in Show, Tenn. Forest Festival, 1994, and many other awards. Mem. Tenn. Watercolor Soc. (David Wade Meml. award 1988, artist mem.), So. Watercolor Soc. (signature mem., merit award 1989), Soc. of Experimental Artists, Friends of Dixon Gallery, Memphis Watercolor Soc., Ga. Watercolor Soc. Presbyterian. Home: 4819 Parkside Ave Memphis TN 38117-6215

MORROW, CHERYLLE ANN, accountant, bankruptcy, consultant; b. Sydney, Australia, July 3, 1950; came to U.S., 1973; d. Norman H. and Esther A. E. (Jarrett) Wilson. Student, U. Hawaii, 1975; diploma Granville Tech. Coll., Sydney, 1967. Acct., asst. treas. Bus. Investment, Ltd., Honolulu, 1975-77; owner Lanikai Musical Instruments, Honolulu, 1980-86, Cherylle A. Morrow Profl. Svcs., Honolulu, 1981—; fin. managerial cons. E.A. Buck Co., Inc., Honolulu, 1981-84; contr., asst. trustee THC Fin. Corp., Honolulu, 1977-84, bankruptcy trustee, 1984-92; v.p., sec., treas. Innervation, Inc., 1989—; panel mem. Chpt. 7 Trustees dist. Hawaii U.S. Depart. Justice, 1988-91; co-chair Small Bus. Hawaii Legislative Action Com., 1990-92. Mem. Small Bus. Hawaii PAC, Lanikai Community Assn., Arts Coun. Hawaii; vol., mem. Therapeutic Horsemanship for Handicapped, program chair, 1990-92, vice chair, 1990—; vol., mem. Small Bus. Adminstrn. Women in Bus. Com. 1987—, vice and program chair, 1990—; vol. tax preparer IRS VITA, 1990—. Mem. AARP (vol. tax preparer TCE 1991—), NAFE, Australian-Am. C. of C. (bd. dir. 1985-92, corp. sec. 1986-92, v.p. 1988-92), Pacific Islands Assn. Women (corp. sec./treas. 1988-90), Pacific Islands Assn. (asst. treas. 1988—). Avocations: reading, music, dancing, sailing, gardening. Office: Innervation, Inc 145 Hekili St Ste 300 Kailua HI 96734-2804

MORROW, ELIZABETH, business owner, sculptress, museum association administrator, educator; b. Sibley, Mo., Feb. 28, 1947; d. Elman A. and Lorine (Hostetter) Morrow; married, 1970 (div. 1979); children: Jan Pawel, Lorentz Arthur. Student, William Jewell Coll., 1958-59, Colo. Coll., 1959-60, U. Okla., 1960-62; BFA, U. Kans., 1964, MFA, 1967; postgrad., U. Minn., 1965, U. Kans., 1968. Pres. E. Morrow Co., Kansas City, Mo., 1966-67; head dept. art U. Hawaii, Honolulu, 1968-69, Tarkio (Mo.) Coll., 1970-74; exec. dir. Pensacola (Fla.) Mus. Art, 1974-76; pres., owner Blair-Murrah Exhbns., Sibley, Mo., 1980—; pres. bd. trustees, chief exec. officer Blair-Murrah Found., Inc., 1991—. Del. White House Conf. on Small Bus., 1986. Lew Wentz scholar U. Okla., 1960-62. Mem. AAUW, Internat. Coun. of Mus., Internat. Coun. Exhbn. Exch., Internat. Soc. Appraisers, Am. Assn. Mus., Nat. Orgn. of Women Bus. Owners, Nat. Assn. Mus. Exhibitions, Ft. Osage Hist. Soc., Friends Art, Internat. Com. Fine Arts, Internat. Com. Conservation, Internat. Sculpture Ctr., DAR, Delta Phi Delta. Republican. Home: Vintage Hill Orch Sibley MO 64088 Office: Blair-Murrah Vintage Hill Orch Sibley MO 64088 also: 7 rue Muzy, PO Box Nr 554, 1211 Geneva 6 Switzerland

MORROW, SUSAN DAGMAR, psychic, educator, writer, consultant; b. Harrisburg, Pa., July 10, 1932; d. William Lime and Margaret Louise (Deckard) Brubaker; m. Henry Taylor Morrow, June 9, 1952 (div. Mar. 1984); children: Quenby Anne, Christopher Brian. Student Carnegie Inst. Tech., 1950-52, U. Ariz., 1952-54, U. Calif., Berkeley Ext., 1960-72, Foothill Coll., 1980-81. Self-employed psychic, psychic tchr., Palo Alto, Calif., 1976-80, Mountain View, Calif., 1980—; medium, psychic, tchr. Seekers Quest Profl. Ctr., San Jose, Calif., 1983—; tchr. Sunnyvale Community Ctr., 1977-87; tchr. San Andreas Health Coun., Palo Alto, 1981-83; lectr. U. Calif., Berkeley, 1978, Foothill Coll., Los Altos, Calif., 1980; lectr. in field; medium, cons. in cases of mental disorientation to psychologists, Palo Alto and Mountain View, 1978—, to detectives and police in cases of missing persons, animals or property, 1983—, pvt. tutor, cons. past lives, archeological information, 1990—. Contbr. articles on psychic awareness to various publs. Mem. Assn. Psychic Practitioners (co-founder, v.p. 1982-83, editor and writer newsletter 1982-83), Assn. Rsch. and Enlightenment, Inst. Noetic Sci., Friends of the Animals. Democrat. Methodist. Avocations: physical mediumship, painting, swimming, sailing.

MORROW, SUSAN H., interior designer; b. Bklyn., Aug. 27, 1943; d. Murray and Roslyn (Benjamin-Polsky) Chalkin; m. Robert Morrow (div.); children: Christopher, Andrew. BFA, Syracuse U., 1964; MA, NYU, 1965; cert. Post Coll. With Bagatelle Assocs., Roslyn, N.Y., 1972-74, The Wallpaper Place, Roslyn, 1974-75, Trio Designs, Huntington, N.Y., 1975-80, SHS Designs, Inc., North Hills, N.Y., 1980—; designer Designs For ..., Manhasset, N.Y., 1981—, ptnr., 1982—; pres. Wallpapers and ..., 1985—; designer Cinderella Project, Bklyn. Union Gas Urban Renewal, 1979, Human Resources, Ind. Living Project, 1982—; designer Designs For..., Roslyn, N.Y.; designer and converter Class Reunion, 1987. Designer Showcase Mansions; contbr. articles to mags. Co-chairperson budget adv. com. Roslyn Schs.; v.p. Norgate Civic Assn., Roslyn. Named Woman of Yr., Hadassah, 1974. Mem. Am. Soc. Interior Designers, 110 Assn. Profl. Women, Assn. Environ. Designers, Mensa, Internat. Platform Assn., LWV (v.p.). Home: PO Box H Sea Cliff NY 11579-0707 Office: Designs For 24 Skillman St Roslyn NY 11576-1183

MORROW, SUSAN LYNNE, psychology educator; b. Baton Rouge, Nov. 18, 1942; d. Howard Marvin and Helen Estella (Morrow) Rodekohr; divorced; children: Andrei Paul, Christina Carla. BA, Concordia Tcrhs. Coll., River Forest, Ill., 1966; M of Counseling, Ariz. State U., 1978, PhD in Counseling Psychology, 1992. Tchr. elem. Luth. Schs., St. Louis and Detroit, 1966-69; educator Am. Soc. Psychoprophylaxis in Obstectrics, Long Beach, Calif., 1970-77; teaching asst. Mesa (Ariz.) C.C., 1976-79; faculty assoc. Ariz. State U., Tempe, 1978-85, 92-93, grad. asst., 1985-87, intern in psychology, 1987-89, grad. rsch. assoc., 1989-90; asst. prof. U. Utah, Salt Lake City, 1993—; counselor, adminstr. Fourth World, Tempe, 1976-93; cons. and speaker in field. Co-author: Living Our Visions: Building Feminist Community, 1984; contbr. articles to profl. jours. Dep. voter registrar Dem. Com., Maricopa County, Ariz., 1983-92. Mem. APA, NOW, AAUW, Am. Counselors Assn., Am. Ednl. Rsch. Assn., Assn. for Women in Psychology (regional coord. 1987-93, conf. coord. 1990), Feminist Therapy Inst. Democrat. Office: U Utah Dept Ednl Psychology 327 Milton Bennion Hall Salt Lake City UT 84112

MORSE, GILLIAN L., bank officer; b. Mineola, N.Y., July 26, 1945; d. Gerry Elden and Martha Putnam (Levis) M.; m. Ronald L. Johnson, Oct. 12, 1991; stepchildren: Christan M. Johnson, Aron J. Johnson. BSBA, Drake U., 1967; MSBA, U. Denver, 1975. Mgr. Minn. Blue Cross, St. Paul, 1968-73; claims analyst Equitable Life Assurance, Mpls., 1973-74; v.p., br. mgr. Bank Western, Denver, 1975-93; br. mgr. Colorado Savs. Bank, Denver, 1994—. Mem. funds allocation com. Mile High United Way, 1988-92. Mem. Rotary Club (pres. 1993-94), West C. of C., Pinehurst Country Club. Republican. Office: Colorado Savs Bank 7575 W Jewell Ave Denver CO 80232

MORSE, HELVISE GLESSNER, physical and life sciences educator; b. Frederick, Md., Sept. 17, 1925; d. George Edward and Rosa May (Durphy) Glessner; m. Melvin Laurance Morse, Jan. 25, 1949; children: Margaret Louise, Laurance Clinton. BA, Hood Coll., 1946; MS, U. Ky., 1949, U. Colo., Denver, 1963; PhD, U. Colo., Denver, 1966. Supr. cytogenetics lab. Children's Hosp., Denver, 1978-79; postdoctoral fellow U. Colo. Med. Ctr., Denver, 1966-67, rsch. assoc., 1968-73, rsch. cytogeneticist, 1974-78, asst. prof. biochemistry, biophysics and genetics, 1979-88, assoc. prof., 1988—; dir. Core cytogenetics lab. U. Colo. Cancer Ctr., Denver, 1988—; Eleanor Roosevelt Inst. Cancer Rsch. fellow U. Colo., Denver, 1979—; mem. cytogenetics subcom. Nat. Children's Cancer Study Group, U.S.A. and Can., 1980-87. Contbr. articles on gene mapping, cytogenetics and Leukemia research to profl. publs., 1970—. Active So. Poverty Law Ctr. Mem. NAACP, Mortar Bd., Sigma Xi. Democrat. Home: 254 S Jasmine St Denver CO 80224-1033 Office: Univ Colo Health Scis Ctr Dept Biochem/Biophys/Genet 4200 E 9th Ave Denver CO 80262-0001

MORSE, KATHLEEN ANN, lawyer; b. Washington, June 23, 1952; d. George Patrick and Margaret Marie (Groeger) M. BA, U. Md., 1976, JD with honors, 1979. Commd. 1lt. U.S. Army, 1982, advance through grades to capt., 1983; assoc. Arent, Fox, Kintner Plotkin & Kahn, Washington, 1979-82; criminal def. counsel (JAG) corps U.S. Army, Nuernberg, Fed. Republic of Germany, 1982-83; criminal trial counsel U.S. Army, Nuernberg, 1983-85; prosecutor, adminstrv. law atty. U.S. Army, Ft. Carson, Colo., 1986-87; asst. atty. gen. Md. State Atty. Gen.'s Office, Balt., 1987-91; chief counsel Balt. City Dept. Social Svcs., 1991—; instr. dept. law USMA West Point, 1990-91. Maj. U.S. Army Res., 1987-91. Recipient Morris B. Myerowitz Moot Ct. award, Atty. Gen.'s Jennifer Lauterbach Robbins award, 1993. Mem. Md. Bar Assn., Order of Coif. Roman Catholic. Office: Balt City Dept Social Svcs Legal Svcs Div 6 St Paul Ctr 20th Flr Baltimore MD 21202-1608

MORSE, KATHLEEN VERNEAL, city official; b. Mankato, Minn., Oct. 9, 1958; d. Leo T. and Alice M. (Maas) Slechta; m. Roger H. Morse, May 12, 1979; children: Crystal, Bridget, Roger. Degree in acctg., Faribault Tech. Coll., 1978. Cert. mcpl. clk. Temp. dep. clk. City of Waterville (Minn.), 1984-85, dep. city clk., 1985-87, city clk., 1987-90; city clk., treas. City of Rice Lake (Wis.), 1992—, grant adminstr., 1993—, dir. mass transit, 1994—. Ex-officio mem. Waterville Sr. Citizens, 1989-91; mem. Civil Def., Waterville, 1987-90; leader Girl Scouts USA, Waterville, 1990-91. Mem. Wis. Clk. Assn., Wis. Treas. Assn., Minn. Clks. Assn., Internat. Instn. Mcpl. Clks., Rice Lake C. of C. Office: City of Rice Lake 11 E Marshall Rice Lake WI 54868

MORTENSEN, CARLA LOUISE, organization executive; b. San Francisco, May 24, 1954; d. Niels Laurids Mortensen and Dorothy Barbara (Sellmer) Paris; m. Robert T. Barrett, June 25, 1994. AB, Occidental Coll., 1976; M Theol. Studies, Harvard U., 1979; postgrad., UCLA, 1980-83; MBA, Simmons Coll., 1993. Fgn. Svc. officer U.S. Dept. State, Copenhagen, 1983-85; legis. asst. AAU, Washington, 1985-87; asst. dir. Office Career Svcs., Cambridge, Mass., 1987-89; asst. dean divsn. continuing edn. Harvard U., Cambridge, 1989-91; dep. dir. sch. pub. health-health policy and mgmt. Harvard U. DCE, Cambridge, 1991-94; exec. dir. Social Investment Forum, Boston, 1994—; cons. Ministry Fgn. Affairs, Bratislava, Slovakia, 1993—; adj. prof. Simmons Coll., Boston, 1994—. Democrat. Office: Social Investment Forum 121 Mount Vernon St Boston MA 02108-1100

MORTENSEN-SAY, MARLYS (MRS. JOHN THEODORE SAY), school system administrator; b. Yankton, S.D., Mar. 11, 1924; d. Melvin A. and Edith L. (Fargo) Mortensen; BA, U. Colo., 1949, MEd, 1953; adminstrv. specialist U. Nebr., 1973; m. John Theodore Say, June 21, 1951; children: Mary Louise, James Kenneth, John Melvin, Margaret Ann. Tchr. Huron (S.D.) Jr. High Sch., 1944-48, Lamar (Colo.) Jr. High Sch., 1950-52, Norfolk Pub. Sch., 1962-63; sch. supt. Madison County, Madison, Nebr., 1963—. Mem. NEA (life), AAUW, Am. Assn. Sch. Adminstrs., Dept. Rural Edn., Nebr. Assn. County Supts., Nebr. Elementary Prins. Assn., N.E. Nebr. County Supts. Assn., Assn. Sch. Bus. Ofcls., Nat. Orgn. Legal Problems in Edn., Assn. Supervision and Curriculum Devel., Nebr. Edn. Assn., Nebr. Sch. Adminstrs. Assn. Republican. Methodist. Home: 4805 S 13th St Norfolk NE 68701-6627 Office: Courthouse Madison NE 68748

MORTENSON, JANICE GAYLE MILLS, business owner, accountant; b. Chgo., Apr. 25, 1949; d. Richard Thomas and Elizabeth Ruth (Sanders) Mills; m. LeRoy A. Mortenson, Apr. 16, 1983 (dec. May 1987); m. James Richard White, Dec. 18, 1993. BA, U. Minn., 1974, BS, 1976; MBA, Seattle U., 1987. CPA, Wash. Co-owner Mortenson Co., Kirkland, Wash., 1984-87; contr. NW Composites, Marysville, Wash., 1987-93; owner Postal Boxes Plus, Bothell, Wash., 1993—, Woodsilk (JMW Enterprises, Inc.), Seattle, 1993—. Mem. Wash. State CPA Soc. (bus. and industry com. 1993-94). Presbyterian. Home: 2202 241st St SE Bothell WA 98021 Office: Woodsilk 754 Aloha St Seattle WA 98109

MORTHAM, SANDRA BARRINGER, state official; b. Erie, Pa., Jan. 4, 1951; d. Norman Lyell and Ruth (Harer) Barringer; m. Allen Mortham, Aug. 21, 1950; children: Allen Jr., Jeffrey. AS, St. Petersburg Jr. Coll., 1971; BA, Eckerd Coll. Cons. Capital Formation Counselors, Inc., Bellair Bluffs, Fla., 1972—; commr. City of Largo, Fla., 1982-86, vice mayor, 1985-86; mem. Fla. Ho. of Reps., 1986-94, Rep. leader pro tempore, 1990-94, minority leader, 1994; Sec. of State State of Fla., 1995—. Bd. dirs. Performing Arts Ctr. & Theatre, Clearwater, Fla.; exec. com. Pinellas County Rep. Com., Rep. Nat. Com. Named Citizen of Yr., 1990; recipient numerous outstanding legislator awards, achievement among women awards from civic and profl. orgns. Mem. Am. Legis. Exch. Coun., Nat. Rep. Legislators Assn., Largo C. of C. (bd. dirs. 1987—, pres.), Largo Jr. Woman's Club (pres., Woman of Yr. award 1979), Suncoast Community Woman's Club (pres., Outstanding Svc. award 1981, Woman of Yr. award 1986), Suncoast Tiger Bay, Greater Largo Rep., Belleair Rep. Woman's, Clearwater Rep. Woman's. Presbyterian. Home: 2860 Vernon Ter Largo FL 34640-4224 Office: Secretary of State State Capitol Rm 2 Tallahassee FL 32399*

MORTILLARO, KAREN G. A., sculptor, educator; b. Rochester, N.Y., Mar. 22, 1943; d. Angelo Joseph and Nellie (Rizzo) M. BFA, Otis Art Inst.,

L.A., MFA. Instr. gifted children's program L.A. City Coll., 1969-70; illustrator gifted children's program Westridge Girls Sch., Pasadena, Calif., 1969-70, West L.A. City Coll., 1970; instr. Isomata, U. So. Calif. Idyllwild Campus, 1970; prof. fine arts Orange Coast Coll., Costa Mesa, Calif., 1970—, asst. div. chmn. dept. fine arts, 1977-82. Neon and anamorphic sculptures exhibited in local, nat. and internat. group shows, 1965—, including Home Savs. and Loan, L.A. (purchase award 1969), La Quinta Art Festival, 1990 (award of excellence 1991), Palm Springs Desert Mus., Calif., 1993 (merit award 1994); U.S. patentee disappearing spheroid display. Ellsie de Wolfe fellow Otis Art Inst., 1968-69, faculty fellow Orange Coast Coll., 1971, 82. Mem. Internat. Sculpture Coun., Nat. Sculpture Soc., Am. Crafts Coun. Office: Orange Coast Coll 2701 Fairview Rd Costa Mesa CA 92626

MORTIMER, ANITA LOUISE, lawyer, consultant, educator; b. Jefferson City, Mo., July 2, 1950; d. Ross Maitland Snell and Viola Alice (Leigh) M.; 1 child, Caleb Ross. BA, Graceland Coll., 1973; JD, Washburn U., 1976; MA in Religion with honors, Park Coll., 1992. Bar: Kans. 1976, U.S. Dist. Ct. Kans. 1976, Mo. 1980, U.S. Dist. Ct. (we. dist.) Mo. 1980, U.S. Ct. Appeals (8th cir.) 1980, U.S. Supreme Ct. 1980. Tng. cons. Orgn. to Counter Sexual Assault, Mo., Iowa, Kans., Ill., 1979-80; asst. dist. atty. Wyandotte County, Kansas City, Kans., 1976-80; asst. U.S. atty. U.S. Dept. Justice, Kansas City, Mo., 1980—; appointee Organized Crime and Drug Enforcement Task Force, 1988; cons. Govs. Task Force on Rape Prevention, Mo., 1979-80; instr. Nat. Coll. Dist. Attys., 1980, various camps and retreats, family-related topics, various seminars for fed. agts.; bd. dirs. SHARE, Inc. Contbr. articles to profl. jours. Bd. dirs. Met. Orgn. to Counter Sexual Assault, Kansas City, 1976-80; apptd. to Presdl. Com. on Status of Women, 1979-80; trustee Independence (Mo.) Regional Health Ctr., 1990-94; mem. Ctr. Stake Strategic Planning Commn. RLDS, 1989-90; apptd. chair World Ch. Task Force on Singles' Ministry RLDS, 1990—; chair del. caucus RLDS World Conf., 1992, 94. Named to Honorable Order of Ky. Cols., Gov., 1980. Mem. ABA, Mo. Bar Assn., Assn. Women Lawyers, Kansas City Met. Bar Assn.; Alumni Assn. Graceland Coll. (bd. dirs. 1987, pres. 1988), John Whitmer Hist. Soc. Mem. Reorganized Ch. of Jesus Christ of Latter Day Saints. Clubs: MOCSA (Kansas City), Friends of Art. Office: US Dept Justice 1201 Walnut St Ste 2300 Kansas City MO 64106-2136

MORTMAN-FRIEDMAN, BETH-LYNN, graphic designer, educator; b. Jersey City, Dec. 17, 1950; d. Abraham and Martha Mortman; 1 child, Alexis Paige. AAS, Queensborough Community Coll., 1972; BS, Buffalo State U., 1975; MS, Pratt Inst., 1988. Cert. art tchr., N.Y. Asst. art dir. Transhigh Corp., N.Y.C., 1976-78; graphic designer/tchr. spl. edn. Lowell Sch., Queens, N.Y., 1978-82; art dir., owner Visual Persuasion Studio, Jericho, N.Y., 1982—; art instr. P.A.C.E. program SUNY Old Westbury, L.I., 1988-93; cons. and lectr. in field. Designer numerous print ads, brochures, logo designs, posters. Recipient numerous nat. design award. Fellow Buffalo State Alumni Assn., Am. Inst. Graphic Artists, Graphic Artists Guild, N.Y. State Art Tchrs. Assn.

MORTON, CAROLINE JULIA, marketing executive; b. N.Y.C.; BS in Edn., U. Pa.; MBA, N.Y. U.; grad. cert. in profl. writing and effective communication, CCNY. Vice pres. mktg. mgmt. V-TEC Corp., Hopewell, Va.; pres. CMR Co., Hopewell; past cons. Advt. Women of N.Y. Mem. AAWU, Am. Mktg. Assn. (past dir.), Advt. Women of N.Y., Fedn. Profl. Bus. Women, Am. Mgmt. Assn., Women in Communications. Contbr. articles to profl. jours. Address: 5705 Courthouse Rd Prince George VA 23875

MORTON, HENRIETTA OLIVE, academic administrator; b. Elbert, Colo., May 22, 1937; d. Henry Oliver and Mary Irene (Wasson) Pearson; m. Wayne Wilbur Morton, Dec. 29, 1956 (div. Aug. 1987); children: Lonnie Wayne, Vicki Rae. BA in Adult Edn. Adminstrn., Loretta Heights Coll., 1984; postgrad., Regis U. Supr. of community edn. and adminstrn. Colo. Northwestern Community Coll., Steamboat Springs, 1975-80; dir. of community edn. Colo. Mountain Coll., Steamboat Springs, 1980—; mchts. coun. mem. Steamboat Chamber Resort Assn., 1985—, econ. devel. coun. mem. V.p., treas. Routt County Sch. Dist. RE-1, 1967-75; vice-chair Rep. Party, 1988—. Mem. Colo. Assn. Sch. Bds. (honor roll 1975), Mountain Plains Adult Edn. Assn., Nat. Coun. Community Svcs. and Continuing Edn., Internat. Toastmistress Club. Republican. Home: 330 Fish Creek Rd Steamboat Springs CO 80477 Office: Colo Mountain Coll 1370 Bob Adams Dr Steamboat Springs CO 80487-5029

MORTON, JANE WILSON, family and consumer sciences specialist; b. Bklyn., Oct. 18, 1925; d. Christopher Adolph and Emily Marie (Werth) Geibel; m. Leroy Victor Wilson, Dec. 22, 1945 (dec. June 1971); children: Stephen Roy, Christopher Robert, Paul Frederic; m. Charles A. Morton, Apr. 7, 1979; 4 stepsons. Student, Skidmore Coll., 1943-46; BA, Queens Coll. City of N.Y., 1970, MS, 1973. Cert. family and consumer scis. specialist. With N.Y. Telephone Co., Freeport, 1942-43; occupational therapy asst. A. Holly Patterson Home for Aged and Infirm, Uniondale, N.Y., 1964-69; high sch. home economist tchr. Bellmore-Merrick (N.Y.) Ctrl. High Sch. Dist., Mepham H.S., 1971-82; entertaining and cookery coord. Great Neck (N.Y.) Pub. Schs., 1982-89; freelance family and consumer scis. specialist Long Island, 1982—; instr. Health Force Operating, Westbury, N.Y., 1987-92. Author, prodr.: (ednl. filmstrips) Basic Sewing Skills, 1983, Cooking for One or Two, 1984; co-author: (cookbook) Fresh Herb Companion, 1994. vol. debt counselor Family Svc. League of Suffolk County, Huntington, N.Y., 1991—; bd. dirs. Cornell Coop. Ext. of Nassau County, N.Y. Mem. Am. Assn. Family and Consumer Scis., N.Y. Assn. Cooking Tchrs., Internat. Assn. Culinary Profls., Culinary Historians of N.Y., N.Y. State Home Econs. Assn. (chair home and community sect. 1993—, pres. L.I. dist. 1983-84, 93-94, bd. dirs. L.I. dist.), Spotlight award L.I. dist.), Local PTA (life).

MORTON, JANICE KENEFAKE, nurse, administrator; b. Mt. Carmel, Ill., Nov. 2, 1951; d. Francis William and Kathleen Helen (Stanley) Kenefake; m. Randy Vilines, Apr. 23, 1973 (div. 1977); m. Danny Joe Morton, Feb. 19, 1979; children: Melissa Ann, Michael Jonothan, Jonothan Edward. ADN, Henderson (Ky.) Community Coll., 1971; BSN, U. Evansville, 1978, MA, 1989. Cert. Nurse Adminstr. Advanced, 1991. Staff nurse Community Meth. Hosp., Henderson, 1971, Vanderbilt U., Nashville, 1971-72, Deaconess Hosp., Evansville, Ind., 1972-73; dir. nursing MEDCO Nursing Home, Henderson, 1973; home health coord. Henderson County Health Dept., 1973-74; staff nurse Fayette County Home Health Agy., Lexington, Ky., 1974-75; staff RN Ft. Logan Hosp., Stanford, Ky., 1975-77; staff nurse Community Methodist Hosp., 1977-79; asst. dir. nursing Community Meth. Hosp., Henderson, 1979-89; chief nursing officer Meadowview Regional Hosp., Maysville, Ky., 1989-94, Colleton Regional Hosp., Walterboro, S.C., 1994—; corneal eye tech. U. Ky., Lexington, 1988-94, U. Louisville, 1988-94; mem. adv. com./nursing Morehead (Ky.) State U., 1990-94; adv. bd. nursing Maysville C.C., 1990-94. Bd. dirs. United Way, Maysville, 1991-94. Named Embassador to Ky. Pk. System Gov. Julian Carrol, 1976. Mem. ANA, Am. Orgn. Nurse Execx., Ky. Orgn. Nurse Execs., S.C. Orgn. Nurse Execs., S.C. Nurses Assn. Home: 208 Greenbay St Walterboro SC 29488 Office: Colleton Regional Hosp 501 Robertson Blvd Walterboro SC 29488

MORTON, JOANNE MCKEAN, computer educator, consultant; b. New London, Conn., Dec. 3, 1953; d. Newton Hubbard and Lucille (Paganetti) McK.; m. Michael McNally Morton, Sept. 16, 1978. BA, Conn. Coll., 1976; MBA, Rensselaer Poly. Inst., 1985. Dept. mgr. Great Atlantic & Pacific Tea Co., Inc., Springfield, Mass., 1976-84; research asst. Hartford Grad. Ctr., Conn., 1985, adj. lectr. Sch. Mgmt., 1986—; lectr. courses in mktg. and computer applications; founder, pres. Morton & Assocs. Income Tax Svcs., 1986—; enrolled agent Dept. Treasury, 1990. Fellow Nat. Tax Practice Inst., Nat. Assn. Enrolled Agts., Conn. Soc. of Enrolled Agts. (bd. dirs.). Home and Office: Morton & Assocs 8 Clifton St Waterford CT 06385-1307

MORTON, LINDA, mayor; b. Dec. 7, 1944; married; 2 children. BA with honors, U. Nebr., 1966. Lic. real estate broker. Tchr. Sunnyvale (Calif.) Elem. Sch., 1967-69, Jefferson County (Colo.) Sch. Dist., 1966-67, 69-70; real estate agt. Crown Realty, Lakewood, Colo., 1979-82, Van Schaack & Co., Lakewood, 1982-83, Re-Max Profls., Lakewood, from 1983. Mem. city council City of Lakewood, 1981-91, now Mayor, Lakewood, Colo., 1991—; represented Lakewood on Bd. Denver Regional Council of Govts., from 1981, chairwoman, 1986-87; chmn. Jefferson C. of C.; appointed by Gov. Colo. to Met. Air Quality Council, 1985; bd. dirs. Nat. Assn. Regional Coun. Govts., 1986-90, CML, 1993—. Office: City of Lakewood 445 S Allison Pky Lakewood CO 80226-3105

MORTON, MALVIN, social welfare administrator, consultant; b. Temeha, Tex., June 24, 1906; d. Charles Newton and Bessie Howell (Warner) M. MA in Social Svcs., U. Pitts., 1945. Caseworker Fed. Emergency Relief Adminstrn., Ft. Worth, 1933-35; program dir. YWCA, Greensboro, N.C., 1935-40; dir. teenage girls program YWCA, Indpls., 1940-43; social work cons. Community Chest Welfare Fedn., Pitts., 1945-47; pub. rels. dir. United Charities, Chgo., 1947-52; exec. dir. Chgo. Fedn. of Settlements & Neighborhood Ctrs., Chgo., 1952-61; publs. dir. Am. Pub. Welfare Assn., Chgo., 1961-71; dir. communications Florence Crittendon Assn. of Am., Chgo., 1971-74, ret., 1974; founder, bd. dirs. Contact Chgo.. Patron Olive Branch Mission, Chgo., 1963—; founder, adviser Citizenship Coun. Greater Chgo., 1956—; exec. dir. Chgo. Mayor's Civic Com. for Jane Addams Centennial, 1960; bd. dir. Friends of Lit., 1978—, pres. 1990-92. Recipient honors Am. Assn. S.W. with Groups, 1993, U. Pitts. Sch. Social Work, 1993, Tex. Wesleyan Univ., 1993. Mem. NASW (life), Am. Med. Writers Assn. (life Chgo. chpt.), Lyric Opera Chgo., Art Inst. Chgo. Democrat. Methodist. Home: 4950 N Ashland Ave # 478 Chicago IL 60640-3417

MORTON, MARGARET ELIZABETH, former state legislator; b. Pocahontas, Va., June 23, 1924; m. James F. Morton. Mem. Conn. Ho. of Reps., 1973-80; mem. from dist. 23 Conn. Senate, 1981-92; vice-chair Conn. Legis. Black and Hispanic Caucus. Del. Dem. Nat. Conv., 1980, 84. Mem. Nat. Council Negro Women (life), NAACP, NOW, Nat. Black Caucus State Legislators. Episcopalian. Home: 25 Margaret E Morton Ln Bridgeport CT 06607-1615 Office: Conn State Senate State Capitol Bldg Hartford CT 06106

MORTON, MARILYN MILLER, genealogy and history educator, lecturer, researcher, travel executive, director; b. Water Valley, Miss., Dec. 2, 1929; d. Julius Brunner and Irma Faye (Magee) Miller; m. Perry Wilkes Morton Jr., July 2, 1958; children: Dent Miller Morton, Nancy Marilyn Morton Driggers, E. Perian Morton Ethridge. BA in English, Miss. U. for Women, 1952; MS in History, Miss. State U., 1955. Cert. secondary tchr. Tchr. English, speech and history Starkville (Miss.) H.S., 1952-58; part-time instr. Miss. State U., 1953-55; mem. spl. collection staff Samford U. Libr., Birmingham, Ala., 1984-92; lectr. genealogy and history, instr. Inst. Genealogy & Hist. Rsch., Samford U., Birmingham, 1985-93, assoc. dir., 1985-88, exec. dir., 1988-93; founding dir. SU British and Irish Inst. Genealogy & Hist. Rsch. Samford U., Birmingham and British Isles, 1986-93; owner, dir. Marilyn Miller Morton Brit-Ire-U.S. Genealogy, Birmingham, 1994—; instr. genealogy classes Samford U. Metro Coll., 1989-94; lectr. nat. conf. Fedn. of Geneal. Socs. Contbr. articles and book revs. to profl. jours. Active Birmingham chpt. Salvation Army Aux., 1982—. Inducted into Miss. U. for Women Hall of Fame, 1952. Fellow Irish Geneal. Rsch. Soc. London; mem. Internat. Soc. Brit. Genealogy and Family History, Nat. Geneal. Soc. (mem. nat. program com. 1988—, lectr. nat. meetings), Assn. Profl. Genealogists, Soc. Genealogists London, Antiquarian Soc. Birmingham (sec., 2d v.p. 1982-84), DAR (regent Cheaha chpt. 1977-78), Dau. Am. Colonists (regent Edward Waters chpt. 1978-79), Phi Kappa Phi (charter mem. Samford U. chpt. 1972). Home and Office: 3508 Clayton Pl Birmingham AL 35216-3810

MORTON, TAMMY B., nurse; b. Westminster, S.C., Oct. 25, 1961; d. Bert Frank and Geraldine (Suttles) Butts; m. Samuel E. Morton Jr., Oct. 5, 1980; children: Micki, Trip. Student, Limestone Coll., Gaffney, S.C., 1986; A degree, Tri-County Tech., Pendleton, S.C., 1989; BSN, Clemson U., 1992, postgrad., 1993—. RN, S.C.; CEN. Psychiatric staff nurse Mt. View Ctr. Anderson (S.C.) Meml. Hosp., 1989; emergency room staff nurse Oconee Meml. Hosp., Seneca, S.C., 1987—; LPN instr. FP Hamilton Career Ctr., Seneca, S.C., 1994—; Lamaze instr. Oconee Meml. Hosp., Seneca, 1994; mem. Vols. in Med. Missions, 1994. EMT Westminster Rescue Squad, 1985-90; county coord. Oconee County Rescue Squads, 1987. Mem. Emergency Nurses Assn., Baptists Nurses Assn., Student Nurses Assn. Tri-County Tech. (co-founder, pres. 1988-89), Sigma Theta Tau, Phi Theta Kappa, Psi Beta. Republican. Baptist.

MORWOOD, BETTY JO, psychiatrist, physician; b. Burlington, Vt., Nov. 8, 1948; d. Nicholas Abraham and Alice (Thamer) M.; 1 child, Sophia Ruth. BA, U. Vt., 1970, MD, 1974, fellow, 1978-80. Diplomate Am. Bd. Psychiatry and Neurology. Resident Stanford (Calif.) U., 1976-77; fellow U. Vt., Burl, 1978-80; med. dir. Cath. Social Services, San Jose, Calif., 1977-78; sr. staff psychiatrist Santa Clara County, San Jose, 1977-78; practice medicine specializing in psychiatry Burlington, 1980—; staff physician Med. Ctr. Vt. Mem. Am. Psychiatry Assn., Vt. Psychiatry Assn.

MOSACK, MARGUERITE ANN, psychologist, educator; b. Garfield Heights, Ohio, May 14, 1951; d. Anthony Joseph and Christine Clarice Mosack. BA, U. Dallas, 1973; MA in Psychology, Duquesne U., 1984. Lic. psychologist, Pa. Psychotherapist Duquesne U. Counseling & Testing Ctr., Pitts., 1985-87; psychol. evaluator Pitts. Assessment and Consultation Ctr., 1985-87; psychology intern Staunton Clinic at Sewickley (Pa.) Valley Hosp., 1987-88; psychologist Northeastern Pa. Counseling Ctr., Kingston, 1988-91; pvt. practice Wilkes-Barre, Pa., 1991—; instr. psychology Community Coll. Allegheny County, Pitts., 1986, Pa. State U., Lehman; grad. instr. mental health referral Inst. Formative Spirituality, Duquesne U., Pitts., 1988; instr. grad. mgmt. Misericordia Coll., Dallas, Pa., 1990; lectr., cons. We Are Remembered Ministry Diocese of Pitts., 1986-87; presenter women's spirituality Luzerne County Women's Conf., Wilkes-Barre, 1989-90, Luzerne County Women's Conf., Wilkes-Barre, 1989-90, 92-93; presenter psychol. issues of elderly Misericordia Coll. Conf., 1989; presenter stress mgmt. ARC, Persian Gulf Support Groups, 1991, breast cancer support group Nesbitt Hosp., 1994; presenter wellness Campus Compact, 1994; instr. assertiveness tng. for educators Pa. State U., 1991. Mem. APA, Northeastern Pa. Psychol. Assn., Pa. Psychol. Assn., Luzerne County Women's Network, NW Pa. Behavioral Health Care Network (pres.-elect bd. dirs. 1994).

MOSAK, BARBARA MARCIA, designer; b. Chgo., Nov. 14, 1950; d. Joseph and Anna (Rabinovitz) M. BA in Design with honors, U. Ill., Chgo., 1976. Tchr. art Temple Emanuel, Chgo., 1973-74; graphic designer Beham & Assocs., Inc., 1974-76, Sta. WFLD-TV, Fox TV, Chgo., 1976-77; graphic artist Sta. WBBM-TV, CBS, Chgo., 1977-87, art dir., 1987-88, design dir., 1988-92; freelance designer Chgo., 1992—. Contbg. author: TV Guide Tune-In Advertising, 1988 (Judge's Choice award 1988). Vol. video artist Communication for Social Change, Chgo., 1974; vol. designer Kidney Found. Ill., 1974-76, NOW, Chgo., 1975; vol. designer, tutor Jewish Vocat. Svc., Chgo., 1981-82. Recipient Desi award Graphics Design: USA, 1981, cert. of leadership YWCA, Chgo., 1983. Jewish. Home and Office: 901 S Plymouth Ct Chicago IL 60605-2059

MOSBY, DOROTHEA SUSAN, municipal official; b. Sacramento, Calif., May 13, 1948; d. William Laurence and Esther Ida (Lux) M. AA in Sociology, Bakersfield (Calif.) Coll., 1966-69; BS in Recreation, San Jose State U., 1969-72; MPA, Calif. State U. Dominguez Hills, Carson, 1980-82. Asst. dept. pers. officer San Jose Pks. and Recreation Dept., 1972-73, neighborhood ctr. dir., 1973-74; sr. recreation leader Santa Monica Recreation and Pks. Dept., 1974-76, recreation supr., 1976-83; head bus. divsn. Santa Monica Recreation and Parks Dept., 1983-88; bus. adminstr. Santa Monica Cultural & Recreation Svcs., 1988-91; dir. pks. and recreation City of South Gate, Calif., 1991—; bd. dirs., officer Santa Monica City Employees Fed. Credit Union, 1980-89, pres. 1986-87; mem. citizens adv. com. L.A. Olympic Organizing Com., 1982-84. Mem. choir, flute soloist Pilgrim Luth. Ch., Santa Monica, 1974—, treas. Luth. ch. coun., 1984-86; vol. driver XXIII Olympiad, Los Angeles, 1984; contbr. local housing assistance U.S. Olympic Com., Los Angeles, 1984; mem. adv. com. Windsor Sq. Hancock Park Hist. Soc., Los Angeles, 1983, dir. Christmas carolling, 1980—, chmn. Olympic com., 1984, bd. trustees, 1984-90, chmn. pub. programs, 1985, co-chmn. pub. programs, 1986, co-vice chair, 1987, chmn., 1988, 89—; L.A. Philharm. Bus. & Profl. Com.; mem. Samuel C. May Grad. Student Rsch. Paper Judging Com., Western Govt. Rsch. Assn., 1994. Recipient Outstanding Profl. of Yr. award Los Angeles Basin Pk. and Recreation Commrs. and Bd. Mems., 1993. Mem. NAFE, Calif. Pk. and Recreation Soc. (bd. dirs. 1979-82, 86, mem. Calif. bd. pk. and recreation pers. 1990-92, Scholarship Found. Bd. 1992—, dist. 10 v.p. 1994), Nat. Recreation and Pk. Assn., Mgmt. Team Assocs. (sec., treas. 1979-83), L.A. World Affairs Coun., Western Govtl. Rsch. Assn., South Gate C. of C., Kiwanis Club, Chi Kappa Rho (pres. 1986), Pi Alpha Alpha, Nat. Assn. Univ. Women. Home: 9329 Elm Vista Dr Apt 103 Downey CA 90242-2992 Office: City of South Gate Dept Pks and Recreation 4900 Southern Ave South Gate CA 90280-3462

MOSELEY, KAREN FRANCES F., school system administrator, educator; b. Oneonta, N.Y., Sept. 18, 1944; d. Albert Francis and Dorothy (Brown) Flanigan; m. David Michael McLaud, Sept. 8, 1962 (div. Dec. 1966); m. Harry R. Lasalle, Dec. 24, 1976 (dec. Feb. 1990); 1 child, Christopher Michael; m. Kel Moseley, Jan. 22, 1994. BA, SUNY, Oneonta, 1969, MS, 1970. Cert. secondary edn. tchr., Fla., Mass., N.Y. Tchr. Hanover (Mass.) Pub. Schs., 1970-80; lobbyist Mass. Fed. Nursing Homes, Boston, 1980-84; tchr., dept. chair Palm Beach County Schs., Jupiter, Fla., 1985—; chair of accreditation Jupiter High Sch., 1990-91; Fulbright tchr., Denmark, 1994—. Author: How to Teach About King, 1978, 10 Year Study, 1991. Del. Dem. Conv., Mass., 1976-84; campaign mgr. Kennedy for Senate, N.Y., 1966, Tsongas for Senate, Boston, 1978; dir. Plymouth County Dems., Marshfield, Mass., 1978-84; Sch. Accountability Com., 1991—; polit cons. Paul Tsongas U.S. Senate, Boston, 1978-84, Michael Dukakis for Gov., Boston, 1978-84. Mem. Nat. Honor Soc. Polit. Scientists, Classroom Tchrs. Assn., Mass. Coun. Social Studies (bd. dirs. Boston chpt. 1970-80), Mass. Tchrs. Assn. (chair human rels. com. Boston chpt. 1976-80), Plymouth County Social Studies (bd. dirs. 1970-80), Mass. Hosp. Assn. (bd. dirs. Boston chpt. 1980-84), Nat. Coun. for Social Studies, Fla. Sch. Supt. Assn. Roman Catholic. Home: 369 River Edge Rd Jupiter FL 33477-9350 Office: Jupiter High Sch 500 Military Trl Jupiter FL 33458-5797

MOSELEY, PATSY LOUISE, counselor, therapist; b. Stuttgart, Ark., Sept. 10, 1947; d. William Vernon and Thelma Charlotte (Taylor) Cantrell; m. William Archia Moseley, June 1, 1969 (div. Nov. 1993); children: Amanda Louise, Randall William. BS in Edn., Ark. State U., 1969, MEd in Counseling, 1989; M in Counseling, Ariz. State U., 1991. Tchr. Memphis City Schs., 1970-72; therapist Wilshire Psychol. Svcs., Phoenix, 1991—; instr. Gateway C.C., Phoenix, 1988-90, Rio Salado C.C., Phoenix, 1992, Ariz. State U., Phoenix, 1991; seminar speaker P.C.M. and Assocs., Phoenix, 1985—; presenter Ctr. Against Sexual Assault, Phoenix, 1986-88; exec. dir. Rising Star, Phoenix, 1991-93, bd. dirs. Mem. adv. bd. Lamplighter Apts. (Severely Mentally Ill Homeless Shelter), Phoenix, 1993—. Mem. Am. Counseling Assn., Assn. for Specialist in Group Work. Home: 4150 E Alan Ln Phoenix AZ 85028-4115

MOSELEY, SHERYL BUCK, nursing administrator; b. Greenville, N.C., Nov. 27, 1955; d. James Earl and Hilda Hatton (Johnston) Buck; m. William Earl Moseley, June 17, 1978. BSN, East Carolina U., 1978, MSN, 1993. Staff nurse rehab. Pitt County Meml. Hosp., Greenville, 1978-80, permanent charge nurse, 1980-81, head nurse rehab., 1981-87, nursing adminstr., 1988—. Co-coord. 514th MP Co. Family Support Group, Greenville, 1991, coord., 1992. Mem. ANA, Assn. Rehab. Nurses (cert.), N.C. Assn. Rehab. Nurses (sec. 1980-81, pres. 1985-86, bd. dirs. 1986-88), N.C. Nurses Assn., Nat. League for Nursing, N.C. Orgn. Nurse Execs., Am. Orgn. Nurse Execs., Sigma Theta Tau (Beta Nu chpt.). Mem. Free Will Baptist Ch. Address: PO Box 846 8 Corbett St Winterville NC 28590-0846 Office: Pitt County Meml Hosp PO Box 6028 2100 Stantonsburg Rd Greenville NC 27835-6028

MOSELEY-BRAUN, CAROL, senator; b. Chgo., Aug. 16, 1947; d. Joseph J. and Edna A. (Davie) Moseley; m. Michael Braun, 1973 (div. 1986); 1 child, Matthew. BA, U. Ill., Chgo., 1969; JD, U. Chgo., 1972. Asst. U.S. atty. U.S. Dist. Ct. (no. dist.) Ill., 1973-77; mem. Ill. Ho. of Reps., 1979-88; recorder of deeds Cook County, Ill., 1988-92; U.S. senator from Ill. Washington, 1993—; mem. fin. com., subcom. on social security and family policy, subcom. on medicare, long-term care and health ins., mem. com. on banking, housing and urban affairs, subcom. on HUD oversight and structure, subcom. on internat. fin. and monetary policy, subcom. on fin. instns. and regulatory relief. Office: US Senate 320 Hart Senate Bldg Washington DC 20510

MOSER, FRANCES H., association executive; b. Holton, Kans., July 12, 1909; d. Albert and Naomi Florence (Hockham) M. BA cum laude, Ottawa U., 1932; MA, Peabody Coll., 1934. Employed girls' sec. YWCA, Waterloo, Iowa, 1935-38; dir. bus. marrieds YWCA, Salt Lake City, 1938-41; dir. bus. girls and coeds YWCA, Des Moines, 1941-44; exec. employed girls divsn. YWCA, Houston, 1944-49; western regional nat. bd. YWCA, San Francisco, 1949-55; student/univ. nat. bd. YWCA, L.A., 1953-55; student/univ. so. region nat. bd. YWCA, Atlanta, 1955-60; co-exec. Wash. U. campus YWCA, St. Louis, 1960-63, exec. com., 1963-66; ctrl. region coord. nat. bd. YWCA, Chgo., 1966-71; assoc. exec. YWCA, N.Y.C., 1971-74, ret., 1974. Bd. dirs. Capitol Hill United Neighborhood, Denver; membership com. YWCA Metro Denver; chair Denver Area Com.; active UNICEF, also numerous polit. campaigns. Recipient Park Hill Neighborhood award Bd. CHUN, Denver, 1993. Democrat. Congregationalist. Home: 1901 E 13th Ave Apt 8G Denver CO 80206

MOSER, JANE WEBB, information specialist; b. Prestonsburg, Ky., Aug. 14, 1950; d. Virgil Alonzo and Nancy Watts (Powers) Webb; m. Robert Wallace Moser, Mar. 2, 1985; 1 child, Robert Douglas. BA in Edn., U. Ky., 1972; MA in Edn., U. Tex., San Antonio, 1975; MLS, San Jose State U., 1992. Reading cons. Provincetown (Mass.)-Truro Schs., 1978-80; sec. in dept. tech. USAF Space Divsn., L.A., 1980-82; mgr. data base USAF Space Systems Div., L.A., 1982-91; tech. info. specialist USAF Space Systems Divsn., L.A., 1982-84, intelligence rsch. specialist, mgr. info. systems, 1984-90; ind. cons., secondary and online rschr. Cypress, Calif., 1992—. Tutor Laubach Literacy, Colorado Springs, Colo., 1975-78; mem. commn. on ch. and soc. Los Altos United Meth. Ch., Long Beach, Calif., 1990-92; founding mem. bd. dirs. Air Force Family Support Ctr., L.A., 1980-81; vol. John Douglas French Ctr. Alzheimer Disease. Recipient Sustained Superior Performance award USAF, L.A., 1982-90; named Space Div. Woman of Yr., Fed. Women's Program, L.A., 1987, Air Force Civilian of Yr., Air Force Assn., L.A., 1988. Mem. Spl. Librs. Assn. (various offices 1984-92, Spl. Achievement award 1989), Calif. Libr. Assn., So. Calif. Online Users Group, North Truro Air Force Sta. Wives Club (hon. pres. 1978-80).

MOSES, BARBARA SMITH, museum education specialist; b. Long Beach, Calif., Apr. 18, 1948. BA, Knox Coll., 1970; MS, U. Memphis, 1994. Interpreter, naturalist Pitts. Zoo, 1971-78; instr. Carnegie Mus. of Natural History, Pitts., 1981-82; curator of edn. Memphis Zoo and Aquarium, Memphis, 1982-90; dir. Moses & Assocs., Memphis, 1990—; instr. Sch. for Profl. Mgmt. Devel. of Zoo and Aquarium Personnel, Wheeling, W.Va., 1984-87, dept. continuing edn. U. Memphis, 1983-86;. Rev. editor Jour. Vol. Adminstrn., Boulder, Colo., 1982-86; author: Volunteers in Zoos and Aquariums, 1981, various guidebooks, 1980—; contbr. articles to profl. jours. Mem. Am. Zoo and Aquarium Assn. (docent adv. 1978-82), Visitors Studies Assn., Southeastern Mus. Conf., Am. Assn. Mus., Phi Beta Kappa.

MOSES, CYNTHIA GLASS, realtor; b. Kittery, Maine, Jan. 27, 1954; d. Park Roy Jr. and Mintie Jane (Eberhart) Glass; m. Robert William Moses, Nov. 26, 1983. BA, U. Md., 1975; MA, U. Va., 1976; postgrad., U. Conn., 1976-79. Cert. residential specialist; cert. relocation profl.; accredited buyer's rep. Owner Cynthia Glass Antiques, Alexandria, Va., 1981-83; assoc. Shannon and Luchs, Bethesda, Md., 1983-89; assoc. broker Re/Max 2000, Rockville, Md., 1990—. Docent Nat. Mus. African Art, Washington, 1979-83. Recipient Rsch. grant U. Conn., Storrs, 1978. Mem. Nat. Assn. Realtors (gov. residential sales coun. 1993—), Md./D.C. CRS Chpt. (pres. 1991-92, Diamond award 1992), Real Estate Buyers Agy. Coun., Montgomery County Assn. Realtors (life mem.). Home: 3 Old Gate Ct Rockville MD 20852 Office: Re/Max 2000 Ste 200 11400 Rockville Pike Rockville MD 20852

MOSES, YOLANDA T., academic administrator; b. Los Angeles, CA; m. James F. Bawek; 2 daughters: Shana and Antonia. BS Sociology, Calif. State Coll., San Bernardino, 1968; M.A., Ph.D Anthropology, UC Riverside, 1976. Dean Coll. of Arts, prof. of soc. sci. Calif. State Polytechnic U., 1982-88; v.p. academic affairs, prof. of anthropology Calif. State U., Dominguez Hills, 1988-93; pres. City Coll. of N.Y./CUNY, 1993—. chair United Negro Coll. Fund Advisory Bd for Service Learning, mem. Women's Forum, Inc.,

Amer. Anthropological Assn (pres. 1995). Office: City Coll of NY/CUNY Office of the Pres Convent Ave at 138th St New York NY 10031*

MOSHER, FRAN ANN, human resources specialist; b. Albuquerque, Nov. 12, 1949; d. George P. and Mary J. (Hotis) Demas; m. Milton H. Mosher, Oct. 4, 1969; children: Peter Aaron, Coleen Denise. Student, N.Mex. State U., 1968-69. Pers. sec. Bank N.Mex., Albuquerque, 1973-76; exec. asst., pers. rep. Broadway Dept. Store, Albuquerque, 1976-78; asst. pers. dir. Amity Leather Products, Albuquerque, 1978-80; local bus. devel. rep., office mgr. Hertz Corp., Albuquerque, 1980-85; pers. coord. Dunhill Temp. Systems, Albuquerque, 1985-88; pers. specialist Hosp. Svcs. Corp., Albuquerque, 1988-90; pers. dir. City of Hobbs, N.Mex., 1990—; cons. in field. Mem. Ctr. for Pers. Rsch. Com., 1995; bd. dirs. Hospice of Lea County; mem. govt. divsn. rep. United Way; instr. N.Mex. Jr. Coll. Mem. Soc. Human Resource Mgmt. (cert. 1994), Job Svc. Employer Com. (state chair 1978—), Internat. Pers. Mgmt. Assn., Rocky Mountain Pub. Employer Labor Rels. Assn. Baptist. Home: 2027 N Adobe Hobbs NM 88240 Office: City of Hobbs 300 N Turner Hobbs NM 88240

MOSHER, SALLY EKENBERG, lawyer; b. N.Y.C., July 26, 1934; d. Leslie Joseph and Frances Josephine (McArdle) Ekenberg; m. James Kimberly Mosher, Aug. 13, 1960 (dec. Aug. 1982). MusB, Manhattanville Coll., 1956; postgrad., Hofstra U., 1958-60, U. So. Calif., 1971-73; JD, U. So. Calif., 1981. Bar: Calif., 1982. Musician, pianist, tchr., 1957-74; music critic Pasadena Star-News, 1967-72; mgr. Contrasts Concerts, Pasadena Art Mus., 1971-72; rep. Occidental Life Ins. Co., Pasadena, 1975-78; v.p. James K. Mosher Co., Pasadena, 1961-82, pres., 1982—; pres. Oakhill Enterprises, Pasadena, 1984—; assoc. White-Howell, Inc., Pasadena, 1984—; real estate broker, 1984—. Contbr. articles to various publs. Bd. dirs. Jr. League Pasadena, 1966-67, Encounters Concerts, Pasadena, 1966-72, U. So. Calif. Friends of Music, L.A., 1973-76, Arroyo Seco Coun., 1991—; bd. dirs. Pasadena Arts Coun., 1986—, pres., 1989-92, chair adv. bd., 1992-93; v.p., bd. dirs. Pasadena Chamber Orch., 1986-88, pres., 1987-88; mem. Calif. 200 Coun. for Bicentennial of U.S. Constn., 1987-90; commr. Endowment Adv. Commn, Pasadena, 1988-90; bd. dirs. Calif. Music Theatre, 1988-90, Pasadena Hist. Soc., 1989-91, I Cantori, 1989-91; bd. dirs. Foothill Area Cmty. Svcs., 1990—, treas., 1991, vice-chair, 1992-94, chair, 1994—. Manhattanville Coll. hon. scholar, 1952-56. Mem. ABA, Calif. Bar Assn., Assocs. of Calif. Inst. Tech., Athenaeum, Kappa Gamma Pi, Mu Phi Epsilon, Phi Alpha Delta. Republican. Home: 1260 Rancheros Rd Pasadena CA 91103-2759 Office: 711 E Walnut St Ste 407 Pasadena CA 91101-1676

MOSHER, SUE A., news technology developer; b. Havre, Mont., Aug. 21, 1953; d. Richard B. and Malinda Grace (Simpson) Billingsley; m. Robert Allen Mosher, June 21, 1986; 1 child, Ann Maura. BA in Sociology, Coll. of William & Mary, Williamsburg, Va., 1974. Asst. music dir. Sta. WOWI-FM, Norfolk, Va., 1974-75; news dir. Sta. WNOR-AM/FM, Norfolk, Va., 1976-77; reporter, editor, writer Sta. WSOC-AM/FM, Charlotte, N.C., 1977-79; editor, writer AP Broadcast Svcs., N.Y.C., 1979-82; asst. broadcast editor Associated Press Broadcast Svcs., N.Y.C., 1982-83; gen. broadcast editor AP Broadcast Svcs., N.Y.C. and Washington, 1983-85; asst. dir. adminstrn. AP Broadcast Svcs., Washington, 1985-87; asst. dir. tech. devel. Associated Press Broadcast Svcs., Washington, 1989-94; prin. Slipstick Sys., Arlington, Va., 1994—. Author: AP NewsDesk User's Manual, 1991. Trustee, Universalist Nat. Meml. Ch., Washington, 1990-91. Mem. Radio-TV News Dirs. (data transmission guidelines com. 1986—).

MOSHER, WENDY JEAN, retail chain official; b. New Bedford, Mass., Feb. 10, 1966; d. Robert Milton and Judith Louise (Rayno) M. Student, Butera Sch. Art, Boston, 1984-85. Cashier Sears, Roebuck & Co., North Dartmouth, Mass., 1984-88; sales mgr. trainee Sears, Roebuck & Co., Dedham, Mass., 1988-90, mgr. automotive svc., 1990-91; mgr. automotive ctr. Sears, Roebuck & Co., Concord, N.H., 1991-93, Sears, Roebuck and Co., Nashua, N.H., 1993—. Mem. NAFE, Merchant's Assn. N.H. (bd. dirs.). Home: 21 Lakeside Ave Lakeville MA 02347 Office: Sears Roebuck and Co 310 Daniel Webster Hwy Ste 102 Nashua NH 03060-5700

MOSHIER, MARY BALUK, patent lawyer; b. Pitts., Aug. 20, 1905; d. Andrew and Johanna (Hlebasko) Baluk; m. Ross Warren Moshier, Sept. 15, 1937; children: Thomas, Stephen. BA, U. Ark., 1929; postgrad., U. Chgo., 1945-46; JD, No. Ky. U., 1962. Bar: U.S. Patent Office 1944, Ohio 1962. Tchr. Gary (Ind.) Pub. Schs., 1930-35; tech. libr. Monsanto Co., Dayton, Ohio, 1936-41, patent chemist, 1942-45, agt., atty., 1949-66; patent adviser U.S. Office of Naval Rsch., San Francisco, 1948-49; patents cons., pvt. practice Scottsdale, Sun City, Ariz., 1969—. Co-author: Anydrous Aluminum Chloride in Organic Chemistry, 1941. Founding mem. Episcopal chs. in Ridgecrest, Calif., 1947, Kettering, Ohio, 1950, Sun City, Ariz., 1974. Mem. AAAS, AAUW, NOW, Lawyers Club of Sun City, Nat. Assn. Ret. Fed. Employees, U.S. Chess Fedn., Phi Alpha Delta Legal Frat. Internat. Democrat. Episcopalian. Home and Office: 17300 N 88th Ave Apt 238 Peoria AZ 85382-3505

MOSIER, MARY C. (CATHY MOSIER), business owner; b. Dayton, Ohio, June 3, 1954; d. Herman Ullery and Cecilia Agnes (Mc Cluskey) Chrowl; m. Ronald Eugene Swank Jr., Jun. 7, 1975 (div. Oct. 1982); children: Angela, Ronald III, Samantha; m. David Michael Neufeld, Aug. 18, 1983 (div. 1991); children: Michael Brent Neufeld, Andrew Jonathan Neufeld; m. Steven Lynn Mosier, Nov. 6, 1992. Mgmt. asst. Air Force Maintenance, Supply and Munitions Mgmt. Engring. Team, Wright-Patterson AFB, Ohio, 1977-82, Air Force Svc. Info. and News Ctr., Kelly AFB, Tex., 1982-88; owner Cat's Crafts, San Antonio, 1988—; pres. Perfect Presentations, San Antonio, 1993—; stock fund mgr., resource advisor 76th Logistics Group, Kelly AFB, 1988—. Leader Webelos and Bear Dens Boy Scouts, 1994—. Recipient Dan Berkant award Air Force Assn., 1985. Mem. NAFE, Fed. Mgrs. Assn., Nat. Assn. Military Comptrollers. Republican. Home and Office: Perfect Presentations 9830 Autumn Silver San Antonio TX 78250

MOSKAL, JANINA, high technology manufacturing executive; b. Czerna, Poland, June 6, 1944; came to U.S., 1963; d. Stanislaw and Agata (Kleczek) Kot; m. Tadeusz J. Moskal, Dec. 29, 1960 (div. 1981); children: Robert R., Thomas L. Student, L.I. U., 1976-78; AAS, Nassau Community Coll., 1980. Machine operator Photocircuits Corp., Glen Cove, N.Y., 1966-70, programmer, 1970-72, supr., 1972-81, engr. process support, 1981-83, systems mgr. laser graphics, 1984-86; gen. mgr., ptnr. NC Design Corp., Williston Park, N.Y., 1983-84; systems mgr. Parlex Corp., Methuen, Mass., 1984-87; mfg. specialist Rothtec Engraving Corp., New Bedford, Mass., 1987—; owner, prin. JM Cons., Glen Cove, 1987—; organizer, instr. tech. courses and seminars, 1980-81, 1986-87. Officer Polish Nat. Home, Glen Cove, 1975-79, Polonia, Glen Cove, 1978. Republican. Roman Catholic. Office: JM Cons Co 109 Shore Rd Glen Cove NY 11542-3428

MOSKOWITZ, RANDI ZUCKER, nurse; b. N.Y.C., Oct. 19, 1948; d. Seymour and Gertrude (Levy) Zucker; R.N., Jewish Hosp. & Med. Center Sch. Nursing, 1969; BA, Marymount Manhattan Coll., 1975; MS, Hunter Coll., 1979; MBA, Columbia U., 1990; m. Marc N. Moskowitz, July 11, 1976. Gen. staff nurse neurosurgery unit, N.Y. Hosp., N.Y.C., 1969-71, sr. staff nurse Recovery Room, 1971-76, nurse coordinator utilization rev., 1976-79; health educator Office of Cancer Communications, Meml. Sloan-Kettering Cancer Center, 1979-81; adminstrv. nurse oncologist Bklyn. Community Hosp. Oncology Program, Meth. Hosp., 1981-83, grants coordinator radiotherapy dept., 1983-86; adminstr. Ambulatory Oncology Ctr., Columbia-Presbyn. Med. Ctr., N.Y.C., 1986-89; adminstr. Surg. Day Hosp., Meml. Sloan-Kettering Cancer Ctr., 1990—; Masters prof. oncology Columbia U. Sch. Nursing. Co-editor Oncology Nursing: Advances, Treatments and Trends into the Twenty-first Century; contbr. articles to profl. jours. Mem. Soc. Ambulatory Care Profl., Oncology Nursing Soc. (sec. N.Y.C. chpt. 1983-87, pres. 1988-89). Home: 446 E 86th St Apt 5-f New York NY 10028-6474 Office: Meml Sloan-Kettering Cancer Ctr 1275 York Ave New York NY 10021-6007

MOSLEY, JONETTA DELAINE, communications consultant; b. Pitts., Jan. 13, 1955; d. Joseph and Auvelia Janet (Williams) Howell; m. Reginald Tederrell Mosley, July 27, 1973 (div. Aug. 1980); 1 child, Kelly Bree. BSEET, Old Dominion U., 1980; JD, So. Meth. U., 1984; MBA, U. Tex., Arlington, 1986. Assoc. elec. engr. Philip Morris, U.S.A., Richmond, Va., 1980-81, Vought Corp., Grand Prairie, Tex., 1981-82; intern patent asst. LTV Corp., Dallas, 1982; briefing asst. Office of Gen. Counsel, Dallas; regional editor EDN Mag., Newton, Mass., 1984-93; pres. Sterling Impression, Inc., Arlington, 1987—; lectr. U. Tex., Arlington, 1994—. Editor newsletter Dataline, 1982-83. Earl Warren Legal Tng. scholar, 1981-84. Mem. Nat. Soc. Profl. Engrs., Nat. Tech. Assn., Profl. Assn. Diving Instrs., Phi Alpha Delta. Democrat. Roman Catholic. Office: 6014 Glenwood Dr Arlington TX 76017-6420

MOSLEY, MARY MAC, retired librarian; b. Rome, Ga., Nov. 11, 1926; d. William McKinley and Mary (Caldwell) H.; m. Samuel A. Mosley, June 12, 1946 (div. 1964); children: Samuel A. Jr., Pamela Ann, James Irwin. Student, Ga. State Coll. for Women, 1943-45; BS, Auburn U., 1947; cert. in teaching, Athens Coll., 1963; M in Library, Emory U., 1968. Tchr. sci. Rome City Schs., 1964-66; extension libr. Tri-County Regional Libr., 1966-67; libr. Shorter Coll., 1967-68, assoc. prof. libr. sci., 1968-76, dir. libr. svcs., 1968-93. Corr. sec. Rome Symphony Women's Guild; pres. Christian Women's Fellowship, 1st Christian Ch., 1992-94. Mem. ALA, AAUW (pres. Rome br.), N. Ga. Assn. Librs., Ga. Libr. Assn., Christian Women's Fellowship, Delta Kappa Gamma. Democrat. Mem. Christian Ch. Home: 24 Rockwood Pl Rome GA 30165-1728

MOSS, ANN MARIE, transportation engineer; b. Detroit, Sept. 18, 1957. Student, U. Detroit, 1975-76, Wayne State U., 1992-93, Oakland C.C., Royal Oak, Mich., 1993-94, Walsh Coll., 1994. Reader, scribe Catherine McAdam, Detroit, 1975—; transp. engr. Nat. Bank of Detroit, 1976—; demonstrator Detroit Sci. Ctr., 1980-85. Learning facilitator for visually impaired Oakland C.C., 1994. Mem. Mich. Assn. CPAs, Inst. Mgmt. Accts., Phi Eta Sigma. Office: Nat Bank of Detroit Transp 611 Woodward Detroit MI 48226

MOSS, CAROLINE GINA, banker; b. Elmira, N.Y., July 21, 1965; d. Francis J. and Gloria A. (Cornacchia) M. BSBA, Bucknell U., 1987; student exec. finance program, London (Eng.) Bus. Sch., 1994—. Trainee, loan officer devel. program Nat. Westminster Bank U.S., N.Y.C., 1987-88, asst. treas., comml. lending officer, 1989-91; asst. v.p., strategic planning officer NatWest Bancorp, N.Y.C., 1991-92; v.p., M&A analyst NatWest Bancorp, Jersey City, 1992-93; v.p., bus. analyst internat. Nat. Westminster Bank PLC, London, Eng., 1994—, personal asst. to the chmn., 1995—. Home: Flat 3 5 Royal Ave, London SW3 4QE, England Office: Nat Westminster Bank, 41 Lothbury, London EC2P 2BP, England

MOSS, CHERYL ANN, trade association official; b. Bronx, N.Y., Nov. 8, 1962; d. Michael A. and Carol (Horn) M. BA in Econs., U. Rochester, 1984, MS in Polit. Sci., 1985. Presdl. mgmt. intern U.S. Dept. Energy, Washington, 1985-86; mem. profl. staff U.S. Senate Energy Com., Washington, 1987-90; program mgr. U.S. Coun. for Energy Awareness, Washington, 1991-93; dir. Nuclear Energy Inst., Washington, 1994—. Mem. U. Rochester Alumni Assn. (exec. com. 1989—). Home: 4620 N Park Ave Apt 811E Chevy Chase MD 20815-4557 Office: Nuclear Energy Inst Ste 400 1776 I St Washington DC 20815

MOSS, ELIZABETH LUCILLE (BETTY MOSS), transportation company executive; b. Ironton, Mo., Feb. 13, 1939; d. James Leon and Dorothy Lucille (Russell) Rollen; m. Elliott Theodore Moss, Nov. 10, 1963 (div. Jan. 1984); children: Robert Belmont, Wendy Rollen. BA in Econs. and Bus. Adminstrn., Drury Coll., 1960. Registrar, transp. mgr. Cheley Colo. Camps, Inc., Denver and Estes Park, 1960-61; office mgr. Washington Nat. Ins. Co., Denver, 1960-61; sec. White House Decorating, Denver, 1961-62; with Ringsby Truck Lines, Denver, Oakland, Calif., and L.A., 1962-67, System 99 Freight Lines, L.A., 1967-69; terminal mgr. System 99 Freight Lines, Stockton, Calif., 1981-84; with Yellow Freight System, L.A., 1969-74, Hayward, Calif., 1974-77; ops. mgr. Yellow Freight System, Urbana, Ill., 1977-80; sales rep. Calif. Motor Express, San Jose, 1981; regional sales mgr. Schneider Nat. Carriers, Inc., No. Calif., 1984-86; account exec. TNT-Can., Nev. and Cen. Calif., 1986-88; mgr. Interstate-Intermodal Divs. HVH Transp., Denver, 1988-89; regional sales mgr. MNX, Inc., Northern Calif., 1989-91; dir. sales Mountain Valley Express, Manteca, Calif., 1992—; chmn. op. coun. for San Joaquin and Stanislaus Counties Calif. Trucking Assn., 1983-84; planning adv. com. Truck Accident Reduction Projects, San Joaquin County, 1987-88. Mem. Econ. Devel. Coun. Stockton C. of C., 1985-86; active Edison High Sch. Boosters, 1982-88. Mem. Nat. Def. Transp. Assn. (bd. dirs. 1986-87), Stockton Traffic Club (bd. dirs. 1982-84, Trucker of Yr.), Ctrl. Valley Traffic Club, Oakland Traffic Club, Delta Nu Alpha (bd. dirs. Region 1 1982-84, v.p. chpt. 103 1984-85, pres. 1985-86, chmn. bd. 1985-87, regional sec. 1987-88, Outstanding Achievement award 1986, 88). Methodist. Home: 455 E Ocean Blvd Apt 602 Long Beach CA 90802-4940

MOSS, JUDITH, mayor, academic administrator; b. Long Branch, N.J., July 11, 1924; d. Louis John and Bryna (Finegold) M. BA, Vassar Coll., 1944; MA, Columbia U., 1947; MS (NSF fellow), Stanford U., 1971. Statistician Statis. Rsch. Group, div. War Rsch., 1944-45; rsch. asst. Nat. Bur. Econ. Rsch., 1945-48; econ. analyst Port of N.Y. Authority, 1948-55, electronics rsch. analyst, 1955-56; electronics rsch. specialist Revlon, Inc., 1956-58; chief integrated data processing City of Phila., 1958-62; sr. system analyst Computer dept., G.E. Co., 1962-64; cons. systems specialist Computer dept., G.E. Co., N.Y.C., 1964-66; sr. ops. rsch. specialist, spl. projects ops., staff cons. Lockheed Missiles and Space Co., Sunnyvale, Calif., 1966-72; rsch. dir., interim vice chancellor pers. San Francisco C.C. Dist., 1972-92; mayor City of Mountain View (Calif.), 1975-77. Trustee Foothill-DeAnza C.C. Dist., 1991—, pres. bd., 1994—; mem. Mountain View City Coun., 1972-80; mem. adv. com. on mgmt. info. sys., chancellor's office Calif. C.C., mem. Trustees Commn. on Futures, 1992; chmn. rsch./devel. commn. Calif. Cmty. and Jr. Coll. Assn.; mem. exec. bd. Health Sys. Agy.; active Jewish Welfare Fedn.; exec. bd. Am. Jewish Com.; past pres. South Peninsula Jewish Cmty. Ctr.; treas. LWV, 1994—. Mem. Inst. Mgmt. Sci. (nat. coun. 1975), Ops. Rsch. Soc. Am., Am. Soc. Pub. Adminstrn., Assn. Calif. C.C. Adminstrs., Western Assn. Schs. and Colls. (accreditation teams mem.), League Calif. Cities, Assn. Bay Area Govts. (alt. exec. bd.). Home: 1943 Mount Vernon Ct # 301 Mountain View CA 94040-2001 Office: 12345 El Monte Ave Los Altos Hls CA 94022-4504

MOSS, MARY LYNN, college administrator; b. Raleigh, N.C., June 29, 1954; d. Zeb and Evelyn (Krause) M. BS, U. N.C., 1977, MEd, 1979, DEd, 1985. Rsch. dir., asst. dir. student activities Meredith Coll., Raleigh, 1979-82; assoc. dean, coach Wingate (N.C.) Coll., 1985-92, dean counseling and acad. devel., 1992—; adminstr. Camp Seafarer, YMCA, Arapahoe, N.C., summers 1982-92; chmn. instl. effectiveness com. Wingate Coll., 1993—. Deacon Wingate Bapt. Ch., 1992. Dupont fellow U. Va., 1982. Mem. ACA, U.S. Tennis Assn., Intercollegiate Tennis Assn., So. Assn. Coll. Student Affairs, N.C. Coll. Pers. Adminstrs., Charlotte Area Ednl. Consortium. Democrat. Baptist. Home: PO Box 105 Wingate NC 28174 Office: Wingate Coll Stegall Adminstrn Bldg Wingate NC 28174

MOSS, SANDRA HUGHES, law firm administrator; b. Atlanta, Dec. 24, 1945; d. Harold Melvin and Velma Aileen (Norton) H.; m. Marshall L. Moss, May 1, 1965; children: Tara Celise, Justin Hughes. Student West Ga. Coll., 1964-65, Ga. State U. Legal sec. Smith, Cohen, Ringel, Kohler & Martin, Atlanta, 1965-78; real estate salesman Century 21-Phoenix, College Park, Ga., 1978-80; office mgr./pers. dir. Smith, Cohen, Ringel, Kohler & Martin, Atlanta, 1980-85; dir. adminstrn. Smith, Gambrell & Russell, Atlanta, 1985—. Bd. dirs., sec. North Clayton Athletic Assn., Riverdale, Ga., 1981-83; sec. E.W. Oliver PTA, Riverdale, 1981; exec. com. E.W. Oliver and N. Clayton Jr. PTA, Riverdale, 1980, 81, 82; den leader Cub Scouts, Pack 959, Riverdale, 1984. Mem. Soc. Human Resource Mgmt., Assn. Legal Adminstrs. (sec. Atlanta chpt. 1988, v.p., pres. 1990-91, regional meetings officer 1992, 93). Home: 200 Deer Forest Trail Fayetteville GA 30214-4016 Office: Smith Gambrell & Russell 1230 Peachtree St NE Ste 3100 Atlanta GA 30309

MOSS, SUSAN, nurse, retail store owner; b. Youngstown, Ohio, Aug. 17, 1940; d. Jarlath G. and Sara G. (Curley) Carney; divorced; children: John P., Jerri Ann Moss Williams. Lic. nurse, Choffin Sch., 1973; AS in Am. Bus. Mgmt., Youngstown State U., 1992. Surg. scrub nurse St. Elizabeth Hosp., Youngstown, 1972-78; office mgr. Moss Equipment Co., North Jackson, Ohio, 1978-83; pvt. duty nurse Salem, Ohio, 1979—; night nurse supr. Gateways for Better Living, Youngstown, 1982-84; owner Laura's Bride and Formal Wear, Salem, 1987—, Strawberry Sunshine Svc. Co., Salem, 1994—; cons. Edith R. Nolf, Inc., Salem. Author: (novelette) Turlaleen. Water therapy aide Easter Seal Soc., Youngstown, 1970-75, bd. trustees, 1973-75; mem. Hear, Now, Denver, 1989. Mem. LPN Assn. Ohio, Bus. and Profl. Women, Youngstown State U. Alumni Club, Short Hills Lit. Soc., Beta Sigma Phi (v.p., Silver Circle award 1986, Order of the Rose 1987). Democrat. Roman Catholic. Office: Laura's Bride & Formal Wear 1271 E Pidgeon Rd Salem OH 44460-4364

MOSS, SUSAN JEAN, interior designer; b. Milw., Nov. 3, 1949. BS in Interior Design, Iowa State U., 1972. Pres. Susan Moss Interiors, Kauai, Hawaii, 1977-85; project designer Richard Crowell Assocs., Honolulu, 1985-90; pres. Trans-Pacific Design, Kamuela, Hawaii, 1991—. Vol. ARC, 1982, mass care vol., 1992; mem. design com. and cmty. rels. North Hawaii Cmty. Hosp., Kamuela, 1993-94; mem. design com. Waimea Main St. Program, Kamuela, 1993. Mem. Am. Soc. Interior Designers (dir., pres. Hawaii chpt., v.p., treas. 1984-91, co-chair design awards 1994, Design Excellence award 1994, Merit award 1987, Fred Harper Cmty. Svc. award 1993, Presdl. citation 1986), AIA (affiliate), Jr. League Honolulu, North Hawaii Rotary Club. Office: Trans-Pacific Design PO Box 190 Kamuela HI 96743

MOSS BOWER, PHYLIS DAWN, medical researcher; b. Waco, Tex., Oct. 27, 1959; d. Phillip Carroll and Teloiv Anita (Marrs) Eddins; m. W. Taylor Moss, Mar. 22, 1980 (div. Aug. 1990); children: Amber Nikkole Moss, Beau Christian Moss; m. Kevin Eugene Bower, May 27, 1992. Student, Tex. Tech. U., 1977-78, 4-C Bus. Coll., 1989-90. Tumor registry Scott & White Hosp., Waco, 1988-92; clin. rsch. in oncology LaGrange (Ill.) Hosp., 1992-93; clin. rsch. asst. pharm. Christie Clinic, Champaign, Ill., 1993—; spirit of Scott & White com. mem. Scott & White Hosp., Temple, Tex., 1992. Leader Girl Scouts USA, Waco, 1983; com. mem. Children's Miracle Network, Temple, 1988-92; breast cancer prevention team Nat. Surg. Adjuvant Bowel and Breast Protocol, LaGrange, 1992-93. Mem. Nat. Tumor Registrars Assn., Tex. Tumor Registrars Assn. (fin. com. mem. 1988-92, membership com. 1989-90), Soc. Clin. Rsch. Assn. (fin. com. mem. 1992—). Methodist. Home: RR 1 Box 71 Villa Grove IL 61956-9714 Office: Christie Clinic 101 W University Ave Champaign IL 61820-3970

MOSTER, MARY CLARE, public relations executive; b. Morristown, N.J., Apr. 7, 1950; d. Clarence R. and Ruth M. (Duffy) M.; m. Louis C. Williams, Jr., Oct. 4, 1987. BA in English with honors, Douglass Coll., 1972; MA in English Lit., Univ. Chgo., 1973. Accredited pub. rels. specialist. Editor No. Trust Bank, Chgo., 1973-75, advt. supr., 1975-77, communications officer, 1977-78; account exec. Hill & Knowlton, Inc., Chgo., 1978-80, v.p., 1980-83, sr. v.p., 1983-87, sr. v.p., mng. dir., 1987-88; staff v.p. comms. Navistar Internat. Corp., Chgo., 1988-93; v.p. corp. comms. Comdisco, Inc., Rosemont, Ill., 1993—; mem. bd. dirs. The Pegasus Players, 1993—. Author poetry, poetry translation. Bd. govs. Met. Planning Coun., Chgo., 1988-94; fellow Leadership Greater Chgo., 1989-90; bd. dirs. New City YMCA, Chgo., 1986-92; corp. devel. bd. Steppenwolf Theatre Co., Chgo., 1988-90; mem. The Chgo. Network, 1994—. Mem. Nat. Investor Rels. Inst. (bd. dirs. 1988-89, 90-93), Arthur W. Page Soc., Pub. Rels. Soc. Am., Internat. Assn. Bus. Comms., Internat. Women's Forum. Office: Comdisco Inc 6111 N River Rd Rosemont IL 60018-5158

MOSZER, IRENE MCCLEAN, information systems executive; b. Phila., Dec. 2, 1943; m. Max Moszer; children: David Christopher, Laura Susan. BS, Drexel U., 1965; MA, Pa. State U., 1967; PhD, Bryn Mawr Coll., 1970. Assoc. prof. econs. Va. State U., Petersburg, 1971-78; dir. forecasting Va. Power, Richmond, 1978-81, mgr. forecasting and econ. analysis, 1981, dist. mgr. East Richmond, 1982, mgr. corp. compensation, 1983, v.p. adminstrv. svcs., 1984-89, v.p. treas., corp. sec., 1990, v.p. info. systems, 1991—; economist Fed. Power Commn., Washington, 1968-70; adj. asst. prof., lectr. econs. Drexel U., Phila., 1966-68; grad. rsch. asst. econs. Bryn Mawr (Pa.) Coll., 1967-68; cons. State Corp. Commn. Va., 1972, 76-77, Bur. Econ. R&D, Val. State Coll., 1970-71; coun. mem. Va. World Trade Coun., Commonwealth of Va., 1988-90. Contbr. articles to profl. jours. Mem. Gov.'s Adv. Commn. on Workers' Compensation, Richmond, 1992-93, Gov.'s Econ. Adv. Bd., Richmond, 1986-90; chmn. Am. Heart Fund, Richmond, 1992; bd. dirs. Leadership Metro Richmond, 1990—; bd. dirs. Jr. Achievement, Richmond, 1990-91, Capital City chpt. Red Cross, Richmond, 1986-89.; mem. human resource planning div. United Way of Greater Richmond, 1986-89. Recipient Exxon Edn. Found. grant Va. State U., 1977, Doctoral fellowship Bryn Mawr Coll., 1966-67, Teaching assistantship Pa. State U., 1965-66, Undergrad. Tuition scholarship Drexel U., 1962-65, Corp. Achievement award Va. Coun. on Status of Women, 1992. Mem. Rotary. Office: Va Power 1 James River Plz 7th and Cary Sts Richmond VA 23219

MOSZKOWSKI, LENA IGGERS, secondary school educator; b. Hamburg, Mar. 8, 1930; d. Alfred G. and Lizzie (Minden); m. Steven Alexander, Aug. 29, 1952 (div. Oct. 1977); children: Benjamin Charles, Richard David, Ronald Bertram. BS, U. Richmond, 1948; MS, U. Chgo., 1953; postgrad., UCLA, 1958. Tchr. Lab. asst. U. Chgo. Ben May Cancer Research Lab., Chgo., 1951-53; biology, sci. tchrs. Bishop Conaty High Sch., Los Angeles, 1967-68; chemistry, sci. tchr. St. Paul High Sch., Santa Fe Springs, Calif., 1968-69; chemistry, human ecology tchr. Marlborough Sch., Los Angeles, 1969-71; tchr. biology and sci. ecology L.A. Unified Sch. Dist., 1971—. Author: Termite Taxonomy Cryptotermes Haviland and C. Krybi, Madagascar, 1955, Ecology and Man, 1971, Parallels in Human and Biological Ecology, 1977, American Public Education, An Inside Journey, 1991-92. Founder, adminstr., com. mem. UCLA Student (and Practical Assistance Cooperative Furniture), Los Angeles, 1963-67; active participant UCLA Earth Day Program, Los Angeles, 1970. Recipient Va. Sci. Talent Search Winner Va. Acad. of Sci., 1946; Push Vol. Tchr. award John C. Fremont High Sch., Los Angeles, 1978. Mem. NEA, Calif. Tchrs. Assn., United Tchrs. L.A., Sierra Club. Democrat. Jewish. Home: 3301 Shelburne Rd Baltimore MD 21208

MOTE, NANCY STAMMELBACH, educator, consultant; b. Pitts., Dec. 6, 1940; d. Albert Edmond and Kathryn (Wain) S.; m. Kenneth Lewis Hoffman, Sept. 3, 1966 (div.); m. James Curtis Mote, Jan. 1, 1977. BA, Grove City Coll., 1962; MEd, Pa. State U., 1965; postgrad., Rutgers U., 1973-81. Tchr. East Orange (N.J.) Bd. Edn., 1962-70; science coordinator, environ. edn. coordinator Livingston (N.J.) Bd. Edn., 1970-86; ednl. cons. McGraw-Hill Book Co., Hightstown, 1988-89, Macmillan/McGraw-Hill, Delran, N.J., 1989—; nat. sci. cons. Macmillan/McGraw Hill, 1993—; dir. Livingston Student Devel. Program, 1974-79; cons. Delta Edn., Nashua, N.H., 1980-86, State Dept. Edn., Trenton, N.J., 1985, McGraw-Hill, Hightstown, N.J., 1986-87. Trustee Hilltop Montessori Sch., Sparta, N.J., 1978-82, Pocono Environ. Edn. Ctr., 1987—. Mem. Nat. Sci. Tchrs. Assn. (exec. com.), N.J. Sci. Tchrs. Assn. (chmn. Elementary Sch. Sci. sect.), Nat. Sci. Suprs. Assn., N.J. Sci. Suprs. Assn. (treas. 1977-78), Assn. for Supervision and Curriculum Devel. Home: Starbuck Hill Rd Chestertown NY 12817 Office: MacMillan-McGraw-Hill Sch Divsn Delran NJ 08075

MOTE, SUE FRANCES, secondary educator; b. Huntsville, Tex., Apr. 13, 1938; d. William James and Angier Faye (Flynt) High; m. Fred Nolan Mote, Aug. 6, 1960; children: Sheree Lynn Mote Klass, John Keith. BA, East Tex. Bapt. Coll., 1959; MA, Sam Houston State U., 1966. Cert. profl. supr., secondary English tchr., Tex. Secondary English tchr. Tex. Pub. Schs., various cities, 1959-85; model tchr. Sam Houston State U., Huntsville, 1972-79; chairperson dept. English Huntsville High Sch., 1980-82; dir. curriculum devel. Huntsville Ind. Sch. Dist., 1985-87, dir. secondary edn., 1987—; cons. Internat. Reading Assn., Little Rock, 1988, Tex. Pub. Schs., Austin, Kingsville, 1990. Bd. dirs. Friends of Pub. Librs., Huntsville, 1994—. Mem. Nat. Coun. Tchrs. English, AAUW, ASCD, Nat. Staff Devel. Coun., Nat. Middle Sch. Assn., Tex. Assn. for Gifted-Talented, Huntsville C. of C. Office: Huntsville Ind Sch Dist 441 FM 2821 E Huntsville TX 77340

MOTES, MONICA ELIZABETH, accountant; b. Columbia, S.C., Jan. 15, 1965; d. James Murray Jr. and Vera M. (Waters) Smith; m. Tommy D. Motes, Feb. 19, 1994. BSBA, U. S.C., Aiken, 1987. Office mgr. Clearweave Hosiery Co., Saluda, S.C., 1983-85; sec., bookkeeper S.C. Aviation, Inc., Ninety Six, S.C., 1985-87; acct. Elliott, Davis & Co., Greenwood, S.C., 1987-90, Commn. of Pub. Works, Greenwood, S.C., 1990-92; prodn. planner, inventory control mgr. So. Brick Co., Ninety Six, S.C., 1992—. Baptist. Home: 1036 Dixired Rd Leesville SC 29070

MOTLEY, CONSTANCE BAKER (MRS. JOEL WILSON MOTLEY), federal judge, former city official; b. New Haven, Sept. 14, 1921; d. Willoughby Alva and Rachel (Huggins) Baker; m. Joel Wilson Motley, Aug. 18, 1946; 1 son, Joel Wilson, III. A.B., N.Y. U., 1943; LL.B., Columbia U., 1946. Bar: N.Y. bar 1948. Mem. Legal Def. and Ednl. Fund, NAACP, 1945-65; mem. N.Y. State Senate, 1964-65; pres. Manhattan Borough, 1965-66; U.S. dist. judge So. Dist. N.Y., 1966-82, chief judge, 1982-86, sr. judge, 1986—. Mem. N.Y. State Adv. Council Employment and Unemployment Ins., 1958-64. Mem. Assn. Bar City N.Y. Office: US Dist Ct US Courthouse Foley Sq New York NY 10007-1501

MOTT, JANET HART, rehabilitation counselor; b. Dallas, Mar. 19, 1939; d. Arthur Joseph and Willa Mae (Millsap) Hart; m. Clyde Edward Mott, Nov. 26, 1971; children: Rebecca, Michael, James, Carol. BA, U. Tex., 1960; MS, Calif. State U., L.A., 1964; PhD, Union Inst., Cin., 1992. Diplomate Am. Bd. Vocat. Experts; cert. rehab. counselor; registered counselor; cert. case mgr. Kindergarten tchr. All Peoples Christian Ch., L.A., 1960-62; social caseworker Bur. Pub. Assistance, L.A., 1962-64; rehab. counselor Dept. Social Welfare, Ventura, Calif., 1964-66, Easter Seal Soc., Worcester, Mass., 1967, U. Wash., Seattle, 1967-68, 69-72, U. Ariz., Tucson, 1968-69, Seattle Opportunities Industrialization Ctr., Seattle, 1967-68; rehab. counselor, case mgr. Mott Rehab. Svcs., Edmonds, Wash., 1972—; regional case mgr. Sunrise Healthcare Corp., 1995—. Mem. Nat. Rehab. Assn., Nat. Rehab. Counseling Assn., Am. Counseling Assn., Am. Rehab. Counseling Assn., Washington Med. Case Mgmt. Assn., Nat. Head Injury Found., Wash. State Head Injury Found., Am. Bd. Vocat. Experts. Home: 22044 99th Pl W Edmonds WA 98020-4540 Office: Mott Rehab Svcs Inc 24007 Edmonds Way Edmonds WA 98026-9161

MOTT, MARY ELIZABETH, educational administrator; b. West Hartford, Conn., July 10, 1931; d. Marshall Amos and Mary Salome (Herman) M. B.A., Conn. Coll. Women, 1953; M.A., Western Res. U., 1963. Cert. tchr., Ohio; cert. computer tchr., Ohio. Mgr. sales promotion Cleve. Electric Illuminating Co., 1953-60; tchr. Newbury Bd. Edn., Ohio, 1960-67, West Geauga Bd. Edn., Chesterland, Ohio, 1967—; chmn. state certification com. in computers ECCO, Mayfield, Ohio, 1983—, exec. bd., 1980—. Asst. dir. West Geauga Day Camp, Chesterland, 1968. Mem. Ednl. Computer Consortium Ohio, West Geauga Edn. Assn. (mem. exec. bd. 1975—), Delta Kappa Gamma. Republican. Clubs: MAC Users Group, Nat. Assn. Playing Card Collectors. Avocations: golf, travel, reading, gardening, computers. Office: Westwood Sch 13738 Caves Rd Chesterland OH 44026-3415

MOTZ, DIANA GRIBBON, federal judge; b. Washington, July 15, 1943; d. Daniel McNamara and Jane (Retzler) Gribbon; m. John Frederick Motz, Sept. 20, 1968; children: Catherine Jane, Daniel Gribbon. BA, Vassar Coll., 1965; LLB, U. Va., 1968. Bar: U.S. Dist. Ct. Md. 1969, U.S. Ct. Appeals (4th cir.) 1969, U.S. Supreme Ct. 1980. Assoc. Piper & Marbury, Balt., 1968-71; asst. atty. gen. State of Md., Balt., 1972-81, chief of litigation, 1981-86; ptnr. Frank, Bernstein, Conaway & Goldman, Balt., 1986-91; judge Md. Ct. of Special Appeals, Md., 1991-94; fed. judge U.S. Ct. Appeals (4th Cir.), Balt., 1994—. Mem. ABA, Md. Bar Assn., Balt. City Bar Assn. (exec. com. 1988), Am. Law Inst., Am. Bar Found., Md. Bar Found., Lawyers Round Table, Fed. Cts. Study Com., Wranglers Law Club. Roman Catholic. Office: Ste 920 101 Lombard St Baltimore MD 21201

MOUDON, ANNE VERNEZ, urban design educator; b. Yverdon, Vaud, Switzerland, Dec. 24, 1945; came to U.S., 1966; d. Ernest Edouard and Mauricette Lina (Duc) M.; m. Dimitrios Constantine Seferis, Dec. 30, 1982; children: Louisa Moudon, Constantine Thomas. BArch with honors, U. Calif., Berkeley, 1969; DSc, Ecole Poly. Fed., Lausanne, Switzerland, 1987. Fed. Register of Swiss Architects. Rsch. assoc. Bldg. Systems Devel., Inc., San Francisco, 1969-70; sr. project planner J. C. Warnecke and Assocs., N.Y.C., 1973-74; archtl. cons. McCue, Boone & Tomsick, San Francisco, 1974-76; asst. to assoc. prof. architecture MIT, Cambridge, Mass., 1975-81; assoc. prof. urban design U. Wash., Seattle, 1981-87, prof. architecture, landscape architecture, urban design and planning, 1987—, dir. urban design program, 1987-93, assoc. dean acad. affairs Coll. Arch. & Urban Planning, 1992-95; dir. Inst. Cascadia Cmty. and Environ., 1993—; lectr. in architecture U. Calif., Berkeley, 1973-75; Ford internat. career chair MIT Sch. Architecture, Cambridge, 1977-79; sec. Assn. Collegiate Schs. of Architecture, 1978-80; sr. researcher Kungl Tekniska Hogskolan, Sch. of Architecture, Stockholm, 1989. Author: Built for Change, 1986; editor: Public Streets for Public Use, 1987, 91, (monograph) Master-Planned Communities, 1990; contbr. articles to profl. jours. Recipient seven rsch. grants Nat. Endowment for the Arts, Washington, 1976-89, individual fellowship, 1986-87, Applied Rsch. award Progressive Architecture, 1983, two rsch. grants Wash. State Dept. Transp., Seattle, 1991-92. Fellow Inst. for Urban Design; mem. Internat. Assn. for the Study of People in Their Phys. Surroundings, Orgn. Women Architects, Tau Sigma Delta. Home: 3310 E Laurelhurst Dr NE Seattle WA 98105-5336 Office: U Wash Urban Design Gould Hall JO-40 Gould Hall Seattle WA 98195

MOUL, MAXINE BURNETT, state official; b. Oakland, Nebr., Jan. 26, 1947; d. Einer and Eva (Jacobson) Burnett; m. Francis Moul, Apr. 20, 1972; 1 child, Jeff. BS in Journalism, U. Nebr., 1969; DHL (hon.), Peru State Coll., 1993. Sunday feature writer, photographer Sioux City Iowa Jour., 1969-71; reporter, photographer, editor Maverick Media, Inc., Syracuse, Nebr., 1971-73, editor, pub., 1974-83, pres., 1983-90; grant writer, asst. coord. Nebr. Regional Med. Program, Lincoln, 1973-74; lt. gov. State of Nebr., Lincoln, 1991-93; dir. Dept. Econ. Devel., Lincoln, 1993—. Mem. Dem. Nat. Com., Washington, 1988-92, Nebr. Dem. State Ctrl. Com., Lincoln, 1974-88; del. Dem. Nat. Conf., 1972, 88, 92; mem. exec. com. Nebr. Dem. Party, Lincoln, 1988-93. Recipient Margaret Sanger award Planned Parenthood, Lincoln, 1991, Champion of Small Bus. award Nebr. Bus. Devel. Ctr., Omaha, 1991, Toll fellowship Coun. State Govts., Lexington, Ky., 1992. Mem. Bus. and Profl. Womem, Nebr. Mgmt. Assn. (Silver Knight award 1992), Nat. Conf. Lt. Govs. (bd. dirs. 1991-93), Nebr. Press Women, Women Execs. in State Govt., Cmty. Devel. Soc., U. Nebr.-Lincoln Journalism Alumni. Democrat. Office: State of Nebr PO Box 94666 Lincoln NE 68509-4666

MOULTON, GRACE CHARBONNET, physics educator; b. New Orleans, Nov. 1, 1923; d. Wilfred J. and Louise A. (Hellmers) Charbonnet; m. William Gates Moulton, June 1, 1947; children: Paul Charbonnet Moulton, Nancy Gates Moulton. BA, Tulane U., 1944; MS, U. Ill., 1948; PhD, U. Ala., 1962. Asst. prof. physics U. Ala., Tuscaloosa, 1962-65; asst. prof. physics Fla. State U., Tallahassee, 1965-74, assoc. prof. physics, 1974-80, prof. physics, 1980—; cons. State Bd. Regents, Fla., 1984-85, Fla. Univ. System, 1989-90. Referee jour. articles Jour. Chem. Physics, Radiation Rsch.; contbr. many sci. rsch. articles to profl. jours. Four Yr. Undergrad. scholar Tulane U., scholar U. Ill.; rsch. grantee NIH. Mem. Am. Phys. Soc., (mem. coun. southeastern sect. 1988—). Office: Fla State U Dept Physics Tallahassee FL 32304

MOULTON, KATHERINE KLAUBER, hotel executive; b. Buffalo, Nov. 28, 1956; d. Murray Joseph and Joanna (Brown) Klauber; m. Michael Arthur Moulton, July, 10, 1982. BS, Cornell U., 1978. Hotel and restaurant designer Cini-Grissom Assoc., Potomac, Md., 1978-82; pres., gen. mgr. Colony Beach & Tennis Resort, Longboat Key, Fla., 1982—; owner Le Tennique, Longboat Key, 1982—; exec. v.p., cons., designer Total Environments, Longboat Key, 1982—. Contbr. articles to restaurant and hotel design mags. Mem. Coquille, Sarasota, Fla., 1982; organizer, fund raiser St. Jude's Children's Rsch. Hosp., 1982; mem. steering com. Girls Inc.; mem. resources com. John and Mabel Ringling Mus.; mem. Sarasota County Tourist Devel. Coun. Recipient Region IV Advocacy award Girls Inc., 1993. Mem. Am. Hotel Motel Assn., Fla. Hotel Motel Assn., Cornell Soc. Hotelmen. Office: Colony Beach & Tennis Resort 1620 Gulf Of Mexico Dr Longboat Key FL 34228-3403

MOULY, EILEEN LOUISE, financial planner; b. Milw., Apr. 18, 1955; d. George Joseph and Gertrude Mary (DuBois) M. MBA in Acctg. summa cum laude, U. Miami, Coral Gables, Fla., 1977, MBA, 1978. CPA, Fla.; cert. fin. planner. Acct. Main Hurdman, CPA's, Miami, Fla., 1979-82, Coopers & Lybrand, CPA's, West Palm Beach, Fla., 1982-83, Pannell Kerr Forster CPA's, Miami, 1983-84; cert. fin. planner Consortium Group, Miami, 1984-86; ptnr., fin. planner Evensky & Brown, Miami, 1986-91; pres. Eileen L. Mouly & Assocs. Inc. Fin. Advisors, Miami, 1991—; instr. U. Miami, 1987-90, Fla. Internat. U., 1987-90; speaker in field. Active Am. Cancer Soc. Mem. AICPA, Fla. Inst. CPAs (bd. dirs. 1991—, sec. South Dade chpt. 1993-94, treas. 1994-95), Internat. Assn. Fin. Planning, Registry Fin. Planning Practitioners, Inst. Cert. Fin. Planners (cert., v.p. greater Miami chpt. 1987-91), Leadership South Dade. Office: Eileen L Mouly & Assocs Inc 290 NW 165th St P800 Miami FL 33169

MOUNT, MARSHA LOUISE, management consultant; b. Newark, May 26, 1962; d. Huston Ellis and Katherine Ellery (Lyman) M. BA, Columbia U., 1984, MBA, 1990. Rsch. asst. Gen. Bd. Global Ministries, N.Y.C., 1984-85; analyst Bristol-Myers, N.Y.C., 1986-88; assoc. staff analyst N.Y.C. Dept. Transp., 1990-94, dep. dir. analytical svcs., 1992-94; mgmt. cons. George S. May Internat. Co., San Jose, Calif., 1994—. Mem. Nat. Mus. Women in Arts, Washington. Recipient Cert. of Merit Nat. Merit Scholarship Corp., 1980, Cert. of Distinction Barnard Coll., N.Y.C., 1984. Mem. NAFE, Am. Soc. Quality Control, Nat. Honor Soc., Beta Gamma Sigma. Home: # K8 206 Lilly Rd NE Olympia WA 98506

MOUNTZ, LOUISE CARSON SMITH, retired librarian; b. Fond Du Lac, Wis., Oct. 20, 1911; d. Roy Carson and Charlotte Louise (Scheurs) Smith; m. George Edward Mountz, May 4, 1935 (dec. Oct. 3 1951); children: Peter Carson, Pamela Teeters Mountz McDonald. Student, Western Coll., 1929-31; AB, The Ohio State U., 1933; MA, Ball State U., 1962; postgrad., Manchester Coll., 1954, Ind. U., 1960-61. Cert. tchr., Ind. Tchr. Monroeville (Ind.) High Sch., 1953-54, Riverdale High Sch., St. Joe, Ind., 1954-55; libr. High Sch., Avilla, Ind., 1955-58; head libr. Penn High Sch., Mishawaka, Ind., 1958-67, Northwood Jr. High Sch., Ft. Wayne, Ind., 1967-69, McIntosh Jr. High Sch., Auburn, Ind., 1969-74; dir. Media Ctr. DeKalb Jr. High Sch., Auburn, Ind., 1974-78; ret., 1978; cons. media ctr. planning Penn-Harris-Madison Sch. Corp., Mishawaka, 1966-67. Author: Biographies for Junior High Schools and Correlated Audio-Visual Materials, 1970; contbr. articles to profl. jours. Bd. dirs. DeKalb County chpt. ARC, 1938-42, 51-53, DeKalb County Heart Assn., 1946-52, DeKalb County Community Concert Assn., 1946-58, Am. Field Svc. Mishawaka chpt., 1960-67; mem Ft. Wayne Philharmonic Orch. Assn., Ft. Wayne Art Mus., Ft. Wayne Hist. Soc., Preservation of Dekalb County Assn., DeKalb Meml. Hosp. Womens Guild. Mem. AAUW, ALA, NEA, World Confedn. Orgns. Teaching Professions, Nat. Coun. Tchrs. English, Ind. Sch. Librarians Assn. (dir. 1963-67), Internat. Assn. Sch. Librarianship, Ind. Assn. Ednl. Communication and Tech., Assn. Ind. Media Educators, Nat. Ret. Tchrs. Assns., Nat. Trust Hist. Preservation, Hist. Landmarks Found. Ind., Delta Kappa Gamma (charter mem., Beta Beta chpt.), Kappa Kappa Kappa (pr. officer 1941-45, pres. Alpha Chi chpt. 1938-40, Garrett Assoc. chpt. 1971-73), Delta Delta Delta (house pres.). Methodist. Lodge: Order Ea. Star. Clubs: Greenhurst Country, Ft. Wayne Women's, Athena Lit. (hon. mem.), Ladies Lit. of Auburn.

MOURAR, LORI LOUISE, nurse; b. Reading, Pa., June 23, 1964; d. Willard Lee and Elizabeth Elaine (Ireson) M. RN, Bryn Mawr Hosp. Sch. Nursing, 1988; student, Ea. Christian Coll., 1992—. RN, Pa., Ariz., S.C. Orthopedics charge nurse Sacred Heart Hosp., Norristown, Pa., 1988-90; pediat. staff nurse Jefferson Park Hosp., Phila., 1990-91; med.-surg. traveling nurse TravCorps, Malden, Mass., 1991-92; vis. nurse Cmty. Health Affiliates, Ardmore, Pa., 1992-94, home care liaison, case mgr., 1994—. Vol. Rep. Hdqs., East Stroudsburg, Pa., 1983. Mem. Main Line Jaycees. Home: 201 E Chelsea Cir Newtown Square PA 19073-2110

MOUSSEAU, DORIS NAOMI BARTON, elementary school principal; b. Alpena, Mich., May 6, 1934; d. Merritt Benjamin and Naomi Dora Josephine (Pieper) Barton; m. Bernard Joseph Mousseau, July 31, 1954. AA, Alpena Community Coll., 1954; BS, Wayne State U., 1959; MA, U. Mich., 1961, postgrad., 1972-75. Profl. cert. ednl. adminstr., tchr. Elem. tchr. Clarkston (Mich.) Community Schs., 1954-66; elem. sch. prin. Andersonville Sch., Clarkston, 1966—, Bailey Lake Sch., Clarkston, 1979—. Cons., rsch. com. Youth Assistance Oakland County Ct. Svcs., 1968-88; leader Clarkston PTA, 1967—; chair Clarkston Sch. Dist. campaign, United Way, 1985, 86; mem. allocations com. Oakland County United Way, 1987-88. Recipient Outstanding Svc. award Davisburg Jaycees, Springfield Twp., 1977, Vol. Recognition award Oakland County (Mich.) Cts., 1984. Fellow ASCD, MACUL (State Assn. Ednl. Computer Users); mem. NEA (del. 1964), Mich. Elem. and Middle Sch. Prins. Assn. (treas., regional del. 1982—, pres.-elect Region 7 1988-89, program planner, pres. 1989-90, sr. advisor, 1990-91, Honor award Region #7 1991), Mich. Edn. Assn. (pres. 1960-66, del. 1966), Clarkston Edn. Assn. (author, editor 1st directory 1963), Women's Bowling Assn., Elks, Spring Meadows Hole-in-One Golf Club, Phi Delta Kappa, Delta Kappa Gamma (pres. 1972-74, past state and nat. chmn., Woman of Distinction 1982). Republican. Home: 6825 Rattalee Lake Rd Clarkston MI 48348-1955 Office: Clarkston Community Schs Bailey Lake Sch 8051 Pine Knob Rd Clarkston MI 48348-3730

MOWDAY, ELAINE WARK, clinical psychologist, educator; b. L.A.. AB, U. Calif., Berkeley, 1967; PhD, Pacific Grad. Sch. Psychology, 1981. Lic. psychologist, Calif. Asst. dir. tng. dept. psychology Children's Hosp., San Francisco, 1975-90, dir. psychology tng., 1990-93; pvt. practice San Francisco, 1978—; cons. psychology Lighthouse for the Blind, San Francisco, 1986-88; oral commr. Psychol. Exam Com., Sacramento, Calif., 1986—; mem. utilization rev. com. Family Svc. Agy., San Francisco, 1990-94, chmn., 1993-94; affiliate staff Calif. Pacific Med. Ctr., San Francisco. Mem. APA. Office: 3663 Sacramento St San Francisco CA 94118 also: 220 Montgomery St # 870 San Francisco CA 94104

MOWERY, ELAINE NICOLE, process consultant; b. Kennewick, Wash., May 24, 1972; d. Johnny C. and Judith Loanne Mowery. BA in Bus. Adminstrn., U. Wash., 1994. Process cons. Andersen Consulting LLP, Seattle, 1994—; student rep. undergrad. program com. U. Wash. Bus. Sch., 1993-94. Student amb. People to People Youth Sci. Exch., Soviet Union, 1989; vol. Goodwill Games, Kennewick, Wash., 1990; student amb. Am. Assembly Collegiate Schs. Bus., Seattle, 1993. Mem. Bus. Info. Tech. Soc. (v.p. membership 1993-94), Am. Mktg. Assn., Alpha Kappa Psi, Sigma Kappa. Home: 3435 Burke Ave N #306 Seattle WA 98103 Office: Andersen Consulting LLP 801 Second Ave Ste 900 Seattle WA 98104

MOY, AUDREY, retail buyer; b. Bronx, N.Y., May 6, 1942; d. Ferdinand Walter Melkert and Stella (Factorow) Schroff; m. Edward Moy, Aug. 16, 1974. BA in Biology, Hunter Coll., 1964, MA in Biology, 1966. Asst. buyer Bonwit Teller, N.Y.C., 1961-68; dept. mgr. Franklin Simon, N.Y.C., 1968; asst. buyer Saks Fifth Ave., N.Y.C., 1968-73; buyer Martins, Bklyn., 1973, Belk Store Svcs., N.Y.C., 1974—. Mem. NAFE. Avocations: cooking, fishing, gardening.

MOY, PEARL MEI-HUNG, antiques dealer; b. Hong Kong, Aug. 2, 1965; came to U.S., 1969; d. Wai Yu Moy and Ping Han Chan. Sales assoc. Polo-Ralph Lauren, Beachwood, Ohio, 1979-83, Stamford, Conn., 1983-85; assoc. product mgr.-men's divsn. Polo-Ralph Lauren, N.Y.C., 1985-92; antiques dealer Phelps-Bancroft Ltd., Tolland, Mass., 1993—. Fund raiser Boys and Girls Club, N.Y.C., 1991; cons. Beautification Com., N.Y.C., 1991; fund raiser Nat. Rep. Party, Washington, 1993, N.Y.C., 1992. Mem. Union League Club, Met. Club.

MOYA, ROSEMARY MERCEDES, mental health administrator; b. Santa Fe, Aug. 11, 1957; d. Willie and Mercedes Sadie Ramona (Rivera) Padilla; m. Raymond Anthony Moya, Aug. 9, 1980; children: Joslyn Monique, Alyssa Nichole. BS in Edn., U. N.Mex., 1979, MPA, 1990. Adminstrv. asst. Hubbard Broadcasting, Albuquerque, 1980; staff asst. N.Mex. Mcpl. League, Santa Fe, 1980-81; staff asst. Div. Mental Health/Dept. of Health, Santa Fe, 1981-82, pers. adminstr., 1982-84, planner, 1981-88, health program mgr., 1988-91, chief community programs bur., 1991—. Parent vol. St. Francis Cath. Sch., 1990—; vol. Am. Cancer Soc., 1993, Easter Seals, Santa Fe, 1991; sec. liturgy com. Santa Maria de la Paz Cath. Com., 1991-94, chair liturgy com., 1994—, mem. bldg. com., 1991-94, mem. art selection com., 1992-94. N.Mex. Mcpl. League scholar, 1987-90; named Woman of Yr., Girls Club, Santa Fe, 1987. Mem. NAFE, Nat. Orgn. for Victim Assistance, Pi Alpha Alpha, Phi Kappa Phi. Democrat. Roman Catholic. Office: Dept Health/Div Mental Hlth 1190 St Francis Dr Santa Fe NM 87502

MOYA, SARA DREIER, municipal government official; b. N.Y.C., June 9, 1945; d. Stuart Samuel and Hortense (Brill) Dreier; m. P. Robert Moya, May 30, 1966; children: J. Brill, Joshua D. BA, Wheaton Coll., Norton, Mass., 1967; postgrad., Mills Coll., Oakland, Calif., 1967-68, Ariz. State U., 1992—. Mem. Paradise Valley (Ariz.) Town Coun., 1986—, vice mayor, 1990-92; chmn. Gov.'s Homeless Trust Fund Oversight Com., 1991—; pres. Ctr. for Acad. Precosity, Ariz. State U., Tempe, 1987—; bd. dirs. Ariz. Assn. Gifted and Talented; participant 3d session Leadership Am., 1990. Mem. Citizens Adv. Bd. Paradise Valley Police Dept., 1984-86, Valley Citizens League Task Force on Edn.; chair Maricopa Assn. Govts. Task Force on Homeless, 1989-92; mem. FEMA bd. Maricopa County and Ariz., 1989—; bd. dirs. Valley Youth Theater, 1990—, Maricopa County Homeless Accomodation Sch., 1991—. Mem. ASPA, Ariz. Women in Mcpl. Govt. (sec. 1988-89, bd. dirs. 1986—, pres. 1989-90), Maricopa Assn. Govts. (regional coun. 1988—, vice-chmn. mag. regional devel. policy com. 1989-91, chair 1992—, mag. joint econ. devel./human resources subcom., mag. youth policy com. 1994—), Maricopa Assn. Govts. (air quality policy com. 1994—), Ariz. Acad., Paradise Valley Country Club, Phi Kappa Phi. Republican. Home: 5119 E Desert Park Ln Paradise Vly AZ 85253-3055 Office: Town Paradise Valley 6401 E Lincoln Dr Paradise Vly AZ 85253-4328

MOYER, CHERYL LYNN, non-profit administrator; b. St. Petersburg, Fla., Apr. 4, 1953; d. Joseph Paul Safko and Doris Marie (Wolf) Sniegocki; m. John Arthur Weber (div. 1982); m. Ross Allen Moyer, June 21, 1983; children: Deborah, Martin, Brian, Spencer. BS, Lock Haven U., 1986; MPA, Pa. State U., 1987. Office mgr. Piper Aircraft Corp., Lock Haven, Pa., 1974-76; radio rep. Sta. WTGC Radio, Lewisburg, Pa., 1976-77; sales rep. Sears, Lycoming Mall, Pa., 1977-83; ptnr., dir. The Trading Post, Williamsport, Pa., 1983-85; mgr., founder Lock Haven U. Day Care, 1985-86; field mgr. Pa. Pub. Interest Coalition, State Coll., Pa., 1987-88; exec. dir. Pa. Assn. Families, Harrisburg, Pa., 1988-91; unit dir.-residential Resources for Human Devel., Phila., 1989-93; mgr. ob-gyn. clinic Meth. Hosp., Phila., 1993-94, bus. analyst, 1994; owner Family Fin. Svcs., 1994—. Grantee Family Planning Svcs., 1994. Mem. Nat. Assn. Dual Diagnosis, Pa. State Alumni Assn., Interfaith Assn., Mensa. Home: 10 Forest Ave Medford NJ 08055 Office: Womens Ctr 2301 S Broad St Philadelphia PA 19148

MOYER, HOLLEY MARKER, lawyer; b. Jamestown, N.Y., Jan. 30, 1947; d. Burdette James and Mary (Novitske) Marker; m. Brent Carlson Blair, June 17, 1967 (div. Dec. 1984); children: Jennifer Kristen, Kendra Elise; m. William Winfield Moyer, Feb. 28, 1987. AAS, Jamestown Community Coll., 1966; BS, Ohio U., 1969; MA, W.Va. U., 1974, JD, 1980. Bar: W.Va. 1980, U.S. Dist. Ct. (so. dist.) W.Va. 1980, Pa. 1982, U.S. Dist. Ct. (we. dist.) Pa. 1982. Tchr. math. various pub. schs., Santa Ana (Calif.), Lakewood (N.Y.) and Morgantown (W.Va.), 1970-77; atty. for students W.Va. U., Morgantown, 1980; assoc. libr., lectr. W.Va. U. Coll. Law, Morgantown, 1980-83; assoc., libr. Jackson, Kelly, Holt & O'Farrell, Charleston, W.Va., 1983-86; cons. Hildebrandt, Inc., Somerville, N.J., 1986-94; dir. customer rels. Lexis-Nexis, Dayton, Ohio, 1994—; speaker at regional, nat. and internat. legal confs. Contbr. articles to profl. jours. Mem. ABA, Am. Assn. Law Libs., N.J. Assn. Law Libs., Phi Delta Phi. Office: Lexis-Nexis Bldg IV 9443 Springboro Pike Miamisburg OH 45342

MOYER, JANE LEA MCMINN, school system administrator; b. Omaha, Dec. 31, 1955; d. H. Samuel and Beverly Jane (Haarmann) McMinn; m. Charles Craig Moyer, June 27, 1981 (div. Nov. 1992); children: Charles Scott, Thomas McMinn. BS in Edn., U. Nebr., 1978; MA in Ednl. Adminstrn., Kearney State Coll., 1985. Cert. adminstr., secondary sch. prin. type D, Colo.; cert. adminstr., supr. secondary endorsed English tchr., reading and mildy-moderately handicapped 7-12, Nebr. Tchr. Omaha Pub. Schs., summers 1978/81, Waverly (Nebr.) Pub. Schs., 1978-79, Millard Pub. Schs., Omaha, 1979-82, Grand Island (Nebr.) Pub. Schs., 1982-93; asst. prin. Grand Junction (Colo.) High Sch., 1993-94, Widefield High Sch., Colorado Springs, 1994—. Bd. dirs. Cen. Nebr. Coun. Alcoholism, Grand Island, 1989-93, sec. 1990-91; bd. dirs. First Presbyn. Ch. Pre-Sch., Grand Island, 1990-93; mem. Grand Island Edn. 2000 Commn., Grand Island Pub. Schs., 1992-93. Mem. Nat. Assn. Secondary Sch. Prins., Colo. Assn. Sch. Execs., Nebr. Assn. Mid. Level Edn. (pres. elect 1993, mem. chmn. 1991-93, bd. dirs. 1991-93), Phi Delta Kappa, Kappa Kappa Gamma (area rush chmn. Nebr. chpt. 1978-93). Republican. Lutheran. Home: 2649 Hatch Circle Colorado Springs CO 80920 Office: Widefield High Sch 615 Widefield Dr Colorado Springs CO 80911

MOYER, JUNE F., critical care nurse; b. Lansdale, Pa., Mar. 14, 1939; d. Marvin D. and Mildred Z. (Kulp) M. BS in Bible, Phila. Coll. of Bible, 1961; diploma, Presbyn. Hosp., 1964; BSN, La Salle U., 1985. Cert. med./surg. nurse, Pa. Staff nurse Presbyn. Hosp. Med. Ctr., Phila., 1964-65; dept. mgr. Grandview Hosp., Sellersville, Pa., 1965—. mem. AACN, Am. Orgn. Nurse Mgrs., Hosp. Assn. Pa., Sigma Theta Tau. Home: 221 W Walnut St Souderton PA 18964-1619

MOYER, NANCY JANE, art educator; b. L.A., Jan. 24, 1938; d. Vernon and Lelia Mae (Sturges) M. BA, U. Southwestern L.A., 1960; MA, La. State U., 1963; PhD, So. Ill. U., 1970. Instr. art S.W. Tex. State U., San Marcos, 1964-66; chair art dept. St. Francis Acad., Joliet, Ill., 1966-67, So. Ill. U., Carbondale, 1968-69, Pan Am. U., Edinburg, Tex., 1972-80; prof. art U. Tex.-Pan Am., Edinburg, Tex., 1969-94, chair art dept., 1994—. One-woman shows include exhbns. for drawing and jewelry; exhibited in over 72 group shows. Recipient Disting. Faculty Achievement award U. Tex.-Pan Am., 1989-90, Outstanding Faculty award, 1990; named Profesora Visitante, Univ. de las Americas, 1989. Mem. NEA, Tex. State Tchrs. Assn., Soc. N.Am. Goldsmiths, Pi Kappa Pi (pres. elect 1995). Home: 6508 N 12th St Mcallen TX 78504-3245

MOYERS, JUDITH DAVIDSON, television producer; b. Dallas, May 12, 1935; d. Henry Joseph and Eula E. (Dendy) Davidson; m. Bill D. Moyers; children: William Cope, Suzanne, John. BS, U. Tex., 1956; LittD (hon.), L.I. U., 1989, SUNY, 1990. Pres., exec. prodr. Pub. Affairs T.V., N.Y.C., 1987—; Bd. dirs. Paine Webber Mut. Funds, Ogden Corp. Exec. prodr. numerous T.V. documentaries (Emmy 1980); contbr. articles to profl. jours., newspapers, mags. Trustee SUNY, 1976-90; commr. U.S. commn. UNESCO, Washington, 1977-80, White House commn. IYC, Washington, 1978-80; mem. judicial selection com. State N.Y., 1992-93. Mem. Century Club. Mem. Congregational Ch. Office: Pub Affairs TV Inc 356 W 58th St New York NY 10019

MOYERS, SYLVIA DEAN, medical record librarian; b. Independence, W.Va., Oct. 22, 1936; d. Wilkie Russell and Ina Laura (Watkins) Collins; m. Paul Franklin Moyers, June 29, 1957; children: Tammy Jeanne, Thomas Paul, Tara Sue. Student, Am. Med. Record Assn., 1977-79. Sec., Teets Lumber Co., Terra Alta, W.Va., 1954-58, Preston County News, Terra Alta, 1958-60; med. record clk. med. record dept. Hopemont (W.Va.) Hosp., 1960-75, dir., 1975-88; sec. The Terra Alta Bank, W.Va., 1990—. Charter mem., past mother advisor Terra Alta Assembly No. 26, Order of Rainbow for Girls, past grand editor Mountain Echoes. Mem. Am. Med. Record Assn., W.Va. Med. Record Assn., Women of Moose. Republican. Methodist. Home: RR 2 Box 273-e Albright WV 26519

MOYLAN, ANN MARIE, critical care nurse; b. Aug. 9, 1964; d. William H. and Ruth E. (Ward) M. BSN, Coll. of New Rochelle, N.Y., 1986; MA in Nursing, NYU, 1990. Staff nurse N.Y. Hosp.-Cornell Med. Ctr., N.Y.C., 1986-89, sr. staff nurse, 1989—. Mem. AACN, ANA, N.Y. State Nurses Assn., Coun. on Computer Applications in Nursing, Nat. Assn. Quality Assurance, Nat. Nurses in Bus. Assn., Sigma Theta Tau.

MOYNAHAN, ELIZABETH REILLY, architect; b. Boston, June 6, 1925; d. Eugene Edward and Mary Eleanor (mcNeese) Reilly; m. Julian Lane Moynahan, Aug. 6, 1945; children: Catherine Maria (dec.), Brigid Elizabeth, Mary Ellen. AB, Radcliffe U., 1946; MArch, Harvard U., 1952. Lic. architect, N.J., Pa., La.; profl. planner, N.J. Architect Ronald Vaughn Assoc., Yardley, Pa., 1958-65, Elizabeth Reilly Moynahan, AIA Architect,

Princeton, N.J., 1965—; commr. N.J. State Bd. Architects, 1976-83. Architect housing, community ctrs., Women's Ctr. for Douglass Coll. N.J. State facilities, restorations, La., N.J., Mass., Pa., Ireland, London. Mem. AIA (Ctrl. chpt. N.J. Soc. Architects sec. 1975, architects housing 1970—), N.J. Soc. Architects (sec. 1984, treas. 1985). Home and Office: 3439 Lawrenceville Rd Princeton NJ 08540-4717

MOYNIHAN, BARBARA ANN, psychotherapist; b. Worcester, Mass.; d. Mario and Linda (Guerrera) DeMarco; 1 child, Michael E. Moynihan. Diploma in nursing, Worcester (Mass.) City Hosp., 1956; BSN, So. Conn. State U., 1977, MS in Counseling, 1981; PhD, U. Conn., 1992; MSN, So. Conn. State U., 1994. RN, Conn.; cert. clin. specialist, adult mental health and psychiat. nursing. Various nursing positions, 1957-62; staff nurse Yale-New Haven Hosp., 1962-71, head nurse emergency svc., 1971-73, staff instr. emergency svc., 1973-76, asst. dir. nursing emergency svc., 1976-80, coord., nurse practitioner, victimology program, 1980-83; founder, dir. rape crisis svc. YWCA of Greater New Haven, 1983-89, founder, dir., 1985-89, founder Teen Connection, 1988; founder Conn. Consortium of Univs. Against Sexual Assault, 1986—; pvt. practice psychotherapist, 1985—; psychotherapist Women's Health and Wellness Ctr. Meriden-Wallingford Hosp., Meriden, Conn., 1990-92; mem. faculty So. Conn. State U. Sch. Nursing, New Haven, 1989—; clin. faculty Concerned Svcs., Guildford, Conn., 1985-88; clin. cons. Yale U. Health Svcs., New Haven, 1983-85; cons., expert witness in civil and criminal cases dealing with sexual assault, 1986—; mem. courtesy faculty Sch. Nursing, Yale U., 1994; cons. PS&D unit West Haven (Conn.) Vets. Hosp. Contbr. numerous articles on sexual assault to profl. jours. Bd. dirs. YWCA, Greater New Haven, 1994. Recipient Elm Ivy award Yale U., 1986. Mem. Office: PO Box 194 Branford CT 06405-0194

MOZER, ANNA CECELIA, design technician; b. Ridley Park, Pa., Aug. 25, 1943; d. Anna Cecelia (Smith) M. Student, Pa. State U. Mem. assembly line Control Switch Co., Folcroft, Pa., 1963-65, mem. machine shop, 1965-66, mem. quality control staff, 1966-67, mem. drafting staff, 1967-69; mem. design staff Wilokinson Electronics, Woodlyn, Pa., 1969-73, Ram Assocs., Glenolden, Pa., 1973-74, Sonobond Corp., West Chester, Pa., 1974-75, M&T Corp., Phila., 1975-78, E.I. DuPont Co., Inc., Newark, Del., 1978—. Mem. bowl-a-thon team Jr. Achievement, Newark, 1994; committeewoman Rep. Orgn., Penn Twp., Pa., 1984093; rescue aux. trustee Kennett Rec., Kennett Sq., Pa., 1988-91; vol. So. Chester County Med., Penn Twp., 1981-88; mem. aux. West Grove (Pa.) Fire Co., 1981-93. Mem. Bus. and Profl. Womens Club, Inc. (1st v.p. Kennett chpt. 1990-91, pres. 1991-92, by-laws chair 1993-95, Women in Govt. awards 1990, 91; 1st v.p. Mid County chpt. 1993-94, pres. 1994-95), Soroptimists. Methodist. Home: PO Box 146 West Grove PA 19390-0146

MOZZOCHI, DEANNA JEAN, interior designer, business owner; b. North Platte, Nebr., Sept. 30, 1938; d. Francis Whitford and Nancy Elizabeth (Hale) Donnell; m. Michael Joseph Mozzochi Jr., Sept. 8, 1962; children: Susan Elizabeth, Michael Joseph III. BA, U. Nebr., 1960; A in Fine Arts, Cottey Coll., 1958; cert. interior design, Paier Coll. Art, 1977. Cert. Nat. Coun. for Interior Design Qualification. Owner DM Interiors, Clinton, Conn., 1978—. Mem. Am. Soc. Interior Designers, Fedn. Garden Clubs Conn., Inc. (chmn. judges coun. 1989-93, membership chmn., 2d v.p. 1993-95), Nat. Coun. State Garden Clubs, Inc. (master flower show judge 1982—), Arbor Garden Club (pres. 1985-88). Home and Office: 16 Shore Rd Clinton CT 06413-2362

MUCCIANO, STEPHANIE LYONS, hospitality, travel, and tourism executive; b. Pitts., Jan. 8; d. Ross Cooper and Catherine Dorothy (Perrone) Lyons; m. Richard Francis Mucciano(dec.); 1 child, Stephanie Lynn. Student St. Petersburg Jr. Coll., 1963-64, Alamogordo Bus. Coll., 1970-71. Sales mgr. Bahama Cruise Line, Tampa, Fla., 1978-82; dir. mktg./sales AAA Holidays/St. Petersburg Motor Club, Fla., 1982-84; dir. mktg./sales Travel and Tourism Resources, Inc., St. Petersburg, 1986, prin., pres., 1986-90; dir. mktg./sales Island Harbor Resort, Cape Haze, Fla., 1984-86; mgr. Radisson-Pan-Am. Ocean Hotel, Miami Beach, Fla., 1986-90; sr. dir. Fla. Restaurant Assn., 1990—; v.p. Europa Tours, 1989—; mktg. cons., bd. dirs., adv. bd. Travel Marketplace, Royal Fiesta Cruises, Clearwater; mem. adv. bd. Culinary Inst., Ft. Lauderdale Art Inst., Acad. Travel and Tourism, Dade County, Fla.; seminar leader, internat. industry speaker. Mem. Fla. Gulf Coast Symphony Guild, St. Petersburg, 1975-86, All Childrens Hosp. Guild, 1975-86, Infinity League to Aid Abused Children, 1981-86, Pinellas Assn. for Retarded Adults, 1975-86, St. Petersburg Internat. Folk Fair Soc. Host Com. Super Bowl XXVIIII; pres. Tampa Bay Mag. Leaders on the Move, 1982, Pinellas County Leaders Move Recipient Cert. of Recognition, George Greer County Commr., Pinellas, 1986; panelist Broward Cultural Arts Coun., Broward City, Fla., 1992-93; state bd. dirs. Am. Heart Assn., 1992-95, v.p. So. Broward chpt., mem. Pub. Affairs Com. State Bd.; bd. dirs. Friends of Jazz City of Hollywood, Fla., 1992-94. Mem. NAFE, Internat. Platform Assn., Pacific Area Travel Assn. (dir.), Sun Coast Travel Industry Assn., Sales and Mktg. Execs. Internat., Travel and Tourism Research Assn., C. of C. (tourism com., chmn. econ. devel. coun.), Women Execs. in Travel, Fla. Assn. Sales Execs., Hotel Sales and Mktg. Assn., Fla. Women's Network, Am. Mktg. Assn., Italian-Am. Club, St. Petersburg Internat. Folk Fair Soc., Assn. Internat. Des Skal Clubs. Avocations: reading, volunteer work. Office: Fla Restaurant Assn 2441 Hollywood Blvd Hollywood FL 33020-6605 also: Europa Tours 2205 Hollywood Blvd Hollywood FL 33020

MUCCIANTE, MARY F., state official; b. Springfield, Ill., Feb. 11; d. Donald R. and Frances Iverne (Cline) M. BA in Legal Studies, Sangamon State U., Springfield, 1984, MPA, 1989. Program planner Ill. Dept. on Aging, Springfield, 1984-86, civil rights coord., 1986-87, program planner, 1987-88; mgr. occupational disease registry Ill. Dept. Pub. Health, Springfield, 1988-92, mgmt. analyst, 1992—. Precinct committeewoman Springfield Rep. Com., 1992; mem. Sangamon County Evening Rep. Club, 1990—, Capitol City Rep. Women, 1992—. Mem. APHA, Ill. Pub. Health Assn. (exec. coun. com. 1991-94), Roman Cultural Soc. Women's Aux. Roman Catholic. Home: 1918 Jeanette Ln Springfield IL 62702-4643

MUCHA, SHIRLEY SEIK, psychiatric clinical nurse specialist; b. Oakdale, Pa., Oct. 1, 1948; d. Glen and Edith Mae (Campbell) Seik; m. George Michael Mucha, Jr., Oct. 6, 1984. BSN, Pa. State U., 1969; MSN, U. Pitts., 1987; postgrad., Western Pa. Family Ctr., 1989-90, 91-92. Cert. clin. specialist child and adolescent psychiat. and mental health nursing, clin. specialist in adult psychiat. and mental health nursing. Nursing supr. Woodville State Hosp., Valleyview Adolescent Ctr., Carnegie, Pa., 1971-82; nursing supr. Mayview Adolescent Ctr., Bridgeville, Pa., 1982-86; nurse clinician Diagnostic and Evaluation Ctr. Western Psychiat. Inst. and Clinic, Pitts., 1986-88; nurse clinician adolescent drug abuse and psychiat. treatment program Western Psychiat. Inst. and Clinic, 1988-90, nurse clinician Adult Mood Disorder Module, 1990-91; nurse clinician adult dual diagnosis program Western Psychiat. Inst. and Clinic, Pitts., 1991—; corp. dir., sec.-treas. Pitts. Mech. Inc., 1993—. Mem. ANA, Nat. Nurses Soc. on Addictions, Sigma Theta Tau. Home: 267 Center Church Rd Mc Murray PA 15317

MUCHMORE, CAROLIN MARIE, real estate corporation officer; b. Aug. 18, 1944; d. Alfred G. and Mary K. (Lang) Columbo; m. Robert W. Muchmore, Mar. 17, 1962; children: Kim A. Wimmer, Dana A., Robert Jr. Cert. real estate broker. Mgr. guest rels. Great Adventure, Jackson, N.J., 1974-79; sales rep. Mut. of Omaha, Ins., Freehold, N.J., 1980-81; sales assoc. Sterling Thompson Realtors, Howell, N.J., 1979-82, Weichert Realtors, Manalapan, N.J., 1982-84; br. mgr. Weichert Realtors, Howell, 1984—; hosting dir. Sister Cities, Howell, 1988—; instr. Cuyohoga Anti-Discrimination, Aberdeen, N.J., 1989, Weichert-Orientation Sch., Aberdeen, 1984-93; v.p. Broker Mgr. Realty Execs. 100, Howell, 1993—. Com. Muscular Dystrophy, Ocean Twp., 1979-85, Spl. Olympics, Monmouth County, 1983-86; chmn. Toys for Tots, Monmouth and Ocean County, 1988-89. Recipient N.J. State Million Dollar Club, N.J. Assn. Realtors, 1981-93, N.J. State Pres. Club, 1985-86. Mem. Grad. Realtors Inst., Women Coun. Realtors (pub. rels. officer), Howell C. of C., Jackson C. of C., BPOE (hon. mem.), Real Estate Brokerage Coun., Nat. Assn. Real Estate Owned Brokers, N.J. Assn. Realtors, Monmouth County Bd. Realtors (dir. 1992—). Home: 2 Cuomo Ct Englishtown NJ 07726-8500

MUCK, RUTH EVELYN SLACER (MRS. GORDON E. MUCK), education educator; b. Buffalo, July 17, 1910; d. Robert A. and Hattie E. (Sheridan) Slacer; B.S., State U. Coll. at Buffalo, 1938, M.S., 1952; Ed.D., State U. N.Y. at Buffalo, 1966; m. Gordon E. Muck, Dec. 27, 1934; 1 child, Linda Mae McGuire. Tchr. pub. schs., Lockport, N.Y., 1931-42; tchr. primary level campus sch. State U. Coll., Buffalo, 1942-66, prof. edn. div. elem., from 1966, now emeritus; cons. tchr. edn. workshops, Minn., Fla. Dir. youth edn. United Meth. Ch., 1960-69; pres. United Meth. Women, Grand Island, N.Y.; bd. dirs. United Meth. Found., West N.Y., 1986—, N.Y. Dist. United Meth. Extension Soc., Buffalo, 1988—; pres. Town of Lockport N.Y. Hist. Soc., 1987—; vol. community svc.; dir. children's used clothing shop. Recipient Mission Recognition award United Meth. Women, 1994. Mem. Assn. Tchr. Educators (state pres. 1972-73), Internat. Reading Assn. (chmn. 1969-71), Delta Kappa Gamma, Pi Lambda Theta. Home: 1091 Stony Point Rd Grand Island NY 14072-2712

MUDD, ANNE CHESTNEY, small business owner, mathematics educator, real estate agent; b. Macon, Ga., June 30, 1944; d. Bard Sherman Chestney and Betty (Bartow) Houston; children: Charles Lee Jr., Richard Chestney, Robert Jason. BA, U. Louisville, 1966, MA, 1976; 1986-90, 1989-92. Math statistician U.S. Bur. Census, Jeffersonville, Ind., 1966-70; instr. math. U. Louisville, 1975-77, Coll. DuPage, Glen Ellyn, Ill., 1978-85, 92; tchr. math and substitute tchr. Lyons Twp. High Sch., La Grange, Ill., 1986-91; realtor First United Realtors, Western Springs, Ill., 1989-92; math tutor Louisville 1969-77, Western Springs, Ill. 1977—. editor: Mathematics Textbook, 1991-92. Mem. steering com. Village Western Springs, 1986-87. Mem. NAFE, Children's Theater Western Springs (bd. dirs. 1987-91), LWV (pres. 1983-85, bd. dirs.), Lyons Twp. High Sch. Com. Student Discipline, Western Springs Hist. Soc., Nat. Coun. Tchrs. Math. Home: 3958 Hampton Ave Western Springs IL 60558-1011

MUDD, SHERYL KAY, secondary school educator, guidance counselor; b. Ft. Thomas, Ky., July 14, 1960; d. Robert Leslie and Marvel Maxine (Youtsey) M.; m. Jackie Elaine Nichols, Lawrence Robert, Gerald Leslie, Randy Kent, Ronald Lee, Rhonda Dee, Michael Todd. BA, Transylvania U., 1982; MEd in Guidance Counseling, Xavier U., Cin., 1988. Cert. elem. tchr., K-12 phys. edn. tchr., Ky. Substitute tchr. Pendleton County Schs., Falmouth, Ky., 1982-84, Campbell County Schs., Alexandria, Ky., 1982-84; tchr. No. Elem. Sch., Butler, Ky., 1984-86; tchr. math. Pendleton Mid. Sch., Falmouth, 1986-88, tchr. reading, 1988-89, tchr. health and phys. edn., 1989-92; tchr. 7th and 8th grades Risk Youth, 1992—. Named to Honorable Order of Ky. Colonels, Commonwealth of Ky., 1979, Tchr. of Yr., Pendleton Mid. Sch., 1989, 93, 94. Mem. ASCD, AAHPERD, Assn. for Advancement Health and Phys. Edn., AACD, Ky. Assn. for Gifted Assn., Ky. Mid. Sch. Assn., No. Ky. Assn. Counseling and Devel. Democrat. Roman Catholic. Home: Tammy Ln Lot 17 Box 166 RR 2 Butler KY 41006-0166 Office: Pendleton County Mid Sch 500 Chapel St Falmouth KY 41040-1410

MUDGE, DOROTHY ELAINE, retired social worker, association executive; d. William and Anne A. (Smith) M. BE, Duluth State Tchrs.' Coll. (now U. Minn. Duluth), 1936; MA, U. Minn. Cert. tchr.; cert. social worker. Dist. supr. adult edn. WPA, Duluth, 1936-42; dir. USO, Warrensburg, Mo., 1942-45, Panama Canal zone, 1945-47; br. dir. YWCA, Akron, Ohio, 1947-49, assoc. dir., 1950-58; br. dir. YWCA, Detroit, 1958-63; dir. YWCA, Tampa, Fla., 1963-66; mem. nat. staff YWCA USA, Atlanta, 1966-77. Named Woman of Yr. Bus. and Profl. Women, Akron, 1956. Mem. AARP (pres. 1991), AAUW. Methodist.

MUEHLNER, SUANNE WILSON, library director; b. Rochester, Minn., June 29, 1943; d. George T. and Rhoda (Westin) Wilson. Student Smith Coll., 1961-63; A.B., U. Calif.-Berkeley, 1965; M.L.S., Simmons Coll., 1968; M.B.A., Northeastern U., Boston, 1979. Librarian, Technische Univ. Berlin, Germany, 1970-71; earth and planetary scis. librarian MIT Libraries, Cambridge, 1968-70, 1971-73; personnel librarian, 1973-74, asst. dir. personnel services, 1974-76, asst. dir. pub. services, 1976-81; dir. libraries Colby Coll., Waterville, Maine, 1981—. Mem. ALA, New Eng. Assn. Coll. and Research Librarians (sec.-treas. 1983-85, pres. 1986-87), Maine Libr. Assn. (chmn. intellectual freedom com. 1984-88, OCLC Users Coun., 1988—), Nelinet (bd. dirs. 1985-91, chair 1989-91). Office: Colby Coll Miller Libr Waterville ME 04901

MUEHRCKE, JULIANA OBRIGHT (JILL MUEHRCKE), publisher, editor; b. Aurora, Ill., Sept. 3, 1945; d. Russell B. and Constance (Rennels) Obright; m. John Evans, Sept. 24, 1965 (div. 1968); 1 child, Andrea Marit; m. Phillip C. Muehrcke, July 22, 1969. Student, U. Colo., 1963-67; BA, U. Wash., 1971. Author textbooks Prentice Hall Textbooks, Englewood Cliffs, N.J., 1967-80, Macmillan Co., N.Y.C., 1973-74, Denoyer-Geppert, Chgo., 1980-82, Harcourt Brace, N.Y.C., 1981-82, Scott Foresman, Glenview, Ill., 1982-83; owner JP Publs., Madison, Wis., 1978—; mng. editor Sunshine Newspaper, Madison, 1981-83, Nonprofit World Jour., Madison, 1983—. Mem. Friends of the Madison Pub. Libr., 1987—, Madison Literacy Coun., 1988—. Mem. Women in Communications Inc. (v.p., membership chair 1987—), Am. Assn. Suicidology (bd. sec. Wis. chpt. 1988—), Alliance for the Mentally Ill, Dane County Mental Health, Univ. League (events chair 1972—). Office: Soc for Nonprofit Orgns 6314 Odana Rd Ste 1 Madison WI 53719-1129

MUELLER, ANNE, legislator; b. Atlanta, Oct. 5, 1929; d. Howard Raymond O'Quin and Bessie Kate (Bell) Brace; m. Hans Kurt Mueller; children: Yvonne Marie Key, Heidi Spivey, Mark Jennings. BS in Zoology, U. Ga., 1951. Registered med. technologist. Med. technologist Grady Hosp., Atlanta, 1953—, St. Joseph Hosp., Atlanta, 1957, Meml. Hosp., Waycross, Ga., 1958-59; legislator Ga. Ho. of Reps., 1983—. Mem. Savannah (Ga.) area Rep. Women, sec., 1980-81, v.p., 1981-82, Ga. Fedn. of Rep. Women, Savannah, dist. dir., 1986—. Republican. Baptist. Home: 13013 Hermitage Rd Savannah GA 31419-2850 Office: GA House of Reps State Capitol Atlanta GA 30334-9003*

MUELLER, BARBARA ALICE, art educator, artist; b. Summit, N.J., July 24, 1937; d. Albert Peter and Mildred Alice (Meekings) M.; m. William Gary Crist, 1978 (div. 1991); 1 stepchild, Julie. BA in Art, Maryville (Tenn.) Coll., 1959; MA in Painting, U. Iowa, 1961; postgrad., Hamline U., 1975, Kunstakademie, Düsseldorf, Germany, 1981, 83. Instr. Maryville Coll., 1961-65, asst. prof., 1965-66; instr. art U. Mo., Kansas City, 1966-68, asst. prof., 1968-77, assoc. prof., 1977-90, prof., 1990—, mem. chancellor's adv. bd. Women's Ctr., 1992—; lectr. in field. Contbr. articles to profl. jours.; one-woman show Unitarian Gallery, Kansas City, 1977, Ward-Nasse Gallery, N.Y.C., 1978, 83, 84-85; 2-person show U. Mo. Gallery Art, 1980; exhibited in numerous group shows Garath Schloss, nr. Düsseldorf, 1983, West Surrey (Eng.) Coll. Art and Design, 1984, including Ark. Arts Ctr., Little Rock, 1985, Trenton State Coll., Knoxville (Tenn.) Mus. Art, 1988, Sioux City (Iowa) Art Ctr., 1989, U. Maine, Presque Isle, 1989, 94, Mulvane Art Mus., Topeka, 1989-90, Del Mar Coll., Corpus Christi, Tex., 1990, William Jewell Coll., Liberty, Mo., 1995, many others. Recipient purchase award William Woods Coll., 1985, Okla. State U., 1987; Fulbright summer faculty seminar grantee, India, 1971; grantee U. Mo., 1978, 81, 82, 88-89, 94, Nat. Endowment for Arts and Kans. Arts Commn., 1986, Faculty Rsch. and Teaching Enhancement Fund, 1990-92, 94, others. Mem. Coll. Art Assn., Women's Caucus for Art. Presbyterian. Office: U Mo Kansas City Dept Art-Art History 5100 Rockhill Rd Kansas City MO 64110-2446

MUELLER, BETTY JEANNE, social work educator; b. Wichita, Kans., July 7, 1925; d. Bert C. and Clara A. (Pelton) Judkins; children—Michael J., Madelynn J. M.S.S.W., U. Wis., Madison, 1964, Ph.D. (E.B. Fred fellow, Nat. Inst. Child Health and Human Devel. fellow), 1969. Asst. prof. U. Wis., Madison, 1969-71; vis. asso. prof. Bryn Mawr (Pa.) Coll., 1971-72; asso. prof., dir. social work Cornell U., Ithaca, N.Y., 1972-78, prof. human services studies, 1978—; nat. cons. Head Start, Follow Through, Appalachian Regional Commn., N.Y. State Office Planning Services, N.Y. State Dept. Social Services, N.Y. State Div. Mental Hygiene, Nat. Congress PTA, ILO. Author: (with H. Morgan) Social Services in Early Education, 1974, (with R. Reinoehl) Computers in Human Service Education, 1989; contbr. articles to profl. jours. Grantee HEW, 1974-76, 79-80, State of N.Y., 1975—, Israeli Jewish Agy., 1985-87, Israeli Nat. Council for Research, 1986-87; Fulbright Research award, 1990. Mem. Am. Sociol. Assn., Internat. Conf. Social Welfare, Nat. Assn. Social Workers, Council Social Work Edn., Chi Omega. Democrat. Unitarian. Home: 11 Forest Ln Ithaca NY 14850-8736 Office: Cornell U Human Services Studies N139MVR Hall Ithaca NY 14853

MUELLER, DIANE MAYNE (DIANE MAYNE), lawyer; b. Milw., Aug. 8, 1934; d. George and Ann (Matuszewski) Markussen; widowed; 1 child, Paul Wilhite; m. Milton W. Mueller, Jan. 1, 1990. AB, Valparaiso U., 1956; MSW, Fla. State U., 1963; JD summa cum laude, DePaul U., 1974. Bar: Ill. 1974, U.S. Dist. Ct. (no. dist.) Ill. 1974, U.S. Dist. Ct. (ea. dist.) Wis. 1977. Assoc. Seyfarth, Shaw, Fairweather & Geraldson, Chgo., 1976-82, ptnr., 1982-86; asst. group counsel LTV Steel Co., Cleve., 1986-93, sr. atty., 1993-95; adj. prof. Northwestern U. Sch. Law, 1984-86. Mem. ABA, Chgo. Club, Chgo. Yacht Club, Univ. Club, Exec. Club of Chgo. (chmn. bd. 1984-85, mem. adv. bd. 1986—), Econ. Club Chgo. Home: 23489 Wimbledon Rd Cleveland OH 44122

MUELLER, GAIL DELORIES, forensic chemist, toxicologist; b. Chgo., Sept. 30, 1957; d. Roger George and Delories B. (Reppert) Johnson; m. Joseph E. Mueller, Jan. 26, 1991. BS in Chemistry, No. Ill. U., 1980. Quality control chemist Standard Pharmacal Corp., Elgin, Ill., 1980; forensic chemist Ill. Racing Bd. Lab., Elgin, 1980-82, Analytical Techs., Inc., Tempe, Ariz., 1982-84; analytical chemist Nichols Inst., San Juan Capistrano, Calif., 1985-87; forensic chemist, toxicologist, GC/MS group leader Damon Reference Labs., Rancho Cucamonga, Calif., 1987-94; forensic chemist, toxicologist Associated Pathologists Labs., Las Vegas, Nev., 1994—. Fellow Am. Inst. Chemists; mem. Am. Chem. Soc., Calif. Assn. Toxicologists. Office: APL Racing Tox Ste 154 4230 S Burnham Ave Las Vegas NV 89119

MUELLER, HEIDI, real estate agent; b. Kaiserslantern, Germany, June 9, 1948; d. Rudolf and Eleonore (Schmitt) M. BA in English, U. Mass., 1972; tchr. credential, San Francisco State U., 1976. Sch. tchr. South San Francisco High, 1975-77; taxi driver DeSoto Cab Co., San Francisco, 1977-87; realtor Prudential Calif. Realty, San Francisco, 1987—; workshop leader The Prosperity Workshop, San Francisco, 1993; personal property coach, 1993—. Mem. NAFE, Nat. Assn. Realtors, Women's Coun. Realtors. Democrat. Home: 125 Hancock St San Francisco CA 94114

MUELLER, JEAN MARGARET, nursing educator; b. Huntington, N.Y., June 3, 1951. Diploma in Nursing, Pilgrim State Hosp., 1973; BSN, SUNY, Stony Brook, 1979; M in Profl. Studies, New Sch. for Social Rsch., 1986. RN, N.Y. Nurses aide Huntington Hosp., N.Y., 1971, LPN, 1972, RN, charge ICU/CCU, MICU/SICU, telemetry, 1973-77; charge nurse, MICU North Shore U. Hosp, Manhasset, N.Y., 1977-78; private duty cases, Holter monitor scanning, 1978-84; dir. nursing svcs., assoc. dir. nursing svcs. Nesconset (N.Y.) Nursing Ctr., 1984-86; nursing edn. instr. St. Charles Hosp., Port Jefferson, N.Y.; labor and delivery nurse SUNY, Stony Brook; teaching and rsch. nurse II Diabetes Ctr., SUNY, Stony Brook; teacing hosp. insvc. educator I SUNY, Stony Brook, 1990—; mem. adj. faculty Sch. of Nursing SUNY, Stony Brook, 1992—, St. Joseph's Coll., 1994; rsch. com. dept. family medicine with E. Stark, E.A.P.; hosp. nursing svcs. cons. office health sys. mgmt. N.Y. State Dept. Health, 1994—; lectr. Med., Emotional and Psychol. Indicators of Family Violence. Contbr. articles to profl. jours. Active Mothers Against Drunk Driving; mem. Suffolk County Family Violence Task Force. Recipient SUNY U. Pres. award for domestic violence tng. programs, 1993, for spl. needs of the elderly tng. programs, 1994. Mem. Nat. Nurses Assn., Sigma Theta Tau. Home: 234 Hallock Rd Stony Brook NY 11790

MUELLER, JULIE LYNN, small business owner; b. Oshkosh, Wis., Sept. 30, 1957; d. Norman David and Arlene Veronica (Robinson) M. Owner, groomer Aurora Kennel, Tulsa. Mem. Am. Saluki Assn. (Breed Challenge Shield award, 1981). Office: 9721 E 61st St Tulsa OK 74133

MUELLER, MARILYN JEAN, insurance company executive; b. Shawano, Wis., Mar. 19, 1946; d. Raymond Walter and Kathryn Ruth (Arveson) M. BA in English, U. Wis., Oshkosh, 1968, BA in Spanish, 1968. CLU; chartered fin. cons. Group rep. Wash. Nat. Ins. Co., Columbus, Ohio, 1968-73, asst. mgr., 1973-79; asst. mgr. Wash. Nat. Ins. Co., Phila., 1979-82, group mgr., 1982—; with Field Mgmt. Coun., Evanston, Ill., 1982-83, sec., 1988, Therapy Dogs, Inc. Tutor Literacy Vols. of Am., Voorhees, N.J., 1986—. Mem. CLU/Chartered Fin. Cons. South Jersey (bd. dirs. 1992-94). Republican. Lutheran. Office: Wash Nat Ins Co Commerce Ctr 1810 Chapel Ave W Ste 260 Cherry Hill NJ 08002

MUELLER, NANCY SCHNEIDER, retired biology educator; b. Wooster, Ohio, Mar. 8, 1933; d. Gilbert Daniel and Winifred (Porter) Schneider; m. Helmut Charles Mueller, Jan. 27, 1959; 1 child, Karl Gilbert. AB in Biology, Coll. of Wooster, 1955; MS in Zoology, U. Wis., 1957, PhD in Zoology, 1962. Instr. zoology U. Wis., Madison, 1966; asst. prof. poultry sci. and zoology N.C. State U., Raleigh, 1968-71; vis. prof. biology N.C. Ctrl. U., Durham, 1971-73, assoc. prof., 1973-79, prof., 1979-93; ret., 1993; vis. scientist U. Vienna, Austria, 1975. Contbr. articles, abstracts to profl. publs. Mem. Am. Soc. Zoologists, Am. Ornithologists Union, Cooper Ornithol. Soc., Wilson Ornithol. Soc., Wis. Acad. Sci., Arts and Letters, N.C. Acad. Sci., LWV (bd. dirs. 1988—, natural resources com. 1988—), Sigma Xi. Home: 409 Moonridge Rd Chapel Hill NC 27516-9385

MUELLER, PEGGY JEAN, dance educator, choreographer, rancher; b. Austin, Tex., June 14, 1952; d. Rudolph George Jr. and Margaret Jean (Locke) M.; m. John Yerby Tarlton, June 24, 1972 (div. June 1983). BS in Home Econs., Child Devel., U. Tex., Austin, 1974. Dance tchr. Shirley McPhail Sch. Dance, Austin, 1972-75; dance tchr. Jean Tarlton Sch. Dance, Alpine, Tex., 1975-77, College Station, Tex., 1977-80; dance tchr. Sul Ross State U., Alpine, 1975-77, Tex. A&M U., College Station, 1977-80, A&M Consol. Community Edn., Coll. Station, 1977-78, Jean Mueller Sch. Dance, Austin, 1980—. U. Tex., Austin, 1980—; dancer, contest judge Gt. Tex. Dance-Off, Austin, 1985-86; mem. equestrian com. Austin-Travis County Livestock Show and Rodeo, 1980-92, chmn. trail ride, 1986—; trail boss, pres. Austin Founders Trail Ride, 1986—; trail boss Bandera Longhorn Cattle Drive and Trail Ride, 1990, 91; choreographer, head cheerleader Austin Texans Pro Football Team, 1981; dance tchr. Austin Ballroom Dancers, 1988; dancer, agt. George Strait/Bud Light Comml. Auditions, 1990; head contest judge Am.'s Ultimate Dance Contest, Austin, 1994; contest judge Two-Stepping Across Am., Austin, 1994; speaker in field. Dancer Oklahoma, Austin, 1969, Kiss Me Kate, Austin, 1970; choreographer, lead role Cabaret, Alpine, 1976. Active Women's Symphony League Austin, 1972—, Settlement Club, Austin, 1987—; recreation chmn. St. Martin's Evang. Luth. Ch., Austin, 1972—; hon. trail boss St. Jude Children's Rsch. Hosp. Trail Ride, Austin and Kyle, Tex., 1991. Recipient Outstanding Trail Rider of Yr. award Wild Horse Trail Ride, Okla., 1984; named Tex. First Lady Trail Boss, Gov. Mark White, Mayor Frank Cooksey, Austin City Coun., 1986, Judge Bill Aleshire, Travis County Commrs., 1989, Outstanding Intramural Sports Team Mgr.-Player, Tex. A&M U., 1978-79. Mem. Tex Assn. Tchrs. of Dancing, Inc., U.S. Twirling and Gymnastics Assn., Univ. Tex. Ex-Students Assn., Tex. Execs. in Home Econs., Am. Vet. Med. Assn. Aux. (v.p. 1978-79, pres. 1979-80), Am. Horse Shows Assn., Internat. Arabian Horse Assn., Austin Women's Tennis Assn. (v.p. 1985-86, pres. 1986-90, spl. events chmn. 1990-92, advisor 1990—, winner 2d ann. Harriet Crosson Outstanding Player & Community Svc. award), Women's Team Tennis of Austin Assn. (pres.-elect 1992-93, pres. 1993-94), Capital Area Tennis Assn. (membership com. 1991, 92), Houston Salt Grass Trail Ride Assn., San Antonio Alamo Trail Ride Assn., Ft. Worth Chisholm Trail Ride Assn., U. Tex. Longhorn Alumni Band, Austin C. of C., Am. Bus. Women's Assn., Austin Alumnae Panhellenic Assn. (1st v.p. 1989-90, rush forum chmn. 1990, pres. 1990-91, parliamentarian 1991-92), Omicron Nu (v.p. 1973-74), Jr. Austin Woman's Club (historian 1990-91), Austin Country Club (team tennis captain 1994—), Zeta Tau Alpha (Austin Alumnae Chpt., alumnae photographer, social advisor 1982-87, treas. 1987-89, publicity chmn. 1989, Easter Seals fundraiser, Honor Cup winner 1990, pres. 1991-92, internat. convention official del. 1988, 92, nominating chmn. 1992-93, mem. yearbook com. 1992-94, 2d v.p. 1993-94). Republican. Clubs: Cen. Tex. Arabian Horse, Capitol Area Quarter Horse Assn., Jr. Austin Woman's, Austin Country. Home: 1506 Hardouin Ave Austin TX 78703-2519 Office: Jean Mueller Sch Dance PO Box 14762 Austin TX 78761-4762

MUFSON, LAURA HELEN, clinical psychologist; b. N.Y.C., July 11, 1961; d. Marvin Robert and Ann Carol (Mauser) M.; m. Bennett P. Leifer, June 11, 1989; 1 child, Joshua Isaac. AB in Psychology, Princeton (N.J.) U., 1983; MA in Psychology, Emory U., 1984, PhD in Clin. Psychology, 1988. Lic. profl. psychologist, N.J., N.Y. NIMH postdoctoral rsch. fellow Columbia U. Coll. of Physicians and Surgeons, N.Y.C., 1988-90; rsch. scientist N.Y. State Psychiat. Inst., 1990—; asst. prof. clin. psychology Col. Coll. of Physicians and Surgeons, N.Y.C., 1990—; dir. tng. and child psychology Babies Hosp., CPMC, N.Y.C., 1990—, asst. clin. dir. childrens anxiety and depression clinic, 1993—; dep. dir., child clin. rsch. ctr. N.Y. State Psychiat. Inst., 1993-94. Co-author: Interpersonal Psychotherapy for Depressed Adolescents, 1993; contbr. articles to profl. jours. Recipient Young Investigator award NARSAD, 1990-92, First award NIMH, 1992—. Mem. Am. Psychol. Assn., Soc. for Rsch. in Children and Adolescents, Assn. for Clin. Psychosocial Rsch., Sigma Xi.f. Office: NY State Psychiat Inst Unit 14 722 W 168th St New York NY 10032-2603

MUFTIC, FELICIA ANNE BOILLOT, consumer relations professional; b. Muskogee, Okla., Feb. 27, 1938; d. Lowell Francois and Geneva Margaret (Halstead) Boillot; m. Michael Muftic, Sept. 6, 1961; children: Tanya Muftic-Streicher, Theodore B., Mariana C. BA, Northwestern U., 1960. Exec. dir. Metro Dist. Atty.'s Consumer Office, Denver, 1973-79; talk show host KNUS, Denver, 1981-83; clk., recorder City and County of Denver, Colo., 1984-91; spl. projects dir. Consumer Credit Counseling, Denver, 1991—; pres. Muftic and Assocs., Denver, 1980-83; commr. Uniform Consumer Credit Code, Colo., 1991—. Author: Colorado Consumer Handbook, 1982. Candidate for mayor, Denver, 1979. Named Media person of Yr., NASW, Colo., 1982; recipient Outstanding Contbrn. in Consumer Affairs award Denver (Colo.) Fed. Exec. Bd., 1982. Mem. Nat. Soc. Fundraising Execs., Inst. Internat. Edn. (bd. mem. 1980—). Democrat. Home: 3671 S Pontiac Way Denver CO 80237-1326 Office: Consumer Credit Counseling 10375 E Harvard Ave Ste 300 Denver CO 80231-3966

MUHA-RONNEAU, CAROL, medical/surgical nurse, critical care nurse; b. East Chgo., Ind., July 24, 1950; d. Joseph Peter and Victoria Magdelene (Biernacki) Muha; m. John Evan Ronneau, Nov. 11, 1989; 1 child, Heather. AAS, Purdue U., 1972, BSN, 1976, MSN, 1988. RN, Ind., Ill.; cert. BLS, ACLS. Staff nurse St. Catherine's Hosp., East Chgo., Ind., 1972-75, unit dir., 1975-76; cardiovascular nurse practitioner Cardiovascular and Renal Cons., Homewood, Ill., 1976-83; vis. instr. Purdue U. North Cen., Westville, Ind., 1984-88, asst. prof., 1988-93, assoc. prof., 1994—; vis. instr. Purdue U./Calumet, Hammond, Ind., 1976-77; cons. On Course Seminars, Valparaiso, Ind., 1991; bd. dirs. ednl. adv. com. Porter County Sch. Corp., 1992-93; chairperson Heartbeats Health Festivals, Westville, Ind., 1989-90, 91. Author: (abstract) Cooperative Learning, 1992, 93, Pocket Care Plans, 1989. Bd. dirs. Am. Cancer Soc., Laporte County, Ind., 1988-90; bd. dirs., officer, Porter County, Ind., 1989—; bd. dirs. Am. Cancer Soc., 1988-90, Am. Heart Assn., Porter County, 1989—, v.p., 1994—. Recipient Best Lect. of Yr. award Purdue U., 1986-87, Vol. of Yr. award Am. Heart Assn., 1991-92, Outstanding Svc. award Am. Heart Assn., 1990-91. Mem. Ind. State Nurses Assn., Purdue U. Nursing Honor Soc. (chairperson elections 1989-92), Sigma Theta Tau. Roman Catholic. Office: Purdue U North Cen 1401 S US 421 Westville IN 46391

MUHLERT, JAN KEENE, art museum director; b. Oak Park, Ill., Oct. 4, 1942; d. William Henry and Isabel Janette (Cole) Keene; m. Christopher Layton Muhlert, Jan. 1, 1966; 1 son, Michael Keene. B.A. in Art and French, Albion (Mich.) Coll., 1964; M.A. in Art History, Oberlin (Ohio) Coll., 1967; student, Neuchatel (Switzerland) U., Inst. European Studies, Paris, Inst. de Phonetique, Acad. Grande Chaumiere. Asst. curator Allen Meml. Art Mus., Oberlin, 1967-68; asst. curator 20th Century painting and sculpture Nat. Collection Fine Arts, Smithsonian Instn., Washington, 1968-73; assoc. curator Nat. Collection Fine Arts, Smithsonian Instn., 1974-75; dir. U. Iowa Mus. Art, 1975-79, Amon Carter Mus., Ft. Worth, 1980—. Author museum brochures, catalogues. Mem. Nat. Mus. Act Adv. Council, 1980-83, vis. com. Allen Meml. Art Mus. of Oberlin (Ohio) Coll., 1987—. Grantee Nat. Endowment Arts-Donner Found., 1979; recipient Friend of Art Edn. award Tex. Art Edn. Assn., 1994. Mem. Assn. Art Mus. Dirs. (trustee 1981-82, 84-86, 92-93, chmn. govt. and art com. 1982-84, chmn. profl. practices com. 1990-92), Western Assn. Art Mus. (regional rep. 1978-79), Am. Assn. Mus. (commn. for new century 1981-84, gen. co-chair 1993 ann. meeting), Am. Arts Alliance (dir. 1980-86, vice-chmn. 1982-84). Office: Amon Carter Mus 3501 Camp Bowie Blvd PO Box 2365 Fort Worth TX 76113

MUIR, BONNIE ANN, computer science educator; b. Watertown, N.Y., May 30, 1959; d. Randall Gregor and Elizabeth Augusta (Cuck) M. BA in Polit. Sci., Am. U., 1982, MS in Tech. Mgmt., 1986. Warehouse mgr. R.G. Muir Distbrs. Inc., Syracuse, N.Y., 1977-79; asst. dir. Georgetown U., Washington, 1979-80; law librarian Pension Benefit Guarantee Corp., Washington, 1980-82; program specialist Am. U., Washington, 1984-87, program mgr., 1984-87, adj. faculty, 1987-91; sr. prin. The Oasis Group Inc., Fairfax, Va., 1985—, also bd. dirs.; project & program mgr. Ogden/ERC Govt. Systems, Fairfax, 1987-91; mem. faculty dept. computer sci. and info. systems Am. U., Washington, 1991-92; cons. U.S. Dept. Health Human Svcs., Washington, 1992—. Mem. IEEE, Assn. for Computing Machinery, Info. Resources Mgmt. Assn., Mid-Atlantic Disaster Recovery Assn., Data Processing Mgmt. Assn., Soc. Applied Learning Tech., Higher Edn. Group Washington, D.C. Coll. Pers. Assn., AAUW. Home: 12622 Glenbrooke Woods Dr Herndon VA 22071-2127 Office: US Dept Health Human Svcs 200 Independence Ave SW Washington DC 20201-0004

MUIR, HELEN, journalist, author; b. Yonkers, N.Y., Feb. 9, 1911; d. Emmet A. and Helen T. (Flaherty) Lennehan; student public schs.; m. William Whalley Muir, Jan. 23, 1936; children: Mary Muir Burrell, William Torbert. With Yonkers Herald Statesman, 1929-30, 31-33, N.Y. Evening Post, 1930-31, N.Y. Evening Jour., 1933-34, Carl Byoir & Assos., N.Y.C., and Miami, Fla., 1934-35; syndicated columnist Universal Svc., Miami, 1935-38; columnist Miami Herald, 1941-42; children's book editor, 1949-56; women's editor Miami Daily News, 1943-44; freelance mag. writer, numerous nat. mags., 1944—; drama critic Miami News, 1960-65. Trustee Coconut Grove Libr. Assn., Friends U. Miami Libr., Friends Miami-Dade Pub. Libr.; vis. com. U. Miami Librs.; bd. dirs. Miami-Dade County Pub. Libr. System; past chmn., mem. State Libr. Adv. Coun., 1979-91, past chmn. Recipient award Delta Kappa Gamma, 1960; Fla. Libr. Assn. Trustees and Friends award, 1973, Coun. Fla. Librs. award, 1990; trustee citation ALA, 1984; named to Fla. Women's Hall of Fame, 1984. Mem. Women in Communications (Community Headliner award 1973), Soc. Women Geographers, Author's Guild. Clubs: Florida Women's Press (award 1963); Cosmopolitan (N.Y.C.); Biscayne Bay Yacht. Author: Miami, U.S.A., 1953, 3d rev. edit., 1990, Biltmore: Beacon for Miami, 1987, 2d rev. edit., 1993. Home: 3855 Stewart Ave Miami FL 33133-6734

MUIR, RUTH BROOKS, counselor, substance abuse service coordinator; b. Washington, Nov. 27, 1924; d. Charles and Adelaide Chenery (Masters) B.; m. Robert Mathew Muir, Nov. 26, 1947; children: Robert Brooks, Martha Louise, Heather Sue. BA in Art, Rollins Coll., Winter Park, Fla., 1947; MA in Rehab. Counseling, U. Iowa, 1979. Cert. substance abuse counselor, Iowa. Program advisor Iowa Meml. Union, Iowa City, 1959-66; counselor, coord. Mid Eastern Coun. on Chem. Abuse, Iowa City, 1976-81; patient rep. Univ. Hosp., Iowa City, 1982-85; rsch. project interviewer dept. psychiatry, U. Iowa Coll. Medicine, 1985-88. Art exhibited at Iowa City Sr. Ctr., 1987, 92, Iowa City Art Ctr., 1989, U. Iowa Hosp., 1991, Great Midwestern Ice Cream Co., 1991; creator, coord. therapeutic series Taking Control, Iowa City Sr. Ctr., 1986-87. Vol. coord. art exhibits Sr. Ctr., Iowa City, 1992-94; treas. bd. dirs. Crisis Ctr., Iowa City, 1975-77; sec. coun. elders Sr. Citizens Ctr., Iowa City, 1976-78; pres. Unitarian-Universalist Iowa City Women's Fedn., 1985; friend of U. of Iowa Mus. Art; mem. Johnson County Arts Coun., Opera Supers, Iowa City Unitarian U.N. Envoy; fgn. rels. coun., bd. dirs. annual changing family conf. U. Iowa, 1986-92; non-govtl. rep. Earth Summit Global Forum, 1992. Mem. AAUW (cultural rep. 1990-92), Iowa City Unitarian Soc. (mem. adult program com. 1993-94, mem. unitarian care com. 1993-94), Pi Beta Phi (v.p. alumnae club), U. Iowa Print and Drawing Study Club. Home and Office: 6 Glendale Ct Iowa City IA 52245-4430

MUJAHED, MARY ELIZABETH, small business owner; b. Cheyenne, Wyo., Mar. 16, 1929; d. Frank Ralph and Elsie Fern (Patterson) Yager; m. Saleh Ramadan Mujahed, July 24, 1952; children: Susan Elizabeth, David Saleh. BA in Liberal Arts, Scripps Coll., 1951. Library asst. Contra Costa (Calif.) County Library System, 1965-69; publisher Orion Pub. Co., Walnut Creek, Calif., 1982—. Editor: How To Stop Smoking, 1982. Mem. Nat. Congl. Rep. Com., Washington, 1977—; sustaining mem. Rep. Nat. Com., 1977—, Nat. Rep. Senatorial Com., 1977-92, Rep. Presdl. Task Force, 1981-88. Recipient Medal Merit Rep. Presdl. Rask Force, 1982; Disting. benefactor Afghan Mercy Fund. Mem. Nat. Acad. Polit. Sci. Methodist.

MUJICA, MARY BERNADETTE, mechanical engineer; b. Red Bank, N.J., Feb. 2, 1963; d. Patrick Peter and Linda Jean (Mohler) McCall; m. Frank Elias Mujica, Apr. 16, 1988; children: Keith Alan, Shannon Yvette, Angela Andrea. BSME summa cum laude, Bucknell U., 1985. Asst. to corp. maintenance mgr. Air Products & Chems., Allentown, Pa., 1985-86; plant maintenance engr. Air Products & Chems., Pasadena, Tex., 1986-87; prodn./quality engr. Air Products & Chems., Pasadena, 1987-88; chem. plant engr., project engr. Shell Oil/Chem., Deer Park, Tex., 1988-90, chem. plant and refinery effluent engr., 1990-92, safety/process safety mgmt. engr., 1992-93, asst. maintenance mgr., reliability engr., 1993—. Asst. leader Jr. Achievement, Allentown, 1985-86; industry sponsor Soc. Women Engrs., Allentown, 1985-86; mem. fin. com. Heritage Park Bapt. Ch., Webster, Tex., 1990-92; firefighter, mem. rescue squad Shell Emergency Response, 1990-94. Kodak scholar, 1982-85. Mem. Tau Beta Pi (sec. 1984). Home: 1001 Glenshannon Ave Friendswood TX 77546 Office: Shell Oil Co PO Box 100 Deer Park TX 77536

MUKHERJEE, BHARATI (MRS. CLARK BLAISE), author, English educator; b. Calcutta, India, July 27, 1940; d. Sudhir Lal and Bina (Banerjee) M.; m. Clark L. Blaise, Sept. 19, 1963; children: Bart Anand, Bernard Sudhir. BA, U. Calcutta, 1959; MA, U. Baroda, India, 1961; MFA, U. Iowa, 1963, PhD, 1969. Instr. in English Marquette U., Milw., 1964-65; instr. U. Wis., Madison, 1965; lectr. McGill U., Montreal, Que., Can., 1966-69; asst. prof. English McGill U., Montreal, Can., 1969-73, assoc. prof., 1973-78, prof., 1978-79; prof. Skidmore Coll., Saratoga Springs, N.Y., 1979-84; assoc. prof. Montclair (N.J.) State College, 1984-87; prof. CUNY, 1987-89, U. Calif., Berkeley; vis. prof. of writing U. Iowa, Iowa City, 1979, 82; vis. prof. Emory U., Atlanta, 1983. Author: The Tiger's Daughter, 1972, Wife, 1975, Kautilya's Concept of Diplomacy, 1976, (with Clark Blaise) Days and Nights in Calcutta, 1977, Darkness, 1985, The Middleman and Other Stories, 1988 (Nat. Book Critics Circle award 1989), The Sorrow and the Terror, 1988, Jasmine, 1989, Political Culture and Leadership in India, 1991, Regionalism in Indian Perspective, 1992, The Holder of the World, 1993; contbr. short stories, essays and book revs. to several jours. Grantee McGill U., 1968, 70, Can. Arts Coun., 1973-74, 77, Shastri Indo-Can. Inst., 1976-77, Guggenheim Found., 1978-79, Can. Govt., 1982; recipient 1st prize Periodical Distbn. Assn., 1980, NEA award, 1986. Mem. PEN. Hindu. Office: U Calif Dept English 322 Wheeler Hall Berkeley CA 94720-4714*

MULAC, PAMELA ANN, priest, pastoral counselor; b. Salem, Ohio, Dec. 6, 1944; d. Elmer John and Dorothy Adelaide (McGee) M.; m. George Robert Larsen, Aug. 8, 1987. Student, Bryn Mawr Coll., 1962-64; AB, U. Chgo., 1966; MDiv, Seabury-Western Theol. Sem., 1974; PhD, Garrett Evang. Theol. Sem., Northwestern U., 1988. Ordained to ministry Episcopal Ch. as priest, 1978. Asst. deacon, priest St. Luke's Ch., Evanston, Ill., 1974-84; asst. priest St. Mark's Ch., Upland, Calif., 1984-88, St. Ambrose Ch., Claremont, Calif., 1988-90; assoc. priest for pastoral care All Saints Ch., Pasadena, Calif., 1991-93; asst. interim pastor St. George's, La Canada, Calif., 1994—; chaplain Foothill Presbyn. Hosp., Glendon, Calif., 1994—; pastoral counselor Swedish Covenant Hosp., Chgo., 1975-84; adj. lectr. Seabury-Western Theol. Sem., Evanston, 1981-82, trustee, 1981-84; pastoral counselor Walnut (Calif.) Valley Counseling Ctr., 1984-89; adj. lectr. marriage and family therapy program Azusa Pacific U., 1988-89, adj. lectr. operation impact, 1991-92; adj. prof. Episc. Theology Sch., Claremont, Calif., 1994. Bd. dirs. Cathedral Shelter Chgo., 1980-84; co-chairperson Leader's Sch. Cursillo, Chgo., 1981-83; mem. Commn. on Alcoholism, Diocese of L.A., 1985-87. Episcopal Ch. Found. fellow, 1978-81. Mem. Am. Assn. Pastoral Counselors (sec. Pacific region 1984-85, treas. 1984-91, fin. chair 1988-91), Assn. Clin. Pastoral Edn. Home and Office: 2964 E Gambrel Gate La Verne CA 91750-2372

MULARSKI, CAROL ANN, librarian, educator; b. McKeesport, Pa., June 14, 1953; d. Ernest and Mary Ann (Long) M. BS, Clarion State Coll., 1975; MLS, U. Pitts., 1981. Cert. music tchr., Pa. Substitute music tchr. Pitts. City Schs., 1976; cashier student accounts U. Pitts., 1976-77, sr. sec. Sch. Edn., 1977-78, adminstrv. aide/data mgr. Sch. Edn., 1978-84; reference libr. Health Scis. Libr. Ohio State U., Columbus, 1984-87, coord. online svcs. and user edn., 1987-91, instr., 1984-90, asst. prof., 1990—, head references svcs., 1992—. Contbr. articles to profl. publs. Mem. Med. Libr. Assn. (cons. editor bull. 1992—). Office: Ohio State U Health Sci Lib 376 W 10th Ave Columbus OH 43210

MULCAHY, LISA MICHELE, financial sales associate; b. Passaic, N.J., Jan. 29, 1962; d. Jack Howard and Dorothy (Fisher) Noonburg; m. Alan Wacyra, Aug. 31, 1986 (div. Apr. 1991); m. James Edward Mulcahy, May 7, 1994. Legal sec. degree, Ct. Reporters Inst., Hackensack, N.J., 1982. Registered series 7 and series 63 N.Y. Stock Exchange; registered with Am. Stock Exchange, Phila. and Pacific Exchanges. Fin. cons. E.F. Hutton & Co., Paramus, N.J., 1982-85; sales assoc. Merrill Lynch, Paramus, 1985—; mem. svc. adv. coun. Merrill Lynch, Paramus, 1992—. Home: 128 Hillman Ave Glen Rock NJ 07452 Office: Merrill Lynch W 115 Century Rd Paramus NJ 07652

MULDAUR, DIANA CHARLTON, actress; b. N.Y.C., Aug. 19, 1938; d. Charles Edward Arrowsmith and Alice Patricia (Jones) M.; m. James Mitchell Vickery, July 26, 1969 (dec. 1979); m. Robert J. Dozier, Oct. 11, 1981. B.A., Sweet Briar Coll., 1960. Actress appearing in: Off-Broadway theatrical prodns., summer stock, Broadway plays including A Very Rich Woman, 1963-68; guest appearances on TV in maj. dramatic shows; appeared on: TV series Survivors, 1970-71, McCloud, 1971-73, Tony Randall Show, 1976, Black Beauty, 1978; star: TV series Born Free, 1974, Hizzoner, 1979, Fitz & Bones, 1980, Star Trek: The Next Generation, 1988-89; NBC miniseries and TV series A Year in the Life, 1986; TV movie Murder in Three Acts, The Return of Sam McCloud, 1989; TV series L.A. Law, 1989-91; motion picture credits include McQ, The Lawyer, The Other, One More Train to Rob, Mati, etc. Bd. dirs. Los Angeles chpt. Asthma and Allergy Found. Am.; bd. advisors Nat. Ctr. Film and Video Preservation, John F. Kennedy Ctr. Performing Arts, 1986. Recipient 13th Ann. Commendation award Am. Women in Radio and TV, 1988, Disting. Alumnae award Sweet Briar Coll., 1988. Mem. Acad. Motion Picture Arts and Scis., Screen Actors Guild (dir. 1978), Acad. TV Arts and Scis. (exec. bd., dir., pres. 1983-85), Conservation Soc. Martha's Vineyard Island. Office: The Artists Group Ltd 1930 Century Park W Ste 403 Los Angeles CA 90067-6803

MULDER, PATRICIA MARIE, educator; b. South Bend, Ind., Dec. 28, 1944; d. Ervin James and Carmen Virginia (Sheeley) Anderson; m. James R. Mulder, Dec. 27, 1964; children: Todd Alan, Scott Robert. BA, Western Mich. U., 1967. Freelance writer, photographer Berrien Springs, Mich., 1980—; tchr. Eau Claire (Mich.) Pub. Schs., 1969-70; staff writer, sales rep. Jour. Era, Berrien Springs, 1979-81; sales rep. Berrien County Record, Buchana, Mich., 1981-82; account exec. WHFB Radio Palladium Pub. Co., St. Joseph, Mich., 1982-86; substitute tchr. Berrien County Intermediate Dist., 1986-89; instr. Southwestern Mich. Coll., Dowagiac, 1989—. Editor The Positive Image newsletter, 1980—, The F Stop, 1982-90; author: Poetry Anthologies, 1989—; staff writer Decision Point, 1988-89; newsletter editor Fernwood Nature Photographers, 1980—. Ofcl. photographer Ind. and Internat. Spl. Olympics, Notre Dame, 1986. Named Emerging Artist Ind. Coun. for the Arts, 1989, Honor award Southwestern Coun. of Camera Clubs, 1988, Photographer of the Yr. Berrien County Photographic Artists, 1987, 90. Mem. Nat. Authors Registry, Southwestern Mich. Coun. Cambera Clubs, Berrien Springs Camera Club (v.p. 1980—), Meth. Profl. Women (sec. 1990—), Berrien County Artists (v.p. 1986), Berrien County Photographic Artists (v.p. 1984). Methodist. Home: 10252 Castner Dr Berrien Springs MI 49103-9602 Office: Southwestern Mich Coll 58900 Cherry Grove Rd # 316L Dowagiac MI 49047-9793

MULFORD, JUDY FORMAN, public relations executive; b. D.C., Oct. 10, 1949; d. George and Amelia (Black) Forman; m. Ralph Kirkman Mulford III, Oct. 5, 1980 (div. Feb. 1991); 1 child, Aimee Marie. Student, N.Mex. State U., 1967-69, U. Md., Ansbach, Germany, 1976-79, U. Mass., 1981-84, 91—. Membership dir. Waterfront Hist. Area League, New Bedford, Mass., 1980-85; project mgr. Mass. Main St. Program, Fall River, 1985-88; pres. Pineapple Hospitality, Inc., New Bedford, 1988-91; dir. cultural devel. City of New Bedford, 1991-92; devel., pub. rels. Kennedy-Donovan Ctr., New Bedford, 1992—; cons. devel. Coastline Elderly, New Bedford, 1992, Assn. for Retarded Citizens, New Bedford, 1992, Kennedy-Donovan Ctr., New Bedford, 1992. Author, editor: Bed and Breakfast Reservations for New England, 1987-91; co-producer: (documentary) Black Heritage, 1993. Active Fall River Celebrates Am., 1990-91; office mgr. New Bedford Mayoral Campaign, 1982-83, 91; campaign worker Bristol County Senate Race, New Bedford, 1992; trustee Zeiterion Performing Arts Theatre; pres. New Bedford Arts Lottery, 1991-92; dist. rep. Mass. Cultural Coun., Boston, 1991-92; dir. Bristol County Travel and Tourism Coun., New Bedford, 1990-92. Polaroid Found. grant for black heritage documentary, 1993. Mem. Am. Bus. Women Assn. (Bus. Person Yr. 1990), Toastmasters, Rotary. Home: 26 Washington St Fairhaven MA 02719-2960

MULHALL, MARY MANNING, consumer foods professional; b. Tampa, Fla., Dec. 9, 1954; d. George Jr. and Dolores Ann (Takash) Manning; m. Thomas P. Mulhall, July 24, 1976. BS in Food and Nutrition, U. Ill., 1976. Assoc. editor The Culinary Arts Inst., Chgo., 1976-78; dir. consumer foods ctr. The Quaker Oats Co., Chgo., 1978—. Editor: Hurry, Let's Eat, 1987, The Pritikin Cookbook, 1991, The Quaker Oats Treasury of Best Recipes, 1992. Student tutor Cabrini Green Tutoring Program/Reading is Fundamental, Chgo., 1984-94. Recipient Cert. of 10-yr. merit Cabrini Green Tutoring Program, Chgo., 1994. Mem. Am. Inst. Wine and Foods, Home Economists in Bus. (treas., newsletter editor 1976-80), U. Ill. Home Econs. Alumni Bd. (dir. 1990—, Merit award 1993), Les Dames d'Escoffier. Office: The Quaker Oats Co 321 N Clark #22-6 Chicago IL 60610

MULICH, MICHELE MARIE, chemical company executive; b. Kansas City, Kans., Oct. 28, 1963; d. Terrence J. and M. Lucille (Graybill) M. BS, Old Dominion U., 1985. Computer operator Va. Internat. Terminals, Norfolk, Va., 1984-85, jr. programmer, 1985-86, programmer, 1986-87, system adminstr., 1987-89, tech. support supr., 1989-90; programmer/analyst Huntsman Chem. Corp., Chesapeake, Va., 1990-92, mgr. mfg. systems, 1992—. Mem. Old Dominion U. Alumni Assn. (pres. Young Alumni Coun. 1993-94, bd. dirs. 1993-94). Roman Catholic. Office: Huntsman Chem Corp 5100 Bainbridge Blvd Chesapeake VA 23320-6502

MULKEY, SHARON RENEE, gerontology nurse; b. Miles City, Mont., Apr. 14, 1954; d. Otto and Elvera Marie (Haglof) Neuhardt; m. Monty W. Mulkey, Oct. 9, 1976; children: Levi, Candice, Shane. BS in Nursing, Mont. State U., 1976. RN, Calif. Staff nurse, charge nurse VA Hosp., Miles City, Mont., 1976-77; staff nurse obstetrics labor and delivery Munster (Ind.) Community Hosp., 1982-83; nurse mgr. Thousand Oaks Health Care, 1986-88; unit mgr. rehab. Semi Valley (Calif.) Adventist Hosp., 1988-89, DON TCU, 1989-91; DON Pleasant Valley Hosp. Extended Care Vacility and Neuro Ctr., 1991-93; dir. nurses Victoria Care Ctr., Ventura, Calif., 1993—. Mem. ANA, Nat. Gerontol. Nursing Assn., Internat. Platform Assn., Alpha Tau Delta (pres. 1973-75), Phi Kappa Phi. Home: 3461 Pembridge St Thousand Oaks CA 91360

MULLAHEY, RAMONA KAM YUEN, land use planner, educator; b. Hilo, Hawaii, Nov. 1, 1945. BA, U. Hawaii, 1967, M Urban and Regional Planning, 1976. Sole proprietor Honolulu, 1976-87; prin. Mullahey & Mullahey, Honolulu, 1987—; nat. speaker on K-12 design edn. to variety internat., nat., regional orgns.; lectr. urban and regional planning U. Hawaii. Author: (book and video) Maintaining A Sense of Place Community Workbook, 1987, Community as a Learning Resource, 1994; editor newsletter Am. Planning Assn. Resources, 1990—. Mem. Rental Housing Trust Fund Commn., Hawaii, 1993—. Recipient Pub. Edn. award Am. Planning Assn., Hawaii chpt., 1993; Nat. Endowment for Arts grantee, Washington, 1986, 92, 94, local grantee; named 1 of 12 Nat. Women Leaders in K-12 Design Edn., The Urban Network. Mem. ASCD, Nat. Trust Historic Preservation (Nat. Preservation Honor award 1988), Am. Planning Assn. (pres. Hawaii chpt. 1992-93, immediate past pres. 1993—, Disting. Leadership award Hawaii Chpt. 1994), Orgn. Am. Leaders (pres. 1990-91), C. of C. of Hawaii (edn. coun.). Home and Office: PO Box 1348 Honolulu HI 96807-1348

MULLAN, SHEILA ANN, pet restaurant owner; b. Toledo, Ohio, Dec. 14, 1956; d. George W. and Mary L. (Dennehy) M. AS, U. Toledo, 1976, BS, 1985. Computer operator Blue Cross-Blue Shield, Durham, N.C., 1985-87; computer programmer Marathon Oil Co., Findlay, Ohio, 1987-92; pres. Puppy Hut Franchising Inc., Toledo, 1992—. Vol. Toledo Humane Soc., 1992—. Office: Puppy Hut Franchising 5201 Monroe St Toledo OH 43623-3139

MULLANEY, DOROTHY MARIE, neonatal nurse; b. Newton, Mass., Dec. 1, 1958; d. James Edward and Evelyn Theresa (Sears) M. BSN, St. Anselm Coll., 1981; M in Health Sci., McMaster U., 1992. Cert. advanced RN practitioner. Staff nurse New Eng. Med. Ctr., Boston, 1981-82, Dartmouth-Hitchcock Med. Ctr., Lebanon, N.H., 1982-91; neonatal nurse practitioner Dartmouth-Hitchcock Med. Ctr., Lebanon, 1991—. Mem. ANA, Nat. Assn. Neonatal Nurses (Vt./N.H. chpt.), Assn. Women's Health, Ob. and Neonatal Nurses, N.H. Nurse Practitioner Assn. (chair prescriptive practice com.). Roman Catholic. Home: 6 Hemlock Hills Enfield NH 03748 Office: Dartmouth-Hitchcock Med Ctr 1 Medical Center Dr Lebanon NH 03756

MULLARKEY, MARY J., state supreme court justice; b. New London, Wis., Sept. 28, 1943; d. John Clifford and Isabelle A. (Steffes) M.; m. Thomas E. Korson, July 24, 1971; 1 child, Andrew Steffes Korson. BA, St. Norbert Coll., 1965; LLB, Harvard U., 1968; LLD (hon.), St. Norbert Coll., 1989. Bar: Wis. 1968, Colo. 1974. Atty.-advisor U.S. Dept. Interior, Washington, 1968-73; asst. regional atty. EEOC, Denver, 1973-75; 1st atty. gen. Colo. Dept. Law, Denver, 1975-79, solicitor gen., 1979-82; legal advisor to Gov. Lamm State of Colo., Denver, 1982-85; ptnr. Mullarkey & Seymour, Denver, 1985-87; justice Colo. Supreme Ct., Denver, 1987—. Recipient Alumni award, Norbert Coll., De Pere, Wis., 1980, Alma Mater award, 1993. Fellow ABA Found., Colo. Bar Found.; mem. ABA, Colo. Bar Assn., Colo. Women's Bar Assn. (recognition award 1986), Denver Bar Assn., Thompson G. Marsh Inn of Ct. (pres. 1993-94). Office: Supreme Ct Colo 2 E 14th Ave Denver CO 80203-2116

MULLEEDY, JOYCE ELAINE, nursing service administrator, educator; b. Paterson, N.J., Aug. 30, 1948; d. Edward and Jane (Van De Weert) Schuurman; m. Philip Anthony Mulleedy, May 14, 1982. BS, Paterson State Coll., 1970. RN, cert. emergency nurse, emergency med. technician, paramedic. Pub. health nurse Vis. Nurse Assn. of No. Bergen County, Ramsey, N.J., 1970-72; health dir. Camp Fowler Assn., Speculator, N.Y., 1973-76; exec. dir. Am. Cancer Soc., Speculator, 1976-77; pub. health nurse Hamilton County Nursing Service, Lake Pleasant, N.Y., 1977-80, supervising pub. health nurse, 1980-82, dir. patient services, 1982-86; quality improvement coord. Susquehanna-Adirondack Regional Emergency Med. Services Program, 1986—; mem. profl. adv. com. Hamilton County Nursing Svc., Indian Lake, N.Y., 1992—. Author instructional booklet: Assessing Your Patients, 1983, (pamphlet) A Note to Parents, 1985. Bd. dirs. Am. Cancer Soc.-Hamilton County Unit, Speculator, 1972-76, Speculator Vol. Ambulance Corps, Inc., 1974-81, ARC-Hamilton County chpt., Lake Pleasant, N.Y., 1981-88; mem. adminstrv. bd. dirs. Grace United Meth. Ch., Speculator, 1982—, Rainbow Christian Children's Ctr., 1992—. Martha Hazen Scholar Am. Legion, 1966; recipient Svcs. award Am. Legion, 1977. Mem. N.Y. State Assn. County Health Ofcls., Adirondack-Appalachian Regional Emergency Med. Svcs. Coun. (chmn. 1982-87, chmn. tng. com. 1982—), Emergency Nurses Assn., Hamilton County Emergency Med. Svcs. Coun. (sec.-treas. 1974-90, instr. 1974—). Republican. Home: PO Box 203 Speculator NY 12164-0203 Office: Susquehanna Adirondack Regional Emergency Med Svcs Prog PO Box 212 Speculator NY 12164-0212

MULLEN, EILEEN ANNE, staff training and development executive; b. Phila., Feb. 14, 1943; d. Joseph Gregory and Helen Rita (Kane) M. BS in English, St. Joseph U., 1967; MA in English, Villanova U., 1978. Cert. tchr., Pa. Tchr., St. Anastasia Sch., Newtown Square, 1960-67, West Cath. Girls High Sch., 1967-74; mgr. staff tng. and devel. ASTM, Phila., 1974—; instr. lit., speech and communications Widener U. Weekend Coll., Chester, Pa. and Wilmington, Del. Author: Speech Command, 1995; contbg. author articles on communications tng. programs; contbr. articles to profl. publs. Mem. ASTD (pres. Phila./Delaware Valley chpt. 1980-81, award for outstanding leadership as pres. 1981), Am. Soc. Assn. Execs. (Delaware Valley chpt.). Democrat. Roman Catholic. Office: ASTM 1916 Race St Philadelphia PA 19103-1180

MULLEN, LAURIE, nurse; b. Ellensburg, Wash., Dec. 22, 1959; d. Gerald James and Kay Barbara (Buchberger) M. BSN summa cum laude, Wash. State U., 1982. RN, Wash. Nurse, with NSI nursing registry Univ. Hosp., Seattle, 1982—; home health nurse Pediatric Home Care, Bellevue, Wash., 1986-93; nurse legal expert witness, Seattle, 1986-93. Mem. Wash. State Nurses Assn., Sigma Theta Tau. Democrat. Roman Catholic. Office: U Wash Med Ctr 1959 Pacific St Seattle WA 98105

MULLEN, REGINA MARIE, lawyer; b. Cambridge, Mass., Apr. 22, 1948; d. Robert G. and Elizabeth R. (McHugh) M. BA, Newton Coll. Sacred Heart, 1970; JD, U. Va., 1973. Bar: Pa., Del., U.S. Dist. Ct. Del., U.S. Ct. Appeals (3d cir.), U.S. Supreme Ct. Dep. atty. gen. State Del. Dept. Justice, Wilmington, 1973-79, state solicitor, 1979-83, chief fin. unit, 1983-88; v.p., counsel MBNA Am. Bank, N.A., Newark, Del., 1988-91, 1st v.p., sr. v.p., counsel, 1991—; Mem. bd. Bar Examiners, State Del., 1979-89; bd. dirs. Del. Cmty. Investment Corp., Wilmington, 1994—, Wilmington Music Festival, 1992—. Mem. fin. com. Chesapeake Bay Girl Scout coun., Wilmington, 1985-94, bd. dirs., 1988-94, v.p., 1990-94, mem. fund devel. com., 1994—; bd. dirs. Comty. Legal Aid Soc., 1994—. Mem. ABA, Del. State Bar Assn. (chair adminstrv. law sect. 1983-85). Democrat. Roman Catholic. Office: 400 Christiana Rd Newark DE 19713-4217

MULLENBACH, LINDA HERMAN, lawyer; b. Sioux City, Iowa, Dec. 25, 1948; d. Verner Wilhelm and Margaretta Victoria (Grant) Herman; m. Hugh James Mullenbach, Aug. 22, 1970; children: Erika Lynn, Linnea Britt. BS in Speech, Northwestern U., 1971, MS in Speech, 1972, JD, 1979. Bar: Ill. 1979, U.S. Dist. Ct. (no. dist.) Ill. 1979, D.C. 1983, U.S. Dist. Ct. D.C. 1983, U.S. Ct. Appeals (7th, D.C. and fed. cirs.), 1983, U.S. Supreme Ct. 1984. Assoc. Jenner & Block, Chgo., 1979-83; assoc. Dickstein, Shapiro & Morin, Washington, 1983-85, prin., 1985-87, ptnr., 1988-93; v.p., assoc. gen. counsel The Md. Ins. Group, Balt., 1994—. Mem. ABA (litigation sect.), D.C. Bar Assn., Women's Bar Assn. D.C., Women's Legal Def. Fund, Assn. Trial Lawyer Am., Mortar Bd., Zeta Phi Eta. Home: 8201 Killean Way Potomac MD 20854-2728

MULLENIX, KATHY ANN, corporate account manager; b. Goodland, Ind., Mar. 8, 1955; d. Boyd Dale and Edith Marie Hoaks; 1 child, Joseph F. Hamburg IV. Diploma, South Newton Jr./Sr. H.S., Goodland, Ind., 1973. Asst. to pres. Planes Moving, Cin., 1981-88; sales mgr. Tru-Pak Moving, Greenville, S.C., 1988-89; corp. acct. mgr. Armstrong Relocation, Atlanta, 1989—. Den leader Cub Scouts, Blue Ash, Ohio, 1982-86; coach's asst. Soccer Assn., Mason, Ohio, 1985-88; treas. PTA Mason Mid. Sch., 1988; tutor Gwinnette Co. Adult Literacy, Lawrenceville, Ga., 1994. Office: Armstrong Relocation 6950 Business Ct Atlanta GA 30340

MULLEN-MENARD, MAUREEN ANNE, artist, arts educator; b. Newton, Mass., June 19, 1961; d. Harold Joseph and Grace Anne (Devlin) Mullen; m. Darius Joseph Menard, July 22, 1989. BFA cum laude, Pratt Inst., 1983; MFA, CUNY, 1987. Curatorial asst. Mus. of Holography, N.Y.C., 1984-85; publs. cons. Exit Art, N.Y.C., 1986; rschr., docent New Mus. of Contemporary Art, N.Y.C., 1985-89; educator Manhattan Montessori Sch., N.Y.C., 1986-88; artist-in-residence Ga. Fine Arts Acad., N.Y.C., 1988; artist, educator The Studio in a Sch. Assn., N.Y.C., 1988-94; arts program developer N.Y.C. Bd. Edn., 1992-94; vis. artist, educator Bklyn. Mus., 1990, The Friends Sem., N.Y.C., 1990-91; staff developer The Studio in Sch. Assn., N.Y.C., 1991-94; arts program developer N.Y.C. Bd. Edn., 1992-94; arts edn. cons. Greenpoint Design Ctr., Bklyn., 1994; guest speaker N.Y.C. Arts Edn. Roundtable, 1994. Artist (paintings) (Women in Visual Arts Merit award 1991); artist (book) Animals in Holography (in Please Touch Mus. for Children, Phila.), 1985; author/developer Citibank Culture in Community Grant, 1994; artist/educator NEA Arts in Edn., 1994; one-woman shows include Pratt Inst., Bklyn., 1982, 83, Hunter Coll. Gallery, N.Y.C., 1987; exhibited in group shows at Pratt Inst., 1984, BACA Downtown Cultural Ctr., Bklyn., 1984, 85, N.Y. State U. Arts and Scis., Potsdam, 1985, Bess Cutler Gallery, N.Y., 1985, City Without Walls Gallery, N.J., 1986, 87, Philip Stansbury Gallery, N.Y.C., 1987, Artists Space, N.Y.C., 1989, 90, 92, The Hudson River Mus., Yonkers, N.Y., 1989, Bloomsburg U. Haas Gallery, Pa., 1989, Mus. Hudson Highlands, N.Y., 1990, Erector Square Gallery, New Haven, Conn., 1991, P.S. 122 Gallery, N.Y.C., 1991, Herron Test Site Gallery, Bklyn., 1992. Recipient William Graf Travel grant Hunt Coll. CUNY, 1987, Pratt Gate award Pratt Inst., 1983, Pratt Ind. Honors Study grant Pratt Inst., 1982, Pilgrim Found. grant, 1979. Fellow Coun. for Basic Edn.; mem. Nat. Art Edn. Assn., Coll. Art Assn. Home: 108 Nassau Ave Brooklyn NY 11222 Office: Maureen Mullen Studio 1205 Manhattan Ave Brooklyn NY 11222

MULLENS, DEBORAH ELAINE, human resources specialist; b. Huntington, W.Va., Nov. 23, 1956; d. Lester Randall and Shirley Eudora (Boggs) M.; 1 child, Eric Zachary Mullens-Steele. BA, Marshall U., 1979; postgrad., Ohio State U., 1986. Interviewer Ohio State U., Columbus, 1982-84, compensation analyst, 1984-86; mgr. compensation and benefits Mt. Carmel East Hosp., Columbus, 1986-87; human resources specialist City of Columbus Health Dept., 1988—. Pres. adv. com. Decision Ctr., Inc. Mem. NAFE. Club: Singles Aware of Christ (Columbus) (pres. 1986-87).

MULLER, ALEXANDRA LIDA, real estate management director; b. N.Y.C., June 9, 1949; d. John William and Elisa (Bianco) M. BA in Math., Western N.E. Coll., 1971; Cert. in Real Estate, NYU, 1982, Cert. as Real Estate Broker, 1991. Lic. notary pub. Ptnr. Raffles, Florence, Italy, 1972-74; bookkeeper Emmeti, Florence, Italy, 1974-76; tchr. English and Italian Berlitz Sch. Langs., Florence, Italy, 1976-77; tchr., interpreter, translator Italy, 1977-84; office mgr. UNICEF, Milan, Italy, 1982-83; dir. Barhite & Holzinger, N.Y.C., 1985-89; dir., office mgr. The Robert-Thomas Co., N.Y.C., 1990-92; assoc. broker The Thomas Campenni Co., N.Y.C., 1992—; ind. real estate broker. Office: The Thomas F Campenni Co 21 W 46th St New York NY 10036

MULLER, CLAUDYA BARBARA, librarian; b. Furth, Germany, Sept. 14, 1946; came to U.S., 1952; d. Ralph Leon and Elfriede Katherine (Hilpert) Burkett; m. William Albert Muller III, Dec. 12, 1965 (div. 1986); 1 child, Martha Genevieve. B.A., Ga. So. Coll., 1967; M.L.S., Emory U., 1968. Asst. to head circulation Ga. State U., 1968-69; asst. dir. War Woman Regional Library, 1970-72; assoc. dir. Ottumwa Heights Coll. Library, Iowa, 1973; bookmobile librarian Gallia County Dist. Library, Ohio, 1976; dir. Jackson County Pub. Library, W.Va., 1976-78, Worcester County Library, Md., 1978-83; state librarian State of Iowa, Des Moines, 1983-86; dir. Suffolk Coop. Library System, 1986-90; exec. dir. Cuyahoga County Pub. Libr., Cleve., 1990—. Editor: University Press Books for Public Libraries, 1979, 80. Tommie Dora Barker fellow Emory U., 1967; recipient Good Citizenship award Rotary, Snow Hill, Md., 1983. Mem. ALA (editor procs. small and medium sized libr. sect. 1981, standards com. 1986-90, mem. architecture for pub. libr. com. 1987-91, com. chair 1989-91), Pub. Libr. Adminstrn. and Mgmt. Assn. (bldg. and equipment sect. bd. dirs., mem.-at-large 1992-94), Pub. Libr. Assn. (chmn. orgn. com. 1983-84, mem. publs. com. 1984-85, chair com. 1985-87, new standards task force), N.Y. Libr. Assn., Ohio Libr. Coun. (govt. affairs com. 1991—). Office: Cuyahoga County Pub Libr 2111 Snow Rd Parma OH 44134*

MULLER, HELEN BATES, retired art educator, artist; b. Mansfield, Ohio, June 28, 1922; d. Vernon Lloyd and Sarah Augusta (Mullett) Bates; m. Peter Paul Muller (dec.); children: Kathryn Noble, Margaret Carr, Peter Paul. Student, U. Mich., 1943; BFA, Ohio State U., 1944; MA, NYU, 1965. Safety dir. F&R Lazarus, Columbus, Ohio, 1942-43; display mgr. Burdines, Miami Beach, Fla., 1943-44; art tchr. Wash. Sch., Port Washington, N.Y., 1958-63; prof., gallery dir. Nassau C.C., Garden City, N.Y., 1963-84, prof. emeritus art, 1984. One-woman shows include Gallery 84, N.Y.C., 1983, 85, 87, 88, 91, Elaine Benson Gallery, 1979, 88, Firehouse Gallery, Nassau C.C., 1979. Bd. dirs. Parrish Art Mus., 1988—, chmn., edn. com., 1985—, trustee, 1987—. Recipient 1st prize for mixed media Guild Hall, 1973, Excellence award L.I. Craftsman Guild, 1972. Mem. Nat. Sculpture Soc. (bd. dirs. 1992—), Southampton Artists (bd. dirs. 1993—).

MULLER, JUDY MARIE, news correspondent; b. Annapolis, Md., Mar. 31, 1947; d. Jack Emerson and Marie (Clark) Mansfield; m. Bruce Albert Muller, June 13, 1969 (div. 1981); children: Kristen Marie, Kerry Ann. BA, Mary Washington Coll., 1969. English tchr. Metuchen (N.J.) H.S., 1970-73; radio newscaster Sta. WHWH Radio, Princeton, N.J., 1975-78, Sta. KHOW Radio, Denver, 1978-81; news corr. CBS News, N.Y.C., 1981-90, ABC News, L.A., 1990—. Contbr. articles to mags. and newspapers. Bd. trustees Forum Theatre, Metuchen, N.J., 1987-89, Middlesex C.C., Edison, N.J., 1988-89. Mem. AFTRA. Office: ABC News LA Bur 4151 Prospect Ave Studio 61 Los Angeles CA 90027

MULLER, KAREN HAGERMAN, psychologist; b. Chehalis, Wash., Apr. 25, 1952; d. William Lee and Nancy (Searle) Hagerman; m. Fred Muller, Oct. 2, 1984; 1 child, Amy Marilyn. BA, U. Oreg.; MA, Calif. State U., Rohnert Park, 1980; PhD, Calif. Sch. Profl. Psychology, Berkeley, 1986. Lic. psychologist, Calif.; lic. marriage, family and child counselor, Calif. Counselor YMCA Youth Devel., Oakland, Calif., 1976-78; dir. tng. Bay Area Women Against Rape, Berkeley, 1978-80; psychologist Calif. Counseling Assocs., Alameda, 1986-92; pvt. practice Hayward, Calif., 1992—; cons. Bay Area Women Against Rape, Berkeley, 1978—. Mem. APA, Calif. Psychol. Assn., Alameda County Psychol. Assn. (info. and referral com.), Assn. for Study of Dreams. Democrat. Jewish. Office: 1345 B St Hayward CA 94542

MULLER, MARGIE H., state bank commissioner; b. L.A., Nov. 30, 1927; d. S. Jack and Marjorie (Ullman) Hellman; m. Steven Muller, June 19, 1951; children: Julie, Elizabeth. BA, UCLA, 1949. Sales promotion asst. Joyce (Calif.) Ltd., London, 1950-51; copywriter Hamrick Advt., Ithaca, N.Y., 1951-54; sr. assoc. Conant and Co., N.Y.C., 1954-57; mgr. advt. and pub. relations Theodore Presser Co., Bryn Mawr, Pa., 1957-58; acct. exec. Laux Advt., Ithaca, 1959-60; asst. v.p. mktg. Tompkins County Trust Co., Ithaca, 1960-71; v.p. Md. Nat. Bank, Balt., 1971-77; sr. v.p. Union Trust Bancorp., Balt., 1977-83; state bank commr. Balt., 1983—. Contbr. articles to profl. jours. Bd. dirs. The Leadership Balt., 1985-87; pres. Balt. Promotion Coun., 1974-75, Health and Welfare Coun., Ctrl. Med., 1982-85; mem. adv. commn. Md. Dept. Econ. and Cmty. Devel., 1975-83; mem. adv. coun. Credit Rsch. Ctr., Krannert Grad. Sch. Mgmt., Purdue U., vice chmn., 1993-94, chmn., 1994—. Mem. Bank Mktg. Assn. (bd. dirs. 1974-78, exec. com. 1977-78, nat. conv. chmn. 1977), Nat. Assn. State Credit Union Suprs. (bd. dirs. 1984-88), Conf. State Bank Suprs. (bd. dirs. 1988-94, vice chmn. 1990-91, chmn. 1991-93), Fed. Fin. Instns. Exam. Coun. (state liaison com. 1991-94, chmn. 1993-94). Office: 501 St Paul Pl 13th Fl Baltimore MD 21202-2272

MULLER, PATRICIA ANN, nursing administrator, educator; b. N.Y.C., July 22, 1943; d. Joseph H. and Rosanne (Bautz) Felter; m. David G. Smith, Mar. 19, 1988; children: Frank M. Muller III, Kimberly M. Muller. BSN, Georgetown U., 1965; MA, U. Tulsa, 1978, EdD, 1983. RN. Staff devel. coord. St. Francis Hosp., Tulsa, 1978-79, asst. dir. for nursing svc., nursing edn., 1979-82, dir. dept. edn., 1982—; presenter various confs. and convs., 1978—. Contbr. articles to profl. jours. Mem. Leadership Tulsa, 1991. Mem. ANA, Nat. League for Nursing, Am. Soc. for Nursing Svc. Adminstrs., Am. Soc. for Health Manpower Edn. and Tng., Okla. Nurses Assn., Okla. Orgn. of Nurse Execs. (pres. 1992-93), Sigma Theta Tau. Office: St Francis Hosp 6161 S Yale Ave Tulsa OK 74136-1992

MULLER, ROBIN ELIZABETH, women's basketball coach; b. Lansing, Mich., July 2, 1963; d. Richard Duncan and Elizabeth Dexter (Blake) M. BA, Kenyon Coll., 1985; MS, Ga. So. Coll., 1988. Asst. women's basketball coach Va. Commonwealth U., Richmond, 1988-93; head coach women's basketball Winthrop U., Rock Hill, S.C., 1993—; head coach Athletes in Action, Moscow, 1993; clinician NCAA Yes Clinic, Fayetteville, Ark., 1994; co-dir. Female Athletes Outreach Program, Rock Hill, 1994—. Mem. Ky. Col. Assn., Women's Basketball Coaches Assn. Episcopalian. Office: Winthrop U Winthrop Coliseum Rock Hill SC 29733

MULLETTE, JULIENNE PATRICIA, television personality and producer, astrologer, author, health center administrator; b. Sydney, Australia, Nov. 19, 1940; came to U.S., 1953; d. Ronald Stanley Lewis and Sheila Rosalind Blunden (Phillips) M.; m. Fred Gillette Sturm, Nov. 24, 1964 (div. Dec. 1969); children: Noah Khristoff Mullette-Gillman, O'Dhaniel Alexander Mullette-Gillman. B.A., Western Coll. for Women, Oxford, Ohio, 1961; postgrad., Harvard U., 1964, U. Sao Paulo, Brazil, 1965, Inst. do Filosofia, Sao Paulo, 1965, Miami U., Oxford, 1967-69. Tchr. English, High Mowing Sch., Wilton, N.H., 1962-64, Stoneleigh-Prospect Hill Sch., Greenfield, Mass., 1964; seminar dir. Western Coll., Oxford, Ohio, 1967-69; pres. Family Tree, The Home Univ., Montclair, N.J., 1978-80; dir. Pleroma Holistic Health Ctr., Montclair, 1980—; dir. Astrological Rsch. Ctr., Sydney, Australia, 1983; hostess (radio talk show) You and the Cosmos Sta. WFMU, East Orange, N.J., 1985, Sta. WJFF, Jeffersonville, N.Y., 1992—, The Juliette Mullette Show, Connections TV, Newark, 1985—, The Juliette Mullette Show Sta. WFDU, Fairleigh Dickinson U., N.J., 1986—, (TV program) You and the Cosmos, Woodstock, N.Y., 1992—; founder Spiritual Devel. Rsch. Group 1986—; pvt. astrology counselor, 1962—; lectr., speaker worldwide, 1968—; guest on radio and TV shows, U.S. and Can., 1962—; host syndicated radio talk show The Juliette Mullette Show, N.Y., N.J., 1987—; host The Juliette Mullette Show You and The Cosmos, WJFF Radio, 1992—, WKNY Radio, 1994—; in charge of programming WPAC Woodstock, 1993—. owner, pres. Moonlight Pond, Woodbourne, N.Y., 1988—; founder The Spiritual Devel. Ctr., 1986—, Pleroma Found. for Astrological Rsch. and Studies, 1990; breeder, trainer llamas, alpacas and other exotic animals; apptd. Woodstock Pub. Access Com., 1993—. Author: The Moon-Understanding the Subconscious, 1973; also articles, 1968—; founding editor KÓSMOS mag., 1968-78, The Jour. of Astrological Studies, 1970; contbg. columnist I Love Cats, 1988—. Founder local chpt. La Leche League, Montclair, 1974. Mem. AAUW (chair cultural affairs Montclair chpt.), Spiritual Devel. Group (founder 1987), Internat. Soc. Astrological Research (founding pres. 1966-78), C.H.A.O.S. (founder 1994—), Am. Fedn. Astrologers (cert.), Société Belge d'Astrologie, Am. Assn. Humanistic Psychology, AAUW (dir. cultural affairs 1987—), NAFE, Internat. Llamas Assn. Avocations: competitive tennis, local theatre, singing. Home: PO Box 65 Bearsville NY 12409

MULLIGAN, DEANNA MARIE, management consultant; b. West Point, Nebr., July 24, 1963; d. Paul Arthur and Judith Maureen (Bottger) Predoehl; m. Stephen Edward Mulligan, Dec. 26, 1985. BS in Bus., U. Nebr., 1985; MBA, Stanford U., 1989. Cons. Woodmen Accident and Life, Hayward, Calif., 1985-87; intern Hewlett-Packard, 1988; dir., corp. planning N.Y. Life, N.Y.C., 1989-90, asst. v.p., 1990-92; assoc. McKinsey & Co., Inc., N.Y.C., 1992—. Vol. Friendly Visitor Program, Napa, Calif., 1987; mem. planning forum, N.Y.C. Nat. Merit scholar, 1981. Office: McKinsey and Co 55 E 52d St New York NY 10020

MULLIGAN, ELINOR PATTERSON, lawyer; b. Bay City, Mich., Apr. 20, 1929; d. Frank Clark and Agnes (Murphy) P.; m. John C. O'Connor, Oct. 28, 1950; children: Christine Fulena, Valerie Clark, Amy O'Connor, Christopher Criffan O'Connor; m. William G. Mulligan, Dec. 6, 1975. BA, U. Mich. 1950; JD, Seton Hall U., 1970. Bar: N.J., 1970. Assoc. Springfield and Newark, 1970-72; pvt. practice, Hackettstown, N.J., 1972; ptnr. Mulligan & Jacobson, N.Y.C., 1973-91, Mulligan & Mulligan, Hackettstown, 1976—; atty. Hackettstown Planning Bd., 1973-86, Blairstown Bd. Adjustment, 1973—; sec. Warren County Ethics Com., 1976-78, sec. Dist. X and XIII Fee Arbitration Com., 1979-87, mem. and chair., 1987-91, mem. dist. ethics com. XIII, 1992—; mem. spl. com. on atty. disciplinary structure N.J. Supreme Ct., 1981—. lectr. Nat. Assn. Women Judges, 1979. Contbr. articles to profl. jours. Named Vol. of Yr. Attys. Vols. in Parole Program, 1978. Fellow Am. Acad. Matrimonial Lawyers (pres.-elect N.J. chpt. 1994—); mem. ABA, Warren County Bar Assn. (pres. 1987-88), N.J. State Bar Assn., Am. Mensa Soc., Kappa Alpha Theta, Union League Club (N.Y.C.), Baltusrol Golf Club (Springfield, N.J.)., Panther Valley Golf and Country Club (Allamuchy, N.J.). Republican. Home: 12 Goldfinch Way Panther Valley Hackettstown NJ 07840 Office: 480 Hwy 517 PO Box 211 Hackettstown NJ 07840-0211

MULLIGAN, ERLINDA RITA, medical/surgical nurse; b. Gallup, N.Mex., June 11, 1954; d. Reginaldo Fred and Maggie (Apodaca) Gallegos; m. Michael Joseph Mulligan,; children: Raymond Fredrick, Margaret Rose, Erin Pablo, Kimberly Edel. ADN, U. N.Mex., Gallup, 1988. RN, N.Mex.; cert. med.-surg. nurse Am. Nurses Credentialing Ctr. Nurse Rehoboth McKinley Christian Hosp., Gallup, 1988-89, nurse I, 1989-90, nurse II, rep. med.-surg. and pediat. units, 1990-91, nurse III, 1991-92, nurse IV, 1992-94, surg. specialist, 1994—. Mem. St. Francis Ch., Gallup, 1954-94, St. Francis Sch. PTO, Gallup, 1982-92, St. Francis Ch. Choir, Gallup, 1991-92; mem. Right to Life Com. of N.Mex., 1992-94, sec. Gallup chpt., 1993-94. Roman Catholic. Home: 205 E Logan Gallup NM 87301

MULLIGAN, ROSEMARY ELIZABETH, paralegal; b. Chgo., July 8, 1941; d. Stephen Edward and Rose Anne (Sannasardo) Granzyk; children: Daniel R. Bonaguidi, Matthew S. Bonaguidi. AAS, Harper Coll., Palatine, Ill., 1982; student, Ill. State U., 1959-60. Paralegal Miller, Forest & Downing Ltd., Glenview, Ill., 1982-91; ind. contractor mcpl. law, 1991—; paralegal seminar educator Harper Coll. Pro-choice activist and mem. Ill. Ho. of Reps., 1993—. Mem. LWV, Am. Planning Assn., Ill. Paralegal Assn., Nat. Women's Polit. Caucus, Ill. Fedn. Bus. and Profl. Women, Ill. Women in Govt., Chgo. Women in Govt. Rels., Ill. Fedn. Bus. and Profl. Women (nat. legis. platform rep. 1991-92, chair Outstanding Working Women of Ill. 1991-92, rep., state treas. Patrick Quinn's Women in Bus. Working Group 1991-92, state membership chair 1989-90, state legis. co-chair, nat. platform rep. 1988-89, state legis. chair, nat. platform rep. 1987-88). Roman Catholic. Home: 346 Cornell Ave Des Plaines IL 60016-2133 Office: Ill Ho of Reps State Capitol Springfield IL 62706*

MULLIKIN, AHYCHEL SOTO, emergency trauma nurse, paramedic; b. Medellin, Colombia, South America, Mar. 18, 1961; d. Luis Norberto and Matilde (Rojas) S. ADN, U. S.C., Spartanburg, 1988. Cert. BLS, ACLS instr., PALS, PHTLS, PEMSTP. Lab technician arterial blood gas Spartanburg Regional Med. Ctr., 1986-87; technician pulmonary lab. Greenville (S.C.) Meml. Med. Ctr., 1981-85, staff nurse oper. rm., 1988-89, trauma nurse, team leader, alt. charge nurse Trauma Ctr., 1988—; active mem. patient care com., Greenville, 1991—, mgmt. adv. com., Greenville, 1992—, EMS com., paramedic clin. instr., Greenville, 1990—. Coord. family support USAR, Greenville, 1992. Mem. Emergency Nurses Assn. Democratic. Roman Catholic.

MULLINEAUX, JEWEL E., retired educator; b. N.Y.C.; d. Aubrey Vibbert and Bertye (Winterling) Brooks; m. Donald Hammond Mullineaux, Sept. 15, 1948. BA in Spanish with honors, Goucher Coll., 1938; postgrad., Temple U., 1938, U. Pa., 1940; MA, U. Md., 1954. Counselor, tchr., interviewer City of Balt., 1938-42; supr., counselor War Man Power Commn., Balt., 1942-48; chief exams. and recruitment Civil Svc. Commn. Balt., 1948-67; assoc. prof. career selection, career counselor Community Coll. Balt., 1967-74; cons. police patrolmen selection, various U.S. cities. Editor Macca Media jour., 1970-73; contbr. articles to profl. jours.; co-author: (novel) Shadow and Shield, 1981; author short stories and poetry. Sec.-treas. Am. Soc. Pub. Adminstrs., Balt., 1950-52; mem. Mid.-Atlantic Assn. Sr. Jr. Colls., 1967-74, Mid-Atlantic Career Counseling Assn., 1967-74, Senator John Marshall Butler's Com. Disting. Women Leaders, 1954; pres. city coun. Beta Sigma Phi, Balt., 1947; all offices local chpt. Beta Sigma Phi, Balt., 1938-50; mentor teenagers Nu Phi Mu, Balt., 1948-50; mem. Halifax Humane Soc., Daytona Beach, Fla., 1980—, Nat. Wildlife Fedn., 1985—. Recipient Cert. Appreciation personnel dept. City of Phila., 1966, Cert. of Award, Ga. State Writing Competition, 1989, Goldkey, Phi Kappa Phi, 1954. Mem. AAUW (mentor creative writers' group, Book award), Halifax River Yacht Club. Christian Scientist. Home: The Landmark 404 S Beach St Apt 202 Daytona Beach FL 32114-5010

MULLINS, BETTY JOHNSON, realtor; b. Killen, Ala., Dec. 29, 1925; d. James E. and Vernie (Muse) Johnson; m. Charles Harvey Mullins, Nov. 18, 1944; children: Charles Harvey Jr., Susan. BS, U. North Ala., 1945. Tchr. Biloxi (Miss.) City Schs., 1945-46, Elizabeth City County Schs., Buckroe Beach, Va., 1946-47, Sheffield (Ala.) City Schs., 1949-58; with family automobile bus., 1958-86; real estate assoc. Neese Real Estate, Inc., Florence, Ala., 1986—. Pres. Project Courtview, Florence, 1980, Heritage Found., Florence, 1994—; mem. Tenn. Valley Art Guild, Tuscumbia, Tenn. Valley Art Ctr., Tuscumbia, Concert Guild, Florence, pres., 1994, Friends of Kennedy Douglas Art Ctr., Florence; v.p. Salvation Army Aux., 1991-92; mem., past pres. United Meth. Women, First Meth. Ch., Florence, mem. adminstrv. and pastor parish and fin. bds.; bd. dirs. Friends of the Libr., Florence, 1993—; mem., past pres. Lauderdale-Colbert-Franklin Foster Grandparent Adv. Bd., Russellville, Ala., Retired Sr. Vol. Program Adv. Bd., past pres.; mem. Pres. Cabinet U. North Ala.; trustee United Way, Shoals, 1992—; mem. Found. Bd. Univ. North Ala., 1994. Recipient Shoals Area Citizen of Yr., 1984, Shoals Area Top Producer Muscle Shoals Area Bd. Realtors, 1991, 92, 93, Community Svc. award U. North Ala., 1994; named Woman of Yr. Bus. and Profl. Women, 1980. Mem. LWV, Shoals-AAUW (pres. 1990-91), Nat. Bd. Realtors, U. North Ala. Alumni Assn. (past pres., bd. dirs., Alumni of Yr. award 1985, Cmty. Svc. award 1994, Found. Bd. 1994), Internat. Fertilizer Devel. Ctr. Century Club (past pres. Muscle Shoals, Ala. chpt.), Shoals C. of C. (past bd. dirs.), Tenn. Valley Hist. Assn., U. North Ala. Sportsman Club, Muscle Shoals Bd. Realtors, Ala. Bd. Realtors. Republican. Methodist. Home: PO Box 70 Florence AL 35631 Office: PO Box 70 Florence AL 35631-0070

MULLINS, MARY ANN, accountant; b. Hazard, Ky., Dec. 10, 1956; d. John Jr. and Stella Mae (Profitt) Pennington; m. Allen Walker, Sept. 17, 1971 (div. 1977); m. Edward Clarence Mullins, Apr. 16, 1983; children: John Douglas, Alison Michelle, Brian David. Payroll, accts. receivable specialist Hazard Express, 1973-77, 79-80, accts. receivable specialist, 1986-89; office mgr. Hazard Explosives, 1980-83; accts. payable/equipment maintenance specialist Lost Mountain Mining, Hazard, 1983-84; adminstrv. asst. Ball Br. Mining, Dwarf, Ky., 1989—. Home: Hwy 1146 PO Box 56 Dice KY 41736 Office: Ball Br Mining Co Inc New Hwy 80 PO Box 450 Dwarf KY 41739

MULLINS, MARY PATRICIA, bank officer; b. Owensboro, Ky, Nov. 30, 1954; d. Paul Michael and Mary Lois (Coomes) Aud; m. James Mark Mullins, Oct. 20, 1973; children: Lori Janel, Scott Anthony. Attended, Owensboro Bus. Coll., 1973, Vanderbilt U., 1986. Loan officer Keesler Fed. Credit Union, Bllo; asst. v.p. Am. Nat. Bank & Trust Co. Chmn. com. Troop 223 Boy Scouts Am., Chattanooga, 1991-94; mem. com. PTA, 1984-94.

MULLINS, OBERA, microbiologist; b. Egypt, Miss., Feb. 15, 1927; d. Willie Ree and Maggie Sue (Orr) Gunn; BS, Chgo. State U., 1974; MS in Health Sci. Edn., Governors State U., 1981; m. Charles Leroy Mullins, Nov. 2, 1952; children: Mary Artavia, Arthur Curtis, Charles Leroy, Charlester Teresa, William Hellman. Med. technician, microbiologist Chgo. Health Dept., Chgo., 1976—, now pers. asst. III. Mem. AAUW, Am. Soc. Clin. Pathologists (cert. med. lab. technician), Ill. Soc. Lab. Technicians. Roman Catholic. Home: 9325 S Marquette Ave Chicago IL 60617-4131 Office: Westtown Neighborhood Health Ctr 2418 W Division Chicago IL 60623

MULLINS, RUTH GLADYS, nurse; b. Westville, N.S., Can., Aug. 25, 1943; d. William G. and Gladys H.; came to U.S., 1949, naturalized, 1955; student Tex. Womans U., 1961-64; BS in Nursing, Calif. State U.-Long Beach, 1966; MNursing, UCLA, 1973; m. Leonard E. Mullins, Aug. 27, 1963; children: Deborah R., Catherine M., Leonard III. Pub. health nurse, L.A. County Health Dept., 1967-68; nurse Meml. Hosp. Med. Center, Long Beach, 1968-72; dir. pediatric nurse practitioner program Calif. State U., Long Beach, 1973—, asst. prof., 1975-80, assoc. prof., 1980-85, prof., 1985—; health svc. credential coord. Sch. Nursing Calif. State U., Long Beach, Calif., chmn., 1979-81, coord. grad. programs, 1985-92; mem. Calif. Maternal, Child and Adolescent Health Bd., 1977-84; vice chair Long Beach/Orange County Health Consortium Divsn. Nursing, 1984-85, chair 1985-86. Tng. grantee HHS, Calif. Dept. Health; cert. pediatric nurse practitioner. Fellow Nat. Assn. Pediatric Nurse Assocs. and Practitioners (exec.

bd., past pres.), Nat. Fedn. Nursing Specialty Orgns. (sec. 1991-93); mem. Am. Pub. Health Assn., Nat. Alliance Nurse Practitioners (governing body 1990-92), Assn. Faculties Pediatric Nurse Practitioner Programs, L.A. and Orange County Assn. Pediatric Nurse Practitioners and Assocs., Am. Assn. U. Faculty, Ambulatory Pediatric Assn. Democrat. Methodist. Author: (with B. Nelms) Growth and Development: A Primary Health Care Approach; contbg. author: Quick Reference to Pediatric Nursing, 1984; asst. editor Jour. Pediatric Health Care. Home: 6382 Heil Ave Huntington Beach CA 92647-4232 Office: Calif State U Dept Nursing 1250 N Bellflower Blvd Long Beach CA 90840-0004

MULLIS, MADELINE GAIL HERMAN, religious studies educator, choir director; b. Lenoir, N.C., Oct. 26, 1936; d. William Richard and Madeline Edythe (Harris) Herman; m. Thad McCoy Mullis Jr., Dec. 18, 1960 (div. Oct. 1978); children: Thad McCoy III, Myra Lynn, Martin Harper. MusB, U. N.C., Greensboro, 1958; MA, Appalachian State U., 1963. Cert. elem., secondary instrumental and choir music tchr. N.C. Jr. choir dir. St. Stephens Luth. Ch., Lenoir, 1969-80, sr. choir dir., 1960—, handbell choir dir., 1970—, deacon, 1980-82, 84-86;, 88-90; Sunday sch. tchr. St. Stephens Luth. Ch., Lenoir, 1983-86; tchr. classroom music, chorus, band Caldwell County Schs., Lenoir, 1958-65, 77—, chair St. Stephens Worship and Music, Lenoir, 1988-93; del. N.C. Synod Conv., Hickory, N.C., 1990; pres. Agape Women's Circle, Lenoir, 1991-92. Chairperson Sesquicentennial Children's Chorus, Caldwell County, 1991; coord. 1st Caldwell County Children's Choral Festival, 1993. Recipient 19 Superior Ratings at Jr. High Sch. Coral Festivals. Mem. NEA, N.C. Ctr. for Advancement of Tchg. (hon.), Assn. Luth. Musicians, N.C. Assn. Educators, Music Educators Nat. Conf., N.C. Music Educators Assn., Am. Orff-Schulwerk Assn., Cmty. Music Club (pres. 1993-95), Alpha Delta Kappa. Republican. Home: 119 Ellison Pl NE Lenoir NC 28645-3716 Office: 1406 Harper Ave NW Lenoir NC 28645-5059 also: Happy Valley Sch Rt 10 Box 639 Lenoir NC 28645

MULLOY-FORKIN, DONNA PATRICE, physical therapist; b. Phila., July 23, 1965; d. Donald Joseph and Barbara Carol (Schroth) Mulloy; m. Thomas Patrick Forkin, Aug. 3, 1991. BA in Chemistry, LaSalle Univ., 1987; M in Phys. Therapy, Temple Univ., 1992. Lic. phys. therapist, Pa. Resident asst. LaSalle Univ., Phila., 1985-87; biochemistry rsch. technician Dept. of Physiology Thomas Jefferson Univ., 1987-89; phys. therapy aide N.E. Phys. Therapy Assocs., Phila., 1991-92; phys. therapist Moss Rehab. Hosp., Phila., 1992-94; sr. phys. therapist Frankford Hosp., Phila., 1994—. Contbr. articles to profl. jours. Vol. Jefferson Univ. Hosp., Phila., 1989, Shriner's Hosp. for Children, 1989. Mem. Am. Phys. Therapy Assn. Home: 3349 Wellington St Philadelphia PA 19149-1615

MULRONEY, MILA, wife of former Canadian prime minister; b. Sarajevo, Yugoslavia, July 13, 1953; d. Dmitrije and Bogdanka Pivnicki; m. (Martin) Brian Mulroney, May 26, 1973; children—Caroline Anne, Benedict Martin, Robert Mark, Daniel Nicolas Dimitri. Faculty of Engring, 1973-76, Concordia U.,Montreal, Que., Can. Hon. chairperson Can. Cystic Fibrosis Found., U. Ottawa Heart Inst.; nat. patron Read Can.; patron Genesis Rsch. Found., Can. Rhett Syndrome Assn.; hon. bd. mem. Women and the Arts Man., Inc.; mem. nat. adv. coun. Tex. Heart Inst. Home: 24 Sussex Dr, Ottawa, ON Canada K1M 1M4 Office: 1981 McGill College Ave # 1100, Montreal, PQ Canada H3A 3C1

MULROONEY, TERESA LEE (TESS MULROONEY), systems analyst; b. Boscobel, Wis., Dec. 30, 1957; d. Edward Paul and Joy Belle (Haas) M.; m. Paul David Eastwood, Dec. 29, 1984. AA, Gateway Tech. Coll., Kenosha, Wis., 1978; BS, Edgewood Coll., Madison, Wis., 1985. Computer programmer Office of Commr. of Ins., Madison, 1979-84; programmer, analyst Wis. Bd. Vocat. Tech. and Adult Edn., Madison, 1984-90; systems analyst, trainer Wis. Dept. Transp., Madison, 1990—. Compiler (book) We Have a Heritage: Brookens Family, 4 vols., 1993-94. V.p., treas. Dunn's Marsh Neighborhood Assn., Madison, 1980-82; co-coord. Madison chpt. NOW, 1988-92, v.p.-exec., 1989-91, vol. conf. coord. Wis. chpt., 1990-91. Mem. Project Mgmt. Inst., Historic Madison Inc., Wis. State Geneal. Soc., Wis. Planned Parenthood, Vilas Neighborhood Assn.

MULTARI, MILLIE, pediatric pulmonary/cardiac nurse, nurse liaison. BSN, Coll. New Rochelle, 1992. Hemodialysis technician Westchester Artificial Kidney Ctr., Valhalla, N.Y.; cardiac and respiratory nurse United Hosp., Portchester, N.Y.; med.-surg. nurse Dobbs Ferry (N.Y.) Hosp.; hosp. staff relief nurse Med. Pers. Pool, White Plains, N.Y.; patient-family educator ventilator-dependent children Blythedale Children's Hosp., Valhalla, 1988-93; community nurse liaison St. Mary's Hosp. for Children, Bayside, N.Y., 1993—; speaker and presenter in field. Mem. Assn. Rehab. Nurses. Christian. Home: 10 N Broadway White Plains NY 10601 Office: St Mary's Hosp for Children Bradhurst Ave Bayside NY 11360

MULVANEY, MARY FREDERICA, systems analyst; b. N.Y., Nov. 27, 1945; d. Michael Joseph and Mary Catherine (Clapper) M. BA, Marymount Coll., 1967; MA, U. Va., 1968. Cert. data processor Inst. Certification of Computer Profls., Ill. Computer systems analyst Dept. of Def., Ft. Meade, Md., 1968-74; sr. programmer analyst Planning Rsch. Corp., McLean, Va., 1974-83; mem. tech. staff Fed. Systems Group TRW Inc., Fairfax, Va., 1983-90; sr. mem. tech. staff GTE Govt. Systems Corp., Rockville, Md., 1990-94; engr., sci. TRW, Inc., Fairfax, Va., 1994—. Mem. IEEE, Data Processing Mgmt. Assn., Computer Measurement Group, Digital Equipment Corp. Users Soc., Cath. Assn. of Scientists and Engrs. Roman Catholic. Office: TRW Sys Integration Group One Federal Systems Park Dr Fairfax VA 22033

MULVEY, HELEN FRANCES, emeritus history educator; b. Providence, Feb. 22, 1913; d. William James and Anna (Nelson) M. A.B., Pembroke Coll., 1933; A.M., Columbia U., 1934; A.M., Radcliffe Coll., 1942; Ph.D., Harvard U., 1949. Instr. history Russell Sage Coll., Troy, N.Y., 1944-46; asst. prof. to prof. history, Conn. Coll., New London, 1946-83, prof. emeritus, 1983—, Brigida Pacchiana Ardenghi chair, 1975-78; vis. prof. Brit. history, U. Wis., Madison, 1971-72; vis. lectr. Yale U., 1974-83; lectr. Irish history, Pfizer Adult Edn., Groton, Conn., 1983-84; vis. scholar Phi Beta Kappa, Washington, 1982-83. Author articles, essays Irish and Brit. history; co-editor bibliog. vol. in A New History of Ireland, 9 vols. Anne Crosby Emery fellow, Brown U., 1933. Mem. Am. Hist. Assn., Am. Conf. for Irish Studies, North Am. Conf. on Brit. Studies, AAUP (chpt. pres. 1962-64), Phi Beta Kappa. Clubs: Harvard. Office: Conn Coll PO Box 5508 New London CT 06320

MULVEY, MARY C., adult education administrator, gerontologist; b. Bangor, Maine, Aug. 17, 1909; d. Michael J. and Ann Loretta (Higgins) Crowley; m. Gordon F. Mulvey, Jan. 25, 1940. BA, U. Maine, 1930; MA, Brown U., 1953; EdD, Harvard U., 1961; LHD (hon.), U. Maine, 1991. Dir. Adminstrn. on Aging, Providence, 1960-63; guidance counselor Providence Sch. Dept., 1963-65; dir. adult edn. City of Providence Sch. Dept., 1965-79; reg. prog. rep. Title V, Older Ams. Act, Nat. Coun. Sr. Citizens, Washington, 1980-94; 1st v.p. Nat. Coun. Sr. Citizens, 1961—; pres. Nat. Sr. Citizens Edn. and Rsch. Ctr., Washington, 1970—; cons. Fed. Housing for the Aging, Washington, 1963-65; del./adv. com. White House Conf. on Aging, 1961, 71, 81, 95, apptd. by Pres. Carter to Fed. Coun. Aging, 1979; charter mem., adv. bd. Coll. Arts/Humanities, U. Maine, 1992—; pres. R.I. State Coun. Sr. Citizens, 1982—; instr. preparing retirement, developer women's program U. R.I., 1963-80; various coms. state and nat. level. Contbr. articles to profl. jours. Numerous hons. including Soroptimists fellow award for rsch. in gerontology, Harvard U., 1955, 57, 59, Cert. of Award as Project Dir. of Sr. AIDES Employment Prog., 1968-78, Medicare award, R.I. State Coun. Sr. Citizens and Nat. Coun. Sr. Citizens, 1985, Disting. Achievement award U. Maine, 1980, Disting. Achievement award Berwick Acad., 1981, Justice for All award R.I. Bar Assn., 1981, Woman of Yr. award Nat. Sr. Pagenat, 1982, R.I. Women First R.I. Sec. of State, 1991, citation Syracuse U., 1991, R.I. Dept. Elderly Affairs, 1993, 25th Anniversary Title V Sr. Employment award Nat. Coun. Sr. Citizens, 1993, Lifetime Achievement award Nat. Coun. Sr. Citizens, 1994; inducted into R.I. Heritage Hall of Fame, 1993. Fellow Gerontol. Soc. Am.; mem. ACA, AAUW, Am. Assn. Adult and Continuing Edn., Harvard U. Alumni Assn. (alumni award R.I. chpt. 1986), U. Maine Alumni Assn., Brown U. Alumni Assn., Pi Lambda Theta, Delta Delta Delta. Home: 95 Plymouth Rd East Providence RI 02914-1943

MUNCEY, BARBARA DEANE, university associate, consultant; b. Welch, W.Va., July 12, 1952; d. Juan Irvin and June Henryetta (Dowse) M. AB, Marshall U., Huntington, W.Va., 1974; postgrad., U. Ill., 1980; postgrad, U. Mich, 1984-85; postgrad., U. Oklahoma, 1987; MA, Western Mich. U., 1994. Cons. Heartside Neighborhood Assn., Grand Rapids, Mich., 1979-80; asst. dir. Muncey Devel. Corp., Grand Rapids, Mich., 1979-80; coord. Northeast Mich. Econ. Devel. Assn., Gayland, Mich., 1980-81; dir. of econ. devel. Grand Rapids Internat Tribal Coun., Mich., 1984-86; dir. Sterling Indsl. Devel. Com., Ill., 1986-89; pres. Muncey Cons. Svcs., 1989-90; grad. asst. coord. office of field experiences Western Mich. U., Kalamazoo, 1990—; mem. grad. studies coun., grad. curriculum com. Western Mich. U., 1992-93, mem. com. to adviser pres. on acad. affairs, 1993; v.p. Sauk Valley Area Econ. Devel. Assn., 1989—; mem. Whiteside County Regional Planning Commn., 1987—. Mem. Rep. Women's Club. Mem. NAFE, Am. Econ. Devel., Ill. Devel. Coun., Mich. Indsl. Devel., Mid-Am. Econ. Devel. Coun. Baptist. Office: Western Mich U Grad Student Adv Com The Grad Coll Kalamazoo MI 49008-5121

MUNCH, JENNIFER CLISE, real estate management executive; b. Keyser, W.Va., Oct. 16, 1947; d. James Dale and Jean (Borror) Clise; m. Thomas Lee Munch, Aug. 19, 1967. BS in Acctg. magna cum laude, U. Balt., 1973. CPA, Md. Mgmt. acct. Monumental Properties Inc., Balt., 1972-73, dir. automated rent system, 1973-74, internal auditor, 1974-75, data processing coordinator, then asst. to controller, 1975-77, acctg. mgr., 1977-79; sr. v.p. and controller Town and Country Mgmt. Corp., Balt., 1979—. Treas. Carroll County Agrl. Ctr., Westminster, Md., 1979-90; mem. allocations com. Balt. United Way, 1983; bd. govs. Carroll County Farm Mus., Westminster, 1985—; chmn. fin. com. Westminster United Meth. Ch., 1985-89, bd. trustees, 1990-91; mem. Carroll County Parks Bd., 1991—; bd. trustees Bowling Brook Sch., 1990—. Mem. Am. Inst. CPA's, Md. Assn. CPA's, Beta Alpha. Republican. Office: Town & Country Mgmt Corp 100 S Charles St Baltimore MD 21201-2725

MUNCY, PAULA ANN, executive search company executive; b. Houston, Jan. 25, 1964; d. Paul I. and L. Jean (Hill) M. MB magna cum laude, U. Miami, 1985. From acct. exec. to dir. Career Advancement Cons., Ft. Lauderdale, Fla., 1987-93; pres. Search Am., Inc., West Palm Beach, Fla., 1993—; exec. dir. RCI Nat. Search, West Palm Beach, 1994—. Adoption counselor, spl. events coord. Humane Soc., Ft. Lauderdale, 1992—. Mem. People for the Ethical Treatment of Animals. Republican. Methodist. Home: 497 Goldenwood Way Wellington FL 33414 Office: RCI Nat Search Ste 600 1655 Palm Beach Lakes Blvd West Palm Beach FL 33401

MUND, GERALDINE, bankruptcy judge; b. L.A., July 7, 1943; d. Charles J. and Pearl (London) M. BA, Brandeis U., 1965; MS, Smith Coll., 1967; JD, Loyola U., 1977. Bar: Calif. 1977. Bankruptcy judge U.S. Cen. Dist. Calif., 1984—. Past pres. Temple Israel, Hollywood, Calif. Mem. ABA, L.A. County Bar Assn. Office: Roybal Bldg 255 E Temple St Los Angeles CA 90012

MUNDORFF SHRESTHA, SHEILA ANN, cardiologist; b. Rochester, N.Y., Dec. 14, 1945; d. Karl Mundorff and Elizabeth Mary (Braun) Ross; m. Buddhi Man Shrestha, June 18, 1988. BS in Biology, Nazareth Coll., Rochester, 1967; MS in Microbiology, U. Rochester, 1984. Lab. technician Eastman Dental Ctr., Rochester, 1967-69, rsch. asst., 1969-71, rsch. assoc., 1971-92, small animal expt. coord., 1984-92, sect. head animal/microbiol. rsch., 1987—, chmn. Instl. Animal Care and Use Com., 1990—, vivarium dir., 1990—, med. emergency program dir., 1991-92, asst. prof., 1992—; mem. animal resource group ADA Health Found., Chgo., 1981-83; cons. working group Sci. Consensus Conf.-Assessment Cariogenic Potential of Foods, San Antonio, 1985; participant, reactor, co-chair animal caries models working groups Conf. on Clin. Aspects of Demineralization of Teeth, Rochester, N.Y., 1994. Patentee in field. CPR instr. ARC, Rochester, 1978—, cert. 1st responder, N.Y.S., 1992—. NIH, Nat. Inst. Dental Rsch. grantee, 1986, 87, 88. Mem. Am. Assn. Dental Rsch. (sec.-treas. Rochester sect. 1977-92). Roman Catholic. Office: Eastman Dental Ctr 625 Elmwood Ave Rochester NY 14620-2989

MUNDY, MARY CAROLYN, administrative assistant; b. East St. Louis, Ill., Mar. 8, 1945; d. Arthur John Hallows and Mary Helen (Berger) Welle; m. Thomas Burke Elliff Sr., Aug. 12, 1964 (dec. June 1989); children: Michael Patrick Elliff, Thomas Burke Elliff Jr. Grad., St. Teresa Acad., 1963. Sec. Brady Donovan & Hatch, 1963-64; housekeeper, 1964-71; sec. H.G. Baker, Jr. Atty. at Law, 1971-81; adminstrv. asst. Armstrong Teasdale, St. Louis, 1981—. Vol. Radio Info. Svc. Recorded for the blind, 1989-90. Office: Armstrong Teasdale 1 Metropolitan Sq Ste 2600 Saint Louis MO 63102-2740

MUNDY, PHYLLIS, state legislator; b. Evansville, Ind., Jan. 31, 1948. BS, Bloomsburg State Coll., 1970. Mem. Pa. Ho. of Reps. Home: 629 Westmoreland Ave Kingston PA 18704 Office: Pa Ho of Reps State Capitol Harrisburg PA 17120 also: Park Bldg Ste 109 400 Third Ave Kingston PA 18704*

MUNGER, JANET ANNE, education administrator; b. N.J., Feb. 27, 1947; d. Victor J. and Ann L. Ferri Munger. BA, Fairleigh Dickinson U., 1968, MA, 1971; EdD, Seton Hall U., 1985. Cert. sch. administr., prin., supr. Tchr. Meml. Sch. No. 11, Passaic, N.J., 1968-70; dir., tchr. Morristown Head Start Program, N.J., 1970-71 (summers); curriculum devel. specialist N.J. State Coun. Arts Grant Program, 1973 (summer); tchr. Ctrl. Sch., Montville, N.J., 1970-73, William Mason Sch., Montville, 1973-81; tchr. gifted and talented William Mason, Valley View and Woodmont Schs., Montville, 1981-82; coord. of curriculum instr. South Plainfield (N.J.) Bd. Edn., 1986-91, supr. fed. and state projects, 1989-92, supr. ednl. programs, 1992-94, prin., 1994—; presenter in field profl. assns.; researcher, writer, cons., 1982—. Mem. ASCD, NEA, Am. Assn. Sch. Adminstrs., N.J. Assn. Sch. Adminstrs., N.J. Edn. Assn., Assn. Secondary Sch. Prins., Prins. and Suprs. Assn., New Eng. Coalition Ednl. Leaders, N.J. Assn. Fed. Program Adminstrs., Phi Delta Kappa, Kappa Delta Pi. Office: S Plainfield Bd Edn Cromwell Pl South Plainfield NJ 07080

MUNHALL, RUTH BEATRICE, business and financial consultant; b. Mendon, Mass., Feb. 8, 1929; d. Lawrence B. and Elsie B. (Gaskill) M. Grad. Salvation Army Officers Coll., Bronx, N.Y., 1951; M.B.A., Calif. Coast U., 1980, Ph.D., D.B.A., 1981. Civilian supr. U.S. Army and VA Hosp., Framingham, Mass., 1946-50; ordained clergywoman; officer Salvation Army centers in Mass., N.Y. and N.J., 1951-64; owner, operator acctg. and real estate firm, N.Y.C., 1964-68; supr. fiduciary and individual taxation Bank of N.Y., N.Y.C., 1968-79; cons. non profit orgns. founder R.M. Scholarship Info. Services, Ark., N.Y., Mass. and Israel, 1981-89; pres., chief exec. officer Munhall, Monahan, Chapman Fiduciary Animal Charities, Inc., 1984—; pres. Munhall Research Sci. Corp., 1985—; cons. in field. Recipient 5 Yr. Civil Def. award Gov. N.Y. State. Author: (booklet) English, French, Hebrew, Spanish for the Traveler, 1990. Mem. DAR, Alumni Assn. Calif. Coast U. Republican.

MUNIZ, NANCY SEVER, speech and language pathologist; b. Carbondale, Pa., June 15, 1955; d. John Paul and Clara Marie (Menart) Sever; m. Robert Louis Muniz, May 24, 1985. BS in Comm. Disorders, Marywood Coll., Scranton, Pa., 1977; MS in Speech Pathology, Idaho State U., 1984; postgrad., Western Wyo. Coll., 1988, U. Nev., Las Vegas, 1993-94. Lic. speech pathologist, Nev., N.Mex. Speech therapy trainee Idaho Dept. Health and Welfare, Pocatello, 1977-78; speech therapist Headstart Sch. Dist. #25, Pocatello, 1978-79; speech therapist Sch. Dist. #55, Blackfood, Idaho, 1979-85; comm. disorders specialist Uinta County Sch. Dist. #1, Evanston, Wyo., 1985-88; speech therapist Roswell (N.Mex.) Ind. Sch. Dist., 1988-92, Clark County Sch. Dist., Las Vegas, 1992—; bilingual speech/lang. diagnostician CCSD, Las Vegas, 1992—; spl. edn. dept. chhmn. Roswell Inst. Sch. Dist., 1989-92; Title VII Indian bilingual tchr./facilitator, Blackfoot, 1984-85. Program dir. and events coord. Spl. Olympics, Evanston, 1985-88; mem. Bruce King Dem. Election Com., Roswell, 1991-92; instr./program coord. CCD, Pocatello, 1980-85. Bilingual Indian Edn. (Title VII) grantee, 1984. Mem. Nev. Speech and Hearing Assn., N.Mex. Speech Lang. and Hearing Assn., Am. Speech Lang. and Hearing Assn., Am.. Slovenian Cath. Women's Union, Clark County Classroom Tchrs. Assn., Am. Slovenian Heritage Soc. Roman Catholic. Home: Apt 2021 1501 Linnbaker Ln H201 Las Vegas NV 89110 Office: Clark County Sch Dist 2625 E St Louis Las Vegas NV 89104

MUNNELL, ALICIA HAYDOCK, economist; b. N.Y.C., Dec. 6, 1942; d. Walter Howe Haydock and Alicia (Wildman) Haydock Roux; m. Thomas Clark Munnell (div.); children: Thomas Clark Jr., Hamilton Haydock; m. Henry Scanlon Healy, Feb. 2, 1980. BA in Econs., Wellesley, 1964; MA in Econs., Boston U., 1966; PhD in Econs., Harvard U., 1973. Staff asst. bus. rsch. div. New Eng. Tel. Co., Boston, 1964-65; teaching fellow econs. dept. Boston U., 1965-66; rsch. asst. for dir. econ. studies program Brookings Instn., Washington, 1966-68; teaching fellow Harvard U., Cambridge, Mass., 1971-73; asst. prof. econs. Wellesley Coll., Mass., 1974; economist Fed. Res. Bank Boston, 1973-76, asst. v.p., economist, 1976-78, v.p., economist, 1979-84, sr. v.p., dir. rsch., 1984-93; asst. sec. for econ. policy Dept. Treasury, Washington, 1993—; mem. Gov.'s Task Force on Unemployment Compensation, Mass., 1975; mem. spl. funding adv. com. for Mass. pensions, 1976; mem. Mass. Retirement Law Commn., 1976-82; staff dir. joint com. on pub. pensions Nat. Planning Assn., 1978; mem. adv. com. for urban inst. HUD grant on state-local pensions, 1978-81; mem. pension rsch. council Wharton Sch. Fin. and Commerce, U. Pa., 1979—; mem. adv. group Nat. Commn. for Employment Policy, 1980-81; mem. adv. bd. Nat. Aging Policy Ctr. in Income Maintenance, Brandeis U., 1980-84; participant pvt. sector retirement security and U.S. tax policy roundtable discussions Govt. Rsch. Corp., 1984; mem. supervisory panel Forum Inst. of Villers Found., 1984; mem. Medicare working group, div. of health policy rsch. and edn. Harvard U., 1984-87; mem. Commn. on Coll. Retirement, 1984-86; mem. com. to plan major study of nat. long term care policies Inst. Medicine, Nat. Acad. Scis., 1984-87; mem. steering com. Am. Assn. Ret. Persons, 1987—; mem. adv. council Am. Enterprise Inst., 1987—; com. mem. Inst. Medicine, Nat. Acad. Scis. Human Rights Com., 1987—; co-founder, pres. Nat. Acad. Social Ins., 1986—; bd. dirs. Pension Rights Ctr.; mem. program rev. com. Brigham and Women's Hosp., 1988—; mem. Commn. to Rev. Mass. Anti-Takeover Laws, 1988-89, econs. vis. com. MIT, 1989—. Author: The Impact of Social Security on Personal Saving, 1974, Future of Social Security, 1977 (various awards), Pensions for Public Employees, 1979, The Economics of Private Pensions, 1982; co-author: Options for Fiscal Structure Reform in Massachusetts, 1975; editor: Lessons from the Income Maintenance Experiments, 1987, Is There a Shortfall in Public Capital Investment?, 1991, (conf. proc.) Retirement and Public Policy, 1991, Pensions and the Economy: Sources, Uses, and Limitations of Data, 1992, co-editor: Pensions and the Economy: Sources, Uses, and Limitations of Data; contbr. articles to profl. jours., chpts. to books. Mem. Inst. Medicine of NAS, Nat. Acad. Pub. Adminstrn. Office: US Treasury Dept Office of Econ Policy 1500 Pennsylvania Ave NW Washington DC 20220

MUÑOZ DONES CARRASCAL, ELOISA, hospital administrator, pediatrician, consultant, educator; b. San Lorenzo, P.R., Oct. 25, 1922; d. Pedro and Maria (Dones) Muñoz; m. José D. Carrascal, Dec. 7, 1962; children: Lilia, Maria. BA in Edn. cum laude, BS in Chemistry cum laude, U. P.R., Rio Piedras, 1943; MD, Tulane U., 1948. Diplomate Am. Bd. Pediatrics. Intern Arecibo Charity Dist. Hosp., 1948-49; resident in pediatrics San Juan (P.R.) City Hosp., 1949-51, chief newborn svc., attending pediatrician, 1951—, dir. neonatal-perinatal medicine, 1965—, dir. fellowship tng. program, 1972—; from instr. to assoc. prof. clin. pediatrics sch. medicine U. P.R., 1951-89, prof., 1989—; courtesy pediatrician neonatologist Tchrs. Hosp., Hato Rey, P.R., 1951-76, Ashford Presbyn. Drs. Hosp., Santurce, P.R., 1951-76, San Jorge H. H. Pavia Fernandez, Santurce, 1951-76; cons. pediatrician neonatologist Tchrs. H. Auxilio Mutuo H., Hato Rey, 1976—, Drs. H. San Jorge H. Ashford, San Juan, 1976—; mem. exec. com. San Juan City Hosp., 1976—, pres. med. faculty, 1976-77, 87-89, mem. instl. rev. bd., mem. ednl. rev. bd., mem. various coms.; lectr. in field. Contbr. articles to profl. jours. U.S. del. Care Orgn. Latin Am., 1962-63. Recipient Bronze medal Brazilian Acad. Human Scis., 1975, Hon. Cert. Internat. Yr. Women, City Mayor Lodo Carlos Romero Barceló, 1975, Hon. Cert. Disting. Svc. to Cmty., Julio Sellés Solá Elem. Sch., 1976; grantee NIH, 1962. Fellow Am. Acad. Pediatrics (neonatal perinatal sect., mem. com. fetus and newborn P.R. chpt. 1956—, sec.-treas. 1962-64, mem. com. history perinatal sect. 1992—, Plaque in Recognition Disting. Pediatrician and Tchr. 1985), Pan Am. Pediatrics; mem. Am. Med. Women Assn., P.R. Med. Assn. (pediatric sect., mem. chamber of dels. 1962-63, Bronze plaque 1967, 91, Gold Pin 1980), P.R. Med. Women Assn. (sec.-treas. 1957-60, pres. 1960-64), Pan Am. Med. Women Assn. (pres. P.R. chpt. 1960-64, P.R. del. VIII Congress Manizales Colombia 1962), Pan Am. Med. Women Alliance (vis. lectr. 1962), Tulane Med. Alumni, London Royal Soc. Health, Colegio de Químicos, Soc. Dominicana de Pediatría (hon., vis. lectr. 1971), Dominican Rep. Soc. (hon.). Home: Duke C 12 Esq Tulane Santa Ana Rio Piedras San Juan PR 00927 Office: Las Americas Profl Ctr Domenech 400 Ste 309 Hato Rey San Juan PR 00918

MUÑOZ-SOLÁ, HAYDEÉ SOCORRO, library administrator; b. Caguas, P.R., Dec. 27, 1943; d. Gilberto Muñoz and Carmen Haydeé (Solá) de Muñoz; m. Juan M. Masini-Soler, Jan. 8, 1966 (div. 1979); children: Juan Martin Masini-Muñoz, Haydeé Milagros Masini-Muñoz. BA in Psychology, U. P.R., Río Piedras, 1965; MLS, U. P.R., Río Piedras, 1970; D in Libr. Sci., Columbia U., 1985. Asst. libr. U. P.R., Río Piedras, 1964-67; dir. libr. Interam. U., Aguadilla, P.R., 1974-75; head svcs. to pub. U. P.R., Aguadilla, 1975-76; cataloguer Cath. U., Ponce, P.R., 1976-79; cataloguer U. P.R., Rio Piedras, 1982-84, head libr. and info. sci. libr., 1984-85, prof. grad. libr. sch., 1986, dir. libr. sys., 1986-93; coord. external resources libr. sys. U. P.R.; mem. Seminar for the Acquisitions of L.Am. Libr. Materials, Miami, Fla., 1982—; dir. P.R. Newspaper Project, Río Piedras, 1986-90; mem. Adv. Com. on Pub. Librs., San Juan, 1987-93; proposal reviewer NEH, 1990—; chmn. Puerto Rican Del. to Nat. White House Conf. on Libr. and Info. Svcs., 1991. Author: La Información y la Documentación Educativa/Informe Sobre la Situación Actual en Puerto Rico, 1991, Memorias: Sequnda Pre-Conferencia de Casa Blanca Sobre Bibliotecas y Servicios de Información en Puerto Rico, 1991; contbr. articles to profl. jours. Mem. Ponce Sport Club, 1976-83, ARC, Ponce, 1978. Recipient plaque White House Pre-Conf. on Libr. and Info. Scis., 1990; French Alps Study Tour scholar Assn. Caribbean Univ. Rsch. and Instl. Librs., 1989, Germany Study Tour scholar Fgn. Rels. Office, Germany, 1991. Mem. ALA, SALALM, Am. Mgmt. Assn., Grad. Sch. Libr. and Info. Sci. Alumni Assn. (pres. 1988-90), Iberoamerican Nat. Librs. Assn. (pres. 1992-93), Puerto Rican Librs. Soc. (coord. So. area 1974, Ponce coord. 1978, Lauro award 1989), Assn. Caribbean U. Rsch. and Instnl. Librs. (Parchment award 1988), Assn. para las Comunicaciones y Tecnología Educativa, Mid. States Assn. Colls. and Schs. (collaborator), Am. Women Assn., Phi Delta Kappa (chair P.R. com. 1988—, pres. pub. rels. 1988-90, Kappan of Yr. 1990), Eta Gamma Delta. Roman Catholic. Office: U of PR Library System PO Box 23302 University Sta San Juan PR 00931-3302

MUNRO, ALICE, author; b. Wingham, Ont., Can., July 10, 1931; d. Robert Eric and Anne Clarke (Chamney) Laidlaw; m. James Armstrong Munro, 1951 (div. 1976); children: Sheila, Jenny, Andrea; m. Gerald Fremlin, 1976. BA, U. Western Ont., 1952, DLitt (hon.), 1976. Author: (short stories) Dance of the Happy Shades, 1968 (Gov.-Gen.'s Lit. award 1969), A Place for Everything, 1970, Lives of Girls and Women, 1971 (Can. Booksellers award, 1972), (short stories) Something I've Been Meaning To Tell You, 1974, Who Do You Think You Are?, 1979 (pub. in U.S. as Beggar Maid: Stories of Flo and Rose, 1984, Gov.-Gen.'s Lit. award 1978), The Moons of Jupiter, 1982, The Progress of Love, 1986 (Gov. Gens. Lit. award 1987), Friend of My Youth, 1990, (short stories) Open Secrets, 1994, A Wilderness Station, 1994; TV scripts: A Trip to the Coast, 1973, Thanks For The Ride, 1973, How I Met My Husband, 1974, 1847: The Irish, 1978. Recipient Can.-Australia Lit. Prize 1994, Marian Engel award, 1986. Home: PO Box 1133, Clinton, ON Canada N0M 1L0 Office: care Alfred A Knopf Inc 201 E 50th St New York NY 10022-7703*

MUNRO, CRISTINA STIRLING, artistic director; b. London, May 22, 1940; m. Richard Munro (div. 1986); children: Alexandra, Nicholas. Attended various artistic schs., London. Mem. ballet corps Sadlers Wells Opera Ballet, London, 1960-62, Het Nederlands Ballet, The Hague, Holland, 1962-63; soloist London Festival Ballet, 1963-72; prin. soloist Eliot Feld Ballet, N.Y.C., 1972-75; prin. dancer, artistic dir. Old Dominion U., Norfolk, Va., 1975; artistic dir. Louisville Ballet Co., 1975-79; ballet mistress Houston Ballet, 1979-85; dir. Munro Ballet Studies, Corpus Christi, Tex., 1985—; artistic dir. Corpus Christi Ballet, 1985—; guest artist and choreographer numerous cos. in U.S. Recipient Giovanni Martini award Louisville, 1978.

Mem. Imperial Soc. Tchrs. of Dance, Royal Acad. Dancing, Brit. Actors Equity Assn., Am. Guild Mus. Artists. Office: Munro Ballet Studios/ Corpus Christi Ballet 5610 Everhart Rd Corpus Christi TX 78411-4905

MUNRO, HEDI See **MESNEY, DOROTHY TAYLOR**

MUNROE, DONNA SCOTT, marketing executive, healthcare and management consultant, educator; b. Cleve., Nov. 28, 1945; d. Glenn Everett and Louise Lennox (Parkhill) Scott; m. Melvin James Ricketts, Dec. 23, 1968 (div. Aug. 1979); 1 child, Suzanne Michelle; m. Peter Carlton Munroe, Feb. 14, 1981. BS in Sociology, Portland (Oreg.) State U., 1976, BS in Philosophy, 1978, MS in Sociology, 1983. Lectr. Portland State U., 1977-79; writing, editorial cons. Worth Pubs., N.Y.C., 1978-79; statis. cons. health scis. U. Oreg., Portland, 1979-82; statis. cons. Morrison Ctr. for Youth and Family Svcs., Portland, 1979-82; writer Equitable Savs. & Loan, Portland, 1981-82; mgr. acct. and projects. Electronic Data Systems, Portland, 1982-87; exec. dir. corp. mktg. and planning CMSI, Portland, 1987—; v.p. mktg. CerikaCorp, Vancouver, Wash., 1993—. Mem. Am. Mgmt. Assn., Am. Mktg. Assn., Am. Soc. for Quality Control, City Club of Portland, Sigma Xi. Democrat. Episcopalian. Home: 536 SW Cheltenham St Portland OR 97201-2602 Office: CerikaCorps 13912 NE 20th Ste 204 Vancouver WA 98686

MUNROE, SHIRLEY ANN, retired hospital association executive, health care consultant; b. Mpls., Mar. 31, 1924; d. Laurence John and Esther (Tuttle) M.; pre-nursing cert. La Sierra Coll., Arlington, Calif., 1943; R.N., Glendale Sanitarium and Hosp. Sch. Nursing, 1946; postgrad. UCLA Extension, 1953-55, Los Angeles City Coll., 1948-51; cert. U. Calif. at Santa Cruz extension, 1971; m. Stanley G. Fjelstrom, Dec. 26, 1954 (div. June 1957). Chief nurse, office mgr. for pvt. practice physicians, Los Angeles, 1946-51; bus. mgr. Bolander Clinic and Emergency Hosp., Van Nuys, Calif., 1951-56, Mendocino Med. Ctr., Ukiah, Calif., 1956; adminstr. Hillside Community Hosp., Ukiah, 1956-78, sec., 1956-78; dir. Ctr. for Small or Rural Hosps., Am. Hosp. Assn., Chgo., 1978-79, dir. constituency programs, 1979-83, exec. dir. constituency sects., 1984-85, v.p., 1985-88; mem. adv. and eval. com. Ukiah Dist. Sch. Vocat. Nursing, 1965-78; faculty U. Calif. extension at Berkeley, Basic Adminstrn. Hosp. Adminstrs. Program, 1966-70; dir., sec. Obs. Investment Co., Ukiah, 1957-67. Asst. dir. pub. relations alumni postgrad. assembly Loma Linda U., Los Angeles, 1949-55; dir. pub. relations world meeting Aerospace Med. Assn., Los Angeles, 1953; chmn. re-edn. nursing com. Calif. Dept. Employment, 1962; cons. lectr. nurse aide edn., adult edn. Willits, Ukiah high schs., 1962; chmn. Career Project for Sr. High Sch. Girls, 1962-64; mem. Mendocino-Lake adv. com. Regional Med. Program, 1969-73; mem. vocat. edn. adv. com. Ukiah Unified Sch. Dist., 1970-73. Soloist, Presbyn. Ch., Ukiah, 1956-69, Ukiah Oratorio Soc., 1958-65; supt. children's edn. Seventh-day Adventist Ch., 1961-64, dir. pub. relations, 1967-78, chmn. fin. com., 1967-78, mem. ch. bd., 1967-78, mem. exec. com. Ill. conf., 1983-89, soloist, 1958-78; mem. ch. bd. Seventh-day Adventist Ch., Elmhurst, 1979-89, dir. music, mem. ch. bd., Roswell, N.Mex., 1989—, dir. ch. ministries, 1990-93, Ch. Elder, 1992—; Choir dir, Westminster Presbyn. Ch., Roswell, 1993—; co-chmn. edn. com. Mendocino County br. Am. Cancer Soc., 1961-62, bd. dirs., 1961-76, pres., 1963-65; mem. steering com. Am. Heart Assn., Mendocino County br. Calif. Heart Assn.; chmn. trustees Tri-County Pre-Payment Medi-Cal Pilot Project, State of Calif., 1969-71; trustee Nor Coa Health, 1967-76, 1st v.p. 1969-71, pres., 1971-72, chmn. South Planning council, 1972-74; mem. Mendocino-Lake counties council, 1966-76; bd. dirs. Mendocino County chpt. ARC, 1968-70; bd. dirs. Blue Cross No. Calif., 1971-78, exec. bd., 1973-78, hosp. provider rep., 1970-78; leader del. People to People Internat. U.S. Citizen Ambassador Program, 1981; mem. bd. Adventist Health System/North, 1981-87, chmn. strategic planning com., 1983-87; mem. bd. Hinsdale Hosp., 1979-94, mem. joint conf. com., 1980-89, chmn. strategic planning com., 1983-88, bd. dirs. fin. com., 1989-94; bd. dirs. Broadview Acad., Lafox, Ill., 1983-86, Roswell Symphony Orch., 1990—, sec.-treas., 1991-93, 2d v.p., 1992-93, 1st v.p. 1993—; 2d v.p. Roswell Symphony Guild, 1993—. Named Trustee of the Year Hinsdale Health System, 1991; recipient Civic Participation award, Outstanding Women in Professions award Calif. Fedn. Bus. and Profl. Women's Clubs, 1965; Outstanding Service award Mendocino-Lake br. Am. Cancer Soc., 1963, 64, 65, Notable Service award, 1968; Walker fellow, 1973; The Ann. Shirley Ann Munroe Leadership Devel. Award named in her honor by Sect. for Small or Rural Hosps. and The Hosp. Rsch. and Ednl. Trust of Am. Hosp. Assn. Mem. Am. Hosp. Assn. (ho. of dels. 1974-78, regional adv. bd. 1974-78, rural resource com. 1976-78, v.p.), Calif. Hosp. Assn. (membership com. 1960-61; legis. liaison 1960, panel hosp. peer rev. adminstrs. 1968-78; mem. ins. com. 1971-78), Redwood Empire Hosp. Conf. (ins. com. 1957-59, exec. com. 1968-71, 1st v.p. 1968, pres. 1969), Hosp. Council No. Calif. (bd. dirs. 1968-77, pres. 1975-76, chmn. com. on program and edn. 1968-70), Assn. Western Hosps. (edn. research found. council 1963Glendale Sanitarium and Hosp. Sch. Nursing Alumni Assn. (pres. Glendale 1947-48), Bus. and Profl. Women's Club (exec. bd. 1957-61, pres. 1959-60, 3d v.p. 1960-61, career advancement com. 1961-62, chmn. personal devel. com. 1962-64, mem. bd. 1962-65, music chmn. Redwood Empire dist. 1960-61), Republican. Club: Soroptimist (pres. Ukiah 1971-72, music chmn. 1962-63, service com. 1961-78, editor bull. 1965-66, Woman of Achievement award 1965, dir. 1970-73). Home: 707 W Mescalero Rd Roswell NM 88201-5226

MUNSELL, SUSAN GRIMES, state legislator, accountant; b. Highland Park, Mich., June 21, 1951; d. Chauncey Gale and Shirley Mabel (Rick) Grimes; m. Frank Edward Munsell, Dec. 5, 1980. BA, Mich. State U., 1973; MBA, U. Mich., 1979. CPA, Mich. Cons. Harris, Kerr, Forster & Co., CPAs, Los Angeles, 1973-76; mgr. Lucky Duck Nursery & Day Care Ctr., Brighton, Mich., 1976-77; tax intern Coopers & Lybrand, CPAs, Detroit, 1978; mem. tax staff Arthur Andersen & Co., CPAs, Detroit, 1979-83; prin. Susan Grimes Munsell, CPA, Fowlerville, Mich., 1983—; mem. Mich. Ho. of Reps., Lansing, 1987—. Dep. treas. Livingston County (Mich.) Reps., 1985-86; active local Girl Scouts U.S. Named One of 10 Outstanding Young People in Mich. Mich. Jaycees, 1986. Mem. LWV (various offices 1976—), NOW (various offices 1977—), Am. Inst. CPA's, Am. Women's Soc. CPA's, Am. Bus. Women's Assn., Mich. Assn. CPA's. Methodist. Home: 209 W Sibley St Howell MI 48843-2220 Office: Mich Ho of Reps State Capitol Bldg Lansing MI 48913*

MUNSEY, BERNICE ANN WILSON, educational counselor; b. Hollywood, Calif., Feb. 2, 1935; d. Allan Marshall and Vero Viola (Erwin) Wilson; m. Everard Munsey, Sept. 20, 1956; children: Wanda, Allan, Andrew, Carolyn. BA, Wellesley Coll., 1956; MA, Hood Coll., 1977; EdD, Va. Poly. Inst., 1986. Asst. Rep. Henry S. Reuss, Washington, 1956, 58-59; asst. office of communications Dem. Nat. Com., Washington, 1970-72; pub. rels. cons. Arlington, Va., 1972-75; asst. Rep. Lindy Boggs, Washington, 1975-76; counselor, tchr. adult edn. Arlington Pub. Schs., 1976; dir. Fgn. Svc. and Ednl. Counseling Ctr., Washington, 1976-79; ednl. counselor U.S. Dept. State, Washington, 1979-81; pvt. practice Washington area, 1979—. Author: Public School Programs in the Washington, D.C. Area, 1979; contbr. articles to profl. jours. Area chmn. Fair Housing Drive, Arlington, 1965; voter registration chmn., Dem. Campaign Com., Arlington, 1964; mgr. office women's affairs Dem. Nat. Conv., N.Y.C., 1976; mem. Arlington Community Svcs. Bd., 1988-91. Mem. ACA, Am. Speech/Hearing/Lang. Assn., Learning Diabilities Assn. Am. (bd. dirs., sec. 1974-75, Pioneer award 1977), Ind. Ednl. Cons. Assn., Sec. Sch. Admission Test Bd., Nat. Assn. Coll. Admission Counselors, Learning Disablities Assn. Va. (founder, pres. 1968-70), Assn. for Gifted, Coun. for Exceptional Children, Orton Dyslexia Sox., Assn. Am. Fgn. Svcs. Women, Swedish-Am. Hist. Soc. (bd. dirs.), VASA of Am. (sec. 1980), Assn. for Psychol. Type, Assn. Profl. Genealogists. Congregationalist. Home and Office: 3623 37th St N Arlington VA 22207-4821

MUNSON, ANNETTE MARLENE, pediatrics nurse; b. Columbia, Mo., Feb. 21, 1964; d. James Derril and E. Ethelene (Bennett) M. BSN, U. Pa., 1986, BS in Econs. and Mgmt., 1986. Cert. pediatric nurse, ANCC, ACLS, Pedriatric Advance Life Support Instr., BCLS Instr., NALS. Commd. 2d lt. U.S. Army, 1986, advanced through grades to capt., 1990; staff nurse in pediatrics Walter Reed Army Med. Ctr., Washington, 1987-89, staff nurse in surg. ICU, 1989-90; staff nurse neonatal ICU William Beaumont Army Med. Ctr., Ft. Bliss, Tex., 1991-92, maternal/child nursing instr. Practical Nurse Course, 1992-95, head nurse pediat., 1995—; instr. coord. infant/child CPR, Safety Class William Beaumont Army Med. Ctr., 1991-93; coord. med. svcs. Area 19 El Paso Spl. Olympics, 1991—. Mem AACN, ANA (coun. on maternal-child health nursing), Tex. Nurses Assn. Office: William Beaumont Army Med Ctr Dept Of Nursing El Paso TX 79920

MUNSON, DEANNA M., textiles educator; b. Topeka, Kans., Apr. 1, 1944; d. Fred and Lucile (Larsen) Michaels; m. Charles E. Munson, Dec. 22, 1968; children: Michelle C., David C. BS, Kans. State U., 1965, MS, 1968, PhD, 1980. Grad. rsch. asst. Kans. State U., Manhattan, 1965-66, asst. instr., 1966-67, instr., 1967-80, asst. prof., 1980-90, assoc. prof. textiles, ext. specialist, 1990—. Group leader 4-H, Geary County, Kans., 1979; ednl. advisor Sch. Dist. 413, Chapman, Kans., 1990-94. Recipient Best Tech. Rsch. Paper award Am. Soc. Heat, Refrigeration and Air Conditioning, 1972, Best Paper award, 1981. Mem. Assn. Coll. Profs. of Textiles and Clothing (assoc. editor 1979-80, editor nat. news 1981-82, scholarship chairperson 1986, registration chairperson 1988), Delta Kappa Gamma (Internat. scholar 1979), Omicron Nu. Republican. Presbyterian. Office: Kans State U 235 Justin Hall Manhattan KS 66506-1423

MUNSON, DEE ALLISON TAYLOR, food marketing executive, consultant; b. Geneva, Ill., Nov. 17, 1936; d. R. Wayne and S. Dorothy (Locke) Allison; m. William Walfred Munson, Aug. 20, 1960 (dec. Jan. 1976); children: Daniel Stewart, Katherine Allison. BS in Food and Nutrition, Purdue U., 1958. Asst. food editor Better Homes & Gardens mag., Des Moines, 1958-60; home economist Calif. Foods Rsch. Inst., San Francisco, 1960-61; food editor Institutions mag., Chgo., 1961-62; ind. food cons. Chgo., 1962-70, 72-75; dir. home econs. Wheat Flour Inst., Chgo., 1970-72; v.p. advt. and consumer edn. Am. Egg Bd., Chgo., 1975-82; v.p. Cole & Weber Advt., Seattle, 1982-85; sr. ptnr. EMB Ptnrs. Inc., Seattle, 1994—; prin., cons. Food Profls., Vashon, Wash., 1985-88; mng. dir. Evans food group Evans Group, Seattle, 1988—; sr. ptnr. EMP Ptnrs., Inc., Seattle, 1994—. Author: Miracle Blender Cook Book, 1965, Culinary Arts Nutrition Cook Book, 1974, 1974, Crepes Cook Book, 1975, Consumer Guide Food Processor Cook Book, 1975. Named Outstanding Alumnae, Purdue U., 1993. Mem. Am. Home Economists Assn., Pub. Rels. Soc. Am. (one of Top 100 Pub. Rels. Profls. 1989), Home Economists in Bus. (program chmn. 1983, nat. chmn.-elect 1986-87, nat. chmn. 1987-89, Outstanding Bus. Home Economist 1992). Baha'i. Home: PO Box 1326 Vashon WA 98070-1326

MUNSON, LUCILLE MARGUERITE (MRS. ARTHUR E. MUNSON), real estate broker; b. Norwood, Ohio, Mar. 26, 1914; d. Frank and Fairy (Wicks) Wirick; R.N., Lafayette (Ind.) Home Hosp., 1937; A.B., San Diego State U., 1963, student Purdue U., Kans. Wesleyan U.; m. Arthur E. Munson, Dec. 24, 1937; children—Barbara Munson Papke, Judith Munson Andrews, Edmund Arthur. Staff and pvt. nurse Lafayette Home Hosp., 1937-41; indsl. nurse Lakey Foundry & Machine Co., Muskegon, Mich., 1950-51, Continental Motors Corp., Muskegon, 1951-52; nurse Girl Scout Camp, Grand Haven, Mich., 1948-49; owner Munson Realty, San Diego, 1964—. Mem. San Diego County Grand Jury, 1975-76, 80-81, Calif. Grand Jurors Assn. (charter). Office: 2999 Mission Blvd Ste 102 San Diego CA 92109-8028

MUNSON, NANCY KAY, lawyer; b. Huntington, N.Y., June 22, 1936; d. Howard H. and Edna M. (Keenan) Munson. Student, Hofstra U., 1959-62; JD, Bklyn. Law Sch., 1965. Bar: N.Y. 1966, U.S. Supreme Ct. 1970, U.S. Ct. Appeals (2d cir.) 1971, U.S. Dist. Ct. (ea. and so. dists.) N.Y. 1968. Law clk. to E. Merritt Weidner Huntington, 1959-66, sole practice, 1966—; mem. legal adv. bd. Chgo. Title Ins. Co., Riverhead, N.Y., 1981—; bd. dirs., legal officer Thomas Munson Found. Trustee Huntington Fire Dept. Death Benefit Fund; pres., trustee, chmn. bd. Bklyn. Home Aged Men Found.; bd. dirs. Elderly Day Svcs. on the Sound. Mem. ABA, N.Y. State Bar Assn., Suffolk County Bar Assn., Bklyn. Bar Assn., NRA, DAR, Soroptimists (past pres.). Republican. Christian Scientist. Office: 197 New York Ave Huntington NY 11743-2711

MUNSON, NORMA FRANCES, biologist, ecologist, nutritionist, educator; b. Stockport, Iowa, Sept. 22, 1923; d. Glenn Edwards and Frances Emma (Wilson) M.; BA, Concordia Coll., 1946; MA, U. Mo., 1955; PhD (NSF fellow 1957-58, Chgo. Heart Assn. fellow 1959), Pa. State U., 1962; postgrad. Ind. U., 1957, Western Mich. U., 1967, Lake Forest Coll., 1971, 72, 78; student various fgn. univs., 1964-71. Tchr., Aitkin (Minn.) High Sch., 1946-48, Detroit Lakes (Minn.) High Sch., 1948-54, Libertyville (Ill.) High Sch., 1955-79; researcher Nutrition, Arthritis, Alzheimer's, Hypoglycemia and Multiple Sclerosis, Libertyville, 1965—; lectr. counseling and nutrition. Author biology lab. manual; contbr. articles to profl. jours. Ruling elder 1st Presbyn. Ch., Libertyville, 1971-77; pres. Lake County Audubon Soc., 1975-79, 82-86, 88-89, Libertyville Edn. Assn., 1964-67; active Rep. Party Ill., Citizens to Save Butler Lake, Citizens Choice, Defenders; mem. U.S. Congl. Adv. Bd., 1985—; bd. dirs. Holy Land Christian Mission Internat.; mem. Heritage Found., Citizens Lake County for Environ. Action Reform, Wilderness Soc. Recipient Hilda Mahling award, 1967, C. of C. award, 1971, Ill. Best Tchr. award, 1974; Biology Tchr. of Yr. award, 1971; NSF fellow, 1957, 58, 60-62, 70-71. Fellow Am. Biog. Inst. Rsch., Internat. Biog. Assn.; mem. Nat. Biology Tchrs. Assn. (rsch. in degenerate diseases, award 1971), AAAS, Am. Inst. Biol. Sci., Ill. Environ. Coun., Nat. Audubon Soc., Ill. Audubon Coun., Nat. Health Fedn., Internat. Platform Assn., Internat. Profl. and Bus. Women, Nat. Wildlife Fedn., N.Y. Acad. Scis., Chgo. Acad. Sci., Parks and Conservation Assn., Concerned Women Am. Nature Conservation, Evanston North Shore Bird Club, Delta Kappa Gamma. Contbr. articles to ednl. jours. Home and Office: 206 W Maple Ave Libertyville IL 60048-2174

MUNSON, VIRGINIA ALDRICH, interior designer, decorator; b. Evanston, Ill., Oct. 10, 1932; d. Jefferson Elliott and Catherine (Stinson) Aldrich; m. John Chester Munson, Feb. 4, 1956; children: Catherine, John Jr., Laura. AA, Bennett Junior Coll., 1952. Owner, pres. Virginia Munson Interiors, Lake Forest, Ill., 1967—. Mem. Lake Forest Ctr. Infant Welfare Soc., 1957-93, pres., 1976-78; active com. candidates caucus, Lake Forest, 1984-87; mem. women's bd. Lake Forest Hosp., 1977—, Guild of Chgo. Hist. Soc., 1990—; bd. dirs. Infant Welfare Soc. Chgo., 1967-93; Ill. Regent Gunston Hall, 1988—. Mem. Am. Soc. Interior Designers (allied 1989—), Nat. Soc. Colonial Dames Am. (pres. State of Ill. br. 1982-84), Soc. Mayflower Descendants, Contemporary Club, Onwentsia Club, Winter Club. Republican. Episcopalian.

MUNZER, CYNTHIA BROWN, mezzo-soprano; b. Clarksburg, W.Va., Sept. 30, 1948; d. Ralph Emerson and Doris Marguerite (Dixon) Brown; 1 dau., Christina Marie. Student, U. Kans., 1965-69. Adj. prof. U. So. Calif.; adj. prof. voice U. So. Calif. Debut, Oxford (Eng.) Opera, 1969, Met. Opera debut, N.Y.C., 1973; performed 1973-94 with: Met. Opera, Phila. Opera, Wolftrap Festival, Washington Opera, Goldovsky Opera, Washington Civic Opera, St. Petersburg Opera, Dallas Opera, Met. Opera-Japan, Boston Concert Opera, Dayton Opera, Chgo. Opera Theatre, Mich. Opera, Kansas City Opera, New Orleans Opera, Houston Grand Opera, Ft. Worth Opera, Florentine Opera-Milw., Minn. Opera, Central City Opera, Aspen Festival, Opera Colo., Boston Festival Orch., Ontario Opera, Salt Lake City Opera, Nev. Opera, Cleve. Opera, Opera Pacific, Des Moines Opera, Ky. Opera, Mobile Opera, Internat. Artist Series in Kuala Lumpur, Penang, Jakarta; Hong Kong Philharmonic, Shanghai Symphony, Singapore Symphony, Philippine Philharmonic, N.Y.C. Ballet, Am. Symphony, Nat. Symphony, Charleston Symphony, Phila. Orch., New Haven Symphony, Houston Symphony, Ft. Wayne Symphony, El Paso Symphony, San Antonio Symphony, Amarillo Symphony, Wichita Symphony, Milw. Symphony, Minn. Orch., Denver Symphony, Phoenix Symphony, Oreg. Bach. Festival, San Francisco Symphony, L.A. Philharm., Louisville Symphony, Rochester Philharmonic, Binghamton Symphony, Rhode Island Symphony, Carmel Bach Festival, Anchorage Symphony, L'Opera de Montreal, Colo. Opera Festival, New York Mozart Bicentennial Festival, Brattleboro Festival, Knoxville Opera, Gold Coast Opera, Hawaii Opera, Augusta Opera, Berkshire Opera, Madison Opera, Chattanooga Symphony. Recipient Frederick K. Weyerhaeuser award, Gramma Fisher Found. award, Goeran Gentele award, Sullivan Found. award, Geraldine Farrar award. Office: PO Box 77332 Los Angeles CA 90007

MUNZINGER, JUDITH MONTGOMERY, investment executive; b. Dayton, Ohio, June 16, 1944; d. Russell Eric and Margaret Lois (Weltzheimer) Montgomery; m. John Stephen Munzinger, May 28, 1977; children—Laurie Anne, Lisa Michelle. B.S. in Edn., Ohio State U., 1966, M.A., 1979, cert. remedial reading, 1980. Cert. tchr., Iowa. Tchr. elem. sch., Lafayette, Ind., 1966-69, Hilliard, Ohio, 1976-79; remedial reading tchr. Sioux City, Iowa, 1979-82; instr., dir. early childhood devel. Briar Cliff Coll.; talented and gifted coordinator, Sioux City, 1982-85; investment exec. Piper Jaffray, Sioux City, 1985—, asst. v.p., 1993; owner Elan Arabians, 1986—. Treas. Siouxlanders for Talented and Gifted; mem. Coalition for Children; judge for Iowa Future Problem Solving Bowl, 1982; sustainer Jr. League; mem. vestry, clk. St. Thomas Episcopal Ch., 1982-84; mem. Children's Hosp. support group, Columbus, Ohio, 1972-79; active Women's Assn. for Columbus Zoo, 1973-76, PTA; asst. Girl Scouts U.S.A., 1980-82.; co-chmn. Sioux City Symphony Debutante Ball, 1990, chmn., 1991. Recipient Service commendation Girl Scouts U.S.A., 1980. Mem. Internat. Arabian Horse Assn., Nat. Show Horse Assn., Ohio State U. Alumni Assn., Delta Zeta. Republican. Home: 3301 W 52nd St Sioux City IA 51108 Office: Piper Jaffray 421 Nebraska St Sioux City IA 51101-1311

MURANAGA, LETICIA ARMIDA, aerospace company buyer; b. L.A., July 28, 1954; d. Antonio and Ernestina (Aguirre) Rodriguez; m. Everardo Alberto Mazadiego, Feb. 3, 1973 (div. Nov. 1979); m. Mark Kenji Muranaga, Nov. 10, 1984; 2 children. AS in Gen. Bus., Glendale (Calif.) C.C., 1986; BSBA, U. Redlands, 1988. Cashier, loan officer Beneficial Fin., L.A., 1972-74; office adminstr. L.A. Unified Sch. Dist., 1974-79; sec. Theodore Barry & Assocs., L.A., 1979-80; office mgr. Zugsmith & Assocs., Studio City, Calif., 1980-81; adminstrv. sec. Lockheed Corp., Burbank, Calif., 1981-83; exec. sec. Lockheed Corp., Calabasas, Calif., 1983-87; procurement asst. Lockheed Corp., Burbank, 1987-92; buyer Lockheed Corp., Calabasas, 1992—. Mem. Nat. Assn. Purchasing Mgmt., Nat. Mgmt. Assn. Office: Lockheed Corp 4500 Park Granada Blvd Calabasas CA 91302

MURCH, CATHERINE HELEN, human resources specialist; b. Bklyn., Feb. 6, 1948; d. Charles Augustine and Catherine Helen (McKinney) Wilton; m. Frank W. Murch Jr., Sept. 26, 1987. Student, ORange County C.C., 1977-79. Asst. dir. personnel Playboy Resort & Country Club, McAfee, N.J., 1972-82, Americana Hotel, McAfee, N.J., 1982-86; dir. personnel Great Gorge Mt. View Resort, McAfee, N.J., 1986-88, Loew's Glenpointe Hotel, Teaneck, N.J., 1988-89; HRIS adminstr. Reckitt & Colman, Wayne, N.J., 1988-90; asst. dir. human resources Seasons Resort, McAfee, 1990—. Mem. Newton Kennel Club (dir. 1988-92, treas. 1992—). Republican. Roman Catholic. Home: 1 Partridge Rd Stockholm NJ 07460-1421 Office: Rt 517 McAfee NJ 07428

MURCHISON, NOLA FAYE, retired librarian; b. Galva, Ill., Mar. 1, 1929; d. John Harold and Eva Mildred (Kling) M.; m. Albert Raisbeck, Aug. 25, 1951 (div. 1955); 1 child, Rory John; m. Richard Lutz, Oct. 8, 1960 (div. 1972); children: Eve Lutz-Smith, Elizabeth Lutz Roush, Lewis. AA, Stephens Coll., 1948; BS in Journalism, U. Ill., 1951; MLS, U. Wis., Milw., 1970; postgrad., U. Wis., Madison, 1976. Library dir. Harvard (Ill.) Pub. Library, 1970-73; librarian Broward County Library, Ft. Lauderdale, Fla., 1974-79, Sheridan (Wyo.) County Library, 1980, Ariz. Dept. Corrections, Tucson, 1981-83; sr. librarian Calif. Dept. Corrections, Chino, 1983-84; librarian, br. head Desert Hot Springs (Calif.) Br. Library, 1984-85, Indio (Calif.) Regional Br. Library, 1985-89; br. head Desert Hot Springs (Calif.) Libr., 1989-94, ret., 1994. Author papers in field. 1st lt. USAF, 1958-59. Recipient John Cotton Dana award ALA, 1980. Mem. ALA, Rotary Internat., DAV, Phi Mu. Unitarian.

MURDOCH-KITT, NORMA HOOD, clinical psychologist; b. Clinton, S.C., May 16, 1947; d. Bernard Constantine and Martha Grace (Hood) Murdoch; m. Jonathan Michael Murdoch-Kitt, Mar. 23, 1974; children: Kelly Michelle, Mark Jason, Sabrina Brittany, Laura Kristina. BA, Wake Forest U., 1969; MS, U. Pitts., 1971, PhD, 1975 . Psychology intern Eastern Pa. Psychiat. Inst., 1972-73; asst. prof., therapist campus counseling center Coll. William and Mary, Williamsburg, Va., 1973-74; staff psychologist child psychiatry dept. Med. Coll. Va., 1974-75; pvt. practice individual psychotherapy and family and marital therapy, Richmond, Va., 1975—. Mem. Richmond Dem. Com., 1976-79, 82-85, 88-89, 91—; v.p. govtl. relations com. Ginter Park Residents Assn., 1987, pres., 1988, 89; mem. Richmond Human Rels. Adv. Commn., 1976-80, Richmond Mayor's Com. on Concerns of Women, 1987—, chair, 1989-93; mem. Richmond Citizens Crime Commn., 1985-88, co-chair police chief sect. com. 1994-95; founder, 1st state chmn. polit. action com. ERA, 1977-78; chief lobbyist ERA Ratification Council, 1977-79; mem. long range planning com. Bapt. Theol. Sch., Richmond, 1993—; Richmond area chair mental health disaster network ARC, 1994—; long range planning com. Bapt. Theol. Seminary, Richmond, 1993—. USPHS fellow, 1969-72. Mem. Am. Psychol. Assn. (steering com. State Leadership Conf. 1986-91, chair 1991, Richmond chair Red Cross/Am. Psychol. Assn. Disaster Mental Health Network), Va. Psychol. Assn. (state legis. lobbyist 1978-79, chmn. legis. com. 1981-83, bd. profl. affairs 1981-85, pres. 1986), Va. Acad. Clin. Psychologists (chmn. profl. affairs com. 1982-84), Va. Breast Cancer Found. (rsch. chair 1992—), Richmond Area Psychol. Assn. (pres. elect 1994, pres. 1995), Chronic Fatigue Assn. (Va chpt.), LWV, ACLU. Presbyterian. Club: Richmond First (chmn. edn. com. 1979-80, dir. 1980-81). Office: Murdoch-Kitt Profl Bldg 3217 Chamberlayne Ave Richmond VA 23227-4806

MURDOCK, MICHELLE MARIE, marketing executive; b. Columbus, Ohio, Nov. 18, 1959; d. Louis Joseph and Barbara Jean (Stites) M. BA in Econs., U. Conn., Stamford, 1982. Membership rep. CUC Internat., Inc., Stamford, 1984-85, membership coord., 1985-86, asst. mgr. account mgmt., 1986-87, asst. mgr. mktg. svcs., 1987, mgr. mktg. svcs., 1987-89, dir. mktg. ops., 1989-90, dir. mktg. systems support, 1990-92; v.p. ops. CRRC, Westport, Conn., 1993; v.p. mktg./sales Sayers Pub. Group, Arvada, Colo., 1994—; cons. on young careerists Bus. and Profl. Women's Club, Inc., Stamford, 1990. Recipient cert. of appreciation Bus. and Profl. Women's Club, Inc., 1990. Mem. NAFE. Office: Sayers Pub Group 5400 Ward Rd Arvada CO 80002-1819

MURDOCK, PAMELA ERVILLA, wholesale travel company executive, retail travel company executive; b. Los Angeles, Dec. 3, 1940; d. John James and Chloe Conger (Keefe) M.; children: Cheryl, Kim. BA, U. Colo., 1962. Pres., Dolphin Travel, Denver, 1972-87; owner, pres. Mile Hi Tours, Denver, 1973—, MH Internat., 1987—, Mile-Hi Advt. Agy., 1986— . Named Wholesaler of Yr., Las Vegas Conv. and Visitors Authority, 1984. Mem. NAFE, Am. Soc. Travel Agts., Colo. Assn. Commerce and Industry, Nat. Fedn. Independent Businessmen. Republican. Home: 5565 E Vassar Ave Denver CO 80222-6239 Office: Mile Hi Tours Inc 2120 S Birch St Denver CO 80222-5043

MURGAS, KATHRYN MARIA, corporate cash manager; b. Milw., Dec. 1, 1964; d. Daniel and Mary Claire Badura. BBA in Fin., U. Wis., 1986; MBA in Corp. Fin., U. Dallas, 1992. Cert. cash mgr. Gen. office clk., asst. to treas. dept. staff Allis-Chalmers Corp., Milw., 1982-86; cash mgmt. adminstr. E-Sys., Inc., Dallas, 1986-93, sr. treasury adminstr., 1993—; presenter in field. Mem. Dallas Treasury Mgmt. Assn. (com. mem.), Sigma Iota Epsilon. Roman Catholic. Office: E-Systems Inc 6250 LBJ Freeway Dallas TX 75240

MURILLO, VELDA JEAN, social worker, counselor; b. Miller, S.D., Dec. 8, 1943; d. Royal Gerald and Marion Elizabeth (Porter) Matson; m. Daniel John Murillo, June 25, 1967 (div. Dec. 1987); 1 child, Damon Michael. BS, S.D. State U., 1965; MA, Calif. State U., Bakersfield, 1980. Cert. marriage, family and child counselor. Social worker adult svcs. Kern County Dept. Welfare, Bakersfield, 1965-78, social worker child protective svcs., 1978-84; asst. coord. sexual abuse program Kern County Dist. Atty., Bakersfield, 1985-91, coord. sexual abuse program, 1991—; Mem. Calif. Sexual Assault Investigators, 1982-84, Kern Child Abuse Prevention Coun., Bakersfield, 1982-84; co-developer, presenter Children's Self Help Project, Bakersfield, 1982-87; cons. mem. Sexual Assault Adv. Com., Bakersfield, 1991—. Mem. Soroptimist Internat. Democrat. Office: Kern County Dist Atty Kern County Dist Atty 1215 Truxtun Ave Bakersfield CA 93301

MUROFF, GLORIA, interior designer; b. N.Y.C., June 22, 1927; d. Harry and Ethel (Levy) Torem; m. Melvin I. Muroff, Mar. 28, 1953; children: Jan Muroff Milestone, Jodi Muroff Goch, Jospeh. BS, NYU, 1949. Interior designer Harry Torem Interiors, Miami, Fla., 1949-61; interior designer, owner, pres. Gloria Muroff Interiors, Miami, 1961—; lectr. Dade Community Coll., Miami, 1968-72, Internat. Coll. of Miami, 1971; mem. bd. Upholstery and Furniture Action Com., Washington, 1973-75. Pub. works in Family Circle, 1966, Who's Who in Multi Family Housing, 1972, Miami News Home and Housing sects., 1979, Ideas Mag., 1980. Co-chair ANTRA, 1985-93, Heart Strings Nat. Touring Co. benefit AIDS victims, Miami, 1989. Recipient award of recognition Euster Merchandise Mart, Miami, 1968, David-Ben Gurion award State of Israel, 1975; named Best in Wallcoverin Design, Sunshine Living, Miami, 1972. Fellow Interior Design Guild of Fla. (bd. dirs. 1983), Internat. Furnishings and Design Assn. (Fla. chpt. pres. 1968-69, nat. pres. 1971-72, v.p. resources Ednl. Found. 1991); mem. Internat. Soc. Interior Designers.

MURPHEY, MARGARET JANICE, marriage and family therapist; b. Taft, Calif., July 24, 1939; d. Glen Roosevelt Wurster and Lucile Mildred (Holt) Lopez; m. Russell Warren Murphey, June 20, 1959; children: Lucinda Murphey Kalbfleisch, Rochelle, Janice So renson. BA in Social Sci., Calif. State U., Chico, 1986, MA in Psychology, 1989. Sec. Folson State Prison, Calif., 1963-66; tchr. Desert Sands Unified Schs., Indio, Calif., 1969-72; claims determiner Employment Development Dept., Redding, Calif., 1976-78; sec. Shasta County Pers., Redding, 1978-79; welfare worker Shasta County Welfare Office, Redding, 1979-85; therapy intern Counseling Ctr. Calif. State U., Chico, 1989-90; therapist Family Svc. Assn., Chico, 1987-90, Butte County Drug and Alcohol Abuse Ctr., Chico, 1989-90; mental halth counselor Cibecue (Ariz.) Indian Health Clinic, 1990—; mem. Community Crisis Response Team, Whiteriver, Ariz., 1991—. Vol. Pacheco Sch., Redding, 1972-76; Sunday sch. tchr., dir. vacation Bible sch. Nazarene Ch., Sacramento, Indio and Redding, 1958-85. Recipient Sch. Bell award Pacheco Sch. Mem. APA, Am. Assn. Marriage and Family Therapists, Psi Chi. Home: PO Box 1114 Show Low AZ 85901-1114 Office: Cibecue Health Ctr Apache Behavioral Health PO Box 1089 Whiteriver AZ 85941-1089

MURPHEY, SHEILA ANN, infectious diseases physician, educator, researcher; b. Phila., July 10, 1943; d. William Joseph and Sara Esther (Mallon) M. AB, Chestnut Hill Coll., 1965; MD, Women's Med. Coll. of Pa., 1969. Diplomate Am. Bd. Internal Medicine, Am. Bd. Infectious Diseases. Intern in internal medicine Mt. Sinai Hosp. of N.Y., 1969-70, resident in internal medicine, 1970-72, instr. internal medicine, 1971-72; fellow infectious diseases U. Pa. Sch. Medicine, Phila., 1972-74, instr. dept. medicine, 1974-75, asst. prof. dept. medicine, 1975-77; chief infectious diseases sect. Phila. Gen. Hosp., 1974-77; attending physician Hosp. U. Pa., Phila. Gen. Hosp., 1974-77; dir. divsn. infectious diseases, asst. prof. medicine Jefferson Med. Coll., Phila., 1977-80, clin. assoc. prof. medicine, 1980—; dir. divsn. infectious diseases Thomas Jefferson U., Phila., 1977-88; infection control officer, attending physician Thomas Jefferson U. Hosp., Phila., 1977—. Contbr. articles to profl. jours. Fellow Coll. Physicians Phila.; mem. Am. Soc. Microbiology, Am. Coll. Physicians, Am. Fedn. Clin. Rsch., Soc. Hosp./Healthcare Epidemiology in Am., Infectious Diseases Soc. Am., Alpha Omega Alpha. Democrat. Roman Catholic. Office: Jefferson Med Coll 1015 Chestnut St Ste 1020 Philadelphia PA 19107-5225

MURPHY, BETTY JANE SOUTHARD (MRS. CORNELIUS F. MURPHY), lawyer; b. East Orange, N.J.; d. Floyd Theodore and Thelma (Casto) Southard; m. Cornelius F. Murphy, May 1, 1965; children: Ann Southard, Cornelius Francis Jr. AB, Ohio State U.; student, Alliance Française and U. Sorbonne, Paris; JD, Am. U., 1958; LLD (hon.), Eastern Mich. U., 1975, Capital U., 1976, U. Puget Sound, 1986; LHD, Tusculum coll., 1987. Bar: D.C. 1958. Corr., free lance journalist Europe and Asia, UPI, Washington; pub. relations counsellor Capital Properties, Inc. of Columbus (Ohio), Washington; atty. Appellate Cts. br. NLRB, Washington, 1958-59; practiced in Washington, 1959-74; mem. firm McInnis, Wilson, Munson & Woods (and predecessor firm); dep. asst. sec., adminstr. Wage and Hour Divsn. Wage and Hour Div. Dept. Labor, 1974-75; chmn. and mem. NLRB, 1975-79; ptnr. firm Baker & Hostetler, 1980—; adj. prof. law Am. U., 1972-80; mem. adv. com. on rights and responsibilities of women to Sec. HEW; mem. panel conciliators Internat. Ctr. Settlement Investment Disputes, 1974-85; mem. Adminstrv. Conf. U.S., 1976-80, Pub. Svc. Adv. Bd., 1976-79; mem. human resouces com. Nat. Ctr. for Productivity and Quality of Working Life, 1976-80; mem. Presdl. Commn. on Exec. Exch., 1981-85. Trustee Mary Baldwin Coll., 1977-85, Am. U., 1980—, George Mason U. Found., Inc., 1990—, George Mason U. Edn. Found., 1993—; nat. bd. dirs. Med. Coll. Pa., bd. corporators, 1976-85; bd. dirs. Ctr. for Women in Medicine, 1980-86; bd. govs. St. Agnes Sch., 1981-87; mem. exec. com. Commn. on Bicentennial of U.S. Constn., chmn. internat. adv. com., 1985-92; vice chmn. James Madison Meml. Fellowship Found., 1989—; bd. dirs. Meridian Internat. Ctr., 1992—, Friends of Congl. Law Libr., 1992—, Friends of Dept. of Labor. Recipient Ohio Gov.'s award, 1980, fellow award, 1981, Outstanding Pub. Service award U.S. Info. Service, 1987; named Disting. Fellow John Sherman Myers Soc., 1986. Mem. ABA (adminstrv. law sect., chmn. labor law com. 1980-83, chmn. internat. and comparative law adminstrv. law sect. 1983-88, chmn. customs, tariff and trade com. 1988-90, employment law sect., 1990), Fed. Bar Assn., Inter-Am. Bar Assn. (editor newsletter 1960-69, Silver medal 1967, co-chmn. labor law com. 1975-83), Bar Assn. D.C., World Peace Through Law Ctr., Am. Arbitration Assn. (bd. dirs. 1985—, editorial bd., 1992), Supreme Ct. Hist. Soc., Am. U. Alumni Assn. (bd. dirs. 1964-65, sec. law sch. 1965-66, pres. 1966-69, chmn. bd. govs. law sch. alumni 1969-73), Mortar Bd., Kappa Beta Pi. Republican. Office: Baker & Hostetler 1050 Connecticut Ave NW Washington DC 20036-5303

MURPHY, BIANCA CODY, psychology educator; b. N.Y.C., June 12, 1950; d. Joseph Thomas and Bianca (Rivoli) Cody. BA, Marymount Manhattan Coll., 1971; MEd, Northeastern U., 1974; EdD, Boston U., 1982. Diplomate Am. Bd. Sexology. Staff psychologist Mystic Valley Mental Health, Winchester, Mass., 1976-81; assoc. prof. psychology Wheaton Coll., Norton, Mass., 1987—; adj. instr. psychology U. Mass., Boston, 1977—; psychologist Newton (Mass.) Psychotherapy Assocs., 1981—. Contbr. articles to profl. jours. Fellow Am. Orthopsychiat. Assn. (chmn. nuclear issues study group 1987-90); mem. APA (com. on women and psychology 1993—, chair 1995), ACA, Assn. for Women in Psychology. Home: 10 Roberts Ave Newton MA 02160 Office: Wheaton Coll Psychology Dept Norton MA 02766

MURPHY, CARYLE MARIE, foreign correspondent; b. Hartford, Conn., Nov. 16, 1946; d. Thomas Joseph and Muriel Kathryn (McCarthy) M. BA cum laude, Trinity Coll., 1968; M in Internat. Pub. Policy, Johns Hopkins U., 1987. Tchr. English, history St. Cecilia Tchr. Tng. Coll., Nyeri, Kenya, 1968-71; reporter Brockton (Mass.) Enterprise, 1972-73; freelance corr. Washington Post, Newsweek, Sunday Times of London, et al, Luanda, Angola, 1974-76; reporter Fairfax County Washington Post, 1976-77, fgn. corr. in South Africa, 1977-82, reporter immigration issues, 1982-85, bur. chief Alexandria, Va., 1985-89; fgn. corr. Mid. East Washington Post, Cairo, 1989-94. Vol. ARC, Washington, 1984, Whitman-Walker Found., Washington, 1988-89. Recipient Courage in Journalism award Internat. Women's Media Found., 1990, George Polk award L.I. U., 1991, Edward Weintal Journalism award Sch. Fgn. Svc., Georgetown U., 1991, Pulitzer prize for internat. reporting, 1991; Edward R. Murrow fellow Coun. on Fgn. Rels., N.Y., 1994-95. Roman Catholic. Office: Washington Post Fgn Desk 1150 15th St NW Washington DC 20071-0002

MURPHY, CATHERINE, painter; b. Cambridge, Mass., 1946. BFA, Pratt Inst., 1967; student, Skowhegan Sch. Painting and Sculpture, 1966. One-woman shows First Street Gallery, N.Y.C., 1972, Piper Gallery, Mass., 1972, Fourcade, Droll, Inc., N.Y.C., 1975, Phillips Collection, Washington, 1976, Xavier Fourcade, Inc., N.Y.C., 1979, 85, J. Rosenthal Fine Arts, Ltd., Chgo., 1988, Lennon, Weinberg, Inc., N.Y.C., 1989, 92; exhibited in group shows at Whitney Mus. Am. Art, N.Y.C., 1972, 73, Indpls. Mus., 1974, Inst. Contemporary Art, Boston, 1976, Mus. Contemporary Art, Chgo., 1977, Am. Acad. and Inst. Arts and Letters, N.Y.C., 1979, 87, 89, 90, 92, Xavier Fourcade, Inc., N.Y.C., 1977, 80, 83, 87, 93, (traveling exhbn.) San Francisco Mus. Modern Art, 1985, Daniel Weinberg Gallery, L.A., 1989, (traveling exhbn.) Cin. Art Mus., 1989, Lennon Weinberg, Inc., N.Y.C., 1989, 90, 91, 93, 94, (traveling exhbn.) Miyaqi Mus. Art, Sendai, Japan, 1991-92, Forum Gallery, N.Y.C., 1993, Koplin Gallery, Santa Monica, Calif., 1993, Tibor de Nagy Gallery, N.Y.C., 1994; permanent collections Chase Manhattan Bank, N.Y.C., Hirshhorn Mus. & Sculpture Garden, Washington, Met. Mus. Art, N.Y.C., Newark Mus., N.J. Art Mus., Trenton, Phillips Collection, Washington, Va. Mus. Fine Arts, Richmond, Weatherspoon Art Gallery, Greensboro, N.C., Whitney, Mus. Am. Art, N.Y.C. Grantee NEA, 1979, 89, Ingram Merrill Found., 1986; Guggenheim fellow, 1982; recipient AAIAL award, 1990. Office: care Lennon Weinberg Inc 580 Broadway Ste 204 New York NY 10012-3223

MURPHY, DEBORAH JUNE, lawyer; b. Clinton, Tenn., Dec. 19, 1955; d. Robert Carlton and Mary Ruth (Melton) M.; m. Charles L. Beach, Dec. 9, 1987. BS, U. Tenn., 1977; postgrad. Vanderbilt U., 1983; JD, Nashville YMCA Law Sch., 1987. Bar: Tenn. 1987. Bank officer C&C Bank, Oak Ridge, 1975-76; tax auditor State of Tenn., Knoxville, 1977-82, Nashville, 1983-85, legal advisor, 1985-86; with office legal services Tenn. Gen. Assembly, Nashville, 1986-87; atty. U.S. Dept. Treasury, 1987—; part time instr. Draughons Coll., Knoxville, 1978-81. Mem. Tenn. Homecoming 1986 Com. Mem. ABA, Tenn. Bar Assn., Assn. Trial Lawyers Am., Tenn. Trial Lawyers Assn., Anderson County Bar Assn., Lawyers Assn. for Women, The Young Lawyers Conf., Sigma Delta Kappa. Democrat. Methodist. Avocation: travel. Home: 512 S Oakwood Ave Clinton TN 37716-2005 Office: 710 Locust St 4th Flr Knoxville TN 37902

MURPHY, DIANA E., federal judge; b. Faribault, Minn., Jan. 4, 1934; d. Albert W. and Adleyne (Heiker) Kuske; m. Joseph Murphy, July 24, 1958; children: Michael, John E. BA magna cum laude, U. Minn., 1954, JD magna cum laude, 1974; postgrad., Johannes Gutenberg U., Mainz, Germany, 1954-55, U. Minn., 1955-58. Bar: Minn. 1974, U.S. Supreme Ct. 1980. Assoc. Lindquist & Vennum, 1974-76; mcpl. judge Hennepin County, 1976-78, Minn. State dist. judge, 1978-80; judge U.S. Dist. Ct. for Minn., Mpls., 1980-94, chief judge, 1992-94; judge U.S. Ct. of Appeals (8th cir.), Minneapolis, 1994—. Bd. editors: Minn. Law Rev., Georgetown U. Jour. on Cts., Health Scis. and the Law, 1989-92. Bd. dirs. Spring Hill Conf. Ctr., 1978-84, Mpls. United Way, 1985—, treas. 1990-94, Bush Found., 1982—, chmn. bd., 1986-91; bd. dirs. Amicus, 1976-80, also organizer, 1st chmn. adv. coun.; mem. Mpls. Charter Commn., 1973-76, chmn., 1974-76; bd. dirs. Ops. De Novo, 1971-76, chmn., 1974-75; mem. Minn. Constl. Study Commn., chmn. bill of rights com., 1971-73; regent St. Johns U., 1978-87, 88—, vice chmn. bd., 1985-87; mem. Minn. Bicentennial Commn., 1987-88; trustee Twin Cities Pub. TV, 1985-94, chmn. bd., 1990-92; trustee U. Minn. Found., 1990—, treas. 1992—; bd. dirs. Sci. Mus. Minn., 1988-94, vice chmn., 1991-94; trustee U. St. Thomas, 1991—; dir. Nat. Assn. Pub. Interest Law Fellowships for Equal Justice, 1992—. Fulbright scholar; recipient Amicus Founders' award, Outstanding Achievement award U. Minn., Outstanding Achievement award YWCA. Fellow Am. Bar Found.; mem. ABA (mem. ethics and profl. responsibility judges adv. com. 1981-88, standing com. on jud. selection, tenure and compensation 1991-94, mem. standing com. on fed. jud. improvements 1994—), Minn. Bar Assn. (bd. govs. 1977-81), Hennepin County Bar Assn. (gov. coun. 1976-81), Am. Law Inst., Am. Judicature Soc. (bd. dirs. 1982-93, v.p. 1985-88, treas. 1988-89, chmn. bd. 1989-91), Nat. Assn. Women Judges, Minn. Women Lawyers, U. Minn. Alumni Assn. (bd. dirs. 1975-83, pres. 1981-82), Fed. Judges Assn. (bd. dirs. 1982—, v.p. 1984-89, pres. 1989-91), Hist. Soc. for 8th Cir. (bd. dirs. 1988-91), Fed. Jud. Ctr. (bd. dirs. 1990-94, 8th cir. jud. coun. 1992-94, mem. U.S. jud. conf. com. on ct. adminstrn. and case mgmt. 1994—), Order of Coif, Phi Beta Kappa. Office: US Dist Ct 684 Courthouse 110 S 4th St Minneapolis MN 55401-2216

MURPHY, DIANE ALYCE, dairy farmer; b. Mpls., Aug. 2, 1949; d. Myles Francis and Anne Mary (Murphy) Timblin; m. Kenneth Hugh Murphy, Aug. 9, 1969; children: Jason, Marie, Lisa, Sarah. Grad. high sch., Delano, Minn. Sec. Advance Machine Co., Spring Park, Minn., 1967-69; city employee Delano (Minn.) Mcpl. Liquour, 1970-82; dairy farmer Murphy Farm, Delano, 1982—. Mem. Watertown Area Women's Bowling Assn. (pres. 1983-94, bd. dirs. 1976-80, Woman Bowler of Yr. 1984). Democrat. Roman Catholic. Home: 7034 Davidson Ave SE Delano MN 55328-9328

MURPHY, DIANE RUTH, database marketer; b. Boston, Jan. 6, 1964; d. Michael Brendon and Ruth Margaret (Johnson) M. BA in Rhetoric, Bates Coll., 1986. Sales mgr. Jordan Marsh, Boston, 1986-87; dir. sales and mktg. Epsilon, Burlington, Mass., 1987—; instr. Bentley Coll., Waltham, Mass., 1992—. Project coord. City Year Serv-a-thon, Boston. Mem. Nat. Coun. for Prescription Drug Programs, New Eng. Direct Mktg. Assn., Toastmasters Internat., Bates Coll. Key Club (fundraiser, class agt. 1989—). Office: Epsilon 50 Cambridge St Burlington MA 01803

MURPHY, DIANE WILLIAMS, public relations executive; b. San Mateo, Calif., Feb. 18, 1949; d. Joseph Percival and Irene Julia (Homchick) Williams; m. William Patrick Murphy, June 17, 1972 (div. Feb. 1985); children: Meghan Elizabeth, Ian Matthew. Student, Northwestern U., 1967-69; BS, Georgetown U., 1972. Press asst., researcher Rep. Nat. Com., Washington, 1972; press asst. Hon. John Rhodes, Washington, 1973-77; acct. exec., media cons. Smith & Harroff, Washington, 1977—. Active Jr. League, Washington, 1982—; membership bd. Friends of Kennedy Ctr., 1982—; v.p. Sgt. Pepper Soc., Washington, 1985. Republican. Episcopalian. Club: Sporting (McLean, Va.). Home: 9225 Vernon Dr Great Falls VA 22066-2229

MURPHY, DONNA, actress. Stage appearances include: (regional theatre) Miss Julie, Pal Joey; (off-Broadway) Song of Singapore, Hey Love: The Songs of Mary Rodgers, Privates on Parade, Showing Off, Birds of Paradise, Little Shop of Horrors, A...My Name is Alice; (Broadway) Hello Again, Passion (Leading Actress in Musical Tony award 1994), They're Playing Our Song, The Mystery of Edwin Drood; TV appearances include Law & Order, All My Children, Another World. Office: Silver Massetti & Assocs 145 W 45th St Ste 1204 New York NY 10036

MURPHY, DONNA LEE, retired dance school owner; b. Mt. Zion, Iowa, Sept. 8, 1941; d. Darrell Othel and Laura Evangeline (Reddick) Loeffler; m. James Barney Murphy; children: Daryl Udell, Michael John. Grad. high sch., Keosauqua, Iowa. Ind. musician, entertainer Iowa, 1959—; instr. dance Donna Lee's Sch. Dance, Eldon and Keosauqua, Iowa, 1959-88; sec., income maintenance worker State of Iowa Dept. Human Services, Keosauqua, 1962-82; office mgr. Barker Wire Co., Keosauqua, 1982-84; instr., choreographer Keosauqua, 1985—; choreographer Van Buren Cmty. Players, Keosauqua, 1963-76; freelance writer feature articles Ottumwa (Iowa) Courier Daily Newspaper, 1988-90, 93—, Fairfield Ledger, Van Buren County Register, 1994—, others; pianist Hist. Hotel Manning, Keosauqua, 1989-93, entertainment dir., 1991-93; sec., computer operator Boley Real Estate, Keosauqua, 1986—. Author: (dance manual series) Tip Top Tapping, 1985—, Jazz & Break Dancing, 1986, Assorted Dance Varieties, 1986. Dir. Flag Corp. Van Buren Sch. Band, Keosauqua, 1986-87. Mem. Nat. Button Soc. Republican. Presbyterian. Home and Office: 1006 5th St PO Box # 562 Keosauqua IA 52565

MURPHY, DONNA MAE, small business owner, social worker, lawyer; b. Phila., Dec. 6, 1955. BA, U. Md., 1978, MSW, 1986, JD, 1989. Lic. social worker, Md.; Bar: Md. 1989, D.C. 1990. Assoc. dir. Young Life, Silver Spring, Md., 1978-83; social worker Rockville (Md.) Dept. Social Svcs., 1987; dir. Springboard Program Mental Health Assn. of Montgomery County, Rockville, 1990-91; owner Heart of Gold Nannies, Rockville, 1993—; vol. Foster Care Rev. Bd., Rockville, 1989—.

MURPHY, EDRIE LEE, hospital laboratory administrator; b. Redwood Falls, Minn., Dec. 4, 1953; d. Melvin Arthur and Betty Lou (Wenholz) Timm; m. David Joseph Murphy, July 28, 1984; children: Michael David, Scott Christopher. BS in Med. Tech. summa cum laude, Mankato State U., 1976; MBA, U. St. Thomas, 1984. Registered med. technologist. Med. technologist Children's Health Care, St. Paul, 1976-81, chemistry supr., 1981-85, lab. mgr., 1985-95, dir. lab. systems, Mpls., St. Paul's Campus, 1995—. Contbr. articles to profl. jours. Charles H. Cooper scholar, 1975. Mem. Am. Soc. Clin. Lab. Scis., Minn. Soc. Clin. Lab. Scis., Am. Assn. Clin. Chemists, Clin. Lab. Mgmt. Assn., Phi Kappa Phi. Club: Elan Vital Ski (v.p. membership 1981-82) (Mpls.). Avocations: photography, sailing, skiing, tennis, travel. Office: Children's Health Care 345 N Smith Saint Paul MN 55102

MURPHY, ELVA GLENN, executive assistant; b. Chickasha, Okla., Aug. 21, 1934; d. Elsie Lee (Murphy) Sommer; m. Calvin E. Morgan, Mar. 11, 1972 (dec. Dec. 1976); m. C. Gordon Murphy, Oct. 17, 1981. Student, UCLA, 1954-55, Columbia U., 1973. Various secretarial positions Calif., 1956-67; fgn. svc. sec. U.S. Dept. State, Paris, 1967-69; exec. asst. to Cyrus R. Vance Simpson Thacher & Bartlett, N.Y.C., 1969-77, 80—, U.S. Dept. State, Washington, 1977-80. Mem. Seraphic Soc. (pres. 1990-92). Democrat. Home: 60 Sutton Pl S # 9HN New York NY 10022 Office: Simpson Thacher & Bartlett 425 Lexington Ave New York NY 10017-3954

MURPHY, ERIN ELIZABETH, editor; b. Balt., Oct. 9, 1965; d. John Joseph and Doris Alice (Metzbower) M. BA in English, U. Miami, Coral Gables, Fla., 1987, BS in Computer Sci., 1987. Assoc. editor IEEE Spectrum Mag., N.Y.C., 1987-90; sr. editor, on-line edutor Omni mag., Greensboro, N.C., 1990—. Mem. Phi Beta Kappa. Office: Omni Mag Ste 200 324 W Wendover Ave Greensboro NC 27408

MURPHY, EVELYN FRANCES, healthcare administrator, former lieutenant governor; b. Panama Canal Zone, Panama Canal Zone, May 14, 1940; d. Clement Bernard and Dorothy Eloise (Jackson) M. AB, Duke U., 1961, PhD, 1965; MA, Columbia U., 1963; hon. degrees, Regis Coll., 1978, Curry Coll., Northeastern U., Simmons Coll., Wheaton Coll., Anna Maria Coll., Bridgewater State Coll., Salem State Coll., Emmanuel Coll.; hon. degree, Suffolk U. Pres. Ancon Assocs., Boston, 1971-72; ptnr. Llewelyn-Davies, Weeks, Forrester-Walker & Bor, London, 1973-74; sec. environ. affairs Commonwealth of Mass., Boston, 1975-79, sec. econ. affairs, 1983-86, lt. gov., 1987-91; mng. dir. Brown Rudnick Freed and Gesmer, Boston, 1991-93; exec. v.p. Blue Cross/Blue Shield of Mass., Boston, 1994—; also bd. dirs. Blue Cross Blue Shield Mass., Boston; vis. pub. policy scholar Radcliffe Coll., 1991; vice chmn./chmn. Nat. Adv. Com. on Oceans and Atmosphere (Presdl. apptd.), 1979-80; bd. dirs. Shawmut Bank of Conn., Shawmut Bank of Mass. Recipient Disting. Svc. award Nat. Sierra Club, 1978, Nat. Govs. Assn. 1978, Outstanding Citizen award Mass. Audubon Soc., 1978; Harvard U. fellow, 1979-80. Mem. Women Execs. in State Govt. (chair 1987). Democrat. Office: Blue Cross Blue Shield Mass 100 Summer St Boston MA 02110-2190

MURPHY, FRANCES LOUISE, II, newspaper publisher; b. Balt.; d. Carl James and L. Vashti (Turley) M.; m. James E. Wood (div.); children: Frances Murphy Wood Draper, James E. Jr., Susan Wood Barnes. BA, U. Wis., 1944; BS, Coppin State Coll., Balt., 1958; MEd, Johns Hopkins U., 1963. City editor Balt. Afro-Am., 1956-57; dir. News Bur., Morgan State Coll., Balt., 1964-71; chmn. bd. dirs. Afro-Am. Newspapers, Balt., 1971-74; assoc. prof. journalism SUNY, Buffalo, 1975-85, Howard U., Washington, 1985-91; editor Washington Afro-Am., 1951-56, pub., 1987—; bd. dirs. Afro-Am. Newspapers, Balt., 1985-87; mem. adv. bd. Partnership Inst., Washington, 1985-91; bd. trustees U. D.C.; treas. African Am. Civil War Meml. Freedom Found., African Am. Leadership Summit. Trustee State Colls. Md., 1971-76, U. D.C., 1993—; bd. dirs. Delta Rsch. and Ednl. Found., 1993—; nat. bd. dirs. NACCP, 1971-76. Named One of 100 Most Influential Black Ams., Ebony mag., 1973, 74, Disting. Marylander, Gov. State of Md., 1975; recipient Ida B. Wells award Congl. Black Caucus, 1989, Public Svc. award African Methodist Episcopal Ch., 1991, Invaluable Svc. award Martin L. King Jr. Found., 1992, Black Women of Courage award Nat. Fedn. Black Women Bus. Owners, 1993, Black Awareness Ach. award Holy Redeemer Catholic Ch., 1993, Bus. of the Yr. award Bus. and Profl. Women's League, 1993, Oustanding Svc. award Capital Press Club, 1993, Black Conscious Com. trophy Unity Nation, 1993, Dedicated Cmty. Svc. award Ward I Cmty. and D.C. Pub. Schs., 1994, Women of Strength award Nat. Black Media Coalition, 1994, Outstanding Woman of Yr. award Alpha Gamma chpt. Iota Phi Lambda, 1994, Art Ctr. Excellence award Capital Press Club, 1994, Excellence in Comm. award Washington Inter-Alumni Coun. United Negro Coll. Fund, 1994. Mem. Nat. Newspaper Pubs. Assn. (editl. com. 1987—, Merit award 1987, 89-93), Soc. Profl. Journalists (Disting. Svc. award 1994), Links, Capital Press Club (exec. bd. 1987—, Outstanding Svc. award 1993), Delta Sigma Theta (Frances L. Murphy II Comm. award Fed. City Alumnae chpt. 1993, Fortitude Image award Prince George's County chpt. 1994). Democrat. Episcopalian. Home: 5709 1st St NW Washington DC 20011 Office: Washington Afro-Am 1612 14th St NW Washington DC 20009-4307

MURPHY, GLORIA WALTER, novelist; b. Hartford, Conn., Feb. 22, 1940; d. Frank and Elizabeth (Lemkin) Walter; m. Joseph S. Murphy; children: William Gitelman, Laurie Gitelman, Daniel Gitelman, Julie Gitelman, Caitlin Murphy. Student, No. Essex Community Coll., Haverhill, Mass., 1979-81, Boston U., 1981-82. Columnist Pandora's Box The Peabody (Mass.) Times, 1975; columnist Murphy's Law The Methuen (Mass.) News, 1979. Author: Nightshade, 1986, Bloodties, 1987, Nightmare, 1987, The Playroom, 1987, the Cry of the Mouse, 1991, Down Will Come Baby, 1991, A Whisper in the Attic, 1992, A Shadow on the Stair, 1993, Simon Says, 1994. Mem. Mystery Writers Am., Authors Guild. Address: Box 670 Ringwood NJ 07456

MURPHY, JANICE K., medical service plan executive. V.p., treas. Kaiser Foun. Health Plan, Oakland, Calif. Office: Kaiser Found Health Plan 1 Kaiser Pl Oakland CA 94612*

MURPHY, JILL LUCILLE, accountant, state official; b. Charlotte, Mich., Jan. 3, 1946; divorced; Gina, Jacqueline. BA, Mich. State U., 1975, MBA, 1977. CPA, Mich. Ops. auditor Mich. Dept. Treasury, Lansing, 1977-78, local govt. auditor, 1979-84; auditor Office Treasury Insp., Lansing, 1978-79; dir. internal audit Mich. Liquor Control Commn., Lansing, 1984-89, Dept. of State, Lansing, 1989—. Honors scholar Lansing Community Coll., 1973. Mem. AICPA, Mich. Assn. CPAs (chair acctg. & auditing 1994-95), Assn. Govtl. Accts. (past pres. Greater Lansing chpt.), Inst. Internal Auditors. Office: Mich Dept State Internal Audit Divsn 124 W Allegan 2d fl Lansing MI 48918

MURPHY, JOAN BARRON, non-profit organization administrator, consultant; b. Troy, Ala., Sept. 30, 1935; d. William Gaston and Mary Eunice (Matthews) Barron; divorced; children: Robert Michael, William Patrick, Pamela Murphy Wright. Student, Troy State Tchrs. Coll., 1952, Mars Hill Coll., 1955, Blue Ridge Tech. Inst., 1980. Sec., bookkeeper City Bd. Edn., Troy, 1952-53; sec. outdoor lighting Gen. Electric Co., Hendersonville, N.C., 1956-57; pub. acct., pub. stenographer Hendersonville, 1957-67; dir. fin. and adminstrn. Western Carolina Cmty. Action, Hendersonville, 1967—; pub. acct. Barrire's Secretarial Service, Hendersonville, 1965-68; fin. sec. St. James Episcopal Ch., Hendersonville, 1966-68; prin. Church St. 66 Service, Hendersonville, 1984-86; bd. dirs. Quality Tire Co., Inc., Hendersonville; fin. cons. Hendersonville County Workshop, Hendersonville, 1966-69, Council on Aging, Hendersonville, 1967-70, Hands and Fingers, Brevard, N.C., 1970-80; cons. Helping Hand Day Care Ctr., Hendersonville, 1967, Play and Learn Day Care Ctr., Hendersonville, 1968-80. Bd. dirs. Henderson County United Way, Hendersonville, 1968-74; mem. Mayor's Disaster Com., Hendersonville, 1971. Mem. Bus. and Profl. Womens Club (pres. 1968-70), Order Ea. Star (assoc. matron 1985-86). Baptist. Home: 913 Kanuga Rd Hendersonvlle NC 28739-9705

MURPHY, JOANNE BECKER, writer; b. Detroit; d. Louis Norman and Gertrude Margaret (Kornmeier) Becker; m. Joseph A. Murphy, Jr., June 24, 1961; children: Michael Ellis, Joseph A. III. BA in Journalism, Mich. State U., 1958; MA in Humanities, Wayne State U., 1975. Communications WBZ TV, Boston, 1958-60, The Jam Handy Orgn., Detroit, 1960-62, Detroit Symphony Orch., 1969-70; freelance writer, editor Detroit, 1980-90, Washington, 1990—. Contbg. writer: Glass: State of the Art, 1989, Affecting Change, 1986; editor: As Parents We Will, 1985 (1st Place award Pub. Svc. Nat. Found. for Alcoholism Communications); writer, editor publs. for arts and human svcs. orgns.; contbr. articles to mags., newspapers. Mem. program bd. Grosse Pointe (Mich.) War Meml., 1987-90; bd. dirs. Detroit Artists Market, 1982-90, Mich. Metro coun. Girl Scouts U.S.A., 1971-78, Family Svcs. Detroit and Wayne County, 1970-76, All Hallows Guild, Washington Nat. Cathedral, 1993—; bd. canvassers Grosse Pointe Sch. Sys., 1986-90. Named one of 50 Outstanding Women Mich. State U., 1958. Mem. Women in Communications Inc. (v.p. pub. rels. D.C. chpt. 1992-93), Washington Ind. Writers, Am. News Women's Club (Washington), Kappa Alpha Theta. Home and Office: 2717 O St NW Washington DC 20007-3128

MURPHY, JOANNE M., computer company executive; b. Holyoke, Mass., Dec. 31, 1957; d. LeRoy Paul and Rose Marie (Danehey) Miller; m. Dennis Francis Murphy III, June 2, 1979; 1 child, Dennis Francis IV. AS in Bus. Studies, Holyoke Community Coll., 1979; BS in Mktg., U. Mass., 1980; postgrad., U. Hartford. Account rep. Xerox Corp., Hartford, Conn., 1980-82; sr. account exec. Exxon Office Systems, Stamford, Conn., 1983-85; area sales cons. ShareTech, Hartford, 1985-86; sr. mktg. rep. Honeywell Info. Systems, Glastonbury, Conn., 1986-87; nat. account exec. Computer Horizons, Inc., 1987-93, dir. bus devel., 1994—. Editor shared tenant newsletter, 1985. Mem. Nat. Orgn. Female Execs., Data Processing Mgmt. Assn., Orgn. for Profls. in Telecommunication. Republican. Roman Catholic. Avocations: skiing, tennis, golf, personal computers. Home: 38 Hillview Ave Madison NJ 07940 Office: Computer Horizons Corp 49 Old Bloomfield Ave Mountain Lakes NJ 07046-1495

MURPHY, JUDITH CHISHOLM, trust company executive; b. Chippewa Falls, Wis., Jan. 26, 1942; d. John David and Bernice A. (Hartman) Chisholm. BA, Manhattanville Coll., 1964; postgrad., New Sch. for Social Research, 1965-68, Nat. Grad. Trust Sch., 1975. Asst. portfolio mgr. Chase Manhattan Bank, N.A., N.Y.C., 1964-68; trust investment officer Marshall & Ilsley Bank, Milw., 1968-72; asst. v.p. Marshall & Ilsley Bank, 1972-74, v.p., 1974-75; v.p., treas. Marshall & Ilsley Invesmtent Mgmt. Corp., Milw., 1975-94; v.p. Marshall & Ilsley Trust Co., Phoenix, 1982—, Marshall & Ilsley Trust Co. Fla., Naples, 1985—; v.p., dir. instnl. sales Marshall & Ilsley Trust Co., Milw., 1994—; coun. mem. Am. Bankers Assn., Washington, 1984-86; govt. relations com. Wis. Bankers Assn., Madison, 1982-88. Contbr. articles to Trusts & Estates Mag., 1980, ABA Banking Jour., 1981, Maricopa Lawyer, 1983. Chmn. Milw. City Plan Commn., 1986—; commr. Milw. County Commn. on Handicapped, 1988-90; bd. dirs. Cardinal Stritch Coll., Milw., 1980-89, Children's Hosp. Wis., Milw., 1989—. Recipient Outstanding Achievement award YWCA Greater Milw., 1985, Sacajawea award Profl. Dimensions, Milw., 1988, Pro Urbe award Mt. Mary Coll., 1988, Vol. award Milw. Found., 1992; named Disting. Woman in Banking, Comml. West Mag., 1988. Mem. Milw. Analysts Soc. (sec. 1974-77, bd. dirs. 1977-80), Fin. Women Internat. (bd. dirs., v.p. 1976-80), Am. Inst. Banking (instr. 1975-78), TEMPO (charter), Profl. Dimensions (hon.), University Club, Woman's Club Wis., Rotary. Democrat. Roman Catholic. Home: 1139 N Edison St Milwaukee WI 53202-3147 Office: Marshall & Ilsley Trust Co 1000 N Water St Milwaukee WI 53202-6025

MURPHY, JULIET ANNE, lawyer; b. Kingston, Jamaica, West Indies, Apr. 22, 1963; came to U.S., 1978; d. Ramon Kirkett and Ouida Vivienne (Bair) M. BA, U. Fla., 1984, JD, 1987. Assoc. Rumberger, Kirk, Etal, Miami, Fla., 1987-89, Law Offices of David Mankin, Ft. Lauderdale, Fla., 1989-93, Law Offices of Peter Stassun, Ft. Lauderdale, 1993—; chair judicial selection Fla. chpt. Nat. Bar Assn., Stuart, 1993—; mem. judicial nominating com. The Fla. Bar, Tallahassee, 1992—, vice chair, 1994—; lemon law arbitrator Atty. Gen. Office. Mem. Nat. Assn. Negro Bus. and Profl. Women (pres. 1994—). Office: Law Offices Peter Stassun 600 S Andrews Ave Ste 200 Fort Lauderdale FL 33301

MURPHY, JUNEANN WADSWORTH, microbiologist, educator; b. Chickasha, Okla., Mar. 13, 1937; d. Evard William and Ann (Adwan) Wadsworth; m. George W. Murphy, Sept. 2, 1967; children: Cynthia Ann Murphy-Erdosh, Sally E. Savino. BS, U. Okla., 1959, MS, 1961, 65, PhD, 1969. Asst. prof. microbiology U. Okla., Norman, 1970-81, dir. med. tech., 1978-82, assoc. prof. microbiology, 1981-86, prof. microbiology, 1986-88, GLC prof. microbiology, 1988-89, GLC prof. microbiology Health Sci. Ctr., 1989—; study section mem. NIH-Div. Rsch. Grants, Bethesda, Md., 1983-87, 92—; vis. asst. prof. U. Okla., Norman, 1969-70; vis. asst. prof. of clin. immunology U. Colo. Health Sci. Ctr., Denver, 1979. Mem. editl. bd. Infection and Immunity, Jour. Med. and Vet. Mycology. Mem. Am. Soc. Microbiology, Am. Assn. Immunologist, Med. Mycology Soc. of Ams., Internat. Soc. Human and Animal Mycology. Democrat. Methodist. Home: 2328 Ashwood Ln Norman OK 73071-7416 Office: Univ Okla Health Sci Ctr PO Box 26901 Oklahoma City OK 73126-0901

MURPHY, KATHLEEN ANN, lawyer; b. Ft. Dix, N.J., May 6, 1953; d. Thomas G. and Nancy K. (Ford) M.; m. Mark V. Kauppi, Aug. 16, 1980; 1 child, Natalie K. BA, Emmanuel Coll., Boston, 1974; MA, U. Colo., 1977; JD, Cath. U. Am., 1993. Bar: Md. 1993. Fgn. Svc. officer Dept. State, Washington, 1980-88; atty.-advisor Armed Svcs. Bd. Contract Appeals, Falls Church, Va. Author: Masked Murder, 1989. Mem. State Bar Md., Women's Bar D.C. Home: 147 Kentucky Ave SE Washington DC 20003

MURPHY, KATHLEEN ANNE FOLEY, advertising agency executive; b. Fresh Meadows, N.Y., Oct. 15, 1952; d. Thomas J. and Audrey L. (Finn) F.; m. Timothy Sean Murphy, Sept. 26, 1992. BA, Marymount Coll., 1974; postgrad., Smith Coll., 1985. V.p. acct. supr., sr. v.p. mgmt. supr., sr. v.p. group dir. Ogilvy & Mather Inc., N.Y.C., 1974-90; sr. v.p., worldwide account dir. Young & Rubicam, San Francisco, 1990-92, sr. v.p., dir. account svcs., 1992—. Mem. San Francisco Advt. Club, Advt. Edn. Fedn. Roman Catholic. Home: One Brookside Ave Berkeley CA 94705 Office: Young & Rubicam 100 1st St San Francisco CA 94105-2634

MURPHY, KATHLEEN JANE, psychologist, educator; b. Worcester, Mass., Nov. 9, 1962; d. Frederick George and Dorothy Jane (McGuiness) M.; m. Gary Lee Tatum, July 3, 1991. BA cum laude, Holy Cross Coll., 1984; MA, Assumption Coll., 1987; PhD, Tex. A&M U., 1991. Lic. profl. counselor, marriage and family therapist. Counselor Tex. Rehab. Commn., College Station, 1988-89, psychometrician, 1989; intern clin. psychology Worcester (Mass.) State Hosp., 1989-90; psychotherapist Sandstone Ctr., College Station, 1991-92, Luth. Social Svc., Bryan, Tex., 1992-93; instr. Blinn Coll., College Station, Tex., 1993—. Editor: Report on Inquiry newsletter, 1988. Mem. APA, Nat. Registere Health Svc. Providers in Psychology, Phi Beta Kappa, Psi Chi, Phi Kappa Phi. Democrat. Roman Catholic. Home: 614 Abbey Ln College Station TX 77845-8141

MURPHY, KATHLEEN MARY, law firm executive; b. Bklyn., Dec. 16, 1945; d. Raymond Joseph and Catherine Elizabeth (Kearney) M. BA in Edn., Molloy Coll., 1971; MS in Edn., Bklyn. Coll., 1975. Cert. elem. sch. tchr., N.Y. Elem. sch. tchr. various parochial schs. L.I., Bklyn., Queens, N.Y., 1969-80; from asst. prin. to prin. parochial sch. Queens, 1980-82; supr.-trainer Davis, Polk, Wardwell law firm, N.Y.C., 1982-88; mgr. Schulte Roth & Zabel, N.Y.C., 1988—; trainer program for new employees, 1984; speaker edn. topics, Bklyn., Queens, 1979-81. Mem. NAFE. Democrat. Roman Catholic.

MURPHY, KATHRYN MARGUERITE, archivist; b. Brockton, Mass.; d. Thomas Francis and Helena (Fortier) M. A.B. in History, George Washington U., 1935, M.A., 1939; M.L.S., Cath. U., 1950; postgrad. Am. U., 1961. With Nat. Archives and Records Service, Washington, 1940-89, ret., supervisory archivist Central Research br., 1958-62, archivist, 1962—, mem. fed. women's com. Nat. Archives, 1974, rep. to fed. women's com. GSA, 1975; docent, 1989—; lectr. colls., socs. in U.S., 1950—; lectr. Am. ethnic history, 1978-79; free lance author and lectr. in field. Founder, pres. Nat. Archives lodge Am. Fedn. Govt. Employees, 1965—, del. conv., 1976, 78, 80, recipient award for outstanding achievement in archives, 1980. Recipient commendation Okla. Civil War Centennial Commn., 1965; named hon. citizen Oklahoma City, Mayor, 1963. Mem. ALA, Soc. Am. Archivists (joint com. hosp. libraries 1965-70), Nat. League Am. Pen Women (corr. sec. Washington 1975-78, pres. chpt. 1978-80), Bus. and Profl. Womens' Club Washington, Phi Alpha Theta (hon.). Contbr. articles on Am. ethnic history to profl. publs. Home: 1500 Massachusetts Ave NW Washington DC 20005-1821 Office: Nat Archives and Records Svc 7th and Pennsylvania Aves NW Washington DC 20408

MURPHY, KATHY A., plan services consultant; b. Tulsa, Jan. 4, 1959; d. Richard D. and Virginia M. Murphy. BBA in Mktg., U. Tex., 1981. Mktg. specialist Hilti, Inc., Tulsa, 1981-82; computer specialist Intrepid Oil & Gas, Dallas, 1983-85; provider rels. rep. Electronic Data Sys., Austin, Tex., 1985-86, claims mgr., 1986-88; sr. mktg. cons. Consultec, Inc., Atlanta, 1988-90; plan svcs. cons. NASCO, Atlanta, 1990—. Chairperson Northside Hosp. Celebration of Lights Fund Raiser, 1994; active St. Andrews Adult Choir, Atlanta, 1990—, St. Andrews Women's Guild, Atlanta, 1993—. Roman Catholic. Office: NASCO Bldg 400 1000 Abernathy Rd Ste 290 Atlanta GA 30328

MURPHY, LINDA SUE, city official; b. Lynchburg, Va., June 7, 1948; d. Carter P. and Dorothy L. (Clark) Tucker; m. Daniel K. Murphy, Mar. 25 1972; 1 child, Krystal Grace. Student, Longwood Coll., 1966-68. Exec. sec. First Nat. Bank of Anchorage, Seward, Alaska, 1976-80; clk. of ct., asst. magistrate Alaska Ct. System, Seward, 1980-81; city clk., pers. officer City of Seward, 1981—. Sec., Seward Concert Assn., 1982; chmn. Seward Sch. Adv. Bd., 1983; v.p. bd. dirs. Seward Life Action Council, 1983-84, pres. bd. dirs., 1984-86; chmn. Seward-Obihiro Sister City Com., 1984; active Lt. Gov. Transition Team, 1995. Named Alaska Mcpl. Official of Yr., 1992. Mem. Internat. Inst. Mcpl. Clks. (bd. dirs. 1992—), Alaska Assn. Mcpl. Clerks (sec. 1984-85, v.p. 1985-86, pres. 1986-87), Alaska Women in Govt. (v.p. 1985-87), Bus. and Profl. Women's Club (v.p. 1988-89, pres. 1989-90), Rotary (bd. dirs. 1989—, treas. 1991-92, v.p. 1992-93, pres. 1994-95). Democrat. Home: Nhn Salmon Rd Seward AK 99664 Office: Seward City Hall PO Box 167 Seward AK 99664-0167

MURPHY, LOIS KAY, management consultant, writer; b. Richmond, Ky., Apr. 7, 1944; d. William Smith and Orla (Dayton) M.; m. Frederick A. Strache, Aug. 11, 1961 (div. 1972); children: Thorne Ann, Sean Myer. BA, U. Ky., 1963; M in Child Psychology, U. Wis., Milw., 1968; PhD, U. Hawaii, 1977; MBA, U. West L.A., 1980. Prof. psychology Alverno Coll., Milw., 1967-69, Chaminad Coll., Milw., 1973-76, U. Hawaii, 1975-77; corp. cons. Olanie Hurst, L.A., 1977-78, Towers Perrin, L.A., 1978-80; mgr. pers. planning Am. Hosp. Supply Corp., Chgo., 1980-81; owner Murphy Mgmt. and Compensation Consulting, Laguna Niguel, Calif., 1981—; presneter bus. and civic orgns., 1973—. Author: Successfully Single, 1992. Pres. LWV, Berea, Ky., 1964-65, Profl. Women's Forum, Lexington, Ky., 1986-87. Mem. APA, Nature Conservancy. Office: Murphy Mgmt & Compensation PO Box 6874 Laguna Niguel CA 92607-6874

MURPHY, LUCY ANN, realtor, broker; b. Toluca, Mont., Jan. 6, 1947; d. Everard Navas and Bertha (Brown) Ferrara; m. (div. June 1990); children: Michael, Amanda, Erin, Aimee. Student, Brigham Young U., 1965-72, U. Utah, 1984-90, San Jose State U., Mont. State U. cert. real estate specialist, realtor land cons. broker. Pres. Med. Mgmt. Assoc., San Jose, Calif., 1979-83; assoc. broker Wardley Corp. Better Homes & Gardens, Park City, Utah, 1992-94; prin. broker Silver Creek Realty, Park City, 1994—. Editor: (newsletter) Snyderville Spirit, 1985-90. Chair Gt. Am. Yard Sale, Park City, 1990; awards acquisition Realtors Clean-Up Day, Park City, 1990-91; scorekeeper Spl. Olympics, Park City, 1990-91; troop leader Girl Scouts Am., Park City, 1985-86; active Rep. Women, Salt Lake City, 1990—; dist. chmn., state del., election judge and registration agt. Rep. Party, 1984—; capt. Park City Camp, Daus. of Utah Pioneers; scoutmaster, den leader, dist. chair Boy Scouts Am., 1980-89; v.p. Calif. Family Women, San Jose; head libr. Summit County Libr. Named to Top 20 Realtors in State, Pres. Club, 1992, 93, 94. Mem. Realtors Land Inst., Park City Bd. Realtors (v.p., edn. com. 1991), Womens Coun. Realtors, Wickman Masters Alumni Assn. Mormon. Office: Silver Creek Realty PO Box 682753 Park City UT 84068-2753

MURPHY, MARGARET HACKETT, federal bankruptcy judge; b. Salisbury, N.C., 1948. BA, Queens Coll., Charlotte, N.C., 1970; JD, U. N.C., Chapel Hill, 1973. Bar: Ga. 1973, U.S. Bankruptcy Ct. Assoc. Smith, Cohen, Ringel, Kohler and Martin, Atlanta, 1973-79; ptnr. Smith, Gambrell & Russell (formerly Smith, Cohen, Ringel, Kohler and Martin), Atlanta, 1980-87; U.S. bankruptcy judge U.S. Dist. Ct. (no. dist.) Ga., Atlanta, 1987—. Office: 1290 US Courthouse 75 Spring St SW Atlanta GA 30303-3367

MURPHY, MARY ANN, human services administrator; b. Salt Lake City, Feb. 13, 1943; d. Wallace L. and Irene (Hummer) Matlock; m. Robert A. Glatzer, Dec. 31, 1977; children: Gabriela, Jessica, Nicholas. BA, U. Wash., 1964; MS, Ea. Wash. U., 1975. House counselor Ryther Child Ctr., Seattle, 1966-67; tchr. presch. Head Start, L.A. and Seattle, 1967-70; tchr. presch. Children's Orthopedic Hosp., Seattle, 1970-71, Washington, 1971-72; mem. faculty Ea. Wash. U., Cheney, 1973-82; exec. dir. Youth Help Assn., Spokane, Wash., 1983-88; mgr. regional ctr. for child abuse and neglect Deaconess Med. Ctr., Spokane, 1988—; pres. Wash. State Alliance for Children, Youth and Families, Seattle, 1985-87; chairperson Gov.'s Juvenile Justice Adv. Commn., Olympia, Wash., 1987-93, Spokane Prevention of Child Abuse and Neglect Coun., Spokane, 1988—. Mem. Nat. Coun. on Juvenile Justice, 1994. Recipient Alumni Achievement award Ea. Wash. U., 1994; named Outstanding Women Leader in Health Care, YWCA, 1992. Home: 1950 W Clarke Ave Spokane WA 99201-1306 Office: Deaconess Med Ctr W 604 6th Spokane WA 99204

MURPHY, MARY C., state legislator. BA, Coll. St. Scholastica; postgrad. U. Minn., Macalester Coll., U. Wis.-Superior, Am. U., Indiana U. H.s. tchr.; mem. Minn. Ho. of Reps., 1976—, mem. com. chair judiciary fin. com., tourism consumer affairs, labor-mgmt. relations coms.; active del. Duluth Central Labor Body AFL-CIO; mem., lector St. Raphael's Parish; dir. State Democratic Farmer-Labor Party, 1972-74, chmn. 8th Dist. credentials com., 1974—, chmn. St. Louis County Legis. Delegation, 1985-86. Mem. Duluth Fedn. Tchrs. (1st v.p. 1976-77, various coms.), Minn. Fedn. Tchrs. (legis. com. 1972-75), Am. Fedn. Tchrs. (del. nat. convs.), Minn. Hist. Soc., Alpha Delta Kappa. Office: State Office Bldg Saint Paul MN 55155

MURPHY, MARY KATHLEEN CONNORS, college administrator, writer; b. Pueblo, Colo.; d. Joseph Charles and Eileen E. (McDermott) Connors; m. Michael C. Murphy, June 6, 1959; children: Holly Ann, Emily Louise, Patricia Marie. AB, Loretto Heights Coll., 1960; MEd, Emory U., 1968; PhD, Ga. State U., 1980. Tchr. English pub. schs., Moultrie, Ga., 1959, Sacramento, 1960, Marietta, Ga., 1960-65, DeKalb County, Ga., 1966; tech. writer Ga. Dept. Edn., 1966-69; editorial asst. So. Regional Edn. Bd., Atlanta, 1969-71; dir. alumni affairs The Lovett Sch., Atlanta, 1972-75, dir. publs. and info. svc., 1975-77; coord. summer series in aging Ga. State U., 1979; dir. devel. found. rels. Ga. Inst. Tech., 1980-87, dir. devel., 1987-89; asst. dir. devel. for spl. gifts U Ga., 1989-91; assoc. v.p. for devel. Oglethorpe U., 1991—; state coord. for Ga., Am. Coun. on Edn. nat. identification program for women in higher edn. administrn., 1983-85; presenter profl. confs.; freelance edn. writer, 1968—; co-author: Fitting in as a New Service Wife, 1966; contbr. and contbg. editor numerous articles on teaching, secondary edn., higher edn., and fund raising to profl. publs.; columnist Daily Jour., Marietta, 1963-67, The Atlanta Constn., 1963-68; editor: Cultivating Found. Support for Edn., 1989, Building Bridges: Fund Raising for Deans, Faculty, and Development Officers, 1992. Bd. advisors Bridge Family Counseling Ctr., 1981-86, Northside Sch. Arts, 1981-83; bd. dirs. Atlanta Women's Network, 1982-84, v.p., 1983-84; prin., bd. dirs. Sch. Religion, Cathedral of Christ the King, 1979-84; mem. devel. com. Archdiocese of Atlanta, 1991-94; publicity chmn. Phoenix Soc. Atlanta, 1981-91, adv. bd., 1988-91; mem. allocations com., exec. com. United Way Met. Atlanta, 1983; bd. counseling Fulton Svc. Ctr., Met. Atlanta chpt. ARC, 1982-83; mem. Leadership Atlanta, class of 1983-84; group facilitator, 1984-85, co-chmn. edn. program, 1987. NDEA fellow, 1965-66; Adminstrn. of Aging fellow, 1977-79; recipient Image Maker award Atlanta Profl. Women's Directory, Inc. 1984. Mem. Coun. for Advancement and Support of Edn. (publs. com., alumni adv. com., 1974-76, dist. III bd., 1981-95, chmn. corp. and found. support conf., N.Y.C., 1985, maj. rsch. conf., Atlanta, 1986, matching gift conf., Tampa, 1989, dist. III conf. chmn. 1986, chair elect 1989-91, chair dist. III bd., 1991-93, past chair and nonminations com. chair, 1993-95, membership svcs. com. 1989-93, Washington bd. dirs. 1992-95, exec. com., trusteeship com., dist. svcs. and governance com., Alice Beeman Writing award, 1994), Coun. of Georsil, Inc. (bd. dir., chair edn. com. planned giving com., 1995—), Nat. Assn. Ind. Schs. (publs. com. 1974-76), Edn. Writers Assn., Nat. Soc. Fund Raising Execs. (v.p. Ga. chpt. 1985, pres. 1986-87, mem.-at-large nat. bd. 1985-89, chmn. pub. rels. com. 1985-87, asst. treas., chair audit com., mem. exec. com. 1988-90), Kiwanis (co-chair membership com. Atlanta club 1990-91, chair program com. 1991-95, dir. 1993-94, asst. sec. 1994-95, sec. 1995—), Phi Delta Kappa, Kappa Delta Pi (pres. 1980-81).

MURPHY, MARY KATHRYN, industrial hygienist; b. Kansas City, Mo., Apr. 16, 1941; d. Arthur Charles and Mary Agnes (Fitzgerald) Wahlstedt; m. Thomas E. Murphy Jr., Aug. 26, 1963; children: Thomas E. III, David W. BA, Avila Coll., Kansas City, 1962; MS, Cen. Mo. State U., 1975. Cert. in comprehensive practice of indsl. hygiene. Indsl. hygienist Kansas City area office Occupational Safety and Health Adminstrn., 1975-78, regional indsl. hygienist, 1979-86; dir. indsl. hygiene Chart Svcs., Shawnee, Kans., 1986-87; dir. indsl. hygiene and hazardous substance control Hall-Kimbrell Environ. Mgmt. and Pollution Control, Lawrence, Kans., 1987-88, mgr. dept. indsl. hygiene div. environ. mgmt. and program control, 1988-89; dir. indsl. hygiene Hazardous Waste divsn. Burns & McDonnell, Engrs., Architects, Kansas City, Mo., 1989-93; mgr. health & safety dept. Burns & McDonnell Waste Cons., Inc., Overland Park, Kansas, 1990-93, dir. indsl. hygiene U.S. Army Corps Engrs., Kansas City, 1993; regional program mgr. environ. & safety region FAA, Kansas City, 1993—; asst. dir. safety office U. Kans. Med. Ctr., 1978-79; adj. prof. continuing edn. divsn. U. Kans.; adj. lectr. Ctrl. Mo. State U. Summer talent fellow Kaw Valley Heart Assn., 1961. Mem. AAAS, Am. Indsl. Hygiene Assn. (sec.-treas. Mid-Am. sect. 1978-79, bd. dirs. 1981, mem. auditcom.), Am. Chem. Soc., Am. Conf. Govt. Indsl. Hygienists (mem. chem. agts. threshold limit value com.), Am. Acad. Indsl. Hygiene, Air and Waste Mgmt. Assn., Environ. Audit Roundtable, N.Y. Acad. Scis., Internat. Soc. Environ. Toxicology and Cancer, Am. Coll. Toxicology, Am. Conf. on Chem. Labeling. Home: 10616 W 123d St Shawnee Mission KS 66213 Office: FAA-ACE 464 OTFO 651 Lou Holland Dr Rm 109 Kansas City MO 64116

MURPHY, MICHELE SUSAN, non-profit agency executive; b. Cleve., Aug. 11, 1949; d. Edward Jerry and Violet Agnes (Lozick) M. BS in Journalism, Ohio U., 1971; M Non-Profit Orgns., Case Western Res. U., 1993. Press rep. Cuyahoga Community Coll. West, Parma, Ohio, 1971-75; pub. info. specialist Cuyahoga Community Coll., Cleve., 1975-76, news bur. mgr., 1976-77, asst. dir. info. svcs., 1977-78, cons., 1979; coord. U.S. Senate Campaign, Cleve., 1981-82; communications liaison Cuyahoga County Bd. Elections, Cleve., 1982-84; exec. dir. Crime Stoppers of Cuyahoga County, Inc., Cleve., 1985-94; founder, dir. West Shore Youth and Family Conflict Resolution Ctr., 1994; cons. in mktg. The City Club, Cleve., 1991. Mem. Leadership Cleve., Greater Cleve. Growth Assn., 1986; editor Rep. News, Cuyahoga County Rep. Orgn., 1983-84. Recipient Appreciation award Greater Cleve. Crime Prevention Com., 1992, Ohio State Chiefs of Police Assn., 1990, Vol. Achievement award CIVAC, Cleve., 1987, Cert. of Appreciation Community Rels. Bd., City of Cleve., 1987, Sports Promotion award Nat. Jr. Coll. Athletic Assn., 1973, 74, 75. Mem. Ohio Mediation Assn., Acad. Family Mediators, Cuyahoga County Police Chiefs Assn. (hon., named Citizen of Yr. 1995).

MURPHY, NANCY L., state legislator; b. Dec. 31, 1929; divorced; children: Michael, Julea, Mark. Mem. Md. Ho. of Dels., from 1982; state senator Md. Senate; mem. Dem. State Cen. Com., 1978-82. Mem. adv. bd. Greater Balt. Med. Ctr. Named Woman of Yr., Bus. and Profl. Women's Club, 1984. Mem. LWV, Md. Assn. Elected Women, Ind. Women's Dem. Club. Methodist. Office: State House Senate Annapolis MD 21401*

MURPHY, PEREGINE LEIGH, clinical researcher, priest; b. Fowler, Calif., Sept. 29, 1954; d. Elbert Thurman Pitcock Jr. and Patricia (Dolan) Olsen. BA in Human Devel., Calif. State U., Hayward, 1979, MS in Clin. Counseling, 1980; MBA, Coll. Notre Dame, Belmont, Calif., 1982; MDiv, Gen. Theol. Sem., 1990. Ordained priest, Episc. Ch., 1991. Parent educator, tchr. Children's Ctr. of Stanford (Calif.) Community, Stanford U., 1980-83; human resource cons. Continental Corp., N.Y.C., 1983-85; v.p. adminstrn. Continental Internat. Life, Continental Corp., N.Y.C., 1985-86; pastoral counselor, chaplain Columbia Presbyn. Med. Ctr., N.Y.C., 1988-89; sr. staff assoc. neuromuscular rsch. N.Y. Neurol. Inst. Columbia Presbyn. Med. Ctr., N.Y.C., 1990—; asst. min. Cathedral Ch. of St. John the Divine, N.Y.C., 1991—; resource cons. in amyotrophic lateral sclerosis N.Y. Neurol. Inst., N.Y.C., 1990—. Contbr. med. articles to profl. jours. Mem. Ctr. for Jewish Christian Rels., Gen. Theol. Sem. Office: NY Neurol Inst 710 W 168th St New York NY 10032-2603

MURPHY, SANDRA ROBISON, lawyer; b. Detroit, July 28, 1949; m. Richard Robin. BA, Northwestern U., 1971; JD, Loyola U., Chgo., 1976. Bar: U.S. Dist. Ct. (no. dist.) Ill. 1976. Assoc. Notz, Craven, Mead, Maloney & Price, Chgo., 1976-78; ptnr. McDermott, Will & Emery, Chgo., 1978—. Mem. ABA (family law sect.), Ill. Bar Assn. (chair sect. family law coun. 1987-88), Chgo. Bar Assn. (chair matrimonial law com. 1985-86), Am. Acad. Matrimonial Lawyers (sec. 1990-91, v.p. 1991-92, pres. Ill. chpt. 1992-93, pres.-elect. 1994-95), Legal Club Chgo.

MURPHY, SHARON MARGARET, university official, educator; b. Milw., Aug. 2, 1940; d. Adolph Leonard and Margaret Ann (Hirtz) Feyen; m. James Emmett Murphy, June 28, 1969 (dec. May 1983); children: Shannon Lynn, Erin Ann. BA, Marquette U., 1965; MA, U. Iowa, 1970, PhD, 1973. Cert. K-14 tchr., Iowa. Tchr. elem. and secondary schs., Wis., 1959-69; dir. publs. Kirkwood C.C., Cedar Rapids, Iowa, 1969-71; instr. journalism U. Iowa, Iowa City, 1971-73; asst. prof. U. Wis., Milw., 1973-79; assoc. prof. So. Ill. U., Carbondale, 1979-84; dean/prof. Marquette U., Milw., 1984-94; provost, v.p. acad. affairs, prof. Bradley U., Peoria, Ill., 1994—; pub. rels. dir., editor Worldwide mag., Milw., 1965-68; reporter Milw. Sentinel, 1967; Fulbright sr. lectr. U. Nigeria, Nsukka, 1977-78. Author: Other Voices: Black, Chicano & American Indian Press, 1971; (with Wigal) Screen Experience: An Approach to Film, 1968, (with Murphy) Let My People Know: American Indian Journalism, 1981, (with Schilpp) Great Women of the Press, 1983; editor: (book, with others) International Perspectives on News, 1982. Bd. dirs. Dow Jones Newspaper Fund, N.Y., 1986—. Recipient Medal of Merit, Journalism Edn. Assn., 1976, Amoco Award for Teaching Excellence, 1977, Outstanding Achievement award Greater Milw. YWCA, 1989; named Knight of Golden Quill, Milw. Press Club, 1977; Nat. headliner Women in Communication, Inc., 1985. Mem. Assn. Edn. in Journalism and Mass Comm. (pres. 1986-87), Internat. Comm. Assn., Tempo, Newspaper Assn. Am. Found. (mem. bd. trustees 1993—), Soc. Profl. Journalists, Nat. Press Club. Democrat. Roman Catholic. Office: Bradley U Office of Provost Peoria IL 61625

MURPHY, SHERYL WARREN, rehabilitation nurse, consultant; b. Meadville, Pa., Mar. 6, 1947; d. Russell A. and Mary (McMaster) Courtney; children: Darren, Heidi; stepchildren: Tonya, Brandon. Diploma, Meadville City Hosp., 1970; BSN, SUNY, Albany, 1988. Cert. in nursing adminstrn. and rehab. nursing and case mgmt. Adminstr. Whole Person Home Health Care, Inc., Erie, Pa.; dir. Pvt. Duty Care, Inc., Erie; med. svcs. cons. Crawford & Co. Health and Rehab. Svcs., Erie; mgr., owner Med. Case Mgmt., Greenville, Pa. Recipient Florence Nightingale and med. awards.

MURPHY, S(USAN) (JANE MURPHY), small business owner; b. Williamsport, Pa., Dec. 26, 1950; d. Jack W. and Edythe J. (Grier) M.; m. Michael J. Sanchez, Dec. 30, 1979. BBA, Pa. State U., 1978. Gen. mgr. Murphy Swift Homes, Hummelstown, Pa., 1970-75; owner, operator Murphy's Home Ctr., Hummelstown, 1975-79, 85-91; mgr. Builder's Emporium, San Diego, 1979-80; entrepreneur Castle in the Sand, San Diego, 1980-83; adminstr. Sohio Constrn., Prudhoe Bay, Alaska, 1983-85; fin. systems analyst Blue Shield, San Francisco, 1991-93; entrepreneur Pacific Bay Svcs., San Francisco, 1993—; owner, operator Murphy's Home Ctr., Hummelstown, Pa., 1994—; cons. in field; dealer Servistar Home Ctrs. Photographs displayed at San Diego Art Inst. Vol. Hershey (Pa.) Free Ch. Donald MacIntyre scholar, 1979, Class of 1920 scholar, 1979, Congressman Kunkel scholar, 1979. Mem. Pa. Hardware Assn., Hummelstown C. of C., Better Bus. Bur. Evangelical Christian. Office: Murphy's Home Ctr Hummelstown PA 17036

MURPHY, SUSAN FULTONBERG, accountant; b. Hartford, Conn., Feb. 23, 1960; d. Donald N. and Arlene (Stahl) Fultonberg; m. Raymond J. Murphy, Aug. 30, 1986; 1 child, William. BS, Pa. State U., 1982. CPA, N.Y. Sr. auditor Ernst & Young (formerly Ernst & Whinney), N.Y.C., 1982-86; computer cons., N.Y.C., 1986-87; mgr. fin. and acctg. Triborough Bridge and Tunnel Authority, N.Y.C., 1987-88, dir. fin. ops., 1988—. Mem. Govt. Fin. Officers Assn., Inst. Mgmt. Accts., Women in Transp. Home: 6050 Boulevard E Apt 12F West New York NJ 07093

MURPHY, SUSAN LYNN JAYCOX, construction executive; b. Bay Shore, N.Y., Aug. 26, 1961. BS, U. Ala., 1984; MBA, Dowling Coll., 1987. Program adminstr. Eaton Corp. Ail Div., Deer Park, N.Y., 1984-87; mgr.

sales adminstrn. Orion Pictures Corp., N.Y.C., 1987-89; pres. Constrn. Materials Testing, Inc., Bethpage, N.Y., 1989—. Mem. ASTM, Am. Soc. Quality Control, Am. Concrete Inst., Delta Mu Delta. Mem. Christian Ch. Home: 30 Oakwood St Blue Point NY 11715-1127 Office: Constrn Materials Testing Inc PO Box 355 Bethpage NY 11714-0355

MURPHY-BARSTOW, HOLLY ANN, financial consultant; b. St. Joseph, Mo., Jan. 16, 1960; d. Roy Edward and Kathryn Louise (Bachle) Murphy; m. Bruce William Barstow, Oct. 1, 1983; children: Brett Murphy, Taylor Lin. Student, U. Mo., 1978-79; BS, N.W. Mo. State U., 1981. Acct. exec. S.C. Johnson, Omaha, Nebr., 1982-83; dir. mktg. YMCA, Omaha, Nebr., 1983-85; fin. cons. Merrill Lynch, Omaha, Nebr., 1985-89, Smith Barney, Omaha, Nebr., 1989—; instr. fin. semin. Creighton U., Omaha, 1993—, Dana Coll., Blair, Nebr., 1993—; fin. corres. KMTV-3, Omaha, 1993—. Pres. Am. Lung Assn. Nebr., Omaha, 1992—; vice chair bd. trustees First Presbyn. Ch., Omaha, 1989—; membership chair bd. mgrs. West YMCA, Omaha, 1991—; mem. Columbian Sch. PTA; campaign chair Toys for Tots, 1994. Mem. Omaha Panhellenic Assn., Leadership Omaha (grad.), River City Roundup (trail boss 1989), Sigma Sigma Sigma. Office: Smith Barney 9394 W Dodge Rd # 250 Omaha NE 68114-3319

MURRAY, ABBY DARLINGTON BOYD, psychiatric clinical specialist, educator; b. Johnstown, Pa., Mar. 1, 1928; d. Frank Reynolds and Marion Gasson (Allen) Boyd; m. Joseph Christopher Murray, Sept. 16, 1950; children: Anne, Joseph Jr., Mary, John, James. BSN, Georgetown U., 1950; MS Edn. in Guidance and Counseling, L.I. Univ., Brookville, N.Y., 1976; MEd Psychiat. Clin. Specialist, Columbia U., 1977; postgrad., Ctr. for Family Learning, New Rochelle, N.Y., 1981-82. Sch. nurse Huntington (N.Y.) Pub. Schs.; with VA Med. Ctr., Northport, Va., 1973-76; prof. U. Md., Balt., 1978-79, L.I. Univ., Brookville, 1979-81; psychiat. clin. specialist VA Med. Ctr., Brooklyn, Va., 1984-87, East Orange, N.J., 1987-89; nurse educator Ft. Monmouth, N.J., 1989—; family therapist Family & Community Counseling Agy., Red Bank, N.J., 1989-91; program planner Ft. Monmouth. Mem. ANA. Republican. Roman Catholic. Home: 91 Tanyard Ln Huntington NY 11743-2421 Office: Fort Monmouth Fort Monmouth NJ 07703

MURRAY, AGNES ELIZABETH, psychologist; b. N.Y.C.; d. Joseph T. and Agnes E. (Higgins) Flynn; m. Thomas C. Murray (dec. Apr. 1991). BA, Fordham U., 1976, MS, 1979, PhD, 1982. Lic. psychologist, N.Y.; cert. sch. psychologist. Pvt. practice Yonkers, N.Y., 1983-91, Bronxville, N.Y., 1991—. Fellow Inst. Rational-Emotive Therapy. Office: 1180 Midland Ave Bronxville NY 10708

MURRAY, ANNE, singer; b. Springhill, N.S., Can., June 20, 1945; d. Carson and Marion (Burke) M.; m. William M. Langstroth, June 20, 1975; children: William Stewart, Dawn Joanne. B.Phys. Edn., U. N.B., 1966, D.Litt. (hon.), 1978; D.Litt. (hon.), St. Mary's U., 1982. Rec. artist for, Arc Records, Can., 1968, Capitol Records, 1969—; appeared on series of TV spls., CBC, 1970-81, 88-93; star CBS spls., 1981-85; toured N. Am., Japan, England, Germany, Holland, Ireland, Sweden, Australia and New Zealand, 1977-82; released 31 albums including: A Little Good News, 1984, As I Am, 1988, Greatest Hits, vols. I, 1981, vol. II, 1989, Harmony, 1987, You Will, 1990, Yes I Do, 1991, Croonin', 1993, others. Hon. chmn. Can. Save the Children Fund, 1978-80. Recipient Juno awards as Can.'s top female vocalist, 1970-81; Can.'s Top Country Female Vocalist, 1970-86; Grammy award as top female vocalist-country, 1974; Grammy award as top female vocalist-pop, 1978; Grammy award as top female vocalist-country, 1980, 83; Country Music Assn. awards, 1983-84; named Female Rec. Artist of Decade, Can. Rec. Industry Assn., 1980, Top Female Vocalist 1970-86; star inserted in Hollywood Walkway of Stars, 1980; Country Music Hall of Fame Nashville; decorated companion Order of Can.; inducted Juno Hall of Fame, 1993. Mem. AFTRA, Assn. Canadian TV and Radio Artists, Am. Fedn. Musicians. Office: Balmur Ltd, 4950 Yonge St Madison Ctr 2400, Toronto, ON Canada M2N 6K1

MURRAY, BARBARA ANN, banker; b. Mitchell, S.D., Apr. 17, 1953; d. John Richard and Shirley Ann (Larson) McNary; m. Wayne Allan Murray, Jan. 25, 1975; children: Corissa Ann, Rebecca Lea, Jeffrey Wayne, Katie Aileen. BS in Edn., Dakota State Coll., 1975. Substitute tchr. Sioux Falls Pub. Schs., S.D., 1975; assoc. Murray Constrn., Sioux Falls, 1975-82; telephone rep. Citibank S.D. NA, Sioux Falls, 1982-83, sr. svc. rep., 1983-84, unit mgr. customer svc., 1984-88, unit mgr. image processing, 1988-89, mgr. corr. svcs., 1989-90, unit mgr., chargeback specialist, 1990-91, unit mgr. cardmem. acctg., 1991-92, unit mgr. nat. accounts payable, 1992-94, mem. gen. ledger implementation mgmt. team, 1994—; owner-operator Hartford Café & Catering, 1994—. Supr. Sunday sch., 1988—, confirmation tchr., 1992-94; mem. bd. edn. First Luth. Ch. Mem. Nat. Assn. Female Execs. Democrat. Lutheran. Clubs: Mothers (pres. 1977-78), Christian Women's (prayer adviser 1980-82). Lodge: Order Eastern Star. Avocations: sewing, camping, hiking, sports. Home: Country Villa Estates 46466 267th St Hartford SD 57033-6917

MURRAY, CHERRY ANN, physicist, researcher; b. Ft. Riley, Kans., Feb. 6, 1952; d. John Lewis and Cherry Mary (Roberts) M.; m. Dirk Joachim Muehlner, Feb. 18, 1977; children: James Joachim, Sara Hester. BS in Physics, MIT, 1973, PhD in Physics, 1978. Rsch. asst. physics dept. MIT, Cambridge, 1969-78; rsch. assoc. Bell Labs., Murray Hill, N.J., 1976-77; mem. tech. staff AT&T Bell Labs., Murray Hill, 1978-85, disting. mem. tech. staff, 1985-87, dept. head low-temperature and solid-state physics rsch., 1987-90, dept. head condensed matter physics rsch., 1990-93, dept. head semicond. physics rsch., 1993—; co-chair Gordon Rsch., Wolfeboro, N.H., 1982, chair, 1984. Contbr. numerous articles to profl. jours. and chpts. to books. NSF fellow, 1969; IBM fellow MIT, 1974-76. Fellow Am. Phys. Soc. (Maria Goeppart-Mayer award 1989), Sigma Xi. Office: AT&T Bell Labs Rm 1D 334 600 Mountain Ave Box 636 New Providence NJ 07974-0636

MURRAY, COLETTE MORGAN, fundraising executive, consultant; b. San Francisco, July 28, 1935; d. Thomas Ralph and Althea L. (Bail) Morgan; m. J. Roger Samuelsen, Sept. 14, 1959 (div. 1969); 1 child, Thea S. Kano; m. Richard Arlan Murray, Nov. 4, 1983. AB, U. Calif., Berkeley, 1959; JD, U. San Francisco, 1964; cert. in mgmt., U. Calif., Davis, 1975, U. Tex., 1989. Cert. fund raising exec. Pvt. practice law Walnut Creek, Calif., 1965-73; exec. dir. Calif. Alumni Assn., Berkeley, 1973-78; asst. chancellor univ. rels. U. Calif., Santa Cruz, 1978-85; v.p. for devel. and alumni U. Louisville, Ky., 1985-88; v.p. for devel. and univ. rels. Tex. Tech. U., Lubbock, 1988-90; corp. v.p. for philanthropy and community devel. Henry Ford Health System, Detroit, 1990—; cons. Coun. for the Advancement and Support of Edn., Washington, 1980—, NSFRE, Washington, 1992-93; bd. mem. Leadership Detroit, Mich., 1992—; pres. Leadership Am. Assn., Washington, 1993-94. Mem. bd. CATCH, Detroit, 1990—. Recipient Dorothy Shaw award Alpha Delta Pi, 1958; named Citizen of Yr., Santa Cruz C. of C., 1981. Mem. NSFRE (pres. 1994), Coun. for the Advancement and Support of Edn. (past chair bd. 1981-82, Hesburgh award 1984), Detroit Athletic Club, Detroit Golf Club. Office: Henry Ford Health System Office of Philanthropy One Ford Pl Detroit MI 48202

MURRAY, CONNIE ANN, artist; b. Grand Junction, Colo., Oct. 1, 1949; d. Otis Wendell and Berniece Anna (Armstrong) Murray; m. John Harold VanGorder; children: Carl Franklin, William John, Chelsie Anne. BFA, Colo. State U., 1971. Consignment artist Imagists Gallery, Ft. Collins, Colo., 1989-91, One West Contemporary Art Ctr., Ft. Collins, 1990—; The Russell Gallery, Denver, 1994—; artist/demonstrator watercolor demonstration Loveland (Colo.) Mus., 1993. Exhibited in group shows at YWCA Gallery, Denver, 1987, Arvada (Colo.) Ctr. for the Arts, 1984, Nat. Watercolor Soc. 70th Ann. Exhbn. Muckenthaler Cultural Ctr., Fullerton, Calif., 1990, Corp. Woods, Overland Park, Kans., 1991, Ariz. Aqueous Traveling Exhbn., Tubac, 1990, Foothills Art Ctr., Golden, Colo., 1983, 85, 86, 87, 89, 93, One West Art Ctr., Ft. Collins, Colo., 1993; in corp. collections Yellow Freight Sys., Inc., Overland Park, Kans., Murray and Thompson, Atty. at Law, Denver. Chairperson fine arts com. Foothills Unitarian Ch., Ft. Collins, 1992—; mem. com. Power Plant Visual Arts Ctr., Ft. Collins, 1986; mem. jury for exbhn. Ft. Collins Gallery, 1986; watercolor instr. City of Ft. Collins Recreation Dept., 1983-84. Recipient Award of Excellence Ariz. Aqueous Exhbn., Tubac, 1990, Gold Medal award Biennial '88, Loveland Mus., 1988. Mem. Nat. Watercolor Soc., Rocky Mt. Nat. Watermedia Soc. Unitarian Universalist.

MURRAY, DAVINA ANN, financial analyst; b. Sabetha, Kans., Nov. 12, 1951; d. Jim R. and Shirley A. (Ellington) Murphy; m. Brian C. Murray, July 2, 1981; 1 child, Bria Lynne. AS in Bus., Point Park Coll., 1992, BS in Acctg., 1992. With Integra Fin. Corp., Pitts., 1978—, past acctg. clk., 1978-79, adminstrv. asst., 1980-86, fin. analyst, 1986—. Mem. com. Pitts. City Sch. Redistricting, 1993. Mem. Internat. Mgmt. Accts., Alpha Sigma Lambda. Office: Integra Fin Corp 4th and Wood St Pittsburgh PA 15278-0001

MURRAY, DEBRA DIANE, new home sales consultant; b. Lawton, Okla., Oct. 9, 1956; d. Jackie Hugh McClung and Edna Mae (Sharp) Fultz; m. Charles Ray Applewhite, Oct. 1979 (div. 1987); children: Aaron Charles, Ashley Diane; m. William Ronald Murray, Aug. 2, 1989. Owner retail bus. South Padre Island, Tex., 1978-85; real estate salesman Preston Real Estate, Dallas, 1985, Abio & Adleta, Dallas, 1986; project mgr. Suburban Am. Homes, Dallas, 1987-88; new home sales cons. Winchester Homes, Clifton, Va., 1989, E.R. Carr & Assocs., Alexandria, Va., 1989-92, Carrhomes, Inc., Annandale, Va., 1993—. Recipient Gold award Nat. Assn. Home Builders, 1990, Platinum award, 1991, 92, 93. Office: Carrhomes Inc 7535 Little River Tpke Annandale VA 22003-2937

MURRAY, DIANE ELIZABETH, librarian; b. Detroit, Oct. 15, 1942; d. Gordon Lisle and Dorothy Anne (Steketee) LaBoueff; m. Donald Edgar Murray, Apr. 22, 1968. AB, Hope Coll., 1964; MLS, Western Mich. U., 1968; MM, Aquinas Coll., 1982; postgrad., Mich. State U., East Lansing, 1964-66. Catalog libr., asst. head acquisitions sect. Mich. State U. Librs., East Lansing, 1968-77; libr. tech. and automated svcs. Hope Coll., Holland, Mich., 1977-88; dir. librs. DePauw U., Greencastle, Ind., 1988-91; acquisitions libr. Grand Valley State U., Allendale, Mich., 1991—; sec., vice chair, chairperson bd. trustees Mich. Libr. Consortium, Lansing, 1981-85. Vice pres. Humane Soc. of Putnam County, Greencastle, 1990-91. Mem. ALA. Methodist. Office: Grand Valley State U Zumberge Libr Allendale MI 49401

MURRAY, ELEANOR F., educator, freelance writer; b. Omaha, Nov. 30, 1916; d. Fred Blatchford and Calista June (Reynolds) Greusel; m. Jack Earl Buckley, June 15, 1970 (dec. Nov. 1977); m. Hubert Larkin Murray; children: Thomas M. B. Hicks, Mary E. Sharp, Barbara R. Wilke. BS in Edn., U. Nebr., 1939. Cert. tchr. of English. Newswriter Etowah Observer, Alabama City, Ala., 1939-40; feature writer Stars 'n Stripes, Tokyo, 1947-51; columnist Japan Times, Tokyo, 1949-51; in pub. relations Am. Internat. Underwriters, Tokyo, 1948-51; writer news and features Paterson (N.J.) Evening News, 1952-54; tchr. Riverdale (N.J.) Sch., 1954-55, Panama Canal Zone Schs., 1955-60, Skokie (Ill.) Schs., 1961-66; freelance writer Sebring, Fla., 1980—. Author: (non-fiction) Bend Like the Bamboo, 1982, Growing Up In Aunt Molly's Omaha, 1990; (poetry) Cherokee County Summer, 1981, God's Green Valley, 1983; author articles. Democrat. Presbyterian. Home: 1418 NE Lakview Dr Sebring FL 33870

MURRAY, ELLEN ROSANNE, artist, educator; b. Raleigh, N.C., June 19, 1947; d. William Don and Sarah Wilson (Elliott) M.; m. Lonnie Dean Meissinger, Jan. 10, 1975; children: Logan Don, Jordan Daniel. BFA, U. N.C., Greensboro, 1969, MFA, 1971. Prof. art Okla. State U., Stillwater, 1971-86, Ariz. State U., Tempe, 1986—; vis. artist U. North Tex., Denton, 1992, Arrowmont Sch. Arts and Crafts, Gatlinburg, Tenn., 1991, 93, 94. Exhibited works at Nat. Watercolor Soc. Ariz. Invitational, 1991, Watercolor Now III, 1991, Watercolor Now IV, 1993, others. Mid-Am. Arts Alliance travelling exhbn. grantee, 1987. Mem. Watercolor USA Honor Soc. (pres. 1993-95, bd. dirs. 1987-90), Nat. Watercolor Soc. Office: Ariz State U Sch Art Tempe AZ 85287-1505

MURRAY, FLORENCE KERINS, state supreme court justice; b. Newport, R.I., Oct. 21, 1916; d. John X. and Florence (MacDonald) Kerins; m. Paul F. Murray, Oct. 21, 1943; 1 child, Paul F. AB, Syracuse U., 1938; LLB, Boston U., 1942; EdD, R.I. Coll. Edn., 1956; grad., Nat. Coll. State Trial Judges, 1966; LLD (hon.), Bryant Coll., 1956, U. R.I., 1963, Mt. St. Joseph Coll., 1972, Providence Coll., 1974, Roger Williams Coll., 1976, Salve Regina Coll., 1977, Johnson and Wales Coll., 1977, Suffolk U., 1981. Bar: Mass. 1942, R.I. 1947, U.S. Dist. Ct. 1948, U.S. Tax Ct. 1948, U.S. Supreme Ct. 1948. Sole practice Newport, 1947-52; mem. firm Murray & Murray, Newport, 1952-56; assoc. judge R.I. Superior Ct., 1956-78; presiding justice Superior Ct. R.I., 1978-79; assoc. justice R.I. Supreme Ct., 1979—; staff, faculty adv. Nat. Jud. Coll., Reno, Nev., 1971-72, dir., 1975-77, chmn., 1979-87, chair emeritus, 1990—; mem. com. Legal Edn. and Practice and Economy of New Eng., 1975—; former instr. Prudence Island Sch.; legal adv. R.I. Girl Scouts; sec. Commn. Jud. Tenure and Discipline, 1975-79; apptd. by Pres. Clinton to bd. dirs. State Justice Inst., 1994—; participant, leader various legal seminars. Mem. R.I. Senate, 1948-56; chmn. spl. legis. com.; mem. Newport Sch. Com., 1948-57, chmn., 1951-57; mem. Gov.'s Jud. Coun., 1950-60, White House Conf. Youth and Children, 1950, Ann. Essay Commn., 1952, Nat. Def. Adv. Com. on Women in Service, 1952-58, Gov.'s Adv. Com. Mental Health, 1954, R.I. Alcoholic Adv. Com., 1955-58, R.I. Com. Youth and Children, Gov.'s Adv. Com. on Revision Election Laws, Gov.'s Adv. Com. Social Welfare, Army Adv. Com. for 1st Army Area; mem. civil and polit. rights com. Pres.'s Commn. on Status of Women, 1960-63; mem. R.I. Com. Humanities, 1972—, chmn., 1972-77; mem. Family Ct. Study Com., R.I. com. Nat. Endowment Humanities; bd. dirs. Newport YMCA; sec. Bd. Physicians Service; bd. visitors Law Sch., Boston U.; bd. dirs. NCCJ; mem. edn. policy and devel. com. Roger Williams Jr. Coll.; trustee Syracuse U.; pres. Newport Girls Club, 1974-75, R.I. Supreme Ct. Hist. Soc., 1988—; chair Supreme Ct. Mandatory Continuing Legal Edn. Com., 1993—. Served to lt. col. WAC, World War II. Decorated Legion of Merit; recipient Arents Alumni award Syracuse U., 1956, Carroll award R.I. Inst. Instn., 1956, Brotherhood award NCCJ, 1983, Herbert Harley award Am. Judicature Soc., 1988, Melvin Eggers Sr. Alumni award Syracuse U., 1992, Merit award R.I. Bar Assn., 1994; named Judge of Yr. Nat. Assn. Women Judges, 1984, Outstanding Woman, Bus. and Profl. Women, 1972, Citizen of Yr. R.I. Trial Lawyers Assn.; Newport courthouse renamed in her honor, 1990. Mem. ABA (chmn. credentials com. nat. conf. state trial judges 1971-73, chair judges adv. com. on standing com. on ethics and profl. responsibility 1991—, joint com. on jud. discipline of standing com. on profl. discipline 1991-94), AAUW (chmn. state edn. com. 1954-56), Am. Arbitration Assn., Nat. Trial Judges Conf. (state chmn. membership com., sec. exec. com.), New Eng. Trial Judges Conf. (com. chmn. 1967), Boston U. Alumni Coun., Am. Legion (judge adv. post 7, mem. nat. exec. com.), Bus. and Profl. Women's Club (past state v.p., past pres. Newport chpt., past pres. Nat. legis. com.), Auota Club (past gov. internat., past pres. Newport chpt.), Alpha Omega, Kappa Beta Pi. Office: RI Supreme Ct 250 Benefit St Providence RI 02903

MURRAY, JEANNE See STAPLETON, JEAN

MURRAY, JEANNE EVELYN, insurance executive; b. Phoenix, Dec. 20, 1932; d. Thomas Lott and Bernice O. (Lockhart) Pettus; m. Richard C. Murray, May 2, 1952; children: Donn R., Susan Murray Hopkins. Student, Lamson Bus. Coll., Phoenix, 1950-52, Phoenix Jr. Coll., 1953-54, Scottsdale Community Coll., Ri, Phoenix, 1954. Sec. E. R. Livermore Adjustment Co., Phoenix, 1952-54, Allstate Ins. Co., Phoenix, 1954-56, State Farm Ins., Phoenix, 1956-60; claim adjuster, investigator, pvt. investigator Panarello Adjustment Co., Scottsdale, 1966-88; ins. exec. Farmers Ins. Group, Scottsdale, 1991-93; claim examiner Insurtx, Scottsdale, 1993—. Fundraiser Am. Cancer Soc., Phoenix, 1975-90, Am. Heart Assn., 1975—; vol. in reading program Scottsdale Pub. Schs. Mem. Ariz. Ins. Claims Assn., Ariz. Pvt. Investigation Assn., U.S. Tennis Assn., Amateur Athletic Assn., Scottsdale Racquet Club. Republican. Methodist. Home: 8407 E Monterey Way Scottsdale AZ 85251-5923 Office: Insurtx Scottsdale AZ 85257-3777

MURRAY, JOAN BROOKS, sorority house director; b. St. Ignatius, Mont., Aug. 19, 1933; d. A.C. and Avice Katherine (Smock) Brooks; children: Marsha, Mary Katherine, Scott. BA in Journalism, U. Mont., 1955. Various positions U. of Mont., 1955-57; asst. to assoc. dean of students Maurine Clow, 1958-59; legis. bill writing staff Dept. of Instrn., Helena, 1961; legal sec., bookkeeper, 1961-65; reporter The Daily Inter Lake, 1967-69, 78-80, news editor; house dir. Delta Gamma, U. Wash., 1992—. First woman chair bd. trustees Sch. Dist. 5-Flathead High Sch. Bd., Kalispell, mem. com. to hire supt., chair of com. to develop pers. policies for dist., chair labor negotiations, chair of com. to establish sabbatical leave policies; leader numerous advs. bds.; bd. dirs. Flathead County Libr. Bd.; bd. deacons First Presybn. Ch., clk. of session, chair of deacons, elder, past chair centennial com.; Flathead County precinct committeewoman; newsletter editor Flathead County Rep. Women's Club; PTA leader, rm. mother, others. Mem. AAUW (Mont. divsn. bd., state bull. editor, Kalispell br. pres., others); Beta Sigma Phi (Lady of Yr. 1980). Home: 2012 NE 45th Seattle WA 98105

MURRAY, JULIA KAORU (MRS. JOSEPH E. MURRAY), occupational therapist; b. Wahiawa, Oahu, Hawaii, 1934; d. Gijun and Edna Tsuruko (Taba) Funakoshi; m. Joseph Edward Murray, 1961; children: Michael, Susan, Leslie. BA, U. Hawaii, 1956; cert. occupational therapy U. Puget Sound, 1958. Therapist, Inst. Logopedics, Wichita, Kans., 1958; sr. therapist Hawaii State Hosp., Kaneohe, 1959; part-time therapist Centre County Ctr. for Crippled Children and Adults, State College, Pa., 1963; vice chmn. adv. bd. Hosp. Improvement Program, East Oreg. State Hosp., Pendleton, 1974; v.p. Ind. Living, Inc., 1976-79; job search instr.; mem. adv. com. Oreg. Ednl. Coordinating Commn., 1979-82; mem. Oreg. Bd. Engring. Examiners, 1979-87; supr., occupational therapist Fairview Tng. Ctr., Salem, Oreg., 1984-94; occupational therapist U.S. Naval Hosp., Okinawa, Japan, 1994—. Rep. from Umatilla County Commrs. to Blue Mountain Econ. Devel. Council, 1976-78; mem. Ashland Park and Recreation Bd., 1972-73; vice chmn. adv. bd. LINC, 1978; mem. exec. bd. Liberty-Boone Neighborhood Assn., 1979-83. Mem. Am. Occupational Therapy Assn., Oreg. Occupational Therapy Assn., Hawaii Occupational Therapy Assn. (sec. 1960) Occupational Therapy Assn., LWV (bd. dirs. Pendleton 1974, 77-78, pres. 1975-77; bd. dirs. Oreg. 1979-81, Ashland 1967-71, v.p. 1970). Office: Medically Related Svcs US Naval Hosp Okinawa Japan PSC 482 FPO AP 96362-1600

MURRAY, KIM MARIE, editor, pharmacist; b. Seattle, May 5, 1961; d. Jack Lloyd and Barbara Jean (Prospek) M. BS in Pharmacy, U. Wash., 1984, PharmD, 1986. Registered pharmacist. Resident in pharmacy Harborview Med. Ctr., Seattle, 1984-86; clin. asst. prof. coll. pharmacy U. S.C., Columbia, 1986-94, adjunct clin. asst. prof. sch. medicine, 1987-94; pharmacist, staff devel. Richland Meml. Hosp., Columbia, 1994; sr. editor Gold Std. Multimedia, Inc., Gainesville, Fla., 1994—. Contbr. articles to profl. jours. Vol. pharmacist Columbia Free Clinic. Mem. Am. Coll. Clin. Pharmacy, Am. Soc. Hosp. Pharmacy, Am. Pharm. Assn., S.C. Soc. Hosp. Pharmacists. Home: 5400 NW 39th Ave J-72 Gainesville FL 32606 Office: Gold Std Multimedia Inc 235 S Main St Gainesville FL 32601

MURRAY, MARY, early childhood and elementary educator; b. Beverly, Mass.; d. Edward James and Anne (Dowd) M. AS in Nursing, Endicott Coll.; AB, Boston Coll., 1985; MSEd in Early Childhood & Elem. Edn., Wheelock Coll., 1993. Cert. tchr., Mass. Tchr. Glen Urquhart Sch., Beverly Farms, Mass., 1982-87, kindergarten asst., 1982-83; kindergarten tchr., 1983-85, first grade tchr., 1985-87; dir. extended day program Glen Urquhart Sch., Beverly Farms, Mass., 1982-85, coord. summer camp program, 1984-86; lower sch. assoc. Shady Hill Sch., Cambridge, Mass., 1987-88; rsch. asst. Wheelock Coll., Boston, 1987-91; tchr. kindergarten, curriculum coord. Prospect Hill Parents' and Childrens' Ctr., Waltham, Mass., 1988-91; substitute tchr. Marblehead (Mass.) Mid. Sch., 1993—; ednl. cons. Beverly Farms, Mass., 1992—; substitute tchr. Shore Country Day Sch., Beverly, Mass., 1992—; founder, dir. Summer Enrichment at Lanesville, Mass., 1987-89; certification cons., adv. bd. Power Industries, Wellesley Hills, Mass., 1989—; cons. Activities Club, Inc., Waltham, 1989-91, NSA, Inc., Woburn, Mass., 1991-92; mem. Early Childhood Adv. Coun., Medford, Mass., 1990-93; lifeguard supr. West Beach Corp., 1980-86; mem. faculty Summer Compass program Lesley Coll. Grad. Sch., Cambridge, Mass., 1993—; mem. certification team Nat. Assn. Educators Young Children, 1989-91; mem. cert. team Ind. Sch. Assn. Mass., 1983-88; presenter workshops. Author curriculum materials, activity kits for children. Tchr. Confraternity of Christian Doctrine program St. Margaret Parish, Beverly Farms, 1970—, dir., coord., 1989—; synod group leader Archdiocese of Boston, 1987; water safety instr. ARC; coach Christian Youth Orgn. Girls Basketball, St. Joseph Parish, Medford, Mass., 1991-93; active Mass. Spl. Olympics. Wheelock Coll. grad. grantee, 1993. Mem. ASCD, Nat. Assn. Edn. Young Children, New Eng. Assn. Edn. Young Children, Ind. Sch. Assn. Mass., Assn. Childhood Edn. Internat., Young Alumni Club Boston Coll. (program coord. 1988-90), Cath. Alumni Club of Boston, Ste. Chretienne Acad. Alumnae Assn., Wheelock Coll. Alumni Assn. Democrat. Roman Catholic. Home and Office: 650 Hale St Beverly Farms Beverly MA 01915-2117

MURRAY, MARY MCFARLANE, entrepreneur; b. Tulsa, Dec. 28, 1947; d. John Robert Kincaid and Letha Nadine (Robertson) Hansen; m. Richard Walter Berge, Feb. 21, 1965 (div. 1972); children: Renae Marie Gerhardstein, Rachelle Ann Dunne; m. Timothy Winslow Murray, Feb. 14, 1987. Student, Grossmont Coll., 1977, U. Md., Berlin, 1983; AA, Fresno City Coll., 1988; BS, Fresno State U., 1990. Various positions Dept. Motor Vehicles, Sacramento, Calif., 1971-74; various positions acctg. Calif. Bd. Equalization, Sacramento, 1975-79; asst. tax collector, treas. County of Madera, Calif., 1985-87; corp. bookkeeper J&S Corp., Madera, 1991-93, Classic Roasters, Inc., Madera, 1991-93; owner Computer Cons. Ctrl. Calif., Madera, 1993—, Kincaid & Kincaid, 1993—. Served as sgt. U.S. Army, 1980-86. Mem. Madera County Genealogy Soc. (treas. 1990), Taxpayers Assn. of Madera County (pres. 1990), Rebekah Madera Lodge. Home: 53-B Brookdale Dr Merced CA 95348 Office: 2340 W Cleveland # 321 Madera CA 93637-8710

MURRAY, PAMELA ALISON, business executive; b. Phila., Sept. 22, 1955; d. Everett Hickman Jr. and Laura Frances (Lautenbach) M. BA in Math. cum laude, Gettysburg (Pa.) Coll., 1977; MBA in Mktg., Temple U., 1986; postgrad., U. Del., 1978-80. Asst./assoc. systems programmer Burroughs Corp., Paoli, Pa., 1977-79, cost acctg. analyst, gen. acctg. analyst, 1979-80, sr. tech. analyst, 1980-82, mgr. data ctr. tech. support, 1982-83; mgr. software product assurance Unisys Corp./Burroughs Corp., Paoli, Pa., 1983-86; mgr. product assurance Unisys Corp., Devon, Pa., 1986-88; sr. staff engr. Unisys Corp., Blue Bell, Pa., 1988-90, system quality mgr., 1990-91; mgr. quality assurance Unisys Corp., Paoli and Blue Bell, 1991-92; mgr. requirements assurance Unisys Corp., Paoli, 1992-93; mgr. Bus. Excellence Unisys. Corp., Paoli, 1993—; instr. after-jours tng. Burroughs Corp./Unisys, 1983-86; examiner Chmn.'s Total Quality Award, 1992, Pa. Quality Leadership Awards, 1994. Mem. Pa. Quality Leadership Bd. Examiners, 1994; fundraiser Am. Heart Assn., 1987—, Am. Cancer Soc., 1989, March of Dimes, 1987, 89; active Phila. Soc. Preservation Landmarks, Phila. Mus. Art. Recipient Young Alumni Achievement award Gettysburg Coll., 1989, Phila. Alumni Club Silver Plate, 1988, Svc. award, 1989. Mem. Am. Soc. Quality Control, PHila. Area Coun. for Excellence, Gettysburg Coll. Alumni Assn. (chmn. alumni reunion com. 1992-93, treas. 1991-93, chmn. alumni ctr. task force 1990-93, career rep. 1988—), Phila. Alumni Club (pres. 1986-90, v.p. 1984-86), Jr. League Phila. (chmn. cookbook sales com. 1990-92, 92-93), Temple U. Alumni Assn. Republican. Mem. Christian Ch. Home: 404 Danor Ct Wayne PA 19087-1232

MURRAY, PATTY, senator; b. Seattle, Wash., Oct. 11, 1950; d. David L. and Beverly A. (McLaughlin) Johns; m. Robert R. Murray, June 2, 1972; children: Randy P., Sara A. BA, Wash. State U., 1972. Sec. various cos., Seattle, 1972-76; citizen lobbyist various ednl. groups, Seattle, 1983-88; legis. lobbyist Orgn. for Parent Edn., Seattle, 1977-84; instr. Shoreline Community Coll., Seattle, 1984—; mem. Wash. State Senate, Seattle, 1989-92; U.S. senator from Washington, 1993—. Mem. bd. Shoreline Sch., Seattle, 1985-89; mem. steering com. Demonstration for Edn., Seattle, 1987; founder, chmn. Orgn. for Parent Edn., Wash., 1981-85; lst Congl. rep. Wash. Women United, 1983-85. Recipient Recognition of Svc. to Children award Shoreline PTA Coun., 1986, Golden Acorn Svc. award, 1989; Outstanding Svc. award Wash. Women United, 1986, Outstanding Svc. to Pub. Edn. award Citizens Ednl. Ctr. NW, Seattle, 1987. Democrat. Home: PO Box 7191 Arlington VA 22207-0191 Office: US Senate 302 Hart Senate Bldg Washington DC 20510-4704

MURRAY, REBECCA BRAKE, lawyer; b. Kingsport, Tenn., Jan. 31, 1949; d. Joseph Albert and Marie (Stinnett) Brake; m. David W. Murray III, Sept. 18, 1971; children: Allison Marie, David W. IV. BS, cert. in phys. therapy,

U. Mich., 1971; MS in Health Scis., Case Western Res. U., 1978; postgrad., Cleve. State Law Sch., 1981-83; JD, U. Tenn., 1985. Bar: Tenn. 1985, U.S. Dist. Ct. (ea. dist.) Tenn. 1986, U.S. Ct. Appeals (6th cir.) 1988. Instr. phys. therapy full time assisting program Cuyahoga C.C., Cleve., 1974; law clk. Neurenberg Plevin, Cleve., 1983, Kennerly Montgomery & Finley, P.C., Knoxville, Tenn., 1984-85; assoc. Kennerly Montgomery & Finley, P.C., Knoxville, 1985-90, shareholder, 1991—. Editor: (law rev.) Cleve. State Law Sch., 1983. Mem. ABA, Tenn. Bar Assn., Knoxville Bar Assn., Def. Rsch. Inst., Tenn. Def. Lawyers Assn. Office: Kennerly Montgomery & Finley PC 550 Main St Knoxville TN 37902

MURRAY, REBECCA LOIS, academic counselor; b. Caddo, Okla., Aug. 24, 1957; d. Pleaz and Iris Algene (Glendinning) Whisenhunt; 1 child, Jennifer Leigh. BA in Psychology, Southeastern Okla. State U., 1979, M in Behavioral Studies, 1980; EdS in Counseling, U. Ala., 1993. Cert. counselor, Ala. Co-owner Bryan County Star, Caddo, Okla., 1978-80; counselor Southeastern Okla. State U., Durant, 1978-80; counselor, adminstrv. liaison Shadow Mountain Inst., Tulsa, 1981-82; tchr., sponsor Verden (Okla.) Pub. schs., 1982-83; tchr., libr., sponsor Indiahoma (Okla.) Pub. Schs., 1983-85; coord. career planning U. Ala., Birmingham, 1986-88, pro counselor, 1992; counselor, chairperson coms. Greenwood Elem., Bessemer, Ala., 1988—; mem. cirsis mgmt. team Bessemer City Schs., 1989—, chairperson com., 1988—; cons. in field. Bd. dirs. Greenwood Elem. PTSO, 1989—; counselor Greenwood Bapt. Ch., 1990-93. Named Outstanding Young Woman Am., 1987. Mem. ACA, Assn. Multicultural Counseling & Devel., Assn. for Spirtual, Ethical & Religious Values in Counseling, Ala. Counseling Assn., Ala. Sch. Counseling Assn., Ala. Assn. Specialists in Group Work, Ala. Assn. Religious and Value Issues in Counseling, Ala. Assn. Multicultural Counseling & Devel. Baptist. Home: 3412 Hartwood Cir Apt 2 Hoover AL 35216

MURRAY, SONIA YVETTE, newswriter; b. Ft. Ord, Calif., Jan. 23, 1968; d. Oliver Eddie and Mattie (Leggett) M. BA in Print Journalism, Howard U., 1989. Staff writer Intown Extra Atlanta Jour./Constn., 1989-90, staff writer bus., 1990-92, staff writer arts, 1992—. Named Overall Print Journalist by Atlanta Assn. Media Women, 1994; Nev. fellow U. Nev., Reno, 1992. Mem. Alpha Kappa Alpha. Home: 1285 Heatherland Dr Atlanta GA 30331 Office: Atlanta Journal Constitution Entertainment Desk 72 Marietta St NW Atlanta GA 30303

MURRELL, DONNA MARIE, airline company executive; b. Birmingham, Ala., Sept. 19, 1941; d. Dudley Cleo and Louise Christine (Sampson) Adams; m. Francis Boney Jordan, Feb. 2, 1973 (dec. 1977); 1 child, Wendy Michele; m. Norman K. Murrell, Dec. 17, 1988. Student, U. Ala., 1958-60. With Southtrust Bank, Birmingham, 1958-63, United Airlines, 1963—; city mgr. United Airlines, New Orleans, 1977-78; mgr. sales and svc. United Airlines, Birmingham, 1978-86; mgr. sta. ops. United Airlines, 1986-88, gen. mgr., 1988—. Pres. Bon Vivants of Ala., Birmingham, 1973-75; bd. dirs. Nat. Arthritis Found., Birmingham, 1986-87; account mgr. United Way, Birmingham, 1980-81. Republican. Episcopalian. Home: 1512 Parkside Ct Homewood AL 35209 Office: United Airlines Municipal Airport Birmingham AL 35212

MURRELL, ESTELLE C., elementary school educator; b. Warren County, Ky., Feb. 13, 1931; d. James B. and Mary Ellen (Johnson) Clark; m. Allen Leslie Murrell, Mar. 14, 1953; children: Leslie Allen, Lisa Ellen. BS, Western Ky. U., 1956. Cert. elem. tchr., Ky. 5th grade tchr. Bowling Green (Ky.) Ind. Bd. Edn.; 6th grade tchr. Warren County Bd. Edn., Bowling Green; 4th grade tchr. Hardin County Bd. Edn., Elizabethtown, Ky.; 4th, 6th and 7th grades tchr. lang. arts Bowling Green Bd. Edn.; tchr. Draughon's Jr. Coll., Bowling Green, Ky. Named to Leader of Am. Elem. Edn., 1971, 73. Mem. NEA, Ky. Edn. Assn., Bowling Green Edn. Assn. (membership chair), Nat. Coun. Tchrs. of English, Ky. Coun. Tchrs. of English Lang. Arts, Internat. Reading Assn., Ky. Coun. Reading Assn. Home: 1404 Woodhurst St Bowling Green KY 42104-3322

MURRELL, JUDITH ANN, oil service company executive; b. Des Moines, Iowa, Dec. 28, 1940; d. James E. and Shirley (Hardman) Stimson; m. Fred L. Murrell, Nov. 16, 1962 (dec. Oct. 1972). MBA, So. Methodist U., 1980. Investor relations mgr. Dresser Industries, Inc., Dallas, 1975-85; investor relations dir. Lone Star Techs., Inc., Dallas, 1985-87, v.p. corp. relations, 1987—, also treas., 1992—. Mem. Nat. Investor Relations Inst. (bd. dirs. 1982-86, v.p. edn. 1984—, v.p. membership 1985). Republican. Congregationalist. Office: Lone Star Techs Inc 5501 LBJ Freeway Dallas TX 75240

MURRY, FRANCIE ROBERTA, special education educator; b. Waukegan, Ill.. BA, Ctrl. Wash. U., 1980, MEd, 1988; PhD, U. Va., 1991. Cert. tchr., Wash. Spl. edn. tchr. Adna (Wash.) Sch. Dist., 1980-81; itinerant spl. edn. tchr. Ellensburg Sch. Dist., Kittitas, Wash., 1981-85; dist. cons., spl. edn. tchr. Ellensburg (Wash.) Sch. Dist., 1985-86, at-risk project cons./coord., 1987-88; dist. cons., spl. edn. tchr. Yelm (Wash.) Sch. Dist., 1986-87; grad. asst. Commonwealth Ctr. Edn. of Tchrs., Va. Behavior Disorders, Charlottesville, Va., 1988-89; grad. instr. U. Va., Charlottesville, 1990, grad. intern, 1990; asst. prof. U. Wyo., Laramie, 1991-93, U. No. Colo., Greeley, 1993—; adj. instr. Ctrl. Wash. U., Ellensburg, 1987-91; cons. Ellensburg Sch. Dist., 1987, Yelm Sch. Dist., 1989, Hampton (Va.) City Schs., 1989, U. Va., Behavior Disorders Project, 1990, Auburn (Ala.) U., 1991, Niobrara Sch. Dist., 1991, 92, 93; in-svc. presenter; nat. and internat. conf. speaker. Contbr. articles to profl. jours. Mem. North Ctrl. Evaluation Team, Wyoming Indian High Sch., 1992. Grantee N.W. Spl. Edn., 1980, Vocat. Edn. Spl. Project, 1982, Title VI-B, 1982, Wash. Edn. Rsch. Assn., 1988, Wash. Mental Health, 1988, Region 10, Va. Commonwealth Div., 1989; Dean's fellow, Curry Sch. Edn., U. Va., 1990, U. Va. Deptl. fellow, 1989; recipient Outstanding scholarship Assn. Colls. and Schs. Edn. in State Univs. and Land Grant Colls., 1992. Mem. ASCD, Am. Ednl. Rsch. Assn., Coun. for Exceptional Children (Va. chpt. v.p. 1990), Coun. for Exceptional Children with Behavior Disorders (pres., Wyo. rep. 1992, 93), Coun. for Exceptional Children with Devel. Delays, Tchr. Educators of Children with Behavior Disorders (pres. 1992, v.p. 1993), Ea. Ednl. Rsch. Assn., Phi Delta Kappa. Office: 310 McKee Hall U of No Colo Greeley CO 80639

MURTAUGH, NANCY BROWN, volunteer; b. Winchester, Mass., Aug. 4, 1941; d. David Samuel and Edith Elizabeth (Hayes) Brown; m. Rodger Waldo Murtaugh, June 26, 1965; children: Jennifer Jean, Elizabeth Lynn, Thomas Rodger, Michelle Kathleen. BS in Edn., U. Wis., 1963; postgrad., Northwestern U., Chgo., 1964-66. Cert. tchr. N.Y., Ill. Tchr. U.F. Sch. Dist. 1, Katonah, N.Y., 1963-64, Skokie (Ill.) Sch. Dist. 69, 1964-68; sales assoc., asst. mgr. Crawford Corp., Rolling Meadows, Ill., 1992-93. Vice-pres. Bd. Edn. Community Consol. Sch. Dist. 15, Palatine, Ill., 1992-95; pres. Friends of Harper Coll., Palatine, 1991-95; active United Way of Palatine, Inverness and Rolling Meadows, Ill., 1989-91; mem. PTA, Palatine, 1973-95; vol. deputy voter registrar, Cook County, Ill., 1991-95; chmn. Friendship Grove of Harper Coll., 1991-94; trustee Ednl. Found. of Community Consol. Sch. Dist. 15, 1991-95; mem. Am. 2000 Goals com., 1991-95, others. Named Master Sch. Bd. mem. Ill. Assn. Sch. Bds., Springfield, 1993, award of merit Ill. State Bd. Edn., 1993. Mem. AAUW (chmn. Initiative for Ednl. Equity 1990-93, designated named gift honoree Arlington Heights, Ill. br. 1983, pres. 1978-82), LWV. Republican. Presbyterian. Home: 1655 Clover Dr Inverness IL 60067

MUSE, VONCEIL FOWLER (MRS. BERT C. MUSE), school librarian, educator; b. Tyler, Tex., July 12, 1915; d. Dennis Cleveland and Elva Mary (Wallace) Fowler; m. Bert Cromwell Muse, Dec. 28, 1938 (dec. Jan. 1983). B.A., Tex. Coll., 1936; M.S.L.S., U. So. Calif., 1953; postgrad. NDEA seminars (grantee) Tex. Women's U., 1965. Cert. profl. all levels, Tex. Elem. tchr. Jasper (Tex.) Schs., 1936-37, Trinidad (Tex.) Schs., 1937-39; tchr.-librarian Stanton Rural High Sch., Whitehouse, Tex., 1940-46; co-owner, Tyler (Tex.) Tribune, 1946-49; tchr.-librarian Tyler Schs., 1949-52; sch. librarian Dallas Pub. Schs., 1952-78; past dir. Women's Southwest Fed. Credit Union, Dallas, 1975-80; yearbook chmn. Dallas Sch. Librarians, 1976; mem. social com. Dallas Ret. Tchrs., 1979. Founder, Glenview Neighbors Assn., Dallas, 1980; mem. Mental Health Assn. Dallas County, 1978, Community Connection, Dallas, 1983, South Central Dallas Civic Group, 1984; mem. Maria Morgan br. YWCA, Friends Vis. Nurses Assn. (charter Dallas chpt.), Mus. African Am. Life and Culture, Women's Ctr. of Dallas, Dallas Classroom Tchrs. (bldg. rep. 1969-78), Dallas Ret. Tchrs. Assn., Am. Assn. Ret. Persons (Red Bird chpt. bd. dirs. 1984-85), United Tchrs. Tex. State Tchrs. Assn. (life), NEA (life), Tex. Ret. Tchrs. Assn. (life), Tex. Library Assn., ALA, Tex. and Southwestern Cattle Raisers Assn., Mitchell County Hist. Commn., Tex. Coll. Nat. Alumni, (life), Tex. Coll. Alumni Assn. of Dallas, Alpha Kappa Alpha life). Democrat. Mem. Christian Methodist Episcopal Ch. Lodge: Court of Calanthe.

MUSGRAVE, PEGGY BREWER, economics educator; b. Maldon, Essex, Eng., Jan. 3, 1924; came to U.S., 1945, naturalized, 1953; d. Herbert Rogers Everard and Blanche Rebecca (Wedlock) Brewer; m. Bennett Richman, Mar. 20, 1945 (div. 1964); children—Pamela Jane Clyne, Roger Michael Richman, Thomas Russell Richman; m. Richard Abel Musgrave, June 6, 1964. B.A., Am. U., 1960, M.A., 1960; Ph.D., Johns Hopkins U., 1962. Sr. research assoc. Columbia U., N.Y.C., 1962-63; asst. prof. U. Pa., Phila., 1963-65; sr. research assoc., internat. tax program Harvard U. Law Sch., 1965-67; assoc. prof., then prof. Northeastern U., Boston, 1967-79; prof. econs. U. Calif., Santa Cruz, 1979-92, provost Crown Coll., 1986-89; cons. various govt. and pvt. orgns., 1962—. Author: Taxation of Foreign Investment Income, 1963; also numerous articles. Mem. Am. Econ. Assn., Nat. Tax Assn., Internat. Inst. Pub. Fin., Phi Beta Kappa. Home: 760 Western Dr Santa Cruz CA 95060

MUSGRAVE, THEA, composer, conductor; b. Edinburgh, Scotland, May 27, 1928; m. Peter Mark, 1971. Ed., Edinburgh U., Paris Conservatory; Mus.D. (hon.). Composer: (opera) The Abbot of Drimock, 1955, The Decision, 1964-65, The Voice of Ariadne, 1972-73, Mary, Queen of Scots, 1975-77, A Christmas Carol, 1978-79 (first performed Va. Opera Assn., 1979), An Occurrence at Owl Creek Bridge, 1981, Harriet, The Woman Called Moses, 1981-84 (1st performed Va. Opera 1985), Simón Bolívar, (ballet) Beauty and the Beast, 1969, Scorpius, 1972, (symphony and orchestral music) Divertimento, 1957, Obliques, 1958, Perspectives, 1961, Noctures and Arias, 1966, Concerto for orch., 1967, Clarinet Concerto, 1968, Night Music, 1969, Scottish Dance Suite, 1969, Memento Vitae, 1969-70, Horn Concerto, 1971, Viola Concerto, 1973, Orfeo II, 1975, Soliloquy II and III, 1980, From One to Another, 1980, Peripeteia, 1981, The Seasons, 1988, (marimba concerto) Journey through a Japanese Landscape, (bass-clarinet concerto) Autumn Sonata, (chamber and instrumental music) Prelude, 1956, String Quartet, 1958, Colloquy of Piano Sonatas #1 & #12, 1960, Trio for flute, oboe and piano, 1960, Monologue, 1960, Serenade, 1961, Chamber Concerto No. 1, 1962, Chamber Concerto No. 2, 1966, Chamber Concerto No. 3, 1966, Music for horn and piano, 1967, Impromptu No. 1, 1967, Soliloquy I, 1969, Elegy, 1970, Impromptu No. 2, 1970, Space Play, 1974, Orfeo I, 1975, Fanfare, 1982, Pierrot, 1985, Narcissus, 1987, Niobe, 1987, (vocal and choral music) Two Songs, 1951, Four Madrigals, 1953, Six Songs: Two Early English Poems, 1953, A Suite O'Bairnsangs, 1953, Cantata for a Summer's Day, 1954, Song of the Burn, 1954, Five Love Songs, 1955, Four Portraits, 1956, A Song for Christmas, 1958, Triptych, 1959, Sir Patrick Spens, 1961, Make Ye Merry For Him That Is To Come, 1962, Two Christmas Carols in Traditional Style, 1963, John Cook, 1963, Five Ages of Man, 1963-64, Memento Creatoris, 1967, Primavera, 1971, Rorate Coeli, 1973, Monologues of Mary, Queen of Scots, 1977-86, O Caro M'e Il Sonno, 1978, The Last Twilight, 1980, Black Tambourine, 1985, For the Time Being, 1986, Echoes Through Time, 1988, Wild Winter for Viols & Voices, 1993. Office: VA Opera Assn PO Box 2580 Norfolk VA 23501

MUSHIK, CORLISS, state legislator; b. Hillsboro, N.D.; d. Kenneth M. and Edith (McDonald) Dodge; m. William Mushik, 1950; 1 child, Ross Dodge. Student, Coll. of St. Benedict's, 1941-42. Realtor; mem. N.D. State Ho. of Reps., 1971-84; now senator N.D. State Senate. Chmn. N.D. Am. Revolution Bicentennial Com. Mem. LWV, PEO. Democrat. Address: 608 3rd St NW Mandan ND 58554-3025 Office: Senate House State Capitol Bismarck ND 58505*

MUSHINSKY, MARY M., state legislator; b. New Haven; m. Martin J. Waters; children: Martin Waters, Edward Waters. Student, So. Conn. State U., Fla. Atlantic U., Wesleyan U. Mem. Conn. Ho. of Reps., 1985—, asst. majority leader, mem. environ., fin., revenue and bonding com., mem. planning and devel. com. Democrat. Home: 188 S Cherry St Wallingford CT 06492-4016 Office: Conn Senate State Capitol Hartford CT 06106*

MUSICH, PAULA JO, journalist; b. Joliet, Ill., Jan. 4, 1957; d. Frank Joseph and Doris (Pohlers) M. BA in Journalism and Mass Comm., U. Wis., 1979; MS in Pub. Rels., Boston U., 1982. Comm. cons. Energy Rsch. Group, Waltham, Mass., 1982-83; account exec. Nigberg Corp., Framingham, Mass., 1983-84; editor Hyatt Rsch., Andover, Mass., 1985-86; sr. editor IDG Comm., Framingham, 1987; sr. writer Ziff Comm., Medford, 1988-93, sr. editor, 1993—. Office: PC Week 10 Presidents Landing Medford MA 02155

MUSIL, CARYN MCTIGHE, educational administrator, educator; b. Bryn Mawr, Pa., May 20, 1944; d. Desmond John and Mary Lawrence (Wilson) McTighe; m. Robert K. Musil, June 15, 1968; children: Rebecca McTighe, Emily Kirkland. BA in English, Duke U., 1966; MA in English, Northwestern U., 1967, PhD, 1974. Instr. Wright Jr. Coll., Chgo., 1967-68; assoc. prof. La Salle U., Phila., 1971-87; sr. fellow Assn. Am. Colls., Washington, 1991-92; sr. rsch. assoc. Assn. Am. Colls. & Univs., Washington, 1992—; exec. dir. Nat. Women Studies Assn., College Park, Md., 1984-91; vis. prof. George Washington U., Washington, 1991; mem. adv. bd. The Washington Ctr. Multiculturalism in Am. Seminar, Washington, 1994; cons. The Ford Found., N.Y.C., 1992-94, other orgns. Editor: The Courage to Question: Women's Studies and Student Learning, 1992, Students at the Center: Feminist Assessment, 1992. Pres. bd. dirs. Building Blocks: Child Devel. Ctr., Phila., 1975-82; bd. dirs. Cmty. Women's Edn. Project, Phila., 1983-87, Lincoln-Westmoreland Housing Corp., Washington, 1992—, Shaw Cmty. Ministry, Washington, 1994—. NEH Summer Seminar fellow, 1982, Pa. Commonwealth fellow Pa. Com. for Humanities, 1987; named Pa. Woman of Distinction, Pa. Women's Campaign Fund, 1987. Mem. Nat. Coun. Rsch. on Women. Democrat. Home: 8600 Irvington Ave Bethesda MD 20817-3604 Office: Assn Am Colls & Univs 1818 R St NW Washington DC 20006-2201

MUSSELMAN, DONNA MCGEOGH, medical/surgical nurse, nursing educator; b. Washington, Sept. 3, 1954; d. James Edward and A. Marguerite (marett) McGeogh; 1 child, Maureen Lynn. BSN, U. Md., Balt., 1976; MS in Med./Surg. Nursing, Va. Commonwealth U., 1981. Staff nurse St. Mary's Hosp., Richmond, Va., 1976-82; instr. med./surg. nursing Richmond Meml. Hosp. Sch. Nursing, 1981-83, coord. med./surg. nursing, 1983-84; clin. nurse Vis. Nurse Assn. Washington D.C., Rockville, Md., 1987-88, clin. supr., 1988-90, acting unit mgr., 1989; assoc. prof. Howard Community Coll., Columbia, Md., 1990—; nurse cons. local law firm, Richmond, 1985-86; state bd. review instr., Richmond, 1987. Mem. PTA, 1985—, corr. sec., 1992-93. Mem. ANA, Md. Nurses Assn., Sigma Theta Tau (chmn. bylaws com. 1983-85, program com. 1984-85). Home: 4512 Boastfield Ln Olney MD 20832-2068

MUSSELMAN, TRUDI TAYLOR, management executive; b. N.Y.C., June 14, 1947; m. Ronald L. Musselman, Dec. 28, 1983. BS, U. Hartford, 1969. U.S. sales mgr. Courtaulds Fabrics, N.Y.C., 1973-79; div. mgr. Avon Products, Kansas City, Mo., 1980-83, Newark, Del., 1987-91; br. mgr. Adia Pers. Svcs., St. Louis and Lancaster, Pa., 1984-86; pres. Mgmt. Dynamics, Lancaster, 1991—; cons. U.S. and Can., 1991. Author: (manuals) Dynamic Presentations, 1992, Seven Steps to Practically Perfect Presentations, 1993, Service With Style, 1993. Pole watcher Dem. Com., Lancaster, 1992. Mem. ASTD.

MUSSELWHITE, LAURA GILSTRAP, history educator; b. Spartanburg, S.C., Mar. 27, 1967; d. Claud Jerry and Linda Ann (Jenkins) G.; m. Harry Austin Musselwhite, July 13, 1991. BA, Berry Coll., Rome, Ga., 1989; MA, U. Ga., 1991. Asst. in charge of spl. projects Registrar's Office Berry Coll., 1989; cataloguer main libr. U. Ga., Athens, 1990, grad. asst. dept. history, 1989-91; lectr. history Berry Coll., 1991; instr. history Floyd Coll., Rome, 1991—; Coord. Emphasis on Women's History Month, Floyd Coll., 1993; judge History Day U. Ga., 1990. 91; student tchr. West Rome High Sch., 1989; editor Social Sci. Rev., Berry Coll., 1987, 88; mem. search com. polit. sci. position Floyd Coll., extended learning com., acad. progress com., minority enrichment com. Mem. Am. Historical Assn., Ga. Assn. Historians, So. Historical Assn., So. Assn. Women Historians, Phi Alpha Theta. Democrat. Episcopalian. Office: Floyd Coll Us Hwy 27 Rome GA 30162

MUSSER, MARGARET MORRIS, marketing professional; b. N.Y.C., Nov. 1, 1962; d. John Daniel and Jean Bingham (MacCollom) M.; m. Gary E. Musser Jr., May 1, 1993. BA in English, Georgetown U., 1984. Mem. staff mktg. programs AT&T Nat. Fed. Mktg., Arlington, Va., 1985; mktg. tech. cons. AT&T Nat. Fed. Systems, Washington, 1985-87; tech. cons. computer mktg. Cin. Bell Tel. Co., 1987-89, mktg. tech. cons., 1989—; tutor (vol.) Ptnrs. in Edn.; dist. Nutrition for Life Internat., 1995—. Editor: (newsletter) District Action Project RAP, 1981-82. Intern Citizen's Complaint Ctr., Washington, 1981-82. Mem. NAFE, Nat. Network of Women in Sales (pres. Cin. chpt., bd. dirs.), Cin. Updowntowners, Soroptimist Internat., Telephone Pioneers Am. Office: Cin Bell Tel Co 201 E 4th St Rm 102-1180 Cincinnati OH 45202-4122

MUSTARD, MARY CAROLYN, financial executive; b. North Bend, Nebr., Sept. 21, 1948; d. Joseph Louis and Rosalie Margaret (Emanuel) Smaus; m. Ronald L. Mustard, Apr. 19, 1969 (div. 1988); children: Joel Jonathan, Dana Marie. Student, Creighton U., 1966-67, C.E. Sch. Commerce, 1967-68, Coll. of St. Mary, 1983-84, Met. C.C., Omaha, 1988-90, Bellevue U., 1991-92. With Platte County Dept. Pub. Welfare, Columbus, Nebr., 1968-69; sec. to plant mgr. B.L. Montague Steel Co., Sumter, S.C., 1969-70; property disposal technician Property Disposal Office, Shaw AFB, S.C., 1970-71; libr. technician Hdqs. Strategic Air Command Librarian, Offutt AFB, Nebr., 1971-76; sec.-steno Hdqs. Strategic Air Command Communications/Frequency Mgmt., Offutt AFB, Nebr., 1976-79; security specialist/program analyst Hdqs. Strategic Air Command Security Police, Offutt AFB, Nebr., 1979-88; budget analyst Hdqs. Strategic Air Command Fin. Mgmt., Offutt AFB, 1988-92; funds control analyst Hdqs. Air Mobility Command, Scott AFB, Ill., 1992-93, chief hdqs. and comm. account, 1993-94, chief hdqs. relocation assistance transition assistance and, 1994—. Mem. Am. Soc. Mil. Comptrollers (SAC Budget Analyst of Yr. 1990). Democrat. Roman Catholic. Office: AMCFSS/FMBO 402 Scott Dr Unit 1K1 Scott AFB IL 62225-5311

MUSTONE, AMELIA P., state legislator; b. Salem, Mass., July 16, 1928; d. Udo A. and Alberta (Durand) Poppey; m. John J. Mustone, 1950; children: John, Lisa, Mary Ellen, Paul, Anastasia, Jessica. B.A., Goddard Coll., Vt. Pres., Meriden Bd. Edn., Conn., 1974-78; mem. Conn. State Senate from 13th Dist., 1979—, dep. majority leader, 1987—. Mem. Nat. Conf. State Legislators, Council on State Govts., Caucus New Eng. State Legislators, Conn. Women's Polit. Caucus; mem. Martin Luther King Jr. Commn.; active YMCA. Recipient Citizen of Yr. award Civitan Club, 1978, 1st Eleanor Roosevelt award NOW. Mem. AAUW, Meridan LWV, Latin Am. Soc. (hon.), Am. Assn. Retail Persons, NAACP. Roman Catholic. Lodge: Soroptimist Internat. Home: 24 Tunxis Cir Meriden CT 06450-7401*

MUTH, MARCIA, folk artist, educator; b. Ft. Wayne, Ind., Sept. 27, 1919; d. Frank O. Miller and Margaret Althea (Welker) Newland. AB, U. Mich., 1949, MA in LS, 1953. Cert. law libr., Mich., Mo. Law libr. U. Mich., Ann Arbor, 1954-61, U. Mo., Columbia, 1961-66; instr. elderhostel program Coll. of Santa Fe, mem. adv. coun. creative writing dept., 1991-93. Author: How to Paint and Sell Your Art, 1984, Thin Ice, 1987, Sticks and Stones, 1993; solo show at Fine Art Gallery, Coll. Santa Fe, 1992; group shows at Jewish Heritage Ctr., Balt., 1990, Swen Parson Gallery at No. Ill. U. DeKalb, Wright Mus. Art at Beloit (Wis.) Coll., Ea. Ill. U., Charleston, Purdue U., West Lafayette, Ind., The Gov.'s Gallery/Mus. N.Mex., 1994, others; represented in permanent collections Mus. Fine Arts, N.Mex., Jewish Mus., N.Y.C., Mus. Native Art, Paris. Jewish. Home and Studio: 2336 Camino Carlos Rey Santa Fe NM 87505-5209

MUZEKARI, THOMASINE DABBS, educational consultant; b. Columbia, S.C., Dec. 4, 1941; d. Jesse Thomas and Margaret Salina (Scott) Dabbs; m. William Muzekari, May 7, 1966; children: Laura DuRant, William Theodore. Student, U. S.C., 1961-62, EdD, 1994; BA, Columbia Coll., 1983, MEd, 1987. Cert. tchr., S.C. Tchr. Richland One Sch., Columbia, 1983-89; staff devel. cons. Richland One Sch., 1989—; co-chair Dist. Challenger Space Ctr. Curriculum Com., 1994; pvt. cons. specializing in learning styles, integrated curriculum, active learning, 1993—. Writer, producer, narrator televised recert. course for tchrs. Middle School Today, 1991. S.C. Dept. Edn. grantee, 1992—. Mem. S.C. ASCD, S.C. Mid. Sch. Assn., S.C. Assn. Tchr. Educators, S.C. Network Women Adminstrs. in Edn. (regional chairperson 1994-95), Nat. Staff Devel. Coun., S.C. Staff Devel. Coun. (governing com. 1994-95), Alpha Delta Kappa (sgt.-at-arms 1988-90). Republican. Methodist. Office: Richland One 1616 Richland St Columbia SC 29201-2657

MUZYKA-MCGUIRE, AMY, marketing professional, nutrition consultant; b. Chgo., Sept. 24, 1953; d. Basil Bohdan and Amelia (Rand) Muzyka; m. Patrick J. McGuire, June 3, 1977; children: Jonathan, Elizabeth. BS, Iowa State U., 1975, postgrad., 1978—; registered dietitian, St. Louis U., 1980. Cert. dietitian. Home economist Nat. Livestock and Meat Bd., Chgo., 1975-77; dietary cons. various hosps. and nursing homes, Iowa, 1978-79; supr. foodsvc. Am. Egg Bd., Park Ridge, Ill., 1980-83; assoc. dir., mgr. foodsvc. Cole & Weber Advt., Seattle, 1984-85; prin., owner Food and Nutrition Comms., Federal Way, Wash., 1986—. Co-author: Turkey Foodservice Manual, 1987; editor: (newsletter) Home Economists in Business, 1975-77, Dietitians in Business and Industry, 1982-85; contbr. articles to profl. jours. Active Federal Way Women's Network, 1986-87. Named Outstanding Dietitian of Yr. North Suburban Dietetic Assn., 1983. Mem. Am. Dietetic Assn., Internat. Foodsvc. Editorial Coun., Consulting Nutritionists, Vegetarian Nutrition, Home Economists in Bus. Roman Catholic. Home: 5340 315th St Federal Way WA 98023

MUZZILLO, RACHEL EVELYN SHEELEY, reporter; b. Richmond, Ind., Nov. 22, 1966; d. Lysle Leavitt and Alecia Eilene (Hindsley) S. BA, Franklin Coll. of Ind., 1989. Intern, writer weekend dept. Indpls. Star, 1988; intern, writer Brandon (Man., Can.) Sun, 1989; intern, writer Palladium-Item, Richmond, 1986-89, reporter, 1989—. Winner first prize Bulwer-Lytton Fiction Contest, San Jose State U., 1988, 3rd pl. spot news Best Gannett Corp. award. Mem. Women in Communications, Soc. Profl. Journalists, Phi Alpha Theta. Home: 516 Riley Rd New Castle IN 47362 Office: Palladium-Item 1175 N A St Richmond IN 47374-3226

MYATT, SUE HENSHAW, nursing home administrator; b. Little Rock, Aug. 16, 1956; d. Bobby Eugene and Janett Lanell (Ahart) Henshaw; m. Tommy Wayne Myatt; children: James Andrew, Thomas Ryan. BS in Psychology, Old Dominion U., 1978, MS in Ednl. Counseling, 1982. Cert. activity cons. Nat. Cert. Coun. of Activity Profls., gerontol. activity therapy cons., Va. Dir. activity Manning Convalescent, Portsmouth, Va., 1983-84, Camelot Hall, Norfolk, Va., 1984-86; coord. activities Beverly Manor, Portsmouth, 1986-87, Gerogian Manor Assisted Living Facility, 1989-90; dir. activities Huntington Convalescent Ctr., Newsport News, Va., 1990-91; nursing home adminstr.-in-tng. Bayview Healthcare Ctr., Newport News, 1991-92; adminstr. Evangeline of Gates, Gatesville, N.C., 1992—, Mary Washington Health Ctr., Colonial Beach, Va., 1993—; instr. Tidewater Community Coll., 1990. Mem. Nat. Assn. Activity Profl. (cert. legis. com.), Va. Assn. Activity Profl. (v.p. 1986-87, creator logo), Hampton Roads Activity Profls. Assn. (sec. 1985-86, pres. 1986-87, v.p. 1987-88). Home: 219 3d St Colonial Beach VA 22443

MYCKANIUK, MARIA ANNA, elementary and special education educator; b. Denver, July 1, 1955; d. Mykola and Stafania (Iwachiw) M. BA, U. No. Colo., 1977; MEd, The Citadel, 1990. Cert. tchr., S.C., Fla. Tchr. kindergarten, 3rd grade St. Catherine's Sch., Denver, 1977-81; remedial tchr. St. Vincent's Home and Sch., Denver, 1978-80; tchr. kindergarten, coord. day camp La Petite Learning Ctr. and Little People's Landing Ctr., Littleton, Colo., 1982-83; tchr. exceptional children Randall-Moore Accelerated Sch., Denver, 1982-83; tchr. 1st grade Bonner Elem. Sch., Macedonia, S.C., 1983-84; tchr. 2nd grade Westview Elem. Sch. Berkeley County Sch. Dist., Goose Creek, S.C., 1984-90; tchr. primary edn. learning disabled Old Kings Elem. Sch. Flagler County Sch. Dist., Palm Coast, Fla., 1990—; mem. adv. com. spl. edn. dept. The Citadel, Charleston, S.C., 1989-90; ednl. cons. Child Find Study Team, 1990—. Active Nat. Wildlife Fedn., 1980—, Gibbs Art Mus., Charleston, 1987-90; tutor Adult Literacy Program, Charleston, 1988-90; co-

coord. children's program Piccolo/Spoleto Festival, Charleston, 1989; bd. dirs. Palm Coast Taxpayers Assn., 1991—; active Spl. Olympics, Odessey of the Mind. Recipient Critical Need Tchr. award State of Fla., 1990-91. Mem. Coun. for Exceptional Children, Alpha Delta Kappa, Phi Delta Kappa. Home: 8 Prince Michael Ln Palm Coast FL 32137-7154

MYERBERG, MARCIA, investment banker; b. Boston, Mar. 25, 1945; d. George and Evelyn (Lewis) Katz; m. Jonathan Gene Myerberg, June 4, 1967 (div. Mar. 1994); 1 child, Gillian Michelle. BS, U. Wis., 1966. Corp. trust adminstr. Chase Manhattan Bank, N.Y.C., 1966-67; asst. cashier Glore Forgan, Wm. R. Staats, Phoenix, 1967-68; bond portfolio analyst Trust Co. of Ga., Atlanta, 1969-72; asst. v.p. 1st Union Nat. Bank, Charlotte, N.C., 1973-78; dir. cash mgmt. Carolina Power & Light Co., Raleigh, N.C., 1978-79; sr. v.p., treas. Fed Home Loan Mortgage Corp., Washington, 1979-85; dir. Salomon Bros. Inc., N.Y.C., 1985-89; sr. mng. dir. Bear, Stearns & Co. Inc., N.Y.C., 1989-93; mng. dir. Bear, Stearns Home Loans, London, 1989-93; chief exec. Myerberg & Co., L.P., N.Y.C., 1994—. Home: Apt P18A 120 E 87th St New York NY 10128 Office: 780 3d Ave New York NY 10017

MYERS, CATHERINE R., academic administrator; b. East Orange, N.J., Jan. 5, 1934; d. Joseph Brown and Charlotte (Metzger) Rodgers; m. Franklin G. Myers, Aug. 11, 1966; children: K.C., Anna Marie. BA, Bryn Mawr (Pa.) Coll., 1955; MA, Oxford U., 1961; PhD, Brown U., 1963. Grad. asst. Brown U., Providence, 1957-59; instr., then asst. prof. Bryn Mawr Coll., 1959-67; assoc. prof. to prof. Mahattanville Coll., Purchase, N.Y., 1968—, head Dept. English, 1974-77, dean of studies, 1980-81, dean of faculty, 1981-86, provost, 1986-92; cons. NEH, 1972, 83, 84, Ednl. Testing Service, Princeton, N.J., 1964-82; examiner U. Mid-Am., 1976; project dir. Improvement of Post-Secondary Edn., 1991—; reviewer U.S. Dept. Edn., 1991—. Author (books) Time in the Narrative of the Faerie Queen, 1973, Magic Makers, 1978, (study guides) Paradise Lost, 1966, The Canterbury Tales, 1967, The Faerie Queen, 1968; co-author The Heroic Spirit, 1978. Bd. dirs. A Better Chance in Ridgefield, Conn., 1987. Fulbright scholar, 1955-57; fellow Bryn Mawr Coll., 1963, NEH, 1978. Mem. AAUP, MLA, Am. Assn. Higher Edn., Westchester Consortium Internat. Studies (pres.). Office: Manhattanville Coll Founders 2900 Purchase St Purchase NY 10577

MYERS, CONNIE JEAN, real estate professional; b. Portland, Oreg., Mar. 16, 1946; d. Thomas Arthur and Jennie Maifair (Saunders) M. BS, Oreg. State U., 1968. Asst. contr. Builders Resources Corp., San Mateo, Calif., 1971-73; contr. Little & Blackwell, Menlo Park, Calif., 1973-76; v.p. Landsing Property Corp., Menlo Park, 1976-82; v.p. reg. ptnr. Landsing Property Corp., Denver, 1982-85; cons. Denver, 1985; sr. v.p. De Anza Assets, Inc., Beverly Hills, Calif., 1985-87; v.p., dir. of asset mgmt. Holden Real Estate, Inc., L.A., 1987-88; pres. First Capital Ptnrs. (North) Inc., Bellevue, Wash., 1988-92; v.p. First Capital Ptnrs., Kirkland, Wash., 1993—. Author: (procedure manuals) Apartment and Mobilehome Communities, 1986, General Management, Leasing & Marketing, Maintenance & Disaster. Mem. Inst. Real Estate Mgmt. (CPM 1980), Wash State Bd. Real Estate (broker 1989), Wash. State Comml. Assn. of Realtors, Comml. Real Estate Women. Republican. Office: First Capital Ptnrs PO Box 452 Kirkland WA 98083

MYERS, DARLENE MARIE, dance studio owner, choreographer; b. Schenectady, N.Y., July 25, 1950; d. Raymond Charles and Marie (Walsh) M. Grad. high sch., Schenectady, N.Y. Dancer Pa. Ballet Co., Phila., 1968-70; tchr., choreographer Schenectady Civic Ballet, 1970-76, Electronic Body Arts, Albany, N.Y., 1978-79; dir. dance Schenectady Arts Council, 1978-79; ballet mistress, choreographer Saratoga Ballet Co., Saratoga Springs, N.Y., 1980-81; artistic dir. Guilderland (N.Y.) Ballet Workshop, 1980-84; head dance program SUNY, Albany, 1981-85; founder, dir. Myers Studio and Art Gallery, Schenectady, 1985—; adj. prof. arts Union Coll., Schenectady, 1980-84, adj. prof. dance; cons. Proctors Theater, Schenectady, 1985—; dir. Myers Dance Co., Schenectady, 1985—, annual summer dance camp hiring guest tchrs. from. N.Y.C. Ballet; artistic dir. N.E. Ballet Co.; choreographer, producer annual full-length Nutcracker, Schenectady. Contbr. (jour. collection) Ariadne's Thread, 1982; choreographer ann. full-length Nutcrackers and a spring concert of new repetoire. Grantee CETA, 1978, 80, Adirondack Jr. Ballet, 1982, 83. Mem. Albany League of Arts. Office: 1020 Barrett St Schenectady NY 12305-1102

MYERS, DEBORAH BUMBAUGH, government relations executive; b. Harrisonburg, Va., Mar. 8, 1952; d. Martin L. and Isabel (Martin) Bumbaugh; m. Laurent E. Myers, Aug. 28, 1971. BS cum laude in Health Svcs. Adminstrn., U. Cin., 1977; postgrad., Xavier U., 1983. Pers. analyst City of Cin., 1977-81, asst. to city mgr., 1982-84; dep. dir. presdl. vols. U.S. Presdl. Inaugural Com., Washington, 1984-85; co-dir. nat. nosocomial program U.S. HHS, Washington, 1985-86, dep. dir. intergovernmental affairs, 1986-89; govt. rels. mgr. CIBA-GEIGY Corp., Washington, 1989—. Asst. office coord. Reagan/Bush regional office, Cin., 1984; asst. to treasury div. nat. Reagon/Bush campaign, Washington, 1984. Recipient Community Leadership award, 1977, Quality Govt. Svc. award City of Cin., 1980. Mem. Women in Govt. Rels. (co-dir. state affairs com. 1989), Washington Area State Rels. Group, Am. League of Lobbyists, Pharm. Mfrs. Assn. Office: CIBA-GEIGY Corp 1747 Pennsylvania Ave NW Ste 7 Washington DC 20006-4604

MYERS, GLORIA J., elementary education educator; b. Atlantic, Iowa, Feb. 14, 1949; d. Louis E. Sr. and Jean M. (Horacek) M. BA in Elem. Edn., U. No. Iowa, 1971, MA in Spl. Edn., 1978. Cert. tchr., K-14 endorsements in behavioral disorders and mental disabilities, Iowa. Title I remedial reading tchr. Council Bluffs (Iowa) Pub. Schs., 1971-75; K-12 multicategorical resource tchr. Walnut (Iowa) Community Sch., 1975—. Mem. planning com. for annual transition fair for S.W. Iowa, Pottawattamie County, 1987—. Recipient Outstanding Achievement award Loess Hills Area Edn. Agy., 1989, Excellence in Edn. award, 1992. Mem. NEA, Iowa Edn. Assn. (local chpt. pres., v.p., sec., treas.), Walnut Edn. Assn. (pres. local chpt., co-chmn.), Delta Kappa Gamma Soc. Internat. Home: PO Box 301 Walnut IA 51577-0301 Office: PO Box 528 Walnut IA 51577-0528

MYERS, GRETCHEN HARDY GODAR, lawyer; b. Webb City, Mo., Dec. 6, 1958; d. William Claude Jr. and Carlyn (Merryman) M.; m. Daniel Joseph Godar, Oct. 11, 1985. BA with honors, U. Mo., 1981, JD, 1984. Bar: Mo. 1984, U.S. Dist. Ct. (we. dist.) Mo. 1984, Calif. 1985, U.S. Dist. Ct. (ea. dist.) Mo. 1985, Ill. 1986, U.S. Ct. Appeals (8th cir.) 1989. Law clk. to justice U.S. Dist. Ct. Mo., St. Louis, 1984-85; prin. The Hullverson Law Firm, St. Louis, 1985—; moderator, lectr. various orgn. and univ. programs; judge trial practice jury trial Wash. U., 1988-89. Author: A Separate Cause of Action for Contribution Among Joint Tortfeasors, 1983, (with others) Antitrust Textbook, 1982; contbr. articles to legal jours. Named one of Outstanding Young Women of Am. Mem. ABA, ATLA (spkr. seminar), Mo. Bar Assn. (mem. spl. com. alternative dispute resolution, vice chair tort law com., mem. civil rules study com., civil practice com., iss. com. and Supreme Ct. rules study com.), Bar Assn. Met. St. Louis (mem. jud. facilities com.), Mo. Assn. Trial Attys. (exec. com. bd. govs., student div. pres. 1983-84, mem. continuing edn. com., fundraising com. and legis. com., mem. bd. govs. 1988—, exec. com. speaker 1988, 89, 90, 91, spl. mem. 1989, chair pub. rels. com. 1989—, chair membership com. 1990—), Women Lawyers Assn. St. Louis (pres.), Mo. Law Rev., Lawyers Assn. St. Louis., Order of Barristers. Office: The Hullverson Law Firm 1010 Market St Ste 155 Saint Louis MO 63101

MYERS, HELEN PRISCILLA, music educator; b. Palo Alto, Calif., June 5, 1946; d. Henry Alonzo Myers and Elsie (Phillips) Myers-Stainton; children: Ian Alister Woolford Myers, Adam Robert Woolford, Sean Patrick Woolford. MusB, Ithaca Coll., 1967; M in Mus. Edn., Syracuse U., 1971; MA, Ohio State U., 1975; PhD, U. Edinburgh, Scotland, 1984; MPhil, Columbia U., 1993. Cert. instrumental mus. K-12, N.Y. Clarinettist Am. Wind Symphony Orch., Pitts., 1966-67; rsch. fellow Columbia U., N.Y.C., 1973-75, lectr., 1975-76; lectr. Goldsmiths' Coll. U. London, 1981-89; assoc. prof. Trinity Coll., Hartford, Conn., 1989—, St. Anthony Hall prof., 1994—; Ford Found. lectr. ethnomusicology Nat. Ctr. Performing Arts, Bombay, India, 1988; vis. assoc. prof. music Columbia U., N.Y.C., 1993; ethnomusicologist cons. Oxford U. Press, London, 1981-83, The New Grove Dictionary of Music, 7th edit., London, 1993—; resident ethnomusicologist Grove's Dictionaries of Music and Musicians, 1976-89; guest lectr. Guildhall Sch. of Music, London, 1982-89. Author: Felicity, Trinidad: Musical Portrait of a Hindu Village, 1984, (with Bruno Nettl) Folk Music in the United States: An Introduction, 1976; author introductions to facsimile reprints of Alice Cunningham Fletcher's Omaha Indian Music, 1994, Indian Games and Dances, 1994, Native Songs, 1994, others; editor, contbr.: Ethnomusicology: An Introduction, 1992, Ethnomusicology: Historical and Regional Studies, 1993; gen. editor, contbr. South Asia Vol. VI, The Garland Ency. of World Music. Grantee Am. Inst. Indian Studies, 1986-87, 88-89, Brit. Acad., 1988-89, Ford Found., 1988, Am. Philosophical Soc., 1989-90, Wenner-Gren Found. for Anthropological Rsch., 1989-90. Mem. Am. Anthropol. Assn., Am. Musicological Soc., Soc. Ethnomusicology (coun. mem. 1992—), Assn. Asian Studies, Internat. Coun. Traditional Music, Indian Musicological Soc., Sangeet Natak Akademi, Earthwatch, English Folk Dance and Song Soc. (editorial bd. Polk Music Jour.), Phi Kappa Lambda. Home: 207 Old Main St Rocky Hill CT 06067-1505 Office: Trinity Coll Music Dept 300 Summit St Hartford CT 06106-3100 also: Grove Dictionaries, Macmillan Press, 4 Little Essex St, London WC2R 3LF, England

MYERS, IONA RAYMER, real estate and property manager; b. Guymon, Okla., Sept. 18, 1931; m. Harold Rudolph Myers, Mar. 28, 1953; children: Richard Galen, Sandra Dawn, Paula Colleen. BS magna cum laude, So. Nazarene U., 1952; MEd, U. Okla., 1959; postgrad., McNeese State U., 1970. Tchr. home econs. Can. County Pub. Schs., Mustang, Okla., 1952-53; tchr. elem. Oklahoma City Pub. Schs., 1955-61, Transylvania County Pub. Schs., Brevard, N.C., 1961-67; elem. tchr., student tchr. supr. Allen Parish Pub. Schs., Oakdale, La., 1967-71; tchr. elem. and jr. high history Lafourche Parish Pub. Schs., Raceland and Lockport, La., 1974-76; tchr. elem. sci. Jefferson Parish Pub. Schs., Metairie, 1976-80; treas. Harold R. Myers Engring. (divsn. Harold R. Myers, Inc.), Metairie, 1993—; mgr. Harion Properties, L.L.C., Metairie, 1994—; vol. founding bd. dirs. Jefferson Performing Arts Soc., Metairie, 1977-83; vol. founding mem. community adv. coun. East Jefferson Gen. Hosp., Metairie, 1980-87. Vol. scout leader S.E. La. Girl Scouts U.S. coun., Metairie, 1977-89, fund raising com., 1992-93; vol. tchr. music Harold Keller Elem. Sch., Metairie, 1981-83; life mem. Rep. Nat. Com., Washington, 1980-91, mem. fin. com., 1988; jubilee chmn., fundraiser Jefferson Performing Arts Soc., Metairie, 1987; candidate La. Ho. of Reps. Dist. 88, Baton Rouge, 1991. New Orleans Mus. of Art fellow, 1984—, So. Nazarene U. fellow, 1985-94; recipient Rice in the Ear award S.E. La. Girl Scouts U.S., 1982, Great Lady/Great Gentleman award Ladies Aux. East Jefferson Gen. Hosp., 1987, Commendation award Jefferson Performing Arts Soc., 1988, Women as Winners award YWCA New Orleans, 1993. Mem. AAUW (pres. 1988-90, vol. coord. Metairie chpt. 1990-91, del. 4 nat. and 4 regional convs. 1987-94, corr. sec. La. chpt. 1989-91, scholar and grantee 1989, Magnolia editor 1991—, chair nominating com. 1992-93, grant honoree La. 1994), Jefferson Hist. Soc. (life), La. Landmarks Soc. (life), Nat. Assn. Parliamentarians, La. Bus. and Profl. Women (auditor, legis. chmn. 1990-91, rec. sec. 1991-92, membership v.p. 1992-93, pres. Jefferson Parish chpt. 1980-82, 1st v.p. 1993-94, pres.-elect 1994—, program v.p. 1993-94, Vision editor 1993—, Jefferson Parish Voice editor 1993—, Outstanding Dist. Dir. award 1985, Nike award 1991, Highest Mem. honor 1992-93, Best Membership Recruiter 1993-94), Metairie Woman's Club (corr. sec. 1994—). Methodist. Home: 4701 Chastant St Metairie LA 70006-2059

MYERS, JANET LOUISE, management consultant; b. Alliance, Ohio. BS with honors, Kent State U., 1962; MA in Info. Systems, U. Denver, 1968; MBA, Northwestern U., 1974. Comml. banker First Nat. Bank Chgo., 1970-75; dir. mktg. and sales Data Resources, Inc., 1975-80; regional dir. Omega Cons., 1980-84; pres. Dearborn Bus. Group, West Lafayette, Ind., 1984—; lectr. in field. Contbr. articles to profl. jours. Office: Dearborn Bus Group 2878 Bridgeway Dr West Lafayette IN 47906-5251

MYERS, JENNIFER PATSY, accountant; b. Mytho, Vietnam, Nov. 27, 1962; d. Joseph and Ann (Shu) Tieu; m. Elwin R. Myers, Dec. 22, 1990. BBA, Tex. A&M U., 1991, MBA, 1992. CPA, Tex. Acct. Knox & Co., Corpus Christi, Tex., 1992-93; tax acct. Jennings, Hawley & Cederberg, Corpus Christi, 1993—. Mem. AICPA, Inst. Mgmt. Accts. (v.p. profl. edn. 1991—). Home: 6402 Weber Rd M-4 Corpus Christi TX 78413

MYERS, LISA M., broadcast journalist. Washington, DC corr. The Chicago Sun-Times, 1977-79; White House corr. The Washington Star, Washington, DC, 1980-81; with NBC News, 1981—, named Diplomatic Corr., 1988; now Chief Congl. Corr. recipient: Humanitas award; two-time honoree, Amer. Women in Radio and TV. Office: NBC News Washington Bur 4001 Nebraska Ave NW Washington DC 20016-2733*

MYERS, MARY ELIZABETH, police officer; b. Akron, Ohio, Aug. 5, 1953; d. Robert A. and Helen M. (Cassidy) M. BA in Edn., U. Akron, 1975, BA in Arts and Sci., 1975; MA in Counseling, Kent State U., 1990, postgrad., 1994. Lic. social worker, Ohio; cert. fgn. lang. instr.; cert. peace officer instr., Ohio. Tchr. Spanish and French Triway Local High Sch., Wooster, Ohio, 1976-77; with Akron Police Dept., 1977—, police sgt., homicide detective supr., 1991—; instr. U. Akron, 1983—, prof., 1993—; counselor trainee supr. Kent (Ohio) State U., 1992-93; speaker and presenter in field. Contbr. articles to profl. jours. Mem. Blossom Music Ctr. Action Coun.; co-chair Summit Medina Regional Critical Incident Stress Debriefing Team. Recipient numerous shooting awards, 1980-87; named Gov.'s Top Twenty Shooters Team, Gov. of Ohio, 1986, 87. Mem. NRA, ACA, Internat. Assn. Women Police, Nat. Law Enforcement Trainers Assn., Fraternal Order of Police, Chi Sigma Iota. Home: 1239 Hilltop Dr Akron OH 44310 Office: Akron Police Dept 217 S High St Akron OH 44308

MYERS, MARY KATHLEEN, publishing executive; b. Cedar Rapids, Iowa, Aug. 19, 1945; d. Joseph Bernard and Marjorie Helen (Huntsman) Weaver; m. David F. Myers, Dec. 30, 1967; children: Mindy, James. BA in English and Psychology, U. Iowa, 1967. Tchr. Lincoln High Sch., Des Moines, 1967-80; editor Perfection Learning Corp., Des Moines, 1980-84, product mgr., 1985-87, v.p., editor-in-chief, 1987-93; pres. Advanced Practical Thinking Tng., Des Moines, 1992—; founding ptnr. orgn. designed to promote Edward de Bono thinking methods, 1992—; founder Edward de Bono Creative Fource, 1994. Editor: Retold Classics, 1988-91, (ednl. program) Six Thinking Hats, 1991, Lateral Thinking, 1993; originator numerous other sch. products and programs. Mem. Gov.'s Commn. to Enhance Ednl. Leadership Iowa, Dept. of Edn., 1991-93. Mem. ASTD, Am. Creativity Assn., Am. Soc. Quality Control, Assn. for Quality and Participation. Home: 4315 Urbandale Ave Des Moines IA 50310 Office: APT/T 10520 New York Ave Des Moines IA 50322

MYERS, MICHELE TOLELA, academic administrator; b. Rabat, Morocco, Sept. 25, 1941; came to U.S., 1964; d. Albert and Lilie (Abecassis) Tolela; m. Pierre Vajda, Sept. 12, 1962 (div. Jan. 1965); m. Gail E. Myers, Dec. 20, 1968; children: Erika, David. Diploma, Inst. Polit. Studies, U. Paris, 1962; MA, U. Denver, 1966, PhD, 1967; MA, Trinity U., 1977; LHD, Wittenberg U., 1994. Asst. prof. speech Manchester Coll., North Manchester, Ind., 1967-68; asst. prof. speech and sociology Monticello Coll., Godfrey, Ill., 1968-71; asst. prof. communication Trinity U., San Antonio, 1975-80, assoc. prof., 1980-86, asst. v.p. for acad. affairs, 1982-85, assoc. v.p., 1985-86; assoc. prof. sociology, dean Undergrad. Coll. Bryn Mawr (Pa.) Coll., 1986-89; pres. Denison U., Granville, Ohio, 1989—; comm. analyst Psychology and Comm., San Antonio, 1974-83; bd. dirs. Am. Coun. on Edn., Fed. Res. Bank of Cleve.; mem. pres.'s commn. Nat. Collegiate Athletic Assn., 1993—. Author: (with Gail Myers) The Dynamics of Human Communication, 1973, 6th and internat. edits., 1992, transl. into French, 1984, Communicating When We Speak, 1975, 2d edit., 1978, Communication for the Urban Professional, 1977, Managing by Communication: An Organizational Approach, 1982, transl. into Spanish, 1983, internat. edit., 1982. Trustee Phila. Child Guidance Clinic, 1988-89; trustee assoc. The Bryn Mawr Sch., Balt., 1987-89; v.p., bd. dirs. San Antonio Community Guidance Ctr., 1979-83; bd. dirs. Sherman Fairchild Found., Inc., 1992—. Am. Coun. Edn. fellow in acad. adminstrn., 1981-82. Mem. Am. Coun. Edn. (commn. women in higher edn. 1990-92, bd. dirs. 1993—), Speech Comm. Assn., Internat. Comm. Assn., San Antonio 100 Club,. Home: 204 Broadway W Granville OH 43023-1120 Office: Denison U Office of the President Granville OH 43023

MYERS, SHARON DIANE, auditor; b. Lawrence, Kans., Sept. 18, 1955; d. Richard Paul and Helen Carol (Overbey) M. AA, Mt. San Antonio Coll., Walnut, Calif., 1981; BSBA, Calif. State U., Pomona, 1983; MBA, Poly. U., Pomona, 1986. Revenue agt. IRS, Glendale, Calif., 1984-85; auditor Def. Contract Audit Agy., L.A., 1985-92; auditor Office Inspector Gen. Resolution Trust Corp., Newport Beach, Calif., 1992—; instr. Azusa (Calif.) Pacific U., 1987, 88, West Coast U., San Diego, 1992. Musician, Sunday sch. supt. Covina (Calif.) Bapt. Temple, 1975—. Mem. Assn. Govt. Accts. Republican. Home: 1630 E Colver Pl Covina CA 91724-2602

MYERS, SHIRLEY DIANA, art book editor; b. N.Y.C., Jan. 6, 1916; d. Samuel Archibald and Regina (Edelstein) Levene; m. Bernard Samuel Myers, Aug. 11, 1938 (dec. Feb. 1993); children: Peter Lewis, Lucie Ellen. BA, NYU, 1936, MA, 1938. Editorial asst. Am. Dancer mag., N.Y.C., 1936-38; asst. to dir. Nat. Art Soc., N.Y.C., 1938-42; freelance, art book editor N.Y.C. and Austin, Tex., 1947—. Editor: Modern Art in the Making, 1950, 59, Mexican Painting in Our Time, 1956, The German Expressionists, 1957, 63, Understanding the Arts, 1958, 63, Bruegel, 1976, Manet, 1977, (with B.S. Myers) Dictionary of 20th Century Art, 1974; asst. editor Ency. of Painting, 1955, 70, 79; asst. editor, contbr. McGraw-Hill Dictionary of Art, 5 vols., 1960-69; contbg. editor: Art and Civilization, 1956, 67; coord., picture editor Ency. World Art: Supplement, Vol. XVI, 1982, 83. Vol. archives New Sch. for Social Rsch. Libr., 1993—. Mem. NOW, Older Women's League (recording sec. Greater N.Y. chpt. 1993-95), Inst. for Ret. Profls.

MYERS, SUE BARTLEY, artist; b. Norfolk, Va., Aug. 22, 1930; d. Louis and Rena M. Bartley; m. Bertram J. Myers, Nov. 24, 1949; children: Beth R., Mark F., Alyson S. Student, Stephens Coll., Va. Wesleyan. V.p. Jamson Realty Inc., Myers Realty Inc.; ltd. ptnr. Downtown Plaza Shopping Ctr., Warwick Village Shopping Ctr., Suburban Park Assocs. Solo shows at Village Gallery, Newport News, 1988, Artist at Work Gallery, Virginia Beach, Va., 1991, Va. Wesleyan U., Virginia Beach, 1991, 92, Will Richardson Gallery, Norfolk, Va., 1993, 94. Pres. adv. coun. Va. Wesleyan U., 1982-94; mayor's del. Sister Cities, Norwich, Eng., 1984, Kidikushu, Japan, 1982, Edinburgh, Scotland, 1991, Toulon, France, 1992; mem. entertainment com. Azalea Festival Norfolk, 1984; founder art scholarship Va. Wesleyan. Mem. Tidewater Artists Assn., Art Odyssey. Jewish. Home: 7338 Barberry Ln Norfolk VA 23505

MYERS-BRUCKENSTEIN, MARY ELIZABETH, nurse; b. Yonkers, N.Y., Dec. 17, 1945; d. Stuart Fredrick and Elizabeth Jane (Bettker) Myers; m. Joseph Bruckenstein, Oct. 2, 1983; stepchildren: Mark David, Kenneth Alan. AA, NYU, 1972, BS in Health Edn, Nursing Arts, 1975; MPA, C.W. Post U., 1981. RN, N.Y. Staff nurse Rusk Inst. Rehab. Medicine, N.Y.C., 1966-68; Peace Corps vol. Princess Teshai Hosp., Addis, Ethiopia, 1968-70; team leader Univ. Hosp., N.Y.C., 1970-75; community health nurse Vis. Nurse Svc. N.Y., Queens, 1975-82; rehab. nurse specialist Menorah Nursing Home, Bklyn., 1982-84; nursing supr. Comprehensive Home Care, Smithtown, N.Y., 1984-87; dir. patient svcs. CHHA Quality Care, Smithtown, N.Y., 1987-88; nursing supr. United Presbyn. Home, Syosset, N.Y., 1988-91; charge nurse L.I. State Vets. Home, Stony Brook, N.Y., 1991—. Phone polls Carter for Pres. Campaign, Ea. Seaboard; union rep. United Fedn. Tchrs., Astoria, Queens. Mem. ACLU, NOW, Amnesty Internat., Returned Peace Corps Vols. Roman Catholic. Home: 6 Burgoyne Ct Coram NY 11727 Office: LI State Vets Home 100 Patriots Rd Stony Brook NY 11790-3318

MYHRE, KATHLEEN RANDI, nurse; b. Everett, Wash., Apr. 18, 1952; d. Richard Alvin and Beverley Jeanette (Nesbit) M. LPN, Bellingham (Wash.) Tech. Sch., 1970; ADN, Lane C.C., Eugene, Oreg., 1988. RN, Oreg. LPN night charge nurse Island's Convalescent Ctr., Friday Harbor, Wash., 1970-75; LPN float Sacred Heart Gen. Hosp., Eugene, Oreg., 1975-87; charge nurse urgent care unit Eugene Clinic, 1987—. Democrat. Home: 80687 Lost Creek Rd Dexter OR 97431-9742

MYLES, MARGARET JEAN, real estate appraiser; b. Detroit, Oct. 26, 1952; d. William Thompson and Patricia (Maclean) M.; 1 child, Tessa Maria. Student, Western Mich. U., 1973, Oakland U., 1974; AA, Coastline C.C., 1986. Unit sec. Hoag Meml. Hosp., Newport Beach, Calif., 1976-80, buyer, 1981-86; real estate appraiser P.M. Myles & Assocs., Irvine, Calif., 1980-89, MJM Appraisal Svc., Irvine, Calif., 1989—. Home: 4531 Wyngate Cir Irvine CA 92714-2345 Office: MJM Appraisal Svc 4531 Wyngate Cir Irvine CA 92714-2345

MYLROIE, WILLA WILCOX, transportation engineer, regional planner; b. Seattle, May 30, 1917; d. Elgin Roscoe and Ruth B. (Begg) Wilcox; m. John Ellis Mylroie (dec. 1947); children: Steven Wilcox Mylroie, Jo Mylroie Sohneronne; m. Donald Gile Fassett, Dec. 30, 1966. BS in Civil Engring., U. Wash., 1940, MS in Regional Planning, 1953. Lic. profl. civil engr. Civil engr. U.S. Engring. Dept. C.E., Seattle, 1941-46; affiliate prof. civil engring. U. Wash., Seattle, 1948-51, research asst. prof. civil engring., 1951-56; assoc. prof. civil engring. Purdue U., Lafayette, Ind., 1956-58; research engr. and planner Wash. State Dept. Hwys., Olympia, 1958-69, head research and spl. assignment div., 1969-81; cons. civil engring. and regional planning Olympia, 1981—; cons. King County Design Commn., Seattle, 1981-89; advisor Coll. Engring. U. Wash., 1978-86, affiliate prof. civil engring., 1981-84; advisor Wash. State U. Coll. Engring., Pullman, 1977-85. Active Girls Scouts U.S. coun., Boy Scouts Am., Olympia, Renton, 1950-66; pres. high sch. PTA, Olympia; commr. Thurston County Planning Commn., Olympia; U.S. Coast Guard Auxilliary, 1982-89, U.S. Power Squadron, 1967—; citizen amb. People to People Trip, Moscow, St. Petersburg, Russia and Muensk, Bolarus. Recipient Profl. Recognition award Women's Transp., Spokane, Spl. Svc. award Transp. Rsch. Bd. Coun., Washington, U. Wash. Coll. Engring. Alumni Achievement award, 1993. Fellow ASCE (ad hoc vis. com. engring. coun. for profl. devel., Edmund Friedman Profl. Recognition award 1978), Inst. Transp. Engrs. (hon. mem., internat. bd. dirs., Tech. Coun. award 1982); mem. Planning Assn. Wash. (bd. dirs.), Sigma Xi. Home and Office: 7501 Boston Harbor Rd NE Olympia WA 98506-9720

MYNSTER, PATRICIA ANN, insurance company executive; b. Grundy, Va., July 26, 1951; d. Albert and Zella (Coleman) Casey; m. Merel Lester Mynster, Dec. 6, 1969. BA, Otterbein Coll., 1988. Mem. staff office of investments Nat. Ins. Co., Columbus, Ohio, 1969—, dir. securities investment, 1991—. Mem. Columbus Coun. World Affairs, Columbus Coun. on Ethics in Econs. Mem. Assn. for Investment Mgmt. and Rsch. (hon. mem.), Treasury Mgmt. Assn., Ctrl. Ohio Treasury Mgmt. Assn. Mem. United Ch. of Christ. Office: Nationwide Ins Co 1 Nationwide Plz Columbus OH 43215-2220

MYRDAL, ROSEMARIE CARYLE, state official, former state legislator; b. Minot, N.D., May 20, 1929; d. Harry Dirk and Olga Jean (Dragge) Lohse; m. B. John Myrdal, June 21, 1952; children: Jan, Mark, Harold, Paul, Amy. BS, N.D. State U., 1951. Registered profl. first grade tchr., N.D. Tchr. N.D., 1951-71; bus. mgr. Edinburg Sch. Dist., 1974-81; mem. N.D. Ho. of Reps., Bismarck, 1984-92, mem. appropriations com., 1991, 92—; lt. gov., State of N.D., Bismarck, 1992—; sch. evaluator Walsh County Sch. Bds. Assn., Grafton, N.D., 1983-84; evaluator, work presenter N.D. Sch. Bds. Assn., Bismarck, 1983-84; mem. sch. bd. Edinburg Sch. Dist., 1981-90; adv. com. Red River Trade Corridor, Inc., 1989—. Co-editor: Heritage '76, 1976, Heritage '89, 1989. Precinct committeewoman Gardar Twp. Rep. Com., 1980-86; leader Hummingbirds 4-H Club, Edinburg, 1980-83; bd. dirs. Camp Sioux Diabetic Children, Grand Forks, N.D., 1980-90, N.D. affiliate Am. Diabetes Assn., Families First-Child Welfare Reform Initiative, Region IV, 1989-92; dir. N.D. Diabetes Assn., 1989-91; chmn. N.D. Ednl. TelecommunicationsCoun., 1989-90; vice chmn. N.D. Legis. Interim Jobs Devel. Commn., 1989-90. Mem. AAUW (pres. 1982-84 Pembina County area), Pembina County Hist. Soc. (historian 1976-84), Northeastern N.D. Heritage Assn. (pres. 1986-92), Red River Valley Heritage Soc. (bd. dirs. 1985-92). Lutheran. Club: Agassiz Garden (Park River) (pres. 1968-69). Home: # 302 121 E Arikara Ave Bismarck ND 58501 Office: 600 E Boulevard Ave Bismarck ND 58505

MYRENT, DEBRA KAREN, photographer; b. Chgo., Aug. 15, 1951; d. Carl and Sylvia (Gusinow) M.; m. James Carl Ruebsamen, Aug. 26, 1984; 1 child, Rebecca. BS, U. Ill., 1973. Book sales rep., in-charge of out of print book search John Gach Bookshop, Balt., 1974-75; plumber apprentice Fort Sheridan (Ill.) Engring. Dept., 1975-77; photographer, prodn. tech. The F/Stop, Inc., Chgo., 1977-79; photographer intern L.A. Times, 1982-83, news photographer, 1990-93; news photographer UPI, L.A., 1985-90, L.A. Daily

News, 1983-85; photographer Ventura, Calif., 1993—; photographer J. Paul Getty Trust, L.A., 1993—. Photographer Hallmark Greeting Card, 1987. Vol. Don Drowty Youth Found., Santa Monica, 1983-86. Recipient 2nd Pl. Best Features Photo Calif. Newspapers Publishers Assn., 1988, Cert. of Merit Kodak Internat. Newspaper Snapshot Awards, 1983. Mem. NOW (bd. dirs. 1992-93, pub. svcs. referral coord., historian), Nat. Press Photographers Assn., Press Photographers Assn. of Greater L.A. (past v.p.). Democrat. Jewish. Home: 729 Alverstone Ave Ventura CA 93003-1122

MYRICK, SUE, congresswoman, former mayor; b. Tiffin, Ohio, Aug. 1, 1941; d. William Henry and Margaret Ellen (Roby) Wilkins; m. Jim Forest (div.); children: Greg, Dan; m. Wilbur Edward Myrick Jr., Sept. 11, 1977. Student, Heidelberg Coll., 1959-60. Exec. sec. to mayor and city mgr. City of Alliance, Ohio, 1962-63; dir. br. office Stark County Ct. of Juvenile and Domestic Rels., Alliance, 1963-65; pres. Myrick Agy., Charlotte, N.C., 1971—; mayor of Charlotte, 1987-91; mem. 104th Congress from 9th N.C. District, Washington, D.C., 1995—; candidate for U.S. Senate from N.C., 1992; mem. U.S. Ho. of Reps., 1994; active Heart Fund, Multiple Sclerosis, March of Dimes, Arts and Scis. Coun. Fund Dr.; past mem. adv. bd. Uptown Shelter, Uptown Homeless Task Force, bd. dirs. N.C. Inst. Politics; v.p. Sister Cities Internat.; mem. Pres. Bush's Affordable Housing Commn.; founder, coord. Charlotte vol. tornado relief effort; bd. dirs. Learning How; former mem. adv. bd. U.S. Conf. Mayors; mem.-at-large Charlotte City Coun., 1983-85, Strengthening Am. Commn.; lay leader, Sunday sch. tchr. 1st United Meth. Ch.; treas. Mecklenburg Ministries; former trustee U.S. Conf. of Mayors. Recipient Woman of Yr. award Harrisonburg, Va., 1968; named one of Outstanding Young Women of Am., 1968. Mem. NAFE, Women's Polit. Caucus, Charlotte C. of C., Beta Sigma Phi. Republican. Home: 310 W 8th St Charlotte NC 28202-1704 Office: US House Reps 401 Cannon House Office Bldg Washington DC 20515-3309 also: Myrick Advt 505 N Poplar St Charlotte NC 28202-1729

NABORS, HARRIET DAVIS, marketing professional; b. Fayette, Ala., July 13, 1966; d. James Melton and May Elba (Otts) Davis. B in Bus. Studies, Barry U., Miami, Fla., 1990; MBA, Nova U., 1992. Customer svc. rep. Fla. Nat. Bank, Ft. Lauderdale, 1986-87; sr. customer svc. rep. Centrust Bank, Pompano Beach, Fla., 1987-89; telephone svc. rep. Am. Express TRS Co., Inc., Ft. Lauderdale, 1989-91; mktg. mgr. Nova Southeastern U., Ft. Lauderdale, 1991—. Grad. Leadership North Broward, Pompano Beach, 1992-93, mem. edn. com., 1993-94. Group Study Exchange scholar Rotary Internat., 1994. Mem. Am. Mktg. Assn., Pompano Beach Bus. and Profl. Women (1st v.p. 1993-94, 94—, young careerist 1992, corr. sec. 1991-92, 93-94, individual devel. speak-off winner 1993). Home: PO Box 2023 Pompano Beach FL 33061-2023 Office: Nova Southeastern U 3301 College Ave Fort Lauderdale FL 33314-7721

NACHTIGAL, PATRICIA, equipment manufacturing company executive, general counsel; b. 1946. BA, Montclair State U.; JD, Rutgers U.; LLM, NYU. With Ingersoll-Rand Co., Woodcliff Lake, N.J., 1979—. Office: Ingersoll-Rand Co 200 Chestnut Ridge Rd Woodcliff Lake NJ 07675

NACOL, MAE, lawyer; b. Beaumont, Tex., June 15, 1944; d. William Samuel and Ethel (Bowman) N.; children: Shawn Alexander Nacol, Catherine Regina Nacol. BA, Rice U., 1965; postgrad., S. Tex. Coll. Law, 1966-68. Bar: Tex. 1969, U.S. Dist. Ct. (so. dist.) Tex. 1969. Diamond buyer/appraiser Nacol's Jewelry, Houston, 1961—; pvt. practice law, Houston, 1969—. Author, editor ednl. materials on multiple sclerosis, 1981-85. Nat. dir. A.R.M.S. of Am. Ltd., Houston, 1984-85. Recipient Mayor's Recognition award City of Houston, 1972; Ford Found. fellow So. Tex. Coll. Law, Houston, 1964. Mem. Houston Bar Assn. (chmn. candidate com. 1970, chmn. membership com. 1971, chmn. lawyers referral com. 1972), Assn. Trial Lawyers Am., Tex. Trial Lawyers Assn., Am. Judicature Soc. (sustaining), Houston Fin. Coun. Women. Presbyterian. Office: 600 Jefferson St Ste 850 Houston TX 77002-7325

NADEAU, KELLY HAMPTON, critical care nurse, educator; b. Charleston, W.Va., July 12, 1958; d. Robert Clarence and Louise Evelyn (Witt) Hampton; m. Marc Alphonse Nadeau, Sept. 10, 1988. BSN, W.Va. Wesleyan Coll., 1980; MN, Emory U., 1986. Clin. nurse I-II Charleston (W.Va.) Area Med. Ctr., 1980-84, chief nurse recruiter, 1982-83, charge nurse med. ICU, 1983-84; nursing instr. critical care VA Med. Ctr., Augusta, GA., 1986-88; trauma nurse coord. DeKalb Med. Ctr., Decatur, Ga., 1989—; instr. BSN dept. Clayton State Coll., Morrow, Ga., 1992—; educator, instr. critical care courses DeKalb Med. Ctr., Rockdale Hosp., 1989—, affiliate faculty BCLS, Am. Heart Assn., Ga., 1990—, ACLS, 1990—; clin. preceptor grad. students Emory U., Atlanta, 1989—, Ga. State U., Atlanta, 1992—. Reviewer: Textbook of Critical Care Nursing, 1990. Recipient scholarship VA Health Profls. Sch., 1984-86, Louise Mellen Fellowship for Critical Care Nursing, 1984-86. Mem. AACN (CCRN, educator, instr. CCRN rev. courses Atlanta area, Augusta chpt. 1986—, com. chair Atlanta chpt. 1990-91, sec. 1991-92, edn. cons. Region 6, 1992-94), Soc. Critical Care Medicine, Emergency Nurses Assn., Sigma Theta Tau (past chpt. pres.). Methodist. Home: 1511 Marshall Ln Conyers GA 30208 Office: DeKalb Med Ctr 2701 N Decatur Rd Decatur GA 30033 Office: Clayton State Coll BSN Dept PO Box 696 Morrow GA 30260

NADELSON, CAROL COOPERMAN, psychiatrist, educator; b. Bklyn., Oct. 13, 1936; m. Theodore Nadelson, July 16, 1965; children—Robert, Jennifer. B.A. magna cum laude, Bklyn. Coll., 1957; M.D. with honors, U. Rochester, N.Y., 1961. Dir. med. student edn. Beth Israel Hosp., Boston, 1974-79, psychiatrist, 1977; assoc. prof. psychiatry Harvard U. Med. Sch., Boston, 1976-79; research scholar Radcliffe Coll., Cambridge, Mass., 1979-80; prof., vice chmn., dir. tng. and edn. dept. psychiatry Tufts-New Eng. Med. Ctr., Boston, 1979-93. Editor: The Woman Patient, Vols. 1, 2 and 3, 1978, 82; Treatment Interventions in Human Sexuality, 1983; Marriage and Divorce: A Contemporary Perspective, 1984, Women Physicians in Leadership Roles, 1986, Training Psychiatrists for the '90s, 1987; editor-in-chief Am. Psychiatric Press, Inc., 1986—; contbr. articles to profl. jours. Trustee Menninger Found., 1988—. Recipient Gold Medal award Mt. Airy Psychiat. Ctr., 1981, award Case Western Res. U., 1983; Picker Found. grantee, 1982-83. Fellow Ctr. for Advanced Study in the Behavioral Scis.; mem. Am. Psychiat. Assn. (pres. 1985-86, Seymour D. Vestermark award 1992), Am. Coll. Psychiatrists, AMA (impaired physicians com. 1984), Group for Advancement of Psychiatry (bd. dirs. 1984). Office: 30 Amory St Brookline MA 02146-3909

NADLER-HURVICH, HEDDA CAROL, public relations executive; b. Bronx, N.Y., June 15, 1944; d. Julius Louis and Julia (Nemzer) Cohen; m. David George Nadler, Oct. 3, 1965 (div. 1979); 1 child, Laura Lee Nadler; m. Burton Earl Hurvich, Dec. 8, 1984. BBA, Baruch Coll., 1965. V.p., sec. Irving L. Straus Assocs., Inc., N.Y.C., 1965-80; exec. v.p. Mount & Nadler Inc., N.Y.C., 1980—. Office: Mount & Nadler 425 Madison Ave New York NY 10017-1110

NADZICK, JUDITH ANN, accountant; b. Paterson, N.J., Mar. 6, 1948; d. John and Ethel (McDonald) N.; B.B.A. in Acctg., U. Miami (Fla.), 1971. Staff accountant, mgr. Ernst & Whinney, C.P.A.s, N.Y.C., 1971-78; asst. treas. Gulf & Western Industries, Inc., N.Y.C., 1979-83, asst. v.p., 1980-82, v.p., 1982-83; v.p., corp. controller United Mchts. and Mfrs. Inc., N.Y.C., 1983-85, sr. v.p., 1985-86, exec. v.p., chief fin. officer, 1986—, also bd. dirs. 1987—. C.P.A., N.J. Mem. Am. Inst. CPAs, Nat. Assn. Accts., N.Y. State Soc. CPAs, U. Miami Alumni Assn., Delta Delta Delta. Roman Catholic. Home: 2 Lincoln Sq Apt 15G New York NY 10023-6205

NAESER, NANCY DEARIEN, geologist, researcher; b. Morgantown, W.Va., Apr. 15, 1944; d. William Harold and Katherine Elizabeth (Dearien) Cozad; m. Charles Wilbur Naeser, Feb. 6, 1982. BS, U. Ariz., 1966; PhD, Victoria U., Wellington, New Zealand, 1973. Geol. field asst. U.S. Geol. Survey, Flagstaff, Ariz., 1966; sci. editor, New Zealand Jour. Geology and Geophsyics, New Zealand Dept Sci. and Indsl. Research, Wellington, 1974-76; postdoctoral rsch. assoc., U. Toronto, Ont., Can., 1976-79; postdoctoral rsch. assoc. U.S. Geol. Survey, Denver, 1979-81, geologist, 1981—; adj. prof. Dartmouth Coll., Hanover, N.H., 1985—, U. Wyo., Laramie, 1984—. Editor: Thermal History of Sedimentary Basins - Methods and Case Histories, 1989; contbr. articles on fission-track dating to profl. jours., 1977—. Docent Denver Zoo. Fulbright fellow New Zealand, 1967-68. Fellow Geol. Soc. Am.; mem. Am. Assn. Petroleum Geologists, Soc. Econ. Paleontologists and Mineralogists, Geol. Soc. New Zealand, Mortar Bd., Phi Kappa Phi. Republican. Methodist. Office: US Geol Survey Mail Stop 981 12201 Sunrise Valley Dr Reston VA 22092

NAFFIE, MARY JEAN, accountant; b. Muskegon, Mich., Oct. 31, 1964; d. Leo J. and Meryln J. (Narowitz) O'Connor; m. Dominic R. Naffie Jr., Sept. 6, 1986; 1 child, Dominic R. III. AA in Acctg./ Data Processing, Baker Coll., 1984. Asst. contr. Stationery Supply Co., Muskegon, 1984-85; owner O'Connor's Cupboard, Muskegon, 1985-86; dep. clk. Egelston Twp., Muskegon, 1986-88; fin. mgr. Muskegon Econ. Growth Alliance, 1988—. Bd. dirs. West Mich. Children's Mus., Muskegon, 1994—, Muskegon Twp. Planning Commn., 1994—; mem. allocations bd. United Way, Muskegon, 1992—, loaned exec., 1991—. Mem. Govt. Fin. Officers Assn. Roman Catholic. Home: 868 S Quarterline Rd Muskegon MI 49442-3834 Office: Muskegon Econ Growth Alliance PO Box 1087 Muskegon MI 49443-1087

NAFZIGER, PATTIE LOIS, state legislator; b. Phoenix; married; 4 children. Attended, Colo. Coll., 1947-48, U. Ariz., 1948-50, Ariz. State U., 1967-70, Coll. So. Idaho, 1970-72. Former ptnr. Sunshine Farms; mem. Idaho Ho. of Reps., 1990—. Asst. leader 4-H; active Jr. League of Phoenix. Home: 1787 E 3100 South Wendell ID 83355 Office: Idaho Ho of Reps State Capitol Boise ID 83720*

NAGASE, TAKAKO, electron microscopist, Japanese language educator; b. Tokyo, Apr. 5, 1936; d. Nobuyoshi and Tomiko Maeda; m. Goro Nagase, Dec. 30, 1965; children: Terumi, George. BS in Biology, Tohoku U., Sendai, Japan, 1959, MS in Zoology, 1961; MA in Musicology, Morgan State U., 1993. Instr. Showa Med. Sch., Tokyo, 1961; electron microscopist U. Del., Newark, 1969—; instr. Lincoln U., Pa., 1988—; instr. Japanese Ctrl. Ednl. Telecom. Network, Washington, 1991-93. Author: Scott Joplin Ragtime Selection, 1980; translator: Biological Aspects of Water Pollution, 1975; contbr. articles to profl. jours. Bd. dirs. Christiana Cultural Arts Ctr., Wilmington, Del., 1980-85. East-West Ctr. scholar U. Hawaii, 1961-63. Mem. Ctrs. for Black Music Rsch. Home: 1013 Baylor Dr Newark DE 19711 Office: Lincoln U Dept Langs and Linguistics Lincoln University PA 19352

NAGDIMON, ELLEN TARA, artist, educator; b. N.Y.C., Dec. 13, 1957; d. Jeoash Morris and Evelyn (Uretzky) N.; m. J. Martin Kahn, June 7, 1994. BA, CUNY, 1981; cert. legal asst., Adelphi U., 1982. Studio liaison N.Y. Feminist Art Inst., N.Y.C., 1985-88; gallery asst. Studio K Gallery, L.I. City, N.Y., 1986-88; instr., cons. Children's Art Carnival, N.Y.C., 1990-92; instr. Forest Hills (N.Y.) Adult Edn., 1988—; chair, treas. Arts Anon Tools, Forest Hills, N.Y., 1993-94. Exhibitions include Ceres Gallery, N.Y.C., 1985-87, NYU, 1985, 88, Emerging Collector, N.Y.C., 1986—. Recipient exhbn. support Artists' Space, 1985, assistanceships DCA, 1985; fellow Vt. Studio Ctr., Johnson, 1991. Mem. Orgn. Ind. Artists, Art Initiatives, Smithsonian, Adult Children (local chair), Coll. Art Assn. Home: 144-75 Melbourne Ave # 1C Flushing NY 11367

NAGEL, DIANA, tax specialist; b. Milw., Nov. 28, 1941; d. Arthur E. and Hazel (Schultz) Meyer; m. Thomas E. Nagel, Aug. 31, 1940; 1 child, Dawn M. Ins. claims rep. Employers of Wausau, Wis., 1969-72; tax preparer H&R Block, Inc., Milw., 1978-80, pub. info. specialist, 1980-83; owner Diana Tax Svc., Wauwatosa, Wis., 1983—; tchr. H&R Block, Inc., Wauwatosa, 1980-83. Home: 2221 N 83d St Wauwatosa WI 53213

NAGEL, PATRICIA JO, non-profit public policy administrator, lawyer; b. Billings, Mont., Sept. 24, 1942; d. Robert Mark and Evelyn Margaret (Lipsack) McKeown; m. Robert Wells Nagel, Aug. 18, 1963; children: Stacia, Susanna. BA in Polit. Sci., N.Mex. State U., 1965; JD, U. Wyo., 1983. Bar: Wyo. 1984. Interior designer Nassif's Interiors, Cedar Rapids, Iowa, 1965-67, Cedar Rapids Paint, 1973-74; law clk. to presiding justice 7th jud. dist., Casper, Wyo., 1983-84; sole practice Casper, 1984—; dir. Wyo. Futures Project, Casper, 1986-88; ptnr. Nagel & Nix, Casper, 1988—; elected to Wyo. State Ho. of Reps., 1992—. Sr. editor Land and Water Law Rev., 1982-83. Vice chair Wyo. Community Devel. Authority; mem. planning commn. City of Casper, 1980; pres., bd. dirs. Friends of the Libr., Casper, 1980; pres. Meadowlark Montessori Sch., Casper, 1979; sec. Casper Bicentennial Com., 1976; v.p. Nicolaysen Art Mus., Casper, 1985-86; sec., bd. dirs. Hospice Cancer Treatment Ctr., Casper, 1985-86. Republican. Presbyterian. Home: 1105 S Durbin St Casper WY 82601-4327

NAGI, CATHERINE RASEH, educational administrator, financial planner; b. Bklyn., Oct. 13, 1940; d. Massed and Catherine (Irato) N. BS, Bklyn. Coll., 1962, MS, 1964, postgrad., 1965-67, 76; postgrad., Hofstra U., 1967-76, St. Johns U., Queens, N.Y., 1976-78. Cert. dist. sch. adminstr., supr., prin., asst. prin., tchr. health/phys. edn., N.Y.; CFP. Tchr. health/phys. edn. Jr. High Sch. 211-Dist. 18, Bklyn., 1962, Bay Ridge High Sch., Bklyn., 1962-63; tchr., acting chair Jr. High Sch. 78-Dist. 22, Bklyn., 1963-70; acting asst. prin. Intermediate Sch. 302-Dist. 19, Bklyn., 1970-71; narcotics edn. tchr. trainer Dist. 19 Bd. of Edn., Bklyn., 1971-73, supr. health/drug edn./svcs., 1973-75; supr. reimbursable programs Dist. 22 Bd. of Edn., Bklyn., 1975-79, supr. comprehensive planning, 1979-84, dep. supt., 1984-90; acting prin. Pub. Sch. 217-Dist. 22, Bklyn., 1980; sch. supt. Dist. 28 Bd. of Edn., Queens, N.Y., 1990—; tchr. Adult Edn./Community Ctrs., N.Y.C., 1959-65; presenter N.Y.C. and N.Y. State Ednl. Confs., Univs.; grant writer N.Y.C. Bd. Edn., 1973—. Co-author, cons. (math. workbook) Get Ahead in Math, 1985; creator, editor (ednl. mag.) Gateways to Learning, 1977-90; creator, developer ednl. data system, 1976; developer first N.Y.C./N.Y. State early identification learning disabilities program, 1975. Named Educator of Yr. Assn. Tchrs. N.Y., 1980; recipient City Coun. Proclamation N.Y.C. Coun., 1991, Legis. resolution N.Y. State Assembly/Senate, 1991, Congl. Record recognition U.S. Congress, 1991, Recognition award Forestdale Foster and Adoptive Parents Assn., Queens, 1992. Mem. ASCD, Am. Assn. Sch. Adminstrs., N.Y.C. Assn. Supts., N.Y.C. Adminstrv. Women in Edn., Bklyn./N.Y. State Reading Coun./Assn., Thomas Jefferson Dem. Club, Kings County Dem. Com. Office: Dist 28 10855 69th Ave Flushing NY 11375-3854

NAGLE, JEAN SUE, sociologist, psychologist; b. Detroit; d. Peter and Hedy (Grusczynski) Karabacz; Student U. Chgo., 1953-55; M.A., N.Mex. Highlands U., 1960, M.S., 1967; Ph.D., Union Grad. Sch., 1977; postgrad. Bryn Mawr Inst. Women in Higher Edn. Adminstrn., 1981, U. Chgo.; m. Robert D. Nagle, Nov. 20, 1956; children—Carl A., Sonya L., Paula E. Diagnostic technician Vocat. Counseling Inst., Detroit, 1952; research technician United Auto Workers-CIO, Detroit, 1958; clin. psychology intern N.Mex. State Hosp., Las Vegas, 1962-63; clin. psychology trainee VA Hosp., Omaha and Lincoln, Nebr., 1963-64; instr. sociology N.W. Mo. State U., Maryville, 1966-70, prof. sociology and psychology, 1971—. Bd. dirs. Inst. Discourse. N.W. Mo. State U. grantee, 1981, 82. Mem. Am. Psychol. Assn., Am. Sociol. Assn., Midwest Sociol. Soc., Psychology/Sociology Club, Mo. Psychol. Assn., World Federalists, Psi Chi, Pi Gamma Mu. Home: 10301 NW Mirror Lake Dr Kansas City MO 64152-2549 Office: NW Mo State U Dept Psychology/Sociology Maryville MO 64468

NAGLE, JOAN GETTIG, engineering writer; b. Altoona, Pa., July 3, 1932; d. William Henry and Dora Eleanor (Goss) Gettig; m. Elliott Valentine Nagle, Mar. 7, 1954; children: Emily Katharine Nagle Green, Laura Elizabeth Nagle Bailey. ScB, Dickinson Coll., 1953. Analytical chemist E.I. duPont de Nemours & Co., Charlestown, Ind., 1953-54; tech. writer U.S. Army Chem. Corps, Dugway, Utah, 1955-56; pub. rels. coord. Wilkinsburg (Pa.) Sch. Dist., 1968-74; engr. publs. Westinghouse Electric Corp., Pitts., 1974-90; mgr. NPR publs. Westinghouse Savannah River Co., Aiken, S.C., 1991-92, mgr. QA support svcs., 1992-93; publications cons. Aiken, 1993—. Contbr. articles to conf. procs. Mem. Gen. Commn. Comm. United Meth. Ch., Nashville, 1989—. Mem. IEEE (editor Transactions Profl. Comm. 1976-89, mem. com. comm. and info. policy, Alfred N. Goldsmith award 1989), Profl. Comm. Soc. of IEEE (mem. adminstrv. com. 1987—). Home and Office: 104 Crane Ct Aiken SC 29803

NAGY, ADRIENNE, chemist; b. Passaic, N.J., Oct. 5, 1959; d. Andrew Paul and Elizabeth (Dugalin) N. BS, Seton Hall U., 1981; postgrad., Dowling Coll., 1992—. Cert. tchr., N.J. Lab. technician, fragrance evaluator Ungerer & Co., Lincoln Park, N.J., 1982-86; sci. instr. North Bergen (N.J.) H.S., 1987-88; assoc. chemist Beecham Products, Parsippany, N.J., 1988-89; R & D chemist Mennen Co., Morristown, N.J., 1989-90; product devel. chemist Estee Lauder, Melville, N.Y., 1990—. Supporter Hungarian Scout Assn., Garfield, N.J. Mem. NAFE, Soc. Cosmetic Chemists, Nat. Honor Soc. Republican. Roman Catholic. Office: Estee Lauder Inc 125 Pinelawn Rd Melville NY 11747

NAGY, CHRISTA FIEDLER, biochemist; b. Marienbad, Czech Republic, July 8, 1943; d. Herbert A. Fiedler and Anna C. (Gluth) Rathmann; m. Bela Imre Nagy, Aug. 22, 1969; 1 child, Byron. BS in Biology, Fairleigh Dickinson U., 1967, MS in Biochemistry, 1974; PhD in Biochemistry, Rutgers U., 1981. Assoc. scientist Hoffmann-La Roche Inc., Nutley, N.J., 1975-80, sr. scientist, 1981-88, assoc. rsch. investigator, 1988—. Mem. AAAS, N.Y. Acad. Scis., Am. Soc. Biol. Chemists, Soc. for Investigative Dermatology, Inflammation Rsch. Assn. Roman Catholic. Office: Hoffmann LaRoche Inc 340 Kingsland St Nutley NJ 07110-1150

NAGY, CHRISTINE LEE, geriatrics, rehabilitation and home care nurse; b. N.Y.C., July 11, 1961; d. Augustus Richard Monturo and Martha Kay Childress Ferris; m. William John Nagy, Aug. 19, 1989; 1 child, Alexander Christopher. BA in Communications, BSN, Cleve. State U., 1990. Cert. in gerontology, rehab. and nursing adminstrn. Staff/charge nurse Metrohealth Med. Ctr., Cleve., 1988-90; charge nurse Jackson Meml. Hosp., Miami, Fla., 1990-92; unit mgr. geriatric rehab. and long term care Saginaw (Mich.) Community Hosp., 1992; charge nurse, nursing home care and rehab. unit Saginaw VA Hosp., 1992-93; unit mgr. geriatric rehab. unit Mt. Sinai Med. Ctr., Miami Beach, Fla., 1993-94; home care rehab. coord. Marymount Hosp., Garfield Heights, Ohio, 1994—; mem. policy, procedure, nurses wk., long term care coms. and behavior modification team Saginaw Community Hosp., 1992—. BLS instr. ARC/Am. Heart Assn., Cleve., Miami, 1990, 91; active Broward County Schs. PTA, 1993, 94, Garfield Heights Schs. PTA, 1994; cub scout den leader, coach Seminole Dist. and Greater Cleve. Dist. Boy Scouts Am.; vol. Lakewood Meals on Wheels, Ohio, 1987-90. Mem. ANA, Nat. League for Nursing, Assn. Rehab. Nurses, Mich. Nurses Assn., Fla. Nurses Assn., Ohio Nurses Assn., Nat. Spinal Cord Nurses. Republican. Roman Catholic.

NAGY, SUZANNE CSIKOS, artist, gallery owner; b. Budapest, Hungary, Mar. 2, 1947; came to U.S., 1979; d. Bela Csikos-Nagy and Lili Kneppo; m. Steve Mati, May 11, 1977 (dec. May 1990); m. R. Edward Townsend, Jr., May 18, 1991; 1 child, Lina N. Degree in econs., Budapest U., 1967; degree in media and art, Acad. of Art and Film, Budapest, 1977. Economist Technoimpex, Budapest, 1968-69; head internat. bus. BUBIV, Budapest, 1969-72; owner Gallery Les Looms, N.Y.C., 1984—. One woman shows include Madison Ave. Matignon Gallery; exhibited in group shows in N.Y., Pa., Conn.; represented in permanent collections Budapest Nat. Gallery, Budapest Mus. Contemporary Art; author, artist: (art book) Tale of the Clock, 1994; contbr. articles to mags. Mem. Yale Club. Home: 22 W 26th St New York NY 10010 Office: Gallery Les Looms 1050 2nd Ave New York NY 10022-4063

NAGYS, ELIZABETH ANN, environmental issues educator; b. St. Louis; d. Dallas and Miriam (Miller) Nichols; m. Sigi Nagys, Feb. 7, 1970; children: Eric M., Jennifer R., Alex E. BS., So. Ill. U. Extenstion, Edwardsville, 1970. Cert. tchr., Mo., Ill. Announcer Sta. KMTY, Clovis, N.Mex., 1970-71; substitue tchr. Ritneour Sch. Dist., Overland, Mo., 1977-78; instr. biology, environ. issues Southwestern Mich. Coll., Dowagiac, Mich., 1988-92; exec. v.p. Profl. Sound Designers, Goshen, Ind., 1994—; reviewer textbooks Harcourt, Brace & Co., 1993. Bd. dirs. United Meth. Ch., Marvin Park, 1979-84; coord. United Meth. Women, 1980-87; mem. Hazardous Waste Com. for Elkhart County, Ind., 1991-94; charter mem. Holocaust Meml. Mus.; assoc. mem. Art Inst. Chgo.; active Nat. Arbor Day Found. Mem. AAUW (v.p. Goshen 1994-95), Nat. Audubon Soc., Sierra Club, Welcome Wagon Club.

NAHIGIAN, ALMA LOUISE, technical documentation administrator; b. Peabody, Mass., Sept. 17, 1936; d. Walter Daniel and Alma Edith (Knowles) Higgins; m. Franklin Roosevelt Nahigian, April 30, 1961; children: Ellen Elise, Dana Leigh, Catherine Elizabeth. AA, Boston U., 1956, BS, 1958, MS in Journalism, 1963. Editor nat. and spl. projects Boston U. News Bur., 1959-61, 63-64; writer, editor Nutrition Found., N.Y.C., 1961-63; writer, editor, cons. Cambridge (Mass.) Communicators, Tech. Edn. Research Ctr., Harvard U., Cambridge, Smart Software, Inc., Belmont, Mass., 1970-82; tech. editor Digital Equipment Corp., Bedford, Mass., 1979-84; prin. tech. writer, editor Wang Labs, Inc., Lowell, Mass., 1984—, documentation sect. mgr. editorial, 1984-93; sr. adv. tech. editor Dun & Bradstreet Software, Westborough, Mass., 1993—; instr. Harvard U., Cambridge, 1988, Radcliffe Coll., Cambridge, 1979; mem. adj. faculty Northeastern U., Boston, 1989—, guest lectr., 1979, 88. Contbr. numerous articles to profl. pubs. Active LWV, Arlington, Mass., 1963-73. Mem. Soc. for Tech. Comm. (bd. dirs. Boston chpt., pres. 1992-93, Tech. Pubs. Competition Excellence award 1989, 93, 94, co-mgr. soc.-level com. 1993—, Art Competitions Excellence award 1992, judge internat. level competitions 1993—). Democrat. Roman Catholic. Home: 30 Venner Rd Arlington MA 02174-8028 Office: Dun & Bradstreet Software 9 Technology Dr Westborough MA 01581

NAJAR, ROBIN MANNING, publishing consultant; b. Dover, Del., Apr. 10, 1958; d. Richard Edward and Harriet Laws (Fisher) Manning; m. Robert Najar, Sept. 14, 1985; children: William Manning, Hannah Fisher. BS in Forestry, U. Maine, 1980. Trails coord. Appalachian Mountain Club, Gorham, N.H., 1983-85; acting conservation dir. Appalachian Mountain Club, Boston, 1985; sales rep. Macmillan Publ. Co., N.Y.C., 1986-90, regional sales mgr., 1990-94; pub. cons., 1994—. Democrat. Roman Catholic. Office: Macmillan Publ Co 866 3rd Ave New York NY 10022-6221

NAJAVITS, LISA MARIANNE, clinical psychologist, researcher; b. New Brunswick, N.J., Jan. 24, 1961; d. Joseph Samuel and Magdalena (Kaufmann) N. BA cum laude, Columbia U., 1983; PhD, Vanderbilt U., 1990. Lic. clin. psychologist, Mass. Pub. policy intern N.Y.C. Bd. Edn., 1983; rsch. asst. Payne Whitney Clinic, N.Y.C., 1983-85; rsch. rater Ctr. for Psychotherapy Rsch. Vanderbilt U., Nashville, 1986-88; rsch. asst. McLean Hosp.-Harvard Med. Sch., Belmont, Mass., 1990—; project dir., asst. psychologist McLean Hosp. and Mass. Gen. Hosp., Belmont, Mass., 1992—; psychology instr. Harvard U. Med. Sch., Boston, 1992—; psychol. examiner Assessment and Cons. for Schs., Nashville, 1988-89; project cons. Vancerbilt U., Nashville, 1991; presenter Am. Psychiat. Assn., New Orleans, 1990, APA, Boston, 1990, Atlanta, 1988, Soc. for Psychotherapy Rsch., Pitts., 1993, Wintergreen, Va., 1990, Santa Fe, 1994, Toronto, Can., 1989, Lyons, France, 1991, Assn. for Advancement of Behavior Therapy, San Diego, 1994, among others. Contbr. articles to profl. jours. Grantee Nat. Inst. Drug Abuse, 1993—. Mem. Am. Assn. for Advancement of Behavior Therapy, Soc. for Psychotherapy Rsch. Office: McLean Hosp 115 Mill St Belmont MA 02178-1048

NAK, CAROL LOUCKS, psychologist; b. Peru, Ind., Oct. 8, 1947; d. William Norris and Elaine (Jenkins) Loucks; m. Charles John Nak, Aug. 24, 1966 (div. May 1974); children: Charles John, Stephanie Nak Mason, Michael Lawrence. BS in Psychology/Sociology, U. Utah, 1976; ms in Secondary Edn., Ind. U., 1977, MS in Counseling and Counselor Edn., 1987, PhD in Counseling Psychology, 1990. Lic. pscyhologist, Fla.; marriage and family therapist, Mont. Tchr., counselor Marmalade Hill Sch., Salt Lake City, 1972-77, Harmony Sch., Bloomington, Ind., 1977-83; supr. student tchrs. and counselors Ind. U., Bloomington, 1984-87; counseling intern Butler U., Indpls., 1986-87; counselor Stetson U., Peland, Fla., 1987-90; therapist Peninsula Med. Ctr., Ormond Beach, Fla., 1990-91; resident, therapist Atlantic Shores Hosp., Daytona Beach, 1992-93; therapist Kelly Ferguson & Assocs., Ormond Beach, 1990-94; pvt. practice Ormond Beach, 1994—. Author: Correlates of EEG Hermispheri Integration, 1990. Edn. fellowship Ind. U., 1985; scholarship Delta Theta Tau. Mem. Am. Psychol. Assn., Assn. Am. Marriage and Family Therapists. Office: 770 W Granada Blvd Ste 206 Ormond Beach FL 32174-5188

NAKAGAWA, JEAN HARUE, diversified corporation executive; b. Honolulu, Sept. 21, 1943; d. Herbert Haruo and Dorothy Mitsue (Nishimura) Yorita; m. Melvin Katsumi Nakagawa, July 16, 1966; 1 child,

Lisa. BBA, U. Hawaii, 1965, MBA, 1968. Rsch. asst. First Hawaiian Bank, Honolulu, 1965-68; dir. planning AMFAC, Inc., Honolulu, 1968-73; v.p. Island Fed. Savings and Loan, Honolulu, 1973-75; dir. rsch. and planning Servco Pacific Inc., Honolulu, 1975—, asst. v.p., 1975-77, v.p., 1977-79, group v.p., 1979-84, sr. v.p., 1984-88, exec. v.p., 1988—; bd. dirs. Servco Pacific Inc., Servco Fin. Corp. Trustee Honolulu Theater for Youth, 1982-89, Hawaii Pub. Employees Health Fund, 1985-89; mem. devel. com. Hawaii Baptist Acad.; bd. dirs. ARC; mem. Pacific Asian Affairs Coun., Hawaii Econ. Edn. Coun., Hawaii Fgn. Rels. Coun. Mem. Hawaii Soc. Corp. Planners (v.p., pres.), Hawaii Econ. Assn. (pres., v.p.), Planning Execs. Inst. (pres.), Orgn. Women Leaders (v.p.). Club: Plaza. Office: Servco Pacific Inc 900 Fort St Mall #600 Honolulu HI 96813

NAKAJIMA, YASUKO, medical educator; b. Osaka, Japan, Jan. 8, 1932; came to U.S., 1962, 69; d. Isao and Taeko Nakagawa; m. Shigehiro Nakajima; children: Hikeko H., Gene A. MD, U. Tokyo, 1955, PhD, 1962. Intern U. Tokyo Sch. Medicine, 1955-56, resident, 1956-57, instr., 1962-67; assoc. prof. Purdue U., West Lafayette, Ind., 1969-76, prof., 1976-88; prof. anatomy and cell biology U. Ill. Coll. Medicine, Chgo., 1988—; vis. rsch. fellow Coll. Physicians and Surgeons, Columbia U., N.Y.C., 1962-64; asst. rsch. anatomist UCLA Sch. Medicine, 1964-65; vis. rsch. fellow Cambridge U., 1967-69. Contbr. articles to sci. jours. Fulbright travel grantee, 1962-65. Mem. AAAS, Soc. Neurosci., Am. Soc. Cell Biology, Am. Assn. Anatomists, Biophys. Soc., Marine Biol. Lab. Corp. Office: U Ill Coll Medicine at Chgo Dept Anatomy-Cell Biology m/c 512 808 S Wood St Chicago IL 60612

NAKAYAMA, PAULA AIKO, justice; b. Honolulu, Oct. 19, 1953; m. Charles W. Totto; children: Elizabeth Murakami, Alexander Totto. BS, U. Calif., Davis, 1975; JD, U. Calif., 1979. Bar: Hawaii 1979. Dep. pros. atty. City and County of Honolulu, 1979-82; ptnr. Shim, Tam & Kirimitsu, Honolulu, 1982-92; judge 8th cir. State of Hawaii, Oahu, 1992—. Mem. Am. Judicature Soc., Hawaii Bar Assn., Sons and Daughters of 442. Office: Ali'iolani Hale 417 S King St Honolulu HI 96813 Address: PO Box 2560 Honolulu HI 96804

NAKER, MARY LESLIE, export transportation company executive; b. Elgin, Ill., July 6, 1954; d. Robert George and Marilyn Jane (Swain). BS in Edn., No. Ill. U., 1976, MS in Edn., 1978, postgrad., 1980; postgrad., Coll. Fin. Planning, 1990. Cert. tchr., Ill., fin. paraplanner. Retail sales clk. Fin'n Feather Farm, Dundee, Ill., 1972-75; self-employed tchr. South Elgin, Ill., 1974-78; teaching asst. Sch. Dist #13, Bloomingdale, Ill., 1976-78, substitute tchr.; office mgr. Tempo 21, Carol Stream, Ill., 1978-82, LaGrange, Ill., 1982-85; sales coord. K&R Delivery, Hinsdale, Ill., 1986-89; fin. planner coord. Elite Adv. Svcs., Inc., Schaumburg, Ill., 1989-90; adminstrv. coord. Export Transports, Inc., Elk Grove Village, Ill., 1990—. Leader Girl Scouts U.S.A., 1972-77, camp counselor, 1972-79. Recipient Music Scholarship PTA, U. Wis., 1967, PTA, U. Iowa, 1968-69. Mem. Nat. Geographic Soc., Smithsonian Assn. Lutheran. Home: 2020 Clearwater Way Elgin IL 60123 Office: Export Transports Inc 1660 Carmen Dr Elk Grove Village IL 60007-6504

NAKHOST, ZAHRA, food scientist; b. Tehran, Iran, Aug. 14, 1948; came to U.S., 1975; d. Ali and Batool (Zarinkolah) N.; m. Ahmad Reza Kamarei, Aug. 24, 1971; chldren: Arzhang, Golbahar. BS, Coll. of Nutrition, Tehran, Iran, 1970; MS, Tehran U., Karaj, Iran, 1975, MIT, 1979. Rsch. specialist dept. of nutrition and food sci. MIT, Cambridge, Mass., 1979-86, rsch. assoc. dept. applied biol. scis., 1986-89; rsch. assoc. Applied BioTechnology Inc., Cambridge, Mass., 1989-90; rsch. scientist The Quaker Oats Co., Barrington, Ill., 1992—. Contbr. numerous sci. articles to profl. jours. and chpt. to book. Recipient Cert. of Recognition, NASA, 1991, Tech. Brief award, 1991. Mem. AAAS, NAFE, Am. Chem. Soc., Inst. Food Technologists, Sigma Xi. Office: The Quaker Oats Co 617 W Main St Barrington IL 60010

NALEWAJA, DONNA, state legislator; m. John Nalewaja; 4 children. BA, U. Minn. Realtor; mem. N.D. Ho. of Reps., 1983-85; now state senator N.D. Senate. Mem. N.D. Coalition Adult Literacy. Mem. N.D. State Union Women's Club. Home: 1121 11th St N Fargo ND 58102-3522 Office: State Senate State Capitol Bismarck ND 58505*

NALEWAKO, MARY ANNE, corporate secretary; b. Johnstown, Pa., Aug. 15, 1934; d. Charles and Margaret (Timothy) Rooney; m. Michael S. Nalewako, Apr. 8, 1961; 1 child, Michael. BSBA, Coll. St. Elizabeth, Convent Station, N.J., 1987. Adminstrv. asst. to chmn. Gen. Pub. Utilities, Parsippany, N.J., 1975-88, corp. sec., 1988—. Recipient Twin award Central (N.J.) YWCA, 1989, award Exec. Women of N.J., 1992. Mem. Am. Soc. Corp. Secs., Seraphic Soc., Spring Brook Country Club. Office: Gen Pub Utilities Corp 100 Interpace Pky Parsippany NJ 07054-1113

NALL, LUCIA LYNN, controller; b. Jackson, Miss., Nov. 22, 1954; d. Aldert S. and Jean (Eaves) Nall. BA in History, Belhaven Coll., 1975, BS in Acctg., 1981; MBA, Miss. Coll., 1994. Acct. Miss. State Bd. Health, Jackson, 1979-85; asst. contr. Miller-Wills Aviation, Jackson, 1985-87; contr. Alston, Rutherford, Tardy & Van Slyke, Jackson, 1987—; owner real estate bus., 1982—; fin. cons. for various bus., 1991—; mgr. individual stock programs, 1992-94. Mem. NAFE. Home: 930 N Livingston Rd Jackson MS 39213-9207 Office: Alston Rutherford Tardy & Van Slyke 121 N State St Jackson MS 39201-2811

NALLEY, ELIZABETH ANN, chemistry educator; b. Catron, Mo., July 8, 1942; d. Arthur E. and Thelma L. (King) Frazier; m. Robert L. Mullican, Jan. 2, 1986; 1 child, George L. BS, Northeastern Okla. State U., 1965; MS, Okla. State U., 1969; PhD, Tex. Woman's U., 1975. High sch. tchr. Muskogee (Okla.) Ctrl. High Sch., 1964-65; instr. Cameron U., Lawton, Okla., 1969-72; asst. prof. Cameron U., Lawton, 1972-75, assoc. prof., 1975-78, prof., 1978—. Contbr. articles to profl. jours. Mem. AAAS, Assn. for Advancement of Computers in Edn., Am. Chem. Soc. (councilor 1980—, sec. div. profl. rels. 1987—, Okla. Chemist award 1992), Am. Inst. Chemists (nat. bd. dirs.), Phi Kappa Phi (regent 1981-89, nat. v.p. 1989-92, nat. pres.-elect 1992-95, nat. pres. 1995—, Disting. Faculty award 1978), Sigma Xi, Sigma Pi Sigma, Iota Sigma Pi. Home: RR 3 Box 176-1 Chickasha OK 73018-9544 Office: Cameron U Dept of Chemistry 2800 W Gore Blvd Lawton OK 73505-6320

NAMEROW, SUSAN ROBBINS, legal administrator; b. Binghamton, N.Y., Oct. 8, 1945; d. Mayer and Esther (Rotenberg) Robbins; children: Lisa B., Lori A., Lynne E. Various positions Day, Berry & Howard, Hartford, Conn., 1983-87; legal adminstr. Cummings & Lockwood, Hartford, Conn., 1987—. V.p. Jewish Community Living Aux., 1992-93, 93-94; bd. dirs. Jewish Children's Svc. Orgn.; co-chair family-to-family program Jewish Family Svc., 1991-92, 92-93. Mem. Assn. Legal Adminstrs. (v.p. Nutmeg chpt. 1993-94, program co-chairperson 1992-93). Office: Cummings & Lockwood City Place I Hartford CT 06103-3495

NANAGAS, MARIA TERESITA CRUZ, pediatrician, educator; b. Manila, Jan. 21, 1946; came to U.S., 1971; d. Ambrosio and Maria (Pasamonte) Cruz; m. Victor N. Nanagas, Jr.; children: Victor III, Valerie, Vivian. BS, U. of the Philippines, 1965, MD, 1970. Diplomate Am. Bd. Pediat. Intern, resident St. Elizabeth's Hosp., Boston, 1971-74; fellow in ambulatory pediat. North Shore Children's Hosp., Salem, Mass., 1974-75; active staff medicine Children's Med. Ctr., Dayton, Ohio, 1976—, head divsn. gen. pediat., 1988-90, co-interim head ambulatory pediat., 1989-90, med. dir. ambulatory pediat., dir. ambulatory svcs., 1990—; clin. asst. prof. pediat. Wright State U., Dayton, 1977-83, clin. assoc. prof. pediat., 1983—, head divsn. gen. pediat., 1993—, selective dir., 1989—; dir., preceptor Wright State U. resident's family clinic Children's Med. Ctr., 1989—, attending physician family practice programs, 1978—. Active Miami Valley Lead Poisoning Prevention Coalition, 19926. Fellow Am. Acad. Pediat.; mem. Western Ohio Pediat. Soc. Office: Children's Med Ctr Health Clinic 1 Children's Plz Dayton OH 45404-1815

NANAVATI, GRACE LUTTRELL, dancer, choreographer, instructor; b. Springfield, Ill., Oct. 2, 1951; d. Curtis Loren and Mary Grace (Leaverton) Luttrell; m. P.J. Nanavati, May 11, 1985; 1 child, William P. BA, Butler U., 1973; MA, Sangamon State U., 1978. Owner, dir. Dance Arts Studio, Springfield, 1973—; artistic dir. Springfield (Ill.) Ballet Co., 1975—; compulsary arts programing com. Sch. Dist. 186, Springfield, 1990—; dance panel Ill. Arts Coun., 1990-92. Vol. Meml. Med. Ctr., Springfield, 1980-88. Named Women of Yr., YMCA, Springfield, 1982; recipient Mayor award for Arts, City of Springfield, 1985, Best of Springfield award Ill. Times, Springfield, 1990. Home: 1501 Williams Blvd Springfield IL 62704 Office: Dance Arts Studio 2820 So MacArthur Springfield IL 62704

NANCE, BETTY LOVE, librarian; b. Nashville, Oct. 29, 1923; d. Granville Scott and Clara (Mills) Nance. BA in English magna cum laude, Trinity U., 1957; AM in Library Sci., U. Mich., 1958. Head dept. acquisitions Stephen F. Austin U. Library, Nacogdoches, Tex., 1958-59; librarian 1st Nat. Bank, Fort Worth, 1959-61; head catalog dept. Trinity U., San Antonio, 1961-63; head tech. processes U. Tex. Law Library, Austin, 1963-66; head catalog dept. Tex. A&M U. Library, College Station, 1966-69; chief bibliographic services Washington U. Library, St. Louis, 1970; head dept. acquisitions Va. Commonwealth U. Library, Richmond, 1971-73; head tech. processes Howard Payne U. Library, Brownwood, Tex., 1974-79; library dir. Edinburg (Tex.) Pub. Library, 1980-91; pres. Edinburg Com. for Salvation Army. Mem. ALA, Pub. Library Assn., Tex. Library Assn., Hidalgo County Library Assn. (v.p. 1980-81, pres. 1981-82), Pan Am. Round Table of Edinburg (corr. sec. 1986-88, assoc. dir. 1989-90), Edinburg Bus. and Profl. Womens Club (founding bd. dirs., pres. 1986-87, bd. dirs. 1987-88), Alpha Lambda Delta, Alpha Chi. Methodist. Club: Zonta Club of San Antonio (bd. dirs. West Hidalgo club 1986-88). Home: 5359 Fredericksburg Rd # 806 San Antonio TX 78229

NANCE, MARTHA MCGHEE, rehabilitation nurse; b. Huntington, W.Va., Jan. 24, 1944; d. Orme Winford and Sadie Mae (Dudley) McGhee; m. John Edgar Nance, Mar. 17, 1990; children: Laura Beckner, Suzie Brickey. RN, St. Mary's Sch. Nursing, Huntington, W.Va., 1980; student, Marshall U., Huntington, W.Va., 1978-88. Cert. rehab. nurse. Surg. head nurse Huntington Hosp. Inc., nursing supr.; quality assurance dir. Am. Hosp. for Rehab., Huntington, 1988-89, DON, 1989-90; rehab. charge nurse Am. Putnam Nursing and Rehab. Ctr., Hurricane, W.Va., 1990—; nursing case mgr. Mountain State Blue Cross & Blue Shield, Charleston, W.Va., 1991. Mem. Assn. for Practitioners in Infection Control. Home: RR 4 Box 100 Hurricane WV 25526-9351

NANCE, MARY JOE, secondary education educator; b. Carthage, Tex., Aug. 7, 1921; d. F. F. and Mary Elizabeth (Knight) Born; m. Earl C. Nance, July 12, 1946; 1 child, David Earl. BBA, North Tex. State U., 1953; postgrad., Northwestern State U. La., 1974; ME, Antioch U., 1978. Tchr., Port Isabel (Tex.) Ind. Sch. Dist., 1953-79; tchr. English, Tex., 1965, Splendora (Tex.) High Sch., 1979-80, McLeod, Tex., 1980-81, Bremond, Tex., 1981-84. Vol. tchr. for Indian students, 1964-65, 79. Served with WAAC, 1942-43, WAC 1945. Recipient Image Maker award Carthage C. of C., 1984; cert. bus. educator. Mem. ASCD, NEA, Nat. Bus. Edn. Assn., Tex. Tchrs. Assn., Tex. Bus. Tchrs. Assn. (cert. of appreciation 1978), Nat. Women's Army Corps Vets. Assn., Air Force Assn. (life), Gwinnett Hist. Soc., Hist. Soc. Panola County, Panola County Hist. & Geneal. Assn., Coun. for Basic Edn., Nat. Hist. Soc., Tex. Coun. English Tchrs. Baptist.

NANGLE, CAROLE FOLZ, counselor; b. Evansville, Ind.; d. Francis Jacob Jr. and Mary Josephine (Metzger) Folz; m. James Francis Nangle Jr., Nov. 21, 1953; children: Cynthia Nangle Bitting, Mary Nangle Boughton, Catherine Nangle Howland. BS, Maryville Coll. Sacred Heart, 1953; MA in Counseling, Webster U., 1985. Substitute tchr. All Saints Cath. Parish, 1962-66; counselor, tchr. Cath. Women's League Day Care Ctr., 1965-74; asst. tchr. art St. Joseph Inst. for Deaf, 1980-81; tutor, counselor St. Vincent German Home, 1979-82; counselor Cath. Family Svcs., 1985—; project Rachel Archdiocese of St. Louis, 1989—. Fundraiser Cath. Women's LEague, 1965-68, fundraiser chmn., 1966, bd. dirs., 1965-71; bd. dirs. Washington U. St. Louis-Newman Club, 1969-74; mem. aux. bd. St. Louis Hosp., 1981-83; mem. alumnae bd. Villa Duchesne Acad. of Sacred Heart, 1963-70, 80-86; weekly fin. accts. Christ the King Parish, 1958-60; bd. govs. Lake Forest Subdivsn., 1982-84, directory, 1982; alumnae class rep. Maryville Coll., 1960-69; bd. dirs. Scholar Program St. Louis, 1966-68, co-chmn., 1967. Mem. Am. Counseling Assn., Assn. Adult Devel. and Aging, Mensa (nat. scholar program 1981-82, chmn. nat. scholar program 1981). Roman Catholic.

NANGLE, JANE ADAMS, lawyer; b. Richmond, Va., Aug. 15, 1944; d. Emil John and Valerie Florence (Sipe) Adams; m. James E. Caldwell, Aug. 16, 1963 (div. Apr. 1971); children: Martha Jane, James E. Jr.; m. John Francis Nangle, June 7, 1986. BA, Webster U., 1975; JD, Washington U., 1979. Bar: Ill. 1980, Mo. 1979, Ga. 1990, U.S. Dist. Ct. (ea. dist.) Mo., U.S. Tax Ct., U.S. Ct. Appeals (8th cir.), U.S. Supreme Ct. Ptnr. The Stolar Partnership, St. Louis, 1978-90; counsel, 1991—. Contbr. articles to profl. jours. Active PTA St. Louis area schs., 1970-86; vol. ARC, Scott AFB, Ill.; den mother Boy Scouts Am., 1977-78. Mem. ABA, Mo. Bar Assn., Ill. State Bar Assn., Ga. Bar Assn., Bar Assn. Met. St. Louis, Mo. Soc. Hosp. Attys., Mo. Sch. Bd. Assn. Republican. Presbyterian. Office: The Stolar Partnership 911 Washington Ave Saint Louis MO 63101-1243

NANK, LOIS RAE, financial executive; b. Racine, Wis., Jan. 6; d. Walter William August and Lanora Elizabeth (Freymuth) N. BS in Econs., U. Wis., 1962; postgrad. in profl. mgmt., Fla. Inst. Tech., 1977. Contract specialist U.S. Naval Ordnance Sta., Forest Park, Ill., 1963-66, U.S. Army Munitions Command, Joliet, Ill., 1966-72; plans/program specialist U.S. Army Munitions Command, Joliet, 1972-73, U.S. Army Armament Command, Rock Island, Ill., 1973-77; chief budget office U.S. Army Auto Log Mgmt. System Act, St. Louis, 1977-81; sr. budget analyst U.S. Army Materiel Command, Alexandria, Va., 1981-87; sr. fin. mgr. Def. Mapping Agy., Reston, Va., 1987-93; cons. Springfield, Va, 1993—. Coun. mem. chairperson bldg. com. Bread of Life Luth. Ch., Springfield, Va., 1986-90, Christ Luth. Ch., Fairfax, Va., 1990—; bd. dirs. Cedar Wood Homeowners' Assn., Bettendorf, Iowa, 1975-77, Oak Homeowners' Assn., Chesterfield, Mo., 1980-81. Mem. NAFE, Am. Soc. Mil. Comptrollers, Va. Assn. Female Execs., Order of Ea. Star. Office: 7812 O'Dell St Springfield VA 22153-2747

NANNA, ELIZABETH ANN WILL, librarian, educator; b. Rahway, N.J., Nov. 21, 1932; d. Rudolph Julius and Dorothy Ada (Haulenbeck) Will; m. Antonio Carmine Nanna, June 15, 1963. Cert. in bus. with honors, Stuart Sch. Bus. Adminstrn., 1963; AA, Ocean County Coll., 1980; BA with honors, Georgian Ct. Coll., 1984, MA, 1984, postgrad., 1984-85; postgrad., Jersey City State Coll., 1988, Montclair State Coll., 1988-89. Cert. art, early childhood and spl. edn., media specialist, supr., N.J. Entrepreneur Ye Olde Cedar Inn, Toms River, N.J., 1963-78; tchr. art and history Monsignor Donovan High Sch., Toms River, 1980-82; tchr. art Whiting (N.J.) Elem. Sch./Manchester Twp. Sch. Dist., 1983-84, Ridgeway Elem. Sch./Manchester Twp. Sch. Dist., Manchester, 1985-87; gifted and talented program tchr., coord., 1984-86; tchr. spl. edn. New Egypt (N.J.) Elem. Sch./Plumsted Twp. Sch. Dist., 1988, libr. media specialist, 1988—. Author: Fostering Cognitive Growth Through Creativity, 1984; contbr. articles to profl. jours. Mem. Mounmouth Park Ball Com., Monmouth County, N.J., 1974—; dir. teen charm sch. Rutgers U. Extension Svc., Ocean County, N.J., 1965; chmn. Ocean County Fair Queen, 1967-84, Ocean County Heart of Hearts Charity Ball, 1976. Recipient Leadership and Svcs. award Ocean County Fair, Ocean County Heart Fund Assn., 1977. Mem. N.J. Reading Assn. (state coun.), N.J. Middle Sch. Assn., N.J. Libr. Assn., N.J. Edn. Assn., Ednl. Media Assn. N.J., Ocean County Artists Guild, Georgian Ct. Coll. Alumni Assn. Republican. Roman Catholic. Home: 15 Mitchell Dr Toms River NJ 08755-5179 Office: Plumsted Twp Sch Dist 44 N Main St New Egypt NJ 08533-1316

NANNEY, SONDRA TUCKER, dance school executive, small business owner; b. Knoxville, Tenn., Dec. 11, 1937; d. Willard Woodrow and Mary Lou (Pollard) Tucker; m. Red Celestine Nanney, March 11, 1960; children: Stacy Leigh Nanney Courtney, Kristin Kaye. Grad. high sch., Knoxville, 1955. Bookkeeper Miles Siegel, CPA, Knoxville, 1955-56; sales sec. Sta. WBIR-TV, Knoxville, 1956-64, Knoxville News Sentinel, 1965-67; owner Concord Farragut Sch., Knoxville, 1974-79, Knoxville Sch. Dance, 1979-94, Images Dancewear, Knoxville, 1989-94; pres. Knoxville Met. Dance, 1982-94. Mem. Knoxville Symphony League (officer 1982-94, pres. 1989-90, chmn. showcase 1993, nominating com. 1992), Knoxville Met. Dance Theatre (pres. 1994). Republican. Office: Knoxville Sch Ballet Arts PO Box 23841 Knoxville TN 37933-1841

NANTO, ROXANNA LYNN, career planning administrator, consultant; b. Hanford, Calif., Dec. 17, 1952; d. Lawson Gene Brooks and Bernice (Page) Jackson; m. Harvey Ken Nanto, Mar. 23, 1970; 1 child, Shea Kiyoshi. A, Chemeketa Community Coll., 1976; B, Idaho State U., 1978. PBX operator Telephone Answer Bus. Svc., Moses Lake, Wash., 1965-75; edn. coord. MimiCassia Community Edn., Rupert, Idaho, 1976-77; office mgr. Lockwood Corp., Rupert, Idaho, 1977-78; cost acct. Keyes Fibre Co., Wenatchee, Wash., 1978-80; acctg. office mgr. Armstrong & Armstrong, Wenatchee, Wash., 1980-81; office mgr. Cascade Cable Constrn. Inc., East Wenatchee, Wash., 1981-83; interviewer, counselor Wash. Employment Security, Wenatchee, 1983-84; pres. chief exec. officer Regional Health Care Plus, East Wenatchee, 1986-88; dist. career coord. Eastmont Sch. Dist., East Wenatchee, 1984-90; prin. Career Cons., 1988-90; exec. dir. Wenatchee Valley Coll. Found., 1990-91; ednl. cons. Sunbelt Consortium, East Wenatchee, 1991-93; cons. CC Cons. Assocs., 1993—; dir. cmty. and organl. devel. Mktg. and Mgmt. Resouce Group, Wenatchee, Wash., 1994—; speaker North Cen. Washington Profl. Women, Wenatche, 1987, Wen Career Women's Network, Wenatchee, 1990, Wenatchee Valley Rotary, 1990, Meeting the Challenge of Workforce 2000, Seattle, 1993; cons., speaker Wash. State Sch. Dirs., Seattle, 1987; speaker Wenatchee C. of C., 1989; sec. Constrn. Coun. of North Cen. Washington, Wenatchee, 1981-83; bd. dirs. Gen. Vocat. Adv. Bd., Wenatchee, 1986-88, Washington Family Ind. Program, Olympia, 1989—; mem. econ. devel. coun. Grant County, 1992—. Mem. at large career Women's Network, 1984—, mem. Econ. Devel. Coun. of No. Cen. Washington; mem. Steering Com. to Retain Judge Small. Grantee Nat. Career Devel. Guidelines Wash. State, 1989; named Wenatchee Valley Coll. Vocat. Contbr. of Yr., 1991. Fellow Dem. Women's Club; mem. Nat. Assn. Career Counselors, Nat. Assn. Pvt. Career Counselors, Nat. Coun. Resource Devel., NCW Estate Planning Coun. Home: 704 Larch Ct Wenatchee WA 98802-5052 Office: CC Cons Assn 704 Larch Ct Ste B East Wenatchee WA 98802-5052

NAPHOLZ, LINDA, psychiatric mental health nurse and educator; b. Milw., July 21, 1955. BSN, U. Wis., Milw., 1978; MSN, U. Wis., Oshkosh, 1980; PhD in Counseling Psychology, U. Wis., 1988. Contract nurse Kimberly Nurses Quality Care Nursing, Milw., 1979—; occupational health nurse practitioner GM, Milw., 1979-88; mental health cons. nurse Day 1/CSP Adult Day Treatment Ctr., Milw., 1980-85, Belwood Ltd., Milw., 1981; faculty, lectr. U. Wis. Sch. Nursing, Milw., 1981-88; exam. for credit examiner Med. Coll. of Wis. Sch. Nursing, Milw., 1984-85; asst. prof. U. Wis. Sch. Nursing, Milw., 1988—; presenter in field. Contbr. articles to profl. jours. Vol. CPR intr., good grooming instr. ARC, 1980-86. Grantee U. Wis. Grad. Sch., Milw., 1991, U. Wis. Sch. Nursing, 1989, 90, 91; Post-Baccalaureate Faculty fellow U. Wis., Milw., 1987-88. Mem. Nat. League for Nursing, Wis. League for Nursing (newsletter com. co-editor 1984-85), Primary Care Nurse Practitioners Assn., Wis. Nurses Assn. (primary care nurse practitioners coun. treas. 1983-85), Am. Assn. for Marriage and Family Therapists (clin.), Sigma Theta Tau (rsch. com. Eta Nu chpt. 1992). Home: 2138 E Lafayette Pl # 2 Milwaukee WI 53202 Office: U Wis Sch Nursing PO Box 413 Milwaukee WI 53201

NAPIER, LOIS CHRISTINE, elementary education educator; b. Cheshire, Ohio, June 28, 1942; d. Walter W. and Pauline (Athey) Rife; m. Lark Napier, Mar. 23, 1963 (div. 1979); children: Lark Jr., Kevin T. BS, Ohio U., 1974. Elem. cert. learning disabilities, educatable mentally retarded. Trainable tchr. Guiding Hand Sch., Cheshire, 1972-74; elem. tchr. Kyger Creek Local Sch., Cheshire, 1974; devel. handicapped tchr. Gallia County Sch., Gallipolis, Ohio, 1974; tchr. learning disabled/developmentally handicapped Addaville Elem. Sch., 1992—; treas. Gallia County Local Edn. Assn., 1981-83, pres., 1984-87, v.p., 1993-94; vice chmn., 1991—. Twp. chmn. Gallia County Rep. Club, 1985-86, Flora Pomona Grange, Pomeroy, Ohio, 1985-87, Cires #778 Star Grange, Dexter, Ohio, 1989-91. Mem. AAUW (pres. 1986-88, sec. 1991-94), Ohio Edn. Assn., Southeastern Ohio Edn. Assn., Gallia County Local Edn. Assn. (pres. 1984-87), Coun. for Exceptional Children, Nat. Soc. DAR, French Colony (vice regent 1992-95). Methodist. Home: 2036 Jessie Creek Rd Bidwell OH 45614-9484 Office: Addaville Elem Sch 1333 Brick School Rd Gallipolis OH 45631-8782

NAPIERALSKI, LINDA BINGAMAN, critical care nurse, educator; b. Reading, Pa., Aug. 13, 1954; d. Frederick William and Dorothy Evelyn (Deck) Bingaman; m. Thomas John Napieralski, Nov. 19, 1983; children: Lisa, Jennifer. Diploma in nursing, Thomas Jefferson U., 1975; BSN, U. Pa., Phila., 1981, MSN in Adult Health, 1983. RN, N.J., Pa.; cert. in med.-surg. nursing; cert. ACLS. Staff nurse, adv. staff nurse Thomas Jefferson U. Hosp., Phila., 1975-78; staff nurse, primary nurse II Hahnemann Hosp., Phila., 1978-81; clin. nurse III U. Pa. Hosp., Phila., 1981-85; instr. Sch. Nursing, student adviser Bryn Mawr (Pa.) Hosp., 1985-86; ICU staff nurse West Jersey Hosp., Voorhees, 1986—; clin. instr. Thomas Jefferson U., Phila., 1991-93; adj. prof. Gloucester County Coll., Sewell, N.J., 1991—. Mem. Osage Parent Faculty Orgn., Voorhees, 1990—. Mem. AACN. Presbyterian. Home: 133 Abbey Rd Voorhees NJ 08043-2003 Office: Gloucester County Coll Dept of Nursing Deptford Twp Sewell NJ 08080

NAPLES, JEAN MARIE, physician; b. Suffern, N.Y., Apr. 27, 1955; d. Ralph Peter and Antoinette (Toscano) N. BS in Med. Tech., Phila. Coll. Pharmacy and Sci., 1977; MPH, U. Calif., Berkeley, 1981; MD, U. Md., 1989; PhD in Tropical Medicine, Johns Hopkins U., 1989. Diplomate Am. Bd. Family Physicians. Lab. dir. Peace Corps USA, Wouakchott, Mauritania, West Africa, 1977-79; lab. tech., food ctr. dir. Med. Vols. Internat., Somalia, 1980-81; med. lab. tech. Church-Home-Hosp., Balt., 1982-89; family medicine resident La. State U. Med. Ctr., Shreveport, 1989-92; high-risk obstetrics fellow Tacoma (Wash.) Family Medicine, 1992-93; resident gen. surgery La. State U. Med. Ctr., Shreveport, 1993—; med. lab. tech. Johns Hopkins Infectious Disease Lab., Balt., 1984-85. Patentee in field. Blood donor ARC, Shreveport, 1989-94; mem. Physician Com. for Responsible Medicine, Washington, 1993. Mem. Am. Med. Women's Assn., Am. Acad. Family Practice, Am. Soc. Clin. Pathologists, Alpha Omega Alpha, Alpha Delta Theta (v.p. 1976-77). Democrat. Roman Catholic. Office: La State Univ Med Ctr 1501 Kings Hwy Shreveport LA 71103-4228

NAPLES, LESLIE ANN, nursing director; b. Fairview, Ohio, May 17, 1961; d. Janette Stanley and Alice May (Roepke) N. Diploma in Nursing, Timken Mercy Med. Ctr., Canton, Ohio, 1982; BA in Healthcare Adminstrn., Capital U., 1991; MBA, Baldwin-Wallace Coll., 1993. Lic. nurse, Ohio. Charge nurse divsn. urology svcs. Parma (Ohio) Community Gen. Hosp., 1982-84; charge nurse divsn. trauma and emergency svcs. Deaconess Hosp. of Cleve., 1984-90, nursing dir., 1990-92; crisis intervention nurse, clin. coord. The Plastic Surgery Ctr., Richfield, Ohio, 1989-92; infusion specialist part-time Baxter Healthcare Corp., Deerfield, Ill., (Cleve. ter.), 1992; nursing dir. emergency svcs. St. John West Shore Hosp., Westlake, Ohio, 1992—. Mem. Westlake (Ohio) Rotary Club. Home: 1430 Crossings Pky Westlake OH 44145 Office: Saint John West Shore Hosp 29000 Center Ridge Rd Westlake OH 44145

NAPOLES, MARTA MARIA, mortgage consultant; b. Miami, Fla., Apr. 23, 1958; d. Oscar and Juana Dolores (Fleites) Sanjurjo; (div. Aug. 1985); children: Janel-Maria, Tania-Kristy. Student, Miami Dade C.C., 1978-79, Barry U., 1989. Asst. dir. pers. Biscayne Bay Marriott Hotel, Miami, 1983-85; dir. human resources Grove Isle Yacht and Tennis Club, Coconut Grove, Fla., 1985-86, Doral Saturnia Internat. Spa Resort, Miami, 1986-87; dir. corp. human resources Royal Caribbean Cruises Ltd., Miami, 1988-91; residential lending loan mgr. Chase Fed. Bank, Sunrise, Fla., 1991-94; mortgage cons. CitiBank FSB, Miami, 1994—; ops. cons. Carrillon Hotel and Resort/R.T.C.-Capital Investment Corp., 1987; dir. ops. for 4 hotels Art Deco Properties, Miami Beach, 1987-88; customer svc. cons. Fed. Express Corp., 1987-88; employment specialist SER Jobs for Progress, Inc., Miami, 1991; unemployment compensation hearing rep. A.D.P., Miami, 1991. Mem. Coral Gables C. of C. (mem. real estate com.). Republican. Roman Catholic. Home: 700 Sea Way Hollywood FL 33024-7126

NAPOLITANO, GRACE F., state legislator; b. Brownsville, Tex., Dec. 4, 1936; d. Miguel and Maria Alicia Ledezma Flores; m. Frank Napolitano, 1982; 1 child, Yolando M., Fred Musquiz Jr., Edward M., Michael M.,

Cynthia M. Student, Cerritos Coll., L.A. Trade Tech, Tec Southwest Coll. Mem. Calif. Assembly, 1993—. Councilwoman City of Norwalk, Calif., 1986-92, mayor, 1989-90; active Cmty. Family Guidance. Mem. Cerritos Coll. Found., Lions Club. Democrat. Roman Catholic. Home: 12946 E Belcher St Norwalk CA 90650 Office: Calif Assembly State Capitol Sacramento CA 95814 also: PO Box 942849 Sacramento CA 94249-0001*

NAPOLITANO, JANET ANN, prosecutor; b. N.Y.C., Nov. 29, 1957; d. Leonard Michael and Jane Marie (Winer) N. BS, U. Santa Clara, Calif., 1979; JD, U. Va., 1983. Bar: Ariz. 1984, U.S. Dist. Ct. Ariz. 1984, Ct. Appeals (9th cir.) 1984, U.S. Ct. Appeals (10th cir.) 1988. Law clk. to presiding judge U.S Ct. Appeals (9th Cir.), 1983-84; ptnr. Lewis & Roca, Phoenix, 1984-93; U.S. atty. Dist. Ariz., Phoenix, 1993—; mem. Atty. Gen.'s adv. com., 1993—. Vice-chair Ariz. Dem. Party, 1991-92; mem. Dem. Nat. Com., 1991-92; State Bd. Tech. Registration, 1989-92; Phoenix Design Standards Rev. Com., 1989-91; bd. dirs. Ariz. Cmty. Legal Svcs. Corp., 1987-92; bd. regents Santa Clara U., 1992—. Truman Scholarship Found. scholar, 1977. Mem. ABA, Am. Law Inst., Ariz. Bar Assn., Maricopa County Bar Assn., Am. Judicature Soc., Ariz. State Bar (chmn. civil practice and procedure com. 1991-92), Phi Beta Kappa, Alpha Sigma Nu. Office: US Attys Office 4000 US Courthouse 230 N 1st Ave Phoenix AZ 85025-0230

NAPOLITANO, VIRGINIA MARY, accountant; b. Chgo., Dec. 3, 1956; d. Alex Marvin and Erminia Mary (DeMarco) Burney; m. Felix Peter Napolitano, Dec. 8, 1973; children: Jennifer Elena, John Marcus. Cert. in Mgmt., Sauk Valley Coll., Dixon, Ill., 1989, student, 1989—. Bookkeeper Rock Falls (Ill.) Nat. Bank, 1976-90; acct. City of Rock Falls, 1990—; acct. Rock Falls Police Pension Fund, 1991—, Rock Falls Fire Pension Fund, 1991—. Roman Catholic. Office: City of Rock Falls 603 W 10th St Rock Falls IL 61071

NAPPER MCNEECE, JANET LYNN, marketing professional; b. Chelsea, Mass., Oct. 5, 1956; d. David Emrys and Jean Ann (Monahan) Napper. BA in Psychology with distinction, U. Colo., 1980. Asst. buyer Target Stores, Mpls., 1981-83; order adminstr. Menswear Internat., N.Y.C., 1983-84; v.p. List Maintenance Corp., Armonk, N.Y., 1984-92; account supr., database mktg. Wunderman Cato Johnson, N.Y.C., 1992—. Active Rombout Village Recreation Com., Beacon, N.Y., 1992. Mem. Women's Direct Response Group, Phi Beta Kappa. Democrat. Presbyterian. Office: Wunderman Cato Johnson 675 6th Ave New York NY 10010-5100

NAQUIN, PATRICIA ELIZABETH, employee assistance consultant; b. Houston, Jan. 28, 1943; d. Louie Dee and Etha Beatrice (English) Price; m. Hollis James Naquin, Mar. 23, 1961; children: Price Naquin, Holli Campbell. BS, U. Houston, 1969, MS, 1982; PhD, Tex. Woman's U., 1988. Lic. profl. counselor; lic. chem. dependency counselor; nat. cert. counselor; cert. chem. dependency specialist; cert. employee assistance profl. Purchasing agt. Internat. Affairs U. Houston, 1966-68; elem. sch. tchr. Pasadena (Tex.) Ind. Sch. Dist., 1969-82; spl. edn. counselor Alvin (Tex.) Ind. Sch. Dist., 1982-85, drug-free schs. coord., 1988-92; marriage and family therapist Lifespan Counseling, Pasadena, 1985-92; employee assistance cons. DuPont, LaPorte, Tex., 1992—; adv. com. mem. Sam Houston U., Huntsville, Tex., 1983; trainer and instr. Bay Area Coun. on Drugs and Alcohol, Houston, 1988-92; cons. Alvin Ind. Sch. Dist., 1989-92, DuPont Valuing People Core Team, 1993—; supr. State Bd. of Profl. Counselors, Houston, 1988—. Co-author: Life is for Everyone Manual, 1990. Com. co-chair Alvin S.A.P. Task Force, 1988-92; com. mem. Tri-Dist. Task Force, Alvin, 1990-91; com. chmn. Alvin Bus./Edn. Partnership, 1992; bd. dirs. Brazoria (Tex.) County Coun. Drugs and Alcohol, 1991. Mem. Am. Assn. Marriage and Family Therapists, Tex. Assn. Counselors of Alcohol and Drug Abuse, Am. Counseling Assn., Employee Assistance Program Assn., Nat. Disting. Svc. Registry/Libr. of Congress, Phi Delta Kappa. Republican. Methodist.

NARAD, JOAN STERN, psychiatrist; b. N.Y.C., June 21, 1943; d. Victor and Grete (Metzger) S.; m. Richard M. Narad; children: Christine, Laurie, Michael. BA, NYU, 1964; MD, Woman's Med. Coll., Pa., 1968. Diplomate Am. Bd. Psychiatry, Am. Bd Child Psychiatry. Intern pediatrics Stanford (Calif.) U. Hosp., 1968-69; resident adult psychiat. Med. Coll., Phila., 1969-71, chief resident in child psychiatry, 1971-73; grad. in psychoanalysis and child psychoanalysis Phila. Psychoanalytic Inst., 1978; practice medicine specializing in child and adolescent psychiatry Westport, Conn., 1979—; chief Adolescent and Young Adult Svc., Silver Hill Found., New Canaan, Conn., 1980-84, 89-93, sr. adolescent cons., 1993-94; unit chief Riverview Hosp. for Children and Youth, Middletown, Conn., 1994—; cons. Cath. Home Girls, Phila., 1971-78, Germantown Friends Sch., 1973-79; asst. prof. Child Psychiat. Med. Coll. Pa., 1975-79; asst. clin. prof. Yale Child Study Ctr., 1979-92, assoc. clin. prof., 1992—. Fellow NIMH, 1968. Fellow Am. Acad. Child and Adolescent Psychiat.; mem. Am. Psychiat. Assn., AMA, Alumnae Assn. Med. Coll. Pa., Am. Psychoanalytic Assn., Western New Eng. Psychoanalytic Soc., Conn. Coun. Child Psychiatry. Home and Office: 3 Colony Rd Westport CT 06880-3703

NARANJO, CAROLYN R., lawyer; b. Far Rockaway, N.Y., Nov. 28, 1954; d. Anthony J. and Mary (Lautazi) Spina; m. James Naranjo, Apr. 28, 1989. BA summa cum laude in Spl. & Elem. Edn., Bklyn. Coll., CUNY, 1976; JD, Temple U., 1981; student, Fordham U., 1980-81. Asst. counsel to head regional counsel First Am. Title Insurance, N.Y.C., 1981-82; legal counsel Creative Abstract Corp., N.Y.C., 1982-84; assoc. firm Friedman & Kornheiser, N.Y.C., 1982-84, Quinn, Cohen, Shields & Bock, N.Y.C., 1984-85; mng. ptnr. Collier, Cohen, Crystal & Bock, N.Y.C., 1990-94; pvt. practice Baldwin, N.Y., 1994—. Office: 746 Merrick Rd Baldwin NY 11510

NARASIMHAN, PADMA MANDYAM, physician; b. Bangalore, India, Mar. 19, 1947; came to U.S., 1976; d. Alasingracher Mandyam and Alamela Mandyam Narasimhan; m. Mandyam N. Venkatesh, Mar. 28, 1981 (div.) 1 child, Ravi. Student, Delhi U., New Delhi, 1964, MBBS, 1969; MD, Maulana Azad Med. Coll., New Delhi, 1970. Diplomate Am. Bd. Internal Medicine. Intern in internal medicine Flushing Hosp., N.Y.C., 1976-77; resident in internal medicine Luth. Med. Ctr., N.Y.C., 1977-79; fellow hematology, oncology Beth-Israel Med. Ctr., N.Y.C., 1979-81; asst. prof. King Drew Med. Ctr., L.A., 1983-87, Harbor UCLA, Torrance, 1987—. Mem. editorial bd. Jour. Internal Medicine, 1986—. Mem. ACP, Am. Soc. Clin. Oncology, So. Calif. Acad. Clin. Oncology. Hindu. Home: 6604 Madeline Cove Dr Palos Verdes Peninsula CA 90274-4608 Office: Harbor UCLA 100 W Carson St Torrance CA 90509

NARDI, THEODORA P., state legislator; b. Warwick, R.I., Aug. 28, 1922; widow; 4 children. Attended, Manhattanville Coll. Mem. N.H. Ho. of Reps.; mem. appropriations com. Chmn. Hills County Dem. Com., 1977-78; pres. N.H. Owl, 1979-80; chmn. Manchester (N.H.) Legis. Del., 1979-82; bd. dirs. N.H. Soup Kitchen, 1985—, New Horizons Soup Kitchen, 1989—; active N.H. Cath. Charities, 1986—, Manchester Housing Coun., 1986—. Democrat. Roman Catholic. Home: 776 Chestnut St Manchester NH 03104-3012 Office: NH Ho of Reps State Capitol Concord NH 03301*

NARDINI, RITA LYNN, mental health nurse; b. Chgo., Nov. 21, 1947; d. Arthur and Julia Rae (Edbrooke) N. ADN, Southwestern Mich. Coll., 1985; student, Mennonite Bibl. Sem., 1987, U. Indpls., 1994—. RN, Ind., Mich.; cert. BLS Am. Heart Assn., crisis prevention intervener, Ind. Staff nurse Michiana Community Hosp., South Bend, Ind., 1985-86; charge nurse psychiat. unit St. Jopseph's Hosp., Mishawaka, Ind., 1986-87, Elkhart (Ind.) Gen. Hosp., 1987-88, Oaklawn Hosp., Goshen, Ind., 1988-90; evening supr., charge nurse adolescent psychiat. unit Charter Hosp., Indpls., 1990-92; weekend charge nurse geriatric psychiat. unit Lockerbie Healthcare, Indpls., 1992—; charge nurse child and adolescent psychiatry Midwest Med. Ctr. (Winona Hosp.), Indpls., 1992-93; child/adolescent psychiat. nurse Koala Hosp., Indpls., 1994—; nurse cons. Growth Innovations, Inc., Berrien Springs, Mich., 1988-89. Mem. ANA (cert. psychiat. nurse), Nat. League Nursing (cert. addictions nurse), Am. Psychiat. Nurses' Assn., Amnesty Internat. Republican. Episcopalian. Office: Koala Hosp 1404 State Ave Indianapolis IN 46203

NARDI RIDDLE, CLARINE, judge, association administrator; b. Clinton, Ind., Apr. 23, 1949; d. Frank Jr. and Alice (Mattioda) Nardi; m. Mark Alan Riddle, Aug. 15, 1971; children: Carl Nardi, Julia Nardi. AB, Ind. U., 1971, JD, 1974; LHD (hon.), St. Joseph Coll., 1991. Bar: Ind. 1974, Conn. 1979, U.S. Dist. Ct. Ind. 1974, Fed. Dist. Ct. Conn. 1980, U.S. Ct. Appeals (2d cir.) 1986, U.S. Ct. Appeals (D.C. cir.) 1994, U.S. Supreme Ct. 1980. Staff atty. Ind. Legis. Svc. Agy., Indpls., 1974-78, legal counsel, 1978-79; dep. corp. counsel City of New Haven, 1980-83; counsel to atty. gen. State of Conn., Hartford, 1983-86, dep. atty. gen., 1986-89, acting atty. gen., 1989, atty. gen., 1989-91; judge Superior Ct. State of Conn., 1991-93; sr. v.p. for govtl. affairs, gen. counsel Nat. Multi-Housing Coun., Nat. Apartment Assn.; asst. counsel state majority Conn. Gen. Assembly, Hartford, 1979, legal rsch. asst. to prof. Yale U., New Haven, 1979; legal counsel com. on law revision Indpls. State Bar Assn., 1979; mem. Chief Justice's Task Force on Gender Bias, Hartford, 1988-90; mem. ethics and values com. Ind. Sector, Washington, 1988-90. Bd. visitors Ind. U., Bloomington, 1974-92; mem. Gov.'s Missing Children Com., Hartford, Conn. Child Support Guidelines Com., Gov.'s Task Force on Justice for Abused Children, Hartford, 1988-90. Named Conn. History Maker Women's Bur. & Permanent Commn. on Status of Women, U.S. Dept. Labor, 1989; recipient Citizen award Nat. Task Force on Children's Constl. Rights. Mem. ABA, Conn. Bar Assn. (chair com. on gender bias, Citation of Merit women and law sect. 1989), Nat. assn. Attys. Gen. (chair charitable trusts and solicitation 1988-90), New Haven Neighborhood Music Sch. (bd. dirs.), Am. Arbitration Assn. (arbitration panel 1994). Democrat. Presbyterian.

NASER, JOANN LYNN, fundraising executive; b. Brownsville, Pa., Apr. 28, 1959; d. Joseph and Margaret Anne (Bodnar) Sarkett; m. James Bennett Naser, Oct. 5, 1991; 1 child, Jonathan Bennett. BA in English and Sociology, Washington and Jefferson U., 1981; MA in English, California U. of Pa., 1988. Lifestyles editor Brownsville (Pa.) Telegraph, 1981-85; grad. asst. California U. of Pa., 1985-87, dir. devel., 1991—; dir. devel. Try-Again Homes, Washington, Pa., 1987-91, Mon Yough Human Svcs., McKeesport, Pa., 1991; dir. of devel. Calif. U. of Pa., 1991—. Mem. Nat. Soc. Fund-Raising Execs., Coun. for Advance and Support of Edn., Brownsville Hist. Soc., Rotary. Home: 315 Low Hill Rd Brownsville PA 15417 Office: California U of Pa 250 University Ave California PA 15419

NASH, ALANNA KAY, critic, writer; b. Louisville, Aug. 16, 1950; d. Allan and Emily Kay (Derrick) N. BA, Stephens Coll., 1972; MS, Columbia U., 1974. Music critic Louisville Courier Jour., 1977; writer, producer Sta. WHAS, Louisville, 1980; pres. Alandale Prodns., Louisville, 1981—; freelance writer specializing in the arts Stereo Rev., Esquire, N.Y. Times, Entertainment Weekly, TV Guide, Ms., Glamour, Working Woman, Saturday Evening Post, Video Rev., 1964—. Author: Dolly, 1978, rev. edit. Dolly Parton: The Early Years, 1994, Behind Closed Doors: Talking with the Legends of Country Music, 1988, Golden Girl: The Story of Jessica Savitch, 1988, Elvis Aaron Presley: Revelations from the Memphis Mafia, 1995; (ghostwriter) Elvis: From Memphis to Hollywood, 1992; co-producer: (TV documentary) The Deaners: Cause without a Rebel; writer, producer: network and syndicated specials; contbr. to books. Recipient Nat. Prodn. awards Alpha Epsilon Rho, 1971. Mem. Soc. Profl. Journalists (bd. dirs. Louisville chpt. 1987—, v.p. 1992-93, pres. 1993-94, Nat. Mem. of Yr. award 1994, Howard Dubin award 1994), Authors Guild, Am. Soc. Journalists and Authors, Country Music Assn. Republican. Methodist. Home and Office: 703 Alta Vista Rd Louisville KY 40206-2940

NASH, ANDREA CAROL, state agency analyst; b. Indpls., Feb. 15, 1951; d. Harry Ritter and Alma Margaret (McIntyre) Flowers; divorced; children: Jennifer Nash, Andrea Elizabeth Bentler. BA, Purdue U., 1972, MS, 1973. Cert. jr. and sr. high sch. tchr. Math tchr. Attica (Ind.) Sch. Dist., 1972-73; analyst State of Calif., San Diego, 1974—. Fiesta worker Ascension Cath. Parish, San Diego, 1984-94; girl scout cookie chmn. Sr. Troop, 1984—, girl scout co-leader, San Diego, 1993—. Mem. Purdue Alumni Assn., Kappa Delta Pi.

NASH, CLARICE ALDINE HAYES, family nurse practitioner, critical care nurse; b. Chgo., May 12, 1952; d. Clarence Jesse and Beatrice Ann (Bevers) Hayes; m. Robert James Nash, Aug. 8, 1981; children: Christopher Robert, Jesse Daniel, Sara April. BSN, U. Tex., El Paso, 1974; MSN, U. South Ala., 1991; FNP, Miss. U. for Women, 1991. RN, Tex., Calif., Miss., Wash.; cert. FNP, ANCC. Staff nurse Sun Towers Hosp., El Paso, Tex., 1974-76; head nurse CCU, St. Joseph Hosp., El Paso, 1976-77; staff nurse MICU/SICU Grossmont Dist. Hosp., La Mesa, Calif., 1984-86; staff nurse CCU, Sharp Meml. Hosp., San Diego, 1984-86, Gulf Coast Community Hosp., Biloxi, Miss., 1987-89; staff nurse critical care Analytical Med. Enterprises, Gulfport, Miss., 1991; nurse practitioner Kitsap County Health Dist., Bremerton, Wash., 1991-93; family nurse practitioner Peninsula Family Med. Ctr., Gig Harbor, Wash., 1994—; adj. faculty ADN program Olympic Coll., Bremerton, Wash., 1991—. With Nurse Corps USN, 1977-83, comdr. USNR. Mem. ANA, AACN, Wash. Nurse's Assn., Nat. League for Nursing, Am. Acad. Nurse Practitioners, Assn. Mil. Surgeons of U.S. Lutheran. Office: Peninsula Family Med Ctr 4700 Pt Fosdick Dr Ste 202 Gig Harbor WA 98335

NASH, JANET RAE, geriatrics nurse; b. Taylorville, Ill., Aug. 12, 1953; d. Rayford C. and Dorothy L (Chlebus) Hurtte; m. James V. Nash, Sept. 17, 1976; children: Cherise, Brian, Brandon, Amanda. Diploma, Decatur Meml. Hosp. Sch. Nsg., 1975. RN, Ill. Staff nurse, charge nurse Decatur (Ill.) Meml. Hosp., 1976-81; clin. coord./head nurse long term care Decatur Meml. Hosp., 1985-91; dir. nursing Americana Healthcare Ctr., Decatur, 1981, Lincoln Manor Nursing Home, Decatur, 1991-92, Cedarwood Healthcare Ctr., Decatur, 1993-94; nurse restorative nursing Ea. Star Home, Macon, Ill., 1992-93; dir. nursing Pershing Estates Psychiat. Facility, Decatur, 1994; supr. Friendship Manor, Mt. Zion, Ill., 1994-95, Fairhaven's Christian Home, Decatur, Ill., 1995—.

NASH, JOYCE DONOVAN, psychologist, health educator, author; b. Carnegie, Pa., Aug. 2, 1940; d. James Stanley and Eleanor M. (Schafer) Donovan; m. John Nash, Sept. 10, 1960 (div. 1964); m. Morgan W. White, Feb. 6, 1983. BS, So. Ill. U., 1972; MA, Stanford U., 1975, PhD, 1977, Pacific Grad. Sch. of Psychology, 1993. Dir. tng. Weight Watchers, San Francisco, 1979-81; health educator Carmel Profl. Assocs., Calif., 1983-85; cons. in field. Author: Taking Charge of Your Weight and Well Being, 1978, Taking Charge of Your Smoking, 1981; (audiocassette album) Taking Charge of Health, 1984, Maximize Your Body Potential, 1986, Now That You've Lost It, 1992. Recipient Nat. Research Service award Dept. Health and Human Services, 1978-79. Mem. Am. Psychol. Assn., Soc. Behavioral Medicine, Assn. Advancement of Behavioral Medicine, Calif. Psychol. Assn. Republican. Office: 1122 Hopkins Ave Woodside CA 94062

NASH, JUNE CAPRICE, anthropology professor; b. Salem, Mass., May 30, 1927; d. Joseph and M. Josephine (Salloway) Bousley; children: Eric, Laura; m. Herbert Menzel, July 1, 1972. BA, CUNY, 1948; MA, U. Chgo., 1953, PhD, 1960. Asst. prof. Chgo. Tchrs. Coll., Chgo., Ill., 1960-63, Yale U. New Haven, Conn., 1963-68; assoc. prof. NYU, 1968-72; prof. CUNY, 1972—; disting. vis. prof. Am. U., Cairo, 1978, U. Colo., Boulder, 1988—; vis. prof. SUNY, Albany, 1988-89; disting. prof. CUNY, N.Y.C., 1990. Author: In the Eyes of the Ancestor, 1970, We Eat the Mines and the Mines Eat Us: Dependency and Exploitation in Bolivian Mining Communities, 1979, From Tank Town to High Tech: The Clash of Community and Industrial Cycles, 1989; editor: Crafts in the World Market: The Impact of Global Exchange on Middle American Artisans, 1993. Mem. Soc. for the Anthropology of Work (pres. 1988—), Assn. Polit. and Legal Activities (pres. 1983), Am. Anthropology Assn., Am. Ethnographic Soc., Assn. for Feminist Anthropology (pres. 1990-93). Home: 2166 Broadway 18D New York NY 10024 Office: CUNY 137th Convent New York NY 10031

NASON, DOLORES IRENE, computer company executive, counselor, eucharistic minister; b. Seattle, Jan. 24, 1934; d. William Joseph Lockinger and Ruby Irene (Church) Gilstrap; m. George Malcolm Nason Jr., Oct. 7, 1951; children: George Malcolm III, Scott James, Lance William, Natalie Joan. Student, Long Beach (Calif.) City Coll., 1956-59; cert. in Religious Edn. for elem tchrs., Immaculate Heart Coll., 1961, cert. teaching, 1962, cert. secondary teaching, 1967; attended, Salesian Sem., 1983-85. Buyer J. C. Penney Co., Barstow, Calif., 1957; prin. St. Cyprian Confraternity of Christian Doctrine Elem. Sch., Long Beach, 1964-67; prin. summer sch. St. Cyprian Confraternity of Christian Doctrine Elem. Sch., Long Beach, 1965-67; pres. St. Cyprian Confraternity Orgn., Long Beach, 1967-69; dist. co-chmn. L.A. Diocese, 1968-70; v.p. Nason & Assocs., Inc., Long Beach, 1978—; pres. L.A. County Commn. on Obscenity & Pornography, 1984—; eucharistic minister St. Cyprian Ch., Long Beach, 1985—; bd. dirs. L.A. County Children's Svcs., 1988—; part-time social svcs. counselor Disabled Resources Ctr., Inc., Long Beach, 1992—; vol. Meml. Children's Hosp., Long Beach, 1977—; mem. scholarship com. Long Beach City Coll., 1984-90, Calif. State U., Long Beach, 1984-90. Mem. adv. bd. Pro-Wilson 90 Gov., Calif., 1990; mem. devel. bd. St. Joseph High Sch., 1987—; pres. St. Cyprian's Parish Coun., 1962—; mem. Long Beach Civic Light Opera, 1973—, Assistance League of Long Beach, 1976—. Mem. L.A. Fitness Club, U. of the Pacific Club, K.C. (Family of the Month 1988). Republican. Roman Catholic.

NASON, THELMA STEIN (TEMA NASON), writer, teacher; b. N.Y.C.; d. Gerson and Bella (Czernitzski) Stein; m. Alvin Nason, Oct. 18, 1944 (dec. Jan., 1978); children: Deborah R., Steffi R., Jean L., Gerson S., Benjamin M. BA, Bklyn. Coll., 1941; postgrad. U. Chgo., 1941-42; MA, Johns Hopkins U., 1968. Instr. econs. Williams Coll., Williamstown, Mass., 1942-43; wage and disputes analyst War Labor Bd., Chgo., N.Y.C., 1943-44; labor rep. CIO, N.Y.C., Washington, San Francisco, 1944-47; cons. Md. Planning Commn., 1952-53; instr. writing Johns Hopkins U., Balt., 1969-78; freelance writer, Balt., 1958—; sr. research assoc. sociology Brandeis U., Waltham, Mass., 1980—. Author: A Stranger Here, Myself, 1977, Ethel: The Fictional Autobiography of Ethel Rosenberg, 1990, Full Moon, various short stories. Contbr. articles to jours., newspapers. Vis. scholar Bunting Inst., Radcliffe Coll., Cambridge, Mass., 1979-80, Frances Shaw award Ragdale Found. Fellow MacDowell Colony, Yaddo, Va. Ctr. for Creative Arts, Sweetbriar. Mem. PEN, Poets and Writers Assn., Nat. Writers Union. Avocations: theatre, reading, music, swimming, walking. Office: Brandeis U Dept Sociology Waltham MA 02254

NASSER, MERRY LYNN, lawyer; b. N.Y.C., Apr. 2, 1952; d. Ezra H. and Evelyn (Miller) N.; 1 child, Michael Nasser Petegorsky. BA, U. Pa., 1972; JD, Boston U., 1976. Ptnr. Nasser & Greenman, Springfield, Mass., 1977-80, Nasser & Schnall, Springfield, 1980-81, Lesser, Newman, Souweine & Nasser, Northampton, Mass., 1981—; lectr. U. Mass., Amherst, 1978; adj. prof. law We. New Eng. Sch. Law, Springfield, 1981-86. Bd. dirs. We. Mass. Family Planning, Northampton, Necessities/Necessidades, Northampton; mem. child sexual abuse task force, Northampton, 1988—; head steering com. Parents and Children in Transition program, Northampton, 1993—. Mem. Nat. Lawyers Guild, Mass. Bar Assn., Women's Bar Assn., Hampshire County Bar Assn. (co-chair probate ct. com. 1988—). Jewish. Democrat. Office: Lesser Newman Souweine & Nasser 39 Main St Northampton MA 01060

NASSIF, SISTER ROSEMARIE, university president; b. 1941. BSc in phys. chemistry summa cum laude, Notre Dame Coll., St. Louis, 1963; PhD in phys. chemistry, Catholic U., Washington, 1970. Chemistry educator, 1963-65; assoc. prof. chemistry Notre Dame Coll., 1970-77, St. Louis Coll. Pharmacy, 1977-83; provincial councilor Sch. Sister Notre Dame, St. Louis, 1983-87; co-vicar Religious Archdiocese of St. Louis, 1987-90; exec. v.p. Coll. Notre Dame Md., Balt., 1990-92, pres., 1992—; chair faculty senate St. Louis Coll. Pharmacy; mem. strategic planning team Notre Dame Coll.; bd. dirs. St. Louis Province Sch. Sisters Notre Dame, Inter-Congregational Ctr. Personal Growth; bd. trustees Coll. Notre Dame Md., 1987-90. Named Outstanding Educator Am., 1971; grantee U.S. Atomic Energy Commn.; fellow Am. Coun. Edn., 1991-92. Sch. Sisters of Notre Dame, 1959—. Office: Coll of Notre Dame Md Office of the President 4701 N Charles St Baltimore MD 21210

NASVIK-DENNISON, ANNA, artist; b. St. Paul; d. Peter Olson and Hattie Mathilda (Swenson) Nasvik; m. Roger Bennett, Nov. 7, 1936; children: Lynne, Kristin. Student, Coll. of St. Catherine, St. Paul, 1925, St. Paul Sch. of Art, 1927, Art Student's League, 1932. Tchr. art St. Joseph's Acad., St. Paul, 1926-30; freelance fashion illustrator N.Y.C., 1930-64; artist syndicated page The Fashion Syndicate, N.Y.C., 1934-38; mem. nat. art bd. Nat. League Am. Pen Women, 1990-92. One woman shows include Colbert Galleries, Sherbrooke St., Mont., Can., 1979, Gallery Milhalis, Sherbrooke St., Mont., 1984, T. Eaton Foyer des Arts, Mont., 1982-87, Venable-Neslage Gallerie, Washington, 1979-84, Lido Galleries, Scottsdale, Ariz., 1988, Hilltop Galleries, Nogales, Ariz., 1991 (top painting award, People's Choice award), 1995, Maiden Ln. Gallery, San Francisco, 1991; represented Newman Galleries, Scottsdale, Ariz. Named Woman of Art, Foyer des Arts, 1982; winner 3 top awards Ariz. juried show, Nat. League Am. Pen Women, 1989; recipient 3 People's Choice award Hilltop Galleries, 1991. Mem. Nat. Mus. Women in Arts, Santa Cruz Valley Art Assn., Lakeshore Assn. of Art, Nat. League of Pen Women (3 Top awards 1989, nat. bd. dirs. 1990—), Pen Women Sonora Desert. Home and Office: 231 W Paseo Adobe Green Valley AZ 85614-3462

NATHAN, ANNETTE RAQUEL, physician, educator; b. Mexico City, Mex., Apr. 6, 1961; d. Paul and Shirley (Rosenstein) N. BS, Rensselaer Polytechnic Inst., 1982; MD, Albany Med. Coll., 1984. Resident in gen. surgery Tripler Army Med. Ctr., Honolulu, 1984-86, emergency physician, 1986-88; resident in emergency medicine Madigan Army Med. Ctr., Tacoma, Wash., 1988-91; mem. emergency medicine staff Darrall Army Community Hosp., Killeen, Tex., 1991-93, St. John's Hosp., Queens, N.Y., 1992-93; paramedic/EMT prof. Ctrl. Tec. Coll., Killeen, 1992-93; asst. prof. Tex. A&M U., 1992; physician Cmty. Hosp., Springfield, Ohio, 1993—; mem. affiliate faculty Mil. Tng. Network, Killeen, 1991-93; med. advisor Clark State Cmty. Coll. paramedic program. Contbr. articles to profl. jours. Mem. AMA, Am. Coll. Emergency Physicians (disaster sect. 1992), Women in Emergency Medicine. Democrat. Jewish. Home: 2244 Old Oak Ln Springfield OH 45503-1763

NATHAN, JACQUELINE SUSANNE, gallery director; b. Chgo., Nov. 3, 1950; d. Eric and Ruth (Löwenstein) N. BA in Art, No. Ill. U., 1973; MA in Cmty. Arts Mgmt., Sangamon State U., 1984. Counselor Lifeworks Reality Project, Rockford, Ill., 1975-79; program asst. Clayville Mus., Pleasant Plains, Ill., 1980; spl. asst. Ill. Arts Coun., Chgo., 1981; dir. audience devel. Great Am. People Show, Petersburg, Ill., 1981; interim dir. Springboard Arts Coun., Springfield, Ill., 1981-82; exec. dir. Wassenberg Art Ctr., Van Wert, Ohio, 1982-85; exhbn. program adminstr. fine arts ctr. Bowling Green (Ohio) State U., 1985—; panelist visual arts Ohio Arts Coun., Columbus, 1989-92, % for Art core com., 1993-94; juror Toledofest, 1994, Crosby Gardens Art Fair, Toledo, 1989. Curator numerous exhbns. including African American Self Portraits, 1991, Art of the Americas, 1992, AtTension to the Moment, 1993, Russian Necro Realism, 1992. Grantee Ohio Arts Coun., 1992, 94, 86-90, Toledo Arts Commn., 1986-88, Ohio Joint Arts/ Humanities Program, 1992. Mem. Wood County Humane Soc. (assoc. treas., bd. dirs. 1989—), Black Swamp Arts Festival (bd. dirs., co-chair 1992-94). Office: Bowling Green State U Fine Arts Center Galleries Bowling Green OH 43403

NATHANSON, LINDA SUE, publisher, author, technical writer, software trainer; b. Washington, Aug. 11, 1946; d. Nat and Edith (Weinstein) N.; m. James F. Barrett. BS, U. Md., 1969; MA, UCLA, 1970, PhD, 1975. Tng. dir. Rockland Research Inst., Orangeburg, N.Y., 1975-77; asst. prof. psychology SUNY, 1978-79; pres. Cabri Prodns., Inc., Ft. Lee, N.J., 1979-81; research supr. Darcy, McManus & Masius, St. Louis, 1981-83; mgr. software tng., documentation On-Line Software Internat., Ft. Lee, 1983-85; pvt. practice cons. Ft. Lee, 1985-87; founder, exec. dir. The Edin. Group, Inc., Gillette, N.J., 1987—; founder, pres. Edin Books, Inc., Gillette, N.J., 1994—. Author: (with others) Psychological Testing: An Introduction to Tests and Measurement, 1988; pub. A Funny Thing Happened at the Interview (G.F. Farrell), 1995, Job Hunting From A to Q (G.F. Farrell), 1995; contbr. articles to mags., newspapers and profl. jours. Recipient Research Service award 1978; Albert Einstein Coll. Medicine Research fellow, 1978-79. Jewish. Home and Office: 102 Sunrise Dr Gillette NJ 07933-1944

NATION, LAURA CROCKETT, electrical engineer; b. Ft. Worth, Dec. 1, 1957; d. Donald Ray and Cora Lee (Holt) Crockett; m. David Hunter Nation, Aug. 23, 1986. BA, U. Tex., Arlington, 1980, BSEE, 1984. Registered profl. engr., Tex. With engring. coop. TU Electric, Dallas, 1981-84; assoc. engr. TU Electric, Euless, Tex., 1984-85, Irving, Tex., 1985-87; engr. TU Electric, Dallas, 1987-91; staff engr. TU Electric, Ft. Worth, 1991-92,

Ctr. for Electron Devices and Systems, U. Tex., Arlington, 1993—. Vol. United Way, Ft. Worth, 1992, Muscular Dystrophy Assn., Dallas, 1987-91. Scholar Mogul Corp., Canton, Ohio, 1976. Mem. IEEE (vol. Discover "E"), NSPE. Republican. Missionary Alliance. Home: 1303 Brittany Ln Arlington TX 76013-2320 Office: U Tex at Arlington Elec Engring Dept 416 Yates St Arlington TX 76010-1539

NATORI, JOSIE CRUZ, apparel executive; b. Manila, May 9, 1947; came to U.S., 1964; d. Felipe F. and Angelita A. (Almeda) Cruz; m. Kenneth R. Natori, May 20, 1972; 1 child, Kenneth E.F. BA in Econs., Manhattanville Coll., 1968. V.p. Merrill-Lynch Co., N.Y.C., 1971-77; pres. The Natori Co., N.Y.C., 1977—; bd. dirs. Dreyfus Third Century Fund, Calyx and Corolla. Bd. dirs. Philippine Am. Found., Jr. Achievement, Inc., 1992, Ednl. Found. for Fashion Industries; trustee Manhattanville Coll. Recipient Human Relations award Am. Jewish Com., N.Y.C., 1986, Harriet Alger award Working Woman, N.Y., 1987, Castle award Manhattanville Coll., Purchase, 1988, Galleon award Pres. Philippines, N.Y.C. Asian-Am. award, Friendship award Philippine-Am. Found., Hall of Fame award Mega Mags. Mem. CFDA, Young Pres.'s Orgn., Fashion Group, Com. of 200. Home: 45 E 62nd St New York NY 10021-8025 Office: Natori Co 40 E 34th St Fl 18 New York NY 10016-4401

NATOW, ANNETTE BAUM, nutritionist, author, consultant; b. N.Y.C., Jan. 30, 1933; d. Edward and Gertrude (Jackerson) Baum; m. Harry Natow, Nov. 30, 1955; children: Allen, Laura, Steven. BS, CUNY Bklyn. Coll., 1955; MS, SUNY Coll. Plattsburg, 1960; PhD, Tex. Women's U., 1963. Registered dietitian, N.Y. Asst. prof. SUNY Coll. Plattsburg, 1967-69, CUNY Coll. Lehman, N.Y.C., 1969-70; assoc. prof., chmn. dept. SUNY Downstate Med. Ctr., Bklyn., 1970-76; prof., dir. nutrition programs Adelphi U., Garden City, N.Y., 1976-90, prof. emerita, 1991—; intern Montreal Diet Dispensary, March of Dimes, 1980; pres., writer, cons. NRH Nutrition Cons., Inc., Valley Stream, N.Y., 1980—. Author: No-Nonsense Nutrition, 1978, Geriatric Nutrition, 1980, Nutrition for the Prime of Your Life, 1983, No-Nonsense Nutrition for Kids, 1985, Megadoses: Vitamins as Drugs, 1985, Nutritional Care of the Older Adult, 1986, Pocket Encyclopedia of Nutrition, 1986, The Cholesterol Counter, 1989, 1988, 2d edit., 1989, The Fat Counter, 1989, The Fat Attack Plan, 1990, The Diabetes Carbohydrate and Calorie Counter, 1991, The Pregnancy Counter, 1992, The Iron Counter, 1993, The Sodium Counter, 1993, The Antioxidant Vitamin Counter, 1994, The Fast Food Counter, 1994; editor Jour. Nutrition for Elderly, 1983—; mem. editorial bd. Environ. Nutrition Newsletter, 1985—; mem. editorial adv. bd. Prevention, 1984-86; contbr. numerous articles to profl. jours. United Hosp. Fund grantee, 1978. Mem. Am. Dietetic Assn., N.Y. State Dietetic Assn., N.Y. State Nutrition Coun. (sec. 1973-74). Home: 100 Rosedale Rd Valley Stream NY 11581-2802 Office: NRH Nutrition Cons Inc 100 Rosedale Rd Valley Stream NY 11581-2802

NATTIEL, CHRISTINE HENRY, minister; b. Orlando, Fla., Feb. 22, 1939; d. Frank and Willie (Lee) Henry; m. Willie Lee Nattiel; children: Gale Frances, Willie Jr., Frank Henry, Timothy David, Dorothy Jeanne, Elizabeth. Diploma, Mebane High Sch., Alachua, Fla., 1957. Ordained to ministry Baptist Ch., 1976. Minister Bapt. Ch., Gainesville, Fla., 1976—. Fundraiser, Citizens for Martin Luther King Day, Gainesville, 1986. Named Outstanding Fundraiser, Citizens for Martin Luther King, 1986. Republican. Home: RR 3 Box 170 Newberry FL 32669-9682

NATURALE, APRIL JULIA, hospital administrator, psychotherapist; b. Englewood, N.J., Apr. 22, 1960; d. Daniel and Patricia Angela (Peters) N. BS, Ramapo Coll., 1982; MSW, Columbia U., 1984. Accredited cert. social worker. Med. social worker Englewood Hosp., 1982-88; psychiatric social worker N.Y. State Office Mental Health, Orangeburg, 1988-92; asst. adminstr. Ramapo Ridge Psychiatric Hosp., Wyckoff, N.J., 1992—. Bd. dirs. Consumers in Action, Rockland County, N.Y., 1990—, Alliance for Mentally Ill, Bergen County, N.J., 1993—. Recipient Cmty. Svc. award N.Y. State Senate, 1990, Advocacy award N.Y. State Alliance for Mentally Ill, 1990. Mem. Am. Mental Health Adminstrs., Nat. Assn. Social Workers. Home: 194 Saddle River Rd Monsey NY 10952 Office: Ramapo Ridge Psychiatric Hosp 301 Sicomac Ave Wyckoff NJ 07481

NATZKE, PAULETTE ANN, manufacturing executive; b. Wausau, Wis., Oct. 23, 1943; d. Milton L. and Geraldine J. (Henrichs) Marth; m. Kenneth A. Natzke, June 29, 1963; children: Jerome E., Julie J. Sec. Marth Wood Shavings Supply, Marathon, Wis., 1973-85; pres. Marth Wood Shavings Supply, Marathon, 1985—; v.p. Marth Transp. Inc., Marathon, 1984—; bd. dirs. Marth Found., Marathon; owner Privacy Point on Lake Nokomis, Tomahawk, Wis., 1992—. Mem. Cen. Wis. Ceramic Assn. (cert. tchr., Best Show award 1981, Best Booth Show award 1982). Republican. Lutheran. Home: 6752 St Hwy 107N Marathon WI 54448 Office: Marth Wood Shavings Supply Inc Marathon WI 54448-9802

NAUDZIUS, RUTH WINTERS, image consultant, home economist; b. Georgetown, Ill., May 5, 1929; d. Ernest Bruce and Melba Meryl (Shepler) Winters; m. Donald Anthony Naudzius, July 1, 1949; children: Laura Kay Naudzius Miller, Lonn Colin. BS with honors, U. Ill., 1951, MEd, 1956; postgrad., Paris, 1990. Cert. home econs. tchr., Ill. Home econs. asst. broadcaster Sta. WILL, Urbana, Ill., 1949; home econs. extension specialist U. Ill., 1951; tchr. home econs. Sch. Dist. of Matoon, Ill., 1951-52, Deland-Weldon, Ill., 1952-54, Sch. Dist. 64, Park Ridge, Ill., 1963-79; image cons. Color 1 Assoc., Park Ridge, 1983—; assoc., 1987—; guest lectr. Oakton Coll., 1986—. Contbr. articles to profl. jours. Morava scholar U. Ill., 1948-51. Mem. Women in Mgmt. (chmn. fundraising Chgo. chpt. 1988—, Woman of Achievement award 1991), AAUW (membership com.), 20th Century Club, Antique Rovers, Omicron Nu. Republican. Mem. Soc. of Friends. Office: Color 1 Assoc 414 S Lincoln Ave Park Ridge IL 60068-3816

NAUGHTON, EILEEN SLATTERY, state legislator; b. Warwick, R.I., Dec. 29, 1945; m. William C. Naughton; children: Christine, William S. BA, Annhurst Coll., 1967. Farmer; mem. R.I. Ho. of Reps.; mem. judiciary com. Mem. Warwick Hist. Soc., Am. Sheep Assn. Home: 100 Old Homestead Rd Warwick RI 02889 Office: RI Ho of Reps State House Providence RI 02903*

NAUGHTON, ELIZABETH ANNE, sales executive; b. Cloquet, Minn., Oct. 6, 1962; d. Willard George and Margaret Anne (Zangle) Hershey; m. Luke F. Naughton, Sept. 1, 1990. BBA in Mktg., U. Wis., Whitewater, 1985; MBA in Mktg., Webster U., 1992. Salesperson Carpenter Tech., Melrose Park, Ill., 1985-86; territory mgr. Metal Goods Svc. Ctrs., St. Louis, 1986-92; sales rep. Barmet Aluminum, Akron, Ohio, 1992; regional sales mgr. Cressona Aluminum, St. Louis, 1993—. Mem. Assn. Women in Metals Industry, Beta Sigma Phi. Roman Catholic.

NAUGHTON, MARIE ANN, corporate executive; b. Boston, Feb. 19, 1954; d. Robert J. and Beatrice T. (McDonald) N. BS in Speech magna cum laude, Emerson Coll., 1976; MA, Ind. U., 1977; Cert. spl. studies bus. and adminstrn. Harvard U., 1989. Speech-lang. pathologist Dedham (Mass.) pub. schs., 1977-79, Mass. Gen. Hosp., Boston, 1979-81; speech pathologist Mt. Auburn Hosp., Cambridge, Mass., 1982-84; v.p. Curtis-Newton Corp., 1984—. Author: A Coarticulation Manual for the Remediation of /S/, 1979. Elected Dedham Sch. Com., 1993—. Fellow Soc. for Ear, Nose and Throat Advances in Children; mem. LWV (dir. at large), Am. Speech, Lang. and Hearing Assn. (cert. clin. competence), Northeastern Retail Lumber Assn., Zeta Phi Eta. Home: 77 Circuit Rd Dedham MA 02026-3605 Office: 41 River St Dedham MA 02026-2935

NAULT, FELICIA, dietitian, nutritionist; b. Panama City, Colon, Panama, Feb. 15; d. Sydney L. and Violet (Samuels) Fennell; m. Frank J. Nault, Jr., July 18, 1991; children: Miles Alexander, Jasmine. BS, Calif. State Poly. Inst., Ponoma, 1979; MBA, U. Phoenix, Costa Mesa, Calif., 1985. Registered dietitian, Calif. Coord. client program San Gabriel Pomona Red. Ctr., West Covina, Calif., 1978-88, cons. nutritionist, 1990—; pub. health nutritionist Orange County, Santa Ana, Calif., 1988—; nutritionist La Clinica Familiar, East Los Angeles, Calif., 1978-81; cons. nutritionist Devel. Disabilities Ctr., Orange, Calif., 1991—; guest Radio Labio, L.A., 1993; participant Hispanic and Latino U.S. Surgeon Gen. Health Conf., Washington, 1992. Health advisor Orange County chpt. March of Dimes, Costa Mesa, 1990; sec.-treas. Orange County Perinatal Coun., 1991. Named Faculty Mem. of Yr., Fairview Devel. Ctr., 1992. Mem. So. Calif. Pub. Health Assn. (chmn. nutrition 1992), Orange County Dietetic Assn. (chmn. community nutrition 1991, Vol. of Yr. award 1992).

NAUMAN, RUTH EILEEN, author; b. San Diego, May 24, 1946; d. James Earl and Ruth May (Cramer) Gent; m. David Gene Nauman, June 16, 1973. Grad., British Inst. Homeopathy, 1994, 94. Homeopathic practitioner pvt. practice, Cottonwood, Ariz., 1970—; freelance writer Cottonwood, Ariz., 1980—; adj. prof. Union Inst., 1992—; tchr. British Inst. Homeopathy, London, 1992—. Author: Interpreting Your Novien Moon, 1979, The American Book of Nutrition and Medical Astrology, 1980, Colored Stones and Their Meaning, 1990, Medical Astrology, 1992, Soul Recovery and Extraction, 1992, Bach Flower Remedies and Astrology, 1992, Homeopathy: 21st Century Medicine, 1993, numerous romance novels. Firefighter West Point (Ohio) Vol. Fire Dept., 1983-86. With USN, 1964-67. Mem. Am. Fedn. Astrologers. Office: Blue Turtle Publishing PO Box 2513 Cottonwood AZ 86326-2513

NAUTS, HELEN COLEY, health science association administrator; b. Sharon, Conn., Sept. 2, 1907; d. William Bradley and Alice (Lancaster) Coley; m. william Boone Nauts, Sept. 22, 1928; children: Nancy Coley, Phyllis Lancaster. Student sch. landscape architecture, Columbia U., 1927-28; D Sci. (hon.), Hartwick Coll., 1986. Pvt. practice landscape architecture N.Y. and Conn.; founder, exec. dir. Cancer Research Inst., N.Y.C., 1953-82, dir. Sci. Med. Communications, 1982—; exec. dir. Brearley Alumnae Assn., N.Y.C., 1940-48, mng. editor Brearley Bulletin, 1946-48; trustee Cancer Research Inst., 1953-66; lectr. cancer cofs. France, Germany, Eng., Japan, China, U.S., Sweden. Author, editor scientific papers in cancer research, 1946-89, monographs on cancer immunology, 1953-84. Recipient William B. Coley Meml. award, 1985, Commandeur de l'Ordre Nat. de Merite Pres. Valery Giscard d'Estaing, 1981, Francis Riker Davis Alumnae award Brearley Sch., 1980. Democrat. Presbyterian. Club: Cosmopolitan (N.Y.C.). Home and Office: Cancer Research Inst 1225 Park Ave New York NY 10128-1758

NAVA, CYNTHIA D., state legislator. BS, Western Ill. U.; MA, Ea. Ill. U. Dir. spl. edn. Godsden Pub. Sch.; mem. N.Mex. Senate; mem. edn. and rules com. Home: PO Box 493 Mesquite NM 88048 Office: NMex Senate State Capitol New Mexico State Capitol NM 87503*

NAVARRO, BLANCA FELICIA, counselor; b. Havana, Cuba, Feb. 5, 1958; came to U.S., 1963; d. Antonio Manuel and Marta Magdalena (Carvajal) N. BA cum laude, S.W. Tex. State U., 1982; MEd, U. Houston, 1993. Sec. Phi Sigma Iota, San Marcos, Tex., 1982; instr. English as a second lang. Houston C.C., 1988-91; student intern Montrose Counseling Ctr., Houston, 1992-93; adminstrv. sec. U. Tex. Health Sci. Ctr., Houston, 1983-94; counselor U. Tex. Mental Sci. Inst., Houston, 1994—. Vol. Pvt. Sector Initiatives, Houston, 1994; pres., founder Grupo De Amigos Latino Americanos, St. Cyril's Ch., Houston, 1987-88; mem. Environ. Def. Fund, People for the Ethical Treatment of Animals, Casa Argentina de Houston, Citizen's Houston Police Acad., 1994, Inst. Hispanic Culture, Rails to Trails Conservancy. Mem. Internat. Assn. Addictions and Offenders Counselors, Am. Counseling Assn., Am. Coll. Counseling Assn., Am. Mental Health Counseling Assn., Am. Coll. Pers. Assn., U. Houston Alumni Assn., Inst. Noetic Scis., Nat. Wildlife Fedn., Nat. Parks and Conservation Assn., NOW, Tex. Parks and Wildlife, Am. Volksport Assn., S.W. Tex. U. Alumni Assn., Golden Key, Psi Chi, Phi Sigma Iota, Alpha Kappa Delta, Sigma Delta Pi, Sierra Club, Houston Bicycle Club, Citizen's Houston Police Acad. Alumni Assn. Christian Ch.

NAVARRO, JANYTE JANENE, environmental educator; b. LaJara, Colo., Apr. 14, 1935; d. John Charles Blissard and Mary Margaret (Mathias) Tedesco; m. Daniel David Myers (div. 1968); children: Kelli, Keith, Kim; m. Rafael Fowler Navarro (div. Sept. 1994); children: Eric, Marshall, Laura Lynne, Mitchell. Student, Colo. U., 1954-55, U. N.Mex. Owner Poodle Breeding Bus., Albuquerque, 1964-67, Jan-Knits, Albuquerque, 1973-74, Sharing is Caring, Albuquerque, 1980—; managing partner Land-Ho Enterprises, 1988—; bd. dirs. Fiesta de Shaklee, Albuquerque, Sondia Ctr. Producer: (video) The Sponsoring Process, 1981; articles, newsletters in field. Mem. Rio Grande Sales Leaders Assn. (pres. 1984, 86). Home and Office: 1505 Gretta St NE Albuquerque NM 87112-4319

NAVEDO, CHRISTELLA, psychologist; b. San Juan, P.R., June 16, 1961; d. Miguel Navedo and Julia M. Galindez de Santiago; m. Modesto Figueroa, Oct. 8, 1988; children: Amanda Marie, Gabriel Omar. A with honors, U. P.R., Bayamon, 1981; B with honors, U. P.R., Rio Piedras, 1983, MA, 1985, PhD, 1994. Lic. psychologist, P.R. Indsl. psychologist III P.R. Telephone Co., San Juan, 1985—. Mem. APA (assoc.; mem. indsl./orgnl. psychology div.), Assn. Interamericana de Psicologia, Assn. de Psicologos de P.R., Assn. de Ex-Alumnos U. P.R. Roman Catholic. Home: Valle Verde III Praderas DF-9 Bayamon PR 00961 Office: P R Telephone Co GPO Box 360998 San Juan PR 00936-0998

NAVEIRAS, CAROLINA FABIOLA, school system administrator; b. Havana, Cuba, Mar. 21, 1951; came to U.S., 1961; d. Leonardo R. and Carolina (Orta) N. AA, Miami Dade Jr. Coll., 1972; BS, Fla. Internat. U., 1974, MS, 1979; postgrad. pub. sch. mgmt., 1986, 90-92. Cert. tchr., adminstr., supr. K-6. Tchr. Dupuis Elem. Dade County Pub. Schs., Hialeah, Fla., 1974-75; 6th grade tchr. North Hialeah Elem. Dade County Pub. Schs., 1976-77, 2nd and 3rd grade tchr. Flamingo Elem., 1977-79, 5th grade tchr. Shadowlawn Elem., 1979-80, 5th grade tchr. Meadowlane Elem., 1980-81, 1st grade tchr., 1981-82, 4th grade tchr., 1982-83, 6th grade tchr., 1983-84, kindergarten tchr., 1984-85, asst. prin. J.H. Bright Elem., 1986-92, dir. sch. bd.- sch. ops., 1992—. Mem. Assn. Hispanic Educators, Dade County Adminstrs. Assn. Home: 7225 W 16th Ave Hialeah FL 33014

NAVEJA-ELLIS, FRANCESCA ANGELA, mental health services administrator, psychotherapist; b. N.Y.C., June 23, 1939; d. Antonio and Jeannette Marie (Thomas) Naveja; m. David H. Ellis, Oct. 21, 1957; children: Theresa Fae Ann Zendejas, David Cary. AA with Honors, Allan Hancock Coll., 1985; BS, Columbia Pacific U., 1988; MA, U. San Francisco, 1989. Adminstr. Community Ministry Ctr., Chino, Calif., 1977-79; bus. mgr. Humanistic Mental Health, Santa Maria, Calif., 1984-85; med. sec. A. Edward Hoctor, MD., Santa Maria, 1985; bus. mgr. Affiliated Psychotherapist, Santa Maria, 1985-87; founder, exec. dir., psychotherapist Community Counseling Ctr., Santa Maria, 1988—; program dir. Safe Interventions, Santa Maria, Case Mgmt. and Consulting Assocs., Santa Maria; mem. adj. faculty Columbia Pacific U., Sierra U.; founder, dir. Trias Inst., Santa Maria, 1984—, AP Inst., Santa Maria, 1986-87; bd. dirs. Friends of Ruth Women's Shelter, Santa Maria, 1985; cons. St. Joseph's High Sch., 1990; CEO Cen. Coast Cons. Assocs., 1991—. Editor, author quar. newsletter Pride, 1990—. Vol. Dem. Women's Caucus 1986; mem. Women's Network, Santa Maria, 1986-89; mental health adv. coun. Santa Barbara County, 1990, with domestic violence edn./elimination svcs., 1992—. Mem. Am. Mental Health Counseling Assn., Assn. Christian Therapists (regional coord., 1988-90), Calif. Assn. Marriage Family Therapists, Cen. Coast Jung Soc., Western Assn. Spiritual Dirs., Cen. Coast Hypnosis Soc. Mem. Am. Assn. Prof. Hypnotherapists. Office: Valley Counseling Ctr 220 E Clark Ave STe B Santa Maria CA 93455 also: Safe Interventions 210 W Main St Ste 6 Santa Maria CA 93454 also: Case Mgmt & Consulting Assn 210 Main St Ste 6 Santa Maria CA 93454

NAVRATILOVA, MARTINA, former professional tennis player; b. Prague, Czechoslovakia, Oct. 18, 1956; came to U.S., 1975, naturalized, 1981; d. Miroslav Navratil and Jana Navratilova. Student, schs. in Czechoslovakia. Profl. tennis player, 1975-94. Author: (with George Vecsey) Martina, 1985, (with Liz Nickels) The Total Zone, 1994. Winner Czechoslovak Nat. singles, 1972-74, U.S. Open singles, 1983, 84, 86, 87, U.S. Open doubles, 1977, 78, 80, 83, 84, 87, U.S. Open mixed doubles, 1987, Va. Slims Tournament, 1978, 83, 84, 85, 86, Wimbledon singles, 1978, 79, 82, 83, 84, 85, 86, 87, 90, Wimbledon women's doubles, 1976, 79, 81, 82, 83, 84, 86, Wimbledon mixed doubles, 1985, 94, French Open singles, 1982, 84, Australian Open singles, 1981, 83, 85, Australian Doubles (with Nagelsen), 1980, (with Shriver), 1982, 84, 84, 85, 87, 88, 89, Grand Slam of Women's Tennis, 1984; named Hon. Citizen of Dallas, AP Female Athlete of Yr., 1983. Mem. Women's Tennis Assn. (dir., exec. com., pres.). Address: IMG 1 Erieview Pla Cleveland OH 44114*

NAYLON, BETSY ZIMMERMANN, artist; b. Buffalo, Jan. 27, 1934; d. Gerard M. and Marion G. (McDonald) Zimmermann; m. Bernard M. Naylon, Aug. 11, 1956; children: Lisa, Bernard, Claire. BA, Rosary Hill Coll., 1955; postgrad., Daeman Coll., 1976; studied with, William Paden, N.Y.C., 1986. instr. Daeman Coll., Buffalo, 1969-70, SUNY, Buffalo, 1974-79, Niagara U., 1981-83, Trinity Ch., 1990-91; art exhbn. judge Internat. Children's Art Exhibit, Niagara Falls, Ont., Can., 1991, Lewiston Art Festival, Buscaglia-Castellani Art Gallery, Niagara U., Grand Island Art Group Exhibit, Niagara on the Lake, Ont., Niagara Falls Soc. Artists, 1992. Commd. artworks CECOS Internat. Inc., 1981, Browning Ferris Industries, Niagara Falls, N.Y., 1982, Mader Corp., Buffalo, 1983, Synder Tank Co., Internat. Harvester Co., Ohio, 1985, Peller & Mure Co., Buffalo, 1985, Carborundum Abrasives, N.Y., Ohio, Va., 1984, Bantam, Doubleday Dell Publ. Co., 1989, 90, Studio Arena Theater, 1988, 92, Martha W. Bennett, 1991, J. & M. Broderick, 1990, Dr. & Mrs. Palumbo, 1994; exhbns. Albright-Knox Gallery, Buffalo, 1980, 91, 93, 94, Stella Niagara Ednl. Park, 1994-95, Burchfield Art Ctr., Buffalo, 1981, O'Keefe Ctr., Toronto, Can., 1982, AAO Galleries, Buffalo, 1984; various solo exhibits including Kenan Gallery, Lockport, N.Y., 1989—, Niagara Falls Meml. Hosp., 1995. Mem. Nat. Assn. Women Artists (traveling printmaking exhibit U.S. 1987-89, traveling painting exhibit India 1989-90), Nat. League Am. Penwomen (1st Place award 1991, Merit award 1989), Nat. Mus. Women in the Arts, Nat. Women's Caucus for Art, Niagara Coun. Arts (bd. dirs. 1983-84), Niagara Frontier Watercolor Soc. (Painting award 1989, 1st prize 1994). Home: 25 Melbourne Pl Buffalo NY 14222 Studio: Stella Niagra Ednl Pk Stella Niagra NY 14144

NAYLOR, JEAN ANN, controller, accountant; b. Pomona, Calif., Oct. 21, 1948; d. Paul Woodrow and Urdelle Cecile (Sparlin) Waters; 1 child, Tamara LeAron. AA in Legal Sec., Shasta Coll., Redding, Calif., 1976; AA in Computer Acctg., Reno Bus. Coll., 1985, BA in Acctg., 1986. Cert. instr. acctg., Nev. Stunt rider King's Motordome, San Jose, Calif., 1968-74; owner, mgr. House of Wigs, Redding, 1974-81; bookkeeper, counselor Shasta County Women's Refuge, Redding, 1981-83; revenue auditor Reno Hilton, 1983-85; instr. Reno Bus. Coll., 1986—; acct. Western Village, Reno, 1985—; acctg. mgr. Eddie's Fabulous 50's, 1986; contr. The Gold Club, 1987; sr. acct. Silver Club Hotel/Casino, Sparks, Nev., 1988-92; asst. contr. Sta. KTVN-TV, Sparks, 1992—; distbr. Amway, 1993—. Campaign dir. Jon Lyons for County Auditor, Redding, 1982. Mem. Nat. Acctg. Assn., Showfolks of Am., Toastmasters.

NAYLOR, PHYLLIS REYNOLDS, author; b. Anderson, Ind., Jan. 4, 1933; d. Eugene Spencer and Lura Mae (Schield) Reynolds; m. Thomas A. Tedesco, Jr., Sept. 9, 1951 (div. 1960); m. Rex V. Naylor, May 26, 1960; children: Jeffrey, Michael. Diploma, Joliet Jr. Coll., 1953; BA, Am. U., 1963. Author: 86 books including Crazy Love: An Autobiographical Account of Marriage and Madness, 1977, Revelations, 1979, A String of Chances, 1982 (ALA notable book), The Agony of Alice, 1985 (ALA notable book), The Keeper, 1986 (ALA notable book), Unexpected Pleasures, 1986, Send No Blessing, 1990 (YASD best book for young adults), Shiloh, 1991 (ALA notable book, John Newbery medal, 1992). Recipient Golden Kite award Soc. Children's Book Writers Am., 1985, Child Study award Bank St. Coll., 1983, Edgar Allan Poe award Mystery Writers Am., 1985, Internat. book award Soc. Sch. Librs., 1988, Christopher award, 1989, Newbery award ALA, 1992, Nat. Endowment of Arts Creative Writing fellow, 1987. Mem. Children's Book Guild of Washington (pres. 1974-75, 83-84), Soc. Children's Book Writers, Authors Guild, PEN, Council for a Livable World, SANE, Physicians for Social Responsibility, Amnesty Internat. Unitarian. Home and Office: 9910 Holmhurst Rd Bethesda MD 20817-1618

NEACSU, MARIA, artist; b. Manoleasa, Romania, Aug. 15, 1948; d. Ioan and Valeria (Busuioc) Grosu; m. Marius C. Neacsu, Aug. 15, 1970; 1 child, George Mircea. BSBA, Acad. Econ. Study, Bucharest, 1973; BS in Art, U. Calif., Berkeley, 1993; postgrad., U. Calif., 1993—. Econ. Iprochim, Bucharest, 1973-81; sr. acct. Bechtel, Inc., San Francisco, 1981-83; acctg. mgr. West Mgmt. Co., Oakland, Calif., 1983-86; sr. acct. Kaiser Engring. Inc., Oakland, 1986-89; artist Walnut Creek, Calif., 1989—. Jack K. and Gertrude Murphy fine arts fellow San Francisco Found., 1994. Republican. Home: 505 Pimlico Ct Walnut Creek CA 94596

NEAL, BARBARA MARIE, association executive; b. Memphis, Aug. 31, 1935; d. John Sr. and Margaret Henrietta (Thornton) N. BA in Social Scis., LeMoyne-Owen Coll., 1960. Ctr. dir. women's activities City of Memphis Recreation Dept., 1957-60; from dir. teenage programs to exec. dir. Sarah Brown Br. YWCA, Memphis, 1960-73; cons. youth constituencies so. region Nat. Bd. YWCA of U.S.A., Atlanta, 1973-75, cons. programs so. region, 1975-78; cons. pers. Nat. Bd. YWCA of U.S.A., N.Y.C., 1978-85, dir. ea. region, 1985-90; pers. specialist Nat. Bd. YWCA of U.S.A., Memphis, 1990-92; interim exec. dir. Nat. Bd. Leadership Corp. YWCA, Memphis, 1992—; mem. faculty Leadership Devel. Ctr. YWCA Nat. Bd., N.Y., Phoenix, 1985-92, cons. devel. edn., N.Y., 1989-92, coord. overseas internship, nat. career devel. program, N.Y., 1986-88, chair affirmative action review team, N.Y., 1990-92; trainer YWCA, 1949—, co-chair nat. exhibit, 1994—. Contbg. writer manuals, brochures, poster YWCA, 1980—. Organist Miss. Blvd. Christian Ch., Memphis, 1958-73; co-chair Memphis City Beautiful Commn., 1970-73; sec. Ky.-Tenn. Coalition YWCAs, 1993—, Coalition of 100 Black Women, mem. action audit com., 1993-94, constn. com., 1994—; mem. World of Difference race reduction campaign B'nai B'rith, N.Y.C., 1989-92; fundraiser Memphis Arts Coun., 1993-94. Named one of Outstanding Young Women in Am. by State of Tenn., 1971; recipient E. Sadler Fri Leadership award YWCA-Memphis, 1993, Outstanding Svc. awd. Nat. Network Postal Women, 1993, Vol. Svc. Recognition award Women in Cmty. Svc. & City Schs., Memphis, 1972; listed for Outstanding Nat. Staff Svc. YWCA Nat. Bd., 1991. Mem. NAFE, LeMoyne-Owen Alumni Assn., Zeta Phi Beta. Democrat. Mem. Christian Methodist Episcopal Ch. Home: 1505 S Wellington St Memphis TN 38106-5423

NEAL, BONNIE JEAN, real estate professional; b. Kansas City, Mo., Apr. 24, 1930; d. David Ira and Juanita Mae (Duncan) Johnson; m. Howard Stranton Neal, July 24, 1948 (div. Oct. 1972); children: Randall Stranton, William Scott, Douglas Kelly. Student, U. Omaha, 1980-86, Londay Sch. Real Estate, Omaha, 1987. Data processing supr. Enron Corp., Omaha, 1980-85, adminstrv. support analyst, 1985-86; real estate sales agt. Allen, Young Assocs., Omaha, 1987, Home Real Estate (merger Allen Young Assocs. and Wurdeman & Maenner), Omaha, 1988; with Coldwell Banker Action Real Estate, 1988-91, Coldwell Banker BJ Brown, La Vista, Nebr., 1991-92. Active PTA, Council Bluffs, Iowa, 1957-59; vol. March of Dimes, Council Bluffs, 1963; mem. Realtors Polit. Action Com. Fellow Omaha Bd. Realtors, Women's Bowling Assn., Order Eastern Star (25-yr. award 1980); mem. Women's Coun. Realtors. Democrat. Baptist. Home and Office: Home Real Estate 14250 W Maple Rd Omaha NE 68164

NEAL, CYNTHIA KAREN, clinical psychologist; b. Detroit, Dec. 30, 1952; d. Gaston O. and Evelyn Jewel (Dunn) N.; m. Thomas Anthony Vittiglio, July 10, 1988; 1 child, Anthony. BA, Wayne State U., 1975, MA, 1977, PhD, 1983. Licensed psychologist. Clin. researcher Sinai Hosp., Detroit, 1977-78; clin. asst. Dept. Neuropsychology Lafayette Clinic, 1974-75; faculty mem. Inst. for Sex Rsch., Bloomington, Ind., 1975, 80; sch. psychologist Lakeshore Pub. Schs., St. Clair Shores, Mich., 1979-80; staff psychologist Ednl. Resources, St. Clair Shores, 1979—; consulting psychologist St. John Hosp., Detroit, 1983—. Mem. Jr. Coun., Founders Soc., Detroit, 1985—, Cranbrook Women's Soc., Bloomfield Hills, Mich., 1987—, Am. Ballet Soc., N.Y.C., 1980—. Recipient Grad. Fellowship Wayne State U., 1988. Mem. APA, DAR (Louise St. Clair chpt.). Republican. Home: 986 W Lincoln St Birmingham MI 48009-3010 Office: Ednl Resources 19900 Ten Mile Saint Clair Shores MI 48009

NEAL, DARWINA LEE, government official; b. Mansfield, Pa., Mar. 31, 1942; d. Darwin Leonard and Ina Belle (Cooke) N. BS, Pa. State U., 1965; postgrad., Cath. U, 1968-70. Registered landscape architect. Landscape architect nat. capital region Nat. Pk. Svc., 1965-69, office of White House liaison, 1969-71, office of profl. services, 1971-74, div. design svcs., 1974-89, chief design svcs., 1989—; judge numerous award juries. Contbr. articles to profl. jours.; co-author sects. of profl. bull., mag.; author introduction to book Women, Design and the Cambridge School; columnist: Land monthly, 1975-79. Mem. Women's Coun. on Energy in Environment. Recipient Merit award Landscape Contractors Met. Washington; recipient hon. mention Les Floralies Internationales de Montreal, 1980 Alumni Achievement award Pa. State U. Arts and Architecture Alumni Soc., 1981. Fellow Am. Soc. Landscape Architects (v.p. 1979-81, pres. elect 1982-83, pres. 1983-84, trustee 1976-77, nat. treas. 1977-79, legis. coordinator 1975-79, sec. Coun. Fellows 1988-90, (del. to Internat. Fedn. Landscape Architects, del. 1989—, ex-officio rep. to U.S./internat. com. on monuments and sites, liaison to historically black coll. and univ. program Dept. Interior, recipient Pres.' medal 1987); mem. Landscape Archtl. Accreditation Bd. (roster vis. evaluators), Nat. Recreation and Parks Assn., Nat. Soc. Park Resources (bd. dirs. 1978-80), Nat. Trust Hist. Preservation, Pa. State U. Alumni Assn. (Washington met. chpt. trustee 1972-74), Am. Arbitration Assn. (nat. panel arbitrators), Com. 100 for the Fed. City, Preservation Action, Nat. Assn. Olmsted Parks, Beekman Pl. Condominium Assn. (bd. dirs. 1985-91, archtl. control com.), Nat. Parks and Conservation Assn., Alliance for Historic Preservation, World Watch, Worldwide. Office: Nat Pk Svc Nat Capitol Reg Dept Interior Divsn Design Svcs 800 N Capitol St NW Ste 790 Washington DC 20242

NEAL, GAIL FALLON, physical therapist, educator; b. New Haven, May 6, 1938; d. Edward Francis and Ruth Alexina (Hutchinson) Fallon; m. Marcus Pinson Neal Jr.; children: Sandra Neal Dawson, Marcus Pinson III, Ruth-Catherine E. Student, Mary Washington Coll., 1955-57; BS in Phys. Therapy, Med. Coll. Va., 1959. Lic. phys. therapist. Staff phys. therpist Univ. Hosps., U. Wis., Madison, 1959-61; chief phys. therapy Stoughton (Wis.) Cmty. Hosp., 1961-63; vol. phys. therapy Cerebral Palsy Ctr., Richmond, Va., 1963-64; pvt. practice in phys. therapy Richmond, 1965-68; interim dir. Stuart Cir. Hosp., Richmond, 1968-69; phys. therpist on call St. Mary's Hosp., Richmond, 1968-74; pres., owner Capital Phys. Therapy Assocs., Richmond, 1989—; part-time phys. therapist St. Mary's Hosp., Richmond, 1975-88; lectr. Med. Coll. Va., Richmond, 1992, 93, John Tyler C.C., Richmond, 1992, 93, 94; mem. adv. bd. phys. therapy Va. State Bd. Medicine, 1990—, vice chmn., 1992—. Mem. adv. bd. Va. Opera, 1979—; bd. visitors Mary Washington Coll., Fredericksburg, Va., 1980-82, rector bd. visitors, 1982-84; pres. Richmond Symphony Orch. League, 1986-88. Named Clubwoman of Yr., Richmond Newsleader, 1972. Mem. Am. Phys. Therapy Assn., Richmond Acad. Medicine Aux. (pres. 1967-68), Med. Soc. Va. Alliance (pres. 1980-81), Med. Coll. Va. Hosps. Aux. (pres. 1973-75), Va. Cultural Laureate Soc. Home: 4607 Stratford Rd Richmond VA 23225 Office: Capital Phys Therapy Assocs 1919 W Huguenot Rd Ste 201 Richmond VA 23235

NEAL, JOYCE OLIVIA, utility company executive; b. Jamaica, N.Y., Aug. 11, 1943; d. Nathaniel Grant and Ernestine (Wilson) Thomas; m. Robert Lee Neal Jr., Dec. 16, 1959 (div. Dec. 1972); children: Cheryl Ann, Robin Crystal, Sylvia Lenore. AAS, SUNY, Farmingdale, 1979; BBA, Hofstra U., 1983. Keypunch operator E.B.S. Data Processing, Amityville, N.Y., 1968-71, asst. supr., 1971-72; keypunch operator Long Island Lighting Co., Hicksville, N.Y., 1972-78, asst. systems designer, 1978-79, assoc. systems designer, 1979-81, systems designer, 1981-84, systems analyst, 1984-85, project leader, 1985-89, sect. supr., 1989—. Tutor Literacy Vols. Am., Nassau County, N.Y., 1988-90; vol. United Negro Coll. Fund, Nassau County, 1985—; bd. dirs. Suffolk County Housing Authority, Hauppauge, N.Y., 1985. Walter A. Lynch scholar SUNY, Farmingdale, 1979; recipient Cert. Appreciation, U.S. Assn. Evening Students, 1978-82, nat. sec. 1982. Mem. NAFE, NAACP, Coll. Scholarship Svc. (Cert. Appreciation, Talent Roster 1979), Black Women's Alliance Inc. (co-founder, pres. 1979-81, 84-85, 90-92, treas. 1986-89, sec. 1994-95, Appreciation award 1989), Take Off Pounds Sensibly (founder Amityville chpt., leader 1974-78, 81-84, 86-87), Phi Theta Kappa, Alpha Beta Gamma, Alpha Sigma Lambda. Baptist. Office: Long Island Lighting Co 175 E Old Country Rd Hicksville NY 11801-4257

NEAL, JULIA TURNER, lawyer; b. Kinston, N.C., Dec. 9, 1954; d. Aubrey Williams and Julia Dean (Sandlin) Turner; m. Merley B. Neal III, Apr. 24, 1993. BA in History, Meredith Coll., 1975; cert. litigation, Inst. Paralegal Tng., 1976; student, John Marshall Sch. Law, 1978-79; JD, Wake Forest U., 1981. Bar: N.C. 1981, U.S. Dist. Ct. (mid. dist.) N.C. 1981. Atty. Robert Tally, Winston-Salem, N.C., 1981-82, Habegger and Johnson, Winston-Salem, 1982-83; pvt. practice Winston-Salem, 1983-85; atty. Womble, Carlyle, Sandridge & Rice, Winston-Salem, 1985-86; sr. atty. Integon Corp., Winston-Salem, 1987-90; v.p., gen. counsel, corp. sec. Strickland Ins. Group, Inc., Goldsboro, N.C., 1990—. Mem. Am. Soc. Corp. Secs., Inc., N.C. Bar Assn., N.C. Assn. Def. Attys., Def. Rsch. Inst. Home: 127 Woods Mill Rd Goldsboro NC 27534 Office: Strickland Ins Group Inc 1107 Parkway Dr Goldsboro NC 27533

NEAL, LEORA LOUISE HASKETT, social services administrator; b. N.Y.C., Feb. 23, 1943; d. Melvin Elias and Miriam Emily (Johnson) Haskett; m. Robert A. Neal, Apr. 23, 1966; children: Marla Patrice, Johnathan Robert. BA in Psychology and Sociology, City Coll. N.Y., 1965; MS in Social Work, Columbia U., 1970, cert. adoption specialist, 1977; IBM cert. community exec. tng. program, N.Y., 1982. Cert. social worker N.Y. state. Caseworker N.Y.C. Dept. Social Service, 1965-67, Windham Child Care, N.Y.C., 1967-73; exec. dir. Assn. Black Social Workers Child Adoption Counseling and Referral Service, N.Y.C., 1975—; cons. adoption, adoption tng. N.Y. State Dept. Social Svc., Columbia U. Sch. Social Work, N.Y.C. Human Resources Adminstrn., U. La., New Orleans; founder Haskett-Neal Publs., Bronx, N.Y., 1993. Co-author: Transracial Adoptive Parenting: A Black/White Community Issue, 1993. Child Welfare League Am. fellow, 1976; recipient cert. No Time to Lose cert. N.Y. State Dept. Social Svcs., 1989. Mem. NAFE, Columbia U. Alumni Assn., CCNY Alumni Assn., Missionary Com. Revival Team (outreach chairperson 1982-88). Democrat. Office: Assn Black Social Workers 1969 Madison Ave New York NY 10035-1549

NEAL, LOUISE KATHLEEN, life insurance company executive, accountant; b. Seattle, Nov. 25, 1951; d. Paul Bradford and Ruth Catherine (Park) Johnson; m. William Steven Neal, Oct. 25, 1974. B.A. in Bus. Adminstrn. and Acctg., U. Wash., 1974. Sr. acct. Touche Ross & Co., Seattle, 1974-77; internal auditor No. Life Ins. Co., Seattle, 1977-83; auditor Northwestern Nat. Life Ins. Co., Mpls., 1983-84, 2d v.p., auditor, 1984-88; sr. v.p., gen. auditor Transam. Occidental Life Ins. Co., L.A., 1988-89, sr. v.p., 1990-92, sr. v.p., chief adminstrv. officer, 1992-95; pres. USA Admin. Svcs. Inc. sub. Transam. Occidental Life Ins. Co., Overland Park, Kans., 1995—. Fellow Life Mgmt. Inst.; mem. AICPA. Office: USA Admin Svcs Inc PO Box 2948 Overland Park KS 66201-1348

NEAL, LOVETT LADELLE, elementary educator; b. Gilmore, Ark., May 15, 1925; d. Thomas Addison Binford and Roxie Anna Lovett Tatum; m. George Howard Neal, June 4, 1950 (dec. Feb. 28, 1993); children: Debora, Stephen, Patricia Kaczmarek, Michael. BS, Ea. Mich. U., 1966; MA in Edn., Wayne State U., 1973. Lic. tchr., grades K-8. Sec. Richman Crosby, Memphis, 1943, Army Supply Depot, Memphis, 1943-44; med. sec. VA Hosp., Memphis, 1944-52, Weather Bur., East Lansing, Mich., 1961; exec. sec. C. of C., Ypsilanti, Mich., 1965; elem. tchr. Ypsilanti Pub. Schs., 1967-70, Detroit Pub. Schs., 1970—. Mem. Grosse Point (Mich.) Women's Dem. Club, 1980-93; precinct del. Dem. Party, 1982-88. Mem. AAUW, Coalition of Labor Union Women, Am. Fedn. Tchrs. (bldg. rep.), Detroit Fedn. tchrs. Baptist. Home: 595 Barrington Rd Grosse Pointe MI 48230-1721

NEAL, MARGARET RUTH, librarian; b. Murray, Ky., Jan. 29, 1944; d. Thomas Harrison and Ruth (Overbey) Crider; m. Roger Alan Neal, Aug. 7, 1966; children: Roger Thomas, Alana Rene. BSc., Murray State U., Ky., 1966; MSc., U. Ill., Urbana, 1970. Libr. skills tchr. Danville (Ill.) Community Consol. Sch. Dist. #118, 1966-68; libr. East Park Jr. High, Danville, Ill., 1968-71; part-time ref. libr. Danville Pub. Library, Ill., 1972-75; libr. North Ridge Jr. High Sch., Ill., 1972-76; eng. tchr. East Park Middle Sch., Danville, Ill., 1976-87; head libr. Danville (Ill.) High Sch., 1987—; sch. dist. rep. Instrl. TV, Urbana, Ill., 1987-91; chair Catlin high sch. Curriculum Com.,m 1989-91, rep. regional Ill. White House conf. on Libr. and Info. Svcs., 1990; mem. com. career fair, 1991; dist. rep. Libr. Grant Writing Network, 1991—; co-panelist Country Ednl. Summit, 1992; mem. Sch. Restructuring Com., 1992—; workshop presenter Sch. Reviewer for Sch.; guest panelist Ill. State Libr. Assn. Convention, 1993. Reviewer for Sch. Library Journal Book Review, How a Horse Grew Course. Co-pres. Booster Club, Catlin, Ill., 1986-91; sponsor Libr. Guild, 1991-92. Recipient Computer Circulation System award Chap. II, 1986-89, Ill. Area IV Grant, 1989; grantee Ill. State Sch. Bd., 1993. Mem. NEA, Ill. Edn. Assn., Danville Edn. Republican. Baptist. Office: Danville High Sch Libr 202 E Fairchild St Danville IL 61832-3196

NEAL, TERESA SCHREIBEIS, secondary education educator; b. Wheatland, Wyo., Mar. 19, 1956; d. Gene L. and Bonnie Marie (Reed) Schreibeis; m. Michael R. Neal, Apr. 7, 1990; 1 child, Rianna Michelle. BA in Am. Studies and English Edn., U. Wyo., 1978; MA in History, U. So. Calif., 1989, PhD, 1994. Cert. secondary edn. tchr., Wyo., Colo. Tchr. lang. arts and social studies, asst. coach Carbon County Sch. Dist. 1, Rawlins, Wyo., 1978-86; asst. lectr. freshmen writing program U. So. Calif., L.A., 1986-90; prof. history Palomar (Calif.) Community Coll., San Diego, 1991; software support specialist Dynamic Data Systems, Westminster, Colo., 1992-93; tchr. humanities/gifted and talented classes Arvada (Colo.) West High Sch., 1993—; participant critical thinking and humanities secondary edn. project NEH, Wyo., 1985-86. Mem., chair Reading Is Fundamental Program, Rawlins, 1983-85. Mem. AAUW, Western Assn. Women Historians, G. Autrey Mus. Western Art, Phi Beta Kappa. Office: 11325 Allendale Dr Arvada CO 80004-4477

NEAL-BAMBENEK, CARA DAWN, medical/surgical nurse and army officer; b. Gallipolis, Ohio, Apr. 2, 1962; d. Earl Edward and Karen Aileen (Parks) Neal; m. John Charles Bambenek III, June 9, 1990. BSN, U. Cin., 1984. Commd. Capt. U.S. Army, 1984-88; staff nurse orthopaedics, gen. surgery and psychiatry Walter Reed Army Med. Ctr., Washington, 1984-88, charge nurse Eisenhower Exec. Ste., 1988-90; staff nurse med./surg. Keller Army Cmty. Hosp., West Point, N.Y., 1990-91, head nurse same day surgery, 1991-92; head nurse med./surg. unit Keller Army Cmty. Hosp., West Point, 1992—. Recipient Meritorious Svc. medal Walter Reed Army Med. Ctr., 1990, meritorious svc. medal with first oak leaf cluster, 1994. Home: 1561 Tan Tara Circle Lake Charles LA 70611 Office: Army Reserves 400th Hosp Sect 2 1850 Old Spanish Trl Houston TX 77054

NEALE, GAIL LOVEJOY, educational administrator; b. Detroit, Feb. 8, 1935; d. Elijah Parish and Jane Appleton (Howell) Lovejoy; m. Richard Potter (div.); m. Anthony Astrachan (div.); children: Owen Lovejoy, Joshua Howell; m. Robert Edward Neale, June 23, 1984. Student, Vassar Coll., 1952-54. Rsch. aide, dir. devel., corp. sec., v.p. Hudson Inst., Inc., Croton on Hudson, N.Y., 1962-76; v.p. Aspen Inst., N.Y.C., 1976-78; dir. external affairs Middlebury (Vt.) Coll., 1978-80; pres. Hudson Inst., Croton on Hudson, 1980-82; corp. sec. Commonwealth Fund, N.Y.C., 1983-86; project adminstr. Mt. Holyoke Coll., South Hadley, Mass., 1986-88; dir. devel. Hampshire Coll., Amherst, Mass., 1988-91; exec. v.p., COO Salzburg Seminar, Middlebury, Vt., 1991—; bd. dirs. JL Found., L.A., Capital Income Builder, L.A., Capital World Growth and Income Fund, L.A., AmcapFund, L.A., Fundamental Investors, L.A., Vera Inst. for Justice, N.Y.C. Bd. dirs. Conern for Dying, N.Y.C., 1986-90. Mem. Origami Soc. Am., Cosmopolitan Club. Democrat. Episcopalian. Home: RD 4 Box 472 Middlebury VT 05753 Office: Salzburg Seminar PO 886 Marbleworks Middlebury VT 05753

NEARY, PAMELA, state legislator; b. Mar. 16, 1955; m. Court Storey; 4 children. BS in Biology and Polit. Sci., Ft. Lewis St. Coll.; MA in Pub. Affairs, Humphrey Inst. Mem. Minn. Ho. of Reps., 1992—; mem. health and human svcs. com., mem. regulated industries and energy com., mem. transp. and transit com. Active Citizens League. Mem. Minn. Women's Polit. Caucus, Minn. Women's Consortium. Democrat. Home: 1033 Indian Trl S Afton MN 55001-9705 Office: Minn Ho of Reps State Capitol Saint Paul MN 55155*

NEARY, PATRICIA ELINOR, ballet director; b. Miami, Fla.; d. James Elliott and Elinor (Mitsitz) N. Corps de ballet Nat. Ballet of Can., Toronto, Ont., 1957-60; prin. dancer N.Y.C. Ballet, 1960-68; ballerina Geneva Ballet (Switzerland), 1968-70, ballet dir., 1973-78; guest artist Stuttgart Ballet, Germany, 1968-71; asst. ballet dir., ballerina West Berlin Ballet, 1970-73; ballet dir. Zurich Ballet (Switzerland), 1978-86, La Scala di Milano ballet co., Italy, 1986-88; tchr., Balanchine ballets, Balanchine Estate, 1987—.

NEASE, JUDITH ALLGOOD, marriage and family therapist; b. Arlington, Mass., Nov. 15, 1930; d. Dwight Maurice Allgood and Sophie (Wolf) Allgood Morris; student Rockford Coll., 1949-50; BA, NYU, 1953, MA, 1954; MS, Columbia U. Sch. Social Work, 1956; m. Theron Stanford Nease, Sept. 1, 1962; children: Susan Elizabeth, Alison Allgood. Social worker Bellevue Psychiat. Hosp., N.Y.C., 1956-59; psychiat. social worker St. Luke's Hosp., N.Y.C., 1959-62; asst. psychiat. social work supr. N.J. Neuropsychiat. Inst., Princeton, 1962-64; group co-leader Ctr. for Advancement of Personal and Social Growth, Atlanta, 1973-76, asst. dir., social work supr., group co-leader Druid Hills Counseling Ctr., Columbia Theol. Sem., 1973-82; marriage and family therapist Cath. Social Svcs., Atlanta, 1978-87; chief Community Mental Health Svc., Ft. McPherson, Atlanta, Ga., 1987-92; master's level clinician Ctr. for Psychiatry, Smyrna, Ga., 1990-92; pvt. practice marriage and family therapy. Mem. NASW, Acad. Cert. Social Workers, Am. Assn. Marriage and Family Therapy, Am. Group Psychotherapy Assn. Republican. Episcopalian. Home: 4678 Cedar Park Way Stone Mountain GA 30083-1887

NEBLETT, CAROL, soprano; b. Modesto, Calif., Feb. 1, 1946; m. Philip R. Akre; 3 children. Studies with, William Vennard, Roger Wagner, Esther Andreas, Ernest St. John Metz, Lotte Lehmann, Pierre Bernac, Rosa Ponselle, George London, Jascha Heifetz. Soloist with Roger Wagner Chorale; performed in U.S. and abroad with various symphonies; debut with Carnegie Hall, 1966, N.Y.C. Opera, 1969, Met. Opera, 1979; sung with maj. opera cos. including Met. Opera, N.Y.C., Lyric Opera Chgo., Balt. Opera, Pitts. Opera, Houston Grand Opera, San Francisco Opera, Boston Opera Co., Milw. Florentine Opera, Washington Opera Soc., Covent Garden, Cologne Opera, Vienna (Austria) Staatsoper, Paris Opera, Teatro Regio, Turin, Italy, Teatro San Carlo, Naples, Italy, Teatro Massimo, Palermo, Italy, Gran Teatro del Liceo, Barcelona, Spain, Kirov Opera Theatre, Leningrad, USSR, Dubrovnik (Yugoslavia) Summer Festival, Salzberg Festival, others; rec. artist RCA, DGG, EMI; appearances with symphony orchs., also solo recitals, (film) La Clemenza di Tito; filmed and recorded live performance with Placido Domingo, La Fancivla del West; numerous TV appearances. Office: New Century Artist Mgmt Inc PO Box 802 Tuxedo Park NY 10987

NECCO, E(DNA) JOANNE, school psychologist; b. Klamath Falls, Oreg., June 23, 1941; d. Joseph Rogers and Lillian Laura (Owings) Painter; m. Jon F. Puryear, Aug. 25, 1963 (div. Oct. 1987); children: Laura L., Douglas F.; m. A. David Necco, July 1, 1989. BS, Cen. State U., 1978, MEd, 1985; PhD in Applied Behavioral Studies, Okla. State U., 1993. Med.-surg. asst. Oklahoma City Clinic, 1961-68; spl. edn. tchr. Oklahoma City Pub. Schs., 1978-79, Edmond (Okla.) Pub. Schs., 1979-83; co-founder, owner Learning Devel. Clinic, Edmond, 1983-93; asst. prof. profl. tchr. edn. U. Ctrl. Okla., Edmond, 1993—; adj. instr. Cen. State U., Edmond, 1989-93, Oklahoma City U., 1991-93; mem. rsch. group Okla. State U., Stillwater, 1991-93. Contbr. articles to profl. jours. Mem. Edmond Task Force for Youth, 1983-87, Edmond C. of C., 1984-87. Mem. Nat. Assn. for Sch. Psychologists, Am. Bus. Women's Assn., Coun. for Exceptional Children, Assn. for Children & Adults with Learning Disabilities, Okla. Assn. for Children & Adults with Learning Disabilities, Golden Key Nat. Honor Soc., Phi Delta Kappa. Republican. Home: 17509 Woodsorrel Rd Edmond OK 73003-6951 Office: U Ctrl Okla Coll Edn 100 N University Dr Edmond OK 73034

NECKAR, CHARLAINE FRANCES, community health nurse; b. Blackwell, Okla., May 23, 1962; d. Charles Franklin and Karen Kaye (Klein) Keltch; m. Milton Neckar Jr., Apr. 24, 1982; children: Ruby Kaye, Rachel Ann, Kit Everet. ADN, San Antonio Coll., 1983; BSN, Incarnate Word Coll., 1993. RN, Tex.; cert. in cmty. health. Staff nurse N.E. Bapt. Hosp., Hospice San Antonio; field PCH supr. Home Nursing and Therapy, San Antonio; quality assurance coord. ABC Home, San Antonio, Brit Tex. Home Health, San Antonio. Office: Brit Tex Home Health Ste 240 1600 NE Loop 410 #220 San Antonio TX 78209

NEDDERMAN, NORMA FAYE SANDBERG, government official; b. Kansas City, Mo., Oct. 15, 1954; d. Max B. and Lillian Beatrice (Walters) Holt; m. Steven Dale Sandberg, Nov. 20, 1976 (div. Feb. 1984); 1 child, Gregory Louis; m. Jeff Paul Nedderman, July 27, 1990; 1 child, Wade Howard. BS in Environ. Health, U. Kans., 1975, MS in Environ. Sci., 1977. Environ. engr. Kans. Dept. Health and Environ., Topeka, 1976-79, EPA, Kansas City, Kans., 1979-87; chief safety and environ. mgmt. br. Gen. Svcs. Adminstrn., Ft. Worth, 1987-91; mgr. Ark.-La. Airport Devel. Office, FAA, Ft. Worth, 1991—; exec. bd. Dallas/Ft. Worth Fed. Safety Coun., Arlington, 1989-90; lectr. in field. Arbitrator Better Bus. Bureau, Kansas City, Mo., 1985-87; active PTA, Arlington, 1987—. NASA fellow, 1976; named one of Outstanding Young Women of Am., 1978. Mem. LWV, Exec. Women in Govt. (v.p. 1991, pres. 1993-94), Air and Waste Mgmt. Assn., Fed. Women's Program Com. (program chmn. 1990—), Fed. Bus. Assn. (v.p. 1992, chmn. scholarship com. 1992-94), Nat. Fire Protection Assn., Toastmasters (pres. 1990, Competetent Toastmaster award 1988, Able Toastmaster award 1992). Methodist. Home: 6200 Meachum Blvd Arlington TX 76016 Office: FAA 4400 Blue Mound Rd Fort Worth TX 76106-1927

NEDERVELD, RUTH ELIZABETH, retired real estate executive; b. Hudsonville, Mich., Oct. 29, 1933; d. Ralph and Hattie (Ploeg) Schut; m. Terrill Lee Nederveld, June 6, 1952; children: Courtland Lee, Valerie Lynn Nederveld Heisey, Darwin Frederic. Degree in Real Estate, U. Mich., 1979; student, Pa. State U., Centre Hall, 1973, Aquinas Coll., Grand Rapids, Mich., 1974; degree, Grad. Realtors Inst., 1979. Cert. residential specialist; registered securities agt. With sales dept. Field Enterprises, Lancaster, Pa., 1962-72; sales assoc. E. James Hogan, Lancaster, 1972-74, C-21 Packard, Grand Rapids, Mich., 1974-80; assoc. broker comml. div. Markland Devel., Inc., Grand Rapids, 1980-86, Am. Acquest Realty, Inc., Grand Rapids, 1986-89; broker, owner R.E. Nederveld Realtors, Ada, Mich., 1989-94; ret., 1994. Pres. Civic Nucomers of Grand Rapids, 1978; trustee, elder Forest Hills Presbyn. Ch., Cascade, Mich., 1983-86. Mem. Nat. Assn. Realtors (mem. comml. dept. 1973—), Mich. Assn. Realtors, Grand Rapids Real Estate Bd., Woman's Council Realtors (corr. sec. 1986-87), Nat. Assn. Female Execs., Assn. Sales and Mktg. Execs. (exec. dir. internat. chpt. 1977-84, pres. Grand Rapids chpt. 1986-87). Republican. Lodge: Order of Eastern Star.

NEDZA, SANDRA LOUISE, manufacturing executive; b. Chgo., Aug. 20, 1951; d. Thomas and Ina Louise (Wilson) Ingle; m. James Owen Earnest, May 5, 1973 (div. Nov. 1984); m. Ronald Edward Nedza, Nov. 22, 1986; 1 child, Thomas Edward. Student acctg., Met. Sch. Bus., Chgo., 1970. Accounting clk. Gane Bros. & Lane, Inc., Chgo., 1967-72; advanced from expeditor to buyer Hammond Organ Co., Chgo., 1972-84; purchasing/prodn. control supr. IRP-Profl. Sound Products, Elk Grove Village, Ill, 1984-94, Bensenville, Ill., 1994—. Mem. Jobs Daughters, 1967—. Mem. Lion, Alpha Iota (scholarship key 1970). Lutheran. Clubs: Juke Box Sno-Riders (sec. 1986-87) (Fox Lake, Ill.), Lakeview Sno-Riders. Lodge: Lioness (v.p. 1985-88, pres. 1988-89) (Chgo.). Home: 1418 S Robert Dr Mount Prospect IL 60056-4542 Office: IRP-Profl Sound Products 321 Bond St 1111 Tower Ln Bensenville IL 60106

NEE, LINDA ELIZABETH, health facility professional; b. Boston, Dec. 29, 1938; d. Thomas Markham and Ellen Thomas (Jamieson) Nee. BA, Russell Sage Coll., 1961; MS in Social Work, Va. Commonwealth U., 1968. Social worker, social svc. dept., N.Y. Neurol. Inst., Columbia Presbyn. Med. Ctr., N.Y.C., 1961-66; med. social worker Tb San., Med. Coll. Va., Richmond, summer 1967; clin. social worker social work dept. Clin. Center, NIH, Bethesda, Md., 1968-74, clin. rsch. social worker sect. exptl. therapeutics, lab. clin. sci., NIMH, Bethesda, 1974-84, clin. genetics rsch. assoc. Nat. Inst. Neurol. Disorders and Stroke, 1984, social sci. analyst, 1984—; mem. ethics com. Md. State Bd. Social Work Examiners, 1979—. Adv., organizer, bd. dirs. Met. D.C. chpt. Alzheimer's and Related Diseases Assn., 1979-88, pres., 1982-86; mem. sci. bd. Familial Alzheimer's Disease Rsch. Found., Tulsa, 1987—; bd. dirs. Friends of Clin. Ctr., Bethesda, 1989—, pres., 1992; trustee The Sage Colls., Troy, N.Y., 1993—. Mem. NASW (chmn. ethics and grievances 1977-79; pres. Met. Washington 1975-77). Editor: Jour. Social Work Met. Washington, 1975-77; columnist: The Bulletin newsletter Nat. Assn. Social Workers, 1975-77; contbr. articles to profl. jours. Office: Clin Ctr NINDS Bethesda MD 20892

NEECE, OLIVIA HELENE ERNST, real estate developer, business consultant; b. L.A., Jan. 3, 1948; d. Robert and Beatrice Pearl Ernst; m. Huntley Lee Bluestein, 1967 (div. 1974); children: Melissa Dawn, Brendon Wade; m. Anthony Ray Neece, Mar. 20, 1977. Cert. interior design, UCLA, 1972-75; BSBA, U. So. Calif., 1990; MBA, UCLA, 1993. Cert. interior designer Calif. Coun. for Interior Design; lic. gen. contractor, real estate broker, Calif. Staff designer Frances Lux Designs, L.A., 1974; project designer Yates Silverman Inc., L.A., 1974-77; owner Olivia Neece Planning & Design, Tarzana, Calif., 1977-86; v.p. project devel. Design Services/Aircoa, Englewood, Colo., 1986-87; v.p. project adminstrn. Hirsch-Bedner Assoc., Santa Monica, Calif., 1987-88; treas.-sec. EON Corp., L.A., 1980—; owner Olivia Neece Planning & Design, Tarzana, 1988-93; dir. ops. The Ernst Group, L.A., 1980—; ptnr. Neece Assocs., L.A., 1993—; prof. Calif. State U., Northridge, part-time, 1994—; speaker in field; instr. ext. program UCLA, 1981-83. Co-author: A Step by Step Approach to Hotel Development, 1988; conbtr. articles to profl. jours. Mem. fund raising and edn. coms. L.A. Music Ctr. Opera League; mem. L.A. Music Ctr. 100; charter mem. Los Angeles County Mus. Art; vol. restoration of San Diego R.R. Mus., 1985-92. Recipient Holiday Inn Devel. award, Foster City, Calif., 1986, Warwick, R.I., 1988, 1st and 2d place awards Lodging Hospitality Designers Circle, 1987, Gold Key award Russell St. Inn, 1986. Mem. Am. Soc. Interior Designers (1st pl. portfolio competition 1974), Inst. Bus. Designers (profl., v.p., bd. dirs.), Nat. Restaurant Assn., Urban Land Inst., Am. Hotel and Motel Assn., Decorative Arts Coun., Nat. Coun. Interior Design Qualifications. Office: Neece Assoc 18200 Rosita St Tarzana CA 91356-4622 also: The Ernst Group 12401 Helena St Los Angeles CA 90049-3907

NEEDHAM, BRENDA LYNN, school system administrator; b. Lebanon, N.H., June 1, 1950; d. Stillman Lucius and Ruth Ellen (Houghton) N.; m. Arthur Dale Garges, Aug. 19, 1979; 1 child, Kali Needham. BS, U. Conn., 1972; MEd, U. Vt., 1979; CAGS, Castleton Coll., 1991. Cert. sch. supt. Supr. Perkins Sch., Lancaster, Mass., 1976-77; co-dir. Developmental Ctr., Bethel, Vt., 1977-78, dir., 1978-81; program coord. Woodstock (Vt.) Learning Clinic, 1981-84; edn. cons. Dept. Edn., Montpelier, Vt., 1985-86; dir. spl. edn. SAU # 32, Lebanon, 1986-89, dir. spl. svcs., 1989-91, asst. supt., 1991-94; supt. East Granby (Conn.) Pub. Schs., 1994—. Office: East Granby Pub Schs 33 Turkey Hill Rd East Granby CT 06026

NEEDHAM, KATHLEEN ANN, gerontology educator, consultant; b. Saginaw, Mich., Aug. 30, 1944; d. George Whitcomb and Ann (Drensky) N.; m. Kenneth Edward Cassady, June 19, 1982. BA, Olivet (Mich.) Coll., 1967; MA, Mich. State U., 1970, postgrad., 1972-76, 90—; cert., U. Mich., 1977. Cert. tchr., Mich. High sch. tchr. Pontiac (Mich.) schs., 1968-72; grad. asst. Mich. State U., East Lansing, 1972-76; asst. prof., chmn. dept. gerontology Madonna U., Livonia, Mich., 1981-90; mem. faculty Madonna Coll., Livonia, Mich, 1991—; grant project dir. Adminstrn. on Aging, Washington, 1977-83, Mich. Dept. Labor, Lansing, 1985-86; grant project supr. NIMH, Washington, 1981-83; cons. in field. Producer tapes in field. Del. Mich. White House Conf. on Aging, Dearborn, 1981; mem. com. Mich. Offie Svcs. to Aging, Lansing, 1983-92; bd. dirs. United Community Svcs., 1985-94, mem. health svcs. com., 1991—; chmn. Mich. Minimum Stds. for Aging, 1987; vol. Focus Hope, Detroit, Mich. Lupus Found.; mem. Mich. Task Force on Older Worker, Lansing, 1987, Mich. Exec. Commn. on Older Learner Summit, 1990-93; chair Mich. Gov.'s Conf. on Aging, 1991; cons. to bd. Mich. Assoc. Svc. Orgns., 1991-93. Recipient Svc. award Internat. Healthcare Assn., 1988, 89. Mem. Gerontol. Soc. Am., Detroit Women's Econ. Club, Mich. Soc. Gerontology (bd. dirs. 1987), Assn. Gerontology in Higher Edn. (membership com. 1982—, pub. policy com. 1988, pub. rels. and fund raising 1992, 93), Am. Soc. Aging. Presbyterian. Home: 22760 Clear Lake Dr Farmington MI 48335-3834 Office: Madonna Univ 36600 Schoolcraft Rd Livonia MI 48150-1176

NEEDHAM, NANCY JEAN, management consultant; b. Chgo., July 21, 1941; d. Robert Leonard and Grace Irene (Bennett) N.; children: Thomas,

Charles, Catharine, Jessica. BA, Wellesley Coll., 1964; MBA, Harvard U., 1972, DBA, 1977. Pubs. specialist MIT, Cambridge, Mass., 1964-65; editor SRA, Chgo., 1966; sr. editor Ency. Britannica, Chgo., 1967; cons. ABT Assocs., Cambridge, 1968; program mgr. Am. Sci. & Engring., Boston, 1969; faculty Harvard Bus. Sch., Cambridge, 1973-75; cons. CRI, Cambridge, 1977-78; prof. mgmt. Poly. U. N.Y., N.Y.C., 1986—; assoc. dir. Ctr. for Advanced Tech. in Telecommunications, N.Y.C., 1986—; pres. ICGS Inc., Boston, 1978—. Contbr. articles to profl. jours. Mem. Am. Soc. Macro Engring. (bd. dirs. 1984-92), C.G. Jung Found. (bd. dirs. 1988-94), Phi Beta Kappa. Presbyterian. Home: RR 2 Box 191 B Delhi NY 13753-9643

NEEL, EULA BARNEYCASTLE, state purchasing agent; b. Votaw, Tex., Feb. 24, 1928; d. Elzie and Susan Viola (Bass) Barneycastle; m. Walter Lee Neel, Dec. 18, 1953 (dec.). Student, Durham's Bus. Coll., 1945-46. Lic. Real Estate Agent, Utah. Sec. E.I. Du Pont Co., La Porte, Tex., 1947-49, asst. to plant buyer, 1949-70, sr. buyer, 1970-76, regional buyer, 1976-78; vol. missionary LDS Ch., Nitro, W.Va., 1979-80; civic/religious activist Salt Lake City, 1980-84; dept. corrections purchasing technician State of Utah, Draper, 1984-87; purchasing agt. State of Utah, Salt Lake City, 1987—; bd. dirs. Vista Mont. Homeowners Assn.; com. chair UCI Furniture Mfg.-State, Salt Lake City, 1988—; mgr. Pharm. Com.-State, Salt Lake City, 1988—. Author: (contract) Rotenone-Treatment of Water Reservoirs, 1991 (Hero Award); composer: (pub.) Development and Self-Esteem, 1975 (hon. mention). Pres. LDS Young Women, Houston, 1962-78; advancement chair Boy Scout of Am., Sandy, Utah, 1985-86. Mem. Nat. Assn. Purchasing Mgmt. Republican. Mem. LDS Ch. Office: State of Utah Purchasing 3150 S State St Salt Lake City UT 84115-3835

NEELY, SALLY SCHULTZ, lawyer; b. L.A. BA Stanford U., 1970, JD, 1971. Bar: Ariz. 1972, Calif. 1977. Law clk. to judge U.S. Ct. Appeals (9th cir.), Phoenix, 1971-72; assoc. Lewis and Roca, Phoenix, 1972-75; asst. prof. Harvard U. Law Sch., Cambridge, Mass., 1975-77; assoc. Shutan & Trost, P.C., Los Angeles, 1977-79, ptnr., 1979-80, Sidley & Austin, L.A., 1980—; faculty ABA Chapt. 11 Bus. Reorgns., 1989—, Bankruptcy Law Inst. and Bankruptcy Litigation Inst., 1987-92, Nat. Conf. Bankruptcy Judges, 1988, 90, Fed. Jud. Ctr., 1989, 90, 94—, Workshop Bankruptcy and Bus. Reorganization NYU, 1992—; rep. 9th cir. jud. conf., 1989-91; mem. Nat. Bankruptcy Conf., 1993—. Chair Stanford Law Sch. Reunion Giving, 1986; bd. visitors Stanford Law Sch., 1990-92. Fellow Am. Coll. Bankruptcy; mem. ABA, Calif. State Bar Assn. (debtor-creditor rels. and bankruptcy subcom. bus. law sect. 1985-87). Office: Sidley & Austin 555 W 5th St Ste 4000 Los Angeles CA 90013

NEES, ELIZABETH, artist; b. Pasadena, Calif., Feb. 3, 1952. BFA in Drawing and Painting cum laude, Calif. State U., Long Beach, 1989, post-grad., 1990-91. Instr. Tai-Chi Chuan, 1993. Exhibited in solo and group shows including South Bay Contemporary Mus. Art, 1991, Orange County Ctr. Contemporary Art, 1993, Torrance Joslyn Fine Arts Gallery, 1994, 3-Sveneteen Gallery, 1995. Fine arts affiliates scholar in visual art Calif. State U., 1988-89. Mem. Women's Caucus for Arts. Studio: 4205 E 11th St Long Beach CA 90804

NEFF, ANNE ROYALL, counselor, psychiatric clinical nurse specialist; b. Richlands, Va., Sept. 14, 1963; d. Joseph Marion Jr. and Mary Jane (Royall) Brown; m. Mitchell David Neff, Oct. 27, 1990. BA, Mary Baldwin Coll., Staunton, Va., 1985; BSN, U. Va., 1987; MS in Edn., Old Dominion U., 1990. RN, Va.; nat. cert. counselor; lic. profl. counselor; cert. psychiat. clin. nurse specialist. Nurse asst. U. Va. Med. Ctr., Charlottesville, 1985-86; nurse Tidewater Psychiat. Inst., Virginia Beach, Va., 1988-89, Norfolk (Va.) Gen. Hosp., 1990—; mental health counselor Crossroads Clin. Svc., Virginia Beach, 1989-93; counselor, nurse, clin. specialist Pembroke Counseling Svc., Virginia Beach, 1989-93; nurse clin. specialist Sentara Norfolk Gen. Hosp., 1990—; profl. counselor, nurse clin. specialist Virginia Beach Psychiat. Inst., 1993—; pvt. practice, 1993—. Recipient Prism Community Svc. award Sentara Norfolk Gen. Hosp., 1993. Mem. ANA, ACA, Mental Health Assn. Tidewater, Mid-Atlantic Group Psychotherapy Soc., Tidewater Acad. Psychiat. Clin. Nurse Specialists, Lic. Profl. Counselors Hampton Roads. Home: 140 Seaside Ln Virginia Bch VA 23462-7642

NEFF, BONITA DOSTAL, communication developmental facilitator; b. Grinnell, Iowa, Aug. 16, 1942; d. Lester Ernest and Mary Margaret (Hudnut) Dostal; m. Gregory Pall Neff, Apr. 27, 1974; 1 child, Kristiana. BA, U. N. Iowa, 1964, MA, 1966; PhD, U. Mich., 1973; AA cum laude, Lansing (Mich.) C.C., 1980. Edn. leadership fellow George Washington U., Washington, 1976-77; specialist Mich. State U., East Lansing, 1977-80, co-investigator family and child inst. energy rsch. team, 1980-82; asst. prof. comm. Purdue U., Hammond, Ind., 1982-87; pres. Pub. Comm. Assocs., Munster, Ind., 1986—; asst. prof. comm. Valparaiso (Ind.) U., 1991—; presenter more than 80 rsch. papers to regional, nat. and internat. profl. confs.; cons. in field. Mem. adv. bd., reviewer Jour. Applied Comm. Rsch.; reviewer Mgmt. Comm. Quar.: An Internat. Jour.; editor procs. on accreditation for nat. conf.; contbr. chpts. to books, profl. articles and poetry to jours. Chancellor's rep. Calumet (Ind.) N.W. Forum Econ. Devel., 1982-84; mem. Lake County (Ind.) Community Devel. Com., 1984—; bd. dirs. Big Bros. and Big Sisters N.W. Ind., 1984, 87; pres., chmn. bd. dirs. N.W. Ind. Youth Chorus. Faculty rsch. grantee U. Mich., 1971, Consumer Product Safety Coun. grantee, 1976-77, Ind. Arts Commn./Nat. Endowment for Arts grantee, 1990-92; recipient top rsch. honors regional confs. Mem. Internat. Comm. Assn. (pub. rels. dir. Pub. Rels. Interest Group, chmn. task force on accreditation 1988), Internat. Pub. Rels. Assn., Speech Comm. Assn. (chmn. commn. for pub. rels. 1988, chmn. nat. Pub. Rels. Rsch. awards com. PRIDE 1988, nat. com. on convs. allied orgns., task force on nat. policy, nat. legis. coun. rep. 1993—), Cen. State Comm. Assn. (chmn. 1988-89, pub. rels. officer 1989-92), Internat. Assn. Bus. Comm., Women in Comm. (pres. Calumet chpt. 1985-90, advisor Valparaiso Student WICI, Inc., Outstanding Communicator 1990), Assn. Educators in Journalism Mass Comm. (charter, mem. internat. com.), World Comm. Assn. Democrat. Roman Catholic. Home: 8320 Greenwood Ave Hammond IN 46321-1813 Office: Pub Comm Assocs 8320 Greenwood Ave Hammond IN 46321-1813

NEFF, DIANE IRENE, naval officer; b. Cedar Rapids, Iowa, Apr. 26, 1954; d. Robert Mariner and Adeline Emma (Zach) N. BA in Psychology and Home Econs., U. Iowa, 1976; MA in Sociology, U. Mo., 1978; MEd in Ednl. Leadership, U. West Fla., 1990. Contract compliance officer, dir. EEO, City of Cedar Rapids, 1979-81; commd. ensign USN, 1981, advanced through grades to lt. comdr.; asst. legal officer Naval Comm. Area Master Sta., Guam, 1982-83; comm. security plans and requirements officer Comdr.-in-Chief US Naval Forces in Europe, London, 1983-85; dir. standards and evaluation dept. Recruit Tng. Command, Orlando, Fla., 1985-89; rsch. and analysis officer Naval Res. Officers Tng. Corps Office Chief Naval Edn. and Tng., Pensacola, Fla., 1989-91; tech. tng. officer Recruit Tng. Command, Great Lakes, Ill., 1991-92, mil. tng. officer, 1992-93, dir. apprentice tng., 1993—. Founding mem. Unity of Gulf Breeze, Fla., 1990; performer various benefits for chs., mus., also others, Orlando, 1988, 91. Fellow Adminstrn. on Aging, 1977. Mem. ASTD, Women Officers Profl. Assn. Unitarian.

NEFF, KATHY S., educator; b. Rochester, Ind., Apr. 24, 1959. Cert. pool operator. With Rochester Community Sch. Corp., 1988-90, head coach girls swimming & diving, 1988—, aquatic dir., swimming and water safety instr., 1988; aquatic supr. Culver (Ind.) Mil. Summer Camps, 1992, 93 summers; coach I.U. Swim Analysis Camp, 1993—; asst. swim coach Culver Mil. Acad., 1993-94; bd. dirs. Rochester Royals Swim Team, 1992—; asst. men's swim coach Culver Mil. Acad., 1993-94; swimming and diving official Indiana High Sch. Athletic Assn., 1991—. Mem. Nat. Fedn. Interscholastic Officials Assn., North Ctrl. Ind. Athletic Officials Assn., Profl. Diving Coaches Assn., Am. Swim Coaches Assn. Office: Rochester Community Schs 650 Zebra Ln Rochester IN 46975-7944

NEHRING, WENDY MARIE, pediatrics nurse; b. Waukegan, Ill., Aug. 17, 1957; d. Virgil M. and R. Allene (Nelson) Nehring. BSN, Ill. Wesleyan U., Bloomington, 1979; MS, U. Wis., Madison, 1983; PhD, U. Ill., Chgo., 1989. Primary nurse level III pediatrics Evanston (Ill.) Hosp., 1979-81; staff/charge nurse pediatrics Kishwaukee Community Hosp., DeKalb, Ill., 1981; staff/charge nurse geriatrics Madison (Wis.) Convalescent Ctr., 1982; instr. parent-child nursing Ill. Wesleyan U., Bloomington, 1983-85; clin. nurse specialist/rsch. asst. U. Ill. Chgo. and Peoria, Coll. Nursing, 1985-87; rsch. asst./nurse cons. U. Ill. at Chgo., Early Intervention Project, 1987-89; sr. rsch. specialist, project dir. U. Ill. Chgo. U. Affiliated Prog. in Devel. Disabilities, 1989-90; sr. rsch. specialist child and family studies U. Ill. at Chgo., Coll. Nursing, Ctr. for Narcolepsy Rsch., 1990-92; pediatric clin. instr. U. Ill., Chgo., 1992, asst. prof. maternal-child nursing, 1992—, coord. undergrad. pediatric nursing program, 1994—; lectr. in field; conductor workshops in field; cons. in field. Contbr. articles to profl. jours. HEW traineeship, 1981-82, 82-83; Downs Syndrome Rsch. fund grantee, 1988, 93—; Nat. Rsch. Svc. awardee, Nat. Ctr. Nursing Rsch.-NIH, 1989, others. Mem. Ctrl. Ill. Down Syndrome Orgn., Nat. Down Syndrome Congress (profl. adv. com. 1988—), Nat. Assn. on Down Syndrome (adv. bd. 1990—, 2d v.p. 1991-94), Am. Assn. on Mental Retardation (prevention com. 1989-92, nursing divsn. pres. 1992-94), Midwest Nursing Rsch. Soc., Soc. for Pediatric Nurses, Alpha Tau Delta, Sigma Theta Tau. Office: U Ill 845 Damen Ave Rm 816 Chicago IL 60612-3750

NEIBURG, SALLY SUE, nursing educator; b. LaGrange, Ga., Nov. 7, 1944; children from previous marriage: Patricia Anne, Elizabeth Sue, James Burton Jr. AA, DeKalb Coll. Nursing, 1973; BA, Ga. State U., Atlanta, 1971, MEd, 1978; EDS, U. Ga., 1987; BSN, Clayton State Coll., 1994. RN. Sr. health educator Ga. Dept. Human Resources, Lawrenceville, 1975-88; asst. dir. staff devel. ARC, Atlanta, 1988; with Atlanta Eye Screening, 1988-89; outreach coord. Cataract Inst., Atlanta, 1989-90; tng. coord. S.E. Regional Ctr. For Drug-Free Schs. & Communities, 1990; tng. planner Atlanta Community Prevention Coalition, 1991-92; sole propr. Healthy Lifestyles, 1992—; nursing instr. Griffin Tech. Sch., 1992-93; sr. nurse Clayton Ctr., Jonesboro, Ga., 1993—; adminstrv. supr. Peachtree Regional Hosp., 1994—; clin. nursing instr. Gordon Coll. Nursing Students, 1995—; chmn. bd. dirs. Canine Vision, Inc. Author: 6 manuals; contbr. articles to profl. jours. Mem. NAFE, Ga. Fedn. Profl. Health Educators, ASTD, AAHPERD, UDC (state chmn. 1988-90, nat. chmn. of pages 1989), Internat. Platform Assn., Daus. of 1812 (local officer 1989—, state officer 1992—), Continental Soc., Daus. of Indian Wars (nat. officer, state officer 1990—), DAR (organizing regent chpt. 1982-84, nat. spkrs. staff 1986-89), Daus. Am. Colonists (chpt. regent 1988-91, state officer 1991—), Colonial Dames of XVII Century (local registrar), Ga. Soc. Magna Charta Dames (state officer 1986—), First Families of Ga., Lions (1st female mem. Atlanta club, chmn. sight and vision 1989-90, officer 1990-91). Episcopalian. Home: 2305 Luther Bailey Rd Senoia GA 30276

NEIDIGK, DIANNE, management consultant; b. Monette, Ark., June 28, 1945; d. William Thomas and Thelma Elizabeth (Wells) Wilkerson; m. Lester Dale Neidigk, Feb. 28, 1964; children: Tami Elizabeth, Scott Alan, Lance Dale, Byron Ross. Student, Sam Houston State U., 1963-65, U. Houston, 1969-70. Sub. tchr. Tomball Ind. Sch. Dist., Tex., 1970-74; owner Total Image & Assocs., Houston, 1980—; dir. Colorific, Houston, 1983-85; v.p. L.D. Neidigk Inc., Magnolia, 1978—; dir. pub. relations, corp accounts Travel Depot, Tomball, 1987—; bd. dirs. The Discovery Fields, 1987; pres. Excel Tng. Dynamics, 1987-94; CEO Am. Inst. Learning and Productivity, 1994—. Author: Scarves: How to Tie One On, 1987, 1987; (newspaper) Total Image, 1984; Total Image, 1986. Mem. ASTD, NAFE, Exec. Women's Network, Assn. Image Cons., Tomball Bus. and Profl. Women, Tomball C. of C., Fedn. Profl. Women, Internat. Platform Assn. (bd. dirs.). Beta Sigma Phi. Republican. Club: Study (Tomball). Avocations: private pilot; tennis; sewing; reading. Home: 1543 Virgie Magnolia TX 77355 Office: Total Image & Assocs 718 W Main St Tomball TX 77375-5540

NEIGER, JUDITH ANNE, marketing professional; b. Bay Shore, N.Y., Aug. 22, 1940; d. Kenneth D. and Hazel (White) Percival; m. John J. Rozuat II, Sept. 25, 1960 (div. Dec. 1972); 1 child, John J. III. BS in Mgmt./Computer Sci., Rochester Inst. Technology, 1979. Mktg. rep. Hewlett-Packard, Rochester, N.Y., 1979-84; product mktg. mgr. Vidar Sys., Herndon, Va., 1984-87; mktg. mgr. Hewlett-Packard, Rockville, Md., 1987-92; mktg. specialist Hewlett-Packard, Falls Church, Va., 1992—; mktg. mgr. Vidar Systems, Herndon, Va., 1984-87. Mem. Direct Mktg. Assn. (speaker 1990-92). Episcopalian. Home: 8423 Hunt Valley Park Vienna VA 22182 Office: Hewlett-Packard 3191 Fairview Park Dr Falls Church VA 22042-4502

NEIL, SANDI SMITH (P. J. NEIL), columnist, poet; b. Plainfield, N.J., Jan. 2, 1962; d. Marcellus Drummond, Jr. and Zenobia Rosmond (DeVore) Smith; m. William Henry Neil, Jr., Apr. 9, 1988; 1 child, Beatrice Evangeline. BA, Glassboro State Coll., 1985. Co-mgr. The Ltd., Sizes Unltd. Divsn., Upper Darby, Pa., 1987-88; svc. rep. Bell Atlantic, Bell of Pa. divsn., Phila., 1990-93; adminstrv. asst. Powelton Mantua Ednl. Fund, Phila., 1994; writer Weekly Press, Phila., 1993-94; columnist, reporter The Valley Informer, Huntsville, Ala., 1994—; graphics operator Sta. WAFF-TV, Huntsville, 1994—; graphics/font operator Sta. WAFF-TV 48, Huntsville, 1994—. Author: Reflections of a Black Life, 1991, Bee-Bee Bunny's Great Big Surprise, 1991, I Can Make That Sound, 1991, Cry, a Celebration of Black Life, 1993, A Good Question, 1993, Cries, a Celebration of Black Life, 1994. Advisor Locust Towers Tenants Assn., 1994; former mem. Young Adult Usher Bd., 1992-94; mem. media com. Stop the Violence Task Force, Huntsville, 1994—; mem. Ala. New South Coalition, Huntsville, 1994—; mem. pub. awareness com. Get Out the Vote Task Force, Huntsville, 1994—; mem. Cmty. Pub. Access TV Com., Huntsville, 1994—; vol. tutor Coalition for At Risk Minority Males Program, Huntsville, 1994; vol. reader/computer tutor kindergarten Rolling Hills Elem. Sch., Huntsville, 1994-95; media subcom. sec. Ala. Breast and Cervical Cancer Control Coalition, Montgomery, 1994—; vol., pathfinder, adventure counselor 1st Seventh Day Adventist Ch., Huntsville, 1994—; vol. Jr. Adventist Youth Soc. Program Coord., Huntsville, 1995—. Mem. North Ala. African-Am. C. of C., Huntsville Press Club. Adventist. Office: PO Box 3585 Huntsville AL 35810-0585 Office: The Valley Informer PO 3585 Huntsville AL 35810-0585

NEILL, LOIS ALENE, realtor, religious educator; b. Davenport, Nebr., Sept. 18, 1936; d. John and Wilda Irene (Bates) Surber; m. Terry Marvin Dowe, Aug. 5, 1956 (dec. Feb. 1969); m. Everett Philip Neill, June 10, 1971; children: Alan Dean, JoAnn, Theodore Marvin, Ross Owen (dec.). Sub. tchr. Los Lunas (N.Mex.) Sch. System; missionary Ch. of Christ, Auckland, New Zealand, 1973-78, Whangavei, N.Z., 1978-86; realtor O'Conor, Piper, Flynn, Westminster, Md., 1987-92, Haines Realty, Westminster, 1992-93, Long & Foster Realtors, Westminster, 1993—. Bible tchr. Ch. of Christ, Westminster, 1986—; vol. March of Dimes, Westminster, 1991, 92, 95, Shephard Staff, Westminster, 1992-95. Mem. Carroll County Assn. Realtors, Hanover/Adams County Assn. Realtors. Home: 208 Garden Way Westminster MD 21157-4600

NEILL, RITA J., elementary school educator; b. Lincolnton, N.C., Oct. 20, 1950; d. George William and Mozelle (Boyles) Jarrett; m. Randy William Neill, Nov. 27, 1970; children: Jennifer Neill Huffman, Julie. AB, Lenoir Rhyne Coll., 1972; MA, Gardner Webb, 1987. Kindergarten tchr. Troutman Elem. Sch., Statesville (N.C.)/Iredell County Schs. Mem. ASCD, Assn. Edn. Young Children (treas. Iredell County 1994—), N.C. Assn. Edn. (sec. 1986-88). Home: 308 Wiggins Rd Mooresville NC 28115-9502

NEILSON, JANE SCOTT, mathematics educator; b. Oakland, Calif., July 29, 1919; d. George Robert and Ethel Genevive (Smith) Scott; m. James Drake Neilson II, Sept. 24, 1955 (dec.). Student in engring., U. Mich., 1937, student in lit. and art, 1938-40; BA in Elem Edn., Calif. State U., Northridge, 1960; postgrad. in secondary edn., UCLA, 1966-67. Process engr. Brigs Mfg. Co., Detroit, 1941-43; mathematician dept. purchasing Detroit GM, 1943-44; mathematician Chrysler Corp., Highland Pk., Mich., 1944-45; dir. recreation ARC, Europe and Korea, 1945-54; assoc. engr. Dr. Betando, Santa Monica, Calif., 1954-56; tchr. math. Las Virgines Unified Sch. Dist., Calabasas, Calif., 1961-79, subs. tchr., 1984-93. Docent Getty Mus., Malibu, Calif., 1982-94. Home: 29095 S Lakeshore Dr Agoura Hills CA 91301

NEIMAN, JERI ANNE, therapist; b. Berkeley, Calif., Jan. 20, 1951; d. Alfred D. Wallace and Marjorie E. (Nordheim) Stevens; m. Roy A. Neiman, June 12, 1969 (div. Aug. 1977); children: Lorien, Arwen. AA, Palomar Jr. Coll., 1977; BA in Psychology with distinction, Calif. State U., Long Beach, 1979, MA in Psychology with distinction, 1981; postgrad. Human Sexuality Program, UCLA, 1991-92. Lic. marriage, family, child therapist, Calif.; cert. community coll. instr., counselor; cert. sex therapist. Rsch. asst. Calif. State U., 1978-82; tchr. Artesia (Calif.)-Bellflower-Cerritos Unified Sch. Dist., 1982-83; dir. Am. Learning Corp., Huntington Beach, Calif., 1983-85; social worker Los Angeles County Children's Protective Svcs., Long Beach, 1986-88; sr. social worker Orange County Social Svc. Agy., Orange, Calif., 1988-90; therapist Cypress Mental Health, Cypress, Calif., 1988—, cons., 1990—; cons., 1990—; group chair, leader Adults Abused as Children, Los Altos Hosp., Long Beach, 1991—, Coll. Hosp., Cerritos, 1993—; speaker, presenter in field. Mem. Child's Sexual Abuse Network, Orange, 1988—; mem. legis. com. Child Abuse Coun. of Orange County, 1988. Women's League scholar, 1980-81. Mem. AAUW, Am. Assn. Marriage, Family Therapists, Calif. Assn. Marriage, Family Therapists, Am. Profl. Soc. for Abused Children, Calif. Profl. Assn. for Abused Children, Phi Kappa Phi, Psi Chi. Republican. Methodist. Office: Cypress Mental Health 5300 Orange Ave Ste 216 Cypress CA 90630

NEIMAN, NORMA, insurance agent; b. Louisville, Mar. 12, 1923; d. Sam and Sarah (Bordofsky) Berlin; m. Jacob B. Neiman, July 26, 1942 (dec. Mar. 24, 1993); children: Bennett A., Anna L. Bever, James C. Student, U. Louisville, 1941-43; student creative writing program, U. Cin., 1975. Asst., gen. support Diversified Coverage Brokerage Agy., 1956-87, gen. agt. various ins. cos., 1987—; gen. agt. Sovereign Life, First Colony Life Inst., Jackson Life Ins. Contbr. poetry to anthologies. Tutor Matthew Duvall Elem. Sch., Cin., 1990-92, Jane Hoop Elem. Sch., Cin., 1993; charter mem. Citizens Against Govt. Waste, 1990. Mem. NAFE, Pan Am. Soc. Cin. (co-founder), Internat. Platform Assn., Internat. Soc. Poets.

NEIMAN, TANYA MARIE, lawyer; b. Pitts., June 28, 1949; d. Max and Helen (Lamaga) N. AB, Mills Coll., 1970; JD, U. Calif. Hastings Coll. of Law, San Francisco, 1974. Bar: Calif. 1975. Law assoc. Boalt Hall U. Calif., Berkeley, 1974-76; pub. defender State of Calif., San Francisco, 1976-81; assoc. gen. counsel, dir. vol. legal services Bar Assn. San Francisco, 1982—; bd. dirs. Jack Berman Advocacy Ctr. Tanya Neiman Day proclaimed in her honor by Mayor of San Francisco, 1991. Mem. ABA (mem. ABA Commn. on Homelessness 1993—, speaker 1985—, Harrison Tweed award 1985), Calif. Bar Assn. (exec. com. 1984—, legal svcs. sect., chair steering com. State Bar Legal Corps), Golden Gate Bus. Assn. Found. (v.p. grant making 1985—), Nat. Conf. Women and Law (speaker 1975—), Nat. Lawyers Guild. Office: Bar Assn San Francisco 685 Market St San Francisco CA 94105-4200

NEIRA, THELMA, lawyer; b. Buenos Aires, Oct. 28, 1958; came to U.S., 1963, naturalized, 1969; d. Oscar Benito and Ageles Estella Neira. BA in Criminal Justice summa cum laude, L.I. U., 1980; JD, Union U., Albany, N.Y., 1983. Bar: N.Y. 1984. Law clk. Office N.Y. State Atty. Gen., Albany, 1982; assoc. Zinman and Chetkof P.C., Jericho, N.Y., 1983-84, Robert D. Frankfort, Deer Park, N.Y., 1984-92; with Town of Huntington(N.Y.)/Town Atty.'s Office, 1992—. Mem. N.Y. State Bar Assn., Suffolk County Bar Assn. Democrat. Roman Catholic. Home: 120 Eastwood Ave Deer Park NY 11729-2804 Office: Office Huntington Town Atty 100 Main St Huntington NY 11743

NEITZ, CORDELIA MILLER, librarian, retired; b. Millersburg, Pa., Mar. 27, 1911; d. John Benjamin and Jalania Alverta (Neagley) Miller; m. John Donald Neitz, Aug. 10, 1940 (dec. June 1968). BS in Libr. Sci., Syracuse U., 1931; postgrad., Susquehanna U., 1934-35; MS in Edn., Temple U., 1968. Organizing sch. libr. Pa. State Libr., Harrisburg, Pa., 1933-34; sr. file clk. Govs. Office, Harrisburg, 1935; cataloger, libr. U.S. Dept. Agrl., Washington, 1936; libr. asst. Pa. State Univ., State College, 1937; libr. cataloger U.S. Dept. of State, Washington, 1938-40; sr. cataloger Columbia Univ. Libr., N.Y.C., 1943-63; catalog libr. Dickinson Coll., Carlisle, Pa., 1963-71; acting libr. Dickinson Coll., Carlisle, 1971-72, catalog libr., from asst. prof. to assoc. prof., 1973-76; libr. Cumberland County Hist. Soc., Carlisle, 1977-83; ret., 1983. Editor: Index to Biographical Annals of Cumberland County, 1983. Vol. Cumberland County Hist. Soc., Carlisle, 1983—. Recipient grant R & D com. Dickinson Coll., Carlisle, 1974. Mem. ALA, AAUP, Pa. Libr. Assn., Cumberland County (Pa.) Hist. Soc., Dauphin County (Pa.) Hist. Soc., Cumberland/Perrry Assn. for Retarded Citizens, Met. Opera Guild. Home: 304 S Pitt St Carlisle PA 17013-3816

NEKRITZ, LEAH KALISH, dean, college administrator; b. N.Y.C., Apr. 6, 1932; d. Jacob Joseph and Anna (Feldman) Kalish; m. Richard Nekritz. BA, Bklyn. Coll., 1953; MLS, Cath. U. Am., 1963. Libr. Prince George's C.C., Largo, Md., 1961-67, dir. libr. svcs., 1967-71, dir. learning resources, 1971-77, assoc. dean for learning resources, 1977-90, dean of learning resources, 1991—; mem. adv. com. State Libr. Resource Ctr., Md., 1976; mem. Met. Washington Coun. of Govts. Libr. Coun., 1976-77, 79-81; mem. bd. advisors Libr. System Coop. in Mid Atlantic, Washington, 1985-88; exec. dir. Md. Congress Acad. Libr. Dirs., 1989-90. mem. adv. com. State Libr. Resource Ctr., Md., 1976; mem. libr. coun. Met. Washington Coun. Govts., 1976-77, 79-81; mem. bd. advisors Libr. Sys. Coop. in Mid Atlantic, Washington, 1985-88; exec. dir. Md. Congress Acad. Libr. Dirs., 1989-90; mem. acad. librs. adv. bd. U. Md. CLIS, 1994. Mem. AAUP, ALA (sec. cmty. and jr. coll. sect. 1974), Md. Libr. Assn., Assn. for Ednl. Comm. and Tech. (treas. 1974, chmn. post-secondary guide 1981). Home: 417 N Fairfax St Alexandria VA 22314-2321 Office: Prince Georges Coll 301 Largo Rd Upper Marlboro MD 20772-2199

NELIPOVICH, SANDRA GRASSI, artist; b. Oak Park, Ill., Nov. 22, 1939; d. Alessandro and Lena Mary (Ascareggi) Grassi; m. John Nelipovich Jr., Aug. 19, 1973. BFA in Art Edn., U. Ill., 1961; postgrad., Northwestern U., 1963, Gonzaga U., Florence, Italy, 1966, Art Inst. Chgo., 1968; diploma, Accademia Universale Alessandro Magno, Prato, Italy, 1983. Tchr. art Edgewood Jr. High Sch., Highland Park, Ill., 1961-62, Emerson Sch. Jr. High Sch., Oak Park, 1962-77; batik artist Calif., 1977—; illustrator Jolly Robin Publ. Co., Anaheim, Calif., 1988—; supr. student tchrs., Oak Park, 1970-75; adult edn. tchr. ESL, ceramics, Medinah, Ill., 1974; mem. curriculum action group on human dignity, EEO workshop demonstration, Oak Park, 1975-76; guest lectr. Muckenthaler Ctr., Fullerton, Calif., 1980, 92, Niguel Art Group, Dana Point, Calif., 1989, Carlsbad A.A., 1990, ARt League, Oceanside Art Group, 1992; 2d v.p. Anaheim Hills Women's Club, 1990-91, rec. sec. 1991-92; fabric designer for fashion designer Barbara Jax, 1987. One-woman show include Lawry's Calif. Ctr., L.A., 1981-83, Whittier (Calif.) Mus., 1985-86, Anaheim Cultural Ctr., 1986-88, Ill. Inst. Tech., Chgo., 1989, Muckenthaler Cultural Ctr., Fullerton, 1990; also gallery exhibits in Oak Brook, 1982, La Habra, Calif., 1983; represented in permanent collections collections McDonald's Corp., Oak Brook, Glenkirk Sch., Deerfield, Ill., Emerson Sch., Oak Park, galleries in Laguna Beach, Calif., Maui, Hawaii, Mich., N.J.; poster designer Saratoga Fine Arts; illustrator The Magic Vineyard, 1994. Active Assistance League, Anaheim, Calif., 1992—. Recipient numerous awards, purchase prizes, 1979—; featured in Calif. Art Rev., Artists of So. Calif., Vol. II, Nat. Artists' Network, 1992. Mem. AAUW (hospitality chmn. 1984-85), Assistance League Anaheim, Oak Park Art League, Orange Art Assn. (jury chairperson 1980), Anaheim Art Assn., Muckenthaler Ctr. Circle, Anaheim Hills Women's Club. Roman Catholic. Home and Office: 5922 E Calle Cedro Anaheim CA 92807-3207

NELLERMOE, LESLIE C., lawyer, partner; b. Oakland, Calif., Jan. 26, 1954; d. Carrol Wandell and Nora Ann (Conway) N.; m. Darrell Ray McKissic, Aug. 9, 1986; 1 child, Devin Anne. BS cum laude, Wash. State U., 1975; JD cum laude, Willamette U., 1978. Bar: Wash. 1978, U.S. Dist. Ct. (ea. dist.) Wash. 1979, U.S. Dist. Ct. (we. dist.) Wash. 1983. Staff atty. Wash. Ct. Appeals, Spokane, 1978-79; asst. atty. gen. Wash. Atty. Gen. Office, Spokane, 1979-83, Olympia, 1983-85; assoc. Syrdal, Danelo, Klein, Myre & Woods, Seattle, 1985-88; ptnr. Heller Ehrman White & McAuliffe, Seattle, 1989—. Bd. dirs. Campfire Boys & Girls, Seattle, 1991—. Mem. ABA, Wash. State Bar Assn., King County Bar Assn. Office: Heller Ehrman White & McAuliffe 6100 Columbia Ctr Seattle WA 98104

NELLIS, BARBARA BROOKS, trust company executive; b. Akron, Ohio, Mar. 16, 1935; d. Frank and Alice (Woodhall) Brooks; m. William J. Waltenbaugh, Oct. 31, 1953 (div. 1965); children: Bonnie, Becky, Brooks; m. Robert E. Nellis, June 25, 1971; children: Cheryl, Jack Lori, Kathryn, Robert. Student, Kent State U., 1964, Akron U., 1965, Purdue U., 1977, Malone Coll., 1978-88. Sec. Goodyear Tire and Rubber Co., Akron, 1952-62; exec. sec. Morgan Adhesives Co., Stow, Ohio, 1969-71; mgmt. cons. Brouse McDowell Hunsicker and Assocs. Law Firm, Akron, 1971-88; real estate agt. Kallstrom Realty, Akron; pres. TMI and D Co. Inc., Akron,

1978-88, T.M. Investment and DUP'T, Akron, 1978-88; real estate agt. Marting Realty, Akron, 1982, McInnis Realty, Akron, 1987; sales mgr. McInnis Coldwell Banker. Recipient Presdl. citation, 1988. Fellow Akron Area Com., Nat. Assn. Realtors, Ohio Assn. Realtors. Democrat. Home: 664 Pebble Beach Dr Akron OH 44333-2849 Office: TMI & D Co Inc 2331 E Market St Apt 519 Akron OH 44312-1478

NELMS, PATRICIA FLANAGAN, education supervisor; b. Tampa, Fla., Jan. 29, 1938; d. Herman Chester and Thelma Lucille (Goodbread) Flanagan; m. Warren B. Nelms, Sept. 6, 1958; children: David Warren, Sandra Patricia Nelms Moore. BA in Edn. with high honors, U. Fla., 1959; M in Reading, U. South Fla., 1973. Cert. elem. reading, supervision and adminstrn., Fla. Elem. tchr. Pinellas County Sch. System, St. Petersburg, Fla., 1969-71; specialist reading and lang. arts Pinellas County Sch. System, St. Petersburg, 1973-82, supr. elem. reading and lang. arts, 1983—. Recipient Cert. of Appreciation for Leadership in Reading, Pinellas Reading Coun., 1985; State grantee, 1972-73. Mem. Internat. Reading Assn., Phi Kappa Phi, Phi Delta Kappa, Delta Kappa Gamma (treas. 1989-91), Kappa Delta Pi. Democrat. Methodist. Home: 16209 McGlamery Rd Odessa FL 33556 Office: Pinellas County Schs Adminstrn Bldg 301 4th St SW Largo FL 34649-2942

NELSEN, LINDA SUE, food scientist; b. Racine, Wis., Mar. 22, 1967; m. Steven J. Nelsen, Sept. 5, 1992. BS in Food Sci., U. Wis., 1990. Rsch. technologist Universal Foods Corp., Milw., 1990-93, assoc. scientist, 1993—. Mem. Inst. Food Technology. Office: Universal Foods Corp 6143 N 60th St Milwaukee WI 53218-1606

NELSON, ALICE ELIZABETH HILL, museum docent; b. Oakland, Calif., Jan. 19, 1921; d. George Clayton Hill and Netha Alice (Hall) Hill-Kinkead; m. James Walter Nelson, Jr., June 13, 1942; children: James W. III, Georgeanne Cusic, Susan Brewster, Karen McCormick, Marjorie Moon. BA, U. Calif., Berkeley, 1942; BFA, Cardinal Stritch Coll., 1968. Pres. Literary League, Meadville, Pa., 1972-74; docent Milw. Art Mus., 1978—, lectr. Art History, 1984—; docent Villa Terrace 18th C Decorative Arts Museum, Milw., 1990—; artist in residence Herb Soc. Am., Milw., 1975-85. One woman show, paintings, sculptures Studio San Damiano, Milw., 1968; two women show, paintings, sculptures Meadville, Pa., 1973. Bd. dirs. Milw. Symphony Women's League, 1960-69. Named Docent of Year Milw. Art Mus., 1984. Mem. League of Milw. Artists, AAUW (bd. dirs., sec. Wis. chpt. 1963-66), Women's Club of Wis. (Art Com. 1987-89, docent 1991—), Alpha Omicron Pi, Prytanean (pres. 1941-42). Republican. Episcopalian. Home: 3366 N Lake Dr Milwaukee WI 53211-2909 Studio: N67 W32426 Wildwood Pt Rd Hartland WI 53029

NELSON, ANNE ELIZABETH, financial consultant; b. N.Y.C., Feb. 14, 1949; d. John Joseph and Elizabeth Norma (Kemnitzer) O'Connor; divorced. BA with honors, Johnson State Coll., 1986; MPA, Harvard U., 1988. Owner Etna (N.H.) Store, 1973-75; with Hopkins Ctr. for Performing Arts Dartmouth Coll., Hanover, N.H., 1980-83, asst. dir. Nelson A. Rockefeller Ctr., 1983-87; cons. group assoc. Smith Barney, N.Y.C., 1988—, 1st v.p., 1994—. Author: Democratic Presidential Debate, 1994. Bd. dirs., treas. Carondelet Found., 1990—; bd. dirs. Tucson Symphony Orch., 1990—; mem. Jr. League of Tucson, 1990—; bd. dirs., dean Fine Arts U. Ariz., 1992—, bd. dirs. major gifts com., 1992—. Recipient Cmty. Svc. award Hispanic Profl. Action Com., 1993; named Vol. Fundraiser of Yr. Nat. Assn. Fundraising Execs., 1993. Mem. Assn. Profl. Investment Consultants, Inst. for Investment Mgmt. Consultants, Harvard Club of Boston. Office: Smith Barney Ste 5550 5285 E Williams Cir Tucson AZ 85711-7410

NELSON, BARBARA ANNE, lawyer; b. Mineola, N.Y., Jan. 16, 1951; d. Richard William and Dorothee Helen (Thorne) N. BA, Inter Am. U. P.R., 1972; JD, New Eng. Sch. Law, 1975. Legal editor Prentice Hall Pub. Co., Englewood Cliffs, N.J., 1976-77; assoc. Antonio C. Martinez Law Firm, N.Y.C., 1977-79, Pollack & Kramer, N.Y.C., 1979-83; pvt. practice N.Y.C., 1983-94. Author, speaker tng. film. Mem. ACLU, Am. Immigration Lawyers Assn., Legal Aid Soc. N.Y., Amnesty Internat., Asia Soc. Home: 324 W 14th St Apt 5A New York NY 10014-5003 Office: 132 Nassau St Ste 219 New York NY 10038-2400

NELSON, BARBARA JONES, food service professional; b. Augusta, Ga., Feb. 3, 1954; d. Robert F. and Margaret H. (Hill) Jones; divorced; children: Candice, Russell. Diploma, Dallas Fashion Mdse. Coll. Sec., treas. Bo-Mar, Inc., Gallup, N.Mex., 1975-93, pres., 1993—. Mem. McKinley County Rep. Party, Gallup, 1991—. Named Employer of Yr. by Connections/Nat. Assn. Retarded Citizens, Durango, Colo., 1991. Mem. NAFE, BPW, Soroptimist, Am. Mgmt. Assn., Nat. Restaurant Assn., Nat. Fedn. Ind. Bus., Gallup C. of C. (bd. dir.). Episcopalian. Office: Bo-Mar Inc 914 E 66 Ave Gallup NM 87301

NELSON, BARBARA KAY, insurance agent, financial services consultant; b. Dayton, Ohio, May 20, 1947; d. Orville James and Catherine Ann (Pentenburg) Weber; m. Theodore Joseph Nelson II, Nov. 8, 1969 (div. Nov. 1990); children: Theodore Joseph III, Jason Michael. BA, U. Dayton, 1969; MA, Webster U., 1985. CLU. TV co-host Sta. WHIO-TV, Dayton, 1969; dept. mgr. Elder-Beerman, Dayton, 1969-70; customer service rep. Ohio Bell Telephone, Dayton, 1970; adminstrv. coordinator AmeriSource, San Antonio, 1984-86; agt. N.Y. Life Ins., 1986-89; sales mgr. John Hancock Fin. Svcs., 1989-93; dir. tng. San Antonio regional mktg. office Lincoln Nat., 1993—. chair bd. San Antonio Women's C. of C. Tex., 1988-91; sec. bd. dirs. Network Power Tex., 1987-90. Mem. exec. bd. Oak Grove Elementary Sch. PTA, San Antonio, 1981-83; mem. San Antonio Assn. Life Underwriters, San Antonio C. of C., local govt. com., 1991—; mem. religious edn. com. St. Mark's Ch., San Antonio, 1983-84; mem. North San Antonio Chamber/Pub. Art, 1984-85. Mem. NAFE, Women Life Underwriters Confederation (pres. 1992—). Club: FLW Officers Wives (pres. 1980-81). Avocations: art; jogging; bicycling; racquetball; reading.

NELSON, CHARLOTTE BOWERS, public administrator; b. Bristol, Va., June 28, 1931; d. Thaddeus Ray and Ruth Nelson (Moore) Bowers; m. Gustav Carl Nelson, June 1, 1957; children: Ruth Elizabeth, David Carl, Thomas Gustav. BA, Duke U., 1954; MA, Columbia U., 1961; MPA, Drake U., 1983. Instr. Beaver Coll., 1957-58, Drake U., Des Moines, 1975-82; office mgr. LWV of Iowa, Des Moines, 1975-82; exec. asst. Iowa Dept. Human Svcs., Des Moines, 1983-85; exec. dir. Iowa Commn. on Status of Women, Des Moines, 1985—. Bd. dirs., pres. LWV, Beloit, Wis., 1960-74; bd. dirs. LWV, Des Moines, 1974-82, Westminster House, Des Moines, 1988—. Named Visionary Woman, Young Women's Resource Ctr., 1994. Mem. Am. Soc. Pub. Adminstrn. (pres. exec. coun. 1984-86, past pres., Mem. of Yr. 1993). Home: 1141 Cummins Cir Des Moines IA 50311 Office: Human Rights Dept Lucas State Office Bldg 321 E 12th St Des Moines IA 50319

NELSON, CLARA SINGLETON, aerospace company executive; b. Union Ridge, Tenn., Apr. 10, 1935; d. Ernest Caldwell and Willie Emma (Hord) Singleton; m. Joe Edward Nelson, July 26, 1953; children: Drexel Edward, Dorissia Lynett. Student Tenn. State U., 1961-62, Middle Tenn. State U., 1984; AS, Motlow Coll., 1978; BS in Edn. with highest honors U. Tenn., Knoxville, 1991. Cert. personnel specialist. Sec., adminstrv. asst. Bedford County Sch., Shelbyville, Tenn., 1957-64; sec., personnel asst. Aro, Inc., Arnold Air Force Sta., Tenn., 1964-71; mem. pub. relations staff, job interviewer Employment Security, Shelbyville, 1971-81; mgr. employment EEO Calspan Corp., Arnold Air Force Sta., 1981-94; with Micro Craft Tech, 1994—; mem. adv. bd. Tenn. Area Vocat. Sch., Shelbyville, 1979—, Bedford Moore Vocat. Ctr., Shelbyville, 1979—; cons., dir. Career Devel. Workshops, Shelbyville. Chmn. adv. commn. Equal Employment Opportunity, 1983—, chmn. employer com. Tullahoma Job Service, Tenn., 1985—; mem. Tenn. Gov.'s Better Schs. Com., 1985—; mem. Patrons Council Argie Cooper Library, Shelbyville; Bus. Adv. Group Motlow State Coll., Tullahoma; trustee Motlow Coll. Found.; mem. Shelbyville Regional Planning Commn. Recipient cert. of appreciation ARC, 1985. Mem. Am. Mgmt. Assn., Highland Rim Resource Mgmt. Assn. (treas. 1983-84, 87, sec. 1988, 94, chair program com. 1989, 1994—), Nat. Assn. Female Execs. (network dir. 1985), Nat. Mgmt. Assn., Nat. Assn. Bus. and Profl. Women's Clubs, Inc. (chair membership 1991—), Am. Assn. Affirmative Action, Tenn. State U. Cluster (chmn. com. 1984—), Tenn. Coll. Placement Assn. Club: Better Homes and Gardens Shelbyville. Methodist. Avocations: reading, gardening. Home: 118 Scotland Hts Shelbyville TN 37160-2912 Office: Micro Craft Tech 690 2d St Arnold AFB TN 37389-4300

NELSON, CONNIE RAE, pharmacy director, educator; b. Lewistown, Mont., Aug. 19, 1950; d. Ward Wallace and Violet May (Charette) Dickson; m. Alan C. Nelson, July 23, 1977; children: Russell Robert, Nicole Elaine. Pharmacy asst. level A degree, Clover Park Vocat. Tech. Inst., Tacoma, 1979; student in pharmacology Bates Vocat. Tech. Inst., Tacoma, 1982. Lic. pharmacy asst. level A. Druggist clk. Thrifty Drugs, Tacoma, 1972-79; intern in hematology, oncology, pediatrics Madigan Army Med. Ctr., Tacoma, 1979-80; pharmacy asst. A, St. Joseph Hosp., Tacoma, 1979-84; pharmacy instr. Clover Park Vocat. Tech. Inst., Tacoma, 1984-93; pharmacy dept. dir. Eton Tech. Inst., Federal Way, Wash., 1993—; ednl. task force pharmacy bd. Wash. State, 1993—, co- chmn. Wash. State Ednl. Task Force, 1995; pharmacy curriculum cons., 1993—. Archtl. and land development West Tapps Maintenance Co., Sumner, Wash., 1979-86, legal and pub. affairs mem., 1984-86, pres., 1985-90. Mem. Wash. State Soc. Pharmacy Assts., Pharmpac (legis. rep. for assts. 1986), Wash. State Soc. Hosp. Pharmacists (pres. Pharmacy Asst. chpt. 1984—), Wash. State Soc. Pharmacy Assts. (founder, pres. 1985—, legal and pub. affairs chmn. 1987—, legis. chmn. 1987—, exec. dir. 1991—). Avocations: lecturing, camping, horticulture. Home: 18710 58th St E Sumner WA 98390-6808 Office: 31919 6th Ave S Auburn WA 98003

NELSON, CYNTHIA KAYE, training professional; b. Kearney, Nebr., May 8, 1949; d. LeRoy J. and W. Eileen (Schmidt) Wacker; m. James C. Nelson (div. 1987); children: Alexis Ann, Whitney Eileen. BA, U. No. Iowa, 1971; postgrad., No. Ill. U., 1973. Cert. tchr., Ill., Mo. Tchr. Dixon (Ill.) Pub. Schs., 1972-74, Maplewood (Mo.)-Richmond Heights Sch. Dist., 1974-75; counselor Mo. Bus. Men's Clearing House, St. Louis, 1975-76; dir. edn. Deltex Co., Naperville, Ill., 1982-84; trainer Electronic Data Systems Co., LaGrange, Ill., 1985-86; learning technologist Bellcore Tng. and Edn. Ctr., Lisle, Ill., 1988-90; tng. instr. Fujitsu Network Switching, Raleigh, N.C., 1990—. Mem. ASTD, AAUW, Nat. Soc. Performance and Instrn., Alpha Chi Omega, Beta Sigma Phi. Republican. Lutheran. Office: Fujitsu Network Switching 4403 Bland Rd Raleigh NC 27609-6288

NELSON, DEBRA JEAN, journalist, public relations executive, consultant; b. Birmingham, Ala., Nov. 12, 1957; d. James Eric Nelson. BA, U. Ala., Tuscaloosa, 1980. Dir. pub. affairs Sta. WSGN Radio, Birmingham, 1980-84, news anchor, reporter, 1982-84; dir. community affairs Sta. WBRC-TV, Birmingham, 1984-88, producer, anchor, 1986-88; instr. spl. studies U. Ala., Birmingham, 1988—; dir. media rels. U. Ala. System, Tuscaloosa, 1991-94; adminstr. external affairs Mercedes-Benz U.S. Internat., Inc., Tuscaloosa, 1994—. Pub. affairs prodr./host Sta. WUAL-FM/WQPR, Tuscaloosa, 1991—. Pres.- elect Found. Women's Health in Ala., Inc., 1993—; mem. U.S. libr. literacy rev. panel Dept. Edn., Washington, 1987-92; mem. Leadership Birmingham, 1991-92; bd. dirs., mem. exec. com. Ala. affiliate Am. Heart Assn., 1986-91; mem. U.S. Mil. Rev. Panel for 6th Congl. Dist., 1987; mem. gen. campaign com. Ala. campaign United Negro Coll. Fund., 1992; pres.-elect. Found. for Women's Health in Ala., 1993—. Recipient award of distinction Internat. Assn. Bus. Communicators, Birmingham, 1985, Disting. Leadership award United Negro Coll. Fund., Birmingham, 1985, 87, 88, Outstanding Achievement award Delta Sigma Theta, 1986, Outstanding Vol. Svc. award ARC, Birmingham, 1987, Woman of Distinction award Iota Phi Lambda, Birmingham, 1987. Mem. Assn. Black Women in Higher Edn. (bd. dirs. 1993—, chair com. on pub. rels.), Am.-Japan Soc., Coun. for Advancement and Support of Edn. Home: 2654 Briarberry Dr Birmingham AL 35226-3815 Office: Mercedes-Benz US Int Inc Ste G3E 1657 N McFarland Blvd Tuscaloosa AL 35406

NELSON, DOREEN KAE, reserve military officer, human resources specialist; b. Duluth, Minn., Oct. 18, 1957; d. Norman G. Nelson and Carola Gerene (Sunneli) Cooper. B Applied Scis., U. Minn., 1983; MS in Human Resources Mgmt. Devel., Chapman U., 1988; MAEd in Mental Health Counseling, Western Ky. U., 1995. Commd. 2nd lt. U.S. Army, 1983, advanced through grades to capt., 1987; pers. officer 62nd Med. Group U.S. Army, Ft. Lewis, Wash., 1987-88; med. pers. officer Acad. Health Scis. U.S. Army, Ft. Sam Houston, Tex., 1989, chief adminstrv. svcs. div. Med. Dept. Ctr. and Sch., 1989-92; med. advisor Readiness Group Knox, Ft. Knox, Ky., 1992-94; counselor intern Ireland Army Hosp., Ft. Knox, 1995. Lutheran. Home: 1130 N Logsdon Pkwy Radcliff KY 40160

NELSON, DOROTHY PATRICIA, health policy analyst, educator; b. Herrin, Ill., July 4, 1921; d. Hugh and Catherine (Disney) Mercer; m. John Robert Nelson, Aug. 18, 1945; children: Eric Mercer, William John. BS, So. Ill. U., 1942; MPH, Yale U., 1946; MBA, Boston U., 1977, PhD, 1984. Dir. edn. Children's Hosp., Boston, 1971-74; asst. prof., adminstr. sch. medicine Boston U., 1974-76; dir. planning Carney Hosp., Boston, 1976-83; mgr. planning Tex. Med. Ctr., Houston, 1985-86; spl. asst. to pres. U. Tex. Health Scis. Ctr., Houston, 1986-88; assoc. prof. health care Tex. Women's U., Houston, 1985-87; pres., exec. dir. Health Access Tex. Inc., Houston, 1988—; adj. prof. health mgmt. U. St. Thomas, Houston, 1988—; nat. bd. dirs. Health Planning Forum, Washington. Founder, pres. Neighbors of Hermann Park, Houston, 1991-93; bd. dirs. The Planning Forum, 1988-94. Recipient Health Security award Sen. Edward Kennedy, 1968. Mem. APHA, FACHE, Yale Club Houston (bd. dirs. 1991—), Rotary Club Houston. Democrat. Methodist. Office: Health Access Tex 1111 Hermann Dr Ste 19A Houston TX 77004-6930

NELSON, DOROTHY WRIGHT (MRS. JAMES F. NELSON), federal judge; b. San Pedro, Calif., Sept. 30, 1928; d. Harry Earl and Lorna Amy Wright; m. James Frank Nelson, Dec. 27, 1950; children: Franklin Wright, Lorna Jean. B.A., UCLA, 1950, J.D., 1953; LL.M., U. So. Calif., 1956; JD honoris causa, Georgetown U., 1993, U. So. Calif., 1993, U. Santa Clara, 1993, Western State U., 1993; hon. degree, Whittier U. Bar: Calif. 1954. Research assoc. fellow U. So. Calif., 1953-56; instr., 1957, asst. prof., 1958-61, assoc. prof., 1961-67, prof., 1967, assoc. dean., 1965-67, dean., 1967-80; judge U.S. Ct. Appeals (9th cir.), 1980—; cons. Project STAR, Law Enforcement Assistance Adminstrn.; mem. select com. on internal procedures of Calif. Supreme Ct., 1987—; co-chair Sino-Am. Seminar on Mediation and Arbitration, Beijing, 1992; dir. Dialogue on Transition to a Global Soc., Weinacht, Switzerland, 1992. Author: Judicial Adminstration and The Administration of Justice, 1973; Contbr. articles to profl. jours. Co-chmn. Confronting Myths in Edn. for Pres. Nixon's White House Conf. on Children, Pres. Carter's Commn. for Pension Policy, 1974-80, Pres. Reagon's Madison Trust; bd. visitors U.S. Air Force Acad., 1978; bd. dirs. Council on Legal Edn. for Profl. Responsibility, 1971-80, Constnl. Right Found., Am. Nat. Inst. for Social Advancement; adv. bd. Nat. Center for State Cts., 1971-73; chmn. bd. Western Justice Ctr., 1986—; mem. adv. com. Nat. Jud. Edn. Program to promote equality for woman and men in cts. Named Law Alumnus of Yr. UCLA, 1967; recipient Profl. Achievement award, 1969; named Times Woman of Yr., 1968; recipient U. Judaism Humanitarian award, 1973; AWARE Internat. award, 1970; Ernestine Stalhut Outstanding Woman Lawyer award, 1972; Coro award for edn., 1978, Pax Orbis ex Jure medallion World Peace thru Law Ctr., 1975, Hollzer Human Rights award, 1988, Gold medal UCLA, 1993; Lustman fellow Yale U. 1977. Fellow Am. Bar Found., Davenport Coll., Yale U.; mem. Bar Calif. (bd. dirs. continuing edn. bar commn. 1967-74), Am. Judicature Soc. (dir., award 1985), Assn. Am. Law Schs. (chmn. com. edn. in jud. adminstrn.), Am. Bar Assn. (sect. on jud. adminstrn., chmn. com. on edn. in jud. adminstrn. 1973-89), Phi Beta Kappa, Order of Coif (nat. v.p. 1974-76), Jud. Conf. U.S. (com. to consider standards for admission to practice in fed. cts. 1976-79). Office: US Ct Appeals Cir PO Box 91510 125 S Grand Ave Pasadena CA 91105-1652

NELSON, ELAINE EDWARDS, lawyer; b. Waco, Tex., Sept. 16, 1947; d. Bedford Duncan and Joyce (Harlan) Edwards; m. David A. Nelson, Apr. 12, 1969; children: Carol Christine, Harlan Claire. BA, Baylor U., 1969, JD, 1978. Gen. counsel Austin Industries, Inc., Dallas, 1978—. Office: Austin Industries Inc 3535 Travis St Ste 300 Dallas TX 75204

NELSON, ETHELYN BARNETT, civic worker; b. Bessemer, Ala., Jan. 16, 1925; d. Laurence McBride and Ethel Victoria Fortesque (King) Barnett; student Huntingdon Coll., 1943, U. Ala., 1948, George Washington U., 1948-49, 74; m. Stuart David Nelson, May 6, 1949; children—Terryl Lynn, Cynthia Dianne, Jacqueline Margo. Sec., U.S. Air Force, Montgomery, Ala. and Panama Canal Zone, 1944-49; sec. to dep. undersec. U.S. Dept. State, Washington, 1951-53, U.S. Ho. of Reps. and U.S. Senate, 1959-60; adminstrv. asst. editorial div. Nat. Geog. Soc., Washington, 1962-65; rec. sec. Dist. IV, Nat. Capital Area Fedn. Garden Clubs, Inc., Washington, 1981-83. Mem. Women's Com. Nat. Symphony Orch., The English-Speaking Union, Vols. for Washington Ballet, Washington Opera Guild. Mem. Salvation Army Aux., Suburban Hosp. Assn. Republican. Clubs: Landon Woods Garden (pres. 1978-80), Congressional Country; Capital Speakers (Washington). Patentee. Home: 6410 Maiden Ln Bethesda MD 20817-5612

NELSON, FREDA NELL HEIN, librarian; b. Trenton, Mo., Dec. 16, 1929; d. Fred Albert and Mable Carman (Doan) Hein; m. Robert John Nelson, Nov. 1, 1957 (div. Apr. 1984); children: Thor, Hope. Nursing diploma, Trinity Luth. Hosp., Kansas City, Mo., 1950; B. Philosophy, Northwestern U., 1961; MS in Info. and Libr. Sci., U. Ill., 1986. RN. Operating rm. nurse Trinity Luth. Hosp., Kansas City, Mo., 1950-52, Johns Hopkins Hosp., Balt., 1952, Wesley Meml. Hosp., Chgo., 1952-58, Tacoma Gen. Hosp., 1958-59, Chgo. Wesley Hosp., 1959-61; libr. asst. Maple Woods Campus Met. Community Colls., Kansas City, 1987-89, libr., libr. mgr. Blue Springs Campus, 1989—; co-founder Coll. for Kids, Knox Coll., Galesburg, Ill., 1982. Nurses scholar Edgar Bergen Found., 1947; recipient Award of Merit, Chgo. Bd. Health, 1952. Home: 7000 N Elm St Plsnt Vlly MO 64068-9571 Office: Blue Springs Campus Libr 1501 W Jefferson St Blue Springs MO 64015-7242

NELSON, GWENDOLYN DIANE, choral, vocal educator; b. Little Rock, Nov. 13, 1950; d. Milton Donaghey and Dora Elizabeth (Gillespie) N. BBA, U. Ark., 1972; MBA, Calif. State U., Dominguez Hills, 1979, postgrad. in voice/piano, 1980-81; postgrad. in acctg., UCLA, 1973-84. Adminstrv. asst. Ark. Plan, Inc., Little Rock, 1969-73; acct. Hughes Aircraft Co., L.A., 1973-80, ops. auditor, 1986-90, property mgmt. specialist, 1990-93; dir. music dept. Baldwin Hills Baptist Ch., L.A., 1979—; choral, vocal instr. Crossroads Acad. Arts and Sci.; auditor Baldwin Hills Baptist Ch., 1983—; cons. Air Force Procurement, Contractor Ops. Revs., L.A., 1984-88. Author music: (Christian mus. drama) Wings Like Eagles, 1988, mus. dir., L.A., 1988-89; playwright: Dissin' Your Body, 1993. Founder, exec. dir. Christian Action Now Is Good Econs., a visual and performing arts orgn. for at-risk youth, 1993; founder, pres. By Faith Cons. and Publishing, 1993; exec. dir. Change, performing arts orgn. for at-risk youth. Mem. Heritage Music Found., Nat. Property Mgmt. Assn. (cert. profl. property specialist, invited speaker seminars and workshops), Mu Phi Epsilon, Alpha Kappa Alpha (grad. advisor 1978-79, del. 1980-81). Home: 227 E Plymouth St Inglewood CA 90302-2315

NELSON, HEDWIG POTOK, financial executive; b. Detroit, Oct. 6, 1954; m. Richard Alan Nelson. BA with honors, U. Mich., 1976; MBA, Am. U., 1980. Fin. asst. antitrust div. U.S. Dept. Justice, Washington, 1979-80; fin. analyst corp. treasury Martin Marietta Corp., Bethesda, Md., 1980-81, fin. adminstr. aggregates div., 1981-83, sr. fin. adminstr. bus. devel. data systems div., 1983, mgr. fin. planning and analysis, 1983-85; mgr. mergers and acquistions M/A-COM Devel. Corp., Rockville, Md., 1985-88; sr. analyst group fin. Marriott Corp., Bethesda, 1988-89, mgr. bus. planning, hotel div., 1989-90; mgr. planning and analysis, geon vinyl div. BF Goodrich, Cleve., 1990-91, bus. contr. molding, geon vinyl div., 1991-93; bus. mgr. extrusions The GEON Co., Cleve., 1993—. Mem. NAFE (treas. Montgomery County chpt. 1987-88). Home: 325 Middlebush Cir Akron OH 44321-2778 Office: The GEON Co 6100 Oak Tree Blvd Cleveland OH 44131-2508

NELSON, HELAINE QUEEN, lawyer; b. Hamtramck, Mich., Mar. 15, 1945; d. Willard Myron and Helen Victoria (Nebraska) Bowers; m. William Michael Nelson, Apr. 19, 1970; 1 child, Lindsey Paige. BS, Western Mich. U., 1969, MS, 1971; JD, U. Detroit, 1977. Bar: Ohio 1977, U.S. Dist. Ct. (no. and so. dists.) Ohio 1978, Ill. 1985. Corp. counsel Beverage Mgmt., Inc., Columbus, Ohio, 1977-79, assoc. gen. counsel, 1979-80, gen. counsel, 1980-84; sr. atty. Abbott Labs., Abbott Park, Ill., 1984-87; div. counsel Abbott Labs., Columbus, 1987—. Mem. Ohio Bar Assn., Am. Corp. Counsel Assn. Unitarian. Office: Ross Products Divsn 625 Cleveland Ave Columbus OH 43215-1754

NELSON, JANE D., opera company executive. Artistic dir. Dayton Opera Assn., Dayton, Ohio. Office: Dayton Opera Assn Memorial Hall 125 E First St Dayton OH 45402*

NELSON, JENNIFER MAY, physical therapist; b. Gilroy, Calif., Nov. 11, 1955; d. Lesley Leo and Janice May (Bongard) H.; m. John Richard Nelson, Aug. 13, 1994. BA cum laude, Westminister Coll., Salt Lake City, 1977; grad., U. Calif., San Francisco, 1981. Cert. phys. therapist, Calif. Phys. therapist Mt. Zion Hosp., San Francisco, 1981-82, Calif. Pacific Med. Ctr., San Francisco, 1982-85, St. Mary's Spine Ctr., San Francisco, 1985-86, Vis. Nurses and Hospice, San Francisco, 1986-90, North Bay Phys. Therapy, Novato, Calif., 1990-92, S. Wagner & Assocs., Greenbrae, Calif., 1992-94; Pace Therapy, Inc., Cypress, Calif., 1994—. Mem., tchr., minister Ch. of Divine Man, 1988—; mem., counselor, tchr. Ch. of Aesclepion Healing, 1991. Home: 24 Skylark Dr Apt 10 Larkspur CA 94939-1261 Office: Pace Therapy Inc 11215 Kush Ave Ste A Cypress CA 90630

NELSON, KAREN, legislative staff director. Staff mem. U.S. Commn. on Civil Rights, Fed. Programs Divsn., 1965-66, Office of Mgmt. and Budget, 1966-70; chief of office of program planning and evaluation Dept. Health, Edn. and Welfare, 1970-74; profl. staff mem. Com. Interstate and Fgn. Commerce, 1974-75; staff dir. Subcom. Health & the Environment, House Com. Energy & Commerce, Washington, 1980—. Office: Subcom on Health & Environment 2424 Rayburn House Office Bldg Washington DC 20515*

NELSON, KARIN BECKER, child neurologist; b. Chgo., Aug. 14, 1933; d. George and Sylvia (Demansly) Becker; m. Phillip G. Nelson, Mar. 10, 1955; children: Sarah Nelson Hammack, Rebecca Nelson Miller, Jenny Nelson Walker, Peter. MD, U. Chgo., 1957; Student, U. Minn., 1950-53. Cert. child neurology Am. Bd. Psychiatry and Neurology. Intern rotating Phila. Gen. Hosp., 1957-58; asst. resident neurology U. Md. Sch. Medicine, Balt., 1958-59; resident neurology George Washington U. Sch. Medicine, Washington, 1959-62; cons. in med. neurology St. Elizabeth's Hosp., Washington, 1960-62; registrar to outpatients Nat. Hosp., Queen Sq., London, 1963; med. officer perinatal rsch. br. Nat. Inst. of Neurol. Disorders and Blindness, NIH, 1964-67; asst. prof. neurology George Washington U., Washington, 1970-72; assoc. neurologist Children's Hosp. of D.C., Washington, 1967-71; instr. neurology George Washington U., Washington, 1967-70; attending neurologist Children's Hosp., Washington, 1971-73, 78—; assoc. clin. prof. neurology George Washington U., Washington, 1972—; cons. Nat. Inst. Child Health and Human Devel., 1975-80, orphan products devel. initial rev. group FDA, 1983-86, Boston Collaborative Drug Surveillance Group, 1985-86, vaccine Am. Acad. Pediatrics, 1985, 87, Dept. Health, State of Calif. Birth Monitoring Group, 1986—, Ctr. for Disease Control Birth Defects Monitoring Com., 1987; med. officer Nat. Inst. Neurol. Disorders and Blindness, NIH, Bethesda, 1972—; med. staff Children Hosp., Washington, 1962—; mem. adv. bd. Internat. Sch. Neuroscis., Venice, Italy, Little Found./World Fedn. Neurology, 1992—, rev. bd. Nat. Inst. Aging; mem. epidemiology steering com. NIH, 1993—. Editor: Workshop on the Neurobiological Basis of Autism, 1979, (with J.H. Ellenberg) Febrile Seizures, 1981; editorial bd. Pediatric Neurology, 1984-90, Brain and Development, 1984—, Neurology, 1985-88, Paediatric and Perinatal Epidemiology, 1987—, Developmental Medicine and Child Neurology, 1988; field editor Epilepsy Advances; contbr. papers to profl. jours. Recipient Spl. Recognition award USPHS, 1977, Spl. Achievement award 1981, United Cerebral Palsy Weinstein-Goldenson Rsch. award 1990, Dirs. award NIH, 1992. Fellow Am. Acad. Neurology (exec. bd. 1989-91, councillor); mem. Soc. Perinatal Obstetricians (hon.), Child Neurology Soc. (program chmn. 1973, liaison nat. Inst. of Neurol. and Communicative Disorders and Blindness 1975-80, ethics com. 1985-87, by-laws com. 1990—, ad hoc com. for concensus statement of DPT immunications and the cen. nervous system 1990, long range planning com. 1991—, Hower award 1991), Am. Acad. for Cerebral Palsy and Devel. Medicine (program chmn. 1985), Am. Epilepsy Soc. (Disting. Basic Neuroscientist Epilepsy Rsch. award 1992), Am. Neurol. Assn. (membership com. 1994—), Internat. Child Neurology Assn. (sci. selection com. 1993-94), Can. Assn. Child Neurology (hon.), Soc. Perinatal

Obstetricians (hon.), Baltic Child Neurology Soc., Dana Alliance Brain Initiatives, Alpha Omega Alpha. Democrat. Jewish. Office: NIH 7550 Wisconsin Ave Rm 700 Bethesda MD 20814-3559

NELSON, KATHERINE J., psychologist, educator; b. Mpls., Apr. 18, 1930; d. Sherman E. and Evelyn (Hedin) Johnson; m. Richard R. Nelson, Sept. 6, 1952; children—Margo E., Laura C. B.A., Oberlin Coll., 1952; M.A., UCLA, 1964, Ph.D., 1968. Postdoctoral fellow Yale U., New Haven, 1968-70, research assoc., 1970-74, asst. prof. psychology, 1974-75, assoc. prof., 1975-78; prof. psychology CUNY, N.Y.C., 1978-86; disting. prof. psychology Grad. Ctr. CUNY, 1986—. Author: Making Sense: The Acquisition of Shared Meaning, 1985; (with Lucia A. French) Children's Understanding of Relative Terms, 1985, Event Knowledge: Structure and Function in Development, 1986, Narrative From the Crib, 1989. Fellow Am. Psychol. Assn., Am. Psychol. Soc., N.Y. Acad. Scis.; mem. Soc. Research in Child Devel. (gov. council 1983-89). Office: CUNY Grad Ctr Devel Psychology 33 W 42nd St New York NY 10036-8003

NELSON, KATHERINE MACTAGGART, educator; b. Mattoon, Ill., Aug. 27, 1953; d. Leonard John and Wandalee Mae (Clodfelder) Stabler; m. John Robert Nelson; children: Scott MacTaggart, Robert John, Matthew David. BS in Edn., Eastern Ill. U., 1973; postgrad., Carroll Coll., 1989—. Tchr. Owen Valley Schs., Spencer, Ind., 1974-76; acad. support coordinator Whitefish Bay Schs., Milw., 1976-80; dir. research Sullivan, Murphy Assoc., Milw., 1980-81; tng. specialist Northwestern Ins., Milw., 1981-84; tng. coordinator Cath. Knights Ins. Soc., Milw., 1984-87; tchr. Pewaukee (Wis.) High Sch., 1988—. Pres. Cushing Elem. Sch. Parent Tchrs. Orgn., 1994—; mem. Milw. Zool. Soc., Womens Fellowship Bd., Cushing PTO Bd.; founder Mgmt. Resources Exec. Sec. Roundtable, Milw., 1986; vol. com. mem. Wis. Make-A-Wish Found.; mem. Congl. Ch., Christian edn. com. 1990—, Bible sch. dir., 1990, 91; vol. Cross for State Supt. campaign. Recipient Leadership award YMCA, 1986. Mem. NEA, ASTD (bd. dirs., chmn. pub. rels. 1984, vol. trainer 1982—), Internat. Assn. Personnel Women (chmn. pub. rels. 1984-85, chmn. membership and registrar, nominating com., by-laws com., vol. trainer, 1981—), Pewaukee Edn. Assn. (exec. com. 1990-93), Law Wives Assn. (v.p. membership and soc. coms., PYC sidestays fin. com.), Milw. Athletic Club, Pewaukee Yacht Club, Wis. Club, P.E.O. Sisterhood (guard, chaplain). Republican. Home: N23w28796 Louis Ave Pewaukee WI 53072-5029 Office: Pewaukee High Sch 510 Lake St Pewaukee WI 53072-3698

NELSON, KATHY ANN, foundation administrator; b. Williamsport, Pa., Sept. 21, 1954; d. Dan LeRoy and Shirley Joann (Klein) Hoover. BS in German Edn., Ind. U. of Pa., 1976; postgrad., Pa. State U., 1978-83. Tchr. German Hollidaysburg (Pa.) Area Sch. Dist., 1977-85; adminstr. Carlisle (Pa.) Project, 1985; dir. fin. devel. and pub. relations Am. Lung Assn., York, Pa., 1986; chief profl. officer Adams County United Way, Gettysburg, Pa., 1987—. Press sec. Nancy Kulp's campaign for 9th Congl. Dist., Pa., 1984; mem. Downtown Gettysburg, 1987—, 125th Battle of Gettysburg Anniversary Commn., 1988; treas. Adams County Christmas Dinner, 1987-90; bd. dirs. Adams County Coun. Community Svcs., 1987—, Pa. State Club of Adams County, 1989-91; mem. adv. bd. Adams County Job Ctr., 1989—, Minority Youth Ednl. Inst., 1988-91, Intercultural Resource Ctr., Gettysburg Coll., 1989-91; mem. Adams Area Postal Customer Coun., 1987-89; dir. Adams Community TV, 1988-89; mem. profl. adv. coun., chair small cities task force United Way of Pa., 1990—, network com. 1992-94, UWLC, 1995. Fulbright/Goethe Haus scholar, Stuttgart, Fed. Republic of Germany, 1982. Mem. NAFE, Bus. and Profl. Women, Ctrl. Pa. Assn. Women Execs. (charter), Kiwanis (Historic Gettysburg chpt. pres. 1991-92, dist. conv. chmn. Pa. chpt. 1992, dist. maj. emphasis program chair 1992-93), Pa. State Alumni Assn. (life), Alpha Omicron Pi (endowment chair 1993—). Democrat. Lutheran. Home: 2566 Old Route 30 Orrtanna PA 17353-9759 Office: Adams County United Way PO Box 3545 Gettysburg PA 17325-0545

NELSON, KAY ELLEN, speech and language pathologist; b. Milw., Apr. 14, 1947; d. John A. and Margaret B. (Janke) Strobel; m. Kuglitsch Dale, Mar. 2, 1974 (div. Dec. 1981); 1 child, Ashley Lara. BA with distinction, U. Wis., Madison, 1969; MA, U. Wis., Milw., 1972. Speech and lang. pathologist Sch. Dist. 146, Dolton, Ill., 1970-71, Waukesha County Handicapped Children's Edn. Bd., Waukesha, Wis., 1972-77, 79-80, Kettle Moraine Area Schs., Wales, Wis., 1980-94; dir. speech/lang. pathology MJ Care, Inc., Fond du Lac, Wis., 1994—; pvt. practice Dousman, Wis., summers 1991-93. Fellow Herb Kohl Found., 1993. Mem. AAUW, NEA,m. Speech, Lang. and Hearing Assn. (cert. of clin. competence, ACE awards 1990, 91, 92, 94), Wis. Edn. Assn. Coun., Wis. Speech, Lang. and Hearing Assn. (sch. rep. dist. VII 1991—, chmn. sch. svcs. com. 1992-94, v.p. sch. svcs. 1994-95), United Lakewood Educators, Internat. Soc. for Augumentive and Alternative Comm., U.S. Soc. for Augumentive and Alternative Comm., Wis. Soc. for Augumentive and Alternative Comm. (sec. 1990-92, membership chmn. 1990-93, v.p. profl. affairs 1993). Unitarian. Office: MJ Care Inc All About Life Rehab Ctr 115 E Arndt St Fond du Lac WI 54936-0428

NELSON, LEANN LINDBECK, small business owner; b. McCook, Nebr., Jan. 27, 1937; d. Clifford Roy Lindbeck and Elizabeth J. (Downs) Rollstin; m. Lawrence L. Nelson, June 21, 1958; children: Glen Lindbeck, Todd Alan. BS in Dietetics, U. Tex., 1960. Dietitian Parkview Bapt. Hosp., Yuma, Ariz., 1960-61; instr. foods and nutrition Jefferson County Schs., Lakewood, Colo., 1969-71; dir. education and consumer programs, cons. nutrition Dairy Coun., Inc., Denver, 1971-74; coord. low-income foods and nutrition programs Emily Griffith Opportunity Sch., Denver, 1974-76; dir., asst. dir. edn./info. and product publicity Am. Sheep Prodrs. Coun., Denver, 1976-83; pres. Natural Accents, Denver, 1983-90; cons. fixed income counseling program City of Denver, Denver County, 1975-76, comm. cons., 1989—; prin. LeAnn Nelson Presents, 1988—; co-chairperson Home Econs. Nat. Task Force on Profl. Unity and Identity, 1992-93; prof. home econs., mem. adv. com. Coll. Applied Human Scis., Colo. State U., 1994—. Author: Accessories... What a Finish!, 1988. Chmn. home econs. adv. com. U. No. Colo., 1980-82; v.p. Clock Tower Mchts. Assn., Denver, 1983-85; chmn., buyer Denver Symphony Guild Gift Shop, 1984-87; mem. adv. bd. State Bd. Cmty. Colls. Occupational Edn., Home Econ. Tech. Adv. Com., 1986—, Coll. Applied Human Scis. Colo. State U., Ft. Collins, 1986-87. Named Colo. Home Economist of Yr. Colo. Home Econs. Assn., 1979, Colo. Bus. Home Economist of Yr. Colo. Home Econs. Assn., 1980; recipient Leadership award Colo. Home Econs. Assn. Mem. Nat. Assn. Women Bus. Owners, Home Economists in Bus. (nat. chmn.-elect 1981-82, nat. chmn. 1982-83, Nat. Bus. Home Economist of Yr. 1986), Colo. Assn. of Profl. Saleswomen, Profl. Aux. Assistance League of Denver, Denver Fashion Group (regional dir. 1984-86), Am. Women in Radio & TV (treas. Denver chpt. 1978-79). Clubs: Penrose, Executive. Home and Office: 1250 Humboldt St Apt 1001 Denver CO 80218-2416

NELSON, LINDA CAROL, corporate chief executive; b. Knoxville, Tenn., Feb. 18, 1954; d. Solon Morris and Dorothy Thelma (Randles) Woods. BA in Polit. Sci. and Psychology magna cum laude, U. Tenn., 1975; BS in Acctg. summa cum laude, Ga. State U., 1978. Cert. of mgmt. acct.; enrolled agt. Pvt. investigator Hanover Security Systems, Knoxville, 1968-74; office mgr. Dale Carnegie Inst., Knoxville, 1969-75; instr. Dale Carnegie course and profl. devel. series Dale Carnegie Inst., Atlanta, 1980-88; legal asst. office of regional atty. H.E.W., Atlanta, 1975; tech. support staff Dist. Conf. U.S. Treasury Dept., Atlanta, 1976, instr., tng. analyst continuing profl. edn., 1976-88; internal revenue agt., tax technician of exam. div. IRS, Atlanta, 1976-79; recruiter U.S. Treasury Dept., Atlanta, 1979-86, team coord. large case exam, 1980-85, resident lead instr. S.E. Region, 1984, coord. Joint Com. Taxation in Congress, 1986-87, fed. racketeering investigator strike force program, 1987; consolidations tax dept. staff mgr. Bellsouth, Atlanta, 1984-85; ind. mgmt. cons. Ga., 1980-86; pres., CEO Exec. Svcs. Inc., Atlanta, 1988—; active Speakers' Bur., Atlanta, 1993—. Hospitality com. mem. Atlanta Women's Network, 1990-92; vol. worker Eagles Boy's Ranch, Atlanta, 1986—; vol. counselor Atlanta Home for Abused Children, 1980-83; Sunday sch. tchr., choir, nursery, various chs., 1975—; fundraiser Atlanta Symphony Orch., 1985-86; cons. adopt-a-student program, 1985-86; vol. missions program 1st Bapt. Ch., Atlanta, 1986; key person United Way Atlanta Combined Fed. Campaign, 1978-84; calling com. Norcross (Ga.) United Meth. Ch., 1983-84; coord. blood drive ARC, Atlanta, 1984; vol. counselor Helen Ross McNabb Ctr., Knoxville, 1970-72; campaign com. mem. Senator Paul Coverdell. Recipient citation U.S. Sec. Labor Brennan, Superior Instr. award Dale Carnegie, 1988; named one of Outstanding Young Women of Am., 1984. Mem. ASTD (vol. placement com. 1988-92), NAFE, Inst. Mgmt. Accts. (program speaker Atlanta chpt., bd. dirs. 1989), High Mus. Art Young Career Mems. Guild, Young Women of the Arts, Nat. Assn. Enrolled Agts., Nat. Soc. Tax Profls., Profl. Info. Network (mem. spkr.'s bur.), Gwinnett County Leads Network (founder), Women's Life Underwriters' Assn. (program spkr.), Atlanta C. of C., Ga. State U. Alumni Assn., U. Tenn. Alumni Assn., Golden Key Nat. Honor Soc., Mortar Bd., U.S. Tennis Assn., Atlanta Lawn Tennis Assn., So. Bicycle League, Sierra Club, Phi Beta Kappa, Beta Alpha Psi, Pi Sigma Alpha, Pi Kappa Phi, Alpha Lambda Delta, Delta Gamma (social chair), Chi Phi Little Sisters (pres.). Home: 6001 Meadowbrook Dr Norcross GA 30093-3729 Office: Exec Svcs Inc PO Box 450822 Atlanta GA 31145-0822

NELSON, LINDA SHEARER, child development and family relations educator; b. New Kensington, Pa., Dec. 8, 1944; d. Walter M. and Jean M. (Black) Shearer; m. Alan Edward Nelson, Dec. 29, 1973; children: Amelia (Amy), Emily. BS in Home Econs. Edn., Pa. State U., 1966; MS in Child Devel. and Family Rels., Cornell U., 1968; PhD in Higher Edn. and Child Devel., U. Pitts., 1982. Head tchr.-lab. nursery sch. Dept. of Psychology, Vassar Coll., Poughkeepsie, N.Y., 1968-69; instr. child devel. dept. home econs. edn. Indiana U. Pa., 1969-72, asst. prof., 1972-77, assoc. prof., 1977-84, prof., 1984—, dept. chair, 1991-93, with human devel. environ. studies dept., 1993—; cons., trainer Head Start Programs, Pa., 1970—, Child Care Programs and Agys., Pa., 1970—; child devel. assoc. rep. Coun. for Early Childhood Profl. Recognition, Washington, 1989-91; field rep. Keystone U. Rsch. Corp., Erie, 1990-91; keynote/guest spkr. Child Devel./Child Care and Home Econs. confs., Pa. and nat., 1985—. Mem. adv. bd. Early Childhood Edn., Annual Edits., 1985—, Interface: Home Econs. and Tech. Newsletter, 1993—; contbr. articles to profl. jours. Bd. dirs. Indiana County Child Care Program, 1970-92; guest spkr. Delta Kappa Gamma, Indiana, 1990, Bus. and Profl. Women, Indiana, 1991. Grantee in field, 1985—. Mem. AAUW, Nat. Assn. for the Edn. Young Children, Pitts. Assn. for the Edn. Young Children (conf. co-chair 1983-85), Assn. Pa. State Coll. and Univ. Faculties, Kappa Omicron Nu. Democrat. Presbyterian. Office: Indiana U of Pa Human Devel and Environ Studies Dept 207 Ackerman Hall Indiana PA 15705

NELSON, LOIS ANNE, education specialist; b. Phila., July 22, 1948; d. Thore Andrew and Anna Nicoletta (Country) Moluf; m. James Joseph Nelson, Mar. 21, 1970 (div. Oct. 1993); children: Christopher Thore, Elizabeth Anne, Rachel Sarah, Joseph. BA, Trenton (N.J.) State Coll., 1970; MA, Villanova U., 1972. Cert. in secondary edn., N.J. English tchr. Audubon (N.J.) High Sch., 1970-73, Warrior Run Middle Sch., Turbetville, Pa., 1973-74; prof. English Santa Fe C.C., Gainesville, Fla., 1985-93; lit. liaison Sch. Bd. of Alachua County and Gainesville Housing Authority, Gainesville, 1994—; adult literacy tchr. Vol. Ctr., Gainesville, 1993—; libr. vol. Millhopper Br. Libr., Gainesville, 1991—. Collector Gainesville Harvest, St. Francis House, 1992—; parish coun. mem., 1986-94, Eucharistic minister, 1992—, lector, 1993—, Rite of Christian Initiation of Adults instr., 1994—. Mem. Gainesville Woman's Club, People of Praise, WINGS, Phi Delta Kappa. Republican. Roman Catholic. Office: Gainesville Housing Authority 1900 SE 4th St Gainesville FL 32643

NELSON, MARGARET VIOLA, internist, educator; b. Elbow Lake, Minn., Mar. 2, 1941; d. Elmer Lawrence and Roxy Viola (Ellison) N.; m. children: Bertram, Emily Johnson. BA, U. Minn., 1962, BS, 1964, MD, 1966. Diplomate Am. Bd. Internal Medicine. Intern Orange County Med. Ctr., Orange, Calif., 1966-67; resident U. Wis., Madison, 1967-70; asst. clin. prof. Hennepin County Med. Ctr., Mpls., 1974-75; physician, med. dir. Oneida (Wis.) Health Svcs., 1976-78; physician Univ. Health Svcs., Madison, Wis., 1980—. Home: 2202 W Lawn Ave Madison WI 53711-1952

NELSON, MARGUERITE HANSEN, special education educator; b. S.I., N.Y., June 23, 1947; d. Arthur Clayton and Marguerite Mary (Hansen) Nelson. AB magna cum laude, Boston Coll., 1969; MS in Edn., SUNY, Plattsburgh, 1973; post master's cert. in gerontology, Yeshiva U., 1982; postgrad., Fordham U., N.Y.C. Cert. elem. and spl. edn. tchr., N.Y. Pre-primary tchr. Pub. Sch. 22R S.I., N.Y.C. Bd. Edn., 1969-70; primary tchr. Oak Street Sch., Plattsburgh, N.Y., 1971-73, Laurel Plains Sch., Clarkstown Cen. Schs., New City, N.Y., 1973-78, Resource Rm. Lakewood Sch., Congers, N.Y., 1978—; mem. adj. faculty St. Thomas Aquinas Coll., Sparkill, N.Y., 1985-89, 95, Fordham U., Lincoln Ctr., N.Y.C., 1990; presenter in field at internat. and nat. confs., seminars. Author: Teacher Stories, 1993, Research on Teacher Thinking, 1993; contbr. articles to profl. jours. and textbooks. Recipient Impact II Tchr. Recognition award, 1984; grantee Chpt. II, 1983-84, Clarkstown Ctr. Schs., 1986-91, Office of Spl. Edn., 1992, 95. Mem. Am. Ednl. Rsch. Assn., Assn. for Children with Learning Disabilities, N.Y. State Congress of Parents and Tchrs. (hon. life), Nat. Assn. for Poetry Therapy, Assn. for Retarded Citizens, AAUW. Home: PO Box 135 Congers NY 10920-0135 Office: Lakewood Elem Sch 77 Lakeland Ave Congers NY 10920-1733

NELSON, MARTHA JANE, magazine editor; b. Pierre, S.D., Aug. 13, 1952; d. Bernard Anton and Pauline Isabel (Noren) N. BA, Barnard Coll., 1976. Mng. editor Signs: Jour. of Women in Culture, N.Y.C., 1976-80; editor Ms. Mag., N.Y.C., 1980-85; editor-in-chief Women's Sports and Fitness Mag., Palo Alto, Calif., 1985-87; exec. editor Savvy, N.Y.C., 1988-89, editor-in-chief, 1989-91. Editor: Women in the American City, 1980, In Style Mag., N.Y.C., 1993-95; cons. editor Who Weekly, Sydney; asst. mng. editor: People, 1993; contbr. articles to profl. jours. Bd. dirs. Painting Space 122, N.Y.C., 1982-85, Urban Athletic Assn. Mem. Am. Soc. Mag. Editors, Women in Film.

NELSON, MARY CARROLL, artist, author; b. Bryan, Tex., Apr. 24, 1929; d. James Vincent and Mary Elizabeth (Langton) Carroll; m. Edwin Blakely Nelson, June 27, 1950; children: Patricia Ann, Edwin Blakely. BA in Fine Arts, Barnard Coll., 1950; MA, U. N.Mex., 1963. Juror Am. Artist Golden Anniversary Nat. Art Competition, 1987, Don Ruffin Meml. Art Exhbn., Ariz., 1989, N.Mex. Arts and Crafts Fair, 1989; guest instr. continuing edn. U. N.Mex., 1991; conf., organizer Affirming Wholeness, The Art and Healing Experience, San Antonio, 1992, Artists of the Spirit Symposium, 1994. Group shows include N.Mex. Mus. Fine Arts Biennial, 1987, N.Mex. Lightworks, 1990, Level to Level, Ohio Layering, 1987, Artist as Shaman, Ohio, 1990, The Healing Experience, Mass., 1991, A Gathering of Voices, Calif., 1991, Art is for Healing, The Universal Link, San Antonio, Tex., 1992, Biennial, Fuller Lodge Art Ctr. Los Alamos, N.Mex., 1993, Layering, Albuquerque, 1993, Crossings, Bradford, Mass., 1994, The Layered Perspective, Fayetteville, Ark., 1994; represented in pvt. collections in: U.S., Fed. Republic of Germany, Eng. and Australia; author: American Indian Biography Series, 1971-76, (with Robert E. Wood) Watercolor Workshop, 1974, (with Ramon Kelley) Ramon Kelley Paints Portraits and Figures, 1977, The Legendary Artists of Taos, 1980, (catalog) American Art in Peking, 1981, Masters of Western Art, 1982, Connecting, The Art of Beth Ames Swartz, 1984, Artists of the Spirit, 1994, (catalog) Layering, An Art of Time and Space, 1985, (catalog) Layering/Connecting, 1987; contbg. editor Am. Artist, 1976-91, Southwest Art, 1987-91; editor (video) Layering, 1990; arts correspondent Albuquerque Jour., 1991-93. Mem. Albuquerque Arts Bd., 1984-88. Mem. Soc. Layerists in Multi-Media (founder 1982). Home: 1408 Georgia St NE Albuquerque NM 87110-6861

NELSON, MARY ELLEN DICKSON, actuary; b. Mpls., Mar. 24, 1933; d. William Alexander and Laura Winona (Baxter) Dickson; m. David Aldrich Nelson, Aug. 25, 1956; children: Frederick Dickson, Claudia Baxter, Caleb Edward. BA, Vassar Coll., 1954; postgrad., Cambridge (Eng.) U., 1954-55. Enrolled actuary joint bd. Dept. Labor and Dept. Treas. Rsch. assoc. N.Am. Life & Casualty Co., Mpls., 1955-56; actuarial asst. John Hancock Mut. Life Ins. Co., Boston, 1956-58; actuary David R. Kass & Assocs., Cleve., 1973-74; pres. Nelson & Co., Cleve., 1975, Conrad, Nelson & Co., Cleve., 1975-81, Nelson & Co., Cleve. and Cin., 1981—; bd. dirs. Blount, Inc., Montgomery, Ala., Cin. Bell Inc., Union Ctrl. Life Ins. Co., Cin. Fulbright scholar, 1954-55. Fellow Soc. Actuaries, Phi Beta Kappa; mem. Am. Acad. Actuaries, Cin. Actuaries Club, Midwest Benefits Conf. (chair 1991), Bankers Club. Republican. Office: 105 W 4th St Cincinnati OH 45202-2735

NELSON, MARY S., former state legislator; b. Boston, May 3, 1943; children: John, Michael, Jamie. Tchr. Perkins Sch. Blind, 1967-77; lectr. River Coll., 1977-78; selectman Nashua, N.H., 1983-85; mem. N.H. Ho. of Reps., 1983-85, N.H. State Senate, 1986-92; del. Dem. State Conv., 1982, 84; cons. on employment and tng. of handicapped, 1977—. Talk show host Sta. WMVU. Mem. N.H. Order of Women Legislators (pres. 1986—), Phi Delta Kappa. Democrat. Roman Catholic. Home: 18 Stanley Ln Nashua NH 03062-3237

NELSON, MICHELE KILLOUGH, clinical psychologist, educator; b. Washington, Jan. 19, 1965; d. Ralph Arnold and Jane Louise (Babb) Killough; m. Evan Stewart Nelson, June 23, 1990. BA with honors, U. N.C., Chapel Hill, 1987; MS, Purdue U., 1990, PhD, 1992. Lic. psychologist, Va. Fellow in health psychology Med. Coll. Va., Richmond, 1992-93, asst. prof. psychiatry, clin. psychologist, 1993—, infectious disease clinic psychologist, 1993—, mem. psychologist kidney-transplant teams, 1993—; presenter Agoraphobics Bldg. Ind. Lives, Richmond, 1992, 93, Cath. Divorce Support Groups, Richmond, 1993, Nursing AIDS Symposium, Richmond, 1993. Author: (with others) Beyond Face: Working with AIDS Patients, 1993; contbr. articles to profl. jours. Grantee HIV Care Consortium, 1992. Mem. APA (presenter 1993, health physiology sect., clin. psychology sect.). Democrat. Office: Med Coll Va PO Box 268 Richmond VA 23298

NELSON, NETTE ADALINE, finance company executive; b. Hood River, Oreg., June 23, 1939; d. Burt Cheney and Ethel Gertrude (Taylor) Nelson; m. Charles Luther Blaylock, July 1961 (div. 1968); children: Charles Wayne, Dennis Ray, Meri Jo. Student, Oreg. State U., 1957-59; BA, U. Nebr., 1983; MPA, Harvard U., 1984. With Lockheed, Sunnyvale, Calif., 1959-62; asst. to mgr. Fairchild Semiconductor, Mountain View, Calif., 1962-68; asst. to state planner Office of Gov., Salem, Oreg., 1968-69; assoc. planner Daniel, Mann, Johnson & Mendenhall, Portland, 1969-74; exec. asst. to dir. Dept. Land Conservation & Devel., Portland/Salem, Oreg., 1974-75; dir. statewide progs. Exec. Dept., State of Oreg., Salem, 1975-80; dir./cons. Nebr. Telecom & Info. Ctr., Lincoln, 1984-87; v.p. Nebr. R&D Authority, Lincoln, 1987-89, pres., 1989-90; pres. The Nelson Group, Lincoln, 1991—; lobbyist various orgns. Contbr. articles to profl. jours. V.p., bd. dirs. Heartland Ctr. for Leadership Devel., Lincoln, 1988—; bd. dirs. Network Nebr., 1991—, Nebr. Venture Group, 1990, Prairie Fire, 1987-90; advisor to Legis. New Horizons for Nebr. project, Lincoln, 1987-90; chmn. Nebr. Edn. Tech. Consortium, Lincoln, 1984—; mem. New Seeds for Nebr. project, Lincoln, 1988-90. Recipient Tribute to Women, Lincoln YWCA, 1994. Mem. Cmty. Devel. Soc., Women's Inst. Theology, Torch Club. Office: 411 S 44th St Lincoln NE 68510-1862

NELSON, NEVIN MARY, interior designer; b. Cleve., Nov. 5, 1941; d. Arthur George Reinker and Barbara Phyllis (Gunn) Parks; m. Wayne Nelson (div. 1969); children: Doug, Brian. BA in Interior Design, U. Colo., 1964. Prin. Nevin Nelson Design, Boulder, Colo., 1966-70, Vail, Colo., 1970—; program chmn. Questers Antique Study Group, Boulder, 1969. Coord. Bob Kirscht for Gov. campaign, Eagle County, Colo., 1986; state del. Rep. Nat. Conv., 1986-88; county coord. George Bush for U.S. Pres. campaign, 1988, 92; chmn. Eagle County Reps., 1989-93. Mem. Am. Soc. Interior Designers. Episcopalian. Home: PO Box 1212 Vail CO 81658-1212 Office: 2498 Arosa Dr Vail CO 81657-4276

NELSON, PAMELA A., state legislator; m. Vic Nelson; 2 children. Former mem. S.D. State Ho. of Reps.; now senator S.D. State Senate; Democrat. Roman Catholic. Home: 2505 S Marion Rd Sioux Falls SD 57106-0842 Office: State Senate State Capital Pierre SD 57501*

NELSON, SARAH MILLEDGE, archaeology educator; b. Miami, Fla., Nov. 29, 1931; d. Stanley and Sarah Woodman (Franklin) M.; m. Harold Stanley Nelson, July 25, 1953; children: Erik Harold, Mark Milledge, Stanley Franklin. BA, Wellesley Coll., 1953; MA, U. Mich., 1969, PhD, 1973. Instr. archaeology U. Md. extension, Seoul, Republic Korea, 1970-71; asst. prof. U. Denver, 1974-79, assoc. prof., 1979-85, prof. archaeology, 1985—, chair dept. anthropology, dir. women's studies program, 1985-87; vis. asst. prof. U. Colo., Boulder, 1974. Co-editor: Powers of Observation, 1990, Equity Issues for Women in Archaeology, 1994; author: Archaeology of Korea, 1993; editor: The Archaeology of Northeast China, 1995. Active Earthwatch, 1989—. Southwestern Inst. Rsch. on Women grantee, 1981, Acad. Korean Studies grantee, Seoul, 1983, Internat. Cultural Soc. Korea grantee, 1986, Scholarly Communication award People's Republic of China, NAS, 1988; recipient Outstanding Scholar award U. Denver, 1989. Fellow Am. Anthrop. Assn.; mem. Soc. Am. Archaeology, Assn. Asian Studies, Royal Asiatic Soc., Sigma Xi (sec.-treas. 1978-79), Phi Beta Kappa. Democrat. Home: 5878 S Dry Creek Ct Littleton CO 80121-1709 Office: U Denver Dept Anthropology Denver CO 80208

NELSON, SUE A., legislative staff member. BA, U. Mich., 1974; MPA, U. Tex., 1980. Rsch. asst. Multi-Ethnic Curriculum Revision Project, Ann Arbor, Mich., 1975; program mgr. Capital Area Planning Coun., Austin, Tex., 1977-78; presdl. mgmt. intern Treasury Dept., 1980-82; budget analyst Office Mgmt. and Budget, 1982-85; dir. budget rev. Senate Budget Com., 1985—; assoc. dir. Nat. Econ. Commn., 1988-89. Office: Com Budget 613 Senate Dirksen Office Bldg Washington DC 20510*

NELSON, TANNIS FLYNN, piano instructor; b. Wilmington, N.C., July 8, 1952; d. Floyd W. and Ila (Blake) Flynn; m. R. Michael Nelson, Aug. 4, 1973; children: Laura Bethany, Steven Michael. Student, U. N.C., 1970-74. Piano instr. Wilmington, N.C., 1968—. Active bd. mgrs. N.C. Congress of Parents and Tchrs., Raleigh, 1989—, 1st v.p., 1994—; pres. New Hanover County Coun. PTAs, Wilmington, 1992—. Recipient Vol. Svc. award Gov. of N.C., 1990, 91, 92, Ann. Vol. Action award President Bush, 1992; named Most Outstanding Sch. Vol., Nat. Assn. Vols. and Ptnrs. in Edn., 1993. Mem. Nat. Assn. Parliamentarians, Wilmington C. of C. (edn. coun. 1993—). Baptist. Home: 211 Gregory Rd Wilmington NC 28405

NELSON, TERI LYNN, social worker; b. Anderson, Ind., Jan. 22, 1956; d. Gordon Dey and Carolyn Jean (Hasler) N. BA, Anderson (Ind.) U., 1978; MSW, Ind. U., Indpls., 1985. Cert. clin. social worker, Ind. Pub. liaison A Better Way, Inc., Muncie, Ind., 1979-80; substance abuse counselor Aquarius House, Inc., Muncie, 1980-85; staff therapist Community Mental Health Ctr., Inc., Lawrenceburg, Ind., 1985, program dir. recovery svcs., 1985—; mem. Ind. Substance Abuse Task Force, Indpls., 1985—, co-chairperson, 1991-94; presenter 5th Ann. Gov.'s Conf. on Mental Health, Indpls., 1985, conf. co chair,presenter Ind. State Ann. Addictions Conf., 1992—; mem. adv. bd. Gov.'s Commn. for a Drug-Free Ind., S.E. region, Jeffersonville, Ind., 1988-92; clin. supr. Community Mental Health Ctr., Inc., Lawrenceburg, 1989—; adj. faculty Union Inst., Cin., 1993—; mem. conf. faculty Midwest Inst., Kalamazoo, Mich., 1992—; mem. adv. bd. Addiction Counselor Tng. Partnership, Indpls., 1993—, training cons. Fairbanks Rsch. and Training Inst. Indpls., 1994—. contbr. to profl. jours. Vol. Crisis Intervention Ctr., Muncie, 1979-84, bd. sec., 1979-82; bd. sec. Family Svcs. Delaware County, Muncie, 1980-84; chairperson Dearborn County Citizens Against Substance Abuse, Lawrenceburg, Ind., 1990. Recipient Citations, VA Med. Ctr., 1985, Am. Bus. Women's Assn., 1985. Mem. NASW, Acad. Cert. Social Workers, Native Am. Legal Def. Assn. Office: Community Mental Health Ctr 285 Bielby Rd Lawrenceburg IN 47025-1055

NELSON, VALERIE JOY, accountant; b. Coeur d'Alene, Idaho, May 20, 1959; d. Darroll Dean Wells and Janet Elizabeth (Dahl) Thomas. BBA in Acctg., Boise State U., 1984; MBA, U. Portland, Oreg., 1990. CPA. Auditor State of Idaho, Boise, 1985-87; chief acct. U. Portland, 1987-90; auditor Far West Fed. Bank, Portland, 1990; fin. analyst Tektronix, Inc., Beaverton, Oreg., 1991, acctg. mgr., 1991-93; acctg. supr. Planar Systems, Inc., Beaverton, 1993—. Mem. Inst. Mgmt. Accts. Office: Planar Systems Inc 1400 NW Compton Dr Beaverton OR 97006

NELSON, VIRGINIA SIMSON, pediatrician, educator; b. L.A.; d. Jerome and Virginia (Kuppler) Simson; children: Eric, Paul. AB, Stanford U., 1963, MD, 1970; MPH, U. Mich., 1974. Diplomate Am. Bd. Pediatrics, Am. Bd. Phys. Medicine and Rehab. Pediatrician Inst. Study Mental Retardation and Related Disabilities, U. Mich., Ann Arbor, 1973-80; mem. faculty phys. medicine and rehab. dept. U. Mich. Med. Ctr., Ann Arbor, 1980-83, resident

PM&R, 1983-85, chief pediatric PM&R, 1985—. Contbr. articles to profl. jours. Office: Univ Mich Med Ctr F7822 Mott Hospital Ann Arbor MI 48109-0230

NELSON, VITA JOY, editor, publisher; b. N.Y.C., Dec. 9, 1937; d. Leon Abraham and Bertha (Sher) Reiner; m. Lester Nelson, Aug. 27, 1961; children: Lee Reiner, Clifford Samuel, Cara Ritchie. BA, Boston U., 1959. Promotion copywriter Street & Smith, N.Y.C., 1958-59; asst. to mng. editor Mademoiselle Mag., N.Y.C., 1959-60; mcpl. bond trader Granger & Co., N.Y.C., 1960-63; founder, editor, pub. Westchester Mag., Mamaroneck, N.Y., 1968-80, L.I. Mag., 1973-78; found., editor, pub., pres. Moneypaper, Mamaroneck, N.Y., 1981—. Bd. dirs. Westchester Tourism Council, Westchester County, N.Y., 1974-75, Sackerpath Council Girl Scouts U.S.A., White Plains, N.Y., 1976-79; bd. govs. v.p. Am. Jewish Com., Westchester, N.Y., 1979-89. Recipient citation Council Arts, 1972; Media award Pub. Rels. Soc. Am., 1974. Mem. Women in Communications (Outstanding Communicator award 1983), Sigma Delta Chi. Democrat. Home: Pleasant Ridge Rd Harrison NY 10528-1004 Office: Temper of the Times Comm 1010 Mamaroneck Ave Mamaroneck NY 10543-1660

NELSON, WENDY SEIKKULA, financial manager; b. Duluth, Minn., July 4, 1956; d. Robert W. and Barbara L. (Laibl) Seikkula; m. Kenneth A. Nelson, Feb. 1, 1986; children: Amber, Brian. AA, North Hennepin C.C., Mpls., 1976; BSB in Acctg., U. Minn., 1978. CPA; cert. mgmt. acct. Sr. acct. Olsen Thelen & Co., St. Paul, 1978-82, Schreir Heimer Kosbab, St. Paul, 1982-83; fin. acctg. mgr. Pako Corp., Plymouth, Minn., 1983-85; asst. contr. United Mailing, Inc., Chanhassen, Minn., 1985-93; CFO Prairie Knights Casino, Bismarck, N.D., 1993—. Mem. Am. Inst. CPAs, Minn. Soc. CPAs, N.D. Soc. CPAs, Inst. Cert. Mgmt. Accts. Office: Prairie Knights Casino HC1 Box 26 A Fort Yates ND 58538

NELSON-MAYSON, LINDA RUTH, art museum curator; b. Vincennes, Ind., Jan. 9, 1954; d. Robert Arthur and Darleen Marie (Andrews) N.; m. William A. Mayson, June 12, 1982; 1 child, Eric Nelson. BFA, Miami U., Oxford, Ohio, 1976; MFA, Ohio State U., 1981. Co-dir. Artreach Gallery, Columbus, Ohio, 1980-82; art instr., gallery asst. Ohio U., Chillicothe, 1982-83; asst. curator Ross County Mus., Chillicothe, 1982-83; art dir. Aaron Copland Music & Arts Program, White Plains, N.Y., 1982-85; artist-in-edn. Nebr. Arts Council, Omaha, 1983-85; curator Art Mus. South Tex., Corpus Christi, 1985-89; curator collections Columbia (S.C.) Mus. Art, 1989-92, dep. dir. curatorial svcs., 1992-94; ind. curator, cons. New Hope, Minn., 1994—; juror art exhibits Corpus Christi Arts Found., 1986-88, Hardin Simmons U., 1987, Anderson Coll., 1989, Hilton Head Art League, 1994; mem. pub. art select panel S.C. Arts Coun., 1990; mem. steering com. South Tex. Regional Arts Conf., 1986-88; adj. lectr. art history U. S.C., 1989-94. Grantee NEA, S.C. Arts Coun., Tex. Coun. on Arts, Kress Found., Inst. Mus. Svcs. Mem. Am. Assn. Mus. (co-chair exhibits competition 1991-93, chair curator's com. 1993-95, chair of chairs 1994-95, nominating com. 1994-95), Southeastern Mus. Conf. (chmn. curator's com. 1991-93, local program com. chair 1992, mem. program com. 1992-93). Democrat.

NELSON-WALKER, ROBERTA, estate planner; b. N.Y.C., Sept. 1, 1936; d. Richard E. and Esther (McBride) Martin; m. Robert L. Nelson, July 20, 1957 (div.); children: Carol, Craig, Robert H.; m. Dan Walker, Nov. 1978 (div.). BA, DePaul U., 1976, MS in Mgmt. with distinction, 1977. Dir. devel. Ray Graham Assocs., Elmhurst, Ill., 1970-76; dir. human resources Nat. Easter Seal Soc., Chgo., 1979-81; v.p. Butler Walker Inc., Oak Brook, Ill., 1981-85; pres. CNR, Inc., Oak Brook, 1985-91; spl. agt. Prudential Ins., Oak Brook, 1991—; lectr. master's program DePaul U., Chgo., 1978-80; condr. seminars on disability, 1973-77, on estate planning, 1991-93; author, project dir. DuPage County Commn., 1976, Gov.'s Coun. on Develop. Disabilities, 1978-79. Author: Creating Acceptance for Handicapped People, 1975, Creating, Planning, and Financial Housing for Handicapped People, 1979. Founder, organizer Found. for Handicapped, 1970-76,; pres. DuPage County Pub. Health Coun., 1974; bd. dirs. DuPage County Mental Health Assocs., 1970, Forest Found. DuPage County, 1976-86, Shakespeare Globe, London and Chgo., 1982—; mem. DuPage County Bd. Health, 1975, Ill. Gov.'s Com. for Handicapped, 1976, women's coun. Chgo. Heart Assn., 1979—. Recipient Meritorious Svc. award, Chgo. Heart Assn., 1968, 70, Fond du Cer award AHA, 1968, Cursade of Mercy Achievement awards, 1974-76, State of Ill. procalmation by Gov. James Thompson, Ill. Epilepsy Assn., 1978. Office: Prudential Ins 1901 S Meyers Rd Oak Brook Terrace IL 60181

NEMETH, PATRICIA MARIE, lawyer; b. Flint, Mich., Sept. 18, 1959; d. Gyula Nemeth and Marie (Glaska) Adkins. BA, U. Mich., 1981; JD, Wayne State U., 1984, LLM, 1990. Bar: Ill. 1987, Mich. 1984, U.S. Ct. Appeals (6th cir.), U.S. Dist. Ct. (ea. dist.) Mich., U.S. Dist. Ct. (we. dist.) Mich. Teaching asst. Wayne State U., Detroit, 1982; intern. U.S. Dist. Ct. (ea. dist.) Mich., Detroit, 1983; assoc. Bloom & Bloom, Birmingham, Mich., 1984-85, Stringari, Fritz, Kreger, Ahearn, Bennett & Hunsinger, Detroit, 1985-92; prin. Patricia Nemeth, Atty. & Counselor, Detroit, 1992—; lectr. labor law seminar Inst. Continuing Legal Edn., 1990; adj. prof. Walsh Coll., 1992-94. Contbr. articles to profl. jours. Mem. ABA (labor sect.), Mich. Bar Assn. (labor sect.), Nat. Order Barristers, Nat. Assn. Women Bus. Owners, Women Lawyer's Assn. Mich., Detroit Bar Assn. Roman Catholic. Office: 243 W Congress Ste 350 Detroit MI 48226-3901

NEMIROFF, MAXINE CELIA, art educator, gallery owner, consultant; b. Chgo., Feb. 11, 1935; d. Oscar Bernard and Martha (Mann) Kessler; m. Paul Rubenstein, June 26, 1955 (div. 1974); children: Daniel, Peter, Anthony; m. Allan Nemiroff, Dec. 24, 1979. BA, U. So. Calif., 1955; MA, UCLA, 1974. Sr. instr. UCLA, 1974-92; dir., curator art gallery Doolittle Theater, Los Angeles, 1985-86; owner Nemiroff Deutsch Fine Art, Santa Monica, Calif.; leader of worldwide art tours; cons. L'Ermitage Hotel Group, Beverly Hills, Calif., 1982—, Broadway Dept. Stores, So. Calif., 1979—, Security Pacific Bank, Calif., 1978—, Am. Airlines, Calif. Pizza Kitchen Restaurants; art chmn. UCLA Thieves Market, Century City, 1960—, L.A. Music Ctr. Mercado, 1982—; lectr. in field. Apptd. bd. dirs. Dublin (Calif.) Fine Arts Found., 1989; mem. Calif. Govs. Adv. Coun. for Women, 1992. Named Woman of Yr. UCLA Panhellenic Council, 1982, Instr. of Yr. UCLA Dept. Arts, 1984. Mem. L.A. County Mus. Art Coun., UCLA Art Coun., UCLA Art Coun. Docents, Alpha Epsilon Phi (alumnus of yr. 1983). Democrat. Jewish.

NENNER, VICTORIA CORICH, nurse; b. Marshall, Tex., Jan. 17, 1945; d. Bernard Paul and Mary DeLayne (Bowen) Corich; BSN (Regents scholar, Krost-Freeman scholar, Mary Gobbs Jones Nursing scholar), Tex. Women's U., 1966; cert. U. Paris, summer 1966; MSN, U. San Diego, 1984; m. Paul Edwin Nenner, Aug. 12, 1970. Mem. nursing staff St. Thomas Hosp., London, 1966-67, Parkland Meml. Hosp., Dallas, 1967-68; coord. nursing continuing edn. Scripps Meml. Hosp., La Jolla, Calif., 1974-85; pres. Marvik Ednl. Svcs., Inc.; mem. part-time faculty U. Calif., San Diego; mem. vis. faculty U. B.C.; mem. Inservice Council San Diego and Imperial Counties, 1974-80, pres., 1976-77; mem. San Diego Community Colls. Health Edn. Adv. Bd., 1976-84. Served to capt. Nurse Corps, USAF, 1968-73. Named Tex. Student Nurse of Year, 1966. Mem. NAFE, Am. Soc. Health Edn. and Tng., Nat. League Nursing, Am. Nurses Assn., Calif. League for Nursing (pres. 1993-94), Sigma Theta Tau. Author articles in field; producer oncology nursing ednl. videotapes. Home: 167712 Los Altos Rd San Diego CA 92109

NENSTIEL, SUSAN KISTHART, insurance professional office administrator; b. Hazleton, Pa., Aug. 21, 1951; d. Frank W. and Mary A. (Price) Kisthart; m. David W. Nenstiel, June 4, 1977. BS, Pa. State U., 1973; MBA, Wilkes (Pa.) Coll., 1982. Control mgr. Barrett, Haentjens & Co., Hazleton, 1973-79, export mgr., 1979-86; exec. dir. Leadership Hazleton, 1986-87; devel. officer Planned Parenthood of NE Pa., Wilkes-Barre, 1986-87; ins. broker, office mgr. Nenstiel & Nenstiel, West Hazleton, Pa., 1988—. Pres. YWCA, Hazleton, 1983-85, Women's Coalition of Greater Hazleton, 1987-91; sec. Govt. Study Commn., Hazleton, 1984-85; bd. dirs. United Way Greater Hazleton, 1986; trustee Hazleton Area Pub. Libr., sec., 1987-89, v.p., 1990-91, pres., 1991-93; chmn. Luzerne County Commn. for Women, 1988-91; mem., chmn. Hazleton City Zoning Bd., 1988-92; treas. Pa. Women's Campaign Fund, 1987-91, pres., 1991-92; mem. Leadership Hazleton Adv. Coun., 1988-92; mem. Pa. Pub. Libr. Project, 1992094; bd. dirs. Hazleton Health Care Found., 1992—, chairperson, 1994—. Named one of Outstanding Women Penns Woods Coun. Girl Scouts U.S.A., 1977, Outstanding Young Women in Am., 1985, Woman of Yr. Soroptomist Internat., 1984, Greater Hazleton Jaycee Disting. Svc. award, 1990; recipient Luzerne County Pathfinder's award, 1990. Mem. AAUW (br. pres. 1977-79, state sec. 1981-83, state treas. 1983-85, state pres. 1992—, Br. Outstanding Woman of Yr. 1980, assn. women's issue com. 1989-91, chairperson assn. conf. state pres. 1994, mem. state bd. 1989—), LWV, NAFE, Nat . Assn. Ins. Women. Republican. Home: 21 Poolside Dr Hazleton PA 18201-9409

NEOS, PERI FITCH, painting contractor, small business owner; b. San Pedro, Calif., Apr. 27, 1938; d. William Roosevelt Fitch and Adele (Russell) Kane; m. Thomas Harold Holston, May 27, 1957 (div. 1969); children: Kevin T. Russell, Kelly J. Russell, Adele H. Breedlove; m. Konstantinos Demetrios Neos, July 3, 1981. BSL, Western State U. Coll. Law, 1975, JD, 1976. Process piping designer The Fluor Corp., L.A., 1965-68; sr. designer CF Braun, L.A., 1968-70; sr. designer, contractor various enginr./constrn. firms L.A., 1970-81; painting contractor, owner El Greco Painting, Hanford, Calif., 1981—; substitute tchr. Kings and Tulare County Sch. Dists., 1992—. Mem. Kings County Citizens Adv. Bd. on Alcohol and Other Drug Programs, Hanford, 1991—; mem. City of Hanford Hist. Resources Commn., 1994—. With USN, 1956-58. Mem. AAUW, Nat. Assn. Women in Constrn., Hanford C. of C., Mensa. Home and Office: El Greco Painting 293 E Adrian Way Hanford CA 93230-1233

NERO, SHIRLEY MAE, real estate executive; b. Marietta, Ga., Apr. 26, 1936; d. Harvey Herbert and Ruby Lois (Waldrop) Dooley; m. Buford Sammy Freeze, May 10, 1954 (dec. Feb. 1973); children: Peggy Eisenhauer, Michael Freeze, Melodie Freeze Hudson, Jeffery Freeze; m. Curt Turner Clark, Nov. 3, 1973 (div. Apr. 1984); m. Robert J. Nero, Apr. 2, 1988. Student, Sch. Mortgage Banking, Chgo., 1965-66. Lic. real estate broker, Ga.; cert. gen. real estate appraiser, real estate agt., Fla. Bookkeeper, payroll clk. Marietta Hosiery Co., 1954-61; bookkeeper, mortgage loan servicing adminstr. The McNeal Cos., Smyrna, Ga., 1961-68; bookkeeper, office mgr. Pulte Homes of Ga. Corp., Marietta, 1968-71, Personality Homes, Inc., Smyrna, 1971-77; real estate agt. Jack W. Boone & Co., Smyrna, 1978-79; bookkeeper Devin Mgmt. Co., College Park, Ga., 1979-80; co-owner, corp. treas. Tube Analysis, Inc., Mableton, Ga., 1979-84; owner, mgr. S.C. Properties, Lithia Springs, Ga., 1984-86; ptnr., appraiser Clark & Assocs., Acworth, Ga., 1986-88; appraiser W.H. Benson & Co., Melbourne, Fla., 1988—. Pres. Parents Without Ptnrs., Douglasville, Ga., 1985-86, treas. Peach St. Regional Council, 1987, conf. chmn. 1987. Named Mem. of Yr., Douglas County Parents Without Ptnrs., 1986. Mem. Appraisal Inst., Women of Moose. Home: 2237 Granville St NE Melbourne FL 32907-2608 Office: WH Benson & Co 4031 Dixie Hwy Melbourne FL 32905

NESBIT, PHYLLIS SCHNEIDER, judge; b. Newkirk, Okla., Sept. 21, 1919; d. Vernon Lee and Irma Mae (Biddle) Schneider; m. Peter Nicholas Nesbit, Sept. 14, 1939. BS in Chemistry, U. Ala., 1948, BS in Law, 1958, JD, 1969. Bar: Ala. 1958. Ptnr. Wilters, Brantley and Nesbit, Robertsdale, Ala., 1958-74; pvt. practice, Robertsdale, 1974-76; dist. judge Baldwin County Juvenile Ct., 1977-88; supernumerary dist. judge and juvenile ct. judge Baldwin County, 1989—. Bd. dirs. Baldwin Youth Services; bd. dirs., v.p. women's activities So. Ala. chpt. Nat. Safety Council, 1978-83; chmn. quality assurance com. The Homestead Retirement Vill., 1992—. Mem. Nat. Assn. Women Lawyers, Nat. Assn. Women Judges, N.Am. Judges Assn., Ala. Dist. Judges Assn., Ala. Council Juvenile Judges, Am. Judicature Soc., Baldwin County Bar Assn., Spanish Fort, Fairhope Bus. and Profl. Women's, Phi Alpha Delta. Democrat. Methodist.

NESBITT, DEETTE DUPREE, volunteer worker; b. Houston, May 5, 1941; d. Raymond Benjamin DuPree and Alice Lula (Cade) Foster; children: Alice L., Charles S. Massey Nesbitt; m. Ernest V. Nesbitt, Aug. 20, 1971. Student, Sam Houston State U., 1960-61, U. Houston, 1961-62, 81-83. Lic. real estate, Tex. Adminstrv. asst. Tex. Iron Works, Inc., Houston, 1963-76, Gulf Coast Real Estate Co., Houston, 1976-78, Schubert Real Estate, Houston, 1980-81; dir., sec. Dad's Club YMCA, Competitive Swim Team, Houston, 1981-83; vol. adminstrv. asst. numerous orgns., Houston. Contbr. articles to various publs. Bd. trustees Pace Soc. Am., Inc., Ladies Oriental Shrine N.Am., Inc.; bd. dirs. Evergreen Friends, Inc., 1991—. Recipient Varina Howell Davis medal Mil. Order Stars and Bars, 1992, Silver Good Citizenship award SAR, 1992; featured on Eyes of Texas, NBC, 1992. Mem. Nat. Soc. DAR, Huguenot Soc., S.C. Soc. Descendants of the Colonial Clergy, Nat. Soc. Magna Charta Dames (colony historian), Plantagenet Soc., Col. Order of the Crown, The Sovereign Colonial Soc. Am. Royal Descent, Order of Hereditary Descendants of Kings of Scotland (life), Nat. Jamestown Soc. (mem. coun. 1993—), First Tex. Co. Jamestowne Soc. (lt. gov., gov. 1985-93, hon. gov. life), Soc. First Families of Ga. 1733-1797 (v.p. gen. Tex. State Soc. 1987—), Soc. First Families of S.C. 1670-1700 (life), Order of First Families of Va. 1607-1624/5 (life), Order of First Families of Miss. 1699-1817 (life), Daus. Rep. Tex. (Tex. Star chpt.), Colonial Dames Am. (pres. chpt. VIII 1995—), United Daus. Confederacy (Jefferson Davis chpt., chmn. Confederate Ball com. 1985—, co-chmn. ball 1988, advisor to chmn. 1989, 90, Jefferson Davis Hist. award, Winnie Davis medal, Spl. Recognition award), Sons and Daus. of Pilgrims (chmn. nat. awards), Freedoms Found. Valley Forge (George Washington Honor medal 1994). Republican. Episcopalian. Home: 15411 Old Stone Trl Houston TX 77079-4206

NESBITT, LENORE CARRERO, federal judge; m. Joseph Nesbitt; 2 children: Sarah, Thomas. A.A., Stephens Coll., 1952; BS, Northwestern U., 1954; student U. Fla. Law Sch., 1954-55; LLB, U. Miami, 1957. Rsch. asst. Dist. Ct. Appeal, 1957-59, Dade County Cir. Ct., 1963-65; pvt. practice Nesbitt & Nesbitt, 1960-63; spl. asst. attorney gen., 1961-63; with Law Offices of John Robert Terry, 1969-73; counsel, Fla. State Bd. Med. Examiners, 1970-71; with Petersen, McGowan & Feder, 1973-75; judge Fla. Cir. Ct., 1975-82, U.S. Dist. Ct. (so. dist.) Fla., Miami, 1983—. Bd. trustees U. Miami; bd. dirs. Miami Children's Hosp. Mem. FBA, Fla. Bar Assn., U.S. Jud. Conf. Com. on Criminal Law and Probation Adminstrn. Office: US Dist Ct 301 N Miami Ave Miami FL 33128-7701*

NESBITT, RUTH, retired association executive; b. Newton, Mass.; d. Samuel Frederick Nesbitt and Lulu Hunt (Glazier) Snow. BA, Wellesley Coll., 1939; MBA, NYU, 1958. Actuarial asst. George B. Buck, N.Y.C., 1939-43, 46-50; club dir. ARC, Pacific Ocean area, 1943-46; asst. to v.p. Melpar Inc., Alexandria, Va., 1950-53; asst. to pres. Daystrom, Inc., Murray Hill, N.J., 1953-60; bus. adminstr. Nat. Bd. YWCA, N.Y.C., 1960-82. Home: 375-4T South End Ave New York NY 10280

NESBITT, VERONICA A., management executive; b. Henderson, Tenn., June 10, 1959; d. Hiawatha Daniel and Laura Mae (Green) Thompson; m. Darryl L. Nesbitt, Nov. 12, 1992; children: Shemenya A. Davis, Maleka L. Cert. stenographer, Miller-Hawkins B. Coll., 1979; Cert. data transcriber, IRS, Memphis, Tenn., 1981; Cert. computer operator, U.S. Army, Newport News, Va., 1985, Cert. computer programmer, 1987; postgrad., Columbia Coll., 1990. Stenographer Memphis & Shelby County Health Dept., Memphis, 1979-80; cash clk./data transcriber IRS, Memphis, 1980-82; data transcriber U.S. Army, Fort Sheridan, Ill., 1982-83; work order clk. U.S. Army, Fort Sheridan, 1984-85, quality control clk., 1985-89, mgmt. asst., 1989—; data transcriber Selective Svc., North Chicago, Ill., 1983-84; telemarketer Allstate Ins. Co., Northbrook, Ill., 1986-88; unit supr. Allstate Ins. Co., Glenview, Ill., 1988-92; employee coun., 1994; total quality facilitator Allstate Ins. Co., Glenview, Ill., 1992; mgmt. asst. Hdqs. US Army Recruiting Command, Ft. Knox, Ky., 1994—; chmn. task force Allstate, Glenview, 1990. Mem. Am. Heart Disease Found., 1991-92, Easter Seal Soc., 1991-92, March of Dimes, 1991-92, Nat. Heart Rsch., 1991-95, Nat. Cancer Rsch., 1991-95, fed. women's program mgr., 1995—. Mem. NAFE, Am. Cancer Soc., Am. Heart Disease Prevention Found., Jack Anderson Internat. Platform Assn. Baptist. Office: CMR 431 233d Base Support Battalion APO AE 09175 also: HHC 440th Signal BN CMR 431 Box 2557 APO AE 09175

NESMITH, FRANCES JANE, education consultant; b. Tulsa, Nov. 6, 1926; d. George W. and Frances Pearl (Hendrix) N. BA, U. Houston, 1947; MA in Polit. Sci., Columbia U., 1951; postgrad., U. Tex., 1957, 58, 61-64; EdD, Columbia U., 1968. Cert. ednl. adminstr. Tchr. Houston Ind. Sch. Dist., 1947-58; lectr. U. Houston, 1956-58; tchr. Austin (Tex.) Ind. Sch. Dist., 1958-69; instr. Columbia U., N.Y.C., 1964-66, Austin Community Coll., 1973-74; coord. secondary social studies Austin Ind. Sch. Dist., 1969-86; adj. assoc. prof. Coll. Edn. U. Tex., Austin, 1986—; edn. cons. Austin, 1986—; cons. Addison-Wesley Pub. Co., Menlo Park, Calif., 1987—, State Bar Tex., Austin, 1989—, Learned & Tested, Inc., Orlando, Fla., 1986. Author: Texas Teacher Appraisal Systems-Economics, 1987, World History, 1988, Economics, U.S. History and Government—A Law-Related Education Resource Guide, 1992; co-auuthor: The Story of Texas, 1963; guest editor Southwestern Jour. Social Edn., 1981. Pub. mem. Citizens and Law Focused Edn. Com. State Bar Tex., Austin, 1983-86; mem. adv. coun. Lifetime Learning Inst., Austin, 1989—. Heft scholar Columbia U., N.Y.C., 1966; recipient Leon Jaworski award Tex. Young Lawyers, State Bar Tex., Austin, 1986, George Washington medal Freedoms Found., Valley Forge, Pa., 1986. Mem. Nat. Coun. Social Studies, Tex. Coun. Social Studies, Austin Coun. Social Studies (exec. sec. 1969-86), Tex. Tchrs. Assn. (life), Tex. Hist. Assn., Delta Kappa Gamma (internat. fellow 1965), Phi Delta Kappa. Democrat. Methodist. Home and Office: 2605 Salado St Austin TX 78705-3911

NESMITH, SUSANNA KATHLEEN, secondary educator; b. Billings, Mont., Aug. 8, 1959; d. James Wilburn and Susanna Kay (Bach) D.; m. Jeffrey Thomas Nesmith, June 29, 1980 (div. Aug. 1984); children: James D., Christopher R. AA, Olympic Coll., 1986; BS, Ctrl. Wash. U., 1987, MEd, 1991. Bus. tchr. Eton Tech. Inst., Port Orchard, Wash., 1987-89; substitute tchr. various schs., Wash., 1990-91; bus. tchr., advisor North Beach High Sch., Ocean Shores, Wash., 1991—; adj. computer instr. Olympic Coll., Bremerton, Wash., 1988-89; adj. bus. tchr. Grays Harbor Coll., Aberdeen, Wash., 1992—. Advisor North Beach Future Bus. Leaders chpt., Ocean Shores, 1991—; regional advisor Capitol Region Future Bus. Leaders of Am., Olympia, 1991-93; den leader, com. mem., merit badge counselor Boy Scouts Am., Ellensburg, Port Orchard, Ocean Shores, 1989—; treas. North Beach Youth Soccer Assn. With U.S. Army, 1979-82. Mem. Future Bus. Leaders of Am. (advisor, regional advisor capitol region), Nat. Bus. Edn. Assn. Home: PO Box 1365 Ocean Shores WA 98569-1365 Office: North Beach High Sch PO Box 969 Ocean Shores WA 98569-0969

NESWALD, BARBARA ANNE, advertising executive; b. N.Y.C., Jan. 14, 1935; d. Edward and Veronica (Presby) Lutz; m. Ronald Neswald, Nov. 15, 1952 (div. Jan. 1957); children: Kurt Thomas, Linda Neswald Hunt, Elizabeth Williams Gann. Student Hunter Coll. Media dir. R.M. Klosterman Inc., Los Angeles, 1960-64, copy writer, Los Angeles, 1964-73; copy chief Broadway Dept. Stores, Los Angeles, 1973-76; creative dir. Lucky Stores, Inc., Buena Park, Calif., 1976-79; v.p. advt. and communications Top Value Enterprises Co., Dayton, Ohio, 1979-82; sales promotion dir. Strawbridge & Clothier Clover div., Phila., 1982—; mem. adv. bd. Los Angeles Trade Tech. Coll., 1976-77. Bd. dirs. Logan Sq. Neighborhood Assn., 1984-94, Pa. chpt. UNICEF, 1985-89, Am. Poetry Ctr., 1985-92, Women in Transition, Inc., Friends of the Children, 1993-94; bus. and profl. funding com. Acad. Vocal Arts; alumna Community Leadership Seminars, Phila. Recipient various advt. awards; N.Y. Regents scholar, 1952-53. Mem. Am. Mktg. Assn., Women in Communications, Inc., Internat. Mass Retailing Assn. (chair steering retail com. advt., mktg. and sales promotion 1988-93, named Retail Advertiser of Yr. 1990), Soroptomists (bd. dirs. Phila. chpt. 1989-91). Office: 801 Market St Philadelphia PA 19103

NETHERS, ELENA SOTO, lawyer; b. St. Louis, Mar. 20, 1963; d. Alberto Arturo and Maria (Vila) Soto; m. Mark Raymond Nethers; children: Patricia Elena, Alexander Mark. BA in Internat. Rels., Newcomb Coll., 1985; JD, Wash. U., St. Louis, 1989. Counsel Mut. of Omaha Ins. Co., 1989-92, sr. counsel, 1992—. Bd. dirs. YWCA, Omaha, 1993. Mem. Nebr. Bar Assn. (exec. com. corp. counsel 1993). Office: Mutual of Omaha Ins Co Mutual of Omaha Plz Omaha NE 68175

NETTER, VIRGINIA THOMPSON, produce company owner; b. Hardyville, Ky., Nov. 2, 1931; d. Duluth Sydnor and Vera (Asbury) Thompson; m. S. Mitchell Netter, Oct. 4, 1947; children: Ronald Lee, Candace Netter Harrison. BA, U. Louisville, 1982; MA in Counseling/Clin. Psychology, Spalding U., 1989. Owner, Netter Produce Co., Louisville, 1954—, Big Four Farms, Belmont, Ky., 1959—. Named to Hon. Order Ky. Cols., 1982. Mem. AAUW, Woodcock Soc., Psi Chi, Phi Kappa Phi. Avocations: ballroom dancing, riding, golf, travel. Home: 1029 Alta Vista Rd Louisville KY 40205-1727 Office: Netter Produce Co 331-335 Produce Plz Louisville KY 40202

NETTESHEIM, CHRISTINE COOK, judge; b. 1944. AB, Stanford Univ., 1966; JD, Univ. of Utah, 1969. Law clk. to chief judge U.S. Court of Appeals, 10th circuit, Salt Lake City; trial atty. Dept. of Justice Honors Program, Foreign Litigation Unit, Ct. of Claims Sect. of Civil Div., 1970-72; team leader atty. FTC, 1972-74; with Hogan & Hartson, D.C., 1974-76; spl. counsel Pension Benefit Guaranty Corp., 1976-80; dep. gen. counsel U.S. Railway Assn., 1980-82; with Shack & Kimball, D.C., 1980-82; judge U.S. Ct. of Fed. Claims, D.C., 1982—. Mem. D.C. Bar Assn., Calif. State Bar. Office: US Court of Federal Claims 717 Madison Pl NW Ste 709 Washington DC 20005*

NETTROUR, LILA GROFF, biology educator; b. San Francisco; d. Arthur and Mary Ellen (Anderson) Groff; m. Lewis F. Nettrour, Oct. 22, 1966; children: John, Barbara. BA, St. Olaf Coll., 1964; MEd, U. Pitts., 1966. Microbiologist Mayo Clinic, Rochester, Minn., 1964-65; sci. tchr. Dover Eyota (Minn.) High Sch., 1966-67; part-time instr. Community Coll. Allegheny County, Pitts., 1980-90, asst. prof. biol. scis., 1991—. Dir. YMCA North Hills, Pitts., 1974-80, chmn. 1980; bd. dirs. St. John's Luth. Ch. Living Gifts and Meml. Fund, Pitts. Mem. AAUW, North Hills Environ. Coun. Office: Community Coll Allegheny Co 8701 Perry Hwy Pittsburgh PA 15237-5353

NETZBAND, DELORIS HARRISON, English language educator, school counselor; b. Bedford, Va., Feb. 4, 1938; d. Ernest and Lucy J. (Hall) Harrison; 1 child, Germaine Auguste. BA in English, St. Joseph's Coll., Bklyn., 1958; MA in English, NYU, 1963; M in Counselor Edn., Plymouth State Coll., 1994. Tchr. English De Witt Clinton High Sch., Bronx, N.Y., 1961-68; lectr. English CCNY, 1969-70; asst. prof. English Dartmouth Coll., Hanover, N.H., 1970-72, Windham Coll., Putney, Vt., 1972-74; tchr. English/drama Orford (N.H.) High Sch., 1974-78; tchr. English Hanover High Sch., 1978-80, Cairo Am. Coll., 1982-93; sch. counselor intern Sunapee (N.H.) Mid. Sch., High Sch., 1993-94, Ray Elem. Sch., Hanover, 1994; mentor Black Student Union, Plymouth (N.H.) State Coll., 1994—. Author: We Shall Live In Peace, 1968, Bannekers of Bannaky Springs, 1970, Journey All Alone, 1971. Fulbright Tchr. fellow, 1966-67. Mem. Phi Delta Kappa. Home: 20 Ledyard Ln Hanover NH 03755

NETZER, LANORE A(GNES), retired educational administration educator; b. Laona, Wis., Aug. 27, 1916; d. Henry N. and Julia M. (Niquette) Netzer; m. Glen G. Eye, 1979. Diploma, Oconto County Normal Sch., 1935; BS, State Tchrs. Coll., Oshkosh, Wis., 1943; MS, U. Wis., 1948, PhD, 1951. Tchr. Goldhorn Rural Sch., Pound, Wis., 1935-36; tchr. Goldfield Sch., Pound, 1936-37, tchr., acting prin., 1937-39; tchr., prin. Spruce (Wis.) Grade Sch., 1939-41; tchr. pub. schs. Neenah, Wis., 1943-46; demonstration and critic tchr. Campus Sch. State Tchrs. Coll., Oshkosh, 1946-48; supr. student tchrs.' coll. instrn. State Tchrs. Coll., Milw., 1950-55; teaching asst. U. Wis., Madison, 1948-50; assoc. prof. edn. U. Wis., Milw., 1955-63; prof. ednl. adminstrn. U. Wis., Madison, 1963-77, emeritus prof., 1977—; rsch. assoc. U.S. Office Edn., 1963-66; supr. student tchrs. coll. instrn. State Tchrs. Coll., Milw., 1950-55; mem. curriculum adminstrn. com. Wis. Coop. Curriculum Planning Program, 1945-52; mem. Wis. Joint Com. on Edn., 1957-59, E.B. Fred Fellowship Com., U. Wis., 1966—; ednl. cons. Educators Progress Svc., 1970—. Author: The Use of Industry Aids in Schools, 1952, (with Glen G. Eye) Supervision of Instruction: A Phase of Administration, 1965, 2d. edit., 1971, (with others) Interdisciplinary Foundations of Supervision, 1969, (with G. Eye) School Administrators and Instruction, 1969, (with others) Education Administration and Change, 1970, (with others) Supervision of Instruction, 1971, Strategies for Instructional Management, 1977; contbr. articles to profl. jours. Rsch. grantee Hill & Knowlton, Inc., N.Y.C., 1949; grantee Wis. Mfrs. Assn., 1954; recipient award of Distinction Nat. Coun. of Adminstrv. Women in Edn., 1975. Mem. AAUP, Wis. Edn. Assn. (life), So. Wis. Edn. Assn., Nat. Assn. Supervision and Curriculum Devel., Wis. Assn.

Supervision and Curriculum Devel., Southwestern Assn. Supervision and Curriculum Devel., Wis. Elem. Sch. Prins. Assn., Am. Assn. Sch. Adminstrs., Wis. Assn. Sch. Dist. Adminstrs., Am. Edn. Rsch. Assn., Wis. Edn. Rsch. Assn., Univ. Coun. Ednl. Adminstrn., U. Wis. Alumni Assn. (life), U. Wis. Meml. Union (life), Phi Beta Sigma, Kappa Delta Pi, Pi Lambda Theta, Phi Delta Kappa. Home: 110 S Henry St Apt 1506 Madison WI 53703-3168 Office: U Wis Dept Ednl Adminstrn 1025 W Johnson St Madison WI 53706-1706

NEU, ELIZABETH ANN, city administrator; b. Ft. Wayne, Ind., Feb. 8, 1956; d. Richard Eugene and Elizabeth Joan (Ankenbruck) Meyer; m. Terrence Lee Neu, May 14, 1977; children: Amanda, Andrew. BA, Ind. U., 1979; grad. Econ. Devel. Inst., U. Okla., 1985. Assoc. planner N.E. Ind. Regional Coordinating Coun., Ft. Wayne, 1979-83; econ. devel. specialist Allen County Plan Commn., Ft. Wayne, 1983-89; v.p. Greater Ft. Wayne C. of C., 1989-90; dir. City of Ft. Wayne Dept. Econ. Devel., 1990—; bd. dirs. N.E. Ind. Bus. Assistance Corp., Ft. Wayne, 1992—, N.E. Ind. Pvt. Industry Coun., Ft. Wayne, 1986-90, Community Devel. Corp., Ft. Wayne, 1988-90; thesis cons. Econ. Devel. Inst., Norman, Okla., 1989—. Bd. dirs. Ft. Wayne Philharm., 1992-93. Mem. Am. Econ. Devel. Coun., Ind. Econ. Devel. Assn. (bd. dirs., chair legis. com. 1989—). Roman Catholic. Office: City of Ft Wayne Dept Econ Devel 840 City-County Bldg Fort Wayne IN 46802

NEUFELD, ELIZABETH FONDAL, biochemist, educator; b. Paris, Sept. 27, 1928; U.S. citizen; m. 1951. Ph.D., U. Calif., Berkeley, 1956; D.H.C. (hon.), U. Rene Descartes, Paris, 1978; D.Sc. (hon.), Russell Sage Coll., Troy, N.Y., 1981, Hahnemann U. Sch. Medicine, 1984. Asst. research biochemist U. Calif., Berkeley, 1957-63; with Nat. Inst. Arthritis, Metabolism and Digestive Diseases, Bethesda, Md., 1963-84, research biochemist, 1963-73, chief sect. human biochem. genetics, 1973-79, chief genetics and biochem. br., 1979-84; prof., chmn. dept. biol. chemistry UCLA Sch. Medicine, 1984—. Named Paasano Found. sr. laureate, 1982, Calif. Scientist of the Yr., 1990; recipient Dickson prize U. Pitts., 1974, Hillebrand award, 1975, Gairdner Found. award, 1981, Albert Lasker Clin. Med. Rsch. award, 1982, William Allan award, 1982, Elliott Cresson medal, 1984, Wolf Found. prize, 1988, Christopher columbus Discovery award for biomed. rsch., 1992, Nat. Medal of Sci., 1994. Fellow AAAS; mem. NAS, Inst. Medicine of NAS, Am. Acad. Arts and Scis., Am. Soc. Human Genetics, Am. Chem. Soc., Am. Soc. Biochemistry and Molecular Biology (pres. 1992-93), Am. Soc. Cell Biology, Am. Soc. Clin. Investigation. Office: UCLA Sch Medicine Dept Biol Chemistry Los Angeles CA 90024

NEUGARTEN, BERNICE LEVIN, social scientist; b. Norfolk, Nebr., Feb. 11, 1916; d. David L. and Sadie (Segall) Levin; m. Fritz Neugarten, July 1, 1940; children: Dail Ann, Jerrold. B.A., U. Chgo., 1936, Ph.D., 1943; D.Sc. (hon.), U. So. Calif., 1980; PhD (hon.), Cath. U., Nijmegen, 1988. Rsch. assoc. Com. on Human Devel., U. Chgo., 1948-50; asst. prof. U. Chgo., 1951-60, assoc. prof., 1960-64, prof., 1964-80, chmn., 1969-73, prof. social svc. adminstrn., 1978-80, mem. com. on policy studies, 1979-80, Rothschild disting. scholar, prof. emeritus, 1988—; prof. human devel. and social policy Northwestern U., 1980-88; mem. council U. Chgo. Senate, 1968-71, 72-75, 78-80, chmn. council com. on univ. women, 1969-70; nat. adv. council Nat. Inst. on Aging, 1975-76, 78-81, Fed. Council on Aging, 1978-81; dep. chmn. White House Conf. on Aging, 1980-81. Author: (with R.J. Havighurst) American Indian and White Children: A Social-Psychological Investigation, 1955, reprint, 1969, (with R.J. Havighurst) Society and Education, 1957, rev., 1962, 67, 75, (with Assocs.) Personality in Middle and Late Life, 1964, reprint, 1980, (with J.M.A. Munnichs et al) Adjustment to Retirement, 1969, (with R.P. Coleman) Social Status in the City, 1971, Middle Age and Aging, 1968; co-editor: (with H. Eglit) Age Discrimination, 1981, Age or Need? Public Policies for Older People, 1982; assoc. editor Jour. Gerontology, 1958-61, Human Devel., 1962-68; adv. or cons. editor other profl. jours., 1959—; author monographs, research papers and reports. mem. various adv. bodies. Recipient Am. Psychol. Found. Disting. Tchg. award, 1975, Disting. Psychologist award Ill. Psychol. Assn., 1979, Sandoz Internat. Prize for Gerontol. Rsch., 1987, Ollie Randall award Nat. Coun. on Aging, 1993, Gold Medal award for lifetime contbn. as a psychologist in the public interest Am. Psychol. Found., 1994. Fellow AAAS, Am. Psychol. Assn. (coun. rep. 1967-69, 73-76, Disting. Sci. Contbn. award 1980, honoree Women's Heritage Exhibit 1992, Gold Medal award 1994), Am. Sociol. Assn., Gerontol. Soc. Am. (pres. 1968-69, Kleemeier award 1971, Brookdale award 1982, Disting. Mentor award 1988), Am. Acad. Arts and Scis., Internat. Assn. Gerontology (governing coun. 1975-78, chmn. N.Am. exec. com. 1983-85, disting. creative contrbn. to gerontology award); mem. Inst. Medicine of NAS. Home: 5801 S Dorchester Ave Chicago IL 60637-1731

NEUGEBAUER, MARCIA, physicist, administrator; b. N.Y.C., Sept. 27, 1932; d. Howard Graeme MacDonald and Frances (Townsend) Marshall; m. Gerry Neugebauer, Aug. 25, 1956; children: Carol, Lee. B.S., Cornell U., 1954; M.S., U. Ill., 1956. Grad. asst. U. Ill., Urbana, 1954-56; vis. fellow Clare Hall Coll., Cambridge, Eng., 1975; sr. research scientist Jet Propulsion Lab. Calif. Inst. Tech., Pasadena, 1956—; vis. prof. planetary sci. Calif. Inst. Tech., Pasadena, 1986-87; mem. com. NASA, Washington, 1960—, NAS, Washington, 1981—; Regents lectr. UCLA, 1990-91. Contbr. numerous articles on physics to profl. jours. Named Calif. Woman Scientist of Yr. Calif. Mus. Sci. and Industry, 1967; recipient Exceptional Sci. Achievement medal NASA, 1970, Outstanding Leadership medal NASA, 1993. Fellow Am. Geophys. Union (sec., pres. solar planetary relationships sect. 1979-84, editor-in-chief Rev. Geophysics 1988-92, pres.-elect 1992-94, pres. 1994-96). Democrat. Home: 1720 Braeburn Rd Altadena CA 91001-2708 Office: Calif Inst Tech Jet Propulsion Lab/MS 169-506 4800 Oak Grove Dr Pasadena CA 91109-8001

NEUGROSCHL, JILL PAULETTE, financial planning company executive; b. N.Y.C., Mar. 25, 1949; d. Irving and Lillian (Berkowitz) Satler, m. Edward Neugroschl, May 28, 1972; 1 child, Dara Satler. BA in Elem. Edn., Farleigh Dickinson U., 1970; MS in Spl. Edn., Coll. New Rochelle (N.Y.), 1974. Cert. fin. planner; registered securities and investment advisor. Tchr. elem. schs. Yonkers, N.Y., 1970-77; v.p. fin. planning Finesco Assocs., Inc., Brewster, N.Y., 1978—; tchr. Brewster (N.Y.) Adult Edn., 1986. Chairperson Conn. Pub. TV Auction Co., New Milford, 1986-89, Temple Sholom Sch. Bd., New Milford, 1987-89, treas., exec. bd., 1989-90, v.p., 1990-91, pres., 1991—; commn. mem. Joseph Eisner Camp Inst. for Living Judaism, Gt. Barrington, Mass., 1991—; bd. dirs. UAHC N.E. Coun., 1994—. Mem. Internat. Assn. Fin. Planning, Inst. Cert. Fin. Planners. Democrat. Jewish. Home: 25 Dean Rd New Milford CT 06776-3824 Office: Finesco Assocs Inc Starr Ridge Rd Brewster NY 10509

NEUHAUS, JO-ANN, urban planner; b. N.Y.C., Nov. 28, 1942; d. Arthur and Betty (Zimmermann) N.; m. Arthur James Nolan, Sept. 9, 1979; children: Grant Alexander Nolan, Seth Zachary Nolan. Student, Ohio Wesleyan U., 1960-62; BA, George Washington U., 1964, MA in Urban and Regional Planning, 1971. Rsch. asst. The Urban Land Inst., Washington, 1964-65; realty asst. D.C. Redevelopment Land Agency, Washington, 1966-67, urban planner, 1967-71, downtown urban planner, 1971-76; project mgr. Pa. Ave. Development Corp., Washington, 1976-80, asst. dir. comml., 1980-82, project mgr., 1982-85, chief project mgmt., 1985-87, dir. proj. devel., 1987—. Mem. Mohigan Hills Citizens Assn., Bethesda, Md., 1980—; treas. Pa. Quater Neighborhood Assn., 1988-94, sec.-treas. 1994—. Mem. Comml. Real Estate Women, Am. Planning Assn., Lambda Alpha Internat. (chmn. land devel. com. 1991-93, v.p. mem. 1993—). Office: Pa Ave Devel Corp 1331 Pennsylvania Ave NW Washington DC 20004

NEUHAUS, SYDNEY ANN, public relations executive. Grad., Cornell U. With med. comms. group Daniel J. Edelman Pub. Rels.; asst. dir., project mgr. Sutton Pub. Rels., 1990; v.p. Medicus Intercon Pub. Rels., 1991-92; sr. v.p., dir. pub. rels. Harrison Star Wiener & Beitler Pub. Rels., 1992—. Office: Harrison Star Wiener & Beitler Pub Rels 16 W 22nd St New York NY 10010

NEUHÄUSER, MARY HELEN, artist, writer, playwright; b. San Antonio, Feb. 17, 1943; d. Gotthelf Friedrich and Edna Earl (Walling) N.; m. Federico Andrea Canuto, Jan. 6, 1972 (div. June 1981. Student, Cath. U. Am., 1957-58; student of drama, Cath. U., 1957-58; student, Carnegie-Mellon U., 1962-64, Studio Nera Simi, Florence, Italy, 1964-65. Official portraits in FBI Bldg., Rayburn House Reps. Office Bldg., Trinity Coll., Sidwell Friends Sch., Washington; one-person shows include Potters House Gallery, Washington, AAUW, Bethesda, Md., Martha Washington Library, Alexandria, Va., Thirty-Year Retrospective, Friendship Gallery, Chevy Chase, 1989; exhibited at Nat. Mus. Fine Arts, Smithsonian Instn., Nat. Cathedral, Lincoln Meml., Corcoran Gallery of Art, Monroe House, Arena Stage, Nat. Dem. Club, Veerhoff Galleries, Washington, Curl Gallery, Washington, Capricorn Galleries, Bethesda, Md., Lorenz Gallery, Bethesda, Gallery Orlov, Alexandria, Seloff Gallery of Fine Art, Brownsville, Tex., Art and Design Gallery, Chantilly, Va., 1994-95; work reproduced in newspapers The Washington Post (1st place 1961, 64), The Washington Daily News, The Evening Star, Capitol Hill Roll Call; represented in numerous pvt. collections; contbr. op-ed articles to Washington Post, Bethesda Almanac, Am. Enterprise Inst. Mag.; author: (plays) The Great Sin, 1993, Awkwright and Murgatroyd, 1994. Active St. Joseph's Home for Boys, Washington, 1965-66, Lincolnia (Va.) Day Care Ctr., 1966-67, Meriwether Home for Children, Washington, 1969-70, congl. campaign of Stewart Bainum; active supporter, writer Dem. Presdl. campaign, 1988, 92; vol. with Vietnam casualties, Nat. Naval Med. Ctr., Bethesda ARC, 1970-71; active supporter and writer on homeless, 1984—; health care advocate writer, U.S. Senate, 1986—; donator art works to Fed. City Shelter, Washington; vol. 3 shelters for homeless, Washington and Md., 1984—; health care advocate, writer U.S. Senate; writer campaign for Nat. Health Ins. Act, 1989—. Recipient Best-in-Show award, first profl. competition, 1961, 11 awards for abstracts, numerous others; ofcl. portraits in FBI Bldg., Rayburn Ho. of Rep. Office Bldg., Trinity Coll., Sidwell Friends Sch. Mem. DAR. Democrat. Mem. Ecumenical Ch. Home and Studio: 4602 Chevy Chase Blvd Chevy Chase MD 20815-5301

NEUMAN, BETH ELLEN, special education educator; b. Litchfield, Minn., Nov. 12, 1952; d. Jerome Andrew and Jean Eleanor (Stoetzel) N. BA, Tex. Woman's U., 1974; MS, Minot State U., 1976. Instr. English Munich (N.D.) Pub. Sch., 1976-80; spl. edn. educator Lake Region Spl. Edn., Devils Lake, N.D., 1980—. Guardian ad litem civic govt., Devils Lake, 1990; bd. dirs., publicity chair Pioneer Players, 1989; mem. Tchr. Ctr. Bd., 1988-92; pres. No. Lights Community Theatre, 1988-90. Mem. AAUW (pres. N.D. 1992-94). Office: Warwick Pub Sch PO Box 7 Warwick ND 58381-0007

NEUMAN, LINDA KINNEY, state supreme court justice; b. Chgo., June 18, 1948; d. Harold S. and Mary E. Kinney; m. Henry G. Neuman; children: Emily, Lindsey. BA, U. Colo., 1970, JD, 1973. Lawyer Betty, Neuman, McMahon, Hellstrom & Bittner, 1973-79; v.p., trust officer Bettendorf Bank & Trust Co., 1979-80; dist. ct. judge, 1982-86; supreme ct. justice State of Iowa, 1986—; mem. adj. faculty U. Iowa Grad. Sch. of Social Work, 1981; part-time jud. magistrate Scott County, 1980-82; mem. Supreme Ct. continuing legal edn. commn. Dir. Nat. Assn. Women Judges. Recipient Regents scholarship. Fellow ABA (chair appellate judges conf., mem. appellate standards com., JAD exec. coun.); mem. Am. Judicature Soc., Iowa Bar Assn., Iowa Judges Assn., Scott County Bar Assn. Office: Iowa Supreme Court State Capitol Des Moines IA 50319

NEUMAN, NANCY ADAMS MOSSHAMMER, civic leader; b. Greenwich, Conn., July 24, 1936; d. Alden Smith and Margaret (Mevis) Mosshammer; BA, Pomona Coll., 1957, LLD, 1983; MA, U. Calif. at Berkeley, 1961; LHD, Westminster Coll., 1987; m. Mark Donald Neuman, Dec. 23, 1958; children: Deborah Neuman Metzler, Jennifer Neuman Joye, Jeffrey Abbott. William A. Johnson Disting. lectr. Am. govt. Pomona Coll., 1990; disting. vis. prof. Washington and Jefferson Coll., 1991, 94, Bucknell U., 1992. Pres., Lewisburg (Pa.) area League Women Voters, 1967-70; bd. dirs. LWV Pa., 1970-77, pres., 1975-77; bd. dirs. LWV U.S., 1977-90, 2d v.p., 1978-80, 1st v.p., 1982-84, pres., 1986-90; bd. dirs., pres. Pathmakers, Inc., 1993—; mem. Pa. Gov.'s Commn. on Mortgage and Interest Rates, 1973, Pa. Commonwealth Child Devel. Com., 1974-75, Nat. Commn. on Pub. Svc., 1987-90; bd. dirs. Housing Assistance Council, Inc., Washington, 1974—, pres., 1978-80; bd. dirs. Nat. Council on Agrl. Life and Labor, 1974-79, Nat. Rural Housing Coalition, 1975—, Pa. Housing Fin. Agy., 1975-80, Jud. Inquiry and Rev. Bd. Pa., 1989-93; Disciplinary Bd. Supreme Ct. Pa., 1980-85; mem. Pa. Gov.'s Task Force on Voter Registration, 1975-76, Nat. Task Force for Implementation Equal Rights Amendment, 1975-77; mem. adv. com. Pa. Gov.'s Interdepartmental Council on Seasonal Farmworkers, 1975-77; mem. Appellate Ct. Nominating Commn. Pa., 1976-79; mem. Fed. Jud. Nominating Commn. Pa., 1977-85, chmn., 1978-81, 82-83; mem. Pa. Gov.'s Study Commn. on Pub. Employee Relations, 1976-78; del. Internat. Women's Yr. Conf., 1977; bd. dirs. ERAmerica, Inc., 1st v.p., 1977-79, Nat. Low Income Housing Coalition, 1979-82; Rural Am., 1979-81, Fed. Home Loan Bank Pitts., 1979-82; mem. Nat. Adv. Com. for Women, 1978-79; mem. nat. adv. com. Pa. Neighborhood Preservation Support System, 1976-77; bd. dirs. Pa. Women's Campaign Fund, 1984-86, 92—, pres., 1992—, Rural Coalition, Washington, 1984-90, Com. on the Constitutional System, 1988-90, Am. Judicature Soc., 1989-93; exec. com. Leadership Conf. Civil Rights, 1986-90; bd. dirs. Pennsylvanians for Modern Cts., 1986— trustee Citizen's Rsch. Found., 1989—; mem. mid. dist. Pa. adv. com. judicial and U.S. atty nominations, 1993-94. Virginia Travis lectureship Bucknell U., 1982. Recipient Disting. Alumna award MacDuffie Sch. for Girls, 1979, Liberty Bell award Pa. Bar Assn., 1983, Barrows Alumni award Pomona Coll., 1987, Thomas P. O'Neill Jr. award for exemplary pub. svc., 1989; named Disting. Daughter of Pa., 1987 Woodrow Wilson vis. fellow, 1993—. Mem. ABA (com. election law and voter participation, 1986-90, accreditation com. 1990—), Am. Arbitration Assn. (bd. dirs. 1986-90). Home: 132 Verna Rd Lewisburg PA 17837-8747

NEUMAN, SUSAN CATHERINE, public relations and marketing consultant; b. Detroit, Jan. 29, 1942; d. Paul Edmund and Elsie (Goetz) N.; AB, U. Miami (Fla.), 1964; MBA, Barry U., Miami Shores, Fla., 1985. APR (PRSA), 1973. Journalist, writer The Miami Herald (Fla.), 1962-65; editor Miamian Mag., 1965-69; pres. Susan Neuman Inc., Miami, 1969—. Mem. Fla. Gov.'s Pub. Relations Adv. Council, 1978-86. Mem. Pub. Relations Soc. Am. (accredited, past officer, bd. dirs. Miami chpt.), Ins. Exchange of Ams. (founding mem.), Econ. Soc. South Fla. (past officer, bd. dirs.), Miami C. of C., Counselor's Acad. Democrat. Roman Catholic. Clubs: Miami City (founder), Miami Internat. Press (charter, founder, pres. 1985-86) (Miami). Home: 13540 NE Miami Ct Miami FL 33161-2739 Office: Susan Neuman Inc Pla Venetia 25th Fl 555 NE 15th St Apt 25K Miami FL 33132-1405

NEUMANN, DIANE, lawyer, mediator; b. New Britain, Conn., Dec. 7, 1947; d. Paul and Nancy (Vinci) Patania; m. Peter A. Neumann, June 14, 1969 (div.); children: Brian, Stacey. MA, Framingham (Mass.) State U., 1982; JD, New Eng. Sch. Law, 1991. Bar: Mass. Therapist; tax rep. IRS; owner, mgr. Divorce Mediation Svcs., Framingham, 1981—. Author: Divorce Mediation: How To Cut Cost and Stress of Divorce, 1989. Mem. Acad. Family Mediation (bd. dirs. 1991—), Divorce Mediation Tng. Assn. (pres. 1988—). Democrat. Unitarian. Home: 1081 Centre St Newton MA 02159-1536 Office: Divorce Mediation Svcs 42 Lincoln St Framingham MA 01701-8239

NEUMARK, GERTRUDE FANNY, materials science educator; b. Nuremberg, Germany, Apr. 29, 1927; came to U.S., 1935; d. Siegmund and Bertha (Forchheimer) N.; m. Henry Rothschilld, Mar. 18, 1950. BA, Barnard Coll., 1948; MA, Radcliffe Coll., 1949; PhD, Columbia U., 1951. Advanced rsch. physicist Sylvania Rsch. Labs., Bayside, N.Y., 1952-60; sr. mem. tech. staff Philips Labs., Briarcliff Manor, N.Y., 1960-85; prof. materials sci. Columbia U., N.Y.C., 1985—; cons. Am. Inst. Physics, N.Y.C., 1968-69; NSF vis. prof., 1982; panelist NRC; panelist, reviewer NSF. Contbr. Encyclopedia of Advanced Materials, numerous articles to sci. jours., chpt. to books; patentee in field. Rice fellow, 1948, Dana fellow, 1948, AAUW Anderson fellow, 1951. Fellow Am. Phys. Soc. (Goeppert-Meyer award com. 1987-89); mem. Materials Rsch. Soc., Electrochem. Soc. (sr.), Soc. Women Engrs. (sr.), Am. Chem. Soc. Office: Columbia U 1137 SW Mudd Bldg New York NY 10027

NEUMEISTER, SUSAN MARY, librarian; b. Buffalo, May 23, 1958; d. Edward John and Regina Mary (Winnicki) N. BA in Geography, SUNY, Buffalo, 1980, MLS, 1982. Clk. Health Scis. Library SUNY, Buffalo, 1978-81, grad. asst., 1981-82, cataloging libr., 1932-91, head bibliog. control, cen. tech. svcs., 1991—. Librarian Buffalo chpt. ARC, 1983—. Grantee, 1987-88. Mem. ALA, SUNY Librs. Assn., Online Audiovisual Catalogers (editor-in-chief newsletter). Democrat. Roman Catholic. Home: 240 N Long St Williamsville NY 14221-5353 Office: SUNY Cen Tech Services Lockwood Libr Bldg Buffalo NY 14260

NEUNZIG, CAROLYN MILLER, middle school educator; b. L.I., May 5, 1930; kd. Stanley and Grace (Walsh) Miller; m. Herbert Neunzig, May 28, 1955; children: Kurt Miller, Keith Weidler. BA, Beaver Coll., Glen Side, Pa., 1953; MSSc, Syracuse U., 1989; postgrad., Adelphi U.; Cert., N.C. State U., Raleigh. Reading tchr. grades K-6 St. Timothy's Sch., Raleigh, N.C., 1971-83, 5th grade tchr., 1983-88, 5th grade lead tchr., 1986-88; tchr. English and geography 7th grade St. Timothy's Mid. Sch., Raleigh, 1991—; tchr Am. govt. 12th grade St. Timothy's Mid. Sch./Hale High Sch., Raleigh, 1991-93; instr. continuing edn. program history Meredith Coll., Raleigh, 1990-91, 95—, spl. high sch. registration commr., 1991-93; elected mem. Ctr. for the Study of the Presidency, 1994; charter mem. Libr. Congress, 1994. Mem. Am. Acad. Polit. and Social Sci., Acad. Polit. Sci., Nat. Coun. for Social Studies, Nat. Coun. Tchrs. English.

NEUSTADT, BARBARA MAE, artist, illustrator, etcher; b. Davenport, Iowa, June 21, 1922; d. David and Cora (Wollensky) N.; children: Diane Elizabeth Walbridge Wheeler, Laurie Barbara Meyer Hall. B.A., Smith Coll., 1944; postgrad., U. Chgo., 1945-46; Art Student's League scholar, Ohio U. Sch. Fine Arts, 1952. Art dir., designer Shepherd Cards, Inc., N.Y.C., 1956-63; dir., instr. Studio Graphics Workshop, Woodstock, N.Y., 1970—; lectr. on printmaking; participant artist in schs. program N.Y. State Schs., 1972-74; Bd. dirs., editor bull. LWV of Woodstock, 1969-70. Illustrator: The First Christmas, 1960, A Dream of Love (by Joseph Langland), 1986 (exhibited in Sarasota, Fla., 1986, Ga. So. Coll., Statesboro, 1987); commd. etching edits to Collectors Am. Art, N.Y.C., 1956, 58, 61, Internat. Graphic Arts Soc., N.Y.C., 1960, N.Y. Hilton Art Collection, N.Y.C., 1961; one-man shows include Ruth White Gallery, N.Y.C., 1958, Phila. Art Alliance, 1959, Portland (Maine) Mus. Art, 1965, L.I. U., Bklyn., 1973, Smith Coll., Northampton, Mass., 1974, Manatee Art League, Fla., 1980, 91, Sarasota, Fla., 1985, 86, Unity Gallery, Sarasota, 1994; group shows include Mus. Modern Art, N.Y.C., 1958-59, Yale U. Art Gallery, New Haven, 1960, Soc. Am. Graphic Artists nat. and internat. exhbns., 1954, 55, 57, 59, 60, 61, 73, 75, 76, 78, L'Antipoete Galerie Librairie, Paris, 1961, Quito, Ecuador, S.Am., 1987, Fla. Printmakers, 1987, 88, So. Printmakers, U. of S. Ala., 1988, Springfest '89, Bradenton, Fla., 1989, Invitational Manatee Art League, Bradenton, 1992, 93, 94, Soc. Exptl. Artists, Longboat Key, juried 1992, juried Shreveport, La., 1993, Nat. Mus. Women Arts, Washington, 1993-94, Longboat Key Art Ctr., 1994; represented in permanent collections including Met. Mus. Art, N.Y.C., Library of Congress, Nat. Gallery Art, Washington, Phila. Mus. Art, USIA, Bonn, Germany, N.Y. Public Library N.Y.C., Rare Book Rm., William A. Neilson Libr., Smith Coll., Henderson Libr., Ga. So. Coll. Found., Statesboro, Ga., McFarlin Libr., Spl. Collections, U. of Tulsa, 1990, Ward Meml. Collection, Gilkey Ctr. for Graphic Arts, Portland (Oreg.) Art Mus., 1992, Nat. Mus. Women Arts. Recipient prize Boston Printmakers, 1957, Joseph Pennell Meml. medal Phila. Watercolor Club, 1972; Yasuo Kuniyoshi Meml. award, 1978; Am. the Beautiful Fund of N.Y. of Natural Area Council grantee, 1973. Mem. Soc. Am. Graphic Artists (prize 1954, 78), Phila. Water Color Club (prize 1972), Soc. Exptl. Artists Fla., Fla. Printmakers, The So. Graphics Coun., Art Uptown Inc. Gallery (Sarasota, Fla.), Gallery Two (Rockville, Md.). Studio: Graphic Workshop Pleiades Press/ Studio 3014 Ave C Holmes Beach FL 34217

NEUWIRTH, BEBE, dancer, actress; b. Newark, Dec. 31; d. Lee Paul and Sydney Anne Neuwirth; m. Paul Dorman. Student, Juilliard Sch., 1976-77. Appeared on Broadway and internationally as Sheila in A Chorus Line, 1978-81; other stage appearances include West Side Story, 1981, Little Me, 1982, Upstairs at O'Neal's, 1982-83, The Road to Hollywood, 1984, Just So, 1985, Sweet Charity, 1985-87 (Tony award for Best Supporting Actress in a Musical 1985-86), Waiting in the Wings: The Night the Understudies Take the Stage, 1986, Showing Off, 1989, Chicago, 1992, Kiss of the Spider Woman (London), 1993, Damn Yankees, 1994; prin. dancer Dancin', 1982; choregrapher, leading dance role Kicks, 1984; TV series Cheers, 1984-93 (Emmy award for Best Supporting Actress in a Comedy Series 1990, 1991); TV guest appearences Frasier, 1994; TV movies Without Her Consent, 1990, Unspeakable Acts, 1990, Wild Palms, 1993; films Say Anything, 1989, Green Card, 1990, Penny Ante, 1990, Bugsy, 1991, Malice, 1993. Vol. performances for March of Dimes Telethon, 1986, Cystic Fibrosis Benefit Children's Ball, 1986, Ensemble Studio Theater Benefit, 1986, Circle Repertory Co. Benefit, 1986, all in N.Y.C. Democrat. Office: Internat Creative Mgmt 8942 Wilshire Blvd Beverly Hills CA 90211 Office: Internat Creative Mgmt 40 W 57th Str New York NY 10019*

NEUWIRTH, JESSICA ANNE, lawyer; b. N.Y.C., Dec. 10, 1961; d. Robert Samuel and Gloria (Salob) N. BA, Yale U., 1982; JD, Harvard U., 1985. Bar: Mass. 1986, N.Y. 1987. Prodr. Concerts for Human Rights Found., N.Y.C., 1987-90; assoc. Cleary, Gottlieb, Steen & Hamilton, N.Y.C., 1990-93, Kridel & Neuwirth, N.Y.C., 1993—; exec. dir., pres. Equality Now, N.Y.C., 1992—. Mem. nat. adv. com. Physicians for Human Rights, Boston, 1986—. Mem. Assn. of Bar of City of N.Y. (mem. com. on sex and law 1992—, mem. com. on internat. human rights 1988-91), Amnesty Internat. (legal advisor 1985-90, mem. com. on internat. devel. 1990-94). Office: Equality Now Columbus Circle Sta PO Box 20646 New York NY 10023

NEUWIRTH, MARY-ELIZABETH JOAN, librarian; b. Quincy, Mass., Jan. 4, 1933; d. Angelo L. and Margaret (Reynolds) Bianchi; m. Jerome H. Neuwirth, Mar. 10, 1957; children: Roanne Margaret, Jessica Loren. BA, U. Mich., 1955; MS, Simmons Coll., 1959. Libr. Boston Pub. Libbr., 1955-59, Rutgers Preparatory Sch., New Brunswick, N.J., 1959-62; indexer Storrs, Conn., 1962-78; libr., media specialist Bolton (Conn.) Pub. Schs., 1978—; learning resources and tech. facilitator State of Conn. and Bolton Pub. Schs., 1980—. Mem. ALA, Conn. Ednl. Media Assn., Ea. Conn. Librs. Home: 54 Bundy Lane Storrs CT 06269 Office: Bolton Pub Schs 72 Brandy St Bolton CT 06043

NEVANS-PALMER, LAUREL SUZANNE, rehabilitation counselor; b. N.Y.C., Aug. 1, 1964; d. Roy N. and Virginia (Place) Nevans; m. Russell Baird Palmer III, Oct. 12, 1991. BA in English, Secondary Edn. cum laude, U. Richmond, 1986, postgrad., 1989-92; MA in Edn. & Human Devel., George Washington U., 1991, cert. in job devel. and placement, 1992. Group leader S.E. Consortium for Spl. Svcs., Larchmont, N.Y., 1980-85; vocat. instr. Assn. for Retarded Citizens Montgomery County, Rockville, Md., 1986-89; edn. specialist George Washington U. Out of Sch. Work Experience Program, Washington, 1989-90; rsch. asst. George Washington U. Dept. Tchr. Prep. & Spl. Edn., Washington, 1989-91; employability skills tchr., rsch. intern Nat. Rehab. Hosp. Rehab. Engring. Dept., Washington, 1991; vocat./ind. living skills specialist The Independence Ctr., Rockville, Md., 1991-93; leadership team mgr. Career Choice project The Independence Ctr. of No. Va., Arlington, 1993-94; program dir. United Cerebral Palsy of D.C. and No. Va., Washington, 1994—; teaching asst. Rehab. Counseling Program, George Washington U., 1991. Recipient traineeship GWU Counseling Dept., 1990, 91. Mem. Nat. Rehab. Assn., Nat. Rehab Counselors Assn., Nat. Career Devel. Assn., Nat. Career Devel. Assn., Nat. Employment Counseling Assn., Nat. Assn. Ind. Living, Am. Assn. Counseling and Devel., Am. Rehab. Counseling Assn. Democrat. Home: 611 Woodside Pky Silver Spring MD 20910-4247 Office: United Cerebral Palsy 3531 8th St NE Washington DC

NEVELS, SUE POGUE, counselor; b. London, Ky., May 8, 1962; d. William Gerald and Lois Faye (Beckner) Pogue; m. Joety Wayne Nevels, Aug. 3, 1985; 1 child, Tyler Danial. BA in Edn., U. Ky., 1984; MA in Counseling, Ea. Ky. U., 1989, postgrad., 1990. Elem. tchr. Sci. Hill (Ky.) Sch., 1984-89; sch. counselor Pulaski County Schs., Somerset, Ky., 1989—; chair Student Tchr. Asst. Team, Somerset, 1993-94; mem. Transformation Com., Somerset, 1993-94. Author: (learning game) Sticky Situations, 1993. Mem. ACA, NEA, Ky. Sch. Counselors Assn. (membership chair 1993-94, exec. bd. 1993-94), Ky. Counseling Assn. (mem. strategic planning com.), Ky. Assn. Sch. Administrs., Mid-Cumberland Counseling Assn. (pres.-elect), Ky. Edn. Assn., Assn. Assessment Counseling Ky. (sec.-treas.). Democrat. Home: 612 Woodview Dr Somerset KY 42501-6808 Office: Nancy Elem Sch 240 Highway 196 Nancy KY 42544-8824

NEVERS, ELIZABETH EILEEN, substance abuse counselor; b. Wichita, Kans., Feb. 27, 1947; d. Michael Henry and Mary Frances (Compton) Carney; m. Larry Joseph Nevers, Aug. 24, 1968; children: Noel Eileen, Michael Alexander Nawrocki. BS in Edn. summa cum laude, U. Wis., Whitewater, 1973; MSE, U. Kans., 1992. Cert. substance abuse counselor. Adminstrv. instr. Sawyer Coll., Milw., 1974-78; office mgr. Nat. Replacement, Inc., Kansas City, 1978-81, K.C. Racquet Club, Inc., Merriam, Kans., 1982-88; instr. Brown Mackie Coll., Overland Park, Kans., 1989-91; Stop Teen Outpatient program dir. Columbia Health Sys. Inc., Overland Park, Kans., 1992—. Pack leader Boy Scouts Am., Lenexa, Kans., 1985-86; troop leader Girl Scouts USA, Lenexa, Kans., 1981-84. Mem. Am. Counseling Assn., Am. Assn. Marriage and Family Therapists, Assn. for Multicultural Counseling and Devel., Internat. Assn. of Marriage and Family Counselors, Internat. Assn. Addictions and Offender Counselors, Kans. Assn. Marriage and Family Therapists. Roman Catholic. Office: Stop Teen Outpatient Prog 10114 W 105 Ste 100 Overland Park KS 66212

NEVIDJON, BRENDA MARION, nursing administrator; b. Norwalk, Conn., Dec. 22, 1950; d. Carl James and Rosemary (Bibby) N.; m. Benjamin C. Staples, Feb. 28, 1983; 1 child, Jameson. BSN magna cum laude, Duke U., 1972; MSN, U. N.C., 1978. Staff nurse Duke U. Med. Ctr., Durham, N.C., 1972-73, 77-78, nurse clinician, 1973-75; staff nurse Kantonsspital, Basel, Switzerland, 1975-76; head nurse Duke U. Med. Ctr., 1978-81; clin. nurse specialist Cancer Control Agy British Columbia, Vancouver, Can., 1981-83, dir. nursing, 1983-85; mgr. cancer program Providence Med. Ctr., Seattle, 1985-88; clin. dir. cancer ctr. U. Wash. Med. Ctr., Seattle, 1988-89; clin. nurse specialist Virginia MAson Med. Ctr., Seattle, 1989-91; dir. nursing medicine/oncology Duke U. Med. Ctr., 1991-94, assoc. chief oper. officer nursing, 1994—; clin. assoc. Duke U. Sch. Nursing, 1992—; clin. instr. U. Wash. Sch. Nursing, Seattle, 1987-91; asst. prof. U. B.C. Sch. Nursing, 1983-84; clin. instr. Duke U. Sch. Nursing, 1980-91. Editor, ONS News, 1989—; contbr. chpts. to books, articles to profl. jours. Vol., bd. dirs. Am. Cancer Soc., Seattle, 1985-88, ARC, Durham, 1991—. Mem. Am. Orgn. Nurse Execs., N.C. Orgn. Nurse Execs., Oncology Nursing Soc., Internat. Assn. Nurse Editors, Sigma Theta Tau. Democrat. Episcopalian. Office: Duke U Med Ctr Box 3543 Durham NC 27710

NEVILLE, MARGARET COBB, physiologist, educator; b. Greenville, S.C., Nov. 4, 1934; d. Henry Van Zandt and Florence Ruth (Crozier) Cobb; m. Hans E. Neville, Dec. 27, 1957; children: Michel Paul, Brian Douglas. BA, Pomona Coll., 1956; PhD, U. Pa., 1962. Asst. prof. physiology U. Colo. Med. Sch., Denver, 1968-75, assoc. prof., 1975-82, prof., 1982—, dir. med. scientist tng. program, 1985-94. Editor: Lactation: Physiology, Nutrition, Breast Feeding, 1983 (Am. Pubs. award 1984), Human Lactation I, 1985, The Mammary Gland, 1987; contbr. numerous articles to profl. jours. Recipient Rsch. Career Devel. award NIH, 1975, NIH merit award, 1993. Mem. AAAS, Am. Physiol. Soc., Am. Soc. Cell Biology, Internat. Soc. Rsch. in Human Milk and Lactation, Phi Beta Kappa. Office: U Colo Dept Physiology PO Box 240C Denver CO 80262

NEVILLE, MONICA MARY, state assembly program executive; b. Phila., Jan. 4, 1949; d. Edward Joseph and Mary Monica (Auletta) N.; m. William H. Pickens III, May, 1993; children: Jennifer Kathryn Gamber, John Blair Gamber, Jr. Student, Rutgers U., 1967-69; AB, U. Calif., Berkeley, 1977. Intern Gov.s' Office, Sacramento, Calif., 1976-77; press asst. Gov. Edmund G. Brown, Jr., Sacramento, 1977-80; pub. info. officer Protection and Adv., Inc., Sacramento, 1980-81; asst. press sec. Calif. Assembly Speaker Willie L. Brown, Jr., Sacramento, 1981-84; press sec. Speaker Willie L. Brown, Jr., Sacramento, 1984-86, spl. asst., 1986-88; prin. cons. Assembly Floor Analysis Unit, Sacramento, 1988-91; dir. Calif. Assembly Fellows Program, Sacramento, 1991—; coord. Calif. Assembly Intern Program, Sacramento, 1991—. Editor: Jesse Marvin Unruh Assembly Fellowship Jour., 1991—. Mem. Calif. Studies Assn., Sacramento, 1992-94, Sacramento (Calif.) Symphony Assn., 1992-94. Mem. Sacramento Press Club, U. Calif. Berkeley Alumni Assn. (life mem.). Home: 9706 Mira Del Rio Dr Sacramento CA 95827-1321 Office: Assembly Fellow Program Legis Office Bldg 1020 N St Ste 402 Sacramento CA 95814-5624

NEVILLE, PHOEBE, choreographer, dancer, educator; b. Swarthmore, Pa., Sept. 28, 1941; d. Kennith R. and Marion (Eberbach) Balsley. Student, Wilson Coll., 1959-61. Cert. practitioner body-mind centering; registered movement therapist. Instr. Bennington (Vt.) Coll., 1981-84, 87-88; vis. lectr. UCLA, 1984-86. Dancer, choreographer Judson Meml. Ch., N.Y.C., 1966-70, Dance Uptown Series, N.Y.C., 1969, Cubiculo Theatre, N.Y.C., 1972-75, Delacorte Dance Festival, N.Y.C., 1976, Dance Umbrella Series, N.Y.C., 1977, Riverside Dance Festival, N.Y.C., 1976, 78, N.Y. Seasons, 1979—; dancer, artistic dir. Phoebe Neville Dance Co., N.Y.C., 1975—, Jacob's Pillow Splash! Festival, 1988, Dance Theater Workshop Winter Events, 1988. Recipient Creative Artist Public Svc. award, 1975; Nat. Endowment for Arts fellow, 1975, 79, 80, 85-87, 92-94, Choreographic fellow N.Y. Found. for Arts, 1989. Mem. Laban Inst. Movement Studies, Dance Theater Workshop, Body-Mind Centering Assn. (cert. practitioner and tchr.), Internat. Movement Therapy Assn. (registered), Internat. Assn. Healthcare Practitioners. Buddhist. Club: Recluse.

NEVIN, JEAN SHAW, knitwear and jewelry designer; b. Bklyn., Dec. 21, 1934; d. Marshall Robert and Dorothy Frances (Brown) Shaw; m. Robert Stephen Nevin, Dec. 9, 1955. BA in English, SUNY, Albany, 1956. Textbook and freelance editor, 1959-74; printmaker, papermaker Jean Nevin Graphics, Indpls., 1969-84; owner, mgr., knitwear designer Chameleon, Indpls., 1985-88; pres., knitwear designer Knitting Machine Shop, Inc., Indpls., 1988-91; owner Knitwearables, Albuquerque, 1991—; instr. print and paper making Indpls. Art League, 1974-83, exhibits coord., 1969, 73, edn. coord., 1979-80, editor Artifacts, 1968-69, 72-73; editor, pub. Swatchnotes, 1987-91. Exhibited to nat. group shows and galleries prints and handmade paper, 1970-84, garments and jewelry, 1992—; designer wearable art. Mem. Facets Studio Designers. Home and Office: 9641 Mendoza Ave NE Albuquerque NM 87109-6614

NEVINS, LYN, educational supervisor, trainer, consultant; b. Chelsea, Mass., June 9, 1948; d. Samuel Joseph and Stella Theresa (Maronski) N.; m. John Edward Herbert, Jr., May 1, 1979; children: Chrissy, Johnny. BA, U. Mass., 1970; MA, George Washington U., 1975. Cert. tchr., trainer. Tchr. Greenwich (Conn.) Pub. Schs., 1970-74; rschr. Conn. State Dept. Edn., Hartford, 1975-76; rschr., coord. Area Coop. Edn. Svcs., Hamden, Conn., 1976-77; program mgr., trainer Coop. Edn. Svcs., Fairfield, Conn., 1977-83, 87—; trainer, mgr., devel., Beginning Educator Support and Tng.program State Conn., Fairfield, Conn., 1987—; supr. Sacred Heart U., Fairfield, 1992—; mem. bias com. Conn. State Dept. Edn., Hartford, 1981—; mem. vision com. Middlesex Mid. Sch., Darien, Conn., 1993—; mem. ednl. quality and diversity com. Town of Darien, 1993—; cons., trainer Cohen and Assocs., Fairfield, 1981—, Farren Assocs., Annandale, Va., 1992—; freelance cons., trainer, Darien, 1983-87; presenter Nat. Conf. GE, 1980, Career Edn., 1983, Am. Edn. Rsch. Assn., 1991; lectr. in field. Coach, mem. Spl. Olympics, 1993—. Mem. NOW (founder, state coord. edn. 1972-74), ASCD. Home: 4 Hollister Ln Darien CT 06820 Office: Coop Ednl Svcs 785 Unquowa Rd Fairfield CT 06430

NEVINS, SHEILA, television programmer and producer; b. N.Y.C.; d. Benjamin and Stella N.; B.A., Barnard Coll., 1960; M.F.A. (Three Arts fellow), Yale U., 1963; m. Sidney Koch; 1 son, David Andrew. TV producer Great Am. Dream Machine, NET, 1970-72, The Reasoner Report, ABC, 1973, Feeling Good, Children's TV Workshop, 1975-76, Who's Who, CBS, 1977-78; v.p. documentary and family programming HBO, N.Y.C., 1978-82, dir. documentary programming Home Box Office, N.Y.C., 1986—. Bd. dirs. Women's Action Alliance. Recipient Peabody award, 1986, 92, Acad. Award Documentary, 1993, Emmy award, 1994; named Woman of Achievement YWCA, 1991. Mem. Writers Guild Am., Women in Film.

NEW, ANNE LATROBE, public relations, fund raising executive; b. Evanston, Ill., May 10, 1910; d. Charles Edward and Agnes (Bateman) N.; m. John C. Timmerman, Sept. 30, 1933; 1 child, Jan LaTrobe. AB, U. S.C., 1930; postgrad., Hunter Coll., 1930-31, NYU, 1932-33. APR (Accredited Pub. Relatons Practitioner). Editorial asst. Pictorial Review Mag., N.Y.C., 1930-32; copy asst. J. Walter Thompson Co., N.Y.C., 1932-33; sub editor Cosmopolitan Mag., N.Y.C., 1933-37; with Girl Scouts of the U.S., N.Y.C., 1937-57, chief pub. rels. officer, 1945-57; dir. pub. info. edn. Nat. Recreation and Park Assn., 1957-66; special asst. gen. dir. Internat. Social Svc. Am. Branch, N.Y.C., 1966-68; dir. devel. Nat. Accreditation Coun. for Agys. Serving Blind and Visual Handicapped, N.Y.C., 1969-78; pres. Timmerman & New Inc., Mamaroneck, N.Y., 1980—; cons. dept. pub. adminstrn. Baruch Coll., CUNY, 1987—. Author: Service For Givers, The Story of the National Information Bureau, 1983, Raise More Money for Your Nonprofit Organization, 1991; contbr. articles to profl. jours. Mem. Westchester Dem. Com. Westchester County, 1963-67, 89—; bd. dirs. Mamaroneck N.Y. United Fund, 1963-64; chmn. nominating com. LWV, Mamaroneck, 1988, chmn. by-law com., 1989; warden emerita, vestery mem. St. Thomas' Episc. Ch., Mamaroneck. Mem. Pub. Rels. Soc. Am. (bd. dirs. N.Y. chpt. 1958-72), Women Execs. Pub. Rels. (sec. 1962--63), Nat. Soc. Fund Raising Execs. (bd. dirs. greater N.Y. chpt. 1978-84), Phi Beta Kappa (Scarsdale/Westchester Phi Beta Kappa Assn.). Democrat. Office: Timmerman & New Inc 235 S Barry Ave Mamaroneck NY 10543-4104

NEW, CLAUDIA MOSS, hospice social worker; b. Mexia, Tex., Oct. 17, 1941; d. William Thomas and Viola (Reynolds) Moss; m. Noah Edward New Jr., Sept. 22, 1963; 1 child, Courtney Page. AA, Coll. of the Mainland, 1969; BS in Psychology, U. Md., 1984; M in Social Svc. Work, U. Tex., Arlington, 1991. Lic. master social worker, Tex.; cert. biofeedback therapist. Vol. caseworker ARC, Seoul, Korea, 1984-85; exec. dir. DeSoto (Tex.) Community Outreach, 1987-90. Mem. NASW, Assn. for Applied Psyhophysiology and Biofeedback North Tex., Bus. and Profl. Women (pres.), DeSoto Jr. Svc. League, LaMarque Jaycee-ettes (pres.), Pilot Club, Alpha Delta Mu. Democrat. Methodist. Home: 136 Highridge Dr De Soto TX 75115-6222 Office: Vis Nurse Assn 211 W Mulberry Kaufman TX 75142

NEW, ROSETTA HOLBROCK, home economics educator, nutrition consultant; b. Hamilton, Ohio, Aug. 26, 1921; d. Edward F. and Mabel (Kohler) Holbrock; m. John Lorton New, Sept. 3, 1943; 1 child, John Lorton Jr. BS, Miami U., Oxford, Ohio, 1943; MA, U. No. Colo., 1971; PhD, Ohio State U., 1974; student Kantcentrum, Brugge, Belgium, 1992. Cert. tchr., Colo. Tchr. English and sci. Monahans (Tex.) High Sch., 1943-45; emergency war food asst. U.S. Dept. Agr., College Station, Tex., 1945-46; dept. chmn. home econs., adult edn. Hamilton (Ohio) Pub. Schs., 1946-47; tchr., dept. chmn. home econs. East High Sch., Denver, 1948-59, Thomas Jefferson High Sch., Denver, 1959-83; mem. exec. bd. Denver Pub. Schs.; also lectr.; exec. dir. Ctr. Nutrition Info. U.S. Office of Edn. grantee, 1971-73. Mem. Cin. Art Mus., Nat. Trust for Historic Preservation. Mem. Am. Home Econs. Assn., Am. Vocat. Assn., Embroiders Guild Am., Hamilton Hist. Soc., Internat. Old Lacers, Ohio State U. Assn., Ohio State Home Econs. Alumni Assn., Fairfield (Ohio) Hist. Soc., Republican Club of Denver, Internat. Platform Assn., Phi Upsilon Omicron. Presbyterian. Lodges: Masons, Daughters of the Nile, Order of Eastern Star, Order White Shrine of Jerusalem.

NEWBERG, DOROTHY BECK (MRS. WILLIAM C. NEWBERG), portrait artist; b. Detroit, May 30, 1919; d. Charles William and Mary (Labedz) Beck; student Detroit Conservatory Music, 1938; m. William C. Newberg, Nov. 3, 1939; children: Judith Bookwalter Bracken, Robert Charles, James William, William Charles. Trustee Detroit Adventure, 1967-71, originator A Drop in Bucket Program for artistically talented inner-city children. Bd. dirs. Bloomfield Art Assn., 1960-62, trustee 1965-67; bd. dirs. Your Heritage House, 1972-75, Franklin Wright Settlement, 1972-75, Meadowbrook Art Gallery, Oakland U., 1973-75; bd. dirs. Sierra Nevada Mus. Art, 1978-80; bd. dirs. Nat. Conf. Christians and Jews, Gang Alternatives Partnership. Recipient Heart of Gold award, 1969; Mich. vol. leadership award, 1969, Outstanding Vol. award City of Reno, 1989-90. Mem. Nevada Mus. Art, No. Nev. Black Cultural Awareness Soc. (bd. dirs.), Hispanic 500 C. of C. No. Nev., Sierra Art Found, Serra Club of Reno. Roman Catholic. Home: 2000 Dant Blvd Reno NV 89509-5193

NEWBERRY, ALICE MABEL, psychologist, educator; b. Colo., Aug. 10, 1954; m. P. Andrew Newberry, July 29, 1972. BA in Philosophy, Colo. State U., 1979, BS in Computer Sci., 1980; MS in Psychology, U. Utah, 1987, PhD in Clin. Psychology, 1991. Lic. psychologist, Utah. Systems analyst Colo. Divsn. Eastman Kodak, Windsor, 1980-84; computer and statistics cons. Divsn. Social Sci. Rsch. U. Utah, Salt Lake City, 1985-87, Marriner S. Eccles rsch. fellow, 1988-90, postdoctoral fellow Counseling Ctr., 1991-92; psychologist Intermountain Health Care, Salt Lake City, 1992—; adj. asst. prof. psychology U. Utah, Salt Lake City, 1992—. Author: (with others) Women in Families, 1989, Interviewing: The Family Therapy Collection, 1987, Semiotics 1981, 1983; contbr. articles to profl. jours. Mem. APA, Utah Psychol. Assn., Phi Beta Kappa. Democrat. Office: Wasatch Canyons Ctr Counseling 5770 S 1500 W Salt Lake City UT 84123

NEWBERRY, CATHARINE ST. JOHN, human resources specialist; b. Barberton, Ohio, Oct. 3, 1950; d. David K. and Catharine G. (St. John) Davies; m. Veechwin Li, Aug. 9, 1975 (div. Dec. 1980); m. Milton G. Newberry, Aug. 30, 1986. BA in History, Swarthmore Coll., 1973; MS in Human Resource Devel., Am. U., 1983. Asst. dir. admissions Inst. for Paralegal Tng., Phila., 1973-77; tng. and devel. adminstr. Scott Paper Co., Chester, Pa., 1977-79; human resources adminstr. SmithKline Beckman Corp., Phila., 1980-81, site pers. mgr., 1981-82, mgr. tng. and orgn. devel., 1982-87, dir. human resources, 1987-89; v.p. human resources Connaught Labs., Inc., Swiftwater, Pa., 1989—. Mem. bd. dirs. Monroe County United Way, Stroudsburg, Pa., 1992—. Mem. Pharm. Mfrs. Assn. (program chmn. 1992-93, chairperson 1993-94). Home: PO Box 28 Stroudsburg PA 18360-0028 Office: Connaught Labs Inc HC 1 Swiftwater PA 18370

NEWBERRY, ELIZABETH CARTER, greenhouse and floral company owner; b. Blackwell, Tex., Nov. 25, 1921; m. Weldon Omar Newberry, Sept. 24, 1950 (dec. Nov. 1984); 1 child. Student Hardin Simmons U., 1938-39. Office mgr. F. W. Woolworth, Abilene, Tex., 1939-50; acct. Western Devel. & Investment Corp., Englewood, Colo., 1968-72; owner, operator Newberry Bros. Greenhouse and Florist, Denver, 1972—; bd. dirs. Western Devel. and Investment Corp. Englewood, Colo., 1979-87. Pres. Ellsworth Elem. Sch. PTA, Denver, 1961-62; v.p. Hill Jr. High Sch. PTA, Denver. Home: 201 Monroe St Denver CO 80206-5505 Office: Newberry Bros Greenhouse 201 Garfield St Denver CO 80206-5518

NEWBERY, ILSE SOFIE MAGDALENE, German language educator; b. Darmstadt, Germany, Nov. 15, 1928; came to U.S., 1965; d. Otto and Charlotte (Brill) Brusius; m. A.C.R. Newbery, Dec. 28, 1954; children: Martin Roger, Frances Janet. Diplom akad. gepr. Übersetzer, U. Mainz, Germany, 1949; Staatsexamen Höh. Lehrfach, U. Frankfurt, Germany, 1954; PhD, U. B.C., Vancouver, Can., 1964. Part-time lectr. Queen's U., Belfast, Ireland, 1955-56; grad. asst. U. B.C., 1958-62; lectr. U. Calgary, Can., 1964-65; asst. prof. Georgetown (Ky.) Coll., 1965-67, assoc. prof., 1968-83, prof. German, 1983—, chair langs. dept., 1989-94; examiner Goethe Inst., 1983-87; oral proficiency tester ACTFL, 1985-87; rsch. in German exile lit. Author software in field, 1989. Founding mem. internat. folk ensemble Singing Hons, Lexington, 1977—. Recipient KCTFL Project award, Ky. Coun., 1994, Rollie Graves Tech. Excellence award, 1993. Mem. Am. Assn. Tchrs. German (v.p. Ky. chpt. 1979-81, pres. 1981-83), Am. Coun. Tchrs. Fgn. Langs., Ky. Coun. Tchrs. Fgn. Langs. (bd. dirs. 1979-83).

NEWBILL, SALLIE PULLER, state senator; b. Roanoke Rapids, N.C., June 23, 1940; d. Timberlake Meredith and Mary Gillam (Williams) Puller; m. Thomas Carroll Newbill, July 2, 1966; children: Sallie Gillam, Thomas Carroll III. MA, U. Va., 1961; MEd, Ga. State U., 1972. Tchr. San Diego Unified Sch. System, 1961-63, Tauranga Girls Coll., New Zealand, 1963-64, Bangkok Internat. Sch., Thailand, 1964-65; journalist Richmond (Va.) Times Dispatch, 1965-66; tchr. Fulton County, Atlanta, 1966-68; research writer Ga. State Dept. Edn., Atlanta, 1968-70; state senator Ga. Gen. Assembly, 1986—; v.p. S&N Enterprises, Atlanta, 1984-86; state news dir. Rep. House Caucus, Atlanta, 1983-86. First woman Rep. elected to Ga. Senate, 1986; v.p. Rep. Women, Atlanta, 1985-86, Fulton County Reps., Atlanta, 1985-86. Mem. Sandy Springs C. of C. Methodist. Clubs: Greater Marietta Rep. Womens; Rep. Women of Northside. Office: GA State Senate State Capitol Atlanta GA 30334*

NEWBORN, KAREN B., lawyer; b. Cleve., Oct. 30, 1944. BA, Goucher Coll., 1966; JD summa cum laude, Cleve. State U., 1976. Bar: Ohio 1976, U.S. Dist. Ct. (no. dist.) Ohio 1976, U.S. Ct. Appeals (6th cir.) 1978, U.S. Dist. Ct. (ea. dist.) Mich. 1984, U.S. Supreme Ct. 1988. Ptnr. Baker & Hostetler, Cleve.; asst. law dir. City Cleve., 1976-79; adj. instr. teaching trial advocacy, 1987. Mem. ABA, Ohio State Bar Assn., Cleve. Bar Assn. (bd. trustees 1989-92, chair commn. women in the law 1987-90), Inn of Ct. Office: Baker & Hostetler 3200 Nat City Ctr 1900 E 9th St Cleveland OH 44114-3303

NEWBRAUGH, KATHERINE DRIVER, elementary school counselor; b. Harrisonburg, Va., Sept. 11, 1949; d. Ira Joseph and Virginia Milton (McIlhany) Driver; m. John Steiner Newbraugh, May 6, 1972; children: Sarah Katherine, Kathryn Anne. BS in Home Econs., Madison Coll., Harrisonburg, 1971; MA in Counseling, W.Va. U., 1992. Cert. sch. counselor. Tchr. RESA VIII, Martinsburg, W.Va., 1971-74, Project Headstart, Berkeley Springs, W.Va., 1978-79; tchr. kindergarten Morgan County Schs., Berkeley Springs, W.Va., 1980-90, elem. sch. counselor, 1990—. Sec. Teen Action Bd., Berkeley Springs, 1990—; cons. Morgan County Child Sexual Abuse Task Force, Berkeley Springs, 1993—; bd. dirs. Boys and Girls Club. Mem. W.Va. Counseling Assn. Democrat. Methodist. Office: Morgan County Schs 200 Myers Street Ext Berkeley Springs WV 25411-1043

NEWBURGE, IDELLE BLOCK, psychotherapist; b. Bklyn.; m. Lawrence G. Newburge; children: Geri, Scott. AB magna cum laude, U. Miami, 1972, MEd, 1973. Lic. mental health counselor; nat. cert. counselor. Acting supr., lead counselor Office Vocat. Rehab., Miami, 1973-79, supr. mental health unit, 1985-87; vocat., edn. specialist Spectrum Programs, Inc., Miami, 1979-81, outpatient supr., 1981-85; psychotherapist Alan Jaffe, PhD and Assoc., Lauderhill, Fla., 1985-88, A.C.S. Pvt. Counseling, Plantation, Fla., 1988-91, KPK Counseling Svcs., Plantation, 1992—; community adv. bd. Fellowship House, Miami, 1985-87; chmn., com. mem. Parent Resource Ctr., Miami, 1979-82. Active Nat. Museum for Women in the Arts (charter), Washington, 1991—, U.S. Holocaust Meml. Museum (charter), Washington, 1991—, Greenpeace, Humane Soc., Nat. Wildlife Fedn., NOW. Fellow Am. Bd. Cert. Managed Care Providers (cert. rehab. counselor); mem. NASW, ACA, Am. Mental Health Counselors Assn., Fla. Alcohol and Drug Abuse Assn., Fla. Soc. Psychotherapists, Mental Health Assn. Broward County (Listen to Children Program cons. 1988—), Mental Health Assn. Broward County (bd. dirs., 1st vice chair), Fla. Soc. Clin. Hypnosis, Lauderhill C. of C. (charter), Plantation C. of C., Women's Forum (charter). Office: KPK Counseling Services 8030 Peters Rd D106 Plantation FL 33324

NEWCOMB, KATHY RAE, elementary education educator; b. Warren, Ohio, Nov. 4, 1952; d. Richard Franklin and Thelma Pearl (Dawson) Palmer; m. Thomas Lee Newcomb, July 28, 1984; 1 child, Matthew Ray. BS, Kent State U., 1975; MEd, Westminster Coll., 1982. Cert. elem. educator, Ohio. Tchr. 1st grade Bloomfield-Mesopotamia Local Schs., Mesopotamia, Ohio, 1975-79; tchr. 3rd grade Bloomfield-Mesopotamia Local Schs., Mesopotamia, 1979-82, tchr. 1st grade, 1982—. Active Parkman (Ohio) Congl. Ch., 1984—; mem. James A. Garfield Scholarship Fund, Garrettsville, Ohio, 1990—. Recipient Class Act Tchr. award, 1994; grantee several tchr. grants Bloomfield-Mesopotamia Schs., 1978—. Mem. Ohio Edn. Assn., Parkman (Ohio) C. of C., N. Am. Wildlife Park Found. Office: Bloomfield-Mespo Local Schs 4466 Kinsman Rd Mesopotamia OH 44439

NEWCOMB, NANCY S., bank executive; b. 1945. Joined Citicorp, N.Y.C., 1967, various mgmt. positions, 1967-82, sr. credit officer N.Am. Investment Bank, 1982-85, sr. exec. v.p. AMBAC, 1986-87, sr. corporate officer, 1988-92, exec. v.p., 1992—. Office: Citicorp 1 Penns Way New Castle DE 19720-2437*

NEWCOMBE, BARBARA TRIPNER, librarian, indexer; b. L.A., June 17, 1923; d. Ferdinand and Gladys Elizabeth (McCleary) Tripner; m. Jack Newcombe, Apr. 14, 1946 (div. 1975); children: Laura, Scott, Tod, Polly. BA magna cum laude, Pomona Coll., Claremont, Calif., 1945; MA, U. Calif., Berkeley, 1946; MLS, Cath. U. Am., 1976. Libr. asst. European Communities Delegation, Washington, 1970-73; libr., div. editor Chgo. Tribune, 1973-85; libr. Ctr. for Investigative Reporting, San Francisco, 1986—. Author: Paper Trails, 1990; contbr. articles to profl. jours. Pomona Coll. alumni scholar, 1945, U. Calif.-Berkeley Chinese Cultural scholar, 1945; named Libr. of the Yr. Soc. Profl. Journalists of No. Calif., 1992. Mem. Spl. Librs. Assn., Calif. Libr. Assn., Am. Soc. Indexers (editor Golden Gate chpt. 1986-89), Progressive Librs. Guild, Phi Beta Kappa. Home: 539 Merritt Ave #4 Oakland CA 94610

NEWELL, BARBARA WARNE, economist, educator; b. Pitts., Aug. 19, 1929; d. Colston E. and Frances (Corbett) Warne; m. George V. Thompson, June 15, 1954 (dec. 1954); m. George S. Newell, June 9, 1956 (dec. 1964); 1 dau., Elizabeth Penfield. BA, Vassar Coll., 1951; MA, U. Wis., 1953, PhD, 1958, D. Pub. Svc.; LHD, Trinity Coll., 1973, Lesley Coll., 1978; LLD, Central Mich. U., 1973, Williams Coll., 1974, Rollins Coll., 1981, Butler U., 1983, Monmouth Coll., 1986; DLitt, Northeastern U., 1974, Mt. Vernon Coll., 1975, Lesley Coll., 1978, Denison U., 1978, Eckerd Coll., 1982, Gettysburg Coll., 1982, Dennison U., 1978; D.Adminstrn., Purdue U., 1976; DSc, Fla. Inst. Tech., 1981; LHD, Eckerd Coll., 1982; LLD, Butler U., 1983; D Pub. Service, Alaska Pacific U., 1986; DsPS, U. Md., 1987. Govt. intern NLRB, 1948, Hudson Shore Labor Sch., 1949; research, teaching asst. U. Wis., 1951-54, asst. to chancellor, 1965-67; research, teaching asst., assoc. U. Ill., 1954-59; asst. prof., then assoc. prof. econs. Purdue U., 1959-65; asst. to pres., assoc. prof. econs. U. Mich., Ann Arbor, 1967-71, acting v.p. student affairs, 1968-70; prof. econs., assoc. provost grad. study and research U. Pitts., 1971; pres. Wellesley (Mass.) Coll., 1972-79; U.S. rep. with rank ambassador to UNESCO, Paris, 1979-81; chancellor State U. System Fla., Tallahassee, 1981-85; Regents prof. Fla. State U., 1985—; vis. scholar Harvard U., 1985-86, vis. lectr., 1986-87; cons. Fla. Dept. Labor, 1991—, State Job Tng. Coordinating Com., 1991; mem. Fla. Supreme Ct. Racial and Ethnic Bias Study Commn., 1990-92. Author: Chicago and the Labor Movement, 1961, (with Lawrence Senesh) The Pulse of the Nation, 1961, Our Labour Force, 1962; editorial bd.: (with Lawrence Senesh) Labor History, 1975—; mem. editorial bd. Jour. for Higher Edn. Mgmt., 1984—; contbr. articles and revs. to profl. jours. and mags. Mem. Disting. Review Panel Gov's. Challenge to State Colls. of N.J., 1985-87; mem. Task Force on Edn. at Earlham Coll., 1985-86; mem. Gov's. Council on High Technology, Fla., 1983-85; mem. Council of 100, Fla., 1981-85; steering com. of pres. to assist the Boston Sch. Dept., 1975-79; U.S. del. World Conf. on Women Leaders, Israel, 1979, Conf. on Women's Edn., Orgn. of Am. States, Buenos Aires, 1973; sec. County of Dane (Wis.) Community Action Council, 1964-66; bd. overseers Boston Symphony Orch., 1974-79, bd. dirs. WGBH-TV, Boston, 1974-79, County of Dane (Wis.) Community Welfare Council, 1964-66; Consortium on Financing Higher Edn., 1974-76, vice chmn., 1975-76; mem. ad hoc com. Future of State Univs. Nat. Assn. State Univs. and Land Grant Colls., N.Y., 1984-85, Internat. U. Consortium for Telecommunications in Learning, 1985-86; chmn. Nat. Commn. on Med. Care for Women of Am. Coll. Ob-Gyn, 1970-72; advisor to bd. of trustees Wesleyan U., Middletown, Conn., 1970-74, So. Regional Edn. Bd., 1981-85; trustee U. Pitts., 1973-76, Brookings Inst., 1973-79, Carnegie Endowment for Internat. Peace, 1973—, Carnegie Found. for the Advancement of Tchg., 1976-79, , Am. Coll. of Paris, 1980, UN Internat. Research and Tng. Inst. for the Advancement of Women, 1986—, Com. for Econ. Devel., 1979—; mem. Pres.'s Commn. on Future of U. Mass., 1988-89; bd. dirs. Mass. Mutual Life Ins. Co., 1981-86, DeVry Corp., 1985-87, Americans for thr Universality of UNESCO, 1984—; mem. Fla. Edn. and Employment Coun. for Women and Girls, 1992—. Wells fellow, 1981. Mem. Soc. for Values in Higher Edn., Nat. Assn. Ind. Colls. and Univs. (bd. dirs. 1977-80), Assn. Am. Colls. (mem. task force on presdl. selection and career devel. 1974). Club: Cosmopolitan (N.Y.C.). Office: Florida State U Dept of Econ Tallahassee FL 32306-2045

NEWELL, CHARLDEAN, public administration educator; b. Ft. Worth, Oct. 14, 1939; d. Charles Thurlow and Mildren Dean (Looney) N. BA, U. North Tex., 1960, MA, 1962; PhD, U. Tex., 1968; cert., Harvard U., 1988. Instr. U. North Tex., Denton, 1965-68, asst. prof., 1968-72; assoc. prof., dir. Fedn. North Tex. Area Univs., Denton, Dallas, 1972-74; assoc. prof., assoc. v.p. acad. affairs U. North Tex., Denton, 1974-76, assoc. prof., chair dept. polit. sci., 1976-80, prof. polit. sci., 1980-92, assoc. v.p., spl. asst. to chancellor, 1982-92, regents prof. pub. adminstrn., 1992—; cons. Miss Bd. Trustees State Instns. Higher Learning, Jackson, 1983-84, Ednl. Testing Svc., Princeton, N.J., 1980, 82, 85; bd. dirs. Mcpl. Clks. Ednl. Found., San Dimas,

Calif.; bd. regents Internat. City/County Mgmt. Assn., U. Washington. Author: (with others) Essentials of Texas Politics, 1995, Texas Politics, 1993, The Effective Local Government Manager, 1993, City Executives: Leadership Roles, Work Characteristics and Time Management, 1989; contbr. articles to profl. jours. Chair charter rev. com. City of Denton, 1978-79; mem. adv. com. Ann's Haven Hospice, Denton, 1981-85; mem. exec. coun. Epsic. Diocese Dallas, 1985-88; mem. Civil Svc. Commn., City of Denton, 1989—, chmn., 1992—. Recipient Elmer Staats Career Pub. Svc. award Nat. Assn. Sch. Pub. Affairs Adminstrn., 1993. Mem. Am. Soc. Pub. Adminstrn. (sect. chmn. 1982-83, mem. editorial bd. 1985-88), Internat. Pers. Mgmt. Assn. (regional program com. 1982-83), Am. Polit. Sci. Assn., Southwestern Polit. Sci. Assn. (sec., treas. 1975-79), Denton C. of C., Denton Tennis Assn., Pi Sigma Alpha (exec. coun. 1988-92). Democrat. Home: 709 Mimosa Dr Denton TX 76201-0858 Office: U North Tex PO Box 5367 Denton TX 76203-0367

NEWELL, MARY-BETH CHRISTINA, nursing administrator; b. Homestead, Pa., Feb. 22, 1961; d. Albert Peter Skowronek and Loretta H. (Gayda) Davis; m. Randy Lee Newell, Sept. 22, 1984 (div. 1986); children: Haley Christine, Brian Augustus. Diploma, Washington (Pa.) Hosp. Sch. Nursing, 1982; student, Am. River Coll., 1989-91. RN, Calif. Psychiat. nurse I Woodville State Hosp., Carnegie, Pa., 1982-83; staff nurse Timken Mercy Med. Ctr., Canton, Ohio, 1983-87; staff nurse II Woodland (Calif.) Meml. Hosp., 1987-91; nurse cons. Scott Health Care, Sac, Calif., 1991-93; dir. nursing svcs. Fairmont Rehab. Hosp., Lodi, Calif., 1993—; preceptor Timken Mercy Med. Ctr., Canton, 1985-87; CPR instr. Woodland Meml. Hosp., 1989-91; advisor Lodi (Calif.) Unified Sch. Dist., 1993—. Instr. cmty. edn. Spkrs. Bur., Woodland, Calif., 1990. Mem. Nat. Assn. Dirs. Nursing Adminstrs., Coun. Long Term Nurses (membership chairperson), Wound, Ostomy and Continence Nurses. Republican. Roman Catholic. Office: Fairmont Rehab Hosp 950 S Fairmont Ave Lodi CA 95240

NEWELL, NANCY LEE, solid waste process engineer; b. Roxboro, N.C., Dec. 16, 1948; d. Hayden Wheeler Jr. and Doris (Smith) N.; m. Russell Kent Clayton, May 31, 1969 (div. Nov. 1993); children: Matthew James Clayton, Marianna B. Clayton Long. Student, Meredith Coll., 1967-69; BA in Botany, U. N.C., 1978; BS in Civil Engring., N.C. State U., 1985. Registered profl. engr., N.C. Asst. engr. W.M. Piatt &Co., Durham, N.C., 1986-88; solid waste process engr. City of Durham Sanitation, 1988—. Mem. Eno River Assn., Durham, 1993-94, Pinecone Traditional Music, Raleigh, N.C., 1990-94. Mem. ASCE, Solid Waste Assn. N.Am., N.C. Recycling Assn., Durham Engrs. Club (treas. 1990-93, pres. 1993-94), Chi Epsilon. Office: City of Durham 101 City Hall Plaza Durham NC 27701

NEWELL, REBECCA GAIL, psychiatric nurse; b. Savannah, Ga., July 4, 1953; d. Henry Morgan and Julia (Rogers) Grimes; m. E. Andrew Newell, June 14, 1980. AA, Armstrong State Coll., 1973, BS in Nursing, 1980; postgrad. Sch. Grad. Nursing, Med. Coll. Ga., 1980-81; cert. psychiat. nurse. RN, Ga. With Charter Savannah (Ga.) Behavioral Health Sys., staff nurse, 1973-74, head nurse, 1974-75, coord. utilization rev. and staff devel., 1975-80, asst. dir. nursing, dir. quality assurance and risk mgmt., 1980-82, dir. nursing, 1982-89, adminstr. adult psychiat. svcs., 1989-91, nursing adminstr., 1991-93, chief nursing officer and adminstr. patient care svcs., 1993, adminstr. clin. svcs., chief nursing officer, 1993—; mem. adj. faculty Armstrong Coll. Sch. Nursing, 1982, Coun. Recruitment and Retention of Nurses, 1978—; profl. staff exchange cons. Named one of Outstanding Young Women Am., 1984, 85; mem. adv. coun. Sta. WGEC-FM Radio; mem. pers. com. Calvary Bapt. Temple. Recipient Leadership award Vocat. Indsl. Clubs Am., 1971, cert. of merit U. Ga. Mem. Ga. Orgn. Nurse Execs., Ga. Hosp. Assn., Armstrong State Coll. Hon. Soc. for Nursing, Ga. So. Coll. Hon. Soc. for Nursing, Concerned Women For Am., Ga. Right to Life Assn., Am. Ctr. for Law and Justice, Sigma Theta Tau. Baptist. Home: 11 Ramsgate Rd Savannah GA 31419-3215 Office: 1150 Cornell Ave Savannah GA 31406-2702

NEWELL, SHARON LYNN, physical education educator; b. Oxnard, Calif., Feb. 14, 1950; d. Ruth Nana (Pool) Horton; 1 child, Amber Lynn Gould. BA, Calif. Bapt. Coll., Riverside, 1971; MS, Azusa Pacific U., 1985. Cert. tchr., Calif. Tchr. phys. edn. Mission Mid. Sch., Riverside, 1971—, dept. head, 1987—; tchr. spl. edn. Summer Sch., Riverside County Schs., 1989—; tchr. Teens Learn Choices Mission Mid. Sch., 1986—; tennis coach; softball, track and intramural sports coach. Democrat. Home: 1440 W Edgehill Rd Apt 36 San Bernardino CA 92405-5144 Office: Mission Mid Sch 5961 Mustang Ln Riverside CA 92509-4260

NEWHALL, JANE WARD, psychologist; b. South Orange, N.J., Feb. 16, 1940; d. Norman S. Ward and Dorothy Ward (Williams) Gordon; m. John Harrison Newhall, July 15, 1961; children: Carol, Thomas, Daniel. BA, Bryn Mawr Coll., 1962, MA in Edn. and Child Devel., 1984, PhD in Human Devel., 1987; respecialization in clin. psychology, Pacific Grad. Sch. Psychology, 1989. Cert. sch. psychologist; lic. psychologist. Staff psychologist Bryn Mawr (Pa.) Child Study Inst., 1986-87; psychologist Agoraphobia & Anxiety Treatment Ctr., Bala Cynwyd, Pa., 1990-91; staff psychologist Phila. Child Guidance Ctr., 1991-93, psychology tng. faculty, 1991—, unit mgr., 1993—; clin. assoc. faculty dept. psychiatry U. Pa. Sch. Medicine, Phila., 1993—; pvt. practice specializing in therapy, psychol. testing and consulting Profl. Svcs. Group, Phila. Child Guidance Ctr., 1991—. Mem. APA, Pa. Psychol. Assn., Orton Dyslexia Soc., Gulph Mills Golf Club, Merion Cricket Club. Home: 414 Righters Mill Rd Narberth PA 19072 Office: Phila Child Guidance Ctr 34th St and Civic Ctr Blvds Philadelphia PA 19104-4322

NEWHOUSE, NANCY RILEY, newspaper editor; b. Bellingham, Wash.; d. Fenwick Charles and Elizabeth (Grace) Riley; m. John Newhouse, Sept. 27, 1961 (div. 1970); m. Michael Iovenko, Mar. 6, 1983. BA, Vassar Coll., 1958. Sr. editor N.Y. Mag., N.Y.C., 1970-75, House & Garden Mag., N.Y.C., 1976; successively home editor, style editor and travel editor N.Y. Times, N.Y.C., 1976—. Editor: Hers: Through Women's Eyes, 1985; editor Hers column N.Y. Times, 1976-92; mem. adv. bd. Vassar Quar., Poughkeepsie, N.Y., 1985—. Recipient Penney-Mo. Newspaper award U. Mo. Sch. Journalism, 1982-83. Mem. The Century Assn. (admissions com.), Women's Forum N.Y. Office: NY Times Co 229 W 43rd St New York NY 10036-3913

NEWKIRK, INGRID, animal rights activist; b. Surrey, Eng., 1949; m. Steve Newkirk, 1967 (div. 1980). Poundmaster D.C., 1978; dir. cruelty investigations Washington Humane Soc., D.C., 1978-80; co-founder (with Alex Pacheco) People for the Ethical Treatment of Animals, D.C., 1980—, also nat. dir. Author: Save the Animals! 101 Easy Things You Can Do, 1990. Office: PETA Box 42516 Washington DC 20015*

NEWLAND, RUTH LAURA, small business owner; b. Ellensburg, Wash., June 4, 1949; d. George J. and Ruth Marjorie (Porter) N. BA, Cen. Wash. State Coll., 1970, MEd, 1972; EdS, Vanderbilt U., 1973; PhD, Columbia Pacific U., 1981. Tchr. Union Gap (Wash.) Sch., 1970-71; ptnr. Newland Ranch Gravel Co., Yakima, Wash., 1970—, Arnold Artificial Limb, Yakima, 1981-86; owner, pres. Arnold Artificial Limb, Yakima and Richland, Wash., 1986—; ptnr. Newland Ranch, Yakima, 1969—. Mem. Yakima Greenway Found., Ctr. Marine Conservation, Public Citizen, We The People, Nat. Humane Edn. Soc., Ams. Responsible TV; contbg. mem. Dem. Nat. Com.; charter mem. Nat. Mus. Am. Indian. George Washington scholar Masons, Yakima, 1967. Mem. NAFE, NOW, Am. Orthotic and Prosthetic Assn., Internat. Platform Assn., Nat. Antivivisection Soc. (life), Vanderbilt U. Alumni Assn., George Peabody Coll. Alumni Assn., Columbia Pacific U. Alumni Assn., World Wildlife Fund, Nat. Audubon Soc., Greenpeace, Irish Nat. Caucus Found. (contbg.), Mus. Fine Arts, Humane Soc. U.S., Wilderness Soc., Nature Conservancy, People for Ethical Treatment of Animals, Amnesty Internat., Pub. Citizen, Wilderness Soc., The Windstar Found., Rodale Inst., Sierra Club (life), Emily's List. Democrat. Home: 2004 Riverside Rd Yakima WA 98901-9526 Office: Arnold Artificial Limb 9 S 12th Ave Yakima WA 98902-3106

NEWLANDS, SHEILA ANN, consumer products company executive, controller; b. Worcester, Mass., Mar. 8, 1953; d. Joseph and Doris Edna (Bachand) N.; m. Domenic V. Testa Jr., Oct. 2, 1976 (div. 1983). BA summa cum laude, Worcester State Coll., 1975; cert. interior design, Bunkerhill Community Coll., 1976; MS, Simmons Coll., 1976; MBA, Suffolk U., 1983. Cert. real estate broker, Mass.; CPA, Wash. Dir. health scis. library Lynn Hosp., Mass., 1976-78, Mt. Auburn Hosp., Cambridge, 1978-81; assoc. fin. analyst Data Gen., Westboro, Mass., 1981-82, fin. analyst, 1982-84, sr. fin. analyst, 1984; fin. analyst Stimson Lane Wine and Spirits, Woodinville, Wash., 1985-86, dir. fin., 1986-91, v.p., contr., 1991—; guest lectr. Simmons Coll. Sch. Library Sci., Boston, 1980-81. Mem. Burlington (Mass.) Conservation Commn., 1978-84. Mem. Fin. Mgmt. Honor Soc., Phi Alpha Theta. Home: PO Box 514 Issaquah WA 98027-0514 Office: Stimson Lane Wine & Spirits One Stimson Ln Woodinville WA 98072

NEWMAN, BARBARA MAE, retired special education educator; b. Rockford, Ill., July 16, 1932; d. Greene Adam and Emma Lorene (Fields) N. BS Edn., No. Ill. U., 1973. Cert. elem. edn. K-8 tchr., spl. edn. (blind and p.s.) K-12 tchr. Exec. sec. Rockford Art Assn., 1961-70; tchr. Title 1 Rockford Pub. Sch. Dist. #205, 1975-76, tchr. vision impaired, 1977-91. Feature editor (Rock Valley Coll. newpaper) The valley Forge, 1970; contbg. writer (Rockford Coll. history) A Retrospective Look, 1980. Alto St. Bernadette adult choir, Rockford, 1958—; holder 5 offices Am. Bus. Women's Assn., Forest City chpt., 1963-70; vol. Winnebago Ctr. for the Blind, Rockford, 1965-70. Named Woman of Yr., Am. Bus. Women's Assn., Forest City chpt., Rockford, 1966; scholar Ill. State Scholarship Commn., No. Ill. U., 1970-73. Mem. Ill. Ret. Tchrs. Assn., Cath. Woman's League of Rockford, Womanspace. Roman Catholic.

NEWMAN, BARBARA POLLOCK, journalist and author TV and print; b. N.Y.C., June 15, 1939; d. Irving G. and Jeanne (Ginsberg) Pollock; div.; 1 child, Penelope. BA, Mount Holyoke Coll., 1960; MA, Columbia U., 1962. Legis. asst. Rep. James Scheuer, Washington, 1964-65, Mayor John Lindsay, N.Y.C., 1965-67; mem. President's Nat. Adv. Commn. on Civil Disorders, Washington, 1967-79; reporter, interviewer Nat. Pub. Radio, N.Y.C., 1971-78; investigative reporter, producer "20/20" ABC News, Washington, 1978-81; exec. producer Jack Anderson Confidential, Washington, 1982-83; pres. Praetorian Productions, Inc., Washington, 1984—; moderator Nat. Town Meetings, Pub. TV, 1975-78; Hostess McNeill Lehrer Report, Aug. 1977; mem. adv. bd. Washington Journalism Review, 1977-80. Author: The Covenant: Love and Death in Beirut, 1989; contbr. news and editl. articles to newspapers and popular jours.; sr. prodr. Now It Can Be Told, 1991; prodr. documentaries for investigative reports Arts and Entertainment Network; prodr. Channel 4 and Ctrl. TV, London. Recipient Peabody award thorugh Nat. Pub. Radio, 1972, Ohio State award, 1973, 74, 76, Silver Gavel award, ABA, 1974, Cadmus award, Am. Lebanese League, 1981; Emmy nominee, 1981 for investigative reporting. Home: 5336 29th St NW Washington DC 20015-1332

NEWMAN, BETTY LOUISE, accountant; b. Llano, Tex., Dec. 1, 1946; d. Travis Alger and Edith Lucile (Tate) N.; m. Vernon George Mangold (div. July 1981); 1 child, Ian Keith. Student, San Antonio Jr. Coll., 1965-66; BBA, U. Tex., San Antonio, 1985. Data claims analyst Blue Cross/Blue Shield, San Antonio, 1980-82; regional sec., acct. BioMed. Applications, San Antonio, 1982-83; with acctg. dept. Comprehensive Bus. Services, Boerne, Tex., 1983-84; acct. Cadwallader Ins. Agy., San Antonio, 1986, Data Processing Support, Inc., San Antonio, 1986-87, Archive Retrieval Systems, Inc., San Antonio, 1986-87; pvt. practice acctg. San Antonio, 1987—; acct. atty., 1989-92. Vol. Boy Scouts Am., San Antonio, 1978-89, unit commr., 1989; bd. dirs. San Antonio Met. Ministries, 1987-90. Scholar Women in Bus., 1983. Mem. NAFE, Nat. Assn. Accts. (assoc. bd. dirs. 1988-90), Inst. Mgmt. Accts., Leon Springs Bus. Assn., Am. Luth. Women. Home and Office: 25403 Brewer Dr San Antonio TX 78257-1139

NEWMAN, CAROL L., lawyer; b. Yonkers, N.Y., Aug. 7, 1949; d. Richard J. and Pauline Frances (Stoll) N. AB/MA summa cum laude, Brown U., 1971; postgrad. Harvard U. Law Sch., 1972-73; JD cum laude, George Washington U., 1977. Bar: D.C., 1977, Calif., 1979. With antitrust div. U.S. Dept. Justice, Washington and L.A., 1977-80; assoc. Alschuler, Grossman & Pines, L.A., 1980-82, Costello & Walcher, L.A., 1982-85, Rosen, Wachtell & Gilbert, 1985-88, ptnr., 1988-90; ptnr. Keck, Mahin & Cate, 1990-94; pvt. practice, L.A., 1994—; adj. prof. Sch. Bus., Golden Gate U., spring 1982. Candidate for State Atty. Gen., 1986; city commr. L.A. Bd. Transp. Commrs., 1993—. Mem. ABA, State Bar Calif., L.A. County Bar Assn., L.A. Lawyers for Human Rights (co. pres. 1991-92), Log Cabin (bd. dirs. 1992—), Calif. Women Lawyers (bd. dirs., bd. govs. 1991-94), Order of Coif, Phi Beta Kappa.

NEWMAN, CLAIRE POE, corporate executive; b. Jacksonville, Fla., Dec. 12, 1926; d. Leslie Ralph and Gertrude (Criswell) Poe; student Fla. State Coll. for Women, 1944-45, Tulane U., 1971-73; m. Robert Jacob Newman, July 3, 1948; children—Leslie Claire, Robert, Christopher David. Co-owner Vineyards in Burgundy, France. Mem. various coms. New Orleans Mus. Art. Mem. Women's com. New Orleans Philharmonic Symphony Assn., 1961—, chmn. orch. rels. com., 1961-63; chmn. New Orleans Easter Seal Drive, 1963; La. trustee Nat. Soc. Crippled Children and Adults, 1963-65. Mem. Women's Aux. C. of C., New Orleans Soc. Archeol. Inst. Am. (v.p. 1972-74), Confrérie des Chevaliers du Tastevin, Sigma Kappa. Club: Metairie Country, Kitzbuehel (Austria) Golf, Golden Skibook (Kitzbuehel), Pass Christian (Miss.) Yacht; Ski (Arlberg). Home: 1111 Falcon Rd Metairie LA 70005-4129 Other: Tiemberg, Kitzbuehel Austria

NEWMAN, CONSTANCE BERRY, museum administrator; b. Chgo., July 8, 1935; d. Joseph Alonzo and Ernestine (Siggers) B.; m. Theodore Roosevelt Newman, July 25, 1959 (div. 1980). AB, Bates Coll., 1956; BSL, U. Minn., 1959; JD (hon.), Bates Coll., 1972, Amherst Coll., 1980; LHD (hon.), Central State U., 1991. Dir. VISTA, Washington, 1971-73; commr. Consumer Product Safety Commn., Washington, 1973-76; asst. sec. U.S. HUD, Washington, 1976-77; pres. The Newman & Hermanson Co., Washington, 1977-82; cons. Govt. of Lesotho, 1987-88; dir. nat. voter coalition Bush-Quayle '88, Washington, 1988; dir. Office Pers. Mgmt., Washington, 1989-92; under sec. Smithsonian Instn., Washington, 1992—; mem. adj. faculty John F. Kennedy Sch. Govt., Harvard U., Cambridge, Mass., 1979-82. Contbr. articles to profl. jours. Mem. Adminstrn. Conf. U.S., Washington, 1973-76, 1989—; commr. M.L. King Fed. Holiday Commn., Washington, 1989; chmn. Def. Adv. Com. on Women in the Svcs., Washington, 1985-86; trustee Community Coll. Balt., 1985-89; adv. to chmn. 1988 Rep. Nat. Conv., New Orleans, 1988; bd. overseers Morehouse Coll. Sch. Medicine, Atlanta, 1976-77; dir. Radio Free Europe, Radio Liberty, Washington, 1979-82. Recipient Pub. Svc. award Ohio State U., 1991. Mem. NAACP, Exec. Women in Govt. (founding mem.), Evaluation Rsch. Soc. (founding mem.). Office: Smithsonian Inst 1000 Jefferson Dr SW Rm 219 Washington DC 20560*

NEWMAN, DIANA S., community foundation executive; b. Toledo, June 15, 1943; d. Fred Andrew and Thelma Elizabeth (Hewitt) Smith; m. Dennis Ryan Newman, Feb. 15, 1964; children: Barbara Lynn Newman LaBine, John Ryan, Elizabeth Anne. Student, Oberlin Coll., 1961-64. Asst. treas. Marble Cliff Quarries Co., 1964-68; community vol., 1968-83; dir. Ohio Hist. Found., Columbus, 1983-90; v.p. advancement The Columbus (Ohio) Found., 1990—. Chair governing com. First Community Ch., 1983-88; bd. dirs. LWV, 1968-72, Ohio Mus. Assn., 1985-90, Nat. Soc. Fundraising Execs. Cen. Ohio chpt., Columbus, 1983-88, Crittenton Family Svcs., Columbus, 1992—; founder Franklin County Com. on Criminal Justice, Columbus, 1972; past pres. Jr. League Columbus. Mem. Ctrl. Ohio Planned Giving Coun. (bd. dirs. 1990—), Columbus Female Benevolent Soc. (bd. dirs. 1984—). Home: 1944 Chatfield Rd Columbus OH 43221-3702 Office: The Columbus Foundation 1234 E Broad St Columbus OH 43205-1463

NEWMAN, JANE, advertising agency executive; b. Woking, Surrey, Eng., Oct. 22, 1947; came to U.S., 1978; d. Ronald William and Victoria (Brady) N.; 1 child. BA, Sussex U., Eng., 1969; MA, Lancaster U., Eng., 1970. Account planner Boase Massimi & Pollitt, London, 1970-78; account mgr. Needham Harper & Steers, Chgo., 1978-79, Ammirati & Puris, N.Y.C., 1979-81; vice chmn. Chiat/Day Advt., N.Y.C., 1981-93; ptnr. Merkley Newman Harty Advt. Agy., N.Y.C., 1993—. Office: Merkley Newman Harty 200 Varick St New York NY 10014-4810

NEWMAN, JANET ELAINE, elementary education educator; b. Savannah, Ga., Dec. 4, 1947; d. Oral Kenneth and Mary Gertrude (Flynn) N. AA, R.I. Jr. Coll., Providence, 1967; A in B., R.I. Jr. Coll., 1976; BA, Mt. St. Joseph Coll., 1969. Elem. tchr. Coventry (R.I.) Sch. Dept., 1970-73; supr. elec. soldering Harwood Mfg., Providence, 1973-80; elem. tchr. Providence Sch. Dept., 1980—; mem. Legal/Edn. Partnership, 1990—, CAP/CAST Team, 1993—; mem. adv. bd. West Broadway Schoolwide Project, 1994—, Sch. Improvement Project, 1994—. Bd. dirs. Woodland Estates Condominium Assn., 1988—; tchr. CCD, St. Martha's Ch., 1985-87. Fellow R.I. Writing Consortium, 1990, Taft Inst. at R.I. Coll., 1991. Roman Catholic. Home: 1145 Hartford Ave Johnston RI 02919-7128 Office: Providence Sch Dept 797 Westminster St Providence RI 02903-4018

NEWMAN, JANICE MARIE, business owner, lawyer; b. N.Y.C., Aug. 11, 1951; d. Robert and Clara (White) Swindler; m. Roger Kevin Newman, Jan. 20, 1972 (div. 1980); 1 child, Germaine M. Swindler-Newman (dec.). BA, Smith Coll., 1973; JD, Rutgers U., 1980. Bar: N.J. 1983, U.S. Supreme Ct. 1987. Adminstrv. asst. Corp. Ann. Reports, N.Y.C., 1972-73; pub. rels. asst. Lippincott & Margulies, N.Y.C., 1973; journalist Essex Forum Newspaper, East Orange, N.J., 1973; pub. info. officer City of Newark, 1974-82; producer, host Newark and Reality TV show, Newark, 1974-85; asst. communications dir. Mayor's Office, Newark, 1982-86; legis. liaison, publ. info. officer N.J. Div. on Women, Trenton, 1988-90, acting dir., 1990, women svcs. coord., 1990-91; environ. issues specialist N.J. Dept. Environ. Protection and Energy, Trenton, 1991-92; comm. specialist Dept. Environ. Protection, Lawrenceville, N.J., 1992—; pvt. practice South Orange, N.J., 1994—; mem. working group N.J. Supreme Ct. Domestic Violence, 1994; pres. JM Newman & Assocs.; chair Interest on Lawyers Trust Accounts, 1995—, mem., 1986—. Mem. editorial bd. N.J. Lawyer mag., 1987—, The Voice, Episcopal Diocese of Newark, 1992-95; design editor: The Voice, 1993-94; contbr. articles to mags. Bd. dirs. Instrns. Exposures Experiences, 1983-87, Greater Newark Conservancy; 2d v.p. Women's Polit. Caucus, N.J., 1991-92, 1st v.p., 1992-93; appt. to N.J. Supreme Ct. Com. on Women in the Cts., 1990—, Com. on Character, 1992—, N.J. Women Vets. Adv. Com., 1993-94; lay reader, eucharistic lay min., parliamentarian, 1992-94, Episc. Diocese of Newark; sr. warden, House of Prayer Espisc. Ch., Newark, 1992. Recipient Pub. Svc. award N.J. Voice Newspaper, 1977, Achievement award Minority Contractors and Craftsmen Trade Assn., 1982, award Nat. Council Negro Bus. and Profl. Women Legal Achievement, 1987, award N.J. Unit Nat. Assn. Negro Bus. and Profl. Women's Clubs, 1987; named to Outstanding Young Women Am. U.S. Jaycees, 1984. Mem. Nat. Assn. Media Women (rec. sec. 1985-87, Media Woman of Yr. award 1985, pres. N.J. cpt. 1986-88), N.J. State Bar Assn. (Young Lawyers Div. Community Svc. award 1989, mem. pub. rels. com. 1987—, 2d vice-chair women's rights sect., 1990-92, 1st vice chair women's rights sect., 1992-93, chair, 1993-95, bd. trustees minorities in the profession sect.), N.J. State Bar Found. (trustee 1994—), N.J. Women Lawyers Assn. (pres. 1986-88, bd. trustees pub. rels. com., entertainment & arts com., Essex County Bar Assn., Nat. Coun. Negro Women, Garden State Bar Assn., Essex County Women Lawyers (trustee 1991-94). Democrat. Episcopalian. Home: 355 Scotland Rd South Orange NJ 07079 also: 4 Sloan St South Orange NJ 07079-1714

NEWMAN, JEANNE JOHNSON, sociolinguistic educator, researcher; b. Twin Falls, Idaho, Dec. 8, 1939; d. Glen Everett Johnson and Alta Ruth (Egbert) Kizer; children: Ronald, Javier. BA, Calif. State U., 1986, MA, 1988; PhD, U. Pa., 1993. ESL tchr., coord. edn. dept. Tulare County Community Action Agy., Visalia, Calif., 1967-69; dir. community devel., dir. planning and evaluation Kings County Community Action Orgn., Hanford, Calif., 1970-75; program planner Community Action Program Tulare County, Visalia, Calif., 1975-79; edn. rev. instr., program specialist, tchr. PROTEUS Adult Tng., Inc., Visalia, Calif., 1979-84; student asst., tutor Calif. State U., Fresno, 1985-86, rsch. asst., 1986-87; rsch. asst. U. Pa., Phila., 1988-89; tchr., workshop facilitator Svc., Commitment, Success Bus. and Tech. Sch., Phila., 1990-93; rsch. assoc. Vocational Rsch. Inst., divsn. Jewish Employment & Vocational Svcs., Phila., 1993—; rsch. papers presented Second Lang. Rsch. Forum, Eugene, Oreg., L.A., 1989, 90, Boston U. Lang. Devel., 1989, 90, TESOL Internat., N.Y.C., 1991, Balt., 1994, Pa. chpt. PENN-TESOL East, 1994; cons. SCS Bus. and Tech. Sch., Phila., 1990—; mem. staff Literacy Rsch. Ctr., newsletter editor, 1990; contbg. mem. Working Papers in Edml. Linguistics, editor, 1989-91. Author rsch. papers. Visitor Presbyn. Home Elderly, Phila., 1988-91; mem., organizer Tri-County Sr. Citizens, Commn. on Aging, Fresno, Kings and Tulare County, 1980-85. Calif. State U. Alumni Assn. scholar, 1987-88, U. Pa. Grad. Sch. Edn. scholar, 1988-93. Mem. TESOL Internat. (vol. Pa. chpt. 1989-94), Am. Assn. Ret. Educators, Am. Assn. Applied Linguistics, AAUW, NAFE, Internat. Platform Assn., Modern Lang. Assn. Home: 4918 Osage Ave Philadelphia PA 19143-1609 Office: Vocat Rsch Inst Ste 1502 1528 Walnut St Fl 1502 Philadelphia PA 19102-3619

NEWMAN, JOAN CLASSETTI, college administrator; b. L.A., July 3, 1955; d. Benny and Irene Classetti; m. J. Stephen Newman, Oct. 4, 1974. BEd, U. Tenn., Knoxville, 1978, EdS in Ednl. Psychology, 1984. Supply/substitute tchr. Knox Bd. Edn., Knoxville, 1978-81; counselor, educator, dir. State Tech. Inst. of Knoxville, 1981-87; dir. acad. assessment and advisement Pellissippi State Tech. C.C., Knoxville, 1987—; mem. adv. com. Tech. Access Ctr., Knoxville, 1994—; primary advisor Phi Theta Kappa, Knoxville, 1983—. GED Preparation grantee Tenn. Divsn. of Edn., 1991, ABE Profl. Devel. grantee, 1992. Mem. Am. Coll. Counseling Assn., Learning Disabled Assn. (bd. dirs.), Full Circle (adv. com. 1992), Assn. on Higher Edn. and Disability, Tenn. Assn. Adults and Continuing Edn. Office: Pellissippi State Tech CC 10915 Hardin Valley Rd Knoxville TN 37932-1412

NEWMAN, JOAN MESKIEL, lawyer; b. Youngstown, Ohio, Dec. 12, 1947; d. John F. and Rosemary (Scarmuzzi) Meskiel; m. Charles Andrew Newman, Aug. 8, 1971; children: Anne R., Elyse S. BA in Polit. Sci., Case-Western Reserve U., 1969; JD, Washington U., St. Louis, 1972, LLM in Taxation, 1973. Bar: Mo. 1972. Assoc. Lewis & Rice, St. Louis, 1973-80, ptnr., 1981-90; ptnr. Thompson & Mitchell, St. Louis, 1990—; adj. prof. law Washington U. Sch. Law, St. Louis, 1975-92; past pres., mem. Midwest Pension Conf., St. Louis chpt.; lectr. in field. Chmn. bd. dirs. Girl Scout Coun. Greater St. Louis, 1988-92, officer, 1978-92; mem. bd. dirs. and exec. com. Girl Scouts of U.S.A., 1993—; chmn. bd. dirs. Met. Employment and Rehabilitation Svcs., 1994—; bd. dirs. Jewish Fedn. St. Louis, 1991—, Jewish Ctr. Aged, 1990-92; chmn. bd. dirs. Women of Achievement, 1993—; mem. community wide youth svcs. panel United Way Greater St. Louis, 1992—; fin., futures task force Kiwanis Camp Wyman, 1992-93; mem. nat. coun. Washington U. Sch. Law, 1988-91; chmn. staff blue ribbon fin. com. Sch. Dist. Clayton, 1986-87; vol. Women's Self Help Ctr. Named Woman of Achievement St. Louis, 1991. Mem. Mo. Bar Assn. (staff pension and benefits com. 1991—), Bar Met. St. Louis (past chmn. taxation sect.), St. Louis Forum, Order of Coif (hon.). Office: Thompson & Mitchell 1 Mercantile Ctr Ste 3300 Saint Louis MO 63101-1622

NEWMAN, JULLIANA, marketing executive; b. Huntington, N.Y., June 5, 1957; d. Coleman and Lillian (Saboe) Newell; m. John Sherfy Newman, Nov. 7, 1988; children: Ana, Anders, Hayley. AA, Suffolk County Community, Selden, N.Y., 1978; BA, Queens (N.Y.) Coll., 1980; postgrad., CUNY, 1980-82. Prodn. editor Plenum Press, N.Y.C., 1982-83; mng. editor LeJacq Pub., N.Y.C., 1984-86; mng. editor/project dir. Audio Visual Med. Mktg., N.Y.C., 1986-88; editorial dir. Haymarket Doyma, N.Y.C., 1988-90; dir. healthcare communication Macmillan Healthcare Info., Florham Park, N.J., 1990-91; communications specialist PCS, Inc., Scottsdale, Ariz., 1991-93; v.p. mktg. Diagnostek, Inc., Albuquerque, N.Mex., 1993—; founder Jour. of Outcomes Mgmt., 1994; editl. dir. Diagnostek Report, 1993—, PRN: Information as Needed, 1993—; cons. Nat. Asthma Edn. Program, Bethesda, Md., 1991, Asthma and Allergy Found., Washington, 1991, Pres.'s Coun. on Phys. Fitness and Sports, Washington, 1991. Cert. editor of Life Scis. Vol. Pres.'s Coun. on Phys. Fitness and Sports, Washington, 1991—. Ednl. grantee Connaught Labs., 1991, Allen & Hanburys, Research Triangle Park, N.C., 1991, 92. Mem. Coun. of Biology Editors, Am. Med. Writers Assn., NAFE, Am. Heart Assn., Arthritis Found., Nat. Council on Prescription Drug Programs. Democrat. Lutheran. Office: Diagnostek Inc 4500 Alexander Blvd NE Albuquerque NM 87107

NEWMAN, KATHARINE DEALY, author, consultant; b. Phila., Aug. 17, 1911; d. Creswell Victor and Harriet Elizabeth (Hetherington) Dealy; m. Morton Newman, May 11, 1946 (div. 1968); children: Deborah Silverstein, Blaze. BS in Edn. summa cum laude, Temple U., 1933; MA in English, U.

Pa., 1937, PhD in English, 1961. Cert. secondary and coll. English educator, Commonwealth of Pa. Tchr. Phila. High Schs., 1933-46, 49-50; asst. prof. U. Minn., Mpls., 1946-47, Temple U. C.C., Phila., 1959; assoc. prof. Moore Coll. Art, Phila., 1961-63; tchr. Abington (PA.) High Sch., 1963-67; prof. West Chester (Pa.) State U., 1967-77; cons. Inst. for Ethnic Studies, West Chester U., 1975-77; exch. prof. Cheyney State (Pa.) U., 1971, San Dieguito Adult Sch., 1993-94; cons. in field. Author: The Gentleman's Novelist: Robert Plumer Ward, 1765-1846, 1961, The American Equation: Literature in a Multi-Ethnic Culture, 1971, Ethnic American Short Stories, 1975, The Girl of the Golden West, 1978, Never Without a Song, 1995; contbr. articles to profl. jours. Named Outstanding Bd. Mem. Jr. League, 1987; Coordinating Coun. Literary Mags. Editor fellow, 1980. Mem. MLA (emeritus), Soc. for Study of Multi-Ethnic Lit. of U.S. (founder, officer 1973, editor newsletter 1973-77, editor MELUS jour. 1977-81, editor emeritus 1983—, Contbn. award 1982), Inst. for Ethnic Studies (founder, chmn. 1975-77), Episc. Svc. Alliance (co-founder 1978, bd. dirs. 1978-87, v.p. 1982, 86, pres. 1983-84, cert. appreciation 1987). Democrat. Episcopalian. Home: 910 Bonita Dr Encinitas CA 92024-3805

NEWMAN, KATHLEEN TERESA, administrator; b. Denver, Apr. 21, 1949; d. Richard Edwin and Helen Virginia (Sweetland) N. BS in Microbiology, Calif. State Polytech U., 1971. Med. tech. blood bank Swedish Med. Ctr., Englewood, Colo., 1971-73; lab. dir. Littleton (Colo.) Large Animal Clinic, 1973-87; lab. mgr. Vet. Svcs. Inc., Broomfield, Colo., 1987—. Mem. Am. Soc. Clin. Pathology, Colo. Assn. Clin. Med. Labs., Vet. Lab. Assn., Arabian Horse Registry. Office: Vet Svcs Inc 2150 W 6th Ave # F Broomfield CO 80020-7116

NEWMAN, LINNAEA ROSE, horticulturist; b. Milw., Sept. 23, 1953; d. Arthur Fred and Katherine Elnora (Cook) N. BS, U. Wis., 1977. Cert. interior horticulturist, cert. performax cons. Grower Shroeder's Flowerland, Green Bay, Wis., 1977-78; with installation Tropical Plant Rentals, Inc., Prarie View, Ill., 1978, with spl. svc., 1978-84, mgr. edn. and rsch., 1984-88; pres. Linnaea Newman & Assocs., Mundelein, Ill., 1989—. Author: Interior Horticulture A Training Manual, 1990, (with others) Retail Store Planning and Design Manual, 1986; contbr. articles to profl. jours. Named one of Outstanding Young Women Am., 1985. Mem. Entomol. Soc. Am., Internat. Soc. Arboriculture, Nat. Assn. Women in Horticulture (v.p. 1986-87), Nat. Coun. Interior HortiCulture Cert. (bd. gov. 1982-88, vice chmn. 1985-86, chmn. 1986-88), Ohio Florists Assn. (mem. planning com. 1983, bd. dirs. 1990-93), Assoc. Landscape Contractors Am. (interior plantscape divsn., edn. com. 1987—). Home: 1051 N Midlothian Rd Mundelein IL 60060-1234 Office: Linnaea Newman Assocs 1051 N Midlothian Rd Mundelein IL 60060-1234

NEWMAN, MARGARET ANN, nursing educator; b. Memphis, Oct. 10, 1933; d. Ivo Mathias and Mamie Love (Donald) N.; BSHE, Baylor U., 1954; BSN, U. Tenn., Memphis, 1962; MS, U. Calif., San Francisco, 1964; PhD, NYU, 1971. Dir. nursing, asst. prof. nursing Clin. Research Center, U. Tenn., 1964-67; asst. prof. N.Y.U., 1971-75, assoc. prof., 1975-77; prof. in charge grad. program and research dept. nursing Pa. State U., 1977-80, prof. nursing, 1977-84; prof. nursing U. Minn., 1984—; disting. resident Westminster Coll., Salt Lake City Utah, 1991. Travelling fellow New Zealand Nursing Ednl. & Rsch. Fund, 1985; Am. Jour. Nursing scholar, 1979-80; recipient Outstanding Alumnus award U. Tenn. Coll. Nursing, 1975, Disting. Alumnus award NYU Div. Nursing, 1984; Disting. Scholar in Nursing award NYU Div. Nursing, 1992, Sigma Theta Tau Founders Rsch. award, 1993, Nursing Scholar award St. Xavier U., 1994. Fellow Am. Acad. Nursing. Author: Theory Development in Nursing, 1979; Health as Expanding Consciousness, 1986, 2nd edit., 1994; editor: (with others) Source Book of Nursing Research, 1973, 2d edit., 1977. Research on patterns of person-environment interaction as indices of health as expanding consciousness; also models of profl. practice. Office: 6-101 Health Scis Unit F 308 Harvard St SE Minneapolis MN 55455-0353

NEWMAN, MARY ALICE, county official; b. Newark, Mar. 8, 1946; d. Stanley L. and Estelle C. (Forrest) Senk; m. Jack David Newman, Oct. 7, 1967; children: Jonathan Christopher, Alison Marie. AA, Newark State Coll., Union, N.J., 1967. Editor R.L. Polk, Portland, Oreg., 1969-71; clk. U.S. Forest Svc., Portland, 1971-74; sec. Def. Contract Adminstrn., Portland, 1974-76; vets. svcs. clk. VA, Portland, 1976-82; intake officer Clackamas County Community Corrections, Oregon City, Oreg., 1982-84; vets. svc. officer Clackamas County Vets. Svcs., Oregon City, 1984—. Co-author: The Horsekeeper, 1985; editor Union Label newsletter, 1980-82, VA Employee newsletter, 1980-82. Mem. Clackamas County Horse Adv., 1989—; judge Oreg. 4-H Horse Program, 1990—; chmn. dressage program Clackamas County 4-H Horse Program, 1989—; chmn. Oreg. State 4-H Dressage Program, 1991—; dist. commr. Lake Oswego Pony Club, Oregon City, 1989—; treas. Oreg. region U.S. Pony Clubs, Oregon City, 1988-92; leader 4-H Club, 1985—. Recipient Minuteman Flag and Star award U.S. treas. Dept., 1980, Svc. award West Linn VFW Post, 1987,. 4-H Leader of Yr. award Clackamas County 4-H Ext., 1990, 92; named County Vets. Svc. Officer of Yr. Oreg. Dept. Vets. Affairs, 1993. Mem. Oreg. County Vets. Svc. Officers (exec. bd. 1988-90, v.p. 1990-91, pres. 1991-94), Nat. Assn. Atomic Vets., Western Paraders Assn. (3d v.p. 1988-92, 2d v.p. 1993—). Home: 20500 S Ridge Rd Oregon City OR 97045-9645 Office: Clackamas County Vets Svcs 719 Main St Oregon City OR 97045-1814

NEWMAN, MURIEL KALLIS STEINBERG, art collector; b. Chgo., Feb. 25, 1914; d. Maurice and Ida (Nudelman) Kallis; m. Albert H. Newman, May 14, 1955; 1 son by previous marriage, Glenn D. Steinberg. Student, Art Inst. Chgo., 1932-36, Ill. Inst. Tech., 1947-50, U. Chgo., 1958-65. hon. life trustee, benefactor Met. Mus. Art, N.Y.C., mem. vis. com. dept. 20th Century Art, mem. acquisitions com., 1981—, mem. decorative arts com., 1989; also Costume Inst. Dir., 20th Century Painting and Sculpture Com., Art Inst. Chgo., 1955-80, governing mem. inst., 1955—, major benefactor, 1979—; pioneer collector Am. abstract expressionist art, 1949—, major show of collection, Met. Mus. Art, N.Y.C., 1981, also show of personal collection of costumes and jewelry, 1981. Bd. govs. Landmarks Preservation Council, Chgo., 1966-78; mem. woman's bd. U. Chgo., 1960-81, Art Inst. Chgo., 1953—; trustee Mus. Contemporary Art, 1970—, benefactor, 1970—; trustee Chgo. Sch. of architecture Found., 1971—, Archives Am. Art, 1976—; mem. bd. Bright New City Urban Affairs Lecture Series, 1966—. Recipient Scroll Recognition of Public Service U.S. Dept. State, 1958. Mem. Antiquarian Soc. of Art Inst. Chgo., Chgo. Hist. Soc. (mem. guild 1958—). Clubs: Arts (Chgo.), Casino (Chgo.).

NEWMAN, NANCY MARILYN, ophthalmologist, educator, consultant, inventor, entrepreneur; b. San Francisco, Mar. 16, 1941. BA in Psychology magna cum laude, Stanford U., 1962, MD, 1967. Diplomate Am. Bd. Ophthalmology. NIH trainee neurophysiology Inst. Visual Scis., San Francisco, 1964-65; clin. clk. Nat. Hosp. for Nervous and Mental Disease, London, 1966-67; intern Mount Auburn Hosp., Cambridge, Mass., 1967-68; NIH trainee neuro-ophthalmology, from jr. asst. resident to sr. asst. resident to assoc. resident dept. ophthalmology sch. medicine Washington U., St. Louis, 1968-71; NIH spl. fellow in neuro-ophthalmology depts. ophthalmology and neurol. surgery sch. medicine U. Calif., San Francisco, 1971-72, clin. asst. prof. ophthalmology sch. medicine, 1972; asst. prof., chief divsn. neuro-ophthalmology Pacific Med. Ctr., San Francisco, 1972-73, assoc. prof., chief, 1973-88; physician, cons. dept. neurology sch. medicine U. Calif., VA Med. Ctr., Martinez, Calif., 1978—; prof. dept. spl. edn. Calif. State U., San Francisco, 1974-79; vis. prof. Centre Nat. D'Ophtalmologie des Quinze-Vingts, Paris, 1980; clin. assoc. prof. sch. optometry U. Calif., Berkeley, 1990—; bd. dirs., adv. bd. Frank B. Walsh Soc., 1974-91, Rose Resnick Ctr. for the Blind and Handicapped, 1988-92, Fifer St. Fitness, Larkspur, 1990-92; Internat. Soc. for Orbital Disorders, 1983—, North Calif. Soc. Prevention of Blindness, 1978-88, North African Ctr. for Sight, Tunis, Tunisia, 1988—; pres., CEO Minerva Medica; cons. in field. Author: Eye Movement Disorders; Neuro-ophthalmology: A Practical Text, 1992; mem. editoral bd. Jour. of Clin. Neuro-ophthalmology, Am. Jour. Opthalmology, 1980-92, Soc. Francaise d'Ophtalmogie, Ophthalmology Practice, 1993—; contbr. numerous articles to profl. jours. Recipient NSPI award Sch. Instrnl. Materials Ophthalmology, Merit award Internat. Eye Found., fellow 1971; Smith-Kettlewell Inst. Vis. Scis. fellow, 1971-72. Mem. AMA (leader Calif. del. continuing med. edn. 1982, 83), San Francisco Med. Soc., Calif. Med. Assn. (sub com. med. policy coms. 1984—, chair com. on accreditation continuing med. edn. 1981-88, chair quality care rev. commn. 1984), Assn. for Rsch. in Vision and Ophthalmology, Pan Am. Assn. of Ophthalmology, Soc. of Heed Fellows, Pacific Coast Oto-Ophthalmology Soc., Lane Medical Soc. (v.p. 1975-76), Internat. Soc. of Neuro-Ophthalmology (founder), Cordes Soc., Am. Soc. Ophthalmic Ultrasound (charter), Orbital Soc. (founder), West Bay Health Systems Agy., Oxford Opthalmology Soc., Pacific Physician Assocs., Soc. Francaise D'Ophtalmologie (mem. editorial bd. jour.). Home: 819 Spring Dr Mill Valley CA 94941-3924

NEWMAN, PATRICIA ANNE, nurse anesthesia educator; b. New Orleans, Aug. 25, 1941; d. Merwyn James and Yvonne Louise (Cannon) Woodson; m. Robert Charles Newman Sr., Dec. 9, 1967 (div. Dec. 1975); 1 child, Robert Charles Jr. Diploma in nursing, Mercy Hosp., New Orleans, 1961; cert. in nurse anesthesia, Charity Hosp., New Orleans, 1963; BA in Health Care, Edn., Ottawa U., 1978; MS in Nurse Anesthesiology, Xavier U., 1992. Cert. RN anesthetist. Staff nurse anesthetist Hotel Dieu Hosp., New Orleans, 1963-70, Oschsner Found. Hosp., New Orleans, 1970-71, Houston Anesthesia Assocs., 1976-81, East Jefferson Hosp., Metairie, La., 1971-76; staff nurse anesthetist, chief nurse anesthetist Stamford (Conn.) Anesthesia Assocs., 1981-91; instr. clin. anesthesia Charity Hosp./Xavier U. Sch. Nurse Anesthesiology, New Orleans, 1991—; adj. instr. in grad. sch. Xavier U., New Orleans, 1992—. Mem. Coun. for Pub. Interest in Anesthesia (chair 1991-92), Am. Assn. Nurse Anesthetists (mgmt. com. 1991-92, nominating com. 1988-89, minutes com. 1985-86, 92-93), La. Assn. Nurse Anesthetists (pub. rels. com. 1992), Conn. Assn. Nurse Anesthetists (pres., v.p., various chairs coms.). Roman Catholic. Home: 4007 Saint Elizabeth Dr Kenner LA 70065-1642 Office: Xavier U Charity Hosp Sch Nurse Anesthesiology 1532 Tulane Ave New Orleans LA 70112-2802

NEWMAN, PAULINE, federal judge; b. N.Y.C., N.Y., June 20, 1927; d. Maxwell Henry and Rosella N. B.A., Vassar Coll., 1947; M.A., Columbia U., 1948; Ph.D., Yale U., 1952; LL.B., NYU, 1958. Bar: N.Y. 1958, U.S. Supreme Ct. 1972, U.S. Ct. Customs and Patent Appeals 1978, Pa. 1979, U.S. Ct. Appeals (3d cir.) 1981, U.S. Ct. Appeals (fed. cir.) 1982. Research chemist Am. Cyanamid Co., Bound Brook, N.J., 1951-54; mem. patent staff FMC Corp., N.Y.C., 1954-75; mem. patent staff FMC Corp., Phila., 1975-84, dir. dept. patent and licensing, 1969-84; judge U.S. Ct. Appeals (fed. cir.), Washington, 1984—; bd. dir. Research Corp., 1982-84; program specialist Dept. Natural Scis. UNESCO, Paris, 1961-62; mem. State Dept. Adv. Com. on Internat. Indsl. Property, 1974-84; lectr. in field. Contbr. articles to profl. jours. Bd. dirs. Med. Coll. Pa., 1975-84, Midgard Found., 1973-84; trustee Phila. Coll. Pharmacy and Sci., 1983-84. Mem. ABA (council sect. patent trademark and copyright 1983-84), Am. Patent Law Assn. (bd. dirs. 1981-84), U.S. Trademark Assn. (bd. dirs. 1975-79, v.p. 1978-79), Am. Chem. Soc. (bd. dirs. 1972-81), Am. Inst. Chemists (bd. dirs. 1960-66, 70-76), Pacific Indsl. Property Assn. (pres. 1979-80). Clubs: Vassar, Yale. Office: US Ct Appeals 717 Madison Pl NW Washington DC 20439-0002*

NEWMAN, PHYLLIS, adult education educator, psychologist; b. N.Y.C., June 23, 1931; d. Arthur and Augusta (Cohen) Deutsch; m. Stan Newman, Dec. 10, 1967; 1 child, Allen. BS in Indsl. Labor Rels., Cornell U., 1952; MS in Edn.-Psychology, profl. diploma, St. John's U., Jamaica, N.Y., 1976. Tchr. N.Y.C. Bd. Edn., 1963-83, psychologist, 1983-86; instr. adult edn. Pima Community Coll., Green Valley, Ariz., 1988—, Pima County Adult Edn., Tucson, 1989—; psychologist, counselor, N.Y.C., 1978-86; owner, mgr. Transitions Assocs., seminar condrs., N.Y.C. and Green Valley, 1991—. Author: Transitions: A Woman's Guide to Successful Retirement, 1991. Precinct committeewoman Green Valley Dem. Com., 1989—; del. Ariz. Dem. Com., 1989—. Mem. AAUW (chmn. ednl. fund 1989—). Home and Office: 1545 Calle del Media Tucson AZ 85704

NEWMAN, RACHEL, magazine editor; b. Malden, Mass., May 1, 1938; d. Maurice and Edythe Brenda (Tichell) N.; m. Herbert Bleiweiss, Apr. 6, 1973 (div. Apr. 1989). B.A., Pa. State U., 1960; cert., N.Y. Sch. Interior Design, 1963. Accessories editor Women's Wear Daily, N.Y.C., 1964-65; designer, publicist Grandoe Glove Corp., N.Y.C., 1965-67; assoc. editor McCall's Sportswear and Dress Merchandiser mag., N.Y.C., 1967; mng. editor McCall's You-Do-It Home Decorating, 1968-70, Ladies Home Jour. Needle and Craft mag., N.Y.C., 1970-72; editor-in-chief Am. Home Crafts mag., N.Y.C., 1972-77; fashion dir. Good Housekeeping mag., N.Y.C., 1977-78; home bldg. and decorating dir. Good Housekeeping mag., 1978-82; editor-in-chief Country Living mag., 1978—; founding editor Country Cooking mag., 1985—, Dream Homes mag., 1989—, Country Kitchens mag., 1990—, Country Living Gardener Mag., 1993—. Pa. State U. Alumni fellow, 1986; recipient Cir. of Excellence award IFDA, 1992, YMCA Hall of Fame, 1992; named Disting. Alumni Pa. State U., 1988. Mem. N.Y. Fashion Group, Nat. Home Fashions League, Am. Soc. Interior Designers, Am. Soc. Mag. Editors. Office: Country Living 224 W 57th St New York NY 10019-3203

NEWMAN, SHARON ANN, principal; b. Denver, Sept. 25, 1946; d. Paul G. and Agnes J. (Hillesheim) Schneible; m. John G. Newman, June 30, 1973; children: Michael, Lisa. BA in Speech, Coll. Mt. St. Joseph, Cin., 1969; MAT in Liberal Studies, Lewis and Clark Coll., Portland, Oreg., 1992. Textbook editor Nat. Textbook Co., Chgo., 1972; tchr. speech and drama Seton High Sch., Cin., 1968-69; tchr. 6th grade St. Therese Sch., Aurora, Colo., 1979-70; tchr. speech and English Seton High Sch., Pueblo, Colo., 1970-71; tchr., head speech dept. Jefferson County Pub. Schs., Denver, 1971-74; tchr. grades 7 and 8 Shakopee (Minn.) Cath. Middle Sch., 1983-84; tchr., team leader Regis High Sch., Denver, 1985-87; dir. admissions Jesuit High Sch., Portland, 1988-90; prin. St. Thomas More Sch., Portland, 1992—; speaker, cons. in field. Author newspaper columns, booklets, books for local use. Mem. Cin. Human Rels. Commn., 1967. Mem. ASCD, AAUW, Nat. Assn. Elem. and Secondary Prins., Nat. Cath. Edn. Assn., Nat. Middle Level Assn., N.W. Women in Ednl. Adminstrn., Confedn. Oreg. Sch. Adminstrs., Oreg. Middle Level Assn. Home: 3790 River's Edge Dr Lake Oswego OR 97034 Office: St Thomas More Sch 3521 SW Patton Rd Portland OR 97034

NEWMAN, SUZANNE DINKES, advertising agency executive; b. Bklyn., Apr. 28, 1949; d. Philip and Natalie (Hollander) Dinkes; m. Ralph Michael Newman, Mar. 9, 1975. Student, Cooper Union, 1967-71, Sch. Visual Arts, N.Y.C., 1971-72. Asst. art dir. Lincoln Ctr. Programs, N.Y.C., 1973-74; art dir. BimBamBoom Mag., Yonkers, N.Y., 1974, Fairfax Advt., N.Y.C., 1974-75; dir. ops. TBE Advt., Yonkers, 1975-87, CEO, 1987-94; prin. R.S. Newman & Assocs., Inc., Yonkers, 1994—; art dir. Time Barrier Express, Yonkers, 1975-80; CEO R.S. Newman & Assocs., Yonkers, 1994— concert coordinator Classic Harmony Prodns., N.Y.C., 1975; spl. event planner The Left Bank, Mount Vernon, N.Y., 1980-81; spl. event cons. Glen Island Casino, New Rochelle, N.Y., 1984-85; event coord., Top Brass, Yonkers, 1986-87; art dir., cons. various music publs., 1974-80. Mem. Yonkers Citizen's Adv. Group, Yonkers Mayorial Transition Com., 1991-92, Alliance Devel. Com., Yonkers Sch. and Bus. Alliance, 1991—, program com., 1991—; mem. Yonkers Coun. Pres.'s Citizens Adv. group, 1992—, Yonkers Dem. Com., dist. leader, 1991-93; jour. chair gala com. Hudson River Mus., 1992; mem.Yonkers Local Bus. Adv. Coun., 1992—; mem. Yonkers Pvt. Industry Coun., 1992—, sec. 1993—; promotion chair Yonkers Hudson Riverfest, 1992-93; bus. adv. com. Yonkers Econ. Devel. Zone, 1993-94; active Yonkers Waterfront Task Force, 1993—; bd. dirs. Youth Theater Interaction, 1994; bd. dirs. Westchester divsn. Jewish Guild for Blind, 1994—. Editor: Rockin' in the Fourth Estate, 1979-80. Art dir.: White and Still All Right!, 1977, Sun Records, 1980, The Buddy Holly Story, 1979. Recipient Disting. Leadership and Service award Westchester County C. of C., 1985, Westchester award, Westchester Small Bus. Coun., 1989. Mem. Westchester Small Bus. Council (communications chmn. 1984-85, Westchester winner 1989), Westchester Assn. Women Bus. Owners, Am. Women Entrepreneurs, Yonkers C. of C., Council for Arts Westchester. Democrat. Jewish. Avocations: reading; antiques; gardening. Office: RS Newman & Assocs 72 Highview Ter Yonkers NY 10705

NEWMAN, TERRIE LYNNE, advertising and marketing executive; b. Boston; d. Joseph and Clara (Bistry) N.; m. Fredric Aron Kerstein, June 18, 1978. BA in English, U. Mass., Boston, 1973. Copywriter Vanda Beauty Counselor, Inc., N.Y.C., 1973-75; creative dir. Vanda Beauty Counselor, Inc., 1975-76; sr. writer Avon Products, Inc., N.Y.C., 1976-79; copywriter Hume, Smith, Mickelberry Advt., Inc., Miami, Fla., 1979-80, Beber, Silverstein & Ptnrs., Advt., Miami, 1980-81; pres., creative dir. Terrie Lynne Newman, Inc., Miami, 1981-92, Terrie Newman Communs., Miami, 1992—. Recipient Internat. Gold Echo award Direct Mktg. Assn., 1987, 88, Internat. Bronze Echo award, 1987, Gold Award for Excellence in Mktg., Gold Coast chpt. Am. Mktg. Assn., 1987, First Place Gold medallion Broadcast Promotion & Mktg. Execs., 1986, Clio award, 1981, Emmy award, 1981, others. Home and Office: 6970 SW 125th St Miami FL 33156-6240

NEWMAN, WINIFRED H., retired educator, association executive; b. Oakland, Md., Jan. 30, 1904; d. Charles J. and Harriett Lucretia (White) N. AB in Elem. Edn., Marshall Coll., 1929; MA in Supervision and Adminstrn., W.Va. U., 1936; EdD (hon.), Morris Harvey Coll., 1953, Marshall Coll., 1954. Tchr. elem. edn. Kanawha County Schs., Charleston, W.Va., 1929-35; prin. Capitol & Lincoln Schs., Charleston, 1935-40; asst. supt. in charge of elem. schs., spl. edn., pers., Charleston-Kanawha County Schs., 1940-69. V.p. Charleston YWCA, 1927—, mem. nat. bd. dirs., 1953-55; sch. supt. Christ Ch. Meth., Charleston, 1955, tchr. Sunday sch.; vol. hosps. Recipient award Christ Sch. Bd. Edn., 1992, Recognition award Coun. Jewish Women, 1991. Mem. AAUW (pres.), W.Va. Elem. Prins. Assn. (pres. 1938-40), Pilot Club Internat. (pres. 1953-54, gov. Ky.-Ohio-W.Va. 1948), Order Eastern Star (hon.), Delta Kappa Gamma (hon.). Home: 1559 Lee St E Charleston WV 25311-2403

NEWPORT, L. JOAN, clinical social worker; b. Ponca City, Okla., July 5, 1932; d. Crawford Earl and Lillian Pearl (Peden) Irvine; m. Don E. Newport, July 9, 1954 (div. July 1971); children: Alan Keith, Lili Kim. BA cum laude, Wichita State U., 1955; MSW, U. Okla., 1977. Diplomate in clin. social work Acad. Cert. Social Workers; lic. social worker, Okla. Dir. children's work Wesley United Meth. Ch., Oklahoma City, 1969-71; social worker Dept. Human Svcs., Newkirk, Okla., 1972-77; in-sch. suspension counselor Kay County Youth Svcs., Ponca City, Okla., 1977; med. social worker St. Joseph Med. Ctr., Ponca City, 1977-78, dir. social work, 1978-83; pvt. practice Ponca City, 1979—; med. social worker Healthcare Svcs., Ponca City, 1983-84; sponsor, organizer Kay County Parents Anonymous, Ponca City, 1976-83; vice chair Okla. State Bd. Lic. Social Workers, Oklahoma City, 1988-90; presentor, lectr. in field. Mem. Okla. Women's Network, 1989—; mem. adv. bd. Displaced Homemakers, Ponca City, 1985-89; mem. adv. bd. Kay County Home Health, 1979-83, chair, 1979-81. Named Hon. State Life Mem. Burbank PTA, Oklahoma City, 1971; scholar Wichita (Kans.) Press and Radio Women, 1953, Conoco, Inc., Houston, 1951. Mem. NASW (pres. Okla. chpt. 1988-90, Social Worker of Yr. 1987), Child Abuse Prevention Task Force (pres. dist. 17 1986-88), Zeta Phi Eta. Democrat. Methodist. Home: 109 N Walnut Ave Newkirk OK 74647-2036 Office: 619 E Brookfield Ponca City OK 74601

NEWS, KATHRYN ANNE, editor, educator, writer; b. McPherson County, Kans., Mar. 16, 1934; d. Henry J. and Mary J. (Kauffman) Goering; m. Albert D. Klassen Jr. (div. June 1976); children: Teresa C., Jean A., Eric P., Rachel S.; m. Francis W. News, Mar. 4, 1982. Student, Bethel Coll., 1952-54, Washburn U., 1964-67; BA, Roosevelt U., 1968; MA, Ind. U., 1971. Assoc. editor Holiday mag. Curtis Pub. Co., Indpls., 1973-74, mng. editor, 1974-77; travel page cons. Sat. Evening Post, 1976-77, Country Gentleman, 1976-77; editor Going Places mag. Chilton Publs., Radnor, Pa., 1977-79; mng. editor Réalités mag., 1979-81, Spring mag. Rodale Press, 1981-82; assoc. prof. communications Temple U., Phila., 1982—. Author: Great Escapes: An Executive's Guide to Fine Resorts, 1980. Recipient cert. of merit Atlantic Monthy, 1958; 1st Place Fellowship award Ind. U. Writers Conf., 1970, Golden Basset award, 1973, Chilton Editorial award, 1978. Office: Temple U Dept Journalism Philadelphia PA 19122

NEWSOM, CYNTHIA MAYE, computer programmer, educator; b. Lusk, Wyo., Jan. 19, 1960; d. Warren Eugene Coleman and Susanne Rae (Burnham) Cross; m. James William Newsom Jr., June 10, 1983; children: Don Blaine, James William III. BS in Computer Sci., U. Ark., 1993. Sec. Linda Phillips, Lusk, 1984-87; clk., flr. supr. Pamida, Inc., Sheridan, Wyo., 1988-89; accounts payable clk. Mitchell Oil Co., Fayetteville, Ark., 1991-92; clk. Tom's One Stop, Fayetteville, 1992-93; paraprofessional High Plains Ednl. Coop., Ulysses, Kans., 1993—. Stevens County committeewoman, v.p. Stevens County Dems. Mem. Assn. Computing Machinery (life mem. local chpt.). Democrat. Episcopalian. Home: 705 S Jefferson St Hugoton KS 67951-2717

NEWSOM, DOUGLAS ANN JOHNSON, author, journalism educator; b. Dallas, Jan. 16, 1934; d. J. Douglas and R. Grace (Dickson) Johnson; m. L. Mack Newsom, Jr., Oct. 27, 1956 (dec.); children: Michael Douglas, Kevin Jackson, Nancy Elizabeth, William Macklemore; m. Bob J. Carrell, 1993. BJ cum laude, U. Tex., 1954, BFA summa cum laude, 1955, M in Journalism 1956, PhD, 1978. Gen. publicity State Fair Tex., 1955; advt. and promotion Newsom's Women's Wear, 1956-57; publicist Auto Market Show, 1961; lab. instr. radio-tv news-writing course U. Tex., 1961-62; local publicist Tex. Boys Choir, 1964-69, nat. publicist, 1967-69; pub. rels. dir. Gt. S.W. Boat Show Dallas, 1966-72, Family Fun Show, 1970-71, Horace Ainsworth Co., Dallas, 1966-76; pres. Profl. Devel. Cons., Inc., 1976-89; faculty Tex. Christian U., Ft. Worth, 1969—, prof. dept. journalism, chmn. dept., 1979-86, adviser yearbook and mag., 1969-79; dir. ONEOK Inc., diversified energy co., 1980—; Fulbright lectr. in India, 1988. Author: (with Alan Scott) This is PR, 1976, 3d edit., 1984, (with Alan Scott and Judy Van Slyke Turk) 4th edit., 1989, 5th edit., 1992, (with Bob Carrell) Writing for Public Relations Practice, 4th edit., 1994, (with Jim Wollert) Media Writing, 1984, 2d edit., 1988; mem. editorial bd. Pub. Rels. Rev., 1978—. Sec.-treas. Pub. Rels. Found. Tex., 1979-80, also trustee; pub. rels. chmn. local Am. Heart Assn., 1973-76, state pub. rels. com. 1974-82, chmn., 1980-82; trustee Inst. for Pub. Rels. Rsch. and Edn., 1985-89; mem. Gas Rsch. Adv. Coun., 1981—. Fellow Pub. Rels. Soc. Am. (chmn. Coll. Fellows 1992, nat. edn. com. 1975, chmn. 1978, nat. faculty adviser, chmn. edn. sect.); mem. Assn. Edn. in Journalism and Mass Communication (pres. pub. rels. div. 1974-75, nat. pres. 1984-85), Women in Communications (nat. conv. treas. 1967, nat. pub. rels. chmn. 1969-71), Tex. Pub. Rels. Assn. (dir. 1976-84, v.p. 1980-82, pres. 1982-83), Mortar Bd. Alumnae (adviser Tex. Christian U. 1974-75), Phi Kappa Phi, Kappa Tau Alpha, Phi Beta Delta. Episcopalian. Home: 4237 Shannon Dr Fort Worth TX 76116-8043 Office: Tex Christian U Dept Journalism PO Box 32930 Fort Worth TX 76129

NEWSOME, MARY DE SÉVIGNÉ, psychoanalyst; b. South Bend, Ind., Dec. 23, 1929; d. Herman Lafayette and Irene Aurora (de Sévigné) N. BA, U. Chgo., 1950; MD, U. Ill., 1959. Mem. faculty Inst. Psychoanalysis, Chgo., 1989—; lectr. U. Chgo., 1993—; assoc. prof. psychiatry Rush Med. Coll., Chgo., 1993—. Contbr. articles to sci. jours. incl. The Annual of Psychoanalysis, Psychoanalytic Inquiry and Progress in Self Psychology. Office: Inst Psychoanalysis 180 N Mich Ave Chicago IL 60601

NEWSOME, SANDRA SINGLETON, elementary education educator, reading specialist, consultant; b. Bayboro, N.C., Apr. 4, 1948; d. John Wilson Singleton and Cora Lee (Beasley) Hatchel; m. Edward Newsome Jr., Feb. 14, 1971. BS, Elizabeth City State U., 1970; MS, Bowie State U., 1979; EdD, Pensacola Christian Coll., 1992. Cert. tchr., Washington. Tchr. D.C. Pub. Schs., Washington, 1970-80, reading tchr., 1980-82, reading specialist, 1982—; asst. prin. Calvary Temple Christian Sch., Sterling, Va., 1985-86; prof. Bowie State U., 1994—; adminstrv. intern Roper Mid. Sch. of Math. Sci. and Tech., Washington, 1993-95; cons. Bowie State Spl. Interest Coun., 1991-92, D.C.-Dakar Friendship Coun., 1991-92; mem. adv. bd. Walk In Faith mag., Washington, 1991-92; dir. Acad. Tutorial Program, Temple Hills, Md., 1990-91. Contbr. to profl. publs. Mentor Teen Parenting, Inc., Hyattville, Md., 1989, Valuettes, Washington, 1990-92; dir. Adult Literacy Coun., Temple Hills, 1990; asst. dir. Jr. Toastmasters, Brightwood, 1993; program developer and dir. Visions: A Tour into Values, Washington, 1993; pres. Hellen Lee Dr. Civic Assn., Clinton, 1994—; dir. Christian edn. Alexandria (Va.) Christian Ctr., 1994—. Recipient Save Our Youth Am. award Soya, Inc., Washington, 1989, Literacy award Bowie State U., 1991; Teacher-to-Teacher grantee, 1990-92; fellow Cafritz Found., 1991. Mem. ASCD, AFT, AAUW, LEAD Program, Nat. Black Child Devel. Inst., Bowie State Spl. Interest Orgn., Alexandria Christian Ctr., Hellen Lee Dr. Civic Assn. (pres. 1994—). Home: 6206 Hellen Lee Dr Clinton MD 20735-3431 Office: Brightwood Elem Sch 13th And Nicholson St NW Washington DC 20011

NEWTON, ELLEN PHILLIPS, accountant; b. Lumberton, N.C., May 9, 1960; d. Edward Franklin Phillips and Hallie Leigh (Bunnell) Brown; m.

Thomas Kim Newton, May 10, 1980; 1 child, Kyle Thomas. BS in Bus. Mgmt., Pembroke State U., 1982. Jr. acct. Haigh, Byrd & Lambert, Fayetteville, N.C., 1982-84; acct. Broadwell Land Co., Fayetteville, N.C., 1984—. Named Asset of Yr. Meth. Coll. Acctg. Club, Fayetteville, 1986. Mem. Inst. Mgmt. Accts. (v.p. membership 1985). Home: 43 N Old Stage Rd Saint Pauls NC 28384-1445 Office: Broadwell Land Co 903 Hay St Fayetteville NC 28305

NEWTON, LEILANI L., bank executive. BA, U. Wis.; MA, U. Mich. Credit mgr. for Austria and Ea. Europe Dow Chemical, Vienna, 1973-77; computer programmer Export-Import Bank of the U.S., 1977-90, asst. to the treas.-controller, 1990—. Mem. Women in Internat. Trade, Profl. Banker's Assn. Office: Export Import Bank of the US 811 Vermont Ave NW Washington DC 20571*

NEWTON, LISA HAENLEIN, philosophy educator; b. Orange, N.J., Sept. 17, 1939; d. Wallen Joseph and Carol Bigelow (Cypiot) Haenlein; m. Victor Joseph Newton, June 3, 1972; children: Tracey, Kit, Cynthia Perkins, Daniel Perkins, Laura Perkins. Student, Swarthmore Coll., 1957-59; BS in Philosophy with honors, Columbia U., 1962, PhD, 1967. Asst. prof. philosophy Hofstra U., Hempstead, N.Y., 1967-69; asst. prof. philosophy Fairfield U., Conn., 1969-73, assoc. prof., 1973-78, prof., 1978—, dir. program in applied ethics, 1983—, dir. program in environ. studies, 1986—; lectr. in medicine Yale U., 1984—; lectr., cons. in field. Author: Ethics in America; co-author: Watersheds, Wake-up Calls; co-editor: Taking Sides: Controversial Issues Business Ethics; contbr. articles to profl. jours. Mem. exec. bd. Conn. Humanities Council, 1979-83. Mem. Am. Soc. Value Inquiry (past pres.), Am. Philos. Assn., Am. Soc. Polit. and Legal Philosophy, Acad. Mgmt., Am. Soc. Law and Medicine, Soc. Bus. Ethics (past pres.), Phi Beta Kappa. Home: 4042 Congress St Fairfield CT 06430-2041 Office: Fairfield U Dept Philosophy Fairfield CT 06430-7524

NEWTON, RHONWEN LEONARD, writer, microcomputer consultant; b. Lexington, N.C., Nov. 13, 1940; d. Jacob Calvin and Mary Louise (Moffitt) Leonard; children: Blair Armistead, Allison Page, William Brockenbrough III. AB, Duke U., 1962; MS in Edn., Old Dominion U., 1968. French tchr. Hampton (Va.) Pub. Schs., 1962-65, Va. Beach (Va.) Pub. Schs., 1965-66; instr. foreign lang. various colls. and univs., 1967-75; foreign lang. cons. Portsmouth (Va.) Pub. Schs., 1973-75; dir. The Computer Inst., Inc., Columbia, S.C., 1983; pres., founder The Computer Experience, Inc., Columbia, 1983-88, RN Enterprises, Columbia, 1991—. Author: WordPerfect, 1988, All About Computers, 1989, Microsoft Excel for the Mac, 1989, Introduction to the Mac, 1989, Introduction to DOS, 1989, Introduction to Lotus 1-2-3, 1989, Advanced Lotus 1-2-3, 1989, Introduction to WordPerfect, 1989, Advanced WordPerfect, 1989, Introduction to DisplayWrite 4, 1989, WordPerfect for the Mac, 1989, Introduction to Microsoft Works for the Mac, 1990, Accountant, Inc for the Mac, 1992, Introduction to Filemaker Pro, 1992, Quicken for the MAC, 1993, Quicken for Windows, 1993, WordPerfect for Windows, 1993, Advanced WordPerfect for Windows, 1993, Lotus 1-2-3 for Windows, 1993, Introduction to Quick Books, 1994, Quick Book for Windows, 1994. Mem. Columbia Planning Commn., 1980-87; bd. dirs. United Way Midlands, Columbia, 1983-86; bd. dirs. Assn. Jr. Leagues, N.Y.C., 1980-82; trustee Heathwood Hall Episcopal Sch., Columbia, 1979-85. Republican. Episcopalian. Home and Office: 1635 Kathwood Dr Columbia SC 29206-4509

NEWTON, VIRGINIA, archivist, historian, librarian; b. Walters, Okla., Oct. 5, 1938; d. John Walter and Reba Catherine (Mawdsley) N.; m. Gary J. Mounce, Dec. 27, 1963 (div. 1982). Student, Inst. Tecnológico y de Estudios Superiores de Monterrey, Nuevo Leon, Mex., 1957; AA in Bus. Adminstrn., Stephens Coll., 1958; BA in History, Okla. State U., 1960; M of Librarianship, U. Wash., 1963; cert. in libr. sci., U. Tex., 1968, MA in History Archives and Libr. Sci., 1975, PhD in History, Archives and Libr. Sci., 1983. Libr. Inst. Pub. Affairs U. Tex., Austin, 1963-65, libr. Art Libr., 1965-67; coord. Sr. Community Svcs. Program Econ. Opportunities Devel. Corp., San Antonio, 1968-69; archivist, spl. collections libr. Trinity U., San Antonio, 1969-73; spl. collections and reference libr. Pan Am. U., Edinburg, Tex., 1974-77; archivist, records analyst Alaska State Archives and Records Svc., 1983-84, dep. state archivist, 1984-87; state archivist Alaska State Archives & Records Mgmt. Svcs., 1988-93; dir. Columbus Meml. Libr. OAS, Washington, 1993—; archives cons. Ford Found. for Brazilian Archivists Assn., 1976, Soc. for Ibero-Latin Thought, 1980, Project for a Notarial Archives Computerized Guide, 1980; reviewer grant proposal NEH, 1978—; chair Alaska State Hist. Records Adv. Bd., 1988-93, coords. steering com., 1991-93. Author: An Archivists' Guide to the Catholic Church in Mexico, 1979; contbr. articles to profl. publs. founder jail libr. Bexar County Jail, San Antonio; hon. dep. sheriff Bexar County, 1972-75; mem. Dem. party; chair Dems. Abroad in Mex., 1979-81; mem. Dems. Abroad Del. The Dem. Nat. Conv., N.Y., 1980; vice- chair Bill Egan Forum Greater Juneau Dem. Precinct, 1986-88. Recipient Commendation award Gov. of Alaska William Sheffield, 1985, Masonic Scholarship for internat. rels. George Washington U., 1960-61; univ. fellow U. Tex.-Austin, 1982-83, post masters fellow U.S. Dept. Edn.-U. Tex., Austin, 1967-68; scholar Orgn. Am. States, 1980, 81, Fulbright-Hays scholar, 1979, 80, scholar Nat. Def. Fgn. Lang.-U. Tex., Austin, 1978-79, scholar Calif. State Libr., 1962-63. Mem. AAUW (bd. dirs. 1983-86, scholar 1983), Nat. Assn. Govt. Archives and Records Adminstrs. (bd. dirs. 1989-93, chair membership com. 1989-93), Alaska Hist. Soc. (bd. treas. 1988-94), Alaska Libr. Assn., Acad. Cert. Archivists (cert. 1989), Rotary, Phi Kappa Phi. Democrat. Quaker. Home: 2801 Park Center Dr A909 Alexandria VA 22302 Office: Columbus Meml Libr OAS 19th & Constitution Ave NW Washington DC 20006-4499

NEWVINE, WENDY MARIE, office manager; b. Syracuse, N.Y., Aug. 9, 1968; d. Ronald Gene and Diane Barbara (Boysen) N. AAS in Bus. Adminstrn., Alfred State Coll.; student, LeMoyne Coll. Accounts payable staff Am. Internat., Syracuse, 1988-90; office mgr. A.C. Legnetto Constrn., Syracuse, 1990-92, Sure-Way Sys., Syracuse, 1992-93, B-Sure Sys., Syracuse, 1993—. Mem. Inst. Mgmt. Accts., Accting. Soc., Internal Auditors. Office: B-Sure Systems Inc 107 Pickard Dr Syracuse NY 13211

NEZU, CHRISTINE MAGUTH, clinical psychologist, educator; b. Passaic, N.J., June 18, 1952; d. Frank Joseph and Alice Anna (Hingstmann) Maguth; m. Arthur Maguth Nezu, June 12, 1983; children: Frank, Alice, Linda. BA, Fairleigh Dickingson U., Rutherford, N.J., 1977; MA, Fairleigh Dickingson U., Teaneck, N.J., 1981, PhD, 1987. Lic. psychologist, N.Y., N.J., Pa. Psychology intern Beth Israel Med. Ctr., N.Y.C., 1985-86; coord. rsch. and clin. supervision Project NSTM, Fairleigh Dickinson U., Teaneck, 1986-87; clin. asst. prof. and supervising psychologist Beth Israel Med. Ctr., Mt. Sinai Sch. Medicine, N.Y.C., 1987-89; asst. prof. Hahnemann U., Phila., 1989-93, assoc. prof., dir. intern tng., 1993—, dir. intern tng., 1989-94; dir. Phila. mental retardation-sex offender project Hahnemann U., 1991—. Co-author: Problem Solving Therapy, 1989; co-editor Clinical Decision-Making, 1989, Psychotherapy of Persons with Mental Retardation: Clinical Guidelines for Assessment and Treatment, 1992; contbr. articles to profl. jours. Mem. Phila. Mus. of Art, Mus. of the U. of Pa.; vol. Winter Shelter Program for the Homeless, Phila., 1991—. Recipient Bd. Trustees fellowship award Fairleigh Dickinson U., 1985, rsch. fellowships, 1983-86. Fellow Pa. Psychol. Assn.; mem. Am. Psychol. Assn., Am. Assn. on Mental Retardation, Assn. for the Advancement of Behavior Therapy (chair com. on acad. tng. 1990-93, coord. acad. and profl. issues 1993—). Lutheran. Home: 2426 Fitler Walk Philadelphia PA 19103 Office: Hahnemann U Broad And Vine Philadelphia PA 19102

NGUYEN, ANN CAC KHUE, pharmaceutical and medicinal chemist; b. Sontay, Vietnam; came to U.S., 1975; naturalized citizen; d. Nguyen Van Soan and Luu Thi Hieu. BS, U. Saigon, 1973; MS, San Francisco State U., 1978; PhD, U. Calif., San Francisco, 1983. Teaching and research asst. U. Calif., San Francisco, 1978-83, postdoctoral fellow, 1983-86; research scientist U. Calif., 1987—. Contbr. articles to profl. jours. Recipient Nat. Research Service award, NIH, 1981-83; Regents fellow U. Calif., San Francisco, 1978-81. Mem. AAAS, Am. Chem. Soc., N.Y.Acad. Scis., Bay Area Enzyme Mechanism Group, Am. Assn. Pharm. Scientists, Am. Assn. Dental Rsch., Internat. Assn. Dental Rsch. Roman Catholic. Home: 1488 Portola Dr San Francisco CA 94127-1409 Office: U Calif Box 0989 San Francisco CA 94143

NICCOLINI, DIANORA, photographer, artist; b. Florence, Italy, Oct. 3, 1936; came to U.S., 1946, naturalized, 1960; d. George and Elaine (Augsbury) N. Student Hunter Coll., 1955-62, Art Students League, 1960, Germain Sch. Photography, 1962. Med. photographer Manhattan Eye, Ear and Throat Hosp., 1963-65; organizer med. photography dept., 1st chief med. photographer Lenox Hill Hosp., 1965-67; organizer, head dept. med. and audio visual edn. St. Clare's Hosp., N.Y.C., 1967-76; mem. Third Eye Gallery, N.Y.C., 1974-76; owner Dianora Niccolini Creations, 1976—; instr. photography Camera Club N.Y., 1978-79, Germain Sch. Photography, 1978-79, N.Y. Inst. Photography, 1981-83; one woman shows 209 Photo Gallery, Top of the Stairs Gallery, Third Eye Gallery, 1974, 75, 77, West Broadway Gallery, N.Y.C., 1981, Camera Club N.Y., 1982, Photographics Unltd. Gallery, N.Y.C., 1981, Overseas Press Club, N.Y.C., 1983, Impulse Gallery, Provincetown, Mass., 1992; exhibited in group show at Jacob Javits Fed. Bldg., N.Y.C., 1992, Neikrug Gallery, N.Y.C., 1993, Ward-Nasse Gallery, Internat. Salon, N.Y.C., 1994; project dir. Photography over 65, N.Y.C., 1978; pub. portfolios; author: Women of Vision, 1982, Men in Focus, 1983; editor: P.W.P. Times, 1981-82; contbr. to photog. books, 1979, 80; designer greeting cards Flashcards, Inc., 1988-90; contbg. editor Functional Photography, 1979-80, N.Y. Photo Dist. News, 1980; listed in numerous anthologies. Mem. Women Photographers N.Y. (founder 1974), Biol. Photog. Assn., Internat. Ctr. Photography, Am. Soc. Mag. Photographers, Am. Soc. Picture Profls., Profl. Women Photographers (coord. 1980-84), Unity Ctr. Practical Christianity. 1982. Home: 356 E 78th St New York NY 10021-2239

NICEWONDER, SUZANNE HIGGINS, electrical engineer, mechanical engineer; b. Charleston, W.Va., Apr. 7, 1964; d. Owen Shannon and Frances Cornelia (Walker) Higgins; m. Steven Gary Nicewonder, Sept. 12, 1987; children: Bryan Gary, Derek Steven, Scott Frederick. BSEE, W.Va. U., 1986, BSME, 1986. Registered profl. engr. Va., W.Va. Sales asst. Electronic Specialty Co., Dunbar, W.Va., 1982-86; mech. engr. Hayes, Seay, Mattern & Mattern, Roanoke, Va., 1986-88, elec. engr., 1993-95; elec. engr. Hercules, Inc., Radford, Va., 1988-92; elec. dept. head Spectrum Engrs., Roanoke, Va., 1995—; instr. Va. Western C.C., Roanoke, 1991—; engring. cons. local firms, Roanoke, 1992-93. Bd. dirs. Hercules' Community Svcs. Fund, Radford, 1990-92; mem. Women of Radford Army Ammunitions Plant, 1991-92. Mem. NAFE, Elec. League of S.W. Va.

NICHOLAS, CAROL LYNN, lawyer; b. Berkeley, Calif., July 28, 1938; d. Frederick Mortimer and Carolyn (Wright) Nicholas; m. Donald Herrick Maffly, Aug. 24, 1958 (div. 1973); children: Donald Herrick, Brian A. E., Elizabeth Lynn. Student, Conn. Coll., 1956-58; AB, U. Calif., Berkeley, 1971; JD, U. San Francisco, 1975; LLM, Georgetown U., 1982. Bar: Calif. 1976, Utah 1991. Staff atty. SEC, San Francisco, 1976-79, Crocker Nat. Bank, San Francisco, 1979-81, Fed. Home Loan Bank, San Francisco, 1983-84; assoc. Rosen, Wachtell & Gilbert, San Francisco and Los Angeles, 1984-86, Lewis, D'Amato, Brisbois & Bisgaard, L.A., 1986-88, Gaston & Snow, San Francisco, 1988-90; asst. atty. gen. State Utah, 1991—. Contbr. book revs. and articles to profl. jours. Mem. ABA (fed. regulation of securities com.). Democrat. Episcopalian. Office: 115 State Capitol Salt Lake City UT 84114-1202

NICHOLAS, MARTHA ANN, college librarian; b. Memphis, Apr. 15, 1936; d. Hubert Ethridge and Beatrice Marie (Black) Williams; m. Doyne Jackson Nicholas, Aug. 29, 1954. BS in Edn., Ark. State U., 1958; MEd, North Tex. State U., 1964. Elem. music tchr. Gideon (Mo.) Pub. Schs., 1955-58; elem. music./6th grade tchr. Ft. Worth Pub. Schs., 1958-61; elem. tchr. Aubrey (Tex.) Pub. Schs., 1961-64; elem. libr. Lewisville (Tex.) Pub. Schs., 1964-65; elem. tchr. Riverside (Calif.) Pub. Schs., 1965-66; head libr. Williams Bapt. Coll., Walnut Ridge, Ark., 1966—. Mem. adv. com. Lawrence Co. Consumer Health Edn., Walnut Ridge, 1973; tchr., soloist, pianist So. Bapt. chs. Tenn., Mo., Tex., Ark., 1954—. Named Alumna of Yr. Williams Bapt. Coll., 1973. Mem. Ark. Libr. Assn. (membership com. 1970-71), So. Bapt. Libr's. Assn., Ark. Found. Assoc. Colls. Com. (pres. 1970-72, sec. 1967-68), Williams Bapt. Coll. Women's Club (past pres.), Nat. Federated Music Club (leader 1966-75). Home: Williams Bapt Coll Box 3597 Walnut Ridge AR 72476 Office: Williams Bapt Coll PO Box 3667 Walnut Ridge AR 72476

NICHOLAS, NICKIE LEE, industrial hygienist; b. Lake Charles, La., Jan. 19, 1938; d. Clyde Lee and Jessie Mae (Lyons) N.; B.S., U. Houston, 1960, M.S., 1966. Tchr. sci. Pasadena (Tex.) Ind. Sch. Dist., 1960-61; chemist FDA, Dallas, 1961-62, VA Hosp., Houston, 1962-66; chief biochemist Baylor U. Coll. Medicine, 1966-68; chemist NASA, Johnson Spacecraft Center, 1968-73; analytical chemist TVA, Muscle Shoals, Ala., 1973-75; indsl. hygienist, compliance officer OSHA, Dept. Labor, Houston, 1975-79, area dir., Tulsa, 1979-82, mgr., Austin, 1982—; mem. faculty VA Sch. Med. Tech., Houston, 1963-66. Recipient award for outstanding achievement German embassy, 1958, Suggestion award VA, 1963, Group Achievement award Skylab Med. Team, NASA, 1974, Personal Achievement award Dept. Labor Fed. Women's Program, 1984, Career Achievement award Federally Employed Women, Inc., 1988, Meritorious Performance award DOL-OSHA, 1990, Disting. Career Svc. award Dept. Labor, 1991, Sec.'s Exceptional Acievement award Dept. Labor, 1991, Cert. Appreciation, OSHA, 1991. Mem. Am. Chem. Soc. (dir. analytical group Southeastern Tex. and Brazosport sects. 1971, chmn. elect 1973), Am. Assn. Clin. Chemists, Am. Conf. Govtl. Indsl. Hygenists, Am. Ind. Hygiene Assn., Am. Soc. Safety Engrs., Am. Harp Soc., Fed. Exec. Assn. (pres. 1984-85), Kappa Epsilon. Home: 1002 Sundance Ridge Dr Dripping Springs TX 78620-9501 Office: 903 San Jacinto Blvd Ste 319 Austin TX 78701

NICHOLIA, IRENE KAY, organization administrator; b. Tanana, Alaska, Oct. 6, 1956; d. Peter P. and Susie (John) N. Attended, Sheldon Jackson Coll., 1975-77. Bilingaul aide Yukon Sch. Dist., Nenana, 1978-84; programs adminstr. Tanana IRA Native Coun., 1984—. Sch. bd. mem. Tanana Sch. Bd., 1988-90; adv. Yukon Salmon Treaty Negotiation, Can./Alaska, 1990-92; bd. dirs. Alaska Fedn. of Natives, Anchorage, 1990-92; task force mem. Tanana Chiefs Subsistence Task Force, Fairbanks, 1990-92. Democrat. Episcopalian. Office: State of Alaska State Capitol Juneau AK 99801*

NICHOLS, ALICE MARSHALL, manufacturing executive; b. Phila., Aug. 19, 1947; d. Thomas John and Elizabeth (Morris) Marshall; m. John Slocum Nichols, Jan. 5, 1970; children: James Treadwell, Christopher Grosvenor. BA, Wheaton Coll., 1969; MA, Brown U., 1977. Tchr. Gordon Sch., East Providence, R.I., 1978-82, head middle sch., 1980-82; founder, pres. Up Country, Inc., Rumford, R.I., 1982—. Mem. mission com. Gen. Congl. Ch. Mem. Agawan Hunt Club (mem. squash team. Home: 94 Congdon St Providence RI 02906-1413 Office: Up Country Inc 9 Newman Ave Rumford RI 02916-1944

NICHOLS, AVIS B., state legislator; b. Waterbury, Vt.; married; 3 children. Student, Burdett Bus. Coll., U. N.H. Mem. N.H. Ho. of Reps.; mem. ways and means com.; former tchr. Burdett Bus. Coll.; former pvt. sec. Mem. Merrimack County Rep. com. and exec. com., Rep. state com., state boiler adv. coun., Kearsarge Regional Sch. Bd., 1976-89, Warner budget com., 1977-83; co-chair Warner br. ARC, 1972-82, dir. swimming program; former marshal and fin. chair Rebekah Assembly N.H.; mem. Girl Scouts U.S. Mem. Welcome Rebekah Lodge (former noble grand). Home: RR 2 Box 817 Warner NH 03278-9202 Office: NH Ho of Reps State Capitol Concord NH 03301*

NICHOLS, CAROL D., real estate professional, association executive. BA, U. Pitts., 1964; cert. in advanced mgmt., U. Chgo. From mgmt. trainee to buyer May Dept. Stores Co., Pitts., 1964-70; various mgmt. positions, then mng. dir. mortgage and real estate div. Tchrs. Ins. and Annuity Assn. Am., N.Y.C., 1970—; instr. real estate div. continuing edn. Marymount Manhattan Coll., N.Y.C., 1975-76, Woman's Sch. Adult Edn. Ctr., N.Y.C., 1976-77; v.p. instn. owners div. Real Estate Bd. N.Y., past chmn. fin. com., mem. seminar and gen. meetings coms. Mem. resource com. Girls, Inc.; trustee, mem. investment com. Nat. Jewish Ctr. for Immunology and Respiratory Medicine; bd. dirs. N.Y. region NCCJ. Recipient Nat. Humanitarian award Nat. Jewish Ctr. for Immunology and Respiratory Medicine, Nat. Brotherhood award NCCJ. Mem. Assn. Real Estate Women (past pres.), Urban Land Inst. (trustee, chmn. urban devel. and mixed use coun., coun. coord. and inner city). Home: 165 Winfield St East Norwalk CT 06855-1622 Office: Teachers Ins & Annuity Assn 730 3rd Ave New York NY 10017-3206

NICHOLS, ELAINE C., business manager; b. Blue Ridge, Ga., Jan. 12, 1947; d. Carlos J. and Artie L. (Ross) Chambers; m. Johnny L. Nichols, Mar. 12, 1971; children: Shannon, Jerry. Student, North Ga. Tech. and Vocat., Clarksville, 1966, Tri-County Community Coll., Murphy, N.C. Cert. CPS. Adminstrv. asst. Arbor Acres Farm, Inc., Blairsville, Ga., 1966-85; asst. mgr. store Duncan Oil, Hayesville, N.C., 1994—. Treas. Clay County Heritage Book Com., 1993. Mem. NAFE. Avocations: sewing, reading, gardening.

NICHOLS, GERRY LYNN, occupational therapist; b. Larned, Kans., Nov. 18, 1951; d. James H. and Dorthea (Griffith) Sooby; m. William P. Hesley, July 1975 (div. July 1981); m. Douglas J. Nichols, Oct. 9, 1987; 1 child, Rebecca. BS in Occupl. Therapy, San Jose State U., 1980; MBA, U. Dallas, Irving, Tex., 1990. Lic. occupl. therapist; cert. case mgr. Mgr. occupl. therapy Meth. Med. Ctr., Dallas, 1985-87; pvt. practice Dallas, 1981-89; occupl. therapist Progressive Rehab. Inst. of Dallas for Ergonomics, Dallas, 1987-88; v.p. bus. devel./strategic planning and devel., dir. rehab., dir. ops., occupl. therapist Am. Rehab. Ctr./Rehab. Sys., Inc., Dallas, 1989-91; pres. GSN Cons., Inc., Carrollton, Tex., 1991—; pres., CEO WorkWell Sys., Inc., Carrollton, 1994—. Contbr. articles to profl. jours. Mem. adv. bd. Home Health Svcs., Inc., 1990—. Mem. Am. Occupl. Therapy Assn. (roster of evaluators 1993—), Tex. Occupl. Therapy Assn. (dist. chairperson, bd. dirs. 1984-88, Cert. of Appreciation 1989), Metrocrest C. of C. Democrat. Home: 2208 Sunrise Ln Carrollton TX 75006 Office: WorkWell Sys Inc 1925 E Beltline Rd # 320 Carrollton TX 75006

NICHOLS, IRIS JEAN, illustrator; b. Yakima, Wash., Aug. 2, 1938; d. Charles Frederick and Velma Irene (Hacker) Beisner; (div. June 1963); children: Reid William, Amy Jo; m. David Gary Nichols, Sept. 21, 1966. BFA in Art, U. Wash., 1978. Freelance illustrator, graphic designer Seattle, 1966—; med. illustrator, head dept. illustration Swedish Hosp. Med. Ctr., Seattle, 1981-86; owner, med. and scientific illustrator Art for Medicine, Seattle, 1986—; part-time med. illustrator U. Wash., Seattle, 1966-67; part-time med. illustrator, graphic coord. dept. art The Mason Clinic, 1968-78; instr. advanced illustration Cornish Coll. Arts, Seattle, 1988—. Illustrator various books including Bryophytes of Pacific Northwest, 1966, Microbiology, 1973, 78, 82, 94, Introduction to Human Physiology, 1980, Understanding Human Anatomy and Physiology, 1983, Human Anatomy, 1984 Regional Anesthesia, 1990, and children's books on various subjects; exhibited in group shows at Seattle Pacific Sci. Ctr., summer 1979, 82, Am. Coll. Surgeons (1st prize 1974), N.W. Urology Conf. (1st prize 1974, 76, 2d prize 1975). Pres. West Seattle Arts Coun., 1983; active Seattle Art Mus. Named to West Seattle High Sch. Alumni Hall of Fame, 1986, Matrix Table, 1986-95. Mem. Assn. Med. Illustrators (Murial McLatchie Fine Arts award 1981), Nat. Mus. Women in the Arts (Wash. state com., bd. dirs. 1987-93), Women Painters of Wash. (pres. 1987-89), U. Wash. Alumni Assn., Lambda Rho (v.p. 1981-82, pres. 1995), Alpha Chi Omega.

NICHOLS, KYRA, ballerina; b. Berkeley, Calif., July 2, 1958. Studied with Alan Howard, Pacific Ballet, Sch. Am. Ballet, N.Y.C. With N.Y.C. Ballet, 1974—, prin. dancer, 1979—. Created roles in Tricolore, 1978, A Sketch Book, 1978, Jerome Robbins' Four Seasons, 1979, John Taras' Concerto for Piano and Wind Instruments, Stravinsky Centennial Celebration, 1982, Jacques d'Amboise's Celebration, 1983; performed in N.Y.C. Ballet's Balanchine Celebration, 1993. Ford Found. scholar; recipient Dance Mag. award, 1988. Office: Peter S Diggins Assocs 133 W 71st St New York NY 10023-3834 also: NYC Ballet Inc NY State Theater Lincoln Ctr Pla New York NY 10023

NICHOLS, LEE ANN, library media specialist; b. Denver, Apr. 27, 1946; d. Bernard Anthony and Margaret Mary (Pughes) Wilhelm; m. Robert Joseph Nichols, July 12, 1975; children: Rachel, Steven, Sarah. BS in Edn., St. Mary of the Plains, Dodge City, Kans., 1968; MA in Edn., Colo. U., 1978. Cert. type B profl. tchr., Colo. Tchr. So. Tama Sch. Dist. Montour, Iowa, 1968-70, Strasburg (Colo.) Sch. Dist., 1970-73; svc. rep. Montain Bell, Denver, 1973-75; libr., tchr. Simla (Colo). Sch. Dist., 1976-78; dir. Simla Br. Libr., 1978-81; dir. Christian edn. St. Anthony's Ch/, Sterling, Colo., 1983-84; libr. cons. Rel Valley Sch., Iliff, Colo., 1984—, Plateau Sch. Dist., Peetz, Colo., 1986—; mem. Colo. Coun. for Libr. Devel., Denver, 1986-92, chmn. 1991; instr. Northeastern Jr. Coll., Sterling; del. Gov.'s Conf. on Libr. and Info. Scis., 1990. Contbr. articles to profl. jours. Active Sterling Arts Coun., sec., 1982-85, v.p., 1985, pres., 1986-87; chair Northeastern Jr. Coll. Found., Sterling, 1983-87, mem. 1981-91; mem. community adv. coun. Northeastern Jr. Coll., 1991-93, chair, 1993; bd. dirs. Wagon Wheel chpt. Girl Scouts Am., 1975-78. Mem. ALA, Am. Assn. Sch. Librs., Assn. Libr. Svcs. to Children, Colo. Ednl. Media Assn., Colo. Libr. Coun., Internat. Reading Assn. (Colo. Coun.). Home: 12288 Rd 370 Sterling CO 80751 Office: Caliche Jr High Sch Rte 1 Iliff CO 80736

NICHOLS, LISA ANN, technical writer; b. Wilmington, Del., Aug. 4, 1959; d. Raymond Albert and Jean Burchall (Cooling) N. BA, U. Del., 1980, MA, 1983. Dir., curator Old Swedes Found., Wilmington, Del., 1984-90; instr. Ziff Technologies, Wayne, Pa., 1990-93; tech. writer Profl. Tng. Svcs., King of Prussia, Pa., 1993—; cons. Rockwood Mus., Wilmington, 1984—, Hist. Soc. Del., Wilmington, 1983-87. Active Red Clay Presbyn. Ch., Wilmington, 1991—, pres. Chancel Choir, 1988—. Mem. Am. Assn. Mus., Am. Assn. State and Local History, Nat. Trust for Historic Preservation, Mid-Atlantic Assn. Mus., Am. Hist. Assn., Phi Alpha Theta. Home: 4618 Pickwick Dr Wilmington DE 19808

NICHOLS, MARCI LYNNE, gifted education coordinator, educator, consultant; b. Cin., July 7, 1948; m. James G. Nichols, June 19, 1970; children: Lisa, Jeanette. B in Arts & Sci., Miami U., 1970, MEd, 1990, postgrad. Cert. Secondary English, elem. gifted edn., computer edn., Ohio. Secondary English tchr. West Clermont Local Schs., Cin., 1970-71; coord. gifted edn. and tchr. Batavia (Ohio) Local Schs., 1981—; speaker, cons. Local Gifted Orgns., Cin., 1988—; vis. instr. dept. ednl. psychology Miami U., Oxford, Ohio, 1991—; presenter Nat. Rsch. Symposium on Talent Devel., 1991. Author, presenter: (videotape series) Parenting the Gifted Parts I and II, 1992; contbr. Resources for Everyday Living; contbr. articles to profl. jours. Speaker Christian Women's Club, Ohio, Ind., Ky., W.Va., 1981—; deacon First Presbyn. Ch. of Batavia, Ohio, 1986-88. Recipient Douglas Miller Rsch. award Miami U., 1991. Mem. ASCD, Am. Ednl. Rsch. Assn., Nat. Assn. for Gifted Children, Consortium Ohio Coords. of Gifted. Home: 110 Wood St Batavia OH 45103-2923 Office: Batavia Local Schs 800 Bauer Ave Batavia OH 45103-2837

NICHOLS, MARY PEROT, writer, educator; b. York, Pa., Oct. 11, 1926; d. Charles Poultney and Dorothy (Leonard) Perot; m. Robert Brayton Nichols, Oct. 11, 1953 (div. 1967); children: Kerstin, Duncan, Eliza. BA in Polit. Sci., Swarthmore Coll., 1948. Reporter, polit. columnist Village Voice, N.Y.C., 1958-66, city editor, columnist, 1968-75; dir. pub. rels. N.Y.C. Parks, Recreation and Cultural Affairs Adminstrn., 1966-68; free-lance journalist, investigative columnist Boston Herald Am., 1975-76; dir. communications Office of Mayor, Boston, 1977-78; pres. Sta. WNYC Radio/TV Communications Group, pub. broadcasting stas. assoc. Nat. Pub. Radio and Pub. Broadcasting System, 1978-80; dir. communications U. Pa., Phila., 1980-83; pres. WNYC Communications Group, N.Y.C., 1984-90; vis. prof. journalism NYU, 1990-91, adj. prof. journalism, 1991-92; adj. prf. social studies N.Y.U., 1992—; bd. dirs. Citizen's Union. Contbr. articles to various publs., including Barron's, New Republic. Trustee Broadcasting Found. Am., 1978-80, Citizens for Arts in Pa., Parks Coun. N.Y.C., 1969-75; bd. dirs. Citizens Union; mem. adv. bd. Adham Ctr. for TV Journalism, Am. U. in Cairo. Recipient Rosebuds award for investigation of organized crime, journalism rev. More, 1973. Mem. City N.Y. Club, Women's City Club (bd. dirs. 1972-74). Democrat. Home: 505 Laguardia Pl Apt 30D New York NY 10012-2005 Office: 532 Laguardia Apt 233 New York NY 10012-1428

NICHOLS, SALLY ANN, graphic artist; b. Wolfeboro, N.H., Apr. 16, 1959; d. Alfred Harley and Eleanor (Deveneau) N.; m. David Karl Jacke, June 21, 1986; 1 child, Emily. BA in Fine Arts, Keene State, 1981. Graphic artist The Wing Press, Framingham, Mass., 1982-83; adminstrv. asst. Audubon Wildwood Camp, Greenfield, N.H., 1983; graphic artist Eastern

Mountain Sports, Peterborough, N.H., 1983-87; carpenter Nichols-Jacke Home, Jaffrey, N.H., 1987-89; graphic artist Mullein Graphics, Jaffrey, N.H., 1987—; massage therapist pvt. practice, Jaffrey, N.H., 1989—; bd. dirs. Landtrust at Gap Mountain, Jaffrey, 1986—. Recipient Wentworth scholarship Gov. Wentworth Assn., 1980; grantee Fed. Govt., 1978-81. Home and Office: 9 Old County Rd Jaffrey NH 03452

NICHOLS, VICKI ANNE, financial consultant, librarian; b. Denver, June 10, 1949; d. Glenn Warner and Loretta Irene (Chalender) Adams; B.A., Colo. Coll., 1972; postgrad. U. Denver, 1976-77; m. Robert H. Nichols, Oct. 28, 1972 (div.); children—Christopher Travis, Lindsay Meredith. Treas., controller, dir. Polaris Resources, Inc., Denver, 1972-86; controller InterCap Devel. Corp, 1986-87; treas., controller, dir. Transnat. Cons., Ltd., 1986-91; head of reference and adult svcs. Jefferson County (Colo.) Pub. Library, 1986—; dir., owner Nichols Bus. Services. Home: 4305 Brentwood St Wheat Ridge CO 80033-4412 Office: 7706 W Bowles Ave Littleton CO 80123

NICHOLS, VIRGINIA VIOLET, insurance agent, accountant; b. Monroe County, Mo., Oct. 26, 1928; d. Elmer W. and Frances L. (McKinney) N.; student Belleville (Ill.) Jr. Coll., 1959-60, Rockhurst Coll., 1964-65, Avila Coll., Kansas City, Mo., 1981-84. Sec., Panhandle Eastern Pipeline Co., Kansas City, Mo., 1964-65, St. Louis County Dept. Revenue, 1965-69, Forest Park Community Coll., 1969-71, Nooney Co., St. Louis, 1971-77, J. A. Baer Enterprises, St. Louis, 1979; acct. Panhandle Eastern Pipe Line Co., Kansas City, Mo., 1979-85. Vol., ARC, 1965—. Mem. Profl. Secs. Internat. (Sec. of Year 1969, sec. Mo. div. 1975-76), Jr. Women's C. of C. (Girl of Year 1975, pres. 1974-75), Soroptimist's Internat. (treas. Kansas City chpt. 1990-91). Republican. Catholic. Home: PO Box 5832 Kansas City MO 64171-0832

NICHOLSON, ELLEN ELLIS, clinical social worker; b. Boston, Apr. 1, 1940; d. George Letham and Mary Stirling (Money) McIver; divorced; 1 child, Matthew Norman Ellis. Dental Hygienist, Forsyth Coll., 1959; BS, Northeastern U., 1973, MEd in Counseling, 1974; MSW, Boston U., 1984. Registered dental hygienist, Mass. Dental hygienist, 1959-66; clin. coord., pvt. dental practice Forsyth Dental Ctr., Boston, 1966-70; dir. vol. counseling Solomon Mental Health Ctr., Lowell, Mass., 1974-75; social worker East Boston Social Ctrs., Inc., 1976-77, dir. youth family counseling, 1977-79; supr. family svc. Boston Housing Authority, 1979-81; social worker Mass. Soc. Prevention Cruelty to Children, Hyannis, 1984-86, supr., 1986-93, clinic dir., 1993—; psychotherapist Riverview Sch., Sandwich, Mass., 1989-93. Advisor youth group Christ Episcopal Ch., Needham, Mass., 1960-64, St. Paul's Ch., Newburyport, Mass., 1964-65; vol. counselor Soloman Mental Health Ctr., Lowell, 1972-74; chair Barnstable County Children's Task Force; chair adv. com. Barnstable County Sexual Abuse Intervention Network. Mem. NASW, Am. Profl. Soc. on Abuse of Children, Sigma Phi Alpha, Sigma Epsilon Rho, Kappa Delta Pi. Office: Mass Soc Prevention Cruelty to Children 206 Breeds Hill Rd Hyannis MA 02601-1881

NICHOLSON, MARILYN LEE, arts administrator; b. San Jose, Calif., Feb. 7, 1949; d. John Hart Nicholson and Betty Ann (Price) Shepardson; m. Neal Luit Evenhuis. BA in English and History, U. Ariz., 1972; BFA in Studio, U. Hawaii-Manoa, Honolulu, 1977, MA in English, 1977, AS, 1984. Edn. coord., dir. Bishop Mus. Arts and Crafts Sch., Honolulu, 1977-79; owner Fiber Arts Store, Kailua, Hawaii, 1978-82; field coord. Hawaii State Found. on Culture and Arts, Honolulu, 1981-85; exec. dir. Sedona (Ariz.) Arts Ctr., 1986-92, Volcano (Hawaii) Art Ctr., 1992—; mem. bd. artist selection com. Ariz. Indian Living Treasures, 1988-92; bd. dirs., treas. Sedona Cultural Arts Ctr., 1987-92; conf. speaker Nat. Assembly Arts Agys., 1988. Founding Chmn. Sedona Gallery Assn., 1990-92; mem. com. Sedona Acad., 1986-92; mem. steering com. community plan City of Sedona, 1989-91; commr. Arts & Cultural Ctr., Sedona, 1989-91; mem. exec. com. planning Volcano Community Assn., 1993—. Recipient Mayor's award for Disting. Svc., Sedona City Coun., 1992. Mem. Cooper Ctr. Coun. (bd. dirs. 1992—), Aloha Festivals-Hawaii Island (bd. dirs. 1992—). Office: Volcano Art Ctr PO Box 104 Hawaii National Park HI 96718-0104

NICHOLSON, MYREEN MOORE, artist, researcher; b. Norfolk, Va., June 2, 1940; d. William Chester and Illeen (Fox) Moore; m. Roland Quarles Nicholson, Jan. 9, 1964 (dec. 1986); children: Andrea Joy, Ross (dec. 1965); m. Harold Wellington McKinney II, Jan. 18, 1981; 1 child, Cara Isadora. BA, William and Mary Coll., 1962; MLS, U. N.C., 1971; postgrad. Old Dominion U. 1962-64, 64-67, 75-85, 86-92, 94-95. The Citadel, 1968-69, Hastie Sch. Art, 1968, Chrysler Mus. Art Sch., 1964. English tchr., Chesapeake, Va., 1962-63; dept. head, Portsmouth (Va.) Bus. Coll., 1963-64; tech. writer City Planning/Art Commn., Norfolk, 1964-65; art tchr. Norfolk pub. schs., 1965-67; prof. lit., art Palmer Jr. Coll., Charleston, S.C., 1968; tchr. Penn Sch. John's Island, S.C., 1968; librarian Charleston Schs., 1968-69; asst. to asst. dir. City Library Norfolk, 1970-72, art and audio-visual librarian, 1972-75, rsch. librarian, 1975-83, librarian dept. fiction, 1983-90; dir. W. Ghent Arts Alliance, Norfolk, 1978—. Poet-in-schs., Virginia Beach, Va., 1987. Book reviewer Art Book Revs., Library Jour., 1973-76; editor, illustrator Acquisitions Bibliographies, 1970—; juried exhibits various cities including Grand Hyatt, Mayflower, Washington, 1987, by Joan Mondale, John Russell, Nohra Haime, curator of Freer Gallery, U.S. Senate; asst. curator, White House; contbr. art and poetry to various publs. Mem. Virginia Beach Arts Ctr., 1978-93, Hampton Art League, 1990—, Suffolk Art League, 1990—; bd. dirs. W. Ghent Art/Lit. Festival, 1979; poetry reader Poetry Soc. Va., Va. Ctr. for Creative Arts, Sweetbriar, 1989, Walden Books, 1991, Christopher Newport U., 1994, Caberet Voltaire, 1994, Statues St. Mark's Cath. Ch., 1991-92; graphics of hundreds of celebrities from life; curator Va. Winter Show Life Saving Mus., 1991-92; judge Bornstein art scholarship Chrysler Mus., 1992. Recipient various art and poetry contests; Coll. William and Mary art scholar, 1958, Tricentenial award for Contbns. to the Arts in Va., 1993; recipient Cert. for Vol. Contbns. to Va. by Gov., 1994; Nat. Endowment Arts grantwriter, 1975; bd. dirs. Tidewater Literacy Coun., 1971-72. Mem. ALA (poster sessions rev. com. 1985-95, pub. relations judes, subcom. communications 1988-90), Pub. Library Assn. (com. bylaws and orgns 1988-90), Va. Library Assn. (pub. relations com. 1984-86, grievance and pay equity com. 1986-88, Logo award 1985, chair elect, 1991-92, chair Pub. Documents Forum, 1992-93, sec. 93-94), Southeastern Library Assn. (Rothrock award com. 1986-88, com. on coms. 1991-92), Poetry Soc. Va. (ea. pres. 1986-89, nominating com. 1989-90, state corr. sec., editor newsletter 1990-93, dir. publicity 1993—), Art Libraries Soc. N.Am., Tidewater Artists Assn. (bd. dirs. 1989—, chair grantwriting com. 1990—, pres. 1991-92), Southeastern Coll. Art Assn., Acad. Am. Poets, Irene Leache Soc., Internat. Platform Assn. (artists assn.), Old Dominion U. Alumni Assn. (artistic dir. Silver Reunion), Southeastern Soc. Archtl. Historians, Ikara (pres. 1989—), D'Art Ctr. (Dockside art rev., bd. dirs. 1991—), Ex Libris Soc. (charter), Va. Writers Club. Home and Office: 1404 Gates Ave Norfolk VA 23507-1131

NICHOLSON, PRISCILLA WRIGHT, artist; b. Columbus, Ohio, Apr. 30, 1965; d. Harry III and Louise Taylor Wright; m. Stephen James Nicholson, May 18, 1991. BA, Smith Coll., 1987; postgrad., Am. U. Publs. asst. Triad Advt., Columbus, Ohio, 1988-89; cultural exch. Fougeres and Troncais, France, 1989-90; English tchr. Yokohama, Japan, 1991-93; sales asst. Courtyard Gallery, Alameda, Calif., 1993-94. Vol. Alameda (Calif.) Meals on Wheels, 1993-94. Home: 1027 Bellview Rd # 2 Mc Lean VA 22101

NICHOLSON, SHELIA ELAINE, account manager; b. Bklyn., Jan. 20, 1963; d. Emmett Sr. and Louise (Ashford) Caldwell; m. Gerard Nicholson, Aug. 2, 1986. BS, Hampton U., 1985. Cert. in CPR. Adminstrv. asst. Lazar Mgmt. Techs. Inc., N.Y.C., 1985-86; mgr. print prodn. The Wessel Co./Horah Graphics, N.Y.C., 1986-87, 88—; acctg. clk. The Howard Marlboro Group, N.Y.C., 1987-88. Mem. NAACP, NAFE, Congress of Racial Equality. Democrat. Baptist. Home: 743 Greene Ave Brooklyn NY 11221-1904 Office: Horah Graphics 274 Madison Ave New York NY 10016-0701

NICHOLS-YOUNG, STEPHANIE, lawyer; b. Kansas City, Mo., Dec. 23, 1956; d. Jack Lee and Martha Jayne (Johns) Nichols; m. Roger A Young, Mar. 22, 1980. BA in Radio-TV, U. Ariz., 1978, JD with distinction, 1985. Bar: Ariz. 1985, U.S. Dist. Ct. Ariz. 1985, U.S. Ct. Appeals (9th cir.) 1985. With news and prodn. dept. Sta. KZAZ-TV, Tucson, 1977-79; photgrapher, reporter, coord. weekend news coverage Sta. KVOA-TV, Tucson, 1979-81; coord. news coverage and writing Sta. KNST, Tucson, 1981-82; developer pub. access tng. program Cox Cable Comms., Tucson, 1982-83; rsch. asst. to prof. U. Ariz. Coll. Law, Tucson, 1983; atty. Wentworth & Lundin, P.A., Phoenix, Ariz., 1985-87, Gallagher & Kennedy, P.A., Phoenix, 1987-94; sole practice Phoenix, 1994—; law clk. Wentworth & Lundin, P.A., Phoenix, summer 1984. Vol. Lawyers Program; bd. dirs. Animal Legal Def. Fund, Environ. Fund for Ariz. Mem. Maricopa County Bar Found. (bd. dirs.), U. Ariz. Law Coll. Assn. (bd. dirs.). Office: 125 E Coronado Phoenix AZ 85004-3020

NICKEL, JANET MARLENE MILTON, geriatrics nurse; b. Manitowoc, Wis., June 9, 1940; d. Ashley and Pearl (Kerr) Milton; m. Curtis A. Nickel, July 29, 1961; children: Cassie, Debra, Susan. Diploma, Milw. Inst., 1961; ADN, N.D. State U., 1988. Nurse Milw. VA, Wood, Wis., 1961-62; supervising nurse Park Lawn Convalescent Hosp., Manitowoc, 1964-65; newsletter editor Fargo (N.D.) Model Cities Program, 1970-73; supervising night nurse Rosewood on Broadway, Luth. Hosps. and Homes, Fargo, 1973-92; assoc. dir. nursing Elim Nursing Home, Fargo, 1992-94, night supr., 1994—. Mem. Phi Eta Sigma. Home: 225 19th Ave N Fargo ND 58102-2352 Office: 3534 S University Dr Fargo ND 58104-6228

NICKEL, ROSALIE JEAN, reading specialist; b. Hooker, Okla., Oct. 10, 1939; d. Edwin Charles and Esther Elizabeth (Wiens) Ollenburger; m. Ted W. Nickel, June 3, 1960; 1 child, Sandra Jean. BA, Tabor Coll., 1961; MA, Calif. State U., Fresno, 1970. Cert. tchr., Calif. Elem. tchr. Visalia (Calif.) Pub. Schs., 1961-62; overseas tchr. Kodaikanal Internat. Sch., Madras State, India, 1963-65; tchr. Mendota (Calif.) Jr. High Sch., 1966; elem. tchr. Fresno Pub. Schs., 1966-68, reading specialist, reading resource tchr., 1987—; elem. tchr. Inglewood (Calif.) Pub. Schs., 1968-73; spl. reading tchr. Tulsa Pub. Schs., 1974-81; salesperson, mgr. Compaq, Marion, Kans., 1981-85; gifted student tchr. Wichita (Kans.) Pub. Schs., 1986; reading specialist Fresno Pub. Schs., 1986—; evaluator State Textbook Com., Tulsa, 1976, 78; mem. quality rev. team Birney Elem. Sch., Fresno. Newsletter editor Marion County Arts Council, 1981-82. Co-dir. Am. Field Service, Tulsa, 1980-81; v.p. Women's Federated Clubs Am., Marion, 1985-86; pres. Butler Mennonite Brethern Women's Fellowship, 1989—. Mem. Internat. Reading Assn., Tulsa Reading Assn., Fresno Area Reading Council. Home: 2821 W Compton Ct Fresno CA 93711-1181 Office: Fresno Unified Schs Tulare And M St Fresno CA 93701

NICKELL, MARGARET CONRAD, educational coordinator, technology educator; b. Falmouth, Ky., June 1, 1947; d. Chester Clay and M. Eloise (Vice) Conrad; m. Robert W. Nickell, Sept. 2, 1967 (div. June 1990); children: James Conrad, Cara Lee Nickell Lindon. AB in English, Morehead State U., 1970, postgrad., 1981. Cert. secondary tchr., Ky., S.C. 8th grade English tchr. Beaufort (S.C.) Bd. Edn., 1970-71; English tchr. Morgan County Bd. Edn., West Liberty, Ky., 1971—, sch. writing resource tchr., 1992—, dist. tech. coord., 1990—; mem. Ky. Writing Program Adv. Com., Frankfort, 1993—, writing cons. Bd. dirs. Ky. H.S. Speech League, 1980-81; active Commonwealth Inst., Frankfort, 1988-89; NEH participant, 1992-93. Ky. Dept. Edn. grantee, 1986-93. Mem. NEA, Ky. Edn. Assn., Ky. Coun. Tchrs. English, Ky. Mid. Sch. Assn., KSC-Internat. Reading Assn., Ky. Assn. Tech. Coords. (regional rep. 1992-94). Office: Morgan County Bd Edn PO Box 489 West Liberty KY 41472

NICKELSON, KIM RENÉ, internist; b. Chgo., Feb. 13, 1956; d. Robert William and Carolynn Lucille (Marts) N.; m. Louis Peter Sguros; 1 child, Brian Louis. BS in Chemistry, U. Ill., 1978; MD, Loyola U., Maywood, Ill., 1981. Diplomate Am. Bd. Internal Medicine. Intern and resident in internal medicine Luth. Gen. Hosp., Park Ridge, Ill., 1981-84; pvt. practice Oakbrook, Ill., 1984-87, Plantation, Fla., 1987—; adj. attending staff Rush-Presbyn. St Luke's Med. Ctr., Chgo., 1984-87; assoc. attending staff Hinsdale (Ill.) Hosp., 1984-87, Humana Bennett Hosp., Plantation, Plantation Gen. Hosp., Universal Med. Ctr., Plantation. Musician Elk Grove (Ill.) Community Band, 1978-87, Hollywood (Fla.) Symphony Orch., 1987—, Sunrise (Fla.) Pops Symphony, 1987—, Deerfield (Fla.) Community Band, 1987—. Mem. ACP, Internat. Horn Soc. Office: Internal Medicine Assocs 499 NW 70th Ave Ste 200 Plantation FL 33317-7573

NICKERSON, CYNTHIA DAWN, journalist; b. Hyannis, Mass., July 25, 1949; d. Arnold Clayton and Joan Louise (Nicol) N. BA, Coe Coll., 1971; MA, U. Denver, 1979. Feature writer, home editor Cape Cod Times, Hyannis, 1984—. Recipient Arts and Entertainment Reporting award New Eng. Press Assn., 1993. Republican. Office: Cape Cod Times 319 Main St Hyannis MA 02601

NICKERSON, RUTH, sculptor; b. Appleton, Wis., Nov. 23, 1905; d. Robert Wellington and Kate Mary (Ellis) N.; m. Edmund Greacen, Jr., Dec. 30, 1935; children: Elizabeth Ruth, Barbara Eleanor. Ed., Simcoe Collegiate Inst., 1921-23, Nat. Acad. Schs., 1928-32. Works represented in permanent collections, Newark Mus., Cedar Rapids (Iowa) Mus. Art, ew Brunswick, N.J., Eden Post Office, N.C., children's br. Bklyn. Pub. Library, New Rochelle City Hall, Grasslands Hosp., Valhalla, N.Y., Montclair (N.J.) Mus. Art, Interchurch Center, N.Y.C. Mem. White Plains Civic Arts Commn., 1948-60, Mitchell Wolfson Mus., Miami, Fla., Queensborough Pub. Libr., Jamaica, N.Y., permanent and pvt. collections. Recipient Nat. ARts Club medal, 1933, Saltus Gold medal N.A.D., 1933, Montclair Mus. medal, 1936, Am. Artists Profl. League medal, 1947, Allied Artists Religious award, 1981, Therese Wright Richard award Nat. Sculpture Soc., 1982, Bertelson prize N.A.D., 1993; Guggenheim fellow, 1946-47. Fellow Nat. Sculpture Soc. (council 1981-83); mem. N.A.D. (diplomate, council mem. 1978-81), Audubon Artists. Address: 30 Lake St Apt 8K White Plains NY 10603-4002

NICKSE, RUTH SPEIRS, psychologist; b. Yonkers, N.Y., June 30, 1931; d. John Yates and Ina (Weeks) Speirs; m. Robert Nickse, 1953 (div. 1964); children: Stephen, Robert, Gail; m. Robert Weieter Balluffi, June 1, 1974; children: Andrew, Barbara, Frank. BS, Cornell U., 1968, MA, 1970, PhD, 1972. Asst. prof. SUNY, Cortland, 1971-74; project dir. Syracuse (N.Y.) Rsch. Corp., 1973-76; fellow Nat. Inst. Edn., Washington, 1976-77; assoc. prof. U. Mass., Boston, 1979-81; pres. Nickse Assocs., Ithaca, N.Y., 1978-79, Brookline, Mass., 1989—; instr. Havard Univ. Extension, Cambridge, Mass., 1981-83; rsch. dir. Adult Svcs./Mass. State Edn. Dept., Quincy, 1979-83; assoc. prof. Boston U., 1983-89; sr. cons. ABT Assocs., Inc., Cambridge, 1990—; vis. scholar Sch. of Edn., Latrobe U., Melbourne, Australia, summer 1993; U.S. del., participant spkr. 1st Internat. Family Literacy Conf., UNESCO, Paris, 1994; mem. external diploma adv. com. program Am. Coun. Edn., 1995—. Author: (book) Assessing Life Skills Competence, 1980, (monograph) Family and Intergenerational Literacy Practice, 1990; co-author: (book) Community Collaborations for Family Literacy, 1993; editor: Beyond Competency Testing: Competency Based Education, 1981; contbr. articles to profl. jours. Named Outstanding Adult Educator, Mass. Assn. Adult and Continuing Edn., 1989. Mem. Am. Psychol. Assn., Am. Edn. Rsch. Assn., Mass. Coalition for Adult Literacy (founding mem.), Internat. Reading Assn., Am. Assn. Adult and Continuing Edn. (prog. devel. award 1985), Internat. League for Social Commitment in Adult Edn. Office: Nickse Assocs 58 Monmouth St Brookline MA 02146-5607

NICOL, ALICE JEAN, counselor; b. Alexandria, Va., Dec. 6, 1949; d. John Calvin and Carlyn Blake Davison; m. Fred Nicol Jr., June 15, 1975; children: Flo, Laurie, Julie. MA in Counseling, U. Mont., 1974; BA in Psychology, Ohio U., 1971; EdS in Adult Edn., U. Wyo., 1995. Lic. profl. counselor, Wyo.; nat. bd. cert. counselor. Counselor Lander (Wyo.) Pub. Schs., 1974-78, Wind River Pub. Schs., Kinnear, Wyo., 1979-87; counselor, dir. placement Ctrl. Wyo. Coll., Riverton, 1987—. vol. advocate, bd. dirs. Fremont County Alliance Against Family Violence, Riverton, 1989-94. Mem. ACA, Am. Coll. Pers. Assn., Wyo. Counselor Assn. (McNeel award 1993). Methodist. Office: Ctrl Wyo Coll 2660 Peck Ave Riverton WY 82501

NICOL, JESSIE THOMPSON, librarian; b. Cleveland, Tenn., Dec. 26, 1931; d. Franklin Monroe and Lucile Geneva (Bagby) Thompson; m. Andrew Emerson Helms, July 30, 1953 (div. 1970); children: Diana Sue, Arthur William; m. William Kennedy Nicol, Jan. 1974 (dec. 1990). BFA, U. Houston, 1972; MLS, U. Tex., 1975; postgrad., U. Tenn., 1985-87. Cert. libr., Va. Libr., archivist Am. Nat. Ins. Co., Galveston, Tex., 1973-77; libr., head acquisitions U. Tenn., Chattanooga, 1977-87, Va. Poly. Inst. and State U., Blacksburg, 1987-91; libr., cons. Info. Emporium, Cleveland, 1991—; libr. Davis Conservation Libr., League City, Tex., 1972-73; substitute tchr. La Marque Ind. Sch. Dist., 1968-73; women's editor Tex. City Sun, 1962. Contbr. articles to profl. jours. Active La Marque PTA, 1957-68, Tex. City Art League, Boy Scouts Am., Little League Am.; vol. Galveston County Hosp. Aux.; asst. leader Girl Scouts Am. Mem. ALA (LAMA fiscal and bus. officers discussion group 1985-89), Southeastern Libr. Assn. (legis. com. 1987-88, 89-90, interstate cooperative com. 1987-88). Methodist. Home and Office: 471 Weatherly Switch Rd SE Cleveland TN 37323-9218

NICOL, MARJORIE CARMICHAEL, research psychologist; b. Orange, N.J., Jan. 6, 1929; d. Norman Carmichael and Ethel Sarah (Siviter) N. BA, Upsala Coll., MS, 1978; MPh, PhD, CUNY, 1988. Mgr. advt. prodn. RCA, Harrison, N.J., 1950-58; advt. mgr., writer NPS Advt., East Orange, N.J., 1960-67; pres. measurement and eval., chief exec. officer, psychol. evaluator Nicol Evaluation System, Millburn, N.J., 1967—; chief exec. officer., dir. Rafiki, Essex County, N.J., 1965—. Author: Nicol Index, Nicol Evaluation System, 1991. Officer Montclair Rehab. Orgn., 1981—; founder, patron Met. Opera at Lincoln Ctr. Republican. Presbyterian. Home: 85 Linden St Millburn NJ 07041-2160 Office: PO Box 111 Millburn NJ 07041-0111

NICOL, NOREEN HEER, dermatology nurse practitioner, educator; b. Jamestown, N.D., July 16, 1955; d. Clifford Howard and Lois Ann (Smith) Heer; m. Robert Bruce Nicol, June 18, 1983; children: Brent Jeffrey, Erica Marie. BSN, U. No. Colo., 1977; MS in Nursing, U. Utah, 1981. RN, Colo., N.D., Utah; lic. nurse practitioner, Utah; cert. tchr., Colo. Sch. nurse, tchr. health Weld County Sch. Dist. 6, Greeley, Colo., 1977-78; nurse coord. emotionally disturbed summer camp program, charge nurse chem. dependency unit N.D. State Hosp., Jamestown, 1978-79; pediatric clin. specialist, charge nurse U. Utah Med. Ctr., Salt Lake City, 1979-81, dir. pediatric dialysis dept., nurse practitioner, adminstr., intermountain pediatric and adolescent renal disease program, 1981-84; instr. clin. nursing Loretto Heights Coll., Denver, 1984-86; dermatology clin. specialist, nurse practitioner Nat. Jewish Ctr. for Immunology and Respiratory Medicine, Denver, 1986—; clin. instr. Coll. Nursing, U. Utah, 1982-85, assoc. instr. dept. pediatrics Coll. Medicine, 1983-85; mem. adj. faculty Loretto Heights Coll., Denver, 1987-88; clin. sr. instr. U. Colo. Health Sci. Ctr. Sch. Nursing, Denver, 1989—; nurse clinician home intravenous therapy and nutrition Travenol Labs., Inc., Denver, 1984-86; speaker, presenter in field. Contbr. articles to profl. jours., chpts. to books. Mem. Weld County Drug and Alcohol Coun., 1977-78. Nursing scholar U. No. Colo., 1975-77. Mem. Nat. Fedn. for Splty. Nursing Orgns. (edn. com. 1991, health policy com. 1991-92, treas. 1992-93, pres. 1993-94), Colo. Nurses Assn. (Garnet Milhone scholar 1976-77), Dermatology Nurses Assn. (edn. com. 1987, liaison for Colo. 1987-88, nat. edn. vice chmn. 1988, chmn. nat. conv. 1988, nat. bd. dirs. western region dir. 1989-90, nat. bd. dirs. 1991—, nat. pres.-elect 1991, nat. pres. 1992—), Am. Acad. Allergy and Immunology, Skin Phototrauma Found., Sigma Theta Tau (hosp. liaison 1991—). Office: Nat Jewish Ctr Immunology and Respiratory Medicine 1400 Jackson St Denver CO 80206-2762

NICOLAÏ, JUDITHE, international business trade executive; b. Lawrence, Mass., Dec. 15, 1945; d. Victor and Evelyn (Otash) Abisalih. Student in photography, L.A. City Coll., 1967, UCLA, 1971; AA in Fgn. Langs., Coll. of Marin, 1983; hon. degree, Culinary Inst., San Francisco, 1981. Photographer Scott Paper Co., N.Y.C., 1975; owner, operator restaurant The Raincheck Room, West Hollywood, Calif., 1976; prin., pres., chief exec. officer, photographer fashion Photographie sub. Nicolaï Internat. Svcs., Nice, France, 1977—; prin., pres., chief exec. officer, instr. catering and cooking Back to Basics sub. Nicolaï Internat. Svcs., San Francisco, 1980—; chief photographer exhibit and trade show, chief of staff food div. Agri-Bus. U.S.A., Moscow and Washington, 1983; head transp. U.S. Summer Olympics, L.A., 1984, interpreter for Spanish, French, Portuguese, and Italian, 1985; prin., pres., chief exec. officer, interpreter Intertrans subs. (Nicolaï Internat. Svcs.), San Francisco, 1985—; founder, pres. Nicolaï Internat. Svcs., San Francisco, 1985—; pres., CEO Cyprus Personal Care Products, 1994—. Contbr. column on food and nutrition to jour., 1983-84. Mem. Alpha Gamma Sigma. Office: Nicolai Internat Svcs 1686 Union St Ste 203 San Francisco CA 94123-4509 Mailing Address: 2269 Chestnut St Ste 237 San Francisco CA 94123-2600

NICOLAY, JANICE, state legislator; b. Watertown, S.D.; m. Jerry Nicolay. MEd, S.D. State U. Mem. S.D. Ho. of Reps., 1983—; chair appropriations com., pub. sch. adminstr.; bd. dirs. 1st Bank S.D. Mem. United Way. Recipient Leadership award YWCA. Mem. Nat. Edn. Assn., S.D. Edn. Assn. Republican. Home: 1401 Suburban Dr Sioux Falls SD 57103-3762 Office: SD House of Reps Office of House Mems Pierre SD 57501*

NICULESCU, DEBBIE EIDE, business management consultant, writer; b. Owensboro, Ky., Sept. 19, 1956; d. Harry Stur and Jane Annabelle (Willis) Eid; children: Yori Alexander, Danielle Marianna. BA in Psychology, Calif. State U., 1986. Research asst. Essex County Youth Services, Belleville, N.J., 1980-81; evaluator Merritt Personnafax, Montclair, N.J., 1981-82; staff asst. Archdiocese of Newark, 1982-84; sr. assoc. The Plotkin Group, San Bernardino, Calif., 1984—. Mem. Exec. Women's Internat., Am. Soc. Tng. and Devel., West End Exec. Assn., Exec. Assn. San Bernardino, Soc. Human Resources Mgmt, No. Calif. Human Resources Coun. Methodist. Lodge: Zonta. Office: The Plotkin Group 661 N Arrowhead Ave San Bernardino CA 92401-1105

NIEDERMEIER, MARY B., retired nutrition educator; b. Webster Groves, Mo., Oct. 20, 1914; d. Albertus and Daisey May (Christman) Wickersham; m. Walter H. Niedermeier, Sept. 9, 1939; children: Gail Santarelli, Bart Niedermeier. BS, Mich. State U., 1937; MA, Columbia U., 1957, profl. diploma, 1959. Cert. in dietetics, Miami Valley Hosp., Dayton, Ohio, 1938. Dist. nutritionist N.J. State Dept. of Health, Newark; instr. nutrition edn. Sch. of Dentistry Fairleigh Dickinson U., Teaneck, N.J.; instr. nutrition edn. Sch. of Nursing St. Louis U. Pres. PTA, Oradell (N.J.) Pub. Sch., 1954-57; bd. dirs. Rancho Bernardo (Calif.) Oaks North Community Ctr., 1974-76; bd. deacons Rancho Bernardo Presbyn. Ch., 1975-77; treas. PEO-TV chpt., Rancho Bernardo, 1990. Grace McCloud fellow 1957-59 Columbia U. Mem. AAUW, AAUP, Am. Dietetic Assn., Calif. Dietetic Assn., N.J. Dietetic Assn., Alpha Omicron Pi. Republican. Home: 17411 Plaza De La Rosa San Diego CA 92128-2223

NIEDRACH, MARTHA KAY, maternity care nurse; b. Neptune, N.J., July 2, 1950; d. Frank Bailey and Junia C. (Jones) Marchion; m. Craig Alan Niedrach, May 14, 1972; children: Curtis, J. Eric, Carrie, Jennifer, Anne. Diploma, Ann May Sch. Nursing, 1972; student, Trenton State Coll., 1975-81; BSN, SUNY, Albany, 1983; MSN, Rutgers U., 1988. RN, N.J.; RN cert. Nat. Certification Corp., internat. bd. cert. lactation cons., cert. BCLS instr. Staff nurse Jersey Shore Med. Ctr., Neptune, N.J., 1972-85, asst. nurse mgr., 1985-87, perinatal nurse clinician, 1987-88, perinatal clin. nurse specialist, 1988-94; pvt. practice Perinatal Nurse Cons.; mem. N.J. Task Force to Promote Breastfeeding, 1991—; assoc. clin. prof., Ocean County Coll. Mem. ANA, AWHONN, Perinatal Assn. N.J., Regional Perinatal Ctr. of Monmouth Ocean County, Inc. (edn. subcom.), Internat. Lactation Cons. Assn., Sigma Theta Tau., Lambda Delta. Home: 1 Maryland Dr Jackson NJ 08527-2132

NIEHAUS, DEBORAH ANN, post anesthesia care nurse; b. Hillsboro, Ohio, Sept. 17, 1949; d. Francis E. and Eleanor M. (Rosselott) Stephens; m. Raymond R. Niehaus, Nov. 28, 1970; children: Tiffany Renata, Ryan Robert. Diploma, Bethesda Hosp. Sch. Nursing, Cin., 1970; BS in Nursing/Mgmt. cum laude, Coll. Mt. St. Joseph, Cin., 1989. Cert. post-anesthesia nurse. Staff nurse med./surg. Highland Dist. Hosp., Hillsboro, Ohio; splty. team leader, relief charge nurse, pediatric, ICU Bethesda Oak Hosp., Cin., staff nurse surg. PACU; staff clin. nurse III Bethesda North Ambulatory Surg. Ctr., Cin.; speaker in field. Contbr., contbg. editor Post Anesthesia Nursing textbook. Mem. Am. Soc. Post Anesthesia Nurses (pres. 1990-91), Assn. Oper. Rm. Nurses, Am. Pain Mgmt. Nurses.

NIELSEN, JANICE ANN, program analyst; b. Indpls., Mar. 14, 1950. BS with distinction, Purdue U., 1972; postgrad., Harvard U., 1979-84, Ga. Tech. U., 1991, Air U., Maxwell AFB, Ala., 1990. Interior designer Upshaw & Assocs., Architects, Lafayette, Ind., 1972, Charles R. Sutton, Architects,

Honolulu, 1972-74, USAF Pacific, Hickam AFB, Hawaii, 1974-77; asst. mgr. interior design program USAF Europe, 1977-84, mgr. interior design program, 1984-87; dir. interior design program USAF, 1987-91; spl. housing mgmt. project officer Office Dep. Asst. Sec. Def. in Policy and Logistics, Washington, 1991; head environ. resource mgmt. team USAF, Washington, 1991-94, budget analyst Dept. Def., 1993-94; program analyst, Air Force Base Conversion Agy. USAF, Arlington, Va., 1994—; speaker at various govt. and industry nat. and internat. confs., symposiums and workshops worldwide; founding bd.. dirs. Fed. Interior Design Found.; mem. fed. constrn. coun. NAS. Named Disting. Alumni, Purdue U.; recipient notable achievement award USAF, outstanding recognition U.S. Army C.E. Mem. Coun. Fed. Interior Designers (bd. dirs. 1989-91, nat. regional chmn., chmn. directory com., outstanding recognition award), NAFE, Dept. Def. Profl. Women's Assn., Airplane Owners and Piliots Assn., 99's Women's Pilot Assn. Home: 3105 Courtside Rd Mitchellville MD 20721-2535 Office: AFBCA/CE 1700 N Moore St Ste 2300 Arlington VA 22209-2805

NIELSEN, JOYCE, former state legislator; b. Askov, Minn., Nov. 20, 1933; d. Clarey Burnhardt and Dorothy Elaine (Saastad) Jensen; m. Eric Hans Nielsen, June 11, 1955; 1 child, Cindy. Grad., Cloquet (Minn.) H.S. Fin. cons. Nielsen Fin. Cons., Inc., Cedar Rapids, Iowa, 1984-88; mem. Iowa Ho. of Reps., Des Moines, 1989-93; facilitator Parenting Edn. Programs 1993—. Bd. dirs., treas. Peoples Ch., Cedar Rapids, 1983; bd. dirs., sec. UN Assn., Cedar Rapids, 1988; bd. dirs., mem. exec. com. United Way, Cedar Rapids. Named Woman of Yr., Coalition of Women's Groups; recipient Outstanding Svc. award YWCA, Community Action Agy. Mem. LWV (bd. dirs.). Democrat. Mem. Unitarian Ch. Home: 2702 Q Ave NW Cedar Rapids IA 52405

NIELSEN, KAREN OLIVIA, telecommunications analyst, researcher; b. Summit, N.J., Nov. 2, 1962; d. Donald David Cooney and Nancy Ann Nielsen Spatz. BA, Muhlenberg Coll., Allentown, Pa., 1984; MA, U. Pa., 1988. Sr. analyst, rsch. mgr. Link Resources, N.Y.C., 1988-91, No. Bus. Info., N.Y.C., 1991—. Contbr. articles to profl. jours. Mem. NAFE, Phi Sigma Iota.

NIELSEN, LYNN CAROL, lawyer, educational consultant; b. Perth Amboy, N.J., Jan. 11, 1950; d. Hans and Esther (Pucker) N.; m. Russell F. Baldwin, Nov. 22, 1980; 1 child, Blake Nielsen Baldwin. BS, Millersville U., 1972; MA, NYU, 1979; JD, Rutgers U., 1984. Bar: N.J. 1984; cert. tchr. handicapped, reading specialist, learning disability tchr. cons., elem. edn. supr. Instr. Woodbridge (N.J.) Twp. Bd. Edn., 1972-83; legal intern appellate sect. divsn. criminal justice Atty. Gen. State N.J., Trenton, 1983, dep. atty. gen. divsn. civil law, 1985; assoc. Kantor & Kusic, Keyport, N.J., 1984-86, Kantor & Linderoth, Keyport, N.J., 1986-92. Officer Fords (N.J.) Sch. # 14 PTO, 1974-75; elder First Presbyn. Ch. Avenel, N.J., 1985-88; bd. dirs. New Beginnings Nursery Sch., Woodbridge, 1989-90, Flemington (N.J.) Presbyn. Nursery Sch., 1991-93. Mem. ABA, N.J. Bar Assn., Monmouth County Bar Assn., Hunterdon County Bar Assn. Home and Office: 3 Buchanan Way Flemington NJ 08822

NIELSEN, NANCY, publishing executive; b. Jeffersonville, Ind., 1950. BA, Univ. Calif., Berkeley, 1975. Asst. city editor, weekend mag. editor Dallas Times Herald, 1975-77; cons. McKinsey & Co. Inc.; dir. office of comm. Capital Cities/ABC Inc., N.Y.C., 1984-86; deputy dir. corp. rels. The N.Y. Times Co., N.Y.C., 1986-88, dir. corp. rels./Pa., 1987-93, v.p. corp. comm., 1992—; bd. dir. Inst. of Journalism Edn. Recipient Alumni Assn. award for outstanding performance in journalism Univ. Calif. Berkeley. Office: The New York Times Co 229 W 43rd St New York NY 10036*

NIELSEN, VERA BAGLEY, retired teacher, librarian; b. Greenwich, Utah, Oct. 13, 1916; d. James Alvin and Diantha Matilda (Anderson) Bagley; m. Byron Woodland, May 17, 1941 (dec. Feb. 1944); 1 child, Kathleen Myrle; m. Leland Nielsen, Sept. 12, 1952 (dec. Jan. 1993); 1 child, James Cary. AB magna cum laude, Brigham Young U., 1937, MA, 1949. Cert. tchr. 1st class elem., librarian, media specialist, supervisory/adminstrn. Tchr., librarian Franklin Sch., Provo, Utah, 1937, Maeser Sch., Provo, 1944-45, Wasatch Sch., Provo, 1952-58, Provost Sch., Provo, 1959-62; demonstraton tchr. Lab. Sch. Brigham Young U., Provo, 1945-49, tchr. film classics, 1957-58; media specialist Grandview Sch., Provo, 1949-52, Rock Canyon Sch., Provo, 1962-83; instr. libr. Coll. Edn., Provo, summers; instr. Coll. Edn. U. Utah, Salt Lake City, 1958-59; subtitute tchr. Cyprus High Sch., Magna, Utah, 1944; cons. workshops Salt Lake City Sch. Dist., 1957, Utah Edn. Assn., Salt Lake City, 1982-93. Contbr. articles to profl. publs.; editor Family Bull., Bagley Family Orgn., 1976-93; cons. Fascinating Tales Series, ARO Pub. Co., 1981-82. Sec. Orem (Utah) Boosters City Coun., 1970-80; with publicity Miss Orem Scholarship Pageant, 1984-94; sec. Utah County Dem. Party, 1984-92, treas., 1992-95. Recipient Disting. Svc. award Kiwanis Club, Provo, 1978, Vol. Svc. award Utah Gov.'s Commn., Salt Lake City, 1993. Mem. AAUW (br. pres., 1944, 76, state pres. 1968-70, regional dir. 1987-89, editor state bull. 1975-79, 90-94, Disting. Woman award Utah State chpt. 1986,), Assn. Childhood Edn. (pres., historian 1970), Ret. Sch. Employees (unit pres., 1983, , NRTA state coord. 1983-87, state pres. 1993-95), Gen. Federated Women's Clubs (state treas., 1992-94, v.p. 94—), Women's Divsn. C. of C. (sec. 1994, treas. 95), Women's Coun. Provo (pres. 1985-87, Delta Literary honor, 1991, parliamentarian, 1992), League of Women Voters, Phi Delta Kappa (treas., officer 1980, Kappan of Yr. Brigham Young U. chpt. 1987). Mormon.

NIELSON, CAROL ANN, medical records supervisor; b. Rochester, Minn., May 22, 1959; d. Raymond and Rita (Pyfferoen) Rhoten; m. Donal O. Nielson, June 26, 1988. B of Applied Studies, U. Minn., 1983. Ins. biller Hennepin Faculty Assocs., Mpls., 1985-91; supr. med. records dept. Found. for Health Care Evaluation, Bloomington, Minn., 1991—. Mem. Assn. Record Mgrs. and Adminstrs. (dir. arrangements spring conf. 1993-94, 94-95, program dir. Twin Cities NAFE Network 1993-94, Rookie of the Yr. 1993). Roman Catholic. Office: Found for Health Care Eval 2901 Metro Dr Ste 400 Bloomington MN 55425-1558

NIELSON, NORMA LEE, business educator; b. Augusta, Ga., Dec. 26, 1953; d. Norman Lyle and Betty Lou (Buckner) Parrott; m. Mark G. Nielson, Nov. 20, 1985 (div. 1988); 1 child, Eric Gordon. BS, Northwest Mo. State U., 1974; MA, U. Pa., 1976, PhD, 1979. CLU. Asst. prof. Iowa State U., Ames, 1977-79, U. So. Calif., L.A., 1979-84; cons. profl. Mercer-Meidinger, L.A., 1984-85; assoc. prof. Oreg. State U., Corvallis, 1985-90; prof. Oreg. State U., 1990—; bd. examiners Internat. Bd. Standards and Practice for Cert. Fin. Planners, 1991—. Developer software; contbg. author: Handbook for Corporate Directors, 1985; contbr. articles to profl. publs. Vol. Linn-Benton Food Share, Corvallis; bd. dirs. Corvallis Cmty. Dare Care, Inc., 1988-91; candidate for Oreg. Ho. of Reps., 1994. Andrus Found. rsch. grantee, 1989-91. Mem. Am. Risk and Ins. Assn. (bd. dirs. 1990—, officer 1993—), Western Risk and Ins. Assn. (officer 1981-84), Risk and Ins. Mgmt. Soc. Office: Oreg State U Coll Bus Bexell Hall 200 Corvallis OR 97331-2603

NIEMANN, BIRGIE ANN, development adminstrator; b. Ainsworth, Nebr., Aug. 28, 1951; d. Ralph Sidney and Norma June (Smith) Collins; m. Michael Victory Houston, Aug. 20, 1971 (div. Dec. 1992); children: John, Mark; m. Scott Thomas Niemann, Dec. 11, 1993. AA in Speech, York Coll., 1971; BA in Communication, Pepperdine U., 1975; MS in Counseling, Calif. State U., 1982. Sec., adminstrv. asst. Pepperdine U., Malibu, Calif., 1971-75; asst. dean of students Pepperdine U., Malibu, 1976; bus. mgr. Wayne-Ferrell, Inc., Iowa City, 1980-82; parent counselor Systems Unlimited Inc., Iowa City, 1982-84; adminstrv. asst. U. Iowa Found., Iowa City, 1984-87; assoc. dean of students Mich. Christian Coll., Rochester Hills, Mich., 1987-89, dean of students, 1989-91; asst. to pres., 21st century advance campaign dir. York (Nebr.) Coll., 1991—. Contbr. articles to profl. jours. Vol. Drug Free Comty. Task Force, Oakland County, 1989; lectr., guest speaker Ch. of Christ, Calif., Iowa, Ohio, Mich., Nebr., Kans., Mo., Tex., 1976—; bd. dirs. United Way. Mem. York County Writers Guild. Mem. Ch. of Christ. Office: York Coll 9th And Kipplinger York NE 68467

NIEMEIER, CYNTHIA LEE, critical care nurse; b. Phila., Feb. 13, 1952; d. David Baine and Norma June (Beucus) Johnston; m. Rodger Craig Niemeier, June 15, 1975; 1 child, Seth Christian. ADN with honors, Sinclair C.C., 1981. Cert. provider BLS; cert. instr. BCLS, cert. provider ACLS Am. Heart Assn. Staff nurse Miami Valley Hosp., Dayton, Ohio, 1982; staff nurse CCU St. Elizabeth Med. Ctr., Dayton, 1982-84; staff nurse med.-surg. ICU/CCU Humana Hosp., Lexington, Ky., 1984; staff nurse med. ICU VA Hosp., Lexington, 1984-85; staff nurse surg. ICU Good Samaritan Hosp., Lexington, 1985-88; staff nurse PACU Swedish Hosp., Seattle, 1988-90; staff nurse PACU Polyclinic Surgery Ctr., Seattle, 1990—, nurse polyclinic code team, 1994—; staff nurse ICU, CCU CIC Providence Med. Ctr., Seattle, 1992; mem. polyclinic code team, 1994—; instr. BCLS Am. Heart Assn., Ky., 1988-89, ARC, Dayton, 1983-84; ACLS provider Am. Heart Assn., Wash., 1991—. Mem. Caledonian and St. Andrews Soc., Phi Theta Kappa. Republican. Office: Polyclinic Surgery Ctr 1145 Broadway Seattle WA 98122

NIEMI, BEATRICE NEAL, social services professional; b. Fitchburg, Mass., July 23, 1923; d. Albert G. and Florence E. (Copeland) Neal; m. Walter V. Niemi, Oct. 21, 1944 (div. 1970); children: Karen Smith-Gary, Gail Niemi Shaw. AS, Colby-Sawyer Coll., 1942; BS in Psychology, Northeastern U., 1972; MA in Counseling Psychology, Assumption Coll., 1974. Dir. homemaker svcs. Children's Aid and Family Svcs., Inc., Fitchburg, 1965-73; founder, exec. dir. Home Health Aide Svc. of North Cen. Mass., Inc., Fitchburg, 1973-85, Ctr. for Well Being, Inc., Fitchburg, 1985—; instr. Touch for Health Found., Pasadena, Calif., 1977—, The Radiance Technique Assn., St. Petersburg, Fla., 1986—; Gateway Outreach trainer The Monroe Inst., Faber, Va., 1990—; v.p. Mass. Coun. for Homemaker-Home Health Aide Svcs., Inc., 1973-81. Pres. Children's Aid and Family Svcs., Inc., Fitchburg, 1964-65; bd. dirs. United Way of Greater Fitchburg, Inc., 1964-70, Leominster (Mass.) Vis. Nursing Assn, 1972-78; chmn. adv. bd. Salvation Army, Fitchburg, 1970-72; v.p. Fitchburg Coun. of Girl Scouts. Fellow Acad. Holistic Health Practitioners; mem. AACD, NASW, Am. Mental Health Counselors Assn., Mass. Assn. Community Health Agys. (bd. dirs. 1970-83), Radiance Technique Assn. Internat., Mass. Mental Health Counselors Assn., Assn. for Transpersonal Psychology, Nat. Guild Hynotists, also others. Office: Ctr for Well Being Inc 70 Bond St Fitchburg MA 01420-2251

NIEMI, CAROL S., advertising company executive, writer; b. Bethesda, Md., Mar. 8, 1948; d. Irving Joseph and Marjorie Elizabeth (Coté) Superfine; m. Kevin John Niemi, Mar. 21, 1978; 1 child, Madeline Ann. Cert. in French, U. Paris, 1969; BA in English and French, Fla. State U., 1970; MA in English, U. Ga., 1976, PhD in English, 1982. Editor Trunklines Del. State Rep. Party, Wilmington, 1982; freelance writer Wilmington, 1982-83; copywriter Lyons, Inc., Wilmington, 1983-85; sr. copywriter Shimer von Cantz, Phila., 1985-86; assoc. creative dir. Sawyer Riley Compton, Atlanta, 1986-88, v.p., creative dir., 1988-93; assoc. creative dir. Tucker Wayne/Luckie, Atlanta, 1993-94; writer, planner, creative dir. specialist for high tech and telecoms. Intelligent Advt., Atlanta, 1994—; former assoc. prof. Goldey Beacom Coll.; former lectr. U. Ga.; adv. commn. Atlanta Art Inst., 1992—; speaker numerous advt. orgns. Vol. polit. campaign Sen. Bill Roth, Wilmington, 1982; pres. Plum Run Civic Assn., Wilmington, 1984; vol. Wesleyan Sch., Atlanta, 1994—; vol. promotional writer for fund raiser Wesleyan Sch., 1994—. Recipient Peach awards Bus., Mktg. Assn. S.E., 1986-93, ProComm. award Bus. Mktg. Assn., 1987-93, Silver Effie award Am. Mktg. Assn., 1991, award Nat. Agri-Mktg. Assn., O&R award Am. Bus. Press, others; named One of Atlanta's Top Three Creative Dirs. Atlanta Bus. Chronicle, 1991, One of Ten Women to Watch, 1992. Mem. Atlanta Ad Club (Addy award 1988, 89, 90), Creative Club Atlanta (Show South award 1992). Republican. Unitarian. Office: Intelligent Advertising 2410 Kimbrough Ct Atlanta GA 30350

NIEMI, JANICE, lawyer, former state legislator; b. Flint, Mich., Sept. 18, 1928; d. Richard Jesse and Norma (Bell) Bailey; m. Preston Niemi, Feb. 4, 1953 (divorced 1987); children—Ries, Patricia. BA, U. Wash., 1950, LL.B., 1967; postgrad. U. Mich., 1950-52; cert. Hague Acad. Internat. Law, Netherlands, 1954. Bar: Wash. 1968. Assoc. firm Powell, Livengood, Dunlap & Silverdale, Kirkland, Wash., 1968; staff atty. Legal Service Ctr., Seattle, 1968-70; judge Seattle Dist. Ct., 1971-72, King County Superior Ct., Seattle, 1973-78; acting gen. counsel, dep. gen. counsel SBA, Washington, 1979-81; mem. Wash. State Ho. of Reps., Olympia, 1983-87, chmn. com. on state govt., 1984; mem. Wash. State Senate, 1987-95; sole practice, Seattle, 1981—; mem. White House Fellows Regional Selection Panel, Seattle, 1974-77, chmn., 1976, 77; incorporator Sound Savs. & Loan, Seattle, 1975. Bd. dirs. Allied Arts, Seattle, 1971—, Ctr. Contemporary Art, Seattle, 1981-83, Women's Network, Seattle, 1981-84, Pub. Defender Assn., Seattle, 1982-84; bd. visitors dept. psychology U. Wash., Seattle, 1983-87, bd. visitors dept sociology, 1988— . Named Woman of Yr. in Law, Past Pres.'s Assn., Seattle, 1971; Woman of Yr., Matrix Table, Seattle, 1973, Capitol Hill Bus. and Profl. Women, 1975. Mem. Wash. State Bar Assn., Wash. Women Lawyers. Democrat. Home: PO Box 20516 Seattle WA 98102-1516

NIENHIUS-HORNER, CAROLYN JOANNE, educator, counselor, consultant; b. Akron, Ohio, Oct. 26, 1948; d. James Patrick and Pauline Elizabeth (Beretics) Kintz; m. Ronald Jay Nienhius, Aug. 23, 1970 (div. Dec. 1979); children: Nathan Jeremy, Seth Michael; m. Karl Ford Horner, Jr., Nov. 3, 1983. BS, Ohio State U., 1972; M in Tech. Edn. Guidance, U. Akron, 1988, M in Counseling, 1990. Lic. social worker, Ohio; cert. employee assistance profl.; trained in divorce mediation. Employee devel. trainer Sum County Dept. Human Svcs., Akron, 1984-90; employee assistance counselor Tri-County Employee Assistance Progam, Akron, 1989-90; intrvention program coord. Community Drug Bd., Akron, 1990-91; counselor, consultant, trainer Hop To It (pvt. practice), Hartville, Ohio, 1991—; instr., trainer, practicum supr., program developer, writer Stark Tech. Coll., Canton, Ohio, 1990—; cons. Child Support Enforcement Agy. Akron, 1989—; in-svc. trainer Wadsworth (Ohio) City Schs.; presenter Ohio Welfare Conf., Toledo, 1989, Ohio Counselors Conf., Columbus, 1990; curriculum writer Case Western Res. U. Mandel Sch. Applied Social Scis. Vol. ARC, Akron, 1967-88, Risk Reduction Health Promotion Task Force, Akron, 1984-89, Side Stream Smoke Task Force, 1984-89; coord. Tri County Disabled Citizens Activities, Akron, 1988-89; recorder Stark Tech. Coll. Adv. Bd., 1990—; mem. citizen ambassador program mgmt. Tng. and Incentive Delegation to Russia and Ukraine, 1992. Mem. AACD, ASTD, Ohio Coun. for Self Esteem, Internat. Assn. for Addictions and Offender Counselors, Toastmasters Internat., Chi Sigma Iota (program chmn. Alpha Upsilon chpt. 1989-90, Pres. award, Akron, 1990). Home and Office: Hop To It 7052 Pinedale St NE Hartville OH 44632-9392

NIENOW, AMY JO, interior designer; b. Menomonee Falls, Wis., Sept. 12, 1965; d. Donald Arthur and Dorothy Patricia (Krutz) N. BS, U. Wis., Stevens Point, 1987. Interior designer Forrer Bus. Interiors, Milw., 1987—. Vol. Sojourner Truth House, Milw., 1994—. Mem. Am. Soc. Interior Designers. Methodist. Home: 2543 N 65th St Wauwatosa WI 53213-1408

NIENSTED, SERENA MAY, art educator, reading consultant; b. St. Louis, Jan. 17, 1916; d. August Henry and Serena May (Kidd) Schult; m. John Leonard Niensted, Nov. 13, 1938 (dec. Nov. 1986); children: Timothy John, Rose Mary Niensted Jackson, Ann Marie Niensted Peacock. AB, Washington U., St. Louis, 1937; MS in Edn., No. Ill. U., 1967. Cert. tchr., Ill. English and history tchr. Prairie Home (Mo.) H.S., 1955-56; English tchr. Jamestown (Mo.) H.S., 1956-58, De Kalb (Ill.) H.S., 1960-63; reading tchr. Carl Sandburg Jr. H.S., Palatine, Ill., 1964-65; reading cons. Wood Dale (Ill.) Schs. Dist. 7, 1966-83; art instr. Coll. of Du Page, Glen Ellyn, Ill., 1987—, tutor People Educating People, 1987-89. One-woman shows include The Edge, 1985-90, 93-94; author numerous poems; contbr. articles to profl. jours. Vol. chapel organist Bensenville (Ill.) Home Soc., 1969—; mem. Bensenville Friends of the Arts, past pres., sec. Named Ms. DuPage Sr. Am., 1990. Mem. Phi Beta Kappa. Democrat. Home: 3 E Memorial Rd Bensenville IL 60106-2541

NIERADTKA, KIRSTEN, human resources specialist; b. Troy, Mich., Oct. 31, 1962; d. Adam and Uta (Kaestner) N. BS, Georgetown U., 1982; MBA, U. Mich., 1992. Credit trainee Mfrs. Hanover Trust Co., N.Y.C., 1984-85, sr. credit analyst, 1985-87; legal asst. Sullivan & Cromwell, N.Y.C., 1988-89; project mgr. City of N.Y.-Real Estate, 1989-90; asst. broker F. Steven Indsl. Real Estate, São Paolo, summer 1990; human resources analyst FMC Corp., Chgo., 1992-94, human resources mgr., 1994—. Deacon, coun. sec. St. Matthews Luth. Ch., Hoboken, N.J., 1986-90. Mem. Chgo. Coun. Fgn. Rels. (com. fgn. affairs 1993). Office: FMC Corp 200 E Randolph Rd Chicago IL 60601

NIES, HELEN WILSON, federal judge; b. Birmingham, Ala., Aug. 7, 1925; d. George Earl and Lida Blanche (Erckert) Wilson; m. John Dirk Nies ; children: Dirk, Nancy, Eric. BA, U. Mich., 1946, JD, 1948. Bar: D.C. 1961, U.S. Supreme Ct. 1962. Atty. Dept. Justice, Washington, 1948-51, Office Price Stblzn., Washington, 1951-52; assoc. Pattishall, McAuliffe and Hofstetter, Washington, 1960-66, resident ptnr., 1966-77; ptnr. Howrey & Simon, Washington, 1978-80; judge U.S. Ct. Customs and Patent Appeals, 1980-82; cir. judge U.S. Ct. Appeals Fed. Cir., 1982—; chief judge U.S. Ct. Appeals (fed. cir.), 1990-94; mem. jud. conf. U.S. Com. on Bicentennial of Constitution, 1986-92; mem. pub. adv. com. trademark affairs Dept. Commerce, 1976-80; mem. adv. bd. BNA's Patent Trademark and Copyright Jour., 1976-78; bd. visitors U. Mich. Law Sch., 1975-78; bd. visitors U. Mich. Law Sch., 1975-78; adv. for restatement of law and unfair competition Am. Law Inst., 1986—; speaker World Intellectual Property Orgn., Forum of Judges, Calcutta, 1987, European Judges Conf., Hague, 1991, Kyoto (Japan) Comparative Law Ctr., 1992, others. Recipient Athena Outstanding Alumna award U. Mich., 1987, Jefferson medal N.J. Patent Law Assn., 1991, Judicial Honoree award Bar Assn. D.C., 1992, D. of Laws, Honoris Causa, John Marshall Law Sch., Chgo., 1993. Mem. ABA (chmn. com. 203, 1972-74, com. 504, 1975-76), Bar Assn. D.C. (chmn. patent trademark copyright sect. 1975-76, dir. 1976-78), U.S. Trademark Assn. (chmn. lawyers adv. com. 1974-76, bd. dirs. 1976-78), Am. Patent Law Assn., Fed. Bar Assn., Nat. Assn. Women Lawyers (Woman Lawyer of Yr. 1980), Women's Bar D.C., Order of Coif, Phi Beta Kappa, Phi Kappa Phi. Office: US Ct Appeals Fed Cir 717 Madison Pl NW Washington DC 20439

NIEZGODA, KAREN ANN, program analyst; b. Mt. Pleasant, Pa., Sept. 30, 1965; d. George Edward and Barbara Jane (Chuey) N. BS summa cum laude, U. Pitts., 1993. Cert. mgmt. acct. Staff asst. U.S. Bur. Mines, Pitts., 1988-93, program analyst, 1993—; mem. supervisory com. MEM Fed. Credit Union, Pitts., 1989—, chair, 1994—. Mem. women's program com. Pitts. Fed. Exec. Bd., 1987-92, mem. Hispanic employment program com., 1987-92. Scholar U. Pitts., 1991. Mem. Inst. Mgmt. Accts. (Cert. of Disting. Performance 1994). Roman Catholic. Office: US Bur Mines PO Box 18070 Pittsburgh PA 15236

NIGHTINGALE, BARBRA LYNNE, English language educator, poet; b. Chgo., Aug. 6, 1949; d. Arthur Alfred and Jeri Louise (Smith) Evans; m. Oscar Allen, Aug. 3, 1968 (div. 1970); 1 child, Kimberly Beth; m. Preston S. Nightingale, Nov. 23, 1977. AA, Delgado Jr. Coll., New Orleans, 1974; BS in Health Adminstrn., Fla. Internat. U., 1980; MA in English, Fla. Atlantic U., 1985; EdD in Higher Edn., Fla. Internat. U., 1991. Assoc. prof. English Broward C.C., Pembroke Pines, Fla., 1983—; advisor south campus Phi Theta Kappa, Pembroke Pines, 1988—; coord. south campus Honors Inst., Pembroke Pines, 1992—. Author: (book of poetry) Lovers Never Die, 1981, Prelude to a Woman, 1986, Lunar Equations, 1993. Recipient Grand prize poetry Nat. Fedn. of State Poetry Socs., 1991. Mem. NEA, Hannah Kahn Poetry Found. (pres. 1994—). Home: 2231 N 52nd Ave Hollywood FL 33021-3310 Office: Broward Community Coll 7200 Pines Blvd Pmbk Pines FL 33024-7225

NIGHTINGALE, ELENA OTTOLENGHI, geneticist, physician, administrator; b. Livorno, Italy, Nov. 1, 1932; came to U.S., 1939; d. Mario Lazzaro and Elisa Vittoria (Levi) Ottolenghi; m. Stuart L. Nightingale, July 1, 1965; children—Elizabeth, Marisa. A.B. summa cum laude, Barnard Coll., 1954; Ph.D., Rockefeller U., 1961; M.D., NYU, 1964. Asst. prof. Cornell U. Med. Coll., N.Y.C., 1965-70, Johns Hopkins U., Balt., 1970-73; fellow in clin. genetics and pediatrics Georgetown U. Hosp., Washington, 1973-74; sr. staff officer NAS, Washington, 1975-79, sr. program officer Inst. Medicine, 1979-82, sr. scholar in residence, 1982-83; spl. advisor to pres. Carnegie Corp. N.Y., N.Y.C., 1983-94, sr. program officer, 1989-94; scholar-in-residence Nat. Acad. Scis., Washington, 1995—; vis. assoc. prof. Harvard U. Med. Sch., Boston, 1980-84, vis. lectr., 1984—; adj. prof. pediatrics Georgetown U. Med. Ctr., 1983—, George Washington U. Med. Ctr., 1994—; mem. recombinant DNA adv. com. NIH, Bethesda, Md., 1979-83. Editor: The Breaking of Bodies and Minds: Torture, Psychiatric Abuse and the Health Professions, 1985, Prenatal Screening, Policies and Values: The Example of Neural Tube Defects, 1987; co-author: Before Birth: Prenatal Screening for Genetic Disease, 1990, Promoting the Health of Adolescents: New Directions for the 21st Century, 1993; contbr. numerous sci. articles to profl. publs. Bd. dirs. Ctr. for Youth Svcs., Washington, 1980-84, Sci. Svc. Inc., Washington, 1985—, Amnesty Internat., U.S.A., 1989-91. Sloan Found. fellow, 1974-75. Fellow AAAS (chmn. com. on sci. freedom and responsibility 1985-88), N.Y. Acad. Scis., Royal Soc. Medicine; mem. Harvey Soc., Am. Soc. Microbiology, Am. Soc. Human Genetics (social issues com. 1982-85), Genetics Soc. Am., Inst. Medicine of NAS (chmn. com. on health and human rights 1987-90), Phi Beta Kappa, Sigma Xi. Office: Nat Acad Scis 2101 Constitution Ave NW Washington DC 20418

NIKOLAIDIS, MERLENE, chemist; b. Hanover, Jamaica, Jan. 10, 1952; came to U.S., 1979; d. Joseph Ethelbert and Mavis Adassa (Gray) Blenheim; m. Louis Bunts, Nov. 1, 1979 (div. Feb. 1984); m. Aris James Nikolaidis, Jan. 1, 1994. BS in Chemistry, Lawrence Tech. U., 1987; postgrad., U. Detroit, 1994—. Lab. technician BASF Corp., Hamtramck, Mich., 1984-87, chemist, 1987-88, quality assurance supr., 1988-91; developmental chemist BASF Corp., Southfield, Mich., 1991—; motivational spkr. Impact for Youth, Detroit, 1991-94. Fellow Am. Chem. Soc.; mem. Detroit Soc. Coating Tech. Home: 5662 Cherry Ln West Bloomfield MI 48324 Office: BASF Corp 26701 Telegraph Rd Southfield MI 48034-2442

NIKOLAY, PATRICIA ANN, special education educator; b. Hanna, Ind., Dec. 20, 1950; d. George Franklin Weckerly and Loretta Joan (Kauchak) Weckerly-Daffron; m. Jerry Lynn Haynes, Oct. 30, 1970 (div. Mar. 1977); m. Steven James Nikolay, July 17, 1987 (div. 1994); children: Abigail Patricia, James Steven. BS, Wright State U., 1977; MS, U. Wis., 1990. Cert. tchr., Wis., Ind. Tchr. learning disabled Wilmington (Ohio) Schs., 1977-78, Pewaukee (Wis.) Schs., 1978-80; tchr. learning disabled, emotionally disabled, EMR Abbotsford (Wis.) Schs., 1986-88; tchr. emotionally disabled, learning disabled Little Chute (Wis.) Schs., 1988—. Mem. NEA, Wis. Edn. Assn., Little Chute Assn. Democrat. Roman Catholic. Home: 736 Peppergrass Ln Neenah WI 54956 Office: Little Chute Schs 1402 N Freedom Rd Little Chute WI 54140

NILES, BARBARA ELLIOTT, psyanalyst; b. Boston, Jan. 31, 1939; d. Byron Kauffman and Helen Alice (Heissler) Elliott; m. John Denison, June 25, 1960 (div. 1981); children: Catherine, Andrew. AA, Briarcliff Coll., 1958; BA, SUNY, 1984; MSW, Hunter Coll., 1986. Cert. social worker; cert. in psychotherapy and psychoanalysis Inst. Contemporary Psychotherapy and Psychoanalysis, 1990. Exec. com. Legal Aid Soc. Women's Aux., N.Y.C., 1965-67; sec. Water Quality Task Force Scientists' Com. for Pub. Info., N.Y.C., 1973-74; founding dir., sec. Consumer Action Now Inc., N.Y.C., 1970-77; dir. devel. Consumer Action Now's Council Environ., N.Y.C., 1976-77; dir. 170 Tenants Corp., N.Y.C., 1979-81; mem. pub. interest com. Cosmopolitan Club, N.Y.C., 1979-82; dir. INFORM Inc., N.Y.C., 1978-84; pvt. practice psychotherapy and psychoanalysis N.Y.C., 1986—; mem. faculty metro ctr. Empire State Coll., N.Y.C., 1987—. Editor: biography: Off the Beaten Track, 1984. Mem. Nat. Assn. Social Workers. Clubs: Cosmopolitan (N.Y.C.), The Vincent (Boston). Office: 230 Central Park W New York NY 10024-6029

NILLES, JAIME MARIE, educator; b. Coshocton, Ohio, July 6, 1961. BA, Ohio No. U., Ada, 1983; MA, U. Akron, 1992. Tchr. 7th grade sci. Norton (Ohio) City Schs., 1985—; coach, mem. athletic coun. Norton City Schs. Mem. NEA, Ohio Edn. Assn. Home: 4379 Greenwich Rd Norton OH 44203 Office: Norton City Schs 4128 S Cleveland-Massillon Norton OH 44203

NIMAN, DOROTHY I., artist; b. Lewiston, Idaho, Dec. 6, 1950; d. Allen and Edith (Niman) Sundstrom; m. Pete Kassel, Dec. 4, 1967 (div. 1980); children: Claricia, Katherine, Pete II. Degree in applied art and sci., Walla Walla C.C., Clarkston, Wash., 1985. Freelance artist Kamiah, Idaho. Home and Office: 212 Hill St PO Box 535 Kamiah ID 83536

NINTEMANN, TERRI, legislative staff member; b. Rochester, Minn., Mar. 16, 1963; d. John F. and Janice A. (Blair) Nintemann; m. Vincent J. Kiernan, Aug. 27, 1994. BS, U. Minn., 1985. Legis. asst. Farm Credit Svcs., St. Paul, Minn., 1986; intern, receptionist U.S. Senator Rudy Boschwitz, Washington, 1985, legis. corr., 1986-87, legis. asst., 1987-91; legis. dir. U.S. Rep. Dave Camp, Washington, 1991-92; profl. staff mem. Senate Agrl. Com., U.S. Senate, Washington, 1992—. Mem. U. Minn. Alumni, FFA Alumni (life mem.), Rep. Women of Capital Hill. Republican. Roman Catholic. Office: Senate Agrl Com 328 A Russell Senate Office Bldg Washington DC 20510

NIPERT, DONNA ANN See **BARRETT, JESSICA**

NISHITANI, MARTHA, dancer; b. Seattle, Feb. 27, 1920; d. Denjiro and Jin (Aoto) N. B.A. in Comparative Arts, U. Wash., 1958; studied with, Eleanor King, Mary Ann Wells, Perry Mansfield, Cornish Sch., Conn. Coll. Sch. Dance, Long Beach State U. Founder, dir. Martha Nishitani Modern Dance Sch. and Co., Seattle, 1950—; dance dir. Helen Bush Sch. and Central YWCA, 1951-54; choreographer U. Wash. Opera Theater, 1955-65, Intiman Theater, 1972—; dance instr. Elementary and Secondary Edn. Act Program, 1966; dance specialist spl. edn. program Shoreline Pub. Schs., 1970-72; condr. workshops and concerts King County Youth Correctional Instns., 1972-73; Dance adv. counsel Wash. Cultural Enrichment Program; dance adv. bd. Seattle Parks and Recreation. Dancer Eleanor King Co., Seattle, 1946-50, dance films, 1946-51, Channel 9, Ednl. TV, 1967-68; lectr. demonstrator numerous colls., festivals, convs., childrens theater.; author articles on dance; one of the subjects: A Celebration of 100 Years of Dance in Washington, 1989. Trustee Allied Arts Seattle, 1967. Recipient Theta Sigma Phi Matrix Table award, 1968, Asian Am. Living Treasure award Northwest Asian Am. Theater, 1984; listed Dance Archives, N.Y.C. Libr., 1991, N.Y.C. Lincoln Ctr. Dance Archives, 1991, U. Wash. Libr. Archives, 1993, exhibit of Japanese Am. Women of Achievement, Burke Mus., 1994, 40th Anniversary of Martha Nishitani Modern Dance Sch. Mem. Am. Dance Guild (exec. com. 1961-63), Com. Research in Dance, Seattle Art Mus., Internat. Dance Alliance (adv. council 1984), Smithsonian Assos., Progressive Animal Welfare Soc. Address: 4205 University Way NE PO Box 45264 Seattle WA 98145-0264

NISSENSON, NORMA, clinical psychologist; b. Frankfort, Ky., Nov. 18, 1917; d. Jacob and Pearl (Klass) Rosen; m. Marc Nissenson, July 6, 1940; children: Carol, Mary. BS, Northwestern U., 1938, MA, 1948. Cert. clin. psychologist, Ill. Exec. dir. Guidance Agy. Adolecents, Chgo., 1946-52; assoc prof. Roosevelt U., Chgo., 1962-70; gen. practice psychology Nissenson Assocs. Ltd., Chgo., 1962—. Bd. dirs. Moraine council Girl Scouts USA, Moraine PTA, Operation Higher Edn. Pays; pres. N. Shore Film Soc.; lectr., participant TV talk shows, Chgo., 1962—. Fellow Am. Orthopsychiat. Assn., Internat. Council Sex Edn. and Parenthood; mem. Am. Psychol. Assn., Ill. Psychol. Assn., Chgo. Psychol. Assn. (pres. 1982), Am. Assn. Counseling and Devel. (life), Am. Assn. Marriage and Family Therapist, Ill. Commn. Human Relations (state adv. council). Home: 966 Princeton Ave Highland Park IL 60035-2380 Office: 1971 2nd St Ste 600 Highland Park IL 60035-3134

NIX, BARBARA LOIS, real estate broker; b. Yakima, Wash., Sept. 25, 1929; d. Martin Clayton and Norma (Gunter) Westfield; A.A., Sierra Coll., 1978; m. B.H. Nix, July 12, 1968; children—William Martin Dahl, Theresa Irene Dahl; step-children—Dennis Leon, Denise Lynn. Bookkeeper, office mgr. Lakeport (Calif.) Tire Service, 1966-69, Dr. K.J. Absher, Grass Valley, Calif., 1972-75; real estate sales and office mgr. Rough and Ready Land Co., Penn Valley, Calif., 1976-77, co-owner, v.p., sec., 1978—, also of Wildwood West Real Estate and Lake of the Pines Sales, Gateway Real Estate. Youth and welfare chmn. Yakima Federated Jr. Women's Club, 1957; den mother Cub Scouts, 1959-60; leader Girl Scouts, 1961-62; mem. Friends of Hospice; mem. Sierra, Nev. Meml. Hosp. Found.; adv. bd. dirs. Roots and Wings Ednl. Found., mini-grant co-chair. Recipient Pres.'s award Sierra Coll., 1973; others. Mem. Penn Valley C. of C., Nat. Assn. Female Execs., Antique Soc. Penn Valley (founder, pres. 1978), Sierra Nevada Meml. Hosp. Aux. Democrat. Roman Catholic. Clubs: Job's Daus. (life). Home: 19365 Wildflower Dr Penn Valley CA 95946-9720 Office: PO Box 191 Rough and Ready CA 95975

NIX, CLAUDIA PUGH, retail executive; b. Cleve., Apr. 21, 1944; d. Robert Edward and Elinor Joy (Pitman) Pugh; m. Carl Michael Nix, May 9, 1970. BA, Warren Wilson Coll., 1969. Counselor for traveler's aid Family Counseling Svcs., Asheville, N.C., 1970-72; social work youth svcs. N.C. Dept. Corrections, Swannanoa, 1972-73; program dir. for health and phys. edn. YWCA, Asheville, N.C., 1973-75; movement edn. specialist Buncombe County Schs., Asheville, 1975-76; instr. adult basic edn. Asheville-Buncombe Tech. Coll., 1976-84; co-owner Liberty Bicycles, Asheville, 1984—. Bd. dirs. Riverlink, Asheville, 19906; mem. Bikeways Task Force of U.AMPO, Asheville, 1989—; founder, bd. dirs. Blue ridge Bicycle Club, Asheville, 1974; area rep. Kenilworth Residence Assn., Asheville, 1977; founder Rape Crisis Ctr. of Asheville, 1976. Rated as Top 100 dealer in U.S., Bicycle Dealers Showcase mag., 1994. Mem. Nat. Bicycle Dealers Assn., Am. Lung Assn. (western region, Vol. of Yr. 1992),. Office: Libery Bicycles Inc 1987 Hendersonville Hwy Asheville NC 28803

NIX, SUZANNE DEE, science educator; b. Providence, June 3, 1945; d. William Herbert Guyer and Edith (Stuhltrager) Kellogg; m. Robert G. Nix Jr., Aug. 29, 1980 (div. Oct. 1989); children: Stephanie VanPelt Ouverson, Rob, Craig Nay, Lara. A degree, Bucks County C.C., 1971; BS summa cum laude, Trenton State U., 1972; MS, Nova S.E. U., 1993. Cert. tchr., Fla. Exec. sec. McGraw-Hill, Inc., Hightstown, N.J., 1966-69; tchr. Parkway Mid. Sch., Ft. Lauderdale, Fla., 1973-75, Parkway Elem. Sch., Wilkesboro, N.C., 1976-78; sci. tchr., dept. chair Olsen Mid. Sch., Dania, Fla., 1979—. Recipient Alumni Practicum Honors award Nova S.E. U., 1994. Mem. ASCD, AAUW, Am. Bus. Women's Assn., Sister Schs. Internat., Inc. (sec. 1992—, bd. dirs.). Methodist. Home: 3001 SW 36th Ave Hollywood FL 33023

NIXON, CAROL HOLLADAY, state administrator; b. Salt Lake City, Dec. 25, 1937; d. Earl Parnell and Mary Regina (Harris) H.; m. William Lynn Nixon, Sept. 9, 1957; children: William H., Joan Turley, Michael L., Jennifer Campbell, Jacqueline Le Cheminant, John Nixon. Student, Brigham Young U. Aide Senator Herman Welker, Washington, 1956-57, Senator Henry Dworshak, Washington, 1959-62, Senator Len Jordan, Washington, 1962-64; asst. Mayor Eddie Pedersen, Idaho Falls, 1965-66; exec. dir. Senator Orrin Hatch, Salt Lake City, 1977-80, dep. campaign mgr., 1982; dir. Utah Arts Coun., 1985-91; from dep. to chief of staff Gov. Norman H. Bangerter, State of Utah, 1992-93; dir. div. of community devel. State of Utah, 1993—; chair Utah State Homeless Coordinating com., 1993—, Utah Housing Devel. Adv. Bd., 1993—, Utah Pvt. Activity Bond Rev. Bd., 1993—; mem. Salt Palace Renovation and Expansion Com., 1991—; commr. Utah Statehood Centennial Commn., 1992—; mem. cabinet Gov. Michael O. Leavitt, 1993—; bd. dirs. Utah Families Found., Utah Sci. Authority. Mem. community adv. bd. Jr. League of Salt Lake City, 1986-90; bd. dirs. Promised Valley Playhouse, 1988-90, Salt Palace/Fine Arts Adv. Bd., 1985-88, Pioneer Theatre Co., 1985-87, Univ. of Utah Instnl. Coun., 1985, Utah Symphony, 1983-84, Nat. Fedn. of Rep. Women, 1984-85; pres. Utah Symphony Guild, 1983-84, Utah Fedn. of Rep. Women, 1984-85; Utah co-chair Women for Reagan-Bush, 1984; mem. Coun. of State Community Devel. Agencies. Named Outstanding Rep. Women Utah Fedn. of Rep. Women, 1993; recipient Music Svc. award State Ofcl. of Edn., 1986. Mem. Ch. LDS.

NIXON, FREDRICA ANN, jeweler, smoking therapist; b. New Britain, Conn., Dec. 18, 1940; d. Frederick Michael and Dora (Cararini) Palmieri; m. Nicholas Albert Pezzulo, Sept. 12, 1964 (dec. July 1976); children: Paul F., Marc P., Erica Ann; m. Leon Earl Nixon, July 16, 1989. Student, Centenary Coll., 1959-61, Berghof Sch Acting, 1961, Gemological Inst. Am., 1990—. Pres., founder Goldilock's Ltd., Williamsville, N.Y.; pres. Stop Smoking Plan, East Amherst, N.Y., 1981—, Stop Smoking Internat., East Amherst, 1986—, Ricki & Co., Williamsville. Author: Stop Smoking Program, 1984. Mem. N.Y. State Jewelers Assn., Jewelers Bd. of Trade, Gemological Inst. Am. Alumni Assn. Republican. Roman Catholic. Home and Office: 79 Britannia Dr East Amherst NY 14051 Office: Ricki & Co 7954 Transit Rd Ste 231 Williamsville NY 14221

NIXON, JOYCE ELAINE, chiropractor, educator, consultant; b. Corning, N.Y., Feb. 17, 1925; d. Douglas Lewis and Mina Phiolana (Barnes) Williams; m. Lewis Earl Nixon, June 21, 1946 (div. Nov. 1958); 1 child, Deborah Joy. BA, Webster U., 1945; postgrad., SUNY, Geneseo, 1952-53; student, PBTS Bible Inst., 1946. Adminstr., chiropractic technician Dr. DeLue, Nunda, N.Y., 1958-85, cons., 1986—; instr. Sacro Occipital Research Soc. Internat., Inc., Omaha, 1966-79. Active Genessee Valley Council on Arts, Geneseo, 1967—; pres., bd. dirs. Nunda Community Home, Inc., 1983—. Mem. Internat. Platform Assn., N.Y. State Chiropractic Women's Aux., Nat. Assn. for Female Execs. (N.Y. State chpt.), Sacro Occipital Research Soc. (internat. sec. 1965-70, officer 1976, Disting. Profl. Service Founder's award 1976, Pres.' award 1980), N.Y. State Bus. and Profl. Women's Assn. (bd. dirs. 1963-71), Internat. Fedn. Bus. and Profl. Women, Geneva Bus. and Profl. Womens Clubs Inc. Republican. Home: 49 Golden Pond Est Akron NY 14001-9548

NIXON, MARNI, singer; b. Altadena, Calif., Feb. 22, 1930; d. Charles and Margaret (Wittke) McEathron; m. Ernest Gold, May 22, 1950 (div. 1969); children: Andrew Maurice, Martha Alice, Melani Christine; m. Lajos Frederick Fenster, July 23, 1971 (div. July 1975); m. Albert David Block, Apr. 11, 1983. Student opera workshop, Los Angeles City Coll., UCLA, U. So. Calif., Tanglewood, Mass. Dir. vocal faculty Calif. Inst. Arts, Valencia, 1970-72; pvt. tchr., vocal coacn, condr. master classes, 1970—, pvt. voice tchr., coach, condr. master classes, 1970—; head apprentice div. Santa Barbara Music Acad. of West, 1980; formerly dir. opera workshop Cornish Inst. Arts, Seattle.; tchr. in field; judge Met. Opera Internat. Am. Music Awards, Nat. Inst. Music Theatre, 1984, 85-86, 87; panelist New Music, Nat. Assn. Tchrs. Singing, pres. (N.Y. chpt.), 1994—; dialect dir., opera recs. Child actress Pasadena (Calif.) Playhouse, 1940-45, soloist Roger Wagner chorale, 1947-53, appeared with New Eng. Opera Co., Los Angeles Opera Co., also Ford Found. TV Opera, 1948-63, San Francisco Spring Opera, 1966, Seattle Opera, 1971, 72, 73; classical recitals and appearances with symphony orchs. throughout U.S., Can., also Eng., Israel, Ireland; appeared on Broadway as Eliza Doolittle in My Fair Lady, 1964; in motion picture as Sister Sophia in Sound of Music, 1964; also in numerous TV shows and night clubs; star children's ednl. TV show Boomerang, ABC-TV, from 1975; off-Broadway show Taking My Turn, from 1983, Opal, from 1992; appeared in (stage plays) Romeo & Juliet, N.Y.C.; taped for Great Performances PBS-TV Role of Edna, 1994; voice dubbed in for musical motion pictures My Fair Lady, The King and I, An Affair to Remember, West Side Story, and others; rec. artist for Columbia, Mus. Heritage Records, Capital, RCA Victor, Ednl.Records, Reference Recs., Varese-Sarabande, Nonesuch; played violin at age 4; studied in youth orch., 10 yrs; studied voice at age 10. Recipient 4 Emmy awards for best actress, 2 Action for Childrens TV awards, 1977; nominee Drama Desk award; recipient Chgo. Film Festival award, 1977, Gold Record for Songs from Mary Poppins, 2 time Grammy award nominee Nat. Acad. Rec. Arts and Scis. (1st rec. Cabaret Songs and Early Songs by Arnold Schoenberg, RCA, 1977 and 1st rec. Emily Dickinson Songs by Aaron Copland, Reference Recs., 1988. Mem. Nat. Assn. Tchrs. Singing (pres. N.Y. chpt. 1994—).

NIXON, SHIRNETTE MARILYN, pharmaceutical company administrator; b. N.Y.C., Apr. 14, 1947; d. Clifford Bernard and Edna Lucille (Anglin) N. BA in English, Bklyn. Coll., 1969. Pers. asst. Mut. N.Y., N.Y.C., 1969-73; editorial asst. Franklin Watts Inc., N.Y.C., 1973-76; adminstrv. sec. for pers. Pfizer, Inc., N.Y.C., 1976-82, adminstrv. sec. for tax, 1982—, oral communication specialist, 1988—; instr. to exec. secs. Prizer, 1988, 89, Mabel Dean Bacon H.S., 1990; leader N.Y. Care Team, 1994. Mem. YWCA Helpline. Recipient Spl. Recognition Letter Mayor David Dinkins. Mem. AAUW, Internat. Tng. in Communication, Bklyn. Coll. Alumni Assn. Democrat. Office: Pfizer Inc 235 E 42nd St New York NY 10017-5703

NIXON, TAMARA FRIEDMAN, banker; b. Cleve., June 3, 1938; d. Victor and Eva J. (Osteryoung) Friedman; m. Daniel D. Nixon, June 14, 1959; children: Asa Joel, Naomi Devorah, Victoria Eve. BA with honors in econs. (Wellesley scholar), Wellesley Coll., 1959; MBA, U. Pitts., 1961. Asst. economist Fed. Res. Bank, N.Y.C., 1959-60, 61-62; economist R.P. Wolff Econ. Rsch., Miami, Fla., 1972-75; econ. cons., Miami, 1975-79; sr. v.p. Washington Savs. & Loan Assn., Miami Beach, Fla., 1979-81; pres. T.F. Nixon Econ. Cons. Inc., 1982—; sr. v.p. CenTrust Savs. Bank, 1984-89; dir. fin. instn. svcs. Keyes Asset Mgmt., Inc., 1991—; real estate feasibility cons.; Budget adv. com. City of Miami Beach, Fla. Fellow U. Pitts., 1961. Land use chmn. Dade County chpt. LWV, 1975-76. Mem. Econ. Soc. S. Fla. (v.p. programs, dir.), Am. Econ. Assn. Office: Sun Bank Internat Ctr 1 Southeast 3rd Ave Miami FL 33131-1704

NIZZE, JUDITH ANNE, physician assistant; b. L.A., Nov. 1, 1942; d. Robert George and Charlotte Ann (Wise) Swan; m. Norbert Adolph Otto Paul Nizze, Dec. 31, 1966. BA, UCLA, 1966, postgrad., 1966-76; grad. physician asst. tng. program, Charles R. Drew Sch. Postgrad., L.A., 1979; BS, Calif. State U., Dominguez, 1980. Cert. physician asst., Calif. Staff rsch. assoc. I-II Wadsworth Vet. Hosp., L.A., 1965-71; staff rsch. assoc. III-IV John Wayne Clinic Jonsson Comprehensive Cancer Ctr., UCLA, 1971-78; clin. asst. Robert S. Ozeran, Gardena, Calif., 1978; physician asst. family practice Fred Chasan, Torrance, Calif., 1980-82; sr. physician asst. Donald L. Morton prof., chief surg. oncology Jonsson Comprehensive Cancer Ctr., UCLA, 1983-91; administrv. dir. clin. rsch. John Wayne Cancer Inst., Santa Monica, Calif., 1991—. Contbr. articles to profl. jours. Fellow Am. Acad. Physician Assts., Am. Assn. Surgeons Assts., Calif. Acad. Physician Assts.; mem. Assn. Physician Assts. in Oncology, Am. Sailing Assn. Republican. Presbyterian. Home: 13243 Fiji Way Unit J Marina Dl Rey CA 90292-7079 Office: John Wayne Cancer Inst St John's Hosp & Health Ctr 1328 22nd St Santa Monica CA 90404-2091

NOAH, JULIA JEANINE, librarian; b. Craig, Mo., July 14, 1932; d. Hiram Curtis and Eloise Julia (Puckett) True; m. Raymond Laverne Noah, Sept. 5, 1954; children: David Scott, Danny Ray, Deborah Jill, Douglas True. BS, U. Ill., 1953; MA in Library Sci., U. South Fla., 1983. Asst. rsch. librarian Parke, Davis & Co., Detroit, 1953-55; cataloging librarian U. Mo., Columbia, 1955-57; sch. librarian High Point Elem. Sch., Clearwater, Fla., 1968; library aide Clearwater High Sch., 1973-78; reference asst. Dunedin (Fla.) Pub. Library, 1978-84, dir. info. svcs., 1984-88, library dir., 1988-94. Mem. ALA, AAUW, DAR, Fla. Libr. Assn., Phi Kappa Phi, Beta Phi Mu. Republican. Presbyterian.

NOAKES, BETTY L., elementary school educator; b. Oklahoma City, Okla., Aug. 28, 1938; d. Webster L. and Willie Ruth (Johnson) Hawkins; m. Richard E. Noakes, Apr. 22, 1962 (dec.); 1 child, Michele Monique. Student, Oklahoma City U., MEd, 1971; BS, Cen. State U., 1962. Cert. therapeutic recration specialist, Okla. Elem. tchr. Merced (Calif.) Pub. Schs., 1966-67, Oklahoma City Schs., 1971-73, Mid-Del Schs., Midwest City, Okla., 1973—. 2nd v.p. PTA, Pleasant Hill, 1991, cert. recognition 1992-93; active Nat. PTA, 1991-92. Recipient Cert. Appreciation YMCA, 1992-92, Disting. Svc. award Mid-Del PTA, 1992. Mem. NEA, ASCD, AAUW, NAACP, Nat. Therapeutic Recreation Assn., Okla. Edn. Assn., Okla. Reading Assn., Okla. Therapeutic Recreation Assn., Nat. Mus. Am. Indian (charter), Smithsonian Inst., Oklahoma City U. Alumni Assn., Meth. Women Assn., Ctrl. State U. Alumni Assn., Okla. Ea. Star (charter mem. Lilly of Valley chpt.), Zeta Phi Beta, Phi Del Kappa. Home: 5956 N Coltrane Rd Oklahoma City OK 73121-3409 Office: 4346 NE 36th St Oklahoma City OK 73121-5400

NOBLE, ADELAIDE, association executive, social worker; b. Buffalo, Aug. 21, 1907; d. Joseph Wilcox and Mary Fassett (Grosvenor) N. BA, Wellesley Coll., 1929; MSW, U. Buffalo, 1951. Program dir. YWCA, Hartford, Conn., 1929-35, Richmond, Va., 1935-38, Niagara Falls, N.Y., 1938-42; br. exec. dir. YWCA, Buffalo, 1942-51; exec. dir. YWCA, Erie, Pa., 1951-57; assoc. exec. dir. YWCA, Buffalo, 1957-68; mem. Bd. Examiners of Cert. Social Workers, N.Y. State, 1966-69. Mem. NASW (chmn. Niagara Falls chpt. 1942, chmn. Erie chpt. 1951, award 1956, chmn. Buffalo chpt. 1957, award 1965). Republican. Presbyterian. Home: 800 Lake Port Blvd Apt C401 Leesburg FL 34748-7660

NOBLE, AMY JO, buyer; b. Longview, Wash., Aug. 16, 1960; d. Leon Thomas and Mary Rae (Baker) N. BA in Mktg., BA in Textiles & Clothing, Univ. Puget Sound, 1982. Customer svc. mgr. Jafco div. Best Products, Bellevue, Wash., 1982-83, buyer giftware and tabletop, 1983-85; assoc. buyer toys Best Products Co. Inc., Richmond, Va., 1985-86, buyer toys, 1986-89, sr. buyer toys, 1989-93; buyer toys Wal-Mart Stores, Inc., Bentonville, Ark., 1993—. Named Univ. Greek Woman of Yr. Mem. Mortar Bd., Alpha Phi, Phi Kappa Phi. Office: Wal-Mart Stores Inc 702 SW 8th St Bentonville AR 72714

NOBLE, CHERRIE SAILE, librarian; b. Lawrence, Kans., Nov. 29, 1953; d. Jack Felix and Donna Jane (King) Saile; m. Michael Charles Noble, May 23, 1992. BA, U. Kans, 1979; MLS, Emporia (Kans.) State U., 1980. Rsch. and instrn. libr. U. Kans. Sch. Bus., Lawrence, 1980—. Mem. ALA, Spl. Librs. Assn. (nominating com. 1992, 93), Kans. Libr. Assn., Phi Alpha Theta, Phi Kappa Phi. Office: 103 Summerfield Hall U Kans Sch Bus Lawrence KS 66045

NOBLE, DEE, artist; b. Roanoke, Ala.; d. Lester Braxton and Edna (Chatman) N.; children from previous marriage: Jay Souza, Jon Souza; m. Warren Brown; 1 child, Christopher. AA, Atlanta Art Inst., 1961; postgrad., Santa Monica Coll., 1976-80, UCLA, 1983-86; cert. of art, Royal Coll. of Art, London, 1985. Illustrator Dept. of the Army, Washington, 1961-62; fashion model various fashion houses, 1962-72; tchr. John Robert Powers Modeling Sch., L.A., 1970-72, Barbizon Modeling Sch., Atlanta, 1972-74; tchr. quilting and interior design Learning Tree, Chatsworth, Calif., 1984-87, Everywoman's Village, Van Nuys, Calif., 1984-89, Glendale (Calif.) C.C., Santa Monica Coll., 1984-94; artist, designer Dee Noble Studio, L.A. and Wrightwood, Calif., 1974-94; owner quilt shop Purple Cow, Wrightwood, 1986-94; owner gourmet shop Aubergine, Wrightwood, 1991-94; owner Cross Creek Farms of Appalachia, Tenn., 1994—; art tutor West High acad. decathlon team Torrance (Calif.) Unified Sch. Dist., 1987; participant Royal Acad. Summer Art Exhbn., London, 1993, 94, Dee Noble Sculpture Tour, U.S., Great Britain, Australia, 1994—; dir. and coord. Carmel (Calif.) Outdoor Summer Art Festival, 1994; owner Cross Creek Farms of Appalachia, Tenn. One-woman shows include Kottler Galleries, N.Y.C., 1981, Keri's Art Gallerie, World Trade Ctr., 1983, Cunningham Art Gallery, Bakersfield, Calif., 1982 (1st prize); exhibited in group shows at various galleries U.S., London, Ireland, 1974—; author short stories; designer children's toys, stage clothes (Best of Show award 1984). Dir., coord. Carmel (Calif.) Outdoor Summer Art Festival, 1994. Recipient Watercolor award Inglewood Art Assn., 1978, Affair in the Gardens, Beverly Hills, Calif., 1981, Top Art award Tosco Corp., 1983. Mem. Internat. Platform Assn. (2nd place award Nat. Art Competition 1994). Home and Studio: Dee Noble Studio Carmel CA 93921

NOBLE, MARION ELLEN, retired home economist; b. Blanchardville, Wis., Feb. 18, 1914; d. Dwight Eldridge and Doris Edna (Parkinson) Baker; m. B. Frank Smyth (dec. 1979); children: William, Ann Smyth Marris, Robert, Larry, Margaret Smyth Decker; m. George C. Noble, 1981. BS, U. Wis., Madison, 1936. V.p. Smyth Bus Systems, Canton, Ohio, 1950; womens editor Radio Station WFAH, Alliance, Ohio, 1952-58; home economist extension svc. Stark County, Ohio State U., Canton, 1961-70. Contbr. articles to profl. jours. Named Woman of the Year Urban League, Canton, 1964. Mem. AAUW, Nat. Assn. Extension Home Economists, Pacific Pioneer Broadcasters, Home Econs. Club, Thimble Collectors Internat., Ladies Oriental Shrine of North Am., Phi Upsilon Omicron, Epsilon Sigma Phi. Republican. Methodist. Home: 3240 San Amadeo # A Laguna Hills CA 92653-3037

NOBLE, MARY CATHERINE, physical therapist, nurse; b. Hamilton County, Kans., Mar. 20, 1920; d. Hartwell John and Margaret Katherine (Williamson) N. Diploma in Nursing, Paradise Valley Sch. Nursing, National City, Calif., 1945; BS in Nursing Edn., Pacific Union Coll., Angwin, Calif., 1950; student, Royal Coll. Nursing, London, 1953, Loma Linda U., 1955. RN, Calif.; registered phys. therapist, Calif., Colo., Kans. Supr. nursing Paradise Valley Hosp., National City, 1946-49; sister tutor, matron Andrews Meml. Hosp., Kingston, Jamaica, 1950-51; clin. supr. Washington Adventist Hosp., Takoma Park, Md., 1954-59; asst. chief therapist Loma Linda (Calif.) San and Hosp., 1960-62; chief therapist Paradise Valley Hosp., 1962-64; clinic therapist Med.-Dental Clinic, Eugene, Oreg., 1964-68; pvt. practice Action Assocs., Eugene, 1968-72; chief therapist Atlanta West Hosp., 1972, Battle Creek (Mich.) Adventist Hosp., 1972-74, Madison (Tenn.) Hosp., 1974-81; pvt. practice Action Assocs., Johnson, Kans., 1982—. Co-author: Hydrotherapy and Massage, 1964; co-editor: Stanton County History, 1987; columnist Life and Health, 15 yrs. Sec.-treas. Stanton County Hist. Soc., Johnson, Kans. Mem. Am. Phys. Therapy Assn. Republican. Seventh-day Adventist. Office: Action Assocs Phys Therapy 116 S Main St Johnson KS 67855

NOBLE, SUNNY A., business owner; b. Moorhead, Minn., May 22, 1940; m. Eric Scott Noble, Apr. 11, 1980. MBA, U. Calif., Berkeley, 1960; qualified parapsychologist, U. Minn., 1979. Mgr. Spear & Hill Attys., N.Y.C., 1969-70; mgr. exec. property mgmt. May Co. Dept. Stores, La Jolla, Calif., 1981-82; owner, pres. The Computer Tutor, L.A., 1984—. Author: (newspaper column) That Computes, 1984-88, The Storyteller, 1987-91. Mem. Internat. Platform Assn., Toastmasters Internat. (ednl. v.p. 1988), Mensa, Beta Sigma Phi. Home and Office: 4152 West Ave L-2 Quartz Hill CA 93536-4216

NOBLES, LORRAINE BIDDLE, dietitian; b. Washington, Apr. 27, 1926; d. Norton William and Lorraine Verna (Tabler) Biddle; m. Stevens Henry Nobles, Dec. 28, 1961 (dec. Apr. 1987). BS, Ohio U., 1952; MSHE, East Carolina U., 1973, MS, 1989. Asst. adminstr. dietitian Emergency Hosp., Washington, 1952-56; asst. supr. sch. lunch program Arlington (Va.) County, 1956-66; chief dietitian Pitt County Meml. Hosp., Greenville, N.C., 1966-91; adj. prof. East Carolina U., Greenville, 1969-91. Mem. Am. Dietetic Assn., N.C. Dietetic Assn. (chmn. ann. meeting 1982), Ea. N.C. Dist. Dietetic Assn. (pres. elect 1977-78, pres. 1978-79, sec. 1988-90), Am. and Mid-Atlantic Soc. Parenteral and Enteral Nutrition (2d Pl. Pearls session 1988), Tau Delta Epsilon, Phi Omicron Nu, Kappa Delta Pi. Republican. Episcopalian. Home: 205 Country Club Dr Ayden NC 28513-9545

NOBLITT, NANCY ANNE, aerospace engineer; b. Roanoke, Va., Aug. 14, 1959; d. Jerry Spencer and Mary Louise (Jerrell) N. BA, Mills Coll., Oakland, Calif., 1982; M.S. in Indsl. Engring., Northeastern U., 1990. Data red specialist, Universal Energy Systems, Beaver Creek, Ohio, 1981; aerospace engr. turbine engine div. components br. turbine group aero-propulsion lab. Wright-Patterson AFB, Ohio, 1982-84, engine assessment br. spl. engines group, 1984-87; lead analyst cycle methods computer aided engr. Gen. Electric Co., Lynn Mass., 1987-90, Lynn PACES project coord., 1990-91; software systems analyst Sci. Applications Internat. Corp., with artificial intelligence Sci. Applications Internat. Corp., Mc Lean, Va., 1991-92, software engrng. mgr., intelligence applications integration, Sci. Applications Internat. Corp., Hampton, Va., 1992-93, mgr. test engrng. and systems support, 1993-94, mgr. configuration mgmt., 1994, mgmt. asst. to TBMCS program mgr., 1994—. Math and sci. tutor Centerville Sch. Bd., Ohio, 1982-86, math. and physics tutor Marblehead Sch. Bd., Mass., 1988-90; rep. alumnae admissions Mills Coll., Boston area, 1987-91. Recipient Notable Achievement award U.S. Air Force, 1984; recipient Special award Fed. Lab. Consortium, 1987. Avocation: book collecting, weight training. Home: 58 Hopkins St Newport News VA 23601 Office: Sci Applications Internat Corp Hampton VA 23666

NOBOA-STANTON, PATRICIA LYNN, corporate executive; b. Cin., Sept. 6, 1947; d. William Emile and Marie Virginia (Ballbach) Hakes; m. Donald R. Stanton, Nov. 10, 1987; children from previous marriage: Aric Israel, Rene Carlos. Diploma Presbyn.-St. Luke's Sch. Nursing, Chgo., 1967, Nat. Inst. Real Estate, 1989, No. Va. Community Coll., 190. Supr. patient care Alexandria Hosp., Va., 1976-78; pres. Renaissance Reprographics, Inc., Reston, Va., 1985-89; pres. Va. Leasing & Copying Inc., Reston, 1978-89; realtor Wellborn Comml., 1989-91; dir. ops., publ. and health cons. Atlantic Resources Corp., 1991-93, dir. ops. and adminstrn., 1991—; exec. v.p. Mark Moseley's Travel, 1993—. Pres. Reston Bd. Commerce, 1985, founding bd. dirs. 1982-85, v.p. 1984, sec. 1983; v.p. Planned Community Archives, Inc., 1985-88; mem. regional com. United Way, 1985-87; Dulles Area Regional Council steering com., 1985-88; pres. Mytерra Home-owners Assn., 1990—; bd. dirs. N. Va. Local Devel. Corp., 1987—; bd. dirs. Fairfax Symphony,

Reston Bd. Commerce, 1989. Named Reston Citizen of Yr., 1985; named Small Bus. Person of Yr. Fairfax County Commn. for Women, 1985-87. Mem. Northern Va. Assn. Realtors, Nat. Assn. Realtors, Va. Assn. Realtors, Nat. Assn. Quick Printers (bd. dirs. Capital chpt. 1984—, vice chair 1987—), Internat. Platform Assn., Fairfax County C. of C. (bd. dirs. 1985-86, 87—), Herndon C. of C., Washington-Dulles Task Force. Episcopalian. Lodge: Rotary. Avocations: computers, music, flying. Office: Mark Moseley's Travel 4000 Legato Rd Ste 200 Fairfax VA 22033

NOCHMAN, LOIS WOOD KIVI (MRS. MARVIN NOCHMAN), educator; b. Detroit, Nov. 5, 1924; d. Peter K. and Annetta Lois (Wood) Kivi; AB, U. Mich., 1946, AM, 1949; m. Harold I. Pitchford, Sept. 6, 1944 (div. May 1949); children: Jean Wood Pitchford Horiszny, Joyce Lynn Pitchford Undiano; m. Marvin A. Nochman, Aug. 15, 1953; 1 child, Joseph Asa. Tchr. adult edn., Honolulu, 1947, Ypsilanti (Mich.) High Sch., 1951-52; spl. instr. English, Wayne State U., Detroit, 1953, 54; tchr. Highland Park (Mich.) Coll., 1950-51, instr. English, 1954-83. Mem. exec. bd. Highland Park Fedn. Tchrs., 1963, 64, 65, 66, 71, 72, mem. 1st bargaining team, 1965-66, 73, del. to Nat. Conv., 1964, 71, 72, 73, 74, rep. higher edn. to Mich. Fedn. Tchrs. Exec. Com., 1972, 73, 74, 75, 76; mem. faculty adv. com. Gov.'s Commn. on Higher Edn., 1973—. Tchr. Baha'i schs., Davison, Mich., 1954, 55, 58, 59, 63, 64, 65, 66, Beaulac, Que., Can., 1960, Greenacre, Maine, 1965; sec. local spiritual assembly Baha'is, Ann Arbor, 1953, sec., Detroit, 1954, chmn., 1955; mem. nat. com. Baha'is U.S., 1955-68; sec. Davison Bahai Sch. Com. and Council, 1956, 58, 63, 64, 65, 66, 67, 68; Baha'i lectr. Subject of local TV show Senior Focus, 1992. Mem. Modern Lang. Assn., Nat. Coun. Tchrs. English, Mich. Coll. English Assn., Am. Fedn. Tchrs., Nat. Soc. Lit. and Arts, Women's Equity and Action League (sec. Mich. chpt. 1975-79), Alpha Lambda Delta, Alpha Gamma Delta. Contbr. poems to mags. Recipient Women's Movement plaque Women Lawyers Assn. Mich., 1975, Lawrence award Mich. Masters Swimming, 1991, 4 World Master Records In Age Group, Indpls. Short Course Meters, 1994. Avocation: U.S. Swimming Master Champion.

NODDINGS, NEL, educator, writer; b. Irvington, N.J., Jan. 19, 1929; d. Edward A. Rieth and Nellie A. (Connors) Walter; m. James A. Noddings, Aug. 20, 1949; children: Chris, Howard, Laurie, James, Nancy, William, Sharon, Edward, Vicky, Timothy. BA in Math., Montclair State Coll., 1949; MA in Math., Rutgers U., 1964; PhD in Edn., Stanford U., 1973. Cert. tchr., Calif., N.J. Tchr. Woodbury (N.J.) Publ Schs., 1949-52; tchr. math. dept. Matawan (N.J.) High Sch., 1958-62, chair, asst. prin., 1964-69; curriculum supr. Montgomery Twp. Pub. Schs., Skillman, N.J., 1970-72; dir. precollegiate edn. U. Chgo., 1975-76; asst. prof. Pa. State U., State College, 1973; from asst. prof. to assoc. prof. Stanford (Calif.) U., 1977-86, prof., 1986—, assoc. dean, 1990-92, acting dean, 1992-94, Lee L. Jacks prof. child edn., 1992—; bd. dirs. Ctr. for Human Caring Sch. Nursing, Denver, 1986-92; cons. NIE, NSF and various other sch. dists. Author: Caring: a Feminine Approach to Ethics and Moral Education, 1984, Women and Evil, 1989, (with W. Paul Shore) Awakening the Inner Eye: Intuition in Education, 1984, (with Carol Witherell) Stories Lives Tell, 1991, The Challenge to Care in Schools, 1992, Educating for Intelligent Belief or Unbelief, 1993; mem. adv. bd. Am. Jour. Edn., Ednl. Theory, Sci. and Edn.; contbr. articles to profl. jours. Mem. disting. women's adv. bd. Coll. St. Catherine. NSF fellow Rutgers U., 1962-64; recipient medal for disting. svc. Tchrs. Coll. Columbia, 1994. Fellow Philosophy of Edn. Soc. (pres.-elect 1990-91, pres. 1991-92); mem. Am. Ednl. Rsch. Assn., Am. Philos. Assn., John Dewey Soc. (pres. 1994—), Phi Beta Kappa (vis. scholar), Kappa Delta Pi. Office: Stanford U Sch of Edn Stanford CA 94305

NODEEN, JANEY PRICE, computer scientist; b. Scotland Neck, N.C., Nov. 7, 1959; d. Wade Hampton and Joyce Ann (Councill) P.; m. Thomas Nodeen. BS in Computer Sci., Christopher Newport Coll., 1987. Engring. analyst Newport News (Va.) Shipbldg., 1978-86; mgr. submarine info. resources and computer ops. Dept. of the Navy, Washington, 1986—. Home: 6915 Ashbury Dr Springfield VA 22152-3221 Office: Naval Sea Systems Command Sea # 92x2 Washington DC 20362

NOE, ELNORA (ELLIE NOE), retired chemical company executive; b. Evansville, Ind., Aug. 23, 1928; d. Thomas Noe and Evelyn (West) Dieter. Student Ind. U.-Purdue U., Indpls. Sec., Pitman Moore Co., Indpls., 1946; with Dow Chem. Co., Indpls., 1960-90, pub. rels. asst. then mgr. employee comm., 1970-87, mgr. community rels., 1987-90, DowBrands Inc., 1986-90; vice chmn. corp. affairs discussion group, 1988-89, chmn., 1989-90; mem. steering com. Learn About Bus. Recipient 2d pl. award as Businesswoman of Yr., Indpls. Bus. and Profl. Women's Assn., 1980, Indpls. Profl. Woman of Yr. award Zonta, Altrusa, Soroptomist & Pilot Svc. Clubs, 1985, DowBrands Great Things Community Svc. award, 1991. Mem. Am. Bus. Women Assn. (Woman of Yr. award 1965, past pres.), Ind. Assn. Bus. Communicators (hon., communicator of yr. 1977), Women in Comm. (Louise Eleanor Kleinhenz award 1984), Zonta (dist. pub. rels. chmn. 1978-80, area dir. 1980-82, pres. Indpls. 1977-79, bd. dirs. 1993—), Dow Indpls. Retiree Club (pres. 1995—).

NOE, MARY CHERYL, adult education educator; b. Monroe, Wis., Mar. 15, 1945; d. John and Irma Valerie (Schlittler) Marty; children: Steven, David, Renee, Scott. BS in Secondary Edn., Lakeland Coll., 1966; MS in Vocat. Edn. summa cum laude, U. Wis., Stout, 1992. Instr. Lindbergh Schs., St. Louis, 1966-68, part-time and substitute tchr., 1968-75; instr., team leader Oreg. (Wis.) Schs., 1975-77; tutor Beaver Dame (Wis.) Schs., 1977-78; mem. customer svc. staff St. Francis State Bank, Milw., 1979-82; instr. adult basic edn. Waukesha County Tech. Coll., Pewaukee, Wis., 1983—, lead instr. workplace edn., 1990—. Bd. dirs., editor Greater Milw. Literacy Coalition, 1989—; leader cub scouts Boy Scouts Am., Milw., 1978-82; mem. religious orgns., 1963—; mem. Wis. Workplace Partnership Programs. Mem. Wis. Vocat. Assn., Am. Vocat. Assn., Am. Assn. Women in Community and Jr. Colls. Office: Navistar Edn Ctr Perkins Ave Waukesha WI 53186

NOEL, BARBARA HUGHES MCMURTRY, music educator; b. Mt. Vernon, Wash., Feb. 27, 1929; d. Lowell Robinson and Mary Evelyn (Hayton) Hughes; children: Sarah Kathleen, Martha Elizabeth. BM, U. Ky., 1951, MM, 1952; PhD, U. Ill., 1972; student, Oberlin Conservatory, 1947-49. Instr. music Union Coll., Barbourville, Ky., 1952-54; instr. music and fine arts Annie Wright Sem., Tacoma, Wash., 1957-63; organist, choirmaster Episc. churches, Calif., Wash., 1954-66; chmn. music dept. U. Richmond (Va.), 1971-76, Mankato (Minn.) State U., 1976-78; dean coll. humanities and fine arts Tex. Woman's U., Denton, 1978-81; dean coll. visual and performing arts U. Mass. Dartmouth, North Dartmouth, 1981-89; prof. music U. Mass., Dartmouth, 1990—; cons. for various music orgns. and univs., 1976—, textbook pubs., 1980—; reviewer Nat. Endowment for the Humanities. Book reviewer Providence Sunday Jour., 1984—; contbr. articles to music jours.; contbr. New Grove Dictionary of Music, 1974. Bd. dirs. Community Symphony Orchs., Mankato, 1976-78, New Bedford, Mass., 1981-87. Grad. fellow Danforth Found., U. Ill., 1966-71. Mem. Coll. Music Soc. (treas. 1983-87, v.p. 1979-83, coun. mem.), Nat. Assn. Schs. Music (undergrad. commr. 1978-81). Episcopalian. Home: 73 Tucker Ln North Dartmouth MA 02747-3529 Office: U Mass Dartmouth North Dartmouth MA 02747

NOEL, MARGARET ELLEN, social worker; b. Beverly, Mass., July 4, 1939; d. William Francis and Sarah Ellen (Northrop) Norris; m. Albert Edmund Noel, Sept. 30, 1962 (div. 1980); 1 child, Scott Charles Noel; m. Marvin Levine, Feb. 17, 1990. AB, Boston U., 1962. Social worker Dept. Family and Children Svcs., Augusta, Ga., 1966-68; children's svcs. worker County Social Svcs., Santa Barbara, Calif., 1968-89, tng. supr., 1989-91, children's svcs. cons., 1991-93; exec. bd. dirs., founder PACT (Protecting and Caring Together), Santa Barbara, 1978-82; mem. PACT/CALM (Child Abuse Listening Mediation) Merger Com., 1982; exec. bd. dirs., sec., fundraising com., liaison Santa Barbara County social svcs. dept., pers. com. CALM, Santa Barbara, 1982-87; organizing com. SART (Sexual Abuse Response Team), Santa Barbara, 1983-89; mem. attendance rev. bd. Santa Barbara City Schs., 1970s, Santa Barbara County Schs., 1984-90. Founding mem. Santa Barbara Women's Polit. Com., 1988—; active Nat. Women's Polit. Caucus, Nat. Women's Health Network, Ams. United for Separation of Ch. and State, Svc. Employees Internat. Union, 1970-91, chpt. pres., 1973; mem. campaign Barbara Boxer for U.S. Senate, 1992-93. Mem. NOW. Democrat.

NOËL, NANCY ELLEN, emergency physician; b. Ithaca, N.Y., Jan. 15, 1959; d. Donald L. and Virginia (Lee) N. BS in Med. Sci., U. Wis., Milw., 1981; MD, Med. Coll. Wis., 1985. Diplomate Am. Bd. Emergency Medicine, Nat. Bd. Med. Examiners; cert. ACLS provider and instr., pediatric advanced life support provider. Resident in emergency medicine, asst. clin. instr. St. Francis Med. Ctr.-U. Ill. Coll. Medicine, Peoria, 1985-88; attending staff physician St. Mary Hosp., Quincy, Ill., 1989-93; clin. assoc. instr. dept. family practice So. Ill. U. Sch. Medicine, 1989-93; attending physician U. Hosp. and Clinics U. Mo., Columbia, 1994—; lectr. in field. Contbr. articles to med. jours. Vol. Big Bros.-Big Sisters, Quincy, 1990-91; mem. Quanada Sexual Assault Adv. Com., Quincy, 1991-93; bd. dirs. Quincy Area Habitat for Humanity, 1991-93; mem. WomenStrength Tri-County Sexual Assault Adv. Com., 1986-88. Fellow Am. Coll. Emergency Physicians; mem. Am. Assn. Women Emergency Physicians, Physicians for Social Responsibility, Phi Beta Kappa, Sigma Eta Sigma, Phi Eta Sigma. Episcopalian. Home: 1203 Sandstone Ter Lake Saint Louis MO 63367

NOEL, TALLULAH ANN, healthcare industry executive; b. Detroit, Oct. 21, 1945; d. Harry Carababas and Ruby Dimple (Gentry) Caruso; m. Vernon E. Noel (div. 1965); children: Cynthia L. Robbins, Kimberly J. Wise. AA in Nursing, Morton Coll., Cicero, Ill., 1976; BS, Coll. St. Francis, Joliet, Ill., 1983; MS in Mgmt., Nat.-Louis U., Evanston, Ill., 1990. RN. Staff nurse Mt. Sinai Hosp., Chgo., 1976-78, head nurse, 1978-79, critical care nurse, 1979-80, oncology clinician, 1980-82; head nurse McNeal Hosp., Berwyn, Ill., 1982-84; dir. nursing Nursefinders of Elmwood Park (Ill.), 1984-86; dir. profl. svcs. Nursefinders of Chgo., Elmwood Park, 1986-87, v.p. profl. svcs., 1987-88, v.p. ops., chief oper. officer, 1988-90; area v.p. Nursefinders, Inc., Hillside, Ill., 1990-91; v.p. Amserv Healthcare, Inc., Riverside, Ill., 1992-94; pres., owner Staffing Team Internat., Inc., Oak Brook, Ill., 1994—. Bd. dirs. Morton Coll. Found., 1987-88, Chgo. Heart Assn., 1985—, Grant Works Children's Ctr., Cicero, 1982-85. Mem. Women's Health Exec. Network, Nat. League Nursing, Oncology Nursing Soc., Am. Fedn. Home Health Agys., Assn. Critical Care Nurses, others. Democrat. Roman Catholic. Office: Staffing Team Internat Inc 1100 Jorie Blvd Ste 234 Oak Brook IL 60521

NOETH, CAROLYN FRANCES, speech and language pathologist; b. Cleve., July 21, 1924; d. Sam Falco and Barbara Serafina (Loparo) Armaro; m. Lawrence Andrew Noeth Sr., June 29, 1946; children: Lawrence Andrew Jr. (dec.), Barbara Marie. AB magna cum laude, Case Western Res. U., 1963; MEd, U. Ill., 1972; postgrad., Nat. Coll. Edn., 1975—. Lic. speech and lang. pathologist, Ill. Speech therapist Chgo. Pub. Schs., 1965; speech, lang. and hearing clinician J. Sterling Morton High Schs., Cicero and Berwyn, Ill., 1965-82, tchr. learning disabilities/behavior disorders, 1982, dist. ednl. diagnostician, 1982-84; Title I Project tchr., summers 1966-67, lang. disabilities cons., summers 1968-69, in-service tng. cons., summer 1970, dir. Title I Project, summers 1973-74, learning disabilities tchr. W. Campus of Morton, 1971-75, chmn. Educable-Mentally Handicapped-Opportunities Tchrs. Com., 1967-68, spl. edn. area and in-sch. tchrs. workshops, 1967—. Precinct elections judge, 1953-55; block capt. Mothers March of Dimes and Heart Fund, 1949-60; St. Agatha's rep. Nat. Catholic Women's League, 1952-53; collector various charities, 1967, 93-94; mem. exec. bd. Morton Scholarship League, 1981-84, corr. sec., 1981-83; vol. Am. Cancer Soc., 1985—; vol. judge Ill. Acad. Decathlon, 1988—. First recipient Virda L. Stewart award for Speech, Western Res. U., 1963, recipient Outstanding Sr. award, 1963. Mem. Am. (certified), Ill. Speech, Language, and Hearing Assns., Council Exceptional Children (divsn. for learning disabilities, pioneers divsn., chpt. spl. projects chmn., exec. bd. 1976-81, chpt. pres. 1979-80), Council for Learning Disabilities, Profls. in Learning Disabilities, Internat. Platform Assn., Kappa Delta Pi, Delta Kappa Gamma (chmn., co-chmn. chpt. music com. 1979—, mem. state program com. 1981-83, chpt. music rep. to state 1982—, chmn. chpt. promotion com. 1993-94). Roman Catholic. Clubs: St. Norbert's Women's (Northbrook, Ill.), Case-Western Res. U., U. Ill. Alumni Assns., Lions (vol. Northbrook, 1966—). Chmn. in compiling and publishing Student Handbook, Cleve. Coll., 1962; contbr. lyric parodies and musical programs J. Sterling Morton High Sch. West Retirement Teas, 1972-83. Home and Office: 1849 Walnut Cir Northbrook IL 60062-1245

NOETH, LOUISE ANN, journalist; b. Evergreen Park, Ill., Nov. 17, 1954; d. Cy John and Alice Rose (Bobrovich) N.; m. Michael T. Lanigan, Aug. 29, 1992. Editor Petersen Pub. Co., Inc., Calif., 1980; assoc. pub., editor Autoscene Mag., Westlake Village, Calif., 1981; investigative editor Four Wheeler Mag., Canoga Park, Calif., 1982—; owner, founder Landspeed Productions, 1985—; automotive writer, columnist Press-Courier Newspaper, Oxnard, Calif., 1992-94; Ventura County Newspapers, 1994—, Car Craft Mag., 1994—; with EG&G, Inc., 1992; auto writer, columnist Ventura County Newspapers, 1994—; cons. Spirit Am. World Speed Record Team, Pontiac Motor Divsn., Land Rover of N.Am., others; mem. Green Mamba Racing Team, Reseda, Calif., 1978—, Spirit of Am. World Speed Racing Record; graphic art commns. for Wallenius Lines, Colony Harbortown Resort, GTE, Ferro Corp., Nikon Profl. Svcs., Kodak Profl. Network, Forbes mag., SEA Sailing. Author: Ventura County Destination Guide: Channel Islands Harbor Retrospect; editor: Hot Rod Performance and Custom, 1979; prodr.: Renewing Pride, Schoolroom in Paradise, Heritage Square; contbr. articles to numerous automotive mags.; photography exhibited at Ventura Village Art Gallery, 1994, Ventura County Mus. History and Art, 1991, Ventura County Nat. Bank, 1990, 92, Ventura County Fair, 1990 (Spl. Non-Competition award Profl. Category); represented in permanent collection Harbor Town Marina Resort Gallery. Mem. project R.A.F.T. Russians and Ams. for Teamwork, Buffalo Bill's West Show. Recipient Moto award in investigative news category, Automotive Journalism Conference, 1983-84, 86. Mem. Tallship Californian Quarter deck Comm., Oxnard C. of C., Edn. Comm. Youth Edn. Motivation Program, Internat. Motor Press Assn. (sec. 1986—), Specialty Equipment Market Assn. (pub. relations com. 1983, suspension and tire com. 1984-85), Am. Auto Racing Writers and Broadcasters Assn.

NOLAN, CATHERINE T., state legislator; m. Gerard Marsicano. Grad. cum laude, NYU. Apptd. ombudsman Dept. of State.; mem. N.Y. State Assembly, 1984—; chair real property taxation com., mem. vets. com., ins. com., corps., authorities and commns. com., commerce, industry and econ. devel. com., chair mass transit subcom., women vets. subcom., apptd. capital planning review bd. MTA; chair N.Y. State Legis. Women's Caucus; mem. Assembly's Hispanic task force Somos Uno. Co-founder Queens Displaced Homemakers Program; bd. dirs. Ridgewood Property Owners and Civic Assn.; bd. trustees Wyckoff Heights Hosp.; active supporter United Forties Civic Assn., Dutch Kills Civic Assn., Farmer's Oval Civic Assn., Hunter's Point Cmty. Coun., Queensbridge Tenant Assn., Youth Patrol and Tenant Patrol, Ravenswood Tenant Assn., Lincoln Block Assn., 56th Street Block Assn., 68th Rd. Block Assn., Cornelia Street Block Assn., Queens Spl. Olympics, Vol. Ambulance Corps., Queens Outreach Project, Ridgewood Vol. Ambulance Corps., Irish Immigration Reform Movement; adv. bd. Borden Ave. Vets. Shelter; Conrad Weiser post Steuben Soc.; mem. Queens Coalition for Political Alternatives; del. Dem. Nat. Conv., 1988. Recipient Pres.' medal LaGuardia C.C., 1989. Mem. NAACP (Astoria-L.I. City chpt.), Sunnyside C. of C., Astoria Kehillah, Sunnyside Kiwanis, Irish-Am. Legis. Club, Italian-Am. Legis. Club, Ridgewood Dem. Club (bd. dirs.), Anoroc Dem. Club, West Queens Ind. Dem. Club. Home: 60-11 Woodbine St Flushing NY 11385 Office: NY State Assembly State Capitol Albany NY 12224*

NOLAN, JEAN, federal agency official; b. Collingdale, Pa., Oct. 25, 1959; d. John Thomas and Elizabeth (Gillan) N.; m. Robert Schwaninger, Mar. 3, 1984 (div. Sept. 1989). BA, Temple U., 1981. Reporter Inside Radio, Cherry Hill, N.J., 1978-82; staff reporter Phila. Bus. Jour., 1982-84, Washington Bus. Jour., Tysons Corner, Va., 1984-85, Housing & Devel. Reporter, Washington, 1985-89; dir. publs. Enterprise Found., Columbia, Md., 1989-91, dir. comms., 1991-93; asst. sec. pub. affairs U.S. Dept. HUD, Washington, 1993—. Mem. Comms. Affinity Group Coun. Found. Democrat. Office: US Dept HUD 451 7th St SW Rm 10032 Washington DC 20410

NOLAN, LINDA JEAN, accountant, controller; b. Washington, Nov. 11, 1958; d. John Thomas and Adeline (Radtke) N. BS in Bus., U. Colo., Boulder, 1984; MS in Acctg., U. Colo., Denver, 1992. CPA, Colo. Acct. Cadnetix Corp., Boulder, 1984-89; mgr. acctg. Mountain Wine (E & J Gallo Winery), Denver, 1989-90; supr. acctg. Sundstrand Fluid Handling, Arvada, Colo., 1990-93; contr. JBH Travel Audit, Inc., Denver, 1993-95. Mem. AICPA, Colo. Soc. CPA's, Inst. Mgmt. Accts., Boulder County CFO Roundtable. Democrat. Lutheran.

NOLAN, LINDA P., arts administrator; b. Wasseon, Ohio, Dec. 22, 1948; d. Robert Wallace and Miriam Myrtle (Ward) Merrell; divorced; children: Wendy Lorraine, April Rene Dawn. AA in Bus. Mgmt., OWJC, Niceville, Fla., 1974; BFA, Fla. State U., 1981, MS in Arts Edn./Therapy, 1983, PhD in Arts Adminstrn., 1989. Art therapist Fla. State U., Tallahassee, 1984-85, art program dir., 1982, 84; arts adminstr. Dept. of State, Tallahassee, 1985; exec. dir. LeMoyne Art Found., Tallahassee, 1985-87; mem. faculty Sch. of Architecture, Fla. A&M U., Tallahassee, 1987-93; exec. dir. Very Spl. Arts of Ind., Indpls., 1993—; arts in edn. artist Dept. of State, Tallahassee, 1983; arts coord. Fla. State U. Conf., Tallahassee, 1985, 88; art cons. Very Spl. Arts Fla., Tallahassee, 1988-93; art edn. cons. So. Assn. Colls. and Schs., Tallahassee, 1992. Arts rep. Dept. Edn., Tallahassee, 1988, 93; co-chair art edn. com. Mus. Art, Tallahassee, 1992-93; sec. 621 Gallery, Tallahassee, 1992-93. Staff sgt. USAF, 1967-71. Adminstrn. grantee City of Tallahassee, 1987, arts grantee City of Tallahassee, 1988, Dept. of State, Tallahassee, 1990. Mem. Arts Adminstrn. and Pub. Policy Nat. Art Edn. Assn. (treas. 1991-93), Am. Assn. Museums, Nat. Art Edn. Assn. Democrat. Office: Very Spl Arts of Ind Inc 1605 E 86th St Indianapolis IN 46240

NOLAN, LOUISE MARY, school system administrator, author; b. Boston, Sept. 28, 1947; d. John Joseph and Helen (Spiers) N. BA, Regis Coll., 1969; MEd, Boston U., 1971 postgrad., 1981-82; postgrad Fitchburg State Coll., 1972-74, Salem State Coll., 1977-79; PhD, Boston Coll., 1986, MIT, 1992. Counselor Camp Thoreau, Inc., Concord, Mass., 1964-68; tchr., chmn. sci. dept. John F. Kennedy Meml. Jr. High Sch., Woburn, Mass., 1969-86; asst. supt. schs. for curriculum and instrn. Woburn Pub. Schs., 1986—; instr. Boston Coll., 1992—; adj. assoc. prof. sch. edn. 1992—; initiator Woburn-Sci. Specialist Program Middlesex Acad. League, Let's Take Sci. Home Program; co-owner Ruth and Louise Silkscreening, Lexington, Mass., Fancypants, Carlisle, Mass.; bd. dirs. ecology program Curry Coll., Milton, Mass., 1977, Mass. Mid. Sch. Sci. Olympics, North Shore Math and Sci. Collaborative, Newspaper in Edn. Boston Globe; mem. MIT High/Middle Sch. Math Sci. Tchr. Program; mem. new standards project Mass. Ednl. Assessment Program Com. Author: Y.E.S.-A Comprehensive Guide to Students Education Youth in Environmental Sciences; Bioluminscence-An Experimental Guide; Marine Plankton; Health Physical Science, 1983, 87, Physical Science: A Problem Solving Approach, 1991, Using Literature to Teach Science. Active New Eng. League Mid. Schs., Nat. League Mid. Schs. Past vice chmn. Mass. Sci. Fair Com.; bd. dirs. North Shore Sci. and Math. Collaborative, Newspaper in Edn. program The Boston Globe. Sci. & engring. fellow MIT Inst. for Mid. and High Sch., 1992; NSF grantee, 1972-73, 77-79, 81-82; chemistry fellow Boston U., 1983-84, edn. fellow MIT, 1992; For a Cleaner Environ. grantee, 1984-86. Mem. NEA, AAAS, Mass. Tchrs. Assn., Nat. Assn. Sci. Tchrs., Mass. Assn. Sci. Tchrs., Nat. Assn. Biology Tchrs., Nat. Assn. Rsch. in Sci. Teaching, Middlesex County Tchrs. Assn., Biology Roundtable, Woburn Tchrs. Assn., Mass. Supts. Assn., Beta Beta Beta, Pi Lambda Theta, Mus. Fine Arts Club, Concord Art Assn. Club, Mus. of Sci. Club. Democrat. Roman Catholic. Home: 9 Stevens Rd Lexington MA 02173-4126 Office: Adminstrn Offices 33 Locust St Woburn MA 01801-4033

NOLAND, ANNGINETTE ROBERTS, sales executive; b. Stillwater, Okla., Sept. 30, 1930; d. Cecil Andrew and Gladys Leah (Woods) Roberts; m. Thomas Vaughan Noland, June 11, 1949; children: Nanette Noland Crocker, Thomas Vaughan Noland, Bruce Andrew Noland. Student, Okla. State U., 1948-49; cert. in planning, U. Wis. Chpt. advisor Kappa Delta Sorority, Stillwater, 1953-54, Baton Rouge, 1956-59; province pres. Kappa Delta Sorority, Miss., 1970-77; chpt. dir. II Kappa Delta Sorority, 1977-84, nat. dir. scholarship program, 1984-87, past mem. evaluation com., chmn. conv. scholarship banquet com., 1985, chmn. fellowships evaluation com., 1984-87; accounts receivables clk. Sta. WLOX-TV, Biloxi, Miss., 1973-76, sales asst., 1976-82, nat. sales asst. and polit. sales, 1982-84, nat. sales supr., 1984—. Parliamentarian Harrison County Rep. Women. Recipient award Order of the Emerald Kappa Delta Sorority, 1988. Mem. NAFE, DAR (treas. Biloxi chpt. 1983-89, corr. sec. 1989—), S.C. Geneal. Soc., Okla. Geneal. Soc., Colonial Dames XVII Century (corr. sec. local chpt. 1985-87, pres. 1987-89, 2d v.p. 1989-90, corr. sec. 1991—, state chmn. Colonial Heritage Week 1989-91, state chmn. yearbooks 1991-93, state organizing sec. 1993—, corr. sec. 1993—), Daughter Am. Colonists (charter mem. local chpt., 1st v.p. local chpt. 1993—), UDC (1st v.p. local chpt. 1990-94, dist. dir., state conv. chmn. 1992, state fin. com. chmn. 1993-94, chpt. pres. 1994—, state recorder crosses mil. svc. 1994—), Sons and Daughters of Pilgrims (state sec. 1995—), Biloxi Yacht Club (aux. corr. sec. 1986-88, sec. 1989-90). Republican. Episcopalian. Home: 2441 Old Bay Rd Biloxi MS 39531-2113 Office: Sta WLOX-TV PO Box 4596 Biloxi MS 39535-4596

NOLAND, CHRISTINA A., judge. BA, La. State Univ., JD. Law clk. to Hon. John V. Parker U.S. Dist. Ct. (La. mid. dist.), 5th circuit; magistrate judge U.S. Dist. Ct. (La. mid. dist.), 5th circuit, Baton Rouge, 1987—. Mem. Am. Bar Assn., La. State Bar, La. Trial Lawyers Assn., Baton Rouge Bar Assn. Office: Russell B Long Fed Bldg & Courthouse 777 Florida St Rm 265 Baton Rouge LA 70801-1713*

NOLAND, MARIAM CHARL, foundation executive; b. Parkersburg, W.Va., Mar. 29, 1947; d. Lloyd Henry and Ethel May (Beare) N.; m. James Arthur Kelly, June 13, 1981. BS, Case Western Res. U., 1969; M in Edn., Harvard U., 1975. Asst. dir admissions, fin. aid Baldwin-Wallace Coll., Berea, Ohio, 1969-72; asst. dir. admissions Davidson (N.C.) Coll., 1972-74; case writer Inst. Edn. Mgmt., Cambridge, Mass., 1975; sec., treas., program officer The Cleve. Found., 1975-81; v.p. The St. Paul Found., 1981-85; pres. Community Found. for S.E. Mich., 1985—; vice chair, bd. trustees Coun. of Mich. Founds., Grand Haven, Mich., 1988—. Trustee Leadership Detroit, 1988-94, Henry Ford Health Systems, 1994—, Alma Coll., 1994—. Mem. Detroit Com. Fgn. Rels., Detroit Econ. Club. Office: Community Found Southeastern Mich 333 W Fort St Ste 2010 Detroit MI 48226-3134

NOLAND, MARIE FLOWERS, county tax assessor, collector; b. Karnack, Tex., Apr. 7, 1942; d. Bilbo and Mildred Marie (Blaylock) Flowers; m. James C. Noland, June 12, 1965; 1 child, Jamie Marie. Grad. h.s., Marshall, Tex. Clk., dep. assessor Harrison County Tax Office, Marshall, Tex., 1960-76; tax collector (elected) Harrison County, Marshall, 1977-96. Mem. Tax Assessor Assn. (sec.). Democrat. Baptist. Home: 3200 Harris Lake Rd Marshall TX 75670 Office: Office of Tax Collector Harrison County Courthouse Marshall TX 85670

NOLAND, MONICA GAIL, elementary school educator; b. Macon, Ga., Oct. 14, 1950; d. Millard Joseph and Josephine Francis (Gawrysiak) Parrish; m. Wayne Douglas Noland, Aug. 16, 1973; children: Bryce Douglas, Karyn Marie. BA in Edn. with honors, Ariz. State U., 1972; postgrad., U. Nev., Las Vegas, 1973-80, U. Nev., Reno, 1985; MA in Elem. Edn., Adams State Coll., 1989; student U.S. Space Acad., Kennedy Space Ctr. Cert. tchr., Nev., Colo. Tchr. elem. sch. Clark County Sch. Dist., Las Vegas, 1972-75, 86-87, Nye County Sch. Dist., Tonopah, Nev., 1985, Mancos (Colo.) Sch. Dist., 1987-92, Montezuma-Cortez (Colo.) Sch. Dist., 1992—; vice-chair Mancos Curriculum Coordinating Coun., 1989-92; bd. dirs. Noland Electric, Inc. Dist. rep. REACH Com. (educating gifted & talented). Climax fellow Amoco Melibdenum Edn. Found., 1988. Mem. ASCD, Nat. Coun. Tchrs. Math., Nat. Assn. Edn. of Young Child, VFW Aux. Office: Montezuma-Cortez Sch Dist RE 1 Cortez CO 81321

NOLES, TAMMY GAYE, writer; b. Fairfield, Calif., Oct. 11, 1965; d. Ellen LaVon (Aldridge) N. AS, Northlake Coll., Irving, Tex., 1986; BA, U. North Tex., Denton, 1989. Intern Las Colinas Weekly, Irving, 1988; freelance reporter Irving Community TV Network, 1987—; pub. rels. exec. Laurey Peat & Assocs. Inc., 1995—; staff writer, news editor, editor Las Colinas People newspaper, Irving, 1992, advt./media rels. coord. H.D. Vest Fin. Svcs., 1990-95. Mem. NAFE, Press Club of Dallas, Alpha Epsilon Rho. Baptist.

NOLLEN, MARGARET ROACH, financial analyst; b. St. Louis, May 3, 1963; d. Jerry Burns and Mary Judith (Moreau) Roach; m. Frederick Walter Nollen II, Jan. 16, 1988; children: Jacob Burns, Patrick James. BBA in Fin.,

U. Tex., 1984; MBA, S.W. Tex. State U., 1990. Mktg. officer First City-Clear Lake, Houston, 1984-85; corp. svcs. officer, mgr. point of sales svcs. First City-Austin, Tex., 1985-87; investment officer NCNB Tex. Nat. Bank, Austin, 1987-89; fin. analyst U. Tex. System, Austin, 1989-91; dir. adminstrn. for external affairs Rice U., Houston, 1991-92; sr. fin. analyst for corp. fin., risk mgmt. and pensions Transco Energy Co., Houston, 1992—. Patentee in field of comml. monetary payment. Mem. NAFE, U. Tex. Exes, S.W. Tex. State U. Alumni Assn. Home: 10510 Great Plains Ln Houston TX 77064-7100 Office: Transco Energy Co Corp Fin 2800 Post Oak Blvd Houston TX 77056-6106

NOLTE, JUDITH ANN, magazine editor; b. Hampton, Iowa, Sept. 17, 1938; d. Clifford P. and Sigrid M. (Johnson) N.; m. Randers H. Heimer, May 7, 1971. BS, U. Minn., 1960; MA in English, NYU, 1965. Tchr. English Middletown (N.Y.) High Sch., 1960-62, High Sch. of Commerce, N.Y.C., 1962-64; merchandising editor Conde Nast Publs., N.Y.C., 1964-69; editor-in-chief Am. Baby Mag., Cahners Pub. Co., N.Y.C., 1969—, Weight Watchers mag., 1980-83; editorial dir. Cahners Childcare Group, N.Y.C., 1990—; hostess Am. Baby Cable TV Show. Chmn. media adv. bd. N.Y. chpt. March of Dimes. Mem. Am. Soc. Mag. Editors (pres. 1986-88), Mortar Bd., Delta Gamma (pres. 1960). Office: Am Baby/Healthly Kids Cahners Publishing Company 249 W 17th St New York NY 10011

NOON, JEAN MCDONOUGH, artist; b. Cambridge, Mass., Apr. 10, 1949; d. James Oltman and Rosamond (Poole) McDonough; m. William F. Noon; children: Preston Marcel, Aaron Miles. BA, Goddard Coll., 1971; BS in Art Edn. summa cum laude, U. So. Maine, 1990. Cert. art tchr., Maine. Artist, 1970—; owner, operator Noon Family Sheep Farm, Springvale, Maine, 1971—; art tchr., 1990—; chmn. suprs. York County Soil and Water Conservation Dist., Sanford, Maine, 1994-95, supr., 1985—. Home: RFD Box 630 Springvale ME 04083

NOONAN, JACQUELINE ANNE, pediatrics educator; b. Burlington, Vt., Oct. 28, 1928. BA, Albertus Magnus Coll., 1950; MD, U. Vt., 1954, DSc (hon.), 1980. Diplomate Am. Bd. Pediatrics, Am. Bd. Pediatric Cardiology. Intern N.C. Meml. Hosp., Chapel Hill, 1954-55; resident in pediatrics Children's Hosp., Cin., 1955-57; rsch. fellow Children's Med. Ctr., Boston, 1957-59; asst. prof. pediatrics State U. Iowa Sch. Medicine, 1959-61; asst. prof. pediatrics cardiology U. Ky. Coll. Medicine, Lexington, 1961-64, assoc. prof., 1964-69, prof., 1969—, chmn. dept. pediatrics, 1974-92; mem. embryology and human devel. study sect. NIH, 1973-78; mem. U.S.-USSE Symposium on Congenital Heart Disease, 1975; mem. sub. bd. pediatric cardiology Am. Bd. Pediatrics, 1977-82; examiner, mem. test. com. Nat. Bd. Med. Examiners, 1984-90, exec. com., 1991—; participant various confs. in field; vis. prof. Vanderbilt U., Nashville, 1987; spkr. in field. Contbr. articles, revs. to med. publs.; mem. editl. bd. Am. Jour. Diseases Children, 1970-80, Am. Jour. Med. Edn., 1975-78, Pediatric Cardiology, 1978-90, Am. Heart Jour., 1994—, Clin. Pediatrics, 1990—. Mem. AMA, Am. Acad. Pediatrics (cardiology sect. chmn. 1972-74), Am. Coll. Cardiology (gov. Ky. chpt. 1989-92), Am. Fedn. Clin. Rsch., Assn. Med. Sch. Pediatric (dept. chmn. exec. com. 1978-81), Fayette County Med. Soc., Irish-Am. Pediatric Soc., Am. Pediatric Soc., Ky. State Med. Assn., NIH Alumni Assn., Soc. Pediatric Rsch., So. Soc. Pediatric Rsch. (pres. 1972). Office: U Ky Med Ctr Pediatrics Ky Clinic Lexington KY 40536-0284

NOONAN, MELINDA DUNHAM, women's health nurse, educator; b. Peoria, Ill., Feb. 19, 1954; d. Emmett Maxwell Dunham and Dixie Maurine (DeCounter) Widner; m. Robert Joseph Noonan; children: Alissa, Meris. Diploma, Ravenswood Hosp. Sch. Nursing, 1977; BSN cum laude, U. Ill., Chgo., 1989. Med. asst. James J. Hines, M.D., S.C., Chgo., 1973-76; staff nurse Northwestern Meml. Hosp., Chgo., 1978-79, asst. head nurse, 1979-80, staff nurse, 1980-86, perinatal and women's health educator, 1983—, coord. Health Learning Ctr., 1989-92; coord. Women's Ctr., Prentice Women's Hosp., Chgo., 1992-94; dir. women's programs Columbus Hosp., Chgo., 1994—; founder, bd. dirs. Mothers Organized for Mut. Support, Chgo., 1981-89; creator, coord. Beyond The Birth Experience Program, Chgo., 1983-91. Contbg. author: Drugs, Alcohol, Pregnancy and Parenting, 1988, Clinical Issues of Perinatal and Women's Health Nursing, 1991. Bd. dirs. Mothers Organized for mut. Support, 1981-88; troop leader Girl Scouts U.S., Chgo., 1991-93. Mem. Internat. Order of Odd and Rebekahs; mem. Assn. Women's Health, Obstet and Neonatal Nurses (consumer edn. com. 1992-93, edn. com. 1994-95). Democrat. Roman Catholic. Lodge: Rebekah (v. grand 1981-82, noble grand 1982-83). Home: 3414 W Glenlake Ave Chicago IL 60659-3420 Office: Columbus Hosp 2520 N Lakeview Ave 11N Chicago IL 60614

NOONAN, NORINE ELIZABETH, academic administrator, researcher; b. Phila., Oct. 5, 1948; d. Alaric Edwin and Norine (Radford) Freeman. BA, summa cum laude, U. Vt., 1970; MA, Princeton U., 1972, PhD, 1976. Asst. prof. Coll. Vet. Medicine, U. Fla., Gainesville, 1976-81, assoc. prof., 1981; research assoc. prof. Georgetown U., Washington, 1981-82; Am. Chem. Soc. sci. fellow U.S. Senate Commerce Com., Washington, 1982-83; program and budget analyst Office Mgmt. and Budget, Washington, 1983-87, acting br. chief sci. and space programs, 1987-88, br. chief, 1988-92; v.p. rsch. Fla. Inst. Tech., Melbourne, 1992—, dean grad. sch., 1993—; bd. advisors U.S. Found. for the Internat. Space U., 1989-90; disting. lectr. MITRE Corp. Inst., 1991; vis. faculty Exec. Seminar Ctrs., Office Personnel Mgmt.; cons. Am. Chem. Soc. com. chem. and pub. affairs; mem. NASA space sci. adv. com.; mem. com. Antarctic policy & sci. NRC; councilor Oak Ridge Assn. Univs.; trustee Southeast Univs. Rsch. Assn., also chair finance com. Contbr. articles to sci. jours. Vol. Balt. City Fair, 1982-91. Bd. dirs. Brevard Symphony Orchestra, 1993—, Wolf Trap Farm Pk. Assocs., Wolf Trap Farm Pk. for the Performing Arts, 1988-92, exec. com. 1990-92, exec. vice chmn., 1991-92, treas., 1992; mem. adv. coun. Brookings Instn. Ctr. for Pub. Policy Edn., 1989-93; treas. White House Athletic Ctr., 1990-92, Potomac Basset Hound Club, Space Coast Tiger Bay Club. Recipient Spl. Performance award Office Mgmt. and Budget, 1987, 88; grantee Fla. div. Am. Cancer Soc., 1977, NIH, 1979, NSF, 1979. Fellow AAAS (mem. at large sect. gen. interest in sci. and tech. 1994—, mem. sci., engring. and pub. policy com.); mem. Am. Soc. Cell Biology, Sigma Xi, Phi Beta Kappa (pres. Fla. chpt. 1980-81). Mem. United Ch. of Christ. Avocations: running, purebred dogs, fishing, cooking, aerobics. Home: 2480 Grassmere Dr Melbourne FL 32904-9715 Office: Fla Inst Tech 150 W University Blvd Melbourne FL 32901-6967

NOONAN, SANDRA JANE, legislative aide; b. Waterville, Maine, Dec. 15, 1957; d. Vernal Estes and Alberta (Bachelder) Glidden; m. Anthony Joseph Noonan, Mar. 25, 1983; children: Miles Arthur, Cole Alex. AAS, Thomas Coll., 1988. Cost acct. Gannett Graphics, Augusta, Maine, 1983-86; gen. ledger acct. C.F. Hathaway, Waterville, Maine, 1986-87; legis. aide House Majority Office, Maine State Legislature, Augusta, 1987-94, Maine Spkr. House Reps., Augusta, 1993—; legis. aide to Rep. Dan. A. Gwadosky, Fairfield, Maine, 1990-93; monitor Legis. Joint Standing Com. on Edn., Augusta, 1992-94. Chair Fairfield (Maine) Community Fest, 1990-95; sec. Fairfield Town Dems., 1990-93, Lawrence High Sch. Alumni, Fairfield, 1991-93, also mem. exec. com., 1993-94. Named Outstanding Young Woman of Am., 1987. Roman Catholic. Home: 76 Martin Stream Rd Fairfield ME 04937-3010 Office: Speaker's Office State St # 2 Augusta ME 04333-4598

NOONAN, SUSAN ABERT, public relations counselor; b. Lancaster, Pa., May 10, 1960; d. James Goodear and Carole (Althouse) Abert; m. David Lindsay Noonan, July 28, 1986; children: Caroline du Pont, Elizabeth Augusta. BA, Mt. Holyoke Col., 1982. Account exec. Merill Lynch, N.Y.C., 1982-83; sr. v.p. Cameron Assocs., N.Y.C., 1983-88; pres., founder Noonan/Russo Comm., N.Y.C., 1988—. Mem. Nat. Investor Rels. Inst. Office: Noonan/Russo Comm Inc 220 5th Ave New York NY 10001

NORCEL, JACQUELINE JOYCE CASALE, educational administrator; b. Bklyn., Nov. 19, 1940; d. Frederick and Josephine Jeanette (Bestafka) Casale; m. Edward John Norcel, Feb. 24, 1962. BS, Fordham U., 1961; MS, Bklyn. Coll., 1966; 6th yr. cert. So. Conn. State U., 1980; postgrad. Bridgeport U. Elem. tchr., pub. schs., N.Y.C., 1961-80; prin. Coventry Schs., Conn., 1980-84, Trumbull Schs., Conn., 1984—; guest lectr. So. Conn. State U., 1980—; cons. Monson Schs., Mass., 1984; mem. adj. faculty Sacred Heart U., Fairfield, Conn., 1985—, adj. faculty So. Conn. State U., summer 1991. Editor: Best of the Decade, 1980; mem. editorial adv. bd. Principal Matters; contbr. articles to profl. jours. Chmn. bldg. com. Trumbull Bd. Edn., 1978-80; chmn. Sch. Benefit Com., Trumbull, 1985-86; catechist Bridgeport Diocese, Roman Cath. Ch., Conn., 1975-85, youth minister, 1979-84, coord., evaluator leadership tng. workshops for teens and adults, 1979-84; mem. St. Stephen's Parish Coun., 1993—. Recipient Town of Trumbull Service award, 1982, Nat. Disting. Prin. award, 1988, Joseph Formica Disting. Svc. award EMSPAC, 1994. Mem. N.E. Regional Elem. Prins. Assn. (rep. 1984-86, sec. 1986-87), Elem. Mid. Sch. Prins. Assn. (pres. 1985-86, Citizen of Year award, 1991, Pres.'s award 1981-85, state elected rep. 1989-90, fed. rels. coord. 1990—), Adminstrn. and Supervision Assn. (sec. 1980-81, pres. 1981-82, exec. bd. 1982-93), Hartford Area Prins. and Suprs. Assn. (local pres. 1981-82), Nat. Assn. Elem. Sch. Prins. (zone I dir. 1987-90, Conn. State Prin. Acad. Adv. Bd. 1986-88, del. to gen. assemblies 1984-90, bd. dirs. 1987-90), Assn. Supervision and Curriculum Devel., Conn. Assn. Supervision and Curriculum Devel., Trumbull Adminstrs. Assn. (pres.-elect 1989-91, pres. 1991-93), Eastern Conn. Council of Internat. Reading Assn., New Eng. Coalition Ednl. Leaders, Associated Tchrs. of Math. in Conn., Phi Delta Kappa (Disting. Fellow award 1992, v.p. rsch. and projects 1993—), Pi Lambda Theta (Beta Sigma chpt.), Delta Kappa Gamma. Republican. Home: 5240 Madison Ave Trumbull CT 06611-1016 Office: Tashua Sch 401 Stonehouse Rd Trumbull CT 06611-1651

NORD, DEANNA LYNN, marketing company executive, consultant; b. Detroit Lakes, Minn., Apr. 20, 1956; d. Donald Harris Steen and Ellen Marie (Bratlien) N. BA, Macalester Coll., St. Paul, 1980; postgrad., U. Minn., 1981-82, St. Catherine's Coll., St. Paul, 1985. Rsch. asst. Minn. Energy Agy., St. Paul, 1977-79; mgr. product devel. Control Data, Mpls., 1980-83, mgr. mktg., 1983-85, account mgr., edn., 1985-86; pvt. practice pub. rels., mktg. cons. Mpls., 1986—; pres., bd. dirs. Self Reliance Ctr., Mpls., 1980-87; mem. U. Minn. Inst. Agrl. Adv. Council, Mpls., 1984-88; sr. cons. Internat. Bus. Cons., St. Paul, 1985-87. Contbr. articles to profl. jours. and mags. Founder, mem. Mpls. Food Policy Task Force, 1985-87, Minn. Solar Sustenance Team, Mpls., 1978-80; participant Nat. Gov.'s Task Force Image of Agrl. Project, Mpls, 1985. Mem. Minn. Women for Agr. (pres. 1982-84), Minn. Food Assn. (rsch. com., community involvement com.), NAFE, Upper Midwest Flute Assn. Home: 210 W Grant St Minneapolis MN 55403-2241

NORDEN, MARILU KENT, artist, actress; b. Calais, Maine, July 28, 1925; d. Carey McCune and Mary (Kent) Young; m. David Philip Jones, May 18, 1946 (div. Aug. 1951); children: Philip Carey, Kristin Zhivago; m. N. Thomas Norden, Feb. 18, 1959; children: Michael Thomas, Christopher Kent, Nicholas Kimbro. Student, Syracuse U., 1944-45. TV vocalist CBS-TV, N.Y.C., 1948-49; artist, narrator Atlantis Documentary Films, Hollywood, Calif., 1954-56; vocalist Leighton Noble Orch., L.A., 1957-58; actor, singer Starlight Opera, Old Globe Theatre, San Diego, 1966-75; founder, dir., actress Stratford Studio Theatre, Del Mar, Calif., 1970-80; print model, TV comml. actress Artists' Mgmt., San Diego, 1970-89; voice-over artist Internat. Children's Recording Co., Del Mar, 1980-85; producer, writer, narrator Once Upon a Tide TV Documentary, Del Mar, 1986-87; profl. artist, painter Creative Edge Prodns. and M.K. Norden Studio, Santa Fe, 1989—. Bd. dirs. Civic Assn., Del Mar, 1970-75, founder, bd. dirs. Channel 37 Del Mar Cable TV, 1975-84, North Coast Repertory Theatre, Solana Beach, Calif., 1980-86; officer, bd. dirs. San Dieguito Little Theatre, Del Mar, 1968-80; mem., creative fund raiser Greer Garson Theatre Steering Coun., Coll. of Santa Fe, 1992—. Recipient Best Actress award San Diego Cmty. Theatre Assn., 1969, San Dieguito Little Theatre, 1968, 69, 70, 72. Mem. Nat. Women in the Arts, Nat. Watercolor Soc. (assoc.), N.Mex. Watercolor Soc. (assoc.), Women's Guild Home of Guiding Hands. Home: Overlook Rd Rte 7 Box 124 PS Santa Fe NM 87505

NORDGREN, SHARON L., state legislator; b. Chgo., Oct. 21, 1943; m. Richard Nordgren; 2 children. Student, U. Minn. N.H. state senator, mem. appropriations com.; mem. Hanover Bd. Selectman, 1979-88, chmn., 1982-88. Trustee Montshire Mus. Sci., 1984-92, chair, 1991-92; chmn. Cmty. Substance Abuse Com., 1989—; bd. dirs. N.H. Women's Lobby, 1992—; mem. Children's Trust Fund, 1990—, State Leadership Team Abuse and Neglect, 1991—, Hanover H.S. Coun., 1983—; cmty. mem. Hanover Inn Bd. Overseers, 1985—. Named Citizen of Yr., Hanover C. of C., 1992. Mem. Ch. of Christ. Home: 23 Ropeferry Rd Hanover NH 03755-1404 Office: NH State Senate State Capitol Concord NH 03301*

NORDHAGEN, HALLIE HUERTH, nursing home administrator; b. Sarona, Wis., Apr. 2, 1914; d. Mathias James and Ethel Elizabeth (Fann) Huerth; B.Ed., U. Wis., Superior, 1938, M.A., 1949; m. Carl E. Nordhagen, May 24, 1947; children: Bruce Carl, Brian Keith. Prin., tchr. Wis. Public Schs., 1932-46; supervising tchr. Wis. Community Coll., 1946-48; psychiat. adminstr. Trempealeau County Health Care Center, psychiat. nursing home, Whitehall, Wis., 1959—; mem. Wis. Nursing Home Adminstrs. Examining Bd.; fellow Menninger Clinic, Topeka, 1979-81; cons. to the bishop Evangelical Lutheran Ch., Wis. Chairperson BRAD Assn./Acohol & Drug Abuse, mem. Trempealeau County Alliance Drug Free Youth; mem. com. cons. to bishop Evangelical Luth. Ch. Am. Recipient Disting. Service award in edn. and hosp. adminstrn., London, 1967, award for services to human services programs Wis. Assn. Human Services, 1972, award for outstanding services to exceptional children Assn. Retarded Children, 1978, award for accomplishments in human resources Trempealeau County Conservation Service, 1981; Wis. State Senate citation, 1983; citatioin Wis. Gov., 1984. Mem. Wis. Assn. County Homes, Wis. Edn. Assn., Wis. Assn. Human Services Programs, Internat. Platform Assn., Am. Lutheran Ch. Women. Clubs: Whitehall Country, Women's. Author: Wisconsin Indians, 1966. Home: 2220 Claire St Whitehall WI 54773-9726

NORDIN, PHYLLIS ECK, sculptor, designer, consultant; b. Chgo. Student Beloit Coll., Wayne State U.; B.S., U. Toledo, 1963, BA cum laude, 1972, MLS, 1992; BA, Sch. Design Toledo Mus. Art, 1972. Design and art cons. various builders, chs., businesses and individuals, 1972—; instr. Lourdes Coll. Sylvania, Ohio, 1986-89, U. Toledo, 1986-89. Prin. works include large bronze sculptures Lucas County Main Library, Toledo, Christ figure St. Joan of Arc Ch., Maumee, Ohio, Ronald McDonald House, Toledo, First English Evangel. Luth. Ch., Grosse Pointe Woods, Mich., Christ Presbyn. Ch., Covenant Presbyn. Ch., Toledo, Toledo Hosp., Reynolds Br. Libr., Toledo, Port Clinton and Defiance (Ohio) Librs. , stone wall mural Epworth United Methodist Ch., Toledo, Beloit Coll., Wis., bronze fountain U. Toledo, bronze life-size children Treasure Coast Mall, Stuart, Fla., Kingston, Tenn. Pub. Libr., welded steel sculpture Town Ctr. Mall, Port Charlotte, Fla., Carey (Ohio) Bank, Toledo Bank, Bi-Centennial Park, Toledo, wood wall carvings 1st Meth. Ch., LaGrange, Ill., ferro-cement abstract Flower Hosp., Sylvania, Ohio, Rossford (Ohio) Meth. Ch.; numerous others; exhibited Allied Artists Am., Salmagundi Club, Audubon artists, N.Am. Sculpture exhibit; numerous others. Represented by Collectors Corner Toledo Mus. Art, 1970—. Recipient Alpha award Foothills Art Ctr., 1983, 1st prize Ann. Nat. Art Exhbn., 1978, also numerous others. Mem. Nat. Assn. Women Artists, Nat. Sculpture Soc., Ohio Designer Craftsmen, Ohio Liturgical Art Guild, Catharine Lorillard Wolfe Art Club, Phi Kappa Phi (hon.). Home and Studio: 4035 Tan Tara Dr Toledo OH 43623-3311

NORDMEYER, MARY BETSY, educator; b. New Haven, May 19, 1939; d. George and Barbara Stedman (Thompson) N. ABPhil, Wheaton Coll., Norton, Mass., 1960; MA, San Jose State U., 1968; AS in Computer Sci., West Valley Coll., 1985. Cert. tchr. spl. edn., Calif.; cert. secondary tchr., Calif. Instr. English Santa Clara (Calif.) Unified Sch. Dist., 1965-77, vocat. specialist, 1977—, dir. project work ability, 1984—, also mem. community adv. com.; facilitator Project Work-Ability, Region 5, 1985-86, sec., 1988-90. Author poetry, 1960, Career and Vocat. Edn. for Students With Spl. Needs, 1986; author/designer Career English, 1974, Career Information, 1975. Recipient Outstanding Secondary Educator award, 1975, Award of Excellence, Nat. Assn. Vocat. Edn., 1984; named Tchr. of Yr. in Spl. Edn., Santa Clara Unified Sch. Dist., 1984-85. Mem. Calif. Assn. Work Experience Educators, Sierra Club, Epsilon Eta Sigma. Democrat. Home: 14920 Sobey Rd Saratoga CA 95070-6236 Office: Santa Clara Unified Sch Dist 1889 Lawrence Rd Santa Clara CA 95051-2166

NORDQUIST, SANDRALEE RAHN, lay worker; b. Chgo., Dec. 5, 1940; d. Herbert Henry and Elinor Gertrude (Duben) Rahn; m. George Leczewski, Oct. 13, 1962 (div. Dec. 1968); 1 child, Peter George (dec.); m. David Arthur Nordquist, July 19, 1969; children: Kerilinn D., Sharianne R. AA, Harper Coll., 1982; BS in English, Elmhurst (Ill.) Coll., 1985, BS in Theology, 1988; postgrad., Northestern Ill. U., Chgo., Drake U. Cert. tchr. English, history, learning disordered, behaviorally disordered, Ill. Tchr. English Luther High Sch. Summer Sch., Chgo., 1990, 92-94; confirmation tchr. Evang. Luth. Ch. of the Holy Spirit, Elk Grove, Ill., 1990-91, leader adult Bible study, 1991-93; guild pres., adv. trinity preaching Evang. Luth. Ch. of the Holy Spirit, 1990-91; tchr. English, gen. music and spl. edn. Foreman High Sch., Chgo., 1990—; feature writer Daily Herald, Paddock Publs., 1991—; lector, greeter, actress Drama Guild. Columnist (newspaper) Pulitzer Pubs. Notebook, 1986-90. Leader Girl Scouts U.S., Chgo. and Elk Grove, 1968-70, 77-81; v.p. Dist. 59 Orch. Assn., Elk Grove Village, Ill., 1985-87; pres. Sch. Dist. 59 Project 444, Elk Grove Village, 1981. Mem. Nat. Coun. Tchrs. of English, Ill. Assn. Tchrs. of English, Sigma Tau Delta. Home: 639 Sycamore Dr Elk Grove Village IL 60007-4624 Office: Foreman High Sch 3235 N LeClaire Ave Chicago IL 60641

NORDYKE, ELEANOR COLE, population researcher, public health nurse; b. Los Angeles, June 15, 1927; d. Ralph G. and Louise Noble (Carter) Cole; m. Robert Allan Nordyke, June 18, 1950; children: Mary Ellen Nordyke-Grace, Carolyn Nordyke-Cozzette, Thomas A., Susan E., Gretchen Nordyke Worthington. BS, Stanford U., 1950; P.H.N. accreditation, U. Calif.-Berkeley, 1952; MPH, U. Hawaii, 1969. RN. Pub. health nurse San Francisco Dept. Health, 1950-52; nurse-tchr. Punahou Sch., Honolulu, 1966-67; clinic coordinator East-West Population Inst., East-West Ctr., Honolulu, 1969-75, population rschr., 1975-82, rsch. fellow, 1982-92; cons. Hawaii Commn. on Population, Honolulu, 1970-83; mem. Hawaii Policy Action Group for Family Planning, Honolulu, 1971-89, chmn., 1976-77. Author: The Peopling of Hawaii, 1977, 2d rev. edit., 1989, A Profile of Hawaii's Elderly Population, 1984, (with Robert Gardner) The Demographic Situation in Hawaii, 1974, mem. editorial bd. Hawaiian Jour. History, 1980—; contbr. articles to profl. jours. Bd. dirs. YMCA, Honolulu, 1970—, vice-chmn. 1978-79, chmn. YMCA Camp Edman, 1989-92; bd. dirs. Hawaii Planned Parenthood, 1974-78, Friends of Libr. of Hawaii, 1985-87; trustee Hawaiian Hist. Soc., 1978-82, Arcadia Retirement Residence, Honolulu, 1978-87; bd. dirs. Hawaii Pacific U., 1988—, mem. liberal arts coun. Mem. Population Assn. Am., Population Reference Bur., Hawaii Pub. Health Assn., Am. Statis. Assn., Hawaii Econ. Assn., Hawaiian Hist. Soc., Friends of East-West Ctr., Friends of Univ. Hawaii Sch. Medicine, Stanford Nurses Alumni Assn., Phi Beta Kappa. Democrat. Congregationalist. Clubs: Stanford of Hawaii, Gen. Fed. Women's History (Honolulu). Home: 2013 Kakela Dr Honolulu HI 96822-2158

NOREIKA, ALMA MARIA, optometrist; b. Michigan City, Ind., Sept. 18, 1963; d. Joseph and Diana E. (Zutautas) N. B Optometry, Ind. U., 1985; D Optometry, Ind. U. Sch. Optometry, 1988. Lic. optometrist, Ind., Ill. Optometrist MH Healthcare, Indpls., 1988—. Mem. Beta Sigma Kappa. Republican. Roman Catholic. Home: 6009 Allisonville Rd Indianapolis IN 46220-5246 Office: MH Healthcare 7160 Shadeland Station Way Indianapolis IN 46256-3915

NOREK, FRANCES THERESE, lawyer; b. Chgo., Mar. 9, 1947; d. Michael S. and Viola C. (Harbecke) N.; m. John E. Flavin, Aug. 31, 1968 (div.); 1 child, John Michael. B.A., Loyola U., Chgo., 1969, J.D., 1973. Bar: Ill. 1973, U.S. Dist. Ct. (no. dist.) Ill. 1973, U.S. Ct. Appeals (7th cir.) 1974. Assoc. Alter, Weiss, Whitesel & Laff, Chgo., 1973-74; asst. states atty. Cook County, Chgo., 1974-86; assoc. Clausen, Miller, Gorman, Caffrey & Witous P.C., 1986—; mem. trial practice faculty Loyola U. Sch. Law, Chgo., 1980—; judge, evaluator mock trial competitions, Chgo., 1978—; lectr. in field. Recipient Emil Gumpert award Am. Coll. Trial Lawyers, 1982. Mem. Chgo. Bar Assn. (instr. fed. trial bar adv. program young lawyer's sect. 1983-84). Office: Clausen Miller Gorman Caffrey & Witous PC 10 S La Salle St Chicago IL 60603-1002

NOREN-IACOVINO, MARY-JO PATRICIA, insurance company executive; b. N.Y.C., Feb. 20, 1951; d. James Pierce and Grace Virginia (Keating) Keelty; m. Louis T. Iacovino, Sept. 23, 1989. Student, CUNY, 1971-72. Asst. v.p. Huntoon, Paige & Co., Inc., N.Y.C., 1972-79; v.p. Merrill Lynch Capital Mkts., N.Y.C., 1979-85, Security Pacific Merchant Bank, N.Y.C., 1985-89, Oxford Resources Corp., Woodbury, N.Y., 1989-90; securities products coord. Equitable Life, N.Y.C., 1990-94. Mem. Oratorio Soc. N.Y. (bd. dirs., mktg. dir. 1993), Women's Life Underwriters Coun., Nat. Assn. Life Underwriters. Home: 17 Park Ave # 9A New York NY 10016 Office: The Equitable 1221 Ave of the Americas 32nd Fl New York NY 10020

NORKIN, CYNTHIA CLAIR, physical therapist; b. Boston, May 6, 1932; d. Miles Nelson and Carolyn (Green) Clair; m. Stanislav A. Norkin, Feb. 19, 1955 (dec. 1970); 1 child, Alexandra. BS in Edn., Tufts U., 1954; cert. phys. therapy Bouve Boston Coll., 1954; MS, Boston U., 1973, EdD, 1984. Instr. Bouve-Boston Coll., 1954-55; staff phys. therapist New Eng. Med. Center, Boston, 1954-55; staff phys. therapist Abington Meml. Hosp., Abington, Pa., 1965-70, Eastern Montgomery County Vis. Nurse Assn., 1970-72; asst. prof. phys. therapy Sargent Coll., Boston U., 1973-84; assoc. prof. phys. therapy, dir. Sch. Phys. Therapy, Ohio U., Athens, 1984—; cons. Boston Center Ind. Living, Cambridge Vis. Nurse Assn., Mass. Medicaid Cost Effectiveness Project, 1978; sec. Health Planning Council Greater Boston, 1976-78; book, manuscript reviewer F.A. Davis Co., 1986—; mem. arthritis adv. com. Ohio Dept. Health. Trustee Brimmer and May Sch., 1980. Mem. AAAS, Am. Phys. Therapy Assn. (on site evaluator commn. on accreditation 1986—), Mass. Phys. Therapy Assn. (chmn. Mass. quality assurance com. 1980-83), Am. Public Health Assn., Mass. Assn. Mental Health, Athens County Vi. Nurse Assn. (sec. adv. council 1984—). Episcopalian. Author: (with P. Levangie) Joint Structure and Function: A Comprehensive Analysis, 1983, 2d edit., 1992; (with D.J. White) Joint Measurement: A Guide to Goniometry, 1985, 2d edit., 1995.

NORLIST See LUST, ELENORE

NORMAN, ALLINE L., health facility administrator; b. Homerville, Ga., Dec. 20, 1938; d. John F. and Alline D. N. BS, Ga. Coll., 1960; cert. Sch. for Med. Records, U.S. Pub. Health Svc., 1961. U.S. pub. svc. offcr. U. Cin., 1961-65; asst. chief and chief med. records U.S. Pub. Health Svc. Hosps., New Orleans, Chgo., Norfolk, 1965-70; chief med. info. section, Med. Adminstrn. Svc. VA Med. Ctr., N.Y., 1970-72, Miami, 1972-75; asst. chief Med. Adminstrn. Svc. VA Med. Ctr., East Orange, N.J., 1975-80, Miami, 1980-83; chief Med. Adminstrn. Svc. VA Med. Ctr., Augusta, Ga., 1983-85; chief field ops. divsn., Med. Adminstrn. Svc. VA Med. Ctr., Atlanta, 1988-89; from dep. dir. to dir. Med. Adminstrn. Svc. VHA, 1990-93, dir. Adminstrn. Svc. Office, 1993—. Recipient Fed. Leadership award, 1992, cert. achievement Fed. Women's Interagency Bd., 1993. Mem. Vets. Health Adminstrn. (chair combined fed. campaign 1991, co-chair chief med. dir. adv. com. on diversity 1992-94, mem. task force subcom. on recommendations of the commn. on the future structure of vets. health care 1992, mem. White House nat. health care task force on integration of govt. systems 1993, sec's. adv. group on sexual harassment, 1993, interagency inst. 1993-94), mem. bd. dirs. sr. exec. assn. 1994). Methodist. Office: Dept Vet Affairs Rm 932 810 Vermont Ave NW Washington DC 20420*

NORMAN, ARLENE PHYLLIS, principal; b. Seattle; d. Samuel Edward and Connie Solveig (Jorgensen) Hendricksen; m. Charles Edward Norman; children: Tamara, Mark, Todd, Lisa. BA, Wash. State U.; MAT, Lewis and Clark Coll., 1980; postgrad., Portland State U. Tchr. Salem (Oreg.) Sch. Dist., 1956; tchr. Beaverton (Oreg.) Sch. Dist., 1973-83, prin. Terra Linda Sch., 1984-94; prin. Aloha Park Sch., 1994; presenter children's seminar Nat. Coun. Tchrs. Eng. Confs. Contbr. articles to mags. Mem. selection com. Associated Oreg. Industries, 1994, 95. Named Prin. of Sch. of Excellence, Assoc. Oreg. Industries, 1991. Mem. NASEP, N.W. Women in Ednl. Adminstrn., Profl. Assistance Com. for State of Oreg., Toastmasters (pres.), Phi Delta Kappa, Pi Lambda Theta (pres.).

NORMAN, CHRISTINA REIMARSDOTTER, language educator; b. Stockholm, Jan. 7, 1947; came to U.S., 1968; d. Leif Reimar and Hilma Birgitta (Berg) Norman; m. Geoffrey Robert Norman, May 27, 1968; children: Catarina Louise, Camilla Elizabeth. Fil. Mag., Stockholm U., 1968; MA, SUNY, Albany, 1973. Cert. tchr., N.Y., Conn. Tchr. French Our Lady of Grace Sch., Stratford, Conn., 1970-71; tchr. French, German Burnt

Hills (N.Y.)-Ballston Lake Jr. High Sch., 1971-74; tchr. English Colegio Ayalde, Lujua, Vizcaya, Spain, 1975-78; tchr. French, English, Spanish Hillcrest Jr. High Sch., Trumbull, Conn., 1979-83; tchr. Spanish, French Saxe Mid. Sch., New Canaan, Conn., 1983-94; tchr. Spanish New Canaan H.S., 1994—. Mem. Conn. Orgn. Lang. Tchrs. Office: New Canaan High Sch Farm Rd New Canaan CT 06840

NORMAN, MARSHA, playwright; b. Louisville, Sept. 21, 1947; d. Billie Lee and Bertha Mae (Conley) Williams; m. Michael Norman (div. 1974); m. Dann C. Byck Jr., 1978 (div.); m. Timothy Dykman; 2 children: Angus, Katherine. B.A., Agnes Scott Coll., 1969; M.A.T., U. Louisville, 1971. Author: (plays) Getting Out, 1977 (John Gassner New Playwrights medallion, Outer Critics Circle award 1979, George Oppenheimer-Newsday award 1979), Third and Oak, 1978, Circus Valentine, 1979, The Holdup, 1980, 'Night, Mother, 1982 (Susan Smith Blackburn prize 1982, Tony award nomination for best play 1983, Pulitzer Prize for Drama 1983, Elizabeth Hull-Kate Warriner award Dramatists Guild 1983), Traveler in the Dark, 1984, Sarah and Abraham, 1987, D. Boone, 1992; (book of musical, lyrics) The Secret Garden, 1991 (Tony award for best book of musical 1991, Tony award nominee for best original score 1991, Drama Desk award for best book of musical 1991); (screenplay) 'Night, Mother, 1986; (teleplays) It's the Willingness, 1978, In Trouble at Fifteen, 1980, The Laundromat, 1985, Third and Oak: The Pool Hall, 1989, Face of a Stranger, 1991; (novel) The Fortune Teller, 1987; (collection) Four Plays by Marsha Norman, 1988. NEA grantee, 1978-79, Rockefeller playwright-in-residence grantee, 1979-80, Am. Acad. and Inst. for Arts and Letters grantee; recipient Lit. Lion award N.Y. Pub. Libr., 1986. Office: Jack Tantleff 375 Greenwich St Ste 700 New York NY 10013-2338*

NORMAN, MARY MARSHALL, counselor, therapist; b. Auburn, N.Y., Jan. 10, 1937; d. Anthony John and Zita Norman. BS cum laude, LeMoyne Coll., 1958; MA, Marquette, U., 1960; EdD, Pa. State U., 1971. Cert. Alcoholism Counselor. Tchr., St. Cecilia's Elem. Sch., Theinsville, Wis., 1959-60; vocat. counselor Marquette U., Milw., 1959-60; dir. testing and counseling U. Rochester (N.Y.), 1960-62; dir. testing and counseling, dean women, asso. dean coll., asst. dean students, dir. student activities, asst. prof. psychology Corning (N.Y.) C.C., 1962-68; rsch. asst. Center for Study Higher Edn., Pa. State U., University Park, 1969-71; dean faculty South Campus, C.C. Allegheny County, West Mifflin, Pa., 1971-72, exec. dean, coll. v.p., 1972-82; pres. Orange County C.C., 1982-90; sr. counselor The Horton Family Program, 1990—. cons. Boricua Coll., N.Y.C., 1976-77; reader NSF, 1977-78; mem. govtl. commn. com. Am. Assn. Cmty. and Jr. Colls., 1976-79, bd. dirs., 1982—; mem. and chmn. various middle state accreditation teams. Bd. dirs. Orange County United Way; bd. dirs. Orange County Alcoholism and Drug Abuse Coun., 1993—. Mem. Am. Assn. Higher Edn., Nat. Assn. Women Deans Counselors, Am. Assn. Women in Community and Jr. Colls. (charter, Woman of Yr. 1981), Pa. Assn. Two-Yr. Colls., Pa. Assn. Acad. Deans, Pitts. Council Women Execs. (charter), Am. Council on Edn. (Pa. rep. identification women for adminstrn. 1978—), Pa. Council on Higher Edn., Orange County C. of C., Gamma Pi Epsilon. Contbr. articles to profl. jours. Home: 8 Crabapple Ln Middletown NY 10940-1006 Office: 115 South St Middletown NY 10940-6441

NORMAN, ROBIN GOLD, educational administrator; b. Boston, Aug. 11, 1947; m. Michael A. Norman, Aug. 10, 1980; children: Josh, Brad. BA in Sociology and Psychology, Syracuse U., 1969; MEd in Learning Disabilities, Boston U., 1973. Cert. elem. edn., elem. sch. prin., moderate spl. needs, generic specialist, adminstr. spl. edn., Mass. Tchr. learning disabled Franklin Elem. Sch., Newton, Mass., 1969-70; asst. to Coord. of Learning Disabilities, Newton, Mass., 1970-73, 79-81; spl. edn. diagnostic Duke U. Med. Ctr., Devel. Evaluation Clinic, Pediatrics, Durham, N.C., 1973-74; team leader spl. needs program Warren Jr. High Sch., Newton, 1976-79, Brown Jr. High Sch., Newton, 1981-84; dir., asst. to Coords. Spl. Edn., Newton, 1984—; chpt. 1 dir. Brown Jr. High Sch., 1984—; instr. Lesley Coll., Cambridge, Mass., 1977; presenter and workshop leader in field; pres. Minn. Assn. Children Learning Disabilities, 1975-76. Bd. dirs. Countryside Elem. Sch., Brown Mid. Sch., Mewton South High Sch. Mini Leave grantee, 1988-89; recipient Charles E. Brown fellow award, 1992. Mem. Assn. Children LEarning Disabilities, Coun. Generic Tchrs., Coun. Adminstrs. Compensatory Edn., Alpha Kappa Delta. Office: Newton Pub Schs 100 Walnut St Newtonville MA 02160-1314

NORMILE, SUSAN ANN, counselor, consultant, educator; b. St. Genevieve, Mo., Apr. 17, 1958; d. Glennon L. and Loretta M. (Roth) Wright; m. William R. Normile, Aug. 21, 1982; children: Katherine M., Patrick J. B in Edn., U. Mo., 1980, MEd, 1982. Lic. profl. counselor, Colo.; cert. rehab. counselor. Counselor, rschr. Harry S. Truman Vets. Hosp., Columbia, Mo., 1979-82; counselor Gray & Assocs., Denver, 1982-83; co-owner Career Potentials, Colorado Springs, 1983-89; counselor, mgr. Olson Vocat. Svcs., Colorado Springs, 1988-93; instr., cons. Pikes Peak Cmty. Coll., Colorado Springs, 1993—. Mem. Am. Counseling Assn., Nat. Career Devel. Assn., El Paso Assn. of Lic. Profl. Counselors, Kappa Delta Pi. Democrat. Roman Catholic.

NORRELL, MARY PATRICIA, nursing educator; b. Seymour, Ind., Jan. 3; d. William C. and Mary Elizabeth (Elkins) Ulrey; m. Robert Gerald Norrell, Aug. 17, 1974; children: Shannan, Richard, Trisha. BSN, Ball State U., 1971; postgrad., Ind. U. Cert. neonatal resuscitation, inpatient obstetrics. Team leader Mt. Sinai Med. Ctr., Miami Beach, Fla., 1971-73; charge nurse Jackson County Schneck Meml. Hosp., Seymour, 1971, 73-74; nurse Camp Matoaka, Oakland, Maine, 1973; master instr. Ind. Vocat. Tech. Coll., Columbus, Ind., 1974—; item writer Nat. Coun. Licensure Exam. for Practical Nurses, 1992. Mem. Assn. of Women's Health, Obstetric and Neonatal Nurses, Ind. Soc. for Healthcare Edn. and Tng. Home: 572 Shawnee Ct Seymour IN 47274-3117

NORRIS, ANDREA SPAULDING, art museum director; b. Apr. 2, 1945; d. Edwin Baker and Mary Gretchen (Brendle) Spaulding. BA, Wellesley Coll., 1967; MA, NYU, 1969, PhD, 1977. Intern dept. western European arts Met. Mus. Art, N.Y.C., 1970, 72; rsch. and editorial asst. Inst. Fine Arts NYU, 1971, lectr. Washington Sq. Coll., 1976-77; lectr. Queens Coll. CUNY, 1973-74; asst. to dir. Art Gallery Yale U., New Haven, 1977-80, lectr. art history, 1979-80; chief curator Archer M. Huntington Art Gallery, Austin, Tex., 1980-88; lectr. art history Dept. Art U. Tex., Austin, 1984-88; dir. Spencer Mus. Art U. Kans., Lawrence, 1988—. Co-author: (catalogue) Medals and Plaquettes from the Molinari Collection at Bowdoin College, 1976; author: (exhbn. catalogues) Jackson Pollock: New-Found Works, 1978; exhbn. The Sforza Court: Milan in the Renaissance 1450-1535, 1988-89. Mem. Renaissance Soc. Am., Coll. Art Assn., Assn. Art Mus. Dirs., Phi Beta Kappa. Office: Spencer Mus Art U Kans Lawrence KS 66045

NORRIS, CARLA SUE TODD, university admissions and recruitment supervisor, software specialist; b. Crawfordsville, Ind., Apr. 27, 1962; d. Walter Parker Jr. and Violet Rose (Hedger) T.; m. Jeffrey Wayne Norris, Nov. 8, 1986; 1 child, Sarah Rose. BA, Ind. State U., 1984, MS, 1992. Data entry oper. Ind. State U., Terre Haute, 1984-86, supr. admissions, recruitment, software specialist, 1986—; mem. banner implementation team Ind. State U., 1994. Treas. Take Off Pounds Sensibly (TOPS), Inc., Riley, Ind., 1993—; co-leader Daisy Scouts Girl Scouts USA, Riley, 1993-94; leader Brownie Troop # 362, Riley, 1994—; active PTO, Riley Elem. Sch., 1993—. Mem. Am. Coll. Counseling Assn., Am. Counseling Assn., Alpha Kappa Delta. Democrat. Baptist. Home: 11251 S Harbor Ln Terre Haute IN 47802 Office: Ind State U Grad Office Alumni Hall Rm 144 Terre Haute IN 47809

NORRIS, CAROL SPOHN, legislative staff administrator; b. Newark, Ohio, Oct. 16, 1949; d. Harold Edwin and Erma Luella (Lallathin) Spohn; m. Alan E. Norris, Nov. 10, 1990. BA, Ohio State U., 1971, MA, 1972. Legis. intern Ohio Legis. Svc. Commn., Columbus, 1972-73; legis. aide Ohio Ho. of Reps., Columbus, 1973-78, legis. rsch. dir., 1979-83, legis. staff dir., 1984-94; speaker Inst. of Politics, Kent, Ohio, 1981. Bd. dirs. Columbus Area Women's Polit. Caucus, Columbus, 1974; legis. rep. Race for the Cure, 1993—. Mem. Conf. for Women in Pub. Svc. (legis. rep. 1994—), Ohio Rep. Womens Polit. Campaign Fund. Republican. Methodist. Office: Ohio Ho of Reps 77 S High St Columbus OH 43266

NORRIS, ELIZABETH DOWNE, archivist; b. White Plains, N.Y., Apr. 25, 1914; d. Albro Farwell and Alice Elizabeth (Morse) Downe; B.A., Smith Coll., 1936; M.Div., Yale U., 1939; M.L.S., Columbia U., 1955; 1 son, Donald E. Norris. Asst. residence dir. New Haven YWCA, 1940-42; religious edn. librarian Union Theol. Sem., N.Y.C., 1953-57; librarian NCCJ, N.Y.C., 1957-63; head librarian Nat. Bd. YWCA of the U.S.A., N.Y.C., 1963—, dir. Nat. Bd. Archives Project, 1976—, YWCA historian, 1980—, project dir. traveling exhbn. Women First for 135 Years, 1993—. Recipient Henry Foote Lewis prize in religion, 1934. Mem. Spl. Libraries Assn., Soc. Am. Archivists. Mem. United Ch. Christ. Editor: Feminine Figures: Selected Facts about American Women and Girls, 1968-72; Subject Headings on Women, 1973; Recent Trends in Professionalism, 1973; The YWCA Advances Women's Rights, 1855-1989, 1989; Dairy of a Volunteer, 1983; Women and Children First; a Century of YWCA Services to Children, 1984, The YWCA Secretary Searches for Professionalism 1889-1955, 1989; contbg. librarian Mental Health Book Rev. Index, 1961-72; editor, mem. adv. com. Books for Brotherhood, ann. 1957-76; co-editor Reunion: Newsletter for Retired Staff, 1994—; contbr. articles to jours. Home: 505 Laguardia Pl New York NY 10012-2001 Office: 726 Broadway New York NY 10003

NORRIS, GENIE M., political organization executive; b. N.Y.C., July 15, 1951; d. Eugene and Peggy (Carter) Martell; m. Larry Specht, Apr. 22, 1982; children: Amanda Michele, Joshua Albert, Rachel Elizabeth. Adminstr. Senator Patrick Moynihan, N.Y.C., 1976; exec. asst. U.S. Senate, Washington, 1982-86; dep. field dir. Carter/Mondale Presdl. Campaign, Washington, 1979; dep. dir. Dem. Nat. Com., Washington, 1980-81; dir., sr. assoc. Francis Assocs., Ltd., Washington, Germany, 1981-82; exec. asst. Senator Patrick Moynihan, Washington, 1982-86; guest lectr. USIA, Washington, 1987-90; mgr. Amb. Residence, Bonn, Germany, 1987-90; sr. assoc. FMR Group, Washington, 1990; dep. exec. dir. Dem. Congl. Campaign Com., Washington, 1990-91, exec. dir., 1991-94; dep. Asst. Sec. for ops. Dept. of State, Washington, 1995—; com. rep. Dem. Nat. Com. South Africa, 1980, Dem. Congl. Campaign Com., Republic of China, 1992; Peace Corp. transistion team leader Pres. Transition Team, Washington, 1992-93; South Africa elections obs. UN, 1994. With U.S. Army, 1975-78. Democrat. Roman Catholic. Home: 1630 Davidson Rd Mc Lean VA 22101 Office: Dept of State Washington DC 20520

NORRIS, JOAN CLAFETTE HAGOOD, elementary school educator; b. Pelzer, S.C., June 26, 1951; d. William Emerson and Sarah (Thompson) Hagood; divorced; 1 child, Javiere Sajorah. BA in History and Secondary Edn., Spelman Coll., 1973; MA in Teaching in Edn., Northwestern U., 1974; MA in Adminstrn. and Supervision, Furman U., 1984. Cert. elem. edn. tchr., elem. prin., social studies tchr., elem. supr., S.C.; notary pub., S.C. Clk. typist Fiber Industry, Greenville, S.C., 1970, Spelman Coll. Alumni Office, Atlanta, 1970-73; tchr. Chgo. Bd. Edn., 1973-74, Greenville County Pub. Schs., Greenville, S.C., 1974—; chair Black History Com., Armstrong Elem. Sch., Greenville, 1991, Am. Edn. Com., Armstrong Elem. Sch., 1992. Contbr. articles to profl. jour. Sec. Webette's Templw # 1312, Greenville, 1985, parliamentarian, 1986; mem. Coun. Negro Women, Greenville, 1988—, NAACP, Greenville, 1989-92. Alliance of Quality Edn. grantee, 1989-90; selected to Potential Adminstrs. Acad., Furman U., 1991; named Tchr. of the Yr., Armstrong Elem. Sch., 1981-82, 90-91. Mem. NEA, AAUW (Greenville chpt. exec. bd. cmty. rep. 1993-94, v.p. for programs 1994—), Internat. Reading Assn., S.C. Network for Women Adminstrs. in Edn., S.C. Alliance of Black Educators, Greenville County Tchrs. Math., Greenville County Tchrs. Sci., Greenville County Tchrs. English, Spelman Alumni Assn., Northwestern Alumni Assn., Phi Kappa Delta (sec. chpt. 1993-94), Phi Delta Kappa (chpt. alt. del. 1992-93). Democrat. Baptist. Home: 219 Barrett Dr Mauldin SC 29662-2030 Office: Armstrong Elem Sch 20 Martin Dr Greenville SC 29611

NORRIS, JUNE RUDOLPH, minister; b. Trinidad, Colo., June 30, 1922; d. Ernest Ellsworth and Bessie Mildred (Dawson) Rudolph; m. Willard M. Norris, Feb. 12, 1938 (div. Sept. 1966); children: Gene Curtis, Paul Martin, Dixie June. Student, East L.A. Coll., 1968-74, Samaritan Bible Sch., L.A., 1972-74. Lic. Universal Fellowship Met. Community Chs., 1973, ordained 1974. Staff clergy Met. Community Ch., L.A., 1972-80; pastor Met. Community Ch., Fayetteville, N.C., 1980-81, St. John's Met. Community Ch., Raleigh, N.C., 1981-88, Ch. Holy Spirit of Met. Community Ch., Des Moines, 1989-93; office mgr. W.M. Norris Constrn., Orlando, Fla., 1961-66; clk. outpatient div. Fla. Hosp., Orlando, 1966-67; supr. White Meml. Med. Ctr., L.A., 1968-76; mem. staff Met. Community Ch., San Diego, 1993—. Contbr. articles to Front Page jour. Mem. team to testify state legis. com. for gay/lesbian rights St. John's Met. Community Ch., 1985. Recipient Disting. Svc. award Universal Fellowship Met. Community Ch., 1991, appreciation White People Healing Racism, 1991. Mem. Hosp. Credit Mgrs. Assn. (pres. 1970-71), Mensa. Office: Met Community Ch PO Box 33291 San Diego CA 92163

NORRIS, LOIS ANN, elementary school educator; b. Detroit, May 13, 1937; d. Joseph Peter and Marguerite Iola (Gourley) Giroux; m. Max Norris, Feb. 9, 1962 (div. 1981); children: John Henry, Jeanne Marie, Joseph Peter. BS in Social Sci., Ea. Mich. U., 1960, MA, 1960; cert. adminstr., Calif. State U., Bakersfield, 1983. Kindergarten tchr. Norwalk-LaMirada Unified Sch. Dist., 1960-62; tchr. various grades Rialto Unified Sch. Dist., 1962-66; kindergarten tchr. Inyokern (Calif.) Sch., 1969-82; 1st grade tchr. Vieweg Basic Sch, 1982-92, kindergarten tchr., 1992—; head tchr. Sierra Sands Elem. Summer Sch.; adminstrv. intern Sierra Sands Adult Sch., master tchr., head tchr., counselor. Ofcl. scorekeeper, team mother, snack bar coord. China Lake Little League; team mother, statistician Indian Wells Valley Youth Football; bd. mem. PTA; pres. Sch. Site Coun.; treas. Inyokern Parents Club; run coord. City of Hope; timekeeper, coord. Jr. Olympics; mem. planning com. Sunshine Festival; active Burros Booster Club. Recipient Hon. Svc. award PTA, 1994. Mem. Desert Area Tchrs. Assn., Assn. Calif. Sch. Adminstrs., Inyokern C. of C. (sec.), Am. Motorcycle Assn., NRA, Bakersfield Coll. Diamond Club. Republican. LDS Ch. Home: PO Box 163 201 N Brown Rd Inyokern CA 93527 Office: Sierra Sands Unified Sch 113 W Felspar Ave Ridgecrest CA 93555-3520

NORRIS, PAMELA, school psychologist; b. Springfield, Mass., May 11, 1946; d. William Henry Jr. and Loretta Agnes (Houck) N. BA in English, Keuka Coll., 1968; MA in Philosophy, U. Mass., 1969; MEd in Guidance and Counseling, Westfield (Mass.) State Coll., 1973; MA in Clin. Psychology with distinction, Am. Internat. Coll., 1991. Nat. cert. sch. psychologist; cert. sch. psychologist, Mass., Conn.; lic. ednl. psychologist, Mass.; lic. real estate broker, Mass.; cert. guidance counselor, Mass.; cert. English tchr., Mass., Conn. English tchr. Agawa Pub. Schs., Feeding Hills, Mass., 1970-87, sch. psychologist, 1987—. Telephone operator Springfield (Mass.) Hotline, 1970-72; telephone operator, counselor Falmouth (Mass.) Emergency and Referral Svc., 1971, SPAN Ctr., Feeding Hills, Mass, 1972-73, CHEC-Line, West Springfield, Mass., 1974-75; occupational therapist Monson (Mass.) State Hosp., 1976-77. Mem. APA (assoc.), Nat. Assn. of Sch. Psychologists, New Eng. Psychol. Assn., Mass. Sch. Psychology Assn., Western Mass. Sch. Psychology Assn., Sigma Tau Delta, Pi Delta Epsilon. Office: Agawa Pub Schs 1305 Springfield St Feeding Hills MA 01030-2180

NORRIS, REBECCA, design firm executive; b. Balt., Sept. 29, 1955; d. Ray Norman and Peggy Jean (Weeks) N. BA, Bob Jones U., 1977. Designer World Wide Advt.-J. Walter Thompson, Balt., 1978; designer, art dir. M.J. Seidel, Balt., 1979-81; designer Johns Hopkins U., Balt., 1981-86; art dir. Norris, Reynolds & Denham, Balt., 1986—. Vol. Transplant Resource Ctr., Balt., 1990-91, Johns Hopkins Women's Bd., Balt., 1992. Recipient design awards Print mag., 1983, N.Y. Soc. Scribes, 1984, Univ. and Coll. Designers Assn., 1985, Graphis, 1992, others. Mem. Printing Industries Md., Md. Hist. Soc., The Daguerreian Soc., Nat. Trust for Historic Preservation. Office: Norris Reynolds & Denham 112 N Beechwood Ave Baltimore MD 21228

NORRIS, SUSAN ELIZABETH, social worker; b. Lubbock, Tex., Oct. 8, 1952; d. William Oxford and Katherine Burton (Sydnor) N. BA, U. Tex., Arlington, 1974; MSW, U. Conn., 1987. Child protective svcs. social worker Tex. Dept. Human resources, Ft. Worth, 1978-82; temp. word processor various cos., 1983-85; rsch. cons. Hartford, Conn., 1986-89; dir. child care svcs. United Way Conn., Hartford, 1987-92, dir. program svcs., 1992-93; faculty/assoc. dir. child and family studies, pediatrics U. Conn. Health Ctr., Farmington, 1993-94; dir. Americorps CARE, Nat. Assn. of Childcare Resource & Referral Agy's., 1994—. Bd. dirs., sec. Hartford Interval House, 1989-93; pres. bd. dirs. Hartford Area Child Collaborative, 1992-94. Democrat. Office: NACCRRA 1319 F St NW Washington DC 20004

NORRIS, SUSAN FETNER, bank examiner; b. Lansing, Mich., Feb. 3, 1949; d. R. Scott Sr. and Joann (Louckes) Fetner; m. Robert B. Norris, Sept. 26, 1987. BA, Mich. State U., 1971. Teller Mich. Nat. Bank, Lansing, 1971-74; supr. new accounts Grand Rapids (Mich.) Bank N.Am., 1974-75; bank examiner Office of the Comptroller of the Currency, Nat. Bank Examiners Bd., Kalamazoo, Mich., 1975-82; policy analyst Office of the Comptroller of the Currency, Nat. Bank Examiners Bd., Washington, 1982-86; asst. field office dir. Office of the Comptroller of the Currency, Nat. Bank Examiners Bd., Kansas City, Mo., 1986-87; mgr. examination support Office of the Comptroller of the Currency, Nat. Bank Examiners Bd., Dallas, 1988-93; compliance mgr. northeast dist. Office of the Comptroller of the Currency, Nat. Bank Examiners Bd., Washington, 1994—. Contbg. author: The Banker's Handbook, 1988. Home: 11344 Woodbrook Ln Reston VA 22094-1333 Office: 1025 Connecticut Ave NW Ste 708 Washington DC 20036

NORSTRAND, IRIS FLETCHER, psychiatrist, neurologist, educator; b. Bklyn., Nov. 21, 1915; d. Matthew Emerson and Violet Marie (Anderson) Fletcher; m. Severin Anton Norstrand, May 20, 1941; children: Virginia Helene Norstrand Villano, Thomas Fletcher, Lucille Joyce. BA, Bklyn. Coll., 1937, MA, 1965, PhD, 1972; MD, L.I. Coll. Medicine, 1941. Diplomate in neurology and geriatric psychiatry Am. Bd. Psychiatry and NEurology. Med. intern Montefiore Hosp., Bronx, N.Y., 1941-42; asst. resident in neurology N.Y. Neurol. Inst.-Columbia-Presbyn. Med. Ctr., N.Y.C., 1944-45; pvt. practice Bklyn., 1947-52; resident in psychiatry Bklyn. VA Med. Ctr., 1952-54, resident in neurology, 1954-55, staff neurologist, 1955—, asst. chief neurol. svc., 1981-91; neurol. cons. Indsl. Home for Blind, Bklyn., 1948-51; clin. prof. neurology SUNY Health Sci. Ctr., Bklyn., 1981—; attending neurologist Kings County Hosp., Bklyn., State U. Hosp., Bklyn. Contbr. articles to med. jours. Recipient spl. plaque Mil. Order Purple Heart, 1986, Spl. Achievement award PhD Alumni Assn. of CUNY, 1993, others. Fellow Am. Psychiat. Assn., Am. Acad. Neurology, Internat. Soc. Neurochemistry, Am. Assn. U. Profs. Neurology, Am. Med. EEG Soc. (pres. 1987-88), Nat. Assn. VA Physicians (pres. 1989-91, James O'Connor award 1987), N.Y. Acad. Scis., Sigma Xi. Republican. Presbyterian. Home: 7624 10th Ave Brooklyn NY 11228 Office: Bklyn VA Med Ctr 800 Poly Pl Brooklyn NY 11209-7104

NORSWORTHY, ELIZABETH KRASSOVSKY, lawyer; b. N.Y.C., Feb. 26, 1943; d. Leonid Alexander and Wilma (Hudgens) Krassovsky; m. John Randolph Norsworthy, June 24, 1961 (div. 1962), m. Nov. 26, 1977 (div. 1984); 1 child, Alexander. AB magna cum laude, Hunter Coll., CUNY, 1965; MA, U. N.C., 1966; JD, Stanford U., 1977. Bar: D.C. 1978, Mass. 1992. Atty. applications, disclosure rev. and investment adviser regulation, divsn. investment mgmt. SEC, Washington, 1978-79, 80-82, atty. operating brs. and disclosure policy divsn. corp. fin., 1979-80, chief, spl. counsel office of regulatory policy divsn. investment mgmt., 1983-86; assoc. Kirkpatrick & Lockhart, Washington, 1986-90; ptnr. Sullivan & Worcester, Boston, 1990-92; pvt. practice Norfolk, Mass., 1992—. Trustee St. Andrew's Endowment Com., Arlington, Va., 1989—, Boston Region SEC Alumni Assn., 1992—; clk. of the vestry St. Paul's, Millis, Mass.; mem.-at-large exec. com. Millis Cmty. Chorale, 1994—. Mem. ABA (internat. law com., securities com. 1986—, investment adviser investment co. subcom. 1990—, law practice mgmt. sec. 1992—), Western Norfolk County Bar Assn., N.Y. '40 Acts Com., MSPCA, Union Club of Boston, Trustees of the Reservations, Phi Beta Kappa, Phi Alpha Theta. Democrat. Episcopalian. Office: 69 Medway St Norfolk MA 02056-1348

NORTH, ANITA, secondary education educator; b. Chgo., Apr. 21, 1963; d. William Denson and Carol (Linden) N. BA, Ind. U., 1985; MS in Edn., Northwestern U., 1987. Cert. tchr., Ill. High sch. social studies and English tchr. Lake Park High Sch., Roselle, Ill., 1987-89; high sch. social studies tchr. West Leyden High Sch., Northlake, Ill., 1989—; exch. program coord. West Leyden High Sch., 1989—, head coach boys' tennis team, 1989—, asst. coach girls' tennis team, 1989—, asst. speech coach, 1992-93. Recipient Fern Fine Teaching award West Leyden High Sch., 1992. Mem. AAUW, Nat. Coun. for Social Studies, Ill. Coun. for Social Studies, Orgn. Am. Historians, Ill. Tennis Coaches Assn., Phi Delta Kappa. Christian.

NORTH, CAROL SUE, psychiatrist, educator; b. Keokuk, Iowa, May 6, 1954; d. Ray Stemen and Doris Ethelyn (Wood) N. BS in Gen. Sci., U. Iowa, 1976; MD, Wash. U., St. Louis, 1983, M in Psychiatric Epidemiology, 1993. Resident in psychiatry Barnes Hosp., Washington U. Med. Sch., St. Louis, 1983-87; rsch. fellow dept psychiatry Washington U., St. Louis, 1987-90, instr. dept. psychiatry, 1987-89, asst. prof. dept. psychiatry, 1989—; staff psychiatrist Grace Hill Neighborhood Health Ctr., St. Louis, 1987—, Midwest Psychiatry, 1993—, Adapt of Am., 1995—. Author: Welcome, Silence, 1987, Multiple Personalities, Multiple Disorders: Psychiatric Classification and Media Influence, 1993; contbr. articles to profl. jours. Bd. dirs. St. Louis Met. Alliance for the Mentally Ill., 1992—; trustee Rosati Stblzn. Ctr., for homeless and mentally ill. Nat. Inst. Alcoholism and Alcohol Abuse grantee, 1988-93, Nat. Hazards Rsch. Applications Info. Ctr. grantee, 1987-88, NIMH grantee, 1991-95. Mem. Am. Psychiat. Assn., Life History Rsch. Soc., Ea. Mo. Psychiat. Soc. (exec. coun.), Presbyn. Serious Mental Illness Network (at-large steering com.), Am. Psychopathol. Assn., Am. Acad. Clin. Psychiatrists, Nat. Alliance for Mentally Ill, St. Louis Track Club. Presbyterian. Office: Washington U Sch Medicine Dept Psychiatry 4940 Childrens Pl Saint Louis MO 63110-1002

NORTH, DORIS GRIFFIN, physician, educator; b. Washington, Nov. 30, 1916; d. Edward Lawrence and Ruth Gladys (Spray) Griffin; m. Victor North, Nov. 2, 1940 (dec. 1984); children: James, Daniel, Frederick. BA, U. Kans., 1938; MT, Kans. State U., 1939, MD, 1947. Med. tech. Ralph G. Ball, M.D., Manhattan, Kans., 1939-40, St. Francis Hosp., Pitts., 1940-41, John Mincer, M.D., Washington, 1941-43; intern Wesly Hosp., Wichita, Kans., 1947-48; resident in pediat. and internal medicine Sedgwick Hosp., Wichita, 1948-49; pvt. practice family physician Wichita, Kans., 1951—; clin. asst. prof. medicine Kans. State U. Sch. Medicine, Wichita, 1974—. Mem. AMA, Am. Acad. Family Practice, Kans. Med. Soc., Med. Soc. Sedgwick County, Phi Beta Kappa, Alpha Omega Alpha. Home: 1000 S Woodlawn Apt 408 Wichita KS 67218 Office: 1148 S Hillside Wichita KS 67211

NORTH, EVA LOIS BATES, environmental technician; b. Corydon, Ind., July 19, 1955; d. Cova and Emma Lee (Snider) Bates; m. Larry North, June 27, 1975 (div. Nov. 1987); 1 child, Nolan Travis. BA, Ind. U.-Purdue U., Indpls., 1986. Clk. Transp. Office, Dept. Def., Indpls., 1977-78; police officer VA Med. Ctr., Indpls., 1978-80, sec. psychiatry svc., 1980-83, motor vehicle operator, 1983-90, program asst. environ. mgmt. svc., 1990-93; environ. mgmt. career intern VA Med. Ctr., Louisville, 1993-94; program analyst VA Med. Ctr., 1994—. Master sgt. U.S. Army, 1974-77, USAR, 1982—. Named Hon. nurse, VA Med. Ctr., Indpls., 1993. Mem. NOW, Women Vets. Orgn. Home: 2012 Edgeland Ave Apt 3 Louisville KY 40204 Office: VA Med Ctr 800 Zorn Ave Louisville KY 40206

NORTH, JULIA B., telecommunications executive. V.p. customer svcs. Bellsouth Telecom., Atlanta. Office: Bellsouth Telecom 675 W Peachtree St NW Atlanta GA 30308*

NORTH, KATHRYN E. KEESEY (MRS. EUGENE C. NORTH), retired educator; b. Columbia, Pa., Jan. 25, 1916; d. Isaac and Elizabeth (French) Keesey; B.S., Ithaca Coll., 1938; M.A., N.Y. U., 1950; m. Eugene C. North, Aug. 18, 1938. Dir. music Cairo (N.Y.) Central Sch. Dist., 1938; music edn. cons. Argyle (N.Y.) Central Sch. Dist., 1939; dir. gen. music curriculum Hartford (N.Y.) Central Sch. Dist., 1939; mem. staff Del. Dept. Pub. Instrn., Dover, 1943; dir. music edn. Herricks (N.Y.) Pub. Schs., 1944-71; ret., 1971. Vis. lectr. Ithaca Coll., summers 1959, 60, 62-65, Fairleigh-Dickinson U., Rutherford, N.J., summer 1966, Albertus Magnus Coll., New Haven, summer 1968; instr. Adelphi Coll., 1954-55, Sch.. Edn., N.Y.U., 1964-65. Mem. Music Educators Nat. Conf., N.E.A., N.Y. State Sch. Music Assn., N.Y. State Tchrs. Assn., Nassau Music Educators Assn. (exec. bd. 1947-58), N.Y. State Council Adminstrs. Music Edn. (chpt. v.p. 1967-68), Herricks

Tchrs. Assn. (pres. 1948), Sigma Alpha Iota. Mem. Order Eastern Star. Home: 1645 Calle Camille La Jolla CA 92037-7107

NORTH, PENNA REARDON, school librarian; b. Stonington, Conn., Jan. 19, 1939; d. Walter Eugene and C. Ruth (Monjo) Reardon; m. John Hollister North, Jan. 17, 1957; children: Edward, Steven, Andrew. BA summa cum laude, Kean Coll., 1972, MA in Liberal Studies, 1980. Cert. elem. tchr., sch. libr. Elem. tchr. Holmdel (N.J.) Schs., 1972-73; libr. media specialist Matawan (N.J.)-Aberdeen Schs., 1973—; cons. Sci. Rsch. Assocs., Chgo., 1980-82. Author: (with others) Women View, 1976. Mem. affirmative action com. chairperson Matawan-Aberdeen Schs., 1980-84. Mem. AAUW, DAR (com. chairperson 1984-92), N.J. Edn. Assn., Monmouth County Edn. Media Assn., Holmdel Hist. Soc., Mensa, Alpha Sigma Lambda (past pres.), Phi Alpha Theta (1st prize for conf. paper 1980), Phi Kappa Phi. Democrat. Office: Matawan-Aberdeen Sch Dist Crest Way Matawan NJ 07747

NORTH-ABBOTT, MARY ANNE, training coordinator; b. Norristown, Pa., July 12, 1961; d. Daniel Arthur and Shirley Anne (Stuckart) North; m. Douglas Milton Abbott, June 24, 1989; children: Gwenn Anne, Douglas Milton Jr. BS in Petroleum Enging., Mont. Coll. Mineral Sci./Tech., 1985. Pumper, operator Conoco, Inc., Odessa, Tex., 1985-87; control rm. operator Conoco, Inc., Billings, Mont., 1987-89; lab. rsch. asst. MSE, Inc., Butte, Mont., 1989-91; tng. coord. MSE, Inc., Butte, 1991—. Mem. Dept. Energy Records and Info. Mgmt. Ad Hoc Com., US Masters Swimming. Roman Catholic. Office: MSE Inc CDIF Butte Indsl Pk Butte MT 59701

NORTHCUFF, WANDA L., state legislator; b. Stuttgart, Ark., Apr. 21, 1937; 4 children. Farmer Hildebrand Farm, Inc., Stuttgart; mem. Ark. Ho. of Reps., 1985—, mem. edn., agr. and econ. devel. coms. Democrat. Baptist. Office: Ark State Rep State Capitol Little Rock AR 72201*

NORTHCUTT, MARIE ROSE, educator; b. White Plains, N.Y., Feb. 2, 1950; d. Carlo and Marcelline Marie Rose (Benoit) DeMarco; m. Kenneth Walter Northcutt, Mar. 17, 1984; children: James Lee, Thomas Joseph. BA, Lynchburg Coll., 1972; MA, Columbia U., 1977. Cert. elem. and secondary tchr., N.Y. Tchr. Petersburg (Va.) Pub. Schs., 1972-74; asst. relocation mgr. Ticor Co., White Plains, 1974-75; 3d grade tchr. Resurrection Sch., Rye, N.Y., 1975-76; 6th grade tchr. Harrison (N.Y.) Cen. Sch. Dist., 1976-78, learning disabilities specialist, 1981—; tchr. of emotionally handicapped N.Y.C. Schs., 1978-80; learning evaluator Empire State Coll., White Plains, 1981-82; ind. evaluation cons., White Plains, 1981—; chair Mid. States Subcom. Active Harrison High Sch. PTA. Mem. Assn. for Children with Learning Disabilities, Westchester County Assn. for Children with Learning Disabilities, Orton Soc., Phi Delta Kappa. Roman Catholic. Home: 81 Griffin Pl White Plains NY 10603-3609 Office: Harrison Cen Sch Dist Union Ave Harrison NY 10528-2108

NORTHUP, ANNE MEAGHER, state legislator; b. Louisville, Jan. 22, 1948; d. James L. and Floy Gates (Terstegge) Meagher; m. Robert Wood Northup, Apr. 12, 1969; children: David, Katherine, Joshua, Kevin, Erin, Mark. BA in Econs., St. Mary's Coll. Notre Dame, South Bend, Ind., 1970. Mem. Ky. Ho. of Reps., Frankfort, 1987—; mem. fin. adv. bd. EPA, 1989-93. Recipient Cath. Schs. Disting. Alumni award, U. Notre Dame award of the yr. Ky. Alumni Assn., Clearing the Air award Am. Lung Assn. of Ky., 1991. Mem. Nat. Order Women Legislators, Nat. Conf. State Legislators, Nat. Republican Legis. Conf., So. Legis. Conf. (alternat from Ky. to fiscal affairs and governmental com.). Roman Catholic. Home: 3340 Lexington Rd Louisville KY 40206-3050 Office: Ky Ho of Reps State Capitol Frankfort KY 40601*

NORTHUP, KAREN FRANCES, environmental planner; b. Columbia, Mo., June 24, 1961; d. William Carlton and Betty Rose (Sullivan) N. B in Gen. Studies, U. Mo., 1984; M in Landscape Architecture, Kans. State U., 1990. Cert. land use planning. Landscape designer Master Lawn and Landscape, Manhattan, Kans., 1989; instr. Kans. State U., Manhattan, 1988-90; landscape architect U. Mo., Columbia, 1990-91; land reclamationist Mo. Dept. National Resources, Jefferson City, 1991-92, environ. specialist, 1992-93; planner, 1993—; ptnr. Nikomis Art and Design, Hartsburg, Mo., 1992-93. Advisor Conservation Fedn., Jefferson City, Mo., 1993—. Recipient Design Charette First Place award Kans. Am. Inst. of Architecture Students, 1989, Grad. Rsch. award Kans. State U. Coll. Architecture, 1990. Mem. Nat. Assn. State Land Reclamationists, Lake Area Judo Club, Sigma Lambda Alpha. Home: RR 2 Box 251D Eldon MO 65026-9531

NORTHWAY, WANDA I., realty company executive; b. Columbia, Mo., July 11, 1942; d. Herman W. and Goldie M. (Wood) Proctor; m. Donald H. Northway, June 12, 1965; 1 child, Michelle D. Student U. Mo., 1966. Lic. real estate agt., Mo.; grad. Realtors Inst. Realtor, assoc. Gentry Real Estate Co., Columbia, 1969-80; realtor Griffin Real Estate Co., 1980-81; pres., realtor, ptnr. House of Brokers Realty, Inc., Columbia, 1981—; pres., organizer Realtor-Assoc. Sales Club, Columbia, 1975; pres. Columbia Bd. Realtors, 1982. Contbr. articles to realty mags. Sunday sch. tchr., girls' aux. leader Baptist Ch.; vol. ARS, local hosp; campaign worker for Columbia legislators; mem. allocation com. United Way; active vol. Am. Cancer Soc. and Heart Assn. Named Realtor Assoc. of Yr., Columbia Bd. Realtors, 1974, Realtor of Yr., 1980. Mem. Mo. Assn. Realtors (state dir. 1974-77, Realtor Assoc. of Yr. award 1977), Realtors Nat. Mktg. Inst. (cert. residential specialist 1978), Nat. Assn. Realtors, (nat. dir. 1977), Epsilon Sigma Alpha (state corr. sec., local pres.). Republican. Baptist. Clubs: Million Dollar (life); Federation of Women's (pres. Mo. 1980). Office: House of Brokers Realty Inc 1515 Chapel Hill Rd Columbia MO 65203

NORTON, ANDRE ALICE, author; b. Cleve., Sept. 17, 1912; d. Adalbert and Bertha Stemm N. Librarian Cleve. Public Library, until 1951. Author: 125 books including The Sword is Drawn (Dutch Gov. award 1946) 1944, Sword in Sheath (Ohioana Juevenile award Honor Book 1950) 1949, Starhunter (Hugo award nomination World Sci. Fiction Convention 1962) 1961, Witch World (Hugo award nomination World Sci Fiction Convention 1964) 1963, Night of Masks (Boy's Club of Am. Certificate of Merit 1965) 1964; series include Swords Trilogy, Star Ka'at Sci. Fiction Series, Witch World Fantasy Series. Recipient Invisible Little Man award Westercon XVI, 1963, Phoenix award 1976, Gandalf Master Fantasy award World Sci. Fiction Convention, 1977, Andre Norton award Women Writers of Sci. Fiction, 1978, Balrog Fantasy award 1979, Ohioana award, 1980, Fritz Leiber award, 1983, E.E. Smith award, 1983, Nebula Grand Master award Sci. Fiction Writers of Am., 1984, Jules Verne award, 1984, Second Stage Lensman award, 1987; named to Ohio Hall of Fame, 1981. Mem. PEN Women, Sci. Fiction Writers Am., Theta Sigma Phi (Headliner award 1963).

NORTON, ELEANOR HOLMES, congresswoman, lawyer, educator; b. Washington, June 13, 1937; d. Coleman and Vela (Lynch) Holmes; m. Edward W. Norton (div.); children: Katherine, John H. BA, Antioch Coll., 1960; MA in Am. Studies, Yale U., 1963, LLB, 1964; LLD (hon.), Cedar Crest Coll., Allentown, Pa., 1969, Bard Coll., Annandale-on-Hudson, N.Y., 1971, Princeton U., 1973, Marymount Coll., 1974, CCNY, 1975, NYU, 1978, Howard U., 1978, Brown U., 1978, Wilberforce U., 1978, Wayne State U., 1980, Syracuse U., 1981, Yeshiva U., 1981, Lawrence U., 1981, Emanuel Coll., 1981, Spelman Coll., 1982, U. Mass., 1983, Smith Coll., 1983, Med. Coll. Pa., 1983, Tufts U., 1984, Bowdoin Coll., 1985. Bar: Pa., 1965, U.S. Supreme Ct., 1968. Law clk. presiding justice Fed. Dist. Ct., 1964-65; asst. legal dir. ACLU, 1965-70; exec. asst. to mayor N.Y.C., 1971-74, chmn. commn. humanities, 1970-77; chmn. commn. humanities EEOC, 1977-81; sr. fellow Urban Inst., 1981-82; prof. law Georgetown U., 1982—; chmn. nat. adv. coun. ACLU; elected del. from D.C. to U.S. Congress, 1990, 92. Author: (with others) Sex Discrimination and the Law: Causes and Remedies, 1975; contbr. articles to profl. jours. Trustee Community Found. Greater Washington, Rockefeller Found., Yale Corp.; bd. dirs. A. Philip Randolph Inst., Bethune Mus. and Archives Nat. Historic Site; catalyst Ctr. Nat. Policy, Manpower Demonstration Research Corp., Martin Luther King, Jr. Ctr. Social Change, Nat. Black Leadership Roundtable, Nat. Polit. Congress Black Women, Nat. Urban Coalition, Pitney Bowes Corp., So. Christian Leadership Conf.; adv. bd. Nat. Women's Polit. Caucus, Women's Law and Policy Fellowship, Workplace Health Fund; chmn. Commn. Future of Women in Workplace, Nat. Adv. Council ACLU; mem. Am. Council Edn., Council Minority Edn., Council Fgn. Relations, U.S. Citizens Com. Monitor Helsinki Accords, exec. panel Ford Found. Project Future of Welfare State, Nat. Acad. Scis. Com. Effects Tech. Change Employment and Working Environment. Recipient Young Woman of Year award Jr. C. of C., 1965; One of 25 Most Influential Women in Am. award Newspaper Enterprise Assn., 1977; Louise Waterman Wise award Am. Jewish Congress, 1971; Harper fellow Yale Law Sch., 1976; vis. Phi Beta Kappa scholar, 1985. Mem. Nat. Acad. Scis. (numerous coms.). Office: 1415 Longworth Washington DC 20515 also: Georgetown U Law Ctr 600 New Jersey Ave NW Washington DC 20001

NORTON, ELIZABETH WYCHGEL, lawyer; b. Cleve., Mar. 25, 1933; d. James Nicolas and Ruth Elizabeth (Cannell) Wychgel; m. Henry Wacks Norton Jr., July 16, 1954 (div. 1971); children: James, Henry, Peter, Fred; m. James Cory Ferguson, Dec. 14, 1985 (div. Apr. 1988). BA in Math., Wellesley Coll., 1954; JD cum laude, U. Minn., 1974. Bar: Minn. 1974. Summer intern Minn. Atty. Gen.'s Office, St. Paul, 1972; with U.S. Dept. Treasury, St. Paul, 1973; assoc. Gray, Plant, Mooty, Mooty & Bennett, P.A., Mpls., 1974-79, prin., 1980-94, of counsel, 1995—; mem. Minn. Lawyers Bd. Profl. Responsibility, 1984-89; mem. U. Minn. Law Sch. Bd. Visitors, 1987-92. trustee YWCA, Mpls., 1979-84, 89-91, co-chmn. deferred giving com., 1980-81, chmn. by-laws com., bd. dirs., 1976-77, lectr.; treas. Minn. Women's Campaign Fund, 1985, guarantor, 1982-83, budget and fin. com. bd. dirs., 1984-87; trustee Ripley Meml. Found., 1980-84; treas. Johnes-Harrison Home, 1967, bd. dirs., 1962-69, 2d v.p., chmn. fin., 1968-69; mem. Sen. David Durenberger's Women's Network, 1983-88. Durant scholar. Fellow Am. Bar Found.; mem. ABA (mediation task force family law sect. 1983-84), Minn. Bar Assn. (human rights com. family law sect., task force uniform marital property act 1984-85), Minn. Bar Found. (dir. 1991-94), Hennepin County Bar Assn. (pres. 1987-88, chmn. task force on pub. edn. 1984, chmn., mem. exec. com. family law sect. 1979-94), Minn. Inst. Legal Edn., Minn. Women's Lawyers (exec. com.), U. Minn. Law Sch. Alumni Assn. (dir. 1975-81, exec. com. 1981-83), Wellesley Club, Phi Beta Kappa. Home: 4980 Dockside Dr # 204 Fort Myers FL 33919-4657 Office: Gray Plant Mooty Mooty & Bennett 33 S 6th St Ste 3400 Minneapolis MN 55402-3796

NORTON, GALE A., state attorney general; b. Wichita, Mar. 11, 1954; d. Dale Bentsen and Anna Jacqueline (Lansdowne) N.; m. John Goethe Hughes, Mar. 26, 1990. BA, U. Denver, 1975, JD, 1978. Bar: Colo. 1978, U.S. Supreme Ct. 1981. Jud. clk. Colo. Ct. of Appeals, Denver, 1978-79; sr. atty. Mountain States Legal Found., Denver, 1979-83; nat. fellow Hoover Instn. Stanford (Calif.) U., 1983-84; asst. to dep. sec. U.S. Dept. of Agr., Washington, 1984-85; assoc. solicitor U.S. Dept. of Interior, Washington, 1985-87; pvt. practice law Denver, 1987-90; atty. gen. State of Colo., Denver, 1991—; Murdock fellow Polit. Economy Rsch. Ctr., Bozeman, Mont., 1984; sr. fellow Ind. Inst., Golden, Colo., 1988-90; policy analyst Pres. Coun. on Environ. Quality, Washington, 1985-88; lectr. U. Denver Law Sch., 1989; transp. law program dir. U. Denver, 1978-79. Contbr. chpts. to books, articles to profl. jours. Participant Rep. Leadership Program, Colo., 1988, Colo. Leadership Forum, 1989; past chair Nat. Assn. Attys. Gen. Environ. Com.; co-chair Nat. Policy Forum Environment Coun. Named Young Career Woman Bus. and Profl. Wome, 1981, Young Lawyer of Yr., 1991. Mem. Federalist Soc., Colo. Women's Forum, Order of St. Ives. Republican. Methodist. Office: Colo Dept of Law 1525 Sherman St 5th Fl Denver CO 80203

NORTON, KAREN ANN, accountant; b. Paynesville, Minn., Nov. 1, 1950; d. Dale Francis and Ruby Grace (Gehlhar) N. BA, U. Minn., 1972; postgrad. U. Md., 1978; cert. acctg. U.S. Dept. Agr. Grad. Sch., 1978; MBA, Calif. State Poly. U.-Pomona, 1989. CPA, Md. Securities transactions analyst Bur. of Pub. Debt., Washington, 1972-79, internal auditor, 1979-81; internal auditor IRS, Washington, 1981; sr. acct. World Vision Internat., Monrovia, Calif., 1981-83, acctg. supr., 1983-87; sr. systems liaison supr., Home Savs. Am., 1987—; cons. (vol.) info. systems John M. Perkins Found., Pasadena, Calif., 1985-86. Author (poetry): Ode to Joyce, 1985 (Golden Poet award 1985). Second v.p. chpt. Nat. Treasury Employees Union, Washington, 1978, editor chpt. newsletter; mem. M-2 Prisoners Sponsorship Program, Chino, Calif., 1984-86. Recipient Spl. Achievement award Dept. Treasury, 1976, Superior Performance award, 1977-78; Charles and Ellora Alliss scholar, 1968. Mem. Angel Flight, Covenant Ch. Avocations: flying, chess, racquetball, whitewater rafting.

NORTON, RUTH ANN, education educator; b. Sioux City, Iowa, Mar. 7, 1947; d. Burton Ellwood and Mildred Ruth (Schneider) N.; m. Jack William Moskal, May 30, 1985. BA, U. No. Iowa, 1969; MS, Syracuse U., 1984, EdD, 1985. Cert. tchr., Iowa, Vt. Tchr. Cedar Falls (Iowa) Unified Sch. Dist., 1969-79; asst. didr. Area 7 Tchr. Ctr., Waterloo, Iowa, 1979-80; tchr. Moretown (Vt.) Elem. Sch., 1980-81; doctoral candidate Syracuse (N.Y.) U., 1981-85; prof. Calif. State U., San Bernardino, 1985—, dir. student teaching, 1985—; cons. tech. tng. inst. Calif. State U., San Bernardino, Constl. Heritage Inst.; trainer supervision workshops Calif. State U., San Bernardino; cons. Lime St. Elem. Sch., Hesperia, Calif.; bd. dirs. Redlands Ednl. Partnership Found.; chairperson Reflections Com. for Redlands PTA Coun. Contbr. articles to profl. jours. Recipient Affirmative Action Faculty Devel. grant Calif. State U., 1986, Profl. Devel. Monetary grant Calif. State U., 1987, Meritorious Performance & Profl. Promise award Calif. State U., 1988. Mem. ASCD, Am. Ednl. Rsch. Assn., Assn. Tchr. Educators, Calif. Assn. for Supervision and Curriculum Devel., Calif. Coun. for Social Studies, Nat. Coun. for Social Studies, So. Calif. Assn. Tchr. Educators, Phi Delta Kappa. Office: Calif State U 5500 University Pky San Bernardino CA 92407-2318

NORTON, VIRGINIA SKEEN (MRS. JOHN H. NORTON, JR.), civic worker; b. Atlanta, June 1, 1907; d. Lola Percy and Rebecca (Baldwin) Skeen; A.B., Agnes Scott Coll., 1928; student Columbia U., 1934-35; m. John Hughes Norton, Jr., Dec. 16, 1938; children—Virginia Skeen Norton Kraft, John Hughes III. With personnel dept. Retail Credit Co., Atlanta, 1929-31, sec. to v.p., gen. mgr. Davison-Paxon, Co., Atlanta, 1931-34; with Aluminium Ltd., N.Y.C., 1935-41, sec. to pres., 1937-41; sec. to pres. Colonial Williamsburg, Inc., N.Y.C., 1943-44. Bd. dirs. North Shore Assos. Chgo. Commons, 1951-54, Infant Welfare Soc. Chgo., 1953-54, Catherine Morrill Day Nursery, Portland, Maine, 1956-59. Mem. Loch Haven Arts Soc., Winter Park Meml. Hosp. Aux., Morse Art Gallery Assocs. (dir. 1982-84), Nat. Soc. Colonial Dames Am. Episcopalian. Address: 1620 Mayflower Ct Apt A-606 Winter Park FL 32792-2577

NORVILLE, DEBORAH, news correspondent; b. Aug. 8, 1958; m. Karl Wellner; 2 children: Karl Nikolai, Kyle Maximilian. BJ, U. Ga., 1979. Reporter Sta. WAGA-TV, Atlanta, 1978-79, anchor, reporter, 1979-81; anchor, reporter Sta. WMAQ-TV, Chgo., 1982-86; anchor NBC News, N.Y.C., 1987-89; news anchor Today Show, NBC, N.Y.C., 1989, co-anchor, 1990-92; corr. Street Stories, CBS, N.Y.C., 1992-94; co-anchor America Tonight, CBS, N.Y.C., 1994; anchor Inside Edition, King World Prodns., 1994—; contbg. editor McCall's, N.Y.C. Bd. dirs. Greater N.Y. coun. Girl Scouts U.S. Recipient Outstanding Young Alumni award Sch. Journalism, U. Ga., Emmy award, 1985-86, 89; named Person of Yr., Chgo. Broadcast Advt. Club, 1989, Anchor of Yr. 2000, Washington Journalism Rev., 1989. Mem. Soc. Profl. Journalists. Office: Inside Edition 402 E 76th St New York NY 10021*

NORWALK, KELLI CURRAN, retail executive, entrepreneur; b. Cleve., Sept. 25, 1949; d. Paul Joseph and Ella (Eylar) Curran; m. Keith Otto Norwalk, Apr. 3, 1970; children: Keith Curran, Alyssa Barr. BA, Butler U., 1978. Exec. dir. Heritage Place, Indpls., 1975-77; social worker Americana Health Care, Indpls., 1978-81; pres., prin. Down By the Ducks, Inc., Indpls., 1982-85; chief exec. officer, prin. The Tarkington Tweed, Inc., Indpls., 1985—. Mem. Butler Tarkington Neithborhood Assn., Indpls., 1978—, Arts, Ind. Mem. 500 Festival Assocs., Indpls. C. of C. Democrat. Roman Catholic. Home: 5534 Bay Landing Ct Indianapolis IN 46254 Office: The Tarkington Tweed Inc 5631 N Illinois St Indianapolis IN 46208-1554

NORWOOD, CAROL RUTH, research laboratory administrator; b. N.Y.C., Oct. 10, 1949; d. John Theodore and Ruth Arnold (Shields) Gundlach; m. Christian K.-H. Schneider; 1 child, from previous marriage, Jonathan Blair. BA, U. Colo., 1971, PhD (Biophysics), 1975. Rsch. assoc. div. biochemistry MIT, Cambridge, 1974-76; rsch. assoc. dept. cardiac surgery Children's Hosp., Boston, 1976-83; instr. dept. surgery Harvard U. Med. Sch., Boston, 1980-83; asst. prof. U. Pa. Sch. Medicine, Phila., 1984-87; dir. Cardiothoracic Surgery Rsch. Labs. Children's Hosp. Phila., 1984-94; dir. General Surgery Rsch. Labs. Children's Hosp. Phila., 1994—. Contbr. articles to sci. jours., chpts. to books. Mem. Am. Chem. Soc. (biochemistry divsn, pub. outreach), Am. Heart Assn. (cardiovascular disease in young coun.). Office: Children's Hosp Phila 34th St And Civic Ctr Philadelphia PA 19104

NORWOOD, CAROLE GENE, middle school educator; b. Odessa, Tex., Feb. 27, 1943; d. Perry Eugene and Jeffie Lynn (Stephens) Knowles; m. James Ralph Norwood, Aug. 4, 1973. BA, U. Tex., 1966; MA, U. North Tex., 1975; cert. ESL, Our Lady of the Lake U., San Antonio, 1988. Student intern Dept. of the Interior, Washington, 1962; English instr. Universidade Mackenzie, Sao Paulo, Brazil, 1966-67, Uniao Cultural Brasil-Estados Unidos, Sao Paulo, 1966-67; tchr. Terrell (Tex.) Jr. Sr. High Sch., 1967-68, Agnew Jr. High Sch., Mesquite, Tex., 1968-70; teaching asst. U. North Tex. Denton, Tex., 1970-71; sec. to pres. The Village Bank, Dallas, 1971-72; tchr. Plano (Tex.) High Sch., 1972-74, Brentwood Middle Sch., San Antonio, 1975-90; instructional specialist Gus Garcia Jr. High Sch., San Antonio, 1990—, interdisciplinary team leader, 1992-93. Mem. World Wildlife Fund, Audubon Soc., Nat. Wildlife Fedn., Nature Conservancy, San Antonio Museum Assn., San Antonio Zoological Soc. Named Outstanding Young Woman of Am., 1972. Mem. AAUW, NEA, ASCD, Nat. Coun. Tchrs. English, San Antonio Area Coun. Tchrs. English, Tex. State Tchrs. Assn., Delta Kappa Gamma. Presbyterian. Office: Edgewood Ind Sch Dist Gus Garcia Jr School San Antonio TX 78228

NORWOOD, DEBORAH ANNE, law librarian; b. Honolulu, Nov. 12, 1950; d. Alfred Freeman and Helen G. (Papsch) N.; 1 child, Nicholas. BA, U. Wash., 1972; JD, Willamette U., 1974; M in Law Librarianship, U. Wash., 1979. Bar: Wash., U.S. Dist. Ct. (we. dist.) 1975, U.S. Ct. Appeals (9th cir.) 1980. Ptnr. Evans and Norwood, Seattle, 1975-79; law librarian U.S. Courts Library, Seattle, 1980-89; state law librarian Wash. State Law Libr., Olympia, 1989—, reporter of decisions, 1994—; adv. bd. mem. U. Wash. Library Automation Cert. Program, Seattle, 1988-89. Mem. Am. Assn. Law Librs., Am. Libr. Assn. Office: Wash State Law Libr PO Box 40751 Temple of Justice Olympia WA 98504-0751

NORWOOD, JANET LIPPE, economist; b. Newark, Dec. 11, 1923; d. M. Turner and Thelma (Levinson) Lippe; m. Bernard Norwood, June 25, 1943; children—Stephen Harlan, Peter Carlton. BA, Douglass Coll., 1945; MA, Tufts U., 1946; PhD, Fletcher Sch. Law and Diplomacy, 1949; LLD (hon.), Fla. Internat. U., 1979; LL.D. (hon.), Carnegie Mellon U., 1984. Instr. Wellesley Coll., 1948-49; economist William L. Clayton Ctr. William L. Clayton Ctr. Tufts U., 1953-58; with bur. labor stats. Dept. Labor, Washington, 1963-91; dep. commr., then acting commr. bur. labor stats. Dept. Labor, 1975-79, commr. labor stats. bur. labor stats., 1979-92; sr. fellow The Urban Inst., Washington, 1992—; dir. Republic Nat. Bank, CIESIN, chair adv. coun. unemployment compensation, 1993—; mem. com. on nat. stats. Nat. Acad. Sci. Author papers, reports in field. Trustee CIESIN, 1994—. Recipient Disting. Achievement award Dept. Labor, 1972, Spl. Commendation award, 1977, Philip Arnow award, 1979, Elmer Staats award, 1982, Pub. Svc. award, 1984; named to Hall Disting. Alumni, Rutgers U., 1987; recipient Presdl. Disting. Exec. rank, 1988. Fellow AAAS, Am. Statis. Assn. (pres. 1989), Royal Statis. Soc., Nat. Assn. Bus. Economists; mem. Am. Econ. Assn., Indsl. Rels. Rsch. Assn., Women's Caucus in Stats., Com. Status Women Econs. Profession, Internat. Statis. Inst., Internat. Assn. Ofcls. Stats., Nat. Acad. Pub. Adminstrn. (vice chair bd. trustees), Nat. Inst. Statis. Sci. (bd. trustees); mem. Cosmos Club (v.p.), Douglas Coll. Soc. Disting. Achievement. Home: 6409 Marjory Ln Bethesda MD 20817-5805 Office: The Urban Inst 1000 Wilson Blvd # 2710 Arlington VA 22209-3901

NORWOOD, JOY JANELL, real estate executive; b. Barnes, Kans., Aug. 25, 1936; d. Howard Clayton and Gladys Melveno (Wells) Cook; divorced; 1 child, Rebecca. Student, U. Colo., 1958-63; grad., Realtors Inst. Ohio State U., 1977. Lic. real estate broker, Ohio. Registered rep. First Investors Corp., Boston, 1966-68; area supr. Wohl Shoe Co., Boston, 1968-70; residential real estate broker Coldwell Banker, Cin., 1970-78, comml. real estate broker, 1978-80; comml. real estate broker Rubloff, Cin., 1980-82; real estate rep. Ky. Fried Chicken/Zantigo, Louisville, 1982-86; v.p. Otto Realty Corp., Cin., 1987-89; pres. Joy Norwood & Assocs., Westchester, Ohio, 1989—. Jr. high sch. tchr. Mason (Ohio) Ch. Christ, 1986—, mem. choir., 1986—. Served with U.S. Army, 1955-58. Mem. Nat. Assn. Corp. Real Estate Execs., Internat. Council Shopping Ctrs., Cin. Bd. Realtors (polit. affairs com. 1974, Million Dollar Club award, 1972-79), Cin. Hist. Soc. Republican. Club: Flying Neutrons (Cin.). Office: Joy Norwood & Assocs 8547 Ashwood Dr West Chester OH 45069-3035

NOTTLEY, CAROL ANN, nonprofit foundation executive; b. Detroit, Apr. 14, 1940; d. William A. Nottley and Mary M. Osborne Baker; m. L. Schneider (div. 1966); m. D. Boles (div. 1974); children: Beth, David, Laura, William, Janet, Kathryn. AA, Macomb County C.C., Warren, Mich., 1974; BA, U. San Francisco, 1990; MA, Webster U., 1994. Cert. bus. adminstrn., pub. affairs. Bus., bldg. mgr. Feminist Econ. Network, Inc., Detroit, 1974-77; asst. exec. dir. The Center, L.A., 1978-79, Alcoholism Ctr. for Women, L.A., 1980-81; exec. dir. People in Progress, L.A., 1981-86; CEO Clare Found., Santa Monica, Calif., 1986-91, AIDS Found., San Diego, 1993—; asst. adminstr. Alcohol and Drug divsn., Dept. Health Svcs., County of San Diego, 1991-93; vice chair HIV Care Coalition, San Diego, 1993—; active Regional Adv. Bd. on AIDS, San Diego, 1992—, San Diego County Planning Coun. Title I, 1993—, State of Calif. Office on AIDS Title I Working, Sacramento, 1994—. Trustee City of San Diego Housing Trust Fund, 1994—; cons., trainer Support Ctr., San Diego, 1991—. Recipient Commendation award for pub. svc. Calif. Senate, 1986, Commendation award for exemplary leadership, 1991; named Outstanding Contbr. in field of alcohol and drugs Calif. Legis. Assembly, 1986. Mem. NAFE. Office: AIDS Found San Diego 140 Arbor Dr San Diego CA 92103

NOVAK, BARBARA, art history educator; b. N.Y.C.; d. Joseph and Sadie (Kaufman) N.; m. Brian O'Doherty, July 5, 1960. B.A., Barnard Coll., 1951; M.A., Radcliffe Coll., 1953, Ph.D., 1957. TV instr. Mus. Fine Arts, Boston, 1957-58; mem. faculty Barnard Coll., Columbia U., N.Y.C., 1958—; prof. art history Barnard Coll., Columbia U., 1970—, Helen G. Altschul prof., 1984—; adv. council Archives of Am. Art, NAD. Editorial bd.; Am. Art Jour.; co-editor Next to Nature, 1980; author: American Painting of the 19th Century, 1969, Nature and Culture, 1980, The Thyssen-BBornemisza Collection 19th Century American Painting, 1986, Alice's Neck, 1987, (play) The Ape and the Whale: Darwin and Melville in Their Own Words, 1987 (performed at Symphony Space, 1987), Dreams and Shadows: Thomas H. Hotchkiss in 19th Cen. Italy, 1993. Commr. Nat. Portrait Gallery; trustee N.Y. Hist. Soc. Fulbright fellow Belgium, 1953-54; Guggenheim fellow, 1974; Nat. Book Critics nominee, 1980; Los Angeles Times Book Award nominee, 1980; Am. Book Award paperback nominee, 1981. Fellow Soc. Am. Historians, Phila. Atheneum; mem. Soc. Am. Historians, Am. Antiquarian Soc., Coll. Art Assn. (dir. 1974-77), N.Y. Hist. Soc. (trustee), PEN. Office: Barnard Coll Art History Dept 606 W 120th St New York NY 10027-5706

NOVAK, JO-ANN STOUT, chemical engineer; b. Glen Ridge, N.J., June 25, 1956; d. Herbert Austin and Anna (Messina) Stout; m. John Robert Novak Jr., Oct. 30, 1976; B. in Chem. Enging., Ga. Inst. Tech., 1977; MBA, Oakland U., 1984. Cert. engr.-in-tng., Ga.; registered profl. engr., Mich. Trainee AC Spark Plug div. GM, Flint, Mich., 1977-78, chemist, 1978-79, exptl. chemist, 1979-81, mfg. engr., 1981-84, sr. mfg. engr., 1984-87; sr. mfg. project engr., 1987-89, mgr. bus. and engring. processes, 1989-90, program planning mgr., 1990-92; supr. engring.-info. & sys., 1992-94, staff engr. chemical and metall. processes, 1994—. Mem. AIChE, Enging. Soc. Detroit, Nat. Soc. Profl. Engrs., Am. Electroplaters Soc. (dir. Saginaw Valley br. 1981-83, ednl. chmn. 1984-85, sec.-treas. 1985-86, 2d v.p. 1986-87, 1st v.p. 1987-88, pres. 1988-89), Soc. Mfg. Engrs. Office: AC Delco Sys Divsn GMC 1300 N Dort Hwy Flint MI 48556-0002

NOVAK, JULIE COWAN, nursing educator, researcher, clinician; b. Peoria, Ill., Oct. 2, 1950; m. Robert E. Novak, 1972; children: Andrew, Christopher, Nicholas. BS in Nursing, U. Iowa, 1972, MA in Nursing, 1976; D.N.Sc., U. San Diego, 1989. RN. Charge nurse U. Iowa Hosp. and Clinics, 1972-73; instr. med. sur. nursing St. Luke's Sch. Nursing, Cedar Rapids, Iowa, 1973-

74; instr. family and community health U. Iowa Coll. of Nursing, 1974-75; perinatal nurse clinician U. Iowa Hosps., 1976-77; pediatric nurse practitioner Chicano Community Health Ctr., 1978-80; lectr., asst. prof. nursing San Diego State U., 1977-79; child health N.P. program coord. U. Calif., San Diego, 1978-82; pediatric nurse practitioner San Diego City Schs., 1980-82; coord. infant spl. care ctr. U. Calif., San Diego, 1982-83, assoc. clin. prof. intercampus grad. studies, 1983-90, dir. health promotion div. community and family medicine, 1985-90; assoc. clin. prof. dept. community family medicine U. Calif. Divsn. Health Care Sci., San Diego, 1990-94; assoc. prof. San Diego State U. Sch. Nursing, 1990-94, Calif. Nursing Students Assn. faculty advisor, 1992-94; pediatric nurse practitioner Naval Hosp., 1990-92, Comp. Health Clinic, 1990-94; prof., dir. FNP, PNP, WHNP program U. Va. Schs. Nursing & Medicine, Charlottesville, 1994—; cons. child health San Diego State U. Child Study Ctr.; mem. accident prevention com. Am. Acad. Pediatrics; lectr. in field. Contbr. numerous articles to profl. jours. and book chpt. to 6 texts; co-author: Ingall's & Salerno's Maternal Child Nursing, 1995, Mosby Year Book. Chair Ann. Refugee Clothing Drive, East San Diego, ESL Program, Car Seat Roundup U. Calif., San Diego, 1983-85; mem. telethon March of Dimes; mem. steering com. Healthy Mothers/Healthy Babies Coalition; chair ways and means com. Benchley-Weinberger Elem. Sch. PTA, 1985-87, pres., 1988-90; v.p., pres. Friends Jamul Schs. Found.; co-chair teen outreach program Jr. League San Diego, 1987-88, chair, 1989-90, bd. dirs., 1990-92; educator presch. health San Carlos Meth. Ch.; mem. Head Start Policy Coun., 1992-94, San Diego County Dropout Prevention Roundtable, 1991-93. Recipient Svc. award Benchley-Weinberger Elem. Sch. PTA, 1988, Hon. Youth Svc. award Calif. Congress Parents and Tchrs., Loretta C. Ford Award for excellence as an nurse practitioner in edn. U. Colo. Mem. ANA, Nat. Assn. Pediatric Nurse Practitioners Assoc. (chpt. pres., program com., coord. legis. field, nat. cert. chair 1992—), Calif. Nurses Assn., Pi Lambda Theta, Sigma Theta Tau (mem. nominations com. 1990-91, pres.-elect Gamma Gamma chpt. 1993-94). Home: 2415 Harmony Dr Charlottesville VA 22901-8990

NOVAK, KIM (MARILYN NOVAK), actress; b. Chgo., Feb. 13, 1933; d. Joseph A. and Blanche (Kral) N.; m. Richard Johnson, April 1965 (div.); m. Robert Malloy, Jan. 1977. Student, Wright Jr. College, Chgo.; A.A., Los Angeles City College, 1958. appeared in: (films) The French Line, 1953, Pushover, 1954, Phffft, 1954, Five Against the House, 1955, Son of Sinbad, 1955, Picnic, 1955, The Man with the Golden Arm, 1956, The Eddie Duchin Story, 1956, Jeanne Eagles, 1957, Pal Joey, 1958, Vertigo, 1958, Bell, Book and Candle, 1958, Middle of the Night, 1959, Strangers When We Meet, 1960, Pépé, 1960, Boys' Night Out, 1962, The Notorious Landlady, 1962, Of Human Bondage, 1964, Kiss Me Stupid, 1964, The Amorous Adventures of Moll Flanders, 1965, The Legend of Lylah Clare, 1968, The Great Bank Robbery, 1969, Tales That Witness Madness, 1973, The White Buffalo, 1977, Just a Gigolo, 1979, The Mirror Crack'd, 1980, Liebestraum, 1991; (TV movies) Third Girl from the Left, 1974, Satan's Triangle, 1975, Malibu, 1983. Named one of 10 most popular movie stars by Box-Office mag. 1956, All-Am. Favorite 1961, Brussels World Fair poll as favorite all-time actress in world 1958. Office: 24700 Outlook Dr Carmel CA 93923*

NOVELLO, ANTONIA COELLO, United Nations official, former U.S. surgeon general; b. Fajardo, P.R., Aug. 23, 1944; d. Antonio and Ana D. (Flores) Coello; m. Joseph R. Novello, May 30, 1970. BS, U. P.R., Rio Piedras, 1965; MD, U. P.R., San Juan, 1970; MPH, Johns Hopkins Sch. Hygiene, 1982; DSc (hon.), Med. Coll. Ohio, 1990, U. Ctrl. Caribe, Cayey, P.R., 1990, Lehigh U., 1992, Hood Coll., 1992. Diplomate Am. Bd. Pediatrics. Intern in pediatrics U. Mich. Med. Ctr., Ann Arbor, 1970-71, resident in pediatrics, 1971-73, pediatric nephrology fellow, 1973-74; pediatric nephrology fellow Georgetown U. Hosp., Washington, 1974-75; project officer Nat. Inst. Arthritis, Metabolism and Digestive Diseases NIH, Bethesda, Md., 1978-79, staff physician, 1979-80; exec. sec. gen. medicine B study sect., div. of rsch. grants NIH, Bethesda, 1981-86; dep. dir. Nat. Inst. Child Health & Human Devel., NIH, Bethesda, 1986-90; surgeon gen. HHS, Washington, 1990-93; spl. rep. for health and nutrition UNICEF, N.Y.C., 1993—; clin. prof. pediatrics Georgetown U. Hosp., Washington, 1986, 89, Uniformed Svcs. U. of Health Scis., 1989; mem. Georgetown Med. Ctr. Interdepartmental Rsch. Group, 1984—; legis. fellow U.S. Senate Com. on Labor and Human Resources, Washington, 1982-83; mem. Com. on Rsch. in Pediatric Nephrology, Washington, 1981—; participant grants assoc. program seminars Nat. Inst. Arthritis, Diabetes and Digestive and Kidney Diseases, NIH, Bethesda, 1980-81; pediatric cons. Adolescent Medicine Svc., Psychiat. Inst., Washington, 1979-83; nephrology cons. Met. Washington Renal Dialysis Ctr. affiliate Georgetown U. Hosp., Washington, 1975-78; phys. diagnosis class instr. U. Mich. Med. Ctr., Ann Arbor, 1973-74; chair Sec.'s Work Group on Pediatric HIV Infection and Disease, DHHS, 1988; cons. World Health Orgn., Geneva, 1989; mem. Johns Hopkins Soc. Scholars, 1991. Contbr. numerous articles to profl. jours. and chpts. to books in field; mem. editorial bd. Internat. Jour Artificial Organs, Jour. Mexican Nephrology. Served to capt. USPHS, 1978—. Recipient Intern of Yr. award U. Mich. Dept. Pediatrics, 1971, Woman of Yr. award Disting. Grads. Pub. Sch. Systems, San Juan, 1980, PHS Commendation medal HHS, 1983, PHS Citation award HHS, 1984, Cert. of Recognition, Div. Research Grants NIH, 1985, PHS Outstanding medal HHS, 1988, PHS Unit Commendation, 1988, PHS Surgeon Gen.'s Exemplary Svc. medal, 1989, PHS Outstanding Unit citation, 1989, DHHS Asst. Sec. for Health cert. of commendation, 1989, Surgeon Gen. Medallion award, 1990, Alumni award U. Mich. Med. Ctr., 1991, Elizabeth Blackwell award, 1991, Woodrow Wilson award for disting. govt. svc., 1991, Congrl. Hispanic Caucus medal, 1991, Order of Mil. Med. Merit, 1992, Washington Times Freedom award, 1992, Charles C. Shepard Sci. award, 1992, Golden Plate award, 1992, Elizabeth Ann Seton award, 1992, Ellis Island Congrl. Medal of Honor, 1993, Legion of Merit medal, 1993, Athena award Alumnae Coun., 1993, Nat. Citation award Mortar Bd., 1993, Disting. Pub. Svc. award, 1993; named Health Leader of Yr., COA, 1992. Fellow Am. Acad. Pediatrics (Excellence Pub. Svc. award 1993); mem. AMA (Nathan Davis award 1993, Meritorious Svc. award 1993), Internat. Soc. Nephrology, Am. Soc. Nephrology, Latin Am. Soc. Nephrology, Soc. for Pediatric Rsch., Am. Pediatric Soc., Assn. Mil. Surgeons U.S., Am. Soc. Pediatric Nephrology, Pan Am. Med. and Dental Soc. (pres.-elect, sec. 1984), D.C. Med. Soc. (assoc.), Johns Hopkins U. Soc. Scholars, Alpha Omega Alpha. Home: 1315 31st St NW Washington DC 20007-3334 Office: UNICEF Rm 634 3 United Nations Plaza New York NY 10017

NOVER, NAOMI, journalist, editor, author; b. Buffalo; d. B.B. and Rebecca (Shane) Goll; m. Barnet Nover. Student, U. Buffalo; BS, N.Y. State Tchrs. Coll.; MA, George Washington U., 1951. News, features, editorial asst. Buffalo Times; tchr. pub., pvt. schs. Buffalo Park Sch. (demonstration sch. of U. Buffalo), Snyder, N.Y.; music critic Denver Post at Goethe Music Festival, Aspen, Colo.; news corr., columnist Washington Bur. Denver Post; editor, bur. chief Nover News Bur., Washington, 1972—; corr. mission to Europe Portland Oregonian, Italian Peace Treaty Conf., Luxembourg Palace, Paris, Ladybird Johnson trips to nat. parks, 1963; attended various econ. summits; White House corr. Pres. Ford European tour, Switzerland, Spain, Finland, England, France, Germany, Poland, 1975, Pres. Ford trips to China, South Korea, Indonesia, Japan, Philippines, Hawaii, 1978, Pres. Carter trips to India, Saudi Arabia, Israel, Egypt, S.Am., Africa, Eng., Europe, Japan, etc., 1978, Pres. Reagan trips to Peoples Republic of China, Europe, Cen. Am., Caribbean, Iceland, Bali, Indonesia, Finland, 1988, Pres. Bush's trips to Italy, The Vatican, Poland, Hungary, France, NATO, London, Costa Rica, Fed. Republic Germany, Belgium, The Netherlands, 1989, to Finland for Bush-Gorbachev Summit, 1990, Can., Martinique, Bermuda, Paris, London, Athens, Crete, Greece, Ankara, Turkey, Istanbul, Turkey, 1991, Moscow, Kiev, Russia, 1991, Honolulu, Sydney, Australia, Canberra, Australia, Melbourne, Australia, Singapore, Seoul, Korea, Osaka, Japan, Tokyo, 1992, Pres. Clinton trip to UN, N.Y., 1993. Writer, dir. plays produced in Buffalo; participated radio and television plays; producer: nationally syndicated radio program Views and Interviews; author: nationally syndicated feature stories and column Washington Dateline, 1952—; contbr. articles to mags. Formerly active ARC, U.S Treasury War Bonds; chmn. Kalorama area Community Chest, 1947-49; originator embassy participation groups, jr. hostess, chmn., originator embassy tour Goodwill Industries; past chmn., producer program with 1,000 Girl Scouts at Pan Am. Union; past mem. council Girl Scouts U.S.A.; chmn. program com. Columbian Women of George Washington U., 1953-56; nat. chmn. War Nurses Meml.; mem. women's bd. George Washington U. Hosp. Recipient award pin U.S. Treasury Dept.; Silver Eagle award Girl Scouts U.S.A.; chosen to christen ship SS Syosset for vol. and charity activities; named honor citizen Colonial Williamsburg (Va.). Mem. White House Corrs. Assn., State Dept. Corrs. Assn., Congl. Press Galleries Corrs. Assn., U.S. Capitol, AAUW, U.S. Capitol Hist. Soc., U.S. Supreme Ct. Hist. Soc., Founding Friend of Blair House, The Circle of Nat. Gallery of Art, Nat. League Am. Pen Women, Smithsonian Assocs., U.S. Archives, Hist. Preservation, Libr. of Congress Assocs., Women in Radio and TV Assn., Women in Arts Mus., Am. Hist. Assn., Welcome to Washington, Ikebana, Phi Beta Kappa Assocs., Sigma Delta Chi, Pi Lambda Theta (past corr. ofcl. publ., nat. scholastic honors). Office: Nat Press Bldg Washington DC 20045

NOVETZKE, SALLY JOHNSON, former ambassador; b. Stillwater, Minn., Jan. 12, 1932; married; 4 children. Student, Carlton Coll., 1950-52; HHD (hon.), Mt. Mercy Coll., 1991. Amb. to Malta, Am. Embassy, Valletta, 1989-93. Past mem., legis. rep. Nat. Coun. on Vocat. Edn.; past mem. adv. coun. for career edn., past mem. planning coun. Kirkwood C.C.; bd. dirs., lifetime trustee Cedar Rapids (Iowa) Community Theater; bd. dirs. James Baker III Pub. Policy Inst. Rice U.; trustee Shattuck/St. Mary's Sch., Faribault, Minn.; vice chmn., lifetime trustee, exec. com. Hoover Presdl. Libr.; past precinct chmn. Iowa Rep. Com., 1976-88, mem. cen. com., 1982-85; state chmn., 1985-87; chmn. Linn County Rep. Com., 1980-83; adv. bd. Iowa Fedn. Rep. Women, 1987-89; vice chmn. campaign adv. bd. Nat. Fedn. Rep. Women, 1987-89; co-chmn. V.P. Bush Inauguration, 1980; Iowa co-chmn. George Bush for Pres., 1988; bd. dirs. Greater Cedar Rapids Found., also chmn. grants com., Coun. of Am. Ambs.; bd. dirs. Ambs. Forum; trustee Shahuck/St. Mary Sch., Fairmont, Minn. Decorated dame Order of Knights of Malta; recipient Disting. Alumnus award Stillwater High Sch., 1991; Disting. Alumni award for outstanding achievement Carleton Coll., 1994. Office: 4747 Mount Vernon Rd SE Cedar Rapids IA 52403-3941

NOVOGROD, NANCY ELLEN, editor; b. N.Y.C., Jan. 30, 1949; d. Max and Hilda (Kirschbaum) Gerstein; m. John Campner Novogrod, Nov. 7, 1976; children: James Campner, Caroline Anne. AB, Mt. Holyoke Coll., 1971. Sec. fiction dept. The New Yorker, N.Y.C., 1971-73, reader, 1973-76; asst. editor Clarkson N. Potter, Inc., N.Y.C., 1977-78, assoc. editor, 1978-80, editor, 1980-83, sr. editor, 1984-86, exec. editor, 1987; sr. editor HG (formerly House and Garden mag.), N.Y.C., 1987-88, editor-in-chief, 1988-93; editor-in-chief Travel & Leisure, N.Y.C., 1993—. Bd. dirs. N.Y. Bot. Garden, 1991, Mount Holyoke Coll., 1992—. Office: Travel & Leisure 1120 Ave of the Americas New York NY 10036

NOVOTNY, DEBORAH ANN, consultant; b. Oak Lawn, Ill., Sept. 23, 1964; d. Russell Anthony and Barbara J. (Doran) N. BA in Econs., Northwestern U., 1986; postgrad., U. Minn., 1988-91. Lic. mutual fund mktg. analyst. Mgr. lab., cons. Northwestern U., Evanston, Ill., 1983-86; asst. mgr. microcomputer services Sara Lee Corp., Chgo., 1986; sr. cons. Lante Corp., Chgo., 1987-88; fin. exec. IDS Fin. Svcs., Inc., Mpls., 1988-91; fin. system coord. Met. Water Reclamation Dist. of Greater Chgo., Chgo., 1991-92; mgmt. systems cons., pres., CEO Deborah A. Novotny, Inc., Chgo., 1992—; cons. Powersoft Corp., Concord, Mass., 1993—; invited Comdex Trade Show spkr. Active teen retreat team St. Michael's Ch., Orland Park, Ill., 1978-84. Ill. State scholar. Mem. MacIntosh Users Group, Chi Omega Rho (charter, chmn. housing assn. 1986-91).

NOVOTNY, SUSAN M., judge; b. Norfork, Nebr., June 13, 1951; d. Richard J. and Blanche M. (Mensik) N.; m. Scott R. Laidig, Jan. 22, 1978. BA cum laude, Cath. Univ. of Am., D.C., 1973; JD, Cath. Univ. of Am. Law Sch., D.C., 1979. Bar: Fla. 1980, Escambia Santa Rosa 1980. Adminstrv. asst., paralegal specialist Dept. of Justice, D.C., 1973-79; trial atty. Criminal Div. Fraud Sect. U.S. Dept. of Justice, D.C., 1979-80; assoc. Kerrigan, Estess & Rankin, Pensacola, Fla., 1980-82; asst. state atty. Pensacola, Fla., 1982-84, asst. U.S. atty., 1984-86; magistrate judge U.S. Dist. Ct. (no. dist.) Fla., Pensacola, 1986—; adj. prof. Pensacola Jr. Coll., 1980-85, Law Enforcement Tng. Acad., 1981-85; instr. Nat. Inst. of Trial Advocacy, 1984-88, Emory Law Sch. Trial Techniques Program, Atlanta, 1985, Atty. Gen.'s Advocacy Inst., Dept. of Justice, 1985-89. Recipient Spl. Achievement award U.S. Dept. of Justice, 1985, Cert. of Appreciation U.S. Dept. of Treasury Bureau of Alcohol, Tobacco & Firearms, 1985. Mem. Am. Bar Assn., Fla. Bar Assn., Escambia Santa Rosa Bar Assn. Office: US Courthouse 100 N Palafox St Rm 204 Pensacola FL 32501-4839*

NOWACKI, DAWN, political science educator, researcher; b. Spokane, Wash., May 24, 1954; d. Everett K. and Patricia (Thiebes) Plumb; m. Robert J. Jamison, June 2, 1984 (div. 1989); 1 child, Alexandra; m. D. Michael Nowacki, Aug. 24, 1991, 1 child, Heather. BA, U. Wash., 1977, MA, 1981; PhD, Emory U., 1995. Staff analyst Radio Free Europe/Radio Liberty, Inc., Paris, 1981-84; asst. editor Soc. for Ctrl. Asian Studies, London, 1985-88; grad. rsch. asst. Emory U., Atlanta, 1988-91; vis. asst. prof. polit. sci. U. S.C., Columbia, 1993-94; asst. prof. polit. sci. Linfield Coll., McMinnville, Oreg., 1994—; mem. mentoring network, women's student svcs. U. S.C., 1993-94. Contbr. articles to profl. jours. U.S. Office Edn. fgn. lang. and area studies fellow, 1991-93, Hewlet grad. fellow Carter Ctr. of Emory U., 1990; Am. Coun. Tchrs. Russian grantee, 1992. Mem. Am. Polit. Sci. Assn., Am. Assn. for Advancement of Slavic Studies, Assn. for Study of Nationalities (Eurasia and Eastern Europe), Phi Beta Kappa. Office: Linfield Coll Dept Polit Sci Mcminnville OR 97128

NOWAK, CAROL A., city official; b. Buffalo, Mar. 5, 1950; d. Walter S. and Stella M. (Gurowski) N. AAS in Bus. Adminstrn., Erie Community Coll., Buffalo, 1986; BS in Bus. Mgmt., SUNY, Buffalo, 1991. With Liberty Nat. Bank/Norstar, Buffalo, 1968-70; with City of Buffalo, 1970-74, asst. adminstrn. and fin., 1974-82, pension clk., adminstr. city police and fire pension fund, city clk., 1982-90, sr. coun. clk., city clk., 1990—. Artist, designer holiday greeting cards, 1984—. Mem. Nat. Notary Assn., SUNY Alumni Assn., Golden Key, Alpha Sigma Lambda. Home: 422 Dingens St Buffalo NY 14206-2321 Office: City of Buffalo City Clerk's Office 1308 City Hall Buffalo NY 14202-3313

NOWAK, JACQUELYN LOUISE, retirement home administrator, realtor, consultant; b. Harrisburg, Pa., Sept. 2, 1937; d. John Henry and Irene Louise (Clark) Snyder; children: Andrew Alfred, IV, Deirdre Anne. Student, Pa. State U., 1973-74; BA, Lycoming Coll., 1975. Editorial writer Patriot News Co., Harrisburg, Pa., 1957-58; dir. West Shore Sr. Citizens Ctr., New Cumberland, Pa., 1969-72; exec. dir. Cumberland County Office Aging, Carlisle, Pa., 1972-80; bur. dir. Bur. Advocacy, Pa. Dept. Aging, Harrisburg, 1980-88; exec. asst. to Pa. Senator John D. Hopper, Senate Com. on Aging and Youth, 1989; owner D&J Prodns., Art and Handcrafted Teddy Bears 1986, Ted E. Bear's Emporium, Harrisburg, 1988-92; assoc. Century 21 Piscioneri Realty, Inc., Camp Hill, Pa.; spl. projects coord. Pa. div. Am. Trauma Soc., 1991-93; adminstr. Country Meadows of West Shore II. Mechanicsburg, Pa., 1993—; recorder Pa. Gov's. Coun. Aging Cen. Region, 1972-74; chmn. pub. rels., 1973-74; mem. state planning com. Pa. State Conf. Aging, 1974, panelist, 1975-78; mem. state bd. Pa. Coun. Homemakers-Home Health Aide Svcs., 1972-80, v.p., 1975, chmn. ann. meeting, 1973-75; sr. citizens subcom. chmn. Pa. Atty. Gens. Commn. to Prevent Shoplifting, 1983; mem. adv. com. Tri-County Ret. Sr. Vol. Program, 1972-74; bd. dirs. Coun. Human Svcs. Cumberland, Dauphin, and Perry Counties, 1973-74; mem. svc. com. Family and Children's Svc. Harrisburg, 1970-74, mem. policy com., 1973-74, bd. dirs. Cumberland County unit Am. Cancer Soc., 1964-76, state del., 1964-66, chmn. county pub. rels., 1965-66, cancer crusade chmn., 1964. Recipient Herman Melitzer award, Pa. Conf. Aging, 1978; named Woman of the Yr. Sta. WIOO Radio, Carlisle, Pa., 1979. Mem. Nat. Assn. Area Ags. on Aging (bd. dir. 1975-80, pres. 1976-77; sec. 1978-79), Pa. Watercolor Soc., Harrisburg Art Assn., Mechanicsburg Art Ctr. (pres. 1987-90, bd. dirs. 1984—), Gerontol Soc. Am., Am. Trauma Soc. (Pa. div. state bd. 1985-88), Older Women's League (founder chpt.), Lycoming Coll. Alumni Assn. (exec. bd. 1987-89), Pa. Fedn. of Women's Club (div. chmn. 1972-76), Torch Club (pres. 1987-88, 2d v.p. 1985-86), Zonta Internat. (sec. 1986-89). Home: 15 Paddock Ln Camp Hill PA 17011-1268

NOWAK, JUDITH ANN, psychiatrist; b. Albany, N.Y., Feb. 18, 1948; d. Jacob Frank and Anne Patricia (Romanowski) N. BA, Cornell U., Ithaca, N.Y., 1970, MD, 1974. Bd. cert. Psychiatry. Resident Univ. Va. Hosp., Charlottesville, 1974-77; fellow in psychiatry Cornell U. Med. Coll. Westchester Div., White Plains, N.Y., 1977-78, clin. affiliate, 1k978-79; staff psychiatrist Chestnut Lodge Hosp., Rockville, Md., 1979-81; med. officer psychiatry St. Elizabeth's Hosp., Washington, 1981; pvt. practice Washington, 1981—; clin. asst. prof. of psychiatry, George Washington U., Washington, 1981-89; clin. assoc. prof. psychiatry, George Washington U. 1989-94, clin. prof. psychiatry, 1994—. Mem. Am. Psychiat. Soc., Washington Psychiat. Soc. (sec. 1989-90, pres. 1991-92), Am. Psychoanalytic Soc., D.C. Med. Soc. Office: 908 New Hampshire Ave NW Washington DC 20037-2346

NOWAK, KIMBERLY ANN, clinical social worker, nurse; b. Springfield, Mass., Jan. 1, 1965; d. Ralph Mitchell and Cynthia L. (Meyer) N. AA with honors, Holyoke (Mass.) C.C., 1986; BA with honors, Mount Holyoke Coll., 1989; MSW, Springfield Coll., 1991; ASN, Springfield (Mass.) Tech. C.C., 1994. Lic. ind. clin. social worker, Mass., RN. Psychiatric crisis clinician Mount Tom Inst. for Human Svcs., Holyoke, Mass., 1990-92; psychiatric cons. Specialized Geriatric Svcs., Ipswich, Mass., 1992-93; supr. psychiatric crisis team and respite unit 3d shift Psychiatric Crisis Svc., Springfield, Mass., 1993-94; pres. Alphabet Ltd., West Springfield, Mass., 1993—; coord. social svcs. for Providence Sys. Charles River West Hosp., Chicopee, Mass., 1994—; nurse crisis stabalizaiton unit Psychiat. Crisis Svc., Springfield, 1994—; charge RN psychiat. unit Cooley Dickenson Hosp., Northampton, Mass. Recipient scholarship Mount Holyoke Coll., 1987. Mem. NASW, Sigma Xi. Democrat.

NOWAK, NANCY STEIN, judge; b. Des Moines, Sept. 17, 1952; d. Russell D. and Christine (Evanoka) Stein; m. Raymond A. Nowak, May 26, 1973. BA, Drake Univ., Iowa, 1974, MA, 1976; JD, George Washington Univ., D.C., 1980. Bar: D.C. 1980, Iowa 1982, Tex. 1986. Briefing atty. Judge Jamie Boyd, 1983-84, Judge Edward Prado, 1984-87; asst. U.S. atty., 1987-88, asst. U.S. trustee, 1988-89; magistrate judge U.S. Dist. Ct. (Tex. we. dist.), 5th circuit, San Antonio, 1989—. Office: US Courthouse 655 E Durango Blvd San Antonio TX 78206*

NOWELL, GLENNA GREELY, librarian, consultant; b. Gardiner, Maine, Apr. 15, 1937; d. Bion Mellon and Faith Louise (Hutchings) Greely; m. Dana Richard Nowell, Sept. 1, 1956 (div. 1971); children: Dana A., Mark R., Dean E. BA in English, U. Maine, 1986. Dir. Gardiner Pub. Libr., 1974—; bd. dirs. Gardiner Bd. Trade; mem. Maine Libr. Commn., 1980-88, Gov.'s Commn. Employment of Handicapped, 1978-81; mem. adv. bd. Gardiner Savs. Bank, 1986—; trustee J. Walter Robinson Welfare Trust, 1986—. Creator, editor Who Reads What publ., 1988—. Mem. Gardiner Econ. Devel. Com., 1989—; interim city mgr. City of Gardiner, 1991. Recipient Hugh Hefner 1st Amendment award Playboy Found., 1987, Outstanding Libr. award Maine Libr. Assn., 1993, Cmty. Svc. award Kennebec Valley C. of C., 1993. Mem. Rotary (pres. Gardiner chpt. 1993-94). Office: Gardiner Pub Libr 152 Water St Gardiner ME 04345-2195

NOWIK, DOROTHY ADAM, medical equipment company executive; b. Chgo., July 25, 1944; d. Adam Harry and Helen (Kichkaylo) Wanaski; m. Eugene Nicholas Nowik, Aug. 9, 1978; children: George Eugene, Helen Eugene. A.A., Columbia Coll., 1980. Cert. lactation counselor, lactation edn. Sec., adminstrv. asst. to pres. Zenco Engring Corp., Chgo., 1970-71; sales rep. Medizenco USA Ltd., Chgo., 1971-73; ptnr. Pacific Med. Systems, Inc., Bellevue, Wash., 1973-76, pres., 1976—. Mem. NAFE, Pacific Mothers Support, Inc. (pres. 1991). Mem. Orthodox Ch. Am. Home: 303 126th Ave NE Bellevue WA 98005-6182 Office: 1407 132nd Ave NE # 10 Bellevue WA 98005-2259

NOXON, MARGARET WALTERS, community volunteer; b. Detroit, Dec. 16, 1903; d. George Alexander and Ethelwyn (Taylor) Walters; grad., Liggett Sch. for Girls, Det., 1922; life teaching certificate Wayne State U., 1925; student Columbia Tchrs. Coll., 1939-40; m. Herbert Richards Noxon, July 15, 1926 (dec. Aug. 4, 1971). Bd. dirs. Coll. Club, Detroit, 1925-30; mem. Salvation Army Aux., Detroit, 1926—; mem. Coll. Club, Summit N.J., 1941—; historian D.A.R., N.Y.C., 1943-46, vice regent, 1946-49; dir. New Eng., Women, 1961-64; dir. Woodycrest-Five Points Child Care, 1961-77; bd. dirs. ARC, Summit, N.J., service com. chmn. uniforms and insignias, 1943-45; v.p. N.Y. Infirmary Aux., N.Y.C., 1948-58, bd. dirs., 1959-80. Recipient award for meritorious personal service ARC, 1945. Mem. Nat. Inst. Social Scis., Grand Jury Assn. N.Y. County, D.A.R. (dir. 1950-70), St. David's Soc. State N.Y., English-Speaking Union, Daus. Am. Colonists, AAUW, Southampton Colonial Soc., Nat. Woman's Farm and Garden Assn. (dir. met. br. 1975—, dir. N.Y. State div. 1978-80, mem. nat. council 1978-80), Ch. Women's League for Patriotic Service, Women's Bible Soc. N.Y., Alpha Sigma Tau. Republican. Presbyterian. Clubs: Southampton (N.Y.) Bath and Tennis, City Gardens (dir. 1963-68, mem. adv. com. 1968-74, dir. 1974-80, adv. bd. 1980-83), York (bd. govs. 1965-66, 73-77), Barnard (trustee 1979-81), Sorosis (v.p. 1979-81), Regency (N.Y.C.). Home: c/o Virginia W Rider 634 Silvermine Rd New Canaan CT 06840-4324

NOYES, JUDITH GIBSON, library director; b. N.Y.C., Apr. 19, 1941; d. Charles II and Alice (Klauss) Gibson; m. Paul V. Noyes, June 1, 1991; children from previous marriage: Andrea Elizabeth Green, Michael Charles Green. BA, Carleton Coll., 1962; MLS, U. Western Ont., London, Can., 1972. Librarian edn. U. New Brunswick, 1972-86; libr. Can. Inst. Sci. and Tech. Info., Ottawa, Ont., Can., 1975-86; univ. librarian Colgate U., Hamilton, N.Y., 1986—; mem. OCLC Adv. Com. on Coll. and Univ. Librs., 1991—; pres. bd. trustees Ctrl. N.Y. Libr. Resources Coun., 1992—. Mem. ALA, Am. Coll. and Rsch. Librs. (nominating com. 1988-89, 92-93, legis. com. coll. libr. sect. liaison 1989-91, chair task force on intellectual freedom, 1992-94), Internat. Standards Orgn. (tech. com. 46, 1981-89). Office: Colgate U Everett Needham Case Libr 13 Oak Dr Hamilton NY 13346-1379

NOZIGLIA, CARLA MILLER, forensic scientist; b. Erie, Pa., Oct. 11, 1941; d. Earnest Carl and Eileen (Murphy) Miller; m. Keith William Noziglia, Nov. 21, 1969; children: Pama Noziglia Cook, Kathryn Noziglia Volpi. BS, Villa Maria Coll., 1963; MS, Lindenwood Coll., 1984. Cert. med. technologist, Am. Soc. Clin. Pathologists. Med. technologist Monmouth (N.J.) Gen. Hosp., 1963-64; spl. chem. med. technologist Hamot Hosp. Med. Ctr., Erie, Pa., 1965-69; pathologist's assoc. Galion (Ohio) Comm. Hosp., 1969-75; dir. crime lab. Mansfield (Ohio) Police Dept., Richland County Crime Lab., 1978-81; crime lab. supr. St. Louis County Police, Clayton, Mo., 1981-84; dir. crime lab. Las Vegas (Nev.) Met. Police, 1984-88, dir. lab. svcs., 1988-93, dir., cons. forensic scis., 1993—. Tech. abstracts editor Jour. Police Sci. and Adminstrn., 1983-91; editorial bd. Jour. Forensic Identification, 1988—; contbr. to (book) Journal of Police Science, 1989, Encyclopedia of Police Science, 1989. Mem. Gov.'s Com. on Testing for Intoxication, Las Vegas, 1984-93; mem. adv. bd. Nev. Bd. Pharmacy, 1988-93; recruiter United Blood Svcs., Las Vegas, 1986-93; bd. dirs., pres. Cmty. Action Against Rape, Las Vegas, 1987-94; co-founder So. Nev. Sexual Assault Protocol, 1986. Recipient award Ohio Ho. of Reps., 1981, Alumni of Yr. award Villa Maria Coll., 1981; named Outstanding Cath. Erie Diocese N.W. Pa., 1988, Woman of Achievement Las Vegas C. of C., 1989. Fellow Am. Acad. Forensic Sci. (bd. dirs. 1988-91, sec. Criminalistics sect. 1986, sect. chmn. 1987, Sect. award 1995); mem. Am. Soc. Crime Lab Dirs. (emeritus, bd. dirs. 1980-87, treas. 1981-82, 88-91, pres. 1986-87), Internat. Police Assn., Internat. Assn. for Identification (emeritus), S.W. Assn. Forensic Scientists, Am. Bus. Women's Assn. (Woman of Yr. 1988, one of top Bus. Women 1993). Republican. Roman Catholic. Office: Forensic Scis 1025 Pagosa Way Las Vegas NV 89128-3348

NUCE, MADONNA MARIE, military officer; b. Denver, Jan. 15, 1952; d. Donald William and Marie Dorothy (Ruscio) N.; m. Edward Ray Geron, Oct. 9, 1982; 1 child, Maria Louise. BA, U. No. Colo., 1974; grad., Command and Gen. Staff Coll., Ft. Leavenworth, 1993. Enlisted U.S. ANG, 1973; commd. 2d lt. U.S. Army, 1981, advanced through grades to lt. col., 1993; adminstrv. supply tech. Colo. Army Nat. Guard, Denver, 1974-79; supply technician Colo. Army Nat. Guard, Golden, Colo., 1979-81; tng. officer Colo. Army Nat. Guard, Aurora, Colo., 1981-84, adminstrv. officer, 1984-85; maintenance officer Colo. Army Nat. Guard, Golden, Colo., 1985-86, asst. supply officer, 1986-91, data processing chief, 1991-92, supply mgmt. officer, 1992-93, comptroller, 1993-94, maintenance officer, 1994—; Mem. Colo. Nat. Guard Assn. (sec. 1981-83, bd. dirs. 1983-85), Assn. of the U.S. Army (treas. 1986-88), Colo. Artists Assn. Group leader 5th grade Archdiocese of Denver Jr. Great Books Program, St. Anne Sch., 1987-89, group leader 7th grade Holy Family, 1991-92; bd. dirs. 9 Health Fair, Denver, 1985-90. Decorated Meritorious Svc. medal, Army Commendation medal, Army Achievement medal. Mem. NAFE, AAUW, Colo. Nat Guard Assn. (sec. 1981-83, bd. dirs. 1983-85), Assn. of U.S. Army (treas. 1986-88). Roman Catholic. Office: Colo Army Nat Guard 6848 S Revere Pky Englewood CO 80012

NUCKLOS, SHIRLEY, medical administrator, consultant; b. Canton, Ohio, Aug. 30, 1949; d. Boyd Alexander and Julia Lillian (Hood) Curtis; m. Nucklos, Mar. 11, 1972; children: Túere, Tené, Tiombé, Nigina, Khari Oji-Lee. BS in Edn., Cen. State U., Wilberforce, Ohio, 1970; MA, Ohio State U., 1971. Cert. elem. tchr., guidance counselor. Guidance counselor Scioto Village High Sch., Powell, Ohio, 1973-78; acad. advisor Franklin U., Columbus, Ohio, 1980-82, acting asst. dir. records, 1982-83, asst. registrar, 1983-90; registrar Ohio Dominican Coll., Columbus, 1990-93; dir. human resources Mid-Am. Phys. Medicine & Exec. Med., Inc., Westerville, Ohio, 1994—; adminstrv. advisor to Black Student Union, Franklin U., 1982-85; human resource cons. Mid-Am. Phys. Medicine, Exec. Med., Inc., Westerville, Ohio, 1989-93, dir. human resources/bus. mgr., 1993—. Vol. tchr. Umoja Sasa Shule, Columbus, 1971-74; booster Mid-west Gymnastic and Cheerleading, Dublin, Ohio, 1988-93; active various com. for minority concerns. Mem. Ohio Assn. Collegiate Registrars and Admissions Officers (sec. 1991-93, Cert. Appreciation 1985, 93), Am. Assn. Collegiate Registrars and Admissions Officers, Nat. Assn. Coll. Deans, Registrars and Admissions Officers, Ohio Assn. Women Deans, Adminstrs. and Counselors, Nat. Assn. Women Deans, Adminstrs. and Counselors, Am. Assn. Univ. Adminstrn., Va. Admissions Counselors for Black Concerns, Ohio Health Info. Mgmt. Assn. (pres. 1994—). Democrat. Mem. Church of God in Christ. Office: Mid Am Phys Medicine & Exec Med Inc 575 Copeland Mill Rd Ste 2F Westerville OH 43081 also: 254 Woodland Ave Ste 105 Columbus OH 43203

NUELL, CHRISTIE LONG, graphic arts educator; b. Oxford, Eng., Feb. 1, 1951; came to U.S., 1971; d. Reginald and Elizabeth (Hutchison) Kissack; m. Franklin Hunt Long, Aug. 7, 1971 (div. 1980); m. Leon Richard Nuell, Apr. 7, 1983; children: Isaac Gregory Elon, Aaron Benjamin. Student, U. Sussex, Falmer, Eng., 1969-71; BA, SUNY, Geneseo, 1971-77; MFA, U. Ga., 1980. Instr. Bethany Coll., Lindsborg, Kans., 1980-81; assoc. prof. Mid. Tenn. State U., Murfreesboro, 1981—. Recipient Purchase award Mid-Am. Biennial Exhbn., Owensboro (Ky.) Mus. Fine Arts, 1982, Juror's Purchase award Internat. Prints Pratt Graphics Ctr., 1986, Turebengtz Meml. Purchase award 41st N.Am. Print Exhbn., The Boston Printmakers, 1989, Purchase award 31st Ann. Tenn. All State Exhbn., Parthenon Galleries, Nashville, 1991. Mem. Soc. Am. Graphic Artists, So. Graphics Assn. Office: Mid Tenn State U PO Box 181 Murfreesboro TN 37133-0181

NUESSLE, SALLY JANE, pharmacoeconomist, pharmacist; b. Balt., July 19, 1959; d. Charles August and Betty Lee (Hull) N. BS in Zoology, U. Md., 1981, PharmD, 1985. Registered pharmacist, Calif.; cert. pharmacotherapy specialist. Poison info. specialist Md. Poison Info. Ctr., Balt., 1983-85; geriatric clin. pharmacist UCLA Med. Ctr., 1986-88; staff pharmacist U. Calif. Med. Ctr., San Francisco, 1988-92; supr. drug info. group Syntex Labs., Inc., Palo Alto, Calif., 1989-92; pharmacoeconomist, drug utilization evaluation pharmacist King Faisal Specialist Hosp. and Rsch. Ctr., Riyadh, Saudi Arabia, 1992—; clin. clerkship preceptor U. Calif., San Francisco, 1985-86; pharmacy resident program preceptor UCLA, 1986-88. Contbr. articles to profl. jours. Spkr. Com. on Drug Abuse Edn., Balt., 1982-83, Elder Edn. Program, Balt., 1982-85; mem. spkrs. bur. Arthritis Found., San Francisco, 1986. Mem. Am. Coll. Clin. Pharmacists, Am. Soc. Hosp. Pharmacists, Drug Info. Assn. Democrat. Home: 3138 Brookmede Rd Ellicott City MD 21042

NUGENT, JANE KAY, utility executive; b. Detroit, Aug. 31, 1925; d. Albert A. and Celia (Betzing) Kay; m. Robert L. Nugent, Apr.3, 1991. BS, U. Detroit, 1948; MA, Wayne State U., 1952; MBA, U. Mich., 1963. Sr. personnel interviewer employment Detroit Edison Co., 1948-60, personnel coord. for women, 1960-65, office employment adminstr., 1965-70, gen. employment adminstr., 1970-71, dir. personnel svcs., 1971-72, mgr. employee rels., 1972-77, asst. v.p. employee rels., 1977-78, v.p. employee rels., 1978-82, v.p. adminstrn., 1982-90, ret., 1990; bd. dirs. First Am. Bank-SE Mich., 1986-90, Bon Secours of Mich. Healthcare System, Inc., 1984-93, Detroit Exec. Svc. Corp.; tchr. U. Detroit Evening Coll. Bus. and Adminstrn., 1963-75; seminar leader div. mgmt. edn. U. Mich., 1968-74, Waterloo Mgmt. Edn. Centre, 1972-77. Mem. Mich. Employment Security Adv. Coun., 1967-81; chmn. bd. dirs. Detroit Inst. Commerce, 1976-79; exec. bd. NCCJ, 1980-91, nat. trustee, 1984-88; bd. dirs. Childrens Home Detroit, 1991—, also 1st v.p. Recipient Alumni Tower award U. Detroit, 1967, Headliner award Women Wayne State U., 1970, Wayne State U. Alumni Achievement award, 1974, Career Achievement award Profl. Panhellenic Assn., 1973, Bus. Achievement award Assn. Bus. Deans, 1989; named one of Top Ten Working Women of Detroit, 1970, Alumnus of Yr., U. Detroit, 1981, Woman of Yr. Am. Lung Assn., 1991, Sr. Profl. in Human Resources Soc. Human Resource Mgmt.; cert. Adminstrv. Mgr. Am. Mgmt. Soc.; inducted in Mich. Women's Hall of Fame, 1988. Mem. Internat. Assn. Personnel Women (pres. 1969-70), Women's Econ. Club (v.p. 1971-72, pres. 1972-73), Am. Soc. Employees (bd. dirs. 1979-90), Personnel Women Detroit (pres. 1960-61), U. Detroit Alumni Assn. (pres. 1964-66), Phi Gamma Nu (nat. v.p. 1955-57), Boys and Girls Club S.E. Mich. (pres. 1987-89), Econ. Club Detroit (v.p. 1981-90), Internat. Womens Forum.

NUMANN, PATRICIA JOY, surgeon, educator; b. Bronx, N.Y., Apr. 6, 1941. BA, U. Rochester, 1962; MD, SUNY Health Sci. Ctr., Syracuse, 1965. Intern, resident SUNY Health Sci. Ctr., Syracuse, 1970, from asst. prof. to assoc. prof. surgery, 1970-89, assoc. dean Coll. Medicine, 1978-84, assoc. dean Coll. Medicine Clin. Affairs, prof. surgery, 1989—; dir. breast care program SUNY Health Sci. Ctr., Syracuse, 1986—; presenter in field. Contbr. chpts. to books, articles to profl. jours. Found. bd. dirs. Vera House, Syracuse, 1993-94; hon. bd. dirs. F.A.C.T., Syracuse, 1994. Named one of Women of Distinction, N.Y. State Gov. Mario Cuomo, 1994; recipient Disting. Surgeon award Assn. Women Surgeons, 1991. Mem. AMA (coun. sci. affairs), ACS (com. on cancer grad. med. edn. com.), Am. Bd. Surgeons (bd. dirs. 1994—), Am. Assn. Endocrine Surgeons (v.p. 1992, pres. 1985), Assn. for Surg. Edn., Corinthian Club. Office: SUNY Health Sci Ctr 750 E Adams St Syracuse NY 13210

NUNLEY, MALINDA VAUGHN ANN, retired elementary school educator; d. William D. and Callie (Ross) Vaughn; m. Harry H. Nunley, Dec. 24, 1940 (dec.); chidlren: Jerry Michael, Sally Coleen. BS in Edn., Mid. Tenn. State U., 1961; MEd in Psychology, Middle Tenn. State U., 1972; postgrad., U. Tenn., Chattanooga, 1974-80, Mid. Tenn. State U. Cert. art tchr., spl. edn. tchr., guidance counselor and cons., individual testing and diagnostics in spl. edn. Tenn. Tchr. Panama Canal Co, Balboa, Panama Canal Zone, 1954-56; adult tchr. U.S. Army, Ft. Davis, Panama Canal Zone, 1956-60; elem. tchr. Ancon Elem. Panama Canal Zone Sch., Tenn., 1961-64; tchr. South Pitts. High Sch., 1964-66, Normal Park Elem. Sch., Chattanooga, Tenn., 1966-71; spl. edn. tchr. Griffith Creek Elem. Sch., Tenn., 1971-83; ret. Tenn.; tutor and substitute tchr., Tenn.; homebound tchr. for alcohol and drug abuse adolescents, 1989-90; spl. speaker to class groups 4th-7th, 1993-94. Mem. NEA, Tenn. Edn. Assn., Marion County Tchrs. Assn., Tenn. Ret. Tchrs. Assn., Chattanooga Edn. Assn. (past faculty rep.). Home: 6555 Hwy 27 Chattanooga TN 37405-9601

NUNN, MURIEL THEONE, guidance counselor; b. Austin, Minn., Sept. 8, 1935; d. Frank Warren and Gladys Christine Pechacek; m. Gerald Keith Robinson, June 4, 1953 (div. Apr. 1983); children: David, Dick, Nancy, Sue Ann, Tahirih; m. William Hiestand Nunn, May 26, 1987. BA, U. No. Iowa, 1964, MA, 1967. Cert. elem. tchr., Iowa; cert. elem. and secondary guidance counselor, Minn. Tchr. kindergarten Cedar Falls (Iowa) Pub. Schs., 1963-66; elem. guidance counselor Prairie Community Schs., Cedar Rapids, 1967-69; tchr. spl. edn. Delano (Minn.) Pub. Schs., 1969-72; tchr. spl. edn. Westonka Pub. Schs., Mound, Minn., 1973-75, guidance counselor mid. level, 1975—. Contbr. articles to profl. jours. Mem. ACA, Minn. Assn. Mid. Level Educators (sec. 1986, v.p. 1987, pres. 1988, treas. 1993, newsletter columnist 1983-93), Minn. Sch. Counselors Assn. (v.p. 1990-92), Minn. Assn. Counseling and Devel. (Minn. Mid. Level Educator of Yr. award 1991). Democrat. Lutheran. Home: 5036 S Lakeshore Dr Maple Plain MN 55359-9676 Office: Mound Westonka High Sch 5905 Sunnyfield Rd E Mound MN 55364-8250

NUNNELLY, LILLIAN BLACK, adult education administrator; b. Hagerstown, Md.; m. Donald A. Nunnelly, July 5, 1952; children: Martha Sue Royster, David, Mark. AB, Lynchburg Coll., 1951; M in Religious Edn., Lexington Theol. Sem., 1954. Ordained min. Disciples of Christ. Substitute tchr., 1955-76; dir. adult basic edn. Henderson C.C., 1976-80; interim assoc. min. Disciples of Christ, Frankfort, Ky., 1981, 83; dir. Ky. Coalition for Literacy, 1982-83, Thorn Hill Learning Ctr./Literacy, Frankfort, 1986—; bd. dirs. Lexington Theol. Sem. Mem. Ky. Assn. for Continuing Edn. Office: Thorn Hill Edn Ctr 700 Leslie Ave Frankfort KY 40601-1238

NURSE, MARY ANNE, project manager; b. Birmingham, Ala., Aug. 26, 1961; d. Robert Leroy and Dorothy Maxine (Barnes) N. BS in Mktg., N.W. Mo. State U., 1983, MBA, 1984; postgrad., Keller Grad. Sch. Mgmt., Mesa, Ariz. Cert. flex-trainer Franklin Quest, Salt Lake City, 1992—; cert. Myers Briggs type indicator trainer Nat. Computer Sys., Mesa, 1993—. Budget analyst Majers Mktg. Rsch. Co., Omaha, 1985; edn. specialist J & K Computer Sys., Mesa, 1985-87, br. edn. supr., 1988; tng. supr. Nat. Computer Sys., Mesa, 1988-90, project mgr., 1990-92, sr. project mgr., 1992—. Author: (planning guide) Project Planning Guide, 1992. Republican. Home: 619 W Palo Verde St Gilbert AZ 85233-5836 Office: Nat Computer Systems Inc 1201 S Alma School Rd Ste 9500 Mesa AZ 85210-2081

NUSBACHER, GLORIA W., lawyer; b. N.Y.C., July 22, 1951; d. Murray and Doris (Togman) Weinberg; m. Burton Nusbacher, Aug. 4, 1974; 1 child, Shoshana. BA, Barnard Coll., 1972; JD, Columbia U., 1975. Bar: N.Y. 1976. Assoc. Hughes Hubbard & Reed, N.Y.C., 1975-83, counsel, 1983-91, ptnr., 1991—; atty. specializing in exec. compensation and employee benefits; lectr. in field. Contbr. articles to profl. jours. Troop leader Girl Scouts Am. Mem. ABA (employee benefits and exec. compensation com. 1987—, fed. regulation securities com., subcom. employee benefits and exec. compensation 1983—, task force exec. compensation, chmn. subcom. fed. and state securities laws of com. employee benefits and exec. compensation 1994—), Phi Beta Kappa. Office: Hughes Hubbard & Reed 1 Battery Park Plz New York NY 10004

NUSBAUM, ALEXIS ROSENOER, clinical psychologist, substance abuse services professional; b. London, Nov. 8, 1959; came to U.S., 1967; d. Victor Michael and Leonie Maureen (Lister) Rosenoer; m. Mark Nathaniel Nusbaum, Dec. 3, 1989; 1 child, Olivia Lior. BA in Women's Studies, Goucher Coll., 1981, BA in Psychology, 1981; MPhil in Clin. Psychology, George Washington U., 1986, PhD in Clin. Psychology, 1988. Psychology assoc. The Walter P. Carter Ctr., Balt., 1988-90, staff psychologist, 1990-91; coord. inpatient substance abuse treatment program Ft. Howard (Md.) VA Med. Ctr., 1991-93, coord. outpatient substance abuse treatment program, 1993—; assoc. dir. predoctoral psychology internship tng. program Balt. VA Med. Ctr. Consortium, Ft. Howard, 1994—; cons. C.E.G.O.- Group Rels. Tng. Program, Washington, 1986-92; chairperson rsch. com. Ft. Howard VA Med. Ctr., 1993—. Instr. CPR tng. Am. Heart Assn., Md., 1994—. Dean Van Meter fellow Goucher Coll., 1982, George Washington U. fellow, 1983. Mem. Am. Psychol. Assn. (divsn. addictions), Nat. Register Health Svc. Providers in Psychology, Md. Psychol. Assn., Phi Beta Kappa. Home: 14533 Almanac Dr Burtonsville MD 20866 Office: 525 Main St Ste 205 Laurel MD 20707

NUSBAUM, MARLENE ACKERMAN, marketing professional; b. Portsmouth, Va., June 13, 1949; d. Martin and Betsy Freda (Katz) Ackerman; m. Robert Collier Nusbaum Jr., June 27, 1971; 1 child, Jessica Lynn. Deuxième Degré, Université d"Orléans Tours, 1970; BA magna cum laude, Rutgers U., 1971; MA, Brown U., 1973, PhD with distinction, 1980. Tchr. French Dana Hall Sch., Wellesley, Mass., 1974-75; master French and German Groton (Mass.) Sch., 1975-80; French instr. dept. humanities MIT, Cambridge, 1981; assoc., product mgr. Digital Equipment Corp., Maynard, Mass., 1981-83; mktg. mgr. interactive video Digital Equipment Corp., Bedford, Mass., 1983-85; pvt. practice mktg. cons. Newton, Mass., 1985-91; bus. devel. dir. BIS Strategic Decisions, Norwell, Mass., 1991—; mem. mktg. adv. com. Global-Sports Ltd., Boston, 1989-90; cons. editor Heinle & Heinle Pub., Boston, 1981. Author: (with Verdier) Parlez Sans Peur!, 1983, (with Holden-Avard and Verdier) Le Français Sans Peur, 1991, (with Beyer) Beth Israel Hosp. Children's Doctor's Kit for Good Health, 1990. Organizer class size PTA Com., Newton, 1986-88, chairperson roundtable exec. com., 1987-88. Chairperson roundtable, exec. com. Newton PTA Coun., 1987-88. Mem. N.E. Conf. Tchrs. of Fgn. Langs., Am. Coun. Tchrs. Fng. Langs., Mass. Fgn. Lang. Assn. Office: BIS Strategic Decisions 1 Longwater Cir Norwell MA 02061

NUSIM, ROBERTA, publisher; b. N.Y.C., Dec. 1, 1943; d. Seymour and Rae (Weiner) N.; m. Stephen Jablonsky, 1965. BA in English, CCNY, 1964; MA, CUNY, 1966. Tchr. N.Y.C. Bd. Edn., 1964-73; v.p. program devel. Mind, Inc., Westport, Conn., 1973-76; pres. Mind Media, 1976-78; founder, pres. Lifetime Learning Systems, Fairfield, Conn., 1978-90; founder dir. The Film Study Guild, 1979-90; founder, pres. The Work & Family Pub. Group, Inc., 1991—; pres. Youth Mktg. Internat. Ltd. Editor: Let's Talk About Health, 1980. Mem. ASCD, NAFE, TESOL, Internat. Assn. Tchrs. of English Fgn. Lang., Am. Film Inst., Women in Communications, Ednl. Press Assn. Am., Ptnrs. for Global Edn. (founder). Avocations: reading, painting. Office: Youth Mktg Internat Ltd PO Box 305 Easton CT 06612-0305

NUSS, BARBARA GOUGH, artist; b. Washington, Apr. 11, 1939; d. Gaines Homer Gough and Edwerta Barbara (Beyer) Barber; m. Frederick A. Johnson, Sept. 30, 1968 (div. 1975); 1 child, Mark Eugene; m. Fred Dean Nuss, Dec. 18, 1982. BFA, Syracuse U., 1960; postgrad., Schuler Sch. Fine Arts, Balt., 1986-87. Art dir. Chappell's Dept. Store, Syracuse, N.Y., 1960-62, 66; mgr., illustrator Holman Anderson & Moore, Washington, 1967-70; art dir., advt. mgr. Ad-Media & Howard Advt. Assocs., Columbia, Md., 1970-75; acct. exec. Graphic Arts Inc., Alexandria, Va., 1975-77; sales mgr. The Jour. Newspapers, Washington, 1977-82; tchr., adult edn. Montgomery Coll., Rockville, Md., 1984-85; pvt. tchr. fine arts, Woodbine, Md., 1982—; chmn. Montgomery County Juried Art Exhibit, Rockville, 1988; pres. Nuss Fine Arts, Inc., 1992—. One person shows include Pa. State U., 1986, NIH, Bethesda, Md., 1989, 90, Md. Nat. Capital Park and Planning Commn., 1991, Art League Gallery, Alexandria, Va., 1992; exhibited in group shows at Art League at the Torpedo Factory, 1987-92, Heritage Gallery Classical Realism, 1989-90, Art Barn Gallery, Washington, 1990 Carmen's Gallery, 1991—, Art Showcase 100 Md. Artists, 1991-92, Assn. pour la Promotion du Patrimoine Artistique Francais, Galerie Jean Lammelin, Argenteuil, France, 1991, Salmagundi Club 14th Ann. Exhibition, 1991, Atrium Gallery Georgetown U., Washington, 1991; represented in permanent collections inlcuding Nat. Park Found., NIH, Am. Coun. Edn., Bell Atlantic, Electronic Industries Assn., Amb. Saudi Arabia, Amb. Portugal. Recipient 1st prize for watercolor C&O Canal Show, 1987, 1st prize for oil painting Rockville Art League, 1987, Montgomery County Art Assn., 1983, 89, Gaithersburg Fine Arts Assn., 1988, grand champion award for oil painting Howard County Fair, 1989, One of Top 100 award for oil painting Nat. Arts for Parks, 1989, 91, 92 (two images selected), image selected for notecard Nat. Parks and Conservation Assn.; image selected for Owen Co. in phone book U.S. Dept. State, 1994-95. Mem. Nat. League Am. Pen Women (sec. Bethesda, Md. 1989), Balt. Watercolor Soc., Art League Torpedo Factory. Home: 3132 Cabin Run Woodbine MD 21797-7933

NUSSBAUM, KAREN, federal agency administrator; b. Chgo., Apr. 25, 1950. BA, Goddard Coll., 1973. Exec. dir. 9 to 5 Nat. Assn. of Working Women, 1993; pres. dist. 925 Svc. Employees Internat. Union, 1993. Co-author: Solutions for the New Work Force: Policies for a New Social Contract, 9 to 5: The Working Woman's Guide to Office Survival. Named to Ohio Women's Hall of Fame, 1984. Office: Dept of Labor Women's Bur 200 Constitution Ave NW Washington DC 20210*

NUSSBAUM, MARTHA CRAVEN, philosophy and classics educator; b. N.Y.C., May 6, 1947; d. George and Betty (Warren) Craven; m. Alan Jeffrey Nussbaum, Aug., 1969 (div. 1987); 1 child, Rachel Emily. BA, NYU, 1969; MA, Harvard U., 1971, PhD, 1975; LHD (hon.), Kalamazoo Coll., 1988, Grinnell Coll., 1993. Asst. prof. philosophy and classics Harvard U., Cambridge, 1975-80, assoc. prof., 1980-83; vis. prof. philosophy, Greek and Latin Wellesley (Mass.) Coll., 1983-84; assoc. prof. philosophy and classics Brown U., Providence, R.I., 1984-85, prof. philosophy, classics and comparative lit., 1985-87, David Benedict prof. philosophy, classics and comparative lit., 1987-89, univ. prof., 1989—; rsch. advisor World Inst. Devel. Econs. Rsch., Helsinki, Finland, 1986-92; vis. prof. law U. Chgo., 1994. Author: Aristotle's De Motu Animalium, 1978, The Fragility of Goodness, 1986, Love's Knowledge, 1990, The Therapy of Desire, 1994; editor: Language and Logos, 1983; (with A. Rorty) Essays on Artistotle's De Anima, 1992, (with A. Sen) The Quality of Life, 1993, (with J. Brunschwig) Passions and Perceptions, 1993. Soc. Fellows Harvard U. jr. fellow, 1972-75, Humanities fellow Princeton U., 1977-78, Guggenheim Found. fellow, 1983, NIH fellow, vis. fellow All Souls Coll., Oxford, Eng., 1986-87; recipient Brandeis Creative Arts award, 1990, Spielvogel-Diamondstein award, 1991; Gifford lectr. U. Edinburgh, 1993. Fellow Am. Acad. Arts and Scis. (membership com. 1991-93, coun. 1992—); mem. Am. Philos. Assn. (exec. com. Ea. divsn. 1985-87, chair com. internat. coop., ex-officio mem. nat. bd. 1989-92, chair com. on status of women 1994—), Am. Philol. Assn., PEN. Office: Brown U Depts Philosophy & Classics PO Box 1918 Providence RI 02912-9000

NUSZ, PHYLLIS JANE, fund raising consultant, meeting planner; b. Lodi, Calif., Dec. 16, 1941; d. Fred Henry and Esther Emma (Enzminger) N. BA, U. Pacific, 1963, MA, 1965; EdD, Nova Southwestern U., 1987. Cert. fund raising exec. Prof. speech comm. Bakersfield (Calif.) Coll., 1965-86; from asst. dir. student activites to found. exec. dir. Bakersfield (Calif) Coll., 1988—; mgmt. seminar dir. Delta Kappa Gamma Soc. Internat., Austin, Tex., 1983-86; loaned exec. United Way San Joaquin County, Stockton, Calif., 1990; fund raising cons. PJ Enterprises, Lodi, Calif., 1987—. Bd. dirs. U. Calif. Sch. Medicine Surg. Found., San Francisco, 1989—; mem. Heritage Circle and Chancellor's Assn., U. Calif. San Francisco, 1987—. Recipient archives award of merit Evang. Luth. Ch. in Am., 1988; fellow Calif. Luth. U., 1985—. Mem. Nat. Soc. Fund Raising Execs. (chmn. mentor program Calif. Capital chpt. 1991, bd. dirs. 1988-91, chmn. acad. fund raising 1991, chmn. mentor program Golden Gate chpt. 1991, founding, pres. San Joaquin chpt. 1992-93, Pres.'s award for Meritorious Svc., Golden Gate chpt. 1991), U. Pacific Alumni Assn. (bd. dirs. 1974-82), Calif. Tchrs. Assn., Nat. Assn. Parliamentarians, Rotary (North Stockton bd. dirs. 1993—), Delta Kappa Gamma (internat. scholar 1986). Republican. Lutheran. Office: PJ Enterprises 1300 W Lodi Ave Ste A11 Lodi CA 95242-3000

NUTTER, ZOE DELL LANTIS, public relations executive, retired; b. Yamhill, Oreg., June 14, 1915; d. Arthur Lee Lantis and Olive Adelaide (Reed) Lantis-Hilton; m. Richard S. West, Apr. 30, 1941 (div. Nov. 1964); m. Ervin John Nutter, Dec. 30, 1965. Assoc. in Bus., Santa Ana Jr. Coll., 1944. Cert. gen. secondary sch. tchr., Calif. Promoter World's Fair & Comml. Airlines Golden Gate Internat. Expn., San Francisco, 1937-39; pirate theme girl, official hostess Treasure Island's World Fair, San Francisco, 1939-40; prin. dancer San Francisco Ballet, 1937-41; artist, 1941-45; program dir. Glenn County High Sch., Willows, Calif., 1952-58; pub. rels. Monarch Piper Aviation Co., Monterey, Calif., 1963-65; pilot, pub. rels. Elano Corp., Xenia, Ohio, 1968-85; bd. dirs. Nat. Aviation Hall of Fame, Dayton, Ohio, pres., chmn., 1989-92, bd. trustees, 1976—, chmn. bd. nominations, 1992—; bd. trustees Ford's Theatre, Washington, Treasure Island Museum, San Francisco; charter mem. Friends of First Ladies, Smithsonian, Washington, 1990-93. Assoc. editor KYH mag. of Shikar Safari Internat., 1985-87; contbg. columnist Scripps Howard San Francisco News, 1938. Bd. dirs. Cin. May Festival, 1976-80; cen. com. Glenn County Rep. Party, Willows, 1960-64; state cen. com. Rep. Party, 1962-64; adv. bd. Women's Air & Space Museum, Dayton, 1987-94. Warrant officer, Civil Air Patrol, 1967-69. Recipient Civic Contbn. Honor award Big Brothers/Big Sisters, 1991, John Collier Nat. award Camp Fire Girls & Boys, 1988, Tambourine award Salvation Army, 1982, State of Ohio Gov.'s award for Volunteerism, 1992; named Most Photographed Girl in World, News Burs. & Clipping Svcs., 1938-39. Fellow Pres.'s Club U. Ky., Ohio State U., Wright State U.; mem. 99's Internat. Women Pilots Orgn. (life, hospitality chmn. 1968), Monterey Bay Chapter 99's (mem. chmn. 1964-65), Walnut Grove Country Club, Lost Tree Country Club, Windstar County Club (Naples, Fla.), Rotary (Paul Harris fellow 1987), Old Port Yacht Club, Shikar Safari Internat. (host com. 1976). Home: 986 Trebein Rd Xenia OH 45385-9534

NUZUM, JANET, federal commissioner. BA, Smith Coll., 1978; JD, Georgetown U., 1983. Bar: D.C., 1983. Legal asst. Arnold Porter, 1978-80, law clerk, 1981-82; prof. staff mem. House Com. on Ways & Means, 1983-91; commr. Internat. Trade Commn., 1991—. Editor: Law and Policy in International Business. Mem. Women in Internat. Trade (mem. bd. dirs. 1990—). Office: Internat Trade Com 500 E St NW Ste 702 Washington DC 20436*

NWA, WILLIA L., special education educator; b. Cleve., July 20; d. Thurman and Josephine (Deadwyler); m. Umoh U. Nwa, Sept. 4, 1971; children: Idara Umoh, Jakitoro Deadwyler, Ayama Nseabasi, Ifiok Odudu, Uko Obong. BS, Ohio State U., 1971; MS, U. Akron, 1975, PhD, 1992. Cert. elem. and secondary edn. tchr., spl. edn. tchr., spl. edn. supr., Ohio. Pianist/organist 7th Ave Community Bapt. Ch., Columbus, Ohio, 1970-71; educator N.E. Local Schs., Springfield, Ohio, 1971-74; supr. U. Akron, Ohio, 1989; educator Canton (Ohio) City Schs., 1975—; presenter, instructor 13th and 14th ann. internat. confs. critical thinking and ednl. reform Sonoma State U., Rohnert Park, Calif., 1993-94, 7th Internat. Conf. Career Devel. and Transition, Albuquerque, 1993, 41st Ann. Conf. Connecting Edn./Collaboration, Toledo, 1993, 8th Internat. Conf. Collaboration/Cooperation in Edn., Lewis & Clark Coll., Portland, Oreg., 1994, 4th Internat. Conf.: Mental Retardation and Devel. Disabilities, Arlington Heights, Ill., 1994. Co-author: (grant) Reading for Survival, 1988; author: The Extent of Participation in Extracurricular Activities with Exceptional Children, 1992. Mem. Bapt. Student Union, Ohio State U., Columbus, 1969-71, mem. choir, 1969-71. Recipient Charles S. Seelback scholarship Forest City Foundaries, Cleve., 1966, Alice A. White scholarship Ohio State U., 1970, Univ. scholarship, U. Akron, 1989; Kurdziel Found. grantee, 1995. Mem. ASCD, NEA, Am. Edn. Rsch. Assn., Nat. Alliance of Black Sch. Educators, Coun. Exceptional Children (exec. com., Outstanding Contbn. in Edn. recognition 1993), Ohio Edn. Assn., East Ctrl. Ohio Edn. Assn., Canton Profl. Educators Assn., Leila Green Alliance of Black Sch. Educators, Deaconess Bd., Missionary Soc., Kappa Delta Pi (presenter 38th biennial convocation Memphis 1992), Pi Lambda Theta (presenter Great Lakes region II profl. conf. Beechwood, Ohio 1994). Office: Canton City Schs 521 W Tuscarawas St Canton OH 44702

NWE, KHIN MAY, physician, educator; b. Rangoon, Burma, Sept. 6, 1941; came to U.S., 1972; d. Unga Fawn and Shu Tin (Chan) Kyin; m. Maling Tin Aye, June 10, 1965 (div. 1972); 1 child, Timothy Maling Aye. BM, BS, Inst. Medicine, Rangoon, 1964. Asst. prof. Temple U., Phila., 1978-82; chief anesthesiologist VA Med. Ctr., Wilmington, Del., 1982—. Office: VA Med Ctr 1601 Kirkwood Hwy Wilmington DE 19803

NYCUM, SUSAN HUBBELL, lawyer. B.A., Ohio Wesleyan U., 1956; J.D., Duquesne U., 1960; postgrad., Stanford U. Bar: Pa. 1962, U.S. Supreme Ct. 1967, Calif. 1974. Sole practice law Pitts., 1962-65; designer, adminstr. legal research system U. Pitts., Aspen Systems Corp., Pitts., 1965-68; mgr. ops. Computer Ctr., Carnegie Mellon U., Pitts., 1968-69; dir. computer facility Computer Ctr., Stanford U., Calif., 1969-72, Stanford Law and Computer fellow, 1972-73; cons. in computers and law, 1973-74; sr. assoc. MacLeod, Fuller, Muir & Godwin, Los Altos, Los Angeles and London, 1974-75; ptnr. Chickering & Gregory, San Francisco, 1975-80; ptnr.-in-charge high tech. group Gaston Snow & Ely Bartlett, Boston, NYC, Phoenix, San Francisco, Calif., 1980-86; mng. ptnr. Palo Alto office Kadison, Pfaelzer, Woodard, Quinn & Rossi, Los Angeles, Washington, Newport Beach, Palo Alto, Calif., 1986-87; sr. ptnr. Baker & McKenzie, Palo Alto, 1987—; trustee EDUCOM, 1978-81; mem. adv. com. for high tech. Ariz. State U. Law Sch., Santa Clara U. Law Sch., Stanford Law Sch., U. So. Calif. Law Ctr., law sch. Harvard U., U. Calif.; U.S. State Dept. del. OECD Conf. on Nat. Vulnerabilities, Spain, 1981; invited speaker Telecom, Geneva, 1983; lectr. N.Y. Law Jour., 1975—, Law & Bus., 1975—, Practicing Law Inst., 1975—; chmn. Office of Tech. Assessment Task Force on Nat. Info. Systems, 1979-80. Author:(with Bigelow) Your Computer and the Law, 1975, (with Bosworth) Legal Protection for Software, 1985, (with Collins and Gilbert) Women Leading, 1987; contbr. monographs, articles to profl. publs. Mem. Town of Portola Valley Open Space Acquisition Com., Calif., 1977;

mem. Jr. League of Palo Alto, chmn. evening div., 1975-76. NSF and Dept. Justice grantee for studies on computer abuse, 1972—. Mem. ABA (sect. on sci. and tech. chmn. 1979-80, chmn. elect 1978-79), Internat. Bar Assn. (U.S. mem. computer com. of corps. sect.), Assn. Computing Machinery (mem. at large of council 1976-80, nat. lectr. 1977—, chmn. standing com. on legal issues 1975—, blue ribbon com. on rationalization of internat. proprietary rights protection on info. processing devel. in the '90s, 1990—), Computer Law Assn. (v.p. 1983-85, pres. 1986—, bd. dirs. 1975—), Calif. State Bar Assn. (founder first chmn. econs. of law sect., vice chmn. law and computers com.), Nat. Conf. Lawyers and Scientists (rep. ABA), Strategic Forum on Intellectual Property Issues in Software of NAS. Address: 35 Granada Ct Portola Vally CA 94028-7736

NYE, MIRIAM MAURINE BAKER, writer; b. Castana, Iowa, June 14, 1918; d. Horace Boies and Hazel Dean (Waples) Hawthorn; B.A., Morningside Coll., 1939, postgrad., 1957-58; postgrad. U. Ariz., 1973, U. S.D., 1975-77, New Coll., U. Edinburgh (Scotland), 1974; m. Carl E. Baker, June 21, 1941 (dec. 1970); children—Kent Alfred, Dale Hawthorn; m. 2d, John Arthur Nye, Dec. 25, 1973. Tchr. jr. high sch., Rock Falls, Ill., 1939-41, Moville (Iowa) Community Sch., 1957-62, Woodbury Central Community Sch., Climbing Hill, Iowa, 1962-64; homemaking columnist Sioux City (Iowa) Jour.'s Farm Weekly, 1953-81; author: Recipes and Ideas From the Kitchen Window, 1973; But I Never Thought He'd Die: Practical Help for Widows, 1978; contbg. author Between the Rivers: A History of the United Methodist Ch. in Iowa, 1986; speaker, Iowa, Nebr., Minn., S.D. Counselor, Iowa State U., 1972—; county adv. Iowa Children's and Family Services, 1980-84; mem. public relations com. Farm Bur., Woodbury County, 1980-82; advisor nat. orgn. for help to widows THEOS, Sioux City chpt., 1981-90; lay del. Iowa United Meth. Conf., 1981-83; mem. Archives History Commission of Iowa Methodist Ch., 1991—. Recipient Alumni award Morningside Coll., 1969, Service award Woodbury County Fair, 1969, Friend of Extension award Iowa State U., 1981. Mem. AAUW, Iowa Fedn. Women's Clubs (dist. creative writing chmn. 1978-80), Alpha Kappa Delta, Sigma Tau Delta. Methodist. Home and Office: PO Box 419 Moville IA 51039-0419

NYLANDER, JANE LOUISE, museum director; b. Cleve., Jan. 27, 1938; d. James Merritt and Jeannette (Crosby) Cayford; m. Daniel Harris Giffen, Nov. 30, 1963 (div. 1970); children: Sarah Louise, Thomas Harris; m. Richard Conrad Nylander, July 8, 1972; 1 child, Timothy Frost. AB, Brown U., 1959; MA, U. Del., 1961; postgrad., Attingham (Eng.) Summer Sch., 1970; PhD (hon.), New England Coll., 1994. Curator Hist. Soc. York (Pa.) County, 1961-62, N.H. Hist. Soc., Concord, 1962-69; instr. New England Coll., Henniker, N.H., 1964-65, Monadnock Community Coll., Peterborough, N.H., 1966-69; curator of textiles and ceramics Old Sturbridge (Mass.) Village, 1969-85; adj. assoc. prof. Boston U., 1978-85; sr. curator Old Sturbridge Vill., 1985-86; dir. Strawbery Banke Mus., Portsmouth, N.H., 1986-92, Soc. Preservation New England Antiquities, Boston, 1992-93; pres. Soc. for Preservation of New Eng. Antiquities, 1993—; adj. asst. prof. U. N.H., Durham, 1987-92; adj. prof. art history and Am. studies Boston U., 1993—; trustee Worcester (Mass.) Hist. Mus., 1978-84, Hist. Deerfield (Mass.), Inc., 1981-94, Hist. Mass. Inc., 1992-93, Decorative Arts Trust, 1991—, Portsmouth Athenaeum, 1988-90, Japan Soc. N.H., 1988-92; mem. adv. bd. Concord (Mass.) Mus., 1986-94, Wentworth-Coolidge Commn., 1991—, Coun. Colonial Soc. Mass., 1993—; mem. adv. bd. dept. Am. decorative arts Mus. of Fine Arts, Boston, 1972—; cons. in field. Author: Fabrics for Historic Buildings, 4th edit., 1990, Our Own Snug Fireside: Images of the New England Home 1760-1860, 1993, paperback edit., 1994; mem. editorial bd. Hist. New Hampshire; 1993—; contbr. numerous articles to profl. jours. Mem. adv. bd. New Eng. Heritage Ctr., 1993—; active State House Adv. Com., Boston, 1984-85, Gov.'s Coun. for Wentworth Coolidge Mansion, Concord, 1964-66; mem. Com. for Preservation of N.H. State Flags, 1989-92. Recipient Charles F. Montgomery Prize Decorative Arts Soc., 1985. Mem. Am. Antiquarian Soc., Am. Assn. for State and Local History, Nat. Trust Hist. Preservation, Royal Oak Assn., Portsmouth Athenaeum Colonial Soc. Mass., New Eng. Mus. Assn., Trustees of Reservations, Soc. Winterthur Fellows, Hist. Mass., Soc. Preservation of N.H. Forests, N.H. Audobon Soc., N.H. Humanities Coun., New Eng. Hist. Geneal. Soc., Hist. Houses Trust New South Wales, Costume Soc. Am. (bd. dirs. 1977-83), Dublin Seminar, Nat. Soc. Colonial Dames in N.H. (bd. dirs. 1967-73), Nat. Soc. Colonial Dames in Mass. (courtesy 1993—), Cos. Colonial Soc. Mass. (coun. 1993—), Brown Club N.H. (trustee 1988-93). Episcopalian. Home: 17 Franklin St Portsmouth NH 03801-4501 Office: Soc Preservation New England Antiquities 141 Cambridge St Boston MA 02114

NYMAN, GEORGIANNA BEATRICE, painter; b. Arlington, Mass., June 11, 1930; d. Daniel Eugene Nyman and Irene Krans (Müller) Lombardi; m. David Aronson, June 10, 1956; children: Judith, Benjamin, Abigail. Diploma, Boston Mus. Sch. Art., 1952, student, 1952-54; postgrad., Longy Sch. Music, Cambridge, Mass., 1965-73. Portraits displayed in Brookline (Mass.) Hosp., Inst. Critical Care Medicine, U. Pitts., McClosky Inst. Voice Therapy, Boston, U.S. Supreme Ct., Washington, New Eng. Sch. of Law, Boston, 1991, Milton (Mass.) Acad., Boston Acad. Music; group exhbns. include Shore Studio Gallery, Boston, 1960, 61, Lee Nordness Gallery, N.Y.C., 1963, Copley Soc. Boston, 1980, Nat. Acad. Design, N.Y.C., 1990; solo exhbns. include Nancy Lincoln Gallery, Brookline, 1990; represented in permanent collections Rose Art Mus., Brandeis U., U. Pitts. Sch. Medicine; commd. portraits include Justice Sandra Day O'Connor, Mr. and Mrs. Pieh-headmaster of Milton Acad., 1992, Justice Harry A. Blackmun, 1993, Julie Harris, American actress, 1994, Hon. James R. Lawton, 1994, Richard Conrad, opera singer, dir.-Boston Acad. Music, 1994, Justice Clarence Thomas, 1995. Jurist Art and Mental Illness--An Itinerary Boston U., 1989; active in LeMoyne Found., Fla., 1989. Recipient Boit prize, 1951, cert. of merit NAD, 1992; Kate Morse fellow Boston Mus. Fine Arts, 1953. Mem. Women's Indsl. Inst. (life), Mass. Soc. Mayflower Descendants. Home and Studio: 137 Brimstone Ln Sudbury MA 01776-3203 also: RR 2, Cornwall, PE Canada C0A 1HO

NYQUIST, KATHLEEN A., publishing executive; b. Biloxi, Miss., May 14, 1955; d. Clarence and Marianne M. (Mahoney) Boehm; m. John D. Nyquist, Nov. 5, 1983; children: Lindsay, Eric. BS in Edn., Miami U., Oxford, Ohio, 1977. High sch. biology tchr. Ill., 1978-79; home tutor Fed. Homebound Program, Ill., 1980; from sci. editor to editorial v.p. Scott Foresman & Co., Glenview, Ill., 1981-89, creative dir., 1990, pub., 1992, pres., 1993—. Parent rev. com. mem. Sch. Dist. 96, Buffalo Grove, Ill., 1991-92. Mem. ASCD, Nat. Coun. Tchrs. Math., Nat. Sci. Tchrs. Assn., Chgo. Book Clinic. Office: Scott Foresman & Co 1900 E Lake Glenview IL 60025

OAK, JANE, accountant, teacher English as second language; b. Salt Lake City, Nov. 23, 1971; d. Eugene and Joan (Park) Oh. BS in Acctg., Mich. State U., 1992. Acctg. mgr. Voice of Korea, Inc., Southfield, Mich., 1992—; tchr. ESL Lang. Ctr. Internat., Southfield, 1993—; ESL dir. World Friends, Royal Oak, Mich., 1993—. Mem. Nat. Assn. Mgmt. Accts. Home: 18250 Hunting Sq N Apt 1826 Birmingham MI 48025 Office: Voice of Korea Inc 5000 Town Ctr Apt 405 Southfield MI 48075-1112

OAKES, ELLEN RUTH, psychotherapist, health institute administrator; b. Bartlesville, Okla., Aug. 19, 1919; d. John Isaac and Eva Ruth (Engle) Harboldt; m. Paul Otis Oakes Sr., June 12, 1937 (div. April 1974); children: Paul Otis Jr., Deborah Ellen, Nancy Elaine Masters; m. Siegmar Johann Knopp, Nov. 24, 1975. BA in Sociology, Psychology summa cum laude, Oklahoma City U., 1961; MS in Clin. Psychology, U. Okla., 1963, PhD, 1967. Lic. clin. psychologist, Okla. Chief psychometrist Okla. U. Guidance Ctr., Norman, 1962; psychology trainee VA Hosp., Oklahoma City, 1962-64, Cerebral Palsy Ctr., Norman, Okla., 1964-65; psychology intern Guidance Service, Norman, 1965-66, staff psychologist, 1966-67; asst. prof. psychology Okla. U. Med. Sch., Oklahoma City, 1967-70; supr. psychology interns Okla. Univ. Health Scis. Ctr., 1967-80; founder, dir. Timberridge Inst., Oklahoma City, 1970-90, pres., 1980-90; pvt. practice clin. psychologist Oklahoma City, 1970-92; instr. Okla. U. extension course, Tinker AFB, Oklahoma City, 1963, U. Okla., 1965-66; discussion leader Inst. for Tchrs. of Disadvantaged Child Oklahoma City Sch. System, 1966; leader group therapy sessions Asbury Meth. and Westminster Presbyn. Chs., Oklahoma City, 1966; mem. psychology team confs. for hearing disorders, Okla. U. Med. Sch., 1967-70; cons. Oklahoma City Pub. Schs., 1970-72; cons., group leader halfway house, 1972; lectr. chs., PTAs, hosps.; reviewer Am. Psychol. Assn. Civilian Health and Med. Program of the Uniformed Svcs., 1978-89. Workshop conductor on Shame & Sexuality, Zurick Jungian Inst. winter seminar, 1992; attended Européen Congrés de Gestalt Thérapie in Paris, 1992; contbr. articles to profl. jours. Speaker Okla. County Mental Health Assn. Annual Worry Clinic, St. Luke's Ch., Oklahoma City, 1968-92, psychology dept. Sorosis Club, St. Luke's Ch.. Mem. Am. Psychol. Assn. (peer rev. project with CHAMPUS, 1978-89), Okla. Psychol. Assn. (pres. 1975-76). Address: 18 Basore Dr Bella Vista AR 72714

OAKES, MARIA SPACHNER, nurse; b. Cinn., Mar. 27, 1947; d. A. William and Roberta Mae (Linville) Stevens; m. John Cullwell Oakes, Nov. 27, 1976; children: John Cullwell II, Laura Suzann. Diploma Sch. Nursing, King's Daughters' Hosp., 1968; student, Ohio U., Ironton, Morehead U. Cert. med./surg. nurse. Staff nurse Ohio State U. Hosp., Columbus, Lawrence County, Ironton; head nurse, neonatal intensive care King's Daughters' Med. Ctr., Ashland, Ky., staff nurse. Bd. dirs. Am. Cancer Soc.; deacon bd. sessions, pres. Women's Assn. First Presbyn. Ch.; v.p. West Ironton Parent-Tchr. Group; pres. Kingsbury Parents for Better Schs.; asst. children's play dir. Play It Safe, Say No to Drugs; past pres. Kings Daus. Hosp. Sch. Nursing Alumni Assn.; mem. strategic planning com. Ironton City Sch. Dist. Mem. ANA, Ky. Nurses Assn. (state offices nursing practice comm., legis. com., state nominating com., nurse practice commn., past pres., v.p., treas. Dist. 4, former v.p., program chmn., seminar planner, continuing edn. coord., current v.p. Dist. 4, mem. ad hoc com. health care reform). Home: 2210 N 3rd Ave Ironton OH 45638-1068

OAKES, ROSALIE VADEN, retired association executive and social worker; b. Lynchburg, Va., June 17, 1917; d. Jesse Clifford and Mabel Irene (Plunkett) Oakes. BA, U. Richmond, 1939; BDiv, Crozer Theol. Seminary, 1942. Exec. dir. YWCA U. Ky., Lexington, 1942-45; mem. so. region staff USO/YWCA Campus Svcs., Atlanta, 1945-47; so. regional co-dir. coll./univ. divsn. YWCA U.S.A., Atlanta, 1947-54; exec. dir. U. Tex. YWCA, Austin, 1954-58; adv. staff World Affiliated YWCA South Africa, 1958-61, 62-72; world rels. cons. Nat. YWCA U.S.A., N.Y.C., 1972-76, world rels. exec., 1976-82, ret., 1982. Active divsn. overseas ministries Nat. Coun. Chs., N.Y.C., 1972-82; YWCA rep. Coop. in Devel., N.Y.C., 1976-82, Am. Coun. Vol. Agys. for Fgn. Svc., N.Y.C., 1976-82, Washington Office on Africa, 1984-94; mem. vestry Ch. Epiphany, Washington, 1984-87, 93-95, chair outreach com., mem. search com., downtown cluster congregations rep., 1989-91; Dem. precinct activist, 1986-92. Home: 4220 Columbia Pike Apt 2 Arlington VA 22204-3029

OAKLAND, NANCY NELL, geriatrics nurse; b. El Paso, Tex., Apr. 26, 1947; d. Clarence L. and Ruth Alice (King) North; div.; children: Heather Lynn, Joshua Glen. BSN, Tex. Christian U., 1969. RN, Ariz. Staff nurse Tex. Children's Hosp., Houston, 1969-72; office nurse Pediatric Assocs., Houston, 1972-74; staff nurse, charge nurse pediatric unit Good Samaritan Hosp., Phoenix, 1974-75; office nurse Pediatric Clinic, Phoenix, 1975-76; sch. nurse Mesa (Ariz.) Pub. Schs., 1986; staff nurse acute care unit Cosada Villa Nursing Ctr., Mesa, 1986-88; staff nurse Valley Luth. Hosp., Mesa, 1988-89, case mgmt. coord., 1989-93; case mgr. Advance Home Health, Chandler, Ariz., 1993—; preceptor BSN students U. Phoenix, 1991-93. Home: 5928 E Ingram St Mesa AZ 85205-3537

OAKLAND, VELMA LEANE, educator; b. Moorhead, Minn., Dec. 29, 1939; d. Alfred J. and Annie (Klusman) Kuvaas; m. Aug. 17, 1959; 1 child, Terry Lee. BS in Edn., Mayville State U., 1966; MS in Edn., N.D. State U., 1969. Cert. elem. tchr., Minn. Tchr. Granville (N.D.) Pub. Schs., 1960-62, Tappen (N.D.) Pub. Schs., 1962-64, Hughes Elem. Sch., Red Lake Falls, Minn., 1964—. Heat Start dir. Inter County Community Coun., Red Lake Falls, Minn., 1970-73; commr. HUD, 1988; mem. Red Lake County Fair Bd., 1988—; mem. exec. com. 7th Congl. Dist., 1988; mem. N.W. Regional Devel. Commn., 1990—; mem. adv. com. N.W. Minn. Global Studies Inst., 1990-91; pres. Red Lake County Eocn. Devel. Corp., 1991-92; sec.-treas. N.W. Regional Devel. Commn. Enterprise Loan Fund. Named Tchr. of Yr., Red Lake Falls Civic and Commerce Assn., 1985; named Outstanding D.F.L.er Red Lake County, 1994. Mem. Minn. Edn. Assn. (sec. 1979—, treas. 1983—, exec. com. 1983—, Impace bd. dirs. 1994, Creative Leadership award 1993), Red Lake Falls Edn. Assn. (Tchr. of Yr. 1985, pres. 1994-95), Delta Kappa Gamma. Home: 118 Main Ave N Red Lake Falls MN 56750-4008 Office: Hughes Elem Sch Red Lake Falls MN 56750

OAKLEY, CAROLYN COBB, library director, academic administrator; b. Wilson, N.C., Nov. 5, 1946; d. Raymond Earl and Edna Gay (Hardison) Cobb; m. Robert Carroll Oakley, Nov. 25, 1971 (div. Oct. 1988); 1 child, Robert Carroll Oakley, Jr. BS, E. Carolina U., 1969, MEd, 1970; postgrad., U. N.C., 1976-77, N.C. State U., 1986—. Cataloger N.C. Dept. C.C., Raleigh, 1969-70; libr. Vance-Granville C.C., Henderson, N.C., 1970-76, coord. library svcs., 1976-87; dir. Learning Resources Ctr., 1987-88; dept. chair for learning resources Wilson (N.C.) Tech. C.C., 1989—; cons. Rose's Stores, Henderson, 1986-87, Ark. Dept. of Higher Edn., Little Rock, Ark., 1994. Author: Index to Doctoral Theses, 1967-85 (N.C. State U.), 1987. Mem. ALA, N.C. Libr. Assn., Am. Assn. Women in Community Colls., SE Libr. Assn., N.C. Learning Resources Assn. Soc. Democrat. Baptist. Home: 304B Katharine Ct W Wilson NC 27893-2766 Office: Wilson Tech C C PO Box 4305 Woodard Sta Wilson NC 27893

OAKLEY, CAROLYN LE, state legislator, small business owner; b. Portland, Oreg., June 28, 1942; d. George Thomas and Ruth Alveta Victoria (Engberg) Penketh; m. Donald Keith Oakley, June 27, 1965; children: Christine, Michelle. BS in Edn., Oreg. State U., 1965. Educator Linn County (Oreg.) Schs., 1965-76; owner Linn County Tractor, 1965-90; mem. Oreg. Legis. Assembly, Salem, 1989—, asst. majority leader, 1993—, majority whip, 1994; mem. exec. bd. Oreg. Retail Coun., 1987-90. Chmn. Linn County Rep. Ctrl. Com., 1982-84; chmn. bd. dirs. North Albany Svc. Dist., 1988-90; chair Salvation Army, Linn and Benton Counties, 1987—; vice chmn. bd. trustees Linn-Benton C.C. Found., 1987—; pres. Women for Agr., Linn and Benton Counties, 1984-86; mem. STRIDE Leadership Round Table, 1991—; state chair Am. Legis. Exch. Coun., 1991—, nat. bd. dirs., 1992—; mem. Edn. Commn. of the States, 1991—, com. policies and priorities, 1993—; hon. mem. Linn-Benton Compact Bd., 1993—; active Linn County Criminal Justice Coun., 1994—. Named Woman of Yr. Albany chpt. Beta Sigma Phi, 1970. Mem. Nat Conf. State Legislators (chmn. edn. com. 1992—), Albany C. of C. (bd. dirs. 1986-93), Linn County Rep. women (legis. chmn. 1982-91). Republican. Methodist. Home: 3197 NW Crest Loop Albany OR 97321-9627 Office: Oreg Legis Assembly State Capital Salem OR 97310

OAKLEY, DEBORAH JANE, researcher, educator; b. Detroit, Jan. 31, 1937; d. George F. and Kathryn (Willson) Hacker; m. Bruce Oakley, June 16, 1958; children: Ingrid Andrea, Brian Benjamin. BA, Swarthmore Coll., 1958; MA, Brown U., 1960; MPH, U. Mich., 1969, PhD, 1977. Dir. teenage and adult programs YWCA, Providence, 1959-63; editorial asst. Stockholm U., 1963-64; rsch. investigator, lectr. dept. population planning U. Mich., 1971-77; asst. prof. community health programs U. Mich., Ann Arbor, 1977-79, asst. prof. nursing rsch., 1979-81, assoc. prof., 1981-89, prof., 1989—, interim dir. Ctr. Nursing Rsch., 1988-90; prin. investigator NIH-funded Rsch. grants on family planning and women's health, mem. nat. adv. com. nursing rsch., 1993—; co-chair Mich. Initiative for Women's Health, 1993—. Author: (with Leslie Corsa) Population Planning, 1979; contbr. articles to profl. jours. Recipient Margaret Sanger award Washtenaw County Planned Parenthood, 1975; Outstanding Young Woman of Ann Arbor award by Jaycees, 1970, Dist. Faculty award, Mich. Assn. Gov. Bds., 1992. Mem. Am. Pub. Health Assn. (chmn. population sect. council), Internat. Union Sci. Study Population, Midwest Nursing Rsch. Soc., Population Assn. Am., Nat. Family Planning and Reproductive Health Assn. (nat. comms.), Delta Omega. Democrat. Home: 5200 S Lake Dr Chelsea MI 48118-9481 Office: U Mich Sch Nursing Ann Arbor MI 48109

OAKLEY, MARY ANN BRYANT, lawyer; b. Buckhannon, W.Va., June 22, 1940; d. Hubert Herndon and Mary F. (Deeds) Bryant; m. Godfrey P. Oakley, Jr., Sept. 2, 1961; children—Martha, Susan, Robert. A.B., Duke U., 1962; M.A., Emory U., 1970, J.D., 1974. Tchr., Winston-Salem/Forsyth County Schs., N.C., 1961-65; assoc. Margie Pitts Hames, Atlanta, 1974-80; ptnr. Stagg Hoy & Oakley, Atlanta, 1980-83, Oakley & Bonner, Atlanta, 1984-90; pvt. practice, 1990—; adj. prof. trial practice Ga. State U., 1986—; adj. prof. pretrial practice Emory U. Law Sch., 1991, 95; bd. dirs. Nat. Employment Lawyers Assn., 1989-94; founding coodr. NELA, Ga.; mem. Ga. Supreme Ct. Commn. on Racial and Ethnic Bias. Contbr. articles to law jours. Notes and Comments editor Emory Law Jour., 1973-74. Author: Elizabeth Cady Stanton, 1972; Bd. dirs. Atlanta Met. YWCA, 1975-79, 1st v.p., 1978-79; mem. Leadership Atlanta, 1979; bd. dirs. Ga. chpt. ACLU, 1981-83; trustee Unitarian Universalist Congregation Atlanta, 1977-80, pres., 1979-80, mem. Unitarian Universalist Commn. Appraisal, 1980-85; bd. dirs. Unitarian Universalist Service Com., 1984-90, v.p., 1986-88, pres. 1988-90. Nat. Merit scholar, 1958. Mem. ABA, Am. Judicature Soc., State Bar Ga. (chmn. individual rights sect. 1979-81), Atlanta Bar Assn., Lawyers Club Atlanta, No. Dist. Bar Council, 1982-86, Ga. Assn. Women Lawyers, Ga. State Bar Disciplinary Bd. (investigative panel 1985-88, chmn., 1987-88), Gate City Bar Assn., Ga. Bd. Bar Examiners, Ga. Legal Svcs. Program Bd., LWV, Phi Beta Kappa, Order of Coif. Home: 2224 Kodiak Dr NE Atlanta GA 30345-4152 Office: 315 W Ponce De Leon Ave Ste 721 Decatur GA 30030-2441

OAKS, B. ANN, plant physiologist, educator; b. Winnipeg, Man., Can., June 4, 1929; d. H.A. and Bernice (Farlinger) O. BA with honors, U. Toronto, Ont., Can., 1951; MA, U. Sask., Can., 1954, PhD, 1959. Alexander von Humbolt assoc. Rsch. Inst. for Dairying, Freising, Fed. Republic Germany, 1958-60; rsch. assoc. Purdue U., West Lafayette, Ind., 1960-64, Oak Ridge (Tenn.) Nat. Lab., 1964-65; asst. prof. biology McMaster U., Hamilton, Ont., 1965-68, assoc. prof., 1968-74, prof., 1974-89; prof. emeritus McMaster U., Hamilton, 1989—; prof. U. Guelph, Ont., 1989—; vis. prof. Wash. State U., 1979-80, U. Nancy, France, 1980, Chiba U., Japan, 1984; adj. prof. U. Guelph, 1987-89; affiliated scientist NRC Lab., Saskatoon, Sask., 1988-92. Assoc. editor Biochemistry and Cell Biology, 1988-90; mem. editorial bd. Plant Physiology, 1970-89, Jour. Plant Physiology, 1984—, Plant and Cell Physiology, 1989-93; contbr. author various books; contbr. articles to profl. jours. Rsch. grantee in field. Fellow Royal Soc. Can.; mem. Can. Soc. Plant Physiologists (treas. 1974-76, Gold medal 1989), Am. Soc. Plant Physiologists. Office: U Guelph, Dept Botany, Guelph, ON Canada N1G 2W1

OAKS, JULIE YVONNE (VONNIE OAKS), geriatric counselor; b. Greer, S.C., July 24, 1953; d. Glenn Talmadge and Julia Lorraine (Morrow) Taylor; m. Carl Lynn Oaks, Jr., May 28, 1983. BA in Acad. Psychology, U. Tenn., 1988, MS in Ednl. and Counseling Psychology, 1991. Cert. counselor, gerontol. counselor Nat. Bd. Cert. Counselors; lic. profl. counselor. Geriatric counselor John T. O'Connor Sr. Citizen Ctr., Knoxville, Tenn., 1990, Ctr. for Health and Creative Aging, Knoxville, 1991—; founder, owner, geriatric counselor Sr. Adult Counseling Svcs., Knoxville, 1993—; group facilitator Ft. Sanders Park West Hosp., Knoxville, 1991-94. Counselor Knoxville-Knox County Geriatric Screen Team, 1992—; mem. Knoxville-Knox County Coun. on Aging. Mem. ACA, Assn. for Adult Devel. and Aging, Tenn. Assn. for Counseling and Devel., Tenn. Assn. for Gerontology and Geriatric Edn., Mental Heaalth Assn. Knox County. Methodist. Home: 9900 Cedar Croft Cir Knoxville TN 37932-3605 Office: Sr Adult Counseling Svcs PO Box 32063 Knoxville TN 37930-2063

OAKS, M(ARGARET) MARLENE, minister; b. Grove City, Pa., Mar. 30, 1940; d. Allen Roy and Alberta Bell (Pinner) Eakin; m. Lowell B. Chaney, July 30, 1963 (dec. Jan. 1977); children: Christopher Allen, Linda Michelle; m. Harold G. Younger, Aug. 1978 (div. 1986); m. Gilbert E. Oaks, Aug. 3, 1987. BA, Calif. State U., L.A., 1972; religious sci. studies with several instrs. Ordained to ministry Ch. Religious Sci., 1986. Tchr. Whittier (Calif.) Sch. Dists., 1972-74, Garden Grove (Calif.) Sch. Dist., 1974-78; instr. Fullerton Coll., 1974-75; founding min. Community Ch. of the Islands (now Ch. of Religious Sci.), Honolulu, 1978-80; min. Ch. of Divine Sci., Pueblo, Colo., 1980-83; founding min. Ch. Religious Sci., Palo Alto, Calif., 1983-86; min. First ch. Religious Sci., Fullerton, Calif., 1986-94, min. emeritus, 1994—; 2d v.p., chmn., corp. sec. VCC Internat., Anaheim, Calif., 1994—; founder, pres. LaVida Inst., Inc., 1994—; workshop leader Religious Sci. Dist. Conv., San Jose, Calif., 1985, Internat. New Thought Alliance Conf., Las Vegas, 1984, 92, Calgary, Alta., Can., 1985, Washington, 1988, Denver, 1989, Anaheim, Calif., 1990, Golden Valley Unity Women's Advance, Mpls., 1986, 87, Qume Corp., San Jose, 1985; presenter SANTI Conf., 1992-94; guest workshop leader Ctr. for Life Enrichment, 1990-92; speaker to cmty. of Tartarstan, 1993. Author: The Christmas in You, 1983, rev. edit., 1994, Ki Aikido the Inner Martial Art, 1984, Old Time Religion Is a Cult, 1985, 2d rev. edit., 1992, Service the Sure Path to Enlightenment, 1985, Stretch Marks on My Aura, 1987, rev. edit., 1995, Beyond Addiction, 1990, 10 Core Concepts of Science of Mind, 1991, Forgiveness and Beyond, 1992, rev. edit. Christmas for All Seasons, 1994; contbr. articles to profl. jours. Del. Soviet and Am. Citizens Summit Conf., 1988, 89; pres. Soviet-Am. New Thought Initiatives, 1991, chmn. conf. St. Petersburg, 1992, Moscow, 1992, weekly radio program Radio Moscow, The Philippines, 1992—; founder Operation K.I.D.S., La Vida Inst., 1994; founder, bd. dirs. Awakening Oaks Found., 1990; pres. SANTI, 1991-94, founder and pres. La Vida Inst., 1994. Named Outstanding Businesswoman, Am. Businesswomen's Assn., 1989. Mem. Fullerton Interfaith Ministerial Assn. (sec.-treas. 1987-89, pres. 1991-92), United Clergy of Religious Sci. (treas. 1991-92, sec. 1992-93, treas. So. Calif. chpt. 1991-92, v.p. 1993-94, pres. 1994-95), Internat. New Thought Alliance (O.C. chpt. pres. 1990), Soroptomists (chair com. internat. coop. and goodwill 1987-88), Kappa Delta Pi. Republican. Office: LaVida Inst Awakening Oaks Press 1775 E Lincoln Ave Ste 101 Anaheim CA 92805

OATES, JOYCE CAROL, author; b. Lockport, N.Y., June 16, 1938; d. Frederic James and Caroline (Bush) O.; m. Raymond Joseph Smith, Jan. 23, 1961. BA, Syracuse U., 1960; MA, U. Wis., 1961. Instr. English U. Detroit, 1961-65, asst. prof., 1965-67; prof. English U. Windsor, Ont., Can., 1967-87; writer-in-residence Princeton (N.J.) U., 1978-81, prof., 1987—. Author: (short story collections) By the North Gate, 1963, Upon the Sweeping Flood, 1966, The Wheel of Love, 1970, Marriages and Infidelities, 1972, The Hungry Ghosts, 1974, The Goddess and Other Women, 1974, Where Are You Going, Where Have You Been?: Stories of Young America, 1974, The Poisoned Kiss and Other Stories From the Portuguese, 1975, The Seduction and Other Stories, 1975, Crossing the Border, 1976, Night-Side, 1977, All the Good People I've Left Behind, 1978, The Lamb of Abyssalia, 1980, A Sentimental Education: Stories, 1981, Last Days: Stories, 1984, Wild Nights, 1985, Raven's Wing: Stories, 1986, The Assignation, 1988, Heat: And Other Stories, 1991, Where is Here?, 1992, Haunted: Tales of the Grotesque, 1994; (novels) With Shuddering Fall, 1964, A Garden of Earthly Delights, 1967 (Nat. Book award nomination 1968), Expensive People, 1967 (Nat. Book award nomination 1969), Them, 1969 (Nat. Book award for fiction 1970), Wonderland, 1971, Do With Me What You Will, 1973, The Assassins, 1975, Childwold, 1976, The Triumph of the Spider Monkey, 1977, Son of the Morning, 1978, Unholy Loves, 1979, Cybele, 1979, Bellefleur, 1980 (Book Prize in Fiction nomination L.A. Times 1980), A Sentimental Education, 1981, Angel of Light, 1981, A Bloodsmoor Romance, 1982, Mysteries of Winterthorn, 1984, Solstice, 1985, Marya, 1986, You Must Remember This, 1987, (as Rosamond Smith) The Lives of the Twins, 1987, American Appetites, 1989, (as Rosamond Smith) Soul-Mate, 1989, Because It Is Bitter, and Because It Is My Heart, 1990, (as Rosamond Smith) Nemesis, 1990, I Lock My Door Upon Myself, 1990, The Rise of Life on Earth, 1991, Black Water, 1992, (as Rosamond Smith) Snake Eyes, 1992, Foxfire: Confessions of a Girl Gang, 1993, What I Lived For, 1994; (poetry collections) Women in Love, 1968, Expensive People, 1968, Anonymous Sins, 1969, Love and Its Derangements, 1970, Angel Fire, 1973, Dreaming America, 1973, The Fabulous Beasts, 1975, Season of Peril, 1977, Women Whose Lives are Food, Men Whose Lives are Money: Poems, 1978, The Stepfather, 1978, Celestial Timepiece, 1981, Invisible Women: New and Selected Poems, 1970-72, 1982, Luxury of Sin, 1983, The Time Traveller, 1987; (plays) The Sweet Enemy, 1965, Sunday Dinner, 1970, Ontological Proof of My Existence, 1970, Miracle Play, 1974, Three Plays, 1980, Daisy, 1980, Presque Isle, 1984, Triumph of the Spider Monkey, 1985, In Darkest America, 1990, I Stand Before You Naked, 1990; (essays) The Edge of Impossibility, 1972, The Hostile Sun: The Poetry of D.H. Lawrence, 1973, New Heaven, New Earth, 1974, Contraries: Essays, 1981, The Profane Art, 1984, On Boxing, 1987, (Woman) Writer, 1988; editor: Ont. Rev., Scenes from American Life, 1973, The Best American Short Stories, 1979, Night Walks, 1982, First Person Singular, 1983, Story: Fictions Past and Present, 1985, Reading the Fights, 1988, The Sophisticated Cat: An Anthology, 1992; editor, compiler: Scenes from American Life: Contemporary Short Fiction, 1973, (with Shannon Ravenel) Best American Short Stories of 1979, 1979, Night Walks, 1982, First Person Singular: Writer's on Their Craft, 1983, (with Boyd Litzinger) Story: Fictions Past and Present, 1985, (with Daniel

Halpern) Reading and Fights, 1988, The Oxford Book of American Short Stories, 1992; also fiction in nat. mags. Recipient O. Henry Prize Story award, 1967, 73, Rosenthal award Nat. Inst. Arts and Letters, 1968, O. Henry Spl. award continuing achievement, 1970, 86, Award of Merit Lotos Club, 1975, St. Louis Lit. award, 1988, Rea award for the Short Story, 1990, Alan Swallow award for fiction, 1990, Nobel Prize in Lit. nomination, 1993; Guggenhem fellow, 1967-68, NEA grantee, 1966, 68. Mem. Am. Acad. and Inst. Arts and Letters. Office: care Ontario Review Press 9 Honey Brook Dr Princeton NJ 08540*

OATES, SHERRY CHARLENE, portraitist; b. Houston, Sept. 11, 1946; d. Charles Emil and Berniece Faye (Lohse) O. Student, North Tex. State U., 1965-66; student under Martin Kellogg; BA in English, Health and Phys. Edn., Houston Bapt. U., 1968. Cert. art tchr., Tex. Tchr. Jackson Jr. High Sch., Houston, 1968-69, Percy Priest Sch., Nashville, 1969-70, Franklin (Tenn.) High Sch., 1970-84; freelance illustrator Bapt. Sunday Sch. Bd., Nashville, 1978-85, United Meth. Pub. House, Nashville, 1980-85; portraitist in oils, owner Portraits, Ltd., Nashville, 1984—. Portraits include corporate leaders, educators, politicians, historian and equestrian subjects, society figures and children; participated in various exhibits at Bapt. Sunday Sch. Bd. and All State and Ctr. South Exhibit at the Parthenon. Recipient 3d place in graphics Ctrl. South Exhbn. at The Parthenon-Tenn. Art League, 1986. Mem. Tenn. Art League. Republican. Baptist. Studio: 816 Kirkwood Ave Nashville TN 37204

OATHOUT, BRENDA HALM, auditor; b. Tecumseh, Nebr., Aug. 16, 1960; d. William W. and H. Lenore (Bentzinger) B.; m. Randall L. Oathout, Sept. 26, 1992. BSBA, U. Nebr., Omaha, 1983. Clk. Boardwalk Hardware, Omaha, 1976-81; claims auditor Physicians Mut. Ins. Co., Omaha, 1981-87; auditor LaHood & Assocs., Overland Park, Kans., 1987-89; advanced auditor Physicians Mut. Ins. Co., Omaha, 1989-92, sr. auditor, 1992—. Republican. Methodist.

OATNEY, CECILIA KAY, army officer; b. McCall, Idaho, May 18, 1956; d. Cecil Edward and Ruby Ilene (Wine) O.; m. Nelvin Eugene Tyler Jr., Dec. 24, 1991. BBA in Acctg., Idaho State U., 1978; MS in Econs. and Ops. Research, Colo. Sch. Mines, 1987. Commd. 2d lt. U.S. Army, 1978, advanced through grades to lt. col., 1995; platoon leader A, B and C Cos. 8th Signal Battalion U.S. Army, Bad Kreuznach, Fed. Republic of Germany, 1978-81, logistics officer, 1981; promoted to capt., 1982; div. radio officer 142d Signal Battalion U.S. Army, Ft. Hood, Tex., 1982-83, comdr. C Co. 142d Signal Battalion, 1983-85, asst. ops. officer, 1985; chief market analysis 6th Recruiting Brigade U.S. Army, Ft. Baker, Calif., 1987-89; with command and gen. staff coll. U.S. Army, Leavenworth, Kans., 1989-90; promoted to maj., 1990; chief strategic systems plans br. 5th Signal Command U.S. Army, Fed. Republc of Germany, 1990-91, chief plans & programs div., 1991; exec. officer 509th Signal Battalion U.S. Army, Italy, 1991-92; exec. officer office dep. chief staff, info. mgmt. U.S. Army, Germany, 1992-94; dep. brigade comdr. 2d Sig BDE, Germany, 1995—. Pres. 4-H Club, Valley County, Idaho, 1973-74. Mem. Armed Forces Communication-Electronics Assn., Assn. U.S. Army. Home: PO Box 92 Donnelly ID 83615-0092 Office: HQ USAREUR & 7 ARMY CMR 420 Box 1022 APO AE 09063

O'BANNION, MINDY MARTHA MARTIN, nurse; b. Cushing, Okla., Aug. 19, 1953; d. John William and Martha Florence (Vineyard) Martin; student Okla. State U., 1971-73, Oscar Rose Jr. Coll., 1973; grad. St. Anthony Sch. Nursing, 1975; RN, Tex.; m. William Neal O'Bannion, Oct. 9, 1976; children: Mindi Martha Mae, William Neale Aaron. Nursing asst. Cushing Mcpl. Hosp., 1973-75, head nurse surg. fl., 1975-76, charge nurse med. unit, 1978-79, 82-83; staff nurse Met. Hosp., Dallas, 1985; staff nurse med. unit Mesquite (Tex.) Community Hosp., 1985-87; nurse post partum unit partum unit and edn. dept. Trinity Med. Ctr., Carrollton, Tex., 1987—. ind. beauty cons. Mary Kay Cosmetics, Dallas, Tex., 1993—. Mem. social com. Royal Haven Bapt. Ch. Women's Missionary Union, Dallas, 1977-78; mem. extension dept. nursery First Bapt. Ch., Cushing, 1979-82, extension dept. presch., 1982-84; mem. extension dept presch. Royal Haven Bapt. Ch., Dallas, 1986-87; mem. Montgomery Elem. Sch. PTA, Farmers Branch, Tex., 1986-94, Vivian Field Jr. H.S. PTA, Farmers Branch, 1993—; treas., mem. nominating com. Joyce Harms group Women's Missionary Union; clk., charter mem. Brookhaven Bapt. Ch., Farmers Br., 1989-92; mem. Valwood Park Baptist Ch., Farmers Br., 1994—. Mem. Am., Tex., Okla. State Nurses Assns., St. Anthony Hosp. Sch. Nursing Alumnae, Bluebonnet Shelties (founder), Tau Beta Sigma, Alpha Xi Delta (corr. sec. 1973). Baptist. Home: 13505 Onyx Ln Farmers Branch TX 75234-4912

OBASEKI, LOVETTE I., consulting company executive; b. July 4, 1953; d. Samson O. Amba A. (Okai) O. BS, Fla. A&M U., 1979, MEd, 1984; diploma in systems analysis, NYU, 1989. Supr. systems adminstrn. Buccellati Ltd., N.Y.C.; systems mgr. JCCA, N.Y.C., 1988-95; cons. Binam Cons. Svcs., 1995—. Active numerous ch. groups. Recipient Honors awards Fla. A&M U. Mem. NAFE, NOW, AAUW, Assn. Sys. Mgmt. (bd. dirs. 1989—, v.p. 1992-93, Excellence in Sys. Mgmt. award 1994, Outstanding Svc. award 1992-93, Appreciation cert. 1990-91, Honors award), Data Processing Mgmt. Assn., Am. Mgmt. Assn., DAV Comdrs. Club (Bronze Leader 1995). Address: PO Box 901026 Far Rockaway NY 11690-1026

OBERG, MARY KATHLEEN, paramedic/nurse coordinator; d. Roy Edward and Kathleen Anne (Davis) Henson; m. Scott Douglas Oberg; 1 child, Kathleen Eleanor Belcher. AA in Nursing, Imperial Valley Coll., 1988; postgrad., SUNY; BSN, U. Phoenix, 1994. RN, Calif.; CEN; cert. ACLS provider and instr., trauma care nurse, pub. health nurse, BLS, mobile intensive care nurse, first aid instr., pediatric advanced life support instr. and provider. Nurse El Centro (Calif.) Regional Med. Ctr., 1987—, peer educator, 1988—, staff and charge nurse ICU, 1988-90, emergency dept. nurse, 1989—; patient educator, clin. instr. El Centro Regional Med. Ctr., 1991-92; acting assoc. dir. clin. svcs., dir. nurse-client edn. Kimberly Quality Care, El Centro, 1992—, paramedic, nurse coord., 1992—; paramedic, EMT instr. Imperial Valley Coll., 1992—. Vol. tchr. first aid Girl Scouts U.S.A.; tchr. BLS various cmty. groups; participant ARC Health Fair; nurse vol. S.W. med. teams for worldwide outreach of med.-nursing tng. and care. Mem. Emergency Nurses Assn., Am. Assn. Diabetic Educators. Home: 1910 Aurora Dr El Centro CA 92243-4108 Office: PO Box 52069 4615 E Elwood St Phoenix AZ 85040-1936

OBERG, MURIEL CURNIN, community health nurse, health facility manager; b. Bridgeport, Conn., July 12, 1925; d. James P. and Lillian (Bannister) Curnin; m. Leonard E. Oberg, Nov. 9, 1946; 1 child, Douglas P. Diploma in Nursing, St. Vincent's Med. Ctr., Bridgeport, 1946; BSN, U. Bridgeport, 1963, MS, 1972; postgrad., Fairfield U., 1991. RN, Conn.; cert. in nursing adminstrn.; cert. profl. educator. Inservice edn. supr. Bridgeport Hosp., 1963-65, health careers counselor Sch. of Nursing, 1966-69; health careers counselor Quinnipiac Coll., 1970-71; asst. dir. maternal and child health Vis. Nurse Assn., New Haven, 1972-81; dir. pub. health nursing Dept. Health City of New Haven, New Haven, 1981—. Recipient USPH traineeship, 1962. Mem. ANA, Conn. Nurses Assn. Home: 240 Hillside Rd Fairfield CT 06430-2145

OBERHAUSEN, JOYCE ANN WYNN, aircraft company executive, artist; b. Plain Dealing, La., Nov. 12, 1941; d. George Dewey and Jettie Cleo (Farrington) Wynn; m. James J. Oberhausen, Oct. 15, 1966; children: Georgann, Darla Renee Estein Oberhausen Christopher, Dale Henry Estein Oberhausen. Student Ayers Bus. Sch., Shreveport, 1962-63, U. Ala., 1964-65. Stenographer, sec. Lincoln Nat. Life Co., Shreveport, 1965-66; sec. Baifield Industries, Shreveport, 1975-86; internat. art tchr., Huntsville, Ala., 1974—; co-owner Precision Splty. Co., Huntsville, 1966—, Mil. Aircraft, Huntsville, 1979—; pres., owner Wynnson Enterprises, Huntsville, 1983—; owner, artist, designer Wynnson Galleries Pvt. Collections, Florist, Meridianville, 1987; owner North Ala. Wholesale Flowers, 1988—, Wynnson Enterprises Mil. Packaging Co., 1988—. Co-founder Nat. Mus. Women in Arts; active Nat. Mus. Women in Arts. Mem. NAFE, Internat. Porcelain Guild, People to People, Porcelain Portrait Soc., United Artists Assn., Am. Soc. of Profl. and Executive Women Hist. Soc., Nat. Trust Hist. Preservation, Internat. Platform Assn., Met. Mus. Art., Smithsonian Assn., Assn. Community Artists, Rep. Senatorial Inner Circle, Ala. Sheriffs Assn., C. of C., Better Bus. Bur., Huntsville Art League and Mus. Assocs., Avocations: oil painting, antiques, handcrafts, gourmet cooking, horseback riding. Home: 156 Spencer Dr Meridianville AL 35759-2023 Office: Wynnson Enterprises Inc 12043 Highway 231 431 N Meridianville AL 35759-1201

OBERHOLTZER, KATHERINE BLOOMFIELD, psychotherapist, clinical social worker; b. Portland, Oreg., May 14, 1957; d. Theodore Robert and Margery A. (Wald) Bloomfield; m. James Scott Shannon Oberholtzer, May 29, 1988; children: Claire, Joseph. BA cum laude, Wesleyan U., Middletown, Conn., 1978; MSW, Smith Coll., 1983. Bd. cert.diplomate in clin. social work; lic. clin. social worker, Ill. Counselor Sonia Shankman Orthogenic Sch., Chgo., 1978-81; clinician Jewish Family and Community Svc., Highland Park, Ill., 1983-87; founder, pres. TRI Counseling Group, Ltd., Skokie, Ill., 1987—; cons. Refugee Task Force, Dept. Mental Health, Chgo., 1988-90. Contbr. articles to profl. jours. Mem. adv. bd. Chgo. Sch. Profl. Psychology Intercultural Program, 1990—; founder, bd. dirs. Women in Internat. Careers, Chgo., 1989. Mem. NASW (panelist, cons. com. on inquiry 1991—), Employee Assistance Profls. Assn., Soc. for Intercultural Edn., Tng. and Rsch., Human Resource Mgmt. Assn. Office: TRI Counseling Group Ltd 5225 Old Orchard Rd Ste 6 Skokie IL 60007

OBERKIRCHER, DIANE JEAN, mathematics educator, tax accountant; b. Buffalo, June 24, 1950; d. Ralph Arthur and Muriel Carol (Glaeser) O.; divorced. BS in Math. Edn., State Univ. Coll., Brockport, N.Y., 1972, MS in Ednl. Adminstrn., 1974. Cert. in secondary math. edn., N.Y. Uni-Pay clk. Marine Midland Bank, Buffalo, 1968-72; asst. registrar State Univ. Coll., Brockport, 1972-74; home instrn. tutor Clarence (N.Y.) Ctrl. Sr. High Sch., 1974-75; part-time inst. Erie C.C., Buffalo, 1975-86; instr. math. Ednl. Testing Methods, Buffalo, 1984-90, Buffalo Pub. Sch. System, 1974—; mem. curriculum devel. com. Buffalo Pub. Schs., 1988, 92—; cooperating tchr. BRIET-U. Buffalo, 1990—; part-time tax acct. Vol., World Univ. Games, Buffalo, 1993. Mem. AAUP, Women Tchrs. Assn. (bd. dirs., v.p. 1993-94, pres. 1994—), Assn. Math. Tchrs. N.Y. State, Theodore Roosevelt Rough Riders, Nat. Coun. Math. Republican. Methodist. Home: 3015 Bender Ct Hamburg NY 14075-3401 Office: South Park High Sch 150 Southside Pkwy Buffalo NY 14220

OBERLY, KATHRYN ANNE, lawyer; b. Chgo., May 22, 1950; d. James Richard and Lucille Mary (Kraus) O.; m. Daniel Lee Goelzer, July 13, 1974 (div. Aug. 1987); 1 child, Michael W. Student, Vassar Coll., 1967-69; BA, U. Wis., 1971, JD, 1973. Bar: Wis. 1974, D.C. 1981. Law clk. U.S. Ct. Appeals, Omaha, 1973-74; trial atty. U.S. Dept. Justice, Washington, 1974-77, spl. asst., 1977-81, spl. litigation counsel, 1981-82, asst. to Solicitor Gen., 1982-86; ptnr. Mayer, Brown & Platt, Washington, 1986-91; assoc. gen. counsel Ernst & Young, Washington, 1991-94; corp. counsel Ernst & Young, New York, 1994—. Mem. ABA (environ. quality com. sect. on natural resources law), Wis. State Bar Assn., D.C. Bar Assn. Democrat. Office: Ernst & Young 277 Park Ave New York NY 10172-0002*

OBERMEYER, THERESA NANGLE, sociology educator; b. St. Louis, July 25, 1945; d. James Francis and Harriet Clare (Shafer) Nangle; m. Thomas S. Obermeyer, Dec. 23, 1977; children: Thomas Jr., James, Margaret and Matthew (twins). BA, Maryville U., St. Louis, 1967; MEd, St. Louis U., 1970, PhD, 1975. Lic. real estate broker. Dir. student activities Lindenwood Colls., St. Charles, Mo., 1969-70; asst. dean of students Loyola Coll., Balt., 1972-73; asst. dir. student activities St. Louis Community Coll., 1973-78; dir. student activities U. Alaska, Anchorage, 1978-79; instr. sociology Chapman U., Anchorage, 1980—; secondary tchr. McLaughlin Youth Ctr. for Juvenile Delinquents, 1984-90; elected Anchorage Sch. Bd., 1990-94. Contbr. articles to profl. jours. Mem. Anchorage Mcpl. Health Commn., 1980-81. Recipient NDEA scholarship, 1970-72, Title I Grant U. Md. and Loyola Coll., 1972-73, Fed. Women's Equity Act U.S. Dept. Edn. U. Alaska, 1978-79; named Fulbright fellow Project India, 1974, Project Jordan, 1977. Mem. DAR (bd. dirs. Anchorage chpt. 1979—), AAUW (bd. dirs Anchorage br. 1980-81), Am. Soc. Pub Adminstrn. (pres., bd. dirs. south cen. chpt. 1981). Home: 3000 Dartmouth Dr Anchorage AK 99508-4413

OBERNDORF, MEYERA E., mayor; m. Roger L. Oberndorf; children: Marcie, Heide. BS in Elem. Edn., Old Dominion U., 1964. Broadcaster Sta. WNIS, Norfolk, Va.; mem. city coun. City of Virginia Beach, Va., 1976—, vice-mayor, 1986, mayor, 1988—. Mem. exec. bd. Tidewater coun. Boys Scouts Am.; bd. dirs. Virginia Beach Pub. Libr., 1966-76, chmn. bd., 1967-76. Mem. AAUW, U.S. Conf. Mayors, Va. Mcpl. League (exec. bd.), Nat. League Cities (vice-chmn.), Princess Anne Women's Club. Jewish. Home: 5404 Challedon Dr Virginia Beach VA 23462-4112 Office: Office of the Mayor Municipal Ctr City Hall Bldg Virginia Beach VA 23456*

OBERSTAR, HELEN ELIZABETH, cosmetics company executive; b. Ottawa, Ill.; d. Milton Edward and Helen (Herrick) Weiss; m. Edward Charles Oberstar, Feb. 3, 1945 (dec. 1984). BS in Chemistry, Monmouth (Ill.) Coll., 1943; postgrad., Northwestern U., Chgo., 1947-49; LLD (hon.), Monmouth Coll., 1987. Asst. food technologist Standard Brands, Inc., Bklyn., 1943-45; chemist Miner Labs., Midwest div., Arthur D. Little, Chgo., 1946-50; rsch. chemist/rsch. supr. Toni Co., div. Gillette Co., Chgo., 1951-65; group leader rsch. and devel. Shulton, Inc., Clifton, N.J., 1965-72; sect. leader rsch. and devel. Am. Cyanamid, Clifton, 1972-75; mgr. rsch. and devel. Clairol Bristol Myers Internat., Stamford, Conn., 1975-82; dir. tech. Clairol Bristol Myers Squibb Consumer Products Group Internat., Stamford, 1982-93; dir. technology internat. group Clairol, Inc. divsn. Bristol-Myers Squibb, Stamford, 1993—. Patentee in field. Recipient Disting. Alumni award Monmouth Coll., 1986, Hall of Achievement award Monmouth Coll., 1995. Mem. Soc. Cosmetic Chemists (house chmn. 1963-64), Cosmetic Toiletries Fragrance Assn. (internat. com. 1985-95). Episcopalian. Home: 512 Belden Hill Rd Wilton CT 06897-4221 Office: Clairol Inc 2 Blachley Rd Stamford CT 06902-4149

OBERSTEIN, MARYDALE, geriatric specialist; b. Red Wing, Minn., Dec. 30; d. Dale Robert and Jean Ebba-Marie (Holmquist) Johnson; children: Kirk Robert, Mark Paul, MaryJean. Student, U. Oreg., 1961-62, Portland State U., 1962-64, Long Beach State U., 1974-76. Cert. geriatric specialist, Calif. Florist, owner Sunshine Flowers, Santa Ana, Calif., 1982—; pvt. duty nursing aide Aides in Action, Costa Mesa, Calif., 1985-87; owner, activity dir., adminstr. Lovelight Christian Home for the Elderly, Santa Ana, 1987—; activity dir. Bristol Care Nursing Home, Santa Ana, 1985-88; evangelist, speaker radio show Sta. KPRZ-FM, Anaheim, Calif., 1985-88; nursing home activist in reforming laws to eliminate bad homes, 1984-86; founder, tchr. hugging classes/laughter therapy terminally ill patients, 1987—; founder healing and touch therapy Slaughter Therapy, 1991-93; bd. dirs. Performing Arts Ctr.; speaker for enlightenment and healing. Author (rewrite) Title 22 Nursing Home Reform Law, Little Hoover Commn. Bd. dirs. Orange County Coun. on Aging, 1984—; chairperson Helping Hands, 1985—, Pat Robertson Com., 1988, George Bush Presdl. Campaign, Orange County, 1988; bd. dirs., v.p. Women Aglow Orange County, 1985—; evanglist, pub. speaker, v.p. Women Aglow Huntington Beach. Recipient Carnation Silver Bowl, Carnation Svc. Co., 1984-85; named Woman of Yr., Kiwanis, 1985, ABI, 1990, Am. Biog. Soc.; honored AM L.A. TV Show, Lt. Gov. McCarthy, 1984. Mem. Calif. Assn. Residential Care Homes, Orange County Epilepsy Soc. (bd. dirs. 1986—), Calif. Assn. Long Term Facilities. Home: 2722 S Diamond St Santa Ana CA 92704-6013

OBERT, MARLENE ANN, business educator; b. Ft. Branch, Ind., June 2, 1942; d. Clemens H. and Marie M. (Wulf) O. BA, U. Evansville, 1964; MS, Ind. U., 1966. Cert. tchr. secondary edn. Tchr. bus. South Gibson Sch. Corp., Ft. Branch, 1964—, chair dept., 1989—; bd. dirs. Farmers & Merchants Bank, Ft. Branch. Mem. AAUW (pres. 1988-90), Delta Pi Epsilon, Delta Kappa Gamma (state chair coms. 1990), Phi Delta Kappa. Democrat. Roman Catholic.

OBIANWU, MARIAN MARIE, nurse; b. Ft. Hood, Tex., May 1; d. William Edward and Elena (Brisco) Land; m. Anthony O. Obianwu; children from a previous marriage: DeFredrick Chrishane, La Tashea Ari, Roosevelt K.C. Grad. in Vocat. Nursing, Temple (Tex.) Jr. Coll., 1982; student, U. Mary Hardin-Baylor; ASN, McClellan C.C., 1988. RN, Tex.; lic. vocat. and psychiat. nurse; cert. psychiat. and mental health nurse. Vocat. respiratory and neurology nurse Scott & White Hosp., Temple, Tex., 1982-86, staff nurse oncology, 1986-87; staff nurse psychiatry Scott & White Hosp., Temple, 1987-89, John Peter Smith Hosp., Ft. Worth, Tex., 1989-91; program mgr. in adolescents John Peter Smith Hosp., Ft. Worth, 1991-94; nurse adult partial hospitalization program Trinity Springs Pavilion, Ft. Worth, 1994—. Mem. NAFE, Advocates of Adolescent and Child Psychiat. Nursing, Tex. Alliance for Mentally Ill. Baptist. Home: 4007 Rushmoor Dr Arlington TX 76016

O'BRIEN, ANNA BELLE CLEMENT, state senator; b. Scottsville, Ky.; d. Robert S. Clement; m. Charles H. O'Brien; 3 stepchildren. Student McMurry Coll., Abilene, Tex. Former mem. Tenn. Ho. of Reps.; mem. Tenn. State Senate, 1976—. Active Am. Legion Aux., Cumberland County Mental Health Assn., DAR, Cumberland County Beautiful Assn., Hosp. Aux.; adv. council Maccasin Bend Psychiat. Hosp., Chattanooga; bd. dirs. Plateau Mental Health Ctr., Cookeville, Tenn.; bd. dirs. Wharton Nursing Home, Cumberland County, Crossville C. of C. Mem. Bus. and Profl. Women's Club, Democratic Women's Club. Clubs: Top Town Garden, Marie Ervin Home Demonstration, Lake Tansi Village Women's. Baptist. Office: Tenn Senate State Capitol Office of House Mems Nashville TN 37219*

O'BRIEN, BETTY ALICE, theological librarian, researcher; b. Kingsburg, Calif., June 12, 1932; d. Robert Herbert and Alice Dorothy (Larson) Peterson; m. Elmer John O'Brien, July 2, 1966. AA, North Pk. Coll., 1952; diploma, North Pk. Theol. Sem., 1954; BA, Northwestern U., 1956; MLS, U. Calif., Berkeley, 1957. Asst. libr. North Pk. Theol. Sem., Chgo., 1957-69; libr. St. Leonard Coll., Dayton, Ohio, 1971-84; researcher United Theol. Sem., Dayton, 1986—, reference coord., 1991—. Editor: Religion Index 2: Festschriften 1960-69, 1980. Mem. Am. Theol. Libr. Assn. (bd. dirs. 1981-91, editor Summary Proc. 1982-91), Ohio Theol. Libr. Assn. (sec. 1972-76, chairperson 1978-79), Meth. Librs. Fellowship (v.p. 1989-91, pres. 1991-93). Mem. United Meth. Ch. Office: United Theol Sem 1810 Harvard Blvd Dayton OH 45406-4539

O'BRIEN, CAROL JEAN, municipal parks administrator; b. Chgo., June 18, 1939; d. Charles August and Frances Carolyn (Reese) Boeck; m. Thomas Joseph McEvoy, Oct. 18, 1958 (div. Mar. 1982); 1 child, Corrine Marie McEvoy; John Patrick O'Brien, July 18, 1985 (div. Mar. 1988). Grad. high sch., Maywood, Ill., 1957. Cert. leisure profl. Mfrs. rep. Midwest Cen., Chgo., 1969-71; supt. recreation Wood Dale (Ill.) Park Dist., 1977-87, bus. mgr., 1988-89, exec. dir. parks and recreation, 1989—; Medinah Park Dist. commr., 1991—. Mem. Nat. Parks and Recreation Assn., Suburban Parks and Recreation Assn. (chairperson 1983-85, sec. 1985-86, spl. projects com. 1986-87), Ill. Parks and Recreation Assn., Wood Dale C. of C. (dir. and sec. 1989-92). Lutheran. Office: Wood Dale Park Dist 533 N Wood Dale Rd Wood Dale IL 60191-1535

O'BRIEN, CATHERINE LOUISE, museum administrator; b. N.Y.C., July 21, 1930; d. Edward Denmark and Catherine Louise (Browne) O'B.; m. Philip R. James (div.); m. Sterling Noel (div.). B.A., Finch Coll., N.Y.C.; postgrad. Williams Coll., Williamstown, Mass., Marymount Coll. Reprodn. mgr. Met. Mus. Art, N.Y.C., 1975—; dir. sales Simon Pearce Gallery, N.Y.C. Exhibited in group shows at Parrish Art Mus., Southampton, N.Y., 1965-70, Met. Mus. Art, N.Y.C., 1975-85, Guild Hall Exhibit, East Hampton, N.Y., 1965-85. Mem. aux. Southampton Hosp., 1970-85; founder East Hampton Horse Show, Ladies Village Improvement Soc., East Hampton, 1970—; mem. fair coms. St. James Ch., N.Y.C., St. Luke's Ch., East Hampton, 1970-85; mem. alumnae adv. bd. Marymount Coll., N.Y.C., 1984-86, chmn. alumnae event, 1994; mem. Women's Nat. Rep. Club, N.Y.C.; chmn. Landmark and Tree Planting Com. For Madison Ave. Assn., N.Y.C., 1994—. Mem. DAR (vice regent East Hampton chpt. 1974-85), Colonial Dames Am. (archives com. 1980-85), Daus. Brit. Empire (historian 1978-85), United Daus. Confederacy (state historian 1970-85), Daus. Colonial Wars (corr. sec. 1983-85), Sons and Daus. of the Pilgrims (corr. sec. 1983-85), Victorian Soc., Soc. Mayflower Descs. (life), English Speaking Union, New Eng. Soc. (mem. ball com. 1983-86), Daus. of Cin. (historian 1979-85), Squadron "A". Republican. Episcopalian. Clubs: Devon Yacht, Maidstone (East Hampton, N.Y.); Southampton Yacht (N.Y.); Metropolitan (N.Y.C.) (women's com., chmn. debutante ball 1980-84); Reciprocal/India House, St. Anthony Union League (N.Y.C.). Avocations: show horses; dogs. Home: 605 Park Ave New York NY 10021-7016 Office: Met Mus Art Fifth Ave New York NY 10028 also: Simon Pearce Gallery 500 Park Ave New York NY 10022

O'BRIEN, HELEN ANDERSON, health services administrator; b. Worcester, Mass., Apr. 19, 1934; d. Albert and Mary Ellen (Connor) Anderson; m. Charles Gerald O'Brien, Jan. 24, 1955 (div. Apr. 1977); children: Mark, Karen O'Brien Tomko. Diploma in nursing, Mass. Gen. Hosp., Boston, 1956; BSN, Western Conn. State U., 1977; MPH with acad. honors, Yale U., 1979. RN, N.Y., Ohio, Mass., Conn. Nurse, charge nurse various locations, 1960-64; chmn. publicity and community edn. Wausau (Wis.) Hosp., 1966-69; adminstrv. resident Danbury (Conn.) Health Dept., 1978; health svcs. cons., Darien, 1979; pres., CEO, Stratford (Conn.) Vis. Nurse Assn., Inc., 1980—; presenter in field. Mem. Needs of Elderly Commn., Stratford, 1980-87; founder Hospice Program Greater Bridgeport, Conn., 1981—; vol. domestic violence and rape counselor YWCA, Bridgeport, 1990—. Fellow Yale U., 1977-79. Mem. APHA, Am. Mgmt. Assn., Conn. Pub. Health Assn. (bd. dirs. 1980-86), Yale Hosp. Adminstrv. Alumni Assn., Nat. League for Nursing, Assn. Yale Alumni in Pub. Health. Home: 129 Gallows Hill Rd West Redding CT 06896 Office: Stratford Vis Nurse Assn 88 Ryders Landing Stratford CT 06497

O'BRIEN, JANE MARGARET, academic administrator; b. Washington, Nov. 17, 1953; d. Thomas and Edith (Pedersen) O'B; m. James A. Grube, Jan 28, 1975; children: William Howard Grube-O'Brien, Harold Thomas Grube O'Brien. BS in Biochemistry, Vassar Coll., 1975; PhD in Chemistry, U. Del., 1981. Rsch. asst. U. Vt., Burlington, 1978-79; asst. prof. chemistry Middlebury (Vt.) Coll., 1980-88, assoc. provost, 1988-89, assoc. prof. chemistry, 1988-91, dean of faculty, 1989-91; pres. Hollins Coll., Roanoke, Va., 1991—; ednl. chmn. biology task force New Eng. Consortium Undergraduate Sci., 1988-91; project mgr. H. Hughes Med. Inst. Instl. Awards, 1988-91; mem. steering com. Sloan New Liberal Arts Initiative, 1988-91. Implementation com. Vermont EPSCoR, 1989-91; bd. dirs. Coun. Ind. Colls. in Va., 1991—, Va. Found. for Ind. Colls., 1991—; ednl. adv. com. Rainforest All, 1991—. Grad. fellow U. Del., 1975-76, Kellogg fellow W.K. Kellogg Found., 1989-92, Internat. fellow Assoc. Am. Colls., 1990-91, Regional fellow finalist White House Fellowship, 1991. Home: PO Box 9625 Roanoke VA 24020 Office: Hollins Coll Office of the President Hollins College VA 24020*

O'BRIEN, JANET W., state legislator; m. John F. O'Brien; 4 children. BA, Tufts U.; MPA, Harvard U. Mem. Mass. Ho. of Reps.; team mediator Mass. joint labor mgmt. com., 1976-79; mem. Munic adv. bd. Mass. Dept. Personnel Adminstrn., 1984-90; coord. Cleanup North and South Rivers, 1985-89; mem. spl. legis. com. on collective bargaining and dispute resolution, 1985-90, cert. dist. ct. mediator, 1989—. Mem. Hanover Planning Bd., 1974-77; chair Hanover Growth Policy Com., 1976-79, Hanover Bd. Selectmen, 1977-79. Democrat. Home: 128 Washington St Hanover MA 02339-2340 Office: Mass Ho of Reps State Capitol Boston MA 02133*

O'BRIEN, KAREN MARIE, lawyer; b. Syracuse, N.Y., Dec. 7, 1958; d. Nathan Anthony and Barbara Ann (Smith) Marra; m. Michael Dennis O'Brien, Oct. 15, 1983; children: Michael Dennis, John Nathan. BA in Polit. Sci. and Econs., SUNY, Geneseo, 1980; JD, Syracuse U., 1982. Assoc. Dibble & Wright, Rochester, N.Y., 1982-84, Joseph, Greenwald & Laake, Hyattsville, Md., 1984-86; supervising atty. SEC, Washington, 1986-90; gen. counsel N.Am. Securities Adminstrs. Assn., Washington, 1990—. Mem. ABA (subcom. state regulation of securities, com. non-pub. and small bus. offerings). Office: NAm Securities Adminstrs Assn One Massachusetts Ave NW Ste 310 Washington DC 20001

O'BRIEN, KATHLEEN ANNE, special education educator; b. Toledo, Jan. 18, 1952; d. Robert Eugene and Livia Josephine (Marini) O'B. BS of Edn., Bowling Green State U., 1974; MEd, U. Tex., 1981. Cert. elem. edn., mental retardation, visually impaired, physically impaired, early childhood and adminstrn. and supervision. Tchr. pre-sch. handicapped Okeechobee (Fla.) Sch. Bd., 1974-76; tchr. visually impaired Manatee County Sch. Sys., Bradenton, Fla., 1981-82; tchr. varying exceptionalities Sarasota (Fla.) County Sch. Sys., 1976-80, tchr. presch. handicapped, 1982—; selected mem. steering com. Tchr. of Visually Handicapped for State of Fla., Tallahassee, 1978-80; selected mem. Validation Team for State Career Ladder Exam., Tallahassee,

1987; guest lectr. U. South Fla., Sarasota, 1979; presenter conf. for visually impaired presch. children, Tampa, Fla., 1984. Mem. adv. bd. Prevention of Blindness, Sarasota, 1978-81; bd. dirs. Planned Parenthood, Sarasota, 1983-84, United Cerebral Palsy, Sarasota, 1984-94; dir. Jr. League, Sarasota, 1993—. Mem. Fla. Developmental Disabilities (bd. dirs. 1989—, planning coun./gov. appointment), Fla. Assn. for Edn. and Rehab. (pres.-elect, pres. 1988—), State of Fla. Pilot Women Svc. Orgn. (Woman of Yr. 1990). Home: 107 Whispering Sands Cir Sarasota FL 34242-1624

O'BRIEN, KATHRYN DAWN, screenwriter; b. Montreal, Que., Can., Feb. 6, 1958; came to U.S., 1990; d. John Joseph and Lillian Ada (Rogers) O'B. Student, Concordia U., Montreal, Vanier Coll., Montreal. Stage mgr. Showplace Dinner Theatre, Toronto, Ont., Can., 1981-86; talent agt. Talent House, Inc., Toronto, 1986-91; freelance writer L.A., 1991—; entertainment editor, film critic Snowdon Press, Montreal, 1975-78; freelance writer Cinema Can., Montreal, 1977; coord. drama festival Montreal Cath. Sch. Commn., 1980; camera dir. Graham Cable, Toronto, 1983. Author: (TV pilot) 'Till Death Do Us Part, 1978, (plays) The Affair, 1982, Four Play, 1984, (screenplay) In Some Circles, 1993. Vol. Meals on Wheels, Toronto, 1984, Care Ring, Toronto, 1984-85.

O'BRIEN, LEANNE DOROTHY, occupational therapist; b. Prairie du Chien, Wis., July 5, 1963; d. Elmer Lawrence and Carol Yvonne (Heins) Marting; m. Jeffrey Scott O'Brien, Sept. 15, 1990; children: Eryn Lorene, Emily Anne. AA, North Iowa Area C.C., 1983; A in Applied Sci., Kirkwood C.C., 1985; BS, U. Kans., 1989; postgrad., U. Iowa, 1991—. Registered occupational therapist; cert. neuro-devel. treatment therapist. Occupational therapy asst. Faribault (Minn.) Regional Ctr., 1985-86, Truman Med. Ctr., Kansas City, Mo., 1986-88; home health occupational therapist Pinnacle Rehab. Inc., Wichita, Kans., 1989-90; supr. St. Luke's Hops., Cedar Rapids, Iowa, 1992-94, mgr. occupational therapy, 1994—; occupational therapist VHI Health Enterprises, Cedar Rapids, 1994—; instr., lectr. in field, 1990—. Vol. First Luth. Ch., Cedar Rapids, 1990—. Mem. Am. Occupational Therapy Assn., Iowa Occupational Therapy Assn. (chair dist. IV 1985—), Elmcrest Country Club. Republican. Home: 3607 Wenig Rd NE Cedar Rapids IA 52402 Office: St Lukes Hosp 1026 A Ave NE Cedar Rapids IA 52406-3026

O'BRIEN, LIBBY ATKINS, public relations executive; b. N.Y.C., Mar. 17, 1913; d. Richard Travis and Alice Gordon (Quigley) Atkins; grad. Kendall Hall, 1931; m. Richard Thomas O'Brien, June 25, 1935 (dec.); children: Francis DeSales, Sarah Jane O'Brien Prezalor. Car rep. Brady Stannard Motors, Brewster, N.Y., Blanchard Motors, Greenwich, Conn., and Tolm Motors, Darren, Conn., 1940-46; producer TV show Libby O'Brien's Table Toppers, 1946-48; commentator, dir. women's programs WLAD, Danbury, Conn., 1948-51, WSTC, Stamford, Conn., 1951-53; asst. dir. public relations Save the Children Fedn., 1954-55; advt. mgr. Roux Distbg. Corp., 1956-57; public relations mgr. Lily Tulip Cup Corp., 1957-64; owner, mgr. Libby O'Brien Enterprises, Inc., 1964-69; owner, breeder, exporter O'Brien Donkey Farm, promoter of tourism in Kenmare, Ireland, 1969-76; sales person, Chatham, Mass., 1976—; book collaborator; active Utilizing Sr. Energy, Know Your Body-Am. Health Orgn.; publicity chmn. Greenwich Meals on Wheels. Collector, seller old N.Y.C. st. signs; exhibited yarn art in singles shows on the Cape and in Newport, R.I.; shows creating new folk art medium on wire mesh, multi-medium, three-dimensional art works, Mass., R.I., & Conn.; exhibited in group show at R.I. Coun. for the Arts, Warwick Mus., 1990; writing and editing biog. novel on Life in Ireland. Mem. Am. Women in Radio and TV, Public Relations Assn., Public Relations Inst. U.K. Republican. Avocation: creating and showing folk art. Home: 35 Hallett Ln Chatham MA 02633

O'BRIEN, MARGARET HOFFMAN, educator; b. Melrose, Mass., Aug. 22, 1947; d. John Francis and Margaret Mary (Colbert) Hoffman; m. Edward Lee O'Brien, June 13, 1970 (div. Sept. 1988); children: John Hoffman, Elizabeth Lee; m. Michael Ellis-Tolaydo, Mar. 9, 1991. AB, Trinity Coll., Washington, 1969; MA, Cath. U., 1971; PhD, Am. U., 1993; LHD, Georgetown U., 1991; LHD (hon.), Trinity Coll., 1994. English tchr. D.C. Pub. Schs., Washington, 1969-73; edn. coord. Street Law, Georgetown Law Ctr., Washington, 1973-75; owner, mgr. Man in the Green Hat Restaurant, Washington, 1976-81; head of edn. Folger Shakespeare Libr., Washington, 1981-94; dir. Teaching Shakespeare Inst., Washington, 1983-94; dir. edn. programs Corp. for Pub. Broadcasting, Washington, 1994—; mem. faculty Prince of Wales Shakespeare Sch., Stratford on Avon, Eng., 1993; edn. dir. Fairfax (Va.) Family Theatre, 1988-93, Md. Shakespeare Festival, St. Mary's City, 1988-91; head of faculty Atlantic Shakespeare Inst., Wroxton, U.K., 1985-90. Gen. editor: Shakespeare Set Free, 1993. Bd. dirs. Edmund Burke Sch., Washington, 1993—, Capitol Hill Day Sch., 1994—, Fillmore Arts Ctr., Washington, 1991-93, Capitol Hill Arts Workshop, Washington, 1989-91, Horizons Theatre, 1991, Janice F. Delaney Found., 1991—, Hartke Theatre, 1989-90; mem. nat. adv. coun. Nat. Diffusion Network, Washington, 1989-91; site visitor U.S. Dept. Edn., Washington, 1990; mem. nat. adv. bd. Orlando Shakespeare Festival, 1990-93. Mem. English Speaking Union (excellence in English com. 1989-91), Shakespeare Assn. Am., Nat.Coun. Tchrs. English. Office: Corp for Pub Broadcasting 901 E St NW Washington DC 20004-2037

O'BRIEN, MARGARET J., community health nurse; b. N.Y.C., Dec. 5, 1918; d. John J. and Nellie (Coyle) O'B. BS, St.John's U., 1954, MS, 1962; MPH, Columbia U., 1964. With Health Dept., City of New York, 1943-81, assoc. dir. Bur. Pub. Health Nursing, dir. Pub. Health Nursing Svc., asst. commr. pyb. health nursing. Contbr. articles to profl. jours. Named Outstanding alumnae Columbia U. Sch. Pub. Health, 1994. Mem. ANA, APHA, NLN, N.Y. State Nurses Assn., N.Y.C. Pub. Health Assn. Home: 11055 72nd Rd Forest Hills NY 11375

O'BRIEN, MARY DEVON, communications executive, consultant; b. Buenos Aires, Argentina, Feb. 13, 1944; came to U.S., 1949, naturalized, 1962; d. George Earle and Margaret Frances (Richards) Owen; m. Gordon Covert O'Brien, Feb. 16, 1962 (div. Aug. 1982); children: Christopher Covert, Devon Elizabeth; m. Christopher Gerard Smith, May 28, 1983. BA, Rutgers U., 1975, MBA, 1976. Contr. manpower Def. Comm. divsn. ITT, Nutley, N.J., 1977-80, adminstr. program, 1977-78, mgr. cost, schedule control, 1978-79, voice processing project, 1979-80; mgr. project Avionics divsn. ITT, Nutley, 1980-81, sr. mgr. projects, 1981-93, cons. strategic planning, 1983—; pres. Anamex, Inc.; bd. trustees South Mountain Counseling Ctr., 1987—, chmn. bd. trustees, 1994—; bd. dirs. N.J. Eye Inst.; session leader Internet Conf., Florence, Italy, 1992; session moderator, panel mem. MES Conf., Cairo, Egypt, 1993; lectr. in field. Author: Pace: System Manual, 1979, Voices, 1982; contbr. articles to profl. jours. and Maplewood Community calendar. Chmn. Citizens Budget Adv. Com., Maplewood, N.J., 1984-87, chmn. recreation, libr., pub. svcs., 1982-83, chmn. pub. safety, emergency svcs., 1983-84, chmn. schs. and edn., 1984-85; bd. trustees United Way Essex and West Hudson Community Svc. Coun., 1988—; first v.p. Maplewood Civic Assn., 1987-89, pres., 1989-91, sec. 1993-94, bd. dirs., officer, 1984—; chmn. Maple Leaf Svc. award Com., 1987-89, 94—, Community Svc. Coun. of Oranges and Maplewood Homelessness, Affordable Housing, Shelter Com., 1988—; chmn. speaker's bur. United Way, 1989-93; v.p. mktg. United Way Community Svc. Coun. of Orange and Maplewood, 1990-93; mem. Maplewood Zoning Bd. of Adjustment, 1983—; officer, mem. exec. bd. N.J. Project Mgmt. Inst., 1985—, pres., 1987-88, v.p. adminstrn., 1994—; bd. dirs. Performance Mgmt. Assn.; chmn. Charter Com.; chmn. Internat. Project Mgmt. Inst. Jour. and Membership survey, 1986-87, mktg. com., 1986-89, long range planning and steering com., 1987—; bd. dirs., vice chmn. Coun. Chpt. Pres. Interaction Com., 1986-90, chmn., 1991—, pres. Internat. Project Mgmt. Inst., 1991, chmn., 1992, v.p. Region II, 1989-90; adv. bd. Project Mgmt. Jour., 1987-90, N.J. PMI Ednl., 1987—; liaison officer; apptd. fellow Leadership N.J., 1993—, Internat. Project Mgmt. Inst. and Performance Mgmt. Assocs.; mem. MCA/N.J. Blood Bank Drive; chmn. Maplewood Community Calendar, 1990—; trustee community svc. coun. and edn. program United Way Essex and West Hudson, 1988—, also, chmn. leadership div., chmn. speakers bur., 1991— and mem. communications com., v.p. mktg. community svc. coun., Oranges and Maplewood, 1991-93. Recipient Spl. commendation for Community Svc. Twp. Maplewood, 1987; First Place award Anti-Shoplifting Program for Distributive Edn. Club Am., 1981, N.J. Fedn. of Women's Clubs, 1981, 82, Retail Mchts. Assn., 1981, 82; Commendation and Merit awards Air Force Inst. Tech., 1981; Pres.'s Safety award ITT, 1983; State award 1st Pl. N.J. Fedn. of Women's Clubs Garden Show, 1982, Outstanding Pres. award Internat. Project Mgmt. Inst., 1988, Outstanding Svc. and Contbrn. award 1986-87; Cert. Spl. Merit award N.J. Fedn. of Women's Clubs, 1982, Disting. Contbn. award United Way, 1990, Pursuit of Exellence Cost Savings Achievement award ITT Avionics, 1990, Meritorious Svc. Recognition award Internat. Project Mgmt. Inst., 1989-90, Maple Leaf award for outstanding community svc., 1992, Phoebe and Benjamin Shackelford award United Way, 1992, U.S. Ho. Reps. citation, 1992, N.H. Gen. Assembly Senate resolution for Community Leadership and Svc., 1992, resolution of Appreciation Township of Maplewood; N.J. Leadership fellow, 1993. Mem. Internat. Platform Speakers Assn., Grand Jury Assn., Telecommunications Group and Aerospace Industries Assn., Women's Career Network Assn., Nat. Security Indsl. Assn., Assn. for Info. and Image Mgmt., Internat. Project Mgmt. Inst. (liaison officerpres. 1991—), Performance Mgmt. Assn, ITT Mgmt. Assn., NAFE, Rutger's Gr. Alumni Assn., Maplewood LWV (chair women and family issues com., bd. dirs.), Maplewood Women's Evening Membership Div. (pres. 1980-82), Lions (Maplewood dir. 1992-95, program chmn. 1991-92, treas. 1994-95, N.J. dist. 16E zone chmn. 1992-93, cabinet sec. internat. dist., region chmn. 1993-94, trustee Eye Bank N.J., internat. dist. 16-E cabinet sec. 1994-95). Home: 594 Valley St Maplewood NJ 07040-2616 Office: Ste 152 21 Madison Plaza Madison NJ 07940

O'BRIEN, MAUREEN SARAH, special education educator, speech pathologist; b. Hazelton, Pa., June 10, 1941; d. Hugh Vincent and Inez Marie (O'Donnell) O'Donnell: m. Gerald Francis O'Brien, Aug. 17, 1968; children: Erin Marie, Terence Sean. BS, Pa. State U., 1962, MEd, 1964; PhD in Spl. Edn., U. Md., 1987. Speech-lang. pathologist pvt. practice, Laurel, Md., 1969-75, Md. Sch. for Deaf, Columbia, 1975-77; instr. Western Md. Coll., Westminister, 1977-78; cons. Portney & Assocs. Inc., Alexandria, Va., 1980; grad. asst. in spl. edn. U. Md., College Park, 1980-87, coord. rsch. projects in spl. edn., 1987-89; comm. coord. Nat. Inst. Deafness and Other Comm. Disorders Clearinghouse, 1991-93. Mem. Am. Speech, Lang., Hearing Assn. (cert. clin. competence in speech pathology), Coun. for Exceptional Children, Md. Speech, Lang., Hearing Assn., 1968—. Home: 16103 Kenny Ct Laurel MD 20707-2624

O'BRIEN, PATRICIA NEVIN, computer scientist; b. Hanover, Pa., June 13, 1957; d. Malcolm Hugh and Lida Mae (Smith) Nevin; m. Thomas Gerard O'Brien, May 2, 1981; children: Thomas Joseph, Karen Louise. BS in Psychology, Towson State U., 1978, MA, 1980. Rsch. asst. Johns Hopkins U., Balt., 1980-82; programmer-analyst Johns Hopkins U., Towson, Md., 1982; ops. rsch. analyst U.S. Army, Aberdeen, Md., 1983-84, 86-87; officer BDM Corp., Albuquerque, 1984-85; pres. Maverick, Inc., Albuquerque, 1985-86; chief analysis div. Def. Test and Evaluation Support Agy., Albuquerque, 1987-89; ops. rsch. analyst Operational Test and Evaluation Ctr. USAF, Albuquerque, 1989—. Mem. Am. Soc. for Quality Control. Home: PO Box 1060 Tijeras NM 87059-1060 Office: 8500 Gibson Blvd SE Kirtland A F B NM 87117-5544

O'BRIEN JABLONSKI, ROMAINE M., nursing educator; b. Chgo., Aug. 8, 1936; d. John Matthew and Alvina Ann (Schmautz) O'B; m. Daniel Jablonski, May 23, 1993. Diploma, Oak Park Sch. Nursing, 1967; BA in Psychology, De Paul U., Chgo., 1974; BHS, Governors State U., 1977, MSN, 1980. RN. Coord. practical nurse program Thornton Community Coll., South Holland, Ill.; instr. nursing St. Xavier Coll., Chgo.; staff devel. coord. Americana Health Care Ctr., Westmont, Ill.; instr. Oak Forest (Ill.) Hosp.; speaker in field. Eucharistic min. local Roman Catholic Ch., 1985-88, instr. CCD, 1983-85, mem. ministry of care com.; regional pres. Ill.-Ind. Slovenian Women's Union, 1992—. Mem. ANA, Nat. League for Nursing (membership com. 1989-90), Ill. Nurses Assn. (sec. 1981-83, bd. dirs. 1983-85, 89-91, 91—, scholarship com. 1991), Am. Diabetic Assn., Bus. and Profl. Women's Club (del. 1981, 83, 85, 86, scholarship chmn. 1985-86, treas. local dist. 1985-86, rec. sec. 1986-87, chmn. pub. rels. 1987-88, numerous positions, Woman of Yr. 1982, Woman of Achievement 1982), Sigma Theta Tau (Excellence in Edn. award 1991, heritage com. Omicron chpt. 1992), Psi Chi. Home: 7345 W Tiffany Dr Orland Park IL 60462-5203

OBRIG, ALICE MARIE, nursing educator; b. Bklyn., Apr. 1, 1939; d. Gordon A. and Virginia (Morgan) O.; BSN, Cornell U., 1961; MS, Boston U., 1967; MPH, John Hopkins U., 1969; EdD, Tchrs. Coll., Columbia U., 1987. Asst. head nurse N.Y. Hosp., N.Y.C., 1961-62; pub. health nurse N.Y.C. Vis. Nurses, 1962-63; instr. Russell Sage Coll., Troy, N.Y., 1969-72, Yale U., New Haven, 1969-72; asst. prof. Fairfield U., Conn., 1973—; cons. and lectr. in field.; contbr. chpt. to book. Mem. APHA, Am. Coll. Nurse Midwives, Nat. League for Nursing, Conn. Pub. Health Assn., Cornell U.-N.Y. Hosp. SON Alumnae Assn. (sec.), Sigma Theta Tau, Delta Kappa Gamma (mem. nominating com., alpha kappa state). Episcopalian. Home: 50 Lafayette Pl Greenwich CT 06830 Office: Fairfield U N Benson Rd Fairfield CT 06430

OBRINSKI, VIRGINIA WALLIN, retired school psychologist; b. Stanton, Iowa, Sept. 4, 1915; d. John Edward Wallace and Frances Geraldine (Tinsley) Wallin; m. Peter James Obrinski, May 2, 1981 (dec. Mar. 26, 1989). BA, U. Del., 1936; MEd, Duke U., 1941. Lic. psychologist, Del. Sch. psychologist Del. Dept. Pub. Instrn., Dover, 1936-64, various suburban sch. dists., Wilmington, Del., 1964-67, Mt. Pleasant (Del.) Sch. Dist., 1967-68, Stanton (Del.) Sch. Dist., 1968-69, Conrad (Del.) Area Sch. Dist., 1969-78; ret., 1978. Recipient plaque Del. Coun. for Exceptional Children Fedn., 1985. Mem. AAUW, APA, DAR, Del. Psychol. Assn., Coun. for Exceptional Children. Baptist. Home: 102 Westminister Dr Dover DE 19904-8716

O'BROCHTA-WOODWARD, RUBY CATHERINE, orthopedic nurse; b. Waynesburg, Pa., Aug. 9, 1953; d. Thomas Anthony and Betty Lou (Clark) O'Brochta; m. F. Kelley Woodward, July 6, 1985; 1 child, Jesse Thomas Woodward. BSN, U. Pitts., 1975. Cert. orthopaedic nurse. Staff/charge nurse, instr., head nurse Children's Hosp. Pitts., 1975-82; orthopaedic clinician, nursing supr. Oakland Orthopaedic Assocs., 1982-84; orthopaedic clinician John Winter, MD and Thomas Gasser, MD, Cheyenne, Wyo., 1984-90; nurse clinician, orthopaedic coding specialist Orthopaedic Assocs. Ltd., Edina, Minn., 1990-93; orthopaedic nurse clinician Minn. Orthopaedic Foot & Ankle Ctr., 1993—. Mem. ANA, Nat. Assn. Orthopaedic Nurses (cert., past com.), Nat. Assn. Physicians Nurses, Minn. Soc. Orthopaedic Physician Assts. Home: 5797 Fulbright Circle SE Prior Lake MN 55372-1941

O'BRYON, LINDA ELIZABETH, television station executive; b. Washington, Sept. 1, 1949; d. Walter Mason Ormes and Iva Genevieve (Batrus) Ranney; m. Dennis Michael O'Bryon, Sept. 8, 1973; 1 child, Jennifer Elizabeth. BA in Journalism cum laude, U. Miami, Coral Gables, Fla. News reporter Sta. KTVX, Salt Lake City, 1971-73; documentary and pub. affairs producer Sta. WPLG-TV, Miami, Fla., 1974-76; producer, reporter, anchor, news dir. then v.p. for news and pub. affairs, exec. editor, sr. v.p. The Nightly Business Report Sta. WPBT-TV (PBS), Miami, 1976—. Recipient award Fla. Bar, Tallahasse, 1977, 2 awards Ohio State U., 1976, 79, local Emmy award So. Fla. chpt. Nat. Acad. TV Arts and Scis., 1978, award Corp. for Pub. Broadcasting, 1978, Econ. Understanding award Amos Tuck Sch. Bus. Dartmouth Coll., Hanover, N.H., 1980, award Fla. AP, 1981, 1st prize Nat. Assn. Rea Hors, 1986, Bus. News Luminary award Bus. journalism Rev., 1990. Mem. Nat. Acad. TV Arts and Scis. (former So. Fla. bd. dirs.), Radio-TV News Dirs. Assn., Sigma Delta Chi. Republican. Roman Catholic. Office: Sta WPBT 14901 NE 20th Ave Miami FL 33181-1121

OBST, LYNDA ROSEN, film company executive, producer, screenwriter; b. N.Y.C., Apr. 14, 1950; d. Robert A. and Claire (Shenker) Rosen; m. David Obst (div.); 1 child, Oliver. BA, Pomona Coll., 1972; degree in philosophy, Columbia U., 1974. Editor Rolling Stone History of 60's, N.Y.C., 1974-76, New York Times mag., N.Y.C., 1976-79; exec. Polygram Pictures, Los Angeles, 1979-81, Geffen Films, Los Angeles, 1981-83; co-producer Paramount Pictures, Los Angeles, 1983-85, Disney Pictures, Los Angeles, 1986—. assoc. prodr. Flashdance, 1983; co-prodr. Adventures in Babysitting, 1987, Heartbreak Hotel, 1988; prodr. The Fisher King, 1991, This is My Life, 1992; exec. prodr. Sleepless in Seattle, 1993, Bad Girls, 1994; contbr. articles to mags. Mem. Writers Guild Am. Office: Lynda Obst Prodns care 20th Century Fox 10201 W Pico Blvd Los Angeles CA 90035*

O'CALLAGHAN, AILEEN, management consultant; b. N.Y.C., Mar. 2, 1947; d. Patrick F. and Catherine (Gallagher) O'C.; m. Norman R. Lange, Apr. 4, 1987. BA, SUNY, New Paltz, 1968. Pers. officer Citicorp, N.Y.C., 1968-75; sr. cons. Hay Group, Phila., 1975—. Office: Hay Group 229 S 18th St Philadelphia PA 19103-6144

O'CALLAGHAN, PATTI LOUISE, court program administrator; b. Bklyn., Mar. 26, 1953; d. Cornelius Leo and Louise Patricia (Casey) O'C.; m. Mark A. Diekman, Dec. 17, 1977; children: Casey, Brian. BA in Biology, NYU, 1975; MS in Physiology, Colo. State U., 1983. Cert. in program adminstrn. Grad. asst. Colo. State U., Ft. Collins, 1975-78; rsch. technician Iowa State U., Ames, 1978-80; counselor trainer Tecumseh Planned Parenthood, Lafayette, Ind., 1985; program coord. Date-rape Awareness and Edn., Lafayette, 1986-89; dir. Tippecanoe Ct. Apptd. Spl. Advocates, Lafayette, 1989—; mem. adv. commn. Ind. State Supreme Ct., Indpls., 1992—. Editor tng. manuals; contbr. articles to profl. jours. Mem. adv. com. Jour. and Courier, Lafayette, 1992-93; vol. adv. Urban Ministries Homeless Shelter, Lafayette, 1992-93; coach Tippecanoe Soccer Assn., West Lafayette, Ind., 1989—; sec., v.p., pres. West Lafayette Sch. Bd., 1988—. D.A.T.E. grantee Ind. Bd. Health, 1988; named Ind. Child Adv. of Yr., 1992. Mem. Ind. Chpt. for Prevention of Child Abuse, Ind. Advs. for Children (program com. 1991-92), Ind. Sch. Bd. Assn. (legis. com. 1991-92), Ctrl. Ind. Assn. Vol. Adminstrs., Assn. of Women in Sci., Nat. Ct.Apptd. Spl. Adv. Assn., West Lafayette Swim Club (v.p. 1989-92). Democrat. Christian. Home: 927 N Salisbury St West Lafayette IN 47906-2717 Office: Tippecanoe CASA Tippecanoe Superior Ct 3 County Courthouse Lafayette IN 47901

OCCELLI DE SALINAS DE GORTARI, YOLANDA CECILIA, wife of president of Mexico; m. Carlos Salinas de Gortari; children: Cecilia, Emiliano, Juan Cristobal. Address: Residencia Oficial de Los Pinos, Delegación Miguel Hidalgo, 11850 Mexico City Mexico

OCCHIUZZO, LUCIA RAJSZEL, restaurant executive; b. Casablanca, Morocco, Nov. 5, 1951; came to U.S., 1958, naturalized, 1973; d. Tadeusz Joseph and Irmina Elizabeth (Wacholska) Rajszel; m. Joel Occhiuzzo, Dec. 9, 1976. BA, Montclair U., 1974. Owner, pres. Mr. O's, Dallas, 1977-83, L n J's Restaurant & Club, Richardson, Tex., 1984—. Guest star Sta. Telecable TV, 1985; L n J's Restaurant subject of TV program, 1986; contbr. articles to newspapers. Recipient Restaurant of Month award Dallas Times Herald, 1978. Mem. Richardson C. of C., ASCAP. Republican. Roman Catholic. Avocations: music, photography, writing. Home: 156 Hidden Cir Richardson TX 75081-3909 Office: L 'n J's Restaurant & Club 2475 Promenade Ctr Richardson TX 75080-5426

OCHMAN, B. L., public relations executive, writer; b. N.Y.C., Mar. 13, 1949; d. Reuben and Dorothy (Bussel) Friedman. B.A. in Journalism, U. Bridgeport (Conn.), 1968. Account exec. Leo Miller Assocs., Westport, Conn., 1968-74; pub. relations dir. M. Hohner Inc., L.I., N.Y., 1974-76; editorial dir. Ruder & Finn Pub. Relations, N.Y.C., 1976-78; account supr. Ben Kubasik Pub. Relations, N.Y.C., 1978-79; pres. Rent-A-Kvetch, Inc., N.Y.C., 1979—; pres. B.L. Ochman Pub. Relations, N.Y.C., 1979—. Mem. N.Y. C. of C., Pub. Relations Soc. Am., N.Y. Assn. Women Bus. Owners. Democrat. Office: 594 Broadway Rm 809 New York NY 10012-3257

OCHSNER, KAREN THERESA, merchandise planner; b. Madison, Wis., Oct. 12, 1965; d. Jule Lou and Sharron Theresa (Dunphy) G. BBA, U. Wis., 1987. Exec. trainee Famous Barr, St. Louis, 1988, sales mgr., 1988-89, asst. buyer, 1989-90, distbn. coord., 1990-92, planning analyst, 1992, svc. ctr. mgr., 1992-93; merchandising analyst Current, Inc., Colorado Springs, Colo., 1994, merchandise planner, 1994—. Mem. U. Wis. Alumni Assn. (bd. dirs. 1990-93). Home: 4634 Chicory Ct Colorado Springs CO 80917

O'CONNELL, ANTOINETTE KATHLEEN, training executive, consultant, artist; b. Phila., July 15, 1944; d. John Joseph and Genevieve Catherine (Moore) O'C.; m. Edward F. Mannino, June 25, 1993. AB in Psychology, Immaculata Coll., 1966; MA in Psychology and Counseling, Villanova U., 1967; studied with Jack Gates, N.Y., 1974. Training specialist Towers, Perrin, Foster & Crosby Inc., Phila., 1969-72; asst. personnel mgr. Foremost Ins. Co., Grand Rapids, Mich., 1972-74; mgr. mgmt. devel. and training credit J.C. Penney Co., Inc., N.Y.C., 1974-80; asst. v.p. Am. Express Internat. Banking Corp., N.Y.C., 1980-81; v.p. Marine Midland Bank, N.A., N.Y.C., 1981-87; chmn. Training Profls., Inc., Phila., 1988—; with Am. Inst. Banking, N.Y., 1981-87, pres., 1987. Solo shows include Revsin Gallery, Phila., 1989, Art A La Carte, Phila., 1994; group shows include Ariel Gallery, N.Y.C., 1990, Mari Galleries of Westchester, Ltd., 1994, Acad. Natural Scis. Phila., 1994; numerous pvt. collections; contbr. articles to profl. jours. Speaker N.Y. State Bankers' Assn., 1986. Mem. ASTD (bd. dirs. Phila. and Del. Valley chpts. 1989—, pres. elect 1992, pres. 1993), Phila. Human Resources Group (rsch. com. 1991—, community svc. com. 1992—). Office: Tng Profls Inc 1614 Kings Mill Rd PO Box 387 Gwynedd Valley PA 19437

O'CONNELL, CATHERINE ANN, library director; b. Balt., Apr. 8, 1946; d. Timothy Edward and Claire Cecilia (Mewshaw) O'C.; m. C. Michael Helmer, May 28, 1977 (div. June 1980). BA, U. Md., 1968; MS in LS, U. Ill., 1971. Cert. permanent profl. libr., Mich., N.J. Reference asst. Pub. Libr. Annapolis (Md.) and Anne Arundel County, 1968-70, br. libr., 1971-72; head adult svcs. Washington County Free Libr., Hagerstown, Md., 1972-76, asst. dir., 1976-84; dir. Pub. Librs. Saginaw (Mich.), 1984-91, Free Libr. of Woodbridge, N.J., 1991—; cons. Hagerstown Bus. Coll., 1976-79, Woodbridge Cultural Arts Com., 1992—, Woodbridge Cable Com., 1992—. Bd. dirs. Pride, Inc., Saginaw, 1987-91. Recipient Sam Shapiro award U. Ill. Libr. Sch., 1972; Md. Libr. Assn. scholar, 1971. Mem. ALA, Pub. Libr. Assn. (bd. dirs. 1988-91), Mich. Libr. Assn., White Pine Libr. Coop. (bd. dirs. 1984-91), Valley Libr. Consortium (bd. dirs. 1984-91), Mgmt. and Adminstrv. Caucus (bd. dirs. 1988-90), Zonta, Rotary Club of Woodbridge (pres. 1994-95), Beta Phi Mu. Office: Free Pub Libr Woodbridge George Frederick Plz Woodbridge NJ 07095

O'CONNELL, SISTER COLMAN, college president, nun. BA in English, Speech, Coll. St. Benedict, St. Joseph, Minn., 1950; MFA in Theater, English, Cath. U., 1954; PhD in Higher Edn. Adminstrn., U. Mich., 1979; student, Northwestern U., Birmingham U., Stratford, Eng., Denver U., Stanford U., Sophia U., Tokyo. Entered Order of St. Benedict. Tchr. English Pierz (Minn.) Meml. High Sch., 1950-53, Cathedral High Sch., St. Cloud, Minn., 1950-53; chairperson theater and dance dept. then prof. theater Coll. of St. Benedict, St. Joseph, 1954-74, dir. alumnae, parent relations, ann. fund, 1974-77, dir. planning, 1979-84, exec. v.p., 1984-86, pres., 1986—; cons. Augsburg Coll., Mpls., 1983-85, Assn. Cath. Coll. and Univs., 1982, Minn. Pvt. Coll. Council, 1982, SW (Minn.) State U., Marshall, 1980-82, Wilmar (Minn.) Community Coll., 1980-82, Worthington (Minn.) Community Coll., 1980-82, U. Minn., Morris, 1980-82; bd. dirs. Minn. Publ Radio. Chair bd. dirs. Minn. Pvt. Coll. Coun., 1991-92; bd. dirs. St. Cloud Cmty. Found., 1991-94. Mem. Nat. Assn. Ind. Colls. and Univs. (bd. dirs. 1993), St. Cloud Area C. of C. (bd. dirs. 1987-90). Office: Coll Saint Benedict 37 College Ave S Saint Joseph MN 56374-2001

O'CONNELL, GWYNETH PIETA, art educator, graphic artist; b. Portland, Oreg., Nov. 25, 1944; d. Ellis Hedrick and Helen Florence (Newland) Jones; m. Kenneth Robert O'Connell, June 21, 1969; children: Anneka Erin, Marlika Megan, Sean Daugherty. BS in Art Edn., U. Oreg., 1966, MFA in Graphic Arts, 1968, Generalist, 1993. Art instr. Tongue Point Job Corp, Astoria, Oreg., 1968-69, Treasure Valley C.C., Ontario, Oreg., 1969-71, 73-78, U. Oreg., Maude I. Kerns Lane C.C., Eugene, 1972-73, 78-84; art/computer instr. Eugene (Oreg.) Pub. Sch. Dist. 4J, 1984—. Co-author Sch. Arts mag., 1990-94. Bd. dirs. Western Rivers coun. Girl Scouts U.S.A., Eugene, 1984-90, leader, 1978-93, Troop Leader of Yr. 1981). HEW prospective tchrs. fellow, U. Oreg., 1966-68, Maude I. Kern's scholar, 1966. Mem. AAUW (bd. mem. 1978-80). Democrat. Home: 220 W 23rd Ave Eugene OR 97405 Office: 4J South Eugene High School 200 N Monroe 2555 Gilham Eugene OR 97401

O'CONNELL, KATHLEEN LECLEAR, nursing educator; b. Steubenville, Ohio, Jan. 28, 1952; d. E. Robert and Irene (Ciancetta) LeClear; m. Thomas Barry O'Connell, July 1, 1970; children: Christopher Thomas, Ryan

Thomas. ADN, Purdue U., 1978, BSN, 1986; MSN, Ind. U., 1988; post-grad., Ball State U., Ind. U. Staff and charge nurse critical care unit Parkview Meml. Hosp., Ft. Wayne, Ind., 1978-84, patient care mgr. critical care unit, 1984-86; assoc. faculty Ind. U.-Purdue U., Ft. Wayne, 1986-89, asst. prof. nursing, 1990—; nurse cons. Assn. for Retarded Citizens, Ft. Wayne, 1988—; nurse reviewer Lincoln Nat. Corp., Ft. Wayne, 1989-90. Vol. nurse practitioner Matthew 25 Health Clinic, Ft. Wayne, 1988—; bd. dirs Whitley County chpt. Am. Cancer Soc., Columbia City, Ind., 1991—, pres., 1994—, mem. state bd., med. dir. Region 3, 1994—. Mem. AACN (cert., Northeast Ind. chpt. 1978—, treas. 1982-83, pres.-elect 1983-84, pres. 1984-85), ISNA (publs. com. 1994—), Sigma Theta Tau (Alpha chpt. 1988—). Roman Catholic. Office: Ind U Purdue U Ft Wayne 2101 E Coliseum Blvd Fort Wayne IN 46805-1445

O'CONNELL, MARGARET SULLIVAN, lawyer; b. N.Y.C., Feb. 16, 1942; d. Thomas J. and Nora (Ryan) Sullivan; m. Anthony F. O'Connell, May 11, 1968 (dec. Mar. 1975); children: Noreen Anne, Joan Margaret, Alison Marie. Nursing diploma, St. Clare's Hosp. Sch. Nursing, N.Y.C., 1962; BA, Jersey City State Coll., 1973; JD, St. John's U., 1983. Bar: N.Y. 1984; RN, N.Y. Staff nurse St. Clare's Hosp., N.Y.C., 1962-64, head nurse, 1964-67; clin. instr. medicine and surgery St. Clare's Sch. Nursing, N.Y.C., 1967-70; nursing supr. Menorah Home and Hosp., Bklyn., 1974-75; assoc. Costello & Shea, N.Y.C., 1987—. Mem. ABA, N.Y. State Bar Assn., Assn. of Bar of City of N.Y., Am. Assn. Nurse Attys. Democrat. Office: Costello Shea & Gaffney One Battery Park Pla New York NY 10004

O'CONNELL, MARY ANN, state senator, business owner; b. Albuquerque, Aug. 3, 1934; d. James Aubrey and Dorothy Nell (Batsel) Gray; m. Robert Emmett O'Connell, Feb. 21, 1977; children: Jeffery Crampton, Gray Crampton. Student, U. N.Mex., Internat. Coun. Shopping Ctrs. Exec. dir. Blvd. Shopping Ctr., Las Vegas, Nev., 1968-76, Citizen Pvt. Enterprise, Las Vegas, 1976; media supr. Southwest Advt., Las Vegas, 1977—; owner, operator Meadows Inn, Las Vegas, 1985—, 3 Christian bookstores, Las Vegas, 1985—; state senator Nev. Senate, 1985-93; chmn. gov. affairs; vice chmn. commerce and labor; mem. taxation com.; alt. Legis. Commn., 1985-86, mem., 1987-88, 91-93; commr. Edn. Commn. States; rep. Nat. Conf. State Legislators; past vice chair State Mental Hygiene & Mental Retardation Adv. Bd. Pres. explorer div. Boulder Dam Area coun. Boy Scouts Am., Las Vegas, 1979-80, former mem. exec. bd.; mem. adv. bd. Boy Scouts Am.; pres., bd. dirs. Citizens Pvt. Enterprise, Las Vegas, 1982-84, Secret Witness, Las Vegas, 1081-82; vice chmn. Gov.'s Mental Health-Mental Retardation, Nev., 1983—; past mem. community adv. bd. Care Unit Hosp., Las Vegas; past mem. adv. bd. Kidney Found., Milligan Coll., Charter Hosp.; tchr. Young Adult Sunday Sch. Recipient Commendation award Mayor O. Grayson, Las Vegas, 1975, Outstanding Citizenship award Bd. Realtors, 1975, Silver Beaver award Boy Scouts Am., 1980, Free Enterprise award Greater Las Vegas C. of C., Federated Employers Assn., Downtown Breakfast Exch., 1988, Award of Excellence for Women in Politics, 1989, Legislator of Yr. award Bldg. and Trades, 1991, Legislator of Yr. award Nat. ASA Trade Assn., 1991, 94, Guardian of Liberty award Nev. Coalition of Conservative Citizens, 1991, Internat. Maxi Awards Promotional Excellence; named Legislator of Yr., Nev. Retail Assn., 1992. Mem. Retail Mchts. Assn. (former pres., bd. dirs.), Taxpayers Assn. (bd. dirs.), Greater Las Vegas C. of C. (past pres., bd. dirs., Woman of Achievement Politics women's coun. 1988). Republican. Mem. Christian Ch. Home: 7225 Montecito Cir Las Vegas NV 89120-3118 Office: Nev Legislature Senate 401 S Carson St Carson City NV 89701-4747

O'CONNELL, MARY ITA, psychotherapist; b. Balt., July 3, 1929; d. Richard Charles and Ona (Buchness) O'C.; m. Leon Jack Greenbaum, Dec. 28, 1962 (div. Jan. 1986); children: Jessie A., Elizabeth K. BA, U. Md., 1956; postgrad., Am. U., 1960—; M in Creative Arts in Therapy, Hahnemann Med. Coll., 1978. Registered Acad. Dance Therapists. Tchr. Robert Cohan Sch. Dance, Boston, 1958-61; instr., choreographer Wheaton Coll., Norton, Mass., 1959-60, Harvard/Radcliffe Colls., Boston, 1960-62; tchr., performer, choreographer Profl. Studios, Washington, 1962-69; asst. prof., adminstr. Fed. City Coll., Washington, 1969-74; movement psychotherapist Woodburn Ctr. for Community Mental Health, Fairfax, Va., 1975-76, Gundry Hosp., Balt., 1976-77, Prince Georges' Community Mental Health Dept., Capitol Heights, Md., 1978-80; lectr. George Washington U., D.C., 1981-85; pvt. practice psychotherapy Silver Spring, Md., 1977—; sr. movement psychotherapist Regional Inst. for Children and Adolescents, Rockville, Md., 1980-82; movement cons. Ctr. for Youth Svcs., Washington, 1981-83; movement psychotherapist D.C. Mental Health Ctrs., Washington, 1985-87, 90—, Community for Creative Non-Violence Women's Shelter, Washington, 1986, LICSW, Washington, 1989. Choreographer, soloist (dance performance) The Artist: A Theatre Happening, 1963; choreographer, co-dir. (outdoor dance event) Tree Sculpting, 1974; choreographer (dance performance) Excitations, 1967, A Dance Event, 1974; soloist, New England Opera, 1961; performer, choreographer WGBM TV/Laboratory Concert Series, 1961; performer, CBS-TV/Erika Thimey Dance Theatre, 1965; guest artist, Harford Coll. Art Festival, 1967. U. Md. scholar, 1955-56. Mem. Dance Circle of Boston (life, pres. 1959-61), Modern Dance Council of Washington (exec. bd dirs., editor 1965-69), Am. Dance Therapy Assn. (treas. metro chpt. 1977-81), Assn. Humanistic Psychology, Family Therapy Network, Am. Dance Guild, NIH (movement specialist 1978-79). Democrat. Home and Office: 16 Sussex Rd Silver Spring MD 20910-5435

O'CONNOR, BARBARA ANNE, circulation manager; b. Roslyn, N.Y., Sept. 29, 1962; d. Thomas Ronald and Barbara Jane (Bolina) O'C.; m. Stephen LaMantia, July 1, 1988. BA, SUNY, Stony Brook, 1984. Circulation asst. Equal Opportunity Publs., Inc., Greenlawn, N.Y., 1986-87; circulation coord. E.O.P., Inc., Greenlawn, N.Y., 1987-88, circulation mgr., 1988—. Contbr. articles to profl. publs. Vol. Family Svc. League of Suffold County, N.Y., 1991, Friends for Long Island's Heritage, 1994; exhibit organizer West Islip (N.Y.) Pub. Libr., 1991. Mem. NAFE, SUNY Stony Brook Alumni Assn., Heritage Treasures Collectors Club (libr.). Office: Equal Opportunity Publs Inc 150 Motor Pky Ste 420 Hauppauge NY 11788-5145

O'CONNOR, BETTY LOU, service executive; b. Phoenix, Oct. 29, 1927; d. Georg Eliot and Tillie Edith (Miller) Miller; m. William Spoeri O'Connor, Oct. 10, 1948 (dec. Feb. 1994); children: Thomas W., William K., Kelli Anne. Student, U. So. Calif., 1946-48, Calif. State U., Los Angeles, 1949-50. Pres. O'Connor Food Svcs., Inc., Jack in the Box Restaurants, Granada Hills, Calif., 1983—, Western Restaurant Mgmt. Co., Granada Hills, 1986—. Recipient Frannie award Foodmaker, Inc., Northridge, Calif., 1984, First Rate award, 1992. Mem. Jack in the Box Franchisee Assn., Spurs Hon. (sec. U. So. Calif. 1947-48), Associated Women Students (sec. U. So. Calif. 1946-47), Gamma Alpha Chi (v.p. 1947-48), Chi Omega. Republican. Roman Catholic. Office: Western Restaurant Mgmt Co 17545 Chatsworth St Granada Hills CA 91344

O'CONNOR, CELIA, mathematician, software engineer; b. Wilmington, Del., Sept. 18, 1941; d. Louis De Spain and Norma (Longeteig) Smith; m. Thomas R. O'Connor, June 11, 1963; children: Sean, Brian. BS in Math., Mont. State U., 1963; MSEE, Tex. A & I, 1974. Programmer Bank of Hawaii, Honolulu, 1964-65, USN, Nas Barbers Point, Hawaii, 1966-67, SAIC, Lexington Park, Md., 1984; programmer, analyst Cubic Corp., Lexington Park, 1984-85, VERAC, San Diego, 1985-87, Ball Systems Engr., San Diego, 1987-90; mathematician TYBRIN Corp., Shalimar, Fla., 1990—; dir. Mil. Spouse Bus. and Profl. Network, San Diego, 1986-89. Advisor Coronado (Calif.) Sch. Bd., 1985-89. Mem. AAUW (edn. chmn. 1991-92), Delta Gamma Alumnae. Office: 603 Shady Brook Ct Southlake TX 76092-3746

O'CONNOR, DENISE LYNN, marketing communications executive; b. West Palm Beach, Fla., Oct. 29, 1958; d. Joseph John and Ada Colleen (Doyle) Fields; m. William York O'Connor, May 31, 1985. BS in Bus., Fla. State U., 1979; MBA, Fla. Inst. Tech., 1983, postgrad. in elec. engring., 1984-86. Cons. Small Bus. Inst., Tallahassee, 1979; mgr. select accts. Burroughs, West Palm Beach, 1980-81; mgr. mktg. communications Harris-Satellite Communications, Melbourne, Fla., 1981-84; sect. mgr. mktg. communications Gen. Electric Info. Svcs., Rockville, Md., 1984-86; mgr. pub. rels. Mgmt. Sci. Am., Atlanta, 1986-88; pres., owner Mktg. Comms. Cons., Atlanta, 1988-94, Saddle River, N.J., 1995—; cons. Sci.-Atlanta (Ga.), Inc., 1988—. Author (brochure) Genie, 1986 (Disting. award Soc. for Tech. Communications); editor (brochure) Electronic Data Interchange, 1986 (Excellence Soc. for Tech. Communications). Vol. Atlanta (Ga.) Humane Soc., 1988, (mem. auxiliary, 1989—). Recipient Ross Systems Pres. award, 1991. Mem. AAUW, PEO (v.p. reciprocity 1990-91, pres. evening and weekend reciprocity coun. 1991-92, chmn. Internat. Peace scholarship 1990), Soc. Tech. Comm., Atlanta Lawn and Tennis Assn.(pres. B-5 team 1989), Country Club South, Delta Zeta. Republican. Methodist. Home and Office: Mktg Comms 8 Denison Dr E Saddle River NJ 07458

O'CONNOR, ELIZABETH ANN, enterostomal therapy rehabilitation nurse; b. Roanoke, Va., Aug. 12, 1936; d. Joseph John and Regina (Seifert) O'C. RN, DePaul Hosp. Sch. Nursing, Norfolk, Va., 1957; student, Mt. St. Agnes Coll.; cert. in enterostomal therapy, Harrisburg (Pa.) Sch. of, Enterostomal Therapy, 1974. RN, dir. enterostomal therapy Holy Cross Hosp., Silver Spring, Md. Contbr. articles to profl. jours. Named Montgomery County Nurse of Yr., 1982, Enterostomal Therapy Nurse of Yr., 1988. Mem. Wound, Ostomy Continence Nurses Soc. (past pres. Mid-Atlantic region, chair, mem. regional by-laws com.), Metro Md. Ostomy Assn. (bd. dirs.), Am. Cancer Soc. (nursing chair ednl. confs.). Office: Holy Cross Hosp 1500 Forest Glen Rd Silver Spring MD 20910-1460

O'CONNOR, SISTER GEORGE AQUIN (MARGARET M. O'CONNOR), college president, sociology educator; b. Astoria, N.Y., Mar. 5, 1921; d. George M. and Joana T. (Loughlin) O'C. B.A., Hunter Coll., 1943; M.A., Catholic U. Am., 1947; Ph.D. (NIMH fellow), NYU, 1964; LL.D. Manhattan Coll., 1983. Mem. faculty St. Joseph's Coll., Bklyn., 1946—; prof. sociology and anthropology St. Joseph's Coll., 1966—, chmn. social sci. dept., 1966-69, pres., 1969—; Fellow African Studies Assn., Am. Anthrop. Assn.; Bklyn. C. of C. (dir. 1973—), Alpha Kappa Delta, Delta Epsilon Sigma. Author: The Status and Role of West African Women: A Study in Cultural Change, 1964. Office: Saint Joseph's Coll Office of Pres 245 Clinton Ave Brooklyn NY 11205-3688

O'CONNOR, GINGER HOBBA, speech pathologist; b. Poynette, Wis., Apr. 20, 1951; d. Walter Leslie and Mary Elizabeth (Krause) Hobba; m. William Scott Elliott, Dec. 27, 1973 (div. 1984); children: Todd C., William Trent, Tiffany Paige; m. Michael Robert O'Connor, Aug. 11, 1990; 1 child, Tanner Michael O'Connor. BA, Marietta Coll., 1973; MA, Ohio State U., 1974. Speech pathologist Del. (Ohio) Speech/Hearing Ctr., 1974-75; speech pathologist Washington County Bd. Mental Retardation Devel. Disabilities, Marietta, Ohio, 1975—, supr. dept. communications, 1985—; speech pathologist ancillary staff Marietta Hosp., 1975—; cons., lectr. Ohio U., Athens, 1980—, South Eastern Ohio Spl. Edn. Resource Ctr., Athens, 1975—; pres. co-founder MR/DD Speech-Lang.-Hearing Network of Ohio, 1992-94. Bd. dirs. Child Devel. Ctr., Marietta, 1977-80, Washington County ARC; mem. med. adv. bd. Headstart, Marietta, 1984—; dist. program chairperson Boy Scouts Am., Parkersburg, W.Va., 1989—; mem. Ohio Safe Kids Coalition. Mem. Am. Speech Lang. Hearing Assn. (speaker 1979—), Ohio Speech Lang. Hearing Assn. (legis. coun. rep. 1990—), Southeastern Ohio Speech Hearing Assn. (v.p. 1982-83, pres. 1983-84), Profl. Assn. for Retarded Adults, YMCA com. for Internat. Awareness (co-chair 1992—). Methodist. Home: 124 Keyser St Marietta OH 45750-1019 Office: Washington Cty Bd Mental Retardation Devel Disabilities PO Box 702 Marietta OH 45750-0702

O'CONNOR, KAY, state legislator; b. Everett, Wash., Nov. 28, 1941; d. Ernest S. and Dena (Lampers) Wells; m. Arthur J. O'Connor, Sept. 1, 1959; 6 children. Diploma, Lathrop H.S., Fairbanks, Alaska, 1959. Office mgr. Blaylock Chemicals, Bucyrus, Kans., 1981-84; store mgr. Copies Plus, Olathe, Kans., 1984-86; acct. Advance Concrete Inc., Spring Hill, Kans., 1986-92; mem. Kansas Ho. of Reps., 1993—; bd. dirs. Hometel Ltd. Republican. Roman Catholic. Home: 1101 N Curtis Olathe KS 66061 Office: PO Box 2232 Olathe KS 66051

O'CONNOR, KIM CLAIRE, chemical engineering and biotechnology educator; b. N.Y.C., Nov. 18, 1960; d. Gerard Timothy and Doris Julia (Bisagni) O'C. BS magna cum laude, Rice U., Houston, 1982; PhD, Calif. Inst. Tech., Pasadena, 1987. Postdoctoral rsch. fellow chemistry dept. Calif. Inst. Tech., Pasadena, 1987-88; postdoctoral rsch. fellow chem. engring., biochemistry, molecular biology, and cell biology depts. Northwestern U., Evanston, Ill., 1988-90; asst. prof. chem. engring. Tulane U., New Orleans, 1990—, faculty molecular and cellular biology grad. program, Newcomb fellow, 1991—; mem. steering com. molecular and cellular biology grad. program Tulane U., 1993—; mem. Tulane Cancer Ctr., 1994—; cons. in field. Reviewer of profl. jours. Mem. Am. Inst. Chem. Engrs., Am. Soc. Engring. Edn., European Soc. Animal Cell Tech., Soc. In Vitro Biology, Assn. Women in Sci., Sigma Xi, Tau Beta Pi, Phi Lambda Upsilon. Office: Tulane U Dept Chem Engring Lindy Boggs Ctr Rm 300 New Orleans LA 70118

O'CONNOR, MARGE, lawyer; b. Elizabeth, N.J., Nov. 10; d. Joseph N. and Margaret Mary (McEvoy) O'C. BA, Coll. of New Rochelle, 1966; JD, Suffolk U., 1979. Tchr., team leader Lexington (Mass.) Schs., 1971-81; atty. Panhandle Eastern Pipe Line Co., Houston, 1981-88, assoc. gen. atty., adminstr., 1986-88; sr. counsel Mobil Natural Gas Inc., Houston, 1988-92, gen. counsel, 1992—. Director Blue Bonnet Bowl Bd., Houston, 1984-89; bd. dirs. instnl. rev. bd. HCA Med. Ctr., Houston, 1990-91. Office: Mobil Natural Gas Inc 12450 Greenspoint Dr Houston TX 77060-1905*

O'CONNOR, MARY ANN, accountant; b. Lynn, Mass., June 18, 1963; d. Edward DeValle II and Jean Helen (Volante) O'C. BA, Hamilton Coll., 1985; MS in Acctg., Northeastern U., 1986. CPA, Mass. Sr. acct. Laventhol & Horwath, Boston, 1986-89; v.p. Abbott Co., Marblehead, Mass., 1990—; adj. faculty mem., mem. adv. bd. Marian Court Coll., Swampscott, Mass., 1993—; alumni admissions vol. fundraiser Hamilton Coll., Clinton, N.Y., 1996—. Vol. Big Sister Assn. Greater Boston, 1990—. Mem. Corinthian Yacht Club. Home: 17 Mugford St Marblehead MA 01945 Office: Abbott Co PO Box 631 Marblehead MA 01945

O'CONNOR, MAUREEN, public relations executive; b. Plainfield, N.J., Sept. 24, 1948; d. John Vincent and Etta Mary (North) O'C.; m. Stephen Priest, May 28, 1981; 1 child, Danielle C. Priest. BSBA, Rider Coll.; post-grad., Rutgers U. East and west coast dir. publicist Capital Records, N.Y.C.; sr. v.p. Solters/Roskin/Friedman, L.A.; exec. v.p. entertainment Rogers & Cowan, L.A. Mem. NARAS, Publicist Guild. Office: Rogers & Cowna 10000 Santa Monica Blvd Los Angeles CA 90067

O'CONNOR, PATRICIA ERYL, telecommunications consultant; b. Kansas City, Mo., Oct. 16, 1945; d. Jesse Edwin O'Connor and Olive Mae (Geagan) Brooks; m. James Harrie Reed, Dec. 18, 1964 (div. July 1972); 1 child, Jana Diann Reed; m. John Robert Morgan, Sept. 27, 1985. AAS, Pima Community Coll., Tucson, 1982. Cert. Nat. Assn. Broadcast Engrs. Radio, radio-telephone lic. gen. class FCC. Communications technician AT&T, Kansas City, Mo., 1972-79, Tucson, 1979-85, San Francisco, 1985-91, Denver, 1991—; chief exec. officer, cons. Profl. Forum Mgmt./MacCircles, Pleasanton, Calif., 1990-92, Denver, 1992—; co-adminstr. Mac Symposium, Cupertino, Calif., 1987-93. Editor: (electronic mag.) Handshake, 1985-94. Election judge, Tucson, 1979-81; area v.p. CWA Local 8150, Ariz., N.Mex., 1984-84, exec. v.p., 1984-85. Home: 24949 Montane Dr W Golden CO 80401

O'CONNOR, PATRICIA RANVILLE, secondary and special education educator; b. Flint, Mich., Feb. 24, 1951; d. Marcel L. and Ruth Ellen (Smith) Ranville. BS, Ea. Mich. U., 1973, MA, 1978; MS in Adminstrn., Pepperdine U., 1995. Cert. tchr. (life) Calif., severely handicapped and learning handicapped, multiple subject, resource specialist. Spl. edn. tchr. Genessee Intermediate Sch. Dist., Flint, 1974-78, Barstow (Calif.) Unified Sch. Dist., 1978-81, Westport Sch., L.A., 1981-83; resource specialist Culver City (Calif.) Unified Sch. Dist., 1983—, mentor tchr., chmn. dept. spl. edn., coord. sch. improvement program; chair sch. site coun.; team leader dept. edn. program quality rev. State of Calif.; mem. C.A.R.E. Team; reader, scorer Calif. Assessment Program. Recipient Hon. Svc. award PTA. Mem. NEA, Calif. Tchrs. Assn. Home: 5460 White Oak Ave Apt 210C Encino CA 91316-2408

O'CONNOR, PEGGY LEE, communications manager; b. Chgo., Apr. 20, 1953; d. William Stanley and Eleanor Sopie (Levandowski) Czaska; m. Charles B. O'Connor, III, Feb. 14, 1978. BS in Biology, Northeastern Ill. U., 1982; MBA, No. Ill. U., 1985. Emergency med. technologist, 1976-82; instr. Chgo. City Wide Colls., 1976-81; program dir. U. Ill. Hosp. 1979-81; program dir. Fermilab, Roselle, 1978-82; dist. adminstrv. mgr. Decision Data Svc., Schaumburg, Ill., 1981-89; gen. mgr. sales svc. Putman Pub., 1989-91; mgr. fin. and adminstrn. Weyerhaeuser, 1992—; bus. control mgr. Ameritech Cellular, 1993—. Recipient award Summit Club 1987, 88, 89. Mem. NAFE, NWAAR, Women in Bus., Pres's. Club, BPA (chairperson bd. dirs.), Chgo. Credit Mgrs. Assn. Avocation: computers. Office: Ameritech Cellular 2365 N Hicks Palatine IL 60067

O'CONNOR, RUTH SUSAN, physician, educator; b. Augusta, Ga., Apr. 23, 1952; d. Henry and Margaret Adellre (Schreider) Wynstra; m. Thomas Joseph O'Connor, Apr. 23, 1977; children: Samuel, Grace, Anna, Rhoda. Student, Wheaton Coll., 1970-73; MD, Med. Coll. Wis., 1977; cert. family practice, Caraway Meth. Med. Ctr., 1980. Diplomate Am. Bd. Family Practice. Intern Carraway Meth. Med. Ctr., Birmingham, Ala., 1977-78, resident in family practice, 1978-80; fellow family practice Caraway Meth. Med. Ctr., Birmingham, Ala., 1980-81, instr. family practice, 1981-85; pvt. practice Greenville, Ill., 1986-88; instr. family practice Sch. Medicine So. Ill. U., Belleville, 1986-88; staff physician Student Health Ctr. Purdue U., West Lafayette, Ind., 1989—; instr. family medicine Ind. U., Indpls., 1989—. Recipient Achievement citation Am. Women's Med. Soc., 1977. Mem. Christian Med. Soc. Baptist. Home: 714 Kossuth St Lafayette IN 47905 Office: Purdue U 1826 Student Health Ctr West Lafayette IN 47907

O'CONNOR, SABRINA NELSON, property acquisition specialist; b. Albany, Ga., Nov. 3, 1969; d. Wiley Frederick Nelson II and Eve-Anne (Duke) Wall. BS in Mktg., U. Cen. Fla., 1992. Lic. real estate broker, Fla. Realtor, assoc. Duke Properties, Maitland, Fla., 1990-92; Post, Buckley, Schuh and Jernigan, Inc., Winter Park, Fla., 1992—. Mem. NAFE, Internat. Right of Way Assn., Am. Mktg. Assn., Phi Theta Kappa, Mu Kappa Tau, Phi Kappa. Republican. Baptist. Office: Post Buckley Schuh Jernigan 1560 Orange Ave Ste 700 Winter Park FL 32789

O'CONNOR, SANDRA DAY, U.S. supreme court justice; b. El Paso, Tex., Mar. 26, 1930; d. Harry A. and Ada Mae (Wilkey) Day; m. John Jay O'Connor, III, Dec. 1952; children: Scott, Brian, Jay. AB in Econs. with great distinction, Stanford U., 1950, LLB, 1952. Bar: Calif. Dep. county atty. San Mateo, Calif., 1952-53; civil atty. Q.M. Market Ctr., Frankfurt am Main, Fed. Republic of Germany, 1954-57; sole practice Phoenix, 1959-65; asst. atty. gen. State of Ariz., 1965-69; Ariz. state senator, 1969-75, chmn. com. on state, county and mcpl. affairs, 1972-73, majority leader, 1973-74; judge Maricopa County Superior Ct., 1975-79, Ariz. Ct. Appeals, 1979-81; assoc. justice U.S. Supreme Ct., 1981—; referee juvenile ct., 1962-64; chmn. vis. bd. Maricopa County Juvenile Detention Home, 1963-64; mem. Maricopa County Bd. Adjustments and Appeals, 1963-64, Anglo-Am. Legal Exchange, 1980, Maricopa County Superior Ct. Judges Tng. and Edn. Com., Maricopa Ct. Study Com.; chmn. com. to reorganize lower cts. Ariz. Supreme Ct., 1974-75; faculty Robert A. Taft Inst. Govt.; vice chmn. Select Law Enforcement Rev. Commn., 1979-80. Mem. bd. editors Stanford (Calif.) U. Law Rev. Mem. Ariz. Personnel Commn., 1968-69, Nat. Def. Adv. Com. on Women in Services, 1974-76; trustee Heard Mus., Phoenix, 1968-74, 76-81, pres., 1980-81; mem. adv. bd. Phoenix Salvation Army, 1975-81; trustee Stanford U., 1976-80, Phoenix County Day Sch.; mem. citizens adv. bd. Blood Services, 1975-77; nat. bd. dirs. Smithsonian Assocs., 1981—; past Rep. dist. chmn.; bd. dirs. Phoenix Community Council, Ariz. Acad., 1970-75, Jr. Achievement Ariz., 1975-79, Blue Cross/Blue Shield Ariz., 1975-79, Channel 8, 1975-79, Phoenix Hist. Soc., 1974-77, Maricopa County YMCA, 1978-81, Golden Gate Settlement. Recipient Ann. award NCCJ, 1975, Disting. Achievement award Ariz. State U., 1980; named Woman of Yr., Phoenix Advt. Club, 1972. Lodge: Soroptimists. Office: US Supreme Ct Supreme Ct Bldg 1 First St NE Washington DC 20543*

O'CONNOR, SHEILA ANNE, freelance writer; b. Paisley, Scotland, Jan. 20, 1960; came to the U.S., 1988; d. Brian Aubrey Witham and Margaret Kirk (Reid) Davies; m. Frank Donal O'Connor, Aug. 9, 1986; children: David Michael, Andrew James. BA in French and German, Strathclyde U., 1980, postgrad. diploma in office studies, 1981, MBA, 1992. Office asst. BBC, London, 1982-83; asst. to mng. dir. Unimatic Engrs. Ltd., London, 1983-84; freelance word processing operator London, 1984-88; staff asst. Internat. Monetary Fund, Washington, 1988—; prin. Internat. Media Assn., Washington, 1988—. Contbr. numerous articles to various publs. Home and Office: 2531 39th Ave San Francisco CA 94116

O'CONNOR, SHERYL ANN, medical services administrator; b. Rome, Ga., Jan. 26, 1951; d. Robert W. and Phyllis M. (Lambert) Nippler; 1 child, Ashley. BS, Ea. Mich. U., 1972; LPN, Washtenaw Community Coll., Ann Arbor, Mich., 1976; RN, Santa Ana Coll., 1980; MA Bus. Mgmt., U. Redlands, 1983. RN; cert. pub. health nurse, healhcare risk mgr., cert. case mgr., cert. quality assurance/utilization mgmt. Med.-surg./oncology nurse Western Med. Ctr., Santa Ana, Calif.; community health nurse Vis. Nurse Assn., Orange, Calif.; hosp. adminstr. USN Med. Svcs. Corps., Jacksonville, Fla., 1985-88; ins. coord. Blue Cross/Blue Shield Fla., Pensacola, Fla., 1988-90; ctr. dir. Singleday Surgery, Jacksonville, 1990-91; dir. quality mgmt. Humana Hosp., Orange Park, Fla., 1991-92; dir. med. affairs Humana Health Plans, Maitland, Fla., 1992-93; dir. health svcs. PCA/Century Med. Health Plans, Inc., Orlando, Fla., 1993-94; dir. nursing Nations Healthcare Inc., Jacksonville, Fla., 1994—. Exec. officer USNR. Mem. N.E. Fla. Assn. of Health Care Quality, Fla. Assn. of Healthcare Quality, Am. soc. of Healthcare Risk Mgrs., Fla. Soc. of Healthcare Risk Mgrs., Naval Res. Assn. Home: # 923 11247 San Jose Blvd Jacksonville FL 32223

O'CONNOR-PETRIE, CATHERINE, land development company executive, consultant; b. Mahopac, N.Y., Jan. 8, 1947; d. Louis Alphonso and Catherine Theresa (Sammartino) Freda; m. Robert James O'Connor, Sept. 6, 1969 (div. Dec. 1983); 1 child, Matthew Christopher; m. Raymond Scott, July 4, 1985; 1 child, Jared Scott. Student, St. Joseph's U., Phila, 1966-68, Stanford U., 1984. Various adminstrv. positions, 1964-72; supr. human resources Itel, Inc., San Francisco, 1972-73, mgr. human resources, 1973-79, dir. word processing systems, 1978-79; dir. human rels. ADP, Inc., San Ramon, Calif., 1979-87, v.p. human resources, 1987-91; v.p. Peake Devel., Inc., Tappahannock, Va., 1992—, Cat Point, Inc., Warsaw, Va., 1992—; pres. Peake Performance, Tappahannock, 1992—. Mem. Warsaw-Richmond County C. of C. (bd. dirs. 1993), No. Neck Travel Coun. Home: RR 1 Box 127 Warsaw VA 22572-9740 Office: Peake Performance PO Box 2326 Tappahannock VA 22560-2326

O'DANIEL, DONNA LYNN, wildlife biologist; b. Greenport, N.Y., Mar. 16, 1945; d. Clarence Wilson and Eva Althea (Woodward) Jones. M of Biol. Sci., U. Tex., 1987. Field rsch. asst. Togiak Nat. Wildlife Refuge, Dillingham, Alaska, 1988; instr. biology Chemeketa C.C., Salem, Oreg., 1989; biol. technician Bur. Land Mgmt., North Bend, Oreg., 1989; field rsch. asst. Hawaiian Islands Nat. Wildlife Refuge, Honolulu, 1990; biol. technician Alaska Maritime Nat. Wildlife Refuge, Adak, 1990; wildlife biologist Johnston Atoll (Pacific Ocean) Nat. Wildlife Refuge, 1991-93, Peregrine Fund Fish Eagle Project, 1993, Midway Atoll Nat. Wildlife Refuge, 1994, Ecol. Svcs. U.S. Fish and Wildlife Svc., Tinian, 1994—. Contbr. book chpt.: Birds of North America, 1994. Recipient On the Spot award U.S. Fish and Wildlife Svc., 1992—, Outstanding Performance award U.S. Fish and Wildlife Svc., 1993. Mem. Am. Ornithologists Union, Asian Wetland Bur., N.Y. Acad. Scis., Assn. Field Ornithologists, Corp. Ornithologists of Ecuador, Lab. Ornithology, Cornell U., Neotropical Ornithol. Soc., Pacific Seabird Group. Home: 216 W Corral Dr Payson AZ 85541-3117

O'DAY, ANITA BELLE COLTON, entertainer, singer; b. Chgo., Oct. 18, 1919; d. James and Gladys (Gill) C. Student, Chgo. public schs. Singer and entertainer various Chgo. Music Clubs, 1939-41; singer with Gene Krupa's Orch., 1941-45, Stan Kenton Orch., 1944, Woody Herman Orch., 1945, Benny Goodman Orch., 1959; singing tours in U.S. and abroad, 1947—; rec. artist Polygram, Emily records, Verve, GNP Crescendo, Columbia, London, Signature, DRG, Pablo; million-seller songs include Let Me Off Uptown, 1941, And Her Tears Flowed Like Wine, 1944, Boogie Blues, 1945; appeared in films Gene Krupa Story, 1959, Jazz on a Summer's Day, 1960, Zigzag,

1970, Outfit, 1974; TV shows 60 Minutes, 1980; Tonight Show, Dick Cavett Show, Today Show, Big Band Bash, CBS Sunday Morning, CNN Showbiz Today, others. Author: High Times, Hard Times, 1981, rev. edit. 1989; performed 50 yr. anniversary concert Carnegie Hall, 1985, Avery Fisher Hall, 1989, Tanglewood, 1990, Town Hall, 1993, currently touring worldwide; albums include Drummer Man, Kenton Era, Anita, Anita Sings The Most, Pick Yourself Up, Lady is a Tramp, An Evening with Anita O'Day, At Mr. Kelly's, Swings Cole Porter, Travelin' Light, All The Sad Young Men, Waiter Make Mine Blues, With The Three Sounds, I Told Ya I Love Ya Now Get Out, Uptown, My Ship, Live In Tokyo, Anita Sings the Winners, Incomparable, Anita 1975, Live at Mingos, Anita O'Day/The Big Band Sessions, Swings Rodgers and Hart, Time for Two, Tea for Two, In a Mellowtone, At Vine St. Live, Mello'Day, Live at the City, Angel Eyes, The Night Has a Thousand Eyes, The Rules of The Road, 1993, others. Mem. AFTRA, Screen Actors Guild, BMI. Office: 1524 La Baig Ave Los Angeles CA 90028-6406

O'DELL, CHARLENE ANNE AUDREY, lawyer; b. Warwick, N.Y., Feb. 27, 1963; d. Charles Edward and Stella Ruth (Brazil) O'D. Student, Fordham U., 1981-83; BA summa cum laude with distinction, Boston U., 1985; JD, NYU, 1988. Bar: N.Y. 1989, U.S. Dist. (so. and ea. dists.) N.Y. 1989, D.C. 1990. Assoc. Winston & Strawn (previously Cole & Deitz), N.Y.C., 1988-90, Graham & James, N.Y.C., 1990—. Editor Moot Ct., NYU, 1987-88. Recipient Moot Ct. Advocacy award NYU, 1987. Mem. ABA, N.Y. State Bar Assn., N.Y. State Women's Bar Assn., New York County Lawyers' Assn. Office: Graham & James 885 3rd Ave New York NY 10022-4834

O'DELL, JOAN ELIZABETH, lawyer, business executive; b. East Dubuque, Ill., May 3, 1932; d. Peter Emerson and Olive (Bonnet) O'D.; children: Dominique R., Nicole L. BA cum laude, U. Miami, 1956, JD, 1958. Bar: Fla. 1958, U.S. Supreme Ct. 1972, D.C. 1974, Ill. 1978, Va. 1987; lic. real estate broker Ill., Va., DC. Trial atty. U.S. SEC, Washington, 1959-60; asst. state atty. Office State Atty., Miami, Fla., 1960-64; asst. county atty. Dade County Atty.'s Office, Miami, 1964-70; county atty. Palm Beach County Atty.'s Office, West Palm Beach, Fla., 1970-71; regional gen. counsel. U.S. EPA, Region IV, Atlanta, 1971-73, assoc. gen. counsel, Washington, 1973-77; sr. counsel Nalco Chem. Co., Oakbrook, Ill., 1977-78; v.p., gen. counsel Angel Mining, Tenn. and Washington, 1979—; pres. South West Land Investments, Miami, Fla., 1979-88; v.p., gen. counsel Events U.S.A., Washington, 1990—. Bd. dirs. Tucson Women's Found., 1982-84, U. Ariz. Bus. and Profl. Women's Club, Tucson, 1981-85; bd. dirs. LWV Tucson, 1981-85, pres., 1984-85; bd. dirs. LWV Ariz., 1984-85, chmn. nat. security study; bd. dirs. LWV, Palm Beach County, Fla., 1990-92; mem. Exec. Women's Council, Tucson, 1982-85. Mem. Fed. Bar Assn., Fla. Bar Assn., D.C. Bar Assn., Va. State Bar Assn. Avocations: camping, hiking, skiing.

O'DELL, LYNN MARIE LUEGGE (MRS. NORMAN D. O'DELL), librarian; b. Berwyn, Ill., Feb. 24, 1938; d. George Emil and Helen Marie (Pesek) Luegge; student Lyons Twp. Jr. Coll., La Grange, Ill., 1957; student No. Ill. U., Elgin Community Coll., U. Ill., Coll. of DuPage; m. Norman D. O'Dell, Dec. 14, 1957; children—Jeffrey, Jerry. Sec., Martin Co., Chgo., 1957-59; dir. Carol Stream (Ill.) Pub. Library, 1964—; chmn. automation governing com. DuPage Library System, v.p., 1982-85, pres. exec. com. adminstrv. librarians, 1985-86. Named Woman of Year, Wheaton Bus. and Profl. Woman's Club, 1968. Mem. ALA, Ill. Library Assn., Library Adminstrs. Conf. No. Ill. Lutheran. Home: 182 Yuma Ln Carol Stream IL 60188-1917 Office: 616 Hiawatha Dr Carol Stream IL 60188-1616

ODELL, MARY JANE, former state official; b. Algona, Iowa, July 28, 1923; d. Eugene and Madge (Lewis) Neville; m. John Odell, Mar. 3, 1967 (dec.); children: Brad Chinn, Chris Odell; m. Ralph Sigler, Nov. 22, 1987. B.A., U. Iowa, 1945; hon. doctorate, Simpson Coll., 1982. Host public affairs TV programs Des Moines and Chgo., 1953-79; with Iowa Public Broadcasting Network, 1975-79, host Assignment Iowa, 1975-78, host Mary Jane Odell Program, 1975-79; sec. of state State of Iowa, 1980-87; ret., 1987—; tchr. grad. classes in communications Roosevelt U., Chgo., Drake U., Des Moines. Chmn. Iowa Easter Seals campaign, 1979-83; mem. Midwest Com. Future Options; bd. dirs. Iowa Shares; mem. exec. bd. Iowa Peace Inst., 1985-92. Recipient Emmy award, 1972, 75; George Washington Carver award, 1978; named to Iowa Women's Hall of Fame, 1979. Republican. Address: 725 Hickman Rd Des Moines IA 50314-2935

ODEN, JEAN PHIFER, special education educator; b. Chgo., May 2, 1936; d. Dillard James and Lena (Conner) Phifer; m. James Edward Oden, Apr. 26, 1959; 1 child, Eric James. BE, Chgo. Tchrs. Coll., 1958; MEd in Learning Disabilities, Chgo. State U., 1973; postgrad., Nat. Coll. Edn., Evanston, Ill., 1986—, cert. advance studies, 1987; EdD, Nat.-Louis U., 1995. Tchr. elem. schs. Chgo., 1958-73, tchr. learning disabilities elem. schs., 1973-81, cons. spl. edn., ind. edn. program facilitator, 1981; learning disability specialist Phillips High Sch., Chgo., 1982—, Englewood High Sch., Chgo., 1987—; mem. Ill. Guidelines for Learning Disabilities Devel. Com., Springfield, Ill., 1981—, Com. to Devel. State Test for Learning Disabilities Tchrs., Springfield, 1986—; speaker Who's Who Congress, Cambridge, Eng., 1992; mem. del. to Vietnam, 1993, mem. del. to China, 1994. Speaker Nat. Urban League N.Y.C. conf., 1980; mem. Congl. Victory Fund, Chgo., 1985, SCLC Met. Chgo., 1979-81, Mayoral Summit Parent-Community Coun. on Ednl. Reform, 1987—, Chgo. Mayor's Edn. Summit on Sch. Reform, 1988; charter mem. Rep. Presdl. Adv. Task Force, 1989, Rep. Inner Circle, 1991; mem. Coalition Black Trade Unionists, 1991—, cons. pool Nat. Juvenile Justice Resource Ctr., 1991—, NAACP; state chair African Am. Econ. Devel. Task Force, Ill. Legis. Black Caucus, 1992—. U.S. Dept. Edn. grantee, 1986; recipient Citizenship award Chgo. mayor, 1984, Cert. merit NAACP South Side Br., 1978; named state advisor U.S. Congl. Adv. Bd., 1985; speaker edn. seminar 19th Congress on Arts and Communicatiion, Cambridge, Eng. Mem. ASCD (mem. Vietnam delegation 1993), LWV, United Neighborhoods Intertwined for Total Equality (founder, exec. dir., researcher), Assn. for Citizens with Learning Disabilities, Coun. for Exceptional Children (liaison to state bd. Ill. Divsn. for Citizens with Learning Disabilities 1980), Spl. Edn. Tchrs. Assn. (1st pres., founder), Black Parents United for Edn. and Related Svcs. (founder), Kappa Delta Pi, Lehigh Country Club, Thousand Trails Club. Mem. Carter C.M.E. Ch. Clubs: Lehigh Country (Fla.); Thousand Trails (Ottawa, Ill.).

ODENDAHL, NORA VIVIAN, test developer; b. Paris, Feb. 11, 1956; d. Alan Odendahl and Alice Katherine (Stehle) Wallerstein. AB, Dartmouth Coll., 1977; PhD, Princeton U., 1985. Staff writer The Princeton (N.J.) Packet, 1986-87; freelance writer, editor, 1987-92; assoc. examiner Ednl. Testing Svc., Princeton, N.J., 1992—. Recipient Best Feature in Class A award Suburban Newspapers Am., 1987. Democrat. Home: 610 Eagles Chase Dr Lawrenceville NJ 08648-2554 Office: Ednl Testing Svc Rosedale Rd Princeton NJ 08541

O'DONNELL, KAREN DARLENE, education educator; b. Geneva, N.Y., Dec. 27, 1951; d. Frank Carmen and Margaret Marie (Leach) Luciano; m. John Patrick O'Donnell, May 11, 1974; children: Sean Patrick, Christopher David. BA cum laude, St. Bonaventure (N.Y.) U., 1974; MS with highest honors, Purdue U., Hammond, Ind., 1979. Cert. 6-12 tchr., Ill.; cert. permanent K-6, 7-12 tchr., N.Y. Tchr. Gra-Mar Sch. for Retarded, Romulus, N.Y., 1974-75, Holy Ghost Sch., South Holland, Ill., 1976-78, 80-81; mem. adj. faculty South Suburban C.C., South Holland, 1982-84, Prairie State C.C., Chgo. Heights, Ill., 1982-86; instr. Finger Lakes C.C., Geneva, N.Y., 1986-91, coord. literacy project, 1989-92, asst. prof., 1991—; project dir. LIVE Sex Equity Grant, 1993-94. Contbr. articles to profl. jours. Mem. Finger Lakes Speakers Bur., Canandaigua, N.Y., 1991—; pres. St. Francis-St. Stephan's Sch. Bd., Geneva, 1992—. Mem. Internat. Reading Assn., Nat. Coun. Tchrs. English, N.Y. Coll. Learning Skills Assn., N.Y. State Reading Assn. (del. 1990-92), Lake Counties Reading Coun. (pres. 1991-92). Roman Catholic. Home: 17 Larchmont St Geneva NY 14456-1425 Office: Finger Lakes CC Lake Shore Dr Canandaigua NY 14424

O'DONNELL, MARY MURPHY, nurse epidemiologist, consultant; b. Lincoln, Ill., Feb. 21, 1918; d. Thomas Edward and Frances Ward (Hayes) Murphy; m. Maurice A. O'Donnell, Jan. 29, 1942. Diploma St. John's Sch. Nursing, Springfield, Ill., 1939. Registered nurse, Ill., Fla. Asst. to ear, nose and throat specialist, 1939-42; nurse U.S. Govt. Hosp., 1942-43; asst. to gen. practitioner, Springfield, 1943-55; staff nurse City Health Dept., Springfield, 1955-65; dir. tng. and edn. Springfield and Sangamon County Civil Def. Agy., 1965-66; exec., cons. in charge med. self-help Ill. Dept. Pub. Health, 1966-74; nurse epidemiologist St. Joseph Hosp., Port Charlotte, Fla., 1975-91, part-time epidemiologist, 1992-93, retired, 1993, cons. epidemiologist, 1993—. mem. Aids Task Force Charlotte County Dept. Pub. Health, Fla., pres. Charlotte County epidemiology group, 1991; instr. AIDS Program, 1987-93. V.p. S. Central area Ill. Women's Civil Def. Council; mem. Ill. Civil Def. Council; chmn. civil def. activities ARC; v.p., mem. health services adv. com. U.S. Civil Defense Council; ofcl. vol. rep. Am. Social Health Assn. Recipient Spl. award State Dept. of Am. Legion Aux., 1954, Cert. of Honor, hon. life membership U.S. Air Force Air Def. Team, 1959, Silver Wing Bracelet, Ground Observer Corps, 1959, Cert. of Honor, Mayor of City of Springfield, 1966, Pfizer award of merit U.S. Civil Def. Council, 1969, Presidential citation U.S. Civil Def. Council, 1972. Mem. Assn. for Practitioners in Infection Control, SW Regional Infection Control. Republican. Roman Catholic. Avocations: boating; swimming; clog dancing; golf; horses. Home: 819 Napoli Ln Punta Gorda FL 33950-6525

O'DONNELL, ROSIE, comedienne, actress; b. Commack, N.Y., 1962. Attended, Dickinson Coll., Boston Univ. Appearances include (TV series) Gimme A Break, 1986-87, Stand By Your Man, 1992, Women Aloud, 1992, Stand-up Spotlight, VH-1 (American Comedy award nomination best female performer in a TV special 1994, Cable ACE award nomination best entertainment host 1994); (film) A League of Their Own, 1992, Sleepless in Seattle, 1993 (American Comedy award nomination best supporting female in a motion picture 1994), Another Stakeout, 1993 (American Comedy award nomination best actress in a motion picture 1994), Car 54, Where Are You?, 1994, The Flintstones, 1994, Exit to Eden, 1994; (theatre) Grease (Broadway prodn.), 1994. Office: Internat Creative Mgmt 8942 Wilshire Blvd Beverly Hills CA 90211*

O'DONNELL, TERESA HOHOL, software development engineer, antennas engineer; b. Springfield, Mass., Nov. 25, 1963; d. Marion Henry and Lena Ann (Zajchowski) Hohol. BS in Computer Engrng., MIT, 1985, BSEE, 1985, MSEE, MS in Computer Sci., 1986. Rsch. asst. MIT Rsch. Lab for Electronics, Cambridge, 1985-86; lead VHSIC insertion engr. USAF Electronic Systems Div., Hanscom AFB, Mass., 1986-88; intelligent antennas engr. USAF Rome Lab., Hanscom AFB, Mass., 1988-91; software devel. engr. Arcon Corp., Waltham, Mass., 1991—. Composer: (choral mass setting) Mass of Rejoicing, 1989. Performer Zbeide's Harem, Tewksbury, Mass., 1986—; organist/composer St. Theresa's Choir, Billerica, Mass., 1987—. Capt. USAF, 1986-91, selective svc. officer, 1992-94. Decorated 2 Commendation medals, Nat. Def. medal, Selective Svc. System Bronze medl; recipient 2 Air Force Ognl. Excellence award USAF Rome Lab., 1989, 91. Mem. IEEE, Nat. Assn. Pastoral Musicians, Am. Guild Organists, Assn. Computing Machinery, Air Force Assn., Eta Kappa Nu (v.p., 1985-86), Sigma Xi Rsch. Soc. Roman Catholic. Office: Arcon Corp 260 Bear Hill Rd Waltham MA 02154

O'DRISCOLL, MARILYN LUTZ, kindergarten educator; b. L.A.; d. Robert Thomas and Helen Mary (Cardamone) Lutz; m. John P. O'Driscoll Jr., Jan. 15, 1966 (dec. 1978); children: Kelley, John, Patrick. BS in Edn., U. So. Calif., 1961, cert. lang. devel. specialist, 1990. Cert. tchr., Calif. Tchr. kindergarten Montebello (Calif.) Sch. Dist., 1961-64, Garvey Sch. Dist., Rosemead, Calif., 1964—; program quality reviewer San Gabriel Consortium, 1988—; mem. parent bd. Incarnation Sch., Glendale, Calif., 1990-92; pres. Incarnation Parish Coun., 1993—; chmn. sch. site coun., 1990-93; participant ednl. TV program, 1989—. Pres. Incarnation Parish Coun., 1993-94, 94-95. Mem. ASCD, NEA, Garvey Edn. Assn., Calif. Tchrs. Assn., Women of Troy (life), Spirit of Troy (life), Kappa Delta.

ODUM, ELIZABETH MOLNAR, accountant; b. West Chester, Pa., Sept. 16, 1958; d. John and Eleanor H. (Gallery) Molnar; m. John Russell Odum, Aug. 3, 1991; 1 child, Kara Gallery. BS, Boston Coll., 1980; MBA, U. Colo., Denver, 1988. CMA, CPA, Colo.; cert. mgmt. acct. Cost acct. The S.W. Shattuck Chem. Co., Inc., Denver, 1981-82; tax acct. Tele-Communications, Inc., Englewood, Colo., 1983-84; sr. fin. analyst Stearns Catalytic World Corp., Denver, 1984-86; budget analyst U S WEST Advanced Techs., Englewood, 1986-89; analyst regulatory fin. U S WEST Advanced Techs., Denver, 1989-91; mgr. subs. billing U S WEST, Inc., Englewood, 1991-93, mgr. regulatory acctg., 1993—. Mem. AICPA, Inst. Mgmt. Accts. (Peaks Pike chpt.), Colo. Soc. CPAs. Office: US WEST Inc 7800 E Orchard Rd Englewood CO 80155

OEHLER, VALERIE ANN, medical sales representative; b. Boston, Mar. 24, 1966; d. John Joseph and Frances Theodora (Giso) Gill; m. David Arthur Oehler, Oct. 1, 1994. BS, Boston Coll., 1988; postgrad., Northeastern U., 1991—. Ter. mgr. SmithKline Beecham, Pitts., 1988-93; med. sales rep. G.D. Searle, Skokie, Ill., 1993—. Home: 15 Mendelssohn St Roslindale MA 02131

OELER, THERESA ANN, research specialist; b. McKeesport, Pa., Oct. 30, 1956; d. Walter Nicholas and Pauline (Hospodar) O. BS in Biology, Chatham Coll., 1978. Rsch. asst. Westinghouse Corp., Pitts., 1979, Duquesne U., Pitts., 1980; microbiologist II Allegheny County Dept. Labs., Pitts., 1980-89; rsch. specialist U. Pitts., Pa., 1989—. Contbr. articles to profl. jours. Tutor Labach Literacy, Pitts., 1986-90. Republican. Office: Univ Pitts Dept Urologic Surgery 3550 Terr & De Soto Sts Pittsburgh PA 15261

OERTEL, YOLANDA CASTILLO, pathologist, educator, diagnostician; b. Lima, Peru, Dec. 14, 1938; came to U.S., 1966; d. Leonardo A. and Dalila (Ramirez) C.; m. James E. Oertel, Sept. 24, 1969. MD, Cayetano Heredia, Lima, 1964. Diplomate Am. Bd. Pathology. Internat. postdoctoral fellowship NIH, Bethesda, Md., 1966-68; asst. prof. pathology Sch. Medicine George Washington U., Washington, 1975-78, assoc. prof., 1978-84, prof., 1984—; cons. Registry Cytology Armed Forces Inst. Pathology, Washington, 1981—. Author: Fine Needle Aspiration of the Breast, 1987; contbr. chpts. to books and articles to profl. jours. Recipient Francisco A. Camino prize Peruvian Med. Assn., 1965, cert. Meritorious Svc. Armed Forces Inst. Pathology, 1974; named Disting. Alumna Cayetano Heredia Med. Sch., 1989. Mem AMA, Internat. Acad. Cytology, Assn. Mil. Surgeons (hon), Colombian Soc. Pathology (hon), Argentinian Soc. Pathology (hon.), Peruvian Soc. Pathologists (hon.), Argentinian Soc. Cytology, (hon.), Am. Soc. Cytology, Coll. Am. Pathologists, Am. Soc. Clin. Pathologists (coun. on cytopathology 1982-88). Office: George Washington U Med Ctr 901 23d St NW Washington DC 20037

OESTREICH, LINDA LOUISE GARLAND, communications coordinator; b. Bklyn., June 23, 1948; d. Thomas Tennant and Muriel Jessie (Campbell) Garland; m. Patrick Kenneth Oestreich, Mar. 31, 1967 (div. 1979); 1 child, Connie Lynn. BA in English, Am. Lit., U. Calif, San Diego, 1979. Sec. Naval Ocean Systems Ctr., San Diego, 1968-76, tech. writer, 1976-86, supr. tech. writer, 1986-90; corp. writer BMC Software, Inc., Sugar Land, Tex., 1990-93; comm. coord. GX Tech., Houston, 1993—; instr. San Diego Mesa Coll., 1982-87, U. Calif. San Diego ext.; cons. in field; chairperson adv. com. San Diego Cmty. Colls. Dept., 1985-89; instr. U. Houston-Downtown, 1994—. Docent, Houston Zool. Gardens. Fellow Soc. Tech. Comm. (assoc., sec. 1985-86, v.p. programs 1987, pres. 1988-90, bd. dirs. Houston chpt. 1992-94, program chmn. 1995 ann. conf.); mem. ASTD (v.p. comm. 1986, mem. editl. staff 1986-88). Home: 6310 Rancho Mission Rd Apt 243 San Diego CA 92108-1936 Office: GX Tech LP 4605 Post Oak Pl Ste 130 Houston TX 77027

OETINGER, JANET, university official; b. Portland, Oreg, Nov. 11, 1944; d. William C. Jr. and Annis R. (Bailey) O. BA, Stanford U., 1966; MFA, Yale U., 1969. Subscription mgr. Am. Conservatory Theatre, San Francisco, 1970; devel. dir. Chelsea Theater Ctr., N.Y.C., 1971-72; asst. dir. dance program Nat. Endowment for Arts, Washington, 1972-75, panelist, cons., site visitor, 1979—; asst. dir. Hopkins Ctr. for Arts, Dartmouth Coll., Hanover, N.H., 1975-78; cons. in arts mgmt., Hanover, 1978-81; dir. arts and lectures U. Calif., Santa Barbara, 1981—; panelist, site visitor Calif. Arts Coun., Sacramento, 1981-85, 92; panelist Santa Barbara County Arts Commn., 1986-88, Western States Arts Fedn., 1990. Am. Field Svc. exch. student, Santiago, Chile, 1961. Mem. Assn. Performing Arts Presenter (bd. dirs. 1982-85, numerous coms., panels and adv. bds., Fan Taylor award 1989), Western Alliance Arts Adminstrs. (bd. dirs. 1986-88, Disting. Svc. award 1989), Calif. Presenters (bd. dirs., exec. com., editor newsletter 1985-88), Chamber Music Am. Home: 5076 Calle Real # A Santa Barbara CA 93111-1813 Office: U Calif Arts and Lectures Santa Barbara CA 93106

OETTING, MILDRED KATHERINE See SQUAZZO, MILDRED KATHERINE

OETTINGER, BRENDA SUSAN, marketing information specialist; b. N.Y.C., Sept. 16, 1959; d. Ernst and Margrit Ellen (Rodrian) O.; m. George Edward Graber, Jr., Oct. 15, 1994. BS in Atmospheric Scis., SUNY, Albany, 1981, M Pub. Affairs, 1988. Asst. to editor N.Y. Environ. News Atmospheric Scis. Rsch. Ctr., SUNY, Albany, 1978-81, editor N.Y. Environ. News, 1982-86; editor Albany Update SUNY, Albany, 1986-89; market info. specialist Office Recycling Market Devel. N.Y. State Dept. Econ. Devel., Albany, 1989—. Editor newsletter The Market, 1989-94. Commr. Saratoga Lake Protection and Improvement Dist., Saratoga, N.Y., 1987-90. Mem. N.Y. State Assn. for Reuse, Reduction and Recycling, Out of Control Ski Club (bd. dirs. 1994-95). Democrat. Jewish. Home: 133 Raylinsky Rd Ballston Lake NY 12019-1119 Office: NY State Dept Econ Devel Office Recycling Market Dev 1 Commerce Ave Rm 950 Albany NY 12206-2015

OFFHOLTER, JEAN MARY, management consultant; b. Berkeley, Calif., Sept. 14, 1932; d. Clarence Ballard Hills and Frances Desire (Ramsay) Hanna; divorced; children: Cheryl Diane McKibbin, Sally Lynn Hillman. BA, San Jose State Coll., 1954. Tech. exec. U.S. Gen. Svcs. Adminstrn., San Francisco, 1966-70; inventory mgmt. specialist U.S. Gen. Svcs. Adminstrn., Washington, 1971-75, supervisory inventory mgmt. specialist, 1975-76, spl. asst., regional commr., 1977-78, dir. retail svcs. div., 1979-83; dir. supply and contracting divs. U.S. Gen. Svcs. Adminstrn., Kansas City, Mo., 1984-86; ret., 1986; cons. in procurement tng. and course devel. Washington, 1986—. Home: 11566 Rolling Green Ct # 200 Reston VA 22091-2243

OFFUTT, REBECCA SUE, sales executive, designer, calligrapher; b. Wheeling, W.Va., Jan. 20, 1951; d. John Howard and Mary Concetta (Lanzuisi) Warden; m. Denver C. Offutt, Apr. 13, 1970 (div. Dec. 1992); children: Kimberly Dawn, Jody Monroe. Student, W.Va. U., 1968-70, W.Va. State Coll., 1973-75; grad., Real Estate Career Ctr., Huntington, W.Va., 1988. Lic. realtor, W.Va. Eligibility specialist W.Va. Dept. Welfare, Charleston, 1974-78; founder, pres. Marabec, Inc., Charleston, W.Va., 1980-82; realtor, sales assoc. McQuire Realty Co., Huntington, 1988-89; sales assoc. Focus Mktg. Consultants, Charleston, 1987-90; ter. mgr. Quorum Corp., Hurricane, W.Va., 1990—. Developer five-yr. plan Jr. League, Charleston and Huntington, 1984; docent Huntington Galleries; pres. Pea Ridge Elem. PTA, Huntington, 1986-87; del.-at-large Ohio Valley Tennis Assn., 1986-87. Recipient Local, Dist. and Regional winner Ricoh Corp., 1993, finalist, 1994. Home: 203 Saddle Horn Rd Charleston WV 25314-2415

OFFUTT, SUSAN ELIZABETH, economist; b. Newport, R.I., Apr. 17, 1954; d. William Franklin and Carol Dorothy (Chieves) O. BS, Allegheny Coll., 1976; MS, Cornell U., 1980, PhD, 1982. Asst. prof. agrl. econs. U. Ill., Urbana, 1982-87; sect. leader Econ. Rsch. Svc. USDA, Washington, 1987-88; chief agr. br. U.S. Office Mgmt. and Budget, Washington, 1988-92; exec. dir., bd. agr. Nat. Rsch. Coun., Washington, 1992—. Office: Nat Rsch Coun 2101 Constitution Ave Washington DC 20418

O'GARA, BARBARA ANN, soap company executive; b. Newark, Aug. 8, 1953; d. Frank Percy and Rose (Giordano) Stevens. AA, Keystone Jr. Coll., 1973; BS, U. Ariz., 1976. Media buyer Wells, Rich, Green/Townsend, Irvine, Calif., 1977-80; dist. sales mgr. Dial Corp., Phoenix, 1980-82; regional sales mgr. Guest Supply, Inc., North Brunswick, N.J., 1982-85; dir. hotel mktg. and sales Neutrogena Corp., L.A., 1985-92, v.p. hotel mktg. and sales, 1992—. Keystone Jr. Coll. scholar, 1972, Morris County scholar, 1971; recipient Outstanding Sales Accomplishment award Armour-Dial, 1981. Mem. Am. Mktg. Assn., Am. Mgmt. Assn., Am. Hotel and Motel Assn., Network Exec. Women in Hospitality. Republican. Roman Catholic. Avocations: tennis, aerobics, running, skiing, photography. Home: Penthouse A 2218 Main St Santa Monica CA 90405-2273 Office: Neutrogena Corp 5760 W 96th St Los Angeles CA 90045-5544

OGATA, SUSAN NAOMI, psychologist; b. N.Y.C., Mar. 13, 1957; d. Kenneth Kenji and Misako (Koshiyama) Ogata; m. Lawrence Joseph Ledesma, Aug. 3, 1985; children: Evan Sadao, Jason Satoru. BA cum laude, UCLA, 1978; MEd, Harvard U., 1980; PhD, U. Minn., 1988. Client svcs. coord. Work Tng. Program, Woodland Hills, Calif., 1981-82; child therapist Huron Valley Child Guidance Ctr., Ann Arbor, Mich., 1986-87; clin. psychologist Bayshores Med. Group, Inc., Redondo Beach, Calif., 1988—. Contbr. articles to profl. jours. Mem. APA, Calif. Psychol. Assn. Home: 9051 Colbreggan Dr Huntington Beach CA 92646-5813 Office: Bayshores Med Group Inc 23326 Hawthorne Blvd Ste 270 Torrance CA 90505-3731

OGDEN, ANN, editor; b. Kansas City, Mo.; d. Audley W. and Leona R. (Locke) Porter; m. Alvin C. Ogden, Apr. 20, 1954; 1 child, Karen. BS in Tech. Journalism, Kans. State U., 1954; MA in Sec. Edn., U. Mo., Kansas City, 1968. Society editor Lyons (Kans.) Daily News, 1954-56; asst. editor Rose Pubs., Shawnee Mission, Kans., 1962-63; instr. developmental reading U. Mo., Kansas City, 1964-67; journalism tchr. Bishop Miege High Sch., Shawnee Mission, 1966-67; asst. editor Kans. Alumni, Lawrence, 1967-68, Vol. Leader and Trustee of Am. Hosp. Assn., Chgo., 1969-72; asst. editor, directory editor Barks Pubs., Chgo., 1975-81; adj. instr. bus. English Triton Coll., River Grove, Ill., 1981-84; freelance writer, editor, 1973—. Bd. dirs. 2000 Found., Overland Park, Kans., 1991—, Strang hist. display com., 1991—. U. Mo. Kansas City fellow, 1964-65, 65-66. Mem. AAUW (chmn. Shawnee Mission chpt. money matters group 1987-89, chmn. Shawnee Mission chpt. Women Investing Now interest group 1993-94), Women in Comms. (pres. Chgo. chpt. 1973-74, historian-archivist Chgo. chpt. 1971-72, mem. procedures manual com. 1971-72, mem. career conf. com. 1971, mem. vol. bur. com. 1971), Alpha Chi Omega (chpt. Lyre editor 1989-91, historian 1991-93, chaplain 1993—).

OGDEN, JEAN LUCILLE, sales executive; b. Chgo., Jan. 20, 1950; d. George William and Mary Elizabeth (MacKenzie) Anderson; m. Michael Jude Ogden, Aug. 27, 1977 (div. Dec. 1983). BA with honors, U. Calif., Santa Barbara, 1971. Sales rep. Am. Hosp. Supply Co., Irvine, Calif., 1975-77, Abbott Labs., HPD, L.A., 1977-78, Gillette Co., Albuquerque, 1978-79, Unitek Corp., Monrovia, Calif., 1979-86, Nat. Patent Dental Products, San Diego, 1986-87; area mgr. Branson Ultrasonics Corp., L.A., 1987—. Mem., co-chair Nat. Multiple Sclerosis Soc., San Diego, 1983—; mem. Am. Cancer Soc., San Diego, 1985—, Zool. Soc., San Diego, 1984-85. Named one of Outstanding Young Women in Am., 1984. Mem. AAUW, NAFE, Med. Mktg. Assn., Salesmasters Albuquerque, Soroptimist Internat. (officer Carlsbad and Oceanside, Calif. chpt. 1983-85), Alpha Phi (house corp. bd. Long Beach chpt. 1974-75, chpt. advisor 1975-76). Republican. Office: Branson Ultrasonics Corp 12955 E Perez Pl La Puente CA 91746-1414

OGDEN, JENNIFER, film producer. Films include: (assoc. prodr.) Garbo Talks, 1984, Suspect, 1987; (prodr.) The Manhattan Project, 1986, Cookie, 1989; (exec. prodr.) Family Business, 1989, Prelude to a Kiss, 1992. Office: 20th Century Fox 10201 W Pico Blvd Los Angeles CA 90035*

OGDEN, JOANNE, real estate executive; b. Cumming, Ga., Apr. 9, 1941; d. Crafton Kemp Sr. and Mary Evelyn (Willis) Brooks; m. William Rush Williams, Jan. 3, 1961 (div. 1966); 1 child, Paul Rush Williams; m. Cecil Leavern Ogden, Sr.; stepchildren: Cecil Laverne Jr., Michael Vann. Grad. high sch., Cumming. Prin. Ogden & Ogden, Milledgeville, Ga., 1966—. Candidate Baldwin County Commnr., Milledgeville, 1984. Mem. Nat. Geog. Soc., Better World Soc., Cousteau Soc., Audubon Soc., Smithsonian Inst., U.S.C. of C., 700 Club (Virginia Beach). Republican. Methodist. Home: 402 Allen Memorial Dr SW Milledgeville GA 31061-4608 Office: Ogden & Ogden 2600 Irwinton Rd Milledgeville GA 31061-9762

OGDEN, MAUREEN BLACK, state legislator; b. Vancouver, B.C., Nov. 1, 1928; came to U.S., 1930; d. William Moore and Margaret Hunter (Leitch) Black; m. Robert Moore Ogden, June 23, 1956; children: Thomas, Henry, Peter. BA, Smith Coll., 1950; MA, Columbia U., 1963; M in City and Regional Planning, Rutgers U., 1977. Researcher, staff asst. Ford Found., N.Y.C., 1951-56; staff assoc. Fgn. Policy Assn., N.Y.C., 1956-58; mem. Millburn (N.J.) Twp. Com., 1976-81; mayor Twp. of Millburn, N.J., 1979-81; mem. N.J. Gen. Assembly, Trenton, 1982—; chmn. Assembly Environment Com., N.J. Gen. Assembly; chmn. Energy and Pub. Utilities Com., Coun. State Govts., 1991-92; mem. adv. bd. Sch. Policy and Planning, Rutgers Univ., New Brunswick, N.J., 1992—. Author: Natural Resources Inventory, Township of Millburn, 1974. Bd. govs. N.J. Hist. Soc., Newark, 1990—; trustee N.J. chpt. The Nature Conservancy; hon. trustee Paper Mill Playhouse, Millburn, 1990—; former trustee St. Barnabas Med. Ctr., Livingston, N.J.; former pres. N.J. Drug Abuse Adv. Coun. Recipient Citation award Nat. Assn. State Outdoors Recreation Liaison Officers, 1987, John F. Kennedy Ctr. for the Performing Arts cert. appreciation, The Alliance for Arts Edn., 1987, Disting. Svc. award Art Educators N.J., 1987, Annual Environ. Quality award EPA Region II, 1988, Citation, Humane Soc. of the U.S., 1989, N.J. Historic Sites Coun. award, 1989, award of merit N.J. Sch. Conservation, 1990, many others; named Legislator of Yr., Cogeneration Inst. Am. Elec. Engrs., 1990. Republican. Episcopalian. Home: 59 Lakeview Ave Short Hills NJ 07078 Office: 266 Essex St Millburn NJ 07041 Office: NJ State Senate State Capitol Trenton NJ 08625

OGDEN, PEGGY A., personnel director; b. N.Y.C., Mar. 21, 1932; d. Stephen Arnold and Margaret (Stern) O. BA with honors, Brown U., 1953; MA, Trinity Coll., Hartford, Conn., 1955. Asst. dir. YMCA Counseling Svc., Hartford, 1953-55; employment interviewer R.H. Macy & Co., N.Y.C., 1955; asst. pers. dir. Inst. Internat. Edn., N.Y.C., 1956-59; pers. advisor Girl Scouts U.S.A., N.Y.C., 1959-61; store and pers. mgr. Ohrbachs, Inc., N.Y.C., 1961-74; dir. pers. N.Y.C. Tech. Coll. CUNY, Bkyn., 1974—; arbitrator Better Bus. Bur., N.Y.C., 1988—; cons. Girl Scout Coun. N.Y., N.Y.C., 1988-89. Mem APA, Am. Assn. U. Adminstrs., Women in Human Resources, N.Y. Pers. Mgmt. Assn. Home: 1100 Park Ave New York NY 10128-1202 Office: NYC Tech Coll 300 Jay St Brooklyn NY 11201-2902

OGDEN, VALERIA JUAN, management consultant, state representative; b. Okanogan, Wash., Feb. 11, 1924; d. Ivan Bodwell and Pearle (Wilson) Munson; m. Daniel Miller Ogden Jr., Dec. 28, 1946; children: Janeth Lee Ogden Martin, Patricia Jo Ogden Hunter, Daniel Munson Ogden. BA magna cum laude, Wash. State U., 1946. Exec. dir. Potomac Coun. Camp Fire, Washington, 1964-68, Ft. Collins (Colo.) United Way, 1969-73, Designing Tomorrow Today, Ft. Collins, 1973-74, Poudre Valley Community Edn. Assn., Ft. Collins, 1977-78; pres. Valeria M. Ogden, Inc., Kensington, Md., 1978-81; nat. field cons. Camp Fire, Inc., Kansas City, Mo., 1980-81; exec. dir. Nat. Capital Area YWCA, Washington, 1981-84, Clark County YWCA, Vancouver, Wash., 1985-89; pvt. practice mgmt. cons. Vancouver, 1989—; mem. Wash. Ho. of Reps., 1991—; lectr. in field; adj. faculty pub. adminstrn. program Lewis and Clark Coll., Portland (Oreg.) State U., 1979—; mem. Pvt. Industry Coun., Vancouver, 1986. Author: Camp Fire Membership, 1980. County V chair Larimer County Dems., Ft. Collins, 1974-75; mem. precinct com. Clark County Dems., Vancouver, 1986-88; mem. Wash. State Coun. Vol. Action, Olympia, 1986-90; treas. Mortar Bd. Nat. Found., Vancouver, 1987—; chair Clark County Coun. Homeless, Vancouver, 1989—. Named Citizen of Yr. Ft. Collins Bd. of Realtors, 1975; recipient Gulick award Camp Fire Inc., 1956, Alumna Achievement award Wash. State U. Alumni Assn., 1988. Mem. Internat. Assn. Vol. Adminstrs. (pres. Boulder 1989-90), Nat. Assn. YWCA Exec. Dirs. Assn. (nat. bd. nominating com. 1988-90), Women in Action, Philanthropic and Ednl. Orgn., Phi Beta Kappa. Unitarian. Home: 3118 NE Royal Oaks Dr Vancouver WA 98662-7435 Office: John L O'Brien Bldg State Capitol Rm 342 Olympia WA 98504

OGDEN, VIRGINIA ANN, elementary school educator; b. Flushing, N.Y., Apr. 23, 1945; d. James Christopher and Rita Frances (Cullen) McGlinchy; m. William Francis Ogden, Mar. 16, 1974. BA, Trenton (N.J.) State Coll., 1966. Tchr. Willingboro (N.J.) Bd. Edn., 1966—; demonstration tchr. Trenton State Coll., 1971-72, cooperating tchr., 1972-77, 87-90. Mem. NEA, N.J. Edn. Assn., Willingboro Edn. Assn. (rep. 1987-93), Burlington Cunty Edn. Assn., Delta Kappa Gamma. Democrat. Roman Catholic. Home: 104 Dorado Dr Delran NJ 08075 Office: Willingboro Bd Edn Salem Rd Willingboro NJ 08046

OGLESBY, CINDY SUE, accountant; b. Dumas, Tex., Oct. 15, 1963; d. Lawrence Ray Morris and Sue Ellen Shockley; m. James Thomas Oglesby, Jr., Dec. 30, 1984; 1 child, Kathlyna Sue Morris. BBA in Acctg., U. Tex., Tyler, 1988, MBA, 1992. CPA Tex.; CMA. Bookkeeper, office mgr. Mr. "C" Food Store, Dallas, 1982-84; staff acct., accts. payable clk. Lehigh Press, Inc., Dallas, 1984-86; quality control statistician Manpower, Inc. (Trane, Inc.), Tyler, 1986-87; staff acct. Dr.'s Meml. Hosp., Tyler, 1987-89; profit planning acct. Tyler Pipe Industries, Inc., 1989-90, profit planning supr., 1990—. Leader Camp Fire Boys and Girls, Tyler, 1991-94. Mem. AICPA, Tex. Soc. CPAs, Inst. Mgmt. Accts. (dir. newsletter 1991-92, v.p. adminstrn. 1992-93, chpt. pres. 1993-94, dir. CMA programs 1994-95). Home: 10804 County Road 212 Tyler TX 75707-9516 Office: Tyler Pipe Industries Inc PO Box 2027 Tyler TX 75710-2027

O'GRADY, BARBARA VINSON, community health nurse, nursing administrator; b. Alhambra, Calif., July 6, 1928; d. Weston Wright and Merdith Alida (Noble) Vinson; m. Joseph Putnam O'Grady, Oct. 24, 1952; children: Joseph Jr., Jeffrey, Kent, Kimberly, Kathryn. BS, UCLA, 1951; MS, U. Minn., 1972. Staff public health nurse San Diego Health Dept., 1952; staff nurse U. Minn. Hosp., 1954-56; staff public health nurse Family Nursing Svc., St. Paul, 1972; asst. prof. Gustavus Adolphus Coll., St. Peter, Minn., 1972-77; dir. Ramsey County Public Health Nursing Svc., St. Paul, 1977-88; health staff Senator Dave Durenberger, Mpls., 1988; cons. pvt. practice, Waterville, Minn., 1989—; mem. bd. govs. U. Minn. Hosp. and Clinic, Mpls., 1983-91, chair, 1985-87; clin. faculty Sch. Pub. Health, 1984-88. Author: (with others) Computer Applications in Medical Care, 1982, Nursing and Computers, 1989, NCNIP: Models for the Future of Nursing, 1989, Procs. of Impact of DRG's on Nursing Conf., 1988; mem. editl. bd. Jour. Cmty. Health Nursing, 1984-94. Mem. Mpls. Charter Commn., 1967-72; co-chair Minn. GOP Issues Devel., 1968, Minn. GOP Constrn. Com., 19660-70; chair Dick Erdall Campaign Com., 1965-71; bd. dirs. Presbyn. Homes of Minn., St. Paul, 1982-88; bd. dirs. Living at Home/Block Nurse Program, 1986—, chair future directions com., 1988—. Recipient Outstanding Contbn. Midwest Alliance in Nursing, 1984, Outstanding Achievement award Bd, of Ramsey County Commrs., 1987; Annie Yates scholar L.A. County General Hosp. Alumni Assn., 1948; Living At Home grantee The Commonwealth Fund, 1986. Fellow Am. Acad. of Nursing; mem. ANA, APHA, Nat. League for Nursing, Minn. Public Health Assn., Sigma Theta Tau. Republican. Presbyterian. Home and Office: 482 Calle Cadiz Apt A Laguna Hills CA 92653-3964

O'GRADY, BEVERLY TROXLER, investment executive, counselor; b. Greensboro, N.C., Nov. 26, 1941; d. Robert Andrew and Beverly Beam (Barrier) Troxler; m. Robert Edward O'Grady, Aug. 6, 1966. BA, St. Mary's Coll., 1963; MA, Columbia U., 1965. Exec. v.p. Wilkinson & Hottinger Inc., N.Y.C., 1973-94, Helvetia Capital Corp., N.Y.C., 1987-94; pres. Wilkinson O'Grady & Co., Inc., N.Y.C., 1994—; mem. adv. bd. Charles Schwab Fin., San Francisco, 1991-93. Active Women's Nat. Rep. Club, N.Y.C., 1991-94. Mem. Assn. Investment Mgrs., N.Y. Soc. Security Analysts, Women's Bond Club (pres. 1992-94), Univ. Club. Roman Catholic. Office: Wilkinson O'Grady & Co Inc 520 Madison Ave New York NY 10022

O'GRADY, MARY J., editor, foundation consultant; b. Chgo., Sept. 25, 1951; d. Valentine Michael and Lillian Mary (Quinlan) O'G. Student, St. Mary's Coll., Rome, Italy, 1970-71; BFA, Manhattanville Coll., 1973. Assoc. editor Magnum Photos, N.Y.C., 1973-76; asst. picture editor Modern Photography Mag., N.Y.C., 1976-78; freelance photographer N.Y.C., 1978-80; sr. producer Trans-Atlantic Enterprises, N.Y.C., L.A., 1981-82; dir. pub. info. World Wildlife Fund, Washington, 1983-84; sr. analyst Mead Data Cen., Washington, 1985-87; editor photos U.S. News and World Report, Washington, 1987-90; program dir. Sacharuna Found., 1990-92; adminstr. Roland Films, 1991-92; assoc. dir. Info. Programs Family Health Internat., 1994—; cons. Time, Inc., N.Y.C., 1981, Exxon Corp., N.Y.C., 1981-82, U.S. News and World Report, Washington, 1987, The German Marshall Fund of U.S., Conservation Internat., Washington, 1992, W. Alton Jones Found., 1993-94. Asst. editor: The Family of Woman, 1978; producer (TV shows) A Conversation With..., 1982, The Helen Gurley Brown Show, 1982, Outrageous Opinions, 1982; photo editor America's Best Colleges, 1989, 90, Great Vacation Drives, 1989. Recipient Editorial Excellence award Natural Resources Coun. Am., 1984. Mem. Soc. Environ. Journalists, Worldwide Women in Environment.

OHANESIAN, SUSAN MARIE, social services administrator; b. Bridgeport, Conn., Nov. 18, 1949; d. Nicholas Anthony and Jeanette Mary (Aniolowski) Yanosy; m. George Vaughn Ohanesian, Apr. 28, 1973. BA, U. Conn., 1971; MSSW, Columbia U., 1979; Cert. in Social Work Adminstrv., Hunter Coll., 1985. Employment interviewer Conn. Unemployment Dept., Bridgeport, 1971-73; legal asst. Mendes & Mount, N.Y.C., 1973-74; milieu therapist The Bridge, N.Y.C., 1976-77; asst. editor Matthew Bender & Co., N.Y.C., 1974-77; asst dir. mental health Palisades Gen. Hosp., North Bergan, N.J., 1981-85; clinic dir. C.S.S. BRC Human Svcs. Corp., N.Y.C., 1985-86; dir. Social Svc. Project Return Found., Inc., N.Y.C., 1986-88, Artemis/Women's Spl. Svcs. Project Return Found., Inc., N.Y.C., 1988; coord. clin. support svcs. Project Return Found., Inc., N.Y.C., 1988-94, sr. dir. substance abuse, 1994—; pres. HPAE, AFT/AFL-CIO, North Bergen, N.J., 1980-81. Contbr. articles to profl. jours. Panlist N.Y. State Conf. on Substance Abuse-Relapse Prevention, 1987-88. Mem. Acad. Cert. Social Workers, Nat. Assn. Social Workers, N.J. Assn. Social Workers.

O'HARA, CATHERINE, actress, comedienne; b. Toronto, Mar. 4, 1954; m. Bo Welch, 1992. Actress, writer with Second City, Toronto, 1974; co-founder of SCTV, 1976 (Emmy award); films include After Hours, 1985, Heartburn, 1986, Beetlejuice, 1988, Dick Tracy, 1990, Betsy's Wedding, 1990, Home Alone, 1990, Little Vegas, 1990, There Goes The Neighborhood, 1992, Home Alone II: Lost In New York, 1992, The Nightmare Before Christmas, 1993 (voice), The Paper, 1994, Wyatt Earp, 1994, A Simple Twist of Fate, 1994, Tall Tale, 1995; TV, SCTV, Comic Relief, Dream On (dir.); co-writer SCTV, Cinemax, 1984, Really Weird Tales, HBO, 1986. Office: care ICM 8942 Wilshire Blvd Beverly Hills CA 90211*

O'HARA, DELIA IGLAUER, occupational health nurse practitioner; b. Cin., Feb. 5, 1942; d. Arnold and Virginia (Dunn) Iglauer; children: Robert, Matthew, William. BS, Simmons Coll., 1965; Cert. Nurse Practitioner, George Washington U., 1975; JD, Howard U., 1987. Bar: Pa., D.C.; cert. family nurse practitioner. Dir. home care program for cancer patients George Washington U. Med. Ctr., 1975-79; occupational health nurse practitioner Libr. of Congress, Washington, 1979-84; lawyer FTC, Washington, 1987-89; health svcs. mgr. Time-Life Books, Inc., Alexandria, Va., 1990-92; pvt. practice law Washington, 1990—; employee health nurse Georgetown U. Hosp., 1992-93; occupational health nurse practitioner Washington Hosp. Ctr., 1993—. Chmn. D.C. Home Care Task Force. Recipient Trustee's scholarship Howard U. Mem. Am. Acad. Nurse Practitioners (bd. dirs. region 3 rep. 1991-94, rec. sec. 1994—), Nat. Alliance Nurse Practitioners (bd. govs. 1986-88), Nurse Practitioner Assn. of D.C. (rec. sec. 1991, pres. 1992—), Nat. Nurse Practitioner Coalition (steering com. 1993), Capitol Area Network of Nurse Attys. (v.p. 1992-93), Simmons Coll. Alumnae Assn. (class sec. Class of 1964, 1989-94). Home: 4227 37th St NW Washington DC 20008-3148 Office: Washington Hosp Ctr 110 Irving St NW Washington DC 20011

O'HARA, KATHLEEN ELLEN, lawyer; b. Flushing, N.Y., Apr. 27, 1954; d. William Thomas and Maureen Therese (O'Regan) O'H.; m. Gary Allen Judkins, Oct. 6, 1990; 1 child, Alanna M. Judkins. BA cum laude, SUNY, Buffalo, 1980, JD, 1984. Bar: N.Y. 1985. Investigator I.U. Oper. Engrs. #17, West Seneca, N.Y., 1984-85; ptnr. Wyssling & O'Hara, Buffalo, 1985-86; assoc. Wyssling, Schwan & Montgomery, Buffalo, 1986—; participant Vol. Lawyers Project, Inc., Buffalo, 1985—. Treas. Days Park Block Club, Buffalo, 1992—; del. West Side Block Clubs and Churches United, Buffalo, 1993. Mem. ABA, Indsl. Rels. Rsch. Assn., N.Y. State Bar Assn., Bar Assn. Erie County. Office: Wyssling Schwan Montgomery 1230 Delaware Ave Buffalo NY 14209-1491

O'HARE, KATHRYN PETRONE, mayor, educator; b. Providence, Feb. 20, 1948; d. Benjamin Victor and Hellen Stella (Olszowy) Petrone; m. John Joseph O'Hare, Apr. 18, 1970; children: Jonathan, Tricia, Jason, Tara. AA in English, R.I. Jr. Coll., 1967; BA in English and Edn., Mt. St. Joseph Coll., 1969; MA in English, R.I. Coll., 1981; PhD in English, U. R.I., 1989. Cert. secondary tchr. English, R.I. Instr. U. R.I., Kingston, 1981-88, C.C.R.I., 1981-86, Bryant Coll., 1981-88, Providence Coll., 1981-88; dir. documents and pubs. Office Sec. State State R.I., Providence, 1986-88, dir. press and pubs., 1988-90, dir. constituent affairs Office Gov., 1990-92; mayor Town West Warwick, R.I., 1992-94; mem. exec. bd. R.I. League Cities and Towns, 1992-94, U.S. Conf. Mayors, Washington, 1992-94; faculty advisor affinity pre-med group Brown U., Providence, 1994—. Editor: Rhode Island Manual, 1989-90; subject articles R.I. Monthly Mag., 1993, R.I. Parents Mag., 1994; contbr. artlces. to profl. jours., newspapers, mags. Bd. dirs. Kent County Vis. Nurses, Warwick, R.I., 1989-94, R.I. Rape Crisis Ctr., Providence, 1992-94, Big Brothers R.I., Pawtucket, 1992-94. Recipient 1st Disting Svc. award West Warwick C. of C., 1994; named Nat. Woman of Yr. Orchard Lake (Mich.) Ladies Aux., 1993. Mem. R.I. Commn. Women (hon.), R.I. Fisherman's Assn. (hon., lifetime). Democrat. Home: 31 Fairview Ave West Warwick RI 02893

O'HARE, SANDRA FERNANDEZ, educator; b. N.Y.C., Mar. 19, 1941; d. Ricardo Enrique and Rosario de Los Angeles (Arenas) Fernandez; m. S. James O'Hare, Oct. 12, 1963; children: James, Richard, Michael, Christopher. BA, Marymount Coll., 1962; MA, U. San Francisco, 1980. Cert. elem. and coll. tchr.; bilingual and lang. devel. specialist. Instr. adult edn. Guam, 1964-66, Spanish Speaking Ctr., Harrisburg, Pa., 1977-79; tchr. Colegio Salesiano, Rota, Spain, 1973, 84, Alisal Sch. Dist., Salinas, Calif., 1979-81, Liberty Sch., Petaluma, Calif., 1981-85, Cinnabar Sch., Petaluma, 1985—; instr. Chapman U., 1994—; also summer migrant edn. programs Cinnabar Sch., Petaluma, 1990, 91; instr. Santa Rosa (Calif.) Jr. Coll., 1982-83, Chapman U., 1994; mem. math. curriculum com. Sonoma County Office Edn., Santa Rosa, 1988. Translator: Isabel la Catolica, 1962. Mem. Asian relief com. ARC, Harrisburg, 1975, Boy Scouts Am., Petaluma, 1983, Mechanicsburg, Pa., 1974, Monterey, Calif., 1971. SDB fellow Johns Hopkins U., 1990. Mem. NEA, AAUW (chair edn. founds. com. 1985-86), Calif. Assn. Bilingual Educators, Cinnabar Tchrs. Assn., Club Hispano-Americano Petaluma (pres. 1987-89). Roman Catholic. Home: 1289 Glenwood Dr Petaluma CA 94954-4326

OHARENKO, MARIA T., public relations official; b. Louvain, Belgium, Dec. 25, 1950; came to U.S., 1951; d. Vladimir and Lubomyra (Kotz) O. BS, Northwestern U., 1972, MS, 1973. Pub. info. officer U.S. AEC, ERDA, Dept. Energy, Argonne and Chgo., Ill., 1973-79; pub. info. and news media advance officer U.S. Dept. Energy, Washington, 1980-81; corp. pub. info. mgr. Northrop Corp., Los Angeles, 1981—. Mem. Aviation/Space Writers Assn., Women in Communications, Soc. Profl. Journalists. Ukrainian Catholic. Office: Northrop Corp 1840 Century Park E Los Angeles CA 90067-2101

O'HERN, CAROL ANN, publishing company executive; b. Chgo., Jan. 13, 1960; d. Elsie Helene (Ebert) Schiemann; m. Patrick Edward O'Hern, Aug. 13, 1982; 1 child, Patrick Edward II. BA, Northwestern U., 1981; post-grad., Nat. Coll. Edn., Evanston, Ill., 1989—. Radio announcer/pub. affairs dir. WSBW-FM, Sturgeon Bay, Wis., 1981; dir. mktg. Nat. Data Resources, Sturgeon Bay, 1981-83; corp. sec. MicroSearch Inc., Sturgeon Bay, 1983-85; product mgr. Nat. Safety Coun., Chgo., 1985-88, Macmillan Directory Div., Wilmette, Ill., 1988—; cons. computer applications Nat. Safety Coun., 1988—. Office: Macmillan Directory Div 3004 Glenview Rd Wilmette IL 60091-3032

OHMAN, DIANA J., state official, former school system administrator; b. Sheridan, Wyo., Oct. 3, 1950; d. Arden and Doris Marie (Carstens) Mahin. AA, Casper Coll., 1970; BA, U. Wyo., 1972, MEd, 1977, postgrad., 1979—. Tchr. kindergarten Natrona County Sch. Dist., Casper, Wyo., 1971-72; tchr. rural sch. K-8 Campbell County Sch. Dist., Gillette, Wyo., 1972-80, rural prin. K-8, 1980-82, prin. K-6, 1982-84, assoc. dir. instrn., 1984-87; dir. K-12 Goshen County Migrant Program, Torrington, Wyo., 1988-89; prin. K-2 Goshen County Sch. Dist., Torrington, Wyo., 1987-90; state supt. pub. instrn. State of Wyo., Cheyenne, 1991-94, secretary of state, 1995—; chmn. Campbell County Mental Health Task Force, 1986-87; mem. Legis. Task Force on Edn. of Handicapped 3-5 Yr. Olds, 1988-89. State Committeewoman Wyo. Rep. Party, 1985-88. Recipient Wyo. Elem. Prin. of Yr. award, 1990; named Campbell County Tchr. of Yr. 1980, Campbell County Profl. Bus. Woman of Yr. 1984, Outstanding Young Woman in Am., 1983. Mem. Coun. of Chief of State Sch. Officers (Washington chpt.), Internat. Reading Assn., Wyo. Assn. of Sch. Adminstrs., Kappa Delta Pi, Phi Kappa Phi, Phi Delta Kappa. Republican. Lutheran. Office: Sec State Office State Capitol Cheyenne WY 82002-0020

OHMAN, JEAN M., association executive, counselor; b. Mpls., May 10, 1920; d. E. W. and May T. (Anderson) O. BS in Health and Phys. Edn., No. State U., Marquette, Mich., 1943; MSW, U. Minn., 1954; postgrad., Hamline U., 1983. High sch. tchr. gen. sci. Ironwood, Mich., 1943-44; recreation dir. City of Marquette, Mich., 1945; warplant mgr. Arkell Co., Mpls., 1945; phys. edn. program dir. St. Paul YWCA, 1945-57, exec. dir., 1957-82; pvt. practice counseling Mpls. and St. Paul, 1982-89, Tempe, Ariz., 1989—. J. J. Hill scholar J. J. Hill Found., 1954. Mem. NASW, Acad. Cert. Social Workers. Home and Office: 2401 W Southern Ave Lot 78 Tempe AZ 85282-4311

O'KEEFE, BEVERLY DISBROW, state official, federal official; b. Wilton, Conn., Sept. 1, 1946; d. Harry Harbs and Jane Corrine (Young) Disbrow; children: Marcia Corrine, Jennifer Lynn; m. John Patrick O'Keefe, Aug. 1981 (div. 1985). AA, Berkshire Community Coll., 1973; BA in Psychology, U. Mass., 1975; MPA, U. S.C., 1979. Lic. social worker, S.C. Statis. clk. U. S.C., Columbia, 1976-78; pub. adminstr. employment and tng. Office of Gov., State of S.C., Columbia, 1976-78, 88—; project coord. Trident Tech. Coll., Charleston, S.C., 1981-82; office mgr. Med. U. S.C., Charleston, 1983-85; coord. bus. svcs. AMI East Cooper Community Hosp., Mt. Pleasant, S.C., 1985-87; mktg. rep. R.L. Bryan Co., Columbia, 1987; pub. adminstr. S.C. Dept. Social Svcs., Columbia, 1988; pub. adminstr., employment and tng. Office Gov. State S.C., Columbia, 1988-89; mem. employment and tng. staff City of Norfolk (Va.) Div. Soc. Svcs., 1990-91; social sci. analyst Naval Edn. and Tng. Ctr. Family Svc. Ctr., Newport, R.I., 1992—. Editor newsletter Friends of Library, 1982-84. Sec. Friends of Charleston County Libr., 1981-82, pres. 1982-84; bd. dirs. Wando High Sch. Local Adv. Coun., Mt. Pleasant, 1981-84; pres. Wando High Sch. PTA, 1982-83, editor newsletter, 1982-85; vol. Navy-Marine Corps Relief Soc., 1993—. Mem. Am. Counseling Assn., R.I. Counseling Assn., Am. Soc. Pub. Adminstrs., APA, Am. Pub. Welfare Assn., Southeastern Employment and Tng. Assn., Phi Theta Kappa. Democrat. Roman Catholic. Home: 472 Gardiner Rd West Kingston RI 02892 Office: US Dept Def USN Family Svc Ctr Naval Edn and Tng Ctr Newport RI 02841

O'KEEFE, KATHLEEN MARY, state government official; b. Butte, Mont., Mar. 25, 1933; d. Hugh I. and Kathleen Mary (Harris) O'Keefe; B.A. in Communications, St. Mary Coll., Xavier, Kans., 1954; m. Nick B. Baker, Sept. 18, 1954 (div. 1970); children—Patrick, Susan, Michael, Cynthia, Hugh, Mardeen. Profl. singer, mem. Kathie Baker Quartet, 1962-72; research cons. Wash. Ho. of Reps., Olympia, 1972-73; info. officer Wash. Employment Security Commn., Seattle, 1973-81, dir. public affairs, 1981-90, video dir., 1990—; freelance writer, composer, producer, 1973—. Founder, pres. bd. Eden, Inc., visual and performing arts, 1975—; public relations chmn. Nat. Women's Democratic Conv., Seattle, 1979, Wash. Dem. Women, 1976-85; bd. dirs., public relations chmn. Eastside Mental Health Center, Bellevue, Wash., 1979-81; Dem. candidate Wash. State Senate, 1968. Recipient Black Community award for composition The Beaufort County Jail, Seattle, 1975, Silver medal Seattle Creative Awards Show for composing, directing and producing Rent A Kid, TV public service spot, 1979. Mem. Wash. Press Women. Democrat. Roman Catholic. Author: Job Finding In the Nineties, handbook on TV prodn., guide to coping with unemployment; composer numerous songs, also producer Job Service spots. Home: 4426 147th Pl NE # 12 Bellevue WA 98007-3162 Office: 212 Maple Park Ave SE Olympia WA 98501-2240

O'KEEFE, NANCY JEAN, real estate company executive; b. Mpls., Jan. 26, 1926; d. Dana Charles and Bonnie Theresa (Lane) Eckenbeck; m. John Robert O'Keefe, Sept. 11, 1946 (div. June 1977); children: Teresa O'Keefe Ankeny, J. Patrick, Leslie O'Keefe Kelly, Bridget O'Keefe Gidley, Elizabeth O'Keefe Skrivseth, Peter C. BS in Social Welfare, U. Minn., 1973. Cert. real estate specialist, Minn., real estate appraiser, Minn.; grad. Real Estate Inst. Sales agt. Harvey Hansen Realty, Edina, Minn., 1976-87; pres., mgr., agt. 1st Mpls. Realty, Edina, 1987-90. Mem. 5th Dist. Rep. Com., Mpls., 1951-52, Minn. Rep. Cen. Com., 1951-52; dist. chmn. fund drive ARC, Mpls., 1956; city chmn. fund drive March of Dimes, Mpls., 1957, 58; bd. dirs. St. Barnabas Hosp., Mpls., 1960-61; pres. Mpls. League Cath. Women, 1974-75. Mem. Minn. Assn. Realtors (bd. dirs. 1990-92), Greater Mpls. Assn. Realtors (bd. dirs. 1986-89, chmn. arbitration bd. 1988, Super Sales Agt. award 1982), Profl. Women's Appraisal Assn., Am. Arbitration Assn. (panel), Pi Beta Phi. Roman Catholic. Home: 6400 York Ave S Apt 602 Minneapolis MN 55435-2339 Office: Great Mpls Real Estate 5357 Penn Ave S Minneapolis MN 55419-1056

O'KEEFE, PATRICIA M., state legislator; b. Methuen, Mass., Feb. 28, 1955. Attended, U. N.H. Commr. Seabrook Beach Village Dist., 1989-91; mem. N.H. Ho. of Reps.; mem. health, human svcs. and elderly affairs com. Bd. dirs. Seacoast Vis. Nurses, 1992—; active Seabrook Budget Com., 1989-90. Democrat. Roman Catholic. Home: 128 Ocean Blvd Seabrook NH 03874 Office: NH Ho of Reps State Capitol Concord NH 03301*

O'KEEFE, RACHEL THERESE, secondary school education; b. Washington, Feb. 9, 1960; d. John Aloysius and Martha (Tulane) O'K.; m. Steven Jon Bohlin, Dec. 27, 1986. BA, St. Johns Coll., 1982; MPA, U. N.Mex., Santa Fe, 1992. Cert. math. and English tchr., N.Mex. Adminstrv. asst. Wellford, Wegman, Krulwich, Gold & Hoff, Washington, 1982, Chgo. Bd. Trade, Washington, 1983; math. tchr. The Maret Sch., Washington, 1983-85, Immaculata High Sch., Rockville, Md., 1985-86, St. Catherines Indian Sch., Santa Fe, 1986-87; asst. dir. admissions St. Johns Coll., Santa Fe, 1987-90; English tchr. Santa Fe Indian Sch., 1992—; faculty mem. Santa Fe C.C., 1993; intern Commn. on Higher Edn., Santa Fe, 1992. Editor: (mag.) Au Verso, 1980. Tutor ESL Literacy Vol. Am., Santa Fe, 1989, Cath. Charities, Washington, 1981. Recipient Caring and Sharing award Santa Fe Indian Sch., 1993, Indian Sci. Tchr. award Native Am. Sci. Edn. Assn., 1987; Ventures Computer Study mini-grant, 1993. Democrat. Roman Catholic. Office: Santa Fe Indian School Cerrillos Rd Santa Fe NM 87501

O'KEEFFE, MARGARET ELIZABETH, advertising executive for manufacturing company; b. Cork, Cork, Ireland, Apr. 3, 1961; came to U.S., 1973; d. Michael Gabriel and Margaret Mary (Daly) O'K. BA, Vassar Coll., 1983, MA, 1984. Cert. secondary tchr., N.Y. Audiovisual coordinator, internat. coordinator Siboney Advt., N.Y.C., 1984; account coordinator, tv prodn. mgr., asst. account exec. Foote, Cone and Belding, N.Y.C., 1984-85; coordinator advt. Bass Shoe Co., Portland, Maine, 1985-86; dir. advt., sales promotion Bass Shoe Co., Portland, 1987—; cons. mktg. Portland Symphony, 1986—. Active Jr. League. Mem. Internat. Advt. Assn., N.Y., Art Dirs. Club, Advert. Club, Portland, Maine. Office: Bass Shoes 360 US Route 1 Falmouth ME 04105-1312

O'KELLY, CHARLOTTE GWEN, sociology educator; b. Hohenwald, Tenn., Sept. 29, 1946; d. Charlie Park and Helen Frances Anderson; m. Larry Sherman Carney, May 10, 1973; 1 child, Seth Lauchlin. AB, Ctrl. Mich. U., 1968; MA, U. Conn., 1969, PhD, 1975. Instr. U. N.C., Asheville, 1973-75; prof. sociology Providence Coll., 1975—; vis. prof. women''s studies U. Hawaii at Manoa, 1990. Author: Women and Men in Society, 1979, 2d edit., 1986; also articles. Lectr. R.I. Com. for Humanities, Providence, 1990, 93. Fellow NDEA, U. Conn., 1968-71, NEH, summers 1981, 84; Fulbright scholar, Japan, 1983. Mem. Am. Sociol. Assn., Sociologists for Women in Soc., Nat. Women's Studies Assn., NOW. Home: 76 Summit Ave Providence RI 02906-2704 Office: Providence Coll Dept Sociology Providence RI 02918

OKIN, CAROL J., federal agency administrator; b. Calif., June 16, 1946; m. Robert J. Okin. Attended, Trinity Coll. Dir. human resources devel. group Office of Personnel Mgmt., dep. dir. Washington area svc. ctr. Mem. ASPA, Exec. Women in Govt. Office: HR Development Group 1900 E St NW Rm 6484 Washington DC 20415-0001*

OKOSHI, SUMIYE, artist; b. Seattle; d. Masanari and Riyoko (Fukuda) Ushiyama; m. George Mukai, Mar. 21, 1976. Grad. Rikkyo Jogakuin U., Futabakai; postgrad., Seattle U., Henry Fry Mus. Modern Art, Seattle, 1957-59. One-woman shows include Gallery Internat., N.Y.C., 1970, Miami Mus. Modern Art, 1972, Nat. Acad. Sci. Washington, Galerie Saison, Tokyo, 1982, St. Peter's Ch. Living Room Gallery, N.Y.C., 1987, Viridian Gallery, N.Y.C., 1987, 92, Port Washington Pub. Libr., 1989, NAS, Washington, 1991-92; exhibited in group shows Met. Mus. Art, N.Y.C., 1977, World Trade Center, N.Y.C., 1979, Tokyo Nat. Mus., 1979, Pace U. Gallery, Briarcliff, N.Y., 1981, Joslyn Center Arts, Torrance, Calif., Newark Mus., 1983, Bergen Mus. Art and Scis., 1983, Am. Acad. Arts and Scis., 1984, Nassau C.C., 1985-86, Port Washington Pub. Library, L.I., N.Y., 1985, Hudson River Mus., 1985, NAWA Ann. Javits Fed. Bldg., 1986, São Paulo and N.Y. Culture Exchange, 1988, Hyndai Gallery, Pusan, Korea, 1988; represented in permanent collection at Steve Hasegawa Bank of Alaska, Kaplan Fund., N.Y., Mr. & Mrs. K. Yoshikawa, N.Y., Mr. & Mrs. Haruo Yoshida, Conn., Nobart Pub. Co. Inc., The Mitsui & Co., N.Y., Hotel Nikko, Atlanta, Bank of Nagoya, N.Y., Palace Hotel, Guam Island, 1991, Port Washington (N.Y.) Pub. Libr., 1989, Lowe Gallery-U. Miami, Miami Mus. of Modern Art, Nat. Women's Edn. Ctr., Saitama-ken, Japan, Nat. Acad. Sci., Washington 1992, Hammond Mus., N. Salem, N.Y., 1993, The Jane Voorhees Zimmerli Art Mus., N.J., 1994, Permanent Collection NAWA. Mem. Japanese Artists Assn. N.Y., Nat. Women Artists Assn. (Belle Cramer award, Ziuta and Joseph Fund. award, Ralph Mayer Meml. award), Nat. Mus. Women in the Arts (charter mem. 1994). Episcopalian. Office: 55 Bethune St # 226G New York NY 10014-1703

OLANITORI, SANDRA JOYCE, women's health nurse; b. South Norfolk, Va., June 1, 1950; d. Floyd L. and Dorothy M. (Corbett) Brown; m. Peter A. Olanitori; children: Adetola, Peter A. AS in Nursing, Norfolk (Va.) State Coll., 1975, BS, 1979; MS, Old Dominion U., Norfolk, 1985. Cert. CPR instr., neonatal resucitation program instr. Respiratory intensive care tech Norfolk Gen. Hosp., 1977-78, staff nurse, 1978-79, charge nurse, 1979-81, head nurse newborn nursery, 1981-90; adminstr., supr. Sentara Bayside Hosp., 1991-92; nurse mgr. newborn nursery Norfolk Community Hosp., 1992—. Mem. ANA (cert. nursing adminstr.), Va. Pub. Health Assn., Nat. Perinatal Assn., Va. Perinatal Assn. (pres.), Action for Prevention, Chi Eta Phi. Home: 901 Harbour North Dr Chesapeake VA 23320-6516

O'LAUGHLIN, MARJORIE HARTLEY, state official. Student, Ind. U., Bloomington. Formerly city clerk Indpls., clerk Ind. Supreme Ct., Ct. Appeals, treas. of Ind., 1987—; formerly vice-chmn. Marion County Rep. Cen. Com., exec. dir. Greater Indpls. Rep. Fin. Com., treas. Hoosiers for Bob Orr coms., 1980, 84. Mem. Nat. Assn. State Treas., Nat. Fed. Rep. Women, Kiwanis of Indpls., Kappa Alpha Theta. Office: State Treasurer 242 State House Indianapolis IN 46204-2212*

OLD, JEAN CURTIS, stockbroker; b. Norfolk, Va., Feb. 10, 1925; d. Curtis L. and Annie (Gause) O. AB, Sweet Briar Coll., 1947; student, Old Dominion U., 1950-54, Am. Inst. Banking, 1958-62. Sec. Blair Jr. High Sch., Norfolk, 1950-54; stockbroker Wyllie & Thornhill, Norfolk, 1954-58; stockbroker, v.p. Wheat First Butcher Singer, Norfolk, 1958—. Treas. Jr. League Norfolk, 1952-54, Zonta Internat., Norfolk, 1960-62; bd. dirs. Va. Opera Assn., Norfolk, 1978-81, Va. Symphony, Norfolk, 1974-82, Wet Lands City of Norfolk, 1988—; mem. planned giving com. Sweet Briar (Va.) Coll., 1988—. Named Outstanding Profl. Woman Outstanding Profl. Women Hampton Rds., Norfolk, 1982. Republian. Episcopalian. Home: 1603 Claud Ln Norfolk VA 23505-2915 Office: Wheat First Butcher Singer 500 E Main St Ste 1400 Norfolk VA 23510-2206

OLDENBURGER, NORMA JANE, medical/surgical nurse; b. Carrington, N.D., Oct. 13, 1947; d. Joseph and Edna J. (Larson) Hoggarth; 1 child, Kristen Nicole. Diploma, St. Luke's Hosp. Sch. Nursing, Fargo, N.D., 1968; BSN, Mary Coll., Bismarck, N.D., 1978. RN, N.D.; cert. PALS. Staff nurse ICU St. Luke's Hosp., Fargo, insvc. instr. ICU; staff nurse ICU St. Alexius Hosp., Bismarck; instr. ACLS. 1st lt. USAR, 1975-77. Mem. ANA, ACCN (cert. CCRN), Sigma Theta Tau. Home: 3100 Winnipeg Dr Bismarck ND 58501-0451

OLDHAM, LEA LEEVER, business owner, author; b. Cleve., Feb. 8, 1931; d. Harold G. and Virginia K. (Hubbard) Reed; m. John W. Leever, Apr. 16, 1949 (div. June 1977); children: Katherine Gavin, John, Lorraine Brooks, Pattie Buscema, Mary Ella Novotny, Christine Skrynecki; m. Jack R. Oldham (dec.); children: James, Naomi Uchnar. Grad. high sch., Cleve. Assoc. editor Diocese L.A., Garden City, N.Y., 1966-69; sr. writer L.I. Daily Rev., Syosset, N.Y., 1969-74; publs. editor Chemco Photoproducts, Glen Cove, N.Y., 1974-77; owner Images to Impress, Willoughby, Ohio, 1980—; instr., coord. Auburn Career Ctr., Painesville, Ohio, 1985-89; mem. part-time faculty Lakeland C.C., 1979—, Cuyahoga C.C., 1991-94; mem. Pvt. Industry Coun., Painesville, 1986—, mktg. comn., 1986-91; founder, coord. Western Res. Writers and Freelance Conf., 1983—, Cleveland Heights-University Heights Mini Writers Conf., 1992-94; mgmt. cons. various bus. and govtl. agys., 1981—. Author: Teaching Techniques for Non-Credit and Continuing Education of Adults and Seniors, 1995; co-author: Expand Horizons by Understanding Self and Others, 1985, Expand Your Time Use Potential, 1987; editor (newspaper) Mature View, 1993-94; contbr. articles to profl. mags. Sec. Hicksville (N.Y.) Coordinating Coun., 1961; v.p. Hicksville Dem. Club, 1960; advisor to newspaper Richmond Heights H.S.; bd. dirs. Divsn. Lay Ministry, Diocese of Ohio, 1986-91. Recipient Bishop's Cross award Diocese of L.I., 1975, Outstanding Pacesetter award Greater Cleve. Women, 1985. Mem. Women Bus. Owners Western Res. (pres. 1984, achievement award 1988), Nat. League Am. Pen Women, Internat. Mgmt. Coun., Garden Writers Assn. Am., Press Club Cleve. Home and Office: 34200 Ridge Rd Apt 110 Willoughby OH 44094-2954

OLDHAM, MAXINE JERNIGAN, real estate broker; b. Whittier, Calif., Oct. 13, 1923; d. John K. and Lela Hessie (Mears) Jernigan; m. Laurance Montgomery Oldham, Oct. 28, 1941; 1 child, John Laurence. AA, San Diego City Coll., 1973; student Western State U. Law, San Diego, 1976-77, LaSalle U., 1977-78; grad. Realtors Inst., Sacramento, 1978. Mgr. Edin Harig Realty, LaMesa, Calif., 1966-70; tchr. Bd. Edn., San Diego, 1959-66; mgr. Julia Cave Real Estate, San Diego, 1970-73; salesman Computer Realty, San Diego, 1973-74; owner Shelter Island Realty, San Diego, 1974—. Author: Jernigan History, 1982, Mears Geneology, 1985, Fustons of Colonial America, 1988, Sissoms. Mem. Civil Svc. Commn., San Diego, 1957-58. Recipient Outstanding Speaker award Dale Carnegie. Mem. Nat. Assn. Realtors, Calif. Assn. Realtors, San Diego Bd. Realtors, San Diego Apt. Assn., Internationale des Professions Immobilieres (internat. platform speaker), DAR (vice regent Linares chpt.), Colonial Dames 17th Century, Internat. Fedn. Univ. Women. Republican. Roman Catholic. Avocations: music, theater, painting, geneology, continuing edn. Home: 3348 Lowell St San Diego CA 92106-1713 Office: Shelter Island Realty 2810 Lytton St San Diego CA 92110-4810

OLDHAM, PHYLLIS VIRGINIA KIDD, retired librarian; b. Lafayette, Ind., Mar. 19, 1926; d. Hulbert Haven and Grace Ellene (Doup) Kidd; BS, Purdue U., 1948, MS, Butler U., 1966; 1 child, Stephen Kidd. Tchr. English, Jefferson High Sch., Lafayette, 1950; tchr., librarian Tudor Hall Sch., Indpls., 1954-70; librarian Park Tudor Sch., 1970-91; ret. 1991; mem. exec. bd. Central Ind. Area Library Svcs. Authority, sec., 1983-85. Mem. People-to-People Internat., dist. dir. Student Ambassador Program, 1970-80; chmn. bd. Cen. Christian Ch., Indpls., 1979-81, 89-90, bd. trustees, 1991; mem. vol. council Indpls. Zool. Soc. Mem. ALA, Marion County Librarians Assn. (pres. 1969-72), Ind. Media Educators, Kappa Delta Pi, Delta Kappa Gamma (treas. Alpha Eta chpt. 1974-80), Pi Beta Phi. Home: 7015 Warwick Rd Indianapolis IN 46220-1050

OLDMAN, MARILYN, psychologist; b. N.Y., June 11, 1936; d. Barnett and Shirley (Kaplan) Binkowitz; m. Elliott Oldman, Sept. 15, 1962 (div. May 1989); children: Elizabeth Sue, Mark Stanford. BS, NYU, 1958; MEd, Trenton State Coll., 1979; postgrad., Rutgers U., 1979-81; EdD, Fairleigh Dickinson U., 1987. Lic. psychologist, N.J. Counselor East Brunswick (N.J.) Adult and Continuing Edn. Program, 1980-91; instr. Fairleigh Dickinson U., Rutherford, N.J., 1982-83; post doctoral externship Union County Psychiat. Clinic, Plainfield, N.J., 1987-89; pvt. practice Watchung, N.J., 1987—; assoc. mem. Group Psychotherapy Assocs., Cranbury, N.J., 1987-94. Assoc. fellow Inst. for Rational-Emotive Therapy; mem. APA, Soc. Psychologists in Pvt. Practice, N.J. Assn. Cognitive-Behavioral Therapists, N.J. Psychol. Assn., N.J. Assn. Women Therapists, N.J. Acad. Psychology. Office: Shawnee Profl Bldg 10 Shawnee Dr Ste 7A Watchung NJ 07060-5803

OLDS, JACQUELINE, psychiatrist, educator; b. Springfield, Mass., Jan. 4, 1947; d. James and Marianne (Ejier) O.; m. Richard Stanton Schwartz, Aug. 26, 1978; children: Nathaniel Leland, Sarah Elizabeth. BA, Radcliffe Coll., 1967; MD, Tufts U., 1971. Diplomate Am. Bd. Psychiatry and Neurology. Resident in adult psychiatry Mass. Mental Health Ctr., Boston, 1974; resident in child psychiatry McLean Hosp., Belmont, Mass., 1976, asst. attending child psychiatrist, 1979—; psychiatrist-in-charge inpatient unit McLean Hall-Mercer Children's Ctr., Belmont, 1976-79; assoc. child psychiatry Beth Israel Hosp., Boston, 1979—; instr. psychiatry, Harvard U. Med. Sch., Boston, 1976-86, asst. prof. clin. psychiatry, 1986—; cons. North Shore Mental Health Ctr., Salem, 1981-82. Contbr. articles to profl. jours., 1982, 89. Sec. Cambridge (Mass.) Nursery Sch. Bd., 1982-84. Fellow Am. Psychiat. Assn.; mem. Mass. Psychiat. Soc. (ethics com. 1988-93, mem. pub. affairs com. 1992—), Am. Acad. Child Psychiatry, Am. Psychoanalytic Assn., New England Coun. Child Psychiatry, Cambridge Skating Club (bd. dirs. 1989). Democrat.

OLDS, SHARON, poet; b. San Francisco, Nov. 19, 1942. BA, Stanford U., 1964; PhD, Columbia U., 1972. Lectr.-in-residence on poetry Theodor Herzl Inst., 1976-80; Fanny Hurst chair Brandeis U., Waltham, Mass., 1986-87; dir. grad. program in creative writing NYU, 1988-91, assoc. prof. English, 1992—; vis. tchr. poetry Manhattan Theater Club, 1982, Poetry Ctr. for YMCA of N.Y.C., 1982, Poetry Soc. of Am., 1983, NYU, 1983, 85, Sarah Lawrence Coll., 1984, Goldwater Hosp., Roosevelt Island, N.Y., 1985-90, Columbia U., 1986, SUNY, Purchase, 1986; adj. prof. grad. program in creative writing NYU, 1983-92. Author: Satan Says, 1980 (San Francisco Poetry Ctr. award 1981), The Dead and Living, 1984 (Lamont Poetry Selection of the Am. Acad. Poets 1984, Nat. Book Critics Circle award 1985), The Gold Cell, 1987, The Matter of This World, 1987, The Sign of Saturn, 1991, The Father, 1992; contbr. poetry to numerous anthologies. Guggenheim fellow, 1981-82; Nat. Endowment for Arts grantee, 1982-83; recipient Madeline Sadin award N.Y. Quar., 1978, Poetry Miscellany Younger Poets award, 1979. Home: 250 Riverside Dr New York NY 10025 Office: NYU Dept English New York NY 10003*

OLDWINE, BARBARA H., retired social worker, retired association executive; b. Binghamton, N.Y., Feb. 8, 1923; d. William Armstead and Mary Eliza Penrose (Harris) Harris; m. Cornelius V. Oldwine, June 6, 1944; children: B. Eilene Oldwine Carter, Valerie O. Barnes. BA, Fisk U., 1944; advanced mgmt. cert., Syracuse U., 1980. Supr. medicaid and food stamps, caseworker pub. adminstr. Broome County Social Svc., Binghamton, N.Y., 1946-81; lectr. Broome Community Coll., Binghamton, 1980-85. Author: (booklet) Black Americans Who Made America What It Is, 1989, 28 TV vignettes, 1976 (N.Y. State Broadcasters award-Sta. WBNG). Bd. dirs. Opportunities for Broome, Binghamton, 1970s, Nat. Bd. YWCA of U.S.A., 1981; pres. Broome County Urban League Guild, Binghamton, 1981; trustee Sta. WSKG-PBS, Binghamton, 1990—; pres. bd. dirs. Am. Cancer Soc., 1993—, YWCA Broome County, 1973; tchr. All Sts. Episcopal Ch., Johnson City, N.Y., 1990—. Named Bicentennial Women of Yr, Binghamton County, 1976, Citizen of Yr., So. Tier Divsn. NASW, 1989, African Am. Distinction Citizen, Gov. Cuomo N.Y., 1993; recipient Svc. to Mankind award Sertoma Club, Binghamton, 1981, Pres.'s award Delta Sigma Theta, 1985, St. George medal Nat. Am. Cancer Soc., 1989, Nation Gold award 1992. Mem. Daus. Isis (Ill. commandress Aleppo Ct. # 140 1987-88, dep. imperial directress pub. rels. 1989—). Episcopalian. Home: 24 Gaylord St Binghamton NY 13904-1608

O'LEARY, HAZEL R., U.S. secretary of energy, former power company executive, lawyer; b. Newport News, Va., May 17, 1937; d. Russell E. and Hazel (Palleman) Reid; m. John F. O'Leary, Apr. 23, 1980; 1 child, Carl G. Rollins. BA, Fisk U., Nashville, 1959; JD, Rutgers U., Newark, 1966. Bar: N.J. 1967, D.C. 1985; cert. fin. planner. V.p., gen. counsel O'Leary Assocs., Inc., Washington, 1981-89; exec. v.p. corp. affairs No. States Power Co., Mpls., 1989-93, pres., 1993; sec. U.S. Dept. Energy, Washington, 1993—. Mem. Phi Beta Kappa. Office: US Dept Energy Office Sec 1000 Independence Ave SW Washington DC 20585-0001

O'LEARY, KATHERINE, county official; b. Salem, Mass., Sept. 13, 1942; d. Richard Bernard and Helene Katherine (Reddy) O'Keefe; m. Richard Allen O'Leary, Nov. 6, 1966; children: Maureen, Bethann, Richard Jr. BS in Acctg., Bentley Coll., 1964. Acct. George Tsoutsouras, CPA, Ipswich, Mass., 1976-79; chmn. Essex County Retirement Bd., Salem, 1979—; treas. County of Essex, Salem, 1979—; v.p. Mass. Assn. Contributory Retirement Sys., Boston, 1991-93, pres., 1993-95; sec. Commonwealth of Mass. Assn. of County Treas., Cambridge, 1985—. Softball coach Salem State Coll., 1987—. Mem. Ward II Social Club (pres. 1984-86). Democrat. Roman Catholic. Home: 19 Witchcraft Rd Salem MA 01970-1233 Office: Essex County Treas 36 Federal St Salem MA 01970-3445

O'LEARY, TERESA, controller; b. N.Y.C., Jan. 21, 1960; d. Donald James and Frances W. (McGowan) O'L. BS, N.Y. Inst. Tech., 1981; JD, N.Y. Law Sch., 1994. Lic. fin. and ops. prin. Sr. compliance examiner Nat. Assn. Securities Dealers, N.Y.C., 1982-85; asst. v.p., sr. compliance officer Ryan, Beck & Co., West Orange, N.J., 1985-89; v.p., contr. Chapdelaine & Co., N.Y.C., 1989—. Office: Chapdelaine & Co 80 Maiden Ln New York NY 10038-4811

OLEEN, LANA, state legislator; b. Kirksville, Mo., Apr. 26, 1949; d. Robert James and Frances (Primm) Scrimsher; m. Kent E. Oleen; children: Brooke, Bentson. BS in Edn., Emporia State U., 1972, MS in Curriculum. Tchr. Council Grove, Kans., 1972-74, St. George, Kans., from 1978; communications coord. Woodward-Clyde Cons., San Francisco, 1974-75; dir. communication Kans. Dept. Human Resources; senator Kans. State Senate, 1988—; mem. Rep. Precinct Com., 1978—. Active Kans. Rep. Women, Riley County Rep. Women. Mem. NEA, Nat. Coun. Tchrs. of English. Lutheran. Home: 3000 Stagg Hill Rd Manhattan KS 66502-4035 Office: State Senate State Capitol Topeka KS 66612*

OLEKSEY, VICKY JOYCE, business analyst; b. Glasgow, Mont., Dec. 12, 1952; d. Frank Smith Jr. and Mary Helen (Smith) McIntyre; m. John Peter Oleksey, Jr., Aug. 7, 1976 (div. May 1984); 1 child, Kathryn Elizabeth. Student, U. Colo., 1973-76, U. Md., Fed. Republic Germany, 1977-81; BSBA, U. Phoenix, 1984; MBA, Boise State U., 1988. Keytape operator 1st Security Bank, Glasgow, 1968-71; programmer analyst Baldwin Data Svcs., Denver, 1973-76; acctg. technician dept. non-appropriated funds U.S. Govt., Ramstein, Fed. Republic Germany, 1977-79, systems operator dept. non-appropriated funds, 1979-80; programmer analyst II, United Banks Colo., Denver, 1982-85; programmer analyst Moore Fin. Group, Boise, Idaho, 1985-87, career developer, 1987-88; mgr. quality assurance West One Bancorp, Boise, 1988-90; mgr. quality assurance software products Bankers Systems, Inc., St. Cloud, Minn., 1991-93, sr. bus. analyst, 1993—. Mem. personnel com., leader single parents group 1st Presbyn. Ch., Boise, 1988-89. Recipient Outstanding Project Chmn. award, Jaycee of Month award U.S. Jaycees-Idaho, 1989, Staff Officer of Yr., 1991, Project Chmn. of Yr. 1991, Ambassador, 1993; named Statesman Minn. Jaycees, 1993, Single Parent of the Yr., 1994. Mem. Am. Bus. Women's Assn. (v.p. Boise chpt. 1987-88, Woman of Yr. award 1987), Capitol Jaycees (v.p. for mgmt. devel. 1989), Sartell Jaycees (pres. 1992-93, state del. 1993-94). Republican. Episcopalian. Home: 2808 21st Ave S Saint Cloud MN 56301-9000 Office: Bankers Systems Inc PO Box 1457 Saint Cloud MN 56302-1457

OLESKOWICZ, JEANETTE, physician; b. N.Y.C., Oct. 10, 1956; d. John Francis and Helen (Zielinski) O. BA, NYU, 1977; D of Chiropractic, N.Y. Chiropractic Coll., 1982; MS, U. Bridgeport, 1984; MD, U. Medicine & Dentistry N.J., 1990. U.S. immigration officer U.S. Dept. Justice, N.Y.C., 1977; commd. med. officer USAR, 1983; advanced through grades to capt. HPSP, 1990; chief psychiatry U.S. Army Hosp., Vincenza, Italy, 1990—. Am. sponsor for a cripples child's health care in Mid. East. Mem. AMA, Am. Psychiat. Assn. Roman Catholic. Home: CMR 427 Box 2462 APO AE 09630 Office: Army MEDDAC, Chief of Psychiatry, CMR 427 Box 2462 APA AE, 09630 Vicenza Italy

OLIAN, JOANNE CONSTANCE, curator, art historian; b. N.Y.C., d. Richard Edward and Dorothy (Singer) Wahrman; m. Howard Olian; children: Jane Wendy, Patricia Ann. Student, Syracuse U.; BA, Hofstra U., 1969; MA, NYU/Inst. Fine Arts, 1972. Grad. internship Met. Mus., N.Y.C., 1973; asst. curator Mus. of City of N.Y., 1974, curator costume collection, 1975-91; cons. curator Costume Collection, 1992—; lectr. Parsons Sch. Design; vis. lectr. Musée des Arts Decoratifs, Paris, summer 1983, 84, 85. Author: The House of Worth: The Gilded Age, 1860-1918, 1982; editor: Authentic French Fashions of the Twenties, 1990, Everyday Fashions of the Forties, 1992, Children's Fashions from Mode Illustre 1860-1912, 1994; contbr. articles to profl. jours., chpts. to books. Mem. Internat. Council Mus. (costume com.), Costume Soc. Am. (dir. 1976-79, 83-86), Fashion Group (bd. dirs. 1985-86), Centre Internat. d'Etude des Textiles Anciens. Club: Cosmopolitan (N.Y.C.). Home: Shepherds Ln Port Washington NY 11050 Office: Mus City NY 1220 5th Ave New York NY 10029

OLIN, LENA MARIA JONNA, actress; b. Stockholm, Mar. 22, 1955; d. Britta Alice Holmberg; 1 child, August. Actress Royal Dramatic Theatre, Stockholm, Bklyn. Acad. Music; performances include (theater) The Alchemist, Paradisbarnen, Juno and the Peacock, Gross and Klein, Servitore Di Due Padrone, Restoration, King Lear, Nattvarden, Summer, A Dream Play, The Master and Margerita, (films) The Adventures of Picasso, 1978, Karleken, 1980, Fanny and Alexander, 1982, Grasanklingar, 1982, After the Rehersal, 1984, Friends, 1987, The Unbearable Lightness of Being, 1988, Enemies, A Love Story, 1989, Havana, 1990, Mr. Jones, 1993, Romeo is Bleeding, 1994; (mus.) Miss Julie. Office: care ICM/Martha Luttrell 321 Westminster Ave Los Angeles CA 90020-4652*

OLINGER, CARLA D(RAGAN), medical advertising executive; b. Cin., Oct. 8, 1947; d. Carl Edward and Selene Ethel (Neal) Dragan; m. Chauncey Greene Olinger, Jr., May 30, 1981. B.A., Douglass Coll., 1975. Mgr. info. retrieval services Frank J. Corbett, Inc., N.Y.C., 1976-77; editor, proofreader, prodn. asst. Rolf W. Rosenthal, Inc., N.Y.C., 1977-78, copywriter, 1978-80, copy supr., 1980-82, v.p. copy dept., 1982-83; v.p., group copy supr., adminstrv. copy supr. Rolf W. Rosenthal, Inc., div. Ogilvy & Mather, 1984-89, v.p., assoc. creative dir. RWR Advt., 1989; v.p., copy supr. Barnum & Souza, N.Y.C., 1990-92; v.p., copy supr. Botto, Roessner, Horne & Messinger, Ketchum Comm., N.Y.C., 1992—. Editor: Antimicrobial Prescribing (Harold Neu), 1979. Mem. Am. Med. Writers Assn., Ch. Club N.Y., St. George's Soc. N.Y. Office: Botto Roessner Horne & Messinger Ketchum Comm 16 W 22d St New York NY 10010

OLIPHANT, BETTY, ballet school director; b. London, Eng., Aug. 5, 1918. Studied classical ballet under Tamara Karsavina and Laurent Novikoff; student, Queen's and St. Mary's Colls.; LLD (hon.), Queen's U., 1978, Brock U., 1978, U. Toronto., 1980; DLitt, York U., 1992. Prin. dancer and arranger Prince & Emile Littler Prodns., London, 1936-46; dance arranger Howard & Wyndham, London, 1936-46; tchr. ballet London, 1936-40; dancer, dance arranger and ballet mistress Blue Pencils Concert Party, Eng., 1944-46; tchr. ballet Oliphant Sch., Toronto, Can., 1948-59; ballet mistress Nat. Ballet of Can., Toronto, 1951-62; prin. and dir. Nat. Ballet Sch., 1959; asso. artistic dir. Nat. Ballet of Can., 1969-75, artistic dir., 1975-89; founder Nat. Ballet Sch., 1991—; founder reorganized Ballet Sch. of Royal Swedish Opera, 1967, Royal Danish Theatre, 1978; mem. jury Internat. Ballet Competition, Moscow, 1977-81, III Internat. Ballet Competition, Jackson, MIss., 1986. Contbr. articles on dance and teaching to profl. publs. Decorated officer Order of Can., 1972, Companion Order of Can., 1985; recipient Centennial medal, 1967, Molson prize, 1978, Diplome d'Honneur Can. Conf. Arts, 1982, Lifetime Achievement award, Toronto Arts Awards Found., 1989, Order of Napoleon, France, 1990, Commemorative medal 125th Anniversary Can., 1992; fellow Ont. Inst. for Studies in Edn., 1985. Fellow Imperial Soc. Tchrs. of Dancing (examiner), Ont. Inst. Studies in Edn., 1985; mem. Can. Dance Tchrs. Assn. (founder, past pres.), Internat. Soc. of Tchrs. of Dancing, Can. Assn. Profl. Dance Orgns. (founding mem.). Office: Nat Ballet Sch, 105 Maitland St, Toronto, ON Canada M4Y 1E4

OLIPHANT, ERNIE L., safety educator, public relations executive, consultant; b. Richmond, Ind., Oct. 25, 1934; d. Ernest E. and Beulah A. (Jones) Reid; m. George B. Oliphant, Sept. 25, 1955; children: David, Wendell, Rebecca. Student, Earlham Coll., 1953-55, Ariz. State U., 1974, Phoenix Coll., 1974-78. Planner, organizer, moderator confs., programs for various women's clubs, safety assns., 1971-86; nat. field coordinator Operation Lifesaver, Inc., 1986-94; assoc. dir. Operation Lifesaver Nat. Safety Council, Phoenix, 1978-86; cons. Fed. R.R. Adminstrn.; prin. Highway and Rail Cons. Svcs., Phoenix, 1995—. lectr. in field.; adviser Am. Ry. Engring. Assn., Calif. Assn. Women Hwy. Safety Leaders, numerous others. Mem. R.R./Hwy. grade crossing com. Ariz. Corp. Commn.; mem. transp. and system com. Ariz. Gov.'s Commn. on Environment; mem. Ariz. Gov.'s Council Women for Hwy. Safety; mem. motor vehicle traffic safety at hwy.-r.r. grade crossings com., roadway environment com., women's div. com. Nat. Safety Council; mem. Phoenix Traffic Accident Reduction Program; task force mem. U.S. Dept. Transp. on Grade Crossing Safety. Recipient Safety award SW Safety Congress, 1973; citation of Merit Adv. Commn. on Ariz. Environment, 1974; Gov.'s award for hwy. safety, 1978; Gov.'s Merit of Recognition Outstanding Service in Hwy. Safety, 1980. Mem. Assn. R.R. Editors, NAFE, Inc., Pub. Relations Soc. Am., R.R. Pub. Relations Assn., committees Nat. Acad. Scis. (dir. transp. research, planning, adminstrn. of transp. safety com., r.r.-hwy. grade crossing safety com.), Women's Transp. Seminar, Ariz. Fedn. Women's Clubs (named pres. of yr. 1968), Ariz. Safety Assn. (safety recognition award 1975), Gen. Fedn. Women's Clubs (internat. bd. dirs.), Nat. Assn. Women Hwy. Safety Leaders, Soc. Govt. Planners, Inc., Phi Theta Kappa. Republican. Quaker. Author of tech. publs.

OLIPHANT, JODIE JENKINS, secondary school consultant; b. Huntsville, Tex., May 1, 1945; d. Lewis George and Mydusta (McGuire) Jenkins; m. Lou Cal Oliphant, Nov. 8, 1963; children: Rosalind, Patrick, Liranda, Ashley. BS, Tex. So. U., 1970; MEd, Prairie View A&M U., 1972. Cert. sch. adminstr. Tchr. bus. Houston Ind. Sch. Dist., 1970-79, sch. counselor, 1979-85, sch. cons., 1985—; chmn., bd. dirs. Oliphant Found., Houston. Coauthor 7th grade typewriting curriculum, 1979. Vol. Voter Registration Campaign, Houston, 1979, 80, 83, United Negro Coll. Fund, 1983, Girl Scouts U.S., Houston, 1986-94, Jesse Jackson for Pres. Campaign, Houston, 1988, Ann Richards for Gov. Campaign, Houston, 1990; del. State Dem. Conv., Houston, 1988; mem. Brentwood Bapt. Ch., Houston, Dowling Mid. Sch. PTA Bd., 1990-91. Recipient Cert. of Appreciation Mayor of Houston, 1979. Mem. NEA, Am. Pers. and Guidance Assn., Houston Tchrs. Assn., Nat. Bus. Edn. Assn., Nat. Coun. Negro Women (exec. bd. Dorothy I. Heights sect. 1979-80, Svc. award 1977, Human Rels. award 1979, Community Svc. award 1991), Nat. Women of Achievement (v.p. Galena Pk. Metroplex chpt. 1991, Golden Apple Ednl. Svc. award 1993), Eta Phi Beta (past. pres. and cons. Xi chpt., exec. bd. 1973—, nat. fin. sec. 1986-90), Alpha Kappa Alpha (exec. bd. Alpha Kappa Omega chpt. 1979-82, 87), Phi Delta Kappa, Top Ladies of Distinction, Inc. Office: Houston Ind Sch Dist 3830 Richmond Ave Houston TX 77027-5864

OLIVARI, KAREN LYNNE, accountant; b. Gardner, Mass., Dec. 4, 1955; d. Emil A. and Barbara R. (Beaton) Tanguay; m. David M. Olivari, Sept. 10, 1977; children: Melanie A., Samuel D. A in Bus. Adminstrn., Mt. Wachusett C.C., 1993; postgrad., Worcester State Coll., 1994—. File clk. Gardner (Mass.) C. of C., 1969-70; sec. Simplex Time Recorder Co., Gardner, 1973-81, Am. Hoechst Corp., Leominster, Mass., 1981-82; bookkeeper J&W Auto Supply Co., Fitchburg, Mass., 1985-90; enumerator U.S. Dept. Census, Worcester, 1990—. Vol. Levi-Heywood Libr., Gardner, 1991-94; leader Montachusett Girl Scouts, Gardner, 1989-92; organizer Sr.

Summer Days Vols., Gardner, 1992-94. Recipient Kathi Pullen award Mt. Wachusett C.C., 1991, Edn. Found. award Mass. Soc. CPAs, 1994; Big Y Supermarkets scholar, 1993. Mem. Nat. Soc. Pub. Accts., Inst. Mgmt. Accts. (v.p. 1994, pres. 1994-95). Home: 185 Leo Dr Gardner MA 01440

OLIVARIUS-IMLAH, MARYPAT, sales, advertising and marketing executive; b. Bklyn., Oct. 25, 1957; d. Kenneth William Joseph and Ann Marie (Beckley) Olivarius; m. Craig Alexander Olivarius-Imlah, Sept. 18, 1982; children: Christopher Edward, Jamison Robert, Meghan Patricia. BS in Mktg. and Communications, Ramapo State Coll. N.J., 1979; MBA in Mktg. and Mgmt., Fairleigh Dickinson U., 1985. Researcher, pub. rels. MacNeil/Lehrer Report, WNET-TV, N.Y.C., 1977; salesperson Terrace Realty, Montvale, N.J., 1977-79; direct mail advt. copywriter Prentice-Hall, Inc., Englewood Cliffs, N.J., 1979-81; editor, promotional designer Beauty & Barber Supply Inst., Englewood, N.J., 1981-83; nat. dir. advt. and pub. rels. Emerson Radio Corp., North Bergen, N.J., 1983-85; founder, pres. Imagery Print & Advt., Print Brokerage Design Agy.

OLIVAS, THERESA MARIE, behavioral science educator, psychotherapist; b. Denver, Dec. 31, 1960; d. Leroy Donald and Mercy Mary (Jaques-Chavez) O. BA, U. No. Colo., 1983, MA, 1986. Lic. psychotherapist, counselor, Colo. Rsch. asst., part-time faculty North Colo. Family Medicine, Greeley, 1983-86, mem. behavioral sci. faculty, 1986-89, dir. behavioral scis. faculty, 1989—; clinician, mental health cons. Centennial Critical Incident and Stress Debriefing Team, Greeley, 1988—; faculty dept. family medicine U. Colo., Denver, 1987—. Bd. dirs. Consumer Credit Counseling, No. Colo., 1992-93; bd. juvenile rev. com. County Commr.'s Office, Weld County, 1994—. Mem. Internat. Critical Incident Stress Found., Am. Counseling Assn., Am. Mental Health Counseling Assn., Colo. Mental Health Assn., Soc. Tchrs. Family Medicine. Democrat. Roman Catholic. Office: North Colo Family Medicine 1650 16th St Greeley CO 80631

OLIVEIRA, MARY JOYCE, middle school education educator; b. Oakland, Calif., Feb. 16, 1954; d. Joseph and Vivian (Perry) O. BA, U. Calif., Berkeley, 1978; student, Holy Names Coll., Oakland, 1992; grad. in math., Calif. State U., Hayward, 1994. Cert. tchr., Calif. Recreation specialist Oakland Parks and Recreation, 1977-89; substitute tchr. Diocese of Oakland, 1989-90; tutor Oakland Pub. Schs., 1991; substitute tchr. Alameda (Calif.) Unified Sch. Dist., 1992-94, Piedmont (Calif.) Unified Sch. Dist., 1993—; tchr. summer program Wood Mid. Sch., Alameda, Calif., 1993, 94, Chipman Mid. Sch., Alameda, 1994; substitute tchr. Piedmont (Calif.) Unified Sch. Dist., 1993—, Alameda Unified Sch. Dist., 1991—. Creator children's sock toys Oliveira Originals, 1985. Vol. in art therapy oncology ward Children's Hosp., Oakland, 1985; vol. Berkeley Unified Sch. Dist., 1990-91. Mem. Internat. Reading Assn., Nat. Coun. Tchrs. English, Nat. Coun. Tchrs. Math. Home: 3903 Mera St Oakland CA 94601-4222

OLIVER, DIANN, telephone company official; b. Lake Charles, La., Oct. 21, 1951; d. Kermit and Edna (Carlock) O. Grad. high sch., Westlake, La. With South Cen. Bell, Lake Charles, La., 1969-74; switch person South Cen. Bell, New Orleans, 1974-75; supr. electronic switching system South Cen. Bell, Alexandria, La., 1975-88; supr. power systems South Cen. Bell, Shreveport, La., 1988—. Troop leader Cen. La. coun. Girl Scouts U.S.A., 1983-88; bd. dirs., event dir. Alexandria Spl. Olympics, 1981-88; bd. dirs. March of Dimes, Alexandria, 1985-87; rape crisis vol. and trainer Family Counselling Agy., Alexandria, 1985-88; vol., trainer Boys Club, Alexandria, 1986-87; bd. dirs., sports dir. Shreveport Shreveport Spl. Olympics, 1988—; v.p. Alexandria Jaycees, 1984-88; clown Internat. Spl. Olympics, Baton Rouge, 1983. Recipient cert. of appreciation La. Spl. Olympics, 1981-88, La. Spl. Edn. Ctr., 1983, 84; Outstanding Young Woman award Alexandria Jaycees, 1984, Dist. Dir. award, 1985, Presdl. award of honor, 1986, Outstanding Svc. award Alexandria Telephone Pioneers, 1984, 86, recognition award Alexandria Jaycee Women, 1984, 85, Outstanding Community Svc. award Sta. KRRV, 1986, proclamation for outstanding community svc. Alexandria Mayor's Office, 1986. Mem. Shreveport Jaycees. Democrat. Baptist. Home: Little River Rd Birmingham AL 35213-2304 Office: Bell South Svcs 65 Bagby Dr Rm 224 Birmingham AL 35209-3771

OLIVER, ELIZABETH KIMBALL, writer, historian; b. Saginaw, Mich., May 21, 1918; d. Chester Benjamin and Margaret Eva (Allison) Kimball; m. James Arthur Oliver, May 3, 1941 (div. July 1967); children: Patricia Allison, Dexter Kimball. BA, U. Mich., 1940. Tchr. Dexter (Mich.) High Sch., 1940-41; libr. Sherman (Conn.) Libr. Assn., 1966-75; pres. Sherman (Conn.) Libr. Assn., 1983-84; writer, historian, 1976—; reporter Sherman Sentinel, 1965-70; editor newsletter Sherman Hist. Soc., 1977-78; columnist Citizen News, Fairfield County, Conn., 1981-83. Author: History of Staff Wives-AMNH, 1961, Background and History of the Palisades Nature Association, 1964, History and Architecture of Grace United Methodist Church, 1990, Legacy to St. Augustine, 1993. Vol. N.Y. Hist. Soc., N.Y.C., 1961-65; treas. Coburn Cemetery Assn., Sherman, 1976-82; historian Greenbrook-Palisades Nature Assn., Tenafly, N.J., 1962-64; mem. St. Augustine Hist. Soc., Naromi Land Trust (life), Cedar Key Hist. Soc. Mem. AAUW, Friends of Libr. (life), Inst. for Am. Indian Studies, Marjorie Kinnan Rawlings Soc. (charter), St. Augustine Woman's Club (archivist, cert. of appreciation 1990), Sherman Hist. Soc. Republican. Congregationalist. Home: 1500 Bishop Estates Rd 12-B Jacksonville FL 32259

OLIVER, JACQUELINE RAE, elementary education educator; b. Atlanta, Oct. 13, 1949; d. Raymond Walter and Madelyn Lenore (Kirkpatrick) Hurn; divorced; 1 child, Amber Kirkpatrick. BS, So. Nazarene U., 1971; M in Spl. Edn., U. Kans., 1985. Tchr. Putnam City Schs., Oklahoma City, 1971-75, Shawnee Mission Schs., Prairie Village, Kans., 1977—. Mem. Delta Kappa Gamma (rec. sec. 1994-95). Democrat. Nazarene. Home: 10710 W 116th St Overland Park KS 66210

OLIVER, JANET HAZEL, package designer, consultant; b. Newark, Dec. 17, 1931; d. Paul Harold and Hazel Maude (Crawford) O. 3-yr. cert., Newark Sch. Fine-Indsl. Art, 1952; cert. in fine arts, Fontainebleau Sch. Fine Arts, France, 1955; BS in Art Edn., NYU, 1962, MA, 1967. Package designer Egmont Arens Design, N.Y.C., 1952-53; art dir. Vanadia Assocs., Newark, 1953-57; package designer, sr. designer Raymond Loewy/William Snaith Inc., N.Y.C., 1957-64; dir. package design Lily Tulip Cup Corp., N.Y.C., 1964-66; sr. designer, project dir., creative dir. Raymond Loewy Internat., N.Y.C., 1966-77; sr. designer, project dir. Werbin & Morrill, N.Y.C., 1977-83; project dir. Deskey Assocs., N.Y.C., 1983-89; cons., designer Intersight Design, N.Y.C., 1989-91; design cons. Janet Oliver Packaging & Graphics, N.Y.C., 1991—; promotional cons., designer Imperial Impressarios Inc., N.Y.C., 1977-79, for ind. concert artists, N.Y.C., 1977—; artist rep., N.Y.C., 1981-83. Founding officer, sec. Eastside Ind. Dems., N.Y.C., 1974-75; promotional design cons. Louis Sepersky for State Senate, N.Y.C., 1980, 84; mem. arts com. Friends of St. Varten's Park, co-chmn., 1980-81. Mem. Fontainebleau Alumni Assn. (treas. 1978-83, v.p. 1983-89, editor bull. 1985-89). Home and Office: 333 E 34th St New York NY 10016

OLIVER, JANINE MARIE, physical therapist, consultant; b. Fairfax, Va., Aug. 21, 1965; d. James Lake and Freda (Sparks) O.; life ptnr. Zoe Gonzalez Rodriguez; 1 child, Patrick Lake. BS in Phys. Therapy, East Carolina U., 1987. Phys. theraphy staff, chief phys. therapy on chronic pain Rehab. Inst. Sarasota, Fla., 1987-89; pres., chief phys. therapy Rehab. Profls. Inc., Sarasota, 1989-90; home health phys. therapist Olsten-Kimberly Quality Care, Virginia Beach, Va., 1990—; cons. Muscular Dystrophy Assn., Virginia Beach, 1990-91, severe and profound program Pembroke Elem. Sch., Virginia Beach, 1992-93, Edmarc Hospice for Children, Portsmouth, Va., 1990-93. Mem., Virginia Beach city coord. for govt. rels. com. Hampton Roads Lesbian and Gay Pride Coalition, 1993—. Mem. NOW, Am. Phys. Therapy Assn., Va. Phys. Therapy Assn. Home: 410 26th St Virginia Beach VA 23451 Office: Olsten Kimberly Quality Care 4801 Columbus St Ste 302 Virginia Beach VA 23452

OLIVER, JOYCE ANNE, journalist, editorial consultant, columnist; b. Coral Gables, Fla., Sept. 19, 1958; d. John Joseph and Rosalie Cecile (Mack) O. BA in Communications, Calif. State U., Fullerton, 1980, MBA, 1990. Corp. editor Norris Industries Inc., Huntington Beach, Calif., 1979-82; pres. J.A. Oliver Assocs., La Habra Heights, Calif., 1982—; corp. editorial cons. Norris Industries, 1982, Better Methods Cons., Huntington Harbour, Calif., 1982-83, Summit Group, Orange, Calif., 1982-83, UDS, Encinitas, Calif., 1983-84, MacroMarketing, Costa Mesa, Calif., 1985-86, PM Software, Huntington Beach, Calif., 1985-86, CompuQuote, Canoga Park, Calif., 1985-86, Nat. Semicondr. Can. Ltd., Mississauga, Ont., Can., 1986, Maclean Hunter Ltd., Toronto, Ont., 1986-90; Frame Inc., Fullerton, Calif., 1987-88, The Johnson-Layton Co., L.A., 1988-89, Corp. Rsch. Inc., Chgo., 1988, Axon Group, Horsham, Pa., 1990-91, Am. Mktg. Assn., Chgo., 1990-92, Kenzaikai Co., Ltd., Tokyo, 1991, Penton Pub., Cleve., 1991, Bus. Computer Pub., Inc., Peterborough, N.H., 1991-92, Helmers Pub., Inc., Peterborough, 1992, Schnell Pub., Co., Inc., N.Y.C., 1992-93, Diversified Pub. Group, Carol Stream, Ill., 1993; mem. Rsch. Coun. of Scripps Clinic and Rsch. Found., 1987-92. Contbg. editor Computer Merchandising/Resell, 1982-85, Computer Reselling, 1985, Reseller Mgmt., 1987-89; contbg. editor Can. Electronics Engring., 1986-90, west coast editor, 1990, Chem. Bus. mag., 1992-93; spl. feature editor Cleve. Inst. Electronics publ. The Electron, 1986-89; bus. columnist Mktg. News, 1990-92; contbr. articles to profl. jours. and mags. Bd. dirs. Action Comms., 1993—. Mem. IEEE, Internat. Platform Assn., Soc. Photo-optical Instrumentation Engrs., Inst. Mgmt. Scis., Nat. Writers Club (profl.), Internat. Mktg. Assn., Soc. Profl. Journalists, L.A. World Affairs Coun. Republican. Roman Catholic. Office: 2045 Fullerton Rd La Habra CA 90631-8213

OLIVER, KATHY JO, vocational specialist; b. Fremont, Ohio, July 12, 1962; d. Royce Marvin and Patricia Ann (LaFountain) O. BS in Psychology, Heidelberg Coll., Tiffin, Ohio, 1985; MEd, U. Toledo, 1992. Cert. child care worker, Ohio. Residential aide 181 House, Tiffin, 1985; substance abuse aide Ctr. for Change, Tiffin, 1983-85, substance abuse counselor, 1985; direct care worker Flat Rock (Ohio) Children's Home, 1985-88; activity dir. E.C.I., Bettsville, Ohio, 1988-89, residential svc. dir. and counselor trainee, 1989-92; intensive family therapist Sandusky Valley Ctr., Tiffin, Ohio, 1992-93; emergency svcs. therapist, 1993-94; vocat. specialist Pvt. Industry Coun., Fremont, Ohio, 1993—. Mem. Assn. for Spiritual, Ethical and Religious Values in Counseling, Am. Assn. for Counseling and Devel., Chi Sigma Iota. Republican. Methodist. Office: Pvt Industry Coun 2511 Countryside Dr Fremont OH 43420-0621

OLIVER, LEANN MICHELLE, government financial officer; b. Eureka, Calif., Nov. 15, 1955; d. George L. and Laura Maxine (Jennings) O. BS, Willamette U., 1977; MPA, SUNY, Albany, 1980; cert., Nat. Comml. Lending Sch. of Am. Bankers Assn., Albany, 1982. Mgmt. trainee U.S. GAO, Albany, 1979-80; presdl. mgmt. intern U.S. SBA, Washington, 1980-83, fin. analyst, policy and program devel., 1983-89; dep. dir. for program devel. Office Econ. Devel., 1989-92; dep. dir. Office of Rural Affairs and Econ. Devel., 1992-94; acting dir. One Stop Office, Capital Shop Project, 1994; acting dir. Office Rural Affairs and Econ. Devel. SBA, Washington, 1995—; bd. dirs. Lafayette Fed. Credit Union, Washington, asst. treas., 1986—. Mem. Internat. Platform Assn. Roman Catholic. Office: SBA 409 3rd St SW Fl 8 Washington DC 20416-0005

OLIVER, MARIANNE, lawyer; b. Pitts., Oct. 3, 1954; d. George Benjamin and Mary Elizabeth (Worden) O.; m. Ronald A. Kisak, Nov. 3, 1984; children: Andrew, Erin. BS, Pa. State U., 1978; JD, Duquesne U., 1986. Taxpayer svc. specialist, supr. IRS, Pitts., 1976-78, adminstrv. intern, 1978-79; field examiner NLRB, Pitts., 1979-86, atty., 1986-87; of counsel Gilardi & Cooper, Pitts., 1987—. Mem. Allegheny County Bar Assn. (labor and employment sect. 1987—), AFL-CIO (lawyers coord. com. 1989—). Democrat. Roman Catholic. Office: Gilardi & Cooper 808 Grant Building Bldg Pittsburgh PA 15219-2200

OLIVER, MARY, poet; b. Maple Heights, Ohio, Sept. 10, 1935; d. Edward William and Helen Mary (Vlasak) O. Student, Ohio State U., 1955-56, Vassar Coll., 1956-57. Chmn. writing dept. Fine Arts Work Ctr., Provincetown, 1972-73, mem. writing com., 1984;, 1991-96; William Blackburn vis. prof. creative writing Duke U., 1995. Author: No Voyage and Other Poems, 1963, enlarged edit., 1965, The River Styx, Ohio, 1972, The Night Traveler, 1978, Twelve Moons, 1979, American Primative, 1983, Dream Work, 1986, House of Light, 1990, New and Selected Poems, 1992, A Poetry Handbook, 1994, White Pine, 1994, Blue Pastures, 1995; contbr. to Yale U. Rev., Kenyon Rev., Poetry, Atlantic, Harvard mag., others. Recipient Shelley Meml. award, 1970, Alice Fay di Castagnola award, 1973; Cleve. Arts prize for lits., 1979; Achievement award Am. Acad. and Inst. Arts and Letters, 1983; Pulitzer prize for poetry, 1984; Christopher award, 1991, L.L. Winship award, 1991, Nat. Book award, 1992; Nat. Endowment fellow, 1972-73; Guggenheim fellow, 1980-81. Mem. PEN, Authors Guild. Home: care Molly Malone Cook Lit Agy PO Box 338 Provincetown MA 02657

OLIVER, MARY ANNE MCPHERSON, religion educator; b. Montgomery, Ala., Nov. 21, 1935; d. James Curtis and Margaret Sinclair (Miller) McPherson; m. Raymond Davies Oliver, Aug. 28, 1959; children: Kathryn Sinclair, Nathan McPherson. BA, U. Ala., Tuscaloosa, 1956; cert., Sorbonne, Paris, 1958; MA, U. Wis., 1959; PhD, Grad. Theol. Union, Berkeley, Calif., 1972. Vol. tchr., preacher, counselor, 1972—; instr. U. Calif., Berkeley, St. Mary's Coll., Moraga, Calif., 1973; adj. faculty San Francisco Theol. Sem., San Anselmo, 1977-81; lectr. San Jose (Calif.) State U., 1980-81, San Francisco State U., 1985-86; adj. prof. dept. liberal arts John F. Kennedy U., Orinda, Calif., 1987—; vis. prof. Gen. Theol. Sem., N.Y.C., 1995. Author: History of Good Shepherd Episcopal Mission, 1978, Conjugal Spirituality: The Primacy of Mutual Love in Christian Tradition, 1994; contbr. articles to profl. jours. Rep. Ala. Coun. on Human Rels., Mobile, 1958; active deanery, conv. Good Shepherd Episc. Ch., Berkeley, Calif., 1970-75; rep. U. Calif. Fgn. Student Hospitality, Berkeley, 1965-70; vol. tchr. Berkeley pub. schs., 1965-73; bd. dirs. Canterbury Found., Berkeley, 1972-75; chmn. bd. dirs. West Berkeley Parish, Berkeley, 1976-78, adult edn. program St. Mark's Episc. Ch., 1992-93; mentor Edn. for Ministry, Univ. of the South, 1993—. Recipient award French Consulate, New Orleans, 1956; Fulbright grantee, 1956, grantee Mabelle McLeod Lewis Found., 1969. Mem. Am. Acad. Religion, Conf. on Christianity and Lit. Democrat. Home: 1632 Grant St Berkeley CA 94703-1356 Office: John F Kennedy U 12 Altarinda Rd Orinda CA 94563-2689

OLIVER, MARY WILHELMINA, law librarian, educator; b. Cumberland, Md., May 4, 1919; d. John Arlington and Sophia (Lear) O. AB, Western Md. Coll., 1940; BS in Library Sci, Drexel Inst. Tech., 1943; JD, U. N.C., 1951. Bar: N.C. 1951. Asst. circulation librarian N.J. Coll. Women, 1943-45; asst. in law library U. Va., 1945-47; asst. reference, social sci. librarian Drake U., 1947-49; rsch. asst. Inst. Govt., U. N.C., Chapel Hill, 1951-52, asst. law librarian, 1952-55, asst. prof. law, law librarian, 1955-59, asso. prof. law, law librarian, 1959-69, prof. law, law librarian, 1969-84, prof. law and law librarian emeritus, 1984—. Mem. ABA, N.C. Bar Assn., Am. Assn. Law Librs. (pres. 1972-73, Marion Gould Gallagher Disting. Svc. award 1992), Assn. Am. Law Schs. (exec. com. 1979-81), Law Alumni Assn. U. N.C., Order of Coif. Home: 157 Carol Woods Chapel Hill NC 27514 Office: U NC Law Libr Van Hecke Wettach Hall # 064A Chapel Hill NC 27514

OLIVER, PEGGY JO, English language educator; b. Sioux City, Iowa, Apr. 18, 1949; d. Robert Delwin and Alta Marie (Waller) Fish; m. Robert J. Mitchell, July 13, 1968 (div. Dec. 1990); children: Jennifer, Paul; m. Lester M. Oliver, Nov. 24, 1991. BA, Purdue U., 1971, MA, 1974, postgrad., 1974. Cert. sch. adminstr., Tex. Grad. teaching asst. Purdue U., West Lafayette, ind., 1971-76; dir. St. Andrew's Day Sch., Houston, 1987-91; English instr. Wharton County Jr. Coll., Sugarland, Tex., 1990-93; dir. resource and training Initiaves for Children, Houston, 1991-92; English instr. Houston C.C., 1992-93, San Jacinto Coll. South, Houston, 1993—. Mem. Tex. Jr. Coll. Tchrs. Assn., Nat. Coun. Tchrs. English, So. Cen. MLA. Office: San Jacinto Coll South 13735 Beamer Rd Houston TX 77089

OLIVER-WARREN, MARY ELIZABETH, library science educator; b. Hamlet, N.C., Feb. 23, 1924; d. Washington and Carolyn Belle (Middlebrooks) Terry; m. David Oliver, 1947 (div. 1971); children: Donald D., Carolyn L.; m. Arthur Warren, Sept. 14, 1990. BS, Bluefield State U., 1948; MS, South Conn. State U., 1958; student, U. Conn., 1977. Cert. tchr., adminstr. and supr., Conn. Media specialist Hartford (Conn.) Pub. Schs., 1952-86; adj. prof. So. Conn. State U., New Haven, 1972-86, asst. prof. Sch. Libr. Sci. and Instructional Tech., 1987—, mem. dept. curriculum com., 1987—. Author: My Golden Moments, 1988, The Elementary School Media Center, 1990, Text Book Elementary School Media Center, 1991, I Must Fight Alone, 1991, (textbook) I Must Fight Alone, 1994. Mem. ALA, Conn. Ednl. Media Assn., Assn. Ret. Tchrs. Conn., Black and Hispanic Consortium, So. Conn. State U. Women's Assn., Cicuso Club (v.p.), Friends Club (v.p.), Delta Kappa Gamma. Home: 6 Freeman Rd Somerset NJ 08873-2925 Office: So Conn State U 501 Crescent St New Haven CT 06515-1330

OLIVETI, SUSAN GAIL, sales promotion and public relations executive; b. Bklyn., Nov. 1, 1938; d. Peter and Nancy Jane (Wolk) Randolph; m. Fosco Anthony Oliveti, Sept. 18, 1970 (div. 1990); children by previous marriage: Lois, Peter, Elizabeth, Ruben. BBA, CCNY, 1967; student, NYU, 1968-69; diploma in nursing, Jewish Hosp. Sch. Nursing, 1960. Estimator, media rsch. Ogilvy & Mather, N.Y.C., 1966-68; TV rep. Adam Young, Inc., N.Y.C., 1968-69; exec. asst. Paramount Pictures, N.Y.C., 1969-80; mgr. conv. and media events Warner Amex Satellite Enterprise Co., N.Y.C., 1980-83; exhibits and pub. rels. specialist Siemens Med. Systems, Iselin, N.J., 1983-85; meetings and pub. rels. mgr. U.S. Trademark Assn., N.Y.C., 1985; v.p. corp. communications J.R. Heimbaugh, Inc., 1986; mgr. sales promotions, pub. relations meetings, convs. Lightolier, Inc., Secaucus, N.J., 1986-90; exec. v.p. Globefern USA, Inc., 1990—. Recipient spl. honors United Airlines, 1978. Mem. Meeting Profls. Internat. (reception com., edn. com.), Pub. Rels. Soc. Am. Democrat. Jewish. Avocations: knitting, gardening, designing jewelry. Office: PO Box 4110 Vero Beach FL 32964

OLK, FRANCINE LAURA, secondary education educator; b. N.Y.C., Oct. 4, 1946; d. Sidney and Frieda (Sturman) Kaufman; m. Alvin Olk, Mar. 3, 1974; children: Karen Rachel, David Allen. BS, Bklyn. Coll., 1967, M in Biology Edn., 1969; M in Computer Sci., SUNY, 1979. Tchr. biology F.D.R. High Sch., Bklyn., 1967—, testing coord., 1991—; adj. prof. biology Kingsborough C.C., Bklyn., 1988-92. Mem. Am. Psychol. Assn., N.Y. Biology Tchrs. Assn. Home: 172 Amherst St Brooklyn NY 11235-4115 Office: 5800 20th Ave Brooklyn NY 11204

OLKERIIL, LORENZA, English educator; b. Koror, Palau, Oct. 10, 1948; d. Ngiratewid and Modekngei Olkeriil; children: Kevin O. Chin, Renee Chin. BA in Elem. Edn., U. Guam, 1982; MA in Instnl. Tech. in Edn., San Jose State U., 1989. Classroom tchr. Ministry of Edn., Koror, 1972-76, 78—, curriculum specialist, 1976-78, edn. trainer, 1988—, coord. bilingual program, 1988—; chair English dept. Palau High Sch.; tng. dir. Peace Corp, Palau, summer 1987; GED instr., Palauan lang. instr. Micronesian Coll., Koror; cons. to pvt. sch., Koror. Speaker Ngiwal State Legis., Koror, 1992; mem. Ngiwal State Constitution, 1983. San Jose State U. fellow, 1987. Mem. Didil Belau (pres. 1992-93), Ngaraboes (treas.-sec. 1980—). Home: PO Box 966 Palau PW 96940 Office: PO Box 159 Palau PW 96940

OLLIE, PEARL LYNN, artist, singer, songwriter; b. Highland Park, Mich., Oct. 15, 1953; d. Sam and Estelle Theresa (Wasielewska) O.; m. Christopher John Keyes, Nov. 29, 1975 (div. Nov. 1978); 1 child, Shane Michael Fiondella. Student, Henry Ford C.C., Dearborn, Mich., 1988-89, Soc. Arts and Crafts Coll., 1970-74, Ctr. for Creative Study, 1980-81. Tchr. ceramics Detroit Head Start, Mt. Zion, Mich., 1973; logo designer, platemaker, printer and painter Island Art Ctr., St. Simons Island, Ga., 1976-79; sec., receptionist High Performance Tube Inc., St. Simons Island, 1976-79; personal legal sec. State Senator Bill Littlefield, St. Simons Island, 1979; art coord., booking agt. Club Savoy Tivoli, San Francisco, 1979; tchr. art Redmond Hall, Squamakawa, Wash., 1980; artist Hollywood Costumes, Dearborn, Mich., 1980-90; account mgr. ins. Dr. Sheryl A. Ollie, Lynn, Mass., 1990; staff artist, acting, costumes Creative Currents, Ferndale, Mich., 1990—; art tchr. P.O.P. Prodns., Nahant, Mass., 1991—; make-up artist Paramount Costumes (was Hollywood Costumes), Dearborn; art tchr. music St. Lukes Montessori Sch., Detroit; artist Mich. Art and Design, Detroit, Dearborn Awnings, Lincoln Park, Mich. Illustrator: (children's book) Granny Gourd Doll, 1986; make-up artist TV commls. and shows, movies. Helper Nahant Youth Soccer, 1991—; co-pres. Nahant PTO, Johnson Sch., 1991-92. Mem. Cultural Enrichment Com., Northshore Creative Arts Coun. Roman Catholic. Home and Office: POP Prodns 25 Pleasant St Nahant MA 01908

OLMSTEAD, DIANE DULUDE, nurse, child birth educator; b. St. Albans, Vt., Aug. 31, 1956; d. Philip Charles and Beatrice J. (Desranleau) Dulude; m. Michael John Olmstead, Aug. 20, 1977; children: Michael J. II, Nicholas Charles. Student, Fanny Allen Sch. of Practiced Nursing, 1975; AS in Nursing, U. Vt., 1978; BS in Health Edn., Johnson State Coll., 1990; postgrad., U. Vt., 1991-93, Case Western Res. U., 1994—; student, Frontier Sch. Nurse-Midwifery, 1994—. RN, Vt. Lic. practical nurse Kerbs Meml. Hosp., St. Albans, 1975-78; staff registered nurse obstetrics Northwestern Med. Ctr., St. Albans, 1978-81, relief charge nurse obstetrics, 1981-87, charge nurse ambulatory care unit, relief nursing supr., 1987-92; clin. nursing supr. Franklin County Home Health Agy., St. Albans, Vt., 1992-94, childbirth edn. coord., lactation cons., 1994—; educator child birth Franklin County Home Health, St. Albans, 1979-86. Mem. ANA, Am. Coll. Nurse Midwives, Chesamore Honor Soc., Sigma Theta Tau. Democrat. Roman Catholic. Home: 114 High St Saint Albans VT 05478-1535 Office: Franklin County Home Health Agy Saint Albans VT 05478

OLMSTED, AUDREY JUNE, academic administrator; b. Sioux Falls, S.D., June 5, 1940; d. Leslie Thomas and Dorothy Lucille (Else) Perryman; m. Richard Raymond Olmsted; 1 child, Quenby Anne. BA, U. No. Iowa, 1961, MA, 1963; PhD, Ind. U., 1971. Comm. instr. Boston U., 1964-71, acting chair comm., 1972-73, asst. prof. comm., 1971-74; debate coach R.I. Coll., Providence, 1978-92, asst. prof. comm., 1987—, internat. student advisor, 1980—; text editor Prentice-Hall Pub., 1986-88. Recipient Faculty award R.I. Coll. Alumni Assn., 1987. Mem. Nat. Assn. Fgn. Student Advisors, Internat. Comm. Assn. Democrat. Office: RI Coll Dept Comm 600 Mt Pleasant Ave Providence RI 02908

OLMSTED, SUZANNE M., photographer; b. Palo Alto, Calif., Apr. 15, 1956; d. Gerald W. and Frances M. (Barnett) O.; m. Edward A. Gillum, July 6, 1982; children: Gerald, James. BA, U. Calif., Santa Cruz, 1979; MFA, So. Ill. U., 1982. Lectr. in photography Ea. Mont. Coll., Billings, 1983-87; exec. dir. Artlink, Phoenix, 1991; artist-in-residence The City of Tempe, Ariz., 1990-92; photo editor The Current, Phoenix, 1993-94; gallery mgr., ass.t prof. art U. Nev., Reno, 1994—. Exhibits include Ea. N.Mex. U., Portales, 1993, Szabo Fine Arts Gallery, Phoenix, 1992, Tempe Art Ctr., 1992, So. Ill. U., Carbondale, 1991, Photo Art Gallery, Burbank, Calif., 1991, Gallery of Art, Rockford (Ill.) Coll., 1991, Red River Exhbn./Silver Anniversary, Plains Art Mus., Moorhead, Minn., 1990, John Michael Kohler Art Ctr., Sheboygan, Wis., 1990, numerous others; contbr. photographs to numerous publs. including Northern Lights, New Times, Quantum Metaphysics and more. Recipient Eben Demarest award Eben Demarest Trust, Pitts., 1987, Outstanding Young Women of Am. award, 1984. Home: 701 Ruby Ave Reno NV 89503

OLNESS, KAREN NORMA, pediatrics and international health educator; b. Rushford, Minn., Aug. 28, 1936; d. Norman Theodore and Karen Agnes (Gunderson) O.; m. Hakon Daniel Torjesen, 1962. BA, U. Minn., 1958, BS, MD, 1961. Diplomate Am. Bd. Pediatrics, Am. Bd. Med. Hypnosis. Intern Harbor Gen. Hosp., Torrance, Calif.; resident Nat. Children's Hosp. Med. Ctr., Washington; asst. prof. George Washington U., Washington, 1970-74; assoc. prof. U. Minn., Mpls., 1974-87; prof. pediatrics, family medicine and internat. health Case Western Res. U., Cleve., 1987—. Named Outstanding Woman Physician, Minn. Assn. Women Physicians, 1987. Fellow Am. Acad. Pediatrics, Am. Acad. Family Physicians, Am. Soc. Clin. Hypnosis (pres. 1984-86), Soc. Clin. and Exptl. Hypnosis (pres. 1991-93); mem. Soc. for Behavioral Pediatrics (pres. 1991-92), Northwestern Pediatric Soc. (pres. 1977). Office: Case Western Res U 11100 Euclid Ave Cleveland OH 44106-2602

O'LOONEY, PATRICIA ANNE, medical program administrator; b. Bridgeport, Conn., Dec. 2, 1954; d. John Joseph and Marjorie Ellen (Curran) O'L. BA in Molecular Biology, Regis Coll., 1976; MS in Biochemistry, George Washington U., 1978, PhD in Biochemistry, 1982. Rsch. asst. biochemistry dept. George Washington Med. Sch., Washington, 1976-82, teaching asst., 1978-81, rsch. assoc., 1982-84, sr. rsch. scientist, 1984-86, asst. prof. medicine and biochemistry, 1986-88; asst. dir. The Nat. Multiple

Sclerosis Soc., N.Y.C., 1988-90, assoc. dir. rsch. and med. programs, 1990-91, dir. rsch. and med. programs, 1991—; vis. lectr. George Washington Med. Sch., 1988—. Author: Lipoprotein Lipase, 1987; contbr. articles to profl. jours. Recipient New Investigator Rsch. award NIH, 1985. Mem. Am. Soc. for Biochemistry and Molecular Biology, N.Y. Acad. Scis., Assn. for Women in Sci., The Mid-Atlantic Lipid Soc., Sigma Xi, Beta Beta Beta. Republican. Roman Catholic. Office: Nat Multiple Sclerosis Soc 733 3rd Ave New York NY 10017-3204

OLSEN, CANDE JOAN, actuary; b. Orange, N.J., Jan. 3, 1950; d. James John and Helene Elaine (Bodnarchuk) O. Student, Smith Coll., 1968-70; BS in Math., Williams Coll., 1972. Actuarial trainee N.Y. Life Ins. Co., 1972-74, actuarial asst., 1974-77, asst. actuary, 1977-80, assoc. actuary, 1980-82, actuary, 1982-86, corp. v.p., actuary, 1986-90, v.p., actuary, 1990—. Fellow Soc. Actuaries; mem. Am. Acad. Actuaries, Am. Soc. CLU's,. Republican. Club: Actuaries (N.Y.) (v.p. student edn. 1978-79). Office: NY Life Ins Co 51 Madison Ave New York NY 10010-1603*

OLSEN, ELLYN IRENE, minister; b. Massillon, Ohio, Dec. 3, 1941; d. Elwyn Powell and Irene May (Gise) Bowen; m. Emil Samuel Olsen, June 25, 1966 (dec. Aug. 1984); children: Paul Martin, Elizabeth Jayne Olsen Regal, Rebecca Elayne, Joanna Gayle. Student, L.A. City Coll., 1965; AS in Humanities and Social Scis., Rockland C.C., 1991; BS in Organizational Mgmt., Nyack Coll., 1992. Ordained to ministry Assemblies of God Internat. Svc. rep. Ohio Bell Telephone Co., Massillon, 1961-62, Pacific Telephone and Telegraph, Hollywood, Calif., 1963-64, So. Calif. Gas Co., L.A., 1964-65; sec., activities dir. Fgn. Student Outreach First Presbyn. Ch. of Hollywood, 1965-67; writer, editor Bless Israel Today Ministries, Inc., New City, N.Y., 1975—, pres., dir., 1984—; mgr. Nanuet (N.Y.) Bible Bookstore, 1992—; tchr. of Bible Grace Conservative Bapt. Ch., Nanuet, 1985—; group leader Single Mothers Prayer/Support Bible Study, Nyack, N.Y., 1993. Author: God's Blueprint for Mankind, 1984; editor gospel tracts, 1989-92; contbr. articles to religious publs. Pres. Free Church Women's Ministries, New City, 1993-94; mem. missions com. Park Evangel. Free Ch., New City, 1993-94. Recipient gen. scholarship grant Rockland C.C. Found., Suffern, N.Y., 1990.

OLSEN, INGER ANNA, psychologist; b. Copper Mountain, B.C, Can., Dec. 25, 1926; d. Dagmar O.; B.S., Wash. State U., 1954, M.S., 1956, Ph.D., 1962. Psychiat. nurse Provincial Mental Health Services B.C., 1947-51, psychologist, 1956-58; psychologist Vancouver (B.C.) City Met. Health Services, 1958-60, Wash. State U. Student Counseling Center, Pullman, 1960-62; sr. psychologist Met. Health Services, Vancouver, 1962-66; instr. psychology Vancouver Community Coll., 1966-87; docent Vancouver Aquarium Assn. Bd. dirs. Second Mile Soc., 1975-89. Contbr. articles to profl. jours. Mem. Am. Psychol. Assn., Gerontol. Soc. Am., Can. Assn. Gerontology, Phi Beta Kappa, Sigma Xi, Alpha Kappa Delta. Home: 1255 Bidwell St Apt 1910, Vancouver, BC Canada V6G 2K8

OLSEN, KAY DANNEVIG, marketing professional; b. Hartford, Conn., Sept. 3, 1960; d. Olaf T. and Katrine (Dannevig) O. AA, HCW, 1980; BS, Skidmore Coll., 1982; MBA, U. Conn., 1987. Analyst, planning and devel. Heublein Inc., Farmington, Conn., 1982-83, strategic planning analyst, 1983-84, pricing analyst, 1984-85, asst. mktg. mgr., 1985-86, assoc. mktg. mgr. Jose Cuervo, 1986-87, mktg. mgr., new products, 1987-88, mktg. mgr. Black Velvet, 1988-89, sr. mktg. mgr. Black Velvet, 1989-90, sr. mktg. mgr. Almaden Vineyards, 1990-92; sr. mktg. mgr. Super Premium Tequilas, Farmington, Conn., 1992—. Bd. dirs. Fin. chmn. Farmington Rep. Town Com., 1993, fin. chmn., 1990-92, vice chmn., 1992-94; bd. dirs. Farmington Woods Master Assn., 1993—. Home: 51 Crocus Ln Avon CT 06001-4547 Office: Heublein Inc 16 Munson Rd Farmington CT 06032-2000

OLSEN, REBA, counselor; b. Milledgeville, Ga., May 9, 1954; d. Henry S. and Ellen (Stancil) Bales; children: Misty Olsen, Daniel Olsen. BA in Social Work magna cum laude, U. Ga., 1976; MEd in Counseling, West Ga. Coll., 1988. Lic. profl. counselor, Ga. Social worker Fannin County ARC, Blue Ridge, Ga., 1976-79, Gordon County Schs./Spl. Edn. Office, Calhoun, Ga., 1980-87; counselor, evaluator Dalton (Ga.) Coll., 1987—; counselor Dalton Family Care, 1993—; group facilitator Children Cope with Divorce, Whitfield County, 1993—; facilitator grief/loss group First Meth. Ch., Dalton, 1994. Presentor confs. in field. Co-chmn. Drug Free Schs. Adv., Gordon County/Calhoun, 1991-93; mem. troubled children's commn., Gordon City Schs., 1986-87; mem. Calhoun/Gordon County Child Abuse Coun., 1985-87; adv. bd. mem. New Connections, Dalton, 1989-93. Regents scholar State of Ga., 1975. Mem. Am. Coll. Counseling Assn., Ga. Coll. Counseling Assn. (charter mem., exec. bd. 1987-93, various coms., Outstanding New Profl. award 1993), Phi Beta Kappa, Kappa Delta Pi. Home: 109 Northside Dr Calhoun GA 30701

OLSEN, SALLIE MULLIKEN, psychologist; b. Urbana, Ill., July 16, 1942; d. Wallace Mulberry and Jean Christie (Forrest) M.; m. Richard Leon Olsen, July 23, 1942; children: Erik Wallace, Kristin Mahloch. BS, U. Wis., 1965; MS, U. Ill., 1968; PhD, Saybrook Inst., 1980. Clin. specialist nurse San Francisco Cen. Hosps., 1968-70; pvt. practice Livermore and San Francisco, 1972—; asst. clin. prof. U. Calif., San Francisco, 1975-80; staff nurse various hosps., San Francisco, 1984-88; dir. nursing edn. Mt. Diablo Hosp., Concord, Calif., 1982-83; lectr. Hayward (Calif.) State U., 1981; sec. Quality Care Consortium, San Francisco, 1994—. Vol. St. Anthony's Found., 1993—, AIDS Health Project, 1991—. Mem. APA. Office: Del Valle Clinic 1797 4th St Livermore CA 94550-4347 also: 1301 17th Ave San Francisco CA 94122

OLSEN, TILLIE, author; b. Omaha, Nebr., Jan. 14, 1912; d. Samuel and Ida (Beber) Lerner; m. Jack Olsen; children: Karla, Julie, Kathie, Laurie. D.Arts and Letters (hon.), U. Nebr., 1979, Hobart and William Smith Coll., 1984; Litt. D. (hon.), Knox Coll., 1982; L.H.D. (hon.), Clark U., 1985; LittD (hon.), Albright Coll., 1986, Wooster Coll., 1991. Writer-in-residence, vis. faculty English Amherst Coll., 1969-70, Stanford U., 1972, M.I.T., 1973-74, U. Mass., Boston, 1974; internat. vis. scholar Norway, 1980; Hill prof. U. Minn., spring 1986; writer-in-residence Kenyon Coll., 1987—; cons. on lit.; reader and lectr.; Regents lectr. U. Calif. at San Diego, 1977—; commencement speaker English dept. U. Calif., Berkeley, 1983, Hobart and William Smith Coll., 1984 Bennington Coll., 1986; regents lectr. U. Calif. at Los Angeles, 1987. Author: Tell Me A Riddle, 1961 (title story received O'Henry award 1961), Rebecca Harding Davis: Life in the Iron Mills, 1972, Yonnondio: From the Thirties, 1974, Silences, 1978, (play) I Stand Here Ironing, 1981, The Word Made Flesh, 1984; editor: Mother to Daughter, Daughter to Mother, 1984, (with others) Mothers and Daughters, That Special Quality: A Exploration in Photographs, 1989; short fiction published in 138 anthologies; books translated in 11 langs. Recipient Am. Acad. and Nat. Inst. of Arts and Letters award for distinguished contbn. to Am. letters, 1975, Ministry to Women award Unitarian Universalist Fedn., 1980, Brit. Post Office and B.P.W. award, 1980, REA award Dungannon Found., 1994; Ford Found. grantee, 1959, Nat. Endowment for Arts grantee, 1968, MacDowell Colony grantee; Stanford Univ. creative writing fellow, 1956-57, Radcliffe Inst. fellow, 1962-64, Guggenheim fellow, 1975-76, Bunting Inst. Radcliffe Coll. fellow, 1985; Tillie Olsen day designated in San Francisco, 1981. Mem. Authors Guild, PEN, Writers Union. Home: 1435 Laguna St # 6 San Francisco CA 94115*

OLSHAN, KAREN, advertising agency executive. Former v.p., then sr. v.p. Batten Barton Durstine & Osborn (now BBDO), N.Y.C.; exec. v.p., dir. rsch. svcs. BBDO, Inc., N.Y.C., 1989—. Office: BBDO NY 1285 Ave of the Americas New York NY 10019-6095*

OLSON, BARBARA FORD, physician; b. Iowa City, June 15, 1935; d. Leonard A. and Anne (Swanson) Ford; m. Robert Eric Olson, Mar. 21, 1959 (div. Oct. 15, 1973); children: Katherine Gee, Eric, Julie. BA, Gustavus Adolphus Coll., 1956; MD, U. Minn., 1960. Diplomate Am. Bd. Family Practice (cert. added qualifications geriatric medicine). Intern St. Paul-Ramsey Med. Ctr., 1960-61; resident in anesthesiology U. Hosp. Cleve., 1961-62, U. Minn. Hosps., Mpls., 1962-63; pvt. practice anesthesiology St. Johns Hosp. and Devine Redeemer Hosp., St. Paul, 1963-67, Mercy Hosp., Coon Rapids, Minn., 1967-74; staff physician Oak Terrace Nursing Home, Minnetonka, Minn., 1974-88; med. dir. nursing home care unit VA Med. Ctr., St. Cloud, Minn., 1988—. Pres., bd. dirs. Alpha Epsilon Iota Med. Found., Mpls., 1980-86. Mem. Minn. Med. Assn., Minn. Women Physicians (pres. 1981-82). Home: PO Box 7306 Saint Cloud MN 56302 Office: VA Med Ctr 4804 8th St N Saint Cloud MN 56303

OLSON, BETTY-JEAN, elementary education educator; b. Camas, Wash., Apr. 26, 1934; d. Earl Raymond and Mabel Anna (Burden) Clemons; m. Arthur H. Geda, Dec. 31, 1957; children: Ann C. Geda-Wall, Scott A. Geda; m. Conrad A. Olson, June 14, 1980. AA, Clark Coll., 1954; BA in Edn., Cen. Wash. Coll. Edn., 1956; MEd, No. Monn. Coll., 1975. Cert. elem. tchr. class I, Mont., supr. K-9 class III. Supervising tchr., demo. teaching No. Mont. Coll.; kindergarten, 1st grade instr. Glasgow, Mont.; supervisor, head tchr. Reading Lab, Glasgow AFB, Mont.; 1st grade instr., kindergarten tchr., elem. adminstr. K-7 Medicine Lake (Mont.) Dist. 7; certification standards and practices Adv. Coun. to the State Bd. Pub. Edn., Mt. State Bd. Pub. Edn.; mem. bd. examiners Nat. Coun. for Accred. of Tchr. Edn., adv. com. Western Mont. Coll., U. Mont.; workshop leader and presenter in field. Mem. Sheridan County Community Protective Svcs. Com., Mid-Lake Scholarship Com. Mem. NEA, ASCD, Internat. Reading Assn., Nat. Coun. for Social Studies, Nat. Elem. Prin. Assoc., Medicine Lake Edn. Assn. (past pres.), Mont. Edn. Assn. (officerships), Mont. Elem. Prin., Delta Kappa Gamma (chpt. pres., exec. bd., committeeships, internat. exec. bd.). Home: 108 E Antelope Antelope MT 59211-9607

OLSON, BONNIE WAGGONER-BRETERNITZ (MRS. O. DONALD OLSON), civic worker; b. North Platte, Nebr.; d. Floyd Emil and Edith (Waggoner) Breternitz; AB, U. Chgo., 1947; m. O. Donald Olson, May 17, 1944; children: Pamela Lynne, Douglas Donald. Dep. clk. Dist. Ct., Lincoln County, Nebr., 1940-42; advt. researcher Burke & Assoc., Chgo., 1942; contbg. newspaper columnist Chgo. Herald-Am., 1943; social worker A.R.C., Chgo., 1942-44, Sacramento, Calif., 1944, Amarillo, Tex., 1945; exec. sec. Econometrica, Cowles Commn. for Rsch. in Econs., Chgo., 1945-47; interior designer, antique dealer. Col.; participant Chgo. Maternity Ctr. Fund Drive, 1953, Chgo. Coun. on Fgn. Rels., 1948-54; mem. Colo. Springs Community Council, 1956-58, chmn. children's div., 1956-58, mem. exec. bd., 1956-58, mem. budget com., 1957-58; mem. Colorado Springs Charter Assn., 1956-60, mem. exec. bd., 1957-59, sec., 1958; chmn. El Paso County PTA, Protective Svcs. for Children, 1959-61; chmn. women's div. fund drive ARC, 1961; mem. League Women Voters, 1957—, mem. state children's law com., 1961-63; chmn. ad hoc com. El Paso County Citizens' Com. for Nat. Probation and Parole Survey, Juvenile Ct. Procedures and Detention, 1957-61; mem. children's adv. com. Colo. Child Welfare Dept., 1959-63, chmn., 1961; del. White House Conf. on Children and Youth, 1960, 70; sec. Citizens Ad Hoc Com. for Comprehensive Mental Health Clinic for Pikes Peak Region, 1966—; mem. Colorado Springs Human Rels. Commn., 1968-71; sustaining mem. Symphony Guild, 1970-72, Fine Arts Ctr., 1957—; mem. Pikes Peak Mental Health Ctr., 1964-67 (bd. dirs.); Colo. observer White House Conf. on Aging, 1981, Colo. Gov.'s Conf. on Aging, 1981, Dist. Atty.'s Child Abuse Task Force, 1986; panelist career planning documentary film Not Just a Job, Radcliffe Coll. Career Svcs., 1990; counselor Health Info. Needs of Elders (Mass. Shine Program), 1992—. Recipient Lane Bryant Ann. Nat. Awards citation, 1971; alumni citation for pub. service U. Chgo., 1961. Mem. Am. Acad. Polit. and Social Sci., Nat. Trust Historic Preservation, Women's Ednl. Soc. Colo. Coll. (life), Council on Religion and Internat. Affairs. Episcopalian. Clubs: Quadranglar, University (Chgo.). Home: 86 Buckboard Rd Duxbury MA 02332-4701

OLSON, CAROL ANN, librarian; b. Chgo., Dec. 16, 1945; d. Kenneth Carlyle and Marion Heath (Barkway) Nygaard; m. Ray Alan Olson, June 15, 1974; children: Eric Robert, Peter Alan. BA in History, Jamestown (N.D.) Coll., 1968; MALS, U. Minn., 1970. Acquisitions libr. Luther Sem. Library, St. Paul, 1971—. Chair libr. rsch. roundtable, life mem. Vesterheim Norwegian-Am. Mus., Decorah, Iowa, Vesterheim Geneal. Ctr., Madison, Wis. Mem. Am. Theol. Libr. Assn., Minn. Theol. Libr. Assn., Minn. Libr. Assn., Libr. Rsch. Roundtable Divsn. Minn. Libr. Assn., Sons of Norway, Romerike Lag and Landings Lab (editor Landings Lag newsletter 1984-94). Lutheran. Home: 2724 Griggs St N Saint Paul MN 55113-1836 Office: Luther Seminary Libr 2481 Como Ave Saint Paul MN 55108

OLSON, CAROL LEA, lithographer, educator, photographer; b. Anderson, Ind., June 10, 1929; d. Daniel Ackerman and Marguerite Louise Olson. AB, Anderson Coll., 1952; MA, Ball State U., 1976. Pasteup artist Warner Press, Inc., Anderson, 1952-53, apprentice lithographer stripper, 1953-57, journeyman, 1957-63, lithographic dot etcher, color corrector, 1959-73, prepres coord. art dept., 1973-81, prepres tech. specialist, 1981-83, color film assembler, 1983—; part-time photography instr. Anderson Univ.; tchr. photography Anderson Fine Arts Ctr., 1976-79; instr. photography, photographics Anderson U., 1979—; mag. photographer Bd. Christian Edn. of Ch. of God, Anderson, 1973-86; freelance photographer. One person show Anderson U., 1979; exhibited in group shows Anderson U., 1980-90, Purdue U., 1982. Instr. 1st aide ARC, Anderson, 1969-79; sec. volleyball Anderson Sunday Sch. Athletic Assn., 1973—. Recipient Hon. mention, Ann Arbor, Mich., 1977, Anderson Fine Arts Ctr., 1977, 78, 83, 1st Pl., 1983, Hon. Mention, 1983, 2d Pl., 1988, Hon. Mention, 1988, 93, Best of Show, 1983, 91, 92, Best Nature Catagory Anderson Fine Arts Ctr., 1994. Mem. AAUW, Associated Photographer Internat., Nat. Inst. Exploration, Profl. Photographers Am. Mem. Ch. of God. Home: 2604 E 6th St Anderson IN 46012-3725

OLSON, CARY ANNETTE, controller; b. Wausau, Wis., Oct. 30, 1956; d. Orin Sidney and Phyllis Olga (Radtke) O. AS, U. Wis., Waukesha, 1986; BBA in Acctg., U. Wis., Whitewater, 1989; postgrad., U. Wis., 1992-95. Cert. mgmt. acct. Clk.-typist I, II, III Waukesha County Dept. Social Svc., 1974-83; acct. clk. I Northview Nursing Home, Waukesha, 1984; from acct. clk. II, adminstrv. asst.-fiscal mgmt. I, budget technician, sr. fin. analyst to bus. mgr. Waukesha County Health & Human Svcs. Dept., 1984-94; contr. Waukesha County Tech. Coll., Pewaukee, 1994—; mem. acctg. curriculum adv. com. Waukesha County Tech. Coll., 1993—; cons., Sussex, Wis., 1990-93. Vol. Wis. Lutheran Child & Family Svc., Milw., 1989—, Bargain Ctr.-WELS Synod, Milw., 1970-83, Milw. Women's Ctr., 1989-92; vol. tax preparer IRS, Pewaukee, 1989—. Recipient Certificate of Spl. Recognition from Christoph Meml. YWCA Women of Distinction Award Program, 1986. Mem. Inst. Mgmt. Accts. (del. Mid-Am. coun. 1992—, chair corp. & acad. devel. 1994—, co-dir. mem. attendance 1989-90, v.p. comm. 1990-92, v.p. fin. & adminstrn. 1991-92, pres. 1992-93), Southeastern Wis. Fin. Mgrs. Assn. (planning com. 1987-94), Govt. Fin. Officers Assn. (budget reviewer 1994—), Wis. Human Svcs. Fin. Mgrs. Assn. (1st vice chair 1985-94, planning com. 1994—), Assn. Am. Women in C.C. Office: Waukesha County Tech Coll 800 Main St Pewaukee WI 53072

OLSON, DIANA CRAFT, image and etiquette consultant; b. Langley, Va., May 5, 1941; d. Winfred O. and Joyce (Clark) Craft; m. Robert J. Olson, May 30, 1976; stepchildren: Stacey Anr, Kirsten Lowry. BA, U. Tex., 1963; MA, San Francisco State U., 1970; cert. image cons., Fashion Acad., Costa Mesa, Calif., 1979. Tchr. USAF, P.R., 1963-64, Long Beach (Calif.) Unified Sch. Dist., 1964-68, South San Francisco (Calif.) Unified Sch. Dist., 1968-79; pres. Diana's Color Collage & Color Collage Inst., Pasadena, Calif., 1979—; etiquette affiliates Dorthea Johnson and Marjabelle Stewart, Washington, 1988—; cons. Weight Watchers Internat., L.A., Ventura, Calif., 1987-90, Marriott Hotels, Long Beach, 1989, 1st Interstate Bank, L.A., 1990, Ritz Carlton Hotels, 1995. Contbr. articles to mags. Mem. Assn. Image Cons. Internat. (sec. 1989-90, v.p. 1990-92). Republican. Presbyterian. Office: Diana's Color Collage 123 S Los Robles Ave Pasadena CA 91101-2417

OLSON, DIANE LOUISE, secondary education educator; b. Ft. Dodge, Iowa, Dec. 15, 1951; d. Ralph Leroy and Donna Marie (Solbeck) O.; m. Michael John Schroeder, June 1, 1991. BA in English Edn., U. No. Iowa, 1974; MA in English Edn., N.E. Mo. State U., 1986. Cert. tchr., Iowa. Tchr. English, drama, composition and speech Lamoni (Iowa) Community Schs., 1974-76; tchr. English Rockwell (Iowa)-Swaledale Community Schs., 1977-80; tchr. English and skills for adolescence Wayne Community Schs., Corydon, Iowa, 1980—; workshop presenter and speaker in field. Author pamphlets for workshops; editor, writer: The Story of Cambria, 1990; contbr. articles to profl. jours. Mem. adminstrv. bd. Christian-United Meth. Ch., Humeston, 1982—, lay leader, 1994-95; actress, reader Wayne County Arts Coun., Corydon, 1987-93; actress, dir. Humeston Theater Group, 1992. Named Outstanding Young Woman of Am., 1986, Outstanding Writing Tchr., Writing Conf., 1991; State of Iowa grantee, 1980. Mem. NEA, AAUW (pres. 1993-95), Nat. Coun. Tchrs. English, Iowa Edn. Assn., Iowa Coun. Tchrs. English, Wayne Cmty. Edn. Assn., Mormon Trail Chamber and Devel. Corp., Beta Sigma Phi (treas., v.p.). Democrat. Home: 511 Guy Porter St Humeston IA 50123-1004 Office: Wayne Community Schs PO Box 308 Corydon IA 50060-0308

OLSON, ELIZABETH FIELDER, librarian; b. Camden, N.J., Nov. 28, 1959; d. Earl Frederick and Judith (Jefferies) Fielder; m. Lauris Ture Olson, May 31, 1986; children: Charlotte Fielder, Lucinda Meredith. BA, Haverford Coll., 1980; MA, U. Pa., 1982; MS, Drexel U., 1986. Rsch. specialist dept. psychiatry U. Pa., Phila., 1983-85; libr. Biddle Law Libr., U. Pa., Phila., 1985-87, Archer & Greiner, Haddonfield, N.J., 1987—. Contbr. book revs. to Libr. Jour., 1989—. Mem. Am. Assn. Law Librs., Greater Phila. Law Libr. Assn. (chair pub. rels. com. 1988, chair nominating com. 1990). Office: Archer & Greiner 1 Centennial Sq Haddonfield NJ 08033

OLSON, ERNESTINE LEE, nurse; b. Gregory, S.D., Oct. 14, 1952; d. Ervin E. and Nila Lee (Ritterbush) Neiman; divorced; children: Nathan, Candice. BSN, U. Nebr., 1974. RN, Nebr. Charge nurse Perkins County Hosp., Grant, Nebr.; mem. Gov.'s Rural Health Task Force, Region II Mental Health Adv. Com.; instr. CPR. Recipient Writing award Am. Jour. Nursing, 1984. Mem. ANA, VFW, Nebr. Nurses Assn. (continuing edn. reviewer), Am. Heart Assn., Am. Legion Aux. (chmn. unit 40 Girls State), Am. Cancer Soc. S.W. Regional SIDS Coun. Mennonite. Home: 976 Garfield Grant NE 69140 Office: 900 Lincoln Ave Grant NE 69140

OLSON, GAYLE AUGUSTINE, psychology educator; b. St. Louis, Jan. 9, 1945; d. George Edward and Edith Emelie (Alpiser) Augustine; m. Richard D. Olson, Aug. 26, 1967. BA, Butler U., 1966; MS, St. Louis U., 1968, PhD, 1970. Asst. prof. St. Mary's Dominican Coll., New Orleans, 1970-71; from asst. to prof. U. New Orleans, 1970—, assoc. dean Grad. Sch., 1976-78, rsch. prof., 1991—; psychologist De Paul Hosp., New Orleans, 1974-76. Mem. editorial rev. bd. Peptides, 1980—; editor: Learning in the Classroom: Theory & Application, 1971; contbr. over 55 articles to profl. jours. Mem. Charlie Logan scholarship com. Seafarers Internat. Union, Camp Springs, Md., 1977—. Grantee Edward Schlieder Found., La. Ed. Quality Support Fund. Fellow APA, Am. Psychol. Soc.; mem. AAAS, Soc. for Neurosci., Psychonomic Soc., Sigma Xi, Psi Chi. Home: 103 Doubloon Dr Slidell LA 70461-2715 Office: U New Orleans Dept Psychology New Orleans LA 70148

OLSON, GEN, state legislator; b. May 20, 1938. BS in Edn. with distinction, U. Minn., EdD. Mayor Minnetrista, Minn., 1981-82; mem. Minn. State Senate, 1983—. Former mem. Park and Recreation Commn., Planning and Zoning Commn., Police Commn., City Council. Republican. Office: Minn State Senate State Capitol Saint Paul MN 55155*

OLSON, IDA MARY, customer service representative, small business owner; b. Lynwood, Calif., Oct. 18, 1952; d. Danford Joseph and Noellie Louise (Willmott) Dodds; m. Dale C. Olson, Sept. 1979, (div. Oct. 1993); children: James Clark Ashley, Jr., Bevan Rheta, Scott Clifford. Student, Cerritos Jr. Coll., 1970-71, Orange Coast Jr. Coll., 1973. Lic. comml. pilot. Sr. customer svc. agt. Delta Airlines, Phoenix, Ariz., 1975—; owner, founder Cargo Queen, Peoria, Ariz., 1994—. Active Apache (Ariz.) PTSA, 1985—, pres. 1991-92; chairhead, head coord. Young Diplomats, Peoria, 1992-93. Mem. Nat. Assn. Realtors, Phoenix Bd. Realtors, Ariz. Macintosh User's Group. Republican. Office: Cargo Queen 8532 Via Montoya Dr Peoria AZ 85382

OLSON, JEAN LOUNSBURY, psychiatric social worker; b. Detroit, Feb. 19, 1942; d. James Breckinridge and Vivian Beatrice (Thomen) Lounsbury; m. Jerome Garrie Pittman, Oct. 16, 1960 (div. 1976); children: James Gary, David Bern, Patrick Alan; m. David John Olson, Nov. 21, 1984; stepson. Matthew Noah. BS, N.C. State U., Raleigh, 1975, BSW, 1976; MSW, U. N.C., Chapel Hill, 1985. Counselor Drug Action, Raleigh, 1978-82; counselor, supr. Juvenile Restitution, Raleigh, 1978-82; clin. social worker Dorothea Dix Hosp., Raleigh, 1984-91; liaison N.C. State Hosp., Raleigh, 1984-91; pvt. practice, Cary and Raleigh, N.C., 1991—. VISTA vol., Raleigh, 1977-78. Mem. Nat. Assn. Social Workers, N.C. Soc. Clin. Hypnosis, N.C. Soc. Clin. Social Work (program com. 1984—), Am. Assn. U. Women, Am. Group Psychotherapy Assn. Democrat. Presbyterian. Home: 8120 Deer Meadow Dr Apex NC 27502

OLSON, JULIE ANN, systems consultant, educator; b. Oklahoma City, May 14, 1957; d. Willard Alton and Ruth Harriet (Ehlers) O.; m. Kevin Peter McAuliffe, Oct. 12, 1985; children: Scott Andrew, Shannon Elizabeth, Kathryn Victoria. BA in History, Augustana Coll., 1979; MBA, Keller Grad. Sch. Mgmt., Chgo., 1989. Systems analyst Continental Bank, Chgo., 1979-82; sr. systems cons., adminstrv. mgr. Computer Scis. Corp. (formerly Computer Ptnrs.), Oakbrook, Ill., 1982—; instr. data processing Oakton Community Coll., Des Plaines, 1982—, faculty coord. accelerated data processing cert. program, 1983-92. Exec. dir., chmn. scholarship Miss N.W. Communities Inc., Des Plaines, 1984-88. Mem. ASTD, NAFE, Data Processing Mgmt. Assn. (asst. faculty coord. Student chpt. 1985-87). Lutheran. Avocations: classical pianist, reading, flamenco dancing, snow skiing, cross stitch. Home: 401 S Pine St Mount Prospect IL 60056-3723 Office: Computer Sci Corp 2021 Spring Rd Ste 200 Oak Brook IL 60521

OLSON, KATY, state legislator, farmer; b. Rock Rapids, Iowa, Oct. 24, 1928; d. Corneluis and Cornelia (Bakker) Gaalswyk; m. Robert R. Olson, Nov. 13, 1948; children: Cynthia, Shirley, Roberta, Kent, Amy. Student, Luther Coll. Bd. mem. PTA Minn. State, 1968-84; mem. Trimont Sch. Bd., Minn., 1976-86; bd. mem. Edn. Coop. Svc. Unit, Mankato, Minn., 1980-86; commr. Region 9 Devel. Commn., 1982-86; rep. Minn. State Govt., St. Paul, 1986-94; vice chair Edn. Com. in House, St. Paul, 1986-94; asst. maj. leader Minn. House of Reps., 1992-94. Home: R R 2 Box 115 Sherburn MN 56171 Office: Minn State Senate State Capitol Saint Paul MN 55155

OLSON, KAY MELCHISEDECH, magazine editor; b. Mpls., Nov. 16, 1948; d. John William and Carol Louise (Born) Melchisedech; m. John Addison Olson, Sept. 5, 1970 (div. 1988); children: Jennifer Marie, Nathan John. BA, U. Minn., 1971. News editor New Hope-Plymouth Post, Crystal, Minn., 1971-73; features editor Sun Newspapers, Bloomington, Minn., 1973-75; with pub. rels. dept. Nat. Car Rental, Bloomington, Minn., 1975-77; free-lance pub. rels. profl. Mpls., 1977-82; mag. editor Miller Pub., Minnetonka, Minn., 1982-90; exec. editor Flower & Garden mag., Workbasket mag. Easy-Does-It Needework & Crafts mag. KC Pub. Inc., Kansas City, Mo., 1990—. Mem. Garden Writers Assn. Am. Roman Catholic. Home: 4726 W 78th Ter Shawnee Mission KS 66208-4413 Office: KC Pub Inc 700 W 47th St Ste 310 Kansas City MO 64112

OLSON, KELLEY HUGHES, nonprofit association administrator, consultant; b. Flint, Mich., Oct. 12, 1962; d. Herman William and Eugenie Louise (LeBeau) Hughes; m. Scott Robert Olson, Oct. 5, 1985; children: Katherine, Lucie. BS in Communication, Northwestern U., 1984. Publicity assoc. Carol DeChant & Assocs., Chgo., 1985; spl. events coord. Easter Seal Camp Hemlocks, Hebron, Conn., 1986-87, Hartford Easter Seal Rehab. Ctr., Hartford, Conn., 1987-90; v.p. devel. The Easter Seal Soc. Conn., Inc., Hebron, 1990—; telethon producer Easter Seal and Sta. WTNH-TV, Channel 8, New Haven, Conn., 1991—; presenter nationwide staff meeting Nat. Easter Seal Soc., Chgo., 1990, 91. Actor in numerous plays and indsl. films. Mem. Planning Giving Group of Conn. Mem. SAG, Women in Communication, Tri Delta. Roman Catholic. Office: The Easter Seal Soc Conn Inc 147 Jones St Hebron CT 06248-0100

OLSON, MARIAN EDNA, nurse, social psychologist; b. Newman Grove, Nebr., July 20, 1923; d. Edwrd and Ethel Thelma (Hougland) Olson; diploma U. Nebr., 1944, BS in Nursing, 1953; MA, State U. Iowa, 1961, MA in Psychology, 1962; PhD in Psychology, UCLA, 1966. Staff nurse, supr. U. Tex. Med. Br., Galveston, 1944-49; with U. Iowa, Iowa City, 1949-59, supr. 1953-55, asst. dir. 1955-59; asst. prof. nursing UCLA, 1965-67; prof. nursing U. Hawaii, 1967-70, 78-82; dir. nursing Wilcox Hosp. and Health Center, Lihue, 1970-77; chmn. Hawaii Bd. Nursing, 1974-80; prof. nursing No. Mich. U., 1984-88. Mem. Am. Nurses Assn. (mem. nat. accreditation bd. continuing edn. 1975-78), Nat. League Nursing, Am. Hosp. Assn., Am.

Public Health Assn., LWV. Democrat. Roman Catholic. Home and Office: 6223 County 513 T Rd Rapid River MI 49878-9595

OLSON, MARIAN KATHERINE, emergency management executive, consultant, publisher, information broker; b. Tulsa, Oct. 15, 1933; d. Sherwood Joseph and Katherine M. (Miller) Lahman; m. Ronald Keith Olson, Oct 27, 1956, (dec. May 1991). BA in Polit. Sci., U. Colo., 1954, MA in Elem. Edn., 1962; EdD in Ednl. Adminstrn., U. Tulsa, 1969. Tchr. public schs., Wyo., Colo., Mont., 1958-67; teaching fellow, adj. instr. edn. U. Tulsa, 1968-69; asst. prof. edn. Eastern Mont. State Coll., 1970; program assoc. research adminstrn. Mont. State U., 1970-75; on leave with Energy Policy Office of White House, then with Fed. Energy Adminstrn., 1973-74; with Dept. Energy, and predecessor, 1975—, program analyst, 1975-79, chief planning and environ. compliance br., 1979-83; regional dir. Region VIII Fed. Emergency Mgmt. Agy., 1987-93; exec. dir., Search and Rescue Dogs of the U.S., 1993—; pres. Western Healthclaims, Inc., Golden, Co.; pres. Marian Olson Assocs., Bannack Pub. Co.; mem. Colo. Nat. Hazards Mitigation Coun., Colo. Urban Search and Rescue Task Force. Contbr. articles in field. Grantee Okla. Consortium Higher Edn., 1969, NIMH, 1974. Mem. Am. Soc. for Info. Sci., Am. Assn. Budget and Program Analysis, Internat. Assn. Ind. Pubs., Nat. Inst. Urban Search and Rescue (bd. dirs.), Nat. Assn. for Search and Rescue, Colo. Search and Rescue, Search and Rescue Dogs of U.S., Colo. Emergency Mgmt. Assn., Front Range Rescue Dogs, Colo. State Fire Chiefs Assn., Kappa Delta Pi, Phi Alpha Theta, Kappa Alpha Theta. Republican. Home: 203 Iowa Dr Golden CO 80403-1337 Office: Western Healthclaims Inc 203 Iowa Dr Ste B Golden CO 80403

OLSON, NADINE FAYE, foreign language educator, consultant; b. Broken Bow, Nebr., Mar. 7, 1948; d. Warren Wendell and Lois Julia (Kolbo) O. BA in Edn., Ea. Wash. U., 1970; MA in Spanish, U. No. Iowa, 1981; PhD in Romance Langs., U. Ga., 1989. Tchr. English and Spanish Cen. Valley Sch. Dist., Spokane, Wash., 1970-82; instr. in Spanish U. of the South, Sewanee, Tenn., 1986-89; asst. prof. Spanish and fgn. lang. edn. Okla. State U., Stillwater, 1989-94, assoc. prof. Spanish and fgn. lang. edn., 1994—; freelance cons., Okla., 1989—; reader advanced placement Spanish exams. Ednl. Testing Svcs., Princeton, N.J., 1991—. Mem. Am. Coun. Tchg. of Fgn. Langs., Okla. Fgn. Lang. Tchrs. Assn. (exec. bd.), Am. Assn. Tchrs. Spanish and Portuguese, Delta Kappa Gamma (chpt. pres. 1979-81, 94-96), Phi Kappa Phi, Sigma Delta Pi (chpt. treas. 1983-84). Office: Okla State U 237 Math Scis Bldg Stillwater OK 74078

OLSON, NANCY ANNE, computer systems analyst; b. Milw., Aug. 16, 1960; d. Rudolph Raymond and Shirley May (Pelot) O. BA in Geography, U. Wis., Milw., 1981, BA in Anthropology, 1981. Mapping application specialist Advanced Computer Graphics, Milw., 1983-84, tng. coord., 1984-87; Macintosh system mgr. Quad/Graphics, Sussex, Wis., 1987-90; sr. systems analyst City of Milw., 1990—; cons. Tech. Directions, Milw., 1992—; mem. adv. bd. MicroStation Mgr., Santa Fe, 1992—, tech. editor, 1993—; trainer U. Wis. Ctr. for Continuing Engring. Edn., Milw., 1992-94. Author: Inside MicroStation 5, 1993. Home: 7731 W Morgan Ave Milwaukee WI 53220-1150

OLSON, PAMELA FAITH, lawyer; b. Fargo, N.D., July 6, 1954; d. Norman Clifford and Inga (Larson) O.; m. Grant Douglas Aldonas, Apr. 12, 1980; children: Nicole Helen, Kirsten Inga, Noah Grant. BA magna cum laude, U. Minn., 1976, JD, 1980, MBA, 1984. Bar: D.C. 1981. Instr. U. Minn., Coll. Bus. Adminstrn., Mpls., 1979; atty., advisor Office of Chief Counsel, IRS, Washington, 1981-84, spl. asst. to chief counsel, 1984-86; assoc. Skadden, Arps, Slate, Meagher & Flom, Washington, 1986-90, ptnr., 1990—. Precinct chair-woman Ind.-Rep. Party, 1980; coun. mem. Holy Trinity Luth. Ch., Falls Church, Va., 1988-91, pres., 1990; bd. dirs. Arlington (Va.) Forest Club, Inc., 1990-92; trustee Millenium Inst., 1993—. Mem. ABA (vice chmn. employment taxes com. 1988-90, chmn. 1990-92, com. on govt. rels. 1992—, com. on coms. 1992—, com. on women and minorities 1993—, com. on membership and mktg. 1993—, coun. dir. sect. on taxation 1993—), Equipment Leasing Assn., D.C. Bar Assn. (chmn. legis. and regulations com.), U. Minn. Law Sch. Alumi Assn. (bd. dirs. 1992—). Office: Skadden Arps Slate Meagher & Flom 1440 New York Ave NW Washington DC 20005

OLSON, PATRICIA JOANNE, artist, educator; b. Chgo., Aug. 22, 1927; d. Fred William and Fern Leslie (Shaffer) Kohler; m. Paul J. Olson, Jan. 21, 1950 (dec. July 1968); adopted children: Paulette, Dominic; stepchildren: Cinty, Katie, Larry, Daniel. BA, Northeastern Ill. U., 1976; MA, Loyola U., 1981. Advt. art dir. Chas. A. Stevens Dept. Store, Chgo., 1950-55; art dir. McCann, Erickson Advt. Agy., Chgo., 1955-57; pres. Olson Studio, Chgo., 1957-75; dept. chair, mem. faculty Chgo. Acad. Fine Art, 1974-78; exhibiting artist Chicago and Santa Barbara, Calif., 1981—; instr. Old Town Triangle Art Ctr., Chgo., 1978—, Bernard Horwich Ctr., Chgo., 1982-86, Art Inst. Chgo., 1987; prof. Columbia Coll., Chgo., 1978—; panelist Chgo. Cultural Ctr.; spkr., demonstrator Skokie Cultural Ctr., 1992, Joliet Art Ctr., 1992; guest spkr. AAUW, Evanston, Ill., 1991, Columbia Coll. Humanities, Chgo., 1992. Author: Women of Different Sizes, 1981; contbr. poetry to mags.; one woman shows include Artemesia Gallery, 1985, Highland Park H.S., 1987, One Ill. Ctr., 1987, Gallery 6000, 1988, Countryside Gallery of New Work, 1991, Old Town Triangle Gallery, 1991, Loyola U. Gallery, 1991; exhibited in group shows New Horizons, Art Inst. Gallery, 1975, 90, Beverly Art Ctr., 1978, 79, 82, 87, 89, 90, Beacon St. Gallery, 1984, 89, Art Inst. Chgo., 1984, Galex 19 Internat., Galesburg, Ill., 1985, Suburban Art League, 1986, Natalini Gallery, 1987, Societe des Pastellistes de France, 1987, Campanile Gallery, 1987, Artemsia Gallery, 1987, Delora Cultural Ctr., 1988, Alexandrian Mus., 1988, Gallery Genesis, 1988, 89, Adler Cultural Ctr., 1989, Post Rd. Gallery, 1989, Evanston Co-op Gallery, 1990, Pilsen Gallery, 1991, Old Town Triangle Gallery, 1991, Loyola U. Gallery, 1991, Chgo. Soc. Artists, 1992, R.H. Love Gallery, 1992, Chgo. Cultural Ctr., 1992, Wood St. Gallery, 1994, North Lakeside Cultural Ctr., 1994, State of Ill. Bldg. Chi. Il. Sr. Citizen Art Network (award), others. Hostess Rogers Park (Ill.) Hist. Soc., 1993. Named to Sr. Hall of Fame, Mayor Daley, Chgo., 1991. Mem. Chgo. Soc. Artists, Chgo. Womens Caucus for Art (curator 1989-90), North Lakeside Cultural Ctr. (mem. art adv. bd. 1990—), Am. Jewish Art Club (juror, curator, speaker 1991), Wizo (juror 1989), Sr. Citizens Art Network. Democrat. Home: 1955 W Morse Ave Chicago IL 60626

OLSON, RUE EILEEN, librarian; b. Chgo., Nov. 1, 1928; d. Paul H. and Martha M. (Fick) Meyers; m. Richard L. Olson, July 18, 1964; children: Catherine, Karen. Student Herzl Coll., 1946-48, Northwestern U., 1948-50, Ill. State U., 1960-64, Middle Mgmt. Inst. Spl. Librs. Assn., 1985-87. Acct. Ill. Farm Supply Co., Chgo., 1948-59; asst. libr. Ill. Agrl. Assn., Bloomington, 1960-66, libr., 1966-86, dir. libr. svcs., 1986—; bd. dirs. Corn Belt Libr. System, 1989-94, sec., 1991—. Mem. area Com. Nat. Libr. Week, 1971, area steering com., 1972; mem. steering com. Illinet/OCLC, 1985-87; mem. adv. council of librs. Grad. Sch. Libr. Sci. U. Ill., 1976-79; mem. Ill. State Libr. Adv. Com. for Interlibr. Cooperation, 1979-80; del. Ill. White House Conf. on Libr. and Info. Svcs., 1978; coordinator Vita Income Tax Assistance, Bloomington, Ill., 1986-89, preparer 1978—. Mem. Am., Ill., McLean County (pres. 1970-71) Libr. Assns., Spl. Librs. Assn. (pres. Ill. chpt. 1977-78, first to be named Disting. Mem. food, agr. and nutrition div. 1989), Ill. OCLC Users Group (treas. 1988-90, bd. dirs. 1991-92), Internat. Assn. Agrl. Librs. and Documentalists, Am. Soc. Info. Sci., Am. Mgmt. Assn., USAIN, Mended Hearts, Inc. (sec. Ill. chpt. 250, newsletter editor, 1994—), Zonta (pres. 1987-89), Bloomington Club. Office: Ill Agrl Assn 1701 N Towanda Ave Bloomington IL 61701-2040

OLSON, SANDRA DITTMAN, medical, surgical nurse; b. Duluth, Minn., Mar. 27, 1953; d. Donald Gene and Evelyn Mae (Wilson) Dittman; m. Douglas Bruce Olson, Aug. 10, 1974; 1 child, Perryn Douglas. BSN, S.D. State U., 1974. Cert. ACLS. Staff nurse U.S. Army Hosp., Nurnberg, Fed. Republic Germany, 1975-79; dir. staff devel. Oak Ridge Care Ctr., Mpls., 1979-81; staff nurse med.-surg. Profl. Nursing, Metairie, La., 1982-83; staff nurse, weekend spl. Tulane Med. Ctr., New Orleans, 1982-83; charge nurse Meadowcrest Hosp., Gretna, La., 1983, house supr., 1983—; employee activity com. bd. mem. Pharmacy-Nursing Task Force; active numerous workshops on edn., staff devel., coronary and intensive care, infection control, long term care, mgmt. Bd. dirs., sec. Bon Temps Homeowners Assn.; chair ct. of honor Boy Scout Troop #378. Named Spink County Wheat Queen; recipient 1989 LA Great 100 Nurses award; S.D. Gov.'s scholar. Mem. Assn. of Women's Students (chmn. social-publicity), U. Women's Svc. Orgn. (Guidon historian), Sigma Theta Tau, Alpha Xi Delta (chmn. philathropy). Home: 2144 LaSalle Ave Terrytown LA 70056-4515

OLSON, WANDA JEAN, lawyer; b. Ft. Meade, Md., Sept. 4, 1957; d. Donald Leslie and Wanda Ardeen (Phillips) O.; m. Robert Selnick Silverstein, June 6, 1981; children: Joshua Olson Silverstein, Erica Olson Silverstein. BA, Johns Hopkins U., 1978; JD, NYU, 1981. Bar: N.Y. 1982, N.J. 1983. Assoc. Cleary, Gottlieb, Steen & Hamilton, N.Y.C., 1981-89, ptnr., 1990—. Editor Ann. Survey Am. Law, 1979-80, mng. editor, 1980-81. Mem. ABA, Order of Coif, Phi Beta Kappa, Omicron Delta Epsilon. Office: 1 Liberty Plz New York NY 10006-1401

OLSON-HAGAN, ARLENE, parochial school administrator; b. Bklyn., May 30, 1926; d. Carl Bernard and Helen Loretta (Segerdell) Olson; m. Raymond G. Hagan, Feb. 15, 1979; stepchildren: Clifford Charles, David Drew. AB in English, Hofstra U., 1948; MS in Edn., SUNY, New Paltz, 1952; Cert. Adv. Study, Hofstra U., 1976. Tchr. Island Trees (N.Y.) Pub. Schs., 1950-55; tchr., dist. pubs. editor Garden City (N.Y.) Pub. Schs., 1955-82; pub. info. officer Amityville (N.Y.) Pub. Schs., 1982-84; dir. external affairs St. Edward's Sch., Vero Beach, Fla., 1986-93. Editor, layout and design newsletters, spl. brochures for schs. Mem. Nat. Sch. Pub. Rels. Assn., Fla. Pub. Rels. Assn., Ctr. for the Arts. Episcopalian.

OLSON-LINDER, JAN IRENE, school counselor, consultant; b. Primquar, Iowa, June 1, 1946; d. Duane Henry and Mary D. (Maxson) Linder; m. Robert A. Olson, 1967; 1 child, Wesley Scott. BS in Secondary Edn., Ctrl. Mo. State U., 1969, MS in Secondary Edn., 1973, cert. sch. counselor, 1978; cert. secondary principalship, Drake U., 1992. Cert. nat. sch. counselor, peer facilitator, gender/ethnic student achievement trainer; lic. evaluator, Iowa, Minn.; cert. secondary adminstr., Iowa, secondary counselor, Iowa, Mo., Minn., secondary tchr., Iowa, Mo., Minn. Tchr. social studies, coord. social sci. curriculum K-12 Concordia (Mo.) Reorganized Sch. Dist., 1968-76; dir. career edn., sch. counselor K-12 Sweet Springs (Mo.) Reorganized Sch. Dist., 1976-78; coord. guidance svcs., peer facilitator Maurice-Orange City Community Schs., Orange City, Iowa, 1978-87; career counseling/devel. cons. K-14 Bur. Career Edn. Dept. Edn., Des Moines, 1987-89; sch. counselor, peer facilitator East High Sch. Sioux City (Iowa) Community Schs., 1989—; adj. instr. edn. dept. Morningside Coll., Sioux City, 1990-91; secondary prin. intern East High Sch., 1990; mem. Women and Minorities in Ednl. Adminstrn. Mentor Program, 1990; coord. statewide career edn. programs and svcs. Iowa Dept. Edn., chair resource and linkage com. Western Iowa Tech. C.C.; implementor, evaluator East High Peer Helping Program; developer advanced peer facilitator tng. U. Iowa; mem. Governor's Equity Roundtable, Governor's Human Svc. Forum, mem. steering com.; cons. Career Devel. Guideline, Career Counseling/Devel. programs, others. Contbr. articles to profl. jours. Mem. ACA (chair midwest region, strategic planning com., coauthor publs. on career counseling, Profl. Svcs. to Mems. award, Govt. Rels. Cert.), NEA, Am. Sch. Counselors Assn. (v.p. secondary level, v.p. midwest region, chair nat. conf., chair career counseling, co-author Counseling 2000), Nat. Career Devel. Assn. (govt. rels. com.), Nat. Peer Helpers Assn. (bd. dirs.), Nat. Assn. Career Guidance Suprs., Iowa Counseling Assn. (pres., conf. chair, chpt. pres., Peer Helper Adult Facilitator award), Iowa Sch. Counselor Assn. (pres., career counseling chair), Iowa Career Devel. Assn. (pres.), Iowas Peer Helpers Assn. (bd. dirs.), Women in Edtl. Leadership, Iowa Edn. Assn., Iowa Coll. Aid Commn. (adv. bd.), Delta Kappa Gamma. Office: Sioux City Community Sch 5011 Mayhew Sioux City IA 51106

OLSRUD, LOIS CHRISTINE, librarian; b. Havre, Mont., Sept. 21, 1930; d. Oscar Ludwig and Marquerite P. (Martinson) O. BA, Concordia Coll., 1952; postgrad., U. Minn., 1954-64; MA, Ind. U., 1966. Tchr. English, libr. Princeton (Minn.) High Sch., 1952-54; libr. Havre High Sch., 1954-57, West Jr. High Sch., Great Falls, Mont., 1957-66; humanities libr. U. Ariz., Tucson, 1966-77, cen. reference libr., 1977-94, libr. fine arts/humanities, 1994—. Contbr. articles to profl. jours. Mem. ALA (libr. svcs. to aging population com. 1990—), AAUP (chpt. exec. bd. 1987-88), Assn. for Women Faculty, Ariz. Libr. Assn. (various coms.), Ariz. Online Users Group, Univ. Ethics and Committment Com., Delta Kappa Gamma (Upsilon chpt. pres. 1976-78, sec. 1986-88), Pi Lambda Theta, Beta Phi Mu. Lutheran. Home: 2985 E Winterhaven Dr Tucson AZ 85716-1279 Office: U Ariz Libr Cen Reference Dept Tucson AZ 85721

O'MAHONEY, ELIZABETH, librarian, executive; b. South Orange, N.J., Dec. 20, 1947; d. John Joseph and Elizabeth Jane (Farrell) O'M. BA, Caldwell Coll., 1969; MLS, Pratt Inst., 1975. Asst. libr. Marine Midland Bank, N.Y.C., 1969-76; asst. libr. Goldman Sachs & Co., N.Y.C., 1976-80, v.p., libr. mgr., 1981-88, v.p., mgr. support svcs., 1988—. Mem. Spl. Librs. Assn. Office: Goldman Sachs & Co 85 Broad St New York NY 10004-2434

O'MALLEY, KATHLEEN ANN, lawyer; b. Nanticoke, Pa., Oct. 2, 1955; d. Thomas Joseph and Regina Frances (Leyman) O'M. BA with honors, Wilkes Coll., 1976; JD, Dickinson Sch. of Law, 1979. Bar: Pa. 1979, U.S. Ct. Appeals (3d cir.) 1979, Fla. 1986, U.S. Supreme Ct. 1986, U.S. Ct. Appeals (11th cir.) 1984. Assoc. Ball & Skelly, Harrisburg, Pa., 1979-83; asst. U.S. atty. U.S. Dept. Justice, Jacksonville, Fla., 1983—, dep. mng. asst. U.S. atty.; instr. Dept. of Justice Office of Legal Edn., 1994—. Recipient cert. of appreciation U.S. Secret Svc., 1986, Disting. Svc. Citation, 7th Jud. Cir. Fla., 1986, cert. of appreciation Ch. Arson Task Force, 1992, letter of Commendation U.S. Secret Svc., 1994. Mem. Fed. Bar Assn. (treas. Jacksonville chpt. 1988-90, v.p. membership 1990-91, v.p. speakers 1991-92, pres.-elect 1992-93, pres. 1993-94), Jacksonville Bar Assn. (vice chair jud. rels. com. 1991-92, chair criminal law sect. 1992-93, vice-chair 4th jud. cir. pro-bono com.), Cath. Lawyers Guild. Republican. Roman Catholic. Office: Office of US Atty Ste 700 200 W Forsyth St Jacksonville FL 32202-4224

O'MALLEY, KATHLEEN M., federal judge; b. 1956. AB magna cum laude, Kenyon Coll., 1979; JD, Case Western Reserve, 1982. Law clk. to Hon. Nathaniel R. Jones U.S. Ct. of Appeals, 6th circuit, 1982-83; with Jones, Day, Reavis & Pogue, Cleve., 1983-84, Porter, Wright, Morris & Arthur, Cleve., 1985-91; chief counsel, first asst. atty. gen., chief of staff Office of Atty. Gen., Columbus, 1991-94; district judge U.S. Dist. Ct. (Ohio no. dist.), 6th circuit, Cleve., 1994—. Mem. Am. Bar Assn., Fed. Bar Assn., Ohio State Bar Assn., Cleve. Bar Assn. Office: US Courthouse 201 Superior Ave NE Rm 135 Cleveland OH 44114*

O'MALLEY, PATRICIA, critical care nurse; b. Boston, May 13, 1955; d. Peter and Catherine (Dwyer) O'M. BSN, Coll. Mt. St. Joseph, Cin., 1977; MS, Ohio State U., 1984, postgrad., 1990—. Cert. critical care nurse. Primary nurse critical care unit Miami Valley Hosp., Dayton, Ohio, nurse educator, clin. nurse specialist, cons.; adj. faculty Wright State U., Dayton. Contbr. articles to profl. jours., textbooks. Recipient honors Dayton Area Heart Assn., Ohio Ho. of Reps., 1994. Mem. AACN (bd. dirs. Dayton-Miami Valley), Soc. Critical Care Medicine, Sigma Theta Tau. Office: Miami Valley Hosp 1 Wyoming St Dayton OH 45409

O'MALLEY, SUSAN, professional basketball team executive. Degree in Bus. and Finance, Mt. St. Mary's, 1983. Dir. advt. Washington Bullets, 1986-87, dir. mktg., 1987-88, exec. v.p., 1988-91, pres., 1991—. Office: Washington Bullets USAir Arena Landover MD 20785*

OMAN, DEBORAH SUE, health science facility administrator; b. North Platte, Nebr., Aug. 26, 1948; d. Rex Ardell and Opale Louise (Smith) O. BS, Kearney State Coll., 1970; MA in Journalism and Mass Comm., U. Nebr., 1993. Med. technologist Physicians Pathology Labs., Lincoln, Nebr., 1970-71; med. technologist student health Colo. State U., Ft. Collins, 1971-72; supr. hematology lab. Bryan Meml. Hosp., Lincoln, 1972-76; sect. supr. hematology, hemostasis Lincoln N.E. br. Corning Clin. Labs., divsn. Corning Life Scis., 1976—; hemostasis cons. Baxter Diagnostics, Inc., Miami, Fla., 1991—; clin. cons. Med. Lab. Automation, Inc., Pleasantville, N.Y., 1990—; adj. prof. Sch. of Med. Tech. Nebr. Wesleyan U., Lincoln, 1979-85; clin. instr. Sch. Med. Tech., U. Nebr. Med. Ctr., Omaha, 1990-95. Contbr. articles to profl. jours. Mem. Am. Soc. Clin. Pathologists (cert., affiliate, Recognition award 1986), Lancaster Soc. Med. Technologists, Cornhusker Ski Club (pres. 1982-83), Kappa Tau Alpha. Republican. Mem. Christian Ch. Office: Corning Clin Labs Plz Mall South 1919 S 40th St Ste 333 Lincoln NE 68506-5248

OMAR, AMEENAH E.P., college dean; b. Laurel, Miss., Apr. 3, 1941; d. Denothras (Pickens) Pierce; m. Abdul Aziz Omar, Apr. 28, 1979; children: Lakisha, Cheryl. BA in English, U. Detroit, MA in Curriculum Devel., EdS; EdD candidate, Wayne State U. Human resource specialist, personnel specialist U.S. Women Army Corps, 1965-70; tchr. Detroit Pub. Sch., 1972-77; mid. sch. tchr., spl. asst. to supt. Highland Pk. (Mich.) Pub. Schs., 1977-86; dir. coll. placement coop. edn. Highland Park Community Coll., 1986-88, dean student svcs.; sec. H.P. Bldg. Authority. Vice chairperson City of Highland Park Planning Commn.; mem. Highland Park Mothers Club, Parent Adv. Coun. for Gifted and Talented, Highland Park Caucus Club; bd. dirs. Reggie McKenzie Found.; mem. Ferris Sch. PTA; sec. Highland Park Bus. Authority. Recipient Outstanding Svc. to PTA award, 1978, Svc. Beyond Duty award Highland Park Sch. Dist., 1980, Outstanding Svc. award Black History Celebration, 1980, Outstanding Svc. award Mich. Week Celebration, 1980-85, Outstanding Svc. to Class awrd, 1986, Spirit of Detroit award, 1993, Achievement award Black Men Inc., 1993, Outstanding Leadership award City of Highland Park, 1994, Queen Mother award Village of Akwarome, Ghana, 1994; named Outstanding Recruiter in State of Mich., 1970. Mem. Mich. Assn. Collegiate Registrars and Admissions Officers, Mich. Coun. Coll. Placement Officers, United Negro Coll. Fund (grad. landmark edn. forum celebration 50th anniversary), Coun. Coll. Placement Officers, C.C. Employment Network, Coop. Edn. Assn., Nat. Assn. Sch. Execs., Nat. Alliance Black Sch. Educators, Alpha Kappa Alpha (outstanding soror Lambda Pi Omega chpt. 1994), Phi Delta Kappa. Home: 30 Farrand Park Highland Park MI 48203-3350 Office: Highland Pk CC Glendale and Third Aves Highland Park MI 48203

O'MARA, MARILYN MAE, communications executive; b. Willoughby, Ohio, Nov. 15, 1942; d. Peter Milan and Mildred (Babic) Aleksic; m. Richard James O'Mara, Feb. 16, 1963 (div. Feb. 1982); children: Kimberly Ann, Richard James Jr. Student, Oakland Community Coll., 1974-81, Am. Inst. Banking, 1973-77, St. Mary's Coll., 1983-87. Finger print clk. U.S. Dept. Justice FBI, Washington, 1962; sales clk. Sears, Roebuck, & Co., Jacksonville, Fla., 1962-63; asst. mgr. Community Nat. Bank, Pontiac, Mich., 1969-78; office mgr. State Farm Ins. Co., Waterford, Mich., 1978-84; sales sec. Guardian Alarm Co., Detroit, 1984-85; office mgr. Jack McCarthy Restaurant, West Bloomfield, Mich., 1985-86; escrow sec. Conselyea Realtor, Royal Oak, Mich., 1986-87; ins. sec. Meemic Life Ins., Birmingham, Mich., 1987; telemarketing supr. Guest House Hosp., Lake Orion, Mich., 1987-90; field mgr. Internat. Edn. Forum, Clarkston, Mich., 1991-92; postal carrier U.S. Post Office, 1992-93; field mgr. Pace Internat., Independence, Mich., 1993—. Trustee Waterform Dem. Group, 1985-88, del. fin. com., 1985-88, pres. Orchard Lake Ladies Aux., 1987-88, sec. nat. chpt., 1987-88; area coord. Internat. Edn. Forum, 1989-90; treas. chpt. Parents Without Ptnrs., Waterford, 1993-94, treas. ea. Mich. regional coun., 1994-95.

O'MEALLIE, KITTY, artist; b. Bennettsville, S.C., Oct. 24, 1916; d. Earle and Rosa Estelle (Bethea) Chamness; m. John Ryan O'Meallie, June 27, 1939 (dec. Apr. 26, 1974); children—Sue Ryan, Kathryn Bethea; m. Lee Harnie Johnson, Aug. 21, 1976. BFA Tulane U., 1937; postgrad., 1954-59. One-woman shows include Masur Mus., Monroe, La., 1979, Marlboro County Mus. of S.C., 1975, Meridian Mus. Art, Miss., 1981, 85; exhibited in group shows at New Orleans Mus. Art, Contemporary Art Ctr., Meadows Mus., Cushing Gallery, SE Ctr. of Contemporary Art, Art 80, Art Expo West, Art Expo 81. Represented in permanent collections New Orleans Mus. Art, Tulane U. Pan-Am. Life Ctr., Masur Mus. Art, Meridian Mus. Art. Nat. officer Newcomb Coll. Alumnae Assn., 1964-66; lectr. exhibitor for many charitable orgns. Recipient award WYES-TV, 1979, Hon. Invitational New Orleans Women's Caucus, 1986, numerous awards and prizes in competitive exhibitions. Mem. Womens Caucus for Art, New Orleans Womens Caucus for Art, Chi Omega Alumnae Assn. (pres. mothers' club 1964), Town and Country Garden Guild (pres. 1970, 1986). Avocations: birdwatching; bridge. Home and Office: 211 Fairway Dr New Orleans LA 70124-1018

O'MEARA, ANNA M., lawyer; b. Chgo., Aug. 11, 1947. BS cum laude, Loyola U., 1969, JD cum laude, 1984. Bar: Ill. 1984, U.S. Dist. Ct. (no. dist.) Ill. 1984. Ptnr. Mayer, Brown & Platt, Chgo., 1984—. Mem. ABA, Ill. Bar Assn. Office: Mayer Brown & Platt 190 S La Salle St Chicago IL 60603-3410

O'MEARA, NETHA MYRLE, nursing educator; b. Etoile, Tex., Mar. 15, 1935; d. Rufus Mansfield and Daisy Belle (Wooten) Burnaman; m. John Patrick O'Meara, Dec. 16, 1967; children: Sharon, Kathleen, John. Cert. with honors, Bapt. Meml. Hosp. Sch. Nursing, San Antonio, 1955; ADN, Trinity U., 1955; BS in Sociology, U. Houston, 1960; MSN, Tex. Woman'sU., 1979. Cert. sch. health nurse, Tex. Charge nurse, supr. nursing Polly Ryon Meml. Hosp., Rosenberg, Tex., 1955-57; staff and charge nurse Hermann Hosp., Houston, 1957-58, mem. faculty, 1960-62; nursing supr. Med. Arts Hosp., Houston, 1958-60; nursing instr. Galileo Adult Sch. San Francisco Ind. Sch Dist., 1962-64; staff devel. coord. Meml. Hosp. Sys., Houston, 1964; nurse Houston Ind. Sch. Dist., 1964-67; instr. Houston Orgn. for Parent Edn., 1969-79; tchr., nurse Houston Ind. Sch. Dist., 1981-83; relief occupational health nurse various indsl. firms, 1967-82; instr. allied health Houston Community Coll., 1986-88; instr. Coll. Nursing Stephen F. Austin State U., Nacogdoches, Tex., 1988—; realtor Gary Greene Realtors, Better Homes and Gardens, Houston, 1982-83; ind. practitioner and rsch. analyst in field. Mem. membership com. Young Reps., Houston, 1963, coun. PTO for Boone Elem. Sch., Houston, 1978, com. Nacogdoches Spl. Edn. Coun., 1991, Northwood Bapt. Ch., 1992; vol. nursing instr. ARC, San Francisco, 1963-64, Nacogdoches (Tex.) Coalition, 1992. Mem. ANA, Tex. Nurses Assn. (chmn. hosp. com. 1961-62), ARC Nurses, Sharpstown Bapt. Ch. (Sunday sch. tchr, mem. various coms. 1974-84). Home: PO Box 630507 Nacogdoches TX 75963-0507 Office: Stephen F Austin State U PO Box 6156 SFA Sta Nacogdoches TX 75963-0507

O'MEARA, TERESA JEAN KEEFE, elementary school counselor; b. Mt. Pleasant, Iowa, Nov. 6, 1957; d. Thomas William Keefe and Catherine Jean Scott Keefe Beavers; m. Ronald Edward O'Meara, Aug. 8, 1981. BA in Middle Sch./Jr. High Edn./Spl.Edn., U. No. Iowa, 1980, MAE in Sch. Counseling, 1991. Nat. cert. counselor, nat. cert. sch. counselor. Tchr. grades 5-6 Mason City (Iowa) Schs., 1980-81, tchr. K-5 behavior disorders, 1984-87, tchr. grade 1, 1987-88, tchr. grades K-1, 1988-89, elem. counselor grades K-5, 1989-90; elem. counselor grades K-6 West Liberty (Iowa) Schs., 1990-91, North Tama Schs., Traer, Iowa, 1991—; adj. instr. U. No. Iowa, Cedar Falls, 1992—, cadre mem. Dept. Ednl. Adminstrn. and Counseling, 1991—. Bd. dirs. Mental Health Clinic of Tama County, 1992—; mem. Traer Devel. corp., 1993—. Mem. Am. Counseling Assn., Iowa Counseling Assn. (chpt. pres., task force counselor adminstrv. collaboration), Am. Assn. Specialists in Group Work, Iowa Assn. Specialists in Group Work, Am. Sch. Counselors Assn., Iowa Sch. Counselors Assn. Roman Catholic. Home: 305 5th St Traer IA 50675 Office: North Tama County Cmty Schs 605 Walnut Traer IA 50675

OMER, LAURA DIANE (LAURA DIANE PACE), military career officer, educator, nurse; b. Minden, La., Jan. 24, 1946; d. Floyd Curtis and Noble Celestial (Garrett) Pace; m. Lewis M. Omer III, July 26, 1986 (dec.). Diploma in nursing, Ga. Bapt. Hosp. Sch. Nursing, 1968; BSN, Am. U., 1983; MA in Edn. and Human Resource Devel., George Washington U., 1987. Various nursing positions, 1968-77; commd. lt. jr. grade USN, 1977, advanced through grades to comdr.; staff nurse Nat. Naval med. ctr., Bethesda, Md., 1977-81; staff charge nurse Naval Hosp., Guantanamo Bay, Cuba, 1981-82; head edn. and tng. Naval Med. Clinic, Quantico, Va., 1983-86, Naval Med. Command NEREG, Great Lakes, Ill., 1987-89; div. officer edn. and tng. Nat. Naval Med. Ctr., Bethesda, 1989-92, head edn. and tng. dept., 1992-95, dept. head edn. and tng., 1992—. Mem. ASTD, AACN, Assn. Mil. Surgeons of U.S., Sigma Theta Tau, Phi Kappa Phi. Home: 8329 Stockade Dr Alexandria VA 22308-1647 Office: Nat Naval Med Ctr Wisconsin Ave Bethesda MD 20889

O'MORCHOE, PATRICIA JEAN, pathologist, educator; b. Halifax, Eng., Sept. 15, 1930; came to U.S., 1968; d. Alfred Eric and Florence Patricia (Pearson) Richardson; m. Charles Christopher Creagh O'Morchoe, Sept. 15,

1955; children: Charles E.C., David J.C. BA, Dublin U., Ireland, 1953, MB, Bch., BAO, 1955, MA, 1966, MD. Intern Halifax (Yorkshire) Gen. Hosp., Eng., 1955-57; instr., lectr. physiology Dublin U., 1957-61, 63-68; instr. pathology Johns Hopkins U., Balt., 1961-62, 68-72, asst. prof. pathology, 1972-74; rsch. assoc. surgery, pathology Harvard U., Boston, 1962-63; asst. prof. anatomy U. Md., 1970-74; assoc.prof., prof. pathology, anatomy Loyola U. Chgo., 1974-84; prof. pathology, cell and structural biology U. Ill., Urbana, 1984—; head dept. pathology coll. medicine U. Ill., Urbana-Champaign, 1994—; staff pathologist VA Hosp., Danville, Ill., 1989—; assoc. head dept. pathology U. Ill., 1991—; courtesy staff pathologist Covenant Hosp., Urbana, 1984—, Carle Clinic, Urbana, 1990—. Contbr. numerous articles to profl. jours. Mem. Internat. Acad. Cytology, Internat. Soc. Lumphology (auditor 1989-91, exec. com. 1991-93), N.Am. Soc. Lymphology (sec. 1988-90, treas. 1990-92, v.p. 1992-94, pres. 1994—), Am. Soc. Cytology, Am. Assn. Anatomists, Ill. Soc. Cytology. Home: 2709 Holcomb Dr Urbana IL 61801-7724 Office: U Ill Coll Med 506 S Mathews Ave Urbana IL 61801-3618

ONAN, KAREN M, accountant; b. Kalamazoo, Mich., Oct. 28, 1960; d. Philip E. and JoAnne (Anderson) Price; m. Roby J. Onan, June 5, 1982; children: Alyssa, Zachary. BBA, U. Wis., 1984. CPA, Wis.; CMA. Cost acct. U.S. Gypsum Co., Milw., 1985; acctg. supr. Gossen Corp., Milw., 1985-87, contr., 1987-90, CFO, 1990-93, v.p. fin., 1993—; bd. dirs. Gossen Corp. Treas. Cleft Lip and Palate Helpline, Milw., 1993—; bd. dirs. Gossen Corp. Found., 1993—. Mem. Focus (treas. 1994), Inst. Mgmt. Accts. Office: Gossen Corp 2030 W Bender Rd Milwaukee WI 53209-3727

ONARAL, BANU KUM, electrical/biomedical engineering educator; b. Istanbul, Turkey, June 15, 1949; came to U.S., 1974; d. Mehmet Serhan and Sukufe (Demirag) Kum; m. Ibrahim Etem, Sept. 21, 1973; 1 child, Mutlu Can. MSEE, Bogazici U., Istanbul, 1974; PhD, U. Pa., 1978. Postdoctoral fellow U. Pa., Phila., 1979-80; vis. asst. prof. Drexel U., Phila., 1980, asst. prof., 1981-85, assoc. prof., 1985-91, prof., 1991—; vis. asst. prof. Bogazici U., 1980-81; vis. prof. Bogarici U., 1987-88; cons. TOKTEN/UN, Istanbul, 1989. Contbr. articles to profl. jours. Recipient EDUCOM'89 Best Ednl. Tool award; Fulbright scholar Inst. Internat. Edn., 1974-78. Fellow AAAS, IEEE (gen. chair 12th ann. internat. conf. IEEE/EMBS Phila. 1990, tech. meetings coun./TAB Piscataway, N.J. 1991—), Am. Inst. Med. and Biol. Engring.; mem. Soc. Women Engrs. (sr.), Am. Soc. Engring. Edn., Sigma Xi. Home: 2301 Cherry St # 4 0 Philadelphia PA 19103-1029 Office: Drexel U 32d and Chestnut St Philadelphia PA 19104

ONA-SARINO, MILAGROS FELIX, physician, pathologist; b. Manila, May 8, 1940; came to U.S., 1965, naturalized, 1983; d. Venancio Vale Ona and Fidela Torres Felix; m. Edgardo Formantes Sarino, June 11, 1966; children: Edith Melanie, Edgar Michael, Edenn Michele. AA, U. Santo Tomas, Manila, 1959, MD meritissimus cum laude 1964. Diplomate Am. Bd. Pathology; med. licensure N.Y., N.J., W.Va. Rotating intern N.Y. Infirmary, 1965-66; resident in anatomic and clin. pathology Lenox Hill Hosp., N.Y.C., 1966-71, asst. adj. pathologist, 1972-74; assoc. pathologist St. Francis Med. Ctr., Trenton, N.J., 1974-84, Hamilton Hosp., N.J., 1974-84; pathologist, chief pathology and lab. medicine svc. Louis A. Johnson VA Med. Ctr., Clarksburg, W.Va., 1984—; clin. instr. pathology Columbia U. Coll. Physicians and Surgeons, N.Y.C., 1973-85; clin. assoc. prof. pathology, W.Va. U. Sch. Medicine. Fellow Am. Soc. Clin. Pathologists, Coll. of Am. Pathologists; mem. Internat. Acad. Pathology, N.Y. Acad. Scis. (life). Office: Louis A Johnson VA Med Ctr Clarksburg WV 26301

O'NEAL, HARRIET ROBERTS, psychologist, psycholegal consultant; b. Covington, Ky., Dec. 28, 1952; d. Nelson E. and Georgia H. (Roberts) O'N. Student, U. Paris Sorbonne, 1972; BA in Psychology, Hollins Coll., 1974; JD, U. Nebr., 1978, MA in Psychology, 1980, PhD in Psychology, 1982. Program dir., therapist Richmond Maxi Ctr., San Francisco, 1979-81; clin. coord., therapist Pacifica (Calif.) Youth Svc. Bur., 1981-83; staff psychologist Kaiser Permanente Med. Ctr., Walnut Creek, Calif., 1983-91; pvt. practice psychotherapy Pleasant Hill, Calif., 1985—; psycholegal cons., Nebr., 1975-79, Calif., 1979—; oral exam commr. Calif. Bd. Behavioral Sci. Examiners, Sacramento, 1982—; pvt. practice psychotherapy, Pleasant Hill, Calif., 1985—; psycholegal cons., presenter San Francisco State U., 1980, U. Calif., San Francisco, 1980, VA Med. Ctr., San Francisco, 1983. Cons. Nebr. Gov.'s Commn. on Status of Women, 1975, 78. NIMH fellow, 1974-79. Mem. Am. Psychol. Assn., Calif. Psychol. Assn., Phi Beta Kappa, Psi Chi. Club: Commonwealth (San Francisco).

O'NEAL, NELL SELF, principal; b. Glenwood, Ark., Feb. 19, 1925; d. Jewell Calvin and Nannie May (Bankston) Self; m. Billie Kenneth O'Neal, Apr. 1, 1943 (div. Jan. 1976); children: Kenneth Dan O'Neal, Rikki Devin O'Neal, Teresa Lynn Severson. BA, Little Rock U., 1964; MS in Edn., Ark. State Tchrs. Coll., 1965. Cert. tchr. mentally retarded, blind; cert. elem. sch. prin. Spl. edn. tchr. Little Rock Pub. Schs., 1961-65; prin. exceptional unit Ark. Sch. for the Blind, Little Rock, 1965—. Mem. Ark. for Environ. Reform, Little Rock. Mem. NOW, NEA, AAUW, Assn. for the Edn., and Rehab. of Blind and Visually Impaired (J. Max Woolly Superior Svc. award 1990), Ark. Edn. Assn., Sierra club, Nat. Audubon Soc., Alpha Delta Kappa. Democrat. Methodist. Home: 6513 Cantrell Rd Little Rock AR 72207-4218 Office: Ark Sch for the Blind 2600 W Markham St Little Rock AR 72205-5925

O'NEAL, PATRICIA JANE, small business owner; b. Bayard, Nebr., Sept. 8, 1937; d. William B. and Freda (Ebel) Barrett; m. Ralph L. O'Neal, Feb. 4, 1955 (div. Dec. 1978); children: Michael, Douglas, Steven, Darla, Kerry O'Neal McKinley. AA, Golden West Coll., 1975; BA in Mgmt., U. Phoenix, 1987. Cert. adminstrn. mgr.; cert. profl. sec. Pers. adminstr. Elec. Equipment Co., Phoenix, 1976-81; exec. asst. ITT Courier, Phoenix, 1980-81; pers. adminstr. Valley Seed Co., Phoenix, 1981-82; mgr. pers. and adminstrn. Kurta Corp., Phoenix, 1982-92; sole proprietor All Ink, Phoenix, 1992-93; pres. All Ink Corp., Phoenix, 1994—; instr. Rio Salado C.C., Phoenix, 1988—, Phoenix Coll., 1984-87. Chmn. Adopt A Student Program, Julian Intermediate Sch., Phoenix, 1988-90. Mem. Adminstrv. Mgmt. Soc. (pres. 1984-86, Mem. of Yr. 1986), Cert. Profl. Sec. Soc. Ariz. (bd. dirs. 1980-90, founding chmn.), Metro Phoenix Human Resources Assn. (dir. 1992), Phoenix Irish 100. Republican. Office: All Ink Corp 1201 N 54th Ave Ste 123 Phoenix AZ 85043-1775

O'NEIL, CHARLOTTE COOPER, environmental education administrator; b. Chgo., Sept. 21, 1949; d. Adolph H. and Charlotte Waters (Edman) Cooper; m. William Randolph O'Neil, Nov. 18, 1972; children; Sean, Megan. BA in Polit. Sci., Okla. State U., 1969; BS in Edn., U. Tenn., 1988. Cert. tchr., Tenn. Intern Senator Charles H. Percy, Washington, 1969; state treas., state hdqrs. office mgr. Jed Johnson for U.S. Senate, Okla., 1972; mem. acct. staff Pacific Architects & Engrs., Barrow, Alaska, 1973; tchr. social studies Jefferson Jr. High Sch., Oak Ridge, Tenn., 1988; edn. specialsit Sci. applications Internat. Corp., Oak Ridge, Tenn., 1988—; mgr. environ. edn. and info. tech. sect. Sci. Applications INternat. Corp., Oak Ridge, 1994—. Author: Science, Society and America's Nuclear Waste, 1992, Technical Career Opportunities in High-Level Waste Management, 1993, The Environmental History of the Tonawanda Site, 1994; contbr. articles to profl. jours. Mem. ASCD, AAUW, Triangle Coalition, Tenn. Geography Alliance, Nat. Coun. for Social Studies (culture, sci. and tech. com., sci. and society com., sec.-treas. 1991—), Earthwatch, Internat. Alliance for High-Level Radioactive Waste Mgmt., Golden Key, Atomic City Aquatic Club (chair constl. rev. com. 1991—). Office: Sci Applications Internat Box 2502 Oak Ridge TN 37831-4724

O'NEIL, CHLOE ANN, state legislator; m. John G.A. O'Neil (dec.); children: Beth Ann Rice, John A.S. BS in Psychology, SUNY, Potsdam, 1967, MS in Edn. Tchr. Hermon-DeKalb Ctr. Sch.; tchr. SUNY, Canton, N.Y., Potsdam; elem. tchr. Parishville (N.Y.)-Hopkinton Ctrl. Sch.; mem. N.Y. State Assembly, 1993—. Past mem. St. Mary's Sch. Bd. Edn.; active St. Michael's Ch. in Parishville, N.Y. Mem. N.Y. State United Tchrs. Home: Cassidy Rd Hopkinton NY 12940 Office: NY State Assembly State Capitol Albany NY 12224*

O'NEIL, CLEORA TANNER, personnel specialist; b. Roosevelt, Utah, Sept. 1, 1946; d. Frank and Pearl (Mecham) Tanner; divorced; 1 child, Sylvia Boroughs. AA, Drury Coll., 1983; BA, Westminster U., 1985. Sec. USAF, Hill AFB, Utah, 1966-74, U.S. Army, Ft. Leonard Wood, Mo., 1981-83, VA Hosp., Salt Lake City, 1983-86; employee rels. specialist USAF, McClellan AFB, Calif., 1986-90; pers. specialist USAF, Washington, 1990-94; employee rels. specialist, fed. women's program mgr. USAF, McClellan AFB, 1994—; resident in upper managerial tng. Civilian Air Staff Tng., USAF, Washington, 1990—. Recipient Outstanding USAF Civilian Pers. Program Specialist award, 1989. Mem. Toastmasters (v.p. Aerospace chpt. 1989-90, Toastmaster of Yr. 1989, pres. Am. River chpt. 1989-90, Pres.' award 1990, internat. gov. 1989-90).

O'NEIL, JILL ALANE, computer analyst, computer security advisor; b. Irvington, N.J., Sept. 10, 1954; d. Roger Allen and Nancy Jean (Chapman) Remington; m. James Francis O'Neil, Jan. 17, 1954; children: Kelly Michelle, Rebecca Alane, Jessica Nicole. AAS in Computer Sci., Union County Tech. Inst., 1974, BS in Computer Sci., 1979. Programmer asst. Exxon Corp., Florham Park, N.J., 1974, programmer, 1974-76, programmer analyst, 1976-81; project leader fin. systems Exxon Rsch. and Engring., Florham Park, 1981-85; systems analyst Exxon Rsch. and Engring., Annandale, N.J., 1985-88, Unix systems adminstr., 1988—, computer security advisor, 1993—. Active Bethlehem Twp. PTA, 1986—. Mem. Computer Security Inst., Soc. Computer and Info. Protection, Cray User's Group. Office: Exxon Rsch and Engring Co RR 22 Annandale NJ 08801

O'NEIL, KAREN RODGERS, public relations executive; b. Palo Alto, Calif., Mar. 21, 1964; d. Peter Jay Rodgers and Barbara Turk; m. Adam O'Neil, June 6, 1992. BS, Boston U. Sr. account exec. Clarke & Co. Pub. Rels., Boston, 1986-89; dir. pub. rels. Guest Quarters Hotels, Boston, 1989-91, Embassy Stes. Hotels, Dallas, 1991-92, Pearle Vision, Inc., Dallas, 1992—; v.p. Pearle Vision Found., Dallas, 1993—. Mem. Pub. Rels. Soc. Am. Office: Pearle Vision Inc 2534 Royal Lane Dallas TX 75025

ONEIL, SUSAN JEAN, media specialist; b. Decatur, Ill., Nov. 19, 1952; d. Richard Greer and Patricia Jane (Miller) Schenk; m. Kevin E. Oneil, Feb. 10, 1952; children: Erin and Patrick. BA, Ill. Wesleyan U., Bloomington, 1974; MSEd, Northern Ill. U., Dekalb, 1978, Northern Ill. U., Dekalb, 1989. Cert. elem. tchr., secondary tchr., media specialist with supervisory endorsement. Tchr. Waldo Jr. High, Aurora, Ill., 1975-76; commercial loan cons. Control Data, Naperville, Ill., 1978-79; tchr. Braidwood Jr. High, Braidwood, Ill., 1979-80; librarian Forrestville Sch. Dir., Forreston, Ill.; media specialist Byron Middle Sch., Byran, Ill., 1982—; pres. Byron Fedn. Tchrs. Byron, 1984-86. Contbg. author: Teaching Electronic Information Skills: A Resource Guide for Grades K-5, 1995. Bd. dirs. Rockford (Ill.) Symphony Orch., 1994—. Recipient Electronic Reference Grant Franklin Computers Byron, 1989; grantee ISBE Profl. Devel., 1995. Mem. AAUW, NOW, Ill. Edn. Assn., Ill. Sch. Libr. Media Assn. (treas. 1993—), Northwestern Consortium of Media Dir., Rockford Symphony Orch. (bd. dirs.). Democrat. Methodist. Office: Byron Middle Sch Libr Tower Rd Byron IL 61010

O'NEIL, TERESE AILEEN (TERRI O'NEIL), nurse practitioner womens' health; b. Chgo., Jan. 5, 1963; d. Donald Patrick and Colette Cecelia (Koehl) O'N. BSN, Creighton U., 1986; MN, U. Wash., 1994. RN, Wash. Resident dir. Creighton U., Omaha, 1984-86; home hospice nurse Hospice of Juneau, Alaska, 1986-87; sr. advocate Centenary-Wilbur United Meth. Ch., Portland, Oreg., 1987-88; community organizer/human rights educator Coun. for Human Rights in L.Am., Portland, Oreg., 1987-88; staff nurse med./surg./oncology unit U. Wash. Med. Ctr., Seattle, 1988-90; AIDS community liaison nurse/asst. AIDS care coord. Group Health Coop./N.W. AIDS Found., Seattle, 1989-92; women's primary care nurse practitioner, adult nurse practitioner La Clinica De Familia Inc, Las Cruces, New Mex., 1994—; co-developer staff tng. curriculum N.W. AIDS Edn. & Tng. Ctr. and Bailey-Boushay House, Seattle, 1992, Rosehedge House, Seattle, 1992. Contbr. articles to profl. jours. Mem. Women and HIV/AIDS Task Force, Seattle, 1991-94; co-developer and vol. facilitator Women's Safer Sex Home Parties at the N.W. AIDS Found., Seattle, 1990-93; v.p. Seattle Treatment Edn. Project, 1991-92, bd. dirs., 1992-94, mem. sci. rev. com., 1990-94; bd. dir. La Piñon Sexual Trauma Recovery Ctr. 1994—. Recipient Spirit of Creighton award Creighton U., 1986. Mem. Jacob's Inst. Women's Health, New Mex. Nurse Practitioner Coun., Sigma Theta Tau, Alpha Sigma Nu. Home: Gen Delivery Santa Teresa NM 88008 Office: La Clinica De Familia Inc 205 W Boutz Bldg 6 Las Cruces NM 88005

O'NEILL, ALICE See LICHT, ALICE VESS

O'NEILL, ELIZABETH STERLING, association administrator; b. N.Y.C., May 30, 1938; d. Theodore and Pauline (Green) Sterling: m. W.B. Smith, June 18, 1968 (div. Aug., 1978); 1 child, Elizabeth S. Kroese; m. Francis James O'Neill, May 19, 1984. BA, Cornell U., 1958; postgrad. studies, Northwestern U., 1959-60. Social sec. Perle Mesta Ambassador Luxembourg, N.Y.C.; spl. asst. Vivian Beaumont Allen, philanthropist, N.Y.C.; rep. Prentice-Hall Pub. Co., Eastern Europe; exec. dir. New Caanan (Conn.) C. of C., 1986—; speaker various orgns. including Lions Club, Exchange Club, Kiwanis, Rotary, Poinsettia Club. Pres. Newcomers, New Caanan, Conn.; pub. rels. rep. Girl Scouts of U.S., Fairfield County; bd. dirs. Young Women's Rep. Club; mem. Gov. Weicker's Com. for Curriculum Reform; mem. community bd. Waveny Care Ctr., New Caanan. Recipient Service awards New Caanan YMCA, N.Y. ASPCA, certs. of appreciation New Caanan Lions Club, President Bush. Mem. AAUW (bd. dirs. New Canaan chpt.), Kiwanis. Christian Scientist. Home: Indian Waters Dr New Caanan CT 06840 Office: New Caanan C of C 111 Elm St New Caanan CT 06840

O'NEILL, ELIZABETH STONE, writer; b. Wilmington, Del., Sept. 29, 1923; d. Paul David and Winona Adele (Lambert) Stone; m. John Carroll O'Neill, Aug. 26, 1942; children: Adele Nova, Claire Linnaea (dec.). Student, Goucher Coll., 1941-42, Stockton Coll., 1952-54; BA, U. of the Pacific, 1956, MA, 1968. Legal sec. Salisbury, Md., 1942-44; elem. tchr. Lincoln Unified Sch. Dist., Stockton, Calif., 1956-58; elem. tchr. Stockton (Calif.) Unified Sch. Dist., 1959-75, community rels. counselor, 1966-68; freelance writer Groveland, Calif., 1975—. Author: Meadow in the Sky-A History of Yosemite's Tuolumne Meadows Region, 1984, 3d edit., 1992, Mountain Sage-The Life Story of Carl Sharsmith, Yosemite's Famous Ranger/Naturalist, 1988; contbr. articles to profl. jours. and poems to mags. Mem. Sierra Club, Audubon Soc., Wilderness Soc. Office: Albicaulis Press 13521 Clements Rd Groveland CA 95321

O'NEILL, JUNE ELLENOFF, economics educator; b. N.Y.C., June 14, 1934; d. Louis and Matilda (Liebstein) Ellenoff; m. Sam Cohn, 1955 (div. 1961); 1 child, Peter; m. David Michael O'Neill, Dec. 24, 1964; 1 child, Amy. BA, Sarah Lawrence Coll., Bronxville, N.Y., 1955; PhD, Columbia U., 1970. Econs. instr. Temple U., Phila., 1965-68; rsch. assoc. Brookings Instn., Washington, 1968-71; sr. economist Pres.'s Coun. Econ. Advisors, Washington, 1971-76; chief human resources budget Congl. Budget Office, Washington, 1976-79; sr. rsch. assoc. The Urban Inst., Washington, 1979-86; dir. Office Policy and Rsch. U.S. Commn. Civil Rights, Washington, 1986-87; prof. econs. and fin., dir. Ctr. for Study Bus. and Govt. Baruch Coll., CUNY, 1987—; mem. Nat. Adv. Com., The Poverty Inst., U. Wis., 1988—. Contbr. articles to profl. jours. Rsch. grantee, U.S. Dept. Labor, NICHD, Dept. Health & Human Svcs., others. Mem. Am. Econs. Assn. (bd. dirs. com. on status of women). Republican. Jewish. Home: 420 Riverside Dr New York NY 10025-7773 Office: Baruch College CUNY 17 Lexington Ave Box 348A New York NY 10010

O'NEILL, KATHERINE TEMPLETON, journalist, museum administrator, former nursing educator; b. Moline, Ill., Jan. 13, 1949; d. Morris John and Patricia (Collins) Templeton; 1 child by previous marriage, Carolyn Patricia Coquillette; m. William James O'Neill Jr., July 18, 1987; children: Alec, Sara, Jessie, Laura O'Neill. BS in Nursing, U. Mich., 1971; postgrad., St. Clare's Hall, Oxford, Eng., 1971-72; MS in Nursing, Boston U., 1974. RN, Ohio, Mass. Instr. Mass. Gen. Hosp., Boston, 1974-76; assoc. prof. Ursuline Coll., Cleve., 1976-81; dir. devel. and pub. rels. Ohio Coll. Podiatric Medicine, Cleve., 1985-87; dir. Chisholm Halle Costume Wing We. Res. Hist. Soc., Cleve., 1988-90; fashion editor Chagrin Valley Times, 1989—; v.p., bd. dirs. Cleve. Health Edn. Mus., 1983—, Cleve. Music Sch. Settlement, 1983—. Exec. com. bd. dirs. Hathaway Brown Sch., 1981—, pres. alumnae bd. dirs., 1984-86; bd. dirs. Cleve. Ballet, 1987—, Cleve. Inst. Music, 1994—, Cleve. Scholarship Programs, 1995; mem. adv. bd. Francis Paine Bolton Sch. Nursing, Case Western Res. U., Cleve., 1990—, GAMUT, Cleve. State U., 1992-93, Cleve. Publs., 1993—. Office: Clanco Mgmt Pepper Pike OH 44124

O'NEILL, KATHRYN J., librarian, educator; b. Flint, Mich., Oct. 28, 1942; d. Edward Robert and Mary Elizabeth (Day) Zahn; m. A. Michael O'Neill, June 1964 (div. 1984); children: Daniel Sean, Margaret Anne, Matthew M. (dec.). Student, Ctrl. Mich. U., 1960-62; BA in Edn., U. Mich., 1964, MLS, 1969. Tchr. English, Ann Arbor (Mich.) Pub. Schs., 1964-69, libr., media specialist, 1970-71; libr., media specialist Ladue Sch. Dist., St. Louis, 1977—; cons. in field. Mem. Planning and Zoning Commn., Brentwood, Mo., 1987-93; alternate Bd. of Adjustment, Brentwood, 1990—; elder Richmond Heights Presbyn. Ch.; active Brentwood Libr. Com., 1994—. Mem. NEA (pres. Ladue chpt. 1991-93), AAUW (bd. dirs. Ann Arbor and Kirkwood-Webster Groves chpts.), U.S. Orienteering Fedn. (level I coach U.S. Olympic com. 1989—, 4th ranked U.S. woman in masters category 1989, 90, 91, 3d place masters category U.S. championship 1991), St. Louis Orienteering Club (v.p. 1985-87, editor 1990-92), Greater St. Louis Knitting Guild, Hosteling Internat./AYH (trip leader), Alpha Chi Omega, Phi Kappa Phi (hon.), Beta Phi Mu (hon.). Home: 1716 Blue Jay Cv Brentwood MO 63144-1604

O'NEILL, MARGARET E., psychological counselor; b. Youngstown, Ohio, Jan. 23, 1935; d. Julius and Anna (Zakel) Huegel; children: Paul McCann, Kathleen McCann, Kevin McCann; m. Thomas B. O'Neill, Oct. 21, 1971 (div. 1979). BSN, UCLA, 1961, MS in Nursing, 1963; MA in Counseling, Calif. Luth. Coll., Thousand Oaks, 1974; PhD in Psychology, U.S. Internat. U., San Diego, 1986. Cert. hypnotherapist, Calif. Instr. Ventura Coll., Calif., 1965-69, dept. chair, 1969-74, coordinator Women's Ctr., 1974-79, counselor, 1979-91; marriage, family and child psychologist, Ventura, 1981-92, Morro Bay and San Luis Obispo, 1992—; trainer, cons. County of Ventura, 1984-90, County of San Luis Obispo, 1991—. Mem. NAFE, San Luis Obispo Psychol. Assn., Rotary Morro Bay, New Comers Club San Luis Obispo. Democrat. Avocations: reading, dancing, hiking, walking, travel. Office: 895 Napa Ave Ste A4 Morro Bay CA 93442-1945

O'NEILL, MARY BONIFACE, alternative education administrator; b. Limerick, Ireland, Jan. 16, 1916; came to U.S., 1935; d. Daniel J. and Ellen (O'Connor) O'N. BA, Incarnate Word Coll., 1942; MA, U. Tex., 1943, Our Lady of Lake U., 1956, 58. Joined Holy Spirit Sisters, Roman Cath. Ch., 1934. Tchr. St. Peter Claver Acad., San Antonio, 1950-63, prin., 1964-70; exec. dir. Healy Murphy Ctr., San Antonio, 1970—. Recipient Recognition award Nat. Coun. Jewish Women, 1984, Martin Luther King award, Humanitarian award Women in Communications, 1988, Spl. Community Svc. award NAACP, 1988, Pro Ecclesia et Pontiface award Pope John Paul II, 1989, Citation of Excellence cert. Tex. Ho. of Reps., San Antonio Light Woman of Yr. award, Irishman of Yr. Cuchulainn award, 1987, others. Democrat. Office: 618 Live Oak San Antonio TX 78202-1932

O'NEILL, NORAH ELLEN, airline pilot; b. Seattle, Aug. 23, 1949; d. John Wilson and Bertha Ellen (Moore) O'N.; m. Scott Reynolds, Jan. 31, 1970 (div. Apr. 1973)); m. Scott Edward Byerley, Jan. 29, 1983; children: Cameron, Bren Maxey. Student, U. Calif., Santa Barbara, 1967-68, San Diego State U., 1868-70; BS in Profl. Aeros., Embry-Riddle Aero. U. Lic. airline transport pilot (comml., instrument instr.). Flight instr. Reynolds Aviation, Anchorage, 1973; flight instr. Alaska Cen. Air, Fairbanks, 1973-74, mail, commuter, medivac pilot, 1974-76; DC-8 pilot Flying Tigers, L.A., Seattle, N.Y.C., 1976-80; 747 pilot Flying Tigers, Los Angeles, 1980—. Mem. Airline Pilots Assn., 747 Pilot Fed. Express, Women Airline Pilots Soc. (co-founder 1978, v.p. 1979-80), The 99's (hon.). Home: PO Box 1504 Walla Walla WA 99362-0027 Office: Fed Express PO Box 727 Memphis TN 38194

O'NEILL, SHEILA, principal. Prin. Cor Jesu Acad., St. Louis. Recipient Blue Ribbon award U.S. Dept. Edn., 1990-91. Office: Cor Jesu Acad 10230 Gravois Rd Saint Louis MO 63123

O'NEILL BIDWELL, KATHARINE THOMAS, fine arts association executive, performing arts executive; b. Dayton, Ohio, Mar. 23, 1937; d. Charles Allen and Margaret Stoddard (Talbott) Thomas; children: Margaret, Stephen, Thomas; m. J. Truman Bidwell. B.A., Sarah Lawrence Coll., Bronxville, N.Y., 1959. Mng. dir. Met. Opera Assn., 1977-86, v.p., 1979-86; first v.p. Met. Opera Guild, N.Y.C., 1978-79, pres., chief exec. officer, 1979-86; dir. spl. projects Lincoln Ctr., N.Y.C., 1986—; dir. Norlin Corp. Bd. dirs. Lincoln Ctr. for Performing Arts, N.Y.C., Assn. of Mentally Ill Children, 1975-76, Valerie Bettis Sch. of Theater/Dance, 1976-79, Salisbury Sch., Conn., 1982-84; trustee Sarah Lawrence Coll., 1977-86; Westminster Choir Coll., 1986-91, Greenwall Found., 1986, Vol. Cons. Group, 1986. Mem. Assn. Sarah Lawrence Coll. (pres. 1975-77). Republican. Episcopalian. Home: 455 E 57th St New York NY 10022-3065 Office: Lincoln Center 70 Lincoln Center Plz New York NY 10023-6548*

O'NEILL-ROLLINS, ERIN KATHLEEN, interior designer; b. Poughkeepsie, N.Y., Mar. 28, 1960; d. Brian Collins and Ellen Marie (Jones) O'N.; m. Matthew Ameade Rollins, Nov. 30, 1985; children: Morgan Anne, Lauren Christine. AAS, Fashion Inst. of Tech., 1981, BFA, 1983. Project dir. The Express Co., South Kent, Conn., 1983-85; prin., v.p. O'Neill Rollins Interiors, Millbrook, N.Y., 1986—; design cons. Millbrook's Restoration, Ltd., 1986—; interior designer Jiminy Peak Mountain Resort, Hancock, Mass., 1985-93, Country Club of Pittsfield, Mass., 1988, residential design, 1990—. Mem. Am. Soc. Interior Designers. Office: O'Neill Rollins Interiors RR 1 Box 61A Millbrook NY 12545-9721

ONET, VIRGINIA C(ONSTANTINESCU), research scientist, educator, writer; b. Sarmasag, Salaj, Romania, Mar. 17, 1939; came to U.S., 1986; naturalized, 1991; d. Virgil and Eugenia (Marinescu) Constantinescu; m. Gheorghe Emil Onet, Sept. 3, 1981. DVM, U Agriculture Scis., Cluj-Napoca, Romania, 1966; PhD, Coll. Vet. Med., Bucharest, Romania, 1974. From asst. to assoc. prof. Coll. Vet. Medicine, Cluj-Napoca, 1966-81, lectr., 1981-85; pvt. researcher Fed. Republic Germany, 1985-86; ind. cons. Detroit, 1986-88; rsch. group leader Grand Labs., Inc., Larchwood, Iowa, 1988-92, mgr. R&D dept. parasitology, 1992—; mem. profl. bd. Coll. Vet. Medicine, Cluj-Napoca, 1970-72, mem. faculty com., 1980-81; mem. Exam. Bd. for Screening Vet. Medicine Candidates, Cluj-Napoca, 1974-85. Author: Diagnosis Guide for Parasitic Disease, 1983; co-author: Laboratory Diagnosis in Veterinary Medicine, 1978; author 7 textbooks; contbr. over 45 articles to profl. jours. Merit scholar Coll. Vet. Medicine, Bucharest, 1964. Mem. AAAS, Am. Soc. Parasitologists, Am. Vet. Med. Assn., Am. Assn. Vet. Parasitologists, World Vet. Poultry Assn., World Assn. for Advancement Vet. Parasitology, Romanian Vet. Medicine Soc., Romanian Soc. Biologists, World Assn. Buiatrics, N.Y. Acad. Scis. Home: 4509 Mountain Ash Dr Sioux Falls SD 57103-4959 Office: Grand Labs Inc PO Box 193 Larchwood IA 51241-0193

ONO, CHERYL EIKO, controls engineer; b. Chgo., Feb. 26, 1965; d. Mitsuo and Sachiye (Ikeda) O. BS, Eastern Ill. U., 1987, MS, 1988. Grad. asst. Eastern Ill. U., Charleston, 1987-88; intern GE Co., Mattoon, Ill., 1988, mfg./quality engr., 1988-92; controls engr. GE Co., Ravenna, Ohio, 1992-94; process engr. GE Co., Nela Park, Cleve., 1994—. Mem. Am. Soc. Quality Engrs., Epsilon Pi Tau. Office: GE Lighting 1975 Noble Rd Cleveland OH 44112-6300

ONO, YOKO, conceptual artist, singer, recording artist; b. Tokyo, Feb. 18, 1933; U.S. citizen; m. John Ono Lennon, Mar. 20, 1969 (dec. 1980); children: Kyoko, Sean; Student Peers' Sch., Gakushuin U., Tokyo, Sarah Lawrence Coll., Harvard U. One-woman shows include Alchemical Wedding, Albert Hall, London, 1967, Evening with Yoko Ono, Birmingham, 1968, Event, U. Wales, 1969, Everson Mus., Syracuse, N.Y., 1971, others; exhibited Fluxshoe, Sch. Art, Falmouth, Cornwall, Eng., 1972; recorded albums: (with John Ono Lennon) Two Virgins, 1968, Life With Lions, 1969, Wedding Album, 1970, Live Peace In Toronto (1969), 1970, Some Time in New York City, 1972, Double Fantasy, 1980 (Grammy award Album of Yr. 1981), Milk and Honey, 1984; solo albums include Yoko Ono/Plastic Ono Band, Fly, Approximately Infinite Universe, Feeling the Space, Season of Glass, Starpeace, 1985; composer numerous songs including Don't Worry Kyoko, Mummy's Only Looking For Her Hand in the Snow, Walking on Thin Ice (Grammy award nomination Best Female Rock Performance on Single 1981), Don't Be Sad. Author six film scripts, Tokyo, 1964, thirteen film score scores, London, 1967, John & Yoko Calendar, 1970, (book) Grapefruit, 1964, London, 1970, A Hole to See the Sky Through, N.Y., 1971. Office: Studio 1 1 W 72nd St New York NY 10023-3426*

ONORATO, LISA ANNE, psychology educator; b. Nyack, N.Y., Dec. 19, 1960; d. Francis Michael and Bruna Rose (Lenzovich) O.; m. Bryan Charles Trotti, July 24, 1993. BA, Gettysburg Coll., 1982; MA, N.Mex. State U., 1984, PhD, 1989. Prof. psychology Hartwick Coll., Oneonta, N.Y., 1987—. Contbr. chpts. to books, articles to profl. jours. Hartwick Coll. grantee, 1989. Mem. APA, Ea. Psychol. Assn., Software Psychology Soc., Phi Kappa Phi, Psi Chi (pres. 1980-82). Office: Hartwick Coll Dept of Psychol Oneonta NY 13820

ONSTINE WOOD, MARY LOUISE, recreational facility executive; b. Powell, Wyo., Sept. 24, 1963; d. Louis Preston and Mary Susanna (Simpers) O.; m. Dale Raymond Wood, Dec. 29, 1984; children: Mary Elizabeth, William Joseph Preston, James Matthew. Student, Northwest Coll., 1982-83; BS in Microbiology, U. Wyo., 1985. Wyo. 4-H amb. coord. U. Wyo. Coop. Extension Svc., Laramie, Wyo., 1982—; lodge mgr. Two Dot Ranch, Cody, Wyo., 1986—; trip coord. Nat. 4-H Western Roundup, 1992—, U. Wyo. Cooperative Ext. Svc., Laramie. Trea. Wyo. N.G. Aux., 1994—, mem., 1987—; state historian Wyo. 4-H Alumni Assn., 1988-91, state sec., 1991-93, dist. coord., 1993-95; advisor jr. leader Natrona County 4-H, 1991—, bd. dirs. found., 1992-94, sec., 1992-94, v.p. coun., 1994; amb. Nat. 4-H, 1983; asst. dist. dir. Ctrl. Dist. Wyo. State 4-H Coun., 1994-95, dist. dir. Ctrl. Dist., 1995—. Recipient Molly Pitcher award U.S. Field Artillery Assn., Alumni award Natrona County 4-H, 1992, 93, Outstanding 4-H Leader award Natrona County, 1994, Wyo. Vol. in Action award, 1995; J.C. Penny scholar Laramie County 4-H Coun., 1990, Key Bank Corp. scholar Natrona County 4-H Coun. Mem. Am. Legion Aux., Alpha Zeta. Republican. Methodist. Home: 4252 Cabin Creek Rd Casper WY 82604-9245

OOSTDYK, ARLENE ROSA, natural health educator, nurse; b. Oxford, N.J., Oct. 28, 1926; d. Ray William and Helen Anna (Renner) Frey; m. Marinus Joseph Oostdyk, Mar. 20, 1948; children: Darlene B. Oostdyk Haberer, Ray Marinus, James Marinus. Grad., Jersey City Hosp. Sch. Nursing, 1947; naturapathic dr., Bernadeen U., 1983. Cert. nutritionist. Sch. nurse Bur. Maternal and Child Health, Alpha and Harmony, N.J., 1947-48, Hawthorne, N.J., 1948-49; nurse Hunterdon Med. Ctr., Flemington, N.J., 1953-60, Phillipsburg, Philipsany, N.J., 1953-60; sch. nurse Hampton Sch. Bd., 1960, Glen Gardner Sch. Bd., 1960; counselor in nutrition Asbury, N.J., 1981—; regional mgr. Natures Sunshine, Spanish Fork, Utah, 1986, divisional mgr., 1989-91, nat. mgr., 1991—; speaker in field. Clk., judge Election Bd., Asbury, N.J., 1967-87. Recipient Dedication of Classroom award Internat. Gospel League, 1984. Mem. Am. Inst. Preventive Medicine (Cert. 1986), Jersey City Med. Ctr. Alumni Assn., Sch. Natural Healing (Cert. 1986), Nat. Health Fedn. (life, million dollar club). Republican. Baptist. Home and Office: 752 Mountain View Rd Asbury NJ 08802-1026

OPARIL, SUZANNE, cardiologist, educator, researcher; b. Elmira, N.Y., Apr. 10, 1941; d. Stanley and Anna (Penkova) O. AB, Cornell U., 1961; MD, Columbia U., 1965. Diplomate Am. Bd. Internal Medicine. Intern in medicine Presbyn. Hosp., N.Y.C., 1965-66; sr. asst. resident in medicine Mass. Gen. Hosp., Boston, 1967-68, clin. and rsch. fellow in medicine, cardiac unit, 1968-71; asst. prof. medicine Med. Sch., U. Chgo., 1971-75, assoc. prof., 1975-77; assoc. prof. dept. medicine U. Ala., Birmingham, 1977-81, asst. prof. physiology and biophysics, 1980-81, assoc. prof., 1981—, prof. medicine, 1981—, dir. vascular biology and hypertension program, 1985—; mem. vis. faculty Nat. High Blood Pressure Edn. Program, 1974—, Joint Nat. Com. on Detection, Evaluation and Treatment High Blood Pressure, 1991; mem. bd. sci. advisors Sterling Drug, Inc., 1988-91; lectr. in field; Selkurt lectr. Ind. U. Sch. Medicine, 1994; hon. prof. Peking Union Med. Coll., 1994. Author books on hypertension; editor Am. Jour. Med. Scis., 1984-94; assoc. editor Hypertension, 1979-83, mem. editl. bd., 1984—; assoc. editor Am. Jour. Physiology-Renal, 1989-91; mem. editl. bd. Jour. Hypertensioin, 1989—; contbr. over 300 articles to profl. jours., chpts. to books. Recipient Young Investigator award Internat. Soc. Hypertension, 1979, ann. award Med. Coll. Pa., 1984; fellow Am. Coll. Cardiology, 1992. Fellow Am. Coll. Cardiology; mem. Inst. Medicine of NAS (corr. com. on human rights 1992, chmn. com. advise Dept. Def. 1993 Breast Cancer Rsch. Program), AAAS, Endocrine Soc., Inter-Am. Soc. Hypertension, Am. Soc. Hypertension (pub. policy com. 1990—, sci. program com. 1990-92), Assn. for Women in Sci., Am. Heart Assn. (coun. for high blood pressure rsch., 1973—, exec. com. 1985-90, vice chmn. 1986, coun. on basic scis. 1978—, mem.-at-large, exec. com. 1979-81, mem.-at-large bd. dirs. 1992, chmn. Louis B. Katz Prize com. 1984-86, chmn., 1988-90, chmn. budget com. 1990-91, v.p. Ala. affiliate 1986-87, pres.-elect Ala. affiliate 1987-88, 93-94, pres. Ala. affiliate 1988-89, nat. pres.-elect 1993-94, nat. pres. 1994—, Lewis K. Dahl Meml. Lectr. 1993), Am. Physiol. Soc. (clin. physiology adv. com. 1992—), Am. Soc. for Clin. Investigation (sec.-treas. 1983-86), Soc. Exptl. Biology and Medicine (councillor 1993—), So. Soc. for Clin. Investigation (Founder's award 1995), Assn. Am. Physicians, Am. Fedn. for Clin. Rsch. (midwest councillor 1974-75, nat. councillor 1975-78, sec.-treas. 1978-80, pres. 1981-82), Phi Beta Kappa, Sigma Xi, Alpha Omega Alpha (mem. nat. bd. dirs., dir.-at-large 1991, treas. 1993). Office: U Ala Sch Medicine 1034 Zeigler Research Bldg Birmingham AL 35294

OPLINGER, KATHRYN RUTH, computer specialist; b. Wadsworth, Ohio, Apr. 18, 1951; d. Herman Carl and Blanche Ruth (White) Simshauser; m. Douglas E. Oplinger, July 26, 1986; children: Raymond, Karla, Kathleen, Laura Dawn. Student, Washington Coll., 1969-71, Kennesaw (Ga.) State Coll., 1988-89. Pres., chief exec. officer Dawn Enterprises, Inc., Atlanta, 1981—; cons. mgmt. info. systems Procter & Gamble, Atlanta, 1989—, Arthur Andersen, USA, Peat Marwick, Guam, others; software expert, programmer Novell Network & Acctg.; spokesperson, designer Saks Fifth Ave, nationwide, 1981-86. Firestone Found. scholar, 1969. Mem. NAFE, Am. Bus. Women's Assn., Lions Internat. (pres. Woodstock, Ga. chpt. 1986-87). Republican. Methodist. Office: Dawn Enterprises Inc c/o Tiller Stewart & Co CPA 780 Johnson Ferry Rd Ste 325 Atlanta GA 30026

OPPENHEIM, ELLEN W., media director, advertising executive; married; 2 children. BA in Journalism with honors in regional planning, U. N.C., 1975. With media rsch. and planning Young & Rubicam, N.Y.C., 1975-83, group supr., 1983-88; worldwide promotion dir. Time Mag., N.Y.C., 1988-89, U.S. mktg. dir., 1989; mng. dir. custom media Am. Express Pub., N.Y.C., 1989-90; media dir. FCB/Leber Katz Ptnrs., N.Y.C., 1990—. Mem. Am. Assn. Advt. Agys. (mag. com. 1991-92, newspaper com. 1992-94, direct mktg. com. 1994—). Office: FCB Leber Katz Ptnrs 767 5th Ave New York NY 10153-0001

OPPENHEIMER, SUZI, state senator; b. N.Y.C., Dec. 13, 1934; d. Alfred Elihu Rosenhirsch and Blanche (Schoen) O.; m. Martin J. Oppenheimer, July 3, 1960; children: Marcy, Evan, Josh, Alexandra. BA in Econs., Conn. Coll. for Women, 1956; MBA, Columbia U., 1958. Security analyst McDonnell & Co., N.Y.C., 1958-60, L.F. Rothschild Co., N.Y.C., 1960-63; mayor Village of Mamaroneck, N.Y., 1977-85; mem. N.Y. State Senate, Albany, 1985—; ranking mem. transp. com., mem. fin., edn., environ. conservation, consumer protection, vets., and drugs com., chmn. Senate Minority Task Force on Women's Issues, treas. Legis. Women's Caucus. Former pres. Mamaroneck LWV, Westchester County Mcpl. Ofcls. Assn., Westchester Mcpl. Planning Fedn. Recipient Humanitarian Svc. award Am. Jewish Com., 1988, Legis. Leadership award Young Adult Inst., 1988, Legis. award Westchester Irish Com., 1988, Hon. Svc. award Vis. Nurses Svcs., 1989, Humanitarian Svc. award Project Family, 1990, Meritorious Svc. award N.Y. State Assn. Counties, 1990, Friend of Edn. award N.Y. State United Tchrs., 1991; honoree Windward Sch. Ann. Dinner, 1992; named Legislator of Yr., N.Y. State Women's Press Club. Democrat. Jewish.

OPPLIGER, PEARL LAVIOLETTE, alcohol/drug abuse services professional; b. Barre, Vt., Aug. 16, 1942; d. Roland Bernard Sr. and Mae C. (Bouley) Laviolette; m. William Gregory Wotschak, Sept. 8, 1962 (div. Feb. 1983); children: Robin Lee Hillier, Rene Beth Greff, Rana Mae Wotschak; m. Edward Lee Oppliger, Aug. 16, 1988. Student, Ohio State U., 1960-62, 66-67; BSW, Bowling Green State U., 1986. Lic. social worker, Ohio, CCDC II, Ohio. Sec. Ohio State U., Columbus, 1964-66; hostess Welcome Wagon, Bowling Green, Ohio, 1975-76; owner, mgr. children's clothing store Rhymes 'n' Reasons, Bowling Green, 1976-84; bookkeeper Friendly Ice Cream Inc., Bowling Green, 1979-80; sales clk. Wilson's Shoe Store, Bowling Green, 1984-85; alcoholism counselor Wood County Coun. on Alcoholism and Drug Abuse, Inc., Bowling Green, 1985-86, family counselor, 1986, supr., 1986-90, dir. recovery svcs., 1990—; adj. instr. in social work Bowling Green State U., 1988—; co-facilitator Parents Helping Parents, Bowling Green, 1990—. Coun. mem.-at-large City of Bowling Green, 1990-93, mem. planning commn., 1988-89, asst. chmn. Bowling Green Rep. Club, 1989-91, chmn. 1991-92; co-founder Downtown Bus. Assn., Bowling Green, 1980-82. Am. Bus. Women's Assn. scholar. Mem. AAUW (v.p. membership com. Bowling Green br. 1991-93, Outstanding Woman in Cmty. Work 1990), NASW. Roman Catholic. Home: 910 N Main St Bowling Green OH 43402-1819 Office: Wood County Coun Alcoholism 320 W Gypsy Lane Rd Bowling Green OH 43402-4506

OQUENDO, MARIA DE LOS ANGELES, laboratory technician; b. Ponce, P.R., Feb. 8, 1963; d. Natividad and Maria M. (Garcia) O.; m. Jorge R. Lugo, Feb. 14, 1987; children: Amarilis, Jorge Alberto. BS, Cath. U., P.R., 1984. Rsch. technician Cornell Med. Coll., N.Y.C., 1987, rsch. technician II, 1989-91, sr. rsch. technician, 1991-94, rsch. specialist physiology dept., 1994, andrologist, 1994—. Mem. Beta Beta Beta. Home: 453 W 261 St Bronx NY 10471 Office: Cornell Med Coll Ob-Gyn Dept IVF M-902 1300 York Ave New York NY 10021

ORAN, ELAINE SURICK, physicist, engineer; b. Rome, Ga., Apr. 16, 1946; d. Herman E. and Bessye R. (Kolker) Surick; m. Daniel Hirsh Oran, Feb. 1, 1969. A.B., Bryn Mawr Coll., 1966; M.Ph., Yale U., 1968, Ph.D., 1972. Research physicist Naval Research Lab., Washington, 1972-76, supervisory research physicist, 1976-88, sr. scientist reactive flow physics, 1988—; head Ctr. for Reactive Flow and Dynamical Systems, 1985-87; mem. adv. bd. NSF; cons. to U.S. govt., agys., NATO. Author: Numerical Simulation of Reactive Flow, 1987, Numerical Approaches to Combustion Modeling, 1991. Assoc. editor Jour. Computational Physics; mem. adv. bd. Computers in Physics; editl. bd. Prog. Ener. Comb. Sci., Constrn. and Flame; contbr. numerous articles to profl. jours., chpts. to books. Recipient Arthur S. Flemming award, 1979, Women in Sci. and Engring. award, 1988 ; grantee USN, NASA, USAF, Defense Advanced Rsch. Projects Agy. Fellow AIAA (pubs. com. 1986—, v.p. publs. 1993), Am. Phys. Soc. (exec. com. fluid dynamics divsn. 1986, 88, exec. com. computer physics 1989—, chmn. 1991-92); mem. AAAS, Am. Geophys. Union, Combustion Inst. (bd. dirs. 1990—), Internat. Colloquium Dynamic Energy Systems (bd. dirs. 1989—), Sigma Xi. Office: Naval Rsch Lab Code 4404 # 4004 Washington DC 20011

ORAV, HELLE REISSAR, retired dentist; b. Tartu, Estonia, July 10, 1925; came to U.S., 1949, naturalized, 1954; d. Johan and Adele Johanna (Minski) Reissar; m. Arnold Orav, May 30, 1952; children: Ilmar Erik, Hillar Thomas. Student Friedrich Alexander U., Erlangen, West Germany, 1946-49; DDS, NYU, 1952. Practice dentistry, N.Y.C., 1952, 60, 62, 68, Valencia, Venezuela, 1953-68. Counselor, Red Cross, Valencia, 1954-55; past mem. Rotary Ladies Republican. Lutheran. Clubs: Country of Maracaibo (Venezuela); Palm Beach Polo and Country (Fla.); Korp Filiae Patriae (N.Y.C.). Avocations: Pre-Colombian art, bridge, travel, swimming, reading. Address: 44 Cocanut Row Palm Beach FL 33480-4005

ORAZIO, JOAN POLITI, financial planning company executive; b. N.Y.C., Mar. 24, 1930; d. Joseph and Anna B. Politi; B.S., Mercy Coll., 1975; cert. fin. planner Coll. Fin. Planning, 1979; m. Louis D. Orazio, Aug. 24, 1952; children: Louise Orazio Mason, Joanne Orazio Tonkin, Paul, Phyllis Orazio Kearsing. Exec. v.p. Gary Goldberg & Co., Suffern, N.Y., 1977-91; pres. Orazio Fin. Svcs., Suffern, 1991—. instr. Rockland Community Coll., 1977-84 ; workshop leader, seminar speaker various colls., corps. community orgns., 1970—. chairperson/trustee Rockland Community Coll., 1984-95. Mem. Internat. Assn. Fin. Planners, Inst. Cert. Fin. Planners, Nat. Orgn. Italian Am. Women, Nat. Assn. Female Execs., Rockland County Bus. and Profl. Women. Roman Catholic. Lodge: Kiwanis. Home: 79 Wilder Rd Suffern NY 10901-2300 Office: 400 Rella Blvd Suffern NY 10901-4249

ORBACZ, LINDA ANN, physical education educator; b. Schenectady, N.Y., June 29, 1948; d. Victor and Genevieve (Stempkowski) O. AAS, Ulster C.C., Stone Ridge, N.Y., 1969; BS, So. Ill. U., 1972; MA, George Washington U., 1982. Cert. permanent tchr., N.Y. Tchr., coach Ellenville (N.Y.) Ctrl. Sch., 1972-73, New Fairfield (Conn.) Sch., 1973-75, Middletown (N.Y.) City Sch., 1975-84, Liberty (N.Y.) Ctrl. Sch., 1984-86; dir. athletics, phys. edn. tchr., coach Newburgh (N.Y.) Enlarged City Sch., 1986—; alumni adv. Ulster County C.C., Stone Ridge, 1981—. Softball, soccer and basketball coach, Newburgh, 1987-92, softball, field hockey, basketball and cheerleading coach Ellenville, Middletown, New Fairfield, Liberty, 1972-86. Recipient Presdl. Sports award Sports Fitness, Washington, 1988. Mem. Am. Alliance Health, Phys. Edn., Recreation and Dance, N.Y. State Alliance Health, Phys. Edn., Recreation and Dance. Home: 11-E Canterbury Ln Wappingers Falls NY 12590 Office: Gardnertown Fundamental Magnet Sch 6 Plattekill Turnpike Newburgh NY 12550

ORBON, MARGARET J., lawyer; b. Chgo., Jan. 21, 1951. BA cum laude, St. Mary's Coll., 1973; JD, Loyola U., 1976. Bar: Ill. 1976, U.S. Dist. Ct. (no. dist.) Ill. 1976. Ptnr. Clausen Miller, Chgo.; lectr. Loyola U., 1976-87. Mem. ABA, Def. Rsch. Inst., Chgo. Bar Assn. Office: Clausen Miller 10 S LaSalle St Chicago IL 60603

ORD, LINDA BANKS, artist; b. Provo, Utah, May 24, 1947; d. Willis Merrill and Phyllis (Clark) Banks; m. Kenneth Stephen Ord, Sept. 3, 1971; children: Jason, Justin, Kristin. BS, Brigham Young U., 1970; BFA, U. Mich., 1987; MA, Wayne State U., 1990. Asst. prof. Sch. Art U. Mich., Ann Arbor, 1994—; juror Southeastern Mich. Scholastic Art Award Competition, Pontiac, 1992, Scarab Club Watercolor Exhbn., Detroit, 1991, Women in Art Nat. Exhbn., Farmington Hills, Mich., 1991, U. Mich. Alumni Exhbn., 1989-90. One-woman shows Atrium Gallery, Mich., 1990, 91; group shows include Am. Coll., Bryn Mawr, Pa., Riverside (Calif.) Art Mus., Kirkpatrick Mus., Oklahoma City, Montgomery (Ala.) Mus. Fine Arts, Columbus (Ga.) Mus., Brigham Young U., Provo, Utah, Kresge Art Mus., Lansing, Mich., U. Mich., Ann Arbor, Detroit Inst. Arts; works in many pvt. and pub. collections including Kelly Svcs., Troy, Mich., FHP Internat., Fountain Valley, Calif., Swords Into Plowshares Gallery, Detroit. Chairperson nat. giving fund Sch. Art, U. Mich., 1993; Sch. Art rep. Coun. Alumni Socs., U. Mich., 1992—. Recipient 1st Pl. award Swords Into Plowshares Internat. Exhbn., Detroit, 1989, Silver award Ga. Watercolor Soc. Internat. Exhbn., 1991, Pres.'s award Watercolor Okla. Nat. Exhbn., Oklahoma City, 1992, Flint Jour. award Buckham Gallery Nat. Exhbn., 1993, Ochs Meml. award N.E. Watercolor Soc. Nat. Exhbn., Goshen, N.Y., 1993, many state and nat. painting awards. Mem. U. Mich. Alumni Assn. (bd. dirs. 1992—, Sch. Art rep.), U. Mich. Sch. Art Alumni Soc. (bd. dirs. 1989-91, pres.), Mich. Watercolor Soc. (chairperson 1992-93, bd. dirs. adv. 1993-94).

ORDWAY, ELLEN, biology educator, entomology researcher; b. N.Y.C., Nov. 8, 1927; d. Samuel Hanson and Anna (Wheatland) O. B.A., Wheaton Coll., Mass., 1950; M.S., Cornell U., 1955; Ph.D., U. Kans., 1965. Field asst. N.Y. Zool. Soc., N.Y.C., 1950-52; research asst. Am. Mus. Natural History, N.Y.C., 1955-57; teaching asst. U. Kans., Lawrence, 1957-61, research asst., 1959-65; asst. prof. U. Minn., Morris, 1965-70, assoc. prof. biology, 1970-85, prof., 1986—; cooperator and cons. U.S. Dept. Agr. Bee Research Lab., Tucson, Ariz., 1971, 1983. Contbr. articles to sci. jours. Mgr. preserves Nature Conservancy, Mpls., 1975—; lectr. Morris area service clubs, 1972—. Mem. Ecol. Soc. Am., Entomol. Soc. Am., Soc. Systematic Biology, Soc. Study Evolution, Kans. Entomol. Soc., Internat. Bee Research Assn., AAAS, AAUP (v.p. 1975-76, sec.-treas. 1971-73 Morris chpt.), Sigma Xi, Sigma Delta Epsilon. Episcopalian. Avocations: travel, photography, raquetball, exploring natural environments, wilderness, areas, etc. Office: U Minn Div Sci And Math Morris MN 56267

ORDWAY, HEIDI ANN, retail store owner; b. Concord, N.H., Sept. 21, 1968; d. Gary Francis and Judith Ruby (Plumb) O. A in Fashion Merchandising and Retail, Westbrook Coll., 1988; B in Bus. Mgmt., Husson Coll., 1990. Store mgr. AMB Audio/Video, Newport, Maine, 1990-91, store owner, 1991—. Home: 240 Nokomis Rd Saint Albans ME 04971 Office: AMB Audio/Video Rte 2 Newport Plz Newport ME 04953

O'REILLY, ROSANN TAGLIAFERRO, computer educator; b. Bronx, N.Y., July 4, 1948; d. Neil F. and Antoinette C. (Odierno) Tagliaferro; m. James T. O'Reilly, Aug. 26, 1972; children: Jean Marie, Ann Maureen. BA in French, Fordham U., 1970. Cert. tchr., N.Y., Ohio. Asst. supr. EDP audit Deloitte Haskins and Sells, N.Y.C., 1968-72; payroll clk. U. Va., Charlottesville, 1972-74, Great Am. Ins., Cin., 1974-76; computer coord. St. Mary Sch., Cin., 1986—. Pres. Hyde Park Neighborhood Coun., Cin., 1985; founder, pres. Sitters Anonymous, 1978. Mem. Mensa. Roman Catholic. Office: St Marys Sch 2845 Erie Ave Cincinnati OH 45208-2398

O'REILLY, WENDA BREWSTER, writer, researcher; b. Frankfurt, Fed. Republic of Germany, Mar. 29, 1948; d. William Russell Brewster and Harriet Stimson Bullitt; m. James Patrick Brewster O'Reilly, July 18, 1981; children: Andrea Mariele, Noelle Christine, Mariele Angelica. BA in Psychology, U. Wash., 1975; MEd, Harvard U., 1977; MA, Stanford U., 1977, PhD in Edn., 1983. Gen. asst. King Broadcasting Co., Seattle, 1965-66; media buyer Benton & Bowles Advt. Agy., N.Y.C, 1967-68; acct. exec. Young & Rubicam Advt. Agy., Milan, 1969-70; advt. producer McCann-Erickson Advt. Agy., Milan, 1971-73; researcher, scholar Inst. for Research on Women and Gender Stanford (Calif.) U., 1983-91; exec. dir. The Birth Place, Menlo Park, Calif., 1985-87; guest lectr., seminar leader in women in mgmt., communications and childbirth isssues, 1979—; statis. analyst and research asst., Stanford U., 1978-81. Author: The Beautiful Body Book, 1984; contbr. chpts. to books, articles to profl. jours. Mem. adv. coun. Pacific Design Forum, 1991—; v.p., bd. dirs. Calif. Assn. Free-standing Birth Ctrs., 1986-88. Grantee William H. Donner Found. Mem. Mid-peninsula Access Corp. (founding bd. dirs. Calif. chpt., v.p., founding bd. dirs. 1986-87). Democrat. Episcopalian.

O'REILLY-LANDRY, MAUREEN (PATRICIA), psychologist; b. Waterbury, Conn., Sept. 9, 1956; d. John James and Marjorie Veronica (Touponse) O'R.; m. Donald William Landry, Sept. 3, 1978; children: Christopher Donald, Michael Joseph. BA summa cum laude, Radcliffe Coll., 1978; PhD, NYU, 1985, postgrad. in psychoanalysis, 1990—. Lic. psychologist. Clin. psychology intern Cambridge (Mass.) Hosp., Harvard Med. Sch., 1983-84, clin. psychology fellow, 1984-85; pvt. practice N.Y.C., 1986—; staff psychologist Bronx (N.Y.) Lebanon Hosp., 1986-88, supervising psychologist, 1988-89; supervising psychologist St. Lukes/Roosevelt Hosp. Ctr., N.Y.C., 1989-92; asst. clin. prof. psychiatry Albert Einstein Coll. Medicine, Bronx, 1988-89; vis. asst. prof. psychology grad. sch. applied and profl. psychology Rutgers U., Piscataway, N.J., 1988-90; supr., cons. Siena Counseling Ctr., Cath. Archdiocese N.Y., Bronx, 1989-92; adj. supr. Columbia U. Psychol. Svcs., N.Y.C., 1990-92, St. Luke's/Roosevelt Hosp. Ctr., N.Y.C., 1992—. Contbr. articles to profl. jours. Mem. APA, Radcliffe Coll. Club N.Y., Phi Beta Kappa. Roman Catholic. Home: 29 Claremont Ave # 2-S New York NY 10027 Office: 29 Claremont Ave New York NY 10027

OREM, SANDRA ELIZABETH, health systems administrator; b. Balt., Sept. 26, 1940; d. Ira Julius and Mabel Ruth (Peeples) O. Diploma, Ch. Home and Hosp. Sch. Nursing, 1962; BS with honors, The Johns Hopkins U., 1968; MS, U. Md., 1972; MA in Applied Psychology, U. Santa Monica, 1991; cert. in advanced applied psychology, U Santa Monica, 1992. Staff, charge nurse Ch. Home and Hosp., Balt., 1962-63; asst. instr. Ch. Home and Hosp. Sch. Nursing, Balt., 1963-64, instr., 1964-70; clin. nurse specialist Johns Hopkins Hosp., Balt., 1972-77, asst. dir. nursing, 1977-79, dir. nursing, 1979-87; clin. assoc. faculty The Johns Hopkins U. Sch. of Nursing, 1984-87; program dir., instr. intermediate massage course Balt. Sch. Massage, 1987—, instr. advanced massage course, 1991—; network mktg. cons., 1991—; pres. Nursing Edn. and Cons. Service, Inc., Balt., 1976-78, Oasis Health Systems, Inc., Balt., 1987—. Contbr. articles to profl. pubs. Vol. Office on Aging, Balt., 1982-83, Boy Scouts Am., Balt., 1984-85. Mem. NOW, Am. Holistic Nurses Assn., Am. Assn. Nurse Massage Therapists, Balt.-Am. Massage Therapy Assn., Md. Assn. Massage Practitioners (advisor to nurse's coalition 1992), Ch. Home and Hosp. Sch. Nursing Alumni Assn. (treas. 1970-72, pres.-elect 1975-76), Johns Hopkins U. Alumnae Assn., Sigma Theta Tau. Democrat. Episcopalian.

OREMLAND, SALLY, administrator; b. Owatonna, Minn., Aug. 16, 1928; d. Raymond Edward Anderson and Roses (Matthews) Anderson Youngstrom; m. Sheldon Oremland, July 30, 1949. BS in Social Work, Moorhead State U., 1971. Med. social work assoc. Vets. Hosp., Fargo, N.D., 1971-72; field exec. Sakakawea Girl Scout Coun., Bismarck, N.D., 1973-79; advocate Displaced Homemaker Program, Bismarck, N.D., 1979-81; cons. svc. to blind & physically handicapped N.D. State Libr., Bismarck, 1981—; exec. dir. Dakota Radio Info. Svc., treas., 1982—; bd. dirs. Community Access Television. Treas. Mayor's Com. on Handicapped, Bismarck, 1990-95, Burleigh County Planning Com., Bismarck, 1986—, Sakakawea Girl Scout Coun., 1987-93; treas. Kennedy Found., Bismarck, 1993—; vice chair dist. 30 Dem. Ctrl. Com., Bismarck, 1994; candidate for senate N.D. Legis. Assembly, Bismarck, 1992. Mem. AAUW, N.D. Libr. Assn. (bd. dirs., constitution com. chair 1990-94), Mensa. Home: 2201 Sherman Dr Bismark ND 58504

OREMLAND, WENDY KAREN, conference producer; b. N.Y.C., Dec. 17, 1969; d. George Alan and Marilyn Lois (Weiss) O. BA in Econ., Union Coll., 1992. Svc. rep. Manpower, Inc., Poughkeepsie, N.Y., 1988-90; intern Shearson, Lehman, Hutton, Inc., Albany, N.Y., 1990; mktg. rep. City of Schenectady, 1991; intern Chubb Group Ins., Albany, 1991; rsch. analyst, mgmt. cons. Integral, Inc., Cambridge, Mass., 1992-94; conf. producer fin. industry IBC-USA Conferences, Inc., Southboro, Mass., 1994—. Mem. Phi Delta Epsilon.

ORESTANO-JAMES, LORI ESTER, middle school educator; b. Hollywood, Fla., Oct. 11, 1963; d. Arthur Jacob and Ruth Virginia (Moncine) Budoff; m. Bill James, Aug. 16, 1987. MusB in Music Edn., Ithaca Coll., 1986; MS in Edn., SUNY, New Paltz, 1990. Cert. music edn. k-12, N.Y.S., cert. elem. edn., N.Y.S. Tchr. music, vocal, gen. Monticello (N.Y.) Ctrl. Sch., 1985—; dir. theatre, jr. high vocal dir. Monticello Ctrl. Sch., 1986—; advisor Monticello Middle Sch. Builders Club, 1989—. Sec., mem. com. Town of Thompson Rep. Com., 1987—; county chair fashion show Com. to Elect Ben Gilman Congressman, 1994; bd. dirs. Sullivan County Branch Big Bros./Big Sisters, 1987-93; regional pres. Orange, Rockland, Sullivan County Regional Bd. Am. Heart Assn., 1986—. Recipient Deans award for Excellence in Tchg., SUNY; named Vol. of Yr. Am. Heart Assn., 1989, Top 10 Finalist Tchr. of Yr. State Edn. Dept., 1992, Sullivan County Woman of Yr. by Sullivan County Dem., 1993. Mem. N.Y. State Theatre Educators Assn., Sullivan County Music Educators Assn. (corr. sec. 1986—), Bus. and Profl. Women, Music Educators Nat. Conf., N.Y. State Music Educators Assn., Sullivan County Dramatic Workshop, Monticello Elks Ladies Aux., Monticello Hadassah (chair publicity 1992—), Monticello Kiwanis Club (hon.), Mu Phi Epsilon. Jewish. Office: Monticello Middle Sch St John St Monticello NY 12701

ORGANEK, NANCY STRICKLAND, nursing educator; b. Middletown, Conn., June 19, 1937; d. Warren Luther and Anna Augusta (Nordquist) Strickland; m. Joseph Richard Organek, May 27, 1961; children: Melissa Lynne, Kelly Anne. BS with honors, U. Conn., 1959, MS, 1979, PhD, 1985; MEd, U. Buffalo, 1967. RN, Conn. Staff nurse, asst. head nurse VA Hosp., West Haven, Conn., 1959-60, Portland (Conn.) Convalescent Ctr., 1976-78; staff nurse VA Hosp., Newington, Conn., 1961; elem. tchr. Balt. Bd. Edn., 1961-62, Buffalo Bd. Edn., 1962-65, Burlington (Mass.) Bd. Edn., 1965-66, Middletown Bd. Edn., 1966-68; asst. prof. nursing U. Conn., Storrs, 1979—; cons. Mt. Sinai, Hartford, Conn., 1981-90; researcher on adolescent pregnancy; presenter at internat., nat. and local meetings. Contbr. articles to profl. pubs. Advisor Portland Bd. Edn./Health Coun., 1980-84; rep. Task Force on Domestic Violence, Hartford, 1979-80; speaker Portland High Sch., 1981. Mem. ANA, NAACOG, Nat. Assn. Neonatal Nurses, N.Am. Nursing Diagnosis Assn., Ea. Nursing Rsch. Soc., Conn. Perinatal Assn., Conn. Nurses Assn. (Svc. award 1984), Conn. Assn. Neonatal Nurses, Sigma Theta Tau (officer 1985-87), Pi Lambda Theta (honors 1981). Home: 179 E

Cotton Hill Rd Portland CT 06480-1036 Office: U Conn 26u231 Glenbrook Rd Storrs Mansfield CT 06268

ORIANI, ANA GLORIA, public relations executive, insurance agent; b. San Salvador, El Salvador, Nov. 8, 1953; came to U.S., 1978; d. Enrique and Gloria (Peralta) O.; m. Jose Roberto Quinonez, July 11, 1974 (dec. May 1978). BS in Econs., Jose Simeon Canas, San Salvador, 1978; BA in Spl. Edn. with honors, Am. U., 1981, MA in Internat. Devel. and Affairs, 1984. Tchr. spl. edn. Mann's Sch., Washington, 1978-82; asst. dir. dept. edn. and culture Orgn. Am. States, Washington, 1983-85; mgr., supr. Gucci, Inc., Beverly Hills, Calif., 1985-86; dir. mktg. United Design Assocs., L.A., 1986-88; v.p. promotions, pub. rels., spl. projects Orion Internat. Corp., Miami, Fla., 1988-93; pub. rels. cons. Miami, 1994—. Bd. dirs., cons. Clinica para los Ninos contra Cancer, Miami, 1990-91, Soc. for Abused Children, Miami, 1990-91; founder Outreach Community Program, 1990-91; bd. dirs. Big Bros./Big Sisters, 1990-91; mem. Dade Ptnrs. Roman Catholic. Home: 1865 Brickell Ave Miami FL 33129-1621 Office: 1865 Brickell Ave Apt 2107A Miami FL 33129-1606

ORITSKY, MIMI, artist, educator; b. Reading, Pa., Aug. 14, 1950; d. Herbert and Marcia (Sarna) O. Student, Phila. Coll. Art, 1968-70; BFA, Md. Inst. Coll. Art, 1975; MFA, U. Pa., 1979. Artist, supr. subway mural projects Crisis Intervention Network, Phila., 1978-83; instr. painting U. Arts, Phila., 1984, 89-93, Abington Art Ctr., Jenkintown, Pa., 1989—, Main Line Art Ctr., Haverford, Pa., 1993—. One-woman shows include Gross McCleaf Gallery, 1980-82, Callowhill Art Gallery, Reading, Pa., Amos Eno Gallery, N.Y.C., 1986, 89, 91, 94, Hahnemann U. Gallery, Phila., 1988, Kauffman Gallery, Shippensburg U., Pa., 1989, Kimberton (Pa.) Gallery, 1990, Rittenhouse Galleries, Phila., 1992-94; group exhbns. include Current Representational Painting in Phila., 1980, Gross McCleaf Gallery, 1980-82. Recipient Purchase award Pa. Coun. Arts/Beaver Coll., 1983, Reading Pub. Mus., 1984; fellow Artists for Environment Found., 1980, Millay Colony for Arts, 1983. Mem. Coll. Art Assn. Home and Studio: 155 Rex Ave Philadelphia PA 19118

ORLIN, KAREN J., lawyer; b. Washington, Apr. 2, 1948; d. Hyman and Lenore O.; 1 child. AB summa cum laude, U. Pa., 1969; JD, Harvard U., 1972. Bar: N.Y. 1973. U.S. Dist. Ct. (so. and ea. dists.) N.Y. 1973, U.S. Ct. Appeals (2d cir.) 1973, Fla. 1982. Assoc. Kronish, Lieb, Weiner & Hellman, N.Y.C., 1972-81; sr. assoc. Valdes-Fauli, Bischoff, Kriss and Mandler, Miami, 1981-82, ptnr., 1982-83; sr. assoc. Ruden, Barnett, McClosky, Smith, Schuster & Russell, P.A., Ft. Lauderdale, Fla., 1983-85, Shea & Gould, N.Y.C. and Miami, 1985-87; of counsel Thomson, Muraro, Razook and Hart P.A., Miami, 1987-88; sr. v.p.-assoc. counsel, asst. sec. Am. Savs. of Fla., F.S.B., Miami, 1988—. Mem. Trustee's Coun. Penn Women, U. Pa., 1987—. Mem. Fla. Bar (corps. and securities com. 1983—), Am. Mensa, Nat. Auctioneers Assn., U. Pa. Dade Alumni Club (pres. 1993—), Greater Miami C. of C. (lawyers com. bus. revitalization group), Zonta Internat. (Downtown Miami chpt. bd. dirs.), Mortar Bd., Sphinx Soc., Nat. Auctioneers Assn., Phi Beta Kappa. Office: Am Savs of Fla 17801 NW 2nd Ave Miami FL 33169

ORLOV, DARLENE, management consultant; b. Elizabeth, N.J., July 13, 1949; d. Sol and Evelyn (Perlman) O.; m. Geoffrey M. Skolnik, Jan. 19, 1986. BA in English, Secondary Edn., Fairleigh Dickinson U., 1971, MA in English Lit., 1982; MBA in Mgmt. with distinction, N.Y. Inst. of Tech., 1981. Pers. dir. Kayser-Roth Corp., N.Y.C., 1975-76; pers. mgr. Corometrics Med. Systems, Wallingford, Conn., 1976-78; mgr. EEO and communications Internat. Playtex, N.Y.C., 1978-79; pres. Orlov Resources for Bus., Inc., N.Y.C., 1979—; adj. asst. prof. NYU, 1980-88; adj. prof. Marymount Manhattan Coll., N.Y.C., 1981-90. Author: Employee Termination: How to Reduce Your Risk, 1986. Trustee Fairleigh Dickinson U., Madison, N.J., 1989-94; bd. dirs., v.p. The Assoc. Blind, Inc., 1991-94. Mem. Women's Econ. Roundtable, Cornell Club of N.Y. Home and Office: 25 Sutton Pl S New York NY 10022

ORLY, ELVIRA JOLAN, lawyer; b. Berkeley, Calif., Nov. 22, 1948; d. Cyrill Vladimir and Elvira Maria (Erni) O.; m. Joseph A. Jeffrey, Aug. 17, 1979 (dec. June 1990). BS, U. Calif., Berkeley, 1970; MBA, JD, U. Calif., 1975. Bar: Calif. 1976, D.C. 1878. Tax atty. Pettit & Martin, San Francisco, 1975-76; legis. dir. for Senator S.I. Hayakawa, Washington, 1976-80; dir. legis. and regulatory affairs Edison Electric Inst., Washington, 1980-82, Getty (Texaco), Washington, 1982-85, Allied Signal, Washington, 1985-88; Washington counsel Browning-Ferris Industries, 1988-89; v.p. market devel. Browning-Ferris Industries, The Netherlands, 1989-90; v.p. external affairs Browning-Ferris Industries Europe, 1990-93; cons. in pub. and govt. affairs, 1993—. Bd. dirs. Codornices coun. Camp Fire Girls, 1973-75. Mem. U.S. Fencing Team to World Championships, 1974, 75; mem. U.S. Olympic Fencing Squad, 1976. Mem. ABA, Calif. Bar Assn., D.C. Bar Assn., U.S. Fencing Assn. (treas. 1987-92), European Environ. Lawyers Assn., Tax Coalition (bd. dirs. 1983-86, chmn. 1985), Behind the Tree Tax Group (chmn. 1985), Nat. Women's Econ. Alliance, Women in Govt. Rels., Assn. Former Senate Employees, Prytanean Club, Jr. League, Beta Gamma Sigma, Alpha Xi Delta. Home: Avenue de Tervueren 48, 1040 Brussels Belgium

ORMISTON, PATRICIA JANE, educator; b. Flint, Mich., Aug. 22, 1938; d. Elmer A. and Katheryn Lucille (Day) Knudson; m. Lester Murray Ormiston, June 13, 1964; 1 child, Brian Todd. BS, Minot State U., 1962; postgrad., U. Mont., 1963—, Mont. State U., 1963—, Western Mont. Coll., 1987. Elem. tchr. Lowell Sch., Gt. Falls, Mont., 1958, Webster Sch., Williston, N.D., 1958-59, Plaza (N.D.) Pub. Sch., 1959-61, Cen. Sch., Helena, Mont., 1962-63, Elrod Sch., Sch. Dist. 5, Kalispell, Mont., 1963—; core team Onward to Excellence, Sch. Dist. 5, Kalispell, 1989-92; participant Rocky Mountain Nat. Outcome-Based Edn. Conf., Greeley, Colo., 1990; presenter Kendall Hunt Lit. Reading Unit, Phi Delta Kappa, Kalispell, 1991, Mont. Assn. Gifted Talented Edn., 1991, Word Conf., Seattle, 1993; inst. presenter, symposium spkr. Utah Coun. Internat. Reading Assn. 28th Annual State Reading Conf., Salt Lake City, 1994; univ. supr. student tchrs. Montana State U., Bozeman, 1994—; mem. adv. bd. Kendall/Hunt Integrated Lang. Arts program Kendall Hunt Pub. Co., Dubuque, Iowa, 1991—; symposium spkr., mem. reading coun., coun. tchrs. English S.D. State Conf., Mitchell, 1994, Five Valleys Reading Conf. U. Mont., Missoula, 1994; insvc. presenter S. Whidbey Intermediate Sch., Langley, Wash., 1994; author (elem. sch. curriculum) PEGASUS Integrating Themes in Lit. and Lang., 1994. Contbg. author lit. based reading units 2d grade level Kendall Hunt Pub. Co., Dubuque, Iowa, 1989—; author PEGASUS Integrating Themes in Literature and Language Correlated to Dade County Pub. Schs. Competency-Based Curriculum for Language Arts, Grades K-5, 1994. Vol. Conrad Mansion Restoration, Kalispell, 1976—; presenter 34th ann. conv. Lit. Base Reading Internat. Reading Assn., New Orleans, 1989. Named Tchr. of Yr., Kalispell Sch. Dist. 5, 1986; Chpt. 2 grantee, 1987-88; Gertrude Whipple Profl. Devel. grantee IRA, 1988. Mem. NEA, Internat. Reading Assn. (symposium speaker 38th ann. conv. San Antonio 1993), Nat. Coun. Tchrs. English, Kalispell Edn. Assn. (bldg. rep. 1987-88, chmn. profl. acknowledgement com. 1988-93), Nat. Hist. Preservation, Phi Delta Kappa, Delta Kappa Gamma. Home: PO Box 64 Kalispell MT 59903-0064 Office: Elrod Sch 3rd Ave W Kalispell MT 59901-4426

ORNBURN, KRISTEE JEAN, accountant; b. Moberly, Mo., Feb. 24, 1956; d. Lloyd Edward and Ruth Maxine (Major) O. AA, Moberly Jr. Coll., 1976; BSBA magna cum laude, U. Mo., Columbia, 1978. CPA, Mo. Teller City Bank & Trust, Moberly, 1974-78; supr. gen. ledger Orscheln Farm & Home Supply, Moberly, 1978-80, supr. accounts payable, 1980, supr. sr. acctg., 1981-82, mgr. acctg., 1982-86; controller Orscheln Consumer Products Div., Moberly, 1986-93; v.p./controller Orscheln Farm & Home Supply, 1993—. Youth worker Carpenter St. Bapt. Ch., Moberly; adv. coun. mem. Moberly Community Coll. Recipient Youth Leadership award Moberly C. of C., 1974. mem. AICPA, Am. Bus. Women's Assn. (pres.), Mo. Sco. CPAs, U. Mo. Alumni Assn., Bapt. Young Women's Club (Moberly) Phi Theta Kappa. Democrat. Office: Orscheln Farm & Home Supply 339 N Williams St Moberly MO 65270-1553

ORNDOFF, ELIZABETH CARLSON, retired reference librarian, educator; b. Spearville, Kans., Mar. 28, 1918; d. Carl Edward and Laura Rebecca (Pine) Carlson; m. John Delbert Orndoff, Dec. 26, 1942; children: Barbara Kay Orndoff Fazal, David Keith, Richard Lee. BA in Sociology, U. Colo., 1940, BEd, 1940; postgrad., U. So. Calif., 1941. Lic. pvt. pilot; cert. tchr. sociology. Head coll. librarian Trinidad (Colo.) State Jr. Coll., 1940-42, tchr. sociology, 1941-42; reference librarian Los Alamos (N.Mex.) Pub. Libr., 1963-73. Editor: (non-fiction book) All of These Things, 1974. Tchr. Sunday sch. Meth. Ch., Trinidad, 1940-41; den mother Boy Scouts Am., Los Alamos, 1953-55; leader Girl Scouts U.S.A., Los Alamos, 1955-56; charter mem. United Ch. Los Alamos, 1947—, historian, 1994, 95; active Friends Los Alamos Pub. Libr., 1989-90, 94—, Habitat for Humanity, 1994—; active Los Alamos Retirement Ctr., Inc., Blood Mobile, Meals on Wheels. Mem. AAUW (life), ALA, United Ostomy Assn., U. Colo. Alumni Assn., Sr. Citizens, Los Alamos Ski Club, Crohn's Colitis Found. Am., Am. Assn. Ret. Persons. Democrat. Home: 997 B 48th St Los Alamos NM 87544-1831

ORNSTEIN, LIBBIE ALLENE, primary school educator; b. Miami, Fla., Mar. 3, 1949; d. Raymond Gerald and Rose Elaine (Feinberg) Blasberg; m. Morton Jay Ornstein, June 16, 1978; children: Randy Brian, Mark Justin. BEd, U. Miami, Coral Gables, Fla., 1971; MS in Early Childhood Edn., Fla. Internat. U., 1980. Cert. elem., early childhood and spl. edn. tchr., Fla. Spl. edn. tchr. F. Douglas Elem. Sch., Phila., 1973-75; 4th grade tchr. Lorah Park Elem. Sch., Miami, Fla., 1975-76; kindergarten tchr. Charles Drew Elem. Sch., Miami, 1976-79; nursery sch. tchr. Temple Beth Ahm, Cooper City, Fla., 1982-83; 2d grade tchr. Myrtle Grove Elem. Sch., Miami, 1983-86; pk 4 tchr. Univ. Sch., Nova U., Davie, Fla., 1986-88; kindergarten tchr. Pines Lakes Elem. Sch., Pembroke Pines, Fla., 1988—. Cub scout den mother Boy Scouts Am., Plantation, Fla., 1987; mem. ORT, Plantation, 1990. Democrat. Jewish. Home: 145 NW 98th Ter Fort Lauderdale FL 33324-7215

O'ROURKE, JOAN B. DOTY WERTHMAN, educational administrator; b. N.Y.C., June 7, 1933; d. George E. Doty and Lillian G. Bergen; 10 children, 8 stepchildren. BA summa cum laude, Marymount Coll., Manhattan, N.Y., 1953; MA, Columbia U., 1958; PhD, St. John's U., 1971. Tchr. History Marymount High Sch., N.Y.C., 1953-55; hist. instr. Marymount Manhattan Coll., 1957-59; acting chmn. hist. dept. Nassau Community Coll., Mineola, N.Y., 1959-60; prof. History Westchester Community Coll., Valhalla, N.Y., 1963-74; prin. Pius X Sch., Scarsdale, N.Y., 1974-77; assoc. dir. alumni relations Fordham U., N.Y.C., 1980-84; co-founder, dir. Assn. for Profl. Psychol. and Ednl. Counseling, Wilmette, Ill., 1987—; ptnr. O'Rourke and Assocs., 1993—; dir., writer Sta. WFAS Radio, White Plains, 1963-64; adj. prof. social sci. Fordham U., 1974-76. Teaching fellow St. John's U., Jamaica, N.Y., 1968; recipient Alumni award Marymount Coll., 1987-88. Mem. Soc. Mayflowers Descs. Ill., Michigan Shores Club. Democrat. Roman Catholic. Office: 78614 Blooming Ct Sun City Palm Spring CA 92203

O'ROURKE, JOANNE A., state legislator; b. Manchester, N.H., Sept. 4, 1939; m. Thomas F. O'Rourke; 3 children. Attended, N.H. Coll. Formerly with New Eng. Telephone and Telegraph Co.; mem. N.H. Ho. of Reps.; asst. minority leader, 1985-90; Dem. whip N.H. Ho. of Reps., 1990—; mem. appropriations com.; mem. rules com.; mem. state-fed. rels. com. Selectman ward three City of Manchester, 1972-77; bd. dirs. Greater Manchester Mental Health, 1985-91, So. N.H. Svcs., 1985—; co-chmn. State Dem. Policy Coun., 1985-87; chmn. Manchester Legis. Del., 1986-92, Dem. City Com., 1992—; mem. exec. com. Hillsborough County, 1986; vice chmn. Coun. State Govt. Intergovtl. Affairs, 1988, chmn., 1989. Democrat. Roman Catholic. Home: 91 Harrison St Manchester NH 03104-3611 Office: NH Ho of Reps State Capitol Concord NH 03301*

ORPHANIDES, NORA CHARLOTTE, ballet educator; b. N.Y.C., June 4, 1951; d. M.T. and Mary Elsie (Tilly) Feffer; m. James Mark Orphanides, July 1, 1972; children: Mark, Elaine, Jennine. BA, CUNY, 1973; student, Joffrey Ballet Sch., N.Y.C., 1970-75; postgrad., Princeton Ballet Sch., 1976-86. Cert. speech and hearing handicapped tchr. Sr. sales assoc. Met. Mus. Art, N.Y.C., 1970-86; membership asst. Patrons Lounge, M.M.A., N.Y.C., 1987—; mem. faculty Princeton (N.J.) Ballet Sch., 1983—, trustee emeritus, 1992—. Mem. cast Princeton Ballet ann. Nutcracker, 1985-90, now Am. Repertory Ballet Co., 1993—; appeared in Romeo & Juliet, 1995. Fundraising gala chmn. Princeton Ballet, 1985, 86, 91-92, chmn. spl. events, 1987—, trustee, 1986—, chmn. Nutcracker benefit, 1990—, Dracula benefit, 1991; vol. libr. Plainsboro (N.J.) Free Libr., 1985; program solicitation chmn. to benefit Princeton Med. Ctr., 1988, T-shirt chmn. benefit, 1990, 91, publicity chmn. ann. June Fete, 1992; mem. worship and arts commn. Nassau Presbyn. Ch., 1989, 90, dinner chmn. Bach Music Festival, 1989, Cambridge Singers, 1990; vol. Nat. Hdqrs. Recording for the Blind, 1991-93; trustee Princeton Youth Fund, 1991-92; dinner chmn. Nassau Ch. Music Festival, 1992, Handel Festival, Nassau Ch., 1993, Princeton Chamber Symphony, 1993; vol. Community Park Sch. Libr., 1992-93; hon. chmn. Princeton Ballet Gala, 1993; chmn. Christmas Boutique, Princeton Med. Ctr., 1993; trustee, Princeton Med. Ctr. Auxilary Bd., 1992—. Democrat. Home: 35 Brearly Rd Princeton NJ 08540-6767 Office: Sch of Princeton Ballet 262 Alexander St Princeton NJ 08540-7104

ORR, BETSY, business education educator; b. Dermott, Ark., Nov. 24, 1954; d. Doy and Peggy (Johnson) Ogles; m. Gary Orr, July 10, 1976; children: Brent, Shane. BA, U. Ark., 1975, bus. edn. cert., 1978, MEd, 1987, EdD, 1994. Cert. tchr., Ark. Tchr. Springdale (Ark.) High Sch., 1978-89; instr. bus. edn. U. Ark., Fayetteville, 1989-94, asst. prof., 1994—. Mem. Nat. Bus. Edn. Assn., Ark. Bus. Edn. Assn. (editor 1989-92), AAUW, Delta Pi Epsilon (pres. 1992—), Phi Delta Kappa. Home: 1006 Northwest N St Bentonville AR 72712 Office: U Ark Grad Edn 108 Fayetteville AR 72701

ORR, BETTIE SELDEN WATFORD, corporate communications executive; b. Texas City, Tex., June 20, 1948; d. Wilbur Horsley and Bettie Selden (Friedell) Watford; m. John Howard Payne, III, Jan. 24, 1970 (div. 1981); m. Charles Lee Orr, May 23, 1992. BJ, U. Tex., 1970. Pub. rels. dir. Lyndon B. Johnson Sch. Pub. Affairs, U. Tex., Austin 1971-72; pub. info. officer Area II Regional Med. Program, U. Calif. Med. Sch., Davis, 1972-73, acting info. officer Med. Sch., 1973-74; congl. staff asst. Washington, 1975-76; dir. pub. rels. Nat. Soc. Med. Rsch., Washington, 1976-79; dir. office communications and pub. affairs Group Health Assn., Inc., Washington, 1979-83; radio/TV rels. specialist ARC, 1984; mgr. communications and info. svcs. Nat. Mental Health Assn., 1985-86, healthcare communications advisor, 1986-87; dir. corp. communications Am. Psych. Mgmt., Inc., 1987-89, healthcare communications advisor, 1989-91; dir. spl. projects Nat. Found. Infectious Diseases, 1991-94; secretariat die, Nat. Coalition for Adult Immunization, 1994—. Mem. Alpha Omicron Pi. Democrat. Episcopalian.

ORR, EMMA JANE, pharmacist, educator; b. Pennington, Va., Sept. 30, 1956; d. Clyde Wilson and Monnie Lee (Daugherty) O.; m. Allen Emerson Clark, Oct. 24, 1981; 1 child, Katherine Wilson. BS in Pharmacy, Med. Coll. Va., 1979; D of Pharmacy with highest hons., U. Ky., 1981. Registered pharmacist, Va., Ky., Tenn. Asst. dir. pharmacy St. Mary's Hosp., Norton, Va., 1980-84, Norton Community Hosp., 1984-90; clin. coord. Hoston Valley Hosp., Kingsport, Tenn., 1990—; adj. faculty Mountain Empire C.C., Big Stone Gap, Va., 1981—; asst. clin. prof. dept. pharmacy and pharmaceutics Med. Coll. Va., Richmond, 1982—. Tchr., children's spkr. Ch. United Meth. Ch., Duffield, Va., Mountain Empire Older Citizens, Wise, Va., 1983-85. Named Young Career Woman of Yr. Bus. and Profl. Women's Club, 1983. Mem. Am. Soc. Hosp. Pharmacists, Am. Pharm. Assn., Va. Soc. Hosp. Pharmacists. Methodist. Home: 100 Quillen Dr Duffield VA 24244

ORR, LINDA J., gerontologist, health science center executive. BS in Edn., Akron U., 1963; MA, Kent State U., 1978; postgrad., Case Western Res. U. Program specialist dept. corrections and rehab. Ohio Youth Commn., Columbus, 1970-74; asst. exec. dir. Stark County Mental Health and Retardation Bd., Canton, Ohio, 1973-77; program dir. Akron Child Guidance Ctr., 1977-82; exec. dir. Coun. Care Sr. Adult Day Care Ctrs., Pitts., 1982-88; assoc. dir. Fairhill Inst. for the Elderly, Cleve., 1988-90; assoc. dir. Ctr. on Aging and Applied Gerontology Chgo. Med. Sch., 1990-91.

ORR, MAUREEN JANE, legal nurse consultant; b. Altoona, Pa., Apr. 15, 1944; d. James E. and Eileen Dumm; m. Steven D. Orr, May 23, 1968; children: Sean C., Brendan H. Diploma, Mercy Hosp., Johnstown, Pa., 1965; BS in Profl. Arts, St. Joseph's Coll., Windham, Maine, 1992. RN, Fla.; cert. ins. rehab. specialist, Ill.; cert. rehab. provider, Fla.; cert. case mgr. Staff ICU nurse Allegheny Gen. Hosp., Pitts., 1965-67; staff nurse Children's Hosp., Pitts., 1967; nurse advisor U.S. AID, Nha Trang, Vietnam, 1967-68; neonatal nurse Columbia Hosp.-Women, Washington, 1968-69; neonatal head nurse Ariz. Health Sci. Ctr., Tucson, 1970-72; health careers instr. Tribal Health Authority, Whiteriver, Ariz., 1976-78; childbirth instr. Bogotá, Columbia, 1978-80; pub. health nurse Dade County Pub. Health Dept., Miami, Fla., 1980-87; dir. profl. svcs. Upjohn Home Health Svcs., Miami, 1987-88; sr. med. cons., supr. Am. Internat. Health & Rehab. Svcs., Inc., Plantation, Fla., 1988—. UN rep. Another Mother for Peace, N.Y., 1969; sec. Am. Women's Club, Bogotá, 1978-80. Recipient Teenagers Helping Educate Through Advocacy award Phoenix, Ariz. Mem. Am. Assn. Legal Nurse Assn. (pres. Miami chpt.). Home: 11631 SW 125th Ct Miami FL 33186-4923 Office: c/o Am Internat Health & Rehab Svcs Inc 150 S Pine Island Rd # 410 Plantation FL 33324

ORR, SANDRA JANE, civic worker, pharmacist; b. Marion, Ohio, June 27, 1930; d. Lawrence Edward and Wanita Izell (Noyes) Schneider; m. Ross Moore Orr, Jr., Aug. 12, 1951; children: Sandra K. Orr Whiston, Sara L. Orr Cochrane. BS in Pharmacy, Med. Coll. Va., 1952. Pharmacist Atkinson & Howard, Richmond, Va., 1952-54, Schneider's Walgreen Agy., Kenton, Ohio, 1954-73; part-time pharmacist Drug Svc., Bethlehem, Pa., 1954-57, Fastchnacts' Drug, Bethlehem, 1954-57. One-woman shows in oils, pastels and watercolors. Chmn. ball St. Luke's Hosp., Bethlehem, 1985, 87; bd. dirs. Hist. Bethlehem, 1988—; dir. liturgical dance 1st Presbyn. Ch., 1968, 78; instr. needlework YMCA, 1980-81; instr. movement Orff tchrs.; instr. ballet Lehigh U. football team, 1966; docent Allentown Art Mus., 1956-68, Art Goes to Sch., 1960-62. Mem. Jr. League Lehigh Valley. Republican. Presbyterian. Home: 405 High St Bethlehem PA 18018-6103

ORR, SUSAN GRINTON, dean; b. Chgo., Oct. 28, 1943; d. William and Ann (Ahern) Grinton; m. Lawrence E. Orr, III, Sept. 16, 1967 (div. 1988); children: Karen, Jennifer. BA in French, U. Ill., 1965; MA in Environ. Mgmt., U. Tex., San Antonio, 1979; PhD in Urban and Regional Sci., Tex. A&M U., 1981; postgrad., Harvard U., 1993. Grad. rsch. asst. Tex. A&M U., College Station, 1981; part time instr. continuing edn. North Harris County Coll., Houston, 1981-83; sr. rsch. fellow Houston Advanced Rsch. Ctr., The Woodlands, Tex., 1983-84; dir. Woodlands Ctr. for Growth Studies, 1984; program coord. adult edn. North Harris Coll., 1984-92; dean community edn. Tomball (Tex.) Coll., 1992—; cons. Tex. Literacy Coun. Partnership Grant, 1991; mem. adult secondary edn. task force Tex. Edn. Agy., 1991, mem. statewide adv. com. for Project FORWARD, 1990-91, statewide adv. com. for adult edn. through television tech., 1990-91. Contbr. articles to profl. jours. Active Klein Oak Strutters Drill Team Booster Club, 1991-92; stroke and turn judge N.W. Aquatic League, 1981-86; bd. dirs. Northampton Club, 1982-83, mem. long range planning com., 1983. Recipient Excellence in Edn. award Houston N.W. C. of C., 1990. Mem. AICP, Am. Planning Assn., Am. Assn. for Adult and Continuing Edn., Am. Assn. Women in Community and Jr. Colls., Assn. for Computer Educators in Tex., LERN, Nat. Coun. Instrnl. Adminstrs., Tex. Adminstrs. Continuing Edn. for Community Jr. Colls., Tex. Assn. for Community Svc. and Continuing Edn., Phi Kappa Phi. Office: Tomball Coll 30555 Tomball Pkwy Tomball TX 77375-4036

ORR-ANDRAWES, ALISON, psychiatrist, psychoanalyst; b. 1949. BA, Wellesley Coll., 1971; MD, U. Tex. Med. Br., Galveston, 1981. Diplomate Am. Bd. Psychiatry and Neurology. Intern in psychiatry N.Y. Med. Coll./Westchester County Med. Ctr., Valhalla, 1981-82; resident in psychiatry Cornell Med. Coll./N.Y. Hosp., Westchester Divsn., 1982-84; resident in child psychiatry Cornell Med. Coll./N.Y. Hosp., White Plains, 1984-86, clin. instr. in psychiatry, 1986-94, clin. asst. prof. in psychiatry, 1995—; clin. instr. in psychiatry NYU Med. Ctr., N.Y.C., 1985—; Sarah Lawrence Coll. Health Svc. Bronxville, N.Y., 1988-93; pvt. practice psychoanalysis N.Y.C., 1986—; adult psychoanalytic tng. Psychoanalytic Inst., NYU, N.Y.C., 1985-93; child psychoanalytic tng. N.Y. Psychoanalytic Inst., N.Y.C., 1990—. Contbr. articles to profl. publs. Wellesley scholar, 1971. Mem. Am. Psychoanalytic Assn., Am. Psychiat. Assn., NYU-Bellevue Psychiat. Soc., Alpha Epsilon Delta (life). Office: 276 Sound Beach Ave Old Greenwich CT 06870-1626

ORR-CAHALL, CHRISTINA, art gallery director, art historian; b. Wilkes-Barre, Pa., Apr. 12, 1947; d. William R.A. and Anona (Snyder) Boben; m. Richard Cahall. BA magna cum laude, Mt. Holyoke Coll., 1969; MA, Yale U., 1974, MPhil, 1975, PhD, 1979. Curator of collections Norton Gallery Art, West Palm Beach, Fla., 1975-77; asst. prof. Calif. Poly. State U., San Luis Obispo, 1978-81, Disting. prof., 1981; dir. art div., chief curator Oakland (Calif.) Mus., 1981-88; chief exec. officer Corcoran Gallery Art, Washington, 1988-90; dir. Norton Gallery of Art, West Palm Beach, 1990—. Author: Addison Mizner: Architect of Dreams and Realities, 1974, 2d printing, 1993, Gordon Cook, 1987, Claude Monet: An Impression, 1993; editor: The Art of California, 1984. Office: Norton Gallery of Art 1451 S Olive Ave West Palm Beach FL 33401-7162

ORRISON, ALANNAH TERESA, economics educator; b. N.Y.C., June 24, 1955; d. Jack Huffaker and Catherine (Messitt) O.; m. Alan Howard Rosenberg, Dec. 22, 1991. AA in Anthropology, L.A. Valley Coll., Van Nuys, Calif., 1976; BA in History, Immaculate Heart Coll., Hollywood, Calif., 1977; MA in Econs., U. So. Calif., 1980; PhD in Econs., NYU, 1994. Instr. econs. Orange County C.C., Middletown, N.Y., 1983-84, NYU, 1983-89; rsch. fellow C.V. Starr Ctr. for Applied Econs., N.Y.C., 1987-89; asst. prof. econs. Saddleback Coll., Mission Viejo, Calif., 1990-92, chmn. honors program, 1992—, assoc. prof. econs., 1992—; co-advisor S.C. Hillel, Mission Viejo, 1994—. Mem. Am. Econs. Assn., Western Econs. Assn., Nat. Collegiate Honors Coun., Western Regional Honors Coun., Alpha Gamma Sigma (co-advisor 1993—). Office: Saddleback Coll BGS 316 28000 Marguerite Pky Mission Viejo CA 92692

ORSHAN, SUSAN AILEEN, women's health care specialist; b. Somerville, N.J., May 16, 1959; d. Martin Louis and Miriam (Ratner) O. BSN, U. Pa., 1981; MA, NYU, 1985, PhD, 1993. Cert. perinatal nurse ANA, cert. childbirth educator Am. Soc. for Psychoprophylaxis in Pregnancy. Teaching fellow, adj. instr. divsn. of nursing NYU, N.Y.C., 1985-89; adolescent pregnancy counselor St. Mary's Hosp., Hoboken, N.J., 1987-88; childbirth educator St. Vincent's Hosp. and Med. Ctr., N.Y.C., 1987-94, Robert Wood Johnson Univ. Hosp., New Brunswick, 1987-91; pvt. practice childbirth edn. Jersey City, 1987—; test cons. Nat. League for Nursing, N.Y.C., 1990-93; asst. prof. Rutgers Coll. Nursing, Newark, 1993—; mem. planning com. 4th and 5th Rogerian Conf. The Sci. and Art of Nursing Practice, N.Y.C., 1991—. Author: (with others) Springhouse, 1992; contbr. articles to profl. jours. Health profl. adv. coun. N.J. chpt. March of Dimes; mem. Hudson County Perinatal Consortium. Fellow Am. Coll. Childbirth Educators; mem. ANA, N.J. State Nurses Assn., Assn. of Women's Health, Obstet. and Neonatal Nursing (corr. mem. rsch. com., dist. III legis. com.), Am. Soc. for Psychoprophylaxis in Pregnancy/Lamaze, Sigma Theta Tau (pres. Upsilon chpt. 1992-94). Jewish. Home: 45 River Dr S # 1415 Jersey City NJ 07310 Office: Rutgers Coll Nursing University Heights Newark NJ 07102

ORSI-LIROT, ANITA CRISTINA, finance executive; b. Greenwich, Conn., Jan. 25, 1958; d. Domenico Vittorio and Anna Marie Luisa Pia (Bemporad) Orsi; m. Gregory J. Lirot; 1 child, Gregory. BA, Trinity Coll., 1978. Mgmt. trainee Mfrs. Hanover Trust, N.Y.C., 1978-82; asst. v.p. Bank of Montreal, N.Y.C., 1982-84, Can. Imperial Bank of Commerce, L.A., 1984-86; v.p. fin. ING Bank (formerly NMB Bank), N.Y.C., 1986-90; pres. ORSI, Inc., Rowayton, Conn., 1990—. Mem. fin. com. United Way of Norwalk, Conn., 1990—, 1990-91; program chair Am. Cancer Soc., Darien, Conn., 1993.

ORSINI, MYRNA J., sculptor, educator; b. Spokane, Wash., Apr. 19, 1943; d. William Joseph Finch and Barbara Jean (Hilby) Hickenbottom; m. Donald Wayne Lundquist, Mar. 31, 1962 (div. Mar. 1987); children: Laurie Jeanine Winter, Stephanie Lynne Lundquist. BA, U. Puget Sound, 1969, MA, 1974; postgrad., U. Ga., 1987. Tchr. Tacoma (Wash.) Pub. Schs., 1969-78; owner, pres. Contemporary Print Collectors, Lakewood, Wash., 1978-81, Orsini Studio, Tacoma, 1985—. Chair Supt.'s Supervisory Com., Tacoma, 1978-79; lobbyist Citizens for Fair Sch. Funding, Seattle, 1979; art chair Women's Pres. Coun., Tacoma, 1987-88; founder, bd. dirs. Monarch Contemporary Art Ctr., Wash. Recipient 1st pl. sculpture award Pleinair

Symposium Com., Ukraine, 1992, Peron Symposium Com., Kiev, Ukraine, 1993; recognized 1st Am. sculptor to exhibit work in Ukraine, 1993; prin. works include six monumental sculptures worldwide. Mem. N.W. Stone Sculptors Assn. (coun. leader 1989—), Pacific Gallery Artists, Internat. Sculpture Ctr., Tacoma City Club. Office: Orsini Studio 4411 N 7th Tacoma WA 98406

ORTEGA, HEATHER AFFLECK, financial analysis officer; b. Winnepeg, Manitoba, Can., Aug. 2, 1964; came to U.S., 1970; d. Allan Douglas and Anne (Kersey) Affleck. BA, U. Puget Sound, 1986; MBA, Duke U., 1990. Corp. fin. analyst Dean Witter, N.Y.C., 1986-88; fin. analysis officer Seafirst Bank, Seattle, 1990—; cons. in field., 1988-89. Advisor Seafirst's Youth Job Program, 1992—. Democrat. Episcopalian. Home: 510 4th Ave W Apt 303 Seattle WA 98119-4335

ORTEGO, ELIZABETH ANN, computer programmer; b. Ft. Bragg, N.C., July 21, 1952; d. Edwin and Anna Elizabeth (Sistrunk) O. BA, Southeastern La. U., 1974, BS, 1983. Libr. Riverside Acad., Reserve, La., 1974-81; programmer, analyst Digital Computer Systems, Hammond, La., 1984-87; programmer Southeastern La. U., Hammond, 1987-88, sr. programmer, 1988-89, project leader, 1989-92, dir. MIS, 1992—. Mem. Coll. and Univ. Computer Users Conf. Office: Southeastern La U PO Box 409 Hammond LA 70404-0409

ORTEGO, GILDA BAEZA, librarian, information professional; b. El Paso, Tex., Mar. 29, 1952; d. Efren and Bertha (Singh) Baeza; m. Felipe de Ortego y Gasca, Dec. 21, 1986. BA, Tex. Woman's U., 1974, graduate, 1974-75; MLS, U. Tex., 1976, postgrad., 1990-93; cert., Hispanic Leadership Inst., 1988. Stack maintenance supr. El Paso Libr. U. Tex., 1974-75; pub. svcs. libr. El Paso Community Coll., 1976-77; ethnic studies libr. U. N.Mex., Albuquerque, 1977-81; br. head El Paso Pub. Libr., 1981-82; dep. head Mex.-Am. Svcs., El Paso Pub. Libr., 1982-84; libr. Mex.-Am. Studies U. Tex. Libr., Austin, 1984-87; libr. Phoenix Pub. Libr., 1987-89; assoc. libr., west campus Ariz. State U., Phoenix, 1989-90; Proyecto Leer libr. Tex. Woman's U., Denton, 1991-92; dir. div. learning resources Sul Ross State U., Alpine, Tex., 1992—; speaker and cons. in field. Founding editor jour. La Lista, 1983-84; founding indexer Chicano Periodical Index, 1981-86; reviewer jour. Voices of Youth Advocates, 1988-90; contbr. poetry and articles to books and jours. Mem. ALA, MLA, Assn. for Libr. and Info. Sci. Edn., Tex. Libr. Assn., Ariz. State Libr. Assn. (pres. svcs. Spanish speaking Roundtable 1989-90), Reforma (pres. El Paso chpt. 1983, pres. Ariz. chpt. 1989-90, nat. v.p. 1993-94, pres. 1994—), Unltd. Potential, Inc. (treas. 1988-89), Hispanic Leadership Inst. Alumni Assn,.

ORTENBERG, ELISABETH CLAIBORNE See **CLAIBORNE, LIZ**

ORTH-AIKMUS, GAIL MARIE, police chief; b. Kansas City, Dec. 31, 1956; d. Ben Roy and Janet Ferrell (Buckner) O.; m. Frank Henry Aikmus Jr., Oct. 5, 1980 (div. Oct. 1990); 1 child, Brian Russell. Cert. law enforcement officer, Mo.; cert. drug canine handler; cert. vanner. Patrol officer Parkville (Mo.) Police Dept., 1977-78; deputy Platte County Sheriff, Platte City, Mo., 1978-79; patrol officer, sgt., lt. Pleasant Valley (Mo.) Police Dept., 1979-85, police chief, 1985—; bd. dirs. Clay County Investigative, pres. bd. dirs., 1991-93; guest spkr. Clay County Mcpl. Judges Conf.; testified before House Com. with Mo. Ho. of Reps., 1994. Appeared in fraud investigation on ABC 20/20 mag., 1980. Named Officer of Yr. Vets. Fgn. Wars Aux., Kansas City, 1991; recipient Key to Manor Pleasant Valley Manor, 1990, Puppy Trucker award Heart of Am. Van Club, 1994. Mem. Mo. Police Chief's Assn., Mo. Peace Officer's Assn., Kansas City Police Chief's Assn., Kansas City Major Case Squad, Kansas City Women in Law Enforcement, Nat. Assn. Chief's of Police, Nat. Rifle Assn., Weimaraner Club Am., Weimaraner Club Greater Kansas City (pres. 1991—). Home: 8405 Kaill Rd Pleasant Valley MO 64068 Office: Pleasant Valley Police Dept 6801 Sobbie Rd Pleasant Valley MO 64068

ORTIZ, BEVERLY RUTH, ethnographic consultant; b. L.A., Feb. 5, 1956; d. Joseph Antonio and Beverly Rae (Miller) O. BS, U. Calif., Davis, 1974; postgrad, U. Calif., Berkeley, 1993—. Dist. historian Plumas Nat. Forest, Greenville, Calif., 1976; park technician Yosemite Nat. Park, Wawona, Calif., summers 1978-81; naturalist Bay Regional Park Dist., Oakland, Calif., 1980—; ethnographic cons. Walnut Creek, Calif., 1986—; cons. Mount Diablo State Park, Walnut Creek, 1990-93, Healdsburg (Calif.) Mus., 1989, Sonoma State U. Acad. Found., Inc., Calif., 1993-95. Author: It Will Live Forever, 1991; contbr. articles to profl. jours. Pres., bd. mem. Miwok Archeol. Preserve of Marin, 1985-89; chair, commr. Walnut Creek Park and Recreation Commn., 1988-92; founder, bd. dirs., pres. Friends of Creeks in Urban Settings, Walnut Creek, 1984—; mem. adv. com. Oyate, Berkeley, 1990—; mem. Citizens Task Force on Creeks Restoration and Trails Master Plan, 1992-93, Contra Costa County Urban Creeks Task Force, 1986-88, Drainage Area 46 Task Force, 1986-87, Walnut Creek in the Yr. 2000 Subcom. on Open Space and Recreation, 1986. Recipient Cert. of Achievement and Profl. Merit East Bay Regional Parks, 1988. Mem. Phi Kappa Phi. Address: Coyote Hills Regional Park 8000 Patterson Ranch Rd Fremont CA 94555

ORTIZ, GERMAINE LAURA DE FEO, secondary educator, counselor; b. Astoria, N.Y., Aug. 6, 1947; d. Andrew and Germaine Laura (Fournier) De Feo; m. Dennis Manfredo, June 6, 1970 (annulled July 1975); m. Angel Manuel Ortiz, July 11, 1975; 1 child, Germaine Angela. AA, Suffolk County C.C., Selden, N.Y., 1969; BA magna cum laude, SUNY, Stony Brook, 1971, MALS, 1974; MS in Edn. with distinction, Hofstra U., 1989. Cert. N-6, 7-12 social studies tchr., sch. counselor, N.Y.; cert. rank II social studies, jr. coll. tchr., sch. counselor, Fla. Tchr. social studies Connetquot Cen. Sch. Dist. Islip, Bohemia, N.Y., 1971—. Mem. ASCD, NEA, N.Y. State Unified Tchrs., Connetquot Tchrs. Assn., Nat. Coun. for Social Studies, N.Y. Coun. for Social Studies, L.I. Coun. for Social Studies, Hofstra U. Alumni Assn., Suffolk County C.C. Alumni Assn., DAV Aux., Vietnam Vets. Am. Aux. Roman Catholic. Home: 5 Honey Ln W Miller Place NY 11764 Office: Connetquot Cen Sch Dist Islip 780 Ocean Ave Bohemia NY 11716

ORTIZ, JOY, corporation professional; b. Santa Fe, N.Mex., Mar. 18, 1948; d. Willie Velarde and Edith June (Ellis) Ortiz; divorced; children: Kevin M., Dawn M., Christopher D. Grad. high sch., Santa Fe, N.Mex., 1966. Co-owner La Tertulia Restaurant, Santa Fe, 1972—; bd. dirs. Sunwest Bank, Santa Fe; bd. trustees U. N.Mex. Hosp., 1994—; chmn. Hist. Design Rev., 1986; chmn. bd. trustees St. Vincent Hosp., 1988-90; mem. Bd. Med. Examiners, 1992—. Chmn. Cusines Santa Fe Am., Santa Fe Fiesta Found., 1990—, pres., 1993—; chmn. Cancer Soc., 1986; trustee Coll. Santa Fe. Named Woman of Distinction, Girl Scouts Am., 1993. Republican. Roman Catholic. Home: 345 Delgado St Santa Fe NM 87501-2756 Office: La Tertulia Restaurant 416 Agua Fria St Santa Fe NM 87501-2506

ORTIZ, KATHLEEN LUCILLE, travel consultant; b. Las Vegas, N.Mex., Feb. 8, 1942; d. Arthur L. and Anna (Lopez) O. BA, Loretto Hghts. Coll., 1963; MA, Georgetown U., 1966; cert. tchg., Highlands U., 1980; cert. travel, ABQ Travel Sch., 1984. Mgr. Montezuma Sq., Las Vegas, 1966-70; office mgr. Arts Food Market, Las Vegas, 1971-75; tchr. Robertson H.S., Las Vegas, 1976-80; registered rep. IDS Fin. Svcs., N.Mex., 1980-84; travel cons. VIP Travel & Tours, Albuquerque, 1985-86, New Horizons Travel, Albuquerque, 1986-87, All World Travel, Albuquerque, 1987-90, Premium Travel Svcs., Albuquerque, 1990-91; travel cons., group tours Going Places Travel, Albuquerque, 1991—. Contbr. 100 articles to newspapers. Founding mem. Citizens Com. for Hist. Preservation, Las Vegas, 1977-79; fund raiser St. Anthony's Hosp., Las Vegas, 1969-75. Mem. LWV (numerous positions), Internat. Airlines Travel Agent Network, Airlines Reporting Corp. Agent, Georgetown Club of N.Mex. (bd. dirs. at large 1991-94), Ali Lassen Leads Club. Home: 7600 Adele Pl NE Albuquerque NM 87109 Office: Going Places Travel 6400 Uptown Blvd Ste 429E Albuquerque NM 87110

ORTIZ, PAULINA PATRICIA, banker, research analyst; b. Panama City, Panama; came to U.S., 1964; d. Felix Alejandro Córdova and Esther (Burke) Blackburn; m. Philip Ortiz (dec. 1985); 1 child, Vanessa D. Grad. in bus. adminstrn., Excelsior Coll., Jamaica, 1962; student, Staten Island C.C., 1977-80, Bklyn. Coll., 1994, Pace U., 1980-85. Cert. data processor and computer programmer. Sec. Dr. Carlos Ibanez, Balboa, Panama, 1964; claims examiner Associated Hosp. Svcs. Greater N.Y., N.Y.C., 1965-66; comptometer operator Lerner Shops Exec. Office, N.Y.C., 1966-69; interect clk. examiner Citibank, N.A., N.Y.C., 1969-70, investigator, corr. clk., 1970-72, claims examiner, 1973, svc. asst., 1973-76, ombudsperson, 1976-79, couselor, 1979-84, customer svc. rep. for S.Am. and Carribean, 1984-86, rsch. investigator, 1986-93, rsch. analyst, 1993—. Former mem. East Bklyn. Chs. for devel. of Nehemiah Housing Project, 1984; mem. fin. com. Our Lady of Charity, former mem. alter guild, mem. ushers com., bd. trustees, sec. parish coun. on fund raiser com., v.p. and pres. Pastor's Aid Soc., 1986; campaign worker Howard Golden for Bklyn. Borough Pres., Congressman Adolphus Towns, 1986, Dist. Leader DaCosta Headley, 1994, Assemblyman Ed Griffith, 1988; candidate Sch. Bd. Dist. # 19, 1989; chairperson Linden Plz. Leaseholders, 1990-92; co-writer bylaws New Linden Plz. Tenants Assn., 1991-92, active, 1992—; charter mem. Day of Independence Com. of Panamanians in N.Y., 1993—; counselor St. Paul's Ch., 1994; active Divino Niño Jesus, 1994. Recipient Appreciation cert. as charter mem. Dem. Sen. task force Dem. Senatorial Campaign Com., 1994, Appreciation cert. Pres. Bill Clinton for support of Dem. Nat. Com., 1994, Outstanding Cmty. Svc. award Sen. Ada L. Smith, 1994, Third Degree, Grand Lady Carmela Rodriguez, 1993, Merit cert. Fourth Degree Georgiana Evans, Faithful Navigator, Ladies of Grace, 1993, Women's History Month Spl. Recognition award Congressman Adolphus Towns, 1989, Mother of Yr. award Jr. Daus. Ct. 229, 1990, Partner in Edn. award Adopt-a-Class Program N.Y. Bd. Edn., 1992-93, Hon. Trustee cert. Am. Indian Relief Coun., 1994, Citizenship cert. Boys Town, 1994, Silver Leader of Yr. cert. DAV Comdrs. Club, 1994. Mem. Urban Bankers Coalition, Knights of Peter Claver & Ladies' Aux. Ct. (vice grand lady of ct. 229 in Bklyn. 1984, grand lady of ct. 229 in Bklyn. 1985, 86, 87, co-founder chpt. 33, established ct. 333 in Queens, N.Y., area dep. N.Y.C.).

ORTIZ-BUTTON, OLGA, social worker; b. Chgo., July 12, 1953; d. Luis Antonio and Pura (Acevedo) Ortiz; m. Dennis Vesley, Aug. 11, 1976 (div. 1979); m. Randall Russell Button, Nov. 3, 1984 (div. Oct. 1993); children: Joshua, Jordan, Elijah. BA, U. Ill., 1975; MSW, Western Mich. U., 1981. Cert. social worker, sch. social worker, hypnosis. Social svcs. dir. Champaign County Nursing Home, Urbana, Ill., 1976; social svcs. and activity dir. Lawton (Mich.) Nursing Home, 1977; job developer Southwestern Mich. Indian Ctr., Watervliet, 1977-78; staff asst. New Directions Alcohol Treatment Ctr., Kalamazoo, 1978; counselor, instr. Alcohol Hwy. Safety, Kalamazoo, 1978-79; clin. social worker Mecosta County Community Mental Health, Big Rapids, Mich., 1981-84; program dir. substance abuse Sr. Svcs., Inc., Kalamazoo, 1984-85; sch. social worker Martin (Mich.) Pub. Schs., 1985—; owner, therapist Plainwell (Mich.) Counseling Ctr., 1989—; S.W. cons. Med. Pers. Pool, 1993—, G.L. Network Mktg., 1993—. Vol. social worker Hospice-Wings of Hope, Plainwell, 1984-85, mem. QTE bd., 1993—; supporter Students Against Aparteid South Africa, Kalamazoo, 1979-81; mem. World Vision and Countertop Ptnr., 1984—; sponsor, vol. People for Ethical Treatment of Animals, 1986—; vol. helper Sparkies for Awana Club Ch., 1989—, Mich. Post Adoption Svc. System, 1994—. NIMH Rural Mental Health grantee, 1979-81. Mem. NASW, Mich. Assn. Sch. Social Workers. Office: Plainwell Counseling Ctr 211 E Bannister Ste K Plainwell MI 49080

ORTIZ RUIZ, AIDA M., university administrator, educator; b. Barranquitas, P.R., Oct. 3, 1940; d. Higinio and Joaquina (Ortiz) O.; m. William Ruiz; 1 child, Philip. BA, U. P.R., 1971; MA, NYU, 1973; MEd, Columbia U., 1988. Tchr. N.Y.C. Bd. Edn., 1972-74; instr. English Queens Coll., N.Y.C., 1974-78; lectr. English Hostos Community Coll., Bronx, N.Y., 1978-83; asst. dean of faculty Hostos Community Coll., Bronx, 1984-86, assoc. dean of academic affairs, 1988-91; coord. freshman yr. programs CUNY, 1991—; mem. test of std. written English com. Coll. Bd., 1985-90; reader SAT Comp, TOEFL-TWE, 1990—; mem. coun. internat. edn. CUNY, 1989—, campaign fund drive, 1990—, mem. chancellors task force on writing, 1984-88, chair univ. adv. com. on transfer and articulation; grants adminstr. Title III, VEA, Ford UCCTOP, Diamond Found. grant Minority Project for Tchg. Professions, 1993—. Contbr. articles to profl. jours. Mem. Inst. for R.R. Policy, N.Y.C., 1986—, CUNY Womne's Coalition, 1984—. Fellow Ford Found., 1971-73. Fellow ASCD, Acad. Affairs Adminstrs., Coll. Compositions and Comm., TESOL, Assn. Tchrs. English, Acad. for Humanities and Scis., Internat. Platform Assn. Office: Hostos Community Coll 500 Grand Concourse Bronx NY 10451-5323

ORTLIP, MARY KRUEGER, artist; b. Scranton, Pa.; d. John A. and Ida Mae (Phillips) Smale; m. Emmanuel Krueger, June, 1940 (dec. Nov. 1979); children: Diane, Keith; m. Paul D. Ortlip, June 26, 1981. Student, New Sch. Social Rsch., N.Y.C., 1957-59, Margarita Madrigal Langs., N.Y.C., Montclair (N.J.) Art Mus. Sch., 1978-79; Nomina Accademico Conferita, Accademia Italia, Italy, 1986; DFA (hon.), Houghton Coll., 1988. Dancer, dance instr. Fleischer Dance Studio, Scranton, Pa., 1934-38. One-woman shows include Curzon Gallery of Boca Raton, Fla. and London, 1986-93, Galerie Les Amis des Arts, Aix-en-Provence, France, 1987; group exhbns.: Salmagundi Club, N.Y.C., 1980, James Hunt Barker Galleries, Nantucket, Mass. and N.Y.C., 1983, Salon Internationale Musée Parc Rochteau à Revin, France, 1985, 90, Accademia Italia, Milan, 1986, many others in Europe and Am.; permanent collections Musée de parc Rocheteau, Revin, France, Pinacothèque Arduinna, Charleville-Meziéres, France. Named Invité d'Honneur, Le Salon des Nations a Retenu L'oeuvre, Paris, 1983, Artist of the Year, La Cote des Arts, France, 1986; recipient La Medaille d'Or, Du 13ème Salon Internationale al du Parc Rocheau au Revin, France, 1985, Medaille d' Honneur Ville de Marseille, France, 1987, Targo D'Oro, Accademia Italia Premio D'Italia, 1986; Trophy Arts Internationale Exposition de Peinture Marseille, Plaquette d' Honneur, Palais des Arts, 1987, Grand Prix Salon de Automne Club Internationale, 1987, Connaissance de Notre Europa Ardennes Eifel, Revin, France, 1990. Mem. Nat. Mus. Women in Arts, Accademia Italia (charter), Instituo D'Art Contemporanea Di Milano, Nat. Soc. Arts and Letters, Gov.'s Club, Salmagundi Club. Home: 588 Summit Ave Hackensack NJ 07601-1547 Office: The Curzon Gallery 501 E Camino Real Boca Raton FL 33432-6127

ORTON, GERALDINE LEITL, psychology and mental health educator, mental health services professional; b. Pitts., May 16, 1939; d. Meinrad M. and Virginia (Traska) L.; m. Guy M. Orton, June 16, 1962; children: Alisa, Guy Christopher. BS, Ind. U. Pa., 1961; postgrad., Scandinavian Sem. for Cultural Study, Valla Folkhogskola, Linkoping, Sweden, 1961-62; MS, Edinboro U. Pa., 1970; PhD, U. Buffalo, 1978. Cert. in counseling psychology and ednl. adminstrn. Elem. sch. tchr. Ripley (N.Y.) Cen. Sch., 1962-70, elem. sch. counselor, 1970-74; program dir. SUNY, Fredonia, 1974-76; asst. prof. Gannon U., Erie, Pa., 1977-81, assoc. prof., 1981—, mem. grad. faculty, 1990—, dir. mental health counseling, 1991—, dir. gen. studies program, 1991-93, chair dept. human svcs., 1992—; pvt. practice, 1984—; bd. dirs. mental health counseling program Warren State Hosp., 1984-88, supr. of placements in Warren County, 1984-88; bd. dirs. Home Instrn. Tutorial Program Rsch. Found. SUNY, Fredonia, 1975-76, Learn, Experience and Develop Program, 1974-75; cons. Bur. of Guidance N.Y. State Dept. Edn., Albany, 1983, mental health program Chautauqua County BOCES, Fredonia, 1974, career edn. program Westfield (N.Y.) Acad. and Cen. Sch., 1974; therapist Parents Supporting Other Parents in Sorrow, Erie, 1978; mem. numerous Gannon U. coms. and task forces; presenter in field. Contbr. articles to profl. jours. Mem. adv. bd. Perspective on Women Series: Pub. Com. on the Humanities in Pa.; mem. Primary Prevention Task Force-Youth Svcs. Coordination Coun. Erie County; numerous presentations Pa. schs. Mem. Internat. Platform Soc., Am. Counselors Assn., Pi Gamma Mu, Lambda Sigma. Office: Gannon U Dept Mental Health Counseling University Square Erie PA 16541

ORULLIAN, B. LARAE, bank executive; b. Salt Lake City, May 15, 1933; d. Alma and Bessie (Bacon) O.; cert. Am. Inst. Banking, 1961, 63, 67; grad. Nat. Real Estate Banking Sch., Ohio State U., 1969-71. With Tracy Collins Trust Co., Salt Lake City, 1951-54; sec. to exec. sec. Union Nat. Bank, Denver, 1954-57; exec. sec. Guaranty Bank, Denver, 1957-64, asst. cashier, 1964-67, asst. v.p., 1967-70, v.p., 1970-75, exec. v.p., 1975-77, also bd. dirs.; pres., chief exec. officer, dir. The Women's Bank N.A., Denver, 1989—, Equitable Bankshares of Colo., 1980—; vice chmn. Equitable Bank Littleton; chmn. bd., dir. Colo. Blue Cross/Blue Shield, lectr.; bd. dirs. Pro Card, Inc.; mem. bd. dirs. Frontier Airlines; Treas. Girl Scouts U.S.A., 1981-87, 1st. nat. v.p., chair exec. com., 1987-90, nat. pres., 1990—; bd. dirs., chair Rocky Mountain Health Care Corp.; bd. dirs. Ams. Clean Water Found., Denver Improvement Assn.; bd. dirs. Commn. Savings in Am. Recipient Woman Who Made a Difference award Internat. Women's Forum, 1994; named to Colo. Women Hall of Fame, 1988, Colo. Entrepreneur of Yr., Inc. Mag. and Arthur Young and Co., 1989, Woman of the Yr., YWCA, 1989. Mem. Bus. and Profl. Women Colo. (3d Century award 1977), Colo. State Ethics Bd., Denver C. of C., Am. Inst. Banking, Am. Bankers Assn. (adv. bd. edn. found.), Nat. Assn. Bank Women, Internat. Women's Forum (Woman Who Makes a Difference award 1994), Com. of 200. Republican. Mormon. Home: 10 S Ammons St Lakewood CO 80226-1331

ORY, MARCIA GAIL, social science researcher; b. Dallas, Feb. 8, 1950; d. Marvin Gilbert and Esther (Levine) O.; m. Raymond James Carroll, Aug. 13, 1972. BA magna cum laude, U. Tex., 1971; MA, Ind. U., 1972; PhD, Purdue U., 1976; MPH, Johns Hopkins U., 1981. Rsch. asst. prof. U. N.C., Chapel Hill, 1976-77; from adj. asst. prof. to assoc. prof. sch. pub. health U. N.C., 1978-88; rsch. fellow U. Minn., Mpls., 1977-78; asst. prof. Sch. Pub. Health U. Ala., Bham, 1978-80; program dir. biosocial aging and health Nat. Inst. on Aging, Bethesda, Md., 1981-86; chief social sci. rsch. on aging Nat. Inst. on Aging, Bethesda, 1987—. Contbr. articles, editor vols. profl. jours. Mem. several nat. task forces on aging and health issues. Recipient Dept. of Health and Human Svcs. award, 1984, 85, 88, Am. Men and Women of Sci., 1989-90; named Disting. Alumna by Purdue U. Fellow Gerontol. Soc. Am.; mem. APHA (gov. coun. 1986-88, program chmn. 1986, chmn.-elect 1989-91, chmn. 1992-93), Am. Sociol. Assn. (regional reporter 1984—, program com. 1986, nominations com. 1987, councilor-at-large 1992-93), Soc. Behavioral Medicine (program chmn. pub. health track 1988-89, program com. 1991-92), Assn. Health Svcs. Rsch., Phi Kappa Phi, Omicron Nu. Office: Nat Inst Aging Gateway Bldg Ste 533 7201 Wisconsin Ave MSC 9205 Bethesda MD 20892-9205

OSBORN, ANN GEORGE, retired chemist; b. Nowata, Okla., Aug. 1, 1933; d. David Thomas and Alice Audrey (Giles) George; m. Charles Wesley Osborn, Nov. 8, 1958 (dec. Dec. 1977); 1 child, Charles David. BA in Chemistry, Okla. Coll. Women, 1955. Rsch. chemist thermodynamics rsch. lab. Bartlesville (Okla.) Energy Rsch. Ctr., U.S. Dept. Energy, 1957—; ret., 1983. Contbr. articles to profl. jours. Mem. AAAS (emeritus), Am. Chem. Soc. Republican. Mem. Christian Ch. (Disciples of Christ). Home: 647 S Pecan St Nowata OK 74048-4015

OSBORN, FRAN STEVENS, post-anesthesia nurse; b. Brownsboro, Tex., Sept. 10, 1940; d. Larence Edmon and Francis Catherine (Tullos) Stevens; m. C.T. Osborn, Aug. 29, 1957; children: Cindy Frances, Sheri Patrice, Lorri Lajuan, Tammy Jayne. LVN, Tyler (Tex.) Jr. Coll., 1980. RN, Tex. Bookkeeper, officer mgr. Tyler Water Sports, 1975-80; staff nurse East Tex. Med. Ctr., Tyler, 1980—. Mem. Am. Soc. Post Anesthesia Nurses, Am. Orgn. Operating Rm. Nurses, Tex. Assn. Post Anesthesia Nurses (2d v.p. 1987-88, treas. 1988-94, 1st v.p. 1994—), East Tex. Assn. Post Anesthesia Nurses (3d v.p. 1991-92, 2d v.p. 1992-93, pres. 1990-91). Democrat. Baptist. Home: PO Box 276 Brownsboro TX 75756-0276 Office: East Tex Med Ctr 1000 S Beckham Ave Tyler TX 75701-1996

OSBORN, JANET KAY, counselor; b. Spencer, Iowa, May 26, 1944; d. Lawrence Bruce and Dorothy Marguerite (Clapp) Rusk; m. Colin Timothy Carris, Aug. 8, 1964 (dec. 1980); children: Todd Jeffrey Carris, Mark Timothy Carris; m. Thomas Ward Osborn III, Nov. 21, 1981. BS, U. Cin., 1969, Cert. advanced grad. study, 1993; MEd, Xavier U., 1987. Tchr. St. Mary's Elem. Sch., El Paso, Tex., 1965-66; tchr. adult edn. Greenhills Schs., Cin., 1971-74; substitute tchr. Finneytown Schs., Cin., 1975-77; tchr. 3Cb Nursery Sch., Cin., 1978-82; counselor Margaret Conradi, Psychologist, Cin., 1986-87, Cin. Counseling Svc., 1987—; mem. task force, cons. Northwest Schs., Cin., 1994—; presenter in field. Co-pres. soccer backer Finneytown Schs., Cin., 1986; mem. youth leadership team Coll. Hill Presbyn. Ch., Cin., 1987-90, elder, 1987—, mem. congl. care leadership team, 1993—; mem. steering com. Arm in Arm, Cin., 1994—. Mem. ACA, Orthopsychiatric Assn. Home: 400 Deanview Dr Cincinnati OH 45224-1415

OSBORN, JUNE ELAINE, pediatrician, microbiologist, educator; b. Endicott, N.Y., May 28, 1937; d. Leslie A. and Dora W. (Wright) O.; divorced; children: Philip I. Levy, Ellen D. and Laura A. Levy (twins). BA, Oberlin (Ohio) Coll., 1957; MD, Western Res. U., 1961; DSc (hon.), U. Med. Dental Sch. N.J., 1990; DMS (hon.), Yale U., 1992; DSc (hon.), Emory U., 1993, Oberlin Coll., 1993; LHD (hon.), Med. Coll. Pa., 1994; DSc (hon.), Rutgers U., 1994. Intern, then resident in pediatrics Harvard U. Hosp., 1961-64; postdoctoral fellow Johns Hopkins Hosp., 1964-65, U. Pitts. Hosp., 1965-66; practice medicine specializing in pediatrics Madison, Wis., 1966-84; dean Sch. Pub. Health U. Mich., 1984-93, prof. epidemiology, pediatrics and communicable diseases, 1984—; mem. faculty U. Wis. Med. Sch., 1966-84, prof. pediatrics and microbiology, 1975-84, asso. dean Grad. Sch., 1975-84; mem. rev. panel viral vaccine efficacy FDA, 1973-79, mem. vaccines and related biol. products adv. com., 1981-85; mem. exptl. virology study sect. Div. Research Grants, NIH, 1975-79; bd. dirs. Stetler Research Fund Women Physicians, 1971-75; mem. med. affairs com. Yale U. Council, 1981-86; chmn. life scis. associateships rev. panel NRC, 1981-84; mem. U.S. Army Med. Research and Devel. Adv. Com., 1983-85; chmn. working group on AIDS and the Nation's Blood Supply, NHLBI, 1984-89; chmn. WHO Planning Group on AIDS and the Internat. Blood Supply, 1985-86. Contbr. articles to med. jours. Mem. task force on AIDS, Inst. of Medicine, 1986; mem. adv. com. Robert Wood Johnson Found. Health Svcs. Program, 1986-91; mem. nat. adv. com. on the health of the pub. program Pew and Rockefeller Founds.; mem. health promotion and disease prevention bd. IOM, 1987-90, Global Commn. on AIDS WHO, 1988-92; chmn. Nat. Commn. on AIDS, 1989-93; trustee Kaiser Found., 1990—; trustee Case Western Res. U., Cleve., 1993—; mem. coun. Inst. Medicine, 1995—. Grantee NIH, 1969, 72, 74-75, Nat. Multiple Sclerosis Soc., 1971; recipient Scientific Freedom award, Am. Assn. for Advancement of Science, 1994. Fellow AAAS (Sci. Freedom and Reponsibility award 1994), Am. Acad. Arts and Scis, Am. Acad. Pediatrics, Am. Acad. Microbiology, Infectious Diseases Soc. Am.; mem. Am. Assn. Immunologists, Soc. Pediatric Rsch., Inst. Medicine. Office: U Mich Dept Epidemiology Sch Pub Health Ann Arbor MI 48109

OSBORN, MARY JANE MERTEN, biochemist; b. Colorado Springs, Colo., Sept. 24, 1927; d. Arthur John and Vivien Naomi (Morgan) Merten; m. Ralph Kenneth Osborn, Oct. 26, 1950. B.A., U. Calif., Berkeley, 1948; Ph.D., U. Wash., 1958. Postdoctoral fellow, dept. microbiology N.Y. U. Sch. Medicine, N.Y.C., 1959-61; instr. N.Y. U. Sch. Medicine, 1961-62, asst. prof., 1962-63; asst. prof. dept. molecular biology Albert Einstein Coll. Medicine, Bronx, N.Y., 1963-66; asso. prof. Albert Einstein Coll. Medicine, 1966-68; prof. dept. microbiology U. Conn. Health Center, Farmington, 1968—; dept. head U. Conn. Health Center, 1980—; mem. bd. sci. counselors Nat. Heart, Lung and Blood Inst., 1975-79; mem. Nat. Sci. Bd., 1980-86; adv. coun. Nat. Inst. Gen. Med. Sci., 1983-86, divsn. rsch. grants NIH, 1989-94, chair, 1992-94; trustee Biosci. Info. Systems, 1986-91; mem. German Am. Acad. Coun., 1994—; mem. space scis. bd. NRC, 1994—, chair com. space biology and medicine, 1994—. Assoc. editor Jour. Biol. Chemistry, 1978-80; contbr. articles in field of biochemistry and molecular biology to profl. jours. Mem. rsch. com. Am. Heart Assn., 1972-77, chair, 1976-77. NIH fellow, 1959-61; NIH grantee, 1962—; NSF grantee, 1965-68; Am. Heart Assn. grantee, 1968-71. Fellow Am. Acad. Arts and Scis. (coun. 1988-91), NAS (coun. 1990-93, com. sci. engring. and pub. policy 1993—); mem. Am. Chem. Soc. (chmn. divsn. biol. chemistry 1975-76), Am. Fedn. Soc. Exptl. Biology (pres. 1982-83), Am. Soc. Biol. Chemists (pres. 1981-82), Am. Soc. Microbiology. Democrat. Office: U Conn Health Ctr Dept Microbiology Farmington CT 06030

OSBORN, NANCY JO, insurance producer, small business owner; b. Springfield, Ill., Oct. 2, 1950; d. Elmer Charles Jr. and Edna Virginia (Lowe) Forcade; m. Scott Alan Guetterman, Mar. 1, 1969 (div. May 1978); children: Stephanie Ann Bertelsmann, Marsha Lynn.; m. Daniel Francis Osborn, Oct. 13, 1990; 1 chld, Caitlin Elizabeth. Grad. high sch., St. Teresa's Acad., East St. Louis, Ill. Lic. ins. producer. Clk., typist Forcade Ins. Agy., Granite City, Ill., 1972-80, casualty agt., 1980-82, property & casualty ins. agt., 1982—, life & health agt., 1984—, owner, chief exec. officer, 1986—; corp. sec. A-Age Elec. Contractors, Inc., Washington Pk., Ill., 1990—; dir. Kaskaskia Indsl. Devel. Corp., 1992—; dir. Kaskaskia Indsl. Devel. Corp., Redbud, Ill., 1990—. Pres. Collinsville (Ill.) Jaycees, 1987-88, state dir.,

1989-90; publicity chmn. Collinsville Italian Fest, 1992—. Named Outstanding Local Pres., Gateway Region Jaycees, 1987-88, #8 State Dir. of Yr., Ill. Jr. C. of C., 1989-90, Outstanding State Chmn. of 1st Quarter, 1990, Outstanding Membership Devel. State Chmn., 1990-91, Outstanding State Chmn. of Yr., 1990-91, Henry Giessenbier fellow, 1995. Mem. Nat. Model R.R. Assn., U.S. Jr. C. of C. (alumni mem.). Roman Catholic. Office: Forcade Ins Agy 1822 State St Granite City IL 62040-4619

OSBORN, RITA DEISENROTH, public relations executive; b. Louisville, Ky., Jan. 27, 1951; d. Lloyd Henry and Catherine Rita (Nicklies) Deisenroth; children: J. Matthew, Amy. BA in Communications cum laude, Bellarmine Coll., 1990. Office mgr. Most Blessed Sacrament & Ascension Schs., Louisville, 1980-88; program asst. Sta. WKPC-TV, Louisville, 1989; pub. rels. asst. Ky. Hosp. Assn., Louisville, 1990, Vis. Nurse Assn., Louisville, 1989-90; writer, researcher Writer's Inc., Louisville, 1990-91; pub. rels. coord. Archdiocesan Comm. Ctr. Archdiocese of Louisville, 1991—; mem. exec. bd. Lupus Found. Kentuckiana, Inc., Louisville, 1989-91; v.p. communications Assn. Louisville Orch., 1990-91; exec. bd. Women in Communications Inc., Louisville, 1990— (Competitive scholar 1989). Vol. St. Matthew Area Ministries Intervention Svcs., Louisville, 1982-84, WKPC-TV Auction, Louisville, 1989—. Recipient 1st Place News Story, Ky. Intercollegiate Press Assn., 1990; Wilson Wyatt fellow Bellarmine Coll., 1990. Mem. Delta Epsilon Sigma. Democrat. Office: Archdiocesan Comm Ctr 1200 S Shelby St Louisville KY 40203-2600

OSBORN, SUSAN TITUS, editor; b. Fresno, Calif., July 11, 1944; d. Clifford Leland Feldt and Jane (Taylor) Cousings; m. Richard G. Titus, Aug. 28, 1965 (div. Dec. 1990); children: Richard David, Michael Craig; m. Richard A. Osborn, Aug. 22, 1992. BA in Religious Studies, Calif. State U., Fullerton, 1988, MA in Comm., 1993. Svc. rep. Mountain Bell Tel., Colorado Springs, Colo., 1965-67; free-lance writer Fullerton, Calif., 1978—; assoc. dir. Biola U. Writers Inst., La Mirada, Calif., 1986-92; co-dir. Christian Communicators Conf. The Master's Coll., Santa Clarita, Calif., 1993—, adj. prof., 1993—; mem. adv. bd. Christian Writers Fellowship, Huntington Beach, Calif., 1987-93; mem. adv. bd. Christian Communicator, San Juan Capistrano, Calif., 1989-94, mng. editor, 1991-92, editor, 1992—; pub. cons. Ednl. Ministries, Brea, Calif., 1989-91; conf. spkr. numerous cities, 1987—; tchr. India Comm. Inst., Bombay; bd. dirs. Moscow Christian Sch. Psychology, 1992—. Author: Parables for Young Teens, 1986, You Start With One, 1990, Meeting Jesus, 1990, Eyes Beyond the Horizon, 1991, Children Around the World Celebrate Christmas, 1993, The Complete Guide to Christian Writing and Speaking, 1994; editor The Christian Communicator. Bd. dirs. Jr. Ebell Club, Fullerton, 1969-75, Youth Sci. Ctr., Fullerton, 1970-75, YMCA Swim Club, Fullerton, 1976-82; pres. Troy Swim Boosters, Fullerton, 1982-88, Moscow Christian Sch. Psychology, 1992—. Recipient Spl. Recognition award Troy Swim Boosters, 1986. Mem. Presbyn. Writers Guild., Spiritual Overseers Svc. Republican. Evangelical. Office: Master's Coll Dept Comm PO Box 221450 Santa Clarita CA 91322-1450

OSBORNE, CHRISTINE MEGAN, musician, educator; b. Kingsport, Tenn., May 16, 1960; d. Charles Edward and Columbine (Amici) O. MusB, performer's cert., Eastman Sch. Music, 1982; MusM, U. So. Calif., L.A., 1985; postgrad., U. Utah, 1993—. Bassoonist Utah Symphony, Salt Lake City, 1985—; pvt. music tchr., Salt Lake City, 1985—; chamber music performer NOVA chamber music series, Salt Lake Chamber, 1987—; adj. asst. prof. bassoon U. Utah, Salt Lake City, 1992—. Author (op-ed pieces) Salt Lake Tribune, 1989, Deseret News; contbr. articles to profl. jours. Pub. lands chair, pub lands activist Utah Chpt. Sierra Club, Salt Lake City, 1988—; voting dist. chair, del. Dem. Party Utah, Salt Lake City, 1992—. Recipient Concerto Competition winner Music Acad. of the West, Santa Barbara, Calif., 1980; chamber music competition winner Coleman Nat. Chamber Music Competition, Pasadena, Claif. 1983; winner hon. mention Dalmas Nelson Best MPA Paper award 1994. Mem. Am. Fedn. Musicians (shop steward 1993—, bd. dirs. local 104 1994—), Am. Soc. for Pub. Adminstrn., Sierra Club (Utah chpt. exec. com. 1992-93). Office: Utah Symphony 123 W South Temple Salt Lake City UT 84101

OSBORNE, GAYLA MARLENE, sales executive; b. Owenton, Ky., Aug. 9, 1956; d. Frederick Clay and Helen Beatrice (Mason) O. AAS, No. Ky. U., 1982, BS, 1986; cert. in Chinese Mandarin, Def. Lang. Inst., 1975. Pers. clk. Dept. Edn. State Ky., Frankfort, 1974; sec. Dept. Health, Edn., Welfare Nat. Inst. Occupational Safety Health, Cin., 1977-79; specialist sales promotion U.S. Postal Svc., Cin., 1980, coord. customer liaison, task force pub. image, account rep., 1986-87, with stamp distbn. task force, 1993—; reservation sale agt. Delta Airlines, 1987-89. Councilmember Florence City Coun., Ky. 1984-87; vol. Children's Home, Covington, 1982, 87. With USAF, 1974-76. Named to Hon. Order Ky. Cols. Mem. Disabled Am. Veterans, No. Ky. U. Alumni Assn., Nat. Assn. Postmasters U.S., Boone County Fraternal Order Police, Ky. Assn. Realtors, Nat. Bd. Realtors, Women in Mil. Svc. for Am. (charter). Democrat. Baptist. Club: Fraternal Order Police. Home: 8395 Juniper Ln Florence KY 41042-9672

OSBORNE, PHYLLIS ANN, nurse; b. Charlotte, N.C., Jan. 12, 1953; d. Joe Brown and Sarah Ula (Porter) Strube; m. Kenneth Ray Osborne, Sept. 15, 1985; children: Terry Ray, Robbie Lynn, James Patterson, Gregory Alan, Charles Ross. Diploma in Nursing, Presbyn. Hosp. Sch. Nursing, Charlotte, 1974. RN; cert. nurse in infection control. Staff nurse ICU/CCU Presbyn. Hosp., Charlotte, 1974-75; staff nurse in pediats. and allergy Drs. Office, Orlando, Fla., 1975-79; staff nurse pub. health dept. Montgomery County, Clarksville, Tenn., 1979-80; charge nurse Westside Hosp., Nashville, 1980-83; charge nurse Jesse Holman Jones Hosp., Springfield, Tenn., 1983-89, infection control employee health nurse, 1989—. Mem. Assn. Profls. in Infection Control and Epidemiology (rec. sec. 1993), Assn. Hosp. Employee Health Profls. Home: 2901 Driftwood Dr Springfield TN 37172 Office: Jesse Holmes Jones Hosp 509 Brown St Springfield TN 37172

OSBORNE-POPP, GLENNA JEAN, health services administrator; b. East Rainelle, W.Va., Jan. 5, 1945; d. B.J. and Jean Ann (Haranac) Osborne; m. Thomas Joseph Ferrante Jr., June 11, 1966 (div. Nov. 1987); 1 child, Thomas Joseph Osborne; m. Brian Mark Popp, Aug. 13, 1988. BA cum laude, U. Tampa, 1966; MA, Fairleigh Dickinson U., 1982; cert., Kean Coll., 1983. Cert. English, speech, dramatic arts tchr., prin./supr. Tchr. Raritan High Sch., Hazlet, N.J., 1966; tchr. Keyport (N.J.) Pub. Schs., 1968-86, coord. elem. reading and lang. arts, 1980-84, supr. curriculum and instrn., 1984-86; prin. Weston Sch., Manville, N.J., 1986-88, The Bartle Sch., Highland Park, N.J., 1988-91, Orange Ave. Sch., Cranford, N.J., 1991-92; dir. The Open Door Youth Shelter, Binghamton, N.Y., 1992-94; child protective investigator supr. Dept. Health and Rehab. Svcs., Orlando, Fla., 1994—; regional trainer Individualized Lang. Arts, Weehawken, N.J., 1976-86; cons. McDougal/Little Pubs., Evanston, Ill., 1982-83. Contbr. chpt. to: A Resource Guide of Differentiated Learning Experiences for Gifted Elementary Students, 1981. Sunday sch. tchr. Reformed Ch., Keyport, 1975-80, supt. Sunday sch., 1982-84. Mem. Order Ea. Star (Tampa, Fla.), Phi Delta Kappa. Republican. Methodist. Office: 1010 Executive Center Dr Orlando FL 32812

OSBURNE, LEANNE CHRISTY, financial consultant; b. New Castle, Pa., May 2, 1936; d. Leon Roosevelt and Anna Mae (Milsom) Christy; children: John Christy Lind, Patrick James. Student, Jacksonville U., 1953-64, postgrad., 1979, 90; MS in Fin. Svcs., Am. Coll., 1979, MS in Mgmt., 1990. CLU, ChFC; registered securities rep., registered securities prin. Claims examiner, agent Prudential Ins. Co., Jacksonville, Fla., 1953-66; v.p. H.M. Harrell Assocs.-Gulf Life Ins. Co., Jacksonville, 1967-74; prodn. mgr. Travelers Ins. Co., Jacksonville, 1974-82; mktg. officer USF&G Corp., Balt., 1982-92; owner cons. practice Jacksonville, 1993—; owner Annuity Mktg. Inst., Jacksonville, 1992—; mem. pres.'s cabinet USF&G Corp., Balt., 1986-92; bd. dirs. Stelko Corp., Sarasota, Fla.; mem. ins. adv. com. Fla. C.C., Jacksonville, 1975-82. Author: Executive Personal Power, 1990, Annuities, 1992. Recipient Eve award Bus. Woman of Yr., Fla. Pub. Co., 1978, Ins. Exec. of Yr. award Fla. C.C. of Jacksonville and CLU Chpt., 1979. Mem. N.E. Fla. Estate Planning Coun. (bd. dirs. 1979-83), Women's Life Underwriters Conf. (nat. bd. dirs. 1981-83), Jacksonville Assn. Life Underwriters (pres. 1981-82), Jacksonville chpt. CLU and ChFC (pres. 1980-81, Heritage Heubner award 1979), Jacksonville Women's Network (founding bd. dirs. 1979), Torch Club Internat. (pres. Jacksonville chpt. 1982, pres. Balt. chpt. 1988), Bull Snort Forum (treas. 1975-82), Mensa (pres. Jacksonville chpt. 1969-79). Unitarian. Home: # 1043 7701 Baymeadows Cir W Jacksonville FL 32256

OSEGUERA, PALMA MARIE, marine corps officer, reservist; b. Kansas City, Mo., Dec. 29, 1946; d. Joseph Edmond and Palma Louise (Utke) O'Donnell; m. Alfonso Oseguera, Jan. 1, 1977; stepchildren: Kristie M. Daniels, Michelle L. Russell, Lori A. Kelley. BA in Phys. Edn., Marycrest Coll., 1969. Commd. 2d lt. USMC, 1969, advanced through grades to col., 1991; asst. marine corps exch. officer Hdqs. and Hdqs. Squadron, Marine Corps Air Sta., Beaufort, S.C., 1969-71; classified material control officer Hdqs. and Svcs. Battalion, Camp S.D. Butler, Okinawa, 1971-73; adminstrv. officer, marine corps exec. officer Marine Corps Air Sta., El, Toro, Santa Ana, Calif., 1973-76; marine corps exch. officer Marine Corps Air Sta., Yuma, Ariz., 1976-77; asst. marine corps exch. officer Support Batallion, Marine Corps Devel. & Edn. Command, Quantico, Va., 1977-79; marine corps exch. officer Hqrs. Marine Corps, Washington, 1979-80; adminstrv. officer Marine Air Base Squadon 46, Marine Air Group 46, Marine Corps Air Sta., Santa Ana, 1981-83, Hdqs. and Maintanence Squadron 46, Marine Air Group 46, Marine Corps Air Sta., Santa Ana, 1983-85, Mobilization Tng. Unit Calif. 53, Landing Force Tng. Command, Pacific, San Diego, 1985-89, 3d Civil Affairs Group, L.A., 1989; dep. asst. chief of staff G-1 I Marine Expeditionary Force, Individual Mobilization Augumentaee Detachment, Camp Pendleton, Calif., 1990-91; assoc. mem. Mobilization Tng. Unit Del. 01, Del., 1992-94; adminstrn. officer Mobilization Tng. Unit, CA-53, EWTG Pac, NAB, Coronado, San Diego. Mem. choir St. Elizabeth Seaton, Woodbridge, Va., 1978-80, St. Patricks, Arroyo Grande, Calif., 1990—. Mem. AAUW (past libr.), Marine Corps Assn., Marine Corps Res. Officer Assn., Marine Corps Aviation Assn. (12 dist. dir. 1987), Women in Mil. Svc. for Am. Republican. Roman Catholic. Home: 728 Scenic Cir Arroyo Grande CA 93420-1617

OSER, JUDI, lawyer, artist; b. Phila., Sept. 18, 1933; d. James Isadore and Mildred (Greenspan) O.; m. Richard Hunter Hollinger, Nov. 4, 1965 (div. Nov. 1975). BA in English with honors, U. Pa., 1956; JD, New Coll. Calif., 1980; student, Sarah Lawrence Coll., Pa. Acad. Fine Arts. Bar: Calif. 1980, U.S. Dist. Ct. (no. dist.) Calif. 1980, U.S. Ct. Appeals (9th crct.) 1982. Law clk. immigration law unit North Beach-Chinatown br. San Francisco Neighborhood Legal Assistance Found., 1979; immigration atty. Law Offices of Fred C. Hite, San Francisco, 1979-81, Wong, Main and Wu, Palo Alto, Calif., 1981; assoc. Law Offices of C. H. Blagburn, San Francisco, 1981-82; staff atty. Am. Ind. Hist. Soc., San Francisco, 1982; sole practice Piedmont, Calif., 1982—. One-woman shows include Lotus Gallery, Berkeley, Calif., Mus. Coastal Arts League, Spanishtown Galleries, Half Moon Bay, Calif., Clark's Corner, San Francisco, Heart's Content, Lyndell, Pa.; exhibited in numerous group shows and pvt. collections; contbr. articles to profl. jours. Mem. Calif. Lawyers for the Arts (atty.'s ref. panel), Eastbay Watercolor Soc. (2d place award 1992), San Francisco Women Artists (bus. sec., bd. dirs., Merit award 1988, 94), Oakland Art Assn. (corp. counsel, bd. dirs., 1st place award 1991, Merit award 1988, 90, 1st prize 30th ann. exhbn. 1987), Phila. Watercolor Club (signature membership), Pa. Acad. Fine Arts (fellowship mem. alumni assn.), Calif. Bar Assn. Office: PO Box 21342 Piedmont CA 94620

OSGOOD, BARBARA TRAVIS, conservationist, sociologist; b. Nyack, N.Y., Nov. 10, 1934; d. Donald Lovatt and Dorothy Catherine (Hammond) Travis; m. William Milne Osgood, Dec. 26, 1955 (div. 1985); children: Stephen Milne, Donald William. BS, Cornell U., 1956, PhD, 1980; MS, Lehman Coll., 1972. Lectr. Herbert H. Lehman Coll., Bronx, 1972-75; asst. prof. Cornell U., Ithaca, N.Y., 1978; staff scientist Coop. State Rsch. Svc., Washington, 1979; with Soil Conservation Svc., 1980—; asst. div. dir. Soil Conservation Svc., Washington, 1985-88; state conservationist Soil Conservation Svc., Somerset, N.J., 1988-91; liaison to EPA Soil Conservation Soc., Washington, 1991-92, assoc. dir. strategic planning and policy analysis, 1992-94, asst. chief, 1994, spl. asst., 1994—. Co-author: (book chpt.) Yearbook of Agriculture, 1986, Conserving Soil, 1986. Flora Rose fellow Cornell U., 1977. Mem. Rural Sociol. Soc., Soil and Water Conservation Soc., Am. Water Resources Assn., Phi Kappa Phi, Omicron Nu Hon. Soc. Methodist. Office: Soil Conservation Svc PO Box 2890 Washington DC 20013-2890

OSGOOD, CHRISTINE MAYER, early childhood educator, administrator; b. Pitts., Oct. 9, 1954; d. Wilbert Jacob and Shirley Elizabeth (Johnston) Mayer; m. Glenn Karl Burger, July 21, 1978 (div. Feb. 1993); 1 child, Liesl Elizabeth; m. Robert Alexander Osgood, Feb. 11, 1993; stepchildren: Hallie Elissa, Garrett Alexander. BS, Pa. State U., 1975, MEd, 1977; PhD, Iowa State U., 1984. Cert. tchr., Ariz., Iowa, N.C., Pa., C.C. tchr., Ariz. Youth edn. specialist Planned Parenthood, Pitts., 1976-78; asst. dir., tchr. Hickory Grove Child Devel. Ctr., Charlotte, N.C., 1978-79; faculty child devel. Des Moines Area C.C., Ankeny, Iowa, 1979-84; cons., evaluator Fairfax (Va.) County Pub. Schs., 1987-90; asst. prof., dir. Project for Study of Young Children George Mason U., Fairfax, 1984-90; program dir., instr. East Valley Inst. Tech., Mesa, Ariz., 1991-94; instr. Ctrl. Ariz. Coll., 1995—; cons. MacMillan Publ. Co., 1990, Ednl. Testing Svcs., 1990, Israeli Govt. and Tel Aviv U., 1990, Ariz. Dept. Edn., Phoenix, 1993. Contbr. articles and revs. to profl. jours. Vol. Houston Elem. Sch., Gilbert, Ariz., 1993-94. Grantee AAUW, 1986. Mem. NEA, Nat. Assn. for Edn. Young Children, Assn. for Childhood Edn. Internat., Omicron Nu. Democrat. Methodist. Home and Office: 517 E Moore Ave Gilbert AZ 85234

O'SHEA, CATHERINE LARGE, marketing and public relations consultant; b. Asheville, N.C., Feb. 27, 1944; d. Edwin Kirk Jr. and Mary Mitchell (Westall) Large; m. Roger Dean Lower, Dec. 19, 1970 (dec. Sept. 1977); children: Thaddeus Kirk Lower and David Alexander Lower (twins, dec.); m. Michael Joseph O'Shea, Dec. 29, 1980. BA in History magna cum laude, Emory U., 1966. Mktg. staff mem. Time Inc., N.Y.C., 1966-69; mktg. adminstr. Collier-Macmillan Internat., N.Y.C., 1970-71; circulation mgr. Coll. Entrance Exam. Bd., N.Y.C., 1971-73; spl. asst. to pres. Wayne Dressel Assocs. Exec. Search, N.Y.C., 1973-75; freelance writer, editor, pub. rels. Princeton, N.J., 1975-78; dir. constituency rels. Emory U., Atlanta, 1978-80; devel. assoc. U. Del., Newark, 1981-83; asst. to pres. Elizabethtown (Pa.) Coll., 1983-85; assoc. v.p. Beaver Coll., Glenside, Pa., 1985; cons. mktg. and pub. rels. Phila., S.C., 1985—. Co-author: 50 Secrets of Highly Successful Cats, 1994; editor Elizabethtown mag., 1983-85; contbr. articles to nat. mags. and profl. jours. Founder Helping Hands Internat.; Trustee Large Found., Newberry Opera House Found. Mem. Pub. Rels. Soc. Am. (accredited), Mortar Bd., Phi Beta Kappa, Phi Mu.

O'SHEA, LYNNE EDEEN, advertising executive, educator; b. Chgo., Oct. 18, 1945; d. Edward Fisk and Mildred (Lessner) O'S. B.A., B.J. in Polit. Sci. and Advt, U. Mo., 1968, M.A. in Communications and Mktg. Research, 1971; Ph.D. in Internat. Communications, Northwestern U., 1977; postgrad., Sch. Mgmt. and Strategic Studies, U. Calif., 1988. Pres. O'Shea Advt. Agy., Dallas, 1968-69; congl. asst. Washington, 1969-70; brand mgr. Procter & Gamble Co., Cin., 1971-73; v.p. Foote, Cone & Belding, Inc., Chgo., 1973-79; v.p. corp. communications Internat. Harvester Co., Chgo., 1979-82; dir. communications Arthur Andersen & Co., Chgo., 1983-86; v.p. strategic planning Campbell-Ewald, Detroit and Los Angeles, 1986; v.p. bus. devel. Gannett Co., Inc., Chgo., 1987-94; group strategic planning dir. DDB Needham Worldwide, Inc., Chgo., 1995—; prof. mktg. U. Chgo. Grad. Sch. Bus., 1979-80, Kellogg Grad. Sch. Mgmt., 1983-94; disting. vis. prof. Syracuse U., 1982—; mem. bd. dirs. Ben and Jerry's Homemade, Inc., 1995—. Bd. dirs. Off-the-Street Club, Chgo., 1977-86; mem. adv. bd. U. Ill. Coll. Commerce, 1980—, Ctr. for Mature Industries, 1982—, Girl Scouts Am., 1985—, Chgo. Crime Comn., 1987—, Stephenson Rsch. Ctr., 1987—, DePaul U., 1989—, Roosevelt U. Recipient numerous Eagle Fin. Advt. awards, Silver medalist Am. Advt. Fedn., 1989; named Advt. Woman of Yr. Chgo. Advt. Club, 1989; named to Glass Ceiling Commn. 1992-95, Com. 21st Century, 1992. Mem. Internat. Women's Forum (v.p. devel., exec. com., bd. dir.), Chgo. Network, Women's Forum Chgo., Women's Forum Mich., Tarrytown Group, Social Venture Network, Execs. Club Chgo., Mid-Am. Club (bd. govs. 1990—). Office: DDB Needham Worldwide Inc 303 E Wacker Dr Chicago IL 60601-5282

O'SHEA, PATRICIA A., physician, educator; b. Syracuse, N.Y., June 14, 1944; d. John Daniel and Mildred (Olbeter) Allen; m. John S. O'Shea, July 5, 1969. BS summa cum laude, Le Moyne Coll., 1966; MD, Johns Hopkins U., 1970. Diplomate Am. Bd. Pathology, Am. Bd. Anatomic, Clin. and Pediat. Pathology. From intern to resident Duke U. Med. Ctr., Durham, N.C., 1970-74; from asst. to assoc. prof. pathology Brown U., Providence, 1974-90; assoc. prof. pathology Emory U., Atlanta, 1990—; mem. faculty Armed Forces Inst., Washington, 1989; short-course faculty U.S. and Can. Acad. Pathology, Augusta, Ga., 1992—. Contbr. articles to profl. jours. Fellow Am. Acad. Pediats., Coll. Am. Pathologists; m. Soc. Pediat. Pathology (mem. coun.). Office: Egleston Children's Hosp Emory U 1405 Clifton Rd NE Atlanta GA 30322

OSHEROW, JACQUELINE SUE, poet, English language educator; b. Phila., Aug. 15, 1956; d. Aaron and Evelyn Hilda (Victor) O.; m. Saul Korewa, June 16, 1985; children: Magda, Dora, Mollie. AB Magna cum laude, Radcliffe Coll., Harvard U., 1978; postgrad., Trinity Coll., Cambridge U., 1978-79; PhD in English and Am. Lit., Princeton U., 1990. Asst. prof. English U. Utah, Salt Lake City, 1989—. Author: (poetry) Looking for Angels in New York, 1988, Conversations with Survivors, 1994. Recipient Witter Bynner prize Am. Acad. and Inst. Arts and Letters, 1990; Ingram Merrill Found. grantee, 1990. Mem. Poetry Soc. Am. (John Masefield Meml. award 1993). Jewish. Home: 1148 E 100 S Salt Lake City UT 84102-1640 Office: U Utah Dept English 3500 LNCO Salt Lake City UT 84112

OSHINS, GLADYS BARBARA, advertising executive; b. N.Y.C., Sept. 10, 1935; d. Louis and Dorothy (Greenberg) Bernstein; m. Elliot Howard Oshins, Apr. 4, 1965. BA, Bklyn. Coll., 1956. Media supr. The Zlowe Co., Inc., N.Y.C., 1958-68; v.p. assoc. media dir. Marsteller, Inc., N.Y.C., 1968-80; v.p. media dir. Intermarco Advt., Inc., N.Y.C., 1980-83; sr. v.p. assoc. media dir. Della Femina McNamee, Inc., EWDB Worldwide, N.Y.C., 1983-92; sr. v.p. media svc. dir. Hudson Media Group, Divsn. MVBMS/EURO RSCG, N.Y.C., 1993—. Office: Messner Vetere Berger McNamee Schmetterer 350 Hudson St New York NY 10014-4504

OSHIRO, SHARLEEN HATSUKO, lawyer; b. Honolulu, Feb. 12, 1951; d. Richard C. and Lillian S. (Hieda) O.; m. Allen T. Hagio, Oct. 1969 (div. July 1974); 1 child, Juli Ann; m. Rodney Y. Sato, Nov. 6, 1982; children: Samantha, Seanna, Rian. BA, U. Hawaii, 1973, JD, 1980. Bar: Hawaii 1980, U.S. Dist. Ct. Hawaii 1980, U.S. Ct. Appeals (9th cir.) 1981. Dep. atty. gen. Dept. of Atty. Gen., Honolulu, 1980-85; v.p., legal counsel Servco Pacific Inc., Honolulu, 1985—. Mem. Hawaii Bar Assn. Democrat. Home: 95-155 Waikalani Dr Mililani Town HI 96789 Office: Servco Pacific Inc 900 Fort Street Mall Ste 500 Honolulu HI 96813-3777

OSKEY, D. BETH, banker; b. Red Wing, Minn., Dec. 23, 1921; d. Alvin E. and Effie D. (Thompson) Feldman; m. Warren B. Oskey, Sept. 27, 1941; children: Jo Cheryl, Warren A., Peter (dec.), Jeffery L.; student U. Wis., River Falls, 1939-41; B.A., Met. State U., Minn., 1975; grad. degree in banking, U. Wis., 1973, M in banking, 1977; student in interior decorating LaSalle Extension U., Chgo., 1970. Officer Hiawatha Nat. Bank, Hager City, Wis., 1959-91, cashier, 1978-79, pres., 1979, chmn. bd., 1984—, exec. v.p., dir., sec. bd. dirs., 1959—, sec., mem. discount com.; with First Nat. Bank of Glenwood, Glenwood City, Wis., 1965—, pres., exec. v.p., 1979—, dir., sec. bd., 1965—, chmn. bd., 1984—, sec., mem. discount com.; ret., 1991; speaker on women in banking. Mem. banking com. Vo-Tech Sch., Red Wing; former officer civic orgns.; mem. Leisurettes, L.W. Barbershop Belles. Mem. AAUW, Ind. Bankers Am., Wis. Bankers Assn., Am. Bankers Assn., Gen. Fedn. Women's Clubs Internat., Inc. (bd. dirs., pres. 1988-90), Minn. Fedn. Women's Clubs (v.p. 1983-85, pres. dist. III 1988-90, pres. elect 1986-88, pres. 1988-90; Leisure World (in charge of comm., mem. mixed chorus), Mesa, Ariz. (pres. Wis. Club, 1991-92). Republican. Lutheran. Home: 1022 Hallstrom Dr Red Wing MN 55066-3819 also: 1561 Leisure World Mesa AZ 85206 Office: Hiawatha Nat Bank Hager City WI 54014

OSLER, DOROTHY K., state legislator; b. Dayton, Ohio, Aug. 19, 1923; d. Carl M. and Pearl A. (Tobias) Karstaedt; BS cum laude in Bus. Adminstrn., Miami U., Oxford, Ohio, 1945; m. David K. Osler, Oct. 26, 1946; children: Scott C., David D. Mem. Conn. Ho. of Reps., 1973-92. Mem. Greenwich (Conn.) Rep. Town Meeting, 1968—, Eastern Greenwich Women's Rep. Club, 1970—; sec. Conn. Student Loan Found., 1973-83, v.p., 1983-84; mem. Spl. Edn. Cost Commn., 1976-77, Sch. Fin. Adv. Panel, 1977-78, Edn. Equity Study Com., 1980-81, Commn. on Goals for U. Conn. Health Ctr., 1975-76; bd. dirs. ARC, 1975. Mem. Nat. Order Women Legislators (sec. 1987-89), Conn. Order of Women Legislators (sec. 1983-84, pres. 1985-86), LWV (pres. Greenwich chpt. 1965-67, sec. Conn. chpt. 1967-72), AAUW (dir. 1971-73), Mortar Board, Phi Beta Kappa, Alpha Omicron Pi. Republican. Christian Scientist. Bi-weekly columnist local newspaper, 1973-83.

OSLICK, MARLENE TANNENBAUM, accountant, educator; b. Phila., Apr. 13, 1939; d. Harry and Clara Sarah (Sperling) Tannenbaum; m. Harold Oslick, June 14, 1959; children: Marci Lynn, Rochelle, Harvey Raymond, Jeffrey Sheldon. Diploma in teaching, Gratz Coll., 1958; BS in Edn., Temple U., 1960; MBA, Fairleigh Dickinson U., 1985. CPA; cert. secondary, math. and physical sci. tchr., N.J. Tchr. B'nai Aaron, Phila., 1958-59, Temple Beth El, West Hartford, Conn., 1960-63, Temple Beth Hillel, Bloomfield, Conn., 1963-68; co-owner, mgr. Park Crescent, Plainfield, N.J., 1977-78; supr. field ops., instr. bur. census U.S. Dept. Commerce, Elizabeth, N.J., 1980; with bus. and fin. communications Regisgard, Ltd. div. W.E. Connor, Seoul, Republic of Korea, 1983-84; controller Leonard Engring., Inc., Cranford, N.J., 1986-87; sr. staff acct. Lerman & Co. CPAs, now Bederson & Co., West Orange, N.J., 1988-91; CPA Sanford, Holzer & Co. CPAs, Westfield, N.J., 1992-93; site controller Gen. Foam Corp. (div. PMC, Inc.), 1993—; sec. Plainfield Bd. Jewish Edn., 1972-74. Author (mag.) Outlook, 1986; editor (mag.) Bus. Korea, 1984. Leader Girl Scouts U.S., Westfield, N.J., 1968-72; den mother Cub Scouts Boy Scouts Am., Westfield, 1973-74, 78; co-pres. Sisterhood of Temple Beth-El, Cranford, N.J., 1990-93. Mem. AICPA, N.J. Soc. CPAs (acctg. educators and students com., scholarship awards com.), Women's League for Conservative Judaism (nat. social action com.), Seoul Internat. Women's Assn., Nat. Council Jewish Women, Hadassah (Westfield chpt., v.p. fundraising 1978-80), Cedar Mar Yacht Club, Sigma Pi Sigma. Home: 847 Nancy Way Westfield NJ 07090-3424 Office: W 100 Century Rd Paramus NJ 07652

OSMAN, EDITH GABRIELLA, lawyer; b. N.Y.C., Mar. 18, 1949; d. Arthur Abraham and Judith (Goldman) Udem; children: Jacqueline, Daniel. BA in Spanish, SUNY, Stony Brook, 1970; JD cum laude, U. Miami, 1983. Bar: Fla. 1983, U.S. Dist. Ct. (so. dist.) Fla. 1984, U.S. Dist. Ct. (mid. dist.) Fla. 1988, U.S. Ct. Appeals (11th cir.) 1985, U.S. Supreme Ct. 1987, U.S. Ct. Mil. Appeals 1990. Assoc. Kimbrell & Hamann, P.A., Miami, 1984-90, Dunn & Lodish, P.A., Miami, 1990-93; pvt. practice in law Miami, 1993—; spkr. in field. Mem. adv. com. for Implementation of the Victor Posner Judgement to Aid the Homeless, 1986-89; spkr. small firm and solo practitioner Town Hall Meetings, 1993; spkr. Bridge the Gap Seminar, Comml. Litigation, 1994. Mem. ABA (product liability com., corp. counsel com.), Fla. Bar Assn. (budget com. 1989-92, voluntary bar liaison com. 1989-90, spl. com. on formation of All-Bar Conf. 1988-89, chmn. mid-yr. conv. 1989, mem. long range planning com. 1988-90, bd. govs. 1991—, spl. commn. on delivery of legal svcs. to the indigent 1990-92, chair program evaluation com. bd. govs., mem. exec. com. 1992-93, rules & bylaws com. 1993-94, dipciplinary rev. com. 1994—, investment com., 1994—, vice chair rules com., 1994—), Dade County Bar Assn. (fed. ct. rules com. 1985-86, chmn. program com. 1988-89, 90-91, exec. com. 1987-88), Fla. Assn. of Bar Assn. Pres.'s (bd. dirs. 1988-89, treas. 1989-90, v.p. 1990-91, pres. 1991-92), Fla. Assn. Women Lawyers (bd. dirs. 1985-86, v.p. Dade County chpt. 1986-87, pres. 1987-88, pres. elect Fla. chpt. 1988-89, pres. 1989-90), Nat. Coun. of Women's Bar Assn. (dir. nat. conf. 1990-91), Dade County Trial Lawyers Assn. Office: Edith G Osman PA Internat Place 100 SE 2nd St Ste 3920 Miami FL 33131-2148

OSMAN, MARY ELLA WILLIAMS, journal editor; b. Honea Path, S.C.; d. Humphrey Bates and Jennie Louise (Williams) Williams; student Coll. William and Mary, Ga. State Coll. for Women; A.B., Presbyn. Coll., 1939; B.S. in L.S., U. N.C., 1944; m. John Osman, Oct. 22, 1936. Asst. libr. Presbyn. Coll., Clinton, S.C., 1936-38, Union Theol. Sem., Richmond, Va., 1938-44; sr. cataloger, asst. libr. Rhodes Coll., Memphis, 1944-52; asst. test cities project Ford Found. Fund for Adult Edn., N.Y.C., 1952-57, assoc. dir. office of info., 1957-61, exec. asst. to pres., sec. to bd. dirs., 1960-61; asst.

libr. AIA, Washington, 1962-68, asst. editor AIA Jour., 1969-72, assoc. editor, 1972-77, sr. editor, 1978-87. Mem. AIA (hon.), Chi Delta Phi, Kappa Delta. Presbyn. Contbr. to various mags. Home: 3600 Chateau Dr Apt 244 Columbia SC 29204-3971

OSMER-MCQUADE, MARGARET, business executive, broadcast journalist; b. N.Y.C.; d. Herbert Bernard and Margaret Normann (Brunjes) O.; m. Lawrence Carroll McQuade, Mar. 15, 1980; 1 son, Andrew. B.A., Cornell U., 1960. Assoc. producer UN Bur., CBS News, N.Y.C., 1962-69; producer 60 Minutes, N.Y.C., 1969-72; reporter, producer Bill Moyer's Jour., Pub. Broadcasting Service, N.Y.C., 1972-73, Reasoner Report, ABC News, N.Y.C., 1973-75; corr., anchor person Good Morning Am., ABC Morning News, Washington, 1975-77; corr. ABC TV News, Washington, 1977-79; v.p., dir. programs Council on Fgn. Relations, 1979-93; pres., CEO Qualitas Internat., N.Y.C., 1994—; dir. Dime Savs. Bank, 1980—; cons. pub. broadcasting; mem. program com. Ditchley Found. Producer, reporter: TV news shows Come Fly A Kite (Nat. Press Photographer's award 1974), Kissinger, 1970, No Tears for Rachel, 1972, Calder: Master of Mobiles, 1975; moderator, producer World in Focus, publ. TV series for Coun. Fgn. Relations/Sta. WNYC, PBS, Worldnet, 1988-93. Mem. U.S. delegation World Conf. on Cambodian Refugees, Geneva, 1980; mem. Def. Adv. Com. on Women in the Service, 1978-82; trustee Cornell U.; mem. bd. overseers Cornell U. Med. Coll., pres.'s coun. Cornell Women; mem. program com. The Ritchley Found., 1994—, task force N.Y. Sch. Vols., 1994—; vol. Nat. Svc. Learning, 1994—. Recipient Peabody award Staff of 60 Minutes, 1970. Mem. NATAS, Coun. Fgn. Relations, program comm. The Mitching Found., Task Force N.Y. Sch. Vol., Nat. Press Club, Mid. Atlantic Club., vol. Nat. Svc. Learning. Club: Cosmopolitan, Century.

OSNES, PAMELA GRACE, special education educator; b. Burke, S.D., Sept. 10, 1955; d. John Ruben and Dortha Grace (Wilson) O.; m. Trevor F. Stokes, Apr. 2, 1982; children: Jocelyn Fern, Logan John. BS in Spl. Edn., U. S.D., 1977, BS in Elem. Edn., 1977; MA in Clin. Psychology, W.Va. U., 1981. Spl. edn. tchr. Sioux Falls (S.D.) Sch. Dist., 1977-79; instr. psychology dept. W.Va. U., Morgantown, 1982-85; dir. Carousel Preschool Program, Morgantown, 1982-85; assoc. prof. U. South Fla., Tampa, 1986-93; dir. Carousel Psychol., ednl. and Family Svcs., Pasco County, Fla., 1993—. Mem. Assn. for Behavior Analysis, Coun. for Exceptional Children (div. early childhood, div. rsch., tchr. edn. div.), Coun. Adminstrs. Spl. Edn., Coun. for Children with Behavior Disorders.

OSORIO, ROSA ERNESTINA, marketing professional, advertising executive; b. Jinotega, Nicaragua, Sept. 11, 1945; came to U.S., 1979; d. Guillermo and Maria (Reyes) Noguera; m. Ivan L. Osorio, Sept. 5, 1965; children: Ivan G., Claudia M. Student, Cath. U., Managua, Nicaragua, 1964-66. Asst. to pres. Fed. Res. Bank of Nicaragua, Managua, 1963-65; asst. to pres. Alfa Omega SA de Publicidad, Managua, 1965-67, gen. mgr., 1967-74; exec. dir. Continental de Inversiones, SA, Managua, 1974-79; exec. v.p. Edipsa of Miami, 1979-85, Americonsult, Inc., Miami, 1985—. Mem. citizens bd. dirs. U. Miami; dir. L.Am. Adv. Coun., Miami, 1979; promotion dir. Ruben Dario Nat. Theatre, Managua, 1970-79; hon. mem. Nat. Tourist Coun. Nicaragua, 1976; hon. dir. constrn. com. Nicaraguan Children's Hosp., Managua, 1979. Recipient Keys to the Cities of Hialeah (Fla.) and New Orleans. Mem. Camara de Comercio Latina, Bus. and Profl. Womens Club (pres. Managua 1971-76). Republican. Roman Catholic. Office: Americonsult 7855 NW 12th St Ste 221 Miami FL 33126-1819

OSOWIEC, DARLENE ANN, post-doctoral clinical psychology fellow, educator, consultant; b. Chgo., Feb. 16, 1951; d. Stephen Raymond and Estelle Marie Osowiec; m. Barry A. Leska. BS, Loyola U., Chgo., 1973; MA with honors, Roosevelt U., 1980; postgrad. in psychology, Saybrook Inst., San Francisco, 1985-88; PhD in Clin. Psychology, Calif. Inst. Integral Studies, 1992. Mental health therapist Ridgeway Hosp., Chgo., 1978; mem. faculty psychology dept. Coll. Lake County, Grayslake, Ill., 1981; counselor, supr. MA-level interns, chmn. pub. rels. com. Integral Counseling Ctr., San Francisco, 1983-84; clin. psychology intern Chgo.-Read Mental Health Ctr. Ill. Dept. Mental Health, 1985-86; mem. faculty dept. psychology Moraine Valley C.C., Palos Hills, Ill., 1988-89; lectr. psychology Daley Coll., Chgo., 1988-90; cons. Gordon & Assocs., Oak Lawn, Ill., 1989—; adolescent, child and family therapist Orland Twp. Youth Svcs., Orland Park, Ill., 1993; psychology fellow Sch. Medicine, St. Louis U., 1994—. Ill. State scholar, 1969-73; Calif. Inst. Integral Studies scholar, 1983. Mem. AACD, APA, Am. Women in Psychology, Am. Statis. Assn., Ill. Psychol. Assn., Calif. Psychol. Assn., Internat. Assn. Marriage and Family Counselors, Am. Soc. Clin. Hypnosis, Internat. Platform Assn., Chgo. Clin. Hypnosis, NOW (chair legal advocate corps, Chgo. 1974-76). Office: St Louis U Sch Medicine 1221 S Grand Blvd Saint Louis MO 63104

OSSEWAARDE, ANNE WINKLER, real estate developer; b. Dallas, June 2, 1957; d. Lowell Graves and Ruth Lenore (Lind) Winkler; m. Kirk L Ossewaarde, Apr. 27, 1991. BBA in Fin. with honors, Emory U., 1979; MBA in Acctg. and Fin., U. Tex., 1983; MS in Real Estate Devel., MIT, 1988. Mgmt. trainee Citizens & So. Nat. Bank, Atlanta, 1979-81; banking assoc. Continental Ill. Nat. Bank, Chgo. and Dallas, 1983-85; asst. v.p., devel. assoc. Trammell Crow Residential, Dallas, 1985-87, Seattle, 1988-91; devel. mgr. Blackhawk Port Blakeley Cmtys., Seattle, 1991-93; real estate portfolio mgr. Aegon U.S.A. Realty, Atlanta, 1994—. Charles Harritt Jr. Presdl. scholar U. Tex., 1982, Alexander Grant scholar, 1982. Mem. Jr. League of Atlanta, Comml. Real Estate Women, MIT Ctr. for Real Estate Alumni Assn., Alpha Epsilon Upsilon. Methodist. Home: 5510 Mount Vernon Pky NW Atlanta GA 30327-4739

OSTASZEWSKI, ALYCE VITELLA, religion educator; b. Chgo., Apr. 24, 1936; d. Peter Anthony and Cleta Earline (Chastain) Indelli; m. Gerald Earl Nelson (div. 1967); children: Peter J., Maryalice C., William P., Paula A.; m. Stanley Joseph Ostaszewski; children: Vinson Shaw, Stacean V. Grad. high sch., Chgo., 1954. Tchr. religious edn. St. John the Evangelist Ch., Streamwood, Ill., 1962-68; tchr. religious edn., facilitator Rite of Christian Initiation of Adults, St. Thomas More Ch., Elgin, Ill., 1980-86; tchr. religious edn., young adult min. St. Julie Billiart Ch., Newbury Park, Calif., 1987-89, confirmation coord., 1990-91; confirmation asst. coord. St. Paschal Baylon Ch., Thousand Oaks, Calif., 1991-92; master chatechist, basic faith formation educator L.A. Diocese, Santa Barbara Region, 1990-93; com. mem. Santa Barbara Regional Conf., 1988-93; confirmation tchr. Holy Cross Parish, Batavia, Ill., 1993-94; 3rd grade religion edn. tchr., 1994—. Sec. Village of Streamwood Homeowners Assn., 1957-58; bd. dirs. Oak Ridge Estates Homeowners Assn., Newbury Park, Calif., 1986-88; lifetime mem. Streamwood Hist. Soc., 1993—; woman's team 7 C.R.H.P. Witness'er, 1994; mem. choir.

OSTENDORF, JOAN DONAHUE, fund raiser, volunteer; b. Boston, Dec. 9, 1933; d. John Stanley and Genevieve Catherine (Morrissey) Donahue; m. Edgar Louis Ostendorf, Feb. 10, 1962; 1 child, Mary Elizabeth. BA, Marymount Coll., Tarrytown, N.Y., 1956; postgrad., Boston U., 1956. Tchr. Boston pub. schs., 1956-57, Waltham (Mass.) pub. schs., 1957-62. Trustee Cleve. Inst. Music, 1984—, mem. trustees coordianting coun., 1989; mem. Jr. League Cleve., 1964, 1st v.p. 1972-73; founder adv. coun. pub. rels. com. Cleve. Orch., 1974, 1st v.p., 1975-76; mem. del. assembly United Way, 1977-87; chmn. benefits Vis. Nurse Assn., 1987-88, March Dimes, 1982; trustee women's com. U. Hosps. Case Western Res. U. Med. Sch., 1974—; mem. nominating com. Inst. Music, 1990-91; 2d v.p. Music and Drama Club, 1991-93, corresponding sec., 1993—; chair Lyric Opera, 1992, Platform Assn., 1992—; pres. bd. trustees Cleve. Inst. Music, 1980-82, pres. women's com., 1980-82; mem. adv. bd. Women's Community Found., 1991—; v.p. Cleve. Internat. Piano Competition, 1994—. Mem. Internat. Platform Assn., Longwood Cricket Club, Intown Club, Chagrin Valley Hunt Club. Republican. Roman Catholic. Address: 3425 Roundwood Rd Chagrin Falls OH 44022-6634

OSTENDORF, JOELLEN, librarian; b. Blue Island, Ill., Oct. 26, 1951; d. Charles Henry and Mildred MArie (Remig) O. BS in Communications, U. Ill., 1973, MLS, 1976. Cert. libr. Libr. U. Ill., Champaign, 1976, Miss. Libr. Commn., Jackson, 1976-77; head libr. Miss. Libr. Commn. Svc. for Handicapped, Jackson, 1977-87; libr. cons. Ga. Div. Pub. Pinr. Svcs., Atlanta, 1987-91, assoc. dir., 1992—; treas. Miss. Libr. Assn., Jackson, 1986-87; program chmn. Miss. Assn. of Workers for the Blind, Jackson, 1982-84; founder Friends of Handicapped, Jackson, 1981. Contbg. author: School Library Media Services for the Handicapped, 1982, (manuals) Reading Can Bd For Everyone, 1981, GOLD Procedures, 1991; editor: (periodical) DIKTA, 1983. Active Lit. Vols. Am., 1991—; vol. Alliance Theatre, Atlanta, 1990—. Mem. ALA, Southeastern Libr. Assn. (interlibr. use roundtable nominating com. 1991), Ga. Libr. Assn., Ga. Online Database Adv. Com. (chmn. 1988-90), Assn. Specialized and Coop. Libr. Agys. (Interface editorial bd. 1991—), OCLC Users Coun. (del. 1992—), Nat. Wildlife Fedn. Office: Div Pub Libr Svcs 156 Trinity Ave SW Atlanta GA 30303-3600

OSTENSO, GRACE LAUDON, legislative staff director; b. Tomah, Wis., 1932; d. Charles C. and Ruby G. (Lamb) Laudon; m. Ned A. Ostenso, Jun. 29, 1963. BS, U. Wis., Stout, 1954; MS, U. Wis., Madison, 1960, PhD, 1963. Rsch. asst. U. Wis., Madison, 1959-63, prof., 1963-67; assoc. editor Encyclopaedia Britannica, 1967-70; br. chief nutrition and tech. Food and Nutrition Svc., Dept. Agrl., Washington, 1970-73, dir. nutrition and tech., 1973-78; sci. cons. Ho. Com. on Sci., Space and Tech., Washington, 1978-87, staff dir., sub-com. on sci., rsch. and tech., 1987-91, staff dir. sub-com. on sci., 1991—. Contbd. articles to profl. jours. Mem. AAAS, Am. Dietetic Assn., Inst. Food Tech., Am. Inst. Nutrition, Am. Pub. Health Assn. Office: Subcom Sci Research & Tech 2319 Rayburn House Office Bldg Washington DC 20515*

OSTERKAMP, DALENE MAY, psychology educator, artist; b. Davenport, Iowa, Dec. 1, 1932; d. James Hiram and Bernice Grace (La Grange) Simmons; m. Donald Edwin Osterkamp, Feb. 11, 1951 (dec. Sept. 1951). BA, San Jose State U., 1959, MA, 1962; PhD, Saybrook Inst., 1989. Lectr. San Jose (Calif.) State U., 1960-61, U. Santa Barbara (Calif.) Ext., 1970-76; prof. Bakersfield (Calif.) Coll., 1961-87, emeritus, 1987—; adj. faculty, counselor Calif. State U., Bakersfield, 1990—; gallery dir. Bakersfield Coll., 1964-72. Exhibited in group shows at Berkeley (Calif.) Art, Ctr., 1975, Libr. of Congress, 1961, Seattle Art Mus., 1962. Founder Kern Art Edn. Assn., Bakersfield, 1962, Bakersfield Printmakers, 1976. Staff sgt. USAF, 1952-55. Recipient 1st Ann. Svc. to Women award Am. Assn. Women in C.C., 1989. Mem. APA, Assn. for Women in Psychology, Assn. for Humanistic Psychology, Calif. Soc. Printmakers. Home: PO Box 387 Glennville CA 93226 Office: Calif State Univ Stockdale Ave Bakersfield CA 93309

OSTERMAN, CONSTANTINE ELAINE, Canadian legislator; b. Acme, Alta., Can., June 23, 1936; m. Joe Osterman, Oct. 30, 1954; children: Theo, Kurt, Kim, Kelly, Joe Jr. MLA representing Three Hills constituency Alta. Legis. Assembly, 1979-92, party whip, mem. edn. caucus and agr. caucus coms., 1982-86, minister of consumer and corp. affairs, mem. social planning com. of cabinet, cabinet/caucus com. on legis. rev., agr. caucus com., 1986, minister of social svcs. and community health, 1986-89, minister career devel. and employment, chair econ. devel., 1989-92; retired Alta. Legis. Assembly, Three Hills, 1992; served select legis. com. to rev. surface rights issue, lead role in passing of Surface Rights Act, 1983. Active exec. bds. local ch., home and sch. assns., Carstairs, Alta., 1958—, surface rights area; commr., charter mem. Alta. Human Rights Commn., 1973-78; pres. Can. Assn. Statutory Human Rights Agys. Address: RR # 1, Carstairs, AB Canada

OSTERTAG-HOLTKAMP, BARBARA JEAN, librarian, supervisor; b. New Britain, Conn., June 5, 1962; d. Agnes (Borawski) Ostertag; m. Richard Tido Holtkamp, July 21, 1990. BS in Mgmt./Adminstrn. Sci., Cen. Conn. State U., 1985. Reference rm. asst. Cen. Conn. State U., Elibu Burritt Libr., New Britain, Conn., 1981-84; retail sales/mgmt. Sears Roebuck & Co., West Hartford, Conn., 1980-86; libr. asst. U. Conn. Health Ctr., Lyman Maynard Stowe Libr., Farmington, Conn., 1986; acct. rep. Combustion Engring., Windsor, Conn., 1986; evening supr. U. Conn. Health Ctr., Lyman Maynard Stowe Libr., Farmington, 1986-90; tech. svcs. supr. Blackwell North Am., Lake Oswego, Oreg., 1990-92; supr. shelving divsn. Beaverton (Oreg.) City Libr., 1992—. Mem. NAFE. Home: Apt 264 29645 SW Rose Ln Wilsonville OR 97070

OSTROFF MASTROPASQUA, MARIA ISABELLA, guidance counselor; b. Molfetta, Puglia, Italy, July 21, 1953; came to U.S., 1966; d. Lorenzo and Carmenantonia Mastropasqua; m. Saul Joseph Ostroff, Mar. 18, 1979 (div. Mar. 1991); children: Daniel Benjamin Ostroff, Jonathan Jesse Ostroff. BA, Ramapo Coll. N.J., 1976; MEd, U. Ariz., 1982, EdD, 1993. Cert. profl. counselor, Ariz., guidance counselor K-12, art tchr. K-12. Asst. curator collections Tucson Mus. Art, 1978-80; allied health counselor Pima C.C., Tucson, summer 1983; tchr. art and Spanish Oracle (Ariz.) Elem. Sch. Dist. # 2, 1980-84; maternal and child health counselor Cath. Community Svcs., Tucson, 1984-86; guidance counselor Tucson High Magnet Sch. Tucson Unified Sch. Dist., 1985—; participant, mentor Tucson Unified Sch. Dist. Leadership Acad., 1992—; counselor, facilitator Seven-Challenges Program, Tucson, 1992—; presenter in field. Contbr. rsch. articles to profl. publs. Fellow U. Ariz., 1992-93. Mem. ASCD, Am. Assn. Counseling and Devel., N.Am. Soc. Adlerian Psychology, Adlerian Soc. of Ariz. Democrat. Roman Catholic. Home: 4226 E Kilmer St Tucson AZ 85711 Office: Tucson High Magnet Sch 400 N 2d Ave Tucson AZ 85705

OSTROW, RONA LYNN, librarian, educator; b. N.Y.C., Oct. 21, 1948; d. Morty and Jeane Goldberg; m. Steven A. Ostrow, June 25, 1972; 1 child, Ciné Justine. BA, CCNY, 1969; MS in LS, Columbia U., 1970; MA, Hunter Coll., 1975; doctoral student, Rutgers U., 1990—. Cert. libr., N.Y. Br. adult and reference libr. N.Y. Pub. Libr., N.Y.C., 1970-73, rsch. libr., 1973-78; asst. libr. Fashion Inst. Tech., N.Y.C., 1978-80; assoc. dir. Grad. Bus. Resource Ctr., Baruch Coll., CUNY, 1980-90, assoc. prof., 1980-90; assoc. dean of librs. for pub. svcs. Adelphi U., Garden City, N.Y., 1990—. Author: Dictionary of Retailing, 1984, Dictionary of Marketing, 1987; co-author: Cross Reference Index, 1989. Mem. ALA, NAFE, Libr. Info. and Tech. Assn., Assn. Coll. and Rsch. Librs. Office: Swirbul Libr Adelphi South Ave Garden City NY 11530

OSTRY, SYLVIA, academic administrator, economist; b. Winnipeg, Man., Can.; d. Morris J. and B. (Stoller) Knelman; m. Bernard Ostry; children: Adam, Jonathan. BA in Econs., McGill U., 1948, MA, 1950; PhD, Cambridge U. and McGill U., 1954; also 17 hon. degrees. Lectr., asst. prof. econs. McGill U.; research officer Inst. Stats., U. Oxford, Eng.; assoc. prof. U. Montreal, Can.; with dept. stats. Econ. Coun. Can., Ottawa, 1964-72, chmn., 1978-79; chief statistician Stats. Can., Ottawa, 1972-75; dep. minister consumer and corp. affairs Govt. Can., Ottawa, 1975-78, dep. minister internat. trade, coordinator internat. econ. relations, 1984-85, ambassador for multilateral trade negotiations, personal rep. of Prime Minister for Econ. Summit, 1985-88; chancellor U. Waterloo, 1991—; head dept. econs. and stats. OECD, Paris, 1979-83; chmn. U. Toronto, Ont., Can., 1990—; lectr. Per Jacobssen Found., 1987; chmn. nat. coun. Can. Inst. Internat. Affairs, 1990—; western co-chmn. Blue Ribbon Commn. for Hungary's Econ. Recovery, 1990—; chmn. internat. adv. bd. Bank of Montreal; bd. dirs. Power Fin. Corp., mem. internat. adv. coun. UN U. World/World Inst. Devel. Econs. Rsch., Helsinki; expert advisor Commn. Transnat. Corps., UN; mem. internat. com. InterAm. Devel. Bank/Econ. Commn. L.Am.-Carribbean Project; mem. acad. adv. bd. World Orgn. Rehab. through Tng., London. Author: Governments and Corporations in a Shrinking World: The Search for Stability, 1990, The Threat of Managed Trade to Transforming Economies; co-author: (with Richard Nelson) Technonationalism and Technoglobalism: Conflict and Cooperation, 1995; co-editor: (with others) Rethinking Federalism: Citizens, Markets and Governments in a Changing World, 1994; contbr. articles on empirical and policy-analytic subjects to more than 90 profl. publs. Decorated companion Order of Can.; recipient Outstanding Achievement award Govt. of Can., 1987, Hon. Assoc. award Conf. Bd. of Can., 1992; Disting. vis. fellow Volvo, 1989-90, U. Toronto fellow, 1989-90. Fellow Royal Soc. Can., Am. Statis. Assn.; mem. Am. Econ. Assn., Can. Econ. Assn., Royal Econ. Soc. (founding), Ctr. for European Policy Studies (internat. adv. coun.), Group of Thirty, Inst. for Internat. Econs. (adv. bd.). Office: U Toronto Ctr Int Studies, 170 Bloor St W 5th Fl, Toronto, ON Canada M5S 1T9

OSUCH, GWYNETH ERION, minister; b. Milw., Jan. 15, 1926; d. Herman Edward and Florence Louise (Olsen) Erion; m. Carl Osuch, July 31, 1948; children: Christopher, Jonathan, Pamela, Elizabeth. BS, Antioch Coll., 1948; MDiv, Dubuque (Iowa) Theol. Sem., 1970. Ordained minister Presbyn. Ch. Chaplain Dubuque (Iowa) Theol. Sem., 1977-78; pastor United Meth. Ch., Wyoming, Iowa, 1981-82; interim pastor Community United Ch. of Christ, Savanna, Ill., 1983-84; pastoral care Westminster Presbyn., Dubuque, 1986-87; interim pastor First United Ch. of Christ, Clinton, Iowa, 1988, Yoked Parish, United Ch. of Christ, Platteville, Wis., 1988-90, Immanuel United Ch. of Christ, Dubuque, 1990, First Presbyn. Ch., Bellevue, Iowa, 1992-93; adj. prof. Dubuque Theol. Sem., 1994-95; ruling elder Westminster Presbyn. Ch., Dubuque, 1971-74; moderator N.E. Iowa Presbytery, 1975, John Knox Presbytery, 1988. Bd. mem., counselor Pastoral Marriage Counseling Svc., Dubuque, 1970-74; bd. mem. Bethany Home, Dubuque, 1986-91, 93-95, ARC Dubuque Chpt., 1987-88. Mem. AAUW.

O'SULLIVAN, EILEEN ANN, banker; b. Phila., May 7, 1956; d. Thomas and Elisabeth (Kiehl) O'S. Student, Ctr. for Fin. Studies, Fairfield, Conn., 1988, U. Pa., 1994—. Teller trainee Beneficial Savs. Bank, Phila., 1974-75, jr. teller, 1975-80, teller #2, 1980-81, teller #3, 1981-82, head teller, 1982-84, mgmt. trainee, 1984-85, asst. mgr., 1975-87, mgr., 1987—. Co-chmn. Widener Day com. Widener Meml. Sch., 1987—; mem., speaker community workshops 35th Police Dist., 1986—, chmn. holiday meals program, 1988—; sec. Greater Broad and Olney Bus. Assn., 1984-88; assoc. mem. Phila. Orch. Soc., 1987-91, 94—; mem. Smithsonian Inst., 1988—, Univ. Mus. Univ. Pa., 1991, neighborhood improvement coun. Phila. Neighborhood Housing Svcs., 1989, Earthwatch, 1990, Pa. Soc. for Prevention of Cruelty to Animals, 1990. Recipient Community Svc. award Phila. Police Dept., 1987, 88, 89, 91. Mem. Nat. Space-L5 Soc. (life). Democrat. Roman Catholic. Office: Beneficial Savs Bank 2 Penn Ctr Concourse Philadelphia PA 19102-1701

O'SULLIVAN, JUDITH ROBERTA, author, legal association administrator; b. Pitts., Jan. 6, 1942; d. Robert Howard and Mary Olive (O'Donnell) Gallick; m. James Paul O'Sullivan, Feb. 1, 1964; children: Kathryn, James. BA, Carlow Coll., 1963; MA, U. Md., 1969, PhD, 1976; postgrad. in law, Georgetown U., 1992—. Editor Am. Film Inst., Washington, 1974-77; assoc. program coord. Smithsonian Resident Assocs., Washington, 1977-78; dir. instl. devel. Nat. Archives, Washington, 1978-79; exec. dir. Md. State Humanities Coun., Balt., 1979-81, 82-84, Ctr. for the Book, Libr. of Congress, Washington, 1981-82; dep. asst. dir. Nat. Mus. Am. Art, Washington, 1984-87, acting asst. dir., 1987-89; pres., chief exec. officer The Museums at Stony Brook,, N.Y., 1989-92; exec. dir. Nat. Assn. Women Judges, Washington, 1993; clk. Office Legal Advisor U.S. Dept. of State, Greenbelt, 1994—; chair Smithsonian Women's Coun., Washington, 1988-89; mem. editorial advisory bd. Am. Film Inst., 1979—. Author: The Art of the Comic Strip, 1971 (gen. excellence award Printing Industry Am.), Workers and Allies, 1975, (with Alan Fern) The Complete Prints of Leonard Baskin, 1984, The Great American Comic Strip, 1991; editor Am. Film Inst. Catalogue: Feature Films, 1961-70, 1974-77. Trustee Child Life Ctr., U. Md., College Pk., 1971-74; chair Smithsonian Women's Coun., 1988-89. Univ. fellow U. Md., 1967-70, Mus. fellow, 1970-71; Smithsonian fellow Nat. Collection Fine Arts, Washington, 1972-73. Mem. Assn. Assn. Art Mus. Dirs., Am. Assn. Mus., Mid-Atlantic Mus. Conf., AAUW. Home: 17 Ridge Rd # F Greenbelt MD 20770-1749

OSWALD, EVA SUE ADEN, insurance executive; b. Ft. Dodge, Iowa, Feb. 2, 1949; d. Warren Dale Aden and Alice Rae (Gingerich) Aspeslet; m. Bruce Elliott Oswald, Nov. 27, 1976. BBS, U. Iowa, 1972. With Great Am. Ins. Co., 1975—; v.p. mktg. div. Great Am. Ins. Co., Orange, Calif., 1987, v.p. profit ctr., 1988-90; pres. Garden of Eva, Inc., 1990—; mem. Snelling-Selby Bus. Coun. Mem. Nat. Assn. Ins. Women, State Guarantee Fund (bd. dirs. 1986-87), Exec. Women St. Paul, Midway C. of C., White Bear Lake C. of C. Methodist. Office: 1585 Marshall Ave Saint Paul MN 55104

OTAYA, MICHIKO, nurse; b. Iwakuni-City, Japan, Mar. 14, 1949. AA, L.A. City Coll.; BSN, Calif. State U., L.A., 1974, BA in Japanese Lit., 1980. RN, Calif. Nurse trainee to charge nurse ICU L.A. County/U. So. Calif. Med. Ctr., 1975-79; pub. health nurse various clinics, L.A., 1979-87; clinic coord. L.A. County, Cen. Dist. Health Ctr., 1979-92; HIV/Tb rsch. nurse Los Angeles County/U. So. Calif. Med. Ctr., 1992—; speaker in field. Contbr. to The Japanese Jour. for the Pub. Health Nurse. Mem. Calif. Thoracic Soc., Am. Lung Assn. (edn. coms.), So. Calif. Pub. Health Assn., Temple City Toastmasters. Home: 9081 E Duarte Rd San Gabriel CA 91775-2011

OTERO-SMART, INGRID AMARILLYS, advertising executive; b. Santurce, P.R., Jan. 9, 1959; d. Angel Miguel and Carmen (Prann) Otero; m. Dean Edward Smart, May 4, 1991. BA in Communication, U. P.R., 1981. Traffic mgr. McCann-Erickson Corp., San Juan, P.R., 1981-82, media analyst, 1982, asst. account exec., 1982-83, account exec., 1983-84, sr. account exec., 1984-85, account dir., 1985-87; account supr. Mendoza-Dillon & Assocs., Newport Beach, Calif., 1987-89, sr. v.p. client svcs., 1989—. Mem. Youth Motivation Task Force, Santa Ana, Calif., 1989—; bd. dirs. Orange County Hispanic C. of C., Santa Ana, 1989-90; mem. Santa Ana Project P.R.I.D.E., 1993. Office: Mendoza-Dillon & Assocs 4100 Newport Place Dr Ste 600 Newport Beach CA 92660-2451

OTHELLO, MARYANN CECILIA, quality assurance professional; b. N.Y.C., Oct. 23, 1946; d. Alphonse Reasum and Edith (Atwater) O. BS, St. Paul's Coll., Lawrenceville, Va., 1968; MS, Columbia U., 1972. Cert. adoption specialist. Family therapist crisis intervention Dept. Social Svcs., N.Y.C., 1968-72; dir. treatment team Abbott House, Irvington, N.Y., 1972-73; unit chief Manhattan State Psychiat. Facility, N.Y.C., 1973-75; asst. dir., dir. social svcs. St. Peter's Sch., Peekskill, N.Y., 1975-77; dir. Patchwork Svcs. for Children, Santa Ana, Calif., 1977-78; dir. adult and geriatric svcs. Cen. City Community Mental Health, L.A., 1978-79; trainer, facilitator Lifespring, Inc., San Rafael, Calif., 1978-80; sr. mgmt. cons. Nelson Cons. Group, Inc., Mpls., 1980-92; dep. dir. Div. Family Svcs. Dept. of Svcs. to Children, Youth and Their Families, Wilmington, Del., 1992-93; dir. planning and quality assurance Episcopal Community Svcs./Diocese of Pa., Phila., 1993-94; dep. exec. dir. Episcopal Cmty. Svcs./Diocese of Pa., Phila., 1994—; cons. Calif. Dept. Edn., 1977; field instr. casework Hunter Coll. Sch. Social Work, N.Y.C., 1975-77; adj. instr. U. So. Calif., L.A., 1977-78; specialist career devel. Goal for It, L.A., 1977-82; mgmt. devel. cons. Mgmt. Dynamics, Irvine, Calif., 1980-82. Contbr. articles to profl. jours.; was interviewed twice on radio talk show As It Is, U. Calif., Irvine. Bd. dirs., presenter humanitarian awards L.A. Commn. on Assaults Against Women, 1985-87, Lettye's Sisters In Session, Wilmington, 1993—; facilitator Ch. of Religious Scis., Huntington Beach, Calif., 1981-83, NAACP, Urban League; founding mem. Kinship Alliance, Pacific Grove and Tustin, Calif., 1992—; mem. Afro-Am. Mus., Phila., 1993—. Named one of Outstanding Young Women of Am., 1976, 81; N.Y. State Regent scholar, 1968; Marie Antoinette Canon fellow Columbia U., 1972. Fellow Child Welfare League Am. (Adoption Specialist plaque 1976-89); mem. NAFE, Smithsonian Instn., Nat. Soc. for Historic Preservation, Wadsworth Antheneum, Nat. Trust for Hist. Preservation, Assn. for Female Execs. Office: Episcopal Community Svcs Diocese of Pa 225 South Third St Philadelphia PA 19106

OTHERSEN, CHERYL LEE, insurance broker, realtor; b. Bay City, Mich., Aug. 17, 1948; d. Andrew Julius and Ruth Emma (Jacoby) Houthoofd; m. Wayne Korte Othersen, Sept. 5, 1964; 1 child, Angela. Lic. ins., Mich. State U., 1980, lic. realtor, 1981. Owner, operator Glad Rags Boutique, Unionville, Mich., 1976-79; dept. mgr. Gantos, Saginaw, Mich., 1979-80; agt., bookkeeper Othersen Ins. Agy., Inc., Unionville, 1979-81, v.p., 1981—; realtor Osentoski Realty Corp., Unionville, 1981—. Active Mich chpt. Nat. Head Injury Found., Mich. chpt. Crohn's and Colitis Found. Am., Inc., Nat. Mus. In the Arts, Nat. Trust for Hist. Preservation; vol. local Rep. campaigns, 1982, 84, 86; assoc. mem. Am. Mus. Natural History; charter supporter U.S. Holocaust Meml. Mus. Fellow (hon.) John F. Kennedy Libr. Found.; mem. Profl. Ins. Agts., Unionville Bus. Assn., Nat. Mus. Women in the Arts (charter). Mem. Moravian Ch. Club: Sherwood-on-the-Hill Country (Gagetown, Mich.). Home: 4483 S Unionville Rd Unionville MI 48767-9723 Office: Othersen Ins Agy Inc 6639 Center St Unionville MI 48767-9482

O'TOOLE, TARA J., federal official; d. Harold J. and Jeanne (Whalen) O'T. BA, Vassar Coll., 1974; MD, George Washington U., 1981; MPH, Johns Hopkins U., 1988. Diplomate Am. Bd. Internal Medicine, Am. Bd. Preventive/Occupational Medicine. Rsch. asst. Sloan-Kettering Cancer Inst., N.Y.C., 1974-77; resident in internal medicine Yale New Haven (Conn.)

Hosp., 1981-84; physician Balt. Cmty. Health Ctrs., 1984-87; fellow in occupational medicine Johns Hopkins U., Balt., 1987-89; sr. analyst Office Tech. Assessment, Washington, 1989-93; asst. sec. energy for environ., safety and health Dept. Energy, Washington, 1993—. Democrat. Office: Dept of Energy Environ Safety & Health 1000 Independence Ave SE Washington DC 20585

OTT, PAULA NISBET, nursing and emergency medical technician educator; b. Peoria, Ill., Nov. 21, 1944; d. Paul McCracken and Melcena Ellen (Arvin) Nisbet; m. Franklin Leo Ott, Nov. 8, 1966; children: Penelope, Jason, Cynthia. BSN, Ill. Wesleyan Coll., 1966; MEd, Northeast La. U., 1977. Cert. Indsl. Audiometric Tech., ARC Instr. First Aid and CPR, Basic and Advanced EMT Instr. Operating room supr. Glenwood Regional Med. Ctr., West Monroe, La., 1966; staff RN Rockford (Ill.) Meml. Hosp., 1966; mental health community nurse H. Douglas Singer Zone Ctr., Rockford, 1966-69; La.; instr. Delta Ouachita Regional Tech. Inst., West Monroe, 1969-88, dept. head health occupations, 1988—; nursing cons. GM Fisher Guide, Monroe, 1989—. Author: (with others) Cole's Basic Nursing Skills, 1991, Instructor's Guide and Concepts, 1991. La. Lung Assn. scholar, New Orleans, 1980; named Educator of Yr., La. Votech. Tchr. of Yr. State Dept. Edn., Baton Rouge, 1986. Mem. Am. Vocat. Assn. (policy com., region IV educator of yr., 1982), Nat. Assn. Health Occupation Tchrs. (treas., 1980-82, outstanding svc. award, 1983), La. Vocat. Assn. (parlimentary historian exec. coun., outstanding svc. award, 1982), La. Assn. Health Occupations Edn. (pres., past pres., exec. coun., tchr. of year, 1982), La. Soc. EMT Instr. Coords. (edn. com. chair, 1986—), Sigma Theta Tau Internat. Democrat. Mem. Assembly of God Ch. Home: RR 2 Box 198 Farmerville LA 71241-9582 Office: Delta Ouachita Regional & Tech Inst 609 Vocational Pky West Monroe LA 71292-0127

OTTE, MIRIAM CATHERINE, trainer; b. Detroit, May 8, 1946; d. Gilbert Theodore and Edith Catherine (Hildebrand) O.; m. Donald Ernest Johnson, Jan. 1, 1980. BA, Valparaiso U., 1969; MSW, U. Mich., 1971. CPA. Social worker various organizations, Chgo., 1971-77; acct. U. Wash., Seattle, 1981-83; acctg. supr. Seattle C.C., 1985-87; project coord. Nordstrom, Seattle, 1989-91; instr. acctg. City U., Seattle, 1989—; trainer F.Y.I. Tng., Seattle, 1992—. Mem. Nat. Speakers Assn., Am. Soc. Tng. and Devel., Toastmasters (dist. treas. 1993—). Office: F Y I Tng 3227 NE 96th St Seattle WA 98115

OTTO, JEAN HAMMOND, journalist; b. Kenosha, Wis., Aug. 27, 1925; d. Laurence Cyril and Beatrice Jane (Slater) Hammond; m. John A. Otto, Aug. 22, 1946; children: Jane L. Rahman, Mary Ellen Takayama, Peter J. Otto; m. Lee W. Baker, Nov. 23, 1973. Student, Ripon Coll., 1944-46. Women's editor Appleton (Wis.) Post-Crescent, 1960-68; reporter Milw. Jour., 1968-72, editorial writer, 1972-77, editor Op Ed page, 1977-83; editorial page editor Rocky Mountain News, Denver, 1983-89, assoc. editor, 1989-92, reader rep., 1992—; Endowed chair U. Denver, 1992—. Founder, chmn. bd. trustees First Amendment Congress, 1979-85, chmn. exec. com., 1985-88, 89-91, pres. 1991—, mem. bd. trustees, 1979—; founding mem. Wis. Freedom of Info. Council. Recipient Headliner award Wis. Women in Communications, 1974; Outstanding Woman in Journalism award YWCA, Milw., 1977; Knight of Golden Quill Milw. Presss Club, 1979; spl. citation in Journalism Ball State U., 1980; James Madison award Nat. Broadcast Editorial Assn., 1981; spl. citation for contbn. to journalism Nat. Press Photographers Assn., 1981; Ralph D. Casey award, 1984; U. Colo. Regents award, 1985; John Peter Zenger award U. Ariz., 1988; Paul Miller Medallion award Okla. State U., 1990; Colo. SPJ Lowell Thomas award, 1990, Disting. Alumna award Ripon Coll., 1992, Hugh M. Hefner First Amendment Lifetime Achievement award Playboy Found., 1994. Mem. Colo. Press Assn. (chmn. freedom of info. com. 1983-89), Assn. Edn. in Journalism and Mass Communications (Disting. Svc. award 1984), Am. Soc. Newspaper Editors (bd. dirs. 1987-92), Soc. Profl. Journalists (nat. treas. 1975, nat. sec. 1977, pres.-elect 1978, pres. 1979-80, First Amendment award 1981, Wells Key 1984, pres. Sigma Delta Chi Found. 1989-92, chair Found. 1992—), Milw. Press Club (mem. Hall of Fame 1993). Office: Rocky Mountain News 400 W Colfax Ave Denver CO 80204-2694

OTTO, MARGARET AMELIA, librarian; b. Boston, Oct. 22, 1937; d. Henry Earlen and Mary (McLennan) O.; children—Christopher, Peter. A.B., Boston U., 1960; M.S., Simmons Coll., 1963, M.A., 1970; M.A. (hon.), Dartmouth Coll., 1981. Asst. sci. librarian M.I.T., Cambridge, 1963; Lindgren librarian M.I.T., 1964-67, acting sci. librarian, 1967-69, asst. dir., 1969-75, asso. dir., 1976-79; librarian of coll. Dartmouth Coll., Hanover, N.H., 1979—; pres., chmn. bd. Universal Serials and Book Exch., Inc. 1980-81; bd. dirs. Rsch. Libr. Group; trustee Howe Libr., Hanover, 1988—, chair 1992—; mem. Brown Libr. Com., rsch. librs. adv. com. OCLC, 1991—, ARL Com. on Preservation of Rsch. Librs., Materials, , 1993—; Colby Coll. Overseers Visiting Com., 1993—; editorial com. U. Press New Eng., 1993—. Council on Library Resources fellow, 1974; elected to Collegium of Disting. Alumnus Boston U., 1980. Mem. ALA (tsk force on assn. membership issues 1993—, ad hoc working group on copyright issues), Assn. Rsch. Librs. (chair preservation com. 1983-85, bd. dirs. 1985-88, mem. stats com., chair membership com. 1992—), Coun. on Libr. Resources (proposral rev. com. 1992—), Dartmouth Club (N.Y.C.), St Botolph Club (Boston), Grolier Club (N.Y.C.), Sloane Club (London). Home: 16 Dresden Rd Hanover NH 03755-1322 Office: Dartmouth Coll 115 Baker Meml Libr Hanover NH 03755

OUELLETTE, JANE LEE YOUNG, biology educator; b. Charlotte, N.C., Dec. 29, 1929; d. James Thomas and Nancy Isabel (Yarbrough) Young; m. Armand Roland Ouellette, Aug. 3, 1951 (dec. Oct. 1984); children—Elizabeth Anne, James Young, Emily Jane, Frances Lee. B.A., Winthrop Coll., 1950; M.A., Oberlin Coll., 1952; postgrad. Coll. Medicine, Baylor U., 1974, U. Tex.-Houston, 1976-83, Tex. Woman's U., 1980-82. Lic. tchr., Tex. Tchr. Maria Regina High Sch., Hartsdale, N.Y., 1969-70, Spring Ind. Sch. System, Tex., 1972-78; coordinator biology program, prof., North Harris County Coll., Houston, 1979—. Meadow's fellow Baylor Coll. Medicine, 1989. Mem. Internat. Assn. for Study of Pain, Internat. Pain Found., N.Y. Acad. Sci., AAAS, Internat. Chronobiol. Soc., People to People Internat. Democrat. Home: 1619 Big Horn Dr Houston TX 77090-1862 Office: North Harris County Coll 2700 W Thorne Dr Houston TX 77073-3426

OUJESKY, HELEN M., microbiology educator; b. Ft. Worth, Aug. 14, 1930; d. Steve and Lillie (Krivanek) Matusevich; m. Frank P. Oujesky, Dec. 27, 1951; children: Michael Jerome, David Franklin, Christopher Aaron. BA, Tex. State Coll. for Women, 1951; MA, Tex. Christian U., 1965; PhD, Tex. Woman's U., 1968. Cert. profl. tchr., Tex. Chemistry/biology tchr. Ft. Worth Ind. Sch. Dist., 1951-63; grad. teaching asst. Tex. Christian U., Ft. Worth, 1963-65; grad. teaching Tex. Woman's U., Denton, 1965-68, asst. prof., 1968-73; assoc. prof. microbiology U. Tex. at San Antonio, 1973-80, prof. microbiology, 1980—; bd. dirs. Tex. Acad. Sci., 1980—. Contbr. numerous articles to profl. jours. Pres. Altrusa Club San Antonio, 1980-81; bd. dirs. Alamo Regional Acad. Sci. & Engring, San Antonio, 1986—, San Antonio Women's Celebration & Hall of Fame, San Antonio, 1985—. Named to San Antonio Women's Hall of Fame/Sci. & Technology, 1987; recipient Research contract Bur. Land Mgmt., 1977-79, Grants NSF, 1976, 77, 79, 80, 81. Fellow Tex. Acad. Sci.; mem. AAAS, AAUW (pres. 1985-87, pres. Tex. br. 1994—), Am. Soc. for Microbiology, Soc. for Indsl. Microbiology (edn. com. 1976), Sigma Xi (Alamo chpt. pres. 1985-86). Republican. Roman Catholic. Home: 604 Skyforest Dr San Antonio TX 78232-2020 Office: U Tex San Antonio/Alliance for Edn 310 S Saint Marys St # 1416 San Antonio TX 78205-3108

OUREDNIK, PATRICIA ANN, accountant; b. Balt., Oct. 5, 1962; d. John Matthew and Patricia Ann (Ruzicka) O. BS in Acctg., U. Balt., 1984; MS in Mgmt. Info. Sys., Fla. Inst. Tech., 1991. CPA, Md. Acctg. clk. Cello Corp., Havre de Grace, Md., 1981-84; staff acct. KPMG Peat Marwick, Balt., 1984-85; audit supv. Coughlin & Mann, Chartered, Bel Air, Md., 1985-88, 89-92; CFO Kidde Sys., White Marsh, Md., 1988-89, FAMIC Corp., Columbia, Md., 1994—; contr. Top Tools Automation Sys., Timonium, Md., 1992-93; cons. FLS Automation, Timonium, 1994. Cons. Shepherd's Clinic, Balt., 1992—. Mem. Md. Assn. CPAs, Assn. Retarded Citizens. Republican. Methodist. Home: 1618 Bramble Ct Bel Air MD 21015 Office: FAMIC Corp 6740 Alexander Bell Dr Ste 180 Columbia MD 21046

OUTHWAITE, LUCILLE CONRAD, ballerina, educator; b. Peoria, Ill., Feb. 26, 1909; d. Frederick Albert and Della (Cornett) Conrad; m. Leonard Outhwaite, Mar. 1, 1936 (dec. 1978); children—Ann Outhwaite Maurer, Lynn Outhwaite Pulsifer. Student, U. Nebr., 1929-30, Mills Coll., 1931-32; student piano, Paris, 1933-35, Legat Sch., London, 1934, N.Y.C. Ballet, N.Y.C., 1936-41, Royal Ballet Sch., London, 1957-59. Tchr. ballet Perry Mansfield, Steamboat Springs, Colo., 1932, Cape Playhouse, Dennis, Mass., 1937-41, Jr. League, N.Y.C., 1937-41, King Coit Sch., N.Y.C., 1937-41; toured with Am. Ambassador Ballet, Europe and S. Am., 1933-35; owner, tchr. dance sch., Oyster Bay, N.Y., 1949-57. Producer, choreographer ballets Alice in Wonderland, 1951, Pied Piper of Hamlin, 1952. Author: Birds in Flight, 1992, Flowers in the Wind, 1994. Mem. English Speaking Union, Preservation Soc., Alliance Française, Delta Gamma. Republican. Methodist. Clubs: Mills Coll., Spouting Rock Beach, Clambake (Newport, R.I.). Office: Beachmound Bellevue Ave Newport RI 02840

OUZOUNIAN, ARMENUHI, dentist; b. Mosul, Iraq, Feb. 17, 1942; came to U.S., 1974; d. Yervant and Warda (Efram) O. DDS, U. Baghdad, Iraq, 1962, degree in anesthesiology, 1966. Cert. U.S. Bd. Dentistry; lic. dentist, Ill. Resident Fed. Teaching Hosp., Baghdad, 1963-66; anesthesiologist Maternity Hosp., Baghdad, 1966-73; gen. practice dentistry Baghdad, 1967-73; asst. various offices, Chgo., 1975-83; gen. practice dentistry Chgo., 1984—. Active Smithsonian Inst., Washington. Mem. ADA, Internat. Platform Assn., Am. Women Dentists Assn., Ill. Dental Soc., Chgo. Dental Soc., Acad. Polit. Sci., U.S. Naval Acad. Home: 9346 N Greenwood Ave Niles IL 60714-5748 Office: 3647 W 26th St Chicago IL 60623-3823

OVENS, MARI CAMILLE, school system administrator, dietitian; b. Spokane, Wash., June 18, 1954; d. Harold Chester and May Eloise (Gundry) Chapman; m. Dana Preston Ovens, Dec. 18, 1985; children: Dylan Preston, Delaney Camille. BS in Dietetics, Ea. Wash. U., 1976; MS in Home Econs., Wash. State U., 1979. Registered dietitian, Wash. Dietary cood. City of Vancouver, Wash., 1978-83; clin. dietitian Eastmoreland Gen. Hosp., Portland, Oreg., 1983; supr. child nutrition Vancouver Sch. Dist. 37, 1983—; mem. culinary arts adv. bd. Clark Coll., Vancouver, 1983—; mem. task force Am. Heart Assns., Seattle, 1988—. Mem. Am. Sch. Food Svc. Assn., (registered dir., adminstr. III), Am. Dietetic Assn. (Recognized Young Dietitian of Yr. Wash. State 1983), Wash. Sch. Food Svc. Assn. (treas. 1989-91, trainer 1993—), Wash. State Dietetic Assn., Soroptimists (pres. Vancouver 1990-92). Office: Vancouver Sch Dist 37 PO Box 8937 Vancouver WA 98668-8937

OVERBY, MONESSA MARY, clinical supervisor, counselor; b. Staples, Minn., Sept. 7, 1932; d. Joseph Melvin Overby and Marie Frances (Fellman) Vollstedt. BS, Coll. of St. Teresa, 1964; MS, Winona State U., 1978. Entered Franciscan Sisters, Roman Cath. Ch., 1953; nat. cert. counselor, Gestalt therapist, trainer. Elem. and jr. high tchr. Cath. Sch. System, Austin, Tracy, Lake City, Minn., 1955-67; sch. adminstr. McCahill Inst., Lake City, 1964-70; pastoral counselor and adult educator St. Edward's, Austin, Minn., 1970-76; adj. faculty and campus minister Winona (Minn.) State U., 1976-84; psychotherapist Family & Children's Ctr. and Human Devel. Assocs., La Crosse, Wis., 1978-84; family counselor Betty Ford Ctr., Rancho Mirage, Calif., 1987-89, clin. mgr. family and outpatient svcs., 1990—; workshop presenter in field. Mem. Am. Counseling Assn., Assn. for Specialists in Group Work, Minn. Assn. Specialists in Group Work (founding pres.). Democrat. Roman Catholic. Office: Betty Ford Ctr 39000 Bob Hope Dr Rancho Mirage CA 92270-3297

OVERGARD, JAYNE ANN, computer consultant; b. Aberdeen, S.D., July 1, 1958; d. E. Theodore and Joyce Julia (Hoffmeister) Overgard; m. Daniel Bruce Cooper, Sept. 28, 1991; children: Maya Elise Coopergard, Ryan Brennan Coopergard. BS in Math., U. Wis., 1981; student, U. Calif., 1978-80, U. Wis., 1976-77. Head tennis profl. West Lane Tennis Club, Stockton, Calif., 1978; air traffic controller FAA Monterey TRACAB, Monterey, Calif., 1982-85; math. dept. head Concordia High Sch., Oakland, Calif., 1985-89; owner Electric Ledger, Alameda, Calif., 1989—. Bd. dirs. Concordia High Sch. Mem. Aircraft Owners and Pilots Assn., Internat. Orgn. Women Pilots, Air Race Classic, Wildly Successful Women Investment Club (treas. 1993-94). Office: Electric Ledger 305 Sand Beach Rd Alameda CA 94501

OVERSTREET, KAREN A., judge. BA cum laude, Univ. of Wash., 1977; JD, Univ. of Oregon, 1982. Assoc. Duane, Morris & Heckscher, Phila., 1983-86; ptnr. Davis Wright Tremaine, Seattle, 1986-93; bankruptcy judge U.S. Bankruptcy Ct. (we. dist.) Wash., Seattle, 1994—; assoc. editor Oregon Law Review; dir. People's Law Sch.; mem. advisory com. U.S. Bankruptcy Ct. (we. dist.) Wash. Mem. Nat. Conf. of Bankruptcy Judges, Wash. State Bar Assn. (creditor-debtor sec.), Seattle-King County Bar Assn. (bankruptcy sec.), Am. Bar Assn., Wash. Women Lawyers Assn. Office: US Bankruptcy Ct Park Place Bldg 1200 Sixth Ave Rm 406 Seattle WA 98101*

OVERTON, JANE VINCENT HARPER, biology educator; b. Chgo., Jan. 17, 1919; d. Paul Vincent and Isabel (Vincent) Harper; m. George W. Overton, Jr., Sept. 1, 1941; children: Samuel, Peter, Ann. AB, Bryn Mawr Coll., 1941; PhD, U. Chgo., 1950. Rsch. asst. U. Chgo., 1950-52, mem. faculty, 1952-89, prof. biology, 1972-89; prof. emeritus, 1989. Author articles embryology, cell biology. NIH, NSF research grantee, 1965-87. Home: 1700 E 56th St Apt 2901 Chicago IL 60637-1935 Office: U Chgo 1103 E 57th St Chicago IL 60637-1572

OVERTON, ROSILYN GAY HOFFMAN, financial services executive; b. Corsicana, Tex., July 10, 1942; d. Billy Clarence and Ima Elise (Gay) Hoffman; m. Aaron Lewis Overton, Jr., July 2, 1960 (div. Mar. 1975); children: Aaron Lewis III, Adam Jerome. BS in Math., Wright State U., Dayton, Ohio, 1972, MS in Applied Econs. (fellow), 1973; postgrad. N.Y. U. Grad. Sch. Bus., 1974-76; Cert. Coll. Fin. Planning, 1987. CFP. Research analyst Nat. Security Agy., Dept. Def., 1962-67; bus. reporter Dayton Jour.-Herald, 1973-74; economist First Nat. City Bank, N.Y.C., 1974, A.T. & T. Co., 1974-75; broker Merrill Lynch, N.Y.C., 1975-80; asst. v.p. E.F. Hutton & Co., N.Y.C., 1980-84; v.p., nat. mktg. dir. investment products Manhattan Nat. Corp., 1984-86; pres. R.H. Overton Co., N.Y.C., 1986—; ptnr. Brown & Overton Fin. Svcs., 1987—. Named Businesswoman of Yr., N.Y.C., 1976. Mem. Nat. Fedn. Bus. and Profl. Women, Inst. Cert. Planners, Internat. Assn. Fin. Planning, Women's Econ. Roundtable, Gotham Bus. and Profl. Womens Club, Rotary Internat., Wright State U. Alumni Assn., Mensa, Zonta. Methodist. Office: Ste 603 142-05 Roosevelt Ave Flushing NY 11354

OVERTON, SARITA ROSA, psychologist; b. South Haven, Mich., June 7, 1954; d. Samuel Edward and Rosa Jane (McGuire) O. BA in Psychology with honors, Mich. State U., 1976, MA in Rehab. Counseling, 1978, MA in Counseling Psychology, 1987, PhD in Counseling Psychology, 1988. Lic. psychologist, Mich. Dir. Job Club, Capital Area Community Svcs., Lansing, Mich., 1978-84; instr. rehab. counseling master's program Mich. State U., East Lansing, 1981-82, program teaching asst., 1985-87, coord. career assistance project, 1984, 84-85, clin. trainee Counseling Ctr., 1986, rsch. asst. disability mgmt. project, 1985-87; clin. trainee St. Lawrence Hosp., Lansing, 1986-87, psychologist Psychol. Svcs. and Addictions Clinic, 1987-91; psychologist Comprehensive Psychol. Svcs., P.C., East Lansing, 1990—; conf. and clin. presenter in field. Contbr. articles to profl. publs. Recipient Presdl. recognition award Mich. Rehab. Assn., 1986; grantee Nat. Inst. Handicapped Rsch., 1985; dissertation rsch. fellow Mich. State U., 1985. Mem. APA. Democrat. Office: Comprehensive Psychol Svcs 2720 E Lansing Dr East Lansing MI 48823-7754

OWADES, RUTH MARKOWITZ, marketing company executive; b. Los Angeles, Sept. 2, 1944; d. David and Yonina (Graf) Markowitz; m. Joseph L. Owades, Sept. 7, 1969. BA with honors, Scripps Coll., Claremont, Calif., 1966; MBA, Harvard U., 1975; postgrad. U. Strasbourg (France), 1966-67. Exec. asst. Los Angeles Econ. Devel. Bd., N.Y.C., 1968-69; copywriter D'Arcy Advt. Co., St. Louis, 1970-71; asst. program dir. KMOX-AM Radio, St. Louis, 1971-72; assoc. producer WCVB-TV, Boston, 1972-73; mktg. project mgr. United Brands Co., Boston, 1975; mktg. dir. CML Group Inc., Concord, Mass., 1975-78; founder, pres. Gardener's Eden Inc., Boston, 1978-82; pres. Gardener's Eden, div. Williams-Sonoma Inc., Emeryville, Calif., 1982-87; founder, pres. Calyx & Carolla, Inc., 1988— ; dir. Hellenic Breweries S.A., Athens, Greece. Recipient Bausch & Lomb award, 1962; Fulbright scholar, 1966; named student Goodwill Ambassador to Nagoya, Japan, 1960. Mem. Direct Mktg. Assn., Phi Beta Kappa. Club: Harvard (N.Y.C.), Women's Forum West (v.p. and treas.). Home: 2164 Hyde St San Francisco CA 94109-1701 Office: 1550 Bryant St # 900 San Francisco CA 94103-4832*

OWEN, BONNIE MARIE, accountant; b. Memphis, May 24, 1948; d. John Wilson and Alma Marie (Cool) Guthrie; m. Troy Gene Owen, Dec. 27, 1969; children: Jeffrey and Jeremy (twins). BA with distinction, Southwestern-At-Memphis Coll., 1970; postgrad., N.C. State U., 1987. CPA, N.C., Va. Travel cons. Dixie Motor Club AAA, Memphis, 1968-69; admissions analyst U. Houston, 1970-71; sr. transcript analyst Houston C.C., 1972-75; acct. Strickland & Morgan, P.C., Norfolk, Va., 1987-88, Baker & McNiff, P.C., Virginia Beach, Va., 1988—. Mem. Tidewater CPA's, Gideons Aux. (v.p. Chesapeake East chpt. 1993, pres. 1994-95). Baptist. Home: 507 Country Club Ct Chesapeake VA 23320 Office: Baker & McNiff PC 5101 Cleveland St Ste 104 Virginia Beach VA 23462

OWEN, CAROL THOMPSON, artist, educator; b. Pasadena, Calif., May 10, 1944; d. Sumner Comer and Cordelia (Whittemore) Thompson; m. James Eugene Owen, July 19, 1975; children: Kevin Christopher, Christine Celese. Student, Pasadena City Coll., 1963; BA with distinction, U. Redlands, 1966; MA, Calif. State U., L.A., 1967; MFA, Claremont Grad. Sch., 1969. Cert. community coll. instr., Calif. Head resident Pitzer Coll., Claremont, Calif., 1967-70; instr. art Mt. San Antonio Coll., Walnut, Calif., 1968—; dir. coll. art gallery Mt. San Antonio Coll., 1972-73. Group shows include Covina Pub. Libr., 1971, U. Redlands, 1964, 65, 66, 70, 78, 88, 92, Am. Ceramic Soc., 1969, Mt. San Antonio Coll., 1991, The Aesthetic Process, 1993, others; ceramic mural commd. and installed U. Redlands, 1991. Mem. Calif. Scholarship Fedn., Faculty Assn. Mt. San Antonio Coll., Coll. Art Assn. Am., Calif. Tchrs. Assn., Friends of Huntington Library, L.A. County Mus. Art, Heard Mus. Assn., Sigma Tau Delta. Republican. Presbyterian. Home: 534 S Hepner Ave Covina CA 91723-2921 Office: Mt San Antonio Coll Grand Ave Walnut CA 91789

OWEN, CHRISTINA L., lawyer; b. Oakland, Calif., Sept. 22, 1946. BS, U. Calif., Berkeley, 1968; JD, U. So. Calif., 1971. Bar: Calif. 1972. Ptnr. Baker & Hostetler, Long Beach, Calif. Mem. State Bar Calif., Maritime Law Assn. U.S. Office: Baker & Hostetler 300 Oceangate Ste 620 Long Beach CA 90802-6801

OWEN, CYNTHIA CAROL, sales executive; b. Ft. Worth, Oct. 16, 1943; d. Charlie Bounds and Bernice Vera (Nunley) Rhoads; m. Franklin Earl Owen, Oct. 20, 1961 (div. Jan. 1987); children: Jeffrey Wayne, Valeria Ann, Carol Darlena, Pamela Kay; m. John Edward White, Jan. 1, 1988 (div. Sept. 1991). Cert. Keypuncher, Comml. Coll., 1963; student, Tarrant County Jr. Coll., 1974-77; BBA in Mgmt., U. Tex., Arlington, 1981. Keypunch operator Can-Tex. Industries, Mineral-Wells, 1966-67; sec. Electro-Midland Corp., Mineral-Wells, 1967-68; exec. sec. to v.p. sales Pangburn Co., Inc., Ft. Worth, 1972-78; bookkeeper, sec. CB Svc., Ft. Worth, 1978-82; tech. sales support coord. Square D Co., Ft. Worth, 1982—. Mem. NAFE, NOW, AAUW. Baptist. Home: 816 Lee Dr Bedford TX 76022 Office: Square D Co 860 W Airport Frwy Ste 101 Hurst TX 76053

OWEN, KAREN CORDELIA, estate planner; b. Whittier, Calif., Sept. 11, 1943; d. Ralph and Janet Elaine (Benito) O.; m. William Robert Ives, July 24, 1963 (div. Aug. 1976); children: Janet Ellen Ives, JoAnn Elaine Ives. Grad. high sch., Yucaipa, Calif. Owner, operator Ives Electric Cars, Romoland, Calif., 1968-72; cost acct., office mgr. Harvill Machine Co., Perris, Calif., 1972-74; owner LaGrange (Wyo.) Bar, 1974-81; planner, cons. ARCO Securities, Inc., Cheyenne, Wyo., 1982-88; br. mgr. Chatfield Investment Co., Cheyenne, 1988-89; pres. ARCO Securities, Inc., LaGrange, Wyo., 1989—; mem. arbitration bd. Better Bus. Bur., Ft. Collins, Colo., 1985; appt. by gov. Ind. Living Adv. Coun., 1991—. Mem. Gov.'s Adv. Coun. on Ind. Living, 1991—, Gov.'s Adv. Coun. for Vocat. Rehab., 1993—; Rep. committeewoman, LaGrange, 1981. Mem. Nat. Assn. Securities Dealers (fin. ops. prin. 1985, registered rep. 1983, supr. prin. 1983), Calif. Scholastic Fedn. (life), Altrusa Internat. Baptist. Office: ARCO Securities Inc PO Box 51 LaGrange WY 82221-0051

OWEN, RANDI JEAN, counselor; b. Chardon, Ohio, Nov. 15, 1963; d. Alvin Robert and Becky Leighann (Perkins) Elder; m. David Matthew Owen, Nov. 26, 1988; 1 child, Chad. BS, Marietta (Ohio) Coll., 1986; MA, Columbia U., 1988, MEd, 1988. Lic. profl. counselor, Mich.; lic. social worker, Mich.; cert. rehab. counselor. Substance abuse counselor Day Top Villages, Blauvelt, N.Y., 1987-88; social worker Tng. in Community Living, New Rochelle, N.Y., 1988-89; vocat. counselor Gen. Rehab. Assn., Troy, Mich., 1989-90, John Raleeb & Assoc., Southfield, Mich., 1990-92; supr., vocat. counselor Med. Mgmt. & Re-employment, Southfield, Mich., 1992—. Mem. Am. Assn. Counseling and Devel., Mich. Rehab. Assn., Nat. Rehab. Assn. Office: Med Mgmt & Re-employment 30555 Southfield Ste 300 Southfield MI 48076

OWEN, SUZANNE, retired savings and loan executive; b. Lincoln, Nebr., Oct. 6, 1926; d. Arthur C. and Hazel E. (Edwards) O. BSBA, U. Nebr., Lincoln, 1948. With G.F. Lessenhop & Sons, Inc., Lincoln, 1948-57; with First Fed. Lincoln, 1963-91; v.p., dir. personnel, 1975-81, 1st v.p., 1981-87, sr. v.p., 1987-91, ret., 1991; mem. pers. bd. City of Lincoln, 1989—. Mem. Lincoln Human Resources Mgmt. Assn., Lincoln Mgmt. Soc., Phi Chi Theta. Republican. Christian Scientist. Clubs: Wooden Spoon, Exec. Women's Breakfast Group, Community Women's. Lodges: Pi Beta Phi Alumnae, Order of Eastern Star (Lincoln).

OWENS, BEVERLY C., accountant; b. Decatur, Ala., Feb. 13, 1952; d. Edward Maxwell and Veloreese C. (Andrew) Harper; children from previous marriage: Cretice Benefield, James Benefield, Lisa Benefield; m. Steven Ray Owens, Jan. 10, 1989; 1 child, Andrew. Student, U. Ala., Huntsville, 1970, Auburn U., 1971; BA cum laude, Lagrange Coll., 1990. Libr. Auburn (Ala.) U. Libr.; cost acct. Millikan, Gainseville, Ga., 1973-78, 82-84, West Point Pepperell, Valley, Ala., 1990—. Mem. tour choir 1st Bapt. Ch., Huntsville, Ala., 1967-70; mem. choir 1st Bapt. Ch., La Grange, Ga., 1993—. Mem. Inst. Mgmt. Accts., Children Am. Revolution (v.p., pianist 1968-70). Home: 103 Plymouth Dr La Grange GA 30240

OWENS, CAROLE EHRLICH, therapist; b. Mpls., Dec. 7, 1942; d. Jerome D. and Amy Ann (Scott) Schein; B.A., U. Md., 1970, M.A., Cath. U. Am., 1977; D of Social Work Yeshiva U., 1987; children: Todd Frederick, Joseph Eric. Lic. Social Worker, Mass. Youth advocate, leader Montgomery (Md.) County Recreation Dept., 1970-72, counselor, supr. preadjudication diversion program, Crisis Home Program, Family Service, 1972-74, adminstr. Karma House (residential drug treatment), 1974-75; program devel. dir. Jewish Social Service Agy., Montgomery County, 1975-77, United Jewish Appeal Fedn. of Montgomery County, 1977-79; therapist, educator, writer, cons. in field, Englewood, N.J., 1979—; instr. Cath. U. Cons. to Montgomery County Exec. candidate, 1974; appointee Gov.'s Task Force, Md., 1978; bd. dirs. Jewish Community Center, 1981—, Temple Sinai Sisterhood, Bergen County, N.J., 1981—; pres. chpt. LWV, 1983. Mem. Internat. Platform Assn., AAUW, Am. Personnel & Guidance Assn. (cert.), Am. Assn. Marriage and Family Therapy (clin.), Am. Assn. Jewish Communal Workers, Nat. Assn. Social Workers, LWV (pres. 1983-84), N.Y. Acad. Scis. Author: The Berkshire Cottages: A Vanishing Era, 1984, Clinical Vs. Psychometric Judgement of Alcohol Use, 1987, Bellefontaine, 1989; Stockbridge, 1989; author: (play) The Lost Days, 1994; author, editor: The Stockbridge Story; editor: Fund-Raising (Elton J. Kernes); reviewer Kirkus Revs.; contbr. articles in field to profl. jours. Home: PO Box 1207 Stockbridge MA 01262-1207

OWENS, DONNA, state agency administrator, former mayor; b. Aug. 24, 1936. Student, Stautzenberger Bus Coll. Past v.p. Lucas County Bd. Edn., Ohio; mem. Toledo City Council, 1980-84; mayor City of Toledo, 1984-89; dir. commerce dept. State of Ohio, Columbus. Mem. Toledo-Lucas County Council for Human Services, Internat. Inst. Greater Toledo, Lucas County Improvement Corp., Toledo Area Employment and Tng. Consortium, St. Vincent Hosp. and Med. Guild, Ohio Sch. Bd. Assn., Assn. of Two Toledos, Toledo Econ. Planning Council, Criminal Justice Coordinating Council,

Toledo Mus. of Art; mem. exec. com. Toledo Met. Area Council of Govts.; bd. dirs. pub. broadcasting WGTE-TV; bd. mgrs. West Toledo YMCA; bd. dirs. YMCA, Substance Abuse Service, Inc.; adv. bd. U.S. Conf. of Mayors. Recipient Legion of Leaders award YMCA, 1976; Community Service award Post 606 VFW. Office: Commerce Dept 77 S High St 23rd Fl Columbus OH 43266-0544*

OWENS, DORIS JERKINS, insurance underwriter; b. Range, Ala., June 16, 1940; d. Arthur Charles and Jennie (Lee) Jerkins; m. Gilbert Landers Owens, Jan. 29, 1959; 1 child, Alan Dale. Student Massey Draughon Bus. Coll., 1958-59, Auburn U., Montgomery, 1980, 81, 82. Cert. ins. counselor, profl. ins. woman. Exec. sec. Henry C. Barnet, Gen. Agt., Montgomery, Ala., 1959-66; sr. underwriter personal lines So. Guaranty Ins. Co., Montgomery, 1966—. Author: Bike Safety, 1976. Instr. Coop. State Dept. Defensive Driver Instr., 1975, 78; instr. ins. classes; v.p. Montgomery Citizens Fire Safety, 1981; panelist Gov.'s Safety Conf., Montgomery, 1975—; mem., panelist Women Annual Hwy. Safety Leaders, Montgomery, 1976, 78, 80; apptd. mem. Alliance Against Drugs, 1989. Recipient Able Toastmaster award Dist. 48 Toastmasters, 1979, Outstanding Lt. Gov. award, 1981, Outstanding Area Gov. award, 1980; named Ins. Woman of Year, 1979. Mem. Ins. Women Montgomery (pres. 1961, 85-86), Internat. Platform Assn. Home: Rosa L Parks Ave Montgomery AL 36125 Office: So Guaranty Ins Co 2545 Taylor Rd Montgomery AL 36117

OWENS, FLORA CONCEPCION, critical care nurse; b. Manila, Nov. 23, 1949; d. Felix and Marieta (Obsuna) Concepcion; m. George Owens, Feb. 13, 1976. Grad., San Juan de Dios Sch. Nursing, Pasay City, The Philippines, 1970; BSN, Concordia Coll., Manila, 1971. RN, Ill., Ark.; cert. in ACLS; CCRN. Staff nurse San Juan de Dios Hosp., 1970-71, Jefferson Meml. Hosp., Mt. Vernon, Ill., 1972, Russellville (Ark.) Nursing Home Ctr., 1973-76; staff nurse, relief supr. St. Mary's Regional Med. Ctr., Russellville, 1972-74, head nurse med. fl., 1975-76, insvc. coord. and unit mgr. med.-surg. ICU, 1979-90, staff nurse, charge nurse med.-surg. ICU, 1990—; instr. basic coronary care class, 1979—, basic arrythmia class, 1979-91; med.-surg. ICU insvc. coord., 1976-90. Mem. AACCN, CCRN.

OWENS, HILDA FAYE, management/leadership development consultant, human resource trainer; b. Fountain, N.C., Mar. 23, 1939; d. Floyd Curtis and Essie Lee (Gay) O. BS in Edn. and Psychology, East Carolina U., 1961, MA in Edn., 1965; PhD in Higher Edn., Fla. State U., 1973; postgrad., Western Carolina U., 1962, U. Louisville, 1967, U. N.C., 1968. Tchr. New Bern (N.C.) City Schs., 1961-65; dir. counseling svcs., prof. Mt. Olive (N.C.) Coll., 1965-71, dean students, prof., 1973-77; coord. student affairs, rsch. assoc. bd. regents State Univ. System Fla., Tallahassee, 1971-73; assoc. prof. higher edn. U. S.C., Columbia, 1977-83; v.p. acad. affairs, prof. Spartanburg (S.C.) Meth. Coll., 1985-90; exec. asst. to pres. for planning and rsch., cons. Spartanburg (S.C.) Meth. Coll., 1990-91; pres. Excel Resource Assocs., Spartanburg, 1991—; mem. bd. dirs. The Haven; numerous presentations in field; speaker bus., edni., civic and ch. meetings, confs. and workshops. Editor: Risk Management and the Student Affairs Professional, 1984, (with Witten and Bailey) College Student Personnel Administration: An Anthology, 1982; mem. editorial bd. Jour. sTaff, Orgn. and Program Devel., Assn. Student Pers. Adminstrs. Jour., Nat. Assn. Student Pers. Adminstrs. Monograph Bd., Coll. Student Affairs Jour.; contbr. articles to profl. jours.; chpts. to books. Grad. Leadership Spartanburg, 1987; adminstrv. bd. Sunday Sch. Bethel United Meth. Ch.; mem. exec. bd. Tuscarora coun. Boy Scouts Am. Honored by Seymour Johnson AFB, 1976; named One of 45 Outstanding S.C. Women, 1980, Disting. Grad. award Fla. State U., 1981, Outstanding Bus. and Profl. Woman of Yr. Spartanburg Bus. and Profl. Women, 1986, Capital Bus. and Profl. Women, 1982, Mt. Olive Bus. and Profl. Women, 1977; recipient Meritorious Svc. award S.C. Coll. Pers. Assn., 1990. Mem. AMA, ASTD, NAFE, Nat. Assn. Student Pers. Adminstrs. (adv. bd. region III, Disting. Svc. award), Am. Assn. Higher Edn., Carolinas Soc. Tng. and Devel., S.C. Coll. Pers. Assn. (pres.), Bus. and Profl. Women U.S., Bus. and Profl. Women S.C. (pres., bd. dirs. Ednl. Found.), Internat. Platform Assn., Rotary Internat., Spartan West Rotary, Delta Kappa Gamma (1st v.p. Alpha Mu chpt.), Phi Delta Kappa (Greenville/Spartanburg chpt., pres. U. S.C. chpt.). Democrat. Home: 230 Old Towne Rd Spartanburg SC 29301-3555 Office: Excel Resource Assocs PO Box 17248 Spartanburg SC 29301-0103

OWENS, JANA JAE, entertainer; b. Great Falls, Mont., Aug. 30, 1943; d. Jacob G. Meyer and Bette P. (Sprague) Hopper; m. Sidney Greif (div.); children: Matthew N., Sydni C.; m. Buck Owens. Student, Interlochen Music Camp, 1959, Internat. String Congress, 1960, Vienna (Austria) Acad. Music, 1963-64; BA magna cum laude, Colo. Womens Coll., 1965, MusB magna cum laude, 1965. Tchr. music Ontario (Oreg.) Pub. Schs., 1965-67, Redding (Calif.) Pub. Schs., 1969-74; entertainer Buck Owens Enterprises, Bakersfield, Calif., 1974-78, Tulsa, 1979—; concertmistress Boise (Idaho) Philharm., 1965-67, Shasta Symphony, Redding, 1969-74. Rec. artist (violinist, vocalist) Lark Records, 1978—. Home: PO Box 35726 Tulsa OK 74153-0726 Office: Lark Records 4815 S Harvard Ave # 520 Tulsa OK 74135-3069

OWENS, LINDA LOU, retail manager; b. Rutledge, Tenn., Aug. 15, 1951; d. Archie Lee and Edna Dora (Rose) Atkins; m. Larry A. Owens, Nov. 18, 1971. Grad. high sch., Rutledge. Mgr. Minor's Marine, Morristown, Tenn., 1981—. Mem. Cherokee lake User Orgn. (pres.), Brickland Acres Garden Club, Lady Elks Club. Baptist. Office: Minor's Marine 2707 Buffalo Trl Morristown TN 37814-5907

OWENS, LUVIE MOORE, association executive; b. Cleve., July 26, 1933; d. Dan Tyler and Elizabeth (Oakes) Moore; m. Lloyd Owens, Jan. 1, 1955; children: Luvie Owens Myers, Elizabeth, Lloyd H. Student, Smith Coll., Northampton, Mass., 1956. Tchr. Howard Jr. High Sch., Wilmette, Ill., 1971-75; U.S. ops. mgr. Frank T. Ross & Co., Evanston, Ill., 1976-86; dir. Internat. Platform Assn., Winnetka, Ill., 1972—, chief exec. officer, 1986—. Treas., mem. jr. coun. Cleve. Mus. Art, 1964-65; commr. Police and Fire Commn., Winnetka, 1980-86; chmn. bd. Lake Shore Unitarian Ch., Winnetka, 1986-87; mem. alumnae bd. Madeira Sch., Greenway, Va., 1984-88. Mem. Jr. League Club (Chgo.), Rotary. Office: Internat Platform Assn PO Box 250 Winnetka IL 60093-0250

OWENS, MARY JO, electronic guidance services company executive; b. Asheville, N.C., Nov. 26, 1936; d. William James and Mamie Laura (Simms) O.; children: Lolita Omaria, Ionita. BS, N.C. State U., 1963; MS in Edn., Iona Coll., 1973. Prof. English N.C. State U., Greensboro, 1961-62, prof. French, 1962-63; instr. French Phillips Sr. High Sch., Battleboro, N.C., 1963-64, Farmville (N.C.) Sr. High Sch., 1964-65; instr. French, English Jordan Sellars Sr. High Sch., Burlington, N.C., 1965-66; program coord. Project Aware, Fed. Grant Program, Greensboro, 1966-67; instr. French, English Westchester County Schs., Mt. Vernon, N.Y., 1967-88; instr. Spanish evening sch. Bedford Park Acad., Bronx, N.Y., 1976-79; realty broker, owner M.J. Howell and Co. Inc., Stanfordville, N.Y., 1982—; founder, owner Electronic Guidance Svcs. Corp., Hunns Lake, N.Y., 1988—. Author: And No Clouds Over My Sun, 1973 (Female Writers award 1975), Native American Images and Recipes, 1991, Through the Glass, Clearly a Character Study of the Half-Breed in America, 1992. Founder Children of Profls. Orgn., Westchester County, N.Y., 1991—; pres. New Rochelle (N.Y.) Assn. Women Voters, 1981-89. Am. Sch. Honors scholar, 1959; City of Mt. Vernon grantee, 1982-84. Mem. Internat. Culture Club (pres. 1982—), N.Y. Profl. Women (pres. 1990-92), N.Y. State Tchrs. Fedn., N.Y. State Retired Tchrs. Assn., Westchester County Minority Bus. Assn. (pres. 1982—), Westchester County Minority Real Estate Bd. (bd. dirs. 1982—), Cherokee Child Orgn. (chmn. 1988-92, Native Am. Visionary award 1992, Inner Man award 1991). Home: PO Box 310 Hunns Lake NY 12581 Office: Electronic Guidance Svcs PO Box 27 Stanfordville NY 12581

OWENS, SHELBY JEAN, electrologist, writer; b. Flintville, Tenn., Dec. 18, 1936; d. Harvey Chrethton and Emma Lucille (McDonald) Langford; m. David Randall Owens, Mar. 12, 1953 (div. Feb. 1970); children—Karen, Kristie, Kaylon; m. Richard Allen Brewer, May 26, 1977. Diploma Hoffman Electrolysis Inst., N.Y.C., 1968, postgrad. cert., 1972. Cert. clin. electrologist. Tech. typist Thiokol Chem. Corp., Huntsville, Ala., 1957-60; exec. sec. CFW Constrn. Co., Fayetteville, Tenn., 1961-65; pvt. practice electrolysis, Winchester, Tenn., 1968-70, Huntsville, 1970-77, Pensacola, Fla., 1975—; rsch. collaborator U. Ala., Birmingham. Author: About that Hair, 1989; founder, Hirsutes Anonymous Initiating Removal Reform, Inc., 1986—. Recipient Pres.'s award Am. Electrolysis Assn., 1984. Mem. Electrolysis Soc. Fla. (lobbyist 1979-86, pres. 1982-86), Am. Bus. Women's Assn. (Pensacola charter chpt.) (past pres., Woman of Yr. award 1984), Soc. Clin. and Med. Electrologists, Fla. Electrolysis Coun. (chmn. 1994). Democrat. Avocations: sewing, writing. Home: 3801 N 12th Ave Pensacola FL 32503-3161 Office: Owens Pub 213 Brent Ln Pensacola FL 32503-2204

OWENS, VIVIAN ANN, plant science educator, researcher; b. Conway, S.C., Sept. 2, 1948; d. Zack Jr. and Frances (Mishoe) O. BS, Howard U., 1971, MS, 1974; PhD, Cornell U., 1984. Assoc. prof. plant sci. Hampton (Va.) U., 1988—; vis. prof. Purdue U., summer 1994; faculty fellow EPA, Washington, summer 1990. Contbr. articles to profl. jours. Mem. Bot. Soc. Am., Am. Inst. Biol. Scis., Soc. Am. Foresters, Electron Microscopy Soc. Am., Va. Acad. Sci. Baptist. Office: Dept Biology Box 6625 Hampton VA 23668

OWEN-TOWLE, CAROLYN SHEETS, clergywoman; b. Upland, Calif., July 27, 1935; d. Millard Owen and Mary (Baskerville) Sheets; m. Charles Russell Chapman, June 29, 1957 (div. 1973); children: Christopher Charles, Jennifer Anne, Russell Owen; m. Thomas Allan Owen-Towle, Nov. 16, 1973. BS in Art and Art History, Scripps Coll., 1957; postgrad. in religion, U. Iowa, 1977. Ordained to ministry Unitarian-Universalist Ch., 1978. Minister 1st Unitarian Universalist Ch., San Diego, 1978—; pres. Ministerial Sisterhood, Unitarian Universalist Ch., 1980-82; mem. Unitarian Universalist Svc. Com., 1979-85, pres., 1983-85. Bd. dirs. Planned Parenthood, San Diego, 1980-86; mem. clergy adv. com. to Hospice, San Diego, 1980-83; mem. U.S. Rep. Jim Bates Hunger Adv. Com., San Diego, 1983-87; chaplain Interfaith AIDS Task Force, San Diego, 1988—. Mem. Unitarian Universalist Ministers Assn. (exec. com. 1988, pres. 1989-91). Office: 1st Unitarian Universalist Ch 4190 Front St San Diego CA 92103-2098

OWINGS, MARGARET WENTWORTH, conservationist, artist; b. Berkeley, Calif., Apr. 29, 1913; d. Frank W. and Jean (Pond) Wentworth; m. Malcolm Millard, 1937; 1 child, Wendy Millard Benjamin; m. Nathaniel Alexander Owings, Dec. 30, 1953. A.B., Mills Coll., 1934; postgrad., Radcliffe Coll., 1935; LHD, Mills Coll., 1993. One-woman shows include Santa Barbara (Calif.) Mus. Art, 1940, Stanford Art Gallery, 1951, stitchery exhbns. at M.H. De Young Mus., San Francisco, 1963, Internat. Folk Art Mus., Santa Fe, 1965. Commr. Calif. Parks, 1963-69, mem., Nat. Parks Found. Bd, 1968-69; bd. dirs. African Wildlife Leadership Found., 1968-80, Defenders of Wildlife, 1969-74; founder, pres. Friends of the Sea Otter, 1969-90; chair Calif. Mountain Lion Preservation Found., 1987; trustee Environmental Def. Fund, 1972-83; Regional trustee Mills Coll., 1962-68. Recipient Gold medal, Conservation Svc. award U.S. Dept. Interior, 1975, Converation award Calif. Acad. Scis., 1979, Am. Motors Conservation award, 1980, Joseph Wood Krutch medal Humane Soc. U.S., Nat. Audubon Soc. medal, 1983, A. Starker Leopole award Calif. Nature Conservancy, 1986, Gold medal UN Environment Program, 1988, Conservation award DAR, 1990, Disting. Svc. award Sierra Club, 1991. Home: Grimes Point Big Sur CA 93920

OWNBEY, LENORE F. DALY, real estate investment specialist; b. Fremont, Nebr., Feb. 24; d. Joseph E. and Anna R. (Godel) Daly; m. Amos B. Ownbey, June 18, 1948; children: Kenton, Stephen. BBA, U. Nebr. Cert. comml. investment mem. Real estate and comml. investment specialist, 1976—; lectr. in field. Writer, speaker Investment, Business and Personal Skills, Motivational and Inspirational. Recipient Ptnrs. in Excellence Achievement award Colo. Chpt. Nat. Speakers Assn., 1988, Cert. of Proclamation Internat. Women of Yr., 1992-93. Mem. Nat. Assn. Realtors, Colo. Assn. Realtors, Denver Bd. Realtors (life mem.), Comml. Investment Real Estate Inst. (life mem., cert. comml. investment mem.).

OWNBEY, PAMELA JEAN, civil engineer, environmental engineer; b. Eugene, Oreg., Sept. 5, 1953; d. Jelde Gene and Irene Neva (Beshears) Meyer; m. Anthony William Ownbey, May 2, 1972; children: Jill Suzanne, David Timothy. BS in Civil Engring. with high honors, Oregon State U., 1986, MS in Civil Engering., 1987. Registered profl. environ. engr., Oreg. Assoc. engr. Brown & Caldwell, Eugene, Oreg., 1987-89; civil engr. USDA-Willamette NF, Eugene, Oreg., 1989-95; environ. engr. Cascade Group, Eugene, Oreg., 1989—; civil engr. David Evans and Assocs., Bend, Oreg., 1995—. Guest speaker Childrens Miracle Network Telethon, Eugene, 1989; vol. Childrens Relief Nursery, Buena Vista Spanish Sch., Eugene, 1990—; asst. coach Kidsports, Eugene, 1992—. GPOP fellow EPA, 1986. Mem. ASCE, AWWA, WPCF. Home: PO Box 10921 Eugene OR 97440

OWNBY, CHARLOTTE LEDBETTER, anatomy educator; b. Amory, Miss., July 27, 1947; d. William Moss and Anna Faye (Long) Ledbetter; m. James Donald Ownby, Sept. 6, 1969; children: Holly Ruth, Mary Faye. BS in Zoology, U. Tenn., 1969, MS in Zoology, 1971; PhD in Anatomy, Colo. State U., 1975. Instr. Okla. State U., Stillwater, 1974-75, asst. prof., 1975-80, assoc. prof., 1980-84, prof., 1984—, dept. head, 1990—, dir. Electron Microscope Lab., 1977-87. Editor Proc. 9th World Congress Internat. Soc. Toxicology, 1989; editorial bd. Toxion, 1984—. Recipient SmithKline-Beecham award for rsch. excellence, 1992; NIH, USPHS grantee, 1984—. Mem. Okla. Soc. for Electron Microscopy (pres. 1977-78), Pan Am. Soc. on Toxinology (pres. 1984-85), Internat. Soc. on Toxinology (pres. elect 1992), Phi Beta Kappa, Sigma Xi, Phi Kappa Phi. Office: Okla State U Dept Physiol Scis 264 Vet Medicine Stillwater OK 74078

OWSIA, NASRIN AKBARNIA, pediatrician; b. Babol, Iran, Dec. 5, 1940; came to U.S., 1968; d. Ahmad and Hoora O.; m. Behrooz A. Akbarnia, Mar. 19, 1968; children: Halleh, Ladan, Ramin. MD, Tehran (Iran) U., 1966. Intern in pediatrics Berkshire Med. Ctr. Hosp., Pittsfield, Mass., 1968-69; resident in pediatrics Albany (N.Y.) Med. Ctr. Hosp., 1969-72; pediatric gastroenterologist St. Christopher Hosp. for Children, Phila., 1972-73; asst. prof. Albany Med. Coll., 1973-76, Tehran U., 1976-80; asst. prof. St. Louis U. Med. Ctr., 1981-89, clin. assoc. prof., 1989-90; pvt. practice San Diego, 1990—. Bd. mem. Persian Cultural Ctr., San Diego, 1993—. Recipient award AMA. Fellow Am. Acad. Pediatrics; mem. Allergy and Asthma Found., Calif. Med. Soc., San Diego Med. Soc. Office: 8010 Frost St No 414 San Diego CA 92123-4284

OWSLEY, TINA KATHLEEN, special education educator; b. Ponca City, Okla., Apr. 3, 1953; d. Lindsey C. Jr. and Nina Jane (Lotts) O. BA in Edn., Northeastern Okla. State U., 1975, MS in Edn., 1978; cert. in deaf edn., Tex. Woman's U., 1981; cert. in spl. edn. adminstrn., Gallaudet U., Washington, 1984. Cert. speech correction, learning disabilities, Mo., speech therapy, learning disabilites, deaf edn., Okla., speech pathology, learning disabilities, deaf edn., educable mentally handicapped, physically impaired, Kans. Tchr. learning disabilities, speech pathologist Perry County Schs., Perryville, Mo., 1975-77; tchr. learning disabilities Vinita (Okla.) Pub. Schs., 1977-78; cons. hearing impaired Sequoyah County Spl. Edn. Coop., Sallisaw, Okla., 1978-80; tchr. hearing impaired Ft. Gibson (Okla.) Pub. Schs., 1980-83; asst. to the v.p. Gallaudet U., 1983-84; coord., tchr. hearing impaired Shawnee County Spl. Edn. Coop., Topeka, 1984—; parent advisor Project ECHO, Okla. Dept. Edn., Oklahoma City, 1978-83; early interventionist Hearing Cons., Topeka, 1989—. Co-author: Curriculum Guide - Presch. Hearing Impaired Children, 1991. Mem. Nat. Assn. for Edn. of Young Children (Kans. chpt., pres. Topeka Assn. 1988-89), NEA (Kans. chpt., mem. Topeka spl. edn. com. 1991—, polit. action com. 1991—), Coun. for Exceptional Children (pres. Chpt. 204 1989—, v.p. Kans. Fedn. 1991-92, pres.-elect Kans. Fedn. 1992-93, pres. 1993-94, chmn. Spl. Edn. Day at the Legis. Kans. Coun. 1991), Kans. Divsn. Early Childhood (pres. 1989-90, mem. chair 1993—), Kans. Educators of Hearing Impaired (pres. 1989-90), Kans. Commn. for Deaf and Hearing Impaired (chair Early Identification and Intervention Coun. 1990—), Soroptimist Internat. Am. (corr. sec. local chpt. 1991-92, cmty. svc. chair 1991—, del. 1992—, bd. dirs. 1992-93, rec. sec. 1993-94, Soroptimist of the Yr. 1993), Sertoma Internat. (publicity chair 1992-94), Topeka Tots Team (sec. 1991—), Jr. Deaf Club (sponsor 1992—), Camp Fire Coun. (bd. dirs. 1993—, chair program/membership 1993—). Republican. Mem. Christian Ch. (Disciples of Christ). Home: 4711 SE Girard St Topeka KS 66609-1838 Office: Shawnee County Spl Edn Coop 1725 SW Arnold Ave Topeka KS 66604-3306

OXELL, LOIE GWENDOLYN, fashion and beauty educator, consultant, columnist; b. Sioux City, Iowa, Nov. 17, 1917; d. Lyman Stanley and Loie Erma (Crill) Barton; m. Eugene Edwin Eschenbrenner, Aug. 8, 1936 (dec. 1954); children: Patricia Gene, Eugene Edward; m. Henry J. Oxell, Nov. 3, 1956. AS in Fashion Merchandising, Broward C.C., Davie, Fla., 1978. Fashion rep. Crestmoor Suit & Coat Co., St. Louis, 1951-56; cons./instr. Miami-Herald Newspaper Glamor Clinic, Miami, Fla., 1957-72; pres./owner Loie's (Loy's) Inc., Miami, Fla., 1958-71; lectr. tng. seminars nat. meetings of A.C. Sparkplug Divsn. Gen. Motors Exec. Wives, Boca Raton, Fla., 1963-65; instr./lectr. Charron-Williams Coll., Miami, 1973-77; instr. Fashion Inst. Ft. Lauderdale, Fla., 1977-86; pres./owner Image Power Unltd., Plantation, Fla., 1992—; lectr. in field; columnist Sr. Life News, Fla., 1992—. Author: I'd Like You to Meet My Wife, 1964. Vol. The Work Force, The AARP Sr. Cmty. Svc. Program, Ft. Lauderdale, 1993—; mem. com. Miami Children's Hosp. Recipient Cert. of Appreciation Dade County Welfare Dept. Youth Hall, Miami, 1966, Community TV Found., Miami, 1966, 71, Woman of the Yr. award Am. Bus. Women's Assn. (Venice of Am. chpt.), 1976-77, Award for Svc. AARP Sr. Community Svc. Program, 1993. Mem. The Fashion Group Internat. Office: Image Power Unltd 1859 N Pine Island Rd # 339 Plantation FL 33322-5224

OXLEY, ANN, television executive; b. Canton, Ohio, Aug. 3, 1924; d. Edward and Dorothy (Duffy) Adang. B.A. with distinction, Ind. U., 1974, M.P.A., 1982; m. Jack Raymond Oxley, Aug. 10, 1946; children: Kathleen Oxley Wiggins, Maureen Oxley Gaff, Joseph, Jeffrey, Christeen Oxley Rhodes, Daniel, Sister Julie Marie Oxley, Jamie, Kevin, Valerie Oxley Fouch, Amy. Advt. account salesperson Ft. Wayne (Ind.) Jour. Gazette, 1945-47; office mgr. Ind. Equestrian Assn., Ft. Wayne, 1971-73; rsch. dir. Taxpayers Rsch. Assn., Ft. Wayne, 1974-76; exec. dir. Ft. Wayne Pub. TV Inc., 1976-86; founder, owner Akin Assocs., 1987—. Active Bicentennial Com., 1976; adviser Media Arts Panel Ind. Arts Commn. Mem. AAUW, Svc. Corp Retired Execs. (publicity chair., 1986nat. mktg. dir. 1989-90), Mensa Internat., C. of C. (cultural com.), Phi Alpha Alpha. Roman Catholic. Home: 4305 Arlington Ave Fort Wayne IN 46807-2635 Office: SCORE 1300 S Harrison Federal Bldg Fort Wayne IN 46807

OZAWA, MARTHA NAOKO, social work educator; b. Ashikaga, Tochigi, Japan, Sept. 30, 1933; came to U.S., 1963; d. Tokuichi and Fumi (Kawashima) O.; m. May 1959 (div. May 1966). BA in Econs., Aoyama Gakuin U., 1956; MS in Social Work, U. Wis., 1966, PhD in Social Welfare, 1969. Asst. prof. social work Portland (Oreg.) State U., 1969-70, assoc. prof. social work, 1970-72; assoc. rsch. prof. social work NYU, 1972-75; assoc. prof. social work Portland State U., 1975-76; prof. social work Washington U., St. Louis, 1976-85, Bettie Bofinger Brown prof. social policy, 1985—. Author: Income Maintenance and Work Incentives, 1982; editor: Women's Life Cycle: Japan-U.S. Comparison in Income Maintenance, 1989, Women's Life Cycle and Economic Insecurity: Problems and Proposals, 1989; editorial bd. Social Work, Silver Spring, Md., 1972-75, 85-88, New Eng. Jour. Human Svcs., Boston, 1987—, Encyc. of Social Work, Silver Spring, 1974-77, 91—, Jour. Social Svc. Rsch., 1977—, Children and Youth Svcs. Rev., 1991—, Social Work Rsch., 1994—. Grantee Adminstrn. on Aging, Washington, 1979, 84, Nat. Inst. Mental Health, 1990-93. Mem. Nat. Assn. Social Workers, Nat. Acad. Social Ins., Nat. Conf. on Social Welfare (bd. dirs. 1981-87), The Gerontol. Soc. Am., Coun. Social Work Edn., Washington U. Faculty Club (bd. dirs. 1988-91). Home: 13018 Tiger Lily Ct Saint Louis MO 63146-4339 Office: Washington U Campus PO Box 1196 Saint Louis MO 63130-4899

OZER, MARTHA ROSS, school psychologist; b. Richmond, Ky., Sept. 4, 1932; d. Robert Lee and Virginia Eudelle (Hurst) Ross; m. John Dudley Redden, Dec. 27, 1953 (dec. June 1969); children: Mary, Patricia, Robert, Mark; m. Mark N. Ozer, Aug. 12, 1979. BA in Elem. Edn., Georgetown Coll., 1954; MA in Counseling, Murray State U., 1966, MS in Psychology, 1968; EdD in Edn. Adminstrn., U. Ky., 1976. Cert. sch. psychologist with automous functioning, Ky.; lic. sch. psychologist, Va. Elem. tchr. Jefferson County Pub. Schs., Louisville, 1954-58, Hickman County Pub. Schs., Campbellsburg, Ky., 1960-62; tchr. emotional disturbed, dir. psychol. svcs. Paducah (Ky.) Pub. Schs., 1965-70; psychologist, program dir. Louisville Pub. Schs., 1970-74; doctoral intern Bur. Edn. for Handicapped U.S. Dept. Edn., Washington, 1974-75; program dir. project sci. tech. and disability AAAS, Washington, 1975-86; postdoctoral intern NYU Brain Trauma Program NYU Med. Ctr., N.Y.C., 1986-87; program dir., adminstr., asst. prof. dept. rehab. medicine Med. Coll. Va., Richmond, 1987-89; psychologist MCV Pediatric Devel. Ctr., Richmond, 1989; sch. psychologist Fairfax (Va.) County Pub. Schs., 1989—; cons. Am. Coun. on Edn., Washington, 1976—, numerous other profl. and disability orgns. Contbr. articles to profl. jours. on access for persons with disabilities to sci. edn. and careers, contbn. of sci./tech. to persons with disabilities. Advisor Disability Rights, 1975-86. Recipient U.S. Presdl. Pub. Sector award, award Am. Coalition Citizens with Disabilities, 1980, Alumni award Geotgetown Coll., 1985; grantee U.S. Dept. Edn., 1975-86, U.S. Dept. Civil Rights, 1975-90, Grant Found., 1975-77, Exxon Found., 1976, IBM, 1976, NSF, 1977-86, Nat. Inst. for Rehab. Rsch., 1978-84. Mem. NSTA (award), APA (bd. dirs. rehab. sect.), NASP (nat. cert.), Va. Psychol. Assn., Assn. Handicapped Student Svc. Programs in Post-Secondary Edn. (editor jour. 1988-91). Home: 3420 38th St NW Apt A-415 Washington DC 20016

OZI, ELIZABETH, private school administrator; b. São Paulo, Brazil, Aug. 5, 1959; d. Heni and Firmina O. BA in Psychology, U. Las Vegas, 1987; postgrad., NOVA U., Fla., 1989—. Cert. tchr. Tchr. Clark County Sch. Dist., Las Vegas, Nev., 1990-94; owner, sch. dir. Parent's Choice, Las Vegas, Nev., 1993—; dir. Home Base Bus., Las Vegas, Nev., 1993—. Interviewer (Radio Show Series) Recognizing Signs to Prevent Suicide, 1990. Counselor Suicide Prevention, Nev., 1988-90. Mem. Psi Chi. Home: 4646 Grasshopper Dr Las Vegas NV 89122

OZICK, CYNTHIA, author; b. N.Y.C., Apr. 17, 1928; d. William and Celia (Regelson) O.; m. Bernard Hallote, Sept. 7, 1952; 1 dau., Rachel Sarah. BA cum laude with honors in English, NYU, 1949; MA, Ohio State U., 1950; LHD (hon.), Yeshiva U., 1984, Hebrew Union Coll., 1984, Williams Coll., 1986, Hunter Coll., 1987, Jewish Theol. Sem. Am., 1988, Adelphi U., 1988, SUNY, 1989, Brandeis U., 1990, Bard Coll., 1991, Spertus Coll., 1991, Skidmore Coll., 1992. Author: Trust, 1966, The Pagan Rabbi and Other Stories, 1971, Bloodshed and Three Novellas, 1976, Levitation: Five Fictions, 1982, Art and Ardor: Essays, 1983, The Cannibal Galaxy, 1983, The Messiah of Stockholm, 1987, Metaphor and Memory: Essays, 1989, The Shawl, 1989, Epodes: First Poems, 1992, What Henry James Knew, and Other Essays on Writers, 1994, Portrait of the Artist as a Bad Character, and Other Essays on Writing, 1995, (play) Blue Light, 1994; also poetry, criticism, revs., transls., essays and fictions in numerous periodicals and anthologies. Phi Beta Kappa orator, Harvard U., 1985. Recipient Mildred and Harold Strauss Living award Am. Acad. Arts and Letters, 1983, Rea award for short story, 1986; Lucy Martin Donnelly fellow, Bryn Mawr Coll., 1992, Guggenheim fellow, 1982. Mem. PEN, Authors League, Am. Acad. of Arts and Scis., Am. Acad. of Arts and Letters, Dramatists Guild, Académie Universelle des Cultures (Paris), Phi Beta Kappa. Office: care Alfred A Knopf Co 201 E 50th St New York NY 10022-7703

PABON-PEREZ, HEIDI, physicist; b. San Juan, Oct. 6, 1939; d. José Antonio Pabon-Rivera and Tomasa D. (Pérez) Pabon. BS, U. Puerto Rico, 1960; MS, U. Rochester, 1961. Health physicist U. P.R. Nuclear Ctr., 1961-69, Dr. I. Gonzalez Martinez Hosp., San Juan, 1965-69; physicist State Dept. P.R., 1964-77; radiological physicist P.R. Med. Ctr., San Juan, 1969-77; instr. Radiological Scis. U. P.R., 1976-77; cons. Med. Physicist Caguas (P.R.) Nuclear Medicine Lab., 1977; lt. Med. Svc. Corps. USN, 1977-80; acting program dir. U. P.R., 1981-84, asst. prof., 1980-84, 1980—; health physicist VA Med. Ctr., San Juan, 1984—. Mem., treas. P.R. YL Club, San Juan, 1977—. Lt. USN, 1977-80. Home: BC9 Yagrumo St Valle Arriba Heights PR 00983 Office: VA Medical Center One Veterans Pla San Juan PR 00927-5800

PACA, VERONICA, financial consultant, computer programmer; b. New Haven; d. David Paca and Lois P. (Flowers) Lewis; 1 child, Gerald Dávon Hampton II. AS in Computer Sci., South Ctrl. C.C., New Haven, 1981; BSBA, So. Conn. State U., 1984. Founder, CEO, bookkeeper/acct. The Bottom Line, Inc.-Bookkeeping Svcs.; ind. fin. cons. New Haven. Software programmer Miniorty Construction Payroll Monitoring Compliance Recordngs, 1994. Pres. PTO-PTA Davis St. Sch., New Haven, 1993-94; assoc. Urban League South Ctrl. Conn., New Haven, 1994. Mem. Greater New Haven Bus. & Profls. Assn. (bd. dirs. rep. 1994), Greater New Haven C. of C. Office: The Bottom Line Inc 50 Fitch St Ste 226 New Haven CT 06515

PACE, ANN L., psychologist; b. N.Y.C.; d. Pasquale and Celia (Baia) Pascarelli; m. Thomas R. Pace, Sept. 27; children: Anthony, Louis, Thomas Jr. AS, Miami-Dade C.C., 1976; BA, MA in Psychology, Barry U., 1978; PhD in Social Psychology, Clayton U., 1982. Lic. hypnotherapist. Instr. Miami-Dade C.C. and Med. Ctr., 1977—, Dade County Pub. Schs., Miami, 1975—; exec. dir. Singles for Svc., Miami, 1991—; dir. P.A.C.E.S. Program, Miami, 1980—; owner, instr. Syosset (N.Y.) Art Gallery, 1965-74; exec. dir. World Care, Miami, 1989—, Freedom Learning Ctr., Miami, 1976—; psychologist pvt. practice Human Devel. Svcs., Miami, 1987—; dir. No. Miami Beach Coun. Self Esteem, 1990—, Freedom Health Care Svcs., No. Miami Beach, 1983—, P.A.C.E.S. Svc. Clubs, Miami, 1980—. Author: Universal Eye, 1981, Manual of Self-Esteem, 1992, (tng. program and manual) Vulnerability and Power, 1994; contbr. articles to profl. jours. Coord. self-esteem program Juvenile Ct. Remediation Program for Youth Offenders. Grantee Rosenberg Found., 1981; nominated to Fla. Women's Hall of Fame, 1985. Mem. Nat. Coun. Self-Esteem, S.E. Fla. Adult Literacy Educators Assn., Am. Assn. Study of Mental Imagery, Assn. for Advanced Ethical Hypnosis. Office: Human Devel Svcs 909 N Miami Beach Blvd Ste 202 Miami FL 33162-3712

PACE, CAROLINA JOLLIFF, communications executive, commercial real estate investor; b. Dallas, Apr. 12, 1938; d. Lindsay Gafford and Carolina (Juden) Jolliff; student Holton-Arms Jr. Coll., 1956-57; BA in Comparative Lit., So. Meth. U., 1960; m. John McIver Pace, Oct. 7, 1961. Promotional advisor, dir. season ticket sales Dallas Theatre Ctr., 1960-61; exec. sec. Dallas Book and Author Luncheon, 1959-63; promotional and instl. cons. Henry Regnery-Reilly & Lee Pub. Co., Chgo., 1962-65; pub. trade rep. various cos., instl. rep. Don R. Phillips Co., Southeastern area, 1965-67; Southwestern rep. Ednl. Reading Svc., Inc.-Troll Assocs., Mahwah, N.J., 1967-72; v.p., dir. multimedia div. Melton Book Co., Dallas, 1972-79; v.p. mktg. Webster's Internat., Inc., Nashville, 1980-82; pres. Carolina Pace, Inc., 1982—; mem. adv. bd. Nat. Info. Ctr. of Spl. Edn. Materials; mem. materials rev. panel Nat. Media Ctr. for Materials of Severely-Profoundly Handicapped, 1981; mem. mktg. product rev. bd. LINC Resources, 1982, 83, 84, mktg. task force, 1983, adv. bd., 1987; reviewer spl. edn. U.S. Dept. Edn., 1975-79, 85; rev. cons. Health and Humas Svcs., 1982, 83, 84, 86; product rev. task force CEC, 1984, 85, 86; cons. Ednl. Cable Consortium, Summit, N.J., 1982-87. Mem. adv. coun. Grad. System Sch. Libr. and Info. Sci. Found., U. Tex., 1987—; co-vice chair Friends Highland Park Libr., 1989; mem. focus group City Dallas Growth Policy Plan; mem. art and design com. West Downtown Ctrs.; active Dallas City Wide Parking Task Force, Ctrl. Transp. Forum Ctrl. Bus. Dist., Union Sta. Art & Design Com., Downtown Transfer Ctrs., Art and Design Com., West End Task Force, Ctrl. Bus. Dist. Task Force; co-founder Operation TexRec, 1990-91. Mem. Ctrl. Dallas Assn. (transportation com.), Dallas Plan (focus com.), Nat. Audio Visual Assn. (conf. panelist 1979), Internat. Comm. Industries Assn., Assn. Ednl. and Comm. Tech., Assn. Spl. Edn. Tech. (nat. dir., v.p. publicity 1980-82), Women's Nat. Book Assn, Women in Comm., Dallas Founders, Ctrl. Dallas Assn., Friends of the West End (pres. 1988—), West End Assn. Dallas (chmn. subcom. on traffic and parking 1986-87, com. demographic study 1987-88), Pub. Rels. Soc. Am., Coun. Exceptional Children (dir. exhibitors com., chmn. publ. com. 1979 conf., conf. speaker 1981), DAR (Jane Douglas chpt.), Dallas Zool. Soc., Dallas West End Hist. Dist. Assn., Dallas Mus. of Art, Dallas Southern Meml. Tex. Parking Assn., Kimball Art Mus., Alpha Delta Pi. Presbyterian. Producer ednl. videos; contbr. articles to profl. jours. Home: 4524 Lorraine Ave Dallas TX 75205-3613

PACE, KAREN YVONNE, mathematics and computer science educator; b. Jefferson City, Mo., Dec. 29, 1957; d. William John and Georgia (Loesch) Sippel; m. Charles Edward Pace, Dec. 27, 1982. EdB, Mo. State U., 1980; EdM, Drury U., 1985. Cert. secondary tchr. Tchr. Salem (Mo.) Sch. Dist., 1980—, Southwest Bapt. U., Boliver, Mo., 1985—; dist. chair Career Ladder Com., Salem, 1991-92; treas. Community Tchrs. Orgn., Salem, 1992-93; assessment expert Salem (Mo.) Sch. Dist., 1993-94; sr. leader Mo. Assessment Project 2000, 1994-95. Pres. Community Cause Club, Salem, 1994. Mem. Salem Tchrs. Assn. (budget com. chair 1992-94). Democrat. Home: PO Box 795 Salem MO 65560-0795 Office: Salem Sch Dist 1400 W Third St Salem MO 65560

PACE, LAURA DIANE See OMER, LAURA DIANE

PACE, MARY G(AY) B(ARKER), operations research analyst, statistician; b. Alton, Ill., June 14, 1944; d. James Allen and Wilma Augusta (Buck) Barker; m. Jack Arthur Windeler, June 10, 1967 (div. Aug. 1986); m. Jeffrey Stewart Pace, May 30, 1987. AAS, Fashion Inst. Tech., N.Y.C., 1964; BA magna cum laude, Montclair State Coll., 1969; MS, U. Mich., 1974, Purdue U., 1978. Statis. programmer Inst. for Cmty. Design Analysis, N.Y.C., 1974-76; statistician E.R. Squibb and Sons, New Brunswick, N.J., 1978-80; ops. rsch. analyst Tng. and Doctrine Command Analysis Command, U.S. Army, Ft. Leavenworth, Kans., 1980-83; ops. rsch. analyst U.S. Army Combined Arms Combat Devel. Activity, Ft. Leavenworth, 1983-84; sr. ops. rsch. analyst Office of Asst. Sec. of Def., Washington, 1984-85; tech. staff Los Alamos (N.Mex.) Nat. Lab., 1985-88; supervisory ops. rsch. analyst U.S. Army Operational Test and Evaluation Agy., Alexandria, 1989; pvt. practice cons. Alexandria, Va., 1987-90; tech. staff asst. to group v.p. The MITRE Corp., McLean, Va., 1990-91, mem. tech. staff, 1991-94; math. statistician US EPA, Washington, 1994—. Editor: Proceedings of the 55th Military Operations Research Society Symposium, 1987; contbr. author: Systems Analysis and Modeling in Defense, 1984. Recipient univ. fellowship Ohio State U., Columbus, 1972. Mem. Mil. Ops. Rsch. Soc. (dir. 1985-92, sec.-treas. 1988-89, v.p. for adminstrn. 1989-90, pres. 1990-91), Am. Statis. Assn., Assn. Computing Machinery, Washington Ops. Rsch. and Mgmt. Coun., Kappa Delta Pi. Home: 7027 Polins Ct Alexandria VA 22306-1458 Office: US EPA 401 M St SW Washington DC 20460

PACE, NORMA, economist, consulting firm executive. Grad., Hunter Coll., 1941; grad. study, Columbia U.; Ph.D. (hon.), Mich. Tech. U., 1975, Poly. Inst., N.Y., 1976, Cedar Crest Coll., 1977, Grove City Coll., 1980, City U. N.Y., 1981. Staff Econometric Inst.; with U.S. Economics Corp. (bus. adv. cons. service), 1944-71, pres., 1969-71; v.p., dir. indsl. econs. Lionel D. Edie & Co., N.Y.C., 1971-73; sr. v.p. Am. Paper Inst.; pres. ECAP (cons. firm), 1987-92; dir. WEPA Group (cons. firm), 1992—; asst. devel. visual aids for teaching econs. Columbia Visual Lab.; dir. Sears, Roebuck & Co., Ga. Pacific Corp., Englehard Corp., Hasbro Co., 3M Co., A. O. Smith Co.; gov. U.S. Postal Service;. Trustee Com. for Econ. Devel. Named to Hunter Coll. Hall of Fame, 1973. Mem. U.S. C. of C. Address: 100 E 42d St New York NY 10017

PACHAN, MARY JUDE KATHRYN DOROTHY, guidance counselor; b. East Otto, N.Y., Jan. 29, 1933; d. Nicholas and Mary (Podolinsky) P. BS in Edn., Medaille Coll., 1964; MS in Edn., St. Bonaventure U., 1972. Cert. guidance counseling, N.Y., elem. edn. tchr., N.Y. 3d grade tchr. Holy Cross Sch., Buffalo, 1955-56; 3d and 4th grade tchr. Immaculata Heart of Mary Sch., Buffalo, 1956-60; 8th grade tchr. Our Lady of Loretta Sch., Buffalo, 1960-64; tchr. English DeSales High Sch., Lockport, N.Y., 1964-68; counselor campus ministry SUNY, Buffalo, 1968-72; counselor St. Joseph's Collegiate Inst., Buffalo, 1973—; dir. guidance svcs. St. Joseph's Collegiate Inst., Buffalo, 1989—. Grantee in English, Nazareth Coll., Rochester, N.Y., 1965, journalism grantee Wall St., Boston U., 1966. Mem. N.Y. State Pers. and Guidance Assn., Counseling and Devel. Hospice Tng., AACD. Home: 557 Burroughs Dr Amherst NY 14226-3900 Office: St Josephs Collegiate Inst 845 Kenmore Ave Buffalo NY 14223-3195

PACHECO, MARGARET MARY, marketing executive; b. Waterville, Maine, June 9, 1962; d. Louis E. and Jeannine F. (Giguere) DeRosby; m. Joseph Pacheco III, Sept. 2, 1989. BJ, U. Mo., 1984. Staff writer, photographer Gannett Newspapers Corp., Waterville, 1976-79; asst. news dir. Kennebec Broadcasting Co., Waterville, 1979-80; staff writer McClatchy Newspapers Corp., Sacramento, Calif., 1982-84; mktg. dir. Leatherby Mktg. Inc., Sacramento, 1984-85; sr. market rsch. analyst Electronic Data Systems, Dallas, 1985-90; dir. mktg. Power Computing Co., Dallas, 1990-93; pres. Daniel Group, Dallas, 1993—. Jacob Stein Meml. scholar U. Mo., 1984. Mem. Internat. Assn. Bus. Communicators, Soc. Competitive Intelligence Profls., Am. Mktg. Assn. Office: 14180 N Dallas Pkwy Ste 600 Dallas TX 75240

PACK, PHOEBE KATHERINE FINLEY, civic worker; b. Portland, Oreg., Feb. 2, 1907; d. William Lovell and Irene (Barnhart) Finley; student U. Calif., Berkeley, 1926-27; B.A., U. Oreg., 1930; m. Arthur Newton Pack, June 11, 1936; children: Charles Lathrop, Phoebe Irene. Layman referee Pima County Juvenile Ct., Tucson, 1958-71; mem. pres.'s council Menninger Found., Topeka; mem. Alcoholism Council So. Ariz., 1960—; bd. dirs. Kress Nursing Sch., Tucson, 1957-67, Pima County Assn. for Mental Health, 1958—, Ariz. Assn. for Mental Health, Phoenix, 1963—, U. Ariz. Found., Casa de los Niños Crisis Nursery; co-founder Ariz.-Sonora Desert Mus., Tucson, 1975—, Ghost Ranch Found., N.Mex.; bd. dirs. Tucson Urban League, Tucson YMCA Youth Found. Mem. Mt. Vernon Ladies Assn. Union (state vice regent, 1962-84),Mt. Vernon One Hundred (founder), Nature Conservancy (life), Alpha Phi. Home: Villa Compana 6653 E Carondelet Dr Apt 415 Tucson AZ 85710-2153

PACK, SUSAN JOAN, art consultant; b. N.Y.C., June 15, 1951; d. Howard Meade and Nancy (Buckley) P. BA summa cum laude, Princeton U., 1973. Market researcher Case & McGrath Inc., N.Y.C., 1977-78; copywriter Laurence Charles & Free, N.Y.C., 1978-83, Warwick Advt., N.Y.C., 1983-85; sr. copywriter Saatchi & Saatchi Compton, N.Y.C., 1985-88; pres. The Pack Collection, 1989—. Mem. Princeton (N.J.) U. Library Council, 1985—; trustee Pack Found. for Med. Research, N.Y., 1983—; bd. dirs. The Poster Soc., N.Y., 1985-87. Recipient 4 Clio awards, 1981, 1 Clio award, 1982.

PACKARD, BARBARA BAUGH, science institute administrator, physician, physiologist; b. Uniontown, Pa., Mar. 10, 1938; d. Walter Ray and Yolande (Ciarlo) Baugh; m. Lawrence Arthur Krames, Nov. 24, 1963 (div. 1971); m. John E. Packard III, July 14, 1979. B.S., Waynesburg Coll., 1960; M.S., W. Va. U., 1961, Ph.D., 1964; M.D., U. Ala.-Birmingham, 1974. Rsch. assoc. Boston U., 1966; instr. biology, rsch. assoc. in medicine U. Chgo., 1966-67; physiologist myocardial infarction br. Nat. Heart Inst., Bethesda, Md., 1967-71; rsch. assoc. U. Ala., Birmingham, 1971-74; Osler med. intern Johns Hopkins Hosp., Balt., 1974-75; sr. med. scientist adminstr. cardiac disease br. div. heart and vascular disease Nat. Heart, Lung, and Blood Inst., Bethesda, Md., 1975-79, assoc. dir. cardiology, 1979-82, dir. div. heart and vascular diseases, 1980-86, assoc. dir. for sci. program operation, 1986—. Trustee Waynesburg Coll., 1991—. Served with USPHS, 1975—. Decorated USPHS Commendation Medal, Outstanding Svc. medal, 1986, Meritorious Svc. medal, 1988, Disting. Svc. medal 1991; recipient Disting. Pa. Coll. Alumni citation, 1991. Fellow Am. Coll. Cardiology (bd. govs. 1992—); mem. Am. Physiol Soc., Am. Heart Assn., Johns Hopkins Med. and Surgical Soc., Assn. Military Surgeons, Sigma Xi. Office: Nat Heart Lung & Blood Inst Bldg 31 Rm 5A03 9000 Rockville Pike Bethesda MD 20892-0001

PACKARD, BONNIE BENNETT, state legislator; b. Concord, N.H., Nov. 9, 1946; d. James Oliver and Caro Lucia (Arsenault) Bennett; m. David Bartlett Packard, Oct. 1, 1983. Mem. N.H. Ho. of Reps., Concord, 1981-82, 85—, vice chair ho. econ. devel. com., 1992, chair ho. commerce com., 1993—; v.p., treas. Dodd Ins. Agy., Contoocook, N.H., 1984-85; bd. dirs. Bus. Fin. Authority. State pres. N.H. Fedn. Rep. Women, 1982-83; chmn. Merrimack County (N.H.) Rep. Com., 1979-80; mem. Hillsborough County Rep. Com., 1995, chair Hillsborough County Del., 1995—; mem. Bd. Selectmen, New Ipswich, N.H., 1989-90; nat. del. trustee Nat. Kidney Found., 1990-91, 1st v.p. N.H. chpt., 1990-91. Mem. New Ipswich Hist. Soc., Greenville Women's Club. Episcopalian. Home: 6 Joy Ln New Ipswich NH 03071-3610 Office: NH Ho of Reps Legis Office Building Rm 207 Concord NH 03301

PACKARD, MILDRED RUTH, middle school educator; b. Boulder, Colo., Sept. 8, 1947; d. Peter L.M. and Jane G. Packard. BA, Lynchburg Coll., 1969; MS, Va. Poly. Inst. and State U., 1973. Cert. phys. edn. tchr., Va. Tchr., basketball, gymnastics and track coach Osbourn High Sch., Manassas, Va., 1969-73; tchr., coach girls softball, basketball and volleyball Rippon Mid. Sch., Woodbridge, Va., 1973-89, athletic dir., 1982-89; tchr., athletic dir., volleyball coach Lake Ridge Mid. Sch., Woodbridge, 1989—. Mem. NEA, AAHPERD, Va. Edn. Assn., Prince William Edn. Assn., Va. Assn. Health, Phys. Edn., and Recreation. Office: Lake Ridge Mid Sch 12350 Mohican Rd Woodbridge VA 22192-1757

PACKARD, ROCHELLE SYBIL, elementary school educator; b. June 25, 1951; d. Dave Wallace and Jeanette (Goddy) P. BA in Early Childhood Edn., Point Park Coll., 1973; MEd in Elem. Edn., U. Pitts., 1975. Instrnl. II permanent tchg. cert., Pa. Substitute tchr. Pitts. Pub. Bd. Edn., 1973-77, kindergarten tchr., 1977—. Chair Israel Day Parade, Pitts., 1981; mem. Hadassah, Pitts., 1983—, Pioneer Women, Pitts., 1982—, ORT, Pitts., 1975—. Mem. Pitts. Fedn. Tchrs., Pitts. State Edn. Agy. Democrat. Jewish. Home: 1405 Browning Rd Pittsburgh PA 15206

PACKER, DIANA, reference librarian; b. Cleve., Sept. 4; d. Herman and Sabina (Hochman) Reich; m. Herbert Packer, June 21, 1964 (dec.); children: Cynthia, Jeremy, Todd. BA, Case Western Res. U., 1951, MLS, 1952. Libr. Horizons Rsch. Inc., Cleve., 1952-64, Cleveland Heights (Ohio) University Heights Pub. Libr., 1969—. Officer Cleveland Heights PTA, 1971-84; bd. dirs. LWV, Cleveland Heights, 1974—. Mem. Ohio Libr. Assn. Home: # 522 2201 Acacia Park Dr Lyndhurst OH 44124

PACKER, JACLYN, social psychologist; b. N.Y.C., Nov. 18, 1955. BA, Queens Coll., 1976; MA, CUNY, 1986, PhD, 1990. Rsch. assoc. Am. Found. Blind, N.Y.C., 1978-85; rsch. cons. N.Y.C., 1989-92; dep. dir. rsch. Med. and Health Rsch. Assn. N.Y.C., Inc., 1992-94; project dir. Am. Found. Blind, 1994—. Predoctoral fellow Ednl. Testing Svcs., Princeton, N.J., 1986; Grace LeGendre fellow Bus. & Profl. Women's Club of N.Y., 1986. Mem. APA, APHA, Am. Assn. Pub. Opinion Rsch. Office: Am Found Blind 15W 16th St New York NY 10011

PACKER, JOAN GARRETT, librarian; b. Houston, June 20, 1947; d. Julius Benjamin and Irma Dorothy (Fonville) Garrett; m. Giles Andrew Packer, Sept. 27, 1979. BA, U. Tex., 1968, MLS, 1969; MA in History, Cen. Conn. State U., 1980. Corp. libr. Houston Lighting and Power Co., 1969-70; asst. curriculum libr. Cen. Conn. State U., New Britain, 1971-81, head reference libr., 1981—; abstractor Hist. Abstracts, Santa Barbara, Calif., 1980-88; reviewer CHOICE jour., Middletown, Conn., 1984—, RQ jour., Chgo., 1987—; cons. Conn. Bank & Trust, Hartford, 1982. Author: Margaret Drabble: An Annotated Bibliography, 1988, Rebecca West: An Annotated Bibliography, 1991. Libr. sci. fellow U. Tex., 1968. Mem. ALA. Office: Cen Conn State U 1615 Stanley St New Britain CT 06050

PACKER, REKHA DESAI, lawyer; b. N.Y.C., Apr. 20, 1955; d. Rajanikant C. and Santosh (Nagpaul) Desai; m. Michael Benjamin Packer, Aug. 11, 1979. AB magna cum laude, Harvard U., 1976, JD, 1979. Bar: Mass. 1979, U.S. Dist. Ct. Mass. 1979, U.S. Tax. Ct. 1980. Assoc. Gaston & Snow, Boston, 1979-87, ptnr., 1987-91; sr. ptnr. Hale and Dorr, Boston, 1991—; speaker Fed. Tax Inst., 1987—, World Trade Inst., 1986—. Mem. Internat. Bar Assn. (mem. com. on investment cos., funds and trusts 1989—), ABA (mem. com. on regulated investment cos., labor law sect. 1986—, com. on U.S. activities of foreigners 1988—), Boston Bar Assn. (labor law sect. 1987—, co-chmn. internat. tax. com. 1987-89), Phi Beta Kappa. Office: Hale and Dorr 60 State St Boston MA 02109-1803

PACKERT, GAYLA BETH, lawyer; b. Corpus Christi, Tex., Sept. 25, 1953; d. Gilbert Norris and Virginia Elizabeth (Pearce) P.; m. James Michael Hall, Jan. 1, 1974 (div. 1985); m. Richard Christopher Burke, July 18, 1987; children: Christopher Geoffrey Makepeace Burke Packert, Jeremy Eliot Marvell Packert Burke. BA, La. Tech. U., 1973; MA, U. Ark., 1976; postgrad., U. Ill., 1975-81, JD, 1985. Bar: Ill. 1985, U.S. Dist. Ct. (no. dist.) Ill. 1985, U.S. Ct. Appeals (7th cir.) 1987, Va. 1988, U.S. Dist. Ct. (we. dist.) Va. 1989. Assoc. Jenner & Block, Chgo., 1985-88; law clk. U.S. Dist. Ct. Va. (we. dist.), Danville, 1988-89; asst. commonwealth atty. Commonwealth of Va., Lynchburg, Va., 1989—. Notes and comments editor U. Ill. Law Rev., 1984-85. Mem. ABA, Phi Beta Kappa. Home: 3900 Faculty Dr Lynchburg VA 24501-3110

PACKHAM, MARIAN AITCHISON, biochemistry educator; b. Toronto, Ont., Can., Dec. 13, 1927; d. James and Clara Louise (Campbell) A.; m. James Lennox Packham, June 25, 1949; children: Neil Lennox, Janet Melissa. BA, U. Toronto, 1949, PhD, 1954. Sr. fellow dept. biochemistry U. Toronto, 1954-58, lectr. dept. biochemistry, 1958-63, 66-67; rsch. assoc. dept. physiol. scis. Ont. Vet. Coll., U. Guelph, 1963-65; rsch. assoc. blood and cardiovascular disease rsch. unit U. Toronto, 1965-66; asst. prof. U. Toronto dept. biochemistry, 1967-72, assoc. prof., 1972-75, prof., 1975-89, acting chmn. dept. biochemistry, 1983, univ. prof., 1989—. Contbr. articles to profl. jours. Royal Soc. Can. fellow, 1991; recipient Lt. Govs. Silver medal Victoria Coll., 1949; co-recipient J. Allyn Taylor Internat. prize in Medicine, 1988. Mem. Can. Biochem. Soc., Am. Soc. Hematology, Can. Soc. Hematology, Am. Assn. Pathologists, Can. Soc. Clin. Investigation, Coun. Thrombosis of Am. Heart Assn., Internat. Soc. Thrombosis and Haemostasis, Can. Atherosclerosis. Office: U Toronto, Dept Biochemistry, Toronto, ON Canada M5S 1A8

PACKLICK, KATHLEEN ANN, artist, gallery owner; b. Pittsfield, Mass., Aug. 2, 1950; d. Frank Stanley and Barbara Jean (Brown) P.; m. Daniel Rhodes Murphy, June 14, 1985. BFA, U. Mass., 1972; MFA, Sch. of Art Inst. of Chgo., 1976. Instr. fiber dept. Sch. Art Inst. Chgo., 1975-76; art instr. Belvoir Terr., Lenox, Mass., 1977; freelance paste-up artist Houston City Mag., 1978-80; geol. drafting specialist Dorchester Oil Co., Houston, 1978-80, Pennzoil, Houston, 1980-84; owner, framer K. Packlick Framing, Houston, 1984-87; owner, dir. West End Gallery, Houston, 1991—; spl. instr. Kansas City Art Inst., 1994; affiliate artist U. Houston, 1993; visual artist resident Vt. Studio Ctr., Johnson, 1994. Illustrator for mag. Progressive Architecture, 1986 (Advt. award). Recipient Fiber award Beaux Arts Designer/Craftsman '75, 1975, Best of Show award New Horizons in Art, 1976, Honorable Mention award Assistance League, 1990, Jurors Merit award Tex. Fine Art Assn., 1994. Democrat. Roman Catholic. Office: West End Gallery 5427 Blossom St Houston TX 77007-5150

PACKMAN, VICKI SUE, assessment analyst; b. Piqua, Ohio, Dec. 8, 1948; d. Charles Richard Packman and Norma Jean (Zimpher) Westerveld. BA in Psychology, Calif. State U., Long Beach, 1977, MS in Indsl. Psychology, 1983. Ind. contractor, cons. L.A., Lafayette and Rosemead, Calif., 1981-83; sr. assessment analyst Salt River Project, Phoenix, 1983—. Pres. Tempe (Ariz.) Soroptimists, 1986. Mem. ACA, APA, Nat. Career Devel. Assn., Pers. Testing Coun. (co-founder, past pres., bd. dirs. 1989—), Ariz. Career Devel. Assn. (sec. 1993-94, v.p. edn. 1995), Soc. Indsl. and Orgnl. Psychology, Phi Kappa Phi. Home: 6333 E Carolina Dr Scottsdale AZ 85254 Office: Salt River Project CRF 205 PO Box 52025 Phoenix AZ 85072-2025

PADBERG, HARRIET ANN, mathematics educator; b. St. Louis, Nov. 13, 1922; d. Harry J. and Marie L. (Kilgen) P. AB with honors, Maryville Coll., St. Louis, 1943; MMus, U. Cin., 1949; MA, St. Louis U., 1956, PhD, 1964. Registered music therapist; cert. tchr. math. and music, La., Mo. Tchr. elem. math. and music Kenwood Acad., Albany, N.Y., 1944-46; tchr. secondary math. Acad. of Sacred Heart, Cin., 1946-47; instr. math. and music Acad. and Coll. of Sacred Heart, Grand Coteau, La., 1947-48; secondary tchr. music Acad. Sacred Heart, St. Charles, Mo., 1948-50; instr. math. and music Acad. and Coll. Sacred Heart, Grand Coteau, 1950-55, Maryville Coll., St. Louis, 1955-56; tchr. elem. and secondary math. and music Acad. Sacred Heart, St. Louis, 1956-57; asst. prof. Maryville Coll., St. Louis, 1957-64, assoc. prof., 1964-68, prof. math., 1968-92, prof. emeritus, 1992—; music therapist Emmaus Homes, Marthasville, Mo., 1992—. Recipient Alumni Centennial award Maryville Coll., St. Louis, 1986; grantee Danforth Found., Colorado Springs, 1970, Tallahassee, 1970, Edn. Devel. Ctr., Mass., 1975, U. Kans., 1980. Mem. Assn. Women in Math., Am. Math. Soc., Math. Assn. Am., Nat. Coun. Tchr. Math., Mo. Acad. Sci., Delta Epsilon Sigma (sec. local chpt. 1962), Pi Mu Epsilon (sec. local chpt. 1958), Sigma Xi.

PADBERG, HELEN SWAN, violinist; b. Shawnee, Okla.; d. Frank P. and Birdie B. (Rudell) Swan; AA, Stephens Coll., 1938; Mus.B., U. Okla., 1940; Mus.M., Northwestern U., 1941; student Jacques Gordon; m. Frank Padberg, Feb. 6, 1943; children: Frank, Kristen. Solo performances and concerts, 1932—; mem. faculty string quartet and symphony soloist Stephens Coll., 1937-38; violinist Oklahoma City Symphony Summer Concerts, 1940; soloist Northwestern U. Symphony, 1941; USO performer, 1941-43; violinist Nat. Orchestral Assn. and Am. Youth Orch., N.Y.C., 1944-46; tchr. strings Maywood (Ill.), 1946-47; asst. concertmaster West Suburban Symphony, Chgo., 1947-48; mem. Chgo. Women's Symphony, Chgo. Civic Orch. and chamber music groups, 1947-51; violinist Ark. String Trio, 1952-58; concertmaster Ark. Symphony and Little Rock Philharmonic, 1953-57, Marjorie Lawrence TV Series, Ark., 1953-54; pvt. tchr. violin, Little Rock, 1953-66; accompanist and performer on piano, harp. Pres., Ark. Med. Soc. Aux., 1962-63, historian, 1963-94; co-founder Little Rock Chamber Music Soc., 1954; pres. bd. dirs. Vis. Nurse Assn. of Pulaski County, Ark., 1967-69; bd. dirs. Internat. Visitors Ctr., Chgo., 1988—, Stephens Coll. Alumna Assn. Bd.; elder, trustee Presbyn. ch. Mem. Am. Harp Soc., Chgo. Harp Soc. (sec. 1979-84), Am. Fedn. Musicians, Am. Opera Soc. (historian 1987—), Am. Opera Soc. of Chgo. (v.p. and program chmn. 1981-82, pres. 1984-87), Internat. Women Assocs. (chmn. 1988-91), Pi Kappa Lambda, Mu Phi Epsilon, Pi Beta Phi (pres. Little Rock Alumnae Club). Clubs: Aesthetic (pres. Little Rock); Womens' Athletic of Chgo. Home: 175 E Delaware Pl Chicago IL 60611-1756

PADDOCK, PAULA J., geriatrics nurse; b. Rochester, N.Y., Oct. 26, 1956; d. Eugene J. and Marguerite R. (Bailey) O'Brien; m. Wayne W. Paddock, Jan. 3, 1981; children: Keith Allen, Eric William. AAS in Nursing, Community Coll. Finger Lakes, 1977. RN, N.Mex., N.Y. Float nurse, charge nurse emergency Lovelace Bataan Med. Ctr., Albuquerque, 1978-79; asst. head nurse pediatrics, charge surg. specialist St. Joseph Hosp., Albuquerque, 1979-83; head nurse Ontario County Health Facility, Canadaigua, N.Y., 1983-86; head nurse, relief supr. Hurlbut Nursing Home, Rochester, N.Y., 1986-88; nurse mgr. Episcopal Ch. Home, Rochester, 1988-90; asst. v.p. nursing, nurse mgr. Thompson Nursing Home, Canandaigua, 1990—; nurse trainer pediatrics in field. Mem. CNA (program coord., program instr., clin. evaulator), Nat. Nurses Assn. Home: 2115 Elton Rd Ionia NY 14475-9701

PADEN, CAROLYN EILEEN BELKNAP, dietitian; b. Takoma Park, Md., Dec. 10, 1953; d. Donald Julius and Lydian Allyne (Plyer) Belknap; m. Raymond Louis Paden, Dec. 29, 1985; 1 child, Matthew Louis. BS in Home Econs. cum laude, Southern Coll., 1977; MS in Nutrition, Loma Linda (Calif.) U., 1983. Registered dietitian. Dietitic tech. Loma Linda U. Med. Ctr., 1978-82, nutritional support dietitian, 1982-84; clin. dietitian Mercy Meml. Med. Ctr., St. Joseph, Mich., 1984-86, mgr. clin. nutrition svcs., 1986—; instr. dietetics Andrews U., Berrien Springs, Mich., 1986—; researcher nutritional status of hospitalized patients Mercy Meml. Med. Ctr., St. Joseph, 1986, 87; cons. nutritional support various Berrien County hosps., 1984—. Mem. Am. Dietetic Assn., Am. Soc. Parenteral and Enteral Nutrition. Adventist. Home: 195 Knott Rd Niles MI 49120-9025 Office: Mercy Meml Med Ctr 1234 Napier Ave Saint Joseph MI 49085-2158

PADGETT, GAIL BLANCHARD, lawyer; b. Douglasville, Ga., Aug. 20, 1949; d. William David and Dorothy Rose (Bennett) P. BA, Ga. State U., 1971, MD, 1974; JD, Georgetown U., 1981. Bar: Va., Ga., D.C., U.S. Supreme Ct. Tchr. Clayton Co. Bd. Edn., Jonesboro, Ga., 1971-77; spl. asst. to dir. Community Rels Svc., Chevy Chase, Md., 1977-81, gen. counsel, 1981-89, assoc. dir., 1989—. chmn. community bd. Countryside, Va., 1983-85; chmn. adminstrn. bd. Galilee Methodist Ch., Sterling, Va., 1985-87. Recipient Disting. Svc. award Atty. Gen. of the U.S., 1992. Mem. Soc. Profls. in Dispute (officer 1988-90). Home: 12 Carrollton Rd Sterling VA 20165 Office: Com Relations Svc Dept Justice Rm 330 5550 Friendship Blvd Bethesda MD 20815

PADGETT, JOY, state legislator; m. Don Padgett; 1 child, Walter. BS, Kent State U. Mem. Ohio Ho. of Reps.; owner Main Off Supply. Mem. YWCA. Recipient Don K. Wales award CORC Joint Policy Bd., 1990,

Tchr. of Yr. award Southwestern Ohio, 1992. Mem. Coshocton, Holmes and Muskingum C. of C., Farm Bur., Coshocton Area Personnel Assn. Republican. Home: 871 Walnut St Coshocton OH 43812-1649 Office: OH Ho of Reps State House Columbus OH 43215*

PADICH, DIANNE S., rehabilitation counselor; b. Detroit, Feb. 26, 1948; d. Myron J. and Jessie E. (Wratten) Wolf; m. Robert A. Padich, Sept. 2, 1972; 1 child, Bryan S. AA, Highland Park C.C., 1968; BA, N.Mex. Highlands U., 1975; MA, U. Ala., 1980. Cert. rehab. counselor. Vocat. evaluator Goodwill Industries, Cin., 1980-82; placement specialist JOY Ctr., Cin., 1982-84; rehab. counselor IKRON, Cin., 1984-85, 86-87; psychol. asst. Geri-Tech., Cin., 1985-86; indsl. rehab. case mgr. Ohio Bur. of Workers' Compensation, Cin., 1987—. With USN, 1969-72. Mem. ACA, Nat. Rehab. Assn. Office: Ste 400 8500 Governors Hill Dr Cincinnati OH 45249-1389

PADOVANO, KATHRYN, dean; b. Hackensack, N.J., Feb. 8, 1948; d. Carl E. and Kathryn (Sellarole) Padovano; m. Edwin Hughes, Feb. 8, 1969; children: Carrie Padovano Hughes, Jamie Padovano Hughes. BA, Felician Coll., Lodi, N.J., 1970; MA, Montclair State Coll., 1974, NYU, 1977; PhD, UCLA. Cert. art tchr. K-12; prin. supr. K-12; sch. adminstrn. supr. Elem. K-6. Art tchr, elem. dept. chair Dumont Sch., N.J., 1970-76; dir. rsch. and planning Long Island U., Greenvale, N.Y., 1983-84; dir. edn. The Queens Mus., Flushing, N.Y., 1987-89; asst. dean edn. Dowling Coll., Oakdale, N.Y.; dean edn. Dowling Coll., Oakdale. Mem. Kappa Delta Pi (Outstanding Svc. award 1994), Phi Delta Kappa (Leader of the Yr 1994). Office: Dowling Coll Idlehour Blvd Oakdale NY 11769-1999

PADVE, MARTHA BERTONNEAU, urban planning and arts consultant, fundraiser; b. Scobey, Mont., Feb. 22; d. Henry Francis and Marie (Vaccaro) Bertonneau; m. Jacob Padve, May 9, 1954 (div. 1980). Student, Pasadena Jr. Coll., 1938-40; cert., S.W. U. Bus. Coll., L.A., 1940-41, Pasadena Inst. for Radio, 1946-47; student, Claremont Colls., 1972-74, U. So. Calif., 1983-84, Community Coll., Pasadena, 1987-88. Juvenile roles Pasadena (Calif.) Community Playhouse, 1935-37; ptnr., bus. mgr. restaurant devel. ventures, Pasadena, 1940-50; club dir. Red Cross, Nfld., Can., 1944-45; leading roles Penthouse Theatre, Altadena, Calif., 1946-48; club dir. armed forces spl. svcs. Red Cross, Austria, 1949-52; head dept. publs. Henry E. Huntington Libr., San Marino, Calif., 1953-57; cons. art planning Model Cities program, Omaha, 1975; founding instr. contemporary art collecting class, 1979-80; dir. devel. Bella Lewitzky Dance Found., L.A., 1980-81; instr. Art. Ctr. Coll. Design, Pasadena, 1981-82, assoc. dir. devel., 1981-83; instr. Coll. Continuing Edn. U. So. Calif., L.A., 1983-84; urban planning and arts cons. The Arroyo Group, Pasadena, 1979—; cons. in field, 1984—; developer edn. program Mus. Contemporary Art, L.A., 1984-86. Contbr. articles to newspapers; author (the arts segment) Pasadena Gen. Plan, 1980-83. Trustee, v.p. Pasadena Art Mus., 1967-74; co-chmn. bldg. fund Norton Simon Mus. Art, Pasadena 1968-70; chmn. Pasadena Planning Commn., 1973-81, Pasadena Street Tree Plan, 1975-76, Pasadena High Rise Task Force, 1979, San Gabriel Valley Planning Coun., 1977-78; mem. Pasadena Downtown Urban Design Plan, 1980-83; founding mem. Arts, Pks. & Recreation Task Force, 1978-80; vice-chmn. Pasadena Design Review Commn., 1974-78; founding chmn. So. Calif. Fellows of Contemporary Art, 1976-78; mem. adv. com. U. So. Calif. Art Galleries, 1976-82, UCLA oral history program contemporary art, 1983—; chmn. audit com. L.A. County Grand Jury, 1986-87; founder Pasadena Robinson Meml. Fund, Inc., 1990-92, bd. dirs. 1992-95; curator Vroman's Art on the Stairwell, 1992—; mem. exec. com. St. Andrew's Sch. Bd., 1993-94; co-chmn. restoration adv. com. St. Andrew's Ch., 1994; judge Pasadena Tournament of Roses, 1994. Named Woman of the Yr., Pasadena Women's Civic League, 1980; recipient Gold Crown award Tenth Muse, Pasadena Arts Coun., 1983, Commendation awards Pasadena City Dirs., 1975, 80, 82, 83, Commendation award L.A. County Bd. Suprs., 1987, Graphic Arts award Southern Calif. Fellows Contemporary Art, 1978. Republican. Roman Catholic. Home and Office: 350 Olympic View Ln Friday Harbor WA 98250-9662

PAELINCK, LORI KELLER, financial planner; b. Concord, N.C., June 19, 1964; d. William Leroy Jr. and Linda (Liverman) Keller; m. Peter Paelinck, Mar. 1, 1986 (div. Jan. 1994). AA summa cum laude, Peace Coll., 1984; BA in English magna cum laude, U. N.C., 1985; postgrad., Rivier Coll., 1986-90. Bookkeeper Barco Industries, Charlotte, N.C., 1984-86; sec. Phoenix Home Life, Nashua, N.H., 1986-88; adminstrv. mgr. Weisman & Tessier Assoc., Nashua, N.H., 1988—. Actress in cmty. theatre prodns., 1990—. V.p., bd. dirs. Am. Stage Festival, Milford, N.H., 1993—; pres. Gate City Striders, Nashua, 1992-94; cmty. rels. United Way, Nashua, 1991-92; race dir. Santa Fund, Nashua, 1991—. Recipient Lifetime Achievement award Gate City Striders, 1993. Mem. Nat. Assn. Life Underwriters, Nashua Theatre Guild (sec./treas. 1991-93), N.H. Cmty. Theatre Assn. (bd. dirs. 1991-92). Republican. Methodist. Home: 17A Stark St Nashua NH 03060-6224 Office: Weisman & Tessier Assoc 1 Indian Head Plz Ste 502 Nashua NH 03060-3466

PAETZOLD, RAMONA LEE, management educator; b. LaPorte, Ind., Feb. 5, 1953; d. A. Eugene and Mildred (Good) Bowers; m. Steven Boughton, June 11, 1993. BA, Ind. U., 1974, MBA, 1977, MA, 1979, DBA, 1990; JD, U. Nebr., 1990. Prof. Carnegie-Mellon U., Pitts., 1979-81, U. Md., College Park, 1981-86; prof. mgmt. Tex. A&M U., College Station, 1990—. Sr. articles editor Jour. Legal Studies Edn., 1994—; staff editor Am. Bus. Law Jour., 1993—; co-author: The Statistics of Discrimination: Using Statistical Evidence in Discrimination Cases, 1994; contbr. articles to profl. jours. Mem. APA, Acad. Legal Studies in Bus., Am. Statis. Assn., Acad. Mgmt., Order of Coif, Beta Gamma Sigma. Office: Tex A&M U Dept Mgmt College Station TX 77843-4221

PÁEZ, LETICIA, academic administrator, consultant, association executive; b. El Paso, Tex., Jan. 16, 1953; d. Marcos Luciolo and Delia (Rojas) P. BS in Criminal Justice, U. Tex., El Paso, 1973, M in Sociology, 1976, MPA, 1987. Supr. youth divsn. Dept. Human Devel., El Paso, 1978-81; temp. dir. high sch. equivalency program U. Oregon, Eugene, 1981; assoc. dir. high sch. equivalency program U. Tex., El Paso, 1979-82; behavioral sci. coord. dept. pediatrics Sch. Medicine Tex. Tech U., 1982-85; field coord. area health edn. ctr. Tex. Tech U., 1985-86; site dir. Karenet Project Sch. Nursing Tex. Tech U., 1986-90; assoc. dir. ednl. planning area health edn. ctr. Sch. Medicine Tex. Tech U., 1986-90, west region adminstr.-operation, Health Edn. Training Ctr. Alliance Tex., 1990—; project cons. HHS, Washington, 1989, merit reviewer, 1990—; internat. leadership cons. Windrock Internat., Conway, Ark., 1992-93; lectr. leadership seminars. Active Adelante Mujer Hispana Planning com., 1984-88; pres. Centro Medico del Valle, El Paso, 1985-89, chmn., 1986-90; active Sr. Companion Program Adv. Com., 1987-89; apptd. mem. Lower Valley Health Care Task Force, 1989—; adv. bd. U.S. Congress Panel on Youth Issues, 1990-92; apptd. mem. Mayor's Hispanic Roundtable, 1990-91; El Paso chpt. pres. YWCA, 1991-93; nat. nom. com. YWCA of U.S.A., 1991—, nat. local relations task force, 1992—, nat. bd. dirs., 1993-94; mem. nom. com. Am. Heart Assn., 1991; apptd. mem. Sec.'s Coun. on Health Promotion and Disease Prevention HHS, Washington, 1992—; juvenile justice adv. com. El Paso Juvenile Justice Sys., 1992-93; active United Way Allocations Task Force, 1993, Tex. Rural Health Assn.; past chmn. Hispanic Health Issues Task Force. Recipient Leadership El Paso award Greater El Paso C. of C., 1985, Liberty Bell award El Paso Young Lawyers' Assn, 1993; named Vol. of Yr., El Paso Ind. Sch. Dist. Project Redirection, 1987, Woman of Yr.-Health Issues, El Paso Women's Polit. Caucus, 1988; W.K. Kellogg Found. fellow 1989-92. Mem. ASPA (v.p.), Am. Assn. for Social Workers, Nat. Coun. for Internat. Health, Profl. Women's Network, Exec. Forum (v.p. adminstrn. 1992-93), U. Tex. El Paso Alumni Assn. Office: Tex Tech Sch Medicine 4800 Alberta Ave El Paso TX 79905

PAFFENHÖFER, ERICA S., management consultant; b. Tuscaloosa, Ala.; 1 child, Claire Marie. BS, U. Ala., 1979; MEd, Ga. State U., 1987. With Harco Drug Co., Northport, Ala., 1973-78; mktg. coord. Savannah and Statesboro (Ga.) Pub. Sch. Sys., 1979, 82-89; dept. mgr., buyer Belk Dept. Store, Savannah, 1980-82; exec. dir. Pvt. Industry Coun., Savannah, 1989-91; workplace specialist Royce Learning Ctr., Savannah, 1992-93; mgmt. cons. Erica S. Paffenhofer, Mgmt. Cons., Savannah, 1993—. Named Most Outstanding Leader, Nat. Youth Leadership Inst., 1976, Leadership Devel. Inst., 1977; recipient Instrnl. Devel. award United Teaching Professions, 1983. Mem. Internat. Mgmt. Coun., Savannah Area C. of C., Rotary Savannah West, Ga. State U. Alumni Assn., U. Ala. Alumni Assn. Office: Erica S Paffenhofer Mgmt Co 24 Norwood Pl Savannah GA 31406-5153

PAGAN, CAROLE CHRISTINE, cable communications administrator; b. Evanston, Ill., July 12, 1956; d. John Russell Stannard and Marjorie Jane (Garner) Suckow; 1 child from previous marriage, Emma Christine Gabor; m. Rubin Pagan, Jan. 1, 1995. Student, Roosevelt U., Chgo., 1985-87, Oakton Community Coll., 1985-87. Mgr. Stuarts, Niles, Ill., 1974-76; saleswoman Joannies Gift Boutique, Skokie, Ill., 1976-78; instr. Fred Astaire Dance Studios, Wilmette, Ill., 1979-81; asst. mgr. Fashionation, Skokie, 1981-83; with cash processing dept. Zayre's, Chgo., 1983-84; office mgr. TCI Ill., Skokie, 1984-87; exec. dir. N.W. Mcpl. Cable Coun., Arlington Heights, Ill., 1987—; conf. participant, 1988—. Mem. Des Plaines (Ill.) Youth Commn., 1988-91. Mem. Nat. Assn. Telecommunications Officers and Advisors (assoc., co-chmn. pub. rels. com. Ill. chpt. 1990). Republican. Office: NW Mcpl Cable Coun 1420 Miner St Rm 402 Des Plaines IL 60016

PAGANI, BEVERLY DARLENE, retired government administrator; b. Compton, Calif., Aug. 29, 1937; d. Donald Marshell Cameron and Irene Von (Kirkendoll) Good; m. Albert Louis Pagani, Feb. 21, 1971; children: Penelope Collins, Deborah Anne, Michael Stuart. BS, So. Oreg. Coll., 1967; MBA, So. Ill. U., Edwardsville, 1972. Cert. cost estimator and analyst. Enlisted USAF, 1959, advanced through grades to capt., 1962, resigned, 1971; chief mgmt. analysis USAF, Mildenhall, Eng., 1974-76; personnel classifier USAF, Scott AFB, Ill., 1979-80; housing mgmt. analyst USAF, Scott AFB, 1980-81, cost analyst, 1981-85; chief manpower analyst USN, Moffett Field, Calif., 1985—; chief mgmt. support office Army Aviation Research and Tech. Activity, Moffett Field, Calif., 1986-88; project control mgr. NASA-AMES Rsch. Ctr., Moffett Field, Calif., 1988-94; retired, 1994. Mem. Soc. Logistic Engrs., Inst. Cost Analysts, Am. Soc. Mil. Comptrollers, Soc. Cost Estimating and Analysis. Republican. Roman Catholic. Office: Numerical Aerodynamic Simulation Systems NASA-AMES Rsch Ctr Moffett Field CA 94503-1099

PAGE, ANNE RUTH, gifted education educator, education specialist; b. Norfolk, Va., Apr. 13, 1949; d. Amos Purnell and Ruth Martin (Hill) Bailey; m. Peter Smith Page, Apr. 24, 1971; children: Edgar Bailey, Emmett McBrannon. BA, N.C. Wesleyan Coll.; student, Fgn. Lang. League; postgrad., N.C. State U.; student, Overseas Linguistic Studies, France, Spain, Eng., 1978, 85, 86. Cert. tchr., N.C. Tchr. Cary (N.C.) Sr. High Sch., 1971-72; tchr., head dept. Daniels Mid. Sch., Raleigh, N.C., 1978-83; chmn. fgn. lang. dept. Martin Mid. Gifted and Talented, Raleigh, N.C., 1983—; leadership team Senate Bill 2 Core co-chair; dir. student group Overseas Studies, Am. Coun. for Internat. Studies, France, Spain, Eng., 1982, 84, 86, 88; bd. dirs. N.T.H., Inc., Washington; cert. mentor tchr. Wake County Pub. Schs., 1989; dir. student exchs. between Martin Mid. Sch. and Sevigné Inst. of Compiegne, France. Sunday sch. tchr. Fairmont United Meth. Ch., Raleigh, 1983-85. Mem. Alpha Delta Kappa. Democrat. Home: 349 Wilmot Dr Raleigh NC 27606-1232 Office: Martin Mid Sch GT 1701 Ridge Rd Raleigh NC 27607-6737

PAGE, BERNADETTE RYAN, emergency physician; b. Chgo., Feb. 10, 1946; d. Frank James and Bernadette Rosamund (Halm) Ryan; m. Jack R. Page, Dec. 23, 1967; children: Jeremy, Sara, Alex, Rachel. MD, Loyola U., 1970. Diplomate Am. Bd. Emergency Medicine. Rotating O intern San Bernardino (Calif.) Hosp., 1970-71; resident in pediat. Orange County Med. Ctr., Anaheim, Calif., 1971-72; staff physician emergency rm. Kaiser Permanente, Bellflower, Calif., 1972-73, St. Mary's Hosp./Long Beach (Calif.) Cmty., 1973-76, Appalachian Regional Hosp., Beckley, W.Va., 1976-78, Charleston (W.Va.) Area Med. Ctr., 1978-82; staff physician, owner Doctors Urgent Care, Charleston, 1982-88; staff physician Orange Chatham Comp. Health, Carrboro, N.C., 1988-91; attending physician emergency rm. Duke U. Med. Ctr., Durham, N.C., 1991—; chair violence prevention com. Am. Assn. Women Emergency Physicians, Durham, 1994—; mem. adv. coun. family violence AMA, 1994; mem. nat. faculty Advanced Cardiac Life Support Am. Heart Assn., 1976-82. Active Durham City-County Violence Prevention Com., 1993-94, North Carolinians for Gun Control, 1993—. Fellow Am. Coll. Emergency Physicians. Democrat. Roman Catholic. Office: Duke U Med Ctr PO Box 3096 Durham NC 27710

PAGE, DOZZIE LYONS, vocational school educator; b. Tiptonville, Tenn., Apr. 13, 1921; d. Lessie LeRoy and Carrie (Oldham) Lyons; children: Rita, Gerald. BS in Edn., Chgo. Tchrs. Coll., 1968; MS in Psychology, Counseling and Guidance Chgo. State U., 1976; MA in Bus. Edn., Govs. State U., 1979. Cashier receptionist Unity Mut. Life Ins. Co., Chgo., 1939-47; sec. United Transport Service Employees Union, Chgo., 1951-53; sec., office mgr. Joint Council Dining Car Employees AFL CIO, Chgo., 1957-59; sr. stenographer Chgo. Police Dept., 1962-65; tchr. office practice Manpower Devel. Tng. Act, Chgo. Bd. Edn., 1965-67; tchr. office occupations Dunbar Vocat. High Sch., Chgo., 1968-71, tchr., coord. distributive edn., 1971-90; mem. NAACP, DuSable Mus. African-Am. History. Mem. Office Occupations Club, Distributive Edn. Assn., Assn. for Supervision and Curriculum Devel., Chgo. Urban League, Chgo. Bus. Edn. Assn. (exec. bd. 1983—, Enos Perry award 1987, pres. 1991-92), Ill. Pers. and Guidance Assn., Am. Pers. and Guidance Assn., Am. Vocat. Assn., Chgo. Urban League, Nat. Bus. Edn. Assn., Ill. Bus. Edn. Assn., Chgo. Bus. Edn. Assn., Chgo. State U. Alumni Assn., Governor's State U. Alumni Assn., Phi Delta Kappa. Home: 6127 S Justine St Chicago IL 60636-2327

PAGE, JUDITH ANNE, marriage and family therapist; b. Boston, Sept. 2, 1936; d. Richard S. and Hope (Rider) Cole; m. Thomas E. Barker, July 13, 1957 (div. 1974); children: Dianne, Paul, Sheryl Barker Holman; m. Merlyn J. Page, Nov. 29, 1974; 1 adopted child, Charlene; stepchildren: Pattie, Ken, Carol, Donna Page Evans, Cliff, Mary. BS in Sociology, Bridgewater State U., 1976, MEd in Counseling, 1984. Lic. social worker, marriage and family therapist, mental health counselor and rehab. counselor, Mass.; cert. secondary tchr., Mass. Tchr. Plymouth (Mass.) Carver Regional Sch., 1976-79; sr. social worker Dept. of Social Svcs., Brockton, Mass., 1979-85; asst. dep. compact adminstr. Dept. of Social Svcs., Boston, 1985-86; tchr. Carver (Mass.) High Sch., 1986-88; dir., counselor Displaced Homemakers, Brockton, 1988-90; staff assoc. Career Access Program in Nursing, Fall River, Mass., 1990-92; counselor, job placement Indsl. Svcs. Program, Boston, 1992-93; owner, therapist A Forward Step, North Easton, Mass., 1989—; developer workshops on career, stepparenting, for women after loss of spouse after div. or death, and following domestic violence and chronic med. problems. Mem. Drug Coalition, Woburn, Mass., 1970-73; mem. mktg. com. Town of Plymouth, 1976-80. Mem. ACA, Nat. Career Devel., Internat. Assn. Marriage and Family Counselors, Mass. Assn. Marriage and Family Therapists, Adlerian Soc. Home: 23 Dela Park Ln North Easton MA 02356 Office: A Forward Step 859 Washington St South Easton MA 02375

PAGE, JUDITH LYNNE, data processing manager; b. Green Bay, Wis., Feb. 2, 1948; d. Donald Joseph and Jane Marilee (Hockstock) P.; m. Gerald O. Gunderson, Aug. 2, 1969 (div. July 1974). BA, U. Wis., 1970. Adminstrv. asst. Office Lt. Gov., Madison, Wis., 1972-77; office mgr. Office of Gov., Madison, 1977-78; policy analyst Dept. Health and Social Svc., Madison, 1978-80, sys. developer, 1980-88, area mgr., 1988-93, sect. chief, 1993—. Mem. Assn. Career Employees (bd. dirs. 1992-94). Office: State Wis Dept Health Social Svc Box 7850 1 W Wilson Madison WI 53707

PAGE, KAREN ANN, publisher; b. Warren, Mich., May 8, 1962; d. George L. and Joan (Banaszewski) P. B.A., Northwestern U., 1983; MBA, Harvard U., 1989. Researcher, Com. of 200, Chgo., 1981; founder, pres. Cakes Unlimited, Evanston, Ill., 1980-83; corp. analyst Shearson Lehman Brothers, N.Y.C., 1983-85; mag. devel. staff Time Inc., N.Y.C., 1985; mgr. FDP Assocs., N.Y.C., 1985-86; group bus. mgr. Fairchild Publs., N.Y.C., 1986-87; sr. assoc., Braxton Assoc., 1989-92; exec. v.p., Silver Eagle Pub., Country Music Mag.; exec. v.p., mgn. dir., Media Devel. Corp., Westport, Ct., 1992—. Co-author: On Becoming a Chef, 1995. Steering com. Women's Health Symposium N.Y. Hosp. Grantee NEH, 1981, General Mills/AAUW Found. fellow 1988-89. Mem. Nat. Assn. Young Profl. Women (nat. pres., bd. dirs., founder 1984-87, recipient Susan B. Anthony award N.Y.C., 1988), Women's Econ. Round Table, Harvard Bus. Sch. Network of Women Alumnae (pres., bd. dirs., founder 1992—), Coun. 100, Founders' Com., Capital Cir., Leadership Cir., Women's Campaign Fund.

PAGE, LINDA KAY, banking executive; b. Wadsworth, Ohio, Oct. 4, 1943; s. Frederick Meredith and Martha Irene (Vance) P. Student Sch. Banking, Ohio U., 1976-77; cert. Nat. Pers. Sch., U. Md.-Am. Bankers Assn., 1981; grad. banking program U. Wis., Madison, 1982-84; BA Capital U. Asst. v.p., gen. mgr. Bancohio Corp., Columbus, Ohio, 1975-78, v.p., dist. mgr., 1979-80, v.p., mgr. employee rels., 1980-81, v.p., divsn. mgr., 1982-83; commr. of banks State of Ohio, Columbus, 1983-87, dir. Commerce, 1988-90; pres., CEO Star Bank Cen. Ohio, Columbus, 1990-92; state dir. FMHA-USDA, 1993—. Bd. dirs. Clark County Mental Health Bd., Springfield, Ohio, 1982-83, Springfield Met. Housing, 1982-83; bd. advisers Orgn. Indsl. Standards, Springfield, 1982-83; trustee League Against Child Abuse, 1986-90; treas. Ohio Housing Fin. Agy., 1988-90; vice chair Fed. Reserve Bd.-Consumer Adv. Coun., 1989-91. Bd. dirs. Pvt. Industry Coun. Franklin County, 1990—, Ohio Higher Edn. Facilities Commn., 1990-93; trustee, treas. Columbus State Community Coll. Found., 1990—; bd. dirs. Columbus Urban League, 1992—. Recipient Leadership Columbus award Sta. WTVN and Columbus Leadership Program, 1975, 82, Outstanding Svc. award Clark County Mental Health Bd., 1983. Mem. Nat. Assn. Bank Women (pres. 1980-81), Am. Bankers Assn. (govt. rels. coun. 1990-92), Women Execs. in State Govt., LWV, Conf. State Bank Suprs. (bd. dirs., sec./treas. 1985-90), dist. chmn. 1984-85), Ohio Bankers Assn. (bd. dirs. 1982-83, 91-92), Internat. Womens Forum, Zonta. Democrat. Avocations: tennis, animal protection, reading, golf. Home: 641 Mirandy Pl Reynoldsburg OH 43068-1602 Office: 200 N High St Columbus OH 43215-2408

PAGE, LISA WEST, secondary school educator; b. Daytona Beach, Fla., Feb. 17, 1958; d. Clarence Clinton and Helen Elizabeth (Goodwin) West; m. Frank Louis Page, June 21, 1981 (div.). BA, Stetson U., 1979; MS, Nova U., 1994. Cert. tchr., Fla.; cert. counselor, Fla. Tchr. Dr. Phillips Elem., Orlando, Fla., 1980-87, Lawton Elem. Sch., Oviedo, Fla., 1987-90, Jackson Heights Mid. Sch., Oviedo, Fla., 1990-94; guidance counselor Tuskawilla Middle Sch., Oviedo, Fla., 1994—; amb. Laurel Oaks Hosp., Orlando, 1991. Named Teacherrific finalist Walt Disney World, 1993; grantee Seminole County Schs., 1992, Drug Edn. Recognition award, 1993. Mem. Am. Counseling Assn., Fla. Assn. for Counseling, Fla. Sch. Counselors Assn., Fla. Mental Health Counselors Assn. Methodist. Office: Tuskawilla Mid Sch Oviedo FL 32765

PAGE, MARY STANCILL, insurance agency executive; b. Greenville, N.C., July 8, 1958; d. William Samuel and Viola (Sutton) Stancill; m. Edward Russell Page, June 26, 1977; children: Andrew, Rusty, Derrick. Grad., high sch., 1976. CPCU; cert. profl. ins. woman, ins. counselor, assoc. in underwriting, accredited advisor in ins. Bookkeeper The Fixture House, Greenville, 1979; ins. agt., officer mgr. Bill Clifton Agy., Greenville, 1979-83; personal and comml. lines agt. Mid-Atlantic Ins., Greenville, 1983-84; clk., personal lines agt. Tadlock Ins. Agy., Inc., Greenville, 1974-79, personal and comml. lines agt., 1984-88, mgr. comml. lines, 1988-91, v.p. ops., 1991—; instr. Ind. Ins. Agts. of N.C., Raleigh, 1991—. Recipient several scholarships. Mem. Nat. Assn. Ins. Women, N.C. Assn. Ins. Women (v.p. 1990-91, pres.-elect 1991-92, pres. 1992-93), Soc. CPCU's (continuing profl. devel. program 1993, pres. Downeast subchpt. N.C. chpt. 1989—), Carolina Assn. Profl. Ins. Agts., Ind. Ins. Agts. N.C., Soc. Cert. Ins. Counselors, Pitt County Assn. Ins. Profls. (sec. 1987-88, pres. 1988-89, com. chmn.), Kiwanis. Democrat. Baptist. Office: Tadlock Ins Agy Inc 320 S Evans St Greenville NC 27835-5047

PAGE, MYRA MANTIUS, investment executive; b. Phoenix, Dec. 9, 1949; d. Philip Karcher Mantius and Cornelia Stuyvesant (Dickinson) Lebens; m. Robert William Page, Aug. 25, 1968; children: John Frederick, Ralph Stuyvesant. BS in Fin., Ariz. State U., 1983. Registered rep., registered investment advisor rep. Account exec. Dean Witter Reynolds, Sun City, Ariz., 1984-88; asst. v.p. Kidder Peabody, Phoenix, 1988—. Mem. met. exec. bd. Valley of the Sun YMCA, Phoenix, 1993—, chmn. Glendale (Ariz.) YMCA, 1992-93; mem. Valley Leadership Class VII, Phoenix, 1986; past chmn. Maricopa County Parks & Recreation Commn., Phoenix, 1981-93; elder, trustee 1st Presbyn. Ch. Democrat. Presbyterian.

PAGE, PENNY BOOTH, librarian; b. Atlanta, Mar. 1, 1949; d. Howard Douglas and Edith Ann (Pennington) Booth; m. Danny F. Page, Dec. 27, 1966 (div. Mar. 1978); 1 child, Scott Matthew; m. Mark E. Lender, July 30, 1983. BA, Rutgers U., 1977, MLS, 1978. Rsch. asst. Rutgers Ctr. Alcohol Studies, Piscataway, N.J., 1978-81, libr., 1981—; co-dir. N.J. Alcohol/Drug Resource Ctr., Piscataway, 1988-90, dir., 1991—. Author: Alcohol Use and Alcoholism: A Guide to the Literature, 1986, Children of Alcoholics: A Sourcebook, 1991; contbr. articles to profl. jours. Mem. ALA, N.J. Libr. Assn. (treas. history and bibliography sect. 1988-90, chair scholarship com. 1994-95, Rsch. award 1989), Substance Abuse Librs. and Info. Specialists (chair 1984-85). Office: Rutgers Ctr Alcohol Studies Smithers Hall Allison Rd Piscataway NJ 08855

PAGE, VALDA DENISE, epidemiologist, researcher, nutritionist; b. Houston, Jan. 23, 1958; d. Ulysses and Dorothy Lee (Sells) P. BS in Food Sci. and Tech., Tex. A&M U., 1981; BS in Nutrition and Dietetics, U. Tex., Houston, 1985, MPH, 1991. Registered and lic. dietitian. Clk. various temp. svcs., Houston, 1980-86; nutritionist, nutrition coord., asst. dir. W.I.C., pub. health analyst Harris County Health Dept., Houston, 1986-93; planner Harris County Juvenile Probation Dept., Houston, 1993—; dietary cons. Deer Park (Tex.) Hosp., 1987-89; clin. instr. U. Tex., Houston, 1986-93. Chmn. health and welfare ministry Windsor Village United Meth. Ch., 1989-94; mem. Windsor Village AIDS Ministry, Houston, 1989—; team capt. March of Dimes Walk Am., Houston, 1988-93; mem. Pres.'s Former Student Adv. Com. on Black Issues, College Station, Tex., 1989—. Mem. APHA, Am. Dietetic Assn., Am. Diabetes Assn. (affiliate, minority initiative task force), Am. Heart Assn. (Speaker's Bur. 1986-93), Inst. Food Technologists, Soc. Epidemiologic Rsch., Nat. Perinatal Assn., Network Blacks in Dietetics and Nutrition. Democrat. Home: 9421 Rosehaven Dr Houston TX 77051-3128 Office: Harris County Juvenile Probation Dept Rsch Planning And Evaluation 3540 W Dallas Houston TX 77019-1796

PAGELER, PATTY JO, accountant; b. Sioux City, Iowa, Mar. 31, 1956; d. Walter Ludwig and Darlene C. (Trometer) Roehrich; m. Gary Allen Pageler, Oct. 29, 1977 (div. Nov. 1988); children: Justin, Ashley. BS, Morningside Coll., 1991. Sr. acct. Mid-Bell Music, Sioux City, 1992-94; corp. acct. St. Luke's Med. Ctr., Sioux City, 1994—. Treas. Hinton Parent Assn., Iowa, 1994—, Loess Hills Audubon Soc., Sioux City, 1992—. Mem. Inst. Mgmt. Accts. Lutheran. Home: 517 Gemini Hinton IA 51024

PAGENKOPF, ANDREA LESUER, university official; b. Hamilton, Mont., July 28, 1942; d. Andrew and Martha Gail (Thompson) LeSuer; m. Gordon Kyle Pagenkopf, June 12, 1964 (dec. Feb. 1987); 1 child, Sarah Lynn. BA, U. Mont., 1964; PhD, Purdue U., 1968. Registered dietitian; lic. nutritionist. Asst. prof. Purdue U., West Lafayette, Ind., 1968, U. Ill., Champaign, 1968-69; asst. prof. Mont. State U., Bozeman, 1969-76, assoc. prof., 1976-86, prof. nutrition, 1986-91, dir. extension, 1991—, vice provost for outreach, 1993—. Author: (with others) Grow Healthy Kids, 1980. Worship commn. chair United Meth. Ch., Bozeman, 1989-90; cons. Gallatin Hospice, Bozeman, 1986-91. Recipient Excellence in Nutrition Edn. award Western Dairy Coun., 1987, Silver Buffalo award Mont. Extension, 1989, Mid-Career award Extension Hon., 1988; named Home Econs. Leader, Mont. Home Econs. Assn., 1990. Mem. Am. Dietetic Assn., Soc. Nutrition Edn. (interest group chair 1990-91), Am. Home Econs. Assn. Office: Mont State U Extension 211 Montana Hall Bozeman MT 59717

PAGLIA, CAMILLE, writer, humanities educator; b. Endicott, N.Y., 1947; d. Pasquale John and Lydia (Colapietro) P. BA in English summa cum laude with highest honors, SUNY, Binghamton, 1968; MPhil, Yale U., 1971, PhD in English, 1974. Mem. faculty Bennington (Vt.) Coll., 1972-80; vis. lectr. Wesleyan (Conn.) U., 1980; prof. humanities U. Arts, Phila., 1984—; vis. lectr. Yale U., New Haven, 1980-84, Wesleyan U., Middletown, Conn., 1980. Author: Sexual Personae: Art and Decadence from Nefertiti to Emily Dickinson, 1990, Sex, Art, and American Culture, 1992, Vamps and Tramps: New Essays, 1994. Office: Univ Arts 320 S Broad St Philadelphia PA 19102

PAGOTTO, LOUISE, English language educator; b. Montreal, June 22, 1950; came to U.S., 1980; d. Albert and Elena (Tibi) P. BA, Marianopolis Coll., Montreal, 1971; TESL Diploma, U. Papua New Guinea, 1975; MA, McGill U., 1980; PhD, U. Hawaii at Manoa, Honolulu, 1987. Tchr. Yarapos High Sch., Wewak, Papua New Guinea, 1971-73, Electricity Commn. Tng. Coll., Port Moresby, Papua New Guinea, 1975-76, Coll. of the Marshall Islands, Majuro, summers 1973-91, Leeward C.C., Pearl City, Hawaii, 1988-89, Kapiolani C.C., Honolulu, 1989—; presenter at confs. Contbr. articles to profl. jours. McConnell fellow McGill U., 1979, Can. Coun. fellow, 1980-83; recipient Excellence in Teaching award Bd. of Regents, 1993. Mem. AAUW, Linguistic Soc. Am., Nat. Coun. Tchrs. English, Hawaii Coun. Tchrs. English. Office: Kapiolani CC 4303 Diamond Head Rd Honolulu HI 96816-4421

PAIGE, ANITA PARKER, retired English language educator; b. Valparaiso, Ind., Feb. 5, 1908; d. Eugene Mark and Grace Agnes (Noon) Parker; m. Robert Myron Paige, Aug. 12, 1933 (dec. 1965); children: Susan Marlowe Paige Morrison, Amy Woods Paige Dunker, Caroline Parker Paige McClennan. AB, Vassar Coll., 1929; MA, U. Chgo., 1930, postgrad., 1931-32. Instr. English Hillsdale (Mich.) Coll., 1930-31, asst. prof., 1931-33; bd. edn. Anglo-Am. Schs., Athens, 1948-51; tchr. secondary sch. Am. Sch., Teheran, Iran, 1957-58; instr. English Republic of China Mil. Cartographic Sec. group, Taipei, Taiwan, 1960-61; instr. dept. English Nat. Taiwan U., Taipei, 1961-62; intermittent lectr., 1988—; bd. dirs. Ginling Girls Mid. Sch., Taipei, 1960-62. Bd. dirs. Cmty. (Presbyn.) Ch., Teheran, 1957-58. Mem. LWV (chmn. Cook County, Ill. child welfare dept. 1933-36, mem. bd. Overseas Edn. Fund 1966-68), Diplomatic and Consular Officers Ret., Am. Women's Group of Paris, Assn. Am. Fgn. Svc. Women, Asian Am. Forum (founding mem.), Friends of Soochow U., Phi Beta Kappa. Democrat.

PAIGE, NORMA, lawyer, corporate executive; b. Lomza, Poland, Oct. 11, 1922; came to U.S., 1927; d. Morris and Edith (Kachourek) Zelaso; children: Holly Paige Russek, Madelyn Paige Givant. BA, NYU, 1944, JD, 1946; postgrad. in bus. adminstrn., CCNY, 1953, NYU, 1969. Bar: N.Y. 1946, U.S. Supreme Ct. 1951. Ptnr. Paige and Paige, N.Y.C., 1948—; v.p., bd. dirs. Astronautics Corp. Am., Milw., 1959—, chmn. bd., 1984—; exec. v.p., bd. dirs. Kearfott Guidance & Navigation Corp., Wayne, N.J., 1988—; bd. dirs. Astronautics C.A., Ltd., Israel, Astronautics GmbH, Fed. Republic Germany. Recipient Jabotinsky Centennial medal Prime Minister of Israel, 1980, Tribute to Women in Indsl. Industry Twin II award YWCA, 1981. Mem. N.Y. Women's Bar Assn. (pres. 1958-59). Office: Astronautics Corp Am 4115 N Teutonia Ave Milwaukee WI 53209*

PAIGE, SANDRA KRISTINE, psychologist; b. Chgo., Dec. 3, 1961; d. Lesly Wade and Barbara Ann (Chambers) Johnson; m. Ray Anthony Paige, Nov. 9, 1991. BA in Psychology, U. Detroit, 1983, MA in Clin. Psychology, 1985, PhD in Clin. Psychology, 1988. Lic. clin. psychologist, Mich. Psychology trainee Mt. Carmel Mercy Hosp., Detroit, 1984-85; clin. intern Oakland County Ct., Pontiac, Mich., 1985-86, Harper-Grace Hosp., Detroit, 1986-87; sr. clin. psychologist State Jud. Counsel, Detroit, 1987—; assoc. psychologist Clark & Assocs., P.C., Southfield, Mich., 1988-94; cons. psychologist Children's Hosp., Detroit, 1988-89, Detroit Counseling Ctr., 1991—, Detroit Police Dept., 1993—; self-employed clin. supr., Detroit, 1993—. Guest commentator radio talk shows, 1991, 92. Mem. APA, Nat. Assn. Self Employed, Govt. Adminstr.'s Assn. (Appreciation award 1989, 91, 92), Zonta Internat., Alpha Kappa Alpha. Democrat. Office: S K Paige PhD Psychol Svcs 3800 Woodward Ave # 518 Detroit MI 48201

PAIGE, SUSANNE LYNN, financial consultant; b. Bklyn., Feb. 25, 1950; d. Abraham and Florence Roslyn (Rosenfeld) P.; divorced. BA cum laude, C.W. Post Coll., 1972, postgrad., 1975. Lic. mortgage broker, N.Y. Buyer B. Gertz and Sons, Inc., Jamaica, N.Y., 1973-76; nat. field sales mgr. LeVison Care Products, Inc., New City, N.Y., 1976-82, Am. Vitamin Products, Inc., Lakewood, N.J., 1984-85; prin. Paige & Assocs., Scarsdale, 1982-87; loan officer and fin. cons. Bayside Fed. Savs. and Loan, Jericho, N.Y., 1987-88; prin. Paige Capital Enterprises, Inc., Rye, N.Y., 1988—; mem. Comml. Investment Divsn./Westchester Bd. Realtors, White Plains, N.Y.; pub. spkr. and lectr. in field. Author: Closing the Deal in Today's Volatile Market, 1994; satarist/polit. cartoonist C.W. Post Coll. News and Editorial, Brookville, N.Y., 1968-72; contbr. articles to profl. jours. Recipient award for Best Original Essay, Newsday Harry F. Guggenheim award, Garden City, N.Y., 1967, Hon. Mention award C.W. Post Coll. Gallery, 1982, Hon. Mention (sculpture) Fresh Meadows (N.Y.) Merchant's Assn., 1971, meritorious notation Real Estate Weekly, 1991-93; selected as Comml. Deal-Maker of Yr., N.Y. Real Estate Jour., 1992, Real Estate Personality, 1993, Northeast Fin. Work-Out Specialist N.Y. and New Eng. Real Estate Jours., 1990-93, also meritorious notation, 1990-93. Mem. Alumni Assn. C.W. Post Coll., 60's East Realty Club, Westchester Bd. Realtors, White Plains, N.Y., Assn. Commercial Real Estate. Office: Paige Capital Enterprises Inc PO Box 1234 Scarsdale NY 10583-9234

PAIN, BETSY M., lawyer; b. Albertville, Ala., Aug. 29, 1950; d. Charles Riley and Jean Faye (Rains) Stone; m. William F. Pain, Nov. 18, 1977; children: Taylor Holland, Emily Anne Pain. AA, Northeastern Okla. A&M, Miami, Okla., 1970; BA, U. Okla., 1974, JD, 1976. Bar: Okla. 1977; U.S. Dist. Ct. (we. dist.) 1979. Staff atty. Okla. Dept. Corrections, Oklahoma City, 1978-79; gen. counsel Okla. Pardon and Parole Bd., Oklahoma City, 1979-84, exec. dir., 1984-88; corp. counsel Roberts, Schornick & Assocs., Inc., Norman, Okla., 1990—. Editor: (newsletter) RSA Environmental Report, 1991—. With extended family program Juvenile Svcs., Inc. Cleveland County, Okla., 1983-91. Mem. Okla. Bar Assn. (environ. law sect. 1977—), Am. Corp. Counsel Assn. Democrat. Methodist. Office: Roberts Schornick & Assoc Inc 3700 W Robinson Ste 200 Norman OK 73072

PAINTER, JANET FERN, secondary education educator; b. Hickory, N.C., July 13, 1963; d. Hanley Hayes and Lorene (Huffman) P. BA in Classics and Psychology, Lenoir-Rhyne Coll., 1985; MEd, U. N.C., Charlotte, 1988. Cert. secondary social sci. and Latin tchr., N.C. Tchr. classical lang. Charlotte (N.C.)-Mecklenburg Schs., 1985—; adj. prof. edn. Davidson (N.C.) Coll., 1990—. Named 1st Union Master Tchr., 1st Union Nat. Bank, 1994; Fng. Study scholar Lenoir-Rhyne Coll., 1983. Mem. ASCD, NOW, ACLU, Am. Classical League, Nat. Coun. Social Studies, Vergilian Soc. Am., N.C. Classical Assn., Fgn. Lang. Assn. N.C. Democrat. Home: 606 B Bertonley Ave Charlotte NC 28211

PAINTER, JULIA BUDJAN, promotional advertising executive; b. Pitts., Mar. 6, 1961; d. Stephen Jr. and Marjorie Ann (Smith) B.; m. David William Painter, Dec. 21, 1984 (div. Nov. 1989); children: Alyson Lowe, Hayden Louise. Editorial asst. AIME Iron & Steelmaker, Pitts., 1979-81; asst. to dir. of bus. devel. Am. Bridge Engring., Pitts., 1982-85; branch adminstr., tech. writer Comp-U-Staff, Pitts., 1988-89; contract tech. writer Davy McKee Engring., Pitts., 1989-91; ind. salesperson promotional advtg. Raleigh, N.C., 1991—. Mem. Advtg. Specialty Inst. Republican. Episcopalian. Home: 1508 Wedgeland Dr Raleigh NC 27615

PAINTER, LINDA ROBINSON, physics educator, dean; b. Lexington, Ky., May 4, 1940; d. J. Kenneth and Juanita Marie (Crosier) R.; m. Roy Allen Painter, May 6, 1967; children: Holly Suzanne, Brent Allen. BS in Physics, U. Louisville, 1962; MS in Physics, U. Tenn., 1963, PhD in Physics, 1968. Asst. prof. physics U. Tenn., Knoxville, 1968-75, assoc. prof. physics, 1975-82, prof. physics, 1982—, asst. dean, Grad. Sch., 1985-88; assoc. dean, 1988—; cons. Health Physics Div., Oak Ridge (Tenn.) Nat. Lab., 1967-77; adj. rsch. and devel. participant, Health and Safety Rsch. Div., Oak Ridge Nat. Lab., 1977-83, part-time employee, 1983-89; bd. dirs. Consultec Scientific, Inc. Contbr. numerous articles to profl. jours. Named Outstanding Young Woman of the Yr., Tenn., Outstanding Young Women of Am., 1974; recipient grants, U.S. Atomic Energy Commn., U.S. Energy Rsch. and Devel. Agy., U.S. Dept. Energy, 1968-89. Fellow Am. Phys. Soc.; mem. Tenn. Conf. Grad. Schs. (pres. 1990-91, editor 1985—), Radiation Rsch. Soc. (assoc. editor 1984-88), Coun. So. Grad. Schs. (publs. com. 1988-90, com. issues and planning 1991—). Baptist. Home: 7708 Devonshire Rd Knoxville TN 37919-8019

PAIVA WEED, M(ARIE) TERESA, state legislator; b. Newport, R.I., Nov. 5, 1959. B.A., magna cum laude, Providence Coll., 1981; J.D., Catholic Univ. of America, 1984. Bar: R.I., 1984. Former asst. city solicitor city of Newport; now mem. R.I. State Sen. Mem. Newport County Bar Assn., Rhode Island Bar Assn., ABA. Office: RI State Senate State Capitol Providence RI 02903*

PAJUNEN, GRAZYNA ANNA, electrical engineer, educator; b. Warsaw, Poland, Dec. 15, 1951; d. Romuald and Danuta (Trzaskowska) Pyffel; m. Veikko J. Pajunen (div. 1990); children: Tony, Thomas, Sebastian. MSc, Warsaw Tech. U., 1975; PhD in Elec. Engring., Helsinki (Finland) U., 1984. Grad. engr. Oy Stromberg Ab, Helsinki, 1974; design engr. Oy Stromberg Ab, 1975-79; teaching/rsch. asst. Helsinki U. Tech., 1979-85; vis. asst. prof. dept. elec. and computer engring. Fla. Atlantic U., 1985-86, asst. prof. elec. and computer engring., 1986-90, assoc. prof. elec. engring., 1990—; vis. asst. prof. dept elec. engring. UCLA, 1988-89; cons. in field; lectr. in field. Author: Adaptive Systems - Identification and Control, 1986; contbr. articles to profl. jours. Grantee Found. Tech. in Finland, Ahlstrom Found., 1982, Wihuri Found., 1982, Foun.d Tech. in Finland, 1983, Acad. Finland, 1984, EIES Seed grantee, 1986, Finnish Ministry Edn., 1985, NSF, 1988-89, 93-94, State of Fla. High Tech. and Industry Coun., 1989. Mem.IEEE, Control Sys. Soci., N.Y. Acad. Sci., AAUW, SIAM, Control and Sys. Theory Group. Roman Catholic. Office: Florida Atlantic Univ Dept Elec Engring Boca Raton FL 33431

PALACIO, JUNE ROSE PAYNE, professor of nutritional science; b. Hove, Sussex, Eng., June 14, 1940; came to U.S., 1949; d. Alfred and Doris Winifred (Blanch) P.; m. Moki Moses Palacio, Nov. 30, 1968. AA, Orange Coast Coll., Costa Mesa, Calif., 1960; BS, U. Calif., Berkeley, 1963; PhD, Kans. State U., 1984. Registered dietitian. Asst. dir. food svc. and res. halls Mills Coll., Oakland, Calif., 1964-66; staff dietitian Servomation Bay Cities, Oakland, 1966-67; commissary mgr. Host Internat., Inc., Honolulu, 1967-73; dir. dietetics Straub Clinic and Hosp., Honolulu, 1973-80; instr. Kans. State U., Manhattan, 1980-84; prof. and program dir. Calif. State U., L.A., 1984-85; prof., program dir. Pepperdine U., Malibu, Calif., 1985—; instr. Kapiolani Community Coll., Honolulu, 1973-79, U. Hawaii, Honolulu, 1975-80, Ctr. for Dietetic Edn., Woodland Hills, Calif., 1986—; cons. Clevenger Nutritional Svcs., Calabasas, Calif., 1985—, Calif. Mus. Sci. and Industry, L.A., 1989—, Calif. State Dept. Edn., Sacramento, Calif., 1985—. Author: Foodservice in Institutions, 1988. Mem. Am. Dietetic Assn. (del. 1977-80, 86-89, reviewer 1986—), Calif. Dietetic Assn. (pres. 1992-93), L.A. Dist. Dietetic Assn., Foodsvc. Systems Mgmt. Edn. Coun., Dietetic Educators of Practitioners, Gamma Sigma Delta, Omicron Nu, Phi Upsilon Omicron. Republican. Episcopalian. Home: 24319 Baxter Dr Malibu CA 90265-4728 Office: Pepperdine U 24255 Pacific Coast Hwy Malibu CA 90263-0001

PALAST, GERI D., federal agency administrator. BA in Polit. Sci., Stanford U., 1972; JD, NYU, 1976. Atty., legis. program analyst Am. Fedn. State County and Mcpl. Employees, Washington, 1976-77; legal counsel, field rep. Nat. Treasury Employers Union, Washington, 1977-79; dir., supervising atty. Nat. Employment Law Project, Washington, 1979-81; dir. politics and legislation Svc. Employees Internat. Union, AFL-CIO, Washington, 1981-93; asst. sec. congrl. and intergovtl. affairs Dept. Labor, Washington, 1993—. Office: Dept Labor Congl & Intergovtl Affairs 200 Constitution Ave NW Washington DC 20210-0001

PALAZZO, ROSEMARY ELIZABETH, marketing manager; b. Hoboken, N.J.; d. Nicholas Anthony and Sophie Palazzo. BS in Mktg., St. Peters Coll., 1979; MBA in Mktg. Mgmt., Pace U., 1991. With Mktg. and Systems Devel. Corp., Lyndhurst, N.J., 1980-82; v.p. advt. and sales promotion Chase Manhattan Personal Fin. Svcs., Inc., N.Y.C., 1982—. Mem. Am. Mktg. Assn. (Am. Mktg. awards 1979, 91), Direct Mktg. Assn., Fin. Comm. Soc., Delta Mu Delta. Office: Chase Manhattan Personal Fin Svcs Inc One Chase Manhattan Plz 22 New York NY 10081

PALECEK, SANDRA MARIE, reading education specialist; b. Ashland, Wis., Oct. 31, 1940; d. Francis Joseph and Martha Evelyn (Verville) Bonneville; m. John Allan Palecek, Oct. 3, 1964; children: Stephanie Lynn, Michael John. BS in Elem. Edn., U. River Falls, 1971; MS in Reading, U. Superior, 1981. Tchr. grades 2 and 3 Spring Valley (Wis.) Sch., 1959-62; tchr. grade 2 Pleasant Hill Sch., Waukesha, Wis., 1962-64; tchr. grades 2 and 3 Glidden (Wis.) Sch., 1964-65; Chpt. I tchr. Butternut (Wis.) Sch., 1966-68; Chpt. I reading specialist Glidden Schs., 1968—; amb. of reading People to People to China, 1993. Pres. Chequmegon Reading Coun., Park Falls, Wis., 1981. Herb Kohl fellow, 1994; recipient Outstanding Svc. award Title I Program, Glidden, 1980, Significant Contbns. award Chpt. I Program, Madison, Wis., 1990; named Dist. Tchr. of Yr., Dept. Pub. Instrn., Madison, 1980, 94, Exemplary Remedial Reading award, 1989. Mem. Internat. Reading Assn., Wis. State Reading Assn., Glidden Fedn. Tchrs. Union (v.p., then pres.). Home: N15517 Town Hall Rd Park Falls WI 54552-8069 Office: Glidden Sch Glidden WI 54527

PALEKAR, ALKA SHARAD, pathologist, researcher; b. Bombay, Sept. 15, 1943; came to U.S., 1970; d. Nilkanth Dattatraya and Manjyla Vishnu (Pandit) Sabnis; m. Sharad Dattaram Palekar, Dec. 28, 1974; children: Priya, Omkar. S.S.C., Balmohan Vidhyamandir, Bombay, 1959; grad. in int. sci., Bombay U., 1961; M.B.B.S., Grant Med. Coll., Bombay, 1966, MD, 1970. Diplomate Am. Bd. Pathology, Am. Bd. Cytopathology. Lect. pathology and bacteriology Grant Med. Coll., 1968-70, reader pathology and bacteriology, 1970; resident pathology Atlantic City Hosp., 1971-73, Shadyside Hosp., Pitts., 1973-75; pathologist Shadyside Hosp., 1975—; rschr., pathologist with NSABP U. Pitts., 1977—. Contbr. articles and sci. papers to profl. jours. Mem. Pitts. Pathology Soc. Hindu. Office: Shadyside Hosp Inst Pathology 5230 Centre Ave Pittsburgh PA 15232

PALERMO, JUDY HANCOCK, elementary school educator; b. Longview, Tex., Sept. 7, 1938; d. Joseph Curtis and Bennie Lee (Deason) Hancock; m. Donald Charles Palermo, Apr. 1, 1961; 1 child, Donald Charles Jr. (dec.). BS in Secondary Edn., 1960. Cert. secondary and elem. edn. tchr., Tex. Art tchr. Dallas Ind. Sch. Dist., 1960-62, 65-67; asst. dir. freshmen orientation program North Tex. State U., Denton, summer 1969, dormitory dir. Oak St. Hall, 1968-71, tchr. part-time, 1970-77; substitute tchr. Denton Ind. Sch. Dist., 1975-78, tchr. 5th grade, 1979-87, art tchr., 1987—; tchr. kindergarten Kiddie Korral Pre-Sch., Denton, 1978-79; trained gifted tchr. Woodrow Wilson Elem. Sch., Denton, 1980, grade level chmn., 1980; grade level chmn. Eva S. Hodge Elem. Sch., Denton, 1988-89, 92-93; mem. rsch. bd. advisors Am. Biog. Inst., 1991—. Active Denton Humane Soc., 1982—, Denton Educators Polit. Action Com., 1984-85; Eva S. Hodge historian PTA, 1992—. Mem. NEA, NAFE, Tex. State Tchrs. Assn., Denton Classroom Tchrs. Assn. (faculty rep. 1984-85), Denton Edn. Assn., Denton Area Art Edn. Asn. (program chmn. 1990-91), Greater Denton Arts Coun., Numismatic Assn. (sec. Greater Denton chpt.), Denton Sq. Athletic Club, Denton Greter Univ. Dames Club (treas. 1970), Bus. and Profl. Women's Assn. (treas. 1990-91, chair audit com. 1992-93, chmn. comm. com. 1993—), Delta Kappa Gamma (treas. 1986-88). Democrat. Home: 1523 Pickwick Ln Denton TX 76201-1290

PALESKY, CAROL EAST, tax accountant; b. Orange, N.J., May 13, 1940; d. Neil Norell and Marie R. Reiss; m. Jacob Palesky; children: Donna, Lewis. AB, Am. Inst., Pleasantville, N.J., 1973; postgrad., Am. Inst., Portland, Maine, 1980; student, Atlantic C.C., Mays Landing, N.J., 1971-73. With mgmt. First Nat. Bank of South Jersey (now First Fidelity), Pleasantville, N.J., 1967-74; loan officer Maine Savs. Bank, Portland, 1980-81; acct., owner East Assocs., Topsham, Maine, 1985—. Treas., bd. dirs. Congl. Term Limits Coalition, Topsham, 1993—; bd. dirs. Maine Citizens Rev. Bd., Portland, 1993—. Scholar Nat. Taxpayer Union, 1992, 94; recipient United to Serve Am. award, 1992. Mem. Nat. Assn. Small Business Owners, Maine Taxpayers Action Network (pres. 1990—), Topsham Taxpayer Assn. (pres. 1991—). Roman Catholic. Home and Office: 24 Sokokis Cir Topsham ME 04086

PALEY, GRACE, author, educator; b. N.Y.C., Dec. 11, 1922; d. Isaac and Mary (Ridnyik) Goodside; m. Jess Paley, June 20, 1942; children: Nora, Dan.; m. Robert Nichols, 1972. Ed., Hunter Coll., NYU. Formerly tchr. Columbia, Syracuse U.; ret. mem. lit. faculty Sarah Lawrence Coll., Stanford, Johns Hopkins, Dartmouth. Author: The Little Disturbances of Man, 1959, Enormous Changes at the Last Minute, 1975, Leaning Forward, 1985, Later the Same Dy, 1985, Long Walks and Intimate Talks, 1991, New and Collected Poems, 1992, The Collected Stories, 1994; stories published in Atlantic, Esquire, Ikon, Genesis West, Accent, others. Sec. N.Y. Greenwich Village Peace Center. Recipient Literary award for short story writing Nat. Inst. Arts and Letters, 1970, Edith Wharton award N.Y. State, 1988, 89, Rea award for short story, 1993, Vt. Gov.'s award for Excellence in the Arts, 1993, award for contbn. to Jewish culture Nat. Found. Jewish Culture; Guggenheim fellow. Mem. Am. Acad. and Inst. Arts and Letters. Office: Box 620 Thetford Hill VT 05074

PALLADINO, LUCY JO, communications executive, psychologist; b. N.Y.C., Oct. 13, 1950; d. John Michael and Lucy Nancy (Caravella) P.; m. Arthur A. Cormano, July 1, 1979; children: Julia, Jennifer. BS summa cum laude, Fordham U., 1972; MA, Ariz. State U., 1975, PhD, 1978. Lic. psychologist, Calif. Rsch. assoc. Ariz. State U., Tempe, 1973-75; psychology fellow Southwestern Med. Sch., Dallas, 1976-77; pvt. practice psychology Encinitas, Calif., 1977—; mem. faculty U. Ariz. Med. Sch., Tucson, 1979-87; prodr. edn. programs Cox Cable, McCaw Cable, Tucson, 1984-87; rsch. dir. Good Health Communications, Tucson, 1985-87. Contbr. articles to profl. jours.; author: (video) Relaxercise, 1986; (audiotape) Psychology of Fitness, 1990. Recipient Small Business Innovation Rsch. award Dept. Health and Human Svcs., 1985; Tucson Community Cable Corp. grantee, 1985. Mem. Am. Psychol. Assn., Nat. Register Psychologists, San Diego Psychol. Assn., Acad. San Diego Psychologists, Phi Beta Kappa. Office: Ste F-8 162 S Rancho Santa Fe Rd Encinitas CA 92024-4364

PALLADINO-CRAIG, ALLYS, museum director; b. Pontiac, Mich., Mar. 23, 1947; d. Stephan Vincent and Mary (Anderson) Palladino; m. Malcolm Arnold Craig, Aug. 20, 1967; children—Ansel, Reed, Nicholas. BA in English, Fla. State U., 1967; grad., U. Toronto, Ont., Can., 1969; MFA, Fla. State U., 1978, ABD, 1993. Editorial asst. project U. Va. Press, Charlottesville, 1970-76; instr. English Inst. Franco Americain, Rennes, France, 1974; adj. instr. Fla. State U., Tallahassee, 1978-79, dir. Four Arts Ctr., 1979-82, dir. U. Mus. of Fine Arts, 1982—. Curator, contbg. editor various articles and exhbn. catalogues, 1982—, including Nocturnes and Nightmres, Monochrone/Polychrome, and Chroma; gen. editor Athanor I-XIII, 1980—; represented in permanent collection Fla. Ho. of Reps., Barnett Bank, IBM. Individual artist fellow Fla. Arts Coun., 1979. Mem. Am. Assn. Mus., Fla. Art Mus. Dirs. Assn. (sec. 1989-91), Phi Beta Kappa. Democrat. Home: 1410 Grape St Tallahassee FL 32303-5636 Office: Fla State U Mus of Fine Arts 250 Fine Arts Bldg Tallahassee FL 32306-2055

PALLAS, STELLA, author, artist; b. Chgo.; d. Pericles Dimitrios and Chrissa (Ratsines) P. BA, N.E. Ill. U., 1967; MA, Calif. State U., L.A., 1979. Cert. elem., adult edn., jr. coll. art tchr., Calif. Elem. sch. tchr. East Whittier (Calif.) City Sch. Dist., 1967-80; substitute elem. sch. tchr. La Habra (Calif.) City Sch. Dist., 1980-86; gifted/talented edn. cons. East Whittier City Sch. Dist., 1980-85; presenter Calif. Assn. for Gifted/Talented, 1986-89. Author: Dig for Dinosaurs, 1981, 2d edit., 1989, Pondering Plants, 1982, Thinking Cat's Guide to Birds, 1983, 2d edit., 91, Eric-Clearinghouse on Handicapped and Gifted Children, 1989, (manual) Art/Teachers, 1983, also abstract in field. Mem. AAUW, Calif. Ret. Tchrs. Assn., Calif. State U.-L.A. Alumni Assn., Kappa Pi, Delta Kappa Gamma. Greek Orthodox.

PALLENIK, CHRISTINE M., lawyer; b. Cleve., Mar. 9, 1957; d. Joseph and Marie Theresa (Kubik) P. BA in History, Seton Hill Coll., 1979; JD, Gonzaga Sch. of Law, 1982. Bar: Tex. Gas buyer United Gas Pipeline Co., Houston, 1984-85; sr. gas buyer Tex. Gas Transmission, Houston, 1985-88; sr. atty. United Gas Pipeline Co., Houston, 1988-93; sr. counsel Panhandle Eastern Corp., Houston, 1993—. Mem. Am. Assn. Corp. Counsel, Fed. Energy Bar Assn. Office: Panhandle Ea Corp 5400 Westheimer Ct Houston TX 77056-5310

PALLMEYER, REBECCA RUTH, federal judge; b. Tokyo, Sept. 13, 1954; came to U.S., 1957; d. Paul Henry and Ruth (Schrieber) P.; m. Dan P. McAdams, Aug. 20, 1977; children: Ruth, Amanda. BA, Valparaiso (Ind.) U., 1976; JD, U. Chgo., 1979. Bar: Ill. 1980, U.S. Ct. Appeals (7th cir.) 1980, U.S. Ct. Appeals 11th and 5th cirs.) 1982. Jud. clk. Minn. Supreme Ct., St. Paul, 1979-80; assoc. Hopkins & Sutter, Chgo., 1980-85; judge adminstrv. law Ill. Human Rights Commn., Chgo., 1985-91; magistrate judge U.S. Dist. Ct., Chgo., 1991—; mem. jud. resources com. Jud. Conf. of U.S., 1994—. Bd. govs. Augustana Ctr., 1990-91. Mem. Fed. Bar Assn., Nat. Assn. Women Judges, Fed. Magistrate Judge's Assn., Chgo. Bar Assn. (past chair devel. of law com. 1992-93, David C. Hilliard award 1990-91), Valparaiso U. Alumni Assn. (bd. dirs. 1992—). Lutheran. Office: US Dist Ct Rm 2414 219 S Dearborn St Chicago IL 60604-1802*

PALLOTTI, MARIANNE MARGUERITE, foundation administrator; b. Hartford, Conn., Apr. 23, 1937; d. Rocco D. and Marguerite (Long) P. BA, NYU, 1968, MA, 1972. Asst. to pres. Wilson, Haight & Welch, Hartford, 1964-65; exec. asst. Ford Found., N.Y.C., 1965-77; corp. sec. Hewlett Found., Menlo Park, Calif., 1977-84, v.p., 1985—; bd. dirs. Overseas Devel. Network. Bd. dirs. N.Y. Theatre Ballet, N.Y.C., 1986—, Consortium for Global Devel., 1992, Miramonte Mental Health Svcs., Palo Alto, Calif., 1989, Austin Montessori Sch., 1993. Mem. Women in Founds., No. Calif. Grantmakers, Peninsula Grantmakers. Home: 532 Marine World Pky # 6203 Redwood Shores CA 94065 Office: William & Flora Hewlett Found 525 Middlefield Rd Ste 200 Menlo Park CA 94025-3495

PALL-PALLANT, TERI, paleontologist, inventor, behavioral scientist, design engr., advt. agy. exec.; b. Somerville, N.J., Jan. 6, 1927; d. Stanley and Milicent P.-P.; BA, Imperial Coll., London, 1948, MS, 1949; PhD, London U., 1954; postgrad. Warren Sch. Aeros., Los Angeles, 1950, Calif. Inst. Tech., 1951; PhD Columbia U., 1963, London U., 1966, ScD, London Inst. Applied Research, 1973; cert. rehab. counselor U. So. Calif., 1975; student UCLA, 1955. Design engr. Simmonds Aerocessories Ltd., London, 1949, dir. vocat. rehab., 1950; founder, owner Teri Pall Advt. Agy., Los Angeles, 1951—, Pall Indsl. Surveys, Pasadena, Calif., 1952—, Pall Tech. Industries, Tarzana, Calif., 1979—; chmn. bd. Pall Industries, Ltd., Taipei, Taiwan and Tarzana, Calif., 1980—; vertebrate paleontologist Am. Mus. Natural History, N.Y.C., 1965-69; leader Teri Pall Trio, Los Angeles, 1951-69; exec. dir. Hoffman House, Long Beach, Calif., 1970-72; sr. adminstrv. analyst Econ. and Youth Opportunities, Los Angeles County, 1973-74; dep. dir. Head Start Program Los Angeles County, 1974-75; assoc. dir. Casa de las Amigas, Pasadena, dir. research and evaluation projects Nat. Inst. Alcohol Abuse and Alcoholism, Washington, 1977; pvt. practice vocat. rehab. counseling, Beverly Hills, Calif., 1977; exec. dir. Little House Los Angeles County, 1978; robotics cons. JPL, Pasadena, 1974-95. Fossil exhibit contbr. Los Angeles County Mus., 1968-77; chmn. Mayor's Commn. on Barrier-Free Architecture, 1978—; vice chmn. research and coordinating com. Gov.'s Commn. on Safe Energy Alternatives, 1979—; mem. Cancer Research Coordinating Com., 1979—; lectr. Long Beach Hosp., 1978; office bd. Inventor's Workshop Internat. Edn. Found., 1980—, Am. Guild of Inventors, 1990—. Recipient Spl. Contbns. award Engring. and Grading Constructors Assn., 1968, Interkamera Gold award Cannes Art Festival, 1969, Speaker of Year award Toastmasters Calif., 1971, Woman of Year for Civic Leadership award Long Beach, 1971, Outstanding Achievement award Am. Cancer Soc., 1979, others. Mem. Statis. Quality Control Engrs. (sec. 1951—), Assoc. Bus. Publs., AAUW, Nat. Rehab. Counseling Assn., Architects and Engrs. Inst., Nat. Soc. Vertebrate Paleontologists, Phi Beta Kappa. Republican. Episcopalian. Author: (play) El Rancho Verde, 1951; (novel) With Banners Flying, 1953; Chinese and Western Worlds from 1800 B.C. to Modern Times, 1950; 4000 Years of Egyptian History, 1950; The Integrating Power Meter, 1956; About the Mammoth, 1962; Look, a Travelogue in Time, 1967; The History of Our Calendar, 1977; designer robotics exhibit Calif. Mus. of Sci. and Industry, L.A., 1990. Developer 2-mile cordless telephone, 1978, wrist chronograph calculator, 1979, Etch-A-Sketch, 1962, AC-DC multimeters, 1954, Miniaturized transcutaneous nerve stimulator, 1969, Electronic remote control system, 1972.

PALMA, ADRIENNE CHRISTINE, gifted and talented educator; b. Staten Island, N.Y., Aug. 22, 1961; d. Salvatore Anthony and Adrienne (Coviello) P. BA in Econs., Fordham U., 1985; postgrad., Georgian Ct. Coll., 1995. Buyers asst. JC Penny Co., N.Y.C., 1979-88; sales rep. Babyfair Inc., N.Y.C., 1988-92; substitute tchr. Belmar and Colts Neck (N.J.) Pub. Schs., 1993; tchr. gifted and talented/reading enrichment Fredon Twp. Sch., Newton, N.J., 1993—; curriculum writer Fredon Twp. Sch., 1993—. Vol. Vol. Ctr. of

Monmouth County (Synergy). Mem. ASCD, N.J. Reading Assn. Office: Fredon Twp Sch 459 State Route 94 S Newton NJ 07860-5018

PALMER, ALICE J., state legislator; b. Indpls., June 20, 1939; m. Edward Palmer; 2 children. BS in English and Sociology, Indiana U.; MA in Urban Studies, Roosevelt U.; PhD in Ednl. Adminstrn., Northwestern U. Former exec. dir. Chgo. Cities in Schs.; senator dist. 13 Springfield, Ill., 1991—. Co-author: The Mature Student's Guide to Reading and Compostion. Founding dir. Met. Chgo. YMCA Youth and Govt. Program. Office: Senate House State Capitol Springfield IL 62706*

PALMER, BEVERLY BLAZEY, psychologist, educator; b. Cleve., Nov. 22, 1945; d. Lawrence E. and Mildred M. Blazey; m. Richard C. Palmer, June 24, 1967; 1 child, Ryan Richard. PhD in Counseling Psychology, Ohio State U., 1972. Lic. clinical psychologist, Calif. Adminstrv. assoc. Ohio State U., Columbus, 1969-70; research psychologist Health Services Research Ctr. UCLA, 1971-77; commr. pub. health Los Angeles County, 1978-81; pvt. practice clin. psychology Torrance, Calif., 1985—; prof. psychology Calif. State U., Dominguez Hills, 1973—. Reviewer manuscripts for numerous textbook pubs; contbr. numerous articles to profl. jours. Recipient Proclamation County of Los Angeles, 1972, Proclamation County of Los Angeles, 1981. Mem. Am. Psychol. Assn. Office: Calif State U Dominguez Hills Dept Psychology Carson CA 90747

PALMER, DAISY ANN, marketing professional; b. Burkburnett, Tex.; d. Leroy Evans and Christine Cleo (Givens) Walker; children: Christy Ann Yazdi, Cyndi Ann Thornhill. Cert. in Human Rels., Oreg. Coll. Edn., 1976; BA, cum laude in Liberal Studies, Edwards U., Tex., 1983; MBA, Calif. Coast U., 1989, PhD, 1993. Cert. interpreter for hearing impaired, Tex. and U.S. Mgr., R.R. Realty/Ins., Wichita Falls, Tex., 1973-75; cons. state agys., 1975-85; asst. coord. Travis County Services for Deaf, Austin, 1979-81; adminstr. Tex. Assn. Deaf, Austin, 1981-85; promotion dir. McGregor Studios, Austin, 1981-92; mktg. coord. Tex. Mcpl. League, Austin, 1985—; sr. field svcs. rep.; interpreter, legis. communicator VISTA, 1981-82. Editor: Tex. Assn. Deaf Directory of Services, 1984; rschr. and author of statis. studies; interpreter for first Japan-U.S. Conf., 1985. Chmn. Gov.'s Communication Barriers Council, 1984; vice chair Austin St. Sch. Adv. Council, 1984-86. Recipient Golden Hand award Nat. Assn. Deaf, Toastmasters Internat. Communication Leadership award, 1976. Mem. Nat. Registry Interpreters, Tex. Assn. Deaf (Golden Hand award for legis. activities 1983), Austin Bus. League. Home: 7301 Ferndale Cove Austin TX 78745-6526 Office: Tex Mcpl League 211 E 7th St Ste 300 Austin TX 78701-3218

PALMER, ELIZABETH, retired association executive; b. N.Y.C., Apr. 17, 1913; d. Augustus Embury and Elizabeth Hepburn (Berdan) P. BSc, Columbia U., 1940; HHD (hon.), MacMurray Coll., 1979. Various positions Ctrl. br. YWCA, N.Y.C., 1935-41; dir. YWCA USO Nat. Bd. YWCA of U.S.A., Conn., 1941-42; gen. sec. YWCA Gt. Britain, Manchester, Eng., 1942-45; various positions World YWCA, Geneva, 1945-56, gen. sec., 1956-78; hon. mem. nat. bd. YWCA of U.S.A, N.Y.C., 1979—, trustee, 1980—. Democrat. Episcopalian.

PALMER, JUDITH, artist; b. Oakland, Calif., Dec. 10, 1934; d. Bean Mark and Laurine (Mattern) P.; m. Robert Ballard Herschler, Aug. 1, 1959 (div. Nov. 1971); children; Matthew, Mark, Sarah, Stephen; m. Ben Frank Stoltzfus, Nov. 8, 1975. BA, U. Calif., Berkeley, 1957; MA, Claremont Grad. Sch., 1971. Photoetching series include Surfaces, 1986, Constructions, 1987, Assemblages, 1987, Romoland, 1988, Proving Ground, 1990, Inscriptions, 1992; cover art for New Novel Rev., 1994, Red, White and Blue novel by Ben Stoltzfus, 1994, Alaluz poetry jour. U. Calif., Riverside. Recipient Purchase Prize Galleries Elect, Venice, Calif., 1987, printmaking award Artists' Liaison, Los Angeles, 1986, 87, Jurors award Dulin Gallery, Knoxville, Tenn., 1987. Mem. Los Angeles Printmakers Soc. Studio: 2040 Arroyo Dr Riverside CA 92506-1609

PALMER, JUDITH GRACE, university adminstrator; b. Washington, Ind., Apr. 2, 1948; d. William Thomas and Laura Margaret (Routt) P. BA, Ind. U., 1970; JD cum laude, Ind. U., Indpls., 1973. Bar: Ind. 1974, U.S. Dist. Ct. (so. dist.) Ind. 1974. State budget analyst State of Ind., Indpls., 1969-76, exec. asst. to gov., 1976-81, state budget dir., 1981-85; spl. asst. to pres. Ind. U., 1985-86, v.p. for planning, 1986-91, v.p. for planning and fin. mgmt., 1991-94, v.p., chief fin. officer, 1994—; bd. dirs. Ind. Fiscal Policy Inst., Washington Park Cemetery Assn. Bd. dirs., sec.-treas. Columbian Found., 1990-94; bd. dirs. Columbia Club, 1989—, v.p., pres.-elect, 1994; bd. dirs. Commn. for Downtown, 1984, mem. exec. bd., 1989-92, chmn. cmty. rels. com., 1989-93; mem. State Budget Commn., 1981-85. Named one of Outstanding Young Women in Am., 1978; recipient Sagamore of the Wabash award, 1977, 85, Citation of Merit, Ind. Bar Assn. of Young Lawyers, 1978, Appreciation award, 1980. Mem. ABA, Ind. Bar Assn., Indpls. Bar Assn. Roman Catholic. Office: Ind Univ Bryan Hall Rm 204 Bloomington IN 47405

PALMER, KRISTINE MARGARET, elementary school counselor; b. Wilmington, Del., Apr. 19, 1963; d. Robert Lewis and Rosemary Ann (Piazza) Phillips; m. G. Gregory Palmer, Nov. 2, 1991. BS, Elizabethtown Coll., 1985; MEd, West Chester U., 1990. Cert. sch. counselor, Pa. Psychiat. technician Rockford Ctr., Wilmington, Del., 1985-87; mental health assoc. Meadowwood Hosp., New Castle, Del., 1987-88; sch. counselor Avon Grove Elem. Sch., West Grove, Pa., 1991-93, Tri-Cmty. Elem. Sch., Steelton, Pa., 1993—. Mem. AACD, Am. Sch. Counselor's Assn., Assn. Specialists in Group Work, Pa. Sch. Counselors Assn., Phi Delta Kappa, Kappa Delta Phi. Office: Tri Community Elem 255 Cypress St Steelton PA 17113-3138

PALMER, KRISTINE NELSON, accounting educator; b. Corning, Iowa, Aug. 22, 1953; d. George Leland and Gertrude Iola (Ross) Nelson; m. William Ray Harbour, Dec. 28, 1973 (div. 1992); children: Jason William, Matthew Ross, Stephanie Lynne; m. Glenn Dean Palmer, Apr. 18, 1992. BS in Bus. Adminstrn., Longwood Coll., 1980; MBA, Va. Commonwealth U., 1982. CPA, Va. Instr. acctg. Longwood Coll., Farmville, Va., 1983-87, asst. prof. acctg., 1987—; adj. instr. Longwood Coll., 1980-83; staff acct. II Charles M. Terry Co., CPAs, Richmond, Va., summer 1985, 86; cons. Small Bus. Devel. Ctr., Farmville, 1989-93. Recipient Faculty of Excellence award Profl. Fraternity Assn., 1992; named Women of Yr., Farmville Bus. and Profl. Women's Club, 1989. Mem. AICPA, Am. Acctg. Assn., Inst. Mgmt. Accts., Va. Soc. CPAs (coop. mem. state com. 1986—), Delta Sigma Pi (faculty advisor, vice chair nat. advisors com. 1989-91, chair 1991-93, Nat. Advisor of Yr. 1988, 91, Regional Advisor of Yr. 1986, 87, 88, 89, 91, 94). Home: Rte 1 Box 20C Rice VA 23966 Office: Longwood Coll 201 High St Farmville VA 23909

PALMER, MARCIA ANN, healthcare management consultant, pharmacist; b. Hammond, Ind., Aug. 26, 1951; d. John J. and Millee (Ivan) P. BS in Pharmacy, Purdue U., 1974; MBA, Loyola U., 1984. Lic. pharmacist, Ind., Ill., Ariz., Fla. Staff pharmacist St. Margaret Hosp., Hammond, Ind., 1974-75; drug info. pharmacist to clin. coord. Ingalls Meml. Hosp., Harvey, Ill., 1975-77; dir. pharmacy Ingalls Meml. Hosp., Harvey, 1977-89; pres. Palmer Assocs., Healthcare Mgmt. Cons., Munster, Ind., 1989—; asst. prof. Purdue U., West Lafayette, Ind., 1972-89, teaching assoc. U. Ill. Chgo., 1979-89. Named Pharmacist Yr., Ill. Council Hosp. Pharmacists, 1988. Mem. Am. Soc. Hosp. Pharmacists, Am. Pharm. Assn., Am. Soc. Cons. Pharmacists, Acad. Managed Care Pharmacy, Am. Soc. Parenteral and Enteral Nutrition. Home: 1514 Cardinal Ct Munster IN 46321-3801 Office: Palmer Assocs 9245 Calumet Ave Ste 202 Munster IN 46321-2807

PALMER, MARIANNE ELEANOR, real estate broker, educator; b. Glen Ridge, N.J., Jan. 28, 1945; d. Charles Norman and Eleanor Ednetta (Adamus) Zimmermann; m. Jack Garner Palmer, Nov. 25, 1975. Student, Cornell U., 1965; BA, Jacksonville U., 1967; postgrad., U. Cin., 1970-71, U. North Fla., 1981; grad., Real Estate Inst., 1987. Lic. real estate broker, Fla.; cert. site agt.; GRI; cert. elem. tchr., Fla. Kindergarten tchr. Pickett & Dinsmore Elem. Sch., Jacksonville, Fla., 1965-68, Lake Forest Elem. Sch., Jacksonville, 1968-69; 1st grade tchr. North Avondale Elem. Sch., Cin., 1969-70, Hilltop Sch., Wyoming, Ohio, 1970-72; 1st and 4th grade tchr. Jacksonville Country Day Sch., 1972-76; substitute tchr. Duval County Pub. Schs., Jacksonville, 1976-80; sch. prin. Christ Episcopal Day Sch., Ponte Vedra Beach, Fla., 1980-84; substitute tchr. Duval and St. John's County Pub. Schs., Jacksonville, 1984-90; kindergarten tchr. Ponte Vedra-Palm Valley Elementary Sch., 1990—; broker-salesman Watson Realty Corp., Ponte Vedra Beach, 1984—. Mem. Nat. Assn. Realtors, Fla. Assn. Realtors, Ponte Vedra Beach Bd. Realtors, N.E. Fla. Builders Assn. (sales and mktg. coun.), Nat. Assn. Tchrs., Fla. Assn. Children Under 6, Fla. Kindergarten Coun., Real Estate Inst. (GRI), Ponte Vedra Club, Multi-Million Dollar Club and Exec. Com., Delta Delta Delta. Episcopalian. Home: 65 San Juan Dr Ponte Vedra Beach FL 32082-1319 Office: Watson Realty Corp 615 Hwy A1A Ponte Vedra Beach FL 32082 also: Ponte Vedra Palm Valley Elem Sch 630 Hwy AIA Ponte Vedra Beach FL 32082

PALMER, MARTHA JANE, computer specialist; b. Sellersburg, Ind., Jan. 5, 1947; d. James William and Dorotha (Townsend) Peyton; m. John Edward Palmer, Mar. 10, 1973; children: Rebecca Lin, Elizabeth Jane. BA in Math., Coll. of St. Francis, Joliet, Ill., 1986. Cert. secondary math. and comprehensive computer sci. tchr., Ill. With tng. and devel. dept. Silver Cross Hosp., Joliet, 1967-73; instr. Lockport (Ill.) Twp. Park Dist., 1975-77; tchr. math. Deer Creek Jr. High Sch., University Park, Ill., 1987-88; tchr., head coach math. team Crete (Ill.)-Monee High Sch., 1988-89; supr. & instr. Computer Lab., adj. instr. math. Joliet Jr. Coll., 1989-92, adminstr. sr. and alumni programs, 1989-91; computer specialist, regional dir. support staff Info. Systems Ctr. VA Hosps., 1992—; oralist judge River Valley Conf., 1989—; sch. del. Ill. Gifted Conf., 1987. Sec. Lockport Planning Commn., 1989-91, Lockport Heritage and Architecture Commn., 1989-93; mem. bd. advisors Lockport Main Street Program, 1991—. Recipient Disting. Svc. award Taft Dist. 90 PTA, Lockport, 1981. Mem. Nat. Coun. Tchrs. Math., Ill. Coun. Tchrs. Math. (del. 1988), Nat. Soc. DAR (registrar Louis Joliet chpt. 1983—, regent 1987-89), Nat. Soc. Daus. War of 1812, Nat. Soc. Colonial Dames XVII Century (pres., bd. dirs. Sarah Hodsdon Morrill chpt. 1989-91, mem., registrar Thomas Hooker chpt. 1994—), Peyton Soc. Va. (life), Nat. Soc. New Eng. Women (life, corr. sec. 1990-94), Nat. Soc. Children Am. Revolution (sr. pres. Ill. Prairie Soc. 1991—, sr. state treas. 1993—), Nat. Soc. Dames of Ct. of Honor, Nat. Soc. Daus. Colonial Wars (pres. Ill. soc. 1995—), Lockport Women's Club (scholarship com. 1991-94), Towsend Soc. Am. (life), Nat. Soc. Daus. Am. Colonists, Nat. Soc. Women Descendents of Ancient and Honorable Artillary Co., Kappa Mu Epsilon. Home: 1520 Johnson St Lockport IL 60441-4483 Office: Region Direct Support Group PO Box 7008 Bldg 37 Hines IL 60141-7008

PALMER, MARTHA MARIA, manufacturing company owner; b. Decatur, Ill., Jan. 21, 1932; d. Emmett J. and Ruth Ann (Donovan) McGowan; m. Thomas W. Palmer, Sept. 15, 1956; children: Jane, Julie, James. Student, Millikin U., 1954. Owner Irrigation Specialties, Gering, Nebr., 1971—. Vol. mem. City Coun., Scottsbluff, Nebr., 1986—. Mem. Soroptomist. Roman Catholic. Home: 1019 E 38th St Scottsbluff NE 69369 Office: PO Box 1306 Scottsbluff NE 69361

PALMER, MILDRED EUNICE, botanical gardens director, horticulturist; b. Kansas City, Mo., Sept. 9, 1911; d. George Lee and Georgia Marie (Murer) Sevedge; m. George Kenneth Palmer, Aug. 24, 1940. Student Kansas City Jr. Coll., 1929-30; cert. horticulture St. Petersburg Vocat., 1948. Licensed nurseryman, landscaper. Owner Palmers' Garden and Nursery, St. Petersburg, Fla., 1945—; garden writer St. Petersburg Times, 1967-69; founder, pres. Suncoast Bot. Garden, Inc., Largo, Fla., 1962-90, designer, dir., 1962-91, pres. emeritus, 1991—; lectr. horticulture, flower arranging, landscape, St. Petersburg, 1951—; dir. horticulture shows, tours, St. Petersburg, 1947—. Author: Hibiscus Unlimited, 1954. Editor The Buds, 1952-91, Life Judge, 1992—. Mem. Garden Writers Assn. Am. (2d place award 1968), Fla. Fedn. Garden Clubs (life, life judge 1958—, Outstanding Svc. award 1977). Democrat. Baptist. Clubs: Woodside Garden (St. Petersburg). Avocations: photography, botanical painting, wild flowers, plant collecting. Home and Office: 5063 Dartmouth Ave N Saint Petersburg FL 33710-8243

PALMER, PATRICIA ANN TEXTER, English language educator; b. Detroit, June 10, 1932; d. Elmer Clinton and Helen (Rotchford) Texter; m. David Jean Palmer, June 4, 1955. BA, U. Mich., 1953; MEd, Nat.-Louis U., 1958; MA, Calif. State U.-San Francisco, 1966; postgrad. Stanford U., 1968, Calif. State U.-Hayward, 1968-69. Chmn. speech dept. Grosse Pointe (Mich.) Univ. Sch., 1953-55; tchr. South Margerita Sch., Panama, 1955-56, Kipling Sch., Deerfield, Ill., 1955-56; grade level chmn. Rio San Gabriel Sch., Downey, Calif., 1957-59; tchr. newswriting and devel. reading Roosevelt High Sch., Honolulu, 1959-62; tchr. English, speech and newswriting El Camino High Sch., South San Francisco, 1962-68; chmn. ESL dept. South San Francisco Unified Sch. Dist., 1968-81; dir. ESL Inst., Millbrae, Calif., 1978—; adj. faculty New Coll. Calif., 1981—, Skyline Coll., 1990—; Calif. master tchr. ESL Calif. Coun. Adult Edn., 1979-82; cons. in field. Past chair Sister City Com. Millbrae. Recipient Concours de Francais Prix, 1947; Jeanette M. Liggett Meml. award for excellence in history, 1949. Mem. AAUW, NAFE, TESOL, ASCD, Am. Assn. of Intensive English Programs, Internat. Platform Assn., Calif. Assn. TESOL, Nat. Assn. for Fgn. Student Affairs, Computer Using Educators, Speech Commn. Assn., Faculty Assn. of Calif. C.C., U. Mich. Alumnae Assn., Nat.-Louis U. Alumnae Assn., Ninety Nines (chmn. Golden West chpt.), Cum Laude Soc., Soroptimist Internat. (Millbrae-San Bruno Women Helping Women award 1993), Peninsula Lioness Club (pres.), Rotary Club (Millbrae), Chi Omega, Zeta Phi Eta. Home: 2917 Franciscan Ct San Carlos CA 94070-4304 Office: 450 Chadbourne Ave Millbrae CA 94030-2499

PALMER, ROSLYN WOLFFE, small business co-owner; b. Bainbridge, Ga., May 4, 1952; d. Jake and Bella (Turetzky) Wolffe; m. A. Jackson Palmer, Mar. 27, 1976; 1 child, Mycla Ann. BA in Journalism, U. Ga., 1974. Women's editor The Post Searchlight, Bainbridge, Ga., 1974-78; news editor, dir. WAZA Radio, Bainbridge, Ga., 1978-84; co-owner Jake's Pawn Shop, Bainbridge, Ga., 1984—; adv. bd. First Port City Bank, Bainbridge, 1992—; dir. Downtown Devel. Authority, Bainbridge, 1993—, S.W. Ga. Regional Libr., Bainbridge, 1989—. Vol., bd. dirs. Am. Cancer Soc., 1978-90; councilwoman Bainbridge City Coun., 1988—; chmn. Ga. Mcpl. Assn. Cmty. and Human Devel. Policy Com., Atlanta, 1992-94; pres. C. of C., Bainbridge, 1993; Leadership Ga. participant, 1992. Recipient Ga. Downtown award Dept. Cmty. Affairs, 1992, Cmty. Involvement award 4-H Club, 1987. Mem. Ga. Power Adv. Coun., Bainbridge Rotary, Jr. Woman's Club (pres. 1977-78). Jewish. Home: 2505 Twin Lake Dr Bainbridge GA 31717-5247 Office: PO Box 262 Bainbridge GA 31717-0262

PALMER, TEKLA FREDSALL, retired dietitian, consultant; b. Harwinton, Conn., Sept. 1, 1918; d. Frank Albert and Bertha Elena (Weingart) Fredsall; m. Charles Peter Palmer, Apr. 13, 1946; children: Peter F., Karen F. BS, Pratt Inst., 1945; MA, Columbia U., 1947; postgrad., NYU, 1964, Syracuse U., 1968, U. Rochester, 1976. Instr. nutrition Pratt Inst., Bklyn., 1945-48; cons. dietitian Grace Clinic, Bklyn., 1952-55; instr. Skidmore Coll. U. Hosp., N.Y.C., 1955-56; chief clin. dietitian Beth Israel Hosp., N.Y.C., 1966; lectr. Keuka (N.Y.) Coll., 1970-71, Rochester (N.Y.) Inst. Tech., 1975; lectr. nutrition Roberts Wesleyan Coll., Rochester, 1975-81; cons. Buffalo Regional Health Dept., 1967-75. Author: (lab. manual) Nutrition, Diet Therapy and Foods, 1954; com. chmn. The Long Island Diet Manual, 1st edit., 1966. Pratt Inst. scholar, Bklyn., 1943-44; Gen. Foods grantee, 1944-45. Mem. Am. Dietetic Assn. (registered), Va. Dietetic Assn., Richmond Dietetic Assn. (legis. chair 1989), Genesee Dietetic Assn. (pres. 1970-71), L.I. Dietetic Assn. (chair diet therapy 1965-66), Oxford Civic Assn., Nat. Parks and Conservation Assn. Methodist. Home: 8033 Ammonett Dr Richmond VA 23235-3201

PALMER-CARFORA, LINDA LOUISE, special education educator; b. Derby, Conn., Mar. 6, 1950; d. Robert Roy and Ruth Mae (Borcherding) Palmer; m. John Michael Carfora, July 22, 1972; 1 child, Rachel Ellen. BS, So. Conn. State U., 1972; M of Edn. of the Deaf, Smith Coll., 1987. Learning disabilities tchr. Melissa Jones Sch., Guilford, Conn., 1972-76; tchr. Nat. Soc. for Autistic Children, London, 1977-79; clinician The Developmental Ctr., London, 1979-80; tchr. The Benhaven Sch., New Haven, Conn., 1982-84, Woodstock (Vt.) Developmental Ctr., 1984-86; ednl. cons. Willie Ross Sch. for the Deaf, Bloomington, Mass., 1994—; writer, edn. cons. Bloomington, Ind., 1994—; spl. edn. cons. Dalton (Mass.) Pub. Schs., 1990. Vol. clinician Elmira (N.Y.) Coll. Speech Clinic, 1968-69; vol. tutor New Haven Regional Ctr. for Mentally Retarded, 1969-70. Mem. Coun. for Exceptional Children, Smith Coll. Alumnae Assn. Congregationalist. Home and Office: 1311 Prairie Dr Bloomington IN 47408-9249

PALMER-HASS, LISA MICHELLE, state official; b. Nashville, Sept. 4, 1953; d. Raymond Alonzo Palmer and Anne Michelle (Jones) Davies; m. Joseph Monroe Hass, Jr. BSBA, Belmont Coll., 1975; AA in Interior Design, Internat. Fine Arts Coll., 1977; postgrad., Tenn. State U., 1991—. Interior designer Lisa Palmer Interior Designs, Nashville, 1977-84; sec. to pres. Hermitage Elect. Supply Corp., Nashville, 1981-83; sec. to dir. Tenn. Dept. Mental Health and Mental Retardation, Nashville, 1984-86; transp. planner Tenn. Dept. Transp., Nashville, 1986—. Mem. Nat. Arbor Day Found. Recipient cert. of appreciation Tenn. Dept. Mental Health and Mental Retardation, 1986; named Hon. Mem. Tenn. Ho. of Reps., 1990. Mem. NAFE, Nat. Wildlife Fedn., Profl. Secs. Internat. (cert.), Nashville Striders Club, The Music City Bop Club, Music City Bop Club Dance and Exhibn. Team, Mensa. Republican. Mem. Disciples of Christ Ch. Office: Tenn Dept Transp Environ Planning Office 505 Deaderick St Ste 900 Nashville TN 37219-1402

PALMISANO, MYRA ANN, nurse; b. Thibodaux, La., Oct. 21, 1948; d. Eddie Peter and Marie Louise (Adams) Toups; m. John Joseph Palmisano Jr., Dec. 8, 1973; children: Lisa Marie, Laura Louise, John Joseph III. Diploma, Charity Hosp. Sch. Nursing, 1970. RN, La. Staff nurse respiratory ICU Charity Hosp., New Orleans, 1970-71, head nurse respiratory ICU, 1971-72, asst. supr. med. ICU/coronary care unit, 1972-74; head nurse ICU-recovery rm. St. Claude Gen., New Orleans, 1974-75; staff nurse ICU Lakeside Hosp., Metairie, La., 1976-79; staff nurse endoscopy Lakeside Hosp., Metairie, 1979-80, acting head nurse ICU, 1980-81, nurse edn. instr., 1981-82, prenatal instr., 1982-84, staff edn. coord., 1984—. Active PTA, St. Lawrence Sch., Metairie, 1982-94; brownie leader Girl Scouts Am., New Orleans, 1983-85; cub scout leader Boy Scouts Am., New Orleans, 1990-93. Named to Great 100 Nurses, New Orleans (La.) Dist. Nurses' Assn., 1993. Mem. Nat. Nursing Staff Devel. Orgn., Am. Heart Assn., New Orleans Health Edn. Tng. Soc., Elenian Italian Culture Club. Democrat. Roman Catholic. Office: Lakeside Hosp 4700 I-10 Service Rd Metairie LA 70001

PALMISANO, SISTER MARIA GORETTI, principal; b. Balt., Nov. 6, 1929; d. Theodore Michael and Agnes Marie (Wheeler) P. BS in Edn., Duquesne U., 1966; MEd in Adminstrn. and Supervision, Towson State U., 1974; postgrad., Loyola Coll., 1976-83. Cert. advanced profl., Md. Tchr. St. Michael Sch., Forstburg, Md., 1952-59; music tchr. Holy Name Sch., Pitts., 1959-64; music tchr., tchr. jr. high St. Margaret Mary Sch., Harrisburg, Pa., 1964-69; prin. St. Brigid Sch., Balt., 1969-73, Bishop John Neumann Sch., Balt., 1973-83; adminstr. SSND Motherhouse, Balt., 1983-91; prin. St. Mary Sch., Hagerstown, Md., 1991—; mem. St. Maria Goretti Recruitment, Hagerstown, 1992—. Named Woman of Yr., Highlandtown Exch. Club, 1983. Mem. ASCD, Nat. Cath. Prins. Assn., Elem. Sch. Prins. Assn.-Archdiocese of Balt. (v.p. 1979-83). Home: 218 W Washington St Hagerstown MD 21740 Office: Saint Mary Sch 218 W Washington St Hagerstown MD 21740

PALMORE, CAROL M., former state government official; b. Owensboro, Ky., Jan. 13, 1949; d. P.J. and Carrie Alice (Leonard) Pate; m. John Stanley Palmore Jr., Jan. 1, 1982. BS in History and Polit. Sci., Murray State U., 1971; JD, U. Ky., 1977. Social worker Dept. Human Resources, Frankfort, Ky., 1971-74; assoc. atty. Rummage, Kamuf, Yewell & Pace, Owensboro, 1977-81; hearing officer Ky. Bd. Claims, Frankfort, 1980-81; gen. counsel Ky. Labor Cabinet, Frankfort, 1982-83, dep. sec. labor, 1984, 1986-87, sec. labor, 1987-90, 91-94; ptnr. Palmore & Sheffer Attys., Henderson, Ky., 1984-86; chmn. Ky. Safety & Health Stds. Bd., Frankfort, 1987-90, 91-94; co-chmn. Ky. Labor Mgmt. Adv. Coun., Frankfort, 1987-90, 91-94; bd. dirs. Ky. Workers' Comp Funding Commn., Frankfort, 1987-90, 91-94, Community Svc. Commn., Frankfort, 1993-94, Ky. Info. Resources Mgmt. Commn., Frankfort, 1994, Sch.-to-Work Partnership Coun., Frankfort, 1994; ex-officio bd. dirs. Pub. Employees Collective Bargaining Task Force, Frankfort, 1994, Ky. Workforce Partnership Coun., Frankfort, 1994. Labor liaison Jones for Gov., Lexington, 1990-91; del. Dem. Nat. Conv., N.Y.C., 1992; mem. inaugural class Ky. Women's Leadership Network, Frankfort, 1993; bd. dirs. Alliant Health Systems Adult Oper. Bd., Louisville, 1992—, Ky. Commn. Homeless, Frankfort, 1993-94; candidate for Sec. State Commonwealth Ky., 1994—. Mem. Ky. Bar Assn. (del. ho. dels. 1985-86, chair law day/spkr. bur. 1985-86, mem. 1986-90), Ky. Bar Found. (bd. dirs. 1985-92, sec. 1986-89, pres. elect 1989-90, pres. 1990-91), Rotary (program chair Frankfort chpt. 1992-93). Episcopalian. Home: 2310 Peaks Mill Rd Frankfort KY 40601 Office: Ky Labor Cabinet 1047 US Hwy 127 S Ste 4 Frankfort KY 40601

PALMQUIST, CAROL ANN, curriculum coordinator; b. Grand Saline, Tex., Mar. 6, 1943; d. Sam Houston and Erdine (Sellman) Dennington; m. Richard Norman Palmquist, May 23, 1987. BS, U. North Tex., 1965, MEd, 1970. Cert. supr., Tex. Tchr. Midland (Tex.) Ind. Sch. Dist., 1965-69; tchr. Port Arthur (Tex.) Ind. Sch. Dist., 1969-85, elem. supr., 1985-89; elem. curriculum coord. Mineral Wells (Tex.) Ind. Sch. Dist., 1990-92, curriculum coord., 1993—. Bd. dirs., officer Port Arthur Little Theatre, 1970's, Tex. Artist Mus. Soc., 1970's. Recipient Presdl. Svc. award Tex. Artist Mus. Soc. Mem. ASCD, Delta Kappa Gamma, Phi Delta Kappa. Methodist. Office: Mineral Wells Ind Sch Dist 906 SW 5th Ave Mineral Wells TX 76067

PALUMBO, RUTH ANN, state legislator; b. Lexington, Ky., July 7, 1949; d. James Keith and Dorothy Calvin (Carrier) Baker; m. John Anthony Palumbo II, June 29, 1974; children: John A. III (dec.), Joseph Edward, James Thomas, Stephen Baker. BA in Secondary Edn., U. Ky., 1972. Sales Chez Lissette Boutique, Leysin, Switzerland, 1966; sales, shoes Purcell's Dept. Store, Lexington, Ky., 1966-70; organist Ctrl. Bapt. Ch., Lexington, Ky., 1968; clk. Good Samaritan Hosp., Lexington, Ky., 1968-73; sec. Dr. Joseph Keith, Lexington, Ky., 1971-73; senate clk. aide Ky. Gen. Assembly, Frankfort, Ky., 1974; pub. rels. Palumbo Properties, Lexington, 1974-92; state rep. Ky. Gen. Assembly, 1991-92; mem. LWV, Lexington, 1990-92, Ky. Women's Polit. Caucus, Louisville, 1991-92, NAt. Order Women Legislators, Washington, 1992; sec. Ctrl. Ky. Caucus, Lexington, 1991-92. Mem. Greater Lexington Dem. Women, fin. v.p., 1982; mem. Nat. Order of Women Legislators, Washington, 1992; legis.liaison ACS Breast Cancer Detection Task Force, Ky., 1992; adv. coun. Bryan Sta. Youth Svcs. Ctr., Lexington, 1992; ball chmn. Lexington Philharmonic Women's Guild, 1990; govt. affairs Am. Symphony Orch. League Vol. Coun., Washington, 1992; bd. dirs. Philharmonic Women's Guild, pres., 1986-88; bd. dirs. Am. Cancer Soc., pres., 1988-89; bd. dirs. Lexington Phulharmonic Soc. Recipient Dorothy Moomaw Miles Svc. award Sayre Sch., 1986, Govs. Vol. Activist award Gov. Wallace G. Wilkinson, 1989, named Lexington's Outstanding Young Woman Bluegrass Jr. Woman's Club, 1982, Leadership Lexington, C. of C., 1988, Leadership Am. Found. for Women's Resources, Washington, 1989. Fellow U. Ky. Devel. Coun.; mem. Jr. League LExington (sec. 1989-90), Prof. Women's Forum, Gamma Phi Veta (pres. 1980-82). Baptist. Home: 10 Deepwood Dr Lexington KY 40505-2106 Office: House of Reps State Capitol Anx Frankfort KY 40601

PAMER, TREVA LOUISE, chemistry educator; b. Doylestown, Ohio, Sept. 22, 1938; d. Henry and Helen (Fetter) P.; m. Anthony M. Masulaitis, Oct. 14, 1978. BS in Chemistry, Kent State U., 1960; MS in Chemistry, CUNY, 1963; PhD in Biochemistry, N.Y. Med. Coll., 1969; MS in Computer Sci., Stevens Inst., Hoboken, N.J., 1983. Chemist Klett Mfg., N.Y.C., 1960-63; rsch. chemist Chas. Pfizer, Bklyn., 1963-64; rsch. assoc. N.Y. Med. Coll., N.Y.C., 1964-68; prof. chemistry Jersey City State Coll., 1968—; chair chemistry dept. Jersey State Coll., 1989—; rsch. Brookhaven Labs., Upton, N.Y., 1973-83. Mem. AAAS, Am. Chem. Soc., Chem. Intersociety Color Coun., Hudson Bergen Chem. Soc. (treas. 1990—), Am. Fedn. Tchrs. (pres. 1970), Rutherford Garden Club (pres. 1982-85). Office: Jersey City State Coll Dept Chemistry 2039 Kennedy Blvd Jersey City NJ 07305

PAMPUSCH, ANITA MARIE, academic administrator; b. St. Paul, Aug. 28, 1938; d. Robert William and Lucille Elizabeth (Whaley) P. BA, Coll. of St. Catherine, St. Paul, 1962; MA, U. Notre Dame, 1970, PhD, 1972. Tchr. St. Joseph's Acad., St. Paul, 1962-66; instr. philosophy Coll. of St. Catherine, St. Paul, 1970-76, assoc. acad. dean, 1979, acad. dean, 1979-84, pres., 1984—; Am. Council Edn. fellow Goucher Coll., Balt., 1976-77; bd. dirs. St.

Paul Cos.; head Women's Coll. Coalition, 1988-91. Author: (book rev.) Philological Quarterly, 1976; contbr. articles to profl. jours. Mem. adv. com. Instl. Leadership project, Columbia U., 1986—; dist. chmn. Rhodes Scholarship Selection com., Mo., Neb., Minn., Kans., N.D., S.D., 1987—; exec. com. Women's Coll. Coalition, Washington, 1985—. Mem. Coun. for Ind. Colls. (bd. dirs. 1987—, chair 1991—), Am. Philos. Assn., St. Paul C. of C. (bd. dirs. 1986—), St. Paul's Athletic Club, Mpls. Club, Phi Beta Kappa. Roman Catholic. Office: Coll of St Catherine Office of the President 2004 Randolph Ave Saint Paul MN 55105-1789

PAMUKCU, SIBEL, civil engineering educator; b. Istanbul, Turkey, Feb. 10, 1956; came to U.S., 1979, naturalized, 1994; d. Necmi an dMediha (Ardal) Taboglu; m. Derya Pamukcu, June 23, 1979; children: Deniz Ozan, Erin Melis. BS in Civil Engring., Bogazici U., Istanbul, 1978; MS in Civil Engring., La. State U., 1981, PhD in Civil Engring., 1986. Project engr. Dept. Hwys./Transp., Istanbul, 1978-79; teaching asst. La. State U., Baton Rouge, 1979-83, rsch. asst., 1983-86; asst. prof. Lehigh U., Bethlehem, Pa., 1986-92, assoc. prof., 1992—; advisor Lehigh U. chpt. Soc. Women Engrs., 1994. Contbr. book chpts., articles to profl. jours. Mem. ASCE, Am. Soc. Testing and Materials, Am. Soc. Engring. Edn., Transp. Rsch. Bd. (sec. com. soil and rock 1988-95, chair com. soil and rock 1995—), Internat. Soc. for Soil Mechanics and Found. Engring., Sigma Xi, Phi Beta Kappa. Muslim. Office: Lehigh U Dept Civil and Environ Engring 13 E Packer Ave Bethlehem PA 18015

PAN, AIQIN ANGELINA, computer scientist; b. Guangzhou, China, Sept. 11, 1963; came to U.S., 1987; d. Kaiwen and Wing Mui (Lin) P. BS, Zhongshan U., Guangzhou, 1984; MS, U. Ala., Birmingham, 1988, PhD, 1990. With Data Base Tech. Inst. IBM, Almaden Rsch. Ctr., San Jose, Calif., 1990-93; with Mitsubishi Electric Rsch. Lab., Sunnyvale, Calif., 1993-94, Borland Internat., Scotts Valley, Calif., 1994-95; dir. R&D Penknowledge, Inc., Birmingham, Ala., 1995—. Author: A Trip Around the World, 1992, Angel's Story, 1993. Named Bay Area Outstanding Individual, Soc. San Francisco Bay Area Engrs., 1993, Profl. Woman of Yr., Disting. Am. Women Computer Scientists, 1991. Mem. IEEE Computer Soc., Assn. for Computing Machinery, Phi Kappa Phi. Home: 5290 Country Oak Ct San Jose CA 95136-3607

PAN, LORETTA REN-QIU, retired educator; b. Changzhou, China, Oct. 1, 1917, came to U.S., 1951, naturalized, 1965; d. Ke-jun and Mei-ying (Xue) P.; B.A. in English Lit., Ginling Coll., 1940; cert. English Lit., Mt. Holyoke Coll., 1952. Instr. English, Nanking U., 1940-41; instr. English and Chinese, St. Mary's Girls Sch., Shanghai, 1941-44; instr. English, Ginling Coll., 1944-45; sr. translator info. dept. Brit. Embassy, Shanghai, 1945-48; Chinese editor U.S. Consulate Gen., Hong Kong, 1949-51; researcher, editorial asst. modern China project Columbia U., 1955-60, lectr. Chinese, 1960-67, sr. lectr., 1968-87. Methodist. Contbr. to various profl. publs. Home: 600 W 111th St New York NY 10025-1813

PAN, MARIA WEIYEI, company executive; b. Beijing, China, June 19, 1943; came to U.S., 1965; d. Po Han Liu and Lillian Shufen Lee; m. Kochang Casey Pan, Sept. 21, 1968; 1 child, Julie Marie. BSBA, Nat. Taiwan U., Tapei, Taiwan, Republic of China, 1965; MS in Math. Stats., U. Iowa, 1967. Biostatician U. Iowa, Iowa City, 1967-69; mathematician Modern Woodmen of Am., Rock Island, Ill., 1969-73; real estate agent Nelson Realty, Davenport, Iowa, 1974-77; math. U.S. Army, Picatinny Arsenal, N.J., 1978-83; dir. Bus. Plus Corp., N.Y.C., 1989-91; real estate agent New Century Assocs.,, East Hanover, N.J., 1983—; dir. LPC Corp., Alhambra, Calif., 1987—; v.p. Handsome Enterprises of N.Y., N.Y.C., 1980-91; pres. BusinessPlus Corp. of N.J., Pine Brook, 1990—. Mem. NAFE, Am. Def. Preparedness Assn., Internat. Two Ten Found., N.J. Assn. Women Bus. Owners, Nat. Contract Mgmt. Assn. U.S. Army. Republican. Office: BusinessPlus Corp NJ 98 Ford Rd Ste 3C Denville NJ 07834

PAN, MARY AGNES, banker; b. Hong Kong, Oct. 20, 1951; came to U.S., 1970; d. Andrew and Priscilla (Ho) Tse; m. Henry Y.M. Pan, June 14, 1974; children: Lincoln, Gregory. BBA with honors, U. Hawaii, 1974. Asst. v.p. Citibank, Hong Kong, 1974-79; v.p. Bankers Trust Co., Hong Kong, 1979-84, Bank of Am., Palo Alto, Calif., 1984-86, Midlantic Nat. Bank, Metro Park, N.J., 1987-88; fin. cons. Merrill Lynch, Lawrenceville, N.J., 1988; v.p. Citibank, N.Y.C., 1988-94; 1st v.p. Republic Nat. Bank of N.Y., N.Y.C., 1994—. Home: 460 Baneswood Cir Kennett Square PA 19348-2550

PANACCIONE, VICKI F., psychologist; b. Fort Campbell, Ky., Oct. 18, 1954; d. Jerome Louis Feuer and Gilda (Rosenberg) Phillips; m. John Panaccione Jr., Aug. 1, 1976; 1 child, Alexander Colin. Student, Brandeis U., 1972-74; BA, Rutgers U., 1976; MA, U. Tenn., 1980, PhD, 1983. Lic. psychologist, Fla. Dir. counseling Waltham (Mass.) Group, 1972-74; state liason Collier Group Home, Red Bank, N.J., 1976; county social worker Monmouth County, Red Bank, 1976; exec. dir. Girls Club Inc., Knoxville, Tenn., 1976-77; pvt. practice social work counselor, 1977-78; vocat. counselor Goodwill Industries, Knoxville, 1978-80; attendance referral counselor Knoxville (Tenn.) City Schs., 1980; pvt. practice lic. psychol. examiner Knoxville, 1982-83; psychologist Seven Counties Svcs., Louisville, 1983-84; pvt. practice psychologist Louisville, 1984-91, Melbourne, Fla., 1991—; clin. intern U. Louisville Sch. Medicine, 1981-82; lectr. Spalding U., Louisville, 1984-85; assoc. med. staff Holmes Regional Med. Ctr., Melbourne, 1992—; affiliated med. staff Children's Psychiat. Ctr., Palm Bay (Fla.) Hosp., 1992—; adj. prof. Fla. Inst. Tech., Melbourne, 1992-93; cons., affiliated staff mem. DeVereux Hosp., Melbourne, 1993-94; cons. early intervention program Holmes Regional Med. Ctr. Active Pacesetters, Melbourne, 1991—. Named Young Career Woman of Yr., Knoxville (Tenn.) Profl. Bus. Women, 1977. Mem. APA, South Brevard Profl. Women's Network, Phi Beta Kappa, Psi Chi. Office: Ste 207 95 Bulldog Blvd Melbourne FL 32901

PANASCI, NANCY ERVIN, speech pathologist, cookbook writer, communications consultant; b. Fairborn, Ohio, Mar. 24, 1954; d. Lindsay James and Frances E. (Erickson) Ervin; m. Ernest James Panasci, Aug. 7, 1976; children: Caitlin Alba, Adele Frances, Carissa Anne. BS, Colo. State U., 1976; MA, Cath. U., Washington, 1979. Tchr. Montessori Sch., Rome, N.Y., 1971-72, Fairfax (Va.) Sch. Dist., 1976-77; speech pathologist Littleton (Colo.) Pub. Schs., 1979-92, pvt. practice, 1992—; communication cons. speech pathology Trial Attys., Denver, 1986—. Com. chairperson. Jr. League in Denver, 1982-91; com. chmn. Make-A-Wish Found. of Colo., 1991; com. chairperson. Denver Victims Svc. Ctr., Share Our Strength, Nat. Kidney Found. Named Best Cook in West, Rocky Mountain Newspaper, Denver, 1982. Mem. Am. Speech Hearing Lang. Assn. (cert. clin. competence 1980), Colo. Speech Hearing Assn. (com. chairperson 1982-86), Cherry Hills Country Club. Roman Catholic. Home: 5191 S Hanover St Englewood CO 80111-6244 Office: Littleton Pub Schs Littleton CO 80120

PANATIER, PATRICIA ELLEN, physics tutor; b. N.Y.C., Sept. 15, 1954; d. James Michael and Irene Elizabeth (Delmore) P.; m. Roger Louis LeBlanc, Dec. 11, 1981; children: Theresa Panatier LeBlanc, Evan Panatier LeBlanc. BS in Physics, SUNY, Stony Brook, 1981. Engring. aide Sperry Corp., Great Neck, N.Y., 1977-80; nuclear engr. LILCO, Shoreham, N.Y., 1982-86; pres. PEP Tutoring, Dix Hills, N.Y., 1989—. Mem. PTA Signal Hill Elem. Sch., Dix Hills, 1991—. Mem. NOW, ACLU, Am. Phys. Soc., Am. Phys. Soc. Forum on Edn., L.I. Forum for Tech. (emeritus scientist). Democrat. Home: 72 Carman Rd Dix Hills NY 11746

PANCAKE, EDWINA HOWARD, science librarian; b. Butte, Mont., Nov. 10, 1942; d. Robert Evan and Edwina Howard (Handfield) P. Student, Miami U., 1960-63; BS in Biology, Baylor U., 1967; MLS, U. Tex., 1969. Sci. info. specialist U. Va., Charlottesville, 1969-73, acting dir. sci. and tech. info. ctr., dir. sci. and engring libr., 1974-93, assoc. prof. emeritus, 1994—. NDEA fellow U. Tex., 1967-68. Fellow Spl. Libraries Assn. (bd. dirs. 1979-81, 83-84, 85-88, pres. 1994-95), Mensa. Episcopalian.

PANCHAL, JOAN, nursing educator; b. Pitts., Feb. 25, 1947; d. Edward and Gertrude (Kaminski) Dauginikas; m. Pravin D. Panchal, Aug. 20, 1970; children: Nita, Sheila, Lisa. A.D., Community Coll. Allegheny, Pitts., 1970; BSN, Pa. State U., 1981; MPH, U. Pitts., 1982, PhD, 1987. Surg. nurse South Side Hosp., Pitts., 1965-70; staff nurse-med. VA Hosp., Bronx, N.Y., 1970; head nurse Jewish Home and Hosp., Bronx, 1970-71; rehab. coord. Negley House, Pitts., 1978-81; instr. nursing Pa. State U., University Park, 1982-85, asst. prof., 1987—, grad. faculty, 1994—; cons., Pitts., 1978-88; with Pa. Dept. Health Nursing, Pub. Health Adminstrn., Pitts., 1982. Author book revs., course; author: (ednl. instrn.) Teaching the Cardiac Patient, 1991. Named for Edn. Excellence, Nightengale fo Pa., 1991. Mem. Pa. League for Nursing (pres. 1992-94, bd. dirs. 1989), NLN, ANA (item writer for cert. 1989), Pa. Nurses Assn. (provider unit 1990, bd. dirs. 1992—). Roman Catholic. Home: 200 Highland Rd Pittsburgh PA 15238 Office: Pa State U 201 Health and Human Devel University Park PA 16802

PANETTA, DEBRA CAROL, finance company executive; b. Stoneham, Mass., Mar. 31, 1962; d. Richard John and Carol Ann (Schirl) Mancini; m. Mark Stephen Panetta, Oct. 5, 1986. BSBA in Acctg. magna cum laude, Suffolk U., 1983; MBA, Northeastern U., 1991. Acct. Hennenberg & Hennenberg, Cambridge, Mass., 1981-90; team acct. Winn Mgmt., Boston, 1983-84; chief acct. Brown, Rudnick, Freed & Gesmer, Boston, 1984-87; sr. tech. acct. John Hancock, Boston, 1987-90, sr. fin. officer, 1990—; owner, mgr. Windsurfer, Winthrop, Mass., 1992—. Activities chair United Way, Boston, 1993-94. Fellow Inst. Managerial Accts., GBO Comm. Team, Assocs. in Customer Svc., Toastmasters, Delta Mu Delta, Beta Gamma Sigma. Office: John Hancock PO Box 111-b-12 Boston MA 02117

PANG, JOANNA (JOANNA ATKINS), dancer, actress, choreographer, director; b. Berkeley, Calif., Feb. 9; d. Joseph H. Panganiban Sr. and Lynette Stevens DeFazio; m. Richard Atkins, 1982; 1 child, Davy Steven Atkins. Student, San Francisco State Coll., 1964-65. Child performer, dancer with ptnr. and brother Joey; with San Francisco Ballet and San Francisco Opera Co., 1952-63; appeared on The Ted Randall Dance Party, San Francisco, 1959-61, Dick Stewart Dance Party, San Francisco, 1961-62, Art Laboe Show, and Earl McDaniel Show, L.A., 1959, Lawrence Welk show, 1961; appeared with U.S. Govt. Mil. Shows, 1954-56, N.Y.C. Ballet, 1955; prin. dancer nat. and internat. tours Toy-Wing Oriental Dance Co., 1965-70; mem. faculty Ballet Arts, Oakland, 1963-64; instr., prin. performer Robicheau Ballet, Boston, 1969-72; cons., guest lectr., artist-in-residence N.J. State Coun. on Arts, 1994—. Appeared on stage in South Pacific, West Stide Story, Music Man. Song of Norway, numerous others; appeared on TV shows Saturday Night Live, CBS Daytime 90, Edge of Night, The Doctors, All My Children; in films Voices, Once A Thief, Stardust Memories, others; appeared in TV commls. Mem. SAG, AFTRA, Actors Equity Assn. Home and Office: 149 Ridgedale Ave Florham Park NJ 07932

PANICELLO, ARLENE TERESA, early childhood educator; b. July 26, 1950; came to U.S., 1950; d. Joseph John and Erminia Dorothy (Rampone) P. BA in Psychology with highest honors, Richmond Coll., S.I., N.Y., 1973; MS in Elem. Edn. with highest honors, CUNY, 1974. Personal home sec. Dr. Joyce Brothers, 1970-72; tchr. Pub. Sch. 189, Bklyn., Pub. Sch. 194, Bklyn., 1975—; educator, acting dir. Lillian Sklar Filler Sch., Bklyn., 1976—; sch. coord. Easter Seals, Bklyn.; student tchr. trainer Kingsborough Coll., Bklyn. Author: (short stories for children) Rejected, 1980, 82 (Letters of Recognition 1985), Do, Re, Mi, 1985; contbr. articles to Christian mags. Chariasmatic leader Resurrection Ch., Bklyn., 1992-94. Roman Catholic. Home: 3021 Avenue W Brooklyn NY 11229-5563 Office: Lillian Sklar Filler 49 Avenue W Brooklyn NY 11223-5640

PANICH, DANUTA BEMBENISTA, lawyer; b. East Chicago, Ind., Apr. 9, 1954; d. Fred and Ann Stephanie (Grabowski) B.; m. Nikola Panich, July 30, 1977; children: Jennifer Anne, Michael Alexei. A.B., Ind. U., 1975, J.D., 1978. Bar: Ill. 1978, U.S. Dist. Ct. (no. dist.) Ill. 1978, U.S. Dist. Ct. (cen. dist.) Ill. 1987, U.S. Ct. Appeals, 1987. Assoc. Mayer Brown & Platt, Chgo., 1978-86, ptnr., 1986—. Mem. ABA, Ill. State Bar Assn. Republican. Roman Catholic. Office: Mayer Brown & Platt 190 S La Salle St Chicago IL 60603-3410

PANICO, ELAINE HARTMAN, nurse; b. Phila., July 13, 1924; d. Edward Earl and Eleanor Mayo (Adams) Hartman; children: Frederick, Robert, Eleanor, Lorne, Earl, John, William, Richard, Louise. BSN, State Coll. and Med. Ctr., 1946; BS in Edn., State Tchrs. Coll., 1946; postgrad., U. Pa., 1946-49. RN Summer Boys Camp, Winnekee, N.H., 1948; instr. Glassboro (N.J.) State Coll., 1948; coll. nurse, asst. Dean State Coll., Glassboro, 1946-48; asst. dir. nurses Osteo. Hosp., Phila., 1948-49, instr. pharm. math., 1948-49; eye surg. nurse Cornell-N.Y. Hosp., N.Y.C., 1949-50; surg. supr. Balt. City Hosps., 1950-52; nurse in charge Taj Mahal Med. Office, Atlantic City, N.J., 1990; surg. office nurse Ventnor, N.J., 1960—; pub. health speaker elem. schs., Boston, 1950; RN internat. confs., Stony Brook, N.Y., 1980-85, A.C. Med. Ctr. Eye Clinic, Atlantic City, 1987-90; creator earliest post-operative surg. intensive care unit, Balt. City Hosps., 1950-52. Cert. classic ballet, 1932-42. Bd. dirs. PTA, Ventnor, 1960-83, Atlantic Performing Arts Ctr., Atlantic City, 1970-90; mem. Holy Spirit Mothers Assn., Absecon, N.J., 1966-83; sponsor South Jersey Regional Theatre, Atlantic Community Concerts, Stockton Coll. Performing Arts; fin. sec. Atlantic City Med. Ctr. Aux., 1963; chmn. spl. projects Miss. Am. Pageant Scholarship Found., Very Important Hostess (V.I.H.), 1967—. Recipient Lifetime Recognition award Great Books Found., 1966-67, 15-yr. Gold award Miss Am. Pageant, 1982. Mem. AAUW, Atlantic County Med. Aux. (pres. 1984-90), U.S. Golf Assn., Internat. Platform Assn., RNs Cancer Heart Meml. Fund. (bd. dirs.), Hydrangea Club (chmn. 1964, Silver 15 Yr. award). Home: 102 S Dudley Ave Ventnor City NJ 08406-2837 Office: 12 S Somerset Ave Ventnor City NJ 08406-2846

PANKEY, ELIZABETH WEEKS, humorous illustrator; b. Norfolk, Va., Feb. 18, 1950; d. Charles S. and Virginia W. Weeks; m. P. Roger Pankey, May 22, 1971; 1 child, Virginia Marie. AS, Shoreline C.C. Tchr. cartooning Seattle; caricaturist e.w.p.Originals, Seattle; cons. E.W.P. Originals, Seattle; artist P.R. Cards and Postcards, 1986-94. Illustrator: What Can You Do With a See-Thru Fig Leaf, 1984; creator P.R.Cards and P.R.Postcards. Co-editor Chimes Trinity Parish Episc. Ch., Seattle, 1991-94. Mem. Cartoonists Northwest (pres. 1990-91, Toonie 1992), Graphic Artists Guild (Soc. Profl. Graphic Artists chpt., nat. rep. 1994—), Snohomish County Women Bus. Owners Assn. (treas.), Internat. Women in Boating (Seattle chpt. 1993), U. Ariz. Alumni (past pres., recruiter).

PANNKE, PEGGY M., insurance agency executive; b. Chgo., Oct. 26; d. Victor E. and Leona (O'Leary) Stich; m. Helmut Pannke, Sept. 1, 1961; children: Thomas Scott, David Savonne, Heidi Mireille, Peter Helmut. Office mgr. DeHaan & Richter P.C., Chgo. and Des Plaines, Ill., 1983-86; v.p. long term care ins. Sales & Seminars, Des Plaines, 1986-90; pres., founder. Nat. Consumer Oriented Agy., Des Plaines, 1990—; cons. on long-term care ins. The Travelers, Tchrs. Ins. & Annuity Assocs., and numerous other ins. cos., N.Y.C., Hartford, Conn. and throughout U.S.; speaker Exec. Enterprises, N.Y.C., 1988-93. Contbr. articles on long-term care ins. to profl. jours. Sponsor Ill. Alliance for Aging, Chgo., 1990—, Ill. Assn. Homes for Aging, 1990-91; bd. govs. St. Matthew Luth. Home, Park Ridge, Ill., 1993—. Recipient Speakers awards Health Ins. Assn. Am., Washington, 1990, Retired Officers Assn., Glenview, Ill., 1991, 93, Nat. Assn. Sr. Living Industries, Denver, 1992, Exec. Enterprises, N.Y.C., 1993. Mem. Nat. Assn. Sr. Living Industries, Ctr. for Applied Gerontology, Nat. Coun. on Aging, Mature Ams. Ad Hoc Com., Am. Mensa of Ill. (program dir. 1983-85), Kiwanis (bd. dirs. Park Ridge 1992—). Office: Nat Consumer Oriented Agy 2200 E Devon Ave Des Plaines IL 60018-4503

PANNULLO, DEBORAH PAOLINO, manufacturing company executive; b. Providence, Apr. 2, 1953; d. Joseph and Lena (Wilde) Paolino; m. Michael J. Pannullo, Apr. 23, 1971 (div. 1973); 1 child, Melissa Jean. BA in Econs., R.I. Coll., 1977; cert. in mfg. mgmt., Bryant Coll., 1982, MBA, 1987; post-grad., Roger Williams U. Payroll analyst Bostitch/Textron, East Greenwich, R.I., 1977-79, cost analyst, 1979-80, U.S. mfg. coordinator, 1980-82, quality circles mgr., 1982-85; productivity mgr. Stanley Fastening Systems, East Greenwich, 1985-87; dir. quality assurance-productivity improvement Stanley-Bostitch, East Greenwich, 1987-91, plant mgr., 1991—; part-time instr. Bryant Coll.; cons. Sml. Bus. Devel. Ctr. Bd. dirs. R.I. Anti Drug Coalition. Named outstanding Woman of Yr. WMCA, 1985. Mem. NAFE, Am. Soc. Quality Assurance, Internat. Assn. Quality Circles (pres.1984-85, bd. dirs. R.I. chpt. 1985—), R.I. Tech. Coun. (chairperson quality assurance sub-com.), R.I. Coll. Alumni Assn. (exec. bd. dirs.), Delta Mu Delta. Roman Catholic. Home: 17 Hawkins St Greenville RI 02828-3103

PANTER, TERRY EVE, accountant; b. Copperhill, Tenn., Apr. 30, 1957; d. Wallace Lloyd Panter and Lelia Louise (Burk) Baggett. BBA, Kennesaw (Ga.) Coll., 1983. CPA, Ga. Owner Panter Acctg. Svcs., Marietta, Ga. Mem. AICPA, Kennesaw Coll. Alumni Assn. Mem. Ch. of Christ. Home: 727 Bonnie Dell Dr Marietta GA 30062 Office: Panter CPAs 2329 Windy Hill Rd NW Marietta GA 30067

PANZONE-HUBBARD, LISA MARIE GINA, tax consultant and specialist, financial planner, tax accountant; b. Phila., Feb. 26, 1960; d. Frank Vincent Sr. and Lisa Veronica (De Pierro) P. BA in Acctg., Rowan Coll., 1981; MS in Taxation, Widener U., 1983. CPA, Pa. Acct. Robert O'Connel & Co. (name now Touche Ross Co.), Phila., 1981; sr. acct., tax acct. Robert B. Burke, Phila., 1981-86; supr. sr. acct. Keystone Orgn., Phila., 1984-85; sr. tax acct. K.M.G. Main Hurdman, Phila., 1985-86; asst. tax dir. I.M.S., Inc., Phila., 1986-87; pvt. practice Phila., 1986—; tax specialist, co-owner Inches Off, Cherry Hill, N.J., 1985—; dir. ops. Cherry Hill Security Solutions, Mt. Laurel, N.J., 1988—. Vol. Community Accts., 1987—; treas., treas. Mt. Laurel Twp., 1984. Mem. Am. Soc. Women Accts., Contemporary Record Soc. (treas. Broomall, Pa. chpt. 1988—), GRASP (treas. Phila. chpt. 1988—). Home: 12 The Ellipse Ste 259 Mount Laurel NJ 08054 Office: 3009 Mt Ephraim Ave Mount Laurel NJ 08054

PAOLO, SUSAN BARKER, psychologist; b. Tripoli, Libya, Aug. 2, 1962; came to the U.S., 1963; d. James Berton Barker and Elizabeth Bell (Barker) Smith; m. Anthony Manuel Paolo, Oct. 6, 1990; 1 child, Helen Elizabeth. BA, Wellesley Coll., 1984; MA, U. Kans., 1987, PhD, 1990. Lic. psychologist, Kans., Mo. Summer intern L.A. (County) Dept. Mental Health, 1983; tchg. asst. psychology dept. U. Kans., Lawrence, 1984-85; childen's caregiver Ctr. for Applied Behavioral Analysis, Lawrence, 1985-86; psychotherapy trainee U. Kans. Psychol. Clinic, Lawrence, 1985-87; psychotherapist Profl. Assocs. in Clin. Psychology, St. Joseph, Mo., 1987; psychology trainee VA Med. Ctr., Knoxville, Iowa, 1987; psychotherapist N.E. Kans. Mental Health and Guidance Ctr., Leavenworth, 1988-89; psychology intern Okla. Health Scis. Ctr., Oklahoma City, 1989-90; staff psychologist, mental health clinic coord. VA Med. Ctr., Kansas City, 1990—. Reviewer: Jour. Hosp. and Cmty. Psychiatry, 1992—; contbr. articles to profl. jours. Co-chair membership growth com. St. Paul's United Meth. Ch., Lenexa, Kans., 1993. Mem. APA, Sigma Xi (assoc. mem.). Office: VA Med Ctr Psychology Svc 4801 E Linwood Blvd Kansas City MO 64128-2226

PAOLONI, VIRGINIA ANN, insurance company executive; b. Scranton, Pa., July 26, 1961; d. Edmund James and Virginia (Borick) P. BS in Mktg., King's Coll., 1983. Underwriter Reliance Ins., Phila., 1983-85; account exec. The Walsh Co., Phila., 1984-87; pres. Paoloni Ins. Agy., Olyphant, Pa., 1987%. Participant Leadership Lackawanna, Scranton, 1991—; bd. dirs. fin. planning Holy Named of Jesus Ch., Scranton, 1990—; mem. allocation steering com. United Way, 1992—; bd. dirs. Am. Heart Assn.; pub. rels. com. Habitat for Humanity, 1993—. Mem. Greater Scranton Ins. Assn. (bd. dirs., chair edn. com. 1989—, 1st v.p.), Jr. League. Republican. Roman Catholic. Home: 1611 Wyoming Ave Scranton PA 18509 Office: Paoloni Ins Agy 766 N Valley Ave Olyphant PA 18447-1716

PAOLUCCI, ANNE ATTURA, playwright, poet, English and comparative literature educator; b. Rome; d. Joseph and Lucy (Guidoni) Attura; m. Henry Paolucci. BA, Barnard Coll; MA, Columbia U., PhD, 1963. Mem. faculty English dept. Brearley Sch., N.Y.C., 1957-59; asst. prof. English and comparative lit. CCNY, 1959-69; univ. research prof. St. John's U., Jamaica, N.Y., 1969—; prof. English St. John's U., 1975—, acting head dept. English, 1973-74, chmn. dept. English, 1982-91, dir. doctor of arts degree program in English, 1982—; Fulbright lectr. in Am. drama U. Naples, Italy, 1965-67; spl. lectr. U. Urbino, summers 1966-67, U. Bari, 1967, univs. Bologna, Catania, Messina, Palermo, Milan, Pisa, 1965-67; disting. adj. vis. prof. Queens Coll., CUNY; bd. dirs. World Centre for Shakespeare Studies, 1972—; spl. guest Yugoslavia Ministry of Culture, 1972; rep. U.S. at Internat. Poetry Festival, Yugoslavia, 1981; founder, exec. dir. Council on Nat. Lits., 1974—; mem. exec. com. Conf. Editors Learned Jours.-MLA, 1975—; del. to Fgn. Lang. Jours., 1977—; mem. adv. bd. Commn. on Tech. and Cultural Transformation, UNESCO, 1978—; vis. fellow Humanities Research Centre, Australian Nat. U., 1979; rep. U.S. woman playwright Inter-Am. Women Writers Congress, Ottawa, Ont., Can., 1978; organizer, chmn. profl. symposia, meetings; TV appearances; hostess Mags. in Focus, Channel 31, N.Y.C., 1971-72; mem. N.Am. Adv. Council Shakespeare Globe Theatre Center, 1981—; mem. Nat. Grad. Fellows Program Fellowship Bd., 1985—; mem. Nat. Garibaldi Centennial Com., 1981; mem. Nat. Grad. Fellows Program, 1985—; trustee Edn. Scholarship, Grants Com. of NIAF, 1990—; guest speaker with E. Albee Ohio No. State U., 1990. Author: (with H. Paolucci) books, including Hegel On Tragedy, 1962, From Tension to Tonic: The Plays of Edward Albee, 1972, Pirandello's Theater: The Recovery of the Modern Stage for Dramatic Art, 1974, Poems Written for Sbek's Mummies, Marie Menken, and Other Important Persons, Places, and Things, 1977, Eight Short Stories, 1977, Sepia Prints, 1985, 2nd edit., 1986; plays include Minions of the Race (Medieval and Renaissance Conf. of Western Mich. U. Drama award 1972), Cipango!, 1985, pub. as book, 1985, 86, videotape excerpts, 1986, 1992, Three Short Plays, 1994; performed N.Y.C. and Washington, 1987-88, Winterthur Mus., U. Del., 1990; The Actor in Search of His Mask, 1987, Italian tranl. and prodn., Genoa, 1987; poems Riding the Mast Where It Swings, 1980, Gorbechev in Concert, 1991; contbr. numerous articles, revs. to profl. jours.; editor, author: introduction Dante's Influence on American Writers, 1977; gen. editor tape-cassette series China, 1977, 78; founder Coun. on Nat. Lit.; gen. editor series Rev. Nat. Lits, 1970—, CNL/Quar. World Report, 1974-76, semi-annual 1977-84, annual 1985—; full-length TV tape of play Cipango! for pub. TV and ednl. TV with original music by Henry Paolucci, 1990. Bd. dirs. Italian Heritage and Culture City-wide com., 1986—; Pres. Reagan appointee Nat. Grad. Fellows Program Fellowship Bd., 1985-86, Nat. Coun. Humanities, 1986—, Ann. award, FIERI, 1990; pres. Columbus: Countdown, 1992 Fedn.; mem. Gov. Cuomo's Heritage Legacy Project for Schs., 1989—; bd. dirs. Am. Soc. Italian Legions of Merit (chmn. cultural com. 1990—). Named one of 10 Outstanding Italian Ams. in Washington, awarded medal by Amb. Rinaldo Petrignani, 1986; named Cavaliere Italian Republic, 1986, "Commendatore" of the Italian Republic Order of Merit, 1992; recipient Notable Rating for Mags. in Focus series N.Y. Times, 1972, Woman of Yr. award Dr. Herman Henry Scholarship Found., 1973, Amita award, 1970, award Women's Press Club N.Y., 1974, Order Merit, Italian Republic, 1986, Gold medal for Quincentenary Can. trustee NIIAF, 1990, ann. awards Consortium of Italian-Am. Assns., 1991, Am.-Italian Hist. Assn., 1991, 1st Columbus award Cath. Charities, 1991, Leone di San Marco award Italian Heritage Coun. of Bronx and Westchester Counties, 1992, Children of Columbus award Order of Sons of Italy in Am., 1993, 1st Nat. Elena Cornaro award Order of Sons of Italy, 1993; Columbia U. Woodbridge hon. fellow, 1961-62; Am. Council Learned Socs. grantee Internat. Pirandello Congress, Agrigento, Italy, 1978. Mem. Internat. Shakespeare Assn., Shakespeare Assn. Am., Renaissance Soc. Am., Renaissance Inst. Japan, Internat. Comparative Lit. Assn., Am. Comparative Lit. Assn., MLA, Am. PEN, Hegel Soc. Am., Dante Soc. Am. (v.p. 1976-77), Am. Found. Italian Arts and Letters (founder, pres.), Pirandello Soc. (pres. 1978—), Nat. Soc. Lit. and Arts, Nat. Book Critics Circle, Am. Soc. Italian Legions of Merit (bd. dirs. 1990—). Office: St John's U Jamaica NY 11439

PAONE, PATRICIA, secondary school educator; b. Altoona, Pa., Jan. 24, 1951; d. Anthony Nicholas and Catherine Mary (Laura) P. BS, Clarion U., 1972; MEd, Penn. State U., 1975. Tchr. Blacklick Valley Sch. Dist., Nanty Glo, Pa., 1972—. Mem. NEA, Pa. State Edn. Assn. (bldg. rep., v.p.), Blacklick Valley Edn. Assn. (v.p.), Blacklick Valley Bus. & Profl. Women's Club (chmn. pub. rels., Dist. 5 Young Careerist award 1980, mem. of yr. 1992), Penn. State Club of Johnstown (exec. bd.), Clarion Alumni Assn. (life), Penn. State Alumni Assn. (life). Democrat. Roman Catholic. Home: 231 Circle Dr Ebensburg PA 15931 Office: Blacklick Valley Sch Dist 155 Birch St Nanty Glo PA 15943

PAPE, ELIZABETH CLARK, advertising executive; b. Plainfield, N.J., Oct. 26, 1948; d. Earl George and Blanche (Conneran) Clark; m. Robert Frederick Pape, June 20, 1970; 1 child, Jonathan Clark. BA in Journalism, Douglass Coll., 1970. Jour. editor Cahners Pub., Boston, 1980-83; account exec. J.W. Thompson Recruitment Advt., Waltham, Mass., 1983, Ingalls

Assocs., Boston, 1983-85; mgmt. supr. Bertsch & Co. Advt., N.Y.C., 1985-86; gen. mgr. Bertsch & Co. Advt. New Eng., Wellesley, Mass., 1986-88; mgmt. supr. Bozell, Jacobs, Kenyon, Eckhardt, Boston, 1988; owner recruitment advt., pub. rels. cons. Pape Communications, South Natick, Mass., 1988—; dir. Boston Human Resources Assn., Cambridge, Mass., 1992—; editorial cons., Cahners Pub., Boston, 1984-85. Treas, Plowshares Day Care Ctr., Newton, 1978, pres., 1979-84. Office: Pape Communications 205 Union St South Natick MA 01760

PAPE, PATRICIA ANN, social worker, consultant; b. Aurora, Ill., Aug. 2, 1940; d. Robert Frank and Helen Louise (Hanks) Grover; children: Scott Allen, Debra Lynn. BA in Sociology, Northwestern U., 1962; MSW, George Williams Coll., 1979. Cert. addictions counselor, Ill.; lic. clin. social worker, sch. social worker, Ill. Pvt. practice family counseling, 1979—; coord. community resources DuPage Probation Dept., Wheaton, Ill., 1977-80; dir. The Abbey Alcoholism Treatment Ctr., Winfield, Ill., 1980-81; prin. Pape & Assocs., Wheaton, 1982—; dir. alcoholism counselor tng. program Coll. of DuPage, Glen Ellyn, Ill., 1982-87; Chgo. affiliate Employee Assistance Program, 1982—; cons. Luth. Soc. Services Ill., 1979-82. Contbr. articles to profl. jours. Mem. alcohol drug task force Ill. Synod Luth. Ch. Am., Chgo., 1985—. Named Woman of Yr., Entrepreneur Women in Mgmt., Oak Brook, Ill, 1986. Mem. Assn. Labor-Mgmt. Adminstrs. Cons. Alcoholism (women's issues com. 1984—), Acad. Cert. Social Workers, Am. Assn. Marriage Family Therapists, Nat. Assn. Soc. Workers, Women in Mgmt. Home: 26W 360 Churchill Rd Winfield IL 60190 Office: Pape & Assocs 618 S West St Wheaton IL 60187-5038

PAPIN, NANCY SUE, educational computer coordinator; b. Long Beach, Calif., Apr. 5, 1951; d. Emil Richard and Marjorie (Wright) DeSmet; m. Robert N. Papin, Oct. 5, 1971; children: Karina L., Brianne M. Student, Apple Computer Co., 1987-91. Sec. Sebring Products, Inc., L.A., 1970-74, bus. owner, 1970—; bus. owner Sebring Internat. of Hollywood, Calif., 1971-74; computer coord. Centralia Sch. Dist., Buena Park, Calif., 1986—; Apple edn. advisor Apple Computer Co., 1993—; mem. edn. tech. com. Centralia Sch. Dist., Buena Park, 1991-95; mem. sch. site coun. Los Coyotes Sch., La Palma, Calif., 1986-92, San Marino Sch., Buena Park, 1991-94; mem. grant writing com. Kennedy H.S., La Palma, 1991; mem. Vision 21 coordinating counsel Centralia Sch. Dist.; mem. sch. site coun. Walker Jr. H.S., 1994—. Author: History/Social Science Frameworks Correlation, 1991. Mem. sch. site coun. Walker Jr. High Sch., 1994—. Republican. Roman Catholic. Office: San Marino Sch 6215 San Rolando Buena Park CA 90620

PAPINEAU, PATRICIA MARY, dancer, educator; b. Rutland, Vt., July 9, 1951; d. Richard Burt and Mary Elizabeth (Qua) P. Student, Green Mountain Coll., 1970, Ind. U., 1976. Owner, dir. Patrician Acad. of Ballet, Rutland, 1965-76; tchr. dance Svetlova Dance Ctr., Dorset, Vt., 1970—; owner, dir. Pati Papineau Performing Arts Ctr., Clifton Park, N.Y., 1978-85; tchr. dance Green Mountain Coll., 1978-80, Albany (N.Y.) Acad., 1978-80, Schenectady (N.Y.) County C.C., 1978-81, Niskyuna High Sch., Schenectady, 1978-80, Albany-Shaker High Sch., Latham, N.Y., 1978-80, Shendehowah High Sch., Clifton Park, 1978-82. Dir. pageants Miss Greater Eastern N.Y., 1987, N.Y.'s Beautiful Baby, 1988, N.Y.'s Natural Miss, 1987-88, Miss Capital Dist./Miss Am., 1987; nat. producer Am.'s Natural Miss, 1988; dir., choreographer Springfield, Vt., Hosp. Debutante Cotillion. Pageant dir. Uncle Sam Parade Orgn., Troy, N.Y., 1987-90; bd. dirs. Rensselaer County Rape Crisis, Troy, 1991-92; N.Y. State bd. dirs. Miss Am. Pageant, 1988; hon. chair Vt. Heart Assn., 1970. Named Miss Green Mountain Coll., 1970, Miss Vt. Miss Am. Pageant, 1970, Miss Vt. Miss World USA, 1972. Methodist. Office: PO Box 2156 Clifton Park NY 12065-9156

PAPPACHRISTOU, JOYCE FLORES, dietitian, educator; b. Springfield, Mass., May 15, 1932; d. Hector and Henrietta (Hemerling) Flores; divorced; children: Dianne, Donna, Paul Jr., Gary. AA, Nassau Community Coll., 1970; BA in Math., Sci. and Home Econs. with honors, Queens Coll., 1973; MA, MS in dietetics/nutrition, NYU, 1976; postgrad., Nova U., 1989—. Cert. tchr., N.Y.C., N.Y., tchr. home econs., health edn., sci., Fla.; lic. dietitian, nutritionist Fla. Tchr. Roslyn High Sch., Elmont Meml. High Sch.; dietician L.I. (N.Y.) Jewish Hosp., St. Mary's Hosp.; instr. nutrition Cath. Med. Ctr. Nursing, 1974-76; chief dietician Jamaica (N.Y.) Hosp., 1976-80; tchr. Broward Coutny (Fla.) Bd. Educators, 1981—; adj. prof. Nassau Community Coll., Fla. Internat. U., 1976-80. Contbr. articles to profl. jours. Mem. Am. Dietetics Assn., Am. Home Econs. Assn. (cert.), Fla. Dietetics Assn., Fla. Assn. Computer Educators, Fla. Correctional Edn. Assn., Fla. Assn. Alternative Educators, Phi Beta Kappa, Kappa Delta Pi.

PAPPALARDO, VIRGINIA BIANCO, art educator, researcher; b. White Plains, N.Y., July 13, 1933; d. Ernest Oreste and Kate A. (Salerno) Bianco; m. Louis James Pappalardo, Dec. 26, 1955; children: Lisa Clare Foster, Jeffrey Louis. BA in Fine Arts, Coll. of Mt. St. Vincent, Riverdale, N.Y., 1954; MA in English Edn., Fairfield U., 1985; postgrad., Union Inst., 1993—. Art tchr. St. Helena's H.S., Bronx, N.Y., 1954-55; art tchr. Westport (Conn.) Pub. Schs., 1972-93, art coord., 1985-89, gifted tchr., 1985-92; adj. prof. art methods Pace U., White Plains, N.Y., 1994; assessor Conn. State Dept. Edn., 1994—; cons. art edn. Pub. Sch. Dists., 1986—; participant curriculum devel. inst. Getty Ctr. for Edn. in Arts, L.A., 1989-91; intern Yale U. Art Gallery, New Haven, Conn., 1993—; cons. art edn. Improving Visual Arts Edn., 1991-92. Mem. Conn. Art Edn. Assn. (past v.p. 1988-90, Art Educator of Yr. 1990), Nat. Art Edn. Assn., Nat. Mus. Women in Arts, Mus. Modern Art, Yale U. Art Gallery.

PAPPAS, EFFIE VAMIS, English and business educator, writer; b. Cleve., Dec. 26, 1924; d. James Jacob and Helen Joy (Nicholson) Vamis; m. Leonard G. Pappas, Nov. 3, 1945; children: Karen Pappas Morabito, Leonard J., Ellen Pappas Daniels, David James. BBA, Western Res. U., 1948; MA in Edn., Case Western Res. U., 1964; MA in English Lit., Cleve. State U., 1986; postgrad., Indiana U. Pa., 1979-80, 81-86. Cert. elem. and secondary tchr., Ohio. Tchr. elem. schs., Ohio, 1963-70; office mgr. Cleve. State U., 1970-72, adminstr. pub. relations, 1972-73; med. adminstr. Brecksville (Ohio) VA Hosp., 1974-78; lectr. English, bus. mgmt., math., comm., composition Cuyahoga C.C., Cleve., 1978-92; lectr. bus. and comms. Cleve. State U., 1980; participant Am. Inst. Chemists Del. to Republic of China, 1984, Inter-Cultural Exch. in the Soviet Union, 1989; teaching asst. Case Western Res. U., 1979-80, Ind. U. Pa., 1979, 80. Feature writer The Voice, 1970-78; editor, writer Cleve. State U. newsletter and mag., 1970-73. Den mother Cub Scouts Am., Brecksville, 1960; mem. local coun. PTA, 1965-70; sec. St. Paul's Coun., 1990-91; tchr. Sunday sch., 1960-65; mem. choir Brecksville United Ch. of Christ, 1975-76, mem. bd. missions, 1966-67; mem. membership com., 1993; mem. Nat. Trust for Hist. Preservation; mem. planning com. Case Western Res. U. Edn. Forum, 1992, 93, 94, 95, Greater Cleve. Project Teaching/Learning '94-95; mem. Ohio Hist. Soc.; charter mem. Nat. Mus. Women in Arts. Profl. devel. grantee Cuyahoga Community Coll., 1982. Mem. NAFE, AAUW (del. Internat. Fedn. of U. Women triennial meeting Stanford U. 1992, legis. chair, del. Ohio meetings 1993, 94, del. Ohio Coalition for Change 1993, 94, mem. Ohio and Cleve. br., del. AAUW Gt. Lakes regional meeting 1994, internat. co-chair Cleve. br. 1994), Ohio Edn. Assn. (rep. assembly Columbus 1994), Am. Assn. Ret. Persons, Nature Conservancy, Smithsonian Instn., Nat. Women's Hall of Fame. Home: 8681 Brecksville Rd Cleveland OH 44141-1912

PAPPAS, GWENDOLYN BENNETT (MRS. PHILLIP MILLER PAPPAS), public relations executive, author; b. Birmingham, Ala.; m. Phillip Miller Pappas; 6 children. DHL (hon.), L'Universite Libre, Asie, 1972. V.p. pub. rels. Super-Chef Mfg. Co., Houston. Author: A Love Letter to my Children, The Heart Reader, 1961, A Heart Breaks So Quietly, 1962, I Miss You Tonight and I'm Lonely, 1969, Sam Houston Returns to Texas, 1969, Night Comes So Early This Time of Year, 1970, Love Me Darling in the Old Way, 1970. Founding dir. Jones Hall; mem. pres. advisors Houston Bapt. Coll.; active Women of Sovereign Christian Svcs., English Speaking Union, L'Alliance d'Francaise d'Houston, Inst. Hispanic Culture of Houston, Internat. Platform Com., Pres. Club Rice U., Houston Ballet Soc., Flagg Opportunity Ctr., Zool. Soc., Smithsonian Soc. Recipient Keys to City, Houston, Marshall, Tex., Christian Svc. and Civic Contbns. Cross Order of St. John of Jerusalem, Disting. Contbn. award Chroniclers Internat., 2 Gold Laurel/Wreath crowns Poet Laureate Internat.; Gwendolyn Bennett Pappas Day held in her honor at U. Houston, Jan. 12, 1963; elected Poet Laureate of Tex., 1963. Mem. Magna Carta Dames (life, Knights of Garter (life), Descendants Order of Washington (life), Am. of Royal Descent (life), Sovereign Colonial Order of Crown (life), Lady Washington DAR, Colonial Dames XVII Century, Huguenots, Daus. Am. Colonists, New Eng. Women, Augustan Soc., Freedom Found., Daus. Brit. Empire, Poet Laureate Internat., Harris County Heritage Soc., Women's Forum, Shephard Soc., Women's Bldg. Assn., Current Lit. Soc., Tuesday Mus. Soc., Southwood Garden Club, Pin Oak's Sponsor Club. Home: 1118 Sugar Creek Blvd Sugar Land TX 77478

PAPPAS, MARIA ELENI, nurse; b. Encino, Calif., Oct. 1, 1960; d. Nicholas Constantine and Helen Cleo (Tannors) P. BSN, U. San Francisco, 1985; M in Nursing, UCLA, 1991. Cert. critical care nurse, pub. health nurse. Staff med./surg. nurse VA Med. Ctr., West L.A., 1985-87; staff nurse ICU VA Med. Ctr., San Francisco, 1987-88; staff nurse SICU St. Mary's Hosp., San Francisco, 1988-89; staff nurse ICU St. Joseph's Hosp., Burbank, Calif., 1989-91; clin. nurse specialist Northridge (Calif.) Hosp. Med. Ctr., 1991-95; asst. clin. prof. Sch. Nursing, UCLA, 1993-94. Co-author: (manual) Brain Death Policy Manual, 1993. VA scholar U. San Francisco, 1984, Reynolds Estate scholar UCLA, 1991. Mem. Sigma Theta Tau (Outstanding Contbn. award 1989). Greek Orthodox. Home: 8012 Comanche Ave Winnetka CA 91306

PAPPAS, SANDRA LEE, state senator; b. 1949; m. Neal Gosman, 1986; 3 children. BA, Met. State U., 1986; MPA, Harvard U., 1994. Former mem. Minn. Ho. of Reps.; now mem. Minn. State Senate; part-time coll. instr. Mem. Dem. Farmer Labor Party. Home: 182 Prospect Blvd Saint Paul MN 55107-2136 Office: Minn State Senate Capitol G-27 Saint Paul MN 55155

PAPPAS PARKS, KATHERINE LOUIS, artist; b. Detroit, June 1, 1942; d. Louis Epaminonda and Effie (Amolhitou) Pappas; m. William Lee Parks, Oct. 12, 1969; 1 child, Leah Yvonne. BFA, Wayne State U., 1965, cert., 1967, MA, 1972. Cert. secondary tchr., Mich., Wis. Art tchr. Willistead Art Sch., Windsor, Can., 1966-67, Bloomfield Hills (Mich.) Pub. Schs., 1967-69; art instr. Gertrude Herbert Art Inst., Augusta, Ga., 1969-70; art tchr. Solomon Schector Elem. Sch., Skokie, Ill., 1979-80; art instr. Mayer Kaplan Jewish Community Ctr., Skokie, 1978-81, Evanston (Ill.) Art Ctr., 1990; presenter art workshop Evanston Twp. H.S., 1988-90; adj. faculty Oakton C.C., Des Plaines, 1980—, Truman Coll., Chgo., 1989-90, 93; curator, exhibitor Suburban Fine Arts Ctr., Highland Park, 1992. One-woman shows include Kemper Group Gallery, Long Grove, Ill., 1980, Oakton C.C.-Koenline Gallery, 1990, Atrium Gallery, Chgo., 1991, Space 900, Chgo., 1992, Truman Coll., Chgo., 1993; group exhbns. include Palais de Congres, Paris, 1976, Tex. Tech U., 1977, Northwestern U., Evanston, Ill., 1979, 82, 85, West Hubbard Gallery, Chgo., 1980, ARC Gallery, Chgo., 1981, 82, 83, 84, 94, Artemesin Gallery, Chgo., 1984, 87, 89, Chgo. Cultural Ctr., 1984, Name Gallery, Chgo., 1985, 88, Contemporary Art Workshop, Chgo., 1985, Ill. State Mus., Springfield, 1985, Beacon St. Gallery, Chgo., 1987, Paper Press Gallery, Chgo., 1988, Zypher Gallery, Louisville, 1990, Cortesy Gallery, Highland Park, Ill., 1992, numerous others. Counselor Vista-Home Peace Corp., Chgo., 1974-75. Grantee Ill. Arts Coun. of Chgo., 1981; recipient Purchase award Truman Coll., Ill. Percent for the Arts, 1988, Purchase award Kemper Group, 1979. Mem. NEA, Coalition Artists of Chgo., Space 900 (exhibitor), Artists Residence Chgo. (curator raw space libr. 1981, dir. exhbns. Navy pier, exhibitor). Greek Orthodox. Home: 1626 Washington St Evanston IL 60202-1630 Office: Oakton CC 1600 E Golf Rd Des Plaines IL 60016

PAPPENFUS, MABEL LOUISE, retired educator; b. Porter, Minn., Sept. 21, 1926; d. Clarence Nels and Sadie Elizabeth (Gillespie) Rasmussen; m. Ben Pappenfus, June 13, 1957 (dec. Sept. 1989); 1 child, Bettyann. BS, St. Cloud (Minn.) State U., 1956. Elem. tchr. pub. schs., Aurora, Minn., 19544-56, Hutchinson, Minn., 1956-57; elem. tchr. Benton County Rurala Schs., Foley, Minn., 1957-62, Sch. Dist. 742, St. Cloud, 1968-85; supt. schs. Benton County, 1962-68; dir. Sch. Bd. Dist. 51, Foley, 1985-93; ret., 1993. Mem. coun. Gethsemane Luth. Ch., Oak Park, Minn., 1975—, also treas. Ch. Women and other offices; dir. Benton County Dem.-Farmer-Labor Party, 1983—. Recipient Friend of Edn. award Ea. Minn. Univserv, 1992. Mem. NEA (life), Minn. Edn. Assn. (life), Future Farmers Am. (hon. mem. Foley chpt.), Benton County 4-H Leaders Assn. (Pioneer award 1989), Kiwanis. Home: 1128 Laurel Ave Saint Paul MN 55104

PAQUETTE, ELISE GOOSSEN, rehabilitation nurse; b. Mt. Kisco, N.Y., Nov. 20, 1956; d. Frederick Lawrence and Angela Rita (Menichelli) Goossen; m. J. Steven Paquette, Aug. 20, 1977; children: Justin, Gregory, Courtney. Diploma in Nursing, Albany Med. Ctr. Sch. Nursing, N.Y., 1977. CRRN. Staff nurse orthopedics Hahnemann Hosp., Phila., 1977-78; staff nurse rehab. Thomas Jefferson U. Hosp., Phila., 1978-79; staff nurse orthopedics, day charge arthritis unit Presbyn. U. Hosp., Pitts., 1979-82; orthopedic nurse to pvt. phys. practice Oakland Orthopedic Assocs., Pitts., 1982-84; sr. rehab. staff nurse George Washington U. Hosp., Washington, 1984-89, asst. head nurse, 1989-90; cons. Comprehensive Rehab. Assocs., Vienna, Va.; unit coord. (head nurse) New Medico Head Injury, Lynn, Mass., 1991; dir. orthopedic rehab. program Reconditioning Program Northeast Rehab. Hosp., Salem, N.H., 1992-94, cons. to clin. programs, 1994—, facilitator cmty. amputee support group, 1992; mem. arthritis sub-com. Presbyn. U. Hosp., Pitts., 1987. Mem. com. Boy Scouts Am., Boxford, Mass., 1990-94; bd. dirs. Topsfield/Boxford Newcomers Club, 1991-92. Mem. Assn. Rehab. Nurses, Inst. Children's Lit. Office: Northeast Rehab Hosp 70 Butler St Salem NH 03079

PARA, ELIZABETH MARIE, social worker; b. Denville, N.J., Oct. 19, 1956; d. John Thomas and Mary Helen (Ofsonka) P. BA, Seton Hall U., 1978; MSW, Rutgers U., 1983. Counselor adolscent Morris County Youth Shelter, Morristown, N.J., 1979-82; rsch. asst. Dr. L. Iffy, Summit, N.J., 1983-87; rehab. cons. Crawford Rehab. Svcs., Totowa, N.J., 1984-86; social worker St. Vincent's Nursing Home divsn. St. Joseph's Hosp., Montclair, N.J., 1987—. Active Slovak Cath. Sokols, Boonton, N.J., 1956—. Mem. NASW. Democrat. Roman Catholic. Office: St Vincent's Nursing Home 45 Elm St Montclair NJ 07042-3297

PARALEZ, LINDA LEE, technology management consultant; b. Raton, N.Mex., Oct. 29, 1955. AS, Amarillo Coll., 1975; student West Tex. State U., 1975-77, BBA, Century U., Beverly Hills, Calif., 1984, MBA, 1987, PhD in Bus. Mgmt. and Econ. Century U. Teaching asst. Amarillo (Tex.) Coll., 1974-75; drafter natural gas div. Pioneer Corp., Amarillo, 1975-76, sr. drafter exploration div. Amarillo Oil Co. 1976-77; drafting supr., engrng. svcs. supr., dir. speakers' bur. Thunder Basin Coal Co., Atlantic Richfield Co., Wright, Wyo., 1977-86; ptnr., tech. and adminstrv. cons. Rose Enterprises, 1986—; prof. U. Phoenix, Utah; adj. prof. Weber State U., Ogden, Utah; tech. writer Eaton Corp., Riverton, Wyo., 1986-88; cons. State Wyo. Office on Family Violence and Sexual Assault, Cheyenne, 1986-89; Diamond L Industries, Inc., Gillette, Wyo., 1986-88; tech. writer, pubs. cons. Thiokol Corp., Brigham City, Utah, 1987-89, design specialist space ops., 1989-90, mgr. total quality mgmt. ctr. space ops., 1990—, cons. organizational effectiveness and quality mgmt. principles; cons. incident investigation team NASA Solid Rocket Booster Program, Huntsville, Ala.; cons. Microsoft Corp., Puget Power, Pub. Svc. Co. of Colo., W.R. White Co. Author: (poetry) God was Here, But He Left Early, 1976, Gift of Wings, 1980, Solo, 1987, 89; columnist Wytech Digest; contbr. numerous articles to profl. jours. Vol. NASA Young Astronauts Program Adv. Com., 1991—; bd. dirs. Campbell County Drafting Adv. Coun., 1984-85; sec. bd. dir. exec. com. Am. Inst. Design and Drafting, 1984-85, tech. publ. chairperson, 1984-85; vol. educator, data specialist child abuse prevention coun. Ogden. Named Most Outstanding Woman, Beta Sigma Phi, 1980, 81; recipient Woman in the Industry recognition Internat. Reprographics Assn., 1980; grand prize winner Wyo. Art Show with painting titled Energy, 1976. Mem. AAUW, NAFE, NOW, Am. Soc. Quality Control, Am. Productivity and Quality Coun., Am. Legion Aux., Ocean Rsch. Edn. Soc., Gloucester, Mass. (grant proposal writer, 1984), Soc. Tech. Communications, 4-H Club. Home: 2888 N 1300 E Ogden UT 84414-2607

PARAS, SOFIA DIMITRIA, counselor, writer, editor; b. Delaware, Ohio, Dec. 31, 1943; d. James Peter and Fotini Dimitria (Dellios) Stoycheff; m. Nicholas Andrew Paras, Dec. 8, 1968; 1 child, Alexandra Nicholas. BA, Ohio Wesleyan U., 1965; cert., Adelphi U., 1987. Tchr. Upper Arlington Schs., Columbus, Ohio, 1966-68; asst. tng. coord. personnel dept. Ohio State U. Hosps., Columbus, 1968-69, art fair coord., 1969; asst. tng. coord. personnel dept. New Eng. Deaconess Hosp., Boston, 1969-70; tng. coord. nursing dept. Meml. Hosp. of Sloan Kettering, N.Y.C., 1970-71; real estate salesperson Gen. Devel. Corp., 1971-72; adminstrv. asst. Ippocampos Maritime and Internship Fin. and Investments, Piraeus, Greece, 1976-81; office mgr. Internapa Fin. Svcs., Athens, Greece, 1981-86; adminstrv. dir. lawyer's asst. program Adelphi U., West Hempstead, N.Y., 1987-88, admissions counselor lawyer's asst. program, 1988—; cons. interior decorator hotel complex Paramount Tourist and Devel. Ltd., Paralimni, Cyprus, 1981-84; nat. nursing conf. coord. Meml. Hosp. Sloan Kettering, St. Louis, 1971. Editor Women's Internat. Club, Athens, 1978-84; author: (poetry) Observations, 1990, (screenplays) Contract I, 1990, Contract II, 1991; editor: Traditional Hellenic Tastes (in Greek and English langs.), 1994. Theatre dir. Am. Farm Sch., Salonica, Greece, 1974; program coord. choir recitals St. Nicholas Greek Orthodox, Babylon, N.Y., 1989—; v.p. Internat. Women's Orgn. of Greece, Salonica, 1973-74; sec. Christian Orthodox Fellowship, Inc. Mem. NAFE, Nassau/Suffolk Neighborhood Network, L.I. Ctr. for Bus. and Profl. Women, Kappa Kappa Gamma, Theta Alpha Phi.

PARCH, GRACE DOLORES, librarian; b. Cleve., May ; d. Joseph Charles and Josephine Dorothy (Kumel) P. B.A., Case Western Res. U., 1946, postgrad., 1947-50; B.L.S., McGill U., 1951; M.L.S., Kent State U., 1983; postgrad., Newspaper Library Workshop, Kent State U., 1970, Cooper Sch. Art, 1971-72, API Newspaper Library Seminar, Columbia U., 1971, Coll. Librarianship, U. Wales, 1984, 85. Cert. literacy instr., Ohio. Publicity librarian Spl. Services U.S. Army, Germany, 1951; post librarian Spl. Services U.S. Army, Italy, 1952; USAF base librarian, 1953-54; br. librarian Cleveland Heights (Ohio) Pub. Library, 1954-63; asst. head reference div. Va. State Library, Richmond, 1964; dir. Twinsburg (Ohio) Pub. Library, 1965-70; dir. newspaper library Cleve. Plain Dealer, 1970-83; county librarian N.C., 1987-92; cons. Cath. Library Assn., 1961-64; mem. home econs. adv. com., Summit County, 1969, books/job com., 1968; mem. adv. com. Guide to Ohio Newspapers, 1793-1973, 1971-74. Contbr. articles to Plain Dealer, N. Summit Times, Twinsburg Bull., Sun Press; author: Where In the World But in the Plain Dealer Library, 1971; Editor: Directory of Newspaper Libraries in the U.S. and Canada, 1976. Recipient MacArthur Found. award, 1988, Libr. of Am. award, 1988. Mem. McGill U. Alumnae Assn. (sec. 1973), Kent State U. Alumni Assn., ALA (rep. on joint com. with Cath. Library Assn. 1967-70), John Cotton Dana award 1967, Library Pub. Rels. Coun. award 1972), Cath. Library Assn. (co-chmn. 1960-63), Spl. Libraries Assn. (chmn. newspaper library directory com. 1974-76, chmn. pub. relations Cleve. chpt. 1973, chmn. edn. com. newspaper div. 1982-83, mem. edn. com. nominating com. 1984), Ohio Library Assn., Western Res. Hist. Soc., Am. Soc. Indexers, Cleve. Mus. Art Assn., Coll. and Research Librarians, Nat. Micrographic Assn., Women Space, Women's Nat. Book Com., Nat. Trust Hist. Preservation. Roman Catholic. Clubs: Cleve. Athletic, Cleve. Women's City. Home: 688 Jefferson St Bedford OH 44146-3711

PARDINGTON, ANNE SIMPSON, counselor; b. Ruston, La., Nov. 23, 1938; d. Ralph Thomas and Frances Lillian (Banks) Simpson; m. George Palmer Pardington III, June 7, 1965; children: Robert William, Suzanne Elizabeth. BA, U. Ark., 1960; M in Christian Edn., Austin Presbyn. Theol. Sem., Tex., 1964; MA in Counseling Psychology, Lewis and Clark Coll., Portland, Oreg., 1981. Lic. profl. counselor, Oreg.; cert. nat. counselor. Dir. Christian edn. Presbyn. Chs., Okla, Tex., 1961-64; hosp. chaplain Tex., N.Y., 1964-66; instr. math. and English Southeastern La. U., Hammond, 1966-68; at home family care Va., Oreg., 1968-94; instr. history and women's studies Averett Coll., Danville, Va., 1976-78; counselor YWCA and S.E. Youth Svc. Ctr., Portland, Oreg., 1978-81; pvt. practice Portland, Oreg., 1982-89; coord. counseling and displaced homemaker program Women's Ctr., Oregon City, Oreg., 1983-85; counselor, instr. life and career options Clackamas C.C., Oregon City, Oreg., 1985—. Columnist women's issues Danville Register, 1977-78; co-author monograph; contbg. author book rev. Mem. ACA, Am. Mental Health Counselors Assn., Oreg. Counseling Assn., Oreg. Mental Health Counselors Assn., Oreg. Assn. for Adult Devel. and Aging, Phi Beta Kappa. Democrat. Presbyterian.

PARDINI, SHARON KAY BROWN, architectural and interior designer; b. Grand Junction, Iowa, Apr. 15, 1938; d. Loyal Melvin Blanshan and Frances Mildred (Brown) Manen; m. Frederick Brown, Oct. 19, 1957 (div. Apr. 1963); 1 child Randal Alan; m. Joseph Leslie Pardini, Nov. 11, 1975; 1 child, Tiana Margaret. BA in Cosmetology, Lee Ann Acad., 1957; AA, U. Calif., Berkeley, 1966; BBA, U. Calif. Owner Sharon's Hair Fashions Salons, Oakland, Calif., 1958-80; v.p., sec., treas. Western Container Transp. Inc., 1978-87; pres. Par-West Inc. Design Firm, 1983—; mem. adv. bd. Bd. Cosmetology, Oakland, 1965-69; owner The Collection Designer Gallery, Lafayette, Calif., 1987-93. Mem. Republican Task Force, Washington, 1981-89; mem. svc. league Santa Catalina Sch., Monterey, Calif., 1986. Mem. Calif. Cosmetologist Assn. (v.p. 1973-75, bd. dirs. 1970-77), Mission Hills Country Club.

PARDUE, MARY LOU, biology educator; b. Lexington, Ky., Sept. 15, 1933; d. Louis Arthur and Mary Allie (Marshall) P. B.S., William and Mary Coll., 1955; M.S., U. Tenn., 1959; Ph.D., Yale U., 1970; D.Sc. (hon.), Bard Coll., 1985. Postdoctoral fellow Inst. Animal Genetics, Edinburgh, Scotland, 1970-72; assoc. prof. biology MIT, Cambridge, 1972-80; prof. MIT, 1980—; summer course organizer Cold Spring Harbor Lab., N.Y., 1971-80; mem. rev. com. NIH, 1974-78, 80-84, nat. adv. gen. med. scis. coun., 1984-86, sci. adv. com. Wistar Inst., Phila, 1976—; mem. health and environ. rsch. adv. com. U.S. Dept. Energy, 1987-94. Mem. editorial bd. Chromsoma, Molecular and Cellular Biology, Biochemistry; contbr. articles to profl. jours. Mem. rev. com. Am. Cancer Soc., 1990-93, Howard Hughes Med. Inst. Adv. Bd., 1993—. Recipient Esther Langer award Langer Cancer Rsch. Found., 1977, Lucius Wilbur Cross medal Yale Grad. Sch., 1989; grantee NIH, NSF, Am. Cancer Soc. Fellow AAAS, NAS (chmn. genetics sect. 1991-94), Am. Acad. Arts and Sci. (coun. mem. 1992—, exec. com. 1994—); mem. NRC (bd. on biology 1989—), Genetics Soc. Am. (pres. 1982-83), Am. Soc. Cell Biology (coun. 1977-80, pres. 1985-86), Phi Beta Kappa, Phi Kappa Phi. Office: MIT Dept Biology 68-670 77 Massachusetts Ave Cambridge MA 02139-3594

PARELL, MARY LITTLE, federal judge, former banking commissioner; b. Fond du Lac, Wis., Aug. 13, 1946; d. Ashley Jewell and Gertrude (McCoy) Little; m. John Francis Parell, May 28, 1972 (div. 1990); children: Christie, Morgan, Shawn, John Brady. AB in Polit. Sci. cum laude, Bryn Mawr Coll., 1968; JD, Villanova U., 1972; LLD (hon.), Georgian Ct. Coll., 1987. Bar. N.J. 1972. Assoc. McCarter & English, Newark, 1972-80, ptnr., 1980-84; commr. N.J. Dept. Banking, Trenton, 1984-90; assoc. gen. counsel Prudential Property & Casualty Ins. Co., Holmdel, N.J., 1991-92; judge U.S. Dist. Ct. N.J., 1992—; chmn. bd. Pinelands Devel. Credt Bank. Bd. trustees Exec. Commn. Ethical Standards, Trenton, 1984-90, Corp. Bus. Assistance, Trenton, 1984-91, N.J. Housing & Mortgage Fin. Agy., Trenton, 1984-90, N.J. Cemetery Bd. Assn., 1984-90, N.J. Hist. Soc., 1976-79., YMCA of Greater Newark, 1973-76, Diocesan Investment; mem. Supreme Ct. N.J. Civil Practice Com., 1982-84, Supreme Ct. N.J. Dist. Ethics Com., 1982-84; lay assesor Ecclesiastical Ct. Episc. Diocese Newark, 1980-84. Fellow Am. Bar Found.; mem. ABA, N.J. Bar Assn., Princeton Bar Assn. Office: US Courthouse 402 E State St Rm 252 Trenton NJ 08605-0515*

PARENT, LOUISE MARIE, lawyer; b. San Francisco, Aug. 28, 1950; d. Jules D. and Mary Louise (Bartholomew) P.; m. John P. Casaly, Jan. 5, 1980. AB, Smith Coll., 1972; JD, Georgetown U., 1975. Bar: N.Y. 1976, U.S. Dist. Ct. (so. dist.) N.Y. 1976. Assoc. Donovan Leisure, N.Y.C., 1975-77; various positions, then gen. counsel Am. Express Info. Svcs. Corp., N.Y.C., 1977-92; dep. gen. counsel Am. Express Co., N.Y.C., 1992-93, exec. v.p., gen. counsel, 1993—; mem. legal adv. com. N.Y. Stock Exch. Bd. dirs. A Better Inc., Cook Found. Sp.. Edn. Mem. ABA (com. depts. corp. law). Home: 1170 Fifth Ave New York NY 10029-6527 Office: Am Express Co Am Express Tower World Fin Ctr New York NY 10285

PARENTI, KATHY ANN, sales professional; b. Gary, Ind., Sept. 24, 1957; d. Lee Everett Huddleston and Barbara Elizabeth (Daves) Tilley; m. Michael A. Parenti, Mar. 31, 1979 (div. Sept. 1990). Student, Ind. U., Gary, 1977; cert., U. Nev., Las Vegas, 1978; diploma, Interior Design Inst., Las Vegas,

1984. Supr. Circus Circus Hotel, Las Vegas, 1980-87; owner Interior Views, Las Vegas, 1984-87; sales rep. Win-Glo Window Coverings, 1987-88; owner Dimension Design, 1988-90; sales rep. Sidney Goldberg & Assoc., Las Vegas, 1990—. Mem. NAFE, Am. Soc. Interior Designers, Internat. Interior Design Assn., Network of Exec. Women in Hospitality, Design Inst. Soc., Rep Network.

PARETSKY, SARA N., writer; b. Ames, Iowa, June 8, 1947; d. David Paretsky and Mary E. Edwards; m. S. Courtenay Wright, June 19, 1976; children: Kimball Courtenay, Timothy Charles, Philip William. BA, U. Kans., 1967; MBA, PhD, U. Chgo., 1977. Mgr. Urban Rsch Ctr., Chgo., 1971-74, CNA Ins. Co., Chgo., 1977-85; writer, 1985—. Author: (novels) Indemnity Only, 1982, Deadlock, 1984 (Friends of Am. Writers award 1985), Killing Orders, 1985, Bitter Medicine, 1987, Blood Shot, 1988 (Silver Dagger award Crime Writers Assn., 1988), Burn Marks, 1990, Guardian Angel, 1992, Tunnel Vision, 1994, also numerous articles and short stories. Pres. Sisters in Crime, Chgo., 1986-88; dir. Nat. Abortion Rights Action League Ill., 1987—. Named Woman of Yr. Ms mag., N.Y.C., 1987. Mem. Crime Writers Assn. (Silver Dagger award 1988), Mystery Writers Am. (v.p. 1989), Authors Guild, Chgo. Network. *

PARHAM, BETTY ELY, credit bureau executive; b. Drumright, Okla., Aug. 14, 1928; d. Wayne Albert and Edith May (Ledgerwood) Bingamon; m. Richard D. Ely, Dec. 22, 1946 (dec. Jan. 1971); children: Richard Wayne, Stephen Wyatt; m. Billy S. Parham, Mar. 10, 1991. BS, East Cen. U., Ada, Okla., 1962, M Teaching, 1965. Office mgr. Louis M. Long, Loans, Ada, 1946-78; owner Credit Bur. Ada, 1956—, mgr., 1978—. Mem. Soc. Cert. Credit Bur. Execs., Assoc. Credit Burs. Okla. (bd. dirs. 1980—, pres. 1990), AAUW (cert. of achievement 1989), Ada Bus. and Profl. Women (chmn. YC, Pres.'s award 1991), Toastmasters (pres. Ada 1984, Presdl. Excellence award 1984), Kiwanis (bd. dirs. Ada 1990-92). Democrat. Home: PO Box 506 Ada OK 74821-0506 Office: Credit Bur Ada 304 E 12th St Ada OK 74820-6510

PARHAM, ELLEN SPEIDEN, nutrition educator; b. Mitchells, Va., July 15, 1938; d. Marion Coote and Rebecca Virginia (McNiel) Speiden; m. Arthur Robert Parham, Jr., Dec. 16, 1961; children: Katharine Alma, Cordelia Alyx. BS in Nutrition, Va. Poly. Inst., 1960; PhD in Nutrition, U. Tenn., 1967, MEd in Counseling, 1994. Registered dietitian. Asst. prof. to prof. No. Ill. U., DeKalb, Ill., 1966—; coord. programs in dietetics No. Ill. U., DeKalb, 1981-86, 90—, coord. grad. faculty in Human and Family Resources, 1985-87; cons. on nutrition various hosps., clins. and bus., Ill., 1980—; founder, dir. Horizons Weight Control Program, DeKalb, 1983-91; founder, leader "Escaping the Tyranny of the Scale" Group, 1994—; co-chair Nutrition Coalition for Ill., 1989-90; ptnr., mgr. Design on Fabric, 1986—. Bd. editors Jour. Nutrition Edn., 1985-90, Jour. Am. Dietetic Assn., 1991—; contbr. articles to profl. jours. Mem. Am. Inst. Nutrition, Soc. Nutrition Edn., Am. Dietetic Assn., Am. Home Econs. Assn., Soc. Nutrition Edn. (treas. 1991-94), N.Am. Assn. Study Obesity.

PARHAM, IRIS ANN, gerontology educator; b. Orange, Tex., Nov. 14, 1948; d. George Kevlin and Nina Mabel Parham; m. Edward Swarbrick, Aug. 9, 1975; 1 child, Erin Elsbeth. B.A., U. Tex., 1970; M.S., W. Va. U., 1973; Ph.D., U. So. Calif., 1976. Asst. prof. gerontology Va. Commonwealth U., Richmond, 1976-81, assoc., 1981-91, prof., 1991—; exec. dir. Va. Geriatric Edn. Ctr. Co-editor: Modular Gerontology Curriculum, 1982, vol. II, 1984, Access, 1990, Resource Guides-Geriatrics, 1990, Gerontological Social Work, 1992; Jour. Social Issues, 1980; spl. editor: Jour. Minority Aging, 1984. Grantee Adminstrn. on Aging, 1978-79, 79-82, 85-87—, Adjusting to Widowhood Va., 1978-79, Temple U., 1983-84, Health Resources and Services Adminstrn., 1985-90, 91—. Mem. Am. Psychol. Assn., So. Gerontol. Soc. (treas. 1984-87), Assn. Gerontology in Higher Edn., Sigma Xi. Avocation: photography. Office: Va Commonwealth U Gerontology Dept Med Coll Va MCV Box 980228 Richmond VA 23298

PARIAG, HAIMWATTIE RAMKISTODAS, medical records administrator; b. Golden Fleece, Guyana, Aug. 31, 1967; came to U.S., 1977; d. Ramkisto Das and Surujpati Ramkistodas; m. Moolchand Pariag. BS in Med. Records Adminstrn., C.W. Post Coll., 1988. Registered records adminstr. Med. records clk. Mary Immaculate Hosp., Jamaica, N.Y., 1986-87; coder Parkway Hosp., Forest Hills, N.Y., 1987, adminstrv. coord., 1987-88, dir. med. records, 1988-91; dir. med. records Massapequa Gen. Hosp., Seaford, N.Y., 1991—. Mem. Am. Health Info. Mgmt. Assn., N.Y. Health Info. Mgmt. Assn., L.I. Health Info. Mgmt. Assn., Health Info. Mgmt. Assn. N.Y.C. Democrat. Hindu. Home: 253 Trouville Rd Copiague NY 11726

PARIGINI, LEDA ENI, human resources specialist; b. Maracay, Venezuela, May 15, 1953; came to the U.S., 1966; BA in Spanish, Fairleigh Dickinson U., 1977. Personnel and customer svc. mgr. Korvettes, Paramus, N.J., 1978-80; dir. human resources K-Mart Fashions, North Bergen, N.J., 1981—. Mem. Soc. for Human Resource Mgmt., Phi Omega Epsilon. Office: K-Mart Fashions 7373 Westside Ave North Bergen NJ 07047

PARILLO, SUSAN KATHAN, rehabilitation coordinator; b. Woonsocket, R.I., June 14, 1966; d. William Allan and Clare Ann (Rivard) Smith; m. Richard Michael Parillo, Dec. 26, 1988; children: Brandon Michael, Tiffani Amber. BS in Phys. Edn., R.I. Coll., 1988. Lic. phys. therapy asst., cert. educator. Rehab. coord. Phys. Therapy Plus, Woonsocket, 1988—; mem. adult task force Gov.'s Coun. on Health and Fitness, Providence, 1993—. Bd. dirs. Young Women of the Yr., East Providence, R.I., 1984—; dir. preliminary pageant Miss. R.I., Johnston, 1992—. Recipient Nat. Outstanding Health and Phys. Edn. award Nat. Assn. Health, Phys.Edn., Recreation, and Dance, 1988; winner in several pageants. Mem. Health and Phys. Edn. Club (treas. 1986-88). Roman Catholic. Home: Clearview Estates 24 Jasmine Ln Johnston RI 02919 Office: Phys Therapy Plus 16 Arnold St Woonsocket RI 02895-2902

PARIS, MARY JEAN, clinical psychologist; b. L.A., Feb. 18, 1950; d. Michael Joseph and Rosina (Grispino) P. BA summa cum laude, U. Hawaii, 1985; MA, Calif. Sch. Profl. Psychology, Berkeley, 1987, PhD, 1991. Intern Letterman Hosp., Presidio, Calif., 1987-89; postdoctoral intern Kentfield (Calif.) Rehab. Hosp., 1991-92; clin. psychologist Fin. Dist. Psychol. Svcs., San Francisco, 1991—; cons. United Cerebral Palsy, San Francisco, 1991—, Multiple Sclerosis Soc., San Francisco, 1994—, Nat. Brain Tumor Found., San Francisco, 1991—. Mem. APA. Office: 235 Montgomery St Ste 939 San Francisco CA 94104-3002

PARISEAU, PATRICIA, state senator; b. St. Paul, Aug. 10, 1936; d. James Martin and Mary Margaret (May) Wright; m. Kenneth Edward Pariseau, July 9, 1960; children: Susan M., Douglas C., Penny A., Linda D., Barbara J., Jacqueline. RN, Ravenswood Hosp. Sch. Nursing, Chgo., 1957. Staff nurse Ravenswood Hosp., Chgo., 1957-58, St. Joseph's Hosp., St. Paul., 1958-59, Office of Drs. Roy & Hilker, St. Paul., 1959-60; aide to U.S. Senator Rudy Boschwitz, St. Paul., 1982-88; mem. Minn. Senate, St. Paul., 1989—. Mem. adv. bd. St. Paul chpt. ARC, 1986-88; vol., officer Minn. Ind. Rep. Com., 1972-83; bd. dirs. Ind. Sch. Dist. 192, Farmington, Minn., 1976-79. Mem. Minn. Waterfowl Assn., Farmington C. of C., Dakota Arts Coun., Ducks Unltd., Eagles Aux., Am. Legion Aux. (sec. Farmington chpt.), VFW Aux., So. Dakota County Sportsmen Club. Office: Minn Senate 151 State St Saint Paul MN 55107-1410*

PARISH, SYNTHIA LEE, special education educator; b. Pullman, Wash., Aug. 27, 1958; d. Curtis Lee and Maureen (Bonham) P.; m. Max W. Williams, Sept. 9, 1978 (div. June 1986); children: Jeremiah James, Sarah Rose. AA, Wenatchee (Wash.) Valley Coll., 1978; BA in Edn., Cen. Wash. U., 1981; postgrad., various colls., Wash., 1981—. Tchr. art and spl. edn., dir. spl. edn. Creston (Wash.) Sch. Dist., 1981-84; tchr. spl. edn. and music, dir. spl. edn., track coach Bickleton (Wash.) Sch. Dist., 1984-85; tchr. spl. edn. Wapato (Wash.) Sch. Dist., 1985—, social skills program instr., dir., 1992—; instr. Upward Bound., Yakima, Wash., 1990. Tutor Equal Opportunities Program, Ellensburg, Wash., 1980-81; actress, singer Creston Community Players, 1981-84; dir. Miss Creston Pageant, 1983-84; coach Spl. Olympics, Wapato, 1989—; cheerleading coach, pep club advisor Creston Sch. Dist., 1981-84; cheerleading coach, jr. class advisor Bickleton Sch. Dist., 1984-85; counselor AIDS Coalition, Yakima, 1988-90; bd. dirs. March of Dimes, Yakima, 1989—, sec., 1991—; bd. dirs. Health Profls. Adv. Coun., Yakima, 1990, co-chmn., 1991—. Mem. NEA, Wash. Educators Assn., Eagles. Home: 1853 Weikel Rd Yakima WA 98908-8857 Office: Wapato Sch Dist PO Box 33 Wapato WA 98951-0033

PARISH-MCCURRY, PATSY, librarian; b. Gilmer, Tex., Dec. 31, 1933; d. Marion Stanley and Ila Ree (Wells) Parish; m. Neal Wendell McCurry, Dec. 23, 1955; children: Marty Neal, Nela Louise. BS in Elem. Edn., East Tex. State U., 1953, MS in Elem. Edn., 1958. Cert. media specialist. Elem. tchr. Union Hill Ind. Sch. Dist., Gilmer, Tex., 1953-83, all-level libr., 1983—. Mem. PTA. Republican. Baptist. Home: Rte 2 Box 680 Gilmer TX 75644 Office: Union Hill ISD Hwy 2088 PO Box 370 Gilmer TX 75644

PARISO, JEAN BRUNNER, real estate professional; b. Reinholds, Pa., Dec. 26, 1925; d. Emory Lutz and Rachel Ebling (Keith) Brunner; m. Jesse Francis Pariso, Aug. 11, 1956; 1 child, Penelope Ann. BA, Cedar Crest Coll., Allentown, Pa., 1947; postgrad., Columbia U., 1948-50. Social caseworker Edwin Gould Found., Inc., N.Y.C., 1947-50; asst. dir. pub. rels. Toy Guidance Coun., N.Y.C., 1950-51; sec. to pres. Charles Schlaifer & Co., N.Y.C., 1951-52; legal sec., asst. prod. ABC, N.Y.C., 1952-54; dir. pub. rels. Cushman & Wakefield, Inc., N.Y.C., 1954-62; asst. dir. Coun. Community Svcs., Princeton, N.J., 1970-72; dir. pub. rels. The Princeton (N.J.) Ballet Soc., 1972-81; sales assoc. Richard A. Weidel Corp. Realtors, Hopewell, N.J., 1987—; pub. info. cons. Community Guidance Ctr., Mercer County, 1988-89. Mem. Montgomery Twp. Bd. Edn., Skillman, N.J., 1962-65; mem. Somerset County Bd. Elections, Somerville, N.J., 1987—; co-chmn. Citizens Com. to elect Kennedy-Johnson, Montgomery Twp., 1960. Democrat. Lutheran. Home: 404 Skillman Rd Skillman NJ 08558-1523 Office: Richard A Weidel Corp 45 W Broad St Hopewell NJ 08525-1901

PARK, ALICE MARY, genealogist; b. Loda, Ill., Oct. 4, 1901; d. Frederick Adam and Sarah Elizabeth (Clemens) Crandall; m. Lee I. Park, Aug. 29, 1925 (dec. Aug. 24, 1978); children: Lee Crandall, Nancy Park Kern. BS, U. Chgo., 1924. Tchr. U. Chgo. Lab. Sch., 1924-25; genealogy rschr. Washington, 1925—. Author: Park/e/s and Bunch on the Trail West, 1974, rev. edit., 1982, Schenck and Related Families in New Netherlands, 1992. Pres. Falls Church (Va.) PTA, 1941-42, LWV, Fairfax, Va., 1947-48. Mem. Chevy Chase Club, Metro. Club. Home: 4200 Cathedral Ave NW Washington DC 20016

PARK, BEVERLY GOODMAN, public relations professional; b. Boston, Nov. 10, 1937; d. Morris and Mary (Keller) Goodman; divorced; children: Glynis Forest, Seth, Elyse. BS, Simmons Coll., 1959; MS, Ea. Conn. State U., 1968; postgrad., Western N.E. Coll. Law, 1994—. Asst. dir. comty. svc. Hartford (Conn.) Courant, 1976-79; mayor Borough of Colchester, Conn., 1979-83; lifestyle editor Chronicle, Willimantic, Conn., 1980-82, suburban editor, 1982-84; dir. pub. rels. U. Conn. Health Ctr., Farmington, 1984—; selected team mem. radiation exposure info. study Belorussia, 1993; mem. adv. bd. Hosp. News; mem. women's affairs com. U. Conn. Health Ctr. Women's Networking Task Force; mem. Univ. Adminstrv. Staff Coun.; mem. minority awards com. U. Conn. Health Ctr., mem. John N. Dempsey hosp. disaster plan com. Designer: (libr. studies curriculum) Classroom Instruction on the Use of Books and Libraries, 1972; pub.: (ednl. booklets) Have You Made Plans for the Future?, 1977-78; editor of edn. holiday and bridal supplements The Chronicle, 1980-84; editor: U. Conn. Health Ctr. Anniversary Mag., 1986, U. Conn. Health Ctr. Med. Catalog, 1986—, (ann. pub.) Salute, 1988—, U. Conn. Health Ctr. 30th Anniversary Supplement, 1991. Bd. dirs. Ea. Conn. Found. for Pub. Giving, Norwich, 1990—; women's club officer Dem. Town Com., Colcheester, 1963—; active Hadassah, Coolchester, 1963-92, Women's League for Conservative Judaism. Recipient Lifestyle Page award New Eng. Press Assn., 1980, Media Excellence in Covering Human Svcs. award Conn. chpt. NASW, 1982, Ragan Report Arnold's Admirables award for excellence in graphics and typography, 1985, Gold award Healthcare Mktg. Report, 1987, award for video ACS, 1990. Mem. NOW (membership com. Southeastern chpt., mem. legis. task force, Meritorious Svc. award Southeastern Conn. chpt. 1985), Am. Soc. for Hosp. Mktg. and Pub. Rels., Am. Mktg. Assn., Assn. Am. Med. Colls. (group on pub. affairs), Conn. Hosp. Assn. (hosp. pub. rels. conf.), State of Conn. Pub. Info. Coun. (steering com.), New Eng. Hosp. Pub. Rels. and Mktg. Assn. (bd. dirs. 1987, 88), Conn. Fedn. Dem. Women's Clubs (program chair Colchester chpt.). Home: 201 W Bass Ln Suffield CT 06078

PARK, CAROLE ROPER, state legislator; b. Kansas City, Mo., Sept. 18, 1939; d. Rudolph Joseph and Rose (Mus) Roper; m. William Basil Park, Apr. 24, 1960 (div. May 1962); 1 child, Jennifer. BA in Edn., U. Mo., 1964. Cert. tchr., Mo. Asst. buyer Rothschild's & Harzfelds, Kansas City, 1959-62; tchr. Kansas City Pub. Schs., 1964-76; mem. Mo. Gen. Assembly, Jefferson City, 1977—; mem. state task force on Alzheimers Disease, com. indigent health care. Recipient Monsignor Elmer H. Berhrmann award for Outstanding Contbns. to Mental Retardation and Devel. Disabilities, Disting. Svc. award Meritorial Svcs. Mental Health Assn., Legis. Leadership award Mo. State Coalition Community Mental Health Ctrs., Lawmaker award Mo. Mental Health Commn., Profl. award Ark of Life, Project Life, award Neiborhood Coun., award for Outstanding Svc. C. of C.; Carole Roper Park Day named in her honor City of Independence, Mo., Oct., 1994. Mem. NCSL (task force on disabilities), Am. Fedn. Tchrs., Nat. Order Women Legislators, Mo. Order Women Legislators, Friends of Truman Campus, U. Mo. Kansas City Alumni Assn., Sugar Creek Dem. Club. Roman Catholic. Home: 11415 Gill St Sugar Creek MO 64054 Office: Mo Ho of Reps State Capitol Rm 313C Jefferson City MO 65101

PARK, ESTHER, retired association executive; b. Democratic People's Republic of Korea, Oct. 18, 1902; came to U.S., 1904; d. Chong Soo and Kyung Kun (Kim) P. BA, U. Hawaii, 1926; postgrad., UCLA, 1936; ACSW cert., Western Res. U., 1941; PhD (hon.), Ewha Womans U., Seoul, Korea, 1964. Tchr. pub. jr. high sch. Hilo, Hawaii, 1926-28; teenage sec. Honolulu YWCA, 1928-40, bus. and profl. women sec., 1947-69; Am. adv. sec. to Korea YWCA internat. divsn. YWCA U.S.A., N.Y.C., 1947-80; internat. vol. Nat. YWCA Korea, 1970-80; ret., 1980. Contbr. weekly articles to The Times, 1964-68. Mem. Korea Child Welfare Com., 1952-62, USO Coun., 1956—; v.p., treas. Korea com. World Univ. Svc., 1955; active Fulbright Commn., 1955-69; mem. adv. com. Korea Ch. World Svc., 1963-70; com. mem. social welfare bur. KNCC, 1964. Recipient citation Nat. Reconstruction Movement Korea and Ewha Womans U., 1962, Pub. Welfare medal Pres. of Republic of Korea, 1966, Seongru medal, 1972, Moran medal, 1980, Korean Coun. Women award, 1968, Mother of Yr. award Saessak Children's Assn., 1971, Nat. YWCA award, 1972, Plaque of Appreciation, U.S. Govt., AID, 1980; named Hon. Citizen, City of Seoul, 1969. Mem. NASW (cert.), BPW, Korea Assn. Vol. Agys. (adviser 1955-80), Royal Asiatic Soc., Am. Women's Club. Republican. Congregationalist. Home: 1434 Punahou St # 732 Honolulu HI 96822

PARK, MARILYN MCKAY, mental health nurse; b. Grand Junction, Colo., Mar. 21, 1931; d. James Arthur and Mabel Frances (Ward) McKay; m. Ellas R. Park, Mar. 20, 1955; children: Robert Earl, Richard James. BSN, U. Colo., 1954; MS, U. Utah, 1967; grad. cert. in public admin., U. UTah, 1983, PhD, 1986. RN, Utah; lic. psychiat. mental health nurse, marriage and family therapist, Utah. Staff nurse Denver Gen. Hosp., 1954, VA Hosp., Salt Lake City, 1954-63; pub. health nurse Salt Lake County, 1963-65; mental health adminstr. Utah State Div. of Mental Health, Salt Lake City, 1967-87; authorization of psychiat. svcs. Utah State Dept. of Health, Salt Lake City, 1987-90; medicare surveyor Psychiat. Hosps. Health Care Financing Adminstrn., Balt., 1984—; rsch. investigator evaluation of Utah prepaid mental health plan U. Minn., 1992-93; dir. QI CPC Olympus View Hosp., 1993—. Contbr. Planned Parenthood Assn., Salt Lake City. Recipient scholarship U. Colo., 1949. Mem. ANA, Utah Nurses Assn. (advanced practice com. 1992, membership com. 1992, coun. specialists in mental health nursing 1975—, chmn. community liaison 1992, bd. dirs. nursing interest group 1990-92), Nat. Alliance for Mentally Ill, Mental Health Assn. Utah. Democrat. Presbyterian. Home: 1731 E Imperial Park Ln Salt Lake City UT 84106

PARK, MARY WOODFILL, information consultant; b. Nevada, Mo., Nov. 20, 1944; d. John Prosser and Elizabeth (Devine) Woodfill; m. Salil Kumar Banerjee, Dec. 29, 1967 (div. 1983); children: Stephen Kumar, Scott Kumar; m. Lee Crandall Park, Apr. 27, 1985; stepchildren: Thomas Joseph, Jeffrey Rawson. BA, Marywood Coll., 1966; postgrad., Johns Hopkins U., 1983, Goucher Coll., 1986. Asst. to dir. U. Pa. Librs., Phila., 1968-69; investment libr. Del. Funds, Phila., 1969-71; investment officer Investment Counselors Md., Balt., 1980-84, 1st Nat. Bank Md., Balt., 1984-85; founder Info. Consultancy, Balt., 1985—; lectr. Villa Julie Coll., Balt., 1989, Loyola Coll., Balt., 1991-92, Cath. U., 1993. Editor, contbr. to profl. pubs. Vol. Internat. Visitors' Ctr., Balt., 1979-80, 91; del. White House Conf. on Librs.; v.p. bd. dirs. Friends of Goucher Libr., 1988-90; mem. industry applications com. Info. Tech. Bd., State of Md., 1993—. Mem. Spl. Librs. Assn. (pres. Balt. chpt. 1991-92, mem. network coord. coun. Sailor project 1993—), Am. Soc. Info. Sic., Assn. Ind. Info. profls., Md. Libr. Assn., Assn. Info. and Dissemination Ctrs., Info. Futures Inst., Hamilton St. Club (bd. dirs. 1989-92). Office: Info Consultancy 308 Tunbridge Rd Baltimore MD 21212-3803

PARK, PATRICIA WEILL, controller; b. N.Y.C., June 30, 1939; d. Harold and Lisbeth (Goldmann) W.; m. Richard Alan Rosenthal, June 10, 1962 (div. 1985); children: Pamela Gail Rosenthal, Mark Carroll Rosenthal; m. Richard Darrow Park, Jan. 9, 1992; 1 child, Heather. BS in Publs., Simmons Coll., 1961; postgrad., Northeastern U., 1981-82; Cert. in Acctg., Bentley Coll., 1987. Assoc. editor various TV and fan mags., N.Y.C., 1961-62; free-lance writer N.Y.C., N.J. and Mass., 1962-78; asst. to mgr. credit/receivables Dodge Co., Cambridge, Mass., 1980-83; asst. controller Edward R. Marden Corp., Allston, Mass., 1983-86; controller Aarlan, Inc., Cambridge, 1986-87; asst. controller SDK Healthcare Info. Systems, Boston, 1987—. Vol. tutor Adult Literacy Program, Brighton, Mass., 1988—; pres., bd. mgrs. condominium assn., 1987-89, v.p., 1991-92, pres. 1993-94. Mem. Mensa. Office: SDK Healthcare Info Systems 1550 Soldiers Field Rd Brighton MA 02135-1183

PARK, SOPHIA S., real estate agent, administrator; b. Busan, Korea, Sept. 5, 1968; d. Martin K. and Connie (Kim) P. AA, El Camino Coll., 1989; postgrad., Calif. State U., Long Beach, 1990—. Lic. real estate agt. Mgr. Capri Motel & Apts., Colorado Springs, 1983-86; realtor assoc. Century 21 Torrance (Calif.) Realty, 1987-91, Prudential Dale Marks, Torrance, 1991-92, Re/Max Beach Cities, Torrance, 1992-93; asst. mgr. Clover Maintenance, Carson, Calif., 1988—; realtor assoc. Tarbell Realty, Torrance, 1993, First Choice Realty & Invest, Huntington Beach, Calif., 1993—; western region adminstr. Data Switch Corp., Long Beach, 1990-94; nat. adminstr. Network Systems Corp., Irvine, Calif., 1994—. Mem. Korean Am. Coalition, L.A., 1993; participant White House Fellowship, Washington, 1992. Mem. NAFE, Korean Am. Coalition. Republican. Presbyterian. Home: 21901 Moneta Ave Apt 23 Carson CA 90745-2855

PARKAS, IVA RICHEY, educator, historian, curator, paralegal; b. Comanche County, Tex., June 28, 1907; d. Andrew J. Richey and Pearl Lucretia (Kennedy) Richey; grad. Wayland Coll., 1927; B.A., Tex. Tech. U., 1935; M.Litt., U. Pitts., 1950; postgrad. UCLA, 1960, Pa. State U., 1961, U. Calif., Berkeley, 1962, Duquesne U., 1963, Carnegie-Mellon U., 1968; m. George Eduardo Parkas, May 5, 1945. Curator, historian Fort Pitt Blockhouse, Pitts., 1946-52, asst. curator-historian, 1964-84; tchr. U.S. history Pitts. sr. high schs., 1953-72; paralegal Allegheny County (Pa.) Law Dept., 1977-82. Del., White House Conf. on Children and Youth, Washington, 1960, 70; World Food Conf., Rome, 1974; U.S. Congl. Sr. Citizens intern, Washington, 1984. Named Disting. Alumnae, U. Pitts., 1978; recipient Classroom Tchr.'s medal Freedoms Found. Valley Forge, 1960; Henry Clay Frick Ednl. fellow; NDEA grantee; Greater Pitts. Air Force Squadron scholar, Pitts. Press scholar, 1960. Mem. NEA (life), AAUW (pres. Pitts. br. 1974-76), Hist. Soc. Western Pa., Western Pa. Council Social Studies (pres. 1969-71), DAR (regent Pitts. chpt. 1986-89), U. Pitts. Alumnae Assn. (bd. dirs. 1978—, v.p. 1984), Pa. Retired Pub. Sch. Employees Assn. (chairperson Am. revolution bicentennial 1974-76), Western Pa. Hist. Soc., Allegheny County Bicentennial Commn., Greater Pitts. Commn. for Women, Delta Kappa Gamma, Phi Alpha Theta. Commonwealth editor: So Your Children Can Tell Their Children, 1976; contbr. articles on hist. subjects to newspapers, mags. Home: 5520 5th Ave Apt C5 Pittsburgh PA 15232-2342

PARKE, JO ANNE MARK, publishing company executive; b. Rochester, Pa., Mar. 8, 1941; d. Robert Kleckner and Alice (Dowling) Mark; m. William Ernst Parke III, May 6, 1963 (div. 1988); children: Alicia Ann, William Ernst IV; m. Robert Arnott Gerhardt, Oct. 19, 1991. Student, U. Strasbourg, France, 1962; BA, Pa. State U., 1963. Reporter Beaver County (Pa.) Times, summers 1959-61, Washington (D.C.) Star, 1963-64; writer Pa. State Dept. Pub. Info., Univ. Park, 1964-65; reporter Centre Daily Times, State College, Pa., 1965-67; editor Spenley Newspapers, Pitts., 1971-72, St. Petersburg (Fla.) Times, 1972-73; freelance writer Phila. Inquirer, 1974-77; editor, assoc. publisher Bus. Digest, Phila., 1978-81; editor Phila. Bus. Jour., 1981-84; v.p. editorial dir. N.Am. Pub. Co., Phila., 1984-93, pres. conf. and seminar divsn., corp. editor-at-large, 1993—; bd. dirs. Graphic Arts Assn. Neographics, Phila., 1984—. Author: All Gods' Children, 1977. Bd. dirs. Mayor's Small Bus. Coun., Phila, 1980-83, C. of C. Small Bus. Coun., Phila., 1980-83. Mem. Women in Communications, Soc. Profl. Journalists (bd. dirs. Phila. chpt. 1990—), Am. Soc. Bus. Press Editors, N.Y. Bus. Press Editors, French-Am. C. of C., Alliance Francaise. Office: N Am Pub Co 401 N Broad St Philadelphia PA 19108-1013

PARKE, M. LESLIE, artist; b. White Plains, N.Y., July 2, 1952; d. William More and Mildred Louise (Lochner) P. BA, Bennington Coll., 1974, MA, 1976. Lila Wallace-Reader's Digest Artist-in-Residence, Giverny, France, 1994. Exhibited in group shows at Centro Cultural Recoleta, Buenos Aires, Argentina, Galerie Etienne Causans, Paris, A.I.R. Gallery, N.Y.C., Schick Art Gallery, Saratoga SPrings, N.Y., St. Lawrence U., Canton, N.Y., 1994, U. West Fla., Pensacola, 1994, Arnot Art Mus., Elmira, N.Y., 1994, Laguna Gloria Art Mus., Austin, Tex., 1994, others. Recipient Honor award Visual Arts award Interfaith Forum Art & Archtl., Washington, 1992, Itzhak Sankowsky award Main Line Art Ctr., Haverford, Pa., 1994.

PARKER, ADRIENNE NATALIE, art educator, art historian, lecturer; b. N.Y., May 23, 1925; d. Benjamin and Bertha (Levine) Lefkowitz; m. Norman Richard Parker, July 22, 1945; children: Dennis, Jonathan W., Steven L. BA cum laude, Hunter Coll., 1945; MFA, Montclair Coll., 1975; postgrad., Instituto Des Artes, San Miguel, Mex., 1987. Instr. art, English Granby High Sch., Norfolk, Va., 1945-46; instr. art Mahwah (N.J.) Bd. Edn., 1970-75, Daus. of Miriam Home for the Aged, Clifton, N.J., Fedn. Home, Paterson, N.J.; instr. art, history Bergen C.C., Paramus, N.J., 1980—. One-woman show Bergen C.C.; exhibited in group shows N.J. Art Educators, Bergen County Art Educators, N.J. Tercentenary (1st place), Pine Libr., Sara Delano Roosevelt House, Hunter Coll., Woodstock Art Assn., 1990-95, Fair Lawn Art Assn., 1991 (award), Palisade Guild Spinners and Weavers, 1994, Bergen C.C., 1994, 95. Editor Fairlawn H.S. PTA, Thomas Jefferson Jr. H.S.; pres. The Comty. Sch., Fairlawn, 1983-86, bd. dirs.; mem. art adv. exhbn. com. Pine Libr., 1992, 93, 94, 95. Mem. N.J. Art Educators, Bergen County Art Educators, Wood Stock Art Assn., Fairlaw Art Assn., Hunter Coll. Alumni Assn. (bd. dirs. no. N.J. chpt. 1970—, pres. 1977-79, program chmn./v.p. 1993-94), Palisade Guild Spinners and Weavers (founder, editor, charter) Phi Beta Kappa. Home: 3827 Fair Lawn Ave Fair Lawn NJ 07410-4395

PARKER, ALICE, composer, conductor; b. Boston, Dec. 16, 1925; d. Gordon and Mary (Stuart) P.; widowed; children: David, Timothy, Katharine, Mary, Elizabeth. BA, Smith Coll., Northampton, Mass., 1947; MS, Julliard Sch., N.Y.C., 1949; MusD (hon.), Hamilton U., Clinton, N.Y., Macalester Coll., St. Paul, Bluffton (Ohio) Coll. Arranger Robert Shaw Chorale, N.Y.C., 1948-66; freelance composer, condr. N.Y.C., 1960—; tchr., workshop leader Westminster Choir Coll., Princeton, N.J., summers 1972—; artistic dir. Melodious Accord, N.Y.C., 1985—. Composer 4 operas, 27 cantatas, 6 song cycles and numerous anthems and suites. Recipient Composer's Serious award ASCAP, 1968—, Barlow Endowment, 1992, Spl. award Nat. Endowment Arts, 1975, Founders award Chorus Am., 1994. Mem. Am. Choral Dirs. Assn., Am. Condrs. Guild, Chorus Am., Hymn Soc. Am., Sigma Alpha Iota. Office: Melodious Accord Inc 801 W End Ave Apt 9D New York NY 10025-5363

PARKER, BARBARA L., educator; b. Phila., Dec. 8, 1933; d. Benjamin and Nettie Vivian (Rademan) Parker. BA, UCLA, 1957; MA, CCNY, 1970; PhD, NYU, 1982. Adj. asst. prof. English Baruch Coll. CUNY, N.Y.C., 1982-89; asst. prof. English The William Paterson Coll. N.J., Wayne, N.J., 1989—. Editor: Ecology of Endemic Diseases in the Dez Irrigation Pilot Area: A Report to the Govt. of Iran, 1962; author: A Precious Seeing: Love and Reason in Shakespeare's Plays, 1987; contbr. articles to profl. jours. Active Friends of N.Y. Pub. Library, 1983—, Friends of Bobst Library, 1982—, Bklyn. Hts. Assn., 1975—, Village Ind. Democrats, N.Y.C., 1960-64. Mem. MLA, N.Y. Shakespeare Assn., Renaissance Soc. Am., Shakespeare Assn. Am., Columbia U. Seminars, Nat. Coun. Tchrs. English. Home: 145 Hicks St Apt 26B Brooklyn NY 11201-2333

PARKER, BARBARA Z., bank executive. Trust and investment mgr. Midlantic Corp., Edison, N.J. Office: Midlantic Corp 499 Thornall St Edison NJ 08837*

PARKER, CAROL JEAN, psychotherapist, consultant; b. Plant City, Fla., Sept. 4, 1946; d. Fennimore Blaine and Verna Melissa (Robinson) Bowman; m. Charles Bridges, June 1, 1968 (div. 1979); children: James, Nova. AA, Hillsborough C.C., Tampa, Fla., 1979; BA, Internat. Coll., L.A., 1981, MA, 1983. Asst. Dr. Clarke Weeks, Plant City, 1964-65; med. transcriber Tampa Gen. Hosp., 1965-71, St. Joseph's Hosp., Tampa, 1976-80; psychotherapist Discovery Inst., Tampa, 1980-85; owner, dir. Ananda Counseling Ctr., Tampa, 1985—; clinician Human Devel. Ctr., New Port Richey, Fla., 1979-81; clin. cons. The Manors, Tarpon Springs, Fla., 1992—, exec. dir. womens choice unit. Participant Task Force on Prostitution and Female Offender Diversion Program, Tampa, 1988. Mem. ACA, Am. Assn. on Mental Health, Internat. Soc. for Study Multiple Personality Disorders and Dissociation, Tampa Bay Assn. Women Therapists, Tampa Bay Study Group on Multiple Personality Disorders and Dissociation (chmn. bd. 1990—, Outstanding Mem. award 1991). Office: Ananda Counseling Ctr 420 W Platt St Tampa FL 33606-2244

PARKER, CONSTANCE MARILYN, geophysicist; b. Sarnia, Ontario, Can., Oct. 31, 1945; came to U.S., 1967; d. William Halley and Mary Anne (Munday) MacBain; m. Deane Norman Parker, June 17, 1967; children: Alexander, Jonathan. BA, U. Western Ontario, 1967. From geophys. programmer to staff geophysicist Arco Oil and Gas Co., Plano, Tex., 1968-91; dir. processing Arco Exploration and Prodn. Tech., Plano, Tex., 1992—. Mem. Soc. Exploration Geophysicists (assoc.). Office: Arco Exploration & Prodn Tech 2300 W Plano Pky Plano TX 75075-8427

PARKER, CYNTHIA MARY, economist, educator; b. Oct. 31, 1957; d. Gene Albert and Minna Edna Fabbri; m. Jeffrey Alan Parker, Apr. 15, 1982; 1 child, Lisa Marie. BA in Econ., Calif. State U., Fullerton, 1980, MBA in Econ., 1989. Estimator Gen. Dynamics Corp., Pomona, Calif., 1980-81; administrv. asst. Jeffrey A. Parker, Montclair, Calif., 1982—; instr. skating Skate Junction, West Covina, Calif., 1986-94; rsch. economist, cons. Formuzis & Pickersgill, Inc., Santa Ana, Calif., 1987-90; instr. econ. Sunny Hills H.S., Fullerton, Calif., 1991-93, Calif. State U., Fullerton, 1991-93; cons. econ. QED Rsch., Inc., Palo Alto, Calif., 1992—; instr. econ. and fin. Nat. U., Riverside, Calif., 1993—; instr. econ. Chaffey Coll., Rancho Cucamonga, Calif., 1993—, Mt. San Antonio Coll., Walnut, Calif., 1994—, mem. paralegal adv. com., 1994—. Mem. Nat. Assn. Bus. Economists, Nat. Assn. Forensic Economists, Omicron Delta Epsilon, Zeta Tau Alpha Alumni.

PARKER, DEBORAH L. ROBERTS, counselor; b. Meridian, Miss., Mar. 15, 1952; d. Bernice (Roberts) Pringle; m. Curtis Edward Parker, Nov. 25, 1972; 1 child, Shana. BS, U. So. Miss., 1978; MEd, Miss. State U., 1980, postgrad. Lic. profl. counselor; nat. cert. counselor. Asst. PBX op., with client admissions dept. Weems Mental Health Ctr., Meridian, 1972-75, counselor children's svcs., 1981-86; career facilitator Meridian Pub. Schs., 1978-80; dir. gov.s youth grant Lauderdale County Juvenile Ctr., Meridian, 1980-81; adolescent counselor, case mgr. Laurel Wood Pscychiat. and Recovery Ctr., Meridian, 1986-89, adolescent program dir., 1989-93; counselor single parent/displaced homemaker Meridian C.C., 1993-94, acad. counselor, 1994—. Named one of Outstanding Young Women of Am., 1983. Mem. AAUW, Alpha Lambda Delta, Delta Sigma Theta, Phi Delta Kappa. Roman Catholic. Home: 411 45th Ct Meridian MS 39301-1126 Office: Meridian Cmty Coll Hwy 39 N Hwy 19 N Meridian MS 39307

PARKER, EDNA G., federal judge; b. Johnston County, N.C., 1930; 1 child, Douglas Benjamin. Student, N.J. Coll. for Women (now Douglass Coll.); B.A. with honors, U. Ariz., 1953; postgrad., U. Ariz. Law Sch.; LL.B., George Washington U., 1957. Bar: D.C. Law clk. U.S. Ct. Claims, 1957-59; atty.-advisor Office of Gen. Counsel, Dept. Navy, 1959-60; trial atty. civil and tax div. Dept. Justice, 1960-69; administrv. judge Contract Appeals Bd., Dept. Transp., 1969-77; spl. trial judge U.S. Tax Ct., 1977-80, judge, 1980—. Mem. ABA, Fed. Bar Assn., D.C. Bar, D.C. Bar Assn., Women's Bar Assn. of D.C., Nat. Assn. Women Lawyers, Nat. Assn. Women Judges. Office: US Tax Ct 400 2nd St NW Washington DC 20217-0002*

PARKER, JAN FRANCES, library manager; b. Huntington, Ind., Sept. 28, 1949; d. James Eugene and Eloise Lucille (Allman) P. BS in Elem. Edn., St. Francis Coll., 1973; MA in Pastoral Studies, U. St. Thomas, St. Paul, 1984; M in Libr. and Info. Sci., U. Wis., Milw., 1991. Dir. media ctr. Diocese of Ft. Wayne (Ind.)-South Bend, 1973-87; exec. sec. Diocesan Pastoral Coun. Diocese of Ft. Wayne (Ind.)-South bend, 1983-85; dir. media svcs. Diocese of Toledo, 1987-88; libr. mgr. St. Lawrence Sem., Mt. Calvary, Wis., 1988—; co-dir. assocs. Congregation of Sisters of St. Agnes, Fond du Lac, Wis., 1994—. Media cons. Our Sunday Visitor, Huntington, Ind., 1983-85; mem. justice, peace ecology com. Congregation of Sisters of St. Agnes, Fond du Lac, Wis., 1991—; mem. Nat. Women's History Project. Mem. AAUW, Pax Christi, Beta Phi Mu. Office: St Lawrence Sem 301 Church St Mount Calvary WI 53057-9605

PARKER, JANET ELIZABETH, psychotherapist, educator; b. Seattle, Mar. 21, 1945; d. John Randall and Margaret Ann (Reed) Walker; m. Robert Charles Parker, July 31, 1966 (div. Dec. 1974); life ptnr. David Albert Mycko. BA in Psychology, Fla. Internat. U., 1973; MA in Clin. Psychology, Lone Mountain Coll., 1976. Lic. mental health counselor. Exec. sec. Deltona Corp., Miami, Fla., 1967-69; adminstrv. asst. House of Bishops-Episcopal Ch., Miami, Fla., 1970-73; adminstrv. asst. Luth. campus ministry U. Fla., 1973-74; counselor, asst. mgr. Spectrum Programs, Miami, 1974-78; instr. Miami-Dade C.C., 1979-84; pvt. practice Miami, 1978—. Editor Dromenon Newsletter. Mem. Dr. Jean Houston's Mystery Sch., 1990—; founder Fla. Women's Polit. Caucus; mem. United Way Citizens Rev., Grove Park Homeowners Assn., also sec., Dade County Dem. Exec. Com., Young Dems., also v.p.; bd. dirs. Switchboard of Miami; Sunday sch. tchr. Holy Comforter Episcopal Ch.; vol. aide Rep. Claude Pepper; vol., hostess Am. Field Svc.; active St. John's on the Lake Meth. Ch. Recipient Outstanding Svc. award United Way and Mental Health Assn. Mem. ARC, NOW, Fla. Counselors Assn., Assn. Transpersonal Psychology, Assn. for Humanistic Psychology, Union of Concerned Scientists, Noetic Scis., Sierra Club, Nature Conservancy, Greenpeace, Habitat for Humanity. Home and Office: 1458 NW South River Dr Miami FL 33125

PARKER, JOAN, public relations executive; b. N.Y.C., Oct. 13, 1935; d. Albert and Elizabeth (Durgin) P.; m. Francis Shea (div. 1964); 1 child, Sarah Young; m. Dale Coenen; children: Stephen, Alison. Student, Hood Coll., 1953-55, Tobé Coburn Sch., 1956. Asst. to pub. relations dir. Elizabeth Arden, N.Y.C., 1956-57; acct. exec. Rowland Co., N.Y.C., 1958-60; owner pub. relations firm N.Y.C., 1969-81; dir. consumer products pub. relations N.W. Ayer Pub. Relations Co., N.Y.C., 1981-82, dir. pub. relations, 1982—; EVP, dir. Ayer & Ptnrs., 1994—. Dir. House of Vision, Chgo., 1983-85, Wolverine Worldwide, Grand Rapids, Mich., 1983—. Recipient Director's Choice award NWEA, 1990. Mem. Pub. Relations Soc. Am. (acad. counselor), Tobé Coburn Alumni Assn. (Most Disting. Alumni 1980), Fashion Group, Women's Jewelry Assn. Office: Ayer Pub Rels 825 8th Ave New York NY 10019-7416

PARKER, KIMBERLY JANE, non-profit association executive, paralegal; b. Ann Arbor, Mich., Sept. 24, 1958; d. John Richard and Jane Eleanor (Twichell) P. BA in Polit. Sci., U. Redlands, 1980; Cert. in Legal Assistantship, U. Calif. Irvine, 1983, Cert. in Non-Profit Exec. Mgmt., 1990; Cert. in Adminstrn. Non-Profit Programs, Calif. State U. Long Beach, 1991. Hostess Disneyland, Anaheim, Calif., 1976-80; legal sec., asst. John R. Parker Law Corp., Orange, Calif., 1976-81; legal asst. C.D. Daly Law Corp., Newport Beach, Calif., 1981-83; exec. dir. Christian Conciliation Svc., Anaheim, 1983—. Editor: Peacemaker's Handbook; contbr. articles to profl. jours. Bd. dirs. YWCA Ctrl. Orange, 1991—; mem. So. Calif. Head Injury Found., Downey, 1990—; chair women's forum Trinity United Presbyn. Ch., 1992-93; grad. Leadership Orange, 1993. Recipient Cert. of Appreciation, County of Orange, 1992; grantee Christian Conciliation, 1985. Mem. Christian Legal Soc., Christian Ministry Mgmt., So. Calif. Mediation Assn., County Assn. Dispute Resolution, Christian Conciliation Svc. (bd. dirs. 1983—), Vol. Ctr. of Orange County. Republican. Presbyterian. Office: Christian Conciliation Svc 18002 Irvine Blvd Ste 170 Tustin CA 92680-3301

PARKER, LEE FISCHER, sales executive; b. Chgo., Nov. 28, 1932; d. Meyer Louis and Lena (Raphael) Fischer; m. Joseph Schwartz, Mar. 18, 1950 (div. Jan. 1986); 1 child, Steven Darryl; m. Robert K. Parker, Jan. 13, 1991. Student, Mallinkroudt Coll., Wilmette, Ill., 1976. Freelance fashion model Chgo., 1958-78; sales assoc. Neiman-Marcus, Northbrook, Ill., 1978-79; owner Keystone Svcs., Woodale, Ill., 1969-82; sales assoc. Marshall Field's, Skokie, Ill., 1986-94; fashion coord. Arnie's Restaurant, Chgo., 1964-68, Blackhawk Restaurant, Chgo., 1964-66, Jim Conway TV Show, Chgo., 1968-70. Mem. Brandeis Women's Aux., Holocaust Mus. Democrat. Jewish.

PARKER, LYNDA MICHELE, psychiatrist; b. Phila., Sept. 28, 1947; d. Albert Francis and Dorothy Thomasinia (Herriott) P.; B.A., C. W. Post Coll., 1968; M.A. (Martin Luther King Jr. scholar 1968-70), N.Y.U., 1970; M.D., Cornell U., 1974; postgrad. N.Y. Psychoanalytic Inst., 1977-82. Intern, N.Y. Hosp., N.Y.C., 1975; resident in psychiatry Payne Whitney Clinic, N.Y.C., 1975-78; psychiatrist in charge day program Cabrini Med. Center, N.Y.C., 1978-79, attending psychiatrist, 1978—; admitting psychiatrist inpatient psychiat. treatment Payne Whitney Clinic, N.Y.C., 1978—, supr. psychiatry residents, 1978—, supr. long-term psychotherapy, 1980-82; attending psychiatrist N.Y. Hosp., Cornell Med. Center, 1979—; practice medicine specializing in psychiatry, N.Y.C., 1979—; instr. psychiatry Cornell U. Med. Coll., 1979-86, asst. prof., 1986—; instr. psychiatry, N.Y. Med. Coll., 1978—; psychiat. cons. Bldg. Service 32BJ Health Fund, 1983-89, Inwood House, N.Y.C., 1983-86, Time-Life Inc., 1986—, Ind. Med. Examiners, 1986—, Epilepsy Inst., 1986-87, asst. med. dir., 1987-88, med. dir., 1988; ind. med. examiner Rep. Health Care Rev. Scis. Mem. adv. bd. St. Bartholomew Community Preserve, N.Y.C. Mem. Am. Psychiat. Assn., Am. Womens Med. Assn. Episcopalian. Office: 219 E 69th St Apt 1J New York NY 10021-5453

PARKER, MARGARET MAIER, physician; b. Portland, Maine, Dec. 8, 1950; d. Paul and Miriam Deibler (Slack) M.; m. Robert Ingalls Parker, Nov. 2, 1974; children: Robert Ingalls Jr., Christopher Maier, Timothy Sumner, Matthew Paul. BS, Brown U., 1973, MD, 1977; cert. in critical care, 1987. Diplomate Am. Bd. Internal Medicine. Intern, resident Roger Williams Gen. Hosp., Providence, 1977-80; fellow critical care medicine NIH, Bethesda, Md., 1980-82, sr. staff physician, 1982-91; assoc. prof. pediat. SUNY, Stony Brook, 1991—; assoc. clin. prof. medicine George Washington U., Washington, 1983-91. Contbr. articles to profl. jours. Deacon Rockville Presbyn. Ch., 1985-88, elder, 1990-91. Fellow ACP, Am. Coll. Critical Care Medicine; mme. Am. Med. Women's Assn., Am. Fedn. Clin. Rsch., Soc. Critical Care Medicine (chair program com. 1995, coun. 1995—). Republican. Presbyterian. Office: SUNY Dept Pediatrics Stony Brook NY 11794-8111

PARKER, MARGO B., employee relations professional; b. Detroit, Feb. 17, 1950; d. Jack Lewis and Shelia Rader. BA, UCLA, 1971; MBA, Pepperdine U., 1984. Mgr. human resources Chief-Tech Ind/& May Co., 1968-78; mgr. human resource devel. Northrop Elec./Mech. Div., Anaheim, Calif., 1977-83, v.p. human resources, 1983-88; v.p. employee rels./comm. Northrop Grumman Corp., Century City, Calif., 1988—. Adv. bd. North/South Orange County YWCA; bd. govs. Human Rels. Commn. Orange County; adv. com. Chapman U., Orange County, others. Named '93 Corp. honoree BEEM Found. Scholarship, L.A., 1993, Woman of Yr., YWCA's Tribute to Women in Industry, 1981; recipient Community Svc. award County of L.A., 1993. Mem. Nat. Assn. Christians and Jewis (exec. bd. dirs.), U. So. Calif. Ctr. for Effective Orgn. (sponsor). Office: Northrop Grumman Corp 1840 Century Park E Los Angeles CA 90067-2101

PARKER, MARTHA ANN, public relations specialist; b. Gainsville, Fla., Jan. 25, 1948; d. Morris Evans and Marian A. (Hickey) Paddick. BA in Communications, U. Ill., 1970; MS in History, U. R.I., 1988. Advt. asst., then advt. mgr. R.I. Host. Trust Nat. Bank, Providence, 1971-74; legis. asst. Congresswoman Pat Schroeder (D. Colo.), Washington, 1974-76; spl. asst. to dean Sch. Architecture U. New Haven, 1977-83; researcher Union Pacific Corp., Omaha, 1983-86; dir. pub. rels. Gorman & Assocs., Providence, 1986-88; account supr. pub. rels. FitzGerald & Co., Cranston, R.I., 1988-89, v.p. pub. rels., 1989-91; dir. Environ. Comm. Group; sr. v.p., dir. account planning and svc., dir. environ. comms. group, ptnr., lectr. Etex Environ. Conf., Washington, 1992, New Eng. Environ. Expo, 1992. Author book revs. for Master Plots, Groher Pub., 1979, 80, 81, 82. Mem. Pub. Rels. Soc. Am. (accredited, mem. Counselors Acad.), Am. Hist. Soc., Orgn. Am. Historians. Office: FitzGerald & Co 105 Sockanosset Cross Rd Cranston RI 02920-5560

PARKER, MARY ALTHEA, art educator; b. Oxford, N.C., Nov. 20, 1906; d. Richard Joseph and Lottie Lee (Barnes) P. BA, Rhodes Coll., 1928; MA, Case Western Res. U., 1944; postgrad., Cleve. Sch. Art, 1942-44, Hans Hofmann Sch. Art, 1950, 54. Psychiat. and occupational therapy nurse Highland Hosp., Asheville, N.C., 1931-42; prof. art history Colby-Sawyer Coll., New London, N.H., 1944-72; tchr. art Kingswood-Cranbrook, Bloomfield Hills, Mich., summer 1948, 49, Brevard (N.C.) Music Ctr., 1951-55; prof. art Claflin Coll., Orangeburg, S.C., 1973-77; prof. sr. grad. faculty workshop Western Carolina U., Cullowhee, N.C., 1990-93, prof. sr. grad. faculty workshop in painting, 1991-93; ret., 1993; bd. dirs. Black Mountain (N.C.) Coll. Arts Mus. One-woman show at World Gallery, Asheville, N.C., 1990; exhibited in group shows at Art Gallery, Newbern, N.C., Zone One Contemporary, Asheville. Group mem. Sister City-Russia, Black Mountain, 1989—. Fellow Va. Ctr. for Creative Arts, The McDowell Colony; mem. LWV, Women's Internat. League for Peace and Freedom. Democrat. Mem. Religious Soc. of Friends. Home: 21 Wagon Trail Black Mountain NC 28711

PARKER, MARY ANN, lawyer; b. Pitts., Jan. 6, 1953; d. Harry N. Sr. and Mary (Sperl) P.; 1 child, Nickolas Parker Palacios. BS cum laude, SUNY, Buffalo, 1975; JD, U. Tenn., 1977. Bar: Tenn. 1978, U.S. Dist. Ct. (mid. dist.) Tenn. 1978, U.S. Ct. Appeals (5th cir.) 1980, U.S. Supreme Ct. 1982, U.S. Ct. Appeals (6th cir.) 1987. Asst. Dist. Atty. Gen., Ashland City, Tenn., 1977-78; sole practice Nashville, 1978—; instr. Nat. Trial Advocacy Coll., 1983-84. Cmty. svcs. vol. St. Henry's Women's Club, Nashville, 1984—; mem. Women's Polit. Caucus, Nashville, 1986—, Tenn. Dem. Polit. Com., 1988—, Tenn. Dem. Fin. Coun., 1991, 92, 93; mem. Dem. Leadership Coun., 1991—, bd. dirs., 1992—. Mem. ABA, Assn. Trial Lawyers Am. (del. 1983-86, sec. 1985-86, young lawyer's sect. sec. 1982-83, 2d vice chairperson 1983-84, 1st vice chairperson 1984-85, chairperson 1985-86, women's caucus sec. 1981-83, 1st vice chairperson 1983-84, chairperson motor vehicles, accidents, premises and govtl. libaility sect. 1989-90, sec. torts sect. 1988-89, named Del. of Yr. 1986), Tenn. Trial Lawyers Assn. (bd. govs. 1978-86, chairperson consumer and victims coalition com. 1986-87), Trial Lawyers Pub. Justice (bd. govs. 1982—, treas. 1990-92, v.p. 1992-93, pres. elect 1993-94, pres. 1994—), Nashville Bar Assn. (ethics com. 1983—, chair and cir. ct. com. 1993—), Tenn. Bar Assn., Pa. Trial Lawyers Assn. Roman Catholic. Home: 5113 Fountainhead Dr Brentwood TN 37027 Office: Parker & Allen Law Offices 207 3d Ave N 3d Fl Nashville TN 37201

PARKER, NANCY KNOWLES (MRS. CORTLANDT PARKER), publishing executive; b. Buffalo, Aug. 30, 1929; d. Ward Emerson and Barbara Louise (Bull) Knowles; student Chevy Chase Jr. Coll., 1949; m. Cortlandt Parker, Sept. 8, 1951; children: Elizabeth, Cortlandt, Stephen, Nancy Gray. Copy girl Washington Evening Star, 1947-49; reporter Newark Evening News, 1949-51; asst. pub. relations dir. Newark Community Chest, 1951-52; writer Suburban Life mag., Summit, N.J., 1952-55; co-founder, assoc. editor Observor Tribune, Mendham, N.J., 1955-59; woman's editor, Recorder Pub. Co., Bernardsville, N.J., 1959-84, v.p., 1960—; editor New Eng. Wine Gazette, Finger Lakes Wine Gazette. Former trustee Somerset Hills Community Chest, North Jersey Tng. Sch., Totowa, Morris-Somerset chpt. UN Assn., Bonnie Brae Ednl. Ctr., Millington, N.J. Vis. Homemaker Svc. of Somerset County (N.J.); now trustee, mem. bd. dirs. Camp Brett-Endeavor, Clinton, N.J., N.J. Hist. Soc., Newark, Morristown (N.J.) Meml. Hosp. Mem. Glen Manor House Com., Portsmouth, R.I. Mem. Bus. and Profl. Women, Nat. Soc. Arts and Letters, Southeastern New Eng. Grape Growers Assn., Jr. League, Pen and Brush N.Y.C., New Eng. Wine Coun. (sec.), Friends of Whitehall Colonial Dameses Am. (bd. dirs. R.I. chpt.), Colonial Dames of Am. (bd. dirs. R.I. chpt.), Newport (R.I., bd. dirs.) Garden Club (bd. dirs., pres.), English Speaking Union (Newport chpt.). Episcopalian. Home: 582 Wapping Rd Portsmouth RI 02871 also: Greenvale Farm & Vineyard 582 Wapping Rd Portsmouth RI 02871 Office: 17 Morristown Rd Bernardsville NJ 07924

PARKER, NIKKI RIDDLE, financial consultant; b. Sale Lake City, Oct. 22, 1956; d. Harmel Guy and Vida (Vidalakis) Riddle. BS, Utah State U., 1977; postgrad. in sociology/econs., U. Utah, 1979. Account exec./bus. news corres. Bache Halsey, Salt Lake City, 1981-82; sr. cert. fin. mgr. Merrill Lynch, Denver, 1982-88; 2d v.p., fin. cons. Smith Barney, Denver, 1988—. Trustee The Gathering Place Endowment Fund, Denver, 1992—, pres. bd. exec. bd. dirs.; 1st v.p. Ch. Coun., St. Catherine Greek Orthodox Ch., 1990-93, mem. long-range planning com. Office: Smith Barney 370 17th St # 1100 Denver CO 80202

PARKER, REBECCA HATCH, stockbroker; b. Live Oak, Fla., Nov. 18, 1955; d. Donald James and Marilyn Webb (Blackmon) Hatch; m. Thomas Parker, June 15, 1991. BA, Fla. State U., 1977. Asst. dir. Fla. House, Washington, D.C., 1977-78; sec. Sci. and Tech. Commn. U.S. Ho. Reps., Washington, 1978-79; loan originator Cameron Brown Co., Annandale, Va., 1979-81; salesperson, mgr. Dictaphone Corp., Alexandria, Va. and Cin., 1981-83; mktg. rep. Computer Consoles, Inc., Reston, Va., 1983-85; account exec. Dean Witter Reynolds, Inc., McLean, Va., 1985-88, Johnston, Lemon and Co., Alexandria, Va., 1988-89, Ferris, Baker, Watts, Washington, 1989—. Bd. dirs. Cardinal Forest Homeowners Assn., fin. com., 1989-93, treas., 1990-91; mem. Jaycees, Washington, 1989-90; mem. coun. on ministries Messiah Ch., 1989—, chmn., 1993—, fin. com., mem. adult coun., pers. and nominations; vol., fin. counselor Fairfax County Ednl. Ctr., 1991-93; co-chair Sml. Bus. Week, 1994, Club 100, 1993—, Small Bus. Ednl. DEvel., 1994—. Mem. Prince William Bd. Realtors, Fla. State Soc., Washington Tennis Patrons, Fairfax C. of C., Fla. State U. Alumni Club (pres. 1978-79, treas. 1986-87, v.p. 1987—), Nat. Assn. Securities Dealers and Secs. (lic. stockbroker, registered rep.), Washington Ski Club (MAST com., budget and fin. com. 1989-92), Delta Zeta Alumni Assn. Democrat. Methodist. Home: 7719 Bellington Ct Springfield VA 22151-2705

PARKER, SARA ANN, librarian; b. Cassville, Mo., Feb. 19, 1939; d. Howard Franklin and Vera Irene (Thomas) P. B.A., Okla. State U., 1961; M.L.S., Emporia State U., Kans., 1968. Adult svcs. librarian Springfield Pub. Libr., Mo., 1972-75, bookmobile dir., 1975-76; coord. S.W. Mo. Libr. Network, Springfield, 1976-78; libr. developer Colo. State Libr., Denver, 1978-82; state librarian Mont. State Libr., Helena, 1982-88, State Libr. Pa., Harrisburg, 1988-90; Pa. commr. librs., dep. sec. edn. State of Pa., Harrisburg, 1990—; cons. and lectr. in field. Author, editor, compiler in field; contbr. articles to profl. jours. Sec., Western Coun. State Librs., Reno, 1984-88, mem. Mont. State Data Adv. Coun., 1983-88, Mont. Telecommunications Coun., 1985-88, WLN Network Coun., 1984-87, Kellogg ICLIS Project Mgmt. Bd., 1986-88. Recipient President's award Nature Conservancy, 1989, Friends award Pa. Assn. Ednl. Communications and Techs., 1989; fellow Inst. Ednl. Leadership, 1982. Mem. ALA, Chief Officers State Libr. Agys. (chair N.E. 1991-92, v.p., pres. elect 1994—), Mont. Libr. Assn. (bd. dirs. 1982-88), Mountain Plains Libr. Assn. (sec. chmn. 1980, pres. 1987-88). Home: 226 A Erford Rd Camp Hill PA 17011 Office: State Libr Pa PO Box 1601 Harrisburg PA 17105-1601

PARKER, SARAH ELIZABETH, judge; b. Charlotte, N.C., Aug. 23, 1942; d. Augustus and Zola Elizabeth (Smith) P. AB, U. N.C., 1964, JD, 1969. Bar: N.C. 1969, U.S. Dist. Ct. (mid., ea. and we. dists.) N.C. Vol. U.S. Peace Corps, Ankara, Turkey, 1964-66; pvt. practice Charlotte, 1969-84; former judge N.C. Ct. Appeals, Raleigh; now assoc. justice N. C. Supreme Ct., Raleigh. Bd. dirs. YWCA, Charlotte, 1982-85; pres. Mecklenburg County Dem. Women, Charlotte, 1973. Mem. ABA, Inst. Jud. Adminstrn., N.C. Bar Assn. (v.p. 1987-88), Mecklenburg County Bar (sec.-treas. 1982-84), Wake County Bar Assn., Charlotte City Club, Capital City Club. Episcopalian. Office: NC Ct Appeals 1 W Morgan St Raleigh NC 27601-1393*

PARKER, VIRGINIA ANNE, ranch administrator; b. Brockton, Mass., Apr. 24, 1918; d. John and Jennie (Krusas) Salus; student Bryant Stratton Coll., Boston, 1938, Columbia U., 1941; computer skills diploma Computer Skills Tng., 1993; m. John Glendon Parker, Feb. 1942 (div. 1952); one dau., Deborah Anne. Sales supr. Reuben H. Donnelley Corp., N.Y.C., 1944-46; traveling sales rep. Elizabeth Arden Inc., N.Y.C., 1946-47; advt. salesperson Park East Pub. Co., N.Y.C., 1947-48; point of sale display work Parker Kleinhans Assos. and V.A. Parker Co., N.Y.C., 1950-55; merchandising coordinator WGBS Radio Sta., Miami, 1957-59; lighting cons. Verd-A-Ray Corp., Miami, 1960-63; string writer, advt. salesperson Palm Beach Post Times, Fla., 1963-65; advt. salesperson Avon Park Sun, Fla., and Sebring News, Fla., 1965-67; sales mgr. radio sta. WJCM, Sebring, and advt. salesperson radio sta. WIPC, Lake Wales, Fla., 1967-69; office mgr., trustee asst., exec. sec. Griffith Ranch Inc., Okeechobee, Fla., 1969-80, semi-ret., 1980, now vol. worker with retarded and handicapped, also with ret. vol. sr. programs Nu-Hope. Mem. Bus. and Profl. Women Miami (2d v.p., rec. sec. 1958-60, state award for nat. security 1960), Parents Without Ptnrs. Fla. (news editor 1962-63). Club: Advt. Miami. Address: 415 Mat-Lo Ave PO Box 1112 Sebring FL 33871

PARKER, VIRGINIA CARLSON, librarian, museum curator; b. Logan, Utah, Nov. 28, 1923; d. John Wilford and Ina Elvina (Sorensen) Carlson; m. Lewis Leonard Parker, Aug. 14, 1946 (dec. May 1993); children: Ben Scott, Jeffrey C., Lee Ford, Julie Ann. BA, Stanford U., 1945; MLS, U. Calif., Berkeley, 1948; MA in Am. Studies, Utah State U., 1983. Asst. reference dept. Henry E. Huntington Libr., San Marino, Calif., 1945-46; libr. Calif. Hist. Soc., San Francisco, 1948-51, Logan (Utah) Bus. Coll., 1984-90; catalog libr. U. Utah, Salt Lake City, 1959-63; cataloger Butte County Libr., Oroville, Calif., 1966-79; spl. collections libr. Merrill Libr., Utah State U., Logan, 1990—; curator, dir. Daus. Utah Pioneers Cache Mus., Logan, 1990—; advisor, curator brochures and exhibits Oroville Chinese Temple, 1966-79. Trustee Oroville Pub. Libr., 1969-71; libr. Oroville Med. Ctr. Libr., 1970-79; commr., chmn. Oroville Parks Dept. Lott Hist. Home and Chinese Temple, 1975-79; dir. 7th Ward Irrigation Co., Logan, 1980—; mem. Logan Mayor's Libr. Study Commn., 1991; trustee Butte County Hist. Soc., Oroville, 1971-75, editor Diggin's, 1971-79. Recipient award of merit Chinese Hist. Soc. Am., 1975, Butte County Hist. Soc., 1971, 79, plaque for svc. City of Oroville, 1979, Woman Over 65 Achievement award Utah State U., 1990. Mem. ALA, AAUW (various offices, Butte County Woman of Yr. award 1978), Nat. League Am. Pen women, Daus. Utah Pioneers, Hist. Soc. Calif., Hist. Soc. Utah, Libr. Assn. Calif., Stanford U. Alumni Assn., Utah State U. Alumni Assn., U. Calif.-Berkeley Alumni Assn., Am. Assn. for State and Local History. Home: 41 S 400th E Logan UT 84321

PARKER-DALY, SAMANTHA, journalist; b. Metuchen, N.J., Apr. 14, 1960; d. Bud and Gladys (Hoffman) Parker; m. Philip Anthony Daly, Apr. 16, 1989; children: William George, Robert Jason, Jennifer Lynn. BA in English, Drew U., 1982; M of Journalism, U. Calif., Berkeley, 1984. Copy editor San Francisco Daily Tribune, 1985-86, news writer, 1986-88; freelance writer N.Y.C., 1988-90; columnist Liner Notes Mag., Washington, 1991—. Author: Singing Out Loud: A History of Women in Popular Music, 1992. Chair fundraising com. Planned Parenthood, San Francisco, 1986-88; vol. Safe Haven Runaway Shelter, N.Y.C., 1989. Mem. NOW (v.p. D.C. area chpt. 1994—), Nat. Assn. Music Writers, D.C. Area Writers Assn. (Golden

Quill award 1993). Address: Werik Gardens 2853 Ontario Rd NW Ste 120 Washington DC 20009-2235

PARKER PAPILLON, SUSAN VICTORIA, financial administrator; b. Lowell, Mass., Aug. 18, 1948; d. Arthur Lemuel and Bertha Elizabeth (Tracey) P.; m. John Joseph Kane, June 14, 1970 (div. June 1984); m. Theodore Earl Papillon, Nov. 22, 1986. BA in Math., Barnard Coll., 1970; AA in Acctg., U. Calif., San Diego, 1972; BS in Acctg., Fairleigh Dickinson U., 1974, MBA in Fin., 1980. CPA; cert. mgmt. acct. Staff acct. Coranado (Calif.) Hosp., 1970-74; bus. mgr. Riverside Hosp., Boonton, N.J., 1974-79; fin. mgr. Healthcare Bus. Systems, Marlboro, Mass., 1980-84; bus. mgr. Harvard Multispeciality Group, Boston, 1984-87; asst. controller Hubbard Regional Hosp., Webster, Mass., 1987-90; bus. mgr. Atlanta Hematology and Oncology Assn., 1990-94; practice adminstr. North Atlanta Neurol. Assoc., P.C., 1994—; owner, cons. Papillon Bus. Svcs., Acworth, Ga., 1990—. Mem. Med. Group Mgrs. Assn., Healthcare Fin. Mgrs. Assn., Ga. Soc. Oncology Practice Mgrs., Piedmont Office Mgrs. Assn., Inst. Mgmt. Accts. Home: 5643 Bay Island Cay Acworth GA 30101-7608

PARKHILL, MIRIAM MAY, retired librarian; b. Ada, Ohio, July 8, 1913; d. Thomas Jefferson Jr. and Cora Anita (Kemp) Smull; m. Edwin Hamilton Parkhill, Oct. 4, 1935 (div. July 1966); children: Diane Paget Parkhill Seils, Thomas Hamilton. AB, Ohio No. U., 1934; MA, Ohio State U., 1935; MA in Libr. Sci., U. Mich., 1963; student, Detroit Bus. Inst., 1937. Staff mem. Nat. Youth Adminstrn., Ada, 1937-38; asst. supr. Nat. Youth Adminstrn., Lima, Ohio, 1939-40; libr. staff mem. Ohio No. U., Ada, 1959-62, asst. libr., instr., 1963-68, catalog dept. head, asst. prof., 1969-72, catalog dept. head, assoc. prof., 1973-78, assoc. prof. emerita, 1980—. Vol. Ada Pub. Libr., 1980—. Mem. AAUW, DAR, Ohio Libr. Coun., Acad. Libr. Assn. of Ohio, Colonial Dames XVII Century, Hardin County Mus., Inc., Alpha Phi Gamma, Zeta Tau Alpha. Republican. Presbyterian. Home: 301 S Main St Ada OH 45810-1415

PARKINS, KELLY ANN, fertilizer company consultant; b. Lawrence, Kans., July 16, 1961; d. Bowen Edward and Ruth Joann (Pope) P. BA in Biol. Sci., U. Del., 1984; postgrad., Calif. Poly. U., Pomona, 1990—. Registered pest control advisor, Calif. Pesticide applicator ChemLawn Svcs., Warminster, Pa., 1984-86; pesticide applicator ChemLawn Svcs., Thousand Oaks, Calif., 1986-87, asst. gen. mgr., 1987-88; sales mgr. ChemLawn Svcs., Orange, Calif., 1988-89; pest control advisor Robinson Fertilizer Co., Anaheim, Calif., 1990—. Bd. dirs., treas., pres. Benchmark Villas Homeowner Assn., Lake Forest, Calif., 1992—. Mem. Calif. Agrl. Production Cons. Assn., Sports Turf Mgrs. Assn. Republican.

PARKINSON, GEORGINA, ballet mistress; b. Brighton, Eng., Aug. 20, 1938. Studied with Royal Ballet Sch. Mem. Royal Ballet, London, from 1955, soloist, from 1959, then prin.; ballet mistress Am. Ballet Theatre, N.Y.C., 1978—. Created roles in: La Belle Dame Sans Merci (Andree Howard), The Invitation (Kenneth MacMillan), Romeo and Juliet (Kenneth MacMillan), Mayerling (Kenneth MacMillan), The Concert (Jerome Robbins), Enigma Variations (Sir Frederick Ashton), Daphnis and Chloe (John Cranko), Everlast (Twyla Tharp). Office: care Am Ballet Theatre 890 Broadway New York NY 10003-1211*

PARKINSON, MARIA LUISA, entertainment employment executive; b. Burbank, Calif., July 27, 1951; d. Roy Wilbur (Parky) and Serafina Antonia (Sorzano) P. AA, Pasadena City Coll., 1973; student, Acad. Stage and Cinema Arts, Los Angeles, 1973-76, The Living History Center, Augoura, Calif., The Second City, 1989—. Career counselor Apple One Employment Agy., Marina Del Rey, Calif., 1977-80, Good People, Inc., Los Angeles, 1980-83, Friedman Personnel Agy., Inc., Los Angeles, 1983-84; owner Parkinson Entertainment Agy., Hollywood, Calif., 1984—; lectr. in field, 1978—. Sponsor Latin Legal Ctr., Santa Monica, 1987—; charter mem. Mus. Contemporary Art. Mem. SAG, Am. Film Inst., Women in Show Bus. (publicity chair), Acad. Sci. Fiction, Fantasy and Horror Films, Hollywood C. of C. (entertainment com.), Entertainment Coun., Count Dracula Soc. (bd. govs.). Democrat. Roman Catholic. Office: Parkinson Entertainment Agy 6922 Hollywood Blvd Ste 514 Los Angeles CA 90028-6125

PARKO, KAREN LYNN, neurologist, public health service officer; b. Farmington, N.Mex., Feb. 18, 1963; d. John James Parko and Betty Jean (Wick) Vigil; m. Andrew McCartney Lowry, June 8, 1991. BA in Psychobiology, NYU, 1986; MD, Uniformed Svcs. U. Health Sci., 1991. Diplomate Nat. Bd. Med. Exams.; cert. BLS instr., ACLS provider, pediatric advanced cardiac life support, advanced trauma life support provider. EKG technician Multiphasic Med. Ctr., N.Y.C., 1983-84; neurosci. rschr. Rockfeller Med. Inst., N.Y.C., 1985-86; EMT Rocky Mountain Health Care, Aurora (Colo.) Presbyn. Hosp., 1986; dr.'s asst. Denver Indian Health Bd., 1986-87; commd. sr. asst. surgeon USPHS, 1987; resident in internal medicine Washington Hosp. Ctr., 1991-92; resident in neurology U. Calif., San Francisco, 1992-95. Active Am. Women's Hosp. Svcs., Washington, 1989—. Mem. Am. Med. Women's Assn., Commd. Officers Assn. USPHS. Office: U Calif 505 Parnassus Ave M-794 San Francisco CA 94143

PARKS, ARVA MOORE, historian; b. Miami, Fla., Jan. 19, 1939; d. Jack and Anne (Parker) Moore; m. Robert Lyle Parks, Aug. 19, 1959 (div. May 1986); children: Jacqueline Carey, Robert Downing, Gregory Moore; m. Robert Howard McCabe, June 20, 1992. Student, Fla. State U., 1956-58; BA, U. Fla., 1960; MA in History, U. Miami, Coral Gables, 1971. Tchr. Rolling Crest Jr. High Sch., West Hyattsville, Md., 1960-63, Miami Edison Sr. High Sch., Fla., 1963-64; grad. asst. U. Miami, Coral Gables, 1964-65; tchr. Everglades Sch. for Girls, Miami, 1965-66; cons., 1966-70; free-lance research historian Miami, 1970-86; adj. prof. U. Miami, Coral Gables, 1986-87; pres. Arva Parks & Co., Miami, 1986—; cons. thematic and interpretive rsch. and design Harry S. Truman Little White House, Key West, Fla., 1989-91; pres. Centennial Press, 1991—. Author: Miami the Magic City, 1981, rev. edit., 1991, The Forgotten Frontier, 1977, Harry Truman and the Key West Little White House, 1991; editor Tequesta Jour. Hist. Soc. Fla., 1986—; writer: (film) Our Miami: The Magic City, 1994. Trustee Miami-Dade C.C., 1984-90; bd. advs., Nat. Trust for Hist. Preservation, 1984-93, chmn. so. region, 1990-91; mem. Bi-Racial, Tri-Ethnic Adv. Bd., Miami, 1984—; exec. com. New World Sch. of Arts, Miami, 1986-90; bd. dirs. Louis Wolfson Media History Ctr., Miami, 1985-90, community adv. Dade Heritage Trust, Miami, 1988—, Orange Bowl Com., 1989—; bd. dirs. Bapt. Health Systems of Miami, Inc., 1992—; trustee U. Miami, 1994—. Recipient Historic Preservation award AIA, 1993, Outstanding Women of History award Cuban Am. Women's Club, 1992, Women Helping Women award Soroptimists, 1992, Am. History award DAR, 1987, Pathfinder's award Women's Com. 100, 1985, Outstanding Citizen award Coral Gables C. of C., 1983, Outstanding Preservationist award Dade Heritage Trust, 1983, Good Faith award Black Archives and Research Found., 1981, Mus. of Sci. award, 1981, Community Headliner award Women in Communications, 1980, Humanitarian award Urban League Guild, 1980, award City of Coral Gables Historic Preservation Bd., 1978; named to Alumni Hall of Fame Dade County Pub. Schs., 1985, Fla. Women's Hall of Fame, 1986, one of Women Who Made a Difference YWCA, 1988, Woman of Distinction award Soroptimist Internat. of Ams. Mem. Internat. Women's Forum, Jr. League. Democrat. Methodist. Home and Office: 1601 S Miami Ave Miami FL 33129-1103

PARKS, CARRIE STUART, artist, forensic artist; b. Missoula, Mont., Feb. 15, 1952; d. Edwin Zaring and Mary Evelyn (McCandless) Stuart; m. Rickie Steven Parks, Sept. 9, 1989. BS in Art/Social Sci. with honors, Lewis and Clark Coll., 1992. Fine artist Art Studio of the Coeur d'Alenes, Cataldo, Idaho, 1974—; forensic artist North Idaho Regional Crime Lab., Coeur d'Alene, 1981-89, Stuart Parks Forensic Cons., Cataldo, 1981—; profl. speaker Art Talk Programs, Cataldo, 1990—; instr. composite and forensic art Inst. for Police Tech. and Mgmt., Jacksonville, Fla., 1989—; instr. crime scene Law Enforcement TV Network, Tex., 1991; instr. composite and forensic art law enforcement agys. throughout U.S., 1988—. Artist, showing watercolors at Coeur d'Alene Resourt, Halikulana Wakikai, Boise Cascade, Idaho Dept. Parks and Recreation, others; author articles; subject of article. Artist-in-residence Citizens Coun. for the Arts in Elem. Schs., No. Idaho Sch. Dist., 1991—. Recipient Spirit of the Am. Woman award J.C. Penneys-Career Excellence, 1994. Mem. Idaho Watercolor Soc. (numerous awards), Internat. Assn. for Identification Art (forensic art sub-com.), Am. Soc. for Law Enforcement Trainers, N.W. Speakers Assn. Unitarian. Home: PO Box 73 Cataldo ID 83810-0073 Office: Art Studios of the Coeur d'Alenes PO Box 73 Cataldo ID 83810-0073

PARKS, CORRINE FRANCES, insurance agency owner; b. Pulaski, Ill., May 23, 1934; d. Elizabeth (Stanfield) Daniels; m. Charles Robert Parks, July 6, 1957; children: Reginald, Pierre. BA, Chgo. State U., 1976; student, Columbia Coll., 1986-87; MA, Gov.'s State U., 1981; postgrad., Chgo. U. Sem., 1990—. Exec. rep. Marsh & McLennon, Inc., Chgo., 1970-74; account exec. Internat. Ins. Cons., Chgo., 1974-77; mktg. rep. Alexander & Alexander, Chgo., 1977-79; v.p. AABACA Ins. Agy., Chgo., 1981; pres. AA& A Ins. Agy., Chgo., 1981—; radio show host Sta. WBEE, Chgo., 1985—; bd. dirs. Unity Chgo., Chgo. Urban Day Sch. Sec. Englewood Redevel. Group, Chgo., Butter's Career Acad., Chgo., 1987; rep. State Sun. Sch., N.I. Juris. Mem. Ind. Ins. Agts. Ill., Women in Radio and TV, Chgo. Bd. Underwriters, Chgo. Mus. Sci. and Industry, Group V Video Club (dir. 1986), Order of Eastern Star (treas. 1983). Democrat. Home: 100 Park Ave Calumet City IL 60409-5065 Office: AA & A Ins Agy 10615 S Halsted Chicago IL 60628

PARKS, JANE DELOACH, law librarian, legal assistant; b. Atlanta, June 7, 1927; d. John Keller and Martha Lorena (Lee) deLoach; m. James Bennett Parks, Dec. 28, 1951 (dec. Sept. 1983); children: Carrie Anne Parks-Kirby, Susan Jane, Lora Beth Parks-Maury. BA magna cum laude, Vanderbilt U., 1949; postgrad., Emory U., 1950-51; tchr. cert., U. Chattanooga, 1954; postgrad., U. Tenn., Chattanooga, 1971-73. Med. rsch./writing dept. surgery Emory U., Atlanta, 1949-51; sec. to med. dir. Tenn. Tuberculosis Hosp., Chattanooga, 1951-53; tchr. Signal Mountain (Tenn.) Elem. Sch., 1954-55; tchr., dean jr. sch. Cleve. (Tenn.) Day Sch., 1963-70; law firm libr., legal asst. Stophel, Caldwell & Heggie, Chattanooga, 1972-85, Caldwell, Heggie & Helton, Chattanooga, 1985-93, Heiskell, Donelson, Bearman, Adams, Williams & Caldwell, Chattanooga, 1993-94, Baker, Donelson, Bearman & Caldwell, Chattanooga, 1994—; tchr. various seminars on legal rsch. and writing, organizing one-person librs. and ch. librs., Chattanooga Legal Secs. Assn., Chattanooga-Hamilton County Bicentennial Libr. Editor (mag.) The Gadfly, 1947-49; editorial asst.: Studio Collotype, 1988 and to profl. jours., 1949—. tchr. Chattanooga Area Literacy Movement, 1984-86; mem. exec. coun. Friends of Chattanooga-Hamilton County Bicentennial Libr., 1989-94; del. Gov.'s Conf.-White House Conf. on Librs. and Info. Svcs., Nashville, 1990; libr. vol. Tenn. Aquarium.; mem. allocations com. United Way, 1994—. Mem. Tenn. Paralegal Assn., Chattanooga Area Libr. Assn. (2d v.p. 1989-90, sec. 1992-93), Non-Atty. Profl. Assn. (chmn. 1989-93), Phi Beta Kappa, Mortar Bd. Republican. Methodist. Office: Baker Donelson Bearman & Caldwell 1800 Republic Ctr 633 Chestnut St Chattanooga TN 37450-0001

PARKS, JULIA ETTA, retired education educator; b. Kansas City, Kans., Apr. 5, 1923; d. Hays and Idella Long; BEd, Washburn U., 1959, MEd, 1965; EdD, U. Kans., 1980; m. James A. Parks, Aug. 10, 1941; 1 child, James Hays. Tchr., concert vocalist Lowman Hill Elem. Sch., 1959-64; faculty Washburn U., Topeka, Kans., 1964-93, prof. edn. 1981-92, mem. pres.'s adv. council, 1981-84, chair edn., phys. edn., health and recreation div., multicultural com., dept. edn., 1986-92; insvc. lectr. reading instrns. Kans. Pub. Schs., 1960-93; lectr. Topeka Pub. Schs. Mem. acad. sabbatical com., Washburn U., 1987-90, vis. teams Nat. Council for Accreditation of Tchr. Edn., 1974-86, prof. emeritus, 1993. Bd. dirs. Children's Hour, 1981-84, Mulvane Art Ctr., 1974-78; judge, All Kans. Spelling Bees, 1982-86; sec. Brown Decision Sculpture Com., 1974-85; oral record account of experiences as a miniority student in integrated Topeka High Sch., 1984. Mem. multicultural non-sexist com. Topeka Pub. Sch., 1967—; apptd. to Kans. Equal Edn. Opportunities Adv. Com., 1988; marshall Washburn U. Commencements, 1980-92; mem. State of Kans. Task Force in Edn., 1991-92; presenter in field. Recipient Educator's award Living the Dream com., Local award for Excellence and Equity in Edn., The Brown Found.; named to Topeka High Sch. Hall of Fame, 1991; The Julia Etta Parks Honor Award created in her honor, Edn. Dept. Washburn Univ. Mem. Kans. Intergenerational Network, Washburn U. Alumni Assn. (contbr. alumni mag. 1989, recipient Teaching Excellence award 1983), Internat. Reading Assn., Kans. Inst. Higher Edn. (mem. pres. adv. council, 1981-83), Kans. Reading Assn., Kans. Reading Profls. Higher Edn., Topeka High Sch. Hist. Soc., Links Club (pres. 1982-84, chairperson scholarship com. 1984—, Topeka Back Home Reunion Club (historian, v.p. 1991—), Delta Kappa Gamma, Phi Delta Kappa, NONOSO Women's Hon. Sorority. Methodist. Office: Washburn U Dept Edn 1700 SW College Ave Topeka KS 66621

PARKS, MADELYN N., nurse, retired army officer, university official; b. Jordan, Okla.. Diploma, Corpus Christi (Tex.) Sch. Nursing, 1943; B.S.N., Incarnate Word Coll., San Antonio, 1961; M.H.A. in Health Care Adminstrn, Baylor U., 1965. Commd. 2d lt. Army Nurse Corps, 1943, advanced through grades to brig. gen., 1975; basic tng. Fort Meade, Md., 1944; staff nurse eye ward Valley Forge (Pa.) Gen. Hosp., 1944; served in India, Iran, Italy, 1944-45; gen. duty staff nurse Fort Polk, La., 1951; nurse eye clinic Tripler Army Med. Center, Hawaii, 1951-54; staff nurse eye, ear, nose and throat ward Brooke Army Med. Center, San Antonio, 1954-57; ednl. coordinator Fort Dix, N.J., 1957-58; instr., supr. enlisted med. tng. U.S. Army Med. Tng. Center, Fort Sam Houston, Tex., 1959-61; chief nurse surg. field hosp. 62d Med. Group, Germany, 1961-62, sr. nurse coordinator, 1962-63; adminstrn. resident Letterman Gen. Hosp., San Francisco, 1964-65; dir. clin. specialist course Letterman Gen. Hosp., 1965-67; chief nurse 85th Evacuation Hosp., Qui Nhon, Vietnam, 1967-68; asst. chief nursing sci. div., asst. prof. Med. Field Service Sch., U.S. Army-Baylor U. Program in Health Care Adminstrn., 1968-72; chief nurse surgeons office Hdqrs. Continental Army Command, Fort Monroe, Va., 1972-73; chief dept. nursing Walter Reed Army Med. Center, Washington, 1973-75; chief Army Nurse Corps, Office of Surgeon Gen., Dept. Army, Washington, 1975-79; ret. Army Nurse Corps, Office of Surgeon Gen., Dept. Army, 1979; faculty assoc. adminstr. U. Md., 1974-78. Decorated D.S.M., Army Commendation medal with 2 oak leaf clusters, Legion of Merit, Meritorious Service medal; recipient Alumna of Distinction award Incarnate Word Coll., 1981. Mem. Ret. Officers Assn., AMEDD Mus. Found. Address: 5211 Metcalf Dr San Antonio TX 78239

PARKS, PATRICIA JEAN, lawyer; b. Portland, Oreg., Apr. 2, 1945; d. Robert and Marion (Crosby) P.; m. David F. Jurca, Oct. 17, 1971 (div. 1976). BA in History, Stanford U., 1963-67; JD, U. Penn., Phila., 1967-70. Bar: N.Y. 1971, Wash. 1974. Assoc. Milbank, Tweed, Hadley & McCoy, N.Y.C., 1970-73; assoc. Shidler, McBroom, Gates & Lucas, Seattle, 1974-81, ptnr., 1981-90; ptnr. Preston, Thorgrimson, Shidler, Gates & Ellis, Seattle, 1990-93; pvt. practice Seattle, 1993—. Active Vashon Allied Arts, Mountaineers, N.W. Women's Law Ctr., Wash. State Women's Polit. Caucus. Mem. NOW, ABA, Wash. State Bar Assn. (past pres. tax sect., past chair gift and estate tax com.), Washington Women in Tax, Washington Women Lawyers, Seattle-King County Bar Assn., Employee Stock Ownership Plan Assn., Western Pension Conf., Pension Roundtable, Wash. Athletic Club. Home: 14028 Glen Acres Rd SW Vashon WA 98070 Office: 1301 5th Ave Ste 3800 Seattle WA 98101

PARKS, SABRA LITTLETON, postmaster, nurse; b. Nassawadox, Va., Feb. 27, 1951; d. Elmer Randolph and Betty Ayres (Colonna) Littleton; m. Daniel Reade Parks, June 4, 1969 (div. 1977); children: Hillery Anne, Daniel Reade Jr. LPN, Sch. Practical Nursing, Nassawadox, 1971-72. Dep. supr. Accomack County Nursing Home, Parksley, Va., 1974-86; clk. U.S. Postal Svc., Hallwood, Va., 1985-89; officer in charge U.S. Postal Svc., Jenkins Bridge, Va., 1986-89; clk. U.S. Postal Svc., Bloxom, Va., 1989-90; postmaster U.S. Postal Svc., Locustville, Va., 1990-93, Hallwood, 1993—; charge nurse Accomack County Nursing Home, Parksley, 1990—. Mem. Citizens for a Better Eastern Shore, Exmore, Va., 1989, Soc. for Preservation of Locustville Acad., 1991. Mem. Nat. Assn. Postmasters of U.S. (vice chair 1990-92). Home: PO Box 13 16435 Lankford Hwy Nelsonia VA 23414-0013 Office: US Postal Svc 27497 Main St Hallwood VA 23359-9998

PARKS, SALLIE ANN, county official, public relations executive, marketing professional; b. Detroit, Sept. 5, 1936; d. Bert A. Rennie and Edna V. (Lampman) Moran; m. Donald K. Parks, Aug. 22, 1959 (div. 1983); children: Sheri Lynn, Steven Rennie. BA, Cen. Mich. U., 1959; postgrad., Mich. State U., 1962. Cert. accredited pub. relations profl. Editor Pinellas Classroom Tchrs. Assn., Clearwater, Fla., 1967-73; sub. tchr. Pinellas County Schs., Fla., 1972-74; real estate mgmt. Clearwater, 1971-74, bus. mgr., 1974-76; exec. dir. Pinellas County Arts Coun., Clearwater, 1976-81; dir. community relations Mease Health Care, Dunedin, Fla., 1981-86; pub. relations cons., tchr. Tokyo, Japan, 1986-87; dir. pub. rels. and mktg. Mease Health Care, Dunedin, 1987-92; county commr. Pinellas County, Clearwater, Fla., 1992—; chair long term care subcom. Nat. Assn. Counties; bd dirs. Fla. Assn. Counties; chair Dist. V Juvenile Justice Bd.; mem. Met. Planning Orgn. Pinellas County, Pinellas County Arts Coun., Pinellas Suncoast Transit Authority, Cmty. Health Purchasing Alliance Dist. V, Tampa Bay Regional Planning Coun. Area Agy. on Aging and Long Term Care subcom., Pinellas County Juvenile Boot Camp Task Force, Success by Six Task Force. Pres. Am. Heart Assn., Suncoast chpt., Clearwater, 1990-92; vice chairperson Clearwater Pub. Libr. Found., 1989; pres. LWV, Clearwater, 1972, PEO Sisterhood, Clearwater, 1975; trustee Pinellas Marine Inst. Recipient Athena award, Women in Communications, 1983, Leadership in the Arts award, Soroptimist Internat., 1980. Mem. Nat. Press Women, Fla. Pub. Rels. Assn. (past pres.). Republican. Presbyterian. Office: Office Bd Commrs 315 Court St Clearwater FL 34616

PARKS MCKAY, JANE RAYE, publicist, marketing specialist; b. Atlanta, Sept. 15, 1952; d. William Ransom and Betsy Barbara (McMillan) Parks; m. Tim Dunn McKay, Sept. 3, 1977. AA in Liberal Arts, West Valley Coll., Saratoga, Calif.; student, San Jose State U., 1981-83; BA in Cmty. Studies, U. Calif., Santa Cruz, 1992. Formerly profl. model; image cons. San Francisco and Monterey Bay, Calif., 1974-93; spkr. in field; media interviewee. Author: The Make-Over--A Teen's Guide to Looking and Feeling Beautiful, 1985, William Morrow. Pres.' Undergrad. fellow U. Calif., Santa Cruz. Democrat. Office: 4715 Opal Cliff Dr Santa Cruz CA 95062

PARLOW, SUSAN ELIZABETH, clinical psychologist, psychotherapist; b. Boston, July 18, 1948; d. Sydney and Lois Faye (Collier) P. BA, New Sch. for Social Rsch., 1977, PhD in Clin. Psychology, 1987; cert., NYU, 1994. Lic. psychologist, N.Y. Asst. clin. prof. Columbia U., N.Y.C., 1990-93; asst. prof. psychology NYU, 1991-93; pvt. practice N.Y.C., 1987—; lectr. in field. Asst. rev. editor Psychoanalytic Dialogues, 1991-93. Vol. food for the homebound Ch. of Francis Xavier, N.Y.C., 1992-93. Mem. APA (divsn. 39), Met. Canoe & Kayak Club. Office: 26 W 9th St Apt 10B New York NY 10011-8920

PARMA, FLORENCE VIRGINIA, magazine editor; b. Kenilworth, N.J., Aug. 30, 1940; d. Howard Frank and Mildred Faye (Lister) von Finkel; m. Wilson Henry Parma, June 15, 1973 (div. Aug. 1986). Studies with pvt. tutor, Chaumont, France, 1961-62; student, NYU, 1962-63. Copywriter Schless & Co., N.Y.C., 1963-65; editor, researcher Barnes Lab., Stanford, Calif., 1969-73; adminstrv. exec. Crater Inc., Honolulu, 1974-79; mgr., editor Off Duty mag., Honolulu, 1979—; v.p. Mapasa, Inc. (dba The Prides of New Zealand), 1992—. Editor: Welcome to Hawaii Guide, 1985—; co-editor: Serotonin and Behavior, 1972; freelance columnist. Republican. Episcopalian. Home and Office: Off Duty Hawaii 3771 Anuhea St Honolulu HI 96816-3849

PARMENTER, KATHLEEN HOGAN, advertising executive; b. N.Y.C., Jan. 14, 1941; d. Robert Aloysius and Helen Marie (Scanlon) Hogan; m. Henry R. Parmenter, Nov. 27, 1965; children: Debra, Pamela. BA, Fordham U., 1963. Sales asst. Blair Cos., N.Y.C., 1959-63; exec. asst. Metromedia Inc., N.Y.C., 1963-71; v.p., gen. mgr. Family Media Inc., N.Y.C., 1971-83; dir. advt. Weight Watchers mag., N.Y.C., 1983-89, v.p. advt., 1989—. Mem. Women Communications, Nat. Acad. TV Arts and Scis., Woodlawn Heights Taxpayers Assn. Home: 4313 Kepler Ave Bronx NY 10470-2047

PARONI, GENEVIEVE MARIE SWICK, retired science educator; b. Eureka, Nev., July 27, 1926; d. William Jackson and Myrtle Rose (Smith) S.; m. Walter Andrew Paroni, Dec. 26, 1954; 1 child, Andrea Marie. BA, U. Nev., Reno, 1948; MEd, U. Idaho, 1978; postgrad., MIT, Oreg. State U., U. Oreg., U. Wash., Ft. Wright Coll., U. Portland. Cert. elem. and secondary sect., Nev. Tchr., vice prin. Eureka County High Sch., 1948-66; coast geodetic U.S. Govt., Eureka, 1950's; tchr. biol. and phys. scis., facilitator Pub. Schs. Dist. #393, Wallace, Idaho, 1968-91; ret., 1991; regional dir. NSTA, Idaho, Panhandle, 1982-90; chmn. in svc. adv. State Dept. Edn., Boise, Idaho, 1980-83, mem. state sci. commn., 1981-82; mem. Idaho Sci. Curriculum Guide Com., 1987, Univ. Idaho Commn. on Math/Sci. Edn., 1988-89, Inland Empire Physics Alliance, 1989-90, Idaho Sci. Alliance Com., 1990. Contbr. history articles to profl. jours. Active Wallace City Coun., 1970-80; bd. dirs. Wallace Pub. Libr., 1983—, Silver Valley Arts and Crafts Assn., 1991, Greater Wallace, 1980-93, Wallace Dist. Arts Coun., 1993; mem. citizen's adv. bd. Idaho Nat. Engring. Lab., 1994—; Rep. precinct chairperson, Wallace, 1970-80; bishop's warden area Episc. Ch., 1990-94; mem. coun. Episc. Diocese Spokane, 1992—. Grantee Idaho Power, 1985; named Outstanding Tchr., Dist. #393. 1975; finalist Presdl. awards in High Sch. Sci. Teaching. Mem. NEA, AAUW (pres. 1970s), Wallace Edn. Assn. (sec. 1970s), Bus. and Profl. Women Assn. (v.p. Nev. chpt. 1953-55), Pythian Sisters (Grand Guard 1950), Order Ea. Star (matron Nev. chpt.), Delta Kappa Gamma (pres. 1980-82), Phi Delta Kappa. Home: PO Box 229 Wallace ID 83873-0229

PARR, CAROLYN MILLER, federal judge; b. Palatka, Fla., Apr. 17, 1937; d. Arthur Charles and Audrey Ellen (Dunklin) Miller; m. Jerry Studstill Parr, Oct. 12, 1959; children: Kimberly Parr Trapasso, Jennifer Parr Turek, Patricia Audrey. BA, Stetson U., 1959; MA, Vanderbilt U., 1960; JD, Georgetown U., 1977; LLD (hon.), Stetson U., 1986. Bar: Md. 1977, U.S. Tax Ct. 1977, D.C. 1979, U.S. Supreme Ct. 1983. Gen. trial atty. IRS, Washington, 1977-81, sr. trial atty. office of chief counsel, 1982; spl. counsel to asst. atty. gen. tax divsn. U.S. Dept. Justice, Washington, 1982-85; judge U.S. Tax Ct., Washington, 1985—. Nat. Def. fellow Vanderbilt U., 1959-60; fellow Georgetown U., 1975-76; recipient Spl. Achievement award U.S. Treasury, 1979. Mem. ABA, Md. Bar Assn., Nat. Assn. Women Judges, D.C. Bar Assn., Women Judges Fund for Justice (bd.). Office: US Tax Ct 400 2nd St NW Washington DC 20217-0002*

PARR, SANDRA HARDY, government affairs administrator; b. Atlanta, Dec. 30, 1952; d. Raymond William Hardy and Ruth (Berry) Yancey; m. James Parr Jr., Apr. 14, 1978; 1 child, James Andrew Parr III. Student, Lurleen B. Wallace Jr. Coll., 1972. Sales adminstr. Etec Corp., Hayward, Calif., 1976-77; adminstrv. sec. Cities Svc. Co., Atlanta, 1977-82; sales and planning coord. Intermodal Transp. Co., Norcross, Ga., 1982-83; freelance temp. sec. Atlanta met. area, 1983-86; freelance word processor, cons. Amoco Container Co., Norcross, 1986-88; psychiat. rev. asst. Am. Psychiat. Assn., Atlanta, 1988-89; support svcs. mgr. Parkside Health Mgmt. Corp., Atlanta, 1989-90; med. staff coord. C.P.C. Parkwood Hosp., Atlanta, 1991—; health svcs. asst. Ciba Vision Corp., 1991-93. Del. internat. nursing conf., citizen amb. program to People's Republic China, Seattle Washington People to People, Beijing, 1989; part-time exercise instr. Mem. NAFE. Home: 1301 Eugenia Ter Lawrenceville GA 30245-7437 Office: CPC Parkwood Hosp 1999 Cliff Valley Way NE Atlanta GA 30329-2420 Address: Philip Morris USA Govt Affairs 3 Ravinia Dr Ste 1560 Atlanta GA 30346

PARRAMORE, BARBARA MITCHELL, education educator; b. Guilford County, N.C., Aug. 29, 1932; d. Samuel Spencer and Nellie Gray (Glosson) Mitchell; m. Lyman Griffis Worthington, Dec. 23, 1956 (div. 1961); m. Thomas Custis Parramore, Jan. 22, 1966; children: Lisa Gray, Lynn Stuart. AB, U. N.C., Greensboro, 1954; MEd, N.C. State U., 1959; EdD, Duke U., 1968. Counselor, thcr. Raleigh City Schs., 1954-59, sch. prin., 1959-65; prof. dept. of curriculum and instrn. N.C. State U., 1970—; acad. specialist Office Internat. Edn., U.S. Info. Svcs., sec. sch. initiative program, The Philippines, 1987. Author: The People of North Carolina, 1972, 3rd edit. 1983. Japan Inst. Social and Econ. Affairs fellow, 1980; N.C. AAUW award for juvenile lit., 1973, Holladay medal for excellence N.C. State U., 1994. Mem. ASCD, N.C. ASCD (pres. 1994—), N.C. Coun. for Social Studies (pres. 1985-87), Assn. Tchr. Educators, Delta Kappa Gamma, Kappa Delta Pi. Home: 5012 Tanglewood Dr Raleigh NC 27612-3135

PARRAVANO, AMELIA ELIZABETH, recording industry executive; b. Providence, Apr. 5, 1951; d. Olindo Luigi and Violet Carmella (Russo) Izzo; m. Grimaldo Antonio Parravano, July 4, 1979; children: Peter Paul, Paula

Elizabeth. AA, Roger Williams Coll., 1972; postgrad., R.I. Coll., 1972-73. Owner, operator Aura Arts & Crafts, Cranston, R.I., 1985-88; pres. Peridot Music, Cranston, 1990—; freelance artist Artist Letters League, Cranston, 1992—; singer, songwriter, musician. Active PTA, Cranston, 1991-92; artist mem. R.I. State Coun. on Arts, Providence, 1986-92; active Pawtucket (R.I.) Arts Coun., 1986-92. Mem. Am. Soc. Composers, Authors and Pubs., Songwriters Guild Am., Gospel Music Assn., County Music Assn., Country Music Showcase Internat. Home: 17 Woodbine St Cranston RI 02910

PARRIGIN, ELIZABETH ELLINGTON, lawyer; b. Colon, Panama, May 23, 1932; d. Jesse Cox and Elizabeth (Roark) Ellington; m. Perry G. Parrigin, Oct. 8, 1975. BA, Agnes Scott Coll., 1954; JD, U. Va., 1959. Bar: Tex. 1959, Mo. 1980. Atty. San Antonio, 1960-69; law libr. U. Mo., Columbia, 1969-77, rsch. assoc., 1977-82; atty. pvt. practice, Columbia, 1982—. Elder, clk. of session First Presbyn. Ch., Columbia; mem. permanent jud. commn. Presbyn. Ch. U.S., 1977-83, mem. advisory com. on constitution, 1983-90. Mem. ABA, Mo. Bar Assn. (chmn. sub-com. revision of Mo. trsut law 1988-92). Democrat. Presbyterian. Home: 400 Conley Ave Columbia MO 65201-4219 Office: 224 N 8th St Columbia MO 65201-4844

PARRINO, CHERYL LYNN, state agency administrator; b. Wisconsin Rapids, Wis., Jan. 21, 1954; m. Jack J. Parrino, Sept. 1, 1990; 1 child, George. BBA in Acctg., U. Wis., 1976. Auditor Pub. Svc. Commn. Wis., Madison, 1976-82, dir. utility audits, 1982-86, exec. asst. to chmn., 1986-91, commr., 1991—, chmn., 1992—; mem. adv. bd. Bellcore, 1991; vice chmn. bd. dirs. Wis. Ctr. Demand Side Rsch., Madison, 1991-92; chmn. bd. dirs. Wis. Pub. Utility Inst., Madison, 1992—; mem. Fed. State Joint Bd., 1993. Mem. Gov.'s Task Force Gross Receipts Tax, Madison, 1991-92, Gov.'s Task Force Alternative Fuels, Madison, 1992—, Gov.'s Task Force Clean Air, Madison, 1992—, Gov.'s Task Force Telecom., Madison, 1993-94. Mem. Nat. Assn. Pub. Utility Commrs. (mem. exec. com. 1991, chair comm. com. 1992—). Republican. Lutheran. Office: Pub Svc Commn Wis PO Box 7854 610 N Whitney Way Madison WI 53709

PARRIS, DONNA SANDS, secondary school educator; b. Winter Haven, Fla., July 30, 1951; d. Maxwell Lloyd and Thelma Desmond (Darby) Sands; 1 child, Brad; m. Jack Andy Parris, June 5, 1992; 1 stepchild, Andy. BS in Edn., Western Carolina U., 1973. Cert. tchr., N.C. Mgr. Alfredo's Restaurant, Maggie, N.C., 1981-85; tchr. health, phys. edn. Haywood County Schs., Waynesville, N.C., 1973-81, 89—, tchr. dropout prevention, 1985-88, mentor, trainer, 1989—, mem. staff devel. cadre, 1991—; health, phys. edn. and 7-8 lang. arts tchr. Ctrl. Haywood H.S., 1994—. Co-author: (textbook) Making Life Choices; editor ednl. handbooks and teaching resources. Named N.C. Health Tchr. Yr., N.C. Assn. Health Edn., 1992. Mem. AAHPERD, ASCD, N.C. Assn. Educators (officer various coms. including polit. action com. for edn. 1974-81), Waynesville Bus. and Profl. Women. Democrat. Methodist. Office: Haywood Ctrl HS PO Box 249 Clyde NC 28721

PARRISH, ALMA ELLIS, elementary school educator; b. Peoria, Ill., Mar. 28, 1929; d. William Edward and Marie (Allton) Ellis; m. Clyde R. Parrish, Jr., Nov. 20, 1949; children: Clyde R. III, Charles, Donald, Royce, Christopher. BS, Bradley U., Peoria. Cert. elem. tchr., S.C., Ill. Tchr. Community Consol. Sch. Dist. 59, Elk Grove Village, Ill., Sipp Sch. Dist., Peoria, Kershaw County Sch. Dist., Camden, S.C. Mem. KCRA, S.C. Edn. Assn., Tchrs. Coun. Dist. 59 (pres., com.), Kershaw County Edn. Assn. (sec., PACE com.), Ill. Ret. Tchr.'s Assn., S.I. Coun.

PARRISH, FLORENCE TUCKER, writer, retired government official; b. Greenville, Miss.; d. Victor Amos and Martha Buchannan (Binkley) Denslow; m. Joseph Nathaniel Tucker Jr., Nov. 9, 1946 (dec.); children: Joseph Nathaniel III, Frederick Steven, James Denslow; m. Noel Francis Parrish, June 25, 1983 (dec. Apr. 1987). Diploma piano, Ward-Belmont Coll., Nashville, 1945; studied piano with Michael Field, N.Y.C., 1945-46; B of Music Edn., Delta State U., Cleveland, Miss., 1960; MS in Counseling, U. So. Miss., 1971; EdD, George Washington U., 1983. Tchr. music Gulfport (Miss.) pub. schs., 1959-63; recreation therapist VA Hosp., Gulfport, 1964-70; edn. counselor USAF, Miss. and Japan, 1971-74, edn. svcs. officer, Republic of Korea, 1974-75, asst. dir. sr. tng. CAP nat. hdqrs., 1975-77; EEO officer D.C. Dept. Labor, 1977-80; bur. chief complaints processing and adjudication Office EEO, U.S. Geol. Survey, Reston, Va., 1980-82, mgr. human resources, Dept. Interior, 1982-84; internat. forum coord. Pres.'s Com. on Employment of Handicapped, 1985; commr. Alexandria Commn. on Aging, Va., 1985-88, chmn. edn. and cultural affairs com., 1985-88, sec., 1987-88; lead scholar pilot project Nat. Coun. on Aging; vis. prof. Kunsan Tchrs. Coll., Kunsan Jr. Coll., 1974-75; apptd. mem. del. People-to-People Internat. Amb. Program, Beijing, Peoples Republic China and Hong Kong, 1988; mem. steering com. Va. Home Care Alliance, 1990-92; mem. exec. bd. Washington Opera Guild, 1992-94; chmn. Night in Old Vienna benefit ball Embassy of Austria, Washington, 1993, co-chair, 1994; mem. adv. bd. Inst. Conflict Analysis and Resolution George Mason U., 1993—, vice chair 1995—, delegate to Arms Ctrl. Negotations in the Middle East, Athens, Greece, 1994; mem. ofcl. delegation 8th Internat. Helicopter Olympic Competition, Moscow, 1994; workshop leader, cons. and lectr. in field; bd. dirs. Wake Assocs., Ltd., Washington, 1980-84. Columnist on aging issues, Alexandria (Va.) Gazette-Packet, feature writer, 1986—; contbr. articles to profl. jours. Organizer, pres. Gulfport chpt. Parents-Without-Ptnrs., 1962-64; charter mem. Westminster Presbyn. Ch., Gulfport, 1961; active Nat. Coun. on Aging, Military Classics Seminar; officer, bd. dirs. Stonehurst IV Homeowners Assn. Recipient Outstanding Vis. Prof. award Kunsan Tchrs. Coll., 1974, Kunsan Jr. Coll. award for promoting tchr. exchange program, also certs. of commendation, Brigadier Gen. Noel F. Parrish award The Nat. Tuskegee Airmen, Inc., commendation for organizing art show Alexandria Commn. on Aging. Mem. Women in Comm., Washington Opera Guild, USAF Assn. (v.p. for community programs Gen. Charles Gabriel chpt. 1991—, Woman of Distinction award), Air Force Assn. (Thomas Anthony Chpt.), NATO Def. Coll. Anciens Assn., Am. Inst. Wine and Food, World Affairs Coun., Va. Assn. on Aging, Nat. Press Club (events and oral history coms., chmn. oral history com.), Miss. Soc. Washington, Ret. Officers Assn., Tex. Soc. Washington, Friends of Kennedy Ctr., Smithsonian Assocs., The Nat. Tuskegee Airmen Inc. Orgn. Home: Stonehurst 9302 Arlington Blvd Fairfax VA 22031-2503

PARRISH, M. JEANNE, psychologist; b. Nashville, Sept. 28, 1924; d. Charles Lee and Marguerite Patricia (Martin) P. BA, Fontbonne Coll., St. Louis, 1951; MEd, St. Louis U., 1956, MS, 1963. Cert. secondary tch. in math., bus. edn. and adminstrn., Mo.; lic. psychologist, Mo. Nurses aid St. Thomas Hosp., Nashville, 1941-43; elem. tchr. St. Stephen Sch., New Orleans, 1945-48, St. Vincent de Paul Sch., San Francisco, 1949-52; secondary tchr. Laboure High Sch., St. Louis, 1952-61; adminstr. Child Ctr. of Our Lady, St. Louis, 1963-66, Marillac Sch. and Residence, Kansas City, Mo., 1966-72; prin. Laboure High Sch., St. Louis, 1972-74; cons. Daus. of Charity-West Ctrl., St. Louis/Midwest States, 1974-80; staff psychologist Kenrick Sch. Theology, St. Louis, 1980-94; bd. dirs. Guardian Settlement Assn., St. Louis, 1984—, Cath. Family Svcs., 1984—. Contbr. articles to profl. jours. Recipient Key to Kansas City, Mo., 1972, Key to New Orleans, 1975. Mem. APA, Nat. Cath. Edn. Assn., Assn. for Theol. Field Educators, Midwest Assn. Spiritual Dirs., Cath. Assn. for Theol. Field Educators. Democrat. Roman Catholic. Home: 7800 Natural Bridge Rd Saint Louis MO 63121 Office: Marillac Provincialate 7800 Natural Bridge Saint Louis MO 63121

PARRIS-HICKLIN, INGRID, recreation specialist; b. Flushing, N.Y., Jan. 18, 1952; d. Alfred and Elizabeth Parris; m. Christopher C. Hicklin, July 13, 1974; children: Kevin, Colin. BA, CCNY, 1975; postgrad., George Washington U., 1975-76, Corcoran Sch. Art, 1980-81. Bi-centennials coord. Nat. Pk. Svc., Manhattan, N.Y., 1973-75; tchr. Marjorie Daw Sch., Alexandria, Va., 1977-78, Alexandria (Va.) Pub. Schs., 1978-80; youth ctr. dir. Fairfax (Va.) County Dept. Recreation, 1977-84, area supr., 1984-85; dir. Huntington Community Ctr., Alexandria, 1985-88; program planner Fairfax (Va.) County Pk. Authority, 1988-91; supr. community ctr. ops. Fairfax (Va.) County Dept. Recreation, 1991—. Lay Eucharistic min. Holy Family Cath. Ch., Dale City, Va., 1991-94. Mem. Va. Recreation and Pk. Soc. (no. dist. ethnic-minority chair 1989-91, profl. task force 1992-93), Jack and Jill Am. Inc. (v.p. 1981-84, pres. 1984-86, 91-93, Disting. Mother award 1992), Links, Inc. (Old Dominion chpt.). Democrat. Office: Fairfax County Cmty & Recreation Svcs 12011 Government Ctr Pkwy Fairfax VA 22035

PARR-JOHNSTON, ELIZABETH, academic administrator; b. N.Y.C., Aug. 15, 1939; d. Ferdinand Van Siclen and Helene Elizabeth (Ham) Parr; m. David E. Bond, Dec. 28, 1962 (div. July 1975); children: Peter, Kristina Aline; m. Archibald F. Johnston, Mar. 6, 1982; children: James, Heather, Alexandra, Margaret. BA, Wellesley Coll., 1961; MA, Yale U., 1962, PhD, 1973; postgrad., Harvard U., 1986. Various positions Govt. of Can., Ottawa, Ontario, 1973-76, INCO Ltd., Toronto, Ontario, 1976-79; chief of staff, sr. policy advisor Govt. Can., 1979-80; various positions Shell Can. Ltd., Calgary, Alberta, 1980-90; pres., vice chancellor Mt. St. Vincent U., Halifax, Nova Scotia, 1991—; pres. Parr-Johnston & Assocs., Calgary, 1990-92; instr. U. Western Ontario, London, Ont., 1964-67, U. B.C., Vancouver, 1967-71; vis. scholar Wesleyan U., Middletown, Conn., 1971-72; acad. rsch. assoc. Carleton U., Ottawa, 1972-73; bd. dirs. Nova Scotia Power, Bank of Nova Scotia, Fishery Products Internat., The Empire Co., Investment Dealers Assn.; spkr. and presenter in field. Mem. editorial bd. Can. Econ. Jour., 1980-83; contbr. articles to profl. jours. Bd. dirs. Dellcrest Home, 1980-84, Calgary Southwest Fed. Riding Assn., 1985-91, The Learning Ctr., Calgary, 1989-91, Halifax United Way, 1991-92, North/South Inst., 1992—, Vol. Planning Nova Scotia, 1992-93, John Howard Soc., planning chmn., 1980-84; mem. nat. innovations adv. com. to min. employment and immigration, 1991-94, policy adv. com. C.D. Howe, 1980-85; mem. Ont. Econ. Coun., 1981-84. Woodrow Wilson fellow, 1962. Mem. Assn. Atlantic Univs. (chair 1994—), Assn. Univs. Colls. in Can. (bd. dirs., mem. exec. com. 1994—), Inter-Am. Orgn. Higher Edn. (adv. com. 1991—), Corp. Higher Edn. Forum (bd. dirs.), Nat. Innovations Adv. Counc. (Fed. Minister Emplyment and Immigration 1991-94), Women in Acad. Adminstrn. (adv. bd. 1991—), Calgary Coun. Advanced Tech. (exec. 1990-91), Can. Econs. Assn., Inst. Pub. Adminstrn. Can., Sr. Women Acad. Administrs. Can., Women in Ednl. Adminstrn. Nova Scotia, Can. Soc. Study Higher Edn., Phi Beta Kappa. Anglican. Office: Mount Saint Vincent U, Office of the Pres and Vice Chancellor, Halifax, NS Canada B3M 2J6

PARROTT, NANCY SHARON, lawyer; b. Atoka, Okla., Jan. 11, 1944; d. Albert L. and Willie Jo (Parkhill) Furr. BA, Okla. U., 1967; MA, No. Tex. U., 1974; JD, Okla. City U., 1982. Bar: Okla. 1984, U.S. Supreme Ct. 1984. Ptnr. Chapman & Chapman, Oklahoma City, 1984-85; chief legal asst. marshal Okla. Supreme Ct., Oklahoma City, 1985—. Mem. Leadership Oklahoma, Oklahoma City; bd. dirs. Am. Cancer Soc. Mem. ABA, Okla. Bar Assn., Okla. County Bar Assn. Briefcase, Am. Adjudicature Soc., Okla. Bar Assn. (chmn. awards com.). Office: Okla Supreme Ct State Capital Bldg 245 Oklahoma City OK 73105

PARRY, RUTH ELAINE, health services research administrator; b. Salisbury, Md., Apr. 10, 1952; d. Robert Owen and Margaret Elsie (Elburn) P. BA, Washington Coll., Chestertown, Md., 1974; MA, Conn. Coll., 1981; M in Adminstrv. Sci., Johns Hopkins U., 1983; JD, U. Md., 1989. Human factors scientist BDM Services Co., Ft. Ord, Calif., 1975-76; research coordinator sch. pub. health Johns Hopkins U., Balt., 1980-83; research assoc. sch. medicine U. Md., Balt., 1983-87; health sci. specialist dept. vet. affairs VA Med. Ctr., Perry Point, Md., 1987-90; cons. in health svcs. rsch. Balt., 1990—; mgr. health svcs. R&D rsch. initiatives and ops. U.S. Dept. Vets. Affairs, Washington, 1992-94, asst. dir. health svcs. rsch. and devel. svc., 1994—. Co-contbr. articles to profl. jours., 1983, 84, 88. Research and devel. com. mem. Md. High Blood Pressure Commn., 1983-86. Recipient spl. contbn. award VA, 1993, 94. Mem. APHA (health law forum), Am. Soc. Law, Medicine and Ethics, Assn. Health Svcs. Researchers. Democrat. Home: 9900 Tailspin Ln Apt I Baltimore MD 21220-2618

PARSHALL, JANET DIFRANCESCA, broadcaster; b. Evanston, Ill., May 4, 1950; d. Vince and T. Margaret (Paul) DiF.; m. Craig Littleton Parshall, May 22, 1971; children: Sarah, Rebekah, Samuel, Joseph. BA, Carroll Coll., 1972. Cert. tchr. Tchr. pub. schs., Waukesha, Wis., 1972-74; broadcaster Sta. WKSH, Brookfield, Wis., 1986-88, Sta. WVCY, Milw., 1988-90, Sta. WYLO, Milw., 1990-92; broadcaster, spl. asst. to pres. Concerned Women for Am., Washington, 1993—; rep., appointee Wis. Women's Coun., Madison, 1990-93, Gov.'s Commn. on Women, Madison, 1991-93; columnist Family Voice Mag., 1992. Author: (with others) Who Will Save the Children? 1991. Sub. host broadcaster Pat Buchanan Show, Washington, 1993—; mem. panel PBS To the Contrary, Owenings Mills, Md. Recipient Gov.'s award for bravery, Gov. of Wis., 1966. Office: Concerned Women for Am 370 L'Efant Promenade SW Ste 800 Washington DC 20024

PARSON, BEVERLY A., foundation administrator; b. Saint Louis, Nov. 10, 1952; d. William Porter and Lovie (Woods) West; m. Edward Kenneth Parson, Mar. 25, 1972; 1 child, Leslie Nicole. B Liberal Studies, St. Louis U., 1983. Cons. dental practice mgmt. Dental Directions Svcs., St. Louis, 1983-87; dir. program and svcs. ea. Mo. chpt. Arthritis Found., St. Louis, 1987—; cons. dental practice mgmt. multi specialty groups, Mo., Ill., 1983-87; developer-medically underserved ednl. programming, St. Louis, 1989-93; cons. Guide to Working with Medically Underserved Populations, Atlanta, 1990-93; creator First Com. for Medically Underserved Population, St. Louis, 1990-93; bd. mem. Mo. State Task Force Arthritis in the Working Years, 1990-93; mem. patient svcs. subcom. Nat. Arthritis Found., 1992-93; mem. adv. bd. Mo. Boothill Edn. Program, 1993. Advocate, speaker St. Louis U.-Geriatric Summer Inst., St. Louis, 1992, United Way, St. Louis, 1990-93, Gov.'s Conf. on Aging, St. Louis, 1993; bd. dirs. Grace Hill Wellness Initiative, 1991-93. Recipient award of excellence Nat. Arthritis Found., Atlanta, 1992, Profl. Achievement award, 1993, Yes I Can award Sentinel Newspaper, St. Louis, 1993. Mem. Arthritis Found. Staff Assn. (grants and recognition com. 1991-93, profl. achievement award 1993). Democrat. Home: 810 Leonard Dr Saint Louis MO 63119-1330 Office: Arthritis Found Ea Mo 8390 Delmar Blvd Saint Louis MO 63124-2100

PARSON, SARAH JANE, account executive-insurance; b. Phila., Nov. 11, 1931; d. Harry and Dorothy (Beatty) P. Grad. high sch., Phila., 1949. Typist, clk. Hartford Steam Boiler I & I Co., Phila., 1949-69, underwriter, 1969-86, sr. mktg. exec., 1986-93; acct. exec. Murray Ins. Agy., Scranton, Pa., 1994—. Contbr. articles to profl. jours. Recipient Ins. Women of Yr. award Greater Scranton Ins. Women, 1991, Rep. award Ins. Systems Unltd., 1991. Mem. Northeastern Pa. Ins. Assn. (past pres. 1991-92), The Scranton Club, Order of Eastern Star (worthy matron 1966-67, 81-82, 90-91). Democrat. Baptist. Home: 6817 Guyer Ave Philadelphia PA 19142-2518

PARSONNET, MIA, physician, writer; b. Vienna, Austria, Jan. 19, 1924; came to U.S., 1939; d. Oser and Sabine (Huebscher) Eimer; m. Victor Parsonnet, June 22, 1950; children: Jeffrey, Brian, Julie. AB, UCLA, 1943; MD, Med. Coll. Pa., 1951. Intern Newark Beth Israel Med. Ctr.; resident in internal medicine Newark City Hosp.; fellowship in therapeutics NYU, Bellevue; physician Millburn, N.Y. Author: What's Really in Our Food, 1991. Home: 113 Sagamore Rd Millburn NY 07041

PARSONS, DARLENE M., psychotherapist, consultant; b. Denver, June 3, 1953; d. Mary Lou Roth; m. Britt Parsons, June 26, 1987; 1 child, Tiffany; 1 child from a previous marriage, Angela Wills. BA magna cum laude in Transpersonal Psychology, Met. State Coll., Denver, 1986; MA in Counseling Psychology and Counselor Edn., U. Colo., 1992. Cert. pre-sch. tchr.; cert. dir. qualified day-care adminstrn.; cert. suicide prevention tng.; cert. critical incident stress debriefing. Pre-sch. tchr. Englewood, Colo., 1982-89; adminstrv. asst. So. Denver Cardiac Rehab., 1989-92; psychotherapist, supr. Adams Community Mental Health Ctr. Cities in the Schs., Commerce City, Colo., 1992—; cons. Premarital Relationship Enhancement Program, Aurora, Colo., 1992—; psychotherapist resdl. group homes Adams Cmty. Mental Health Ctr., 1993—; master trainer Aggression Replacement Tng. Colo. scholar Met. State Coll., 1984-86. Mem. Am. Assn. Counseling and Devel. (Colo. state br.), Am. Mental Health Counseling Assn., Internat. Assn. Marriage and Family Counselors, Colo. Mental Health Counseling Assn., Chi Sigma Iota, Beta Alpha Omega (exec. counsel 1991, 92). Office: Adams Community Mental Health Ctr 7840 Pecos St Denver CO 80221-3859

PARSONS, ESTELLE, actress; b. Lynn, Mass., Nov. 20, 1927; d. Eben and Elinor (Mattson) P.; m. Richard Gehman, Dec. 19, 1953 (div. Aug. 1958); children: Martha and Abbie (twins); m. Peter L. Zimroth, Jan. 2, 1983; 1 child, Abraham. B.A. in Polit. Sci., Conn. Coll. Women, 1949; student, Boston U. Law Sch., 1949-50. Stage appearances include: Happy Hunting, 1957, Whoop Up, 1958, Beg, Borrow or Steal, 1960, Threepenny Opera, 1960, Mrs. Dally Has a Lover, 1962, Ready When You Are C.B, 1964, Malcolm, 1965, Seven Descents of Myrtle, 1968, And Miss Reardon Drinks a Little, 1971, Mert and Phil, 1974, The Norman Conquests, 1975-76, Ladies of the Alamo, 1977, Miss Margarida's Way, 1977-78, The Pirates of Penzance, 1981, The Shadow Box, 1994; adapted, dir., performer Orgasmo Adulto Escapes from the Zoo, 1983, The Unguided Missile, Baba Goya, 1989, Shimada, 1992; film appearances include: Bonnie and Clyde, 1966; Rachel, Rachel, 1967, I Never Sang for My Father, 1969, Dick Tracy, 1990, Boys On The Side, 1995; TV appearances include: Roseanne, 1990—; artistic dir. N.Y. Shakespeare Festival Players, 1986. Recipient Theatre World award, 1962-63, Obie award, 1964; recipient award Motion Picture Acad. Arts and Scis., 1967; Recipient Medal of Honor, Conn. Coll., 1969. Home: 505 West End Ave New York NY 10024-4320

PARSONS, HELGA LUND, writer; b. Seattle, Sept. 5, 1906; d. Gunnar and Marie Pauline (Vognild) Lund; m. Durwin David Algyer, June 6, 1937 (dec. 1971); children: Deanne Algyer Mathisen, Marilyn A. McIntosh; m. James Stewart Parsons, Sept. 30, 1972 (dec. 1988). Grad., Columbia Coll. Expression, Chgo., 1926. Lead actress Repertory Playhouse, Seattle, 1929-34; assoc. prof. drama U. Wash., 1931-32; dir. apprentice group Repertory Playhouse, Seattle 1932-34; writer, anchor radio programs Bon Marche Dept. Store, Seattle 1933-35; v.p. creative dir. Norwegian Am. Mus., Decorah, Iowa 1960-66. Author: Norway Travel Newspaper Series, Seattle, 1930, Concert Touring, Monodramas, 1936, (novelized version) Blondie and Dagwood King Features, 1946; script writer serials for WOR, CBS, NBC, N.Y.C.; appeared in Solid Gold Cadillac, I Remember Mama; editor Surfsedge Newsletter. Activities chmn. Glenview, Naples. Mem. Norwegian Am. Mus. (life), MIT (hon.). Republican.

PARSONS, MARCIA PHILLIPS, judge. Bankruptcy judge U.S. Bankruptcy Ct. (Tenn. ea. dist.), 6th circuit, Greeneville, 1994—. Office: US Courthouse 101 Summer St West Greeneville TN 37743*

PARSONS, MARILYN TABOR, school librarian; b. Bluefield, W.Va., Aug. 12, 1949; d. Marvin Alvin and Blanche Marie (Hill) Tabor; m. Jackie Lee Parsons, Aug. 14, 1971. BA, Marshall U., 1971; MA, Tenn. Tech. U., 1989. Cert. elem. tchr., K-12 libr. sci., K-8 adminstrn. and supervision, all Tenn. Tchr. McDowell County Schs., Welch, W.Va., 1971-72; elem. libr. Binghamton (N.Y.) City Schs., 1972-74, Tazewell (Va.) County Schs., 1974-78, Anderson County Schs., Clinton, Tenn., 1978—; mem. Anderson County Schs. Core Tech. Team, Clinton, 1993—. Active libr. com. Bearden Meth. Ch., Knoxville, Tenn., chancel choir. Mem. Tenn. Assn. Sch. Librs. (chair conf. com. 1992), Tenn. Libr. Assn., ALA, NEA, Tenn. Edn. Assn., Tenn. Reading Assn., Anderson County Reading Assn., Anderson County Elem. Librs. Assn. (elem. coord. 1978—), West Oaks Community Club (sec. 1978—, past pres., past v.p.), Alpha Delta Kappa (pres. 1992—, past historian, past pres.-elect). Democrat. Home: 7716 Luscombe Dr Knoxville TN 37919

PARSONS, MINDY (MINDY ENOS), magazine editor; b. Cin., May 18, 1962; d. Max Allen and Margery Ann (White) Enos; m. Judd Lewis Parsons, Sept. 4, 1993; children: Cody Robert and Savannah Anne (twins). AA in Liberal Arts, Brevard Community Coll., 1983; BSBA, Fla. Inst. Tech., 1986; MBA, N.Y. Inst., Boca Raton, Fla., 1992. Mem. adminstrv. support staff IBM, Boca Raton, 1980, 81; dir. mktg. Progressive Pub., Melbourne, Fla., 1986; owner, pub. Echelon Pub. Inc., Melbourne, 1986-87; editor Keuthan Communications Inc., Melbourne, 1987-89; staff writer First Mktg. Corp., Pompano Beach, Fla., 1989-90; assoc. editor Billboard Publs. Inc., Coral Springs, Fla., 1990-92, Caribbean Clipper, Inc., Clearwater, Fla., 1992-93; reporter South Fla. News Network, Coral Springs, 1993-94; owner Creative Communications, Delray Beach, Fla., 1993—. Author: How to Save for Your Child's Education, 1990; editor: Soccer for Children, 1988, History of Bahamas, 1990; contbr. articles to profl. publs. Vol. Humane Soc. of Broward County, Coral Springs, 1990-91. Recipient Best Defensive Player award Hotlanta Volleyball Classic III, 1991. Mem. NAFE, Soc. Am. Bus. Editors and Writers, NOW. Republican. Methodist. Home: 221 SE 34th Ave Boynton Beach FL 33435-8632 Office: PO Box 1711 Delray Beach FL 33447

PARSONS, SCOTTIE, artist; b. Watonga, Okla., Nov. 6, 1925; d. Robert Lee and Flora Elizabeth (Tuel) Hatcher; m. Frank Duane Stewart, Dec. 22, 1948 (dec.); children: Mark Duane, Mary Jan Stewart McDonald; m. Clyde Wallace Parsons Jr., Nov. 6, 1971. BS in Art Edn., Midwestern State U., 1968, student, 1968, 69, 84; student, So. Meth. U., Dallas, 1982-83. Tchr. art Wichita Falls (Tex.) Pub. Schs., 1969-70; owner Fine Arts Gallery, Wichita Falls, 1971; tchr. in field; studio artist, Wichita Falls, 1978—. One-person shows include LewAllen Gallery, 1991, William Campbell Contemporary Gallery, 1992, 94; exhibited in group shows at Invitational Fund Raiser Exhbn., 1988-94, LewAllen Gallery, Santa Fe, 1988—, William Campbell Contemporary Gallery, Ft. Worth, 1989—, Horwitch LewAllen Gallery, 1994, 95, Arlington (Tex.) Mus. Fine Art, 1993. Named to Women's Hall of Fame, North Tex. Com., 1988. Mem. Tex. Fine Arts Assn. (bd. dirs. 1988-94, Citation winner 1978, 80, 83, 84, 85, Juror's Choice award, 1983), Wichita Falls Art Assn. (pres. 1987-89, 91-93), Alum Santa Fe Inst. Fine Arts Alumni Assn. Republican. Presbyterian. Home: 2614 Amherst Dr Wichita Falls TX 76308 Office: Studio Artist Atelier 2629 Plaza Pkwy Wichita Falls TX 76308

PARSONS-SALEM, DIANE LORA, lawyer; b. Arlington, Mass., Apr. 17, 1945; d. Hugh Crocker and Tryphena Grace (Reader) Parsons; m. William Stephen Holloway, Mar. 20, 1993; 1 child, Nicole D. Salem. BA, Boston U., 1967; JD, Suffolk U., 1970. Bar: Mass. 1970, U.S. Dist. Ct. Mass. 1972, U.S. Supreme Ct. 1979. Atty. Allstate Ins. Co., Weston, Mass., 1970-72; assoc. Haig Der Manuelian, Boston, 1972-80; sr. assoc. Widett, Slater & Goldman, P.C., Boston, 1980-84; real estate atty. Friendly Ice Cream Corp., Wilbraham, Mass., 1984-87; asst. gen. counsel Hardee's Food Systems, Inc., Rocky Mount, N.C., 1987-90, dep. gen. counsel, 1990—. Mem. ABA, Mass. Bar Assn. Home: 724 Eagles Ter Rocky Mount NC 27804-6404 Office: Hardees Food Systems Inc 1233 Hardees Blvd Rocky Mount NC 27804-2815

PARTEE, BARBARA HALL, linguist, educator; b. Englewood, N.J., June 23, 1940; d. David B. and Helen M. Hall; m. Morriss Henry Partee, 1966 (div. 1971); children: Morriss M., David M., Joel T.; m. Emmon Werner Bach, Nov. 2, 1973. BA with high honors in Math., Swarthmore Coll., 1961; PhD in Linguistics, MIT, 1965; DSc (hon.), Swarthmore Coll., 1989, Charles U., Prague, Czechoslovakia, 1992. Asst. prof. UCLA, 1965-69, assoc. prof., 1969-73; assoc. prof. linguistics and philosophy U. Mass., Amherst, 1972-73, prof., 1973-90, Disting. Univ. prof., 1990—, head dept. linguistics, 1987-93; fellow Ctr. for Advanced Study in Behavior Scis., 1976-77; mem. bd. mgrs. Swarthmore Coll., 1990—. Author: (with Stockwell and Schachter) The Major Syntactic Structures of English, 1972, Fundamentals of Mathematics for Linguists, 1979, (with ter Meulen and Wall) Mathematical Methods in Linguistics, 1990; editor: Montague Grammar, 1976; co-editor: (with Chierchia and Turner) Properties, Types and Meaning, Vol. I: Foundational Issues, Vol. II: Semantic Issues, 1989; mem. editoral bd: Language, 1967-73, Linguistic Inquiry, 1972-79, Theoretical Linguistics, 1974—, Linguistics and Philosophy, 1977—. Recipient Chancellor's medal U. Mass., 1977; NEH fellow, 1982-83; Internat. Rsch. and Exchanges Bd. fellow, 1989-90. Mem. NAS (chair anthropology sect. 1993—), Linguistic Soc. Am. (pres. 1986), Am. Philos. Assn., Assn. Computational Linguistics, Am. Acad. Arts and Scis., Sigma Xi. Home: 50 Hobart Ln Amherst MA 01002-1321 Office: U Mass Dept Linguistics Amherst MA 01003

PARTHEMORE, JACQUELINE G., physician, educator; b. Harrisburg, Pa., Dec. 21, 1940; d. Philip Mark and Emily (Buvit) Parthemore; m. Alan Morton Blank, Jan. 8, 1967; children: Stephen Eliot, Laura Elise. BA, Wellesley Coll., 1962; MD, Cornell U., 1966. Research edn. assoc., asst. prof. med. Veterans Adminstn. Hosp., San Diego, Calif., 1974-78; asst. prof. Sch. of Medicine U. Calif., San Diego, 1974-80; staff physician Veterans Adminstrn. Med. Ctr., San Diego, La Jolla, 1978-79; assoc. prof. medicine, 1980-85; asst. chief, med. service, staff physician Veterans Adminstrn. Med. Ctr., San Diego, La Jolla, 1979-80; acting chief, med. service VA Med. Ctr.,

La Jolla, 1980-81, chief of staff, 1984—; prof. medicine, assoc. dean U. Calif. Sch. Medicine, San Diego, 1985—; ex officio representing chief med. dir. VA, NIH. Contbr. articles to profl. jours. Recipient Bullock's 1st Annaul Portfolio award, 1985, San Diego Pres.'s Council Woman of Yr. award, 1985, Calif. Women in Govt. award, 1985, YWCA Tribute to Women in Industry award, 1987. Mem. Endocrine Soc., Am. Fedn. Clin. Rsch., Am. Bone and Mineral Soc., Nat. Assn. VA Chiefs of Staff (pres. 1989-91), Am. Assn. Clin. Endocrinologists, Wellesley Coll. Alumnae Assn. (1st v.p. 1992—). Office: VA Med Ctr 3350 La Jolla Village Dr San Diego CA 92161-0002

PARTON, DOLLY REBECCA, singer, composer, actress; b. Sevier County, Tenn., Jan. 19, 1946; d. Robert Lee and Avie Lee (Owens) P.; m. Carl Dean, May 30, 1966. Country music singer, rec. artist, composer, actress, radio and TV personality; entrepreneur, owner entertainment park Dollywood, established 1985. Radio appearances include Grand Ole Opry, WSM Radio, Nashville, Cass Walker program, Knoxville; TV appearances include Porter Wagoner Show, from 1967, Cass Walker program, Bill Anderson Show, Wilburn Bros. Show, Barbara Mandrell Show; rec. artist, Mercury, Monument, RCA , CBS record cos.; star movie Nine to Five, 1980, The Best Little Whorehouse in Texas, 1982, Rhinestone, 1984, Steel Magnolias, 1989, Straight Talk, 1991; albums include Here You Come Again (Grammy award 1978), Real Love, 1985, Just the Way I Am, 1986, Portrait, 1986, Think About Love, 1986, Trio (with Emmylou Harris, Linda Ronstadt) (Grammy award 1988), 1987, Heartbreaker, Great Balls of Fire, Rainbow, 1988, White Limozeen, 1989, Home for Christmas, 1990, Eagle When She Flies, 1991, Slow Dancing with the Moon, 1993 (Grammy nomination, Best Country Vocal Collaboration for Romeo (with Tanya Tucker, Billy Ray Cyrus, Kathy Mattea, Pam Tillis, & Mary-Chapin Carpenter), (with Tammy Wynette and Loretta Lynn) Honky Tonk Angels, 1994; composer numerous songs including Nine to Five (Grammy award 1981, Acad. award nominee and Golden Globe award nominee 1981); author: Dolly, 1994. Recipient (with Porter Wagoner) Vocal Group of Yr. award, 1968; Vocal Duo of Yr. award All Country Music Assn., 1970, 71; Nashville Metronome award, 1979; Am. Music award for best duo performance (with Kenny Rogers), 1984; named Female Vocalist of Yr., 1975, 76; Country Star of Yr., Sullivan Prodns., 1977; Entertainer of Yr., Country Music Assn., 1978; People's Choice award, 1980, 88; Female Vocalist of Yr., Acad. Country Music, 1980; Dolly Parton Day proclaimed, Sevier County, Tenn., designated Oct. 7, 1967, Los Angeles, Sept. 20, 1979; recipient Grammy awards for best female country vocalist, 1978, 81, for best country song, 1981, for best country vocal performance with group, 1987; co-recipient (with Emmylou Harris and Linda Ronstadt) Acad. Country Music award for album of the yr., 1987; named to Small Town of Am. Hall of Fame, 1988, East Tenn. Hall of Fame, 1988. Address: c/o Maureen O'Connor Rogers & Cowan 10000 Santa Monica Blvd Los Angeles CA 90067-7007*

PARTRIDGE, CONNIE R., advertising executive; b. Bklyn., Apr. 10, 1941; d. Nicholas and Teresa (Monteleone) Sorrentino; m. Vincent Richard Partridge, Dec. 17, 1960 (div. Aug. 1983); children: Jean Marie, Marianne, James. Student, Coll. New Rochelle (N.Y.), 1958-60; BA, Coll. Old Westbury, 1979. Sr. account exec. Finesse Promotions, Queens Village, N.Y., 1979-84; pres. Partridge Promotions, Wheatley Heights, N.Y., 1984—. Pres. Taukomas Sch. PTA, Wheatley Heights, N.Y., 1972-74; v.p. Half Hollow Hills Coun., Dix Hills, N.Y., 1974-76; campaign mgr. Half Hollow Hills Sch. Bd. Elections, 1978; dir. Suffolk County Women's Bus. Enterprise Coalition, 1989—; mem. program adv. bd. Sta. WLIW/Channel 21. Recipient Jenkins Meml. award N.Y. State PTA, 1974. Mem. NAFE, Nat. Assn. Women Bus. Owners (L.I. chpt. founder 1985, corr. sec. 1986, v.p. 1989, pres. 1994—), L.I. Assn./Small Bus. Coun., L.I. Advt. Club, L.I. Ctr. Bus. and Profl. Women, Splty. Advt. Assn. Internat. (cert. advt. specialist), Splty. Advt. Assn. Greater N.Y. (scholarship award), Pres.'s Roundtable. Democrat. Roman Catholic. Office: 55 Waterford Dr Wheatley Heights NY 11798

PARTYKA, DEBORAH ANN, laboratory administrator; b. Independence, Ohio, June 9, 1961; d. Chester and Henrietta E. (Peldyak) P. BS in Clin. Arts and Sci., Hiram Coll., 1983. Lic. med. technologist. Med. technologist Cleve. Clinic Found., 1983-89; supr. hematology Meridia Huron Hosp., Cleve., 1989—, coord. total quality mgmt., 1989—. Mem. Clin. Lab. Mgmt. Assn. (OHio divsn.), Am. Soc. Clin. Pathologists. Republican. Roman Catholic. Office: Meridia Huron Hosp 13951 Terrace Rd Cleveland OH 44112

PASCH, SUZANNE HARRIET, dean, educator; b. Milw., Aug. 20, 1943; d. Nathan Franklin and Rose Helen (Tolkan) P.; children: Lori Michelle Wiviott Tishler, Stephen Daniel Wiviott. BS in English with highest honors, U. Wis., 1965, MS in Edn. Psychology, 1966, PhD in Ednl. Psychology, 1970. Asst. prof. ednl. psychology U. Wis., Milw., 1972-74, assoc. prof. ednl. psychology, 1975-93, acting dir. Ctr. for Women's Studies, 1984-86, dir. Ctr. Teaching Edn., 1988-93; dean Sch. Edn., prof. Trenton State Coll., 1993—. Contbr. numerous articles to profl. jours. Mem. Am. Ednl. Rsch. Edn., Am. Assn. Colls. of Tchr. Edn., Assn. Teacher Educators, Assn. Advancement Internat. Edn. Home: 17 Wilkinson Way Princeton NJ 08540 Office: Trenton State Coll Hillwood Lakes CN 4700 Trenton NJ 08650

PASCHAL, BEVERLY JO, lawyer; b. Birmingham, Ala., Aug. 21, 1955; d. Arthur Buel and Nellie Jo (Weaver) P.; m. Richard F. Poston, Aug., 1992. BA with honor, U. North Ala., 1976; JD, Birmingham Sch. Law, 1982. Bar: Ala. 1982, U.S. Dist. Ct. (no. dist.) Ala. 1982, U.S. Ct. Appeals (11th cir.) 1983. Assoc. St. John & St. John, Cullman, Ala., 1982-84; pvt. practice Cullman, 1984-85, 92—; ptnr. Paschal & Collins, Cullman, 1986-92. Pres. Cullman County Hist. Soc., 1986-87. Named one of Outstanding Young Women Am., 1984; recipient Citiation of Honor, Young Career Women Program, 1989. Mem. ABA, Assn. Trial Lawyers Am., Ala. Trial Lawyers Assn., Cullman County Bar Assn., Pilot Club Internat. (Sweetheart award Cullman 1985), Cullman Bus. and Profl. Women's Assn. (young careerist award). Home: 1797 County Rd 972 Cullman AL 35055-8866 Office: 905 2nd Ave SW Ste D 905 Cullman AL 35055

PASCOE, PATRICIA HILL, writer, state senator; b. Sparta, Wis., June 1, 1935; d. Fred Kirk and Edith (Kilpatrick) H.; m. D. Monte Pascoe, Aug. 3, 1957; children: Sarah, Ted, Will. BA, U. Colo., 1957; MA, U. Denver, 1968, PhD, 1982. Tchr. Sequoia Union High Sch. Dist., Redwood City, Calif. and Hayward (Calif.) Union High Sch. Dist., 1957-60; instr. Met. State Coll., Denver, 1969-75; instr. Denver U., 1975-77, 81, research asst. bur. ednl. research, 1981-82; tchr. Kent Denver Country Day, Englewood, Colo., 1982-84; freelance writer Denver, 1985—; mem. Colo. Senate, Denver, 1989-92, 95—; commr. Edn. Commn. of the States, Denver, 1975-82. Contbr. articles to numerous publs. and jours. Bd. dirs. Samaritan House, 1990-94, Cystic Fibrosis Found., 1989-93; pres. East High Sch. Parent, Tchr. and Student Assn., Denver, 1984-85; mem. Moore Budget Adv. Com., Denver, 1966-72; legis. chmn. alumni bd. U. Colo., Boulder, 1987-89; del. Dem. Nat. Conv., San Francisco, 1984, N.Y.C., 1992. Mem. Soc. Profl. Journalists, Common Cause (bd. dirs. Denver chpt. 1986-88), Phi Beta Kappa. Presbyterian.

PASCOLINI, DONNA, accountant; b. Pitts., Sept. 28, 1967; d. Mario Carl and Christa Agnes Pascolini. BS in Acctg., U. Akron, 1989; MBA, John Carroll U., 1994. Mktg. ops. acct. Babcock & Wilcox, Barberton, Ohio, 1989-90, fin. forecaster and analyst, 1990-93, cost ledger acct., 1993-94, replacement parts acct., 1994—. Mem. Inst. Mgrl. Accts. (student pres., dir. advt. 1987-90), U. Akron Ski Club (v.p. 1985-89).

PASE, MARILYN NELSEN, nurse, educator; b. Brigham City, Utah, Feb. 13, 1943; d. Daniel Clarence Nelsen and Aldine (Anderson) Nelsen Johns. BSN with high honors, U. Ala., Huntsville, 1974, BS in Biology with high honors, 1984; MSN, Vanderbilt U., 1975. RN, Ala., Utah, N.Mex. Staff nurse Med. Ctr. Hosp., Huntsville, 1974-77, LDS Hosp., Salt Lake City, 1977 summer; clin. preceptor for grad. students U. Ala., Birmingham, 1978; instr. nursing, then asst. prof. U. Ala., Huntsville, 1975-83; mem. nursing faculty Oakwood Coll., Huntsville, 1985-86; infection control nurse, employee health nurse Crestwood Hosp., Huntsville, 1984-86; staff nurse Meml. Med. Ctr., Las Cruces, N.Mex., 1987-91; asst. prof. dept. nursing N.Mex. State U., Las Cruces, 1988—. Contbr. to profl. publs., reviewer. Mem. ANA, AACN (chpt. pres. 1991-92), N.Mex. Nurses Assn. (exec. bd. Dist. 14 1994, dist. pres. 1990-93, Nurse Researcher award 1994), Sigma Theta Tau, Delta Kappa. Mem. LDS Ch. Office: Dept Nursing N Mex State U Las Cruces NM 88003

PASHLEY, MARY MARTHA, corporate finance educator; b. Oak Ridge, Tenn., May 12, 1956; d. John Hamilton and Wilogene (Queener) P. BA, Vanderbilt U., 1976; MS, U. Tenn., 1978, MBA, 1985, PhD, 1986. Teaching asst. U. Tenn., Knoxville, 1978-82, rsch. asst., 1982-83, lectr., 1983-85; asst. prof. fin. Tenn. Tech. U., Cookeville, 1986-93, assoc. prof., 1993—, assoc. dir. honors program; textbook reviewer Scott, Foresman & Co., 1988; ad hoc referee Fin. Mgmt., 1988, Applied Fin. Econs., 1991—, Fin. Rev., 1988—. Treas Mastersingers Community Chorus, 1988-89. Walter Melville Bonham Meml. scholar U. Tenn., 1982-93. Mem. Am. Bus. Women's Assn. (charter v.p. Chilhowee Bandstand chpt. 1984), Fin. Mgmt. Assn. (faculty liason 1986—, presenter 1980, 82, 87, 94), Nat. Collegiate Hons. Coun., Mensa proctor 1990-94, registrar 1992, 94, Mid Tenn.), Beta Gamma Sigma, (chpt. sec.-treas. 1987-88, pres. 1988-89), Phi Kappa Phi, Omicron Delta Kappa. Office: Tenn Tech U Dept Econs and Fin Cookeville TN 38505

PASKAWICZ, JEANNE FRANCES, anesthesiologist; b. Phila., Mar. 3, 1954; d. Alex and Lillian (Pyluck) P. BSc, Phila. Coll. Pharmacy; MA, Villanova U., 1973; postgrad., St. Joseph U., 1979; PhD, Kensington U., 1984. Mem. anesthesiology staff Einstein Med. Ctr., Phila., 1990-94, Temple U. Hosp., 1994—; mem. detox./rehab. staff Presbyn. Med. Ctr., Phila., 1984—; house officer MCD-Elkins Park (Pa.) Campus, 1990—; mem. psychiatry staff Hahnemann U. Hosp., Phila., 1984-90; hostage negotiator Office of Mental Health, Phila., 1984-90; mem. surgery/anesthesiology staff Mt. Sinai Hosp., Phila., 1989-91. Bd. dirs. Phila. Coll. Pharmacy, St. Joseph U. Mem. NAFE, Nat. Parks Conservation Assn., North Shore Animal League, Amvets, DAV Comdrs. Club, Lambda Kappa Sigma.

PASS, CAROLYN JOAN, dermatologist; b. Balt., May 14, 1941; d. Isidore Earl and Rhea (Koplowitz) P.; B.S., U. Md., 1962, M.D., 1966; m. Richard Malcolm Susel, June 23, 1963; children—Steven, Gary. Rotating intern USPHS Hosp., Balt., 1966-67; med. resident St. Agnes Hosp., Balt., 1967-68; dermatology resident and fellow U. Md. Sch. Medicine Hosps., 1968-71; pvt. practice specializing in dermatology, Balt. and Ellicott City, Md., 1971—; mem. staff James Lawrence Kernan, St. Agnes; vol. dermatology clinics U. Md., St. Agnes hosps.; asst. clin. prof. dermatology U. Md. Sch. Medicine, 1978—; mem. exec. com. adv. bd. Nat. Program in Dermatology, 1975. Diplomate Am. Bd. Dermatology. Mem. AMA, Med. and Chirurgical Soc. State Md. (del.), Balt. City Med. Soc. (del. 1974, pub. rels. com., 1992-94, alternate del. 1994—), Am. Women's Med. Assn., Am. Acad. Dermatology (award exhibit 1970), Soc. Investigative Dermatology, Md. Dermatology Soc. (sec.-treas. 1974-76, pres. 1976-77), Soc. Contemporary Medicine and Surgery, U. Md. Sch. Medicine Alumnae Assn. (bd. dirs. 1987—). Jewish. Clubs: Suburban Country (Balt.); Country Garden. Gourmet. Home: Timberlane 8410 Park Heights Ave Baltimore MD 21208-1716 Office: Pine Heights Med Ctr 1001 Pine Heights Ave Ste 301 Baltimore MD 21229-5291

PASS, LISA KEI, psychologist; b. Reidsville, N.C., Feb. 1, 1957; d. Josephus Garland and Mary Frances (Burroughs) P.; m. John Halebian, Sept. 5, 1987; 1 child, Samantha Whitney. BA cum laude, Clark U., 1979; MA in Sch. Psychology, NYU, 1982, PhD in Sch. Psychology, 1988. Lic. psychologist, N.Y.; cert. sch. psychologist, N.Y. Psychology intern Jewish Child Care Assn., N.Y.C., 1982-83; grad. asst./teaching fellow grad. dept. ednl. psychology NYU, N.Y.C., 1983-84; sch. psychologist Shield Inst., N.Y.C., 1984-87; staff psychologist Schneider Children's Hosp., New Hyde Park, N.Y., 1988-94; pschol. cons. in pvt. practice N.Y.C., 1994—; psychol. cons. Cons. on Call, N.Y.C., 1991. Mem. APA, Nat. Assn. Sch. Psychologist, N.Y. State Psychol. Assn. Democrat. Unitarian. Home and Office: 250 E 73d St 16E New York NY 10021

PASSALACQUA, ANGELA VIRGINIA, lawyer; b. Sao Paulo, Brazil, Mar. 26, 1961; came to U.S. 1973; d. Giuseppe and Ilda (Correa Peixoto) P.; m. Leonard Samuel Baker, Jan. 24, 1987; children: Joshua Mathew, Marc Alexander, Virginia Ilda. BA, Rutgers U., 1982, JD, 1985. Bar: N.J. 1985, U.S. Dist. Ct. N.J. 1985, Pa. 1985. Jud. law clk. Judge Superior Ct., Camden, N.J., 1985-86; asst. dep. pub. advocate div. mental health advocacy Pub. Advocate's Office, Camden, 1986-89; asst. pub. defender Camden County, N.J., 1991—; adj. prof. legal rsch. and writing, Rutgers U., Camden, N.J., 1990-92, dir. legal rsch. and writing program, 1992—. Office: Rutgers Law Sch-Camden 5th and Penn St Camden NJ 08102

PASSI, BETH, school administrator. Dir. Blake Lower Sch., Hopkins, Minn., 1982—. Recipient elem. sch. recognition award U.S. Dept. Edn., 1989-90, 93-94, Bush prin. leadership fellow, 1993-94. Office: Blake Lower Sch 110 Blake Rd Hopkins MN 55343

PASSONS, DONNA JANELLE, academic administrator; b. Ft. Benning, Ga., Apr. 15, 1951; d. Robert James and Mary Anita (Morris) P.; m. Phillip Michael Holmes, Oct. 27, 1989. BA in Govt., U. Tex., 1980, MBA, 1989. Adminstrv. asst. Gov.'s Div. Planning Coord., Austin, Tex., 1972-74, Commn. on Pub. Edn., Tex. Ho. of Reps., Austin, 1975, Med. Profl. Liability Study Commn., Austin, 1975-77; adminstrv. asst. U. Tex. Sch. of Law, Austin, 1977-80, conf. coord. Office Continuing Legal Edn., 1980-84; asst. dir. U. Tex. Sch. Law, Austin, 1984-85, dir., 1985-89, asst. dean Office Continuing Legal Edn., 1989-94; exec. dir. Tex. Inst. Continuing Legal Edn., Austin, 1994—; pres. Specialized Profl. Insts., Inc., 1992—. Mem. ABA, Assn. CLE Adminstrs. (bd. dirs.-at-large 1984-85, treas. 1985-86, sec. 1986-87, pres.-elect 1987-88, pres. 1988-89), Meeting Planners Internat. (bd. dirs. Hill Country chpt. exec. com. 1985-86, 91), Am. Assn. Law Schs. (bd. dirs. CLE com. 1991-92, sec. CLE com. 1992-93, chmn.-elect 1993-94, chmn. 1994—), Tex. Soc. Assn. Execs. Office: PO Box 4646 Austin TX 78765-4646

PASSWATER, BARBARA GAYHART, real estate broker; b. Phila., July 10, 1945; d. Clarence Leonard and Margaret Jamison; m. Richard Albert Passwater, June 2, 1964; children: Richard Alan, Michael Eric. AA, Goldey-Beacom Coll., 1963; BA, Salisbury State U., 1982. Notary pub., Md. Sec. DuPont, Wilmington, Del., 1963-65, Nuclear-Chgo., Silver Spring, Md., 1965-67; office mgr. Montgomery County Sch. System, Wheaton, Md., 1977-79; adminstrv. asst. Solgar Nutritional Rsch. Ctr., Berlin, Md., 1979—; assoc. broker Prudential-Groff Realty, Berlin, Md., 1983-87, ReMax, Inc., Berlin, Md., 1987-88; broker, mgr. River Run Sales Ctr., Berlin, Md., 1988—. Treas. Ocean Pines (Md.) Vol. Fire Dept. Aux., 1981-84; emergency med. tech. Ocean Pines (Md.) Vol. Fire Dept., 1983—; sec. Ocean Pines (Md.) Fire Dept., 1990—; mem. Foster Care Review Bd., Snow Hill, Md., 1984—. Mem. Beta Sigma Phi, Phi Kappa Phi. Office: River Run 11433 Beauchamp Rd Berlin MD 21811

PASTER, JANICE D., state legislator; b. St. Louis, Aug. 4, 1942. BA, Northwestern U., 1964; MA, Tufts U., 1967; JD, U. N.Mex., 1984. Pvt. practice, 1984—; mem. N.Mex. State Senate from 10th dist. Democrat. Home: 5553 Eakes Rd NW Albuquerque NM 87107-5529 Address: Senate House State Capitol Sante Fe NM 87503*

PASTERNACKI, LINDA LEA, critical care nurse; b. Green Bay, Wis., May 26, 1947; d. Paul John and Marion M. (Zagzebski) P.; (div.); children: Sam, Dan, Rachel Marie. Nursing diploma, St. Francis Sch. Nursing, Wichita, Kans., 1968; BS, Coll. St. Francis, Joliet, Ill., 1981, MS in Health Adminstrn., 1986. RN med.-surg. St. Francis Hosp., Wichita, 1968-70; RN ICU-critical care unit Sunrise Hosp., Las Vegas, Nev., 1970-72; RN critical care unit Presbyn. Hosp., Albuquerque, 1972-75; RN med. ICU, surg. ICU VA Hosp., Albuquerque, 1976-81; RN emergency rm. Univ. Heights Hosp., Albuquerque, 1981-82; RN ICU, critical care unit Lovelace Med. Ctr., Albuquerque, 1982-86; RN ICU, emergency rm., surg. cornary care, intensive recovery room Presbyn. Hosp., Albuquerque, 1986—; RN emergency rm., ICU, critical care unit St. Joseph Med. Ctr., Albuquerque, 1992—; hyperbaric therapy instr. Presbyn. Hosp., Albuquerque, 1975; clin. instr. U. N.Mex. EMT Sch., Albuquerque, 1980. Mem. AACN. Home: 10605 Central Park Dr NE Albuquerque NM 87123 Office: Presbyn Hosp 1100 Central SE Albuquerque NM 87103

PASTERNAK, JOANNA MURRAY, special education educator; b. Houston, Feb. 9, 1953; d. Lee Roy and Evelyn Mary (Kirmss) Murray; children: Sheila Ann Tanner, Lawrence Ross Tanner IV; m. Allen Pasternak, Jan. 9, 1993. BA in Liberal Arts with honors, Our Lady of the Lake, San Antonio, 1990. Acctg. clk. The Houston Post, 1981-85; owner, art cons. Tanner Fine Art, Houston, 1985-92; spl. edn. tchr. Houston Ind. Sch. Dist., 1991—; art cons. Plz. Gallery, Houston, 1985; mem. benefits com. Houston Ind. Sch. Dist., 1992—. Campaign worker Dem. Party, 1993—; mem. precinct and state del. Dem. Senate, 1994; vol. Nat. Health Care Campaign. Mem. Am. Assn. Children with Learning Disabilities, Tex. Fedn. Tchrs. (bd. dirs. quality ednl. stds. in teaching 1993), Houston Fedn. Tchrs. (chair legis. liaison com. 1993, v.p. 1992—), Greater Houston Area Reading Coun., Delta Mu Delta. Democrat. Home: 2141 Colquitt St Houston TX 77098-3310 Office: Houston Fedn Tchrs 3202 Weslayan St Ste 102 Houston TX 77027-5748

PASTINE, MAUREEN DIANE, university librarian; b. Hays, Kans., Nov. 21, 1944; d. Gerhard Walter and Ada Marie (Hillman) Hillman; m. Jerry Joel Pastine, Feb. 5, 1966. AB, in English, Ft. Hays State U., 1967; MLS, Emporia State U., 1970. Reference librarian U. Nebr.-Omaha, 1971-77; undergrad. libr. U. Ill., Urbana, 1977-79; reference librarian, 1979-80; univ. libr. San Jose State U.-Calif., 1980-85; dir. librs. Wash. State U., Pullman, 1985-89; ctrl. univ. libr. So. Meth. U., 1989—; mem. adv. bd. Foothill Coll. Libr. 1983-85; leader ednl. del. librs. to People's Republic of China, 1985, Australia/New Zealand, 1986, Soviet Union, 1988, East & West Germany, Czechoslovakia, Hungary, Austria, 1991, Rio de Janeiro, 1993. Co-author: Library and Library Related Publications: A Directory of Publishing Opportunities, 1973; asst. compiler: Women's Work and Women's Studies, 1973-74, 1975; compiler procs. Teaching Bibliographic Instruction in Graduate Schools of Library Science, 1981; editor: Integrating Library Use Skills into the General Education Curriculum, 1989; co-editor: In the Spirit of 1991: Access to Western European Libraries and Literature, 1992; contbr. articles to profl. publs. Recipient Disting. Alumni Grad. award Emporia State U., 1986, Dudley Bibliog. Instruction Libr. of Yr. award, 1989. Mem. ALA (chmn. World Book-ALA Goal awards jury 1984-85), Assn. Coll. and Rsch. Librs. (editorial adv. bd. BIS Think Tank 1982-85, chmn. bibliographic instrn. sect. 1983-84, editorial bd. Choice 1983-85, chmn. Miriam Dudley Bibliographic Instrn. Libr. of Yr. award com. 1984-85, mem. task force on librarians as instrs. 1986—, chair task force internat. rels. 1987-89, BIS Libr. of Yr. 1989, rep. to AAAS/CAIP, 1989—, chair internat. rels. com. 1990-94, rsch. libr. of yr. award's com. 1994—, ALA pay equity com. 1994—), Libr. Adminstrn. and Mgmt. Assn. (chmn. stats. sect. com. on devel., orgn., planning and programming 1982-83, sec. stats. sect. exec. com. 1982-83, mem. at large 1986—), ALA Library Instrn. Round Table (long range planning com. 1986—), ALA Libr. Rsch. Round Table, Wash. Libr. Assn., Assn. Libr. Collections & Tech. Svcs. Divsn., Libr. and Info. Tech. Assn., Assn. Specialized and Coop. Libr. Agencies (chair multi-lincs internat. networking discussion group 1990-92), Libr. Rsch. Roundtable, Women's Studies Sect., Eng. and Am. Lit. Studies Discussion Group, Tex. Libr. Assn., Pacific N.W. Libr. Assn., Phi Kappa Phi, Beta Phi Mu. Home: 8720 Hanford Dr Dallas TX 75243-6416 Office: So Meth U Cen Univ Librs Fondren Libr Dallas TX 75275-0135

PASTORKOVICH LENGEL, DIANE, secondary education counselor; b. Charleroi, Pa., June 26, 1962; d. Joseph David and Erminia Rose (Manzini) Pastorkovich; m. Elliott Gordon Lengel, May 6, 1989. BA, Calif. (Pa.) U., 1984, MEd, 1986; postgrad., Slippery Rock U., 1991-92. Cert. ednl. specialist in secondary sch. guidance, Pa.; cert. instr. elem. edn., Pa. Coord. teen parenting program Midwestern Intermediate Unit 4, Grove City, Pa., 1986-88; consultation and edn. coord. Community Counseling Ctr. Mercer County, Hermitage, Pa., 1989-90; counselor, instr. Women's Ctr., New Options Program and Office Transfer Svcs. C.C. of Allegheny County, Pitts., 1992-93; secondary sch. counselor Sharon (Pa.) High Sch., 1993—. Mem. AAUW (Grove City/Slippery Rock Br.), Am. Counseling Assn., Pa. Sch. Counselors Assn., Mercer County Sch. Counselor's Assn. (pres. 1994—), Kappa Delta Pi. Democrat. Roman Catholic. Office: Sharon City Sch Dist 1129 E State St Sharon PA 16146

PATACK, MELISSA B., lawyer; b. Albany, N.Y., Sept. 25, 1956; d. Marvin E. and Sandra R. (Cohen) P. BS in Indsl. and Labor Rels., Cornell U., 1978; JD, Boston U., 1981. Assoc. Friedman & Koven, Chgo., 1981-84, Sachnoff Weaver, Chgo., 1985-87; minority counsel judiciary subcom. cts. U.S. Senate, Washington, 1987-89, minority chief counsel, 1991-94, counsel Sen. Mitch McConnell, 1994—; lobbyist Am. Israel Pub. Affairs Com, Washington, 1987-89. Pres. divsn. young leadership Jewish United Fund, Chgo., 1986-87; bd. dirs. Jewish Community Coun. Washington, 1993—. Republican. Jewish. Office: US Senate Subcom Cts & Adminstrv Practice 120 Russell Office Bldg Washington DC 20510

PATANO, PATRICIA ANN, health and fitness professional, marketing and public relations specialist; b. Chgo., June 14, 1950; d. Thomas Vincent and Gladys Estelle (Olejniczak) P. Student, Los Angeles Pierce Coll., 1968-70, UCLA, 1974-84. Pub. relations mgr. Motel 6, Inc., Century City, Calif., 1974-77; mgr. corp. communications 1st Travel Corp., Van Nuys, Calif., 1977-79; mktg. pub. relations mgr. Unitours, Inc., Los Angeles, 1979-81; asst. v.p. pub. relations Los Angeles Olympic Com., 1981-84; pres., co-owner PaVage Fitness Innovations, Playa del Rey, Calif., 1984-88; dir. spl. projects J.D. Power and Assocs., Agoura Hills, Calif., 1988—; trustee Nat. Injury Prevention Found., San Diego, 1983—; cons. Dick Clark Productions, Burbank, Calif., 1985, Reebok USA Ltd., Boston, 1983—. Co-author: MuscleAerobics, 1985; contbr. articles to profl. jours. Vol. Motion Picture Hosp., Woodland Hills, Calif., 1968-70; bd. dirs. Los Angeles Boys and Girls Club, 1984—; mem. council San Fernando Natural History Mus., 1987-89; big sister Pride House, Van Nuys, 1987-89; active juvenile delinquent program Pride House. Recipient Corp. award Pres.'s Council Phys. Fitness, 1983; fellow Alfred North Whitehead Leaderships Soc.-U. Redlands, 1995. Mem. L.A. Advt. Club, Nat. Injury Prevention Found. (trustee 1984-87), Child Shelter Homes: A Rescue Effort (bd. dirs.), Mid Valley Athletic Club (Reseda, Calif.), Marina City (Marina del Rey, Calif.). Republican. Presbyterian. Clubs: Mid Valley Athletic (Reseda, Calif.); Marina City (Marina del Rey, Calif.). Office: JD Power & Assocs 30401 Agoura Rd Agoura Hills CA 91301-2084

PATE, JACQUELINE HAIL, retired data processing company manager; b. Amarillo, Tex., Apr. 7, 1930; d. Ewen and Virginia Smith (Crosland) Hail; student Southwestern U., Georgetown, Tex., 1947-48; children: Charles (dec.), John Durst, Virginia Pate Edgecomb, Christopher. Exec. sec. Western Gear Corp., Houston, 1974-76; adminstr., treas., dir. Aberrant Behavior Ctr., Personality Profiles, Inc., Corp. Procedures, Inc., Dallas, 1976-79; mgr. regional site svcs programs Digital Equipment Corp., Dallas, 1979-92, ret. 1992. Active PTA, Dallas, 1958-73. Mem. Daus. Republic Tex. Methodist. Home: 7232 Timberidge Fort Worth TX 76180

PATE, MARY RUCZKO, realtor; b. Augusta, Ga., Feb. 15, 1960; d. Leonard Vincent and Sara Margaret (Trimmier) Ruczko; m. Timothy Earl Pate, Mar. 24, 1984; children: Timothy Alexander, Sara Elizabeth. AA, Anderson Coll., 1980; BA in Elem. Edn., Clemson U., 1982. Cert. residential specialist. Realtor Crowell & Co Realtors, North Augusta, S.C., 1992—. Mem. Nat. Assn. Realtors, S.C. Assn. Realtors, North Augusta/Belvedere Bd. Realtors (pres. 1993, mem. million dollar club 1992), North Augusta Mothers Club (treas. 1992-93). Republican. Roman Catholic. Home: 1911 Green Forest Dr North Augusta SC 29841-2159 Office: Crowell & Co Realtors 454 W Martintown Rd North Augusta SC 29841-3106

PATE, SHARON SHAMBURGER, educator; b. Kenosha, Wis., Mar. 30, 1954; d. Thomas Benjamin and Ruth (Penny) Shamburger; m. Johnny Lee Pate, July 23, 1976. BS, Miss. U. Women, 1975; MEd, Miss. State U., 1980; postgrad., Fla. State U., 1994—. Cert. tchr., Fla. Mgr. Cato Dept. Stores, West Point, Miss., 1975-76; area mgr. Wal-Mart Stores, West Point, 1976; tchr. home econs. South Sumter High Sch., Bushnell, Fla., 1977-78; instr. community edn. Riverdale (Fla.) High Sch., 1982-84; substitute tchr., asst. to dean North Ft. Myers (Fla.) High Sch., 1982-84, tchr. home econs., 1978-80, 84—, instr. community edn., 1980-81, 84—; mktg. instr. Mosley High Sch., Panama City, Fla, 1992—; mgmt. trainee J.C. Penney Co., Ft. Myers, 1980-81; sponsor Future Homemakers Am., Cypress Lake High Sch., Ft. Myers, 1984-90, instr. community edn., interior decorating; tchr. mktg. edn., fashion mktg. Mariner High Sch., Cape Coral, Fla. Mem. Fla. Vocat. Assn., Fla. Assn. Mktg. Educators, Distributive Edn. Clubs Am. (advisor 1989-93), Elite Modeling Club (advisor 1990-92). Republican. Pentecostal. Home:

309 Foxmoor Ln Panama City FL 32405 Office: Mosley High Sch 501 Mosley Dr Lynn Haven FL 32444

PATEL, MARILYN HALL, federal judge; b. Amsterdam, N.Y., Sept. 2, 1938; d. Lloyd Manning and Nina J. (Thorpe) Hall; m. Magan C. Patel, Sept. 2, 1966; children: Brian, Gian. B.A., Wheaton Coll., 1959; J.D., Fordham U., 1963. Bar: N.Y. 1963, Calif. 1970. Mng. atty. Benson & Morris, Esq., N.Y.C., 1962-64; sole practice N.Y.C., 1964-67; atty. U.S. Immigration and Naturalization Svc., San Francisco, 1967-71; sole practive San Francisco, 1971-76; judge Alameda County Mcpl. Ct., Oakland, Calif., 1976-80, U.S. Dist. Ct. (no. dist.) Calif., San Francisco, 1980—; adj. prof. law Hastings Coll. of Law, San Francisco, 1974-76. Author: Immigration and Nationality Law, 1974; also numerous articles. Mem. bd. of visitors Fordham U. Sch. of Law. Mem. ABA (litigation sect., jud. adminstrn. sect.), ACLU (former bd. dirs.), NOW (former bd. dirs.), Am. Law Inst., Am. Judicature Soc. (bd. dirs.), Calif. Conf. Judges, Nat. Assn. Women Judges (founding mem.), Internat. Inst. (bd. dirs.), Advs. for Women (co-founder). Democrat. Office: US Dist Ct PO Box 36060 450 Golden Gate Ave San Francisco CA 94102*

PATEOS, KAREN ELIZABETH, sports specialist; b. Akron, Ohio, Aug. 16, 1966; d. Jim George and Genevieve anne (Stoddard) P. BA in History, U. Akron, 1989, MPA, 1992. Sec. Akron (Ohio) Standard, 1984; student asst. U. Akron, 1984-89, intern in corp. challenge, 1992; site dir. Recreation Bur. City of Akron, 1992—. Vol. Am. Cancer Soc., Akron, 1991. Mem. ASPA, Internat. City Mgrs. Assn., Ohio Parks and Recreation, Phi Alpha Theta. Home: 211 N Portage Path # 104 Akron OH 44303-1131

PATERSON, EILEEN, radiation oncologist, educator; b. Bklyn., Oct. 16, 1939; d. John Alexander and Frances (Rabito) P.; m. Bruce Leroy Benedict, Jan. 2, 1981. BA, Wilson Coll., Chambersburg, Pa., 1961; MD, Woman's Med. Coll. Pa., 1965. Diplomate Am. Bd. Radiation Oncology, Am. Bd. Nuclear Medicine. Intern Highland Hosp., Rochester, N.Y., 1965-66; resident radiology (radiation therapy) U. Rochester, 1966-69; asst. prof. radiation oncology U. Rochester, N.Y., 1970-83, assoc. prof., 1983—; chief dept. radiation oncology Rochester Gen. Hosp., 1983—; cons. Arnot Ogden Hosp., Elmira, N.Y., 1970-74, Genesee Hosp., Rochester, 1983—. Contbr. articles to med. jours. Mem. Am. Coll. Radiology, Am. Soc. Therapeutic Radiology and Oncology. Office: Rochester Gen Hosp 1425 Portland Ave Rochester NY 14621-3001

PATI, PATRICIA ANN, psychologist; b. Queens Village, N.Y., Feb. 15, 1949; d. Charles and Helen (Annis) P.; m. Carlson Andrews Theodore, Sept. 9, 1989. BA, Loyola U., L.A., 1972, MA, 1974; PhD, U.S. Internat. U., 1982. Counselor Careunit, Laguna Beach, Calif., 1978-83; psychologist Humanistic Therapy Inst., Irvine, Calif., 1981-85, Orange County Substance Abuse Agy., Santa Ana, Calif., 1984-85; pvt. practice psychology San Diego, 1985-87, Poway, Calif., 1987—. Mem. APA, San Diego Psychol. Assn., Nat. Register Health Svc. Providers, Employee Assistance Profls. Assn. (bd. dirs., editor newsletter 1991-92), Psi Chi. Office: 15706 Pomerado Rd Ste 210 Poway CA 92064

PATILLO, SYLVIA JANE, human resources executive, educator; b. Kansas City, Mo., Nov. 15, 1946; d. John W. and Lola Mae (Williams) Jamierson; divorced; children: Rochelle D. Brown, Jason L. Patillo. AA, Penn. Valley Community Coll., Kansas City, 1981; BS, Park Coll., 1988; MA, Ottawa U., 1992. Computer operator Interstate Brands Corp., Kansas City, 1976-85, sec., 1986-88, personnel asst., 1988-89; employment specialist Gov. Employees Hosp. Assn., Independence, Mo., 1989—. Recording sec. Nat. Black MBA Assn., Kansas City, 1993—; vol. Urban League of Kansas City, 1986—; bd. dirs. Rose Brooks Ctr. Shelter for Women, Kansas City, 1987-90. Recipient scholarship Am. Bus. Womens Assn., 1987, 88. Mem. Soc. Human Resource Mgrs. Office: Van Kampen Am Capital 7501 Tiffany Springs Pky Kansas City MO 64153

PATRICK, CAROL LEE, psychologist; b. Rochester, N.Y., Jan. 27, 1953; d. Walter Frank and Frances Marcella (Johnston) Chappelle; m. John V. Patrick, Aug. 16, 1975; 1 child, Kimberly Sue. BA, Ohio Northern U., 1975; MA, Wright State U., 1977; PhD, Purdue U., 1985; postgrad., Wright State U., 1985-87. Lic. psychologist. Adminstrv. asst. Allen County Children Svcs. Bd., Lima, Ohio, 1980-81; teaching asst. Purdue U., Lafayette, Ind., 1982-83; intern Med. Coll. Ohio, Toledo, 1986-87, Bruce Kline & Assocs., Dayton, Ohio, 1985-87; clin. devel. psychologist Bruce Kline & Assocs., 1987-89; pvt. practice Lima, 1989—; faculty Ohio Northern U., Ada, 1988, Ohio State U., Lima, 1988, Sinclaire C.C., 1988; cons. Crossroads Crisis Ctr., Lima, 1989-91, Allen County Mentally Retarded/Devel. Disabled Bd., Lima, 1989-92, Blanchard Valley Ctr., 1990-91. Mem. APA, World Conf. for Gifted and Talented, Nat. Assn. for Gifted Children, Ohio Psychol. Assn., Ohio Assn. for Gifted Children, Play Therapy Assn. Office: 1037 W Market St Lima OH 45805-2729

PATRICK, EVA BERT, nurse; b. Pinehurst, N.C., July 25, 1953; d. John Patrick and Clara Elizabeth (Byrd) Pope; m. W. Ward Patrick, Mar. 29, 1986; children: Eric Quinn Bates, Scarlet Marie Bates, Ellen Elizabeth. Lic. practical nurse cert., Sandhills Community Coll., 1973, ADN in Nursing, 1983. RN, N.C. Charge nurse Sandhills Nursing Ctr., Pinehurst, 1977-78; mem. recovery room staff S.W. Miss. Regional Med. Ctr., McComb, 1978-80; head nurse Manor Care of Pinehurst, 1983-85; staff nurse emergency dept. Cen. Carolina Hosp., Sanford, N.C., 1985-86; home health nurse St. Joseph's Home Health Agy., Southern Pines, N.C., 1986-87, patient care coord., 1987; respite care coordinator Dept. Aging Moore County, Carthage, N.C., 1986-87; staff nurse Moore Regional Hosp., Pinehurst, N.C., 1989-91; home care coord. St. Joseph Home Health Agy., Southern Pines, N.C., 1991—. Democrat. Presbyterian. Home: 702 Sunset Dr PO Box 1062 Carthage NC 28327 Office: St Josephs Home Health Agy 590 Central Dr Southern Pines NC 28387-2812

PATRICK, GWENDOLYN HUNTER, buyer; b. Nashville, Apr. 27, 1947; d. Champ Jr. and Marguerite (Pullen) Hunter; m. Thomas Emory Patrick, Aug. 20, 1970 (div. Sept. 1993); children: Terence Edward, Ragan Leigh. BS, Tenn. State U., 1969; postgrad., U. Tenn., 1973. Cert. purchasing mgr. Jr. trainee retail Abraham & Straus Co., Bklyn., 1968; adminstrv. asst. Tenn. State U., Nashville, 1969-74, Meharry Med. Coll., Nashville, 1974-76; purchasing asst. E.I. duPont de Nemours, Inc., Nashville, 1976-79; sr. buyer Textron Aerostructures, Nashville, 1979—; project bus. cons. Jr. Achievement, NAshville, 1988. Recipient 3d Pl. trophy RRCA Women's Distance Festival, 1994. Mem. NAFE, Nat. Mgmt. Assn., Tenn. State U. Alumni Assn., Alpha Kappa Alpha (25 Yr. Silver medallion 1993). Democrat. Mem. Ch. of Christ. Office: Textron Aerostructures PO Box 210 Nashville TN 37202-0210

PATRICK, JANE AUSTIN, association executive; b. Memphis, May 27, 1930; d. Wilfred Jack and Evelyn Eudora (Branch) Austin; m. William Thomas Spencer, Sept. 11, 1952 (ddec Apr. 1970); children: Anthony Duke, ToniLee Candice Spencer Hughes; m. George Milton Patrick, Oct. 1, 1971. Student Memphis State U., 1946-47; BSBA, Ohio State U., 1979. Service rep. So. Bell Tel. and Tel., Memphis, 1947-52; placement dir. Mgmt. Pers., Memphis, 1965-66; pers. asst. to exec. v.p. E & E Ins. Co., Columbus, Ohio, 1966-69; Ohio exec. dir. Nat. Soc. for Prevention of Blindness, Columbus, 1969-73; regional dir. Ohio and Ky. CARE and MEDICO, Columbus, 1979-87; v.p. Career Execs. of Columbus, 1987-91; owner, pres. Patricks, 1987—; lectr., cons. in field. Mem. choir 1st Community Ch., Columbus, Ohio State Univ. Svc. Bd.; bd. dirs. Columbus Coun. on World Affairs, 1980-92, sec., 1983-91, chmn. devel. com.; chmn. pers. com. Ohio Hunger Task Force, 1989-90. Recipient commendations Nat. Soc. Prevention Blindness and Cen. Ohio Lions Eye Bank, 1973. Plaques for Svc. award Upper Arlington Pub. Schs., 1986. Mem. Non-Profit Orgn. Mgmt. Inst. (pres.), Nat. Soc. Fund-Raising Execs. (cert., nat. dir.), Pub. Rels. Soc. Am. (cert., membership com. chairperson), Ins. Inst. Am. (cert.), Mensa Internat., Columbus Dental Soc. Aux. (historian and publicity chair), Alpha Gamma Delta, Epsilon Sigma Alpha (pres.). Home: 2511 Onandaga Dr Columbus OH 43221-3619

PATRICK, JANET CLINE, medical society administrator; b. San Francisco, June 30, 1934; d. John Wesley and Edith Bertha (Corde) Cline; m. Robert John Patrick Jr., June 13, 1959 (div. 1988); children: John McKinnon, Stewart McLellan, William Robert. B.A., Stanford U., 1955; postgrad. U. Calif.-Berkeley, 1957, George Washington U., 1978-82. English tchr. George Washington High Sch., San Francisco, 1957, K.D. Burke Sch., San Francisco, 1957-59, Berkeley Inst., Bklyn., 1959-63; placement counselor Washington Sch. Secs., Washington, 1976-78, asst. dir. placement, 1978-81; mgr. med. personnel service Med. Soc. D.C., 1981-89, pres. Med. Pers. Svcs. Inc., 1989— . Chmn. area 2 planning com. Montgomery County Pub. Schs. (Md.), 1974-75; mem. vestry, corr. sec., Christ Ch., Kensington, Md., 1982-84, vestry, sr. warden, 1984-85, vestry, chmn. ann. giving com., 1986-89; chmn. long-range planning com., 1989-92, sec., 1992-93, jr. warden, 1994; fin. com. Montgomery County Pvt. Industry Coun. Mem. Met. D.C. Med. Group Mgmt. Assn., Phi Beta Kappa. Republican. Episcopalian. Club: Jr. League (Washington). Home: 5206 Carlton St Bethesda MD 20816-2306 Office: Med Personnel Svcs Inc 1707 L St NW Ste 250 Washington DC 20036-3804

PATRICK, LESLIE DAYLE, hydrologist; b. Grand Island, Nebr., Nov. 20, 1951; d. Robert Norman and Charlotte Ruth (Thomas) Mayfield; m. Jeffrey Rogan Patrick, July 1, 1972. BA in Geology, U. Alaska, Anchorage, 1975, MS in Mgmt., 1991. Data base mgr. U.S. Geol. Survey, Anchorage, 1975-78, with digital modeling, 1980-85, with water use studies, 1978-91, chief computer sect., systems analyst, 1985-91, asst. dist. chief mgmt. ops., 1991—. Mem. Alaska Groundwater Assn. (sec./treas. 1980). Office: US Geol Survey Water Resources Div 4230 University Dr Ste 201 Anchorage AK 99508-4626

PATRICK, SUE FORD, diplomat; b. Union Springs, Ala., Nov. 9, 1946; d. Oscar Ford and Mildred (Hunter) Ford Carter; m. Henderson M. Patrick, Dec. 24, 1973; 1 child, Lauren. BA, Coll. Notre Dame of Md., 1967; postgrad., U. Va., 1967-69, 70-72; MA, Boston U., 1982; postgrad., Nat. War Coll., Washington, 1991-92. Joined Fgn. Svc., Dept. State; vice-consul Am. Consulate, Udorn, Thailand, 1973-74; desk officer Dept. State, Washington, 1976-78, 1st sec., 1981-84, spl. asst. refugee programs, 1984-85; 2d sec. U.S. Embassy, Nairobi, Kenya, 1978-81; 1st sec. polit. affairs U.S. Embassy, Abidjan, Ivory Coast, 1985-88; dep. chief of mission U.S. Embassy, Kigali, Rwanda, 1988-91, Nat. War Coll., Washington, 1991-92; adv. on NATO policy Office of Sec. of Def., The Pentagon, Washington, 1992-93, dir. office of fgn. civil. mil. affairs, 1993-94; congl. affairs advisor Office Regional Security Policy Dept. State, Washington, 1994—. Mem. Am. Fgn. Svc. Assn. Roman Catholic. Home: 2715 Colt Run Rd Oakton VA 22124-1101 Office: Office Regional Security Policy EAP/RSP Rm 5313 Dept State Washington DC 20520

PATRONE-BLACK, LAURA MAY, cell and molecular biologist, biomedical researcher; b. Upper Nyack, N.Y., June 29, 1962; d. Joseph Atillio and Elaine Ellen Patrone; m. Andrew Thomas Black, July 9, 1994. BA magna cum laude, U. N.C., Greensboro, 1984; MA, Coll. William and Mary, 1988; PhD, SUNY, Binghamton, 1992. Postdoctoral rsch. fellow Mayo Clinic, Scottsdale, Ariz., 1992-94, Chem. Industry Inst. Toxicology, Research Triangle Park, N.C., 1994—. Author: (with others) Animal Test Alternatives: Refinement, Reduction, Replacement, 1995; contbr. articles to periodicals. Mem. Assn. Women in Sci., N.C. Soc. Toxicology, Phi Beta Kappa, Phi Sigma, Beta Beta Beta, Sigma Xi (assoc.). Roman Catholic. Home: 4607E Hope Valley Rd Durham NC 27707 Office: Chem Industry Inst Toxicology 6 Davis Dr Research Triangle Park NC 27709

PATTEE, PAMELA VALENTINE, counselor; b. New Haven, Conn., Jan. 22, 1927; d. Louis Everett and Hazel Mae (Noone) Valentine; m. William Hascall Pattee, Apr. 24, 1954; children: William E., Timothy H. BA, U. Ga., 1948; MAT, Jacksonville U., 1969; postgrad., Fla. State U., 1974. Cert. guidance counselor, Fla. Sec. to pres. Jacksonville (Fla.) U., 1948-53; adminstrv. staff Stetson U., De Land, Fla., 1953-55; co-owner antique shop Jacksonville, 1963-66; tchr. Duval County Sch. Bd., Jacksonville, 1965-74, counselor, 1974—; presenter in field. Legislative liaison Duval County Counselors, 1979—. Recipient Lucille Crysell award in recognition of excellence and dedication in delivery of guidance svcs. in Duval County, 1994. Mem. Elem. Counselors of Duval County (pres. 1978-79), Duval Assn. for Counseling and Devel. (pres. 1979-80, exec. bd. 1993-94), Am. Counselors Assn., Huxley Inst. for BioSocial Rsch., Jacksonville Alumni Assn. Episcopalian. Home: 4111 Trieste Pl Jacksonville FL 32244-2324

PATTEN, ETHEL DOUDINE, retired hematologist; b. N.Y.C., Feb. 21, 1942; d. Ethel (Campbell) Bruno; m. Bernard M. Patten, June 27, 1964; children: Allegra, Craig. BA, Barnard Coll., 1963; MD, N.J. Coll. Medicine, 1967. Diplomate Am. Bd. Internal Medicine, Am. Bd. Pathology. Intern USPHS Hosp., S.I., N.Y., 1967-68, resident in internal medicine, 1968-70; fellow in hematology NYU Med. Sch., N.Y.C., 1970-71, NIH, Bethesda, Md., 1971-72; fellow in blood banking Am. Nat. Red Cross, Washington, 1972-73; dir. blood bank U. Tex. Med. Br., Galveston, 1974-93; assoc. prof. medicine and pathology U. Tex. Med. Br., 1974-94; ret., 1994. Contbr. sci. papers and abstracts to numerous publs. Sugreon, USPHS, 1967-73. Nat. Heart, Lung and Blood Inst. transfusion medicine grantee, 1985-90. Fellow ACP; mem. South Cen. Assn. Blood Banks (pres. 1981-82), AMA, Am. Assn. Blood Banks.

PATTERSON, ANITA MATTIE, union administrator; b. Birmingham, Ala., Feb. 19, 1940; d. John Evans Patterson and Flora Ella (Paul) Patterson/Mitchell; m. LeRoy Harold Walden, Mar. 19, 1958 (dec. Apr. 1966); children: Christopher Ann, DeRoy, Chanita. Student, Wayne State U., 1968-72, 72-78, Wayne State U., 1976-79. Sr. counselor City of Detroit, 1965-79; area dir. AFSCME, Washington, 1979—; exec. bd. Coalition Labor Union Women, Washington, exec. dir., 1975-77; chair nat. women's com. Coalition Black Trade Unionists, Washington, 1985—; tchg. fellow AFL-CIO Organizing Inst., Washington, 1992—; ofcl. election observer South Africa Election, 1994. Active So. Regional Coun., Atlanta, 1992—; mem. social svcs. com. Salem Bapt. Ch., Atlanta, 1990—. Recipient Cmty. Svcs. award A. Philip Randolph Inst., 1990, Cmty. Svcs. award So. Christian Leadership Coun., 1991, Leadership award Ga. State Legis. Black Caucus, 1992, Disting. Recognition award City of Detroit, 1989, Sojourner Truth award Coalition of Black Trade Unionists, 1994, Operation PUSH Labor award, 1994; named Addie L. Wyatt Woman of Yr., Coalition of Black Trade Unionists, 1990. Mem. Nat. Coun. Negro Women (ad hoc labor com. 1986—, Recognition award 1989, Svc. award 1988), Marracci Ct. # 32. Democrat. Office: AFSCME Internat Area Office 1720 Peachtree St Ste 150B Atlanta GA 30309

PATTERSON, BEVERLEY PAMELA GRACE, accountant; b. London, Feb. 6, 1956; came to U.S., 1975; d. Ernest Charles and Barbara (Wiseman) Patterson; children: Tamara, Russell, Stuart. AAS with honors, Tacoma C.C., 1978; BBA with honors, U. Puget Sound, 1980. CPA, Wash. Accounts payable clk. Hillhaven Corp., Tacoma, 1975-76, staff acct., 1980-83, acquisition analyst, 1984-86; contr., chief fin. officer Tacoma Luth. Home and Retirement Community, 1987—; cons. in field, 1984—. Bd. dirs., treas. YWCA, 1992-94. Mem. AICPA, Wash. Soc. CPAs (healthcare com. 1993-95), Am. Soc. Women Accts. (chmn. bd. dirs. Tacoma chpt., mem. edtl. bd. The Woman CPA mag. 1989-92, pres. 1991-92), Healthcare Fin. Mgmt. Assn. Home: PO Box 1507 Gig Harbor WA 98335-3507 Office: Tacoma Luth Home & Retirement Community 1301 N Highland Pky Tacoma WA 98406-2116

PATTERSON, BEVERLY ANN GROSS, fund raising consultant, social services administrator; b. Pauls Valley, Okla., Aug. 5, 1938; d. Wilburn G. Jack and Mildred E. (Steward) Gross; m. Kenneth Dean Patterson, June 18, 1960 (div. 1976); children: Tracy Dean, Nancy Ann Patterson-McArthur, Beverly Jeanne Patterson-Wertman. AA, Modesto (Calif.) Jr. Coll., 1958; BA in Social Sci., Fresno (Calif.) State U., 1960; M in Community Counseling, Coll. Idaho; postgrad., Stanislaus State Coll., Turlock, Calif., U. Idaho, Boise (Idaho) State U. Cert. secondary tchr., Calif., Idaho, lic. real estate agt., Idaho. Secondary tchr. Ceres and Modesto Calif., Payette and Weiser Idaho, Ontario Oreg., 1960-67; dir. vol. svcs. mental retardation and child devel. State of Idaho, 1967-70, cons. dir. vol. svcs. health and welfare, 1970-72; dir. Ret. Sr. Vol. Program, Boise, 1972-74; exec. dir. Idaho Nurses Assn., Boise, 1974-76; community svcs. adminstr. City of Davis, Calif., 1976-78; devel. dir. and fundraising Mercy Med. Ctr., Nampa, Idaho, 1978-85; exec. dir. St. Anphonsus Med. Ctr. Found., Boise, 1985-87; dir. devel. and gift planning Idaho Youth Ranch, Boise, 1989-94; fund devel. cons. Mercy Housing, Nampa, Idaho, 1994—, Pratt Ranch Boys Home, Emmett, Idaho, 1994—, Northwest Childrens Home, Lewiston, Idaho, 1994—, Idaho Spl. Olympics, Boise, 1994—, Idaho Fund for Parks & Lands, 1994—; incorporator, pres. Nonprofit Svcs., Inc., 1995—; founder Fellowship Christian Adult Singles, Boise, 1974; cons., exec. dir. Boise Hotline, 1988-90; cons., fundraiser Cmty. Resources and Devel., 1980; co-dir., proprietor, ACOA workshop leader Child Within Concepts, Inc., Boise, 1987—; cons., coord. Rural Hosp. Edn. Consortium, 1988; cons. hosp. fund devel. and cmty. resources Gritman Meml. Hosp., Moscow, Idaho, 1987-88; cons., conf. coord. State of Idaho, 1987-88; counselor Adult Children of Alcoholics, 1991. Coord. Idaho Golf Angels Open Pro-Am Tournament, Boise, 1989-91; founding exec. v.p. of Coll. Fund for Students Surviving Cancer, 1993—; bd. dirs.Arthritis Found., IDaho, 1984-86, Idaho Mental Health Assn., 1985-87; charitable fund raising coord., 1978—. Named Idaho Statesman Disting. Citizen, 1985. Mem. Nat. Assn. for Hosp. Devel. (treas. 1980, accreditation chmn. 1984-86, conf. chmn. 1982, 85). Mem. Community Christian Ch. Home: 315 W Maple Ave Meridian ID 83642-2268 Office: Mercy Housing Idaho PO Box 8538 1512 12th Ave Rd Nampa ID 83686 also: Child Within Concepts 2920 Raindrop Dr Boise ID 83706-4840

PATTERSON, CATHERINE MARIE, lawyer; b. Livonia, Mich., June 12, 1963; d. Donald Craig and Dorothy Jean (McInroy) P. BS, Madonna U., 1985; JD, Detroit Coll. Law, 1992. Legal asst. Bleakley & McKeen, Detroit, 1984-85, Miller, Canfield, Paddock and Stone, Detroit, 1985-89; employee and civil rights compliance system adminstr. United Technologies Automotive Inc., Dearborn, Mich., 1989-90; assoc. Miller, Canfield, Paddock and Stone, Detroit, 1990—; mem. coop./employer edn. bd. Madonna U., Livonia, Mich., 1993—. Mem. ABA, Fed. Bar Assn., Mich. Bar Assn., Detroit Bar Assn., Oakland Bar Assn., Woman's Bar Assn. Mich., Nat. Cath. Coll. Grad. Honor Soc., Kappa Gamma Pi. Office: Miller Canfield Paddock and Stone PLC 150 W Jefferson Ste 2500 Detroit MI 48226

PATTERSON, CHASSON MICHELLE, municipal official. BSBA in Fin. and Mktg., U. Denver, 1989. Investment acct. Regional Transp. Dist., Denver, 1987-89, investment mgr., 1989—. Mem. Assn. Investment Mgmt. and Rsch., Treasury Mgmt. Assn. (cert. cash mgr.), Denver Soc. Security Analysts. Office: Regional Transp Dist PO Box 46530 Denver CO 80201-6530

PATTERSON, CLAIRE ANN, vocational educator; b. Cin., Dec. 28, 1950; d. Lloyd E. and Ruth T. (Flaherty) Lachtrupp; m. Calvin Stanley Patterson, Jr., July 14, 1973; children: Christopher, Alicia. BS, U. Cin., 1973, MEd, 1980. Cert. elem. tchr., elem. supr., secondary math, secondary prin., Ohio, Va., P.R. Third grade tchr. Acadamia de Aguidilla, P.R., 1973-74; fifth grade tchr. Our Lady of the Rosary, Norfolk, Va., 1974-76; jr. high math and sci. tchr. Yavneh Hebrew Day Sch., Cin., 1976-79; math tchr. Winton Woods City Schs., Cin., 1979-80; math. coord. Great Oaks Inst. of Tech. and Career Devel., Cin., 1980-86, benefits coord./personnel profl., 1986-88, career devel. mgr., 1987-93, asst. dir., 1993—; ednl. cons. schs. in Ohio, 1988—. Author: Let's Celebrate Math, 1991; contbr. articles to profl. jours. Recipient Career Coord. award State of Ohio, 1993. Mem. Ohio Vocat. Assn. (com. chmn. 1990-93, OVA Pacesetter award 1991, 92, 93), Career Edn. Assn. (pres. 1992-93), Nat. Coun. Local Adminstrs., Southwest Career Coun. (pres. 1991-92). Republican. Roman Catholic. Office: Great Oaks Inst Tech and Career Devel 3254 E Kemper Rd Cincinnati OH 45241

PATTERSON, CLARA DALE, administrative assistant; b. Louisville, Dec. 9, 1955; d. Gilbert Dale and Claudia M. (Burke) Lynch; m. Clinton Nim Patterson, Mar. 21, 1976; children: Christopher Lawrence, Lucas Paul. Degree in Cosmetology, Laurel County Vocat. Tech. Sales Howard Bros. Discount, Corbin, Ky., 1971-73; nurses aid Southeast Ky. Bapt. Hosp., Corbin, 1974-75; adminstrv. asst., bookkeeper Tom Alexanders, Corbin, 1976-77; cosmetologist, stylist New Image, Corbin, 1982, Martha's Beauty, Corbin, 1982-83; cosmetologist, owner Clara's Hair Loft, Corbin, 1983-86; adminstrv. asst, mgr. Nearly New Shop, Corbin, 1987-93; adminstrv. asst, acct., bookkeeper United Waste Sys., Corbin, 1993—. Instr. cheerleading Woodbine Elem. Sch., Corbin, 1983-86; instr. vacation Bible Sch., Corbin, 1976-93; vol. Whitley County Mid. Sch., 1992, sec./v.p., 1992; sec. Whitely County H.S., 1988-92, vol., 1992. Republican. Baptist. Home: 1864 Bacon St Corbin KY 40701 Office: United Waste Sys Inc/HSI Hwy 1232 PO Box 281 Gray KY 40734

PATTERSON, DAWN MARIE, dean, consultant, writer; b. Gloversville, N.Y., July 30; d. Robert Morris and Dora Margaret (Perham) P.; m. Robert Henry Hollenbeck, Aug. 3, 1958 (div. 1976); children: Adrienne Lyn, Nathaniel Conrad. BS in Edn., SUNY, Geneseo, 1962; MA, Mich. State U., 1973, PhD, 1977; postgrad., U. So. Calif. and Inst. Ednl. Leadership. Librarian Brighton (N.Y.) Cen. Schs., 1962-67; asst. to regional dir. Mich. State U. Ctr., Bloomfield Hills, 1973-74; grad. asst. Mich. State U., East Lansing, 1975-77; cons. Mich. Efficiency Task Force, 1977; asst. dean Coll. Continuing Edn., U. So. Calif., Los Angeles, 1978-84; dean, assoc. prof. continuing edn. Calif. State U., Los Angeles, 1985—; CEO Acclaims Enterprises Internat.; pres. Co-Pro Assocs. Mem. Air Univ. Bd. Visitors, 1986-90, Commn. on Extended Edn. Calif. State U. Calif., 1988-91; Hist. Soc., Los Angeles Town Hall, Los Angeles World Affairs Council. Dora Louden scholar, 1958-61; Langworthy fellow, 1961-62; Edn. Professions Devel. fellow, 1974-75; Ednl. Leadership Policy fellow, 1982-83; Leadership Calif., 1992, Leadership Am., 1994. Mem. AAUW (pres. Pasadena br. 1985-86), Am. Assn. Adult and Continuing Edn. (charter), Nat. Univ. Continuing Edn. Assn., Internat. Assn. Continuing Edn. and Tng. (bd. dirs. 1990—), Calif. Coll. and Mil. Educators Assn. (pres.), Los Angeles Airport Area Edn. Industry Assn. (pres. 1984), Rotary Club of Alhambra (bd. dirs.), Fine Arts (Pasadena), Zonta (pres. 1994—), Kappa Delta Pi, Phi Delta Kappa, Phi Beta Delta, Phi Kappa Phi. Republican. Unitarian. Office: 5151 State University Dr Los Angeles CA 90032-4221

PATTERSON, ELIZABETH JOHNSTON, former congresswoman; b. Columbia, SC, Nov. 18, 1939; d. Olin DeWitt and Gladys (Atkinson) Johnston; m. Dwight Fleming Patterson, Jr., Apr. 15, 1967; children: Dwight Fleming, Olin DeWitt, Catherine Leigh. BA, Columbia Coll., 1961; postgrad. in polit. sci., U. S.C., 1961, 62, 64; LLD (hon.), Columbia Coll., 1987; D Pub. Svc. (hon.), Converse Coll., 1989. Pub. affairs officer Peace Corps, Washington, 1962-64; postgrad. VISTA, OEO, Washington, 1965-66; D Pub. Svc. Head Start and VISTA, OEO, Columbia, 1966-67; tri-county dir. Head Start, Piedmont Community Actions, Spartanburg, S.C., 1967-68; mem. Spartanburg County Coun., 1975-76, S.C. State Senate, 1979-86, 100th-102nd Congresss from 4th S.C. dist., 1987-93. Trustee Wofford Coll., 1975-81; bd. dirs. Charles Lea Ctr., 1978-90, Spartanburg Coun. on Aging; pres. Spartanburg Dem. Women, 1968; v.p. Spartanburg County Dem. party, 1968-70, sec., 1970-75; trustee Columbia Coll., 1991—. Mem. Bus. and Profl. Women's Club, Alpha Kappa Gamma. Methodist. Office: PO Box 5564 Spartanburg SC 29304-5564

PATTERSON, HELEN CROSBY, clinical psychologist; b. Jackson, Miss., Nov. 12, 1947; d. Thomas Atkinson and Helen Elizabeth (Crosby) Patterson; m. Fred C. Craig, July 7, 1967 (div. July 1970); 1 child, Erin Crosby. BA in Psychology, Millsaps Coll., 1972; MS in Clin. Psychology, U. Wyo., 1976, PhD in Clin. Psychology, 1978. Lic. clin. psychologist, Miss., N.Mex., Del. Coord. supervisions and internships N.E. Grad. Sch., Keene, N.H., 1979-80; sr. clinician Jackson (Miss.) Mental Health Ctr., 1980-82; pvt. practice in Miss. and N.Mex., 1981-93; clin. dir. Pain Mgmt. Ctr. St. Vincent Hosp., Santa Fe, N.Mex., 1990-91; psychol. cons. disability determination svcs., Jackson, 1983—, Albuquerque, 1988-90, 91-93, Wilmington, Del., 1993—; cons. So. Beverage Co., Jackson, 1986-91, St. Vincent Hosp., Santa Fe, 1990-91. Mem. Hinds County Assn. for Children with Learning Disabilities, Jackson, 1985-88, Hinds County Mental Health Assn., Jackson, 1980-83. Mem. APA. Address: 3817 Don Juan Ct Albuquerque NM 87107

PATTERSON, JANICE P., community and geriatrics health nurse; b. Riobamba, Ecuador, Oct. 7, 1941; d. Michael James and Ella Catherine (Patzsch) Ficke; m. Michael Milton Patterson, June 11, 1966; children: Michael Shane, Shad Milton. Diploma, West Suburban Hosp., Oak Park, Ill., 1963; BSN, U. Iowa, 1968. Emergency rm., ICU staff nurse Bloomington (Ind.) Hosp.; operating rm. staff nurse VA Hosp., Iowa City; operating rm. supr. Kirksville (Mo.) Osteopathic Hosp., 1973-77; clinic coord. Cancer Screening Clinic County Health Dept., Athens, Ohio, 1987-93; supr.

Hickory Creek Nursing Ctr., The Plains, Ohio, 1989-90; dir. nursing Arcadia Nursing Ctr., Coolville, Ohio, 1990-93; staff nurse Integrated Health Svcs. of Kansas City at Alpine North, Riverside, Mo., 1993—. Mem. Ohio Dir. Nursing Assn., Sigma Theta Tau (Lambda Omega chpt. 1990—). Home: 4837 NW 57 Ct Kansas City MO 64151

PATTERSON, KAREN ANNE, communications executive, author; b. Pitts., Mar. 7, 1948; d. Frederick John, Jr., and Gladys Mary (Steinhardt) Killmeyer; m. John H. Patterson, Sept. 6, 1987; children by previous marriage: Jesse Frank, Joshua Kane. Student speech and drama Penn Hall Jr. Coll., 1966-67; BA in Broadcast and Sociology, Marquette U., 1970. Assoc. editor Nat. Safety Council, Chgo., 1970-72; editor, research asst. U.S. Savs. and Loan League, Chgo., 1972; editor, dir. pub. relations Nat. Eye Research Found., Chgo., 1972-73; editorial dir. Red Bud Publs., Columbus, Ohio, 1974-76; pres., creative dir. Pace Media, Columbus, 1976-83; dir. communications Price Waterhouse, Columbus, 1983-85; dir. pub. relations and devel. Med. Ctr. Hosp., Chillicothe, Ohio, 1985-87; pres. Pace Communications, Chillicothe, 1987—; cons.; freelance writer, contbr. trade and comml. publs.; books include: Construction: Principles, Materials and Methods, 1972; City Slicker's Guide to Self Sufficiency, 1981-82; Heavenly Herbs, 1982; Borden: A Price Waterhouse Perspective, 1984; also novels, 1979-80. Recipient Communicators award Gt. Lakes Regional Com., 1983. Mem. Am. Mktg. Assn., Pub. Rels. Soc. Am., Assn. Women in Communications, Pres.'s Club of Am. Mgmt. Assn., Penn Hall Alumni Club, Marquette U. Alumni Club. Office: Pace Communications 36 N Walnut St Chillicothe OH 45601-3114

PATTERSON, LINDA A. DEARMOND, process engineer, material science consultant; b. Monmouth, N.J., May 25; d. Charles and C. Frances (Trocchia) DeArmond; m. David J. Patterson, Feb. 25, 1984. BS in Chemistry, N.Mex. State U., 1983; student, U. Calif., Irvine, 1983, U. Tex., Arlington, 1990—. With Dept. Def., White Sands Missile Range, N.Mex., 1979-83; teaching asst. U. Calif., Irvine, 1983; analytical chemist Pfizer Pharm., Groton, Conn., 1985-88; process engr. Tex. Instruments, McKinney, 1988—; cons., co-owner Patterson Profl. Group, Prosper, Tex., 1994—; site facilitator Tex. Instruments Women's Initiative, 1992—. Vol. Univ. Nursing Home, McKinney, 1992—, Heard Mus. & Wildlife Sanctuary, McKinney, 1992—. Mem. Am. Chem. Soc.

PATTERSON, LYDIA ROSS, industrial relations specialist, consulting company executive; b. Carrabelle, Fla., Sept. 3, 1936; d. Richard D. Ross and Johnnie Mae (Thomas) Kelley; m. Edgar A. Corley, Aug. 1, 1964 (div.); 1 child, Derek Kelley; m. Berman W. Patterson, Dec. 18, 1981. BA, Hunter Coll., 1958. Indsl. rels. specialist U.S. Dept. Energy, N.Y.C., 1966-68; regional dir./mgr. Div. Human Rights State of N.Y., N.Y.C., 1962-66, 68-76; v.p. Bankers Trust Co., N.Y.C., 1976-87; pres., chief exec. officer Extend Cons. Svcs., N.Y.C., 1985—; v.p., mgr. Merrill Lynch and Co. Inc., N.Y.C., 1987-90; seminar speaker Columbia U., Wharton Sch. Bus., Harvard U., Duke U., Cornell U., 1976-85; mem. conf. bd. Cornell U., Bus. Policy Rev. Coun., Exec. Leadership Coun. Bd. dirs. Project Discovery Columbia U., 1988, CUNY, Vocat. Edn. Adv. Coun., 1990. Mem. Am. Soc. Pers. Adminstrn., N.Y. and Nat. Urban League, Employment Mgrs. Assn., Fin. Women's Assn. (govt. and community affairs com. 1986-87), Women's Forum, Employment Dissemination of Info., Wellington Community Edn. Found. (bd. dirs. 1992—). Office: 12689 Coral Breeze Dr West Palm Beach FL 33414-8070

PATTERSON, MABEL SUE, small business owner; b. Elizabethtown, Ky., Dec. 28, 1957; d. H. and M. (Florence) Sloan; m. Paul Lee Patterson II, Dec. 17, 1978; 1 child, Paul Lee III. BS in Home Econs., Edn., U. Ky., 1978. Home econs., early childhood educator; co-owner, office mgr. Patterson Eye Care Ctrs., Inc., Campbellsville, Ky., 1982—; bd. dirs. Patterson Eye Care Ctrs., Inc. Mem. NAFE, Ky. Optometric Auxillary (state pres. 1991-93), Kappa Delta Pi, Phi Upsilon Omicron. Democrat. Baptist.

PATTERSON, MARGARET MARY, advertising executive, communications consultant; b. Lancaster, Wis., Dec. 24, 1959; d. John Francis and Charlotte Marie (Osterhaus) P.; m. Richard Joseph Mehalic, Sept. 12, 1992. BS in Journalism, U. Wis., 1982. Mng. editor, prodn. mgr. Nat. Dairy News, Madison, 1982-84; copywriter Deere & Co., Moline, Ill., 1984-88; product group advt. specialist Ford New Holland (Pa.), 1988-90; comms. mgr. Massey Ferguson, Racine, Wis., 1990-93; copy and account contact Rhea & Kaiser Advt., Naperville, Ill., 1993—; comms. cons. Packaging Corp. of Am., Evanston, Ill., 1993—, Bellwether Comms., Racine, 1993. Mem. Nat. Agri-Mktg. Assn. (awards chmn. 1994-95). Democrat. Roman Catholic. Home: 183 Mistwood Ln North Aurora IL 60542-3000 Office: Rhea & Kaiser Advt 400 E Diehl Naperville IL 60563

PATTERSON, MARIA JEVITZ, microbiology-pediatric infectious disease educator; b. Berwyn, Ill., Oct. 23, 1944; d. Frank Jacob and Edna Frances (Costabile) Jevitz; m. Ronald James Patterson, Aug. 22, 1970; children: Kristin Lara, Kier Nicole. BS in Med. Tech. summa cum laude, Coll. St. Francis, Joliet, Ill., 1966; PhD in Microbiology, Northwestern U., Chgo., 1970; MD, Mich. State U., 1984. Diplomate Am. Bd. Med. Examiners, Am. Bd. Pediatrics. Lab. asst., instr. med. microbiology for student nurses Med. Sch. Northwestern U., Chgo., 1966-70; postdoctoral fellow in clin. microbiology affiliated hosps. U. Wash., Seattle, 1971-72; asst. prof. microbiology and pub. health Mich. State U., East Lansing, 1972-77, assoc. prof., 1977-82, assoc. prof. pathology, 1979-82, lectr. dept. microbiology and pub. health, 1982-87, resident in pediatrics affiliated hosps., 1984-85, 86-87, clin. instr. dept. pediatrics and human devel., 1984-87, assoc. prof. microbiology-pub. health-pediatrics-human devel., 1987-90, prof., 1990—; staff microbiologist dept. pathology Lansing Gen. Hosp., 1972-75; dir. clin. microbiology grad. program. Mich. State U., 1974-81, staff microbiologist, 1978-81; postdoctoral fellow in infectious diseases U. Mass. Med. Ctr., Worcester, 1985-86; asst. dir. pediatrics residency Grad. Med. Edn. Inc., Lansing, 1987-90; med. dir. Pediatrics Health Ctr. St. Lawrence Hosp., Lansing, Mich., 1987-90, Ingham Med. Ctr., 1990-94; cons. clin. microbiology Lansing Gen. Hosp., 1972-75, Mich. State U., 1976-82, Ingham County Health Dept., 1988—, Am. Health Cons., 1993; cons. to editorial bd. Infection and Immunity, 1977; presenter seminars. Contbg. author: Microbiology: Principles and Concepts, 1982, 3d edit., 1991, Pediatric Emergency Medicine, 1992; contbr. articles to profl. jours. and publs. Mem. hon. com. Lansing AIDS Meml. Quilt, 1993. Recipient award for teaching excellence Mich. State U. Coll. Osteo. Medicine, 1977, 78, 79, 80, 83, Disting. Faculty award Mich. State U., 1980, Woman Achiever award, 1985, excellence in pediatric residency teaching award, 1988, Alumni Profl. Achievement award Coll. of St. Francis, 1991; grantee renal disease divsn. Mich. Dept. Pub. Health 1976-82. Fellow Pediatric Infectious Diseases Soc., Am. Acad. Pediatrics; mem. Am. Coll. Physician Execs., Am. Soc. Microbiology, Am. Soc. Clin. Pathologists (affiliate, bd. registrant), South Ctrl. Assn. Clin. Microbiology, Infectious Diseases Soc. Am., Mich. Soc. Infectious Diseases, N.Y. Acad. Scis., Kappa Gamma Pi, Lambda Iota Tau. Roman Catholic. Home: 1520 River Ter East Lansing MI 48823-5314 Office: Mich State Univ Microbiology/Pub Health East Lansing MI 48824-1101

PATTERSON, MARION LOUISE, photographer, educator; b. San Francisco, Apr. 24, 1933; d. Morrie Leslie and Esther Elizabeth (Parker) P. BA, Stanford U., 1955; MA, Calif. State U., San Francisco, 1970. Clk. Best's Studio (Ansel Adams Gallery), Yosemite, Calif., 1958-61; asst. to photography editor Sunset Mag., Menlo Park, Calif., 1961-64; freelance photographer Oaxaca, Mex., 1964-66; communications cons. Projects to Advance Creative in Edn., San Mateo, Calif., 1966-68; instr. in photography, chair photography dept. Foothill Coll., Los Altos Hills, Calif., 1968—. One woman shows include West German Embassy in the Hague, Bayreuth, Republic of Germany, Kasteel Hoensbroeck, Netherlands, Daxaca, Mex., San Francisco Mus. of Modern Art, Focus Gallery, San Francisco, Oakland Mus., Monterey County Mus., Stanford U., Ansel Adams Gallery, Yosemite, and others; exhibited in group shows MIT, George Eastman House, Polaroid Corp., Art in the Embassies, Ind. U., U. of Ala., Critics Choice Traveling Exhibit, New Light, New Directions, Reclaiming Paradise, and others; contbr. photographs and articles in books and magazines. Mem. Am. Soc. Mag. Photographers, Soc. for Photographic Edn. Office: Foothill Coll 12345 El Monte Ave Los Altos CA 94022-4504

PATTERSON, MARTHA ELLEN, artist, art educator; b. Anderson, Ind., Mar. 12, 1914; d. Clarence and Corrine Ringwald; m. John Downey, Nov. 27, 1935 (div. 1946); 1 child, Linda Carol; m. Raymond George Patterson, May 6, 1947. Student, Dayton (Ohio) Art Inst., Bendell Art Sch., Bradenton, Fla. Beauty operator WRENS, Springfield, Ohio, 1932-40; co-owner Park Ave. Gallery, Dayton; window decorator, art tchr.; tchr. art; judge art shows. One-woman shows include N.C.R. Country Club, Bill Turner Interiors, U. Dayton, High Street Gallery, Trails End Club, The Designerie, Riverbend Park, Statesman Club, State Fidelity Bank, Wygerson's Garden Ctr., Pebble Springs, Backstreet, First City Fed. Bank, Bradenton, Fla., Alley Gallery, Merrill-Lynch, Miami U., Gem City Bank, Dayton, Ohio, Winters Bank, Dayton, Sherwin-Williams, Howard Johnsons, Dayton Woman's Club, Bergamo, Dayton Meml. Hall, Bob and Arts, Del Park Med. Soc., The Dayton Country Club, Christ Methodist Ch., Unitarian Ch., The Metropolitan, Rikes, Dr. Pavey's, Dr. Chaney's, Dayton Convention Ctr., The Yum Yum, Jan Strunk Interiors, Park Avenue Gallery; artist: (water colors, oils, acrylics, inks and pastels) exhibitions include: Dayton Art Inst., Meml. Hall of Dayton, Dayton Country Club, Bergamo, Womens Club of Dayton, Am. Watercolor Soc., Riverbend Park, First City Fed., NCR Country Club, Springfield (Ohio) Mus., Longbaat Key Art Ctr., others; in private collections of Mr. and Mrs. Richard Nixon, Virginia Graham, Les Brown, Paul Lynde, Air Force Mus. at Wright Patterson, Mr. and Mrs. Charles Lange of NCR, U. Dayton-Ohio, Stephen House, Doug Yeager, and others. Vol. Christian Woman's Soc. of Am., Twig Children's Hosp., Dayton, The Utopians; mem. Tri Art Dayton, Long Boat Key Art Ctr., Fla. Recipient first prize Dayton Soc. Painters and Sculptors Show Rikes, First Prize, 1976, 77, First Prize, Best in Show, 1978, Beavercreek Art Assn. First Place, Best in Show, Artist and Sculpture Yearly Show, 1966, 68 2d place, Dayton Art Inst. 2d prize, Tri County Hon. Mention, Walker Motor Sales 2d place, Bendell Art Gallery 2d and 3d, Montgomery County Fair Best in Show. Mem. Art League of Manatee, Nat. Mus. Women in Art, Springfield Mus. Art, Dayton Soc. Painters, N.Y. Watercolor Soc., Ohio Water Color Soc., Western Ohio Water Color Soc. Republican. Methodist. Home: 3853 Lawrenceville Dr Springfield OH 45504 Address: 5920 7th Ave W Bradenton FL 34209-3519

PATTERSON, MARY-MARGARET SHARP, writer, editor, media strategist; b. Fairmont, W.Va., July 12, 1944; d. H. Sutton Sharp and Columbia Strock; m. David Sands, June 15, 1968; 1 child, Scott Sutton. BA cum laude, Ohio State U., 1966, MA, 1967. Media coordinator Am. Hosp. Assn., Chgo., 1969; feature and mag. writer Chgo. Today newspaper, 1969-70; reporter Houston Chronicle, 1971-73; instr. journalism U. Houston, 1974-76; asst. prof. Utica (N.Y.) Coll. U. Syracuse, 1976-78; dir. undergrad. studies coll. journalism U. Md., College Park, 1978-82, editor, 1982; dir. information and devel. Audubon Naturalist Soc. Cen. Atlantic States, Inc., Chevy Chase, Md., 1982-89; dir. media rels. Defenders of Wildlife, Washington, 1989-90; resident Johns Hopkins-Nanjing U. Ctr. for Chinese and Am. Studies, Nanjing, China, 1990-91; sr. writer, editor Am. Assn. Ret. Persons, Washington, 1993—; cons. project Africa Carnegie Mellon U. Pitts., 1969; newspaper div. head summer journalism inst. Trinity U., San Antonio, 1979-81; columnist San Antonio Mag., 1976-79; cons. Callahan & Assoc., Washington, 1992—. Contbr. numerous articles and book revs. to newspapers and mags. Mem. Chevy Chase Presbyn. Ch. Choir, Washington, 1980—, ruling elder, 1993—. Recipient Reporting Excellence award The Newspaper Fund, Cleve., 1966; Univ. Grad. fellow Ohio State U., 1966, Nat. Grad. fellow Women in Communications, 1967. Mem. Soc. Profl. Journalists, Mortar Bd., Washington Ind. Writers, Inc., Kappa Tau Alpha. Democrat.

PATTERSON, NONA SPARKS, small business owner; b. Tipton Hill, N.C., Sept. 9, 1935; d. Fred and Mary Jane (Byrd) Sparks; m. J. M. Patterson, Apr. 24, 1960; children: James Stacy, Jonathan Sparks. BS in Elem. Edn. and History, Berry Coll., 1958; postgrad., U. Ga. Tchr. Floyd County Sch. Sys., Ga., 1959-60; H.S. English tchr. Gwinnett County Sch. Sys., Ga., 1960-67; v.p. Furniture Village, Lawrenceville, Ga., 1967—. Past pres. Lawrenceville (Ga.) Elem. Sch., 1976-78, Lawrenceville Mid. Sch., 1978-80, Ctrl. High Sch., 1980-89; Sunday sch. tchr. United Meth. Ch., Lawrenceville, 1980—; bd. dirs. Swinnett Fine Arts Ctr., Duluth, Ga., 1984—; vol. Olympic Com.; del. Dem. Conv., Atlanta, 1984; mem. exec. bd. Swinnett (Ga.) Dem. Com., 1988—; active Jr. Svc. League, Atlanta, 1978—, Atlanta Children's Theatre, 1978-89, Atlanta Symphony Assn., 1989—. Mem. Ga. Home Furnishing Assn. (bd. dirs.). Home: 1946 New Hope Rd Lawrenceville GA 30245 Office: Furniture Village 194 Gwinnett Dr Lawrenceville GA 30245

PATTERSON, PATRICIA ANNE, law librarian; b. Phila., May 12, 1938; d. Stanley J. and Jane T. (Walsh) Compton; m. Keith C., Mar. 11, 1972; 1 child, Brian J. BA, St. Mary Coll., 1970; MLS, U. Denver, 1980. Tax librarian Baker & McKenzie, Chgo., 1981-82; reference librarian Schiff Hardin & Waite, Chgo., 1982-84, law librarian, 1984-87, dir. legal info. svcs., 1987—; mem. faculty Am. Bankers Assn., Nat. Grad. Trust Sch., Evanston, Ill., 1987—; bd. mem. West Pub. Co., St. Paul, 1987—. Reviewer books include American Law Publishing, 1984, Commercial Law, 1987; contbr. articles to profl. jours. Mem. ABA, Am. Assn. Law Librs. (exec. bd.), Chgo. Assn. Law Librs., Spl. Librs. Assn., Assn. Records Mgrs. and Adminstrs., Beta Phi Mu. Roman Catholic. Office: Schiff Hardin & Waite 7200 Sears Towers Chicago IL 60606

PATTERSON, PEGGY, judge; b. 1950. BA, Centre Coll. of Ky., 1972; JD, Univ. of Ky., 1976. With Ogden, Sturgill & Welch, Ashland; magistrate judge U.S. Dist. Ct. (Ky. ea. dist.), 6th circuit, Ashland, 1990—. Office: Carl D Perkins Federal Bldg 1405 Greenup Ave Rm 210 Ashland KY 41101-7542*

PATTERSON, POLLY REILLY (MRS. W. RAY PATTERSON), civic worker, retired communications company executive; b. Wilkinsburg, Pa., 1906; d. Thomas L. and Margaret (Coughey) Reilly; m. W. Ray Patterson, Sept. 2, 1943. Student, U. Pitts. With Bell Telephone Co. of Pa., Pitts., 1925-71, clk., mgmt. positions, 1935-64, assoc. pub. rels. staff, 1965-71. Asst. treas. Allegheny County (Pa.) Soc. for Crippled Children, 1962-66, v.p., 1966-70; bd. dirs. Jr. Achievement, Inc., SW Pa., 1950-71, Pa. Soc. Crippled Children and Adults, 1960-68, Pitts. YWCA, 1964-72, Chatham Village Homes, Inc., 1973-76; mem. Allegheny County United Way, 1972—, nat. ho. of dels. Nat. Soc. for Crippled Children and Adults, 1965-67. Named Pitts. Advt. Woman of Yr., 1958, one of Pitts.'s Ten Outstanding Women, Pitts. Sun Telegraph, 1959; recipient Crystal Prism award Am. Advt. Fedn., 1972, 75. Mem. Assn. Pitts. Clubs (bd. dirs. 1946-81, pres. 1952-53), Altrusa Internat. (pres. Pitts. Club 1950-51), Pitts. Advt. Club (v.p., sec. 1929-69), Pitts. Bus. and Profl. Women's Club, Telephone Pioneers Am. Home: 402 Olympia Rd Pittsburgh PA 15211-1308

PATTERSON, SHELIA FAY, accountant; b. Montgomery, Ala., Mar. 2, 1962; d. Tom Woods and Leanna (McPherson) Provo; m. John Patterson, May 10, 1986; 1 child, Zayauna De'Shaye. BS in Acctg., U. Ala., 1984. Acct. Fairview Med. Ctr., Montgomery, 1985-86, Birmingham (Ala.) Water Works Bd., 1987—; trainer acctg. co-op students Birmingham Water Works Bd., 1990—, safety com. mem., 1990—. Ensemble choir mem. New Pilgrim Bapt. Ch., Birmingham, 1993-94. Mem. Inst. Mgmt. Accts., Beta Gamma. Baptist.

PATTERSON, TRUDY JENKINS, librarian; b. Eunice, La., Feb. 2, 1951; d. Jack Gordon and Bettie (Brunson) Jenkins; m. Donald Ray Patterson, Feb. 9, 1979; children: Daniel Alan, Abby Elizabeth. B.A. in English Edn., U. Southwestern La., 1972; M.L.S., La. State U., 1974. Adminstrv. librarian Richland Parish Library, Rayville, La., 1974-77, Webster Parish Library, Minden, La., 1978-79; head reference dept. Lafayette (La.) Pub. Library, 1979-80; tech. services librarian Calcasieu Parish Pub. Library, Lake Charles, La., 1981-82; adminstrv. librarian Jefferson Davis Parish Library, Jennings, La., 1982—. Mem. Preservation Resource Ctr. New Orleans. Mem. ALA, La. Library Assn., Southeastern Library Assn., Nat. Trust for Historic Preservation, Pub. Libr. Assn. Democrat. Methodist. Home: PO Box 127 Elton LA 70532-0127 Office: Jefferson Davis Parish Libr 118 W Plaquemine St Jennings LA 70546-5856

PATTERSON, VEDA MALIA, equal opportunity specialist; b. Greensboro, N.C., Nov. 9, 1954; d. Walter and Dorothy Martelle (Dusenbury) P. BA, Howard U., 1976; MS, Am. U., 1987. Claims svc. rep. State Farm Ins. Co., Alexandria, Va., 1978-83; substitute tchr. Fairfax County, Arlington County and Alexandria City Schs., 1983-88; cons. pub. rels. United Black Fund, Washington, 1985-87; equal opportunity specialist U.S. Dept. Agriculture, Washington, 1988—; participant U.S. Dept. Agriculture Mgmt. Devel. Program, Washington, 1993-94; cons. in field. Co-founder No. Va. chpt. Nat. Polit. Congress of Black Women. Mem. Continental Socs., Inc. (No. Va. chpt. v.p. 1993—), Jr. League No. Va., Howard U. Alumni Assn. (No. Va. chpt. charter mem., past sec.), Alpha Kappa Alpha. Democrat. Presbyterian. Home: 2000 Huntington Ave #501 Alexandria VA 22303

PATTERSON, VICKI ROBYN, public relations professional; b. Rocky Mount, N.C., June 19, 1952; d. Norman Wheeler and Jane Cummings (Taylor) P. Student, Brenau Coll., Gainesville, Ga.; BA in Journalism, U. S.C., 1979. Adminstrv. asst. Columbia Area Mental Health Ctr., 1979-85; circulation mgr. Bobbin Internat., 1985-86, prodn. coord., 1985-86; freelance writer, 1986-89; pub. info. coord. Babcock Ctr., 1989-91; asst. dir. community edn. S.C. Dept. Disabilities and Spl. Needs, 1991—; pub. rels. coord. Spay-Neuter Assn., Columbia, S.C., 1981; publicity chair Westminster Presbyn. Ch., Columbia, 1991; com. chair St. Patrick's Day Celebration, Columbia, 1991. Author newsletters Money Works, 1986-89, Brick Talk, 1986-89; editor, photographer Key to Columbia mag., 1986-91; editor 50 Most Eligible Men in Columbia, 1980; assoc. editor: Services for People with Mental Retardation, 1992. Bd. dirs. Very Spl. Arts S.C., Columbia, 1992-93; deacon Westminster Presbyn. Ch., 1989-91. Recipient 1st place award 4th Ann. Datsun Student Advt. Contest, 1979. Mem. Vol. Profls. Cultural Coun. (sec. 1990-91, treas. 1991-92, 1st vice chair 1992-93), Toastmasters Internat. (publicity chair 1992, sgt.-at-arms 1992), Media Club, State Govt. Info. Officers, Alpha Gamma Delta. Home: 3004 Exmoor Rd Columbia SC 29204-7712 Office: SC Dept Disabilities Spl 4706 Harden St Ext Columbia SC 29240

PATTERSON, VIRGINIA GOODWIN, social worker; b. Nashville, Feb. 21, 1917; d. Marsh and Lena Grace (Givens) Goodwin; BS, Peabody Coll., 1968; MSW, U. Tenn., 1970; lic. pvt. social work practitioner; lic. social worker; m. Fletcher Woodall Patterson, June 17, 1940; 1 child, Judith Ellen Patterson Murphy. Various secretarial positions, 1934-43; dir. day camp Cumberland Valley Girl Scout council, Nashville, summers 1953-62; sec. Centenary Methodist Community Center, Nashville, 1961-64; dir. resident camp Sycamore Hills, Ashland City, Tenn., summers 1963-65; case worker United Methodist Community Center, 1970-71; social case worker, dir. day care for elderly Sr. Citizens, Inc., Nashville, 1971-88; ret., 1988; v.p. Cumberland Valley Girl Scout council, 1963-64; youth tchr., counselor Dalewood Meth. Ch., 1950—, pres. Women's Soc. Christian Service. Pres. Isaac Litton High Sch. PTA, Nashville, 1959-61; dir. Ind. Svcs. Sr. Citizens, 1985; pres. United Meth. Women, 1990, 94; mem. choir Dale United Meth., 1990—; mem. adminstrv. bd. Coun. on Ministries. Recipient Thanks badge Girl Scouts, 1961. Mem. Nat. Assn. Social Workers (past chpt. registrar, corr. sec.), Tenn. Fedn. Aging (pres. 1982-84, sec. 1984-86, 91, bd. dirs. 1992-94), Nat. Council Aging, Pi Gamma Mu (past chpt. sec.). Republican. Lodges: Soroptimists of Nashville (pres. 1986), Civitan (pres. 1990-91, bd. dirs. 1992-94). Contbr. articles to profl. jours. Home: 1709 Sherwood Ln Nashville TN 37216-4023 Office: 1801 Broadway Nashville TN 37203

PATTERSON, VIVIAN JANE, gemologist; b. Sedalia, Mo., May 20, 1937; d. Raymond W. and Emma M. (Ossenschmidt) Chapin; m. Herbert G. Patterson, Aug. 28, 1965; children: Cynthia Laura, Brian Chase. Student, South Tex. Jr. Coll., Houston, 1963-64; grad., Gemological Inst. Am., 1982. Various secretarial positions Houston area, 1956-69; mgr., co-owner G.E.M. Jewelry, Webster, Tex., 1982-91, 93; co-owner G.E.M. Jewelry and Gifts, Port Richey, Fla., 1993—; frequent speaker womens' orgns., Houston area. Sponsor Clear Lake City (Tex.) Youth Soccer, 1985-86, Bay Area Baseball Leagues, Houston, 1983-86; judge Distributive Edn. Clubs Am., 1987; mem. Cmty. Svc. Coun. Pasco County. Mem. Accredited Gemologist Assn., Gemological Inst. Am. (cert.), Jewelers of Am., Fla. Jewelers Assn., Calusa Bus. and Profl. Women's Assn., West Pasco C. of C. (amb.), Prof. Svcs. Networking Group (sec.), Masons (Job's Daughters, hon. mem.). Republican. Methodist.

PATTERSON-DEHN, CATHLEEN ERIN, nurse, hospital administrator; b. Akron, Feb. 25, 1958; d. James Edward and Doris Elizabeth (Boyd) P.; m. James Keith Dehn, June 27, 1981. BSN, U. Akron, 1980; MSN, Case Western Res. U., 1988; MA in Dance, Case Western Reserve U., 1992; postgrad., NYU, 1994—. RN, Ohio; cert. pediatric nurse practitioner ANCC. Nurse technician Children's Med. Ctr. Akron, 1978-80, staff nurse, 1980-81; pediatric and advanced clin. nurse, asst. head nurse, clin. nurse specialist Rainbow Babies and Children's Hosp., Cleve., 1981-91, edn. coord., 1991-94, project dir., 1989-91; dir., pediatric nurse practitioner The Child Health Ctr., Bklyn., 1994—; lectr. Frances Payne Bolton Sch. Nursing, Case Western Res. U., Cleve., 1990—, project dir., 1991—; project dir. Dance Cleve., 1990-91; mem. nat. faculty Neonatal Resuscitation Program, Am. Heart Assn., Am. Acad. Pediatrics; instr. Nursing Child Assessment Satellite Tng. U. of Washington, 1991—, Nursing Systems Toward Effective Parenting of Pre-Term Infants, 1992. Co-founder Sick Kids Need Involved People, Cleve., 1987; pres. Friends Footpath, Cleve., 1989-90; team-walk capt. March of Dimes, Cleve., 1989— (Edn. grantee 1991); mem. Nat. Mus. Women in Arts. Recipient Samuel E. and Rebecca Elliott award for Community Svc. Case Western Res. U., 1988; named One of Outstanding Young Women of Am., 1988; Fed. Profl. Nurse Trainee scholar, 1986-87. Mem. Midwest Nursing Rsch. Soc., NAFE, Womens City Club, Sigma Theta Tau. Home: 15 Washington Pl #4A New York NY 10003 Office: The Child Health Ctr 209 York St Brooklyn NY 11201

PATTERSON-WENGER, PAMELA ANN, physical therapist; b. Clay Center, Kans., Oct. 10, 1954; d. Nolan John and Rachel Ann (Dinsmore) Patterson; m. James Donald Wenger, Dec. 8, 1979; 1 child, Patrick Nolan. Student, U. Kans., Lawrence, 1972-75; BS in Physical Therapy, U. Kans., Kansas City, 1976. Lic. physical therapist, Iowa, Kans., Nebr., Mo. Physical therapist dir. Profl. Physical Therapy Svcs., Hamburg, Iowa, 1977-81; physical therapist Physical Therapy Svcs., Hamburg, 1981-83; dir. physical therapy Restorative Health Svcs., Hamburg, 1983-86, Red Oak, Iowa, 1986-87; dir. physical therapy Community Hosp., Fairfax, Mo., 1987—, Community Hosp. Assn. Home Health Agency, 1992—; cons. Stanton (Iowa) Care Ctr., 1984-87, Malvern (Iowa) Care Ctr., 1984-85, Vista Garden Care Ctr., Red Oak, 1984-87, Good Samaritan Care Ctr., Red Oak, 1984-87, Red Oak Rehab. Agy., 1985-87, Bethesda Care Ctr. Tarkio, Mo., 1988—. Active First Presby. Ch., Clay Center, 1976-83, United Trinty Ch., Hamburg, 1977—, Omaha Ballet, 1978—, Opera Omaha, 1978—, Hamburg Community Arts Council, 1985—. Mem. Am. Physical Therapy Assn., Orthopedic and Geriatric sections Am. Physical Therapy Assn., Iowa Physical Therapy Assn., Mo. Physical Therapy Assn. Republican. Home: 1510 Argyle St Hamburg IA 51640-1402 Office: Community Hosp Assn US Hwy 59 Fairfax MO 64446

PATTON, CINDY ANNE, biology educator; b. Portsmouth, Va., Aug. 31, 1956; d. James Clark and Nancy Elizabeth (Bell) P. BS in Biology, Fitchburg (Mass.) State Coll., 1986; M in Health Edn., Worcester (Mass.) State Coll., 1993. Cert. sci., biology, gen. sci. and health tchr., Mass. Tchr. earth sci. Leominster (Mass.) High Sch., 1987-88; tchr. sci. Grey Jr. High Sch., Acton, Mass., 1989-93, cheerleading coach, 1989-93; tchr. South Mid. Sch., Braintree, Mass., 1993-94, student coun. advisor, 1993-94; biology prof. Middlesex C.C., Bedford, Mass., 1994—; advisor tennis intramurals, Acton, 1990-93. Bd. dirs. Minutemen Assn. Retarded Citizens, Concord, Mass., 1989; coach Acton Cmty. Basketball, 1990-93; EMT, 1991—; CPR instr. Am. Heart Assn., 1993—; mem. Acton (Mass.) Bd. Health, 1994—. Recipient resolution Mass. Ho. of Reps., 1991, Portrait of Tchr. award Campbell Soup Co., 1991, Am. Hero in Edn. award Reader's Digest, 1991. Mem. NAST. Office: Middlesex CC Springs Rd Bedford MA 01730

PATTON, MARCIE JANE, political science educator; b. Rochester, Pa., Apr. 8, 1953; d. James Richardson and Jane (Snitger) P. BA, Trinity U., San Antonio, 1975; MA, U. Chgo., 1977, PhD, 1989. Instr. Elmhurst (Ill.) Coll., 1984-86, asst. prof., 1986-92; asst. prof. polit. sci. Fairfield (Conn.) U., 1992—; bd. dirs. Found. on Democratization and Polit. Change in the Middle East, Washington, 1991—; mem. adv. com. Midwest Faculty Seminar Program, Chgo., 1990-94; cons. Bennett Assocs., Chgo., 1991-93. Author book revs. and articles. Fairfield U. grantee, 1993, 94—, Am. Inst. Maghribi Studies grantee, 1991, Elmhurst Coll. grantee, 1987, 90. Mem.

Am. Polit. Sci. Assn., Middle East Studies Assn. Office: Fairfield U Dept Politics N Benson Rd Fairfield CT 06430

PATTON, NANCY MATTHEWS, elementary education educator; b. Pitts., Apr. 7, 1942; d. Thomas Joseph and Sara Theresa (Jocunskas) Matthews; m. Jack E. Patton, July 20, 1974; children: Susan, Steven. BS in Edn., Ind. U. of Pa., 1963; grad. student, U. Pitts. 4th grade tchr. Elroy Sch., Pitts., 1980-91; 6th grade tchr. Brentwood Middle Sch., Pitts., 1991—; sponsor Brentwood Middle Sch. newspaper; coach Brentwood Varsity Cheerleaders, 1981-93. Councilperson Brentwood Borough Coun., 1988—, v.p., 1994—; sec. Brentwood Dem. Com., 1989—. Mem. NEA, Nat. Sci. Tchrs. Assn., Pa. State Edn. Assn., Brentwood Century Club. Democrat. Roman Catholic. Home: 105 Hillson Ave Pittsburgh PA 15227-2941

PATTY, ANNA CHRISTINE, middle school educator; b. Atlanta, Aug. 25, 1937; d. Henry Richard and Gertrude (Smith) Johnson; children: Robert E., C. Wayne Jr., Christine E. BS in Math., U. Ga., 1959; MA in Edn., Va. Poly. Inst. and State U., 1991. Cert. tchr., Va. Mgr. Steak and Ale Restaurants, Inc., Dallas, 1982-84; bus. mgr. Nova Plaza Corp., Charlotte, N.C., 1984-86; asst. mgr. WoodLo, Inc., Charlotte, 1986-87; food activity mgr. Army and Air Force Exch. Svc., Schweinfurt, Fed. Republic Germany, 1987-89; substitute tchr. Montgomery County Schs., Christiansburg, Va., 1989-91; rsch. asst. Va. Poly. Inst. and State U., Blacksburg, 1990-91; math. and sci. middle sch. tchr. Hampton (Va.) City Schs., 1991—. Mem. NEA, Va. Educators Assn., Nat. Sci. Tchrs. Assn. (summer inst. participant 1992), Va. Middle Sch. Assn., Va. Sci. Tchrs., Nat. Coun. Tchrs. Math. Republican. Unitarian. Home: 121 Signature Way Apt 315 Hampton VA 23666-5939

PATZKOWSKI, CAROLYN SUE, nursing consultant; b. Enid, Okla., Aug. 12, 1954; d. Esther Leola (Beckwith) P. Diploma, Hillcrest Hosp., Tulsa, 1976; BSN, West Tex. State U., 1980. Cert. pediatric ICU nurse. Pediatric staff nurse Bass Hosp., Enid, 1979; post-partum staff nurse Okla. Meml. Hosp., Oklahoma City, 1980, med.-surg. staff nurse, 1981; ind. cons. Enid, 1981—. Mem. internation mission Marilyn Hickey Ministries, London, 1993. Home: 734 N Davis St Enid OK 73701-3415

PATZOLD, LORETTA ANN, counselor; b. Crawfordsville, Ind., Feb. 10, 1947; d. Kenneth Edward and Doris (Taylor) Smith; m. William Earl Patzold, May 25, 1990. BS, Ind. U., Kokomo, 1970, MS, 1971, K-12 reading endorsement, 1980; counselor cert., Ind. U., Indpls., 1990. Elem. tchr. No. Cmty. Schs., Sharpsville, Ind., 1970-72, 85-90, tchr. kindergarten, 1972-85, elem. and jr. H.S. counselor, 1990—; tutor, Kokomo, 1970-88; reading clinician Ind. U., Kokomo, summer 1983. EMT, Indian Heights Fire Dept., Kokomo, 1984-87; clown for nursing homes Miles of Smiles, Kokomo, 1990—. Mem. ACA, Ind. Counseling Assn. (regional sec.-treas. 1992-94), Am. Sch. Counselors Assn., Ind. Sch. Counselors Assn. (com. 1992-93), Ind. Sch. Women's Club, Delta Kappa Gamma (chpt. pres. 1992-94, state conf. treas. 1994, scholar 1990), Pi Lambda Theta (regional rep. 1980-86). Home: 2032 E Boulevard Kokomo IN 46902-2451 Office: No Cmty Schs 2115 W 500 N Sharpsville IN 46068

PAUL, ALIDA RUTH, arts and crafts educator; b. San Antonio, May 30, 1953; d. Richard Irving and Anne Louise (Holman) Paul. B.S. in Edn., Southwest Tex. State U., 1975; M.Ed., U. Houston, 1984. Cert. tchr., Tex. Tchr. art and crafts Houston Ind. Sch. Dist., 1975—. Republican. Episcopalian. Home: 16830 Grampin Dr Houston TX 77084-1945

PAUL, BARBARA MARIA, insurance executive; b. Balt., Jan. 16, 1952; d. Edward Leonard and Alice B. (Zengro) Fraczkowski; m. Wayne Allen Paul, Sept. 12, 1980. BA in Bus. Adminstrn., Coll. Notre Dame of Md., Balt., 1980, MA in Mgmt., 1987. Analsyt Blue Cross/Blue Shield, Balt., 1972-76, trainer, 1977-80, coord., 1980-83, project mgr., 1983-85, mgr. account installation, 1985-89; v.p. ops. Dental Mgmt. Corp., Balt., 1989—; adj. faculty Coll. Notre Dame of Md., Balt., 1987—. Mem. Historic Hampton, Balt., 1987—. Mem. ASTD, Am. Mgmt. Assn., Chesapeake Human Resource Assn., Exec. Women's Network, Delta Mu Delta, Baltimore County C. of C. Office: Dental Mgmt Corp 1 W Pennsylvania Ave Ste 800 Towson MD 21204-5025

PAUL, BARBARA SIMMONS, management accountant; b. Needham, Mass., Jan. 18, 1934; d. Charles Edward and Mary (Cornell) Simmons; m. Warren I. Paul, 1962 (div. 1978); children: David Dickson Paul, Brice Cornell Paul. Student, N.E. Bapt. Hosp. Sch. Nursing, Boston, 1951-53; BS in Bus. Adminstrn. summa cum laude, U. So. Maine, 1979. Agy. cashier Paul Revere Life Ins. Co., Worcester, Mass., 1953-59; flight attendant Ea. Air Lines, N.Y.C., 1960-62; agy. cashier Bankers Life Co., N.Y.C., 1962-64; relief nurse various agys., Columbus, Ohio, 1966-69; acct. clk. Kans. State U., Manhattan, 1971-74; clerical temp. various agys., Portland, Maine, 1974-79; cost acct. Maine Nat. Bank, Portland, 1980-83; v.p. Casco Bay Island Devel. Assocs., 1981-92; fin. analyst Maine Savings Bank, Portland, 1983-86; pres. Mgmt. Info. Sys. Svc., Yarmouth, 1986—; team leader household contbns. United Way Campaigns, Portland, 1982, employee contbns., 1984, corp. contbns., 1986; participant various cost acctg. seminars Greater Portland Area, 1984-94; owner, mgr. summer camp resort, Casco Bay, Maine. Mem. Mcpl. Planning Bd., Manhattan, 1971-74; leader cub scouts and boy scouts Boy Scouts Am., Yarmouth, Maine, 1974-78; elected Yarmouth Town Coun., 1985-88; mem. land acquisition com. Yarmouth Open Space, 1988-90; treas. Yarmouth Hist. Soc., 1988-92; originator, mgr. Citizens for Sensible Taxes, Yarmouth, 1990-94; elected Yarmouth Sch. Com., 1994—. Scholar N.E. Bapt. Sch. Nursing, 1951. Mem. Inst. Mgmt. Accts. Home and Office: Mgmt Info Sys Svc RR 1 Box 129A Homewood Village Yarmouth ME 04096

PAUL, CAROL ANN, academic administrator; b. Brockton, Mass., Dec. 17, 1936; d. Joseph W. and Mary M. (DeMeulenaer) Bjork; m. Robert D. Paul, Dec. 21, 1957; children: Christine, Dana, Stephanie, Robert. BS, U. Mass., 1958; MAT, R.I. Coll., 1968, Brown U., 1970; EdD, Boston U., 1978. Tchr. biology Attleboro (Mass.) High Sch., 1965-68; asst. dean., mem. faculty biology North Shore Community Coll., Beverly, Mass., 1969-78; master planner N.J. Dept. for Higher Edn., Trenton, 1978-80; assoc. v.p. Fairleigh Dickinson U., Rutherford, N.J., 1980-86; v.p. acad. affairs Suffolk Community Coll., Selden, N.Y., 1986—; faculty devel. cons. various colls., 1979—, title III evaluator, 1985—. Author: (lab. manual and workbook) Minicourses and Labs for Biological Science, 1972 (rev. edit., 1975); (with others) Strategies and Attitudes, 1986; book reviewer, 1973-77. V.p. League of Women Voters, Beverly, 1970-74, Cranford, N.J., 1982-83; alumni rep. Brown U., Cranford, 1972—. Commonwealth Mass. scholar, 1958; recipient Acad. Yr. award NSF, 1968-69, Proclamation for Leadership award Suffolk County Exec., 1989. Mem. AAHE, AAWCC, Profls. and Orgn. Developers (planning com. 1977-79, nat. exec. bd. 1979-80), Nat. Coun. for Staff, Phi Theta Kappa, Pi Lambda Theta. Roman Catholic. Home: 75 Fairview Circle Middle Island NY 11953-2340 Office: Suffolk Community Coll 533 College Rd Selden NY 11784-2851

PAUL, CHARLOTTE P., nursing educator; b. Clarendon, Tex., Jan. 13, 1941; d. William Clyde Peggram and Sibyl (Rattan) Jones; m. Robert M. Paul, Apr. 4, 1964; children: Peter, Lauraine. Diploma, St. Anthony's Hosp. Sch. Nursing, Amarillo, Tex., 1961; student, Amarillo Coll., 1958-65; BS, Syracuse U., 1972, MS, 1973, PhD in Edn. Adminstrn., 1979; postgrad., Wright State U., 1977-79, U. Tex., El Paso, 1983-86. Nurse St. Anthony's Hosp., Amarillo, Tex., 1961-65; evening charge nurse Upstate Med. Ctr. SUNY, Syracuse, 1966-68, VA Hosp. Gen. Hosp., Syracuse, 1965-66; asst. to head nurse Meml. Hosp., Syracuse, 1966-68; nurse IV therapy Community-Gen. Hosp., Syracuse, 1968-72; instr. Syracuse Cen. Sch. System, 1972; asst. dir. insvc. edn. House of Good Samaritan Hosp., Watertown, N.Y., 1973-74; instr. SUNY Sch. Nursing, Syracuse, 1974-75, Syracuse U. Sch. Nursing, 1975-76; asst. dean Wright State U., Dayton, Ohio, 1977-79; assoc. prof. Edinboro U. Pa., 1979-86, prof., 1986—, chairperson dept. grad. studies, 1980-82, chairperson dept. nursing, 1987-89; coord. quality assurance William Beaumont Army Med. Ctr., Ft. Bliss, Tex., 1982-85; adj. assoc. prof. U. Tex., El Paso, 1982-85; cons. in field. Contbr. articles to profl. jours., papers in field. Bd. dirs. ARC, Syracuse, 1970-77, Erie County Emergency Mgmt. Agy.; chairperson Lake Erie Higher Edn. Coun., 1972-74, cons., 1987—; mem. Coun. on Aging Com. on Long Term Care, Dayton, 1977-78. Lt. col. USAR. Recipient Unit Citation award CAP, 1968, Excellence in Nursing Edn. award, 1992, Leadership and Svc. award Lake Area Health Edn. Ctr., 1994; Gladys Post scholar, 1958-61, Rodney Horle scholar, 1971-72, Nellie Hurly scholar, 1971-72; grantee HEW, 1977, Wright State U., 1977-78, William Beaumont Army Med. Ctr., 1986, Edinboro U. Pa., 1979-80, 91; Nightingale Soc. fellow, 1988; named to Internat. Profl. and Bus. Women's Hall of Fame, 1994. Mem. APHA, Gerontol. Soc. Am., St. Anthony's Hosp. Sch. Nursing Alumni Assn., Syracuse U. Alumni Assn., N.Y. Acad. Sci., Assn. Mil. Surgeons U.S., Nat. Ski Patrol (life), Nightengale Soc., Kiwanis (bd. dirs. Edinboro club 1987-95, pres. 1988-89, v.p. 1987-88), Sigma Theta Tau (advisor), Pi Lambda Theta (pres. local chpt. 1973-75). Republican. Office: Edinboro U Pa 139 Centennial Hall Edinboro PA 16412

PAUL, EVE W., lawyer; b. N.Y.C., June 16, 1930; d. Leo I. and Tamara (Sogolow) Weinschenker; m. Robert D. Paul, Apr. 9, 1952; children: Jeremy Ralph, Sarah Elizabeth. BA, Cornell U., 1950; JD, Columbia U., 1952. Bar: N.Y. 1952, Conn. 1960, U.S. Ct. Appeals (2nd cir.) 1975, U.S. Supreme Ct. 1977. Assoc. Botein, Hays, Sklar & Herzberg, N.Y.C., 1952-54; pvt. practice Stamford, Conn., 1960-70; staff atty. Legal Aid Soc., N.Y.C., 1970-71; assoc. Greenbaum, Wolff & Ernst, N.Y.C., 1972-78; v.p. legal affairs Planned Parenthood Fedn. Am., N.Y.C., 1979—, v.p., gen. counsel, 1991—. Contbr. articles to legal and health publs. Trustee Cornell U., Ithaca, N.Y., 1979-84; mem. Stamford Planning Bd., Conn., 1967-70; bd. mem. Stamford League Women Voters, 1960-62. Harlan Fiske Stone scholar Columbia Law Sch., 1952. Mem. ABA, Conn. Bar Assn., Assn. of Bar of City of N.Y., Stamford Bar Assn., U.S. Trademark Assn. (chairperson dictionary listings com. 1988-90), Phi Beta Kappa, Phi Kappa Phi. Office: Planned Parenthood Fedn 810 7th Ave New York NY 10019-5818

PAUL, EVELYN ROSE, critical care nurse; b. New Bern, N.C., May 10, 1953; d. Robert Austin and Sadie Marie (Simpson) P. BSN, U. N.C., 1975. Cert. critical care nurse, ACLS. Staff nurse Beaufort County Hosp., Washington, N.C., 1975-79; chief nurse, nurse clinician, staff nurse surg. ICU Med. U. S.C., Charleston, 1979-85; staff/charge nurse cardiac surgery Pitt County Meml. Hosp., Greenville, N.C., 1985-89, asst. nurse mgr. cardiac surgery, 1989-95, RN IV, 1995—. Mem. AACN (pres. elect Heart of the East chpt. 1991-92).

PAUL, GRACE, retired medical technologist, author; b. Liberal, Kans., Mar. 12, 1908; d. David and Myrtle Helen (Brewer) P.; student, Tulsa U., 1930-36, Auburn U., 1948, Columbia U., 1949-51. Med. technologist St. Johns Hosp., Tulsa, 1930-36, VA Hosp., Wadsworth, Kans., 1947-48; plant quarantine insp. U.S. Dept. Agr., N.Y.C., 1948-51; claims examiner Social Security Adminstrn., Balt., 1956-71; market rsch. interviewer Response Analysis, Princeton, N.J., 1973-76. Vol. worker United Way of Temple (Tex.), 1974-84, Cultural Activities Center, Youth Services Bur., Ret. Sr. Vol. Program, 1973—; active CAC Humanities Council of Temple, 1972-86; vol. Retired Sr. Vol. Program. Served with WAC, 1944-46. Recipient Jefferson award for Central Tex., 1983; named Outstanding Vol. in Temple Chs., 1985, tax counselor Vol. Income Tax Assistance and Tax Counselling for Elderly. Mem. Am. Soc. Med. Technologists, Entomol. Soc. Am., Internat. Platform Assn., Bus. and Profl. Women's Club, Kans. Authors Club. Presbyterian. Author: Your Future in Medical Technology, 1962; A Short Course in Skilled Supervision, 1965; contbr. to Environ. Engr.'s Handbook, vol. III, 1975. Home: 209 W 8th Ave # 2 Hutchinson KS 67501-4646

PAUL, MARY MELCHIOR, human resources professional; b. Tipton, Ind., Apr. 29, 1952; d. John A. and Inez Marie (Clark) Meyer; 1 child, Regina. BS, U. Evansville, 1974; MBA, So. Ill. U., 1987. Mgr. The Children's Shops, St. Louis, 1980-86; cons., trainer Edison Bros. Stores, St. Louis, 1987; program mgr. Anheuser-Busch Cos., 1988-94; human resources devel. mgr. Campbell Taggart, Inc. (divsn. Anheuser-Busch Cos. Inc.), St. Louis, 1994—. Mem. Coro Found. Mem. ASTD, Profl. Woman Network, Women in Leadership Alumnae. Home: 530 Lafayette Dr Belleville IL 62220-3664

PAUL, NANCY ELIZABETH, psychiatric-mental health nurse; b. Summit, N.J., Mar. 5, 1943; d. Victor Carl and Lois Emily (Procter) Bonardel; m. Richard Edward Paul, Apr. 8, 1967; children: Deborah, Michael, Kimberly. BS in Nursing, Skidmore Coll., 1965; MA in Counseling, Framingham State Coll., 1991. RN, Mass.; ANA cert. psychiat.-mental health nurse, clin. specialist; lic. mental health counselor. Head nurse Mass. Mental Health Ctr., Boston, 1965-68; nurse Cushing Hosp., Framingham, Mass., Charles River Hosp., Wellesley, Mass., 1969-72; staff nurse Leonard Morse Hosp., Natick, Mass., 1979—; outpatient clinician Counseling Ctr., 1993—. Mem. Mass. Nurses Assn. Home: 933 Old Connecticut Path Framingham MA 01701-7750

PAUL, RHONDA ELIZABETH, university program director, career development counselor; d. John and Vivian (Griffin) P. BA, Mich. State U., 1977; MA, Atlanta U., 1979; postgrad., Wayne State U., 1982—. Cert. counselor, Mich.; nat. cert. career counelor; lic. profl. counselor. Counselor, student affairs dept. Spelman Coll., Atlanta, 1978-79; life/career devel. specialist Wayne State U., Detroit, 1979-81, minority devel. counselor, 1981-83; prog. dir. recruitment dept. Wayne State Sch. of Medicine, Detroit, 1983—; cons./proprietor RP Career Assocs., Detroit, 1990—. Recipient Award of Pride, Mich. State U., Lansing, 1977, Spl. Recognition award Nat. Bd. for Cert. Counselors, 1993. Mem. Am. Assn. Counseling and Devel., Mich. Assn. Counseling and Devel., Mich. Assn. Multicultural Counseling and Devel., Nat. Career Devel. Assn., Nat. Coalition of 100 Black Women (bd. dirs.), NAACP, Alpha Kappa Alpha. Home: 4068 Cortland St Detroit MI 48204-1506 Office: Wayne State U H N J 1-East Detroit MI 48202

PAUL, SUSMITA (MISTY PAUL), chiropractor; b. Calcutta, India, Jan. 10, 1963; came to U.S., 1971; d. Pradip Kumar and Chandra (Saha) P.; m. George Arthur Emilio, Aug. 20, 1988. BS in Biology, Union Coll., 1985; D of Chiropractic, Logan Coll. Chiropractic, 1988. Lic. chiropractor, Tex., Calif., Mo., Colo. Assoc. Chiropractic Health Ctr., Columbus, Miss., 1988-90; owner Ctrl. Valley Chiropractic, Sacramento, 1991-93; assoc. United Chiropractic, San Antonio, 1993—. Pres., bd. dirs. Leads Club, Carmichael, Calif., 1992; mem. Network Profl., Fair Oaks, Calif., 1991-92. Recipient Sigma Chi award Union Coll., 1981. Mem. Am. Chiropractic Assn., Tex. Chiropractic Assn., Toastmasters Internat.

PAULEY, JANE, television journalist; b. Indpls., Oct. 31, 1950; m. Garry Trudeau; 3 children. BA in Polit. Sci, Ind. U., 1971; D. Journalism (hon.), DePauw U., 1978. Reporter Sta. WISH-TV, Indpls., 1972-75; co-anchor WMAQ-TV News, Chgo., 1975-76, The Today Show, NBC, N.Y.C., 1976-90; corr. NBC News, N.Y.C., 1976—; prin. writer, reporter NBC Nightly News, 1980-82, substitute anchor, 1990—; co-anchor Early Today, NBC, 1982-83; prin. corr. Real Life With Jane Pauley, NBC, 1990; co-anchor Dateline NBC, 1992—. Office: NBC News 30 Rockefeller Plz New York NY 10112*

PAULEY, RHODA ANNE, communications and marketing executive; b. Elizabeth, N.J., Nov. 26, 1939; d. Isadore and Jean Litin Manheim. BA magna cum laude, Smith Coll., 1961; postgrad. in Am. lit. Stanford U., 1961-63. Editorial asst. Edn. and World Affairs, N.Y.C., 1963-65; tech. writer Data Processing div. U.S. Life Ins. Corp., N.Y.C., 1965-67; dir. publs. and mktg. Diebold Group, Inc., N.Y.C., 1967-72; gen. mgr. Direct Mail/Mktg. Assn., Inc., N.Y.C., 1972-75; cons. on new bus. and orgn. devel., 1975-76; v.p. comm. and clearinghouse Work Am. Inst., Scarsdale, N.Y., 1976-81; dir. comm. svcs. Girl Scouts U.S.A., 1981-90; dir. comm. YWCA of the U.S.A., 1990-92; cons. Strategic Comm. 1992—; chmn. com. for Liaison on Advt. and Sales Promotion, 1974. Chmn., Task Force on Employee-Mgmt. Rels. and Quality of Working Life, Transp. Rsch. Bd./NRC, 1979-82. Editor: The Student in Higher Education, 1968. Bd. dirs. West Side One Stop for Coord. Sr. Svcs. Mem. Am. Mktg. Assn. (pres. not-for-profit coun., 1990-91, v.p. pub. rels., N.Y. women in com. 1990-92), N.Y. Women in Comm. (chair strategic planning 1992-94), Nat. Coun. Chs. (bd. mgrs.). Home: 233 E 69th St New York NY 10021-5414

PAULIK, MARY THERESA, municipal government official, researcher; b. Flushing, N.Y., Sept. 17, 1939; d. Joseph Percival and Gertrude Veronica (Mahony) Melanson; m. William Paul Paulik, Jan. 21, 1961. AA in Social Scis., Suffolk Community Coll., Brentwood, N.Y., 1979; BA in Human Rels. in Mgmt., St. Joseph's Coll., Patchoque, N.Y., 1980; MPA, L.I. U., 1986. Teller, clk. Chase Manhattan Bank, Flushing, 1957-58; adminstrv. corp. sec. Ginn & Co./Ednl. Textbooks, N.Y.C., 1960-61, regional supervisory mgr., 1961-66; various per diem positions Writing/Rsch. Cos.-Bus. Firms, L.I., N.Y., 1967-70; adminstrv. sec. Town of Islip, Brentwood Water Dist., 1972-88, water dist. coord., 1988—; officer bus. and polit. orgns.; mem. environ. groups. Contbr. articles to profl. jours. Fundraiser United Way, Suffolk, N.Y., 1987-88, team coord., 1989—, assn. for retarded, 1987-88, unit coord., 1989—; fundraiser March of Dimes; mem. Bayshore Rep. Club, N.Y., 1989—, pres., 1992; mem. Islip Rep. Women, 1989—. Mem. AAUW, Bus. and Profl. Women (mem. exec. bd. Bay Shore chpt. 1989—, pres. 1994, Woman of Yr. 1994), Cousteau Soc. (environmentalist), Nat. Audubon Soc., Nat. Geog. Soc. (environmentalist), Nat. Wildlife Soc. (environmentalist), Wilderness Soc., Sigma Iota Chi. Roman Catholic.

PAULIN, AMY RUTH, civic activist, consultant; b. Bklyn., Nov. 29, 1955; d. Ben and Alice Lois (Roth) P.; m. Ira Schuman, May 25, 1980; children: Beth, Sarah, Joseph. BA, SUNY, Albany, 1977, MA, 1978, postgrad., 1979—. Instr. SUNY, Albany, 1978, Queens (N.Y.) House of Detention, 1979; fundraiser United Jewish Appeal Fedn., N.Y.C., 1979-83; dir. devel. Altro Health & Rehab., Bronx, N.Y., 1983-86; fundraising cons. N.Y.C., 1986-88; pres. LWV, Westchester, N.Y., 1992-95; trustee Scarsdale Village, 1995—. Mem. Town Club Edn. Com., 1983-89, mem. Scarsdale Bowl Com., 1992—, chair, 1994—; mem. Scarsdale Japanese Festival, 1992-93; mem. Westchester Women's Equity Day, 1987-92; mem. nominating com. Heathcote Neighborhood Assn., 1991-92, bd. dirs.; mem. Westchester County Bd. Legislators Task Force on Women and Youth at Risk, Updating Voting Equipment; founding mem. Women for Justice and Safety; mem. steering com. POW'R Coalition; co-chair Parent Tchr. Coun. Sch. Budget Study; future planning chair Kids Base Bd.; chair parking and traffic sub-com. Villiage Downtown Devel. Com.; bd. dirs. Scarsdale Village Youth Bd., Scarsdale Open Soc. Assn., United Jewish Appeal Fedn. Scarsdale Womens Campaign; troop leader Girl Scouts Am. Home: 12 Burgess Rd Scarsdale NY 10583-4410

PAULIN, JEANIE MARIE, accountant; b. Louisville, Mar. 14, 1963; d. Anita Marie P.; 1 child, Anita Christene. BSBA, U. Louisville, 1985; postgrad., U. Tex., 1988-92. CPA, CMA. Acctg. asst. Ky. Fried Chicken, Louisville, 1982-86; store mgr. Ky. Fried Chicken, Ft. Worth, 1986-87; acctf. asst. Meridian Oil Inc., Ft. Worth, 1987-88, acct., 1988-90; acct. Atlas Powder Co., Dallas, 1990-91; sr. acct. I GTE Directories, Dallas Ft. Worth Airport, 1991-93; sr. acct. II GTE Directories, Dallas, Ft. Worth, 1993-94, supr. NYPS sales billing, 1994—. Vol. Dallas Police Dept., 1990-91, Ft. Worth Police Dept., 1988-90. Mem. Am. Soc. Personnel Adminstrs., Tex. Soc. CPA's, Inst. Mgmt. Accts. Roman Catholic. Office: GTE Directories PO Box 618910 Dallas TX 75261

PAULK, ANNA MARIE, office manager; b. Columbia, Tenn., Feb. 5, 1959; d. Earl Gaston Woodard, Sr. and Anna Genette (McCuin) Woodard Tison; m. John Eason Paulk III, June 6, 1982 (div. June 1992); children: Erica Marie, Aimee Renae, Janna Elizabeth. AAS, Abraham Baldwin Coll., 1988; BBA cum laude, Ga. Southwestern U., 1992. Office mgr. E.J. Tison, D.D.S., P.C., Ashburn, Ga., 1979—. Pres. PTO/Tiftarea Acad., 1993—. Mem. Gamma Beta Phi. Republican. Mem. Ch. of Christ. Home: 283 Lakeview Dr Sycamore GA 31790 Office: EJ Tison DDS PC 372 E College Ave Ashburn GA 31714-1209

PAULL, LINDY, legislative staff director; b. Miami, Nov. 22, 1948. BBA in Acctg., Fla. Internat. U., U. Fla., 1974; JD, U. Fla., 1980, LLM, 1980. Sr. tax specialist Laventhol & Horwath CPAs, Coral Gables, Fla., 1974-77; instr. legal writing and tax rsch. U. Fla. Coll. of Law, 1979-80; atty.- advisor Judge Herbert L. Chabot, U.S. Tax Ct., 1980-82; tax assoc. Sutherland, Asbill & Brennan, Washington, 1982-86, tax counsel, mem. minority staff, 1986, minority dep. chief counsel, 1987; minority dep. staff dir., chief tax counsel Senate Com. on Fin., Washington, 1988—. Office: Com on Fin Rm 205 Senate Dirksen Office Bldg Washington DC 20510*

PAULSON, MARY ALICE, psychologist; b. Columbus, Ohio, July 23, 1962; d. H. William and Carol Joan (Phillips) P.; m. Andrew Edward Kerr, Dec. 23, 1990. Student, Newbold Coll., Berkshire, Eng., 1982, Columbia Union Coll., 1980-83; BA in Psychology, Mt. Vernon (Ohio) Nazarene Coll., 1986; MA, Andrews U., 1990, postgrad., 1993. Lic. prof. counselor. Chem. lab. technician Ashland Chem., Dublin, Ohio, 1986-88; intern Children's Hosp. Guidance Ctr., Columbus, 1989, MT. Carmel Hospice, Columbus, 1989; grad. asst. Andrews U., Berrien Springs, Mich., 1989-90; psychotherapist Family Learning Ctr., South Bend, Ind., 1990-92; psychologist intern St. Lawrence Hosp., Lansing, Mich., 1992—. Author children's books; originator FOOI Therapy. Mem. APA (presenter at conf.) ACA, Pi Lambda Theta, Psi Chi. Office: St Lawrence Hosp Outpatient Behavioral Medicine Svcs 1210 W Saginaw St Lansing MI 48915

PAULSON-EHRHARDT, PATRICIA HELEN, laboratory administrator; b. Moses Lake, Wash., June 10, 1956; d. Luther Roanoke and Helen Jane (Baird) Paulson; m. Terry Lee Ehrhardt, Mar. 12, 1983. Student, Pacific Luth. U., 1974-76; BS in Med. Tech., U. Wash., 1976; BS in Biology, MS in Biology, Eastern Wash. U., 1982. Med. technologist Samaritan Hosp., Moses Lake, 1979-81; lab. supr. Moses Lake Clinic, Kalispell Regional Hosp., Mont., 1987-88; with Kalispell (Mont.) Regional Hosp., 1987; account exec. Pathology Assocs. Med. Lab., Spokane, Wash., 1988—; mem. med. lab. tech. adv. com. Wenatchee (Wash.) Valley Coll., 1984-85, chmn., 1985-86. Mem. Flathead Valley Community Band, 1987-90. Mem. ASCLS, CLMA (Inland N.W. chpt. pres. 1993-94, bd. dirs. 1994-95), Am. Soc. Clin. Pathologists (cert.), Pan Players Flute Soc., Flathead Tennis Assn., Sigma Xi, Kappa Delta (pledge class pres. 1976). Republican. Lutheran. Home: Bldg #118 2901 Kendall Rd Walla Walla WA 99362

PAULU, FRANCES BROWN, international center administrator; b. Hastings, Minn., June 22, 1920; d. Thomas Andrew and Florence Ida (Tuttle) Brown; m. Burton Paulu, June 29, 1942; children: Sarah Leith Paulu Boittin, Nancy Jean Paulu Hyde, Thomas Scott. BA magna cum laude, U. Minn., 1940. Case worker Family Welfare Assn. Mpls., 1943-45; interviewer Community Health and Welfare Council, Mpls., 1963; sch. social worker Project Head Start, Mpls., 1966; program dir. Minn. Internat. Ctr., Mpls., 1970-72, exec. dir., 1972-89, cons., 1989; mem. tourism adv. com. City of Mpls., 1976-83; mem. adv. council Minn. World Trade Ctr., 1984-86. Pres. UN Rally, 1970-72; chmn. Mpls. Charter Commn., 1972-74; bd. dirs. Urban Coalition of Mpls., 1967-70; dir. Minn. World Trade Week, 1977-81; participant Intercultural Communication Project, Japan, 1974; mem. mgmt. team Minn. Awareness Project, 1982-89—. DeWitt Jennings Payne scholar, 1939-40; Sch. Social Work fellow U. Minn., 1942-44; recipient Nat. People to People Disting. Membership award, 1987, Schmoker award YMCA Internat. Program Svcs., 1991. Mem. Nat. Council for Internat. Visitors (officer and/or exec. com. mem. 1975-81, leader fact-finding team North Africa, Middle East, India 1978, conf. chair 1989), Nat. Assn. for Fgn. Student Affairs, People to People Internat., LWV (pres. Mpls. 1967-69), UN Assn. Minn. (adv. coun. 1979-92, sec. 1994—), Mpls.-St. Paul Com. on Fgn. Rels., Nat. Coun. World Affairs Orgns. (participant Taipei-Manila Study Tour 1988), Alliance FranÇaise (dir. 1991-94), U. Minn. Women's Club (pres. 1992-94), Phi Beta Kappa, Alpha Omicron Pi, Lambda Alpha Psi. Home: 5005 Wentworth Ave Minneapolis MN 55419-1302

PAULUS, NORMA JEAN PETERSEN, lawyer, state school system administrator; b. Belgrade, Nebr., Mar. 13, 1933; d. Paul Emil and Ella Marie (Hellbusch) Petersen; LL.B., Willamette Law Sch., 1962; LL.D., Linfield Coll., 1985; m. William G. Paulus, Aug. 16, 1958; children: Elizabeth, William Frederick. Sec. to Harney County Dist. Atty., 1950-53; legal sec., Salem, Oreg., 1953-55; sec. to chief justice Oreg. Supreme Ct., 1955-61; admitted to Oreg. bar, 1962; of counsel Paulus and Callaghan, Salem, mem. Oreg. Ho. of Reps., 1971-77; sec. state State of Oreg., Salem, 1977-85; of counsel firm Paulus, Rhoten & Lien, 1985-86; supt. pub. instrn. State of Oreg., 1990—; Oreg. exec. bd. US West, 1985—; adj. prof. Willamette U. Grad. Sch, 1985; mem. N.W. Power Planning Com., 1986-89. Fellow Eagleton Inst. Politics, 1971; mem. Pacific NW Power Planning Council, 1987-89; adv. com. Defense Adv. Com. for Women in the Service, 1986, Nat. Trust for Hist. Preservation, 1988—; trustee Willamette U., 1978—; bd. dirs. Benedictine Found. of Oreg., 1980—, Oreg. Grade. Instn. Sci. and Tech.,

1985—, Mid Willamette Valley council Camp Fire Girls, 1985-87; overseer Whitman Coll., 1985—; bd. cons. Goodwill Industries of Oreg.; mem. Salem Human Relations Commn., 1967-70, Marion-Polk Boundary Commn., 1970-71; mem. Presdl. Commn. to Monitor Philippines Election, 1986. Recipient Distinguished Service award City of Salem, 1971; Path Breaker award Oreg. Women's Polit. Caucus, 1976; named One of 10 Women of Future, Ladies Home Jour., 1979. Woman of Yr., Oreg. Inst Managerial and Profl. Women, 1982, Oreg. Women Lawyers, 1982, Woman Who Made a Difference award Nat. Women's Forum, 1985. Mem. Oreg. State Bar, Nat. Order Women Legislators, Women Execs. in State Govt., Women's Polit. Caucus Bus. and Profl. Women's Club (Golden Torch award 1971), Zonta Internat., Delta Kappa Gamma.

PAVALON, DONNA MAE, librarian; b. Hutchinson, Minn., May 11, 1948; d. Loraine Frances and Lucy Gertrude (Woller) Schandel; m. Norman B. Pavalon, Aug. 27, 1977; children: Kerri A., Kelli L. BS, U. Wis., Milw., 1973; MS, libr. cert., U. Nev., Las Vegas, 1988. Cert. reading specialist, libr. specialist. Tchr. Milw. Pub. Schs., 1974-78; tchr., libr. Clark County Sch. Dist., Las Vegas, Nev., 1978-86; libr. Clark County Sch. Dist., Las Vegas, 1987—. Mem. ALA, Nev. Libr. Assn., Clark County Sch. Librs. Assn. (pres. elect 1990-91, pres. 1991-92). Home: 2357 Viewcrest Rd Henderson NV 89014-3628

PAVEK, BRYN CARPENTER, director arts administration; b. Phoenix, Mar. 7, 1955; d. John Leon and Lenore Maxine (Stapp) Carpenter; m. Charles Christopher Pavek, Dec. 18, 1977. BFA in Theatre magna cum laude, Ariz. State U., 1977; student, U. Ariz., 1973. Freelance designer Phoenix, 1973-77; box office mgr. Ariz. State U. Theatre, Tempe, 1976; creative drama specialist City of Phoenix, summer 1976; box office ticketing asst. U. So. Calif., L.A., 1977; co. and stage mgr. Hartford (Conn.) Stage Co. Youth Theatre, 1978, adminstrv. mgr., 1979-80; budget analyst U.S. Naval Mil. Command, Arlington, Va., 1981; prodn. supr. Arlington County Visual & Performing Arts, 1981-84; dep. dir. McLean (Va.) Community Ctr., 1984-87; exec. dir. Reston (Va.) Community Ctr., 1987—; prodn. chair Southeastern Theatre Conf., Arlington, 1984; mem. Drug Free Recreation for Youth Task Force, Fairfax, Va., 1988—, Dogwood Edn. Task Force, Reston, 1989—. Mem. com. Fairfax County Coun. of the Arts, 1987—, Purple Sage Cluster Assn. Social Commn., Reston, 1988; mem. organizing com. Fairfax County Summit Youth Issues, 1989. Recipient Human Rights award Fairfax County, Va., 1991. Mem. Va. Assn. Female Execs., Cultural Alliance Greater Washington, Pk. and Recreation Assn. Democrat. Unitarian. Home: 12149 Purple Sage Ct Herndon VA 22070-5622

PAVELKA, ELAINE BLANCHE, mathematics educator; b. Chgo.; d. Frank Joseph and Mildred Bohumila (Seidl) P.; B.A., M.S., Northwestern U.; Ph.D., U. Ill. With Northwestern U. Aerial Measurements Lab., Evanston, Ill.; tchr. Leyden Community High Sch., Franklin Park, Ill.; prof. math. Morton Coll., Cicero, Ill.; invited speaker 3d Internat. Congress Math. Edn., Karlsruhe, Germany, 1976. Recipient sci. talent award Westinghouse Elec. Co. Mem. Am. Edn. Research Assn., Am. Math. Assn. 2-Year Colls., Am. Math. Soc., Assn. Women in Math., Can. Soc. History and Philosophy of Math., Ill. Council Tchr. of Math., Ill. Math. Assn. Community Colls., Math. Assn. Am., Math. Action Group, Ga. Center Study and Teaching and Learning Math., Nat. Council Tchrs. of Math., Sch. Sci. and Math. Assn., Soc. Indsl. and Applied Math., Northwestern U. Alumni Assn., U. Ill. Alumni Assn., Am. Mensa Ltd., Intertel, Sigma Delta Epsilon, Pi Mu Epsilon. Home: PO Box 7312 Westchester IL 60154-7312

PAVLICK, PAMELA KAY, nurse, consultant; b. Topeka, Aug. 16, 1944; d. Cy Pavlick and June Lucille (Arnold) (dec.) Dull. Diploma nursing, St. Luke's Hosp., Kansas City, Mo., 1966; BA in Psychology magna cum laude, U. North Fla., 1982, MS in Health Adminstrn. summa cum laude, 1987. RN, Mo., Ill., Fla.; cert. ins. rehab. specialist; lic. rehab. providor, Fla. Clin. instr. St. Luke's Hosp., Kansas City, 1966-70; instr. lic. practical nursing Springfield (Ill.) Sch. Bd., 1970-72; nursing supr. Jacksonville Beach (Fla.) Hosp., 1972-74; pub. health nurse State of Fla., Ocala, 1974-76; dir. nursing Upjohn Health Care, Jacksonville, Fla., 1976-77, mem. adv. com.; med. rep. Travelers Ins. Co., Jacksonville, 1977-84; rehab. cons. Aetna Life & Casualty, Jacksonville, 1985—, rep. nurse cons. adv. coun., 1988-90. Mem. Am. Nurses Assn., Am. Assn. Rehab. Nurses, Nat. Assn. Rehab. Providers, Phi Kappa Phi. Republican. Episcopalian. Home: 14023 Tontine Rd Jacksonville FL 32225-2025 Office: Aetna Life & Casualty PO Box 2200 Jacksonville FL 32203-2200

PAVLIK, NANCY, convention services executive; b. Hamtramck, Mich., July 18, 1935; d. Frank and Helen (Vorobojoff) Phillips; m. G. Edward Pavlik, June 30, 1956; children: Kathleen, Christine, Laureen, Michael, Bonnie Jean. Student, U. Ariz., 1956-80. Exec. sec. Mich. Bell, Detroit, 1951-56, RCA, Camden, N.J., 1956-58; owner, pres. Southwest Events Etc., Scottsdale, Ariz., 1969—. Chmn. hospitality industry com. Scottsdale City Coun., 1989—; bd. dirs. Scottsdale Curatorial Bd., 1987-89. Mem. Soc. Incentive Travel Execs., Meeting Planners Internat., Am. Soc. Assn. Execs., Indian Arts and Crafts Assn., Scottsdale C. of C. (bd. dirs., tourism steering com. 1984-88), Contemporary Watercolorists Club. Democrat. Roman Catholic. Home: 7500 E Mccormick Pky # 33 Scottsdale AZ 85258-3454 Office: SW Events Etc 8233 E Paseo Del Norte A-600 Scottsdale AZ 85258

PAXTON, ALICE ADAMS, artist, architect and interior designer; b. Hagerstown, Md., May 19, 1914; d. William Albert and Josephine (Adams) Rosenberger; m. James Love Paxton Jr., June 26, 1942 (div.); 1 child, William Allen III (dec.). Student, Peabody Inst. Music, Balt., 1937-38; grad., Parson's Sch. Design, N.Y., 1940; studies with J. Laurie Wallace, 1944-46; studies with Augustus Dunbier, 1947-48, Sylvia Curtis, 1949, Milton Wolsky, 1950, Frank Sapousek, 1951. Freelance work archtl. renderings and interior design, N.Y., 1937-40; interior designer, designer spl. furnishings, muralist Orchard and Wilhelm, Omaha, 1940-42; tchr. art classes Alice Paxton Studio, Omaha, 1957-64; tchr. mech. drawing, archtl. rendering and mech. perspective Parson's Sch. Design, N.Y., 1937-40. Designer (interior) Chapel Boys' Town, Nebr., 1942; one-woman show of archtl. renderings Washington County Mus. Fine Arts, Hagerstown, 1944; exhibited group shows at Joslyn Mus., Omaha, 1943-44 (1st place), Ann. Exhbn. Cumberland Valley Artists, Hagerstown, 1945; represented in permanent collections at No. Natural Gas Co. Bldg., Omaha, Swanson Found., Omaha; also pvt. collections; vol. designer, decorator: recreation room Omaha Blood Bank, ARC, 1943, recreation room Creighton U., 1943, lounge psychiat. ward Lincoln (Nebr.) Army Hosp., 1944; planner, color coordinator Children's Hosp., Omaha, 1947, painted murals, 1948, decorated dental room, 1950; designed Candy Stripers' uniforms; painted and decorated straw elephant bag presented to Mrs. Richard Nixon, 1960; contbr. articles and photographs to Popular Home mag., 1958. Co-chair camp and hosp. coms. ARC, 1943-45, mem. county com. to select and send gifts to servicemen, 1943-46; mem. Ak-Sar-Ben Ball Com., Omaha, 1946-48, Nat. Mus. Women in the Arts, The Md. Hist. Soc.; judge select Easter Seal design, Joslyn Mus., 1946; mem. council Girl Scouts U.S., Omaha, 1943-47; spl. drs. chmn. Jr. League, Omaha, 1947-48, chair Jr. League Red Cross fund dr., 1947-48; bd. dirs., vol. worker Creche, Omaha, 1954-56; mem. Omaha Jr. League; chmn. Jr. League Community Chest Fund Dr., 1948-50; co-chair Infantile Paralysis Appeal, 1944; numerous vol. profl. activities for civic orgns., hosps., clubs, chs., community playhouse, and for establishing wildlife sanctuary. Recipient three teaching scholarships Parson's Sch. Design, 1937-40, presdl. citation ARC activities, 1946, 1st prize Ann. Midwest Show Joslyn Mus., 1943. Mem. Associated Artists Omaha (charter), Internat. Platform Assn., U.S. Hist. Soc., Nat. Mus. Women in Arts (charter), Md. Hist. Soc., Fountain Head Country Club. Republican. Episcopalian. Home: 19614 Meadowbrook Rd Hagerstown MD 21742

PAXTON, J. WILLENE, retired university administrator; b. Birmingham, Ala., Oct. 30, 1930; d. Will and Elizabeth (Davis) P. AB, Birmingham So. Coll., 1950; MA, Mich. State U., 1951; EdD, Ind. U., 1971. Nat. cert. counselor, lic. profl. counselor, Tenn. Dormitory dir. Tex. Tech U., Lubbock, 1951-53; counselor Mich. State U., East Lansing, summer 1951, 52; dir. univ. ctr. and housing SUNY, Fredonia, 1953-56, assoc. dean of students, 1956-57; asst. dean of women U. N.Mex., Albuquerque, 1957-63; dean of women East Tenn. State U., Johnson City, 1963-68, 70-78, dir. counseling ctr., 1978-92; ret., 1992. Sec. adminstrv. bd. Meth. Ch., 1983-86, chmn., 1994—, chmn. social concerns com., 1991-93, program chmn. Good Timers fellowship, 1995, pres. Sunday Sch. class, 1994; tng. dir. Contact Teleministries, Inc., 1983-87, chair, 1988, 95, vice chair, 1993-94; bd. dirs. Asbury Ctrs., chmn. policy com. 1995. Mem. AAUW (br. pres.), APA, ACA, Tenn. Psychol. Assn., Assn. Univ. and Coll. Counseling Ctr. Dirs. (convention planning com. 1991), Am. Coll. Pers. Assn. (media bd., newsletter editor), Nat. Assn. Women Deans, Adminstrs. and Counselors, Tenn. Assn. Women Deans and Counselors (state pres., v.p., program chmn.), Delta Kappa Gamma (chpt. pres. 1974-76, state rec. sec. 1977-79, v.p. 1979-81, chmn. nominating com. 1981-83, chmn. leadership devel. com. 1983-85, internat. rsch. com. 1982-84, chmn. self study com. 1985-87, chmn. com. to study exec. sec. 1987-89, state pres. 1989-91, parliamentarian 1991-93, internat. constn. com. 1992-94, mem. awards com. 1993-95, chair internat. convention meal functions com. 1994, State Achievement award 1987), East Tenn. Edn. Assn. (chair guidance divsn.), Gen. Federated Woman's Club (pres. 1980-81, 88-89, 2nd v.p. 1991-95), Univ. Women's Club (v.p. 1993-94, pres. 1994—). Home: 1203 Lester Harris Rd Johnson City TN 37601-3335

PAXTON, LAURA BELLE-KENT, English language educator, management professional; b. Lake Charles, La., Feb. 8, 1942; d. George Ira and Gladys Lillian (Barrett) Kent.; m. Kenneth Robert Paxton Jr., Jan. 2, 1962. BA, McNeese U., Lake Charles, 1963, MA in English, 1972; EdD, East Tex. U., 1983. cert. English, social studies instr., prin., supt., ednl. adminstr., Ariz. Tchr. Darrington (Wash.) High Sch., 1966-70; English instr. Maricopa Community Coll., Phoenix, 1974-92; migrant program instr. Phoenix Union High Sch., 1984-88; English instr. Embry-Riddle Aeronautical U., Luke AFB, Ariz., 1985-87; sales rep. Merrill Lynch Realty, Phoenix, 1985-88; co-owner Paxton Mgmt. Co., Phoenix, 1985—; asst. prof. English Western Internat. U., Phoenix, 1992—; Editor Ariz. corr. courses, 1987-88; presenter migrant worker program confs., 1987—; reviewer Prentice-Hall, 1985. Author: A Handbook for Middle Eastern Dancers, 1978, The Kent Family History From 1787-1981, 1981, A Handbook of Home Remedies, 1981, Elements of Effective Writing, 1993; contbr. articles and poems to mags. and profl. jours. Mem. Everett, Wash. Opera Guild, 1966-70, Ariz. State U. Opera Guild, Tempe, 1978-80; mem. City of Darrington Council, 1969-70; ESL instr. Friendly House, Phoenix, 1978-79. Mem. Ariz. English Assn., Phi Delta Kappa. Home: 8415 N 32d Ave Phoenix AZ 85051

PAYETTE, PATRICIA LESPERANCE, association executive, physical educator; b. Two Rivers, Wis., Oct. 11, 1941; d. Kenneth C. and Norma M. (Beitzel) Lesperance; m. Ronald Mitchell Payette, June 15m 1963; 1 child, Kevin Lesperance. BS in Edn., U. Wis., 1963. Cert. tchr. K-12, Ind., Ill., Wis.; lic. real estate broker. Asst. dir. Monroe City Pre-Sch. for Devel. Disabled, Bloomington, Ind., 1965-67; tchr. Wauconda (Ill.) Pub. Schs., 1963-64; tchr. head start Columbus (Ind.) Pub. Schs., 1967; tchr. Bement (Ill.) Pub. Schs., 1969-70, Monticello (Ill.) Pub. Schs., 1970-72; dir. adult devel. unit United Cerebral Palsy, Green Bay, Wis., 1974-78; supr. data comm. ctr. A. C. Nielsen, Green Bay, 1979-81; dir. respite care program Brown County Assn. Retarded Citizens, Green Bay, 1981-84; real estate broker, asst. sales mgr. Skogg Co., Green Bay, 1984-89; exec. dir. YWCA Green Bay-DePere, 1989—; also bd. dirs. YWCA Green Bay. Bd. dirs. Cerebral Palsy Inc., Green Bay; mem. citizens advocacy bd. Brown County Assn. Retarded Citizens; active Vision for Race Unity, Violence Free Initiative. Fellow Green Bay Rotary; mem. Zonta Internat. (bd. dirs.). Home: 813 W Saint Francis Rd De Pere WI 54115-3538 Office: YWCA of Green Bay-Depere 230 S Madison St Green Bay WI 54301-4504

PAYNE, ALMA JEANETTE, English educator and author; b. Highland Park, Ill., Oct. 28, 1918; d. Frederick Hutton and Ruth Ann (Colle) P. BA, Wooster (Ohio) Coll., 1940; MA, Case Western Res. U., 1941, PhD, 1956. Tchr. English, history, Latin Ohio Pub. Schs., Bucyrus and Canton, 1941-46; from instr. to prof. English and Am. studies Bowling Green (Ohio) State U., 1946-79, dir. Am. studies program, 1957-79, chair Am. culture PhD program, 1978-79, prof. emerita English, Am. studies, 1979—; adj. prof. Am. studies U. South Fla., 1982—. Author: Critical Bibliography of Louisa May Alcott, 1980, Discovering the American Nations, 1981; contbr. articles to profl. jours.; editor Nat. Am. Studies Assn. Newsletter; contbr. articles to profl. jours. Nat. Coun. for Innovation in Edn. grantee, Norway, U.S. Embassy and Norwegian Dept. Ch. and State, 1978-79. Mem. AAUW (pres. 1982-84), Soc. Descendants of the Mayflower in Fla. (state treas. 1985), Nat. Am. Studies Assn. (v.p. (1977-79), Phi Beta Kappa, Phi Kappa Phi, Kappa Delta Pi, Alpha Lambda Delta. Republican. Presbyterian. Home and Office: 11077 Orangewood Dr Bonita Springs FL 33923-5720

PAYNE, ANITA HART, reproductive endocrinologist, researcher; b. Karlsruhe, Baden, Germany, Nov. 24, 1926; came to U.S., 1938; d. Frederick Michael and Erna Rose (Hirsch) Hart; widowed; children: Gregory Steven, Teresa Payne-Lyons. BA, U. Calif., Berkeley, 1949, PhD, 1952. Rsch. assoc. U. Mich., Ann Arbor, 1961-71, asst. prof., 1971-76, assoc. prof., 1976-81, prof., 1981—, assoc. dir. Ctr. for Study Reprodn., 1989-94; vis. scholar Stanford U., 1987-88; mem. reproductive biology study sect. NIH, Bethesda, Md., 1978-79, biochem. endocrinology study sect., 1979-83, population rsch. com. Nat. Inst. Child Health and Human Devel., 1989-93. Assoc. editor Steroids, 1987-93; contbr. book chpts., articles to profl. jours. Recipient award for cancer rsch. Calif. Inst. Rsch. Cancer, 1953, Acad. Women's Caucus award U. Mich., 1986. Mem. Endocrine Soc. (chmn. awards com. 1983-84, mem. nominating com. 1985-87, coun. 1988-91), Am. Soc. Andrology (exec. coun. 1980-83), Soc. for Study of Reprodn. (bd. dirs. 1982-85, sec. 1986-89, pres. 1990-91). Office: U Mich Steroid Rsch Unit Lab L1225/0278 Womens Hosp Ann Arbor MI 48108-0278

PAYNE, ANN LEITH PATTON, supervisor education; b. Talladega, Ala., Aug. 14, 1942; d. Roy Knox and Isabel (Mathes) Patton; m. Lanny Terrell Payne, Aug. 2, 1963; children: Charles Knox, David Thomas. BS, U. Ala., 1963; MS, U. Tenn., 1974. Tchr. Tenn. Sch. for Deaf, Knoxville, 1963-70, 74-85, vocat. coord., 1985-87, high sch. supr., 1987—. Mem. AAUW, DAR, Tenn. Edn. Assn. (bd. dirs. 1976-79), Scottish Soc. Knoxville, Delta Kappa Gamma (pres. 1984-86). Republican. Presbyterian. Home: 12405 Hound Ears Pt Knoxville TN 37922-2408 Office: Tenn Sch for Deaf 2725 Island Home Blvd Knoxville TN 37920-2700

PAYNE, CHRISTINE BABCOCK, career psychologist; b. Junction City, Kans., Jan. 14, 1943; d. David Edward and Dorothy (Viner) Babcock; m. James R. Payne, Oct. 16, 1982; children: Terrence Thomas, Melanie Payne Tate. AA, Stephens Coll., 1963; BA, Parsons Coll., 1966; MS, Calif. Coast U., 1993, postgrad., 1993—. Tchr. Page-Park Sch., St. Louis, 1966-68; assoc. buyer Famous-Barr Dept. Store, St. Louis, 1968-70; pers. asst. Gimbel's Dept. Store, N.Y.C., 1970-71; tng. dir. Gimbel's East, N.Y.C., 1971-72; employment mgr. Hosp. for Spl. Surgery, N.Y.C., 1972-73; pers. dir. J.B. Ivey & Co., Orlando, Fla., 1973-75; dir. employer rels. Okla. Employment Security Commn., Tulsa, 1980-84; pers. dir. Sanger-Harris Dept. Store, Tulsa, 1982; dir. career devel. Women's Ctr. U. Tulsa, 1988-93; pres., owner Transitions Counseling Ctr., Tulsa, 1992—; counseling dir. career and ednl. svcs. Resonance Ctr. for Women, Tulsa, 1993; coord. dislocated worker program Ctrl. Okla. Vo-Tech Sch., Drumright, 1984-86. Author: Tearing Down the Walls: An Adult Woman's Guide to Education and Financial Aid, 1993. Speech writer State Senator Ted V. Fisher, Okla., 1986; pres. Vol. Svc. Coun., St. Louis, 1975-79. Recipient Mayor's Pinnacle award for Outstanding Contbn. in Area of Edn., Mayor's Commn. on Status of Women, Tulsa, 1993. Mem. ACA, NAFE, Nat. Career Devel. Assn., Nat. Assn. Fin. Aid Adminstrs., Adult Career Devel. Network, Assn. for Measurement Evaluation in Counseling Devel. Office: Transitions Counseling Ctr 4821 S Sheridan Ste 222 Tulsa OK 74145

PAYNE, DEBORAH ANNE, medical company officer; b. Norristown, Pa., Sept. 22, 1952; d. Kenneth Nathan Moser and Joan (Reese) Dewhurst; m. Randall Barry Payne, Mar. 8, 1975. AA, Northeastern Christian Jr. Coll., 1972; B in Music Edn., Va. Commonwealth U., 1979. Driver, social asst. Children's Aid Soc., Norristown, Pa., 1972-73; mgr. Boddie-Noell Enterprises, Richmond, Va., 1974-79; retail food saleswoman Hardee's Food Systems, Inc., Phila., 1979-81; supr., with tech. tng. and testing and computer depts. Cardiac Datacorp., Phila., 1981-95. Mem. bd. advisers Am. Biog. Inst., 1989. Mem. NAFE, Delta Omicron (pres. Alpha Xi chpt. 1978-79, pres. Epsilon province 1980-85, chmn. Eastern Pa. alumni 1986-88, Star award 1979), Am. Soc. Profl. and Exec. Women. Republican. Home: 4301 Chippendale St Philadelphia PA 19136-3628

PAYNE, ELIZABETH ANN THOMAS, food service business owner; b. South Pittsburgh, Tenn., Jan. 9, 1951; d. Horace Lee and Elizabeth Pearl (Short) Thomas; m. John Edward Payne, May 9, 1969; children: John Brenton, William Ethan, Amanda Ann. Pvt. student apprentice to chef, Lucerne Sch., Switzerland, 1981-82; cert. in basic mgmt. and suprervison, Cooking and Hospitality Inst., Chgo., 1988; apprenticeship to Chrsistine Bryant, 1987-89. Cert. in health svcs.; cert. in mgmt. Marrriott Corp. Mgr. Cheese Keg, Bartlesville, Okla., 1981-83; catering bus. Stavanger, Norway, 1983-85; asst. chef, cons. Coffee and Tea Market, Valparaiso, Ind., 1987-89; catering mgr. Marriott at Samford U., Birmingham, Ala., 1990-92; asst.mgr. R & S Mgmt., Charlotte, N.C., 1993; owner The Art of Food, Birmingham, Ala., 1994—; owner, prop. food svc. delivery and catering bus., Chatom, Ala., 1994—. Photographer travel publ. Fund raiser Tchrs. Orgn., Stavanger, 1984. Republican. Mem. Ch. of Christ. Home and Office: Rt 1 Box 75 Bridgeport AL 35740

PAYNE, ELIZABETH ELEANORE, surgeon, otolaryngologist; b. Detroit, Mar. 17, 1945; d. Richard Franklin and Eleanore Grace (Dieterich) P.; 1 child from previous marriage, Julia Elizabeth Komanecky. Student, St. Olaf Coll., 1962-64; MD, U. Iowa, 1968. Cert. Am. Bd. Otolaryngology, Am. Acad. Otolaryngic Allergy; lic. in medicine, Minn., Iowa. Intern Phila. Gen. Hosp., 1968-69; resident gen. surgery U. Minn., Mpls., 1969-70; resident otolaryngology U. Minn., 1970-74, clin. asst. prof. dept. otolaryngology, asst. clin. prof. dept. family practice and community health; pvt. practice, Mpls., 1974—; mem. med. staff North Meml. Med. Ctr., Mpls., Children's Med. Ctr., AbbottNorthwestern Hosp. Contbr. articles to profl. jours. Mem. AMA, Am. Acad. Otolaryngology Head and Neck Surgery, Am. Acad. Otolaryngic Allergy, Minn. State Med. Assn., Minn. Acad. Otolaryngology Head and Neck Surgery (coun. mem.), Minn. Acad. Medicine, Hennepin County Med. Assn. Office: Affiliated Otolaryngologists 3366 Oakdale Ave N Ste 307 Minneapolis MN 55422-2985

PAYNE, FLORA FERN, social service administrator; b. Carrollton, Mo., Sept. 25, 1932; d. George Earnest and Bernadine Alice (Schaefer) Chrisman; m. H.D. Matticks, Oct. 20, 1950 (div. Oct. 1959); children: Dennis Don, Kathi D.; m. S.L. Freeman, Nov. 25, 1960 (div. Jan. 1973); 1 child, Gary Mark; m. Vernon Ray Payne, Mar. 18, 1988. Student, S.E. C.C., Burlington, Iowa, 1976-77; cert. stenographer, Corr. Sch., Chgo., 1960-61; social svc. designee, Mo. Sch. Nursing, 1991. Sec. to v.p. Moore Co., Marceline, Mo., 1973-75; steno to trainmaster A.T. & S.F. Rlwy. Co., Fort Madison, Iowa, 1975-88; with social svc. Brookfield (Mo.) Nursing Ctr., 1990—. Mem. NAFE, MOSS. Republican. Home: 206 East St Bucklin MO 64631 Office: Brookfield Nursing Ctr 315 Hunt St Brookfield MO 64628

PAYNE, FRANCES ANNE, literature educator, researcher; b. Harrisonburg, Va., Aug. 28, 1932; d. Charles Franklin and Willie (Tarvin) P. B.A., Shorter Coll, 1953, B.Mus., 1953; M.A., Yale U., 1954, Ph.D., 1960. Instr. Conn. Coll., New London, 1955-56; instr. U. Buffalo, 1958-60, lectr., 1960, asst. prof., 1960-67; assoc. prof. SUNY, Buffalo, 1967-75; prof. English and medieval lit. SUNY, 1975—; adj. fellow St. Anne's Coll., Oxford, Eng., 1966-67, 68-69. Author: King Alfred and Boethius, 1968; Chaucer and Menippean Satire, 1981. Contbr. articles to scholarly publs. AAUW fellow, Oxford, 1966-67; Research Found. grantee SUNY Central, Oxford, 1967, 68, 71, 72; recipient Julian Park award SUNY-Buffalo, 1979. Mem. Medieval Acad. Am., Internat. Arthurian Soc., New Chaucer Soc., Internat. Soc. Anglo-Saxonists, Pi Kappa Lambda. Office: SUNY-Buffalo 306 Clemens Hall Buffalo NY 14260

PAYNE, LINDA COHEN, business owner; b. N.Y.C., Jan. 9, 1953; d. Gerald Theodore and Bianca (Joselson) Cohen; m. Stephen George Payne, Mar. 20, 1977; 1 child, Joshua Theodore Cohen. BA, Hunter Coll., 1981. Brokerage asst. Harris, Upham & Co., N.Y.C., 1974-75; dept. head cen. inquiry Standard & Poor's Corp., N.Y.C., 1976-87; owner, mgr. Payne Fin. Rsch., N.Y.C., 1988—. Mem. ALA, NOW, Spl. Libr. Assn., Libr. Mgmt. Assn., Exec. Females. Home and Office: Payne Fin Rsch 27 Norchester Dr Princeton Junction NJ 08550-1225

PAYNE, LISA MOSSMAN, middle school educator; b. Chula Vista, Calif., May 9, 1966; d. William George Jr. and Lynne (Burke) Mossman; m. Charles Alan Payne, June 2, 1990; children: Molly Alexandra, Max Emerson. BA in English, U. Calif., Irvine, 1988; MA in English, Chapman U., 1990. Cert. jr. coll. tchr., Calif. Tchr. Chapman U., Orange, Calif., 1989-90, Orange Coast Coll., Costa Mesa, Calif., 1990, Riverside (Calif.) C.C., 1990; tchr. English, head dept. St. John's Sch., Rancho Santa Margarita, Calif., 1990-94, dir. middle sch. summer program, 1993; leader Jr. Great Books Found., Chgo., 1992—; mem. Middle Sch. Restructuring Team, 1993; Library Accreditation Team, 1993-94. Author curriculua in field; writer children's books. Mem. Soc. Children's Bookwriters and Illustrators. Home: 183 Cornell Irvine CA 92715

PAYNE, LUCY ANN SALSBURY, law librarian, educator, lawyer; b. Utica, N.Y., July 5, 1952; d. James Henry and Dorothy Eileen (Seavy) Salsbury; m. Albert E. Payne, June 2, 1973 (div. 1983); 1 child, Joni Eileen. MusB, Andrews U., 1974; MA, Loma Linda (Calif.) U., 1979; JD, U. Notre Dame, Ind., 1988; MLS, U. Mich., 1990. Bar: Ind. 1988, Mich. 1988, U.S. Dist. Ct. (no. and so. dists.) Ind. 1988, U.S. Ct. Appeals (7th cir.) 1992. Rsch. specialist Kresge Libr. Law Sch. U. Notre Dame, 1988-90; asst. libr. Kresge Libr. Law Sch., 1990-91; assoc. libr. Kresge Libr. Sch. U. Notre Dame, 1991—. Contbr. articles to profl. jours. Mem. ABA, Am. Assn. Law Librs., Mich. Bar Assn., Ind. Bar Assn., Ohio Regional Assn. Law Librs., Mich. Assn. Law Librs., St. Joseph County Bar Assn. Adventist. Office: U Notre Dame Law Sch Kresge Law Libr Notre Dame IN 46556

PAYNE, MARGARET MARILYN, pediatric nurse practitioner; b. Buffalo, July 10, 1940; d. Joseph J. and Ruth (Esler) Kane; m. William Delano Payne, Sept. 8, 1960; children: Michael, Kelly, John, Joseph. Diploma, Millard Fillmore Hosp. Sch. Nursing, 1972; BS in Nursing, D'Youville Coll., 1974; MS in Child Health and Nursing Adminstrn., cert. as Pediatric Nurse Practitioner, SUNY, Buffalo, 1979; postgrad., Cornell U., 1980-81, Buffalo Sch. of the Bible, 1981-85. Enlisted USAR, 1975, advanced through grade to lt. col., 1992; asst. chief nurse 455th Gen. Hosp., Providence, 1985-92, AGR 324th Gen. Hosp., Perrine, Fla., 1992-94; ednl. svcs. adminstr. Gaymar Industries, Inc., Orchard Park, N.Y., 1994—; lectr. in field; adj. clin. instr. Grad. Sch. Nursing, SUNY, Buffalo, 1979-83, asst. prof. occupational therapy, 1979-82; staff nurse Millard Fillmore Hosp., Buffalo, 1971-73; pvt. duty nurse Manpower Nursing Svc., 1973-74; staff nurse, team leader Erie County Dept. Pub. Health, 1974, coord. child health assurance program, 1976-78, sr. nurse practitioner, 1978-79, dir. well child clinics, 1979-82, dir. patient svcs., 1982-83; part-time marriage and family counselor, Full Gospel Tabernacle; active Nat. Pressure Ulcer Adv. Bd. Active Marriage Encounter, 1979-85; adv. bd. AGAPE, a Christian Parents group for handicapped children, 1979-85. Decorated Army Commendation medal (2). Mem. ANA, Assn. Mil. Surgeons U.S., AACCN, Wound Ostomy and Continence Nurses Soc., Am. Assn. Nurse Anesthesia, Post Anesthesia Nurses Assn., N.Y. State Nurses Assn. Home: 5293 Ellicott Rd Orchard Park NY 14127

PAYNE, MARTHA HELEN, secondary education educator; b. Elk City, Okla., Mar. 30, 1946; d. Glenn Warren and Rula Helen (Rorabaugh) Anderson; m. Larry D. Payne, Sept. 4, 1965; children: Timothy Don, Steven Warren. BS in Edn., Tulsa U., 1979; M of Edn., Northeastern State U., 1988. Cert. tchr. math. Tchr. Owasso (Okla.) Mid. Sch., 1979-84, Owasso High Sch., 1984—. Mem. Nat. Coun. Tchrs. Math. (com. chair). Office: Owasso High Sch 12901 E 86th St N Owasso OK 74055

PAYNE, PAULA MARIE, minister; b. Waukegan, Ill., Jan. 13, 1952; d. Percy Howard and Annie Maude (Canady) P. BA, U. Ill., 1976; MA, U. San Francisco, 1986; MDiv, Wesley Theol. Sem., 1991. Ordained to ministry United Meth. Ch., 1990. Chaplain for minority affairs Am. U., Washington, 1988-89; chaplain, intern NIH, Bethesda, Md., 1989-90; pastor Asbury United Meth. Ch., Charles Town, W.Va., 1990—; supt. ch. sch. United Meth. Ch., Oxon Hill, Md., 1989-90; mem. AIDS task force Wesley Theol. Sem., Washington, 1988-89; mem. retreat. com. Balt. Conf., 1990—; chair scholarship com. Asbury United Meth. Ch., 1990—. Bd. dirs. AIDS Task Force Jefferson County, Charles Town, 1991—, Community Ministries, Charles Town, 1991—. Tech sgt. USAF, 1984-88; chaplain Army N.G., Md.

Recipient Cert. of Recognition, Ill. Ho. of Reps., 1988, 20th Century award of Achievement Internat. Biog. Ctr., Cambridge, Eng., 1993, 1st Five Hundred, Cambridge, 1994, Citizen's citation, City of Balt., 1994, others; Ethnic Minority scholar United Meth. Ch., 1988-89, Brandenburg scholar, 1988-89, Tadlock scholar, 1989-90, Calvary Fellow scholar Calvary United Meth. ch., 1989-90. Mem. U. Ill. Alumni Assn. (bd. dirs. 1987-88), Alpha Kappa Alpha (pres. local chpt. 1974-76, v.p. 1973). Democrat. Home: 1711 Lakeside Ave Baltimore MD 21218

PAYTON, ANTOINETTE SHIELDS, realtor; b. Miles City, Mont., Mar. 9, 1926; d. Claude M. and Odie (Waddell) Shields; m. Robert J. Iholts, Mar. 30, 1946 (dec. Oct. 1957); children: Robert C., Marilyn Tracy; m. Donald Glen Payton, Dec. 5, 1959. BA, U. Mont., 1959; postgrad., U. Nev., 1960-71. Cert. tchr., libr., Nev.; lic. realtor, Nev. Tchr. Reno Pub. Schs., 1960-64; libr. Billinghurst Jr. High Sch., Pine Mid. Sch., Reno, 1964-85; realtor, co-owner, sec. Century 21 All Seasons, Reno, 1985—, also bd. dirs. Recipient Disting. Svc. award Washoe County Tchrs. Assn., 1985. Mem. AAUW, PTA (life Reno), Nat. Assn. Realtors, Nev. Assn. Realtors, Reno/Sparks Assn. Realtors, DAR, Mayflower Descendants Soc., Order of the Crown of Charlemayne in the U.S.A., Alpha Delta Kappa (pres., treas. 1975-82), Beta Sigma Phi (life, officer 1950-95). Office: Century 21 All Seasons 1595 S Virginia St Reno NV 89502-2826

PAYTON, JACQUELINE N., mathematics educator; b. Louisa, Va., Aug. 7, 1937; d. Floyd R. and Juanita B. (Johnson) Nelson; m. Richard W. Payton, June 24, 1961; children: Richard Jr., Glennis, Charles, Sheree. BS, Va. State U., 1958, MEd, 1971; EdD, U. Va., 1987. Instr. math. Lancaster (Va.) County Sch. Bd., 1958-69, Chesterfield (Va.) County Sch. Bd., 1971-72, 73-74; assoc. prof. math. Va. State U., Petersburg, 1974—; instr. math. U. Va., Charlottesville, 1985, 86; project dir. Upward Bound Math. and Sci. Ctr. Va. State U., Petersburg, 1991—. Mem. Nat. Coun. Tchrs. Math., Internat. Soc. Tech. in Edn., Va. Coun. Tchrs. Math., Ea. Ednl. Rsch. Assn., Phi Delta Kappa, Kappa Mu Epsilon. Office: Va State U 306 S Hunter Mcdaniel Petersburg VA 23803

PAYTON ROE, JOY, museum coordinator; b. Conshocton, Ohio, Dec. 10, 1960; d. George Scott and Grace Eileen Guldenschuh Payton; m. Thomas Bryan Roe, Sept. 18, 1993. BFA, Syracuse U., 1983. Asst. edn. dept. Cin. Art Mus., 1984-85, asst. mgr. pubs. and photographic svcs., 1985-89, acting mgr., 1989-90, assoc. coord., 1990-93, coord. photographic svcs., rights and reprodns., 1993—; exec. com., chair fundraising, coord. membership Cin. Artists' Group Effort, Cin., 1988-92; adv. bd. Arts Cin. '94, 1994. Author: (short stories) USA Weekend, 1991, I Never Believed in Ghosts Until..., 1992; exhibited in group shows at Bicentennial Commons, Cin., 1987, C.A.G.E. Gallery, Cin., 1990—, Alternative Gallery, Cin., 1991-93, Carnegie Art Ctr., Covington, Ky., 1991, Semantics Gallery, Cin., 1992. Active Salvation Army, Cin., 1985, 86; speaker various civic orgns. Grantee Spellman Trust Found., 1981. Mem. R.O.A.R.R. Artists' Alliance (founding, fin. officer 1990-92, artists open studio tour 1992), Am. Soc. Media Photographers, Visual Resource Assn. Democrat. Office: Cin Art Mus Eden Park Cincinnati OH 45202-1596

PAZANDAK, CAROL HENDRICKSON, liberal arts educator; b. Mpls.; d. Norman Everard and Ruth (Buckley) Hendrickson; m. Bruce B. Pazandak (dec. 1986); children: David, Bradford, Christopher, Eric, Paul, Ann; m. Joseph P. O'Shaughnessy, May 1991. PhD, U. Minn., 1970. Asst. dir. admissions U. Minn., Mpls., 1970-72, asst. dean liberal arts, 1972-79, asst. to pres., 1979-85, office of internat. edn., acting dir., 1985-87, asst. prof. to assoc. to prof. liberal arts, 1970—; vis. prof. U. Iceland, Reykjavik, 1984, periods in 1983, 86, 87, 88, 89, 90-92, 93, 94; vis. rsch. prof. U. Oulu, Finland, 1993; exec. sec. Minn.-Iceland Adv. Com., U. Minn., 1984—; cons. U. Iceland, 1983—; co-chair Reunion of Sisters-Minn. and Finland Confs., 1986—. Editor: Improving Undergraduate Education in Large Universities, 1989. Past pres. Minn. Mrs. Jaycees, Mpls. Mrs. Jaycees; formerly bd. govs. St. John's Preparatory Sch., Collegeville, Minn.; former bd. trustees Coll. of St. Teresa, Winona, Minn.. Recipient Partnership award for contbn. to advancing shared interests of Iceland and Am., 1994; named to Order of the Falcon, Govt. of Iceland, 1990. Mem. Internat. Coun. Psychologists, Am. Psychol. Assn., Am. Coun. Edn. (former steering com. Nat. Identification Program for Women in Higher Edn. Adminstrn. 1983-86), Soc. Advancement of Scandinavian Studies. Home: 1361 Prior Ave S Saint Paul MN 55116-2656 Office: U Minn N 247 Elliott Hall 75 E River Rd Minneapolis MN 55455-0432

PEABODY, LAURA ELLEN, information technology administrator; b. Torrence, Calif., Oct. 8, 1960; d. Laurence C. and Harriett Laura (Bamford) P.; m. Mark Stephen Park, Nov. 14, 1981. AB in Econs., U. Calif., Berkeley, 1981; MBA in Info. Systems, Golden Gate U., 1990. Cert. computer profl. Benefit authorizer Social Security Adminstrn., Richmond, Calif., 1981-84; programmer analyst Letterman Army Med. Ctr., San Francisco, 1984-86; computer specialist Naval Hosp., Oakland, Calif., 1986-90; MIS mgr. City of Fairfield, Calif., 1990—. Mem. Mcpl. Info. Systems Assn. Calif. (No. region pres.-elect 1992-93, pres. 1993—), Data Processing Mgmt. Assn., Internat. Assn. for Certification of Computer Profls. Episcopalian. Office: City of Fairfield 1000 Webster St Fairfield CA 94533

PEABODY, SYLVIA ROCKWOOD, community health nurse, agency administrator; b. Chester, Vt., June 12, 1919; d. Arthur Cochran and Gladys Ina (Davis) P. BS, Columbia U., 1946; RN, Children's Hosp. Sch. Nursing, Boston, 1943; MS, Simmons Coll., 1954; postgrad., Harvard U., 1974. RN, R.I., Mich., Mass., N.Y. Staff nurse, team leader Vis. Nurse Svc. N.Y., N.Y.C., 1944-47, Barry County Health Dept., Hastings, Mich., 1947-49; pediatric nursing cons. Mich. Crippled Children's Commn., Marquette, 1949-50; pub. health instr. Children's Hosp. Sch. Nursing, Boston, 1950-53; sr. nurse, supr., asst. dir. Vist. Nurse Assn. Met. Detroit, 1954-64, exec. dir., 1964-78; exec. dir. Vis. Nurse Svc. Newport (R.I.) County, 1979-85; part-time charge nurse John Clarke Nursing Ctr., Middletown, R.I., 1989-95; incorporator, bd. dirs. Island Hospice, Newport, 1982-85. Pres. Newport County, Lit. Vols. Am., 1986-93; vol. Island Hospice, Newport, 1985—; buddy Project AIDS of R.I., 1986—; tutor ESL, 1986—. Mem. APHA (chmn. pub. health nursing sect. 1958-64, newsletter editor 1958-64, v.p. 1968-72), Nat. League for Nursing (pres. 1975-77), Am. Assn. Retired Persons (vol. tax. counselor 1984—). Episcopalian. Home: 400 Bellevue Ave Apt 101 Newport RI 02840-6922

PEACH, PEGGY, mental health therapist, chemical dependency counselor; b. Middletown, Ohio, Sept. 14, 1946; children: Christina, Scott. BS in Edn., Ohio U., 1971; MA, U. Cin., 1987; PhD, Union Inst., Cin., 1994—. Pers. mgr. Import Store, Lebanon, Ohio, 1971-75; trainer Ohio Dept. Transp., Lebanon, 1975-80; family therapist Greene Hall, Xenia, Ohio, 1987-88; counselor, clin. dir. County Drug and Alcohol, Lebanon, 1989-90; therapist Bergamo, Dayton, Ohio, 1992; crisis counselor Eastway, Dayton, 1991-92; therapist A.V.O.I.S.E., Cin., 1991-94, Dartmouth Hosp., Dayton, 1992-94; condr. workshops in field. Mem. Ctrl. Com., Rep. Party, Warren County, Ohio, 1988; den mother cub scouts Boy Scouts Am., 1981; vol. Children's Svcs., Lebanon, 1986, Women Helping Women, Cin., 1987. Mem. Am. Counselors Assn., Assn. for Religious and Value Issues in Counseling, Nat. Cert. Reciprocity Consortium Alcohol and Other Drug Abuse. Roman Catholic.

PEACHER, GEORGIANA MELICENT, poet, educator; b. Syracuse, N.Y., Nov. 13, 1919; d. William Catlett and Georgiana (Ruckman) P. BS, Syracuse U., 1941, MS, 1943; PhD, Northwestern U., 1946. Dir. speech therapy Neuro-Phys. Rehab. Clinic, Phila., 1946-47; prof. speech pathology and psychology Temple U. Med. Sch., Phila., 1948-67; dir. speech therapy N.Y. Hosp., Cornell U., N.Y.C., 1953-56; ind. rschr. various cities, Russia, Eng., Scotland, 1967-75, C.G. Jung Inst., Zürich, Switzerland, 1975-76; prof. speech and psychology John Jay Coll. CUNY, 1976-90; prof. emerita John Jay Coll. CUNY, 1990—; pres. Pearl Shedding Press, South Portland, Maine, 1990—. Author: (book) How to Improve Your Speaking Voice, 1966, Mary Stuart's Ravishment Descending Time, 1976, (play) Hatshepsut, 1982, (poem) Elizabeth of Mariana, 1992; contbr. articles to profl. jours. Grantee for performance of Indira India, CUNY, 1988, 89. Fellow Am. Speech Hearing Lang. Assn.; mem. Baxter Soc. (sec. 1991-93). Democrat. Home and Office: 245 Broadway South Portland ME 04106

PEACO, JOYCE LORANE, elementary school educator; b. Wilmington, Del.; d. James Wesley and Rosa Juanita (Petty) P. BA, Howard U., 1961; MA, U. Del., 1968; EdD, Nova U., 1984. Elem. tchr. Sarah Webb Pyle Sch., Wilmington, 1963, George Gray Sch., Wilmington, 1963-76, Shipley Sch., Wilmington, 1976-85, Lombardy Sch., Talleyville, Del., 1985—; cooperating tchr. Wilmington Pub. Sch. System, 1970, 80. Leader Chesapeake Bay Girl Scouts, Wilmington, 1969—. Recipient Green Angel award Chesapeake Girl Scouts, 1988, Outstanding Leader award Chesapeake Girl Scouts, 1988, Community Svc. award Martin Luther King Dinner Com., 1989. Mem. NEA, AAUW, Nat. Assn. Univ. Women, Kappa Delta Pi, Delta Kappa Gamma, Nat. Sorority Phi Delta Kappa Inc., Sigma Gamma Rho. Home: 8 Colony Blvd Wilmington DE 19802-1465 Office: Brandywine Sch Dist Lombardy Elem Sch 412 Foulk Rd Wilmington DE 19803-3880

PEACOCK, JUDITH ANN See ERWIN, JUDITH ANN

PEACOCK, MARY WILLA, magazine editor; b. Evanston, Ill., Oct. 23, 1942; d. William Gilbert and Mary Willa (Young) P. B.A., Vassar Coll., 1964. Assoc. lit. editor Harper's Bazaar mag., N.Y.C., 1964-69; staff editor Innovation mag., N.Y.C., 1969-70; editor in chief, co-founder, sec.-treas., pres. Rags mag., N.Y.C., San Francisco, 1970-71; co-founder, features editor Ms. mag., N.Y.C., 1971-77; pub., pres. Rags mag., N.Y.C., 1977-80; sr. editor Village Voice, N.Y.C., 1980-85, style editor, 1985-89; editor-in-chief Model mag., N.Y.C., 1989—, editorial cons., 1991—; fashion dir. Lear's Mag., N.Y.C., 1992-94; dep. editor In Style Mag., 1994, Mirabella mag., 1994—.

PEACOCK, VALERIE LYNN, paralegal; b. Tallahassee, Nov. 6, 1962; d. William Stanley and Valerie Jo (Tate) P. AA with honors, Tallahassee Community Coll., 1982; BS in Bus. Communication, Fla. State U., 1986. Cert. legal asst., Ga. With Fla. House of Reps., Tallahassee, 1980-84; with office of registrar Fla. State U., Tallahassee, 1984-85; tchr. Leon County Sch. Bd., Tallahassee, 1986-87; legal asst. Dept. of Ins.-Receivership, Tallahassee, 1987-88, B.K. Roberts, Baggett, LaFace & Richard, Tallahassee, 1988; paralegal specialist criminal div. Fla. Atty. Gen., Tallahassee, 1988—; mem. adv. bd. Nat. Ctr. Paralegal Tng., Miami and Ft. Lauderdale, Fla., 1990—; with paralegal studies program Rollins Coll. Ctr. for Lifelong Edn., 1992—. Mem. Jr. League of Tallahassee, 1992—, bd. dirs. 1993—, community pub. rels. chmn., 1993—, chmn. internat. pub. rels. com., 1992-93; vol. missionary local ch. to Port-au-Prince, Haiti, 1985; mem. adminstrv. bd. local ch., Tallahassee, 1988—; atty. gen. rep. Ptnrs. in Excellence, Tallahassee, 1990; bd. dirs. Am. Heart Assn., 1992—; chmn. Children's Miracle Network, 1993, mem. community bd., 1994—. Mem. Fla. Supreme Ct. Hist. Soc., Friends of Maclay Gardens, Pi Kappa Phi, Phi Sigma Soc., Phi Theta Kappa. Republican. Office: Atty Gen Criminal Div The Capitol Tallahassee FL 32399-1050

PEALE, RUTH STAFFORD (MRS. NORMAN VINCENT PEALE), religious leader; b. Fonda, Iowa, Sept. 10, 1906; d. Frank Burton and Anna Loretta (Crosby) Stafford; m. Norman Vincent Peale, June 20, 1930; children: Margaret Ann (Mrs. Paul F. Everett), John Stafford, Elizabeth Ruth (Mrs. John M. Allen). AB, Syracuse U., 1928, LLD, 1953; LittD, Hope Coll., 1962; LHD (hon.), Milw. Sch. Engring., 1985, Judson Coll., 1988; LHD, Milw. Sch. Engring., 1985. Tchr. math. Cen. High Sch., Syracuse, N.Y., 1928-31; nat. pres. women's bd. domestic missions Ref. Ch. Am., 1936-46; sec. Protestant Film Commn., 1946-51; chmn. Am. Mother's Com., 1948-49; pres., editor-in-chief, gen. sec., CEO, chmn. bd. dirs. Peale Ctr. for Christian Living, 1940—; nat. pres. bd. domestic missions Ref. Ch. in Am., 1955-56; mem. bd. N. Am. Missions, 1963-69, pres., 1967-69; mem. gen. program council Ref. Ch. in Am., 1968—; mem. com. of 24 for merger Ref. Ch. in Am. and Presbyn. Ch. U.S., 1966-69; v.p. Protestant Council N.Y.C., 1964-66; hon. chancellor Webber Coll., 1972—; co-founder, pub. Guideposts, N.Y.C., 1945—, pres., 1985-92, chmn. bd., 1992—; pres. Fleming H. Revell, Tarrytown, N.Y., 1985-92; founder Ruth Stafford Peale Ctr., Syracuse, 1989—. Appeared on: nat. TV program What's Your Trouble, 1952-68; Author: I Married a Minister, 1942, The Adventure of Being a Wife, 1971, Secrets of Staying in Love, 1984; founder, pub. (with Dr. Peale) Guidepost mag., 1957—; co-subject with husband: film One Man's Way, 1963. Trustee Hope Coll., Holland, Mich., Champlain Coll., Burlington, Vt., Stratford Coll., Danville, Va., Lenox Sch., N.Y.C., Interchurch Center Syracuse U., 1955-61; bd. dirs. Cook Christian Tng. Sch., Lord's Day Alliance U.S.; mem. bd. and exec. com. N.Y. Theol. Sem., N.Y.C.; sponsor Spafford Children's Convalescent Hosp., 1966—; bd. govs. Help Line Telephone Center, 1970—, Norman Vincent Peale Telephone Center, 1977; mem. nat. women's bd. Northwood Inst., 1981. Named New York State Mother of Yr., 1963, Disting. Woman of Yr. Nat. Art Assn., Religious Heritage Am. Ch. Woman of Yr., 1969; recipient Cum Laude award Syracuse U. Alumni Assn. N.Y., 1965, Honor Iowans' award Buena Vista Coll., 1966, Am. Mother's Com. award religion, 1970, Disting. Svc. award Coun. Chs., N.Y.C., 1973, Disting. Citizen award Champlain Coll., 1976, Disting. Svc. to Community and Nation award Gen. Fedn. Women's Clubs, 1977, Horatio Alger award, 1977, Religious Heritage award, 1979, joint medallion with husband Soc. for Family of Man, 1981, Soc. Family of Man award, 1981, Alderson-Broaddus award, 1982, Marriage Achievement award Bride's Mag., 1984, Gold Angel award Religion in Media, 1987, Adela Rogers St. John Roundtable award, 1987, Disting. Achievement award Am. Aging, 1987, Paul Harris award N.Y. Rotary, 1989, Leader's award Arthritis Found. Dutchess County, 1992, Norman Vincent Peale award Internat. Platform Assn., 1994, The Dave Thomas Well Done! award, 1994, Norman Vincent Peale award for positive thinking, 1994. Mem. Insts. Religion and Health (bd. exec. com.), Am. Bible Soc. (bd. trustees 1948-93, hon. trustee 1993—), United Bible Soc. (v.p.), The Interchurch Ctr. (bd. dirs. 1957-92, chair 1982-90), Nat. Coun. Chs. (v.p. 1952-54, gen. bd.; treas. gen. dept. United Ch. Women, vice chmn. broadcasting and film commn. 1951-55, program chmn. gen. assembly 1966), N.Y. Fedn. Women's Clubs (chmn. religion 1951-53, 57-58), Home Missions Coun. N.A. (nat. pres. 1942-44, nat. chmn. migrant com. 1948-51), Nat. League Am. Pen Women (hon. life), PEO, Alpha Phi (Frances W. Willard award 1976). Republican. Office: Peale Ctr Christian Living 66 E Main St Pawling NY 12564-1409

PEARCE, DRUE, state legislator; b. Fairfield, Ill., Apr. 2, 1951; d. H. Phil and Julia Detroy (Bannister) P. AB, Ind. U., 1973; MPA, Howard U., 1984. Sch. tchr. Clark County, Ind., 1973-74; curator Louisville Zoo, 1974-77; dir. Summerscene, Louisville, 1974-77; asst. v.p. Alaska Nat. Bank of the North, 1977-82; legis. aide to Alaska State Rep. John Ringstad, 1983; mem. Alaska Ho. of Reps., 1984-88; state senator Alaska Senate, 1988—. Mem. Alaska Resource Devel. Coun., Alaska Women's Polit. Caucus. Mem. DAR, Alaska C. of C. Republican. Home: 6035 Tanaina Dr Anchorage AK 99502-1832 Office: Office of the State Senate State Capitol Juneau AK 99811*

PEARCE, ELIZABETH ANNE, financial analyst; b. San Francisco, Nov. 10, 1959; d. Henry Milton and Joanne Margaret (Rodley-Coleman) P. AB, U. Calif., Berkeley, 1983. Chartered fin. analyst. Dividend dept. mgr. Emmett A. Larkin Co., San Francisco, 1982-84; portfolio mgmt. assoc. Tuttle & Noroian, San Francisco, 1984-86; v.p., portfolio mgr. Noroian & Assocs., San Francisco, 1986-88; dir. rsch. Anderson Capital Mgmt., San Francisco, 1988-94; v.p., sr. equity analyst Merus Capital Mgmt., San Francisco, 1994—; bd. dirs. Marin Stonewall Alliance. Mem. scholarship com. U. Calif. Alumni, Marin County. Mem. San Francisco Security Analysts, Bay Area Career Women, San Francisco Women's Club, Fin. Women's Club. Home: 104 Wisteria Way # 3 Mill Valley CA 94941 Office: Merus Capital Mgmt 309 Carrera Dr San Francisco CA 94111

PEARCE, JEANNIE, writer, insurance administrator; b. Casa Grande, Ariz., Sept. 24, 1948; d. Johnnie E. and Barbara (Dismukes) Pearce; m. Bryce Hallice Storseth, Aug. 15, 1981; 1 child, Michael Scott. B.S., U. Ariz., 1979. Mktg. rep. Group Health Coop., Seattle, 1981-83; dist. mgr. Health Plus/Blue Cross, Seattle, 1983-84; mktg. dir. Personal Health, Seattle, 1984-85; sales dir. Cigna Health Plan, Seattle, 1985-88; real estate agent John L. Scott Real Estate, Seattle, 1988-92; freelance writer, 1992—; prin. Bus. Writers Northwest, Seattle, 1994—. Avocations: oil painting, writing. Office: Bus Writers Northwest PO Box 66003 Seattle WA 98166

PEARCE, JENNIFER SUE, real estate appraiser; b. Jacksonville, Fla., Nov. 1, 1954; d. Marvin William and Betty Mae (White) Robinson; m. James Zenous Pearce Jr., Mar. 30, 1974; children: Keith Bryan, Kevin Patrick. Student, Baylor U., 1983, U. Ga., 1985; cert., Jacksonville U., 1986. Cert. residential and comml. real estate appraiser, Fla. Broker, sales Watson Realty Corp., Jacksonville, 1979-82; sr. resdl. appraiser Page Aspinwall Appraiser, Jacksonville, 1982-90; owner Jennifer Pearce Appraiser, Jacksonville, 1991—; instr. real estate appraisal Fla. Community Coll., 1987; commissioned by Ednl. Testing Svc. to establish exam for certification of appraisers in state of Fla. Mem. Appraisal Inst., Am. Acad. State Cert. Appraisers (charter), Daus. of the Nile. Home: 4807 Avon Ln Jacksonville FL 32210-7505 Office: 1938 Blanding Blvd Jacksonville FL 32210-3263

PEARCE, JOAN DELAP, research company executive; b. Oakland, Calif., June 13, 1930; d. Robert Jerome and Wilhelmina (Reaume) DeLap; m. Gerald Allan Pearce, June 18, 1953; 1 child, Scott Ford. Student, U. Oreg., 1948-55. Research assoc. deForest Research, Los Angeles, 1966-78; dir. research Walt Disney Prodns., Burbank, Calif., 1978; assoc. dir. deForest Research, Los Angeles, 1978-92; pres., bd. dirs. Joan Pearce Rsch. Assocs., 1992—; lighting dir. Wilcoxen Players, Beverly Hills, Calif., 1955-60, Theatre 40, Los Angeles, 1960-66. Bd. advisors Living History Ctr., Marin County, Calif., 1982-89, bd. dirs., 1989—. Mem. Am. Film Inst. Democrat. Avocations: photography; travel; theater; swimming. Home: 2621 Rutherford Dr Los Angeles CA 90068 Office: Joan Pearce Rsch Assocs 8111 Beverly Blvd Ste 308 Los Angeles CA 90048

PEARCE, MARGARET TRANNE, law librarian; b. San Bernadino, Calif., Mar. 20, 1946; d. Paul Nelson and Margaret (Buchanan) Gregory; m. Ronald Wayne Pearce, Jan. 13, 1973; 1 child, Alice. BA in Edn., U. Kans., 1968; MLS, Emporia State U., 1969; postgrad., Washington U., 1982-83. Asst. libr. Kans. State U., Manhattan, 1969-73; assoc. law libr. Washington U., St. Louis, 1974-80; ct. libr. Mo. Ct. Appeals (ea. dist.), St. Louis, 1981-83; libr. 8th Cir. Libr., Kansas City, Mo., 1983—. Guardian ad litem Ct. Appointed Spl. Advocates, Johnson County, Kans., 1984-88. Mem. Am. Assn. Law Librs., Mid-Am. Assn. Law Librs., Kansas City Assn. Law Librs. (bd. dirs. 1992-93, sec. 1995—). Home: 8408 W 113th St Overland Park KS 66210 Office: US Cts Libr 811 Grand Ave Kansas City MO 64106-1909

PEARL, HELEN ZALKAN, lawyer; b. Washington, Sept. 12, 1938; d. George and Harriet (Libman) Zalkan; m. Jason E. Pearl, June 27, 1959; children: Gary M., Esther H., Lawrence J. BA with hons., Vassar Coll., 1959; JD, U. Conn., 1978. Bar: Conn. 1978, U.S. Dist. Ct. Conn. 1978. Mkt. rsch. analyst Landers, Frary & Clark, New Britain, Conn., 1960-61; managerial statistician Landers, Frary & Clark, 1961-62; real estate salesperson Denuzze Co., New Britain, 1966-70; property mgr. self-employed New Britain, 1970-75; legal asst. Atty. Gen. Office, State of Conn., Hartford, 1978; assoc. Weber & Marshall, New Britain, 1978-83; ptnr. Weber & Marshall, 1983—; hearing officer Commn. on Human Rights & Opportunities, State of Conn., 1980—; spl. master State of Conn. Judicial Dept., 1986—. New Britain rep. to Cen. Conn. Regional Planning Agy., 1973-75, 84—, chmn., 1990-92; mem. New Britain Bd. Fin. and Taxation, 1973-77; founder, mem. Conn. Permanent Commn. on Status of Women, 1975-82; also others. Recipient Women in Leadership award, YWCA of New Britain, 1988, Book award for torts, Am. Jurisprudence, 1976, Econs. prize, Vassar Coll., 1959. Mem. AAUW (pres. 1970-72), Conn. Bar Assn. (family law sect., women and the law sect.), New Britain Bar Assn., League Women Voters (Conn. specialist 1987—), Hartford Vassar Club, Phi Beta Kappa. Democrat. Jewish. Home: 206 Hickory Hill Rd New Britain CT 06052-1010 Office: Weber & Marshall PO Box 1568 New Britain CT 06050-1568

PEARL, LAUREN HEIDI, foreign language educator; b. Springfield, Mass., Feb. 4, 1950; d. Abraham Benjamin and Lindy (Pessin) Feinstein; m. Jeffrey Tobey Pearl, Feb. 24, 1974; children: Edward Lee, Lisa Sue. BA in French/Spanish, Simmons Coll., Boston, 1971; MA in Romance Langs., Boston Coll., 1972. Cert. fgn. lang. tchr., Md. Fgn. lang. tchr. J.F. Kennedy Jr. High Sch., Springfield, Mass., 1972-74; fgn. lang. tchr./chmn. dept. B. Tasker Middle Sch., Bowie, Md., 1974—; fgn. lang. cons. Prince Georges County pub. schs., 1976—; pres. Lauren's Laminates, 1976—. Author/editor supplementary workbook: Latin is Not Dead, 1978. Tchr. Hebrew, Temple Solel, Bowie, Md., 1986—. Home: 2907 Traymore Ln Bowie MD 20715 Office: B Tasker Middle School 4901 Collington Rd Bowie MD 20715

PEARMAN, SARA JANE, librarian; b. Dallas, Sept. 6, 1940; d. Lormor Allen and Dorothy Edna (Linge) P.; widowed. BA, U. Wichita, 1962; MA, U. Kans., 1964; PhD, Case Western Res. U., 1974. Instr. art history Kearney (Nebr.) State Coll., 1964-66; slide libr. Cleve. Mus. Art, 1968—; asst. prof. Kent (Ohio) State U., 1984—; cons. Art and Arch. Thesaurus, Williamston, Mass., Getty Art History Program, Malibu, Calif.; owner Venerable Bead, Cleve., 1993—. Author various publs. on slide librs., iconography, graphic design, other publs. in field. Mem. Historians of Netherlands Art, Art Librs. of N. Am. (pres. Ohio chpt. 1986-87). Office: Cleve Mus of Art 11150 East Blvd Cleveland OH 44106-1711

PEARSON, CAROL LYNN, writer; b. Salt Lake City, Sept. 27, 1939; d. Lelland Rider and Emeline (Sirrine) Wright; m. Gerald Neils Pearson, Sept. 9, 1966 (div. July 1979); children: Emily, John, Aaron, Katy. BA in Drama, Brigham Young U., 1961, MA in Drama, 1962. Author: (poems) Beginnings, A Growing Season, A Widening View, I Can't Stop Smiling, Women I Have Known and Been; (autobiography) Goodbye, I Love You, 1986; (play) Mother Wove the Morning, 1989. Safe home provider Battered Women's Alternatives, Walnut Creek, 1979—. Recipient 1st place Bay Area Poets, 1984; named Outstanding Young Woman of Utah, 1967. Mormon. Home: 1384 Cornwall Ct Walnut Creek CA 94596-2338

PEARSON, DEBORAH ANN, psychologist, educator; b. New Bedford, Mass., Apr. 23, 1957; d. Harry Jr. and Louise Agnes (Dalmar) P.; m. John Crawford Woodhouse II, Sept. 4, 1982. BA, Wesleyan U., 1979; MA, Rice U., 1982, PhD, 1986. Lic. psychologist, Tex. Rsch. asst. Rice U., Houston, 1979-82, Tex. Children's Hosp., Houston, 1983-86; vis. asst. prof. Rice U., Houston, 1986; asst. prof. U. Tex. Med. Sch., Houston, 1987—; adj. asst. prof. Rice U., Houston, 1986; advisor Assn. of Retarded Citizens, Houston, 1989—; cons. Attention Deficit Hyperactivity Disorder Assn., Houston, 1989—. Author: (with others) The Development of Attention: Research and Theory, 1990; contbr. articles to profl. jours.; mem. editorial bd. Jour. Child & Family Studies, 1994—. Elder St. Thomas Presbyn. Ch., Houston, 1986-88. Numerous rsch. grants, 1987—. Mem. APA, Houston Psychol. Assn., Soc. Rsch. in Child Devel., Am. Assn. Mental Retardation, Assn. for Women in Sci., Soc. Pediatric Psychology. Office: U Tex Med Sch 1300 Moursund St Houston TX 77030-3497

PEARSON, GERTRUDE BOOTH, state legislator; b. Quincy, Mass., Apr. 16, 1918; d. Gilbert Alexander and Grace Ripley (Dunn) Booth; m. Gray Waite Pearson, Apr. 10, 1947 (dec. Dec. 1970); children: Grace Pearson Lilly, Gray Waite Pearson Jr. Student, Simmons Coll., Boston, 1935-37; BEd, Keene (N.H.) State Coll., 1960, MEd, 1970. Tchr. Thayer High Sch., Winchester, N.H., 1960-63, Keene (N.H.) High Sch., 1963-82; mem. N.H. Legis., Concord, 1989—. Chmn. Cheshire County Delegation, Keene, 1992—; treas. N.H. Fedn. Rep. Women, Concord, 1990—. Named Keene State Coll. President's Outstanding Woman of N.H., 1992. Mem. N.H. Ret. Tchrs. Assn. (pres. 1990-92), Friends of the Keene Pub. Libr. (pres. 1988-89). Home: 445 Park Ave Apt 5 Keene NH 03431 Office: N H General Ct Concord NH 03301

PEARSON, LOUISE MARY, retired manufacturing company executive; b. Inverness, Scotland, Dec. 14, 1919 (parents Am. citizens); d. Louis Houston and Jessie M. (McKenzie) Lenox; grad. high sch.; m. Nels Kenneth Pearson, June 28, 1941; children—Lorine Pearson Walters, Karla. Dir. Wauconda Tool & Engring. Co., Inc., Algonquin, Ill., 1950-86; reporter Oak Leaflet, Crystal Lake, Ill., 1944-47, Sidelights, Wilmette, Ill., 1969-72, 79-82. Active Girl Scouts U.S.A., 1955-65. Recipient award for appreciation work with Girl Scouts U.S., 1965. Clubs: Antique Automobile of Am. (Hershey, Pa.), Vet. Motor Car (Boston), Classic Car of Am. (Madison, N.J.). Home: 125 Dole Ave Crystal Lake IL 60014-5837

PEARSON, MARGARET DONOVAN, mayor; b. Nashville, Oct. 29, 1921; d. Timothy Graham and Nelle Ligon (Schmidt) Donovan; m. Jimmie Wilson

Pearson, Aug. 2, 1946 (dec. Oct. 1978). BS, Vanderbilt U., 1944, MA, 1950; MS, U. Tenn., 1954. Cryptanalysist Army Signal Corps, Washington, 1944-45; phys. edn. tchr. Nashville Bd. Edn., 1945-46; tchr. English, phys. edn. White County Bd. Edn., Sparta, Tenn., 1946-57; spl. edn. supr. Tenn. Dept. Edn., Cookeville, 1957-65; staff devel. dir. Tenn. Dept. Edn., Nashville, 1965-84; 1st woman alderman City of Sparta, 1987-91, 1st woman mayor, 1991—. Mem. Tenn. Gov.'s Com. Employment of Disabled, 1989—, U.S. Ret. Sr. Vol. Program, 1985—. Am. Speech, Lang. and Hearing Assn. fellow, 1971; Ky. Col.; Tenn. Col. Mem. Tenn. Mcpl. League (dist. dir. 1987-94, 1st woman elected as v.p.), Sparta C. of C., Rotary (1st woman elected pres.). Methodist. Home: 114 Highland Dr PO Box 22 Sparta TN 38583-0022 Office: PO Box 30 Sparta TN 38583-0030

PEARSON, PATRICIA KELLEY, marketing/staff coordinator; b. Carrollton, Ga., Jan. 21, 1953; d. Ben and Edith (Kelley) Rhudy; m. Ray S. Pearson, June 4, 1976; children: Chad, Jonathan, Kelly. BA in Journalism, Ga. State U., 1974; BSN, West Ga. Coll., 1990. RN Ga., Fla. Pub. rels. asst. Grady Meml. Hosp., Atlanta, 1974-77; editorial asst. Childers & Sullivan, Huntsville, Ala., 1977-78; sales rep. AAA Employment Agy., Huntsville, 1978-80; editor Wright Pub. Co., Atlanta, 1980-82; elect./electronic drafter PRC Cons., Atlanta, 1980-87; researcher Dept. Nursing at West Ga. Coll., Carrollton, 1989-90; med./surg. nurse Tanner Med. Ctr., Carrollton, Ga., 1989-90, Delray Community Hosp., Delray Beach, Fla., 1990-91, Innovative Med. Svcs., 1991-94; with staff devel., employee rels. Beverly Oaks Rehab. and Nursing Ctr., 1994—. All-Am. scholar U.S. Achievement Acad., 1990, recipient Nat. Coll. Nursing award, 1989. Mem. NOW, Ga. Nursing Assn., Omicron Delta Kappa. Democrat. Home: 229 Cedar Ave Cocoa Beach FL 32931

PEARSON, SUSAN WINIFRED, educational administrator; b. Wasco, Calif., Oct. 8, 1941; d. Gerald Thomas and Maxine (Jensen) P.; B.S., Tex. Christian U., 1963, M.Ed., 1971; Ed.D., U. Houston, 1982. Tchr. history, chmn. dept. Spring Branch Ind. Sch. Dist., Houston, 1963-68; personnel asst. Tenneco Inc., Houston, 1969-70; grad. asst. Tex. Christian U., 1970-71; dir. student activities Navarro Jr. Coll., Corsicana, Tex., 1972-73; dir. counseling svcs. North Harris County Coll., Houston, 1973-84, div. head bus., communications and fine arts, developmental studies and counseling, 1984-86, dean instrn./student svcs., 1986—; ednl. cons., 1994—. Mem. Am. Pers. & Guidance Assn., Am. Coll. Pers. Assn., Nat. Assn. Women Deans, Adminstrs. and Counselors, So. Coll. Pers. Assn., Tex. Assn. Women Deans, Adminstrs. and Counselors, Tex. Assn. Coll. and Univ. Student Pers. Adminstrs., Tex. Assn. Jr. Coll. Instructional Adminstrs., Tex. Assn. Community Coll. Chief Student Pers. Adminstrs., Phi Kappa Phi, Delta Gamma. Presbyterian. Author articles in field.

PEART, ELIZABETH R., developmental disabilities nurse; b. Paterson, N.J., Mar. 4, 1946; d. Frederick M. and Regina J. (Looss) Brown. Diploma, Meth. Hosp. Sch. Nursing, Bklyn., 1967; student, Miami Dade Community Coll., 1992—. Asst. head nurse Adventist Nursing Home, Livingston, N.Y., 1981-84; dir. nursing Pine Haven Home, Philmont, N.Y., 1984-85; med. coord. Miami (Fla.) Cerebral Svcs., Inc., 1985-87; office nurse Dr. Charles A. Kosove, Homestead, 1987-89; quality assurance Barnwell Nursing Facility, Chatham, N.Y., 1990; med. review supr. Gulf Coast Home Health Svcs., St. Petersburg, Fla., 1990-91; staff devel. quality assurance Miami (Fla.) Cerebral Palsy Svcs., Inc., 1991-94; adminstr. Miami Cerebral Palsy Residential Svcs., Inc., 1994—; cons. Miami Cerebral Palsy Residential Svcs., 1987-90; pvt. duty rehab. and patient teaching; insvc. educator. Vol. Health Fair, Homestead, Fla., 1989. Svc. award Miami Cerebral Palsy, 1987, 94. Mem. Devel. Disabilities Nursing Assn., Nat. Fire Protection Assn., Am. Bus. Women's Assn., Fla. Nurses Assn. Presbyterian. Home: 26225 SW 130 Ct Homestead FL 33032 Office: Miami Cerebral Palsy Svcs 5100 Hallandale Beach Blvd Hollywood FL 33023

PEART, MARGARET FARNUM, speech pathologist, social worker, psychotherapeutic clinician; b. Keene, N.H., June 23, 1945; d. Franklin Sprague and Dorothy Beatrix (Priest) P. BA, U. N.H., 1969; MEd, Boston U., 1972, MSW, 1994. Lic. speech-lang. therapist, Mass.; lic. social worker. Speech therapist Manchester (N.H.) Easter Seals, Inc., 1969, Springfield (Mass.) Pub. Schs., 1969-71; speech pathologist Governor Med. Ctr., Providence, 1972-74, New Bedford (Mass.) Pub. Schs., 1974-94; intern in social work John C. Corrigan Mental Health Ctr., Fall River, Mass., 1993-94; dir. student support group Boston U., Fall River, 1993-94. Mem. adv. bd. Headstart, New Bedford, 1975-77; facilitator loss and grief group Hospice of St. Luke's Hosp., New Bedford, 1985-93, vol., 1981-93; caregiver InterCh. Coun., New Bedford, 1977-78; psychotherapist Project Care, Ctr. for HIV and AIDS, New Bedford, 1994—. Named Outstanding Vol., St. Luke's Hospice, 1991. Roman Catholic.

PEART, SHERRY HARTMAN, lawyer; b. Houston, Jan. 13, 1951; d. Earl Creston and Alice Marie (Johnson) Hartman; m. John Edward Peart, Mar. 29, 1987; 1 child, Christopher Johnson. BA, U. Tex., 1973, JD, 1975; cert. Modern English Law, London Sch. Econ., 1974. Bar: Tex. 1976. Assoc. Jordan, Ramsey & Hill, Dallas, 1976-77; atty. Sun Oil Co. (Del.), Dallas, 1977-84; sr. atty. Sun Exploration and Prodn. Co., Dallas, 1984-90; chief counsel Oryx Energy Co., Dallas, 1990—; dir., v.p. Oryx Credit Union, Dallas, 1988-91. Mem. Dallas Bar Assn. Office: Oryx Energy Co 13155 Noel Rd Dallas TX 75240-5067

PEASE, DENISE LOUISE, state bank regulator; b. Bronx, N.Y., Mar. 15, 1953; d. William Henry Jr. and Louise Marion (Caswell) P. BA, Columbia U., 1978, postgrad., 1981-82; postgrad., Baruch Grad. Sch Pub Adminstrn., 1982-83, Institut Européen d'Administration des Affaires INSEAD, 1990. Exec. spl. asst. to county exec. N.J. Office of the County Exec., County of Essex (N.J.), 1982-83; urban analyst III State of N.Y. Dept. Banking, 1983-86, exec. asst. to the supt. of banks, 1986-87; dep. supt. of banks State of N.Y. Dept. Banking, N.Y.C., 1987—; mem. N.Y. State Gov.'s Econ. Devel. Sub-cabinet. Adv. bd. Cornell U. Coop. Extension; mgmt. program adv. bd. Sch. Bus. SUNY, 1990; mem. Alfred U. Devel. Com., mentoring program N.Y. State Women in Govt.; U.S. del. Europe Am. Emerging Leaders Conf., 1993. Named to Salute to Outstanding African Am. Bus. and Profl. Women, Dollar & Sense Mag., 1990, one of Outstanding Young Women in Am., 1979-81; recipient N.Y. State Assembly Citation of Merit, 1988, Profl. Achievement award Nat. Assn. Negro Bus. and Women's Club, 1981, Cmty. Svc. award N.Y. State Black and Puerto Rican Legislators Assn., 1993; Nat. Urban fellow, 1982-83, Charles H. Revson fellow Columbia U., 1981-82. Mem. NAACP (life mem.), Nat. Coun. of Negro Women (life mem.), Coalition of 100 Black Women, Fin. Women's Assn. N.Y. (bd. dirs.). Office: NY State Banking Dept 2 Rector St Fl 18 New York NY 10006-1819

PEASE, ELLA LOUISE, elementary education educator; b. Kokomo, Ind., May 31, 1928; d. James E. and Carrie Alice (Ringer) Earnest; m. Harold Edwin Pease, Aug. 10, 1985; children: Charles Miller, James Miller, Ricky Ensley, Wanda Cisna. BS, Ball State U., 1956, MA, 1959; postgrad., Ind. U., Ft. Wayne. Tchr. 1st grade Union Twp. (Ind.) Pub. Schs., 1953-56, Wells City (Ind.) Pub. Schs., Forest Park Sch., Ft. Wayne, Ind., 1956-93. Docent Ft. Wayne Art Mus.; libr. Simpson United Meth. Ch., Ft. Wayne. Mem. NEA-R, Internat. Reading Assn., Ret. Ind. Tchrs. Assn., Ft. Wayne Ret. Tchrs. Assn. Home: 5108 E State Blvd Fort Wayne IN 46815-7467

PEASLEE, MARGARET MAE HERMANEK, zoology educator; b. Chgo., June 15, 1935; d. Emil Frank and Magdalena Bessie (Cechota) Hermanek; m. David Raymond Peaslee, Dec. 6, 1957; 1 dau., Martha Magdelena Peaslee-Levine. A.A., Palm Beach Jr. Coll., 1956; B.S., Fla. So. Coll., 1959; med. technologist, Northwestern U., 1958, M.S., 1964, Ph.D., 1966. Med. technologist Passavant Hosp., Chgo., 1958-59; med. technologist St. James Hosp., Chicago Heights, Ill., 1960-63; asst. prof. biology Fla. So. Coll., Lakeland, 1966-68, U. S.D., Vermillion, 1968-71; assoc. prof. U. S.D., 1971-76, prof., 1976, acad. opportunity liaison, 1974-76; prof., head dept. zoology La. Tech. U., Ruston, 1976-90, assoc. dean, dir. grad. studies and rsch., prof. biol. scis. Coll. Life Scis., 1990-93; v.p. for acad. affairs U. Pitts. at Titusville, Pa., 1993—. Contbr. articles to profl. jours. Fellow AAAS; mem. AAUP, Am. Inst. Biol. Scis., Am. Soc. Zoologists, S.D. Acad. Sci. (sec.-treas. 1972-76), N.Y. Acad. Scis., Pa. Acad. Sci., La. Acad. Sci. (sec. 1979-81, pres. 1983), Sigma Xi, Phi Theta Kappa, Phi Rho Pi, Phi Sigma, Alpha Epsilon Delta. Office: U Pitts at Titusville Titusville PA 16354-0287

PEAT, WANDA JEAN, critical care nurse; b. Sioux Center, Iowa, July 6, 1956; d. Ralph and Arlene (Rozeboom) Punt; m. Alex Peat, June 11, 1976; children: Jennifer, Daniel, Bethany, Michael. Student, Buena Vista Coll., Storm Lake, Iowa, 1974-75; RN with distinction, Laramie County Community Coll., Cheyenne, Wyo., 1988. Cert. advanced cardiac life support. Staff nurse med./surg. unit DePaul Hosp., Cheyenne, 1988; staff nurse emergency rm. Home Hosp., Lafayette, Ind., 1988-89; high tech. pediatric home health nurse Hosp. Home Health Care of Midlands, Omaha, 1989-91; charge nurse, pvt. duty nurse Nursefinders, Inc., Omaha, 1989-91; pub. health nurse Sioux County Pub. Health, Orange City, Iowa, 1991-92. Mem. Am. Nurses Assn., Student Nurses Assn. (treas., fundraiser chmn.).

PEAVEY, FRANCES JEAN, social change worker; b. Twin Falls, Idaho, Aug. 16, 1941; d. Thomas C. and Dorothy (Carpenter) P. MA, San Francisco State U., 1957. tchr. Calif. Inst. Integral Studies, San Francisco, 1993-94. Author: Heart Politics, 1985, A Shallow Pool of Time, 1989, By Life's Grace, 1994. Cons. Sankat Mochen Found., Varanasi, India, 1980—. Recipient Giraffe award Giraffe Project, 1994. Mem. Interhelp (founding). Home and Office: 3181 Mission St # 30 San Francisco CA 94110

PEAVLER, NANCY JEAN, editor; b. Kansas City, Mo., Dec. 19, 1951; d. Elmer Alfred and Ruth Lenoris (Peterson) Zimmerli; m. Craig Eugene Peavler, Dec. 6, 1975; 1 child, Matthew Dean. Assoc., Kansas City (Kans.) Community Coll., 1976. Staff writer The Kansas City Kansan, 1972-73; assoc. editor Capper's Stauffer Communications, Topeka, 1976-87, editor, 1987—. Precinct com.-woman Shawnee County Rep. Party, Topeka, 1985-87. Mem. Women in Communications (chair chpt. publicity, chair freedom of info. com. 1991-92, v.p. membership/recruitment 1992-93), Beta SIgma Phi (sec. 1978-79, chpt. v.p. 1979-80). United Methodist. Office: Capper's 1503 SW 42nd St Topeka KS 66609

PEBBLES, SUSAN ELIZABETH, physical therapist; b. Tonawanda, N.Y., July 16, 1963; d. Howard Patrick and Elizabeth Catherine (Buckley) P. BS in Phys. Therapy, SUNY, Buffalo, 1985. Lic. phys. therapist. Staff phys. therapist Our Lady of The Lake Hosp., Baton Rouge, La., 1985-87; dir. phys. therapy Healthfocus, Wharton, Tex., 1987-90; pvt. practice Pineville Phys. Therapy, Charlotte, N.C., 1990—; mem. Ind. Practicing Phys. Therapists, Charlotte, 1990—; stockholder Rehab. Svcs. Network, Charlotte, 1993—. Contbr. articles to profl. jours. Scholar Ashland Oil Refinery, 1981. Mem. Am. Phys. Therapy Assn., Charlotte Women Bus. Owners, Charlotte C. of C., Nat. Honor Soc. Democrat. Roman Catholic. Home: 6027 Kingstree Dr Charlotte NC 28210 Office: Pineville Phys Therapy 6548 Carmel Rd Ste 108 Charlotte NC 28226

PECK, DEANA S., lawyer; b. Wichita, Kans., Nov. 6, 1947; d. Richard Rector Williams and Elva Alene (Davis) Williams; m. Frederick Page Peck, June 16, 1967 (div. Nov. 1981); 1 child, Paige. BA, Wichita State U., 1970; JD, U. Kans., 1975. Bar: Ariz. 1975, U.S. Dist. Ct. Ariz. 1975, U.S. Ct. Appeals (9th cir.) 1981, U.S. Ct. Appeals (10th cir.) 1990, U.S. Ct. Appeals (fed. cir.) 1991. Assoc. Streich Lang, Phoenix, 1975-80, ptnr., 1980—; vis. lectr. U. Kans. Sch. of Law, Lawrence, 1985. Mem. ABA, Maricopa County Bar Assn., State Bar Ariz. (antitrust coun.), Kans. U. Law Soc. (bd. govs. 1980-82). Office: Renaissance One 2 N Central Ave Phoenix AZ 85004-2391

PECK, DIANNE KAWECKI, architect; b. Jersey City, June 13, 1945; d. Thaddeus Walter and Harriet Ann (Zlotkowski) Kawecki; m. Gerald Paul Peck, Sept. 1, 1968; children: Samantha Gillian, Alexis Hilary. BArch, Carnegie-Mellon U., 1968. Architect, P.O.D. Research & Devel., 1968, Kohler-Daniels & Assocs., Vienna, Va., 1969-71, Beery-Rio & Assocs., Annandale, Va., 1971-73; ptnr. Peck & Peck Architects, Occoquan, Va., 1973-74, Peck, Peck & Williams, Occoquan, 1974-81; corp. officer Peck Peck & Assos., Inc., Woodbridge, Va., 1981—; chief exec. officer, interior design group Peck Peck & Assoc., 1988—. Work pub. in Am. Architecture, 1985. Vice pres. Vocat. Edn. Found., 1976; chairwoman architects and engrs. United Way; mem. Health Systems Agy. of No. Va., commendations, 1977; mem. Washington Profl. Women's Coop.; chairwoman Indsl. Devel. Authority of Prince William, 1976, vice chair, 1977, mem., 1975-79; developer research project Architecture for Adolescents, 1987-88; mem. inaugural class Leadership Am., 1988, Leadership Greater Washington; mem. D.C. Coun. Metrication, 1992—, D.C. Hist. Preservation League, Rep. Nat. Com. Recipient commendation Prince William Bd. Suprs., 1976, State of Art award for Contel Hdqrs. design, 1985, Best Middle Sch. award Coun. of Ednl. Facilities Planners Internat., 1989, Creativity award Masonry Inst. Md., 1990, First award, 1990, Detailing award, 1990, Govt. Workplace award for renovations of Dept. of Labor Bldg., 1990, Creative Use of Materials award Inst. of Bus. Designers, 1991, 1st award Brick Inst. Md., 1993, award Brick Inst. Va., 1994; named Best Instl. Project Nat. Comml. Builders Coun.; subject of PBS spl.: A Success in Howard Co. Mem. Soc. Am. Mil. Engrs., Prince William C. of C. (bd. dir.). Republican. Roman Catholic. Club: Soroptimist. Research on inner-city rehab., adolescents and the ednl. environ. Office: 2050 Old Bridge Rd Woodbridge VA 22192

PECK, ELISABETH CRAFT, decorative painter; b. Rochester, N.Y., Oct. 11, 1960; d. A. Burr and Elisabeth Pritchard (Wells) Craft; m. Edmund Eugene Peck, July 19, 1986; 1 child, Elisabeth Maria. Student, Rungsted Statskolen, Denmark, 1978-79, U. Copenhagen, 1982; BA, State U. Coll. at Potsdam, N.Y., 1983. Owner, prin. Elisabeth Craft Peck: Decorative Painting, Boston, 1987—; instr. Cambridge (Mass.) Ctr. for Adult Edn., 1987—, Boston Ctr. for Adult Edn., 1987—; studio art instr. New Eng. Sch. of Art and Design, 1995—. Nat. Merit scholar, 1978. Office: Peck Decorative Painting 15 Park St Boston MA 02136-3139

PECK, ELLIE ENRIQUEZ, retired state administrator; b. Sacramento, Oct. 21, 1934; d. Rafael Enriquez and Eloisa Garcia Rivera; m. Raymond Charles Peck, Sept. 5, 1957; children: Reginaldo, Enrico, Francisca Guerrero, Teresa, Linda, Margaret, Raymond Charles, Christina. Student polit. sci. Sacramento State U., 1974. Tng. services coord. Calif. Div. Hwys., Sacramento, 1963-67; tech. and mgmt. cons., Sacramento, 1968-78; expert examiner Calif. Pers. Bd., 1976-78; tng. cons. Calif. Pers. Devel. Ctr., Sacramento, 1978; spl. cons. Calif. Commn. on Fair Employment and Housing, 1978; community svcs. rep. U.S. Bur. of Census, No. Calif. counties, 1978-80; spl. cons. Calif. Dept. Consumer Affairs, Sacramento, 1980-83, project dir. Golden State Sr. Discount Program, 1980-83; dir. spl. programs for Calif. Lt. Gov., 1983-90, ret., 1990; pvt. cons., 1990—; cons., project dir. nat. sr. health issues summit Congress Calif. Srs. Edn. and Rsch. Fund, 1995; project dir. SSI/QMB Outreach Project, 1993-94. Author Calif. Dept. Consumer Affairs publ., 1981, U.S. Office Consumer Edn. publ., 1982. Bd. dirs Sacramento/Sierra Am. Diabetes Assn., 1989-90. Author: Diabetes and Ethnic Minorities: A Community at Risk. Trustee, Stanford Settlement, Inc., Sacramento, 1975-79; bd. dirs. Sacramento Emergency Housing Ctr., 1974-77, Sacramento Community Svcs. Planning Coun., 1987-90; v.p. Calif. Advs. for Nursing Home Reform, 1990—; v.p. bd. dirs. Calif. Advocates; campaign workshop dir. Chicago/Latino Leadership Conf., 1982-95; v.p. Comision Femenil Nacional, Inc., 1987-90; del. Dem. Nat. Conv., 1976; mem. exec. bd. Calif. Dem. Cen. Com., 1977-89; chairperson ethnic minority task force Am. Diabetes Assn., 1988-90; steering com. Calif. Self-Esteem Task Force Minority Steering Com., 1990-93. Recipient numerous awards including Outstanding Community Svc. award Comuicaciones Unidos de Norte Atzlan, 1975, 77, Outstanding Svc. award, Chicano/Hispanic Dem. Caucus, 1979, Vol. Svc. award Calif. Human Devel. Corp., 1981, Dem. of Yr. award Sacramento County Dem. Com., 1987, Outstanding Advocate award Calif. Sr. Legis., 1988, 89, Calif. Assn. of Homes for Aging, Advocacy award, 1989, Resolution of Advocacy award, League Latin-Ams. Citizens, 1989, Meritorious Svc. to Hispanic Community award Comite Patriotico, 1989, Meritorious Svc. Resolution award Lt. Gov. of Calif., 1989, Cert. Recognition award Sacramento County Human Rights Commn., 1991, Tish Sommers award Older Women's League/Joint Resolution Calif. Legislature, 1993, Latino Eagle award in govt. Thomas Lopez Meml. Found., 1994. Mem. Hispanic C. of C., CongressCalif. Srs., Sacramento Gray Panthers, Latino Dem. Club Sacramento County (v.p. 1982-83). Home and Office: 2667 Coleman Way Sacramento CA 95818-4459

PECK, JOAN KAY, systems engineer; b. Cedar Rapids, Iowa, Sept. 22, 1959; d. Leonard Allen and Mildred Jane (Keller) P. BS in Indsl. Engring., Iowa State U., 1983; MS in Space Tech., Fla. Inst. Tech., 1986; clergy student, River City Met. Cmty. Ch., Sacramento, 1993—. Student intern Rockwell-Collins, Cedar Rapids, 1979; coop. student Amana (Iowa) Refrigeration, 1981; sr. engr. Harris Govt. Aerospace Systems, Palm Bay, Fla., 1983-88; sr. systems engr. McDonnell Douglas Space Systems Co., Kennedy Space Ctr., Fla., 1988-94. V.p. programming Inst. Indsl. Engrs., Ames, 1982-83; victim advocate Sexual Assault Victims Svcs., Fla. State Attys. Office, Brevard County, 1991-92. Recipient Group Achievement award NASA, 1991.

PECK, MARIE JOHNSTON, Latin American area studies consultant; b. New Haven, Aug. 15, 1932; d. James Howard and Marie Anna Christina (Voigt) Johnston; m. Austin Monroe Peck, July 9, 1952 (div. 1959). AS, Larson-Quinnipiac, 1952; BA, U. N.Mex., 1968, PhD, 1974. Writer, coord. bilingual edn. coll. edn. U. N.Mex., Albuquerque, 1976-78; pres., owner Southwestern Images, Inc., Shawnee Mission, Kans., 1978—; lang. cons. The Warren Found., Seattle, 1990—; Vis. scholar U. N.Mex., Albuquerque, 1983; vis. instr. Wofford Coll., Spartanburg, S.C., 1984; adj. instr. humanities Johnson County Community Coll., Overland Park, Kans., 1985-86, coord. Brown V. Topeka Conf., 1986; cons. Brown V. Topeka Project, Merriam, Kans., 1984-88; bd. dirs. Op. SER, Colorado Springs, Colo., Midcoast Radio, Inc., Kansas City; curriculum writer Albuquerque Pub. Schs., 1980-81. Contbr. articles to profl. jours. Mem. Internat. Trade Task Force Greater Kansas City. Fulbright scholar, 1981-82; Fgn. Lang. fellow HEW, 1967-71, Rsch. fellow Orng. Am. States, 1970. Mem. NAFE, Puget Sound Grants Writers Assn., Fulbright Alumni Assn., Tchrs. of English to Speakers of Other Langs., Nat. Assn. for Bilingual Edn., Phi Beta Kappa. Home and Office: 8300 Phillips Rd SW Apt 123 Tacoma WA 98498

PECK, MARY MARGARET, banker; b. Breckenridge, Minn., Nov. 1, 1966; d. Francis J. and Veronica M. (Ciesynski) Ficenec; m. Robert W. Peck, Aug. 21, 1986. AA, Blue Mountain C.C., Pendleton, Oreg., 1987; BA, Western Oreg. State Coll., 1990; M of Mgmt., Willamette U., 1992. Auditor LaSalle Bus. Credit Inc., Lake Owsego, Oreg., 1992-94; sr. loan analyst Bank Am., Portland, Oreg., 1994—. Dean's Merit scholar Willamette U., 1990-92. Mem. Inst. Mgmt. Accts., Team Am., Lions Club. Office: Bank Am 1001 SW 5th Ave Portland OR 97204

PECKHAM, MARIKO HAMANO, nurse; b. Otaru, Hokkaido, Japan, Feb. 3, 1949; came to the U.S., 1970; d. Shingo and Hideko (Hanagami) Hamano; m. James Michael Peckham, May 18, 1970 (div. Aug. 1984); children: Samuel Eigi, Angela Louise. A in English, Kanto Gakuin Jr. Coll., Yokohama, Japan, 1970; ADN, Yakima (Wash.) Valley C.C., 1987; BSN, Wash. State U., 1992. RN, Wash.; cert. med.-surg. nurse. Staff LPN St. Elizabeth Med. Ctr., Yakima, 1982-87, staff RN, 1987—. Recipient scholarship Yakima (Wash.) Med. Soc., 1991. Mem. Wash. Nurses Assn. Republican. Office: Providence Yakima Med Ctr 110 S 9th Ave Yakima WA 98902-3315

PEDEN, EDITH SWEETSER, public relations executive; b. Tulsa, Mar. 9, 1934; d. Eric Camp and Mary Sweetser (Smith) Stahl; m. James C. Peden Jr., Feb. 27, 1960 (div. 1984); children: Katherine Stewart, Eric Camp, Margaret Girard. Student, Wells Coll., 1952-54; AB in Polit. Sci., U. Calif., Berkeley, 1956; postgrad., Washington U., St. Louis, 1983-84, Tulsa U., 1985, U. Center Tulsa, 1991. Sec. dept. econ. def. Dept. of State, Washington, 1957-58; adminstrv. asst. Okla. congressman Page Belcher, Washington, 1958; adminstrv. asst. to pub. rels. rep. Douglas Aircraft Co., Washington, 1958-60; asst. to pvt. investor St. Louis, 1960-61; communications aide Philbrook Art Ctr., Tulsa, 1984; founder, prin. Environ. Pub. Rels., Inc., Tulsa, 1987—. Active Philbrook Art Soc., Gilcrease Mus., Jr. League; mem. Women's Coun., Bladon, Oxfordshire, Eng., 1962; tutor to area minority students, St. Louis, 1975; mem. LWV, participant urban renewal program, 1971, chairperson environ. com., 1990; asst. supt. ednl. program local Presbyn. ch., 1965; mem. communications com. First Presbyn. Ch., 1990; mem. Women's Task Force on Edn., Tulsa C. of C. Recipient spl. recognition of authored papers, Harvard Bus. Sch., 1984, Okla. Gov. David Walters and Sam Walton of Wal-Mart, 1991. Mem. Women in Comm., Inc., Pub. Rels. Soc. Am. (environ. sect.), Women's Found. of Tulsa, Petroleum Club of Tulsa, Kappa Kappa Gamma. Republican. Office: Box 563 4308 S Peoria Ave Tulsa OK 74105-3922

PEDEN, LYNN ELLEN, marketing executive; b. L.A., Mar. 1, 1946; d. Orlan Sidney and Erna Lou (Harris) Friedman; m. Ernest Peden, Aug. 1994. Student UCLA, 1963-65, 71-72, Willis Bus. Coll., 1965-66, Fin. Schs. Am., 1982, Viewpoints Inst., 1970-71. Office mgr. Harleigh Sandler Co., L.A., 1965-67; customer svc. Investors Diversified Svcs., West L.A., Calif., 1968-76; exec. sec. McCulloch Oil Corp., West L.A., 1976; mgr. publs. Security 1st Group, Century City, Calif., 1976-80; office mgr. Morehead & Co., Century City, 1980-81; dir. mktg., mgr. customer svc. Ins. Mktg. Services, Santa Monica, Calif., 1981-82; v.p. Decatur Petroleum Corp., Santa Monica, 1982-83; asst. v.p., broker svcs., dir. Angeles Corp., L.A., 1984-87; asst. to pres. Pacific Ventures, Santa Monica, 1988-90; La Grange Group, West L.A., 1990—. Mem. Migi Car Am. Club (sec., newsletter editor). Fin. and ins. writer; contbr. poetry to UCLA Literary Mag., 1964. Home: 4365 McLaughlin Ave # 12 Los Angeles CA 90066-5957

PEDERSON, CARRIE ANN, programmer, analyst; b. Port Townsend, Wash., Dec. 12, 1957; d. Joe Dell and Shirley Ann (Harris) Wall; m. Joseph Allen Bauer, May 5, 1979 (div. 1986); m. Roald Leif Pederson, May 23, 1987. AS in Computer Programming, So. Ohio Coll., 1981; cert. in data processing, Live Oaks Joint Vocat. Sch., Milford, Ohio, 1976; BBA in Info. Systems, Dallas Bapt. U., 1993. Programmer Procter & Gamble Co., Cin., 1976-87; systems analyst AMP Inc., Harrisburg, Pa., 1987-89; computer sys. cons. James Rich Computing, Corsicana, Tex., 1989-91; programmer/analyst Guardian Industries, Corsicana, 1991-93; project mgr. Intrix Systems Group, Sacramento, 1993—; prof. Navarro Coll., Corsicana, 1989-93. Vol. Updowntowners, Cin., 1986-87; sponsor Ind. Order Odd Fellows Children's Home, Corsicana, 1989-90. Mem. Newcomers Club (corr. sec. 1990). Democrat. Mem. Christian Ch. Home: 110 Kershaw Ct Folsom CA 95630-8611

PEDERSON, KATHRYN MARIE, instructional technology administrator; b. Minot, N.D., Apr. 28, 1958; d. Clifford Artine and Leona (Schlecht) Lang; m. Robert Norman Pederson, Oct. 11, 1986. BA, Minot State U., 1984; MA, U. Mary, 1989. Mgr. Answer Dakota Answering Svc., Minot, 1980-82; legal sec. Teevens, Johnson, Montgomery, Minot, 1982-86; acctg. clk. Interstate Brands Corp., Minot, 1986; data input operator N.D. Legis. Coun., Bismarck, N.D., 1986-87; asst. Bismarck Pub. Schs./Tech. Enabling Disabled Individuals, Bismarck, 1987-89; state tech. dir. Dept. Pub. Instrn., Bismarck, 1989-92. Editor: (newsletter) CEC Newsletter, 1987-89, TEDIgram, 1987-89, Superintendent's Report, 1990-92; author: (newsletter) TecTalk, 1990—. Fin. com. Faith United Meth. Ch., Minot, 1986. Mem. N.D. Edn. Assn., N.D. Libr. Assn., Assn. Instrnl. Tech., N.D. Ednl. Telecommunications Coun. (exec. dir. 1989-92), Okla. State U. Satellite Program (adv. coun. 1989-92), Satellite Ednl. Resources Consortium (adv. coun. 1989-92), Jaycees (Outstanding Fundraiser 1989, Jaycee of Month 1989, Outstanding Com. chmn. 1989, Project of Yr. 1989, Top Mem. Recruiter 1990). Methodist. Office: Prairie Pub TV Prairie Sch Divsn PO Box 3240 Fargo ND 58108-3240

PEDERSON, MAI, noncommissioned air force officer; b. Kuwait, May 27, 1960; d. Moheb Abbas-Helmy al Sadat and Amira. BS in Occupational Edn., Southern Ill. U., 1986; AAS in Pers. Adminstrn., Community Coll. Air Force, 1988; AAS in Comm. Applications Tech., C.C. USAF, 1993. Enlisted USAF; telecommunications specialist Air Force Cryptologic Support Ctr., Kelly AFB, 1980-81; traffic analysis, telecommunications ops. specialist Air Force Communications Squadron, Norton AFB, 1981-82; with USAF, Kalkar Air Station, Fed. Republic of Germany, 1983-85; info. systems ops. specialist Robins AFB, Ga., 1985-86, base career advisor, 1986-89; non-commd. officer-in-chg. re-enlistments USAF, Ga., 1990-91, non-commd. officer-in-chg. Separations, 1990-91, non-commd. officer-in-charge Outbound Assignments, 1991; non-commd. officer-in-charge Customer Support Ctr. USAF, Robins AFB, Ga., 1992; non-commd. officer-in-charge Quick Response Debriefing Team USAF, Vogelweh AFB, 1993-94, non-commd. officer-in-charge formica ops., 1994—; sole translator Operation Restore Hope USAF, Cairo West AFB, Egypt, 1993-94. Vol. tchr. ESL, Robins AFB, 1986; lay leader Baha'i Faith, Robins AFB, 1985-92; field rep. for Women in Mil. Svc. for Am. Meml., 1991—. Mem. Air Force Assn. (life),

Non-Commd. Officers Assn. (life), Rambling Robins Volksmarch Club (pres. 1987-91). Office: 2605F/DOHA Unit 8995 Box 545 APO AE 09094-0545

PEDERSON, RENA, newspaper editor. Editorial page editor Dallas Morning News. Office: The Dallas Morning News 508 Young St Dallas TX 75265*

PEDERSON, SUZANNE HUBER, civic worker; b. Louisville, Apr. 4, 1931; d. Kenneth Klemmer and Marguerite (Agne) Huber; m. Bernhardt L. Pederson, Jan. 31, 1953; children: Elise Pederson Morrison, Bernhardt L. II, Thomas W., Suzanne Pederson Kowalkoski. BS, U. Mich., 1953. Office mgr. Pederson Women's Clinics, Bay City, Mich., 1980—. Pres. Bay City Sch. Bd., 1976-78, 94-95, trustee, 1976-78, 93-94; trustee Bay Area Family YMCA, 1986—, Health Edn. Found., 1988—; trustee, pres. Bay Med. Ctr. Aux., 1987; vestrywoman Trinity Episcopal Ch., 1974—, also lay reader, chalice adminstr. Mem. AMA Aux. (nat. com. 1990-93), Mich. Med. Soc. Aux. (pres. 1989-90). Home: 6327 Golf Lakes Ct Bay City MI 48706 Office: Pederson Women's Clinics 2108 16th St Bay City MI 48708

PEDRAM, MARILYN BETH, reference librarian; b. Brewster, Kans., Apr. 3, 1937; d. Edgar Roy and Elizabeth Catherine (Doubt) Crist; m. Manouchehr Pedram, Jan. 27, 1962 (Oct. 28, 1984); children: Jaleh Denise, Cyrus Andre. BS in Edn., Kans. State U., 1958; MLS, U. Denver, 1961. Cert secondary educator, Mo. 7th grade tchr. Clay Ctr. (Kans.) Pub. Schs., 1958-59, Colby (Kans.) Pub. Sch. System, 1959-60; reference libr. Topeka (Kans.) Pub. Libr., 1961-62, extension dept. head, 1963-64, reference libr., 1964-65; br. libr. asst. Denver Pub. Libr., 1965-67; reference libr. Kansas City (Mo.) Pub. Libr., Plaza Br., 1974-79, Kansas City (Mo.) Main Libr., 1979—. Mem. ALA, Mo. Libr. Assn., Kans. City Assn. Law Librs., Am. Assn. Ret. Persons, NAFE, Gluten Intolerance Group of N.Am., Celiac Sprue Assn., Kans. State U. Alumni Assn., Kans. City Online Users Group, Nat. Parks and Conservation Assn. Office: Kansas City Pub Libr 311 E 12th St Kansas City MO 64106-2412

PEDZICH, (CAROL) JOAN, law librarian; b. Utica, N.Y., Oct. 8, 1948; d. Rodger Albert and Mary (Cunningham) Kendrick; m. Robert John Pedzich, Aug. 15, 1970; children: Keith Justin, Adam Andrew. BS, SUNY, Oswego, 1970; MLS, SUNY, Geneseo, 1980. Asst. libr. Rochester (N.Y.) Mus. & Sci. Ctr., 1978-81; chief archivist Internat. Mus. of Photography, Rochester, 1981-85; head reference svcs. Nixon Hargrave Devans & Doyle, Rochester, 1985-88; law libr. Harris Beach & Wilcox, Rochester, 1988—; book reviewer Libr. Jour., N.Y.C., 1989-95; reference books contbg. reviewer Law Libr. Jour., N.Y.C., 1994-95. Co-curator (exhbn.) Rochester, An American Photographic Ctr., 1984; contbr. articles to profl. jours. Mem. Am. Assn. Law Librs., Assn. Law Librs. Upstate N.Y. (bd. dirs. 1993-94, editor newsletter 1991-92), Pvt. Law Librs. (spl. interest sect.). Democrat. Home: 90 Harbor Hill Dr Rochester NY 14617 Office: Harris Beach & Wilcox 130 Main St E Rochester NY 14604-1687

PEEK, KIMBERLY KAYE, accountant; b. Lubbock, Tex., Oct. 17, 1964; d. Kenneth Reed and Sharron Ann (Bradshaw) P.; m. Timm R. Johnson, Sept. 2, 1989. BS in Acctg., No. Ariz. U., 1986. CPA, Ariz.; cert. mgmt. acct. Rotational employee-forecasting and budgeting Motorola, Phoenix, 1986, rotational employee-cost acctg., 1986-87, rotational employee-internal audit acct., 1987, rotational employee-internat. acct., 1987-88, cost acct. LATG, 1988-89, cost acct. CPSTG, 1989-91, capital projects analyst, 1991—. Active Food Bank, Jr. Achievement, Adopt-a-Family, Christmas in April. Mem. Inst. Mgmt. Accts. (employment and advt. 1989-90, treas. 1990-91, v.p. adminstrn. 1991-92, v.p. comm. 1992-93, v.p. membership 1993-94, pres. chpt. 1994—). Libertarian. Baptist. Home: 1730 E Carson Rd Phoenix AZ 85040 Office: Motorola 5005 E McDowell Rd Phoenix AZ 85008

PEEK, LINDA OLIVE, materiel specialist; b. East Orange, N.J., Jan. 25, 1949; d. Carl Henry Peek and Helen Florence (Dewar) Wutke; div. 1970; children: Michelle Ann Foust, Engle Robert Carlton Foust II. Grad., Long Beach Evening High Sch., 1971. Lab receptionist Long Beach (Calif.) Meml. Hosp. Med. Ctr., 1969-71; office mgr. Dr. Francis A. Hurtubrise MD, Inc., Long Beach, 1971-72; lab. technician Long Beach Meml. Hosp. Med. Ctr., 1972-79, St. Mary's Hosp., Grand Junction, Colo., 1980-89; materiel specialist Antelope Valley Hosp. Med. Ctr., Lancaster, Calif., 1991—. Mem. "I Count" (lab. rep. 1992—), Employee's Assn. (mem.-at-large 1993-94). Democrat. Home: 44753 18th St W Lancaster CA 93534-2711 Office: Antelope Valley Hosp Med 1600 W Avenue J Lancaster CA 93534-2894

PEELER, BRENDA CARRIE, chemical engineer; b. Concord, Mass., Apr. 23, 1957; d. George David Monroe and Carolene Elizabeth (Rink) P. BSChemE, U. Lowell, 1979. Process engr. Hess Oil V.I. Corp., St. Croix, 1979-83, sr. engr., 1983-92, group leader, chem. engr., 1992—; mem. sea turtle hatching and watch survey Nat. Park Svc., St. Croix, 1988. Mem. AIChE. Home: Box 2577 Kingshill Saint Croix VI 00851

PEEPLES, AUDREY RONE, association executive; b. Chgo., May 22, 1939; d. John Drayton and Thelma (Shepherd) Rone; m. Anthony Alonzo Peeples, Aug. 14, 1971; children: Jennifer Lynn, Michael Anthony. BA, U. Ill., 1961; MBA, Northwestern U., 1978. Trust adminstr. Continental Bank, Chgo., 1961-72; assoc. regional dir. Girl Scouts of U.S.A., Chgo., 1973-76; asst. exec. dir., then exec. dir. Girl Scouts of Chgo., 1976-87; exec. dir. YWCA Met. Chgo., 1987—; corp. sec. Maja, Inc., Chgo. Mem. nat. bd. alumni 21st Century com. Girl Scouts U.S.; bd. dirs. Chgo. Network, 1988—, pres., 1992-94; bd. dirs. United Way Chgo., 1987-92; mem. adv. bd. Women In Bus. Yellow Pages, 1988—, Mus. Sci. and Industry, Black Creativity Gala; bd. dirs. Chgo. Found. for Women. Recipient St. Annes award, Archdiocese of Chgo., 1985, Black Rose award, League Black Women, Chgo., 1987. mem. Chgo. Alliance Collaborative Effort (v.p. 1990—, chair 1994, bd. dirs. 1st Trust 1990-95), Econ. Club Chgo., Univ. Club Chgo. (com. on admissions 1994—). Democrat. Roman Catholic. Home: 9339 S Hoyne Ave Chicago IL 60620-5606 Office: YWCA Met Chgo 180 N Wabash Ave Chicago IL 60601-3608

PEEPLES-CARTER, RACHEL JAYNE, marketing educator; b. Atlanta, Nov. 4, 1952; d. Gholston William Sr. and Janie Mae (Peters) P.; m. Timothy O. Carter, Sept. 20, 1986. Student, Mercer U., U. Miami, Fla., Ft. Valley State Coll. Computer tech. specialist DeKalb Bd. Edn., Decatur, Ga., 1979-80, interrelated resource educator, 1980—; mktg./network rep. Lewis, Peeples, Carter, Atlanta, 1982—. Vol. YMCA, Atlanta & DeKalb, 1984-86; mem. Gainesville (Ga.) Civic Assn., 1976-77. Mem. NAFE (rschr. 1984-89), NAACP, Community Club. Baptist. Home: Rt 744 Pine Lake GA 30072

PEINDL, KATHLEEN SHALER, research associate; b. Dec. 13, 1946; d. Robert Miles and Edna Grace (Sherman) Fawcett; 1 child, Lee Andrew Peindl. BS in Biology, Westminster Coll., 1968; MS in Microbiology, Duquesne Univ., 1971; PhD, U. Pitts., 1993. Lab. coord. biology dept. Point Park Coll., Pitts., 1968-71; rsch. assoc. Sch. of Dental Medicine, Univ. of Pa., Phila., 1971-75, Peoria Sch. of Medicine, U. Ill., 1975-76; owner, mgr. Scrimshaw, Inc., 1978-81; chemistry instr. C.C. of Beaver County, Monaca, Pa., 1981-86; rsch. asst. Western Psychiat. Inst. and Clinic, U. Pitts., 1986-88; project coord., sr. rsch. assoc. U. Pitts., 1988—; sr. rsch. assoc. Case Western Res. U., Cleve., 1994—. Contbr. articles to profl. jours. Doctoral fellowship Nat. Inst. of Alcohol and Alcoholism. Mem. AAUW, Am. Suicide Found., Fry Glass Soc., Am. Soc. Microbiology, Assn. of Women in Sci., Chi Omega, Beta Beta Beta, Phi Sigma. Home: 138 Orchard Dr Beaver PA 15009-1117 Office: Case Western Res U Dept Psychiatry Triangle Bldg Ste 200 Cleveland OH 15213-2593

PEIRCE, GEORGIA WILSON, public relations executive; b. Newton, Mass., Jan. 6, 1960; d. Norris Ridgeway and Anne (McCusker) P. BA, Duke U., 1982. Intern to Speaker of Ho. of Reps., Washington, 1981; prin. PR, etc., Quincy, Mass., 1987-94; dir. media rels. The Mass. Gen. Hosp., Boston, 1994—; cons. Mass. Group Insur. Commn., 1985. Contbr. articles to profl. jours. Mem. community rels. com. Vis. Nurse Assn./Hospice of South Shore; mem. com. to elect Mondale-Ferraro, Mass., coord. speakers bur., 1984; mem. charitable trust com. Maj. John F. Regan; com. mem. City of Quincy Recycling Com.; del. Mass. Dem. Conv., 1982, 83; v.p. South Shore Ad Club, 1990-91, mem.-at-large, 1991-92. Recipient 9th Wave awards 1989, 1st pl. in Pub. Rels. award, 1989, merit awards, 1992. Mem. NAFE, South Shore C. of C., Small Bus. Assn. New England, Women's Golf Assn. Mass., Publicity Club New England (Merit Bell Ringer award), Rotary Internat., Eastward Ho! Country Club Chatham (club champion 1977-81, 83, 91, 93), Wollaston Golf Club. Democrat. Roman Catholic. Home: 71 Bayfield Rd N Quincy MA 02171-2005 Office: Mass Gen Hosp Office of Pub Affairs Fruit St Boston MA 02114

PEISEN, DEBORAH JEAN, systems analyst, engineer, aviation planner; b. L.A., May 11, 1947; d. Walter Lewis and Florence Isabel (Hinchcliff) Hall; m. Jan W. Pritchard, Nov. 8, 1969 (div. Oct. 1981); 1 child, Jennifer Pritchard. BS, Calif. State Poly. U., 1970; MA, Calif. State U., L.A., 1976. Lic. helicopter pilot. Mgr. catering svc. Marriott Hotels, L.A., 1977-79; mgr. Gulliver's Restaurant, San Diego, 1979-80; sec. Crocker Nat. Bank, L.A., 1980-83; aviation planner Hoyle, Tanner & Assocs., Bedford, N.H., 1985-87; sr. engr. Systems Control Tech., Inc., Arlington, Va., 1987—; coord. Model Ordnance Working Group, Alexandria, Va. ,1987-92; mem. FAA/Industry, 1988-92, sec. vertiport/heliport working group, 1988-94; mem. steering group Civil Rotocraft Initiative, Washington, 1991-92; chmn. Heliport Tech. Planning Com., Alexandria, 1991-92. Contbr. articles to profl. publs. Mem. Am. Helicopter Soc., Helicopter Assn. Internat. (lectr. joint Ga. Tech. Coll. heliport planning course 1987-92), Internat. Women Helicopter Pilots (sec. 1987-88), Mid-Atlantic Helicopter Assn. (sec. 1991-92, bd. dirs. 1990—, chairperson heliport com., pres. 1994—), Ninety-Nines (sec. 1986-87). Office: SAIC/SCT Group Ste 1500 1213 Jefferson Davis Hwy Arlington VA 22202

PEISER, DONNA PEARL, office administrator; b. Freeport, Tex., Dec. 30, 1941; d. Norman Atword Bellard and Dorothy Evelyn (Graham) Calhoun; m. Donald Lawrence Peiser, July 8, 1983; children: John Troy McMinn, William Cory McMinn, Jeanna Lynn Mazza. BSBA, Pacific Western U., 1991. Stenographer Dow Chem. USA, 1960-67, sec., 1973-79, adminstrv. sec., 1980-83, sr. office adminstr., 1983-92; adminstrv. asst. Brazosport Coll, Lake Jackson, Tex., 1968-72. Past alderman Village Jones Creek; coord. Parent Vol. Program Brazosport High Sch., 1990; mem. instrl. adv. coun. Brazosport Ind. Sch. Dist., co-chmn., 1989-90; elder Gulf Prairie Presbyn. Ch., chmn. policy com., mem. pastoral nomination search com. Home: 6426 Bryan Rd Freeport TX 77541-9410

PELCYGER, GWYNNE ELLICE, mental health services professional; b. Bklyn., May 18, 1959; d. Iran and Elaine (Morley) P.; m. Aaron Blum, Dec. 21, 1991. BA, Hofstra U., 1981; MS, St. John's U., 1987. Cert. sch. psychologist, N.Y. Case mgr. Cath. Charities, N.Y.C., 1986-87; program mgr. Profl. Svc. Ctr. for Handicapped, N.Y.C.; consulting psychologist Graham Windom, N.Y.C., 1987-89; edn. specialist Assn. for Neurologically Impaired Brain Injured Children, N.Y.C., 1987-88; sch. psychologist N.Y.C. Bd. of Edn., 1988-92, Okeechobee (Fla.) County Sch. Bd., 1994—. Mem. APA, AACD, Nat. Assn. Sch. Psychologists, N.Y. ACD, Fla. Assn. for Sch. Psychologists, Treasure Coast Counselors Assn., PhysChi Nat. Honor Soc.

PELESKY, CATHY A., clinical psychologist; b. N.J., Apr. 20, 1957. BA, Villanova U., 1979; MA, Wayne State U., 1983, PhD, 1986. Lic. psychologist. Psychologist, clin. specialist Newton (N.J.) Meml. Hosp., 1986—; clin. psychologist Family Treatment Assocs., Stroudsburg, Pa., 1989—. Mem. APA, Pa. Psychol. Assn. Office: Family Treatment Assocs 720 C Phillips St Stroudsburg PA 18360-2224

PELFREY, DEANNA KAYE WEDMORE, public relations and marketing executive, educator; b. Cin., June 9, 1941; d. Irvin John and Ann Lee (Barone) Wedmore; divorced; 1 child, Danielle Newland Wedmore Pelfrey. BA in English, Coll. of Mt. St. Joseph, Ohio, 1964; postgrad., U. Poitiers, LaRochelle, France, 1966; MA in English and Am. Lit., Xavier U., 1972; postgrad., U. Louisville, 1977. Tchr. world lit. Wyoming High Sch., Cin., 1964-66; youth fashion coord. H&S Pogue Co., Cin., 1966-69; dir. fashion program Internat. Sch. for Young Ams., Cin., Europe, 1969-71; pres. Pelfrey Assocs., Inc., Louisville, 1976—; chmn. bd dirs. Youth Arts Coun., Louisville, 1988-91; bd. dirs. Walden Theatre, Louisville, 1988—; pres. alumni bd. dirs. Coll. of Mt. St. Joseph, Cin., 1991—; mem. Edn. and Workforce Inst., 1991—. Chair Louisville Zoo Commn., 1977-84; pres. Louisville Zoo Found., 1979-81, chair Metazoo Captial campaign, 1981, co-chair herpetarium/aquarium capital campaign, 1982-84; mem. arts in edn. task force Jefferson County Pub. Schs., 1981-83; founding mem. planning team Ky. Inst. for Arts in Edn., 1982, mem. adv. com. planning team, 1983-87; bd. trustees Louisville Collegiate Sch., 1983-84, pres. parent's coun., 1983-84, mem. long range planning adv. com., 1984, mem. internat. adv. com., 1989-90; bd. dirs. Louisville Internat. Cultural Ctr., 1992—; mem. priority programs fund com. Metro United Way, 1992. Recipient 4 Citizen Contribution awards Mayor of Louisvile, 1981-91. Mem. Am. Assn. Zool. Pks. and Aquariums (conf. del. 1975-84, 91), Pub. Rels. Soc. Am. (chair com. 1991—, bd. dirs. Bluegrass chpt. 1992—, exec. steering com. internat. sect. 1993—), Direct Mktg. Assn. (com.), Counselors Acad., Fashion Group Internat. Fashion I (founder 1976, pres. 1977-78, advisor 1978-79, chair fashion seminar 1978, Stanley Mžrcus event 1980, co-chair fall fashion event 1983), Jr. League of Louisville (bd. dirs. 1977-80). Home: 711 W Main St Louisville KY 40202-2657 Office: Pelfrey Assocs Inc 730 W Main St Louisville KY 40202-2653

PELHAM, FRAN O'BYRNE, writer, teacher; b. Phila., Oct. 16, 1939; d. Frederick Thomas and Frances Rebecca (Johns) O'Byrne; m. Donald Lacey Pelham, June 15, 1968; children: Mary Frances, Michael. BA, Holy Family Coll., 1967; M in English Edn., Trenton Coll., 1974; EdD, U. Pa., 1993. Cert. secondary tchr. Tchr. Sch. Dist. Bristol (Pa.) Twp., 1967-70; feature writer various publs., Phila. and others, 1980—; prof., dir. Writing Ctr. Holy Family Coll., Phila., 1982-89; asst. prof. lit. and writing LaSalle U., Phila., 1989—; dir. tech. communications Internat. Chem. Co., Phila., 1985-90; speaker, workshop leader various orgns. Author: Search for Atocha Treasure, 1989, Downtown America: Philadelphia, 1989; contbr. articles to mags. Participant Home and Sch. Assn., Jenkintown, Pa., 1983, Jenkintown Arts Festival, 1984, Campus Ministry Team Holy Family Coll., Phila., 1986-89, Alliance for a Living Ocean, 1991—, Phila. Children's Reading Roundtable, Authors Guild. Recipient Citation Mayor's Commn., 1988. Mem. Nat. Coun. Tchrs. Eng., Am. Conf. Irish Studies, Nat. League Am. Pen Women (br. pres. 1982-84), Phila. Writers' Conf. (bd. dirs. 1982-86), Pi Lambda Theta, Lambda Iota Tau, Phi Delta Kappa. Democrat. Roman Catholic. Office: LaSalle U Olney Ave Philadelphia PA 19120

PELHAM, JUDITH, hospital administrator; b. Bristol, Conn., July 23, 1945; d. Marvin Curtis and Muriel (Chodos) P.; m. Jon N. Coffee, Dec. 30, 1992; children: Rachel, Molly, Edward. BA, Smith Coll., 1967; MPA, Harvard U., 1975. Various govt. postions, 1968-72; prin. analyst Urban Systems, Cambridge, Mass., 1972-73; dir. devel. and planning Roxbury Dental and Med. Group, Boston, 1975-76; asst. to dir. for gen. medicine and ambulatory care Peter B. Brigham Hosp., Boston, 1976-77, asst. dir. ambulatory care, 1977-79; asst. v.p. Brigham and Women's Hosp., Boston, 1980-81; dir. planning and mktg. Seton Med. Ctr., Austin, Tex., 1980-82, pres., 1982-92, chief exec. officer, 1987-92; pres., chief exec. officer Daughters of Charity Health Services, Austin, 1987-92; pres. Mercy Health Svcs., Farmington Hills, Mich., 1993—; cons. Robert W. Johnson Found., 1979-80; bd. dirs. Mercy Health Svcs., 1993—, Am. Healthcare Systems, 1993—, Healthcare Rsch. adn Devel. Inst., Inc., 1993—; bd. trustees Mercy Health Found., 1993-94, Mercy Internat. Health Svcs., 1993-94. Author: Financial Management of Ambulatory Care, 1985; contbr. articles to profl. jours. Trustee A. Shivers Radiation Therapy Ctr., Austin, 1982-92, Marywood Maternity and Adoption Agy., 1982-86; bd. dirs. Quality of Life Found., Austin, 1985, Austin Rape Crisis Ctr., adv. bd., 1986-88; bd. dirs., trustee League House, 1982-93, Seton Fund, 1982-93; mem. Gov's Job Tng. Coordinating Council, 1983-85; adv. council U. Tex. Social Work Found., 1983-85; charter mem. Leadership Tex., Austin, 1983-93. Recipient Leadership award YWCA, Austin, 1986. Mem. Am. Coll. Healthcare Execs., Am. Hosp. Assn., Tex. Hosp. Assn. (mem. various couns. 1982-87), Austin Area Rsch. Orgn., Cath. Health Assn. (bd. dirs. 1987—, com. on govt. rels. 1984-91), Tex. Conf. Cath. Health Facilities (bd. dirs. 1985-89, pres. 1988), Cath. Health Assn. (sec., treas. 1982—, chair fin. com. 1992—). Office: Mercy Health Svcs 34605 Twelve Mile Rd Farmington Hills MI 48331

PELIAS, NATALIE ANNE, employment consultant; b. New Orleans, Oct. 31, 1950; d. James Michael and Esther (Daley) Pelias; m. David Michael Herman, Dec. 11, 1991. Diploma, U. Grenoble, France, 1966; student, U. New Orleans, 1968-72. Adminstrv. asst. Prudential Bache, New Orleans, 1976-78; account exec. Acctg. Pers. Cons., New Orleans, 1978-80; ptnr. Glover-Pelias, New Orleans, 1980-82; pres. Pelias & Assocs., New Orleans/Louisville, 1982—; condr. workshops and seminars in field. Vol. WYES Pub. TV, New Orleans, 1976-78. Recipient Citizenship award DAR, 1964; named to Hon. Order of Ky. Cols., one of Outstanding Young Women of Am., 1984. Mem. Nat. Assn. Pers. Cons. (cert. CPC, life). Greek Orthodox.

PELL, MARY CHASE (CHASEY PELL), civic worker; b. Binghamton, N.Y., May 23, 1915; d. Charles Orlando and Mary (Lane) Chase; m. Wilbur F. Pell, Jr., Sept. 14, 1940; children: Wilbur F., Charles Chase. BA, Smith Coll., 1937. Case worker Binghamton State Hosp., 1937; sociology tchr. Charles W. Wilson Meml. Hosp., Johnson City, N.Y., 1938; commentator travel and industry, sta. WSVL, Shelbyville, Ind., 1962-67. Contbr. articles to publs. Chmn. Ind. Fund Raising Com. for Smith Coll., Indpls., 1961; bd. dirs. Nat. Mental Health Assn., 1961-79, pres. 1976-77; pres. Ind. Mental Health Meml. Found., Indpls., 1964-65, Mental Health Assn. Ind., Indpls., 1962-63, bd. dirs., 1951-70; commr. Ind. Mental Health Planning Commn., Indpls., 1964-65; mem. Central Ind. Task Force on Mental Health Planning, 1965-66; mem. Ind. Com. on Nursing, Indpls., 1965-66, Central Ind. Regional Mental Health Planning Com., 1968; chmn. Manpower Conf. on Mental Health, Washington, 1969; del. Ind. Republican Conv., 1951; vice chmn. Shelbyville Rep. Com., 1951; sec. Ind. Com. for Rockefeller, 1969-70; pres. Indpls. Smith Coll. Club, 1969-70; participant Nat. Health Forum of Nat. Health Council, N.Y.C., 1971; mem. adv. bd. Isaac Ray Ctr. Rush Presbyn. St. Luke Medical Ctr., 1978-91; mem. gov.'s Task Force on the Future Mental Health in Ill., 1986-87; mem. commn. to revise the mental health code of Ill., 1988; pres. Mental Health Assn. Ill., Springfield, 1975; mem. Gov.'s Commn. for Revision of Mental Health Code Ill., 1975-76; v.p. for N.Am., World Fedn. for Mental Health, 1977-87; bd. dirs. Vis. Nurse Assn. Evanston (Ill.), 1975-87, v.p. 1981-84, pres., 1984-86; community mental health adviser Jr. League of Chgo., 1979-83; mem. Ill. Guardianship and Advocacy Commn., 1978-86, chmn., 1981; gov. Task Force on Future of Mental Health in Ill., 1986-87; mem. gov. commn. to revise mental health code; mem. home health adv. com. to Dept. Pub. Health, State of Ill., 1982-87; adv. com. Ill. Mental Health Svcs. System, 1992-93; pres. Mental Health Assn. Greater Chgo., 1983-84, mem. pub. policy com., 1987-92; pres. Smith Coll. Alumni of Chgo., 1984-86 (alumni award medal) ; mem. Women's Bd. Northwestern U., Aux. of Evanston and Glenbrook Hosps., University Guild of Evanston, Jr. League Evanston, pres. Ind. Lawyers' Wives, Indpls., 1959-60; treas. Nat. Lawyers' Wives, 1961-62; mem. commn. to rev. and revise Ill. Mental Health Code, 1987-90. Recipient Outstanding Citizen award Shelby County C. of C., 1959-60, Outstanding Vol. of Yr. award Indpls. Jr. League, 1962, Leadership award Mental Health Assn. Ind., 1971, Arts and Humanities award, Shelbyville Rotary Club, 1981, alumnae medal Smith Coll., 1993; named One of Ten Most Newsworthy Women In Ind., Indpls. News, 1962, Disting. Leader in Vol. Mental Health Movement, Ill. Ho. of Reps., 1976, Miss. Col., 1976, Ala. Lt. Gov., 1980. Presbyterian. Clubs: Fortnightly (Chgo.); Garden of Evanston, Jr. League of Evanston. Home: 1427 Hinman Ave Evanston IL 60201-4636

PELL, PYRMA DAPHNE TILTON, civic worker; b. N.Y.C., Feb. 5, 1909; d. Newell Whiting and Mildred Olive (Bigelow) Tilton; student Queens Coll., London, 1921-26, Kunst Akademie, Vienna, Austria, 1927-28; m. John Howland Gibbs Pell, Sept. 3, 1929; children—Sarah Gibbs, John Bigelow. Active in preservation and restoration Fort Ticonderoga, N.Y., 1950-87, also coordinator spl. events, 1950-87; treas. Friends of Chung Ang U., Korea, 1965-71. Recipient Spl. award Friends of Chung Ang U., 1971, First award Historic Preservation, Garden Club Am., 1973. Mem. Am. Acad. Poets (co-founder), Colonial Dames Am., Assn. Churchill Fellows of Westminster Coll., Colony Club, Knickerbocker Club, Alpha Xi Delta. Christian Scientist. Home (summer): Pelican Pl Bellevue Ave Newport RI 02840

PELLE, BEVERLY SHARON, accountant; b. Denver, Dec. 30, 1958; d. Walter A. and Ruth L. (Beakey) Piltz; m. Michael Gerard Pelle, June 27, 1981; children: Miranda Rae, Michelle Lynn. BS in Psychology, U. Denver, 1981; cert., Barnes Bus. Coll., Denver, 1984; A in Acctg., Red Rocks C.C., Lakewood, Colo., 1987. Sales assoc. Denver Dry Goods, Lakeside, 1977-83; circulation clk. Penrose Libr., U. Denver, 1978-79; sales clk. Sayco Industries, Denver, 1984; acctg. technician Goodwill Industries Denver, 1985-86, co-dir. acctg., 1986-87, dir. acctg., 1987—; cons. property mgmt., Denver, 1992-93. Troop leader Mile High coun. Girl Scouts U.S., 1992—. Office: Goodwill Industries Denver 6850 N Federal Blvd Denver CO 80221

PELLEGRIN, HELEN, healthcare administrator, marketing consultant, association executive. PhD, Stanford U., 1978. Acting dir. comm. program Grad. Sch. Bus. Stanford U., 1983-84; dir. comm. Career Action Ctr., Palo Alto, Calif., 1984-89; media liaison Menlo Sch. & Coll., Atherton, Calif., 1989-90; case mgr. TBI project Santa Clara Valley Med. Ctr., San Jose, Calif., 1991-92; pub. edn. specialist Cmty. Assn. for Rehab., Palo Alto, 1992—. Editor: The Libertine, 1978. Founder Headway Unltd., Palo Alto, 1990; bd. dirs. Family Survival Project, San Francisco, 1992-94, Svcs. for Brain Impaired, San Jose, 1991—; mem. Citizens Adv. Com., Palo Alto, 1991-93, Leadership Palo Alto, 1990; co-pres. Mid-Peninsula YWCA, Palo Alto, 1993—. Mem. Phi Beta Kappa. Home: 291 Parkside Dr Palo Alto CA 94306 Office: Cmty Assn for Rehab Inc 525 E Charleston Rd Palo Alto CA 94306

PELLEGRINO, VICTORIA GRAZZIELLA, marketing professional; b. Roma, Italy, May 5, 1962; came to U.S.A., 1970; d. Antonio and Maria Caterina (Surianello) P. Postgrad., Melrose Bty. Acad., 1980, American R.E. Acad., Waltham, Mass., 1981; BS, Boston Coll., 1984. Co-owner, prin. Monica Styles Hair Salon, Stoneham, Mass., 1980-; r.e salesperson Century 21 Small Real Estate, Malden, Mass., 1981-83; co-owner, founder Tantastix Suntanning Salon, Stoneham, Mass., 1984-; account exec. Allstates Air Cargo, Inc., E. Boston; nat. account exec. Exhibit Express Allied, Lexington, Mass., 1989--. Mem. Nat. Assn. Hairdressers, Nat. Assn. Realtors, Mass. Assn. Realtors, Middlesex Bd. Realtors, Internat. Exhibitors Assn. Home: 2 Barberry Rd North Reading MA 01864-2125 Office: Exhibit Express Inc 15 Elm St # 2 Bedford MA 01730-2136

PELLER, MARCI TERRY, real estate executive; b. Upland, Pa., Nov. 5, 1949; d. Max Maclyn and Lucille Eugenia (Zucker) P. AA, Harcum Jr. Coll., Bryn Mawr, Pa., 1971; student, Villanova U., 1971-73. With sales dept. William H. Cartwright Real Estate, North Palm Beach, Fla., 1985-91; realtor-assoc. Fin. Realty Group, Lake Park, Fla., 1991—. Republican. Jewish. Address: 5420 N Ocean Dr Singer Island FL 33404 Office: Fin Realty Group 9498 Alternate A1A Lake Park FL 33403

PELLETIER, MARSHA LYNN, state legislator, secondary school educator; b. Mt. Pleasant, Mich., July 29, 1950; d. Eugene Russell and Mary Ellen (Edde) Mingle; m. Arthur Joseph Pelletier, May 19, 1973; 1 child, John Frederick. BS in Home Econs. and Edn., Kans. State U., 1971, MS in Edn. Guidance and Counseling, 1972. By what organization are you certified as real estate broker (CER section)?. Conf. coord., guidance counselor Kans. State U., Manhattan, 1971-73; home econs. tchr. Franklin (Mass.) High Sch., 1974, Exeter (N.H.) High Sch., 1974-75, Barrington (N.H.) Mid. Sch., 1975-81, Pentucket Regional Jr. High Sch., West Newbury, Mass., 1981-82; realtor assoc. Century 21 Ocean and Norword Realty, Portsmouth, N.H., 1983-86; interior design tchr., cons. U. N.H., Durham, 1986-87; home econs. tchr. Dover Jr. High Sch., 1983—; rep. Dist. 12 Dover N.H. Ho. of Reps., Concord, 1992-94; ind. real estate broker Dover, 1986—. mem. Health Task Force, Dover and Concord, 1993-94; mem. bd. trustees St. John's Meth. Ch., 1995—. Mem. NEA (local pres. negotiator, membership chair, leadership exec. com., rep. 1979—), Nat. Coalition for Consumer Edn., Alpha Delta Kappa. (v.p. historian altruistic chmn. 1984-89). Democrat. Home: 94 Back River Rd Dover NH 03820

PELLETIER, NANCY ANNE, obstetrics/gynecology nurse, educator; b. St. Louis, June 16, 1951; d. David Cooper Hill and Cenith Lorraine Gore; m. Russell Dean Pelletier, June 16, 1972; children: Kyle, Lindsay, Bradley. Cert. in practical nursing, Alexandria Hosp. Sch. of Practical Nursing, 1971; cert. in health edn., U. Md., 1973; AAS magna cum laude, No. Va. C.C., 1984. LPN, Va.; RN, Va. LPN in pediatrics Alexandria (Va.) Hosp., 1971-72, LPN in medications, 1972-73, LPN in post partum and intensive care nursery, 1977-84, nurse post partum and float pool, 1984-85, childbirth educator, 1978—; sch. nurse, tchr. health edn. Alexandria City Pub. Schs., 1973-76; lead nurse Ob-Gyn Assocs. No. Va., Alexandria, 1984-91; lead ob-gyn nurse Kaiser Permanente of Mid-Atlantic Region, Woodbridge, Va., 1991—; advisor Vocat. Edn. Clubs Am., Washington, 1974. Author: (pamphlet) A Nurse Discusses Your Cesarean Delivery, (teaching tool) Test Your Pregnancy Knowledge. Mem. NAACOG, Am. Soc. for Psychoprophylaxis in Obstetrics (cert. ACCE), Phi Theta Kappa.

PELLEY, DEBRA ANN, legislative policy analyst; b. Portsmouth, Ohio, Oct. 29, 1959; d. Harry Thomas and Faye Ann (Lewis) Herdman; m. Jeffrey Wayne Pelley, Aug. 21, 1982. BS in Psychology, Ohio State U., 1982, M of Labor and Human Resources, 1989; MA in Psychology, Duquesne U., 1983. Compensation/tng. intern Ohio Office Collective Bargaining, Columbus, 1985-86; grad. rsch. assoc. Labor Edn. and Rsch. Svc. Ohio State U., Columbus, 1986-89; legis. policy analyst Ohio Legis. Budget Office, Columbus, 1989—. Co-author: Unemployment Resources Guide, 1987; author newsletter articles. Mem. Soc. for Human Resource Mgmt., Nat. Women's Studies Assn., Beta Gamma Sigma, Phi Kappa Phi. Mem. Disciples of Christ Ch. Home: 126 E Tulane Rd Columbus OH 43202 Office: Ohio Legis Budget Office 77 S High St 8th Fl Columbus OH 43266-0347

PELLEY, SHIRLEY NORENE, library director; b. Raymondville, Tex., Oct. 9, 1931; d. Llloyd Marshall and Lillian Norene (Southall) Ayres; m. May 14, 1954 (div.); children: Michael, Cynthia, Katheryne. BA in Music Edn., Bethany Nazarene Coll., 1954; MLS, U. Okla., 1966. Tchr. Hilldale Elem. Sch., Oklahoma City, 1954-56; music tchr. self-employed, Okla., Mo., 1956-64; circulation clk. Bethany (Okla.) Pub. Libr., 1964-65; libr. reference U. Okla. Libraries, Norman, 1966-83; dir. learning resource ctr. So. Nazarene U., Bethany, 1983—. Mem. ALA, Okla. Libr. Assn., Assn. Coll. and Rsch. Librs., Met. Librs. Network of Ctrl. Okla., Assn. Christian Librs. Republican. Nazarene. Office: So Nazarene U Learning Resource Ctr 4115 N College Ave Bethany OK 73008-2671

PELLICAN, DONNA MARGUERITE, primary school educator; b. Leoti, Kans., Aug. 7, 1934; d. Earl August and Ella May (Bivins) Halfman; m. Steven Thomas Pellican, Aug. 23, 1954; children: Diane, Debra. BA in Edn., Wester State Coll., Gunnison, Colo., 1957; MA in Early Childhood Edn., U. No. Colo., 1978. Kindergarten tchr. Uravan (Colo.) Pub. Schs., 1957-59, Weld County Sch. Dist. 6, Greeley, Colo., 1960-93; mem. com. Head Start program, 1968, kindergarten program revision, 1965; curriculum writer math., sci. and reading, 1960-90. State del. Rep. Delegation., Greeley, 1983; rep. to Greeley Edn. Assn. United Way, 1990-91. Mem. AAUW, Greeley Edn. Assn. (pres. 1981-83, local del. to state 1981-93, appreciation award 1982, valuable svc. award 1984, spl. recognition award 1985, shiny apple award 1988), Colo. Edn. Assn. (state, regional del. to nat. 1980-83), High Country Champs R.V. Club (sec.-treas. 1985-94), Alpha Delta Kappa (pres. Alpha Epsilon 1965-68, silver sister award 1990). Home: 1804 45th Ave Greeley CO 80634

PELLICCIOTTI, PATRICIA M., management consultant, financial analyst; b. Phila.. V.p., dir. regional sales EGR Commnications Inc., N.Y.C., 1975-77; pres. Pellicciotti Assocs., Northfield, N.J., 1977-83; registered rep. IDS/Am. Express, Mpls., 1981-85; v.p. Herzog, Heine, Geduld Inc., N.Y.C., 1984-85; pres. Fin. Cons. Group Inc., Phila., 1985—; registered rep. Rothschild Registry Inc., N.Y.C., 1986—; founder, bd. dirs. Woman to Woman Seminars; founder Word-For-Word Court Reporting, 1991—. Producer, hostess radio talk show WWDB-FM Woman to Woman, Phila.; author: Renting Money; founder, artistic dir. performance group Power in the Children. Pres. bd., exec. dir. Upward Bound; bd. dirs. Girl Scouts U.S. Recipient Recognition award Vice Pres. George Bush. Mem. Mktg. Communications Execs. Internat. (past v.p.), Nat. Assn. Securities Dealers (registered rep., cert. real estate appraiser), Nat. Econ. Round Table, SBA (adv. Pres. Carter's Interagy. Task Force for Women, cons. Active Corp Execs.). Club: Toastmasters. Office: Financial Cons Group Inc 618 S 2nd St Philadelphia PA 19147 also: Financial Cons Ghoulinc c/o Lu Ro, Residanza Faggi, 541 Milano Basiglio Italy

PELOQUIN, EMELIE FLEURETTE, nursing administrator; b. Woonsocket, R.I., Dec. 6, 1953; d. Gerard H. and Marielle (Berube) P. ADN, Community Coll. of R.I., Lincoln, 1979. RN, R.I.; cert. in med.-surg. nursing. Staff RN Landmark Med. Ctr., Woonsocket, 1980-88; asst. clin. mgr. R.I. Hosp., Providence, 1988-90; asst. nurse mgr. Landmark Med. Ctr., Woonsocket, 1992-94, nursing coord., 1990-92; asst. nurse mgr. Rehab. Hosp. of R.I., N. Smithfield, 1994—. Treas. Woonsocket Hosp. Local 5067, 1985-88; bd. trustees Woonsocket Tchrs. Guild, 1987-88. Recipient Landmark Med. Soc. Scholarship award Aux. Soc., 1992. Mem. AACN, R.I. State Nurses Assn., Am. Assn. Neurosci. Nurses, Nat. Assn. Orthopedic Nurses, R.I. Coun. Nurse Mgrs., Phi Theta Kappa. Home: 92 Avenue B Woonsocket RI 02895-6262

PELOQUIN, LORI JEANNE, clinical psychologist; b. Milw., Sept. 21, 1957; d. Wayne Joseph Peloquin and Jeanne Audrey (Ehlers) Driessen; m. Allen Theodore Retzlaff Jr., May 5, 1990; 1 child, Austin Miles Retzlaff. Student, U. Wis., Eau Claire, 1975-76; BA summa cum laude, U. Minn., 1978; MA, U. Rochester, 1982, PhD, 1985. Lic. psychologist, N.Y. Teaching asst. U. Rochester, N.Y., 1981-83, instr. psychology, 1984; co-dir. Early Intervention Specialist Tng. Program Strong Ctr. for Devel. Disabilities Rochester Sch. Medicine, 1992-94; instr. depts. pediatrics and psychiatry (psychology) U. Rochester Sch. Medicine and Dentistry, N.Y., 1984-93; sr. instr. dept. pediatrics and psychiatry U. Rochester Sch. Medicine and Dentistry, 1993—; pvt. practice Rochester, 1985—; cons. Rochester Children's Nursery and Bd. Coop. Ednl. Svcs., 1986-90, Hillside Children's Ctr., Rochester, 1985-87; planning coord. Crisis Intervention Program, Rochester, 1985-86; mem. steering com. Early Childhood Intervention Coun. Monroe County, 1989-90; mem. profl. adv. bd. Greater Rochester Attention Deficit Disorder Assn. Contbr. chpts. to books, articles to profl. publs. Mem. APA, Psychologists for Social Responsibility, Rochester Area Assn. Clin. Psychologists (v.p. 1987-89, pres. 1989-90, exec. com. 1990-91, ann. banquet com. chair 1991), Genesee Valley Psychol. Assn. (program com. 1991-93), Coalition for Svcs. to Parents with Devel. Disabilities (com. chmn. 1985-90, coord. 1988-90), N.Y. State Psychol. Assn., Assn. for Advancement of Psychology, Mental Health Assn., Phi Beta Kappa. Presbyterian. Office: 247 Park Ave Rochester NY 14607-2723

PELOSI, NANCY, congresswoman; b. Balt., Mar. 26, 1941; d. Thomas J. D'Alesandro Jr.; m. Paul Pelosi; children: Nancy Corinne, Christine, Jacqueline, Paul, Alexandra. Grad., Trinity Coll. Former chmn. Calif. State Dem. Com., 1981; committeewoman Dem. Nat. Com., 1976, 80, 84; fin. chmn. Dem. Senatorial Campaign Com., 1987; mem. 99th-102d Congresses from 5th Calif. dist., 1987-1992, 103rd Congress from 8th Calif. dist., 1993—; mem. appropriations com., subcoms. labor, HHD & edn., fgn. ops., D.C.; intelligence (select) com., standard official conduct com. Office: US Ho of Rep 240 Cannon Bldg Washington DC 20515-0508

PELT, JUDY ANN LOBDILL, artist; b. Grand Island, Nebr., Oct. 21, 1939; d. Oran Russell Lobdill and Sylvia Salome (Dobbs) Acola; m. Thomas Hanna Pelt, Sept. 11, 1960 (div. Feb. 1986); children: Gregory, Paige, Brooke. Student, North Tex. State U., 1957-58, Tex. Christian U., 1958-59, Tex. Tech. U., 1959-60. Tchr. workshops Longview, Tex., 1987-89; tchr. Imagination Celebration, Ft. Worth, 1990-92, Ft. Worth Womans Club, 1987—. Mem. Pastel Soc. Am. (Master Pastelist 1987), Pastel Soc. Southwest, Knickerbocker Artists U.S.A., Salmagundi Club (assoc.). Home: 2204 Ridgmar Pla #2 Fort Worth TX 76116-2340

PELTON, VIRGINIA LUE, small business owner; b. Utica, Kans., Apr. 15, 1928; d. Forrest Selby and Nellie (Simmons) Meier; m. Theodore Trower King Jr., Oct. 27, 1956 (div.); m. Harold Marcel Pelton, July 11, 1970; children: Mary Virginia Joyner, Diana Jean. Student, Kans. State U., 1946-47, Ft. Hays U., 1947-48, Washington U., St. Louis, 1950-51. Instr. Patricia Stevens Modeling Sch., Kansas City, Mo., 1948-50; model various cos., Calif. and N.Y., 1951-53; fashion cons. Giorgio, Beverly Hills, Calif., 1967-68, Cellas Gallay, Beverly Hills, 1975-77, Dorso's, Beverly Hills, 1977-79; buyer, mgr. giftware Slavick's, Laguna Hills, Calif., 1980-83; owner P.J. Secretarial Svcs., Laguna Hills, 1980—; v.p. H.P. Fin. Inc., Laguna Hills, 1983—. Editor Profl. Network newsletter, 1980—. Sec. Leukemia Soc. Am., Santa Ana, 1985—; mem. Laguna Beach Art Mus., 1986—. Mem. Profl. Network Assn. (sec. 1986—), Market Plus The Consumer Network, Saddleback C. of C., Laguna Hills Club, Kappa Delta. Republican. Methodist. Home: 24942 Georgia Sue Laguna Beach CA 92653-4323

PELTZ, ALICE JEAN, bacteriologist; b. Astoria, N.Y., Apr. 7, 1950; d. John Christopher and Alice Rose (Faltin) Rauth; m. Lowell J. Peltz, Oct. 12, 1974 (dec. Mar. 1987); adopted children: Laura Jean Scruggs, Randall Michael, James Julius. AAS in Biol. Tech., SUNY, Farmingdale, 1970; BA in Natural Sci., Adelphi U., 1989; MPA, L.I. U., 1992, cert. in gerontology, 1994. Lab. technician toxicology lab. drug abuse sect. Suffolk County Dept. Health Svcs., Hauppage, N.Y., 1973-81, bacteriologist pub. & environ. health lab. water bac. sect., 1981—; presenter confs. and workshops Adelphi U., Garden City, N.Y., 1992, 93, Hofstra U., Hempstead, N.Y., 1993, N.Y. Inst. Tech., Old Westbury, 1993, Suffolk Acad. Law, 1993, 94, Suffolk County C.C., Brentwood campus, 1994. Active Suffolk County Rep. Women, 1993, Huntington Breast Cancer Action Coalition, Family Svc. League Suffolk County, Inc.; intern Cath. Charities Meals on Wheels Program, 1994; mem. Nassau Assn. Continuing Cmty. Edn. Mem. NAFE, Am. Soc. for Pub. Adminstrn. (mem. environ. and natural resources sect.), Soc. Forensic Toxicologists, Inc., N.Y. State Pub. Health Assn., Suffolk County Assn. Mcpl. Employees (mem. polit. action com., sec.-treas., med. examiners' unit), Pi Alpha Alpha. Lutheran. Home: 114A Wells Rd Northport NY 11768 Office: Suffolk County Med Examiner Bldg 487 North Complex Hauppage NY 11787

PELTZ, DIANE PETERSON, distance learning executive; b. Duluth, Minn., June 1, 1941; d. Charles Victor and Hazel Rayetta (Lind) Peterson; m. Steven Kenneth Peltz, Aug. 8, 1969 (div. Jan. 1984); children: Joshua Steven, Jessica Lind. BA, U. Minn., Duluth, 1966; BS in Edn., Marymount U., 1974; MEd, U. Minn., Mpls., 1993. English tchr. Fairfax (Va.) County and Falls Church Sch. Sch., 1977-83; chief page designer, writer Connection Newspapers, Reston, Va., 1983-85; pres., owner David Prodns., Reston, 1983-88; designer, coord. Conservative Digest-Viqurie County, Falls Church, Va., 1985; editor-in-chief Buyers Guide Newspaper, Annandale, Va., 1986; asst. dir. consumer affairs Nat. Turkey Found., Reston, 1986-87; supr. editorial svcs. Unisys-TAD, McLean, Va., 1987-89; mem. faculty comm. U. Minn., St. Paul, 1989-93; dir. media devel. Advance, Inc., Arlington, Va., 1993—; cons. N.W Calbe TV, Mpls., 1990-93, also various bus., Mpls. Author: (book) Book of Songs, 1983; author, composer operas Addictions, 1981, Patterns, 1979, Separations, 1977, others; contbr. articles to profl. jours. Mem. com. Parents Adv. Com., Fairfax, 1979; chair media AAUW, Washington, 1977-78; nat. chair NOW, Washington, 1974. Unitarian Universalist Ch. grantee, 1983; recipient Classics II award PRSA, 1990, 1st Pl. Publs. award Agrl. Com. in Edn., 1990, Best in Mid-West TV award Garden Communicators, 1991, 92, 93; ednl. grantee AAUW, 1980. Mem. SAG, ASCAP, Internat. Teleconferencing Assn. (program com., award 1991, 92, 93), U.S. Distance Learning Assn. Office: Advance Inc 2200 Wilson Blvd # 700 Arlington VA 22201

PELTZ, PAULETTE BEATRICE, corporate lawyer; b. Bklyn., May 30, 1954; d. Joseph and Margaret P. BA, SUNY, Binghamton, 1976; JD, Am. U., 1979. Bar: D.C. 1980, Va. 1982, Md. 1986. Atty. U.S. EPA, Washington, 1979-83; assoc. Mahn, Franklin & Goldenberg, Washington, 1983-85, Deso, Greenberg & Thomas, P.C., Washington, 1985-87; corp. gen. counsel Western Devel. Corp., Washington, 1987-91; v.p. and corp. gen. counsel Mills Corp., 1992-94; v.p. legal Charter Oak Ptnrs., Vienna, Va., 1994—. Home: 11012 Beach Mill Rd Great Falls VA 22066-3026 Office: Chareter Oak Ptnrs 8000 Towers Crescent Dr Ste 950 Vienna VA 22182

PELZER, JOAN KATHLEEN, supplier relations executive; b. Manhasset, N.Y., June 28, 1967; d. Albert William and Rosalind Kathleen (Muratore) P. BA in Comms., SUNY, Oswego, 1989; MBA Internat. Fin., Fordham U., 1995. Supplier rels. mgr., minority bus. mgr. NYNEX, N.Y.C., 1989—; mem. campaign Cmty. Quality Coun. N.Y.C., 1993—. Vol. Clinton Presidential Campaign, N.Y.C., 1992. Mem. NAFE, NOW, Nat. Assn. Purchasing Mgrs. (chairperson pub. rels. N.Y.C.), Am. Soc. for Quality Control, Am. Women's Econ. Devel. Corp., Assn. Mgmt. Women, Minority Mgmt. Assn. Democrat. Roman Catholic. Home: 1506 Gilford Ave New Hyde Park NY 11040 Office: NYNEX Corp 240 E 38th St New York NY 10016-2708

PELZL, BEVERLY RUTH, perioperative nurse; b. Springer, N.Mex., Sept. 11, 1943; d. Earnest W. and Pauline F. Weir; m. Robert M. Pelzl, Dec. 18, 1965; 1 child, Virginia. Diploma, Regina Sch. Nursing, 1964. RN, N.Mex.; cert. oper. rm. nurse, RN first asst. Clin. nurse specialist III gen. surgery, gynecology, laparoscopy and urology St. Joseph Hosp., Albuquerque. Mem. Assn. Operating Room Nurses.

PEMBERTON, BOBETTE MARIE (HARMAN), nursing administrator; b. San Mateo, Calif., Oct. 20, 1952; d. William Adolph and Agnes Marie (Costa) Harman; m. William Charles Pemberton (div. Sept. 1993). BSN, U. San Francisco, 1975, PHN. RN, Calif., Hawaii, Fla.; cert. pub. health nurse, flight nurse, OR nurse. Recreation supr. Burlingame (Calif.) Recreation Ctr., 1968-74; nursing asst. III Stanford U. Med. Ctr., Palo Alto, Calif., 1974-75, staff nurse, 1976-78; clin. edn. supr., mobile ops. supr. Irwin Meml. Blood Bank, San Francisco Med Soc., 1978-87; OR staff nurse U. Calif., Davis, 1987-88; asst. dir. blood svcs. ARC, Farmington, Conn., 1988-89; coord. blood bank St. Anthony's Med. Ctr., St. Petersburg, Fla., 1989-90; dir. donor svcs. Hunter Blood Ctr., Clearwater, Fla., 1990-93; dir. nursing svcs. Blood Bank of Hawaii, Honolulu, 1993—; chairperson nursing edn. com. Calif. Blood Bank System, No. Calif. region seminar Irwin Meml. Blood Bank; mem. sci. com. Blood Bank Nurses Calif., Calif. Blood Bank System; nursing rep. Local 535; lectr. in field. With USAFR, 1983—. Mem. NAFE, Am. Bus. Women's Assn. (rec. sec., chairperson spring conf. Burlingame charter chpt., del. Kansas City conv.), Am. Assn. Blood Banks, Calif. Blood Bank Soc. (nursing and donor svcs. com.), Air Force Assn., Air Force Res. Officers Assn. Republican. Roman Catholic. Home: 1717 Mott-Smith Dr Apt 2405 Honolulu HI 96822 Office: Blood Bank of Hawaii 2043 Dillingham Blvd Honolulu HI 96819

PENA, MODESTA CELEDONIA, retired principal; b. San Diego, Tex., Mar. 3, 1929; d. Encarnacion E. and Teofila (Garcia) P.; BA, Tex. State Coll. for Women, 1950, MA, 1953, cert. supr., 1979; cert. prin. Tex. A&I U., 1961, cert. supt., 1981. Tchr. English, San Diego (Tex.) High Sch., 1950-76; asst. supt. curriculum and instrn. San Diego Ind. Sch. Dist., 1976-80; gifted edn. resource tchr. William Adams Jr. High Sch., Alice, Tex., 1980-83, asst. prin. for instrn., 1983-88; faculty Bee County Coll., 1975-76. V.p., San Diego PTA, 1963; charter mem. Duval County Hist. Commn., 1975—; reporter Duval Co. Hist. Com., 1988—. Newspaper Fund Inc. fellow, 1964; recipient Adolfo Arguijo Day award, 1990; named Outstanding Sr. of Duval County, Grayfest, 1992. Mem. Tex. State Tchrs. Assn. (rec. sec. 1952-53, 63-64, 1st v.p. 1957-58, 66-67 pres. 1961), Delta Kappa Gamma (rec. sec. chpt. 1972-74, first v.p. 1974-76, pres. 1976-78, achievement award 1985, chpt. parlimentarian, 1984-88, state com. Eula Lee Carter Meml. Fund, state com. constn., area coord. state com. pers., state recording sec.), Phi Delta Kappa (treas. chpt. 1978-79, rec. sec. chpt. 1983-84). Home: PO Box 353 306 W Gravis Ave San Diego TX 78384-2604

PENALOZA, BETTY RAQUEL, buyer; b. Lima, Peru, Oct. 4, 1947; came to U.S., 1970; d. Hernan and America (Ortiz) P.; m. Ray D. Roy Sr., Mar. 23, 1974 (div. Feb. 1989). BBA, U. St. Thomas, 1992, postgrad., 1993—. Adminstrv. asst. Petroperu, Lima, 1968-70; adminstrv. asst. Petroperu, Houston, 1970-74, buyer, 1974-88; buyer, owner Serpimpex, S.A., Houston, 1991-93; owner Am. Victoria Trading Co., Houston, 1994—. Vice-chair Loop Program, End Hunger Network, 1993; vol. Mayor's Office, NAFTA Liaison, 1993. Named First Woman Elected Sec. of the Consular Corps, Consular Corps Houston, 1987.

PENCEK, CAROLYN CARLSON, educator; b. Appleton, Wis., June 13, 1946; d. Arthur Edward and Mary George (Notaras) Carlson; m. Richard David Pencek, July 10, 1971; children: Richard Carlson, Mallory Barbara Rowlinds. BA in Polit. Sci., Western Coll., 1968; Ma in Polit. Sci., Syracuse U., 1975; postgrad., Temple U., 1991—. Investment analysts asst. Bankers Trust Co., N.Y.C., 1969-71; substitute tchr. Lackawanna Trail Sch. Dist., Factoryville, Pa., 1971-81; instr. polit. sci. Keystone Jr. Coll., La Plume, Pa., 1972-73; USGS coding supr. Richard Walsh Assocs., Scranton, Pa., 1975-76; instr. polit. sci. Pa. State U., Dunmore, 1976-77; treas. Creative Planning Ltd., Dunmore, 1988—; bd. trustees Lourdesmont Sch., Clarks Summit, Pa., 1989—. Bd. dirs. Lackawanna County Child and Youth Svcs., Scranton, 1981—, pres., 1988-90; founding mem., sec. Leadership Lackawanna, 1982-84; bd. dirs. N.E. Pa. Regional Tissue and Transplant Bank, Scranton, 1984-88, Vol. Action Actr., Scranton, 1986-91; founding mem. Women's Resource Ctr. Assn., Scranton, 1986—, pres., 1986-87. Named Vol. of Yr. nominee, Vol. Action Ctr., 1985; Temple U. fellow, Phila., 1991-92. Mem. AAUW (sec. 1973-75, state sel. com. 1979-81), Assn. Jr. Leagues (area II coun. mem. 1978-79), Jr. League Scranton (v.p. 1980, pres. 1981-83, Margaret L. Richards award 1984), Philharmonic League (v.p. 1976, pres. 1977). Episcopalian. Home: RR 2 Box 2489 Factoryville PA 18419 Office: Creative Planning Ltd 1100 Dunham Dr Dunmore PA 18512

PENDERGAST, PAULA BROWN, personnel consultant; b. Cin., Nov. 17, 1943; d. Everett Raymond and Gayle (Hosutt) Brown; m. Michael Stewart Colvin, July 1962 (div. Aug. 1972); children: Kimberly Elaine, Barbara Gayle; m. Joseph Barry Pendergast, Apr. 1975; 1 child, Patrick Alexander. AS, SUNY, Hartsdale, 1990. Office adminstr. Eastman Kodak, Washington, 1961-63; pers. cons. Weatherby Assocs., Stamford, Conn., 1972-76; pres. Human Resources, Inc., Stamford, 1980—; mem. adv. bd. Amity Bancorp; bd. dirs. Conn. Community Cares, Inc., Norwalk. Mem. Nat. Assn. Temp. Svcs. (pres. Conn. chpt. 1990-91, Nat. Assn. Pers. Women (v.p. Conn. chpt. publs. 1986-87), Nat. Assn. Pers. Cons. Republican. Congregationalist. Office: Human Resources Inc 25 Van Zant St Norwalk CT 06855-1713

PENDL, ANNE LYNN, journalist; b. Mishawaka, Ind., Aug. 8, 1938; d. James Graham and Lonnette (Eutzler) McCollam; m. Gene Richard Pendl, June 18, 1960; children: John Graham, Daniel Stuart, Elizabeth Lynn, Ann-Marie, Thomas Christopher. Student, St. Mary's Coll., Notre Dame, Ind., 1956-58, Ind. U., South Bend, 1988-89. With divsn. sales & reservations United Airlines, South Bend, 1958-60; syndicated columnist Copley News Svc., San Diego, 1992-94. Docent Snite Mus. Art, Notre Dame, 1983—, lectr., 1990, storyteller, 1990—, mem. Friends of the Snite Mus. Bd., 1992—, chairperson edn. com., 1983—; docent South Bend Regional Mus. Art, 1993—; art history educator for children and storyteller TV Channel 46 WHME, Mishawaka, Ind., 1990—; pres. Bethany Guild Sacred Heart Parish, Notre Dame, 1982-83, treas., 1992-94. Roman Catholic. Home and Office: 703 Peashway South Bend IN 46617

PENDLETON, ELSA LOUISE, librarian; b. Lakewood, Ohio, Feb. 26, 1937; d. Roy Paul and Sara Eleanor (Cadwell) Walther; m. Robert Leon Pendleton, Jan. 25, 1958; children: Bryan Whittier, Phillip Clarke. BA, Oberlin Coll., 1958; MSLS, La. State U., 1970. Libr. City of Whittier (Calif.) Pub. Libr., 1972-80; libr., automation coord. Kern County Libr., Bakersfield, Calif., 1980-82; libr. Simutech, Inc., Ridgecrest, Calif., 1982-84, CTA, Inc., Ridgecrest, 1984-87; data ctr. mgr. Computer Scis. Corp., Ridgecrest, 1987-90; tech. documentation mgr. Boeing Info. Svcs., Ridgecrest, 1990—; Author book revs. Libr. Jour., 1975—, Pubs. Weekly, 1993—. Pres. bd. dirs. Women's Ctr. High Desert, Inc., Ridgecrest, 1993—. Mem. AAUW (pres. Ridgecrest br. 1984-86), Assn. for Imaging and Info. Mgmt., Res. Officers Assn. Ladies, Friends of the Ridgecrest Libr. (founder, first pres. 1988), Altrusa. Home: PO Box 129 Ridgecrest CA 93556-0129 Office: Boeing Info Svcs PO Box 369 Ridgecrest CA 93556-0369

PENDLETON, GAIL RUTH, newspaper editor, writer; b. Franklin, N.J., May 8, 1937; d. Waldo A. and Ruby (Bonnett) Rousset; m. John E. Tyler, Mar. 10, 1956 (div. 1978); children: Gwenneth, Victoria, Christine; m. Jeffrey P. Pendleton, Oct. 1, 1978 (dec. 1992). BA, Montclair (N.J.) State Coll., 1959; M in Div., Princeton (N.J.) Theol. Sem., 1973. Ordained minister Presbyn. Ch., 1974. Tchr. Epiphany Day Sch., Kaimuki, Oahu, Hawaii, 1956-58; editor Women's Sect. Daily Record, Morristown, N.J., 1959-62, reporter, 1963-65; tchr. Hardystown Twp. Sch., Franklin, 1968-69; asst. pastor First Presbyn. Ch., Sparta, N.J., 1973-74; reporter N.J. Herald, Newton, 1976-78, editor lifestyle sect., 1978-93, editor Friday eneternatinment sect., 1993—. Recipient Ruth Cheney Streeter award Planned Parenthood N.W. N.J., 1985. Mem. N.J. Press Assn. (family sect. layout award 1985, 87, 88, 89, 91, 2nd feature columns award 1986), Zonta. Office: NJ Herald 2 Spring St Newton NJ 07860-2077

PENDLETON, JOAN MARIE, microprocessor designer; b. Cleve., July 7, 1954; d. Alvin Dial and Alta Beatrice (Brown) P. BS in Physics, Elec. Engring., MIT, 1976; MSEE, Stanford U., 1978; PhDEE, U. Calif., Berkeley, 1985. Sr. design engr. Fairchild Semiconductor, Palo Alto, Calif., 1978-82; staff engr. Sun Microsystems, Mountain View, Calif., 1986-87; chief exec. officer Harvest VLSI Design Ctr. Inc., Palo Alto, 1988—; dir. engring. Silicon Engring. Inc., Scotts Valley, Calif., 1994—; dir. engring. Silicon Engring., Inc., Scotts Valley, Calif., 1994—; cons., designer computer sci. dept. U. Calif., Berkeley, 1988-90. Contbr. articles to profl. jours.; inventor, patnetee serpentine charge transfer device. Recipient several 1st, 2d and 3d place awards U.S. Rowing Assn., Fairchild Tech. Achievement award, 1982, 1st place A award Fed. Internat. Soc Aviron, 1991. Mem. IEEE, Assn. for Computing Machinery, Lake Merritt Rowing Club, Stanford Rowing Club, U.S. Rowing Assn. Home: 1950 Montecito Ave Apt 22 Mountain View CA 94043-4334

PENDLETON, MARY CATHERINE, foreign service officer; b. Louisville, Ky., June 15, 1940; d. Joseph S. and Katherine R. (Toebbe) P. BA, Spalding Coll., 1962; MA, Ind. U., 1969; cert., Nat. Def. U., 1990; D (hon.), U. N. Testemitanu, Moldova, 1994. Cert. secondary tchr., Ky. Tchr. Presentation Acad., Louisville, 1962-66; vol. Peace Corps, Tunis, Tunisia, 1966-68; employment counselor Ky. Dept. for Human Resources, Louisville, 1969-75; gen. svcs. Am. Embassy, Khartoum, Sudan, 1975-77; counsular officer Am. Embassy, Manila, Philippines, 1978-79; adminstrv. officer Am. Embassy, Bangui, Cen. African Republic, 1979-82, Lusaka, Zambia, 1982-84; post mgmt. officer Dept. of State Bur. European and Can. Affairs, Washington, 1984-87; adminstrv. counselor Am. Embassy, Bucharest, Romania, 1987-89; dir. adminstrv. tng. divsn. Fgn. Svc. Inst., Arlington, Va., 1990-92; ambassador Am. Embassy, Chisinau, Moldova, 1992—. Bd. dirs. Am. Sch. of Bucharest, 1987-89. Named to Honorable Order of Ky. Cols., 1988. Democrat. Roman Catholic. Home and Office: Am Embassy Chisinau Dept of State Washington DC 20521-7080

PENDLEY, HOLLY ANN, industrial design company executive; b. Walnut Creek, Calif., Sept. 15, 1962; d. Carl David Jaramillo and Dolores Ann (Zulaica) Williams; m. Alan David Pendley, July 21, 1991; 1 child, Logan Charles Tillman. BA in History, U. Calif., Berkeley, 1991. Legal sec. Airola, Williams & Dietrich, San Francisco, 1983-90; artistic cons. Micro Indsl. Design, Lagunitas, Calif., 1990-91; art dir. Aqualina divsn. Micro Indsl. Design, Petaluma, Calif., 1992—. Instr. Literacy Vols. Am., Petaluma, 1994; steward United Ch. Christ, Petaluma, 1994. Office: Aqualina divsn Micro Indsl Design 1364 N McDowell # 25 Petaluma CA 94954

PENGELLY, VALERIE BONANINI, public health nurse, program director; b. Butte, Mont., July 6, 1955; d. Prospero Dante and Maria Pasqualina (Bonanni) Bonanini. Student, Mont. Inst. Tech., 1973-74, St. Mary Coll., 1974-75; LPN, Butte Vocat.-Tech. Ctr., 1977; AD in Nursing, No. Mont. Coll., 1985. RN, Mont. Staff LPN St. James Community Hosp., Butte, 1980-83, nurse obstetric intensive care nursery, 1985-90; nurse St. Peters Community Hosp., Helena, Mont., 1985; traveling nurse intensive care nursery Torrance (Calif.) Meml. Med. Ctr., 1991, Children's Hosp. Oakland, Calif., 1991; pub. health nurse, dir. supplemental nutrition program for women, infants and children Butte-Silver Bow, Powell County, Beaverhead County Butte-Silver Bow Health Dept., 1991—; office nurse Butte Pediatrics, 1992-93. Bd. dirs. Safe Space; active Big Bros. and Sisters Butte. Mem. Mont. Nurss Assn. Office: Butte-Silver Bow Health Dept 25 W Front St Butte MT 59701-2865

PENKALA, ANTOINETTE MARIE, administrative assistant; b. N.Y.C., July 12, 1952; d. Peter Paul Michael and Mary Ann (Popu) P.; m. Richard Williams, May 27, 1978 (div. June 1981). BA in Econs., Albertus Magnus Coll., 1974. Credit and collections clk. State Nat. Bank, Bridgeport, Conn., 1976-77; supr. accounts payable, accounts receivable Sanitas Svc. Corp.,

Bethany, Conn., 1977-78; supr. work order control Textron Lycoming, Stratford, Conn., 1978-93; asst. to accessory merchandise mgr. Wayside of Milford, Conn., 1993-94; asst. to dir. facilities U. New Haven, 1994—. Democrat. Roman Catholic. Home: 201 North St Milford CT 06460

PENKOFF, DIANE WITMER, communications educator; b. Pasadena, Jan. 20, 1945; d. Stanley Lamar and Mary Evelyn Witmer; m. Robert D. Joyce (div. 1987); 1 child, David William Penkoff. AA, Golden West Coll., Huntington Beach, Calif., 1977; BS in BA, U. LaVerne (Calif.), 1980; MS in Sys. Mgmt., U. So. Calif., L.A., 1989; MA in Communication Arts, U. So. Calif., 1993, PhD in Orgnl. Comm., 1994. Dir. pub. rels. Weight Watchers, Santa Ana, Calif., 1980-84; dir. comm. March of Dimes, Costa Mesa, Calif., 1986-90; prin. Penkoff Comm. Resources, L.A., 1990-92; instr. Calif. State U., Fullerton, 1990-94; asst. lectr. comm. arts and scis. U. So. Calif., University Park, 1991-94; asst. prof. Purdue U., West Lafayette, Ind., 1994—. Editor, The Paper Weight, 1981-84. Chmn. awd. com. March of Dimes, Costa Mesa, nat. vol., 1980—. Mem. Bach Chorale, Pub. Rels. Soc. Am. (acredited mem.), U. So. Calif. Alumni Assn.

PENN, DAWN TAMARA, entrepreneur; b. Knoxville, Tenn., July 22, 1965; d. Morton Hugh and Virginia Audra (Wilson) P. AS, Bauder Fashion Coll., Atlanta, 1984; postgrad., U. Tenn., 1986; grad., Rasnic Sch. Modeling, Knoxville, 1986. Gen. mgr. Merry-Go-Round, Knoxville, 1984-86; mgr., dancer Lady Adonis Inc. Performing Arts Dance Co., Knoxville, 1987-90; owner, pres. Lady Adonis, Inc. Performing Arts Dance Co., Knoxville, 1990—, also chmn.; owner/pres. Penn Mgmt. and Investment Co. Comml. Real Estate, Knoxville, 1989—; deputized bonded rep. Knox County Sheriff's Dept., Knoxville, 1989-90; fgn. dance tours include Aruba, Curacao, Caracas, Barbados, Ont., Que., Montreal, Nfld., Labrador, N.S., New Brunswick; cons. The John Reinhardt Agy., Winston-Salem, N.C., 1987—, Gen. Talent Agy., Monroeville, Pa., 1990—, Xanadu, Inc., Myrtle Beach, S.C., 1991—. Author, editor: Lady Adonis Performing Arts promotional mag., 1988; TV and motion picture credits include: Innocent Blood, 1992, The Phil Donahue Show, N.Y.C., 1989, 91. Coord. bridal fair Big. Bros./Big Sisters Knox County, Knoxville, 1985, 86; judge Southeastern Entertainer of Yr. Pageant, Knoxville, 1992—, Miss Knoxville U.S.A. Pageant, Knoxville, 1990—; active Knoxville Conv. and Visitors Bur., 1993-94. Recipient 1st Pl. award for swimsuit TV comml. and runway modeling Internat. Model's Hall of Fame, 1986, 1st Pl. award for media presentation Modeling Assn. Am. Internat., 1986; nominee The Pres.'s Commn. on White House Fellowships, U.S. Office Pers. Mgmt., 1994-95. Mem. Internat. Platform Assn., Profl. Assn. Diving Instrs. (cert.). Methodist. Home: 5109 Ridgemont Dr Knoxville TN 37918-4539 Office: Lady Adonis Inc/Penn Mgmt Ste 4 7320 Old Clinton Hwy Knoxville TN 37921-1064

PENN, LYNN SHARON, materials scientist; b. Iowa City, June 18, 1945; d. Robert Joseph and Dorothy Evelyn (Etsinger) Johnson; m. Arthur Leon Penn, June 24, 1968; 1 child, Ethan. AB, U. Pa., 1966; MA, Bryn Mawr Coll., 1970, PhD, 1974. Chemist Lawrence Livermore Nat. Lab., Livermore, Calif., 1974-78; sr. scientist Textile Rsch. Inst., Princeton, N.J., 1978-80, Ciba-Geigy Corp., Ardsley, N.Y., 1980-83; prin. scientist Midwest Rsch. Inst., Kansas City, Mo., 1983-86; rsch. prof. Polytechnic U., Bklyn., 1987-91; prof. U. Ky., Lexington, 1991—; chair Gordon Rsch. Conf. on Sci. of Adhesion, 1992. N.Am. editor Internat. Jour. Adhesion and Adhesives; contbr. articles to profl. jours. Mem. Am. Soc. Testing Materials, Soc. Adv. Materials and Process Engring., Fiber Soc., Adhesion Soc. (sec. 1982-90), Kappa Kappa Gamma. Jewish. Home: 31 Division Ave Nyack NY 10960-4405

PENNA, CAROLYN MARIE, legal association administrator, lawyer; b. Flushing, N.Y., Aug. 23, 1952; d. Gilbert Russell Jr. and Lovetta (MacNaughton) Hoffman; m. Joseph N. Penna, May 6, 1978; 1 child, Justin Scott. BA, CUNY, 1974; JD, N.Y. Law Sch., 1984. Supr. communications Hosp. for Spl. Surgery, N.Y.C., 1978-81; editor of court decisions Am. Arbitration Assn., N.Y.C., 1981-86, regional v.p., 1986-92, gen. counsel, 1992—; commr. Bergen County State Superior Ct., Hackensack, N.J., 1986-87. Contbr. articles to profl. jours. Mem. ABA, N.Y. State Bar Assn., N.J. State Bar Assn., Assn. of Bar of City of N.Y., Morgan Horse Assn. of N.J. Lutheran. Office: Am Arbitration Assn 140 W 51st St New York NY 10020-1203*

PENNEY, ALEXANDRA, magazine editor-in-chief, writer; married; 1 child. Grad., Smith Coll.; MA, Hunter Coll., 1977. Editor health and beauty Glamour mag.; editor at large Bantam Doubleday; editor-in-chief Self mag., 1989—. Author: How to Make Love to a Man, 1981, Great Sex, 1985, How to Keep Your Man Monogamous, 1989; contbr. articles to N.Y. Times Mag., Vogue, others. Office: Self Magazine Conde Nast Publs Inc 350 Madison Ave New York NY 10017-3704*

PENNEY, SHERRY HOOD, university chancellor, educator; b. Marlette, Mich., Sept. 4, 1937; d. Terrance and B. Jean (Stoutenburg) Hood; m. Carl Murray Penney, July 8, 1961 (div. 1978); children: Michael Murray, Jeffrey Hood; m. James Duane Livingston, Mar. 30, 1985. BA, Albion Coll., 1959, LLD (hon.), 1989; MA, U. Mich., 1961; PhD, SUNY, Albany, 1972. Vis. asst. prof. Union Coll., Schenectady, N.Y., 1972-73; assoc. higher edn. N.Y. State Edn. Dept., Albany, 1973-76; assoc. provost Yale U., New Haven, Conn., 1976-82; vice chancellor acad. programs, policy and planning SUNY System, Albany, 1982-88; acting pres. SUNY, Plattsburgh, 1986-87; chancellor U. Mass., Boston, 1988—; chmn. bd. dirs. Nat. Higher Edn. Mgmt. Systems, Boulder, Colo., 1985-87; mem. commn. on higher edn. New Eng. Assn. Schs. and Colls., Boston, 1979-82, Middle States Assn. Schs. and Colls., Phila., 1986-88; mem. commn. on women Am. Coun. Edn., Washington, 1979-81, commn. on govt. rels., 1990-94; bd. dirs. Boston Edison Co., Carnegie Found. for Advancement of Teaching, 1994—. Author: Patrician in Politics, 1974; editor: Women in Management in Higher Education, 1975; cons. editor Change mag. and Jour. Higher Edn. Mgmt.; contbr. articles to profl. jours. Trustee Berkeley Div. Sch., Yale U., 1978-82, John F. Kennedy Libr. Found.; bd. dirs. Albany Symphony Orch., 1982-88, U. Mass. Found., 1988—, Mcpl. Rsch. Bur., Boston, 1990—, New England Coun., New England Aquarium, Boston Plan for Excellence; corp. mem. United Way, 1990—, active One on One Leadership Coun., Hers Mid Atlantic Adv. Bd., NASULGC Commn. Urban Affairs, The Ednl. Resource Inst., 1994. Recipient Disting. Alumna award Albion Coll., 1978. Mem. Am. Assn. Higher Edn., Orgn. Am. Historians, Internat. Assn. Univ. Pres., Nat. Assn. State Univs. and Land Grant Colls., Greater Boston C. of C. (bd. dirs.), Yale Club (N.Y.C.) St. Botolph Club, Comml. Club (Boston). Unitarian. Office: U of Mass Office of the Chancellor 100 Morrissey Blvd Boston MA 02125

PENNIMAN, LINDA J. (LYN PENNIMAN), health scientist, occupational/environmental health nurse; b. Springfield, Mass., Sept. 1, 1952; d. Raymond J. and Mildred (Lanier) P.; m. Donald J. Connors, May 30, 1993. ADN, Springfield Tech. C.C., 1977; BSN, U. Vt., 1986; MPH, Johns Hopkins U., 1987. RN, Vt. Staff/charge nurse Pub. Health Svc. Hosp., Kotzebue, Alaska, 1978-81; nurse mgr. Med. Ctr. Hosp. Vt., Burlington, 1981-86; staff nurse Johns Hopkins Hosp., Balt., 1986-89, rsch. asst. sch. hygiene and pub. health, 1987; health scientist OSHA, Washington, 1988—. Co-chair bd. dirs. Casa Md., Takoma Park, 1993-94. Mem. APHA. Home: 816 Colby Ave Silver Spring MD 20912 Office: DOL/OSHA Rm N 3718 200 Constitution Ave NW Washington DC 20210

PENNINGER, FRIEDA ELAINE, retired English language educator; b. Marion, N.C., Apr. 11, 1927; d. Fred Hoyle and Lena Frances (Young) P. AB, U. N.C., Greensboro, 1948; MA, Duke U., 1950, PhD, 1961. Copywriter Sta. WSJS, Winston-Salem, N.C., 1948-49; asst. prof. English Flora Macdonald Coll., Red Springs, N.C., 1950-51; tchr. English Barnwell, S.C., 1951-52, Brunswick, Ga., 1952-53; instr. English U. Tenn., Knoxville, 1953-56; instr., asst. prof. Woman's Coll., U. N.C., Greensboro, 1956-58, 60-63; asst. prof., assoc. prof. U. Richmond (Va.), 1963-71; chair., dept. English Westhampton Coll., Richmond, 1971-78; prof. English U. Richmond, 1971-91, Bostwick prof. English, 1987-91; ret., 1991. Author: William Caxton, 1979, Look at Them, 1990, Chaucer's "Troilus and Criseyde" and "The Knight's Tale": Fictions Used, 1993; compiler, editor: English Drama to 1660, 1976; editor: Festschrift for Prof. Marguerite Roberts, 1976. Fellow Southeastern Inst. of Mediaeval and Renaissance Studies, 1965, 67, 69. Democrat. Presbyterian. Home: 2701 Camden Rd Greensboro NC 27403-1438

PENNINGTON, BEVERLY MELCHER, financial services company executive; b. Vermillion, SD, Feb. 8, 1931; d. Cecil Lloyd and Phyllis Cecelia (Walz) M.; m. Glen D., Sept. 1, 1965 (dec. Aug. 1986); 1 child, Terri Lynn. BS, U. S.D., Vermillion, 1952. Enrolled agt. cert. IRS 1989. Sec. budget dept. Bur. of Indian Affairs, Aberdeen, S.D., 1952-53, pvt. sec., 1953-54; pvt. sec. U.S. P.H.S. Indian Health, Aberdeen, 1954-55; adminstr. asst. U.S. Pub. Health Svc., Anchorage, 1955-58, U.S. Pub. Health, Dental Pub. Health, Washington, 1958-61; grant adminstr. Dental Pub. Health, Washington, 1961-65; co-owner Penn Mel Marina, Platte, S.D, 1965-74; co-owner Pennington Tax Service, Platte, 1974-86, owner, 1986-93; pres., CEO, White Tiger Fin. Svc., Inc., Platte, 1994—. Contbr. articles to profl. jours. Mem. Platte Women's Club, sec., 1965-68, pres., 1968-70, 89-91; mem. Libr. Bd., sec., 1982-85. Fellow Am. Soc. Tax Profls. (sec. 1989-91); mem. NAFE, Platte C. of C. (v.p. 1989, pres. 1990), Lyric Theatre Mus. Soc. (pres. 1988-92), U.S. C. of C., Washington Dakota Ctrl. Com. Republican. Presbyterian. Office: White Tiger Fin Svc Inc 420 Main Platte SD 57369

PENNY, JOSEPHINE B., retired banker; b. N.Y.C., July 7, 1925; d. Charles and Delia (Fahey) Booy; student Columbia U., Am. Inst. Banking; grad. Sch. Bank Adminstrn. U. Wis., 1975; m. John T. Penny, July 15, 1950 (div.); children—John T., Charleen Penny DeMauro, Patricia Penny Paras. With Prentice-Hall, N.Y.C., 1942-43; with Trade Bank & Trust Co., 1943-52, 61-70; with Nat. Westminster Bank U.S.A., 1970-85, v.p., dep. auditor, 1978-85. Mem. Bank Adminstrn. Inst. (chpt. dir. 1983-85), Inst. Internal Auditing, Nat. Assn. Bank Women (chpt. chmn. 1980-81). Home: 221A Manchester Ln Jamesburg NJ 08831-1711

PENROD, ANN MARIE, chemist; b. Portland, Oreg., Jan. 16, 1947; d. John Joseph and Henrietta Katherine (Roth) Plescher; divorced; 1 child, Paula Ann. Student, N.Mex. Inst. Mining and Tech., 1965-67, U. Akron, 1967-68; BS in Chemistry, Walsh Coll., 1989. Lab. technician Phillips Petroleum, Akron, Ohio, 1967-69, Akron City Hosp., 1970-72; analytical chemist, thermal analyst Teledyne Monarch Rubber, Hartville, Ohio, 1972-90; quality engr., lab. mgr. Uniroyal Chem. Co., Inc., Painesville, Ohio, 1990—. Recipient scholarship Walsh Coll., 1989. Mem. Internat. Mgmt. Coun., North Coast Thermal Analysis Soc. (sec. 1987-89, v.p. 1989-91, pres. 1991-92). Eastern Orthodox. Office: Uniroyal Chem Inc 720 Fairport Nursery Rd Painesville OH 44077

PENROSE, CYNTHIA C., health plan administrator, consultant; b. Manila, Nov. 24, 1939; came to U.S., 1940; d. Douglas Lee Lipscomb Cordiner and Jane (Sturgeon) Edises; m. Douglas Francis Penrose, July 11, 1959 (div. 1981); children—Vicki Lynn, Lee Douglas; m. Alan Harrison Magazine, Aug. 30, 1984. B.A., U. Calif.-Berkeley, 1963; M.B.A., U. Santa Clara, 1977. Cert. social services. Vice pres and dir. employment Resource Ctr. for Women, Palo Alto, Calif., 1973-78; bus. planner Raychem Corp., Menlo Park, Calif., 1979; adminstrv. mgr. Electric Power Research Inst., Palo Alto, 1979-83; dir. ops. Utility Data Inst., Washington, 1984-85; dir. ops. Randmark, Inc., 1986-87; coordinator mkt. devel. for Mid-Atlantic States Kaiser Foundation Health Plan, Washington, 1987-88, asst. to Assoc. regional mgr., 1988—; sr. ptnr. MB Assocs., Washington, 1983-88; bd. dirs. and treas. Unique Enterprises, Washington, 1985-87; sec. Wesley Property Mgmt. Co., 1987-89; bd. dirs. Wesley Housing Devel. Corp., 1988-89. Bd. dirs., v.p. LWV, Berkeley and Palo Alto, 1966-73; chmn. program adv. council Resource Ctr. for Women, Palo Alto, 1980-83; mem. Affirmative Action Adv. Com. Palo Alto, 1975-76. Mem. Exec. Women's Roundtable (Washington, founder), Peninsula Profl. Women's Network (v.p. 1981-82), U. Calif. Alumni Assn., AAUW (Bicentennial br. sec. 1986-88), Nat. Wellness Coalition, Med. Group Mgmt. Assn., United Srs. Health Coop., LWV. Democrat. Episcopalian. Avocations: swimming; nutrition and health; reading. Home: 1302 Chancel Pl Alexandria VA 22314-4707 Office: Kaiser-Permanente 2101 E Jefferson Rockville MD 20849

PENRY, DEBORAH L., biological oceanographer, educator; b. Fort Dix, N.J., Feb. 28, 1957. BA in Biol. Sci. with High Honors and Distinction, U. Del., 1979; MA in Marine Sci., Coll. William and Mary, 1982; PhD in Oceanography, U. Wash., 1988. Rsch. asst. dept. invertebrate ecology Va. Inst. Marine Sci., Gloucester Point, 1979-82; rsch. assoc. U.S. Dept. Energy program brine disposal monitoring McNeese State U., Lake Charles, La., 1982-83; lab. chemist Core Labs., Inc., Lake Charles, 1982-83; rsch. asst. Sch. Oceanography U. Wash., Seattle, 1983-88, postdoctoral rsch. assoc., 1988-90; rsch. assoc. Horn. Point Lab. U. Md., Cambridge, 1990-92; asst. prof. dept. integrative biology U. Calif., Berkeley, 1991—. Contbr. articles to profl. jours. Recipient Alan T. Wterman award NSD, 1993, Young Investigator award; fellow NSF; H. Rodney Scharp scholar U. Del., Whitson scholar U. Wash.; grantee NAS Frontiers of Sci. Organizing Com., NAS German Am. Frontiers of Sci. Organizing Com. Mem. AAAS, Am. Geophys. Union, Am. Soc. Limnologists and Oceanographers, Oceanograpy Soc., Phi Beta Kappa, Phi Kappa Phi, Beta Beta Beta. Office: Univ of Calif Dept of Integrative Biology Berkeley CA 94720-3140

PENTZ, SARA, cosmetics executive, former television journalist; b. Columbus, Ohio, Oct. 4, 1937; d. Jack Burdett and Lucille Elaine (Watrous) P.; m. Charles Robert Coulter, Oct. 8, 1977 (div. Aug., 1985). BA, Ohio State U., 1959; postgrad., Columbia U., N.Y.U. Asst. news editor, reporter Sta. WBNS-TV, Columbus, 1959-60; picture editor TV Guide Mag., N.Y.C., 1961-65; news reporter Sta. WNEW-TV (now Sta. WNYC-TV), N.Y.C., 1969-75; v.p. mktg. Swensen's Ice Cream, San Francisco, 1975-79; news reporter CNN, L.A., 1983, Sta. KTUL-TV, Tulsa, 1984; editor Art Gallery Mag., Tulsa, 1984-85; ptnr. Image Dynamics, Dallas, 1987-89; cultural affairs editor Sta. WFAA-TV, Dallas, 1986-93; owner, mgr. Sara Pentz Prodns., Dallas, 1988-93; pres., clinic owner, distributor Sara Pentz, Inc. doing bus. as Mont-Ro Skin Care, Southern Calif., 1993—; host Sta. KUCI talk radio, Irvine, Calif.; speaker, lectr., panelist at numerous meetings and seminars for charitable groups; instr. North Lake Community Coll. (Continuing Edn. Program), 1986, '87, '88. Bd. dirs. Dallas Theater Ctr., Shakespeare Festival of Dallas, Infant Intervention Ctr., Irving, Tex., Irving Ballet Co. (ex officio), Irving YWCA (ex officio), Darco Drug Rehab. Inc. (ex officio), Dallas; adv. bd. Shakespeare Festival of Dallas, 20th Anniversary, Tex. Theatre Hist. Soc., Inc., Dallas; bd. trustees Irving Symphony Orch. Assn.; chmn. Cultural Affairs Coun. of Irving Festival of Trees, 1987; chmn. advt. and publicity Irving Hosp. Found. Texasfest, 1989; vol. Children's Hosp., Orange County; many other civic roles. Named Media Person of Yr., Tex. Early Childhood Intervention Program, Austin, 1991, Bd. Mem. of Yr. Infant Intervention Ctr., Irving, 1990-91, Outstanding Vol. of Yr., Vol. Ctr. Dallas, 1991; recipient High Spirited Citizen award, Irving, 1991; nominee Barbara Jordan award Tex. Govs. Com. for Disabled Persons, 1989, Best Community Svc. by Individual Female award Irving unit Am. Cancer Soc., 1992. Mem. Nat. Assn. Women Bus. Owners (Outstanding Achievement award Dallas chpt. 1991), Women in Communications (Matrix award Dallas chpt. 1990), Dallas Friday Group, Irving C. of C. (pub. rels. com.), North Dallas C. of C., Newport Harbor C. of C. Home: 3711 Channel Pl Newport Beach CA 92663 Office: Mont-Ro Skin Care Sara Pentz Inc 1000 Bristol St N Ste 6 Newport Beach CA 92660

PEPE, TERI-ANNE, development chemist; b. Oakland, N.J., Sept. 9, 1967. BS in Physics, Fairfield U., 1989; MS in Chemistry, Fairleigh Dickinson U., 1993, MBA in Fin., 1994. Cert. profl. tutor chemistry, physics, math., N.J., Conn., N.Y. Analytical chemist L&F Products, Inc., Montvale, N.J., 1989-91; sr. devel. chemist new products group Lever Bros. Co., Edgewater, N.J., 1991-94, prin. sr. devel. chemist new products laundry detergents, 1994—; summer intern detergents lab. L&F Products, Inc., Montvale, 1987, summer intern analytical lab., 1988; work reengring. task force mem., 1990—; judge Regional Sci. Fair, Hackensack, N.J., 1990-91. Advt. mgr. Mirror Newspaper, Fairfield, Conn., 1987-89. Recipient award for piano excellence Trinity Coll. of London, achievement award for outstanding acads. in physics, 1987. Mem. Am. Chemical Soc., Am. Oil Chemists Soc., Am. Inst. Physics, Liberty Sci. Ctr. (edn. com.), Sigma Pi Sigma, Pi Mu Epsilon. Home: 88 Seminole Ave Oakland NJ 07436

PEPLOWSKI, CELIA CESLAWA, librarian; b. Mont., Que., Can., June 4, 1918; came to U.S., 1923; d. Stanley and Wladyslawa (Fabisiak) P. BA and BS with honors, Tex. Woman's U., 1953; MALS, U. Wis., 1955. Substitute libr. Shorewood (Wis.) Pub. Libr., 1955; cataloger, libr. periodical svcs. Arlington (Tex.) State Coll., 1955-56; head libr. English sect. U. of the Sacred Heart, Tokyo, 1956-57; base libr. Sioux City (Iowa) Air Base/USAF, 1957-59; substitute libr. Milw. Sch. Bd., 1959-61; head tech. svcs. Milw. Downer Coll., 1961-63; cataloger, reference libr. Sterling Mcpl. Pub. Libr., Baytown, Tex., 1964-67, acting city libr., 1964-65; asst. extension supr. Mobile (Ala.) Pub. Libr., 1967-68, adminstrv. asst., pers. officer, 1968-69, internat. trade ctr. libr., 1969-70, supr. main libr., 1970-87. Mem. AAUW (com. chmn. Mobile br.), ALA (subscription books rev. com. 1973-75), Wis. U. Alumni Assn., Tex. Woman's U. Alumni Assn., Pi Lambda Theta, Beta Phi Mu. Home: 217 Berwyn Dr W # 209 Mobile AL 36608-2119

PEPPE, KATHRYN KLUSS, pediatrics nurse, educator; b. Akron, Ohio, Mar. 4, 1947; m. Michael G. Peppe, May 15, 1976. BSN, Ohio State U., 1969, MS in Pediatric Nursing Edn., 1971. RN, Ohio. From nurse gen. surgery to burn unit nurse Ohio State U. Hosps., Columbus, 1969-70; instr. Orient (Ohio) State Inst., 1971, Ohio State U., Columbus, 1971-75; asst. nursing dir. Div. Maternal and Child Health Ohio Dept. Health, Columbus, 1975-77, adminstrv. staff nurse cons. Divsn. Maternal and Child Health, 1977-89, asst. chief Divsn. Maternal and Child Health, 1989-93, acting chief Divsn. Maternal and Child Health, 1993-94, chief Divsn. Maternal and Child Health, 1994—; mem. Ohio Devel. Disabilities Planning Coun., 1980-94. Co-author numerous publs.; editorial bd. mem. Infants and Young Children, 1991—. Grantee Ohio Dept. Health 1980, 83-86, 85-86. Fellow Am. Acad. Nursing; mem. ANA (Coun. on Maternal-Child Nursing nominating com. 1989-91), Am. Assn. on Mental Retardation (fellow 1982, chair Nat. Task Force 1973-75, chair nursing div. Ohio chpt. 1972-75), Ohio Nurses Assn. (liaison com. with Ohio State Med. Assn. and Ohio Osteopathic Assn. 1988—, selection com. March of Dimes, 1982, 85, 89—, Maternal-Child Nurse of Yr. 1981), Mid-Ohio Dist. Nurses Assn. (bd. dirs. 1980-84, bylaws com. 1973, 84, 88, nominating com. 1976, scholarship com. 1983—, methods/resources com. Office: Ohio Dept Health Div Maternal-Child Health PO Box 118 Columbus OH 43266-0118

PEPPER, DOROTHY MAE, nurse; b. Merill, Maine, Oct. 16, 1932; d. Walter Edwin and Alva Lois (Leavitt) Stanley; m. Thomas Edward Pepper, July 1, 1960; children: Walter Frank, James Thomas. RN, Maine Med. Ctr. Sch. Nursing, Portland, 1954. RN, Calif. Pvt. duty nurse Lafayette, Calif.; staff nurse Maine Med. Ctr., Portland, 1954-56, Oakland (Calif.) VA Hosp., 1956-58; pvt. duty nurse, dir. RN's Alameda County, Oakland. Mem. Profl. Nurses Bur. Registry.

PEPPER, MARY JANICE, educational consultant; b. Pearsall, Tex., Oct. 1, 1942; d. Muriel Newton and Jane (Harbour) Moore; m. Clifton Gail Pepper, Feb. 19, 1961; children: John David, James Newton, Jeffery Michael. Student, U. Tex., 1960, 65, 76. Bus. mgr. Natalia (Tex.) Independent Sch. Dist., 1967-71; statistician Tex. Edn. Agy., Austin, 1971-72; mgr. bookkeeping div. Tex. Ednl. Cons. Svc. Inc., Austin, 1972-76, adminstrv. v.p., 1976-82, v.p., COO, 1982-93, pres., 1993—; team tchr. edn. program. U. Tex., Austin, 1985; lectr. Tex. Assn. Secondary Sch. Prins., Austin, 1988. Editor: Sch. Fin. Newsletter, Update for Sch. Adminstrs. Sec. Community Indsl. Found., Natalia, 1969-71, Medina County Water Control and Improvement, Natalia, 1970-71; mem. adv. com. Tex. Edn. Agy. Mem. Tex. Assn. Sch. Bus. Ofcls. (instr. 1987-88, chair coord. task force on sch. acctg. Tex. Edn. Agy. 1991-93), Mended Hearts (sec. 1989-90, newsletter editor 1990-91). Baptist. Home: 16048 Hamilton Pool Rd Austin TX 78738-7401 Office: Tex Ednl Consultative Svcs Inc PO Box 18898 Austin TX 78760-8898

PEPPER, NORMA JEAN, mental health nurse; b. Ellington, Iowa, Nov. 7, 1931; d. Victor F. and Grace Mae (Tate) Shadle; m. Bob Joseph Pepper, Dec. 28, 1956 (dec. Oct. 4, 1985); children: Joseph Victor, Barbara Jean, Susan Claire (dec.). Diploma in Nursing, Broadlawns Polk County Hosp., 1950-53; BSN, U. Iowa, 1953-55; MSN, U. Colo., 1955-60. Cert. mental health nurse. Head nurse Colo. Psychiatric Hosp., Denver, 1956; head nurse, Psychiatry Denver General Hosp., 1958-60; with Nurses Official Registry, Denver, 1960-73; staff nurse VA Med. Ctr., Denver, 1974-94; counselor VA Hosp. Employee Assistance Com., Denver, 1987-94. Mem. Colo. Nurses Assn. Home: 4836 W Tennessee Ave Denver CO 80219-3130

PERANIO, JOANNE CELESTE, psychiatrist; b. Paterson, N.J., Oct. 5, 1951; d. Alfred Joseph and Marie Theresa (D'Agostino) P.; m. Michael Francis Triolo, Aug. 16, 1970 (div. Oct. 1982); children: Bobbi Triolo, Michael Triolo. BA, Montclair State Coll., 1973; MS, William Paterson Coll., 1985; MD, N.J. Med. Sch., 1989. Bd. eligible psychiatrist. Tchr. biology and chemistry DePaul H.S., Wayne, N.J., 1974-77, Passaic Valley H.S., Little Falls, N.J., 1980-82; tchr. 7th grade Westwood (N.J.) Mid. Sch., 1984-85; intern Morristown (N.J.) Meml. Hosp., 1989-90; resident physician Univ. Hosp., Newark, N.J., 1990-93; pvt. practice, staff mem. Hackensack (N.J.) Med. Ctr., 1993—. Roman Catholic. Office: Ste 15 140 Prospect Ave Hackensack NJ 07601

PERATA, VERONICA LUCILLE, realtor; b. Oakland, Calif., May 25, 1944; d. Robert Paul and Lucille Veronica (Victorino) Marks; m. Eugene Anjos Santos, Sept. 15, 1962 (div. 1973); children: Ronald Eugene, David Robert, Veronica Jean; m. Robert Domingo Perata, Apr. 27, 1974. Lic. realtor, cosmetologist, Calif. Cosmetology operator Kut & Kurl, Fremont, Calif., 1963-67; realtor assoc. Tri-City Brokers, Fremont, 1968-70, Look Realty, Fremont, 1970-74, Gygax Realty, Fremont, 1974-93; co-owner Bob's Athletic Club, Fremont, 1974-93. Mem. Tri-City Mktg. Assn. (sgt. at arms 1990-93), Women's Coun. Realtors (v.p. 1991-93). Home: 38731 Sobrante St Fremont CA 94536-4452 Office: Galaxy Realty 41051 Mission Blvd Fremont CA 94539-3859

PERDREAU, CORNELIA RUTH WHITENER, English as a second language educator, international exchange specialist; b. Beacon, N.Y.; d. Henry Kato Whitener and Mazie Althea (Martin) Whitener-Johnson; m. Michel Serge Yves Perdreau, June 14, 1969; 1 child, Maurice Laurence Henri. BA, SUNY, Potsdam, 1969; MA, Ohio U., 1971, 72. French/Latin tchr. Walt Whitman Jr. High Sch., Yonkers, N.Y., 1969-70; French teaching asst. Ohio U., Athens, 1970-71, ESL tchr., 1976—; English/French tchr. Lycee de Chambery, France, 1972; English tchr. Acad. de Paris, France, 1984; study abroad coord. Ohio U., Athens. Contbr. articles to profl. jours. Chair Tri-County Community Action Agy., Sugarcreek, Ohio, 1982; mem. bd. Dairy Barn Arts Ctr., Athens, 1985-91; trustee Ohioana Bd. Trustees, Columbus, 1987—. Mem. TESOL (chair rules and resolutions com. 1993—), Ohio TESOL (pres. 1986-87), Internat. Black Profls. in TESOL (founder, chair 1991—), Internat. Assn. Black Profls. in Internat. Affairs (founder), Assn. Internat. Educators (pres.-elect 1995—), Adminstrs. and Tchrs. in ESL (chair 1992—). Office: Ohio Program Intensive English 201 Gordy Hall Athens OH 45701

PERDUE, BEVERLY MOORE, state legislator, geriatric consultant; b. Grundy, Va., Jan. 14, 1948; d. Alfred P. and Irene E. (Morefield) Moore; children: Garrett, Emmett. BA, U. Ky., 1969; MEd, U. Fla., 1974, PhD, 1976. Pvt. lectr., writer, cons., 1980-86; pres. The Perdue Co., New Bern, N.C., 1985—; rep. N.C. State Gen. Assembly, Raleigh, 1986-90; senator N.C. Gen. Assembly, Raleigh, 1990—. Bd. dirs. Nations Bank, New Bern, 1985—, N.C. United Way, Greensboro, 1990-92; exec. mem. N.C. Dem. Party, Raleigh, 1989—; bd. mem. N.C. Equity, Raleigh, 1992; mem. N.C. travel bd. Nat. Conf. of State Legislators. Named Outstanding Legislator, N.C. Aging Network, 1989, 92, Toll fellow Nat. Conf. State Legislators, Lexington, Ky., 1992. Mem. Nat. Coun. on Aging, Bus. and Profl. Women, Rotary. Episcopalian. Home: 211 Wilson Point Rd New Bern NC 28562-7519 Office: Perdue & Co PO Box 991 421 Craven St New Bern NC 28562 also: NC Senate House State Capitol Raleigh NC 27611*

PERDUE, THEDA, history educator, author; b. McRae, Ga., Apr. 2, 1949; d. James Howard and Ouida (Davis) P. AB, Mercer U., 1972; MA, U. Ga., 1974, PhD, 1976. From asst. prof. to assoc. prof. history Western Carolina U., Cullowhee, N.C., 1975-83; prof. history Clemson (S.C.) U., 1983-88, U. Ky., Lexington, 1988—; editor Indians of S.E., U. Nebr. Press, Lincoln, 1985—; cons. Smithsonian Instn., Washington, 1989; Fulbright lectr., N.Z., 1988. Author: Slavery and the Evolution of Cherokee Society, 1979, Native Carolinians, 1985, The Cherokee, 1988; editor: Nations Remembered, 1980, Cherokee Editor, 1983; co-editor: Southern Women, 1993; mem. editorial bd. Jour. Women's History, 1988—, Ethnohistory, 1992—. Newberry Libr. fellow, 1978, Rockefeller Found. fellow, 1980-81. Mem. Am. Hist. Assn., Orgn. Am. Historians, Am. Soc. for Ethnohistory, So. Hist. Assn., So. Assn.

for Women Historians (pres. 1985-86). Democrat. Office: U Ky Dept History Pot # 1715 Lexington KY 40506

PEREIRA, CELINA ANTONIETA, physician; b. Bombay, India, Dec. 21, 1941; came to U.S., 1967; d. João Costa and Adelina (DeSousa) P.; m. Donald Andrew McGowan; children: Malini, Meena. MD, Grant Med. Coll., Bombay, 1965. Resident in pediats. Boston City Hosp., 1967-69, R.I. Hosp., Providence, 1969-70; instr. in pediats. Brown U., Providence, 1973-75; staff physician U. R.I., Kingston, 1975—. Contbr. articles to profl. jours. Vol. hospice VNA, Wakefield, R.I., 1994; active World Spiritual U. Fellow Am. Acad. Pediats. (diplomate), R.I. Med. Soc., Washington County Med. Soc. Roman Catholic. Office: U RI Health Svcs Kingston RI 02881

PERELLA, SUSANNE BRENNAN, librarian; b. Providence, Mar. 19, 1936; d. Laurence J. and Harriet E. (Delaplane) Brennan. B.A., U. Conn., 1960; M.L.S., U. Mich., 1967. Head M.B.A. Library, Univ. Conn., Hartford, 1964-66; asst. librarian Cornell Univ. Grad. Sch. Bus., Ithaca, N.Y., 1967-72; head reader's services FTC Library, Washington, 1972-79; library dir. FTC Library, 1979-92; asst. dir. Libr. and Info. Svcs. U.S. Treasury, Washington, 1992—. Mem. Law Librarians Soc., Spl. Libraries Assn., Am. Assn. Law Libraries, Fed. Library and Info. Ctr. Com. Office: US Dept Treasury Libr 1500 Pennsylvania Ave NW Washington DC 20220-0002

PERES, JUDITH MAY, journalist; b. Chgo., June 30, 1946; d. Leonard H. and Eleanor (Seltzer) Zurakov; m. Michael Peres, June 27, 1972; children: Dana, Avital. BA, U. Ill., 1967. Acct. exec. Daniel J. Edelman Inc., Chgo., 1967-68; copy editor Jerusalem (Israel) Post, 1968-71, news editor, 1971-75, chief night editor, 1975-80, editor, style book, 1978-80; copy editor Chgo. Tribune, 1980-82, rewriter, 1982-84, assoc. fgn. editor, 1984-90, nat. editor, 1990-95, nat./fgn. editor, 1995—. Office: Chicago Tribune 435 N Michigan Ave Chicago IL 60611

PERES, VALARIE JEAN, paralegal; b. Great Falls, Mont., July 3, 1955; d. Ferdinand Nels and Jean Allison (Ackerman) P.; m. Daniel Joseph Jaraczeski (div. 1983); 1 child, Brandon John Jaraczeski. AS in Paralegal, Coll. Great Falls, 1991. Lic. pvt. investigator. Paralegal Kenneth R. Olson Law Firm, Great Falls, 1991—; paralegal Great Falls, 1992—, pvt. investigator, 1993—. Bd. dirs. Great Falls Electrics Baseball, 1993—; active Alliance for Youth, Great Falls, 1989—; football coach Salvation Army Flag Football, Great Falls, 1984-88. Mem. Am. Trial Lawyers Assn., Mont. Big Sky Paralegal Assn. (editor newsletter 1993). Roman Catholic. Office: Kenneth R Olson Law Office 600 Central Ave Ste 316 Great Falls MT 59401-3141

PERETTI, ELSA, jewelry designer; b. Florence, Italy, May 1, 1940. Tchr. French and Italian pvt. schs.; mem. staff Dado Torrigiani (Architect), Milan, Italy; fashion model Spain, France, Gt. Britain, U.S.; jewelry designer Halston, Giorgio Sant'Angelo, from 1969; designer jewelry accessories, perfume creator Tiffany & Co., N.Y.C., 1974—. Represented in permanent collections Mus. Fine Arts, Boston, Mus. Fine ARts, Houston. Recipient Coty award, 1971, Pres.' Fellow award R.I. Sch. Design, 1981, Spirit Achievement award Albert Einstein Coll., 1982, Fashion Group Night of the Stars award, 1986. Address: care Tiffany & Co 727 Fifth Ave New York NY 10022

PERETTI, MARILYN GAY WOERNER, volunteer management professional; b. Indpls., July 30, 1935; d. Philip E. and Harriet E. (Meyer) Woerner; children: Thomas A., Christopher P. BS, Purdue U., 1957. Nursery sch. lab. asst. Mary Baldwin Coll., Staunton, Va., 1957-58; tchr. 1st grade, nursery sch. No. Ill. area schs., 1958-61; asst. tchr. of blind Glenbard E. High Sch., Lombard, Ill., 1978-80; adminstrv. asst. Elmhurst Coll., 1980-81; dir. vol. svcs. DuPage Convalescent Ctr., Wheaton, 1981—; developer new vol. pos. for vis. the non-verbal handicapped, 1994; prodr. 4 ednl. slide programs on devel. countries, 1988-91; initiator used book collection for library project U. Zululand, S. Africa, 1993-94. Editor, designer newsletter Our Developing World's Voices, 1994—. Bd. dirs. Lombard YMCA, 1977-83, pres. 1980; vol. Chgo. Uptown Ministry, 1979; midwest educator for Our Developing World, 1989—; participant fact finding trips El Salvador, 1988, Honduras, 1989, Nicaragua, 1989, Republic of South Africa, 1991. Mem. Coun. Dirs. Hosp. Vols. Met. Chgo., DuPage Assn. Vols. Adminstrn., Assn. Vol. Adminstrn. Office: DuPage Convalescent Ctr Wheaton IL 60187

PERETZ, MILDRED, educator; b. Phila., May 3, 1923; d. Israel and Bessie (Cohen) Arinsberg; m. Louis Peretz, Oct. 15, 1950; children: Stephen Clark, David Maxwell. BA, Rutgers U., 1945. Tchr. Latin, English Woodstown (N.J.) High Sch., 1945-46; tchr. Latin, French Plainfield (N.J.) High Sch., 1947-50; edn. educator Long Beach (Calif.) State U., 1981; tchr. algebra Nat. U., Palm Springs, Calif., 1987; tchr. drama Ft. Lewis Coll., Durango, Colo., 1991, 92; book reviewer, chair Brandeis U. Nat. Women's Com., 1992—, v.p., current events chair, 1981-94. Performer (leading roles) Ghosts, The Importance of Being Earnest, Hamlet, Edward My Son, January Thaw, Bloody Mad to Cry, The Matchmaker, Look Homeward Angel, The Glass Menagerie, others.

PEREZ, ANN ELISABETH, critical care nurse; b. Johnstown, Pa., Apr. 21, 1951; d. Bernard John and Mary Jo (Coshun) Kessler; m. Walter William Steeley (div. 1971); m. Rafael C. Perez, Jr. (div. 1979); 1 child, Benjamin K. Perez. LPN, Greater Johnstown Vocat. Tech., 1970; RN, Conemaugh Sch. of Nursing, 1982; BS in Health-Related Professions, U. Pitts., 1991. RN; CCRN. LPN Lee Hosp., Johnstown, 1971-72; ICU/CCU/open heart/trauma Conemaugh Hosp., Johnstown, 1982—. Mem. YMCA, Johnstown, 1990—. Lt. USNR, 1972—. Mem. Am. Heart Assn. (ACLS), Am. Lung Assn., Am. Cancer Soc., Res. Officers Assn., Assn. Mil. Surgeons U.S. Home: 551 Ruby St Johnstown PA 15902

PEREZ, JANET MARY WETZKA, medical-surgical/transplant nurse; b. Metairie, La., Nov. 13, 1964; d. Anselm and Aline (Ruffina) Wetzka; m. Michael Joseph Perez, Aug. 22, 1987. BSN, La. State U. Med. Ctr., 1986. RN, La.; cert. med.-surg. Staff nurse Ochsner Found. Hosp., New Orleans, 1986-91, conf. coord. and chair unit quality assurance com., 1989-91, chair nursing resource com., 1990-94, patient care coord., 1991—; CPR instr., 1988—. Mem. Beverly Hills Civic Assn., Metairie, 1990—. Mem. Internat. Transplant Nurses Soc. (pres. La. chpt.), Internat. Urol. Scis., Inc., Sigma Theta Tau. Roman Catholic. Home: 6100 Irving St Metairie LA 70003-2843 Office: Ochsner Found Hosp 1516 Jefferson Hwy New Orleans LA 70121-2484

PEREZ, JULIE ANNA, audio engineer; b. Miami, Fla., Sept. 2, 1961; d. Miguel Angel and Dorothy Elizabeth (Headford) P. Student, U. Miami, 1979-83. Audio engr. NBC, Inc., N.Y.C., 1984—; asst. music mixer (TV shows) Saturday Night Live, 1987-93, Late Night with David Letterman 7th Anniversary Spl., 1989; music mixer Late Night with David Letterman, summer 1989, Late Night with Conan O'Brien, 1993—; audio engr. Later with Bob Costas, Friday Night Videos, Brokaw Reports; co-founder TECHNET; sem. chair AES Women in Audio, 1991. Editor: Music Engring. Tech. newsletter, 1983; audio engr. TV talk-show Donahue, 1985-87 (Emmy nomination). Contbr. Planned Parenthood Fedn. Am., 1986—, Women in the Arts. Recipient Down Beat award Down Beat mag., 1982, Best Engineered Live Performance award Down Beat mag. Mem. NARAS, NOW, ACLU, NATAS, (Emmy nomination for sound mixing 1986), Acad. TV Arts and Scis. (Emmy nomination for sound mixing 1993), Audio Engring. Soc., Nat. Assn. Broadcast Employees and Technicians, Women in Music. Democrat. Home: 18 Harriot Ave Harrington Park NJ 07640 Office: NBC Inc 30 Rockefeller Plz Rm 240 New York NY 10112-0001

PEREZ, LUZ LILLIAN, psychologist; b. Ponce, P.R., Aug. 7, 1946; d. Emiliano and Maria D. (Torres) P.; children: Vantroi, Maireni. BA, Herbert H. Lehman Coll., 1974; PhD, NYU, 1989. Lic. psychologist, N.Y. Staff psychologist Soundview Throgs Neck Community Mental Health Ctr., Bronx, 1980-88; coord. early childhood program Crotona Park Cmty. Mental Health Ctr., Bronx, 1988-91; cons. psychologist Highbridge Adv. Coun. Presch. Program, Bronx, N.Y., 1991-93, Coalition for Hispanic Family Svcs., Bklyn., N.Y., 1991—, Marathon Child Devel. Ctr., Queens, N.Y., 1993-94, Bronx Orgn. for Learning Disabled, 1993—, Village Child Devel. Ctr., N.Y.C., 1994—, Graham-Windham Svcs. to Families and Children, 1994—. Grantee NIMH, 1974-77. Mem. APA, Assn. Hispanic Mental Health Profls.

PEREZ, MARIA PILAR, artist, educator; b. Bogota, Colombia, Mar. 28, 1953; came to U.S. 1988; d. Jaime Ernesto and Sofia (Dussan) P. BA in Fine Arts, U. Jorge Tadeo Lozano, Bogota, 1977; postgrad. diploma in conservation, Instituto Interamericano, Mexico City, 1978. Conservator/restorer Art Restoration by Demetrios, Bogota, 1978-86, N.Y.C., 1990-91; conservator/restorer Theodore Nightwine & Assocs., Sarasota, Fla., 1991-92; dir. fine arts and restoration Art Studio Tampa, Fla., 1992—. Illustrator: (book for children) Globo Magico 3, Bogota, 1984. Orgn. Am. States scholar, 1977-78. Mem. Tampa Tchrs. Group. Home: 1705 E Kirby St Apt A Tampa FL 33604-3535 Office: Art Studio Tampa 1705 E Kirby St Apt B Tampa FL 33604-3535

PEREZ, ROSIE, actress, choreographer; b. Bklyn.; d. Ismael Serrano and Lydia Perez. dramatic appearances include: (T.V.) 21 Jump Street, WIOU, (film) Do the Right Thing, 1989, White Men Can't Jump, 1992, Night on Earth, 1992, Untamed Heart, 1993, Fearless, 1993 (Acad. award nom. Best Supporting Actress 1994), It Could Happen To You, 1994. Office: CAA 9830 Wilshire Blvd Beverly Hills CA 90212*

PÉREZ-STABLE, MARIA ADELAIDA, librarian; b. Havana, Cuba, Nov. 2, 1954; came to U.S. 1960; d. Diego Javier and Maria Luisa (Dominguez) Perez-Stable. BA magna cum laude, Miami U., Oxford, Ohio, 1976; MSLS, Case Western Res. U., Cleve., 1977; MA in History w/hons., Western Mich. U., 1986. Catalog libr. Western Res. Hist. Soc., Cleve., 1977-79; catalog libr. Western Mich. U., Kalamazoo, 1979-84, edn. libr., 1984-91, social scis. libr., 1991—. Co-author: Peoples of the American West, 1989, Understanding American History Through Children's Literature: Instructional Units and Activities for Grades K-8, 1994; editor: Directory of Michigan Academic Libraries, 1984. Mem. ALA, Mich. Library Assn., Orgn. Am. Historians, Nat. Trust for Historic Preservation, Phi Beta Kappa, Phi Kappa Phi, Beta Phi Mu. Democrat. Roman Catholic. Office: Waldo Libr Western Mich U Kalamazoo MI 49008

PEREZ-VALDES, YVONNE ANN, nurse, educator; b. Tampa, Fla., May 18, 1946; d. Raimundo Abal and Encarnita (Perez) P. ASN, St. Petersburg Jr. Coll., 1978. Med./surg., ob-gyn and pediatric ICU nurse; RN, Fla. Nurse St. Joseph Hosp., Tampa, Fla., 1966-71, cardiologist office nurse mgr., 1976-78; coronary care unit nurse U. Community Hosp., Tampa, Fla., 1978-80; emergency rm. charge nurse, ICCU asst. head nurse Centro Asturiano Hosp., Tampa, Fla., 1980-85; mem. faculty, head dept. nursing Tampa Coll., 1985-88; supr., dir. edn. Oakwood Nursing Home, Tampa, 1988-89; instr. health Hillsborough County Schs., Tampa, 1989-95; dir. staff devel. Meadowbrook Manor Tampa, 1995—; faculty mem., Health Industry Adv. Bd., Learey Ctr., 1992-95. Author: Cry Out, I'm Listening. Mem.-at-large Nat. Rep. Com., Washington, 1991-95; mem. Presdl. Com., Washington, 1991-92, Senatorial Com., Washington, 1991-92. Name included Benefactor's Wall Am. Nursing Found. Bldg., Washington. Mem. ANA, Nat. ARC Nurse Diabetes Assn., Am. Cancer Assn., Am. Hispanic Nurses (chmn. 1992), Fla. Nurses Assn., Tampa Nurses Assn., Dist. 4 St. Joseph's Hosp. Devel. Coun., Nat. Audubon Soc. Democrat. Roman Catholic. Office: Hillsborough County Schs Ctr for Tng 5410 N 20th St Tampa FL 33610-8213 Also: Meadowbrook Manor of Tampa 8720 Jackson Spring Rd Tampa FL 33615

PERFIDO, RUTH S., lawyer; b. Pitts., Oct. 10, 1941. BA, Newcomb Coll., 1963; JD, U. Pitts., 1977. Bar: Pa. 1977. Ptnr. Reed Smith Shaw & McClay, Pitts. Office: Reed Smith Shaw & McClay Mellon Sq 435 6th Ave Pittsburgh PA 15219-1886

PERHACS, MARYLOUISE HELEN, musician, educator; b. Teaneck, N.J., June 15, 1944; d. John Andrew and Helen Audrey (Hosage) P.; m. Robert Theodore Sirinek, Jan. 27, 1968 (div. Jan. 1975). Student, Ithaca (N.Y.) Coll., 1962-64; BS, Juilliard Sch., 1967, MS, 1968; postgrad., Hunter Coll., 1976, St. Peter's Coll., Jersey City, N.J., 1977. Cert. music tchr., N.Y., N.J. Instr. Carnegie Hall, N.Y.C., 1966-69; program developer, coord., instr. urban edn. program Newburgh (N.Y.) Pub. Sch. System, 1968-69; adj. prof. dept. edn. St. Peter's Coll., Jersey City, 1976-92; tchr. brass instruments Indian Hills High Sch., Oakland, N.J., 1976; tchr. Jersey City Pub. Schs., 1976-77, N.Y.C. Pub. Sch., Bronx, 1980-84; pvt. tchr. Cliffside Park, N.J., 1976—; vocal music tchr. East Rutherford, N.J., 1990; tchr. music Bergen County Spl. Svcs. Sch. Dist., 1990-91; tchr. gen. music Little Ferry (N.J.) Pub. Schs., 1991-92; tchr. mid. sch. instrumental Paramus (H.J.) Pub. Schs., 1993-94; singer, trumpeter Norwegian Caribbean Lines, 1981-82, Jimmy Dorsey Band, Paris and London, 1974; music and edn. lecture cir., 1992—. Singer with Original PDQ Bach Okay Chorale, N.Y.C., 1966, Ed Sullivan Show, N.Y.C., 1970, St. Louis Mcpl. Opera, 1970; music and edn. lecture cir., 1992—; singer, dancer, actress (Broadway shows) Promises, Promises, 1969-71, Sugar, 1971-72, Lysistrata, 1972; trumpeter (Broadway shows) Jesus Christ Superstar, 1973, Debbie!, N.Y.C., 1976, Sarava!, 1979, Sophisticated Ladies, 1982, Fiddler on the Roof, Lincoln Ctr., 1981; writer, host series on women in music Columbia Cable/United Artists, 1984. Cons. to cadette troop Girl Scouts U.S., Jersey City, 1967-68. Mem. NEA, AFTRA, Actors Equity Assn., Am. Fedn. Musicians (mem. theatre com. local 802 1972—, chmn. 1973), Music Educators Nat. Conf., N.J. Music Educators Assn., N.J. Sch. Music Assn., N.J. Edn. Assn., Music Educators Bergen County, Internat. Women's Brss Conf. (charter), Internat. Trumpet Guild (charter, Woman of Accomplishment 1992), Mu Phi Epsilon. Democrat. Episcopalian. Home and Office: 23 Crescent Ave Cliffside Park NJ 07010-3003

PERI, WINNIE LEE BRANCH, educational director; b. Dallas; d. Floyd Hamilton and Eula Dee (Richardson) Branch; m. Fred Ronald Peri; children: Kenneth Michael, Michael Anthony, Desiree Denise. BA in Psychology, Calif. State U., Long Beach, 1978, English teaching credential, 1988; social sci. teaching credential, Calif. State U., Northridge, 1979. Republic of South Africa tchr. Internat. Sch. Svcs., Princeton, N.J., 1980-82; tchr. English, St. Jeanne de Lestonnac Sch., Tustin, Calif., 1988-91; dir. edn. Sylvan Learning Ctr., Mission Viejo, Calif., 1993-94; self-employed as tutor, 1994—; facilitator Rainbows for All God's Children, 1989; mem. team experience sch. evaluation com. WASC/WCEA. Mem. adv. bd. Thomas Paine Sch. PTA; dep. sheriff Los Angeles County. Mem. Psi Chi.

PERINE, MARTHA LEVINGSTON, banker; b. Mobile, Ala., June 27, 1948; d. George H. and Martha C. (Matthews) Levingston; m. David A. Perine, June 14, 1969; children: David Andrew Jr., Alissa Lynette, Alison Lynette. BS in Bus. Adminstrn., Clark Coll., 1969; MA in Econs., Washington U., St. Louis, 1971. Mgmt. trainee Fed. Res. Bank of St. Louis, 1971-72, adminstrv. asst., 1973-74, asst. mgr., 1975-77, mgr., 1977-78, asst. v.p., 1978-81, v.p., 1981-83, v.p., controller, 1983—. Mem. allocation com. United Way, St. Louis, 1987-89, Conf. Edn.'s Statewide Task Froce on Tchr. Edn., 1987-88, community outreach task force, 1994—; vol. United Negro Coll. Fund., chairperson ann. fundraising dinner 1984, 86, co-chair, 1983, 85; bd. mgrs. Monsanto br. YMCA, St. Louis, 1981—, v.p. fin., 1983; sec. Jackson Park PTO, St. Louis, 1982-83, pres., 1982-84, treas., 1985-86; pres. Brittany Woods PTO, St. Louis, 1986-87, treas., 1987-88; fin. sec., bd. dirs. Holy Met. Missionary Bapt. Ch.; mem. Mayorial Fin. Task Force, 1993—. Mem. NAACP (life), Iota Phi Lambda (v.p. 1987—), Alpha Kappa Alpha (nat. treas. 1990-94, ctrl. regional dir. 1994—). Democrat. Office: Fed Reserve Bank St Louis PO Box 442 Saint Louis MO 63166

PERKINS, AGNES REGAN, retired English language educator; b. Helena, Mont., Apr. 28, 1926; d. Thomas Patrick and Agnes Woodworth (Dickerson) Regan; m. William David Perkins, July 26, 1950; children: Todd, Aaron, Stuart. BA, U. Mont., 1947, MA, 1949. Prof. English Ea. Mich. U., Ypsilanti, 1961-86; ret., 1986. Co-author (With Helbig): Dictionary of American Children's Fiction, 1859-1959, 1985, Dictionary of American Children's Fiction, 1960-1984, 1986, Dictionary of British Children's Fiction, 2 vols., 1989, Dictionary of Children's Fiction from Australia, Canada, India, New Zealand, and Selected African Countries, 1992, Dictionary of American Children's Fiction, 1985-1989, 1993, The Phoenix Award of the Children's Literature Association, 1993, This Land Is Our Land: A Guide to Multicultural Literature for Children and Young Adults, 1994; co-complier anthologies of poems, 1974, 77, 81. Mem. Children's Lit. Assn., U. Mich. Women's Rsch. Club. Democrat. Home: 2565 W Ellsworth Rd Ann Arbor MI 48108

PERKINS, DEBORAH ANNE, interior designer; b. Mineola, N.Y., Mar. 8, 1954; d. Arthur Cudner and Maria (Risko) P.; 1 child, Olivia Anne Perkins. AAS in Interior Design magne cum laude, Chamberlayne Sch., Boston, 1975. Cert. fitness instr. YMCA. Film admissions coord. Gen. Cinema Corp., Chestnut Hill, Mass., 1976-78; tchr. adult edn. Kennedy Community Sch., Cambridge, Mass., 1976; interior design cons. Jordan Marsh Co., Quincy, Mass., 1978-81; freelance interior designer Honduras, Central Am., 1981; sales rep. New Eng. territory LaFrance (S.C.) Fabrics, 1982-84; owner, designer The Design Studio, Watertown, Mass., 1985—. Mem. Boston Soc. Architects Task Force for Homeless, 1988-90; big sister YWCA, Boston, 1985—; participant Grace Chapel Nursing Home Ministry, Lexington, Mass., 1989-90, Intermission Performing Arts, 1989-90. Mem. NAFE, Women Entrepreneurs Homebased, Am. Soc. Interior Designers, Alpha Nu Omega. Home and Office: 101 Arsenal St Watertown MA 02172-2638

PERKINS, DOROTHY A., marketing professional; b. Weiser, Idaho, Aug. 13, 1926; d. Ross William and Josephine Stanford (Gwilliam) Anderson; m. Leonard Taylor Perkins, Nov. 16, 1948; children: Larry Taylor, Michael A., Drew A., Nancy. Grad. high sch., Boise, Idaho. Sec. Meadow Gold Dairies, Boise, 1944-46; sec. to supt. Idaho State Police, Boise, 1946-48, Idaho State Dept. Edn., Boise, 1952-56; sec. to maintenance engr. Idaho State Dept. Hwys., Boise, 1956-58; adminstrv. sec., asst. mgr. Casper (Wyo.) C. of C., 1962-72, exec. v.p., 1972-91; mktg. rep. World Wide Travel, Casper, 1991—. Mem. Wyo. Ho. of Reps., 1982—, chmn. house labor, health and social svcs. com., 1990—; found. bd. dirs., pres. Nat. Hist. Ctr., 1995. Mem. Wyo. C. of C. Execs. (sec.-treas. 1978-91, past pres.), Mountain States Assn. (bd. dirs. 1979-91, past pres.), Wyo. Hwy. Users Fedn. (bd. dirs. 1978—, pres. 1993—). Republican. Home: 1014 Surrey Ct Casper WY 82609-3270 Office: World Wide Travel PO Box 9370 Casper WY 82609-0370

PERKINS, ELIZABETH ANN, actress; b. Queens, N.Y., Nov. 18, 1960; d. James Perkins and Jo Milton. Grad., Goodman Theatre, Chgo., 1981. Films include: About Last Night, 1986, From the Hip, 1987, Sweet Hearts Dance, 1988, Big, 1988, Love at Large, 1990, Enid is Sleeping, 1990, Avalon, 1990, He Said/She Said, 1991, The Doctor, 1991, Indian Summer, 1993, The Flinstones, 1994, Miracle on 34th Street, 1994; TV film: For Their Own Good, 1992. Office: Creative Artists Agy 9830 Wilshire Blvd Beverly Hills CA 90212-1825*

PERKINS, GLADYS PATRICIA, retired aerospace engineer; b. Crenshaw, Miss., Oct. 30, 1921; d. Douglas and Zula Francis (Crenshaw) Franklin; m. Benjamin Franklin Walker, Sept. 26, 1952 (dec.); m. William Silas Perkins, Sept. 16, 1956 (dec.). BS in Math., Le Moyne Coll., 1943; postgrad., U. Mich., 1949, U. Calif., L.A., 1955-62. Mathematician Nat. Adv. Com. for Aeronatics (now NASA), Hampton, Va., 1944-49, Nat. Bur. of Standards, L.A., 1950-53, Aberdeen Bombing Mission, L.A., 1953-55; assoc. engr. Lockheed Missiles Systems Div., Van Nuys, Calif., 1955-57; staff engr. Hughes Aircraft Co., El Segundo, Calif., 1957-80; engring. specialist Rockwell Internat., Downey, Calif., 1980-87, ret., 1987. Contbr. articles to profl. publs. Named Alumnus of Yr. Le Moyne-Owen Coll., 1952; recipient Nat. Assn. for Equal Opportunity in Higher Edn. award Le Moyne-Owen Coll. Mem. Soc. of Women Engrs., Assn. of Computing Machinery, Le Moyne-Owen Alumni Assn. (pres. 1984), U. Mich. Alumni Club, Alpha Kappa Alpha. Democrat. Congregationalist. Home: 4001 W 22nd Pl Los Angeles CA 90018-1029

PERKINS, KARON ELAINE, lawyer; b. Lexington, Ky., Nov. 9, 1959; d. John Robert and Sharon Lynn (Cook) P. BA, Purdue U., 1980; cert. of proficiency, Pushkin Inst. Russian Lang., Moscow, 1980; JD, Ind. U., 1983. Bar: Ind. 1984, U.S. Dist. Ct. (so. dist.) Ind. 1984, U.S. Dist. Ct. (no. dist.) Ind. 1990. Internt. mktg. specialist Ind. Dept. Commerce, Indpls., 1980-81; law clk. Mendelson, Kennedy, Miller, Muller & Hall, Indpls., 1981-83; assoc. Jewell, Crump & Angermeier, Columbus, Ind., 1983-86; ptnr. Dalmbert, Marshall & Perkins, Columbus, 1986-92; pvt. practice Columbus, Ind., 1992—; asst. city atty. City of Columbus, 1985—; town atty. Town of Hope (Ind.), 1987-89; course coord. law for non lawyers Ind. U.-Purdue U., Columbus, 1985—; course coord. inst. law Sr. Citizen Ctr., Columbus, 1990; author, speaker continuing legal edn. seminar, 1988, 89, 90, 91, 92, 94; bd. dirs., sec. Bartholomew Area Legal Aid, 1984—. Mem. Leadership Bartholomew County, Columbus, 1986; bd. dirs. Salvation Army, Columbus, 1986-92, Columbus Dance Workshop; chmn. Bartholomew County Young Reps., 1986-88, 2d dist. Young Reps., 1987-91; treas. Columbus Task Force on Poor Relief, 1985-90. Recipient Outstanding Female Young Rep., Ind. Young Rep. Fedn., 1987, cert. of appreciation Ind. Tsk Force on Poor Relief, 1987; faculty alumni fellow Ind. U., 1983. Mem. ABA (del. young lawyers div. 1986-87), Ind. Bar Assn. (council, bd. dirs. young lawyers sect., sec.-treas., chair), Bartholomew Bar Assn. (sec., sec.-treas. 1984-90), Ind. Assn. Trial Lawyers, Columbus Jaycees (v.p. 1986, Outstanding New Mem. award 1985), Columbus Jaycees (bd. dirs. 1987), Zonta Club (parliamentarian Columbus 1986-88), Kiwanis. Baptist. Home: 15830 E Lakeshore Dr N Ct Hope IN 47246 Office: Ste 204 404 Washington St Columbus IN 47201

PERKINS, MARIE MCCONNELL, real estate executive; b. Mobile, Ala., June 26, 1938; d. Emanuel and Mary Thelma (Lyons) Andrews; m. Michael Reid Perkins, Jan. 23, 1993; children: Angela Denise McConnell Young, Robin McConnell Wade, Dana McConnell Scott. Grad. high sch., Mobile. Lic. real estate broker. Sales assoc. Roberts Bros. Inc., Mobile, 1974-78, broker assoc., 1978-79; real estate cons. Century 21 Regional Staff South, Mobile, 1979-80; broker, owner ERA Marie McConnell Realty, Inc., Mobile, 1980—, Baldwin County, Ala., 1989—; state dir. Relo-Inter-City Relocation, 1984—. Contbr. articles to mags., newspapers. Bd. dirs. Mobile Cystic Fibrosis Assn., 1987, Penelope House, 1990-94, 92 Cath. Social Svcs.; chmn., organizer Adopt-A-Family program, Mobile, 1984-94; mem. Regional Adv. Coun. for State of Ala., SBA, also chair Women in Bus. for State of Ala. Recipient Career Woman award Gayfers Career Club, Mobile, 1979, Small Bus. of Yr. award C. of C., 1989, Leadership award Scholarship Women's Coun. Realtors, 1993; named Sales Person of Yr., Am. Real Estate Inst., 1978, Broker of Yr., 1980, First Lady of Mobile, 1990. Mem. Nat. Assn. Realtors, Ala. Assn. Realtors (state dir. 1983-85, 88-90), Mobile County Bd. Realtors (bd. dirs., organizer Crime and Missing Children watches, staff instr., Realtor of Yr. 1983), Mobile and Baldwin County Assn. Realtors, Mobile Area C. of C. (exec. com., vice chmn. communication, chmn. Pride Involvement Coun. 1991-92, Small Bus. of Yr. 1989), Women's Coun. Bd. Realtors (Mobile chpt. pres. 1994), Mobile & Baldwin County Home Builder's Assn., Bienville Club. Republican. Baptist. Office: ERA Marie McConnell Realty Inc 824 Western American Dr Mobile AL 36609-4183

PERKINS, NANCY JANE, industrial designer; b. Phila., Nov. 5, 1949; d. Gordon Osborne and Martha Elizabeth (Keichline) P. Student, Ohio U., 1967-68; BFA, U. Ill., 1972. Indsl. designer Peterson Bednar Assocs., Evanston, Ill., 1972-74, Deschamps Mills Assos., Bartlett, Ill., 1974-75; dir. graphic design Cameo Container Corp., Chgo., 1975-76; indsl. design cons. Sears Roebuck & Co., Chgo., 1977-88; cons. indsl. design, 1988—; founder Perkins Design Ltd., Anna Wagner Keichline Gallery, Bellefonte, Pa.; adj. prof. grad. design seminar U. Ill. Chgo., 1982, 88, 91, 93, adj. instr. undergrad. design, 1984, 88, 91, 93; adj. instr. Ill. Inst. Tech., 1987, 91; vis. assoc. prof. Carnegie-Mellon U., 1991; juror annual design rev. Indsl. Design mag., 1986; mem. tech. rev. com. Ben Franklin Partnerships, 1991—; keynote speaker several major U.S. design groups; speaker Design in Am. symposium, Nagoya, Japan, 1989. Contbr. articles to profl. jours.; patentee marine, automotive and consumer products. Co-leader Cadette troop DuPage County coun. Girl Scouts U.S., 1978-79. Recipient Outstanding Alumni award U. Ill. Alumni Jour., 1981, Goldsmith award, 1992; profiled in Indsl. Design mag., 1986, Feminine Ingenuity (by Anne L. Macdonald), 1992, Dun & Bradstreet Reports, 1993; featured in Chgo. Atheneaum "33 plus 20", 1993, Pratt Manhattan Gallery, N.Y.C., 1994. Fellow Indsl. Designers Soc. Am. (treas. Chgo. chpt. 1977-79, vice chmn. 1979-80, chmn. 1981, mem. dist. membership com. 1982, mem. ann. conf. com. 1983, mem. publs. com. 1985-86, dir.-at-large 1987-88, v.p. Midwest dist. 1989-90, nat. sec.-treas. 1991-92, del. Internat. Coun. of the Socs. Indsl. Design 1989, speaker Mideast Conf.). Home and Office: Perkins Design Ltd 111 W Maple St #1002 Chicago IL 60610

PERKINS, NINA ROSALIE, social worker; b. Huntington, W.Va., July 17, 1953; d. Lloyd William and Violet Macil (Elkins) Fowler; m. Homer Chester Bartoe, Jan. 30, 1972 (div. Dec. 1979); m. Gary Michael Lovejoy, Aug. 9, 1982 (div. Mar. 1989); m. Raymond Wesley Perkins, Apr. 14, 1989 (div. Nov. 1989); 1 child, Homer David. BSW, Marshall U., 1982; postgrad., W.Va. U., 1989, 91, 94; 1988-90. Lic. social worker, W.Va.; cert. personal care provider. Child care worker Charles W. Cammack Children's Ctr., Huntington, 1983-84; ins. underwriter Mut. of Omaha, Shreveport, La., 1984-86; banquet mgr. Ramada Inn, Shreveport, 1986-87; ctr. coord. Cabell County Community Svcs. Orgn., Inc., Huntington, 1987-90, case mgr. sr. svcs., 1990-92; minority AIDS program coord. W.Va. Dept. Health, Charleston, 1988-90, cons. instr., 1990-92; social worker Marshall U. Sch. Medicine, Frank E. Hanshaw Geriatric Ctr., Huntington, 1990—; owner, adminstr. Sr. Care Mgmt. Svcs., Huntington, W.Va., 1991-92; dir. social svcs. Wayne Continuous Care Ctr., 1992—; charter mem. Cabell County Com. for Drug Info., Huntington, 1990—; mem. Huntington Area AIDS Task Force, 1988—; social work cons. for Region 2, Area Agy. on Aging Adv. Com.; cons. and guest lectr., 1991—. Mem. Dem. Women's Club, Cabell County. Recipient Cert. for Concerned Citizenship, State of W.Va., 1982. Mem. Am. Mgmt. Assn., W.Va. Assn. Dirs. Sr. Programs, NAFE, Internat. Plaform Assn. Democrat. Baptist. Office: Frank Hanshaw Geriatric Ctr 2900 1st Ave Huntington WV 25702-1271

PERKINS, SUE DENE, journalism educator; b. Wichita Falls, Tex., Jan. 12, 1946; d. Darrye Clayton and Josephine Marie (Hall) P. BA, North Tex. State U., 1968; MA, Stephen F. Austin State U., 1980; postgrad., Angelo State U., 1979. Cert. tchr., Tex. Mag. editor Haire Pubs., N.Y.C., 1968-69; women's editor Arlington (Tex.) Daily News, 1970, police reporter editor, 1972; mag. editor Tex. Assn. Bus., Houston, 1972-74; editor in ho. pubs. P.R. Am. Assn. Respiratory Therapy, Dallas, 1974-76; asst. employee pub. rels. Gen. Telephone, San Angelo, 1976-79; dir. student publs. Stephen F. Austin State U., Nacogdoches, Tex., 1980-83, founder Women in Comm. chpt., 1982; instr. journalism Tex. A&M Univ., College Station, 1983-84; owner photo supply Photo-Graphics Co., Lufkin, Tex., 1985-88; adv. student pubs. Diboll (Tex.) Ind. Sch. Dist., 1987—; computer cons. Deep East Tex. Coun. Govt., Lufkin, 1990, Region VII Edn. Svc. Ctr., Kilgore, Tex., 1994. Editor: (mags.) Handbags & Accessories, 1968-69, Tex. Industry, 1972-74, (newspaper) Arlington Daily News, 1970-72, (newsletter) Am. Assn. for Respiratory Therapy Bull., 1974-76. Pres. Wheeler Cemetery Assn., Corrigan, Tex., 1992, v.p., 1993; sec. Youth for Christ, Diboll, Tex., 1993—. Named Outstanding Ex-Student Electra (Tex.) Alumni Assn., 1981-82. Mem. Journalism Educators Am., Tex. Journalism Edn. Assn., Tex. Classroom Tchrs.Assn., Order Ea. Star. Baptist. Home: Rt 1 Box 106 Corrigan TX 75939 Office: Diboll Ind Sch Dist 1000 E Harris Diboll TX 75941

PERKINS-CARPENTER, BETTY LOU, fitness company executive; b. Rochester N.Y., Jan. 22, 1931; d. Edward C. and Bertha M. (Loeser) Kalmn; m. Floyd F. Perkins, Jan. 31, 1951 (div. 1979); children: Cheryl Lee, F. Scott; m. Marcellus Chipman Carpenter, Oct. 10, 1981. BS in Phys. Edn. Adminstrn., Empire State Coll., N.Y., 1979; MS in Early Childhood Edn. Adminstrn., Nova U., 1983; cert. in Gerontology, St. John Fisher Coll., 1992. Tchr., coach Rochester YWCA, 1954-59, Perkins Swimming Sch., Penfield, N.Y., 1959-64; pres. Perkins Swim Club, Inc., Rochester, 1964—, Lic. Corp. Fit By Five, Inc., Rochester, 1969—, Child Fitness Prodns., Inc. d/b/a Sr. Fitness Prodns., Rochester, 1983—, Penfield Fit By Five, Rochester, 1984—; diving coach Olympic Games, Montreal, 1976; mem. adv. com. N.Y. State Task Force Phys. Fitness and Sports, 1978-82; bd. dirs. U.S. Olympic Diving Com., 1976-80, The Wesley Group; cons. European sports facilities, 1969-83, Pres.'s Council on Phys. Fitness and Sports, 1986-89; mem. adv. com. Community Savs. Bank, Rochester, 1976-79; mem. adv. bd. O.A.S.I.S.; exercise cons. U. Rochester Pepper Study, 1992—. Author: The Fun of Fitness-A Handbook for the Senior Class, 1988, How to Prevent Falls-Introducing the Balance System, 1989; Am. editor: Teaching Babies to Swim, 1979; contbr. articles to profl. jours. Exec. producer audio-visual instructional materials. Vice-chmn., bd. dirs. Regional Coun. on Aging; judge Athena Awards. Served with USAF, 1948-51. Recipient Gold medal Inst. Achievement of Human Potential, Brazil, 1973, Mike Malone Meml. Diving award, 1977, Cady Diving award, 1977, Honor award ARC, 1991; named to Monroe County Athletes Hall of Fame, Rochester, 1979; named Sports Woman of Yr., U.S. Olympic Diving Commn., 1979, Citizen of Yr., Rotary, 1988, Healthy Am. fitness Leader, Rochester Small Bus. Person of Yr., 1990. Mem. U.S. Diving Assn. (life, numerous offices), Rochester Assn. Edn. of Young Children, Nova U. Alumnae Assn., Oak Hill Country Club, Order Eastern Star (life), Sigma Phi Omega (mem. Alpha Lambda chpt.). Republican. Avocations: swimming, cross-country skiing, reading, travel. Office: Fit By Five Inc 1606 Penfield Rd Rochester NY 14625-2394

PERKINSON, DIANA AGNES ZOUZELKA, import company executive; b. Prostejov, Czechoslovakia, June 27, 1943; came to U.S., 1962; d. John Charles and Agnes Diana (Sincl) Zouzelka; m. David Francis Perkinson, Mar. 6, 1965; children: Dana Leissa, David. BA, U. Lausanne (Switzerland), 1960; MA, U. Madrid, 1961; MBA, Case Western Res. U., 1963; cert. internat. mktg. Oxford (Eng.) U., 1962. Assoc. Allen Hartman & Schreiber, Cleve., 1963-64; interpreter Tower Internat. Inc., Cleve., 1964-66; pres. Oriental Rug Importers Ltd., Cleve., 1979—; pres. Oriental Rug Designers, Inc., Cleve., 1980—; pres. Oriental Rug Cons., Inc., Cleve., 1980—; chmn. Foxworthy's Inc., Ft. Myers, Naples, Sanibel, Fla.; bd. dir. Beckwith & Assocs., Inc., Cleve., Secura Inc., Dallas, Dix-Bur Investments, Ltd., Real Estate By Design. Trustee, Cleve. Ballet, 1979, exec. com., 1981; mem. Cleve. Mayor's Adv. Com.; trustee Diabetes Assn. Greater Cleve.; mem., chmn. grantsmanship Jr. League of Cleve., 1982; mem. mem. Cleve. Found.-Women in Philanthropy, 1982; trustee Ft. Myers Symphony, 1990. Mem. Women Bus. Owners Assn., Oriental Rug Retailers Am. (bd. dir. 1983), Cleve. Racquet Club, Recreation League, The League Club (Naples, Fla.), Hillbrook Club, Univ. Club (Ft. Myers, Fla.), Captiva Yacht Club. Republican. Roman Catholic. Home: Ravencrest PO Box 477 Sanibel FL 33957-0477 Office: Oriental Rug Importers Ltd Inc 2430 Periwinkle Way Sanibel FL 33957-3207 also: 17001 Captiva Rd Captiva Island FL 33924

PERLESS, ELLEN, advertising executive; b. N.Y.C., Sept. 9, 1941; d. Joseph B. and Bertha (Messinger) Kaplan; m. Robert L. Perless, July 2, 1965. Student, Smith Coll., 1958-59, Bard Coll., 1959-62. Copywriter Doyle, Dane Bernbach, N.Y.C., 1964-70, Young & Rubicam, N.Y.C., 1970-74; creative supr. Young & Rubicam, 1974-76, v.p., creative supr., 1977, v.p., assoc, creative dir., 1978, sr. v.p., assoc. creative dir., 1979-84; v.p., assoc. creative dir. Leber Katz Ptnrs., 1984-85, sr. v.p., creative dir., 1986-87; sr. v.p., sr. creative dir. FCB/Leber Katz Ptnrs., N.Y.C., 1987-93, sr. v.p., group creative dir., 1994—. Recipient Clio awards, Andy awards, awards Art Dirs. Club N.Y., N.Y. Festivals. Mem. One Club for Art and Copy (awards), N.E. Harbor Fleet Marine Club. Home: 37 Langhorne Ln Greenwich CT 06831-2611 Office: FCB/Leber Katz Ptnrs 767 5th Ave New York NY 10153-0001

PERLMAN, SANDRA LEE, playwright, consultant; b. Phila., June 18, 1944; d. Sidney Henry and Betty (Lee) P.; m. Henry Lewis Halem, Sept. 10, 1969; 1 child, Jessica Ariel. BA, Am. U., 1966. Actress st. theatre Soc. Hill Theatre/Phila. Recreation, 1968; rsch. editor Prof. Harvey Littleton, Madison, Wis., 1968-69; speech and advt. writer Sta. WMTV-Channel 15, Madison, 1969; English tchr. Garfield High Sch., Akron, Ohio, 1969-72; producer, writer PBS Channels 45/49, Kent, Ohio, 1975-81; communications cons. Halem Studios, Inc., Kent, 1981—; chmn. bd. Halem Studios, Kent, 1988—; promotions dir. Stas. NPR/WKSU-FM, Kent, 1985-87; playwright in residence Cleve. State U., 1993—; playwright, dir. Massillon (Ohio) Mus., 1988-89. Editor: Glassblowing: A Search for Form, 1968. Bd. dirs. Bicentennial Commn., Kent, 1976, Kent Hist. Soc., 1977-87. Ohio Arts Coun. fellow, 1983, 86, Ohio Arts Coun./OHC Joint Program fellow 1989. Mem. Ohio Theatre Alliance (bd. dirs., playwriting chair), Dramatists Guild , Ohio Arts Coun. (new works panel 1987-89), First Internat. Women Playwrights Conf. (ops. dir. 1988). Home and Office: Halem Studios Inc 429 Carthage Ave Kent OH 44240-2303

PERLMAN, SUSAN GAIL, organization executive; b. N.Y.C., Dec. 29, 1950; d. Philip and Pearl Perlman; ed. Hunter Coll., N.Y.C., 1967-71. Copywriter, Blaine Thompson Advt., N.Y.C., 1968-71; copywriter J.C. Penney Co., N.Y.C., 1971-72; assoc. exec. dir. Jews for Jesus, San Francisco, 1972—, bd. dirs., also editor Issues mag.; speaker, cons. in field; steering com. mem. Lausanne Consultation on Jewish Evangelism, Copenhagen, Denmark; del. Bapt. Gen. Conf.; mem. Lausanne Com. for World Evangelization, Oxford, Eng. Mem. editorial bd. Evang. Missions Quar. Mem. Am. Jewish Congress, Interdenominational Fgn. Missions Assn. (mem. exec. com.). Democrat. Baptist. Office: 60 Haight St San Francisco CA 94102-5802

PERLMUTTER, BARBARA S., public relations executive; b. Hartford, Conn., Oct. 7, 1941; d. Leon and Ethel (Zinman) Sondik; m. Louis Perlmutter, Dec. 11, 1966; children: Kermit, Eric. BA, Smith Coll., 1963; MA in History, Columbia U., 1965; MBA, NYU, 1979. Analyst Celanese Internat. Co., N.Y.C., 1965-69; sr. econ. analyst Nat. Econ. Rsch. Assoc., White Plains, N.Y., 1979-85; dir. pub. affairs Marsh & McLennan Companies, Inc., N.Y.C., 1985-88, v.p. pub. affairs, 1988—. Office: Marsh & McLennan Companies 1166 Ave of The Americas New York NY 10036-2774

PERLMUTTER, DIANE F., communications executive; b. N.Y.C., Aug. 31, 1945; d. Bert H. and Frances (Smith) P. Student, NYU Grad. Sch. of Bus., 1969-70; AB in English, Miami U., Oxford, Ohio, 1967. Writer sales promotion Equitable Life Assurance, N.Y.C., 1967-68; adminstrv. asst. de Garmo, Inc., N.Y.C., 1968-69, asst. account exec., 1969-70, account exec., 1970-74, v.p., account supr., 1974-76; mgr. corp. advt. Avon Products, Inc., N.Y.C., 1976-79, dir. communications Latin Am., Spain, Can., 1979-80, dir. brochures, 1980-81, dir. category merchandising, 1981-82, group dir. motivational communications, 1982-83, group dir. sales promotion, 1983-84, v.p. sales promotion, 1984, v.p. internat. bus. devel., 1984-85, area v.p. Latin Am., 1985, v.p. advtg. and campaign mktg., 1985-87, v.p. U.S. operational planning, 1987; cons. N.Y.C., 1987-88; sr. v.p. Burson-Marsteller, N.Y.C., 1988-90, exec. v.p., mng. dir. consumer products, 1991-93, bd. dirs., 1992—, co-chief operating officer, 1993-94, chief operating officer, 1994—; chairperson ann. meeting Direct Selling Assn., Washington, 1982; v.p. Nat. Home Fashions League, N.Y.C., 1975-76; adj. instr. SUNY/Fashion Inst. Tech., 1992—; bd. dirs. Double L.P. Industries, Inc. Founding bd. mem. Am. Red Magen David for Israel, N.Y.C., 1970-75; mem. adv. coun. Miami Sch. Bus., 1986—, Miami Sch. Applied Scis., 1978-81. Mem. Pub. Rels. Soc. Am., Advt. Women of N.Y., Women in Communications, Miami U. Alumni Assn. (pres., chair 1986), Publicity Club N.Y. (bd. dirs. 1994—), Beta Gamma Sigma. Office: Burson-Marsteller 230 Park Ave S New York NY 10003-1513

PERLMUTTER, DONNA, music and dance critic; b. Phila.; d. Myer and Bessie (Krasno) Stein; m. Jona Perlmutter, Mar. 21, 1964; children: Aaron, Matthew. BA, Pa. State U., 1958; MS, Yeshiva U., 1959. Music and dance critic L.A. Herald Examiner, 1975-84, L.A. Times, 1984—; dance critic Dance Mag., N.Y.C., 1980—; music critic Opera News, N.Y.C., 1981—, Ovation Mag., N.Y.C., 1983-89; panelist, speaker various music and dance orgns. Author Shadowplay: The Life of Antony Tudor, 1991. Recipient Deems Taylor award for excellence in writing on music ASCAP, 1991. Mem. Music Critics Assn. Home: 10507 Le Conte Ave Los Angeles CA 90024-3305

PERLOFF, MARJORIE GABRIELLE, English and comparative literature educator; b. Vienna, Austria, Sept. 28, 1931; d. Maximilian and Ilse (Schueller) Mintz; m. Joseph K. Perloff, July 31, 1953; children—Nancy Lynn, Carey Elizabeth. A.B., Barnard Coll., 1953; M.A., Cath. U., 1956, Ph.D., 1965. Asst. prof. English and comparative lit. Cath. U., Washington, 1966-68; asso. prof. Cath. U., 1969-71; asso. prof. U. Md., 1971-73, prof., 1973-76; Florence R. Scott prof. English U. So. Calif., Los Angeles, 1976—; prof. English and comparative lit. Stanford U., Calif., 1986—, Sadie Dernham prof. humanities, 1990—. Author: Rhyme and Meaning in the Poetry of Yeats, 1970, The Poetic Art of Robert Lowell, 1973, Frank O'Hara, Poet Among Painters, 1977, The Poetics of Indeterminacy; Rimbaud to Cage, 1981, The Dance of the Intellect: Studies in the Poetry of the Pound Tradition, 1985, The Futurist Moment: Avant-Garde, Avant-Guerre and the Language of Rupture, 1986, Poetic License: Essays in Modern and Postmodern Lyric, 1990, Radical Artifice: Writing Poetry in the Age of Media, 1991; editor: Postmodern Genres, 1990; co-editor: John Cage: Composed in America, 1994; contbg. editor: Columbia Literary History of the U.S., 1987; contbr. preface to Contemporary Poets, 1980; A John Cage Reader, 1983. Guggenheim fellow, 1981-82, NEA fellow, 1985; Phi Beta Kappa scholar, 1994-95. Mem. MLA (exec. coun. 1977-81, Am. lit. sect. 1993—), Comparative Lit. Assn. (pres. 1993-94), Lit. Studies Acad. Home: 1467 Amalfi Dr Pacific Palisades CA 90272-2752 Office: Stanford U Dept English Stanford CA 94305

PERLOWITZ, VALERIE WIENSLAW, information systems executive, consultant; b. Queens, N.Y., Feb. 10, 1962; d. Arthur Eugene and Natalia (Pasichnyk) Wienslaw; m. William Bryan Perlowitz, July 25, 1987. BSEE in Elec. Engring./Computer Engring., Northeastern U., 1986. Cert. engr.-in-tng., Mass. Simulation engr. Sikorsky Aircraft, Stratford, Conn., 1986-87; engr. Bite, Inc., Manassas, Va., 1987-88; cons. Aerotek, Inc., Reston, Va., 1988-89, Comsys, Inc., Rockville, Md., 1989; pres. Reliable Integration Svcs., Inc., Fairfax, Va., 1989—. Apptd. to Opportunity Va. Commn., Commonwealth of Va. Mem. IEEE, Computer Soc. of IEEE, NAFE, Network of Entrepreneurial Women, Women in Tech., Inc. (co-founder, pres.), No. Va. Tech. Coun., Art Deco Soc. of Wash., Fairfax C. of C. (Leadership Fairfax Class 1991), George Mason Incubator Program. Office: Reliable Integration Svcs 2214 Rock Hill Rd Ste 300 Herndon VA 22070-4005

PEROTTI, ROSE NORMA, lawyer; b. St. Louis, Aug. 10, 1930; d. Joseph and Dorothy Mary (Roleski) Perotti. B.A., Fontbonne Coll., St. Louis, 1952; J.D., St. Louis U., 1957. Bar: Mo. 1958. Trademark atty. Sutherland, Polster & Taylor, St. Louis, 1958-63, Sutherland Law Office, 1964-70; trademark atty. Monsanto Co., St. Louis, 1971-85, sr. trademark atty., 1985-91, assoc. trademark counsel, 1991-94, trademark counsel, 1994—. Honored with dedication of faculty office in her name, St. Louis U. Sch. Law, 1980. Mem. Mo. Bar Assn., Bar Assn. Met. St. Louis, ABA, Am. Judicature Soc., Smithsonian Assocs., Friends St. Louis Art Museum, Mo. Bot. Garden.

PERREAULT, ALISON MARIE, artist; b. Rochester, N.Y., July 16, 1963; d. Bernard Nicholas Perreault and Angela Theresa Stipo. Student, Rochester Inst. Tech., 1982-85; BFA with distinction, Calif. Coll. Arts and Crafts, 1988. art instr. Hayward (Calif.) Adult Edn., Laurel Ctr., 1987-88, MiraCosta Coll., Palomar Coll., 1990-94; exhbn. awards juror Olde Ramona Hotel Gallery, 1990, 93; freelance illustrator designer. One-woman shows include Kruglak Gallery, Mira Costa Coll., Oceanside, Cafli., 1992, Hyde Gallery, Grossmont Coll., San Diego, 1994, Union Gallery U. Utah, 1994; exhibited in group shows at Isabel Percy West Gallery, Calif. Coll. Arts and Crafts, Oakland, 1988, The Art Gallery, San Francisco, 1988, Oceanside Civic Ctr. Opening Competition, Oceanside, 1990, MiraCosta Coll., Oceanside, 1993, Cypress Coll. Invitational, Cypress, Calif., 1993; juried exhbns. include San Diego Art Inst. Gallery, 1990, Coal Army-Navy Acad. Show, Carlsbad, Calif., 1990, Calif. Mus. Art, Santa Rosa, 1991, San Diego Art Inst. Awards Show, 1992, South Fair, Del Mar, Calif., 1993. Mem. Chgo. Arts Coalition, Nat. Artists Equity Assn., Artists Equity Assn. (pres. San Diego chpt. 1993, v.p. 1992), Bowling Gorilla Artists Group. Home and Office: PO Box 520995 Salt Lake City UT 84152-0995

PERRETT, RHONDA ALLISON, elementary school educator; b. Miami Beach, Fla., Apr. 13, 1961; d. Carlton and Betty (Schachter) Fredericks; m. William Montague Perrett IV, Nov. 3, 1984. BS in Speech Comm., No. Mich. U., 1984; postgrad., Mt. St. Mary U., 1995. New patient educator Mountainview Med., West Nyack, N.Y., 1985-86; med. office mgr. Dr. Zack Zepher, New City, N.Y., 1986-87, Dr. H. K. Chaudhry, Montgomery, N.Y., 1989-92; spl. edn. para-profl. Valley Ctrl. Schs., Walden, N.Y., 1992—; media mail cons. Dr. Ronald Hoffman, N.Y.C., 1991—. Mem. Kappa Delta Pi, Delta Zeta. Republican. Jewish. Home: 89 Borden Rd Walden NY 12586

PERRIN, GAIL, editor; b. Boston, Oct. 14, 1938; d. Hugh and Helen (Baxter) P. B.A., Wellesley Coll., 1960. Copy girl Washington Daily News, summers, 1954-57, reporter, 1958, 60-61, acting women's editor, food editor, 1961-62, rewrite reporter, 1963-65; reporter Honolulu Star Bull., 1959; women's editor Boston Globe, 1965-71, asst. met. editor, 1971-74, food editor, 1974-92; food cons., free-lance writer, 1992—. Mem. Assn. Food Journalists, Women's Culinary Guild.

PERRIN, JANICE HELEN DAVIS, special education educator; b. Port Arthur, Tex.; d. Albert Otho and Helen (Anderson) Davis. BS in Early Childhood Edn./Reading, U. So. Miss., 1978; M. Elem. Edn., Mansfield U., 1987, spl. edn. K-12 cert., 1987, reading specialist cert., 1987. Cert. reading elem., early childhood and spl. edn., Pa., N.Y., early childhood edn., MS, W.Va., Mo, reading, elem. edn., Mo. Adult basic edn./GED tchr. JTPA, Mansfield (Pa.) U.; remedial reading and math. tchr. Columbia (Miss.) Pub. Schs., 1979-81; remedial reading tchr. Sikeston R-6 Sch., Morehouse, Mo., 1978-79; optional I spl. edn. tchr. Corning Painted Post Sch. Dist., Painted Post, N.Y., 1985-86, 88-89; optional IV spl. edn. tchr. Bur. of Coop. Ednl. Svcs., Williamsport, Pa., 1989-90; tchr. Apalachin (N.Y.) Alternative Learning Program Broome-Deware-Tioga Bur. Coop. Ednl. Svcs., 1991, 92-93; opt. II tchr. Bur. Coop. Ednl. Svcs.-Broome-Tioga Chenago Forks Sch. Dist., Binghamton, N.Y., 1992—; presenter on children's safety issues. Mem. N.Y. State U. Tchrs., Am. Fedn. Tchrs., Internat. Student Affairs (past pres., v.p.), Order of Rainbow for Girls (past worth advisor). Home: 33 Lori Dr Apalachin NY 13732

PERRIN, SARAH ANN, lawyer; b. Neoga, Ill., Dec. 13, 1904; d. James Lee and Bertha Frances (Baker) Figenbaum; m. James Frank Perrin, Dec. 24, 1926. LLB, George Washington U., 1941, JD, 1964. Bar: D.C. 1942. Assoc. atty. Mabel Walker Willebrandt, law office, Washington, 1941-42; atty. various fed. housing agys., 1942-69, asst. gen. counsel FHA, Washington, 1959-60, asst. gen. counsel HUD, Washington, 1960-69; sec. Nat. Housing Conf., Washington, 1970-80; rsch. cons. housing and urban devel., Palmyra, Va., 1970-76; acting sec. Nat. Housing Rsch. Coun., Washington, 1973-80; bd. dirs. Nat. Housing Conf., 1972—. Mem. Rep. Presdl. Adv. Commn., 1991-92; trustee Found. for Coop. Housing, 1975-80; mem. Blue Ridge Presbytery Div. Mission, Presbyn. Ch., 1979-80, Friends of Fluvanna County Libr. Mem. ABA, Fed. Bar Assn., Women's Bar Assn. D.C. (pres. 1959-60), Nat. Assn. Women Lawyers, George Washington Law Assn., Charlottesville Area Women's Bar Assn., Fluvanna County Bar Assn., Fluvanna County Hist. Soc. (pres. 1973-75, exec. com. 1985-89), Order Eastern Star, Presbyn. Women (pres. Fork Union chpt. 1972-80, sec. 1980-94), Phi Alpha Delta (internat. pres. 1955-57, internat. adv. bd.). Home: Solitude Plantation Palmyra VA 22963

PERRIS, ELIZABETH L., federal judge; b. 1951. AB, U. Calif., 1972; JD, U. Calif., Davis, 1975. Admitted to bar, 1976. Bankruptcy judge U.S. Dist. Ct. Oreg., 1984—. Office: US Dist Ct 900 Security Pacific Plz 1001 SW 5th Ave Portland OR 97204-1118*

PERRONE, RUTH ELLYN, university administrator; b. Hearne, Tex., July 2, 1951; d. John Paul Perrone and Ellen Gayle (Sullivan) Perrone-Robertson. BS, Stephen F. Austin State U., 1973; MPA, Tex. A&M U., 1986. Social worker Tex. Dept. Pub. Welfare, Nacogdoches, Tex., 1974-76; licensing rep. Tex. Dept. Human Resources, Bryan, 1976-85; spl. asst. to vice chancellor for state affairs Tex. A&M Univ. System, Austin, 1987-90; asst. to pres. Tex. A&M U., College Station, 1990-92, dir. external rels., 1992—; advisor legis. study group Tex. A&M U., 1992—. Chair governing bd. John Ben Shepperd Pub. Leadership Found., Odessa, Tex., 1993-94; bd. dirs. Tex. Lyceum, Austin, 1992—; assoc. mem. St. Joseph Hosp. Aux., Bryan, 1993—. Mem. Nat. Assn. State Univ. and Land Grant Coll. (coun. on govtl. affairs), Coun. for Advancement and Support of Edn., Bryan/College Station C. of C. (coun. on govtl. affairs). Office: Texas A&M University Office of President 805 Rudder Tower College Station TX 77843

PERROW, CECELIA ROTON, history educator; b. Texarkana, Ark., Jan. 25, 1945; d. William F. and M. Louise (Mashaw) Roton; m. Michael P. Perrow, Aug. 26, 1967; children: Kristin Laura, Karen Perrow McMains. BA, Coll. of William and Mary, 1967; MA, U. N.Mex., 1979; PhD in History, No. Ariz. U., 1994. Tchr. Duxbury (Mass.) H.S., 1967-68; Peace Corps vol. Nyanchwa Sec. Sch., Kisii, Kenya, 1969-70; tchr. N.Mex. State U., Grants, 1973-91, prof. history, 1991—, coord. Adult Learning Ctr., 1984, coord. acad. studies, 1986-90; chmn. Resource Ctr., Inc., Grants, 1985-88. Voter registrar Cibola County, N.Mex., 1984—. Fulbright scholar, Amsterdam, The Netherlands, 1988, internat. scholar Delta Kappa Gamma, 1992-93. Mem. Western Polit. Sci. Assn., Phi Beta Kappa.

PERRY, ANDREA SUSAN, information systems specialist; b. Miami, Fla., Sept. 21, 1962; d. David Livingstone and Florence May (Brinkmann) P. BS, M in Info. Scis., Fla. State U., 1984. Bus. assoc. Electronic Data Systems, Tallahasse, Fla., 1984-85; systems engr. Electronic Data Systems, Dallas, 1985-87, systems supr., 1987-92; implementation mgr. Electronic Data Systems, Providence, 1992-93, dep. account mgr., 1993—; mentor for leadership trainees Electronic Data Systems, Dallas, 1991-93. Server Ministries for the Homeless, Dallas, 1990-91. Mem. Health Ins. Assn. Am. Avocation: Republican. Office: Electronic Data Systems 1471 Elmwood Ave Cranston RI 02910

PERRY, BLANCHE BELLE, physical therapist; b. New Bedford, Mass., Sept. 2, 1929; d. Joseph Rudolph and Beatrice (Faria) Andrews; BS, Ithaca (N.Y.) Coll., 1951; MA, Assumption Coll., Worcester, Mass., 1978; m. Louis Perry, Nov. 26, 1953; (dec. 1980); children: Marcia, Susan, Tracey, Evelyn. Office and hosp. phys. therapist, Mass. and N.Y., 1961-65; dir. rehab. svcs. St. Luke's Hosp., New Bedford, 1967-89; ret, 1989; profl. adv. com. Vis. Nurse Assn. Wareham, 1980; mem. faculty continuing edn. Newbury Coll., 1986; corporator New Bedford Five Cents Savs. Bank, Compass Bank for Savs. Chmn. Mattapoisett Sch. Com., 1970; vice chmn. Mass. Sch. Commn. Area IV, 1972-75; sec. Old Colony Regional Vocat. Sch. Com., 1973—; trustee Abner Pease Scholarship Found.; chmn. com. opportunity ctr. CARF, New Bedford, 1987. Grantee Elks Nat. Found., 1965. Mem. Am. Phys. Therapy Assn., Nat. Rehab. Adminstrs. Assn., Delta Kappa Gamma. Republican. Club: Mattapoisett Women's. Home: 41 Aucoot Rd Mattapoisett MA 02739-2401

PERRY, BRENDA L., college administrator; b. New Bedford, Mass., Nov. 8, 1948; d. Frank Andrade and Mary Mendes; m. Clyde L. Perry, Jan. 18, 1965; children: Lisa Marie, Scott Anthony. AA, Middlesex Community Coll., Bedford, Mass., 1975; MA, Goddard Coll., 1977; BA, Stonehill Coll., 1981. Cert. alcohol and drug addiction counselor. Social worker Dorchester Child Devel. Ctr., Boston, 1971-75; coord. Mass. Advocacy Ctr., Boston, 1975-76; asst. dir. Roxbury Multi Svcs. Girls Residential Treatment Ctr., Boston, 1976-78, Commonwealth of Mass. Female Svcs. Dept Youth, Boston, 1978-81; monitor evaluator Commonwealth of Mass. Dept. Social Svc., Boston, 1981-83; asst. dir. admissions Rollins Coll., Winter Park, Fla., 1983—. Poetry pub. in 1988 Anthology of Poems, Am. Poetry Assn. Bd. dirs. Seminole County Mental Health Assn., Altamonte Springs, Fla., 1983-85. Mem. Nat. Assn. of Wildlife Fedn., Smithsonian Inst., Nat. Arbor Day Found., Nat. Assn. of Black Sch. Educators, Nat. Assn. Coll. Admission Counselors, Nat. Assn. Fgn. Students, So. Assn. Coll. Admission Counselors. Democrat. Mem. Theosophical Soc. Home: 810 S Riverside Dr New Smyrna Beach FL 32168-7448 Office: Rollins Coll Holt Ave Winter Park FL 32789

PERRY, CATHERINE D., judge; b. 1952. BA, Univ. of Okla., 1977; JS, Wash. Univ. Sch. of Law, 1980. Sec., law clk. Gillespie, Perry & Gentry, Sentinel, Okla., 1970, 77-78; with Armstrong, Teasdale, Kramer & Vaughn, St. Louis, 1980-90; magistrate judge U.S. Dist. Ct. (Mo. ea. dist.), 8th circuit, St. Louis, 1990-94, district judge, 1994—. Mem. Fed. Magistrate Judges Assn., Nat. Assn. of Women Judges, Am. Bar Assn., Mo. Bar Assn., Bar Assn. of Metropolitan St. Louis, Women Lawyers Assn. of Greater St. Louis. Office: US Courthouse 1114 Market St Rm 840 Saint Louis MO 63101-2043*

PERRY, CYNTHIA NORTON SHEPARD, diplomat; b. Terre Haute, Ind., Nov. 11, 1928; d. George William and Flossie (Phillips) N.; m. James O. Shepard, Nov. 2, 1946 (div. June 1970); children: Donna Ross, James O. Jr., Milo Kent, Mark; m. James O. Perry, Mar. 20, 1971; children: Paula

Lucille, James O. Jr. BS in Polit. Sci., Ind. State U., 1967, DCL (hon.), 1987; EdD, U. Mass., 1972; LLD (hon.), U. Md., 1984, Coppin State Coll., 1991; LHD (hon.), Chatham Coll., 1988; D of Pub. Svc., U. Mass., 1989. Sec. Nichols Investment Corp., Terre Haute, 1956-61; ednl. rep. Ohio region IBM Corp., Terre Haute, 1962-68; dir. tchrs. corps U. Mass., Amherst, 1968-71; assoc. prof. edn. Tex. So. U., Houston, 1971-74, dean internat. student affairs, 1978-82; cons., lectr., U. Nairobi U.S. Peace Corps, Kenya, 1974-76; staff devel. officer UN Econ. Com. for Africa, Addis Ababa, Ethiopia, 1976-78; chief edn. and human resources div. AID, Washington, 1982-86; amb. to Sierra Leone, Am. Embassy, Freetown, 1986-89; amb. to Burundi, Am. Embassy, Bujumbura, 1989-93. Contbr. articles to profl. jours. Bd. dirs. Inst. for Internat. Edn. Bd. Bols., 1984, World Affairs Coun., 1984, Houston Internat. Festival, 1994, Houston Model UN, 1994, Nat. Coun. for Internat. Vis., 1994; mem. Houston Commn. on Fgn. Rels., 1984, Houston Consular Corps, 1984, Greater Houston Partnership, 1993-94; diplomat in residence Furr H.S., 1993-94. Recipient Disting. Alumni award U. Mass., 1981, Ind. State U., 1987, Exceptional Diplomacy award U. Burundi, Ctrl. Africa, 1993, Superior Honor award U.S. Dept. State, 1993, Hon. Consul Republic of Senegal, 1994. Mem. Praeclarus, Nat. Bus. and Profl. Women, Internat. Coun. for Ednl. Devel. (bd. dirs. 1984-86), Altrusan Soc. (bd. dirs. 1981-82), Delta Sigma Theta (pres. Houston chpt. 1982-83). Republican. Home and Office: 3602 S Macgregor Way Houston TX 77021-1504

PERRY, DORIS ELIZABETH, banker; b. Montgomery, Ala., Nov. 18, 1949; d. Thomas Brantley and Billie Jo (Perry) P. BS, Math. U. Montevallo, 1972; MDiv, Asbury Theol. Seminary, 1984; postgrad., Am. Inst. Banking, 1992. Computer programmer Liberty Nat. Life Ins. Co., Birmingham, 1972-81; circulation mgr. United Meth. Comm., Birmingham, 1986-90; clk. quality control AmSouthBank, Birmingham, 1990—. Author: Creative Expressions; contbr. articles to United Meth. Christian Advocate, 1986-90. Clin. pastoral educator Carraway Meth. Med. Ctr., Birmingham, 1983; mem. coun. ministries, adminstrv. bd. Cahaba Heights United Meth. Ch., 1987—, dir. comm., 1989-94, alt. del. ann. conf., 1995—; trained leader, participant Disciple Bible Study, Birmingham, 1993. Home: 4016 Meadowview Cir Birmingham AL 35243

PERRY, E. ELIZABETH, social worker, real estate manager; b. Balt., Oct. 2, 1954; d. James Glenn and Pearl Elizabeth (Christopher) P.; 1 child, Linden Andrew. AA, C.C. of Balt., 1973; B in Art, Psychology, Social Work, U. Md., Balt., 1975, MSW, 1978. Asst. grant coord. Md. Conf. Social Concern, Balt., 1975; dir. social svcs. West Balt. Community Health Care Corp., Balt., 1978-80; tng. counselor NutriSystem Inc. of Md., Balt., 1983-86; counselor/psychotherapist Switlik Elem. Sch., Marathon, Fla., 1988-89; program dir. emergency shelter Children's Home Soc., Miami, 1990-91; health educator, spokesperson Rape Treatment Ctr., Miami, 1991-94; CEO, pres. bd. Child Assault Prevention Project, Miami, 1993—; self-employed in real estate rehab. and mgmt., 1980—; pub. speaker on women's and children's issues/sexual assault issues, 1990—. Bd. dirs. Partnership Way, 1993—, ACHIEVE, 1995; pub. citizen Dem. Nat. Com. Mem. AAUW, NOW (bd. dirs. Dade County 1994-95), Nat. Abortion Rights Action League, Amnesty Internat., People for the Am. Way, Psi Chi, Phi Theta Kappa. Democrat. Home: San Marco Island 1505 NE 13th Pl Miami FL 33139 Office: Child Assault Prevention Project PO Box 398442 Miami FL 33139

PERRY, EVELYN REIS, communications company executive; b. N.Y.C., Mar. 9; d. Lou L. and Bertl (Wolf) Reis; m. Charles G. Perry III, Jan. 7, 1968; children: Charles G. IV, David Reis. BA, Univ. Wis., 1963; student Am. Acad. Dramatic Arts, 1958-59, Univ. N.Mex., 1963-64. Lic. real estate broker, N.C. Vol. ETV project Peace Corps, 1963-65; program officer-radio/tv Peace Corps, Washington, 1965-68; dir. Vols. in Svc. to Am. (VISTA), Raleigh, N.C., 1977-80; exec. dir. CETA Program for Displaced Homemakers, Raleigh, 1980-81; cons. exec. dir. to Recycle Raleigh for Food and Fuel, Theater in the Park, 1981-83, Artspace, Inc., Raleigh, 1983-84; pres., chief exec. officer Carolina Sound Communications, MUZAK, Charleston, S.C. and 12 counties in S.C., 1984—; pub. rels. account exec. various cos., Washington, Syracuse, N.Y., 1969-71; cons. pub. rels. and orgn. Olympic Organizing Com., Mexico City, 1968; cons. pub. rels., fundraising, arts mgmt. pub. speaking, Ill., Pa., N.C., 1971-77; organizational and pub. speaking cons. Perry & Assocs., Raleigh, 1980—. Mem. adv. bd. Gov.'s Office Citizen Affairs, Raleigh, 1981-85; mem. Involvement Coun. of Wake County, N.C., Raleigh, 1981-84; mem. Adv. Coun. to Vols. in Svc. to Am., Raleigh, 1980-84; mem. Pres.'s adv. bd. Peace Corps, Washington, 1980-82; v.p., bd. dirs. Voluntary Action Ctr., Raleigh, 1980-84, bd. dirs., Charleston, 1988-94; sec. bd. dirs. Temple Kahil Kadosh Beth Elohim, 1987-89, sec. fin., 1989-90, v.p. programming, 1990-93, v.p. adminstrn. 1993—; bd. dirs. Chopstik Theater, Charleston, 1989-90; del., chmn. S.C. Delegation White House Conf. Small Bus. Mem. N.C. Coun. of Women's Orgns. (pres., v.p. 1982-84), Charleston Hotel and Motel Assn., N.C. Assn. Vol. Adminstrs. (bd. dirs. 1980-84), S.C. Restaurant Assn., Nat. Assn. Women Bus. Owners, Internat. Planned Music Assn. (bd. dirs. 1986—, newsletter editor), NAFE, Nat. Fedn. Ind. Businesses (mem. adv. bd. 1987—, chmn. guardian adv. coun. 1994—), Internat. Platform Assn., Theaterworks (bd. dirs. 1994—), Charleston C. of C. Office: Carolina Sound Comm Inc 1023 Wappoo Rd Ste 27B Charleston SC 29407-5960

PERRY, FREDERICKA MAE (FREDI PERRY), writer, publisher, insurance salesperson; b. Kirkland, Wash., July 18, 1938; d. Arthur John Bates and Dorothea H. (Workosky) Speed; m. Lincoln R. Perry, May 9, 1965; children: Andrea Lee, Kenneth R., Pamela E. BA, Wash. State U., 1960. Sales exec. Lincoln R. Perry and Assocs., Bremerton, Wash., 1967—; author, pub. Perry Pub., Bremerton, Wash., 1989—. Author, editor: Kitsap County: Year of the Child, 1979; author, pub.: Kitsap County: A Centennial History, 1979, Port Madison: 1854-1889, 1989, Seabeck: Tide's Out; Table's Set, 1993; editor: Kitsap County: A History, 1977. Mem. Kitsap County Hist. Soc., Silverdale, Wash., 1972—, Wash. State Hist. Soc., Tacoma, 1976—, Pacific NW Historians Guild, Seattle, 1985—. Home and Office: 5788 Lene'a Dr NW Bremerton WA 98312

PERRY, HELEN, educator, nurse; b. Birmingham, Ala., Mar. 4, 1927; d. Van Mary Ellenol (Thornton) Curry; m. Charlie Pitts, May, 1960; 1 child, Charlenia; m. George Perry (dec. 1989); children: Hattie Mae (dec.), George Jr., Jose. Student, LaSalle Extension U., Chgo., 1968, Georgetown U., 1979; Doctorate/Mayanuis Mosaic Soc., Duke Univ., San Antonio, 1979. Lic. practical nurse; paramedic. Supply tchr. City Bd. Edn., Birmingham, 1977—; notary pub., Ala., 1975—; nurse home health U. Ala. at Birmingham Hosp., 1988—. Vol. ARC, Birmingham, 1970—; mem. crime watch Am. Police, Washington, 1989; mem. Hall of Fame Pres. Task Force, Washington, 1983-91; nominee Nat. Rep. Com., Washington, 1991, 92; selected VIP Guest delegate Rep. Nat. Conv., Houston, 1992, fin. com. fundraiser Middleton for Congress Campaign '94, Dist. # 59 Bd. Reps.; life mem. Rep. Presdl. Task Force, Washington, 1992; trustee Nat. Crime Watch, 1989, adv. bd. Am. Security Coun., Va., Washington, 1969-91; mem. Nat. Congl. Com. Adv. Bd., Washington; mem. Nat. Law Enforcement Assn., 1989; min. Greater Emmanuel Temple Holiness Ch., Birmingham, 1957—, ordained elder, vice-champion of mother bd.; mem. Coalition for Desert Storm, various others. Recipient cert. of appreciation Pres. Congl. Task Force, 1990, Diamond award U.S.A. Serve Am., 1992, award Ala. Sheriff Assn., 1989, Navy League, 1989-91, Rep. Presdl. award Legion of Merit, 1994, cert. of appreciation Rep. Nat. Commn., 1994, nominated Presdl. Election Registry Rep. Presdl. Task Force, 1992; named Good Samaritan Law Enforcement Officers, Royal Proclamation Royal Highness Kevin, Prince Regent of Hutt River Province, 1994, Royal Ceremonial Jewel. Mem. LaSalle Extension U. Alumni (life mem.), Ala. Nurses Assn., Nat. Assn. Unknown Players. Home: 201 W Ann Dr SW Birmingham AL 35211-4935

PERRY, JACQUELIN, orthopedic surgeon; b. Denver, May 31, 1918; d. John F. and Tirzah (Kuruptkat) P. B.E., U. Calif., Los Angeles, 1940; M.D., U. Calif., San Francisco, 1950. Intern Children's Hosp., San Francisco, 1950-57; resident in orthopedic surgery U. Calif., San Francisco, 1951-55; orthopedic surgeon Rancho Los Amigos Hosp., Downey, Calif., 1955—; chief pathokinesiology Rancho Los Amigos Med. Ctr., 1961—; chief stroke service Rancho Los Amigos Hosp., 1972-75; mem. faculty U. Calif. Med. Sch., San Francisco, 1966—; clin. prof. U. Calif. Med. Sch., 1973—; mem. faculty U. So. Calif. Med. Sch., 1969—, prof. orthopedic surgery, 1972—, dir. polio and gait clinic, 1972—; Disting. lectr. for hosp. for spl. curgery and Cornell U. Med. Coll., N.Y.C., 1977-78; Packard Meml. lectr. U. Colo. Med. Sch., 1970; Osgood lectr. Harvard Med. Sch., 1978; Summer lectr., Portland, 1977; Shands lectr.; cons. USAF; guest speaker symposia; cons. Biomechanics Lab. Centinela Hosp., 1979—. Served as phys. therapist U.S. Army, 1941-46. Recipient Disting. Svc. award Calif. Assn. Rehab. Facilities,1981, Pres.'s award, 1984, Milton Cohen award Nat. Assn. Rehab., 1993, Isabelle and Lenard Goldensen award for tech. United Cerebral Palsy Assn., 1981, Jow Dowling award, 1985, Profl. Achievement award UCLA, 1988, Armistad award Rancho Los Amigos Med. Ctr., Calif., 1990; named Woman of Yr. for Medicine in So. Calif., L.A. Times, 1959, Alumnus of Yr., U. Calif. Med. Sch., 1980, Physician of Yr. Calif. Employment Devel. Dept., 1994. Mem. AMA, Am. Acad. Orthop. Surgeons (Kappa Delta award for rsch. 1977), Am. Orthop. Assn. (Shands lectr. 1988), Western Orthop. Assn., Calif. Med. Soc., L.A. County Med. Soc., Am. Phys. Therapy Assn. (hon. Golden Pen award 1965), Am. Acad. Orthotists and Prosthetists (hon.), Scoliosis Rsch. Soc., LeRoy Abbott Soc., Am. Acad. Cerebral Palsy. Home: 12319 Brock Ave Downey CA 90242-3503 Office: Rancho Los Amigos Med Ctr 7601 Imperial Hwy Downey CA 90242-3456

PERRY, JEAN LOUISE, dean; b. Richland, Wash., May 13, 1950; d. Russell S. and Sue W. Perry. BS, Miami U., Oxford, Ohio, 1972; MS, U. Ill., Urbana, 1973, PhD, 1976. Cons. ednl. placement office U. Ill., 1973-75; adminstrv. intern Coll. Applied Life Studies, 1975-76, asst. dean, 1976-77, assoc. dean, 1978-81, asst. prof. dept. phys. edn., 1976-81; assoc. prof. phys. edn. San Francisco State U., 1981-84, prof., 1984-90, chair, 1981-90; dean Coll. of Human and Community Scis. U. Nev., Reno, 1990—. Named to excellent tchr. list U. Ill., 1973-79. Mem. AAHPERD (fellow research consortium, pres. 1988-89), Am. Assn. Higher Edn., Am. Ednl. Research Assn., Nat. Assn. Phys. Edn. in Higher Edn., Nat. Assn. Girls and Women in Sports (guide coordinator, pres.), Delta Psi Kappa, Phi Delta Kappa. Home: 3713 Ranchview Ct Reno NV 89509-7437 Office: U Nev Coll Human and Community Scis Mail Stop 136 Reno NV 89557

PERRY, KIMBERLY KAY, university administrator; b. Spencer, Iowa, Feb. 14, 1961; d. Thomas Austin and Carolyn Lucille (Runneberg) Perry; m. Carey Lee Gilbert, Nov. 28, 1992. BA, U. No. Iowa, 1984, MA, 1990. Grad. teaching asst. U. No. Iowa, Cedar Falls, 1984-86; resident coord. Briar Cliff Coll., Sioux City, Iowa, 1986-88; area coord. Ctrl. Mo. State U., Warrensburg, 1988-89; dir. univ. housing U. Dubuque, Iowa, 1989-92; asst. dir. residence life and instr. U. Wis., Green Bay, 1992—. Mem. Dubuque Chorale, 1989-92. Named to Outstanding Young Women of Am.; recipient Brindley Individual Events Outstanding Speech award U. No. Iowa, 1984, Persuasive Speaking award Interstate Oratorical Assn., 1984, Persuasive, Poetry, Prose award Nat. Forensic Assn., 1984. Democrat. Methodist. Home: 624 Van Caster Dr Green Bay WI 54311-7131

PERRY, LOIS WANDA, safety consultant; b. Seattle, Dec. 29, 1937; d. William and Ethel Lenora (Benson) Abrahamson; m. S. Peter Perry, Jan. 12, 1991; stepchildren: Christopher, Tony. BA, Pacific Luth. U., 1962; postgrad., Gonzaga U., 1984. Cert. vocat. rehabilitaton counselor. Claims rep. Social Security Adminstrn., Calif. and Oreg., 1962-69; field rep. Oreg. Dept. of Labor and Industries, Salem, Oreg., 1969-72; safety cons. and trainer, regional safety coord. Wash. Dept. of Labor and Industries, Spokane, 1987—. Guardian Ad Litem Spokane County Juvenile Ct., 1989—. Mem. AAUW (membership v.p. Valley br. 1992-94, program v.p., co-chair 1994—, com. chair Downtown br. 1989-90, bd. dirs. 1989-90), ASTD (bd. dirs. Spokane-Inland N.W. chpt. 1992), Spokane Tng. Consortium. Democrat. Lutheran. Home: 914 S Mckinzie Rd Liberty Lake WA 99019-9752 Office: Wash State Dept Labor & Industries 901 N Monroe St Ste 100 Spokane WA 99201-2148

PERRY, MARGARET, librarian, writer; b. Cin., Nov. 15, 1933; d. Rufus Patterson and Elizabeth Munford (Anthony) P. AB, Western Mich. U., 1954; Cert. d'etudes Francaises, U. Paris, 1956; MSLS, Cath. U. Am., 1959. Young adult and reference librarian N.Y. Pub. Library, N.Y.C., 1954-55, 57-58; librarian U.S. Army, France and Germany, 1959-63, 64-67; chief circulation U.S. Mil. Acad. Library, West Point, N.Y., 1967-70; head edn. library U. Rochester, N.Y., 1970-75, asst. prof., 1973-75, assoc. prof., 1975-82, asst. dir. libraries for reader services, 1975-82, acting dir. libraries, 1976-77, 80; univ. libr. Valparaiso U., Ind., 1982-93; ret., 1993; mem. Task Force on Coop. Edn., Rochester, 1972. Author: A Bio-bibliography of Countee P. Cullen, 1903-1946, 1971, Silence to the Drums: A Survey of the Literature of the Harlem Renaissance, 1976, The Harlem Renaissance, 1982, The Short Fiction of Rudolph Fisher, 1987; also numerous short stories; contbr. articles to profl. jours. Bd. dirs. Urban League, 1978-80. Recipient 1st prize short story contest Armed Forces Writers League, 1966; 2nd prize Frances Steloff Fiction Prize, 1968, 1st prize short story Arts Alive, 1990, 2nd prize short story Willow Rev., 1990; seminar scholar Schloss Leopoldskron, Salzburg, Austria, 1956. Mem. ALA, NOW. Democrat. Roman Catholic. Home: 15050 Roaring Brook Rd Thompsonville MI 49683

PERRY, MARGARET N., academic administrator; b. Waynesboro, Tenn., Apr. 23, 1940; m. Randy L. Perry; 2 children. BS in Home Econs., U. Tenn., Martin, 1961; MS in Nutrition, U. Tenn., Knoxville, 1963, PhD in Nutrition and Food Sci., 1965. NDEA fellow depts. food sci. and nutrition U. Tenn., Knoxville, 1961-64, part-time instr. dept. food sci. Coll. Home Econs., 1963-64, asst. prof. food sci. and food systems adminstrn., asst. to dean, 1966-68, asst. dean Coll. Home Econs., 1967-68, assoc. dean, 1968-73, dean for grad. studies, assoc. prof., 1973-79; assoc. v.p. for acad. affairs Tenn. Tech. U., 1979-86, dir. Joe L. Evins Appalachian Ctr. for Crafts, 1982-83; chancellor U. Tenn., Martin, 1986—; mem. exec. com. Council Grad. Schs. in U.S., Washington, 1974-77, chair nominating com., 1977; mem. exec. com. So. Conf. Grad. Schs., 1975-78; bd. dirs. Knoxville Early Child Devel. Ctr., 1975-78, corr. sec., 1976-77; apptd. mem. team Am. educators to visit and study univs. in Iraq, 1977; mem. Tenn. planning com. Identification Women in Higher Edn. Programs, Am. Council on Edn., 1978-86, chair, 1979-81, mem. Nat. Forum on Women in Higher Edn., Athens, Ga., 1978, mem. Commn. on Women in Higher Edn., Washington, 1979-82, resource person Nat. Forum on Women in Higher Edn., Princeton, N.J., 1981; rep. to N.E. U. Tech., Shenyang, Peoples Republic China, 1984; mem. internat. com. Am. Assn. State Colls. and Univs., 1986—; ofcl. visit and renewal sister univ. agreement Hirosaki U., Japan, 1989, English tng. Konohana-Gakuen High Sch., 1989; lectr. in field. Mem. editorial bd.: Grad. Programs and Admissions Manual, 1975-78; contbr. articles to profl. publs. Mem. U. Tenn. Alumni Bd. Govs., 1969-71, adv. com. Univ. Day Care Ctr., 1984-86, Tenn. 4-H Club Found., Inc., 1990, JOBS adv. coun. Dept. Human Svcs. State of Tenn., 1990, Tenn. Adv. Com., Lower Miss. Delta Devel. Commn., 1989—; chair Tenn. Tech. U. United Way Drive, 1979-82, dept. leader, 1983-86; tchr. Sunday sch. Collegeside Ch. of Christ, 1979-86; bd. dirs. Putnam County United Way, 1981-85; chair Weakley County United Way, 1987. Nat. Endowment for Arts grantee, 1979-83. Mem. Am. Assn. State Colls. and Univs. (state rep. 1989-90), Profl. and Organizational Devel. Networks in Higher Edn., Inst. Food Technologists, Am. Home Econs. Assn., Tenn. Home Econs. Assn., Am. Men and Women in Sci., Tenn. Women's Forum, Omicron Nu, Sigma Xi, Phi Kappa Phi, Omicron Delta Kappa, Delta Kappa Gamma. Club: U. Tenn. at Knoxville Faculty (bd. dirs. 1974-77). Home: Chancellor's Residence Martin TN 38238 Office: U Tenn Office of the Chancellor 325 Adminstrn Martin TN 38238*

PERRY, MARILYN See **WIDNEY, MARILYN EDITH**

PERRY, MARSHA GRATZ, legislator, professional skating coach; b. Niagara Falls, N.Y., Dec. 9, 1936; d. William Henry and Margarett Edna (Barr) Gratz; m. Robert X. Perry, Jr., Jan. 28, 1961; children: Robert, Margarett, David. Student, Elmira Coll., 1954-57; BILR, Cornell U., 1959. Coll. recruiter Inmont, N.Y.C., 1959-61; skating dir. City of Bowie (Md.), 1971-86; skating coach Benfield Pines Ice Rink, Millerville, Md., 1974—; mem. Md. Ho. of Dels.; mem. Md. Ho. of Dels.; summer hockey & skating coach Washington Capitals, Landover, Md., 1986—; co-dir. Prostart Hockey Programs. Dist. dir., v.p., planning zoning dir. Crofton (Md.) Civic Assn., 1974-86; pres. West County Fedn. Cmty. Assn.; mem. AACO Drug & Alcohol adv. coun.; bd. dirs. Am. Cancer Soc., Am. Heart Assn., YMCA, Md. Hall Creative Arts. Named Citizen of Yr. Crofton Civic Assn., 1986. Mem. Assn. Women Legislators (exec. bd.). Home: 1605 Edgerton Pl Crofton MD 21114-1504 Office: MD Ho of Dels State Capital Annapolis MD 21401

PERRY, MARY ELLA, transportation executive; b. Charleston, W.Va., Feb. 20, 1941; d. Harry Keith and Anna Gayle (Hatfield) Dempsey; m. Jim D. Perry; 1 child, Alicia Ann. BA, Morris Harvey Coll., 1975; MA, Coll. of Grad. Studies, 1992. Tng. officer W.Va. Dept. of Transp., Charleston. Literacy tutor Literacy Vols. of Am.; vice chair W.Va. State Employees Combined Campaign. Recipient Make It Shine award for environ. work State of W.Va., 199-92. Mem. Putnam County C. of C. Home: 329 E Maplewood Estates Scott Depot WV 25560

PERRY, MAXINE LEWIS, state official; b. Sterling, Colo., Sept. 13, 1933; d. William Merrill Lewis and Florence Elizabeth (Boudreaux) Perry; m. Lowell Wesley Perry, Jan. 30, 1956; children: Lowell Wesley Jr., Scott Tyler, Merrideth Lynne. BA in English, Wayne State U., 1960; JD, Detroit Coll. Law, 1980. English and journalism tchr. Detroit Pub. Schs., 1960-74, cons., 1989; dep. dir. civil host com. Rep. Nat. Conv., Mich., 1980; adminstrv. commr. Mich. Liquor Control Commn., Lansing, 1980-89, chairwoman, 1991—; dir. corporate and found. programs Oakland U., Rochester, Mich., 1989-90; mem. nat. adv. com. SBA, also mem. bus. and econ. devel. com. for Great Lakes Region. Del. to Rep. Nat. Conv., 1980; bd. dirs. Boysville, Boys and Girls Clubs of Am.; mem. coun. Internat. Yr. of the Family, Lansing, 1994. Recipient citation Booker T. Washington Businessmen's Assn., 1980, Cmty. award Mich. Grocers Assn., 1980, Market Watch Leaders award 1994, Mich. State Safety Commn. award, 1994. Mem. NAACP (life), Nat. Alcohol Beverage Control Assn. (bd. dirs., pres.-elect 1993-94, pres. 1994—), U. Mich. Pres. Club. Roman Catholic. Home: 29336 E Chanticleer Dr Southfield MI 48034 Office: Mich Liquor Control Commn PO Box 30005 7150 Harris Dr Lansing MI 48909

PERRY, MOLLY MARIE, museum director; b. Ludington, Mich., Aug. 9, 1955; d. Robert Charles and Millicent Marie (Rosewarne) Middleton; m. Philip Edward Perry, Oct. 16, 1982; stepchildren: Timothy Edward, Andrew Michael. Associates degree, West Shore C.C., Scottville, Mich., 1975; BS in Animal Sci., Mich. State U., 1977, BS in Agrl. Comm., 1979; postgrad. in bus. adminstrn., Lake Superior State U., 1991. Mus. dir., pub. info. dir. Mason County Hist. Soc., Ludington, 1979-87; mus. dir. Grand Haven Area Hist. Soc., Grand Haven, Mich., 1987-91; mus. cons. Drummond Island, Mich., 1991—; mus. dir. Marquette Mission Park and Mus, Ojibwa Culture, St. Ignace, Mich., 1994—. Editor: Historic Mason County, Michigan, 1980. Upper Peninsula Quilt Rsch. grantee Capitol City Quilt Guild, 1994, Upper Peninsula Quilt Rsch. grantee Nat. Quilting Assn., 1994. Mem. Am. Assn. Mus., Am. Assn. State and Local History, Mich. Mus. Assn. (bd. dirs. 1994—), Mich. Quilt Network (bd. dirs. and newsletter editor 1991-94), West Shore C.C. Alumni Assn. (bd. dirs. and newsletter editor 1988—). Home: HC 52 Box 95 Drummond Island MI 49726 Office: Marquette Mission Park & Mus Ojibwa Culture 500 N State St Saint Ignace MI 49781

PERRY, NANCY ESTELLE, psychologist; b. Pitts., Oct. 30, 1934; d. Simon Warren and Estelle Cecelia (Zaluski) Reichard; m. John Cleveland; children: Scott, Karen, Elaine. BS, Ohio State U., 1956, MA in Psychology, 1969, PhD in Psychology (EPDA fellow), 1973. Nurse, various locations, 1956-63; sch. psychologist Public Schs. Columbus (Ohio), 1970-72; human devel. specialist Madison County (Ohio) Schs., 1972-75; pvt. practice clin. psychology, cons. psychology, Worthington, Ohio, 1975-80; tchr. U. Wis. Sch. Nursing, Milw., 1980-88, Milw. Devel. Center, 1980-83; pvt. practice Assoc. Mental Health Services, 1983-87; pvt. practice Glendale Clinic for Stress Mgmt. and Mental Health Clinics, 1987—; faculty Wis. Profl. Schs.; adj. faculty U. Wis., Milw. Ohio Dept. Edn. grantee, 1973-76. Mem. APA, Wis. Psychol. Assn., Am. Soc. Clin. Hypnosis, Internat. Soc. Study of Dissociation, Am. Assn. Marriage and Family Therapists. Home: 2210 W Charter Mall Thiensville WI 53092-5451 Office: 5225 N Ironwood Ln Milwaukee WI 53217-4906

PERRY, NANCY TROTTER, former telecommunications company executive; b. Cleve., Jan. 1, 1935; d. Charles Hanley and Mable Dora (Lowry) Trotter; m. Robert Anthony Perry, Apr. 27, 1957. Student, Dunbarton Coll., 1952-53, W.Va. U., 1953-55. Svc. rep. C&P Telephone Co., Balt., 1956-60, adminstrv. asst., 1960-67, staff supr., 1967-69; staff mgr., 1969-79; mgr. consumer affairs C&P Telephone Co., Balt., 1979-91. Bd. dirs., founding dir. Balt. Mus. Industry, Md. Info. and Referral Providers Coun., Learning Ind. Through Computers, Inc., 1991, pres., 1994—; bd. dirs. Md. Gerontol. Assn., Md. Consumer Coun., chair, 1994—, Fgn.-Born Info. and Referral Network, Hearing and Speech Agy., 1989-94, founding dir. Tele-Consumer Hotline, 1986-92; vice-chair United Way Survival Needs Allocation Panel, 1994—. Mem. AAUW, Soc. Consumer Affairs Profls. in Bus., Md. Ctr. for Ind. Living, Nat. Fedn. of Blind, Alliance for Pub. Technology, Sons of Italy. Home: 3701 Chatham Rd Ellicott City MD 21042-5105

PERRY, NICOLA JANE, restaurant executive; b. Sydney, Australia, June 7, 1959; came to U.S., 1981.; d. George Edward and Doreen Audry (Davies) P. Student, Purcell Sch. Music, Art Ednl. Trust. Tea lady Stock Exch., London, 1977; waitress Barcave Group, London, 1978-80; waitress, mgr. Great Am. Health Bar, N.Y.C., 1981-84; waitress Union Sq. Cafe, N.Y.C., 1985-87; waitress, maitre di, bookkeeper Barocco, N.Y.C., 1988-91; owner Tea and Sympathy, N.Y.C., 1991—. Address: 96 Greenwich Ave # 2 New York NY 10011 Office: Tea and Sympathy 108 Greenwich Ave New York NY 10011

PERRY, RHODA E., state legislator. Now mem. R.I. State Senate. Office: Senate House State House Providence RI 02903*

PERRY, RUTH EARLENE, physician; b. Phila., July 25, 1956; d. William Earl and Ruth Ann (Woodland) P.; m. Frederick Montgomery Walton, Sept. 20, 1986; children: Kendall Taylor, Courtney Eleanora. BA in Biology, Swarthmore Coll., 1978; MD, Temple U., 1982. Diplomate Am. Bd. Internal Medicine; diplomate Am. Bd. Emergency Medicine. Intern Med. Coll. Pa., 1982-83; resident in internal medicine Med. Coll. Pa., 1983-85; attending physician emergency rm. Albert Einstein Med. Ctr., Phila., 1985-92, dir. occupational health, 1991-92; med. dir. Bristol (Pa.) Site and Corp. Engring. Rohm & Haas Co., 1992—. Fellow Am. Bd. Emergency Medicine; mem. Am. Coll. Emergency Medicine, Am. Coll. Occupational Medicine, Pa. Med. Soc., Opera Guild. Home: 702 Dominion Dr Moorestown NJ 08057 Office: Rohm & Haas DVI Inc State Rd & Rte 413 Bristol PA 19007

PERRY, SARAH TERESA ANDERSON (TERI PERRY), nurse manager, critical care nurse; b. Flushing, N.Y., Jan. 14, 1957; d. John Thomas and Dorothy Reu (James) Anderson; m. Dennis Michael Perry Sr., Oct. 17, 1981; children: John Thomas, Clayton Foster. ADN, Augusta (Ga.) Coll. Sch. Nursing, 1979; BSN, Med. U. of S.C., 1985, MSN, 1987. Shift supr. ICU U. Hosp., Augusta, Ga.; staff nurse III Roper Hosp., Charleston, S.C.; nurse mgr. Med. U. of S.C. Med. Ctr., Charleston; mem. biomed. ethics com. U. of S.C. Med. Ctr., Charleston, 1988-94; nurse mgr. CCU Med. Coll. of Ga., Augusta, 1994—; registry coord. Nat. Registry of Myocardial Infraction 2, 1994—. Mem. AACN (pres. Charleston chpt. 1989-90), S.C. Nurses Assn., Sigma Theta Tau. Home: 1976 Neptune Dr Augusta GA 30906

PERRY, SUSAN E., accounting educator; b. Milw., Feb. 24, 1950; d. Lloyd C. and Catherine M. (Hughes) P. BS, U. Wis., 1986, MBA, 1989, PhD, 1990. CPA; CMA. Ops. mgr. J.C. Penney, Co., Milw., 1976-81; prin. Sun Designs, Milw., 1981-86; asst. prof. acctg. U. Va., Charlottesville, Va., 1990—. Contbd. articles to profl. jours. Treas. bd. dirs. Sexaul Assault Resourse Agy., Charlottesville, Va., 1993-94. Deloitte & Touche fellow, 1990. Mem. Ill. CPA Soc., Am. Acctg. Assn., Josephson Ethics Inst., Inst. Mgmt. Accts. Office: U Va McIntire Sch Commerce 233 Monroe Hall Charlottesville VA 22901

PERRY, VALERIE ANN, city clerk; b. Pawtucket, R.I., Mar. 18, 1944; d. Robert Llewelyn and Rose Claudette (DeLuca) Conroy; m. Robert S. Perry, III, June 27, 1964; children: Elizabeth Anne, Catherine Frances, Robert S. IV. Grad. high sch., East Providence, R.I. Clk. typist Atlantic Yarns, Providence, 1961-65; sec. East Providence (R.I.) Sch. Dept., 1978-86; adminstrv. asst. City of East Providence, 1986-90, city clk., 1990—. Co-chair East Providence Charity Ball, 1992—; mem. East Providence High Sch. Hall of Fame Com., 1987-90, 93. Mem. R.I. Town and City Clks. Assn. (membership chair 1991-92, legis. com. 1992—, exec. bd. 1993), R.I. Fedn. Bus. and Profl. Women's Clubs (recording sec. 1983-85, treas. 1985-87, 89-90, 1st v.p. 1990-91, pres. 1991-92), East Providence Bus. & Profl. Women's Club (pres. 1982-83, Woman of Achievement 1990). Home: 30 Wannamoisett Rd East Providence RI 02914-3119 Office: City of E Providence 145 Taunton Ave East Providence RI 02914-4530

PERRY-PLATT, ROSE MARIE, management specialist, decorator consultant; b. Tallahassee, June 17, 1946; d. Riley and Lillie Mae (Colson) Clack; m. Leroy Perry, Aug. 24, 1968 (div. July 1982); m. Ricardo Anthony Platt, Apr. 27, 1986. Grad., Lincoln High Sch., 1963; student, Fayetteville State U., 1975-81, Shaw U., 1992. Sec./bookkeeper Pineview Elem. Sch., Tallahassee, 1963-71; personnel asst. Fayetteville (N.C.) State U., 1971-78, personnel technician, 1978-88, position mgmt. specialist, 1988—. Mem. State Employees Assn. N.C. (memberhsip chair 1990-91, vice chair 1991-92, dist. chair 1992-93, region membership 1993—, Mem. of Yr. 1991, Outstanding Mem. 1992, Outstanding Svc. 1993), Am. Bus. Womens Assn. (hospitality chair 1985-90), N.C. Coll./Univ. Personnel Assn. Home: 5225 Delco St Fayetteville NC 28311-2331 Office: Fayetteville State Univ 1200 Murchison Rd Fayetteville NC 28301-4298

PERSCHBACHER, DEBRA BASSETT, lawyer; b. Pleasanton, Calif., Oct. 28, 1956; d. James Arthur and Shirley Ann (Russell) Bassett; m. Rex Robert Perschbacher, June 4, 1989. BA, U. Vt., 1977; MS, San Diego State U., 1982; JD, U. Calif., Davis, 1987. Bar: Calif. 1987, D.C. 1990, U.S. Dist Ct. (no. and ea. dists.) Calif. 1988, U.S. Ct. Appeals (9th cir.), 1988, U.S. Supreme Ct., 1991. Guidance counselor Addison Cen. Supr. Union, Middlebury, Vt., 1982-83, Milton (Vt.) Elem. Sch., 1983-84; assoc. Morrison & Foerster, San Francisco, 1986; jud. clk. U.S. Ct. Appeals (9th cir.), Phoenix, 1987-88; assoc. Morrison & Foerster, Walnut Creek, Calif., 1988-92; sr. atty. Calif. Ct. Appeal (3d appellate dist.), Sacramento, 1992—; tutor civil procedure, rsch. asst. U. Calif., Davis, 1985-87. Sr. articles editor U. Calif. Law Rev., Davis, 1986-87; editor, 1985-86. Bd. Dirs. Episcopal Cmty. Svcs., 1994—. Mem. AAUW, ABA (vice chmn. ethics com. young lawyers divsn. 1989-91, exec. com. labor and employment law com. 1989-90), Sacramento County Bar Assn., Women Lawyers of Sacramento. Democrat. Home: 1438 41st St Sacramento CA 95819-4041 Office: Ct Appeal 914 Capitol Mall Sacramento CA 95814-4811

PERSINGER, CLARA M., insurance agent; b. Atlanta, July 26, 1942; d. Henry Wilson and Ellie Mae (Norred) Barnes; m. Gene E. Persinger Sr., Aug. 26, 1964 (div. 1986); 1 child, Suzanne Geraldine Persinger Clinger; m. Leroy Wagler, Dec. 29, 1990; 2 children. Student, West Georgia Coll., 1960-62. Pres. Persinger Ins. Co., Bradenton, Fla., 1978—. Pres. Altrusa Internat. of Bradenton, 1987, active, 1986-93; active Gulfcoast Girl Scouts, Sarasota, Fla., 1986-91, United Way of Manatee County, Bradenton, 1986-93. Named Small Bus. Person of Yr., Bradenton C. of C., 1986. Mem. Ind. Ins. Agts. Assn. (pres. 1983-84), Manatee County Life Underwriters (pres. 1988-89, John A. Wooten Life Underwriter 1989). Republican. Baptist. Home: PO Box 10320 Bradenton FL 34282

PERSINGER, MILDRED EMORY, association volunteer; b. Roanoke, Va., Apr. 28, 1918; d. Edward Bourke and Mildred Price Spiers; m. Richard Burwell Persinger, June 20, 1942; children: Louise Tilghman Persinger Montgomery, Richard Emory, Philip Burwell. AB, Hollins Coll., 1939; postgrad., Bryn Mawr Coll., 1940-41. Mem. faculty Ala. Poly. Inst. (name now Auburn U.), Auburn, 1941-42; nat. bd. dirs., mem. exec. com. YWCA U.S.A., 1952-70; mem. World YWCA Coun., Ghana, Can., Greece, Singapore, 1971-83; Congl. testimony. Contbr. articles, editorials to profl. jours. including N.Y. Herald Tribune, YWCA Mag.; guest editor/cons. Good Housekeeping Mag., 1985. Active Pres.'s Commn. UN, 1970-71, Nat. Commn. Internat. Women's Yr., 1976-78; organizer internat. tribune Internat. Women's Yr., Mexico City, 1975, chair internat. com. Nat. Women's Conf., Houston, 1977; founder, pres. Internat. Women's Tribune Ctr., 1976-82; UN rep. World YWCA, Geneva, 1976-95; active YWCA, White Plains and Yonkers, N.Y.; mem. U.S. com. UN Devel. Fund Women, bd. dirs., 1992-95; bd. dirs. UN Assn. U.S.A., 1970-76, Non-Govtl. Orgns. Com. Disarmament, bd. dirs., 1980-94, mem. exec. com. Commn. Study Orgn. Peace, 1971-79; active World Population Conf., Bucharest, 1974, World Women's Confs. Mex., 1975, Copenhagen, 1980, Nairobi, 1985; initiator, convenor Women's Mid-Decade Dialogue, 1979-82; pub. mem. U.S. Pres.'s Commn. on the Status of Women, 1962-64; chair conf. UN Reps., 1969-72; bd. dirs. Conf. Non-Govtl. Orgns. in Consultative Status with UN Econ. and Social Coun., 1976-80, 94-95; nat. bd. dirs. overseas edn. fund LWV, 1977-81, Am. br. Internat. Social Svc.; bd. dirs. Pub. Affairs Com., 1975-82; sec. Nat. Com. Against Discrimination in the War Effort, 1943-45; mem. N.Y. State Com. Against Discrimination in Housing, 1950-53, N.Y. State Gov.'s Consumer Adv. Coun., 1957-58, Jr. League Westchester on Hudson, 1951-58, bd. dirs., 1953-55. Recipient Eleanor Schnurr award UN Assn. U.S.A., 1993; named hon. mem. nat. bd. dirs. YWCA U.S.A., 1973-95. Mem. LWV (adv. com. bd. edn. 1951-52, bd. dirs. 1948-56, 90-92). Democrat. Presbyterian. Home: 26 Judson Ave Dobbs Ferry NY 10522-3011

PERSON, PAULA (MRS. P. BARRY PERSON), social skills organization executive, entrepreneur; b. Worcester, Mass., Feb. 19, 1935; d. Leo Joseph and Imelda Mary (Elmore) Barry; married; children: Suzanne Elizabeth Person Tapley, John Lloyd III, Christian Barry. BA in Edn. and Spanish, Marymount Coll., 1957; postgrad., Harrington Inst. Interior Design, 1974-75. Cert. elem. tchr., N.Y. Founder, tchr. Post Nursery Sch. U.S. Forces, Aschaffenburg, Fed. Republic Germany, 1958, Post Kindergarten Sch. U.S. Forces, Aschaffenbrug, 1959-62; tchr. King Solver Sch., Ft. Knox, 1963-64, Model Sch., Louisville, 1964-66; free lance interior designer Chgo., 1974-79; pres., founder The Children's Spoon, Winnetka, Ill., 1979—, London, 1985—; co-founder Aschaffenburg Players, 1960-90, creater of cultural events for children U.S./Eng., 1980—. Author, designer The Children's Spoon Coloring Book of Manners for Boys and Girls, 1985; creater 9 musical ditties for program and cassete tape. Bd. dirs. Chinese Am. Internat. Woman's Coun. Chgo.; active presdl. campaigns., 1972, 80; swimming instr. Red Cross, Milton, Vt., Marymount Coll.; fund raiser UNICEF Children with AIDS, 1993, 94. Named Showcase House Designer, Park Ridge Youth Campus Fundraiser, 1982, 84, 85. Mem. Internat. Platform Assn., Internat. Women Assocs. Internat. Visitor's Ctr., The English Speaking Union (Chgo. chpt.), Marymount Coll. Alumnae Assn. (pres. 1977-80). Office: The Children's Spoon PO Box 148 Winnetka IL 60093-0148

PERSYN, MARY GERALDINE, law librarian, law educator; b. Elizabeth, N.J., Feb. 25, 1945; d. Henry Anthony and Geraldine (Sumption) P. AB, Creighton U., 1967; MLS, U. Oreg., 1969; JD, Notre Dame U., 1982. Bar: Ind. 1982, U.S. Dist. Ct. (no. and so. dists.) Ind. 1982. Social scis. librarian Miami U., Oxford, Ohio, 1969-78; staff law librarian Notre Dame (Ind.) Law Sch., 1982-84; dir. law library Valparaiso (Ind.) U., 1984-87, law librarian, assoc. prof. law, 1987—. Editor Journal of Legislation, 1981-82; mng. editor Third World Legal Studies, 1986—. Mem. ABA, Ind. State Bar Assn., Am. Assn. Law Libraries, Ohio Regional Assn. Law Libraries (pres. 1990-91). Roman Catholic. Home: 1308 Tuckahoe Park Dr Valparaiso IN 46383-4032 Office: Valparaiso U Law Libr Sch Law Valparaiso IN 46383

PERTHOU, ALISON CHANDLER, interior designer; b. Bremerton, Wash., July 22, 1945; d. Benson and Elizabeth (Holdsworth) Chandler; m. A.V. Perthou III, Sept. 9, 1967 (div. Dec. 1977); children: Peter T.R., Stewart A.C. BFA, Cornish Coll. Arts, 1972. Pres. Alison Perthou Interior Design, Seattle, 1972—, Optima Design, Inc., Seattle, 1986-89; treas. Framejoist Corp., Bellevue, Wash., 1973-90; pres. Classics: Interiors & Antiques, Inc., 1988—; cons. bldg. and interiors com. Children's Hosp., Seattle, 1976—; guest lectr. U. Wash., Seattle, 1980-81. Mem. bd. trustees Cornish Coll. Arts, Seattle, 1973-80, sec. exec. com., 1975-77; mem. procurement com. Patrons of N.W. Cultural and Charitable Orgn., 1985—, mem. antiques com., 1991—. Mem. Am. Soc. Interior Design, Seattle Tennis Club (mem. house and grounds com. 1974-75), City Club. Office: 4216 E Madison St Seattle WA 98112-3237

PERTILLAR-BREVARD, LISA ANN, researcher; b. Hartford, Conn., Mar. 9, 1968; d. Lawrence Sr. and Edna Pearl (Roberts) P. BA with honors, Smith Coll., 1991; PhD, Emory U., 1995. Apprentice dance anthropologist Artists' Collective, Hartford, 1982-85; asst. mgr. Galt Toys-Hartford Civic Ctr., 1985, 87; intern Smithsonian Instn., Washington, 1987, 88, 89; academic peer asst. Community Coll. Connections Smith Coll., Northampton, Mass., 1990; intern coord. Smithsonian Instn., Washington, 1992—; researcher Afro-Am. Studies dept., Smith Coll., Northampton, 1988-89, liaison, 1989—, peer counselor Fin. Aid Office, Smith Coll., 1989; instr. Emory U., 1993-94; vis. scholar Smithsonian Inst., 1993. Author: A Selected, Annotated Bibliograpy on Black American Gospel Music and Related Subjects, 1992, Madame Emma Azalia Smith Hackley (1867-1922): Preserver and Transmitter of African-American Folk Music, 1994; co-author: Wade in the Water Teacher's Guide, 1994, Wade in the Water: African-American Sacred Music Traditions, 1994; prodr., dir., narrator video documentaries Common Games of Black Inner-City Girls, 1988, Portrait of a Black Family, 1988. Pres. Smith Coll. Choir Omega, 1987-88; liaison fin. aid Smith Coll., 1987-88, career devel. Smith Coll., 1989-90. Named one of Glamour Mag.'s Top Ten Coll. Women, 1990, Maybelline Cosmetics Top Ten Coll. Women, 1991. Mem. Internat. Alumnae Orgn. Smithsonian Inst., Loomis Chaffee Alumnae Orgn.

PESIN, ELLA MICHELE, journalist, public relations professional; b. North Bergen, N.J., Aug. 29, 1956; d. Edward and Helene Sylvia (Rattner) P. BA, Sarah Lawrence Coll., 1978. Press rep. CBS-TV News and Entertainment, N.Y.C., 1978-80; publicist Newsweek Mag., N.Y.C., 1980-81; prin. Pesin Pub. Rels., N.Y.C., 1980-94; freelance journalist N.Y.C., 1981—; publicist Universal Studios MCA Inc., L.A., 1982-83; with publicity and mktg. NBC-TV News, N.Y.C., 1985-86; media exec. Burson Marsteller Pub. Rels.-Press/Media Execs., N.Y.C., 1986-87; speaker in field. Contbg. editor Cable Age mag., TV Radio Age mag., Advt. Forum, Facts Figures & Film, Advt. Compliance Svc.; contbr. columns to newspapers. Active Israel Bonds/United Jewish Appeal, N.Y.C., Rudolph Giuliani for N.Y.C. Mayor campaign. Mem. Pub. Rels. Soc. Am., Am. Soc. Journalists and Authors, N.Y. Fin. Writers Group, N.Y. Venture Group, Women Comm., Women Bus., Publicity Club N.Y. Home and Office: 401 E 80th St Apt 11J New York NY 10021

PESLAK HYMAN, VICTORIA, graphic designer; b. Bridgeport, Conn., Mar. 18, 1954; d. Chester Stanley and Jeanne Victoria (Roberts) P.; m. Steven Lynn Hyman, Oct. 27, 1984. B of Communication Design, Parsons Sch. Design, 1976. Graphic designer Vogue Mag., N.Y.C., 1976; art dir. Brides Mag., N.Y.C., 1977-81, Seventeen Mag., N.Y.C., 1981-84, Harper's Bazaar Mag., N.Y.C., 1984-85; pres. Platinum Design, Inc., N.Y.C., 1985—; speaker in field. Art dir.: (book) True Reauty, 1994. Mem. Am. Inst. Graphic Arts, Am. Craft Mus. (assoc.), Art Dirs. Club, Graphic Artists Guild, Soc. Publ. Designers, Fashion Group. Office: Platinum Design Inc 14 23d St New York NY 10010

PETERING, JANICE FAYE, hotel executive; b. Covington, Ky., Feb. 10, 1950; d. Edward Charles Petering Sr. and Shirley Ellen (McKenzie) Petering Brancucci. Student, Eastern Ky. U., 1969; cert., Ramada Mgmt. Inst., 1982. Cert. hotel adminstr. Night auditor Caesars Palace Hotel, Las Vegas, Nev., 1970-77; chief rack clk. Caesars Palace Hotel, Las Vegas, 1979-80, supr. accounts receivable, 1980-82, casino comptr., 1982-83, ops. comptr., 1983-85; exec. asst. to hotel mgr. Tropicana Hotel & Country Club, Las Vegas, 1977-79, hotel mgr., 1985-86; hotel mgr. MGM Marina Casino and Hotel, Las Vegas, 1986-87; dir. hotel ops. MGM MArina Casino and Hotel, Las Vegas, 1987-90; hotel mgr. Vacation Village, Las Vegas, Nev., 1991-93; internal controller, fin. analyst Continental Hotel Casino, Las Vegas, 1993—. Mem. Internat. Assn. Hospitality Accts., Las Vegas Hotel-Motel Assn., Las Vegas Hotel Mgrs. Assn., Network of Exec. Women in Hospitality. Roman Catholic. Office: Hotel Continental Inc 4100 Paradise Rd Las Vegas NV 89109

PETERMAN, DONNA COLE, communications executive; b. St. Louis, Nov. 9, 1947; d. William H. Cole and Helen A. Morris; m. John A. Peterman, Feb. 7, 1970. BA in Journalism, U. Mo., 1969; MBA, U. Chgo., 1984. Mgr. employee comm. Sears Merchandise Group, Chgo., 1975-80; dir. corp. comm. Sears, Roebuck and Co., Chgo., 1982-85; affairs and mktg. comm. Seraco Real Estate, Chgo., 1980-82; sr. v.p., dir. corp. comm. Dean Witter Fin. Svcs. Group, N.Y., 1985-88; sr. v.p., mng. dir. Hill and Knowlton, Inc., Chgo., 1988-94; exec. v.p. Hill and Knowlton, Inc., N.Y.C., 1994—. Media chmn, DeKalb County Comm, Georgia, 1975, media dir., Mo. Atty. Gen., 1971, copywriter, Govt. of Mo., 1971, media dir, Rep. Govs. Conf., 1974; trustee Met. Planning Coun. Mem. Internat. Assn. Bus. Communicators, Pub. Relations Soc. Am., Chgo. Coun. Fgn. Relations, Columbia Yacht Club, City Midday Club, Huguenot Yacht Club, Univ. Club. Republican. Catholic.

PETERS, ANN LOUISE, accounting manager; b. Knoxville, Tenn., Jan. 26, 1954; d. William Brown and Louise (Emerson) Nixon; m. Raymond Peters, July 11, 1975. BBA, Miami U., Oxford, Ohio, 1976; MBA, Xavier U., 1985. Cert. internal auditor. Acctg. officer Soc. Bank (formerly Citizens Bank), Hamilton, Ohio, 1977-85; internal auditor Procter & Gamble Co., Cin., 1985-86, audit sect. mgr., 1986-88, sr. cost analyst, beauty care, 1988-90; plant fin. mgr. Procter & Gamble Mfg. Co., Phoenix, 1990-92; sr. fin. analyst, beauty care Procter & Gamble Co., Cin., 1992-93, group mgr., gen. acctg., 1993—. Mem. Inst. Internal Auditors, Inst. Mgmt. Accts. Republican. Congregationalist. Home: 7889 Ironwood Way West Chester OH 45069 Office: Procter & Gamble Co 2 P & G Plaza TE-11 Cincinnati OH 45202

PETERS, BARBARA HUMBIRD, writer, editor; b. Santa Monica, Calif., Sept. 26, 1948; d. Philip Rising and Caroline Jean (Dickason) Peters. AA, Santa Monica Coll., 1971; BS, San Diego State U., 1976; postgrad. UCLA, 1981-82, 84. Ptnr. Signet Properties, L.A., 1971-85; tech. editor C. Brewer & Co., Hilo, Hawaii, 1975; editor The Aztec Engineer mag., San Diego, 1976-77; regional publicist YWCA, San Diego, 1977-78; campaign cons. Rep. Congl. and Assembly Candidates San Diego; Pollster, Los Angeles Times, 1983; pres., dir. Humbird Hopkins Inc., San Clemente, Calif., 1978-91; pub. rels. cons. ASCE, San Diego, 1975-76, Am. Soc. Mag. Photographers, San Diego, 1980. Author: The Layman's Guide to Raising Cane: A Guide to the Hawaiian Sugar Industry, 1975, The Students' Survival Guide, 1976, 2d edit. 1977. Mem. Mayor's Coun. on Librs., L.A., 1969; mem. Wilshire Blvd. Property Owners Assn., Santa Monica, 1972-78; docent Mus. Sci. and Industry, L.A., 1970; founding mem. Comml. and Indsl. Properties Assn., Santa Monica, 1982-89. Recipient Acting award Santa Monica Coll., 1970. Mem. NAFE, Internat. Assn. Bus. Communicators, Sales and Mktg. Execs. Assn. Avocations: travel, opera, puns.

PETERS, BERNADETTE (BERNADETTE LAZZARA), actress; b. Queens, N.Y., Feb. 28, 1948; d. Peter and Marguerite (Maltese) Lazzara. Student, Quintano Sch. for Young Profls., N.Y.C. Ind. actress, entertainer, 1959—. Appeared on TV series All's Fair, 1976-77; frequent guest appearances on TV; films include The Longest Yard, 1974, Silent Movie, 1976, Vigilante Force, 1976, W.C. Fields and Me, 1976, The Jerk, 1979, Pennies from Heaven, 1981 (Golden Globe Best Actress award), Heart Beeps, 1981, Tulips, 1981, Annie, 1982, Slaves of New York, 1988, Pink Cadillac, 1989, Impromptu, 1990, Alice, 1990; stage appearances include The Most Happy Fella, 1959, Gypsy, 1961, This is Google, 1962, Riverwind, 1966, The Penny Friend, 1966, Curly McDimple, 1966, Johnny No-Trump, 1967, George M!, 1968, Dames at Sea, 1968, La Strada, 1969, W.C., 1971, On the Town, 1971, Tartuffe, 1972, Mack and Mabel, 1974, Sally and Marsha, 1982, Sunday in the Park with George, 1983 (Tony nomination 1983), Song and Dance, 1985, Into the Woods, 1987, The Goodbye Girl, 1993; TV films David, 1988, Fall From Grace, 1990, The Last Best Year, 1990; rec. artist: (MCA Records) Bernadette Peters, 1980, Now Playing, 1981. Recipient Drama Desk award for Dames and Sea, 1968, for Good-Bye Girl, 1993; Drama Desk award nomination, 1987, 88, Tony award nominee, 1971, 74, 83, 85, Tony award for Best Actress in Song and Dance, 1986, Theatre World citation for George M!, 1968, Drama Desk award, 1986, Hasty Pudding Theatrical award, 1987 woman of the Yr., Sara Siddons Actress of Yr. award, 1993-94. Office: Judy Katz PR 1790 Broadway Ste 1600 New York NY 10019

PETERS, CAROL ANN DUDYCHA, counselor; b. Ripon, Wis., Dec. 23, 1938; d. George John and Martha (Malek) Dudycha; m. Milton Eugene Peters, Aug. 27, 1960. AB, Wittenberg U., 1960, MEd, 1963; leadership devel. cert., Ctr. for Creative Leadership, Greensboro, N.C., 1986; postgrad., U. Toledo, 1973—. Lic. profl. counselor, Ohio; nat. cert. counselor, nat. cert. career counselor Nat. Bd. Cert. Counselors, Inc. Tchr. Springfield (Ohio) City Schs., 1960-62, Mad River-Green Local Schs., Springfield, 1962-63; counselor Napoleon (Ohio) City Schs., 1963-70, Findlay (Ohio) City Schs., 1970—; field counselor Career Relocation Corp. Am., Valhalla, N.Y., 1992—; cons., prin. Peters and Peters, Findlay, 1979—; leader Creative Edn. Found., Buffalo, 1980-91, colleague, 1985—; founder ednl. corp. Career Info. Bur. Hancock County, 1974. Pres. Big Bros./Big Sisters Hancock County, 1982-83; bd. dirs. Citizens Opposing Drug Abuse (C.O.D.A.), Findlay, 1982—; advisor, leader Hancock Addictions Prevention for Youth (H.A.P.P.Y.), 1985-91; mem. Hancock County Community Devel. Found. Edn. Com., 1990—, Findlay/Hancock County Am. 2000 New Sch. Design Team, 1991-92; mem. Hancock County Crisis Response Team, 1991—. Named One of Outstanding Young Women of Am., 1967; named Outstanding Woman in Edn., Bus. and Profl. Women, 1983; recipient Outstanding Citizenship award The Lincoln Ctr., Findlay, 1989, Meritorious Svc. award Big Bros./Big Sisters Hancock County, 1988. Mem. ACA, AAUW (Findlay br.), NEA (life), Am. Sch. Counselor Assn., Nat. Career Devel. Assn., Ohio Edn. Assn., Ohio Counseling Assn., Ohio Sch. Counselor Assn., Findlay-Hancock County C. of C. (sec. edn. com. 1984-90). Lutheran. Office: Findlay City Schs 227 S West St Findlay OH 45840-3377

PETERS, CAROL BEATTIE TAYLOR (MRS. FRANK ALBERT PETERS), mathematician; b. Washington, May 10, 1932; d. Edwin Lucius and Lois (Beattie) Taylor; B.S., U. Md., 1954, M.A., 1958; m. Frank Albert Peters, Feb. 26, 1955; children—Thomas, June, Erick, Victor. Group mgr. Tech. Operations, Inc., Arlington, Va., 1957-62, sr. staff scientist, 1964-66; supervisory analyst Datatrol Corp., Silver Spring, Md., 1962; project dir. Computer Concept, Inc., Silver Spring, 1963-64; mem. tech. staff, then mem. sr. staff Informatics Inc., Bethesda, Md., 1966-70, mgr. systems projects, 1970-71, tech. dir., 1971-76; sr. tech. dir. Ocean Data Systems, Inc., Rockville, Md., 1976-83; dir. Informatics Gen. Co., 1983-89; pres. Carol Peters Assocs., 1989—. Mem. Assn. Computing Machinery, IEEE Computer Group. Home and Office: 12311 Glen Mill Rd Potomac MD 20854-1928

PETERS, CAROLJEAN NATALIE, elementary education educator; b. Belleville, Ill., Mar. 6, 1931; d. Frederick Henry and Florence Louise (Spies) Zwetschke; m. Arthur Henry Peters, Dec. 26, 1953; children: Julia Lynn, Thomas Arthur, Douglas Frederick. AA, Belleville Area Coll., 1950; AB, BS summa cum laude, Millikin U., 1952; MEd summa cum laude, So. Ill. U., 1984. Cert. elem. tchr. Elem. tchr. Roxana (Ill.) Dist., 1952-53; elem. tchr. Dist. 118, Belleville, 1954-56, substitute tchr., 1969-79; freelance storyteller, book reviewer Belleville, 1966-82, tchr. reading, 1983-87; reading improvement assistance tchr./chpt. 1 tchr. Wolf Br. Dist. 113, Belleville, 1984-94; reading cons. and diagnostician Belleville, 1994—; young authors conf. presenter St. Clair Region & State, Bloomington, Ill., 1986-91; in-service programmer E. St. Louis Schs., 1983, 85, Illini Grant Dist., Fairview Hghts., Ill., 1988, Wolf Br., 1989, 90, regional supts./prins. meeting, 1990; mem. state assessment project, 1991-92; presenter Belleville Area Arts Coun., 1985, Madison County Arts Coun., 1989, St. Clair; in-svc. portfolio presenter Dist. 113, 1992. Editor, feature writer: (church newsletter) Our St. Paul News, 1984-92. Leader, trainer River Bluffs coun. Girl Scouts U.S., Belleville, 1965-69; broadcaster Radio Info. Svc., Belleville, 1973-83; bd. dirs., sec., pres. Call for Help, Inc., Belleville and East St. Louis, 1978-82, 84-88, 89-91; bd. dirs., life mem. Meml. Hosp. Aux., Belleville, 1957—, YMCA Belleville, 1967-72; sec. ch. coun. St. Paul United Ch. of Christ, Belleville, 1981-84, v.p., 1984-85, pres., 1985-86. Recipient St. Clair Sq. Golden Apple award. Mem. Ill. Reading Coun., Internat. Reading Assn., Lewis & Clark Reading Coun., AAUW, Pi Mu Theta, Phi Kappa Phi, Kappa Delta Pi. Republican. Office: Wolf Br Sch 125 Huntwood Rd Belleville IL 62221-1999

PETERS, CATHY J., nurse practitioner, education consultant; b. Niagara Falls, N.Y., Dec. 9, 1951; d. Walter Anthony and Phyllis (La Barber) P. BSEd, SUNY, Cortland, 1973; AAS, SUNY, Syracuse, 1975; MS in Nursing, U. Rochester, 1981. Cert. adult nurse practitioner, N.Y. Nursing instr. SUNY, Brockport, 1981-82; dir. health edn. Group Health of Blue Cross/Blue Shield, Rochester, N.Y., 1985-88; dir. edn. Health Psychology Assocs., Rochester, 1988-91; nurse practitioner AC Rochester/GM, 1991-92; condr. stress mgmt. workshops, Rochester; editor, grant writer, dept. women's health and ob-gyn. Rochester Gen. Hosp., 1991-93; cons. health edn. adv. bd. Monroe County Health Dept., Rochester, 1989-90; mem. med. team Inst. for Shipboard Edn., U. Pitts., 1993. Vol. Blessed Sacrement Ch., Rochester, 1991—. Robert Wood Johnson grantee, 1979-81; Civil Svc. Employees' Assn. scholar, 1975. Mem. APHA, N.Y. State Coalition Nurse Practitioners, Internat. Patient Edn. Coun. Home and Office: PO Box 18555 Rochester NY 14618-0555

PETERS, DOLORES YVONNE, neonatal clinical nurse specialist; b. Washington, Aug. 9, 1951; d. Lewis Bradford and Thelma Beatrice (Walker) P. BSN cum laude, U. Md., 1975; MSN in Nursing of Developing Families, Catholic U. Am., 1989; BA in Biology cum laude, Western Md. Coll., 1973. RN, Va., D.C., Md.; cert. neonatal nurse practitioner. Obstet. staff nurse Sibley Meml. Hosp., Washington, 1975-76; nursery ednl. coord. Nat. Naval Med. Ctr., Bethesda, Md., 1980-82, neonatal clin. nursing specialist, 1982-90; neonatal clin. nurse specialist Washington Hosp. Ctr., 1990—; resource applications faculty C.V. Mosby Co., 1990-93. Am. Lung Assn. of Md. nursing rsch. fellow, 1987-88. Mem. Nat. Assn. Neonatal Nurses, Washington Met. Area Neonatal Nurses, Assn. of Women's Health, Obstet. and Neonatal Nurses, Sigma Theta Tau, Beta Beta Beta. Home: 2337 Massanutten Dr Silver Spring MD 20906-6178

PETERS, ELEANOR WHITE, mental health nurse; b. HIghland Park, Mich., Aug. 11, 1920; d. Alfred Mortimer and Jane Ann (Evans) White; m. William J. Peters, 1947 (div. 1953); children: Susannah J., William J. (dec.). RN, Christ Hosp. Sch. Nursing, Jersey City, 1941; BA, Jersey City State Coll., 1968; postgrad., U. Del., 1969-70; MS, SUNY, New Paltz, 1983. RN, N.J., N.Y. Mem. staff various area hosps. N.J., 1941-58; indsl. nurse Abex, Mahwah, N.J., 1958-68; sch. nurse Liberty (N.Y.) Ctrl. Sch., 1971-76; coord. practical nurse program Hudson County C.C., Jersey City, 1979-80; community mental health nurse Letchworth Village, Thiells, N.Y., 1981—. Mem. AAUW (pres. 1988-92), Alpha Delta Kappa (sec. Mu chpt. 1973-75), Sigma Theta Tau (Kappa Eta chpt.). Republican. Lutheran. Home: PO Box 224 Saddle River NJ 07458 Office: Letchworth Village Main St Devel Disabil Svcs Office PO Box 823 South Fallsburg NY 12779

PETERS, ELIZABETH ANN HAMPTON, nursing educator; b. Detroit, Sept. 27, 1934; d. Grinsfield Taylor and Ida Victoria (Jones) Hampton; m. James Marvin Peters, Dec. 1, 1956; children: Douglas Taylor, Sara Elizabeth. Diploma, Berea Coll. Hosp. Sch. Nursing, 1956; BS in Nursing, Wright State U., Dayton, Ohio, 1975; MS in Nursing, Ohio State U., Columbus, 1978. Therapist-RN Eastway, Inc., Dayton, Ohio, 1979-81; therapist family counseling svc. Good Samaritan-Community Mental Health Ctr., Dayton, Ohio, 1981-83; instr. Wright State U. Sch. Nursing, Dayton, 1983-84; clin. nurse specialist, pain mgmt. svcs., pain mgmt. program UPSA, Inc., Dayton, 1983-86; staff nurse Hospice of Dayton, Inc., 1985-86, dir. vol. svcs., 1986-89, dir. bereavement svcs., 1986-87; asst. prof. Community Hosp. Sch. Nursing, Springfield, Ohio, 1990-93, prof., 1993—. Author: (with others) Oncologic Pain, 1987. Mem. Clark County Mental Health Bd., Springfield, 1986—; mem. New Carlisle (Ohio) Bd. Health, 1990—. Mem. ANA, Ohio Nurses Assn. (pres. Tecumseh Trail dist.), Sigma Theta Tau. Home: 402 Flora Ave New Carlisle OH 45344-1329

PETERS, ELLEN ASH, state supreme court chief justice; b. Berlin, Mar. 21, 1930; came to U.S., 1939, naturalized, 1947; d. Ernest Edward and Hildegard (Simon) Ash; m. Phillip I. Blumberg; children: David Bryan Peters, James Douglas Peters, Julie Peters Haden. BA with honors, Swarthmore Coll., 1951, LLD (hon.), 1983; LLB cum laude, Yale U., 1954, MA (hon.), 1964, LLD (hon.), 1985; LLD (hon.), U. Hartford, 1983; Georgetown U., 1984; LLD (hon.), Yale U., 1985, Conn. Coll., 1985, N.Y. Law Sch., 1985; HLD (hon.), St. Joseph Coll., 1986; LLD (hon.), Colgate U., 1986, Trinity Coll., 1987, Bates Coll., 1987, Wesleyan U., 1987, DePaul U., 1988; HLD (hon.), Albertus Magnus Coll., 1990; LLD (hon.), U. Conn., 1992; LLD, U. Rochester, 1994. Bar: Conn. 1957. Law clk. to judge U.S. Circuit Ct., 1954-55; assoc. in law U. Calif., Berkeley, 1955-56; prof. law Yale U., New Haven, 1956-78; adj. prof. law; assoc. justice Conn. Supreme Ct., Hartford, 1978-84; chief justice Conn. Supreme Ct., 1984—; adj. prof.

law Yale U., 1978-84. Author: Commercial Transactions: Cases, Texts, and Problems, 1971, Negotiable Instruments Primer, 1974; contbr. articles to profl. jours. Bd. mgrs. Swarthmore Coll., 1970-81; trustee Yale-New Haven Hosp., 1981-85, Yale Corp., 1986-92; mem. conf. Chief Justices, 1984—, pres. 1994; hon. chmn. U.S. Constl. Bicentennial Com., 1986-91; mem. Conn. Permanent Commn. on Status of Women, 1973-74, Conn. Bd. Parsons, 1978-80, Conn. Law Revision Commn., 1978-84; bd. dirs. Nat. Ctr. State Cts., 1992—, chmn., 1994. Recipient Ella Grasso award, 1982, Jud. award Conn. Trial Lawyers Assn., 1982, citation of merit Yale Law Sch., 1983, Pioneer Woman award Hartford Coll. for Women, 1988, Disting. Svc. award U. Conn. Law Sch. Alumni Assn., 1993. Mem. ABA, Conn. Bar Assn. (Jud. award 1992), Am. Law Inst. (coun.), Am. Acad. Arts and Scis., Am. Philos. Soc. Office: Conn Supreme Ct Drawer N Sta A 231 Capitol Ave Hartford CT 06106

PETERS, ESTHER CAROLINE, aquatic toxicologist, pathobiologist, consultant; b. Greenville, S.C., May 9, 1952; d. Otto Emanuel and Winifred Ellen (Bahan) P.; m. Harry Brinton McCarty, Jr., May 27, 1984; children: Rachel Elizabeth, William Brinton. BS, Furman U., 1974; MS, U. South Fla., 1978; PhD, U. R.I., 1984. Rsch. asst. Environ. Rsch. Lab., U.S. EPA, Narragansett, R.I., 1980-81; grad. rsch. asst. U. R.I., Kingston, 1981-84; assoc. biologist JRB Assocs., Narragansett, 1984-85; postdoctoral fellow Dept. of Invertebrate Zoology, Nat. Mus. Natural History, Washington, 1985-86, resident rsch. assoc., 1986-89; rsch. fellow Registry Tumors in Lower Animals, Nat. Mus. of Natural History, Washington, 1987-91; sr. scientist Tetra Tech, Inc., Fairfax, Va., 1991—; sci. adv. panel Project Reef-keeper, Am. Littoral Soc., Miami, Fla., 1988—; courtesy asst. prof. Dept. Marine Sci., U. South Fla., St. Petersburg, 1987—; cons. The Nature Conservancy, Arlington, Va., 1991. Author: (with others) Pathobiology of Marine and Estuarine Organisms, 1993, Disease Processes of Marine Bivalve Molluscs, 1988; contbr. articles to profl. jours. Recipient Nat. Rsch. Svc. postdoctoral tng. fellowship NIH, Bethesda, Md., 1987-91. Mem. AAAS, Am. Fisheries Soc., N.Y. Acad. Scis., Soc. for Environ. Toxicology and Chemistry, Soc. Invertebrate Pathology, Sigma Xi. Office: Tetra Tech Inc 10306 Eaton Pl Ste 340 Fairfax VA 22030-2201

PETERS, FRANCES ELIZABETH, librarian; b. Phila., Nov. 25, 1915; d. Alexander and Sarah Mower (Scott) P. BSEd, U. Pa., 1936, MA in Latin, 1938; BSLS, Drexel Inst. Tech., 1940; MLS, Drexel U., 1966. Br. libr. Free Libr. Phila., 1951-52, 57-62, asst. in office of work with adults, 1953-57, asst. in art dept., 1945-48, asst. extension div., 1941-45; libr. Holiday mag. Curtis Pub. Co., Phila., 1948-51; asst. libr. Pedagogical Libr., Sch. Dist. Phila., 1962-63; libr. Cheltenham High Sch., Wyncote, Pa., 1963-66, Community Coll., Temple U., Phila., 1966-67; head libr. Pa. Coll. Podiatric Medicine, Phila., 1968-82, libr., 1982—. Mem. Salvation Army Aux. Mem. AAUW, DAR, Victorian Soc., Nat. Soc. Daus. 1812, Classical Assn. Atlantic States, Phila. Classical Assn., Hist. Soc. Pa., Cruiser Olympia Assn., Pa. Classical Assn., Pi Lambda Theta, Eta Sigma Phi, Beta Phi Mu, Phi Delta Gamma, Phi Kappa Phi. Republican. Baptist. Home: 600 E Cathedral Rd Apt 505H Philadelphia PA 19128-1931 Office: Charles E Krausz Libr Pa Coll Podiatric Medicine Race At 8th St Philadelphia PA 19107

PETERS, JEAN THERESA, sales executive; b. Boulder, Colo., July 22, 1944; d. Barney Clifford and Frances Kathrine (Tholen) Neff; m. Ford Gordon Peters Jr., Jan. 29, 1982; 1 child, Christopher Samuel. Student, U. Colo., 1962-63; lic., Brown Radio-TV Sch., 1975. Reception clk. first aide and water safety dept. Denver chpt. ARC, 1960-62; reception clk. Takcom Jewelry, N.Y.C., 1963-64; mem. promotion staff Calla Records, N.Y.C., 1965-67; detail sales rep. Alright Med. Labs., N.Y.C., and R.I., 1971-74; engr., tech. dir. WTNH-TV, New Haven, 1975-76, KWGN-TV, Denver, 1976-79; engr. KBTV (name now KUSA-TV), Denver, 1976; adminstrv. asst., v.p. sales broadcast equipment G.P. Enterprises, Inc., Arlington, Tex., 1980—. Mem. Bowie High Sch. PTSA, Arlington, 1991—. Mem. Soc. Motion Picture and TV Engrs., World Wildlife Fund, Humane Soc. U.S., Wilderness Soc., Arlington Herb and Garden Club. Office: G P Enterprises Inc PO Box 912 Arlington TX 76004-0912

PETERS, KAREN RONELL, public administrator; b. Topeka, Kans., June 20, 1944; d. Ralph Keller and Mary Jean (Meyers) Keller Wynn; 1 child, Lisa Renee. BA, U. Okla., 1966; MA in Spanish, Wichita State U., 1970; postgrad., U. Calif., Irvine, 1971-74, cert. in hazardous materials mgmt., 1986; JD, Western State U., 1993. Adminstrv. analyst I program planning div. County of Orange, Calif., 1976, adminstrv. analyst II program coordination div., 1976-79, staff analyst III program coordination div., 1979-80, mgr. adminstrv. services div. environ. mgmt. agy., 1980-84; sr. staff analyst Hazardous Materials Program/CAO, 1984-86; adminstrv. mgr. I hazardous materials program Orange County Fire Dept., 1986-94, adminstrv. mgr. I facilities mgmt., 1995—; guest lectr. U. Calif., 1989. Co-chmn. issue briefing com. North Orange County chpt. NOW, 1983-84, state pres. Calif. 1979-81, chmn. polit. action task force, 1983-85, treas., 1983, numerous offices; sec. ERA-Orange County, 1982-83, treas. 1977-79; chmn. Community Devel. Coun., Inc., 1977-78, vice-chmn., 1976-77, chmn. project rev. and program devel. com., 1976-77; v.p., bd. dirs. Chateau Orleans Homeowners Assn., 1983-84, pres., 1977-78, treas., 1994—; active numerous polit. campaigns, 1976-84, prevention week activities Child Abuse Coun. Recipient numerous civic awards including Woman of Distinction award Soroptimist Internat. of Orange, 1989, Progress for Women award Santa Ana Coll., 1986, Cert. of Achievement for Leadership award North Orange County YWCA, 1986, Woman of Achievement award Women in Communications, Inc., 1983, Golden Key award Dem. Women Orange County, 1983, and many others. Mem. NOW, Calif. Hazardous Waste Assn., Am. Soc. Pub. Adminstrn. (exec. coun. Orange County chpt. 1977-81, treas. 1978-79, chmn. task force 1976-77), U. Okla. Alumni Assn. (life), Wichita State U. Alumni Assn., Unitarian Soc. Orange County, Nat. Women's Polit. Caucus, Sigma Delta Pi. Home: 2525 N Bourbon St Apt 2M Orange CA 92665-3012 Office: Orange County Fire Dept 180 S Water St Orange CA 92666-2123

PETERS, LAURALEE MILBERG, diplomat; b. Monroe, N.C., Jan. 28, 1943; d. Arthur W. and Opal I. (Mueller) Milberg; m. Lee M. Peters, May 30, 1964; children: David, Evelyn, Edward, Matthew. BA with highest honors, U. Kans., 1964, postgrad., 1965-67; student, Fgn Svc. Inst., 1975. Asst. pub. info. officer NAS, Washington, 1967-69; joined Fgn. Svc., Dept. State, 1972, commd. sr. fgn. svc. officer, 1985; chief visa sect. Am. Embassy, Saigon, Vietnam, 1972-74; internat. fin. officer Dept. State, Washington, 1975-79; U.S. rep. to Econ. and Social Commn. for Asia and Pacific, UN, Bangkok, Thailand, 1979-81; devel. fin. officer Dept. State, Washington, 1981-82; econ. officer Israel, West Bank, Gaza, 1982-84; dir. Office Monetary Affairs Dept. State, Washington, 1984-86; econ. counselor Am. Embassy, Islamabad, Pakistan, 1986-88; career devel. officer Dept. State, Washington, 1988-89, dep. asst. sec. for personnel, 1989-91; mem. Sr. Seminar, 1991-92; U.S. Ambassador to Sierra Leone, 1992—. Various leadership positions Boy Scouts Am., 1977-88. Recipient Disting. award of merit Nat. Capitol Area Coun. Boy Scouts Am., 1986. Mem. Am. Fgn. Svc. Protective Assn. (v.p. 1981-84), Consular Officer's Assn. (sec. 1974-75), Phi Beta Kappa. Home: 6205 Mori St Mc Lean VA 22101-3150 Office: Am Embassy, Walpole & Siaka Stevens Sts, Freetown Sierra Leone*

PETERS, MARILYN PULAWSKI, training manager; b. Dunkirk, N.Y., Apr. 22, 1953; d. Mack and June (Fishburn) Pulawski; m. Brian D. Kerr, May 25, 1993; children: Breanne, Sarah. BA in Theatre/English, SUNY, Fredonia, 1975; MBA in Mgmt., Russell Sage Coll., 1986. Costume designer George St. Theatre, New Brunswick, N.J., 1975-76; profl. faculty theatre dept. SUNY, Albany, 1976-78; restaurant owner Gemini Jazz Cafe, Albany, 1978-80; asst. prof. Jr. Coll. Albany, 1980-86; tng. cons. Corp. Resource Assocs., Redwood City, Calif., 1988-90; tng. developer Genentech, Inc., Intel Corp., AT&T, Motorola, Inc., 1988-90; sr. curriculum developer Oracle Corp., Redwood City, 1990-91; customer svc. tng. mgr. Intuit, Inc., Palo Alto, Calif., 1991—. Regents scholar N.Y. State Bd. Regents, Albany, 1971. Home: 54 Lafayette Ave Hayward CA 94544-8154

PETERS, MERCEDES, psychoanalyst; b. N.Y.C. Student Columbia U., 1944-45; BS, L.I. U., 1945; MS, U. Conn., 1953; tng. in psychotherapy Am. Inst. Psychotherapy and Psychoanalysis, 1960-70; cert. in Psychoanalysis Postgrad. Ctr. For Mental Health, 1976; PhD in Psychoanalysis, Union Inst., 1989. Cert. psychoanalyst Am. Examining Bd. Psychoanalysis; cert. mental health cons. Social worker various agys., pub. instns., 1945-63; sr. psychotherapist Community Guidance Svc., 1960-75; staff affiliate Postgrad. Ctr. for Mental Health, 1974-76; pvt. practice psychoanalysis and psychotherapy, Bklyn., 1961—. Contbr. articles to profl. jours. Bd. dirs. Brookwood Child Care Assn.; mem. vestry Grace Ch., Brooklyn Heights. Fellow Am. Orthopsychiat. Assn.; mem. LWV, NAACP, NASW, Postgrad. Psychoanalytic Soc., Assn. For Psychoanalytic Self Psychology, Wednesday Club. Office: 142 Joralemon St Brooklyn NY 11201-4709

PETERS, PATRICIA LYNN, administrator; b. N.Y.C., July 2, 1950; d. Hans and Gloria (Trachtenberg) P.; m. Bradford Carter Steele, Dec. 9, 1977 (div. Aug. 1981). BFA, Boston U., 1972. Travel agt. Chestnut Hill (Mass.) Travel, 1972-74; cons. TWA Tour Ops., N.Y.C., 1974-75; mgr. systems tech. Heritage Travel, Cambridge, Mass, 1975-92; dir. automation, tng. The Lawyer's Travel Svc., N.Y.C., 1992-93; ops. mgr. JourneyCorp Travel Mgmt., N.Y.C., 1993—; cons. in field. Mem. NAFE, Boston Sabre Club. Home: 445 E 80th St 2C New York NY 10021 Office: JourneyCorp Travel Mgmt 488 Madison Ave New York NY 10022

PETERS, ROBERTA, soprano; b. N.Y.C., May 4, 1930; d. Sol and Ruth (Hirsch) P.; m. Bertram Fields, Apr. 10, 1955; children: Paul, Bruce. Ed. privately; Litt.D., Elmira Coll., 1967; Mus. D., Ithaca Coll., 1968, Colby Coll., 1980; L.H.D., Westminster Coll., 1974, Lehigh U., 1977; D.F.A., St. John's U., 1982; LittD, Coll. New Rochelle, 1989. Author: Debut at the Met; Met. Opera debut as Zerlina in Don Giovanni, 1950; recorded numerous operas; appeared motion pictures; frequent appearances radio and TV; sang at Royal Opera House, Covent Garden, London, Vienna State Opera, Munich Opera, West Berlin Opera, Salzburg Festival, debuts at festivals in Vienna and Munich; concert tours in U.S., Soviet Union, Scandinavian countries, Israel, China, Japan, Taiwan, South Korea, debut, Kirov Opera, Leningrad, USSR, sang at Bolshoi Opera, Moscow (1st Am. to receive Bolshoi medal). Trustee Carnegie Hall; dir. Met. Opera Guild; chmn. Nat. Inst. Music Theater, 1991—; apptd. by Pres. Bush to Nat. Coun. Arts, 1992. Named Woman of Yr. Fedn. Women's Clubs, 1964; honored spl. ceremony on 35th anniversary with the Met. Opera Co., 1985; was 1st Am. to receive Bolshoi medal. Office: ICM Artists Ltd 40 W 57th St New York NY 10019-4070

PETERS, SARAH WHITAKER, art historian, writer, lecturer; b. Kenosha, Wis., Aug. 17, 1924; d. Robert Burbank and Margaret Jebb (Allen) Whitaker; m. Arthur King Peters, Oct. 21, 1943; children: Robert Bruce, Margaret Allen, Michael Whitaker. BA, Sarah Lawrence Coll., 1954; MA, Columbia U., 1966; student, L'Ecole du Louvre, Paris, 1967-68; diplome, Ecole des Trois Gourmandes, Paris, 1968; PhD, CUNY, 1987. Freelance critic Art in Am., N.Y.C.; lectr. Bronxville (N.Y.) Adult Sch., Internat. Mus. Photography, 1979, Tufts U., 1979, Madison (Wis.) Art Ctr., 1984, Meml. Art Gallery, Rochester, N.Y., 1988, 91, Caramoor Mus., Katonah, N.Y., 1988, Yale U. Art Gallery, New Haven, Conn., 1989, The Cosmopolitan Club, N.Y.C., 1977, 91, Sarah Lawrence Coll., Bronxville, N.Y., 1992, The Phillips Collection, Washington, 1993, Mpls. Inst. Arts, 1993, Whitney Mus. Am. Art, Champion, 1994, U. Wis., Parkside, 1994, Nat. Wildlife Art Mus., Jackson Hole, Wyo., 1995; lectr-in-residence Garrison Forest Sch., Owings Mills, Md.; adj. asst. prof. art history C.W. Post, U. L.I. Author: Becoming O'Keeffe: The Early Years, 1991; contbr. articles to profl. jours. Mem. Coll. Art Assn., Bronxville Field Club, The Cosmopolitan Club. Home: 14 Village Ln Bronxville NY 10708

PETERS, SHIRLEY ANN, pediatrics nurse; b. Burbank, Calif., July 25, 1948; d. Frank F. and Marion Belle (Thorn) P. Diploma, Kaiser Found. Sch. Nursing, 1970; BS in Health Sci., Chapman Coll., 1978, MS in Health Sci., 1981. RN, Calif.; cert. pediatric nurse practitioner. Pediatric nurse practitioner Kaiser-Permanente Med. Ctr., Panorama City, Calif.; rsch. nurse practitioner Pharmacology Rsch. Inst., Van Nuys, Calif.; pediatric nurse practitioner, infection control practitioner Granada Hills (Calif.) Community Hosp.; pediatric nurse practitioner Med. Ctr. of North Hollywood, Calif., CIGNA Health Plans of Calif., North Hollywood; patient care coord., quality improvement/utilization rev. Alternative Health Care, Chatsworth, Calif.; pediatric nruse practitioner Childrens Hosp. of L.A., L.A. Mem. United Nurse's Assn. Calif. (clinic co-chair, parliamentarian, negotiator, NAPNAP, Assn. Infection Control Practitioners.

PETERS, VIRGINIA, actress; b. Los Angeles, July 15, 1924; d. Peter and Tessie (Skiller) Stetzenko. Grad., Pasadena (Calif.) Playhouse, 1944; student, Los Angeles City Coll. Tchr. Burbank (Calif.) Little Theatre, 1978-80, Burbank Acad. Performing Arts, 1979—. TV appearances in Night Strangler, 1972, Love American Style, 1973, Rita Moreno Show, 1977, Laverne and Shirley, 1977, 78, Happy Days, 1977, Dallas, 1980, The Waltons, 1981, House Detective, 1985, Knight Rider, 1985, Murder She Wrote, 1986, Hunter, 1986, Hardcastle and McCormick, 1986, Cavanaughs, 1986, Paper Chase, 1986, also Days of Our Lives, Divorce Court, Grace Under Fire, 1993; film appearances include The Arrangement, 1968, The Cat People, 1981, Fast Times at Ridgemont High, 1982, Rat Boy, 1985, The Deacon Street Deer, 1985, My Demon Lover, Mr. President, The Judge, Stripped to Kill II, 1988, Hero, My Girl II; appeared in: TV movie The 11th Victim, 1979; TV pilot We Got It Made; also numerous commls. Mem. Masquers Club (past dir.), Pasadena Playhouse Alumni Assos. (past dir.). Democrat. Roman Catholic.

PETERS BOGNANNI, CATHLEEN LORRAINE, computer graphic artist; b. Balt., Mar. 17, 1968; d. Ronald Edward and Rosemary Lorraine (Johnston) Peters; m. Anthony John Bognanni, Oct. 19, 1991. BS, Towson State U., 1991. Graphic designer The Harford Edition, Bel Air, Md., 1991-92, The Harford Impulse, Bel Air, 1991-92; computer artist Mid Atlantic Label, Inc., Forest Hill, Md., 1993—; free-lance artist, Bel Air, 1991—. Artist series drawings Matisse I-IV, 1989, photographic series Atrophy I-IV, 1991. Democrat.

PETERSEN, ANNE C(HERYL), foundation administrator, educator; b. Little Falls, Minn., Sept. 11, 1944; d. Franklin Hanks and Rhoda Pauline (Sandwick) Studley; m. Douglas Lee Petersen, Dec. 27, 1967; children: Christine Anne, Benjamin Bradfield. BA, U. Chgo., 1966, MS, 1972, PhD, 1973. Asst. prof., rsch. assoc. Dept. Psychiatry U. Chgo., 1972-80, assoc. prof., rsch. assoc., 1980-82; prof. human devel., head Dept. Individual and Family Studies Pa. State U., University Park, 1982-87, dean Coll. Health and Human Devel., 1987-92; dean Grad. Sch., v.p. for rsch. U. Minn., Mpls., 1992-94, prof. adolescent devel. and pediatrics, 1992—; dep. dir. NSF, Arlington, Va., 1994—; vis. prof., fellow Coll. End. and Devel. Psychology, Roosevelt U., Chgo., 1973-74; cons. Ctr. for Health Adminstrn. Studies U. Chgo., 1976-78, Ctr. for New Schs., Chgo., 1974-78, Robert Wood Johnson Found. Mathtech, Inc., 1987-89; coord. clin. rsch. tng. program Michael Reese Hosp. and Med. Ctr., Chgo., 1976-80, dir. Lab. for Study of Adolescence, 1975-82; mem. faculty Ill. Sch. for Profl. Psychology, 1978-79; statis. cons. Coll. Nursing U. Ill. Med. Ctr., 1975-83; assoc. dir. health program MacArthur Found., 1980-82, also cons. health program, 1982-88; chair sr. adv. bd. NIMH, 1987-88. Reviewer Jour. of Youth and Adolescence, 1975-80, Devel. Psychology, 1979—, Sci., 1979—, Jour. of Edn. Psychology, 1979—, Child Devel., 1980—, Jour. Edn. Measurement, 1980, Ednl. Researcher, 1980, Am. Ednl. Rsch. Jour., 1981—, Jour. of Mental Imagery, 1982-92, Sex Roles, 1984—; cons. editor Psychology of Women Quar., 1978-82, assoc. editor, 1983-86; adv. editor Contemporary Psychology, 1985-86; editorial bd. various profl. jours. Bd. overseers Lewis Coll., Ill. Inst. Tech., 1980-82; mem. adv. bd. longitudinal data archive project Murray Ctr., Radcliffe Coll., 1985-91, mem. sci. adv. bd., 1983-91. Mem. NAS (nat. forum on future children and their families 1987-91, chmn. panel on child abuse and neglect 1991-93), fellow AAAS, APA (chmn. task force on reproductive freedom 1979-81, program chmn. 1981-82, chmn. task force on long range planning 1986-89, pres. div. 7 1992-93), Am. Ednl. Rsch. Assn. (various offices), Assn. Women in Sci., Behavior Genetics Assn., Psychometric Soc., Acad. Europaea, Soc. for Rsch. on Adolescence (pres. 1990-92, past pres., chmn. nominations com. 1992-94). Home: 11166 Harbor Ct Reston VA 22091 Office: NSF 4201 Wilson Blvd Ste 1205 Reston VA 22091

PETERSEN, CATHERINE HOLLAND, lawyer; b. Norman, Okla., Apr. 24, 1951; d. John Hays and Helen Ann (Turner) Holland; m. James Frederick Petersen, June 26, 1973 (div.); children: T. Kyle, Lindsay Diane. B.A., Hastings Coll., 1973; J.D., Okla. U., 1976. Bar: Okla. 1976, U.S. Dist. Ct. (we. dist.) Okla. 1978. Legal intern, police legal advisor City of Norman, 1974-76; sole practice, Norman, 1976-81; ptnr. Williams Petersen & Denny, Norman, 1981-82; pres. Petersen Assocs., Inc., Norman, 1982—; adj. prof. Okla. City U. Coll. Law, 1982, U. Okla. Law Ctr., 1987; instr. continuing legal edn. U. Okla. Law Ctr., Norman, 1977, 79, 81, 83, 84, 86, 89-94. Bd. dirs. United Way, Norman, 1978-84, pres., 1981; bd. dirs. Women's Resource Ctr., Norman, 1975-77, 82-84; mem. Jr. League, Norman, 1980-83, Norman Hosp. Aux., Norman, 1982-84; trustee 1st Presbyn. Ch., 1986-87. Named to Outstanding Okla. Women of 1980's, Women's Polit. Caucus, 1980, Outstanding Women Am., 1981, 83. Fellow Am. Acad. Matrimonial Lawyers (pres. Okla. chpt. 1990-91, bd. govs. 1991-95); mem. Cleve. County Bar Assn., Okla. Bar Assn. (chmn. family law sect. 1987-88, seminar instr. 1986-94), Phi Delta Phi. Republican. Home: 4716 Sundance Ct Norman OK 73072-3900 Office: PO Box 1243 314 E Comanche St Norman OK 73069-6009

PETERSEN, CYNTHIA LOIS, controller; b. N.Y.C., Sept. 22, 1945; d. Edward John and Esther (Ettinger) Kilgus; m. Carl J. Petersen Jr., July 3, 1965; children: Carl John III, Debra Dawn. Student, Hunter Coll., 1962-66; B of Profl. Studies with distinction, Pace U., 1980. Cost acct. LeCroy Rsch., Spring Valley, N.Y., 1981; from cost acct. to contr. Am. Tack and Hardware Co., Inc., Monsey, N.Y., 1981—. Den mother Boy Scouts Am., Monsey, 1976; leader Girl Scouts Am., Monsey, 1978-83. Mem. Inst. Mgmt. Accts. Episcopalian. Home: 7 Park Ln Monsey NY 10952

PETERSEN, ELLEN ANNE, artist; b. N.Y.C., Dec. 18, 1930; d. William George and Dina (Bochmeier) Heinrich; m. Ralph Lamon Petersen, Dec. 14, 1952; children: William, Bryan. BS, NYU, 1968, MS, 1970. Art educator Paramus (N.J.) High Sch., 1969-85; tchng. artist William Carlos Williams Ctr. for Arts, Rutherford, N.J., 1989-91; studio artist Parrish Mus., Southampton, N.Y., 1988—; artist workshops Guild Hall Mus., East Hampton, N.Y., 1992—; Video interview "Women in the Arts" Fairleigh Dickinson U., Teaneck, N.J., 1977, LTV-local TV, East Hampton, 1991. Represented in permanent collection Guild Hall Mus., East Hampton, N.Y. Bd. dirs. Jimmy Ernst Artists' Alliance, East Hampton, N.Y., 1985-92; mem. edn. com. Parrish Art Mus., Southampton, 1989—; curator Springs Invitational Art Exhbn., East Hampton, 1994. Recipient hon. mention Guild Hall Mus., 1994, 1st prize N.J. state Exhbn., East Orange, N.J., 1967, award Springs-Ashawagh Hall Invitational, East Hampton, 1993, Juried Exhbn., Parrish Mus., 1992. Mem. Nat. Women's Caucus of Art, Artists' Equity, Jimmy Ernst Artists' Alliance (treas. 1988-90, v.p. 1990-92), Art Students' League (life), Women's Caucus for Art (v.p. Dallas chpt. 1987-88). Home and Studio: 7 South Pond Rd East Hampton NY 11937

PETERSEN, JACQUELINE ANN, school nurse; b. Council Bluffs, Iowa, Jan. 18, 1938; d. Lafe Roundy and Lauretta Jean (Nuzum) Robertson; m. Karl Roy Petersen, May 25, 1958; children: Kirk Dean, Jeffrey Lynn, Kris Eugene. ADN, Nebr. Meth. Hosp. Nursing, 1958. RN, Iowa; ordained priest Reorganized Ch. of Jesus Christ of Latter Day Saints, 1991. Charge nurse ICU Meth. Hosp., Omaha, 1958-59, recovery rm. nurse, 1959-60; nursing home nurse Rose Vista Home, Woodbine, Iowa, 1964-66, 68-70; pvt. duty nurse Logan, Iowa, 1973-76; sch. nurse Lo-Ma Cmty. Schs., Logan, 1976—; mem. wellness com. Lo-Ma Schs., Logan, 1987-94, level I investigator, 1989-94, AIDS coord., 1992-94; chmn., mem. Sch. Drug Free Com., Logan, 1987-94. Vol. ARC Bloodmobiles, Woodbine and Logan, 1960—; active neighborhood club Jolly Makers, Magnolia, Iowa, 1964-95; scout leader, den mother Boy Scouts Am., Logan, 1968-70; Sunday sch. tchr. RLDS Ch., Woodbine, 1970-85; women's leader Worship Commn. Ch., Woodbine, 1978, chair, 1987-93; pres. Parent Music Assn., Logan, 1983-84. Mem. NEA, Philanthropic Ednl. Orgn. (treas. 1986-88). Home: RR 2 Box 150 Logan IA 51546

PETERSEN, MAUREEN JEANETTE MILLER, management information consultant, former nurse; b. Evanston, Ill., Sept. 4, 1956; d. Maurice James and M. Joyce (Mielke) Miller; m. Gregory Eugene Petersen, July 7, 1984; 1 child, Trevor James. BS in Nursing cum laude, Vanderbilt U., 1978; MS in Biometry and Health Info. Systems, U. Minn., 1984. Nurse U. Iowa Hosps. and Clinics, Iowa City, 1978-82; research asst. Sch. Nursing, U. Minn., Mpls., 1982-83; mgr. Arthur Andersen/Andersen Cons., Mpls., 1984—. Mem. Women in Biocomputing, Mensa. Methodist. Home: 1050 County Rd C2 W Saint Paul MN 55113-1945 Office: Andersen Cons 45 S 7th St Minneapolis MN 55402-1607

PETERS-MCDOWELL, DWAN RENEÉ, actress, employment executive; b. Wahiwa, Hawaii, June 23, 1964; d. Shelton Von and Barbara Jean (Carter) Peters; m. Paul Richard McDowell, Apr. 14, 1990. BA in Speech Commn., U. Fla., 1988; postgrad., Lisa Maile Profl. Actors' Sch., 1993, Bill Einsiedel Prodns., 1993—. Exec. asst. Office Congl. Liaison/Pentagon, Dept. of Army, Washington, 1989-90; client svcs. specialist The Firm Inc., Orlando, Fla., 1994—; focus group moderator on interpersonal comm. and AIDS rsch. study U. Fla., 1988. Featured actress KVG Prodns., 1993, Einsiedel Prodn., 1993, 88 Daze Short Film, 1994. Mem. program com. African Am. Women Summit, Orlando, 1994. Mem. NAFE.

PETERSON, BARBARA ANN BENNETT, history educator; b. Portland, Oreg., Sept. 6, 1942; d. George Wright and Hope (Chatfield) Bennett; m. Frank Lynn Peterson, July 1, 1967. BA, BS, Oreg. State U., 1964; MA, Stanford U., 1965; PhD, U. Hawaii, 1978; PhD (hon.), London Inst. Applied Rsch., 1991. Prof. history U. Hawaii, Honolulu, 1967—, chmn. social scis. dept., 1971-73, 75-76, asst. dean, 1973-74; prof. Asian history and European colonial history and world problems Chapman Coll. World Campus Afloat, 1974; prof. European overseas exploration, expansion, and colonialism U. Colo., Boulder, 1978; assoc. prof. U. Hawaii-Manoa Coll. Continuing Edn., 1981; Fulbright prof. history Wuhan (China) U., 1988-89; Fulbright rsch. prof. Sophia U., Japan, 1967; lectr. Capital Speakers, Washington, 1987—. Co-author: Women's Place is in the History Books, Her Story, 1962-1980: A Curriculum Guide for American History Teachers, 1980; author: America in British Eyes, 1988; editor: Notable Women of Hawaii, 1984, (with W. Solheim) The Pacific Region, 1990, 91, American History: 17th, 18th, and 19th Centuries, 1993, America: 19th and 20th Centuries, 1993; assoc. editor Am. Nat. Biography; contbr. articles to profl. publs. Participant People-to-People Program, Eng., 1964, Expt. in Internat. Living Program, Nigeria, 1966; chmn. 1st Nat. Women's History Week, Hawaii, 1982; pres. Bishop Mus. Coun., 1993-94; active Hawaii Commn. on Status of Women. Recipient state proclamations Gov. of Hawaii, 1982, City of Honolulu, 1982, Outstanding Tchr. of yr. award Wuhan (China) U., 1988, Medallion of Excellence award Am. Biog. Assn., 1989, Woman of Yr. award, 1991; Fulbright scholar, Japan, 1967, China, 1988-89; NEH-Woodrow Wilson fellow Princeton U., 1980. Fellow World Literary Acad (Eng.), Internat. Biog. Assn., (Cambridge, Eng. chpt.); mem. AAUW, Am. Studies Assn. (pres. 1984-85), Fulbright Alumni Assn. (founding pres. Hawaii chpt. 1984-88, mem. nat. steering com. chairwomen Fulbright Assn. ann. conf. 1990), Am. Hist. Assn. (mem. numerous coms.), Am. Coun. on Edn., Maison Internat. des Intellectuals, Hawaii Found. History and Humanities (mem. editorial bd. 1972-73), Hawaii Found. Women's History, Hawaii Hist. Assn., Nat. League Am. Pen Women (contest chairperson 1986), Women in Acad. Adminstrn., Fulbright Assn., Pi Beta Phi, Phi Kappa Phi. Home: 1341 Laukahi St Honolulu HI 96821-1407 Office: U Hawaii 874 Dillingham Blvd Honolulu HI 96817

PETERSON, CAROL ANNA, accountant; b. Overland Park, Jan. 4, 1960; d. Carl Arlin and Anita JoAnn (Moeller) P. BS in Acctg. and Bus. Adminstrn., U. Kans., 1982; MBA, Rockhurst Coll., 1989. Cert. integrated resources mgr., prodn. and inventory mgr. Acct. Harold E. Goss & Assocs., Overland Park, 1983-84; cost acct. Murphy Industries, North Kansas City, Mo., 1984-85; mgr. mfg. sys. and traffic Target Products, Inc., Kansas City, 1985-90; mgr. cost acctg. Sanofi Animal Health, Inc., Overland Park, 1990—. Mem. Am. Soc. Women Accts. (bd. dirs., sec. 1985), Am. Prodn. and Inventory Control Soc. (v.p., bd. dirs. 1994—), Inst. Mgmt. Accts. Office: Sanofi Animal Health Inc 7101 College Blvd Ste 610 Overland Park KS 66210

PETERSON, CAROL BROOKE, psychologist, educator; b. San Francisco, June 20, 1964; d. Kent Richard and Dale (Clyde) P.; m. Darren Lorne Acheson, Sept. 5, 1992. BA in Psychology magna cum laude, Yale U., 1986; PhD in Clin. Psychology, U. Minn., 1993. Freshman counselor Yale U., New Haven, 1985-86, predoctoral psychology intern Med. Sch., 1991-92;

rsch. asst. in child and adolescent psychiatry U. Minn., Mpls., 1987-88, psychotherapist, 1987-91, 93—, predoctoral fellow eating disorders program dept. psychiatry, 1988-91, neurobehavioral pharmacology trainee, 1989-90, postdoctoral fellow, 1993—; crisis counselor Walk-In Counseling Ctr., Mpls., 1988-89; assessment clk. U. Minn. Hosp., 1988. Contbg. author: Psychiatric Disorders in Children and Adolescents, 1990. Vol. Yale-New Haven Hosp., 1983-84. Mem. APA, Am. Psychol. Soc., Soc. for Psychotherapy Rsch., Nat. Abortion Rights Action League, NOW (vol.), World Wildlife Fund, Amnesty Internat., Phi Beta Kappa, Sigma Xi, Phi Kappa Phi. Democrat. Office: U Minn Dept Psychiatry UMHC Box 393 Minneapolis MN 55455

PETERSON, DONNA KAY, business consultant; b. Chgo., July 7, 1960; d. Richard Lavern and Donna Kay (Menthe) P. BS in Gen. Engring., U.S. Mil. Acad., 1982. Commd. 2d lt. U.S. Army, 1982, advanced through grades to capt., 1986; helicopter pilot U.S. Army, Ft. Hood, Tex., 1983-86, chief of protocol, 1986-87; resigned U.S. Army, 1987; freelance author, 1988-90; freelance bus. cons. Orange, Tex., 1991—; mem. Svc. Acad. Selection Bd., State of Tex., 1992—. Author: Dress Gray: A Woman at West Point, 1990; contbr. articles to mil. and polit. jours. Maj. USAR, 1987—. Named Outstanding Female Vet. of Tex., Tex. Vet.'s Land Bd., 1988; Capt. Donna Peterson Day proclaimed in Orange County, Tex., 1988. Mem. Am. Legion, Vietnam Vets. Am. (life., hon. award 1990), Houston West Point Soc. (1st female mem.), Women Mil. Pilots, Inc., Tex. Bus. and Profl. Women's Club (Young Careerist award 1987). Republican. Home: PO Box 158 Orange TX 77631

PETERSON, DOROTHY LULU, artist, writer; b. Venice, Calif., Mar. 10, 1932; d. Marvin Henry and Fay (Brown) Case; m. Leon Albert Peterson, June 21, 1955; 1 child, David. AD, Compton (Calif.) Coll., 1950. Artist Moran Printing Co., Lockport, N.Y., 1955-59; caricature artist West Seneca and Kenmore Creative Artist Socs., 1973-86; commd. artist in pvt. practice, 1986—; comml. artist Boulevard Mall, Kenmore (N.Y.) Arts Soc., 1974—. Works include portraits of Pres. and Mrs. Reagan in Presdl. Libr. Collection, also portraits of Geraldine Ferraro, Presidents Clinton, Bush, Nixon, Ford, also Bette Davis, Lucille Ball, Bing Crosby, Elizabeth Taylor, 1971-94; author articles. Recipient awards West. Seneca Art Soc., 1975, Kenmore Art Soc., 1982, 86. Democrat. Baptist. Home: 55 Raintree Is Tonawanda NY 14150-9516

PETERSON, EILEEN M., state agency administrator; b. Trenton, N.J., Sept. 22, 1942; d. Leonard James and Mary (Soganic) Olschewski; children: Leslie, Valerie, Erica. Student, Boise State U. Adminstrv. sec. State Ins. Fund, Boise, 1983-85; legal asst. Bd. Tax Appeals, Boise, 1985-87, exec. asst., 1987-92, dir., 1992—. Vol. Boise Art Mus., Idaho Refugee Svc. Mem. Mensa, Investment Club (pres.), Mountains West Outdoor Club, Idaho Rivers United. Home: 3317 Mountain View Dr Boise ID 83704 Office: Idaho State Bd Tax Appeals 1109 Main St Boise ID 83702

PETERSON, ELSA VICTORIA, photo and permissions editor; b. San Francisco, Nov. 15, 1952; m. John H. Turner, Oct. 15, 1994. BA with highest honors, U. Calif., Riverside, 1976; MA, Case Western Res. U., 1979. Proofreader Composers Recs. Inc., N.Y.C., 1979-80; editorial asst. Otto Luening, N.Y.C., 1979-80; adminstrv. asst. C.F. Peters, N.Y.C., 1980-81; copyright adminstr. European Am. Music, Totowa, N.J., 1981-83; freelance photo and permissions editor Elsa Peterson Ltd., N.Y.C., 1984—; stock photographer Design Conceptions, N.Y.C., 1989-91, D. Donne Bryant Stock, Baton Rouge, 1991—, Stock, Boston, 1994—; instr. Greenwich (Conn.) Adult and Continuing Edn., Greenwich, 1992—. Mem. Am. Adoption Congress, Washington, 1987—. Recipient Grad. Alumni award Case Western Res. U., Cleve., 1978. Mem. Am. Soc. Picture Profls. (sec. N.Y. chpt. 1994-95), Editorial Freelancers Assn., Entrepreneurial Woman's Network.

PETERSON, ETHEL MARIE, education educator; b. Dodge City, Kans., Oct. 31, 1933; d. Henry Lindberg and Myrtle May (Smith) P. AA, Dodge City C.C., 1955; BS in Edn., Ft. Hays State U., 1960, MS in Edn., 1967, postgrad., 1977. Cert. elem. tchr., sch. counselor. Tchr. 5th & 6th grades Sch. Dist. #1, Kismet, Kans., 1955-57, tchr. 7th grade, 1957-58; tchr. 5th grade Unified Sch. Dsit. 443, Dodge City, Kans., 1958-76, counselor elem. sch., 1976-94, coord. guidance, 1989-94; western Kans. coord. tchr. edn. Kans. Newman Coll., Wichita, 1994—. Sec., bd. dirs. New Chance, Inc., Dodge City, 1988-94; del. nat. conv. Dem. Nat. Conv., N.Y.C., 1992, chair Ford County Dems., Dodge City, 1982-90.; bd. dirs. United West Community Credit Union, Dodge City, 1993—. Named Kans. Master Tchr. Emporia State U., 1992; inducted into Kans. Tchrs. Hall of Fame, 1992. Mem. NEA (nat. bd. dirs. 1975-81, Kans. bd. dirs. 1972-83, Dodge City exec. com. 1968-71, 90-94, pres. 1969-70, Kans. del. 1972-83, 90-94), Bus. and Profl. Women;s Club (parliamentarian 1994—), Phi Delta Kappa (alternate del. 1994—). Home: 2315 Melencamp Dodge City KS 67801 Office: Kans Newman Coll PO Box 1058 Dodge City KS 67801

PETERSON, GINGER GAIL, advertising and film executive, business owner; b. Corpus Christi, Tex., Oct. 28, 1960; d. James Harland and Lucia Gail P. BA in Comm., U. Hawaii, 1982. Advt. agency owner Peterson Advertising & Assocs., Kamuela, Hawaii, 1988—; v.p. Big Island Film and Video, Hawaii, 1990-94. Film prodn. coord. Playboy, 1992; location mgr./coord. Bobby Brown Music Video, 1992; TV film prodn. mgr. Tom Selleck (Discovery Channel), 1992; feature film location mgr. Waterworld/Universal Studios, 1993-95. Recipient PELE award Advt. Fedn. Hawaii, 1988. Mem. Film and Video Assn. Democrat. Baptist. Home: PO Box 1629 Kamuela HI 96743

PETERSON, HELEN HOFF, retired association executive; b. Centerville, N.J., June 3, 1902; d. David Cox Reading and Frederica Sutherland (Anderson) Hoff; m. Alvah Peterson, Aug. 18, 1928 (dec. 1972); children: Jon Alvah, David Hoff. BA, Brown U., 1923; cert., YWCA Sch. Profl. Workers, 1925; MA, Ohio State U., 1933. Sec. girl res. YWCA, Burlington County, N.J., 1925-28; sec. Ohio State U. YWCA, Columbus, 1929; adminstr. job tng. YWCA, Columbus, 1938; instr. pub. affairs YWCA Nat. Profl. Sch., Painsville, Ohio, 1953-57; exec. Ohio dist. YWCA, Columbus, 1957-61; chair indsl. com. YWCA, Columbus, 1930; bd. dirs. Nat. YWCA, 1946. Deacon 1st Congrl. Ch., 1970-74. Recipient award Racial Justice Urban League, 1968, Mistard Seed award Ch. Women United, 1968; named one of Valiant Women, Nat. Ch. Women United, 1972, one of Women of Achievement, YWCA, 1987; named to Ohio Women's Hall of Fame, 1991. Mem. Univ. Women's Club (art group 1928—). Democrat. Home: 2039 Collingswood Rd Columbus OH 43221

PETERSON, JANE WHITE, nursing educator, anthropologist; b. San Juan, P.R., Feb. 15, 1941; d. Jerome Sidney and Vera (Joseph) Peterson; 1 child, Claire Marie. BS, Boston U., 1968; M in Nursing, U. Wash., 1969, PhD, 1981. Staff nurse Visiting Nurse Assn., Boston, 1964-66; prof. Seattle U., 1969—, dir. nursing home project, 1990-92, chair pers. com., 1988-90; chair dept. Community Health and Psychiat. Mental Health Nursing, 1987-89; sec. Coun. on Nursing and Anthropology, 1984-86; pres. Wash. League Nursing, Seattle, 1988-90; pres. bd. Vis. Nurse Svcs., Seattle, 1988-90; contbg. cons. CSI Prodn., Okla., 1987; cons. in nursing WHO/U. Indonesia, Jakarta, fall 1989. Contbr. articles to profl. jours., chptrs. to books. Mem. Seattle Art Mus., 1986—. Fellow: Soc. for Applied Anthropology; mem. Am. Anthropological Assn., Soc. for Med. Anthropology, Nat. League for Nursing, Am. Ethological Soc. Office: Seattle U Sch Nursing Broadway and Madison Seattle WA 98122

PETERSON, JOANNE ELIZABETH, instructional media specialist; b. Colby, Wis., Sept. 24, 1947; d. Willard J. and Alice A. (Miller) Becherer; m. Gary Lee Peterson, Aug. 19, 1972; 1 child, Nicole. BS in Edn., U. Wis., LaCrosse, 1969; MA, U. Wis., Milw., 1975. Libr. Sparta (Wis.) Pub. Schs., 1969-71; instructional media specialist Wauwatosa (Wis.) Pub. Schs., 1971—. Registration & fin. chair Wis. State AAUW Conv., 1994. Mem. AAUW, Nat. Edn. Assn., Met. Libr. Assn. Milw., Wis. Ednl. Media Assn., Beta Phi Mu. Lutheran. Office: Wauwatosa Pub Schs 11100 W Center St Wauwatosa WI 53222-4286

PETERSON, JUDITH ANN, county official; b. Springfield, Pa., Dec. 24, 1940; d. Hamilton Mileson and Mae Louise (Waldron) Artley; m. George Irwin Peterson, July 1, 1961 (div. Apr. 1979); children: Gail E., Robert M. BS, Mich. State U., 1962; MPA, Western Mich. U., 1978. Head blood bank dept. Bronson Meth. Hosp., Kalamazoo, Mich., 1962-63; asst. to city mgr. City of Springfield, Mich., 1978-81; purchasing mgr. Kalamazoo County, 1981-86; county coord. Barry County, Hastings, Mich., 1986—. Mem. Mich. Assn. County Adminstrv. Officers (bd. dirs. 1993—), Mich. Assn. Fin. Officers, Purchasing Assn. Mich., Exch. Club of Hastings (bd. dirs. 1990-93). Episcopalian. Home: 2028 Hubble Rd Hastings MI 49058 Office: County of Barry 220 W State St Hastings MI 49058

PETERSON, KRISTEN, photographer; b. Tarrytown, N.Y., Oct. 3, 1952; d. John and Carolyn (Wells) P. BA in Art and Photography, Hamline U., 1974. Pres. Photography by Kristen Peterson, St. Louis, 1974—; suburban life editor Ingersoll Suburban Papers/Town & Country mag./AT&T, St. Louis, 1975-87; lectr. in field. Works pub. in Town and Country mag., U.S. News and World Report, Better Homes and Gardens, Newsweek, N.Y. Daily News, Women's Wear Daily, Chgo. Tribune, People Mag., Ency. Britannica, Washington Star, St. Louis Symphony, St. Louis Art Mus., Coca-Cola, Pet Inc., Variety Club, Webster U., Wedgewood, Mosanto; also included in book Images of St. Louis. Recipient Color Grand prize Kodak Internat. Newspaper Snapshot contest, 1972, numerous other awards. Mem. Mo. Press Women (pres. 1982-84, v.p. 1980-82, treas. 1978-80, 40 awards in communications contests), Nat. Fedn. Press Women (numerous awards), Nat. Press Photographers Assn. Home: 41 Countryside Ln Saint Louis MO 63131-3310

PETERSON, KRISTINA ANN, international trade finance banker; b. Boston, Oct. 4, 1963. BSBA, Boston U., 1985; postgrad., MIT, 1987-88; MBA, U. Chgo., 1990. Rsch. cons. MIT, Cambridge, Mass., 1986-88; mktg. summer intern Am. Express TRS Co., 1989; mgr. Citibank Global Trade Fin. Div., 1990-92; asst. v.p. Citicorp N.Am. Structured Trade Fin., Chgo., 1992-94; v.p. ABN AMRO Bank NV., Structured Trade Fin., Chgo., 1994—. Home: 2909 N Sheridan Rd Apt 1709 Chicago IL 60657-5908 Office: ABN AMRO Bank NV 135 S LaSalle Ste 611 Chicago IL 60603

PETERSON, LINDA S., lawyer; b. Grand Forks, N.D., Mar. 15, 1952. BA summa cum laude, U. N.D., 1973; JD, Yale U., 1977. Bar: N.D. 1977, D.C. 1978, U.S. Dist. Ct. D.C. 1979, U.S. Ct. Appeals (D.C. cir.) 1979, U.S. Ct. Appeals (3d cir.) 1982, Calif. 1986, U.S. Ct. Appeals (fed. cir.) 1986. Law clk. Ct. of Appeals for D.C., Washington, 1977-78; ptnr. Sidley & Austin, L.A. Dep. counsel Webster Commn., 1992. Mem. L.A. County Bar Assn. (conf. dels. 1987-90), State Bar Calif. (rules of ct. com. 1988-91), Women Lawyers Assn. L.A. (bd. dirs. 1989-94), Phi Beta Kappa. Office: Sidley & Austin 555 W Fifth St Ste 4000 Los Angeles CA 90013-1010

PETERSON, MILLIE M., state legislator; b. Merced, Calif., June 11, 1944. BS, U. Utah, 1979, MSW, 1984. Mem. Utah State Senate from 12th dist., 1991—. Mem. NASW, Assn. Am. Med. Colls. Democrat. Address: 7131 W 3800 S West Valley City UT 84120-3416 Office: Senate House State Capitol Salt Lake City UT 84114*

PETERSON, NANCY ANN, real estate broker; b. Fargo, N.D., Sept. 18, 1947; d. Simar Kristian and Rhoda Alice (Anderson) Nelson; m. John William Peterson, Oct. 20, 1967 (dec. Aug. 1979); 1 child, Dauvin John. BS, Moorhead State U., 1979, MA, 1994; student Real Conservatorio, Madrid, Spain, 1981. Cert. comml. investment mgr. Owner, pres. Circle Realtors Inc., Fargo, 1971—; bd. dirs. Town & Country Realty; Honorarium prof. Classical Guitar Moorhead State U. Bd. dirs. Plains Art Mus., Moorhead, Minn., 1983—, pres., 1987—; mem. devel. council Moorhead State U., 1987; treas. O'Rourke-Plains Mus., Moorhead, 1984-85, v.p., 1986-87; pres. O'Rourke-Plains Arts Assn., 1987-88; pres. Plains Art Mus., 1987-88; mentor Women's Network for Entrepreneuial Tng., 1989-92; bd. dirs. Fargo-Moorhead Youth Symphony. Mem. Nat. Assn. Realtors, Fargo-Moorhead Bd. Realtors, Women's Council Realtors (pres. 1977), Fargo-Moorhead Home Builders, Linden Assoc., Fargo-Moorehead Black History Orgn. (com. dir. 1989), Women's Network for Entrepreneurial Tng. (mentor 1989-92). Lodge: Zonta. Avocations: classical guitar, fishing, scuba diving, skiing, glider flying. Office: Cir Realtors Inc 1220 Main Ave Fargo ND 58103-8201

PETERSON, PATRICIA ELIZABETH, library network administrator, educator; b. Iowa City, July 25, 1942; d. Gregory Raymond and Ruth Elizabeth (Green) Patterson; m. Sylvan Johnathan Peterson, June 14, 1964; children: Deborah Lynn, Christine Elizabeth. BS, Mayville State Coll., 1963; MS, St. Cloud State U., 1979. Tchr., libr. Nekoma (N.D.) High Sch., 1963-67, Gackle (N.D.) High Sch., 1967-70; tchr. Lester Prairie (Minn.) High Sch., 1971-78; dir. media Kimball (Minn.) High Sch., 1978-83; dir. Cen. Minn. Librs. Exch., St. Cloud, 1983—; pres. Coun. Coop. Librs., St. Paul, 1987-88, 94-95. mem. ALA, AAUW, Assn. for Ednl. Comm. and Tech., Forum of Exec. Women, Friends of the Libr. Devel. and Svcs. Libr., Friends of the Great River Regional Libr., Minn. Libr. Assn., Minn. Ednl. Media Orgn. (v.p. 1992-94), Minn. Assn. Libr. Friends, Cold Spring Lioness Club, Phi Delta Kappa. Home: 591 Central Ave SE Richmond MN 56368-8117 Office: Ctrl Minn Librs Exch Bldg Ch 61 St Cloud State U Saint Cloud MN 56301

PETERSON, PATTI MCGILL, college president; b. Johnstown, Pa., May 20, 1943; d. Earl Frampton and Helen G. McGill; m. Luther D. Peterson, Aug. 31, 1968; 1 son, Lars-Anders. B.A. in Polit. Sci., Pa. State U., 1965; M.A. in Polit. Sci., U. Wis., 1968, Ph.D. in Polit. Sci. and Ednl. Policy, 1974; cert. advance study, Harvard U., 1977; D.Litt (hon.), Le Moyne Coll., 1983. Asst. prof. polit. sci., dean of freshman women Schiller Coll., Ger., 1968-69; asst. prof. polit. sci. SUNY-Oswego, 1971-72, asst. to pres., adj. prof., 1972-77, v.p. acad. services and planning, assoc. prof., 1978-80; pres. Wells Coll., Aurora, N.Y., 1980-87, St. Lawrence U., Canton, N.Y., 1987—; bd. dirs. Nia. Mo. Power Corp., Security Mut. Life Ins. Co. OnBank. Author numerous articles in field. Trustee Nat. Women's Hall of Fame; trustee Northwood Sch. Sta. WCNY-TV-FM; mem. bd. overseers The Nelson A. Rockefeller Inst. Govt., 1988; trustee Assn. Am. Colls., 1987; chmn. Pub. Leadership Edn. Network, 1983-85; mem. Gov.'s Com. on Vol. Enterprise, 1983-85; pres. Assn. Colls. and Univs., N.Y., 1984-86; chair Women's Coll. Coalition, 1983-85, U.S.-Can. Fulbright Com., 1990—; mem. Com. on Nat. Challenges in Higher Edn., 1986-88. Carnegie fellow Harvard U., 1977. Mem. Am. Coun. Edn. (chmn. com. on leadership devel. and acad. adminstrn. 1982-84), Mid. States Assn. Colls. and Schs. (cons., chmn.). Home: 54 E Main St Canton NY 13617-1419 Office: St Lawrence U Office of the President Canton NY 13617*

PETERSON, PAULETTE ELIZABETH, biochemist; b. Fresno, Calif., June 25, 1957; d. Carl Benjamin and Lila Irene (Orvik) P.; m. Bruce Eric Kirkpatrick, Aug. 9, 1987. BS in Biochemistry, U. Calif., Davis, 1979; postgrad., U. Calif., Santa Clara, 1979-80; MFA, San Jose State U., 1994. Teaching asst., grad. asst. U. Calif., Santa Cruz, 1979-80; rsch. & devel. chemist I, II & III SYVA, Palo Alto, Calif., 1981-86; sr. chemist, project leader Biotrack, Mountain View, Calif., 1986-90; sr. scientist, project mgr. Cholestech, Hayward, Calif., 1990-93; practicing artist, art instr. pvt. practice, Santa Clara, Calif., 1993—. Patentee, inventor in field; contbr. articles to profl. jours. Mem., activist, coord. Com. Against U.S. Intervention in El Salvador, Palo Alto, 1984. Recipient hon. mention Olympiad of the Arts, Los Gatos, Calif., 1994; winner illustration competition Applied Materials Internat., 1992.

PETERSON, SALLY LU, communications executive; b. Waukegan, Ill., July 23, 1942; d. George C. and Luella Alice (Flood) P. BA, Govs. State U., Park Forest, Ill., 1983; MA, Calif. Grad. Sch. Theology, 1994; grad., United Christian Bible Inst.; postgrad., Internat. Seminary, 1993—. Ordained to ministry United Christian Ch. Ministerial Assn., 1990. V.p. Cabac TV, Gurnee, Ill., pres.; producer, dir. WHKE Channel 55, Wis.; outreach to Moscow, Jerusalem, Europe and Africa; founder, organizer, pres. radio ministry Trumpet Ministries, 1991—. Evangelist, founder, organizer TV ministry Calling Revival, 1977—, producer, dir. TV programming for Northern Ill., 1983—; co-founder, co-organizer TV ministry Interfaith Community Svc. Prayer for Peace. Mem. Cabac Cable TV Producers of Lake County Ill. (pres. 1984, 88—), Order Ea. Star (Worthy Matron of Waukegan 209, 1968), Warren-Newport Woman's Afternoon Club of Gurnee (pres. 1982-84, 86-80). Home and Office: 33712 S Oplaine Rd Gurnee IL 60031-3416

PETERSON, SHARON LYNN CRAIG, managed care services executive; b. Decatur, Ill., July 7, 1945; d. Corwin Moore and Evelyn Marie (Oye) Craig; 1 child, Karla Christina Johnson. Diploma in nursing, Decatur Macon County Hosp., 1967; BS, MSN, 1975; MHSN, Gov. State U., 1977. RN, Mo., Ill., Ark. Head nurse med./surg. unit St. Mary's Hosp., Kankakee, Ill., 1967-74, 78-85; mental health adminstr. Manteno (Ill.) Mental Health Ctr., 1974-85; rehab., med. case mgr. Upjohn Co., Springfield, Mo., 1985-89; rehab. and med. mgr., dist. mgr. Fortis Corp., Springfield, Mo., 1989-93; managed care and cost containment specialist exec. ADVO-CARE, 1993—. Mem. Am. Assn. Occupl. Health Nurses, Assn. Rehab. Nurses, Case Mgmt. Soc. Am., Ind. Case Mgmt. Assn. Home: RR 4 Box 3090 Reeds Spring MO 65737

PETERSON, SOPHIA, international studies educator; b. Astoria, N.Y., Nov. 24, 1929; d. George Loizos and Caroline (Hofstetter) Yimoyines; m. Virgil Allison Peterson, Dec. 28, 1951; children: Mark Jeffrey, Lynn Marie. BA, Wellesley (Mass.) Coll., 1951; MA, UCLA, 1956, PhD, 1969. Instr. Miami U., Oxford, Ohio, 1961-63; with W.Va. U., Morgantown, 1966—, assoc. prof., 1972-79, prof., 1979—, dir., internat. studies maj., 1980-92; dir. W.Va. Consortium for Faculty & Course Devel. in Internat. Studies, Morgantown, 1980—. Author: monograph Monograph Series in World Affairs, 1979. Recipient gold medal semi-finalist CASE Prof. of Yr. award Coun. for Advancement and Support of Edn., 1987, Outstanding Tchr. award W.Va. U., W.Va. U. Coll. Arts and Scis., 1988, finalist Prof. of Yr. award W.Va. Faculty Merit Found., 1991. Mem. Internat. Studies Assn. (v.p. Mid-Atlantic chpt. 1978-86), W.Va. Polit. Sci. Assn. (pres. 1984-85), AAAUP (pres. W.Va. U. chpt. 1976-78). Democrat. Home: 849 Vandalia Dr Morgantown WV 26505-6247 Office: WVa U Dept Polit Sci Morgantown WV 26506

PETERSON, STACEY MICHELLE, financial and management professional; b. Tulsa, Nov. 29, 1963; d. Paul Eldon and Carolyn Kay (Hughes) P. BS, Cornell U., 1986; MBA, U. Pa., 1991. Comml. banking officer Bank of Am., L.A., 1986-89; fin. analyst intern Amoco Corp., Chgo., 1990; fin. analyst Atlantic Richfield Co., Dallas, 1991-93; sr. fin. analyst Atlantic Richfield Co., L.A., 1993—. Mem. Wharton Alumni Assn. So. Calif., Cornell Alumni Assn. So. Calif., Phi Kappa Phi, Kappa Delta. Home: 13928 Tahiti Way # 116 Marina Del Rey CA 90292 Office: Atlantic Richfield Co 515 S Flower St Los Angeles CA 90071

PETERSON, SUZETTE MARIE, educator; b. Madison, Wis., May 9, 1959; d. Kermit Norman and Dorothy Eugenia (Terre) P. BS in Elem. Edn., No. Mont. Coll., 1985. Tchr. Stepping Stone Preschool, Middleton, Wis., 1986-88, Caring Ctr., Verona, Wis., 1988-90, World Ednl. Ctr., Naha City, Japan, 1990-91, St. Therese Sch., Albuquerque, 1991-92; camp dir. Girl Scouts Assn., Mayhill, N.Mex., 1991-92; tchr. St. Peters (Minn.) Pub. Schs., 1992-93, Milan Elem. Sch., Grants, N.Mex., 1993—. Bd. dirs. Milton (Wis.) Coll. Alumni, 1989-90. Recipient Ikebona award Okinawan Ikebona Soc., Japan, 1990. Mem. NAFE, Vegetarian Soc. Democrat. Roman Catholic. Home: 6801 Los Volcanes # J-12 Albuquerque NM 87121

PETERSON, TRUDY HUSKAMP, national archivist; b. Estherville, Iowa, Jan. 25, 1945. BS, Iowa State U., 1967; MA, U. Iowa, 1972, PhD, 1975. Various positions Nat. Archives, Washington, 1968-87, asst. archivist, 1987-93, dep. archivist of U.S., 1993—, acting archivist, 1993—; Fulbright lectr. in Am. studies, 1983-84; commr. U.S.-Russia Joint Commn. on MIA/POWs, 1992—; sec. Internat. Conf. on Round Table on Archives, 1992-93, pres., 1993—. Author: Agricultural Exports, Farm Income and the Eisenhower Administration, 1979, Basic Archival Workshop Exercises, 1982, Archives and Manuscripts: Law, 1985; editor: Farmers, Bureaucrats and Middlemen: Historical Perspectives on American Agriculture, 1980; mem. editl. bd. The Am. Archivist, 1978-81; contbr. articles to profl. jours. Pres. Capitol Hill Restoration Soc., 1987-88. Fellow Soc. Am. Archivists (mem. coun. 1984-87, pres. 1990-91, held various offices, Gondos Meml. award 1973, Fellows Posner prize 1987); mem. Agrl. History Soc. (mem. exec. com. 1982-85, pres. 1988-89), Soc. History in Fed. Govt. (mem. exec. com. 1987-89). Office: Nat Archives & Records Adminstrn 8th & Pennsylvania Ave NW Washington DC 20408

PETERSON, VIRGINIA BETH, counselor; b. Oak Park, Ill., July 19, 1946; d. Edward Henry and Lorraine Minnie (Hermann) Schmidtke; m. Roger Alan Peterson, Aug. 20, 1966; children: Mark Alan, Ross Edward, Ryan David. BS, U. Wis., Stevens Point, 1972, M in Edn. Profl. Devel., 1984; cert. in Guidance and Counseling, U. Wis., Stout Menomonie, 1987, EdS in Guidance and Counseling, 1993. Cert. K-8 tchr., K-12 counselor, Wis. Tchr. elem. sch. Deerfield (Wis.) Community Schs., 1966-68; tchr. elem. sch. Nekoosa (Wis.) Pub. Schs., 1972-86, tchr. elem. sch., dir. alcohol and drug program, 1986-90, dir. dist. alcohol and drug program, elem. sch. counselor, 1990-91; dist. counselor for at risk dist. alcohol and drug dir., elem. sch. counselor Wausau (Wis.) Pub. Schs., 1991—; apptd. mem. Citizens Coun. on Alcohol and Other Drugs, Madison, Wis., 1989-94; trainer, cons The Wood Group, Port Edwards, Wis., 1990—; apptd. mem. State Coun. on Alcohol and Other Drugs/Edn. Prevention Com., 1994—. Contbg. author: SOS (Study on Suicide), 1989. Chmn., vice-chmn., mem. Reaching Others on Alcohol and Drugs, Nekoosa, 1986-91; bd. dirs. Wood County Partnership, Wisconsin Rapids, Wis., 1988-91, Family Counseling Svcs., Wausau, 1992—, U. Wis. Clearinghouse, Madison, 1987—, reviser pamphlets and booklets, 1987—. Recipient Drug Buster for Wis. award USA Today, 1989, Dirs. Community Leaders award FBI, 1990. Mem. AACD, Am. Sch. Counselor Assn., Wis. Sch. Counselor Assn., Wisconsin Rapids Area C. of C. (drug free task force 1989-91). Lutheran. Home: 802 E Lakeshore Dr Wausau WI 54401-8500 Office: GD Jones Elem Sch 1018 S 12th Ave Wausau WI 54401-5382

PETERSON-CARDENAS, ANITA ANN, educational evaluator; b. Shell Lake, Wis.; m. Emery J. Cardenas II, July 26, 1982. BA, Marquette U., 1983; MEd, Harvard U., 1987; postgrad., U. So. Calif. Cert. family and marriage therapist. Pvt. practice counseling and cons., Boston, 1987-88; cons., evaluator State of Hawaii, Honolulu, 1988-89; ednl. evaluator Kamehameha Schs., Bishop Estate, Honolulu, 1990—; cons., Honolulu, 1988—. Author: Development of a Criterion-Referenced, Performance-Based Assessment of Reading Comprehension in a Whole Literacy Program, 1991, Performance Based Assessment in the KEEP Whole Literacy Curriculum, 1992, Integrating Assessment into the Whole Literacy Curriculum, 1993, Teacher Change in a Whole Literacy Curriculum, 1994. Rep. Com. on Human Svcs., Honolulu, 1989; active neighborhood bd., 1992. Mem. ASCD, Am. Ednl. Rsch. Assn., Nat. Soc. Study Edn., Polit. Edn. Assn., Harvard Club (v.p. Hawaii chpt.) Phi Delta Kappa. Office: Kamehameha Schs EED Eval Kapalama Heights Honolulu HI 96817

PETERSON-HARRIS, NANCY JANE, special education services professional; b. Wauseon, Ohio, June 13, 1950; d. Maurice Ray and Edna Lucille (Merillat) Hootman; m. James Robert Harris Jr., Apr. 11, 1990; children: Stephanie Peterson, Sarah Harris. BA, Adrian Coll., Mich., 1972; Postgrad., Bowling Green State, 1979-82, Owens Community Coll., Toledo, Ohio, 1993—. Cert. qualified mental retardation profl., moderate severe profound retardation profl. Tchr. Tiffin Developmental Ctr., Tiffin, Ohio, 1979-84; cons., owner Positive Outlooks, Oregon, Ohio, 1986-88; adminstr. Garden Farms, Oak Harbor, Mich., 1984-87; habilitation coord. Luther Home of Mercy, Williston, Ohio, 1987-88; residential dir. Blanchard Valley Residential Ctr., Findlay, Ohio, 1988-93.

PETIT, BRENDA JOYCE, credit bureau sales executive; b. Houston, Dec. 8, 1939; d. Clyde and Bess (Dobbin) McBee; m. Emile Petit, June 20, 1958 (div. 1972); children: Michael, Melinda. Student, Coll. of the Mainland, Texas City, Tex., 1986. Sec. La Marque ISD, La Marque, Tex., 1966-77; employment counselor Snelling & Snelling, Texas City, 1977-78; exec. asst. M. Lackey, Inc., Galveston, Tex., 1978-84; mgr. MPMS Credit Bur., Galveston, 1984-88, TRW, Houston, 1988—; speaker at colls., convs., clubs; bd. dirs. Consumer Credit Counseling Svcs. Galveston County. Lifetime mem. Galveston County Fair and Rodeo Assn., Santa Fe, Tex., 1980—; mem. U. Tex. Med. Br. Women's Aux., Galveston, 1984—; bd. dirs. City of La Marque Tax Reinvestment Zone, 1990—; bd. dirs. Internat. Credit Assn. Mem. NAFE, Internat. Credit Assn. Galveston County (bd. dirs.). Democrat. Baptist. Home: PO Box 173 La Marque TX 77568-0173 Office: TRW 450 Gears Rd Ste 130 Houston TX 77067-4512

PETIT, DEBORAH LYNN, banker, analyst; b. Stockton, Calif., July 23, 1963; d. James Arneil Petit and Mildred Edwyna (Gordon) Hurt; m. Michael Kasimoff, May 28, 1988 (div. May 1990); 1 child, Trevor James. BS in Agrl. and Managerial Econs., U. Calif., Davis, 1985. Mgr. WSSI, Carmichael, Calif., 1986-89, Genesis Microsys., Santa Rosa, Calif., 1990; agrl. mgmt. specialist USDA-FmHA, Santa Rosa, 1990-91; agrl. mgmt. specialist USDA-FmHA, Salinas, Calif., 1991—, v.p. EEO com., 1992—. Mem. Camber Ski Club (bd. dirs. activities com.). Home: 946 W Alisal # 5 Salinas CA 93901 Office: USDA-FMHA 635 S Sanborn Rd # 18 Salinas CA 93901

PETITAN, DEBRA ANN BURKE, educator, education counselor, design engineer, writer, author; b. Chgo., Mar. 12, 1932; d. James Marcellus and Susan Florence (Hines) Burke; m. Kenneth Charles Petitan, Aug. 9, 1952; 1 child, Susan Florence. AA, Wilson Jr. Coll., Chgo., 1951, N.Y. Inst. Photography, 1952; BS in Primary Edn., Chgo. State U., 1956, MS in Indsl. Edn., 1967; DSc in Applied Sci. and Tech., London Inst. Tech., 1971; postgrad., U. Wis., Bradley U., U. Calif., U. Ill.; grad., Inst. Children's Lit., West Redding, Conn., 1991. Tchr. Chgo. Bd. Edn., 1958-71, guidance counselor, 1976-84, now tchr., cons.; nat. dir. edn. Nation of Islam, 1971-75; design engr. Fed. Sign and Signal Corp., Chgo., 1975-76; mem. nat. adv. bd. Nat. Right to Work Orgn., 1976-85; cons. ednl. devel., 1978; computer libr. cons.; owner, CEO, Fayzah's Fin. Svcs., Fayzah's Creative Prodns., Inc.; participant summer writing festival U. Iowa, 1991. Photographer VISTA News, 1969-70; writer children's lit. Dir. Christian Edn. Trinity United Ch. Christ, Chgo., 1978-81, family counselor, 1978-81, organizer, leader family counseling ministry, lic. lay Eucharistic minister Episcopal Ch. St. Edmund, 1989; chmn. Career Women for Johnson/Humphrey, Chgo., 1965; navigator, pub. rels. officer 1L Wing, Squadron 8, capt. Civil Air Patrol, 1953-56. Named Woman of Yr. Iota Phi Lambda, 1978; recipient 250 Hr. medal Ground Observer Corps, 1952, 25 Yr. Service medallion Chgo. Bd. Edn., 1987. Mem. Off-Campus Writer's Workshop (editor newsletter Green River Writers), Soc. of Children's Book Writers, Children's Reading Roundtable, Green River, Ky. Writers, Epsilon Pi Tau. Office: Chgo Bd Edn 1839 W Pershing Rd Chicago IL 60609-2317

PETITTO, BARBARA BUSCHELL, artist; b. Jersey City; d. John Edward and Anna (Barnaba) Buschell; m. Joseph Bruno Petitto, Feb. 1, 1964; children: Vincent John, Christopher Joseph. Student, Fairleigh Dickinson U., 1969-70; studio art cert., N.J. Ctr. Visual Arts, Summit, 1985; student, Art Students League, N.Y.C., 1980, 89-92, Montclair Art Mus., 1991-93. Represented by Ward-Nasse Gallery, N.Y.C.; artist-in-resident art faculty Acad. St. Elizabeth, Convent Station, N.J., 1989, 90, 91; art faculty Morris County Art Assn., Marristown, N.J., 1989; curator Olcott Studio Gallery Art Show, Bernardsville, N.J., 1985; demonstrator Acad. St. Elizabeth, Convent Station, 1989, 90; dir. Student's Art Festival WNET/Thirteen, Acad. St. Elizabeth, 1989. One-woman shows include Ariel Gallery, N.Y.C., 1987, 88, Corner Gallery World Trade Ctr., N.Y.C., 1989, 90, Montserrat Gallery, N.Y.C., 1992; juried show N.J. Ctr. Visual Arts, Summit, 1985, 92; exhibited in group shows at Ward-Nasse Gallery, 1989-94, Artworks-Trenton, N.J., 1989, 92, Jain Gallery, N.Y.C., 1989, 91, Blackwell St. Gallery, Dover, N.J., 1993, Ben-Shahn Gallery, William Paterson Coll., 1992, 94, Jain-Marounouchi Gallery, N.Y.C., 1992, 93, Cmty. Arts Assn., Ridgewood, N.J., also corp. and pvt. collections; contbr. articles to profl. jours. Named Miss Livingston N.J., Livingston C. of C., 1956; recipient Rudolph A. Voelcker Meml. award Art Ctr. N.J., 1982, Excellence award Hunterdon Art Mus., 1988, award for excellence Artists League Ctrl. N.J., 1989, Cornelius Low House, Middlesex County Mus., Montclair Art Mus., 1990, award for mixed media Millburn-Short Hills Art Assn., 1989, First Pl. award N.E. Caldwell Art Festival, 1989, award Nabisco Brands, Inc., East Hanover, N.J., 1990, Excellence award Ann. Tri-State Artists League Ctrl. N.J., 1991, 92, Winsor & Newton Plaque, Visual Arts League, Edison, N.J., 1992, Excellence award Manhattan Arts Internat. Cover Art Competition, 1994. Mem. Artworks, Nat. Soc. Painters in Casein and Acrylic, Nat. Assn. Women Artists, Inc., Artists Equity, Visual Arts League, N.J. Ctr. Visual Arts, Nat. Mus. Women in Arts, Jersey City Mus. Office: PO Box 515 Whippany NJ 07981-0515

PETOW, JOAN CLAUDIA, orthopedic nurse; b. Spokane, Wash., Mar. 5, 1946; d. August and Ella (McHargue) P. Diploma summa cum laude, Deaconess Hosp. Sch. Nursing, Spokane, 1967; BSN cum laude, Pacific Luth. U., 1969. RN, Wash.; cert. orthopedic nurse. Staff nurse orthopedic unit Deaconess Med. Ctr., Spokane, 1969-70, nurse ICU, 1970-72, asst. head nurse adult surg. unit, 1972-73, head nurse orthopedics unit, 1973-83; staff nurse Valley Hosp. and Med. Ctr., Spokane, 1984—; orthopedic quality assurance rep. Valley Hosp. and Med. Ctr., Spokane, 1988-90. Chmn. Spokane Coun. Christian Bus. and Profl. Women, 1976-77. Mem. Nat. Assn. Orthopedic Nurses (cert.), Sigma Theta Tau.

PETRAITIS, KAREL COLETTE, lawyer; b. Chgo., Apr. 4, 1945; d. Ferdinand John and Dolores (Karroll) P.; B.A., U. Md., 1967, postgrad., 1967-68; J.D., George Washington U., 1971. Bar: Md. 1972, U.S. Supreme Ct. 1977. Law clk. Prince George's County Office of Law (Md.), 1971-72, atty., 1972-80; real estate atty. Harloff & Perkins, Riverdale, Md., 1978-82; pvt. practice law, College Park, Md., 1980—; past pres., v.p., treas, bd. dirs. Coll. Park Bd. Trade. Youth coord. Agnew for Gov., 1966, Mathias for Senate, 1968, Beall for Senate, 1970; nat. committeewoman Md. Young Reps., 1971-79, dir., 1979-81, legal counsel, 1972-79; mem. bd. trustees Elizabeth Seton H.S., 1991—. Recipient cert. appreciation Prince George County Circuit Ct., 1979; cert. public service Prince George County, 1980; pres. Friends of Md. Summer Inst. for Creative and Performing Arts, 1983-86, trustee, 1986—. Mem. AAUW, Md. Bar Assn., Prince George County Bar Assn., George Washington Law Alumni Assn. (bd. dirs. 1979-81, 87—, sec. 1982-84, pres. Md. chpt. 1985-87), U. Md. Alumni Assn. (pres. young alumni 1978-80, pres. Prince George's 1986-88, bd.dirs. 1988—). Roman Catholic. Home: 7307 Radcliffe Dr College Park MD 20740-3023 Office: 4321 Hartwick Rd # 201L College Park MD 20740-3210

PETRE, DONNA MARIE, county judge; b. Joliet, Ill., Apr. 21, 1947; d. James Jacob and Catherine (Hedrick) P.; m. Dennis Michael Styne, Sept. 4, 1971; children: Rachel Catherine, Jonathan James, Juliana Claire, Aaron Coopersmith. BA, Clarke Coll., 1969; MA, Northwestern U., 1971; JD, U. Calif., San Francisco, 1976. Bar: Calif. 1976. Jud. clk. Calif. Ct. Appeals, San Francisco, 1976-77; instr. legal rsch. and writing Hastings Coll. Law, U. Calif., San Francisco, 1976; dep. atty. gen. criminal appeals dept. State of Calif., San Francisco, 1977-80, dep. atty. gen. consumer fraud dept., 1980-83; dep. atty. gen. med. fraud dept. State of Calif., Sacramento, 1983-86; judge Yolo County Mcpl. Ct., Woodland, Calif., 1986-89, Yolo County Superior Ct., 1990—; adj. prof. trial practice U. Calif., Davis; mem. criminal justice commn. Marin County Bd. Suprs., 1982; mem. adv. com. Jud. Coun. on Adminstrv. Justice in Rural Counties, 1988—. Mng. editor Hastings Constl. Law Quar., 1975-76. Bd. dirs. Woodland Literacy Coun., 1986—; active LWV. Mem. AAUW, Calif. Judges Assn. (mem. commn. on studying problems with driving under influence of alcohol and other drugs), Yolo County Bar Assn., Women Lawyers Calif., Sacramento Women Lawyers, Bus. and Profl. Women (co-chairperson legis. 1986—), Davis C. of C., Yolo C. of C., Woodland C. of C. Republican. Office: Yolo County Superior Ct 725 Court St Woodland CA 95695-3436

PETRILLI, MICHELLE LESLIE, lawyer; b. Bridgeport, Conn., Sept. 3, 1953; d. Russell Moreton and Patricia Aldona (Yasonis) Cory; m. Jeffrey S. Welch, May 24, 1978 (div.); 1 child, Stephanie Cory. BA in Biol. Sci., U. Del., 1976; JD, Del. Law Sch., Widener U., 1979. Bar: Del. 1979, Pa. 1980. Law clk. Schmittinger & Rodriguez, P.A., Wilmington, Del., 1977-79; jud. clk. Del. Ct. Chancery, Wilmington, 1980-81; assoc. legal counsel Bank of Del. and Bank of Del. Corp., Wilmington, 1981-84, gen. counsel, V.P., 1984—; mem. exec. com. bd. dirs. Industry Coun. for Tangible Assets, Washington, 1983-86; state rep. Conf. of State Bank Suprs., 1986—. Elected bd. dirs. New Castle County Econ. Devel. Corp., chmn. affordable housing com.; apptd. chair Gov.'s Pub. Safety Coun. Mem. ABA, Del. Bar Assn., Fin. Women Internat., Del. Valley Corp. Counsel Assn. (bd. dirs. 1986-89), Lawyers Forum, Del. Bankers Assn. (govt. affairs com.), Del. State C. of C. (elected dir. 1989). Republican. Roman Catholic. Home: 2618 Tonbridge Dr Wilmington DE 19810-1217 Office: Bank of Del 222 Delaware Ave Wilmington DE 19899-1621*

PETRILLO, ANNA, elementary school educator; b. Roccoromana, Caserta, Italy, July 21, 1952; came to U.S., 1954; d. Carmine Antonio and Anna (Ricciardi) P. BS in Edn., Youngstown State U., 1974; MEd, U. Houston, 1982, cert. supervision and mid-mgmt., 1991, postgrad., 1986—; endorsement ESL, Tex. So. U., 1984. Cert. elem. tchr., ESL tchr., supr., midmgmt. adminstr., Tex. Tchr. ESL for adults Girard (Ohio) Pub. Schs., 1976-78; tchr. 3d and 4th grades Diocese of Youngstown, Ohio, 1975-78; tchr. 1st grade, math. specialist, reading specialist Houston Ind. Sch. Dist., 1978-86, tchr. technologist, career ladder level III, 1986—; adj. prof. Houston C.C., 1986—; mem. career ladder com. Houston Ind. Sch. Dist., 1984-93, grant writing cons., 1991—, mem. Houston's task force for edn. excellence, 1983-84; textbook reviewer Merrill Pub. Co., 1985. Mem. Houston Proud Community Involvement, 1990—; cert. ombudsman Harris County Area Agy. on Aging, Houston, 1991-92; instr. first aid ARC, Youngstown, 1972-78. Grantee NSF, 1982, Impact II replicator 1984, 91, 94, developer 1985, 87, 89, Houston Bus. Com. for Ednl. Excellence, 1992-93, mini-grantee. Mem. ASCD, Congress of Houston Tchrs., Assn. Tex. Profl. Educators, Houston Assn. for Childhood Edn. (pres. 1992-94, v.p. for later childhood 1990-92), Houston Area Apple Users Group (edn. SIG chair 1985-91), U. Houston Alumni Orgn. (life), Phi Delta Kappa (newsletter editor 1990). Democrat. Roman Catholic. Home: 5327 Beechnut Houston TX 77096 Office: Lovett Elem Sch 8814 S Rice Ave Houston TX 77096

PETRIN, HELEN FITE, lawyer, consultant; b. Bklyn., June 22, 1940; d. Clyde David and Connie Marie Keaton; m. Michael Richard Petrin, June 29, 1963; children: Jennifer Lee, Michael James, Daniel John. BS, Rider Coll. (now Rider U.), 1962, MA, 1980; postgrad., Glassboro (N.J.) Coll. (now Rowan Coll.), 1981; JD, Widener U., 1987. Bar: Pa. 1989, N.J. 1990, U.S. Dist. N.J. 1990. Tchr. bus. edn. Pennsville (N.J.) Meml. High Sch., 1962-66; asst. prof. Salem Community Coll., Carney's Point, N.J., 1977-81; asst. prof. Brandywine Coll. Widener U., Wilmington, Del., 1981-87, asst. prof., adminstr., dir. paralegal program, 1987-88; dir. continuing legal edn. Widener U. Sch. Law, Brandywine, 1987-88; pvt. practice computer cons. Phila., N.J. and Del., Del., Pa., N.J., 1988—; pvt. practice law Salem, N.J., 1989—; prosecutor Pilesgrove Township, N.J., 1990-91; dep. surrogate Salem County, N.J., 1991—; word processing cons. New Castle County (Del.) Pers. Dept., 1983; mem. dist. I ethics com. N.J. Supreme Ct., 1993—. Pres. bd. Salem County YMCA, 1983, bd. dirs., 1980—; col. atty. Phila. Vols. for Indigent Program, 1990—, Camden Legal Svcs., Inc. for Salem County, 1990—; bd. dirs. United Way Salem County, 1991—, treas., 1994-95; mem. III com. Home Ownership and Opportunity for People Everywhere (HOPE), Salem, N.J., 1992—. Mem. ABA (chmn. young lawyers econs. com. 1990-93, vice chmn. mktg. legal svcs. com. gen. practice sect. 1993—), ATLA, N.J. Bar Assn. (exec. com. 1990-93), Pa. Bar Assn., Phila. Bar Assn. (probate adv. panel 1992—), Salem County Bar Assn. (treas. 1991-92, sec. 1992-93, v.p., pres.-elect 1993-94, pres. 1994-95), Delta Pi Epsilon (sec. bd. dirs. 1980-82). Home: 99 Marlton Rd Pilesgrove NJ 08098 Office: 51 Market St Salem NJ 08079-1909

PETRO, JANE A., plastic and reconstructive surgeon; b. Erie, Pa., Dec. 17, 1946; d. William Irwin and Virginia (Douglas) Arbuckle; m. Denis J Petro, Mar. 28, 1969 (div. 1982); 1 child, Noah Edward. BS, Eckerd Coll., St. Petersburg, Fla., 1968; MD, Pa. State U., 1972. Diplomate Am. Bd. Surgery, Am. Bd. Plastic and Reconstrv. Surgery. Gen. surg. resident U. Louisville, 1972-74, Harrisburg Hosp., Pa., 1974-76; plastic surgery resident Pa. State U., Hershey, 1977-79; burn/microsurg. fellow Albert Einstein Coll. Medicine, Bronx, 1979-80; asst. prof. surgery N.Y. Med. Coll., Valhalla, 1981-85; assoc. prof. surgery N.Y. Med. Coll., 1985—; assoc. dir. burns Westchester County Med. Ctr., Valhalla, 1981—. Contbr. articles to profl. jours. Recipient Physicians Recognition award AMA, 1977, 90, 92, McArthur Alumni award for disting. achievement Eckerd Coll., 1980, My Sister's Place Ann. Leadership awrad, 1991. Mem. Am. Assn. med. Colls., Assn. Women Surgeons, Am. Assn. Physicians for Human Rights, AAAS, Am. Burn Assn., Am. Cleft Palate Assn., Am. Med. Womens Assn. (Community Svc. award 1993), Inst. of Soc., Ethics and the Life Scis., Soc. for Health and Human Values, N.Y. Acad. Sci., N.Y. Acad. Medicine, Acad. of Compensation medicine, Am. Assn. for Advancement of the Humanities, Am. Fedn. Clin. Research, Wedstchester County Med. Soc., N.Y. Soc. Plastic and Reconstrv. Surgery, N.Y. Reg. Head and Neck Soc., others. Democrat. Presbyterian. Office: Westchester County Med Ctr Burn Unit Valhalla NY 10595

PETRONZI, JOELLEN, educator, art consultant; b. Newark, Nov. 1, 1952; d. Andrew Frank and Mary Ann (Bongiovanni) Cirlincione; m. Ronald Samuel Petronzi, Sept. 14, 1974; 1 child, Greg. Student, Monmouth Coll., 1972-74; BA, Montclair (N.J.) State Coll., 1977; MA, NYU, 1992. Cert. K-12 art tchr., N.J. Tchr. art Hanover Twp. Schs., Whippany, N.J., 1978-83, Far Brook Sch., Short Hills, N.J., 1988-90, South Orange-Maplewood (N.J.) Sch. Dist., 1990—; freelance illustrator, N.J., 1983-88, 94; art cons. Tiffany & Co., N.Y.C., 1990—. Sch. State of N.J., 1972-74. Mem. Art Educators N.J. (guest speaker 1992, 93), Nat. Art Edn. Assn., Met. Mus. Art, Nat. Trust for Hist. Preservation. Roman Catholic. Home: 23 Rutgers St Maplewood NJ 07040 Office: Columbia HS 17 Parker Ave Maplewood NJ 07040

PETROZZI-JONES, JOANNE, mechanical engineer; b. Boston, Sept. 4, 1956; d. Ferdinando and Gina (DiCenzo) Petrozzi; m. Steven William Jones, Sept. 9, 1978. BS in Mech. Engring., Northeastern U., 1979. Field engr. Power Generation Svc. Gen. Electric, King of Prussia, Pa., 1979-89; installation engr. product svcs. dept. Gen. Electric, Schenectady, N.Y., 1989-91; steam turbine methods engr. Power Generation Svc. Gen. Electric, Schenectady, 1991-92; maintenance sys. mgr.ops. and maintenance Gen. Electric, Springfield, Mass., 1992-93; maintenance planner Power Sys. Gen. Electric, Schenectady, 1993-94, new unit spares project adminstr., 1994—. Home: 815 Herrick Rd Delanson NY 12053 Office: Gen Electric 1 River Rd Bldg 37-2ANX Schenectady NY 12345

PETROZZINO, JANE A., learning consultant; b. Newark, Oct. 5, 1947; d. Anthony Frank and Janet Louise Petrozzino. BA, William Paterson Coll., 1969, MEd, 1974; PhD, Fordham U., 1982. Elem. tchr. Wayne (N.J.) Pub. Schs., 1969-74, learning disabilities specialist, 1974-75, learning cons., 1975-84; pvt. practice as learning cons. Kinnelon and Wayne, N.J., 1981—; supr. spl. edn. Ramapo Ctrl. Sch. Dist., Hillburn, N.Y., 1984-87; prin./asst. to regional exec. dir. spl. edn. Region VII Coun. Spl. Edn., Bergen County, N.J., 1987-88; supr. instrn./asst. to supt. Moonachie Bd. Edn., Bergen County, N.J., 1987-88; supr. spl. svcs. Totowa (N.J.) Bd. Edn., 1988-89; adj. prof. William Paterson Coll., Wayne, 1978—; panelist/cons. U.S. Dept. Edn., Washington, 1982—; lectr., in-svc. staff trainer various bds. edn., N.Y., N.J., 1982—; mem. U.S. world team in field of dyslexia Orton Dyslexia Soc./Pres.'s Com. U.S. Amb. Program, 1993. Mem. N.J. Assn. Learning Cons., N.Y. State Adminstrs. Assn., Orton-Dyslexia Soc., Assn. Children with Learning Disabilities, Fordham U. Sch. Adminstrs. Assn., Phi Delta Kappa. Roman Catholic. Home: 77 Old Cow Pasture Ln Smoke Rise Kinnelon NJ 07405

PETT, VIRGINIA BUSSERT, chemistry educator; b. Chgo., Sept. 8, 1941; d. Elmer Charles and Martha Lavinia (Russell) Bussert; m. Harry Gregory Pett, Sept. 8, 1963 (dec. July 1992); children: Janice Lee, Kathleen Anne, Brian Timothy. BA, Coll. Wooster, 1963; MA, Wayne State U., 1972, PhD, 1979. NIH postdoctoral tng. grantee Inst. for Cancer Rsch., Fox Chase Cancer Ctr., Phila., 1979-81; assoc. prof. chemistry Coll. Wooster, Ohio, 1981—; sabbatical leave Naval Rsch. Lab., Lab for the Structure of Matter, Washington, 1987-88, dpet. biochemistry Case Western Res. Sch. Medicine, Cleve., 1991-92. Recipient Career Advancement award NSF, 1991-94. Mem. AAAS, Am. Crystallographic Assn., Assn. for Women in Sci. Office: The College of Wooster Dept Chemistry Wooster OH 44691

PETTENGILL, URSULA PRATER, college and university administrator; b. Cowden, Ill.; d. Arizona and Edith Rachel (Withem) Prater; m. Frederick B. Pettengill, June 21, 1952 (dec. Nov. 1986). BS, Ind. State U., Terre Haute, 1940; MS, Kans. State U., 1946; postgrad., Syracuse U., 1959. Chmn. dept. home econs. Lovington (Ill.) Twp. High Sch., 1940-42; chmn. dietary dept. William Woods U., Fulton, Mo., 1942-45; dir. food svc. Drake U., Des Moines, 1946-49, Syracuse (N.Y.) U., 1949-71; cons. dietary dept. svcs. various colls. and univs., 1952-92; chief program planning and mgmt. VA Med. Ctr., Syracuse, 1974-81; dir. ops. Mgmt. Svc. Systems Corp., 1972-74; nutrition lectr. Head Start, Minn. Author: American Red Cross Cook Book, 1972; author food manuals, membership directories. Bd. dirs. Girls Club of Ctrl. N.Y., 1972-82, ARC, 1975-79; mem. fin. com., adminstrv. bd. Univ. United Meth. Ch., 1983—, pres. bd. trustees, 1990-93; bd. mem. Syracuse (N.Y.) Home Assn., 1985—, chair house com. and fin. com., 1989—. Mem. AAUW, Am. Sch. Food Svc. Assn., Nat. Restaurant Assn., N.Y. State Assn. Food Dirs. (v.p. 1971), Profl. Women's League (pres. 1983-85), Zonta Club. Syracuse (program chair, fin. chair svc. com., membership chair), Syracuse Women of Rotary (pres. 1986-88, 94—, membership chair 1989-91), Corinthian Club, Corinthian Found. (bd. mem., chair membership com. 1994—), Evening Guild, Gertrude Brown Guild (pres. 1992, 93, nominating chair 1993—), Kappa Pi. Methodist. Home: 308 Hurlburt Rd Syracuse NY 13224-1823

PETTERCHAK, JANICE A., library director; b. Springfield, Ill., Sept. 15, 1942; d. Emil H. and Vera C. (Einhoff) Stukenberg; m. John J. Petterchak, Oct. 5, 1963; children: John A., Julie Gilmour, James. AA, Springfield Coll., 1962; BS, Sangamon State U., 1972, MA, 1982. Supr. hist. markers Ill. State Hist. Soc., Springfield, 1973-74, asst. exec. dir., 1985-87; curator photographs Ill. State Hist. Libr., Springfield, 1974-79, assoc. editor, 1979-83, rep. local history svcs., 1983-85, libr. dir., 1987—; project dir. NEH/Ill. newspaper cataloging project. Author: (booklets) Researching and Writing Local History in Illinois: A Guide to the Sources, 1987; editor: Bibliography of Illinois History, 1994; assoc. editor Illinois Historical Jour.; contbr. articles to profl. jours. Grantee NEH, 1987—. Mem. Ill. State Hist. Soc. (pubs. com.), Ill. Labor History Soc., Abraham Lincoln Assn. (co-editor Papers Abraham Lincoln Assn. 1981-82), Stephen A. Douglas Assn., Sangamon County Hist. Soc. (bd. dirs. 1991-94, v.p. 1994—). Home: 19 Mallard Dr Rochester IL 62563-9753 Office: Ill State Hist Libr 1 Old State Capitol Plz Springfield IL 62701-1512

PETTERSON, LYNNE MATHER, computer company executive, systems analyst; b. Evanston, Ill., Dec. 26, 1953; d. Donald Rahl and Janet (Horn) P. BA, East Carolina U., 1976, MA, 1980; MRP, U. N.C., Chapel Hill, 1985, PhD, 1991. Instr., teaching asst., rsch. asst. U. N.C., Greenville, 1976-80; instr., teaching asst., rsch. asst. U. N.C., Chapel Hill, 1980-84, co-team leader user svcs. statis. and computer lab., 1984-90; mgmt. analyst Sci. Computing/EPA, Research Triangle Park, 1990—. Mem. editorial bd. Carolina Planning, 1980-82; contbr. articles to profl. jours. Mem. NAFE, Assn. Am. Geographers, Am. Planning Assn., Southeastern Regional Svcs. Assn., Regional Svcs. Assn., N.C. Acad. Sci., Women in Mgmt., Toastmasters (v.p. pub. affairs Chapel Hill chpt. 1992-93, sgt.-at-arms 1992-93), Gamma Theta Upsilon. Home: 108 Emerald Cir Durham NC 27713-2413 Office: Sci Computing/US EPA MD-34 77 Alexander Dr Research Triang NC 27711

PETTIETTE, ALISON YVONNE, lawyer; b. Brockton, Mass., Aug. 16, 1952. Student Sorbonne, Paris, 1971-72; BA, Sophie Newcomb Coll., 1972; MA, Rice U., 1974; JD, Bates Coll., 1978. Bar: Tex. 1979, U.S. Dist. Ct. (so. dist.) Tex. 1980, U.S. Ct. Appeals (5th cir.) 1981. Ptnr. Harvill & Hardy, Houston, 1979-83; pvt. practice, Houston, 1983-84; assoc. O'Quinn & Hagans, Houston, 1984-86, Jones & Granger, Houston, 1986-88; pvt. practice, Houston, 1988—. Editor Houston Law Rev. U. Houston, 1976-78. Exercise instr. YWCA, Houston, 1976-81, U. St. Thomas, Houston. NDEA fellow Rice U., Houston, 1972-74; Woodrow Wilson scholar, Tulane U., New Orleans, 1972. Mem. ABA, Assn. Trial Lawyers Am., Tex. Trial Lawyers Assn., Houston Trial Lawyers Assn., Phi Delta Phi, Phi Beta Kappa.

PETTIGREW, L. EUDORA, university president; b. Hopkinsville, Ky., Mar. 1, 1928; d. Warren Cicero and Corrye Lee (Newell) Williams; children: Peter W. Woodard, Jonathan R. (dec.). MusB, W.Va. State Coll., 1950; MA, So. Ill. U., 1964, PhD, 1966. Music/English instr. Swift Meml. Jr. Coll., Rogersville, Tenn., 1950-51; music instr., librarian Western Ky. Vocat. Sch., Paducah, 1951-52; music/English instr. Voorhees Coll., Denmark, S.C., 1954-55; dir. music and recreation therapy W.Ky. State Psychiatric Hosp., Hopkinsville, 1956-61; research fellow Rehab. Inst., So. Ill. U., Carbondale, 1961-63, instr., resident counselor, 1963-66, coordinator undergrad. ednl. psychology, 1963-66, acting chmn. ednl. psychology, tchr. corps instr., 1966; asst. prof. to assoc. prof. dept. psychology U. Bridgeport, Conn., 1966-70; prof., chmn. dept. urban and met. studies Coll. Urban Devel. Mich. State U., East Lansing, 1974-80; assoc. provost, prof. U. Del., Newark, 1981-86; pres. SUNY Coll. at Old Westbury, 1986—; cons. for research and evaluation Hall Neighborhood House Day Care Tng. Project, Bridgeport, 1966-68, coordinator for edn. devel., 1968-69; cons. Bridgeport Public Schs. lang. devel. project, 1967-68, 70; cons. research/evaluation U.S. Eastern Regional Lab., Edn. Devel. Center, Newton, Mass., 1967-69; assoc. prof. U. Bridgeport, 1970, Center for Urban Affairs and Coll. of Edn., Mich. State U., East Lansing, 1970-73; cons. Lansing Model Cities Agy., Day Care Program, Lansing, Mich., 1971; trustee L.I. Community Found.; program devel. specialist Lansing Public Schs. Tchr. Corps program, 1971-73; cons. U. Pitts., 1973, 74, Leadership Program, U. Mich. and Wayne State U., 1975, Wayne County Public Health Nurses Assn., 1976, Ill. State Bd. Edn., 1976-77; chair commn. Africa SUNY, 1994—; lectr. in field; condr. workshops in field; cons. in field. Tv/radio appearances on: Black Women in Edn, Channel 23, WKAR, East Lansing, 1973, Black Women and Equality, Channel 2, Detroit, 1974, Women and Careers, Channel 7, Detroit, 1974, Black Women and Work: Integration in Schools, WITL Radio, Lansing, 1974, others.; Contbr. articles to profl. jours. Recipient Diana award Lansing YWCA, 1977, Outstanding Profl. Achievement award, 1987, award L.I. Ctr. for Bus. and Profl. Women, 1988, Educator of Yr. 100 Black Men of L.I., 1988, Black Women's Agenda award, 1988, Woman of Yr. Nassau/Suffolk Coun. of Adminstrv. Women in Edn., 1989, Disting. Ednl. Leadership award L.I. Women's Coun. for Equal Edn. Tng. and Employment, 1989, L.I. Disting. Leadership award L.I. Bus. News, 1990, Disting. Black Women in Edn. award Nat. Coun. Negro Women, 1991; named Outstanding Black Educator, NAACP, 1968, Oustanding Woman Educator, Mich. Women's Lawyers Assn. and Mich. Trial Lawyers Assn., 1975, Disting. Alumna, Nat. Assn. for Equal Opportunity in Higher Edn., 1990, Woman of Yr., Nassau County League of Women Voters, 1991. Mem. AAAS, Nat. Assn. Acad. Affairs Adminstrs., Internat. Assn. Univ. Pres. (exec. com.), Phi Delta Kappa. Office: SUNY-Old Westbury PO Box 210 Old Westbury NY 11568-0210

PETTIGREW WELCH, DANA MARY, musician, insurance agent; b. Oklahoma City, Jan. 15, 1951; d. Richard Clester and Alice Butler (Sargent) Pettigrew; m. Douglas A. Welch, Aug. 4, 1994; children: Marilyn Yvonne Pettigrew, Lonnie Dean Pettigrew Jr. Student, Oklahoma City U., 1966-68. Cert. profl. ins. agt. Cert. Profl. Ins. Assn. Profl. performance musician Oklahoma City, 1965—, Seattle, 1989—; ind. agt. Pettigrew Ins. Agy., Oklahoma City, 1974-89, Protection Designs, Seattle, 1989—; owner Protection Designs Ins. Agy. Ch. organist Pa. Ave Christian Ch., 1979-89. Life Underwriter Tng. Council fellow, 1984. Mem. NAFE, Oklahoma City Health Underwriters Assn. (bd. dirs., sec. 1986—, v.p. 1987, pres. 1989), Oklahoma City Life Underwriters Assn. (bd. dirs. 1984-85), Seattle Musicians Assn., Renton-Auburn Musicians Assn., Okla. Country Music Assn., Ind. Ins. Agts. Assn., Profl. Ins. Agts. Assn., Cascade Assn. Life Underwriters, Renton C. of C., Kiwanis (sec. Renton chpt. 1988, 89, pianist 1987—). Republican. Mem. Christian Ch. Home and Office: 3511 NE 11th Pl Renton WA 98056-3442

PETTINE, LINDA FAYE, physical therapist; b. New London, Conn., Nov. 11, 1958; d. Robert Anderson and Pauline Priscilla (Johnson) Erwin; m. H. Louis Pettine Jr., Mar. 6, 1982. BS, U. Conn., 1980; student, Quinnipiac Coll., Hamden, Conn., 1989-91. Registered phys. therapist, Conn. Staff phys. therapist Worcester (Mass.) Hahneman Hosp., 1980, Newport (R.I.) Hosp., 1980-82, Middlebury Orthopaedic Group, Waterbury, Conn., 1982; staff phys. therapist Easter Seal Rehab. Ctr. of Cen. Conn., Meriden, 1982-84, hosp. and rehab. ctr. coord., 1984-86; co-founder Pettine & McDiarmid Phys. Therapy, Cheshire and Wallingford, Conn., 1986-88; pres. Keystone Phys. Therapy & Sports Medicine P.C., Cheshire and Wallingford, Conn., 1988—; lectr. Diabetes Edn. Program, Meriden, 1985; cons. Waterbury (Conn.) Nursing Ctr., 1986-87. Mem. adv. bd. Waterbury Continuing Edn. program, 1985; guest speaker Conn. chpt. Am. Diabetes Assn., Meriden, 1986, Arthritis Support Group, Meriden, 1986, Meriden Indsl. Mgr. Assn., 1986. Katherine Wyckoff and Margaret Wyckoff Moore Endowed scholar, 1991. Mem. Am. Phys. Therapy Assn., Conn. Phys. Therapy Assn.

(program com. chair 1991-92). Office: Keystone Phys Therapy & Sports Medicine PC 675 S Main St Cheshire CT 06410-3153 also: 850 N Main Street Ext Wallingford CT 06492-2400

PETTIS, MARY JANE, laboratory manager; b. New Ulm, Minn., Sept. 1, 1956; d. Lowell Eugene and Audrey Jane (Gobler) P. BS, U. Wis., Eau Claire, 1979; postgrad., Kennedy Western U., Boise, Idaho, 1993—. Sanitation supr. Green Giant, St. James, Minn., 1979-80; food technologist Kraft Foods, Beaver Dam, Wis., 1980-82; quality control mgr. Fleur de Lait Foods, New Holland, Pa., 1982-83; lab. mgr. Assoc. Milk Producers, Inc., New Ulm, 1983—, environ. affairs coord. North Ctrl. region, 1990—. Founding pres. Friends of Flandrau St. Park, New Ulm, 1986-90; leader Cadette/Sr. Peacepipe coun. Girl Scouts U.S., Redwood Falls, Minn., 1985-91, trainer sci., math. and tech., 1990—; mem. choir, bd. dirs. New Ulm Chorale, 1985—. Mem. Internat. Assn. Milk, Food and Environ. Sanitarians, Minn. Sanitarians Assn. (v.p. 1993—), Am. Chem. Soc. Roman Catholic. Office: Assoc Milk Producers Inc 312 Center St New Ulm MN 56073

PETTIT, JULIE THERESE, mechanical engineer, small business owner; b. Sioux City, Iowa, Mar. 19, 1967; d. Thomas William and Evelyn Carol (Mandersheid) Lefler. BS in Mechanical Engineering, South Dakota Sch. of Mines and Tech., 1990, MS in Mechanical Engineering, 1992. Rsch. asst. & teaching asst. Mech. Engring. Dept. South Dakota Sch. of Mines, Rapid City, 1990-92; maint. engr. Monsanto Chem. Co., Soda Springs, Idaho, 1993-94; v.p. Precision Prototype, Rapid City, 1994—. Grantee U.S. Dept. Agr., 1994. Mem. ASME, Am. Prodn. & Inventory Control Soc., Am. Soc. Quality Control. Office: Precision Prototype 1007 Sycamore St Rapid City SD 57701

PETTIT, WENDY JEAN, management company executive; b. Gary, Ind., Oct. 6, 1945; d. Wendell E. and Ethel (Binkley) Pettit. BA, MacMurray Coll., 1967; MSBA, Ind. U., 1978, certificate in Acctg. Ind. U., 1992; MBA, Ind. U., 1993. Acctg. clk. J. Walter Thompson USA, Chgo., 1967-68, adminstrv. asst., 1968-72, personnel asst., 1973-74, fin. analyst, 1974-78, office svcs. asst., 1978-80, acctg. dept. mgr., 1980-90; pres. Pettit Acctg. & Mgmt. Svcs., 1990—; asst. contr. Inland Employees Fed. Credit Union, 1993—. Bd. dirs. Miller Citizens Corp., Gary, 1979-86, treas., 1979-82. Named Career Woman of the Year, Bus. and Profl. Women, Gary, 1967. Mem. Nat. Assn. Female Execs., Am. Mgmt. Assn., LWV. Methodist. Avocations: singing, piano, cooking. Home: 8000 Oak Ave Gary IN 46403 Office: 31 W Lincoln Hwy Schererville IN 46375

PETTITT, BARBARA JEAN, pediatric surgeon; b. Niagara Falls, N.Y., Feb. 2, 1952; d. Robert Andrew and Joan Marilyn (Boore) P.; m. Richard Allen Schieber, May 24, 1981; children: Christine Pettitt Schieber, Lucy Pettitt Schieber, Brian Pettitt Schieber. BA in Chemistry magna cum laude, Cen. Coll., Pella, Iowa, 1972; D of Medicine, Northwestern U., Chgo., 1976. Diplomate Am. Bd. Surgery with certificates of spl. competence in pediatric surgery and surg. critical care; lic. pediatric surgeon, Calif., Pa., Ga. Student fellow in rehab. medicine Rehab. Inst. Chgo., spring 1974; intern in straight surgery Los Angeles County-U. So. Calif. Med. Ctr., 1976-77, resident in gen. surgery, 1977-81; resident in pediatric surgery Childrens' Hosp. Pitts., 1982-84; asst. prof. surgery and pediatrics dept. Sch. Medicine Emory U., Atlanta, 1985—; mem. staff Henrietta Egleston Hosp. for Children, Atlanta, 1985-86; mem. staff Grady Meml. Hosp., Atlanta, 1985—, dir. pediatric surg. svc., 1990—; chief of surgery Hughes Spalding Children's Hosp., 1993—; instr. in ATLS, ACLS, PALS; active various coms. Henrietta Egleston Hosp. for children, 1985-86, Grady Meml. Hosp., 1986—; lectr., presenter many profl. and ednl. orgns., 1983—. Contbg. author: (with M. Rowe) Pediatric Surgery, 4th edit., 1986; contbr. articles to profl. publs. Bd. dirs., trustees DeKalb Choral Guild, Atlanta, 1988—; pres. Summit Cmty. Assn., 1992—; chairperson health and safety com. Arbor Montessori Sch. Rsch. grantee Rsch. Corp., summer 1971, NIH, 1983-84; Rollscreen full-tuition scholar, 1969-72; Ruth G. White scholar Calif. State P.E.O., 1974-75; 1st Prize Bernard Baruch Essay Contest, Am. Congress Rehab. Medicine, 1975; named Outstanding Young Woman of Yr., State of Pa., 1984, State of Ga., 1986. Fellow ACS, Am. Acad. Pediatrics (surg. sect., critical care sect.); mem. AMA, Am. Med. Womens' Assn., Southeastern Surg. Congress, Am. Pediatric Surg. Assn., Assn. Women Surgeons, Am. Soc. Parental and Enteral Nutrition, La.A. County-U. So. Calif. Med. Ctr. Soc. Grad. Surgeons, Phi Delta Epsilon (pres. med. sch. chpt. 1974-75, undergrad. midwest regional coord. 1974-75, nat. exec. com. 1976-80, nat. intern-resident liaison com. 1980-85, nat. constn. and bylaws com. 1986—, Isadore Pilot award Chgo. chpt. 1975, nat. svc. award 1976), Soc. Critical Care Medicine, Ga. Surg. Soc., Assn. Surg. Edn. Democrat. Episcopalian. Office: Emory Univ Sch Medicine Dept of Surgery 69 Butler St SE Atlanta GA 30303-3033

PETTORINI, PAULA G., clinical psychologist; b. Waterbury, Conn., Dec. 21, 1946; d. Pasquale Joseph and Anna Mary (Geruch) Galluci; m. James George Pettorini, June 24, 1967; children: James Matthew, Peter David. RN, Yale U., 1967; BA, U. Ill., 1986; D in Psychology, Ill. Sch. Profl. Psychology, 1991. RN; lic. clin. psychologist. Charge nurse Conn. Mental Health Ctr., New Haven, 1967-70; charge nurse newborn intensive care Waterbury (Conn.) Hosp., 1975-80; pvt. duty nurse N.J. Nurse Registry, Dover, 1980-85; staff psychologist Ravenswood Mental Health Ctr., Chgo., 1989-92; clin. case mgr. & supr., psychologist Medco Behavioral Care, Chgo., 1992—; pvt. practice Chgo., 1990—. Mem. APA, Internat. Soc. Psychotherapy Rsch. (presenter), Ill. Psychol. Assn. (health reimbursement com. 1993—). Home: 551 Oakdale Ave Glencoe IL 60022

PETTUS, SALLY LOCKHART, psychologist; b. N.Y.C., Aug. 17, 1937; d. Alfred Sherman and Jane Clay (Zevely) Foote; m. Charlton Messick Pettus, June 21, 1958 (div. 1974); children: Charlton, Cybele; m. William Frank Wyatt Jr., Sept. 10, 1989. Student, Vassar Coll., 1955-58; AB, Roger Williams Coll., 1972; EdD, Boston U., 1977. Lic. Psychologist. Psychol. cons. Ipswich (Mass.) Sch. System, 1975-77, Human Resource Inst., Brookline, Mass., 1975-77, New England Meml. Hosp., Stoneham, Mass., 1977-78; sr. psychologist Newton (Mass.) Guidance Clinic, 1978-82; clin. assoc. East Side Ctr., Providence, 1987-89; sr. psychologist Netrowest Youth Guidance, Framingham, Mass., 1982-91; clin. psychologist Providence, 1989—; clin. supr. Women's Protective Svcs., Framingham, 1987-90; reviewer in field. Mem. Nat. Register Health Svc. Providers in Psychology, Am. Psychol. Assn., Am. Orthopsychiatric Assn., Mass. Psychol. Assn. R.I. Psychol. Assn.

PETTY, MARGE, state senator; b. Ft. Wayne, Ind., Feb. 26, 1946; m. Tyrus C. Petty, 1968; children: Brandon, Megan. Senator, ranking minority, judiciary com., mem. ways & means Kans. State Senate; minority leader Ways & Means Com.; mem. Commerce Com., Fin. Institutions & Ins., Pensions and Investments; Dem. caucus policy chair KPERS Investigating Com. Episcopalian. Home: 106 NW Woodlawn Ave Topeka KS 66606-1241 Address: State Senate State Capitol Topeka KS 66612

PETTYJOHN, SHIRLEY ELLIS, lawyer, real estate executive; b. Liberty, Ky., Aug. 16, 1935; d. Wesley Barker and Ada Lou (Bryant) Ellis; m. Flem D. Pettyjohn, Sept. 24, 1955; children: Deena Renee, Ellisa Denise. BS in Commerce, U. Louisville, 1974, JD, 1977. Bar: Ky. 1978, Ind. 1988; lic. real estate broker, Ky., Ind.; cert. mediator. Pres. Universal Devel. Corp., Ky. and Fla., 1984—, Pettyjohn Inc., Ky. and Ind., 1967—, Ind. Mediation Svcs., Inc., 1990—, Ky. Mediation Svcs., Inc., 1991—; v.p. Continental Investments Corp., 1986—; sr. ptnr. Pettyjohn & Assocs., Attys., 1987—. Editor Law-Hers Jour. Vice-chmn. Louisville and Jefferson County Planning Commn., 1971-75; mem. Gov.'s Conf. on Edn., 1977, jud. nominee, 1981, Met. Louisville Women's Polit. Caucus, Bluegrass State Skills Corp., 1992—, Ky. Opera Assn. Guild; elected mem. Ky. State Dem. Exec. Com., 1988-92; del. Nat. Dem. Conv. and Dem. Nat. Platform Com., 1988; bd. dirs. Ky. Dem. Hdqs., Inc., 1988-92, Pegasus Rising, Inc.; chmn. Okolona Libr. Task Force. Recipient Mayor's Cert. Recognition, 1974, Mayor's Fleur de lis award, 1969-73, Excellence in Writing award Arts Club Louisville, 1986, 87, 93. Mem. ABA, NAFE, Nat. Assn. Adminstrv. Law Judges, Ky. Bar Assn., Louisville Bar Assn., Women Lawyers Assn. of Jefferson County, Am. Judicature Soc., Clark County Bar Assn., Ind. Bar Assn., Ind. Assn. Mediators, Am. Inst. Planners, Women's C. of C. of Ky. (past bd. dirs., chmn. legis. com.), Am. Legion (aux.), Fraternal Order Police Assn. (award 1982), Louisville Legal Secs. (past pres., editor Law-Hers Jour.), Coun. of Women Pres. (past pres., Woman of Achievement award 1974), Louisville Visual Arts Assn. (former bd. dirs.), Louisville Ballet Guild (chair audience devel. 1989-91), Dem. Leadership Coun., Jefferson County Dem. Women's Club (past v.p.), Nat. Fedn. Dem. Women's Clubs, Spirit of 46th Club, Mose Green Club, North End Club, 12th Ward Club, S. End Club, 3rd Ward Club, Highland Pk. Club, Grass Roots Club, Harry S. Truman Club, Beargrass Club, Arts Club of Louisville (past pres.), Sigma Delta Kappa, Chi Thi Theta. Home: 6924 Norlynn Dr Louisville KY 40228-1471 Office: 600 E Court Ave Ste 102 Jeffersonville IN 47130

PETYKIEWICZ, SANDRA DICKEY, editor; b. Detroit, Sept. 23, 1953; d. James Fulton and Alice Diane (Nowak) Dickey; m. Edward W. Petykiewicz, Oct. 17, 1981; 1 child, Kendall Lee. BA, Cen. Mich. U., Mt. Pleasant, 1975. Reporter Big Rapids (Mich.) Pioneer, 1975, Midland (Mich.) Daily News, 1975-77; reporter Saginaw (Mich.) News, 1977-79, feature editor, 1979-80, asst. metro editor, 1980-81; copy editor Washington Post, 1981-82; asst. city editor Balt. News Am., 1982-83; metro editor Jackson (Mich.) Citizen Patriot, 1983-87, editor, 1987—; bd. dirs. Mich. AP, 1987-93, pres., 1990, 91-92; bd. dirs. Mid Am. Press Inst., 1992—; mem. alumni bd. Ctrl. Mich. U., 1992—, mem. journalism adv. bd., 1992—. Pulitzer Prize juror, 1990-92. Mem. Jackson Area Quality Initiative, 1990—. Mem. Am. Soc. Newspaper Editors, AP Mng. Editors, Soc. Profl. Journalists, Bus. and Profl. Women's Club (editor newsletter 1985-86, Young Career Woman of Yr. award 1984), Rotary Club, Jackson Econ. Club (chairwoman 1992), Sigma Delta Chi.

PETZEL, FLORENCE ELOISE, textiles educator; b. Crosbyton, Tex., Apr. 1, 1911; d. William D. and A. Eloise (Punchard) P. PhB, U. Chgo., 1931, AM, 1934; PhD, U. Minn., 1954. Instr., Judson Coll., 1936-38; asst. prof. textiles Ohio State U., 1938-48; assoc. prof. U. Ala., 1950-54; prof. Oreg. State U., 1954-61, 67-75, 77, prof. emeritus, 1975—, dept. head, 1954-61, 67-75; prof., div. head U. Tex., 1961-63; prof. Tex. Tech U., 1963-67; vis. instr. Tex. State Coll. for Women, 1937; vis. prof. Wash. State U., 1967. Effie I. Raitt fellow, 1949-50. Mem. Seattle Art Mus., Oreg. Art Mus., Met. Opera Guild, Portland Opera Assn., Sigma Xi, Phi Kappa Phi, Omicron Nu, Iota Sigma Pi, Sigma Delta Epsilon. Author Textiles of Ancient Mesopotamia, Persia and Egypt, 1987; contbr. articles to profl. jours. Home: 625 NW 29th St Corvallis OR 97330-5255

PETZOLD, ANITA MARIE, psychotherapist; b. Princeton, N.J., June 2, 1957; d. Charles Bernard and Kathleen Marie (McDonald) P.; m. Joseph Santiago, June 13, 1985 (div. Nov. 1991). AS in Bus., Indian River C.C., Ft. Pierce, Fla., 1986; BS in Liberal Studies, Barry U., 1988; MS in Human Svcs. Adminstrn., Nova U., 1989, postgrad., 1989-91; postgrad., LaSalle U., 1994—. Lic. mental health counselor, Fla.; cert. addictions profl.; internat. cert. alcohol and drug abuse counselor; nat. cert. counselor; cert. employee assistance counselor; cert. DUI instr. Admissions asst. The Palm Beach Inst., West Palm Beach, Fla., 1985-86; dir. admissions Heritage Health Corp., Jensen Beach, Fla., 1986-89; divsn. dir. county drug abuse program Martin County Bd. of County Commrs., Stuart, Fla., 1989—; mem. Drug Resource Team for the 12th Congl. Dist., Fla., 1990—, Juvenile Justice Assn. of the 19th Jud. Ct., Fla., 1993—; grant writer in field. Vol. Hist. Soc. Martin County, Stuart, 1986—; mem. United Way Martin County, Stuart, 1993; mem. bd. dirs. Cmty. AIDS Adv. Project, Stuart, 1993; chmn. treatment com. Martin County Task Force on Substance Abused Children, Stuart, 1993—. Recipient Outstanding Cmty. Svc. award United Way Martin County, Stuart, 1993. Mem. NASW, Am. Mental Health Counselors Assn., Nat. Criminal Justice Assn., Nat. Assn. Alcoholism and Drug Abuse Counselors, Nat. Consortium Treatment Alternatives to St. Crime Programs, Am. Coll. Addiction Treatment Adminstrs., Am. Labor-Mgmt. Adminstrs., Fla. Alcohol and Drug Abuse Assn. Republican. Roman Catholic. Office: Martin County Bd County Commrs 400 SE Osceola St Stuart FL 34994-2577

PETZOLD, CAROL STOKER, state legislator; b. St. Louis, July 28; d. Harold William and Mabel Lucille (Wilson) Stoker; m. Walter John Petzold, June 27, 1959; children: Ann, Ruth, David. BS, Valparaiso U., 1959. Tchr. John Muir Elem. Sch., Alameda, Calif., 1959-60, Parkwood Elem. Sch., Kensington, Md., 1960-62; legis. aide Md. Gen. Assembly, Annapolis, 1975-79; legis. asst. Montgomery County Bd. Edn., Rockville, Md., 1980; community sch. coordinator Parkland Jr. High Sch., Rockville, 1981-87; mem. Md. Ho. of Dels., Annapolis, 1987—; mem. transp. planning bd. Nat. Capitol Region, 1989—; vice chair energy and transp. com. Nat. Conf. State Legislatures; exec. com. Montgomery United Way Coun., 1981—. Editor Child Care Sampler, 1974, Stoker Family Cookbook, 1976. Pres. Montgomery Child Care Assn., 1976-78; mem. Md. State Scholarship Bd., 1978-87, chmn. 1985-87; chmn. Legis. Com. Montgomery County Commn. for Children and Youth, 1979-84; mem., v.p. Luth. Social Services Nat. Capitol Area, Washington, 1980-86. Recipient Statewide award Gov.'s Adv. Bd. on Homelessness; recognized for outstanding commitment to children U.S. Dept. HEW, 1980. Mem. AAUW (honoree Kensington br. 1971, honoree Md. div. 1981), Women's Polit. Caucus (chmn. Montgomery County 1981-83), Women's Caucus Md. Legislature. Democrat. Lutheran. Home: 14113 Chadwick Ln Rockville MD 20853-2103

PEYSER, ROXANE D., lawyer; b. Queens, N.Y., June 17, 1959; m. Ted Ross Peyser; children: Rachel Renee, Natasha Tovah, Samuel Aaron. BA in Middle Eastern Studies, George Washington U., 1981; JD, U. Houston, 1987. Bar: Tex., Ala., U.S. Dist. Ct. (so., no. dists.) Tex., U.S. Ct. Appeals (5th cir.). Intern Harris County Dist. Atty's. Office, Houston, 1987; atty. Saccomanno & Clegg, Houston, 1988-90, Graham, Bright & Smith, Dallas, 1990-92; sr. legal counsel Compass Bancshares, Inc., Birmingham, 1992-94; atty. Sirote & Permutt, P.C., Birmingham, Ala., 1994—; participant, grad. Project Corp. Leadership, Birmingham, 1993-94; section mem. meditation com. Ala. Bar Assn., 1993—. Contbr. numerous articles to profl. jours. Mem. bd. dirs. Am. Jewish Congress, Dallas, 1990-91; tchr. Temple Emanu El, Birmingham, 1993—; mem., contbr. Israel Bonds Bd., 1994—, Nat. Coun. Jewish Women, 1993—; mem. steering com. bus. & profl. women section Jewish Fedn., 1994—. Mem. ABA, Am. Corp. Counsel Assn., Tex. Bar Assn., Ala. Bar Assn., Tex. Assn. Bank Counsel. Office: Sirote & Permutt PC 2222 Arlington Ave S Birmingham AL 35205

PEYTON, ELLA LOUISE, association executive, consultant; b. Alexandria, Ind., Dec. 15, 1927; d. Russell Kenneth and Ruth E. (Bowyer) Graham; m. Harold Roy Peyton, June 24, 1949; 1 child, Linda Peyton Clear. AA in Early Childhood Edn., BA in Bus./Acctg., Anderson U., 1978; postgrad., U. Wis., Osh Kosh, 1979. Adminstrv. asst. YWCA, Anderson, Ind., 1975-80; exec. dir. YWCA, Beloit, Wis., 1980-87, Elgin, Ill., 1987-90; interim exec. dir., cons. YWCA, 1993—. Author: (booklet) Stretch Your Dollar, 1976. Life mem. YWCA, 1975—, Friends Judson Coll., bd. dirs., 1989-90; mem. Gov.'s Coun. Domestic Violence, Wis., 1985-87. Recipient Disting. Svc. award C. of C., 1986, Charlotte Danson award Women Mgmt., Inc., 1988; named Diplomat of Yr. women's divsn. C. of C., 1986. Mem. Am. Bus. Women (pres. 1979), Zonta Club (pres., internat. del. 1985), Jobs Daus. (guardian), Order Ea. Star (matron, state pres.), Psi Sigma Alpha (pres.). Baptist. Home (summer): 401 Mohawk Dr Anderson IN 46012 Home (winter): 660 Hook # 15 Clermont FL 34711

PFAELZER, MARIANA R., federal judge; b. L.A., Feb. 4, 1926. AB, U. Calif., 1947; LLB, UCLA, 1957. Bar: Calif. 1958. Assoc. Wyman, Bautzer, Rothman & Kuchel, 1957-69, ptnr., 1969-78; judge U.S. Dist. Ct. (ctrl. dist.) Calif., 1978—. pres., v.p., dir. Bd. Police Commrs. City of L.A., 1974-78; bd. vis. Loyola Law Sch. Named Alumna of Yr. by UCLA Law Sch., 1980. Mem. ABA, Calif. Bar Assn. (local adminstrv. com., spl. com. study rules procedure 1972, joint subcom. profl. ethics and computers and the law coms. 1972, profl. ethics com. 1972-74, spl. com. juvenile justice, women's rights subcom. human rights sect.), L.A. County Bar Assn. (spl. com. study rules procedure state bar 1974). Office: US Dist Ct 312 N Spring St Los Angeles CA 90012-4701*

PFAFF, AMY KAE, small business owner; b. Englewood, N.J., Dec. 11, 1973; d. Ray John and Karen Kay (Southards) P. Grad. high sch. Mgr. Silver Collection, Rockaway, N.J., 1990-93; owner Simply Silver, Lynchburg, Va., 1993—. Active YMCA. Mem. Nat. Assn. Self-employed. Republican. Office: Simply Silver E2 River Ridge Mall Lynchburg VA 24502

PFAFF, VIRGINIA CAROLYN, artistic director; b. Passaic, N.J., Sept. 11, 1935; d. Andrew and Mary (Szabo) Horvath; m. Richard L. Pfaff, Aug. 18, 1956; children: John F., Karen L. Pfaff Reinertson. Grad. high sch., Passaic. Program dir. Wolf Trap Found., Vienna, Va., 1971-78; gen. mgr. Playhouse Sq. Ctr., Cleve., 1979-82; mng. dir. Victory Theatre, Dayton, Ohio, 1982-84, Kahilu (Hawaii) Theatre, 1984—. Mem. Assn. Performing Arts Presenters, Internat. Soc. Performing Arts Adminstrs. (sec. 1987, bd. dirs. 1982-87), Hawaii Assn. Music Socs. (v.p., treas. 1987—), Hawaii Consortia, Performing Arts Presenters of Hawaii (pres.), Western Alliance Performing Arts Adminstrs. Republican. Home: Mamalahoa Hwy Kamuela HI 96743 Office: Kahilu Theatre Parker Ranch Mall Kamuela HI 96743

PFAFFLIN, SHEILA MURPHY, psychologist; b. Pasadena, Calif., July 31, 1934; d. Leonard Anthony and Honora (Shields) Murphy; m. James Reid Pfafflin, Sept. 7, 1957. BA, Pomona Coll., 1956; MA, Johns Hopkins U., 1958, PhD, 1959. Mem. tech. staff AT&T Bell Labs., Murray Hill, N.J., 1959-75; dist. mgr. AT&T, Morristown, N.J., 1975—; Chair sub com. on Women-Com. on Equal Opportunities in Sci. and Tech., NSF, Washington, 1981-85; mem. adv. coun. Math/Sci. Tchr. Supply and Demand, N.J. Dept. Higher Edn., 1982-83; mem. adv. bd. for Maths., Sci. and Computer Sci. Teaching Improvement Grants, N.J. Dept. Higher Edn., 1984-89. Co-editor: Expanding the Role of Women in the Sciences, 1978, Scientific-Technological Change & the Role of Women in Development, 1981, Psychology & Educational Policy, 1987; contbr. articles to profl. jours. Trustee Ramapo Coll. of N.J., Mahwah, N.J., 1984—; adv. bd. Project "SMART", Girls Clubs of Am., N.Y.C., 1984—, Consortium for Ednl. Equity, Rutgers U., New Brunswick, N.Y., 1983—; pres. Assn. for Women in Sci. Ednl. Found., Washington, 1982—. Fellow AAAS, N.Y. Acad. Scis., Am. Psychol. Assn.; mem. Assn. for Women in Sci. (pres. 1980-81, Women Scientist award, Met. Chpt., 1987), Phi Beta Kappa, Sigma Xi. Home: 173 Gates Ave Gillette NJ 07933-1719 Office: AT&T 100 Southgate Pkwy Rm 3F07 Morristown NJ 07960-6441

PFEFFER, JUDITH STADLEN, psychologist; b. Washington, Sept. 28, 1942; d. Morris and Marian (Singerman) Stadlen; m. Philip Elliot Pfeffer, Dec. 22, 1962; children: Charles, Ari, Shira. BA, CUNY, 1963; MEd, Rutgers U., 1965; PhD, Temple U., 1981; cert. cognitive therapy, U. Pa., 1985. Cert. sch. psychologist, Pa.; lic. psychologist, Pa. Tchr. Highland Park (N.J.) Sch. Dist., 1963-66; supr., lectr. Hunter Coll. CUNY, 1968-69; cons. learning disabilities Chgo., Phila., N.Y.C., 1968-74; cons. psychologist, rsch. assoc. Montgomery County Intermediate Unit, Norristown, Pa., 1980-82; supr., lectr. Pa. State U., Abington, 1982-83; pvt. practice Warrington, Pa., 1982—; adj. asst. prof. Temple U., Phila., 1981-82; cons. psychologist Bucks County Intermediate Unit, Doylestown, Pa., 1982—, Bristol Twp. Spl. Edn. Dept., Bristol, Pa., 1987—. Co-author: A Guide to Teaching Children with Learning Disabilities, 1968. Fellow Temple U., 1978. Mem. APA, Pa. Psychol. Assn., Phila. Soc. Clin. Psychologists, Phi Beta Kappa. Home and Office: 812 Lorraine Dr Warrington PA 18976-2218

PFEIFER, ALINE JEANETTE, association executive; b. Alton, Ill., Apr. 30, 1930; d. Herbert Henry and Esther Margaretha (Schuette) Meyer; m. Edward Louis Pfeifer, July 12, 1952 (dec. May 1970); children: David C., Linda L. Pfeifer Smith, Cheryl L. Pfeifer Pelham. BA in Psychology and Social Work, Valparaiso U., 1951; MS in Counseling, So. Ill. U., 1972. Lic. clin. social worker, Mo. Sec. group edn. Assn. Family Living, Chgo., 1952-53; tchr. kindergarten Alton (Ill.) Pub. Schs., 1953-54; clk. U.S. Army, Ft. Leonard Wood, Mo., 1954-55; manpower rep. Ill. State Dept. Labor, Granite City, 1971-74; adminstr. programs Family Svc. and Vis. Nurse, Alton, 1974-83; exec. dir. YWCA of St. Joseph, Mo., 1984—; trainer Ill. Family Planning Coun., Springfield, Peoria, Alton, 1982-83. Leader Girl Scouts Am., Godfrey, Ill., 1962-70; coord. St. Joseph Legis. Network, 1986-93; pres. ch. coun. First Luth. Ch., St. Joseph, 1990-92. Mem. AAUW (bd. dirs. 1988-93), Nat. Assn. YWCA Execs., League Women Voters (bd. dirs. 1988-93), YWCA Investment Club (organizer 1987-93), St. Joseph C. of C (diplomat 1985-93), Sertoma, Altrusa (pres. 1989-91), Women's Career Network (bd. dirs. 1988-91). Office: YWCA 304 N 8th St Saint Joseph MO 64501-1988

PFEIFFER, JANE CAHILL, former broadcasting company executive, consultant; b. Washington, Sept. 29, 1932; d. John Joseph and Helen (Reilly) Cahill; B.A., U. Md., 1954; postgrad., Cath. U. Am., 1956-57; LHD (hon.), Pace Coll., 1978, U. Md., 1979, Manhattanville Coll., 1979, Amherst U., 1980, Babson Coll., 1981, U. Notre Dame, 1991; m. Ralph A. Pfeiffer, Jr., June 3, 1975. With IBM Corp., Armonk, N.Y., 1955-76, sec. mgmt. rev. com., 1970, dir. communications, 1971, v.p. communications and govt. relations, 1972-76, bus. cons., 1976-78; chmn. NBC, Inc., N.Y.C., 1978-80; bus. cons., 1980—; dir. Ashland Oil Co., Mony Fin. Svcs., Internat. Paper Co., J.C. Penney Co.; trustee The Conf. Bd., 1991. Mem. pres.'s adv. com. White House Fellows, 1966, Pres.'s Gen. Adv. Commn. on Arms Control and Disarmament, 1977-80, Pres.'s Commn. Mil. Compensation, trustee Rockefeller Found., U. Md., Carnegie Hall, U. Notre Dame. White House fellow, Washington, 1966; recipient Achievement award Kapppa Kappa Gamma, 1974-80, Eleanor Roosevelt Humanitarian award N.Y. League for Hard of Hearing, 1980, Disting. Alumna award U. Md., 1975, Humanitarian award NOW, 1980, Centennial Alumna Medallion U. Md., 1988. Mem. Council on Fgn. Relations, Overseas Devel. Council. Club: Econ. of N.Y. Office: 90 Field Point Cir Greenwich CT 06830-7011

PFEIFFER, SOPHIA DOUGLASS, state legislator, lawyer; b. N.Y.C., Aug. 10, 1918; d. Franklin Chamberlin and Sophie Douglass (White) Wells; m. Timothy Adams Pfeiffer, June 7, 1941; children: Timothy Franklin, Penelope Mersereau Keenan, Sophie Douglass. A.B., Vassar Coll., 1939; J.D., Northeastern U., 1975. Bar: R.I. 1975, U.S. Ct. Apls. (1st cir.) 1980, U.S. Supreme Ct. 1979. Editorial researcher Time, Inc., N.Y.C., 1940-41; writer Office War Info., Washington, 1941-43, N.Y.C., 1943-45; editorial staff Nat. Geog. Mag., Washington, 1958-59, 68-70; editor Turkish Jour. Pediatrics, Ankara, 1961-63; staff atty. R.I. Supreme Ct., Providence, 1975-76, chief staff atty., 1977-86; mem. Maine Ho. Reps., 1990-94; lectr. U. So. Maine, 1995—. Contbr. in field. Pres., Karachi Am. Sch. (Pakistan), 1955-56; chair, Brunswick Village Review Bd., 1986-89. Home: 15 Franklin St Brunswick ME 04011-2101

PFIFFNER, LINDA JO, psychologist, educator; b. Santa Monica, Calif., Dec. 5, 1959; d. Harold Joseph and Ruth (Albert) P. BA in Psychology summa cum laude, UCLA, 1981; MA in Psychology, SUNY, Stony Brook, 1983, PhD in Clin. Psychology, 1987. Lic. clin. psychologist, Calif. Psychologist child devel. ctr. U. Calif., Irvine, 1987-92, clinic dir., 1991—, asst. prof. in residence dept. pediatrics, 1992—; cons. Stakeholder Plan, Attention Deficit Hyperactivity Disorder, Fed. Resource Ctr. Spl. Edn., U. Ky.; presenter in field. Author: (with others) Attention Deficit Hyperactivity Disorders: A Handbook for Diagnosis and Treatment, 1990, Hyperactivity in Children: A Handbook, 1993; guest reviewer Pediatrics, Behavior Therapy, 1989—; contbr. articles to profl. jours., chpts. to textbooks. Recipient First award NIMH, 1993—; grantee Sigma Xi, 1985, Calif. Coll. Medicine, 1993; Grad. Coun. fellow SUNY, 1981-83. Mem. APA, Assn. Advancement Behavior Therapy, Soc. Rsch. Child and Adolescent Psychopathology, Profl. Group Attention-Related Disorders, Phi Beta Kappa, Psi Chi. Home: 68 Whitman Ct Irvine CA 92715 Office: U Calif Child Devel Ctr 4621 Teller Ste 108 Newport Beach CA 92660

PFISTER, GAIL WILLIAMS, economics educator; b. Seattle, May 6, 1936; d. Randall Smallwood Jr. and Jean (Miller) Williams; m. John S. Williams, Aug. 23, 1958 (div. 1979); children: Eric, Lori; m. Cloyd Harry Pfister, Apr. 24, 1982; stepchildren: Gaby, Cathy, Michael, Romi. AA, Marymount Coll., Rome, 1955; BA in Econs., Oberlin Coll., 1957; MA in History, Fairleigh Dickinson U., 1968; MA in Econs., NYU, 1976. Rsch. assoc., then lectr. Fairleigh Dickinson U., Teaneck, N.J., 1973-79; asst. prof. George Mason U., Fairfax, Va., 1979-82; lectr. U. Md., Heidelberg, Germany, 1982-84, U. Ariz., Tucson, 1984-86, U. South Fla., Tampa, 1986-89, Eckerd Coll., St. Petersburg, Fla., 1986-89; mem. faculty dept. bus. adminstrn. Marymount U., Arlington, Va., 1989—. Author: Multinational Corporations: Problems and Prospects, 1975, Transborder Data Flows and Multinational Enterprise, 1988. Home: 4653 Kirkpatrick Ln Alexandria VA 22311

PFLUEGER, M(ELBA) LEE, academic administrator; b. St. Louis, Sept. 2, 1942; d. Pless and Edna Mae (Russell) Counts; m. Raymond Allen Pflueger, Sept. 14, 1963 (div. June 1972); children: Salem Allen, Russell Counts. BS in Home Econs., Univ. Mo., 1969; MEd in Guidance and Counseling, Washington Univ., St. Louis, 1973. Ednl. psychologist Ozark Regional Mental Health Ctr., Harrison, Ark., 1974-75; from account mgr. to mgr. pers. Enterprise Leasing Co., St. Louis, 1977-79; mgr. employee rels. Eaton Corp., Houston, 1979-80; owner Nature's Nuggets Fresh Granola, St. Louis, 1980-83; dir. corp. ednl. svcs. Maryville Coll., St. Louis, 1983-84; adminstr. mgmt. skills devel. McDonnell Douglas, St. Louis, 1984-85, mgr. employee involvement, 1985-86, prin. specialist human resources mgmt., 1988-89; mgr. human resources McDonnell Douglas, Houston, 1986-88; dir. devel. sch. engring. U. Mo., Rolla, 1989-93, dir. devel., corp. and found. rels., 1992-93; regional dir. devel., assoc. dir. maj. gifts and capital projects Washington U., St. Louis, 1994—; part-time leader trainer Maritz Motivation, St. Louis, 1984-89. Chair United Fund Campaign for U. Mo., Rolla, 1991. Mem. PEO. Office: Washington U Office Maj Gifts and Capital Projects Campus Box 1228 One Brookings Dr Saint Louis MO 63130-4899

PFLUM, BARBARA ANN, pediatric allergist; b. Cin., Jan. 10, 1943; d. James Frederick and Betty Mae (Doherty) P.; m. Makram I. Gobrail, Oct. 20, 1973; children: Christina, James. BS, Coll. Mt. St. Vincent, 1967; MD, Georgetown U., 1971. Cons. Children's Med. Ctr., Dayton, Ohio, 1975—, dir. allergy clinic, 1983-89. Fellow Am. Acad. Pediatrics, Am. Acad. Allergy and Immunology, Am. Coll. Allergy and Immunology; mem. Ohio Soc. Allergy and Immunology, Western Ohio Pediatric Soc. (pres. 1985-86). Roman Catholic. Home: 4502 Lytle Rd Waynesville OH 45068-9483 Office: 201 E Stroop Rd Dayton OH 45429-2825

PFOHL, DAWN GERTRUDE, hospital administrator; b. Balt., June 7, 1944; d. Harry F. Coleman and Gertrude (Stahlin) Scharmer; m. Ronald J. Pfohl, June 18, 1967; 1 child, Shara Lynn. BS, Capital U., 1966; MS, Miami U., Oxford, Ohio, 1972; M Health Adminstrn., Xavier U., 1991. Grad. teaching asst. Mich. State U., East Lansing, 1966-67; rsch. asst. Istituto di Microbiologia, U. Palermo, Italy, 1967-69; grad. rsch. asst. Miami U., 1970-71; microbiology instr. Wilmington (Ohio) Coll., 1972; med. microbiologist McCullough-Hyde Hosp., Oxford, 1972-78, dir. clin. lab. svcs., 1978-93, dir. quality assessment and improvement, safety officer, 1993—. Treas., mem. ch. coun. Faith Luth. Ch., Oxford, 1990-93; parent rep. S.W. Edn. Resource Reg. Coun., Cin., 1986-87; bd. dirs., editor newsletter, pres. Oxford Assn. for Children with Learning Disabilities, 1985-88; active Butler County Local Emergency Planning Com., 1994—, vice chair, 1995—. Mem. Am. Soc. Microbiologists, Am. Soc. Clin. Pathologists, Ohio Assn. Quality in Healthcare, Clin. Lab. Mgmt. Assn. (scholar 1990), Oxford C. of C. Office: McCullough-Hyde Meml Hosp 110 N Poplar St Oxford OH 45056-1292

PHARES, LYNN LEVISAY, public relations communications executive; b. Brownwood, Tex., Aug. 6, 1947; m. C. Kirk Phares, Aug. 22, 1971; children: Laura, Margaret, Adele, Jessica. BA, La. State U., 1970; MA, U. Nebr., 1987. Asst. to advt. mgr. La. Nat. Bank, 1970-71; writer, producer, asst. v.p., account exec. Smith, Kaplan, Allen & Reynolds, Inc., Omaha, 1971-80; assoc. dir. pub. affairs U. Nebr. Med. Ctr., 1980-83; dir. pub. rels. ConAgra, Inc., Omaha, 1985-87, v.p. pub. rels., 1987-90, v.p. pub. rels. and cmty. affairs, 1987—; pres. ConAgra Found. Office: ConAgra Inc 1 Conagra Dr Omaha NE 68102-5094

PHARR, ANN E., public programs administrator; b. N.Y.C., July 25, 1946; d. John B. and Pauline Anna (Hawkins) P. BS, Howard U., 1968, MS, 1972; MPIA, U. Pitts., 1979, PhD, 1988. Instr. psychology Morgan State U., Balt., 1972-73; psychology instr., rsch. asst. Peace Corps Fourah Bay Coll., Sierra Leone, 1973-75; unit adminstr. CARE, Inc., Tunisia, Bangladesh, Liberia, Sierra Leone, 1976-78; adminstr., mgmt. U.S. AID, Tanzania, Uganda, Mali, 1980-83; spl. asst. to dep. commr. D.C. Commn. of Pub. Health, 1986-88; adj. prof. dept. bus., pub. adminstrn., and econs. Bowie (Md.) State U., 1989; mgmt. cons. Pragma Corp., Falls Church, Va., 1989; internat. devel. cons. Roy Littlejohn Assocs., Inc., Washington, 1989-91; internat. tng. cons. Louis Berger Internat., Washington, 1990; pub. health analyst Office Maternal and Child Health, D.C. Commn. Pub. Health, 1990-91; project leader, TOT African Am. HIV/AIDS Edn. Program ARC, Washington, 1991-92; program dir. lead CSAT AIDS tng. for staff serving African Am. drug abusers ARTI, Alexandria, Va., 1992-93; resident advisor AIDSCAP South Africa, Johannesburg, 1993-94; lead facilitator USAID/AED NIS Exch. and Observation al Tour PRAGMA, Falls Church, Va., 1994—; cons., team leader Assn. Black Psychologists Project, 1994-95; cons. World Trade Assn., 1994, Evaluation Assn., 1994-95, Randolp Assn., 1994-95. Coun. mem. Ballou Adolescent Health Care Ctr., Washington, 1990-91, Adv. Coun. SEC, D.C. chpt. ARC, 1989-90; staff liaison Infant Mortality Rev. Bd. Work Group, Commn. of Pub. Health, Office of Maternal and Child Health, Washington, 1990-91; bd. dirs. Child Enrichment Ctr., Washington, 1986—, Home Testing Inst., 1988—, Leadership Roundtable, D.C. Commn. for Women, 1992-93; active D.C. Bd. of Edn. AIDS Task Force, PSI Task Force Project Right On; instr., trainer HIV/AIDS ARC. U. Pitts. scholar, 1979; Commerce Dept. Econ. Devel. Adminstrn. fellow, 1979; recipient Cert. of Appreciation Contbn. to Women's Program Adv. Com., 1987, Award of Appreciation, 1987; Disting. Alumnus award GSPIA U. Pitts., 1993; Martin Luther King/Ceasar Chavez/Rosa Parks fellow U. Mich., 1988. Mem. Am. Soc. Pub. Adminstrn., Nat. Forum of Black Pub. Adminstrs. (asst. chmn. program devel. com. 1987-88), D.C. Urban Mgmt. Assn., Black Profls. in Internat. Affairs, Black Women's Agenda, Black Women's Health Project (rsch. com.).

PHARR, CYNTHIA IVY, public relations executive; b. Laurel, Miss., Oct. 26, 1948; d. J.C. and Corine (Miller) Ivy; m. Thomas L. Pharr, Nov. 24, 1970 (div. 1990); children: Thomas Colin, Jonathan Tyler. BS, Miss. State U., 1968, MA, 1974. Tchr. various schs., Tenn., Fla., Miss., 1969-72; freelance pub. rels. cons. Winnepeg, Can., 1973-75; pub. affairs officer Can. Consulate Gen., Atlanta, 1975-78; pres., co-founder Pharr Cox Comm., Dallas, 1978-86; pres., founder C. Pharr & Co., Dallas, 1986-89; pres. and CEO Tracy-Locke/Pharr Pub. Rels., Dallas, 1989-93; pres. C. Pharr Mktg. Comm., Dallas, 1993—; bd. dirs. Spaghetti Warehouse, Dallas, GuestCare, Inc., ShowBiz Pizza Time, Inc. Bd. dirs. Leadership Dallas Alumni, 1989, Community Adv. Bd., 1990, Susan G. Komen Found., Dallas, 1990-91; trustee So. Meth. U. Named one of 10 Outstanding Working Women Glamour mag., 1985, Outstanding Miss. Woman Pres.'s Coun. on Status of Women, 1991. Mem. Greater Dallas C. of C., Pub. Rels. Soc. Am. (accredited in pub. rels., nat. chmn., 1989, recipient Tex. Star award 1989. Methodist. Office: C Pharr Mktg Comm 3030 LBJ Fwy Ste 1460 Dallas TX 75234

PHARR, JACQUELINE ANITA, biology educator; b. Charlotte, N.C., July 18, 1931; d. Sidney Marion and Gladys Zenobia (Graves) P. BS, Johnson C. Smith U., 1954; MEd, Columbia U., 1961. Tchr., chmn. sci. dept. Mecklenburg Coll., Charlotte, N.C., 1954-64; tchr., chmn. sci. dept. West Charlotte-Charlotte-Mecklenburg Schs., 1964-87, ret., 1987. Mem. Phi Delta Kappa, Alpha Kappa Alpha. Democrat. Methodist. Home: 2501 Senior Dr Charlotte NC 28216-4349

PHELAN, DONNA ANN, career officer; b. Flushing, N.Y., July 26, 1955; d. Robert Gustave and Grace Patricia (McKeough) P. BA in French, Pa. State U., 1977; MA in Internat. Rels., U. Pa., 1978. Commd. 2nd lt. U.S. Army, 1977, advanced through grades to major, 1977-94; intelligence officer 101st Airborne Divsn. U.S. Army, Ft. Campbell, Ky., 1978-81; staff officer Intelligence and Security Command U.S. Army, Arlington, Va., 1982-85; exec. asst. U.S. Pacific Command U.S. Army, Camp H.M. Smith, Hawaii, 1986-89; negotiations officer Def. Intelligence Agy. U.S. Army, Washington, 1990-93, pol.- mil. affairs officer U.S. Arms Control & Disarmament Agy., 1993—. Troop leader Girl Scouts USA, Honolulu, 1987-89, Annandale, Va., 1990-91. Roman Catholic. Office: US Arms Control & Disarmament Agy 320 21st St NW Washington DC 20451

PHELAN, ELISABETH ANN, accountant; b. Miami, Okla., Jan. 12, 1954; d. Chester Owen and Joan Mary (Osborn) Blair; m. Jeffery Lee Phelan, Oct. 13, 1982; children: Dustin Smith, Deborah Smith, Jacqueline, Chad. BBA in Acctg., Langston U., 1994. Cert. mgmt. acct. Credit clk. in acctg. Franklin Supply Co., Bartlesville, Okla., 1981-83; acctg. clk. Phillips Petroleum Co., Bartlesville, 1984-87, GPM Gas Corp (subs. Phillips Petroleum), Bartlesville, 1987-93; acct. Total Compression Inc./Samson Comm., Tulsa, 1994—. Mem. Univ. Ctr. at Tulsa Acctg. Club. Republican. Episcopalian. Office: Total Compression Inc 2 W 2nd St Tulsa OK 74103

PHELAN, ELLEN, artist; b. Detroit, Nov. 3, 1943; d. Thomas Edward and Katherine Louise (Gojlewicz) P; m. Joel Elias Shapiro, Nov. 22, 1978. BFA, Wayne State U., 1969, MFA, 1971. Instr. Wayne State U., Detroit, 1969-72, Fairleigh Dickinson U., 1974, Mich. State U., East Lansing, 1974-75, Calif. Inst. Arts, 1978-79, Bard Coll., 1980, NYU, 1981, Sch. of Visual Arts, 1981-83, Calif. Inst. Arts, 1983; prof. of practice of studio art Harvard U., Cambridge, Mass., 1995—; Milton Avery vis. lectr. Bard Coll., 1994. One-woman exhbns. include Willis Gallery, Detroit, 1972, 74, Artist's Space, N.Y.C., 1975, Susanne Hilberry Gallery, Birmingham, Mich., 1977, 79, 81, 82, 84, 86, 88, 90, 92, 94, Wadsworth Athenaeum, Hartford, Conn., 1979, Ruth Schaffner Gallery, L.A., 1979, The Clocktower, N.Y.C., 1980, Hansen-Fuller-Goldeen Gallery, San Francisco, 1980, 82, Dart Gallery, Chgo., 1981, Barbara Toll Fine Arts, N.Y.C., 1982, 85, 86, 87-88, 89, 90, 92, 93, Asher/Faure, L.A., 1989, 92, 94, Balt. Mus. Art, 1989, Albright-Knox Art Gallery, Buffalo, 1991, U. Mass. Amherst Fine Arts Ctr., 1992, Saidye Bronfman Ctr., Montreal, Que., 1993, Contemporary Mus., Honolulu, 1993, John Stoller, Inc., Mpls., 1993, Cin. Art Mus., 1994; exhibited in group shows at Detroit Inst. Arts, 1970, 80, Willis Gallery, Detroit, 1971, 79, J.L. Hudson Gallery, Detroit, 1972, Cranbrook Acad. Art, Bloomfield Hills, Mich., 1972, 79, 84, Grand Rapids (Mich.) Art Mus., 1974, Paula Cooper Gallery, N.Y.C., 1975, 76, 77, 78, 79, 90, Fine Arts Bldg., N.Y.C., 1976, Acad. der Kunste, Berlin, 1976, Susanne Hilberry Gallery, Birmingham, 1976-77, 83, 85, 91, Willard Gallery, N.Y.C., 1977, Kansas City (Mo.) Art Inst., 1977, N.A.M.E. Gallery, Chgo., 1977, Hallwalls, Buffalo, 1977, Mus. Modern Art, N.Y.C., 1978, 89, 92, Weatherspoon Art Gallery U. N.C., Greensboro, 1979, 92, Albright-Knox Gallery, Buffalo, 1979, Brown U., Providence, 1980, XIII Olympic Winter Games, Lake Placid, N.Y., 1980, Jeffrey Fuller Fine Art, Phila., 1980, Portland (Oreg.) Ctr. for Visual Arts, 1980, The Drawing Ctr., N.Y.C., 1980, 82, Brooke Alexander Gallery, N.Y.C., 1980, Mus. Contemporary Art, Chgo., 1980, 81, P.S. 1 Mus., N.Y.C., 1981, 92, Art Latitude Gallery, N.Y.C., 1981, Leo Castelli Gallery, N.Y.C., 1981, Sutton Place, Guildford, Eng., 1982, Gallerie d'Arte Moderna di Ca'Pesaro, Venice, Italy, 1982, Inst. Contemporary Art of Virgini Mus., Richmond, Va., 1982, Galerie Biedermann, Munich, 1982, Thomas Segal Gallery, Boston, 1983, Fuller-Goldeen Gallery, San Francisco, 1983, 86, William Paterson Coll., Wayne, N.J., 1983, 89, Artist's Space, N.Y.C., 1983, 84, Harborside Indsl. Ctr., Bklyn., 1983, Orgn. Ind. Artists, N.Y.C., 1984, Bernice Steinbaum Gallery, N.Y.C., 1984, Brentwood Gallery, St. Louis, 1984, U. Calif., Irvine, 1984, U. No. Iowa Gallery Art, Cedar Falls, 1984, Hudson River Mus., N.Y.C., 1984, Barbara Toll Fine Arts, N.Y.C., 1984, 85, 86, 87, Detroit Focus Gallery, 1984, Cable Gallery, N.Y.C., 1984, Wayne State U., Detroit, 1984, Matthews Hamilton Gallery, Phila., 1984, Barbara Krakow Gallery, Boston, 1984, BlumHelman Warehouse, N.Y.C., 1984, Pam Adler Gallery, N.Y.C., 1985, Daniel Weinberg Gallery, L.A., 1985, 89, Knight Gallery, Charlotte, N.C., 1985, Bank of Boston, 1986, Whitney Mus. Am. Art, Stamford, Conn., 1987, 89, Scott Hansen Gallery, N.Y.C., 1987, Saxon-Lee Gallery, L.A., 1987, Parrish Art Mus., East Hampton, N.Y., 1987, Curt Marcus Gallery, N.Y., 1988, Loughelton Gallery, N.Y.C., 1988, 90, Whitney Mus. Am. Art, N.Y.C., 1988, 91, Hillwood Art Gallery C.W. Post Campus, Brookville, N.Y., 1989, USIA traveling exbhn., 1989, Edward Thorp Gallery, N.Y.C., 1989, Pine Street Lobby Gallery, San Francisco, 1989, Fuller Gross Gallery, San Francisco, 1989, Solo Press/Soho Gallery, N.Y.C., 1989, Maxwell Davidson Gallery, N.Y.C., 1989, Blum Helman Gallery, N.Y.C., 1989, R.I.S.D., Providence, 1989, Graham Modern, N.Y.C., 1990, Hood Mus. Art Dartmouth Coll., Hanover, N.H., 1990, 92, New Britain Mus. Am. Art, Hartfor, Conn., 1991, Asher-Faure, L.A., 1991, Annina Nosei Gallery, N.Y.C., 1991, Lintas Worldwide, N.Y.C., 1991, Nina Fredenheim Gallery, Buffalo, 1991, Molica Guidarte Gallery, N.Y.C., 1991, Squibb Gallery, Princeton, N.J., 1991, Cleve. State U. Gallery, 1992, Ind. Curators Inc., N.Y.C., 1992, Wexner Ctr. for the Arts, Columbus, Ohio, 1992, Transamerica Corp., San Francisco, 1992, The Gallery Three Zero, N.Y.C., 1992, Haggerty Mus. Art, Milw., Barbara Methes Gallery, N.Y.C., Asher Fauve Gallery, L.A., Hillwood Art Mus., Brookville, N.Y., Pamela Auchincloss Gallery, N.Y.C., Leo Castelli Gallery, N.Y.C.; represented in permanent collections Mus. Modern Art, N.Y.C., Whitney Mus. Am. Art, N.Y.C., Bklyn. Mus., Walker Art Ctr., Mpls., Balt. Mus., Toledo Mus. Art, Hood Mus. Dartmouth Coll., High Mus. Art, Albright-Knox Art Gallery, Moderna Museet, Stockholm, Mus. Contemporary Art, Mexico City, Detroit Inst. Arts, MIT, Whitehead Inst., Philip Morris, Inc., Volvo Corp., Chase Manhattan Bank, Chem. Bank, BankAm., Bank of Am., Prudential Ins. Co., U.S. Trust & Co., Inter Metro Industries, Lannan Found., numerous pvt. collections. Nat. Endowment for Arts grantee, 1978-79.

PHELPS, CARRIE LYNN, communications director; b. Ft. Wayne, Ind., June 18, 1964; d. Richard Claire and Judith Elaine (Potts) P. BA in Journalism/Criminal Justice, Ind. U., 1986. Dir. communications Ind. Mfrs. Assn., Indpls., 1987-89, Ind. Dept. Commerce, Indpls., 1989-90; dir. Gray, Miller & Mitsch, P.R., Indpls., 1990-91; dir. comm. and devel. Wapehani coun. Girl Scouts U.S.A., Daleville, Ind., 1991-94; account exec. Caldwell VanRiper Advt./Pub. Rels., Indpls., 1994—. Contbr. articles to profl. jours., mags., and newspapers. Cons. Offender Aid and Restoration, Indpls., 1988—. Mem. Pub. Rels. Soc. Am. Home: 6903 Challenge Ln Indianapolis IN 46250-3914 Office: Caldwell VanRiper Advt/Pub Rels 1314 N Meridian St Indianapolis IN 46202

PHELPS, FLORA L(OUISE) LEWIS, editor, anthropologist, photographer; b. San Francisco, July 28, 1917; d. George Chase and Louise (Manning) Lewis; m. C(lement) Russell Phelps, Jan. 15, 1944; children: Andrew Russell, Carol Lewis, Gail Bransford. Student, U. Mich.; AB cum laude, Bryn Mawr Coll., 1938; AM, Columbia U., 1954. Acting dean Cape Cod Inst. Music, East Brewster, Mass., summer 1940; assoc. social sci. analyst U.S. Govt., 1942-44; co-adj. staff instr. anthropology Univ. Coll., Rutgers U., 1954-55; mem. editorial bd. Américas mag. OAS, Washington, 1960-82; mng. editor, 1974-82, contbg. editor, 1982-89; N.J. vice chmn. Ams. Dem. Action, 1950; mem. Dem. County Com. N.J., 1948-49. Author articles in fields of anthropology, art, architecture, edn., travel; contbr. Latin Am. newspapers. Mem. AAAS, Am. Anthrop. Assn., Archaeological Inst. Am., Latin Am. Studies Assn., Soc. for Am. Archaeology, Soc. Woman Geographers. Home: Collington # 2212 10450 Lottsford Rd Mitchellville MD 20721-2748

PHELPS, GAIL LANITA, medical/surgical and oncology nurse; b. Guymon, Okla., June 13, 1952; d. Lawrence Mearl and Ulah Mae (Fox) Blackwelder; m. James D. Phelps, Jan. 9, 1976; children: Chandra, Kelly, Codie, Calab, Sean. ADN, Garden City C.C., Kans., 1991. RN, Oreg.; nat. cert. oncology nurse. Nurses aid Tex. County Hosp., Guymon, 1968-70, Edmond (Okla.) Meml. Hosp., 1972-75, St. Catherine Hosp., Garden City, 1980-82, 90-91; staff nurse Rogue Valley Med. Ctr., Medford, Oreg., 1991—; mem. hazardous waste com. Rogue Valley Med. Ctr., 1991-92, mem. quality assurance rev. bd., 1991-92, staff mix com., 1993—, action com., 1993—, controlled quality ins. com. emergency rm. units, 1993—; mem. Inter-Dept. Quality Assurance Task Force, 1994—. Team mom Medford Little League Assn., 1992; guard leader AWANA, Medford, 1991, 92. Mem. ANA, Oreg. Nurses Assn. Democrat. Baptist. Home: 698 S Modoc Ave Medford OR 97504-8037 Office: Rogue Valley Med Ctr 2825 E Barnett Rd Medford OR 97504-8332

PHENIX, GLORIA GAYLE, educational association administrator; b. Dallas, Mar. 4, 1956; d. Joe Raymond and Sondra Lanell (Baskin) Christopher; m. Douglas William Phenix, Aug. 8, 1987; children: David William, Duncan Kenneth. BA, U. North Tex., 1979, postgrad., 1979-81; PhD, ABD, U. Minn., 1981-89. Dean Jordan Coll., Benton Harbor, Mich., 1990; pres. Phenix & Assocs. Tng. Cons., St. Joseph, Mich., 1991—, Topeka, Kans., 1993—. Mem. allocation com. United Way, 1990-92, Literacy Coun., 1991-93; mem. Topeka Race Rels. Task Force, 1994. Fulbright-Hayes fellow Africa, 1990; Hewlett Mellon Found. grantee, 1987, Benton Found. grantee, 1988. Mem. Am. Polit. Sci. Assn., Minn. Polit. Sci. Assn. (bd. dirs. 1989-90), Midwest Polit. Sci. Assn., Am. Assn. Trainers and Developers, Am. Soc. for Quality Control. Presbyterian. Office: Phenix & Assocs 505 Pleasant St # 505 Saint Joseph MI 49085-1269 also: Phenix Assocs 1178 SW College Ave Topeka KS 66604-1453

PHILIPP, ANITA MARIE, computer sciences educator; b. Evergreen Park, Ill., Sept. 7, 1948; d. Benedict Anthony and Anne Therese (Bolf) Butkus; m. Leslie Howard Philipp, Sept. 6, 1975; children: Leslie Aaron, Renée Marie. BA in Elem. Edn., St. Norbert Coll., 1969; MEd in Ednl. Media, U. Okla., 1978; student, Okla. City C.C., 1980-93, U. Ctrl. Okla., 1994—. Cert. tchr., Okla., audio-visual specialist, Okla. Tchr. fifth grade Green Bay (Wis.) Bd. Edn., 1970; social ins. rep. Social Security Adminstrn., Chgo., 1970-73; ops. supr. Social Security Adminstrn., Evanston, Ill., 1973; employee devel. specialist Social Security Adminstrn., Chgo., 1973-76; claims rep. Social Security Adminstrn., Oklahoma City, 1976-77, ops. analyst, 1977-78; adj. instr. computer sci. Okla. City C.C., 1985—; dir. computer edn. St. James Sch., Oklahoma City, 1987-93; ednl. computer cons., 1989—; faculty advisor St. James Light Newspaper; mem. restaurant evaluation team Dunn-Farley Enterprises, San Marcos, Calif., 1978—. EEO counselor Social Security Adminstrn., Chgo., 1972-73, coord. info. and referral svcs., 1982-83; leader Campfire Girls, Oklahoma City, 1986-89; mem. St. James Sch. Bd. Edn., Oklahoma City, 1987 (St. James sch. devel. com. 1990—, chairperson 1994); eucharistic min. St. James Ch. Named among Top 25 Tchrs., Apple Computer/Homeland Stores, 1990. Mem. Okla. Computer Using Educators (pres. 1990—), Moore West Jr. High Best Booster Club. Roman Catholic. Home: 2209 Lane Way Cir Oklahoma City OK 73159 Office: Okla City CC 7777 S May Ave Oklahoma City OK 73159

PHILIPSON, CYNTHIA ANN, geologist; b. Dallas, Oct. 28, 1957; d. Herman Louis, Jr. and Sonia Edith (Topletz) P. Student, Smith Coll., Northampton, Mass., 1976-78; BA, Duke U., 1978-80; BS, U. Tex., Austin, 1980-82. Mktg. mgr. Perutz Enterprises, Dallas, 1984-86; lab. tech. Core Labs., Dallas, 1986-87, rsch. geologist, 1987-89; rsch. and devel. project coord. Core Labs., Houston, 1989-90, supr. tech. pubs. rels., 1990-93, sr. mktg. coord., 1993-94; sr. mktg. coord. Western Atlas Logging Svcs., Houston, 1994—. Author: Automated Pattern Analysis in Petroleum Exploration, 1992; editor (newsletters) In Formation, 1989-91, Encore!, 1989—. Campaigner United Way of Greater Dallas, 1984-85, United Way of Tex. Gulf Coast, 1992, 94; mem. Anti-Defamation League leadership devel. com., Houston, 1992—. Mem. Am. Assn. Petroleum Geologists, Soc. Petroleum Engrs., Soc. Core Analysts, Smith Coll. Club Houston. Office: 10201 Westheimer Bldg 1A Houston TX 77042

PHILLIPS, BARBARA LEE, special education educator; b. Centerville, Iowa, May 9, 1930; d. William Earl and Daisy Ruth (Hinote) Espy; m. Homer Hiatt Phillips, Jan. 18, 1948; children: Kelly, Kerry, Kay Phillips Crabb, Kyle. AA, Centerville (Iowa) C.C., 1970; BSE, N.E. Mo. State U., 1971. Lic. tchr. in elem. and spl. edn. Elem. tchr. Seymour (Iowa) Cmty. Schs., 1971-86, spl. edn. tchr., 1986—. Bd. dirs. Appanoose County Hist. Soc., Centerville, 1986-94, Appanoose County Activity Ctr., Centerville, 1979-85. Named Dist. Conservation Tchr. of the Yr., Wayne County Dist. Conservation Bd. Mem. AAUW (pres. 1991-93), Iowa State Edn. Assn. (sec.-treas. 1979—), Delta Kappa Gamma (pres. 1992-94). Republican. Baptist.

PHILLIPS, B(ARBARA) LORRAINE, association executive; b. Oakdale, Calif., Nov. 4, 1943; d. John Leo and Mary Jane (Istilarte) Bernard; m. Charles Louis Phillip, July 26, 1964 (div. June 1980); 1 child, Addison Page. BA, UCLA, 1972; MA, Calif. State U., Dominguez Hills, 1973. Edn. adminstr. credential, Montessori cert. Dir. Jack 'n' Jill Presch., Baumholder, Germany, 1969-72; tchr. Long Beach (Calif.) State U., 1975-79, Dominguez Hills State U., 1975-79, Monterey (Calif.) Peninsula Coll., 1975-79; coord. child devel. svcs. Ft. Ord and Presidio, Monterey, 1977-80; program dir. Family Resource Ctr., Monterey, 1980-81; adminstr. KTM Svcs., Aptos, Calif., 1981-84; exec. dir. YWCA Watsonville, Calif., 1984—; rschr. I/D/E/A, L.A., 1974-75; cons. Family Resource Ctr., 1982, Watsonville C. of C., 1983. Active Leadership Santa Cruz County, Santa Cruz, Calif., 1985-86; bd. dirs. Family Svc. Assn., Watsonville, 1988-90. Mem. Rotary Internat. (com. chair Watsonville chpt. 1992—, Paul Harris fellowship 1993). Office: YWCA of Watsonville 340 E Beach St Watsonville CA 95076-4838

PHILLIPS, BERNICE CECILE GOLDEN, vocational education educator; b. Galveston, Tex., June 30, 1920; d. Walter Lee and Minnie (Rothsprack) Golden; m. O. Phillips, Mar. 1950 (dec.); children: Dorian Lee, Loren Francis. BBA cum laude, U. Tex., 1945; MEd, U. Houston, 1968. cert. tchr., tchr. coord., vocat. tchr., Tex. Dir. Delphian Soc., Houston, 1955-60; bus. tchr. various private schs., Houston area, 1960-65; vocat. tchr. coord. office edn. program Pasadena (Tex.) Ind. Sch. Dist., 1965-68, Houston Ind. Sch. Dist., John H. Reagan High Sch., 1968-85. Bd. dirs. Regency House Condominium Assn., 1991-93. Recipient numerous awards and recognitions for vocat. bus. work at local and state levels. Mem. AAUW (life mem., bd. dirs. 1987—, v.p. ednl. found. 1987-90, pres. Houston 1992-94), NEA, Nat. Bus. Edn. Assn., Am. Vocat. Assn. (life), Tex. State Tchrs. Assn. (life), Tex. Classroom Tchrs. Assn. (life), Tex. Bus. Edn. Assn., Am. Vocat. Assn. (life), Greater Houston Bus. Edn. Assn. (reporter), Houston Assn. Ret. Tchrs., Tex. Assn. Ret. Tchrs., Delta Pi Epsilon (mem. emeritus), Beta Gamma Sigma. Home: 2701 Westheimer Rd Apt 8H Houston TX 77098-1235

PHILLIPS, BETTY LOU (ELIZABETH LOUISE PHILLIPS), author, interior designer; b. Cleve.; d. Michael N. and Elizabeth D. (Materna) Suvak; m. John S. Phillips, Jan. 27, 1963 (div. Jan. 1981); children: Bruce, Bryce, Brian; m. John D.C. Roach, Aug. 28, 1982. BS, Syracuse U., 1960; postgrad. in English, Case Western Res. U., 1963-64. Cert. elem. and spl. edn. tchr., N.Y. Tchr. pub. schs. Shaker Heights, Ohio, 1960-66; sportswriter Cleve. Press, 1976-77; spl. features editor Pro Quarterback Mag., N.Y.C., 1976-79; freelance writer specializing in books for young people, 1976—; interior designer residential and comml.; bd. dirs. Cast Specialties Inc., Cleve. Author: Chris Evert: First Lady of Tennis, 1977; Picture Story of Dorothy Hamill (ALA Booklist selection), 1978; American Quarter Horse, 1979; Earl Campbell: Houston Oiler Superstar, 1979; Picture Story of Nancy Lopez, (ALA Notable book), 1980; Go! Fight! Win! The NCA Guide for Cheerleaders (ALA Booklist), 1981; Something for Nothing, 1981; Brush Up on Your Hair (ALA Booklist), 1981; Texas ... The Lone Star State, 1989, Who Needs Friends? We All Do!, 1989; also contbr. articles to young adult and sports mags. Bd. dirs. The Children's Mus., Denver; mem. Friends of Fine Arts Found., Denver Art Mus., Cen. City Opera Guild, Alameda County Cancer League. Mem. Soc. Children's Book Writers, Am. Soc. Interior Designers (profl., cert.), Delta Delta Delta. Republican. Roman Catholic. Home: 125 Guilford Rd Piedmont CA 94611-3804

PHILLIPS, BILLY SAXTON, artist, designer, painter; b. Louisville, Nebr., June 20, 1915; d. Charles William and Georgia Hazel (de le Zene) Tremblay; m. John Henry Phillips, Sept. 3, 1937; 1 dau., Terry. Grad., Art Ctr. Coll. of Design, 1950. Free-lance artist L.A., 1951—; package designer Wilson Paper-Disneyland, Anaheim, Calif., 1952-56; inventor Vernon (Calif.) Container Corp., 1952-56; instr. Clatsop Community Coll., Astoria, Oreg., 1990-92; painter Reva-Reva Gallery, Papeete, French Polynesia, 1972-92, Royal Gallery, Lahaina, Maui, Hawaii, 1993-94; artist P.M. Prodns., L.A., 1951-90; instr., motivator Maoridom, New Zealand, 1980—; instr. Art Ctr. Coll. Design, 1952-53. Designer, patentee Ukili, 1967, packages, 1960 (Zipper openings on cardboard containers); designer Disneyland's Tinkerbell; group shows include Royal Art Gallery, Met. Gallery, Lahanina, Maui, Hawaii, 1994, Kona, Hawaii, 1995. Developer Cultural Exchange Program First Ams.-Maori, S.W. Am. Indians and New Zealand Maoris, 1986. Mem. Art Ctr. Alumni (charter, life), Trail's End Art Assn., Lady Elk, Inventors and Scientists Am.

PHILLIPS, CARLA, county official; b. Balt., Nov. 14, 1963; d. Paulo Pereira de Mendonca and June Ann (Lewis) Cortese; m. Wayne Shriver Phillips, Mar. 24, 1990. BS, East Carolina U., 1985; MPA, U. Balt., 1993. Program dir. YMCA of Met. Washington, Alexandria, Va., 1985-86; ctr. supr. Balt. County Govt., Towson, Md., 1986-90, community supr., 1990-92, sr. community supr., 1992-94, asst. therapeutic recreation coord., 1994—. Water safety instr. YMCA of Greater Balt., 1986—, Rosedale Recreation Coun., Balt., 1991, 93; asst. basketball coach Md. Spl. Olympics, Towson, 1994—; mem. 6th Dist. Substance Abuse Adv. Coun., Towson, 1990-92, Villa Cresta PTA, Parkville, MD., 1988-92. Mem. ASPA, Nat. Recreation and Park Assn. (cert. leisure profl.), Md. Recreation and Parks Assn., Soc. for Pub. Affairs and Adminstrn., Kappa Delta Pi, Phi Sigma Pi, Pi Alpha Alpha. Home: PO Box 5052 Timonium MD 21094 Office: Balt County Govt Parks and Recreation 301 Washington Ave Towson MD 21204

PHILLIPS, CYNTHIA ANN, law educator; b. Mpls., Nov. 1, 1947; d. Gordon and Alice Harriet Phillips. BS in Pub. Adminstrn., U. N.D., 1969, MA in Polit. Sci., 1973, JD, 1976. Bar: N.D. 1976, U.S. Dist. Ct. (fed. dist.) 1978. Pub. health exec. N.D. State Dept. Health, Bismarck, 1969-73; atty.

N.D. Art Gallery Assn., Grand Forks, 1977-78; supervising atty. Legal Assistance of N.D., Fargo, 1978-79; asst. prof., then assoc. prof. law Moorhead (Minn.) State U., 1979—, dir. legal asst. program, 1981-85, affirmative action officer, 1985-87. Bd. dirs. Plains Art Mus., Fargo, 1985—, pres. 1991-94; bd. dirs. Rape and Abuse Crisis Ctr., Fargo, 1979-85, Eclectic Co., St. Paul, 1986-89; dist. and precinct officer, del. Dem. Non Partisan League, Fargo, 1986—; founding mem. Law Women's Caucus, U. N.D. Sch. of Lawm 1973, N.D. NOW, 1975, Nat. Rural Women Comm., 1979-81, Nat. Nom. Comm., 1981-84; chair N.D. delegation Nat. Women's Conf., 1977; mem. continuing com. Nat. Women's Conf., 1977-79. Recipient Healing the Hurt award Rape and Abuse Crisis Ctr., 1985, Women Helping Women award Soroptimists, 1981; grantee N.D. State Arts Coun., 1992. Mem. N.D. Bar Assn., Acad. Legal Studies in Bus., Moorhead State Faculty Assn. (grievance officer 1992—), Minn. Interfaculty Orgn. (Woman of Year in the Arts honoree 1994). Office: Moorhead State U Moorhead MN 58563

PHILLIPS, DENISE, critical care nurse; b. Orange, N.J., July 11, 1960; d. James Henry Phillips and Gracie Estelle (Reed) Brown. Diploma in nursing, Riverside Hosp. Sch. Nursing, Newport News, Va., 1985; cert. in paralegal studies, Hampton U., 1990. RN, Va., Fla., Md., N.Y.; cert. BLS instr., ACLS; instr. cert. nurse asst. and LPN programs. Nurse asst. Riverside Hosp., Newport News, 1981-86; Riverside Hosp. Riverside Regional Med. Ctr., Newport News, 1986-91; staff nurse Traveling Nurse Corp., Malden, Mass., 1991-93; dir. staff devel. Va. Health Svcs., Inc., Newport News, 1993—; per diem nurse adminstr. Sentasa Hampton (Va.) Gen. Hosp., 1994—; LPN, cert. nurse asst. instr. Career Devel. Ctr., Newport News, 1989-91; lectr. on decreasing profl. liability for healthcare workers, 1990—. Vol. Williamsburg (Va.) area Girl Scouts U.S., 1990-92. Mem. ACCN, Nat. League of Nursing. Home: 529 F Waters Edge Newport News VA 23606 also: 7402 Vernon Pl Newport News VA 23605 Office: 540 Aberthaw Ave Newport News VA 23601

PHILLIPS, DOROTHY ALEASE, lay church worker, educator, freelance writer; b. Durham, N.C., May 11, 1924; d. Clarence Robert and Addie Lee (Outen) Hicks; m. Chester Raymond Phillips, Oct. 10, 1942; children: Cynthia Kaye, Dean Hayward, Kent Vincent. BS in Edn. and English, Bob Jones U., 1954; M in Edn., East Carolina U., 1970. Cert. secondary tchr., N.C. Former writer, illustrator Sunday sch. lit. Ayden (N.C.) Press.; former nat. youth chmn. women's aux. Free Will Bapts.; dir. pub. rels. and Christian edn. Heritage Bapt. Ch., Johnson City, Tenn., 1980-91; tchr. Four Oaks (N.C.) H.S., 1955-56, Smithfield (N.C.) H.S., 1956-61, Farmville (N.C.) H.S., 1963-65, Rose H.S., Greenville, 1965-76, Univ. H.S., Johnson City, Tenn., 1976-78; participant Blue Ridge Mountain Christian Writers Conf., Black Mountain, N.C.; former thcr. journalism Rose H.S., Greenville, N.C.; mem. choirs, Sunday sch. tchr. various Bapt. chs.; speaker at women's retreats and seminars. Home: 1601 Paty Dr Johnson City TN 37604-7636

PHILLIPS, DOROTHY KAY, lawyer; b. Camden, N.J., Nov. 2, 1945; d. Benjamin L. and Sadye (Levinsky) Phillips; children: Bethann P., David M. Schaffzin. BS in English Lit. magna cum laude, U. Pa., 1964; MA in Family Life and Marriage Counseling and Edn., NYU, 1975; JD, Villanova U., 1978. Bar: Pa. 1978, N.J. 1978, U.S. Dist. Ct. (ea. dist.) Pa. 1978, U.S. Dist. Ct. N.J., 1978, U.S. Ct. Appeals (3d cir.), 1984, U.S. Supreme Ct. 1984. Tchr., Haddon Twp. High Sch. (N.J.), and Haddon Heights High Sch. (N.J.), 1964-70; lectr., counselor Marriage Council of Phila.; lectr. U. Pa. and Hahnemann Med. Schs., Phila., 1970-75; atty. Adler, Barish, Daniels, Levin & Creskoff, Phila., 1978-79, Astor, Weiss & Newman, Phila., 1979-80; ptnr. Romisher & Phillips, P.C., Phila., 1981-86; prin. Law Office of Dorothy K. Phillips, 1986—; faculty Sch. of Law Temple U. Guest speaker on domestic rels. issues on radio and TV shows; featured in newspaper and mag. articles; contbr. articles to profl. jours. Rosenbach Found., Philadanco, Fedn. Allied Jewish Appeal (lawyers. div.), World Affairs Coun.; bd. mem. Anti-Defamation League of B'nai B'rith, Nat. Mus. Jewish History, mem. friends' circle, Athenaeum, Phila., shareholder. Mem. ABA, Assn. Trial Lawyers Am. (membership com. 1990-91), Pa. Trial Lawyers Assn. (chair membership com. family sect. 1989-90), Pa. Bar Assn. (continuing legal edn. com. 1990-92, faculty, lectr. Pa. Bar Inst. Continuing Legal Edn. 1990, panel mem. summer meeting 1991), N.J. Bar Assn., Phila. Bar Assn. (chmn. early settlement program 1983-84, mem. custody rules drafting com. for Supreme Ct. Pa., spl. events speaker on pensions, counsel fees, written fee agreements 1989-91, co-chair mandatory continuing legal edn. 1994), Phila. Trial Lawyers Assn., Montgomery County Bar Assn., Lawyers Club. Office: 1818 Market St Fl 35 Philadelphia PA 19103-3638

PHILLIPS, DOROTHY REID, retired library technician; b. Hingham, Mass., Apr. 21, 1924; d. James Henry and Emma Louise (Davis) Reid; m. Earl Wendell Phillips, Apr. 22, 1944; children: Earl W., Jr., Betty Herrera, Carol Coe. Cert., Durham Vocat. Sch., 1952; B.S. in Comml. Edn., N.C. Central U., 1959; postgrad. U. Colo., 1969; M.Human Relations, Webster Coll., 1979; postgrad. Grad. Sch. Library Sci., U. Denver, 1983. Vocat. nurse Meml. Hosp., U. N.C., Chapel Hill, 1955-59; vol. work, Cairo, Egypt, 1965-67; library technician Base Library, Lowry AFB, Colo., 1960-65, Fitzsimons Med. Library, Aurora, Colo., 1976-94; ret. 1994; mem. Denver Mus. Natural History, Denver Art Mus., Mariners. Mem. AAUW (chpt. community rep. 1982-83, state chmn. edn. found. 1982-84, pres. Denver br. 1984-86), Altrusa Internat. (corr. sec. Denver 1982-83, bd. dirs. 1984-85, pres. Denver chpt. 1988), Friends of Library, Colo. Library Assn., Council Library Technicians, Federally Employed Women, Delta Sigma Theta (corr. sec. Denver 1964-66). Democrat. Presbyterian. Home: 3085 Fairfax St Denver CO 80207-2714

PHILLIPS, ELAINE LEE, psychology educator; b. Atlanta, Nov. 13, 1950; d. Irving Earl and Norma Nadine Young; m. Douglas Dean Chambers. BA summa cum laude, Western Mich. U., 1973, MA, 1975, PhD, 1986. Lic. psychologist, Mich. Sch. psychologist Eastern Svc. Dist., Galesburg, Mich., 1975-77; coord. Family and Children's Svcs. Barry County Mental Health, Hastings, Mich., 1977-82; psychologist Pheasant Ridge Ctr., Kalamazoo, 1982-83, Kalamazoo Regional Psychiat. Hosp., 1983-87; assoc. prof. Western Mich. U., Kalamazoo, 1987—; cons. in field. Contbr. articles to profl. jours. Bd. dirs. Hospice Greater Kalamazoo, 1987—, mem. clin. records evaluation and rev. com., 1987—, mem. program evaluation and adv. com., 1987—, chmn. bereavement evaluation com., 1989—; sec. Commn. on Status Women, 1989-90, pres., 1990-92. Kalamazoo Consortium Higher Edn. grantee, 1989. Mem. APA, Women in Psychology and Clin. Psychology. Office: Western Mich U Kalamazoo MI 49008

PHILLIPS, ELIZABETH JASON, lawyer; b. Boston, Sept. 3, 1936; d. Richard Eliot and Elizabeth Harding (McClure) Jason; m. William Morris Phillips Jr., Mar. 2, 1991; children: Meredith Rowe, William Morris Phillips III, Eleanor Anne, Robert J., Lee B. Stewart. BA in History, U. Mass., 1958; MEd, U. Hartford, 1969; JD, Western New Eng. Coll., Springfield, Mass., 1977. Bar: Mass. 1977, U.S. Dist. Ct. Mass. 1978, Va. 1981, U.S. Dist. Ct. (ea. dist.) Va. 1981, U.S. Dist. Ct. D.C. 1981, U.S. Dist. Ct. (we. dist.) Va. 1982, U.S. Ct. Appeals (4th cir.) 1982, U.S. Supreme Ct. 1984. Ptnr. firm Thompson & Stewart, Ludlow, Mass., 1977-80; adminstr. Office Atty. Gen., Commonwealth of Va., Richmond, 1980-82, asst. atty. gen., 1982-84; dep. Commr. Indsl. Commn. Va., 1984-91; dep. commr., mgr. dispute resolution divsn. Va. Workers' Compensation Commn., Richmond, 1991—. Trustee Ludlow Hosp., 1979-80. Mem. ABA, Richmond Bar Assn., Va. Bar Assn., Ludlow C. of C. (pres. 1980). Episcopalian. Home: 7906 Brays Point Rd Hayes VA 23072 Office: Va Workers' Compensation Commn 1000 Dmv Dr Richmond VA 23220-2036

PHILLIPS, FRANCES A., public relations executive. Graduate, U. Miss.; postgrad., N.Y. Sch. Interior Design. Editor, writer House & Garden Mag.; acct. supr. Gray & Rogers, 1980-83, head consumer group, 1983-84, v.p., 1984-86, assoc. dir. pub. rels., 1986-88, v.p., dir. pub. rels., 1988-89, sr. v.p., 1989-90; sr. v.p., dir. pub. rels. Foote Cone & Belding, Phila., 1991—. Mem. Pub. Rels. Soc. Am., Internat. Furnishings and Design Assn. Office: Foote Cone & Belding 200 S Broad St Philadelphia PA 19102-3803*

PHILLIPS, GAIL, state legislator; b. Juneau, Alaska; m. Walt Phillips; children: Robin, Kim. BA in Bus. Edn., U. Alaska. Mem. Homer (Alaska) City Coun., 1981-84, Kenai Peninsula Borough Assembly, 1986-87; chmn. legis. com. Alaska Mcpl. League, 1; mem. Joint Agy. Task Force on Spruce Beetle-Kenai Peninsula; mem. Alaska Ho. of Reps., 1990, 92, house majority leader, 1993-94; high sch. bus. tchr., Fairbanks, Nome, Alaska; airline agt., exec. sec. and sta. mgr. Alaska Airlines, Western Airlines, Wien Air; owner, mgr. Quiet Sporting Goods; ptnr. Lindphil Mining Co.; pub. rels. cons.; legis. aide to Senate pres. Active Homer United Meth. Ch., Rep. Ctrl. Com. Alaska, Kenai Peninsula Coll. Coun.; past bd. dirs. Homer Soc. Natural History; past mem. com. bd. and race coord. Iditarod Trail Dog Sled Race. Mem. Western States Legis. Coun. (exec. com.), Am. Legis. Exch. Coun. (state chmn.), Resource Devel. Coun. Alaska, U. Alaska Coll. Fellows, Homer Emblem Club, Homer, Seldovia, Anchor Point, Soldotna and Kenai C. of C., Peninsula Coun. Chambers, Kachemak Bay Visitors Assn. Home: PO Box 3304 Homer AK 99603 Office: 126 W Pioneer Ave Homer AK 99603 also: Alaska House of Reps State Capitol Juneau AK 99811*

PHILLIPS, GENEVA FICKER, editor; b. Staunton, Ill., Aug. 1, 1920; d. Arthur Edwin and Lillian Agnes (Woods) Ficker; m. James Emerson Phillips, Jr., June 6, 1955 (dec. 1979). B.S. in Journalism, U. Ill., 1942; M.A. in English Lit., UCLA, 1953. Copy desk Chgo. Jour. Commerce, 1942-43; editorial asst. patents Radio Research Lab., Harvard U., Cambridge, Mass., 1943-45; asst. editor adminstrv. publs. U. Ill., Urbana, 1946-47; editorial asst. Quar. of Film, Radio and TV, UCLA, 1952-53; mng. editor The Works of John Dryden, Dept. English, UCLA, 1964—. Bd. dirs. Univ. Religious Conf., Los Angeles, 1979—. UCLA teaching fellow, 1950-53, grad. fellow 1954-55. Mem. Assn. Acad. Women UCLA, Dean's Coun., Coll. Letters and Scis. UCLA, Friends of Huntington Library, Friends of UCLA Library, Friends of Ctr. for Medieval and Renaissance Studies, Samuel Johnson Soc. of So. Calif., Assocs. of U. Calif. Press., Conf. Christianity and Lit., Soc. Mayflower Descs. Lutheran. Home: 213 1st Anita Dr Los Angeles CA 90049-3815 Office: UCLA Dept English 2225 Rolfe Hall Los Angeles CA 90024

PHILLIPS, GLYNDA ANN, editor; b. Riverside, Calif.; d. Henry Grady and Patricia (Loflin) P. BA in English, Millsaps Coll., 1977. News editor The Magee (Miss.) Courier, 1981-84; editor Miss. Farm Bur. News and MFB Producer Edition, Jackson, 1984—. Contbr. articles to profl. jours. Recipient first place personal column Nat. Fedn. Press Women, 1984, first place personal column Miss. Press Women's Assn., 1984, first place feature articles Miss. Press Women's Assn., 1984.

PHILLIPS, GRETCHEN, clinical social worker; b. Erie, Pa., July 14, 1941; life ptnr. Beverly Campbell, June 10, 1989. BA, Mercyhurst Coll., 1966; MSW, Yeshiva U., 1972; postgrad., Advanced Ctr. Psychotherapy, 1972-73, Washington Sq. Inst., 1973-77. Bd. cert. diplomate clin. social work; lic. social worker, N.Y. Psychiat. social worker, forensic social worker Creedmoor Psychiat. Ctr., Queens Village, N.Y., 1972-80; Med. social worker Bellevue Hosp. Ctr., N.Y.C., 1980-83; intake probation officer N.Y.C. Probation, Family Court, Bklyn., 1983—. Mem. NASW, Am. Group Psychotherapy Assn. Home: 125 Radford St # 3C Yonkers NY 10705-3049 Office: Probation Intake Kings Family Ct 283 Adams St Brooklyn NY 11201-2898

PHILLIPS, JANE BANNING, aviatrix, pilot examiner and flight instructor. BA, U. Calif., Irvine, 1972; AAS in Flight Tech., Lane C.C., Eugene, Oreg., 1988. Cert. multi-engine airline transport pilot, DC-3 Type Rating; FAA designated pilot examiner. Flight instr. Lane C.C., 1988-90; pilot McKenzie Flying Svc., Eugene, 1990-93; asst. chief flight instr. Lane C.C., 1990—; FAA pilot examiner Eugene, 1992—; guest lectr. C. of C., AAUW, sch. and ch. groups, Eugene, 1990—. ESL instr. Lane County Literacy Coun., Eugene, 1993. Amelia Earhart scholar, 1993; Santa Rosa Ninety-Nines scholar, 1987. Mem. Internat. Ninety-Nines, Willamette Valley Ninety-Nines (treas. 1990-91, chmn. 1993-94), Nat. Assn. Flight Instrs., Assn. Ind. Airmen, Airplane Operators and Pilots Assn., Exptl. Aircraft Assn. Office: PO Box 40635 Eugene OR 97404-0104

PHILLIPS, JANET COLLEEN, educational association executive, editor; b. Pittsfield, Ill., Apr. 29, 1933; d. Roy Lynn and Catherine Amelia (Wills) Barker; m. David Lee Phillips, Feb 7, 1954; children—Clay Cullen, Sean Vincent. B.S., U. Ill, 1954. Reporter Quincy (Ill.) Herald Whig, 1951, 52, soc. editor, 1953; editorial asst. Pub. Info. Office U. Ill.-Urbana, 1953-54, asst. editor libr., 1954-61; asst. editor Assn. for Libr. and Info. Sci. Edn., State College, Pa., 1960-61, mng. editor, 1961-89, exec. sec., 1970-89; adminstrv. dir. Interlibr. Delivery Svc. of Pa., 1990—. Mem. AAUW, Assn. for Libr. and Info. Sci. Edn., Embroiderer's Guild Am., Pa. State Blue Course Club, Pa. State U. Women's Club, Theta Sigma Phi, Delta Zeta. Presbyterian. Address: 471 Park Ln State College PA 16803-3208

PHILLIPS, JANET GRACE, elementary school counselor; b. Berwyn, Pa., July 11, 1963; d. Roy Edward and Patricia Kathleen (Berg) Gaunt; m. Todd Allen Phillips, Oct. 6, 1990; 1 stepchild, William Runk. BA in Psychology, U. San Diego, 1987, MA in Marriage, Family, Child Counseling, 1990. Cert. sch. psychologist, 1994, pupil pers. svcs. credential, 1990. Intern in family counseling Family Svc. Assn., San Diego, 1988-90; intern sch. counseling San Diego City Schs., 1989-90; sch. counselor LaMesa/Spring Valley Sch. Dist., LaMesa, Calif., 1990—, mentor tchr., 1994—; instr. edn. U. San Diego, part-time, 1993, 95; supr. counselor interns LaMesa/Spring Valley Sch. Dist., 1992—; chmn. Connecting for Success Conf., 1991—; lectr. in field. Editor U. San Diego Athletic Alumni Newsletter, 1994. Recipient Hon. svc. award PTA, LaMesa, 1994. Mem. APA, Am. Sch. Counselor Assn., San Diego Assn. Counseling and Devel., U. San Diego Sch. Edn. Alumni Assn. (bd. dirs. 1992—), Chi Sigma Iota. Republican. Home: 5375 Via Alcazar San Diego CA 92111-4606 Office: Northmont Elem Sch 9405 Gregory St La Mesa CA 91942-3811

PHILLIPS, JEAN BROWN, public relations consultant; b. Phila.; d. Harold T. and Elizabeth (Ulrich) Brown; m. John Tudor Phillips (dec.); 1 child, Barbara Jean. B.S., Drexel U. Producer, broadcaster Sta. WTVT-TV, Tampa, Fla., 1962-64; pub. relations exec. Frank Shattuck Co., N.Y.C., 1964-68, Creamer Dickson Basford, N.Y.C., 1968-72; editor Good Food mag., N.Y.C., 1972-75; pres. Phillips Communications, N.Y.C., 1976—; producer TV program Our Turn, 1982—. Cons., Displaced Homemaker Program, N.Y.C., 1982—, Midlife Inst., Marymont Manhattan Coll., N.Y.C., 1982—; founder, pres. Manhattan Older Women's League, N.Y.C., 1981. Mem. Am. Women in Radio and TV, Am. Home Econs. Assn. (N.Y. State Spotlight award 1982), Pub. Relations Soc. Am. Club: Overseas Press (N.Y.C.). Home: 360 W 22nd St Apt 2E New York NY 10011-2629

PHILLIPS, JO ANN, secondary school educator; b. St. Ignatius, Mont., Mar. 25, 1954; d. Verne L. and Amelia R. (Rouillier) Harris; m. Lloyd E. Phillips, Aug. 25, 1973; children: Jennifer, Cody. BA, U. Mont., 1976. Cert. secondary sch. tchr., Mont. Office skills tchr. Kicking Horse Job Corps, Ronan, Mont., 1976-88; bus. edn. tchr. Sch. Dist. # 28, St. Ignatius, 1988—; advisor Bus. Profls. Am., St. Ignatius, 1992—, Nat. Honor Soc., St. Ignatius, 1990—; tchr. adult edn., St. Ignatius, 1988—. Advisor food drive Nat. Honor Soc., St. Ignatius, 1993. Mem. Mission Boosters (pres. 1988—), AFT (local sec. 1990—). Roman Catholic. Office: Sch Dist 28 PO Box 400 Saint Ignatius MT 59865-0400

PHILLIPS, JUDY LORRAINE, counselor; b. Olympia, Wash., Sept. 27, 1955; d. Eugene Clarence and Erlyse Irene (Champine) Steinbrenner; m. David Leslie Phillips, Mar. 6, 1976; 1 child, Brett Donald. BA, Pacific Luth. U., 1978, M in Guidance Counseling, 1985. Cert. sch. counselor, K-12. Day treatment therapist Lewis County Mental Health, Chehalis, Wash., 1978-80; family therapist Grays Harbor Youth Home, Elma, Wash., 1980-83; sch. counselor Winlock (Wash.) High Sch., 1985—. Organist St. John's Episcopal Ch., Centralia, Wash.; active Eagles, Centralia, Girl Scouts U.S., Olympia, Wash. Mem. Am. Assn. Counseling and Devel., Am. Sch. Counselor Assn., Wash. Sch. Counselor Assn., Wash. Counseling Assn., Pacific Northwest Assn. of Coll. Admissions Counselors. Episcopalian.

PHILLIPS, JULIA MAE, physicist; b. Freeport, Ill., Aug. 17, 1954; d. Spencer Kleckner and Marjorie Ann (Figi) Phillips. BS, Coll. William and Mary, 1976; PhD, Yale U., 1981. Mem. tech. staff AT&T Bell Labs., Murray Hill, 1981-88, supr. thin film rsch. group, 1988—; program mgr. Consortium Superconducting Elecs., 1989-92. Editor: Heteroepitaxy on Silicon Technology, 1987, Epitaxial Oxide Thin Films and Heterostructures, 1994; prin. editor Jour. Materials Rsch., 1990—; mem. editorial bd. Applied Physics Letters and Jour. Applied Physics, 1992-94; contbr. articles to profl. jours. Fellow APS; mem. Materials Rsch. Soc. (sec. 1987-89, councillor 1991-93, 2d v.p. 1993, 1st v.p. 1994, pres. 1995), Sigma Xi, Phi Beta Kappa. Office: AT&T Bell Labs 600 Mountain Ave New Providence NJ 07974-0636

PHILLIPS, JULIA MILLER, film producer; b. N.Y.C., Apr. 7, 1944; d. Adolph and Tanya Miller; m. Michael Phillips (div.); 1 dau., Kate Elizabeth. B.A., Mt. Holyoke Coll., 1965. Former prodn. asst. McCall's Mag.; later advt. copywriter Macmillan Publs.; editorial asst. Ladies Home Journal, 1965-69; later assoc. editor; East Coast story editor Paramount Pictures, N.Y.C., 1969; head Mirisch Prodns., N.Y., 1970; creative exec. First Artists Prodns., N.Y.C., 1971; founded (with Tony Bill and Michael Phillips) Bill/Phillips Prodns., 1971; founder, producer Ruthless Prodns., Los Angeles, 1971—. Author: You'll Never Eat Lunch in this Town Again, 1990; films include Steelyard Blues, 1972, The Sting, 1973 (Acad. award for best picture of yr.), Taxi Driver, 1976 (Palme d'or for best picture), The Big Bus, 1976, Close Encounters of the Third Kind, 1977, (co-producer) The Beat, 1988; dir. The Estate of Billy Buckner, for Women Dirs. Workshop, Am. Film Inst., 1974. Recipient Katherine McFarland Short Story award, 1963, Short Story award Phi Beta Kappa, 1964. Mem. Acad. Motion Picture Arts and Scis., Writers Guild. Office: care Writers Guild 8955 Beverly Blvd Los Angeles CA 90048-2420*

PHILLIPS, KATHLEEN JOAN, lawyer; b. Jersey City, Apr. 14, 1946; d. Irving S. and Frances (Dunberg) P. BA, U. Rochester, 1968; MA, Boston Coll., 1974; JD, Boston U., 1978. Bar: Mass. 1978. From asst. counsel to assoc. counsel Bank of Boston, 1978-84; sr. counsel Computervision, Bedford, Mass., 1984-88; v.p., gen. counsel, sec. Harris Graphics Corp. subs. Heidelberger Druckmaschineu, Dover, N.H., 1988-90; cons., bus. negotiations, 1990—; bd. dirs. New Eng. Loan Mktg. Corp., Braintree, Mass. Reviewer Drood Rev. of Mysteries, 1993—; columnist and reviewer Mystery Scene Mag.; proprietor Time and Again Books, 1st Edit. Mysteries, others; contbr. to Great Woman Mystery Writers. Mem. ABA, Mass. Bar Assn., Nat. Assn. Corp. Counsel. Home: 364 Main St North Andover MA 01845-3952

PHILLIPS, LINDA, actress; b. Mpls., May 1, 1947; d. Elmer and Alice (Doherty) Johnson; children: William D. Jr., Henry W.; m. Bill Wiley, May 5, 1966. Student, Oxford U., Eng., 1992; grad., Calif. State U., Northridge, 1993, UCLA, 1994. Voice specialist for movies, TV shows and commls. including Pet Sematary (voice of the demon child), As The World Turns, Lonesome Dove, The Lion King; appeared on TV series L.A. Law, CHIPS and on stage. Recipient Robby award for best supporting actress in a comedy, 1982. Episcopalian. Home: 3808 Los Amigos St La Crescenta CA 91214-1611

PHILLIPS, LINDA DARNELL ELAINE FREDRICKS, psychiatric and geriatrics nurse; b. Calgary, Alta., Can., July 23, 1940; came to U.S., 1964; d. Richard and Adeline Ruth (Kuch) Fredricks; m. Marion Rolley Phillips, June 25, 1960 (div. 1962). Cert. in nursing with honors, Broward C.C., Ft. Lauderdale, Fla., 1983. Exec. sec. Grandeur Motor Cars, Pompano Beach, Fla., 1975-80; charge nurse Las Olas Hosp., Ft. Lauderdale, 1983-85; nurse Med. Pers. Pool, Ft. Lauderdale, 1984-85; pvt. duty nurse, Ft. Lauderdale, 1985—; pres., v.p. L.P.R.N. Inc., 1992-93; cons. nurse Waterford Point Condo, Pompano Beach, Fla., 1980-90. Mem. Fla. Nurses Assn., Internat. Platform Assn. Address: 2910 NE 55th St Fort Lauderdale FL 33308

PHILLIPS, LINDA GOLUCH, plastic surgeon, educator, researcher; b. Chgo., Nov. 11, 1951; d. Edward Walter and Rosemarie (Tomasek) Goluch; m. William Anthony Phillips, July 12, 1975; children: Cooper William, Nolan Edward, Spencer Geoffrey, Corinna Lee. BA, U. Chgo., 1974, MD, 1978. Diplomate Am. Bd. Surgery, Am. Bd. Plastic Surgery (mem. qualifying examination team 1993). Resident U. Chgo., 1978-80; intern in gen. surgery Northwestern U., Chgo., 1980-81, instr., surgeon, 1982-83; asst. prof. Wayne State U., Detroit, 1985-88; asst. prof. plastic surgery U. Tex. Med. Br., Galveston, 1988-91, assoc. prof. plastic surgery, 1991—, Truman G. Blocker Jr., MD, Disting. chairperson, chief divsn. plastic surgery, 1994—; mem. consulting med. staff Shriners Burns Inst., Galveston, Tex., 1988—; chmn. basic rsch. grants com. Plastic Surgery Edn. Found., Chgo., 1992—, mem. ednl. assessment com., mem. scholarship com., 1987-92, mem. plastic surgery-in-svc. exam. com., 1987-88, 89-93, mem. instrnl. course com., 1991-92, mem. rsch. fellowship com., mem. rsch. fund proposals com., 1993, 94; parliamentarian Plastic Surgery Rsch. Coun., 1991-93; Morestin lectr. Nat. Med. Assn., 1991; guest speaker Royal Coll. Surgeons, Eng., 1993; speaker in field. Co-author book chpts.; contbr. articles, abstracts to profl. jours. Pres. Blue Marlin Swim Team, Houston, 1993; active Clear Creek Ind. Sch. Dist., Houston, 1992. Grantee in field. Fellow Am. Coll. Surgeons; mem. AMA, Am. Assn. Plastic Surgeons, Am. Burn Assn. (mem. orgn. and delivery of burn care com. 1988-91, mem. ednl. com., 1991-94), Am. Soc. Plastic and Reconstructive Surgeons (mem. program com. 1991-92, mem. exhibits com. 1992, 93, chair, 1993-94, mem. sci. program com. 1994), Am. Soc. Maxillofacial Surgeons (mem. news com. 1992, mem. membership com. 1992-93), Am. Assn. Surgery of Trauma (mem. search com. editor of Jour. Trauma 1992), Am. Soc. Aesthetic Plastic Surgery, Am. Assn. Hand Surgery, Am. Geriatric Soc., Am. Diabetes Assn., Plastic Surgery Rsch. Coun., Surgical Infection Soc., Assn. Women Surgeons (pres. 1992-94, v.p./pres.-elect 1990-92, chair program com. 1990-92, chair membership com. 1988-89, mem. nominating com. 1989-92), Blocker-Lewis Surgery Soc. (exec. sec. 1988-92), Assn. Acad. Chairmen of Plastic Surgery (mem. prerequisite com. 1990, 91), The Wound Healing Soc. (mem. honors and awards com. 1993), Singleton Surg. Soc. (sec.-treas. 1993—), Soc. Head and Neck Surgeons, Tex. Soc. Plastic Surgeons, Assn. Acad. Surgery, N.Y. Acad. Sci., Tex. Med. Assn., Galveston Med. Soc., Sigma Xi. Roman Catholic. Home: 15823 Sylvan Lake Houston TX 77062 Office: U Tex Med Br 6.124 McCullough Bldg Galveston TX 77555-0724

PHILLIPS, MARA MAZACCO, sales management executive; b. Lodi, N.J., May 1, 1965; d. Joseph Anthony Mazacco and Carole Francis (Was) Helton; m. David D. Phillips, May 14, 1988. BA, Eckerd Coll., 1987. Profl. rep. Marion Labs., Hackensack, N.J., 1987-90; cardiovascular sales cons. Marion Merrell Dow, Hackensack, 1990-92; dist. mgr. Marion Merrell Dow, Balt., 1992-94, sr. regional account mgr., 1994—; cardiovascular cons. pilot program Marion Merrell Dow, Hackensack, 1990-91. Recipient first place award for case study Soc. for the Advancement of Mgmt., St. Petersburg, Fla., 1986. Mem. Am. Mgmt. Assn., Condominium Assn. (bd. dirs., v.p. 1988-92). Republican.

PHILLIPS, MARY ELIZABETH, artist, art educator; b. Greenville, Mich., June 28, 1949; d. Frederick Wendell and Rita Agnes (Hubert) P.; m. John Richard Sayre, Aug. 2, 1991. BA, Siena Heights Coll., 1971; MA, No. Ill. U., 1981, MFA, 1986. Prodn. editor Hunter Pub. Co., Chgo., 1973-76; grad. asst. No. Ill. U., De Kalb, 1976-78, grad. staff asst., 1984-86; internat. program co-dir. Studio Angelico Siena Heights Coll., Adrian, Mich., 1979, 87; asst. prof. art Phillips U., Enid, Okla., 1979-83, assoc. prof. art, 1987-93, prof. art, 1993—; chair dept. art Phillips U., 1994—; freelance artist Farmington, Mich., 1983-84; dir. Grace Phillips Johnson Gallery, Enid, 1979-83, 1987—; pres. faculty senate Phillips U., Enid, 1990-91; trustee Enid Arts & Humanities Coun., Enid, 1992—, South San Juan Field Sta., Enid, 1992-93; participant Calligraphy Rev. Workshop, Quartz Mt., Okla., 1993; juror local and regional art shows, No. Okla. Summer Seminar fellow NEH, 1990; recipient Show prize Dodge City (Kans.) Arts Coun., 1993. Mem. Coll. Art Assn. (instl.), Kappa Gamma Pi. Roman Catholic. Office: Phillips U Dept of Art 100 S University Ave Enid OK 73701-6439

PHILLIPS, MARY LEE S., housing finance administrator; b. Lewes, Del., May 30, 1948; d. Leven Thomas and Mary Beatrice (Adams) Shockley; m. James J. F. Phillips, July 6, 1974. AAS, Del. Tech. and C.C., Georgetown, Del., 1969; BS in Bus. Mgmt. magna cum laude, Wilmington Coll., 1994. Vol. Del. Art Mus., Wilmington, 1970-79; bus. mgr. DAST, Dover, Del., 1979-84; freelance bus. mgr., cons., 1984-92; fiscal chief New Castle County Cmty. Devel. and Housing, Wilmington, 1992—. Mem. Young Dem. Club, Wilmington, 1970-73; coord. Youth Confirmation, 1987—; treas. United Meth. Women, 1988-91, v.p., 1992-93, pres., 1993—; mem. staff parish rels. Asbury United Meth. Ch., New Castle, 1990—, active, 1970—; leader Young Women's Retreat, 1992; bd. dirs. Neighborhood House, Wilmington, 1994—; mem. fin. com. Celebration 75, Wilmington, 1994—. Democrat.

Office: New Castle County Cmty Devel Housing 110 S French St Wilmington DE 19801

PHILLIPS, PAMELA KIM, lawyer; b. San Diego, Feb. 23, 1958; d. John Gerald and Nancy Kimiko (Tabuchi) Phillips; m. R. Richard Zanghetti, Sept. 16, 1989. BA cum laude, The Am. U., 1978; JD, Georgetown U., 1982. Bar: N.Y. 1983, Fla. 1983, U.S. Dist. Ct. (so. dist.) N.Y. 1983, U.S. Dist. Ct. (mid. dist.) Fla. 1994. Assoc. Curtis, Mallet-Prevost, Colt & Mosle, N.Y.C., 1982-84, LeBoeuf, Lamb, Greene & MacRae, N.Y.C., 1984-90; ptnr. LeBoeuf, Lamb, Leiby & MacRae, N.Y.C., 1991—. Mng. editor The Tax Lawyer, Georgetown U. Law Sch., Washington, 1980-81. Coun. mem. The Fresh Air Fund, 1991-94. Am. Univ. scholar, Washington, 1976-78. Mem. ABA, Women's Bar Assn., Bar Assn. of City of N.Y. (sec. young lawyers com. 1987-89, chmn. 1989-91, second century com. 1990-93, banking law com. 1991-94), N.Y. Athletic Club, Jacksonville Bar Assn., The River Club. Democrat. Roman Catholic. Home: 108 Putters Way Ponte Vedra Beach FL 32082 Office: LeBoeuf Lamb Greene & MacRae 125 W 55th St New York NY 10019-5369 also: 50 N Laura St Ste 2800 Jacksonville FL 32202-3656

PHILLIPS, PATRICIA A., municipal official; b. Phila., Feb. 22, 1947; d. Randall Horace and Mane Ann (Benderavage) Grissom; m. Charles Thomas Phillips II, Dec. 16, 1967; children: Charles T. III, Kent Jesse. BS in Bus., Old Dominion U., 1969, MBA, 1990. CPA, Va. Staff acct. Coopers & Lybrand, Norfolk, Va., 1970-72, sr. acct., 1972-74, supervisory acct., 1974-75; rsch. coord. City of Virginia Beach, Va., 1975-85, dir. rsch., 1985-92, dir. fin., 1992—; chair supervisory com. Va. Beach Mcpl. Employee Fed. Credit Union, 1980-83. Facilitator Mayor's Com. on Econ. Devel., Virginia Beach, 1990, Dept.-Vol. Coun., Virginia Beach, 1991-93; mem. Old Dominion Edn. Found., Norfolk, 1992-93. Mem. AICPA, Internat. Assn. Accts. (v.p. local chpt. 1971-73). Roman Catholic. Office: City of Virginia Beach Mcpl Ctr Virginia Beach VA 23456

PHILLIPS, PATRICIA JEANNE, retired school administrator, consultant; b. Amarillo, Miss., Jan. 13, 1935; d. William Macon and Mary Ann (Cawthon) Patrick; m. William Henry Phillips, June 22, 1962; 1 child, Mary Jeanne. BA, Millsaps Coll., 1954; MA, Vanderbilt/Peabody U., 1957; EdD, U. So. Miss., 1978. Tchr. Jackson (Miss.) Pub. Schs., 1954-73, prin., 1973-75, asst. prin., 1975-77; dir. ednl. program Eden Prairie (Minn.) # 272, 1977-80; dir. elem. edn. Meridian (Miss.) Pub. Schs., 1980-91, asst. supt. curriculum, 1991, ret., 1991; prof. Miss. Coll., Clinton, part-time 1977, Miss. State U., Meridian, 1981-95; ednl. cons. in field. Co-author: (testing practice) Test Taking Tactics, 1987; contbr. articles to profl. jours. pres. Meridian Symphony Orch., 1987; v.p. Meridian Coun. Arts, 1986; bd. dirs. Meridian Art Mus. Named Boss of Yr., Meridian Secretarial Assn., 1985, Arts Educator of Yr., Meridian Coun. Arts, 1991; recipient Excellence award Program Sch. Improvement, 1993, Excellence award Pub. Edn. Forum, 1994. Mem. Miss. Assn. Women (pres.), Rotary, Phi Delta Kappa (pres. 1986-87). Republican. Methodist. Home: 322 51st St Meridian MS 39305-2013 Office: Miss State Univ Meridian Campus 1000 Hwy 19 S Meridian MS 39302

PHILLIPS, PEPPER ELLEN, psychologist; b. Cin., Oct. 26, 1960; d. Robert Murr and Jerri Phillips. BA, Hanover Coll., 1982; MA, Ind. State U., 1984, PhD, 1990. Tchr., therapist Englishton Park Acad. Remediation and Tng. Ctr., Lexington, Ind., 1981; cons. Energize, Phila., 1981; rsch. asst. Ind. State U., Terre Haute, 1983-84, doctoral fellow, 1984-87, counselor, 1989-90; counseling intern U. Mo., Columbia, 1987-88; staff psychologist, asst. prof. psychology U. Md., College Park, 1990—. Contbr. articles to profl. jours. Mem. APA, Assn. Women in Psychology. Democrat. Office: U Md Shoemaker Hall College Park MD 20742

PHILLIPS, ROSE MARIE L., real estate company owner; b. Flint, Mich., Sept. 17, 1937; d. Milford Neamon and Geraldine Marie (Huntoon) Lessley; m. Robert Spencer Phillips, Jan. 9, 1965; children: Patrick, Michelle. Attended, Ctrl. Mich. U. Sales assoc. The Norwood Group, Bedford, N.H., 1976-80; relocation divsn. mgr. The Norwood Group, Bedford, 1980-82; exec. v.p., co-owner The Norwood Realty, Inc., Bedford, 1982—; bd. dirs. Optima Health. Bd. dirs., past chairwoman Greater Manchester (N.H.) C. of C., 1988-94; bd. trustees Fidelity Health Alliance, Manchester, 1990—, Alliance Resources, Inc., Manchester, 1993—; incorporator N.H. Charitable Found., Concord, 1990—. Named Bus. Leader of Yr. by Bus. N.H. Mag., Manchester, 1992, one of 10 Most Powerful Women in state of N.H. by Network Publs., 1993. Mem. Nat. Assn. Realtors, Relocations Dirs. Coun. (bd. dirs. 1993—), Employee Relocation Coun. Office: The Norwood Realty Inc 176 S River Rd Bedford NH 03110-6925

PHILLIPS, SHARON KELLY, special education educator; b. Petersburg, Va., June 19, 1955; d. Robert Reginald and Lucille (Marjorie) Kelly; m. Dallas Lowell Phillips, July 13, 1980; children: Matthew Dalton, Caitlin Fox. BA, Averett Coll., 1978. Cert. learning disabilities, emotional disturbance, elem. edn. tchr., remedial reading. Learning disabilities self contained tchr. Southampton County Pub. Schs., Courtland, Va.; learing disabilities, emotional disturbance resource tchr. Greensville County Pub. Schs., Emporia, Va. Past coord. Greensville County Spl. Olympics; participant Project Teaching Educators About Mainstreaming. Mem. Emporia Jr. Woman's Club (past edn. dept. chmn.). Home: 24417 Adams Grove Rd Emporia VA 23847

PHILLIPS, SUSAN MEREDITH, financial economist, former university administrator; b. Richmond, Va., Dec. 23, 1944; d. William G. and Nancy (Meredith) P. BA in Math., Agnes Scott Coll., 1967; MS in Fin. and Ins., La. State U., 1971, PhD in Fin. and Economics, 1973. Asst. prof. La. State U., 1973-74, U. Iowa, 1974-78; Brookings Econ. Policy fellow, 1976-77; econ. fellow Directorate of Econ. and Policy Rsch., SEC, 1977-78; assoc. prof. fin. dept. U. Iowa, 1978-83, assoc. v.p. fin. and univ. svcs., 1979-81; commr. Commodity Futures Trading Commn., 1981-83, chmn., 1983-87; prof. fin. dept., v.p. fin. and univ. svcs. U. Iowa, Iowa City, 1987-91; bd. govs. Fed. Res. Bd., Washington, 1991—. Author (with J. Richard Zecher): The SEC and the Public Interest; contbr. articles in field to profl. jours. Office: Fed Res System 20th Constitution St NW Washington DC 20551

PHILLIPS, SUSAN PRESCOTT, critical care nurse; b. Milton, Fla., Apr. 12, 1957; d. John Hansel and Dorothy Lawrence (Wise) Prescott; divorced; 1 child, Heather Denise. Cert. of practical nursing with honors, Pensacola Jr. Coll., 1976; ADN, Jefferson Davis Jr. Coll., 1980; BSN, U. South Ala., 1989, postgrad., 1994—. RN, Fla.; CEN. Relief staff nurse Am. Nurses Svcs., Inc., Pensacola, Fla.; adj. in nursing Pensacola Jr. Coll. Home: 400 E First Ave Jay FL 32565-1048

PHINNEY, BETH, Canadian legislator. Ed., McMaster U., Hamilton Tchrs. Coll. Tchr. Saltfleet, 1961-64, Montreal, Que., Can., 1964-67; tchr. ESL, 1968-74; with ministry of edn. Province of Que., 1974-79, spl. asst. to ministry of regional & econ. devel., 1981; real estate sales rep., 1982; mem. Ho. of Commons, Ottawa, Ont., Can., 1988—, mem. justice com., 1988—. Mem. Royal Can. Legion. Office: House of Commons, Confederation Bldg Rm 713, Ottawa, ON Canada K1A 0A6

PHINNEY, JEAN SWIFT, psychology educator; b. Princeton, N.J., Mar. 12, 1933; d. Emerson H. and Anne (Davis) Swift; m. Bernard O. Phinney, Dec. 11, 1965; children: Peter, David. BA, Mass. Wellesley Coll., 1955; MA, UCLA, 1969, PhD, 1973. Asst. prof. psychology Calif. State U., L.A., 1977-81, assoc. prof. psychology, 1981-86, prof. psychology, 1986—. Editor: Children's Ethnic Socialization, 1987; asst. editor Jour. Adolescence; contbr. articles to profl. jours. NIH grantee. Mem. Am. Psychol. Assn., Soc. for Rsch. in Child Devel., Soc. for Rsch. in Adolescence. Office: Calif State U Dept Psychology 2250 State University Dr Los Angeles CA 90032

PHIPPS, LYNNE BRYAN, interior architect, clergywoman, parent educator; b. Chapel Hill, N.C., Sept. 23, 1964; d. Floyd Talmadge and Sandra Patricia (McLester) Bryan; m. Thomas Otey Phipps, July 18, 1985. BFA, RISD, 1986, B Interior Architecture, 1987; cert. in parent edn., Wheelock Coll., Boston, 1989; postgrad., Andover Newton Theol. Sem., 1991—. Nat. cert. interior arch. Apprentice Thompson Ventulett Stainback, Atlanta, 1983-85; jr. designer Earl Fransberg & Assocs., Boston, 1986-87; sr. designer, prin. Innovative Designs, Duxbury, Mass., 1986—; parent educator, pres. Parenting Puzzle, 1990—; parent educator Families First, Cambridge, Mass.; youth min. St. Andrew's Episcopal Ch., Hanover, Mass., 1992-94; youth and family min. St. Stephen's Episcopal Ch., Cohasset, Mass., 1993—; guest lectr., jurist Auburn (Ala.) U., 1988, RISD, Providence, 1990; assoc. prof. Mass. Bay C.C., Wellesley, 1987-88; guest jurist Wentworth U., Boston, 1988-89. Designer furniture. Mem. Inst. Bus. Designers, Assn. Parent Educators, Jr. League Boston. Office: Innovative Designs The Parenting Puzzle 18 Bay View Rd Duxbury MA 02332

PHOENIX, ANTOINETTE DAVIS, fundraiser; b. Clarksville, Tex., July 26, 1959; d. Robert and Addie (Wilson) Davis; m. Donnell Phoenix, Apr. 25, 1986; 1 child, Brittanie Dionne. AA in Social Sci., Wichita State U., 1989, B of Gen. Studies, 1989. Sales assoc. Henry's Inc., Wichita, 1981-84; with Wichita State U., 1981-90; accounts mgr. United Way of the Plains, Wichita, 1990—; panel spkr. numerous confs. Wichita State U., 1989, 92, 93-94; spkr. Wichita Metro Family Preservation Agy., Inc. Allocation vol. United Way of the Plains, 1990. Mem. NAFE, Wichita Area C. of C. (com. mem. 1991-92), The Chamber, Small Bus. Coun., 1992—, Nat. Assn. for Advancement of Color People, 1990, Bus. and Profl. Women, Tabernacle Bapt. Ch., 1991—. Democrat. Baptist. Office: United Way of the Plains 212 N Market St Ste 200 Wichita KS 67202-2090

PHOTIADIS, DEBORAH ANN, state official; b. Buffalo, Mar. 29, 1954; d. Christie James and Joan Tucker P.; m. Theodore John Berger; children: Paul, Anne, Peter, Katie. MA, St. John's Coll., 1986. Real estate developer Annapolis, Md., 1976-80; v.p. The Gault Corp., Balt., 1980-82; exec. adminstr. Renaissance Plz. Ltd. Partnership, Balt., 1982-85; chief real estate, asst. sec. Dept. Gen. Svcs., State of Md., Balt., 1985-92; exec. dir. privatization coun. Office of Gov., State of Md., Annapolis, 1992—; chair fin. innovations com. U.S. EPA Environ. Fin. Adv. Bd., Washington, 1994—; active Nat. Coun. Pub.-Pvt. Partnerships, Washington, 1992—, Md. Blue Ribbon Panel Tributary Strategies, Annapolis, 1994. Active Arundel Habitat for Humanity, 1994—. Office: State of Md Budget Dept 45 Calvert St Annapolis MD 21401

PI, WEN-YI SHIH, aircraft company engineer, researcher; b. Peiping, People's Republic of China, Feb. 28, 1935; came to U.S., 1959; d. Chih-Chuan and Hsiu-Yun (Yang) Shih; m. William Shu-Jong Pi, July 2, 1961; 1 child, Wilfred. BS, Nat. Taiwan U., Taipei, Republic of China, 1956; MS, Stanford U., 1961, PhD, 1963. Research assoc. Stanford (Calif.) U., 1963-64; engrng. specialist Northrop Corp., Hawthorne, Calif., 1965-83, sr. tech. specialist, 1983—. Contbr. articles to profl. jours. Recipient Silver Achievement award Los Angeles YWCA, 1983; Amelia Earhart Scholar Zonta Internat., 1961-62. Fellow: AIAA (assoc.); mem. Sigma Xi. Office: Northrop Grumman Corp Aircraft Aircraft Divsn One Northrop Ave Dept 3852/63 Hawthorne CA 90250-3277

PIAGESI-ZETT, DIANE CRISTINA, rehabilitation services professional; b. Phillipsburg, N.J., Nov. 21, 1954; d. Raymond Anthony and Betty Lou (Castner) Piagesi; m. Livio Zett, Aug. 28, 1983; children: Alessandra, Francesca. BA, Rutgers U., 1977; MA, U. Conn., 1979, profl. diploma, 1980. Cert. rehab. counselor. Clinician Sussex House Newton (N.J.) Meml. Hosp., 1980-85, asst. dir., programs v.p., 1985-94; dir. transitional svcs. Sussex House Newton (N.J.) Meml. Hosp., 1994—; dir. N.J. Psychiat. Rehab. Assn., Hackensack, N.J., 1984-94, sec., 1989-93; tng. assoc. Boston U. Ctr. Psychiat. Rehab., 1985—; cons. Family Support Group, Newton, 1989-92; rehab. cons. Homestead Nursing Home, Frankford, N.J., 1980-88. Henry Rutgers scholar Rutgers Coll., 1977, Pi Lambda Theta scholar, 1979. Mem. N.J. Psychiat. Rehab. Assn. (bd. dirs., sec. 1984, Appreciation award 1993), Internat. Assn. Psychosocial Rehab. Svcs. Roman Catholic. Office: Sussex House-Newtown Meml Hosp 175 High St Newton NJ 07860

PIASKY, LUCILLE ALICE, insurance professional; b. Scranton, Pa., Nov. 6, 1944; d. Leonard Francis and Lucille Antoinette (Perdyan) P. BA, Pa. State U., 1976; MS, Widener U., 1987. CLU, CPCU. Svc. rep. Bell Telephone of Pa., Scranton, 1962-73; claim rep. State Farm Ins. Co., Dupont, Pa., 1977-81; claim analyst State Farm Ins. Co., Bloomington, Ind., 1981; claim supr. State Farm Ins. Co., Dresher, Pa., 1981-83; underwriting supr. State Farm Ins. Co., Concordville, 1983-88; claim supt. State Farm Ins. Co., Scranton, Pa., 1988—. Pres. Jr. Century Club, Scranton, 1994—. Mem. CPCU of N.E. Pa., CLU of N.E. Pa., Phi Beta Kappa, Phi Kappa Phi. Democrat.

PIAZZA, MARGUERITE, opera singer, actress, entertainer; b. New Orleans, May 6, 1926; d. Albert William and Michaela (Piazza) Luft; m. William J. Condon, July 15, 1953 (dec. Mar. 1968); children: Gregory, James (dec.), Shirley, William J., Marguerite P., Anna Becky; m. Francis Harrison Bergtholdt, Nov. 8, 1970. MusB, Loyola U., New Orleans; MusM, La. State U.; MusD (hon.), Christian Bros. Coll., 1973; LHD honoris causa, Loyola U., Chgo., 1975. Singer N.Y.C. Ctr. Opera, 1948, Met. Opera Co., 1950; TV artist, regular singing star Your Show of Shows NBC, 1950-54; entertainer various supper clubs Cotillion Room, Hotel Pierre, N.Y.C., 1954, Las Vegas, Los Angeles, New Orleans, San Francisco, 1956—; ptnr. Sound Express Music Pub. Co., Memphis, 1987—; bd. dirs. Cemrel, Inc. Appeared as guest performer on numerous mus. TV shows. Nat. crusade chmn. Am. Cancer Soc., 1971; founder, bd. dirs. Marguerite Piazza Gala for the Benefit of St. Jude's Hosp., 1976; bd. dirs. Memphis Opera Co., World Literacy Found., NCCJ; v.p., life bd. dirs. Memphis Symphony Orch.; nat. chmn. Soc. for Cure Epilepsy. Decorated Mil. and Hospitaller Order of St Lazarus of Jerusalem; recipient service award Chgo. Heart Assn., 1956, service award Fedn. Jewish Philanthropies of N.Y., 1956, Sesquicentennial medal Carnegie Hall; named Queen of Memphis, Memphis Cotton Carnival, 1973, named Person of Yr. La. Council for Performing Arts, 1975, named Woman of Yr. Nat. Am. Legion, named Woman of Yr. Italian-Am. Soc. Mem. Nat. Speakers Assn., Woman's Exchange, Memphis Country Club, Memphis Hunt and Polo Club, New Orleans Country Club, Summit Club, Beta Sigma Omicron, Phi Beta. Roman Catholic. Home: #301 Park Pl 5400 Park Ave # 301 Memphis TN 38119

PIAZZA, MARIE THERESA, former secondary education educator; b. N.Y.C., May 26, 1928; d. Anthony and Marie Theresa (Capri) P. BS in Acctg., Fairleigh Dickinson U., 1972. Cert. tchr., N.J. Acctg. clk. N.Y. Life Ins. Co., N.Y.C., 1946-49; stenographer Civil Aeronautics Adminstrn., Kennedy Airport, N.Y., 1949-50; adminstrv. asst. Nipkow & Kobelt, Inc., N.Y.C., 1950-54; sec. to v.p. Schwab Bros. Corp., N.Y.C., 1954-61, adminstrv. asst., 1963-70; sec. to dir. engring. Wellington Electronics, Inc., Englewood, N.J., 1961-62; exec. sec. York Radio Corp., South Hackensack, N.J., 1970-72; bus. tchr. Cresskill (N.J.) High Sch., 1972-91; ret., 1991. Named Tchr. of the Year and recipient grant Gov. Kean's Tchr. Recognition Program, 1986. Mem. Am. Soc. Women Accts. (dir. 1985—), NEA, N.J. Bus. Edn. Assn., Phi Zeta Kappa, Phi Omega Epsilon. Home: 274 Baldwin Ave New Milford NJ 07646-1904

PICARD, NANCY MARIE, writer, multicultural consultant; b. Meadowbrook, Pa., Apr. 18, 1966; d. Salvatore R. and Marlene M. (Delle) P. BA in English, Syracuse U., 1988, BA in Pub. Rels., 1988; postgrad., U. Wis., 1994—. Mag. editor Croftward Publs., London, England, 1988-89; internat. rschr. Internat. City Mgmt. Assn., Washington, 1989-90; vol., English tchr. U.S. Peace Corps., Sopron, Hungary, 1990-92; cross cultural specialist U.S. Peace Corps., Budapest, Hungary, 1992-93; founder, pres., freelance writer, editor Light Resources Cons., 1993—; comm. cons. U.S. Agency for Internat. Devel., Budapest, Hungary, 1994; cons. Ferenczi and Ferenczi Bus. Systems, Budapest, Hungary, 1991—; rsch. aid. psychology clinic U. Wis. Hosp., Madison, 1994—. Advocate vol. Dane County Advocates for Battered Women, Madison, Wis., 1994; vol. Budapest Feminist Network, Hungary, 1993-94. Recipient Golden Key Pub. Rels. award Pub. Rels Soc. of Am., 1988. Mem. Am. Psychological Assn. Democrat. Home: 400 Fairlea Dr Edgewater MD 21037

PICARDI, JENNIFER J., accountant; b. Montgomery County, Md., Oct. 14, 1969; d. Angelo Felix and Elizabeth Jean (Purdie) P. Student, Bentley Coll. Acctg. mgr. Level 1 Techs., Rockland, Mass., 1990—. Mem. Am. Soc. Notaries, Inst. Mgmt. Accts., Nat. Assn. Female Execs.

PICCARD-KRONE, KAREN ALIOTTE, public relations executive, political consultant; b. La Jolla, Calif., Aug. 10, 1959; d. Peter Elliot and Connie (Anaya) Piccard; m. F. William Krone III, Aug., 1980. BA in History, Portland (Oreg.) State U., 1981; degree in law, U. West Los Angeles, 1985; grad. in polit. mgmt., U. Calif., Davis, 1992-94. Radio talk show host So. Calif. KPZE-AM, Laguna Niguel, Santa Ana, Calif., 1986-87; pres. Krones and Assocs., Inc., Portland, 1988—; mem. adv. bd. Pacific N.W. Grantmakers/Grantseekers Conf., 1990-92. Contbr. articles to profl. jours. Com. chmn., mem. adjustment com. Portland Planning Bur., 1991—; chmn. auction com. Oreg. Mus. Sci. and Industry, 1991, PSU "Ultimate Tailgate" Auction, 1994; chmn. steering com. Scanfair, Portland, 1989-90; mem. variance com., Portland, 1989-91; campaign mgr. numerous ballot measures, polit. candidates, 1990-94; exec. dir. Oreg. Non-Profits Assn., 1991—; dir. devel. Oreg. LWV, 1992—; dir. Columbia Symphony Orch., 1993—; chmn. vol. coun. Portland Art Mus., 1995—; dir. Loaves and Fishes, 1994—; pres. Friends of Mystery, 1995—. Charles S. Linderman scholar, 1992; recipient Pub. Svc. award Portland City Coun., 1991. Mem. Soc. Fund Raising Execs. (advocate, non-profit lobbyist, mem. exec. bd.), Portlandia Club, Inc. (bd. dirs., Woman of Yr. 1990), Oreg. Art Inst., Oreg. Nordic Coun. (pres. 1992—), Sherlock Holmes Soc. Portland, Scandinavian Heritage Found., Rotary, Friends of Mystery (pres. 1995—), Optimist Club (pres. 1991-92), City Club Portland (com. mem.). Office: 333 S State St Ste 166 Lake Oswego OR 97034-3959

PICCININI, JANICE, state legislator; b. Balt., Dec. 16, 1945; d. Anthony Joseph and Irene (Knoedler) P. BS, Frostburg State U., 1967; MA, Johns Hopkins U., 1974. Lic. real estate agt., Md. Tchr. Baltimore County Pub. Sch., 1967-79; in real estate, 1974—; pres. Tchrs. Assn. Baltimore County, 1979-81, Md. State Tchrs. Assn., 1981-85; mem. Md. State Senate, Baltimore County's 10th Legis. Dist., 1991—, jud. proceedings com., joint com. on fed. rels., 1991-93; mem. budget and tax com., 1993-95; bd. dirs. Commn. on Infants and Toddlers; cons. in field. bd. dirs. Pub. Sector Labor Rels. Bd. of Md., 1983-85, Exec. Women's Network, 1987-90; mem. Congresswoman Helen D. Bentley's Mil. Acad. Rev. Com. and Edn. Com., 1984—; del. Dem. Nat. Conv., 1984; mem. Nat. Dem. Platform Com., 1984; apptd. mem. Md. Stadium Authority, 1986-88; apptd. mem. Md. State Dem. Ctrl. Com., 1987-90; chair legis. com. Women's Caucus, Md. Gen. Assembly, 1992. Named to Outstanding Young Women of Am., 1981, Educator of Yr., Md. Assn. Elem. Sch. Prins., 1985; recipient Outstanding Leadership award U. Md. Chpt. Phi Delta Kappa, 1983, Outstanding Contbns. to Minority Affairs award MSTA, 1985, Lille Carroll Jackson award, 1985, Am. Com. on Italian Migration award 1986, Shaare Zedek Med. Ctr. (Jerusalem) Pub. Svc. award 1994. Mem. NOW, Nat. Orgn. Women Legislators, Sons of Italy (exec. dir. Md. Order, Ameritan award 1983). Office: 110 College Ave Annapolis MD 21401-1676

PICCIONI, CONSTANCE ELISABETH, retired librarian; b. Boise, Idaho, Oct. 24, 1908; d. Christian Henry and Sophie (Goeke) Lehde; m. Claude Joseph Piccioni, June 14, 1942; children: Steven John, Gerold Claude, Kathryn Maria, Kristine Elise. BS in LS, U. Wash., 1930, BA in Sociology, 1931. Cert. libr., Wash. Acquisitions libr. U. Wash. Libr., Seattle, 1930-36, Oreg. State Coll. Libr., Corvallis, 1936-41, Mont. State U., Bozeman, 1957-67; chief camp libr. U.S. Army Spl. Svcs., Ft. Lewis, Wash., 1941-46; readers' advisor Santa Barbara (Calif.) Pub. Libr., 1948-52; cataloger Tacoma Pub. Libr., 1952-54, King County Pub. Libr., Seattle, 1954-57; acquisitions libr. Wash. State Libr., Olympia, 1967-72; ret., 1972; Vol. Alberta Bair Theater, 1988—. Author: New Ideas for the Mendery, 1936; co-author: Oregon State College Serial Publications, 1938. Driver Yellowstone County Coun. on Aging, Billings, Mont., 1973-88; vol. St. Vincent Hosp., Billings, 1973—; reader tapes for handicapped Sch. Dist. 2, Billings, 1975-88. Mem. AAUW (v.p. 1988-91), Bus. and Profl. Women (pres. 1968-69, v.p. 1980-81). Democrat. Roman Catholic. Home: 1823 Clark Ave Billings MT 59102-4042

PICKARD, AGNES LOUISE, small business executive; b. St. Albans, Maine, Feb. 25, 1933; d. Walter S. Stone and Louise Allen; m. James A. Pickard, Apr. 15, 1950 (dec. June 1971); children: Asa, Jamie, James. Grad., Milo High Sch., 1949. Mgr. Milo (Maine) Hotel, 1947-64; mgr., owner Milo Sport Shop, 1957-76; owner Pickard's Sport Shop, Brewer, Maine, 1976—; owner Dakin Sporting Goods, Brown Tackle Co. Recipient Grand Cross of Color, Rainbow for Girls, 1973, numerous sales awards Johnson Motors, Starcraft Boats, 1969-91. Mem. Order of Eastern Star (sec. Rebakah Lodge 1972, award 1976). Republican. Home and Office: 802 Wilson St Brewer ME 04412-1015

PICKEN, EDITH DARYL, school system administrator; b. Washington, Jan. 19, 1955; d. Edward George and Edith Kellog (Jones) P. BS, Towson State U., 1978; MS, CAS, Johns Hopkins U., 1985. Cert. English tchr., guidance counselor, prin. and supervision, advanced profl. I, Md. English tchr. Balt. City Pub. Schs., 1979-83; guidance counselor Anne Arundel County Pub. Schs., Md., 1994, adminstr., 1994—; counselor Loyola Edn. Counseling Ctr., Balt.; guest speaker and presenter in field. Named Md. Sch. Counselor of Yr., 1989. Mem. NEA, ASCD, ACA, Md. Assn. Counseling and Devel., AAUW, Md. ASCD, Am. Sch. Counselors Assn., Md. Sch. Counselors Assn., Tchrs. Assn. Anne Arundel County, Chi Sigma Iota, Pi Lambda Theta. Office: North County High Sch 10 E 1st Ave Glen Burnie MD 21061

PICKENS, HEATHER JONES, counselor; b. Louisville, July 11, 1966; d. Peter Rhea and Ellen (Miles) Jones; m. Steven Arnold Pickens, Aug. 4, 1990. BA, Mercer U., 1988; MA, U. Ga., 1991. Cert. sch. counselor. Legal asst. Manning and Assocs., Norcross, Ga., 1988-89; sch. counselor Whit Davis Elem., Athens, Ga., 1990-91, Loganville (Ga.) Mid. Sch., 1991-93, Sweetwater Mid. Sch., Lawrenceville, Ga., 1993—. Mem. Am. Assn. Counseling and Devel., Ga. Sch. Counselor Assn., Jr. League, Smoke Rise Bapt. Ch., Kappa Delta Pi, Psi Chi. Democrat. Home: 1925 Tyler Trce Lawrenceville GA 30243-2952

PICKERING, AVAJANE, specialized education facility executive; b. New Castle, Ind., Nov. 5, 1951; d. George Willard and Elsie Jean (Wicker) P. BA, Purdue U., 1974; MS in Spl. Edn., U. Utah, 1983, PhD, 1991. Cert. spl. edn. Co-dir. presch. for gifted students, 1970-74; tchr. Granite Community Edn., Salt Lake City, 1974-79; tchr. coordinator Salt Lake City Schs., 1975-85; adminstrv. dir., owner Specialized Ednl. Programming Svc., Inc., Salt Lake City, 1976—; mem. Utah Profl. Adv. Bd.; adj. instr. U. Utah, Salt Lake City, 1985—; instr. Brigham Young U., 1993—. Rep. del. Utah State Conv., also county conv.; vol. tour guide, hostess Temple Square, Ch. Jesus Christ of Latter-Day Saints, 1983-88. Mem. Coun. for Exceptional Children, Coun. for Learning Disabilities, Learning Disability Assn., Ednl. Therapy Assn. Profl., Learning Disabilities Assn. Utah (profl. adv. bd.), Attention Deficit Coalition Utah (treas.), Hadassah, Delta Kappa Gamma, Phi Kappa Phi. Home: 1595 S 2100 E Salt Lake City UT 84108-2750 Office: Specialized Ednl Programming Svcs 1760 S 1100 E Salt Lake City UT 84105-3430

PICKERING, BARBARA ANN, pharmaceutical sales representative, nurse; b. Crawfordsville, Ind., Mar. 7, 1949; d. Francis Eugene and Mary Katherine (Smith) Weaver; m. James Bruce Pickering, June 13, 1970; children: Michelle Ann, Kara Rachelle. BS, Ind. Cen. Coll., 1969. RN, Ind. Nurse Meth. Hosp., Indpls, 1983-85; sales rep. Johnson & Johnson, Ft. Washington, Pa., 1984-87; restricted card specialist Blue Cross/Blue Shield, Govt., Indpls., 1987-88; med. sales rep. BASF/Knoll Pharm., Mt. Olive, N.J., 1988—. Vol. Am. Cancer Soc., 1993—; active program bd. Project Leadership Svc., Butler U., Indpls., 1990. Recipient Creative Sales award Sweeney & Ptnrs., 1988. Mem. Indpls. Assn. Pharmacists, Indpls. Med. Reps. Soc. Home: 6310 Dahlia Dr Indianapolis IN 46217-3839 Office: BASF/Knoll Pharm 3000 Continental Dr Mount Olive NJ 07828

PICKERING, SHELBIE JEAN, mortgage loan executive; b. Ellisville, Miss., Sept. 5, 1939; d. Robert Lee and Virgie Clyde (Shoemake) Smith; m. James Dale Pickering, Aug. 24, 1958; 1 child, James Stephen. BS in Bus. magna cum laude, William Carey Coll., 1990. Reg. mortgage underwriter; cert. appraisal reviewer. Bd. secretary Jones County Bd. Edn., Laurel, Miss., 1960-63; ins. underwriter Graves/Montgomery Ins. Agy., Laurel, 1963-65; office mgr. Kux Distributors, Laurel, 1965-66; adminstrv. asst. Gen. Electric, Bay St. Louis, Miss., 1966-71; mortgage loan officer Hancock Bank, Gulfport, Miss., 1971—; seminar leader Hancock Bank, Gulfport, 1988-92;

panelist Miss. Mortgage Lenders, Jackson, 1988-91; cons. Equitrust Mortgage, Gulfport, 1987-88; Gulf Coast rep. Nat. Mortgage Lenders, Atlanta, 1978-91. Tutor Adult Literacy Progam of Gulfport, 1989-92; sponsor March of Dimes Walk-a-Thon, Gulfport, 1988-92. Mem. Miss. Gulf Coast Mortgage Lenders Assn. (bd. dirs. 1991-92), Nat. Assn. Reg. Mortgage Underwriters and Cert. Rev. Appraisers, Gulf Coast Bd. Realtors, Garden Park Hosp. Health Mgmt. Resources. Republican. Baptist. Office: Hancock Bank # 1 Hancock Plaza Gulfport MS 39501

PICKERING, VICTORIA, elementary education educator; b. Chamoise, Mo., June 15, 1934; m. Charles David Pickering, May 28, 1955; children: Barbara, Kimberly Kromberg, John. BS with hons., Peru State Coll., 1971, degree in Spl. Edn., 1980. Cert. tchr. spl. edn., elem. edn. Tchr. 4th grade Friend (Nebr.) Pub. Schs., 1956-58; tchr. 1st grade Syracuse (Nebr.)-Dunbar-Avoca Sch. Dist., 1954-56, 58-62, substitute tchr., 1962-79, tchr. 4th-5th-6th grades, 1979-86, tchr. chpt. I reading, 1986—. Supt. Otoe County Fair, Syracuse, 1974-94; active Otoe County Democrats; leader 4-H Club, Syracuse, 1965-82; leader Cub Scouts, mem. C.I.P. com. Girl Scouts Am., Syracuse, 1965-70; mem. Em-A-Non, Syracuse, 1956-76. Recipient Leadership award Town & Country 4-H Club, 1984. Mem. NEA, Apple Valley Reading Assn. (parent involvement chmn. 1992-94), Syracuse-Dunbar-Avoca Edn. Assn. (chmn. profl. growth 1984-94, treas. 1981-82, sec. 1979-80), Nebr. State Reading Assn., Nebr. State Edn. Assn., Otoe County Agriculture Soc., Delta Kappa Gamma. Home: 1449 Mohawk Box 418 Syracuse NE 68446 Office: Syracuse Dunbar Avoca Sch Dist PO Box P Syracuse NE 68446

PICKETT, BETTY HORENSTEIN, psychologist; b. Providence, R.I., Feb. 15, 1926; d. Isadore Samuel and Etta Lillian (Morrison) Horenstein; m. James McPherson Pickett, Mar. 10, 1952. A.B. magna cum laude, Brown U., 1945, Sc.M., 1947, Ph.D., 1949. Asst. prof. psychology U. Minn., Duluth, 1949-51; asst. prof. U. Nebr., 1951; lectr. U. Conn., 1952; profl. assoc. psychol. scis. Bio-Scis. Info. Exchange, Smithsonian Instn., Washington, 1953-58; exec. sec. behavioral scis. study sect. exptl. psychology study sect. div. research grants NIH, Washington, 1958-61; research cons. to mental health unit HEW, Boston, 1962-63; exec. sec. research career program NIMH, 1963-66, chief cognition and learning sect. div. extramural research program, 1966-68, dep. dir., 1968-74, dir. div. spl. mental health programs, 1974-75, acting dir. div. extramural research program, 1975-77; assoc. dir. for extramural and collaborative research program Nat. Inst. Aging, 1977-79; dep. dir. Nat. Inst. Child Health and Human Devel., Bethesda, Md., 1979-81; acting dir. Nat. Inst. Child Health and Human Devel., 1981-82, dir. Div. Rsch. Resources, 1982-88; mem. health scientist adminstr. panel CSC Bd. Examiners, 1970-76, 81-88; mem. coun. on grad. edn. Brown U. Grad. Sch., 1989-91. Contbr. articles to profl. jours. Mem. APA, Am. Psychol Soc., Psychonomic Soc., Assn. Women in Sci., AAAS, Phi Beta Kappa, Sigma Xi. Home: Morgan Bay Rd PO Box 198 Surry ME 04684-0198

PICKLE BEATTIE, KATHERINE HAMNER, real estate agent; b. Henrico County, Va., Sept. 30, 1936; d. Laurance Davis and Susan (Mooers) Hamner; widowed 1969; children: Katherine Carter Beattie, Harry Canfield Beattie IV, Margaret Spotswood Beattie; m. Timothy L. Pickle, III, Dec. 29, 1989. Attended, Va. Commonwealth U. Pres. Varina Wood Products, Inc., Gloucester-Mathews County, 1969-75; real estate agt. Nat. Assn. Bd. Realtors, Gloucester-Mathews County, Richmond, Va., 1975—; pres. Varina Wood Products, Inc., 1969-75. Pres. George F. Baker PTA, 1970; v.p. Varina Women's Club, Henrico, Va., 1969-70; sec. Mathews Women's Club, 1992-94; mem. Rep. Women's Club. Mem. DAR (Cricket Hill chpt.), Va. Lions Club. Episcopalian. Home: PO Box 317 Gwynn's Island VA 23066

PICKLES, LORNA TOSH, women's health nurse; b. Manchester, Eng., Jan. 6, 1953; d. James Paterson Flett and Hilda (Lawton) Tosh; m. Alan Pickles, Aug. 24, 1974; 1 child, Steven Lee. Cert. in nursing with honors, QARANC, Eng., 1975; cert. midwife, Sch. Midwifery, Bolton, Eng., 1976; BSN with honors, Barry U., 1991; postgrad., Miami U., 1994—. cert. health visitor Bolton Inst. Tech. Sch. nurse Bury Area Health Authority, Lancashire, Eng., 1976-77; staff nurse Good Samaritan Hosp., West Palm Beach, Fla., 1984-89; nurse mgr. Palms West Hosp., Loxahatchee, Fla., 1989-90; staff nurse St. Mary's Hosp., West Palm Beach, 1990-94; health visitor Bury and Rochdale Area Health Authority, Lancashire, 1977-84; nurse mgr. obstetrics in field. Cpl. Army, U.K., 1972-75. Mem. NAACOG (cert.), Fla. Nurses Assn., Sigma Theta Tau (Lambda Chi chpt.).

PICKOVER, BETTY ABRAVANEL, retired executive legal secretary, civic volunteer; b. N.Y.C., Apr. 20, 1920; d. Albert and Sultana (Rousso) Abravanel; m. Bernard Builder, Apr. 6, 1941 (div. 1962); children: Ronald, Stuart; m. William Pickover, Aug. 23, 1970 (dec. Nov. 1983). Student, Taft Evening Ctr., 1961-70. Sec. U.S. Treasury Dept., Washington, 1942-43; exec. legal sec. various attys., Bronx, N.Y., 1956-70; exec. legal sec. various attys., Yonkers, N.Y., 1971-83, ret., 1983. Chair Uniongram Sisterhood of Temple Emanu-El, 1975—, Honor Roll, 1975—; sr. citizen cmty. leader Yonkers Office for Aging, 1984—, Westchester County Sr. Adv. Bd., White Plains, N.Y., 1989-92; mem. Mayor's Cmty. Rels. Com. of Yonkers, 1985—, historian, 1988—. Recipient Proclamations from Mayors of Yonkers, 1985, 89, 92, awards from U.S. Ho. of Reps., 1992 (2), awards Mayors of Yonkers, 1985-94, awards from Senator and Assemblymen, N.Y. State, 1987-94, REsolution, City Coun. of Yonkers, 1993, Woman of excellence award Yonkers C. of C., 1993, others; named to Sr. Hall of Fame, Westchester County, 1992. Democrat. Jewish. Home: 200 Valentine Ln Yonkers NY 10705

PICOLOGLOU, SUSAN MARIE, geneticist, molecular biologist, technical editor; b. Mpls., Dec. 5, 1946; d. Walter A. and Enid J. (Evans) Burton; m. Basil Picologlou, Aug. 12, 1972; children: Aliki, Elizabeth. BA, U. Minn., 1967; MS, Purdue U., 1971, PhD, 1975. Geneticist, molecular biologist U. Ill., Chgo., 1979-90; sr. tech. editor Advanced Photon Source Argonne (Ill.) Nat. Lab., 1990—; tchr. biology Coll. of DuPage, Glen Ellyn, Ill., 1991-92. Contbr. articles to sci. jours. Home: 1315 Gilbert Ave Downers Grove IL 60515-4505 Office: Argonne Nat Lab APS Bldg 362 Argonne IL 60439

PIECH, MARGARET ANN, mathematics educator; b. Bridgewater, N.S., Can., Apr. 6, 1942; d. Frederick Cecil and Margaret Florence (Laschinger) Garrett; m. Kenneth Robert Piech, June 19, 1965; children: Garrett Andrew, Marjorie Ann. BA, Mt. Allison U., Sackville, N.B., Can., 1962; PhD, Cornell U., 1967. Asst. prof. SUNY, Buffalo, 1967-72, assoc. prof., 1972-78, prof. math., 1978—; cons. NSF, Washington, 1980-81, Aspen Analytics, Buffalo, 1986—; v.p. Seventy Niagara Svcs., 1990—. Contbr. articles to profl. jours. Woodrow Wilson fellow, 1962-63; grantee NSF, 1976-85, U.S. Army Rsch. Office, 1985-89. Mem. IEEE, Am. Math. Soc., Assn. Computing Machinery, Greater Yellowstone Coalition, Henry's Fork Found. Office: SUNY Diefendorf Hall Buffalo NY 14214

PIECH, MARY LOU ROHLING, medical psychotherapist, consultant; b. Elgin, Ill., Jan. 20, 1927; d. Louis Bernard and Charlotte (Wylie) Rohling; m. Raymond C. Piech, Feb. 12, 1950 (dec. Feb. 1985); 1 child, Christine Piech. BA, U. Ill., 1948, MA, 1953; postgrad., Ill. Inst. Tech., 1966-68, Union Inst., 1991-94. Cert. clin. psychologist, Ill.; diplomate Am. Bd. Med. Psychotherapy. Instr. psychology Elmhurst (Ill.) Coll., 1955-61; asst. prof. psychology North Cen. Coll., Naperville, Ill., 1961-67, Elmhurst (Ill.) Coll., 1968-81; med. psychotherapist Shealy Pain & Health Rehab. Ctr., LaCrosse, Wis., 1977-82, Shealy Inst. Holos Inst. Health, Springfield, Mo., 1982—. Author, editor: (video series) Mental Health, 1982, (audio tape series) Holistic Mental Health, 1983. Recipient award Lilly Found., Elmhurst Coll., Shealy Inst., 1977. Fellow Am. Bd. Med. Psychotherapy; mem. APA, N.Am. Soc. Adlerian Psychology, Assn. Psychol. Type (life), Phi Beta Kappa, Phi Kappa Phi, Mortar Bd. Office: Shealy Inst 1328 E Evergreen St Springfield MO 65803-6204

PIECHOWSKI, LISA DRAGO, psychotherapist; b. Long Beach, Calif., Apr. 13, 1956; d. Alfred Anthony and Winifred Elisabeth (Smith) Drago; m. William Joseph Piechowski, June 23, 1979; children: Dana Marie, Darcie Elizabeth. BA in Spl. Edn. magna cum laude, Providence Coll., 1978; MA in Counseling Psychology, U. Conn., 1981; PhD in Counseling Psychology, U. Mass., 1993. Lic. psychologist. Tchr. spl. edn. Waterford (Conn.) Pub. Schs., 1978-82, parent counselor, 1982-85; family therapist N.E. Parent and Child Soc., Schenectady, 1985-86; psychotherapist Cath. Family Svc., Saratoga Springs, N.Y., 1986-87; pvt. practice psychotherapy, Clifton Park, N.Y., 1987-89; psychol. counselor Berkshire Comm. Coll., Pittsfield, Mass., 1988-92, 93—; adj. prof. Berkshire C.C., Pittsfield, Mass., 1989, 90, 92; psychotherapist Family Ctr. of Berkshires, Berkshire Med. Ctr., Pittsfield, 1993—; staff psychologist South County Psychiatric and Psychotherapy Ctr., Gt. Barrington, Mass., 1995—; adj. prof. Antioch New Eng. Grad. Sch., Keene, N.H., 1991-92; teaching asst. U. Mass., Amherst, spring 1991; presenter in field; manuscript reviewer Families in Soc. jour., 1992. Mem. APA. Democrat. Episcopalian. Home: 71 Pill Dr Becket MA 01223-0080 Office: 20 Lewis Ave Great Barrington MA 01230

PIEL, CAROLYN FORMAN, pediatrician, educator; b. Birmingham, Ala., Oct. 18, 1918; d. James R. and Mary Elizabeth (Dortch) Forman; m. John Joseph Piel, Aug. 3, 1951; children: John Joseph, Mary Dortch, Elzabeth Forman, William Scott. BA, Agnes Scott Coll., 1940; MS, Emory U., 1943; MD, Washington U., St. Louis, 1946. Diplomate Am. Bd. Pediatrics (examiner 1973-88, pres. 1986-87); diplomate Am. Bd. Pediatric Nephrology. Intern Phila. Gen. Hosp., 1946-47; resident Phila. Children's Hosp., 1947-49; fellow Cornell U. Med. Sch., N.Y.C., 1949-51; from instr. to assoc. clin. prof. Stanford U. Sch. Medicine, San Francisco, 1951-59; from asst. prof. to prof. Sch. Medicine, U. Calif., San Francisco, 1959-89, emeritus prof., 1989—. Author, co-author research articles in field. Bd. mem. San Francisco Home Health Service, 1977-83. Emeritus mem. Soc. for Pediatric Research, Am. Pediatric Soc., Am. Soc. for Pediatric Nephrology, Am. Soc. Nephrology, Western Soc. for Pediatric Nephrology (pres. 1960). Democrat. Presbyterian. Home: 2164 Hyde St San Francisco CA 94109-1701 Office: U Calif PO Box 748 San Francisco CA 94143

PIERCE, ANDREA MARIE, biochemist, researcher; b. Worcester, Mass., June 19, 1959; d. George L. Durfee; m. William R. Pierce, Oct. 31, 1981; children: Alyssa M., Matthew R. BS in Clin. Chemistry, Providence, 1981; PhD in Biochemistry, U. Mass., Lowell, 1992. Cert. technologist in chemistry. Med. technologist Cranston (R.I.) Gen. Hosp., 1981; clin. chemistry technician Kollsman Instrument Co., Merrimack, N.H., 1981-86; teaching asst. U. Mass., Lowell, 1987-91; instr. biochemistry U. N.H., Durham, 1992; sr. scientist Instrumentation Lab., Lexington, Mass., 1992—. Adult vol. Girl Scouts Am., Hollis, N.H., 1993. Mem. Am. Soc. Hematology, Am. Assn. Clin. Chemistry. Office: Instrumentation Lab 113 Hartwell Ave Lexington MA 02173

PIERCE, CAROL JEAN, freelance writer, photographer; b. Allentown, Pa., July 7, 1946; d. Russel and Viola (Meck) Brewer; m. Wayne Thomas Pierce, June 15, 1972; children: Alan, Wendy, Russel, Benjamin. BS in Elem. Edn., Kutztown U., 1968; postgrad., Moravian Coll., 1977-81, Writers Dig Sch., Cin., 1985-87. Cert. elem. edn. tchr., Pa. Elem. sch. tchr. Souderton (Pa.) Area Sch. Dist., 1968-84; instr. Williamsport Area Community Coll., Wellsboro, Pa., 1984-85; ch. sec. Trinity United Presbyn. Ch., Tioga, Pa., 1985-88; crew leader U.S. Dept. Commerce, Wilkes-Barre, Pa., 1988-89; freelance writer various newspapers Tioga County, Pa., 1987—; computer cons. New Covenant Acad., Mansfield, Pa., 1991—. Contbr. articles to newspapers, mags., and bus. jours. Bd. dirs. ARC, Wellsboro, 1991—; sec. Tioga Grange # 1223, 1988-91; publicity chairperson Pa. State Laurel Festival, Wellsboro, 1986-91; treas. Presbyn. Women of Presbyery Northumberland; sec. First Presbyn. Women Wellsboro. Mem. NAFE, Am. Legion Aux. Home: RR 2 Box 5 Tioga PA 16946-9504

PIERCE, CAROLE JEAN, artist; b. Dallas, Sept. 7, 1950; d. Bertrum Robert and Dorothy Lillian (Meyer) Brownie; m. Lee Pierce, Mar. 13, 1970; 1 child, Brandon. BFA in Painting and Printmaking, So. Meth. U., 1972; MFA in Printmaking, Calif. Coll. Arts & Crafts, 1994. Advt. prodn. Zale Corp., Dallas, 1972; mgr. direct mail Halle Bros., Cleve., 1973-75; advt. art dir. Sanger Harris, Dallas, 1975-79; photography coord. Neiman Marcus Horchow Collection, Dallas, 1979-81; freelance art & photography coord. San Francisco, 1982-83; writer, researcher Culinary Historians Boston, 1983-85; researcher for curator N.Y. Pub. Libr., N.Y.C., 1985-87; tchr., artist Kala Inst., Berkeley, Calif., 1987—. Solo exhbns. include Jillian Coldiron/Fine Art, San Francisco, 1989, Joan Roebuck Gallery, Lafayette, Calif., 1994, Calif. Coll. Arts and Crafts, 1994; group exhbns. include Kala Inst., Berkeley, Calif., 1989, 92, Accurate Art Gallery, Sacramento, 1989, Matrix Gallery, Sacramento, 1989, Gallery House, Palo Alto, Calif., 1989, Orange County Ctr. Contemporary Art, Santa Ana, 1989, Coll. San Mateo, Calif., 1990, Wichita (Kans.) Art Assn., 1990, Pacific Art League, Palo Alto, 1990, Ford Aerospace Corp., San Jose, Calif., 1990, Artisans Gallery, Mill Valley, Calif., 1991, San Diego Art Inst., 1992, U. Portland, Oreg., 1993, Shidoni Contemporary Gallery, 1993, U. Oreg., Eugene, 1994, Long Beach (Calif.) Arts, 1994, Berkeley (Calif.) Art Ctr. Assn., 1994, Osaka (Japan) Found. Culture, 1994, Columbia (Mo.) Coll., 1995, Southwest Tex. State U., San Marcos, 1995, others; represented in permanent collections U.S. Embassy Nairobe, Kenya, Havana, Cuba, Harvard U., Sandoz Pharm., Vanguard Co., numerous pvt. collections. Vol. Shanti Project, San Francisco, 1989; docent Mus. Modern Art, San Francisco, 1988-91, art express program, 1991-92, art coord. children's program, 1988-90. Recipient Monoprint award Pacific Art League, Palo Alto, Calif., 1990; juror award Hill Country Arts Found., Austin, Tex., 1991, 1st pl. award Calif. Coll. Arts & Crafts, Oakland, 1993, Berkeley Art Ctr. Assn. 10th Ann. Nat. Juried Exhbn., 1994. Mem. Am. Inst. Wine & Food, Internat. Wine & Food Soc., L.A. Printmakers Soc. (Monoprint award 1990). Home: PO Box 1032 Ross CA 94957-1032 Office: Kala Inst 1060 Heinz Ave Berkeley CA 94710-2719

PIERCE, CATHERINE ELAINE, data processing professional; b. Richmond, Calif., Jan. 18, 1948; d. Eugene B. and Jo Beth (Mouser) Cox; m. Larry E. Pierce, May 21, 1968; children: Lisa Marie Cora Pierce, Jamie Gail Motley, Larry Edward Pierce, Jr. Student, Park Coll. Acct. Shawnee, Okla., 1970—; data/configuration mgr. Tinker AFB, Okla., 1985—. Mem. Armed Forces Communicators and Electronics Assn., Air Force Assn., Tinker Mgmt. Assn. Pentecostal. Office: HQ CSC/CMPM 4005 Hilltop Rd Tinker AFB OK 73145-2713

PIERCE, CATHERINE MAYNARD, history educator; b. York County, Va., Oct. 11, 1918; d. Edward Walker Jr. and Cassie Cooke (Sheppard) Maynard; m. Frank Marion Pierce Jr., Oct. 4, 1940 (dec. 1974); children: Frank Marion III, Bruce Maynard. BS in Sec. Edn., Longwood Coll., Farmville, Va., 1939; postgrad., Coll. William and Mary, Williamsburg, 1948, 58, 68. Tchr. York County Pub. Schs., Va., 1939-45; instr. Chesapeake (Va.) pub. schs., 1946-49, 57-74; cons. Vol. Svcs., Williamsburg, Va., 1975—. Author audio-visual hist. narratives for use in pub. schs., 1965-86. Organizer The Chapel at Kingsmill on the James, Williamsburg, 1987—, chmn. governing bd., 1987—. Mem. Pilot Club Internat. (pres. Williamsburg Club 1979-80), DAR (Williamsburg chpt. mem., regent 1980-83). Baptist. Address: Kingsmill on the James 4 Bray Wood Rd Williamsburg VA 23185-5504

PIERCE, DEBORAH MARY, educator; b. Charleston, W. Va.; d. Edward Ernest and Elizabeth Anne (Trent) P.; m. Henry M. Armetta, Sept. 1, 1967 (div. 1981); children: Rosse Matthew Armetta, Stacey Elizabeth Pierce. Student, U. Tenn., 1956-59, Broward Jr. Coll., 1968-69; BA, San Francisco State U., 1977. Cert. elem. tchr., Calif. Pub. relations assoc. San Francisco Internat. Film Festival, 1965-66; account exec. Stover & Assocs., San Francisco, 1966-67; tchr. San Francisco Archdiocese Office of Cath. Schs., 1980-87; with The Calif. Study, Inc. (formerly Tchr's. Registry), Tiburon, Calif., 1988—; pvt. practice as paralegal San Francisco, 1989—; tchr. Jefferson Sch. Dist., Daly City, Calif., 1989-91. Author: (with Frances Spatz Leighton) I Prayed Myself Slim, 1960. Pres. Mothers Alone Working, San Francisco, 1966, PTA, San Francisco, 1979, Parent Teacher Student Assn., San Francisco, 1984; apptd. Calif. State Bd. Welfare Community Rels., Com., 1964-66; active feminist movement. Named Model of the Yr. Modeling Assn. Am., 1962. Mem. People Med. Soc., Assn. for Rsch. and Enlightenment, A Course in Miracles, Commonwealth Club Calif, Angel Club San Francisco. Democrat. Mem. Unity Christ Ch. Home: 1479 48th Ave Apt 2 San Francisco CA 94122-2832

PIERCE, DONNA L., lawyer; b. Bermuda, Dec. 25, 1952; came to U.S., 1953; d. William R. and Joyce (Brewer) P.; m. Dana Austin, Jan. 16, 1976; 1 child, Dylan Pierce Austin. AS, Greenville (S.C.) Coll., 1976; BS, U. S.C., 1978, JD, 1980. Bar: S.C. 1981, U.S. Dist. Ct. (ea. dist.) Tenn. 1981, U.S. Ct. Appeals (4th, 5th, 6th, 11th cirs.) 1981, Tenn. 1982. Trial atty. Tenn. Valley Authority, Knoxville, Tenn., 1981-84; litigation ptnr. Chambliss & Bahner, Chattanooga, 1985-93, Chattanooga Human Rights and Rels. Comsn., 1993; gen. counsel U. of the South, Sewanee, Tenn., 1994; dir. S.E. Tenn. Legal Svcs., Chattanooga, 1988-92; advisor Cleve. State Coll., 1988-92. Mem. Tenn. Sup. Ct. Commn. on CLES and Specialization, 1993—. Mem. ABA, Fed. Bar Assn., S.C. Bar Assn., S.E. Tenn. Lawyers Assn. for Women (pres. 1990), Tenn. Lawyers Assn. for Women (bd. dirs. 1988-90), Tenn. Bar Assn., Chattanooga Bar Assn. (bd. govs. 1988-93, pres. 1992-93), Order of Coif. Office: U of the South 735 University Ave Sewanee TN 37383-1000

PIERCE, ELIZABETH GAY, civic worker; b. N.Y.C., Mar. 26, 1907; d. Martin and Julia (Stone) Gay; AB, Barnard Coll., 1929; m. William Curtis Pierce, June 19, 1929; children: Martin Gay, Elizabeth Gay Pierce Fuchs, Josiah. Vol. worker Boston City Hosp., 1929-30, Community Service Soc., N.Y.C., 1931-32; mem. dependent children's sect. Welfare Council, N.Y.C., 1939-40; chmn. house com. North Shore Holiday House, Huntington, L.I., 1944, pres., 1945; co-chmn. thrift shop com. Knickerbocker Hosp., N.Y.C., 1957-64; mem. exec. com. of women's com. Legal Aid Soc., N.Y.C., 1958-59; mem. Women's Aux. Knickerbocker Hosp. (exec. com. 1960-64); adv. trustee Maine Citizens for Hist. Preservation, 1983-87; trustee Jones Mus. Ceramics and Glass, 1985-89. Mem. Soc. Colonial Dames in State N.Y. (bd. mgrs., 1962-67, corr. sec. N.Y. 1965-67, pres. 1967-70), Nat. Soc. Colonial Dames Am. (pres. 1972-76, nat. pres.), Soc. for Preservation New Eng. Antiquities (Maine council, former chmn. Marrett House, exec. com.), Mayflower Soc. N.Y. (sec. 1985-88), Daus. Founders and Patriots, Nat. Grange (mem. exec. com.). Episcopalian. Club: Colony, Ch. (N.Y.C.). Home: RR 1 Box 5140 West Baldwin ME 04091-9736

PIERCE, GRETCHEN NATALIE, investment company executive; b. Eugene, Oreg., July 7, 1945; d. Nils Bernard and Jewel (Bauman) Hult; m. Howard Walter Pierce, Dec. 26, 1970; children: Eric Nils, Hailey Lynn, . BA, U. Oreg., 1966. Rsch. analyst Boise (Idaho) Cascade Corp., 1966-68, mgr. divs., 1968-84, dir. info. adminstrn., 1984-86; pres., gen. mgr. Hult & Assocs., Eugene, 1986—; bd. dirs. Siuslaw Valley Bank, Florence, Oreg. Trustee U. Oreg., Sacred Heart Hosp., 1987-91; bd. dirs. City Club of Eugene, 1990-91; pres. Eugene Area C. of C., 1992; mem. Oreg. Econ. Devel. Commn., 1993—. Mem. Oreg. Women's Forum, U. Oreg. Alumni (Disting. Alumni award 1984). Republican. Lutheran. Lodge: Rotary. Office: Hult & Assocs 401 E 10th Ave Ste 500 Eugene OR 97401-3367

PIERCE, HILDA (HILDA HERTA HARMEL), painter; b. Vienna, Austria; came to U.S., 1940; 1 child, Diana Rubin Daly. Student, Art Inst. of Chgo.; studied with Oskar Kokoschka, Salzburg, Austria. Art tchr. Highland Park (Ill.) Art Ctr., Sandburg Village Art Workshop, Chgo., Old Town Art Center, Chgo.; owner, operator Hilda Pierce Art Gallery, Laguna Beach, Calif., 1981-85; guest lectr. major art mus. and Art Tours in France, Switzerland, Austria, Italy; guest lectr. Russian river cruise and major art mus. St. Petersburg and Moscow, 1994. One-woman shows include Fairweather Hardin Gallery, Chgo., Sherman Art Gallery, Chgo., Marshall Field Gallery , Chgo.; exhibited in group shows at Old Orchard Art Festival, Skokie, Ill., Union League Club (awards), North Shore Art League (awards), ARS Gallery of Art Inst. of Chgo.; represented in numerous private and corporate collections; commissioned for all art work including monoprints, oils, and murals for Carnival Cruise Lines megaliner M.S. Fantasy, 1990, 17 murals for megaliner M.S. Imagination, 1995, 49 paintings for megaliner M.S. Imagination, 1995; contbr. articles to Chgo. Tribune Mag., American Artist Mag., Southwest Art Mag., SRA publs., others. Recipient Outstanding Achievement award in Field of Art for Citizen Foreign Birth Chgo. Immigrant's Svc. League. Mem. Arts Club of Chgo. Studio: PO Box 7390 Laguna Niguel CA 92607-7390

PIERCE, LISA MARGARET, product and market development manager; b. Nyack, N.Y., June 2, 1957; d. William Twining and Elizabeth (West) P. BA with honors, Gordon Coll., Wenham, Mass., 1978; MBA, Atkinson Sch., Salem, Oreg., 1982. Mgr. 6th Congl. Dist. Carter/Mondale, Manchester, Mass., 1976; investigator Dept. Social Svcs., Nyack, 1977-78; paralegal Beverly, Mass., 1978-79; mgr. Reagan Presdl. Primary, Rockland County, N.Y., 1980; performance analyst Dept. Social Svcs., Pomona, N.Y., 1982; market analyst Momentum Techs., Parsippany, N.J., 1983; cons. Booz Allen & Hamilton, Florham Park, N.J., 1984, Deloitte-Touche, Morristown, N.J., 1985; market researcher, forecaster AT&T, Bedminster, N.J., 1985-87, asst. pvt. line product mgr., 1987-89, Integrated Svcs. Digital Network product mgr., 1989-93; cons., mem. faculty and dept. chair Telecomms. Rsch. Assocs., St. Marys, Kans., 1993—; panelist, contbr. TeleCommunications Assn., San Diego, 1992, Internat. Comm. Assn., Atlanta, Ea. Comm. Forum, N.Y., Nat. Engrng Consortium, Chgo; cons. Sidereal, Portland, Oreg., 1982. Tutor Literacy Vols. Am., Somerville, N.J., 1989-91; mem. Jr. League Am., Morristown, N.J., 1987-90; mem. Internat. Oceanographic Found., Washington. Grantee in field. Mem. Am. Mgmt. Assn. (profl.), Nat. Audubon Soc. Republican.

PIERCE, MARIANNE LOUISE, technology and healthcare products company executive, consultant; b. Atchison, Kans., Apr. 22, 1949; d. James Arthur and Marian Louise (Patton) P.; m. Woodrow Theodore Lewis Jr., June 23, 1973 (div. June 1981). Student, Barnard Coll.; AB, Columbia U., 1970, MBA, 1975. Dep. dir. N.Y. Model Cities, N.Y.C., 1971-73; assoc. corp. fin. Citibank Mcht. Banking, N.Y.C., 1975-77; sr. assoc. N.Y.C., San Francisco, N.Y.C., 1977-82; dep. biotech. dir. Ciba Geigy A.G., Basel, Switzerland, 1982-85; pres., chmn. bd. dirs. Life Scis. Assocs., Ltd., N.Y.C.; Conn.; Basel; Adelaide, Australia, 1985—; mng. ptnr. Patton, Pierce, Brandon & Co., 1986—; pres., CEO, chmn. XXygen, Inc., New Haven, 1991—. Author: (pamphlet) Developing Biotechnology Strategies for Multinational Corporations, 1985, Managing Successful Strategic Alliances, 1990. Mem. Brit. Biotech. Assn., Comml. Devel. Assn., Practicing Law Inst.

PIERCE, PONCHITTA ANNE, television host, producer, journalist; b. Chgo., Aug. 5, 1942; d. Alfred Leonard and Nora (Vincent) P. Student, Cambridge (Eng.) U., summer 1962; B.A. cum laude, U. So. Calif., 1964. Asst. editor Ebony mag., 1964-65, assoc. editor, 1965-67; editor Ebony mag. (N.Y.C. office), 1967-68; chief N.Y.C. editorial bur. Johnson Pub. Co., 1967-68; spl. corr. CBS news div., N.Y.C., 1968-71; contbg. editor McCall's mag., 1971-77; editorial cons. Philps Stokes Fund, 1971-78; staff writer Reader's Digest, 1976-77, roving editor, 1977-80; co-producer, host Today in New York Sta. WNBC-TV, N.Y.C., 1982-87; freelance writer, TV broadcaster; bd. govs. Overseas Press Club. WNBC-TV co-host: Sunday, 1973-77, The Prime of Your Life, 1976-80; author: Status of American Women Journalists on Magazines, 1968, History of the Phelps Stokes Fund 1911-1972; contbg. editor: Parade mag., 1993. Del. to WHO Conf., Geneva, 1973; bd. dirs. Casita Maria, Inc., Dance Theatre of Harlem, Voice Found., Third St. Music Sch. Settlement, Big Sisters, Inc., Unward, Inc., Inner-City Scholarship Fund, Sta. WNET-TV; mem. women's bd. Madison Sq. Boys and Girls Club; mem. Columbia U. Health Scis. Adv. Coun. Recipient Penney-Mo. mag. award excellence women's journalism, 1967; John Russwurm award N.Y.C. Urban League, 1968; AMITA Nat. Achievement award in communications, 1974. Mem. NATAS, Calif. Scholarship Fedn. (life), Nat. Honor Soc., Women in Communications (Woman Behind the News award 1969, Nat. Headliner award 1970), Fgn. Policy Assn. (bd. govs., bd. dirs.), Coun. on Fgn. Rels., Mortar Bd., Alumnae. Clubs: Econs. of N.Y., Lotos.

PIERCE, RHONDA YVETTE, criminologist; b. Tampa, Fla., Dec. 4, 1959; d. Howard Jr. and Olivia (Powell) P. AA in Criminal Justice, Hillsboro C.C., Tampa, 1979; BS in Criminology, Fla. State U., Tallahassee, 1981. Cert. mgr. of housing. With Tampa Housing Authority, 1982—, mgmt. coord., 1988-90, lease enforcement officer, exec. asst., 1991, dir. ops., 1992—. Area youth dir. 11th Episcopal dist. A.M.E. Ch., Tampa, 1991-93; local youth dir. Mt. Olive A.M.E. Ch., Tampa, 1989-91. Recipient Dedicated Christian Svc. award Mt. Olive A.M.E. Ch., 1983. Mem. Nat. Assn. Housing and Redevel. Ofcls. Methodist. Office: Tampa Housing Authority 1514 Union St Tampa FL 33607

PIERCE, SUSAN HOOD, accountant; b. Fort Dodge, Iowa, June 2, 1951; d. Melvin Peter and Illiah Mary (Olson) Hood; m. Dean Clair Pierce, July 26, 1975; children: Aaron Michael, Scott Christopher, Andrew James, Matthew John. BA, U. Iowa, 1972, MA, 1977; BA, Briar Cliff Coll., 1981. CPA, Iowa. Dir. tng. U. Iowa Alcoholism Ctr., Iowa City, 1974-76; asst. dir. Woodbury County Employment Tng. Ctr., Sioux City, Iowa, 1978-79;

bus. mgr. Pierce Moving/Storage, Sioux City, 1980-88; exec. dir. Tax Rsch. Conf., Sioux City, 1988-94; mgmt. cons. Pierce & Assocs., Sioux City, 1994—; instr. Western Iowa Tech. C.C., Sioux City, 1981-82, Briar Cliff Coll., Sioux City, 1986-88. Active United Way, LWV, Coun. on Sexual Assault and Domestic Violence, Jr. League Sioux City, Compassionate Friends, Leadership Sioux City, C. of C. Govtl. Affairs Com., Siouxland Soccer Found., Blessed Sacrament Parish Coun. Recipient Woman of Excellence award, 1992. Mem. Assn. Jr. Leagues Internat. (resolutions com.). Roman Catholic. Office: Pierce & Assocs 117 Pierce St # 108 Sioux City IA 51101

PIERCE, SUSAN RESNECK, academic administrator, English educator; b. Janesville, Wis., Feb. 6, 1943; d. Elliott Jack and Dory (Block) Resneck; m. Kenneth H. Pierce; 1 child, Alexandra. AB, Wellesley Coll., 1965; MA, U. Chgo., 1966; PhD, U. Wis., 1972. Lectr. U. Wis., Rock County, 1970-71; from asst. prof. to prof. English Ithaca (N.Y.) Coll., 1973-83, chmn. dept., 1976-79, 81-82; dean Henry Kendall Coll. Arts and Scis., prof. English U. Tulsa, 1984-90; v.p. acad. affairs, prof. English Lewis and Clark Coll., Portland, Oreg., 1990-92; pres. U. of Puget Sound, Tacoma, 1992—; vis. assoc. prof. Princeton (N.J.) U., 1979; program officer div. ednl. programs NEH, 1982-83, asst. dir., 1983-84; bd. dirs. Janet Elson Scholarship Fund, 1984-1990, Tulsa Edn. Fund, Phillips Petroleum Scholarship Fund, 1985-90, Okla. Math. & Sci. High Sch., 1984-90, Hillcrest Med. Ctr., 1988-90, Portland Opera, 1990-92, St. Joseph's Hosp., 1992—, Seattle Symphony, 1993—; cons. U. Oreg., 1985, Drury Coll., Springfield, Mo., 1986; mem. Middle States and N. Cen. Accreditation Bds.; mem. adv. com. Fed. Women's Program, NEH, 1982-83; participant Summit Meeting on Higher Edn., Dept. Edn., Washington, 1985; speaker, participant numerous ednl. meetings, sems., commencements; chair Frederick Ness Book Award Com. Assn. Am. Colls., 1986; mem. award selection com. Dana Found., 1986, 87; mem. Acad. Affairs Council, Univ. Senate, dir. tchr. edn., chmn. adv. group for tchr. preparation, ex-officio mem. all Coll. Arts and Scis. coms. and Faculty Council on Internat. Studies, all U. Tulsa; bd. dirs. Am. Conf. Acad. Deans; bd. trustees Hillcrest Med. Ctr. Author: The Moral of the Story, 1982, also numerous essays, jour. articles, book sects., book revs.; co-editor: Approaches to Teaching "Invisible Man"; reader profl. jours. Bd. dirs. Arts and Humanities Coun., Tulsa, 1984-90; trustee Hillcrest Hosp., Tulsa, 1986-90; mem. cultural series com., community rels. com. Jewish Fedn., Tulsa, 1986-90; bd. dirs. Tulsa chpt. NCCJ, 1986-90. Recipient Best Essay award Arix. Quar., 1979, Excellence in Teaching award N.Y. State Edn. Council, 1982, Superior Group Service award NEH, 1984, other teaching awards; Dana scholar, Ithaca Coll., 1980-81; Dana Research fellow, Ithaca Coll., 82-83; grantee Inst. for Ednl. Affairs, 1980, Ford Found., 1987, NEH, 1989. Mem. MLA (adv. com. on job market 1973-74), South Ctrl. MLA, Soc. for Values in Higher Edn., Assn. Am. Colls. (bd. dirs.), Am. Conf. Acad. Deans (bd. dirs. 1988-91), Phi Beta Kappa, Phi Kappa Phi, Phi Gamma Kappa. Office: U of Puget Sound 1500 N Warner St Tacoma WA 98416-0001*

PIERCY, JOAN MARY, management consultant; b. Eau Claire, Wis., Nov. 23, 1944; d. Gerald S. and Alice (Erpenback) P. BA in Bus. Adminstrn., U. Wis., 1967. Underwriter Hartford (Conn.) Ins. Group, 1967-74, cons., 1974-76; asst. sec. —, 1976-79, div. dir., corp. sec., 1979-83, v.p. bus. mgmt. group, 1983-85; v.p. Hartford Integrated Techs. Inc., 1985-86; mgr. ins. cons. Deloitte & Touche, Hartford, 1986-94; sr. v.p. customer group Physicians Mut. Ins., Omaha, 1994—; vis. lectr., Advanced Tech. Systems Seminars Carnegie Mellon U., 1990; speaker, Koreau Life Ins. exec. program Coll. Ins., N.Y., 1990; sr. managing insurauer cons., Deloitte & Touche. Vice chmn. bd. dirs. Leadership Greater Hartford, 1990; co-chmn. Women's Exec. Conf., Hartford, 1988; pres. Leadership Greater Hartford Alumni Assn., 1984-85. Recipient Women in Leadership recognition award YWCA, Hartford, 1980. Mem. Improvement Inst., Univ. Club. Roman Catholic. Office: Deloitte Haskins & Sells Physicians Mutual Ins Cos 2600 Dodge St Omaha NE 68131

PIERCY, MARGE, poet, novelist, essayist; b. Detroit, Mar. 31, 1936; d. Robert Douglas and Bert Bernice (Bunnin) P.; m. Ira Wood, 1982. AB, U. Mich., 1957; MA, Northwestern U., 1958. Instr. Gary extension Ind. U., 1960-62; poet-in-residence U. Kans., 1971; disting. vis. lectr. Thomas Jefferson Coll., Grand Valley State Colls., fall 1975, 76, 78, 80; vis. faculty Women's Writers Conf., Cazenovia (N.Y.) Coll.; Elliston poetry fellow U. Cin., 1986; DeRoy Disting. vis. prof. U. Mich., 1992. Author: Breaking Camp, 1968, Hard Loving, 1969, Going Down Fast, 1969, Dance the Eagle to Sleep, 1970, Small Changes, 1973, To Be of Use, 1973, Living in the Open, 1976, Woman on the Edge of Time, 1976, The High Cost of Living, 1978, Vida, 1980, The Moon is Always Female, 1980, Braided Lives, 1982, Circles on the Water, 1982, Stone, Paper, Knife, 1983, My Mother's Body, 1985, Gone to Soldiers, 1988, Available Light, 1988 (May Sarton award 1991), Summer People, 1989, He, She and It, 1991, Body of Glass, 1991 (Arthur C. Clarke award 1993), Mars and Her Children, 1992, The Longings of Women, 1994. Cons. N.Y. State Coun. on Arts, 1971, Mass. Found. for Humanities and Coun. on Arts, 1974; mem. Writer Bd., 1985-86; bd. dirs. Transition House, Mass. Found. Humanities and Pub. Policy, 1978-85, Am. Ha-Yam, 1988—; gov.'s appointee to Mass. Cultural Coun., 1990-91, Mass. Coun. on Arts and Humanities, 1986-89; artistic adv. bd. ALEPH Alliance for Jewish Renewal, Am. Poetry Ctr., 1988—; lit. adv. panel poetry NEA, 1989. Recipient Borenstone Mountain Poetry award, 1968, 74, Lit. award Gov. Mass. Commn. on Status of Women, 1974, Nat. Endowment of Arts award, 1978, Carolyn Kizer Poetry prize, 1986, 90, Shaeffer-Eaton-PEN New Eng. award, 1989, Golden Rose Poetry prize, 1990, Brit ha-Dorot award The Shalom Ctr., 1992. Mem. PEN, NOW, Authors Guild, Authors League, Writers Union, Am. Poetry Soc., Nat. Audubon Soc., Mass. Audubon Soc., New Eng. Poetry Club. Address: PO Box 1473 Wellfleet MA 02667

PIERGIES, BARBARA ALICE, computer scientist; b. Cleve., June 7, 1958; d. Robert William and Mildred Eileene (Fowler) Homan; m. James Douglas Piergies, Jan. 9, 1988; children: Robert James, Mary Catherine. BA, Cleve. State U., 1983, M.Computer and Info. Sci., 1985. Instr. Cleve. State U., 1984-85, Lorain County Community Coll., Elyria, Ohio, 1984; cons. Booz-Allen & Hamilton, Dayton, Ohio, 1985-88; sr. computer scientist Sci. Applications Internat. Corp., Dayton, Ohio, 1988—, instr., 1988-91; configuration control expert Suppressor Simulation System. Co-author computer program: User Friendly Interface, 1992, Information Analysis System, 1988. Asst. Germantown (Ohio) Area Concerned Citizens Assn., 1991; team walk leader March of Dimes, Dayton, 1988-91. Mem. Am. Def. Preparedness Assn., Internat. Test and Evaluation Assn., Phi Eta Sigma, Beta Gamma Sigma. Lutheran. Home: 12701 Air Hill Rd Brookville OH 45309 Office: Sci Applications Internat 101 Woodman Dr #103 Dayton OH 45431

PIERIK, MARILYN ANNE, librarian; b. Bellingham, Wash., Nov. 12, 1939; d. Estell Leslie and Anna Margarethe (Onigkeit) Bowers; m. Robert Vincent Pierik, July 25, 1964; children: David Vincent, Donald Lesley. AA, Chaffey Jr. Coll., Ontario, Calif., 1959; BA, Upland (Calif.) Coll., 1962; cert. in teaching, Claremont (Calif.) Coll., 1963; MSLS, U. So. Calif., L.A., 1973. Tchr. elem. Christ Episcopal Day Sch., Ontario, 1959-60; tchr. Bonita High Sch., La Verne, Calif., 1962-63; tchr., libr. Kettle Valley Sch. Dist. 14, Greenwood, Can., 1963-64; libr. asst. Monrovia (Calif.) Pub. Libr., 1964-67; with Mt. Hood C.C., Gresham, Oreg., 1972—, reference libr., 1983—, chair faculty scholarship com., 1987—; campus archivist Mt. Hood C.C., Gresham, 1994—; mem. site selection com. Multnomah County (Oreg.) Libr., New Gresham br., 1987, adv. com. Multnomah County Libr., Portland, Oreg., 1988-89; bd. dirs. Oreg. Episcopal Conf. of Deaf, 1985-92. Bd. dirs. East County Arts Alliance, Gresham, 1987-91; vestry person, jr. warden St. Luke's Episc. Ch., 1989-92; founding pres. Mt. Hood Pops, 1983-88, orch. mgr., 1983-91, 93—, bd. dirs., 1983-88, 91—. Recipient Jeanette Parkhill Meml. award Chaffey Jr. Coll., 1959, Svc. award St. Luke's Episcopal Ch., 1983, 87, Edn. Svc. award Soroptimists, 1989. Mem. AAUW, NEA, Oreg. Edn. Assn., Oreg. Libr. Assn., ALA, Gresham Hist. Soc. Office: Mt Hood Community Coll Libr 26000 SE Stark St Gresham OR 97030-3300

PIERPOINT, KAREN ANN, marriage-family-child therapist; b. Puyallup, Wash., Sept. 1, 1944; d. Peyton Randolph Winn and Jessie Mae (Kenoyer) Kalmen; m. Randall Dean Pierpoint, Mar. 19, 1966; children: Janet, Wendy, Elizabeth, Nathan. BA, U. Oreg., 1966; MS in Counseling, San Diego State U., 1988. Lic. marriage, family and child counseling, Calif. Elem. tchr. Lane County Dist. 4, Eugene, Oreg., 1966-67, Umatilla County Dist. 19-R, Weston, Oreg., 1967-70; internat. student ministry staff mem. Campus Crusade for Christ, Internat., San Bernardino, Calif., 1970-75; dir. Christian edn. Graeagle (Calif.) Community Ch., 1975-83; dir. women's ministries Pine Valley (Calif.) Community Ch., 1983-87; lectr. counselor edn. dept. San Diego State U., 1988-89; mental health cons. San Diego City Schs., 1988-89; staff therapist Heartland Bibl. Counseling, El Cajon, Calif., 1987-90, Shepperson Psychol. Assocs., Fullerton, Calif., 1990-91; pvt. practice family therapist Fullerton, 1992—; ednl. cons. New Life Acad. Home Edn., San Diego, 1984-90; allied profl. Coastal Communities Hosp., Costa Mesa, 1991; allied health profl. Yorba Hills Hosp., Yorba Linda, Calif., 1991, Calif. Psychiat. Ctr., Santa Ana, 1992—. Columnist Free Indeed Mag., 1976-78. 4-H club leader Mohawk Valley 4-H Club, Plumas County, Calif., 1976-83, Mt. Empire 4-H Club, San Diego County, Calif., 1984-87; 4-H club advisor Mohawk Valley 4-H Club, Plumas County, 1982-83. Named for 4-H Ten Yrs. of Leadership, Mt. Empire 4-H Club, 1986. Mem. Calif. Assn. Marriage and Family Therapists (clin.), Am. Assn. Marriage and Family Therapy (clin.), Christian Assn. for Psychol. Studies (clin.), Internat. Platform Assn., Nat. Parenting Instrs. Assn., Phi Kappa Phi. Republican. Office: 680 Langsdorf Ste 217 Fullerton CA 92631

PIERRI, MARY KATHRYN MADELINE, cardiologist, critical care physician, educator; b. N.Y.C., Aug. 12, 1948; d. Charles Daniel and Margaret Loyola (Pesce) P. BA, Manhattanville Coll., 1969; MD, Med. Coll. Pa., 1974. Med. resident Med. Coll. Pa., Phila., 1974-77; fellow in cardiology N.Y. Hosp., N.Y.C., 1977-79; asst. physician Meml. Hosp., N.Y.C., 1980-89, assoc. physician, 1989—, chief cardiology svc., 1991—; assoc. prof. medicine Cornell Med. Coll., N.Y.C., 1989—. Fellow Am. Coll. Cardiology, N.Y. Cardiological Soc.; mem. ACP, Soc. Critical Care Medicine, Alpha Omega Alpha. Office: Meml Hosp Sloan Kettering Cancer Ctr 1275 York Ave New York NY 10021

PIERRO, GRACE EDNA, mechanical engineer; b. New Brunswick, N.J., Sept. 2, 1960; d. Joseph Laurence Jr. and Elissa Anne (Lucadamo) Kish; m. Gerald Pierro, June 30, 1990; 1 child, Alexis. BSME, N.J. Inst. Tech., 1986. Drafter, designer Brown, Boveri Co., Inc. (BBC), North Brunswick, N.J., 1984-86; prodn. engr. Singer-Kearfott Divsn., Little Falls, N.J., 1986-88; sr. prodn. engr. White Tool Co., Kenilworth, N.J., 1988-89; from application engr. to mgr. prodns. Miniflow Sys., Inc., Watertown, Mass., 1991-94; process engr. Shawmut Mills, West Bridgewater, Mass., 1994—. Mem. ASME. Roman Catholic. Home: PO Box 825 Onset MA 02558-0825

PIERSON, CAROL ANNE, broadcast executive; b. Santa Monica, Calif., Jan. 10, 1945; d. David Waltz and Florence Edith (Hoeg) P.; life ptnr. Janice Lynne Thyer. BA, Antioch Coll., 1975. Pub. affairs dir. Sta. WYSO, Yellow Springs, Ohio, 1973-75, asst. mgr., 1975-76; asst. radio mgr. Sta. WGBH, Boston, 1976-84; program dir. Sta. KQED, San Francisco, 1985-91, dir. radio prodns., 1991—; pres. Media Works, Somerville, Mass., 1976-91. Musician: (rec.) Solid Ground, 1983. Recipient GLAAD media award, San Francisco, 1991. Mem. Western Pub. Radio (sec.), Women's Philharmonic (treas.), Nat. Lesbian and Gay Journalists Assn. (treas.). Office: Sta KQED-FM 2601 Mariposa St San Francisco CA 94110-1400

PIERSON, HELEN HALE, educator; b. Lee County, Va., Aug. 5, 1941; d. James William and Genevieve (Dalrymple) Hale; widowed; children: Christine H., Michael B. BA, Westminster Coll., 1963; MEd, Indiana U. Pa., 1968; cert.community coll. tchr, Glendale Community Coll., 1983. Cert. tchr., Pa. Tchr. Sharon (Pa.) City Schs., 1963-66, York (Pa.) City Schs., 1966-67, Prince George's County Schs., Upper Marlboro, Md., 1967-81; office mgr. Creative Realty, Inc., Phoenix, 1983-85; tchr. Rio Salado Coll., Phoenix, 1983—, N.Am. Coll., Phoenix, 1985-91; dir. edn. N.Am. Coll., 1989—; tchr. Rio Salado Coll., 1990, speaker, dept. transp., 1989; tchr. Glendale Community Coll., 1990—; tchr. Ariz. Dept. Youth Treatment and Rehab., 1991, Ariz. Corrections Edn. Program, 1991-94; edn. dir. Columbia Coll., 1994—. Recipient Outstanding Tchr. award Rio Salado Community Coll., 1990, 92, Most Outstanding Tchr. award Ariz. Pvt. Sch. Assn., 1990. Mem. NCTE, Nat. Bus. Edn. Assn., Indiana U. Pa. Alumni Assn., Chi Omega Alumni Assn. Republican. Home: 2716 W Michelle Dr Phoenix AZ 85023-1727

PIERSON-CHARLTON, CANDACE SUE, public relations consultant; b. Corvallis, Oreg., Dec. 12, 1950. BS in Liberal Studies-Journalism, Oreg. State U., 1973; postgrad., U. Nebr., 1986-88. Traveling cons. Alpha Omicron Pi Sorority, Inc., Nashville, 1974-75; reporter, copyeditor Anchorage (Alaska) Times, 1975-76; pub. rels. specialist Providence Hosp., Anchorage, 1977-83; dir. cmty. rels. Berkshire Med. Ctr., Pittsfield, Mass., 1983-85; pub. rels. dir. Alaska Pacific U., Anchorage, 1985; dir. Nebr. Health Network, Nebr. State Dept. Health, Lincoln, 1989-90; pub. info. officer N.D. Mus. of Art, Grand Forks, 1991-92; cons. Pierson-Charlton Pub. Rels., Grand Forks, 1991—; presenter in field. Editor The Prince's Trust, London, 1986; airwatch reporter KHAR Radio, Anchorage, 1978-81; host producer KSKA Pub. Radio, Anchorage, 1980; contbr. articles to profl. publs. Active Pine To Prairie coun. Girl Scouts U.S.A., 1994—; bd. dirs. Greater Grand Forks Symphony, 1994—, N.D. Ballet Co., 1994—, United Way, 1993—, Friends of N.D. Mus. of Art, 1991-94; chmn. cmty. adv. bd. KFJM Pub. Radio, 1992—; mem. devel. coun. Coll. Liberal Arts, Oreg. State U.; vol. Lied Ctr. for Performing Arts, Lincoln, 1989-90, Bryan Meml. Hosp., Lincoln, 1987-91; mem. film com. Nebr. Commn. on Status of Women, Lincoln, 1990-91; mem. budget reduction com. U. Nebr., Lincoln, 1987. Recipient 1st Pl. Best Cmty. Rels. Program award Alaska Press Club, 1979, 80, 81, 2d Pl. Cmty. Rels. award Alaska Press Club, 1982, 2d Pl. Brochure award Alaska Press Club, 1982, 2d Pl. Ann. Report award Alaska Press Club, 1982; named Mrs. Grand Forks for 1995 Mrs. N.D. Pageant. Mem. PEO, Pub. Rels. Soc. Am. (bd. dirs. Alaska 1982, sec.-treas. 1980-81, 2d Place Cmty. Rels. program Anchorage chpt. 1982), Alpha Omicron Pi (Outstanding Alumna award 1989, Cert. of Honor 1988, chpt. advisor to Zeta chpt. 1990-91, scholarship advisor 1987-89, alumnae programming chmn., 1989-90, pub. rels. com. 1988-89, pres. alumnae chpt. 1988-89). Office: Pierson-Charlton Pub Rels 908 25th Ave S Grand Forks ND 58201

PIERSON-STEIN, MARJORIE MAXINE GORDON, former educator; b. Boston, Feb. 22, 1925; d. David A. and Fannie (Klevansky) Gordon; m. Melvin Pierson, Nov. 10, 1946 (dec. Jan. 1981); children: Frederick, Eric, Jon; m. Daniel Stein, Dec. 4, 1982. AB in Edn., UCLA, 1945. Dir. The Mel Piersons Rec. Club, L.A., Malibu, Calif., 1953-70; adminstr. Property Mgmt. & Investments, San Diego, Malibu, Mexico, Hawaii, 1970—. Clk., judge precinct voting, Studio City, 1980-91, 94—; bd. dirs. Big Bros. L.A.; v.p. membership Valley Cmty. Philharm. Assn., 1994-95. Mem. AAUW, Valley U. Women (v.p. 1994-95, pres. 1992-94), UCLA Women's Sports (bd. dirs.), Bruin Boosters Women's Sports, Jewish Big Bros., Jewish Fedn. Coun. Democrat.

PIETRUS, CAROL LYNN, city official, corporation executive; b. Chgo., Sept. 15, 1948; d. Alfred E. and Nellie V. (Komperda) Cregier; m. Walter Nmn, May 4, 1968; 1 child, Tracey Aileen. High sch. grad., Chgo. Adminstrv. asst. Spector Freight System, Inc., Bensenville, Ill., 1969-80; pres.'s asst. Kidco, Inc., Bensenville, Ill., 1980-82, Lauer Sbarbaro Assocs., Chgo., 1982-83, Cas Co., Lisle, Ill., 1984; pres. The Office Extension, Inc., Chgo., 1985-89, Originals Only, Inc., Ill., 1990-94, Money Mailer Greater Woodfield, Willowbrook, Ill., 1990—, The Mktg. Coaches, Wheaton, Ill., 1995—; town planner Town of Wheaton, Ill., 1994—; speaker on the how-to's of direct mail mktg. and networking for cos., chambers and convs. Author: (office info. series) "If You Asked Me About..."; co-author of 8 cassette series: Bullseye Marketing. Mem. North Suburban Assn. Commerce and Industry (bd. dirs., networkers, mem. mktg. com.), Am. Assn. Franchisers and Dealers, Hoffman Estates C. of C., Profl. Spkrs. of Ill., Nat. Spkrs. Assn. Home: 26w471 Grand Ave Wheaton IL 60187-2963 Office: Office Town Planner 26W471 Grand Ave Wheaton IL 60187-2963

PIETRZAK, SHARON LEE, psychotherapist; b. Blue Island, Ill., July 22, 1945; d. William Valentine and Elaine Alma (Krueger) Kunkel; m. Michael George Pietrzak, May 7, 1966 (div. Mar. 1989); children: Bryan Michael, Mark William. MHA, Prairie State Coll., 1979; MA in Counseling and Psychology, Governor's State U., 1987. Contractual individual mental health counselor, group facilitator Markham (Ill.) Rehab. Workshop, 1980-81; contractual pre-therapist Chgo. Heights (Ill.) Terrace Nursing Home, 1982-85; mental health worker, registry Ingalls Meml. Hosp., Harvey, Ill., 1985-86; from ind. rater to pre-therapy dir. U. Ill., Chgo., 1986-90; contractual mental health counselor Joyce Rheinheimer, PhD & Assocs., Tinley Park, Ill., 1990—; pvt. practice Chgo., Mawteno, Ill., 1986; bd. govs. psychology Gov.'s State U., 1985; contractual pre-therapist Lake Shore Hosp., Chgo., 1981, Deerbrook Nursing Ctr., Joliet, Ill., 1984-85; contractual group facilitator Ill. Dept. Mental Health, Elizabeth Ludeman Ctr., Park Forest, Ill., 1981-86, Chgo. gay population, 1985-86, Southwest Community Svc., Markham, 1985-89; instr. Prairie State Coll., Chgo. Heights, 1985-87; mem. Bridgeport Med. Ctr., Chgo., Printers Square Med. Ctr., Chgo., Bourbonnais (Ill.) Med. Ctr., Peotone (Ill.) Med. Ctr., 1986-91; therapist Glenwood (Ill.) Med. Ctr., Chgo. and Olympia Fields Osteopathic Hosp. Outpatient Psychiatry Clinics, 1986—. Recipient Ill. State Gov.'s Vol. Recognition award, 1979. Mem. NOW, AACD, The Chgo. Soc., Am. Mental Health Counselors Assn., Pub. Citizens Assn., Phi Theta Kappa. Lutheran. Office: 55 E Washington St Ste 621 Chicago IL 60602-2106

PIGNATELLI, DEBORA BECKER, state legislator; b. Weehawken, N.J., Oct. 25, 1947; d. Edward and Frances (Fishman) Becker; m. Michael Albert Pignatelli, Aug. 22, 1971; children: Adam Becker, Benjamin Becker. AA, Vt. Coll., 1967; BA, U. Denver, 1969. Exec. dir. Girl's Club Greater Nashua, N.H., 1975-77; dir. tenant svcs. Nashua Housing Authority, 1979-80; vocat. counselor Comprehensive Rehab. Assocs., Bedford, N.H., 1982-85; specialist job placement Crawford & Co., Bedford, 1985-87; mem. appropriations com. N.H. Ho. of Reps., Concord, 1986-91, asst. minority leader, 1989-92; mem. N.H. State Senate, 1992—; Senate Dem. Whip; mem. appropriations, environ., econ. devel. and pub. affairs com.; del. Am. Coun. Young Polit. Leaders, Germany, 1987. Mem. Nashua Peace Ctr., 1980—; asst. coach Little League Baseball, Nashua, 1987-90; mem. steering com. Gephardt for Pres. Campaign, N.H., 1987-88; del. Dem. Nat. Conv., 1988. Mem. N.H. Children's Lobby, Women's Lobby. Jewish. Home: 22 Appletree Grn Nashua NH 03062-2252 Office: NH State Senate State House Rm 115 Concord NH 03301

PIGOTT, KAREN GRAY, community health nurse, geriatrics nurse; b. Utica, N.Y., May 15, 1956; d. Charles Philip and Pauline (Nelson) Gray; m. James H. Pigott, Apr. 30, 1977; children: William Charles, Christopher McCabe. Diploma, Albany Med. Ctr. Sch. Nursing, 1978; diploma nurse practitioner, SUNY, Syracuse, 1982. Cert. adult nurse practitioner. Staff nurse Albany (N.Y.) Med. Ctr., 1978-79, St. Elizabeth's Hosp., Utica, 1979-80; staff nurse RN Community Meml. Hosp., Hamilton, N.Y., 1980-81; nurse practitioner pvt. office, Waterville, N.Y., 1982-87, VA Med. Ctr., Gainesville, Fla., 1987-90; nurse practitioner pvt. office Balt., 1990—; cons. in field; preceptor for grad. students U. Fla., 1988-90, U. South Fla., 1989-90, U. Md. Vol. health care provider Salvation Army Homeless Clinic, Gainesville, 1989-90, Spl. Olympics Events, Gainesville, 1990. Mem. ANA, Fla. Nurses Assn. (Expert in Clin. Practice award 1990). Presbyterian. Home: 115 Wakely Terr Bel Air MD 21014 Office: 301 St Paul Pl Baltimore MD 21202-2102

PIGOTT, MELISSA ANN, social psychologist; b. Ft. Myers, Fla., Jan. 28, 1958; d. Park Trammell and Leola Ann (Wright) P.; m. David H. Fauss, Jan. 1, 1988. BA in Psychology, Fla. Internat. U., Miami, 1979; MS in Social Psychology, Fla. State U., 1982, PhD in Social Psychology, 1984. Rsch. asst. Fla. Internat. U., 1978-79, Fla. State U., Tallahassee, 1980-84; dir. mktg. rsch. Bapt. Med. Ctr., Jacksonville, Fla., 1984-89; rsch. assoc. Litigation Scis., Inc., Atlanta, 1989-91; sr. litigation psychologist Trial Cons., Inc., Miami, 1991-93; dir. rsch. Magnus Rsch. Cons. Inc., Ft. Lauderdale, 1993—; adj. prof. psychology U. North Fla., Jacksonville, 1985-89, Nova Southeastern U., Ft. Lauderdale, 1995—. Author: Social Psychology: Study Guide, 1990, Social Psychology: Instructors Manual, 1990; contbr. articles to profl. jours. Mem. ACLU, Am. Psychol. Assn., Am. Psychol. Law Soc., Amnesty Internat., Civitan Internat., Southeastern Psychol. Assn., Soc. for Psychol. Study of Social Issues, Soc. Personality and Social Psychology, Greenpeace, Psi Chi. Democrat. Office: Magnus Rsch Cons Inc 3118 N Federal Hwy Ste 177 Lighthouse Point FL 33064

PIHLAJA, MAXINE MURIEL MEAD, orchestra executive; b. Windom, Minn., July 19, 1935; d. Julian Wright and Mildred Eleanor (Ray) Mead; m. Donald Francis Pihlaja, Jan. 4, 1963; children: Geoffrey Blake, Kirsten Louise, Jocelyn Erika. BA, Hamline U., 1957; postgrad., Columbia U., 1957-58. Group worker Fedn. of Chs., L.A., 1956; case worker St. John's Guild Floating Hosp. Ship, N.Y.C., 1957-59; Y-Teen program dir. YWCA, Elizabeth, N.J., 1957-60, Boulder, Colo., 1964-65; spl. svcs. program and club dir. U.S. Army, Ingrandes and Nancy, France, 1960-62; music buyer, salesperson Guinn's Music, Billings, Mont., 1977-78, N.W. Music, Billings, 1978-79; office adminstr. Am. Luth. Ch., Billings, 1979-84; mgr. Billings Symphony Soc., 1984—; substitute tchr. Community Day Care and Enrichment Ctr., Billings, 1971-76. Dir. Handbell choir 1st Presybn. Ch., Billings, 1972—, Am. Luth. Ch., 1981-84, 1st English Luth. Ch., 1982—; mem. Billings Symphony Chorale, 1965-91, Bellissimo!, 1983-93. Mem. Nat. Soc. Fund Raising Execs. (sec. Mont. 1988), Mont. Assn. Female Execs., Am. Guild English Handbell Ringers (state chmn., 1988-89, treas. Area X bd. dirs. 1990-94, membership chmn. 1994—), Mont Assn. Symphony Orchs. (treas. 1987-92). Lutheran. Office: Billings Symphony Orch 401 N 31st St Billings MT 59101-1200

PIIRMA, IRJA, chemist, educator; b. Tallinn, Estonia, Feb. 4, 1920; came to U.S., 1949; d. Voldemar Juri and Meta Wilhelmine (Lister) Tiits; m. Aleksander Piirma, Mar. 10, 1943; children: Margit Ene, Silvia Ann. Diploma in chemistry, Tech. U., Darmstadt, Fed. Republic of Germany, 1949; MS, U. Akron, 1957, PhD, 1960. Rsch. chemist U. Akron, Ohio, 1952-67, asst. prof., 1967-76, assoc. prof., 1976-81, prof., 1981-90; prof. emerita U. Akron, Ohio, 1990—; dept. head U. Akron, Ohio, 1982-85. Author: Polymeric Surfactants, 1992; editor: Emulsion Polymerization, 1982; contbr. articles to profl. jours. Recipient Extra Mural Rsch. award BP Am., Inc., 1989. Mem. Am. Chem. Soc. Home: 3528 Adaline Dr Cuyahoga Falls OH 44224-3929 Office: U Akron Akron OH 44325-3909

PIKE, LYNN LOUISE, group merchandise manager; b. Cedar Rapids, Iowa, Jan. 28, 1957; d. Merrill E. and Marion Louise (Slater) P. A in Optometric Assisting, North Iowa Area C.C., Mason City, 1979. Asst. Dr.'s Myers, Manville, Livin & Teig, Cedar Rapids, Iowa, 1979-82; optician Dr. Robert P. Scholl, Cedar Rapids, 1982-86; retail mgr. LensCrafters, Cedar Rapids, 1986-87; store gen. mgr. LensCrafters, Kansas City, Mo., 1988-90; merchandise mgr. LensCrafters, Cin., 1990-93; spl. assignment merchandising dept. LensCrafters Can., Toronto, 1993-94; group merchandise mgr. LensCrafters, Cin., 1994—; membership chmn. Optometric Assts. Assn. Iowa, 1983-84, v.p., 1984-85. Mem. Am. Bd. Opticianry (cert.). Office: LensCrafters 8650 Governors Hill Dr Cincinnati OH 45249

PIKE, SANDRA LEONG, real estate appraiser, consultant; b. Oakland, Calif., Aug. 15, 1949; d. Tim and Laura (Lau) Leong; 1 child, Wendy Pike. BS, U. Calif., 1970. Cert. sr. residential appraiser. Computer programmer, rschr. On-Line Decisions, Berkeley, Calif., 1970-71; med. rsch. economist Kaiser Found. Health Plan, Oakland, Calif., 1972-79; computer tech. rep. Gen. Electric Info. Svcs., San Francisco, 1979-82; account exec., appraisals Trans Am. Relocation, Walnut Creek, Calif., 1982-85; residential appraiser First Nationwide Bank, Pleasant Hill, Calif., 1985-86; comml. appraiser Home Fed. Savings and Loan of San Francisco, 1986-87; appraiser mgr. First Deposit Nat. Corp., San Ramon, Calif., 1988-89; prin., ind. fee appraiser Sandra L. Pike Assocs., Walnut Creek, Calif., 1989—. Mem. Appraisal Inst. (chpt. treas. 1989-90, edn. com. 1993—). Office: PO Box 845 Lafayette CA 94549

PIKLO, CHARLENE LORRAINE, retail professional; b. Camden, N.J., Sept. 21, 1954; d. John Alfred and Loretta H. (Vogt) P. BS, U. Tampa, 1975. Mgr. trainee Roses Stores Inc., Macon, Ga., 1975-76; asst. mgr. Roses Stores Inc., Onley, Va., 1976; sr. asst. mgr. Roses Stores Inc., Burlington, N.C., 1976-77; merchandiser Roses Stores Inc., Henderson, N.C., 1977-78; asst. buyer Roses Stores Inc., N.Y.C., 1978-79; buyer Roses Stores Inc., Henderson, 1979-83, div. mgr. mdse., 1983-86; gen. mdse. mgr. Conston Corp., Phila., 1986-90; gen. mdse. mgr., v.p. Crystal Brands Retail, Reading, Pa., 1990-93; pres. Creative Giftworks, Reading, 1993—; dir. retail merchandising Disney Direct Mktg. Svcs., Inc., Edison, N.J., 1994—. Recipient Torch of Liberty, Anti-Defamation League, 1988—. Mem. NAFE, Profl.

Bus. Sorority, Phi Gamma Nu. Roman Catholic. Office: 20 Kilmer Rd Edison NJ 08817

PILAT, JOANNE MARIE, telecommunications company executive. BA cum laude, Siena Heights Coll., 1969; MSW, Cath. U. Am., 1974; M of Mgmt., Northwestern U., 1988. Tchr., organizer community services various orgns., Mich., Ill., 1961-72; family therapist Oak Park (Ill.) Family Service and Mental Health Ctr., 1974-75; patient therapist Luth. Ctr. for Substance Abuse, Park Ridge, Ill., 1975-80, dir. social services, 1980-81; dir. med. social services Luth. Gen. Hosp., Park Ridge, 1981-82, dir. clin. social services, 1982-84; mgr., regional mgr. employee assistance program AT&T, Chgo., 1984-88, cons. orgn. devel., 1988-90; mgr. cen. region benefits AT&T, 1990-93, regional mgr. west and ctrl., 1993-94, nat. mgr. retired employees benefits orgn., 1994—; co-chair bus. and industry Internat. Council Alcohol and Addictions, Lausanne, Switzerland, 1984—, co-chair. social work, 1980-84; mem. subcom. White House. Conf. for Drug-Free Am., 1987—; instr. Ctr. Family Studies, Northwestern U., 1980—, Grad. Sch. Social Work, Loyola U., Chgo., 1980—; chair edn. and tng. Ill. Gov.'s Adv. Council Alcoholism, 1980; mem. Ill. Alcoholism Counselors' Cert. Bd.; speakerin field U.S. and abroad. Contbr. chpt. to book, articles to profl. jours. Bd. dirs. Alcohol, Drug Dependence Luth. Social Services, Chgo., 1987—; mem. alumni bd. Northwestern U. Inst. Psychiatry, 1984—. Mem. Assn. Labor/Mgmt. Adminstrs. Cons. (nat. bd. dirs.), Alcoholism, Northwestern U. Mgmt. Club, Women in Mgmt., Alumni Assn. Ctr. for Family (membership chair 1984-87). Office: AT&T 1708 Golf Rd Tower II Ste 400 Rolling Meadows IL 60008

PILCHER, ELLEN LOUISE, rehabilitation counselor; b. Washington, Feb. 5, 1949; d. Donald Everett and Edna Lois (Walker) P.; m. Adam J. Buzon Jr., July 27, 1974 (div. Apr. 1991). BA in Psychology, So. Ill. U., 1971, MA in Rehab. Counseling, 1973. Social svcs. asst. Dept. Army, Ft. Huachuca, Ariz., 1973-74, New Ulm, Germany, 1974-75, Ft. Sill, Okla., 1977-87; counselor Goodwill Industries, Lawton, Okla., 1976-77; ind. living specialist Ariz. Bridge to Ind. Living, Phoenix, 1984-87; disability specialist Samaritan Rehab. Inst., Phoenix, 1987-89; disability cons. Peoria, Ariz., 1989—; founder Problems of Architecture and Transp. to Handicapped, Lawton, Okla., 1976-79; founder, past pres. Polio Echo Support Group, Phoenix, 1985—; co-founder, bd. mem. Disability Network of Ariz., Phoenix, 1986—; disability speaker Easter Seal Soc. and free lance, Phoenix, 1984—; producer, host Cable Community Svc. TV Show, Glendale, Ariz., 1987-91; mem. nat. adv. bd. Polio Support Groups, St. Louis, 1987. Named Ms. Wheelchair Ariz. Good Samaritan Med. Ctr., Phoenix, 1986, Second Runner-Up Ms. Wheelchair Am., Ms. Wheelchair Am. Assn., Richmond, Va., 1986, Outstanding Bus. Person Ariz. Parks/Recreation, 1987; recipient Celebration of Success award Impact for Enterprising Women, Phoenix, 1989, Extraordinary Personal Achievement award Lions Club Found., Phoenix, 1987. Mem. NOW (co-founder Lawton chpt. 1982, Glendale, Ariz. chpt. 1984), Nat. Rehab. Assn., Nat. Rehab. Counselors Assn., Ariz. Rehab. Assn., Ariz. Rehab. Counselors Assn. Democrat. Unitarian.

PILGRIM, DEBORAH ANNICE, psychotherapist; b. Bklyn., Sept. 18, 1956; d. Charles Montague and Nellian Claire (Holloway) P. AB, Smith Coll., 1978; EdM, Harvard U., 1979; EdD, George Washington U., 1986. Rsch. analyst/supr. Crown Hts. Community Corp., Bklyn., summers 1974, 76; supr. Urban League Tutorial Program, Bklyn., summers 1975,77; substitute tchr. Smith Coll. Lab. Campus Sch., Northampton, Mass., 1978; dir. Crown Hts. North Multi-Svc. Ctr. Tutorial Program, Bklyn., summer 1978; psychology extern Cath. U. Am., Washington, 1980-81; psychiat. teaching fellow Boston U. Sch. Medicine, 1981-82; clin. psychology intern Boston City Hosp., 1981-82; psychology teaching fellow Harvard U., Cambridge, Mass., 1987, staff psychologist, 1985—; lectr. and cons. in field. Artist original sculpture in King's Plaza Ctr. in Bklyn., 1971. Prodn. mem. Brookline (Mass.) Community Theater; resident mem. Concerned Black Citizens of Brookline; recruiter/interviewer Smith Coll.; mem. admissions com. Harvard U. Grad. Sch. Edn., 1978-79. NIMH grantee, 1981-82. Mem. APA, Assn. Black Psychologists, Am. Assn. for Counseling and Devel., Assn. for Multi-Cultural Counseling and Devel. (co-chair nat. conv. 1988-89), Phi Delta Kappa. Democrat. Episcopalian. Office: Harvard U Bur Study Counsel 5 Linden St Cambridge MA 02138-5004

PILGRIM, DIANNE HAUSERMAN, art museum director; b. Cleve., July 9, 1941; d. John Martin and Norma Hauserman; divorced. BA, Pa. State U., 1963; MA, Inst. Fine Arts, NYU, 1965; postgrad., CUNY, 1971-74; LHD (hon.), Amherst Coll., 1991, Pratt Inst., 1994. Chester Dale fellow Am. wing. Met. Mus. Art, N.Y.C., 1966-68, researcher, 1971, rsch. cons. Am. paintings and sculpture, 1972-73; asst. to dirs. Pyramid Galleries, Ltd., Washington, 1969-71, Finch Coll. Mus. Art, Washington, 1971; curator dept. decorative arts Bklyn. Mus., 1973-88, chmn. dept., 1988; dir. Cooper-Hewitt Mus., N.Y.C., 1988—; mem. adv. com. Gracie Mansion, N.Y.C., 1980; mem. design adv. com. Art Inst. Chgo., 1988—; mem. Hist. House Trust of N.Y.C., Mayor's Office, 1989—. Co-author, curator: (book and exhbn. catalogue) The American Renaissance 1876-1917, 1979, (book) The Machine Age in America 1918-1941, 1986 (Charles F. Montgomery prize Decorative Arts Soc.). Bd. dirs. Nat. Multiple Sclerosis Soc., 1989. Recipient Disting. Alumni award Pa. State U., 1991. Mem. Art Table, Decorative Arts Soc. (pres. 1977-79). Office: Smithsonian Instn Cooper-Hewitt Nat Design Mus 2 E 91st St New York NY 10128-0606

PILLAERT, E(DNA) ELIZABETH, museum curator; b. Baytown, Tex., Nov. 19, 1931; d. Albert Jacob and Nettie Roseline (Kelley) P. B.A., U. St. Thomas, 1953; M.A., U. Okla., 1963; postgrad., U. Wis., 1962-67, 70-73. Asst. curator archaeology Stovall Mus., Norman, Okla., 1959-60, ednl. liaison officer, 1960-62; research asst. U. Okla., Norman, Okla., 1962; research asst. U. Wis., Madison, 1962-65, cons. archaeol. faunal analysis, 1965—; curator osteology Zool. Mus., Madison, 1965—, chief curator, 1967-92, assoc. dir., 1992—. Bd. dirs. Lysistrata Feminist Coop., Madison, 1977-81, Univ. YMCA, Madison, 1974-77. Mem. Soc. Vertebrate Paleontology, Wis. Archaeol. Soc., Okla. Anthrop. Soc., Am. Assn. Mus., NOW, Stoughton Hist. Soc., Am. Ornithological Union, Friends of Stoughton Libr., Friends of Stoughton Auditorium. Home: 216 N Prairie St Stoughton WI 53589-1647 Office: U Wis Zool Mus 434 Noland Bldg 250 N Mills Rd Madison WI 53706

PILLAI, RAJNANDINI K., management educator; b. Madras, India, Dec. 30, 1956; came to U.S., 1988; d. Krishnamurthy and Mirna Pillai. BS, U. Bombay, 1976, MBA, 1986; PhD, SUNY, Buffalo, 1994. Mgr. State Bank of India, Bombay, 1977-88; instr., rsch. asst. SUNY, Buffalo, 1988-93; asst. prof. mgmt. U. Miami, Coral Gables, Fla., 1993—. Author: (with Susan Stites-Doe) Ancillary to Strategic Human Resources Management, 1993. Pres. Jaycees, Bombay, 1987-88, nat. theme dir., 1982. Recipient teaching and rsch. awards. Mem. Acad. of Mgmt., Eastern Acad. of Mgmt. Hindu. Office: U Miami 414M Jenkins/Sch of Bus Coral Gables FL 33124

PILLING, JANET KAVANAUGH, lawyer; b. Akron, Ohio, Sept. 5, 1951; d. Paul and Marjorie (Logue) Kavanaugh; m. Martin Jolles, Mar. 6, 1987; children: Madeleine Sloan Langdon Jolles, Jameson Samuel Rhys Jolles. BA, Ohio Wesleyan U., 1973; JD, U. Mo., 1976; LLM, Villanova U., 1985. Bar: Pa. 1976, U.S. Tax Ct. 1976, U.S. Dist. Ct. (ea. dist.) Pa. 1976. Atty. Schnader, Harrison, Segal & Lewis, Phila., 1976-83; gen. counsel Kistler-Tiffany Cos., Wayne, Pa., 1983—. Mem. Phila. Estate Planning Coun., Montgomery County Estate Planning Coun., Delaware County Estate Planning Coun., Del. Valley Planned Giving Coun., Chester County Estate Planning Coun. Mem. ABA, Phila. Bar Assn. (probate sect., tax sect.), Pa. Bar Assn., Delaware Valley Planned Giving Coun., Phi Beta Kappa, Phi Delta Phi. Office: Kistler-Tiffany Cos 987 Old Eagle School Rd Ste 70 Wayne PA 19087-1708

PILOSI, JOY ETTA, secondary school educator; b. Scranton, Pa., Apr. 17, 1941; d. Nicholas and Dorothy (Lewis) P. BS, East Stroudsburg U., 1963, MEd, 1966. Cert. tchr., Pa. Phys. edn. tchr. North Pocono High Sch., Moscow, Pa., 1963—, girls' basketball coach, 1964-75, girls' softball coach, 1964-80, girls' volleyball, 1964-90. Inducted Northeastern chpt. Pa. Sports Hall of Fame. Mem. NEA, Pa. State Edn. Assn., North Pocono Edn. Assn. Democrat. Baptist. Office: North Pocono High Sch Church St Moscow PA 18444

PILSNER, JOYCE MARION, health services administrator; b. N.Y.C., Jan. 30, 1925; d. Sol and Estelle (Schaffle) Mayersohn; m. Harry Pilsner, Dec. 20, 1947; 1 child, Toby Jane. AB, Hunter Coll., 1944; MA, Columbia U., 1946; cert, Inst. for Not-for-Profit Mgmt., 1977. Tchr. N.Y.C., 1945-67; rsch. assoc. Inst. Community Studies Sarah Lawrence Coll., Bronxville, N.Y., 1968-69, asst. to dean, 1968-70; rsch. assoc., field coordinator Consortium on Community Crises Cornell U., Ithaca, N.Y., 1970-71; exec. dir. Riverdale Mental Health Ctr., Bronx, N.Y., 1971—. Membership chmn., correspondence sec. Riverdale Community Coun.; mem. dist. bd. Comprehensive Health Planning Agy.; mem., sec. sub-regional com. Bronx Fedn. Mental Health and Mental Retardation Agys.; bd. dirs. Riverdale Sr. Ctr., 1974-82; v.p., sec., bd. dirs. Coalition of Mental Health, Mental Retardation and Alcoholism Agys., 1975-95; mem. Community Bd. 8, Bronx, 1975—, chmn. health com., ethics com., youth com., 2d v.p., 1989, 1st v.p., 1990-93, chmn., 1993—; mem. community adv. bd. North Cen. Bronx Hosp., 1983-89, chmn. health, membership and nominating coms.; mem. Nat. Users Group, Info. Scis. Div. Nathan Kline Inst., 1984-87, exec. com., sec., 1985-86; borough outreach com. Greater N.Y. Fund/ United Way, 1985-89. Named Riverdalian of Yr., 1979; recipient Cert. of Meritorious Svc. N.Y.C. Mayor Edward I. Koch, 1986, Community Svc. award Benjamin Franklin Dem. Club, 1992. Mem. AAUW, LWV, Riverdale Mental Health Assn. (dir. 1965-71, chmn. pub. rels., editor newsletter), UN Assn. (dir. Riverdale chpt., chmn. publicity), Am. Orthopsychiat. Assn., Assn. fellow Adminstrs. Mental Health and Mental Retardation Facilities (dir. 1974—), East Hampton House Owners Ltd. (bd. dirs., v.p. 1986, pres. 1988—), Alumni Assn. Inst. for Not-for-Profit Mgmt. (exec. com. 1987-89), Bronx Mental Health Coun. (chmn. legis. com. 1980—). Home: 4721 Delafield Ave Bronx NY 10471-3311 Office: Riverdale Mental Health Assn 5676 Riverdale Ave Bronx NY 10471-2138

PILVIN, BARBARA JEANNE, librarian; b. Balt., Mar. 4, 1951; d. Harold and Beatrice (Rich) P. AB cum laude, Smith Coll., 1973; MA, Yale U., 1976; MLS, U. Md., 1981. Editorial asst. Libr. of Congress, Washington, 1974; libr. asst. Jewish Community Ctr. of Greater Washington, Rockville, Md., 1978-79; spl. project cataloger U. Pa., Phila., 1982-84; reference libr. Free Libr. of Phila., 1986—; student intern Archives and Manuscripts Dept, McKeldin Libr., U. Md., College Park, 1981, grad. asst. Coll. of Libr. Info. Svcs., 1982. Co-author: Mental and Developmental Disabilities: Directory of Legal Advocates, 1982; co-author, founder, editor newsletter The Alliance, 1987-89; contbr. articles in A New Day: Voices from Across the Land. Reader Broadcaster Radio Reading and Taping Svcs. Washington Ear, Silver Spring, 1974-75, Recs. for the Blind, New Haven, 1977-78, Radio Info. Ctr. for the Blind, Phila., 1983-86; vol. libr. Stanley Meml. Pub. Libr., Laurel, Md., 1982. Mem. NOW (del. nat. conv. Phila. chpt. 1987), Am. Libr. Assn., Am. Printing History Assn., Modern Lang. Assn., Nat. Alliance for the Mentally Ill, Depression and Related Affective Disorders Assn. Democrat. Jewish. Office: Free Libr of Phila 1901 Vine St Philadelphia PA 19103

PIMLEY, KIM JENSEN, financial training consultant; b. Abington, Pa., Apr. 29, 1960; d. Alvin Christian Jensen and Helen Marie (Kairis) Meinken; m. Michael St. John Pimley, Nov. 10, 1988; 1 child, Oliver Jensen Pimley. BA, Emory U., 1982, MA, 1982; postgrad., U. Chgo., 1985—. Mgr. tng. ops. Continental Bank, Chgo., 1986-88, mgr. coll. rels., 1988-90, mgr. client svcs. The Globecon Group, N.Y.C., 1990-92; prin. Pimley & Pimley, Inc., Glencoe, Ill., 1992-93; pres. P&P Tng. Resources, Inc., Glencoe, 1993—. Mem. Chgo. Coun. on Fgn. Affairs, 1990—. Scholarship U. Chgo., 1984. Mem. ACLU, NOW, Oxford and Cambridge Club. Office: P&P Tng Resources Inc 543 Grove St Glencoe IL 60022-1843

PINARD-DARLING, MARJORIE ANN, psychotherapist; b. Midland, Mich.; d. Stanley C. and Felicia J. (Belchak) Yascolt; m. Thomas Pinard, Jan. 14, 1967; children: Tom, Ann. BS in Psychology, Mich. State U., 1964, MA in Psychology, 1966; MA in Psychology, U. Notre Dame, 1990. Ltd. lic. psychologist, Mich.; lic. profl. counselor, Mich., clin. social worker, Ind. Instr. psychology Ferris State U., Big Rapids, Mich., 1967-68, Delta Coll., University Center, Mich., 1969-72, Lake Michigan Coll., Benton Harbor, Mich., 1972-85; psychotherapist U. Notre Dame, Ind., 1987-88, Meml. Hosp., South Bend, Ind., 1988-90, Stress Recovery Ctr., South Bend, 1990-94, Dr. John J. Haskin, MD, PC, Granger, Ind., 1991-94; Dr. Sonego & Assocs., Mishawaka, Ind., 1994—; mem. sex offense staff Madison Ctr., South Bend, 1973-76; developer, presenter mid. sch. program for prevention sexual assault South Bend Mid. Schs., 1985-87; participant, presenter Project C.E.A.S.E. (Childhood Edn. against Sexual Abuse) to preschs. and grade schs. in Michiana, 1985-87. Book reviewer V.O.I.C.E.S., Treating Abuse Today. Planner, developer Alpha program Niles (Mich.) Community Schs., 1975-77, mem. steering com. Southwestern Mich. Consortium on Gifted and Talented, 1983-86; condr. edn. meetings, workshop, publicity campaign on symptoms, phys. and psychol. effects of cystic fibrosis, chmn. fundraising campaigns Cystic Fibrosis Found., Saginaw, Mich., 1981-83. Recipient svc. award Cystic Fibrosis Found., 1983, Hadassah, 1986; disting. alumni scholar Mich. State U., 1960-64; grad. fellow U. Notre Dame, 1986-89. Mem. APA, Assn. for Psychotherapeutic Humor, Victims of Incest Can Emerge Survivors, Mich. Psychol. Assn. Home: 2316 Yankee Niles MI 49120

PINCH, PATRICIA ANN, insurance agent; b. Port Hueneme, Calif., Oct. 8, 1947; d. William Claude and Lois (Monroe) Pinch; m. Vincent J. Lupo, Apr. 6, 1973 (dec. 1975). B.S. in Med. Tech., Med. Coll. Va., 1969. Human cytogenetic researcher Bklyn. Hosp., 1970-72; animal genetic researcher Mt. Sinai Hosp., N.Y.C., 1972-74; med. tech. supr., owner Vee-Jay Clin. Labs., Bklyn., 1974-86; supr. G.J.L. Clin. Lab., Amityville, N.Y., 1986-87; dist. agt. Prudential Ins., 1987-94. Mem. Am. Soc. Clin. Pathologists. Roman Catholic. Office: 124 Kime Ave North Babylon NY 11703-3317

PINCKLEY, LAVERNE CRAIG, education professional; b. Tompkinsville, Ky., Jan. 18, 1929; d. Glen M. and Amie (Proffitt) Craig; m. Thomas Bratton Pinckley, June 6, 1955; children: Teena, Pippa. BA, Western Ky. U., 1952, MA, 1954, Rank I, 1969. Standard cert. for sch. leaders. Pub. sch. tchr. Monroe County Schs., Tompkinsville, 1949, 52-54, 1955-66, instrnl. supr., 1966—; supr. adult basic edn., Monroe County, 1966—; mem. Literacy Coun. Bd., Monreo County, curriculum devel., Monroe County Schs. Mem. campus bd. Western Ky. U.-Glasgow. Mem. Ky. Edn. Assn., Monroe County Edn. Assn., NEA, Ky. Assn. Ednl. Suprs., Ky. Assn. Curriculum Devel., Ky. Assn. Sch. Adminstrs. Home: 1114 Columbia Ave Tompkinsville KY 42167

PINCUS, ANN TERRY, federal agency administrator; b. Little Rock, Sept. 12, 1937; d. Fred William and Cornelia (Witsell) Terry; m. Walter Haskell Pincus, May 1, 1965; children: Ward, Adam, Cornelia Battle. BA, Vassar Coll., 1959. Editorial asst., writer Glamour Mag., 1963; reporter Ridder Pubs., Washington, 1963-66; freelance writer Washington, 1966-76; dir. info. select com. on U.S. population U.S. Ho. Reps., Washington, 1977-79; nat. publicist Nat. Pub. Radio, Washington, 1979-83; press sec. U.S. Sen. Charles Mathias, Washington, 1983-87; profl. staff mem. Senate Com. on Rules, Washington, 1983-87; v.p. communications Stas. WETA-TV/Radio, Washington, 1987-93; dir. Office of Rsch., U.S. Info. Agy., Washington, 1993—; bd. dirs. Wildfowl Trust of N. Am., Graysonville, Md., Fgn. Student Service Council, Washington, Woodley House. Editor: Kennedy Center Cookbook, 1977; contbr. articles to profl. jours. Home: 3202 Klingle Rd NW Washington DC 20008-3403 Office: Office of Rsch US Info Agy 301 4th St Rm 352 Washington DC 20547*

PINCUS, JACQUELINE KRON, library assistant; b. Schenectady, N.Y., July 7, 1936; d. Gabriel and Anna (Mayer) Kron; m. Michael S. Pincus, June 10, 1956; children: Jonathan D., Gregory K. BS in Music Edn., Ithaca (N.Y.) Coll., 1958; postgrad., Mansfield (Pa.) U., 1976-78. Asst. libr. Mansfield Pub. Libr., 1976-80, Staunton (Va.) Pub. Libr., 1980-82; circulation libr. Little Falls (N.J.) Pub. Libr., 1983-87; libr. asst. Charleston (S.C.) County Librs., 1988—. Mem. AAUW (sec. 1989-92), Low Country Women's Coalition (sec. 1990), Newcomers Assn. of the Low Country (sec. 1989-90). Home: 907 E Arctic Ave Box 1589 Folly Beach SC 29439

PINCUS, JILLIAN RUTH, physician; b. Bklyn., May 26, 1947; d. William and Elsa Bronson Pincus. BA, Radcliffe Coll., 1969; MD, Med. Coll. Pa., 1974. Cert. Am. Bd. Internal Medicine, Am. Bd. Nephrology. Intern, resident U. Medicine and Dentistry of N.J.-Robert Wood Johnson Med. Sch., 1974-77, nephrology fellow, 1978-79; nephrology fellow U. Miami Sch. Medicine, 1977-78; attending physician Jewish Inst. Geriatric Care, New Hyde Park, N.Y., 1979-80, L.I. Jewish Hosp.-Hillside Med. Ctr., New Hyde Park, 1980-82; from asst. to assoc. med. dir. Sandoz Pharm., East Hanover, N.J., 1982-88; med. dir. CIBA-Geigy Corp., Summit, N.J., 1988-90, exec. med. dir., 1990-92, clin. head, 1992-93, head, 1993—. Active Nat. Kidney Found. Mem. AMA, Am. Soc. Nephrology, Am. Med. Women's Assn., Women in Nephrology. Home: 1 Plymouth Rd Chatham NJ 07928 Office: CIBA-Geigy Corp 556 Morris Ave Summit NJ 07901

PINCUS, LAURA R., investor, accountant; b. Bklyn., Jan. 19, 1923; d. Sam and Esther (Boimel) Shore; m. William Pincus, Jan. 31, 1942 (dec. Jan. 1994); children: Irene, Stephan. Student, La Salle Inst., N.Y.C., 1940, C.W. Post, L.I. N.Y., 1960-62. Statis. typist Feinberg & Spaulder, N.Y.C., 1939-40, acct., 1948-58; owner Pincus Plumbing, Northport, N.Y., 1958-80; office mgr. James Robinson, N.Y.C., 1960-61; owner Pincus Plumbing, San Diego, 1980-87, Laura's Ltd., Wellington, Fla., 1987—. Youth program dir. Young Men's Hebrew Assn., Bklyn., 1939-41; founder East Northport Jewish Ctr., L.I., N.Y.; active Tifereth Israel Synagogue of San Diego, 1980-87, Tempe Beth Torah-Wellington, 1987—; mem. Nat. Coun. of Jewish Women, Palm Beach sect., 1991—. Mem. Copperfield Assn., B'nai B'rith (life, bd. dirs., pres. Horizon chpt.), Hadassah (life), Brandeis Club (life, auditor Brandeis Palm Beach East chpt.), Am. Red Mogen David for Israel (life, founder San Diego Tikvah chpt. 1982-87, Wellington chpt. 1990, pres. Tikvah chpt. 1982-87, pres. Wellington chpt. 1990—). Home: 12884 Buckland St West Palm Beach FL 33414

PINCUS, PATRICIA HOGAN, nurse; b. Lockport, N.Y., Dec. 4, 1945; d. George W. and Theresa J. (Harrington) Wendel; children: Jennifer, Molly, Peter. RN, Mercy Hosp. Sch. Nursing, Buffalo, 1966; MPH, U. Rochester, 1985; BS, Empire State Coll., Rochester, N.Y., 1977. RN, N.Y.; cert. infection control nurse. Instr. Empire Nine Emergency Med. Tech. Program, Rochester, 1976; infection control practitioner dept. medicine U. Rochester Med. Ctr., 1975-79, asst. nursing practice coord. dept. nursing, 1979-80; tech. assoc. IDU Univ. Rochester, 1980-92, nurse mgr. Clin. Rsch. Ctr., 1992—. Contbr. numerous articles to profl. jours. Mem. ANA, AONE, Nat. Assn. Gen. Clin. Rsch. Ctr. Nurse Mgrs., Genesee Valley Nurses Assn., Assn. for Practitioners in Infection Control (bd. dirs.),Western N.Y. State Infection Control Officers (bd. dirs.). Home: 14 W Jefferson Rd Pittsford NY 14534-1902 Office: Univ Rochester Med Ctr Box 619-13 609 Elmwood Ave Rochester NY 14620-2913

PINCUS, RANDI, advertising executive; b. Bklyn., June 10, 1957. BS, Queens Coll., 1977; cert. in printing, Hofstra U., 1980. Asst. prodn. mgr. Brancy Design & Media, Hicksville, N.Y., 1979-81; asst. advt. mgr. Nature's Bounty Inc., Bohemia, N.Y., 1981-85; advt. mgr. Milgray Electronics Inc., Farmingdale, N.Y., 1985-90; community & profl. liaison New Medico Rehab. Svcs. of Nassau, Great Neck, N.Y., 1990-91; mktg. rep. Ctr. for Rehab., Hauppage, N.Y., 1991-92; advt. profl., dir. advt. Aid Auto Stores, Inc., Westbury, N.Y., 1992—.

PINE, LOIS ANN HASENKAMP, nurse; b. Cheyenne, Wyo., Feb. 21, 1950; d. Clifford Norbert and Julie Adda (Younglund) Hasenkamp; m. Julius William Pine Jr., Feb. 16, 1974; children: Margaret Ann, Julius William III, Lawrence Michael. BS, U. Wyo., 1976, MS in Parent-Child Nursing, 1989. RN. From staff nurse to charge nurse Ivinson Meml. Hosp., Laramie, Wyo., 1976-86; maternal-child nurse cons. Perinatal and Prevention Program, Wyo. Dept. Health, Cheyenne, 1988—. Mem. St. Lawrence Council of Cath. Women, Laramie, 1980—, St. Cecilia's Group, Laramie, 1980—, Albany County PTA, Laramie, 1985-91; mem. health profl. adv. com. Wyo. chpt. March of Dimes, 1988—. Mem. ANA, NAACOG (sect. vice chmn. 1980-86), Wyo. Nurses Assn., Am. Acad. Pediatrics (perinatal pediatrics dist. VIII sect.), Nat. Assn. Neonatal Nurses (charter), Sigma Theta Tau (Alpha Pi chpt. treas. 1990-94, Alpha Pi chpt. corr. sec. 1983-84). Democrat. Home: 1062 Empinado Dr Laramie WY 82070-4873

PINE, PATRICIA PALMER, aging services administrator; b. Portland, Maine, Mar. 14, 1940; d. Maurice George and Elizabeth Wadsworth (Syphers) Palmer; m. James Erlon Hannaford, Oct. 1, 1960 (div. June 1970; Paula L., Brenda J. Hannaford Bryan; m. Vanderlyn Russell Pine, Aug. 9, 1974; stepchildren: Gordon K., Brian T., Daniel R. AB, Vassar Coll., 1972; MA, Columbia U., 1975; PhD, SUNY, Albany, 1993. Dir. Dutchess County Office for the Aging, Poughkeepsie, N.Y., 1976-80; assoc. dir. Hudson Valley Health Systems Agy., Tuxedo, N.Y., 1980-83; exec. dir. Hospice Assn. of Ulster County, Kingston, N.Y., 1983-84; assoc. exec. dir. WellCare N.Y., Kingston and Newburgh, 1984-86; dir. Ulster County Office Aging, Kingston, 1986—; pres. The Gerontol. Inst., 1993—; adj. prof. SUNY, New Paltz, 1973—, Marist Coll., Poughkeepsie, 1976-79, Adelphi U., L.I. City, 1983. Pres. United Way of Ulster County, Kingston, 1989-90; mem. N.Y. State Adv. Commn. on Aging-In Initiative, 1991—; trustee The Kingston Hosp., 1993—. Gerontol. Soc. Am. rsch. fellow, 1987, Paul Harris fellow Rotary Internat., 1989; named Vol. of the Yr., United Way of Ulster County, 1990. Mem. NASW, Nat. Coun. on Aging, Gerontol. Soc. Am., N.Y. State Assn. Area Agys. on Aging (rec. sec. 1978-80, chair statewide conf. 1980, chair tng. com. 1986-88, pres. 1995—). Home: 18 Plattekill Ave New Paltz NY 12561-1917 Office: Ulster County Office Aging 1 Albany Ave # 1800 Kingston NY 12401-2946

PINEDA, MARIANNA, sculptor, educator; b. Evanston, Ill., May 10, 1925; d. George and Marianna (Dickinson) Packard; m. Harold Tovish, Jan. 14, 1946; children: Margo, Aaron, Nina. Student, Cranbrook Acad. Art, summer 1942, Bennington Coll., 1942-43, U. Calif.-Berkeley, 1943-45, Columbia U., 1945-46, Ossip Zadkine Sch. Drawing and Sculpture, Paris, 1949-50. instr. sculpture Newton Coll. Sacred Heart, 1972-75, Boston Coll., 1975-77; vis. assoc. prof. Boston U., 1974, 78, annually 83-87, 89-90; vis. sculptor Sch. of Mus. Fine Arts, Boston, 1990-91; vis. critic Boston U., 1992. One-woman shows include Slaughter Gallery, San Francisco, 1951, Walker Art Ctr., Mpls., 1952, Currier Gallery, Vt., 1954, De Cordova Mus., Lincoln, Mass., 1954, Premier Gallery, Mpls., 1963, Swetzoff Gallery, Boston, 1953, 56, 64, Honolulu Acad. Art, 1970, Alpha Gallery, Boston, 1972, Newton Coll., (Mass.), 1972, Bumpus Gallery, Duxbury, Mass., 1972, Contemporary Art Ctr., Honolulu, 1982, Hanalei Palace, Kona, Hawaii, 1982, Lyman House Mus., Hilo, Hawaii, 1982, Pine Manor Coll., Mass., 1984, Rotenberg Gallery, Boston, 1990, 93, 94, Coll. of William and Mary, 1992, Wiggin Gallery, Boston Libr., 1993, Rotenberg Gallery, Mass., 1994; group shows include Oakland (Calif.) Civic Mus., 1944, Village Art Ctr., N.Y.C., 1944, Albright Art Gallery, Buffalo, 1947, Bklyn. Mus., 1947, Galerie 8 Paris, 1950, Met. Mus. Art, N.Y.C., 1951, San Francisco Mus. of Art, 1955, Inst. Contemporary Art, Boston, 1958, 59, 61, Whitney Mus. Am. Art, N.Y.C., 1953, 54, 55, 57, 59, Boston Arts Festival, 1957, 58, 60, 62, 63, 65, 85, Silvermine Annual Exhibit, Conn., 1957, Pitts. Internat., 1958, Mus. Modern Art., N.Y.C., 1960 (traveling), Art Inst. Chgo., 1959, 61, Dallas Mus. Art, 1961, Nat. Inst. Arts & Letters, 1961, N.Y. World's Fair, 1964, De Cordova Mus., 1963, 64, 1972, 75, 87, Sculptors Guild, N.Y.C., 1967-95, Pine Manor Coll., Mass., Pa. State U., 1974, The Women's Bldg., L.A., 1976, Simmons Coll., Mass., 1980, Helen Schlein Gallery, Boston, 1982, SUNY-Buffalo, 1983, Fitchburg Mus. Art, Mass., 1984, Newton Art Ctr., Mass., 1985, Boston U. Art Gallery, 1986, Shulman Sculpture Pk., White Plains, N.Y., 1986, 87, 88, Fed. Res. Gallery, Boston, Alchemie Gallery, Boston, 1987, 93, Nat. Acad. Design, N.Y.C., 1985-89, 91, 92, 93, 94-95, Boston Visual Artist Union Invitational, 1986, Bunting Inst., Fed. Reserve Gallery, Boston, 1986, Port of History, Phila., 1987, Brockton Art Ctr., Mass., 1987, Judi Rotenberg Gallery, Boston, ann. 1987-93, A.I.R. Gallery, N.Y.C., 1988, Boston Pub. Libr., 1988, Nat. Sculpture Soc., N.Y.C., 1986-89, 90-95, Holyoke Mus., Mass., 1989, Washington Art Assn., Conn., 1989, Bumpus Art Gallery, Duxbury, 1989, Page St. Gallery, San Francisco, 1989, Judi Rotenberg Gallery, Boston, 1990, 91-95, Louis Ross Gallery, N.Y.C., 1990, Shidoni Galleries, 1990, The Contemporary Mus., Honolulu, 1990, Cast Iron Gallery, 1993, Kyoto (Japan) Civic Gallery, 1993, Walsh Art Gallery, Fairfield, Conn., 1991, Wingspread Gallery, Northeast Harbor, Maine, 1991, Judi Rotenberg Gallery, Boston, 1992, NAD Jury exhbn., 1992, 93, World Fin. Ctr. Gallery, 1992, Phila. Sculptors Guild, 1992, Kingsborough C.C., Bklyn., 1994; represented permanent collections, Walker Art Ctr., Mus. Fine Arts, Boston Williams Coll., (Mass.), Dartmouth coll., Hanover, N.H., Addison Gallery, Andover, Mass., Munson-Williams-Proctor Inst., Ithaca, N.Y., Fogg Art Mus., Cambridge, Mass., Radcliff Coll., Boston Pub. Library, Wadsworth Athenaeum, Hartford, Conn. State of Hawaii, NAD,

1983, 84, 85, 87, 88, 90, 91, 92, 93, 94, Muscarelle Mus., Williamsburg, Va.; commd. work, Twirling, Bronze figure group, East Boston Housing for Elderly, The Spirit of Lili'uokalani bronze, Hawaii State Capitol. Recipient award Oakland Civic Mus., 1944, Mather prize Chgo. Art Inst., 1944, Margaret Brown award Ins. Contemporary Art, Boston, 1957, Grand prize Boston Arts Festival, 1960, Lampston prize Nat. Sculpture Soc., N.Y.C., 1986, Gold medal Nat. Sculpture Soc., 1988, Taillex award, 1991; Bunting Inst., Radcliffe Coll. fellow, 1962, 63. Fellow NAD (Gold medal 1987, Artists award 1988, 93). Home: 380 Marlborough St Boston MA 02115-1502 Office: care Judi Rotenberg 130 Newbury St Boston MA 02116-2904

PINEDO, MYRNA ELAINE, psychotherapist, educator; b. Riverton, Wyo., Apr. 28, 1944; d. Pedro Berumen and Ruth Jama (Kuriyama) P.; m. Alan P. Schiesel, Sept. 9, 1964 (div. July 1973); 1 child, Elaine Marie (Schiesel) Thompson; m. Wallace Vern Calkins, Aug. 31, 1990; children: Cary Calkins, Jeff Calkins, Krisi Calkins. BA in Psychology, Calif. State U., Northridge, 1980; MA in Cmty. Clin. Psychology, Calif. Sch. Profl. Psychiatry, 1982, PhD in Cmty. Clin. Psychology, 1987. Lic. marriage, family and child counselor, Calif.; cert. mental health counselor, Wash.; cert. marriage and family therapist, Wash. Pychiat. asst. William Newton, M.D., Marine del Rey, Calif., 1983-84; psychologist Kern County Mental Health, Bakersfield, Calif., 1984-88; alcohol counselor Spl. Treatment Edn. Program Svcs., Bakersfield, 1985-87; marriage and family therapist Jay Fisher & Assocs., Bakersfield, 1986-87; therapist program devel. Correctional Specialties, Bellevue, Wash., 1988-90; pvt. practice HAP Counseling Group, Bellevue, 1990—; adj. faculty Calif. State U., Bakersfield, 1986, Kern County Mental Health, 1987, Bellevue C.C., 1989, Antioch U., 1992, 93; spkr. in field. Panelist EastSide Domestic Violence Com., 1991-93; bd. dirs. Kern County Child Abuse Coun., 1986-88; mem. treatment com. Kern County Child Abuse Task Force, 1985-88; mem. Stop-Abuse by Counselors, 1993—. Mem. Am. Counseling Assn., Wash. Assn. Mental Health Counselors, Assn. Marriage and Family Therapists. Office: HAP Counseling Group 515 116th Ave NE Ste 165 Bellevue WA 98004

PINES, LOIS G., state legislator; b. Malden, Mass., 1940; m. Joseph Pines; 2 children. BA, Barnard Coll., 1960; JD, U. Cin. Law Sch., 1963. Corp. tax atty., 1964-72; alderman City of Newton, Mass., 1971-73; mem. Mass. Ho. of Reps., 1973-78; regional dir. New England Fed. Trade Commn., 1979-81; mem. Mass. State Senate, 1986—. Home: 40 Helene Rd Newton MA 02168-1025 Office: Mass State Senate State Capital Boston MA 02133*

PINGLETON, SAYRA SUE, health facility administrator; b. Springfield, Mo., Mar. 31, 1950; d. W. R. and Helen K. (Dempsey) Davis; m. William Pingleton, Dec. 29, 1988. Diploma, Burge Sch. Nursing, Springfield, 1971; BS, Drury Coll., 1973; MSN, Tex. Women's U., 1979. Instr. Burge Sch. Nursing, Springfield, Graceland Coll., Lamoni, Iowa; dir. nursing North Kans. City (Mo.) Hosp. Mem. AACN. Office: North Kan City Hosp 2800 Clay Edwards Dr Kansas City MO 64116

PINHEIRO, AILEEN FOLSON, secondary education educator; b. Park River, N.D., Oct. 24, 1921; d. Morris Bernard and Clara Christine (Olson) Folson; m. Eugene Arthur Pinheiro, Sept. 9, 1948. BA, Concordia Coll., 1942; MA, Whittier (Calif.) Coll., 1963. Cert. secondary edn. tchr. Tchr. Kiester (Minn.) High Sch., 1942-44, Wasco (Calif.) Jr. High Sch., 1944-45, Taylors Falls (Minn.) High Sch., 1945-47; tchr. Baldwin Park (Calif.) Unified Sch. Dist., 1947-52, 53-73, ret., 1973. Author: (handbook) The Heritage of Baldwin Park, 1981, (pamphlets) The Heritage of Baldwin Park, 1982-88. Volunteer mus. dir. City of Baldwin Park, 1983—. Recipient Older Am. Recognition award L.A. County Bd. Suprs., 1991. Mem. AAUW (pres. 1967-69), Baldwin Park Hist. Soc. (bd. dirs. 1981-91, Trophy 1983, chmn. 1985-94), Baldwin Park C. of C. (Golden Heritage award 1983, Citizen of Yr. award 1993), Baldwin Park Woman's Club (program chmn. 1990-91, treas. 1991-92, internat. chmn. 1989-94, publicity chmn. 1992-94). Presbyterian. Home: 13009 Amar Rd Baldwin Park CA 91706-5702 Office: Baldwin Park Mus 14327 Ramona Blvd Baldwin Park CA 91706-3242

PINHEY, FRANCES LOUISE, physical education educator; b. Canton, Ohio, Apr. 18, 1927; d. Frederick Otto and Rose June (Wolf) Sengleitner; m. Donald Charles Pinhey, June 13, 1952; children: Val Don, Shauna Rae, Kaye Dorrell, Lon Pernell. BA, Muskingum Coll., 1949; MS, U. R.I., 1977; postgrad., Ind. U., 1958. Cert. tchr., Ohio. Tchr. Canton Pub. Schs., 1949-50; instr. Muskingum Coll., New Concord, Ohio, 1950-52; tchr. New Concord Pub. Schs., 1950-52, Barberton (Ohio) High Sch., 1952-53, Ottawa (Ont., Can.) Pub. Schs., 1954-57, Ottawa YMCA, 1954-57; instr. Dakota Wesleyan U., Mitchell, S.D., 1959-63, Wilmington (Ohio) Coll., 1963-67; tchr. New London (Conn.) Pub. Schs., 1967-68; asst. prof. phys. edn., coach Mitchell Coll., New London, 1968—; chair, mem. Conn. Sports Officiating Rating Bd., 1968-78. Nat. ofcl. women's volleyball & basketball, 1958-80; pres. PTA, Wilmington, 1967, PTA mem., New London, Conn., 1968-77; vol. New London Recreation Dept., 1986, Little League, 1970-75; vol. condr. CBA Badminton Tournaments. Inducted into Mitchell Coll. Hall of Fame, 1993. Mem. AAHPERD, Nat. Jr. Coll. Field Hockey Coaches Assn. (pres. 1991—), Nat. Jr. Coll. Men's Tennis Assn., U.S. Badminton Assn., Nat. Assn. Sport and Phys. Edn., Nat. Dance Assn., Nat. Dance-Exercise Instrs. Tng. Assn., Nat. Jr. Coll. Athletic Assn. (chmn. New Eng. region XXI field hockey com. 1975-89, women's field hockey Coach of Yr. region XXI 1975, 78, 79, 80, 81, 82, 83, 84, 90, nat. championships and Nat. Coach of Yr. 1979, 81, 83, 84, 90, Men's Tennis Coach of Yr. Region XXI 1983, 87, 89, 90). Home: 43 Bellevue Pl New London CT 06320-4701 Office: Mitchell Coll 437 Pequot Ave New London CT 06320-4498

PINILLA, ANA RITA, neuropsychologist, researcher; b. N.Y.C., May 20, 1957; d. Louis and Luz Maria (Diaz) P.; m. Jorge Rosado Rosado, Dec. 01, 1979; children: Jorge Javier, Juan Carlos, Ana Mari. BS magna cum laude, U. P.R., Rio Piedras, 1978; MS, Caribbean Ctr., San Juan, P.R., 1980, PhD, 1988. Lic. psychologist, P.R. Prof. psychology Inter-Am. U., San Juan, 1980-91; neuropsychologist Neuropsychol. Svcs. to Developmental Deficiencies Children, Bayamon, P.R., 1987-88; asst. dir. Gov.'s Prevention Program, San Juan, 1988-90; exec. dir. Learning Disability Ctr., San Juan, 1990-94; external evaluator prevention program Roberto Clemente Sports City, Carolina, P.R., 1990—; cons. in ednl. programs Gov.'s Office; adviser, evaluator drug prevention programs, 1994—; cons. in field. Author: Analysis of Wisc-R, 1988; contbr. articles to profl. publs. Mem. Internat. Neuropsychol. Soc., Nat. Acad. Neuropsychology.

PINKAS, CATHERINE IRENE, education program manager; b. Memphis, Tenn., May 15, 1947. MBA, JFK U., 1990. Instr. Diablo Valley Coll., Pleasant Hill, Calif., 1991-94; pres. Tng. Internat., Walnut Creek, Calif., 1990-95; adminstr. human genome project Lawrence Berkeley (Calif.) Lab., 1992-95. Mem. com. Biotech. Edn. Consortium, 1993-94. Mem. Am. Statis. Assn., Women in Internat. Trade (v.p. 1989-94).

PINKHAM, ELEANOR HUMPHREY, retired university librarian; b. Chgo., May 7, 1926; d. Edward Lemuel and Grace Eleanor (Cushing) Humphrey; m. James Hansen Pinkham, July 10, 1948; children: Laurie Sue, Carol Lynn. AB, Kalamazoo Coll., 1948; MS in Library Sci. (Alice Louise LeFevre scholar), Western Mich. U., 1967. Pub. svcs. libr. Kalamazoo Coll., 1967-68, asst. libr., 1969-70, libr. dir., 1971-93, ret. 1993; vis. lectr. Western Mich. U. Sch. Librarianship, 1970-84; mem. adv. bd., 1977-81, also adv. bd. Inst. Cistercian Studies Libr., 1975-80. Mem. ALA, AAUP, ACRL (chmn. coll. libr. sect. 1988-89), Mich. Libr. Assn. (pres. 1983-84, chmn. acad. div. 1977-78), Mich. Libr. Consortium (exec. coun. 1974-82, chmn. 1977-78, Mich. Libr. of Yr 1986), OCLC Users Coun., Beta Phi Mu. Home: 2519 Glenwood Dr Kalamazoo MI 49008-2405

PINKSTON, ISABEL HAY, minister, religious organization administrator; b. Cambridge, Ohio, Oct. 30, 1922; d. Wilmer Martin and Mary Nola (Clark) Hay; m. Benedict George Dudley, Mar. 12, 1969 (dec. Feb. 1974); m. Robert Sherrill Pinkston, May 1, 1984 (dec. Dec. 1985). BA cum laude, Monmouth (Ill.) Coll., 1944; postgrad. in Christian edn., Wheaton (Ill.) Coll., 1948-49; M of Therapeutic Counseling, Open Internat. U., Sri Lanka, 1994. Ordained to ministry Nat. Assn. Congl. Chs., 1985. Instrumental and vocal music tchr. United Presbyn. Mission Sch., Frenchburg, Ky., 1944-48; dir. Christian edn. United Presbyn. Ch., Zanesville, Ohio, 1949-51; Christian edn. dir. A.R. Presbyn. Ch., Augusta, Ga., 1952-55; mem. staff Koinonia Found., Pikesville, Md., 1956-66; min., pres. bd. dirs. Ch. Religious Rsch., Inc., Grand Island, Fla., 1988—; del., participant Internat. Conf. Paranormal Rsch., Ft. Collins, Colo., 1988-89; tchr. psychography course Sancta Sophia Sem., 1991; speaker Conf. of Internat. Inst. of Integral Human Scis. and Spiritual Scis. Fellowship, 1994, Ann. Conf., World U., 1994. Author: (biography) Seed-Sower for God's Kingdom, 1987, Understanding Homosexuality, 1993; co-editor: Psychography, 1990; editor (newsletter), Koinonia Epistle, 1957-66, Religious Rsch. Found., 1988—, Religious Rsch. Press, 1988—. Mem. Internat. Coun. Cmty. Chs. (del. 1988—), Assn. for Past-Life Rsch. and Therapy (workshop leader 1989). Home: PO Box 208 Grand Island FL 32735 Office: Ch Religious Rsch Inc 11134 County Road 44 Leesburg FL 34788-2613

PINN, VIVIAN W., pathologist, federal agency administrator; b. Halifax, Va., 1941. MD, U. Va., 1967. Intern in pathology Mass. Gen. Hosp., Boston, 1967-68, rschr. in pathology, 1968-70; asst. pathologist Tufts U. New England Med. Ctr. Hosp., 1970-77, pathologist, 1977-82; from asst. to assoc. prof. pathology Tufts U., 1971-82, asst. dean student affairs, 1974-82; prof., dept. chair pathology Howard U., 1982-91; first dir. Office Rsch. on Women's Health, NIH, Bethesda, Md., 1991-94, assoc. dir. women's health rsch., 1994—. Office: NIH Office Rsch on Woman's Health 9000 Rockville Pike Bldg 1 Rm 201 Bethesda MD 20892

PINNER, DOROTHY ELAINE, nursing consultant; b. Harrisville, Mich., Jan. 9, 1935; d. Gerald Eugene and Allena Belle (Hile) Wentworth; m. Lester H. Pinner, Jan. 26, 1958 (div. June 1979); children: John, Daniel. BSN, U. Mich., 1956; MSN, Wayne State U., 1962. RN, Mich. Asst. dir. nursing Tulare County Health Dept., Visalia, Calif., 1970-73; dir. nursing Barry-Eaton-Ionia Health Depts., Charlotte, Mich., 1975-79; exec. dir. Vis. Nurses Assn. Mid.-Mich., Midland, 1979-88; health cons. Midland, 1988-90; nurse cons. Mich. Dept. Pub. Health, Lansing, 1990—; mem. adv. bd. MSN outreach program Wayne State U., Detroit, 1980-82; mem. adv. bd. continuing edn. for nursing Delta Coll., Saginaw, 1981-85; mem. adv. bd. BSN and MSN projects Saginaw Valley State U., 1985-88. Bd. dirs. Mich. Home Health Assembly, Lansing, 1978-84. Recipient Ellen Toporek award U. Mich., 1956. Mem. ANA, Nat. League of Nursing, Mich. League of Nursing, Mich. Nurses Assn. (Community Health Nurse of Yr. 1985), Sigma Theta Tau (Excellence in Nursing Practice award Theta Chi chpt. 1989). Home: 315 Village Pky # 3 Gaylord MI 49735 Office: Mich Dept Pub Health 400 Main St Gaylord MI 49735

PINNEY, FRANCES BAILEY, art therapist, artist, consultant; b. Newton, Mass., July 18, 1935; d. Gage and Ellen (Nealley) Bailey; m. Peter T. McKinney, June 7, 1957 (div. Nov. 1981); children—Peter, Karen, David. A.B., Vassar Coll., 1957; M.A., U. Houston-Clear Lake, 1979. Social worker State Bd. Child Welfare, Elizabeth, N.J., 1957-58; art therapist Mental Health and Mental Retardation Authority, Houston, 1979-81; exec. dir. Creative Alternatives, Houston, 1982—. Bd. dirs. Citizens Alliance for Mentally Ill, Houston, 1983, 84, 85; pres. Berkeley County League of Women Voters, 1993-94. Mem. Am. Art Therapy Assn., Nat. Art Edn. Assn., Am. Group Psychotherapy Assn., Am. Assn. Counseling and Devel., Artist's Equity. Episcopalian. Avocation: scuba diving. Home: PO Box 2210 Martinsburg WV 25401-7180 Office: 404 West Burke St Martinsburg WV 25401

PINSKER, PENNY COLLIAS (PANGEOTA PINSKER), television producer; b. Miami, Fla., Aug. 22, 1942; d. Theodore Peter and Agatha Madge (Bridgeman) Collias; m. Raymond Robert Elman , Feb. 19, 1962 (dec. 1967); 1 child, Alan; m. Lewis Harry Pinsker, Oct. 22, 1968. Grad. high sch., Miami, Fla. Operator So. Bell Telephone Co., Miami, 1960-67; asst. dir. pub. affairs Sta. WCKT-TV, Miami, 1968-70; dir. pub. affairs Sta. WOR-AM, N.Y.C., 1971-78; reporter documentary and consumer affairs Sta. WTFM, N.Y.C., 1978-81; dir. editorials and sta. svcs. Sta. WWOR-TV, N.Y.C. and Secaucus, N.J., 1981-87; mgr. community affairs and spl. projects Sta. WWOR-TV, Secaucus, 1987-91, dir. community affairs and spl. projects, 1991—. Author, editor: (resource directory) Sta. WOR on Crime, 1982 (recipient George Washington Medal Honor Freedom Found., Emmy award for Outstanding Editorial, 1981), The Changing Family, 1982 (recipient Broadcast Media award San Francisco State U., Emmy nominated), A Child is Missing, 1983 (recipient Broadcast Media award San Francisco State U., Emmy nominated), Taking the High Out of High School, 1984 (recipient Broadcast Media award San Francisco State U, Angel award Religion Media, Bronze medal Internat. TV and Film Soc.); project mgr. A+ For Kids (Emmy award 1989, also Emmy nomination, named 12th nat. Point of Light, 1989), At For Kids: Project Director National, (Emmy nominations 1989-91; N.Y. Emmy award 1989, 1991; Nat. Edn. Assn. award 1991). Media advisor N.J. Crime Prevention Officers Assn.; mem. comm. com. N.J. affiliation Am. Heart Assn.; bd. dirs. Queensboro Soc. Prevention Cruelty to Children, 1978-83; pub. mem. N.J. Gov.'s Task Force on Child Abuse and Neglect, 1988—; mem. comm. com. Am. Cancer Soc.; bd. dirs. Hoboken Chamber Orch., 1989-90; trustee Assn. for Children of N.J., 1990—; mem. N.J. Coun. on Adult Edn. and Literacy, 1992—; bd. dirs. N.J. Edn. Found., 1991-92. Recipient disting. svc. award N.J. Speech-Lang.-Hearing Assn., 1987, community svc. award Urban League Hudson County, 1986, media award for achievement in preventing child abuse N.J. Child Assault Prevention Project, 1993. Mem. NAFE, Nat. Broadcast Editl. Assn. (bd. dirs. 1986-87), Nat. Broadcast Assn. Cmty. Affairs, Advt. Coun. N.J. (bd. trustees 1986—), N.J. Broadcasters Assn. (bd. dirs. 19926), Meadowlands Regional C. of C. (bd. dirs. 1991-92). Home: Winterwood Farm 449 Kingwood-Locktown Rd Flemington NJ 08822 Office: Sta WWOR-TV 9 Broadcast Plz Secaucus NJ 07094-2913

PINSKY, ELIZABETH LEAR, social worker; b. N.Y.C., Mar. 22, 1940; d. Phillip E. and Dora (H.) Lear; m. Lawrence M. Pinsky, Sept. 9, 1973; children: Stacey F., Caroline R. BS, Simmons Coll., 1961; MSW, Columbia U., 1963. Cert. social worker, N.Y. Intake worker Dept. of Child and Family Welfare, Westchester, N.Y., 1963-64; med. social worker Mt. Sinai Hosp., N.Y.C., 1964-67; psychiatric social worker Epilepsy Found., Nassau County, N.Y., 1968-72; field instr. Hunter Coll. Sch. Social Work, N.Y.C., 1970-72; dir. social svcs. Margaret Teitz Ctr. Nursing Care, Queens, N.Y., 1972-75, Grace Plaza Long Term Care Facility, Great Neck, N.Y., 1982-87; field instr. Adelphi U. Sch. Social Work, Garden City, N.Y., 1982-87; dir. Home Based Counseling Svcs., Great Neck, 1991—; pvt. practice psychotherapist, elder care cons. Great Neck, 1991—. Mem. NASW (exec. dir. Nassau County div. 1979-82), Acad. Cert. Social Workers, Sr. Umbrella Network of Nassau County (co-chairperson).

PINSON, ARTIE FRANCES, elementary school educator; b. Rusk, Tex., June 20, 1933; d. Tom and Minerva (McDuff) Neeley; m. Robert H. Pinson, Dec. 14, 1963 (div. Nov. 1967); 1 child, Deidre R. BA magna cum laude, Tex. Coll., 1953; postgrad., U. Tex., 1956, North Tex. U., 1958, 63, New Eng. Conservatory, 1955, 57, 59, 62; MEd, U. Houston, 1970. Music tchr. Bullock High Sch., LaRue, Tex., 1953-59; music tchr., 9th grade English tchr. Story High Sch., Palestine, Tex., 1959-64; 6th grade tchr. Turner Elem. Sch., Houston, 1964-66; 3d, 5th and 6th grade tchr. Kay Elem. Sch., Houston, 1966-70; 6th grade tchr. Pilgrim Elem. Sch., Houston, 1970-75; 3d to 6th grade math. tchr. Pleasantville Elem. Sch., Houston, 1975-79; kindergarten to 5th grade computer/math. tchr. Betsy Ross Elem. Sch., Houston, 1979—, instrnl. coord.; lead tchr. math./sci. program Shell/Houston Ind. Sch. Dist., 1986-87, Say "Yes" program, 1988-89; math. tchr. summer potpourri St. Francis Xavier Cath. Ch., 1991; math. tchr. sci. and engrng. awareness and coll. prep. program Tex. So. U., 1993, 94; presenter at confs. in field; conducts tchr. tng. workshops. Author computer software in field; contbr. articles to mags. Musician New Hope Bapt. Ch., Houston, 1991—, Sun. sch. tchr.; pianist Buckner Bapt. Haven Nursing Home, Houston, 1990-91. Recipient Excellence in Math. Teaching award Exxon Corp., 1990. Mem. Assn. African Am. Math. Educators (Salute to Math. Tchrs. award 1991, treas. 1991-93, sec. 1993—), Nat. Coun. Tchrs. Math., Tex. Coun. Tchrs. Math. (Excellence in Math. Tchg. award 1988), Houston Coun. Tchrs. of Math. (Excellence in Math. Tchg. award 1993), Heroines of Jericho. Home: 5524 Makeig St Houston TX 77026 Office: Betsy Ross Elem Sch 2819 Bay St Houston TX 77026

PINSON, LINDA JEAN, business book publisher, small business educator; b. Winnemucca, Nev., Mar. 11, 1941; d. F.W. Kelly Pearce and Sue Cohen Area; m. Raymond G. Pinson, Feb. 2, 1963; children: Glenn D., J. Kelley. BS in Edn., U. Nev., Reno, 1963. Cert. instr. Calif. Community Colls. Owner, founder Ray & Linda's Clock Repair, Tustin, Calif., 1979—; ptnr. Out of Your Mind. . .and Into the Market Place, Tustin, 1986-94; owner Out of Your Mind... and Into the Market Place, Tustin, Calif., 1994—; small bus. and pub. cons. throughout U.S., 1986—; tchr. colls., industries, bus. orgns. Co-author: The Home-Based Entrepreneur, 1990, 2d edit., 1993, Target Marketing for Small Business, 1989, 2d edit., 1993, Keeping the Books, 1988, 2d edit., 1993, Steps to Small Busines Start-Up, 1987, 2d edit., 1993, Anatomy of a Business Plan, 1987, 2d edit., 1993, The Woman Entrepreneur, 1992; co-author software program Automate Your Business Plan, 1991, 2d edit., 1993. Mem. coun. Gov. Wilson's Calif. Coun. to Promote Women in Bus., 1993—; mem. adv. coun. U.S. SBA, 1994. Named Small Press Pub. of Yr., Quality Books Inc., 1989, Women in Bus. Advocate of Yr., U.S. SBA, 1991; recipient Ben Franklin award Pub. Mktg. Assn., 1994. Mem. Nat. Assn. Women Bus. Owners (chpt. pres. 1992-93, Calif. state pres. 1994-95), Pubs. Mktg. Assn., COSMEP Pubs. Assn., Nat. Assn. Watch and Clock Collectors, Order Ea. Star, Gamma Phi Beta. Republican. Presbyterian. Office: Out of Your Mind & Into the Marketplace 13381 White Sand Dr Tustin CA 92680-4565

PINT, REBECCA ANNE, pharmacist; b. Akron, Ohio, Apr. 11, 1959; d. James Anthony and Betty Jean (Etling) P. BS in Pharmacy, Ohio State U., 1982. Lic. pharmacist, Ohio. Staff pharmacist Lane Drug Co., Canton, Ohio, 1982-83; pharmacy mgr. K-Mart Corp., Akron, 1983—. Editor: (newsletter) Pharmasummits, 1989-90. Soprano St. Paul Adult Choir, Akron, 1981—; trustee Canal Park Condominium Owners, Akron, 1986-89. Mem. Am. Pharm. Assn., Ohio Pharmacists Assn., Summit Pharm. Assn. (coun. 1990-93), Ohio State U. Alumni Assn. Summit County (bd. dirs. 1990-93, sec., 1991—). Democrat. Roman Catholic. Office: K-Mart 4414 Pharmacy 2975 S Arlington Rd Akron OH 44312-4797

PINTO, CHRISTINE MARIE, fundraising executive; b. Windber, Pa., Nov. 27, 1965; d. Patsy David and Rose Marie (Santucci) Pinto. BA in Journalism magna cum laude, Ind. U. of Pa., 1988. Comm. assoc. United Way, Allentown, Pa., 1989-91; freelance writer Doylestown, Easton, Pa., 1992; field rep. Lehigh Valley Unit Am. Cancer Soc., Allentown, 1993-94; dir. devel. Turning Point of Lehigh Valley, Bethlehem, Pa., 1994—. Vol. Big Brothers/Big Sisters of Lehigh Valley, Inc., Allentown, 1989—, Regional Hospice at Windber, 1992, Lehigh Valley Hospice, 1993. Mem. Women in Comms., Young Profls. Assn. (bd. dirs. 1989-92), Internat. Assn. Bus. Communicators (bd. dirs. 1989—), Bethlehem (Pa.) Area Jaycees. Democrat. Roman Catholic. Office: PO Box 5355 Bethlehem PA 18015

PINTO, ROSALIND, retired educator, civic volunteer; b. N.Y.C.; d. Barney and Jenny Abrams; m. Jesse E. Pinto (dec.); children: Francine, Jerry, Evelyn. BA in Polit. Sci. cum laude, Hunter Coll.; MA in Polit. Sci., History, Columbia U.; postgrad., Queens Coll., LaGuardia Community Coll. Lic. social studies tchr. jr. high sch., N.Y., per diem lifetime substitute; cert. N.Y. State secondary sch. social studies grades 7-12. Substitute tchr., 1966-69, 90, 91—; tchr. social studies I.S. 126Q, L.I. City, N.Y., 1969-88, Jr. High Sch. 217 Briarwood, N.Y.C., 1988-89; ret., 1989; part-time cluster tchr. social studies and communication arts Pub. Sch. 140, Bronx, N.Y., 1990-91, 92; substitute tchr. I.S. 227Q, 1992-93, Dist. 24Q, 1994, 95—; participant numerous personal and profl. devel. seminars and workshops. Author curriculum materials; contbr. chpt. to Study Guide for Regents Competency Test in U.S. History and Govt., 1990; contbr. poems to anthologies, include Tears of Fire, Dance on The Horizon, Outstanding Poets of 1995, Best Poems of 1994, Seasons to Come, poem to rec. The Sound of Poetry, Nat. Libr. of Poetry (editor's Choice award 1993, 94). Enrollment asst. Insight Heart Team, 1989; vol. receptionist Whitney Mus., Manhattan; mem. com. on pub. transp. Cmty. Bd. 6, Queens, 1990—, mem. com. on history, 1990—, chmn. beautification com., 1992—; active Great Smokies Song Chase Warren-Wilson Coll., N.C., 1992; vol. local polit. campaigns. Recipient cert. of appreciation for participation in worksite sponsor program Dept. Probate Cmty. Svc. Project, 1993. Mem. NAFE, Internat. Soc. Poets (lifetime mem. adv. panel, Internat. Poet of Merit award 1993), N.Y. Insight Alumni Assn., Forest Hills Van Ct. Homeowners Assn., ctrl. Queens Hist. Soc., Queens Hist. Soc., Columbia U. Grad. Sch. Arts and Scis. Alumni Assn., Hunter Coll. Alumni Assn., Mcpl. Art Soc. (hon. mention Design 2000 award), Robert F. Kennedy Dem. Assn. (bd. dirs.), Ctr. for Sci. in the Pub. Interest.

PINTO MCLAIN, CELESTE, lawyer; b. Greenwich, Conn., Sept. 10, 1949; d. John H. and Celeste (Solari) Pinto; m. Thomas E. McLain, July 2, 1983; children: John Thomas, Brannack J. BA, Trinity Coll., Washington, 1971; JD, Georgetown U., 1974. Bar: Calif. 1974. Assoc. Omelveny & Myers, L.A., 1974-79; assoc. gen. counsel, asst. gen. counsel, asst. corp. sec. Tiger Internat., L.A., 1979-86; trustee Pilgrim Group Mut. Funds, 1990—; mem. bd. dirs. Calif. Bd. Accountancy, 1985-93; mem. screening panel President's Commn. on White House Fellowships, L.A., 1993—; seminar panelist Duke U., Durham, N.C., 1992. Bd. dirs., com. chmn. Luminaires, L.A., 1991—, Nat. Railroad Passenger Corp., 1994— (apptd. by U.S. Sen.); chmn., mem. steering com. L.A. Women's Forum, 1992—; mem. nat. law alumni bd. Georgetown U., Washington, 1992—. Recipient Leadership Achievement award in bus. YMCA, L.A., 1981. Mem. Calif. Bar Assn., Am. Arbitration Assn. (arbitrator 1981—), Orgn. Women Execs. (pres., bd. dirs. 1984-88), Trinity Coll. Alumnae Assn. (exec. coun. 1972—, mem. bd. dirs. 1994—), Phi Beta Kappa. Office: PO Box 49835 Los Angeles CA 90049-0835

PINZONE, ALISON LYONS, construction engineer; b. Melrose, Mass., Mar. 22, 1957; d. Gilbert Francis and Hilda (Robertson) Lyons; m. Scott Russell Pinzone, Sept. 11, 1982. BS Engrng. in Civil and Urban Engrng., U. Pa., 1979. Engr. Burns & Roe, Oradell, N.J., 1979-81; asst. supt. Turner Constrn., Seattle, 1981-82; estimator Turner Constrn., L.A., 1982-85, asst. supt., 1985-86, purchasing agt., 1986-87; project engr. Turner Constrn., Costa Mesa, Calif., 1987-89; project engr. Turner Constrn., L.A., 1989-91, sr. project engr., 1991-92, project mgr., 1993—. Home: 21060 Timber Ridge Rd Yorba Linda CA 92686-6991 Office: Turner Constrn Co-LA 555 W 5th St 37th Fl Los Angeles CA 90013

PIOTRKOWSKI, CHAYA S., psychologist, researcher; b. Altenmarkt, Germany, Nov. 26, 1946; arrived in Can., 1951; 1 child. BA, U. Calif., Berkeley, 1969; PhD, U. Mich., 1977. lic. psychologist, N.Y. Instr. Wayne State U., Detroit, 1975-77; asst. prof. New Sch. for Social Rsch., N.Y.C., 1977-79, Yale U., New Haven, Conn., 1979-84; assoc. prof. St. John's U., Jamaica, N.Y., 1984-88; dir. Nat. Coun. of Jewish Women Ctr. for the Child, N.Y.C., 1989—; bd. sci. counselors Nat. Inst. for Occupational Safety and Health, CDC, Atlanta, 1992—; bd. trustees Home Instruction Program for presch. children, 1991-93; adv. bd. Miss. Forum on Children and Families, 1992—; conf. leader in field. Author: Work and the Family System, 1979; mem. editl. bd. Am. Jour. Orthopsychiatry, 1989—, Applied Behavioral Sci. Rev., 1992—; assoc. editor Jour. of Occupational Health Psychology; contbr. articles to profl. jours. Jr. faculty fellow Yale U., 1983-84, fellow Ctr. for Study of Human Rights, Columbia U., 1983-84; grantee numerous orgns. including Yale U., 1981, City of N.Y., 1986, U.S. Dept. Edn., 1990-93, U.S. Dept. Health and Human Svcs., 1990-93, Women's Bur., Dept. Labor, 1991-92, David and Lucile Packard Found., 1993—, A.L. Mailman Family Found., 1993-94, Rauch Found., 1992-93, Smith Richardson Found., 1992-93, Carnegie Corp., 1992-94, Ford Found., 1993-94. Fellow Am. Orthopsychiat. Assn.; mem. APA, APHA, Am. Edn. Rsch. Assn., Soc. for Rsch. in Child Devel., Nat. Coun. Family Rels.

PIPER, ANNETTE CLEONE, social services administrator, researcher; b. St. Paul, July 13, 1936; d. Frank Robert Zimmerman; m. Aaron Cleaves Piper, Apr. 17, 1958 (div. 1974); children: Michelle, Renee. BA, Wayne State U., 1960, MSW, 1965, postdoctoral, 1985—. Inst. rsch. Wayne State U., Detroit, 1965-69; program mgr. Ariz. Dept. Econ. Security, Bisbee, 1976-79; tng. and personnel coordinator Mich. Dept. Social Svcs., Detroit, 1971-73, mgr. svcs. sect., 1973-74; program mgr. Mich. Dept. Social Svcs., Pontiac, 1974-76; dep. dir. Sta. WCCYS Mich. Dept. Social Svcs., Detroit, 1979-88; dist. dir.r. Mich. Dept. Social Svcs., Westland, 1988—; ret., 1988; instr., cons. Cochise Community Coll., Douglas, Ariz., 1979. Mem. Nat. Assn. Child Welfare Adminstrs., Nat. Child Welfare Leadership Ctr., Am. Pub. Welfare Assn., Wayne State U. Alumni Assn, Psi Chi. Home: 23010 Webster Oak Park MI 48237-2119

PIPER, CAROL ADELINE, councilman; b. Chgo., Jan. 28, 1924; d. John and Myra May (Hughett) Preston; m. Robert Donald Piper, Dec. 18, 1945;

children: Stephen, Barbara, Bruce, Diane. BA, North Cen. Coll., Naperville, Ill., 1945. Asst. rsch. chemist Quaker Oats Co., Chgo., 1945; office mgr. H. & R. Block, Ridgewood, N.J., 1977-82; councilman City of Naperville, 1987-91; re-elected to Naperville City Council, 1991-95; appointed to Electric Adv. Bd. of Naperville, 1987-91; bd. dirs. Naperville Settlement Mus. Bd., 1991-95. Precinct committeewoman Naperville Rep. Com., 1956-70; mem. Glen Rock (N.J.) Pub. Libr. Bd., 1975, Glen Rock City Coun., 1977-82, 91—; apptd. bd. Naperville City TV, 1991—. Mem. LWV (pres. Glen Rock 1972-74). Home: 104 Devon Ln Naperville IL 60540-5840 Office: City of Naperville 175 W Jackson Ave 400 S Eagle St Naperville IL 60566-7020

PIPER, FREDESSA MARY, school system administrator; b. Monroe, La., June 19, 1945; d. Floyd Preston and Zona Mary (Jones) P.; m. Robert John Parks, Mar. 20, 1969 (div. 1980). BS, Ill. State U., 1964; MEd with distinction, DePaul U., 1972; EdD, Loyola U., Chgo., 1984. Cert. tchr., gen. adminstr., sch. supt., Ill. Tchr. secondary schs. Chgo. Pub. Schs., 1964-73, staff asst., 1974-76, coord., 1977-83, tchr., coord., 1984-87; asst. supt. Ednl. Svc. Region Cook County, Chgo., 1987—; project coord. Malcolm X City Coll., Chgo., 1973-74; coord. Athletes for Better Edn., Chgo., 1975-77; cons. Community Reading is Rewarding Program, Chgo., 1989—; author radio scripts, speeches. Project coord. Local Ward Back to Sch. Fun-Fest, Chgo., 1983—; program coord. Pre-Thanksgiving Day Srs. Dinner, Chgo., 1983—; asst. to chmn. Re-election Campaign, Chgo., 1986, 88; promotional dir. Unity in Community Boat Cruise, Chgo., 1987—. Mem. ASCD, Nat. Alliance Black Sch. Educators, Am. Assn. Sch. Adminstrs., Phi Delta Kappa, Delta Epsilon Sigma. Democrat. Baptist. Office: Ednl Svc Region Cook County 10220 S 76th Ave Bridgeview IL 60455

PIPER, LINDA AMMANN, personnel consulting firm executive; b. Newark, Nov. 29, 1949; d. Ernest D. and Marie (Liccese) Ammann; m. Stephen George Piper; 2 children. BA, W.Va. U., 1972. Cert. pers. cons. Mgr., asst. buyer Gilchrist Co., Boston, 1972-74; mgr. Harvard Coop. Soc., Cambridge, Mass., 1974-77; pers. cons. Wellesley Profl. Corp., Mass., 1977-82; pres. Career Connections, Inc., Nashua, N.H., 1982—. Mem. Nashua C. of C. (amb.), Nat. Human Resource Assn. (bd. dir., ways and means chair), No. New Eng. Assn. Pers. Svcs. (bd. dirs. 1982—, treas. 1983-84, v.p. 1984-85, sec. 1986-88), Nat. Assn. Pers. Svcs., N.E. Human Resources Assn., New Hampshire Assn. Temporary Staffing Svcs., 1994—. Office: Career Connections Inc 74 Northeastern Blvd Nashua NH 03062-3160

PIPER, LINDA S., educational administrator; b. Dec. 8, 1944; m. Michael L. Piper; childen: David, Amanda, Mindy. BS in Bus., Ind. State U., 1967, MS in Vocat. Edn., Adminstrn. and Bus., 1976; postgrad., Sterling Inst., 1992. Tchr. coord. bus. and office edn. North Knox High Sch., Edwardsport, Ind., 1967-70; supr. bus. and office edn., coord. extended svcs. Divsn. Vocat. Edn., Ind. Dept. Edn., 1970-76; dir. postsecondary vocat. edn., mgr. data and info. Commn. on Vocat. and Tech. Edn., 1977-91; exec. dir. Ind. Occupational Info. Coord. Com., Indpls., 1991—; mem. Ind. Leadership Devel. Consortium, 1975; cons. in field.; mem. state plan workshop U.S. Dept. Edn. Mem. Am. Vocat. Assn. (mem. various seminars and confs.), Ind. Vocat. Assn. (mem. handbook revision com.), IETA, INRS, ICVA. Home: 7263 N Audubon Rd Indianapolis IN 46250-2617 Office: INDOICC 10 N Senate Ave Rm 205 Indianapolis IN 46204-2201

PIPER, MARGARITA SHERERTZ, school administrator; b. Petersburg, Va., Dec. 20, 1926; d. Guy Lucas and Olga Doan (Akers) Sherertz; m. Glenn Clair Piper, Feb. 3, 1950; children: Mark Stephen, Susan Leslie Piper Weathersbee. BA in Edn., Mary Washington Coll. of Fredericksburg, 1948; MEd, U. Va., 1973, EdS, 1976. Svc. rep. C&P Telephone, Washington, 1948-55, adminstrv. asst., 1955-56, svc. supr., 1956-62; tchr. Culpeper (Va.) County Pub. Schs., 1970-75, reading lab dir., 1975-80; asst. prin. Rappahannock (Va.) County Pub. Schs., 1980-81, prin., 1981-88, dir. pupil pers., spl. programs, 1988—; chair PD 9 regional transition adv. bd. Culpeper, Fauquier, Madison, Orange and Rappahannock Counties, Va., 1991-94; vice chair Family Assessment and Planning Team, Washington, 1992—. Recipient Va. Gov. Schs. Commendation cert. Commonwealth of Va., 1989-93. Mem. NEA, Va. Edn. Assn., Va. Coun. Adminstrs. Spl. Edn., Va. Assn. Edn. for Gifted, Rappahannock Edn. Assn. Democrat. Episcopalian. Office: Rappahannock County Pub Sch 6 Schoolhouse Rd Washington VA 22747

PIPER, PAT KATHRYN, state senator; b. Delavan, Minn., July 16, 1934; d. Claire I. and Geneva R. (Tibodeau) P. BA, Coll. St. Teresa, Winona, Minn., 1962; MA, Cath. U., 1972. Tchr. St. Augustine Sch., Austin, Minn., 1956-58, St. Francis Sch., Rochester, Minn., 1958-60, St. James (Minn.) Sch., 1960-61; catechist St. Catherine Sch. Ctr., Luverne, Minn., 1961-63, catechist, dir., 1964-67; catechist Area Ctr., Hayfield, Minn., 1963-64; dir. St. Ann's Ctr., Slayton, Minn., 1967-69, Christian Edn. Ctr., Austin, 1969-94; mem. Minn. Ho. of Reps., 1982-84, 84-86, Senate State of Minn., 1986, 90, 92; chair Senate Family Svcs. Com. Contbr. articles to profl. jours. Active United Way, YMCA, Council for Handicapped, Salvation Army. Mem. LWV, Bus. and Profl. Women. Mem. Democrat Farmer Labor Party. Roman Catholic. Lodge: Zonta. Home: 800 1st Dr NW Austin MN 55912-3070 Office: Minn State Senate G-9 State Capitol Saint Paul MN 55155*

PIPERNO, SHERRY LYNN, psychotherapist; b. La Crosse, Wis., Sept. 22, 1953; d. Morris and Leona Jennie (Shelmadine-Hanson) Piperno. BA in Fine Arts, U. N.Mex., 1982, MA in Counseling, 1989. Nat. cert. counselor; lic. clin. mental health counselor. Mental health counselor Bernalillo County Detention Ctr., Albuquerque, 1990—; group facilitator and youth authority Juveinile Probation dept. 2d Jud. Dist. Ct., Albuquerque, 1990-92; program therapist Heights Psychiatric Hosp., Albuquerque, 1990-91; cons. Albuquerque Fire Dept. Mem. ACA, Am. Mental Health Counselors Assn., Internat. Assn. Addictions and Offender Counseling, Fraternal Order of Police. Democrat. Lutheran.

PIPITONE, PHYLLIS L., psychologist, educator, author; b. Chgo.; m. S. Joseph Pipitone, Aug. 28, 1948 (dec.); children: Guy, Daniel, Paul; m. Thomas A. Cox, Jan. 3, 1980. Student Chgo. Conservatory Music, 1941-44, Peabody Conservatory Music, 1945, Chgo. Tchrs. Coll., 1946-47, So. Meth. U., 1951-52; MA, U. Akron (Ohio), 1967; PhD, Kent (Ohio) State U., 1974. With B.S. & H. Advt. Agy., Chgo., 1941-43; instr. piano and theory Music Acad. Chgo.; psychologist, instr. U. Akron and Kent State U., 1970-79; pvt. practice psychology, Akron, 1967—; lectr. in field in U.S and abroad. Served with WAC, AUS, 1944-46. NIMH grantee, 1974, HEW Child Devel. fellow, 1974. Mem. Am. Psychol. Assn., Nat. Assn. Sch. Psychologists, Mensa, Council Exceptional Children, Am. Hypnosis Soc., Kent Psi Research Group, Assn. Study/Dreams, Am. Soc. Psychical Research, Phi Delta Kappa. Clubs: Tuesday Musical, Weathervane Theatre Women's Bd., Akron Women's City, Wadsworth Women's. Home: 224 Pheasant Run Wadsworth OH 44281-2344

PIPPEL, GERANE GODDARD, volunteer; b. Long Beach, Calif., Jan. 16, 1929; d. Philip Hubbard and Ethlyn (Bradley) Goddard; m. John Richard Lawson, Jan. 30, 1946 (dec. 1969); children: Kathleen Lynd Hodges, Dawn Elizabeth Lawson, Susan Doreen Lawson; m. William Harold Pippel Jr., Apr. 4, 1979; children: Mary Ellen Leopard, Dulcy Murchison, Cecilia Anne Andrzewski. AA, Santa Ana Jr. Coll., Calif.; student, Del. State U., 1992—. Adminstrv. sec. Paint Branch Unitarian Ch., Adelphi, Md., 1966-73; asst. dir. field svcs. Americans United for Ch. and State, Silver Spring, Md., 1973-76; exec. sec. to dir. edn. Chemical Mfg. Assn., Washington, 1976-79; sec. Lighthouse Realty, Ocean City, Md., 1981-82; asst. town clk. Fenwick Island Town Hall, Fenwick Island, Del., 1983-84; coun. mem. Persons with Disabilities Dover, Del., 1992—; mem. Universal Health Care Reform, Dover, 1993—, Nat. Assn. Social Workers, Dover, 1994—; co-chair adv. bd. Crossroads Milford, Del., 1994—. Mem. Gov. adv. coun. Svcs. for Aging and Adults with Physical Disabilities, New Castle, Del., 1992—; medicare/medicaid counselor Elderinfo, Dover, Del., 1993—. Mem. World Clown Assn., Del. Agenda for Women (health com.), Ret. Sr. Vol. Program (knitter), Health Care Providers (vol.), Nat. Orgn. for Women (vol.). Democrat. Methodist. Home: 58 Keenwik Rd Selbyville DE 19975

PIRAINO, ANN MAE, seminar trainer, leader, vocational counselor; b. Vancouver, Wash.; d. Elsworth Wallace Schmoeckel and Alice Marie (Blankenbickler) Avalos; m. Michael Salvatore, Nov. 19, 1983. BA in Edn., Seattle U., 1972; MA in Appl. Behavioral Sci., City U. Leadership Inst of Sea, 1987. Cert. rehab. counselor. Sec. to supt. Pasco (Wash.) Sch. Dist. No. 1, 1972-74; adminstrv. asst. Burns and Roe, Inc., Richland, Wash., 1974-81; exec. sec. UNC Nuclear Industries, Inc., Richland, Wash., 1981-83, Fairchild Semiconductor, Inc., Puyallup, Wash., 1984-87; instr. Eton Tech. Inst. (ETI), Federal Way, Wash., 1987-89; trainer, cons. Piraino Prodns., Wash., 1985—; seminar leader and cons. Profl. Sec. Internat., Wash., Alaska and Oreg. state chpts., 1985—; cons. Fed. Way Women's Network and Career Devel. Network, Wash., 1985-88; employment coord. Bus. Computer Tng. Inst., Tacoma, 1989-90; adj. faculty Office Automation Griffin Coll., Tacoma, 1990; vocat. rehab. counselor Total Care Svcs., 1990-92, 94—, Favorite Cons., 1990-94. Editor: (newsletter) The Circuit Writer, 1985-87, (pub. assn. newsletters) Hear Ye, Hear Ye, 1986-88, Training Wheels, 1987-90, Speak Up!, 1991-92, Reflections, 1991—; role expert: (competency study) ASTD Competency and Standards Project, 1988. Co. rep. United Way/Fairchild Semiconductor, Wash., 1986; team co-leader March of Dimes/Fairchild Semiconductor, Wash., 1986; team leader March of Dimes/Town Criers Toastmasters, Wash., 1989, 90. Recipient Xi Alpha Epsilon and Beta Sigma Phi Woman of Yr. award, 1979-81; named Sec. of Yr. Pas-Ric-Ken/Sea Tac Chpts., Profl. Secs. Internat., Richland/Fed. Way, Wash., 1979, 90; Sec. of Yr. Wash.-Alaska Div. Profl. Secs. Internat., Spokane, 1980. Mem. NAFE, ASTD (chpt. v.p. 1988-89, pres. 1990), Profl. Secs. Internat. (chpt. pres. 1985-86, 91-92, pres.-elect Wash./Alaska divsn. 1986-87, pres. 1987-88), Toastmasters (area gov. 1991-92, dean Leadership Inst. dist. 32 1992-94), Nat. Assn. Rehab. Profls. in Pvt. Sector, Wash. Women in Worker's Compensation. Home: 38807 134th Pl SE Auburn WA 98002

PIRET, MARGUERITE ALICE, investment banker; b. St. Paul, May 10, 1948; d. E.L. and Alice P.; children: Andrew, Anne. AB, Radcliffe Coll., 1969; MBA, Harvard U., 1974. Comml. loan officer Bank New Eng. (now Fleet Bank), Boston, 1974-79; mng. dir. Kridel Securities, N.Y.C., 1979-81; pres., founder, dir. Newbury, Piret & Co., Inc., Boston, 1981—; trustee, chmn. audit com. Pioneer Mutual Funds, Boston. Vis. com. mem. Am. decorative arts and sculpture Mus. Fine Arts, Boston, 1982—; mem. nominating com. for candidates for overseer of Harvard U. and for candidates for dir. of Harvard Alumni Assn.; adv. com. on shareholder responsibility Harvard U., 1986-87; trustee, mem. exec. com. Boston U. Med. Ctr. Hosp., 1979—, chmn. fin. com.; trustee Mass. Hosp. Assn., 1983-86, Boston Ballet Ctr. for Dance Edn., 1989-93. Mem. Harvard Club. Office: Newbury Piret & Co Inc One Boston Pl Boston MA 02108

PIRNIE, ABBY J., federal agency administrator; b. N.Y.C., Dec. 17, 1949; d. Duncan and Esther (Lewis) P.; m. Abbott B. Lipsky, Jr., Aug. 20, 1971 (div. 1983); children: Leah M. Lipsky, Alyson B. Lipsky; m. Brian J. Maas, Sept. 22, 1984; children: Brittain M. Maas, Dana P. Maas. AB, Smith Coll., 1971, EdM, 1972. Tchr. Pinewood Sch., Los Altos, Calif., JFK Jr. H.S., Florence, Mass., 1971-75; market adminstr. MCI, Washington, 1976-77; cons. Booz, Allen and Hamilton, Bethesda, Md., 1977-78; spl. asst. to dir. Office of Enforcement and Office of Water EPA, Washington, 1978-84, chief environ. results br. Office Mgmt. Sys. and Evaluation, Office Policy, Planning and Evaluation, 1984-86, dir. info. mgmt. and svcs. divsn. Office Info. Resources Mgmt., Office Adminstrn. and Resources Mgmt., 1986-89, dir. program sys. divsn., 1989-91, dir. Office Coop. Environ. Mgmt., Office Adminstr., 1991—. Office: EPA 401 M St SW Rm 1145 WT Washington DC 20460

PIRONTI, LAVONNE DE LAERE, association executive; b. L.A., Jan. 11, 1946; d. Emil Joseph and Pearl Mary (Vilmur) De Laere; m. Aldo Pironti, May 21, 1977. BA in Internat. Rels., U. So. Calif., L.A., 1967. Commd. ensign USN, 1968-91, advanced through grades to comdr., 1979; pers. officer Lemoore (Calif.) Naval Air Sta., 1972-74; human rels. mgmt. specialist Human Resource Mgmt. Detachment, Naples, Italy, 1975-78; comms. staff officer Supreme Hdqrs. Allied Powers Europe, Shape, Belgium, 1979-83; dir. Navy Family Svc. Ctr. Sigonella Naval Air Sta., Sicily, 1983-85; exec. officer Naval Sta. Guam, Apra Harbor, 1985-87; comms. staff officer NATO Comm. and Info. Sys. Agy., Brussels, Belgium, 1987-89; polit. officer for Guam, trust Territories Pacific Islands Comdr. Naval Forces Marianas, Agana, Guam, 1989-91; store mgr. Sandal Tree, Lihue, Hawaii, 1991-92; CEO, exec. dir. YWCA of Kauai County, Lihue, 1992—. Vice pres. Kauai Sex Abuse Core Group, Lihue, 1993—; co-chair Kauai Human Svcs. Coun., Lihue; steering com. Hawaii Health and Human Svcs. Alliance, Lihue, 1993—; adv. bd. County Family Self-Sufficiency Program, Lihue, 1993—. Decorated Navy Commendation medal, Meritorious Svc. Medal with 1 star, Def. Meritorious Svc. Medal with 2 stars, others; named Fed. Woman of the Yr. Comdr. Naval Forces Marianas, 1986-87. Roman Catholic. Office: YWCA Kauai County 3094 Elua St Lihue HI 96766

PIRSCH, CAROL MCBRIDE, state senator, community relations administrator; b. Omaha, Dec. 27, 1936; d. Lyle Erwin and Hilfrie Louise (Lebeck) McBride; student U. Miami, Oxford, Ohio, U. Nebr., Omaha; m. Allen I. Pirsch, Mar. 28, 1954; children—Pennie Elizabeth, Pamela Elaine, Patrice Eileen, Phyllis Erika, Peter Allen, Perry Andrew. Former mem. data processing staff Omaha Public Schs.; former mem. wage practices dept. Western Electric Co., Omaha; former legal sec., Omaha; former office mgr. Pirsch Food Brokerage Co., Inc., Omaha; former employment supr. U.S. West Communications, Omaha, now mgr. pub. policy; mem. Nebr. Senate, 1979—. Pres. bd. dirs. Omaha Libr.; past pres., bd. dirs. Nebr. Coalition for Victims of Crime. Recipient Golden Elephant award; Outstanding Legis. Efforts award YWCA, Breaking the Rule of Thumb award Nebr. Domestic Violence Sexual Assault Coalition, Cert. of Appreciation award U.S. Dept. Justice. Mem. VASA, Nat. Orgn. Victim Assistance (Outstanding Legis. Leadership award), Freedom Found., Orgn. U.S. West Women, Nat. Order Women Legislators, Tangier Women's Aux., Footprinters Internat., Keystone Citizen Patrol (Keystoner of the Month award), Audubon Soc., Rotary Internat. (bd. dirs.), N.W. Community Club, Benson Rep. Women's Club, Bus. and Profl. Rep. Women Club. Office: State Capitol Lincoln NE 68509

PISCATELLI, NANCY MARIE, educator; b. Boston, Feb. 11, 1953; d. Joseph Murphy and Eleanor Elizabeth (Jeffers) Kelley; m. Thomas George Piscatelli, Apr. 17, 1976; 1 child, Thomas Joseph. BS, Bridgewater State Coll., 1975, MEd, 1979; MEd, Boston Coll., 1977; EdD, Northeastern U., 1989. With sales Wm. Filenes & Sons Co., Boston, 1969-76; tchr. Boston Pub. Schs., 1975—; cons. Tchrs. Corp. Network, 1979-80. Author/editor: (handbook) The Paraprofessional Handbook, 1979; contbr. articles to profl. jours. Campaign worker Dem. Com., Quincy, Mass., 1975—; active sch. vol. pet project of Mrs. George Bush. Mem. Am. Fedn. Tchrs., Nat. Coun. Tchrs. Math., Internat. Reading Assn., Ea. Educators Rsch. Assn., Boston Tchrs. Union, Boston Computer Soc. Roman Catholic. Home: Pheasant Hill 10 Chickadee Dr Norfolk MA 02056-1741 Office: Boston Pub Schs 26 Court St Boston MA 02108-2505

PISCIOTTA, VIVIAN VIRGINIA, psychotherapist; b. Chgo., Dec. 7; d. Vito and Mary Lamia; m. Vincent Diago Pisciotta, Apr. 1, 1951; children: E. Christopher, Vittorio, V. Charles, Mary A. Pisciotta Higley, Thomas Sansone. BA in Clin. Psychology, Antioch U., 1974; MSW, George Williams Coll., 1984; postgrad., Erickson Inst. of No. Ill., 1990. Lic. clin. social worker; diplomate in clin. social work. Short-term therapist Woman Line, Dayton, Ohio, 1976-79; psychotherapist Cicero (Ill.) Family Svcs., 1982-83, Maywood (Ill.) - Proviso Family Svcs., 1983-84, Maple Ave. Med. Ctr., Brookfield, Ill., 1985-88, Met. Med. Clinic, Naperville, Ill., 1986-88; allied staff Riveredge Psychiat. Hosp., Forest Park, Ill., 1986—, Linden Oaks Hosp., Naperville, Ill., 1990; psychotherapist, pvt. practice Oakbrook, Ill., 1988—; psychotherapist, co-founder Archer Austin Counseling Ctr., Chgo., 1988-89; psychotherapist, founder Archer Counseling Ctr., Chgo., 1989—; allied staff Linden Oaks Psychiat. Hosp., Naperville, 1990—; substitute tchr. Chgo. Pub. High Sch., 1981. Author treatment prog., workshops in field. Co-founder Co-org Nursery Sch., Rockford, Ill., 1956; leader Great Books of the Western World series, Piqua, Ohio, 1977, Rockford, 1960-65; leader Girl Scouts U.S., St. Bridget Sch., Rockford, 1968-71. Mem. Assn. Labor-Mgmt. and Cons. on Alcoholism, Soc. Clin. Exptl. Hypnosis, Nat. Assn. Social Workers, Acad. Cert. Social Workers, Nat. social Wk. Register, Antioch Univ. Alumnus Assn. Rockford Coll. Alumnae Orgn. (newsletter contbr. 1972-73), Soc. for Clin. and Exptl. Hypnosis (assoc. mem.), Internat. Soc. for Clin. and Exptl. Hypnosis (assoc. mem.). Republican. Roman Catholic. Office: Archer Counseling Ctr 7002 W Archer Ave Ste 2B Chicago IL 60638-2202 also: Oakbrook Profl Bldg Oakbrook Ctr Mall Ste 214 Oak Brook IL 60521

PISCOTTANO, ANN USCILLA, city official; b. New Haven, Feb. 5, 1954; d. Victor and Martha (Ianotti) Uscilla; m. Louis James Piscottano, Dec. 1, 1989; children: Martin, Louis, Daniel, Anthony, Joseph. Alderwoman City of New Haven; active Airport Adv. Bd., New Haven. Bd. dirs. People Against Violence Everywhere; mem. parish coun. St. Bernadette Ch., New Haven; mem. exec. bd., treas. St. Bernadette Sch.; founder Friends of East Shore. Home: 21 Ira St New Haven CT 06512 Office: Bd of Aldermen City Hall 165 Church St New Haven CT 06510

PISTELLA, CHRISTINE LEY, public health educator; b. Pitts., July 11, 1949; d. David Adam and Mary Louise (Barrett) Ley; m. Frank Joseph Pistella; 1 child, Lauren Nicole. BA in Edn., U. Pitts., 1970, MSW, 1972, MPH, 1977, PhD with distinction, 1979. Lic. social worker, Pa. Program counselor/supr. Transitional Svcs., Inc., Pitts., 1972-74; mental health profl. St. Francis Med. Ctr., Pitts., 1974-75; sr. rsch. social worker Magee-Women's Hosp., Pitts., 1976-78; rsch. assoc. Sch. Pub. Health U. Pitts., 1976-80, rsch. coord. Sch. Social Wk., 1978-79; asst. prof. pub. health U. Pitts. Sch. Pub. Health, 1980—; rsch. cons. USPHS Region V, Chgo., 1985-88, Washington-Greens Human Svcs., 1982-84, Southwestern Pa. Area on Aging, Monessen, 1980-83; rsch. dir. Family Health Coun. of Western Pa., Pitts., 1982-87. Contbr. articles to profl. jours., chpts. to books; editor/co-editor more than 10 rsch. monographs on family health, social wk. Mem. Mayor's Commn. on Families, Pitts., 1988-94, Infant Mortality Rev. Team, Pa. Perinatal Assn., Pitts., 1990-93, Injury Prevention Adv. Bd. of Allegheny County, Pitts., 1989—, Venango-Forest Cmty. Health Action Com., 1992-95; mem. steering com. Pa. Area Health Edn. Ctr., 1994-95. Mem. NASW, APHA, Nat. Rural Health Assn., Pa. Forum for Primary Health Care, Pa. Pub. Health Assn., Assn. of Tchrs. of Maternal and Child Health, Assn. Cert. Social Workers, Greater Pitts. C. of C. (alumni bd. of leadership Pitts. 1991-94), Delta Omega. Democrat. Roman Catholic. Office: U Pitts Grad Sch Pub Health 216 Parran Hall Pittsburgh PA 15261

PITASI, JUDY, nurse; b. Oneida, Tenn., June 29, 1950; d. Roy Vernon and Hattie (Turner) Cadle; m. Joseph Anthony Pitasi, June 29, 1984; children: Lauren Leigh, Marc Andrew. Diploma, U. Tenn., 1970; grad., USAF Flight Nurse Course, 1979, USAF Nursing Mgmt. Sch., 1982, Aeromedical Ground Coord. Sch., 1983. Charge nurse Shepherd Spinal Ctr., Atlanta; supr. Met. Hosp., Atlanta. Mem. Nat. Rep. Senatorial com. Maj. USAF, 1974-87. Named Outstanding Jr. Officer Ga., 1984. Mem. Res. Officers Assn. (v.p. 1982, nat. com. 1980-84), Emergency Dept. Nurses Assn., Assn. Mil. Surgeons U.S. Baptist. Republican.

PITCHER, HELEN IONE, healthcare services administrator; b. Colorado Springs, Colo., Aug. 6, 1931; d. William Forest Medlock and Frankie La Vone (Hamilton) Tweed; m. Richard Edwin Pitcher, Sept. 16, 1949; children: Dushka Myers, Suzanne, Marc. Student, U. Colo., 1962-64, Ariz. State U., 1966, Maricopa Tech. Coll., 1967, Scottsdale C.C., 1979-81. Design draftsman Sundstrand Aviation, Denver, 1962-65; tech. illustrator Sperry, Phoenix, 1966-68; art dir. Integrated Circuit Engring., Scottsdale, Ariz., 1968-71, dir. advt., 1981-92; advt. artist Motorola Inc., Phoenix, 1971-74; pres. Pitcher Tech. Pubs., Scottsdale, 1974-81; nursing cons. Nursing Cons. Connection, Fountain Hills, Ariz., 1993—. Profl. advisor Paradise Valley Sch. Dist., Phoenix, 1984—; mem. bd. advisors graphic arts dept. Ariz. State U., Tempe. mem. Nat. Audio Visual Assn., Bus. Profl. Advt. Assn. (treas. 1982-86), Direct Mktg. Club. Democrat. Mem. Ch. Christ. Home: 13681 N Pima Rd Scottsdale AZ 85260-4105

PITKAPAASI, ELIN LYDIA, construction executive; b. Phila., June 4, 1952; d. Unto and Wilma Helen (Koski) P.; (div. 1981). BA in Psychology, Calif. State U., Fullerton, 1980; postgrad., Drexel U., 1981-86. Sec. Constrn. Coordinated, Inc., Conshohocken, Pa., 1981-82, adminstrv. asst., 1982-83, asst. project mgr., 1983-85, project mgr., 1985—. Vol. coach AMBUCS Spl. Olympics, Conshochocken, 1988-91; vol. Am. Assn. EMT's, Orange County, Calif., 1975-77, CAP, Bryn Mawr, Pa. and Orange County, 1968-73. Democrat. Home: 200 W 4th Ave Conshohocken PA 19428 Office: Constrn Coordinated Inc 101 E 8th Ave Conshohocken PA 19428-1779

PITT, JANE, medical educator; b. Frankfurt, Fed. Republic Germany, Aug. 25, 1938; came to U.S., 1939.; d. Ludwig Friederich and Vera (Aberle) Ries; m. Martin Irwin Pitt, Aug. 12, 1962 (dec. 1980); children: Jennifer, Eric Jonathan; m. Robert Harry Socolow, May 25, 1986; stepchildren: David, Seth. BA, Radcliffe Coll., 1960; MD, Harvard U., 1964. Diplomate Am. Bd. Pediatrics. Resident Children's Hosp. Med. Ctr., Boston, 1964-66; fellow Tufts U. Med. Sch., Boston, 1966-67, Harvard U. Med. Sch., Boston, 1967-69; asst. prof. SUNY Downstate Sch. Medicine, N.Y.C., 1970-71; asst. prof. Coll. Physicians and Surgeons Columbia U., N.Y.C., 1971-75, assoc. prof. Coll. Physicians and Surgeons, 1975—; mem. instl. rev. bd. Columbia Health Scis. Campus, N.Y.C., 1982—. Reviewer Jour. of Infectious Diseases, New Eng. Jour. Medicine, 1976—; contbr. articles to profl. jours. Grantee NIH, 1974, 78, 87, 88, 89. Fellow Infectious Disease Soc.; mem. NIH (grantee study sects.), Pediatric Infectious Disease Soc., Soc. Pediatric Research. Democrat. Jewish. Home: 34 Westcott Rd Princeton NJ 08540-3060 Office: Columbia U Coll Physicians Surgeons 630 W 168th St New York NY 10032-3702

PITTA, PATRICIA JOYCE, psychologist; b. N.Y.C., July 3, 1947; d. John Joseph and Mildred (Gioiosa) P.; m. Eric Eugene Kirk; children: Eric Jon, Kevin. BA, Queens Coll., 1968; MS, Hunter Coll., 1972; PhD, Fordham U., 1975. Recreational therapist Roosevelt Hosp., N.Y.C., 1968-73, psychology intern, 1973-74; staff psychologist NYU Med. Ctr., 1974-78, clin. instr., 1975—; pvt. practice psychology Manhasset, N.Y., 1977—; chief psychologist St. John's Episc. Hosp., Smithtown, N.Y., 1978-79; cons. North Shore U. Hosp., Manhasset, 1979-84; mem. faculty L.I. family therapy div. Inst. Psychoanalysis; supr. psychologist Clin. Psychology Doctoral Program St. John's U., N.Y.; media psychologist, relationship expert Nat. & Local T.V.; mem. bd. dirs., task force head divsn. pvt. practice ADA, 1994—; lectr. in field. Contbr. articles to profl. jours., newspapers. Mem. APA (bd. dirs. ind. practice div.), Nassau County Psychol. Assn. (pvt. practice com. 1986-88, bd. dirs. 1987—, social issues com. 1988—), Working Woman Manhasset, L.I. Ctr. Bus. and Profl. Women, Assn. for Retarded Children (bd. dirs. 1988-92), L.I. Assn. Mariage and Family Therapy (bd. dirs. 1992—, sec. 1993—). Office: 35 Bonnie Heights Rd Manhasset NY 11030-1636

PITTMAN, CAROLYN, artist. Recipient Outstanding Artistic Contbn. certificate City Coun. Balt., 1986, Certificate for devoted and caring way of artistically conveying arts to people of Md., 1986, certificate of hon. citizenship Annapolis, Md., 1988, citizen citation City of Balt., 1986, Gov.'s citation Md., 1986; Carolyn Pittman Day proclaimed by City of Balt., 1986, Impressionist Paintings award Womens Power Inc., Md., 1986, Outstanding Achievements award Anne ARundle County, Md., 1988, Exec. citation, Md., 1988. Address: Character Art Inc 2301 Joplea Ave Baltimore MD 21225-1163

PITTMAN, JACQUELYN, mental health nurse, nursing educator; b. Pensacola, Fla., Dec. 22, 1932; d. Edward Corry Sr. and Hettie Oean (Wilson) P. BS in Nursing Edn., Fla. State U., 1958; MA, Columbia U., 1959, EdD, 1974. Physician asst. Med. Ctr. Clinic, Pensacola, 1953-55; clin. instr., asst. dir. nursing svc. Sacred Heart Hosp., Pensacola, 1955-56; instr.psychiatric nurse Fla. State Hosp., Chattahoochee, 1958, Pensacola Community Coll., 1959-60, 62-63; chmn. div. nursing Gulf Coast Community Coll., Panama City, Fla., 1963-66; asst. prof. U. Tex., Austin, 1970-72, assoc. prof., 1972-80; prof. nursing, coord. curriculum and teaching Grad. Program La. State U. Med. Ctr. Sch. Nursing, New Orleans, 1980—; curriculum cons. Nicholls State U., Thibodaux, La., 1982, Our Lady of the Lake Sch. Nursing, Baton Rouge, 1983; rsch. liaison So. Bapt. Hosp., New Orleans, 1987-89, Med. Ctr. La., 1992—; mem. Sci. Misconduct Inquiry com. La. State U. Med. Ctr., 1992—; adv. bd. Sister Henrietta Guyot Professorship. Tchr. Christian edn. program for mentally retarded St. Ignatius Martyr Ch., 1979-80; tchr. initiation team Rite of Christian Initiation of Adults, Our Lady of the Lake Cath. Ch., Mandeville, La., 1983-86; ethics com., bd. trustee Hotel Dieu Hosp., New Orleans, 1987-91; v.p., bd. dirs. St. Tammany Guidance Ctr., Inc., Mandeville, 1987-91; mem. Dem. Nat. Comm., Presdl. Task Force, 1992, Ctr. for Study of Presidency; judge Internat. Sci. and Engring. Fair Assn., 1990, 92; del. La. State Nurses' Assn. State Conv., 1992; assoc. Libr. of Congress. Mem. ANA, LWV, N.Y. Acad. Scis., Acad. Polit. Sci., Libr. of

Congress Assocs., Nat. Trust for Hist. Preservation, La. Endowment for Humanities, La. Nurses Assn. (archivist 1987—, state task force com. to preserve hist. documents 1987—), So. Nursing Rsch. Soc., Nat. League Nursing, Boston U. Nursing Archives, Women's Inner Cir. Achievement N.Am. Cmtys., Internat. Order of Merit, World Found. Successful Women, Wilson Ctr. Assocs., Kappa Delta Pi, Sigma Theta Tau. Democrat. Roman Catholic. Address: 204 Woodridge Blvd Mandeville LA 70471-2604 Office: La State U Med Ctr 1900 Gravier St New Orleans LA 70112-2262

PITTMAN, KATHERINE ANNE ATHERTON, elementary education educator; b. Baytown, Tex., Aug. 20, 1956; d. William Clifford Sr. and Pauline (High) Atherton; children: Richard Neil, Angela Christine, William Charles. Student, Lee Coll., 1973-75, 76, 87; BA in Liberal Arts and History, Tex. A&M U., 1977; cert. in secondary edn., Stephen F. Austin State U., 1978; cert. elem. and secondary edn., U. Houston, 1989, MS in Elem. Edn., 1991. Cert. elem. and high sch. tchr., Tex. Catalog clk. J.C. Penney Co., Baytown, Tex., 1974-75; substitute tchr. San Augustine (Tex.) Ind. Sch. Dist., 1978; math. tchr. Brookeland (Tex.) Ind. Sch. Dist., 1980-81; substitute tchr. Deer Park (Tex.) Ind. Sch. Dist., 1988-89; tchr. 6th grade Channelview (Tex.) Ind. Sch. Dist., 1989-94; tchr. 7th grade ESL English Houston Ind. Sch. Dist., 1994—; substitute tchr. Goose Creek Consol. Ind. Sch. Dist., Baytown, 1987-89; tchr. ESL, Harris County Dept. of Edn./Lee Coll., Baytown, 1989-90, substitute ESL tchr., 1990-91; customer svc. assoc. Montgomery Ward Co., Baytown, 1988-89. Mem. Assn. Tex. Profl. Educators, Tex. Computer Edn. Assn., Houston Fedn. Tchrs. Office: Stevenson Middle Sch 9595 Winkler Houston TX 77017

PITTMAN, LISA, lawyer; b. Limestone, Maine, Jan. 4, 1959; d. William Franklin and Rowena Paradis (Umphrey) P.; m. Edward Leon Pittman, May 26, 1984; 1 child, Graham Edward Paradis. BA, U. Fla., 1980, MA, 1981, JD, 1984; LLM, George Washington U., 1988. Bar: Fla. 1984, D.C. 1993, U.S Supreme Ct. 1993. Spl. asst. to gen. counsel Nat. Oceanic and Atmospheric Adminstrn., Washington, 1984-85, atty., advisor, 1985-87; minority counsel Com. on Mcht. Marine & Fisheries, Ho. of Reps., Washington, 1987-95; counsel com. on resources U.S. Ho. of Reps., Washington, 1995—. Pres. Ho. of Reps. Child Care Ctr. Parents Assn., Washington. Home: 6123 Ramshorn Dr Mc Lean VA 22101 Office: US Ho of Reps 1320 Longworth HOB Washington DC 20515

PITTMAN, NATALIE ANNE, paralegal; b. Detroit, Apr. 17, 1952; d. George Jack and Catherine Helen (Platusich) Ochenski; children: Erik Garrett Pittman, Jason Christopher Pittman; m. John Robert Pittman, Dec. 16, 1977; stepchildren: Mark Allen, David Robert. AS with highest honors, Cen. Tex. Coll., 1985. Owner, mgr. pet store, Killeen, Tex., 1977-85; paralegal Silverblatt Law Office, Killeen, 1985—; corp. sec. Am. Budgerigar Soc., Inc., Killeen, 1986—; also bd. dirs.; spkr. legal asst. program Ctrl. Tex. Coll., Killeen, 1986—, adv. com., 1989—, instr., 1991—; bd. dirs. Heart of Tex. Hospice; show promoter Thunder in the Hills Drum Corps, 1993—; mem. show promoters task force Drum Corps Internat., 1994—. Editorial advisor Know Your Pet-Budgerigars, 1987. Spokesperson Concerned Citizens Quality Edn., Killeen, 1981; pres. Pebble Sch. PTA, Killeen, 1984; active Killeen H.S. Band Boosters, 1987—, pres., 1991-93; help one student to succeed (HOSTS) tutor Killeen Ind. Sch. Dist., 1993—; umpire state softball tournaments, 1976; active polit. and civic orgns. Mem. State Bar Tex. (legal asst. div.), Nat. Notary Assn., Dallas-Ft. Worth Exhbn. Budgerigar Club (show sec. 1989), Heart 'O Tex. Exhbn. Budgerigar Club (founding). Republican. Roman Catholic. Home and Office: 1704 Kangaroo Ave Killeen TX 76543

PITTMAN, OUIDA SMITH, home economist; b. McComb, Miss., Mar. 29, 1956; d. William D. and Elizabeth M. (Johnson) Smith; married; children: Karmeen, Monnette, Darnella Burkett. BS, Alcorn State U., 1976; MS, U. Miss., 1978. Cert. home economist. Dir. nursery, kindergarten Alcorn State U., Lorman, Miss., 1978; home economist Emergency Land Fund, Jackson, Miss., 1978-80; tchr. Hattiesburg (Miss.) Pub. Sch., 1981-83; extension home economist Coop. Extension Svc., Natchez, Miss., 1984—. Leadership participant C. of C., Natchez, 1993-94; pres. Adams County Inter-Action Agy., Natchez, 1994—, Adams County Child Abuse Team, Natchez, 1994—. Mem. Nat. Coalition Black Devel. in Home Economics, Am. Home Econs. Assn., Miss. Home Econ. Assn., Nat. Resource & Environ. Mgmt., Miss./Nat. Assn. Extension Home Economist, Alcorn State U. Alumni Assn., Heroines of Jerico, Alpha Kappa Alpha, Xi Mu, Epsilon Sigma Phi. Democrat. MEthodist. Office: Coop Extension Svc 301 Loberty Rd Natchez MS 39120

PITTS, BARBARA TOWLE, accountant; b. St. Paul, Minn., Nov. 8, 1944; d. James Francis and Helen (Gorman) Towle; m. E.R. Pitts, Oct. 19, 1965; 1 child, Paris Tucker Pitts. BSBA, U. Ala., 1980. CPA, Wash., Tenn. Prin. Barbara M. Pitts Assocs., Fayetteville, Tenn., 1982-90, Barbara M. Pitts CPA, Seattle, 1990—. Bd. dirs. United Way Lincoln County, Fayetteville, 1989, Lincoln County Bd. Edn., Fayetteville, 1988-90; mem. planning com. Tenn. Hist. Soc., Nashville, 1989. Recipient Cert. of Recognition Tenn. Main St. Program, 1989; named Woman of Yr. Fayetteville Bus. and Profl. Women, 1988. Mem. AICPA, Wash. Soc. CPA, Northwest Watercolor Soc. (treas.). Home: 3515 E Marion St Seattle WA 98122-5258

PITTS, VIRGINIA M., human resources executive; b. Boston, Nov. 22, 1953; d. Harold Francis and Connie (Caico) Cummings; m. Daniel J. Pitts, Mar. 12, 1977. Student, Northeastern U., 1982-85, Lesley Coll. Adminstrv. asst. J. Baker Inc., Hyde Park, Mass., 1980-82, fin. adminstr., 1982-84, dir. human resources, 1984—, 1st sr. v.p., 1991—; trustee New Eng. Joint Bd. AFL-CIO, Quincy, Mass., 1984-89; guest lectr. Aquinas Jr. Coll.; mem. bd. dirs. Boston Crusaders, Drum & Bugle Corps. Instr. Boston Crusaders Drum and Bugle Corps, other marching bands, Mass., R.I., Maine, N.H., 1973-85; regional v.p. 210 Charitable Assn., Watertown, Mass., 1989-90; bd. dirs. Handi-Kids, Boston Crusaders Drum and Bugle Corps; guest lectr. Aquinas Jr. Coll., Milton, Mass. Mem. Am. Mgmt. Assn., Am. Compensation Assn. (cert. profl.), Soc. Human Resource Mgrs. Office: J Baker Inc 555 Turnpike St Canton MA 02021-2724

PITZLER, DONNA LYNN, secondary school educator; b. Edmonton, Alta., Can., Feb. 21, 1945; d. Frederick Walter and Isobel Orra (Wells) Blasius; m. John P. Holleman, Sept. 11, 1965 (div. Oct. 1986); children: Jeffrey P., Erin L.; m. Bruce Lee Pitzler, Nov. 24, 1989. BA, Calif. State U., 1968; MBA, Calif. Luth. U., 1983. Cert. elem. and secondary tchr., Calif. Tchr., dept. head Newhall (Calif.) Sch. Dist., 1975-78; tchr. Oak Park (Calif.) Sch. Dist., 1978-79; tchr., adminstr. Moorpark (Calif.) Sch. Dist., 1979—, cons., 1990-92, mentor tchr., 1984, 92, 94-95; fed. sex equity grant adminstr., 1992-95; registered securities broker, 1993—. Mem. Calif. Assn. Work Experience Educators, Computer Using Educators. Home: 2248 Hollowpark Ct Thousand Oaks CA 91362-1706 Office: 4500 N Tierra Rejada Rd Moorpark CA 93021

PIVER, SUSAN M., lawyer, insurance manager; b. Phila.; d. David and Rosalind (Nicholas) Myers; m. M. Steven Piver; children: Debra, Carolyn, Kenneth. AB, U. Pa.; postgrad., Temple U.; JD, SUNY, Buffalo, 1976. Bar: N.Y. 1977. Spl. counsel fraud and abuse Erie County (N.Y.) Medicaid, Buffalo, 1976-82, atty., dir. medicaid utilization rev., 1982-85; atty., v.p. legal affairs, counsel Children's Hosp. of Buffalo, 1985—; adj. faculty D'Youville Coll. Mem. Brylin Adv. Bd., D'Youville Health Svcs. Adv. Bd.; bd. dirs. Coordinated Care, 1989—, vice chair, 1994—. Mem. Am. Acad. Hosp. Lawyers, Nat. Health Lawyers Assn., N.Y. State Bar Assn. (com. on health care law, 1988—), Erie County Bar Assn. (co-chair health care law com.). Home: 315 Lincoln Pky Buffalo NY 14216-3127 Office: Childrens Hosp of Buffalo 219 Bryant St Buffalo NY 14222-2099

PIVIN, JEANETTE EVA, psychotherapist; b. Fall River, Mass., Feb. 24, 1932; d. Oscar and Ida Antoinette (Gauthier) P. B in Edn., Cath. Tchrs. Coll., 1956; MA in Theology, U. Notre Dame, 1967; cert. clin. pastoral edn., Worcester State Hosp., 1975; cert. interior design, Hall Inst. Tech., 1989. Tchr. St. Matthew Sch., Cranston, R.I., 1956-64; assoc. prof. religious studies Salve Regina U., Newport, R.I., 1967-74; staff counselor La Salette Counseling Svcs., Attleboro, Mass., 1975-80; pastoral counselor Interfaith Counseling Ctr., Providence, R.I., 1975—; pvt. practice Providence, 1980—. Home and Office: 139 Woodbine St Providence RI 02906-2543

PIXLER, SUSAN LYNN, pediatric nurse practitioner; b. Conway, S.C., July 21, 1957; d. Billie Frank Boyd and Sarah Frances (Deevon) Boyd Purrington; m. Curtis Brook Pixler, June 9, 1979. BSN cum laude, Baylor U., 1979; MSN, U. Tex., Arlington, 1990. RN, Tex.; cert. pediatric nurse practitioner Nat. Certification Bd. Pediatric Nurse Practitioners and Nurses. Nursing asst., patient aide Baylor U. Med. Ctr., Dallas, 1977-79; staff, charge to asst. head nurse Hillcrest Bapt. Hosp., Waco, Tex., 1979-82; staff nurse Waco Daignostic Clinic, 1982-83; team leader, staff nurse Scott and White Hewitt (Tex.) Clinic, 1983-88; staff and charge nurse Cook-Ft. Worth Children's Med. Ctr., 1990—; faculty specialist U. Tex., Arlington, 1990—, mem. curriculum com., 1991-92; faculty sec. U. Tex. Arlington, 1992-94, mem. faculty affairs com., 1994—, mem. adv. com. student affairs; mem. pediatric practices coun. Harris Meth. Hosp., Ft. Worth, 1991—; presenter in field. Unit pres., membership and voter registration chair LWV, Ft. Worth and Waco, 1985—; vol. campaign Ann Richards for Gov. Tex., 1989-90, March of Dimes, 1990, Nat. Kidney Found., Ft. Worth, 1991, Paws Across Tex., 1994—. Recipient cert. of merit LWV, 1987; Mary Cunningham scholar, 1975-77. Mem. ANA, Tex. Nurse Practitioners, Assn. for the Care of Children's Health (membership chair), Tex. Nurses' Assn. (nominating and govtl. affairs com., co-chair govtl. affairs com. 1994—), Nat. Assn. Pediatric Nurse Assocs. and Practitioners, Baylor U. Alumni Assn., Sigma Theta Tau (jr. counselor 1993-94, pres.-elect 1994—). Democrat. Baptist. Home: 2501 Clovermeadow Dr Fort Worth TX 76123-1171 Office: U Tex PO Box 19407 Arlington TX 76019

PIZARRO, MARIA DE JESUS, industrial engineer, consultant; b. El Paso, Tex., Aug. 28, 1961; d. Jesus and Rosa (Calvo) P.; m. Gary Davis, June 29, 1991. BS in Indsl. Engring., Tex. A&M U., 1984; postgrad., UCLA, 1993—. Registered profl. engr., Calif. Indsl. engr. I Hughes Aircraft, El Segundo, Calif., 1984-85; indsl. engr. TRW, Redondo Beach, Calif., 1985-87; sr. indsl. engr., mfg. data sys. mgr. Loral Librascope, Glendale, Calif., 1987-92; indsl. engr., acting supr. Eaton Corp., El Segundo, 1992—; cons., dir. M.P. Cons., Pasadena. Mem. Am. Inst. Indsl. Engrs., Soc. Women Engrs., Soc. Mexican Am. Engrings. and Scientists (mentor-tutor cmty. activities 1984—, treas. 1991—, dir. 1991—, Gold medal 1994). Office: Eaton Corp 2338 Alaska Ave El Segundo CA 90245

PIZZA, MARY ANN, physician; b. Blue Island, Ill., Apr. 25, 1956; d. Albert and Florence Isabel (Bucel) P. BS, U. Notre Dame, 1978; MD, U. Chgo., 1982. Diplomate Am. Bd. Internal Medicine. Resident U. Chgo., 1982-85; fellow in gen. internal medicine UCLA, 1985-86, asst. clin. prof. medicine, 1986-87; staff physician Northwestern U. Health Svc., Evanston, Ill., 1989—; instr. medicine Northwestern U., Chgo., 1990—. Recipient Mary Roberts Scott Meml. award U. Chgo., 1982, Acad. Excellence award Am. Med. Women's Assn., 1982. Mem. ACP, Am. Coll. Health Assn., Soc. Gen. Internal Medicine, Internat. Soc. Travel Medicine, Phi Beta Kappa, Sigma Xi, Alpha Omega Alpha. Roman Catholic. Office: Northwestern U Health Svc 633 Emerson St Evanston IL 60208-4000

PIZZAMIGLIO, NANCY ALICE, performing company executive; b. Oak Park, Ill., Aug. 22, 1936; d. Howard Joseph and Marian Louise (Henne) Gilman; m. Ernest George Lovas, May 17, 1957 (div. Nov. 1976); children: Lori Dianne, Randall Gilman; m. Albert Theodore Pizzamiglio, Mar. 27, 1978. Student, North Tex. State U., 1955-56. Stewardess North Cen. Airlines, Chgo., 1956-57; receptionist Leo Burnett Advt. Agy., Chgo., 1957-59; office mgr. Judy Stallons Employment Agy., Oak Brook, Ill., 1973-75; mgr. and escort Prestige Vacations, Inc., Oak Brook, Ill., 1975-76; corp. dir. Al Pierson Big Band U.S.A., Inc., Aubrey, Tex., 1976—, Al Pierson, Ltd., Aubrey, Tex., 1978—; corp. pres. Gilman, Inc. Artists Mgmt., Aubrey, Tex., 1982—; owner Dancing Horse Ranch, Aubrey, Tex., 1983—; bus. mgr. Guy Lombardo's Royal Canadians, Aubrey, Tex., 1989—. Editor: (newsletter) Property Owners Assn., 1972-73; contbr. articles to profl. jours. Recipient expert award NRA, 1952. Mem. U.S. Lipizzan Registry (bd. dirs. 1986-89), Dallas Dressage Club (bd. dirs. 1988-94), Am. Horse Shows Assn., Am. Quarter Horse Assn., U.S. Dressage Fedn. (qualified rider 1989, third/all breeds, first level 1989, first/all breeds, fourth level 1991, third Vintage Cup, fourth level 1991, third all-breeds first level 1992, third vintage cup first level 1992). Republican. Episcopalian. Address: Gilman Inc Artist Mgmt Rte 1 PO Box 149 Aubrey TX 76227

PIZZUTO, DEBRA KAY, secondary school mathematics educator; b. Camden, N.J., Nov. 25, 1957; d. Edward John and Kathryn Mary (Kegolis) Andrews; m. Victor Bruce Pizzuto, Nov. 28, 1981. BA in Bus. Adminstrn., Rutgers U., 1980. Cert. math. tchr., N.J., N.H. Math. tchr. Parkside Jr. High Sch., Manchester, N.H., 1985-87, Cumberland Regional H.S., Seabrook, N.J., 1987-88, St. James High Sch., Carney's Point, N.J., 1988-92, Ocean City (N.J.) High Sch., 1993—; ednl. cons. Newshire Forms, Inc., Bridgeton, N.J. Author, instr. (video tape) "Algebra One" in Superstar Tchr. Series. Named Superstar Tchr. for High Sch. Video Instrn. The Teaching Co. Mem. Math. Assn. Am., Nat. Coun. Tchrs. Math. Roman Catholic. Office: Ocean City High Sch Atlantic Ave Ocean City NJ 08226

PLACEK-ZIMMERMAN, ELLYN CLARE, educator, consultant; b. Chgo., Sept. 3, 1951; d. Clarence Joseph and Jerrine LaMarr (Ruhlow) Placek; m. Allan John Zimmerman, Aug. 10, 1974; 1 child, Alissa Jan. BS, No. Ill., 1973, MS, 1977, CAS, 1978, EdD, 1982. Tchr. Arlington Heights Pub. Sch., Ill., 1973-75, 75-76, dir. libr. and learning ctr., 1976-81, tchr. lang. arts and reading jr. high sch., 1981-84, tchr. kindergarten, 1984-86; prin. Orchard St. Sch., Fox River Grove, Ill., 1988-89, Pritchett Sch., Buffalo Grove, Ill., 1989-90, Round Lake Ill., 1992-93, asst. supt. curriculum and instrn., 1993—; dir. Ill. State grant "At Risk Program" for pre-sch. children, Cary Pub. Schs., 1986-87; mem. part-time faculty Coll. of Edn., Roosevelt U., Chgo., 1983-84, 88-89; tchr. jr. high social, reading & lang. arts studies, 1988; cons. in field; mem. steering com. Curriculum 2000 Conf., De Kalb, Ill., 1985; lectr. in field; mem. registration com. Fall conf. IASCD, 1987; supr. student tchrs. Ill. State U., Normal, 1986, Roosevelt U., Chgo., 1988-89, Elmhurst Coll., 1992; freelance writer Daily Herald newspaper. Contbg. author: Feeling Good About Food. Sec. Scarsdale Estates Homeowners Assn., Arlington Heights, 1983; hon. life mem. PTA; bd. dirs. ABC/25 Found., 1991-92. Mem. Ill. Assn. for Supervision and Curriculum Devel. (triple I arrangements com. 1988, registration com. for fall conf. 1987), Ill. Assn. Tchrs. of English (cons., speaker conf. 1984), Ill. Women Adminstrs. (publicity com. conf. 1985), Phi Delta Kappa (bd. mem. 1992—). Avocation: playing guitar, calligraphy. Home: 402 E Orchard St Arlington Heights IL 60005-2660

PLADERA, LUCRETIA LAURYL, librarian, administrator; b. Kansas City, Mo., June 28, 1937; d. Howard Shuey and Jean (Murduck) Gable; m. Paul Pladera, Aug. 8, 1982. BS in Elem. Edn., U. Kansas, 1959; MLS, U. Hawaii, 1967; DLS, U. So. Calif., 1979. Children's libr. Ewa Beach (Hawaii) Libr., 1971-75; sch. libr. specialist Dept. Edn. sch. libr. svc., Honolulu, 1975-79; program coord. Maui Libr. Dist., Waikuku, Hawaii, 1979-85; dist. adminstr. Hawaii Libr. Dist., Hilo, 1986-91; libr. Kahului (Maui) Libr., 1991-93; dist. adminstr. Kauai Libr. Dist., Lihue, Hawaii, 1993-94; cons. pub. libr. Idaho State Libr., 1994—. Author: Palace, 1983. Pres. Toastmasters Internat. Maui, 1983-84. Mem. AAUW (v.p. program com. 1988-90, v.p. membership com. 1990-91), Hawaii Libr. Assn. (pres. 1979-80), Soroptimist Internat. (pres. Maui chpt. 1985-86, Hilo chpt. 1990-91). Home: 501 E Garden Ave Apt A Coeur D Alene ID 83814 Office: 2201 N Government Way Coeur D Alene ID 83814

PLAIN, BELVA, writer; b. N.Y.C., Oct. 9, 1919; d. Oscar and Eleanor Offenberg; m. Irving Plain, June 14, 1941 (dec. 1982); 3 children. Grad., Barnard Coll. Author: Evergreen, 1978, Random Winds, 1980, Eden Burning, 1982, Crescent City, 1984, The Golden Cup, 1987, Tapestry, 1988, Blessings, 1989, Harvest, 1990, Treasures, 1992, Whispers, 1993, Daybreak, 1994; contbr. short stories to McCall's, Good Housekeeping, Redbook, Cosmopolitan. Office: care Delacorte Press 1540 Broadway New York NY 10036-4094*

PLAINE, LLOYD LEVA, lawyer; b. Washington, Nov. 3, 1947. BA, U. Pa., 1969; postgrad., Harvard U.; JD, Georgetown U., 1975. Bar: D.C. 1975. Legis. asst. to U.S. Rep. Sidney Yates, 1971-72; with Sutherland, Asbill & Brennan, Washington, 1975-82, ptnr., 1982—. Fellow Am. Bar Found., Am. Coll. Trust and Estate Counsel; mem. ABA. Office: Sutherland Asbill & Brennan 1275 Pennsylvania Ave NW Washington DC 20004-2404

PLAISTED, CAROLE ANNE, elementary education educator; b. Meredith, N.H., Apr. 3, 1939; d. Morris Holman and Christina Martin (Dunn) P. BEd with honors, Plymouth (N.H.) Tchrs. Coll., 1960; MA, Columbia U., 1966; cert., N.Y. Inst. Photography, 1990. Cert. tchr., N.H. Tchr. Lang St. Sch., Meredith, 1960-61, Mechanic St. Sch., Laconia, N.H., 1961-62, Wheelock Lab. Sch., Keene, N.H., 1963-94; summer tchr. Cheshire County Headstart, Hinsdale, N.H., 1965; tchr. children's lit. Keene State Coll., 1974, 75; classroom evaluator D.C. Heath Co., Lexington, Mass., 1985-86; dist. trainer for drug edn. supervisory unit, Keene, 1988-94. Author: The Graduates Speak, 1990; co-author curriculum materials; contbr. Kindergarten: A Sourcebook for School and Home, 1984. Trustee Reed Free Libr., Surry, N.H., 1988—; program chair Wheelock Sch. PTA, 1964-65. Named Outstanding Elem. Tchr. of Am., 1973. Mem. Cheshire County Ret. Tchrs. Assn., Delta Kappa Gamma (corr. sec. Alpha chpt. 1972-76, state scholarship chmn. 1985—, Beta Alpha state scholarship 1989).

PLAISTED, JOAN M., diplomat; b. St. Peter, Minn., Aug. 29, 1945; d. Gerald A. and Lola May (Peters) P. Student, U. Grenoble, France, 1965-66, U. Calif., Berkeley, 1966; BA in Internat. Rels., Am. U., 1967, MA in Asian Studies, 1969; graduate, Nat. War Coll., 1988. Korea desk officer Commerce Dept., Washington, 1969-72, Japan desk officer, 1972-73; commercial officer Am. Embassy, Paris, 1973-78; internat. economist Orgn. Econ. Cooperation & Devel., Paris, 1978-80; econ. officer Am. Consulate Gen., Hong Kong, 1980-83; trade negotiator White House Office of Spl. Trade Rep., Geneva, 1983-85; deputy dir. China desk State Dept., Washington, 1985-87; acting deputy chief of mission, chief econ./commercial sect. Am. Inst. in Taiwan, Taipei, 1988-91; chargé d'affaires, deputy chief of mission Am. Embassy, Rabat, Morocco, 1991-94; dir. Thai and Burma affairs Dept. of State, Washington, 1994—. Recipient Lodestar award Am. U., 1993. Mem. Am. Fgn. Svc. Assn., Hong Kong Wine Soc. (founding). Office: Dept of State EAP/TB Rm 4312 Washington DC 20520

PLAISTED, SUZETTE LYNNE, organization executive; b. Butler, Pa., Apr. 30, 1963; d. John James Jr. and Margaret Katherine (Saylor) P. Cert., L'Inst. Catholique, Paris, 1983; BA in Speech Communication, Linfield Coll., 1985; postgrad., Wayne Community Coll., 1988—, Cen. Mich. U., 1989. Intern McMinnville (Oreg.) C. of C., 1984; landscaper, caterer Linfield Coll., McMinnville, 1982-85; 1st asst. mgr. Eat'n Park Restaurants, Inc., Pitts., 1985-87; dir. comm. Girl Scout Coun. Coastal Carolina, Inc., Goldsboro, N.C., 1987-93, dir. fund devel., 1993—. Tutor Wayne County Lit. Ctr., Goldsboro, 1990—; parenting instr., vol. aide, county coord. and support group co-leader Ea. N.C. Child Abuse Prevention Ctr., Kinston, 1988—. Mem. Goldsboro Jaycees (ofcl. photographer Christmas parades 1992, 93, co-chmn. midwest flood relief effort, various awards), Toastmasters (sgt.-at-arms Goldsboro, 1993—), Pi Kappa Alpha, Lambda Lambda Sigma (recorder, historian), Pi Kappa Delta. Office: Girl Scout Coun Coastal Carolina Inc 108 E Lockhaven Dr Goldsboro NC 27534-1714

PLAKANS, SHELLEY SWIFT, social worker, psychotherapist; b. Boston, Aug. 29, 1943; d. William Nye and Phyllis (Childs) Swift; m. John Joseph Guinan Jr. (div. 1975); children: Ashley, Lindsey Guinan, John Jeffrey, Daniel Plakans; m. John Plakans. AB, Wheaton Coll., 1965; MEd, Fitchburg (Mass.) State Coll., 1977; MSW, Simmons Sch. of Social Work, Boston, 1987. Lic. ind. clin. social worker, Mass.; bd. cert. diplomate. Staff psychologist Ayer (Mass.) Guidance Ctr., 1978-81; substance abuse specialist Family Counseling and Guidance Ctrs., Danvers, Mass., 1990-91; pvt. practice psychotherapy Boston North Shore Assocs., Salem, 1985-90, NEPA, Salem, 1990-94. Mediator Lynn (Mass.) Youth Resource Bur., 1986-87, Marblehead Cmty. Counseling Ctr., 1995—. Mem. Nat. Assn. Social Workers, Mass. Acad. Clin. Social Work, Inc., Am. Soc. Clin. Hypnosis, Internat. Soc. Clin. Hypnosis. Office: 1 Pleasant Ln Marblehead MA 01945

PLANK, DONNA MARIE, dean; b. Temple, Tex., Feb. 6, 1953; d. Ecta and Nancy Laura (Weems) Chambers; children: James Aaron, Benjamin Clements. AA, Temple Jr. Coll., 1973; BA, U. Mary Hardin-Baylor, 1985; MS in Edn., Baylor U., 1990. Dir. career planning and placement, dir. student publs. U. Mary Hardin-Baylor, Belton, Tex., 1985-87, assoc. dir. admissions, dir. student publs., 1987-88, dean of women, dir. student publs., 1988-90, assoc. dean of students, 1990—. Mem. AAUW, Tex. Assn. of Coll. and Univ. Student Pers. Adminstrs. Office: U Mary Hardin-Baylor 9th And College Belton TX 76513

PLANT, MARETTA MOORE, public relations and marketing executive; b. Washington, Sept. 4, 1937; d. Henry Edwards and Lucy (Connell) Moore; m. William Voorhees Plant, June 14, 1959; children: Scott Voorhees, Craig Culver, Suzannah Holliday. BS in Bus. Adminstrn., U. Ark., 1959. Owner, mgr. Handcrafts by Maretta, Westfield, N.J., 1966-73; photographer M-R Pictures, Inc., Allendale, N.J., 1973-77; communications asst. United Way-Union County, Elizabeth, N.J., 1977-79; pub. rels. cons. Creative Arts Workshop, Westfield, 1977-81, Coll. Adv. Cons., 1983-89; community rels. coord. Raritan Bay Health Svcs. Corp., Perth Amboy, N.J., 1979-81; dir. pub. rels. St. Elizabeth Hosp., Elizabeth, N.J., 1981-86; dir. mkgt./communications Somerset Med. Ctr., Somerville, N.J., 1986-90; v.p. mktg. and pub. rels. Somerset Med. Ctr., Somerville, 1990—. Trustee Bridgeway House, Elizabeth, 1982-86, Far Hills Race Meeting Assn., N.J., 1989—, pub. rels com. N.J. Hosp. Assn., Princeton, 1982-83, 89-92, coun. auxs., 1988-92, pub. rels. com., 1989-92; committeewoman Union County Rep. Com., Westfield, 1983-85; bd. dirs. pub. affairs com. Morris Mus., Morristown; bd. dirs. communications com. Somerset County United Way, 1992—. Mem. Pub. Rels. Soc. Am., Nat. Fedn. Press Women, N.J. Press Women (chmn. communications contest 1990-92), Am. Soc. Hosp. Mktg. and Pub. Rels. (coun. mem. Region II, membership com.), N.J. Hosp. Mktg. and Pub. Rels. Assn. (corr. sec. 1984-86, pres. 1986-88), Somerset County C. of C. (mag. com. 1988-93), U. Ark. Alumni Assn., Summit-Westfield Assn., Delta Gamma, Coll. Women's (Westfield) Club, Soroptimists (internat., charter). Home: 118 Effingham Pl Westfield NJ 07090-3926 Office: Somerset Med Ctr Rehill Ave Somerville NJ 08876-2546

PLANTIKOW, FRANCES KAY, human resources specialist; b. Lansing, Mich., Jan. 28, 1947; d. Charles Black and Vivian Jane (Francis) Leighton; m. John Steven Plantikow, Feb. 21, 1970 (div.); children: Jennifer Ann, Bertram Jay (dec.). BA, Mich. State U., 1969; MS in Edn., SUNY, Plattsburgh, 1980. Cert. nat. counselor. Program dir. Stop ctr. for domestic violence Clinton County Mental Health Assn., Plattsburgh, 1981-83, community residence supr. Breakthrough II, 1985-86, dir. employee assistance svcs., 1986-93; counselor/advocate, vol. coord. A Woman's Place, Merced, Calif., 1984-85; guest Gov.'s Task Force on Domestic Violence, Albany, N.Y., 1981-83, N.Y. State Coalition Against Domestic Violence, Albany, 1981-83; lectr., cons., trainer in field. Author manual: Domestic Violence Training Guide, 1984; editor manual: Management Training and Supervisors' Training Guide, 1987; author A Woman's Place Newsletter, 1984-85. Founder safe home network for battered women and battered women's support group STOP Domestic Violence, Plattsburg, 1981-83; founer safe home network for battered women A Woman's Place, 1984; founding mem. Ctrl. Calif. Coalition Against Domestic Violence, Merced, Calif., 1984-85; sec. Merced Zool. Soc., 1984-85; deacon, sec. bd. deacons 1st Presbyn. Ch., Plattsburg, 1987-90, sec., chmn. nurture coun., 1986-89, elder, 1993—, chmn. outreach coun., 1992—. With USAF, 1969-71. N.Y. State Dept. Social Svcs. grantee, 1982. Mem. NAFE, AACD, Am. Mental Health Counselors Assn., Soc. Human Resouce Profls. Home: 43 Set Point Plattsburgh NY 12901-1771

PLANTZ, CHRISTINE MARIE, librarian, union officer; b. Moscow, Idaho, July 28, 1946; d. John Albert and Marian Florence (Malm) Holmes; m. Charles Walter Plantz, May 19, 1973. BA, Shimer Coll., 1968; postgrad., U. Chgo. GLS, 1968-72; BS, Chadron State Coll., 1977. Children's libr. Chgo. Pub. Libr., 1969-73; libr. Rushville (Nebr.) Pub. Schs., 1974-77; tchr. Sheridan County Dist. 126, Rushville, 1979; libr. Bur. Indian Affairs, Pine Ridge, S.D., 1980—; pres. local Nat. Fedn. Fed. Employees, Pine Ridge, S.D., 1987-89, 91-92, sec. BIA coun., 1988—, owner LaserPress Desktop Pub., Rushville, 1992—. Mem. Rushville City Coun., 1986-90, Rushville Pub. Libr. Bd., 1974-82; bd. dirs. Family Rescue Shelter, Gordon, Nebr., 1982-88, Black Hills Girl Scout Coun., Rapid City, S.D., 1990—. Episcopalian. Home: PO Box 219 Rushville NE 69360 Office: Laser Press PO Box 219 133 Main St Rushville NE 69360

PLATOU, JOANNE (DODE), museum director; b. Mpls., Jan. 6, 1919; d. Wesley Richmond and Catherine Harriet (Fisher) Pierson; m. Ralph Victor Platou, Jan. 23, 1942 (dec. Sept. 1968); children: Peter Erling, Thomas Stoud, Mary Kirk Platou Marloff. BS, U. Minn., 1939; MFA, Tulane U., 1959. Columnist Mpls. Tribune, 1939-42; med. photographer Ochsner Clinic, New Orleans, 1943-46; tchr. photography Metairie (La.) Pk. Country Day Sch., 1946-51; free lance artist New Orleans, 1953-68; curator edn. New Orleans Mus. Art, 1969-75; chief curator Historic New Orleans Collection, 1976-86, dir., 1986-92, dir. emerita, 1992—; bd. dirs. Arts Coun. New Orleans, 1972-88, Long Vue House and Gardens, New Orleans, 1982-88; tchr. mus. career course Tulane U., New Orleans, 1983-87. Curator exhbns. The Wit of It, 1972, The Art Works, 1972, The Camera, 1974; author catalogue, curator exhbn. Alfred R. Waud, 1979. NEH grantee, New Orleans Mus. Art, 1975. Mem. Am. Mus. Assn., Friends of the Cabildo, Coll. Art Assn., Am. Assn. State and Local History.

PLATT, JAN KAMINIS, former county official; b. St. Petersburg, Fla., Sept. 27, 1936; d. Peter Clifton and Adele (Diamond) Kaminis; m. William R. Platt, Feb. 8, 1962; 1 son, Kevin Peter. B.A., Fla. State U., 1958; postgrad. U. Fla. Law Sch., 1958-59, U. Va., 1962, Vanderbilt U., 1964. Pub. sch. tchr. Hillsborough County, Tampa, Fla., 1959-60; field dir. Girl Scouts Suncoast Coun., Tampa, 1960-62; city councilman Tampa City Council, 1974-78; county commr. Hillsborough County, 1979—; chmn. Hillsborough County Bd. County commrs., 1980-81, 83-84; chmn. Tampa Bay Regional Planning Council, 1982; chmn. West Coast Regional Water Supply Authority, Tampa, 1985; chmn. Hillsborough County Council of Govts., 1976, 79; chmn. Sunshine Amendment Drive 7th Congrl. Dist., Tampa, 1976; chmn. Community Action Agy., Tampa, 1980-81, 83-84; chmn. Tampa Charter Revision Commn., 1975; chmn. Prison Sitting Task Force, Tampa, 1983, Tampa Housing Study Com., 1983, Met. Planning Orgn., Tampa, 1984, Bd. Tax Adjustment, Tampa, 1984; appointee Constitution Revision Commn., Fla., 1977, HRS Dist. IV Adv. Council, Fla.; mem. Hillsborough County Expressway Authority, Taxicab Commn.; vice chmn. steering com. Nat. Assn. Counties Environ. Task Force; Bd. dirs. March of Dimes, Tampa, The Fla. Orchestra, Tampa; trustee Hillsborough County Hosp. Authority, Tampa, 1984-94; pres. Suncoast Girl Scout Council, Citizens Alert, Tampa, Bay View Garden Club; v.p. Hillsborough County Bar Aux.; mem. adv. bd. Northside Community Mental Health Ctr.: Access House, Tampa; active mem. Arts Council of Tampa-Hillsborough County, 1983-85, Drug Abuse Coordinating Council Orgn., Tampa, Bd. Criminal Justice, Tampa, Fla. Council on Aging, Inebriate Task Force, Tampa, Tampa Downtown Devel. Authority Task Force, Tampa Sports Authority, Tampa Area Mental Health Bd., Children's Study Commn., Manahill Area Agy. on Aging, Tampa, Athena Soc., Tampa Area Com. on Foreign Affairs, League of Women Voters. Recipient Outstanding Community Athena Soc. Service award, 1976, First Annual Humanitarian award Nat. Orgn. for Prevention of Animal Suffering, 1981, Spessard Holland Meml. award Tampa Bay Com. for Good Govt., 1979, First Lady of Yr. award Beta Sigma Phi, 1980, Women Helping Women award Soroptimist Internat. Tampa, 1983, Eliza Wolff award Tampa United Methodist Ctrs., 1982, Good Govt. award Tampa Jaycees, 1983, Good Govt. award League of Women Voters, 1983. Mem. Am. Judicature Soc., State Assn. County Commrs. Fla. (at-large dir.), AAUW (bd. dirs.), Mortar Bd., Garnet Key, Phi Beta Kappa, Phi Kappa Phi. Democrat. Episcopalian. Home: 4606 W Beach Park Dr Tampa FL 33609-3705 Office: 4606 Beach Park Dr Tampa FL 33609

PLATT, LESLIE OLIVER, psychologist; b. Atlanta, Jan. 17, 1960; d. Andrew Gordon and Zonna Laurece (Williams) Oliver; m. James William Platt, Aug. 14, 1982. BS, Presbyn. Coll., 1982; MEd, Ga. State U., 1984; PhD, U. Ga., 1993. Cert. sch. psychology, mental retardation, S.C. Spl. edn. tchr. Fulton County Bd. Edn., Atlanta, 1982-83, Alexander City (Ala.) Bd. Edn., 1984-86, Tallassee (Ala.) City Bd. Edn., 1986-88; psychometrist Wilkes County Bd. Edn., Washington, Ga., 1988-89; grad. asst. U. Ga., Athens, 1989-92; psychology intern N.W. Ga. Regional Hosp., Rome, 1992-93; psychologist Beckman Mental Health Ctr., Greenwood, S.C., 1993-94, Whitten Ctr., Clinton, S.C., 1994—. Contbr. articles to profl. jours. Scholar Presbyn. Coll., 1982. Mem. APA, Nat. Assn. Sch. Psychologists, Assn. Mental Retardation, Coun. Exceptional Children, Assn. Retarded Citizens Ea. Elmore County (bd. dirs. 1987-88, chair membership 1987-88), Kappa Delta Pi. Presbyterian. Home: Rt 1 Box 135 Abbeville SC 29620

PLATT, MARCIA ELLIN, gerontologist; b. Astoria, N.Y., Jan. 20, 1947; d. Benjamin and Ethel (Glassberg) Berman; m. Leslie A. Platt, Aug. 10, 1969; 1 child, Bill Lawrence. BS, NYU, 1968, MA, 1972; MA, George Mason U., 1986. Cert. activity cons. Nat. Certification Coun. of Activity Profls. Sr. adult program dir. Reston (Va.) Community Ctr., 1991-92. Mem. No. Va. Assn. of Activity Profls., Am. Psychol. Assn. (assoc.), Psi Chi. Home: 11901 Triple Crown Rd Reston VA 22091-3015

PLATTI, RITA JANE, educator, draftsman, author, inventor; b. Stockton, Calif., Aug. 29, 1925; d. Umbert Ferdinand and Concettina Maria (Natoli) Strangio; m. Elvin Carl Platti, July 27, 1955; 1 child, Kimberley Jane. Student, Dominican Coll., 1943-45; AB in Math, U. Pacific, 1947, postgrad., 1947-52, 68. Cert. sec. tchr., Calif.; lic. real estate agt., Calif. Farmer Escalon, Calif., 1943—; tchr. math St. Mary's High Sch., Stockton, 1947-49, 52, 54; chem. analyst Petri Winery, Escalon, 1949; draftsman Kyle Steel Co., Stockton, 1950-52; pvt. practice as draftsman Stockton, 1952-66; tchr. math Montezuma Sch., Stockton, 1956-57, Davis Elem. Sch., Stockton, 1957-58; with rental bus., 1958-81; tchr. math Amos Alonzo Stagg High Sch., 1961-80, Humphreys Coll., 1981-83, Hamilton Jr. High Sch., 1984-90; owner, involved in prodn. and mktg. R.J. Creations, 1991—; speaker workshops Stanislaus State U., 1992, Calif. Math. Coun., Fresno State U., 1992, Nat. Sci. Found. Conf., 1993; speaker math./sci. conf. Calif. State U., Bakersfield, 1994; evaluator Math. Framework (K-12) Calif. State Dept. Edn. Author: Math Proficiency Plateaus, 1979, author, pub. series, 1979-86; 3 patents in field. Mem. NEA, Calif. Tchrs. Assn. Democrat. Roman Catholic.

PLAWECKI, JUDITH ANN, dean, nursing educator; b. East Chicago, Ind., June 5, 1943; d. Joseph Lawrence and Anne Marilyn (Hamnik) Curosh; m. Henry Martin Plawecki, June 10, 1967; children: Martin H., Lawrence H. BS, St. Xavier Coll., Chgo., 1965; MA, U. Iowa, 1971; PhD, 1974. Asst. prof. Mt. Mercy Coll., Cedar Rapids, Iowa, 1971-73; asst. dept. chmn., assoc. prof., 1974-75; assoc. prof. U. Iowa, 1975-76; asst. dean, assoc. prof. U. Minn., 1976-81; acting dean, assoc. dean and prof. U. N.D., Grand Forks, 1981-82, dean and prof. nursing, 1982-83; dean and prof. nursing Lewis U., Romeoville, Ill., 1983-87; dean, prof. nursing U. South Fla., Tampa, 1987—. Univ. Iowa Fellow, 1973. Mem. ANA, Nat. League for Nursing, Older Women's League, Sigma Xi, Sigma Phi Omega, Sigma Theta Tau, Phi Lambda Theta. Office: U South Fla Coll Nursing MDC 22 12901 Bruce B Downs Blvd Tampa FL 33612-4742

PLAYER, GERALDINE (JERI PLAYER), small business executive; b. Cleve., Mar. 26, 1952; d. Cornelius Millsape and Ola Mae (Maxie) Fisher; m. Van O. Player, Aug. 27, 1970 (dec. Mar. 1975); children—Ricardo T., Van O., Michelle. Student Sawyer Coll. Bus., Mayfield, Ohio, Virginia Marti Sch. Design, Lakewood, Ohio, Inst. Children's Lit., Conn., Case Western Res. U., Fall 1988. Owner, Jeri's Designs, Inc., Cleve., 1970—, Success Writers, Cleve., 1986—; freelance scriptwriter, 1990—; fashion cons. Active adoptive parenting orgn. Mem. Nat. Assn. Female Execs. Club: Back Wall (Beachwood, Ohio). Lodge: Brotherhood (Bklyn.). Avocations: aerobics; photography; theatre; speech. Home: PO Box 12471 Cleveland OH 44112-0471 Office: 1605 N Cahuenga Blvd Ste 211 Los Angeles CA 90028-6281

PLAYER, KIM WILLIAMS, speech language pathologist; b. Moscow, Idaho, Sept. 12, 1955; d. James Elwood and Anna Lue (Nuttall) Williams; m. Rodney Lynn Player, Aug. 12, 1977; children: Shannon, Dayna, Kirk. BS, Utah State U., 1976, MS, 1977. Speech-language pathologist Oneida Sch. Dist., Malad, Idaho, 1977-78, Cache County Sch. Dist., Logan, Utah, 1978-79, Duchesne County (Utah) Sch. Dist., 1983-84, Emery County Sch. Dist., Huntington, Utah, 1985—; mem. task force com. Utah State Office Edn., Salt Lake City, 1989-92, coord. communication disorders, 1992—. Treas. Emery County Dem. Ctrl. Com., Castle Dale, Utah, 1992—. Mem. Utah Speech-Lang.-Hearing Assn. (continuing edn. adminstr. 1977—), Utah Edn. Assn., NEA, Emery Edn. Assn. (sec. 1985—), NOW. Office: Emery Sch Dist PO Box 120 Huntington UT 84528

PLAYER, THELMA B., librarian; b. Owosso, Mich.; d. Walter B. and Grace (Willoughby) Player; B.A., Western Mich. U., 1954. Reference asst. USAF Aero. Chart & Info. Center, Washington, 1954-57; reference librarian U.S. Navy Hydrographic Office, Suitland, Md., 1957-58; asst. librarian, 1958-59; tech. library br. head U.S. Navy Spl. Project Office, Washington, 1959-68, Strategic Systems Project Office, 1969-76. Mem. Spl. Libraries Assn., D.C. Library Assn., AAUW, Canterbury Cathedral Trust in Am., Nat. Geneal. Soc., Internat. Soc. Brit. Genealogy and Family History, Ohio Geneal. Soc., Royal Oak Found., Daus. of Union Vets. of Civil War. Episcopalian. Home: 730 24th St NW Washington DC 20037-2543

PLAYER, WANDA HOPE, accountant; b. Hampton, Va., Oct. 2, 1955; d. Clyde Louis and Mary Janet (Gulledge) P.; m. James G. Pappas, Jr., July 27, 1985. BSBA, U. S.C., 1977. CPA, Va., S.C.; cert. fin. planner. Sr. acct. Peat Marwick, Mitchell & Co., Charlotte, N.C., 1977-80; internal audit mgr. 1st Va. Banks, Inc., Roanoke, Va., 1980-81; dist. mgr. Automatic Data Processing, 1981-82; mgr. Young & Prickitt, P.C. CPAs, 1982-87; prin. W. Hope Player CPA, Roanoke, 1987—; v.p. CPA Affiliates Va., Ltd., 1990-92, pres. 1993-94. Grad. Leadership Roanoke Valley, 1987-88, mem. curriculum com., 1988-93, steering com. 1993—; mem. adv. bd. Women's Ctr., Hollins Coll., 1988; bd. dirs. Voice of Blue Ridge, 1988—. Named Outstanding Young Woman of the Yr., Roanoke Valley, 1992. Mem. AICPA, Nat. Assn. Accts. (bd. dirs. 1988, v.p. 1987-88), Roanoke Regional C. of C. (sml. bus. coun. com., bd. dirs. 1989-90, 92-95, vice chmn. 1993-94), Inst. Cert. Fin. Planners, Va. Soc. CPAs's (chmn. young CPA's com. 1990-91), Porsche Club (treas. 1988-89), Nat. Assn. of Women Bus. Owners (pres. Blue Ridge regional chpt. 1994—), United Way of Roanoke Valley(bd. dirs., 1995—), Better Bus. Bur. (bd. dirs., 1995—). Presbyterian. Home: 2239 Grandin Rd SW Roanoke VA 24015-3529 Office: 316 Mountain Ave SW Roanoke VA 24016

PLAYTON, DONA, lawyer; b. Laramie, Wyo., Nov. 21, 1966; d. Priscilla (Lyons) Moree; m. Roland C. Maldonado, Aug. 11, 1990. BS in Adminstrn. of Justice, U. Wyo., 1989, JD, 1993. Bar: Colo. 1993, Wyo. 1994, U.S. Dist. Ct. Wyo. 1994. Legis. page Wyo. Ho. of Reps., Cheyenne, 1987; legal asst. Protection and Advocacy, Cheyenne, Wyo., 1989-90; mgr. Potter Law Club Bookstore, Laramie, 1990-92; student dir. Univ. Legal Svcs., Laramie, 1992-93; asst. aggy. gen. State of Wyo. Atty. Gen., Cheyenne, 1993—. Mem. ABA, Nat. Assn. Women Lawyers, Wyo. Trial Lawyers Assn. Home: 620 S 13th St Laramie WY 82070-3227

PLESHETTE, SUZANNE, actress, writer; b. N.Y.C., Jan. 31; d. Eugene and Geraldine; m. Thomas Joseph Gallagher III, Mar. 16, 1968. Student, Sch. Performing Arts, Syracuse U., Finch Coll., Neighborhood Playhouse Sch. of Theatre. Founder, prin. The Bedside Manor (later div. of J.P. Stevens). Theatre debut in Truckline Cafe; star in Broadway prodns. Compulsion, The Cold Wind and the Warm, The Golden Fleecing, The Miracle Worker, Special Occasions; star TV series Bob Newhart Show, 1972-78, Suzanne Pleshette is Maggie Briggs, 1984; starred in TV series Bridges to Cross, 1986-87, Nightingales, 1988-89, The Boys Are Back, 1994—; star 30 feature films including The Birds, Forty Pounds of Trouble, If It's Tuesday This Must Be Belgium, Nevada Smith, Support Your Local Gunfighter, Hot Stuff, Oh God! Book II; TV movies include Flesh and Blood, Starmaker, Fantasies, If Things Were Different, Help-Wanted Male, Dixie Changing Habits, One Cooks, The Other Doesn't, For Love or Money, Kojak, The Belarus File, A Stranger Waits, Alone In The Neon Jungle, Leona Helmsley: The Queen of Mean, 1990, Battling for Baby, 1991-92, A Twist of the Knife, 1993; writer, co-creator, producer two TV series. Published author.

PLESS, VERA, mathematics and computer science educator; b. Chgo., Mar. 5, 1931; d. Lyman and Helen (Blinder) Stepen; m. Irwin Pless, June 15, 1952 (div. 1980); children: Naomi, Benjamin, Daniel. PhB, U. Chgo., 1952; PhD, Northwestern U., 1957. Mathematician USAF, Lincoln, Mass., 1962-72; rsch. assoc. MIT, Cambridge, Mass., 1972-75; prof. math. U. Ill., Chgo., 1975—. Author: The Theory of Error Correcting Codes, 1989; contbr. articles to profl. publs. U. Ill. scholar, 1989-92; recipient Tempo All-Professor Team, Sciences, Chicago Tribune, 1993. Mem. Am. Math. Soc. (chair nominating com. 1984), Math. Assn. Am., IEEE (bd. govs. 1985-89), Assn. Women in Math. Office: UIC MSCS (M/C 249) 851 S Morgan 322 SEO Chicago IL 60607-7045

PLIMPTON, PAULINE AMES, civic worker, writer; b. N. Easton, Mass., Oct. 22, 1901; d. Oakes and Blanche Ames; B.A., Smith Coll., 1922; m. Francis T.P. Plimpton, June 4, 1926; children: George Ames, Francis T.P., Oakes Ames, Sarah Gay. Pres., House of Industry, 1940-48; bd. dirs. Inst. World Affairs, 1940-74, Pub. Edn. Assn., 1933-44; chmn. United Campaign Fund for Planned Parenthood of Manhattan and Bronx, 1946-49; chmn. Planned Parenthood Fedn. Am. campaign, 1959-60, bd. dirs. 1959-67, 70-73; chmn. United Campaign, 1964; bd. dirs. Planned Parenthood of N.Y.C., 1965-74; rep. Western Hemisphere region Internat. Planned Parenthood Fedn., 1970-73; fund raiser, vol. coun. Philharm. Symphony Soc. N.Y., N.Y. Legal Aid Soc., ARC; mem. adv. coun. Friends of the Columbia Librs., 1986—. Recipient Planned Parenthood award for devoted service, 1969. Republican. Unitarian. Clubs: Cold Springs Harbor Beach Club, Cosmopolitan, Piping Rock, Ausable (Adirondacks). Contbg. author, editor, compiler Orchids at Christmas, 1975, The Ancestry of Blanche Butler Ames and Adelbert Ames, 1977, Oakes Ames: Jottings of a Harvard Botanist, 1979, The Plimpton Papers: Law and Diplomacy, 1985, A Window on Our World: More Plimpton Papers, 1989, A Collector's Recollections: George Arthur Plimpton, 1993. Home: 131 E 66th St New York NY 10021-6129 also: 168 Chichester Rd Huntington NY 11743-6525

PLISKOW, VITA SARI, anesthesiologist; b. Tel Aviv, Israel, Sept. 13, 1942; arrived in Can., 1951; came to U.S., 1967; d. Henry Norman and Renee (Mushkatel) Stahl; m. Raymond Joel Pliskow, June 30, 1968; children: Tia, Kami. MD, U. B.C., Vancouver, 1967. Diplomate Am. Bd. Anesthesiology. Anesthesiologist Olympic Anesthesia, Bremerton, Wash., 1971-74, ptnr., anesthesiologist, 1974-84; pres., co-founder Olympic Ambulatory Surgery Ctr., Bremerton, 1977-83; ptnr., anesthesiologist Allenmore Anesthesia Assocs., Tacoma, 1983—; staff anesthesiologist Harrison Meml. Hosp., Bremerton, 1971—, Allenmore Hosp., Tacoma, 1983—. Trustee Tacoma Youth Symphony Assn., 1994—; active Nat. Coun. Jewish Women, 1972—. Fellow Am. Coll. Anesthesiologists, Am. Coll. Chest Physicians; mem. Am. Soc. Anesthesiologists (del. Wash. State 1987—), Wash. State Med. Assn. (del. Pierce County 1993-94), Wash. State Soc. Anesthesiologists (pres. 1985-87), Pierce County Med. Soc. (sec.-treas. 1992). Office: 900 Sheridan Rd Bremerton WA 98310

PLOUMIS, ATHENA B. FRATHELLOS, interior designer; b. Bklyn., Dec. 16, 1935; d. Nestor S. and Florence J. (Chakos) Frathellos; m. William Alexander Ploumis, Feb. 12, 1956; children: Eric Jon, Celeste Ann, Vanessa Alyse, Damon Nestor. Student, Case Western Reserve U., 1952-54, Fairleigh Dickinson U., 1964-66; AD, N.Y. Sch. Interior Design, 1969. Singer, actress Little Lake Theater, Cannonsburgh, Pa., 1961-63; tchr. sculptor, painting Teaneck (N.J.) Pub. Schs., 1964-66; prin. designer Harveys, White Plains, N.Y., 1969-71, Bloomingdales, N.Y.C., 1971-73; owner, designer Athena Interiors, Larchmont, N.Y., 1973—. Pres. Larchmont Hist. Soc., 1992-94, co-founder, 1980; pres. Larchmont Womens Club, 1984-86; co-founder Head Start Program, Mamaroneck, N.Y., 1966. Mem. Am. Soc. Interior Design (cert.). Greek Orthodox. Home and Office: 90 Park Ave Larchmont NY 10538

PLOVANICH, PATRICIA ANN, theologian, educator; b. Charleston, W.Va., Mar. 5, 1938; d. John Paul and Roberta Patricia (Rynd) P. BA, Rosary Hill Coll., 1968; MA, Fordham U., 1972, PhD, 1990. H.S. tchr. music and French DeSales High Sch., Columbus, Ohio, 1962-67; asst. to v.p. student affairs Rosary Hill Coll., Buffalo, 1968-70; lectr. Fordham U., Bronx, N.Y., 1974-78; adj. asst. prof. U. Va., Charlottesville, 1979-80; asst. prof. Loyola Coll., Balt., 1981-83, U. San Diego, 1990—. Vol. Erie County Dems., Buffalo, 1984, Soujourners Family Homeless Shelter, Charleston, W. Va., 1989, 90. Recipient Faculty Rsch. grants U. San Diego, 1992, 93; Steber prof., 1994-95. Mem. Am. Acad. Religions (conv. presenter 1994), Coll. Theology Soc. (conv. presenter 1982, 91, 92, 93, 94, 95. conv. sect. head 1992-95). Roman Catholic. Home: 6730 Glidden St Apt M6 San Diego CA 92111-7360 Office: U San Diego 5998 Alcala Park San Diego CA 92110-2429

PLUBELL, ANN MARIE, lawyer; b. Beaver Falls, Pa.. BA cum laude, SUNY, Buffalo; JD, Georgetown U., LLM in Taxation. Bar: N.Y., D.C., U.S. Dist. Ct. D.C., U.S. Ct. Appeals (D.C. cir.), U.S. Tax Ct., U.S. Supreme Ct. With Student Loan Mktg. Assn., Washington, Assoc. gen. counsel, corp. sec., v.p. Vice chmn. Washington Area Lawyers for the Arts; chmn. long range planning com. Nat. Capital chpt. ARC; mem. Corp. Art Acquistion Com., Washington. Mem. ABA, Am. Soc. Corp. Secs. Office: Student Loan Mktg Assn 1050 Thomas Jefferson St NW Washington DC 20007-3837

PLUCINSKI, VERONICA MARY, librarian; b. Bklyn., May 20, 1952; d. Stanley and Helen (Nagorski) P. BA, SUNY, Cortland, 1974; MLS, Queens Coll., 1975. Libr. asst. Pfizer Inc., N.Y.C., 1976-77, asst. libr., 1977-79, libr., 1979-83, chief libr., 1983-88, mgr. libr. svcs., 1988-93, asst. dir. profl. info., 1993—. Mem. Med. Libr. Assn. (N.Y./N.J. chpt. treas. 1988-90, chmn. 1991-93, chair nominating com. 1983, 93-94). Roman Catholic. Office: Pfizer Inc 235 E 42d St New York NY 10017

PLUMMER, CLARA KEMPER, real estate broker; b. N.Y.C., Mar. 27, 1968; d. Wallace Clegg and Melinda (Budge) K. Diploma, Marymount Coll., London, Eng., 1987; student, Colo. U., 1987-90; lic. real estate salesman, Acad. Real Estate, Destin, Fla., 1991, brokers lic., fin. investment analyst, 1993. Sales rep. Puddle Car Wash, Boulder, Colo., 1987-89; mgr. Gas Gauge Plus, Boulder, 1989-90; waitress Monroe's Resturant, New Orleans, 1990-91; sales rep. Abbot Realty, Destin, Fla., 1991—; broker, owner, pres. Emerald Coast Realty, Destin, 1993—; broker, owner, bd. dirs. Emerald Coast Vacation Rentals, Destin, 1993—; owner Realty Assocs. of the Emerald Coast, 1994—; bd. dirs., sec. Holiday Isle Assocs., Destin, 1993-94; ptnr. Crystal Beach Ptnrs. L.C., 1994—. Mem. Nat. Assn. Realtors, Fla. Assn. Realtors, Emerald Coast Assn. Realtors, Destin C. of C. Republican. Episcopalian. Home: 716 Shore Dr Destin FL 32541-4602 Office: Emerald Coast Realty 797 Highway 98 E Destin FL 32541-2425

PLUMMER, EVELYN LEIGH, accounting educator; b. New London, Conn., Sept. 24, 1943; d. John Calvin and Ruth Glover Sitts; m. Albert Edwin Plummer, Apr. 23, 1966; children: Margaret A., Mary A., David G. BS, Ariz. State U., 1970, M in Accountancy, 1985, also postgrad. CPA, Ariz.; cert. cmty. coll. tchg. Acctg. instr., chair acctg. dept. Lamson Jr. Coll., Phoenix, 1985-90; acctg. instr., rsch. intern Maricopa C.C., Phoenix, 1985-91; pvt. practice Phoenix, 1979—; asst. prof. DeVry Inst. Tech., Phoenix, 1992—. Scout leader Girl Scouts Am., Phoenix, 1975-81, Boy Scouts Am., Phoenix, 1981-84. Mem. AICPAs, Ariz. CPAs (mem. continuing profl. edn. com. 1994—), Nat. Bus. Edn. Assn., Inst. Mgmt. Accts., Phi Kappa Phi. Democrat. Methodist. Office: DeVry Inst Tech 2149 W Dunlap Ave Phoenix AZ 85021

PLUMMER, MARCIE STERN, real estate broker; b. Plymouth, Mass., Oct. 28, 1950; d. Jacob and Rosalie (Adelman) Stern; m. John Dillon McHugh II, Oct. 8, 1974 (div.); 1 child, Joshua Stern; m. Louis Freeman Plummer Jr., Sept. 25, 1982; children: Jessica Price, Denelle Boothe. BA, Am. Internat. Coll., 1972, MAT in English, 1973, postgrad., 1974; postgrad., U. Conn., 1974; lic. real estate broker, Anthony Sch. Real Estate, Walnut Creek, Calif., 1985. Educator, chair dept. Windsor Locks (Conn.) Sch. Dist., 1972-74; educator, placement dir. Heald Bus. Coll., San Francisco, 1974-77; educator evening and day divs. Diablo Valley Coll., Pleasant Hill, Calif., 1975-77; real estate agt. Morrison Homes, Pleasant Hill, 1977-78; real estate agt., tract mgr. Dividend Devel., Santa Clara, Calif., 1978-81; real estate agt. Valley Realty, 1981-84; broker, owner Better Homes Realty, 1984-89; real estate broker, owner The Presád Co. Inc. subs. Better Homes Realty, Danville, Calif., 1984-90; owner The Mktg. Group, 1989—. Better Homes Realty rep. for orgn. of Danville 4th of July Parade, City of Danville, 1984-88; publicist San Ramon Valley Little League, Alamo, Calif., 1986—; active Battered Women's Found., Contra Costa County, Calif., 1986—, Yosemite Fund, 1992—, Safe Home Teen Program, 1991—; active rep. voter registration, Walnut Creek, Calif., 1987—; mem. Civic Arts Coun., Walnut Creek, 1988—; drama coach, dir. Advanced Drama Ensemble, 1993-94. Recipient numerous nat., state and regional awards in field, $400 million closed vol. in real estate sales achievement award, 1991. Mem. Bldg. Industry Assn. (Sales vol. award 1978-89), Sales & Mktg. Coun. (sponsor MAME awards banquet 1978-89, Gold sponsor 1986-88), Calif. Assn. Realtors, Contra Costa Bd. Realtors. Jewish. Home: 123 Erselia Trl Alamo CA 94507-1311 Office: Better Homes Realty PO Box 939 Danville CA 94526

PLUMMER, ORA BEATRICE, nursing educator, trainer; b. Mexia, Tex., May 25, 1940; d. Macie Idella (Echols); BS. in Nursing, U. N.Mex., 1961; M.S. in Nursing Edn., UCLA, 1966; children—Kimberly, Kevin, Cheryl. Nurses aide Bataan Meml. Meth. Hosp., Albuquerque, 1958-60, staff nurse, 1961-62, 67-68; staff nurse, charge nurse, relief supr. Hollywood (Calif.) Community Hosp., 1962-64; instr. U. N.Mex. Coll. of Nursing, Albuquerque, 1968-69; sr. instr. U. Colo. Sch. Nursing, Denver, 1971-74; asst. prof. U. Colo. Sch. Nursing, Denver, 1974-76; staff assoc. III Western Interstate Commn. for Higher Edn., Boulder, Colo., 1976-78; dir. nursing Garden Manor Nursing Home, Lakewood, Colo., 1978-79; ednl. coordination Colo. Dept. Health, Denver, 1987—. Active Colo. Cluster of Schs.-faculty devel.; mem. adv. bd. Affiliated Children's and Family Services, 1977; mem. state instl. child abuse and neglect adv. com., 1984—; mem. planning com. State Wide Conf. on Black Health Concerns, 1977; mem. staff devel. com. Western Interstate Commn. for Higher Edn., 1978, minority affairs com., 1978, coordinating com. for baccalaureate program, 1971-76; active minority affairs U. Colo. Med. Center, 1971-72; mem. ednl. resources com. public relations com., rev. com. for reappointment, promotion, and tenure U. Colo. Sch. Nursing, 1971-76; regulatory tng. com., 1989—, gerontol. adv. com., Met. State Coll., 1989—; expert panel mem. Long Term Care Training Manual, HCFA, Balt., 1989; mem. EDAC com. Colo. Dept. of Health. Mem. NAFE, Am. Soc. Tng. and Devel., Am. Nurses Assn., Colo. Nurses Assn. (affirmative action comm. 1977, 78, 79), Phi Delta Kappa. Avocation: pub. speaking, training. Contbr. articles in field to profl. jours. Office: 4300 Cherry Creek South Dr Denver CO 80222-1530

PLUMMER, PATRICIA LYNNE MOORE, chemistry and physics educator; b. Tyler, Tex., Feb. 26; d. Robert Lee and Jewell Ovelia (Jones) Moore; m. Otho Raymond Plummer, Apr. 10, 1965; children: Patrick William Otho, Christina Elisa Lynne. BA, Tex. Christian U., Ft. Worth, Tex., 1960; postgrad., U. N.C., 1960-61; PhD, U. Tex., 1964; grad., Bryn Mawr Summer Inst., 1992. Instr., Welch postdoctoral fellow U. Tex., Austin, 1964-66; postdoctoral fellow Dept. Chemistry, U. Ark., Fayetteville, 1966-68; rsch. assoc. Grad. Ctr., Cloud Phys. Rsch., Rolla, Mo., 1968-73; asst. prof. physics U. Mo., Rolla, 1973-77; assoc. dir. Grad. Ctr. Cloud Phys. Rsch., 1977-79, sr. investigator, 1980-85; assoc. prof. physics U. Mo., 1977-85; prof. dept. chemistry and physics U. Mo., Columbia, 1986—; internat. sci. advisor Symposium on Chemistry and Physics of Ice, 1982—. Assoc. editor Jour. of Colloid and Interface Sci., 1980-83; contbr. articles to profl. jours., chpts. to books. Rsch. grantee IBM, 1990-92, Air Force Office Rsch., 1989-91, NSF, 1976-86, NASA, 1973-78; Air Force Office Rsch. summer fellow, 1988, Bryn Mawr Summer Inst., 1992. Mem. Am. Chem. Soc., Am. Phys. Soc., Am. Geophys. Union, Sigma Xi (past pres.). Democrat. Baptist. Office: Univ of Missouri 314 Physics Bldg Columbia MO 65211

PLUNKERT, DONNA MAE, business owner; b. Pa., Apr. 26, 1951; d. Norman Francis and Rada Mae (Snyder) Dickensheets; m. Bruce Herbert Plunkert, Nov. 2, 1975; 1 child, Gabriel Bruce. Grad., Littlestown (Pa.) H.S., 1969. Sales clk. Colonial Fair, Hanover, Pa., 1970-72, sec., 1972-75; full-time sec. Norm's Auction, Hanover, 1975-79, part-time sec., 1979-84; owner Old Buttermould Patterns Products, Littlestown, 1989—. Reproduced antique buttermolds for gift shops Carroll County Farm Mus., Westminster, Md., Historic Michie Tavern, Charlottesville, Va. Mem. U.S. C. of C., Mus. Store Assn. (assoc.). Mem. Brethren Ch. Home: 315 N Queen St Littlestown PA 17340

POBLETE, RITA MARIA BAUTISTA, physician, educator; b. Manila, May 19, 1954; came to U.S., 1980; d. Juan Gonzalez and Rizalina (Bautista) Poblete. BS, U. Philippines, 1974, MD, 1978. Diplomate Am. Bd. Internal Medicine. Intern, resident Wayne State U./Detroit Med. Ctr., 1982-85, fellow in infectious disease, 1986-87; fellow in infectious disease Chgo. Med. Sch./VA Hosp., North Chicago, Ill., 1985-86; fellow in spl. immunology U. Miami (Fla.)-Jackson Meml. Hosp., 1987-89; adj. clin. instr. dept. of medicine U. Miami, 1989-90, asst. prof. medicine, 1990-94; infectious diseases cons. Cedars Med. Ctr., Miami, 1994—; infectious disease cons. Cedars Med. Ctr., Miami, 1994—. Contbr. articles to med. jours. Mem. Am. Soc. for Microbiology, World Found. Successful Women. Office: Cedars Med Ctr 1295 NW 14th St Ste E Miami FL 33125

PODGOR, ELLEN SUE, lawyer, educator; b. Bklyn., Jan. 30, 1952; d. Benjamin and Yetta (Shilensky) Podgor. BS magna cum laude, Syracuse U., 1973; JD, Ind. U., Indpls., 1976; MBA, U. Chgo., 1987; LLM, Temple U., 1989. Bar: Ind. 1976, N.Y. 1984, Pa. 1987. Dep. prosecutor Lake County Prosecutor's Office, Crown Point, Ind., 1976-78; ptnr. Nicholls & Podgor, Crown Point, 1978-87, instr. Temple U. Sch. Law, 1987-89; assoc. prof. law sch. St. Thomas U., Miami, Fla., 1989-91, Ga. State U., Atlanta, 1991—. Author: White Collar Crime In A Nutshell; assoc. editor Ind. Law Rev., 1975-76; contbr. articles to legal jours.; mem. adv. bd. BNA Criminal Practice Manual. Del. Ind. Dem. State Conv., 1982. Mem. ABA, Ind. Bar Assn., Nat. Assn. Criminal Def. Lawyers. Democrat. Jewish. Office: Ga State U Coll Law PO Box 4037 Atlanta GA 30302-4037

PODHORETZ, HARRIETTE, psychologist, psychoanalyst; b. N.Y.C., Nov. 28, 1932; d. John and Leah (Bressler) Miller; m. Jan. 22, 1958; children: Jane, James. BS in Edn., CCNY, 1953, MA in English Edn., 1966; MA in Psychology, Fordham U., N.Y.C., 1973; PhD, Fordham U., 1974. Lic. psychologist, N.Y.; grad. psychoanalyst. Tchr. N.Y.C. Pub. Schs., 1953-59; psychotherapist Jamaica Ctr. Psychotherapy, N.Y.C., 1968-72; psychotherapist in pvt. practice N.Y.C., 1972-75, pvt. practice psychology, 1975—; pvt. practice psychology Scarsdale, N.Y., 1979—; tng. analyst Nat. Psychol. Assn. for Psychoanalysis, 1976—. Contbr. chpts. to books. Mem. APA, NYCAPS, NPAP. Home: 253 Garth Rd Scarsdale NY 10583-4050 Office: 51 E 42nd St New York NY 10017-5404

PODLES, ELEANOR PAULINE, state senator; b. Dudley, Mass., June 6, 1920; d. Francis and Pauline Magiera; student U. N.H.; m. Francis J. Podles, June 28, 1941; children: L. Patricia Podles Barrett Fogleman, Elizabeth Lee Podles Keegan. Mem. N.H. Ho. of Reps., Concord, 1976-80; selectman City of Manchester, N.H., 1976-81, v.p., 1978—; mem. N.H. State Senate, Concord, 1980—; asst. majority whip, mem. fin. com., chmn. public affairs com., public instns. health and welfare com. Del., N.H. Republican Conv., 1976, 78, N.H. Constl. Conv., 1984; pres. pro tem N.H. Senate, 1986—, chair jud. com., vice chair exec. com., senate fin. com., senate edn. com., health and human services for pub. insts. com.; pres. Manchester Rep. Women's Club, 1979—; bd. dirs. St. Joseph's Community Service, Manchester Vis. Nurse Assn., Mental Health Ctr. Manchester, Senate Edn. Com.; state chmn. Am. Legis. Exchange Council; mem. sen. fin. com., 1995—; sen. pres. pro tem, 1995—. Bd. dirs. Mental Health Ctr. Greater Manchester; mem. N.H. Childrens Trust Fund, 1986—. Mem. Am. Legis. Exch. Coun. (state chmn.), Orgn. Women Legislators, Manchester Vis. Nurse Assn., Manchester Country Club. Club: Manchester Country. Home: 185 Walnut Hill Ave Manchester NH 03104-2136 Office: N H State Senate State Capitol Concord NH 03301

PODMOKLY, PATRICIA GAYLE, typesetting company professional; b. Chgo., May 15, 1940; d. Edwin Paul Baker and Frances (Williams) Popiela. Grad., Jones Comml. Sch., Chgo. Bookkeeper, sec. William C. Douglas & Ralph Falk II, Lake Forest, Ill., 1958—; owner Global Graphics, Inc., Elmhurst, Ill., 1987—. Roman Catholic. Home: 1002 Muir Ave Lake Bluff IL 60044-1538

PODOLEFSKY, RONNIE LYNN, organization executive; b. Bklyn., Jan. 25, 1950; d. Sidney and Jacqueline (Glassman) Shapiro; m. Aaron Mayer Podolefsky, June 3, 1973; children: Noah, Isaac. BS, SUNY, Stony Brook, 1972; cert. nuclear medicine tech., W.Va. U., 1985. Tchr. sci. Brentwood (N.Y.) Pub. Schs., 1971-73; animal technician, chief Brentwood/Bayshore (N.Y.) Animal Hosps., 1973-75; artist, stained glass Mt. Morris, Pa., 1979-86; nuclear med. tech. Monongalia Gen. Hosp., Morgantown, W.Va., 1985-86; asst. radiation safety officer W.Va. U. and Hosp., Morgantown, 1985-86; nuclear med. tech. HCA Greenview Hosp., Bowling Green, Ky., 1988-89; nuclear med. dept. supr., radiation safety officer Graves Gilbert Clinic, Bowling Green, 1989-90; chpt. pres. N.E. Iowa NOW, Cedar Falls, 1992-93; state pres. Iowa NOW, 1993—; cons. Graves Gilbert Clinic, Bowling Green, 1989; speaker in field. Vol. Family and Children's Coun., Waterloo, Iowa, 1991-93; bd. dirs. YWCA, Waterloo, 1992—; field organizer Iowa Women's Equality Campaign, 1992; co-founder Iowans for Social Justice, 1993—; co-founding mem. Iowans for Democracy, Des Moines, 1993—; mem. steering com. Ams. United for Separation of Ch. and State, 1994—. Mem. Soc. Nuclear Medicine (assoc.). Home: 8206 Buck Rdg Cedar Falls IA 50613-9490 Office: Iowa NOW PO Box 674 Cedar Falls IA 50613-0674

PODOS-UNTERMEYER, SALLE, lawyer; b. Bklyn., Oct. 1, 1938; d. David Meyer and Rose (Ifshin) Garber; m. Steven Maurice Podos, June 20, 1959 (div. Dec. 1978); children: Richard Lance Podos, Lisa Beth Podos; m. Walter Untermeyer, Jr., May 2, 1982. BA, Vassar Coll., 1959; MA, Brandeis U., 1960; JD, Columbia U., 1977. Bar: N.Y. 1978. Assoc. Paul, Weiss, Rifkind, Wharton & Garrison, N.Y.C., 1977-79; gen. counsel, v.p., sec. MacAndrews & Forbes Group, Inc., N.Y.C., 1979-81; sr. assoc. Sage Gray Todd & Sims, N.Y.C., 1981-84, Proskauer Rose Goetz & Mendelsohn, N.Y.C., 1984-87; pres., gen. counsel Untermeyer Mace Ptnrs., 1987-89; of counsel Mazur Carp & Rubin, 1989-91; mem. fin. com. Congresswoman Carolyn Maloney, 1994—. Class fund-raising chmn. Vassar Coll., 1977-80; bd. dirs. Vassar Club N.Y., 1978-80; chmn. women's div. U.S. Senate Campaign, 1970; regional chmn. U.S. Presdl. Campaign, 1972; chmn. State Rep.'s Campaign, 1973; del.-elect Interim Dem. Conv., 1974, Lawyers Com. for Gov. Carey, 1978; chmn. Mo. state legis. Nat. Coun. Jewish Women, 1969-75, mem. nat. affairs com., 1969-77, chmn. Mo. juvenile justice project, 1970-75, mem. legis. coordinating com. Midwestern region, 1971-75, mem. nat. task force on constl. rights, 1974-77; v.p., bd. dirs. St. Louis Jewish Community Rels. Coun., 1970-75, chmn. ch.-state and Black Jack Amicus Curiae coms.; v.p., bd. dirs. St. Louis chpt. Am. Jewish Com., 1969-75, chmn. urban affairs and placement for ex-offenders coms., mem. com. on status of women, 1974-77; mem. legis. liaison Coalition for Environment, St. Louis, 1970-74; bd. dirs. St. Louis Jewish Community Ctrs. Assn., 1970-74, chmn. urban affairs and legis. affairs coms.; bd. dirs. St. Louis Jewish Family and Children's Svc., 1972-74, chmn. welfare rights and health svcs. coms.; bd. dirs. Glaucoma Found., 1986—; vol. coord. Poor People's Campaign, 1968; founder, bd. dirs. Consumer's Assn., 1967-69; founder, chmn. Urban Corps program St. Louis Mayor's Com. on Youth, 1969-72; panelist White House Conf. on Children and Youth, 1970, 72, White House Conf. on Aging, 1974; founder, bd. dirs. Mo. chpt. PEARL (Pub. Edn. and Religious Liberty), 1972-75; fundraising chmn. N.Y. Found. Arts, 1992-94; bd. dirs. N.Y. Found. Sr. Citizens. Woodrow Wilson Found. fellow, 1959, NDEA fellow, 1959. Mem. ABA, Assn. of Bar of City of N.Y. (mem. continuing legal edn. com., com. on lecture), N.Y. State Bar Assn., Womens Prison Assn. (bd. dirs.). Home: 950 Park Ave New York NY 10028-0320

POE, (LYDIA) VIRGINIA, reading educator; b. Bklyn., Jan. 19, 1932; d. Harold Waldemar and Lydia Beatrice (Doswell) Lind; m. Harold Weller Poe, Sept. 11, 1954; children: Michael Lind, David Harold, Timothy Claude. BA, Beloit Coll., 1954; MEd, U. Southwestern La., 1961, EdS, 1972; EdD, U. So. Miss., 1983. Cert. tchr., Fla., La., Ill., Wis. Elem. tchr. Caroline Brevard Sch., Tallahassee, 1961-64; supervising tchr. Fla. State U., Tallahassee, 1962-64; elem., supervising tchr. Hamilton Lab. Sch., Lafayette, La., 1965-67; prof. reading U. Southwestern La., Lafayette, 1968—, head Dept. Curriculum and Instrn., 1986-91, assoc. dir. Hawthorne Ctr. Spl. Edn. and communicative disorders, 1988—; co-originator field experiences U. Southwestern La., 1970—; observer in elem. sch. Ecole de Charlemagne, Nancy, France, 1967; cons. Lafayette Parish Schs., 1968—. Editorial review panel The Ednl. Forum, 1992—; contbr. to book: Reading Research Review, 1984; contbr. articles profl. jours., 1985—; presenter papers to profl. orgns. 1968—. Organizer Conf. on Women in Politics, Lafayette, 1976 (recipient scholarship 1974); treas. State of La. ERA United, 1977; organizer, pres. First Luth. Ch. Day Care Ctr., Lafayette, 1977-80; chair quality edn. svcs. Lafayette Parish Year Round Schs. Study Com. Recipient research grant, U. Southwestern U., 1986-87. Mem. ASCD, Internat. Reading Assn., Am. Reading Assn., Coll. Reading Assn., AAUW, (fellowship contribution 1976), United Fedn. Coll. Tchrs., Nat. Assn. Yr. Round Edn., Phi Delta Kappa, Phi Kappa Phi, Kappa Delta Pi, Beta Sigma Phi. Democrat. Lutheran. Office: U Southwestern La PO Box 42051 Lafayette LA 70504-2051

POEHLMANN, JOANNA, artist, illustrator, designer; b. Milw., Sept. 5, 1932; d. Herbert Emil and Lucille (Conover) P. Attended, Layton Sch. Art, 1950-54, K.C. (Mo.) Art Inst., 1954, Marquette U., 1958, U. Wis., 1965, 1985. Solo exhbns. include St. James Gallery, Milw., 1963, (retrospective) Milw. Art Mus., 1966, Bradley Galleries, Milw., 1982, Signature Gallery, John Michael Kohler Art Ctr., Sheboygan, Wis., 1979, 84, Woodland Pattern Book Ctr., Milw., 1988, The Cell Gallery, Rochester, N.Y., 1988, 89, Charles Allis Art Mus., Milw., 1991, Layton Gallery at Cardinal Stritch Coll, Milw., 1993, Univ. Meml. Libr., Madison, Wis., 1993, Wustum Mus. Fine Arts, Racine, Wis., 1994; two-man shows include Bradley Galleries, 1964, 69, 80, 91, Cardinal Stritch Coll., Milw., 1980; invitational group shows include Cudahy Gallery of Wis. Art, Milw. Art Mus., 1962-85, 92, Bradley Galleries, 1967-79, Lakefront Festival of Art, Milw. Art Mus., 1962-63, 70-72, 76-79, Country Art Gallery, Long Island, N.Y., 1963-71, Mount Mary Coll., Milw., 1979, 83, Chosy Gallery, 1980, 81, 86, U. Dallas, 1987, Frick Gallery, Germany, 1991, Spertus Mus. Judaica, Chgo., 1986, World Fin. Ctr., N.Y.C., 1992, Istvan Kiraly Muzeum, Budapest, Hungary, 1992, Artspace, Richmond, Va., 1994, Va. Ctr. For Craft Arts, Richmond, 1994, many others; juried group shows include Milw. Art Mus., 1963, 75, 78, Chgo. Art Inst., 1978, 81, Milw. Fine Arts Gallery, 1980, U. Wis. Fine Arts Gallery, Milw., 1980, The West Pub. Co., St. Paul, 1982, Auburn U., 1983, Zaner Gallery, Rochester, N.Y., 1984, Pratt Graphics Ctr., N.Y.C., 1985, Art 54 Gallery, N.Y.C., 1987, Boston Art Inst., 1987, Bradley U., Peoria, Ill., 1989, Wustum Mus. Fine Arts, 1989, 1992, Trenton State Coll., 1991, numerous others; represented in collections including Victoria & Albert Mus., London, N.Y. Pub. Libr., Mus. Kunsthandwerk, Frankfurt, Germany, Milw. Art Mus., Milw. Pub. Libr., U. Dallas, Orchard Corp. Am., St. Louis, McDonald's Corp., GE Med. Systems Bldgs., Waukesha, Goldhirsh Group, Boston, Marquette U.-Haggerty Mus. Art, others; subject of articles; author: Love Letters, Food for Thought, Cancelling Out. Recipient Merit award Art Dir.'s Club, Milw., 1962, 100 Best award, 1967, 100 Best award Milw. Soc. Communicating Arts, 1973, 76, MGIC award Wis. Painters & Sculptors, 1981, Merit award Illustration Milw. Advt. Club, 1983, 2d award Wustum Mus. Fine Arts, 1983, 4th Purchase Prize award McDonald's Fine Art Collection Competition, 1983, Juror's award Zaner Gallery, 1984, Hopper/Koch award Wustum Mus. Fine Arts, 1985, spl. mention, Purchase award Bradley U., 1985, Purchase award Moravian Coll., 1985, Jack Richeson award Wustum Mus. Fine Arts, 1985, Purchase award U. Del., 1986, Strathmore Paper Co. award Wustum Mus. Fine Arts, 1986, Purchase award U. N.Dak., 1987, Award of Excellence miniature art Metro Internat. Competition, N.Y.C., 1987, 3d award Wustum Mus. Fine Arts, 1987, Purchase award U. Dallas, 1988, Award of Excellence Wustum Mus. Fine Arts, 1992, Individual Art fellowship Milw. County, 1993; Arts Midwest/NEA Regional Visual Artist fellow, 1994—. Roman Catholic. Home and Studio: 1231 N Prospect Ave Milwaukee WI 53202

POE-JACKSON, GERTIE LAVERNE, sales executive; b. Chgo., Feb. 7, 1949; d. L.C. and Gertrude (Winfrey) Poe. BSBA, Roosevelt U., 1978, MBA, 1984. Policy analyst Continental Bank, Chgo., 1971-87; fin. planner IDS/Am. Express, Merrillville, Ind., 1987-89; sales rep. Valic, Chgo., 1990-94, Invest Fin. Svcs., Bridgeview, IL, 1994—. Mem. Sigma Gamma Rho. Baptist. Home: PO Box 19201 Chicago IL 60619 Office: Invest Fin Svcs Bridgeview Bank & Trust 7940 S Harlem Bridgeview IL 60455

POESNECKER, CONNIE JO, insurance agency executive; b. Hettinger, N.D., July 17, 1959; d. Dale Eugene and Josephine Adelia (Kretchmar) Jones; m. Gary Ralph Poesnecker, Mar. 25, 1982. BA, Calif. State U.-Stanislaus, Turlock, 1979. Cert. ins. counselor. Adjudicator La. Dept. Labor, Opelousas, 1983-86; account rep. Arthur A. Watson & Co., Inc., Wethersfield, Conn., 1986-89, account. exec., profl. liability, 1989-90, mgr. profl. liability, 1990-93; asst. v.p. Arthur A. Watson & Co., Wethersfield, Conn., 1993—. Vol. coach Spl. Olympics, New Haven, 1989-91; VIP panelist Easter Seals, New Haven, 1987—. Mem. Hartford Assn. Ins. Women, Conn. Young Ins. Profls. Home: 65 Fairview Ter South Glastonbury CT 06073-3305 Office: Arthur A Watson & Co Inc 225 Spring St Wethersfield CT 06109-3485

POFFENBERGER, KATHRYN IONE, retired librarian, volunteer; b. Vincennes, Ind., Oct. 7, 1908; d. George Horace and Mary Nell (Harber) Purcell; m. John Templeton Poffenberger (dec. 1954). BS, U. Indpls., 1930; MusM, Ind. U., 1951. Cert. libr., Ind.; cert. tchr., Ind. Tchr., libr. Pleasantville (Ind.) Pub. Schs., 1930-33, Glenwood (Ind.) Pub. Schs., 1933-36, Topeka (Ind.) Pub. Schs., 1936-41; tchr., libr. South Bend (Ind.) Community Schs., 1941-76, ret., 1976; rschr. in internat. peace studies Notre Dame (Ind.) U. Mem. ALA, LWV, AAUW (speaker), Am. Assn. Ret. People (tax preparer 1976—), No. Ind. Hist. Soc. (mus. cataloging 1976—), Nat. Ret. Tchrs. Assn., Ind. Ret. Tchrs. Assn., Ind. Libr. Assn., Common Cause, Citizens Action Coalition, UN of U.S.A., Am. Civil Rights Union, Mothers Against Drunk Driving, Met. Opera Guild.

POGREBIN, LETTY COTTIN, writer, lecturer; b. N.Y.C., June 9, 1939; d. Jacob and Cyral (Halpern) Cottin; m. Bertrand B. Pogrebin, Dec. 8, 1963; children: Abigail and Robin (twins), David. A.B. cum laude with spl. distinction in English and Am. Lit, Brandeis U., 1959. V.p. Bernard Geis Assocs. (book pubs.), N.Y.C., 1960-70; columnist The Working Woman column Ladies Home Jour., 1971-81; editor Ms mag., N.Y.C., 1971-87, columnist, editor at large, 1987-89, contbg. editor, 1990—; columnist The N.Y. Times, Newsday, Moment Mag., Wasington Post, Moment Mag., Washington, 1990—; contbg. editor Family Circle, Ms. mag., Tikkun mag.; cons. Free to Be, You and Me projects, 1972—; lectr. women's issues and family politics, changing roles of men and women, friendship in Am., nonsexist child rearing and edn., Judaism and feminism, Mid-East politics. Author: How to Make It in a Man's World, 1970, Getting Yours: How to Make the System Work for the Working Woman, 1975, Growing Up Free, 1980, Stories for Free Children, 1982, Family Politics, 1983, Among Friends, 1986, Deborah, Golda, and Me: Being Female and Jewish in America, 1991; mem. editorial bd. Tikkun Mag.; contbr. articles to N.Y. Times, Washington Post, Boston Globe, The Nation, TV Guide, also other mags., newspapers. Sec. bd. Author's Guild; bd. dirs. Ms. Found., Ams. for Peace Now, New Israel Fund, Jewish Fund for Justice, Commn. on Women's Equality, Am. Jewish Congress, PEN Am.; mem. Task Force on Women Fedn. Jewish Philanthropies, N.Y.C. Commn. on Status of Women. Pointer fellow Yale U., 1982, MacDowell Colony fellow, 1979, 89, 94, Cummington Colony Arts fellow 1985, Edna St. Vincent Millay Colony fellow, 1985. Mem. Nat. Women's Polit. Caucus (a founder), Women's Forum of N.Y. (bd. dirs.). Address: 33 W 67th St New York NY 10023-6224

POGUE, MARY ELLEN E. (MRS. L. WELCH POGUE), youth and community worker; b. Fremont, Nebr., Oct. 27, 1904; d. Frank E. and Mary (Coe) Edgerton; m. L. Welch Pogue, Sept. 8, 1926; children: Richard Welch, William Lloyd, John Marshall. BFA, U. Nebr., 1926; studied violin with Harrison Keller, Boston, 1926-28, Kemp Stillings Master Class, N.Y.C., 1935-37. Mem. Potomac String Ensemble, 1939-80. Historian, Gov. William Bradford Compact, 1966—; vice chmn. Montgomery County (Md.) Victory Garden Ctr., 1946-47; pres. Bethesda Community Garden Club, 1947-48; founder, bd. dirs. Montgomery County YWCA, 1946-50, 52-55; founder Welcome to Washington Music Group, 1947—. Recipient Outstanding Service award Bethesda United Meth. Ch., 1984, Bethesda Community Garden Club, 1985, 93, Devoted Svc. award D.C. Mayflower Soc., 1985, 89. Mem. Soc. Mayflower Descs. D.C. (dir. D.C. 1954—, elder 1971-91, elder emeritus), PEO Sisterhood (pres. 1957-59), Mortar Bd. Alumnae (pres. 1965-67), Nat. Cap. Area Fedn. Garden Clubs, Bethesda United Meth. Women, Nat. Geneal. Soc., New Eng. Geneal. Soc., Ohio Geneal. Soc. (life), Md. Geneal. Soc., Md. Hist. Soc., Conn. Soc. Genealogists, Pilgrim Soc. (life), Plimoth Plantation, Hereditary Order of Descs. Colonial Govs., Nat. Soc. Magna Charta Dames, Colonial Order of Crown, Sovereign Colonial Soc. Ams. Royal Descent, Order of Descs. Colonial Physicians and Chirurgiens, Nat. Soc. Women Descs. Ancient and Hon. Arty. Co., Welcome to Washington Internat. Club, Ind. Agy. Women (assoc.), Capital Speakers Club, The Plantagenet Soc., Soc. Descs. of Knights of the Most Noble Order of the Garter, DAR, Order Ams. Armorial Ancestry, Saybrook Colony Founders Assn., Soc. Founders of Norwich, Conn., Kenwood Country Club, Delta Omicron Music (life). Methodist. Compiler, editor: Favorite Recipes of Mary Edgerton of Aurora, Nebraska, 1963, Edgerton-Coe History, 1965. Home: 5204 Kenwood Ave Bethesda MD 20815-6604

POHL, KATHLEEN SHARON, editor; b. Sandusky, Mich., Apr. 7, 1951; d. Gerald Arthur and Elizabeth Louise (Neukamm) P.; m. Bruce Mark Allen Reynolds, June 11, 1982. BA in Spanish, Valparaiso U., 1973; MA in English, No. Mich. U., 1975. Producer, dir. fine arts Sta. WNMU-FM, Marquette, Mich., 1981-82; instr. communications Waukesha County (Wis.) Tech. Inst., 1983; editor Ideals mag., Milw., 1983-85; editor, mng. editor Raintree Pubs., Milw., 1985-87; mng. editor Country Woman mag., Greendale, Wis., 1987—; exec. editor Country Handcrafts mag., Greendale, 1990-93, Taste of Home Mag., Greendale, Wis., 1993—; editor Talk About Pets, Greendale, 1994—. Author nature book series, 1985-87; mng. editor: Irwin the Sock (Chgo. Book Clinic award 1988). Mem. Internat. Platform Assn., Nat. Mus. of Women in Arts, Alpha Lambda Delta (hon.). Home: N54 W26326 Lisbon Rd Sussex WI 53089 Office: Country Woman Mag 5400 S 60th St Greendale WI 53129-1404

POIANI, EILEEN LOUISE, mathematics educator, college administrator, higher education planner; b. Newark, Dec. 17, 1943; d. Hugo Francis and Eileen Louise (Crecca) P. BA in Math., Douglass Coll., 1965; MS in Math., Rutgers U., 1967, PhD in Math., 1971. Teaching asst., grad. preceptor Rutgers U., New Brunswick, N.J., 1966-67; asst. counselor Douglass Coll., New Brunswick, 1967, 69-70; instr. math. St. Peter's Coll., Jersey City, 1967-70, asst. prof., 1970-74, dir. of self-study, 1974-76, assoc. prof., 1974-80, prof., 1980—, asst. to pres., 1976-80; asst. to pres. for planning St. Peter's Coll., 1980—; chairwoman U.S. Commn. on Math. Instrn., NRC of NAS, Washington, 1983-90; founding nat. dir. Women and Math. Lectureship Program, Washington, 1975-81, mem. adv. bd., 1981—; project dir. Consortium for Advancement of Pvt. Higher Edn., Washington, 1986-88; mem. N.J. Math. Coalition, 1991—, Nat. Seminar on Jesuit Higher Edn., 1990-94, mem. strategic planning com. N.J. Assn. Ind. Colls. and Univs., 1990-92; charter trustee Rutgers U., 1992—. Author: (with others) Mathematics Tomorrow, 1981; contbr. articles to profl. jours. Mem. Newark Mus., Nutley (N.J.) Hist. Soc., Friends of Newark Libr.; trustee Nutley Free Pub. Libr., 1974-77, St. Peter's Prep. Sch., Jersey City, 1986-92; active fee arbitration commn. N.J. Supreme Ct., 1983-86, ct. ethics com., 1986-90; U.S. nat. rep. Internat. Congress Math. Edn., Budapest, Hungary, 1988; mem. statewide planning com. NCCJ, 1988-92; chair evaluation teams Mid. States Assn. Coll. and Schs.; mem. U.S. delegation to Internat. Congress on Math; trustee The Cath. Advocate, 1993—. Recipient Douglass Soc. award Douglass Coll., 1982, Outstanding Cmty. Svc. award Christopher Columbus Found., 1994, Outstanding Svc. award Middle States Assn. Colls. and Schs., 1994, Christopher Columbus award N.J. Columbus Found.; named Danforth Assoc., Danforth Found., 1972-86. Mem. AAUP, Math. Assn. Am. (bd. dirs. lectureship program, gov. N.J. chpt. 1972-79, chair human resources coun. 1991—, Outstanding Coll. Teaching award 1993), Am. Math. Soc., Nat. Coun. Tchrs. Math. (speaker 1974—), Soc. Coll. and Univ. Planning (program com. 1989—, speaker nat. confs. 1986, 88, 89, 90, judge grad. paper competition), Pi Mu Epsilon (1st woman pres. in 75 yrs. 1987-90). Roman Catholic. Office: St Peter's Coll 2641 Kennedy Blvd Jersey City NJ 07306

POINDEXTER, BARBARA GLENNON, secondary school educator; b. Dallas, Oct. 19, 1937; d. Victor and Ruth (Gaskins) Ward; m. Noble Turner Poindexter, Aug. 2, 1994; 1 child, Victoria Angela Glennon Betts. BS, Tex. Woman's U., 1958; postgrad., Kans. State U., 1969-70. Cert. tchr. S.C., Kans., N.Mex., Tex. Drama and English tchr. Linn (Kans.) High Sch., 1968-69; tchr. Mosquero (N.Mex.) High Sch., 1973-74, Sumter (S.C.) Sch. Dist., Maywood Sch., 1974-76, Harleyville (S.C.) High Sch., 1976-78, Hampton (S.C.) High Sch., 1978-79, Centerville Sch., S.C., 1979-80; tchr. English Scurry-Rosser Sch., Scurry, Tex., 1981-82; tchr. French and Spanish Christ the King, Dallas, 1982-83; tchr. French and English, chmn. fgn. lang. dept. Wilmer-Hutchins High Sch., Dallas, 1983—. Mem. Theta Alpha Phi. Democrat. Methodist. Home: 1914 Berkley Ave Dallas TX 75224 Office: Wilmer-Hutchins High Sch 5520 Langdon Rd Dallas TX 75241

POINDEXTER, BEVERLY KAY, media and communications professional; b. Noblesville, Ind., Nov. 12, 1949; d. Wayne Francis and Rosalie Christine (Nightenhelser) Hunter; m. Jerry Roger Poindexter, Dec. 7, 1969; children: Nick Ashley, Tracy Lynne, Wendy Dawn, Cory Matthew. Student, Purdue U. Editor Tri Town Topics Newspaper, 1965-69; reporter, photographer Noblesville Daily Ledger, 1969-70; asst. mgr., sales mgr. sports dir. Sta. WHYT Radio, Noblesville, Ind., 1973-79; gen. mgr., sales mgr., music dir. Sta. WEWZ Radio, Elwood, Ind., 1979-90; acct. exec. Stas. WAXT-WHBU Radio, Anderson, Ind., 1988-89; now news stringer Sta. WRTV-6, Indpls., Sta. WTHR TV, Indpls.; acct. exec. Sta. WLHN Radio, Elwood, Ind.; real estate broker Booker Realty, Cicero, Ind., 1990—. Area rep. Youth for Understanding, Hamilton County, Ind.; pres. bd. dirs. Hamilton Heights Elem. Football, Arcadia, Ind., 1981-83; founder, chmn. Hamilton Heights Elem. Cheerleaders, Arcadia, 1981-87; youth leader, counselor Ch. of the Brethren, Arcadia, 1991-94; active Ch. of Brethren Women's Fellowship. Mem. Nat. Assn. Realtors, Ind. Assn. Realtors, Met. Indpls. Bd. Realtors. Republican. Home: 14645 E 281st St Atlanta IN 46031 Office: Booker Realty PO Box 437 99 S Peru Cicero IN 46034

POINDEXTER, LINDA SUE, laboratory manager; b. Alma, Mich., Jan. 7, 1944; d. Lyle Burton and Eva Marie (Northrup) Bartrem; m. David Lee Poindexter, Aug. 17, 1963 (div. Dec. 1987); children: Eric David, Kristina Marie, Kevin Lynn. BS with honors, Mich. State U., 1965; MBA, Lake Superior State U., 1994. Lic. med. technologist. Med. technologist Sparrow Hosp., Lansing, Mich., 1964-65, Olin Health Ctr., Mich. State U., East Lansing, 1965-68, Otsego County Hosp., Gaylord, Mich., 1969-70; med. technologist, lab. mgr. Thirlby Clinic, Traverse City, Mich., 1977—; mem. profl. adv. panel Med. Lab. Observer, 1991-92; mem. MMC Lab. Quality Com., Traverse City, Mich., 1992-93. Mem. Traverse City State Hosp. Reuse Task Force, 1988-90; participant Traverse City Summitt Conf., 1990. Mem. AAUW (publicity chair 1988-90, br. pres. 1990-92, fundraiser chair 1992-94). Methodist. Home: 3120 College Terrace Ct Traverse City MI 49684-8812 Office: 3537 W Front St Traverse City MI 49684-9689

POINTER, MARTHA MANNING, accounting educator; b. Johnson City, Tenn., June 1, 1949; d. Ambrose N. and Mary Manning; m. Robert L. Pointer, Jr., Aug. 29, 1970; children: Robert L., III, Charlse A. BS, Tenn. Technol. U., 1972; MA, East Tenn. State U., 1977, MBA, 1981; PhD, U. S.C., 1992. CPA, Tenn. CPA Johnson & Davis, Johnson City, 1979-81; contr. Mountcastle Corp., Johnson City, 1985-87; instr. East Tenn. State U., 1981-84, 87-88, asst. prof., 1991—. Contbr. articles to profl. jours. Mem. AICPA, Am. Acctg. Assn., Tenn. Soc. of Pub. Accts., Inst. Mgmt. Accts. Home: 1201 Oakdell Ct Johnson City TN 37604 Office: East Tenn State U PO Box 70710 ETSU Johnson City TN 37614

POKA, HELEN NOBL, writer, artist; b. Hodsagh, Hungary, 1905; came to U.S., 1958, naturalized, 1958; d. Illes and Cecilia (Simon) Nobl; m. Zoltan Vegh, 1927 (div. 1931); m. John Poka, 1958 (dec. 1970). MA, Peter Pazmany U., Budapest, Hungary, 1924, PhD in Scis., 1928. Cert. secondary tchr., N.Y., N.J. Dir. fgn. lang. Budapest Pub. High Sch., 1928-47; tchr. fgn. langs. Elizabeth (N.J.) Sch. System, 1960-70, ret., 1970. Author: Shakespeare's Influence on Szigligeti, 1932, Autumn Leaves, 1993, Reminiscences of a Survivor, and others; contbg. author: Poet's Pen, 1990;. Established Poka scholarship; The Dean's scholar Columbia U., 1947-48. Mem. AAUW, Ret. Tchrs. Assn., People to People, Zonta (Woman of Yr. award 1993). Home: 43 Lafayette St Rumson NJ 07760

POKORNI, ORYSIA, musician; b. Ternopil, Ukraine, Aug. 4, 1938; came to U.S., 1951; d. Gregory and Olha (Moroz) Danylkiw; m. Paul Pokorni, Jan. 25, 1958; children: Daniel, Mark. Student, Cosmopolitan Sch. Music, 1962; AA, Truman Coll., 1984; BA, Northeastern Ill. U., 1989. Mgr. Internat. Theatre of Chgo., 1963—; asst. office mgr. Ravenswood Hosp., Chgo., 1980-83; radio announcer Sta. WEDC, Chgo., 1965-66; tchr. Sch. Ukrainian Studies, Chgo., 1966—, Chgo. Pub. Schs., 1990—; choir dir. Moloda Dumka Children's Choir, Chgo., 1981-85. Accompanist various choirs and soloists, 1960—; composer songs; music arranger for children's plays. Active Ukrainian Women's League, Chgo., 1985. Mem. Ukrainian Congress Com. (chmn. spl. events com. 1984—), Nat. Geographic Soc. Home and Office: 4520 N Richmond St Chicago IL 60625-3826

POKORNY, CATHY A., public relations executive. Grad., Bowling Green State U. Advisor Griswold-Eshleman Co.; v.p. acct. exec. graphics asst.

Edward Howard & Co., 1973-80; v.p. Watt-Jayme Pub. Rels., 1980-81; exec. v.p. Publicom, 1981-83; pres. Proconsul, 1983-89; COO Jayme Orgn., 1989-92, vice chmn., 1992-93, chmn., CEO, 1993—. Mem. Cleve. Adv. Club. Office: 25825 Science Park Dr Cleveland OH 44122*

POKRAS, SHEILA FRANCES, judge; b. Newark, Aug. 5, 1935; m. Norman M. Pokras, 1954; children: Allison, Andrea, Larry. Student, Beaver Coll., 1953-54; BS in Edn., Temple U., 1957; JD cum laude, Pepperdine U., 1969. Bar: Calif. 1970, U.S. Dist. Ct. D.C. 1970, U.S. Dist. Ct. Calif. 1970, U.S. Supreme Ct. 1975. Tchr. elem. and secondary schs. Phila. and Newark, 1957-59; pvt. practice law Long Beach, Calif., 1970-78; city councilwoman Lakewood, Calif., 1972-76; judge Long Beach Mcpl. Ct., 1978-80, L.A. Superior Ct., 1980—; supervising judge, 1986; del. Calif. State Dem. Cen. Com., 1975, Calif. State Conv., 1975; mem. Com. on Gender Bias in Calif. Courts, 1986-89. Advisor Jr. League, 1980-85; mem. early childhood adv. bd. Long Beach City Coll.; bd. dirs. Long Beach Alcoholism Coun., 1979-80, Boys and Girls Club Am., 1981-89, Long Beach Symphony, 1985, Jewish Community Fedn., 1982-86, past mem. community rels. com.; active Nat. Women's Polit. Caucus, LWV. Named Woman of Yr. NOW, Long Beach, 1984; recipient Torch of Liberty award B'nai B'rith Anti-Defamation League, 1974; honoree Nat. Conf. Christians and Jews, 1986. Mem. ABA, AAUW, Nat. Assn. Women Judges (dist. supr. 1986), Calif. Bar Assn. (judges div.), Calif. Judges Assn. (mem. ann. seminar com. 1981-89), Mcpl. Cts. Judges Assn. (mem. Marshall com. 1979-80), L.A. County Bar Assn. (judges div., mem. arbitration com.), Women Lawyers Assn., L.A. (judges sect.), Women Lawyers Assn. Long Beach, Long Beach Legal Aid Found. (v.p. 1976-78), Long Beach Bar Assn. (active various coms., bd. govs. 1977-78, Judge of Yr. 1987), Long Beach C. of C. (bd. dirs.). Office: So Dist Superior Ct 415 W Ocean Blvd Long Beach CA 90802-4512

POL, ANNE, operations executive; b. Cavan, Ireland, Sept. 10, 1947; came to U.S., 1960; d. Patrick John and Margaret (Rahill) McN.; m. Richard Stephen Pol, Dec. 2, 1967; 1 child, Anne Cristin. BA, CCNY, 1971, MA, 1977. Tchr. St. Jude's Sch., N.Y.C., 1971-73; mgmt. intern N.Y.C. Fire Dept., 1973, labor rels. officer, 1974-75, dep. dir. Office of Mgmt. Planning, 1975-77, pers. dir., 1977-78; mgr. labor and employee rels. Becton Dickinson & Co., Franklin Lakes, N.J., 1978-80; mgr. employee rels. planning Ingersoll Rand Co., Woodcliff Lakes, N.J., 1980-81, mgr. manpower and orgn. planning, 1981-82; cons. Oakland, N.J., 1982-84; dir. orgn. planning and exec. staffing Pitney Bowes, Stamford, Conn., 1984-85, dir. of mfg. components, 1985-86, dir. of mfg. assembly, 1986-87, v.p. pers., 1987-90, v.p. mfg. ops., 1990-91; v.p. new product devel. Pitney Bowes, Inc., Stamford, 1991-93, pres. shipping and weighing systems divsn., 1993—; bd. dirs. VGI, Valley Forge, Pa., Arrow Electronics, Inc., Melville, N.Y. Bd. dirs. St. Joseph's Hosp., Stamford, 1988-95. Regents scholar N.Y. State, 1966-71. Office: Pitney Bowes Inc 1 Parrott Dr Shelton CT 06484

POLACCO, PATRICIA, children's author, illustrator. Works include (juvenile) Meteor!, 1987, Rechenka's Eggs, 1988, The Keeping Quilt, 1988, Uncle Vova's Tree, 1989, Boatride with Lillian Two-Blossom, 1989, Thunder Cake, 1990, Just Plain Fancy, 1990, Babushka's Doll, 1990, Some Birthday!, 1991, Appelemando's Dreams, 1991, Picnic at Mudsock Meadow, 1992, Mrs. Katz & Tush, 1992, Chicken Sunday, 1992, The Bee Tree, 1993, Babushka Baba Yaga, 1993, Tikvah Means Hope, 1994, Pink & Say, 1994, My Rotten, Redheaded, Older Brother, 1994; illustrator: Casey at the Bat, 1992. Office: Putnam Pub Group 200 Madison Ave New York NY 10016-3901*

POLACHEK-LIPTAK, MICHELLE, agency executive; b. Cleve., Sept. 21, 1954; d. Mike and Amelia (Giuliano) Polachek; m. George Louis Liptak, Apr. 3, 1976. Grad., Television Workshop, 1984; student, Cuyahoga Community Coll., 1985-86. EMT Ohio, 1990. Co-founder Television Workshop, Beachwood, Ohio, 1982-84; exec. dir. Cleve. Ballet Coun., 1982-86; dir. instrn. John Casablancas, Beachwood, Ohio, 1984-85; pres., chief exec. officer Liptak, Oshaben & Assocs., Inc., Garfield Heights, 1986—; dir. devel. Cleve. Sports Legend Found., 1987-88; soc. editor The Leader Newspaper, Garfield Heights, Ohio, 1988-89; pres., CEO, chairperson of bd. Health Exams, Inc., Garfield Heights, Ohio, 1993; co-founder, co-pres. Prime Life Care Ctr., Inc., Cleve., 1993; dir. pub. rels. Providence House, Cleve., 1987-88, OASIS, Cleve., 1987-88; mem. adv. bd. Harper's Bazaar. Dir. pub. rels. City Club of Cleve., 1983-88 (Pub. Rels. Svc. award 1988); mem. Nat. Mus. Women in Arts; trustee Leukemia Soc. Am. Named One of Most Interested People in Ohio, No. Ohio Live Mag., 1987; proclaimed Michelle A. Liptak Day City of Garfield Heights, 1988. Mem. NAFE, Nordonia Hills C. of C. (dir. pub. rels. 1991-92). Home and Office: 10712 Wadsworth Ave Garfield Heights OH 44125-2255

POLAK, VIVIAN LOUISE, lawyer; b. N.Y.C., Nov. 1, 1952; d. Henri and Greta Etty (Querido) P. BA, Barnard Coll., 1974; JD, Harvard U., 1977. Bar: N.Y. 1978, D.C. 1978, U.S. Dist. Ct. (ea. and so. dists.) N.Y. 1978. Assoc. Donovan, Leisure, Newton and Irvine, N.Y.C., 1977-86; ptnr. LeBoeuf, Lamb, Greene & MacRae, N.Y.C., 1986—. Mem. N.Y. Bar Assn. (sec. antitrust sect. 1991-92, mem. exec. com. 1993—, chmn. internat. trade com. 1985-90). Office: LeBoeuf Lamb Greene and MacRae 125 W 55th St New York NY 10019-4513

POLAN, ANNETTE LEWIS, artist; b. Huntington, W.Va., Dec. 8, 1944; d. Lake and Dorothy (Lewis) P.; m. Arthur Lowell Fox Jr., Aug. 31, 1969 (div. 1994); children: Courtney Van Winkle Fox, Arthur Lowell Fox III. 1st degree, Inst. des Profs. de Francaise, Paris, 1965; BA, Hollins Coll., 1967; postgrad., Corcoran Sch. Art, 1968-69. Vis. artist Art Therapy Italia, Vignale, Italy, 1986; dir. summer program La Napoule Art Found., Chateau de la Napoule, France, 1987, 88, 90; guest lectr. China, Japan, 1989; prof. Corcoran Sch. Art, Washington, 1974—; chmn. painting dept. Corcoran Coll. Art, Washington, 1991—; dir. Washington Project for the Arts. Illustrator: Say What I Am, 1989, Relearning the Dark, 1991; cover designer Doers of the Word, 1995. Bd. dirs. Washington Project for the Arts, 1994—. Mem. Corcoran Faculty Assn. (pres. 1988-89). Office: Corcoran Sch Art 1680 Wisconsin Ave NW Washington DC 20007

POLAN, NANCY MOORE, artist; b. Newark, Ohio; d. William Tracy and Francis (Flesher) Moore; m. Lincoln Milton Polan, Mar. 28, 1934; children: Charles Edwin, William Joseph Marion. AB, Marshall U., 1936. One-man shows include Charleston Art Gallery, 1961, 67, 73, Greenbrier, 1963, Huntington Mus. Art, 1963, 66, 71, N.Y. World's Fair, 1965, W.Va. U., 1966, Carroll Reese Mus., 1967; exhibited in group shows Am. Watercolor Soc., Allied Artists of Am., Nat. Arts Club, 1968-74, 76-77, 86, 87, 91, 92, 93-94, Pa. Acad. Fine Arts, Opening of Creative Arts Center W.Va. U., 1969, Internat. Platform Assn. Art Exhibit, 1968-69, 72-74, 74, 79, 85-86, 88-90, (Gold medal Best of Show 1991, 2d award painting 1994), Allied Artists W.Va., 1968-69, 86, Joan Miro Graphic Traveling Exhbn., Barcelona, Spain, 1970-71, XXI Exhibit Contemporary Art, La Scala, Florence, Italy, 1971, Rassegna Internazionale d'Arte Grafica, Siena, Italy, 1973, 79, 82, Opening of Parkersburg (W.Va.) Art Center, 1975, Art Club Washington, 1992, Pen & Brush, 1992-93, others. Hon. v.p. Centro Studie Scambi Internazionale, Rome, Italy, 1977. Recipient Acad. of Italy with Gold medal, 1979, 86, Norton Meml. award 3d Nat. Jury Show Am. Art, Chautauqua, N.Y., 1960; Purchase prize, Jurors award, Watercolor award Huntington Galleries, 1960, 61; Nat. Arts Club for watercolor, 1969; Gold medal Masters of Modern Art exhbn., La Scala Gallery, Florence, 1975, gold medal Accademia Italia, 1984, 1986, diploma Internat. Com. for World Culture and Arts, 1987, many others. Mem. AAUW, DAR, Nat. Mus. Women Artists (charter), Allied Artists W.Va., Internat. Platform Assn. (3rd award-painting in ann. art exhbn. 1977, Gold medal for Best of Show 1991), Allied Artists Am. (assoc.), Huntington Mus. Fine Arts (life), Tri-State Arts Assn. (Equal Merit award 1978), Sunrise Found., Composers, Authors, Artists Am., Inc., Pen and Brush (Watercolor exhbn. 1993, Grumbacher golden palette mem., Grumbacher award 1978), Am. Watercolor Soc. (assoc.), W.Va. Watercolor Soc. (charter mem.), Nat. Arts Club, Leonardo da Vinci Acad. (Rome), Accademia Italia, Vero Beach Arts Club, Riomer Bay Yacht Club, Guyan Golf and Country Club, Huntington Cotillion (charter mem.) Sigma Kappa. Episcopalian. Address: 2 Prospect Dr Huntington WV 25701-4860 also: 2106 Club Dr Vero Beach FL 32963-2154

POLASCIK, MARY ANN, ophthalmologist; b. Elkhorn, W.Va., Dec. 28, 1940; d. Michael and Elizabeth (Halko) Polascik; B.A., Rutgers U., 1967; M.D., Pritzker Sch. Medicine, 1971; m. Joseph Elie, Oct. 2, 1973; 1 dau., Laura Elizabeth Polascik. Jr. pharmacologist Ciba Pharm. Co., Summit, N.J., 1961-67; intern Billings Hosp., Chgo., 1971-72; resident in ophthalmology U. Chgo. Hosp., 1972-75; practice medicine specializing in ophthalmology, Dixon, Ill., 1975-93; pres. McNichols Clinic, Ltd.; cons. ophthalmology, Jack Mabley Devel. Ctr., 1976-93; mem. staff Katherine Shaw Bethea Hosp. Bd. dirs. Dixon Community Trust Mental Health Ctr., 1977-82. Mem. AMA, Ill. Med. Soc., Ill. Assn. Ophthalmology, Am. Assn. Ophthalmology, Alpha Sigma Lambda. Roman Catholic. Club: Galena Territory.lub: Galena Territory. Office: 1700 S Galena Ave Dixon IL 61021-9677

POLASKI, ANNE SPENCER, lawyer; b. Pittsfield, Mass., Nov. 13, 1952; d. John Harold and Marjorie Ruth (Hackett) Spencer; m. James Joseph Polaski, Sept. 14, 1985. BA in Psychology, Allegheny Coll., 1974; MSW, U. Pa., 1976; JD, George Washington U., 1979. Bar: D.C. 1979, U.S. Dist. Ct. (D.C. dist.) 1980, U.S. Ct. Appeals (D.C. cir.) 1980, Ill. 1982, U.S. Dist. Ct. (no. dist.) Ill. 1982, U.S. Ct. Appeals (7th cir.) 1982. Law clk. to assoc. judge D.C. Ct., Washington, 1979-80; trial atty. Commodity Futures Trading Commn., Chgo., 1980-84, sr. trial atty., 1984, dep. regional counsel, 1984-88; assoc. Gottlieb and Schwartz, Chgo., 1988-91; staff atty. Chgo. Bd. of Trade, 1991-92, sr. atty., 1992-94, asst. gen. counsel, 1994—. Mem. ABA, Chgo. Bar Assn. Office: Chgo Bd of Trade 141 W Jackson Blvd Chicago IL 60604-2904

POLEMITOU, OLGA ANDREA, accountant; b. Nicosia, Cyprus, June 28, 1950; d. Takis and Georgia (Nicolaou) Chrysanthou. BA with honors, U. London, 1971; PhD, Ind. U., Bloomington, 1981. CPA, Ind. Asst. productivity officer Internat. Labor Office/Cyprus Productivity Ctr., Nicosia, 1971-74; cons. Arthur Young & Co., N.Y.C., 1981; mgr. Coopers & Lybrand, Newark, 1981-83; dir. Bell Atlantic Video Svcs. Co., Reston, Va., 1983—; chairperson adv. coun. Extended Day Care Community Edn., West Windsor Plainsboro, 1987-88. Contbr. articles to profl. jours. Bus. cons. project bus. Jr. Achievement, Indpls., 1984-85. Mem. NAFE, AICPAs, Nat. Trust for Hist. Preservation, Ind. CPA Soc., N.J. Soc. CPAs (sec. mems. in industry com.), Princeton Network of Profl. Women. Home: PO Box 2744 Reston VA 22090 Office: Bell Atlantic Video Svcs 1880 Campus Commons Dr Reston VA 22091

POLENZ, JOANNA MAGDA, psychiatrist; b. Cracow, Poland, Oct. 20, 1936; came to U.S., 1961; d. Mieczyslaw and Nusia (Goldberger) Uberall; m. Daryl Louis Polenz, July 8, 1962 (div. 1991); children: Teresa Ann, Daryl Philip, Elizabeth Sophia. MD, U. Sydney, Australia, 1960; MPH, Columbia U., 1992. Diplomate Am. Bd. Psychiatry and Neurology. Intern Bklyn. Hosp., 1961-62; resident Mt. Sinai Med. Ctr., N.Y.C., 1962-65; ednl. fellow Mt. Sinai Med. Ctr., 1965-66, rsch. assoc., 1966-67; med. dir. Tappan Zee clin. Phelps Meml. Hosp., Tarrytown, N.Y., 1968-71, dir. dept. psychiatry, 1972-77; sr. attending psychiatrist Meml. Hosp. Ctr., 1972-93; pvt. practice Briarcliff Manor, N.Y., 1971-91; physician Joint Commn. Accreditation of Healthcare Orgns., Oakbrook Terrace, Ill., 1993—; lectr. in field. Author: In Defense of marriage, 1981; (with other) Test Your Marriage IQ, 1984, Test Your Success IQ, 1985; contbr. articles to profl. jours.; numerous TV appearances including Phil Donahue, 1988, Oprah Winfrey 1984. Grant Found. grantee, 1970. Fellow Am. psychiatric Assn., Royal Soc. for Health; mem. AMA, N.Y. Acad. Scis., Pan Am. Med. Assn., Westchester Psychiatric Assn. (sec. 1982-85, chair person fellowship com. 1989).

POLEVOY, NANCY TALLY, lawyer, social worker, genealogist; b. N.Y.C., May 27, 1944; d. Charles H. and Bernice M. (Gang) Tally; m. Martin D. Polevoy, Mar. 19, 1967; children: Jason Tally, John Gerald. Student, Mt. Holyoke Coll., 1962-64; BA, Barnard Coll., 1966; MS in Social Work, Columbia U., 1968, JD, 1986. Bar: N.Y. 1987. Caseworker unmarried mothers' svc. Louise Wise Svcs., N.Y.C., 1967, caseworker adoption dept., 1969-71; caseworker Youth Consultation Svc., N.Y.C., 1968-69; asst. rsch. scientist, psychiat. social worker dept. child psychiatry NYU Med. Ctr., N.Y.C., 1973-81; adv. ct. apptd. spl. advs. Manhattan Family Ct., N.Y.C., 1981-82; cons. social work, 1981-86; matrimonial assoc. Ballon, Stoll & Itzler, 1987, Herzfeld & Rubin, P.C., 1987-88; pvt. practice, N.Y.C. Contbr. articles on early infantile autism and genealogy to profl. jours. Mem. Parents' Adv. Bd. Riverdale Country Sch., 1988-93; mem. outreach bd. Manhattan divsn. United Jewish Appeal Fedn., 1990-94, exec. bd. Manhattan divsn., 1992, mem. met. campaign cabinet, 1994—; mem. archives com. Cen. Synagogue, 1991—, chmn. 1994—; trustee Am. Jewish Hist. Soc., 1992—. Recipient French Govt. prize, 1963. Mem. Bar Assn. of City of N.Y., N.Y. State Bar Assn. (child custody com. of family law sect.), Nat. Assn. Social Workers, Acad. Cert. Social Workers, Barnard Coll. Alumni Assn. (v.p. 1966). Home and Office: 1155 Park Ave New York NY 10128-1209

POLICH, NANCY JOSEPHINE, engineer; b. Detroit, Sept. 11, 1962; d. Donald Joseph and Barbara Ann (Dana) P.; m. James Kenneth Kyser, Oct. 11, 1985; 1 child, Danielle Nicole. BS in Materials Engr., BSME, U. Mich., 1984; MS in Materials Sci., U. Va., 1992. Sr. assoc. engr. IBM, Manassas, Va., 1985-88; engr. cons. Failure Analysis Assoc., Alexandria, Va., 1988-89; mgr. engring. and spl. projects Alcatel, Reston, Va., 1989—; mem. corp. working group coun. fiber optics Alcatel, Paris, 1993, mem. corp. working group coun. radio space and def., 1990. Bd. dirs. Savas-Rape Crisis Ctr., Mannassas, 1988-89. Mem. Am. Soc. Metals. Office: Alcatel ITS Inc 12030 Sunrise Valley Dr Reston VA 22091

POLICHENE, BRIGET M., general counsel; b. Ravenna, Ohio; m. Charles M. Chamness. BA in Econs., Johns Hopkins U., 1981; JD with honors, Duke U., 1984. Bar: Ga. 1984, D.C. 1987. Atty. Morris, Manning & Martin, 1984-86, Drinker, Biddle & Reath, 1986-88; gen. counsel House Com. on Banking, Fin. and Urban Affairs, 1988—. Recipient U.S. Law Week award. Office: Banking Finance & Urban Affairs 2129 Rayburn House Ofc Buil Washington DC 20515*

POLIN, JANE LOUISE, foundation official; b. N.Y.C., Sept. 30, 1958; d. Raymond and Constance F. (Caplan) P. BA, Wesleyan U., Middletown, Conn., 1980; MBA, Columbia U., 1988. Asst. dir. ann. giving Wesleyan U., 1980-82; centennial fund assoc. Met. Opera Assn., N.Y.C., 1982-84; devel. officer Columbia U., N.Y.C., 1984-88; program mgr., compt. GE Founds., Fairfield, Conn., 1988—. Panelist arts-in-edn. Nat. Endowment for Arts, Washington, 1989-90, 94; adv. bd. mem. Carnegie Hall, N.Y.C., 1992—, Nat. Corp. Theatre Fund, N.Y.C., 1991—, Young Audiences, N.Y.C., 1991—. Mem. Alpha Delta Phi. Office: General Electric Fund 3135 Easton Tpke Fairfield CT 06431-0002

POLING, GAIL ZIEGLER, nurse; b. Weehawken, N.J., Aug. 21, 1956; d. Albert William and Marie L. (Rinaldi) Ziegler; m. Steven Poling, May 30, 1987; 1 child, Matthew. AAS, Bergen Community Coll., 1978; BSN, Felician Coll., 1985. RN. Staff nurse Criticare Support Svcs., Teaneck, N.J., 1984-86; asst. supr. client care Passaic County Elks Adult Tng., Clifton, N.J., 1986-91; rec. review case mgr. World Wide Rehab. Svcs., Lansdale, Pa., 1990—; rehab. cons. Ind. Health Care, Northern N.J., 1990—; mem. adv. bd. Northern N.J. Colls., 1985—. Mem. med. staff N.J. Spl. Olympics, 1983-89. Mem. ANA, ACA, Am. Assn. Rehab. Nurses, Am. Assn. Spical Cord Injury Nurses, Assn. Nurse Healers/Therapeutic Touch.

POLINGER, IRIS SANDRA, dermatologist; b. N.Y.C., Feb. 10, 1943; m. Harvey I. Hyman, Feb. 6, 1972. AB, Barnard Coll., 1964; PhD, Johns Hopkins U., 1969; MD, SUNY Downstate, Bklyn., 1975. Diplomate Am. Bd. Dermatology. Teaching positions various schs. including NYU Coll. Dentistry and Harvard Med. Sch., 1969-73; med. intern Baylor Coll. Medicine, 1975-76, resident in dermatology, 1976-79; pvt. practice dermatology Houston, 1979—. Bd. dirs. Ft. Bend County Women's Ctr., Richmond, Tex., 1993—. Mem. Am. Bus. Women's Assn. (chair scholarship com. 1986—, chair scholarship event com. 1993—). Office: 4915 S Main # 104 Stafford TX 77477

POLINSKY, JANET NABOICHECK, state official, former state legislator; b. Hartford, Conn., Dec. 6, 1930; d. Louis H. and Lillian S. Naboicheck; BA, U. Conn., 1953; postgrad. Harvard U., 1954; m. Hubert N. Polinsky, Sept. 21, 1958; children: Gerald, David, Beth. Mem. Waterford 2d Charter Commn. (Conn.), 1967-68, Waterford Conservation Commn., 1968-69; Waterford rep. Town Meeting, 1969-71, SE Conn. Regional Planning Agy., 1971-73; mem. Waterford Planning and Zoning Commn., 1970-76, chmn., 1973-76; mem. Waterford Dem. Town Com., 1976-92, del. State Dem. Conv., 1976, 78, 80, 82, 84, 86, 90, 92; mem. Conn. Ho. of Reps. from 38th Dist., 1977-92, asst. majority leader, 1981-83, chmn. appropriations com., 1983-85, 87-89, ranking mem., 1985-87, minority whip, 1985-86, dep. speaker, 1989-92; dep. commr. dept. adminstrv. svcs., State of Conn., 1993-94, commr., 1994-95, sec. of state, 1995—. Trustee Eugene O'Neill Meml. Theatre Ctr., 1973-76, 81-92; corporator, Lawrence and Meml. Hosps., 1987—; mem. New Eng. Bd. Higher Edn., 1981-83; mem. fiscal affairs com. Eastern Conf. Council of State Govts., 1983-88. Named Woman of Yr., Waterford Jr. Women's Club, 1977, Nehantic Women's Bus. and Profl. Club, 1979, Legislator of Yr., Conn. Library Assn., 1980. Mem. Order Women Legislators, Delta Kappa Gamma (hon.). Home: 15 Gardner Cir New London CT 06320 Office: 30 Trinity St Hartford CT 06106

POLIRER, DEBRA JOYCE, accountant; b. Mt. Kisco, N.Y., June 13, 1962; d. Frank Mathew and Cynthia Claire (Wertheimer) Gasthalter; m. Peter Ian Polirer, June 26, 1988. Student, Georgetown U., 1980-82; BS in Acctg., Mercy Coll., 1987. CPA, N.Y. Sr. proofreader Pennysaver Corp., Yorktown Heights, N.Y., 1983-87; sr. staff acct. Combe Inc., White Plains, N.Y., 1987-94; tax editor H & R Block, Poughkeepsie, N.Y., 1994—. Contbg. author: Hearts on Fire, 1987, The Poetry of Life: A Treasury of Moments, 1987, Best New Poets of 1987, Editor's Choice, 1988. Mem. Inst. Mgmt. Accts., Delta Mu Delta. Jewish. Home: 186 Spackenkill Rd Poughkeepsie NY 12603

POLITY, LEDDY SMITH, preschool director; b. Wrightsville, Pa., Nov. 6, 1936; d. Michael Kenneth and Vivian Lentz (Birnstock) Smith; m. Richard Milton Polity, Sept. 15, 1956; children: Karen, Bruce, Jennifer. Student, Gettysburg (Pa.) Coll., 1954-56, Kean Coll., 1966-74. Cert. early childhood edn. Tchr. Little Folks Nursery Sch., Woodbridge, N.J., 1966-67; co-founder, tchr. Presbyn. Nursery Sch., Matawan, 1967; dir. Presbyn. Nursery Sch., 1982—; cons. community services bd. Brookdale Community Coll., 1977-82; workshop presentor, various community groups statewide. Contbr. articles to profl. jours.; appeared as TV panelist on N.Y. and N.J. talk shows. Mem. Sch. Aged Child Care Task Force, N.J. Dept. Human Services, 1983; ad hoc citizens adv. bd., N.J. Bur. of Licensing, 1981, 85, 86-87; Sunday sch. tchr., Cross of Glory Luth. Ch., Aberdeen, 1963-73, Sunday Sch. supt., 1974-76, vacation sch. dir., 1976-78; coordinator, Girl Scouts of U.S., Matawan, 1976-79; apptd. to Gov's. Child Care Adv. Council of N.J., 1984—. Mem. N.J. Shore Chpt. Assn. for Edn. of Young Children (pres. 1976-78), N.J. Assn. for Edn. of Young Children (lit. chmn. 1978-80, 1st v.p. 1980-82, state pres. 1982-84, exec. bd. advisor 1984-86), Assn. for Edn. of Young Children (state conf. planner, 1980, 81, 82). Home: 144 Idlebrook Ln Matawan NJ 07747-1747 Office: Presbyn Nursery Sch 33 Hwy 34 Matawan NJ 07747-1957

POLIZZI, JAN CRANDALL, state legislator, community and maternal-women's health nurse; b. St. Louis, June 26, 1949; d. Charles J. and Anne E. (Gray) Crandall; m. Peter J. Polizzi, July 2, 1972; 1 child, Joseph John. ADN, Maryville Coll., St. Louis, 1977; BSN, St. Louis U., 1980; postgrad., So. Ill. U. RN, Mo. Staff nurse neonatal ICU, Cardinal Glennon, St. Louis; perinatal nurse II Grace Hill Neighborhood Svcs., St. Louis, dir. Wellness Inst. Mem. Mo. Ho. of Reps. Recipient Young Alumni award Maryville Coll., 1988, Page One Civic award St. Louis Newspaper Guild, 1989. Mem. ANA (cert. high risk perinatal nurse), Mo. Nurses Assn. (pres. 3d dist., bd. dirs., Nurse of Yr. award 1986), Mo. League for Nursing, Politically Active Nurses Mo. (chmn.). Home: 5953 Shortleaf Ct Saint Louis MO 63128-4306 Office: Mo Ho of Reps State Capitol Jefferson City MO 65101*

POLK, EDRICE JEANNE, career counselor, family counselor; b. Citronelle, Ala., Mar. 2, 1937; d. Scarelle Harris and Cora (Shines) Hawkins; m. Paul G. Polk, Nov. 16, 1957; children: Thomas Eric, Timothy Edward, Jeannette. BS, Ala. State U., 1957; MS, Ctrl. State U., 1968. Lic. profl. counselor, nat. cert. counselor. Tchr. Lawton (Okla.) Pub. Schs., 1958-59; PREP GED tchr. USAEUR GED Ansbach (Germany) Edn. Ctr., 1959-60; tchr. Ansbach Elem. Sch., 1961-63; libr. Ft. Benning (Ga.) Children's Sch., 1964-65, Muscogee County Sch. Dist., Columbus, Ga., 1966-67; dept. head English, social studies tchr. Yellow Springs (Ohio) Sch. Dist., 1969-72; tchr. Ft. Leavenworth (Kans.) Sch. Dist., 1972-73; PREP GED tchr. Army Edn. Ctr., Wertheim, Germany, 1973; English tchr. Bassfield (Miss.) High Sch., 1974-77; guidance counselor Jefferson Davis County Vo-Tech Ctr., Carson, Miss., 1977—; cons. Zinger-Miller, Inc., 1992—, Miss. Stae Dept. Edn., 1980—; pvt. practice, Miss., 1987—, workship presenter T.E.T., P.E.T., Inc., Miss., 1985—; lectr. in field. Author: (video) Problem Solving: A Classroom Model, 1984. Major Miss. State Guard, Jackson, 1989. Mem. NEA, Am. Counselors Assn., Miss. Counselors Assn., Miss. Vocat. Counselors Assn. (Counselor of Yr. 1991-92), Miss. Assn. Women in Ednl. Leadership, Pinebelt Counselors Assn., Jefferson Davis County Assn. Educators. Home: PO Box 1493 Prentiss MS 39474

POLK, MELISSA LEIGH, air force officer; b. Honolulu, Aug. 11, 1965; d. Charles Bland and Mary Elizabeth (Maddux) P. Student, So. Union Jr. Coll., 1983-84; AA, Albany Jr. Coll., 1986; student, Darton Coll., 1986-89; BSN, Albany State Coll., 1992. Nurse East Albany (Ga.) Med. Ctr., 1991, Pub. Health Svc., Albany, 1991-93. With USAF, 1994—. Mem. Ga. Assn. Nursing Students, Nat. League Nursing, Nat. Assn. Nursing Students, Sigma Theta Tau Internat.

POLKINGHORNE, PATRICIA ANN, hotel executive; b. Galveston, Tex., Aug. 17, 1948; d. C.L. and Barbara Ann (Rathke) Hughes; children: Pamela, Christopher. Student, Sam Houston State Tchrs. Coll., Huntville, Tex. Catering mgr. Rodeway Inn, Denver; office mgr. sales dept. Hyatt Regency, Phoenix; asst. to v.p., treas., controller Continental Drilling, Okla. City; asst. to v.p. resort food and beverage The Pointe Resorts Inc., Phoenix; dir. adminstrn. S.W. Audio Visual, Inc.; asst. to dir. and mgr. catering Phoenician Resort, 1991-92, asst. to dir. of travel industry sales, 1992-93, exec. adminstrv. asst. to dir. of food and beverage divsn., 1993—. Mem. NAFE, Assn. for Info. Systems Profls. Republican. Episcopalian. Office: 6000 E Camelback Rd Scottsdale AZ 85251

POLK-MATTHEWS, JOSEPHINE ELSEY, school psychologist; b. Roselle, N.J., Sept. 24, 1930; d. Charles Carrington and Olive Mae (Bond) Polk; m. Donald Roger Matthews, Aug. 29, 1959 (div. 1974); children: John Roger, Alison Olivia; m. William Y. Delaney, Sept. 17, 1994. AB, Mt. Holyoke Coll., 1952; credential in occupational therapy, Columbia U., 1954; MA, U. So. Calif., L.A., 1957; Cert. Advanced Study, Harvard U., 1979, MS, 1980. Cert. elem. edn. life teaching credential, Calif; cert. ednl. adminstrn. life credential, Calif.; cert. pupil personnel svcs., counseling life credential, sch. psychology credential, Calif.; sch. psychology credential, Nev. Occupational therapist VA Hosp., Northport, N.Y., 1953-55, L.A., 1955-57; health svcs. adminstr. John Wesley County Hosp., L.A., 1957-59; elem. tchr. L.A. (Calif.) City Schs., 1959-60, Santa Clara (Calif.) Unified Sch. Dist., 1960-65, 71-74; asst. prof. Sch. Edn., San Jose (Calif.) State U., 1971; asst. prin. Berryessa Union Sch. Dist., San Jose, Calif., 1974-77, 85-86; ednl. cons. Boston (Mass.) U. Sch. Medicine, 1981-83; asst. prin. Inglewood (Calif.) Unified Sch. Dist., 1986-90; sch. psychologist Clark County Sch. Dist., Las Vegas, 1990-94; med. facility developer Commonwealth Mass., Dept. Mental Health, Boston, 1980-81, ednl. liaison, Roxbury Juvenile Ct., 1979. Author: (with others) The New Our Bodies Ourselves, 1983; prodr.: (video) Individualized Rsch., 1971. Commr. Commn. on the Status of Women, Cambridge, Mass., 1981-83; hostess Ctr. for Internat. Visitors, Boston, 1983-84; pers. recruiter L.A. (Calif.) Olympic Organizing Com., 1984; vol. tutor Las Vegas (Nev.) Libr., 1992. Mem. Nat. Assn. Sch. Psychologists, Calif. Assn. Sch. Psychologists, Nev. Assn. Sch. Psychologists, Clark County Assn. Sch. Psychologists, Assn. Black Psychologists, Phi Delta Kappa, Alpha Kappa Alpha. Home: 127 Sandpiper St Newport News VA 23602-6336

POLKOWSKI, DELPHINE THERESA, elementary education educator, speech therapist; b. Chgo., Dec. 13, 1930; d. Harry and Rosalie Eleanor (Swiatkowski) P. BS, U. Ill., 1952; MA, Northwestern U., 1957. Speech therapist Community Unit Sch. Dist. 300, Dundee, Ill., 1952-53, S.W. Cook County Co-op Spl. Edn., Tinley Park, Ill., 1960-61; caseworker Ill. Dept. Pub. Aid, Chgo., 1969-87; tchr. Chgo. pub. schs., 1953-88; proctor City

Chgo., 1973—. Republican. Roman Catholic. Home: 1320 Carlson Dr Streamwood IL 60107-3020

POLLACK, JANE SUSAN, lawyer; b. Newark. BS, U. Pa.; JD, Rutgers U., 1976; LLM, NYU, 1983. Bar: N.J. 1976, U.S. Dist. Ct. N.J. 1976, N.Y. 1982. Assoc. McCarter & English, Newark, 1976-82; labor counsel CBS, Inc., N.Y.C., 1982-84, broadcast counsel, 1984-87; assoc. gen. counsel Athlone Industries, Inc., Parsippany, N.J., 1987-93; v.p., sec., gen. counsel Forstmann & Co., N.Y.C., 1993—. Assoc. trustee U. Pa.; mem. editorial bd. N.J. Lawyer. Mem. ABA, N.J. Bar Assn., Am. Corp. Counsel Assn., Assn. of Bar of City of N.Y.), Trustees Coun. Penn Women, Phi Beta Kappa. Republican. Home: 280 Millburn Ave Millburn NJ 07041-1704 Office: Forstmann & Co Inc 1185 Avenue Of The Americas New York NY 10036-2601

POLLACK, LANA, state senator; b. Ludington, Mich., Oct. 11, 1942; d. Abbie and Genevieve (Siegel) Schoenberger; m. Henry Pollack, 1963; children: Sara (dec.), John. BA, U. Mich., 1965, MA, 1970; postgrad. Am. U., Am. Acad. Performing Arts, 1976.Instr. Washtenaw Community Coll., 1975-81; sr. adminstr. John Howard Compound Sch., Zambia, 1970-71; chmn. Ann Arbor Democratic Party (Mich.), 1975-77; mgr. campaign for State Senate, 1978, campaign for 2d Congl. Dist., 1980; regional coordinator gubernatorial campaign, 1981; mem. Mich. State Senate, 1983—; candidate for Congress, 1988. Trustee, Ann Arbor Bd. Edn., 1979-82. Democrat. Office: 2065 Columbia St Ann Arbor MI 48104-6410 also: Senate House State Capitol Lansing MI 48909*

POLLACK, SONYA A., artist; b. Phila., Nov. 17, 1932; d. Herman and Helene (Spindor) Glick; m. Alfred Pollack; children: Harry, Kenneth, Helena, Daniel. Grad., Pa. Acad. Fine Arts, 1973; BFA, Phila. Coll. Art, 1975. One-woman shows include 3d Street Gallery, Phila., 1982, 84, Woodmere Art Mus., Phila., 1987, Phila. Art Alliance, 1991; represented in juried and invited group shows at Internat. House, Phila., 1972, Univ. Art League, Phila., 1973, Eastern Coll., Bryn Mawr, Pa., 1973, Vendo Nubes Gallery, Phila., 1973, Woodmere Gallery, Phila., 1975, 76, 79, 81, Civic Center Mus., Phila., 1975, 78, 81, Peale House, Phila., 1981, 84, 85, Allentown (Pa.) Mus., 1982, 84, 86, 94, Glassboro (N.J.) State Coll., 1982, Phila. Art Alliance, 1975, 82, 83, 91, Montgomery County Ct. House, Norristown, Pa., 1982, 83, 84, 3d Street Gallery, 1983, 84, 85, Lancaster (Pa.) Coummunity Gallery, 1984, West Chester (Pa.) State Coll., 1984, Noyes Mus., N.J., 1984, Lehigh (Pa.) U., 1984, Woodmere Art Mus., Phila., 1984, 86, 89, 94, Marion Locks Gallery, Phila., 1984, Pa. Acad. Fine Art Fellowship, Phila., 1984, Cheltenham (Pa.) Ann. Painting Exhbn., 1973, 85, 89, 92, 94, Hopkins House Gallery, N.J., 1987, Pa. Acad. Fine Arts, 1972, 87, Port of History Mus., Phila., 1988, Del. Art Mus., Wilmington, 1989, Muhlenberg Coll., Allentown, 1989, 90, The X Gallery, Nantucket, Mass., 1991, 92, 93, Long Beach Island Found. Arts and Scis., 1991, Berman Mus. Art Ursinus Coll., Collegeville, Pa., 1992, Morris Gallery, Phila., 1994; contbr. articles to profl. jours. Recipient Hunt award Artist Equity, Drake Press award Pa. Acad. Fine Arts, 1972, Gimble award Pa. Acad. Fine Arts, 1972, Alexander award Cheltenham Ctr. for Arts, 1989, Curator's Choice award Muhlenberg Coll., 1990, Tobeleah Wechsler award Cheltenham Ctr. for Arts, 1994. Mem. Pa. Acad. Fine Arts Fellowship (v.p. 1981-83, chairperson trust fund 1983-88, bd. dirs.). Home: 609 Fairview Rd Narberth PA 19072

POLLACK, SYLVIA BYRNE, educator, researcher, counselor; b. Ithaca, N.Y., Oct. 18, 1940; d. Raymond Tandy and Elsie Frances (Snell) Byrne; divorced; children: Seth Benjamin, Ethan David. BA, Syracuse U., 1962; PhD, U. Pa., 1967; MA, Antioch U., 1993. Instr. Women's Med. Coll. Pa., Phila., 1967-68; rsch. assoc. U. Wash., Seattle, 1968-73, rsch. asst. prof., 1973-77, rsch. assoc. prof., 1977-85, rsch. prof., 1985—; counselor Sch. Nursing N000, 1993—; asst. mem. Fred Hutchinson Cancer Ctr., Seattle, 1975-79, assoc. mem., 1979-81; mem. study sect. NIH, Washington, 1978-79, 83-85. Contbr. numerous articles to profl. jours.; reviewer for profl. jours. Recipient rsch. grants Am. Cancer Soc., 1969-79, Nat. Cancer Inst., 1973—, Chugai Pharm. Co., Japan, 1985-91. Mem. Am. Counsel Assn., Am. Assn. Immunologists, Soc. Devel. Biology, Soc. Leuc. Biology. Office: Univ Wash SM-20 Seattle WA 98195

POLLAK, (PHILIPPA) BETH, educational consultant; b. Chgo., Apr. 23, 1935; d. Samuel Stewart and Evelyn (Brown) Greenberg; m. Philip Len Pollak, June 1, 1965; children: Scott J., Dale M. BSEd cum laude, U. Ill., 1955. Cert. ednl. cons. Tchr. Fairview Sch., Skokie, Ill., 1955-57; tchr. Chgo. Bd. Edn., 1957-63, Morton Grove, Ill., 1964-65; owner, mgr., counselor Acad. Counseling Svcs., Inc., Munster, Ind., Evanston, Ill., 1978-91; pvt. counselor, ednl. cons. Burr Ridge, Ill., 1991—. Chair women's div. Northwest Ind. Jewish Welfare Fedn., Gary, Ind, 1972, 75; pres. B;nai Brith Women, Morton Grove, 1964; pres. Congregation Beth Israel Sisterhood, Gary, 1970. Mem. Ind. Ednl. Cons. Assn. (past bd. dirs.), Nat. Assn. Cdmission Counselors, Am. Counseling Assn., Delta Phi Epsilon, Kappa Delta Pi. Jewish.

POLLAK, JOANNE E., lawyer; b. Cleve., July 16, 1944. BA magna cum laude, Dickinson Coll., 1965; JD with honors, U. Md., 1976. Bar: Md. 1976. V.p., gen. counsel The Johns Hopkins Health System Corp., Balt. Office: Johns Hopkins Health System Corp 600 N Wolfe St Baltimore MD 21287-1900

POLLAN, CAROLYN JOAN, state legislator; b. Houston, July 12, 1937; d. Rex and Faith (Basye) Clark; B.S. in Radio and TV, John Brown U., 1959; postgrad. NYU, 1959; PhD in Edn., Walden U., 1993. m. George A. Pollan, Jan. 6, 1962; children—Cee Cee, Todd (dec.), Robert. Mem. Ark. Ho. of Reps., 1974—, now sr. Republican mem., asst. speaker pro-tempore, 1993; apptd. by Gov. numerous coms., commns.; ex-officio mem. Workplace Literacy Project Adv. Bd. U.S. Dept. Labor & Ednl. Testing Svc., 1990-93, Nat. Adult Literacy Survey, 1990-93; del. Am. Soviet Seminar, Am. Council Young Polit. Leaders, Exeter, N.H., 1976; co-developer Total Touch Test; owner Patent Model Mus.. Vice chmn. Ark. Rep. Com., 1972-76; del. Rep. Nat. Conv., 1976; bd. dirs. Ark. Cancer Soc., Ark. Easter Seals Soc.; bd. dirs. Greg Kistler Treatment Center for Physically Handicapped, Ark. Found. Assoc. Colls., 4-H Found. for Sebastian County; trustee John Brown U.; mem. legis. adv. com. So. Regional Edn. Bd. Recipient Conservation Legislator of Yr. award Ark. Wildlife Fedn., Nat. Wildlife Fedn., Sears Roebuck & Co., 1976, Outstanding State Legislator of Yr. award Ark. Pub. Employees Assn., 1979, Lifetime Mem. award Ark. PTA, 1994, many others; named 1 of 10 Outstanding Legislators, Assembly of Govtl. Employees, 1980, Legislator of Yr., Ark. Human Service Providers Assn., 1982, Citizen of Yr. by Ark. Social Workers, 1993, Outstanding Women in Ark. Politics by Ark. Dem., 1990, One of 10 Top Legislators in 1993 Ark. Dem. Gazette, 1993, one of Top 100 Women in Ark., Ark. Bus. Publ., 1995; voted 1 of Ft. Smith's 10 Most Influential Citizens, S.W. Times Record Readers, 1979. Mem. Ark. Internat. Woman's Forum (founding mem.), Ft. Smith Car Restoration Assn. Baptist. Address: House of Reps State Capitol Little Rock AR 72201 Office: 400 N 8th St Fort Smith AR 72901-2204*

POLLARD, BRENDA SUE, school nurse; b. San Diego, July 7, 1952; d. Robert Ervin and Bonnie Lucille (Ironside) H.; m. Bobby Sain Pollard, Oct. 26, 1973; children: Timothy Robert, Stephanie Brooke. AAS, Ark. State U., 1972. Staff nurse, 11-7 supr. White County Meml. Hosp., Searcy, Ark., 1972-74; supr., staff Newport (Ark.) Hosp., Inc., 1974-82, infection control nurse, 1982-85; infection control nurse Harris Hosp. and Clinic, Newport, 1985-87; sch. nurse Newark Sch. Dist., 1987—. Sponsor Parent's Resource Inst. of Drug Edn., Newark, 1992-93, 95, Teens Of N.E. Ark., 1992-93, 95. Mem. Nat. Assn. of Sch. Nurses, Ark. Assn. Sch. Nurses, Arks. Assn. of Infection Control Practitioners. Home: PO Box 40 Newark AR 72562 Office: Newark Sch Dist 1500 North Hill St Newark AR 72562

POLLARD, JEAN ANN, author, artist; b. Waterville, Maine, Apr. 3, 1934; d. James Everett and Bertha Stella (Campbell) P.; m. Peter Garrett, Nov. 23, 1973; children: Jessica Elisabeth, Julian James. BFA, Boston U., 1956. One-person shows at Colby, Unity, Bowdoin, Thomas colls., U. Maine, Farmington, Audubon Ctr., Flamouth, Arts Coun. Gallery, Winston-Salem, others; in many group shows including Harlow Gallery, Gardner, Art for Am. Gallery, Newcastle, Waterville Gallery of Fine Arts, Maine Sportsman's Show, Augusta, Unity Coll. Art Gallery, others; author: Polluted Paradise: The Story of the Maine Rape, 1973, author, illustrator The New Maine Cooking, 1987, The Ice Ladder, 1987; contbr. articles to profl. jours. Mem. Natural Resources Coun. Maine, Beyond War, Maine Organic Farmers and Gardners, Sister-City Pairing Project, Kotlas, USSR, Waterville; vol. writer, illustrator teaching Maine studens. Numerous poetry awards, 1986-89; recipient Journalism Category award Writer's Digest, 1982, Article Category award 1987, Short Story Category award 1987. Mem. Poets and Writers, Sci. Fiction Writers Am., Maine Writers and Pub. Alliance, Soc. Children's Book Writers and Illustrators, Union of Maine Visual Artists, Maine Media Women. Home and Office: RR 2 Waterville ME 04901-9802

POLLARD, MARGARET LOUISE, association administrator; b. Leominster, Mass., Nov. 15, 1934; d. Edward Francis and AliceMary (Sosvielle) Sasseville; m. Walter Howard Pollard III, Mar. 10, 1957 (dec. Oct. 1974); children: Caroline Pray, Walter Howard IV, Margaret Peirce, Melissa Anne; m. James L. Baird Jr., Jan. 9, 1993. BS, Simmons Coll., 1956; MS, Boston U., 1983. Editor Hist. Soc. Western Pa., Pitts., 1971-75; mgr. advtr. and promotions F.W. Faxon Co., Westwood, Mass., 1976-80; owner, mgr. Peg Pollard Communications, Boston, 1981-84; dir. comms. Mass. Dental Soc., Natick, 1984-93; coord. vols. Lyman Allyn Art Mus., New London, Conn., 1993—; exec. dir. Norwich (Conn.) Heritage Trrust, 1994—. Editor LWV, Westwood, 1966, pres., Greensburg, Pa., 1968-71; bd. dirs. First Night, Inc., Boston, 1982-89, Friends Boston Ctr. for Arts, 1985-88. Mem. Am. Soc. Assn. Execs., Am. Soc. Med. Writers, New Eng. Soc. Assn. Execs., Publicity Club New Eng. (Bellringer award 1984). Home: 48 Misty View Ave Mystic CT 06355 Office: 93 Broadway Norwich CT 06360

POLLARD, SHIRLEY, employment training director, consultant; b. Brunswick City, Va., July 8, 1939; 1 child, Darryl. Degree in bus. adminstrn., Upper Iowa U., 1978. Adminstr. East. Balt. Community Corp.; tng. coord. Balt. County Concentrated Employment Tng. Program; exec. dir. Park Heights Community Corp., Balt.; dir. Linkages, Inc., Balt. Contbr. articles to Afro Am. newspaper. Pres. Park Hghts. Cmty. Devel. Corp.; active Balt. Urban League, Balt. Welfare Rights Orgn.; pres. United Black Fund Balt., 1989—, Presdl. Task Force, 1992; founder, pres. Balt. County Polit. Action Coalition, 1982—; founder, dir. Linkages, Inc., 1980; founder, dir. Tng. and Placement Svcs., 1989; active United Svc. Orgn., Md. Minority Contractors Assn., U.S. Civil rights Mus. and Hall of Fame, Smithsonian Instn.; founder African Am. Culture Ctr.; co-founder Project Lou, Inc.; founder The Afro Fund, Inc.; active Fund for a Free South Africa's Founding Assocs. Leadership Coun., Nat. Women's Hall of Fame, Nat. Abortion Rights Action League, Srs. Coalition, Md. Edn. Coalition, CORE, So. Christian Leadership Conf, Nat. Trust for Hist. Preservation; presdl. appointment Md. Selective Svc. Bd., 1993. Recipient Outstanding Achievement award Md. Minority Contractors Assn., Mayor's Citation, Martin Luther King Civil Rights award, 1987, Md. State Dept. Edn. award, 1987, Congl. Achievement award, Kool Achiever awards, 1990, Nat. Black Caucus Spl. award, 1990, Congrssional Achievement award, 1988, Svc. award The Writers Club, 1991, USO Meritorious Svc. award, 1991, Gov.'s Vol. award, 1992, Acad. of Excellence award, 1992; Mayor's citation, 1984. Mem. Am. Soc. Pers. Adminstrn., Am. Soc. Health/Manpower/Edn./Tng., Assn. for Providers Employment and Tng., NAACP (founder, pres. Randallstown chpt. 1988—), Balt. Coun. on Fgn. Affairs, Transafrica, USO, Md. Minority Contractors Assn. (Achievement award 1986, bd. dirs. 1984-89), Smithsonian Assoc., Md. C. of C. (greater Balt. com. 1985). Office: PO Box 32051 Baltimore MD 21208-8051

POLLICK, MARTHA FLORENCE, nursing educator; b. Phila., Jan. 27, 1944; d. Abraham L. and Gertrude (Carfrey) Scanlin; m. Thomas E. Pollick Jr. BSN, Columbia Union Coll., 1966; MA in Edn. with distinction, Beaver Coll., 1983; MSN, Villanova U., 1985; EdD, Columbia U., 1993. Cert. in nursing adminstrn.; ACLS. Nurse therapist Psychiat. Day Care Ctr., Takoma Park, Md., 1966-67; staff nurse CCU Washington Sanitarium and Hosp., Takoma Park, Md., 1967-68; asst. head nurse CCU Grad. Hosp. of U. Pa., Phila., 1968-70; instr. Albert Einstein Med. Ctr. Sch. Nursing, Phila., 1970-74; nursing dir. St. Mary Hosp., Phila., 1975-76, 77; instr. Cooper Med. Ctr. Sch. Nursing, Camden, N.J., 1977-79, Episcopal Hosp. Sch. Nursing, Phila., 1980-86; staff nurse float pool Shore Meml. Hosp., Somers Point, N.J., 1988-94; dir. nursing Episcopal Hosp., Phila., 1988-94; program coord. Grad. Nursing Program Rutgers the State U. of N.J., Camden, 1994—; dir. St. Mary Hosp. Sch. Practical Nursing, Phila., 1976-77; instr. Cram Stat, Phila., 1985; co-pres. Continuing Edn. Unltd., Phila., 1985-87; item writer SUNY, Albany, 1986; asst. prof. Trenton State Coll. Sch. Nursing, 1986; adj. faculty dept. nursing LaSalle U., 1986-87, acad. advisor, 1986-87, asst. prof., 1987-89, adj. faculty, 1989-91; lectr. in field. Contbr. articles to profl. jours.; editorial bd. Holistic Nursing Practice. Active Ams. for Restitution and Righting of Old Wrongs, Assn. Am. Indian Affairs; mem. Phila. Elder Abuse Task Force, 1986—; CPR instr. Am. Heart Assn.; bd. trustees Episcopal Hosp., Phila., 1985-88. Mem. NAFE, ANA, AACN, Pa. Nurses Assn. (Phila. dist. chair ad hoc fund raising com.), Delaware VAlley Nurse Educators Assn., Am. Orgn. Nurse Execs., Southeastern Pa. Orgn. Nurse Execs., Nat. League for Nursing, Southeastern Pa. League for Nursing (bd. dirs.), N.Am. Nursing Diagnosis Assn., Am. Heart Assn., Southeastern Pa. Heart Assn. (coun. of nurses), Sigma Theta Tau (mem. chpt. eligibility com.). Office: Rutgers the State U of NJ Grad Nursing Program at Camden 311 N 5th St Camden NJ 08102

POLLOCK, KAREN ANNE, computer analyst; b. Elmhurst, Ill., Sept. 6, 1961; d. Michael Paul and Dorothy Rosella (Foskett) P. BS, Elmhurst Coll., 1984; MS, North Cen. Coll., 1993. Formatter Nat. Data Corp., Lombard, Ill., 1985; computer specialist VA, Hines, Ill., 1985—. Lutheran.

POLLOCK, LORETTA MARIE, elementary education educator; b. Portland, Oreg., Apr. 27, 1939; d. Marion Pierre and Mary Elizabeth (Kies) Mills; m. Wesley Robert Pollock, June 21, 1958; children: Forrest Dale, Andreé Verne, Alexi Marie. BA in Edn., U. Ala., 1976, Master's degree, 1987, postgrad., 1988, 89; postgrad., Western Mich. U., 1991. Cert. Type A tchr., Ala. Tchr. 1st grade Swanson Sch., Palmer, Ala., 1978—; v.p. Valley Reading Coun., 1987, pres., 1988, chair literacy com., 1989; mem. math. curriculum com. Matanuska/Susitna Sch. Dist., 1978, mem. curriculum com., 1985, mem. sci. curriculum com., 1989—, chair, 1993-94, co-organizer Hands-On Sci. Fair, 1991, 92, mem. primary sci. curriculum com., 1991-93, mem. 1st grade outcome com., 1992-93; leader workshops in field. Contbr. articles to profl. jours. Sci. Alive grantee, 1987; NEWEST awardee, 1993. Mem. NSTA (presenter conv. 1992), NEA, Internat. Reading Assn., Ala. State Reading Assn. (sec. 1989-91, state conf. hospitality chair 1990), Ala. Natural Resources and Outdoor Edn. Assn., Ala. Sci. Tchrs. Assn., Matanuska/Susitna Edn. Assn., Alpha Delta Kappa. Roman Catholic.

POLLOCK, MARGARET LANDAU, elementary school educator; b. Jefferson City, Mo., Oct. 18, 1936; d. William Wold and Grace Elizabeth (Creamer) Anderson; m. Charles Walker Nichols, Aug. 10, 1958 (div. Sept. 1970); children: Elizabeth, Charles, Christopher, Jeffrey; m. William Whalen Pollack, Jan. 30, 1993. AA, Stephens Coll., 1956; BS in Elem. Edn., U. Mo., Columbia, 1958; MA in Reading Edn., U. Mo., Kansas City, 1987. Cert. elem. tchr., Mo. Kindergarten tchr. Columbia Schs., 1958-59, Moberly (Mo.) Schs., 1960-62; 1st grade tchr. Kansas City Schs., 1962-63; kindergarten tchr. Independence (Mo.) Schs., 1966-75; chpt. I reading specialist Thomas Hart Benton Elem. Sch., Independence, 1975-93; book reviewer Corpus Christi (Tex.) Caller Times, 1994—; children's libr. Corpus Christi, 1995—; cons., presenter in field. Bd. dirs. Boys and Girls Club, Independence, 1990-93; coord. Independence Reading Fair, 1989-93; coord. books and tutoring Salvation Army, Kansas City, 1990-92. Mem. AAUW, ASCD, Internat. Reading Assn. (People to People del. to USSR 1991, local v.p. 1990-91, pres. 1991-92), Internat. Platform Assn., Austin Writer's League, Archeol. Inst. Am., Earthwatch, Nature Conservancy, Sierra Club, Phi Kappa Phi, Pi Lambda Theta (pres. Beta Upsilon chpt. 1992-93). Home: 3535 Santa Fe St # 3 Corpus Christi TX 78411-1346

POLON, LINDA BETH, elementary school educator, writer, illustrator; b. Balt., Oct. 7, 1943; d. Harold Bernard and Edith Judith Wolff; m. Marty I. Polon, Dec. 18, 1966 (div. Aug. 1983). BA in History, UCLA, 1966. Elem. tchr. L.A. Bd. Edn., 1967—; writer-illustrator Scott Foresman Pub. Co., Glenview, Ill., 1979—, Frank Schaffer Pub. Co., Torrance, Calif., 1981-82, Learning Works, Santa Barbara, Calif., 1981-82, Harper Row Co.; editorial reviewer Prentice Hall Pub. Co., Santa Monica, Calif., 1982-83. Author: (juvenile books) Creative Teaching Games, 1974, Teaching Games for Fun, 1976, Making Kids Click, 1979, Write up a Storm, 1979, Stir Up a Story, 1981, Paragraph Production, 1981, Using Words Correctly, 3d-4th grades, 1981, 5th-6th grades, 1981, Whole Earth Holiday Book, 1983, Writing Whirlwind, 1986, Magic Story Starters, 1987, (teacher's resource guides) Just Good Books, 1991, Kid's Choice/Libraries, 1991. Mem. Soc. Children's Book Writers. Democrat. Home: 11640 Kiowa Ave # 205 Los Angeles CA 90049-6244 Office: L A Bd of Edn 980 S Hobart Blvd Los Angeles CA 90006-1220

POLONITZA, NANCY JEAN, college counselor; b. Bayonne, N.J., Oct. 22, 1948; d. Edmund Henry and Margaret (Mackin) P. AB, Kean Coll., 1970; MEd, U. Del., 1972. Nat. cert. counselor; cert. yoga instr. Counselor SUNY, Plattsburgh, N.Y., 1972-75, Ocean County Coll., Toms River, N.J., 1976—; tech. reviewer Dept. Edn., Washington, 1984-92; yoga instr., 1989—. Staff mem. Peacetrees, Bedford-Stuyvesant, N.Y., 1991, planning group mem., Camden, N.J., 1992. Recipient Svc. awards Ocean County Coll. Disabled Student Svcs. Assn., 1987, Ocean County Juvenile Detention Ctr., 1988. Mem. N.J. Cmty. Coll. Counselors Assn. (pres. emeritus 1988—, Counselor of Yr. 1993), N.J. Counselors Assn., Calif. Yoga Tchrs. Assn. Office: Ocean County Coll Counseling Svcs College Dr Toms River NJ 08754

POLOUKHINE, OLGA, artist; b. Paris, Nov. 1, 1934; came to U.S., 1948; d. Nikita and Sophie (Schidlovsky) Koulomzin; m. Nicolas Poloukhine, Nov. 20, 1960; children: Olga, Michael, Elena. BA, Rutgers U., 1956; MA, Columbia U., 1960. Cert. art tchr. K-12, N.Y. Art tchr. Nyack (N.Y.) Schs., 1957-59, White Plains (N.Y.) Sch. System, 1959-60, Locust Valley (N.Y.) Pub. Schs., 1960-62. Exhibited in group shows at Wunchs Art Gallery, Taller Galeria Forte, Barcelona, Spain, Richard Gallery, Northea. U., Boston Le Chateau Royal de Collioure, France, Hecksher Mus., N.Y., Nassau County Fine Arts Mus., N.Y., Fine Arts Mus. L.I., Long Beach Mus. Art, numerous others; represented in permanent collection at Zimmerli Art Mus., Rutgers U., other corp. and pvt. collections, including IBM, AT&T, N.Y. Tel. Co., NYNEX, O.C.A. Mem. L.I. Graphic Eye Gallery (founder, pres. 1989-91), Nat. Assn. Women Artists, Internat. Graphic Art Found., Manhattan Graphics Ctr., Nat. Mus. of Women in the Arts (charter), N.Y. Soc. Women Artists. Eastern Orthodox. Home: 83 Skidmore Rd Lagrangeville NY 12540

POLSKI, MARGARET MARY, management consultant; b. Mpls., Oct. 18, 1955; d. Philip J. and Catherine A. (Lerum) P. B Elected Studies, U. Minn., 1981; postgrad., Harvard U. Personnel adminstr. Longyear Co., Mpls., 1975-78; personnel mgr. J Mark, Inc., Mpls., 1979; personnel adminstr. BMC Industries, St. Paul, 1979-82, mgr. employee and labor rels., 1982-83, dir. corp. human resources, 1983-84; dir. human resources Santa Cruz Imports, Brisbane, Calif., 1984-85, Check Tech. Corp., St. Paul, 1985-86; v.p., chief fin. officer Americord, Inc., Mpls., 1986-89, chief exec. officer, 1989-93, also bd. dirs.; cons. Minn. Waste Mgmt. Bd., 1988—, William Mitchell Coll. Law, St. Paul, 1988-89. Bd. dirs. Harriet Tubman Women's Shelter, Mpls., 1987-90, pres., 1988-90. Recipient Disting. Svc. award Twin Cities Personnel Assn., 1981, 82. Home: 85 Dunster St Cambridge MA 02138-5926

POLSON, A(LMA) IRENE, educator; b. Princeton, Ill., Oct. 14, 1925; d. Frank William and Ellen Christine (Eckstrom) P. AB, Augustana Coll., 1948; MA, Northwestern U., 1954; postgrad. various colls. and univs. Cert. high sch. tchr., Ill.; cert. tchr., Chgo. Tchr. United Twp. High Sch., East Moline, Ill., 1948-53, York Community High Sch., Elmhurst, Ill., 1954-58, Springfield (Ill.) area High Schs., 1959-63, Harvard (Ill.) Community High Sch., 1963-64, Chgo. High Schs., 1964-76, Maria High Sch., Chgo., 1978-79; substitute tchr. Chgo. High Schs., 1980—; summer camp counselor, tchr., Ill., Wis., N.D., 1960, 64-68, 76; lectr. Le Cercle Français de Chgo., 1981; part-time instr. Richard J. Daley Coll., Chgo., 1982, 94. Author: It's Fun To Ski, 1973; contbr. numerous articles, photographs, and poems to newspapers and mags. Recipient 1st prize Internat. Narrative Poem Poets and Patrons, 1986, others; Nat. Def. Edn. Act fellow U.S. Govt., 1962. Mem. NEA, Ill. Edn. Assn. (dist. rep. 1951), AAUW, Nat. League Am. Pen Women (treas. Chgo. br. 1982-88), Poets and Patrons (treas. 1981-84), Chgo. Sunday Evening Club Chorus, Apollo Mus. Club, Oak Park Ski Club, Illini Ski Club, Elmhurst Ski Club, Nomad Ski Club, Delta Kappa Gamma (chpt. pres. 1962-63). Office: Daley Coll 7500 S Pulaski Rd Chicago IL 60652

POLSON, LAURA LAMKIN, nurse administrator; b. Louisville, Dec. 4, 1962; d. Robert Dane and Martha Louise (Penick) Lamkin; m. Louis Scott Heimann, Dec. 15, 1978 (div. Apr. 1979); m. James Howard Polson, Aug. 25, 1984; children: Amanda Brooke, Morgan Elizabeth, Joshua Dane. AS in Nursing, U. Louisville, 1982; postgrad., Bellarmine Coll., 1994—. CCRN. Staff nurse Sts. Mary & Elizabeth Hosp., Louisville, 1982-85, charge nurse, 1985-87; staff nurse Homecare Ptnrs., Louisville, 1985-86; staff nurse Humana Hosp. Audubon, Louisville, 1987-90, lab. mgt., 1990-91, dir. cardiovascular svcs., 1991-93; dir. invasive cardiovascular svcs. Audubon Regional Med. Ctr., Louisville, 1993—; CCMN mem. Columbia/HCA Healthcare, Inc., 1993—. Mem. Nat. Soc. Profl. Cardiovascular Technologists. Democrat. Home: 5350 Highway 62 NE Corydon IN 47112 Office: Audubon Regional Med Ctr 1 Audubon Plz Louisville KY 40217-1319

POMASKI, ANNE MARIE, accountant; b. Buffalo, Feb. 13, 1962; d. Henry Anthony and Rose Marie (Battista) Panfil; m. Theodore Francis Pomaski, Apr. 20, 1985; children: Emily Anne, Ashley Lynn. BS in Acctg., SUNY, Buffalo, 1985. Jr. acct. Westwood-Squibb Pharm., Inc., Buffalo, 1984-85, mktg./budgeting acct., 1985-86, fin. acct., 1986-89, supr. gen. acctg., 1989-91, mgr. payroll, 1991-93, mgr. internal audit, 1993—. Mem. Inst. Mgmt. Accts. (dir. mem. rels. 1990-91, dir. newsletter 1988-90). Office: Westwood-Squibb Pharm Inc 100 Forest Ave Buffalo NY 14213-1091

POMERANCE, DIANE LINDA, business owner, television, film producer; b. N.Y.C., July 3, 1951; d. Benjamin Louis and Gerda (Reider) Yapko; m. Norman Jerome Pomerance. BA, U. Mich., 1974, MA, 1976, PhD, 1979. Prodn. sec., asst. NBC Sports, N.Y.C., 1977-78; sales asst. NBC, N.Y.C., 1978; prodn. asst., assoc. dir. CBS, N.Y.C., 1978-79; assoc. dir. CBS, NBC and Sta. WNET, N.Y.C., 1978-83, freelance story analyst, reader, 1979-83; segment producer Sta. KTTV-Channel 11, L.A., 1983-84; v.p., account exec. Pub. Info. Network, L.A., 1984-85; exec. producer, co-owner 50/50 Prodns., L.A., 1985-87; exec. producer, owner Polaire Group, Inc., L.A., 1987—. Author: Katherine: A Woman of Vision, 1984. Bd. dirs. MiraMed, Sinay Ballet, Mainstreet Children's Found. U. Mich. fellow, 1974-76. Mem. ASPCA, Dir.'s Guild Am., SAG, AFTRA, Internat. Documentary Assn., Women in Film, Book Publicists of So.Calif. (lectr., speaker L.A. chpt.), Speakers Press Bur. (lectr., speaker), Am. Film Inst. (seminar moderator, coord. L.A. chpt.), World Wildlife Fund, Greenpeace, Nat. Humane Edn. Soc., L.A. Women's Found. (grants review com.). Office: Polaire Group Inc 15760 Ventura Blvd Fl 7 Encino CA 91436

POMERANTZ, RHODA SILVERSTEIN, geriatrician, internist, health center executive; b. Phila., May 6, 1937; d. Alexander Silverstein and Bertha (Joffe) Solomon; m. Marc A. Pomerantz, Aug. 14, 1958 (div. Jan. 1986); children: Lauren, Susan; m. Irwin I. Feinberg, Nov. 16, 1986; stepchildren: Susan, Michael, Jonathan, David, Steven. AB, U. Pa., 1958; MD, Women's Med. Coll., Phila., 1963; MPH, U. Ill., 1976. Diplomate Am. Bd. Internal Medicine, Am. Bd. Geriatric Medicine. Intern Presbyn. St. Luke's Hosp., Chgo., 1963-64, resident in internal medicine, 1964-66, 68-69; mem. attending staff Tri-City Hosp., Oceanside, Calif., 1967, Mile Square Health Ctr., Chgo., 1969-72; mem. adj. attending staff Presbyn.-St. Luke's Hosp., Chgo., 1969-70, med. dir., assoc. adminstr. ambulatory care, 1969-72, asst. attending staff dept. internal medicine, 1970-74, assoc. attending staff internal medicine and preventive care, 1974-82; project dir. Johnston R. Bowman Health Ctr., 1972-76, med. dir., 1976-82; chief Sect. of Geriatric Medicine St. Joseph Health Ctrs. and Hosps., Chgo., 1982—. Editor Geriatric Rehab. Series, 1980-81; mem. editorial bd. The Pharos, 1976-94, Ambulatory Medicine Alert, 1987. Fellow ACP, Gerontol. Soc. Am., Am. Geriatrics Soc. (del. to AMA 1983-90); mem. AMA, Am. Med. Dirs. Assn. (alt. del. to AMA 1990—, cert.), Ill. Geriatrics Soc., Phi Beta Kappa, Alpha Omega Alpha, Delta Omega. Home: 1315 N Sutton Pl Chicago IL 60610-2007 Office: St Joseph Health Ctrs and Hosp 2900 N Lake Shore Dr Chicago IL 60657

POMERANTZ, WILMA MARIAN, nurse, social services administrator; b. Bklyn., Nov. 17, 1944; d. Jacob and Gladys (Shapiro) P. BA, Am. U., 1966;

MA, Kean Coll., 1976, BSN, 1991; AAS, County Coll. of Morris, Randolph, N.J., 1983. Tchr. Newark Bd. Edn., 1966-77; staff nurse Overlook Hosp., Summit, N.J., 1983-84, Newark Beth Israel Med. Ctr., 1984-88; info. specialist N.J. AIDS Hotline, Newark, 1988-91, coord., 1991—. Pres., bd. dirs. No. Lights Alternatives of N.J., Plainfield, 1993—; mem. N.J. women and AIDS Network, New Brunswick, 1991—. Recipient Profl. Practice award Kean Coll., 1991. Mem. ANA, Assn. of Nurses in AIDS Care, (ctrl. N.J. chpt.), N.J. State Nurses Assn., Sigma Theta Tau. Office: NJ AIDS Hotline 201 Lyons Ave Newark NJ 07112-2027

POMMER, FRANCES MIRIAM, insurance company executive; b. Balt.. BA, Moore Inst., Phila., BS, MA. CPCU. Mgr. producer rels. Zurich & Md. Casualty Co., Phila.; agt. Wohlreich & Anderson, N.Y.C., A.W. Topkis & C., Bala Cynwyd, Pa.; v.p. Evans, Conger, Broussard & McCrea, Bala Cynwyd, Pa.; reg. mgr. EDS, Phila., 1978-88; mgr. Electronic Data Systems, Mt. Laurel, N.J., 1988-91; cons. pvt. practice, Barrington, N.J., 1991—; instr., adj. faculty Rutgers U., Camden, 1968-83; nat. faculty CIC, 1978—. Contbr. to CPCU textbooks. Mem. CPCU Nat. Assn., N.Y. CPCU's, Pa. CPCU's, N.J. CPCU's, Profl. Ins. Agts. Assn., NAFE, Ins. Brokers Assn. Office: EDS 522 Du Bois Ave Barrington NJ 08007-1012

POMMIER, BARBARA ELIZABETH, psychiatric nurse, researcher; b. London, Nov. 30, 1947; came to U.S., 1948; d. Ignatius and Maria (Jungst) Wroczynski; m. Gregory Lawler, June 1968 (div. Nov. 1979); children: Sabrina, Nicholas, Alexei; m. Rodney F. Pommier, May 21, 1983. BSN, Oreg. Health Scis. U., 1982. Diplomate Oreg. State Bd. Nursing. Staff cardiology nurse Portland (Oreg.) VA Med. Ctr., 1982-87, charge cardiology nurse, 1984-86, asst. head nurse, 1984-88, staff psychiatry nurse, 1987-90; staff psychiatry nurse N.Y. VA Med. Ctr., N.Y.C., 1990-93; mem. rsch. com. Portland VA Med. Ctr., 1985-90, mem. recruitment and retention com., 1987-90; rschr. in field. Active Friends Pine Mountain Observatory, Eugene, Oreg., 1987-94, Portland Rose Soc., 1994-95. Nursing Rsch. grantee Portland VA Med. Ctr., 1986. Mem. Sigma Theta Tau. Home: 7140 SW Gable Pky Portland OR 97225

POMPEO-MELONE, MARIE ANTOINETTE, medical/surgical nurse, nursing educator; b. Jersey City, Feb. 27, 1961; d. Patrick D. and Antoinette (LeFante) Pompeo; m. Thomas M. Melone, June 20, 1986. Diploma in Nursing, St. Francis Hosp. Sch. Nursing, Jersey City, 1983; BSN, St. Peter's Coll., Jersey City, 1986; MA, Jersey City State Coll., 1990. RN, N.J.; cert. tchr. health edn., sch. nurse, tchr. handicapped. Staff nurse St. Francis Hosp., Jersey City, 1983-86; sch. nurse Jersey City Pub. Schs., 1986—; head cheerleading and dance coach St. Dominic Acad., 1987—, P.S. 8 Biddy Bulldogs, 1991—, St. Peter's Coll., 1991-93. Mem. ANA, NEA, N.J. Edn. Assn., Hudson County Sch. Nurse Assn., N.J. State Nursing Assn., Jersey City Educators Assn., Nat. Fedn. Interscholastic Spirit Assn., Nat. Fedn. Interscholastic Coaches Assn., Am. Assn. Cheer Coaches and Advisors (safety cert.), N.J. Cheerleading Coaches and Assn. Inc (co-dir. state competition 1993, 94, exec. bd. 1992—, coord. drug awareness resistance edn., cheer competition 1994, nat. cheer dance judging cert.).

POMPETTI-SZUL, IRENE CATHERINE, language educator; b. Phila., Jan. 4, 1948; d. Joseph and Catherine (Sortino) Pompetti; m. Casimir Chmielnicki, Feb. 20, 1971 (div. 1983); children: Sonya, Steven; m. Andrij V.R. Szul, Mar. 26, 1988. BA in Spanish, Beloit (Wis.) Coll., 1968; MA in Internat. Rels., U. Pa., 1971, CAS in Edn. Linguistics, 1989; MEd in English Edn., Temple U., 1977; postgrad., SUNY, Albany, 1992—. Cert. tchr. Spanish, English as second lang., and social studies, N.Y. Tchr. Spanish and Latin Am. history Solebury Sch., New Hope, Pa., 1970-71; tchr. English as second lang. Sch. Dist. Phila., 1972-78, bilingual curriculum developer, 1980-84, English as second lang. coord., 1984-85; instr. English and speech communication Penn State Ogontz, Abington, Pa., 1985-87; Spanish tchr. Liberty (N.Y.) High Sch., 1988-89; tchr. English as second lang. Middletown (N.Y.) Jr. High Sch., 1989-91; link program coord., instr. Spanish Orange County Community Coll., Middletown, 1991-92; instr. English as second lang. Sullivan County Community Coll., Loch Sheldrake, N.Y., 1990; asst. prof. ESL and bilingual edn. SUNY, New Paltz, 1990-92; cons. Abington Meml. Hosp., 1987; ESL cons. N.Y. State Edn. Dept., 1993. Author: English: Your Second Language: Readings in ESOL for Secondary Students, 1981. Vol. organizer Clean Air Coun., Phila., 1981; testifier Pa. Govs. Energy Coun., Phila., 1981; active Sullivan County Planning Bd., Monticello, N.Y., 1990; vice chmn. Environ. Mgmt. Coun., Lumberland, N.Y., 1988-89; active Lumberland Fire Dept., 1989-90. Recipient Book prize Columbia Tchrs. Coll., 1968. Mem. N.Y. Tchrs. English as 2d Lang. (asst. coord. Mid-Hudson region 1992), N.Y. Assn. Fgn. Lang. Tchrs., Sierra Club, Nat. Audubon Soc., Phi Sigma Iota. Republican. Roman Catholic. Home: PO Box 3899 Albany NY 12203

POND, PATRICIA BROWN, library science educator, university administrator; b. Mankato, Minn., Jan. 17, 1930; d. Patrick H. and Florence M. (Ruehle) Brown; m. Judson S. Pond, Aug. 24, 1959. BA, Coll. St. Catherine, St. Paul, 1952; MA, U. Minn., 1955; PhD, U. Chgo., 1982. Sch. libr. Minn., N.Y., 1952-62; asst. prof. libr. sci. U. Minn., 1962-63; reference libr. U. Mont., 1963-65; asst. prof. U. Oreg., 1967-72, assoc. prof., 1972-77; prof., assoc. dean Sch. Libr. and Info. Sci. U. Pitts., 1977-85. Mem. ALA (life), Phi Beta Kappa, Beta Phi Mu, Delta Phi Lambda, Kappa Gamma Pi. Home: 14740 SW Forest Dr Beaverton OR 97007-5117

POND, PHYLLIS JOAN, state legislator; b. Warren, Ind., Oct. 25, 1930; d. Clifford E. and Rosa E. (Hunnicutt) Ruble; m. George W. Pond, June 10, 1951; children: William, Douglas, Jean Ann. BS, Ball State U., Muncie, Ind., 1951; MS, Ind. U., 1963. Tchr. home econs., 1951-54; kindergarten tchr., 1961—; mem. Ind. Ho. of Reps. from 15th dist., 1978-82, from 20th dist., 1982-92, from 85th dist., 1992—, majority asst. caucus chmn., vice chmn. ways and means com., 1995. Del. Ind. State Rep. Conv., 1976, 80, 84, del., 1986, 88; alt. del. Rep. Nat. Conv., 1980. Mem. AAUW, New Haven Woman's Club. Lutheran.

PONDER, CATHERINE, clergywoman; b. Hartsville, S.C., Feb. 14, 1927; d. Roy Charles and Kathleen (Parrish) Cook; 1 child, Richard; student U. N.C. Extension, 1946, Worth Bus. Coll., 1948; BS in Edn., Unity Ministerial Sch., 1956. Ordained to ministry, Unity Sch. Christianity, 1958; minister Unity Ch., Birmingham, Ala., 1956-61; founder, minister Unity Ch., Austin, Tex., 1961-69, San Antonio, 1969-73, Palm Desert, Calif., 1973—. Mem. Assn. Unity Chs., Inc. (hon. DD 1976), Internat. New Thought Alliance, Internat. Platform Assn. Clubs: L.A., St. James (Hollywood, Calif.), Petroleum of L.A., Cardinal (Raleigh, N.C.). Author: The Dynamic Laws of Prosperity, 1962, The Prosperity Secret of the Ages, 1964, The Dynamic Laws of Healing, 1966, The Healing Secret of the Ages, 1967, Pray and Grow Rich, 1968, The Millionaires of Genesis, 1976, The Millionaire Moses, 1977, The Millionaire Joshua, 1978, The Millionaire from Nazareth, 1979, The Secret of Unlimited Prosperity, 1981, Open Your Mind to Receive, 1983, Dare to Prosper!, The Prospering Power of Prayer, 1983, The Prospering Power of Love, 1984, Open Your Mind to Prosperity, 1984, The Dynamic Laws of Prayer, 1987. Office: 73-669 Hwy 111 Palm Desert CA 92260

PONNÉ, NANCI TERESA, entertainment promoter; b. Chgo., May 10, 1958; d. Joseph Anthony and Irene Theresa (Nasadowski) P. BA, DePaul U., 1980. Actress, model Chgo., 1978—; pub. Chgo. Talent Directory, 1985—, Spotlight, 1989; pres./owner Chgo. Talent Enterprises Inc., 1991—; producer VIP Forums on Progress in Chgo. Talent Industry, 1990; speaker in field; hypnotist. Prodr.: (radio talk show) The Strange World of Lee Darrow, Sta. WONX-AM, 1993. Dem. vol. to Re-elect Mayor Washington, 1987; Dem. vol. for Clinton/Gore, 1992; Dem. vol. to elect Patrick Quinn to Sec. State, Ill., 1990. Named Miss Chgo., recipient Spl. Judges award Miss America Scholarship Pageant, 1981-82; Goodman Sch. of Drama scholar, 1978. Mem. NATAS, Chgo. Conv. and Tourism Bur., Ice Skating Inst. of Am. (3 Gold medals World Championships, 1994). Universalist Wiccan. Office: Chgo Talent Enterprises PO Box 25644 Chicago IL 60625-0262

PONTZER, LYNDA MARIE, art educator; b. St. Marys, Pa., Jan. 26, 1947; d. Edward Andrew and Orma Marie (Nicklas) P.; 1 child, Dayna Marie. Student, Pa. State Coll., 1964, Mercyhurst Coll., 1964-65, Cleve. Inst. Art, 1965-68; BFA with distinction, U. Ariz., 1970, MEd, 1970; postgrad., Montclair State Coll., 1970-72, U. Ariz. Cert. art tchr., N.J., Pa. Environ. arts tchr. N.J. Pub. Schs., Murray Hill, 1970-72; portrait artist tchr. Sommerset (N.J.) Art Assn., 1972, Denmark Adult Edn., Roskild, Denmark, 1974-76; social worker Adult Rehab. Network, Copenhagen, 1974-76; English instr. Tehran, Iran, 1976-78; substitute tchr. St. Marys (Pa.) Area Sch. Dist., 1978-83, art tchr., 1990-92; pvt. art instr. Pontzer's Portrait Studio, St. Marys, 1985—; art guest spkr. Boy Scouts, Secretaries, St. Marys, 1984, 94; art instr. Picture Lady Program, St. Marys, 1986-89; chairperson People's Choice Art Festival, St. Marys, 1987—; active Elk County Coun. Arts, 1989—. Founder Mother's Day Healthcare YMCA, Ridgway, Pa., 1987-89, active, 1978—; artist ARC, St. Marys, 1987; chairperson Queen of World Festival, 1985—. Mem. Am. Soc. Portrait Artists, Nat. Mus. Women in Arts (charter). Republican. Roman Catholic. Home: 500 Spruce St Saint Marys PA 15857-1767 Office: Pontzer Portrait Studio 500 Spruce St Saint Marys PA 15857-1767

PONZI KAY, MARYLOU, human resources specialist; b. N.Y.C., Oct. 14, 1950; d. Bruno and Constance Louise (DeLuca) P.; m. William J. Kay, Jr., Oct. 24, 1993. BA, SUNY, Geneseo, 1972; MA, U. Iowa, 1974, SUNY, Buffalo, 1979; postgrad., N.Y. Inst. Tech. Pers. adminstr. Michelin Tire Corp., Lake Success, N.Y., 1978-83; tech. recruiter 1st Data Resources, Lake Success, N.Y., 1983-84; mgr. human resources Chem. Bank, Jericho, N.Y., 1984-87; pers. officer J.P. Morgan Inc., N.Y.C., 1987-89; mgr. employment Am. Express Inc., N.Y.C., 1989-92; dir. human resources RockBottom Stores, Inc., 1992-95; asst. dir. human resources Canon U.S.A., Lake Success, N.Y., 1995—; instr. French and Spanish Amityville H.S. Adult Edn., 1986—. Editor: (guidebook) New England Guide, 1982, Canada Guide, 1982. Pres. LeBourget Alliance, Amityville, N.Y., 1995—; mem. bus. adv. coun. Adults and Children with Learning Disabilities, 1994—. Mem. Soc. Human Resources Mgmt. Roman Catholic. Office: 1 Canon Plz Lake Success NY 11042-1198

POOL, MARY JANE, design consultant, author, lecturer; d. Earl Lee Pool and Dorothy (Matthews) Evans. Grad., St. de Chantal Acad., 1942; BA in Art with honors, Drury Coll., 1946. Mem. staff Vogue mag., N.Y.C., 1946-68; assoc. merchandising editor Vogue mag., 1948-57, promotion dir., 1958-66, exec. editor, 1966-68; editor House and Garden mag., 1969, editor-in-chief, 1970-80; cons. Baker Furniture Co., 1981-94, Aves Advt., Inc., 1981-92, bd. dirs.; mem. bd. govs. Decorative Arts Trust; past mem. bd. govs. Fashion Group, Inc., N.Y.C. Co-author: The Angel Tree, 1984, The Gardens of Venice, 1989, The Gardens of Florence, 1992, The Angel Tree-A Christmas Celebration, 1993; editor: 20th Century Decorating, Architecture, Gardens, Billy Baldwin Decorates, 26 Easy Little Gardens. Mem. bus. com. N.Y. Zool. Soc., 1979-86; trustee Drury Coll., 1971—; bd. dirs. Isabel O'Neil Found., 1978—. Recipient award Nat. Soc. Interior Designers, Disting. Alumni award Drury Coll., 1961. Address: 1 E 66th St New York NY 10021-5852

POOLE, ANITA JOYCE, marketing and publishing company executive; b. Galveston, Tex., Oct. 27, 1950; d. Donald Wayne and Mary Alice (Anderson) Lawson; m. Richard Barton Poole, July 31, 1971; 1 child, Brian Andrew. AS in Nursing, Cooke County Coll., Gainesville, Tex., 1978. RN, Tex. Staff nurse Westgate Med. Ctr., Denton, Tex., 1978-84; nursing dir. Brookwood Recovery Ctr., Denton, 1984-86; coord. provider rels. Sanus Tex. Health Plan, Inc., Dallas, 1986-88; pres. Lawson and Lee Pub., Denton, 1987—; dir. mktg. WynRose, Inc., Dallas, 1988-89, Innovative Healthcare Systems, Inc., Dallas, 1989-91; dir. account svcs. CORPHEALTH, Inc., Ft. Worth, 1991-93, v.p. provider devel., 1993—; chmn. profl. staff exec. com. Brookwood Recovery Ctr., Denton, 1985-86; cons. managed healthcare firms, Dallas, 1988. Editor: Finger Theatrics: Fine Motor Development for Young Children, 1988. Co-founder pediatric hosp. orientation program Westgate Med. Ctr., 1983-84; chmn. childsafe program Denton Assn. for Edn. Young Children, 1979-80. Nursing scholar Cooke County Coll., 1976-78. Home: 2004 North Lake Trail Denton TX 76201-0604 Office: CORPHEALTH Inc 1300 Summit Ave Ste 600 Fort Worth TX 76102-4420

POOLE, ARNETTA MARIE, neonatal intensive care nurse; b. Cleve., July 17, 1966; d. Sylvester and Sylvia (Poole) Blue. BSN, Loma Linda U., 1990. Cert. BLS. Relief charge nurse Loma Linda Community Hosp., 1989-91; staff nurse Pomona Valley (Calif.) Med. Ctr., 1990—. Recipient We Care award Loma Linda Community Hosp., 1989-90. Mem. Nat. Assn. Neonatal Nurses, Orgn. for Obstetric, Gynecologic and Neonatal Nurses, Nat. League for Nurses, Sigma Theta Tau. Office: 12480 Iroquois Rd Apple Valley CA 92307

POOLE, EVA DURAINE, librarian; b. Farrell, Pa., Dec. 20, 1952; d. Leonard Milton and Polly Mae (Flint) Harris; m. Tommy Lynn Cole, May 15, 1970 (div. Sept. 1984); 1 child, Tommy Lynn Cole; m. Earnest Theodore Poole, Sept. 22, 1990; 1 child, Aleece Remelle Poole. BA in LS, Tex. Woman's U., 1974, MLS, 1976; postgrad., U. Houston, 1989. Libr. asst. Emily Fowler Pub. Libr., Denton, Tex., 1970-74; children's libr. Houston Pub. Libr., 1974-75, 1st asst. libr., 1976-77; children's libr. Ector County Libr., Odessa, Tex., 1977-80; head pub. svcs. Lee Davis Libr. San Jacinto Coll., Pasadena, Tex., 1980-84; libr. dir. San Jacinto Coll. South, Houston, 1984-90; libr. svcs. mgr. Emily Fowler Pub. Libr., Denton, 1990-93, interim dir., 1993, libr. dir., 1993—. Named to Outstanding Young Women of Am., 1991. Mem. ALA (libr. adminstrn. and mgmt. assn. edn. com. 1993—, conf. program com. 1994—), Pub. Libr. Assn. (conf. program com., 1995), Tex. Libr. Assn. (by-laws com. pub. libr. div. 1993—, ad hoc leadership inst. com. 1995, alumnae 1st class Tex. Accelerated Libr. Leaders 1994), Pub. Libr. Adminstrs. North Tex. (vice chair 1994-95, chair 1995—, pres. 1995), Tex. Mcpl. Libr. Dirs. Assn. (v.p./pres. elect 1994-95, grantee 1993), Denton Rotary Club. Office: Denton Pub Libr 502 Oakland St Denton TX 76201

POOLE, JILLIAN HANBURY, cultural center administrator, educator; b. London, Aug. 11, 1930; came to U.S., 1943; d. Anthony Henry Robert Culling and Una (Rawnsley) Hanbury; m. Richard Armstrong Poole, Nov. 2, 1957; children: Anthony Hanbury, Colin Rawnsley. AB, George Washington U., 1952; MA, George Mason U., 1984. Research asst. to bur. chief Ridder Newspapers, 1958-60; adminstr. Nat. Planning Assn., 1953-57; exec. sec. Nat. Cathedral Assn., Washington, 1960-64; dir. Nat. Cathedral Fund, Washington, 1966-69; mgr. devel. Corcoran Gallery Art, Washington, 1969-71; dir. devel. John F. Kennedy Ctr. Performing Arts, Washington, 1972-90, asst. to chmn., 1987-90; advisor to the chmn. John F. Kennedy Ctr. for the Performing Arts, 1990-92; adj. prof. Am. U., 1978-93. Pres. Fund for the Arts and Culture in Cen. and Ea. Europe, 1991—; trustee N.C. Sch. Arts Found., 1980-84, The Acting Co., N.Y.C., 1981-90, Nat. Bldg. Mus., Washington, 1985-91, George Mason U. Found., 1984—.

POOLER, ROSEMARY S., federal judge; b. 1938. BA, Brooklyn Coll., 1959; MA, Univ. of Conn., 1961; JD, Univ. of Mich. Law Sch., 1965. With Crystal, Manes & Rifken, Syracuse, 1966-69, Michaels and Michaels, Syracuse, 1969-72; asst. corp. counsel Dir. of Consumer Affairs Unit, Syracuse, 1972-73; common counsel City of Syracuse N.Y. Public Interest Rsch. Group, 1974-75; chmn., exec. dir. Consumer Protection Bd., 1975-80; commr. N.Y. State Public Services Commn., 1981-86; staff dir. N.Y. State Assembly, Com. on Corps., Authorities and Commns., 1987-94; judge Supreme Ct., 5th Judicial Dist., 1991-94; district judge U.S. Dist. Ct. (N.Y. no. dist.), 2nd circuit, Syracuse, 1994—; vis. prof. of law Syracuse Univ. Coll. of Law, 1987-88; v.p. legal affairs Atlantic States Legal Found., 1989-90. Mem. Onondaga County Bar Assn., N.Y. State Bar Assn., Women's Bar Assn. of the State of N.Y., Assn. of Supreme Ct. Justices of the State of N.Y. Office: Federal Bldg PO Box 7395 100 S Clinton St Rm 1240 Syracuse NY 13261*

POOR, ANNE, artist; b. N.Y.C., Jan. 2, 1918; d. Henry Varnum and Bessie (Breuer) P. Student, Bennington Coll., 1936, 38, Art Students League, 1935, Acad. Julien, Paris. trustee, gov. Skowhegan Sch. Painting and Sculpture, 1947-61, 89; artist corr. WAC, 1943-45. Illustrator: Greece, 1964. Works exhibited Am. Brit. Art Ctr., 1944, 45, 48, Maynard Walker Gallery, 1950, Graham Gallery, 1957-59, 62, 68-71, 85, Rockland Ctr. for Arts, West Nyack, N.Y., 1982, 83, Terry Distenfass Gallery, N.Y.C.; executed murals, P.O., Gleason, Tenn., DePew, N.Y., South Solon (Maine) Free Meeting House, 1957, others; represented permanent collections, Whitney Mus., Bklyn. Mus., Wichita Mus., Art Inst. Chgo. Edwin Austin Abbey Meml. fellow, 1948; grantee Nat. Inst. Arts and Letters, 1957; recipient Benjamin Altman 1st prize landscape painting N.A.D., 1971, 86, Childe Hassam award, 1972, 77. Mem. Artists Equity Assn., Nat. Inst. Arts and Letters. Office: Terry Distenfass Gallery 50 W 57th St New York NY 10019-3914

POOR, JANET MEAKIN, landscape designer; b. Cin., Nov. 27, 1929; d. Cyrus Lee and Helen Keats (Meakin) Lee-Hofer; m. Edward King Poor III, June 23, 1951; children: Edward King IV, Thomas Meakin. Student, Stephens Coll., 1947-48, U. Cinn., 1949-51, Triton Coll., 1973-76. Pres. Janet Meakin Poor Landscape Design, Winnetka, Ill., 1975—; chmn. bd. dirs. Cgho. Horticultural Soc., Chgo. Botanic Garden. Author, editor: Plants That Merit Attention Vol. I: Trees, 1984; contbr. articles to profl. jours. Participant in longe range planning City of Winnetka, 1978-82, archtl. and environ. bd., 1980-84, beautification commn., 1978-84, garden coun., 1978-82; adv. coun., sec. of agr. Nat. Arboretum, Washington; nat. adv. bd. Filoli, San Francisco; trustee Ctr. Plant Conservation at Mo. Botanical Garden, St. Louis, also mem. exec. com.; mem. adv. coun. The Garden Conservancy, 1989—; trustee Winnetka Congl. Ch., 1978-80. Recipient merit award Hadley Sch. Blind, 1972; named Vol. of Yr. Hadley Sch. Blind. Mem. Chgo. Hort. Soc. (chmn. bd. dirs. 1987-93, medal 1984, gold medal garden design, exec. com., chmn. rsch. com., women's bd., designer herb garden Farwell Gardens at Chgo. Botanic Garden, Hutchinson medal 1994), Am. Hort. Soc. (bd. dirs., Catherine H. Sweeney award 1985), Garden Club Am. (chmn. nat. plant exchange 1980-81, chmn. hort. com. 1981-83, bd. dirs., 1983-85, corresponding sec. 1985-87, Horticulture award Zone X1 1981, Creative Leadership award 1986), Fortnightly Club, Garden Guild (bd. dirs.), Garden Club Am. (v.p. 1987-89, medal awards chmn. 1991-93, Honor medal 1994). Republican.

POOR, SUZANNE DONALDSON, advertising and public relations executive; b. Somers Point, N.J., Oct. 6, 1933; d. James Watt and Roberta (Radford) Donaldson; m. Richard Sumner Poor, Mar. 19, 1955 (div. Sept. 1983); children—Jonathan Scott, Jeffrey Sumner, Sara Suzanne. A.B., Mt. Holyoke Coll., 1955; M.A., Montclair State Coll., 1975; postgrad. NYU, 1977-83, MPhil, Drew U. 1992, postgrad., Drew U., 1994—; photography student New Sch. Social Research, 1979-82. Reporter, copy writer WFLB, WFLB-TV, Fayetteville, NC., 1955-56; dir. public relations Montclair YMCA, N.J., 1965-69; dir. public relations Girl Scouts Greater Essex County, Montclair, 1969-74; assoc. pub. relations dept. Nat. League Nursing, N.Y.C., 1974; freelance public relations, photography, Montclair, 1974-76; dir. communications Insts. Religion and Health, N.Y.C., 1976-78; ptnr., pres. Miller/Poor Assocs., Verona, N.J., 1978—. Pres. bd. trustees Doubletree Gallery, Montclair, 1977-79; trustee Friends of N.J. Network, 1986-93. Mem. Am. Soc. Mag. Photographers, Am. Woman's Econ. Devel. Corp., Nat. Assn. Female Execs., Exec. Women N.J. (bd. dirs. 1980-83), NJ Ad Club (bd. govs. 1983—, editor Ad Talk, 1982—), Am. Soc. Media Photographers (editor Exposure newsletter 1993—). Democrat. Episcopalian. Avocations: bicycling, swimming, tennis, furniture restoration. Home: 30 Plymouth St Montclair NJ 07042-2625 Office: Miller Poor Assocs 280 Bloomfield Ave Verona NJ 07044-2426

POOS, LAURA ELLEN, stockbroker; b. St. Louis, Feb. 20, 1961; d. Robert Van Liew and Carole Lee (Krusen) P. BS, U. Mo., 1983. Beverage/banquet mgr. Sheraton Hotels, St. Louis, 1988; sales rep. Smith-Scharff, St. Louis, 1988; dir. A.T.I. Career Inst., Falls Church, Va., 1988-91; registered rep. Edward D. Jones & Co., Leesburg, Va., 1989-93; investment specialist Riggs Nat. Bank/Ind. Fin. Svcs., Washington, 1993—; instr. adult edn. Pks. and Recreation, Manassas, Va., 1990-91; speaker in field. Author: Bartending and Beverage Management, 1991. Mem. Nat. Soc. DAR, Ducks Unlimited (chairperson 1988—), C. of C. Republican. Roman Catholic. Office: Riggs Nat Bank 4249 Wisconsin Ave NW Washington DC 20016

POPE, ARLETTE FARRAR, insurance company professional; b. Paterson, N.J., Jan. 30, 1958; d. Arthur James Jr. and Mildred Louise (Johnson) Farrar; m. Leonard Pope, Aug. 12, 1990; children: Tyrell D., Trenace D., Leonard II. BSBA, Fairleigh Dickinson U., 1980. Claim svc. rep. State Farm Ins. Co., Paramus, N.J., 1983-88; claim automation and processing specialist State Farm Ins. Co., Wayne, N.J., 1988—; notary pub. State of N.J., 1985—. Trustee The New Beginning Is Now, Paterson, N.J., 1989—; adminstrv. asst. New Christian Tabernacle COGIC, Paterson, 1981—. Mem. Ch. of God in Christ. Home: 189 Union St # 2 Lodi NJ 07644-1115

POPE, INGRID BLOOMQUIST, artist, sculptor, lecturer, poet; b. Arvika, Sweden, Apr. 2, 1918; came to U.S., 1928; d. Oscar Emanuel and Gerda (Henningson) Brostrom; m. Howard Richard Bloomquist, Feb. 14, 1941 (dec. Nov. 1982); children: Dennis Howard, Diane Cecile Connelly, Laurel Ann Shields; m. Marvin Hoyle Pope, Mar. 9, 1985. BA cum laude, Manhattanville Coll., 1979, MA in Humanities, 1981; MA in Religion, Yale Div. Sch. Yale U., 1984. lectr. Nat. Assn. Am. Pen Women, Greenwich, Soroptimist Club, Greenwich, Greenwich Travel Club, Ch. Women United Greenwich, 1st Congl. Ch., Scarsdale, N.Y., 2d Congl. Ch., Greenwich, 1st Congl. Ch., Stamford, Conn., 1st Ch. of Round Hill, St. Mary Ch., Greenwich. Exhbns. include Manhattanville Coll., Purchase, N.Y., Yale Div. Sch., Ch. of Sweden in N.Y.C., Greenwich Arts Coun., Greenwich Arts Soc., First Ch. of Round Hill; author: (poems) Musings, 1994. Past bd. dirs. N.Y.C. Mission Soc., Greenwich YWCA, Greenwich Acad. Mother's Assn.; past trustee First Ch. Round Hill, Greenwich, mem.; pres. Ch. Women United, Greenwich, 1989-91; bd. dirs. Greenwich Chaplaincy. Mem. AAUW, Nat. Assn. Pen Women (v.p.), English Speaking Union, Yale Club N.Y.C. and Greenwich, Stanwich Club, Acad. Am. Poets, Nat. Mus. of Women in the Arts, Travel Club. Home: 538 Round Hill Rd Greenwich CT 06831-2641

POPE, LILLIE, psychologist, educator, writer, consultant; b. N.Y.C., June 22, 1918; d. Isador and Annie (Chusid) Bellin; m. Martin Pope, June 27, 1947; children: Miriam, Deborah Judith. BA, CCNY, 1937, MS in Edn., 1941; PhD, NYU, 1969. Lic. psychologist, N.Y. Psychologist Bklyn. Jewish Hosp., 1957-64; psychologist day treatment program Infants Home of Bklyn., 1959-64; dir. Bur. Edn. & Tng. Job Orientation Neighborhoods, N.Y.C., 1964-65; dir. learning disability clinic Coney Island Hosp., Bklyn., 1965—, assoc. chief child psychiatry, 1986—; adj. prof. Bklyn. Coll., 1972-76; cons., lectr. Head Start and spl. edn. programs, nationwide, 1956—; cons. New Theatre Bklyn., 1983—; mem. edn. adv. bd. Teaching Exceptional Children, Washington, 1980-86; chair adv. bd. McDowell Ctr. for Learning, Bklyn., 1983—. Author: Guideline to Teaching Remedial Reading, 1994. Lectureships U. Anchorage, 1983; bd. dirs. New Theatre Bklyn., 1983—, Ezra Jack Keats Found., Bklyn., 1987—. NIMH fellow, 1968; United Cerebral Palsy Assn. grantee, 1969, N.Y.C. Bd. Edn. grantee, 1967—; recipient Mary Hornby award Atlantic Conf. Nova Scotia, 1981. Fellow Am. Acad. Sch. Psychology; mem. APA (diplomate), Internat. Reading Assn., Coun. for Exceptional Children (Outstanding Svc. award 1990), Orton Soc., Multidisciplinary Acad. Clin. Edn. (charter), Assn. for Children With Learning Disabilities.

POPE, SARAH ANN, elementary education educator; b. Granite City, Ill., Dec. 4, 1938; d. Vance Guy and Lily Lovinia (Fischer) Morgan; m. Thomas E. Pope; children: Robert, Susan, James, John, William. BS in Edn., So. Ill. U., Edwardsville, 1970, MS in Edn., 1976. Lang. arts, humanities, sci., English, reading, math. tchr. Madison (Ill.) Community Sch. Dist., 1970—. Co-founder libr. Harris Elem. Sch., 1990. Fellow Old Six Mile Hist. Soc.; mem. Am. Hemerocallis Soc. Office: Madison Community Unit Sch 1707 4th St Madison IL 62060-1505

POPE, SYLVIA MICHELINA, computer programmer/analyst; b. Mt. Kisco, N.Y., Dec. 5, 1962; d. Frank and Lisa Curra; m. Lawrence Pope; children: Justin Allen, Stephanie Francesca. BS, SUNY, Albany, 1984; MS, Pace U., 1988. Computer programmer/analyst Synergy, Washington, 1989-92, Gen. Rsch. Corp., Vienna, Va., 1992—. With USAFR, 1986—. Roman Catholic.

POPINSKY, SYDELLE, retail executive, librarian, gallery owner; b. Newburgh, N.Y., Nov. 8, 1935; d. George and Molly (Bernstein) Schuman; m. Aug. 29, 1954; children: Diana Hyland, Mitchell. BS, U. Wis., 1957, MLS, 1971. Cert. tchr., Wis., Calif. Tchr. Beloit (Wis.) Sch. System, 1957-58, 1966-68; tchr. Guadalajara-Am. Sch., Guadalajara, Mex., 1964-65, Claremont (Calif.) Sch. System, 1968-69; ref. libr. Rockford (Ill.) Pub. Libr., 1971-72, Pensacola (Fla.) Pub. Libr., 1972-73, No. Ill. Libr. System, Rockford, 1973-76; continuing edn. cons. Tex. State Libr., Austin, 1976-84; adminstr./owner Clarksville Pottery and Galleries, Austin, 1985—; part owner Clarksville Pottery Studio, Inc.; adv. cons. Buyer's Mkt. Niche Mag., 1994—. Mem. Dem. Women's Group, Austin, 1976—. Mem. Am. Craft Retailer Assn. (bd. dirs. 1989-92), Am. Craft Assn. (mem. focus group 1994—). Home: 5101 Crestway Dr Austin TX 78731-5405 Office: Clarksville Pottery The Arboretum Market 9722 Great Hills Dr Austin TX 78759

POPKIN, GERRI CHAPPELL, county official; b. Long Branch, N.J., Nov. 21, 1949; d. Percival Henry and Cecelia Lydia (Biertuempfel) Chappell; m. Joel Popkin, Oct. 11, 1970 (div. 1993); children: David Joel, Michael Lee, Jamie Danielle. AA, Monmouth Coll., 1973; BA, Thomas Edison State Coll., 1985. Registered pub. purchasing ofcl.; cert. profl. pub. buyer, county purchasing ofcl., pub. mgr. Dir. consumer affairs County of Monmouth, Freehold, N.J., 1983, 86, dir. purchasing, 1987—; sr. field rep. N.J. State Lottery Dept. Treasury, Trenton, N.J., 1984-85. Councilwoman Boro of Neptune City, N.J., 1982-88; candidate N.J. State Senate, 1987; teamwalker March of Dimes Walkathon, 1984, 85, 94; rep. mcpl. chairperson Neptune City Reps., 1989—; pres. Monmouth County Fedn. Rep. Women, Monmouth, N.J., 1987-89; bd. dir. Women's Political Caucus of N.J., 1993—; legis. chair WPC-N.J., Monmouth-Ocean County Devel. Coun. Mem. Nat. Inst. Govtl. Purchasing, N.J. Legis. Agenda for Women (trustee 1993), Thomas Edison Alumni Assn., Monmouth Coll. Alumni Assn. Methodist. Home: 50 Sylvania Ave Neptune City NJ 07753 Office: County of Monmouth Hall of Records Freehold NJ 07728

POPKIN, JOYCE GAIL, psychologist; b. Bklyn., Nov. 18, 1947; d. Gilbert and Fally (Mardex) P.; m. Theodore William Hilgeman, July 19, 1987; 1 child, Alexandra Elaine. BA, Queens Coll., 1968; EdM, Temple U., 1970, PhD, 1984. Licensed psychologist, N.Y.; cert. sch. psychologist, N.Y., N.J., Pa. Sch. psychologist Comsewogue Sch. Dist., Port Jefferson Station, N.Y., 1971—; pvt. practice psychology, 1991—; workshop leader Nat. Ctr. for Study Corporal Punishment, 1979-80; mem. Dropout Prevention Com., Comsewogue Schs., 1986—, attendance policy com., 1986-87; supr. Masters and Doctoral Level Interns, Comsewogue Schs., 1988-89. Bd. dirs. Sylvan Gardens Coop., Miller Place, N.Y., 1984-87, 89—. Mem. APA, Suffolk County Psychol. Assn. (sch. psychology com. 1990—), Nat. Assn. Sch. Psychologists. Home: 22 Paul Revere Ln Centerport NY 11721-1610

POPOVICH, HELEN HOUSER, university administrator; b. El Paso, Tex., Nov. 19, 1935; m. James E. Popovich, Oct. 4, 1967 (dec. Apr. 1976); 1 son, Peter Edward; m. Donald G. MacConnel, Oct. 14, 1984. B.A., U. Tex., El Paso, 1955; M.A., U. Tex.-El Paso, 1958; Ph.D., U. Kans., 1965. Asst. prof. to assoc. prof., assoc. dean U. South Fla., Tampa, 1965-78; dean, v.p., acting pres. Winona (Minn.) State U., 1978-83; pres. Fla. Atlantic U., Boca Raton, 1983-89; pres. Ferris State U., Big Rapids, Mich., 1989-94, univ. advancement officer, 1994—. Bd. dirs. Winona LWV, 1980-82, Boca Raton United Way, 1983-89, Med. Investment Trust Fund, 1985-89, Rsch. and Tech. Inst. Amerikam; mem. Minn. Humanities Commn., St. Paul, 1980-83; v.p. Grand Rapids Econ. Coun., 1991. Mem. Am. Assn. Higher Edn., Am. Assn. State Colls. and Univs. (bd. dirs. 1988-93, sec.-treas. 1990-93), Grand Rapids Econ. Club (vice chairperson 1991-92, chairperson 1992-93), Delta Kappa Gamma, Omicron Delta Kappa, Phi Delta Kappa. Office: Ferris State University Big Rapids MI 49307

POPP, CHARLOTTE LOUISE, health development center administrator, nurse; b. Vineland, N.J., July 26, 1946; d. William Henry and Elfriede Marie (Zickler) P. Diploma in Nursing, Luth. Hosp. of Md., Balt., 1967; BA in Health Edn., Glassboro (N.J.) State Coll., 1972; MA in Human Devel., Fairleigh-Dickinson U., 1981. Cert. Sch. Nurse, N.J., Health Educator, N.J. Charge nurse Newcomb Hosp., Vineland, N.J., 1967-71; supr. Vineland Rehab. Ctr., 1971-72; charge nurse Bridgeton (N.J.) Hosp., 1972-73; dir. insvc. edn. Millville (N.J.) Hosp., 1973-76; dir. hosp. insvc. edn. Vineland Devel. Ctr. State of N.J., 1976-78, program asst. Vineland Devel. Ctr., 1978-87; dir. habilitation planning services State of N.J., Vineland Devel. Ctr., 1987—, lead program coord. Vineland Devel. Ctr., 1981—; exam proctor State of N.J. Bd. Nursing, Newark, 1973—. Editorial rev. bd. (jour.) Nursing Update, 1973-77. Instr. basic life support, Am. Heart Assn., bd. dirs. Tri-county chpt., 1979-83, South Jersey chpt., 1983-90. Mem. ANA, N.J. State Nurses Assn., Am. Assn. Mental Retardation, South Jersey Insvc. Exch. (life), Smithsonian Assn., Luth. Hosp. of Md. Alumni Assn., Glassboro State Coll. Alumni Assn., Fairleigh-Dickinson U. Alumni Assn. Lutheran. Office: Vineland Devel Ctr 1676 E Landis Ave Vineland NJ 08360-2901

POPPE, DONNA, music educator; b. Newton, Kans., Feb. 25, 1953; d. Louis Gustav and Dorothy Elizabeth (VanDenBrand) P. Student, Hastings Coll., 1970-72; BA in Music Edn., U. North Colo., 1974; cert. Orff-Schulwerk, U. Denver, 1977; MEd in Curriculum, Seattle Pacific U., 1990, MA in Integrated Arts, 1990. Band, music, orch. tchr. Weld County Sch. Dist., Greeley, Colo., 1974-79; spl. edn. tchr. Franklin Pierce Sch. Dist., Tacoma, Wash., 1979-84; music tchr. Sumner (Wash.) Sch. Dist., 1984—; cons. Seattle Pacific U., 1982; cons., prof. Fla. State U., Tallahassee, 1985-89, U. Ga., Athens, 1988-89; clinician/presenter U. Nebr., Lincoln, 1991; clinician N.W. Orff Conf., 1994. Contbr. articles to profl. jours. Mem. Tacoma Symphony, 1983-85; coord. team Wash. State Tchrs. Strike, 1991; chair dist. Valuing Diversity, 1993-95; drama clinician N.W. Orff Conf., 1994. Am. Orff-Schulwerk Assn. grantee, 1991. Mem. NEA, Nat. Audubon Soc. (newsletter editor 1974-79, field trip leader Seattle 1992), Am. Orff-Schulwerk Assn. (nat. bd. trustees 1987-90, editorial bd. 1984-87, clinician and presenter Cleve. 1983, Denver, 1990), Music Educators Nat. Conf. (rep. 1983-85, rsch. session Olympia, Wash. 1990), Drum Corps Internat. Democrat. Home: 11609 Marine View Dr SW Seattle WA 98146 Office: Sumner Sch Dist 230 Wood Ave Sumner WA 98390-1279

POPPER, VIRGINIA SOWELL, education educator; b. Macon, Ga., Sept. 10, 1945; d. Clifford E. and Hazel (Lewis) Sowell; m. James Clarence Sikes, June 24, 1967 (div. 1989); children: Zachary Andrew, Cristen Elizabeth; m. Joseph W. Popper, Jr., Dec. 28, 1992. AB, Wesleyan Coll., Macon, 1967; MEd, U. North Fla., 1973; PhD, Ga. State U., 1991. Tchr. 6th grade Jones County Schs., Gray, Ga., 1966-67; tchr. 12th grade Richmond County Schs., Augusta, Ga., 1967-68; guidance counselor Aiken County Schs., North Augusta, S.C., 1968-69, asst. prin., 1969-71; dir. Durham (N.C.) campus Kings Coll., 1974-77; rsch. asst. Ga. Dept. Edn., Atlanta, 1983-85; asst. prof. tchr. edn. Mercer U., Macon, 1989—; tchr. cultural studies exch. program Scinanto Gakuin Coll. of Kitakusha, Japan-Mercer U. Contbg. author: Business in Literature, 1986; contbr. articles, reports to profl. publs. Chmn. Mid. Ga. Regional Libr. System, Macon, 1989-91; bd. dirs. Jr. League Macon, Macon YWCA, Macon Intown, Macon Heritage Found., Bibb County Am. Cancer Soc., March of Dimes, Macon Ballet, Friends of Libr., Gladys Lasky Weller Scholarship Found., Mayor's Lit. Task Force. Mem. ASCD, Assn. Tchr. Educators, Ga. Coun. Social Studies, Kappa Delta Lambda, Pi Lambda Theta. Republican. Episcopalian. Home: 798 Saint Andrews Dr Macon GA 31210-4769 Office: Univ Coll Mercer Tift College Dr Forsyth GA 31029

POPPLER, DORIS SWORDS, lawyer; b. Billings, Mont., Nov. 10, 1924; d. Lloyd William and Edna (Mowre) Swords; m. Louis E. Poppler, June 11, 1949; children: Louis William, Kristine, Mark J., Blaine, Claire, Arminda. Student, U. Minn., 1942-44; JD, Mont. State U., 1948. Bar: Mont. 1948, U.S. Dist. Ct. Mont. 1948, U.S. Ct. Appeals (9th cir.) 1990. Pvt. practice law Billings, 1948-49; sec., treas. Wonderpark Corp., Billings, 1959-62; atty. Yellowstone County Attys. Office, Billings, 1972-75; ptnr. Poppler and Barz, Billings, 1972-79, Davidson, Veeder, Baugh, Broeder and Poppler, Billings, 1979-84, Davidson and Poppler, P.C., Billings, 1984-90; U.S. atty. Dist. of Mont., Billings, 1990-93; field rep. Nat. Indian Gaming Commn., Washington, 1993—. Pres. Jr. League, 1964-65; bd. dirs., pres. Yellowstone County Metre Bd., 1982; trustee Rocky Mt. Coll., 1984-90, mem. nat. adv. bd., 1993—; mem. Mont. Human Rights Commn., 1988-90. Recipient Mont. Salute to Women award, Mont. Woman of Achievent award, 1975, Disting. Svc. award Rocky Mt. Coll., 1990. Mem. AAUW, Mont. Bar Assn., Nat. Assn. Former U.S. Attys., Nat. Rep. Lawyers Assn., Internat. Women's Forum, Yellowstone County Bar Assn. (pres. 1990), Alpha Chi Omega. Republican. Office: Nat Indian Gaming Commn 1850 M St NW Ste 210 Washington DC 20005

POPRICK, MARY ANN, psychologist; b. Chgo., June 25, 1939; d. Michael and Mary (Mihalcik) Poprick; B.A., De Paul U., 1960, M.A., 1964; Ph.D., Loyola U., Chgo., 1968. Intern in psychology Elgin (Ill.) State Hosp., 1961-62; staff psychologist, 1962; staff psychologist Ill. State Tng. Sch. for Girls, Geneva, 1962-63, Mt. Sinai Hosp., Chgo., 1963-64; lectr. psychology Loyola U. at Chgo., 1964-67; asst. prof. Lewis U., Lockport, 1967-70, assoc. prof., 1970-75, chmn. dept., 1968-72 (on leave 1972-73); postdoctoral intern in clin. psychology Ill. State Psychiat. Inst., Chgo., 1972-73; pvt. clin. practice David Psychiat. Clinic, Ltd., South Holland Ill., 1973-87; pvt. practice, South Holland, Ill., 1987—; assoc. sci. staff Riveredge Hosp., Forest Park, Ill., 1975-76; ltd. lic. practitioner dept. psychiatry Christ Hosp., Oak Lawn, Ill., 1983—; ancillary staff dept. psychiatry Ingalls Meml. Hosp., Harvey, Ill., 1994—. Co-chmn. commn. on personal growth and devel. Congregation of 3d Order St. Francis of Mary Immaculate, Joliet, 1970-71; clin. resource person Cath. Archdiocese of Chgo., 1977—. Mem. Am. Psychol. Assn. (rep. from Ill. 1985-88), Ill. (sec.-treas. acad. sect. 1975-77, mem. student devel. com. 1975-77, chmn. acad. sect. 1977-78, 78-79, mem. program com. 1977-78, sec. 1979-81, pres.-elect 1981-82, pres. 1982-83, past pres. 1983-84, chmn. program com. 1981-82, awards com. 1983-86, rep. Com. of ET and Minority Affairs 1988-89, rep. Cook County 1989-91), Anxiety Disorders Assn. Am., Midwestern Psychol. Assn. (Cook County rep. 1989-91), Soc. for Sci. Study Religion, AAAS, Chgo. Assn. Psychoanalytical Psychology (rsch. com. 1988), Kappa Gamma Pi, Psi Chi (sec. 1964-65, pres. 1965-66). Home: 547 Marquette Ave Calumet City IL 60409-3316 Office: 16284 Prince Dr South Holland IL 60473-3233

POPS, MARCIA CLAIRE, probation officer, social welfare administrator; b. Hollywood, Calif., Oct. 2, 1941; d. Harry and Ida Toby (Rosen) Wolpin; m. Gerald M. Pops, Aug. 29, 1961; children: Cynthia Frances Wynne, Hillary Anne Bhaskaran, Deborah Gayle Pops. AA in Edn. and Social Work, U. Calif., 1962; BS in Pol. Sci., U. Wis., 1965; MS in Spl. Edn., Syracuse U., 1974. Teaching asst. Syracuse U., 1973-74; cons., social worker II Family Svcs. Assn., Morgantown, W.Va., 1974-75; dir. Monongahela Vol. Action Ctr., Morgantown, W.Va., 1975-77; chief probation officer 17th Judicial Cir. P.O., Morgantown, W.Va., 1977—; v.p., pres.-elect Coun. Internat. Programs, W.Va.; pres. Coun. of Internat. Fellowship-U.S. Branch, 1988-94; chair W.Va. state adv. com. to the U.S. Commn. on Civil Rights, 1985—. Recipient Nat. Pub. Svc. award Am. Soc. for Pub. Adminstrn. and Nat. Acad. Pub. Adminstr., 1989, Outstanding Committment to Pub. Svc. award. Mem. Golden Key Nat. Honor Soc. (hon.). Office: 17th Judicial Cir Probation Office 3d Flr Courthouse Morgantown WV 26505

PORAD, LAURIE JO, jewelry company official; b. Seattle, Dec. 19, 1951; d. Bernard L. and Francine J. (Harvitz) P. BA, U. Wash., 1974; postgrad., Seattle Pacific U., summers 1975-76. Cert. standard tchr., Wash. Substitute tchr. Issaquah (Wash.) Sch. Dist., 1974-77; with data processing dept. Ben Bridge Jeweler, Seattle, 1977-83, auditing mgr., 1983-87, systems mgr., 1987-92, MIS special project mgr., 1992—; mem. adv. bd. computer sci. dept. Highline Community Coll., Midway, Wash., 1985—, mem. tech. prep. leadership com. 1993—. Tchr. religion sch. Temple de Hirsch Sinai, Seattle, 1972-76, 84—, coord. computerized Hebrew learning ctr., 1987-88, coord. of religion sch. city facility, 1988-93, coord. mentor tchr. program, 1993—; tutor Children's Home Soc. Wash., Seattle, 1976-77. Mem. Assn. for Women in Computing (life mem., chmn. chpt. workshop 1985-88, nat. chpts. v.p. 1985-88, nat. pres. 1988-90, nat. chpt. v.p. 1992-93, rep. ind. mems. 1993—), Wash. Women United. Home: 14616 NE 44th St Apt M-2 Bellevue WA 98007-7102 Office: Ben Bridge Jeweler PO Box 1908 Seattle WA 98111-1908

PORITZ, DEBORAH T., state attorney general. Atty. gen. State of N.J. Office: Law & Pub Safety Dept Justice Complex CN 080 Trenton NJ 08625-0080*

PORRECA, BETTY LOU, education educator; b. Cin., Aug. 8, 1927; d. James Long and Hallie Marie (Jacobs) Hackathorn; m. Charles C. Porreca, Aug. 26, 1949 (widowed 1966); 1 child, Zana Sue Porreca Easley. BA, U. Ariz., 1970, MEd, 1973; PhD, Pacific Western U., 1990. Faculty Cochise Coll., Douglas, Ariz., 1973-83, Pima Community Coll., Tucson, 1983—. Author: (poetry) Selected Poems, 1975; contbr. articles to profl. jours. Chairperson Adult Continuing Christian Edn. Catalina Meth. Ch., Tucson, 1990—; vol. Crisis Pregnancy ctr., Tucson, 1989-91. Mem. Modern Lang. Assn., Nat. Coun. Tchrs. English, Pi Lambda Theta. Democrat. Methodist. Office: Pima Community College 1255 N Stone Ave Tucson AZ 85705

PORTANTE, LENORE ANN, army officer; b. Windber, Pa., July 23, 1960; d. Anthony Thomas and Louise Lenore (Cann) P.; m. Michael William Gifford, Mar. 7, 1992. BA in History and Polit. Sci., U. Mary Hardin-Baylor, 1993. Enlisted U.S. Army, 1979-88, commd. 2d lt., 1988, advanced through grades to capt., 1992. Mem. Phi Alpha Theta (historian 1992—), Pi Gamma Mu.

PORTELL, CRISTINA, curator; b. Barcelona, Spain, Apr. 25, 1956; came to U.S., 1990; d. Alberto and Rosa Maria (Cortés) P. MA in Art History, U. Autónoma de Barcelona, 1981; MLS, NYU, 1992. Freelance graphic designer Barcelona, Spain, 1980-86; exec. sec. Fundación Bosch Gimpera, Barcelona, Spain, 1987-90; mus. educator N.Y. Transit Mus., Bklyn., 1990-91; rsch. asst. Mus. Modern Art, N.Y.C., 1992-93; researcher Dahesh Mus., N.Y.C., 1993-94, asst. curator, 1994-95, curator, 1995—. Office: Dahesh Mus 601 5th Ave New York NY 10017

PORTER, BONNIE, photographer; b. Duluth, Minn., Mar. 26, 1959; d. Vernon Ward and Oriole Byrd (Pobanz) P. BA in English and Photojournalism, Boston U., 1981; postgrad., Mass. Coll. Art, Boston, 1987; student, Sch. Mus. Fine Art, 1986-87. Libr. assoc. Mus. Fine Arts, Boston, 1982-90, book preservationist, 1986-90, mus. recorder, 1990—; guest lectr. Sch. of Mus. Fine Arts, Boston, 1988—; guest instr., 1989. One women show Gallery 22P, Boston, 1994; group shows include The Basement Gallery, Boston, 1987, Alchemie Gallery, Boston, 1987, Grossman Gallery, (Disting. award), 1988, 93 (Disting. award), Ariel Gallery, N.Y.C., 1988, Trustman Art Gallery, Boston, 1989, Loft Gallery, Boston, 1990, Fed. Reserve Bank of Boston Gallery, 1990, Attleboro Mus., Mass., 1992, The Danforth Mus., Framingham, Mass., (Purchase award), 1992, Bromfield Gallery, Boston, 1993, 88 Room, Boston, 1994, Mus. Fine Arts, Boston, 1995, Barret House, N.Y., 1995. Exec. bd. Fort Point Artist Community, 1991—. Recipient Finalist award The Artist Found., 1991. Mem. Ctr. for Creative Photography, Photographic Resource Ctr. Home: 34 Farnsworth St 4th Fl Boston MA 02210

PORTER, DIXIE LEE, insurance executive, consultant; b. Bountiful, Utah, June 7, 1931; d. John Lloyd and Ida May (Robinson) Mathis. B.S., U. Calif. at Berkeley, 1956, M.B.A., 1957. Personnel aide City of Berkeley (Calif.), 1957-59; employment supr. Kaiser Health Found., Los Angeles, 1959-60; personnel analyst U. Calif. at Los Angeles, 1961-63; personnel mgr. Reuben H. Donnelley, Santa Monica, Calif., 1963-64; personnel officer Good Samaritan Hosp., San Jose, Calif., 1965-67; fgn. service officer AID, Saigon, Vietnam, 1967-71; gen. agt. Charter Life Ins. Co., Los Angeles, 1972-77, Kennesaw Life Ins. Co., Atlanta, from 1978, Phila. Life Ins. Co., San Francisco, from 1978; now pres. Women's Ins. Enterprises, Ltd.; cons. in field. Co-chairperson Comprehensive Health Planning Commn. Santa Clara County, Calif., 1973-76; bd. dirs. Family Care, 1978-80, Aegis Health Corp., 1977-92, U. Calif. Sch. Bus. Adminstrn., Berkeley, 1974-76; mem. task force on equal access to econ. power U.S. Nat. Women's Agenda, 1977—. Served with USMC, 1950-52. C.L.U. Mem. C.L.U. Soc., U. Calif. Alumni Assn., U. Calif. Sch. Bus. Adminstrn. Alumni Assn., AAUW, Bus. and Profl. Women, Prytanean Alumni, The Animal Soc. Los Gatos/Saratoga (pres. 1987-90), Beta Gamma Sigma, Phi Chi Theta. Republican. Episcopalian.

PORTER, ELISABETH SCOTT (LEEZEE PORTER), political worker; b. Mar. 23, 1942; d. Buford and Mary (Lowe) Scott; 1 child, Erin Lee; m. Paul Henry Nitze, Jan. 1993. Student, Sweet Briar Coll., Pan Am. Bus. Sch. Pres. Antique and Contemporary Leasing, Inc., Washington; founder, dir. Adams Nat. Bank, Washington; mem. Bd. Trade, Washington, Allied Bd. Trade, N.Y.C. Mem. fin. com. Diocese of Washington; mem. adv. bd. WAMU-FM, Washington; founder, profl. mem. Potomac chpt. Inst. Bus. Designers; active PTA; vestry mem. Grace Episcopal Ch., Washington; mem. Georgetown Citizens Assn., Leadership Washington, 1989—; mem. adv. bd. Elk Hill Farm, Va., Urban League; Dem. co-chmn. Women's Campaign Fund, Washington; mem. Dem. Women's Coun.; mem. bd. Women's Campaign Research Fund; v.p. bd. trustees Maret Sch., Washington; v.p. Champs Found.; mem. Leadership Washington, 1989-90. Mem. Washington C. of C., Nat. Assn. Women Bus. Owners, Georgetown Bus. and Profl. Orgn., Capitol Hill Assn. Bus. and Profls. Office: Antique and Contemporary Leasing Inc 709 12th St SE Washington DC 20003-2962

PORTER, ELSA ALLGOOD, writer, lecturer; b. Amoy, China, Dec. 19, 1928; d. Roy and Petra (Johnsen) Allgood; m. Raeford B. Liles, Mar. 19, 1949 (div. 1959); children: Barbara, Janet; m. G. Hinckley Porter, Nov. 22, 1962; children: David, Brian, Wendy. BA, Birmingham-So. Coll., 1949; MA, U. Ala., 1959; M in Pub. Adminstrn., Harvard U., 1971; LHD (hon.), U. Ala., 1986. With HEW, Washington, 1960-73; with U.S. CSC, Washington, 1973-77; asst. sec. Dept. Commerce, Washington, 1977-81; disting. practitioner in residence Washington Pub. Affairs Ctr., U. So. Calif., Washington, 1982-84; sr. mgmt. assoc. The Prodn. Group, Alexandria, Va., 1985-87; project dir. Cathedral Coll. of the Laity, Washington, 1987-89; v.p. R & D The Maccoby Group, Washington, 1990—. Bd. dirs. Delphi Internat. Group, 1981—. Fellow Nat. Acad. Pub. Adminstrs.; mem. Women's Nat. Dem. Club. Home: 1250 S Washington St Alexandria VA 22314-4454

PORTER, HELEN VINEY (MRS. LEWIS M. PORTER, JR.), lawyer; b. Logansport, Ind., Sept. 7, 1935; d. Charles Lowry Viney and Florence Helen (Kunkel) V.; m. Lewis Morgan Porter, Jr., Dec. 26, 1966; children: Alicia Michelle, Andrew Morgan. A.B., Ind. U., 1957; J.D., U. Louisville, 1961. Bar: Ind. and Ill. 1961, U.S. Supreme Ct. 1971. Atty. office chief counsel Midwest regional office IRS, Chgo., 1961-73; assoc. regional atty. litigation center Equal Employment Opportunity Commn., Chgo., 1973-74; practice in Northbrook, Ill., 1974-79, 80-86; ptnr. Porter & Andersen, Chgo., 1979-80, Porter & Porter, Northfield, Ill., 1986—; lectr. Law in Am. Found., Chgo., summer, 1973, 74; assoc. prof. No Ill Coll Law (formerly Lewis U. Coll. Law), Glen Ellyn, Ill., 1975-79. Lectr. women's rights and fed. taxation to bar assns., civic groups. Recipient Disting. Alumni award U. Louisville Sch. of Law, 1986, President's award Nat. Assn. of Women Lawyers, 1985. Fellow Am. Bar Found., Ill. State Bar Found.; mem. Women's Bar Assn. Ill. (pres. 1972-73), ABA (chmn. standing com. gavel awards 1983-85, bd. editors jour. 1984-90, mem. standing com. assn. comm. 1990-93), Fed. Bar Assn. (pres. Chgo. chpt. 1974-75), Ill. Bar Assn. (assembly del. 1972-78), Nat. Assn. Women Lawyers (pres. 1973-74). Home and Office: 225 Maple Row Northfield IL 60093-1037

PORTER, JENNIFER MADELEINE, producer, director; b. Milw., Oct. 3, 1962; d. John Hamlin and Helen Meak (Smith) P. BA in Comm., Bowling Green State U., 1984. Audio visual supr. Liberty Mutual Ins. Group, Berwyn, Pa., 1985-88; sr. prodr. audio visual Prudential Ins. Co., Mpls., 1988-93; proprietor Shoot The Moon Prodns., Mound, Minn., 1993—. Prodr., dir., writer: (audio visual program) Phantom Lake... A Lifetime of Memories, 1991 (Best of Show 1991, Script award Assn. for Multi-Image, Internat. 1991), Vision... The Gamma Phi Beta Foundation, 1992 (First Place award 1993). Mentor U. Minn., Mpls., 1989—; fund raiser Gamma Phi Beta Found. Philanthropy-Spl. Camping for Girls, Minn., Wis., 1991—; chairperson 100th Celebration, Phantom Lake YMCA Camp, Mukwonago, Wis., 1994—. Mem. Assn. for Multi-Image Internat. (exec. bd. local 1986-88), Gamma Phi Beta (internat. officer, pub. rels. speaker/prodr. 1991—). Home and Office: Shoot The Moon Prodns 1764 Heron Ln Mound MN 55364-1252

PORTER, JILL, journalist; b. Phila., Aug. 5, 1946; d. Sidney and Mae (Merion) Chalfin; m. Eric Porter, Mar. 7, 1970 (div. 1975); m. Fred Hamilton, Oct. 28, 1983; 1 child, Zachary. BA, Temple U., 1968. Pub. rels. Manning Smith P.R., Phila., 1968-69; reporter Norristown Times Herald, Norristown, Pa., 1969-72, The Trentonian, Trenton, N.J., 1972-75; reporter The Phila. Daily News, Phila., 1975-79, columnist, 1979—; instr. Temple U., 1976-80. Contbr. articles to numerous mags. Vol. Phila. Futures, 1994. Recipient Keystone Press award Pa. Newspaper Publisher"s Assn., 1985. Home: 715 Stradone Rd Bala Cynwyd PA 19004-2113 Office: Phila Newspapers Inc Phila Daily News 400 N Broad St Philadelphia PA 19130-4015

PORTER, JOAN MARGARET, elementary educator; b. Vernon, Tex., Dec. 25, 1937; d. Elton Lonnie and Clara Pearl (Yeager) Smith; m. Claude Walker Porter, Feb. 13, 1960; children: Jolene Porter Mohindroo, Richard Euin, Vonda Sue, Darla Ailese. BA, Wayland Bapt. U., 1960; M in Elem. Edn., Ea. N.Mex. U., 1981, bilingual endorsement, 1982. cert. classroom tchr., N.Mex. ESL tchr. Jefferson Elem. Sch., Lovington, N.Mex., 1979-81, tchr. first grade, 1981-82; tchr. bilingual first grade Jefferson Elem. Sch., Lovington, 1982-89; tchr. bilingual first grade Highland Elem. Sch., Plainview, Tex., 1989-91, 1992—, tchr. first grade, 1991-92, tchr. bilingual first grade, 1992—; vol. tchr. Cert. Adult Literacy, Lovington. Mem. PTA, Tex. Classroom Tchrs. Assn., Delta Kappa Gamma (profl. affairs. com. chmn., 1991), Phi Kappa Phi. Southern Baptist. Home: 101 Juanita St Plainview TX 79072-7625 Office: Highland Elem Sch 1707 W 11th St Plainview TX 79072-6439

PORTER, JOYCE KLOWDEN, theatre educator and director; b. Chgo., Dec. 21, 1949; d. LeRoy and Esther (Siegel) Klowden; m. Paul Wayne Porter, June 8, 1980; 1 child, David Benjamin. BA in Speech Edn., U. Ill., 1971; MA in Theatre, Northwestern U., 1972; postgrad., Northeastern U., Chgo., 1980, 89, Ill. State U., 1985-90. Prof. theatre, play dir. Moraine Valley Community Coll., Palos Hills, Ill., 1972—, acting theatre coord., 1986-87; adj. faculty Columbia Coll., 1988—; co-owner, tour organizer Chgo. Theatre Arts Tours, Calumet City, Ill., 1988-93; co-owner Porter Video Prodns.; actress, 1972—. Author: (textbook) Humanities on the Go, 1992. Mem. adv. bd. Oak Park (Ill.) Park Dist., 1983; co-chmn. Moraine chpt. Chgo. Area Faculty for nuclear Freeze, Palos Hills, 1985-87; announcer for blind Chgo. Radio Info. Svc., 1982-83; bd. dirs. Festival Theatre, Oak Park, 1989—; mem. play selection com. Village Players of Oak Park. Mem. Assn. for Theatre in Higher Edn., Ill. Theatre Assn., Community Coll. Humanities Assn., Ill. Fedn. Tchrs., Nature Conservancy, Zeta Phi Eta. Office: Moraine Valley Community Coll 10900 S 88th Ave Palos Park IL 60465-0937

PORTER, KAREN COLLINS, non-profit organization administrator, counselor; b. Detroit, Dec. 3, 1953; d. Cecil Allen and Mary Louise (Grzena) Collins; m. Frederick James Porter, Aug. 16, 1975; children: Suzanne Catherine, Kirstin Maureen. Student, Albion Coll., 1971-74, U. Mich., 1975; BA, U. Colo., Boulder, 1976; MA, U. Colo., Denver, 1979. Co-dir. Loveland (Colo.) Resource Ctr., 1982-84; asst. dir. Interim House-YWCA, Detroit, 1985; assoc. dir. First Step, Canton, Mich., 1985—; bd. dirs., sec. Loveland Childbirth Edn. Assn., 1980-82; bd. dirs., chairperson Thompson Valley Presch., Loveland, 1980-84; advocate Larimer County Sexual Assault Team, Loveland, 1982-84; mem. bd. dirs. Samaritan Counseling Ctr., Farmington Hills, Mich., 1985-89, mem. program com., 1985—. Leader Girl Scouts Am., Farmington Hills, 1985-90. Home: 29113 Forest Hl Farmington MI 48331 Office: 44978 Ford Rd Ste C Canton MI 48187-2903

PORTER, LEAH LEEARLE, biological researcher; b. Remington, Va., Sept. 19, 1963; d. James Wallace and Earline Yvonne (Moore) P. BS, U. Md., 1985; MS, Cornell U., 1990, PhD, 1993. Biol. technician U.S. Dept. Agr., Beltsville, Md., 1981-85; agrl. cons. Md. Dept. Agr., College Park, 1985; cons., office mgr. Carpigraphics, Inc., Beltsville, 1985-86; grad. rsch. asst. Cornell U., Ithaca, N.Y., 1986-94; cons., mktg. asst. LeEarle Enterprises, Ithaca, 1988-94; mgr. internat. project Glahe Cons. Group, Washington, 1994—; cons., mktg. asst. Le Earle Enterprises, Ithaca, 1988-93. Md. State Senate scholar, 1984-85; faculty grad. fellow Cornell U., 1986-87. Fellow N.Y. Acad. Scis.; mem. Am. Phytopathological Soc., Assn. Women in Sci., Black Grad. and Profl. Students, Alpha Chi Sigma, Zeta Phi Beta. Democrat. Baptist. Office: 1700 K St NW Washington DC 20006

PORTER, MARSHA KAY, educator, writer; b. Sacramento, Feb. 7, 1954; d. Charles H. and Eileen J. (Miller) P. BA in English and Edn., Calif. State U., Sacramento, 1976, traffic safety credential, 1979, MA in Ednl. Adminstrn., 1982. Cert. lang. devel. specialist, Calif.; cert. first aid instr. ARC. Bookkeeper Chuck's Parts House, Sacramento, 1969-76; substitute tchr. Sacramento City Unified Sch. Dist., 1976-78; coord. Title I, Joaquin Miller Mid. Sch., Sacramento, 1978-81; tchr. ESL and driver's edn. Hiram Johnson H.S., Sacramento, 1981-85, C.K. McClatchy H.S., Sacramento, 1985—; freelance editor, 1981-87; guest lectr. Nat. U., Sacramento, 1992-93. Co-author video movie guide film reference book, pub. annually; contbr. movie revs., short stories and articles to publs. Vol. instr. CPR and first aid ARC, Sacramento, 1986-92; guest writer United We Stand Calif., Sacramento, 1993-94. Gov.'s scholar State of Calif., 1972. Mem. NEA, Calif. Tchrs. Assn., Calif. Assn. Safety Educators, Calif. Writers, Calif. Writers Assn. (sec. 1987-94), Delta Kappa Gamma. Roman Catholic.

PORTER, RHONDA DAVIS, critical care, emergency nurse; b. Cabarrus County, N.C., July 31, 1956; d. Donald Matthew and Margaret Louise (Cauble) Davis; m. Allen Lovejoy Porter, Dec. 15, 1979; children: Jeffrey Allen, Matthew Glenn. Diploma, Mercy Sch. Nursing, Charlotte, N.C., 1977; BSN, U. N.C., Charlotte, 1979. Cert. mobile intensive care nurse, trauma nurse, ACLS. Staff nurse Wesley Long Community Hosp., Greensboro, N.C.; nurse cons. Aetna Life Ins., 1990-92, clin. nurse specialist, 1992—. Mem. Emergency Nurses Assn. Home: 5506 Cobble Glen Ct Greensboro NC 27407-6351

PORTER, ROBERTA ANN, counselor, educator, school system administrator; b. Oregon City, Oreg., May 28, 1949; d. Charles Paul and Verle Maxine (Zimmerman) Zacur; m. Vernon Louis Porter, Dec. 27, 1975. B in Bus. Edn., So. Oreg. Coll., 1971, M in Bus. Edn., 1977; cert. in counseling, Western Oreg. Coll., 1986. Cert. in leadership Nat. Seminars, 1991. Tchr. Klamath Union High Sch., Klamath Falls, Oreg., 1971-73, Mazama Mid.-High Sch., Klamath Falls, 1973-83; instr. Oreg. Inst. Tech., Klamath Falls, 1975-92; counselor Mazama High Sch., Klamath Falls, 1983-93, mem. site based mgmt. steering com., 1991—; vice-prin. Bonanza (Oreg.) Schs., 1993—; presenter Oreg. and Nat. Assn. Student Coun., 1989-92, Oreg. Sch. Bds. Assn., Sch. Counselor Assn., 1995, state mini workshops counselors/adminstrs.; mem. task force for ednl. reform in Oreg., 1993-94; trainer asst. Leadership Devel. Am. Sch. Counselor Assn. Trainer U.S. Army and Marines Recruiters, Portland and Medford, Oreg., 1988-89; master trainer Armed Svcs. Vocat. Aptitude Battery/Career Exploration Program, 1992—; candidate Klamath County Sch. Bd., Klamath Falls. Recipient Promising, Innovative Practices award Oreg. Sch. Counselors, 1990. Mem. NEA, ACA, COSA, ASCD, Oreg. Sch. Counseling Assn. (presenter, v.p. high sch. 1988-91, membership com. 1991-93, pres. 1992-95, parliamentarian 1994-95), Oreg. Edn. Assn., Oreg. Counseling Assn., Oreg. Assn. Student Couns. (bd. dirs. activity advisors 1989-91), Nat. Assn. Student Couns., Klamath Falls Edn. Assn. (bldg. rep. 1990-93, sec. 1991-92, negotiations team 1992-93), Delta Kappa Gamma (exec. bd. Alpha chpt. 1985—, pres. 1990-92, state conv. chmn. 1992, state legis. com. 1991-93, chmn. 1993—, state expansion com.). Home: 3131 Derby St Klamath Falls OR 97603-7313

PORTER, SHARON LYNN, library services professional; b. Gillette, Wyo., Oct. 14, 1954; d. Wayne Laurent and Patricia Jean (Hubbard) Moore; m. Roger Edison Porter, Aug. 1, 1981; children: Russell Edward, Seth Michael. AS, Casper Coll., 1975; BS, U. Wyo., 1977; postgrad., Sheridan Coll., U. Wyo., 1979-92. Rsch./student aide U. Wyo., Laramie, 1977; asst. supr. prodn. control Kerr-McGee Coal Corp., Wright, Wyo., 1977-79; sr. environ. technician Rocky Mtn. Energy Co., Wright, Wyo., 1979-81; investment money mgr. First Wyo. Bank-Wright, 1981-83; sec., prin. Campbell County Sch. Dist., Wright, 1983-85; libr. sub. Campbell County Sch. Dist. and Campbell County Libr., Wright, 1985-93, libr. asst., 1994—; exec. co-owner, bus. mgr. Porter Constrn./Wright Mini-Storage, Wright, 1985-93; cert. instr. Mine Safety Health Adminstrn., Denver, 1980—, ARC MultiMedia FirstAid, Casper, Wyo., 1980-90, Eberline Radiation Protection, Sante Fe, 1980-81; issuing officer work permits State of Wyo./Dept. Labor, Cheyenne, 1984—. 4-H leader Wright Kids, 1990-92; Sunday sch. dir. St. Francis on Prairie, Wright, 1979-82, vestry bd., bishops com., 1992-94; mem.-at-large Parents and childrens Coun., Wright, 1990—; rep. del. Campbell County Conv., 1994. Recipient Life Sci. scholarship Casper Coll., 1974, True Oil Co. scholarship, 1975. Mem. Wright Crafters Club (sec. 1985—), Farmhouse Frat. Aux. (pres. 1976-77, chpt. sweetheart 1977), Wright C. of C., Phi Theat Kappa, Alpha Zeta, Alpha Chi Omega (sec. 1975-77). Republican. Episcopalian. Home: PO Box 197 Wright WY 82732-0197 Office: Porter Constrn Wright Mini Storage 500 Sandcreek Ct Wright WY 82732

PORTER, VERNA LOUISE, lawyer; b. L.A., May 31, 1941. B.A., Calif. State U., 1963; JD, Southwestern U., 1977. Bar: Calif. 1977, U.S. Dist. Ct. (cen. dist.) Calif. 1978, U.S. Ct. Appeals (9th cir.) 1978. Ptnr. Eisler & Porter, L.A., 1978-79, mng. ptnr., 1979-86, pvt. practice law, 1986—; judge pro-tempore L.A. Mcpl. Ct., 1983—, L.A. Superior Ct., 1989—, Beverly Hills Mcpl. Ct., 1992—; mem. state of Calif. subcom. on landlord tenant law, panelist conv., mem. real property law sect. Calif. State Bar, 1983; speaker on landlord-tenant law to real estate profls., including San Fernando Bd. Realtors; vol. atty. L.A. County Bar Dispute Resolution, mem. client rels. panel, fee arbitrator. Editorial asst., contbr. Apt. Owner Builder; contbr. to Apt. Bus. Outlook, Real Property News, Apt. Age; mem. World Affairs Coun., Mem. ABA, L.A. County Bar Assn. (client-rels. vol. dispute resolution and fee arbitration, 1981—), L.A. Trial Lawyers Assn., Wilshire Bar Assn., Women Lawyer's Assn., Landlord Trial Lawyers Assn. (founding mem., pres.), da Camera Soc. Republican. Office: 2500 Wilshire Blvd Fl 1226 Los Angeles CA 90057-4317

PORTH, SUSAN E., medical sevice plan executive; b. 1948. MA, MBA, Harvard U., 1972. Mgr. mktg. Crown Zellerbach Corp., Salt Lake City, 1973-78; with Kaiser Found. Health Plan, 1978—; sr. v.p. finance Kaiser Found. Health Plan/Kaiser Found. Hosps.; also CFO Kaiser Found. Health Plans Ga. and Northwest; sr. v.p. Kaiser Found. Health Plan Conn.; treas. Kaiser Found. Office: Kaiser Found Health Plan 1 Kaiser Pl Oakland CA 94612*

PORTILLO, CAROL DIANE, marketing educator, vocalist; b. Las Cruces, N.Mex., Apr. 29, 1963; d. J. Francisco Tomas and Maria Erlinda (Puentes) P. AA, N.Mex. State U., 1985, BA, 1987, MBA, 1989. Sales-ter. mgr. Cronatron Welding, Norcross, Ga., 1989-90; bus. instr. Fed. Correctional Inst.-La Tuna, Anthony, N.Mex., 1990-91, Nat. Edn. Ctr., San Antonio, 1991-92, Palo Alto Coll., San Antonio, 1992—; asst. mgr. City Savs. & Loan, San Antonio, 1991; prof. St. Mary's U., San Antonio, 1992—. Mem. Am. Mktg. Assn. (faculty advisor 1993—, advisor Women in Bus. 1993-94), Hismapic MBAs. Roman Catholic. Office: St Mary's Univ One Camino Santa Maria San Antonio TX 78238

PORTMAN, SUSAN NEWELL, lawyer; b. El Dorado, Kans., Sept. 12, 1953; d. Richard and Denise (Beaudequin) Newell; m. Glenn A. Portman, Jan. 2, 1987. BS in Math., U. Okla., 1975; JD summa cum laude, Am. U., 1982. Bar: Tex. 1983, U.S. Dist. Ct. (no. dist.) Tex. 1983. Math. statistician U.S. Dept. Labor Bur. Labor Statistics, Washington, 1975-76; assoc. Johnson, Bromberg & Leeds, Dallas, 1983-87; div. counsel Nat. Gypsum Co., Dallas, 1987-88, corp. counsel, 1988-91, sr. corp. counsel and asst. sec., 1991-93. Treas. Lake Highlands Square Homeowners Assn., Dallas, 1991-93. Named Deans fellow Am. U., recipient Mussey Prize. Mem. So. Meth. U. Sch. Law Corp. Coun., 500 Inc. Club, Pi Mu EPsilon, Alpha Lambda Delta. Democrat. Presbyterian. Home and Office: 9503 Winding Ridge Dr Dallas TX 75238-1451

PORTMANN, MICHELE, secondary education educator, counselor; b. Tillamook, Oreg., May 7, 1950; d. Frank Joseph and Goldie Marie (Cahill) P. BS in Math., We. Oreg. State Coll., Monmouth, 1972, MS in Counseling, 1979; MEd in Adminstrn., Ariz. State U., Tempe, 1984. Tchr. Wy'East Jr. H.S., Hood River, Oreg., 1971-72; illustrations/rev. clk. RMC Mgmt., Portland, Oreg., 1972-73; head tchr. UDESEA Prep. Sch., Stuttgart, West Germany, 1973-75; counselor Heppner (Oreg.) High Sch., 1976-83; tchr. math. South Umpqua High Sch., Myrtle Creek, Oreg., 1984-85; counselor, vice prin. Riddle (Oreg.) Sch. Dist., 1985-87; counselor Cottage Grove (Oreg.) High Sch., 1987—; Bd. dirs. Oreg. Assn. Student Couns., 1991—, presentations and camp dir., 1981—. Mem. steering com. Com. to Elect Jim Gilroy, Cottage Grove, 1993-94; mem. Drug Action Coun., Cottage Grove, 1987-91. Mem. Oreg. Edn. Assn., Bohemia Sunriser Kiwanis (pres., sec., lt. gov. 1994-95, Disting. Pres. award 1991), Phi Delta Kappa. Roman Catholic.

PORTNOY, MERI, nurse; b. Afula, Israel, May 8, 1950; came to the U.S., 1974; d. Chaim Giladi and Ruth (Feit) Giladi-Meron; m. Yoav Portnoy, Dec. 26, 1972; 1 child, Edan. RN diploma, Hasharon Hosp., Petach-Tikva, Israel, 1972; B in Liberal Studies, Lesley Coll., 1994. Sec. Israel Legetion, South Africa, 1973-74, Israeli Embassy, Washington, 1974-75; nurse Dr. Evrett Gordon, Washington, 1975-76; nurse Dialysis Clinic Renal Treatment Ctr., Rockville, Md., 1986—; nurse dialysis dept. Shady Grove Adventist Hosp., Rockville, 1991—; nurse Dialysis Clinic, Biomed. Application, Bethesda, Md., 1976-84; cardiac critical care unit nurse George Washington U. Hosp., Washington, 1980; kidney transplant nurse Georgetown U. Hosp., Washington, 1984-86; real estate sales agt. Long and Foster Real Estate, 1986-87. Mem. Jewish Cmty. Ctr., 1975—, Hadassa-Women Orgn. Hebrew Speaking Br., 1992—; sec. Weizman Inst. Funds Raising Office, Washington, 1989; dir. asst., actress Jewish Repertory Theatre, Md., 1994—. Democrat. Home: 6328 Montrose Rd Rockville MD 20852

PORUBCAN, JUDIANN WILKOWSKI, nurse practitioner; b. Milw., May 16, 1953; d. Raymond E. and Elizabeth A. (Dunlap) P. BSN, U. Wis., Milw., 1975; MSN, U. Fla., 1981. RN, Fla., Wis. Staff nurse VAMC, Gainesville, Fla., 1978-87, home health coord., 1987-89, nurse mgr. emergency svcs., 1989-90, nurse practitioner hosp. based home health care, 1990-93; nurse practitioner rehab. and geriatrics Indpls. VAMC, 1993—. Mem. ANA, AACN (cert. adult and gerontol. nurse practitioner), Emergency Nurse's Assn., Fla. Nurse's Assn., Ind. Gerontol. Nurses Assn. (bd. dirs.), Sigma Theta Tau.

POSEN, SUSAN ORZACK, lawyer; b. N.Y.C., Nov. 5, 1945. BA, Sarah Lawrence Coll., 1967; JD, Bklyn. Law Sch., 1978. Bar: N.Y. 1979. Assoc. Stroock & Stroock & Lavan, N.Y.C., 1978-83, 84-86; ptnr. Stroock, Stroock & Lavan, N.Y.C., 1987—; asst. gen. counsel Cablevision Systems Corp., Woodbury, N.Y., 1983-84. Office: Stroock & Stroock & Lavan 7 Hanover Sq New York NY 10004-2616

POSER, JOAN RAPPS, artists agent; b. Plainfield, N.J., Apr. 10, 1940; d. Mandel Max and Marion Davidson Rapps; m. Jay Sanford Poser, Nov. 15, 1964; children: Lester Philip, Toby Anne. BA, U. Conn., 1962. Self-employed travel cons. Lancaster, Pa., 1976-79; tchr. McDonogh Sch., Balt., 1982-90; artist's agt. Joan E. Poser Assocs. Agts. in the Arts, Balt., 1978—; co-owner, v.p. Poser's Apparel, Inc., Pa., 1990-95; co-owner Poser's Accessories Sales Reps., 1995—. Pres. Lancaster Town Fair, 1974, Temple Beth El Sisterhood, 1973-77; pres. and devel. chmn. Md. Assocs. for Dyslexic Adults and Youth, Inc., 1989-91; campaign chair Bus. and Profl. Women, Assoc. Jewish Charities, Balt., 1985; spl. events chair Cultural Arts Inst. Chizuk Amuno Congregation, 1986-90, trustee, 1986-90; bd. dirs. Janus Sch., Lancaster, 1991—, Lancaster Jewish Community Ctr., 1991—, Temple Beth El, 1991—; chmn. Lancaster Jewish Community Ctr. 50th Anniv. Gala, 1994, Temple Beth El 50th Anniv. Gala, 1995. Mem. Hadassah. Democrat. Home: 119 Greenview Dr Lancaster PA 17601-4988

POSEY, ELIZABETH FITZGERALD, university dean, educator; b. Pecos, Tex., Apr. 26, 1940; d. Johnnie S. and Margaret Elizabeth (Duncan) Fitzgerald; m. John Mahoney, Sept. 19, 1959 (div. 1983); children—Teri, Tana; m. Bob Posey, Nov. 19, 1983. B.A., U. Ariz., 1965; M.Ed., Sul Ross State U., 1969; Ed.D., No. Ariz. U., 1979. Tchr. Balmorhea (Tex.) Elem. Sch., 1965-66, Alpine (Tex.) Elem. Sch., 1967-70; vocat. coordinator, cons. West Tex. Edn. Service Ctr., Region XVIII, 1970-71; counselor Ft. Stockton High Sch., 1971-72; career edn. coordinator Demonstration in Career Edn. Project, 1972-74; v.p. Career Edn. Media, Inc., 1974-78; career and affective edn. cons. Edn. Achievement Corp., 1974-75; v.p., mgmt. cons., program developer Synergistic Ednl. Systems, Inc., 1975-79; mem. part-time faculty Rio Salado Coll., Phoenix, 1979; asst. dean student life Sul Ross State U., Alpine, Tex., 1979-82, dean student life, 1982-84, asst. prof. edn., 1979-86; assoc. prof., coordinator field experiences, Ea. N.Mex. U., Portales, 1986-93; counselor Dexter (N.Mex.) Elem. Sch., 1992—; cons. and lectr. in field; counselor Neighborhood Youth Corps, 1969. Mem. adv. bd. Tri County Drug Edn. Program, 1980-81, Alpine Centennial Com., 1980-82. Recipient Sponsor-of-Yr. awards Sul Ross State U. Student Pres.'s Assn., 1981, 82, 83, 84; U.S. Dept. Edn. spl. services grantee, 1982-83, 83—; 4-H Club Parents Award, 1980; cert. of recognition Boy Scouts Am., 1981. Mem. ACA, ASCD (exec. bd. 1993—), Assn. Humanistic Edn. and Devel., Nat. Career Devel. Assn. (del. 1979), Am. Vocat. Assn., Tex. Counseling Assn., N.Mex. Counseling Assn., N.Mex. Assn. Supervision and Curriculum (affiliated pres., exec. bd., excellence in edn. award, 1994), Ea. N.Mex. Research and Study Council, Permian Basin Counselors Assn. (Outstanding Service award, 1986-87), Phi Delta Kappa, Kappa Delta Pi (Omnicron Upsilon chpt. sponsor). Democrat. Contbr. articles to profl. jours. Home: PO Box 307 Hagerman NM 88232-0307 Office: Dexter Consolidated Schs PO Box 159 Dexter NM 88230-0159

POSNER, KATHY ROBIN, communications executive; b. Oceanside, N.Y., Nov. 3, 1952; d. Melvyn and Davonne Hope (Hansen) P. BA in Journalism, Econs., Manhattanville Coll., 1974. Fin. planner John Dreyfus Corp., Purchase, N.Y., 1974-80; corp. liaison Gulf States Mortgage, Atlanta, 1980-82; dir. promotion Gammon's of Chgo., 1982-83; coordinator trade show mktg. Destron, Chgo., 1983-84; pres. Postronics, Chgo., 1984-87; v.p. Martin E. Janis & Co., Inc., Chgo., 1987-90; exec. v.p., chief exec. officer Communications 2000, Chgo., 1990—; pres., chief exec. officer Comm2 Inc. Editor: How to Maximize Your Profits, 1983; contbg. editor Internat. Backgammon Guide, 1974-84, Backgammon Times, 1981-84, Chgo. Advt. and Media; columnist Food Industry News. Bd. dirs. Chgo. Beautification Com., 1987, Concerned Citizens for Action, Chgo., 1987; mem. steering com. Better Boys Found.; campaign mgr. Brown for Alderman, Chgo., 1987. Mem. NOW, Women in Communication, Am. Soc. Profl. and Exec. Women, Mensa, Nat. Acad. TV Arts and Scis., The Acad. of Arts (v.p.), City Club of Chgo., Chgo. Area Pub. Affairs Group, Baderbrau Beer Drinking Soc. (v.p. pub. rels.), Cavendish North Club (bd. dirs. 1984-87), Gammon's Chgo. (bd. dirs. 1980-83 editor newsletter 1982-83), Met. Club, Plz. Club, Monroe Club, 410 Club. Republican. Jewish. Office: Sears Towers Ste 9750 Chicago IL 60606

POSNER, LINDA IRENE, government official; b. Balt., Feb. 6, 1939; d. Morris and Rosabelle (Hankin) Rosen; m. Allan Bernard Posner, Dec. 29, 1957; children: Larry Gregg, Michael Glenn, Robert Ira. BA summa cum laude, Coll. of Notre Dame, 1989. Dir., lectr. Montgomery Ward's Fashion, Modeling and Charm Sch., Md., 1962-66; fashion and pub. rels. dir. Montgomery Ward, Md., 1966-75; freelance writer Balt., 1975-76; pres., co-owner Designer's Circle Ltd., Balt., 1976-78; TV writer, producer Dept. of Def., Ft. Meade, Md., 1979-87; TV mgr. Dept. Def., Ft. Meade, Md., 1980-87, sr. edn. and tng. mgr., 1987-91, performance technologist, 1991-94, multi-media ops. mgr., 1994—; regional dir. The Fashion Group, Balt., 1972-74. Mem. com. March of Dimes, Balt., 1976-78; chairperson Combined Fed. Campaign Com., 1987, U.S. Savs. Bonds, 1989. Dept. of Def. scholar, 1987-88. Mem. Women in Communications, Human Resources Mgmt. Assn., AFTRA. Jewish. Home: 11008 Valley Heights Dr Owings Mills MD 21117-3055

POSS, MARY CANADA, civic leader; b. Dallas, Oct. 25, 1951; d. William Ralph and Eula Belle (Key) Canada; m. James Michael Poss, June 16, 1973. BBA in Mgmt., U. Tex., 1973. Sr. work measurement analyst Mercantile Nat. Bank at Dallas, 1976-78, rsch. and devel. analyst, 1978-80, ops. officer and mgr., 1980, asst. v.p. and mgr., 1980-82; v.p. and dist. calling officer InterFirst Bank Dallas, N.A., 1982-84; dir. Greater Dallas Crime Commn., 1990-92; campaign worker Perot Petition Com., Dallas, 1992; dir. Mayors United on Safety, Crime and Law Enforcement, Dallas, 1992—. Exec. com. Greater Dallas Crime Commn., 1992—; Lakewood Elem. Sch. Community Coun., 1992— (chmn. budget com.); adv. bd. dirs. Tex. Community Bank, 1989-92; v.p. programs Greater Dallas Planning Coun.; candidate for Dallas City Coun., 1989; City of Dallas Internat. Ambassador of Dallas Com., 1990-91; adv. bd. Children's Advocacy Ctr. of Dallas; Mayor Strauss' Coun. on Intergovernmental Affairs, 1989-91, bd. of mgmt. East Dallas C. of C., 1989-91; cons. Dallas chpt. Young Pres.'s Orgn.; bd. dirs. Lakewood C. of C., 1988-91. Recipient Dallas Police Officers' Choice award, 1990, Gov.'s award for Crime Prevention, 1991. Mem. Dallas Friday Group, Dallas Coun. on World Affairs (chmn. mayors' summit juvenile violence 1994), Dallas Mus. of Art, Diana Dean Head Injury Guild, Downtown Dallas Rotary Club. Home: 6405 Mercedes Dallas TX 75214

POST, BARBARA JOAN, elementary education educator; b. Passaic, N.J., June 29, 1930; d. John Ward and Florence Barbara (Barnum) Post; m. Edward Wayne Poppele, Apr. 10, 1954 (dec. Mar. 1978); children: E. Scott Poppele, Sara Elizabeth Poppele, Andrew John Poppele. BSE, William Paterson Coll., 1953; cert. in counseling, Rutgers U., 1981; postgrad., Columbia U., 1983, Northeastern U., 1983. Cert. tchr., N.J. Elem. tchr. Cen. Sch., Glen Ridge, N.J., 1953-55, Middletown (N.J.) Village Sch., 1956, Our Lady of Perpetual Help, Highlands, N.J., 1981-85; reading tchr. Monmouth Reading Ctr., Long Branch, N.J., 1985; tchr. gifted/talented Harmony Sch., Middletown, 1987-88; edn. coord. for Monmouth County Nat. Coun. on Alcoholism, Freehold, N.J., 1988-89; coord. math./sci. consortium Brookdale Community Coll., Lincroft, N.J., 1989-90; tchr., owner Learning Post and Creative Garden of Art for Children, Middletown, 1991—; dir. art Hillel Sch., Ocean, N.J., 1991—; dir.-owner Learning Post, Middletown, 1986—; art tchr. Art Alliance of Monmouth County, Red Bank, N.J., 1986-88. Author: (poem) The Lift, 1988 (short story) Sarah-Grand, 1984, Hooked on the Classics, 1988; artist (program cover) Country Christmas, 1990, 91. Demonstrator Family Reading Fair, Lincroft, 1989; participant Muscular Dystrophy Telethon, Eatontown, N.J., 1986. Mem. AAUW (tchr., mentor for teen women 1989-92, Appreciation award 1989-90), Nat. Soc. DAR (chairperson 1961-62), N.J. Shore Rose Soc. (exhibitor, 2d and 3d prize for roses 1986). Republican. Presbyterian. Home: 14 Oakland St Red Bank NJ 07701

POST, EMILY (ELIZABETH LINDLEY POST), author; b. Englewood, N.J., May 7, 1920; d. Allen L. and Elizabeth (Ellsworth) Lindley; m. George E. Cookman, 1941 (dec. 1943); 1 child, Allen C.; m. William G. Post, Aug. 5, 1944; children: William G., Lucinda Post Senning, Peter L. Grad. high sch. Dir. Emily Post Inst., 1965—. Author: Emily Post's Book of Etiquette for Young People, 1968, Wonderful World of Weddings, 1970, Please Say Please, 1972, Emily Post's Etiquette, 1965, rev. edit. 1992, The Complete Book of Entertaining, 1981, Emily Post's Complete Book of Wedding Etiquette, 1982, rev. edit., 1991, Emily Post Talks with Teens about Manners and Etiquette, 1986, Emily Post on Weddings, 1987, Emily Post on Entertaining, 1987, Emily Post on Etiquette, 1987, Emily Post on Invitations and Letters, 1990, Emily Post on Business Etiquette, 1990, Emily Post on Second Weddings, 1991, Emily Post's Wedding Planner, rev. edit., 1991, Emily Post's Table Manners For Today: Advice For Every Dining Occasion, 1994, Emily Post on Guests and Hosts, 1994; contbg. editor: Good Housekeeping Mag. Republican. Episcopalian. Office: Good Housekeeping Hearst Corp 959 8th Ave New York NY 10019-3737*

POST, JUDY, director of administration; b. Bedford, Ohio, Jan. 12, 1959; d. James Peter and Dorothy Jane (Malley) Kukla; m. Rex W. Post, Aug. 23, 1983 (div. May 1990); 1 child, Taylor Lauren. BS in bus. admin., Baldwin Wallace Coll., 1991. Admin. asst. Fabricated Metal Specialties, Walton Hills, Ohio, 1977-82; admin. asst. Ecotran Corp., Beachwood, Ohio, 1982-84, acct. mgr., 1984-89, dir. adminstrn., 1989—. Mem. Soc. Human Resource Mgmt., The Growth Assn. Republican. Office: Ecocenters Corp 31225 Bainbridge Rd Solon OH 44139

POST, MARKIE, actress; b. Palo Alto, Calif., Nov. 4, 1950; d. Richard and Marylee Post; m. Michael Ross; 1 child, Kate. BA, Lewis and Clark Coll. Researcher TV game show Split Second; assoc. producer game show Double Dare, 1976-77; actress, 1977—. Actress: (stage prodns.) Joe Egg, The Fantastiks, The Hairy Ape, Guys and Dolls, (TV shows) Masquerade Party, Frankie and Annette - the Second Time Around, (TV series) Semi-Tough, 1980, The Gangster Chronicles, 1981, The Fall Guy, 1982-85, Night Court, 1985-92, Hearts Afire, 1992—, (TV movies) Not Just Another Affair, 1982, Triple Cross, 1986, Glitz, 1988, Tricks of the Trade, 1988. Mem. AFTRA, Screen Actors Guild. Office: care Jon Carrasco Sterling/Withers Co 4044 Melrose Ave 3d Flr Los Angeles CA 90069*

POST, ROSE ZIMMERMAN, newspaper columnist; b. Morganton, N.C., Oct. 2, 1926; d. Samuel Sinai and Anna (Pliskin) Zimmerman; m. Edward Martin Post, July 8, 1947; children: David Bruce, Phyllis Post Lebowitz, Samuel Michael, Jonathan Alan, Anna Susan. BA, U. N.C., Greensboro, 1948; postgrad., U. N.C., 1972-74; LittD (hon.), Catawba Coll., 1981. Reporter Salisbury (N.C.) Post, 1951-83, columnist, 1983—; adj. prof. journalism Catawba Coll., Salisbury, 1988-89. Mem. Temple Israel PTA, Salisbury, 1950-80s; bd. dirs. Nat. Coun. Jewish Women; various offices numerous orgns. Recipient Ernie Pyle award Scripps Howard News, 1989, O Henry award N.C. Associated Press News Coun., 1991, 92, N.C. Working Press Excellence in Writing award, 1988, 89, 90, 93; named Citizen of Yr. Salisbury Civitan Club, 1976, Woman of Achievement Salisbury A&PW, 1971. Mem. AAUW, NCCJ, Nat. Assn. Newspaper Columnists (1st pl. for gen. columns 1994), N.C. Press Women (sec. 1983, 2d v.p. 1984, 1st v.p. 1985, pres. 1986), N.C. Press Club. Democrat. Jewish. Home: 125 E Corriher Ave Salisbury NC 28144-2427 Office: Salisbury Post 131 W Innes St Salisbury NC 28144

POSTERARO, CATHERINE HAMMOND, librarian, gerontology educator; b. Hartford, Conn., Nov. 13, 1946; d. Joseph Francis and Elizabeth Claire (Desmond) Hammond; m. Anthony Francis Posteraro, Jr., June 20, 1970; children: Anthony Francis III, Christopher Clarke. AB, Emmanuel Coll., Boston, 1968; MS, Simmons Coll., 1970; MA, St. Joseph Coll., West Hartford, Conn., 1992. Asst. libr. dir., asst. prof. acad. resources St. Joseph Coll., 1986—, lectr. gerontology, 1991—; mem. continuing edn. com. Capitol Region Libr. Coun., Windsor, Conn., 1990—. Recipient Sister Mary Elizabeth Delice award Inst. Gerontology, St. Joseph Coll., 1992. Mem. ALA, Assn. Coll. and Rsch. Librs. (nat. com. Instrn. for Diverse Population 1994-97), Conn. Libr. Assn., Gerontol. Soc. Am., Sigma Phi Omega (nat. acad. hon. soc. gerontology). Home: 24 McDivitt Dr Manchester CT 06040 Office: St Joseph Coll Libr 1678 Asylum Ave West Hartford CT 06117

POST-GORDEN, JOAN CAROLYN, psychology educator; b. Oak Park, Ill., July 3, 1932; d. DeWitt T. and Mary Jane (Lewellen) Post; children: Gregrey Wayne, Jeffrey Scott, Kayle Lynn, Tamara Anne. BS, Manchester (Ind.) Coll., 1964; MS, U. Ga., 1967, PhD, 1970. Lic. psychologist, Colo. Tchr. Clarke County Schs., Athens, Ga., 1964-65; part-time asst. prof. Tex. Tech U., Lubbock, 1968-69; instr. So. Colo. State Coll., Pueblo, 1970-71; asst. prof. U. So. Colo., Pueblo, 1971-76, assoc. prof., 1976-81, prof., 1981—, chmn. dept., 1991—; asst. to city mgr., Champaign, Ill., 1980-81; psychologist So. Ctrl. Ill. Devel. Dist., Flora, 1979-80; dir. scholarly and creative activities U. So. Colo., 1988-91. Contbr. chpt. to book and articles to profl. jours. NDEA fellow, 1964-66, Danforth teaching fellow, 1978, faculty fellow Colo. State Div. Mental Health, 1986-87. Mem. APA, Soc. for Rsch. in Child Devel., Rocky Mountain Psychol. Assn., Colo. Psychol. Assn., Psi Chi, Sigma Xi, Alpha Omicron Pi. Home: 1021 Ruppel St Apt 31 Pueblo CO 81001-2559 Office: U So Colo Dept Psychology Pueblo CO 81001

POSTON, ANN GENEVIEVE, psychotherapist, nurse; b. Sioux City, Iowa, July 28, 1936; d. Frank Earl and Ella Marie (Stanton) Gales; m. Gerald Connell Poston, June 27, 1959; children: Gregory, Mary Ann, Susan. BSN, Briar Cliff Coll., 1958; MA, U. Mo., 1978; postgrad., Family Inst. of Kansas City, Inc., 1989-91. RN, Kans., Mo.; lic. counselor, Mo. Staff nurse, sr. team leader St. Joseph Mercy Hosp., Sioux City, 1958-59; head nurse St. Anthony's Hosp., Rock Island, Ill., 1960, charge nurse, 1966-69; charge nurse St. Mary's Hosp., Mpls., 1970-71, North Kansas City (Mo.) Hosp., 1972-73, Tri-County Mental Health Ctr., North Kansas City, 1973-79; psychotherapist VA Med. Ctr., Kansas City, 1979-84, Leavenworth, Kans., 1984-85; psychotherapist The Kans. Inst., Olathe, 1985-94; psychotherapist, marriage and family therapist Psychiatry Assocs., Overland Park, Kans., 1994—; cons. Synergy House, Parkville, Mo., 1974-75, North Kansas City Hosp., 1978-79, VA Hosps., Kansas City and Leavenworth, 1979-85, Cath. Charities, Kansas City, 1983-87, Olathe Med. Ctr., 1985—, Humana Med. Ctr. Overland Park, Kans., 1986—, St. Joseph Med. Ctr., Kansas City, Mo., 1990—. Author, presenter (video) Depression & Suicide, 1980. Third officer King's Daus., Moline, Ill., 1960-69; campaign worker Rep. Party, Moline, 1963-68; community asst. New Mark Community Affairs, Kansas City, 1972-76; nursing rep. Combined Fed. Campaign, Kansas City, 1982; coord. mental health program com. Midwest Health Congress, Kansas City, 1981. Mem. ACA, ANA (cert.), Internat. Assn. for Marriage and Family Counselors, Am. Assn. Marriage and Family Therapy (clinical), Nat. Bd. Cert. Counselors, Mo. Assn. Marriage and Family Therapy, Sigma Theta Tau. Roman Catholic. Office: The Kans Inst 20375 W 151st St Ste 206 Olathe KS 66061-5360

POSUNKO, BARBARA, elementary education educator; b. Newark, July 17, 1938; d. Joseph and Mary (Prystauk) P. BA, Rutgers U., Newark, 1960;

MA, Kean Coll., Union, N.J., 1973; teaching cert., Seton Hall U., Newark, 1966. Cert. elem. tchr., reading specialist, N.J. Social case worker Newark City Hosp., 1960-65; elem. tchr. Plainfield (N.J.) Bd. Edn., 1966; elem., jr. and sr. high sch. tchr. minimum basic skills and reading Sayreville (N.J.) Bd. Edn., 1966-82; tchr. Chpt. I and minimum basic skills Sayreville (N.J.) Bd. Edn., Parlin, 1982—, cooperating tchr. to student tchrs., 1983—, coord. testing, 1984—; sch. coord. for congressionally mandated study of ednl. growth and opportunity, 1991—; mem. numerous reading coms. Recipient Outstanding Tchr. award N.J. Gov.'s Tchr. Recognition Program, 1988. Mem. NEA, Internat. Reading Assn., N.J. Reading Assn., N.J. Edn. Assn. Home: 17 Drake Rd Mendham NJ 07945-1805

POSUNKO, LINDA MARY, elementary education educator; b. Newark, Dec. 24, 1942; d. Joseph and Mary (Prystauk) P. BA, Newark State Coll., Union, N.J., 1964; MA, Kean Coll., Union, 1974. Cert. permanent elem. tchr., supr., prin., N.J. Elem. tchr. Roselle (N.J.) Bd. Edn., 1964-65; elem. tchr. Garwood (N.J.) Bd. Edn., 1965-92, head tchr., 1974-76, 79-81, head tchr. elem. and early childhood edn., tchr. 1st grade, 1992—; cooperating tchr. to student tchrs.; instr. non-English speaking students and children with learning problems; mem. affirmative action, sch. resource coms.; conductor in-svc. workshops on early childhood devel. practices, 1993. Recipient honor cert. Union County Conf. Tchrs. Assn., 1972-73, Garwood Tchr. of Yr. award, 1983, Outstanding Tchr. award N.J. Gov.'s Tchr. Recognition Program, 1988; named one of 2000 Am. Notable Women. Mem. ASCD, NEA, Internat. Reading Assn. (bd. dirs. suburban coun.), N.J. Edn. Assn., Garwood Tchrs. Assn. (sec., v.p., pres.), High/Scope Ednl. Found. Home: 17 Drake Rd Mendham NJ 07945-1805

POTASEK, MARY JOYCE, physicist, researcher; b. Mpls., Oct. 27, 1945; d. Chester and Millie Potasek. BA in Math., Coll. St. Catherine, 1967; MS in Physics, U. Ill., 1970, PhD, 1974. Research asst. U. Ill., Urbana, 1970-74; research scientist Internat. Bus. Machines, Watson Research Ctr., Yorktown Heights, N.Y., 1974-75; NSF, AAUW postdoctoral fellow Princeton (N.J.) U., 1975-78; NATO postdoctoral fellow Max Planck Inst., Gottingen, West Germany, 1978-80; mem. tech. staff AT&T, Princeton, 1980-86, AT&T Bell Labs., Murray Hill, N.J., 1986-90, Columbia U., N.Y.C., 1990—. Contbr. articles to profl. jours. Mem. AAAS, Optical Soc. of Am., Am. Phys. Soc., Phi Beta Kappa, Pi Mu Epsilon. Home: 197 Dodds Ln Princeton NJ 08540-4105

POTASH, JANE, artist; b. Phila., May 3, 1937; d. Norval and Mary (Fox) Levy; m. Charles Potash, Jan. 21, 1962; children: Andrew Samuel, Dorothy Frances. BA, U. Pa., 1959. One-woman shows include Storelli Gallery, Phila., 1979, Langman Gallery, Jenkintown, Pa., 1979, 81, Phoenix Gallery, N.Y., 1981, A.R.T. Beasley Gallery, San Diego, 1986, Vorpal, N.Y., 1987; exhibited in group shows at Wayne Art Ctr., 1971, Lancaster Summer Arts Festival, 1971, 72, 74, Cooperstown (N.Y.) Nat. Juried Show, 1971, Abington Art Ctr., 1972-74, Phila. Art Alliance, 1975, Allentown Art Mus., 1976, Pa. Acad. Fine Arts, 1978, 80, Butcher and More Gallery, Phila., 1981, Wachs Davis Gallery, Washington, Shayne Gallery, Montreal, Can., 1982, Montreal Mus. Fine Arts, 1982, Source Gallery, San Francisco, 1983, Langman Gallery, 1987, Virginia Miller Gallery, Coral Gables, Fla., 1990; represented in collections at Fox Companies, Blue Cross, Blue Shield of Pa., Subaru, N.J., Nordstrom Stores, Calif., Beaver Ins. Co., San Francisco; represented in pvt. collections in U.S. and Can. Recipient Best of Show award Old York Rd. Studio: 220 Old York Rd Jenkintown PA 19046

POTASH, JEREMY WARNER, public relations executive; b. Monrovia, Calif., June 30, 1946; d. Fenwick Bryson and Joan Antony (Blair) Warner; m. Stephen Jon Potash, Oct. 19, 1969; 1 child, Aaron Warner. AA, Citrus Coll., 1965; BA, Pomona Coll., 1967. With Forbes Mag., N.Y.C., 1967-69, Japan External Trade Orgn., San Francisco, 1970-75; v.p., co-founder Potash & Co. Comm. and Rsch., San Francisco, 1980-87, pres., 1987—; founding exec. dir. Calif.-S.E. Asia Bus. Coun., Oakland, 1991—; exec. dir. Customs Brokers and Forwarders Assn., San Francisco, 1990—; bd. dirs. Judah L. Magnes Mus., Berkeley, 1981-94, co-founder docent program, 1980, pres. Women's Guild, 1980-81; bd. dirs. Temple Sinai, Oakland, 1984-86; pres. East Bay region Women's Am. Orgn. for Rehab. Through Tng., 1985-86. Mem. Am. Soc. Assn. Execs., World Trade Club San Francisco, Book Club Calif., Oakland Women's Lit. Soc. Pres. Women's Guild Judah L. Magnes Mus., Berkeley, 1980-81, co-founder docent program, 1980, bd. dirs., 1981-94; pres. East Bay region Women's Am. ORT, 1985-86. Mem. Am. Soc. Assn. Execs., World Trade Club San Francisco, Book Club Calif., Oakland Women's Lit. Soc. Office: Potash & Co Comm & Rsch 1946 Embarcadero Oakland CA 94606

POTEET, MARY JANE, computer scientist; b. Raleigh, N.C., May 26, 1946; d. Charles William and Geraldine Lucile (Adams) Hampton; m. William Walter Schubert, Dec. 30, 1967 (div. June 1979); children: Kristen, Stephen, Betsy, Kathryn; m. H. Wesley Poteet, Mar. 21, 1991. BA in Math., Park Coll., 1967. Programmer U. Mo. Med. Ctr., Columbia, 1968-72, City and County of Denver, 1979-80; sr. sys. programmer Citicorp Person to Person, Denver, 1980-82; sys. support rep. Software AG, NA, Denver, 1982-83; prin. info. sysm. specialist Idaho Nat. Engring. Lab., EG&G, Idaho Falls, 1983-89; adv. svcs. specialist IBM Profl. Svcs., Albuquerque, 1989-91; field mgr. IBM Svc., Boulder, Colo., 1991-93; project mgr. IBM Cons. & Svcs. SW, Denver, 1993—; presenter career workshop for girls No. Colo. U., Greeley, 1993. Leader Girl Scouts U.S.A., Pocatello, Idaho and Columbia, Mo., 1969-79, Idaho Falls, 1986-89, cluster leader, Rigby, Idaho, 1988-89; mem. Albuquerque Civic Chorus, 1990-91; bd. dirs., mem. LWV, Pocatello, Idaho, 1977-79, 84-85, pres., 1978-79; bd. dirs. Luth. Ch. Women, Pocatello, 1978-79; youth advisor Luth. Ch., Idaho Falls, 1984-89; tchr. Sunday sch. local ch., Albuquerque, 1990-91; youth com. chairwoman local ch., Boulder, Colo., 1994; mem. Ch. Coun., 1994; tchr. 7th grade Sunday sch., 1993-94. Lutheran. Home: 3916 W 104th Pl Westminster CO 80030

POTENZA, DAISY MCKASKLE, newspaper executive; b. Houston, Mar. 5, 1906; d. George Washington and Dora Amy (Crump) McKaskle; student Sinclair Bus. Coll., 1925, Massey's Bus. Coll., 1924-26, U. Houston; m. Julius Orian Potenza, Sept. 26, 1928; 1 dau., Marjorie Ann (Mrs. William L. Hale) (dec.). With Houston Chronicle, 1926-87, adminstrv. asst. to editor-in-chief, 1930-79, adminstrv. asst. to sr. v.p. and cons., 1979-87, cons. for spl. assignments, 1994—. Exec. sec. Houston Endowment, Inc., 1968-69; bd. dirs. Pin Oak Charity Horse Show, 1978, 79, 80, 81, 82, 83, 84. Recipient award United Fund, 1967—; tribute for exec. service to Chronicle, 1983; outstanding ticket sales awardee Pin Oak Charity Horse Show, Tex. Children's Hosp., 1975-83, 84. Mem. Nat., Tex. press women, Women in Communications, Press Club Houston (hon. life). Methodist. Club: Farm and Ranch. Home: 2405 San Felipe St Houston TX 77019-3403 Office: 801 Texas Ave Houston TX 77002

POTTER, CHARLOTTE ANN, health education educator, physical education educator; b. Sept. 21, 1943; d. Charles Douglas and Jessie (Lewallen) Faulkner; m. Gary D. Potter, Dec. 24, 1962; 1 child, Bill Douglas. BS in Health and Phys. Edn., Tex. A&M U., 1972, MS in Health and Phys. Edn., 1975. With Westinghouse Corp., 1965; sec. dept. microbiology U. Ky., 1966-67; sec. dept. poultry sci. Tex. A&M U., 1968-69, tchr. dept. phys. edn., 1973; tchr. health and phys. edn. dept. College Station Ind. Schs., A&M Consolidated High Sch., 1973—, dept. head health and phys. edn., coord. intramurals, 1973—, student tchr. supr., 1974—; guest lectr. Tex. A&M U., College Station, 1993—. Adult leader Equestrian 4-H Club, 1971-83; vol. College Station Little League Baseball, 1971-81; vol. sch. health College Station Ind. Sch. Dist., 1972, com. chmn. PTO South Knoll, 1972-76; cardiopulmonary resuscitation instr. vol., 1972—; vol. Tex. A&M U. Horseman's Assn., 1982—; vol. Phoebe's Home Toy, 1989—. Mem. AAHPER, NEA, Nat. Assn. Secondary Sch. Prins., Am. Heart Assn., Assn. for Advancement Health Edn., Tex. AHPERD, Tex. Edn. Assn., College Station Edn. Assn., Ctrl. Tex. Assn. Student Coun. Sponsors, Tex. Assn. Student Coun. Sponsors, Tex. A&M Assn. Former Students, Am. Sch. Health Assn., Tex. Sch. Health Assn., Ctrl. Tex. Long Ears Assn., Am. Donkey and Mule Assn., S.W. Donkey and Mule Assn., Gulf Coast Donkey and Mule Assn., Delta Psi Kappa, Delta Kappa Gamma. Home: 5609 Straub Rd College Station TX 77845-6966

POTTER, DEBORAH ANN, news correspondent, educator; b. Hagerstown, Md., June 10, 1951; d. Peter R. and H. Louise (McDevitt) P.; m. Robert H. Witten, May 1, 1982; children: Cameron, Evan. BA, U. N.C., 1972; MA, Am. U., 1977. Assignment editor Sta. WMAL-TV, Washington, 1972-73, prodr., 1973-74; reporter Voice of Am., Washington, 1974-77; anchor Sta. KYW, Phila., 1977-78, CBS Radio, N.Y.C., 1978-81; White House corr. CBS News, Washington, 1981-85, state dept. corr., 1985-87, congl. corr., 1987-89, environ. corr., 1989-91; contbg. corr. 48 Hours, 1989-90; host Nightwatch CBS News, Washington, 1991; Washington corr. Cable News Network, Washington, 1991-94; asst. prof. Sch. Comm. Am. U., Washington, 1994—; vis. faculty Poynter Inst. Media Studies. Host (video prodn.) Beyond the Spotted Owl, 1993, Health Beat, 1994. Mem. adv. coun. Environ. Journalism Ctr., Radio and TV News Dirs. Found., Washington, 1994—; lay reader St. Alban's Episc. Ch., Washington, 1988-89. Mem. U. N.C. Alumni Assn. (bd. dirs. 1990-93, Disting. Young Alumna award 1990). Office: Am U Sch Comm 4400 Massachusetts Ave NW Washington DC 20015

POTTER, EMMA JOSEPHINE HILL, language educator; b. Hackensack, N.J., July 18, 1921; d. James Silas and Martha Loretta (Pyle) Hill; m. James H. Potter, Mar. 26, 1949. AB cum laude with honors in Classics (scholar), Alfred (N.Y.) U., 1943; AM, Johns Hopkins U., 1946. Tchr. Latin, Balt. County Pub. Schs., 1943-44; instr. French, Spanish, Balt. Poly. Inst., 1950-83; instr. Spanish adult edn. classes, 1946-48; treas. Bruno-Potter Inc., acctg. Trustee James Harry Potter Gold Medal, ASME. Mem. Johns Hopkins U., Alfred U. alumni assns., Internat. Platform Assn., Johns Hopkins U. Faculty Club. Democrat. Home: 419 3rd Ave Avon By The Sea NJ 07717-1244

POTTER, JUNE ANITA, small business owner; b. La Crosse, Wis., Jan. 22, 1938; d. Christian John and Ethel Marie (Stafslien) Stefferud; m. James Oscar Potter, June 18, 1961; children: Jill Potter Rutlin, Todd. BA in Home Econs., St. Olaf Coll., Northfield, Minn., 1960; postgrad., N.Y. Sch. Interior Design, 1964; MS in Edn., U. Wis., Menomonie, 1977. Sr. high home econs. tchr., FHA advisor Tomah (Wis.) High Sch., 1960-64, Black River Falls (Wis.) High Sch., 1971-83; freelance interior designer Warrens, Wis., 1964—; ptnr., mgr. James Potter Cranberry Marsh, Inc., Warrens, 1968—. Co-pubr.: Warrens Centennial Book, 1968, Cranberry Centennial Book, 1989. Active various charitable orgns.; bd. dirs. Warrens Cranberry Festival, 1984—; mem. Warrens Area Bus. Assn., 1990—; sec. Wis. Cranberry Bd., Inc., 1990—; sec. Warren Mills Cemetery Assn., 1993—; mem. com. Wis. Alice in Dairyland Finale, 1993—; mem. Jellystone Campground and Ministry. Mem. AAUW (v.p. 1989—), NAFE, Wis. State Cranberry Growers Assn. (pub. rels. com. 1994—, mem. centennial com. 1988—), Tomah Pky. Garden Club, Beta Sigma Phi (officer, com. mem. 1962—, Nat. Order or Rose 1983, Silver Cir. award 1985, Girl of Yr.). Lutheran. Home and Office: RR 2 Box 12 Warrens WI 54666-9501

POTTER, KAREN ANN, international management executive, consultant; b. Canandaigua, N.Y., Nov. 2, 1949; d. Floyd John and Isabel Catherine (Bain) P.; m. John Weston Chamberlin, Nov. 17, 1979 (div. 1986). Diploma with honors, U. Rouen, France, 1970; BA in French, St. Lawrence U., 1971; M in Internat. Mgmt. with distinction, Thunderbird U., 1974. Product mgr. The Clorox Co., Oakland, Calif., 1975-81; sr. product mgr. Bacardi Imports Inc., Miami, Fla., 1981-83; acct. mgmt. supr. McCann-Erickson, San Francisco, 1984; v.p. Foremost Dairies Inc., San Francisco, 1985, The Christian Bros. Co., Santa Rosa, Calif., 1985-87; internat. mgmt. cons. San Francisco, 1988—; export devel. advisor Kenya Export Devel. Support Project USAID, Nairobi, Kenya, 1992-94; advisor Kenya Assn. Mfrs., 1992-94, Nairobi, Fresh Produce Exporters Assn., Nairobi, 1992-94, Horticultural Devel. Authority, Nairobi, 1992-94. Author: Burundi's Private Sector, 1991, Kenya's Private Sector, 1992-93; editor: Kenya's Horticultural Sector, 1992, Kenya's Export Markets Series, 1992-93. Mem. NAFE, Am. Bus. Assn., Kenya Mus. Soc.. Home: 344 Birdsall Pkwy Palmyra NY 14522

POTTER, LILLIAN FLORENCE, business executive secretary; b. Montreal, Que., Can., Oct. 19, 1912; came to U.S., 1934; naturalized citizen.; d. Thomas Joseph and Lily Rose (Robertson) Quirk; m. Theodore Edward Potter, July 20, 1932 (dec. Apr. 1980); children: Peter Edward, Stephen Thomas. Grad. high sch., Montreal, 1929, grad., 1931. Sr. sec. S.D. Warren div. Scott Paper Co., Westbrook, Maine, 1955-69, editor indsl. publ. S.D. Warren div., 1969-72; editor Nat. Antiques Rev. mag., Portland, Maine, 1972-77; exec. sec. Humboldt Portland Litho div. Humboldt Nat. Graphics, Inc., Fortuna, Calif., 1977—; free lance writer Guy Gannett Pub. Co., Portland, 1960-64. Author: (children's book) Once Upon an Autumn, 1984 (state 1st pl. award, nat. 3d pl. award), (antiques and collectibles) A Re-Introduction to Silver Overlay on Glass and Ceramics, 1992; co-author: (textbook, tchrs. manual) Foundations of Patient Care, 1981; asst. editor, N.E. dist. The Secretary mag., Profl. Secs. Internat., 1960-62; editor Maine Chpt. Bull., 1963-64. Recipient George Washington Honors medal Freedoms Found., Valley Forge, Pa., 1964, Sec. of Yr. award Portland chpt. Profl. Secs. Internat., 1967, Outstanding Svc. award State of Maine Sesquicentennial, 1970, Outstanding Svc. award Island Pond (Vt.) Hist. Soc. 1978. Mem. Maine Media Women (pres. 1970-71, Woman of Yr. 1973, Communicator of Achievement plaque and prize 1991), Maine Writers and Pubs. Alliance, Women's Lit. Union, Portland Lyric Theater, Island Pond Hist. Soc., Jones Mus. Glass and Ceramics, Westbrook Women's Club, Order Eastern Star (past matron, past pres.). Republican. Episcopalian. Home: 80 Payson St Portland ME 04102-2851

POTTER, LYNDA K., art educator; b. Salamanca, N.Y., Sept. 21, 1942; d. William Glenn and B. Pauline (Atkins) Hogue; m. Steven L. Potter, June 21, 1959; children: Michael William, Marilyne Leigh, Nanette Jeanne, Matthew Christian. AA, Reading Community Coll., Reading, Pa., 1982. Instr. painting Albright Coll. Continuing Edn., Reading, 1980-82; instr. watercolor Rock Run Camps, Coventry, Pa., 1986—; instr. drawing Reading Community Coll., 1989; instr. painting, artist in residence Lynda Potter Art Gallery, City Mktg. Art Ctr., Savannah, Ga., 1991-95; instr. Creative Center, U. S.C., Beaufort, S.C., 1995—; represented by Lynda Potter Art Gallery, City Mktg. Art Ctr., Savannah, Ga., Char-Tel Gallery, Reading, Pink House Gallery, Hilton Head Island, S.C.; pres. Madison Co-op Gallery, Reading, Pa., 1988-89; juried into Gallery 209, Savannah, Ga., 1994; instr. watercolor workshop Hilton Head (S.C.) Art League, 1991-94. One-woman shows include Morgantown Libr., Pa., 1978, Bank of Boyertown, Pa., 1981, Reading Area C.C., Reading, 1986, Wyomissing Inst. Fine Art, Pa., 1983, 87, United Ways of Berks County, Pa., 1979, 89, Foulkeways, Gwynedd, Pa., 1991, Bluffton Libr., S.C., 1991, Hilton Head Art League, S.C., 1991, Kendal at Longwood, Kennett Square, Pa., 1991, U. Club, Wichita Falls, Tex., 1992, Pink House Gallery, Hilton Head, S.C., 1992, Heyward St. Gallery, Bluffton, S.C., 1994; exhibited in group shows at Berks County Art Coun. (award), 1981, Pottstown Art Guild, Pa., (award), 1982, Reading Pub. Mus., Pa., 1982, 83, 89, Penn. State Nitany Lions Show, Pa., 1984, 85, 87, 88, York Art Assn, Pa. (award), 1989, Pa. Watercolor Soc., 1989, (award) 94, Beaufort Art Assn. (award, 1st prize 1993), 1990, 91, 92, 93, Hilton Head Art League (award), 1991, 92, 93, Savannah Art Assn. (4 merit awards), 1992, 93, 94, City Market Art Ctr. Gallery, Savannah, 1990-94, Collectors Choice Gallery, 1993, Visual Arts Ctr., Fla., 1994, Piccolo Spoleto Art Show, Charleston, S.C., 1993, 94, 95; co-author: Bluffton Sketches, 1994. Study chairperson LWV, Lake County, Ill., 1969-70; elder Presbyn. Ch., REading, Pa., 1988-94, Low Country Presbyn. Ch., Bluffton, S.C., 1994—. Mem. Hilton Head Art League (workshop dir. 1990, bd. dirs. 1994), Savannah Art Assn., S.C. Watercolor Soc., Pa. Watercolor Soc., Beaufort Art Assn., Berks Art Alliance (pres. 1981), Beaufort Art Assn., Soc. of Bluffton Artists (pres. 1994-95). Home: 200 Whiteoaks Cir Bluffton SC 29910

POTTER, TANYA JEAN, lawyer; b. Washington, Oct. 30, 1956; d. John Francis and Tanya Agnes (Kristof) P. BA, Georgetown U., 1978, JD, 1981. Bar: D.C. 1982, U.S. Ct. Appeals (D.C. cir.), U.S. Ct. Appeals (fed. cir.), U.S. Dist. Ct. (D.C. dist.), U.S. Ct. Internat. Trade. Assoc. Ragan and Mason, Washington, 1981-88; atty.-adviser Office of Chief Counsel for Import Adminstrn., U.S. Dept. Commerce, Washington, 1989-92; mediator D.C. Superior Ct., 1982-84. Author: Practicing Before the Federal Maritime Commission, 1986, supplement, 1988, Preferentiality under the Proposed Commerce Department Regulations, 1990, Oil Refining in U.S. Foreign-Trade Zones, 1990. Recipient Community Service Recognition award ARC, Washington, 1986. Mem. ABA, Bar Assn. of D.C. (exec. coun. ad law sect. 1985-89).

POTTLE, CONNIE SUE, librarian; b. Denver, Feb. 15, 1953; d. Jack T. and Rita (Whelan) P. BA, U. Oreg., 1974, MLS, 1975. Children's libr. Memphis-Shelby County Pub. Libr., 1975-77, coord. youth svcs., 1988—; children's libr. Dallas Pub. Libr., 1977-81, br. mgr., 1981-87; storyteller Delta Rising, Memphis, 1988—; artist Memphis City Schs., 1990-91; dir. storytelling festival Voices of Excellence, 1984-86. Compiler: Trippin' thru Dallas, 1981; coord., storyteller weekly cable TV show Storytime, 1982; mem. adv. bd. Memphis Parent Newsletter, 1990. Crisis counselor Dallas Working Against Rape, 1977-87; mem. Dallas Pub. Libr. Cable TV Bd., 1982, Mayor's Task Force on Latchkey Children, Dallas, 1985, Memphis-Shelby County Children and Youth Coun., 1989. Recipient Children's and Young Adult Round Table Svc. award Tenn. Libr. Assn., 1994; named Libr. of Yr., Memphis Libr. Coun., 1992. Mem. ALA (notable books com. 1992—, preschool svcs. and parent edn. com. 1989-92, Caldecott award com. 1988), Dallas Storytelling Guild (co-founder, pres. 1985-87), Tejas Storytelling Assn. (bd. dirs. 1985-86, John Henry Faulk Storytelling award 1987). Office: Memphis-Shelby County Pub Libr 1850 Peabody Ave Memphis TN 38104-4021

POTTORFF, JO ANN, state legislator; b. Wichita, Kans., Mar. 7, 1936; d. John Edward McCluggage and Helen Elizabeth (Alexander) Ryan; m. Gary Nial Pottorff; children: Michael Lee, Gregory Nial. BA, Kansas State U., 1957; MA, St. Louis U., 1969. Elem. tchr. Pub. Sch., Keats and St. George, 1957-59; cons., elem. specialist Mid Continent Regional Edn. Lab., Kansas City, Mo., 1971-73; cons. Poindexter Assocs., Wichita, 1975; campaign mgr. Garner Shriver Congl. Camp, Wichita, 1976; interim dir. Wichita Area Rape Ctr., 1977; conf. coord. Biomedical Synergistics Inst., Wichita, 1977-79; real estate sales asst. Chester Kappelman Group, Wichita, 1979—; state rep. State of Kans., Topeka, 1985—. Mem. sch. bd. Wichita Pub. Schs., 1977-85; bd. dirs. Edn. Consol. and Improvement Act Adv. com., Kans. Found. for the Handicapped; mem. Children and Youth Adv. com. (bd. dirs.); active Leadership Kans.; chairperson women's network Nat. Conf., State Legislators; mem. Wichita Children's Home Bd. Recipient Disting. Svc. award Kans. Assn. Sch. Bds., 1983, Outstanding Svc. to Sch. Children of Nation award Coun. Urban Bds., 1984, awards Gov.'s Conf. for Prevention of Child Abuse and Neglect, Kans. Assn. Reading. Mem. Leadership Am. Alumnae (bd. dirs., sec.), Found. for Agrl. in Classroom (bd. dirs.), Jr. League, Vet. Aux. (pres.), Bd. Nat. State Art Agys., Rotary, Chi Omega (pres.). Office: Chester Kappelman Group PO Box 8036 Wichita KS 67208-0036

POTTS, ANNIE, actress; b. Nashville, Oct. 28, 1952. Student, Calif. Inst. of Arts; BFA, Stephens Coll. Appeared in films including Corvette Summer, 1978, King of the Gypsies, 1978, Heartaches, 1982, Crime of Passion, 1984, Ghostbusters, 1984, Stick, 1985, Pretty in Pink, 1986, Jumpin' Jack Flash, 1986, Pass the Ammo, 1988, Who's Harry Crumb, 1989, Ghostbusters II, 1989, Texasville, 1990, Breaking the Rules, 1992; plays include Richard III, Charley's Aunt, Cymbeline; TV appearances include Black Market Baby, 1977, Flatbed Annie and Sweetie Pie: Lady Truckers, 1979, Cowboy, 1983, Why Me?, 1984, Ladies in Waiting; TV series include Goodtime Girls, 1980, Designing Women, 1986-1993, Love and War, 1993— (Emmy nomination, Lead Actress - Comedy Series, 1994). Spokesperson Women for the Arthritis Found.; mem. aux. bd. MADD. Office: care Erwin Stoff 7920 Sunset Blvd Ste 350 Los Angeles CA 90046*

POTTS, BARBARA JOYCE, historical society executive; b. L.A., Feb. 18, 1932; d. Theodore Thomas and Helen Mae (Kelley) Elledge; m. Donald A. Potts, Dec. 27, 1953; children: Tedd, Douglas, Dwight, Laura. AA, Graceland Coll., 1951; grad., Radiol. Tech. Sch., 1953; grad. program for sr. execs. in state and local govt., Harvard U., 1989. Radiol. technician Independence (Mo.) Sanitarium and Hosp., 1953, 58-59, Mercy Hosp., Balt., 1954-55; city coun. mem.-at-large City of Independence, 1978-82, mayor, 1982-90; exec. dir. Jackson County Hist. Soc., 1991—; chmn. Mid-Am. Regional Coun., Kansas City, Mo., 1984-85; bd. dirs. Mo. Mcpl. League, Jefferson City, 1982-90, v.p., 1986-87, pres., 1987, 88; chmn. Mo. Commn. on Local Govt. Cooperation, 1985-90. Author: Independence, 1985. Mem. Mo. Gov.'s Conf. Edn., 1976, Independence Charter Rev. Bd., 1977; bd. dirs. Hope House Shelter Abused Women, Independence, 1982—, Vis. Nurses Assn., 1990-93, Mid-Continent Coun. U.S. Girl Scouts, 1991—; pres. Child Placement Svcs., Independence, 1972-89, Greater Kansas City region NCCJ, 1990—; trustee Independence Regional Health Ctr., 1982-90, 94—, Park Coll., 1989—; mem. Nat. Women's Polit. Caucus, 1978—; mem. adv. bd. Greater Mo. Focus on Leadership, mem. steering com., 1989—. Recipient George Lehr Meml. award for community svc., 1989, Woman of Achievement award Mid-Continent coun. Girl Scouts U.S.A., 1983, 75th Anniversary Women of Achievement award Mid-Continent coun. Girl Scouts, 1987, Jane Adams award Hope House, 1984, Community Leadership award Comprehensive Mental Health Svcs., Inc., 1984, 90, Graceland Coll. Alumni Disting. Svc. award 1991, Disting. Citizen award Independence C. of C., 1993, Outstanding Community Svc. award Jackson County Inter-Agy. Coun., 1994; named Friend of Edn. Indpendence NEA, 1990. Mem. LWV (Community Svc. award 1990), Am. Inst. Pub. Svc. (mem. bd. nominators), Nat. Trust for Hist. Preservation. Mem. Reorganized LDS Ch. Home: 18508 E 30th Ter S Independence MO 64057-1904

POU, LINDA ALICE, interior designer, architectural designer; b. Huntsville, Ala., Oct. 26, 1942; d. Louis and Lillian Maurice (Garvin) Grabensteder; m. Robert LeRoy Pou, Aug. 27, 1965; children: Susan Caroline, Stephanie Lynn. B of Interior Design, Auburn U., 1964; postgrad., Ecoles D'Art Americaines, 1964. Interior designer Martin Interiors, Huntsville, Ala., 1963, Blance Reeves Interiors, Atlanta, 1964-65, Militare, Atlanta, 1965, Loveman's Dept. Store, Huntsville, Ala., 1966, Southeastern Galleries, Charleston, S.C., 1967; draftsman Brown Engring., Huntsville, Ala., 1967-68, Naval Electronics Systems Command, S.C., 1968, Leland Engrs., Charleston, S.C., 1968-69; owner Drafting Svc., Mobile, Ala., 1977-78, The Design Svc., Prattville, Ala., 1980-92; The Design Svc., Savannah, Ga., 1992—. Composer songs including (adult anthems), Sing for Joy, 1983, Sing Hallelujah to the Lord, He's the Rainbow in My Life, 1984, (children's)ûLord of Harvest, 1984, Sing a Song to the Lord of Earth, 1985, (children's musical) Six Myths of Christmas, 1986; compiler and editor book of poetry, Nana's Legacy. Mem. jr. bd. Florence Crittendon Home for Unwed Mothers, Mobile, Ala., 1977-79, Prattville Planning Commn., 1980-92, chmn., 1985-88, vice-chmn., 1988-92; mem. Prattville Hist. Re-devel. Authority, 1988-89; children's choir dir. 1st United MEth. Ch., 1979-83, 87-89, adminstrv. bd., 1987-89, bldg. commn., 1987-89, trustee, 1990-92; mem. Savannah Symphony Women's Guild, 1993—. Mem. ASCAP, Spinners (treas. 1982-83), Prattville C. of C., Garden Club of Savannah, Alpha Gamma Delta. Home and Office: 202 E 45th St Savannah GA 31405-2216

POULIN, MARIE-PAULE, Canadian government official; b. Sudbury, Ont., Can., June 21, 1945; d. Alphonse-Emile and Lucille (Ménard) Charette; m. Bernard A. Poulin, May 21, 1977; children: Elaine, Valérie. BA, Laurentian U., Sudbury, 1966; MSW, U. Montréal, Que., Can., 1969; PhD (hon.), Laurentian U., Sudbury, 1995. Lectr. U. Montreal, 1969-70, Coll. of Gen. and Profl. Instrn., Hull, Que., 1972-73; rschr. Ctr. Social Svcs., Hull, 1972-73; interviewer, rschr. French Radio and TV, Ottawa, Ont., 1973-74; prodr. Sta. CBOF-CBC, Ottawa, 1974-78; founder and dir. svcs. in N.E. and N.W. Ont. Sta. CBON (French Network-CBC), Sudbury, 1978-83; exec. dir. regional programming CBC, Ottawa, 1983-84, assoc. v.p. regional broadcasting, 1984-88, sec. gen., 1988-90, v.p. human resources, 1990-92; dep. sec. for comm. and consultation The Privy Coun. Govt. of Can., Ottawa, 1992-93; chmn. Can. Artists and Prodrs. Profl. Rels. Tribunal, Ottawa, 1993—; bd. dirs. Cité Collégiale, Ottawa, 1988-91. Commr. for French lang. svcs. Province of Ont., 1986-89; regent U. Sudbury, 1981-83; bd. dirs. Laurentian Hosp., Sudbury, 1980-88, Cambrian Coll.Found., Sudbury, 1983-88; v.p. Art Ctr., Ottawa, 1988-90; pres. Regroupement gens d'affaires, Ottawa, 1991-92. Recipient medal for contbn. to Can. Culture, Coun. of French-Am. Life, 1987, Prix Marcel-Blouin for best morning program in Can., 1983, Profl. Woman of Yr. award Reseau des femmes d'affaires professionnelles, 1990. Mem. Assn. Grads. of U. Montréal, Can. Circle (exec.). Home: 100 Pretoria Ave, Ottawa, ON Canada K1S 1W9 Office: 240 Sparks St 8th Fl W, Ottawa, ON Canada K1A 1A1

POULIOT, ASSUNTA GALLUCCI, business school owner and director; b. West Warwick, R.I., Aug. 14, 1937; d. Michael and Angelina (DeCesare) Gallucci; m. Joseph F. Pouliot Jr., July 4, 1961; children: Brenda, Mark, Jill, Michele. BS, U. R.I., 1959, MS, 1971. Bus. tchr. Cranston High Sch., R.I.,

1959-61; bus. dept. chmn. Chariho Regional High Sch., Wood River Junction, R.I., 1961-73; instr. U. R.I., Kingston, 1973-78; founder, dir. Ocean State Bus. Inst., Wakefield, R.I., 1977—; dir. Fleet Nat. Bank, 1985-91; bd. mgrs. Bank of New Eng., 1984-85; commr. Accrediting Coun. Ind. Colls. and Schs., 1995—; speaker in field. Pres. St. Francis Women's Club, Wakefield, 1975; sec. St. Francis Parish Coun., Wakefield, 1980; mem. Econ. Devel. Commn., Wakefield, 1981-85; mem. South County Hosp. Corp., Wakefield, 1978—; fin. dir. Bus and Profl. Women's Club, Wakefield, 1982-84; chmn. Ladies Golf Charity, 1985-91; mem. Computer Info. Systems Com., Chariho Regional Career and Tech. Ctr.; bd. dirs., treas. Galilee Beach Club Assn. Mem. R.I. Bus. Edn. Assn. (newsletter editor 1979-81), New Eng. Bus. Coll. Assn. (sec. 1984-86, pres. 1985-87), R.I. Assn. Career and Tech. Schs. (treas., bd. dirs. 1979—), Eastern Bus. Edn. Assn. (conf. leader), Nat. Bus. Edn. Assn. (conf. leader), Career Coll. Assn. (conv. speaker, pub. rels. com., govt. rels. com., membership com., key mem., nominating com., evaluator), Assn. Colls. and Schs. (COPSA commr. 1994—), R.I. Women's Golf Assn., Am. Cancer Soc., U. R.I. Alumi Assn. (Excellence Bus. award 1992), Phi Kappa Phi, Delta Pi Epsilon (pres., newsletter editor). Roman Catholic. Club: Point Judith Country (past ladies golf chmn.). Avocations: golf, gardening. Home: 137 Kenyon Ave Wakefield RI 02879-4242 Office: Ocean State Bus Inst Mariner Sq Boxes 1&2 140 Point Judith Rd Narragansett RI 02882

POULOS-WOOLLEY, PAIGE M., public relations executive; b. Woodland, Calif., Apr. 26, 1958; d. Paul William Jr. and Frances Marie (Gibson) Poulos; m. John Stuart Woolley, Jr., Feb. 3, 1990. Student, U. Calif., Davis, 1977-80. Mgr. pub. rels. Somerset Wine Co., N.Y.C. and San Martin, Calif., 1982-88; dir. comm. The Beverage Source, San Francisco, 1988-89, Rutherford (Calif.) Hill Winery, 1989-90; pres. Paige Poulos Comm., Berkeley, Calif., 1990—; founder, chmn. WINECOM, 1992—. Pub. rels. editor: Practical Winery & Vineyards, 1994—; wine editor Focus Mag. Mem. Pub. Rels. Soc. Am. (bd. dirs. 1993—, sec. 1994, pres.-elect East Bay chpt. 1994-95, editor newsletter food and beverage sect. 1993-94), Women in Comm., Acad. Wine Comm. (program chair 1994), Internat. Assn. Bus. Communicators. Republican. Episcopalian. Office: Paige Poulos Comm PO Box 8087 Berkeley CA 94707

POULSEN, FERN SUE, special events and public relations consultant; b. Chgo., Sept. 29, 1959; d. Herman and Renee (Greenberg) Bass; m. Gregory Carl Poulsen, May 5, 1953. Ba, N. Ill. U., 1981. Corporate communications staff coordinator Centel Corp., Chgo., 1981-86; mgr. special events Network Mktg. Group, Oak Brook, Ill., 1986-88; pres. Poulsen Promotions, Chgo., 1988—; cons. spl. events and pub. rels. Vol. Easter Seal Soc. and March of Dimes, Chgo., 1987-88, Penny Pullen Campaign Com., Park Ridge, Ill., 1981-83, Am. Cancer Soc., Des Plaines, Ill., 1983; exec. advisor Jr. Achievement, Chgo., 1982-83; active Lincoln Park Cen. Assn., Chgo., 1988. Named Outstanding Woman Student Leader N. Ill. U. Women's Faculty, 1980. Mem. Internat. Assn. Bus. Communicators, Women's Am., ORT, Ad-Net Chgo., Parents and Child Edn. Soc., Omicron Delta Kappa, Phi Kappa Phi.

POULSON, JUDI LYNN, peacemaker; b. Fairmont, Minn., Dec. 27, 1941; d. H.J. and Eleanor Dorothy (Morris) Pieser; m. Donald F. Bernstein, Mar. 31, 1963 (div. Aug. 17, 1989); children: Michael, Andy, Ross Bernstein; m. LeRoy F. Poulson, June 12, 1992; stepchildren: Lori, Mark. BS in Sociology/Psychology, U. Minn., 1963; MS in Peace Studies, Mankato State U., 1983. Caseworker I Ramsey County Welfare Dept., St. Paul, 1963-64; tchr./presenter various locations, 1983—; adj. faculty women's studies Mankato (Minn.) State U., 1989—. Contbr. poetry to books. Bd. dirs. S.W. Ctrl. Consortium on Higher Edn., 1979-82, Prairie Lakes Extended Campus, Mankato State U. Alumni Bd., 1983—; del. state conv. DFL Party, Minn.; mem. energy com. City Coun., Fairmont, Minn.; mem. Cedar Park Planning Com.; mem. com. to plan new high sch. Sch. Dist. 454, Fairmont; pres. Am. Field Svcs., 1987-94; mem. Martin County Preservation Assn. Region 9 Minn. grantee, 1978. Mem. AAUW (Internat. award 1990), Minn. Commonwealth Fund, Toastmasters (pres. 1992-94, CTM award 1991), Friendship Force (treas.). Jewish. Home: 1881 Knollwood Dr Fairmont MN 56031-2303

POUND, E. JEANNE, school psychologist, consultant; b. N.Y.C., Oct. 19, 1949; adopted d. W. James and Thelma (Rendall) P.; div.; 1 child, Courtney Jason Pound. BA in English cum laude, U. Mass., 1971; MS in Social Work, U. Wis., 1973; EdS in Sch. Psychology, U. Ga., 1977. Cert. sch. psychologist, Ga., Mass.; cert. sch. social worker, N.Y. Psychiat. social worker White Mountain Community Mental Health Svcs., Littleton, N.H., 1974; sch. social worker Lake Placid (N.Y.) Ctrl. Schs., 1974-75; sch. psychologist Wilbraham (Mass.) Pub. Schs., 1977-80, Stoneham (Mass). Pub. Schs., 1980-81, Richmond County (Ga.) Pub. Schs., 1981-83, Griffin (Ga.) Regional Ednl. Svc. Agy., Ga., 1984-87; evaluator of innovative program grants Ga. State Dept. Edn., Atlanta, 1987—; supr. sch. psychology interns Ga. State U., Atlanta, 1994. Author: (chpt.) Children's Needs-Psychological Perspectives ("Children and Prematurity"), 1987. Mem. APA, Nat. Assn. Sch. Psychologists (cert.), Ga. Assn. Sch. Psychologists (regional rep. 1991-93), Humane Soc. U.S., World Wildlife Fedn., Kappa Delta Pi, Phi Kappa Phi, Phi Delta Kappa. Home: 150 Bryson Ln Fayetteville GA 30214 Office: Atlanta Pub Schs Divsn of Elem Edn 978 North Ave NE Atlanta GA 30306

POUND, LAVARNE, activist; b. Floral Park, N.Y., Apr. 1, 1927; d. John and Amelia (Hofstetter) Maribu; m. Howard Pound, Sept. 29, 1951; children: Barbara, Russell. Grad., Mrs. Skinner's Bus. Sch., Garden City, N.Y., 1948. With clerical dept. Town of Clarkstown, New City, N.Y., 1968-90. Editor newsletter Town Crier, 1977-89, Local Opinions, 1986-89, Retiree Newsletter, 1993—. Pres. Town of Clarkstown Unit Civil Svc. Employees Assn., New City, 1980-89, Rockland County Local, New City, 1986-89, vice chair retirees exec. bd., Albany, 1991—, pres., 1992— Local 918; chair safety transp. chair adv. coun. Office for Aging, Rockland County, 1992—; co-chair Rockland County Sr. Health Care Coalition, 1993—. Named Woman of Yr., Civil Svc. Employees Assn., 1991, Sr. Citizen of Yr., Office of Aging, Rockland County, 1994. Home: 11 Stratford Pl New City NY 10956

POUNDSTONE, SALLY, library director; m. Robert Bruce Poundstone; children: Nancy Katrina, Holly Megan, Angus Bruce, Alice Heather. BA, U. Ky., 1954, MA in Libr. Sci., 1955. Asst. head ref. dept. Louisville (Ky.) Free Pub. Libr., 1955-59; libr. Folger Shakespeare Libr., Washington, 1959-60; chief acquisition dept. White Plains (N.Y.) Pub. Libr., 1960-62; libr. Bedford Hills (N.Y.) Pub. Elem. Sch., 1965-66; dir. Mamaroneck (N.Y.) Free Libr. and Emelin Theatre, 1966—; instr. libr. sci. N.Y. U., 1968-69, Coll. of New Rochelle (N.Y.), 1970-71; adv. coun. mem. Pratt Inst. Grad Sch. of Libr. and Info. Sci., 1978-87; adminstrv. svcs. chmn. N.Y. Met. Ref. and Res. Libr. Agy., 1977-79, bd. trustees, 1979-88, 2d b.p. and chair, 1984-85, pres., 1985-88; planning and devel. com. mem. Bibliomation, Inc., 1988-90; chair Conn. State Adv. Coun. for Libr. Planning and Devel., 1988-90. Pres. Garden Club of Mamaroneck, 1969-70, Larchmont-Mamaroneck Film Coun., 1971-72, Mamaroneck Hist. soc., 1976-77, bd. mem., 1976-87; vice chmn. Village of Upper Nyack Planning Bd., 1988-89; leadership com. and task force mem. Westchester 2,000, 1984-87; com. mem. Rotary Club of Westport, 1987—, bulletin chair, 1988-90; active Downtown Westport Adv. Com., 1989-90, Rep. Town. Com., Weston, Conn., 1990-93, Westport Bridge & Traffic Com., 1990—, Westports of the World Com., 1991, Westport Telecomm. Com., 1994—, and others. Mem. ALA, Conn. Libr. Assn., Fairfield Libr. Adminstrs. Group, Archons of Colophon, Pub. Libr. Dirs. Assn. Westchester County (various offices and chairs), N.Y. Libr. Assn. (sec. treas. adult librs. assn. 1970-72, pres. pub. librs. sect. 1981-82, chair planning com. 1984-85). Home: 48 Sharp Hill Rd Wilton CT 06897 Office: Westport Lib Assn PO Box 5020 Westport CT 06881-5020

POUPORE, NORMA CAREY, former motel executive; b. Burke, N.Y., Sept. 14, 1929; d. Matthew Gabriel and Laura Anna (Moore) Carey; m. Bernard Charles Poupore, Feb. 16, 1952; children—Kevin, Barry, Casey, Michael. Grad. Adirondack Bus. Sch., 1946. With Marine Midland Banks, Malone and Syracuse, N.Y., 1946-53; legal stenographer local attys. and Office Ct. Adminstrn., State of N.Y., 1954-80; owner, operator Gateway Motel, Malone, 1962-86. Extension Service (bd. dirs.), Grange, Malone C. of C., Hotel-Motel Assn., Catholic Daus. Am. Republican. Roman Catholic. Club: Malone Golf and Country (bd. dirs.). Lodge: Elks. Avocations: golf; bowling; reading, duplicate bridge. Home: 2 Howard Dr Malone NY 12953-2350

POUR-EL, MARIAN BOYKAN, mathematician, educator; b. N.Y.C.; d. Joseph and Mattie (Caspe) Boykan; m. Akiva Pour-El; 1 dau., Ina. A.B., Hunter Coll.; A.M., Harvard U., 1951, Ph.D., 1958. Asst. prof. math. Pa. State U., 1958-62, assoc. prof., 1962-64; mem. faculty U. Minn., Mpls., 1964—; prof. math. U. Minn., 1968—; mem. Inst. Advanced Study, Princeton, N.J., 1962-64; mem. coun. Conf. Bd. Math. Scis., 1977-82, trustee, 1978-81, mem. nominating com., 1980-82, chmn., 1981-82; lectr. internat. congresses in logic and computer sci., Eng., 1971, Hungary, 1967, Czechoslovakia, 1973, Germany, 1983, Japan, 1985, 88, China, 1987; lectr. Polish Acad. Sci., 1974; lecture series throughout Fed. Republic of Germany, 1980, 87, 89, 91, Japan, 1985, 87, 90, 93, China, 1987, Sweden, 1983, 94, Finland, 1991, Estonia, 1991, Moscow, 1992, Amsterdam, 1992; mem. Fulbright Com. on Maths., 1986-89. Author: (with I. Richards) Computability in Analysis and Physics, 1989; author numerous articles on mathematical logic (theoretical computer sci.) and applications to mathematical and physical theory. Named to Hunter Coll. Hall of Fame, 1975; NAS grantee, 1966. Fellow AAAS, Japan Soc. for Promotion of Sci.; mem. Am. Math. Soc. (coun. 1980-88, numerous coms., lectr. nat. meeting 1976, also spl. sessions 1971, 78, 82, 84, chmn. spl. sessions on recursion theory 1975, 84), Assn. Symbolic Logic, Math. Assn. Am. (nat. panel vis. lectrs. 1977—, lectr. nat. meetings 1982, 89), Phi Beta Kappa, Sigma Xi, Pi Mu Epsilon, Sigma Pi Sigma. Office: U Minn Sch Math Vincent Hall Minneapolis MN 55455

POUSSAINT, RENEE FRANCINE, journalist; b. N.Y.C., Aug. 12, 1944; d. Christopher Wallace and Bobbie (Vance) P.; m. Henry J. Richardson III, Sept. 10, 1977. B.A., Sarah Lawrence Coll., 1966; M.A., UCLA, 1971; postgrad., Yale Law Sch., 1966-67, Ind. U., 1971-72; student, Sorbonne, Paris, 1964-65; hon. doctorate, Mt. Vernon Coll., Washington, 1985; cert., Columbia U. Journalism Sch., Michele Clark Fellowship Program for Minority Journalists, 1972. Program dir. AIESEC, N.Y.C., 1968-69; editor African Arts Mag., Los Angeles, 1969-71; reporter WBBM-TV, Chgo., 1974-76, CBS Network News, Chgo., Washington, 1976-78; became anchorperson WJLA-TV, Washington, 1978; now correspondent PrimeTime Live, ABC News, New York; dancer Jean Leon Destine Troupe, N.Y.C., 1966; translator U. Calif. Press, Los Angeles, 1970; tutor Operation Rescue, Washington, 1981—. Hon. dir. Nat. Kidney Found., Washington, 1981—; citizen advisor YWCA, Nat. Capitol Area, 1983—; co-chmn. Nat. Capital Area Lung Assn., 1982; membership chmn. Arthritis Found., 1981-82. Recipient Reporting award Ill. Mental Health Assn., 1976; recipient Reporting award Nat. Assn. Media Women, 1977, Broadcasting Excellence award AAUW, 1979, Emmy awards, 1979, 80, 81, 82, Broadcast award NAACP, 1980, Whitney Young Meml. award Washington Urban League, 1983. Mem. AFTRA, NAACP (life), Capitol Press Club. Office: PrimeTime Live 147 Columbus Ave 3rd Fl New York NY 10023-5900*

POWE, DIANE, nurse anesthetist, educator; b. Elmhurst, N.Y., July 30, 1951; d. Ernest and Dorothy (Bryant) P. BS, Hunter Coll., 1973; MA, Teachers Coll., 1976; postgrad., Va. Tech. U. reg. nurse anesthetist. Commdr. USN, 1976-94; staff nurse anesthetist Kings County Hosp. Ctr., Bklyn., 1984-87, Lewis-Gale Clinic, Salem, Va., 1988—. Mem. Roanoke Symphony Orch. Soc., 1988. Recipient Nat. Defense Svc. medal USN, 1991. Mem. Am. Assn. Nurse Anesthetists, Nat. Employment and Training Assn., Phi Theta Kappa, Omicron Tau Theta. Office: Lewis Gale Clinic Anesthesia Dept 1802 Braeburn Dr Salem VA 24153

POWEL, M. BETH, secondary education educator, medical technologist; b. Ft. McClellan, Ala., Dec. 20, 1954; d. Ben F. and Marie (Taylor) P. BS in Natural Sci., Memphis State U., 1975, BS in Med. Tech., 1976; MEd in Secondary Edn., U. Ala., 1983. Med. tech. Meth. Hosp., Memphis, 1975-76, Guadalupe Regional Med. Ctr., Carlsbad, N.Mex., 1976-77, Univ. Hosps., Birmingham, Ala., 1978-85, Huntsville (Ala.) Hosp., 1986—; tchr. biology Huntsville City Schs., 1985—; rschr. U.S. Army Micom, Redstone Arsenal, Ala., summer 1986—. Woodrow Wilson Nat. Fellowship Found. fellow, 1993. Mem. Ala. Edn. Assn., Huntsville Sci. Tchrs. Assn., Nat. Sci. Tchrs. Assn., Nat. Assn. Biology Tchrs., Tenn. Valley Jazz Soc., Botanical Garden Soc. Office: Grissom HS 7901 Bailey Cove Rd SE Huntsville AL 35802-3303

POWELL, ANICE CARPENTER, librarian; b. Moorhead, Miss., Dec. 2, 1928; d. Horace Aubrey and Celeste (Brian) Carpenter; student Sunflower Jr. Coll., 1945-47, Miss. State Coll. Women, 1947-48; B.S., Delta State Coll., 1961, M.L.S., 1974; m. Robert Wainwright Powell, July 19, 1948 (dec. 1979); children: Penelope Elizabeth, Deborah Alma. Librarian, Sunflower (Miss.) Pub. Library, 1958-61; tchr. English, Isola (Miss.) High Sch., 1961-62; dir. Sunflower County Library, Indianola, Miss., 1962—; mem. adv. coun. State Instl. Library Services, 1967-71; mem. adv. bd. library services and constrn. act com. Miss. Library Commn., 1978-80, mem. pub. library task force, 1986—; mem. Pub. Library Standards Com., 1988—; mem. state adv. coun. adult edn., 1988-92; mem. steering com. NASA community involvement program Miss. Delta Community Coll., 1990, adult edn. adv. com.; mem. Dist. Workforce Coun., 1994. Mem. AAUW, NOW, ALA (speaker senate subcom. on illiteracy 1989, dist. workforce coun., 1994—), Miss. Library Assn. (exec. dir. Nat. Library Week 1975, steering com. 1976, chmn. Right to Read com. 1976, co-chmn., 1987, chmn. legis. com. 1979, chmn. intellectual freedom com. 1975, 80, mem. legis. com. 1973-86, chmn. membership com. 1982, pres. 1984, chmn. nominating com. 1986, chmn. election com. 1989, mem. legis com., mem. registration com., mem. membership com., mem. nominating com. 1994, Peggy May award 1981), Sunflower County Hist. Soc. (pres. 1983-87), Miss. Literacy Assn., Delta Coun., Sunflower County Literacy Coun. (treas.). Methodist. Home: PO Box 310 Sunflower MS 38778-0310 Office: Sunflower County Libr 201 Cypress Dr Indianola MS 38751-2415

POWELL, ANNE ELIZABETH, editor; b. Cheverly, Md., Nov. 11, 1951; d. Arthur Gorman and Barbara Anne (MacAran) P.; m. John Alan Ebeling Jr., 1972 (div. 1983). BS, U. Md., 1972. Reporter Fayetteville (N.C.) Times, 1973-75; home editor Columbus (Ga.) Ledger-Enquirer, 1976; assoc. editor Builder mag., Washington, 1977-78; architecture editor House Beautiful's Spl. Publs., N.Y.C., 1979-81; editor Traditional Home mag., Des Moines, 1982-87, Mid-Atlantic Country mag., Alexandria, Va., 1987-89; editor in chief publs. Nat. Trust for Hist. Preservation, Washington, 1989—. Author: The New England Colonial, 1988. Mem. Nat. Press Club, Am. Soc. Mag. Editors. Home: 707 S Royal St Alexandria VA 22314-4309 Office: Nat Trust for Hist Preservation 1785 Massachusetts Ave NW Washington DC 20036-2117

POWELL, CAROL CHRISTINE, restaurant owner; b. Seattle, Feb. 15, 1941; d. Benjamin Olaf and Lois Carol (Smith) Michel; m. William Fred Roth, Apr. 8, 1961 (div. Dec. 1972); children: Christine Roth Elliott, Fred Roth, Traci Roth Bailey; m. George Benjamin Powell, Dec. 22, 1972 (dec. 1993); children: Kathy Powell Rank, George Benjamin. Grad. high sch., Seattle. Dishwasher Happy Chef, Cherokee, Iowa, 1978; dishwasher, waitress Randall's Cafe, Cherokee, 1978-79, mgr., 1979-82; owner, operator The FoodBroker, Cherokee, 1983-92; with Amway Network Mktg., 1988—; health aide Cherokee (Iowa) County Home, 1994—. Mem. Cherokee C. of C. Democrat. Home and Office: Cherokee County Home 418 N 6th St Cherokee IA 51012-0342

POWELL, CAROLYN WILKERSON, music educator; b. Hamburg, Ark., Oct. 9, 1920; d. Claude Kelly and Mildred (Hall) Wilkerson; m. Charles Luke Powell, Dec. 12, 1923; children: Charles Luke Jr., James Davis, Mark Wilkerson, Robert Hall. AB, Cen. Methodist, Fayette, Mo., 1942; MAT, U. N.C., Chapel Hill, 1970. Life Teaching Cert. Mo. Teaching Cert. N.C. Choral dir. Maplewood Richmond Heights Sch., St. Louis, 1943-45; pvt. piano tchr. Greensboro N.C. Area, Greensboro, 1951-63; organist Presbyterian and Methodist Ch., Greensboro, 1950-61; dir. Ch. Youth Choirs, Greensboro, 1958-61; choral and humanities tchr. Page High Sch., Greensboro, 1963-67; choral dir. Githens Jr. High Sch., Durham, N.C., 1967-80; organist St. Peter's Episcopal Ch., Altavista, Va., 1981-83; chmn. Dist. Choral Festival N.C. Dist., 1968-78; accompanist and music dir. Altavista Little Theatre Altavista, Va., 1981-83. Sunday and vacation schs. tchr., organist Grace Meth. Ch., Greensboro; den mother Boy Scouts Am., Greensboro, 1951-57; mem. Chapel Hill Preservation Soc., 1985—; vol., chapel organist, pediat. tutor U. N.C. Hosps., Chapel Hill, 1984-89. Mem. NEA, AAUW, Music Educators Nat. Conf., Am. Organists Guild, Classroom Tchrs. Assn., Ackland Art Mus. Assn., Chapel Hill Preservation Soc., Nat. Federated Music Club Euterpe, Chapel Hill Country Club, U. Woman's Club, The Carolina Club, Delta Kappa Gamma. Avocations: reading, golf, needlework, gardening, travel and antiques. Home: 2446 Honeysuckle Rd Chapel Hill NC 27514-6821

POWELL, DIANNE, legislative staff director; b. Balt., May 30, 1942; 1 child. Attended, Strayer Coll., 1962. Clerk, typist office of edn. Dept. Health & Human Svcs., 1960-63; sec. Mfg. Chemists Assn., 1963-65; case worker Office of Rep. Kika de la Garza, 1965-81; appt. scheduler chmn. de la Garza House Com. on Agr., 1981-87, dep. staff dir., 1988-90, staff dir., 1990—. Office: Com on Agriculture 1301 Longworth House Office Bldg Washington DC 20515*

POWELL, ELIZABETH PARKER, manufacturing exective; b. Denver, Dec. 5, 1938; d. Everett Humphreys and Clare Gernon (Davis) Parker; m. David George Powell, Sept. 21, 1963; children: Parker Davis, Clare Madeline, Elizabeth Everett. BA, Smith Coll., Northhampton, Ma., 1960; MA, Tufts U., 1962; MBA, Babson Coll., 1976. Lectr. U. Lowell, 1976-78; asst. prof. mgmt. Babson Coll., Wellesley, Ma, 1978-80; seminar leader U. Lowell, Babson Coll., Wellesley Coll., Harvard U. Ctr., 1978-85; co-founder, dir., chair, treas. Diamond Machining Tech., Inc., Marlborough, Ma., 1976—; dir. Mass. Technology Develop. Corp., 1994—; charter trustee Phillips Acad., Andover, Mass., 1980—, chair audit com.; trustee Babson Coll., 1984—, chmn. presdl. search com.; bd. dirs., fin. com. Harvard Community Health Plan, Boston, 1980-86, bd. overseers, 1986—; bd. dirs. Smaller Bus. Assn. New Eng., vice chair, 1994—; bd. dirs. World Wide D-I-Y Coun., vice chair, 1994. Mem. Wellesley Town metting, 1973—; mem. Gov. Dukakis Fiscal Mgmt. Task Force, 1990; Rep. Town Com., Wellesley; sec. Wellesley Free Libr. Needs Com., 1974-76; exec. com. Wellesley Free Libr. Centennial Fund, 1983-86. Mem. Jr. League of Boston, Denver and Phila., Inc., Boston Symphony Vol. Assn., Nat. Fedn. Bus. (Mass. guardian adv. coun. 1987—), Smith Coll. Club of Wellesley (pres. 1975-77, v.p. 1973-75), Wellesley Club, Vincent Club, Union Club. Home: 109 Edmunds Rd Wellesley MA 02181-2722 Office: Diamond Machining Tech. 85 Hayes Memorial Dr Marlborough MA 01752-1831

POWELL, ELIZABETH PEARCE, artist, illustrator; b. Boston, July 23, 1930; d. Ralph Dewey and Eugenia Whitehead (Norris) P.; m. Arthur Polier, Sept. 17, 1955 (dec. Nov. 1986); children: Nicole,David, Elizabeth (dec.), Alison (dec.), Stephen; m. Richard M. Ohmann, July 20, 1990. BA, Oberlin Coll., 1952; MFA, Sch. Visual Arts, N.Y.C., 1988. Art critic Park East, N.Y.C., 1961-73; instr, adult edn. Stamford (Conn.) Bd. Edn., 1973-76; instr. painting, dioramas Stamford Mus. and Nature Ctr., 1973-76; CEO, sculptor, instr. Greenwich (Conn.) Art Barn, 1976-80; high sch. tchr. N.Y.C. Bd. Edn., 1985-86; office asst. Sch. Visual Arts, N.Y.C., 1987-88, office asst. pres., 1988-90; free lance illustrator Middletown, Conn., 1990—; art dir. Radical Tchr. Collective, 1994—; instr. Wesleyan U. Grad. Liberal Studies Program, Middletown, 1992. Illustrator: (book) Citizenship, 1990. Chair marriage and divorce com. NOW, N.Y.C., 1971-73. Mem. Graphic Artists Guild. Democrat. Home and Office: LaBelle Rd Hawley MA 01339

POWELL, JUDITH E., nursing administrator; b. Wheeling, W.Va., Aug. 12, 1939; d. James Paul and Alice Jean (Lisk) Cummins; m. William Allen Powell, Nov. 23, 1984; children: Kimberly, David, Brad, Carrie, Shaun. Diploma, Ohio Valley Gen. Hosp., Wheeling, 1960; BNA, Columbia Pacific U., Mill Valley, Calif., 1981, MBA, M in Nursing Adminstrn., 1983. Cert. in nursing adminstrn. DON Med. Found. of Bellaire, Ohio, dir. health svcs.; DON Meml. Hosp. of Union County, Marysville, Ohio. Mem. adv. bd. Ohio Hi Point Joint Vocat. Sch., Tri-Rivers Sch. Practical Nursing, Marion Tech. Coll. Mem. Am. Acad. Ambulatory Nursing Adminstrn. (charter), Am. Hosp. Assn., Ohio Soc. for Nurse Execs.

POWELL, JULIA GERTRUDE, volunteer; b. Fenton, Mich., Jan. 25, 1907; d. Thomas James and Leila May (Bishop) Selman; m. Ronald Douglas Powell, June 25, 1924 (div. May 4, 1961); 1 child, Delva Dorothea (dec.). BA in Edn., Colo. Coll., 1949, MA in Edn., 1949; M in Adminstrn., UCLA, 1950; postgrad., Chapman Coll. Tchr. kindergarten Garden Grove (Calif.) Elem. Sch., Garden Grove Unified Sch. Dist., 1950-71. Pres. Garden Grove Tchrs. Assn., Calif., 1961, Ebell of Laguna Hills, Leisure World, 1983, Beethoven chpt. Guild, Orange County, 1984; Worthy Matron Hermosa chpt. Eastern Star, Santa Ana, Calif., 1972; Worthy High Priestess White Shrine of Jerusalem, 1976; Queen Merret Temple Daus. of Nile, Anaheim, Calif., 1988-89. Mem. NEA-Am. Assn. Ret. Persons, AAUW, Calif. Ret. Tchrs. Assn. Republican. Presbyterian.

POWELL, KARAN HINMAN, university program administrator; b. Great Lakes, Ill., May 25, 1953; d. David Daniel and Mary Anne (Buretz) Hinman; m. David Leonidas Powell, Feb. 14, 1987; children: Meloni (dec.), Erik. BS, We. Ill. U., 1975; MDiv, Loyola U., Chgo., 1981, B Sacred Theology (hon.), 1981; postgrad., George Mason U., 1994—. Cert. tchr., Ill., Va. Tchr. St. Hugh Cath. Sch., Lyons, Ill., 1975-77; tchr. Lay Ministry Tng. Program, Chgo., 1980-81, Jackson, Miss., 1981-83; adminstr. Inst. Creation Centered Spirituality Mundelein Coll., Chgo., 1978-79; exec. dir. North Am. Forum Catechumenate, Washington, 1983-88; dir. Profl. Devel. Program, tchr. theol. studies, tng. cons., exec. devel., direct contact tng. Georgetown U., Washington, 1988-94, dir. organization devel. program, 1991—; assoc. pastor Annunciation Cath. Ch., Columbus, Miss., 1981-83; cons. dioceses in U.S., Can., 1983—; cons. to fed. govt., profit and non-profit corps. Author: How to Form a Catechumenate Team, 1985; editor: Breaking Open the Word of God series, 1986-88, The Ninety Days, 1989; contbr. articles Cath. mags.; speaker Religious Edn. Congress, L.A., 1987-88, 90. Active on Blessed Sacrament RCIA Team, Alexandria, Va., 1984-86. Recipient tchr.'s scholarship State of Ill., 1971-75, cert. recognition KC, Columbus, Miss., 1982. Mem. Am. Soc. for Tng. and Devel., Assn. Psychol. Type, N.Am. Forum Catechumenate (cons. 1982—), Cath. Edn. Future's Project (mem. com. 1985-88, Va. SIDS Alliance, 1991—, state steering com. 1993-94, bd. dirs., 1993-94, pres. 1994—), Organization Devel. Network. Democrat. Office: 21351 Sweet Clover Pl Ashburn VA 22011

POWELL, LINDA, state education official. Commr. of edn. Minn. Dept. Edn. Office: Edn Dept 712 Capitol Sq Bldg 550 Cedar St Saint Paul MN 55101-2233

POWELL, MARGARET ANN SIMMONS, computer scientist; b. Gulfport, Miss., May 26, 1952; d. William Robert and Nancy Rita (Schloegel) Simmons; m. Mark Thomas Powell, Sept. 11, 1983. AS in Math., N.W. Miss. Jr. Coll., 1972; BS in Edn., Memphis State U., 1977; BS in Computer Sci., U. Md., 1988; MS in Computer Sci., Johns Hopkins U., 1991. Tchr. Sacred Heart Sch., Walls, Miss., 1973-80; office mgr. Hyman Builders Supply, Memphis, 1980-84; tech. instr. Bendix Field Engring. Corp., Greenbelt, Md., 1985-87; software engr. Assurance Technology Corp., Alexandria, Va., 1987-89, Naval Rsch. Lab., Washington, 1989-93; computer scientist Naval Info. Systems Mgmt. Ctr., Washington, 1993—. Bd. dirs. Greenbrook Village Homeowners Assn., 1992—; sec. Greenbelt East Adv. Com., 1994, chair, 1995. Named one of Outstanding Young Women Am., 1977. Mem. IEEE Computer Soc., Assn. for Computing Machinery, Phi Kappa Phi, Kappa Delta Pi, Phi Theta Kappa, Mu Alpha Theta. Roman Catholic. Home: 7810 Somerset Ct Greenbelt MD 20770-3022 Office: NISMC 1225 Jefferson Davis Hwy Arlington VA 22202

POWELL, MARY JO(SEPHINE), nurse; b. Valdosta, Ga., Feb. 16, 1959; d. Tom J. Sr. and Jessie H. Smith. BSN, Valdosta State Coll., 1982. Staff nurse Med. Coll. of Ga., Augusta, 1982-86, Quincy Co., Augusta, 1986-90, RS Data, Augusta, 1990-92; HIV/AIDS staff nurse Quincy Co., Augusta, 1992-93, Aiken (S.C.) Regional Med. Ctr., 1993-94, 94—, St. Joseph's Hosp., Augusta, 1994.

POWELL, MELINDA SUE, food company executive; b. West Islip, N.Y., Feb. 7, 1963; d. Henry Stuart and Barbara L. (Thompson) P. BBA, U. Vt., 1985. Rep. Hershey Chocolate Co., Burlington, Vt., 1985-87, dist. account supr., 1987-90, regional analyst, 1991—. Democrat. Home: 1035 S Artery #504 Quincy MA 02169

POWELL, PATRICIA ANN, mathematics and business educator; b. Covington, Ga., Apr. 6, 1956; d. John Doyle Sr. and Pauline Josephine (Thompson) Dunn; m. Jackie Lee Powell, May 10, 1980; 1 child, Jackie Lee II. BS, Lee Coll., 1978; MEd in Adminstrn. and Supervision, U. Tenn., 1993. Br. loan officer Am. Nat. Bank and Trust, Chattanooga, 1979-81; instr. math., careers Hamilton County Schs., Chattanooga, 1983-85, 93—; customer svc. rep. First Union Nat. Bank, Atlanta, 1986-88; instr. tech. bus., typing DeKalb County Schs., Decatur, Ga., 1989; grad. asst. U. Tenn., Chattanooga, 1991-93; instr. math. Hamilton County Sch. System, 1993—; instr. English, bus. math. and bus. skills Urban League Bus. Skills Tng. Ctr., Chattanooga; adj. faculty Chattanooga State Tech. Community Coll., 1991-92. Co-author: Career Orientation-Grade 8, 1985 (monetary award 1984-85); singer African Americans Against Blood Disorders Benefit, Atlanta, 1994. Singer, Mayor's Office Performing Artists Against Drugs, Atlanta, 1990; vol. Chattanooga Community Kitchen, 1990—; tutor, coord. math., reading United Way's Adult Reading Program, Chattanooga, 1991—; instr. aerobics Am. Heart Assn., Chattanooga, 1991—; vol. Warner Park Zoo, Chattanooga; treas. Looking to the Word Ministries, Inc., 1985—; v.p. parents group First Cumberland Child Devel. Ctr., 1992-94. Outstanding Classroom Tchr. nominee, 1993-94; recipient Black Grad. fellowship U. Tenn., Chattanooga, 1992, 93; named Woman of Yr. and Mrs. Congeniality, Mrs. Chattanooga-Am. Pageant, 1990; Endowment scholar, 1977-78. Mem. AAUW, NAFE, Friends of the Zoo Preservation Group, Chatta, Area Math. Assn., Delta Sigma Theta, Kappa Delta Pi (pres., v.p. 1993—). Mem. Pentecostal Ch. Home: PO Box 24912 Chattanooga TN 37422-4912

POWELL, PHYLLIS LAVERNE, positive organization professional; b. N.Y.C., May 25, 1959; d. Charles Edward and Ruth Naomi (Simmons) P.; children: Norman, Noraema, Norelle, Naquan, Nakeim, Regina. Student, John Jay Coll., 1979-84. Legal asst. Bronx Criminal Ct., N.Y.C., 1979-84; community svc. aide N.Y.C. Parks Dept., 1985-86; pres. Postive Orgn. with Educ-as-a-Reality (POWER), N.Y.C., 1992—. Vol. asst. tchr. Archdiocese Head Start, N.Y.C., 1988-92.

POWELL, ROSALIE, home economist; b. Milw., Oct. 24, 1947; d. William and Daisy P.; BS in Home Econ. Bus., U. Wis., Stout, 1969, MS in Home Econs. Edn., 1974. Extension home economist U. Wis. Extension, Langlade County, 1969-74, Waukesha County, 1976-91, Milw. and Waukesha Counties, 1992-93, family resource mgmt. agent, Milwaukee County, 1994—; instr. U. Wis.-Stout, Menomonie, 1975-76; asst. prof. dept. family devel. U. Wis. Extension, 1976-81, assoc. prof., 1981-87, chmn. family devel. dept., 1984-94, prof., 1987—. Mem. Am. Assn. Family and Consumer Scis., Wis. Assn. Family and Consumer Scis., Nat. Coalition Consumer Edn., Nat. Assn. Extension Home Economists, Wis. Assn. Extension Home Economists, Soc. Nutrition Edn., Wis. Consumers League, Bus. and Profl. Women (chpt. pres. 1970-72), Am. Council on Consumer Interests, Gamma Sigma Sigma (nat. pres. 1975-77), Epsilon Sigma Phi. Home: 403 Sheffield Rd Waukesha WI 53186-6361 Office: 1304 S 70th St West Allis WI 53214

POWELL, SHARON JOYCE, physical education educator; b. Whitehall, Wis., July 28, 1937; d. Melvin William and Erna Judith (Senty) Luethi; m. Lawrence Ray Powell, July 9, 1961; children: Scott, Jeffrey. BS, U. Wis., 1959, postgrad., 1964—. Phys. edn. tchr. grades 1-12 Boscobel (Wis.) Pub. Schs., 1959-61; phys. edn. tchr. grades 7-12 Oelwein (Iowa) Pub. Schs., 1961-62; phys. edn. tchr. grades 9-12 Jefferson (Wis.) Pub. Schs., 1963-67; phys. edn. tchr. elem. and sr. high Wisconsin Dells (Wis.) Pub. Schs., 1967-69; phys. edn. tchr. sr. high Waunakee (Wis.) Pub. Schs., 1969-72; substitute tchr. Tomah (Wis.) Pub. Schs., 1972-77, phys. edn. tchr. grades 10 and 11, 1977—; coach sr. high tennis, Tomah (Wis.) Pub. Sch., 1977-84, sr. high softball, 1977-86. Mem. adminstrv. bd. United Meth. Ch., 1974—; active Monroe County Reps., Sparta, Wis., 1990-93. Mem. NEA, AAUW (sec. 1984-86, v.p. 1988-90, pres. 1990-92), Wis. Edn. Assn., Tomah Edn. Assn. (co-pres. 1994—), Friends of the Libr. Methodist. Home: RR 1 Box 144 Tomah WI 54660-9728 Office: Tomah Pub Schs Hwy 16 Tomah WI 54660

POWELL, SHARON LEE, social welfare organization administrator; b. Portland, Oreg., July 25, 1940; d. James Edward Carson and Betty Jane (Singleton) Powell. BS, Oreg. State U., 1962; MEd, Seattle U., 1971. Dir. outdoor edn. Mapleton (Oreg.) Pub. Schs., 1962-63; field dir. Totem Girl Scout Council, Seattle, 1963-68, asst. dir. field services, 1968-70, dir. field services, 1970-72; dir. pub. rels. and program Girl Scout Council of Tropical Fla., Miami, 1972-74; exec. dir. Homestead Girl Scout Council, Lincoln, Nebr., 1974-78, Moingona Girl Scout Coun., Des Moines, 1978—. Pres. agy. dirs. assn. United Way Cen. Iowa, Des Moines, 1987-88, mem. priorities com., 1986-90, chairperson agy. rels., 1994—, chairperson agy. issues, 1989-90; mem. priority goals task group United Way Found., Des Moines, 1985-92; capt. Drake U. Basketball Ticket Drive, Des Moines, 1983-87; sec. Urbandale Citizens Scholarship Found., 1989-93; mem. ad hoc long-range planning com. Urbandale Schs., 1989, mem. budget rev. task group, mem. year-round sch. task group, 1992-93; mem. gender equity task force State of Iowa, 1993—. Mem. AAUW (mem. gender equity task group), Assn. Girl Scouts Execs. (chair nat. conv. 1985-90, nat. bd. dirs. 1985-87, nat. nominating com. 1982-84, nat. treas. 1987-90, nat. pres. 1991—), Urbandale C. of C. (bd. dirs., chair edn. com.), Animal Rescue League of Iowa (bd. dirs. 1992—, shelter chair 1992—), Des Moines Obedience Tng. Club (pres. 1987-89), Des Moines Golden Retriever Club (bd. dirs., pres. 1992—), Altrusa (treas. Des Moines chpt. 1983-85, cmty. svc. chair 1986-87), Des Moines Kennel Club. Democrat. Office: Moingona Girl Scout Coun 10715 Hickman Rd Des Moines IA 50322-3798

POWELL, STEPHANIE, visual effects director; b. Dayton, Ohio, Sept. 27, 1946; d. Harley Franklin and Evelyn Luella (Reed) Pence. Pres., CEO Video Assist Systems, Inc., North Hollywood, Calif., 1979—, Out of the Blue Visual Effects, 1989; Blue Screen Effects supr. Jurassic Park, Flintstones; Visual Effects supr. MGM's Blown Away, CBS My Brothers Keeper. Supr. visual effects: (motion pictures) Jurassic Park, Flintstones, Blown Away, (TV) Quantum Leap, My Brother's Keeper, various comml.s.; developer using 3/4-inch videotape for broadcast; co-developer color videotap for motion picture work. Mem. Acad. TV Arts and Scis., Acad. Magical Arts and Scis. Office: Video Assist Systems Inc 11030 Weddington St North Hollywood CA 91601-3212

POWER, COLLEEN JOYCE, librarian, author, researcher; b. Lawton, Okla., Oct. 26, 1945; d. Ernest F. and Loyce Aileen (Brooks) P. BS in Zoology, U. Okla., 1966, BA, 1965, MLS, 1967. Dir. fisheries oceanography libr. U. Wash., Seattle, 1967-70; sci. libr. Humboldt State U., Arcata, Calif., 1970-74; sci. collection devel. officer Ariz. State U., Tempe, 1974-78; sci. libr. Calif. State U., Chico, 1978—, coord. regional svcs., 1984—, coord. bibliographer instruction, 1988—; reviewer RQ, Chgo., 1984—, 20th Century Sci. Fiction Readers Guide, Chgo., 1987-90, Sci. Tech. Book Revs., Chgo., 1989—. Author: (chpts.) Online Catalog Revealed, 1984; mem. editorial bd. Tech. Svcs. Qtr., 1984—. Mem. Calif. Acad. Rsch. Librs. (membership dir. 1986-87), Calif. Acad. Rsch. Libr. (sec. 1985-86), ACRL (vice chair, chair elect sci. tech. sect. 1989-90, chair 1990-91, chair extended campus svcs. sect. 1993—), Sci./Engring. Acad. Librs. (pres. 1984-85, statewide pres. 1985-86). Office: Calif State U Meriam Libr Chico CA 95929

POWER, ELIZABETH HENRY, consultant; b. Hickory, N.C., Sept. 28, 1953; d. William Henry Power and Katheryn Otis (Smith) Nelson. Cert. in creative writing, N.C. Sch. Arts, 1971; BA in Sociology, U. N.C., Greensboro, 1977. With adoption and foster home recruitment Davidson County Dept. Human Svcs., Nashville, 1980-81; behavioral cons. Nutri-System Weight Loss Ctr., Nashville, 1982-84; corp. sec., cons. Quantum Leap Cons., Inc., Nashville, 1984-86; pres., owner EPower & Assocs., Brentwood, Tenn., 1980-84, 86—; owner MPD/DD Resource & Edn. Ctr., Nashville, 1991-93; seminar presenter, 1977—; cons. GM/Saturn, 1988—. Author: Getting the Fat Out of Your Head So It Stays Off Your Body, 1987, If Change Is All There Is, Choice Is All You've Got, 1990, Managing Our Selves: Building a Community of Caring, 1992; co-author, editor: Circle of Love: Child Personal Safety, 1984; contbg. author: Nonprofit Policies and Procedures, 1992, More than Survivors: Conversations with Multiple Personality Clients, 1992, also articles. Vol. West Chester (Pa.) Women's Resource Ctr., 1977; vol. instr. theology Lay Acad. Episc. Diocese Western N.C., Asheville, 1976-77; mem. Burke County Coun. Status Women, Morganton, N.C., 1977-79, sec., 1978; vol. Western N.C. Flood Com., 1977-78; exec. dir. N.C. Rape Crisis Assn., Raleigh, 1979, Foothills Mental Health Ctr., Morganton, 1978-79; mem. task force, writer, convener, facilitator N.C. Gov.'s Conf. Mental Health, 1979; trainer, vol. Rape House Crisis Ctr., Nashville, 1979-81; vol, trainer Rape and Sexual Abuse Ctr., Nashville, 1981-82, bd. dirs., 1981-82; mem. quality circles steering com. Tenn. Dept. Human Svcs., 1980-81; program cons. Women's Resource and Assistance Program, Jackson, Ten., 1988-82; vol. devel. cons. AGAPE Christian Counseling Ctr., Nasville, 1988; bd. dirs., Life Challenge Tenn., 1989—. Recipient numerous awards N.C. Dept. Mental Health/Mental Retardation, 1979, State of N.C., 1979, Central Nashville Optimist Club, 1982, Waco YWCA, Waco, Tex., 1985. Mem. AAUW, NAFE, Nat. Mental Health Assn., Nat. Prevention Coalition, Internat. Soc. for the Study of Multiple Personality and Dissociation. Democrat. Home and Office: PO Box 2346 Brentwood TN 37024-2346

POWERS, ALTA ANN, academic counselor; b. Waco, Tex., July 8, 1940; d. Theodore Charles and Thelma Ruth (Guthrie) Lorenz; m. Benny Lloyd Powers, Sept. 2, 1961; children: Michele Ann Powers Johns, Joy Rene Powers Harris, Bryce Lee. BA, Baylor U., 1962; student, East Tex. State U., Commerce, 1973-76; MEd in Counseling, Tarleton State U., 1987. Tchr. Killeen (Tex.) Ind. Sch. Dist., 1964-65, Florence (Tex.) Ind. Sch. Dist., 1966-67, Marble Falls (Tex.) Ind. Sch. Dist., 1967-69; tchr. spl. edn. Valley Mills (Tex.) Ind. Sch. Dist., 1972-90; counselor Whitney (Tex.) Ind. Sch. Dist., 1990—. Mem. ACA, AAUW, PTO, Assn. Tex. Profl. Educators, Tex. Counseling Assn. Office: Whitney Ind Sch Dist 305 San Jacinto Whitney TX 76692

POWERS, CAROL JEAN, preschool educator; b. Dodge City, Kans., Apr. 30, 1950; d. Richard Eugene and Thelma Nadine (Cossman) Maxwell; m. William Edward Powers, June 2, 1972; children: Collin Maxwell, Hayley Jean. AA, Dodge City C.C., 1970; BS, Kans. State U., 1972. Tchr. Geary County Retarded Children's Assn., 1972-73; dir., tchr. Big Lakes Devel. Ctr., 1973-76; substitute tchr. USD 475, 1973-76; day care home provider, 1977-80; program dir. People Care, Wichita, Kans., 1980-81; tchr. Ft. Riley (Kans.) Presch., 1981-93; owner Heartland Deliveries, Junction City, Kans., 1993—. Community rep. Headstart Policy Coun., Junction City, 1993; membership chair Sheridan Sch. PTA, Junction City, 1991-93. Named one of Outstanding Young Women of Am., 1978. Mem. AAUW.

POWERS, CLAUDIA MCKENNA, state government official; b. Key West, Fla., May 28, 1950; d. James Edward and Claudia (Antrim) McKenna; m. Richard Garland Powers, Dec. 27, 1971; children: Gregory, Theodore, Matthew, Thurston. BA in Edn., U. Hawaii, 1972; MA, Columbia U., 1975. Cert. tchr., N.Y. Rep. Greenwich (Conn.) Rep. Town Meeting, 1979-93, sec. bldg. com., 1982-84, sec. legis. com., 1986-88, 90-93; mem. Conn. Ho. of Reps., 1993—, mem. govt. adminstrn. and elections com., 1995—. Campaign chmn. Greenwich Rep. Town Com., 1984, 85, chmn., 1986—; sec. Rep. Round Table, Greenwich, 1988-90; bd. govs. Riverside Assn., Greenwich, 1987-91, sec., 1991-92; class mother Riverside Sch., Greenwich, 1984-90; mem. altor guild Christ Ch., Greenwich, 1990—; adminstrv. coord. Greenwich Teen Ctr., 1990-91; alt. del. Rep. Nat. Conv., New Orleans, 1984—; v.p. LWV of Greenwich, 1990-91. Episcopalian. Home and Office: 15 Hendrie Ave Riverside CT 06878-1808

POWERS, CYNTHIA SALVADORI, bookkeeper, accountant; b. Pitts., Nov. 26, 1953; d. Robert Leo Salvadori and Marion (Scully) Bradley; m. Michael John Powers, Oct. 19, 1973; children: Sarah Kathleen, Morgan Alicia. AAS in Acctg., Adirondack C.C., 1993. Bookkeeper Higgins Candy Co., Glens Falls, N.Y., 1977-79; full charge bookkeeper Adirondack Stihl, Inc., Saratoga Springs, N.Y., 1979-85; jr. acct. Olympia Arenas Inc., Glens Falls, N.Y., 1986-90; full charge bookkeeper Adirondack East Corp., Saratoga Springs, N.Y., 1990-92; bookkeeper accts. payable Ledfoot, Glens Falls, N.Y., 1993—. Roman Catholic.

POWERS, DORIS HURT, engineering company executive; b. Indpls., Jan. 17, 1927; d. James Wallace Hurt Sr. and Mildred (Johnson) Devine; m. Patrick W. Powers, Nov. 12, 1950 (dec. 1989); children: Robert W. Powers, Jaye P., Laura S. Powers. Student, So. Meth. U., 1944-45; BS in Engring., Purdue U., 1949; postgrad., U. Tex., W. Tex., 1952-53, Ecole Normale Du Musique, Paris, 1965-68; grad., Harford County Leadership Acad., 1991. Flight instr. Red Leg Flying Club, El Paso, Lawton, Okla., 1951-57; check pilot Civil Air Patrol, El Paso, Lawton, Okla., 1952-57; ground instr. Civil Air Patrol, Washington, Tex., Okla, 1957-61; exec. v.p. T&E Internat., Inc., Bel Air, Md., 1979-88, pres., 1989-91; exec. v.p. T.E.I.S., Inc, Bel Air, 1979-88, pres., 1989-91; pres. Shielding Technologies, Inc., Bel Air, 1987—. Mem. Northeastern Md. Tech. Coun., 1991—; bd. dirs. Leadership Acad., 1991—. Recipient Svc. award U.S. Army, 1978, Cert. of Appreciation U.S. Army Test and Evaluation Command, 1988. Mem. CAP (lt. maj. 1951-58), Soc. of Women Engrs. (sr., v.p. 1977, treas. 1979, sec. rep. 1986-88, mentor 1986—, speaker 1978—, selected to Coll. of Fellows 1993), Engring. Soc. Balt. (speaker 1980—), 99's (pres. 1951-53), Am. Soc. Indsl. Security, Am. Def. Preparedness Assn., Hartford County Econ. Devel. Coun., Assn. of U.S. Army, Northeastern Md. Tech. Coun. Home: 6 Mcgregor Way Bel Air MD 21014-5631

POWERS, ESTHER SAFIR, design consultant; b. Tel Aviv, Sept. 1, 1948; arrived in Can., came to U.S., 1977; d. Nisan and Batia (Epstein) Safir; children: Jared Barnet, Elliott Robert; m. Richard Michael Drag, May 25, 1986. MusB, McGill U., Montreal, Que., Can., 1969; MusM, Ga. State U., 1982, PhD, 1985. Music tchr. North York Bd. Edn., Toronto, Ont., 1969-77; cons. Ested Mgmt., 1975-77, Mescon Group, Atlanta, 1983-95, PeopleTech, 1995—. Contbr. articles to profl. jours., chpt. to book. Pres. bd. dirs. Montessori Sch., Atlanta, 1978; vol. Nat. Coun. Jewish Women, Atlanta, 1990; mem. Ga. Exec. Womens Network; bd. dirs. Coun. Battered Women, 1994—. Mem. Nat. Coun. Jewish Women, Nat. Assn. Sch. Karate, Nat. Soc. for Performance and Instrn. (pres. Atlanta chpt. 1984-85, conf. mgr. 1983-84, internat. v.p. 1988-90, internat. pres. 1991-92, presdl. citation 1988, presdl. award 1989, leadership award 1990). Office: PeopleTech 1040 Crown Pointe Pky # 570 Atlanta GA 30308

POWERS, JANE ADAIR, medical administrator; b. Laurens, S.C., July 7, 1948; d. Charles Allen and Mary Alice (Bolt) Adair; m. Alvin Dewitt Powers Jr., June 7, 1969; children: Maryanne, Maryellen, Maryelizabeth, Alvin III. BA, Winthrop Coll., 1969. Tchr. Aiken (S.C.) Dist., 1971-73; sec. Self Meml. Hosp., Greenwood, S.C., 1973-76; coord. Upper Savannah Area Health Edn. Consortium, Greenwood, 1976-77; dir. Upper Savannah AHEC, Greenwood, 1977—. Mem. Am. soc. Healthcare Edn. and Tng. Baptist. Home: Rte 4 Box 132 Laurens SC 29360 Office: Upper Savannah AHEC 1325 Spring St Greenwood SC 29646

POWERS, PATRICIA ANN, rehabilitation nurse; b. Balt., July 30, 1950; d. Anthony Albert and Angela Ann (Gorski) Podles; m. Lewis A. Powers (div. Oct. 1978); children: Lewis Anthony, Shane Eric; m. Peter Gregory Swindell, July 13, 1990. AA, Essex Community Coll., 1980; BS in Nursing, U. Md., 1981, MS in Nursing, 1992. Cert. registered rehab. nurse. Primary nurse I, II and III Md. Inst. Emergency Med. Systems Svcs., Balt., 1980-85; unit sup. head trauma patients Montebello Rehab. Hosp., Balt., 1985-88, nurse liaison, 1988-91; community health nurse Bay area Family Care Home Health Svcs., Balt., 1991—; nurse liaision cons. on rehab. potential Montebello Rehab. Hosp., Balt., 1988—. Co-author: Brain Injury Family Handbook, 1988. Mem. Assn. Rehab. Nurses (chairperson nomination com. 1986-88). Home: 1314 Gibbs Ct Bel Air MD 21014 Office: Montebello Rehab Hosp 2201 Argonne Dr Baltimore MD 21218

POWERS, SHARON SHOFFNER, principal; b. Dayton, Ohio, Jan. 12, 1949; d. Timothy C. and Ruby M. (Spradlin) Shoffner; m. Gregory J. Powers, Nov. 8, 1969 (div. July 1981); children: Joshua D., Zachary A. BS, Coll. Great Falls, 1970; MEd, U. Ariz., 1974, Wright State U., 1983. Cert. elem. tchr. and prin., Ohio. Tchr. Skyline Elem. Sch., Great Falls, Mont., 1971; tchr., reading specialist Tucson Unified Sch. Dist., 1971-79; tchr. Donnelsville (Ohio) Sch. Dist., 1979-80; coord. gifted edn. Tecumseh Local Schs., New Carlilse, Ohio, 1980-84; prin. Donnelsville Elem. Sch., 1984-91, McAdams Early Childhood Ctr., New Carlisle, Ohio, 1991—; mem. diversified coop. tng. adv. com. Greene County Career Ctr., 1994-95; speaker in field. Mem. Springfiled/Calrk County Career Edn. Adv. Coun., 1982-83. Recipient Adminstr. of Yr. award Coun. of Exceptional Children, 1980-81, Outstanding Elem. Tchr. Am., 1975; grantee Martha Holden Jennings, Nat. Diffusion Network, Wells Fargo, Ohio Arts Coun. Mem. Ohio Assn. Elem. Sch. Adminstrs., Clark County Elem. Prins. Assn. (sec. 1994-95), Phi Delta Kappa (Responsible Tchr. award 1982). Mem. Ch. of Christ. Office: McAdams Early Chldhood Ctr 1400 Mcadams Dr New Carlisle OH 45344-2449

POWERS, SHIRLEY MARIE, banker; b. Miles City, Mont., Feb. 27, 1930; d. Emil Henry and Karen Elizabeth (Topp) Swanson; m. William Howard Powers Jr., Apr. 5,1952; children: Michael Howard, Thomas Mark. AAS, Coastal Carolina Community Coll, 1969; cert. Sch. Banking, U. N.C., Chapel Hill, 1978. Lic. real estate broker, N.C. Adminstrv. asst. Bank of N.C., Jacksonville, 1974-77; mortgage loan officer Bank of N.C., Raleigh, 1977-82; real estate lending officer N.C. Nat. Bank, Raleigh, 1983; asst. v.p. So. Nat. Bank N.C., Raleigh and Charlotte, 1983-86; v.p. So. Nat. Bank N.C., Charlotte, 1987—. Mem. Home Builders Assn. Charlotte (treas. women's coun. 1988). Democrat. Lutheran. Office: So Nat Bank NC 1263 Arrowpine Dr Ste 301 Charlotte NC 28273-5508

POWERS, SONIA NODLE, psychologist, consultant; b. Canton, Ohio, May 11, 1943; d. George Bernard and Evelyn Lee (Hoyman) Nodle; m. Brad C. Thurman, June 25, 1965 (div. 1977); children: Mark, Ginger, Scott. BS, Calif. State U., 1965; MS, Nat. U., San Diego, 1981; PhD, PSPS, San Diego, 1983. Lic. clin. psychologist, Calif. Foster home supr. Children's Home Soc., Orange County, Calif., 1966-70; salesperson Red Carpet Realtors, Huntington Beach, Calif., 1972-75; mgr. Red Carpet Realtors, Escondido, Calif., 1975-79; owner, pres. Red Carpet Realtors, Lake Forest, Calif., 1979; psychologist in pvt. practice San Clemente, Calif., 1983—; pub. speaker, pres. Power Presentations, San Clemente, Calif., 1989—; dir. Profl. Success Seminars, San Clemente, Calif., 1981—; trainer Police Officers Standards and Tng., State of Calif., 1985—; cons. psychologist for numerous bus. orgns. and state, county and city govt. agencies, 1983—. Contbr. articles to profl. jours.; author: Charismatic Leader....Self Esteem, 1983; co-host TV broadcast various programs. Hon. fire fighter, 1991. Johnston Found. scholar, 1982; Honored Citizen of South Orange County, 1986. Mem. APA, Robbins Rsch. Internat., San Juan Capistrano C. of C. Office: Power Presentations 607 Avenida Acapulco Ste 200 San Clemente CA 92672-2404

POWERS, STEFANIE (STEFANIE FEDERKIEWICZ), actress; b. Hollywood, Calif., Nov. 2, 1945; m. Patrick de la Chenais, April 1, 1993. Film appearances include Among the Thorns, Experiment in Terror, 1962, McClintock, 1963, Fanatic, 1964, Warning Shot, 1967, Herbie Rides Again, 1973, Escape to Athena, 1979, Invisible Stranger, 1984, Mother's Day, 1984; TV movie appearances include Five Desperate Women, 1971, Sweet Sweet Rachel, 1971, Paper Man, 1971, Ellery Queen: Don't Look Behind You, 1971, Hardcase, 1972, Sky Heist, 1975, Return to Earth, 1976, Washington: Behind Closed Doors, 1977, Nowhere to Run, 1978, A Death in Canaan, 1978, Family Secrets, 1984, Mistral's Daughter, 1984, Hollywood Wives, 1985, Deceptions, 1985, At Mother's Request, 1987, (co-producer) Beryl Markham: A Shadow on the Sun, 1988, She Was Marked for Murder, 1988, Love and Betrayal, 1989, When Will I Be Loved?, 1990, The Burden of Proff, 1992, Survive The Night, 1993, Hart to Hart: Old Friends Never Die, 1994; TV series The Girl from U.N.C.L.E., 1966, The Feather and the Father Gang, 1977, Hart to Hart, 1979-84. *

POWIS, CONSTANCE GAIL, legal assistant; b. Lansing, Mich., May 10, 1946; d. Albert Edward Jr. and Vivian Jeanette (Bateman) P.; m. Harry Kuulani Kahale Jr., Mar. 18, 1978 (div. 1981). Assoc. in Bus., Lansing Community Coll., 1977. Cert. profl. legal sec., profl. sec., legal asst. Legal sec. Farhat, Burns and Story, P.C., Lansing, 1966-74, adminstrv. asst., 1975-78; legal sec. various law firms, Las Vegas, Nev., 1978-81, Miller, Canfield, Paddock & Stone, Lansing, 1981; legal asst. Foster, Swift, Collins & Smith, P.C., Lansing, 1981—; mem. adv. com. Lansing Community Coll., 1981—, adj. prof., 1985-86; mem. adv. bd. Davenport Coll., Lansing, 1987—. Mem. State Bar Mich. (legal assts. sect. 1990—, coun. 1990-91), Nat. Assn. Legal Assts., Greater Lansing Estate Planning Coun. (assoc.). Republican. Home: 5647 Harper Rd Holt MI 48842-8615 Office: Foster Swift Collins & Smith PC 313 S Washington Sq Lansing MI 48933-2193

POYNOR, DEBORAH ANN, English language educator; b. Chillicothe, Ohio, Dec. 11, 1952; d. Everett Hershall and Virginia Ann (Stanhope) Keller; m. Raymond Walter Poynor, Aug. 9, 1974; children: Dedra Ann, Brad Raymond, Jessica Renee. AS in Computers, Scioto Tech. Coll., 1973; BS, Ohio U., 1991. Cert. English and secondary edn. tchr., Ohio. Computer operator Med. Ctr. Hosp., Chillicothe, 1973-75; clk. Harrison Twp., Chillicothe, 1980—; substitute tchr. city and county schs., Chillicothe, 1991—. Honorary mem. Ross County Com. for the Elderly, 1985—, Ross County 4-H, 1983—. Mem. Ross County Trustees and Clks. Assn., Ross County Homemakers. Home and Office: Harrison Twp Ross County 9293 Charleston Pike Chillicothe OH 45601-9060

POYNTER, MARION KNAUSS, retired publishing executive; b. Poughkeepsie, N.Y., Apr. 17, 1926; d. Louis Eugene and Rose (Arndt) Knauss; m. Nelson Paul Poynter, May 4, 1970 (dec. 1978). A.B., Vassar Coll., 1946. Librarian, Time, Inc., N.Y.C., 1949-51; research analyst U.S. Govt., Washington, 1952-60; editorial research analyst St. Petersburg Times, Fla., 1961-63, editorial asst./editorial writer, 1963-70, contbg. editor, 1970-78; dir. Times Pub. Co., 1970-91, Poynter Inst. for Media Studies, 1970-91; bd. visitors U. Md. Coll. Journalism, 1990—. Home: The Meadows 6845 Blantyre Rd Warrenton VA 22186-9416

POYTHRESS, STEPHANIE LYNN, editor, writer; b. Rockford, Ill., May 22, 1964; d. William Hull and Georgia Anne (Correnti) P. BA, Oakland U., Rochester, Mich., 1987. Freelance editorial asst. Aegis Group, Troy, Mich., 1986-89, freelance editor, 1988-89; freelance writer Stephanie Poythress, Inc., Rochester, 1987—; editor Entertainment Publs., Inc., Troy, 1990, Cat Companion Mag. Quarton Group Pub., Troy, 1990-92; mng. editor Smart Health Quarton Group Pub., Troy, 1990-92; assoc. editor 21 Mag. Quarton Group Pub., 1990-92; writer, editor Anthony M. Franco, Inc., Detroit, 1992-93; cons. pub. rels. Four Star Marble, Mt. Clemens, Mich., 1989-92; instr. freelance writing Rochester Adult Edn. Editor (airline newsletter) Spl. Agt., 1988-89, (automotive newletter) New Dimensions, 1989; contbg. editor GMAC Quest mag., 1989-90; asst. editor Twenty One mag., Interior Lifestyles mag.; mng. editor Smart Health newsletter; contbr. articles to numerous mags. Mem. Detroit Inst. Arts, 1989—, mem. founders jr. coun. Mem. Internat. Women's Writing Guild, Women in Communications, Inc. Office: Anthony M Franco Inc Ste 600 400 Renaissance Ctr Detroit MI 48243

PRABHAKAR, ARATI, federal administration research director, electrical engineer; b. New Delhi, Feb. 2, 1959; came to U.S., 1962; d. Jagdish Chandra and Raj (Madan) P. BSEE, Tex. Tech U., 1979; MSEE, Calif. Inst. Tech., 1980, PhD in Applied Physics, 1984. Congl. fellow Office Tech. Assessment U.S. Congress, Washington, 1984-86; program mgr. electronic sci. divsn. DARPA, Arlington, Va., 1986-90, dep. dir. defense sci. office, 1990-91, dir. microelectronics tech. office, 1991-93; dir. Nat. Inst. Standards & Tech., Gaithersburg, Md., 1993—. Contbr. articles to profl. jours. Rsch. fellow Calif. Inst. Tech., 1979-84; grad. rsch. program for women Bell Labs., 1979, 80; named Disting. Engr. of 1994, Tex. Tech U.; elected to Tex. Tech Elec. Engring. Acad., 1994. Mem. IEEE, Eta Kappa Nu, Tau Beta Pi. Office: Nat Inst Stds & Tech US Dept of Commerce Rte 270 Bldg 101 Rm A1134 Gaithersburg MD 20899

PRACHICK, TONI THOMAS, librarian; b. Jonesboro, Ark., Mar. 21, 1954; d. John Hayden and Sarah (Doan) Thomas; m. Thomas Paul Prachick, June 19, 1982. BA, U. North Tex., 1977; MLS, Tex. Woman's U., 1991. Libr. asst. Richland Hills (Tex.) Pub. Libr., 1987-88, Flower Mound (Tex.) Pub. Libr., 1989, Fort Worth (Tex.) Pub. Libr., 1989-90; market rsch. libr. intern GTE Telephone Ops., Irving, Tex., 1990-91; staff asst. libr. Am. Eagle Tng. Ctr., DFW Airport, Tex., 1993—. Mem. ALA, Tex. Libr. Assn., Spl. Libr. Assn., N.E. Tex. Online Users Group. Republican. Episcopalian. Home: 34 Devonshire Dr Bedford TX 76021

PRACHT, DRENDA KAY, psychologist; b. Carrollton, Mo., Jan. 15, 1952; d. Ethan Lyle Pracht and Wilma Esteleen (Henderson) Lucas; 1 child, Matthew Kent. BA in Psychology, William Jewell Coll., 1974; MS in Clinical Psychology, Cen. Mo. State U., 1976; postgrad. in clin. psychology, Fielding Inst., Santa Barbara, Calif., 1987—. Lic. psychologist, marriage and family therapist, Minn., Kans.; lic. psychologist, Mo., Minn. Therapist Briscoe Carr Cons., Kansas City, Mo., 1978-79; psychologist Crittenton Ctr., Kansas City, 1979-81, Cen. Minn. Mental Health Ctr., St. Cloud, 1981-85, St. Cloud Hosp., 1985-87; gen. practice psychology St. Cloud, 1985-92, Kansas City, 1992—; cons. St. Benedicts Ctr., Country Manor, 1986-92. Mem. Cen. Minn. Child Abuse Team, St. Cloud, 1981-85; bd. dirs. Cen. Minn. Child Care Assn., St. Cloud, 1982-83. Mem. Am. Psychol. Assn., Cen. Minn. Psychol. Assn. (pres. 1984-85), Minn. Lic. Psychologists, Minn. Psychol. Assn., Alpha Delta Pi Aumni Assn. Presbyterian. Office: Ste 206 1200 E 104th St E-1 Kansas City MO 64131

PRAEGER, SANDY, state legislator; b. Oct. 21, 1944; m. Mark A. Praeger. Student, U. Kans., 1966. V.p. Douglas County Bank; mem. Kans. Ho. of Reps. Vice chmn. Douglas County Rep. Cent. Com.; chmn. Leadership Kans.; pres. bd. dirs. United Way. Home: 3601 Quail Creek Ct Lawrence KS 66047-2134 Office: Kans State Senate State Capitol Topeka KS 66612*

PRAGER, SUSAN WESTERBERG, dean, law educator; b. Sacramento, Dec. 14, 1942; d. Percy Foster Westerberg and Aileen M. (McKinley) P.; m. James Martin Prager, Dec. 14, 1973; children: McKinley Ann, Case Mahone. AB, Stanford U., 1964, MA, 1967; JD, UCLA, 1971. Bar: N.C. 1971, Calif. 1972. Atty. Powe, Porter & Alphin, Durham, N.C., 1971-72; acting prof. law UCLA, 1972-77, prof. Sch. Law, 1977—, Arjay and Frances Fearing Miller prof. of law, 1992—, assoc. dean Sch. Law, 1979-82, dean, 1982—; bd. dirs. Pacific Mut. Life Ins. Co., Newport Beach, Calif. Editor-in-chief, UCLA Law Rev., 1970-71. Trustee Stanford U., 1976-80, 87—. Mem. ABA (council of sect. on legal edn. and admissions to the bar 1983-85), Assn. Am. Law Schs. (pres. 1986), Order of Coif. Office: UCLA Sch Law 405 Hilgard Ave Los Angeles CA 90095-1476

PRAKUP, BARBARA LYNN, communications executive; b. Cleve., Oct. 6, 1957; d. Edward Vincent and Carol Marie (O'Hara) Reese; m. Gary M. Prakup, July 2, 1977; 1 child, Sarah Ellen. BA, Cleve. State U., 1979; MA, Cleve. State U., Ohio, 1981. Cert. Clinical Competence, Ohio. Speech therapist Keystone Local Sch. Dist., LaGrange, Ohio, 1981-82; lang. devel. spl. Cuyahoga County Bd. M.R., Cleve., 1982-86; sr. clinician InSpeech, Inc., Valley Forge, Pa., 1987-88; speech pathologist Middleburg Heights, Ohio; dir. speech pathologists Litchfield Rehab. Ctr., Akron Gen. Med. Ctr., 1988-90; owner Comprehensive Communication Specialists, Medina, Ohio, 1990—. Mem. Am. Sph. & Hrng. Assn., Aphasiology Assn. Ohio, Akron Regional Sph & Hrng Assn. Democrat. Mennonite. Office: Comprehensive Comm Specialists 750 E Washington St # A-6 Medina OH 44256-2137

PRANGE, SALLY BOWEN, artist, potter; b. Valparaiso, Ind., Aug. 11, 1927; d. Milton Matern and Sarah Louise (Mammen) Bowen; m. A.J. Prange Jr., Feb. 4, 1950 (div. Mar. 1993); children: Christine Anne, Martha Louise, Laura Beth, David Elliott. BA, U. Mich., 1950. One-woman shows at Greenwood Gallery, Washington, 1980, Greenwich House Pottery, N.Y.C., 1983, Olson & Larson Gallery, West Des Moines, Iowa, 1984, Contemporary Crafts Gallery, Portland, Oreg., 1986, Gallery Moderne, Syracuse, N.Y., 1987, Durham (N.C.) Art Guild, 1993, Lee Hansley Gallery, Raleigh, N.C., 1993; exhibited in group shows at Greater Reston (Va.) Arts Ctr., 1984, Kyoto (Japan) Crafts Ctr., 1986, Pewabic Pottery, Detroit, 1990, No. Ariz. U., Flagstaff, 1993, Tyndall Gallery, Durham, 1993, Am. Embassy, Tokyo, 1993; represented in permanent collections at So. Progress Corp., Birmingham, Ala., N.C. Mus. History, Raleigh, Everson Mus. Art, Syracuse, N.Y., Victoria & Albert Mus., London, Nat. Mus. Am. Art, Washington, Museo Internazionale della Ceramiche, Faenza, Italy, Glazo Corp, N.C. Mem. Nat. Coun. Edn. in Ceramic Arts, Am. Craft Coun., Piedmont Crafts, Tri-State Sculptors Guild. Home and Studio: 6421 Heartwood Dr Chapel Hill NC 27516

PRASIL, LINDA ANN, lawyer, writer; b. Chgo., July 27, 1947; d. Joseph J. and Helen Marie (Palucki) P.; m. John T. Rank, July 25, 1970; 1 child, Sean Patrick Prasil Rank. BA in Interdisciplinary Studies, Am. U., Washington, 1974, JD, 1977; MALS, Mundelein Coll., Chgo., 1992. Bar: Ill. 1977. Ind. contractor Baker & McKenzie, Chgo., 1977-78; atty. Pretzel, Stouffer, Nolan & Rooney, Chgo., 1978-79; sole practitioner Lincolnshire, Ill., 1979—; atty. Leonard M. Ring, Chgo., 1982; grader Ill. State Bar Examiners, Chgo., 1978-90; organizer Kennedy for Pres., Chgo., 1979-80, NOW-ERA Ill., Chgo., 1980, Ill. Polit. Action Com., Chgo., 1981. Legal advisor Holy Cross Talk of Town, Deerfield, Ill., 1992, 93; tchr. Holy Cross Drug Awareness Program, Deerfield, 1993; religious edn. tchr. Holy Cross, Deerfield, 1983-86. Mem. Ill. State Bar Assn., Internat. Alliance of Holistic Lawyers. Office: 35 Keswick Ct Lincolnshire IL 60069-3425

PRATER, SANDRA JEAN, corporate communications executive, event planner; b. Seattle, May 11, 1944; d. William Northy and Blanche Elvira (Wilson) P. Student, Western Wash. State U., 1962-63. Mktg. svc. rep. Pacific Northwest Bell, Seattle, 1963-66; asst. comm. analyst Seattle-1st Nat. Bank, 1966; comm. cons. Comm. Mgmt., Inc., Seattle, 1966-72; mgr. bus. devel. and adminstrv. sys. Stevens Thompson & Runyan, Inc., Seattle, 1972-75; comm. cons. U.S. West (formerly Pacific Northwest Bell), Seattle, 1975-76, svc. cons., 1976, acct. exec., 1977, market mgr., 1978, mktg. competition analyst, 1978-80, corp. contbns. mgr., 1980-88, program dir. U.S. West Found., 1988-89, mgr. employee comm., spl. events, 1989-93; propr. Prater Writes, Redmond, Wash., 1993—. Editor Review, 1994. Chair Seattle/Tacoma adv. com. Local Initiatives Support Corp., 1983-86, chair fund raising, 1986-87; mem. Seattle Art Mus., King County Sexual Assault Resource Ctr., Wash. Wildlife and Recreation Coalition, 1991-92, Coun. Founds., Coun. Prevention Child Abuse & Neglect, Women in Founds.-Corp. Philanthropy, United Way King County, many others. Recipient numerous civic awards; Washington World Affairs fellow, 1986-87. Mem. Pub. Rels. Soc. Am., City Club (charter), Internat. Assn. Bus. Communicators, Redmond C. of C., Leadership Redmond, Seattle C. of C., Bellevue C. of C. Office: Prater Writes 14009 NE 63d St Redmond WA 98052

PRATHER, DONNA LYNN, psychiatrist; b. Charlotte, N.C., Nov. 4, 1946; d. James Boyd and Ann (Joyner) P. BA, Queens Coll., Charlotte, 1968; MD, U. N.C., 1978. Supr. Meckenburg County Dept. Social Svcs., Charlotte, 1971-74; family practice intern Charlotte Meml. Hosp., 1978-79, resident in family practice, 1979-81; fellow in family medicine U. N.C., Chapel Hill, 1981-82; resident in psychiatry N.C. Meml. Hosp., Chapel Hill, 1982-85; pvt. practice psychiatry Chapel Hill, N.C., 1985—; psychiatrist Person Counceling Ctr., Roxboro, N.C., 1983-92; med. dir. Orange-Person-Chatam Mental Health Ctr., Chapel Hill., 1992—; clin. asst. prof. U. N.C., Chapel Hill., 1985—. Mem. N.C. Psychiat. Assn., N.C. Med. Soc., Am. Psychiat. Assn., N.C. Psychiat. Assn. (chmn., com. for women 1990-91). Office: The Courtyard Ste 27 Chapel Hill NC 27514

PRATHER, LENORE LOVING, state supreme court presiding justice; b. West Point, Miss., Sept. 17, 1931; d. Byron Herald and Hattie Hearn (Morris) Loving; m. Robert Brooks Prather, May 30, 1957; children: Pamela, Valerie Jo, Malinda Wayne. B.S., Miss. State Coll. Women, 1953; JD, U. Miss., 1955. Bar: Miss. 1955. Practice with B. H. Loving, West Point, 1955-60, sole practice, 1960-62, 65-71, assoc. practice, 1962-65; mcpl. judge City of West Point, 1965-71; chancery ct. judge 14th dist. State of Miss., Columbus, 1971-82; supreme ct. justice State of Miss., Jackson, 1982-92; presiding justice State of Miss., 1993—; v.p. Conf. Local Bar Assn., 1956-58; sec. Clay County Bar Assn., 1956-71. 1st woman in Miss. to become chancery judge, 1971, and supreme ct. justice, 1982. Mem. ABA, Miss. State Bar Assn., Miss. Conf. Judges, DAR, Rotary, Pilot Club, Jr. Aux. Columbus Club. Episcopalian. Office: Miss Supreme Ct PO Box 117 Jackson MS 39205-0117 also: PO Box 903 Columbus MS 39703-0903

PRATHER, RITA CATHERINE, psychology educator; b. Marietta, Ohio, Nov. 20, 1948; d. Lloyd R. Sr. and Rita C. (Alkazin) Peters; m. Robert E. Prather, Dec. 20, 1969. BA, U. Cen. Fla., 1983; MA, La. State U., 1985, PhD, 1989. Lic. clin. psychologist, Tex. Asst. prof. Tex. A&M U., College Station, 1988-89; psychologist Psychol. Assn. Tex., P.C., Houston, 1989-90; postdoctoral fellow U. Tex. Med. Sch. Houston, 1990-91, asst. prof. psychology, 1991—; speaker on pub. rels. U. Tex.-Houston, Judge Houston Sci. and Engring. Fair, 1993, 94. Contbr. over 30 articles to profl. jours. and confs. U. Miss. Med. Ctr. rsch. grantee, 1988. Mem. APA (divsn. clin. and health psychology), Houston Psychol. Assn. (speakers bus. 1990—), Soc. Behavioral Medicine, Assn. Advancement Behavior Therapy. Home: PO Box 920814 Houston TX 77292-0814 Office: U Tex Med Sch Psychiatry Dept 1300 Moursund St Houston TX 77030-3406

PRATHER, SUSAN LYNN, public relations executive; b. Melrose Park, Ill.; d. Horace Charles and Ruth Anna Paula (Backus) P.; divorced. BS, Ind. U., 1973, MS, 1975. Arts administr. Lyric Opera Chgo., 1975; jr. account exec. Morton H. Kaplan Assocs., Chgo., 1976-78, sr. account exec., 1978-81; account supr. Ketchum Pub. Relations, Chgo., 1981-83, v.p., 1983-87, v.p., group mgr., 1985-87; v.p., dir. pub. relations Cramer-Krasselt, Chgo., 1987—; cons. Disney-MGM Studios, Velamints, Citicorp Global Payments Div., S.W. Airlines, Beechnut Nutrition Corps., Foster Wheeler, Diners Club, Reading Energy, Kellogg Co., Battle Creek, Mich., 1985—, Village of Rosemont, Ill., 1977—. Singer various recitals; founder, dir. Chgo. Sports Hall of Fame, 1978-81. Mem. archives com. Chgo. Symphony Orch., 1986—, mem. long term planning com., 1987-89; mem. press advance team Papal Visit to Chgo., 1978; mem. White House Press Advance Team, Chgo., 1976-80. Mem. Pub. Rels. Soc. Am. (bd. dirs. Chgo. chpt. 1987—), Internat. Pub. Rels. Assn., Publicity Club (bd. dirs. 1986—, Merit award 1982, Golden Trumpet awards, Silver Trumpet awards), Bus. and Profl. Assn. Lutheran. Home: 3950 N Lake Shore Dr Chicago IL 60613-3434

PRATT, ALICE REYNOLDS, retired educational administrator; b. Marietta, Ohio, Oct. 5, 1922; d. Thurman J. and Vera L. (Holdren) Reynolds. BA, U. Okla., 1943. Reporter, high sch. tchr., 1944-50; asst. dir. Houston office Inst. Internat. Edn., 1952-58, dir. office, 1958-87, v.p., 1976-87, ret. 1987. Decorated Palmes Academiques (France), 1966; Order of Merit (Fed. Republic Germany), 1972; knight Order of Leopold II (Belgium), 1973; named Woman of Yr., Houston Bus. and Profl. Women, 1958; recipient Matrix award Theta Sigma Phi, 1961; Nat. Carnation award Gamma Phi Beta, 1976. Mem. Houston Com. Fgn. Rels., Japan Am. Soc. (Houston), Houston Philos. Soc., Houston-Taipei Soc. (founding mem., pres. 1989-92), Houston-Galveston/Stavanger Sister City Assn. (founding mem.), Sister Cities Internat. (past nat. bd. dirs.), Nat. Coun. Internat. Visitors (past nat. bd. dirs.), Pan Am. Roundtable (bd. dirs.), Inst. Internat. Edn. (bd. dirs. so. regional office), Houston Forum (founding bd. govs.). Republican. Episcopalian.

PRATT, BARBARA IRIS, audit manager; b. Laurel, Miss., Aug. 31, 1950; d. Joseph Eugene and Iris May (Neville) P. BA in Bus. Adminstrn., Minot State U., 1978; M in Acctg., U. N.D., 1979. CPA, N.D.; cert. internal auditor, fraud examiner, mgmt. acct. Acct. City of Grand Forks, N.D., 1980-81; assoc. prof. Minot (N.D.) State U., 1981-84; audit dir. Midwest Fed. Sav. Bank, Minot, 1984-87; contr., v.p. Windtree Fin. Corp., Sherman Oaks, Calif., 1987-90; audit group mgr., v.p. Gt. Western Fin. Corp., Chatsworth, Pa., 1990—. Named Bus. Person of Yr., Phi Beta Lambda, 1987. Mem. AICPAs, Inst. Internal Auditor (sec. 1992-94, exec. v.p. 1994—, Outstanding member San Fernando chpt. 1989), Cert. Fraud Examiners, Inst. Mgmt. Accts. Office: Gt Western Bank 9401 Oakdale Ave Chatsworth CA 91311

PRATT, KATHERINE MERRICK, company executive; b. Alexandria, Egypt, July 4, 1951; d. Theodore and Bettie (Curland) R.; m. Harry Kenneth Todd (div.); 1 child, Kirsten Todd-Pratt. BBA in Mgmt. Systems, U. Iowa, 1980; postgrad., U. Tex., 1985-87. Program data mgr. Rockwell Internat., Dallas, 1981-85; support coord. GTE Govt. Systems, Taunton, Mass., 1987-89, support engr., 1989-93; pres. Enviro-Logistics Inc., Jamestown, R.I., 1993—. Mem. Soc. Logistics Engrs. (officer, mem. standing com. environ. applications, nat. chpt. newsletter judge), U.S. Pony Club (Ctrl. New Eng. championship chairwoman).

PRATT, LINDA, educator; b. Mass., May 28, 1948. BA, U. Mass., 1970, MEd, 1975, EDd, 1978. Cert. elem. edn., reading specialist, reading supr. Prof., dir. grad. reading program Elmira (N.Y.) Coll.; prof. Gonzaga U., Spokane, Wash.; insvc. tchr. U. Mass., Amherst; reading specialist Southwick (Mass.) Pub. Sch. System. Mem. IRA, NCTE, Nat. Reading Conf., Kappa Delta Pi, Phi Delta Kappa, Kappa Delta Gamma. Office: Elmira Coll Elmira NY 14901

PRATT, RENEE, state legislator. BA, Dillard U.; MEd, U. New Orleans. Mem. La. Ho. of Reps. Named Spl. Educator of Yr. Mem. Nat. Honor Soc., Alpha Kappa Mu. Democrat. Roman Catholic. Office: La Ho of Reps State Capitol Baton Rouge LA 70804 Address: 1636 Toledano St Ste 304 New Orleans LA 70115*

PRATT, SONIA L., art educator, artist; b. Mannington, W.Va., Mar. 2, 1949; d. Ralph W. and Irene (Watson) Long; m. Frederick Michael Pratt, Aug. 19, 1972; children: Devin Frederick, Hagan Matthew. BA in Art Edn., Fairmont State Coll., 1972; postgrad., U. Ariz., 1974, W. Va. U., 1976. Advanced profl. cert. in art edn. Art instr. Garrett County Bd. of Edn., Oakland, Md., 1973—; bd. dirs. Garrett County Arts Coun., McHenry, Md.; mem., edn. outreach com. The Art Co., Davis, W.Va.; founding mem. Summit Mt. Artist, Oakland. Active Am. Fedn. Tchrs./Garrett County Fedn. Tchrs., 1980—, St. Peter's Cath. Ch., Oakland, 1982—, NOW. Recipient John Dewey award for Excellence in Edn., Am. Fedn. Tchrs./Garrett County Fedn. Tchrs., 1983; New Forms Regional grantee Pa. Coun. on the Arts, 1994; grantee Nat. Endowment for the Arts, Rockefeller Found., Andy Warhol Found. for the Visual Arts, Inc. Mem. Md. State Art Edn. Assn. (Outstanding Svc. in Art Edn. award 1982, 84). Democrat. Roman Catholic. Home: PO Box 114 Oakland MD 21550

PRAVDA, MURIEL, sculptor, educator; m. Arthur Pravda; childlren: Amy Holland, Don. Cert., Bklyn. Coll., 1947, South Fla. Art Inst., 1993, Atterbury Sculpture Sch., 1976; student, Bruno Lucchese Seminars, 1980—. Cert. art instr. Instr. clay sculpture South Fla. Art Inst., Miami; lectr. sculpture workshops; restorer paintings Lang Gallery, Jamaica Estates, 1970-80. Exhibited in group shows at North Miami Mus., Internat. Boat Show, Miami Beach, Hollywood (Fla.) Art Guild, Community Art Alliance, Hollywood; pvt. commns. include John Kennedy '89; one woman shows include South Fla. Art Inst., 1987, Gallery at Turnberry, North Miami Beach, 1989; faculty show at Discovery Ctr., Ft. Lauderdale; miniature show at Del Bello Gallery, Toronto, Ont., Can., Leonard Art Gallery, Ft. Lauderdale, 1990, many others. Recipient 1st place sculpture award Miami Art League, 1981, Merit award sculpture, 1982, Silver Poet, Writer's Lullaby, 1990, Gold Poet, Song of the World, Editor's Award, The Survivors, nat. Libr. of Poetry, 1993. Mem. Nat. Sculpture Soc., Internat. Sculpture Soc. (assoc.), Women in the ARts, Miami Art League, Nat. Mus. Women Arts (charter mem.). Home: 1655 NE 115th St North Miami FL 33181

PRAY, MERLE EVELYN, nurse psychotherapist, educator; b. Washington, Vt., Apr. 19, 1931; d. Clifton Clough and Dorothy (Wadleigh) P. Diploma in nursing, N.H. Sch. Nursing, Concord, 1952; BSN, Loyola U., Chgo., 1977; MS, U. Ill., Chgo., 1983. RN, Ill.; cert. in addictions nursing Nat. Nurses Soc. on Addictions; cert. clin. specialist in adult psychiat. and mental health nursing ANA. Community placement coord. Ill. Dept. Mental Health and Devel. Disability, Chgo., 1977, mental health adminstr., planning area coord., 1978-81; head nurse VA West Side Med. Ctr., Chgo., 1984, clin. specialist, 1985—; adj. clin. instr. psychiat. nursing U. Ill., 1986—. Mem. ANA, Nat. Nurses Soc. on Addictions, Am. Psychiat. Nurses Assn., Ill. Nurses Assn. Home: 175 E Delaware Pl Chicago IL 60611-1756 Office: VA West Side Med Ctr 820 S Damen Ave Chicago IL 60680

PREBLE, LINDA M., nursing administrator; b. Bangor, Maine, Mar. 1, 1950; d. John and Ruby Mae (Dorr) MacLauchlan; divorced; children: William, Robert. BSN, U. Maine, 1973; M in Healthcare Adminstrn., Quinnipiac Coll., 1988. RN, Conn., Fla. Ob-gyn. staff nurse Yale New Haven Hosp., 1973-79, med. ICU nurse, 1979-83, post anesthesia staff nurse, 1983-88; adminstrv. mgmt. intern Shirley Frank Found., New Haven, 1987-88; clin. nurse adminstr. pain mgmt. Yale U., New Haven, 1988-92; nurse mgr., arthritis and pain ctrs. North Broward Med. Ctr., 1992—. Author: A Manual for Acute Postoperative Pain Management, 1992; author and editor: Acute Pain Mechanisms and Management, 1992; contbr. articles to profl. jours. Mem. Internat. Assn. Study of Pain, Am. Pain Soc., Am. Soc. Post Anesthesia Nurses, Am. Soc. Pain Mgmt. Nurses (founder), Conn. Soc. Post Anesthesia Nurses. Home: 7598 Pinewalk Dr S Margate FL 33063

PREBLE, LOU-ANN M., state legislator; m. Bill Preble. Grad., Tuomey Hosp. Sch. Nursing, 1950, Prima C.C., 1978. RN S.C., 1951-77; physical evaluator Medi-Quik, Tucson, 1978-82; co-owner, mgr. retail apparel store, 1972-75, ret.; mem. Ariz. Ho. of Reps., mem. assignments com. former precinct committeeman, dep. registr.; state committeeman, 1974-92; rep. at large State Exec. Com., 1991-92. Republican. Roman Catholic. Address: 2100 S Cathy Ave Tucson AZ 85710 Office: House of Representatives 1700 W Washington Phoenix AZ 85007*

PREECE, NORMA, executive secretary; b. Kaysville, Utah, May 19, 1922; d. Walter and Wilma (Witt) Buhler; m. Joseph Franklin Preece, July 26, 1946 (dec. 1991); children: Terry Joe, Shannette Preece Keeler. Grad. high sch., Kaysville, 1940. Telephone operator Mountain States Telephone & Telegraph Co., Kaysville, 1940-43; clk. Civil Svc., Ogden, Utah, 1943-50; newspaper corr. Davis County Clipper, North Davis County, Utah, 1954-85; pub. communication dir. Latter-day Saints Ch., Kaysville, 1988-89; exec. sec. Kaysville Area C. of C., Kaysville, 1985-90; stake missionary Latter-Day Saints Ch., Kaysville, 1991—. Publicity chmn. Boy Scouts Am., Kaysville, 1965-69, Am. Cancer Dr., Davis County, 1967, Kaysville Civic Assn., 1960-80; mem. Utah Press Women Assn., Salt Lake City, 1973-75; active publicity Utah Congress PTA, Salt Lake City, 1977—; judge FFA, Davis County, 1968; campaign com. mem. Rep. Party, Davis County, 1990; ordinance worker LDS Temple, Ogden, Utah, 1992-94, Bountiful, Utah, 1995—; co-chmn. Kaysville City Centennial, 1950. Recipient award for outstanding contbn. Davis High Sch., Kaysville, 1979, Total Citizen award Utah C. of C., 1988, Disting. Svc. award Kaysville Arts Coun., 1981; Outstanding Svc. award Kaysville Jaycees, 1972, Disting. Svc. award, 1985, Cmty. Unsung Hero award City of Kaysville, 1994; named Citizen of Yr., City of Kaysville, 1985. Mem. Lit. Club (Athena chpt., sec. 1984, 87, v.p. 1989, pres. 1990), Fine Arts Club (pres. 1964, sec. 1994). Mem. LDS Ch. Home: 347 E 200th N Kaysville UT 84037 Office: Kaysville Area C of C 44 E 100th N Kaysville UT 84037

PREER, JEAN LYON, university administrator, educator; b. Rochester, N.Y., June 25, 1944; d. Henry Gould and Helen Corinne (McTarnaghan) Lyon; m. James Randolph Preer, June 24, 1967; children: Genevieve, Stephen. BA in History with honors, Swarthmore Coll., 1966; MLS, U. Calif., Berkeley, 1967; JD with highest honors, George Washington U., 1974, PhD, 1980. Bar: D.C. 1975. With Henry E. Huntington Libr., San Marino, Calif., 1967-69; Woodrow Wilson Found. teaching intrn Fed. City Coll., Washington, 1969-70; cons. Inst. for Svcs. to Edn., Silver Spring, Md., 1981-82; vol. edn. divsn. Nat. Archives, Washington, 1981-89; adj. prof. U. D.C., 1984-85; adj. prof. Cath. U. Am., Washington, 1985-87, asst. prof. sch. libr. and info. sci., 1987-92, assoc. prof., 1992—, assoc. dean., 1991-93, 94—, acting dean, 1993-94; adj. assoc. prof. George Washington U., 1985-87. Contbr. articles to profl. jours. Mem. governing bd. Nat. Cathedral Sch., Washington, 1987-91. Fellow Nat. Acad. Edn., 1984-85; grantee Nat. Endowment for Humanities. Mem. Order of Coif, Beta Phi Mu. Home: 2900 Rittenhouse St NW Washington DC 20015-1524 Office: Cath U Am Sch Libr and Info Sci Washington DC 20064

PREHLE, TRICIA A., accountant; b. Queens, N.Y., Oct. 17, 1970; d. William G. and Dolores (Cameron) P. BBA in Acctg., CUNY, Baruch Coll., 1992. Cert. mgmt. acct. Acct. Gruntal & Co., Incorporated, N.Y.C., 1992—. Mgr. Community Tax Aid, Inc., N.Y.C., 1992—. Mem. Inst. Cert. Mgmt. Accts., Sigma Alpha (Delta chpt.). Home: 60-48 69th Ave Flushing NY 11385-5140 Office: Gruntal & Co Incorporated 14 Wall St New York NY 10005

PREISS, PATRICIA ELLEN, musician, educator; b. N.Y.C., May 19, 1950; d. Fredric H. and Madeline (Robbins) P.; m. Eric A. Lerner, Nov. 1970 (div. 1975). BA, Harvard U., 1973; MFA, Calif. Inst. Arts, 1987. Performer, bassist Carla Bley Band, Willow, N.Y., 1977-78; instr. piano, composition The Hall Sch., Pittsfield, Mass., 1983-84; instr. music Santa Monica (Calif.) C.C., 1989; tchr. piano The Hackley Sch., Tarrytown, N.Y., 1991; tchr. piano and composition Fraioli Sch. of Music, Greenwich, Conn., 1991—; accompanist SUNY, Purchase, N.Y., 1991—; pvt. piano tchr., N.Y., Conn., Mass., 1980—. Author: Musical Materials, 1987; composer, performer Jamaica's Album, 1984; composer Complete Enlightenment, 1986. Performance grantee Cambridge (Mass.) Arts Coun., 1977, Artists grantee No. Berkshire Coun. on Arts, 1983. Home: 18 Thomas St Cos Cob CT 06807

PREMO, DOLORES ANN, realtor; b. Reedsburg, Wis., July 18, 1935; d. Anthony P. and Juliann C. (Peasall) Hudzinski; m. Stanley David Premo, Sept. 10, 1955. Cert. profl. sec., residential specialist, residential broker. Asst. to county clk. Sauk County, Baraboo, Wis., 1952-55; sec. to pres. Ozier Constrn. Co., Champaign, Ill., 1955-57, Bartelt Engring. Co., Rockford, Ill., 1957-67, Priebe Ins. Co., Rockford, 1967-68; sales rep. Bob Lindgren, Realtor, Rockford, 1969-72; owner Premo & Assocs., Rockford, 1972-75; exec. v.p. Whitehead, Inc., Realtors, Rockford, 1975—. Editor: Focus on Homes, 1983-93. Mem. Rockford Area Assn. Realtors (Outstanding Individual 1978, Outstanding Com. Chmn. 1984, Realtor of Yr. 1990), Rockford East/C.V. Rotary Club (dir.), Paul Harris Found. (fellow). Home: 7223 Tulagi Trl Rockford IL 61108-4454 Office: Whitehead Inc 5100 E State St Rockford IL 61108-2398

PRENDERGAST, ANNE MAYFIELD, secondary education educator; b. Baton Rouge, Dec. 4, 1945; d. Rupert Franklin and Priscilla Annie-Lauri (Sappington) Mayfield; m. William Davis Balis, Jan. 26, 1967 (div. 1972); m. John Goebel Prendergast, Jan. 18, 1975; 1 child, Judith Anne. BS in Bus. Edn., La. State U., 1968; MEd in Higher Edn. Adminstrn., U. New Orleans, 1992. Life cert. vocat. tchr., type A secondary cert., La. Legal sec. various firms, 1968-75; media buyer Ad-Four Advt. Agy., Baton Rouge, 1975; instr. devel. English, Slidell (La.) Tech. Inst., 1978-79, instr., head bus. dept., 1980-86; adminstrv. cons. Apex Employment Cons., New Orleans, 1979-80; instr. English and bus. Slidell Learning Ctr., Delgado C.C., 1987-89, office mgr., 1989-94; tchr. English Slidell H.S., 1994—. Mem. exec. bd. Women's Health Found. La., Slidell, 1993; com. chmn. Project Graduation, Slidell, 1994. Mem. Nat. Coun. Tchrs. English, La. Coun. Tchrs. English, Slidell C. of C., Phi Kappa Delta, Alpha Theta Epsilon, Kappa Delta Pi. Republican. Baptist. Home: 553 Manchester Dr Slidell LA 70461-4917 Office: Slidell HS 1 Tiger Dr Slidell LA 70458

PRENTICE, ANN ETHELYND, academic adminstrator; b. Grafton, Vt., July 19, 1933; d. Homer Orville and Helen (Cooke) Hurlbut; divorced; children: David, Melody, Holly, Wayne. AB, U. Rochester, 1954; MLS, SUNY, Albany, 1964; DLS, Columbia U., 1972; LittD (hon.), Keuka Coll., 1979. Lectr. sch. info. sci. and policy SUNY, Albany, 1971-72, asst. prof., 1972-78; prof., dir. grad. sch. library and info. sci. U. Tenn., Knoxville, 1978-88; assoc. v.p. info. resources U. South Fla., Tampa, 1988-93; dean Coll. of Libr. and Info. Svcs. U. Md., 1993—. Author: Strategies for Survival, Library Financial Management Today, 1979, The Library Trustee, 1973, Public Library Finance, 1977, Financial Planning for Libraries, 1983, Professional Ethics for Librarians, 1985; editor Pub. Library Quar., 1978-81; co-editor: Info. Sci. in its Disciplinary Context, 1990; assoc. editor Library and Info. Sci. Ann., 1987-90. Cons. long-range planning and pers. Knox County Libr. System, 1980, 85-86, Richland County S.C. Libr. System, 1981, Upper Hudson Libr. Fedn., N.Y., State Libr. Ohio, 1986; trustee Hyde Park (N.Y.) Free Libr., treas., 1973-75, pres., 1976; trustee Mid-Hudson Libr. System, Poughkeepsie, N.Y., 1975-78; trustee adv. bd. Hillsborough County Libr., 1991-93. Recipient Disting. Alumni award SUNY, Albany, 1987, Columbia U., 1991. Mem. ALA, Am. Soc. Info. Sci. (exec. bd. 1986-89, conf. chmn. 1989, pres. 1992-93, chmn. info. policy com. 1994-95), Assn. for Libr. and Info. Sci. Edn. (pres. 1986). Office: Univ Md Coll Libr and Info Svcs 4105 Hornbake Bldg College Park MD 20742

PRESCOTT, JANELLE, medical/surgical nurse; b. Uniontown, Pa., Jan. 5, 1965; d. Robert Lee and Pauline (Marcinek) Smith; m. Marvin Levi Prescott, Oct. 14, 1989; 1 child, Aaron Michael. Diploma, Uniontown Hosp. Sch. Nursing, 1988, Finesse Finishing Sch., Uniontown, 1986. RN, Pa. Nurse Uniontown Hosp., 1988—. Mem. U.S. Friendship Ambs., 1987—. Home: PO Box 1381 Uniontown PA 15401-1381

PRESCOTT-RHYMER, STEPHANIE JOY, critical care nurse; b. Mobile, Ala., Nov. 14, 1966; d. Henry Arthur and Joy (Scrivener) P.; m. Spencer O.

Rhymer, Aug. 27, 1993; stepchildren: Brandon, Nathan, Cameran. BSN, U. So. Ala., 1989. RN, Ala.; cert. BLS, ACLS, PALS. Critical care nurse Mobile Infirmary, 1989-90; critical care and float nurse U. South Ala. Med. Ctr., Mobile, 1990-91, nurse in surg. step-down unit, 1991-93; with Homecare Svcs., 1992-93, UMC Burn Unit, 1993-94, St. Agnes Med. Ctr., 1993-94, CCU River Parishes Hosp., La., 1994. Mem. ANA, AACN, Ala. Nurses Assn., Nat. League for Nursing, Am. CC Soc., Sigma Theta Tau. Methodist. Home: 1267 Winwood Dr Mobile AL 36605 Office: River Parishes Hosp 500 Rue de Sante La Place LA 70068

PRESIDENT, TONI ELIZABETH, counselor; b. Charleston, S.C., Aug. 23, 1954; d. Sam and Margaret (Shokes) P.; 1 child, Kayla Javonne. BS cum laude, S.C. State Coll., 1976; MEd, The Citadel, 1984; postgrad., Coll. of Charleston, 1993. Tchr., grade 5 Berkeley Elem. Sch., Moncks Corner, S.C., 1976-77; tchr., grade 2 Ben Tillman Elem. Sch., Charleston, 1977-85; guidance counselor Ronald E. McNair Elem. Sch., Charleston, 1985-92, Jennie Moore Elem. Sch., Mt. Pleasant, 1992-94, Orange Grove Elem. Sch., Charleston, S.C., 1994—. Mem. Ebenezer A.M.E. Ch., Charleston, Charleston YWCA, PTA. Recipient bd. mem. awards Charleston (S.C.) Actors Theatre Soc., 1987, 88, Young Women's Christian Assn., Charleston, 1988; named Best Supporting Actress, Charleston (S.C.) Actors Theatre Soc., 1988. Mem. NEA, AACD, Am. Sch. Counselors Assn., S.C. Sch. Counselors Assn., S.C. Edn. Assn., Charleston County Edn. Assn., Phi Delta Kappa, Alpha Kappa Alpha, S.C. State U. Alumni Assn. (Palmetto project). Office: Orange Grove Elem Sch 1225 Orange Branch Rd Charleston SC 29407

PRESKA, LORETTA A., federal judge; b. 1949. BA, Coll. St. Rose, 1970; JD, Fordham U., 1973; LLM, NYU, 1978. Assoc. Cahill, Gordon & Reindel, N.Y.C., 1973-82; ptnr. Herzog, Calamari & Gleason, N.Y.C., 1982-92; fed. judge U.S. Dist. Ct. (so. dist.) N.Y., N.Y.C., 1992—. Active The Parents League. Mem. ABA, N.Y. State Bar Assn., N.Y. County Lawyers Assn., Assn. Bar City N.Y., Fed. Bar Coun., Fordham Law Alumni Assn. (v.p.). Office: US Courthouse Foley Sq New York NY 10007

PRESKA, MARGARET LOUISE ROBINSON, institute executive; b. Parma, N.Y., Jan. 23, 1938; d. Ralph Craven and Ellen Elvira (Niemi) Robinson; m. Daniel C. Preska, Jan. 24, 1959; children: Robert, William, Ellen Preska Steck. B.S. summa cum laude, SUNY, 1957; M.A., Pa. State U., 1961; Ph.D., Claremont Grad. Sch., 1969; postgrad., Manchester Coll., Oxford U., 1973. Instr. LaVerne (Calif.) Coll., 1968-75, asst. prof., asso. prof., acad. dean, 1972-75; instr. Starr King Sch. for Ministry, Berkeley, Calif., summer, 1975; v.p. acad. affairs, equal opportunity officer Mankato (Minn.) State U., 1975-79, pres., 1979-92; project dir. Kaliningrad (Russia) Mil. Re-Tng., 1992—; Disting. svc. prof. Minn. State U.; pres. Inst. for Effective Teaching, 1993—; bd. dirs. No. States Power Co., Norwest Corp., Mankato, Minn., Wellspring, Southeastern Minn. Pres. Pomona Valley chpt. UN Assn., 1968-69, Unitarian Soc. Pomona Valley, 1968-69, PTA Lincoln Elem. Sch., Pomona, 1973-74; mem. Pomona City Charter Revision Commn., 1972; chmn. The Fielding Inst., Santa Barbara, 1983-86; bd. dirs. Elderhostel Internat., 1983-87, Minn. Agrl. Interpretive Ctr. (Farmam.), 1983-92, Am. Assn. State Colls. and Univs., Moscow on the Mississippi - Minn. Meets the Soviet Union; nat. pres. Campfire, Inc., 1985-87; chmn. Gov.'s Coun. on Youth, Minn., 1983-86, Minn. Edn. Forum, 1984; mem. Gov.'s Commn. on Econ. Future of Minn., 1985—, NCAA Pres. Commn., 1986-92, NCAA Cost Cutting Commn., Minn. Brainpower Compact, 1985; commr. Great Lakes Govs.' Econ. Devel. Coun., 1986, Minn Gov.'s Commn. on Forestry. Carnegie Found. grantee Am. Coun. Edn. Deans Inst., 1974; recipient Outstanding Alumni award Pa. State, Outstanding Alumni award Claremont Grad. Sch., YWCA Leader award 1982, Exch. Club Book of Golden Deeds award, 1987; named one of top 100 alumni, SUNY, 1985, Hall of Heritage award, 1988, Wohelo Camp Fire award, 1989. Mem. AAUW (pres. Mankato 1990-92), LWV, Women's Econ. Roundtable, St. Paul/Mpls. Com. on Fgn. Rels., Am. Coun. on Edn., Am. Assn. Univ. Adminstrs., Zonta, Rotary, Benedicts Dance Club. Unitarian. Home: 476 W Broadway Winona MN 55987 Office: Minn State Univs Inst for Effective Teaching 1125 W Wabasha Winona MN 55987

PRESLEY, JEANNINE C., former secondary education educator; b. Fayetteville, Ark., Sept. 25, 1929; d. Evertt Earl and Evalee McCurdy (Nelson) Campbell; m. Atha Winfield McMurtrey (dec. Oct. 1962); children: Atha Winfield, Ward Gerard, Mark Earl; m. George Henry Presley, Mar. 25, 1978. BSE, U. Ark., 1951; MA, Tex. Woman's U., 1968. Cert. tchr. Tchr. Lake Highlands H.S., Richardson, Tex., 1964-66, Stephen F. Austin Jr. H.S., Garland, Tex., 1966-69, Lincoln (Ark.) H.S., 1969, Farmington (Ark.) H.S., 1970-94. Mem. Ladies of Elks (pres. 1990—), Daughters of Nile (queen 1994-95), Order of Amaranth, White Shrine of Jerusalem, Order of Ea. Star (worthy matron 1986), Beta Sigma Phi (Silver Circle, Preceptor Zeta). Republican. Episcopalian. Home: 808 Vandeventer Fayetteville AR 72701

PRESLEY, PRISCILLA, actress; b. Bklyn., May 24, 1945; m. Elvis Presley, 1967 (div. 1973). Studies with Milton Katselas; student, Steven Peck Theatre Art Sch., Chuck Norris Karate Sch. Prin. Bis and Beau; co-executor Graceland, Memphis. Appearances include (films) The Naked Gun, 1988, The Adventures of Ford Fairlaine, 1990, The Naked Gun 2 1/2, 1991, The Naked Gun 33 1/3, 1994, (TV series) Those Amazing Animals, 1980-81, Dallas, 1983-88, (TV movie) Love Is Forever, 1983; prodr. (TV movie) Elvis and Me, 1988. Office: Graceland PO Box 16508 Memphis TN 38186-0508*

PRESS, AIDA KABATZNICK, writer; b. Boston, Nov. 18, 1926; m. Newton Press, June 5, 1947; children: David, Dina Press Weber, Benjamin Presskreischer. BA, Radcliffe Coll., 1948. Reporter Waltham (Mass.) News-Tribune, 1960-63; freelance writer, 1960-63; editorial cons. Mass. Dept. Mental Health, Boston, 1966-72; Waltham/Watertown reporter Boston Herald Traveler, 1963-70; dir. news and publs. Harvard Grad. Sch. Design, Cambridge, Mass., 1972-78; publs. editor Radcliffe Coll., Cambridge, 1978-81, dir., editor of publs., 1981-83, editor Radcliffe Quar., 1971-93, dir. pub. info., 1983-93; cons. editor Regis Coll. Alumnae Mag., Weston, Mass., 1994. Editor emerita Radcliffe Quar., 1993—; contbr. articles to newspapers and mags. Recipient Publs. Distinction award Am. Alumni Coun., 1974, Top 5 coll. Mag., Coun. for Advancement and Support of Edn., 1984, Top 10 Univ Mags., 1991, Gold medal Coll. Mags., 1991, Alumnae Achievement award Radcliffe Coll., 1994.

PRESSER, BETH MICHELLE, recreational facility executive, gaming educator; b. Las Vegas, Nev., Mar. 31, 1964; d. Robert and Concetta Ann (Fasso) P. Student, Edison C.C., Ft. Myers, Fla., 1982-84; grad., Casino Career Inst., Atlantic City, N.J., 1987-92. State Cert. in Blackjack, Roulette, Craps, Baccarat, Mini-Baccarat, Pai Gow Poker., N.J., 1992. Cashier, dealer, pit mgr. Carnival Cruises, Miami, Fla., 1984-87; rep. Trump Plaza Casino, Atlantic City, N.J., 1988; dealer Ceasars Casino, Atlantic City, N.J., 1988-93; floor supr. Hollywood Casino, Aurora, Ill., 1993-94; games mgr., tng. ctr. adminstr., instr. Sheraton Casino, Robinsonville, Miss., 1994—. Mem. Greenpeace. Democrat. Jewish. Home: 7942 Rocky Creek # 4 Southaven MS 38671 Office: Sheraton Casino 1 Casino Center Dr Robinsonville MS 38664

PRESSER, HARRIET BETTY, sociology educator; b. Bklyn., Aug. 29, 1936; d. Phillip Rubinoff and Rose (Gudowitz) Jabish; m. Neil Nathan Presser, Dec. 16, 1956 (div.); 1 child, Sheryl Lynn. BA, George Washington U., 1959; MA, U. N.C., 1962; PhD, U. Calif., Berkeley, 1969. Statistician Bur. Census, Washington, 1959; research assoc. Inst. Life Ins., N.Y.C., 1962-64; lectr. demography U. Sussex, Brighton, England, 1967-68; staff assoc. Population Council, N.Y.C., 1968-69; asst. prof. sociomed. scis. Columbia U., N.Y.C., 1969-73, assoc. prof. sociomed. scis., 1973-76; prof. sociology U. Md., College Park, 1976—, dir. Ctr. on Population, Gender, and Social Inequality,, 1988—, disting. faculty rsch. fellow, 1993-94; fellow in residence Netherlands Inst. for Advanced Study in Humanities & Social Sci., Wassenaar, The Netherlands, 1994—; fellow Ctr. for Advanced Study in the Behavioral Scis., Stanford, Calif., 1986-87, 91-92; bd. dirs. Population Reference Bur., 1993—; cons. Nat. Inst. for Child Health and Human Devel., 1975—. Editorial bd. Time and Soc., 1991—, Social Forces, 1984-87, Signs, 1975-85; assoc. editor Jour. Health and Social Behavior, 1975-78. Nat. Inst. for Child Health and Devel. grantee, 1972-78, 83-88, Population Coun. grantee, 1976-79, NSF grantee, 1982-83, 90-94, Rockefeller Found. grantee, 1983-85, 88-94, William and Flora Hewlett Found. grantee, 1989—, Andrew W. Mellon Found. grantee, 1994—; named Disting. Alumni scholar George Washington U., 1992-93. Mem. Population Assn. Am. (bd. dirs. 1972-75, 2nd v.p. 1983, 1st v.p. 1985, pres.-elect 1988, pres. 1989), Am. Pub. Health Assn. (council mem. population sect. 1976-79), Am. Sociological Assn. (coun. mem. at large 1990-93, chmn., coun. mem. population sect. 1978-83), Sociological Research Assn. (elected). Office: U Md Dept Sociology College Park MD 20742 also: c/o NIAS, Meijboomlaan 1, 2242 PR Wassenaar The Netherlands

PRESSON, GINA, journalist, news and documentary production company executive; b. Nuremberg, Germany, Sept. 1, 1959; parents Am. citizens; d. Gerald Vann Presson and Gail Anne (Carter) Presson Nichols; m. William Michael Hammesfahr, Apr. 25, 1987. BA cum laude, Duke U., 1981. Intern reporter, field producer Sta. WTVD-TV, Durham, N.C., 1979-81; assoc. producer, producer, writer, fill-in reporter Sta. KXAS-TV, Dallas/Ft. Worth, 1981-84; reporter, anchor Sta. KFDX-TV, Wichita Falls, Tex., 1984-85; reporter, producer Sta. WTVR-TV, Richmond, Va., 1985-86; reporter Sta. WWBT-TV, Richmond, 1986-88; owner, reporter, producer Presson Perspectives, Clearwater, Fla., 1988—; prodr. Tampa (Fla.) Com. of 100, 1989, Poynter Inst. for Media Studies, 1990—, Leadership Am. and A Presdl. Classroom for Young Ams., 1993; reporter, prodr. Sta. WEDU-TV, Tampa, 1988—, Sta. WTSP-TV, 1992, Sta. WUSF-Radio, 1993. Prodr. program Everyday Heroes, PBS, 1994. Mem. Healthy Start Coalition; publicist First Presbyn. Ch. Svc. Com., St. Petersburg, Fla., 1990—, Habitat for Humanity, Richmond, 1987-88, Children's Miracle Network, Richmond, 1986-88. Recipient Gold medallion Broadcast Promotion and Mktg. Execs., 1982, 10th Dist. Addy award (5 states), Ft. Worth Ad Club, 1982, 83, Tops award Dallas Ad Club, 1982, Best Spot award Tex. Assn. Broadcasters, 1982, 83, Tops award Dallas Ad Club, 1982, Best Spot award Tex. Assn. Broadcasters, 1983, 4th Pl. award in News Spl., Internat. N.Y. Fest., 1992, Gabriel award, 1993, Fla. AP award, 1993, 3rd Pl. Green Eyeshade award (5 states), 1994; honoree N.Y. Fest., 1994. Mem. Soc. Profl. Journalists (dept. regional dir. 1990—, pres. Tampa chpt. 1989-90, fund raiser 1988-89, award 1993), Duke U. Alumni Assn., Leadership Am., Alpha Delta Pi. Office: Presson Perspectives 600 Druid Rd E Clearwater FL 34616-3912

PRESTAGE, JEWEL LIMAR, political science educator; b. Hutton, La., Aug. 12, 1931; d. Brudis L. and Sallie Bell (Johnson) Limar; m. James J. Prestage, Aug. 12, 1953; children—Terri, James, Eric, Karen, Jay. B.A., So. U., Baton Rouge, 1951; M.A., U. Iowa, 1952, Ph.D., 1954; LHD (hon.), U. D.C., 1994. Assoc. prof. polit. sci. Prairie View (Tex.) Coll., 1954-55, 56; assoc. prof. polit. sci. So. U., 1956-57, 58-62, prof., 1962—, chairperson dept., 1965-83, dean pub. policy and urban affairs, 1983-89; Honors prof. polit. sci. Banneker Honors Coll., Prairie View U., 1989—, dean, 1990—; chmn. La. adv. com. to U.S. Commn. on Civil Rights, 1975-85; mem., chmn. nat. adv. coun. on women's ednl. programs U.S. Dept. Edn., 1980-82; vis. prof. U. Iowa, 1987-88. Author: (with M. Githens) A Portrait of Marginality: Political Behavior of the American Woman, 1976; contbr. articles to profl. jours. Rockefeller fellow, 1951-52; NSF fellow, 1964; Ford Found. postdoctoral fellow, 1969-70. Mem. Am. Polit. Sci. Assn. (v.p. 1974-75), So. Polit. Sci. Assn. (pres. 1975-76), Nat. Conf. Black Polit. Scientists (pres. 1976-77), Nat. Assn. African Am. Honors Programs (pres. 1993-94), Am. Soc. for Pub. Adminstrn. (pres. La. chpt. 1988-89, mem. nat. exec. coun. 1989-90), Links Inc., Alpha Kappa Alpha. Home: 2145 77th Ave Baton Rouge LA 70807-5508 Office: So Univ PO Box 125 Prairie View TX 77446-0125

PRESTERA, LAURETTA ANNE, newspaper executive; b. Newark, Dec. 15, 1947; d. George Anthony and Carmela (Sallustro) P. BA in Communications, Bridgewater State Coll., 1976; MBA in Mgmt., Fairleigh Dickinson U., 1981. Advt. sales rep. The N.Y. Times, N.Y.C., 1980-81, circulation sales rep., 1981-82, asst. mgr. circulation, 1982-83; home delivery mgr. The N.Y. Times, Torrance, Calif., 1983-84; S.W. mgr. The N.Y. Times, Dallas, 1984-85; west coast mgr. The N.Y. Times, Torrance, 1985-87; nat. sales dir. The N.Y. Times, N.Y., 1987-92; home delivery dir. The N.Y. Times, N.Y.C., 1992—, group dir. distbn., 1992—; treas. The N.Y. Times Distbn. Corp., N.Y. and Calif., 1984-89. Recipient Pub. award The N.Y. Time, 1984. Mem. People for Ethical Treatment of Animals, San Francisco SPCA, L.A. SPCA, Cal-Western Circulation Mgrs., Am. Newspapers Pubs. Assn. Roman Catholic.

PRESTOM, DAWN ELLEN, art director; b. Bklyn., May 14, 1965; d. Gerard Francis Prestom and Marie Elizabeth (Tomasino) Macioce. BFA in Advt., Sch. Visual Arts, N.Y.C., 1988. Jr. art dir. D'Arcy Masius Benton & Bowles, N.Y.C., 1988-89; art dir. Backer Spielvogel Bates, N.Y.C., 1989-91, Chiat/Day, N.Y.C., 1991-93; supervising art dir. Korey Kay & Ptnrs., N.Y.C., 1993—; substitute tchr. Sch. Visual Arts, N.Y.C., 1989-94. Recipient 3 Clio awards, award Internat. Print & Film Festival, Communications Arts Ann.; named one of Adweek's Best 5 Spots of the Yr. Home: 19 Greene St Apt 4R New York NY 10013

PRESTON, ASTRID, artist; b. Stockholm, Sept. 29, 1945; came to U.S., 1952; d. Stanley and Milda E. Borbals; m. Howard J. Preston, Sept. 1, 1943; 1 child, Max. BA, UCLA, 1967. One-woman shows include L.A. Inst. of Contemporary Art, 1982, Newspace, L.A., 1983, 84, 85, Patty Aande Gallery, San Diego, 1986, Krygier/Landau Contemporary Art, L.A., 1987, Laguna Art Mus., Laguna Beach., Calif., 1987, Jan Turner Gallery, L.A., 1989, 91. Bd. dirs. L.A. Contemporary Exhibits, 1984-89, Beyond Baroque, Venice, Calif., 1994—. Grantee Nat. Endowment of the Arts, 1987.

PRESTON, CAROL ANN, special education educator; b. Buffalo, Aug. 11, 1953; m. Robert George Preston, June 7, 1980; children: Nicole, Amy. Student, Keuka Coll., 1971-73; BS, SUNY, Plattsburg, 1975; MS, Russell Sage Coll., 1992. Cert. elem., spl. edn. tchr., N.Y. Program analyst N.Y. State Higher Edn. Svcs. Corp., Albany, 1977-82; tchr. spl. edn. Saratoga Springs (N.Y.) City Sch. System, 1992-94, Schuylerville (N.Y.) Jr./Sr. H.S., 1994—. Daisy Girl Scout leader, 1989-90, Brownie leader Girl Scouts U.S., Clifton Park, N.Y., 1990-93, jr. leader, 1993-94; substance abuse chmn. N.Y. State PTA, Albany, 1992-93, spl. edn. chmn., 1993-95; mem. sch. bd. Shenendehowa Ctrl. Sch. Dist., Clifton Park, 1989-92. Named Honorary Life mem. Shenendehowa PTA Coun., 1990. Mem. Phi Kappa Phi. Home: 15 Turnberry Ln Clifton Park NY 12065-1104

PRESTON, ELIZABETH FLORENCE, government official; b. Athens Twp., Mich., Apr. 2, 1932; d. Aaron Elsworth and Mary Ann Katherine (Lutz) Munn. BS, Columbia Pacific U., 1981, MBA, 1982. Adminstrv./staff asst. Regional Office of Mich. State Farm Ins. Cos., Marshall, 1962-68, U.S. Army Communications Command, Okinawa, Japan, 1968-74; indsl. liaison specialist (TILO)/U.S. Army Material Devel./Readiness Command, Alexandria, Va., 1975-77; adminstrv. and mgmt. officer DPCA/U.S. Army HQ, Ft. Huachuca, Ariz., 1977-79, Shasta Dam/U.S. Dept. Interior, Bur. Reclamation, Redding, Calif., 1979-81; bus. mgr., chief NAF div. U.S. Army Support Group, Bremerhaven, Germany, 1981-83; dir. personnel and community activities DPCA/USMC The Netherlands, Schinnen, The Netherlands, 1983-92. Methodist.

PRESTON, FAITH, college president; b. Boston, Sept. 14, 1921; d. Howard Knowlton and Edith Smith (Wilson) P.; m. Winthrop Wadleigh, Dec. 19, 1970. B.A., Boston U., 1944; M.A., 1945; Ed.D., Columbia U. Tchrs. Coll., 1964. Tchr. Georgetown (Mass.) High Sch., 1945-47; tchr. Stoneham (Mass.) High Sch., 1947-50, Endicott Jr. Coll., Beverly, Mass., 1950-53; dir. research P.R. Jr. Coll., 1953-55; dean adminstrn., 1955-63, v.p., 1963-65; pres. White Pines Coll., 1965-91, pres. emerita, 1991—, also life trustee. Author: David and the Handcar, 1950, Jose's Miracle, 1955, The Silver Box, 1979, A Gift of Love, 1994. Mem. bd. incorporators Cath. Med. Ctr., Manchester, N.H., 1978-89; bd. dirs. Caregivers; pres. bd. dirs. N.H. Assn. for Blind; trustee funds Chester Congl. Bapt. Ch., deacon, 1988—. Kellogg fellow, 1964. Mem. Am. Assn. Jr. Colls., Phi Lambda Theta, Kappa Delta Pi, Delta Kappa Gamma. Republican. Clubs: Univ. Women's (London); The College (Boston); Fortnightly. Home: PO Box 25 Chester NH 03036-0025 Office: White Pines Coll Office of the Pres 40 Chester St Chester NH 03036

PRESTON, JANE, psychiatrist, educator. BS in Biology, Trinity U., 1949; MD, Baylor Coll. of Medicine, 1953. Intern St. Louis City Hosp., 1953-54; resident in internal medicine St. John's (Newfoundland, Can.) Gen. Hosp., 1955-56; resident in internal medicine Baylor Coll. of Medicine, Houston, 1956-57, resident in psychiatry, 1957-60, clin. assoc. prof., 1965—; mem. faculty Austin (Tex.) State Hosp. Residency Program, 1983—; bd. dirs. Samaritan Counseling Ctrs., 1987-90; mem. ad hoc ethics com. Shoal Creek Hosp., 1987-89, chair credentials com., 1987-90; presenter Carrier Found. Symposium, 1984; mem. Task Force on Revision of Insanity Sect. of Tex. State Criminal Code, 1973; chair med. evaluation team Richmond State Sch. for Retarded, 1975-76; mem. ad hoc com. Revisions Mental Health Code of Tex., 1976, 79, 82-85; mem. mental health adv. coun. Tex. Dept. Mental Health and Mental Retardation, 1979-84, mental adv. com., 1984—, chair med. adv. com. subcom. on community mental health ctrs., 1986—; examiner Am. Bd. Psychiatry and Neurology, 1983, 87; project dir. Tex. Telemedicine Project, 1989—; mem. adv. bd. Tex. Tech. Health Sci. Ctr. MedNet Project, 1989-90, cons., 1989—; speaker for medicine Bell Comm. Rsch., 1989, 90; pres. Telemed. Interactive Consultative Svcs., Inc., 1988—; pres. The Am. Telemedicine Assn.; mem. com. high performance computing and comm. Nat. Rsch. Coun.; bd. dirs. Friends of Nat. Libr. of Medicine. Author: The Telemedicine Handbook, 1993; contbr. articles to profl. jours. Elder Presbyn. Ch., USA.; docent The Gov.'s Mansion, Austin; past docent The Bayou Bend Collection, Houston; cons. Cath. Charities, Gulf Coast Presbytery, Jewish Community Ctr., Houston, 1969-79. Recipient resolution honoring rural health contbn. Tex. Ho. of Reps. Fellow Am. Psychiat. Assn. (diplomate, budget com. 1976-82, chair 1981-82, cons. 1982-89, cons. resource and devel. com. 1987-89, chair long range planning com. 1981-82, com. info. systems 1984-87, cons. 1987-89, chair task force on telemedicine 1981, com. telemed. svcs. delivery 1984—, sci. exhibitor 1985, 86, 87, 88); mem. AMA, Am. Group Psychiat. Assn., Am. Coll. Psychiatry, Internat. Platform Assn., Nat. Alliance for the Mentally Ill, Mental Health Assn., Tex. Med. Assn. (sci. exhibitor 1988-90), Tex. Soc. Psychiat. Physicians (pres. 1970-80, chair sci. program devel. com. 1976-79, cons. com. allied disciplines 1976—, co-chair nat. affairs, govt. rels. com. 1977-79), Houston Psychiat. Soc. (pres. 1972), N.Y. Acad. Scis., Alpha Chi, Alpha Epsilon Iota, Alpha Omega Alpha. Office: Telemed Interactive Cons Svc Inc 204 E 4th St Austin TX 78701 also: 1700 One American Ctr 600 Congress Ave Austin TX 78701

PRESTON, JOELLEN, cabinetmaker; b. Tuscola, Ill., May 31, 1959; d. Joseph Earl and Mary Ellen (Canfield) Wachob; m. James Ervin Preston, Sept. 12, 1987 (div. Mar. 1992); children: Joey, Kathryn, Rebecca. BS in Psychology, Ind. State U., Terre Haute, 1991. Analytical technician A.E. Staley/Henkel Corp., Houston, also Decatur, Ill., 1986-89; victim advocate Vigo County Sheriff's Dept., Terre Haute, 1990-91; framing sequencer Schrock Cabinet Co., Arthur, Ill., 1992—. Mem. Dem. Nat. Com., 1993—. Mem. NOW, Psi Chi. Home: 311 S Oak St Arthur IL 61911-1244

PRESTON, LOYCE ELAINE, retired social work educator; b. Texarkana, Ark., Feb. 25, 1929; d. Harvey Martin and Florence (Whitlock) P.; student Texarkana Jr. Coll., 1946-47; B.S., Henderson State Tchrs. Coll., 1950; certificate in social work La. State U., 1952; M.S.W., Columbia U., 1956. Tchr. pub. schs., Dierks, Ark., 1950-51; child welfare worker Ark. Dept. Public Welfare, Clark and Hot Spring counties, 1951-56, child welfare cons., 1956-58; casework dir. Ruth Sch. Girls, Burien, Wash., 1958-60; asst. prof. spl. edn. La. Poly. Inst., Ruston, 1960-63; asst. prof. Northwestern State Coll., Shreveport, La., 1963-73; asst. prof. La. State U., Shreveport, 1973-79; ret., 1979. Chpt. sec. La. Assn. Mental Health, 1965-67, Gov's. adv. council, 1967-70; mem. Mayor's Com. for Community Improvement, 1972-76. Mem. AAUW (dir. Shreveport br. 1963-69), Acad. Cert. Social Workers, Nat. Assn. Social Workers (del. 1964-65, pres. North La. chpt., state-wide com. 1968-69), La. Conf. Social Welfare, La. Fedn. Council Exceptional Children (pres. 1970-71), La. Tchrs. Assn. Home: 9609 Hillsboro Dr Shreveport LA 71118-4804

PRESTON, MEREDITH, public relations executive; b. Long Island, N.Y., Mar. 4, 1952. BA in English Lit., U. of the South, 1974. Legis. aide U.S. Congressman Don Bonker, 1976-77, Senator S.I. Hayakawa, 1977-80; media dir. Bailey-Deardourff Assocs., Inc., 1980; polit. aide Assemblyman Dave Stirling, 1982; acct. exec. Hill & Knowlton, 1983-85, acct. supr., 1985-86, group supr., 1986-87, v.p. and dir. corp. comm. divsn., 1987-91; pres. Preston Pub. Rels., L.A., 1991—. Office: 1116 Pagoda Pl Los Angeles CA 90031*

PRESTON, SUSAN GORDON, social worker; b. Rochester, Pa., Aug. 27, 1955; d. Richard Lee and Betty Pearl (Wallace) Gordon; m. Thomas John Preston, Apr. 4, 1981; 1 child, Bethany Nicole. BSW, Pa. State U., 1976; MSW, U. Pitts., 1981, cert. in family and martial therapy, 1984. Group home worker Care for Youth, Greensburg, Pa., 1977-79; child and family therapist Family Svcs., Bridgewater, Pa., 1979-81, Irene Stacy Mental Health Ctr., Butler, Pa., 1981-82; psychiat. social worker Butler Meml. Hosp., 1982-83; pvt. practice child and family therapy New Brighton, Pa., 1983-88; dir. clin. svcs. Luth. Youth & Family Svcs., Zelienople, Pa., 1984-92; dir. Seneca Ridge of Aliquippa Hosp. Mental Health Svcs., New Brighton, 1992—; trainer Contact, Beaver, Pa., 1986-94. Mem. NOW (v.p. Beaver Valley chpt. 1991-92, pres. 1993, co-pres. 1994). Democrat. Home: 104 Red Fox Dr Beaver Falls PA 15010-4952 Office: Seneca Ridge of Aliquippa Hosp Mental Health Svcs 615 Penn Ave New Brighton PA 15066-1340

PRESTRIDGE, PAMELA ADAIR, lawyer; b. Delhi, La., Dec. 25, 1945; d. Gerald Wallace Prestridge and Peggy Adair (Arender) Martin. BA, La. Poly. U., 1967; M in Edn., La. State u., 1968, JD, 1973. Bar: U.S. Dist. Ct. (mid. dist.) La. 1975, U.S. Dist. Ct. (so. dist.) Tex. 1982, U.S. Ct. Appeals (5th cir.) 1982, U.S. Supreme Ct. 1990. Law clk. to presiding justice La. State Dist. Ct., Baton Rouge, 1973-75; ptnr. Breazeale, Sachse & Wilson, Baton Rouge, 1975-82, Hirsch & Westheimer P.C., Houston, 1982-92; pvt. practice atty. Houston, 1992—. Counselor Big Bros./Big Sisters, Baton Rouge, 1968-70; legal cons., bd. dirs. Lupus Found. Am., Houston, 1984-93; bd. dirs. Quota Club, Baton Rouge, 1979-82, Speech and Hearing Found., Baton Rouge, 1981-82, The Actors Workshop, Houston, 1988-93; active Tex. Accts. and Attys. for the Arts. Recipient Pres.'s award Lupus Found. Am., 1991, cert. of appreciation Assn. Atty. Mediators, 1992. Mem. ABA, La. Bar Assn., Tex. Bar Assn., Houston Bar Assn., Houston Bar Found., Assn. Atty. Mediators (bd. dirs. 1994—, Citation for Outstanding Mems. 1993), Profl. Atty.-Mediators Coop. (v.p., bd. dirs. 1994, pres. 1995), Phi Alpha Delta. Democrat. Eckankar. Home: 908 Welch St Houston TX 77006-1312 Office: Phoenix Tower Ste 3300 PO Box 130987 Houston TX 77219-0987

PRETTYMAN, BARBARA EDMONDS, federal agency administrator; b. Boston, Apr. 16, 1934; d. Vincent J. and Catherine Puorro; m. Henry G. Edmonds, Jr., June 9, 1953 (div. June 1981); children: Leslie L., Jeffrey G., Steven B.; m. George B. Prettyman, Jan. 16, 1982. Student, Wellesley Coll., 1951-53; DES, U. Strasbourg, 1954; BA, U. Md., 1963, MA, 1966, PhD, 1972. Cons. Nat. Bur. Standards, Gaithersburg, Md., 1975, Am. Trade and Fin. Corp., Arlington, Va., 1975. Instr. U. Md., College Park, Md., 1963-74; interpreter/escort Dept. State, Washington, 1972-78; linguist, analyst, divsn. chief, adminstr. Nat. Security Agy., Fort Meade, Md., 1976—. Contbr. articles to profl. jours. Mem. Internat. Affairs Inst. (sec. 1989-91), Wellesley Club, Pen and Cursor Soc., Napoleonic Soc. Am., Phi Kappa Phi. Home: 12835 Folly Quarter Rd Ellicott City MD 21042

PRETTYMAN, PAULA MARIE, critical care nurse, home infusion nurse; b. Dayton, Ohio, Dec. 20, 1964; d. Gene Clifton and Betty Jean (Rasnick) P. AAS, Sinclair Community Coll., Dayton, 1987; BS, U. Cin., 1992. RN, Ohio; cert. BLS instr. Staff nurse Bethany Luth. Village, Centerville, Ohio, 1987-89, shift supr., 1988-89; staff nurse CCU Grandview Hosp., Dayton, 1988-89; staff nurse ICU and relief charge Southview Hosp., Dayton, 1989; staff nurse burn unit U. Cin. Hosp., 1990-92; burn life support instr. Am. Nursing Care/Amerimed, Cin., 1992—; home health care nurse Am. Nursing, Dayton, 1989-91. Office: Am Nursing Care/Amerimed 8044 Montgomery Rd Ste 570 Cincinnati OH 45236

PRETTYMAN-BAKER, SHEILA, pediatrics, neonatal nurse; b. Dayton, Ohio, May 22, 1957; d. Gene Clifton and Betty Jean (Rasnick) Prettyman; m. Stephen Ray Baker, Feb. 4, 1989. AS, Kettering Coll. Med. Arts, 1978, AD in Emergency Med. Tech., 1985. Cert. emergency med. technician-paramedic. Nursing supr. Bethany Luth. Village, Centerville, Ohio; neonatal nursery nurse St. Elizabeth Hosp., Dayton; charge nurse Mercy Hosp.,

Fairfield, Ohio; office nurse Kettering; IV nurse educator St. Elizabeth Hosp., Dayton.

PRETZER, MARY B., small business owner; b. Wakefield, Nebr., Dec. 20, 1955; d. Arthur C. and Marie G. (Putnam) P.; m. Keith W. Welsch, Sept. 5, 1987 (div. Sept. 1991). BS in English, Wayne State U., 1978. Reporter Brush (Colo.) News Tribune, 1978-79; advt. mgr. Limousin Jour., Fort Collins, Colo., 1980-83; ad agy. owner Wood 'n I Prodns., Fort Collins, 1983-84; publs. specialist Colo. State U., Fort Collins, 1984-86; tng. dir. Performance Seminar Group, Bridgeport, Conn., 1988-91; speaker trainer Bus. & Profl. Rsch. Orgn., Aldermaston, Eng., 1990. Editor: In House Graphics, Loveland, 1986-88; co-author: 60 Outstanding Newsletters, 1991; contbr. articles to profl. jours. Mem. Nat. Assn. Self Employed. Office: 823 4th St SE Loveland CO 80537-6426

PREVE, ROBERTA JEAN, librarian, researcher; b. Wilmington, Del., Feb. 27, 1954; d. Burton Hugo Sanders and Betsy (Kan) Klein; m. Thomas Alan Preve, Sept. 23, 1978; children: Stephanie Jean, Melanie Marie. BA, U. N.H., 1975; MLS, Simmons Coll., 1985. Rschr. U. N.H., Durham, 1974-75; rsch. asst. Eikonix Corp., Burlington, Mass., 1976-79; asst. cashier, credit dept. mgr. Dania (Fla.) Bank, 1980-83; rsch. assoc. Ctr. for Strategy Rsch., Cambridge, Mass., 1984-86; info. svcs. Braxton Assocs., Boston, 1986-87; mktg. adminstr. Summit Tech., Waltham, Mass., 1987-90; mgr. market rsch. AT&T Capital Corp., Framingham, Mass., 1991—; co-owner T&R Pest Mgmt., Attleboro, Mass., 1988—. Mem. Spl. Librs. Assn., New England Online (dir., logistics chair 1986-90), Beta Phi Mu. Office: AT&T Capital Corp PO Box 9104 Framingham MA 01701-9104

PREVOR, RUTH CLAIRE, psychologist; b. N.Y.C., June 20, 1944; d. Gustav and Greta (Dreifuss) Strauss; m. Sydney Joseph P., July 4, 1963; children: Joy, Grant, Jed. BA, U. P.R., 1966; PhD, Caribbean Ctr. of Postgrad., Studies, San Juan, 1988. Cert. forensic psychologist. Asst. dean Caribbean Ctr. of Postgrad. Studies, 1986-87; dir. prenatal edn. Ashford Meml. Hosp., San Juan, 1987; pvt. practice San Juan, 1984—; advisor, field faculty Vt. Coll., Norwich U., 1990-91; trustee Caribbean Ctr. for Advanced Studies, San Juan, Miami, Fla., 1990—. Bd. dirs. Jewish Community Ctr., Miramar, P.R., 1986—, bd. dirs. pre-sch., 1990—; pres. Home and Sch./St. John's Prep., San Juan, 1980-81, P.R. chpt. Hadassah Sch., 1972-74; presdl. adv. com., 1990-92. Mem. Am. Psychol. Assn., Assn. of Psychology of P.R. (hon. award 1984), Caribbean Counselors Assn., Caribe Hilton Club, Nat. Assn. Children with Learning Disabilities, Nat. Register Health Svc. Providers in Psychology. Jewish. Office: Ashford Med Ctr San Juan PR 00907

PREW, DIANE SCHMIDT, information systems executive; b. Orange, N.J., Jan. 21, 1945; d. Herman and Elfriede (Witt) Schmidt; m. Jonathan Prew, Jan. 27, 1968; 1 child, Heather Diane. BSBA, U. N.H., 1967. Cert. systems profl. Programmer analyst Eastman Kodak Co., Rochester, N.Y., 1967-70; program and system mgr. Nat. Acad. Scis., Washington, 1970-72; owner Active Info. Systems, Nashua, N.H., 1974-79; dir. info. svcs. City of Manchester, N.H., 1980—; bd. dirs. Manchester Mcpl. Employees Credit Union, v.p., 1993—. Mem. Data Processing Mgmt. Assn. (sec. 1982-84, exec. v.p., 1984-85, pres. 1985-86, treas. 1986—, Bronze award 1988, Silver award 1991), Rotary Club. Home: 50 Mack Hill Rd # 877 Amherst NH 03031-3223 Office: City of Manchester Info Systems Dept 100 Merrimack St Manchester NH 03101-2210

PREWITT, NANCY BROWNER, systems analyst; b. Tulsa, Dec. 20, 1955; d. Harold Dean and Patricia Lucille (Crouch) B.; m. Kenneth Lawrence Prewitt, June 30, 1979 (div. Nov. 1985). BSBA in Acctg., U. S.C., 1978. Auditor S.C. Electric & Gas, Columbia, 1978-80, programmer, 1980-84, programmer analyst, 1985-89, systems analyst, 1989—, coord. employee polit. awareness, 1989-94. Solicitor United Way, Columbia, 1982-94, March of Dimes, Columbia, 1982-94. Recipient scholarship Altrusa Soc., 1976-77. Mem. Columbia C. of C. (solicitor 1982-94), Civitans (sec. Capitol City chpt. 1990-91). Republican. Episcopalian. Home: 3620 Cairnbrook Dr Columbia SC 29210

PREY, BARBARA ERNST, artist; b. Jamaica, N.Y., Apr. 17, 1957; d. Herbert Henry and Margaret (Joubert) Ernst; m. Jeffrey Drew Prey, Jan. 11, 1986; children: Austin William Ernst Prey, Emily Elizabeth Prey. BA with honors, Williams Coll., 1979; MDiv, Harvard U., 1986. Sales staff Tiffany and Co., N.Y.C., summer 1977; summer intern Met. Mus. Art, N.Y.C., summer 1979; personal asst. Prince Albrecht Castell, Castell, Germany, 1980-81; with modern painting dept. Sotheby's Auction House, N.Y.C., 1981-82; sales asst. Marlborough Gallery, N.Y.C., 1982; teaching asst. Boston Coll., 1984, Harvard U., Cambridge, Mass., 1984-85; vis. lectr. Tainan (Taiwan) Coll. and Sem., 1986-87; artist Prosperity, Pa., 1987—; art juror Washington and Jefferson Coll., Washington, Pa., 1990; presenter in field. Illustrator: (books) Boys Harbor Cookbook, 1988, A Dream Became You, (4 book series) A City Grows Up, 1991, (cover) Am. Artist Mag., summer 1994; exhibited paintings in group shows including Mus. of Fine Arts, Nassau County, N.Y., 1988, Nat. Arts Club, N.Y.C., 1988, Gallery One, Rockland, Maine, 1992, Williams Coll., Williamstown, Mass., 1993, Johnstown (Pa.) Art Mus., 1993, Blair Art Mus., Hollidaysburg, Pa., 1993; exhibited in one-woman shows including Harvard-Yale-Princeton Club, Pitts., 1991; represented in many pvt. collections. Class agt. Williams Coll., Williamstown, Mass., 1981-91; bd. mem. Citizens Libr., Washington, 1992-93; active Bethel Presbyn. Ch. Recipient Fulbright scholarship Fulbright Assn., Germany, 1979-80, grant Roothbert Fund, Chatauqua, N.Y., 1982-84, Ch. History award Gordon-Conwell Sem., S. Hamilton, Mass., 1984, Henry Luce Found. grant Henry Luce Found., Taiwan, 1986-87. Mem. Pitts. Watercolor Soc. (Jean Thoburn award 1994), Nat. Mus. Women in the Arts. Republican.

PRICE, AMY ELIZABETH, marketing professional; b. Nashville, Sept. 25, 1957; d. Robert Alden and Emily (Washington) Brown; m. Daniel Edward Price, Oct. 11, 1986; 1 child, Robert Daniel. Student, Vanderbilt U., 1974-76; B Mech. Engring., Ga. Inst. Tech., 1978. Registered engr.-in-tng., Ga. Mech. engr. TVA, Knoxville, 1978-81; applications engr. electricity divsn. Schlumberger Industries, Norcross, Ga., 1981-85, mgr. customer svc. Neptune divsn., 1985-87, mgr. mktg. svcs., 1987-89; mktg. mgr. (Can.) Schlumberger Industries, Mississauga, Ont., 1989-91; program mgr. Schlumberger Industries, Greenwood, S.C., 1991-93, mktg. mgr., 1993—. Bd. dirs. Gwinnett Coun. for Arts, Duluth, Ga., 1991-93. Mem. ASME, Automatic Meter Reading Assn. (bd. dirs., officer 1990-93). Office: Schlumberger Industries Measurement Div 1310 Emerald Rd Greenwood SC 29646

PRICE, ANTOINETTE TUMINELLO, counselor; b. Shreveport, La., July 18, 1929; d. Joseph and Rose (Bonomo) Tuminello; m. Clayton Glenn Price, Dec. 19, 1953; children: Clayton Glenn Jr., Joseph Michael. BS, Centenary Coll. La., 1950; MEd, La. State U., 1953; DEd, Northwestern State U., Natchitoches, La., 1979. Nat. cert. sch. counselor; lic. profl. counselor, La., Tex. Tchr., counselor Fair Park High Sch./Caddo Parish Sch. Bd., Shreveport, 1951-69, summer counselor, 1967-69; ednl. cons. Caddo Parish Sch. Bd., Shreveport, 1969-79; adminstr. After Sch. Ctrs. Caddo Parish Sch. Bd., 1979-80, supr., counseling and testing, 1980—; instr. La. Tech U., Ruston, 1969-91, Northwestern State U., Natchitoches, 1978-88, La. State U., Shreveport, 1983-92; guest lectr. of edn. Centenary Coll. of La., Shreveport, 1980—; mem. sch. accountability adv. com. La. Dept. Edn., Baton Rouge, 1992—. Contbr. articles to profl. jours. Chair literacy and internat. rels. Altrusa Internat., Inc., Shreveport, 1993-94; bd. dirs. La. Profl. Counselors, Baton Rouge, 1990—. Acad. scholar Centenary Coll., 1947-50, Tulane U., New Orleans, 1950-51. Mem. Am. Counseling Assn., Am. Ednl. Rsch. Assn., Am. Sch. Counselors Assn., Assn. Counselor Edn. and Supervision, Am. Assn. for Counseling and Devel. (nat. conv. presenter 1988), Assn. of Tchr. Educators (nat. conv. presetner 1981), La. Assn. for Counseling and Devel. (state conv. presenter 1983, 87), Phi Delta Kappa, Alpha Delta Kappa (past pres. local chpt.). Democrat. Roman Catholic. Home: 533 Dunmoreland Dr Shreveport LA 71106-6115 Office: Caddo Parish Sch Bd 1961 Midway St Shreveport LA 71108-2201

PRICE, BELINDA KATHRYN, hydrogeologist; b. Abergavenny, Gwent, U.K., July 11, 1961; came to U.S., 1983; d. Ronald Frederick and Eileen Megan (Powles) P.; m. William Matthew Dunne, Jan. 20, 1984; 1 child, Elizabeth Kathryn Dunne. BSc in Geology, U. Bristol, U.K., 1982; MSc in Hydrogeology, U. London, 1983. Registered profl. geologist, Calif., Ark., Ga., Tenn., Ky. Statistician, geologist W.Va. Geol. and Econ. Survey, Morgantown, 1984-86; hydrogeologist IT Corp., Pitts., 1986-88; sr. tech. assoc. IT Corp., Knoxville, Tenn., 1988—. Author articles, abstracts, reports in field. Mem. Nat. Ground Water Assn. (mem. editl. bd. Ground Water Jour. 1994—), Daus. of British Empire. Office: IT Corp 312 Directors Dr Knoxville TN 37923

PRICE, BETTY JEAN, legal assistant; b. Matador, Tex., Apr. 25, 1937; d. Parmer Franklin and Sarah Luella (Cantrell) Neal; m. Theodore Frederic Canatis, Dec. 4, 1954 (div. 1968); children: Neal Frederic, Gregory William, Wayne Franklin; m. William Edgar Price, Oct. 11, 1969. AA, Kauai C.C., 1976; B in Gen. Studies magna cum laude, Wichita State U., 1992. Pvt. sec. Dynalectron Corp., Kauai, Hawaii, 1971-79; trial specialist Turner & Boisseau, Wichita, 1979-82; legal sec. David Arst Law Office, Wichita, 1982-84; legal assistant Hershberger, Patterson Jones & Roth, Wichita, 1984—. Contbr. essays on women's issues to newspapers. Vol. Women's Crises Ctr., Wichita, 1993. Mem. Wichita NOW (v.p. 1993-94, pres. 1994—, cmty. organizer for women's history month 1994), Golden Key, Phi Kappa Phi. Democrat.

PRICE, CAROLINE LEONA, personnel consulting company executive; b. N.Y.C., Dec. 13, 1947; d. Richard Gustave and Ruth Leonora (Kling) Schlegel; m. Harold Edmond Price, Sept. 27, 1969; children: Jonathan (dec.), Matthew. AA, Concordia Jr. Coll., Bronxville, N.Y., 1967; student, Wagner Coll., Bregenz, Austria, 1967-68; BA, Lehman Coll., CUNY, 1969. Tchr. Dept. Def. Sch. System, Brindisi, Italy, 1970-71; prin. social welfare exec. Putnam County Dept. Social Svcs., Brewster, N.Y., 1971-75; pers. dir. to patent trader, Mt. Kisco, N.Y., 1976-77; tchr. English as fgn. lang. Arbeiterkammer, Feldkirch, Austria, 1978-84; office mgr. Peachtree Temps., Inc., Peachtree City, Ga., 1984-85; office adminstr. Chip & Dale, Peachtree City, 1985-87; rsch. dir. Borman/Gray, Atlanta, 1987-88; owner, prin. Caprice Cons., Peachtree City, 1988-94; assoc. Ward Howell Internat., Atlanta, 1994—; founding chmn. So. Conservation Trust, Inc., 1993—. Chmn. Peachtree City Planning Commn., 1986-92, McIntosh Recreation Complex Bond Commn., Peachtree City, 1989; mem. Fayette County Solid Waste Com., Fayetteville, Ga., 1989-90, Fayette County Bicentennial Com., 1986; candidate Fayette County Bd. Commrs., 1990; mem. City Coun., Peachtree City, 1992—; founding mem. Peachtree City Compassionate Friends, 1990; bd. dirs. West Fayette YMCA, 1991—. Mem. Atlanta Researcher's Roundtable (sec. 1989-90), Am. Bus. Women's Assn. (pres. McIntosh charter chpt. 1989-90, Woman of Yr. award 1990). Lutheran. Home and Office: Ste 421 2403 Ashford Park Peachtree City GA 30269

PRICE, CINDA LU, psychotherapist; b. Cleve., Jan. 1, 1962; d. William Albert and Betty Lee (Curzon) Benes; m. Benjamin Mark Price, Mar. 7, 1987; children: Jesse Lee, Kaylee Kristine. BS, Kent State U., 1984; MEd, Sam Houston State U., 1989, postgrad., 1992. Lic. profl. counselor, marriage and family therapist, chem. dependency counselor. Supr. Belmont Habilitation Ctr., Barnsville, Ohio, 1984-85; tchr. Klein (Tex.) Ind. Sch. Dist., 1985-87, Conroe (Tex.) Ind. Sch. Dist., 1987-89; psychotherapist Alliance for Healing and Recovery, Houston, 1989-92, Advanced Psychiat. Svcs., Conroe, 1992—; cons. Forest Springs Hosp., Houston, 1990—, Charter Hosp. of Kingwood, Tex., 1993—, Gulf Pines Hosp., Houston, 1993—; owner Advanced Psychiat. Svcs., Conroe, 1992—. Developer First Time Offenders Program, Conroe, 1993, dir., developer intensive outpatient programs for chem. dependency, 1994. Recipient Alumnae Assn. Leadership award Kent State U., 1984. Mem. Tex. Assn. for Counseling and Devel., Am. Assn. Counseling and Devel., Am. Assn. Play Therapy, Am. Assn. Clin. Hypnosis, Internat. Assn. Addiction and Offender Counselors, Tex. Counseling Assn., Kappa Delta Pi, Delta Zeta (v.p. 1982-83, pres. 1983-84). Methodist. Office: Advanced Psychiatric Svcs 1712 N Frazier Ste 213 Conroe TX 77301

PRICE, DEBBIE MITCHELL, journalist, newspaper editor; b. Littlefield, Tex., June 3, 1959; d. Horace A. and Diane (Hall) Mitchell; m. Larry C. Price, May 2, 1981. BFA, So. Meth. U., 1980. Reporter Ft. Worth Star-Telegram, 1980-83, 91, Phila. Daily News, 1983-87, Washington Post, 1988-91; columnist Ft. Worth Star-Telegram, 1991-93, exec. editor, 1993—, v.p., 1994—; free-lance writer, Phila., 1987-88. Recipient 1st place Gen. Column Writing award Tex. AP Mng. Editors, 1991, 1st place Mag. Writing award Women's Sports Journalism, 1989, 1st place award Chesapeake Bay AP Mng. Editors, 1990. Mem. Am. Soc. Newspaper Editors, Soc. Profl. Journalists (Ft. Worth chpt.). Office: Ft Worth Star-Telegram Inc PO Box 1870 400 W 7th St Fort Worth TX 76102*

PRICE, FRANCES KIE, hospital administrator; b. Franklin, Ky., Jan. 30, 1950; d. Atha and Dorothy Louise (Poole) Kie; m. James Lewis Price, Feb. 29, 1981; children: Shelley, Tina, Jeremy, James. Ctrl. svc. tech. Jesse Holman Jones Hosp., Springfield, Tenn., 1986-88, surg. technologist, 1988-90, ctrl. svc. mgr., 1990—, recall and chem. inventory mgr., 1993—. Tng. Agy. mgr. Am. Heart Assn., 1993—. Recipient cert. Excellence ARC, 1993; named Parent of Yr. So. Ky. Head Start, 1987. Mem. NAFE, Internat. Assn. Healthcare Ctrl. Svc. Materials Mgmt., Am. Soc. Healthcare Ctrl. Svc. Personnel (Sterile Bow 1992), Internat. Registry Environ. Engrs. and Profls. (environ. compliance mgr. 1994), Assn. Surg. Technologists, Tenn. Soc. Healthcare Ctrl. Svc. Personnel, Midstate Soc. Healthcare Ctrl. Svc. Personnel, Women's Writers Guild. Office: Jesse Holman Jones Hosp 509 Brown St Springfield TN 37172-2941

PRICE, GAYL BAADER, residential construction company administrator; b. Gothenburg, Sweden, Mar. 1, 1949; came to U.S., 1951; d. Harold Edgar Anderson and Jeanette Helen (Hallberg) Akeson; m. Daniel J. Baader, Nov. 27, 1971 (div. Sept. 1980); m. Leigh C. Price, Feb. 28, 1983; foster children: Heidi, Heather. BA in Fgn. Lang., U. Ill., 1971. Asst. buyer The Denver, 1971-73, buyer, 1973-75; escrow sec. Transam. Title, Evergreen, Colo., 1975-76, escrow officer, 1976-78, sr. escrow officer, 1978-79, br. mgr., 1979-84; sr. account mgr. Transam. Title, Denver, 1984-87, sales mgr., 1987-91, v.p., 1989-94; cmty. mgr. Village Homes of Colo., Littleton, Colo., 1994—. Vol. Safehouse for Battered Women, Denver, 1986—, Spl. Olympics, 1986—, Adult Learning Svcs., 1993—, Kids Cure for Cancer, 1994—. Mem. Home Builders Assn. Met. Denver (bd. dirs. 1989—, exec. com. 1992, assoc. mem. coun. chair 1991, Arthur Gaeth Assoc. of Yr. 1989), Sales and Mktg. Coun. Met. Denver (chair, Most Profl. award 1989), Douglas County Econ. Devel., Zonta Club (Denver II, pres. 1990, Zontian of Yr. 1988), Colo. Assn. of Homebuilders (Assoc. of Yr. 1992). Home: 1975 Linda Ln Evergreen CO 80439 Office: Village Homes 6 W Dry Creek Cir # 200 Littleton CO 80201

PRICE, ILENE ROSENBERG, lawyer; b. Jersey City, July 2, 1951; d. Irwin Daniel and Mildred (Riesberg) Rosenberg; m. Jeffrey Paul Price, Feb. 18, 1973. AB, U. Mich., 1972; JD, U. Pa., 1977. Bar: Pa. 1977, D.C. 1978, U.S. Dist. Ct. D.C. 1979, U.S. Ct. Appeals (D.C. cir.) 1979. Assoc. Haley, Bader & Potts, Washington, 1977-80; staff atty. Mut. Broadcasting System Inc., Arlington, Va., 1980-82, asst. gen. counsel, 1982-85; gen. counsel MultiComm Telecommunications Corp., Arlington, 1985-88; east coast counsel Westwood One, Inc., Arlington, 1988-91; gen. counsel Resource Dynamics Corp., Vienna, Va., 1991—. Mem. ABA, Fed. Communications Bar Assn., Wash. Met. Area Corp. Counsel Assn., Women's Bar Assn. D.C. (bd. dirs. 1984-87). Office: Resource Dynamics Corp 8605 Westwood Center Dr Vienna VA 22182

PRICE, JEANNINE ALLEENICA, clinical psychologist; b. Cleve., Oct. 29, 1949; d. Q. Q. and Lisa Denise (Wilson) Ewing; m. T. R. Price, Sept. 2, 1976. BS, Western Res. U., 1969; MS, Vanderbilt U., 1974; MBA, Stanford U., 1985. Cert. alcoholism counselor, Calif. Health Service coordinator Am. Profile, Nashville, 1970-72; exec. dir. Awareness Concept, San Jose, Calif., 1977-80, counselor, 1989—, exec. dir., 1989-90, v.p. Image Makers (formerly Awareness Concepts), 1991—; mgr. employee assistance program Nat. Semiconductor, Santa Clara, Calif., 1980-81; mgmt. cons. employee assistant programs; counselor Awareness Concept, 1989—, exec. dir., 1989-90. Mem. Gov.'s Adv. Council Child Devel. Programs. Mem. Am. Bus. Women's Assn., NAFE, AAUW, Coalition Labor Women, Calif. Assn. Alcohol counselors, Almaca. Author: Smile a Little, Cry a Lot, Gifts of Love, Reflection in the Mirror, The Light at the Top of the Mountain, The Dreamer, The Girl I Never Knew, An Act of Love, Walk Toward the Light.

PRICE, KAREN OVERSTREET, pharmacist, medical editor; b. South Boston, Va., Oct. 28, 1964; d. Alvin Keith and Catherine Coggin (Marshall) Overstreet; m. David McRoy Price, June 18, 1988. BS in Pharmacy, U. N.C., 1987; MS in Drug Info., L.I. U., 1990. Cert. editor life scis. Bd. Editors in Life Scis. Pharmacist Eckerd, Burlington, N.C., 1988; Lasdon Rsch. fellow Internat. Drug Info. Ctr., Bklyn., 1988-90; drug info. analyst Am. Soc. Hosp. Pharmacists, Bethesda, Md., 1990-91; med. editor Adverceutics, Inc., Laurel, Md., 1991-93; dir. Meniscus Ednl. Inst., Phila., 1993—. Co-author: Athletic Drug Reference, 1991; co-author, co-editor: (computer program) Athletic Drug Reference, 1992; editorial rev. bd. P&T, 1993—; editorial bd. Drugdex Info. Sys., 1994—. Recipient Upjohn award for excellence in rsch. Upjohn Pharms., 1990. Mem. Am. Pharm. Assn. (reviewer 1991—), Am. Med. Writers Assn. (manuscript editor 1991-93, news editor 1994—), Am. Soc. Hosp. Pharmacists, Drug Info. Assn., Rho Chi Honor Soc. Office: Meniscus Ednl Inst Ste 210 105 N 22d St Philadelphia PA 19103

PRICE, KATHLEEN MCCORMICK, book editor, writer; b. Topeka, Kans., Dec. 25, 1932; d. Raymond Chesley and Kathleen (Shoffner) McCormick; m. William Faulkner Black, Aug. 25, 1956 (div. 1961); 1 child, Kathleen Serena; m. William Hillard Price, Aug. 13, 1976. BA, U. Colo., Denver, 1971. Book reviewer Denver Post, 1971-78; book editor San Diego Mag., 1978-92; cons. editor St. John's Cathedral, Denver, 1985—. Author: There's a Dactyl Under My Foot, 1986, The Lady and the Unicorn, 1994. Historian, Altar Guild, St. John's Cathedral, Denver. Mem. PEN Internat., Denver Women's Press Club, Denver Country Club, La Garita Club, Phi Beta Kappa. Episcopalian. Home: 27 Crestmoor Dr Denver CO 80220-5853

PRICE, LEONTYNE, concert and opera singer; b. Laurel, Miss., Feb. 10, 1927; d. James A. and Kate (Baker) P.; m. William Warfield, Aug. 31, 1952 (div. 1973). BA, Central State Coll., Wilberforce, Ohio, 1949, DMus, 1968; student, Juilliard Sch. Music, 1949-52; pupil, Florence Page Kimball; LHD, Dartmouth Coll., 1962, Fordham U., 1969, Yale U., 1979; MusD, Howard U., 1962; Dr. Humanities, Rust Coll., 1968. Profl. opera debut in 4 Saints in 3 Acts, 1952; appeared as Bess in Porgy and Bess, Vienna, Berlin, Paris, London, under auspices U.S. State Dept., also N.Y.C. and U.S. tour, 1952-54; recitalist, soloist with symphonies, U.S., Can., Australia, Europe, 1954—; appeared concerts in India, 1956, 64; soloist, Hollywood Bowl, 1955-59, 66, Berlin Festival, 1960; role as Mme. Lidoine in Dialogues des Carmelites, San Francisco Opera, 1957; opera singer, NBC-TV, 1955-58, 60, 62, 64, San Francisco Opera Co., 1957-59, 60-61, 63, 65, 67, 68, 71, as Aida at La Scala, Milan, 1957, Vienna Staatsoper, 1958, 59-60, 61, Berlin Opera, 1964, Rome Opera, 1966, Paris Opera, 1968, recital, Brussels Internat. Fair, auspices State Dept., 1958, Verona Opera Arena, 1958-59, recitals in Yugoslavia for, State Dept., 1958; rec. artist, RCA-Victor, 1958—, appeared Covent Garden, London, 1958-59, 70, Chgo. Lyric Theatre, 1959, 60, 65, Oakland (Calif.) Symphony, 1980, soloist, Salzburg Festival, 1959-63, Tetro alla Scala, Milano, 1960-61, 63, 67, appeared Met. Opera, N.Y.C., 1961-62, 64, 66, 75, 76; since resident mem., until 1985; soloist, Salzburg Festival, 1950, 60, debut, Teatre Dell'Opera, Rome, 1967, Teatro Colon, Buenos Aires, Argentina, 1969, Hamburg Opera, 1970; recordings include A Christmas Offering with Karajani, God Bless America with Charles Gerhardt, Arias from Don Giovanni, Turandot, Aida, Emani, Messa di Requiem, Trovatore, Live at Ordway, The Prima Donna Collection, A Program of Song with D. Garvey, Right as the Rain with André Previn. Hon. bd. dirs. Campfire Girls; hon. vice-chmn. U.S. com. UNESCO; co-chmn. Rust Coll. Upward Thrust Campaign; trustee Internat. House. Decorated Order at Ment Italy; recipient merit award for role of Tosca in NBC-TV Opera; Mademoiselle mag., 1955; 20 Grammy awards for classical vocal recs. Nat. Acad. Rec. Arts and Scis.; citation YWCA, 1961; Spirit of Achievement award Albert Einstein Coll. Medicine, 1962; Presdl. medal of freedom, 1964; Springarn medal NAACP, 1965; Schwann Catalog award, 1968; Nat. Medal of Arts, 1985; named Musician of Year, Mus. Am. mag., 1961; others. Fellow Am. Acad. Arts and Sci.; mem. AFTRA, Am. Guild Mus. Artists, Actors Equity Assn., Sigma Alpha Iota, Delta Sigma Theta. Office: Columbia Artists Mgmt Inc 165 W 57th St New York NY 10019-2201 also: 1133 Broadway New York NY 10010*

PRICE, LINDA RICE, community development administrator; b. Norman, Okla., Sept. 17, 1948; d. Elroy Leon and Esther May (Wilson) Rice; m. Michael Allen Price, May 17, 1970; children: Justin R, Mathew Lyon. BA in Am. History, U. Okla., 1970, M. Regional and City Planning, 1975. Dir. U. Okla. Crisis Ctr., Norman, 1969-70; cardio-pulmonary technician Bethany Med. Ctr., Kansas City, Kans., 1970-72; mgr. congressional campaign Barsotti for Congress, Kansas City, 1972; planning intern City of Seminole (Okla.), 1973-74, City of Tecumseh (Okla.), 1974-75; planner I City of Norman, 1975-76, planner II, 1975-80, community devel. coord., 1980—; adj. prof. U. Okla., Norman, 1986-93; cons. in field, Norman, 1980—. Past pres., mem. LWV Norman, 1979—; chmn. Norman Arts & Humanities Coun., 1983-86; bd. dirs. Women's Resource Ctr., Norman, 1991-92; v.p. Oakhurst Neighborhood Assn., Norman, 1991-94; mem., past pres. bd. Thunderbird Clubhouse, 1992—. Named to Leadership Norman, Norman C. of C., 1992, for Exemplary Mgmt. Practice, The Urban Inst., 1989, for Outstanding Performance, HUD, 1988; recipient Citation of Merit, Okla. State Hist. Preservation, 1991, Spl. Recognition, Okla. Hist. Soc., 1991. Mem. Am. Inst. Cert. Planners (cert.), Am. Planning Assn. (sec. Okla. chpt. 1980-82), Planning and Women (regional coord. 1987-90), Assn. Cen. Okla. Govt. (areawide planning and tech. adv. com. 1979—), Nat. Community Devel. Assn., (state whip 1988—, chair nat. membership 1994—), Homeless Here Coalition, Social Svcs. Coordinating Coun. Democrat. Presbyterian. Office: City of Norman PO Box 370 Norman OK 73070-0370

PRICE, MONICA LEIGH, sales and marketing executive; b. Durham, N.C., Aug. 31, 1964; d. Jack Washington and June Carol P. BBA in Mktg., Stetson U., Deland, Fla., 1986, MBA, 1987. Account coord. Giorgio Beverly Hills, Atlanta, 1988-89; territory mgr. Calvin Klein Cosmetic Co., Atlanta, 1989-94; sales rep. True Form Intimate Apparel divsn. Maidenform, Inc., Atlanta, 1994—. Mem. Atlanta Lawn Tennis Assn. Home: 337 Akers Ridge Dr NW Atlanta GA 30339-3216

PRICE, PATRICIA ANNE, artist; b. Tulsa, Feb. 4, 1950; d. Max Edward and Katharine (Jordan) P. BA, Oral Roberts U., 1974. Pvt. practice oil and gas lease broker Burleson County, Tex., 1978-84; rsch. and sale clk. The Kiva Indian Arts, Santa Fe, 1984-90; owner, mgr. Singing Coyote-Southwestern Art, Santa Fe, 1992—. Exhibited in Romanian Libr., N.Y.C., 1975, Boston (Mass.) Coll., 1975, S.W. Tex. State, San Marcos, 1977, Ohio State U., Columbus, 1977. East European scholar, S.W. Tex. State U., 1977, Romania Ministry of Tourism scholar, 1976. Mem. Women's Divsn. Aux. C. of C. Santa Fe, The Cherokee Nation (tribal mem.), VFW Women's Aux., Am. Legion Women's Aux. Home and Office: 142 Verano Loop Eldorado Santa Fe NM 87505

PRICE, ROSALIE PETTUS, artist; b. Birmingham, Ala.; d. Erle and Ellelee (Chapman) Pettus; AB, Birmingham-So. Coll., 1935; MA, U. Ala., Tuscaloosa, 1967; m. William Archer Price, Oct. 3, 1936. Instr. Birmingham (Ala.) Mus. Art, 1967-70, Samford U., 1969-70. Painter in watercolors, casein, oil and acrylic; One-man shows include Samford U., 1964, Birmingham Mus. of Art, 1966, 73, 82-83, Town Hall Gallery, 1968, 75, South Central Bell, 1977, Birmingham Southern Coll., 1992; represented in permanent collections Birmingham Mus. Art, Springfield (Mo.) Art Mus., U. Ala. Moody Gallery of Art, many others. Bd. dirs. Birmingham Mus. of Art, 1950-54, vice chmn., 1950-51; bd. trustees Birmingham Music Club, 1956-66, rec. sec., 1958-62. Recipient purchase award Watercolor USA, 1972; named to Watercolor USA Honor Soc., 1986. Mem. Nat. Watercolor Soc., Nat. Soc. Painters in Casein and Acrylic (W. Alden Brown Meml. award 1970, Joseph A. Cain Meml. award 1983), Birmingham Art Assn. (pres. 1947-49, Best Watercolor award 1950, Little House on Linden purchase award 1968), So. Watercolor Soc., Watercolor Soc. Ala. (sec. 1948-49), La. Watercolor Soc., Pi Beta Phi. Episcopalian. Clubs: Jr. League of Birmingham (chmn. art com. 1947-50), Window Box Garden. Home: 300 Windsor Dr Birmingham AL 35209-4338 Office: 2132 20th Ave S Birmingham AL 35223-1002

PRICE, STEPHANIE JO WALLACE, adult probation-parole officer; b. Eastland, Tex., Sept. 17, 1946; d. Matthew James and Ruth Margaret

(Fowler) Wallace; m. Winston Price (div. May 21, 1985). BA, N.Mex. State U., 1985. Lab. technician N.Mex. State Learning Assistance Ctr., Carlsbad, 1986-87; probation-parole officer Corrections Dept., Carlsbad, 1987—. Sec. div. IV, Eddy County Democrats, Carlsbad. Mem. Am. Probation-Parole Assn., AAUW (legal advocacy chair 1990-91, 2d place per capita donation Rocky Mountain region 1991), Altrusa Inc. Internat. of Carlsbad (community svc. chair), Mayor's Drug Task Force. Home: PO Box 1665 Carlsbad NM 88221-1665 Office: Corrections Dept 1305 W Lea St Carlsbad NM 88220-4354

PRICE, TERESA JUNE, city planner; b. Albuquerque, Sept. 15, 1957; d. Wyndel Gene and Peggy June (Cooper) P.; m. John Michael Griesenauer; children: Andrew Price Griesenauer, Nicholas Price Griesenauer. BS in Home Econs., Okla. State U., 1979; M. of Regional and City Planning, U. Okla., 1981. Assoc. planner City of Oklahoma City, 1981-83; exec. dir. Neighborhood Housing Svcs., Inc., Oklahoma City, 1983-85; planning dir. City of O'Fallon, Mo., 1985—; mem. Metro Fair Housing Coun., Oklahoma City, St. Charles (Mo.) County Master Plan Task Force. Bd. dirs. Neighborhood Devel. and Conservation Ctr., Oklahoma City, 1984-85, Comty. Assn. Inst.-St. Louis, 1992-93. Mem. Am. Planning Assn., Mo. Planning Assn., St. Charles County Planning Assn. Office: City of O'Fallon 138 S Main St O'Fallon MO 63366-2867

PRICE, THEODORA HADZISTELIOU, individual and family therapist; b. Athens, Greece, Oct. 1, 1938; came to U.S. 1967; d. Ioannis and Evangelia (Emmanuel) Hadzisteliou; m. David C. Long Price, Dec. 26, 1966 (div. 1989); children: Morgan N., Alkes D.L. BA in History/Archaeology, U. Athens, 1961; DPhil, U. Oxford, Eng., 1966; MA in Clin. Social Work, U. Chgo., 1988; Diploma in Piano Teaching, Nat. Conservatory, Athens, 1958. Lic. clin. social worker; bd. cert. diplomate in clin. social work. Mus. asst. and resident tutor U. Sydney, Australia, 1966-67; instr. anthropology Adelphi U., N.Y.C., 1967-68; archaeologist Hebrew Union Coll., Gezer, Israel, 1968; asst. prof. classical archaeology/art U. Chgo., 1968-70; jr. rsch. fellow Harvard Ctr. Hellenic Studies, Washington, 1970-71; clin. social worker Harbor Light Ctr., Salvation Army, Chgo., 1988-89; therapist Inst. Motivational Devel., Lombard, Ill., 1989-90; caseworker Jewish Family & Community Svc., Chgo., 1989-90; staff therapist Family Svc. Ctrs. of South Cook County, Chicago Heights, 1990-91; pvt. practice child, adolescent, family therapy Bolingbrook, Ill., 1991—; dir. counseling svcs., clin. supr., psychotherapist The Family Link, Inc., Chgo., 1993; therapist children, adolescents and families dept. foster care Catholic Charities, Chgo., 1993-94; individual and family therapist South Ctrl. Cmty. Svcs. Individual-Family Counseling Svcs., Chgo., 1994—; staff therapist Cen. Bapt. Family Svcs., Chgo., 1991, Gracell Rehab., Chgo., 1991-92; casework supr., counselor Epilepsy Found. Greater Chgo., 1992-93; lectr. in field; bd. mem., cons. Naperville Sch. for Gifted and Talented, 1982-84. Author: (Monograph) Kourotrophos Cults and Representations of the Greek Nursing Deities, 1978; contbr. articles to profl. jours. Meyerstein Traveling awardee, Oxford, Eng., 1963, 64; Sophocles Venizelos scholar, 1962-65. Mem. NASW, Nat. Acad. Clin. Social Workers, Ill. Clin. Social Workers (bd. cert. diplomate). Home and Office: 10 Pebble Ct Bolingbrook IL 60440

PRICE BODAY, MARY KATHRYN, choreographer, small business owner, educator; b. Fort Bragg, N.C., May 20, 1945; d. Max Edward and Katharine (Jordan) P.; m. Les Boday (div. 1982); children: Shawn Leon Boday, Irmali Ferecho Boday; m. Richard A. Weil, May 1, 1986. BFA, U. Okla., 1968, MFA, 1970; studies with David Howard, 1972-74. Soloist dancer Mary Anthony Dance Co., N.Y.C., 1971-74, Larry Richardson Dance Co., N.Y.C., 1971-73; dancer Pearl Lang Dance Co., N.Y.C., 1971-73, Gaku Dance Theater, N.Y.C., 1972-74; ballet mistress and soloist dancer St. Gallen Ballet, Switzerland, 1974-75; dancer, tchr. Zurich Ballet, Switzerland, 1975-76; asst. prof. U. Ill., Champaign-Urbana, 1976-79; artist-in-residence Cornish Inst., Seattle, 1979-80; pres. The Dance Works, Inc., Seattle, 1981-90; dir. Seahurst Ballet, 1982-84; pres. The Dance Works, Inc., Erie, Pa., 1990—; dir. dance dept., asst. prof. Mercyhurst Coll., Erie, Pa., 1990-94; dir. Peoria Ballet, 1994—; asst. prof. Bradley U., Peoria, 1994—; tchr. Harkness Ballet N.Y., Mary Anthony Dance Sch., Zurich Ballet, Nat. Acad. Arts Ill., Jefferson High Sch. Performing Arts Portland, also choreographer; tchr. Summer Dance Lab.; choreographer Mary K. Price Dance Co., U. Ill., Nat. Acad. Arts, Cornish Inst., Seahurst Ballet; tchr. Kneeland Workshops, Port Townsend, Wash., 1988; tchr., co-dir. Kneeland Seminars, Las Vegas, Nev., Port Townsend, summers 1989, 90, Oklahoma City U., summer 1990, Am. Coll. Dance Festival, 1991, 92, 93; tchr. Pa. Gov's. Sch. of the Arts, 1991, 92, 94, David Howard summer seminar Mercyhurst Coll., summer 1992, David Howard Summer Workshop with Tulsa Ballet Theatre, 1993, 94; guest artist, asst. prof. Slippery Rock U., 1994. Choreographer 3 ballets Ballet Co. St. Gallen, 1988, dance concert Mary & Friends, Seattle, 1990, The Nutcracker for Warner Theatre Erie; co-choreographer The Nutcracker Ballet, 1991-93, Coppelia, 1993, The Little Mermaid of Lake Erie at the Warner Theater, 1994. Outstanding Dancer award U. Okla., 1968; named one of Outstanding Young Women of Am., 1977. Office: Mary Price Boday Dance Bradley Univ Communications/Fine Arts Peoria IL 61625

PRIDE, MIRIAM R., academic administrator; b. Canton, China, June 6, 1948; d. Richard E. and Martha W. Pride; divorced. Grad., Berea College Found. Sch., 1966, College of Wooster, 1970; MBA, U. Ky., 1989. With sales room Boone Tavern Hotel Berea Coll., Berea, Ky., 1963-70; intern in administrn. in higher edn., head resident College of Wooster, Wooster, Ohio, 1970-72; accounts payable clerk, dir. Boone Tavern Hotel, head resident, dir. student activities Berea Coll., 1972-88; eligibility worker dept. human resources State of Ky., 1975-76; assistantship undergrad. advising coll. bus. U. Ky., 1987-89; asst. to pres. for campus life, v.p. for administrn., pres. Blackburn Coll., Carlinville, Ill., 1989—. Chair United Way Berea, Carlinville, 1989-92; mem. Berea Tourism Commn., Blue Grass Area Devel. Dist., United Way Macoupin Allocation Com., 1989-92; bd. dirs. Girl Scouts, Land of Lincoln, 1993—, Carlinville Area Hosp., 1993—, Assn. Presbyn. Colls. and Univs., Fedn. Ind. Ill. Colls. and Univs., 1993—. Mem. Carlinville C. of C. (bd. dirs.), Rotary. Mem. Federated Ch. Office: Blackburn Coll Office of the President Carlinville IL 62626

PRIEST, HARTWELL WYSE, artist; b. Brantford, Ont., Can., Jan. 1, 1901; d. John Frank Henry and Rachel Thayer (Gavet) Wyse; m. A.J. Gustin Priest, Aug. 4, 1927; children: Paul Lambert, Marianna Thayer. BA, Smith Coll. Former tchr. graphic art Va. Art Inst., Charlottesville; former lectr. on prints and lithography; juror art exhbn. Unitarian Ch., 1993. One-woman shows include Argent Gallery, N.Y.C., 1955, 58, 60, 73, 77, 81, Va., 1969, 71, Nantucket, Mass., 1956, Ft. Lauderdale, Fla. Art Ctr., 1956; Pen & Brush, N.Y.C., 1973, 91, invitational retrospective exhbn. McGuffey Art Ctr., Charlottesville, Va., 1984, Va., N.Y., 1984, 88; work represented in permanent collections Library of Congress, Washington, Norton Gallery, Palm Beach, Fla., Soc. Am. Graphic Artists, Hunterdon County Art Ctr., Longwood Coll., Smith Coll., Va. Mus., Richmond, Carnegie Mellon U. and numerous others; solo exhbn. of prints McGuffey Art Ctr., Charlottesville, Va., 1988, 90, 93, Woodstock Artist Gallery, 1990, Soc. Am. Graphic Artists, 1988-89, 92, Bombay, 1989, U. Va. Hosp., 1989, Bergen Mus. Art and Sci., 1991; represented in group shows McGuffey Gallery, 1988, 94, Gallery Show, Richmond, Va., 1988, Nat. Assn. Women Artists, Florence, Italy, 1972, N.Y.C., 1989, ann. show Ojibway Hotel Club, Pointe au Baril, Georgian Bay, Ont, Can., 1991, Soc. Am. Graphic Arts, N.Y.C., 1989, 92, Woodstock, N.Y. Art Assoc., 1990, McGuffey Art Ctr., Charlottesville, Va., 1990, 94, Pen and Brush ann. Graphic Show, N.Y.C., 1991 (award for etching Spring, Ada Rosario Cecere Meml. award), Bergen Mus., N.J., 1991, Ojibway Club, Ont., Can., 1991; represented in traveling group shows Nat. Assn. Women Artists, Puerto Rico, 1987, India, 1989, N.Y.C., 1994; pvt. collection U. Va. Hosp., Charlottesville, 1989. Recipient awards for lithograph Field Flowers, Longwood Coll., 1965, Nat. Assn. Woman Artists, 1965, lithograph West Wind, A Buell award, 1961, print Streets of Silence, T. Giorgi Meml. award, 1973, lithograph Blue Lichen, Pen & Brush, 1984, award for collage, 1985; 1st award for graphics Blue Ridge Art Show, 1985, Gene A. Walker award for print Glacial Rocks, 1986, award for print Blue Ridge Show, 1987, Philip Isenburg award for graphic PreCambrian Rock Pattern, 1988, Ada R. Cecere Meml. award Pen and Brush, 1991, Art award Piedmont Coun. Arts, 1993. Mem. Nat. Assn. Women Artists (Travelling Printmaking Exhbn. 1987-89), Pen and Brush, Soc. Am. Graphic Artists, Washington Print Club, 2d St. Gallery, Charlottesville, McGuffey Art Ctr. Home: 41 Old Farm Rd Charlottesville VA 22903-4725

PRIEST, MELISSA LENORE, lawyer; b. New Orleans, Mar. 26, 1962; d. Wayne Patrick and Nancy Ann (Dague) P. BA magna cum laude, Southwestern U., 1983; JD, U. Tex., 1986. Bar: Tex. 1986. Asst. dist. atty. Bexar County Dist. Attys. Office, San Antonio, 1987-90, chief grand jury sect., 1990—. Chair bd. dirs. Good Samaritan Ctr., San Antonio, 1988-94; vestry mem. St. Stephens Episc. Ch., San Antonio, 1991-94; vol. mediator Bexar County Dispute Resolution Ctr., San Antonio, 1994. Mem. San Antonio Young Lawyer's Assn., Bexar County Women's Bar Assn. (bd. dirs. 1990-91, sec. 1992, Belva Lockwood Outstanding Young Lawyer award 1990). Democrat. Office: Bexar County Dist Attys Office 300 Dolorosa San Antonio TX 78205

PRIEST, RUTH EMILY, music minister, choir director, composer arranger; b. Detroit, Nov. 7, 1933; d. William and Gertrude Hilda (Stockley) P. Student, Keyboard Studios, Detroit, 1949-52, Wayne State U., Detroit, 1953, 57, Ea. Pentecostal Bible Coll., Peterborough, Ont., 1954-55, Art Ctr. Music Sch., Detroit Inst. Mus. Arts, 1953-54. Legal sec., 1951-90; organist, pianist, vocalist Berea Tabernacle, Detroit, 1943-61; organist Bethany Presbyn. Ch., Ft. Lauderdale, Fla., 1961-67, 69-72; choir dir., organist Bethany Drive-in Ch., Ft. Lauderdale, Fla.; organist First Bapt. Ch., Pompano Beach, Fla., 1967-68, St. Ambrose Episcopal Ch., Ft. Lauderdale, 1969-72; music dir., organist Grace Brethren Ch., Ft. Lauderdale, 1972-75; organist Boca Raton (Fla.) Community Ch., Bibletown, 1975-85; min. music, organist Warrendale Community Ch., Dearborn, Mich., 1985—; ptnr. Miracle Music Enterprises; concert and ch. organist/pianist; organist numerous weddings, city-wide rallies of Detroit and Miami Youth for Christ, Christ for Labor and Mgmt., Holiness Youth Crusade, numerous other civic and religious events; featured weekly as piano soloist and accompanist on Crusade for Christ Telecast, Detroit, 1950-60, CBC-TV, Windsor, Ont., Can.; staff organist Enquire Hotel, Galt Ocean Mile, Ft. Lauderdale, Fla., 1962-67; tchr. piano adult edn. evening sch. program Mich. Pub. Sch. System, 1991—. Ongoing educator in pvt. piano, organ, music theory; Recording artist: Ruth Priest at the Organ, Love Notes from the Heart, Christmas with Ruth. Mem. Am. Guild Organists (past mem. exec. bd. Detroit chpt.). Office: Miracle Music Enterprises PO Box 554 Southfield MI 48037-0554

PRIEST, SHARON DEVLIN, state official; b. Montreal, Quebec, Can.; m. Bill Priest; 1 child, Adam. Tax preparer, instr. H & R Block, Little Rock, 1976-78; account exec. Greater Little Rock C. of C.; owner, founder Devlin Co.; mem. Little Rock Bd. Dirs., 1986—; vice mayor Little Rock, 1989-91, mayor, 1991-93; Sec. of State State of Arkansas, 1994—; bd. dirs. Invesco Inc., New Futures. Bd. dirs., past pres. Metroplan (Environ. Svc. award 1982), YMCA, Southwest Hosp.; mem. Advt. and Promotion commn., Ark. Internat. Visitors Coun., Pulaski Are Transp. Svc. Policy Com., St. Theresa's Parish Coun., Exec. com. for Ark. Mcpl. League, Nat. League of Cities Trans. and Communications Steering Com. and Policy Com., adv. bd. M.M. Cohn., Little Rock City Beautiful Commn., 1980-86; former bd. dirs. Downtown Partnership, Southwest YMCA, 1984, 86, sec.; former mem. Community Housing Resource Bd., 1984-86, Pub. Facilities Bd. Southwest Hosp., 1985-86, Southwest Merchants' Assn., 1985—, 2d v.p., 1985; chmn. Little Rock Arts and Humanities Promotion Commn.; led petition dr. for appropriation for Fourche Creek Plan 7A. Mem. Leadership Inst. Alumni Assn. (4 Bernard de la Harpe awards). Office: Office of Secretary of State State Capitol Bldg 256 Little Rock AR 72201-1411

PRILL, JUDITH DIANE, environmental analyst; b. Derby, Conn., Aug. 17, 1958; d. Paul J. Jr. and Joyce A. (Faber) P.; m. Steven Knauf, June 25, 1983; 1 child, Andrew. BS in Conservation cum laude, U. Conn., 1980; MPA, U. Hartford, 1992. Cert. soil scientist. Resources asst., staff asst. Bur. Forestry Dept. Environ. Protection, Hartford, Conn., 1981-85; caretaker, program asst. Goodwin State Forest Dept. Environ. Protection, Hampton, Conn., 1982-86; land agt., environ. analyst land acquisition and mgmt. div. Dept. Environ. Protection, Hartford, 1985-90, environ. analyst permit re-engring. team Office of Commr., 1993—. Contbr. articles to profl. jours. Recipient Take Pride in Am. Nat. award U.S. Dept. of the Interior, 1989. Mem. Soc. Soil Scientists So. New Eng., Alpha Zeta. Office: Dept Environ Protection 79 Elm St Hartford CT 06106-1632

PRIMO, JOAN ERWINA, retail and real estate consulting business owner; b. Detroit, Aug. 28, 1959; d. Joseph Carmen and Marie Ann (Nash) P. BA, Wellesley Coll., 1981; MBA, Harvard U., 1985. Acct. exec. Michigan Bell, Detroit, 1981-82, AT&T Info. Sys., Southfield, Mich., 1983; planning analyst Gen. Motors, Detroit, 1984; v.p. Howard L. Green & Assocs., Troy, Mich., 1985-89; prin., founder The Strategic Edge, Inc., Southfield, 1989—. Contbr. articles to profl. jours. Founders soc. mem. Detroit Inst. Arts, 1989—. Mem. Internat. Coun. Shopping Ctrs. (faculty, seminar leader 1987—), Wellesley Club Southeastern Mich. (pres. 1994—), Harvard Bus. Sch. Club Detroit (bd. dirs. 1994—), Ivy Club Detroit (bd. dirs. 1994—). Republican. Roman Catholic. Home: 1185 Stonecrest Dr Bloomfield Hills MI 48302 Office: The Strategic Edge 24333 Southfield Rd Ste 211 Southfield MI 48075

PRIMUS, CAROL JO, librarian; b. Frankfort, Germany, Sept. 1, 1955; came to U.S., 1956.; d. Marvin Merle and Dorothy Mae (Worman) Thompson; m. Jeffrey Alan Carlson, Apr. 11, 1981 (dec.); m. David Merrill Primus; children: Jordan, Kristin. BA, U. No. Colo., 1978; MLS, U. Md., 1987. Libr. asst. Silverton (Colo.) Pub. Libr., 1981-82, Grand Rapids (Mich.) Pub. Libr., 1986-87, Fairfax County Pub. Libr., Alexandria, Va., 1987-88; periodicals libr. We. State Coll., Gunnison, Colo., 1988-92; libr. Mesa County Pub. Libr. Dist., Grand Junction, Colo., 1992; resource sharing cons. Three Rivers Regional Libr. System, Glenwood Springs, Colo., 1993—. Active People Opposing Water Export Raids, Gunnison, 1989—. Program grantee Libr. Svcs. and Constrn. Act., Colo. State Libr., 1991. Mem. ALA, Colo. Libr. Assn.

PRIMUS, MARY JANE DAVIS, social worker, author; b. Marion, Iowa, May 31, 1924; d. Lawrence Henry and Verna Leona (Suman) Davis; m. Paul C. Primus, Aug. 23, 1955; children: Kenneth Roy, Donald Karl. BS, Iowa State U., 1950. Asst. cashier First State Bank, Greene, Iowa, 1942-46; tchr. Oskaloosa (Iowa) pub. schs., 1950-52; extension home economist Iowa State U., Oskaloosa-Eldora, 1952-57; homemaker, dist. supr. Iowa Dept. Social Svc., Webster City, 1970-77; substitute tchr. Eldora Pub. Schs., 1966-68; homemaker health aide supr. Mid-Iowa Community Action OEO, Iowa Dept. Social Svc., 1968-69; ptnr. LMAJ Herbs and Spices, Unltd. Author: Through the Window, 1973; Through the Window Twice, 1974; Tracery Windows, 1975; Shuttered Windows, 1977; Wings, 1979; Wings II, 1980; area news corr., 4 newspapers; columnist Iowa Wildlife Fedn.; murals in Steamboat Rock, Iowa H.S. Bldg., Iowa City Hall, Kiwanis Bldg., 1983-94; contbr. poems to various publs. Den mother Boy Scouts Am., Steamboat Rock, Iowa, 1966-71; leader Girl Scouts Am., Steamboat Rock, 1969-72; mem. Iowa State U. Extension Family Living Coun., Hardin County, 1961-65, 82-86, chmn. 1984-86, 90-94; outreach chmn. Iowa Family and Children Svcs., 1966-72; chmn. Hardin County Coun. on Aging, 1989-91; field days women's program chmn. Iowa Soil Conservation, 1968; pres. United Ch. of Christ, 1963-65. Mem. LWV, AAUW, AARP, Nat League Am. Pen Women, Am. Home Econs. Assn., Nat. Council Homemaker-Home Health Aide Services, Nat. Soc. Lit. and the Arts, Soil Conservation Soc. Am., Am. Legion, Internat. Platform Assn., Herb Soc. Am., Hardin County Hist. Soc., Federated Women's Club, PEO, Order Eastern Star.

PRINCE, ANNA LOU, composer, music publisher, construction company executive; b. Isabella, Tenn.; d. Ulysses Gordon and Della Carrie (Hawkins) P.; children: Sandra, Teresa, vandi. Diploma Carolina Sch. Broadcasting, 1966; Zion diploma, Israel Bible Sch., Jerusalem, 1970; diploma S.W. Tech. Coll., 1970; student United Christian Assn., 1976; MusD, London Inst. Applied Rsch., 1991; Diplomatic Diploma, Acad. Argentina de Diplomacia, 1993; PhD (hon.) Australian Inst. Co-ordinated Rsch., Victoria, 1993; Diploma of Honors of Internat. Affairs, Institut Des Affaires Internationales, Paris, 1994. Lic. Bible tchr. United Christian Acad. Songwriter Hank Locklin Music Co., Nashville, 1963-70; entertainer 1982 World's Fair, Knoxville, Tenn., 1982; ptnr., owner Prince Wholesale Bait Co., Canton, N.C., 1976-82, Grad Builders, Canton, 1982-86, Prince TV Co., 1986-94; music publisher Broadcast Music, Inc., Nashville, 1982—; photographer Washington Press Corps., 1991-94; mem. production staff, talent coord. (TV series) Down Home, Down Under, 1989-90. Songs recorded on RCA: I Feel a Cry Coming On, 1965 (#1 in Eng.), Best Part of Loving You, (#1 in Eng.), Anna, 1969 (Billboard 1970, recorded in Ireland 1974, hit in Europe); over 20 songs recorded to date; appeared Grand Ole Opry, 1970; host TV talk show, Cable Channel 19, 1989—. Cand. for county commnr. Democratic party Macon County, N.C., 1984; bd. dirs. Macon County Taxpayers Assn., Inc., 1984, v.p., 1984-86; bd. dirs. Head Start, Topton, N.C., 1969-73. Nominated Disting. Women N.C., N.C. Council on Status of Women, 1984, Jefferson award WYFF TV and Am. Inst. for Pub. Service, Outstanding Bus. Woman Small Bus. Adminstrn., 1984. Mem. BMI, Internat. Parliament Safety and Peace (life, dept. fgn. affairs, dep. mem. assembly), Nashville Songwriters Assn. Internat. (moderator, tchr. 1984-86), Country Music Assn., Reunion Profl. Entertainers, Fraternal Order Police, C. of C., Order of Knight of Templars (dame), Lofsensic Order (dame), Maison Internationales des Intellectuals. Democrat. Office: 313 Gallatin Rd S Madison TN 37115-4006

PRINCE, ANTOINETTE ODETTE, visual artist, art educator; b. Watertown, N.Y., Mar. 18, 1946; d. Clarence Oliver and Marion Eva (Moffatt) Odette; m. George Mather Prince, Aug. 5, 1976 (div. 1981). Grad., Boston Mus. Sch., 1981-82; postgrad., Harvard U., 1986—. Painting instr. Boston Mus. Sch., 1981-82, 86; painting instr. Exptl. Coll. Tufts U., Medford, Mass., 1986; dir. Loading Dock Gallery, Boston, 1982-83; painting instr. Cambridge (Mass.) Art Assn., 1983-85; dir., adminstr., instr. Prince Art Workshops, 1984-92; art instr. Wang Ctr. for Performing Arts, Boston, 1991-92; instr. iterface Mother Earth Art Workshops, 1992—; coord. Art Talk, Cambridge Art Assn., 1983-85, bd. dirs. Exhibited Boston City Hall, 1981, 88, Mus. Fine Arts, Boston, 1982, DeCordova Mus., 1983-84, Habitat Inst. for Environment, 1986, Vernon St. Studios, 1989-94, Grossman Gallery, 1990, 91, 92, Chinese Cultural Inst., 1990, CBS This Morning TV Show, 1992, Tofias Gallery, 1992, Wang Ctr. for the Performing Arts, 1991, 92; work pub. in Jour. Nuclear Medicine, 1991. Recipient Traveling Scholars award Mus. Fine Arts, 1982; Pub. Action for Arts grantee, 1985. Studio: 6 Vernon St Somerville MA 02145

PRINCE, CATHY LONG, neuro-orthopedic nurse administrator; b. McCaysville, Ga., Oct. 6, 1956; d. Joseph H. and Charlene E. (Aaron) Long; m. James Darryl Prince, Aug. 19, 1983; 1 child, Christy Renae McDaniel-Short. Diploma, Dalton Vocat. Sch. Health Occupations, 1979; ASN, North Ga. Coll., 1987. RN, Ga. Nursing asst. Fannin Regional Hosp., Blue Ridge, Ga.; EMT, Gilmer County Emergency Med. System, Ellijay, Ga.; EMT Pickens County Emergency Med. System, Jasper, Ga.; advanced clin. nurse NE Ga. Med. Ctr., Gainesville; DON Mountainside Nursing Home, Jasper, Ga. Mem. Nat. Assn. Orhopaedic Nurses, Ga. Info. Control Network. Home: PO Box 26 East Ellijay GA 30539-0026

PRINCE, FRANCES ANNE KIELY, civic worker; b. Toledo, Dec. 20, 1923; d. John Thomas and Frances (Pusteoska) Kiely; m. Richard Edward Prince, Jr., Aug. 27, 1951; children: Anne, Richard III (dec.). Student U. Louisville, 1947-49; AB, Berea Coll., 1951; postgrad., Kent Sch. Social Work, 1951, Creighton U., 1969; MPA, U. Nebr., Omaha, 1978. Instr. flower arranging Western Wyo. Jr. Coll., 1965, 66; editor Nebr. Garden News, 1983-90. Author poems. Chmn. Lone Troop coun. Girl Scouts U.S.A., 1954-57, trainer leaders, 1954-68, mem. state camping com., 1959-61, bd. dirs. Wyo. state coun., 1966-69; chmn. Community Improvement, Green River, Wyo., 1959, 63-65, Wyo. Fedn. Women's Clubs State Library Svcs., 1966-69, U.S. Constitution Bicentennial Commn. Nebr. 1987-91, Omaha Commn. on the Bicentennial 1987-91; mem. Wyo. State Adv. Bd. on Libr. Inter-Co-op., 1965-69, state libr. bd., 1965-69, Nat. sub com. Commn. on the Bicentennial of the U.S. Constitution, 1986-91; bd. dirs. Sweetwater County Libr. System, 1962-69, pres. bd., 1967-68; adv. coun. Sch. Dist. 66, 1970-79; bd. dirs. Opera Angels, 1971, fund raising chmn., 1971-72, v.p., 1974-80; bd. dirs. Morning Musicale, 1971-82; bazaar com. Children's Hosp., 1970-75; docent Joslyn Art Mus., 1970—; mem. Nebr. Forestry Adv. Bd., 1976—; citizens adv. bd. Met. Area Planning Agy., 1979—; mem. Nebr. Tree-Planting Commn., 1980—; bd. dirs. U.S. Constn. Bicentennial Commn. Nebr., 1987-92, Omaha Commn. on the Bicentennial, 1987-92, Nat. commn. on Bicentennial of U.S. Constitution; bd. dirs. United Ch. Christ, Intermountain, 1963-69, mem. exec. com., 1966-69; bd. dirs. United Ch. Christ, 1985-92. Recipient Libr. Svc. award Sweetwater County Library, 1968; Girl Scout Svcs. award, 1967; Conservation award U.S. Forest Service, 1981; Plant Two Trees award, 1981; Nat. Arbor Day award, 1982; Pres. award Nat. coun. of State Garden Clubs, 1986, 87, 89, Joyce Kilmer award Nat. Arbor Day Found., 1990; awards U.S. Constn. Bicentennial Commn. Nebr., 1987, 91, Omaha Commn. on the Bicentennial, 1987, Nat. Bicentennial Leadership award Coun. for Advancement of Citizenship, 1989, Nat. Conservation medal DAR, 1991, George Washington silver award Nat. commn. on Bicentennial of U.S. Constitution, 1992, Mighty Oak award Garden Clubs of Nebr., 1992. Mem. AAUW (Vol. of Yr. Omaha br. 1989), New Neighbors League (dir. 1969-71), Ikebana Internat., Symphony Guild, Omaha Playhouse Guild, ALA, Nebr. Libr. Assn., Omaha Coun. Garden Clubs (1st v.p. 1972, pres. 1973-75, state bd. dirs. 1979—, mem. nat. council bd. dirs. 1979—, pres. award 1988, 89, 90), Internat. Platform Assn., Nat. Trust for Hist. Preservation, Nebr. Flower Show Judges Coun., Nat. Coun. State Garden Clubs (chmn. arboriculture 1985-90, 93—, chmn. nature conservancy 1991-93), Nebr. Fedn. Garden Clubs (pres. 1978-81), Garden Club (dir. 1970-72, pres. 1972-75). Home: 8909 Broadmoor Dr Omaha NE 68114-4248

PRINCE, KATHY KAY, nurse; b. Panama Canal Zone, July 26, 1957; d. Billy Osbin and Shirley Ann (Weiser) Adams. BSN, U. South Fla., 1980. ACLS; RN, Fla. With Tampa (Fla.) Gen. Hosp., 1979—, mem. nursing standards and practice com., 1980—, nurse, IV therapy coord., exptl. burn and transplant nurse, 1991—, employee exposure task force, 1991—, employee adv. com., 1994-96, chmn. quality of work life com., 1994, chmn. employment adv. com., 1995; selection steering com. Change Team Internat., 1994-95. Contbr. articles to newsletters. Speakcer career week Lanier Elem. Sch., Tampa, 1989—. Mem. ARC, Nephrology Nurses Assn., Intravenous Nurses Assn., Internat. Assn. for Welfare Animals, World Wildlife Fund, Adopt A Manatee, Cir. K (sec. 1977), Sierra Club, Phi Theta Kappa. Democrat. Baptist. Office: Tampa Gen Hosp Box 1289 Tampa FL 33601

PRINCE, LEAH FANCHON, art educator and research institute administrator; b. Hartford, Conn., Aug. 12, 1939; d. Meyer and Annie (Forman) Berman; m. Herbert N. Prince, Jan. 30, 1955; children: Daniel L., Richard N., Robert G. Student, U. Conn., 1957-59, Rutgers U., Newark, 1962; BFA, Fairleigh Dickinson U., 1970; postgrad., Caldwell Coll. for Women, 1973-75, Parsons Sch. of Design, N.Y.C., 1978. Cert. tchr. art, N.J. Tchr. art Caldwell-West Caldwell (N.J.) Pub. Schs., 1970-75; pres. Britannia Imports Ltd., Fairfield, N.J., 1979-89; tchr. religious studies Bohrer-Kaufman Hebrew Acad., Randolph, N.J., 1981-82; co-founder and corp. sec. Gibraltar Biol. Labs., Inc., Fairfield, 1970—; dir. and co-founder Gibraltar Inst. for Rsch. and Tng., Fairfield, 1984—; cons. Internat. Antiques and Fine Arts Industries, U.K., 1979-89; cons. in art exhibitry Passaic County Coll., Paterson, N.J., 1989-93; art curator Fairleigh Dickinson U., Rutherford, N.J., 1972-74; curator history of design Bloomfield (N.J.) Coll., 1990-91. Exhibited in group shows at Bloomfield (N.J.) Coll., 1990, Caldwell Women's Club, N.J., 1991, State Fedn. Women's Clubs Ann. Show, 1992 (1st pl. award 1992), Newark Art Mus., 1992, West (N.J.) Essex Art Assn., 1990, Somerset (N.J.) Art Assn. Ann. Juried Show, 1994, Mortimer Gallery, Gladstone, N.J., 1994, Tewksbury His. Soc. (1st pl. award 1994); one-woman shows include Passaic County Coll., N.J., 1990, Caldwell Coll., N.J., 1990. Chair ann. juried art awards Arts Coun. of Essex Bd. Trustees, Montclair, N.J., 1984-90. Numerous one-woman shows univs. and fin. instns., N.J. Mem. AAUW, Somerset Art Assn., Nat. Mus. of Women in the Arts, Barnegat Light Yacht Club. Republican. Home: 5 Standish Dr Mendham Twp Morristown NJ 07960

PRINCE, PATRICIA LYNN, physician; b. L.A., Feb. 19, 1959; d. Leonard and Bridget (Clarke) P. BS, U. Ottawa, Ont., Can., 1979, MD, 1983. Diplomate Am. Bd. Family Practice. Physician, prin. Nev. Med. Ctr., Las Vegas, 1992—; aviation med. examiner FAA. Mem. AMA, Am. Acad. Family Practice, Nev. Acad. Women Physicians, Clark County Med. Soc. Office: Nev Med Ctr # C-19 601 S Rancho Dr Ste C-19 Las Vegas NV 89106-4825

PRINCE, PHYLLIS EHRLICH, activist, volunteer; b. N.Y.C., Feb. 11, 1927; d. Simon and Gussie (Leichter) Ehrlich; widowed; children: Daniel, Melissa, James. AB in Physiology & Pub. Health, Hunter Coll., 1947; MS in Sci. Edn., U. Bridgeport, 1969; MBA in Mgmt., U. Conn., 1980. Researcher, writer Exploring the Unknown, N.Y.C., 1947-49; spl. projects Standard Brands, Stamford, Conn., 1976-78; mgr. info. svcs. Champion Internat., Stamford, Conn., 1978-86; cons. Arthur D. Little Impact, Cambridge, Mass., 1986-88. Author: Blood Supply Industry, 1987. Founder, pres. Coalition Citizens for Choice, Fairfield, Conn., 1987, Med Assist, Fairfield, 1990; founder Impact, Conn., 1993, Breakfast for All, 1982-86; bd. dirs. Planned Parenthood Conn., New Haven, 1993. Recipient Richardson award United Way, Stamford, 1990, Golden Rule award J.C. Penney, Stamford, 1991. Mem. Nat. Coun. Jewish Women (Hannah Solomon award 1992). Home: 1 Strawberry Hill Ave Stamford CT 06902

PRINCE, SUSAN ELIZABETH, secondary education educator; b. Asuncion, Paraguay, Feb. 20, 1964; came to the U.S., 1982; d. Gilbert Athol and Mabel Deane (Marshall) Nichols; m. John Michael Prince, June 6, 1987; 1 child, Sarah Elizabeth. BS in Edn., Ouachita Bapt. U., 1986. Tchr. Perryville (Ark.) H.S., 1986-87, Barnesville (Ga.) Elem. Sch., 1987-88, Glenwood (Ark.) H.S., 1988—. Democrat. Baptist. Office: Glenwood High Sch PO Box 27 Glenwood AR 71943

PRINCIPAL, VICTORIA, actress; b. Fukuoka, Japan, Jan. 3, 1950; d. Victor and Ree (Veal) P.; m. Harry Glassman, 1985. Attended, Miami-Dade Community Coll.; studied acting with Max Croft, Al Sacks and Estelle Harman, Jean Scott, Royal Acad. Dramatic Arts. Worked as model, including TV commls.; appearences include (film) The Life and Times of Judge Roy Bean, 1972, The Naked Ape, 1973, Earthquake, 1974, I Will I Will For Now, 1976, Vigilante Force, 1976; (TV movies) Last Hours Before Morning, 1975, Fantasy Island, 1977, The Night They Stole Miss Beautiful, 1977, Pleasure Palace, 1980, Not Just Another Affair, 1982, Mistress, 1987, The Burden of Proof, 1990, Just Life, 1992, Beyond Obsession, 1994; exec. prodr., actress Naked Lie, 1989, Blind Witness, 1989, Sparks: The Price of Passion, 1990, Don't Touch My Daughter, 1991, Seduction: Three Tales from the Inner Sanctum, 1993, River of Rage: The Taking of Maggie Keene, 1993; exec. prodr. Midnight's Child, 1992; (TV series) Dallas, 1978-87; (theatre) Love Letters, 1990; author: The Body Principal, 1983, The Beauty Principal, 1984, The Diet Principal, 1987. Office: care Alan Nierob 10000 Santa Monica Blvd Los Angeles CA 90067-7007

PRINCIPE, HELEN MARY, medical case manager; b. Santa Monica, Calif., May 18, 1953; d. William John and Bessie Sylvia (Amsden) McGonagle; 1 child, Francis Edward. AS, Northeastern U., 1978; BSN cum laude, Worcester (Mass.) State Coll., 1981. RN, Mass., Calif. Critical care nurse Mt. Auburn Hosp., Cambridge, Mass.; adminstrv. nurse, critical care nurse, instr. Alta Bates Hosp., Berkeley, Calif.; clin. instr. med.-surg. staff devel., critical care nurse Valley Hosp., Las Vegas, Nev.; med. case mgr., supr. Intracorp, Oakland, Calif.; spl. case cons. Lincoln Nat., Pleasanton, Calif.; with Conservco, Walnut Creek, Calif.; assoc. mgr. PruCare of No. Calif., San Mateo, Calif. Mem. AAUW, Rehab. Ins. Nurses Group, Case Mgmt. Soc. Am. (founding pres. No. Calif. chpt., nat. bd. dirs., chmn. membership com.), Individual Case Mgmt. Assn.

PRINGLE, BARBARA CARROLL, state legislator; b. N.Y.C., Apr. 4, 1939; d. Nicholas Robert and Anna Joan (Woloshinovich) Terlesky; m. Richard D. Pringle, Nov. 28, 1959; children: Christopher, Rhonda. Student, Cuyahoga C.C. With Dunn & Bradstreet, 1957-60; precinct committeewoman City of Cleve., 1976-77; elected mem. Cleve. City Coun., 1977-81; mem. Ohio Ho. of Reps., Columbus, 1982—; vice chmn. pub. utilities com., energy and environment com., pub. safety and hwy. com., transp. and urban affairs com., interagy. coun. on Spanish speaking affairs, power siting bd., communicatively impaired program adv. bd., small bus. com., aging and housing com., fin. and references coms., edn. com. Vol. Cleve. Lupus Steering Com., various community orgns.; charter mem. Statue of Liberty Ellis Island Found. Recipient cert. of appreciation Cleve. Mcpl. Ct., 1977, Exch. Club Bklyn., 1978, Cmty. Recreation Appreciation award City of Cleve., 1978, Key to City of Cleve., 1979, Cleve. Area Soapbox Derby cert., 1976, 77, 81, cert. of appreciation Ward 9 Youth League, 1979-82, No. Ohio Patrolman's Benevolent Assn. award, 1983, Cuyahoga County Firefighters award, 1983, Outstanding Pub. Servant award for Outstanding Svc. to Hispanic Cmty., 1985, Nat. Sr. Citizen Hall of Fame award, 1987, cert. of appreciation Cleve. Coun. Unemployed Workers, 1987, Ohio Farmers Union award, 1990, award of appreciation United Labor Agy., 1993, Susan B. Anthony award, 1995. Mem. Nat. Order Women Legislators, Fedn. Dem. Women of Ohio, Nat. Alliance Czech Catholics, St. Michael Ch. Altar and Rosary Soc., Ward 15 Dem. Club, Polish Falcons. Democrat. Home: 708 Timothy Ln Cleveland OH 44109-3733

PRINSEN, WILLEMINA YVONNE, career counselor and educator; b. Holland, Mich., Aug. 27, 1959; d. Evart Jan and Annie (Schierbeek) P. B of Sci. Edn., Ctrl. Mich. U., 1982; MA in Counselor Edn. & Psychology, Western Mich. U., 1987. Lic. profl. counselor, Mich. Tchr. Cassia County Sch. Dist., Burley, Idaho, 1982-84; coord. of tutors Western Mich. U., Kalamazoo, Mich., 1985-87; counselor Northwestern Mich. Coll., Traverse City, Mich., 1987-88, asst. dir. admissions, 1988-90; tchr. English SCALIA, Lisbon, Portugal, 1991; dir. career and employment svcs. Northwestern Mich. Coll., Traverse City, 1992—; travel advisor Extended Edn. Svcs., Traverse City, 1991—, instr., 1992—. Editor Grand Traverse Counselor, 1991; author (newspaper) Northern Express, 1991. Projects com. Mich. Assn. Coll. Admissions, Traverse City, 1989-90; vice chair Northwestern Mich. Coll. Adminstrs. Coun., Traverse City, 1988-89; coord. events CMU Recreation Club, Mt. Pleasant, Mich., 1980-82. Mem. Mich. Coll. and Univ. Placement, Midwest Coll. Placement, Nat. Career Devel., Mich. Career Devel., Am. Counseling Assn., Grand Traverse Area Counselors, Zonta Club. Office: Northwestern Mich Coll 1701 E Front St Traverse City MI 49684

PRINS-GROSE, LAVONNE KAY, software engineer; b. Sibley, Iowa, Feb. 28, 1957; d. Henry Simon and Katherine (Schram) Prins; m. Dan Matthew Grose, Feb. 6, 1993. BA, S.W. State U., Marshall, Minn., 1982; postgrad., Mankato (Minn.) State U., 1982-84. Instr. math. Mankato State U., 1982-84; computer operator Sathers, Round Lake, Minn., 1985; law records analyst ITT Consumer Fin. Corp., St. Louis Park, Minn., 1985-86; systems programmer Metaphor, Eden Prairie, Minn., 1987-89; pres. Ablazon Unltd. Inc., Ramsey, Minn., 1990—; sr. systems programmer Health Risk Mgmt., Edina, Minn., 1989-91; software engr. Dimensional Medicine, Inc., Minnetonka, Minn., 1992—. Sgt. U.S. Army, 1975-79. Republican. Mem. Reformed Ch. in Am. Home and Office: 5631 164th Ln NW Ramsey MN 55303

PRISCO, SUSAN MARIE, accountant; b. Morristown, N.J., Nov. 28, 1961; d. Salvatore Gerard and Beverly Joyce (Hofmaster) Pastore; m. Michael Peter Prisco, Oct. 6, 1990. BS in Acctg., Seton Hall U., 1984. Acct. Gordon Publ., Randolph, N.J., 1984-85; acct. Safilo USA, Fairfield, 1985-90, sr. acct., 1990-94; mgr. ops. and sales adminstr. Optique Du Monde, Fairfield, 1994—. Mem. Inst. of Mgmt. Accts. Office: Optique Du Monde 1 Gardner Rd Fairfield NJ 07004-2205

PRITCHARD, MARGARET ELIZABETH, community activist; b. Winston-Salem, N.C., Oct. 27, 1936; d. Thomas Hugh and Ruth (Cannoy) Guinn; m. Howard Porter Pritchard; children: Howard Porter, Wilson Cannoy. BS, Wake Forest Coll., 1959; MS, Vanderbilt U., 1962; EdD, Memphis State U., 1993. Rsch. asst. Bowman Gray Sch. of Medicine, Wisnton-Salem, 1959-62; tchr. Memphis City Schs., 1962; bd. dirs. Shelby County (Tenn.) Land Use Control Bd., 1988—; chmn. Memphis Landmarks Commn., 1993—. Chmn. Shelby County Rep. Primary Bd., 1979; sec. Memphis Cmty. Rels., 1968-72. Recipient Preservation award Memphis Heritage, 1993. Mem. Am. Planning Assn., Memphis Symph. League (pres. 1984-85), Woman's Exch. Memphis (pres. 1988). Republican. Presbyterian. Home: 1800 Harbert Ave Memphis TN 38104

PRIVETTE, ROSA LEE MILLSAPS, county official; b. Hartsville, S.C., Sept. 29, 1952; d. Johnnie Arvel and Catherine Elizabeth (Teal) Millsaps; m. Michael Alan Privette, July 4, 1971 (div. Sept. 1976). AB in Acctg., Florence-Darlington Tech. Coll, 1986; BS in Acctg., Coker Coll., 1990. CPR cert.; notary pub. S.C.; lic. life ins. agt. Tax acct. L. R. Redfearn, Jr. Pub. Acct., Cheraw, S.C., 1973-74; jr. fin. officer Chesterfield-Marlboro Econ. Opportunity Coun., Inc., Cheraw, 1974-78; acct. Chesterfield-Marlboro County Commn. Alcohol and Drug Abuse, Cheraw, 1978-86; acct. Marlboro County Commn. on Alcohol and Drug Abuse, Bennettsville, S.C., 1986—, dep. dir., 1986-91, intervention specialist, 1982—, group leader, 1993—; policy advisory mem. Chesterfield-Marlboro Headstart Program, 1979-82; fin. mgmt. team mem. Waccamaw Coun. Project Office of the Gov. Divsn. Econ. Opportunity, 1994. Vol. leader coop. extension svc. Clemson U., 1986—; mem. Pee Dee Coalition Against Domestic and Sexual Assault Marlboro Adv. Coun., 1991—, Marlboro County Treatment Adv. Team S.C. Dept. Social Svcs., 1991—, Marlboro County Inter-Agy. Coun., 1991—. Mem. Am. Lung Assn. (S.C. chpt., bd. dirs.), Am. Cancer Soc. (S.C. chpt., bd. dirs.). Democrat. Baptist. Home: PO Box 57 Patrick SC 29584-0057 Office: Marlboro County Commn Alcohol & Drug Abuse 725 W Main St Bennettsville SC 29512-3116

PRIZIO, BETTY J., property manager, civic worker; b. L.A., Jan. 23, 1928; d. Harry W. and Irene L. (Connell) Campbell; divorced; children: David P., John W., Robert H., James R. AA in Social Sci., L.A. City Coll., 1949. Owner, mgr. indsl. bldgs. and condominiums indsl. bldgs. and condominiums,, Tustin, Calif., 1976—; owner Baskets and Bows by Jean, Tustin, 1994—; ind. mktg. exec., Melaleuca. Bd. dirs. Founders Chpt. Aux., Providence Speech and Hearing Ctr., 1986-88, aux. pres., 1986-89; vol. Western Med. Ctr. Aux., 1985-89, chmn. gift shop com., 1987-88, 2d v.p., 1992, jr. vol. adv., mem. bd. dirs. fund raising group; mem. adv. coun. Chapman Coll., Orange, Calif., 1986-87, bd. mem. Pres. Assocs., 1985-86; bd. dirs. Chapman Music Assocs., 1986—, Tustin Hist. Soc., 1988—, Santa Ana YWCA, 1976-77; mem. adv. coun. Orange County chpt. Freedoms Found. at Valley Forge, 1985—; mem. Orange County chpt. Charter 100, 1985-87; active United Meth. Ch.; others. Mem. Tustin Hist. Soc. (bd. dirs. 1988-90). Republican. Home: 17342 Village Dr Tustin CA 92680-2546

PROBER, JOANNE S., librarian; b. Chgo., Feb. 26, 1938; d. Jacob Meyer and Esther (Wolfson) Shapiro; m. Richard Prober, Aug. 30, 1959; children: Benjamin, Daniel, Joshua. BS, U. Wis., 1959; MSLS, Case Western Res. U., Cleve., 1974. Cert. media specialist K-12. Librarian E. Cleve. Bd. Edn., 1974—. Jennings scholar, 1984. Mem. Ohio Ednl. Libr. Media Assn. Office: Chambers Sch 14305 Shaw Ave Cleveland OH 44112-2707

PROBER, PAULA, therapist; b. Wilmington, Del., Nov. 8, 1951; d. Leonard and Rose (Kreisman) P. BA, Am. U., 1973; MEd, Shippensburg (Pa.) U., 1981; MS, Oreg. State U., 1992. Cert. mental health profl., Oreg. Tchr. elem. 1-8 gifted various schs., Wilmington, Eugene, Oreg., 1973-81, Dillsburg, Pa., 1973-81; pvt. practice Options Counseling Svcs., Eugene, 1992—; leader jour.al writing groups for adults and teens, 1994—; cons. in field; adj. instr. U. Oreg., 1981-92; tchr. gifed children and parents U. Oreg. Super Summer Program, Eugene, 1983-91 summers. Author: Time to Tell, 1993, (manual) Able Learners Strategies for the Classroom, 1987; contbr. articles to profl. jours.; writer, moderator, producer (video) Wounded Healers, 1992 (award 1992). Dir. sr. adult acting group, Eugene, 1986-88. Mem. ACA, Phi Kappa Phi. Home: 1337 E 43rd Ave Eugene OR 97405-5202

PROCHOVNICK, ORA SHELEE, lawyer, educator; b. Chgo., June 4, 1957; d. Ammiel Moses and Payah Ann (Solove) P.; life ptnr. Rena Ann Frantz. Student, Washington U., St. Louis, 1975-78; LLB, New Coll. of Calif., 1984. Bar: Calif. 1984. Intern Nat. Lawyer's Guild, Portland, Oreg., 1982; legal researcher Lesbian Rights Project (now named NCLR), San Francisco, 1982; teaching asst. New Coll. of Calif., San Francisco, 1982-84; legal researcher Nat. Lawyer's Guild, San Francisco, 1984; law clk. West Bay Law Collective, San Francisco, 1983-84; prof. Sch. of Law New Coll. of Calif., San Francisco, 1986—; dir. New Coll. Housing Advocacy Clinic, 1994—; founding ptnr. Bayside Legal Advocates, San Francisco, 1984—; panelist, seminar presenter Vol. Legal Svcs. Program, AIDS Legal Referral Panel, San Francisco, 1986—; legal advisor, cons. Nat. Ctr. Lesbian Rights, San Francisco, 1990—. Author: Landlord-Tenant Practice Manual, S.F.T.U. Tenant Handbook; author, editor: Lesbians Choosing Motherhood, 1991; contbg. author: AIDS Law, 1988, 90. Bd. dirs. AIDS Legal Referral Panel, San Francisco, 1987-93; bd. dirs. ritual com. Congregation Sha'ar Zahav, San Francisco, 1990—; del. World Congress Gay and Lesbian Jews, 1988-89, 93; mediator Comty. Bds., San Francisco, 1990—. Recipient Wiley B. Manual award State Bar Calif., 1992, 93, 94, Pres.'s Pro Bono award State Bar Calif., 1993. Mem. Nat. Lawyers Guild (panelist, seminar presenter 1986—), Bar Assn. San Francisco (panelist, seminar presenter 1986—, Outstanding Law Officer of Yr. 1987, Vol. Atty. of Month 1987, Ann. Pro Bono award 1987, 88, 89, 90, 91, 92, 93), Bay Area Lawyers for Individual Rights (panelist, seminar presenter 1986—). Home: 47 Cuvier St San Francisco CA 94112-1026 Office: New Coll Calif 50 Fell St San Francisco CA 94102

PROCOPIO, MARYLOUISE ELIZABETH, college program director; b. Fountain Hill, Pa., Nov. 30, 1956; d. William Nicholas and Margaret Anastasia (Sekerak) Strobel; m. Thomas Francis Procopio, Aug. 12, 1978 (div. May 1991); children: William Francis, Francesca Ann. BS in Home Econs. Edn., Marywood Coll., 1978; postgrad., Temple U., 1988—. Cert. home economist, nat., cert. TIPS trainer, nat., cert. food exec. Substitute tchr. Salisbury Twp. Sch. Dist., Allentown, Pa., 1979-82, Allentown Sch. Dist., 1979-82; instr. Nat. Edn. Corp.-Allentown Bus. Sch., 1982-87; coord. hosp. edn. Lehigh Carbon C.C., Schnecksville, Pa., 1987—; TIPS trainer HealthComm. Inc., Washington, 1990—; outside agt. Solid Gold Travel Agy., Bethlehem, Pa., 1991—; external auditor Northampton C.C., Bethlehem, 1992; adv. bd. mem. Lehigh County Vo-Tech. Sch., Schnecksville, 1992—. Safety officer Interested Persons Union Terr., Allentown, 1986-87, pres., 1987-90, 94—, advisor, 1990-94; bd. dirs. Union Terr. Athletic Club, Allentown, 1989-90, fin. sec., 1990-91, Big A Booster Club Allen H.S., 1992—, pres., 1993-94; chair bldg. subcom., mem. steering com. Allentown Sch. Dist. Flexible Sch. Calendar Com. Mem. NEA, NAFE, Coun. on Hotel, Restaurant and Instl. Educators, Am. Home Econs. Assn., Pa. State Edn. Assn., Pa. Travel Coun. (edn. com. 1993—), Soc. Travel and Tourism Educators, Pa. Home Econs. Assn. (Mideast dist. treas. 1982-89), Pa. Assn. Two-Yr. Colls. (bd. dirs. 1990-92, v.p. 1992-93, pres. 1993—). Democrat. Roman Catholic. Office: Lehigh Carbon CC ABE site ABE site 600 Hayden Cir Allentown PA 18103-9353

PROCTER, MARIE LOUISE, small business owner, ESL educator; b. Trenton, N.J., Mar. 16, 1933; d. Charles Howard and Marion Jane (Moon) Hazard; m. Bernard S. Weinman, Dec. 30, 1958 (div. Oct. 1960; 1 child, Elizabeth; m. William C. Procter, Dec. 2, 1967; stepchildren: Christopher, Carleton. BA, Guilford (N.C.) Coll., 1955; EdM, Temple U., 1963; postgrad., Sch. Internat. Tng., Brattleboro, Vt., 1988-89. Exec. dir. Lower Bucks Child Day Care Ctr., Bristol, Pa., 1965-73; tchr. Bucks Mont Reevaluation Cmty., Langhorne, Pa., 1976-82; office mgr. Baha'i Internat. Cmty., N.Y.C., 1983-85; owner, mgr. Procter Rentals, Brattleboro, 1989—; ESL tchr. Windham Supervisory Dist., Brattleboro, 1990-91. Editor newsletter Brattleboro Area Baha'is, 1990—; editor, writer for arts jour. Stage and Studio, 1993—. Pres. Hotline for Help, Brattleboro, 1991-94, Arts Coun. Windham County, 1993—; sec. Vt. Com. for Racial Ethnic Harmony, 1990—, Dist. Teaching Com. Baha'is of Vt., 1990-93; trustee Brattleboro Area Drop-In Ctr., 1991-94. Home: 20 Williston St Brattleboro VT 05301 Office: Procter Rentals 20 Williston St Brattleboro VT 05301

PROCTOR, BARBARA GARDNER, advertising agency executive, writer; b. Asheville, N.C.; d. William and Bernice (Baxter) Gardner; B.A. Talladega Coll., 1954; m. Carl L. Proctor, July 20, 1961 (div. Nov. 1963); 1 son, Morgan Eugene. Music critic, contbg. editor Down Beat Mag., Chgo., from 1958; internat. dir. Vee Jay Records, Chgo., 1961-64; copy supr. Post-Keyes-Gardner Advt., Inc., 1965-68, Gene Taylor Assos., 1968-69, North Advt. Agy., 1969-70; contbr. to gen. periodicals, from 1952; founder Proctor & Gardner Advt., Chgo., 1970—, now pres., chief exec. officer. Mem. Chgo. Urban League, Chgo. Econ. Devel. Corp. Bd. dirs. People United to Save Humanity, Better Bus. Bur. Cons. pub. relations and promotion, record industry. Recipient Armstrong Creative Writing award, 1954; awards Chgo. Fedn. Advt. Clubs, N.Y. Art Dirs. Club. Woman's Day; Frederick Douglas Humanitarian award, 1975; named Chgo. Advt. Woman of Year, 1974. Mem. Chgo. Media Women, Nat. Assn. Radio Arts and Sci., Women's Advt. Club, Cosmopolitan C. of C. (dir.), Female Execs. Assn., Internat. Platform Assn., Smithsonian Instn. Assos. Author TV documentary Blues for a Gardenia, 1963. Office: Proctor & Gardner Advt Inc 111 E Wacker Dr Ste 321 Chicago IL 60601*

PROCTOR, GWENDOLYN SAUER, public health administrator; b. Trenton, N.J., Apr. 9, 1946; d. Nicholas William and Genevieve Natalie (Marcy) Sauer; m. R. Lance Bowers, Feb. 11, 1967 (div. Sept. 1972); 1 child, Tammy Lynne; m. Timothy George Proctor, Feb. 23, 1974; 1 child, Timothy Jr. BS, Pasons Coll., 1969; cert. pub. mgr., Rutgers U., 1987, MS in Pub. Adminstrn., 1994. Lic. sanitarian, N.J.; cert. pub. mgr. Field worker Bur. Potable Water div. Water Resources N.J. Dept. Environ. Protection and Energy, 1972; sanitarian trainee Consumer Health Svcs. Div. Family Health Svcs., N.J. Dept. Health, 1972-73, sanitarian Consumer Health Svcs., 1973-78, sr. sanitarian Consumer Health Svcs., 1978-85, exec. asst., 1985-90; exec. asst. N.J. Dept. Health, 1990-92, sr. sanitarian Consumer Health Svcs., 1992-93; exec. asst. Div. Family Health Svcs., N.J. Dept. Health, 1993—; co-coord. How Healthy are New Jerseyans Project, 1984. Mem. Am. Soc. Pub. Adminstrs. Home: 30 Cottage Ct Hamilton Square NJ 08690-3923

PROPHET-COMPTON, DEBBIE JO, pilot; b. Springfield, Mo., Apr. 9, 1956; d. Tom Haggard and Dorothy O. (Leach) Prophet; m. James S. Compton, June 21, 1980. BSN manga cum laude, St. Louis U., 1981, JD, MBA with honorsMBA, 1982. Lic. comml. pilot. Nurse burn unit St. John's Hosp., St. Louis, 1981-85; nurse ICU St. Louis U., 1983-85, utilization mgr., 1986; CEO Brittany Group Inc., St. Louis, 1989-90; owner CFS, Inc., St. Louis, 1991—; chairperson, fin. com. Deaconess Found., St. Louis, 1989-92. Mem. DAR, 1987. Named one of Outstanding Young Women ofAm., 1989. Mem. U.S. Pilot Assn., Mo. Pilots Assn., Women's Pilot Assn. (The 99's), Aircra t Owners and Pilots Assn., Exptl. Aircraft Assn., Pilot/Lawyer Bar Assn., Women's Commerce Assn., Internat. Aerobatic Club. Home: 18025 Deercliff Ct Saint Louis MO 63038 Office: CFS Inc 580 Beechcraft Ave Chesterfield MO 63005

PROPP, GAIL DANE GOMBERG, computer consulting company executive; b. N.Y.C., Mar. 22, 1944; d. Oscar and Goody (Rosenburgh) Dane; BA in Econs., Barnard Coll., 1965; m. Ephraim Propp; children: Eric Wesley, David Marc, Anna Michelle. Instr., programmer IBM Corp., N.Y.C., 1965-66; systems and programmer analyst R.S. Topas Co., N.Y.C., 1966-67; dir. systems and programming Abercrombie & Fitch Co., N.Y.C., 1967-69; dir. corp. data processing and MIS, 1969-77; founder, 1977, pres. Met Data Systems, Inc., N.Y.C., 1977—; founder, pres. Datatype Internat. Inc, 1982—; sr. v.p./CIO Slim-Fast Foods Co., 1991—. Bd. overseers Bar-Ilan U., Israel; mem. adv. bd. KIRUV. Mem. Internat. Coun. Computers in Edn., Women in Info. Processing, Assn. Systems Mgmt., Data Processing Mgmt. Assn., Assn. Systems Mgmt., Assn. Inst. Cert. Systems Profls., Photog. History Soc. Am., Photog. Historic Soc. N.Y. Contbr. articles to profl. jours. Office: 919 3rd Ave New York NY 10022-3903

PROPST, ANNABETH LADNY, statistician; b. Chgo., June 7, 1950; d. Howard E. and Lee Ann (Ladny) P.; m. Joseph R. Compton, Nov. 1, 1969 (div. Aug. 1973); children: Raymond Nelson, Heidi Ann. BS in Mgmt., No. Ill. U., 1976, MS in Applied Scis., 1978. Asst. liaison engr. Borg Warner Corp., Dixon, Ill., 1977-80, mfg. engr., 1980-82, plant statistician, 1982-84; sr. quality assurance engr. Amerock Corp., Rockford, Ill., 1984-86; sr. cons. JDQ Cons., Inc., Rockford, 1986-87; cons. Process Mgmt. Inst., Mpls., 1987-91; owner Quality Transformation Svcs., Chgo., 1991—. Book reviewer Technometrics, 1986—. Advisor Jr. Achievement, Dixon, 1983-84, Rockford, 1985-86; cons. Project Bus., Rockford, 1986. Mem. Am. Soc. for Quality Control (chair conf. 1986, newsletter pub. 1987-90, divsn. treas. 1991—), Am. Statis. Assn. (SPES adv. bd. 1986—), Beta Gamma Sigma, Pi Mu Epsilon, Omicron Delta Kappa. Republican. Presbyterian. Home: 1455 E 54th Pl # 2 Chicago IL 60615-5428

PROROK, CYNTHIA LYNNE, controller, accountant; b. Pitts., Oct. 24, 1959; d. Thomas Martin and Verna Wanda (Wood) P. BS in Econs. and Bus., Pub. Adminstrn., Slippery Rock (Pa.) U., 1982, M in Adminstrn., 1988. Legis. asst. Nat. Tax Limitation Com., Washington, 1980; acct. Butler (Pa.) Conservation Dist., 1981—; sr. internal auditor County of Butler, 1982-84, asst. fin. dir., 1984-85, dep. controller, 1985—, dep. controller, budget coordinator, 1988-93, asst. dir. of audits, 1993—, regional audit mgr./dept. auditor gen., 1989-93. Mem. Butler County Rep. Women, 1985—, Butler County Rep. Task Force, 1987-88, com. Butler County Rep. Party, 1994, chmn. fin. and budget com., 1994. Washington fellow Nat. Leadership Inst./Heritage Found., 1980. Mem. Nat. Assn. Accts. (bd. dirs. tech. programs and profl. devel. 1987—), Govt. Fin. Officers Assn. (conf. com. 1988—), Assn. of Govt. Accts., Assn. Pub. Adminstrs. Republican. Roman Catholic. Home: 2180 Camelot Dr Apt 2A Harrisburg PA 17110-3505 Office: Bur of State-Aided Audits Dept of Auditor General 316-D Finance Bldg Harrisburg PA 17120

PROSSER, JEAN VICTORIA, social worker, therapist; b. Chgo., June 3, 1924; d. Edward and Victoria Isabella (Johnson) P.; m. Aug., 1953 (div.). BA, Roosevelt U., 1948; MSW, U. Ill., 1957. Lic. social worker, therapist, Fla. Caseworker Ill. Dept. of Pub. Aid, Chgo., 1948-54; instr. in med. social work U. Ill. Hosps., Chgo., 1957-60; social worker Firman House Presbytery of Chgo., 1960-65; social worker U. Chgo. Hosps., 1965-69; sch. social worker Sch. Dist. 161, Flossmoor, Ill., 1969-86; part-time social work therapist Ind. Child Abuse Relief Enterprises, Daytona Beach, Fla., 1987-91; pvt. practice Daytona Beach, 1991—; bd. dirs. Daytona Neurol. Assocs. Rehab. Ctr. Active Habitat for Humanity. Mem. NASW (Social Worker of Yr. award 1994), NAACP, , Soc. for Clin. Social Workers, Sigma Gamma Rho. Democrat. Presbyterian. Home: 105A Wood Duck Cir Daytona Beach FL 32119-1345

PROSSER, KATHY, state official; b. Canton, Ohio, Aug. 9, 1950; d. Ralph H. Prosser and Frances Elizabeth Vandall Copeland. MPA, Harvard U., 1987. Exec. asst., dep. treas. Office of Senator John Glenn, Washington, 1973-83, chief of staff, 1983-85; dir. scheduling and advance, campaign com. John Glenn for Pres., Washington, 1983-84; Washington rep. John F. Kennedy Sch. Govt., Harvard U., Cambridge, Mass., 1986; dep. commr. fin. and adminstrn. Mass. Dept. Environ. Mgmt., 1987-89; commr. Ind. Dept. Environ. Mgmt., Indpls., 1989—; bd. dirs. water quality Internat. Joint Commn., Washington, 1989—; chair Recycling Inst. Ind., Indpls., 1989—, Ind. State Emergency Planning Commn., Indpls., 1989—; bd. dirs. Econ. Devel. Coun. Ind., Indpls., 1989—. Mem. Dem. platform com. Mass., 1989. Named one of 100 Most Interesting Women, Boston Woman Mag., 1988, Woman of Distinction, Soroptimist Club Ind., 1993. Mem. Environ. Coun. States (founding, pres. 1993-94), Women Execs. in State Govt. (chair 1993-94), Environ. Law Inst. (bd. dirs., exec. com.). Office: Ind Dept Environ Mgmt PO Box 6015 100 N Senate Ave Indianapolis IN 46206

PROSSER, LISA ALISON, health care consultant; b. Brighton, Mass., Dec. 8, 1966; d. David Ernest and Irene Adriana (Tassy) P. BA in Math., Cornell U., 1988; MS in Mgmt., MIT, 1992, MS in Tech. and Policy, 1992. Info. systems cons. Andersen Cons., Stamford, Conn., 1988-90; cons. The Wilkerson Group, N.Y.C., 1992—. Democrat. Office: The Wilkerson Group 666 3rd Ave New York NY 10017

PROSSER, PAMELA L., controller; b. Milw., Apr. 21, 1964; d. Lawrence Richard and Nancy Ann (Schaf) Schultz; m. Daniel Joseph Prosser, Dec. 19, 1987; children: Emily Carol, Nicholas Scott. BBA in Mktg., U. Wis., Whitewater, 1985. Sales rep. Hormel Foods, St. Louis, 1986; customer svc. rep. Kelch Corp., Cederburg, Wis., 1987, accts. payable analyst, 1988, asst. corp. controller, 1988-90; divsn. controller Kelch Corp., Mequon, Wis., 1990—. Mem. Ours of Greater Milw (treas. 1994—).

PROST, SHARON, lawyer; b. May 24, 1951; m. Kenneth F. Greene, June 24, 1984; 1 child, Matthew Prost-Greene. BS, Cornell U., 1973; MBA, George Washington U., 1975, LLM in Taxation, 1984; JD, Am. U., 1979. Bar: D.C. Labor rels. specialist Office of Personnel Mgmt., 1973-76; with Gen. Acctg. Office, 1976-79; trial atty. Fed. Labor Rels. Authority, 1980-83; atty. chief counsel's office Dept. of Treasury, 1983-84; assoc. solicitor Nat. Labor Rels. Bd., 1984-89; chief minority labor counsel Senate Com. on Labor and Human Resources, 1989-93; minority chief counsel Senate Com. on the Judiciary, 1993—. Office: Com on the Judiciary 147 Senate Dirksen Office Bldg Washington DC 20510*

PROULX, EDNA ANNIE, writer; b. Norwich, Conn., Aug. 22, 1935; d. George Napolean and Lois Nelly (Gill) Proulx; m. James Hamilton Lang,

June 22, 1969 (div. 1990); children: Jonathan Edward Lang, Gillis Crowell Lang, Morgan Hamilton Lang. BA cum laude, U. Vt., 1969; MA, Sir George Williams U., Montreal, Can., 1973; DHL (hon.), U. Maine, 1994. Author: Heart Songs and Other Stories, 1988, Postcards, 1992 (PEN-Faulkner award 1993), The Shipping News, 1993, (Nat. Book award for fiction 1993, Chgo. Tribune Heartland award 1993, Irish Times Internat. Fiction award 1993, Pulitzer Prize for fiction 1994); contbr. more than 50 articles to mags. and jours. Kress fellow Harvard U., 1974, fellow Vt. Coun. Arts, 1989, NEA, 1991, Guggenheim Found., 1992; rsch. grantee Inter.-U. Ctr., 1975; resident Ucross Found., 1990-92; recipient Heartland award Chgo. Tribune, 1993, Internat. Fiction prize Irish Times, 1993. Mem. PEN Am. Ctr., Phi Beta Kappa, Phi Alpha Theta. Office: c/o Scribners Pub Co 866 3rd Ave Fl 7 New York NY 10022-6221

PROVENSEN, ALICE ROSE TWITCHELL, artist, author; b. Chgo.; d. Jay Horace and Kathryn (Zelanis) Twitchell; m. Martin Provensen, Apr. 17, 1944; 1 child, Karen Anna. Student, Art Inst. of Chgo., 1930-31, U. Calif., L.A., 1939, Art Student League, N.Y., 1940-41; D.H.L. (hon.), Marist Coll., 1986. With Walter Lanz Studios, Los Angeles, 1942-43; OSS, 1944-45. Exhibited (with Martin Provensen), Balt. Mus., 1954, Am. Inst. Graphic Arts, N.Y., 1959, Botolph Group, Boston, 1964; exhibited one person shows: Henry Feiwel Gallery, N.Y.C., 1991, Children's Mus., Washington, 1991, Moscarelle Mus. Art, Williamsburg, Va., 1991; books represented in Fifty Books of Yr. Selections, Am. Inst. Graphic Arts, 1947, 48, 52 (The Charge of the Light Brigade named Best Illustrated Children's Book of the Yr., N.Y. Times 1964, co-recipient Gold medal Soc. Illustrators 1960); Author, illustrator: books including Karen's Opposites, 1963, Karen's Curiosity, 1963, What is a Color?, 1967, (with Martin Provensen) Who's In the Egg, 1970, The Provensen Book of Fairy Tales, 1971, Play on Words, 1972, My Little Hen, 1973, Roses are Red, 1973, Our Animal Friends, 1974, The Year at Maple Hill Farm, 1978, A Horse and a Hound, A Goat and a Gander, 1979, An Owl and Three Pussycats, 1981, Town and Country, 1984, Shaker Lane, 1987, The Buck Stops Here, 1990, Punch in New York, 1991 (Best Books N.Y. Times, 1991), My Fellow Americans, 1994; illustrator: (with Martin Provensen) children's books including Mother Goose Book, 1976, Old Mother Hubbard, 1977, A Peaceable Kingdom, 1978, The Golden Serpent, 1980, A Visit to William Blake's Inn, 1981, Birds, Beasts and the Third Thing, 1982, The Glorious Flight, 1984 (Caldecott medal 1984), The Voyage of the Ludgate Hill, 1987; also textbooks.

PROVENZANO, MAUREEN LYNN, secondary educator; b. Anaheim, Calif., Nov. 25, 1963; d. Andrew Eugene and Maura Ann (McGivern) P. BA in English, Loyola Marymount U., L.A., 1986; teaching credential, Calif. State U., Fullerton, 1991; MA in Teaching English to Speakers of Other Langs., Calif. State U., L.A., 1993. Cert. Language Devel. Specialist, Calif.; English teaching credential, Calif.; lic. real estate saleswoman, Calif. Tchr. English, Temple City (Calif.) High Sch., 1991—, supr. Saturday sch., 1991-92; tchr. English lit., intermediate level ESL Temple City Adult Sch., 1994; mem. adv. bd. Peer Listeners, 1991-92; mem. intercultural com. Temple City Unified Sch. Dist., 1994, sr. class advisor, 1994, co-advisor Students Against Drunk Driving, 1993-94. Mem. NEA, Nat. Coun. Tchrs. English, Calif. Assn. Tchrs. English, Southland Coun. Tchrs. English, Calif. Tchrs. Assn., Calif. Tchrs. English to Speakers of Other Languages, Club Europa. Republican. Roman Catholic. Home: 8821 3/4 E Fairview Ave San Gabriel CA 91775-1209

PROWSE, YVONNE RUTH, homeless services administrator; b. Dumont, N.J., Nov. 8, 1962; d. Robert Eliot Prowse and Antoinette Mary Carbone Breazzano. BA in Religious Studies, Fairfield (Conn.) U., 1984. Youth min. St. Patrick's Home for Children, Sacramento, 1984-85; asst. coord. Sacramento Religious Community for Peace, 1985-89, exec. dir., 1989-91; program dir. Loaves & Fishes, Sacramento, 1991—; pub. speaker, events coord. various social justice orgns., Sacramento, 1986—. Contbr. articles to monthly newspaper PeaceWorks; facilitator class for Living Responsibly in the Troubled World, 1987-91; founder, singer Melody and the Matriarchs, 1993—. Vol. Jesuit Vol. Corps, Sacramento, 1984-85; singer, actress, scriptwriter Creative Alternatives, Sacramento, 1991-93; del. Middle East Witness tour of Israel and Palestine, Sacramento Middle East Peace Project, 1990. Office: Loaves & Fishes PO Box 15951 Sacramento CA 95852

PRUD'HOMME, CINDY JO, controller; b. Milw., June 3, 1959; d. James Frederick and Patricia Sharon (Kennedy) P.; m. William Lee Clifton, May 17, 1978 (div. 1982); 1 child, Erica Laine Clifton. Student in bus. mgmt., Santa Monica (Calif.) Coll., 1976, West LA Coll., 1977-80. Acctg. coord. Mega Ins. Agy./Midland Ins., Menlo Park, Calif., 1980-82; prodn. mgr. Corp. Graphics, L.A., 1982-84; acct., adminstv. mgr. Thomson Consumer Products Corp., Culver City, Calif., 1984-87; mgr. acctg. and pers. Hogg Robinson, Inc., L.A., 1987-90; contr. Hogg Robinson, Inc., Saginaw, Mich., 1990-94, Acordia, Inc., Saginaw, 1995—. Contbr. articles to profl. jours. Site leader Clinic Def. Alliance/L.A., 1989-90; active Calif. Abortion Rights Action League, L.A., 1989-90, Amnesty Internat., 1989-90. Named Young Careerist, Glendale (Calif.) Bus. and Profl. Women, 1989. Mem. Calif. Fedn. Bus. and Profl. Women (cert., instr.; Wilshire Bus. and Profl. Women treas.-fin. chair 1988, rec. sec.-treas. 1989); L.A. Sunset Dist. chair PEP/PAC 1989 (rec. sec. 1990, Dist. Individual Devel. winner 1988), Saginaw Bus. and Profl. Women (2d v.p., chair issues mgmt. Dist. II Mich. Fedn. 1991). Democrat. Lutheran. Office: Acordia Inc 5090 State St Ste C Saginaw MI 48603-7705

PRUDOM, MELANIE JOAN, business educator, consultant; b. Rochester, N.Y., Dec. 6, 1955; d. Homer A. and Shirley Myrtle (Konz) P. AAS, SUNY, Alfred, 1976; BBA, St. John Fisher Coll., Rochester, 1979; MBA, U. Rochester, 1983; postgrad., Temple U. Cert. cash mgr. Mktg. officer Mfrs. Hanover Trust Co., Rochester, 1979-82, acctg. officer, 1982-83; asst. v.p., product mgr. Mfrs. Hanover Trust Co., N.Y.C., 1983-86, asst. v.p., sales rep., 1986-87; asst. v.p., sr. product mgr. Fidelity Bank, Phila., 1987-88; asst. v.p., sr. mktg. mgr. First Fidelity Corp., Phila., 1988-90; bus. cons. Temple U. Small Bus. Devel. Ctr., Phila., 1990-92, sr. bus. cons., 1992-93, asst. dir., 1993—; bs. mgr. 7th St. Dance Studio, Bklyn., 1986-87; student advisor U. Rochester, Phila. and N.Y.C., 1983—. Contbr. articles to profl. jours. Com. mem. Nat. Kidney Found., Phila., 1989-91; field mgr. Youth for Understanding, Phila. and N.Y.C., 1985-89; race dir. Lilak 10-K, Rochester, 1980-83. Recipient Honorable mention Nat. Univ. Continuing Edn. Assn., 1992, 1st place regional, 1992. Mem. Am. Mktg. Assn. Office: Temple U Small Bus Devel Ctr Speakman Hall (006-00) Rm 6 Philadelphia PA 19122

PRUITT, ALICE FAY, mathematician, engineer; b. Montgomery, Ala., Dec. 17, 1943; d. Virgil Edwin and Ocie Victoria (Mobley) Maye; m. Mickey Don Pruitt, Nov. 5, 1967; children: Derrell Gene, Christine Marie. BS in Math., U. Ala., Huntsville, 1977; postgrad. in engring., Calif. State U., Northridge, 1978-79. Instr. math. Antelope Valley Coll., Quartz Hill, Calif., 1977-78; space shuttle engr. Rockwell Internat., Palmdale, Calif., 1979-81; programmer, analyst Sci. Support Svcs. Combat Devel. and Experimentaton Ctr., Ft. Hunter-Liggett, Calif., 1982-85; sr. engring. specialist Loral Vought Systems Corp., Dallas, 1985-92; mem. tech. staff Nichols Rsch. Corp., Huntsville, Ala., 1992—. Mem. DeSoto (Tex.) Coun. Cultural Arts, 1987-89. Mem. AAUW (sch. bd. rep. 1982, phone chmn. 1987-89, legal advocacy Fund Chairperson 1989-91), Toastmasters Internat., Phi Kappa Phi. Republican. Methodist. Office: Nichols Rsch Corp PO Box 40002 4040 S Memorial Pkwy Huntsville AL 35815-1502

PRUITT, ANNE ELIZABETH, software engineer, systems consultant; b. Jacksonville, Fla., Aug. 8, 1950; d. Buford Calvin and Hazel Irene (Miller) P.; m. Michael Thomas O'Leary, Dec. 4, 1985; 1 child, Stephen Michael. BA cum laude, Mercer U., 1972; MS, U. Ga., 1977. Psychology technician Ctrl. State Hosp., Milledgeville, Ga., 1972-75; grad. asst. U. Ga., Athens, 1975-80; mfg. supr. E.E. DuPont de Nemours Co., Seaford, Del., 1981-86; microcomputer cons. ABA Centerfield Systems, Springfield, Mass., 1986-94; adj. prof. Am. Internat. Coll., Springfield, 1988-90; software engr. Kemper Mgmt. Svcs., Glastonbury, Conn., 1993—. Supporter WAMC Pub. Radio, Albany, N.Y., 1993, WFCR Pub. Radio, Amherst, Mass., 1994. Mem. NOW, Compuserve Consultant Forum (archivist 1990-91, sect. leader, 1993-94), Ind. Computer Cons. Assn., Consumers Union. Democrat.

PRUITT, J. MICHELE, management executive; b. Bethesda, Md., Nov. 21, 1962; d. Robert Marshall and Jean Alice (Hampton) P. BA in Comm./Bus., High Point U., 1984. Mktg. mgr. BOMA Internat., Washington, 1987-88, dir. sales, 1988-90; dir. mktg. Associated Builders and Contractors, Washington, 1990-92; pres. Atelier West Design, Denver, 1992—; project dir. Convention Mgmt. Group, Fairfax, Va., 1993-94; dir. Internat. Bicycle and Sports Show, Bicycle Industry Orgn., Boulder, Colo., 1994—. Vol. Presdl. Inaugural Com., Washington, 1992-93; docent Corcoran Gallery Art, Washington, 1993. Mem. Internat. Assn. Bus. Communicators, Nat. Trust for Historic Preservation, Am. Soc. Assn. Execs., Jr. League Washington, Smithsonian Young Benefactors, Bravo! for the Washington Opera. Democrat. Presbyterian. Home: 3329 E Bayaud Ave # 1512 Denver CO 80209 Office: Bicycle Industry Orgn 1526 Spruce St Ste 303 Boulder CO 80302

PRUSSING, LAUREL LUNT, state official, economist; b. N.Y.C., Feb. 21, 1941; d. Richard Valentine and Maria (Rinaldi) Lunt; m. John Edward Prussing, May 29, 1965; children: Heidi Elizabeth, Erica Stephanie, Victoria Nicole Johanna. AB, Wellesley Coll., 1962; MA, Boston U., 1964; postgrad., U. Calif., San Diego, 1968-69, U. Ill., 1970-76. Economist Arthur D. Little, Cambridge, Mass., 1963-67, U. Ill., Urbana, 1971-72; mem. county bd. Champaign County, Urbana, 1972-76, county auditor, 1976-92; mem. local audit adv. bd. Office Ill. Compt., Chgo., 1984-92. Contbr. to Illinois Local Government: A Handbook, 1990. Founder Com. for Intelligent Tax Reform, Urbana, 1982—, Com. for Elected County Execs., Urbana, 1986—; state rep. 103d dist. Ill. Gen. Assembly, 1993-95. Named Best Freshman Legislator Ind. Voters Ill., 1994; recipient Friend of Agriculture award Ill. Farm Bur., 1994; named to Legis. Honor Roll Ill. Environ. Coun., 1994. Mem. LWV, Govt. Fin. Officers Assn., U.S. and Can. (com. on acctg., auditing and fin. reporting 1980-88, Fin. Reporting award 1981-91, Disting. Budget award 1986), Nat. Assn. Local Govt. Auditors (charter), Ill. Assn. County Auditors (pres. 1984-85). Democrat. Home: 2106 Grange Dr Urbana IL 61801

PRUZAN, IRENE, arts administrator, music educator, flutist, marketing and public relations specialist; b. Watertown, N.Y., Jan. 3, 1949; d. John Edward and Esther (Coahn) P.; m. Charles G. Ullery, Jan. 30, 1972 (div. 1978); m. Charles Robert Freeman, May 20, 1988. Student, U. Ariz., 1966-68; MusB, U. So. Calif., 1971; postgrad., San Francisco State U., 1972-74, U. Minn., 1976-80. Tchr. flute, coach chamber music MacPhail Ctr. for Arts, U. Minn., Mpls., 1976-85, coordinator instrumental music, 1978-81, program dir. instrumental music, 1982-85, div. head of programs, 1985-86; regional dir. Music On The Move, Inc., Valley Cottage, N.Y., 1986-87; pres. Music On the Move Minn., Inc., St. Paul, 1987—; founding mem. Crocus Hill Trio, 1976—; pub. rels. cons. Sch. of Music, U. Minn., 1991; faculty Nat. Music Camp, Interlochen, Mich., 1983, 84; cons. edn. and festival Ordway Music Theatre, St. Paul, 1985-87; mgr. Sartory String Quartet, Mpls., 1986-93; developer numerous master classes. Writer teaching materials for flute. Mem. Ariz. Chamber Orch., Tucson, 1967, San Gabriel (Calif.) Symphony, 1968-71; extra player St. Paul Chamber Orch., 1977-91; bd. dirs. Twin Cities Friends of Chamber Music, 1982-89; organizer German jazz residency USIA, Minn. and Wis., 1986; cons., program dir. Young Audiences Minn., Mpls., 1986-88. Mem. Nat. Flute Assn. (dir. mktg. 1987-90), Minn. Alliance for Arts in Edn., Twin Cities Musicians Union. Office: Music On The Move Minn Inc PO Box 4125 Saint Paul MN 55104-0125

PRUZZO, JUDITH JOSEPHINE, office manager; b. Oklahoma City, July 11, 1945; d. Joseph Michael and Mary Amelia (Reinhart) Engel; m. Neil Alan Pruzzo, Aug. 20, 1966 (dec. Sept. 1991); children: Maria Pruzzo Richards, Eric Alan, Brian Samuel, Lisa Michelle. BS in Pharmacy, Southwestern Okla. U., 1968. Registered pharmacist, Mo., Okla., Tex.; cert. by Coun. Homeopathy. Nurse's aide Valley View Hosp., Ada, Okla., 1963-64; pharmacy technician Gibson Pharmacy, Ada, Okla., 1966; pharmacist Trinity Luth. Hosp., Kansas City, Mo., 1968-69, Rsch. Hosp., Kansas City, Mo., 1969-73, East Town Osteo. Hosp., Dallas, 1973; office mgr., profl. homeopath Neil A. Pruzzo, DO, P.A., Richardson, Tex., 1975-91; profl. homeopath, nutritional counselor Pruzzo Clinic, Inc., Richardson, 1992—; lectr., presenter homeopathy and weight loss. Mem. Dallas Symphony Assn., 1992—, Stradivarious patron, 1994—. Women's Bowling Assn. scholar, 1963; named Ada Dist. Dairy Princess, Okla. Dairy Princess Contest, 1965. Mem. Internat. Found. Homeopathy, Nat. Ctr. Homeopathy, Am. Pharm. Assn., Homeopathic Assn., Naturopathic Physicians (assoc.), Southwestern State U. Alumni Assn. (life), Kappa Epsilon (life, v.p. 1967-68). Home: 4303 Shadow Glen Dr Dallas TX 75287-6828 Office: Pruzzo Clinic Inc 1910 Firman Dr Ste 100 Richardson TX 75081-1827

PRYCE, DEBORAH D., congresswoman; b. Warren, Ohio, July 29, 1951. BA cum laude, Ohio State U., 1973; JD with honors, Capital U., 1976. Bar: Ohio 1976. Former asst. city prosecutor, asst. city atty., first asst. city prosecutor Columbus, Ohio; former judge Franklin County Mcpl. Ct., Columbus; mem. 103rd Congress from 15th Ohio dist., Washington, D.C., 1993—; mem. coms.: banking, fin. and urban affairs, housing and community devel., fin. instns. supervision, regulations and deposit ins., consumer credit and ins., govt. ops., environment, energy and natural resources. Republican. Presbyterian.

PRYDS, DARLEEN N., historian; b. Oakland, Calif., Mar. 16, 1961; m. Eric Leland Saak, June 1, 1986. BA, U. So. Calif., L.A., 1983, MA, 1985; PhD, U. Wis., 1994. Pub. rels. coord. U. Ariz., Divsn. for Medieval Reformation Studies, Tucson, 1987-89, 91; scholar-in-residence St. Peter's Episcopal Ch., Morro Bay, Calif., 1993; asst. dir. Ctr. for Renaissance Studies, The Newberry Libr., Chgo., 1994—. Translator, editor: University Training in Medieval Europe, 1993; contbr. articles to profl. jours. Creator, organizer summer lectr. series Divsn. of Medieval Reformation Studies, Tucson, 1987-91; lectr. St. Philip's Episcopal Ch., Tucson, 1992. Recipient Haynes fellowship U. So. Calif., L.A., 1983, Fulbright-Hays fellowship Fulbright Commn., Rome, 1989-90, Travel grant U. Wis., Rome, 1991, Conf. grant U. Wis., Louvain-la-Neuve, Belgium, 1992. Mem. Am. Hist. Assn., Am. Soc. Church History, Internat. Medieval Sermon Studies Soc., Medieval Acad. Am., Renaissance Soc. Am., Phi Beta Kappa. Democrat. Episcopalian.

PRYE, ELLEN ROSS, advertising executive; b. Waynesboro, Va., Mar. 12, 1947; d. John Dewey and Betty Lou (Hardman) Ross; m. Warren Douglas Drumheller, June 7, 1969 (div. 1987); children: Amy Heather Drumheller, Warren Daniel Drumheller; m. John Paul Prye, July 24, 1993. BS, James Madison U., 1990. Cert. tchr. art K-12, Va/. Graphic artist The News-Virginian, Waynesboro, 1990-92, advt. prodn./composing mgr., 1992—. Recipient Distinction award Shenandoah Valley Art Ctr., 1989. Mem. Va. Press Assn. (Merit certs. 1991, 93). Presbyterian. Home: 1830 S Talbott Pl Waynesboro VA 22980 Office: The News-Virginian 544 W Main St Waynesboro VA 22980

PRYOR, CAROL GRAHAM, obstetrician-gynecologist; b. Savannah, Ga.; m. Louis O.J. Manganiello, June 11, 1950; children: Carol Helen, Victoria Manganiello Mudano. AB, Ga. Coll., 1943; MD, Med. Coll. Ga., 1947. Rotating intern City Hosps., Balt., 1947-48; asst. resident pathology Baroness Erlanger Hosp., Chattanooga, 1948; intern. obstetrics City Colls., Balt., 1949; coll. physician Ga. State Coll. for Women, Milledgeville, Ga., 1949-50; resident obstetrics City Hosps., Balt., 1950-51; asst. resident gynecology Univ. Hosp., Balt., 1951-52; sr. resident ob-gyn. Univ. Hosp., Augusta, Ga., 1952; pvt. practice ob-gyn. Augusta, 1952—. Mem., former pres. Iris Garden Club, Augusta; mem. coun. on maternal and infant health State of Ga., Atlanta, 1981-90; mem. edn. found. AAUW, 1961-63, state v.p., br. pres., 1963-65. Recipient Cert. of Achievement-Community Leadersip, Ga. div. AAUW, 1982; named Med. Woman of Yr., Ga. br. 51 Am. Med. Women's Assn., 1961. Fellow am. Coll. Surgeons (1st woman mem. Ga. chpt. 1956), Am. Coll. Ob-Gyn.; mem. AMA, Richmond County Med. Soc., So. Med. Assn., So. Surg. Congress, Delta Kappa Gamma. Democrat. Methodist. Office: 2316 Wrightboro Rd Augusta GA 30904

PRZELOMSKI, ANASTASIA NEMENYI, retired newspaper editor; b. Cleve., Dec. 11, 1918; d. Ernest Nicholas and Anna (Ress) Nemenyi; m. Edward Adrian Przelomski, July 4, 1946. A.B., Youngstown State U., 1939; M.Ed., U. Pitts., 1942. Tchr. Youngstown Pub. Sch., Ohio, 1939-42; reporter Vindicator, Youngstown, 1942-57, asst. city editor, 1957-73, city editor, 1973-76, mng. editor, 1976-88, ret., 1988. Named Woman of Yr., Youngstown Bus. and Profl. Women's Club, 1977, bus. category Woman of Yr., YWCA, 1986; recipient Community Service award Youngstown Fedn. Women's Clubs, 1981, Woman of Yr. award YWCA, 1983; named to Ohio Woman's Hall of Fame, 1986. Mem. AP Mng. Editors Assn., UPI Ohio Editors Assn. (bd. dirs. 1984-88), Ohio Assn. AP, Ohio Soc. Newspaper Editors, Youngstown State U. Alumni Assn. (trustee 1978-83), Catholic Collegiate Assn., Phi Kappa Phi. Republican. Roman Catholic. Home: 4000 Logangate Rd Youngstown OH 44505

PRZYBYLSKI, SANDRA MARIE, speech pathologist; b. Berwyn, Ill.; d. Raymond and Julie Marie (Vocelka) Hammers; m. James Przybylski; children: Eric, Sara. BS, U. Iowa, 1968; MA, U. Ill., 1971. Cert. clin. speech pathologist; speech/lang., educable mentally retarded education, learning disabilites and elem. tchr., life, Mo. Speech, lang. pathologist LaPlata (Mo.) Sch. Dist., 1974-87, Maysville (Mo.) Sch. Dist., 1990-92, Bucklin (Mo.) Sch. Dist., 1992—. Named one of Outstanding Young Women of Am., 1980, to Disting. Svc. Registry-Speech and Hearing, 1990. Mem. Am. Speech, Lang., Hearing Assn., Autism Soc. Am., Mo. Edn. Assn.

PSALTIS, HELEN, medical and surgical nurse; b. Rockford, Ill., Nov. 27, 1931; d. Harry and Martha (Triantafelakis) P. Diploma, St. Margaret Hosp., Hammond, Ind., 1953; BSN, DePaul U., 1961; MS in Health Edn., Purdue U., 1971; MSN, Purdue U., Calumet, Ind., 1988. RN, Ind., cert. sch. nurse, Ind. Sch. nurse Pub. Sch. City of E. Chgo., Ind.; asst. supr., staff nurse, instr. St. Catherine Hosp., East. Chgo., Ind.; instr., head nurse, staff nurse St Margaret Hosp., Hammond. Mem. ANA, Nat. League for Nursing, Sigma Theta Tau. Home: 4303 Ivy St East Chicago IN 46312-3026

PSARIS, AMY CELIA, manufacturing engineer; b. Bklyn., June 18, 1963; d. Arnold S. and Ellen Marion (Wachtel) Levitt. BSME, U. Tex., 1985; MBA, U. Mich., 1991. Mfg. engr. BOC Power Train GM, Flint, Mich., 1985-87; balance engr. BOC Power Train GM, Flint, 1987-88; mfg. engr. BOC Power Train GM, Pontiac, Mich., 1988-91; sr. mgr. engr. Orbital Engine Co., Tecumseh, Mich., 1991-92; sr. project engr. Johnson & Johnson Corp., Austin, Tex., 1992-93, prodn. team leader, 1993-94; mfg. engr. Ford Motor Co., 1994—. Mem. vis. com. U. Tex. Mech. Engring. Dept., Austin; lit. vol. Williamson County Literacy Coun., 1992-93; mem. Austin Civic Wind Ensemble; tutor Vols. for Adult Literacy, 1987-88; mem. Friends of Alec (U. Tex. Coll. Engring.), Friends of LBJ Libr., Leadership Round Rock. Mem. ASME, Mich. Soc. Profl. Engrs. (bd. dirs. 1987-90, Young Engr. of Yr. 1988, MathCounts chmn. 1988), Soc. Mfg. Engrs., Saginaw Valley Engrs. Coun. (banquet publicity chmn. 1987-88), Tex. Exes Alumni Orgn. Office: Ford Motor Co Glass Divsn PO Box 555 Tulsa OK 74102

PUC, HEIDI SONYA, physician; b. Bklyn., Dec. 2, 1964; d. Adolf and Frieda (Loser) H. BS, CCNY, 1987; MD, Mt. Sinai Sch. Medicine, 1989. Diplomate Am. Bd. Internal Medicine. Internal medicine intern N.Y. Hosp., N.Y.C., 1989-90, resident in internal medicine, 1990-92; fellow hematology and oncology Meml. Sloan-Kettering Cancer Ctr., N.Y.C., 1992—; presenter in field. Author: (with others) Pathology of the Testis and Adnexa, 1994; contbr. articles to profl. jours. Soc. Women Engrs. scholar. Mem. ACP, Am. Soc. Hematology, Alpha Omega Alpha. Office: Meml Sloan-Kettering Cancer Ctr 1275 York Ave New York NY 10021-6007

PUCEL, JOANNA KAY, speech communication educator; b. Virginia, Minn., Mar. 17, 1947; d. Jack Jacob and Esther Elizabeth (Jackson) Petritz; m. John Charles Pucel, Sept. 9, 1967; 1 child, Janet. BS, St. Cloud State U., 1974; MA, U. Minn., 1985. Asst. prof. St. Cloud (Minn.) State U., 1977—; dir. speech anxiety reduction program St. Cloud State U., 1980—; art chair Communication Apprehension & Avoidance Commn. Speech Communication Assn., 1992; cons. in field. Contbr. articles to profl. jours. Rsch. grantee St. Cloud State U., 1990, 93. Mem. AAUW (pres. 1986-88, coll./univ. rep. 1985—, state bd. dirs. 1994—, grantee 1988), Ctrl. Minn. Community Found. (chair arts divsn. 1991—), St. Cloud Community Arts Coun. (pres. 1984-86), St. Cloud Chpt. Mended Hearts, Inc. (founder, pres. 1985-88), Delta Kappa Gamma (communications chair 1990—). Home: 1481 25th St SE Saint Cloud MN 56304-9500 Office: St Cloud State U Dept Speech Communicat Saint Cloud MN 56301

PUCHTLER, HOLDE, histochemist, pathologist, educator; b. Kleinlosnitz, Germany, Jan. 1, 1920; came to U.S., 1955; d. Gottfried and Gunda (Thoma) P. Cand. med., U. Würzburg, 1944; Md, U. Köln, 1949; MD, U. Küln (Germany), 1951. Rsch. assoc. U. Köln, 1949-51; resident in pathology U. Küln, 1951-55; rsch. fellow Damon Runyon Found., Montreal, Que., Can., 1955-58; rsch. assoc. Med. Coll. Ga., Augusta, 1959-60, asst. rsch. prof., 1960-62, assoc. rsch. prof., 1962-68, prof., 1968-90, prof. emerita, 1990—. Assoc. editor Jour. Histotechnology, 1982—; editl. bd. Histochemistry, 1977-90. Honored at Symposium on Connective Tissues in Arterial and Pulmonary Diseases, 1980. Fellow Am. Inst. Chemists, Royal Microscopical Soc.; mem. Royal Soc. Chemistry, Am. Chem. Soc., Histochem. Soc. Gesellschaft Histochemie, Anatomische Gesellschaft, Ga. Soc. Histotech. (hon.). Office: Med Coll Ga Dept Pathology Augusta GA 30912

PUCKETT, CARLISSA ROSEANN, not-for-profit association executive; b. Effingham, Ill., Jan. 21, 1951; d. Carl Winston and Flora Pauline (Cox) Browning; m. Steve Dawson Puckett, Oct. 27, 1973; children: Heather Nicole, Adam Dawson, Christopher Alex. AS, Lake Land Jr. Coll., Mattoon, Ill., 1972; BA, Ea. Ill. U., 1976; MS, So. Ill. U., 1986. Child care aide Assn. Retarded Citizens Effingham County, Effingham, 1972-74, asst. supr. devel. work activities, 1975-77, residential coord., 1981-84, residential dir., case coord. dir. family support, 1984-88; owner, mgr. Denim's Inn, Effingham, 1977-81; coord. housing Ill. Dept. Mental Health and Devel. Disabilities, Springfield, 1988-89, coord. Community Integrated Living Arrangements, 1989-90; bur. chief Bur. Resource Design, Springfield, 1990-91, Bur. Devel. Field Svcs., 1991-93; exec. dir. Springfield Assn. for Retarded Citizens, 1993—. Named Bus. and Profl. Woman of Yr., Effingham County Jr. Women's Club, 1986. Mem. Am. Assn. on Mental Retardation (membership com. Ill. chpt. 1992), Assn. for Retarded Citizens, Sons and Daus. of Pearl Harbor Survivors (pres. Ill. chpt.), Phi Kappa Phi. Home: 3813 NW Territory Dr Springfield IL 62707 Office: Springfield Assn Retarded Citizens 2719 S 11th St Springfield IL 62703

PUCKETT, CAROL ANN, personnel administrator; b. Ft. Worth, May 23, 1946; d. Harold Woodrow and Marie (Auvenshine) Hallman; m. William Bruce Puckett, May 24, 1974 (div. Aug. 1979); 1 child, Leann Marie. BA in English, Tex. Woman's U., Denton, 1968. Cert. tchr., Tex. High sch. tchr. Krum (Tex.) Ind. Sch. Dist., 1968-69; v.p. Stafford-Lowdon Co., Ft. Worth, 1969-75; various positions Westgate Fabrics, Grand Prairie, Tex., 1975-79; pers. dir. Denton County Govt., Denton, 1980-86; pers. mgr. Denton Pub. Co., 1986—. Bd. dirs. United Way of Denton County, 1987—, campaign chair, 1995; co. organizer Am. Heart Assn., Denton, 1992, 93; vol. local Habitat for Humanity Affiliation. Mem. Denton Pers. Assn. (sec., editor newsletter), Soc. Human Resources Mgrs., Newspaper Pers. Rels. Assn. Mem. Ch. of Christ. Office: Denton Pub Co 314 E Hickory Denton TX 76201

PUCKETT, ELIZABETH ANN, law librarian, law educator; b. Evansville, Ind., Nov. 10, 1943; d. Buell Charles and Lula Ruth (Gray) P.; m. Joel E. Hendricks, June 1, 1964 (div. June 1973); 1 child, Andrew Charles; m. Thomas A. Wilson, July 19, 1985. BS in Edn., Eastern Ill. U., 1964; JD, U. Ill., 1977, MS in L.S., 1977. Bar: Kans. 1978, Ill. 1979. Acquisitions/reader services librarian U. Kans. Law Library, Lawrence, 1978-79; asst. reader services librarian So. Ill. U. Law Library, Carbondale, 1979-81, reader services librarian, 1981-83; assoc. dir. Northwestern U. Law Library, Chgo., 1983-86, co-acting dir., 1986-87; dir./assoc. prof. South Tex. Coll. Law Library, Houston, 1987-89; dir./prof. South Tex. Coll. Law Libr., Houston, 1990-94, U. Ga. Law Libr., Athens, 1994—. Co-author: Evaluation of System-Provided Library Services to State Correctional Centers in Illinois, 1983; co-editor Uniform Commercial Code: Confidential Drafts, 1993. Mem. ABA, Am. Assn. Law Librs. (mem. exec. bd. 1993-96). Office: U Georgia Law Libr Athens GA 30602-6018

PUCKO, DIANE BOWLES, public relations executive; b. Wyndotte, Mich., Aug. 15, 1940; d. Mervin Arthur and Bernice Letitia (Shelly) Bowles; m. Raymond J. Pucko, May 22, 1965; children: Todd Anthony, Gregory Bowles. BA in Sociology, Bucknell U., Lewisburg, Pa., 1962. Accredited in pub. rels. Asst. to pub. rels. dir. Edward C. Michener Assocs., Inc., Harrisburg, Pa., 1962-65; advt./pub. rels. coord. Superior Switchboard & Devices,

Canton, Ohio, 1965-66; editorial dir. women's svc. Hutchins Advt. Co., Inc., Rochester, N.Y., 1966-71; pres. Editorial Communications, Rochester and Elyria, Ohio, 1971-77; mgr. advt. and sales promotion Tappan Air Conditioning, Elyria, 1977-80; mgr. pub. affairs Kaiser Permanente Med. Care Program, Cleve., 1980-85; corp. dir. pub. affairs Keystone Health Plans, Inc., Camp Hill, Pa., 1985-86; v.p., dir. client planning Young-Liggett-Stashower, Cleve., 1986; v.p., dir. pub. rels. Marcus Pub. Rels., Cleve., 1987-91; sr. v.p. Proconsul, Cleve., 1991—, also bd. dirs.; mgr., role model Women in Mgmt. Field Placement program, Cleve. State U., 1983—; prof. advisor Pub. Relations Student Soc. of Am., Kent State U., 1988—. Bd. trustees, mem. exec. com., chmn. pub. rels. adv. com. Ronald MacDonald House of Cleve., 1993—; bd. dirs., chmn. pub. rels. com. Assn. Retarded Citizens, Cleve., 1987-91. Recipient Woman Profl. Excellence award YMCA, 1984, MacEachern award Acad. Hosp. Pub. Rels., 1985, Bell Ringer award Cmty. Rels. Report, 1985, Bronze Quill Excellence award Internat. Assn. Bus. Communicators, 1992, 93, Cleve. Comms. award Women in Comms. Internat., 1993, Tower award Bus./Profl. Advt. Assn., 1993, Creativity in Pub. Rels. award, 1994. Fellow Pub. Rels. Soc. Am. (bd. dirs. 1983-85, 86—, officer 1991—, mem. counselors acad. 1986—, Silver Anvil award 1985, Mktg./Consumer Rels. award East Ctrl. dist. 1992); mem. Press Club Cleve. (bd. dirs. 1989—, v.p. 1990—), Cleve. Advt. Club, Women's City Club Cleve. Republican. Methodist. Home: 656 University Ave Elyria OH 44035-7239 Office: Proconsul 25825 Science Park Dr Cleveland OH 44122-7315

PUDLES, LYNNE, art historian; b. Pitts., July 30, 1951; d. Saul B. and Claire (Marcus) P.; m. Martin Davis, July, 1974 (div. 1978); m. R.B. Duncan, June 10, 1989. BA summa cum laude, U. Pitts., 1973; MA, U. Calif., Berkeley, 1977, PhD, 1987. Vis. instr. art history Humboldt State U., Arcata, Calif., 1977-78, U. Chgo., 1985-86; instr. art history Cleve. State U., 1986-87, asst. prof. art history, 1987; asst. prof. art history Lake Forest (Ill.) Coll., 1987-93, assoc. prof. art history, 1993—; exec. adv. com. Interdisciplinary Nineteenth Century Studies, 1988-91; commr. Winnetka (Ill.) Archtl. Landmarks Preservation, 1992—; advisor Ill. Acad. Fine Arts; cons. in field. Author: (exhbn. catalogue) Roger Snakkers Retrospective Exhbn., 1991, Michael Croydon, "The Love Poems" Exhbn., 1988; contbr. articles to profl. jours. Founder The Pitts. Women's Ctr., 1970-73, Pitts. Rape Crisis Ctr., 1970-73; coord. Letter Drive to Support Reauthorization of NEA, Lake Forest, 1990. Fellow Samuel Kress Found., 1975, U. Calif., Berkeley, Found. and Alumni Assn., 1979-80, Danforth Found., 1974-79, 1981-82, Theodore Rousseau Met. Mus. Art, 1981-82, Belgian Ministry of Edn. and Culture, 1981-82, U. Calif., Berkeley, Grad. Humanities Rsch., 1981-82. Mem. AAUP, Am. Assn. Museums, Soc. for Values in Higher Edn., Midwest Art History Soc., Coll. Art Assn. Am., Phi Beta Kappa (U. Calif. Berkeley fellow 1985, No. Calif. Assn. fellow 1985), Mortar Board Nat. Hon. Soc. Home: 555 N Sheridan Rd Lake Forest IL 60045 Office: Lake Forest Coll Art Dept 555 N Sheridan Rd Lake Forest IL 60045-2338

PUDLIN, HELEN POMERANTZ, lawyer; b. N.Y.C., June 26, 1949; d. George and Claire Pomerantz; m. David B. Pudlin, Dec. 23, 1973; children: Alexander R., Julia H. BA cum laude, U. Pa., 1970, MS, 1971, JD, 1974. Bar: Pa. 1974. Lectr. U. Pa. Law Sch., 1983-87; asssoc. Ballard, Spahr, Andreas & Ingersoll, Phila., 1974-81, ptnr., 1981-89; gen. counsel Provident Nat. Bank, Phila., 1989-93; sr. v.p., dep. gen. counsel PNC Fin. Corp., Pitts., 1992-93; sr. v.p., mng. gen. counsel PNC Bank Corp., Pitts., 1993, sr. v.p., gen. counsel, 1993—; speaker in field. Author: (with others) Review of Antitrust Laws and Procedures, 1983, Criminal Antitrust Litigation Manual, 1983, Pennsylvania Medical Society Handbook, 1989; co-author: Joint Ventures in Healthcare. Active mem. Bd. of Ethics City of Phila., Mayor-Elect's Task Force on Legal Svcs., Com. of Seventy; trustee Lankenau Hosp., Lankenau Hosp. Found.; bd. advisors Pub. Interest Law Ctr. Phila. Mem. ABA (antitrust sect., litigation sect., bus. law sect.), Am. Acad Hosp. Attys., Pa. Bar Assn. (ho. of dels. 1987-90, judiciary com.), Phila. Bar Assn. (bd. govs. 1989-91, fed. cts. com., bus. law sect.), Forum Exec. Women, Acad. Natural Scis. (bd. dirs., trustee), U. Pa. Law Sch. Alumni Soc. (bd. mgrs.), Locust Club. Office: PNC Bank Corp 5th Ave & Wood Sts Pittsburgh PA 15265

PUETZ, PAMELA ANN, human resources executive; b. Lawrence, Mass., Aug. 17, 1949; d. Gregory and Eleanor Christine (Stull) Bedrosian; m. Tracy Barnum Braun, Jan. 26, 1974 (div. 1985); 1 child, Susannah Barnum; m. Dan Lee Puetz, May 31, 1986. AS, Fisher Jr. Coll., Boston, 1969; BS in Mgmt. with high distinction, Babson Coll., Wellesley, Mass., 1973. Br. mgr. First Security Bank of Utah, N.A., Salt Lake City, 1974-76; bus. mgr. U.S. Ski Team, Inc., Park City, Utah, 1976-77; banking specialist Tracy Collins Bank, Salt Lake City, 1980-83; instr. Fitness Inst., LDS Hosp., Salt Lake City, 1983-85; owner/operator Grapevine Svcs., Redondo Beach, Calif., 1987-88; human resources adminstr. PacifiCare Health Systems, Inc., Cypress, Calif., 1988-89, human resources analyst, 1989-91, human resources project mgr., 1991—, human resources info. systems mgr., 1992—; assoc. DLP Constrn. & Devel., Garden Grove, Calif., 1992-94; sr. mgr. human resources systems Mattel, Inc., El Segundo, Calif., 1994—. Mem. Personnel and Indsl. Rels. Assn., Assn. Human Resource Systems Profls.

PUFF, JEAN ELLINGWOOD, civic worker; b. Evanston, Ill., July 25, 1924; d. Lloyd and Margaret (Brown) Ellingwood; m. Henry b. Puff, June 10, 1950; children: James Raymond, Margaret Elizabeth. BA, Northwestern U., 1945, BS in Nursing, 1947. Nurse, student health svc. Northwestern U., Evanston, Ill., 1947-48; pres. Gov. Wentworth Arts Coun., N.H., 1973-81; bd. dirs. Wolfeboro (N.H.) Playhouse, 1975-82; gov. Wentworth Arts Coun.; vol. Delta Gamma vision screening, Buffalo, 1960-65, Buffalo Philharmonic, 1959-69; mem. Huggins Hosp. Aid (Wolfeboro), Friends of Music of the Smithsonian Instn.; life mem. Ridley Coll. Womans Guild, St. Catherine, Ont., Can. Mem. Northwestern U. Med. Sch. Alumni Assn., Northwestern U. Alumni Assn., Rep. Women's Fedn., Ridley Coll. Woman's Guild (life), Wolfeboro Garden Club, Delta Gamma. Presbyterian. Died Dec. 4, 1994. Home: Box 743 Springfield Point Wolfeboro NH 03894

PUFFER, SHARON KAYE, senior residential loan officer; b. Portland, Oreg., June 23, 1944; d. Henry and Linda Katherine (Olsen) Clearwater; m. Arleigh Rocco Puffer, Feb. 5, 1965; children: Michele Lynn, Heidi Leigh. Student, Portland State U., 1962-64. Lic. real estate salesperson. Real estate sales agt. Valley Realty, Dublin, Calif., 1979-82; with real estate sales The Ryness Co., Danville, Calif., 1982-83; sales coord. spl. projects Coldwell Banker, San Ramon, Calif., 1983-86; residential loan officer Coldwell Banker Mortgage, Danville, 1986-87, Glenfed Mortgage, San Ramon, 1987-89; sr. real estate loan officer Bank of America Residential Loan Ctr., Walnut Creek, Calif., 1989—. Membership chmn. Livermore (Calif.) Jr. Women affiliate Nat. Fedn. of Women, 1974-75, pres., 1975-76. Mem. Contra Costa Bd. Realtors. Republican. Home: 330 McCloud Pl Danville CA 94526

PUGH, JOYE JEFFRIES, educational administrator; b. Ocilla, Ga., Jan. 23, 1957; d. Claude Bert and Stella Elizabeth (Paulk) Jeffries; m. Melville Eugene Pugh, Sept. 21, 1985. AS in Pre-law, S. Ga. Coll., 1978; BS in Edn., Valdosta State Coll., 1980, MEd in Psychology, Guidance and Counseling, 1981; EdD in Adminstrn., Nova U., Ft. Lauderdale, Fla., 1992. Cert. tchr., adminstr., supr., Ga. Personnel adminstr. TRW, Inc., Douglas, Ga., 1981-83; recreation dir. Ocilla (Ga.), Irwin Recreation Dept., 1983-84; exec. dir. Sunny Dale Tng. Ctr., Inc., Ocilla, 1984—; pres. and registered agt. Irwin County Resources, Inc., Ocilla, 1988—. Contbr. articles on handicapped achievements to newspapers, mags. (Ga. Spl. Olympics News Media award, 1987, Assn. for Retarded Citizens News Media award, 1988). Mem. adv. bd. Area 12 Spl. Olympics, Douglas, Ga., 1984-88; pres. Irwin County Spl. Olympics, 1984—; exec. dir. Irwin Assn. for Retarded Citizens, Ocilla, 1984—, fund raising chmn., 1984—; arts and crafts chmn. Ga. Sweet Potato Festival, Ocilla, 1985—; chmn. Sweet Tater Trot 5K/1 mile Road Races, 1993—; state bd. dirs. Ga. Spl. Olympics, 1995-98; founder, chmn. Joseph Mascolo Celebrity Events, 1985—. Recipient Spirit of Spl. Olympics award, Ga. Spl. Olympics, Atlanta, 1986, Community Svc. award, Ga. Assn. for Retarded Citizens, Atlanta, 1987, Govs.' Vol. award, Ga. Vol. Awards, Atlanta, 1988, Presidential Sports award, AAU, Indpls., 1988, Humanitarian award Sunny Dale Tng. Ctr., Inc., Ocilla, 1988, Golden Poet award New Am. Poetry Anthology, 1988, Outstanding Coach-Athlete Choice award Sunny Dale Spl. Olympics, Ocilla, 1992, Dist. Coach award, 1993. Mem. Mut. Unidentified Flying Object Network (Ga. state sect. dir., asst. state dir.), Ga. State Assn. for Retarded Citizens, Nat. Assn. for Retarded Citizens, Ctr. Dirs. Ga., Ocilla Rotary Club, Sunny Dale Unified Track Club (founder 1991—). Baptist. Home: 230 Lakeside Cir Douglas GA 31533-9656 Office: Sunny Dale Tng Ctr Inc Box 512 Mascolo Dr Ocilla GA 31774-9801

PUGH, MARION STIRLING, archaeologist, author; b. Middletown, N.Y., May 12, 1911; d. Louis and Lena May (Randall) Illig; m. Matthew Williams Sirling, Dec. 11, 1933 (dec. 1975); children: Matthew Williams, Jr. (dec.), Ariana Stirling Withers; m. John Ramsey Pugh, Aug. 7, 1977 (dec. Mar. 1994). BS, Rider Coll., 1930; postgrad. George Washington U., 1931-33. Office sec. Bur. Am. Ethnology, Smithsonian Instn., Washington, 1931-33; archaeologist with Matthew W. Stirling, Fla., 1934-38, Smithsonian Instn.-Nat. Geog. Soc. archeol. expdn. Mex., 1939-46, Panama, 1948-53, Ecuador, 1957, Costa Rica, 1962. Author: (with Matthew Stirling) Tarqui, an Early Site in Manabi, Ecuador, 1962, El Limon, an Early Tomb Site in Cocle Province, Panama, 1963, Archaeological Notes on Almirante Bay, Bocas del Toro, Panama, 1963, The Archeology of Taboga, Uraba and Taboguilla Islands, Panama, 1963; contbr. articles to Nat. Geog. mag. and Ames. mag. Trustee The Textile Mus., Washington, 1968—, pres. 1984-87. Corecipient Franklyn L. Burr award Nat. Geog. Soc., 1941, Disting. Svc. medal Peruvian Embassy, 1985. Fellow Am. Anthrop. Assn., Gen. Div. Anthropology; mem. Am. Ethnol. Soc., Soc. Latin Am. Anthropology, Washington Anthrop. Soc., Washington Acad. Sci., Soc. Woman Geographers (pres. 1960-63, 69-72, mem. exec. council 1954-74, Gold medal 1975). Avocations: swimming, textiles. Home: 20351 Airmont Rd Round Hill VA 22141

PUGLIESE, KAREN OLSEN, public relations executive; b. S.I., N.Y., Aug. 20, 1963; d. Harold Birger and Janet Midred (Cronk) Olsen; m. John Michael Pugliese Jr., Oct. 21, 1989. BA in Polit. Sci., Union Coll., 1985. Asst. editor Food Mgmt. mag., N.Y.C., 1985-86; account exec. Edelman Pub. Rels., N.Y.C., 1986-87; account exec., sr. v.p., group dir. Creamer Dickson Basford, N.Y.C., 1987—. Recipient Gold quill Internat. Assn. Bus. Communicators, 1991, Internat. Pub. Rels. award Internat. Pub. Rels. Soc., 1993, CIPRA, Inside PR, 1993. Republican.

PUGLIESE, MARIA A., psychiatrist; b. Phila., Sept. 16, 1948; d. Peter Francis and Ida Agnes (Rosa) P.; m. J. Paul Hieble, Sept. 14, 1985; q child, Helen Elisa Hieble. BS, Chestnut Hill Coll., 1970; MD, U. Pa., 1974. Diplomate Am. Bd. Psychiatry and Neurology. Attending psychiatrist Inst. Pa. Hosp., Phila., 1978—, Malvern (Pa.) Inst., 1982—. Office: 111 N 49th St Philadelphia PA 19139

PULASKI, LORI JAYE, career officer; b. Madison, Wis., June 22, 1962; d. Stanley Harold and Phyllis Mabel (Billock) P.; m. Joseph Kawika Kim, Sept. 14, 1986 (div. Aug. 1991). BS, USAF Acad., 1984; MA in Aero. Sci., Imbry Riddle Aero. U., 1995. Commd. 2d lt. USAF, 1984, advanced through grades to capt., 1988; evaluator/instr. pilot USAF, Carswell AFB, Tex., 1986-92; flight safety officer USAF, Edwards AFB, Calif., 1992-94, evaluator/instr. pilot, 1994—. Home: 729 Twinberry Ln Lancaster CA 93534

PULHAMUS, MARLENE LOUISE, elementary school educator; b. Paterson, N.J., Sept. 11, 1937; d. David Weeder and Elfrieda (Ehler) Wemmell; m. Aaron R. Pulhamus, Aug. 20, 1960; children: Steven, Thomas, Nancy. Student, Trenton State U., 1957; BS, William Paterson U., 1959; postgrad., Rutgers U., 1992. Cert. elem. tchr., N.J. Kindergarten tchr. Wayne (N.J.) Bd. Edn., 1959-63; kindergarten tchr. Paterson Bd. Edn., 1974-75, 2d grade tchr., 1975-81; basic skills instr. Paterson Pub. Schs., 1981—; trainer for insvc. groups for learning ctrs. and math. with manipulatives for local pub. schs.; trainer for tchg. using 4MAT (Excel, Inc.)-tchg. to reach all learning styles in classroom. Pres. Friends of Eisenhower Libr., Totowa, N.J., 1975-77; coord. ch. sch. Preakness Reformed Ch., Wayne, 1990—. Recipient Gov.'s award for teaching excellence State of N.J. Commn. Edn., 1991, 4Mation awards, 1995. Mem. ASCD, NEA, Nat. Coun. Tchrs. Math., Nat. Assn. for Edn. Young Children, N.J. Edn. Assn., Passaic County Edn. Assn., Paterson Edn. Assn. (mem. exec. bd., 1985-89, legis. chmn. 1986-89). Home: 47 Easedale Rd Wayne NJ 07470 Office: Paterson Pub Sch 448 Main St Paterson NJ 07501-2818

PULITZER, EMILY S RAUH (MRS. JOSEPH PULITZER, JR.), art consultant; b. Cin., July 23, 1933; d. Frederick and Harriet (Frank) Rauh. AB, Bryn Mawr Coll., 1955; student, Ecole du Louvre, Paris, France, 1955-56; MA, Harvard U., 1963. Mem. staff Cin. Art Mus., 1956-57; asst. curator drawings Fogg Art Mus., Harvard, 1957-64, asst. to dir., 1962-63; curator City Art Mus., St. Louis, 1964-73; mem. painting and sculpture com. Mus. Modern Art, 1975—; chmn. visual arts com. Mo. Arts Council, 1976-81; co-chmn. fellows Fogg Art Mus., 1978—; mem. bd. Inst. Mus. Services, 1979-84; commr. St. Louis Art Mus., 1981-88, vice chmn., 1988; bd. dirs. Pulitzer Pub. Co. Bd. dirs. Forum, St. Louis, 1980—, pres., 1990-94; bd. dirs. Mark Rothko Found., 1976-88, Grand Ctr., 1993—; bd. dirs. arts in transit com. Bi-State Devel. Agy., vice chmn., 1987—; mem. overseers com. to visit Harvard Art Mus., 1990—; trustee Mus. Modern Art, 1994—. Mem. Am. Fedn. Arts (dir. 1976-89), St. Louis Mercantile Libr. Assn. (bd. dirs. 1987-93), Women's Forum of Mo. Home: 4903 Pershing Ave Saint Louis MO 63108-1201

PULITZER, ROSLYN K., social worker, psychotherapist; b. Bronx, N.Y., Apr. 25, 1930; d. George and Laura Eleanor (Holtz) P. BS in Human Devel. and Life Cycle, SUNY, N.Y.C., 1983; MSW, Fordham U., 1987. Lic. clin. social worker, N.Y.; cert. in psychoanalytic psychotherapy of the personality disorders. Clinic dir. Resources Counseling and Psychotherapy Ctr., N.Y.C., 1985-89; social worker, clin. supr. methadone maintenance treatment program Beth Israel Med. Ctr., N.Y.C., 1989—;, 1989-92; cons. therapist, clin. supr. Identity House, N.Y.C., 1980—, exec. dir., 1985, clin. dir., 1993-95. Mem. regional adv. coun. N.Y. State Div. Human Rights, N.Y.C., 1975-76; mem. Community Bd. 6, N.Y.C., 1978-81; founder, legis. chmn. N.Y. State Women's Polit. Caucus, 1978-80. Mem. NASW, Acad. Cert. Social Workers, Soc. Masterson Inst., N.Y. Milton Erickson Soc. for Psychotherapy and Hypnosis (cert.). Home: 110 Bank St Apt 5F New York NY 10014-2168 Office: 250 E 25th St New York NY 10010-3102

PULLEN, LETTIE MAE, health facility administrator; b. Forest, Va., Aug. 21, 1937; d. Victor John Henry and Mary Frances (Younger) Jones; m. Thomas Pullen Jr., Nov. 11, 1961; children: Jerri P. Jones, Jackie P. Carson, Carol A., Thomasena V., JoAnn. Grad. high sch., Bedford, Va., 1958. Cert. site mgr. Bedford Nutrition Ctr., Lynchburg, Va., 1977—. Columnist Bedford Bulletin, 1984; actress Little Town Players, 1985—; singer Bedford Choral Soc., 1985—. Dir. pledge ctr. Muscular Dystrophy Assn., Bedford, 1980—; outreach worker Total Action Against Poverty, 1969-72, Lynchburg Community Action Group, 1973-77. Democrat. Baptist.

PULLEN, NANCY ELLEN, marketing consultant; b. Tucson, Aug. 22, 1949; d. John Paul Pullen and Ellen Lyle (Jorgenson) Pullen Foules; m. David Lynn Preuss; Aug. 22, 1981; children: Donald, Elizabeth. BSBA, Stephen F. Austin State U., 1971; MSBA, U. Denver, 1973. Brand asst. to brand mgr. Procter & Gamble, Cin., 1973-81; mktg. mgr. Heublein Wine Divsn., San Francisco, 1981-82; account dir. Foote, Cone & Belding, S.A., Barcelona, Spain, 1981-85; sr. account dir. Addison Design Cons., San Francisco, 1985-88; exec. v.p. and prin. PSL Mktg. Resources, San Francisco, 1988—; speaker in field. Bd. dirs. Calif./Nev. United Meth. Found., San Francisco, 1993—. Mem. Roundtable for Women in Foodsvcs., Am. Mktg. Assn., San Francisco C. of C. Home: 677 Spruce St Berkeley CA 94707 Office: PSL Mktg Resources Inc 10 Lombard St #400 San Francisco CA 94111

PULLEN, PENNY LYNNE, non-profit administrator, former state legislator; b. Buffalo, Mar. 2, 1947; d. John William and Alice Nettie (McConkey) P.; BA in Speech, U. Ill., 1969. TV technician Office Instructional Resources, U. Ill., 1966-68; community newspaper reporter Des Plaines (Ill.) Pub. Co., 1967-72; legislative asst. to Ill. legislators, 1968-77; mem. Ill. Ho. of Reps., 1977-93, chmn. ho. exec. com., 1981-82, minority whip, 1983-87, asst. minority leader, 1987-93; pres., founder Life Advocacy Resource Project, 1992—; exec. dir. Ill. Family Inst., 1993-94; mem. Pres.'s Commn. on AIDS Epidemic, 1987-88; mem. Ill. Goodwill Del. to Republic of China, 1987. Del. Atlantic Alliance Young Polit. Leaders, Brussels, 1977, Rep. Nat. Conv, 1984; mem. Republican Nat. Com., 1984-88; summit conf. observer as mem. adhoc Women for SDI, Geneva, 1985; former mem. Maine Twp. Mental Health Assn.; active Nat. Coun. Ednl. Rsch., 1983-88. Recipient George Washington Honor medal Freedoms Found., 1978, Dwight Eisenhower Freedom medal Chgo. Captive Nations Com., 1977, Outstanding Legislator awards Ill. Press Assn., Ill. Podiatry Soc., Ill. Coroners Assn., Ill. County Clks. Assn., Ill. Hosp. Assn., Ill. Health Care Assn.; named Ill. Young Republican, 1968, Outstanding Young Person, Park Ridge Jaycees, 1981, One of 10 Outstanding Young Persons, Ill. Jaycees, 1981. Mem. Am. Legis. Exchange Council (dir. 1977-91, exec. com. 1978-83, 2d vice chmn. 1980-83), DAR. Lodge: Kiwanis.

PULLIAM, BRENDA JANE, secondary school educator; b. Griffin, Ga., Jan. 28, 1941; d. Delmus Lawton and Eva Jane (Cobb) P. BA, Tift Coll., 1963; MA in Teaching, Converse Coll., 1972; EdD, Nova U., 1993; postgrad., U. Toulouse, France. Cert. secondary tchr., Ga. Tchr. French Jonesboro (Ga.) H.S., 1963—, chair fgn. langs. dept., 1970—; co-founder KPS Leadership Specialists, 1993—; correlator Harcourt Brace Jovanovich, 1989; speaker So. Conf. Lang. Teaching, 1993, adv. bd. Contbr. articles to profl. jours.; contbr. ednl. papers to ERIC. Chair citizen exchs. Atlanta-Toulouse Sister Cities, 1987—, tour leader, 1989, 94; interpreter Travelers Aid Met. Atlanta, 1989—. Grantee NDEA, 1963; recipient STAR Tchr. award, 1983. Mem. NEA, Am. Coun. Teaching Fgn. Langs., Am. Assn. Tchrs. French, Ga. Assn. Educators, Fgn. Lang. Assn. Ga., Clayton County Edn. Assn., So. Conf. Lang. Teaching. Baptist. Home: 9261 Brave Ct Jonesboro GA 30236-5110 Office: Jonesboro High Sch 7728 Mount Zion Blvd Jonesboro GA 30236-2441

PULLIAM, YVONNE ANTOINETTE, gifted education educator; b. Chgo.; d. Virgil D. Sr. and Velma (Hunter) P. BA in Edn., Lane Coll., 1966; MA in Ednl. Adminstrn. and Supervision, Roosevelt U., 1988. Cert. intermediate tchr. Tchr. Howalton Day Sch., Chgo., 1968-69; actress N.Y.C., 1970-75; tchr. gifted Chgo. Bd. Edn., 1975-78, 81—; tutor Broadway play Raisin, N.Y.C., 1977-78, Annie, N.Y.C., 1980-82; coordinator Adopt-.-Sch. program, Chgo., 1984-85; tchr. rep. PTA O'Keefe Sch., Chgo., 1984-85. cartoonist 1st Nat. Bank Chgo. newsletter 1969; stand-in for Diana Ross In Mahogany, 1976; appeared on All My Children, The Hosp. and indsl. films and voiceovers. Recipient cert. of merit Glamour mag., 1965, award for innovative teaching Bus.Week, 1990; named featured designer V2 Fashions, Chgo., 1967, Essence mag., 1971. Mem. AFTRA, Chgo. Tchrs. Union, Am. Film. Inst., Phi Delta Kappa. Democrat.

PULSIFER, MARGARET BIGWOOD, psychologist; b. Boston, Nov. 16, 1959; d. Harold Smith and Brenda (MacHugh) Bigwood; m. Peter Emery Pulsifer, Aug. 2, 1987. BA, Boston Coll., 1981, MA, 1983; PhD, SUNY, Buffalo, 1989. Lic. psychologist, Md. Clin. psychology extern, St. Elizabeths Hosp., Washington, 1987-88, clin. psychology intern, 1988-89; postdoctoral fellow Johns Hopkins U. Sch. Med., Balt., 1989-90; pediatric psychologist Kennedy Krieger Inst./Johns Hopkins U., Balt., 1990-94; instr. dept. psychiatry Johns Hopkins Sch. Medicine, Balt., 1994—. Mem. Jr. League of Washington, 1989—. Mem. Am. Psychol. Assn., Md. Psychol. Assn., Nat. Acad. Neuropsychology. Office: Johns Hopkins Sch Medicine Dept Psychiatry 600 N Wolfe St-Meyer 218 Baltimore MD 21287

PUMARIEGA, JOANNE BUTTACAVOLI, mathematics educator; b. Coral Gables, Fla., May 27, 1952; d. Ciro Charles and Rosaria Frances (Calabrese) Buttacavoli; m. Andres Julio Pumariega, Dec. 26, 1975; children: Christina Marie, Nicole Marie. BA in Math. and Edn. magna cum laude, U. Miami, 1973, MA in Math., 1974; postgrad., U. Houston, 1991-92. Cert. secondary math. tchr., Tex., Fla., Tenn., N.C. Grad. tchg. asst. U. Miami, Coral Gables, 1973-74; substitute tchr. Dade County Pub. Schs., Miami, 1975; math. instr. Miami Dade C.C., 1975-76; math. and G.E.D. instr. Durham (N.C.) Tech. Inst., 1976-77; math. instr. Durham High Sch., 1977-78, Durham Acad., 1978-80, Univ. Sch. of Nashville, 1980-83; pvt. practice math. instr. Houston, 1984-86; tutor Clear Lake Tutoring Svc., Houston, 1987-90; pvt. practice, S.A.T, lang. inst. League City, Tex., 1990-92; pvt. practice math. and S.A.T. instr. Columbia, S.C., 1992—; instr. lang. Nelson Elem. Sch., Columbia, 1993—; instr. fgn. langs. Lonnie B. Nelson Elem. Sch., Columbia, S.C. Chair bd. edn. St. Mary Parish, League City, 1988-90, lector, 1992; C.C.E. tchr. St. John Neumann Cath. Ch., Columbia, S.C., 1993—; treas. St. Thomas More Women's Club, Houston, 1985-86; v.p., then pres. housestaff med. wives Duke U., Durham, N.C., 1978-80. Mem. Newcomers of Greater Columbia (chair pub. rels. chpt. 1993-94), Newcomers of Greater Colo. (com. chair coord. 1994—), Welcome Neighbors of Bay Area (v.p., program chmn. 1991-92), Tex. Med. Aux., Bay Area Med. Wives, Phi Kappa Phi, Kappa Delta Pi, Alpha Lambda Delta (Woman of Yr. 1972), U. S.C. Faculty Women's Club (v.p. 1993-94, pres. 1994—). Roman Catholic. Home and Office: 2121 Bee Ridge Rd Columbia SC 29223

PUMPHREY, JANET KAY, editor; b. Balt., June 18, 1946; d. John Henry and Elsie May (Keefer) P. AA in Secondary Edn., Anne Arundel Community Coll., Arnold, Md., 1967, AA in Bus. and Pub. Adminstrn., 1976. Office mgr. Anne Arundel C.C., 1964—; mng. editor Am. Polygraph Assn., Severna Park, Md., 1973—; archives researcher Am. Polygraph Assn., Severna Park, 1973—; owner JKP Publication Svcs., 1990—. Editor: (with Albert D. Snyder) Ten Years of Polygraph, 1984, (with Norman Ansley) Justice and the Polygraph, 1985, 2d edit., 1994, A House Full of Love, 1990. Mem. Rep. Nat. Sustaining Com. Mem. NAFE, Am. Polygraph Assn. (hon.), Md. Polygraph Assn. (affiliate), Internat. Platform Assn., Anne Arundel County Hist. Soc., Alumni Assn. Anne Arundel Community Coll. Republican. Methodist. Home: 3 Kimberly Ct Severna Park MD 21146-3703 Office: Am Polygraph Assn PO Box 1061 Severna Park MD 21146-8061

PUMPHREY, LELA DALE (KITTY PUMPHREY), finance educator, consultant; b. Tampa, Fla., June 28, 1941; d. Franklyn Whiting and Colleen L. (Roberts) Ely; m. Bobby Joe McDaniel, Nov. 8, 1963 (div. May 1978); children: Sylvia Colleen Hoke, Joseph Ely McDaniel, John Christopher McDaniel; m. Norman Dean Pumphrey, Aug. 22, 1978. BS in Bus. Adminstrn., U. So. Miss., 1968; MBA, Ark. State U., 1973; PhD, U. Mo., 1984. CPA, CIA, CMA. Staff acct. Wolfe, Roush & McDuff, CPA's, Pascagoula, Miss., 1968-69; internal auditor First Nat. Bank, Paragould, Ark., 1969-70; staff acct. Johnston, Freeman & Jones, CPA's, Jonesboro, Ark., 1970-71; owner Lela D. Pumphrey, CPA, Paragould, Ark., 1971-76; asst. prof. Ark. State U., Jonesboro, 1976-83, U. Arkansas, Little Rock, 1984-88; prof. Idaho State U., Pocatello, 1988—; cons. Idaho Legis. Auditor, Boise, 1989—. Contbr. articles to profl. jours. chmn. Bannock County Rep. Com., Pocatello, 1993—; com. chmn. Pocatello C. of C., 1988—; various chairmanships Gate City Rotary Club, 1989—; elected mem. county gov. body Greene County Quorem Court, Paragould, 1976-77. Mem. AICPA (com. mem.), Am. Acctg. Assn., Idaho Soc. CPA's (com. mem. 1988—), Assn. Govt. Accts. (Nat. Pres's. award 1992, regional v.p. 1994-95), Inst. Internal Auditors (com. mem. 1992—), Inst. Mgmt. Accts. (manuscript dir. 1994). Republican. Lutheran. Home: 2019 Diane Lane Pocatello ID 83201 Office: Idaho State U Campus Box 8020 Pocatello ID 83209

PUMPIAN, BETTY ANN G., advertising executive; b. Balt., Sept. 19, 1935; d. Emanuel Henry and Carlyn Rose (Freudenthal) Goldstone; m. Paul H. Pumpian, June 24, 1956. BS in Mktg., U. Balt., 1956. Network coord., asst. buyer Parkson Advt., N.Y.C., 1957-61; traffic mgr. Sta. KORK, Las Vegas, Nev., 1961; project coord., bookkeeper Art Dept., L.A., 1961-62; network and planning coord. Ogilvy & Mather, L.A., 1962-75, asst. media dir., 1975-78, assoc. media dir., 1978-80, v.p., dir. nat. broadcast and programming, 1980-89; nat./regional broadcast adminstr. Bozell, Inc., L.A., 1989-90; v.p., sr. network negotiator Western Internat. Media, L.A., 1991—; lectr. Adweek Seminars, L.A., 1989-91. Chmn. 1st Coun. Dist. Horsemen's Adv. Com., L.A., 1978-81; chmn. L.A. Equine Adv. Com., 1978-83; pres. Cal-Western Appaloosa Inc., 1981-82, bd. dirs; mem. horse drugging adv. com. Calif. Dept. Food and Agr., Sacramento, 1987—. Recipient Commendation award L.A. City Coun., 1983, Achievement cert. YWCA, L.A., 1976. Mem. Appaloosa Horse Club (dir., chmn. planning and rev. 1987-88, 93-94, chmn. rules 1988-92, chmn. mktg. 1992—, chmn. youth 1992-93, v.p. 1994-95). Republican. Office: Western Internat Media 8544 W Sunset Blvd West Hollywood CA 90069-2387

PUNCHES, JILL PIPER, municipal official; b. Columbus, Ohio, Oct. 22, 1962; d. Larry Dean Maurer and Marcia Piper Swisher; m. Richard Scott Punches, Dec. 11, 1993; 1 child, Madeline Corinne. BA in Econs., Kalamazoo Coll., 1984; student, Universitat Bonn, Germany, 1982-83, Humboldt State U., Arcata, Calif., 1989. Cert. TESL. Student activities coord. Internat. English Lang. Inst., Humboldt State U., 1987-90; properties assoc. Port of Portland, Oreg., 1990-91, airfield ops. supr., 1991-93, supt. terminal and landside ops., 1993—. Mem. Salsa and blue Chips Investment Club (treas. 1993-94), Airport Ground Transp. Assn., Women's Transp. Seminar. Home: 2405 NE 42d St Portland OR 97213 Office: Port of Portland Box 3529 Portland OR 97208

PURACCHIO, SHERYL LEGER, reporter, recycling education consultant; b. Chgo., Mar. 22, 1957; d. Joseph Oscar Leger and Loverle Ester (Coulter) Leger-Siers; m. Mark Alan Puracchio, Sept. 12, 1982; children: Louis, Elise, Scott, Sara. Grad. high sch., River Forest, Ill. Supr. Lyric Opera Chgo., 1977-82; coord. recycling City of Wilmington, Ill., 1991-93; environ. reporter Wilmington Free Press, 1991—; recycling edn. cons., 1993—; coord. model community Cen. States Edn. Ctr., Champaign, Ill., 1990—; presenter success story UN Environ. Programme, 1991. Vice pres. Citizens for Clean Environ., Wilmington, 1990-91. Named Ill. Jr. Woman of Yr., Gen. Fedn. Women's Clubs, 1991; recipient spl. recognition Ill. Ho. of Reps., 1991, cert. of excellence Trailways coun. Girl Scouts U.S.A., 1991. Mem. Worldwide Network, Ill. Fedn. Womens Clubs (chmn. jr. conservation, conservation chmn. dist. 11, 1992-94, Dist. Jr. Woman of Yr. award 1991), Wilmington Jr. Woman's Club (pres. 1988-90, 94-96). Roman Catholic. Home and Office: 1499 Amber Ln Wilmington IL 60481-9308

PURCELL, ANN RUSHING, state legislator, office manager medical business; b. Reidsville, Ga., May 12, 1945; d. William Robert and Katie (Dasher) Rushing; m. Dent Wiley Purcell, May 26, 1966; children: Edwin Wiley, Mieke Ann, Mikki Marie. BS in Edn., Ga. So. Coll., 1966. Cert. secondary tchr. Tchr. math. Evans (Ga.) High Sch., 1966-68; tchr. math., earth and sci. Beaumont Jr. High Sch., Lexington, Ky., 1969-70; substitute tchr. Tallahassee, Fla., 1970's; agt. Noblin Realty, Tallahassee, 1970's; office mgr. Radiation Therapy Assocs., PC, Savannah, Ga., 1979—; state legislator Ho. of Reps. Ga. Gen. Assembly, Atlanta, 1991—. Author: Purcells of South Georgia and Other Related Families, 1976. Bd. dirs. Med. Assn. Ga. Polit. Action Com., Atlanta, 1988-89, Girl Scout Coun. Savannah, 1991—, Ga. So. U. Found., 1992—; mem. adv. com. Effingham County Extension Svc., 1992—; fin. chmn. State YMCA, 1991—; bd. adv. Claxton Youth Detnetion Ctr. Recipient Friend of Medicine award Med. Assn. Ga., 1991, 93, 94, Guardian of Small Bus. award Nat. Fedn. Ind. Bus., 1992, 94. Mem. Aux. to the Med. Assn. Ga. (pres. 1985), Aux. to the Ga. Med. Soc. (pres. 1981-82), Ga. Salzburger Soc., Effingham County Pub. Officials Assn., Rotary. Democrat. Methodist. Home: 410 Willowpeg Way Rincon GA 31326-1295 Office: State Capitol Ste 401 Atlanta GA 30334

PURCELL, CLARE DRIGGS, pediatrician; b. N.Y.C., Aug. 13, 1949; d. Thomas Augustus and Katherine Agnes (Driggs) P.; m. Thomas George Neumann, Oct. 12, 1974; children: John, Elizabeth, William. BA, U. Mich., 1970; MD, Northwestern U., 1974. Diplomate Am. Bd. Pediats. Intern, resident Children's Meml. Hosp., Chgo., 1974-76; infectious disease fellow U. Ill. Hosp., Chgo., 1976-78; pvt. practice Glenview, Ill., 1978—; infectious disease cons. Lake County Health Dept., Waukegan, Ill., 1978-80. Active Am. Family Assn., Tupelo, Miss. Fellow Am. Acad. Pediats.; mem. AMA, DAR (mem. social and nat. def. 1989), Phi Beta Kappa, Alpha Omega Alpha. Home: 1640 S Ridge Rd Lake Forest IL 60045 Office: 2050 Pfingsten Ste 190 Glenview IL 60025

PURCELL, GAIL POURIE, elementary education educator; b. St. Louis, June 22, 1936; d. Edmund Albert and Golda Marie (Clark) Pourie; m. Murray E. Purcell, July 13, 1957; children: Margaret Elizabeth Calaluce, Timothy James, Scott Edmund. BS in Elem. Edn., S.E. Mo. State U., 1959; MEd in Early Childhood Edn., East Tex. State U., 1974; EdS in Early Childhood Edn., U. Mo., 1988. Cert. early childhood specialist, Mo., lifetime teaching cert. pre-kindergarten-grade 8, Mo., Tex. Tchr. grade 1-3 Sims Sch., Audrain County, Mo., 1957-58; tchr. pre-sch. Meth. Ch. Co-op., Mexico, Mo., 1969-71; tchr. grade 1, kindergarten, extended kindergarten, chpt. 1 Mexico Pub. Schs., 1959-60, 75-90, dir. chpt. 1, 1990—. Creator: (ednl. material) Lakeshore Learning Materials. Pres. Area PTA Coun., Sulphur Springs, Tex., 1973-74; active Sisterhood chpt. P.E.O., pres.-elect, 1992-94, Audrain County Child Abuse/Neglect Coun., Mexico, 1990—, Divsn. Family Svcs. Educare Com., Mexico, 1993—; pres. Community Tchrs. Assn. Mexico Pub. Schs., 1987. Mem. NEA, ASCD, Internat. Reading Assn., Delta Kappa Gamma, Alpha Chi Omega. Republican. Mem. Disciples of Christ. Office: Mexico Sch Dist 920 S Jefferson St Mexico MO 65265-2563

PURCELL, LEE, actress; b. N.C., June 15, 1953; m. Gary A. Lowe; 1 child, Gary; 1 stepchild. Student, Royal Acad. Dramatic Art; studies with Margot Lister, Milton Katselas, Jeff Corey, Robert F. Lyons. Appeared in (films) Adam at 6 A.M., 1970, The Toy Factory, 1971, Dirty Little Billy, 1972, Kid Blue, 1973, Mr. Majestyk, 1974, Almost Summer, 1978, Stir Crazy, 1980, Valley Girl, Eddie Macon's Run, 1983, Laura's Dream, 1986, (TV) Highjack, 1973, Stranger in Our House, 1978, Kenny Rogers as the Gambler, 1980, Killing at Hell's Gate, 1981, Magnum P.I., Murder, She Wrote, 1985, My Wicked Wicked Ways: The Legend of Errol Flynn, 1986, Secret Sins of the Father, 1994 (Emmy nomination, Supporting Actress - Special, 1994), (stage) Richard III, A Streetcar Named Desire, The Taming of the Shrew, A Midsummer Night's Dream. Recipient Bronze Halo Career Achievement award So. Calif. Motion Picture Council, 1985. Mem. Actors' Equity Assn., Screen Actors Guild, AFTRA, Acad. Motion Picture Arts and Scis., Acad. TV Arts And Scis. Office: The Artists Group 1930 Century Park W Suite 403 Los Angeles CA 90067*

PURCELL, MARY HAMILTON, speech educator; b. Ft. Worth; d. Joseph Hants and Letha (Gibson) Hamilton; m. William Paxson Purcell, Jr., Dec. 28, 1950; children: William Paxson III, David Hamilton. BA, Mary Hardin-Baylor Coll., 1947; MA, La. State U., 1948; HHD (hon.), Mary Hardin-Baylor Coll., 1986. Instr., dept. speech and dramatic arts Temple U., Phila., 1948-53, 60-61; part-time instr. speech Cushing Jr. Coll., Bryn Mawr, Pa., 1966-78. Pres., Pa. Program for Women and Girl Offenders, 1968-73; pres. Nether Providence Parent Tchr. Orgn., 1975-76; treas. Virginia Gildersleeve Internat. Fund Univ. Women, 1975-81, bd. dirs., 1987-93; bd. dirs. Citizens Crime Commn. of Phila., 1976—; mem. Wallingford-Swarthmore Dist. Sch. Bd., 1977-83; bd. dirs. Nat. Peace Inst. Found., 1983-86, Big Bros./Big Sisters of Am., 1985-90, Pa. Women's Campaign Fund, 1985-88; bd. dirs. Ministers and Missionaries Fund Am. Bapt. Conv., 1985-94, pres., 1995—, Internat. Devel. Conf., 1986—. Named Outstanding Alumna Mary Hardin-Baylor Coll., 1972, Disting. Dau. Pa., 1982, v.p., 1994—; recipient Zeta Phi Eta award excellence in communications, 1983. Mem. AAUW (Pa. div. pres. 1968-70, v.p. middle Atlantic region 1973-77, program v.p. 1979-81, pres. 1981-85, rep. to UN, 1985-89), Internat. Fedn. Univ. Women (1st v.p. 1986-89, pres. 1989-92, rep. to UN 1992—; pres. UN Dept. Pub. Info. Non Govt. Orgn. ann. conf. 1993), Speech Assn. Am., Pi Kappa Delta, Pi Gamma Mu, Delta Sigma Rho, Alpha Psi Omega, Alpha Chi. Democrat. Baptist. Home: 9 Oak Knolls Dr Media PA 19086-6315

PURCELL, MARY LOUISE GERLINGER, educator; b. Thief River Falls, Minn., July 17, 1923; d. Charles and Lajla (Dale) Gerlinger; student Yankton Coll., 1941-45, Yale Div. Sch., 1949-50, NYU, summer 1949; MA (alumni fellow), Tchrs. Coll. Columbia, 1959, EdD, 1963; m. Walter A. Kuyawski, June 9, 1950 (dec. July 1954); children: Amelia Allerton, Jon Allerton; m. 2d, Dale Purcell, Aug. 26, 1962. Teen-age program dir., YWCA, New Haven, 1945-52; dir. program in family rels., asst. prof. sociology and psychology Earlham Coll., Richmond, Ind., 1959-62, conf. coord. undergrad. edn. for women, 1962; chmn. div. home and community Stephens Coll., Columbia, Mo., 1962-73, chmn. family and community studies, 1962-78, dir. Learning Unltd., continuing edn. for women, 1974-78, developer course The Contemporary Am. Woman, 1962, cons., 1962; prof., Auburn (Ala.) U., 1978-88, prof. emerita, 1988—, head dept. family and child devel., 1978-84, spl. asst. to v.p. acad. affairs, 1985-86. chmn. search com. for v.p. acad. affairs, 1984; vis. prof. Ind. U. Summer Sch., 1970. Cons. student personnel svcs., Trenton (N.J.) State Coll., 1958-59, 61. Recipient Alumni Achievement award Yankton Coll., 1975. Mem. AAUW, Am. Home Econs. Assn. (bd. dirs. 1967-69, chair 1st subject matter unit 1969, family relations and child devel. sect. 1986-89), Groves Conf. on Family, Nat. Council Family Relations (dir., chmn.-elect affiliated councils, 1981-82, chmn., 1982-84, nat. program chmn. 1977, chmn. film awards com., chmn. spl. emphases sect., bd. dirs., Ernest G. Osborne award for excellence in teaching 1979), Delta Kappa Gamma. Presbyterian. Contbr. articles to coll. bulls., jours. Home: 120 Belden St Falls Village CT 06031-1112

PURDES, ALICE MARIE, secondary education educator; b. St. Louis, Jan. 8, 1931; d. Joseph Louis and Angeline Cecilia (Mozier) P. AA, Belleville Area Coll., 1951; BS, Ill. State U., Normal, 1953, MS, 1954; PhD, Fla. State U., Tallahassee, 1976. Cert. in music edn., elem. edn., secondary edn., adult edn. Teaching/grad. asst. Ill. State U., 1953-54; music supr. Princeton (Ill.) Pub. Schs., 1954-55; music dir. Venice (Ill.) Pub. Schs., 1955-72, secondary vocal music dir., 1955-72; coord. literacy program Venice-Lincoln Tech. Ctr., 1983-86, chair lang. arts dept., 1983—. Mem. St. Louis chpt. World Affairs Coun., UN Assn.; charter mem. St. Lous Sci. Ctr., Harry S Truman Inst.; contbr. Old Six Mile Mus., 1981, Midland Repertory Players, Alton, Ill., 1991; chair Cystic Fibrosis Spring Bike-A-Thon, Madison, Ill., 1981, Granite City, Ill., 1985. Recipient gold medal Nat Senior Olympics, 1989, Senior World Games, 1992, several scholarships. Mem. AAUW, Music Educators Nat. Conf., Ill. Music Educators Assn., Am. Choral Dirs. Assn., Fla. State Alumni Assn., Ill. Adult and Continuing Educators Assn., Am. Fedn. Tchrs. (pres. 1957-58), Western Cath. Union, Croation Fraternal Union, Nat. Space Soc., Travelers Abroad (pres. 1966-68, 89—), Internat. Platform Assn., Archaeol. Inst. Am., Friends of St. Louis Art Mus., St. Louis Numis. Assn., Madison Rotary Club (internat. amb.), Slavic and East European Friends (life), Lovejoy Libr. Friends, Ill. State U. Alumni Assn. Roman Catholic. Home: PO Box 274 Madison IL 62060-0274 Office: Venice-Lincoln Tech Ctr S 4th St Venice IL 62090-1063

PURDY, SHERRY MARIE, lawyer; b. Billings, Mont., Mar. 12, 1960. Student, U. Mont., 1978-80; BS, Ea. Mont. Coll., 1983; JD, Willamette U., 1987. Bar: Colo. 1987, U.S. Dist. Ct. Colo. 1987. Assoc. Holland & Hart, Denver, 1987-90; sr. atty. Atlantic Richfield Co., Denver, 1990—. Contbr. articles to profl. jours. Mem. ABA, Colo. Bar Assn., Colo. Women's Bar Assn., Colo. Hazardous Waste Mgmt. Soc. (program com. chair 1989-90, v.p. 1990-91), Denver Bar Assn. Office: Atlantic Richfield Co Ste 1600 555 17th St Denver CO 80202-3916

PURKERSON, MABEL LOUISE, physician, physiologist, educator; b. Goldville, S.C., Apr. 3, 1931; d. James Clifton and Louise (Smith) P. A.B., Erskine Coll., 1951; M.D., U. S.C., Charleston, 1956. Diplomate Am. Bd. Pediatrics. Instr. pediatrics Washington U. Sch. Med., St. Louis, 1961-67, instr. medicine, 1966-67, asst. prof. pediatrics, 1967—, asst. prof. medicine, 1967-76, assoc. prof. medicine, 1976-89, prof., 1989—, assoc. dean curriculum, 1976-94; assoc. dean acad. projects, 1994—; cons. in field. Editorial bd. Jour. Am. Kidney Diseases, 1981-87 ; contbr. articles to profl. jours. USPHS spl. fellow, 1971-72. Bd. counselors Erskine Coll., 1971—. Mem. Am. Heart Assn. (exec. com. 1973-81), Council on the Kidney, Am. Physiol. Soc., Am. Soc. Nephrology, Internat. Soc. Nephrology, Central Soc. Clin. Research, Am. Soc. Renal Biochemistry and Metabolism, Sigma Xi (chpt. sec. 1974-76). Avocations: traveling; gardening; photography. Home: 20 Haven View Dr Saint Louis MO 63141-7902 Office: Washington Univ Sch Medicine Renal Div Dept 660 S Euclid Ave St Box 8132 St Louis MO 63110

PURNELL, FLORIE ELIZABETH, trainer; b. Winston-Salem, N.C., Mar. 29, 1955; d. Bernard Owen and Mary Elizabeth (Thompkins) Taylor; m. Rodney James Roundtree, Mar. 9, 1973 (div. Apr. 1978); 1 child, Rodney James; m. Fason Anderson, May 28, 1988; children: Rachel, Jasmin. AAS in Bus. Adminstrn., Forsyth Tech. Coll., Winston-Salem, 1981; BS in Bus. Adminstrn., High Point Coll., Winston-Salem, 1985; MS in Human Resource Counseling, N.C. A&T State U., Greensboro, 1992. Supr. Piedmont Airlines, Winston-Salem, 1974-88; counselor Tokyo English Life Line, Tokyo, 1990-91; trainer Oak Assocs., Tokyo, 1991-92; program dir. Am. C. of C., Tokyo, 1993—. Pres. Girl Talk, Tokyo, 1991-92. Mem. Am. Counseling Assn. Democrat. Baptist. Home: Apt 8 191 Condominium, 191 Jalan Ampang, 50450 Kuala Lumpur Malaysia

PURSELL, CLEO WILBURN, church official; b. Ft. Worth, Feb. 16, 1918; d. Charles P. and Eltrie Lee (Tice) Dalton; m. Paul Edgar Pursell, Feb. 16, 1939 (dec. 1973). Grad. high sch. Ordained to ministry Nat. Assn. Free Will Bapts., 1939. Asst. pastor various chs., Okla., 1939-57; pres. Okla. State Aux., First Okla. and First Mission Dists.; officer Calif. State Aux., 1960; 2nd v.p., youth chmn. Woman's Nat. Aux. Conv. 1946-48, 52-55, nat. study chmn., 1955-57, exec. sec.-treas., Nashville, 1963-85. Author: Missionary Education of Our Youth, 1955, Woman's Auxiliary Manual, 1965, Triumph Over Suffering, 1982, Death and Dying, 1982, Anne, You're Super, 1990; columnist: Words for Women Contact Mag., 1966-70; editor Co-Laborer, 1963-85, (newsletter) The Minister's Wife, 1965-94; contbr. articles to profl. jours. Prominent in youth work, Okla., 1939-57; tchr. dist. and state Sunday Sch. workshops. Mem. Women's Fellowship Federated Women's Missionary Socs. (treas. Bristow, Okla., 1955). Home: 1148 Vultee Blvd Apt 12 Nashville TN 37217-2108

PURSLEY, CAROL COX (CAROL SUE COX-PURSLEY), psychotherapist; b. Chattanooga, Dec. 7, 1951; d. George Edwin and M. Sue (Clarke) Cox; m. James V. Pursley; 1 child, Drew Vinson; stepchildren: Nancy, John. BS, U. Tenn., 1973, MS, 1975; PhD, U. Ky., 1983. Registered rehab. supplier, Ga.; cert. rehab. counselor, ins. rehab. specialist; lic. psychologist, Ky., lic. profl. counselor, Ga. Dir. rehab. Goodwill Industries, Knoxville, Tenn., 1975-77; rsch. and evaluation asst. region IV rehab. continuing edn. U. Tenn., Knoxville, 1977; crisis intervention cons., job placement counselor KACRC, Knoxville, 1977-78; instr., cons. region IV rehab. continuing edn. program U. Tenn., Knoxville, 1978-79; teaching/rsch. asst. U. Ky., Lexington, 1979-80; rehab. specialist Internat. Rehab. Assocs., Louisville, 1980; psychologist and assoc. clin. staff Ea. State Hosp., Lexington, 1981-84; rehab. cons. Southeastern Transitions, Atlanta, 1985-86; pvt. practice rehab. cons. Marietta, Ga., 1986-94; pvt. practice psychotherapy and testing North Atlanta Neurol. Assocs., Marietta and Atlanta, 1994—; allied health profl. Ridgeview Inst., 1994—; vocat. rehab. assessment cons. and counselor Kennestone Hosp. at Windy Hill, Marietta, 1988-92; clin. assoc. Am. Bd. Med. Psychotherapists, 1986—; stragety meeting cons. Sony Music Entertainment, N.Y.; cons. ADA; expert witness Ga. Composite Bd. Profl. Counselors, Social Workers and Marriage and Family Therapists, 1991—; cons. to Gov.'s Rehab. Adv. Com., 1990. Chairperson-elect Vol. State Rehab. Counseling Assn., Knoxville, 1976; mem. Mayor's Adv. Com. for Handicapped, Knoxville, 1974-76. Facility Improvement grantee s.e. region Rehab. Svcs. Adminstrn., 1975-77, Facility Establishment grantee United Cerebral Palsy, 1977. Mem. APA, Am. Counseling Assn., Ga. Psychol. Assn., Ky. Psychol. Assn., Nat. Assn. Rehab. Providers in the Pvt. Sector (rsch. and tng. com. 1988-94), Pvt. Rehab. Suppliers of Ga. (chairperson ethics com. 1989-91, named person of distinction state PRSG chpt. newsletter 1990, ethics com. 1986-92), Nat. Rehab. Assn., Nat. Rehab. Counseling Assn., Menninger Found., Phi Kappa Phi. Office: 2520 E Piedmont Rd Ste F Marietta GA 30062-7208

PURZE, JUDY SUZANNE, real estate executive, consultant; b. Chgo., Aug. 16, 1953; d. Gilbert and Marcia (Waldshine) P. BS in Bus., U. Colo., 1975; M in Internat. Bus., Am. Grad. Sch. Internat. Bus., Glendale, Ariz., 1976. Realtor Century 21, Phoenix, 1975-76; mgr. internat. site selection Britt and Frerichs, Chgo., 1976-78; sr. analyst Real Estate Rsch. Corp., Chgo., 1978-80; devel. dir. Homart Devel. Co., Chgo., 1980-83; real estate mgr. Best Products Co., Richmond, Va., 1983-84; real estate rep. Vol. Shoe Co., Hurst, Tex., 1984-87; real estate mgr. Montgomery Ward Co., Chgo., 1987-89; v.p. real estate Hit or Miss, Inc., Irving, Tex., 1989—. Mem. Internat. Assn. Corp. Real Estate Execs., Internat. Coun. Shopping Ctrs. Office: Hit or Miss Inc 4835 N O'Connor Rd Ste 134-338 Irving TX 75062

PUTA, DIANE FAY, medical staff services director; b. Manitowoc, Wis., Mar. 6, 1947; d. Ruben William and Gertrude Katherine (Novak) P. BSN, Alverno Coll., 1971; MS in Ednl. Adminstrn., U. Wis., Milw., 1979, PhD in Urban Edn., 1991. Staff nurse St. Mary's Hosp., Milw., 1971-72, St. Anthony's Hosp., Milw., 1972-74; nurse coord. Pvt. Initiative in PSRO, Wis., 1974-75; insvc. instr. Deaconess Hosp., Milw., 1975-77, insvc. coord., 1977-81; dir. nursing staff devel./quality assurance Good Samaritan Med. Ctr., Milw., 1981-84, dir. quality assurance, 1984-85, dir. utilization mgmt., 1985-88; mgr. quality mgmt. Sinai Samaritan Med. Ctr., Milw., 1988-89, dir. med. staff svcs. and quality mgmt., 1989—. Author: (with others) Interdisciplinary QA: Issues in Collaboration, 1991; author poem. Mem. Channel 10/36 Friends, Milw., Friends of Pub. Mus., Milw., 1991. Mem. Nat. Assn. for Healthcare Quality, Am. Soc. Quality Control, Alverno Coll. Alumnae Assn., U. Wis. Alumni Assn., Delta Epsilon Sigma, Kappa Gamma Pi. Home: 4050 W Rivers Edge Cir Apt 2 Milwaukee WI 53209-1129 Office: Sinai Samaritan Med Ctr PO Box 342 Milwaukee WI 53201-0342

PUTHOFF, FRANKIE, claims specialist; b. Albuquerque, Oct. 24, 1958; d. Norma Marie (Begley) Hileman; m. Brian W. Puthoff, Dec. 7, 1985; children: James E., Christopher. Student, Wilmington Coll. Cert. in assoc. customer svc., assoc. life and health claims, health ins. assoc. Unit leader Prudential Ins., Cin., 1983-87; claims specialist, team leader Union Ctrl. Life Ins., Cin., 1987-94; sr. risk specialist Unum Ins., Portland, Maine, 1994—. Fellow Life Mgmt. Inst.; mem. Cin. Life, Accident and Health Claim Assn. (sec. 1992-94). Republican. Baptist. Home: 21 Elliot Rd Gorham ME 04038 Office: Unum Ins 2211 Congress St Portland ME 04101

PUTNAM, BARBARA LOU, mental health nurse; b. Ringgold, Ga., Jan. 9, 1945; m. Wayne Miller Putnam, Dec. 14, 1963; children: Charles, Mike, Tim. Student, Mercer U., 1984-86; BSN, Emory U., 1988. Asst. phys. therapist 5th Ave. Nursing Home, Rome, Ga., 1983-84; pvt. duty nurse, home health nurse Am. Patient Care, Rome, 1989—; staff nurse Northwest Ga. Regional Hosp., Rome, 1989—. Home: RR 9 Box 13 Rome GA 30165-9809

PUTNAM, GLENDORA MCILWAIN, retired lawyer, association executive; b. Lugoff, S.C., July 25, 1923; d. Simon Peter McIlwain and Katherine (Stewart) McIlwain; m. Harold B. Putnam, Jr., Nov. 19, 1964 (div. Apr. 1977). Student, Barber-Scotia Jr. Coll, Concord, N.C., 1943; AB, Bennett Coll., 1945, LLD (hon.), 1991; JD, Boston U., 1948; LLD (hon.), Southeastern Mass. U., 1986. Bar: Mass. 1949, U.S. Dist. Ct. Mass., 1962, U.S Supreme Ct. 1965. Atty. Yoffa & Yoffa, Boston, 1949-51; of counsel Vets. Bonus Commn., Boston, 1953-58; contracts adminstr. Craig Systems, Inc., Lawrence, Mass., 1959-61; pvt. practice G.M. Putnam, Atty., Lawrence, Boston, Needham, Mass., 1949-88; asst. atty. gen., chief Divsn. Civil Rights and Liberties Commonwealth Mass., 1963-69; chmn. Mass. Commn. Against Discrimination, 1969-75; dep. asst. sec. Fair Housing and Equal Opportunity HUD, Washington, 1975-77; equal opportunity officer Mass. Housing Fin. Agy., 1977-88; ret., 1988. Pres. YWCA U.S.A., 1985-91, nat. bd. dirs. 1973-94, nat. bd. trustees, 1982—; sec. Rep. Town Com., Methuen, Mass., 1952-66; mem. Rep. State Com., Boston, 1956-67; exec. com. New Eng. Conf. NAACP Brs., 1956—; trustee YWCA Retirement Fund, 1982—, The Boston Conservatory, 1972—, Bennett Coll., 1991—; bd. dirs. NAACP Legal Def. and Ednl. Fund, Inc., 1984—, Mus. Afro-Am. History, 1991—. Recipient humanitarian award Boston Br. NAACP, 1973, Black Women Who Made It Happen award Nat. Coun. Negro Women, 1985, Silver Shingle Disting. Pub. Svc. award Boston U. Law Sch., 1988, Ambassador award YWCA of the U.S.A., 1993; named Woman of Yr., Greater Boston Bus. and Profl. Women's Club, 1969, Woman of Achievement Boston Big Sisters, 1985, Acad. Disting. Bostonians, Greater Boston C. of C., 1988. Mem. Mass. Bar Assn., Mass. Black Lawyers' Assn., Mass. Black Women Attys., Boston Bar Assn., NAACP (Merrimack Valley br.), Boston U. Law Sch. Alumni Assn. (exec. com.), Delta Sigma Theta. Home: Apt 25G 790 Boylston St Boston MA 02199 Office: YWCA of USA 726 Broadway New York NY 10003-9511

PUTNAM, LINDA LEE, communication educator, researcher; b. Frederick, Okla., Aug. 10, 1945; d. Allard Warren and Etta Wanona (Tucker) Loutherback; m. Thomas Milton Putnam III, Mar. 28, 1970; 1 child, Ashley Ann. BA, Hardin-Simmons U., 1967; MA, U. Wis., 1968; PhD, U. Minn., 1977. Instr. U. Mass., Amherst, 1968-69; instr., chair dept. speech-theatre Normandale Community Coll., Bloomington, Minn., 1969-77; prof. communication Purdue U., West Lafayette, Ind., 1977-93; dept. head Tex. A & M Univ., 1993—; vis. scholar Stanford U., U. Calif.-Berkeley, San Francisco, 1984, Harvard U.-Harvard Negotiation Project, 1992. Editor: Communication and Organization, 1983(Best Publ. award 1985), Handbook of Organizational Communication, 1987 (Best Publ. award 1988), Communication and Negotiation, 1992. Del. Dem. State Conv., Mpls., 1972-74; treas. local dist. Dem. Farm Labor Party, Mpls., 1973-74, co-chairperson, 1974-75; block chair Am. Can. Soc. Fund Raiser, West Lafayette, 1986-87. Recipient AMOCO Teaching award Purdue U., 1986, Andersch award Ohio U., 1991, Disting. Alumni award Hardin-Simmons U., 1991, Charles H. Woolbert Rsch. award Speech Comm. Assn., 1993. Mem. Acad. Mgmt. (chair power negotiation, conflict mgmt. com. 1989-91), Speech Comm. Assn. (mem. at large 1984-87), Ctrl. States Speech Assn. (sec. comm. theory com. 1978-79, Scholar Showcase award 1989), Internat. Comm. Assn. (fellow 1986-88), Internat. Assn. for Conflict Mgmt. (bd. dirs. 1990-92, pres.-elect 1993-94).

PUTNAM, LYNNE BUNKER, civil engineer; b. Oakland, Calif., Dec. 4, 1955; d. Edwin Huntington and Evelyn Barbara (Marks) Bunker; m. Jonathan Blair Putnam, May 12, 1990. BSCE, U. Calif., Berkeley, 1978; MPA, Calif. State U., 1987. Registered profl. engr., Calif. Jr. civil engr. Contra Costa County Pub. Works, Martinez, Calif., 1978-80, assoc. civil engr., 1980-84, sr. civil engr., 1984-86; assoc. engr. Ctrl. Contra Costa Sanitary Dist., Martinez, 1986-90, sr. engr., 1990—. Contbr. papers to profl. confs. Named Young Careerist, Bus. & Profl. Women, 1990. Mem. Calif. Water Pollution Control Assn. (chair pub. edn. com. 1992-95, past chair Bay sect.), Talksics Toastmasters Club (charter pres. 1987—). Republican. Office: Ctrl Contra Costa San Dist 5019 Imhoff Pl Martinez CA 94553

PUTNEY, MARY ENGLER, federal auditor; b. Overland, Mo., May 1, 1933; d. Bernard J. and Marie (Kunkler) Engler; children: Glennon (dec.), Pat Michael, Michelle. Student Fontbonne Coll., 1951-52; AA, Sacramento City Coll., 1975; BS in Bus., Calif. State U., 1981; CPA, Calif. Asst. to acct. Mo. Research Labs., Inc., St. Louis, 1953-55, sec. to controller, 1955-56, adminstrv. asst. to pres., 1958-60; sec. to mgr. Western region fin. Gen. Electric Co., St. Louis, 1960-62; sec. to regional v.p. agrl. loans Crocker Nat. Bank, Sacramento, 1962-67, credit analyst No. region, 1967, sec. to v.p. and mgr. capital office, Sacramento, 1967-72; student tchr. Sacramento County Dept. Edn., 1979-81; acctg. technician East Yolo Community Services Dist., 1983; mgmt. specialist USAF Logistics Command, 1984; staff auditor Office Insp. Gen., U.S. Dept. Transp., 1984-92; auditor Adminstrn. for Children Families U.S. Dept. Health and Human Svcs., 1992—. Mem. Sacramento Community Commn. for Women, 1978—, rec. sec., 1980-81, bd. dirs., 1980—; mem. planning bd. Golden Empire Health Systems Agy. Mem. AARP (tax counselor for the elderly), AAUW (fin. officer 1983—), Nat. Assn. Accts. (dir., newsletter editor), Fontbonne Coll. Alumni Assn., Calif. State Alumni Assn., Assn. Govt. Accts. (chpt. officer), Am. Soc. Women Accts., German Geneological Soc. (bd. dirs. 1990—, publicity dir. 1994—), Rio Del Oro Racquet Club, Beta Gamma Sigma, Beta Alpha Psi. Roman Catholic. Home: 2616 Point Reyes Way Sacramento CA 95826-2416 Office: US Dept Health & Human Svcs ACF/OCSE Div of Audits 2989 Fulton Ave Sacramento CA 95821

PUTTERMAN, FLORENCE GRACE, artist, printmaker; b. N.Y.C., Apr. 14, 1927; d. Nathan and Jean (Feldman) Hirsch; m. Saul Putterman, Dec. 19, 1947. BS, NYU, 1947; MFA, Pa. State U., 1973. Founder, pres. Arts Unlimited, Selinsgrove, Pa., 1969—; curator Milton Shoe Collection, 1970—; artist in residence Title III Program Cultural Enrichment in Schs. Program, 1969-70; instr. Lycoming Coll., Williamsport, Pa., 1972-74, Susquehanna U., Selinsgrove, PA, 1984—. Exhibited one-woman shows, Everson Mus., Syracuse, N.Y., 1976, Hagerstown, Md., 1978, Stuhr Mus., Grand Island, N.B., 1979, Muhlenburg Ctr. for the Arts, Pa., 1985, Harmon Gallery, Fla., 1985, The State Mus. of Pa., 1985-86, Segal Gallery, N.Y., 1986, Canton Inst. Fine Arts, Ohio, 1986, Fla. Biennial Polk Mus., Lakeland, Fla., 1987, 89, Artists Choose Artists, Tampa Mus., 1987, Auburn Works on Paper, 1987, Ala., Ruth Volid Gallery, Chgo., 1989, Polk Mus. Art, Lakeland, Fla., 1989, Lowe Gallery, Atlanta, 1990, Mickelson Gallery, Washington, 1990, Palmer Mus., Pa. State U., 1990, Payne Gallery, Moravian Coll., 1991, Everhart Mus., Scranton, Pa., 1991, Lowe Gallery, L.A., 1992, Center Gallery, Bucknell U., Pa., 1993, Lore Degenstein Gallery, Susquehanna U., Selinsgrove, Pa., 1993, Lowe Gallery, Atlanta, 1993, Down Roll Gallery, Sarasota, Fla., Gallery 10, Washington; group shows, Library Congress, Soc. Am. Graphic Artists, Ball State Drawing Ann., Muncie, Ind., Arts Club

N.Y., Colorprint, U.S.A., Smithsonian Traveling Exhbn., Boston Printmakers, N.C. Print & Drawing, Chautauqua Nat., U. Dallas Nat. Print Invitational, Segal Gallery, Rutgers Drawing, Polk Mus., Tampa Mus., Sichaun Fine Art Inst., Mickelson Gallery, Harmon Gallery, Mus. Art U. Ariz., 1988, U. Del., Newark, 1988 Mid Am. Biennial, Owensboro Mus. Art, VCCA Exhbn. Mcpl. Gallery, Regensburg, Federal Republic of Germany, 1989, Erie (Pa.) Art Mus., 1990, 1990 twenty year survey Palmer Mus., Pa. State U., Univ. Park, Payne Gallery Moravian Coll., Bethlehem, Pa., 1991, Everhart Mus., Scranton, Pa., 1991, U. Del. Biennial, Phila. Watercolor Soc., Noyes Mus., N.J., 1992, Erie (Pa.) Mus., 1991, Mus. Fine Arts, Hanoi, 1991, Spanish Embassy, Madrid, 1992, Anita Shapolsky Gallery, N.Y., 1990, American Women's Artists, Foster Harman Gallery Sarasota, Fla., 1993, Humphrey Gallery, N.Y., 1992, Anita Shapolsky Gallery, N.Y., 1993, Fla. Printmakers, Miami, 1993, Fla. Artists Ringling Mus., 1994. Recipient award Silvermine Guild Conn. Appalachian Corridors, Arena, 1976, Gold medal of honor Audubon Artists ann. competition, Whitehead award Boston Printmakers, 1985, Shellenberg award Artists Equity, 1985, award N.C. Print & Drawing, 1985, award Chautauqua Nat., 1985, Johnson & Johnson award 3rd Ann. Nat. Printmaking Council of N.J., 1985, Purchase award N.J. State Mus., 1987, Disting. Alumni award Pa. State U. Sch. Arts & Architecture, 1988, Ethel Klassen Meml. award Fla. Artists Group, 1992, Earl Horter award Phila. Water Color Club, 1992, Stella Drabkin Meml. award Color Print Soc.; Va. Ctr. for the Creative Arts fellow, 1983-84; Nat. Endowment Arts grantee. Mem. Soc. Am. Graphic Artists (v.p.), Nat. Assn. of Women Artists (Nat. Medal of Honor, Elizabeth Blake award). Home: 220 Morningside Dr Sarasota FL 34236

PUTZEL, CONSTANCE KELLNER, lawyer; b. Balt., Sept. 5, 1922; d. William Stummer and Corinne (Strauss) Kellner; m. William L. Putzel, Aug. 28, 1945; 1 son, Arthur William. A.B., Goucher Coll., 1942; LL.B., U. Md., 1945, J.D., 1969. Bar: Md. 1945. Social worker Balt. Dept. Pub. Welfare, 1945-46; atty. New Amsterdam Casualty Co., Balt., 1947; staff atty. Legal Aid Bur., Balt., 1947-49; mem. Putzel & Putzel, P.A., Balt., 1950-89; pres. Constance K. Putzel, P.A., 1989—; instr. U. Balt. Sch. Law, 1975-77, Goucher Coll., 1976-77; chmn. character com. Ct. Appeals for 3d Cir., 1976—. Author: Divorce Organization System, 1984, 3d edit., 1993, Representing the Older Client in Divorce, 1992. Mem. Md. Com. on Status of Women, 1972-76; mem. Com. to Implement ERA, 1973-76; Pres. U. Md. Law Alumni Assn., 1978; bd. dirs. Legal Aid Bur., 1951-52, 71-73. Fellow Am. Acad. Matrimonial Lawyers, Internat. Acad. Matrimonial Lawyers; mem. ABA, Md. Bar Assn. (bd. govs. 1972-73, chmn. family law sect. 1978-79). Home: 8207 Spring Bottom Way Baltimore MD 21208-1859 Office: 29 W Susquehanna Ave Baltimore MD 21204-5201

PYLES, CAROL DELONG, dean, consultant, educator; b. Oil City, Pa., Apr. 6, 1948; d. William J. and Doris (Gresh) DeLong; m. Richard Pyles, Mar. 26, 1980; 1 child, Whitney Dawn. BS, Alderson-Broaddus Coll., Philippi, W.Va., 1966-70; MS in Nursing, Tex. Woman's U., 1982-85; MA, W. Va. U., 1972-73, EdD, 1974-80. RN, W.Va., Tex., Fla.; cert. health edn. specialist; lic. profl. counselor, Tex., Okla.; nat. cert. counselor. Instr. nursing Fairmont (W.Va.) State Coll., 1971-73, asst. prof. nursing edn., 1973-76, asst. dean Com. Coll., 1976-78, prof. nursing, chmn. divsn. health careers, 1978-81; cons., adj. faculty Salem Coll., Clarksburg, W.Va., 1978-81; officer Allied Health Houston Com. Coll. System, 1981-83, chmn. divsn. sales, mktg. & mgmt., 1983-85; dean Coll. Spl. Arts & Scis., prof. health edn. adminstrn. Cen. State U., Edmond, Okla., 1985-87; dean Coll. of Health, Phys. Edn. & Recreation Ea. Ill. U., Charleston, 1987-91, prof. health studies, 1987-91; dean, prof. allied health techs. Miami-Dade (Fla.) C.C., 1991—; bd. dirs. Dade County Area Health Edn. Ctr., Inc.; treas. bd. dirs. Nat. Network for Health Career Programs in Two Yr. Colls.; pres. cons. seminar devel., P & P Assoc., Inc., Houston; coun. pvt. practice for marriage, life crises, behavior & image problems. Author: articles for Issues in Higher Edn. Mem. South Fla. Health Planning Coun., Indigent Health Care Task Force, Met. Dade County, Fla., Dade County Area Health Edn. Ctr., Inc.; chmn. Indsl. Commn., Charleston (Ill.) Recreation Ctr., 1989; bd. dirs. ARC, East Coles County chpt., Reg. United Way, Coalition Against Domestic Violence, Am. Cancer Soc. Named Personality of Am. 1986, Outstanding Young Leader in Allied Health, 1984, Most Outstanding Young Women of Am., 1983; recipient Svc. award Am. Cancer Soc., 1984. Mem. Am. Coun. Edn., Nat. Identification Program, Am. Cancer Soc., Am. Assn. Coll. for Tchrs. Edn. Inst. Rep., Assn. Schs. Allied Health Professions, Fla. Assn. Community Colls., Alliance of 100 (Fla. Hosp. Assn.), Rotary Internat., Sigma Theta Tau. Office: Miami Dade Community Coll Med Ctr Campus 950 NW 20th Med Ctr Miami FL 33127-4693

PYLES, SUSAN KAY, marketing executive; b. Mt. Clemens, Mich., Apr. 29, 1954; d. Paul James Pyles and Charlotte Ettalene Snowden. BA cum laude, U. South Fla., 1976. Copywriter Denton & French, Tampa, Fla., 1977-79, account exec., 1979-81; account rep. J. Walter Thompson, Atlanta, 1981-82; account exec. Liller Neal, Atlanta, 1982-83; account exec. The Bloom Agy., Dallas, 1983-85, sr. account exec., 1985-86, v.p., account supr., 1986-89; sales and mktg. dir. Sta. KSPN-FM, Aspen, Colo., 1989-91, World Wide Ski Corp., Aspen, 1991-93; owner Susan Pyles Mktg., 1993—. Mem. Women's Forum, Aspen. Mem. Phi Kappa Phi. Home: PO Box 8264 Aspen CO 81612-8264 Office: PO Box 8264 Aspen CO 81612-8264

PYM, ANNE LOUISE, speech communication educator; b. Fairbanks, Alaska, Apr. 3, 1945; d. Elwyn Alexander and Caroline Lenora (Benner) Pym; m. Robert Martin Makus, Dec. 12, 1970 (div. Oct. 1991); 1 child, Elijah Robert. BA, U. Wash., 1968, MA, 1970; PhD, Pa. State U., 1987. Tchr. English, speech and debate Mountlake Terrace (Wash.) High Sch., 1968-69; instr., debate coach Green River C.C., Auburn, Wash., 1970-71; dir. childcare program Neighborhood House, Seattle, 1970-73; teaching asst. Pa. State U., University Park, Pa., 1983-87; asst. prof. dept. speech comm. Calif. State U., Hayward, 1987-92, assoc. prof., 1992—, dir. Ctr. for Hermeneutics and Postmodern Thought, 1971-94; co-chmn. Hayward Rhetorical Criticism Conf., 1993—. Contbr. articles to profl. jours. Mem. Hayward Growth Mgmt. Task Force, 1992-93. Recipient meritorious performance award Calif. State U., 1989; Sparks humanities fellow Pa. State U., 1985-86; rsch. scholar and grant Calif. State U., 1992. Mem. Speech Comm. Assn., Rhetoric Soc. Am., Internat. Soc. for History Rhetoric, Western Speech Commn. Assn., Western Speech Assn. (chmn. freedom of speech div. 1989-90, rhetoric and pub. address div. 1992-93). Office: Calif State U Dept Speech Comm Hayward CA 94542

PYTEL, JEANNE MARIE, interior designer; b. Albany, Ga., Aug. 9, 1955; d. Stanley and Eva-Clare (Corcoran) P. Student, Wash. State U., 1974-76; BA in Fine Arts, U. Wash., 1981; BA in Interior Design, Western Wash. U., 1982. Qualified interior designer. Intern in interior designing Zervas Taysi & Assocs., Bellingham, Wash., 1982; archtl. drafter, space planner Drafting Cons., Bellingham, Wash., 1982-85; interior designer Am. Internat. Design Group, Seattle, 1985-86, Facs for Offices, San Francisco, 1987-89; interior designer, cons. Lhe & Assocs., Orinda, Calif., 1989; interior designer Hemmeter Design group, Honolulu, 1989; interior designer, project coord. Bank of Hawaii, Honolulu, 1989—. Vol. space planner Am. Heart Assn., Honolulu, 1993. Mem. Am. Soc. Interior Designers. Home: 1088 Bishop St Ste 1410 Honolulu HI 96813-3119

QUADER, PATRICIA ANN, elementary education educator; b. Pitts., Sept. 9, 1941; d. Andrew and Julia (Gutilla) Supira; m. Walter Anthony Quader, Jan. 15, 1966. BA, Carlow Coll., 1963; MEd, U. Pitts., 1967. Cert. elem. tchr., supt., Pa. Tchr. Diocese of Pitts., 1963-64; tutor Pitts. Tchrs. Tutoring Svc., 1964-65; intern tchr. Burrell Sch. Dist., Lower Burrell, Pa., 1966; tchr. Kiski Area Sch. Dist., Vandergrift, Pa., 1966-91; computer, libr. skills tchr. Vandergrift Elem. Sch., 1991—; instr. Pa. State U., New Kensington, 1970-72; in-svc. instr. in computer literacy Kiski Area Sch. Dist., 1985-91, edited K-3 computer skills curriculum. Co-author: 4th and 5th grade computer literacy curricula for Kiski Sch. Dist.; editor Kiski Area K-6 Computer Skills Curriculum, 1991—. Chmn. Bell-Avon PTA, Salina, Pa., 1988-91. Recipient scholarship Carlow Coll., 1959. Mem. NEA, ASCD, Pa. State Edn. Assn., Kiski Area Edn. Assn., Phi Delta Kappa. Democrat. Roman Catholic. Office: Vandergrift Elem Sch 420 Franklin Ave Vandergrift PA 15690-1311

QUADHAMER, BETTEE COLLEEN, oncological nurse, educator; b. Kearney, Nebr., Sept. 22, 1953; d. Alvin Lynn and Marjorie Bertha (Bishop) Burchell; m. Steven R. Quadhamer, Feb. 26, 1972; children: Chad Lynn, Lindsay Leigh, Colt Thomas. Diploma, St. Francis Sch. of Nursing, 1976; BS in Biology, U. of Nebr., Kearney, 1976; MSN, Bishop Clarkson Coll., 1992. Charge nurse obstetrics Good Samaritan Hosp., Kearney, Nebr., 1976-78; instr. nursing Cen. C.C., Kearney, Nebr., 1978—; cons. health Zion Luth. Sch., Kearney, 1982-89; mem. Oncology Workshop Planning Com., 1992—; adv. bd. mem., sec. St. Lukes Good Samaritan Village, 1993—. Counselor health merit badge Boy Scouts Am., Kearney, 1983-90, dep. leader, 1980-82, mem. scout com., 1983-90; mem., sec. ch. bd. dirs. 1st Christian Ch., Minden, Nebr., 1987-90, 92—, deacon, 1980-94, elder 1995—; sec., v.p., pres. Kearney Swim Assn., 1984-91. Mem. ANA, Nebr. Nurses Assn., Oncology Nursing Soc. Office: Cen Community Coll 512 W 11th St Kearney NE 68847-7336

QUAIFE, MARJORIE CLIFT, nursing educator; b. Syracuse, N.Y., Aug. 21. Diploma in Nursing with honors, Auburn Meml. Hosp; BS, Columbia U., 1962, MA, 1978. Cert. orthopaedic nurse; cert. in nursing continuing edn. and staff devel.; BLS instr. Staff instr. Columbia Presbyn. Hosp., N.Y.C. Contbr. articles to numerous profl. publs. Mem. ANA, N.Y. State Nurses Assn., Nat. Assn. Orthopaedic Nurses, Nat. Assn. Nursing Staff Devel., Sigma Theta Tau.

QUALLIOTINE, ZENOVIA JOY, critical care nurse, educator; b. N.Y.C., Feb. 21, 1953; d. Henry and Yolanda (Gastaldo) Arzt; m. Richard Faust Qualliotine, Oct. 7, 1984; 1 child, Rebecca Amy Todarello. AAS, Suffolk Community Coll., Selden, N.Y., 1980; BSN, Adelphi U., 1982; MPA, C.W. Post Coll., 1989; MSN, SUNY, Stony Brook, 1994. Cert. adult health nurse practitioner; cert. PNP; cert. PALS instr., ACLS instr., CEN, CCRN. Med./surg. float nurse Southside Hosp., Bay Shore, N.Y., 1978-80, ICU staff nurse, 1980-84, staff nurse CCU, 1984-86, quality assurance coord., 1987—, critical care educator, 1978—; com. mem. Hospice of the South Shore, Bay Shore, 1988-92. Contbr. articles to profl. jours. Mem. Am. Heart Assn., Right to Life. Mem. AACN, ANA, N.Y. State Nurse Practitioners Assn., Am. Assn. Nurse Practitioners, Nat. League for Nursing, Emergency Nurse Assn., Nat. Assn. Pediat. Nurse Practitioners. Home: 30 Duval St East Islip NY 11730-2309

QUALLS, ROXANNE, mayor of Cincinnati. Former exec. dir. Women Helping Women; former dir. No. Ky. Rape Crisis Ctr.; former dir. Cin. office Ohio Citizen Action; councilwoman City of Cin., 1991-93, mayor, 1993—; former chairperson Cin. City Council's Intergovtl. Affairs and Environment Com.; former vice chairperson Community Devel., Housing and Zoning Com.; 2d v.p. OKI Regional Coun. Govts.; mem. Gov.'s Commn. on Storage and Use of Toxic and Hazardous Materials, Solid Waste Adv. Com. of State of Ohio, Gov.'s Waste Minimization Task Force; former chair bd. commrs. Cin. Met. Housing Authority; bd. dirs. Shuttlesworth Housing Found. Hon. chair Friends of Women's Studies; mem. Jr. League Adv. Coun. Recipient Woman of Distinction award Girl Scouts U.S., 1992, Woman of Distinction award Soroptomists, 1993, Outstanding Achievement award Cin. Woman's Polit. Caucus, 1993. Office: City Hall 801 Plum St Rm 150 Cincinnati OH 45202*

QUALLS, SOPHRONIA ANITA, elementary school educator; b. Enfield, N.C., Dec. 31, 1955; d. Waldo and Olympia (Solomon) Q.; m. Charles Wayne Foster, Sept. 30, 1989. BA, N.C. Ctrl. U., 1978. Cert. tchr., N.C. Tchr. Orange County Schs., Hillsborough, N.C., 1978-92; Kindergarten tchr. Cobb County (Ga.) Schs., Smyrna, 1992—. Dem. judge Durham (N.C.) County Bd. Election; active Cobb-Marietta Jr. League. Mem. NEA, Nat. Trust for Hist. Preservation, Nat. Coun. Negro Women, N.C. Mus. History, N.C. Ctrl. U. Alumni Assn., Delta Sigma Theta. Home: 3203 Whiteoak Circle Smyrna GA 30082-3363

QUARTERMAN, CYNTHIA LOUISE, lawyer; b. Savannah, Ga., Apr. 6, 1961; d. Rudolph V. and Bernice (Colvin) Q.; m. Pantelis Michalopoulos, Nov. 2, 1993. BS, Northwestern U., 1983; JD, Columbia U., 1987. Atty. Benson & McKay, Kansas City, 1987-88, Steptoe & Johnson, Washington, 1989-93; dep. dir. Minerals Mgmt. Svc., Dept. Interior, Washington, 1993—. Mem. ABA (vice chair programs litigation sect. 1993-94). Home: 1337 21st St NW Washington DC 20036 Office: Dept Interior 1849 C St NW Washington DC 20421

QUARTON, JEAN ELSA RULF, psychologist, sexologist, hypnotherapist; b. Hartford, Conn., Mar. 29, 1942; d. Walter Otto and Elsa Margareta (Blume) Rulf; m. David T. Quarton, Aug. 25, 1973 (div.); m. Conrad L. Bergendoff, Feb. 9, 1980. BFA, R.I. Sch. Design, 1964; MA in Home Econs., U. Iowa, 1968, PhD, 1974. Lic. psychologist, Ill.; cert. advanced clin. hypnotherapist Staff psychologist Riverside Retreat, 1974-76; pvt. practice clin. psychology, Rock Island, Ill., 1976-81; clin. cons. to Quad-cities Indsl. Employee Assistance Programs, Internat. Harvester, 3M, John Deere, J.I. Case, Rock Island arsenal, Army C.E., 1977-81; pvt. practice clin. psychology, LaGrange Park, Ill., 1982—; cons. Quad-Cities Alcoholism Info. Ctrs., 1977-80, Davenport (Iowa) Sch. System, 1977-78; staff psychologist ACP, Chgo., 1982-84; pres. Accredited Affiliated Psychologists, P.C.; clin. cons. Gen. Motors, Reuben Donnelley, Continental Bank, AT&T, United Airlines, McDonald's; adj. prof. psychology Augustana Coll., Rock Island, 1977; mgr. Chgo. Psychol. Assn. Telephone Answering Svc., 1985-92. Mem. Quad-cities Career Women's Network, 1978-81, keynote speaker, 1978; lectr. in field. Spl. Rsch. asst. U. Iowa, 1970-73. Fellow Am. Bd. Sexology (supr. clin. sex. therapists 1992); mem. Rock Island Psychol. Assn. (sec. 1980-81), Chgo. Psychol. Assn. (chmn. newsletter com. 1982-83, editor newsletter 1982-83, sec. 1983-85, pres. 1986-87, chmn. program com. 1985-86), NOW, Bus. Networking Soc. (bd. dirs. Chgo. 1983—). Lutheran. Club: Bus. and Profl. Women's (chmn. pub. rels. 1983-84, named Woman of Achievement 1983), Movers and Shakers in Feminist Thought and Action (co-chair, chmn. publicity midwest regional hypnosis conv. 1992). Contbr. articles to profl. jours. Home and Office: 12 St Mary's Pl Wilmington NC 28403-1144

QUASIUS, CHIYOKO TANINARI, accountant; b. Hiroshima, Japan, Aug. 12, 1948; came to U.S., 1977; d. Isao and Chidori (Yamasaki) Taninari; m. Robert Thomas Quasius, July 22, 1957; 1 child, Marie Elizabeth. Assoc. Sci., South Ga. Coll., 1978; BSBA, Christopher Newport Coll., 1981; MBA, Old Dominion U., 1985. CPA, N.Y. Tour guide for non-Japanese Japan Travel Bur., Hiroshima, 1969-74; project mgr.'s sec. Kaiser Engring., Hiroshima, 1974; freelance interpreter Hiroshima, 1974-76; asst. to project mgr. Shipping Mgmt. S.A.M., Hiroshima, 1976-77; sr. acct. Peat Marwick Main & Co., N.Y.C., 1987-90; tax cons. Price-Waterhouse, N.Y.C., 1990-92, Union, N.J., 1993—. Translator: Hiroshi Oshima Biography. 1st v.p. Denbigh Lioness Club, Newport News, Va., 1986-87. Japan Soc. scholar U. New Orleans, 1979; Univ. fellow Old Dominion U., 1984. Home: 1388 Omara Dr Union NJ 07083-5211

QUAYLE, MARILYN TUCKER, lawyer, wife of former vice president of U.S.; b. 1949; d. Warren and Mary Alice Tucker; m. J. Danforth Quayle, Nov. 18, 1972; children: Tucker, Benjamin, Corinne. BA in Polit. Sci., Purdue U., 1971; JD, Ind. U., 1974. Pvt. practice atty. Huntington, Ind., 1974-77; ptnr. Krieg, DeVault, Alexander & Capehart, Indpls., 1993—. Author: (with Nancy T. Northcott) Embrace the Serpent, 1992. Office: Krieg DeVault Alexander & Capehart 1 Indiana Sq Ste 2800 Indianapolis IN 46204-2017

QUEEN, EVANGELINE PALMER, private school educator, administrator, psychologist; b. S.C., May 15, 1905; d. Laurence Palmer and Daisy Dene (Nix) White; m. Edward Jerome Queen, Feb. 26, 1942; 1 child, Evangeline Marie. AB, Howard U., 1928; MA, Columbia U., 1933; PhD, NYU, 1951. Tchr. elem., jr. and sr. high D.C. Pub. Schs., Washington, 1927-39, rsch. asst. and asst. to chief examiner, 1939-49, asst. prin., 1949-64; founder, owner, dir., tchr. Avalon Montessori Sch., Washington, 1962—; assoc. prof. psychology D.C. Tchrs. Coll., Washington, 1972-75; tutor The Kingsbury Ctr., Washington, 1991—. Mem. St. Anthony Ch., Washington, 1952—, parish coun. rep. Mem. APA (life), AARP, N.Am. Montessori Tchrs. Assn., D.C. Psychol. Assn., Assn. Montessori Internat., Am. Montessori Soc. (life), Nat. Assn. Secondary Sch. Prins., D.C. Assn. Secondary Sch. Prins., Montessori Tchrs. Assn., Washington Montessori Inst. Tchr. Network, Nat. Ret. Tchrs. Assn. (Golden Age mem.), Delta Pi Epsilon (charter), St. Aiden Sch. (charter). Democrat. Roman Catholic. Home: 1424 Girard St NE Washington DC 20017 Office: Avalon Montessori Sch 2814 Franklin St NE Washington DC 20018

QUEEN, EVELYN E. CRAWFORD, judge, law educator; b. Albany, N.Y., Apr. 6, 1945; d. Iris (Jackson) Crawford; m. Charles A. Queen, Mar. 6, 1971; children: Angela, George. BS, Howard U., 1968, JD, 1975. Bar: N.Y. 1976, U.S. Dist. Ct. (D.C. dist.) 1978, U.S. Ct. Appeals (D.C. cir.) 1977, U.S. Supreme Ct. 1980. Park ranger Nat. Park Svc., Washington, 1968-69; pers. specialist NIH, Bethesda, Md., 1969-75; staff atty. Met. Life Ins. Co., N.Y.C., 1975-76; atty. advisor Maritime Adminstrn.-U.S., Washington, 1976-78; att. U.S. atty.-D.C. Justice Dept., Washington, 1978-81; hearing commr. D.C. Superior Ct., Washington, 1981-86, judge, 1986—. Recipient Trifoil award Hudson Valley Girl Scout Coun., Albany, 1988, Spl. Achievement awards HEW, 1975, certs. and plaques of appreciation. Mem. ABA, Nat. Bar Assn., Nat. Assn. Women Judges, Washington Bar Assn. Office: DC Superior Ct 500 Indiana Ave NW Washington DC 20001

QUELER, EVE, conductor; b. N.Y.C.. Student, Mannes Coll. Music, CCNY. Music staff, N.Y.C. Opera, 1958-70, assoc. condr., Ft. Wayne (Ind.) Philharm., 1970-71, founder, music dir., Opera Orch., N.Y., 1968, condr. Lake George Opera Festival, Glen Falls, N.Y., 1971-72, Oberlin (Ohio) Music Festival, 1972, Romantic Festival, Indpls., 1972, Mostly Mozart Festival, Lincoln Center, 1972, New Philharmonia, London, 1974, Teatro Liceu, Barcelona, 1974, 77, San Antonio Symphony, 1975, guest condr., Paris Radio Orch., 1972, P.R. Symphony Orch., 1975, 77, Mich. Chamber Orch., 1975, Phila. Orch., 1976, Montreal Symphony, 1977, Cleve. Orch., 1977 (Recipient Martha Baird Rockefeller Fund for Music award 1968, named Musician of Month, Mus. Am. Mag. 1972), N.Y.C. Opera, 1978, Opera Las Palmas, 1978, Opera de Nice, 1979, Nat. Theatre of Prague, 1980, Opera Caracas, Venezuela, 1981, San Diego Opera, 1984, Australian Opera, Sydney, 1985, Kirov Opera, St. Petersburg, Russia, 1993, Hamburg Opera, Germany, 1994; recording CBS Masterworks, 1974, 76, Hungaroton Records, 1982-85. Office: care Robert J Lombardo 61 5th Ave New York NY 10003-4304 also: Opera Orch NY 239 W 72nd St # 2R New York NY 10023-2734*

QUENNEVILLE, KATHLEEN, lawyer; b. Mt. Clemens, Mich., July 31, 1953; d. Marcel J. and Patricia (Armstrong) Q.; BA, Mich. State U., 1975; JD, Golden Gate U., 1979. Bar: Calif. 1980. Atty. Wells Fargo Bank, San Francisco, 1980-81; staff counsel Calif. State Banking Dept., San Francisco, 1981-83; assoc. Manatt, Phelps, Rothenburg & Tunney, Los Angeles, 1983-84; v.p., assoc. gen. counsel Bank of Calif., San Francisco, 1984—. Asst treas. AIDS Legal Referral Panel of the San Francisco Bay Area, 1986-92. Mem. Calif. State Bar Assn. (bus. law sect. corp. law depts. com. 1988-90), Calif. Bankers Assn. (chair regulatory compliance com.). Office: Bank of Calif 400 California St San Francisco CA 94104-1302

QUERBES, BETTY-LANE SHIPP, interior designer, real estate agent; b. Mayersville, Miss.; d. Byron Cadmus and MaryLucille (Lane) Shipp; m. Andrew C. Querbes Jr., Dec. 21, 1950; children: Renee Lane, Andrew IV, Maura Colette. Student, Centenary Coll., 1949-51, La. State U., Shreveport, 1972-74. Designer, salesperson Dunn Furniture Co., Inc., Shreveport, La., 1976; interior designer, buyer Dunn Furniture Co., Inc., 1977-82, advertising specialist, 1978-82; columnist, feature writer The Times, Shreveport, 1974-87; co-owner, designer Prothro-Querbes Interior Design, Shreveport, 1982—; real estate salesperson, Andrew Querbes, Jr., Inc., Shreveport, 1975—. Mem. orgnl. com. Live Oak Retirement Ctr., Shreveport; active lay resources task force First Meth. Ch. of Shreveport, 1989—, chair lay resources and leadership devel., 1991-92; sec. La. chpt. Am. Lung Assn., 1987-90, v.p., 1990-93, pres., 1993—; mem. Commn. for Bi-Centennial of Constn. of U.S., 1987-91; chmn. Mayor's Com. to Fight Veneral Disease, Shreveport; pub. rels. specialist Shreveport Mental Health Assn.; v.p. Caddo Bossier Day Care Assn.; treas. Jr. League Shreveport, pres. 1971-72; acquisitions chmn. Spring Street Mus., 1988-90, chmn. bd. dirs., 1990-94. Mem. Am. Soc. Interior Designers (v.p. No. La. assn. 1991-92, pres.-elect 1992—), DAR (pelican chpt.), Nat. Soc. Colonial Dames in Am. (sec. Shreveport com. 1987-90, co-chair Shreveport com. 1994—), Shreveport Med. Soc. (tobacco com.), Demoiselle Club Shreveport (past sec., chmn.), Cotillion Cub Shreveport (gen. chmn. 1977), Chi Omega Alumnae (past pres.). Democrat. Methodist. Home: 321 Corinne Cir Shreveport LA 71106-6003 Office: Prothro Querbes 7035 Sand Beach Blvd Shreveport LA 71105-4929

QUESTEL, MAE, actress; b. Bronx, N.Y., Sept. 13, 1908; d. Simon and Frieda (Glauberman) Q.; m. Leo Balkin, Dec. 22, 1930 (dec.); children: Robert (dec.), Richard; m. Jack E. Shelby, Nov. 19, 1970. Student in drama, J.G. Geiger, N.Y.C., 1916-24; scholar, Theatre Guild, N.Y.C., 1923, Columbia U., 1949, Theatre Wing, 1951. Appeared in vaudeville at, Palace Theatre, 1930, on RKO theater circuit, 1931-38; radio shows include Betty Boops Frolics, NBC, 1932; cartoon voices Betty Boop, 1931—, Olive Oyl, 1933—, Mr. Bugs Goes to Town, 1934, Little Audrey, 1946; TV cartoon Winky Dink and You, 1956-60, Popeye (as Olive Oyl), 1981; stage appearances include Dr. Social, 1948, A Majority of One, 1959-61, Come Blow Your Horn, 1963, Enter Laughing, 1963, Bajour, 1964, The Warm Peninsula, 1966, Walk Like A Lion, 1969, Barrel Full of Pennies, 1970, Where Have You Been, Billy Boy, 1969, Betty Boop—60 Yrs., N.Y.C., 1990, Betty Boop (Olive Oyl), U. Nebr., Lincoln, 1990; appeared: films A Majority of One, 1961, It's Only Money, 1962, Funny Girl, 1967, Move, 1969, Zelig, 1983, Hot Resorts, 1984, Who Framed Roger Rabbit?, 1988, New York Stories: A Trilogy, 1988-89, Christmas Vacation, 1989; TV spokeswoman for Scott Paper Co. as Aunt Bluebell films, 1971-78; other commls. include Playtex, 1970-72, Romilar, 1970-72, Folger's Coffee, 1970-72, Speidel Watch Bands, 1980, S.O.S, 1981, Parker Bros. video game Popeye, 1983-84; soap opera Somerset, 1976-77, All My Children, 1983; other TV appearances include Good Morning America, 1980, Good Day Show, 1980, Picture Pages, 1981, Entertainment Tonight, Joan Rivers and Her Friends; also numerous recs. including Good Ship Lollipop; (Troupers award for outstanding contbn. to entertainment 1979, Annie award Internat. Animated Film Soc. 1979). Named Living Legend NYU Sch. Social Work, 1979. Mem. Screen Actors Guild, AFTRA, Actors Equity Assn., Nat. Acad. TV Arts and Scis. (award 1978), Hadassah. Clubs: Troupers (award 1963), Variety. Home: 27 E 65th St Apt 7C New York NY 10021-6556

QUICK, LESLIE VOOGD, psychologist; b. Passaic, N.J., July 23, 1962; d. Clinton Allen and Anne (Sparano) Voogd; m. Hunter Cavin Quick, Mar. 5, 1994. BBA, U. Miami, 1983; MS, Vanderbilt U., 1988. Lic. psychol. assoc. Commodity broker J.C. Bradford & Co., Nashville, 1984-86; psychologist I Specialized Youth Svcs., Charlotte, N.C., 1988-91; psychologist II Dept. Corrections, State of N.C., Charlotte, 1991—; mem. crisis assessment and referral svc. Cedar Springs Hosp., Pineville, N.C., 1990-92; cons. St. Marks, Inc., ICF-MR Adult Group Homes. Mem. Area Client Rights Com., Charlotte, 1992—; chmn. Substance Abuse Client Rights Com., Charlotte, 1993—; com. mem. Coun. for Children, Charlotte, 1991; mem. Mint Mus. of Art, Charlotte, Humane Soc.; mem. disaster assistance ARC. Mem. APA, N.C. Addiction Profls., N.C. Psychol. Assn. Home: 3900 Barclay Downs Rd Charlotte NC 28209

QUIGG, JEAN, principal. Prin. Frostwood Elem. Sch., Houston. Recipient Elem. Sch. Recognition award U.S. Dept. Edn., 1989-90. Office: Frostwood Elem Sch 12214 Memorial Dr Houston TX 77024-6299

QUIGLEY, PATRICIA ANN, educator; b. N.Y.C., Mar. 27, 1955; d. Andrew Patrick and Margaret Mary (Hall) Q. BS, Mercy Coll., 1978; MS, Lehman Coll., 1982. Elem. tchr. St. Mary, Bronx; spl. edn. tchr. Cmty. Sch. 129, Bronx, 1984-87, Cmty. Sch. 44, Bronx, 1987-88, Intermediate Sch. 193, Bronx, 1988-89; resource tchr. I.S. 193, Bronx, 1989-94, staff developer, 1991-94; asst. prin. Intermediate Sch. 193, Dist. 12, Bronx, 1994—. Mem. United Fedn. Tchrs. Roman Catholic.

QUIGLEY, SUSAN LYNN BROKAW, nurse; b. Auburn, N.Y., Mar. 27, 1961; d. Thomas Allen and Elizabeth Edna (Ashbarry) Brokaw; m. Patrick Lawrence Quigley, July 19, 1980; children: Thomas Robert, Tyler Patrick. ADN, Cayuga County C.C., 1991; student, Nazareth Coll. RN, N.Y.; ACLS. Telemetry nurse Clifton Springs (N.Y.) Hosp., 1991-93; staff nurse ICU Newark (N.Y.) Wayne Community Hosp., 1993—.

QUIJADA, ANGÉLICA MARÍA, elementary educator; b. Tijuana, Mex., Mar. 22, 1963; came to U.S., 1967; d. Juan José and Paula (Magallanes) Q. AA, L.A. Harbor Coll., Wilmington, Calif., 1985; BA, Calif. State U., Carson, 1990, MA, 1993. Tchr. asst., tutor L.A. Harbor Coll., 1982-85; elem. tchr. asst., tutor Ambler Avenue Sch., Carson, 1985-90; bilingual elem. tchr. Hooper Avenue Sch., L.A., 1991—. counselor Pathfinders, Carson Seventh Day Adventist Ch., 1980; treas. Carson Spanish Seventh-Day Adventist Ch., 1994. Mem. TESOL, United Tchrs. L.A. (co-chairperson 1994). Democrat. Home: 320 E 181st St Carson CA 90746-1815

QUILTER, JOAN MARY, school system administrator; b. Waterbury, Conn., Jan. 12, 1928; d. Thomas George and Sally Ann (Sakocius) Q. BS in Math. Edn., Boston U., 1958; MA in Counseling, Fairfield U., 1960, CAS in Sch. Psychol. Examining, 1962; PhD in Child Devel./Sch. Psychol. Svcs., St. John's U., Jamaica, N.Y., 1978. Cert. sch. psychologist, counselor, math. tchr., adminstr., Conn. Elem. tchr. St. John Baptiste Sch., N.Y.C., 1955-56, St. Patrick Sch., Stoneham, Mass., 1956-59; math. tchr. Crosby High Sch., Waterbury, Conn., 1959-64; psychol. examiner Waterbury Pub. Schs., 1964-68, sch. psychologist, 1968-70; dir. student svcs. Region 15, Middlebury and Southbury, Conn., 1970—; adj. prof. Teikyo Post U., Waterbury, 1978-93, Sacred Heart U., Fairfield, 1987—. Mem. STS Program Rev. Com., Southbury, 1986-92; bd. dirs. Child Guidance Clinic of Greater Waterbury, 1986-93, sec., 1988-90, v.p., 1990-91, pres., 1991-92; bd. dirs. Family Svc. of Greater Waterbury, 1987—; mem. Commn. for People with Disabilities, Waterbury, 1987-93; early edn. adv. com. Teiyko Post U., 1987—; asst. chair edn. com. NEASC, Bridgeport, 1991, Weston, 1992, Lyman Meml., 1994; chair tchr. preparation program of colls. and univ. State Dept. Edn., 1990 & 92; mem. adv. com. St Joseph Coll., West Hartford, Conn., 1993. Mem. Am. Psychol. Assn., Am. Assn. Mental Retardation, Am. Assn. Sch. Adminstrs., Am. Assn. Counseling and Devel., Coun. Exceptional Children, Assn. Suprs. Curriculum Devel., Litchfield County Dirs. Assn. (pres. 1985-86), Conn. Assn. Pupil Pers. Adminstrs. (treas. 1984-86), AAUW (v.p. 1984-92), Quota Club (sec. Waterbury 1980-81, v.p. 1981-83, pres. 1983-85, treas. 1985-87, lt. gov. 5th dist. Quota Internat. 1986-87, gov. 1987-89, internat. chair of hearing and speech com., 1988-90), Am. Ednl. Rsch. Assn., Conn. Coun. Adminstrs. Spl. Edn., Nat. Assn. Sch. Psychologists, Nat. Assn. Pupil Svcs. Adminstrs., Delta Kappa Gamma (chair membership com. 1982-84). Democrat. Roman Catholic.

QUINDLEN, ANNA, journalist, author; b. Phila., July 8, 1953; d. Robert V. and Prudence Quindlen; m. Gerald Krovatin; children: Quin, Christopher, Maria. BA, Barnard Coll., 1974. Reporter New York Post, N.Y.C., 1974-77; gen. assignment, city hall reporter New York Times, N.Y.C., 1977-81, columnist About New York, 1981-83, dep. met. editor, 1983-85, columnist Life in the 30's syndicated, 1986-89, columnist Public and Private, 1990-94. Author: Living Out Loud, 1988, (novel) Object Lessons, 1991, The Tree That Came to Stay, 1992, Thinking Out Loud, 1993, One True Thing, 1994. Recipient Mike Berger award for Disting. Reporting, 1983, Pulitzer Prize for Commentary, 1992; named Woman of Yr., Glamour mag., 1991. *

QUINN, BARBARA ANNETTE, psychology educator; b. St. Joseph, Mo., Jan. 12, 1960; d. John Wesley and Joycelyn Adele (Pinnell) Dowdy; m. Daryl C. Quinn, Jan. 16, 1982; 1 child, Ryan Spencer. BA, U. Mo., 1981; MA, Wayne State U., 1987, PhD, 1989. Lectr. Wayne State U., Detroit, 1984-87; asst. prof. Madonna U., Livonia, Mich., 1990-93, chair psychology dept., assoc. prof., 1994—. Mem. United Campaign Com., Livonia, 1991. Grantee So. Bapt. Conv., 1987-89; grad. fellow Wayne State U., 1982-83, 85. Mem. APA, Am. Psychol. Soc., Midwestern Psychol. Assn., Soc. for Personality and Social Psychology, Am. Assn. Applied and Preventive Psychology, Soc. for Cmty. Rsch. and Action (student rep. 1982-89), Phi Beta Kappa, Phi Kappa Phi. Office: Madonna U 36600 Schoolcraft Rd Livonia MI 48150-1176

QUINN, ELIZABETH R., elementary education educator; b. Covina, Calif., Oct. 7, 1951; d. John Howard and Rosemary (Branine) Roberts; m. D. Whitney Quinn, July 18, 1980. BA, Ariz. State U., 1973; Marriage, Family and Child Counseling, Azuza Pacific U., 1980; BS, Calif. State U., Fullerton, 1993. Tchr. Saddleback Valley Unified Sch. Dist., Mission Viejo, Calif., 1976—, mentor tchr., 1992—; Cert. life standard elem. credential K-8, Calif. Named Tchr. of Yr. Kiwanis, Mission Viejo, 1992. Mem. Calif. Tchrs. Assn., Saddleback Valley Educators.

QUINN, JANE BRYANT, journalist, writer; b. Niagara Falls, N.Y., Feb. 5, 1939; d. Frank Leonard and Ada (Laurie) Bryant; m. David Conrad Quinn, June 10, 1967; children—Matthew Alexander, Justin Bryant. B.A. magna cum laude, Middlebury Coll., 1960. Assoc. editor Insiders Newsletter, N.Y.C., 1962-65, co-editor, 1966-67; sr. editor Cowles Book Co., N.Y.C., 1968; editor-in-chief Bus. Week Letter, N.Y.C., 1969-73, gen. mgr., 1973-74; syndicated financial columnist Washington Post Writers Group, 1974—; contbr. fin. column to Women's Day mag., 1974—; contbr. NBC News and Info. Service, 1976-77; bus. corr. WCBS-TV, N.Y.C., 1979, CBS-TV News, 1980-87, ABC-TV Home Show, 1991-93; contbg. editor Newsweek mag., 1978—. Author: Everyone's Money Book, 1979, 2d edit., 1980, Making the Most of Your Money, 1991, A Hole in the Market, 1994. Mem. Phi Beta Kappa. Office: Newsweek Inc 251 W 57th St New York NY 10019-1802

QUINN, JANITA SUE, city secretary; b. Breckenridge, Tex., Apr. 14, 1950; d. Doyle Dean and Peggy Joyce (Melton) Allen; m. John Lloyd Rippy, June 27, 1969 (div. Mar. 1976); children: Johna DeAnn, Jason Allen; m. Ervel Royce Quinn, Jan. 31, 1987; stepchildren: Amy Talitha, Jason Ervel. Student, Odessa (Tex.) Jr. Coll., 1968-70, U. Tex. of Permian Basin, Odessa, 1978-79, 85-86. New accts. clk. State Nat. Bank, Odessa, Tex., 1975-76; accts. receivable clk. Woolley Tool Corp., Odessa, Tex., 1976-78; data entry operator M-Bank, Odessa, Tex., 1978-79; asst. county treas. Ector County, Odessa, Tex., 1979-83, county treas., 1983-88; office mgr., co-owner Nat. Filter Svc., Inc., San Antonio, 1988-91; temporary employment Kelly Temporary Svcs., Abilene, Tex., 1991; sec. Pride Refining, Inc., Abilene, Tex., 1991-93; city sec. City of Eastland, Tex., 1993—. Mem., treas., bd. dirs. Family Outreach Svc. Taylor County; vol. tchr. Parenting for Parents and Adolescents; recorder, del. West Tex. Corridor II Com., Eastland and Dallas, 1993; county del. Taylor County dem. Party, Abilene, 1992; state del. Tex. Dem. Party, Dallas, 1991. Mem. Tex. Mcpl. Clks. Assn., County Treas. Alumni Assn. (recorder 1991-93), Rotary Internat. Democrat. Ch. of Christ. Office: City of Eastland 416 S Seaman St Eastland TX 76448-2750

QUINN, JOANNE R., public relations executive; b. N.Y., July 2, 1953. BA in Psychology, Brown U., 1974. Acct. exec., acct. supr., v.p. Edelman Pub. Rels. Worldwide, 1977-80, sr. v.p., 1980-92, dep. mgr., 1983—, creative cons., 1986-92, exec. v.p., gen. mgr. consumer divsn., 1992—. Office: Edelman PR Worldwide 1500 Broadway New York NY 10036*

QUINN, LOIS MARIE, health services administrator; b. Boston; d. Charles Edward and Grace Marie (Lowder) Seabrook; R.N., Boston City Hosp.; B.A., Glassboro State Coll., 1977; M.A., Central Mich. U., 1982; m. Richard Edward Quinn; children—Deborah Marie, Christopher Edward, Erin Elizabeth, Patrick Richard. Pediatric staff nurse Boston City Hosp.; staff nurse, coronary care nurse, supr., patient edn. coordinator, dir. nursing service Rancocas Valley Hosp., Willingboro, N.J., 1967-78; nursing mgmt. cons. Am. Medicorp., Bala Cynwyd, Pa., 1977-78; asst. adminstr. Washington Meml. Hosp., Turnersville, N.J., 1978-80; pres. Lois Quinn Assocs., Nursing Mgmt. Cons., Willingboro, N.J., 1980-83; mgr. nursing services Universal Health Services, Inc., King of Prussia, Pa., 1983-84, dir. mgmt. services, profl. standards, 1984-90, dir. profl. svcs. Am. Healthcare Mgmt., Inc. 1990-93; v.p. profl. affairs, Am. Healthcare Mgnt., Inc., 1993-94; sr. v.p. profl. affairs Primary Health Sys., L.P., 1994—. Cert. nursing adminstr. Mem. Amnesty Internat., Coop. Am., Bread for the World. Mem. Common Cause, Am. Nurses Assn., Pa. Nurses Assn., N.J. Nurses Assn. (coordinator So. N.J. nursing adminstrs. and educators 1975-77), Sigma Iota Epsilon. Roman Catholic. Developer of proprietary automated quality measurement and productivity systems; featured in newspaper articles and nat. publs. Address: 360 Old Forge Crossing Devon PA 19333

QUINN, MARY M., communications executive, marketing director; b. Bklyn., May 28, 1955; d. Raymond Leo and Catherine Mary (Martin) Quinn. BA in Journalism, L.I. U., 1976; MBA in Mktg., Fordham U., 1984; postgrad., U. London, summer 1975. Assoc. editor Modern Floor Coverings Mag., N.Y.C., 1976-77; community rels. asst. Rahway (N.J.) Hosp., 1977-79; asst. dir. pub. rels. Brookdale Hosp. Med. Ctr., Bklyn., Jan. 1979 to May 1979; sales promotion writer Marsh and McLennan Inc., N.Y.C., 1979-81; pub. rels. account exec. Ins. Info. Inst., N.Y.C., 1982-84; 2nd v.p., pub. rels. mgr. Chase Manhattan Bank, L.I., N.Y., 1984-87; pres. Prase Mktg., L.I., N.Y., 1987-92; v.p. corp. comm. Fleet Bank, Melville, N.Y., 1992—; adj. prof. mktg. Concordia Coll., Westchester, N.Y., 1992—. Recipient award for internat. understanding Rotary Found., Fed. Republic Germany, 1987, Gov.'s Vol. Svc. award, 1993; L.I. U. scholar, 1972-76, N.Y. State Regents scholar, 1972-76. Mem. NAFE, Pub. Rels. Soc. Am.

QUINN, SALLY, journalist; b. Savannah, Ga., July 1, 1941; d. William Wilson and Bette (Williams) Q.; m. Benjamin Crowninshield Bradlee, Oct. 20, 1978; 1 child, Josiah Quinn Crowninshield Bradlee. Grad., Smith Coll. Reporter, Washington Post, 1969-73, 74-80; co-anchorperson CBS Morning News, N.Y.C., 1973-74. Author: We're Going to Make You a Star, 1975, (novels) Regrets Only, 1986, Happy Endings, 1991. Address: 3014 N St NW Washington DC 20007

QUINN, TERRY ATKINSON, marketing professional; b. Pitts., Sept. 20, 1955; d. Loid Richard and Pattie Theresa (Royer) Atkinson; m. Harry Joseph Quinn, Aug. 8, 1981; children: Samantha, Christina, Catherine. BA in Comms. and English, U. No. Colo., 1977. Cert. tchr. English and Speech. Tchr. English and speech Deerfield (Kans.) High Sch., 1977-78; social hostess Grand Hotel, Mackinac Island, Mich., 1978; comm. tchr. Oxford (Wis.) Fed. Maximum Security Prison, 1978-79; personnel mgr. The Inn on Mackinac, Mackinac Island, Mich., 1979; sales/mktg. recruiter Mgmt. Recruiters, Milw., 1979-81; asst. mktg. mgr., promo specialist TSR Hobbies, Inc., Lake Geneva, Wis., 1981-84; mktg. specialist Quinn Studio, Lake Geneva, 1984-88; mktg. and promo cons. Lake Geneva, 1988—; 3rd ward alderwoman City of Lake Geneva, 1993—; speaker in field. Co-coord. Walworth County Citizens for Peace, Walworth County, Wis., 1985-87; leader Brownies/Girls Scouts U.S., 1992—. Mem. AAUW (past pres. Geneva Lakes Br. 1988-90, historian Wis. Div. 1990-91). Home and Office: 1203 Center St Lake Geneva WI 53147-1209

QUINN, YVONNE SUSAN, lawyer; b. Spring Valley, Ill., May 13, 1951; d. Robert Leslie and Shirley Eilene (Morse) Q.; m. Ronald S. Rolfe, Sept. 1, 1979. BA, U. Ill., 1973; JD, U. Mich., 1976, MA in Econs., 1977. Bar: N.Y., U.S. Dist. Ct. (ea. and so. dists.) N.Y., U.S. Ct. Appeals (2d, 3d, 4th, 10th and D.C. cirs.), U.S. Supreme Ct. Assoc. Cravath, Swaine & Moore, N.Y.C., 1977-80; assoc. Sullivan & Cromwell, N.Y.C., 1980-84, ptnr., 1984—. Mem. ABA, Assn. of Bar of City of N.Y., India House Club. Office: Sullivan & Cromwell 125 Broad St New York NY 10004*

QUINN-KERINS, CATHERINE, psychologist; b. Neptune, N.J., Mar. 12, 1951; d. James R. and Jane (Forman) Quinn; m. Daniel Kerins, Jan. 14, 1978; children: Katie, Amanda, Benjamin. BA magna cum laude, Fairleigh Dickinson U., 1973; postgrad., Hahneman Med. Coll., 1974-75; MEd, U. Del., 1975; PhD, U. Pa., 1983. Lic. psychologist, Pa. Treatment coord., psychologist St. Gabriel's Hall, Audubon, Pa., 1975-86; clin. psychologist InterPsych Assocs., King of Prussia, Pa., 1985-87; full-time ind. practice Audubon, 1987—; mem. allied health staff Phoenixville (Pa.) Hosp., 1990—; mem. part-time faculty dept. psychology Neuman Coll., Aston, Pa., 1977. V.p. Montessori Children's House of Valley Forge, Wayne, Pa., 1985-87. Mem. APA, Am. Assn. Anxiety Disorders, Obsessive Compulsive Found., Phi Omega Epsilon, Phi Zeta Kappa, Psi Chi. Home: 2018 Blackbird Cir Norristown PA 19403-1845 Office: 2605 Egypt Rd Norristown PA 19403-2317

QUINN-MUSGROVE, SANDRA LAVERN, political science educator; b. Grand Rapids, Mich., Oct. 30, 1935; d. Rex Earl and Lavern Emaline (Conner) Nowland; m. James Fenton Arbing, July 16, 1954 (div. 1966); m. C. John Quinn, Nov. 16, 1966 (div. 1986); children: Joan B., John J., Jane M., Julie T., Sandra M.; m. Freddy G. Musgrove, Oct. 24, 1986. BA, U. Las Vegas, 1975, MA, 1976; PhD, Claremont Grad. Sch., 1978. Interior decorator Montgomery Ward, Grand Rapids, 1964-66; mdse. specialist Montgomery Ward, N.Y.C., 1966-72; asst. community affairs dir. Sta. KORK-TV, Las Vegas, 1975-76; exec. officer Norman Kaye R.E. Inc., Las Vegas, 1976-78; dir. edn., writer Polit. Rsch., Dallas, 1978-80; prof., dept. chmn. San Jacinto Coll., Houston, 1980-88, dir., 1985—; prof. dept. chair Our Lady of Lake U., San Antonio, 1988—; mem. speaker's bur., 1980—; dir. Friendswood Indsl. Devel. Corp., Texas; ptnr. QUIMUS, Tri-County Analysts, Friendswood, 1984—. Co-author: America's Royalty: All the Presidents Children, 2d edit., 1995, How to Pass An Essay Exam, 1983, Texas Government: Its Moral Foundations, 1993, Auctions for Amateurs, 1993; (newspaper columns) On Education, 1984-92, Jus' Thinking 'bout, 1992—, How to Pass Objective Exams, 1991; contbr. articles to profl. jours. Program dir. Am. Bus. Women's Assn., Pearland, Tex., 1982-83; founder Friendswood Literary Forum, 1980; del. Rep. Nat. Conv., 1981; bd. dirs. Terra Genesis, Fort Sam Houston Comml. Dist. Commn. Recipient Outstanding Member award Multiple Sclerosis Assn., Las Vegas, 1977. Mem. AAUP (pres.), Southwestern Social Scis. Assn., Women in Polit. Sci., Southwest Humanities Assn., Southwest Polit. Sci. Assn.; Our Lady of the Lake Univ. Club (pres.). Roman Catholic. Home: 700 Waverly Ave San Antonio TX 78201-6138 Office: Our Lady of the Lake U 24th St San Antonio TX 78285

QUIÑONES, MARTHA IRENE, international business and marketing specialist; b. Bogota, Colombia, Sept. 18, 1952; came to U.S. 1967; m. Mark Karavolos. BS in Internat. Bus. and Mktg., NYU, 1987. Asst. trader Bunge Corp., N.Y.C., 1970-87; export import cons. Export Ease, Park Ridge, N.J., 1988—. Mem. NAFE, Active Core of Exec. (small bus. adminstrn.), World Trade Assn., Internat. Trade Roundtable (bd. dirs.), Tappan Zee Internat. Trade Assn. Office: Export Ease 58 Ormsay St Park Ridge NJ 07656-2205

QUIÑONES KEBER, ELOISE, art historian, educator; b. L.A.; d. Rudy Jr. and Margaret (Romero) Q. BA, Immaculate Heart Coll., 1966; MA, UCLA, 1967, Columbia U., 1979; PhD, Columbia U., 1984. Lectr. Columbia U., N.Y.C., 1984-86; prof. art history Baruch Coll. CUNY, 1986—. Author: Codex Telleriano Remensis: Ritual, Divination, and History in a Pictorial Aztec Manuscript, 1995 (Getty Grant Program Publ. Subvention award 1992); co-author: Art of Aztec Mexico: Treasures of Tenochtitlan, 1983; editor: Chipping Away on Earth: Studies in Prehispanic and Colonial Mexico in Honor of Arthur J.O. Anderson and Charles E. Dibble, 1994; co-editor: The Work of Bernardino de Sahagún, 1988, Mixteca Puebla: Discoveries and Research in Mesoamerican Archaeology and Art, 1994; contbr. articles to profl. jours. Mellon postdoctoral fellow Columbia U., 1984-86, fellow Ford Found./NRC, 1986-87, Am. Coun. of Learned Socs. fellow, 1987-88, 93-94, NEH fellow, 1991, 93-94; grantee Am. Philos. Soc., 1986. Mem. Coll. Art Assn., Assn. Latin Am. Art, Am. Soc. for Ethnohistory. Home: 600 W 115th St New York NY 10025-7701 Office: CUNY Baruch Coll Box E1020 17 Lexington Ave New York NY 10010

QUINTANA, MARAGARET ANN, financial analyst, banker; b. Marianna, Fla., June 21, 1952; d. John Amos and Ella-Margaret Estright (Callin) Dickenson; m. Enrique Quintana Jr., Aug. 25, 1973. AA with honors, Fla. Jr. Coll., Jacksonville, 1982, AS in Banking with honors, 1983; BBA in Acctg. cum laude, U. North Fla., 1985, MBA, 1986. CPA, Fla. Internal auditor Atlantic Nat. Bank, Jacksonville, Fla., 1985; auditor Coopers & Lybrand, Jacksonville, 1986-88; asst. contr. Fla. Physicians Ins. Co., Jacksonville, 1988-92; sr. auditor, tax acct. Grenadier, Appleby, Collins & Co., Jacksonville, 1992-93; fin. analyst Am. Nat. Bank, Jacksonville, 1993—. Mem. acctg. del. to Soviet Union, People to People Amb. Program, 1991; cashier chmn. Jacksonville Jazz Festival, 1992—; mem. adminstrv. coun. Spring Glen United Meth. Ch., Jacksonville, 1992—, chmn. worship com., 1992-93, chmn. children's ministry, 1993—. Recipient 5-Yr. Recognition cert. Am. Express Internat. Banking Corp., 1979, Outstanding Svc. award Alpha Sigma Pi, 1985. Mem. AICPA, Inst. Mgmt. Accts., Inst. Internal Auditors, Fla. Inst. CPAs (Grad. Study scholar 1985), U. North Fla. Alumni Assn. (v.p. 1989-90, Recognition award 1989), Jacksonville Rose Soc. (v.p., treas. 1991-94), Phi Theta Kappa (sec., pres. 1982-84, Recognition award 1983, 84, Most Disting. Alumni Mem. 1984, Honors Inst. scholar 1984, Hall of Honor 1984), Phi Kappa Phi. Home: 5224 Hoof Print Dr Jacksonville FL 32257 Office: Am Nat Bank 1551 Atlantic Blvd Jacksonville FL 32207

QUINTELA, ADRIA ELENA, lawyer; b. Guantanamo, Cuba, Mar. 15, 1967; came to U.S., 1974; d. Israel Francisco and Norma (Lopez) Rodriguez; m. Pablo A. Quintela, Dec. 23, 1989. BBA, U. Miami, 1988; JD, Northwestern U., Chgo., 1991. Bar: Fla. 1991. Assoc. atty. Valdes-Fauli, Miami, 1991-93, Krupnick, Campbell, et al, Ft. Lauderdale, Fla., 1993—. Mem. ABA, Am. Trial Lawyers Assn., Fla. Bar, Broward County Hispanic Bar Assn. (sec. 1993), Broward County Bar Assn., Broward County Trial Lawyers Assn. Office: Krupnick Campbell et al 700 SE 3rd Ave Ste 100 Fort Lauderdale FL 33316

QUIRING, PATTI LEE, search firm owner; b. Indpls.; d. Harold Woodrow and Flora Lee (Hoffman) Dulin; m. David Allen Niederhaus, June 1972; (div. May 1974); m. David Jonathon Quiring, Dec. 7, 1976; 1 child: Erin Ashley. AA, Ball State U., Muncie, 1972, BS, 1975; MBA, Ind. Wesleyan U., 1990. Profl. Sec. Summer employee P. R. Mallory and Co., Inc., Indpls., 1970, 1971; student asst. Ball State U., Muncie, Ind., 1970-72; adminstrv. asst. Ball Corp., Muncie, 1972-74; student asst. Ball State U., Muncie, 1975; adminstrv. asst. P. R. Mallory and Co., Inc., 1975-76; various mgmt. level positions Blue Cross and Blue Shield of Ind., Indpls., 1976-87; exec. recruiter Tech. Resource Group, Indpls., 1988-91; pres. Quiring Assocs., Inc., Indpls., 1991—; Co-facilitator Corporate Bd. Task Force, 1993—. Co-chair venture com. United Way, 1991-93, mem. adv. com. women's div., 1991—, bd. dirs., exec. com., 1993—, mem. goals and priorities com., 1993, agy. rels. cabinet vice-chairperson, 1993-94, chair, 1995—, campaign cluster co-chmn., 1994-95, campaign cabinet, 1995, northeast area team leader, 1995, vol. Pan Am. Games, Indpls., 1987; bd. dirs. alumni rels. Coll. Bus. Ball State U., Muncie, 1988—, mem. alumni coun., 1994—, Heritage Pl. Sr. Citizens Ctr., Indpls., 1988-90, Indpls. YWCA, 1988-90, Feathercove Homeowners Assn., 1990—; corp. capt. Humane Soc., 1990-91; mem. mktg. com. Children's Mus., 1992—, mem. bd. advisors, 1995—; active Equal Opportunity Adv. Bd., 1992—; mem. bd. dirs. Geist Harbors Property Owner's Assn., 1995—. Recipient Blue Cross award of Excellence, Indpls., 1985, City Ctr Vol. award, Indpls., 1985, Salute to Women of Achievement Individual award YWCA, 1993, Network of Women in Business Networker of Yr. award, 1993; named Blue Cross Bus. Women of Yr., Indpls. 1982, 86, Humane Soc. Outstanding Vol., Indpls., 1985. Mem. Ind. Assn. Pers. Svc. Bd., Network of Women in Bus. (pres. 1993), Cen. Ind. Pers. Assn., Ind. C. of C. (Ind. Small Bus. Coun. bd. 1994), Ind. Med. Group Mgmt. Assn., Nat. Assn. Pers. Svcs., Indpls. and Ind. C. of C. Home: 11033 Tenacious Dr Indianapolis IN 46236-9566

QUIRK, DONNA HAWKINS, financial analyst; b. Chgo., Sept. 29, 1955; d. Martin Francis and Monica Mae (Hesslau) Hawkins; m. John James Quirk, Dec. 5, 1981; children: Martin Patrick, Mary Kathleen, Colleen Monica. BS in Commerce, DePaul U., 1977, M.B.A., 1982. With Jewel Food Stores, Melrose Park, Ill., 1977—, acctg. mgr., 1980-85, fin. analyst, 1985—. V.p. St. Tarcissus Sch. Bd. Mem. Assn. M.B.A. Execs., Nat. Assn. Female Execs., Twice as Nice Mothers of Multiples, Beta Gamma Sigma, Delta Mu Delta. Roman Catholic. Home: 5046 N Mason Ave Chicago IL 60630-1947 Office: Jewel Food Stores 1955 W North Ave Melrose Park IL 60160-1101

QUIROZ, CAROLE ELIZABETH, critical care nurse; b. Passaic, N.J., Mar. 20, 1961; d. Masami Okada and Bette (Shizuko) Masuda; m. Richard Quiroz, Oct. 19, 1985; children: Richard Sean, Danielle Elizabeth. AAS, Fashion Inst. Tech., N.Y.C., 1980; BSN, Seton Hall U., 1985, MSN, 1994. ACLS. Staff nurse Overlook Hosp., Summit, N.J., 1985-86; ICU staff nurse Lenox Hill Hosp., N.Y.C., 1986-88; ICU-CCU per diem charge nurse Montclair (N.J.) Community Hosp., 1989-93; critical care per diem nurse Lenox Hill Hosp., N.Y.C., 1988-93; per diem nurse CPACU Morristown Meml. Hosp., $, 1992-93; nurse Critical Care Assocs., Montclair, N.J., 1990-93; adminstrv. supr. The Gen. Hosp. Ctr. at Passaic, Passaic, N.J., 1993-94; adj. prof. Seton Hall U., South Orange, N.J., 1994—; presenter in field. Recipient Nursing Rsch. award Jersey Shore Med. Ctr., 1992. Mem. AACN, N.J. State Nurses Assn., Sigma Theta Tau. Office: Seton Hall U S Orange Ave South Orange NJ 07079

QUISENBERRY, SHIRLEY SABIN, executive level association volunteer; b. Gillette, Wyo., May 12, 1928; d. Donald Roger and Velva Mae (Lewis) Sabin; m. Karl Spangler Quisenberry, Jan. 1, 1949; children: Keith Sabin, Nancy Quisenberry Litvack, David Karl. BA, U. Nebr., 1949. Pres. Houston chpt. UN Assn., 1986-88, pres. Tex. div., 1989-92; chair coun. chpt., div. pres. UN Assn. USA, N.Y.C., 1991-94, sec. bd. govs., 1993—; leadership corps cons. UN Assn. USA, N.Y.C., 1990—. Exec. dir. YWCA, Schenectady, N.Y., 1977; pres. Bd. Edn., Burnt Hills, N.Y., 1970-77; pres. LWV, Ridgefield, Conn., 1978-81. Mem. AAUW (pres. Schenectady br. 1970-71, leadership team cons. 1985-90, state bd. dirs., Named grant 1977, 85, 93). Home: 43 Shady Ridge Ln Asheville NC 28805

QUIST, JEANETTE FITZGERALD, television production educator, choreographer; b. Provo, Utah, July 4, 1948; d. Sherman Kirkham and Bula Janet (Anderson) Fitzgerald; m. G. Steven Quist; children: Ryan, Amy, Michelle, Jeremy. Student, U. Redlands, Calif., 1970; BA, Brigham Young U., 1971; postgrad., Calif. State U., Riverside, 1972, Calif. State U., San Bernardino, 1973. Host, co-producer children's show PBS Sta. KBYU-TV, Provo, 1968-69; buyer ready to wear J.C. Penney & Co., Redlands, 1969-71; tchr. spl. reading program Fontana (Calif.) Elem. Sch. Dist., 1971-73; owner, choreographer Jeanette Quist Creative Dance, Tri Cities, Wash., 1975-79; owner, tchr. Dance Studio, Gridley, Calif., 1979-81; producer, instr. Butte Coll., Oroville, Calif., 1986—; asst. producer Kate Knight Prodn. Co., Chico, Calif., 1987; video producer Gridley Sch. Dist., 1987-88. Prodr., editor promotional video Police Acad., 1986, commls. for Butte Coll., 1987—; prodr., dir. telecourse Interior Designer, 1988—; prodr., hostess TV talk shows Crossroads, 1988—, NVCA Today, BCTV Forum, 1991—; prodr. orientation video Butte Coll., 1989, 90, video series Intro to Telecommunications, video series on Recycling for Butte Environ. Coun., 1995, Early Alert video for Butte Coll., 1995; choreographer Kaleidoscope, 1988, South Pacific, 1989, Fantasticks, 1990, Amahl and the Night Visitors, 1990, An Evening of Song and Dance, Butte Coll., 1991, Kiss Me Kate, Butte Coll., 1992, Hello Dolly, Chico Stake, 1992; chmn. 3D Expo-Fine Arts Festival, 1991; prodr. 2 videos; choreographer Tumbleweeds, Butte Theatre, 1994. State judge Miss. Am. Contest, Provo, 1968; 1st v.p. Friends of Libr., Gridley, 1988; chmn. Regional Fine Arts Festival Tri Cities, 1978; v.p. Gridley High Sch. Parent Club, 1990; chmn. 3D Expo Fine Arts Festival for Oroville, Gridley, and Butte Coll., 1991. Recipient Acad. Excellence award Butte Coll., 1993-94; Mask club scholar Brigham Young U., 1967; Project Maestro grantee, 1994. Mem. AAUW (membership v.p. 1989—, com. for gender equity for Gridley br.), Butte County Arts Coun. (spl. com. 1986), Kaleidoscope Arts Coun., Am. Assn. Women in Community Jr. Colls. Republican., Ch. of Jesus Christ Latter-day Saints.

QUON, CHRISTINE MICHELLE, medical technologist, volunteer; b. Oakland, Calif., Jan. 26, 1950; d. James K.F. and Mildred Anolyn Chun; m. Daniel Albert Quon, July 19, 1975; children: Alexis, Brittany. BS in Biology, U. So. Calif., 1972; med. tech. cert., Sequoia Hosp., 1974. Staff med. technologist Scripps Meml. Hosp., La Jolla, Calif., 1974-79, transfusion svc. supr., 1979-84; cons., 1984-90; lab. dir. Coastal Med. Ctr., Encinitas, Calif., 1990-94; cons. Better Life Inst., San Diego, 1984-90. Mem. allocation com. United Way, San Diego County, 1978-88, Girl Scouts U.S., 1992—; bd. dirs. YWCA, San Diego County, 1975-87, vol., 1976—, pres., 1976-79; nat. bd. dirs. YWCA/U.S.A., 1979-81. Mem. Am. Soc. Clin. Pathology (assoc., registered med. technologist).

RAASH, KATHLEEN FORECKI, artist; b. Milw., Sept. 12, 1950; d. Harry and Marion Matilda (Schwabe) Forecki; m. Gary John Raash, June 13, 1987. BS, U. Wis., Eau Claire, 1972; MFA, U. Wis., Milw., 1978. One, two and three person shows include Sight 225 Gallery, Milw., 1979, 81, Nicolet Coll., Rhinelander, Wis., 1981, Messing Gallery, St. Louis, 1982, Arts Consortium, Cin., 1982, Ctr. Gallery, Madison, Wis., 1982, Otteson Theatre Gallery, Wuakesha, Wis., 1982, Foster Gallery, Eau Claire, 1984, Duluth (Minn.) Art Inst., 1984, West Bend (Wis.) Gallery of Fine Arts, 1987, U. Wis.-Waukesha Fine Arts Gallery, 1988, Marion Art Gallery, Milw., 1990, Layton Honor Gallery, Milw., 1991, West Bend Art Mus., 1995; exhibited in group show at River Edge Galleries, Wis., 1990, 91, 94, Peltz Gallery, Milw., 1990, 91, 92, 93, 94; represented in permanent collections United Bank and Trust of Madison, Fine Arts Gallery U. Wis., Miller Brewing Co., Independence Bank of Waukesha, U. Wis. Home and Studio: W 148 N 7615 Woodland Dr Menomonee Falls WI 53051

RABB, HARRIET SCHAFFER, lawyer, educator; b. Houston, Sept. 12, 1941; d. Samuel S. and Helen G. Schaffer; m. Bruce Rabb, Jan. 4, 1970; children: Alexander, Katherine. BA in Govt., Barnard Coll., 1963; JD, Columbia U., 1966. Bar: N.Y. 1966, U.S. Supreme Ct. 1969, D.C. 1970. Instr. seminar on constl. litigation Rutgers Law Sch., 1966-67; staff atty. Center for Constl. Rights, 1966-69; spl. counsel to commr. consumer affairs N.Y.C. Dept. Consumer Affairs, 1969-70; sr. staff atty. Stern Community Law Firm, Washington, 1970-71; asst. dean urban affairs Law Sch., Columbia U., N.Y.C., 1971-84, prof. law, dir. clin. edn., 1984—; George M. Jaffen prof. law and social responsibility Law Sch., Columbia U., 1991—, vice dean, 1992—; gen. counsel Dept. Health and Human Svcs., Washington, 1993—; mem. faculty employment and tng. policy Harvard Summer Inst., Cambridge, Mass., 1975-79. Author: (with Agid, Cooper and Rubin) Fair Employment Litigation Manual, 1975, (with Cooper and Rubin) Fair Employment Litigation, 1975. Bd. dirs. Ford Found., 1977-89, N.Y. Civil Liberties Union, 1972-83, Lawyers Com. for Civil Rights Under Law, 1978-86, Legal Def. Fund NAACP, 1978-93, Mex. Am. Legal Def. and Edn. Fund, 1986-90, Legal Aid Soc., 1990-93; mem. exec. com. Human Rights Watch, 1991-93; trustee Trinity Episcopal Sch. Corp., 1991-93. Office: Dept Health and Human Svcs 200 Independence Ave SW Rm 722A Washington DC 20201

RABE, ELIZABETH ROZINA, hair stylist, horse breeder; b. Granby, Quebec, Canada, Sept. 28, 1953; d. John J. and Christina Maria (De Vaal) Gluck; m. Oct. 21, 1972 (div. 1981); children: Diana Marie Claire, Michelle Diane. Diploma in hairstyling, Art Inst. Film hairstylist Internat. Alliance Theatrical, Stage Employees and Moving Pictures Machine Operators Local 706, L.A., 1977-94. Recipient Design Patent hock support horse brace U.S. Design Patent Office, Washington, 1994. Home: 522 W Stocker # 1 Glendale CA 91202

RABIDEAU, MARGARET CATHERINE, media center director; b. Chgo., Nov. 24, 1930; d. Nicholas and Mary Agnes (Burke) Oberle; m. Gerald Thomas Rabideau, Nov. 27, 1954; children: Mary, Margaret, Michelle, Gregory, Marsha, Grant. BA cum laude, U. Toledo, 1952, MA in Ednl. Media Tech., 1978. Cert. tchr. K-12 media tech., supr. ednl. media, tchr. English and journalism. Asst. dir. pub. rels. U. Toledo, 1952-55; publicity writer United Way, Toledo, 1974-75; tchr. Toledo Pub. Schs., 1975-80, libr., media specialist, 1980-90; dir. media svcs. Sylvania (Ohio) Schs., 1990—; task force to evaluate coll. programs Ohio Dept. Edn., 1987; on-site evaluation team, Hiram Coll., Ohio, 1991; north ctrl. evaluation team Northwestern Ohio, 1985—. Citizen task force Toledo/Lucas County Libr., Ohio, 1991, mem. friends of the libr., 1990—; task force Sta. WGTE-TV PBS Sta., Toledo, 1993; Toledo botanical gardens instr. U. Toledo, 1990. Mem. ALA, U. Toledo Alumni Assn., Ohio Ednl. Libr. Media Assn. (N.W. dir. 1993—, vocat. dir. 1985-89, Libr. Media Specialist of Yr. 1993), Am. Ednl. Comm. and Tech., Phi Delta Kappa (Outstanding Newsletter Nat. award 1990, pres. Toledo chpt.). Home: 1038 Olson St Toledo OH 43612-2828 Office: Sylvania Schs 6850 Monroe St Sylvania OH 43560-1922

RABII, PATRICIA BERG, church administrator; b. Lynn, Mass., Nov. 7, 1942; d. Clarence Oscar and Naomi Ruth (MacHugh) B.; m. S. Rabii, Oct. 26, 1966 (div. 1988); children: Susan M., Elizabeth L. AA, Green Mtn. Coll., Poultney, Vt., 1962; BA cum laude, U. Pa., 1978. Cons. City of Phila., 1981; fin. svcs. officer U. Pa., Phila., 1981-90; asst. to exec. dir. Psi Upsilon Found., Paoli, Pa., 1990-92; parish adminstr. St. David's (Radnor) Episcopal Ch., Wayne, Pa., 1992—; co-dir. career planning/pub. rels. Resources for Women, Phila., 1978-81. Counselor direct patient and care ARC, St. Louis, 1967-69; bd. dirs. Upper Merion PTA, 1976-78, Dental Clinic, King of Prussia, 1976-78; leader Girl Scouts U.S.A., King of Prussia, 1976-77, 80-81. Recipient ACT 101 Svc. award, Penn Cap, 1989. Mem. AAUW, U. Pa. Women's Club (bd. dirs. 1975-80, v.p. 1979-80). Home: 5 Drummers Ln Wayne PA 19087-1503 Office: St Davids Radnor Episcopal 763 Valley Forge Rd Wayne PA 19087

RABINER, SUSAN, editor; b. Bklyn., May 5, 1948; d. Nathan M. and Gloria (Bodinger) R.; m. Alfred G. Fortunato, Mar. 27, 1974; children: Anna, Matthew. B.A. cum laude, Goucher Coll., 1969. Asst. editor Random House, N.Y.C., 1969-72; editor Oxford U. Press, N.Y.C., 1973-79, sr. editor, 1980-86; sr. editor St. Martin's Press, N.Y.C., 1986-87, Pantheon Books, N.Y.C., 1987-90, Basic Books, Inc., N.Y.C., 1990—; vis. lectr. Yale U., New Haven, 1983, 84. Home: 1009 Brent Dr Wantagh NY 11793-1043 Office: Basic Books Inc 10 E 53rd St New York NY 10022-5244

RABINOVICH, RAQUEL, painter, sculptor; b. Buenos Aires, Argentina, Mar. 30, 1929; came to U.S., 1967, naturalized, 1973; d. Enrique Rabinovich and Julia Dinitz; m. Jose Luis Reissig, Feb. 14, 1956 (div. 1981); children—Celia Karen, Pedro Dario, Nora Vivian. Student U. Córdoba, Argentina, 1950-53, Sorbonne, Paris, 1957, U. Edinburgh, Scotland, 1958-59; lectr. Whitney Mus., 1983-86, Marymount Manhattan Coll., 1984-90. Exhbns. include Hecksher Mus., Huntington, N.Y., 1974, Susan Caldwell Gallery, N.Y.C., 1975, CUNY Grad. Ctr., 1978, The Jewish Mus. Sculpture Ct., N.Y.C., 1979, Ctr. Inter-Am. Rels., 1983, Bronx Mus. Arts, N.Y.C., 1987, Fordham U. Lincoln Ctr., N.Y.C., 1985, Ams. Soc., 1990, Erik Stark Gallery, 1991, Montgomery Ctr., 1992, Trans-Hudson Gallery, 1993, Noyes Mus., 1994, others; represented in collections World Bank Fine Art Collection, Washington, Univ. Art Mus., Austin, Cin. Art Mus., Walker Art Ctr., others. NEA fellow, 1991-92. Avocations: travel; music. Home and Studio: 141 Lamoree Rd Rhinebeck NY 12572

RABINOWITZ, GLORIA, book designer, artist; b. N.Y.C., Nov. 4, 1952; d. Murray and Judith (Levine) R. BA cum laude in Fine Arts, Queens Coll., 1975; MFA in Painting, Boston U., 1977; postgrad., Asethetic Realism Found., N.Y.C., 1983—. painting residency Va. Ctr. for the Creative Arts, Sweet Briar, 1980, 81, 93, MacDowell Colony, Peterborough, N.H., 1980, Millay Colony for the Arts, Austerlitz, N.Y., 1980. One-woman shows include Queens Coll., 1975, Bromfield Gallery, Boston, 1977, Pleiades Gallery, N.Y.C., 1993; exhibited in group shows at Queens Coll., 1973, Boston U., 1976, Cambridge (Mass.) City Hall, 1979, 2d St. Gallery, Charlottesville, Va., 1980, Roanoke (Va.) Mus. Fine Arts, 1981, 22 Wooster Gallery, N.Y.C., 1983, Terrain Gallery, N.Y.C., 1983, Marymount Manhattan Coll., N.Y.C., 1985, Randolph-Macon Coll., Ashford, Va., 1987, Danville (Va.) Mus. Fine Arts, 1987, NYU, 1990, N.Y. Law Sch., 1994; works reproduced in calendar for Am. Mut. Life Ins. Fellow Boston U., 1975, 76. Mem. Sierra Club. Home: Apt 8W 4th St Apt 9 New York NY 10014-2219 Office: Dover Publs Inc 180 Varick St New York NY 10014-4606

RABKE, SUZANNE, computer educator; b. Victoria, Tex., Feb. 1, 1964; d. Leroy Arthur and Erleen Mary (Mudd) Boedeker; m. O'Dell Ray Rabke Jr., Nov. 2, 1985; 1 child, Trent Michael. AS, Victoria Coll., 1984; BS, U. Houston, 1986. Tchr. computer Hallettsville (Tex.) High Sch., 1987—; instr. adult computer literacy classes, 1992-95. Hon. mem. PAL, Hallettsville High Sch., 1992. Office: Hallettsville High Sch PO Box 368 Hallettsville TX 77964-0368

RABUSKA, MICHÈLE JOANNE, customer relations specialist; b. Waterbury, Conn., Dec. 6, 1963; d. Peter Constantine and Joan Elfreida (Bergstrom) R. AA, Capital Community-Tech. Coll., 1993; postgrad., Wesleyan U., 1993—. With bus. office St. Francis Hosp. and Med. Ctr., Hartford, Conn., 1990-93, customer rels. specialist, 1993—; adminstrv. support, personal computer trainer, cons. The 1000 Corp., Hartford, 1993-94; cons., trainer St. Francis Hosp. Profl. Svcs., 1994. Election pollwatcher Hartford Courant newspaper, 1992—; mem. Pub. Concern Found., Washington, 1993—, Amnesty Internat., 1989—. Recipient scholarship Wesleyan U., 1993, 94, Etherington scholarship Wesleyan U., 1993, 94, Conn. State grant, 1993. Mem. St. Francis Hosp. Women's Aux., Phi Theta Kappa, Alpha Zeta Psi. Republican. Russian Orthodox. Home: 942 Main St Apt 815 Hartford CT 06103-1220 Office: St Francis Hosp and Med Ctr 114 Woodland St # 363 Hartford CT 06105-1299

RAC, ANNA M., accountant; b. Gdansk, Poland, Feb. 10, 1949; came to U.S., 1967; m. M. Christopher Rac, Apr. 6, 1973; children: Christopher, Matthew. BA in Liberal Arts, U. Ill., 1972; MS in Acctg., Roosevelt U., 1975. CPA, Ill., cert. internal auditor, bank auditor. Internal auditor Fed. Res. Bank, Chgo., 1975-78; acctg. mgr. Met. Water Reclamation Dist., Chgo., 1978—. Mem. AICPA, Ill. Inst. CPAs, Govt. Fin. Officers Assn., Ill. Govt. Fin. Officers Assn. Roman Catholic. Office: Met Water Reclamation Dist. Greater Chgo 100 E Erie St Chicago IL 60611-2803

RACE, LYNDA SUSAN, school administrator; b. Delhi, N.Y., Dec. 8, 1948; d. Stanley Alton and Norah Wilma (Travel) Hewitt; m. Gregory Arthur Race, July 15, 1972; children: Erin Elizabeth, Krystina Elaine. BS in Edn., Keuka Coll., 1971; MS in Edn., Oneonta State U., 1975; MS in Ednl. Adminstrn. & Policy Studies, Albany State U., 1992. Cert. sch. dist. adminstr. Tchr. elem. edn. Middleburgh (N.Y.) Ctrl. Sch., 1971-72; tchr. elem. edn. South Kortright (N.Y.) Ctrl. Sch., 1972-92, asst. supt., 1992—; presenter ea. regional conf. on inclusive edn. N.Y. State Edn. Dept., 1993, N.Y. State Reading Conf., 1994. Inclusion grantee N.Y. State Edn. Dept., 1992, 93, grantee U. Vt. and N.Y. State Edn. Dept., 1994. Mem. ASCD, Sch. Adminstrs. Assn. N.Y. State, N.Y. State Assn. Sch. Bus. Officials, Delta Kappa Gamma (chair publicity 1992-94). Republican. Presbyterian.

RACE, SUE MARIE, information and management systems specialist; b. Lansing, Mich., Sept. 9, 1952; d. Edward and Lavina Ellen (Watson) Maciatek; m. William Paul Race, Sept. 1, 1973 (div. 1982); 1 child, Casey Sue. AS in Bus., Lansing C.C., 1973, San Diego City Coll., 1984; BSBA, San Diego State U., 1987; MBA, Nat. U., 1989. Adminstrv. asst. electronics divsn. Gen. Dynamics, San Diego, 1983-85, mfg. engrng. analyst, 1985-86, ops. rep., MPL analyst, 1986-88, systems analyst, 1988-90, lead project analyst, 1990-91, sr. mgmt. systems analyst, 1991-92; mgmt. systems specialist GDE Systems, Inc., San Diego, 1992—. Mem. NAFE, Upsilon Pi Epsilon. Office: GDE Systems Inc 16550 W Bernardo Dr San Diego CA 92127

RACHKO, BARBARA GAIL, artist; b. Paterson, N.J., Jan. 22, 1953; d. George and Dorothy Barbara (King) R. BA, U. Vt., 1975. Lic. comml. pilot and Boeing 727 flight engr. One-woman shows include Capitol Hill Art League, Washington, 1992, Cunneen-Hackett Art Gallery, Poughkeepsie, N.Y., 1993, Art League Gallery, Alexandria, Va., 1993, NIH, Bethesda, Md., 1994, Howard C.C., Columbia, Md., 1995, Manhattanville Coll., Purchase, N.Y., 1995; group exhibits include Art Barn Gallery, Washington, 1989, 93, Nat. Arts Club, N.Y.C., 1990, 91, Salmagundi Club, N.Y.C., 1991, 92, Hoyt Inst. Fine Arts, New Castle, Pa., 1991, 93, Sumner Mus., Washington, 1991, Harmon-Meek Gallery, Naples, Fla., 1992, Pensacola (Fla.) Mus. Art, 1992, Foxhall Gallery, Washington, 1992, 93, Pleiades Gallery, N.Y.C., 1992, Muscarelle Mus., Williamsburg, Va., 1992, 94, Cardinal Gallery, Annapolis, Md., 1993, 94, Andre Zarre Gallery, N.Y.C., 1993, Chrysler Mus., Norfolk, Va., 1994, Miami '94 Internat. Art Exposition, Miami Beach, Fla., Roger Lapelle Galleries, Phila., 1994, 479 Gallery, Phila., 1994, others. Served to lt. USN, 1983-89, lt. comdr. USNR, 1989—. Mem. Nat. Artists Equity Assn., Nat. Assn. Women Artists, Knickerbock Artists (assoc.), Allied Artists of Am. (assoc.), Oil Pastel Assn., Orgn. of Ind. Artists, Md. Pastel Assn. Democrat. Roman Catholic. Home: 1311 W Braddock Rd Alexandria VA 22302-2705

RACINE, JEAN DORINE, banker; b. Portland, Oreg., May 23, 1944; m. Bill F. Racine; children: Carmell R., Tawna L. Student, Inst. Fin. Edn., Portland, 1976-83, Portland State U., 1981-82, N.W. Intermediate Banking Sch., Portland, 1987, IFE Asset/Liability Sch., 1989. Bookkeeper escrow closing Bump & Meyer Real Estate, Hillsboro, Oreg., 1965-66; sec. Forest Grove br. Wash. Fed. Savs. Bank, Hillsboro, 1966-70, with loan dept., loan closing, loan svc., 1971-75, mgr. Aloha br., 1975-76, v.p. personnel, 1976-83, v.p. adminstrn., 1983-89, sr. v.p., 1989—; bd. dirs. Washington Fed. Ins. Corp., Hillsboro, Washington Fed. Svc. Corp., Hillsboro, Ward Cook, Inc., Portland; bd. dirs. Oreg. Fin. Inst. Edn. Assn. Bd. dirs. Hillsboro Downtown Bus. Assn.; former sch. bd. chmn. Groner Elem., Hillsboro. Mem. Pacific N.W. Personnel Mgmt. Assn., Western Pension Conf., Oreg. League Fin. Insts. (personnel com.). Office: Wash Fed Savs Bank PO Box 628 Hillsboro OR 97123-0628

RACITI, MARIA CELESTE, psychologist; b. Norristown, Pa., June 15, 1964; d. Grazio and Guiseppa (Torrisi) R.; m. Clarence Allen Thornburg, Feb. 28, 1992; children: Russell, Reece. BS, U. Scranton, 1986; MA, Tex. Tech. U., 1988, PhD, 1991. Lic. clin. psychologist. Clin. psychologist Gloucester, Va., Denbigh, Va.; clin. psychologist Riverside Rehab. Inst., Newport News, Va., 1990-92. Mem. APA.

RADA, MURIEL MARY, English language educator; b. Chgo., Oct. 31, 1950; d. Irwin Charles and Mary Laverne (Andrews) R.; m. John Alexander Falck, Oct. 15, 1994. BA in English/French, St. Mary Coll., Leavenworth, Kans., 1972; MA in English, U. Mo., Kansas City, 1974; PhD in English, U. Nebr., 1991. Part-time instr. U. Mo., Kansas City, 1972-74; mem. faculty Metro C.C., Omaha, 1974—; lectr. in field. Contbr. book revs. to profl. jours. Active drug edn. program Miller Park Sch., Omaha, 1984—, multicultural arts program, 1984—; coord. Adopt-A-Sch. program Metro C.C., Omaha, 1984—, host internat. students, 1990—; leader Girl Scouts USA, 1993—; organizer 4-F Fun Club, 1990—; mem. YWCA. Grantee NEH, 1981. Mem. AAUW, NEA, Nebr. State Edn. Assn., Metro C.C. Edn. Assn., Phi Delta Kappa. Office: Metro CC PO Box 3777 Omaha NE 68103-0777

RADABAUGH, MICHELE JO, sales executive; b. Ashland, Ohio, May 1, 1961; d. James L. and Natalie J. (Barnhart) Sonnett; m. Brett L. Radabaugh, Sept. 22, 1990; 1 child, Natalie M. Assoc. in Advt., Northwood Inst., 1983, BBA, 1984. Xerox operator Nolan, Norton, Inc., Lexington, Mass., 1984-85; instr. Stautzenberger Coll., Findlay, Ohio, 1986-88; acad. coord. Stautzenberger Coll., Findlay, 1988-90, acad. dean, 1990-93; sales rep. Glencoe divsn. McGraw-Hill, 1993—. With USN, 1986. Named Outstanding Educator, C. of C., Findlay, 1988. Mem. Nat. Bus. Edn. Assn. Republican. Office: 1701 Wendell Ave Lima OH 45805

RADAZZO, PAMELA, executive recruiter; b. Stamford, Conn., Aug. 29, 1964; d. Louis Peter and Mona Lisa (Andersson) Raymond. BA in Psychology, U. Conn., 1987. Affiliate rels. assoc. World Wrestling Fedn., Stamford, 1988-89; exec. recruiter The Westen Assocs., Stamford, 1989-93; v.p. internat. exec. search The Delafield Group, Darien, Conn., 1993—. Mem. Darien Rep. Town Com., 1994—. Mem. NAFE, LWV, Nat. Assn. Self Employed, Championship Auto Racing Teams. Roman Catholic. Office: The Delafield Group 972 Boston Post Rd Darien CT 06820

RADCHIK, ISANA, accountant; b. Kiev, Ukraine, Russia, Apr. 16, 1956; came to U.S., 1980; d. Roman and Irene (Usach) R.; m. Roman Kalmykov, Oct. 22, 1977; 1 child, Lillian K. BBA, All Union State Inst., Moscow, 1977; MBA, Pace U., 1984. CPA. Contr. Souzvuzfilm, Moscow, 1977-79; instr. Adelphi Coll., N.Y.C., 1981-84; auditor Glen Ingram and Co., N.Y.C., 1984-85; sr. acct. Time Equities Inc., N.Y.C., 1985-89; contr. RD Mgmt. Corp., N.Y.C., 1989—. Office: RD Mgmt Corp 810 7th Ave New York NY 10019-5818

RADCLIFFE-SMALLWOOD, CYNTHIA, research librarian; b. Ft. Wayne, Ind., Sept. 30, 1946; d. John Carroll and Martha (Kellersberger) Radcliffe; m. Christopher Carroll Smallwood, Sept. 15, 1979. BA, Calif. State U., Hayward, 1975; MLS, U. Md., 1978. Libr. asst. Oakland (Calif.) Pub. Libr., 1974-76; libr. Foley & Lardner, Washington, 1978-80, Morgan, Lewis & Bockius, Washington, 1980-83; head libr. Swidler & Berlin, Washington, 1983-85; rschr. ABC News, Washington, 1985-88, mgr. rsch. libr., 1988-92; mgr. info. ctr. Lexis-Nexis, Dayton, Ohio, 1992—. Mem. Am. Assn. Law Librs. (program planner Washington 1978-85), Spl. Librs. Assn. Libertarian. Episcopalian. Home: 2906 Cobblestone Crossing Ct Spring Valley OH 45370-9154 Office: Lexis-Nexis 9443 Springboro Pike Miamisburg OH 45342-4425

RADEMACHER, BETTY GREEN, counselor, consultant; b. Marion, Ill., June 28, 1935; d. Morris Lee and Elva (Davis) Booth; m. Ronald Green, Aug. 21, 1957 (div. 1972); children: Susan Green Lembke, Karen Green Townsend; m. David Day Rademacher, June 7, 1975. BS, So. Ill. U., 1957, MS, 1959. Cert. profl. in human resources. Counselor So. Ill. U., Carbondale, 1958-60; counselor Ill. State U., Normal, 1972-81, staff psychologist, 1990—; dir. career edn. Ill. Wesleyan U., Bloomington, 1981-90; lectr. various profl. confs. Author: (chpt.) New Horizons in Parenthood, 1982; co-author: Williamson County Schools, 1989; contbr. articles to profl. jours. Bd. dirs. United Campus Christian Found., Normal, 1978—; mem. Womens Div. C. of C., Bloomington, 1989—; mem., com. chair Bloomington-Normal Human Resource Coun., 1981—. Mem. Am. Counseling Assn. (Ill. chpt.), Soc. Human Resource Mgmt., Am. Coll. Pers. Assn., Coll. Placement Coun. (midwest chpt.), Ill. Sml. Coll. Placement Assn. (pres. 1988-90), Phi Kappa Phi, Phi Delta Kappa, Pi Lambda Theta. Democrat. Presbyterian. Home: 702 Broadway St Normal IL 61761-3766 Office: Illinois State Univ Student Counseling Ctr Normal IL 61761

RADER, ELLA JANE See ASHLEY, ELLA JANE

RADER, HANNELORE, library director, consultant; b. Berlin, Germany, Dec. 19, 1937; d. Henry H. and Talia E. (Tramontin) Busch; widowed; 1 child, Ingrid M. BA in Russian, U. Mich., 1960, MA in Libr. Sci., 1968, MA in German Lit., 1971; Degree in Ednl. Leadership, Eastern Mich. U., 1978. Children's librarian Washington D.C. Pub. Libr., 1960-62; asst. humanities librarian Eastern Mich. U., Ypsilanti, 1968-70, orientation librarian, 1970-76, coord. edn., psychology div., 1976-80; libr. dir. learning ctr. U. Wis.-Parkside, Kenosha, 1980-87; dir. univ. libr. Cleve. State U., 1987—; evaluator, libr. instr. Ball State U., Muncie, Ind., 1983; evaluator for self study Calif. State U.-L.A. Libr., 1989, CCNY Libr., 1989. Contbr. articles to numerous jours. Recipient Walter H. Kaiser award Mich. Libr. Assn., 1977, Disting. Alumnus award U. Mich. Libr. Sch., 1984; fellow Coun. Libr. Resources, 1975-76; USIA and West German Libr. grantee, 1987. Mem. ALA (mem. coun. 1980-84, 84-92, 92—), AAUW (pres. Cleve. chpt. 1993-95, Edn. Found. honoree 1994), Assn. Coll. and Rsch. Librs. (pres., bd. dirs. 1985-88, Miriam Dudley Libr. Instrn. award 1993), Spl. Librs. Assn., Ohio Libr. Assn., Rotary. Office: Cleve State U Libr 1860 E 22d St Cleveland OH 44115

RADER, TINA LOUISE, pathologists' assistant; b. Allentown, Pa., Apr. 9, 1959; d. Marlin Robert and Gioconda Maria (Alpago) R. BS in Med. Tech., Bloomsburg U., 1981; M Health Sci., Quinnipiac Coll., 1987. Med. technologist Lehigh Valley Hosp. Ctr., Allentown, Pa., 1981-84, Brigham & Womens Hosp., Boston, 1984-85; pathologists' asst. Dartmouth-Hitchcock Med. Ctr., Lebanon, N.H., 1987-89, New Eng. Med. Ctr., Boston, 1989-91, R.I. Hosp., Providence, 1991-94, Fox Chase Cancer Ctr., Phila., 1994—. Fellow Am. Assn. Pathologists' Assts. (edn. com. chairperson 1990—). Office: Fox Chase Cancer Ctr Dept Pathology 7701 Burholme Ave Philadelphia PA 19111

RADFORD, MARTHA JO, physician, educator; b. Boston, June 21, 1948; d. Edward Parish and Nettie (Garrison) R.; m. Louis George Graff IV, May 10, 1980; children: Louis George Graff V, Alice Elizabeth Graff. BS, U. Calif., Berkeley, 1970, MA, 1973; MD, Harvard U., 1978. Resident in internal medicine Brigham and Women's Hosp., Boston, 1978-81; fellow in cardiovascular disease Duke U. Med. Ctr., Durham, N.C., 1981-84; asst. prof. medicine U. Conn., Farmington, 1984-93, assoc. prof. medicine, 1993—; cons. Conn. Peer Rev. Orgn., Middletown, 1993—. Fellow Am. Coll. Cardiology. Office: U Conn Health Ctr 263 Farmington Ave Farmington CT 06030-1305

RADICE, ANNE-IMELDA, museum director; b. Buffalo, Feb. 29, 1948; d. Lawrence and Anne (Marino) R. A.B., Wheaton Coll., Norton, Mass., 1969; M.A., Villa SchiFanoia, Florence, Italy, 1971; Ph.D., U. N.C., 1976; M.B.A., Am. U., 1984. Asst. curator Nat. Gallery of Art, Washington, 1972-76; archtl. historian U.S. Capitol, Washington, 1976-80, curator Office of Architect, 1980-85; dir. Nat. Mus. Women in the Arts, 1985-89; chief div. of creative arts USIA, 1989-91; sr. dep. chmn. Nat. Endowment for Arts, Washington, 1991-92; acting chmn., 1992-93; exec. v.p. Gray & Co. II, Miami, Fla., 1993; prodr. World Affairs TV Prodn., 1994; assoc. producer Think Tank, 1994; chief spl. projects, confidential adviser Courtney Sales Ross, 1994—; cons. in pub. rels. and TV, 1994—. Contbr. articles to profl. jours.

RADICE, CAROL, editor; b. Rahway, N.J., June 4, 1964; d. Richard Charles and Shirley (Deitz) R. BA, Rutgers U., 1986. Reporter Worrell Pubs., South Orange, N.J., 1986-87; editor Forbes Newspapers, Somerville, N.J., 1987-89, Nat. Assn. Fleet Adminstrs., Iselin, N.J., 1989-91, Whole Foods Comms. Inc., South Plainfield, N.J., 1991-92, Dow Jones Fin. Pub. (formerly Charter Fin.), Shrewsbury, N.J., 1992—. Active Clean Ocean Action Com., Monmouth County, 1993—. Mem. N.J. Press Assn., Women in Prodn., Soc. Profl. Journalists. Office: Dow Jones Fin Pub 179 Ave At The Commons Shrewsbury NJ 07702

RADICE, SHIRLEY ROSALIND, educator; b. Newark, June 2, 1935; d. Gerald Alexander and Pauline Deborah (Baitz) Deitz; m. Richard Charles Radice, Dec. 17, 1955; children: Carol, Richard Neil. BA, Kean Coll., Union, N.J., 1960, MA, 1963; EdD, Rutgers U., 1985. Tchr. Edison (N.J.) Bd. Edn., 1960-64, 70—, trainer, 1990—; instr. grad. sch. edn. Rutgers U., 1992—; mem. grant com. N.J. Dept. Higher Edn., 1988-90; lectr. Rutgers U., 1989—, instr. in edn., 1992—; curriculum/resource coord., Edison, 1994—; ednl. cons. in field. Contbr. articles to profl. jours. Recipient N.J. Gov.'s Recognition award for outstanding contbn. to edn., 1991; grantee Ford Found., 1966, State of N.J., 1973. Mem. Nat. Tchrs. Assn. (del. 1980-87), N.J. Tchrs. Assn., Edison Tchrs. Assn. (co-chmn. legis. com. 1975-76), Kappa Delta Phi.

RADINO, MARGE FRANCES, pharmaceutical company executive; b. Evanston, Ill., Mar. 1, 1962; d. Anthony Vincent and Margery Jane (Kale) Rodino; children: Ashley, Rachel, Tara. BS cum laude, No. Ill. U., 1984. Cert. compensation profl. Ops. mgmt. trainee Harris Trust & Savs. Bank, Chgo., 1984-85, pers. rep., 1985, sr. human resourse profl., 1986-88, human resources cons., employee rels. officer, 1988-89, sr. human resources cons., asst. v.p., 1989-90; human resources policy cons. Boot Pharms., Inc., Lincolnshire, Ill., 1990-92, sr. compensation/human resources policy cons., 1992—. Chair social com. Buffalo Grove (Ill.) Jr. Women's Club, 1990; active local ch. Mem. Am. Compensation Assn., Soc. Human Resource Mgmt. Office: Boots Pharms Inc 300 Tri State Internat Ctr Lincolnshire IL 60090

RADKE, MARGARET HOFFMAN, retired educator; b. Rochester, Minn., Nov. 22, 1923; d. Roy John and Lucille (Denn) Hoffman; m. Frederick H. Radke, Sept. 4, 1946 (dec. Nov. 1977); children: Kathryn, Frederick R., Lori Radke Bessette, Eileen Radke Nokes, Sharon E. BS summa cum laude, Hamline U., 1945; MA in Zoology, U. Calif., Berkeley, 1947; postgrad., U. Maine, 1964-67. Technician bacteriology lab. Mayo Clinic, Rochester, 1943, 44; teaching asst. in zoology U. Calif., 1945-46; instr. chemistry and microbiology Hamline U., St. Paul, 1946-47, 48; instr. zoology Iowa State U., Ames, 1947-49; pvt. techr. piano, voice and clarinet, Orono, Maine, 1960-74; tchr. sci. Old Town (Maine) High Sch., 1968-70; tchr. sci. Bangor (Maine) Sch. System, 1970-88, head dept., 1979-86; ret., 1988; instr., biochemistry technician U. Maine, Orono, 1964-66, summer 1967; asst. music dir. Penobscot Valley Children's Theater, Orono. Author: (poems) Soul Love, 1969. Condr. children's choir United Meth. Ch., Orono, 1964-78; mem. oratoria U. Maine, 1953—, docent Hudson Mus., 1992—; bd. dirs. Maine Noetic Studies, 1993—. New sci. wing dedicated in her honor Bangor High Sch., 1988. Mem. AAUW, NEA, Nat. Sci. Tchrs. Assn., Maine Sci. Tchrs. Assn., Maine Tchrs. Assn., New Eng. Assn. Chemistry Tchrs., Order Eastern Star (soloist 1964-67), Alpha Delta Kappa (coms.). Republican. Methodist. Home: 17 Mainwood Ave Orono ME 04473-1326

RADKOWSKY, KAREN, advertising, marketing research executive; b. Washington, Nov. 8, 1957; d. Lawrence and Florence (Kramer) R. BA, Columbia U., 1979. Rsch. analyst Cosmair, Inc., N.Y.C., 1979-82, sr. rsch. analyst, 1982-84; asst. rsch. mgr. Am. Express Co., N.Y.C., 1984-85; account rsch. mgr. BBDO, Inc., N.Y.C., 1985-88, v.p., assoc. rsch. dir., 1988-94, sr. v.p., assoc. rsch. dir., 1994—.

RADLEY, VIRGINIA LOUISE, humanities educator; b. Marion, N.Y., Aug. 12, 1927; d. Howard James and Lula (Ferris) R. B.A., Russell Sage Coll., 1949, L.H.D., 1981; M.A., U. Rochester, 1952; M.S., Syracuse U.,

1957, Ph.D., 1958. Instr. English Chatham (Va.) Hall, 1952-55; asst. dean students, asst. prof. English Goucher Coll., 1957-59; dean freshmen, asst. prof. English Russell Sage Coll., 1959-60, assoc. dean, assoc. prof. English, 1960-61, prof. chmn. dept., 1961-69; dean coll., prof. English Nazareth Coll., Rochester, N.Y., 1969-73; provost for undergrad. edn., central adminstrn. SUNY, Albany, 1973-74; exec. v.p., provost Coll. Arts and Scis., SUNY, Oswego, 1974-76; acting pres. Coll. Arts and Scis., SUNY, 1976-78; pres. SUNY, Oswego, 1978-88; prof. English and Humanities SUNY, 1988-93; scholar-in-residence Russell Sage Coll., 1993—; vis. prof. Syracuse U., summer 1957-59, Nazareth Coll., summer 1965; cons. N.Y. State Dept. Edn.; chmn. commn. on women Am. Coun. on Edn., 1978-81, sr. assoc. Office of Women, 1990—; trustee Marymount Manhattan Coll., 1988-90; mem. commn. on higher edn. Middle States Assn., 1979-86; disting vis. prof. Russell Sage Coll., 1994-95. Author: Samuel Taylor Coleridge, 1966, Elizabeth Barrett Browning, 1972, also articles. Mem. MLA (chmn. regional sect. Romanticisn 1969), English Inst., Pi Lambda Theta. Republican. Home: RR 1 Box 1697 Poestenkill NY 12140-1706

RADMAN, DEBORAH M., public relations executive; b. Deadwood, S.D., Aug. 23, 1955. Acct. exec. Darcy Comms., 1976-80, The Johnston Group, 1980-81; dir. mktg. & advtg. Van Schaack & Co., 1981-82; pub. rels. acct. mgr. Broyles, Allebaugh & Davis, 1982-83; acct. supr. Servoss, 1983-84, v.p., 1984-91; exec. v.p. Servoss-Barnhart Pub. Rels., 1991-92; pres. Brown Radman Wolper, 1992—. Mem. Pub. Rels. Soc. Am. (pres. Colo. 1987, mem. bd. dirs. 1982-91), Am. Mktg. Assn. Office: Brown Radman Wolper 800 E 19th Ave Denver CO 80218*

RADNOFSKY, BARBARA A., lawyer; b. Broomall, Pa., July 8, 1956; m. Daniel Edward Supkis Jr.; children: Danielle Esther, Max David, Michaela Sarah. BA magna cum laude, U. Houston, 1976; JD with honors, U. Tex., 1979. Bar: Tex. Assoc. Vinson & Elkins, L.L.P., Houston, 1979-87, ptnr., 1987—; mem. faculty intensive trial advocacy program U. Tex. Sch. Law, 1985-86; speaker in field. Contbr. articles to profl. jours. Albert Jones scholar U. Tex. Sch. Law; named Outstanding Young Lawyer Houston, Houston Young Lawyers Assn., 1988-89. Mem. ABA (chmn. Nat. Trial Competition 1983), Tex. Young Lawyers Assn. (Outstanding Young Lawyer Tex. 1988-89), Tex. Assn. Def. Counsel (chmn. rules of evidence com. 1987-89, med. malpractice com. 1984-86), Nat. Health Lawyers Assn. Office: Vinson & Elkins 3300 First City Tower 1001 Fannin Houston TX 77002

RADOJCSICS, ANNE PARSONS, librarian; b. Mansfield, Ohio, Mar. 23, 1929; d. Richard Walbridge Parsons and Iva Pearl (Ruth) Kemp; m. Joseph Michael Radojcsics, July 8, 1950; children: Kurt Joseph, Jo Anne Radojcsics Kent. Diploma, Bethel Woman's Coll., Hopkinsville, Ky., 1949; BS, Miss. State U., 1972, MEd, 1974. Cert. secondary tchr., Miss. Chemist Humphries Borg-Warner Co., Mansfield, 1950-53; asst. reference libr. Mansfield Pub. Libr., 1953-59; libr. media specialist Verona (Miss.) Sch., 1970-92, supr. Verona computer lab., 1985-92; libr. media specialist Pierce St. Elem. Sch., Miss., 1992—; supr. libr. Guntown (Miss.) Sch., 1988-90, Shannon (Miss.) Sch., 1988-92; chmn. assessment project Miss. Libr.-Miss. Dept. Edn., Jackson, 1986-92; coord. region I Miss. Conf. on Libr. and Info. Svc., 1990; mem. Miss. Edn. TV Adv. Coun., 1985—; cons. content instrnl. prodn.-libr. rsch. skills Miss. Ednl. Tv., 1995. Author: Clay Tablets to Media Centers: Library Development from Ancient to Modern Times, 1975. Bd. dirs., past pres. SAFE, Inc., Tupelo, Miss., 1978-92, bd. dirs. emeritus, 1992—; mem. Lee County Adult Lit. Task Force, Tupelo, 1987-90; schs. chmn. Target Tupelo, 1981-85. Recipient Ed Ransdell Instructional TV award, 1991. Mem. AECT, DSMS, AAUW (pres. Tupelo chpt. 1977-81, Miss. div. 1984-86), Miss. Profl. Educators, Mississippians for Ednl. Broadcasting, Miss. Ednl. Computer Assn., Miss. Libr. Assn. (project chmn. com. on sch. librs. 1989, awards chmn. 1987-88, Ednl. Comm. and Tech. Roundtable chair 1993), Miss. Profl. Educators Lee County (pres. 1989-92), Miss. Profl. Educators Tupelo/Lee County (treas. 1993—), Apple Computer User Group (co-organizer). Democrat. Episcopalian. Home: Carr Vista 3 Michael St Tupelo MS 38801-8608 Office: Pierce St Media Ctr 1008 Pierce St Tupelo MS 38801

RADWICK, MELISSA JANE, elementary counselor; b. Memphis, Nov. 26, 1954; d. Nelson Arthur and Mary Jane (Loss) Haas; m. Douglas Martin, Oct. 23, 1976; children: Nathan, Eric. BA in Elem. Edn., Mich. State U., 1975; MA in Health Edn., U. Mich., 1981; counseling endorsement, Ctrl. Mich. U. 6th grade tchr. North Branch (Mich.) Schs., 1976-93, elem. counselor, 1993—; student asst. coord. North Br. Schs., 1991-93, coord. parent class, 1991—, chmn. cmty. teen, 1993—; county schs. rep. Continuum Care Com., Lapeer, Mich., 1992-93. Grantee Genesee Intermediate Dist., 1991, 93. Mem. AAUW, PEO. Republican. Lutheran. Home: 8635 Gera Rd Birch Run MI 48415-9717

RADY, ELSA, artist; b. N.Y.C., July 29, 1943; d. Simon and Lily (Mehlman) R. Attended, Chouinard Art Sch., 1962-66. Designer Interpace, L.A., 1989-94; designer Swid/Powell, N.Y.C., 1989-94. Solo exhbns. include The Am. Hand, Washington, 1979, Impressions Gallery, Boston, 1982, Janus Gallery, L.A., 1981, 84, Jan Turner Gallery, L.A., 1987, 88, Holly Solomon Gallery, 1987, 90, 94, Ochi Gallery, Sun Valley, Idaho, 1990, Isetan Fine Arts, Inc., Tokyo, 1991, Santa Barbara Mus. Art, 1993; group exhbns. include L.A. County Mus. Art, 1966, Contemporary Crafts Mus., N.Y.C., 1969, Pasadena Art Mus., 1968, 71, Phila. Art Alliance, 1973, Tweed Mus. U. Minn., 1975, Craft and Folk Art Mus., L.A., 1977, Phoenix Art Mus., 1980, Smithsonian Inst., Washington, 1980, Smith Anderson Gallery, Palo Alto, Calif., 1982, U. Mo., 1983, Govett-Brewster Gallery, New Plymouth Taranak, New Zealand, 1983, L.A. Mcpl. Gallery, 1984, Barbara Krakow Gallery, Boston, 1984, Garth Clark Gallery, N.Y.C., 1985, Everson Mus. Art, Syracuse, N.Y., 1985, 90, Victoria and Albert Mus., London, 1986, Newark Mus., 1988, Met. Mus. Art, N.Y.C., 1989, Ariz. State U. Art Mus., 1989, Norton Gallery Art, West Palm Beach, Fla., 1991, Espace Lyonnais d'Art Contemporain, Lyons, France, 1993, Patricia Faur, Santa Monica, Calif., 1994; represented in permanent collections UCLA, Disneyland, Anaheim, Calif., Western White House, San Clemente, Calif., Utah Mus. Fine Arts, U. Ariz., Tempe, Smithsonian Inst., Boston Mus. Fine Arts, Victoria and Albert Mus., Bklyn. Mus., Cooper-Hewitt Mus., N.Y.C., Newark Mus., County Mus. Art L.A., Met. Mus. Art, N.Y.C., Denver Art Mus., others. NEA fellow, Washington, 1981; Calif. Arts Coun. co-grantee, 1983. Home and Office: 1500 Andalusia Ave Venice CA 90291

RAE, BARBARA JOYCE, employee placement company executive; b. Prince George, B.C., Can., May 17, 1930; d. Alfred and Lottie Kathleen (Davis) Holmwood; m. George Suart, Feb. 14, 1984; children: Jamie, Glenn, John. MBA, Simon Fraser U., Burnaby, B.C., 1975. Chmn. Adia Can., Ltd., Vancouver, B.C., 1953—; bd. dirs. Can. Imperial Bank of Commerce, Grosvenor Internat. Ltd., B.C. Telephone Co., B.C. Telecom, Noranda, Inc., Seaboard Life Ins. Co., Sta. KCTS 9 Seattle Pubb. TV, Xerox Can., Ltd. Chancellor Simon Fraser U., 1987-93; mem. Jud. Appts. Com., B.C., 1988-90; mem. adv. coun. Imagine Campaign, 1988; mem. Premier's Econ. Adv. Coun., B.C., 1987-91; mem. Price Minister's Com. on Sci. and Tech., B.C., 1989-94; gen. chmn. United Way Lower Mainland, 1987, Salvation Army Red Shield Vancouver Campaign, 1986; bd. dirs. Vancouver Bd. Trade, 1972-76; nat. co-chmn. Can. Coun. Christians and Jews. Decorated Order of Can., Order of B.C.; recipient Simon Fraser U. Outstanding Alumnae award, 1985, Vancouver YWCA Bus. Women of Yr. award, 1986, West Vancouver Achievers award, 1987, B.S. Entrepreneur of Yr. award, 1987, Nat. Vol. award, 1990, Can. Woman Entrepreneur B.C. award, 1992. Home: 2206 Folkestone Way #3, West Vancouver, BC Canada V7S 2X7 Office: Adia Can Ltd, 744-1055 Dunsmuir St POBox 49292, Vancouver, BC Canada V5A 1S6

RAEBURN, SUSAN DELANEY, clinical psychologist; b. N.Y.C., Dec. 1, 1950; d. Boyd and Ginnie Powell Raeburn; m. William Phillip Delaney, May 25, 1991. BA in Psychology, UCLA, 1972; MA in Rsch. Psychology, San Francisco State U., 1974; PhD in Social-Clin. Psychology, The Wright Inst., 1984. Lic. psychologist, Calif. Asst. faculty San Francisco State U., 1973-74; evaluation specialist Model Cities Agy., Office of Mayor, San Francisco, 1975-76; spl. studies coord. Alameda County Health Care Scis. Agy., Oakland, Calif., 1977-78; pub. health planner Alameda County Health Care Svcs. Agy., Oakland, 1980-87; staff psychologist Behavioral Medicine Clinic Dept. Psychiatry Stanford U. Med. Ctr., 1986-92; clin. psychologist pvt. practice Berkeley, Calif., 1987—; clin. assoc. U. Calif., San Francisco, Health Program for Performance Artists, 1988—; psychologist Kaiser Permanente, 1992—. Contbr. articles to profl. jours. Mem. NOW, 1991—, Amnesty Internat., 1991—. Named Calif. State scholar, 1968-72. Mem. APA, Calif. Psychol. Assn., Alameda County Psychol. Assn. Democrat. Office: 2576 Shattuck Ave Berkeley CA 94704

RAEDEKE, LINDA DISMORE, geologist; b. Great Falls, Mont., Aug. 20, 1950; d. Albert Browning and Madge (Hogan) Dismore; m. Kenneth John Raedeke, Dec. 26, 1971 (div. 1982); m. Charles Moore Swift, Jr., Mar. 14, 1992. BA in History, U. Wash., 1971, MS in Geology, 1979, PhD, 1982. Geomorphologist, park planner Corporacion Nacional Forestal and U.S. Peace Corps, Punta Arenas, Chile, 1972-74; glacial geologist Empresa Nacional del Petroleo, Punta Arenas, 1972-75; geologist FAO, UN, Punta Arenas, 1974; geologist Lamont-Doherty Geol. Obs., Columbia U., Tierra del Fuego, Chile, 1974-75; Wetlands evaluation project coord. Wash. Dept. Agr., U. Wash., Seattle, 1975-76; geomorphol. cons. Okanogan County Planning, Oceanographic Inst. Wash., Seattle, 1976; curator Remote Sensing Applications Lab., U. Wash., 1976-77; geol. cons. Amoco, Denver, 1978; petrologist Lamont-Doherty Geol. Obs., 1979; geol. cons. Empresa Minera de Mantos Blancos, Tierra del Fuego, 1980; geol. rsch. asst. U. Wash., Seattle, 1977-81; exploration geologist Chevron Resources Co., Denver, 1981-84; rsch. geologist Chevron Oil Field Rsch. Co., La Habra, Calif., 1984-89; sr. compensation analyst Chevron Corp., San Francisco, 1989-90; staff geologist Chevron Overseas Petroleum, Inc., San Ramon, Calif. 1990-91, project leader, 1991-95, new ventures coord. for the far east, 1995—. Contbr. articles to profl. jours. Recipient Cert. of Achievement YWCA, 1988. Mem. Am. Geophys. Union, Geol. Soc. Am., Am. Assn. Petroleum Geologists (poster chmn. 1987). Office: Chevron Overseas Petroleum Inc PO Box 5046 San Ramon CA 94583-0946

RAEDER, MYRNA SHARON, lawyer, educator; b. N.Y.C., Feb. 4, 1947; d. Samuel and Estelle (Auslander) R.; m. Terry Oliver Kelly, July 13, 1975; children: Thomas Oliver, Michael Lawrence. BA, Hunter Coll., 1968; JD, NYU, 1971; LLM, Georgetown U., 1975. Bar: N.Y. 1972, D.C. 1972, Calif. 1972. Spl. asst. U.S. atty. U.S. Atty.'s Office, Washington, 1972-73; asst. prof. U. San Francisco Sch. Law, 1973-75; assoc. O'Melveny & Myers, L.A., 1975-79; assoc. prof. Southwestern U. Sch. Law, L.A., 1979-82, prof., 1983—, Irwin R. Buchalter prof. law, 1990. Mem. faculty Nat. Judicial Coll., 1993. Prettyman fellow Georgetown Law Ctr., Washington, 1971-73. Author: Federal Pretrial Practice, 1987, ALI, 1989. Fellow Am. Bar Found.; mem. ABA (chmn. com. on fed. rules and criminal procedure criminal justice sect. 1987-93, vice-chair pubs. criminal justice sect. 1994—, trial evidence com. litigation sect. 1980—), Assn. Am. Law Schs. (com. on sects. 1984-87, chairperson women in legal edn. sect. 1982), Nat. Assn. Women Lawyers (bd. dirs. 1991—, pres.-elect 1993, pres. 1994), Women Lawyers Assn. L.A. (bd. dirs., coord. mothers support group 1987—), Order of Coif, Phi Beta Kappa. Office: Southwestern U Sch Law 675 S Westmoreland Ave Los Angeles CA 90005-3905

RAFAEL, RUTH KELSON, retired archivist, librarian, consultant; b. Wilmington, N.C., Oct. 28, 1929; d. Benjamin and Jeanette (Spicer) Kelson; m. Richard Vernon Rafael, Aug. 26, 1951; children: Barbara Martinez Yates, Brenda Elaine. BA, San Francisco State U., 1953, MA, 1954; MLS, U. Calif.-Berkeley, 1968. Cert. archivist, 1989; life credential. Libr. Tchr. San Francisco Unified Sch. Dist., 1956-57; libr. Congregation Beth Sholom, San Francisco, 1965-83; archivist Western Jewish History Ctr. of Judah L. Magnes Mus., Berkeley, Calif., 1968, head archivist, libr., curator of exhibits, 1969-94; ret., 1994; cons. NEH, Washington, NHPRC, Congregation Sherith Israel, San Francisco, Mount Zion Hosp., San Francisco, Benjamin Swig archives project, San Francisco, Koret Found., Camp Swig, Saratoga, Calif.; project dir. Ethnicity in Calif. Agriculture, 1989, San Francisco Jews of European Origin, 1880-1940, an oral history project, 1976, curator exhibits Western U.S. Jewry. Author: Continuum, San Francisco Jews of Eastern European Origin, 1880-1940, 1976, rev. edit., 1977; (with Davies and Woogmaster) poetry book Relatively Speaking, 1981; Western Jewish History Center: Archival and Oral History Collections, Judah L. Magnes Meml. Mus., 1987; contbg. editor Western States Jewish History, 1979—. Mem. exec. bd. Bay Area Library Info. Network, 1986-88. Bur. Jewish Edn. scholar, San Francisco, 1983; NEH grantee, 1985. Mem. ALA, Soc. Am. Archivists, Soc. Calif. Archivists, Calif. Library Assn., No. Calif. Assn. Jewish Librarians (pres. 1975-76), Jewish Arts Council of the Bay (bd. dirs. 1981-83),

RAFFENSPERGER, SHIRLEY ANN, town official; b. Bradford, Pa., Sept. 5, 1932; d. Michael Benjamin and Mabel V. (Swanson) Gallagher; m. Edgar Merrow Raffensperger, Sept. 12, 1953; children: Andrew, Catharine, Thomas. BA, Pa. State U., 1953. Councilwoman Town of Ithaca, N.Y., 1976-89; supr. Town of Ithaca, 1990-93. Active N.Y. State Dem. Com., Albany, 1984-86, 86-88. Home: 139 Pine Tree Rd Ithaca NY 14850

RAFFERTY, CHRISTINE ANN, critical care nurse; b. Passaic, N.J., June 30, 1965; d. James W. and Alice H. (Voss) Havel; m. Michael Rafferty, May 27, 1988; 1 child, Sean. BSN with honors, Rutgers U., 1987. RN, N.J.; cert. BLS, Am. Heart Assn. Nurses' aide, staff nurse, then charge nurse telemetry Beth Israel Hosp., Passaic, 1985-91, staff nurse critical care unit, 1991—; staff nurse telemetry Valley Hosp., Ridgewood, N.J., 1991-92. Asst. leader parent support group Parent Talk, Carlstadt, N.J., 1991-93. Mem. ANA, AACN (nat. chpt. no. N.J.), N.J. Nurses Assn. Presbyterian. Home: 211 Alden St # 314 Wallington NJ 07057 Office: Beth Israel Hosp 70 Parker Ave Passaic NJ 07072

RAFFERTY, NANCY SCHWARZ, anatomy educator; b. Jamaica, N.Y., June 11, 1930; d. Franklin and Louise (Barry) Schwarz; m. Keen Alexander Rafferty, Aug. 7, 1953; children: Burns Arthur, Katherine Louisa. B.S., Queens Coll., 1952; M.S., U. Ill., 1953, Ph.D., 1958. Instr. anatomy Johns Hopkins U., 1963-66, asst. prof., 1966-70; asst. prof. anatomy Northwestern U., Chgo., 1970-72; asso. prof. Northwestern U., 1972-76, prof., 1976-94, prof. emeritus, 1994—; corp. mem., gen. libr. reader Marine Biol. Lab., Woods Hole, Mass. Contbr. articles on cell biology of the crystalline lens to profl. jours. USPHS fellow, 1958-63; USPHS grantee. Mem. Assn. Research in Vision and Ophthalmology, Internat. Soc. for Eye Research, Am. Assn. Anatomists, AAAS, Am. Soc. Cell Biology, Visual Scis. (study sect. of NIH), Sigma Xi, Phi Sigma. Home: 59 Harbor Hill Rd Woods Hole MA 02543-1219 Office: Marine Biol Lab Woods Hole MA 02543

RAFTERY, LAUREL A., research biologist, educator; b. Hilo, HI, Oct. 8, 1956; d. John Cornwell and Helga Ruth (Isakson) R.; m. Jeffrey Allen Casey, Apr. 10, 1982; 1 child, Bret W.R. Casey. AB, U. Calif., Berkeley, 1979; PhD, U. Colo., 1986; postdoctoral, Harvard U., 1986-92. Teaching fellow Harvard Univ., 1988; instr. dept. dermatology Cutaneous Biology Rsch Ctr. Mass. Gen. Hosp. and Harvard Med. Sch., Charlestown, Mass., 1993—; asst. biologist Mass. Gen. Hosp.; instr. Harvard Med. Sch.; speaker in field. Postdoctoral fellowship NIH, 1986-89, Charles A. King Trust, 1989-91. Mem. AAAS, Soc. for Devel. Biology, Genetics Soc. Am. Office: Cutaneous Biology Rsch Ctr MGH-East Bldg 149 13th St Charlestown MA 02129

RAFUSE, WANDA JEANETTE, counselor; b. DeFuniak Springs, Fla., Aug. 7, 1957; d. Ralph Raygene Sr. and Mildred Jeanette (Wyatt) R. BA in Psychology, St. Leo (Fla.) Coll., 1979. Cert. tchr., Fla. Substitute tchr. Pasco County Bd. of Pub. Edn., Dade City, Fla., 1977-86, dep. supr. elections, 1984-86; salesperson Landmark Real Estate, Dade City, 1987-90; office mgr. Jackson & Assocs. Ins., Dade City, 1988; spouse abuse counselor Sunrise Spouse Abuse Shelter, Dade City, 1988; drug rehab. counselor The Women's Ctr., Dade City, 1988-89; rehab. therapist Zephyrhills (Fla.) Correctional Instn., 1989-90; counselor Vocat. Rehab., Cross City, Fla., 1990-92; counselor for deaf Vocat. Rehab., Lakeland, Fla., 1992—. Precinct committee woman Pasco County Dem. Exec. Com., 1984-88; pres. Dade City Area Dem. Club, 1985; Sta. WEDU-Pub. Broadcasting Svc., Polk County Community Svcs. Coun. Southern Scholarship Found. scholar, 1976; recipient First Bapt. Ch. Dade City, 1985, Dedicated Svc. award Zephyrhills Correctional Inst., 1990, Rookie of Yr. award Vocat. Rehab. Dist. III, Gainesville, Fla., 1991. Mem. NAFE, Nat. Rehab. Assn., Nat. Assn. Realtors, Fla. Rehab. Assn., Fla. Assn. Realtors, Dade City Bd. of Realtors. Democrat. Home: 403 E Clinton Ave Dade City FL 33525 Office: Vocat Rehab Box 10 200 N Kentucky Ave Ste 310 Lakeland FL 33801-4993

RAGAN, ANN TALMADGE, media and production consultant, actor; b. Raleigh, N.C., July 6, 1951; d. Samuel Talmadge and Marjorie Lois (Usher) R.; m. L. Worth Keeter III, Aug. 22, 1992. Student, U. N.C., 1969-71, Finch Coll., 1972-73, New Sch. Social Rsch., 1973-74, Western Wash. U., 1978. Acct. estimator Benton & Bowles Inc., N.Y.C., 1971-72, media buyer, 1974-77; speechwriter, press aide Senator Robert Morgan, Wash., 1978-79; asst. producer John F. Murray Inc., N.Y.C., 1979-80; producer, sales dir. Grand Street Films, N.Y.C., 1980-84; ind. producer for various clients N.Y.C., 1984-86; asst. pub. The Pilot, Inc., Southern Pines, N.C., 1986—; also bd. dirs. The Pilot, Inc.; prodn. mgr. Anglo Am. Media Workshops, London, 1988-90. Contbr. articles to newspaper and jour. Mem. Roanoke Island Hist. Assn., Sandhills Little Theatre, actress, 1986-89, Moore county Arts Coun., 1986-89. Mem. AFTRA, SAG, Women in Theatre, Pi Beta Phi. Democrat. Methodist. Home and Office: 4200 Laurel Cyn # 104 Studio City CA 91604-2001

RAGGI, LISA MARGARET MARY, lawyer; b. Jersey City, Aug. 30, 1958; d. Edward James and Tina (Navarchi) R.; m. Richard Winfield Conrad, Mar. 19, 1994. Student, Williams Coll., 1978-79; BA, Wellesley Coll., 1980; JD, Cath. U., 1983. Bar: D.C. 1983, N.Y. 1988. Law clk. D.C. Ct. of Appeals, Washington, 1983-84; sr. atty. divsn. corp. fin. SEC, Washington, 1983-84; assoc. gen. counsel, v.p. Drexel Burnhan Lambert, N.Y.C., 1987-90, Shearson Lehman Bros., N.Y.C., 1990-92; v.p. high yield Lehman Bros. Inc., N.Y.C., 1992—. Mem. Nat. Assn. Securities Dealers (arbitration panel 1988—), D.C. Bar Assn., N.Y. Bar Assn.

RAGGI, REENA, federal judge; b. Jersey City, May 11, 1951. BA, Wellesley Coll., 1973; JD, Harvard U., 1976. Bar: N.Y. 1977. U.S. atty. Dept. Justice, Bklyn., 1986; ptnr. Windels, Marx, Davies & Ives, N.Y.C., 1987; judge U.S. Dist. Ct. (ea. dist.) N.Y., Bklyn., 1987—. Office: US Courthouse 225 Cadman Plz E Brooklyn NY 11201

RAGGIO, LOUISE BALLERSTEDT, lawyer; b. Austin, Tex., June 15, 1919; d. Louis F. and Hilma (Lindgren) Ballerstedt; m. Grier H. Raggio, Apr. 19, 1941; children: Grier, Thomas, Kenneth. B.A., U. Tex., 1939; student, Am. U. Washington, 1939-40; J.D., So. Methodist U., 1952. Bar: Tex. 1952, U.S. Dist. Ct. (no. dist.) Tex. 1958. Intern Nat. Inst. Pub. Affairs, Washington, 1939-40; asst. dist. atty. Dallas County, Tex., 1954-56; shareholder Raggio and Raggio, 1956—. Sec. Gov.'s Commn. on Status of Women, 1970-71; trustee Tex. Bar Found., 1982-86, chmn., 1984-85, chmn. fellows, 1993—, Dallas Women's Found., 1993—, Nat. Conf. Bar Founds., 1986-92. Recipient Zonta award, Bus. and Profl. Women's Club award, So. Meth. U. Alumni award, Woman of Yr. award Tex. Fedn. Bus. and Profl. Women's Clubs, 1985, award Internat. Women's Forum, 1990, Disting. Law Alumni award So. Meth. U., 1992; Disting. Trial Lawyer award, 1993, Outstanding Trial Lawyer award Dallas Bar Assn., 1993, Pacemaker award Nat. Bus. Women Owners Assn., 1994; inducted into Tex. Women's Hall of Fame, 1985. Fellow Am. Bar Found.; mem. ABA (chmn. family sect. 1975-76), State Bar Tex. (chmn. family law sect. 1965-67, dir. 1979-82, citation for law reform 1967, Pres.'s award 1987, Sarah T. Hughes award 1993), Dallas Bar Found. (pres. fellows com. 1991), Am. Acad. Matrimonial Lawyers (gov. 1973-81, trustee found. 1992—), Bus. and Profl. Women's Club (pres. Town North 1958-59), LWV (pres. Austin 1945-46), Phi Beta Kappa (pres. Dallas chpt. 1970-71, 90-92). Unitarian. Home: 3561 Colgate Ave Dallas TX 75225-5010 Office: Raggio and Raggio 3316 Oak Grove Ave Dallas TX 75204-2331

RAGLE, GEORGE ANN, accountant; b. Detroit, Dec. 21, 1946; d. Joseph Theodore and Josephine Theresa (Mastrogiovanni) Gibson; m. James Albert, Sept. 3, 1976; children: Gina Ann, Jeffrey Allen. Assoc. Bus., Oakland C.C., Farmington Hills, Mich., 1974; B Accountancy, Walsh Coll., Troy, Mich., 1975; MBA, Ctrl. Mich. U., 1981. Cert. sch. bus. adminstr., Mich. Tax analyst Burroughs Corp., Detroit, 1976, Robillard & Joyce, St. Clair Shores, Mich., 1977-78; acctg. mgr. Baker Driveaway, Bloomfield Hills, Mich., 1978-79; staff acct. Macomb County Contr., Mt. Clemens, Mich., 1979-80; sr. acct. Macomb Intermediate Sch. Dist., Mt. Clemens, 1980-86; dir. bus. Mt. Clemens Community Schs., 1986-88, Pinconning (Mich.) Area Sch., 1988-90; dir. bus. and pers. St. Clair Intermediate Sch. Dist., Port Huron, Mich., 1990—. Bd. officer, treas. Fraser (Mich.) Pub. Schs. Bd. Edn., 1974-78; bd. mem. Anchor Bay Schs. Bd. Edn., New Baltimore, Mich., 1991—, treas., 1991-92, 94-95. Mem. Assn. Sch. Bus. Ofcls., Mich. Sch. Bus. Ofcls., Mich. Assn. Sch. Pers. Adminstrs., Macomb/St. Clair Sch. Bus. Ofcls. Home: 52134 Charleston Ln New Baltimore MI 48047-1191 Office: St Clair Intermediate Sch Dist 499 Range Rd Port Huron MI 48061

RAGNO, NANCY NICKELL, educational writer; b. Phila., Sept. 2, 1938; d. Paul Eugene and Sara Jane (Mensch) Nickell; m. Joseph Diego Ragno, Aug. 25, 1961; 1 child, Michelle Angela. BA, Lebanon Valley Coll., 1960; MA, NYU, 1968. Cert. tchr., N.J. Tchr. N.J. pub. schs., 1961-68; project editor Prentice-Hall, Inc., Englewood Cliffs, N.J., 1968-70, Harcourt Brace Jovanovich, N.Y.C, 1970-72; sr. editor Silver Burdett Co., Morristown, N.J., 1972-76; editor, writer Houghton Mifflin Co., Boston, 1976-77; sr. editor J.B. Lippincott Co., Phila., 1977-79; sr. author Silver Burdett Ginn, Morristown, 1984—. Author: (textbook series) Silver Burdett English, 1984, World of Language, 1992, (sound filmstrip) The City and the Modern Writer, 1970, Buying on the Installment Plan, 1974. Bassoonist Harrisburg (Pa.) Symphony Orch., 1959, Plainfield (N.J.) Symphony Orch., 1976, Somerset (N.J.) County Orch., 1989, Princeton (N.J.) Community Orch., 1992. Mem. ASCD, Nat. Coun. Tchrs. English, Internat. Reading Assn., Am. Soc. Journalists and Authors, Textbook Authors Assn., Authors Guild, U.S. Power Squadron. Democrat. Mem. Ch. of Christ. Home: 112 Hillcrest Terr Stuart FL 34996

RAGO, DOROTHY ASHTON, retired educator; b. N.Y.C., Oct. 10, 1925; d. Thomas Percy and Isabel (Seddon) Ashton; divorced, 1958; 1 child, Thomas Ashton. BA, Wellesley Coll., 1946; MA, Columbia U., 1964. Cert. early childhood edn. tchr., N.Y. Editor Alford Baby Group mags., N.Y.C., 1948-52; kindergarten tchr. N.Y.C. Bd. Edn., 1964-86; ret. Mem. vestry Chapel of St. John Saunderstown, R.I., 1988-91; mem. Human Rights Com., North Kingstown, R.I., 1988—; treas. Pettaquamscutt Hist. Soc., 1991—. Mem. South County Women's Club (recording sec.), Saunderstown Yacht Club. Republican. Episcopalian.

RAGSDALE, BERTHA MAE See KOLB, BERTHA MAE

RAGSDALE, CHRISTINA ANN, public relations executive, consultant; b. Long Beach, Calif., July 27, 1956; d. David Neal and Mary Lou (Kaiser) Webber; m. Joel Gordon Ragsdale, Mar. 14, 1987. BA in Creative Writing, Lone Mountain Coll., 1978; MA in Communication Studies, Calif. State U., Sacramento, 1983. Instr. communication studies Calif. State U., Sacramento, 1981-84; prodn. mgr. Videomedia, Inc., Sunnyvale, Calif., 1984-85; comm. specialist Mercy Gen. Hosp., Sacramento, 1985-88, community rels. mgr., 1988; owner Ragsdale Comm., Sacramento, 1988-93; water quality info. mgr. County of Sacramento, 1993—; cons. Cablevision of Sacramento, 1982; presenter Calif. Water Pollution Control Assn. conv., 1994, Ideas Unltd. workshop Soc. Healthcare Pub. Rels. and Mktg., 1985. Mem. exec. com. Harry S. Truman Dem. Club, Sacramento, 1990—; active comm. com. Am. Lung Assn., Sacramento, 1988—, chair Clean Air Week, 1993, 94, bd. dirs. Mem. Sacramento Pub. Rels. Assn. (bd. dirs. and sec. 1989-91, numerous awards), Natomas Optimist (charter), Nat. Assn. Profl. Environ. Communicators. Home: 14887 Trinidad Dr Rancho Murieta CA 95683

RAHBAR, ZITA INA, health insurance executive; b. Kaunas, Lithuania, Mar. 15, 1937; came to U.S. 1949; d. Stasys and Ona (Eitkeviciute) Carneckas; m. Vytautas Dudenas, June 20, 1960 (div. 1965); m. Darius Rahbar, Mar. 26, 1970. BA St. Xavier Univ., Chgo., 1957; postgrad. in physiology U. Chgo., 1957-59, MBA, 1978. Mng. editor Lyons & Carnahan div. Meredith Corp., Chgo., 1960-68, mgr. program planning, 1968-73; exec. cons. George S. May Co., Chgo., 1973-75; sr. cons. planning Blue Shield Assn., Chgo., 1975-76, dir. corp. planning Blue Shield/Blue Cross Assn., 1976-78, sr. dir. program devel. and implementation, 1978-81, v.p. mktg. Blue Cross Calif., Los Angeles and Oakland, Calif., 1981-87; pres., Creative Mktg. Solutions, 1987—, CMS Automotive, Inc., 1992—. Bd. dirs. Bethune Ballet, Los Angeles, 1982—; mem. com. Orgn. Women Execs., Los Angeles, 1982—; co-founder Women in Pub., Chgo., 1965; mem. NOW, Town Hall Calif., Chgo. Council Fgn. Relations, World Affairs Council Los Angeles.

Fellow U. Chgo., 1957-58. Mem. Am. Mgmt. Assn., Am. Mktg. Assn., AAAS, Republican. Roman Catholic. Home: 912 Blue Spring Dr Westlake Village CA 91361-2006

RAHILL, MARGARET ANNE, retired museum curator; b. Milw., Feb. 21, 1919; d. Joseph Benedict and Margaret (Scherdan) Schmidt; m. William James Fish, Nov. 14, 1941 (dec. 1945); 1 child, Mary Fish Arcuri; m. Frank M. Rahill, Mar. 14, 1951 (dec. Oct. 1986); children: Marguerite, Laura Rahill Maramba. BA, U. Wis., 1958; student, Mt. Mary Coll., 1958. With pub. rels. Blackland Army Air Base, Waco, Tex., 1942-43; reporter, art critic Milw. Sentinel, 1945-62; with pub. rels. dept. Milw. Art Ctr., 1962-63, Layton Sch. Art, Milw., 1965-68, Bel Canto Chorus, Milw., 1965-68; curator in charge Charles Allis Art Mus., Milw., 1968-91; prin. Book Bay, Milw., 1962-72; vis. instr. journalism Marquette U., Milw., 1972-73; mem. organizing com. Florentine Opera Club, 1962, with pub. rels. dept. 1962-65; mem. organizing com. Wis. Chamber Orch., Milw., 1975-76; v.p. art, councillor-at-large Wis. Acad. Sci. Arts and Letters, Madison, 1981-85; juror numerous art competitions, Wis., 1962-91. Contbr. articles to profl. jours. Active City of Milw. Art Commn., 1982-90, pres., 1984-85. Recipient Gridirm award Milw. Press Club, 1955, 57, 59, 60, Community Svc. award Milw. Art Commn., 1976, Devel. award Milw. County Hist. Soc., 1982, Promotion of Hispanic Culture award Centro de la Communidad Unida, 1988. Mem. AAUW, Wis. Painters and Sculptors (hon.), Wis. Crafts Coun. (hon.). Roman Catholic. Home: 4801 Connecticut Ave Apt 302 Washington DC 20008

RAHL, LESLIE LYNN, risk advisor, entrepreneur; b. N.Y.C., May 16, 1950; d. Myron and Esther (Botwin) Horwitz; m. Jeffrey Mark Lynn, Dec. 20, 1969 (div. 1981); m. J. Andrew Rahl Jr., Apr. 30, 1989; 1 child, Kevin; stepchildren: Kaitlin, Stephen. SB, MIT, 1971, MBA, 1972. V.p. swaps and derivatives Citibank, N.Y.C., 1972-91; pres. Leslie Rahl Assocs., N.Y.C., 1991-94; co-prin. Capital Market Risk Advisors, N.Y.C., 1994—; bd. dirs. Internat. Swap Dealers Assn., N.Y.C., 1988-90; mem. task force WEIRD instruments; presenter in field. Contbr. articles to profl. jours. Bd. dirs., treas. 60 East End Ave. Assn., N.Y.C., 1986—. Recipient On the Rise award Fortune. Mem. Internat. Assn. Fin. Engrs. (bd. dirs. 1993—), Madison Beach Club. Office: Capital Market Risk Advisors 420 Lexington Ave New York NY 10170

RAHM, BARBARA JANE, counselor; b. Waukegan, Ill., Nov. 16, 1941; d. Alton Romeo and Jane Romaine (Gregory) Kaste; m. Kenneth J. Schultz, Aug. 24, 1963 (div. Dec. 1990); children: Annemarie Katharine, Kristin Elise, Carleen Janette. B of Edn., U. Wis., 1963; MA in Guidance, Northeastern U., 1991. Cert. counselor. Audio-visual dir., libr. Sch. Dist. 155, Crystal Lake, Ill., 1984-88; counselor, case mgr. Family Svc. Assn., Elgin, Ill., 1991-93; sch. counselor Simmons Mid. Sch., Aurora, Ill., 1993—. Mem. ACA. Home: 1085 Hecker Dr Elgin IL 60120-4604

RAHM, DIANNE, government and international affairs educator; b. N.Y.C., Sept. 27, 1951; d. Olaf Lennart and Jeanne (Todd) R.; m. Richard R. Valdes, Apr. 23, 1971 (div. 1982); 1 child, Anastasia Rahm Valdes. BA in Liberal Arts, Wichita State U., 1975, MA in Am. History, 1976; MS in Computer Sci., Fitchburg State Coll., 1985; PhD in Pub. Adminstrn., Syracuse U., 1989. Computer sci. instr. Cen. New Eng. Coll., Worcester, Mass., 1979-82; assoc. prof. computer mgmt. Becker Jr. Coll., Worcester, Mass., 1982-86; adj. prof. pub. adminstrn. Syracuse (N.Y.) U., 1987; asst. prof. pub. adminstrn. Pa. State U., 1988-90; assoc. prof. govt. and internat. affairs U. South Fla., Tampa, 1990-93, 1994—, dir. computing, 1991-92; programmer, analyst Data Gen. Corp., Westboro, 1978-79; sr. rsch. assoc. tech. and info. policy program Syracuse U., 1986-88; cons.Mtmg. Info. Systmes and Computer Systems, Worcester, 1980-86, U.S. Gen. Acctg. Office, Washington, 1989, Fla. Dept. Labor and Employment, Tampa, 1991, City of Clearwater, Fla., 1991, City of Pinellas Park, Fla., 1991. Contbr. articles to profl. jours. Mem. Am. Soc. Pub. Adminstrn., Assn. Pub. Policy Mgmt., Policy Studies Orgn., Sci. and Tech. in Govt., So. Polit. Scis. Assn., Union Concerned Scientists. Unitarian. Office: U South Fla Dept Govt & Internat Affairs 4202 E Fowler Ave Tampa FL 33620-9951

RAHM, SUSAN BERKMAN, lawyer; b. Pitts., June 25, 1943; d. Allen Hugh and Selma (Wiener) Berkman; m. David Alan Rahm, Nov. 23, 1972; children: Katherine, William. BA with honors, Wellesley Coll., 1965; postgrad., Harvard U., 1966-68; JD, NYU, 1973. Bar: N.Y. 1974, D.C. 1988. Assoc. Marshall, Bratter, Greene, Allison & Tucker, N.Y.C., 1973-81, ptnr., 1981-82; ptnr. Kaye, Scholer, Fierman, Hays & Handler, N.Y.C., 1982—, chair real estate dept., 1993—. Editor: New York Real Property Service, 1987. Bd. dirs. Girls Inc., 1989-93; mem. aux. bd. Mt. Sinai Hosp., N.Y.C., 1987—. Recipient cert. of outstanding svc. D.C. Redevel. Land Agy., 1969, She Knows Where She's Going award Girls' Clubs of Am., 1987. Mem. ABA, Assn. of Bar of City of N.Y., N.Y. Bar Assn. (real property law com., co-chmn. real-estate devel. . 1987-91), Am. Coll. Real Estate Lawwyers, Comml. Real Estate Women N.Y. (bd. dirs. 1988-94), v.p. 1988-91, pres. 1991-93). Office: Kaye Scholer Fierman Hays & Handler 425 Park Ave New York NY 10022-3506

RAICHEL, GERI WAHRMAN, educator; b. Bklyn., Jan. 13, 1943; m. Daniel Richter Raichel, Mar. 23, 1967; children: Adam Mark, Dina Karen. BA, Bklyn. Coll., 1964; MA, Columbia U., 1967; postgrad., Fordham U., 1972-78. Cert. supr., tchr. Tchr. N.Y.C. (N.Y.) Bd. Edn., 1964-68; tchr. of gifted Harrington Park (N.J.) Bd. Edn., 1979-80, Ridgefield (N.J.) Bd. Edn., 1980-81, Wyckoff (N.J.) Bd. Edn., 1981-83; tchr. gifted, coord. tech. Harrington Park (N.J.) Bd. Edn., 1983—; adj. instr. William Paterson Coll., Wayne, N.J., 1976-80. Bd. mem. Wyckoff (N.J.) Twp. Bd. Edn., 1976-79; founder, bd. mem. Cmty. Learning Ctr., Wyckoff, 1976-81. Mem. ASCD, Harrington Park Edn. Assn. (pres. 1991-92), Gifted Child Soc. (curriculum coord. 1980-84, leadership com. 1992-93, bd. mem.). Office: Harrington Park Sch 191 Harriot Ave Harrington Park NJ 07640-1401

RAIKEN, ESTHER CAGEN, librarian; b. Cleve., Dec. 22, 1907; d. Charles and Ida (Kaufman) Hirsch; m. Samuel Lawrence Cagen, June 18, 1934 (dec. Jan. 1982); children: Lenore, Barbara (dec.), Robert; m. Oscar Harris Raiken, Sept. 18, 1983. BS, Western Res. U., 1962, MLS, 1963. Head children's rm. Lee Br. Libr., Cleveland Heights, Ohio, 1953-57; head Fairfax Sch. libr. Cleveland Heights Sch. Libr. System, 1957-69; instr. children's lit. Case Western Res. U., Cleve., 1964-67, Cleve. State U., 1967-69; dir. pilot media ctr. Belvoir Elem. Sch., Cleveland Heights, 1969-74; libr. Convent of Sacred Heart, San Francisco, 1974-76, Congregation Sherith Israel, San Francisco, 1980—. NDEA scholar Kent (Ohio) U., 1964. Mem. Assn. Jewish Librs. (award presenter 1991, Best Book of Yr. award 1991), AAUW, Beta Phi Mu. Democrat. Jewish. Home: 1900 Jackson St San Francisco CA 94109-2860

RAILSBACK, SHERRIE L., adoption search/reunion consultant; b. Phila., Mar. 12, 1942; children: Ricky, Cindy. BBA, U. Ky., 1981. Sales mgr. Marjo Cosmetics, Ft. Wayne, Ind.; asst. dir. patient fin. svcs. Riverside Meth. Hosp., Columbus, Ohio; cons. Railsback and Assocs., Long Beach, Calif.; adoption search/reunion cons. L.A. Mem. NAFE, ASTD, Book Publicists of So. Calif., Toastmasters.

RAIN, CHERYL ANN, underwriter; b. Alton, Ill., Aug. 22, 1950; d. Robert E. and Mary F. (Miller) Gill; m. William A. Rain Jr., Mar. 31, 1973; children: Nathan A. Rain, Jeremy S. Rain. BA, So. Ill. U., Edwardsville, 1972, MBA, 1992. Tng. mgr. Germania Fed. Savs., Alton, Ill., 1983-86; with St. Louis Commerce Mortage Corp., St. Louis, 1986—, asst. v.p., 1992-94; regional underwriting mgr. Commerce Mortgage Corp., St. Louis, 1994—. Asst. treas. Jr. League of Greater Alton, 1984-85, treas., 1985-86; pres., bd. dirs. Evang. Sch. for Young, Godfrey, Ill., 1982-83; moderator for bd. deacons Elm St. Presbyn. Ch., Alton, 1981-82. Republican. Methodist. Home: 1405 Duval Dr Godfrey IL 62035-1635 Office: Commerce Mortgage Corp 8000 Forsyth Blvd # 606 Clayton MO 63105-1707

RAINES, CHARLOTTE AUSTINE, artist, poet; b. Sullivan, Ill., July 1, 1922; d. Donald Malone and Charlotte (Wimp) Butler; m. Irving Isaack Raines, Sept. 26, 1941; children: Robin Raines Collison, Kerry Raines Lydon. BA in Studio Arts magna cum laude, U. Md., 1966. One woman show at Castle Theatre, 1988, Md., C.T.V. Awards Hall, Md., 1993; exhibited in numerous group shows including Corcoran Gallery, 1980, Md.'s Best Exhbn., 1986, Md. State House, 1990; represented in various pvt. collections; selected works in U.S. Dept. State Arts in Embassies Program; contbr. poems to literary publs. Mem. Artists Equity Assn., Writers' Ctr., Phi Kappa Phi. Studio: 4103 Longfellow St Hyattsville MD 20781-1748

RAINES, JO ANN, academic affairs coordinator; b. Charleston, W.Va., June 17, 1960; d. H. Glenville and Betty (Sheets) R. BA in Polit. Sci., W.Va. State Coll., 1982; MA in Polit. Sci., Ohio U., 1986. Legis. aide Ohio Ho. of Reps., Columbus, 1986-88; legis./pub. affairs W.Va. Higher Edn. Ctrl. Office, Charleston, 1988-92; acad. affairs coord. Marshall U. Sch. of Medicine, Huntington, W.Va., 1992—. Vol. DARE Softball, Charleston, 1993, Neighborhood Watch, Huntington, 1993-94; bd. dirs. Thereuputic Riding for Youth, Huntington, 1994. Home: 2232 Guthrie Ct Huntington WV 25703

RAINES, MARY ELIZABETH, airline executive; b. Tifton, Ga., Nov. 28, 1951; d. Marvin D. and Lou E. (Collins) R. BBA, Coll. William and Mary, 1973; JD with distinction, Emory U., 1979. Bar: Ga. 1979. Atty. Delta Air Lines, Inc., Atlanta, 1980-84, sr. atty., 1984-85, asst. sec., 1985-90, corp. sec., 1990-94, gen. atty., 1994—. Mem. ABA, Am. Soc. Corp. Secs., State Bar Ga. Office: Delta Air Lines Inc Hartsfield Atlanta Internat Airport Atlanta GA 30320

RAINEY, JEAN OSGOOD, public relations executive; b. Lansing, Mich., Apr. 5, 1925; d. Earle Victor and Blanche Mae (Eberly) Osgood; m. John Larimer Rainey, Nov. 29, 1957 (dec. Oct. 1991); children: Cynthia, John Larimer, Ruth. Grad., Lansing Bus. U., 1942. Pub. rels. dir. Nat. Assn. Food Chains, Washington, 1954-59; v.p. pub. rels. Manchester Orgns., Washington, 1959-61; ptnr. Rainey, McEnroe & Manning, Washington, 1962-73; v.p. Manning, Selvage & Lee, Washington, 1973-79, pres. Washington div., 1979-84, sr. counsellor, 1985—; owner Jean Rainey Assocs., Washington, 1986-87; sr. v.p. Daniel J. Edelman Inc., 1987—. Author: How to Shop for Food, 1972. Pres. Hyde Home and Sch. Assn., Washington, 1969-71; co-chmn. Nat. Com. for Reelection of the Pres., 1972. Mem. Pub. Rels. Soc. Am. (accredited), Am. Women in Radio and TV (pres. Washington chpt. 1962-63, mem. nat. bd. 1963-65), Am. News Women's Club (pres. 1973-75). Republican. Episcopalian. Clubs: City Tavern, International. Home: Apt 250B 4000 Cathedral Ave NW Washington DC 20016-5249 Office: Edelman Pub Rels 1420 K St NW Washington DC 20005-2500

RAINS, MARY JO, banker; b. Konawa, Okla., Oct. 27, 1935; d. Albert Wood and Mary Leona (Winfield) Starns; m. Billy Z. Rains, June 17, 1956; 1 child, Nicky Z. Student Okla. Sch. Banking, 1969, Seminole Jr. Coll., 1970-72, E. Central State U., 1978-79, Okla. State U., 1987, Pontotoc County Adult Vocat. Tech. Ctr., 1987; diploma Am. Inst. Banking, 1981, 83. Acctg. divsn. Universal C.I.T., Oklahoma City, 1953-56; cashier Okla. State Bank (name changed to Bancfirst), Konawa, 1957-89, sr. v.p., customer svc. officer, 1989—. Sec. 1st Baptist Ch., Konawa, 1969-79, mem. budgeting com., 1982-92, chmn. fin. com., 1994. Mem. Okla. Bankers Assn. (dir. women's div. 1974-76), Konawa C. of C., Am. Legion., Order Eastern Star. Home: RR 2 Box 28 Konawa OK 74849-9802 Office: PO Box 156 Konawa OK 74849

RAINS, MURIEL BARNES, retired educator, real estate agent; b. Atlanta, Feb. 6, 1916; d. George Washington and Nancy Blodgett (Enos) Barnes; m. David Dean Rains (dec.); children: Rose Muriel, David Dean II. BS, Wilberforce (Ohio) U., 1937; MA, Tex. So. U., 1955; postgrad., Temple U., 1956-81. Cert. tchr., N.J., Tex., Del., Pa.; cert. news reporter, Ohio. News reporter Ohio State News, Columbus, 1937-40; tchr. Houston Pub. Schs., 1950-56, Camden (N.J.) Pub. Schs., 1956-63, various schs., Wilmington, Del., 1963-78; various schs., Claymont, Del., 1978-81; real estate agt., Phila., 1980—; former mem. city profl. growth com. Wilmington Pub. Schs., 1963-67; instr. in physics Brandywine Coll., Wilmington; co-author WOMP (Wilmington Occupational Project). Poetry author; contbr. articles to profl. jours. Active Houston Interracial Commn., 1950-56, State Reception Com., Houston, 1949. Mem. AAUW, Am. Assn. Math. Tchrs., Nat. Hist. Soc., Germantown Civic League (rec. sec. 1986-91), Alpha Kappa Alpha (life). Episcopalian. Home and Office: 6909 Boyer St Philadelphia PA 19119-1908

RAISER, MARY M., chief of protocol; b. Buffalo, Aug. 5, 1942; d. Robert and Eleanor (Verduin) Millonzi; m. Charles Victor Raiser II, Sept. 7, 1963 (dec. July 1992); 1 child, Mary van Schuyler. Student, Smith Coll., 1960-63; BS in Edn., U. Va., 1964; MA, SUNY, Buffalo, 1978; postgrad., George Washington U., 1990—. Tchr. grade 5 Pub. Sch. #56, 1965-66; tchr. grades 5-8 Emwood Franklin Sch., Buffalo, 1973-75; regional dir. western N.Y. office Sen. Daniel P. Moynihan, Buffalo, 1977-79; spl. asst. Sen. Daniel P. Moynihan, Washington, 1979-81; chief of protocol to U.S. Pres., v.p., sec. of state Dept. State and White House, Washington, 1993—. Founder Smith Coll. Club Scholarship; pres. Del. Assn., 1971; chair Quality of Life Task Force, Com. Alternative Forms of Govt., Buffalo, 1976; chair vols. D.C. chpt. ARC, 1985-86, bd. dirs., 1986-90, chair comm. com., 1986-90, mem. mgmt. com. D.C. chpt.; bd. dirs. Cmty. Mus. Sch., Buffalo, 1967-70, Jr. Group, Albright-Knox Gallery, Buffalo, 1967-70, Sasha Bruce House, Washington, 1981-83, Higher Achievement Program, Washington, 1989-90, Ellington Fund of Duke Ellington Sch. for the Arts D.C. Pub. Performing Arts H.S., 1989-92, Nat. Symphony Orch., 1992—; participant, fundraiser local and statewide elections Buffalo, 1970-92; fundraiser Dem. Nat. Com., Congressmen Matsui, LaFalce, Dicks, Nowak, Sens. Gore, Robb, others, 1970-92; mem. fin. com. Moynihan for Sen., 1981-82; mem. arrangements com. Dem. Nat. Conv., 1984, mem. site selection com., 1987-88; mem. Albert Gore Jr. Presdl. Fin. Com., 1987-88; chair devel. com., bd. dirs. Women's Campaign Fund, 1988-90, Dem. chair, 1990-93; founder women's coun. Dem. Senatorial Campaign Com., 1992—. Episcopalian. Office: Office of Protocol Dept State 2201 C St NW Rm 1232 Washington DC 20520

RAITT, BONNIE LYNN, singer, musician; b. Burbank, Calif., Nov. 8, 1949. Student, Radcliffe Coll. Performer blues clubs, East Coast; concert tours in Britain, 1976, 77; albums include Bonnie Raitt, 1971, Give It Up, 1972, Takin' My Time, 1973, Streetlights, 1974, Home Plate, 1975, Sweet Forgiveness, 1977, The Glow, 1979, Green Light, 1982, Nine Lives, 1986, Nick of Time, 1989 (Grammys 1990, Rock-Best Vocal Performance, Female, Pop-Best Vocal Performance, Female, Album of Yr.), I'm in the Mood (with John Lee Hooker) (Grammy 1990, Blues-Best Traditional Record), The Bonnie Raitt Collection, 1990, Luck of the Draw, 1991 (Grammy 1992, Rock-Best Vocal Performance, Female), Longing In Their Hearts, 1994; songs include Something to Talk About (Grammy 1992, Country-Best Vocal Performance, Female), Good Man, Good Woman (with Delbert McClinton) (Grammy 1992, Rock-Best Vocal by a Duo or Group). Recipient numerous Grammy nominations, four Grammy awards 1990, three Grammy awards 1992. Office: PO Box 46037 Los Angeles CA 90046

RAJOPPI, JOANNE, county official; b. Glen Ridge, N.J., Dec. 25, 1947; d. Raleigh and Edna Mildred R.; div.; children: Peter-Anthony, Andrew Leigh. BA, Case Western Reserve U., 1970; MPA, Seton Hall U., 1988. Staff writer Newark Evening News, N.J., 1970-71; editor N.J. Carpenter's Funds, Springfield, 1972-84; mayor, coun. mem. Twp. Springfield, N.J., 1976-78; chmn., mem. Union Co. Bd. Freeholders, Elizabeth, N.J., 1978-80; asst. sec. state State N.J., Trenton, 1981-82; registrar of deeds and mortgages County of Union, Elizabeth, 1984—; lectr. Pol. Sci. Rutgers-The State U., New Brunswick, 1989—. Author: (book) Women in Office: Getting There and Staying There, 1993; contbr. articles to jours. State committeewoman N.J. Dem. Co., 1978—; commr. Presdl. Com. on Scholrs, 1979-81; mem. Dem. County Com., 1989—; mem. Clinton/Gore N.J. Core Group, 1992. Mem. Women's Polit. Caucus N.J. (v.p. 1994—), N.J. Assn. Counties (pres., dir. 1990-91, Achievement award 1987-91), Union County C. of C. (bd. dirs. 1990—), Bus. and Profl. Women (legis. chair 1987-89, Achievement award 1990), Rotary Internat. (bd. dirs. 1991-94). Democrat. Office: Union County Office of the Register 2 Broad St Elizabeth NJ 07207

RAJSKI, PEGGY, film director, film producer; b. Stevens Point, Wis.. Attended, U. Wis. Films include: (prodn. mgr.): Lianna, 1982, Almost You, 1984; (prodr., prodn. mgr.) The Brother From Another Planet, 1984, Matewan, 1987, Eight Men Out, 1988; (prodr.) The Grifters, 1990, Little Man Tate, 1991 (also 2nd. unit dir.), Used People, 1992; (prodr. video) Bruce Springstein's Glory Days; (dir.) Trevor, 1994 (Acad. award for Best Live Action Short Film). Office: 140 Riverside Dr Ste 5E New York NY 10024*

RAKER, IRMA STEINBERG, judge; b. Bklyn., Apr. 28, 1938; d. Manuel J. and Fannie (Rakov) Steinberg; m. Samuel K. Raker, Apr. 3, 1960; 1 child, Mark Stefanie Leslie. BA, Syracuse U., 1959; cert. of attendance (hon.), Hague (The Netherlands) Acad. Internat. Law, 1959; JD, Am. U., 1972. Bar: Md. 1973, D.C. 1974, U.S. Dist. Ct. Md. 1977, U.S. Ct. Appeals (4th cir.) 1977. Asst. state's atty. State's Atty.'s Office of Montgomery County, Md., 1973-79; ptnr. Sachs, Greenebaum & Tayler, Washington, 1979-80; judge U.S. Dist. Ct. Md., Rockville, 1980-82, Cir. Ct. for Montgomery County, Md., 1982-94, Ct. of Appeals of Md., Rockville, 1994—; adj. prof. Washington Coll. Law, Am. U., 1980—; faculty seminar leader child abuse course Nat. Coll. Dist. Attys. at U. Mass., 1977; mem. faculty Md. Jud. Inst., Nat. Criminal Def. Inst., 1980, 81, 82; instr. litigation program Georgetown Law Ctr.-Nat. Inst. Trial Advocacy; mem. legis. com. Md. Jud. Conf., mem. exec. com., 1985-89, mem. commn. to study bail bond and surety industry in Md.; mem. spl. com. to revise article on crimes and punishment State of Md., 1991—; mem. inquiry com. atty. Grievance Commn. Md., 1978-81; chair com. on criminal law and traffic U.S. Dist. Ct. Md., 1981. Past editor Am. U. Law Rev. Treas., v.p. West Bradley Citizens Assn., 1964-68; mem. adv. com. to county exec. on child abuse Montgomery County, 1976-77, mem. adv. com. to county exec. on battered spouses, 1977-78, mem. adv. com. on environ. protection, 1980; mem. citizens adv. bd. Montgomery County Crisis Ctr., 1980. Recipient Outstanding Contbn. awards (2) Montgomery County Govt. Fellow Md. Bar Found.; mem. ABA (del. nat. conf. state trial judges, active various coms.), Md. State Bar Assn. (chairperson coun. criminal law and practice sect., mem. bd. govs. 1981, 82, 85, 86, 90, mem. coun. litigation sect., active coms.), Nat. Assn. Women Judges, Internat. Acad. Trial Judges, Montgomery County Bar Assn. (chairperson criminal law sect. 1978-79, mem. exec. com. 1979-80, active other coms.), Montgomery County Bar Leaders, Women's Bar Assn. Md., Women's Bar Assn. D.C., Hadassah Women's Orgn. (life), Pioneer Women Na'amat (hon. life, Celebration of Women award 1985), Pi Sigma Alpha. Office: Ct of Appeals of Md Judicial Ctr # 305 Rockville MD 20850

RAKOV, BARBARA STREEM, marketing executive; b. Bklyn., Jan. 4, 1946; d. Harold B. and Claire (Colbert) Streem; m. Harris J. Rakov, Nov. 20, 1970 (div. Mar. 1972). BS, Boston U., 1967; postgrad. NYU, 1972-74. Market rsch. analyst, product mgr., mktg. mgr. J.B. Williams, N.Y.C., 1967-77; mktg. mgr. Del Labs., Farmingdale, N.Y., 1977-78; product mgr., sr. product mgr., asst. to office of pres., dir. mktg. and sales Benelux countries, v.p. group mktg., dir., dir. new products, v.p. bus. devel. Joseph E. Seagram & Sons, 1978-90; pres. BSR Assocs., N.Y.C., 1990-92; v.p. mktg. Del Labs., 1992-94; v.p. mktg. Tsumura Internat., Secaucus, N.J., 1994—. Mem. L'Ordre des Coteaux de Champagne, Les Gastronomes de la Mer, Am. Mgmt. Assn. Avocations: tennis, skiing, squash, reading, water skiing. Home: 40 Shady Cove Ln Sag Harbor NY 11963-2407 Office: Tsumura Internat 300 Lighting Way Secaucus NJ 07096-1578

RALIS, PARASKEVY, art educator, artist; b. N.Y.C., Sept. 16, 1951; d. Harry and Katerina (Koumi) R. AA, Miami-Dade Community Coll., 1970; BFA, Fla. Internat. U., 1973; MS, Nova U., 1977. Tchr. Miami (Fla.) Park Elem. Sch., 1973-80; instr. visual arts, photography Am. Sr. High Sch., 1980-81; tchr. Holmes Elem. Sch., 1981-84, Horace Mann Jr. High Sch., 1983-85; instr. magnet program visual arts, photography R.R. Moton South Ctr. for the Expressive Arts, 1984—, head dept. fine arts spl. area, 1986-89, 93-94, magnet lead tchr., 1992-93; magnet dept. head R.R. Moton South Ctr. for the Expressive Arts, Miami, 1993-94; chairperson grant writing com. R.R. Moton Expressive Arts Ctr., 1990; mem. SBM Sch. Cadre, 1993-95, R.R. Moton's Sch. Based Mgmt. Cadre, 1993-95. Prin. works include Twenty-First M. Allen Hortt Meml. Exhbn., Contemporary Reflections of the 19th Century, 1979, Media Plus, 1980, Inception, 1981, Artspace, 1982, Class Impressions, 1983, Southern Exposure, 1986; exhibited in group shows at Met. Mus. Art and Art Ctr., Coral Gables, Fla., 1986, Broward Community Coll. Fine Arts Gallery, 1985, Mus. Art, Ft. Lauderdale, 1979, 84, North Miami Mus. and Art Ctr., 1983, Fla. Internat. U., 1980, Nat. Exhibit Am. Art, Chautauqua, N.Y., 1985, Images I Miami Dade Community Coll., 1988, Omni Internat. Mall Artworks Gallery, 1990, 91, 92, The Ctr. for Visual Comms., 1993, Sheldon Lurie Art Against AIDS Auction IV, Biltmore Hotel, Coral Gables, Fla., 1994 ; inventor first art game in U.S. History, 1978; Photog. of James Brown, 1981. Mem. Dade County Art Tchrs. Assn. (bd. dirs., publicity chmn., Pres.'s award 1984), Fla. Art Educators Assn. (presenter 1994), United Tchrs. of Dade (liaison to Dade Art Educators Assn. 1981-94), Art Edn. Assn. (chair photography com. conv. 1990). Greek Orthodox. Home: 798 NE 71th St Miami FL 33138 Office: RR Moton S Ctr for Excellence Expressive Arts Ctr 18050 Homestead Ave Miami FL 33157-5599

RALPH, JEAN DOLORES, education educator; b. Detroit, Sept. 6, 1923; d. Alfred Heath and Genievieve (Taber) Smith; m. Fred A. Ralph, May 4, 1946 (dec. June 1979); children: Nancy Jean, Ellen Sue, Marty. BA, Ea. Mich. U., 1946; MA, Wayne State U., 1961; edn. specialist, U. Mich., 1973; EdD, Nova U., 1981. Cert. gifted elem. and secondary English tchr., adminstr., supr., reading specialist, Mich., Ariz., Fla. Elem. tchr. pub. schs., Harper Woods, Farmington, Mich., 1954-61; elem. prin. Farmington Pub. Schs., 1961-73; curriculum writer Nogales (Ariz.) Pub. Schs., 1973-74; elem. prin. Miami (Ariz.) Pub. Schs., 1974-75; adminstr. Tucson Hebrew Acad., 1975-76; adminstr., tchr. Santa Cruz Sch. Dist. 28, Nogales, 1976-77; dir. edn. Eckerd Wilderness Camps, Brooksville, Fla., 1977-78; prof. edn. Eckerd Coll., St. Petersburg, Fla., 1978-79; adminstr. edn. program Nova U., Orlando, Fla., 1981-86, prof. edn., 1986-89; prof. edn. Kennesaw State Coll., Marietta, Ga., 1989-91; adj. prof. Ea. Ariz. Coll., Gila County, 1974-75; tchr. gifted Orange County Schs., Orlando, 1979-83, tchr. lang. lab. for migrant children, 1983-86, Chpt. I coord., tchr. reading, 1986-89; edn. cons. Ency. Brit., 1969-73, Ariz. Dept. Edn., Phoenix, 1973-77; reading cons. Holt Winston Rinehart, 1973-75. Mem. Nat. Coun. Tchrs. English, Internat. English Reading Assn., Coun. Exceptional Children, Assn. Supervision and Curriculum Devel. Home: 900 Towne Green Blvd Apt 611 Kennesaw GA 30144-2190

RALSTON, JOANNE SMOOT, public relations counseling firm executive; b. Phoenix, May 13, 1939; d. A. Glen and Virginia (Lee) Smoot; m. W. Hamilton Weigelt, Aug. 15, 1991. B.A. in Journalism, Ariz. State U., 1960. Reporter, The Ariz. Republic, Phoenix, 1960-62; co-owner, pub. relations dir. The Patton Agy., Phoenix, 1962-71; founder, pres., owner Joanne Ralston & Assocs., Inc., Phoenix, 1971-87, 92—; pres. Nelson Ralston Robb Comm., Phoenix, 1987-91; pres. Joanne Ralston & Assoc., Inc., Scottsdale, Ariz., 1992—. Contbr. articles to profl. jours. Bd. dirs. Ariz. Parklands Found., 1984-86, Gov.'s Council on Health, Phys. Fitness and Sports, 1984-86; task force mem. Water and Natural Resources Council, Phoenix, 1984-86; mem. Ariz. Republican Caucus, 1984—, others. Recipient Lulu' awards (36) Los Angeles Advt. Women, 1964—, Gold Quill (2) Internat. Assn. Bus. Communicators, Excellence awards Fin. World mag., 1982-93, others; named to Walter Cronkite Sch. Journalism Hall of Fame, Coll. Pub. Programs Ariz. State U., 1987; name one of 25 Most Influential Arizonians, Phoenix Mag., 1991. Mem. Pub. Relations Soc. Am. (counselor sect.), Internat. Assn. Bus. Communicators, Phoenix Press Club (pres. bd.), Investor Rels. Inst., Phoenix Met. C. of C. (bd. dirs. 1977-84, 85-91), Phoenix Country Club. Republican. Avocations: horses, skiing.

RALSTON, LENORE DALE, academic policy and program analyst; b. Oakland, Calif., Feb. 21, 1949; d. Leonard Earnest and Emily Allison (Hudnut) R. BA in Anthropology, U. Calif., Berkeley, 1971, MPH in Behavioral Sci., 1981; MA in Anthropology, Bryn Mawr Coll., 1973, PhD in Anthropology, 1980. Asst. researcher anthropology inst. internat. studies U. Calif., Berkeley, 1979-82, rsch. assoc. Latin Am. Study Ctr., 1982-83, acad. asst. to dean Sch. of Optometry, 1990—; assoc. scientist, rsch. adminstr. Med. Rsch. Inst., San Francisco, 1982-85; cons. health sci. Berkeley, 1986-90; mem. fin. bd. Med. Rsch. Inst., 1983-84; speaker in field. Co-author: Voluntary Effects in Decentralized Management, 1983; contbr. articles to profl. jours. Commr. Cmty. Health Adv. Com., Berkeley, 1988-90; vice chair, commr. Cmty. Health Commn., Berkeley, 1990-93; mem. bd. safety com. Miles, Inc., Berkeley, 1992—. Grantee Nat. Rsch. Svc. Award, WHO, NIMH, NSF. Fellow Applied Anthropology Assn.; mem. Am. Pub. Health

Assn., Am. Anthropology Assn., Sigma Xi. Home: 1232 Carlotta Ave Berkeley CA 94707-2707

RALSTON, LUCY VIRGINIA GORDON, artist; b. Washington, Sept. 9, 1926; d. Byron Brown and Lucy (Virginia (Gordon) R. Grad., Finch Jr. Coll., 1942; student, Parsons Sch. Design; studied with, Leon Kroll. Freelance artist Tiffany and Co., 1947-48; designer U.S.S. Constution book Am. Bible Soc. and John Jay and Eliza Jane Watson Found. for presentation Bibles to grads. U.S. Naval Acad., USCG Acad., Marchant Marine Acad., 1953—; art tchr. Sr. Citizens of Pelham, 1948-50. One-woman show Pelham (N.Y.) Meml. High Sch., 1939; exhibited in group shows Westchester Fedn. Women's Clubs, Bronxville, N.Y., 1954, Mt. Vernon (N.Y.) Art Assn., 1955, Allied Artists Am., N.Y.C., 1955, others; represented in permanent collections Assn. Jr. Leagues Am., N.Y.C. and tour U.S. and Can., John Jay and Eliza Jane Watson Found., Elizabeth, N.J.; executed mural at Westchester Restaurant, Mamaroneck, N.Y.; commd. portraits of Princess Anne and Prince Charles of Eng., Brit. Am. Soc. Vol. numerous civic orgns., 1942-45. Recipient Popular prize Manor Club, 1947, 48, 2d prize, 1958, 1st prize for graphic art, 1957; Popular prize Westchester Assn. Women's Clubs, 1951, Mt. Vernon Art Assn., 1954, 2d prize Met. Mus., Pelham, 1969. Mem. DAR (registrar Knapp chpt. 1961-63, recording sec. Anne Hutchinson chpt. 1989—), Jr. League Pelham, Daus. of Cin. (registrar 1973-78), Nat. Soc. Colonial Dames State N.Y., Colonial Soc. Ams. Royal Descent, Nat. Soc. Magna Carta Dames, Colonial Soc. Descendants Knights of Garter, Colonial Order Crown, Huguenot Soc. Am., Welcome to Washington Internat. Club. Republican. Episcopalian. Home and Studio: 4784 Boston Post Rd Pelham NY 10803

RALSTON, SHIRLEY ANN, civic leader; b. Pueblo, Colo., Oct. 5, 1936; d. Clay E. and Vivian M. (Cassidy) Klamm; m. Richard N. Ralston, June 15, 1954; children: Gary Allen, Sandra Lynn, Kathryn Fern, William Chester. AA in Bus. Adminstrn., Santa Ana Coll., 1980. Mem. exec. com. Nat. Found. March of Dimes, Orange, Calif., 1966-86, vol. coord., 1974-81, Calif. vol. advisor, 1983-86; vice chmn. Housing Community Devel. Block Grant Adv. Com., Orange, 1975-76; mem. governing bd. Rancho Santiago Coll., Santa Ana, Calif., 1981—; mem. birth defects monitoring program task force Calif. Dept. Health Svcs., 1985-88; bd. dirs. Orange County Fedn. Rep. Women, pres., 1990-91; chair choosing the future com., chair student svcs. and programs Bd. Govs. for Calif. C.C.'s, 1990—, v.p. bd. govs., 1992—; active Calif. Arthritis Found. Coun., others. Named Citizen of Yr., Anaheim Jr. Ebell, 1966, Jr. Woman of Yr., Ctrl. Orange County Panhellenic, 1976, Citizen Politician, Calif. Rep. Com., 1983; recipient commendation C.C. Educators of New Californians, 1991, L.A. C.C. Dist., 1991. Mem. Assn. C.C. Trustees (policy com., fed. rels. com.). Lutheran. Home: 1474 N Cleveland St Orange CA 92667-3707

RAMAGE, PATRICIA G., librarian; b. Austin, Tex., Aug. 20, 1938; d. David Edmund Lewis and Yvonne (Etnyre) Grear; m. Cecil Hugh Ramage, Dec. 21, 1957; children: David Lewis, Jeanne Marie, Michael Christopher. BA in Sociology, U. Tex., El Paso, 1972; MLS, U. Tex., Austin, 1974. Supr. Social Work Libr. U. Tex., Austin, 1975-77, libr. LBJ Sch. Pub. Affairs Libr., 1977-79; serials libr. Biomed. Libr., Mobile, Ala., 1980-84; sys. libr., sr. libr. U. South Ala., Mobile, 1981—. Mem. ALA, NOTIS (libr. users coun. 1993—), Ala. Libr. Assn., Network Ala. Academic Libr. (grant 1985-87, electronic access com. 1990—). Home: 2779 Lynndell Dr Mobile AL 36695 Office: U South Ala Library LB 310 Mobile AL 36688

RAMALEY, JUDITH AITKEN, university president, endocrinologist; b. Vincennes, Ind., Jan. 11, 1941; d. Robert Henry and Mary Krebs (McCullough) Aitken; m. Robert Folk Ramaley, Mar. 1966 (div. 1976); children: Alan Aitken, Andrew Folk. BA, Swarthmore Coll., 1963; PhD, UCLA, 1966; postgrad., Ind. U., 1967-69. Rsch. assoc., lectr. Ind. U., Bloomington, 1967-68, asst. prof. dept. anatomy and physiology, 1969-72; asst. prof. dept. physiology and biophysics U. Nebr. Med. Ctr., Omaha, 1972-74, assoc. prof., 1974-78, prof., 1978-82, assoc. dean for rsch. and devel., 1979-81; asst. v.p. for acad. affairs U. Nebr., Lincoln, 1980-82; prof. biol. scis. SUNY, Albany, N.Y., 1982-87, v.p. for acad. affairs, 1982-85, acting pres., 1984, exec. v.p. for acad. affairs, 1985-87; exec. vice chancellor U. Kans., Lawrence, 1987-90; pres. Portland (Oreg.) State U., Oreg., 1990—; bd. dirs. Bank of Am.; mem. endocrinology study sect. NIH, 1981-84; cons.-evaluator North Cen. Accreditation, 1978-82, 89-90; mem. regulatory panel NSF, 1979-82; mem. Ill. Commn. Scholars, 1980—. Co-author: Progesterone Function: Molecular and Biochemical Aspects, 1972; Essentials of Histology, 8th edit., 1979; editor: Covert Discrimination, Women in the Sciences, 1978; contbr. articles to profl. jours. Bd. dirs. Family Svc. of Omaha, 1979-82, Albany Symphony Orch., 1984-87, mem. exec. com., 1986-87, Urban League Albany, 1984-87, 2d v.p., mem. exec. com., 1986-87, Upper Hudson Planned Parenthood, 1984-87, Capital Repertory Co., 1986-89, Assn. Portland Progress, 1990—, City Club of Portland, 1991-92, Metro Family Svcs., 1993—, Campbell Inst. for Children; bd. dirs. NCAA Pres. Commn., 1991, chair divsn. II subcom., 1994, mem. joint policy bd., 1994; chmn. bd. dirs. Albany Water Fin. Authority, 1987; mem. exec. com. United Way Douglas County, 1989-90; mem. adv. bd. Emily Taylor Women's Resource Ctr., U. Kans., 1988-90; mem. Silicon Prarie Tech. Assn., 1989-90, Portland Opera Bd., 1991-92, Portland Leaders Roundtable, 1991—; mem. bd. devel. com. United Way of Columbia-Williamette, 1991—; active Oreg. Women's Forum, 1991—, Portland Met. Sports Authority; progress bd. Portland-Multinomah County, 1993—. NSF grantee, 1969-71, 71-77, 75-82, 77-80, 80-83. Fellow AAAS; mem. AACU (bd. dirs. 1995—), Nat. Assn. State Univs. and Land Grant Colls. (exec. com., mem. senate 1986-88, vice chair commn. urban agenda 1992—), Endocrine Soc. (chmn. edn. com. 1980-85), Soc. Study Reprodn. (treas. 1982-85), Soc. for Neuroscis., Am. Physiol. Soc., Western Assn. Schs. and Colls. (commr. 1994—), Am. Coun. on Edn. (chmn. commn. on women in higher edn. 1987-88), Assn. Portland Progress (bd. dirs.), Portland C. of C. (bd. dirs. 1995—), Signum Laudis. Office: Portland State U Office of the President PO Box 751 Portland OR 97207-0751

RAMBERG, PATRICIA LYNN, investment specialist; b. Melrose Park, Ill., June 15, 1951; d. Roy Andrew and Elsie Elaine (Lossau) Fricke; m. Richard Lynn Ramberg, May 31, 1980; children: Richard Lynn II, Caitlyn Elizabeth. BS in Bus. Adminstrn. magna cum laude, Elmhurst Coll., 1976; MA in Edn., U. St. Thomas, 1989. Lic. broker. Assoc. dir. ops. Bank Mktg. Assn., Chgo., 1972-75; exec. dir. Soc. Tchrs. Family Medicine, Kansas City, Mo., 1975-78, Minn. Assn. Children with Learning Disabilities, St. Paul, 1979-80; sr. instrnl. designer Applied Learning Systems, Mpls., 1989-90; dir. Upper Midwest Conservation Assn., Mpls., 1990-92; account exec. Dean Witter Reynolds, Inc., Bloomington, Minn., 1992-94; investment specialist FBS Investment Svcs., Inc., Mpls., 1994—; adj. faculty U. St. Thomas, St. Paul, 1990. Developer curriculum materials; contbr. to profl. publs. Mem. NAFE, Am. Soc. Assn. Execs. Lutheran. Home: 10049 Johnson Ave S Bloomington MN 55437 Office: FBS Investment Svcs Inc First Bank Robbinsdale 4000 W Broadway Robbinsdale MN 55422

RAMBO, SYLVIA H., federal judge; b. Royersford, Pa., Apr. 17, 1936; d. Granville A. and Hilda E. (Leonhardt) R.; m. George F. Douglas, Jr., Aug. 1, 1970. BA, Dickinson Coll., 1958; JD, Dickinson Sch Law, 1962; LLD (hon.), Wilson Coll., 1980, Dickinson Sch. Law, 1993. Bar: Pa. 1962. Atty. trust dept. Bank of Del., Wilmington, 1962-63; pvt. practice Carlisle, 1963-76; public defender, then chief public defender Cumberland County, Pa., 1974-76; judge Ct. Common Pleas, Cumberland County, 1976-78, U.S. Dist. Ct. (mid. dist.) Pa., Harrisburg, 1979-92; chief judge Pa. & Md., 1992—; asst. prof., adj. prof. law Dickinson Sch. Law, 1974-76. Mem. Nat. Assn. Women Judges, Pa. Trial Lawyers Assn., Phi Alpha Delta. Democrat. Presbyterian. Office: US Dist Ct Federal Bldg PO Box 868 Harrisburg PA 17108-0868

RAMEY, REBECCA ANN, elementary education educator; b. Dayton, Ohio, Jan. 27, 1948; d. Donald Smith and Margaret Jeanne (Cross) Ingabrand; divorced; 1 child, Joshua David. BS, Miami U., Oxford, Ohio, 1970, MEd in Adminstrn., 1978. Cert. permanent tchr., prin., Ohio. Tchr. social studies and lang. arts Springboro (Ohio) Community Schs., 1970—; dept. head Clearcreek Elem. Sch., Springboro, 1991—. Choir dir. 1st Bapt. Ch., Franklin, Ohio, 1985—, chmn. bd. Christian edn., 1991—; sec. exec. bd. Tamarack Swim Club, Springboro, 1990—, Springboro Band Boosters Assn., 1992. Named Worker of Yr., 1st Bapt. Ch., 1992. Mem. NEA, Ohio Edn. Assn., Springboro Edn. Assn., Order Ea. Star (past matron 1973, 84), Ladies Oriental Shrine N.Am. Republican. Home: 205 Foliage Ln Springboro OH 45066-9312 Office: Clearcreek Elem Sch 750 S Main St Springboro OH 45066-1424

RAMIG, SUSAN WYNNE, physician, anesthesiologist; b. Scottsbluff, Nebr., Dec. 1, 1950; d. Wayne Eugene and Theresa (Green) R.; m. Curt A. Wischmeier, June 5, 1976. Student, Nebr. Western Coll., 1970-72, U. Nebr., 1972-73; MD, U. Nebr., 1976. Diplomate Am. Bd. Anesthesiology. Intern/resident U. Nebr. Med. Ctr., 1976-79; staff Meth. Hosp., Omaha, 1979-81, Medctr. One, Bismarck, N.D., 1981-85, Dalcota Midland Hosp., Aberdeen, S.D., 1985-89; med. dir. anesthesia St. Luke's Midland Regional Med. Ctr., Aberdeen, 1989—; bd. dirs. Aberdeen Area Physicians, 1990—/. Bd. dirs. Aberdeen Community Concert Assn., 1988-91; past v.p. and pres. Land of Oz Questers, Aberdeen; co-chair publicity fo 2d Berggren Gala, No. State U., Aberdeen, 1986-87. Mem. Am. Soc. Anesthesiologists, Internat. Anesthesia Rsch. Soc., Soc. Cardiovascular Anesthesia. Office: St Lukes Midland Reg Med Ctr 305 S State Aberdeen SD 57401

RAMIREZ, MARIA C(ONCEPCIÓN), educational administrator; d. Ines and Carlota (Cruz) R. BA, Incarnate Word Coll., San Antonio, 1966; MEd, U. Tex., Austin, 1979; postgrad., S.W. Tex. State U., San Marcos, 1980. Cert. elem. tchr., bilingual tchr., supr. Elem. tchr. regular and bilingual Edgewood Ind. Sch. Dist., San Antonio, 1966-69; elem tchr. regular and bilingual Austin (Tex.) Ind. Sch. Dist., 1969-74, bilingual program coord., 1974-89; instructional coord. Austin Ind. Sch. Dist., 1989-91, helping tchr., 1991—. Mem. NAFE, ASCD, Tex. Assn. for Bilingual Edn., Austin Area Assn. for Bilingual Edn., Austin Assn. for Pub. Sch. Adminstrs., Hispanic Pub. Sch. Adminstrs.

RAMIREZ, TINA, artistic director; b. Caracas, Venezuela; d. Gloria Maria Cestero and Jose Ramirez Gaonita. Studied dance with Lola Bravo, Alexandra Danilova, Anna Sokolow. Toured with Federico Rey Dance Co.; founder, artistic dir. Ballet Hispanico, N.Y.C., 1970—; panelist NEA, N.Y. Sate Coun. on Arts; mem. advisory panel N.Y.C. Dept. Cultural Affairs; bd. dirs. Dance Theater Workshop. Appearances include (Broadway) Kismet, Lute Song, (TV) Man of La Mancha. Recipient Arts and Culture Honor award Mayor of N.Y.C., 1983, Ethnic New Yorker award N.Y.C., 1986, Gov.'s Arts award N.Y. State Gov. Mario Cuomo, 1987; honoree Nat. Puerto Rican Forum, Hispanic Inst. for Performing Arts. Office: Ballet Hispanico 167 W 89th St New York NY 10024*

RAMO, ROBERTA COOPER, lawyer; b. Denver, Aug. 8, 1942; d. David D. and Martha L. (Rosenblum) Cooper; m. Barry W. Ramo, June 17, 1964. BA magna cum laude, U. Colo., 1964; JD, U. Chgo., 1967. Bar: N.Mex., 1967, Tex. 1971. With N.C. Fund, Durham, N.C., 1967-68; nat. teaching fellow Shaw U., Raleigh, N.C., 1968-70; mem. Sawtelle, Goode, Davidson & Troilo, San Antonio, 1970-72, Rodey, Dickason, Sloan, Akin & Robb, Albuquerque, 1972-74; sole practice law, Albuquerque, 1974-77; dir., shareholder Poole, Kelly & Ramo, Albuquerque, 1977-93; shareholder Modrall, Sperling, Roehl, Harris & Sisk, 1993—; bd. dirs. United N.Mex. Bank of Albuquerque, 1983-88. Bd. dirs., past pres. N.Mex. Symphony Orch., 1977-86; bd. dirs. Albuquerque Community Found., N.Mex. First, 1980-90; trustee Manzano Day Sch., 1975-77; bd. regents U. N.Mex., 1988-94, pres. 1990-93. Recipient Disting. Pub. Svc. award Gov. of N.Mex., 1993. Fellow Am. Bar Found.; mem. Albuquerque Bar Assn. (dir., pres. 1980-81), N.Mex. Bar Assn. (chmn. bus., banking sect. 1979-80, Outstanding Contbn. award 1981, 84), ABA (pres. elect 1994, bd. govs. 1994—, vice chmn. 1981-82, chmn. law practice sect. 1984, ALI/ABA com.), Am. Bar Retirement Assn. (bd. dirs. 1990-94), Am. Judicature Soc. (bd. dirs. 1988-91), Greater Albuquerque C. of C. (bd. dirs. exec. com. 1987-91). Contbr. articles to profl. jours. Address: Modrall Sperling Roehl Harris & Sisk PO Box 2168 Albuquerque NM 87103-2168

RAMO, VIRGINIA M. SMITH, civic worker; b. Yonkers, N.Y.; d. Abraham Harold and Freda (Kasnetz) Smith; B.S. in Edn., U. So. Calif., DHL (hon.), 1978; m. Simon Ramo; children—James Brian, Alan Martin. Nat. co-chmn. ann. giving U. So. Calif., 1968-70, vice chmn., trustee, 1971—, co-chmn. bd. councilors Sch. Performing Arts, 1975-76, co-chmn. bd. councillors Schs. Med. and Engring.; vice-chmn. bd. overseers Hebrew Union Coll., 1972-75; bd. dirs. The Muses of Calif. Mus. Sci. and industry, UCLA Affiliates, Estelle Doheny Eye Found., U. So. Calif. Sch. Medicine; adv. council Los Angeles County Heart Assn., chmn. com. to endow Chair in cardiology at U. So. Calif.; vice-chmn., bd. dirs. Friends of Library U. So. Calif.; bd. dirs., nat. pres. Achievement Rewards for Coll. Scientists Found., 1975-77; bd. dirs. Les Dames Los Angeles, Community TV So. Calif.; bd. dirs., v.p. Founders Los Angeles Music Center; v.p. Los Angeles Music Center Opera Assn.; v.p. corp. bd. United Way; v.p. Blue Ribbon-400 Performing Arts Council; chmn. com. to endow chair in gerontology U. So. Calif.; vice chmn. campaign Doheny Eye Inst., 1986. Recipient Service award Friends of Libraries, 1974, Nat. Community Service award Alpha Epsilon Phi, 1975, Disting. Service award Am. Heart Assn. 1978, Service award U. So. Calif., Spl. award U. So. Calif. Music Alumni Assn., 1979, Life Achievement award Mannequins of Los Angeles Assistance League, 1979, Woman of Yr. award PanHellenic Assn., 1981, Disting. Service award U. So. Calif. Sch. Medicine, 1981, U. So. Calif. Town and Gown Recognition award, 1986, Asa V. Call Achievement award U. So. Calif., 1986, Phi Kappa Phi scholarship award U. So. Calif., 1986, Vision award Luminaires of Doheny Eye Inst., 1994. Mem. UCLA Med. Aux., U. So. Calif. Pres.'s Circle, Commerce Assos. U. So. Calif., Cedars of Lebanon Hosp. Women's Guild (dir. 1967-68), Blue Key, Skull and Dagger.

RAMOS, ELEANOR LACSON, internist; b. Quezon City, The Philippines, Mar. 26, 1956; d. Pol and Evelyn (Manahan) Ramos. BS, Tufts U., 1977; MD, Tufts Med. Sch., Boston, 1981. Diplomate Am. Bd. Internal Medicine, Am. Bd. Nephrology. Resident in internal medicine N.E. Med. Ctr., Boston, 1981-84; fellow in nephrology Brigham & Women's Hosp., Boston, 1984-88, med. dir. renal transplant svc., 1988-90; med. dir. renal transplant svc. U. Fla., Gainesville, 1990-94; assoc. dir. immunology clin. rsch. Bristol-Myers Squibb Pharm. Rsch. Inst., Wallingford, Conn., 1994—. Mem. Am. Soc. Transplant Physicians (chairperson patient care and edn. com. 1994-95, Young Investigation award 1989—), Am. Soc. Nephrology, Internat. Soc. Nephrology, Alpha Omega Alpha. Office: Bristol-Myers Squibb Immunology Clin Rsch 5 Research Pky PO Box 5100 Wallingford CT 06492-7660

RAMOS, LINDA MARIE, endoscopy technician; b. San Jose, Calif., July 8, 1961; d. Albert Sequeira and Catherine Marie (Souza) Vieira; m. John Bettencourt Ramos, June 12, 1982 (div. July 1993). AA, De Anza Coll., 1986; BA, St. Mary's Coll. Calif., Moraga, 1988. Cert. gastrointestinal clinician, aerobic instr. Endoscopy technician O'Connor Hosp., San Jose, 1979-94, Good Samaritan Health Sys., Los Gatos, Calif., 1994—; aerobic instr. Mountain View (Calif.) Athletic club, 1984—, Decathlon Club, Santa Clara, 1991—, Golds Gym, Mountain View, 1994—. Contbr. articles to profl. jours. Vol. O'Connor Hosp., 1975-79; active campaign Santa Clara City Council, 1980-81. Fellow Irmandade Da Festa Do Espirito Santo (sec. 1974-82, queen 1975-76), Soc. Gastrointestinal Assts., No. Soc. Gastrointestinal Assts., Soc. Espirito Santo of Santa Clara, Luso Am. Fraternal Fedn. (state youth pres. 1979-80, youth leader local coun. Santa Clara Mountain View 1979-87, scholar, 1979, founder, organizer Mountain View-Santa Clara chpt. 1980, pres. local region 1980-84, state 20-30 pres. 1984-85, state dir. youth programs 1988-94, state dir. 1994); mem. Aerobics and Fitness Assn. Am. Republican. Roman Catholic. Home: 1618 Roll St Santa Clara CA 95050-4024 Office: Good Samaritan Health Sys 15066 Los Gatos-Almaden Rd Los Gatos CA 95032

RAMOS, MARYANN FERRARA, educator; b. N.Y.C., Mar. 30, 1940; d. Silvio Francis and Anna (Lombardo) Ferrara; m. Robert Anthony Ramos, June 20, 1964; children: Laura Ann, Robert Anthony Jr. BA, Rutgers U., 1973; BS, Touro Coll., 1974; MPH, Columbia U., 1987. Clin. physician asst. VA Med. Ctr., Bklyn., 1974-75, Lyons, N.J., 1975-85; corp. physicians asst., program mgr. Corp. Health Care, Danbury, Conn., 1987-89; occupational med. adminstr. N.Y. Power Authority, White Plains, N.Y., 1989-93; acad. coord., lectr. CUNY/Harlem Hosp. Physicians Asst. Program, N.Y.C., 1993-94; assoc. prof., dir. Nova Southeastern U. Physician Asst. Program, 1994—. Author: (chpt.) Physician Assistant: A Guide to Clinical Practice, 1994. Mem. Greenwich (Conn.) Bd. Health, 1989-94; elected mem. Rep. Town Mtg., Greenwich, 1991-93; chair health care study LWV, Greenwich, 1991-94; town chair Dem. Town Com., Greenwich, 1994. Fellow Am. Acad. Physician Assts., Fla. Acad. Physician Assts.; mem. Am. Coll. Occupational and Environ. Medicine Occupational Physician Asst. (Ind. Physicians Assn.). Roman Catholic. Home: 3049 Perriwinkle Circle Davie FL 33328 Office: Nova Southeastern U Physician Asst Program 1750 NE 167th St North Miami Beach FL 33162-3017

RAMOS-CANO, HAZEL BALATERO, social worker, early childhood educator, food service director, free-lance caterer; b. Davao City, Mindanao, Philippines, Sept. 2, 1936; came to U. S., 1960.; d. Mauricio C. and Felicidad (Balatero) Ramos; m. William Harold Snyder, Feb. 17, 1964 (div. 1981); children: John Byron, Snyder, Jennifer Ruth; m. Nelson Allen Blue, May 30, 1986 (div. 1990); m. A. Richard Cano, June 25, 1994. BA in Social Work, U. Philippines, Quezon City, 1958; MA in Sociology, Pa. State U., 1963, postgrad., 1966-67. Faculty, tng. staff Peace Corps Philippine Project, University Park, Pa., 1961-63; sociology instr. Albright Coll. Sociology Dept., Reading, Pa., 1963-64; research asst. Meth. Ch. U.S.A., State College, Pa., 1965-66; research asst. dept. child devel. & family relations Pa. State U., University Park, Pa., 1966-67; exec. dir. Presbyn. Urban Coun. Raleigh Halifax Ct. Child Care and Family Svc. Ctr., 1973-79; early childhood educator Learning Together, Inc., Raleigh, 1982-83; loan mortgage specialist Raleigh Savings & Loan, 1983-84; restaurant owner, mgr. Hazel's on Hargett, Raleigh, 1985-86; admissions coord., social worker Brian Corp. Nursing Home, Raleigh, 1986-88, food svc. dir., 1989-90; regional dir. La Petite Acad., Raleigh, 1989-90; asst. food svc. mgr. Granville Towers, Chapel Hill, N.C., 1990-92; mgr. trainee Child Nutrition Svcs. Wake County Pub. Sch. System, Raleigh, N.C., 1993-94; food svc. dir. S.W. Va. 4-H Ednl. Conf. Ctr., Abingdon, 1994—; cooking instr. Wake Cmty. Tech. Coll., Raleigh, 1986-92; freelance caterer, 1964—; chair Internat. Cooking Demonstrations Raleigh Internat. Festival, 1990-93. Pres. Wake County Day Care United Coun., 1974-75, N.C. Assn. Edn. Young Children (Raleigh Chpt.), 1975-76; bd. mem. Project Enlightenment Wake County Pub. Schs., 1976-77; various positions Pines of Carolina Girl Scout Council, 1976-85; chmn. Philippine Health and Medical Aid Com., Phil-Am Assn. Raleigh 1985-88 (publicity chmn.); elder Trinity Presbyn. Ch., Raleigh, 1979-81, bd. deacons, 1993-94. Recipient Juliette Low Girl Scout Internat. award, 1953, Rockefeller grant Rockefeller Found., 1958-59, Ramon Magsaysay Presidential award, Philippine Leadership Youth Movement, 1957; Gov.'s Cert. Appreciation State N.C., 1990, Raleigh Mayor's award Quality Childcare Svcs., 1990. Mem. Presby. Women, Raleigh, (historian 1975-76), Penn State Dames (pres. 1968-69). Democrat. Home: 270 Henderson Ct Abingdon VA 24210 Office: SW Va 4-H Ednl Ctr 25236 Hillman Hwy Abingdon VA 24210

RAMPERSAD, PEGGY A. SNELLINGS, sociologist, educational administrator; b. Fredericksburg, Va., Jan. 12, 1933; d. George Daniel and Virginia Riley (Bowler) Snellings; m. Oliver Ronald Rampersad, Mar. 19, 1955; 1 child, Gita. BA, Mary Washington Coll., Fredericksburg, 1953; student, Sch. of Art Inst. of Chgo., 1953-55; MA, U. Chgo., 1965, PhD, 1978. Grad. admissions counselor U. Chgo., 1954-57, adviser to fgn. students, 1958, dir. admissions Grad. Sch. Bus., 1959-63, rsch. project specialist Grad. Sch. Bus., 1970-78, pers. mgr. Grad. Sch. Bus., 1979-80, mgr. organizational devel. Grad. Sch. Bus., 1980-82, adminstr. dept. econs., 1983—; cons. North Ctrl. Assn. Colls. and Secondary Schs., Chgo.,1964-70, Orchestral Assn. of Chgo. Symphony Orch., 1982, Chgo. Ctr. for Decision Rsch., 1982, Harvard U., 1993—. Exhibited paintings in juried shows at Va. Mus. Fine Arts, Art Inst. Chgo., others; editor North Cen. Assn. Quar., 1972; contbr. articles to profl. jours. U. Chgo. grad. fellow, 1963-67. Mem. AAUW, Am. Econ. Assn., Am. Acad. Polit. and Social Sci., Art Inst. Chgo. (museum assoc.), Pi Lambda Theta (past pres.). Episcopalian. Home: 5531 S Kenwood Ave Chicago IL 60637-1755 Office: U Chgo Dept Econs 1126 E 59th St Chicago IL 60637-1539

RAMSAY, KARIN KINSEY, religious educator; b. Brownwood, Tex., Aug. 10, 1930; d. Kirby Luther and Ina Rebecca (Wood) Kinsey; m. Jack Cummins Ramsay Jr., Aug. 31, 1951; children: Annetta Jean, Robin Andrew. BA, Trinity U., 1951. Cert. assoc. ch. edn., 1980. Youth coord. Covenant Presbyn. Ch., Carrollton, Tex., 1961-76; dir. ch. edn. Northminster Presbyn. Ch., Dallas, 1976-80, Univ. Presbyn. Ch., Chapel Hill, N.C., 1987-90, Oak Grove Presbyn. Ch., Bloomington, Minn., 1990-93; coord., ecum. minister Flood Relief for Iowa, Des Moines, 1993; program coord. 1st Presbyn. Ch., Greenbay, Wis., 1994—; mem. Presbytery Candidates Com., Dallas, 1977-82, Presbytery Exams. Com., Dallas, 1979-81; clk. coun. New Hope Presbytery, Rocky Mount, N.C., 1989-90. Author: Ramsay's Resources, 1983—; contbr. articles to jours. in field. Design cons. Brookhaven Hosp. Chapel, Dallas, 1977-78; elder Presbyn. Ch., Carrollton, 1982—; coord. Lifeline Emergency Response, Dallas, 1982-84. Mem. Assn. Presbyn. Ch. Educators. Home: 2420-6 Eastman Ave Green Bay WI 54302 Office: 1st Presbyn Ch 709 Howard St Green Bay WI 54303

RAMSDELL, NANCY STEWART, computer engineering executive; b. N.Y.C., May 12, 1937; d. Charles Francis and Abbie C. (Crawford) Stewart; m. Frank Richey Philpott, July 15, 1961 (div. June 1965); 1 child, Stephanie Kaye; m. Robert A. Ramsdell, July 10, 1982; stepchildren: Paige Leigh, Jason Ralph. BA, Colo. Coll., 1960; MS, Temple U., 1969. Dance instr. Cornell Coll., Mt. Vernon, Iowa, 1960-64, Temple U., Phila., 1966-69; programmer, instr., mgr., staff programmer IBM, Poughkeepsie, N.Y., 1969-83; instr., software engring. mgr., program mgr. Unisys, Salt Lake City, Utah, 1985—; mem. data processing adv. bd. Salt Lake C.C., 1983-84. Modern dance dir., choreographer and dancer numerous concerts, 1961-69. Pastoral nominating com. Community of Grace Presbyn. Ch., Sandy, Utah, 1989-90. Mem. PEO (Utah state bd., 1st v.p. 1994-95, 2d v.p. 1992-94, corr. sec. 1991-92, rec. sec. 1990-91), Women's Investment Group of Sandy (pres. 1989-90). Home: 1992 E Falcon Hurst Cir Sandy UT 84092-3923

RAMSEY, BONNIE JEANNE, mental health facility administrator, psychiatrist; b. Tucson, Dec. 9, 1952; d. William Arnold Jr. and Doris Marie (Gaines) R. BS cum laude, U. S.C., 1971-75, MD, 1981. Diplomate Am. Bd. Psychiatry and Neurology; lic. child and adult psychiatrist S.C., N.C., Ga. Chief resident in psychiatry William S. Hall Psychiat. Inst., Columbia, S.C., 1983, unit dir. adolescent girls, 1986-89; chief child and adolescent inpatient program William S. Hall Psychiat. Inst., Columbia, 1989—, interim dir. child and adolescent div., 1989-92; interim chmn. child and adolescent div. dept. neuropsychiatry U. S.C., Columbia, 1989-92; instr. Sch. of Medicine U. S.C., Columbia, 1986-89, asst. prof. Sch. of Medicine, 1989—. Mem. choir Trinity Meth. Ch., West Columbia, 1981—, vice chmn. bd. trustees, 1989—, trustee, 1990—, mem. at large adminstrn. bd., 1993—; adv. coun. Habitat for Humanity. Named one of Outstanding Young Women of Am., 1985. Mem. AMA (del. residents physician sect. 1983, 84, 86, housing staff sect. 1988—), Am. Psychiat. Assn. (local sec.-treas., pres. 1981—), Am. Acad. Child Psychiatry, S.C. Med. Soc., Columbia Med. Soc., Palmetto Soc. United Way. Methodist. Office: William S Hall Psychiat Inst PO Box 202 Columbia SC 29202-0202

RAMSEY, FRANCES MAE, retired librarian; b. Minneapolis, Kans., Mar. 29, 1925; d. Chester Harold and Phyllis Henrietta (Lott) Ewart; m. Jed Jr. Ramsey, May 31, 1948; children: David Jed, Robert Lynn, Julia Frances Ramsey Lewitt, Daniel Ewart. BS, Kans. State U., 1947; student, Okla. State U., 1964-65, Lamar U., 1966, North Tex. State U., 1969. Cert. libr., Tex.; secondary tchr., Kans. Tchr. sci. Ellis (Kans.) High Sch., 1947-48; tchr. English Culver (Kans.) High sch., 1962, Minneapolis High Sch., 1962-63; libr. aid Okla. State U., Stillwater, 1964-65; jr. high libr. Beaumont (Tex.) Ind. Sch. Dist., 1966, high sch. libr., 1966-90, ret., 1990. Singer Interfaith Choral Soc., Beaumont, 1967-68, 71, 75-79, 86-89, 91; bd. dirs. Habitat for Humanity of Beaumont, 1978—; vol. libr. Calder Bapt. Ch., Beaumont, 1965—. Mem. AAUW, Tex. Libr. Assn., Phi Kappa Phi, Delta Kappa Gamma (pres. 1976-78). Democrat. Baptist.

RAMSEY, INEZ LINN, librarian, educator; b. Martins Ferry, Ohio, Apr. 25, 1938; d. George and Leona (Smith) Linn; m. Jackson Euguene Ramsey, Apr. 22, 1961; children: John Earl, James Leonard. B.A. in Hist. SUNY-Buffalo, 1971; M.L.S., 1972; Ed.D. in Audiovisual Edn., U. Va., 1980. Librarian Iroquois Central High Sch., Elma, N.Y., 1971-73, Lucy Simms Elem. Sch., Harrisonburg, Va., 1973-75; instr. James Madison U., Harrisonburg, 1975-80, asst. prof., 1980-85; assoc. prof. 1985-91, prof. 1991—; mem. Va. State Library Bd., Richmond, 1975-80; cons. contr. to Enclopedia, articles to profl. jours.; author (with Jackson E. Ramsey): Budgeting Basics,

Library Planning and Budgeting; project dir. Oral (tape) History Black Community in Harrisonburg, 1977-78; storyteller, puppeteer. Rsch. grantee James Madison U., Harrisonburg, 1981, Commonwealth Ctr. State Va., 1989. Mem. ALA, Am. Assn. Sch. Librarians, Assn. Edn. Communications Tech. (exec. bd. DSMS 1989—), Higher Edn. Media Assn. (sec., treas. 1989—), Children's Lit. Assn., Puppeteers Am., Nat. Assn. Preservation and Perpetuation of Storytelling, Va. Ednl. Media Assn. (sec. 1981-83, citation 1983 pres. 1985-86, Educator of Yr. award 1984-85, Meritorious Service award 1987-88), Phi Beta Kappa (pres. Shenandoah chpt. 1980-81), Higher Edn. Media Assn. (sec. treas., 1989—), Beta Phi Mu. Home: 282 Franklin St Harrisonburg VA 22801-4019 Office: James Madison U Dept Secondary Edn Sci Harrisonburg VA 22807

RAMSEY, LUCILLE AVRA, small business owner; b. N.Y., Mar. 3, 1942; d. Albert and Mazie (Gordon) Miller; m. Charles Allen Ramsey, Feb. 3, 1968; children: Aaron Ramsey (dec.), Jacqueline Hartigan. BS, U. San Francisco, 1986. Office mgr. Quicksilver Products Inc., San Francisco, 1962-66; exec. sec. Far West Lab. for Educ. Rsch. and Devel., San Francisco and Berkeley, Calif., 1966-68; office mgr. The Ark Pub. Co., Tiburon, Calif., 1973-75; adminstrv. asst. Nat. Coun. Jewish Women, San Francisco, 1979-80; asst. to the chief Tiburon Fire Protection Dist., 1980; exec. dir. Zionist Orgn. Am., San Francisco, 1980-87; asst. dir. Bay Area Coun. for Soviet Jews, San Francisco, 1987-89; exec. dir. Jewish Community Rels. Coun., Oakland, Calif., 1989-91; pres. Ramsey Cons., Mill Valley, Calif., 1991—; leader first ever interreligious task force to the USSR. Author: Concerns of the Jewish Community 1930's/1970's. Civic organizer, planner, chairperson Marin County Clergy Group, San Rafael, Calif., 1975-79; asst. area dir. Am. Jewish Com., San Francisco Bay Area chpt., 1994—. Democratic. Jewish.

RAMSEY, LYNN ALLISON, public relations executive; b. Phila., July 31, 1944; d. Charles Edward and Edna Berry (Whetstone) R. Student, Inst. European Studies, Vienna, Austria, 1964-65; BA, Boston U., 1967. Copy editor Am. Heritage Pub. Co., N.Y.C., 1969-71; prodr., writer Rick Carrier Film Prodns., N.Y.C., 1971-72; mng. editor New Ingenue mag., N.Y.C., 1973-75; freelance writer N.Y.C., 1975-80; mgr. pub. rels. Cunningham and Walsh (acquired by Ayer Pub. Rels. 1987), N.Y.C., 1981—; v.p., mgr. Ayer Pub. Rels., N.Y.C., 1988-95; pres., CEO Jewelry Info. Ctr., N.Y.C., 1995—. Author: Gigolos; The World's Best-Kept Men, 1978; photographer: FLY: The Complete Book of Sky Sailing, 1974; contbr. articles to profl. jours. Mem. Fgn. Policy Assn. 1982-87; sec. U.S.A. Bald Eagle Command, 1975—. Mem. Pub. Rels. Soc. Am. (accredited, bd. dirs. N.Y. chpt. 1993-95), The Fashion Group, Women's Jewelry Assn. (bd. dirs. 1993—, Award for Excellence 1993).

RAMSEY, SALLY ANN SEITZ, retired state official; b. Columbus, Ohio, Feb. 15, 1931; d. Albert Blazier and Mildred (Dodson) Seitz; m. Edward Lewis Ramsey, Apr. 11, 1953 (div. 1962); children: Edward Lewis, Sylvia Ann Mitchell. BA, Ohio State U., 1952, MA, 1955, postgrad., 1963-66; postgrad. St. Mary Coll.-Xavier, Kans., 1962. Rsch. engr., then sr. rsch. engr. N.Am. Aviation, Inc., Columbus, Ohio, and Downey, Calif., 1962-67; legis. intern State of Ohio, 1964-65; rsch. and info. officer Ohio Dept. Urban Affairs, Columbus, 1967-68; adminstrv. specialist Ohio Dept. Devel., Columbus, 1968; assoc. planner, then sr. planner Div. State Planning, Fla. Dept. Adminstrn., Tallahassee, 1968-76; econ. analysis supr., then econ. analyst Fla. Dept. Commerce, 1976-93; ret., 1993; congl. campaign cons., 1966. U.S. Econ. Devel. Adminstrn. fellow, 1978-79. Mem. ASPA, DAR, Fla. Econs. Club, Kappa Kappa Gamma, Pi Sigma Alpha. Episcopalian. Home: 2429 Merrigan Pl Tallahassee FL 32308-2346

RAMSEY, SANDRA LYNN, psychotherapist; b. Camp LeJeune, N.C., Feb. 7, 1951; d. Robert A. and Lola J. (Hann) R.; m. Edward G. Schmidt, July 9, 1988; children: Seth, Sarah, Anna, Rachel. Student, U. Calif., Long Beach, 1969-70, Orange Coast Coll., Costa Mesa, Calif., 1971-72; BA in Psychology with distinction, U. Neb., 1987, MA in Counseling Psychology, 1989. Vol. coord., client adv. Rape/Spouse Abuse Crisis Ctr., Lincoln, 1989-90; mental health therapist Health Am., HMO, Lincoln, 1991-94; pvt. practice, Lincoln, 1994—; contract therapist Lincoln Pediatric Group, 1990-91, Family Svc. Assn., Lincoln, 1990-91, Community Preservation Assocs., Lincoln, 1991-94. Mem. Nebr. Domestic Violence Sexual Assault Coalition. Portenier scholar U. Nebr., 1986-87. Mem. APA (assoc.), Assn. Pvt. Practice Therapists, Nebr. Assn. for Counseling and Devel., Golden Key, Psi Chi. Home: 4831 S 67th St Lincoln NE 68516

RAMSEY, VIRGINIA CAROL MARSHALL, middle school educator; b. Alcoa, Tenn., Aug. 7, 1935; d. Arthur Glenn and Dorothy Alexander (Huff) Marshall; m. David Lawrence Ramsey, July 5, 1957; children—Stephanie Lea, Jennifer Lynne, Thomas Marshall. B.A., Maryville Coll., 1957; Ed.M., W. Ga. Coll., 1981; Ed.S., U. Ga., 1984. Cert. tchr., counselor, art supr., data collector, tchr. art. Instr. art Maryville Coll., Tenn., 1957-58; supr. art Alcoa City Sch. System, Tenn., 1958-59; art instr. Cobb County Pub. Schs., Marietta, Ga., 1972—, Cobb Community Sch., Marietta, 1980-83; bd. dirs. Student Art Symposium, Athens, Ga.; presenter art shows, confs., 1972, 80, 84, 87. Author: Student Teacher Handbook, 1982. Mem. Kennestone Hosp. Guild, Marietta, 1967—; mem. Bells Ferry Homeowners Assn.; mem. Cobb PTA, 1967—, treas., 1974-76, pres., 1970-71, 76-77; mem. Sprayberry High Sch. Booster Club, 1972-86; panelist Gov.'s Conf. on Career Devel., Macon, 1972; leader Girl Scouts U.S.A., 1971-72; v.p. Sprayberry Adv. Council, Marietta, 1981-82, pres., 1982-86; active Robert Woodruff Mus. Art, 1969—, Cobb Arts Coun., 1975—, Marietta/Cobb Fine Arts Orgn., 1970—. Mem. Nat. Art Edn. Assn., Ga. Art Edn. Assn. (mid. sch. chmn. 1984-87, high sch. chmn. 1977-79, Art Tchr. of Yr. State of Ga. 1988-89), Ga. Assn. Educators, Atlanta Area Art Tchrs. Assn., Cobb County Assn Educators, Huguenot Soc. (v.p. Tenn. 1974-75), Delta Kappa Gamma. Republican. Presbyterian. Avocations: photography, hiking, bridge, golf, history, painting. Office: Mabry Sch Cobb County Sch System 2700 Jims Rd Marietta GA 30066-1414

RAMSEY-GOLDMAN, ROSALIND, physician; b. N.Y.C., Mar. 22, 1954; d. Abraham L. and Miriam (Colen) Goldman; m. Glenn Ramsey, June 29,1 975; children: Ethan Ramsey, Caitlin Ramsey. BA, Case Western Res. U., 1975, MD, 1978; MPH, U. Pitts., 1988, DPH, 1992. Med. resident U. Rochester (N.Y.), 1978-81; chief resident Rochester Gen. Hosp., 1981-82; staff physician Univ. Health Svc., Rochester, 1982-83; rheumatology fellow U. Pitts., 1983-86, instr. medicine, 1986-87, asst. prof., 1987-91, co-dir. Lupus Treatment and Diagnostic Ctr., 1987-91; asst. prof. medicine Northwestern U., Chgo., 1991—; dir. Chgo. Lupus Registry, Northwestern U., Chgo., 1991—. Contbr. rsch. articles to profl. jours. Recipient Finkelstein award Hershey (Pa.) Med. Ctr., 1986. Fellow Am. Coll. Rheumatology; mem. Am. Coll. Physicians, Soc. for Epidemiologic Rsch., Ctrl. Soc. Clin. Rsch. Office: Northwestern U Ward 3-315 303 E Chicago Ave Chicago IL 60611

RAN, SHULAMIT, composer; b. Tel Aviv, Oct. 21, 1949; came to U.S., 1963; m. Abraham Lotan, 1986. Studied composition with, Paul Ben-Haim, Norman Dello, Joio, Ralph Shapey; student, Mannes Coll. Music, N.Y.C., 1963-67. With dept. music U. Chgo., 1973—, prof. music; composer-in-residence Chgo. Symphony Orch., 1990—, Lyric Opera of Chgo., 1994—. Compositions include 10 Children's Scenes, 1967, Structures, 1968, 7 Japanese Love Poems, 1968, Hatzvi Israel Eulogy, 1969, O the Chimneys, 1969, Concert Piece for piano and orchestra, 1970, 3 Fantasy Pieces for Cello and Piano, 1972, Ensembles for 17, 1975, Double Vision, 1976, Hyperbolae for Piano, 1976, For an Actor: Monologue for Clarinet, 1978, Apprehensions, 1979, Private Game, 1979, Fantasy-Variations for Cello, 1980, Excursions for violin, cello, piano, 1980, A Prayer, 1982, Verticals for piano, 1982, String Quartet No. 1, 1984, (for woodwind quintet) Concerto da Camera I, 1985, Amichai Songs, 1985, Concerto for Orchestra, 1986, (for clarinet, string quartet and piano) Concerto da Camera II, 1987, East Wind, 1987, String Quartet No. 2, 1988-89, Symphony, 1989-90, Mirage, 1990, Inscriptions for solo violin, 1991, Chicago Skyline for brass and percussion, 1991, Legends for Orch., 1992-93, Invocation, 1994; commd. pieces include for Am. Composers Orch., Phila. Orch., Chgo. Symphony, Chamber Soc. of Lincoln Ctr., Mendelssohn String Quartet, Da Capo Chamber Players, Sta. WFMT; composer, and soloist for 1st performances Capriccio, 1963, Symphonic Poem, 1967, Concert Piece, 1971. Recipient Acad. Inst. Arts and Letters award, 1989, Pulitzer prize for music, 1991, Friedheim award for orchestral music Kennedy Ctr., 1992; Guggenheim fellow, 1977, 90. Office: U Chgo Dept Music 5845 S Ellis Ave Chicago IL 60637-1404

RANCOURT, BARBARA R., political advisor; b. Erie, Pa., June 14, 1952; d. Robert Allan and Sarah Elizabeth (Shaw) Schrader; m. Charles S. Rancourt; 1 child, Alison. BA, Wheaton Coll., Mass. Assoc. Mahoney, Hawkes & Goldings, Boston; confidential asst. Gov. of Mass., Boston; del. Rep. Conv.; bd. dirs. French Libr. of Boston, Zoo Com./Gov.'s Coun., Boston. Unitarian. Home: 315 Longfield Cir Lake Mary FL 32746-4015

RAND, JOELLA MAE, nursing educator; b. Akron, Ohio, July 9, 1932; d. Harry S. and Elizabeth May (Miller) Halberg; m. Martin Rand; children: Craig, Debbi Stark. BSN, U. Akron, 1961, MEd in Guidance, 1968; PhD in Higher Edn. Adminstrn., Syracuse U., 1981. Staff nurse Akron Gen. Hosp., 1953-54; staff-head nurse-instr. Summit County Receiving, Cuyahoga Falls, Ohio, 1954-56; head nurse psychiat. unit Akron Gen. Hosp., 1956-57; instr. psychiatric nursing Summit County Receiving, Cuyahoga Falls, 1957-61; head nurse, in-service instr. Willard (N.Y.) State Hosp., 1961-62; asst. prof. Alfred (N.Y.) U., 1962-76, assoc. prof., assoc. dean, 1976-78, acting dean, 1978-79, dean, 1979-90, dean coll. profl. studies, 1990-91, prof. counseling, 1991—; cons. N.Y. State Regents Program for Non-Collegiate Sponsored Instrn., 1984; cons. collegiate programs N.Y. State Dept. Edn., 1985, Elmira Coll., 1991, U. Rochester, 1992-93; accreditation visitor Nat. League for Nursing, 1984-92; ednl. cons. Willard Psychiat. Hosp., 1992-93; mem. profl. practice exam. subcom. Regents Coll., 1990-95. Recipient Teaching Excellence award Alfred U., 1977, Mary E. Gladwin Outstanding Alumni award Akron U. Coll. Nursing, 1983, Alfred Alumni Friends award, 1989, Grand Marshall commencement Alfred U., 1993. Mem. N.Y. State Coun. of Deans (treas. 1984-88), Genesee Regional Consortium (v.p.), Western N.Y. League Nursing (bd. dirs. 1991-93), Genesee Valley Edn. Com. (chair 1984-86), Sigma Theta Tau (treas. Alfred chpt. 1984-85). Office: Alfred U 343 Myers Hall Alfred NY 14802

RAND, KATHY SUE, public relations executive; b. Miami Beach, Fla., Feb. 24, 1945; d. William R. and Rose (Lasser) R.; m. Peter C. Ritsos, Feb. 19, 1982. BA, Mich. State U., 1965; M in Mgmt., Northwestern U., 1980. Asst. editor Lyons & Carnahan, Chgo., 1967-68; mng. editor Cahners Pub. Co., Chgo., 1968-71; pub. rels. writer Super Market Inst., Chgo., 1972-73; account supr. Pub. Communications Inc., Chgo., 1973-77; divisional mgr. pub. rels. Quaker Oats Co., Chgo., 1977-82; exec. v.p., dep. gen. mgr. Golin/Harris Communications, Chgo., 1982-90; exec. v.p. Lesnik Pub. Rels., Northbrook, Ill., 1990-91; mng. dir. Manning, Selvage & Lee, Chgo., 1991—. Dir. midwest region NOW, 1972-74; mem. Kellogg Alumni Adv. Bd.; bd. dirs. Jr. Achievement of Chgo. Mem. Pub. Rels. Soc. Am. (Silver Anvil award 1986, 87), Pub. Club Chgo. (Golden Trumpet awards 1982-87, 90, 94), Northwestern Club Chgo., Kellogg Alumni Club, Beta Gamma Sigma. Home: 400 Riverwoods Rd Lake Forest IL 60045-2547

RANDALL, CAROLYN MAYO, chemical company executive; b. Atlanta, June 11, 1939; d. Frank and Winifred (Layton) Mayo; m. James Allen Hall, Dec. 28, 1960 (dec. 1973); children: James Allen Hall Jr., Christopher Mayo Hall, Charlotte Ann Hall; m. Thomas E. Randall, Feb. 2, 1978. BA, U. Ga., 1959. Ptnr. Mayo Chem. Co., Marietta, Ga., 1989—. Bd. dirs. Mayo Edn. Found; active Alliance Theater Atlanta, Salvation Army Aux., Voters Guild Met. Atlanta, Friendship Force Atlanta, Kennestone Hosp. Cancer Group, Am. Cancer Soc. Mem. Cobb County Gem & Mineral Soc. (trustee), S.E. Fedn. Mineralogical Soc. (historian), Atlanta Preservation Soc., Nat. Trust Historic Preservation, Ga. Trust Hist. Preservation, Nat. Meml. Day Assn., Better Films Assn. Met. Atlanta (bd. dirs.), Ret. Officers Assn. (ladies aux. bd. dirs.), Ga. Mineral Soc., Native Atlantians Club, 100 Club (pres.), The Frog Club, Terrell Mill Estates Women's Club (bd. dirs.), Dobbins AFB Officers Wives Club (bd. dirs.), Alpha Chi Omega. Republican. Episcopal. Home: 3244 Beechwood Dr SE Marietta GA 30067

RANDALL, CATHARINE, French educator; b. Lafayette, Ind., Apr. 14, 1957; d. E.V. Jr. and Sally (Shaw) R.; m. W.R. Coats, Nov. 1, 1986 (div. June 1994); 1 child, Sara Shaw Coats. BA in History, Ohio Wesleyan Coll., 1978; MA in French, Boston Coll., 1981; MPhil. in French, Yale U., 1982; PhD in French, U. Pitts., 1987. Asst. prof. French Montclair (N.J.) State Coll., 1988-89, Rutgers U., New Brunswick, N.J., 1989-91; assoc. prof. French, dir. Intermediate Lang. Program Barnard Coll., N.Y.C., 1991—; presenter papers in field, 1986—; spkr. 16th Century Studies Conf., 1991, 92, 93; organizer, presenter confs.; cons. lang. texts dept. Houghton-Mifflin Pub. Co. Author: Subverting the System: d'Aubigné and Calvinism, 1990, (Em)bodying the Word: Textual Resurrections in the Martyrological Narratives of John Foxe, Jean Crespin, Théodore de Bèze, and Agrippa d'Aubigné, 1992; editor (with Daniel Russell) Simon Bouquet's Imitation et traduction des cent dix-huit emblèmes d'Alciat, 1994; contbr. chpts. to books, numerous articles to profl. jours.; reviewer. Princeton Ctr. Theological Inquiry fellow, 1994—, Folger Shakespeare Libr. fellow, 1990-91, Newberry Libr. Rsch. fellow, 1989; grantee Princeton U., 1992, NEH grantee Duke U., 1992, Dartmout Sch. Criticism and Theory grantee, 1986. Mem. Phi Beta Kappa, Phi Sigma Iota, Phi Alpha Theta. Republican. Episcopalian. Home: 323 Fairfield Ave Ridgewood NJ 07450 Office: Barnard Coll 3009 Broadway New York NY 10027

RANDALL, CLAIRE, church executive; b. Dallas, Oct. 15, 1919; d. Arthur Godfrey and Annie Laura (Fulton) R. A.A., Schreiner Coll., 1948; BA, Scarritt Coll., 1950; DD (hon.), Berkeley Sem., Yale U., 1974; LHD (hon.), Austin Coll., 1982; LLD, Notre Dame U., 1984. Assoc. missionary edn. Bd. World Missions Presbyterian Ch., U.S., Nashville, 1949-57; dir. art Gen. Council Presbyterian Ch., U.S., Atlanta, 1957-61; dir. Christian World Mission, program dir., assoc. dir. Ch. Women United, N.Y.C., 1962-73; gen. sec. Nat. Council Ch. of Christ in U.S.A., N.Y.C., 1974-84; nat. pres. Ch. Women United, N.Y.C., 1988-92; ret., 1992—. Mem. Nat. Commn. on Internat. Women's Yr., 1975-77, Martin Luther King Jr. Fed. Holiday Commn., 1985. Recipient Woman of Yr. in Religion award Heritage Soc., 1977; Empire State Woman of Yr. in Religion award State of N.Y., 1984; medal Order of St. Vladimir, Russian Orthodox Ch., 1984. Democrat. Episcopalian. Home: 13427 W Countryside Dr Sun City West AZ 85375-4711

RANDALL, ELIZABETH (LISA RANDALL), state agency administrator; d. Harry Randall, Jr. BA, Smith Coll., 1975; JD, Wake Forest U., 1978. Bar: N.J. Former dep. atty.; former asst. counsel Gov. Tom. Kean, N.J.; trial atty. Essex County Prosecutor's Office, N.J., 1979-81; former atty. Borough of Hillsdale; former mcpl. prosecutor Boroughs of Dumont and Park Ridge; ptnr. Randall, Randall and Stevens, Westwood, N.J., 1985-91; rep. 39th Legis. Dist. N.J. State Assembly, 1985-91; counsel County of Bergen, N.J., 1991-94; commr. Dept. of Banking Govt. of N.J., 1994—; served as vice chair fin. instns. com. and edn. com., mem. judiciary com. N.J. State Assembly; minority whip, then majority whip N.J. State Assembly, 1986; adj. prof. pub. policy Sch. Adminstrn. and Bus. Ramapo Coll., 1991; sec., treas. N.J. Assn. County Counsels, 1992-94. Former bd. dirs. TWIN Mgmt. Forum; mem., bd. dirs., vice chair venture grants com. United Way Bergen County. Mem. N.J. Bar Assn., Bergen County Bar Assn., Bergen County Women Lawyers. Office: Banking Dept CN 040 20 West State St Trenton NJ 08625-0040

RANDALL, ELIZABETH ELLEN, personnel manager; b. Maple Hill, Kans., Mar. 21, 1915; d. Edwin and Ann (Scott) Sage; m. George Albert Randall, May 29, 1941; children: Cheryl Ann, Rebecca Lynn. Student, Kans. State U., 1932-34. Tchr. elem. sch Maple Hill, Kans., 1932-34, Dover, Kans., 1934-46; reader Luce Press Clippings, Topeka, 1959-63, supr., 1964, office mgr., 1964—. Tchr. Jr. High Ch. Sch., 1949-61; mem. pastoral com. Dover Federated Ch., 1991—. Mem. Dover 4-H Club (leader 1960-62), Dover Rebekah Lodge, Eastern Star, Am. Leg. Aux., Disabled Am. Vets. Aux., 14th Armored Divsn. Aux. Democrat. Home: 5731 SW 22nd Ter Topeka KS 66614-1831 Office: Luce Press Clippings 912 S Kansas Ave Topeka KS 66612-1211

RANDALL, HERMINE MARIA, power plant engineer; b. Vienna, Austria, July 22, 1927; came to U.S., 1948; d. Heinrich Georg Adametz and Maria Antonia (Paul) Safranek; m. May 25, 1948 (div. 1975); children: George Eugene, Dorothy Maria. Lic. 1st class stationary engr., Mass. Shift supr. Stony Brook Generating Sta. Mass. Mcpl. Wholesale Electric Co., Ludlow, 1980-82; chief engr. power plant U. Mass., Amherst, 1982-87, mgr. utility generation and distbn., 1987-90, acting dir. engring., 1990-91; dir. engring., 1991—. Recipient spl. achievement award Region I, U.S. Dept. Labor, 1980, Chancellor's Citation U. Mass., 1990, Citation for Outstanding Performance, Commonwealth of Mass., 1990. Mem. Nat. Assn. Power Engrs. (pres. Springfield chpt. 1989-90), Assn. Energy Engrs., Am. Inst. Plant Engrs. Republican. Home: 4 Popes Way Hadley MA 01035-9749 Office: U Mass Phys Plant Amherst MA 01003

RANDALL, LINDA LEA, biochemist, educator; b. Montclair, N.J., Aug. 7, 1946; d. Lowell Neal and Helen (Watts) R.; m. Gerald Lee Hazelbauer, Aug. 29, 1970. BS, Colo. State U., 1968; PhD, U. Wis., 1971. Postdoctoral fellow Inst. Pasteur, Paris, 1971-73; asst. prof. Uppsala (Sweden) U., 1975-81; assoc. prof. Washington State U., Pullman, 1981-83, prof. biochemistry, 1983—; guest scientist Wallenberg Lab., Uppsala U., 1973-75; study section NIH, 1984-88. Editorial bd. Jour. of Bacteriology, 1982—; co-editor: Virus Receptors Part I, 1980; contbr. articles to profl. jours. Recipient Eli Lilly Award in Microbiology and Immunology, Am. Soc. Microbiology, Am. Assn. Immunologists, Am. Soc. Exptl. Pathology, 1984, Faculty Excellence Award in Rsch., Washington State U., 1988, Disting. Faculty Address, 1990. Mem. Am. Microbiol. Soc., AAAS, Am. Soc. Biol. Chemists, Protein Soc. Office: Washington State U. Biochemistry/Biophysic Dept Pullman WA 99164-4660

RANDALL, LYNN ELLEN, librarian; b. Chgo., Oct. 10, 1946; d. Ward W. and Hazel A. (Nettles) R. BA, King's Coll., 1970; MA, Seton Hall U., 1973; MLS, Rutgers U., 1978. Libr. N.J. Inst. Tech., Newark, 1970-75; libr. dir. N.E. Bible Coll., Essex Fells, N.J., 1975-81; reference libr. Seton Hall U., South Orange, N.J., 1983-85; dir. libr. svc. Berkeley Coll. Bus., West Paterson, N.J., 1985-89, libr. dir. Caldwell Coll., 1989—; reference librarian, instr. Morris (N.J.) County Coll., 1981-83. Co-author: N.J. Online Directory, 1983; editor N.J. Librs., fall 1984, spring 1986, winters 1990, 91; chair N.J. region III resource sharing com. Mem. Union County (N.J.) Heritage Commn., 1975-76. Mem. ALA (treas. Libr. Instrn. Round Table 1989-90, chair libr. instrn. roundtable, Libr. Sch. Task Force 1992—), Assn. Coll. and Resource Librs. (chair evaluation B1 Handbook task force 1991—), Middle States Assn., Am. Assn. Bible Colls. (evaluator 1977, 79, 84, 92), N.J. Libr. Assn. (chair automated libr. svcs. sect. 1986-88, conf. program editor 1987-89, chair exhibits com. 1989-91, 94—, chair adminstrv. sect. 1990-92, chair coll. & univ. sect. 1990-91, conf. chair 1991-94, editor coll. and univ. sect. newsletter 1982-84, 87-92, 2d v.p. 1992-94), N.J. Libr. Network (pres. Region II 1987-89, chair resource sharing com. 1993, info. svcs. com. 1994). Office: Jennings Libr Caldwell Coll 9 Ryerson Ave Caldwell NJ 07006-6195

RANDALL, PATRICIA MARY, temporary employment firm executive; b. Boston, June 12, 1948; d. Alfred Earl Randall and Evangeline A. (McHugh) Blackwell; m. Richard Paul James, June 26, 1982 (div. 1989); children: David, Jennifer; m. Scott Darren Graff, Jan. 1, 1990. BA in Philosophy, Bridgewater (Mass.)State Coll., 1980. Owner, mgr. The Indoor Garden, Brockton, Mass., 1972-78; dining room mgr. Red Coach Grill Cambridge, Mass., 1981-82, Boston Ramada, Allston, Mass., 1982-85; br. mgr. The Resource Group, Cambridge, 1985-90; sr. tech. specialist Brandon Systems Corp., Boston, 1990—. Roman Catholic. Home: PO Box 381361 Cambridge MA 02238-1361 Office: Brandon Systems Corp 1 Exeter Pla 699 Boylston St Boston MA 02116

RANDALL, PRISCILLA RICHMOND, travel executive; b. Arlington, Mass., Mar. 19, 1926; d. Harold Bours and Florence (Hoefler) Richmond; m. Raymond Victor Randall, Mar. 2, 1946; children: Raymond Richmond, Priscilla Randall Middleton, Susan Randall Geery. Student, Wellesley Coll., 1943-44; Assoc., Garland Coll., 1946; student, Winona State U., 1977-81. Pub. relations dir. Rochester Meth. Hosp., Rochester, Minn., 1960-69; dir. pub relations Sheraton Rochester, 1969-71; pres. Med. Charters, Rochester, 1970-75, Ideas Unltd., Rochester, 1969-77; chief exec. officer Randall Travel, Rochester, 1977-89; pres. Randall Travel Delray, Delray Beach, Fla., 1989—; pres. Bar Harbour Apts. Inc., Delray Beach, 1989. Editor, Inside Story, 1960-69, Rochester Meth. Hosp. News, 1960-69; producer Priscilla's World, 1972-75. Pres. Rochester Meth. Hosp. Aux., 1957-59, Downtown Bus. Assn., Rochester, 1985. Recipient Woman of Achievement Bus. YWCA, Rochester, 1983, Golden Door Knob, Bus. and Prfl. Women, Rochester, 1979. Mem. Inst. Cert. Travel Agts. (life), Assn. Retail Travel Agts. (life, nat. bd. 1988-90, sec. to bd. 1988-90, sec.-treas. Arlington, Va. nat. bd. 1990), Am. Soc. Travel Agts., Pacific Area Travel Agts., Minn. Exec. Women in Travel, Cruise Line Internat. Assn. (master cruise counselor), Women's Golf Com. Little Club (Gulfstream, Fla.) (sec.), Hibiscus Garden Club (Delray Beach, Fla.) (sec.). Home: 86 Macfarlane Dr Apt 2C Delray Beach FL 33483-6901 Office: Randall Travel Delray Inc 1118 E Atlantic Ave Delray Beach FL 33483-6936

RANDALL, ROMAINE M., accountant; b. Charleston, W.Va., Oct. 8, 1957; d. Blanchard and Lorraine (Manny) R. BS, Plymouth State Coll., 1979; MBA, Northeastern U., 1986. CPA, CMA, FLMI, CLU. With pub. records divsn. Sec. of State, Boston, 1980-83; with tax dept. Feeley & Driscoll, Boston, 1983-84; fin. analyst Tex. Instruments, Dallas, 1985; CPA Gray, Gray & Gray, Boston, 1987-90; fin. analyst John Hancock Ins. Co., Boston, 1990—; prin. Romaine M. Randall, CPA, Belmont, Mass., 1990—.

RANDALL, SHERRI LEE, accountant; b. Burlington, Vt., Dec. 21, 1959; d. Robert Dale and Carolyn Sue (Ferguson) Schaffner; m. Cleve Hadley Randall, Feb. 11, 1981 (div. Mar. 1992); 1 child, Clayton James. BBA with high honors, Idaho State U., 1985. CPA, Idaho. Staff acct. Price Waterhouse, Anchorage, 1985-87; acct. Little-Morris, Boise, Idaho, 1987—; mem. acctg. alumni adv. panel Idaho State U., Pocatello, 1989-90. Vol. coord. Caribou Nat. Forest, Pocatello, 1984; treas. Assn. for Retarded Citizens Ada County, Boise, Idaho, 1989-91, mem. fin. com., 1989-92. Scholar Idaho State U., 1983-84, Crawford-Moore Found., 1984. Mem. AICPA, Idaho Soc. CPAs, Inst. Mgmt. Accts. (bd. dirs. acad. resl. ednl. projects 1992-94, v.p. and edn. & profl. devel. 1994-95), Phi Kappa Phi, Beta Gamma Sigma, Beta Alpha Psi. Office: Little-Morris 350 N 9th St Ste 200 Boise ID 83702-5469

RANDINELLI, TRACEY ANNE, magazine editor; b. Morristown, N.J., Apr. 6, 1963; d. Andrew R. and Patricia Ann (Brenner) R. BA in Comm., U. Del., 1985. Copywriter Macy's N.J., Newark, 1985-86; edit. asst. Globe Comms. Corp., N.Y.C., 1986-87; from asst. editor to assoc. editor Scholastic Math and DynaMath Mags. Scholastic, Inc., N.Y.C., 1987-89, editor Scholastic Math Mag., 1989—. Mem. Soc. Children's Book Writers, Ednl. Press Assn. Am. (Disting. Achievement award feature article divsn. 1991). Office: 555 Broadway New York NY 10012-3999

RANDISI, ELAINE MARIE, law corporation executive, educator; b. Racine, Wis., Dec 19, 1926; d. John Dewey and Alveta Irene (Raffety) Fehd; AA, Pasadena Jr. Coll., 1946; BS cum laude (Giannini scholar), Golden Gate U., 1978; m. John Paul Randisi, Oct. 12, 1946 (div. July 1972); children: Jeanine Randisi Manson, Martha Randisi Chaney (dec.), Joseph, Paula, Catherine Randisi Carvalho, George, Anthony (dec.); m. John R. Woodfin, June 18, 1994. With Raymond Kaiser Engrs., Inc., Oakland, Calif., 1969-75, 77-86, corp. acct., 1978-79, sr. corp. acct., 1979-82, sr. payroll acct., 1983-86, acctg. mgr., Lilli Ann Corp., San Francisco, 1986-89, Crosby, Heafey, Roach & May, Oakland, Calif., 1990—; corp. buyer Kaiser Industries Corp., Oakland, 1975-77; lectr. on astrology Theosophical Soc., San Francisco, 1979—; mem. faculty Am. Fedn. Astrologers Internat. Conv., Chgo., 1982, 84. Mem. Speakers Bur., Calif. Assn. for Neurologically Handicapped Children, 1964-70, v.p. 1969; bd. dirs. Ravenwood Homeowners Assn., 1979-82, v.p., 1979-80, sec., 1980-81; mem. organizing com. Minority Bus. Fair, San Francisco, 1976; pres., bd. dirs. Lakewood Condominium Assn., 1984-87; mem., trustee Ch. of Religious Sci., 1992—; treas. First Ch. Religious Sci., 1994—. Mem. Am. Fedn. Astrologers, Nat. Assn. Female Execs., Calif. Scholarship Fedn. (life), Alpha Gamma Sigma (life). Mem. Ch. of Religious Science (lic. practioner pres. 1990-91, sec. 1989-90). Initiated Minority Vendor Purchasing Program for Kaiser Engrs., Inc., 1975-76. Home: 742 Wesley Way Apt 1C Oakland CA 94610-2338 Office: Crosby Heafey Roach & May 1999 Harrison St Oakland CA 94612-3515

RANDLE, ELLEN EUGENIA FOSTER, opera and classical singer, educator; b. New Haven, Conn., Oct. 2, 1948; d. Richard A.G. and Thelma

Lousie (Brooks) Foster; m. Ira James William, 1967 (div. 1972); m. John Willis Randle. Student, Calif. State Coll., Sonoma, 1970; studied with Boris Goldovsky, 1970; student, Grad. Sch. Fine Arts, Florence, Italy, 1974; studied with Tito Gobbi, Florence, 1974; student, U. Calif., Berkeley, 1977; BA in World History, Lone Mountain Coll., 1976, MA in Performing Arts, 1978; studied with Madam Eleanor Steber, Graz, Austria, 1979; studied with Patricia Goehl, Munich, Fed. Republic Germany, 1979; MA in Counseling and Psychology, U. San Francisco, 1990, MA in Marriage, Family, Child Counseling, 1991; MA in Marital and Family Therapy, U. San Francisco, 1991—, 1994. Clin. case mgr. Oakland, Calif., 1991—; MA in Marriage Family Therapy, 1994; instr. East Bay Performing Art Ctr., Richmond, Calif., 1986, Chapman Coll., 1986; clin. case mgr. Kairos Unlimited Group Home, Oakland. Singer opera prodns. Porgy & Bess, Oakland, Calif., 1980-81, LaTraviata, Oakland, Calif., 1981-82, Aida, Oakland, 1981-82, Madame Butterfly, Oakland, 1982-83, The Magic Flute, Oakland, 1984, numerous others; performances include TV specials, religous concerts, musicals; music dir. Natural Man, Berkeley, 1986; asst. artistic dir. Opera Piccola, Oakland, Calif., 1990—. Art commr. City of Richmond, Calif. Recipient Bk. Am. Achievement award. Mem. Music Tchrs. Assn., Internat. Black Writers and Artists Inc. (life mem., local #5), Nat. Coun. Negro Women, Nat. Assn. Negro Musicians, Calif. Arts Fedn., Calif. Assn. for Counseling and Devel. (mem. black caucus), Nat. Black Child Devel. Inst., The Calif.-Nebraskan Orgn., Inc., San Francisco Commonwealth Club, Gamma Phi Delta. Democrat. Mem. A.M.E. Zion Ch. Home: 5314 Boyd Ave Oakland CA 94618-1112

RANDOLPH, BEVERLEY, production stage manager; b. Norristown, Pa., Aug. 26, 1951; d. Robert Lyman Kratz and Sarah Randolph (McDonnell) DaCosta. BFA magna cum laude, Ithaca Coll., 1973. Prodn. supr. Follies in Concert, Lincoln Ctr., 1985, Uptown It's Hot, Phila., 1985, Queenie Pie, Duke Ellington Mus., Phila. & Washington, 1987, Jerome Robbins Broadway, Nat. Tour, Japan, L.A., 1990-91, Tony Awards, 1992, Sansho the Bailiff, Bklyn. Acad. Music, 1993; prodn. stage mgr. Merrily We Roll Along, N.Y.C., 1981, A Doll's Life, L.A., N.Y.C., 1982, Gala Opening of Ky. Ctr. of Performing Arts, Louisville, 1983, End of the World, Washington and N.Y.C., 1984, Grind, 1985, Cabaret, N.Y.C., 1988, Jerome Rubbin's Broadway, 1989-90, Kiss of the Spider Woman, Purchase, 1990, N.Y., 93, Metro, N.Y.C., 1992, Falsettos, N.Y.C., 1992, Passion, 1994; stage mgr. Chapter Two, 1979. Stage mgr. Nat. Inst. of Music Theatre, N.Y.C., 1986-87; participant Broadway Cares. Mem. Actors Fund (life), Actor's Equity Assn.

RANDOLPH, ELIZABETH S. (MRS. JOHN DANIEL RANDOLPH), former educational administrator; b. Farmville, N.C.; d. John Hagans and Pearl (Johnson) Schmoke; A.B., Shaw U., 1936, H.H.D. (hon.), 1979, LHD (hon.); M.A., U. Mich., 1945; postgrad. U. N.C., 1964, DrPub Svc. U. N.C. at Charlotte; m. John Daniel Randolph, June 7, 1950 (dec. Dec. 1963). Tchr., English and French, New Hope High Sch., Rutherfordton, N.C., 1936-37; tchr. librarian DuBois High Sch., Wake Forest, N.C., 1937-43, Jordan Sellars High Sch., Burlington, N.C., 1943-44; tchr. English, adminstrv. asst. W. Charlotte (N.C.) High Sch., 1944-58; prin. University Park Elem. Sch., Charlotte, 1958-68; dir. ESEA activities Charlotte-Mecklenburg Schs., 1968-73, adminstrv. asst. for sch. ops., 1973-76, asst. supt., 1976-77, asso. supt., 1977-82. Mem. bd. trustees Found. for the Carolinas, The Salvation Army; trustee Shaw U., N.C. Agrl. and Tech. State U., Davidson Coll., Queen's Coll., Planned Parenthood Greater Charlotte, Pub. Libr. Charlotte and Mecklenburg County; bd. Christian edn. 1st Bapt. Ch. West; co-chair Friends of Johnson C. Smith U.; bd. dirs. Mus. of the New South, Programs for Accessible Living, Afro-Am. Cultural Ctr., Gethsemane Enrichment Program. Mem. AAUW, NEA (life), ASCD (pres. 1977-78), Nat. Coun. Negro Women, Links, NAACP, Phi Delta Kappa, Delta Kappa Gamma, Alpha Kappa Alpha (Mid-Atlantic regional dir. 1964-68, chmn. standards com., nat. parliamentarian 1974-76). Home: 1616 Patton Ave Charlotte NC 28216-5417

RANDOLPH, LILLIAN LARSON, medical association executive; b. Spokane, Wash., May 3, 1932; d. Charles P. and Juanita S. (Parrish) Larson; m. Philip L. Randolph, Nov. 12, 1952; children: Marcus, Andrew. BA, U. Wash., 1954, MA, 1956; PhD, U. Calif., Berkeley, 1966; EdD, N.Mex. State U., 1979. Researcher U. Wash., Seattle, 1954-59; asst. prof. Calif. State U., Hayward, 1964-68, U. Tex., El Paso, 1972-74; dir. S.W. Conservatory of Music, El Paso, 1972-74; adj. prof. Loyola U. and DePaul U., Chgo., 1974-78; asst. prof. DeVry Inst. Tech., Lombard, Ill., 1982-84; mgr. AMA, Chgo., 1985—; cons. Weber Co., Chgo., 1979-85. Author: Fundamentals of Government Organizations, 1971, Third Party Settlement of Disputes, 1973. Mem. AAUP, Phi Beta Kappa. Home: 408 W Wilshire Dr Wilmette IL 60091-3154

RANDOLPH, LINDA JANE, mathematics educator; b. Ypsilanti, Mich., Feb. 25, 1942; d. Roy Lawrence and Sarah (Jefferson) Robinson; m. Jerry F. Basler; children: Deborah L. Bolton, Sandra A. Randolph. BS in Teaching and Math., Ea. Mich. U., 1983, M in Math., 1989, postgrad., 1989—. Math. tutor Ea. Mich. U., Ypsilanti, 1980-82, supr. adult edn., tchr., 1983-94, instr. math.; substitute tchr. Tecumseh (Mich.) Pub. Sch., 1983-91; instr. math., program coord. UAW-FORD/EMU Milan Plastic Plant, 1991-94; peer-advisor Acad. Svcs. Ctr., Ea. Mich. U., 1979-83; lecturer computer sci. dept. Ea. Mich. U., 1986-89, equity program, 1990-91. Mem. Am. Math. Assn., Mich. Math. Assn., Bus. and Profl. Women (v.p. chpt. 1991-92, sec. 1994-95), Nat. Edn. Computing Conf., Mich. Assn. Computer Users in Learning, Ea. Mich. U. Alumni Assn. (bd. dirs.). Home: 1414 Collegewood Ypsilanti MI 48197-1672 Office: Ea Mich U 34 N Washington Ypsilanti MI 48197

RANDOLPH, NANCY ADELE, nutritionist, consultant; b. St. Louis, Sept. 7, 1941; d. Robert Andrew and Mary Jane (Hilliker) R.; m. John Reginald Randolph-Swainson, Sept. 16, 1989. BS, U. Ariz., 1963; MEd, Boston U., 1971; postgrad., Harvard U., 1983. Intern instn. adminstrn. Mills Coll., Oakland, Calif., 1963-64; staff dietitian St. Lukes Hosp., St. Louis, 1964-65; clin. dietitian New England Deaconess Hosp., Boston, 1965-66; dietitian mgr. The Seiler Corp., Waltham, Mass., 1966-67; instr., acting dir. Whidden Hosp. Sch. Nursing, Everett, Mass., 1967-72; instr. nutrition Northeastern U. Coll. Nursing, Boston, 1972; renal/rsch. dietitian Lemuel Shattuck Hosp., Jamaica Plain, Mass., 1979-81; New England regional dietitian coord. Beverly Enterprises, Virginia Beach, Va., 1985-88; state nutritionist, surveyor Mass. Dept. Pub. Health/Health Care Quality, Boston, 1988-89; cons. nutritionist Randolph Assocs., West Palm Beach and Sarasota, Fla., 1990—; cons. dietitian Jewish Rehab Ctr., Swampscott, Mass., 1972-79, Lenox Hill Rehab. Ctr., Lynn, Mass., 1972-79, Jesmond Nursing Home, Nahant, Mass., 1972-88, numerous other health care facilities in New England, 1972-88. Mem. Am. Dietetic Assn. (cert.), Fla. Dietetic Assn., Cons. Nutritionists Practice Group, Cons. Dietitians in Health Care.

RANDOLPH-CLARK, PATRICIA ANN, nursing educator; b. Plainfield, N.J., Apr. 7, 1951; d. William H. and Betty Ann (Day) Randolph; m. Thomas G. Clark, Jan. 4, 1986; children: Alexander, Elizabeth Evelyn. AAS, Somerset County Coll., 1973; BSN, Rutgers U., 1976; MA, NYU, 1981. Cert. ANA clin. specialist in adult psychiat.-mental health nursing, clin. specialist in med.-surg. nursing. Pub. health nurse Saranac Lake, N.Y.; in-service educator Somerville, N.J.; nursing instr. Jersey City; assoc. prof. North County Community Coll., Saranac Lake; pvt. practice in psychotherapy. Mem. ANA, N.Y. State Nurses Assn. Home: 103 Riverside Dr Saranac Lake NY 12983-2319

RANEY, MIRIAM DAY, actress; b. Florence, S.C., Sept. 30, 1922; d. Lewie Griffith and Iola Lewis (Edwards) Day; m. Robert William Raney, Mar. 31, 1946 (div. Sept. 1976); children: Robert William Jr., Miriam, Kevin Paige, Megan. BSM in Voice, Music Edn., U. N.C., Greensboro, 1939-43; student (summers), Julliard Sch. Music, 1942-43; BA in Music History, U. Ark., Little Rock, 1978-81; Certificate, Adam Roarke Film Actors Lab., Irving, Tex., 1989. Singing chorus N.Y.C. Ctr. Opera Co., 1943-44; understudy, singing chorus Oklahoma, Theater Guild, N.Y.C., 1944-45; ingenue lead Connecticut Yankee, Geosan Subway Cir., N.Y.C., 1945; understudy, singing chorus Up In Central Park, Michael Todd, N.Y.C., 1945-46; beauty cons. Mary Kay Cosmetics, Inc., Dallas, 1993-94. Author: slide sound synchronized show Ark. Women in Music, 1982; composer, lyricist: The Bend and the Willows, 1982, Ballad of Petit Jean, 1983; recent stage appearances include Hedda Gabler (Reponde de Capite repertory), 1990, Time of Your Life (Community Theatre of Little Rock), 1991, Our Town, 1991, Evening with Women II (Regional Theatre of Cen. Ark.), 1991, 1988; appeared in TV program Unsolved Mysteries, 1988; film Killing Time With Aunt Olene, 1988; also commercials, tng. films, 1987-92; print model, Little Rock, Memphis, Ft. Worth, 1988-92. Ch. soloist, various protestant chs., Little Rock, 1946-55; music dir., leader Ouachita Girl Scout Coun., Little Rock, 1963-70; choir mem. adminstrv. bd., adult ch. sch. tchr. Pulaski Heights United Meth. Ch., Little Rock, 1970-76; mem. Speakers Bur. Coalition of Womens Clubs for ERA, Little Rock, 1974-75; bd. dirs. Local 266, AFM, Little Rock, 1980-83. Named Illustrious Alumna, U. N.C. at Greensboro, 1945; recipient Thanks Badge Oachita Coun. Girl Scouts U.S., Little Rock, 1965. Mem. AAUW (Little Rock legis. com. 1973-79, program com. 1973-79, state rep. for cultural interests 1976-79), Musical Coterie (Little Rock), Cen. Ark. Guild of Organists (pres. student chpt. 1977-80). Democrat. Home: 25 Valley Forge Dr Little Rock AR 72212-2613

RANFT, ELIZABETH ELAINE, advertising director; b. Mount Ayr, Iowa, May 5, 1956; d. John Phillip and Ethel Elaine (Drage) D.; m. Jan Pieter Ranft, Aug. 30, 1992. BA with honors, U. B.C. Writer Scali, McCabe, Sloves, Vancouver, B.C., 1977-81; sr. writer Young and Rubicam, San Francisco, 1981-83; assoc. creative dir. Hayhurst, Vancouver, 1983-84; prin. Elizabeth Dawson Addirections, Vancouver, 1984-86; assoc. creative dir. McCann-Erickson, Vancouver, 1986-90, creative dir., 1990—. Recipient Cable Car award San Francisco Ad Club, 1982, Clio awards Cannes Comml. Festival, 1987, 88, Mktg. awards Mktg. Mag., Toronto, 1988-90, Lotus awards Vancouver Ad Club, 1990-91. Mem. Alpha Gamma Delta. Office: McCann-Erickson Advt of Canada, 355 Burrard St, Vancouver, BC Canada V6C 3H2*

RANKAITIS, SUSAN, artist; b. Cambridge, Mass., Sept. 10, 1949; d. Alfred Edward and Isabel (Shimkus) Rankaitis; m. Robbert Flick, June 5, 1976. B.F.A. in Painting, U. Ill., 1971; M.F.A. in Visual Arts, U. So. Calif., 1977. Rsch. asst., art dir. Plato Lab., U. Ill., Urbana, 1971-75; art instr. Orange Coast Coll., Costa Mesa, Calif., 1977-83; chair dept. art Chapman Coll., Orange, Calif., 1983-90; Fletcher Jones chair in art Scripps Coll., Claremont, Calif., 1990—; represented by Ruth Bloom Gallery, Santa Monica, Calif.; represented by Ruth Bloom Gallery, Santa Monica, Calif., Robert Mann Gallery, N.Y.C.; overview panelist visual arts Nat. Endowment for Arts, 1983, 84. One-woman shows include Los Angeles County Mus. Art, 1983, Internat. Mus. Photography, George Eastman House, 1983, Gallery Min. Tokyo, 1988, Ruth Bloom Gallery, Santa Monica, 1989, 90, 92, 95, Schneider Mus., Portland, Ore., 1990; Ctr. for Creative Photography, 1991, Robert Mann Gallery, N.Y.C., 1994, Mus. Contemporary Photography, Chgo., 1994; represented in permanent collections U. N.Mex. Art, Santa Monica Coll., Ctr. for Creative Photography, Mus. Modern Art, Santa Barbara Mus. Art, Los Angeles County Mus. Art, Mpls. Inst. Arts, San Francisco Mus. Modern Art, Security Pacific Bank, Mus. Modern Art, Lodz, Poland, Princeton U. Art Mus., others. Active L.A. Ctr. for Photographic Studies, 1988—, mem. adv. bd. trustees. Nat. Endowment for Arts fellow, 1980, 88, U.S./France fellow, 1989, Agnes Bourne fellow in Painting and Photography, Djerassi Found., 1989; recipient Graves award in Humanities, 1985. Mem. Coll. Art Assn., L.A. Contemporary Exhbns. (adv. trustee L.A. Ctr. for Photographic Studies), L.A. County Mus. Art. Studio: Studio 5 1403 S Santa Fe Ave Los Angeles CA 90021-2531

RANKIN, BONNIE LEE, insurance executive; b. Lancaster, Pa., June 27, 1953; d. E. Lee and Mary Jane (Weaver) R. BA in Liberal Arts, Millersville (Pa.) U., 1975; postgrad., U. Pa., 1994—. Cert. ins. counselor, 1986; CPCU, 1981. Claim adjuster Nationwide Ins. Co., Phila., 1975-76; comml. underwriter Nationwide Ins. Co., Harrisburg, Pa., 1976-78; sr. comml. underwriter Harleysville (Pa.) Mut. Ins. Co., 1978-79, tng. coord., 1979-81, br. underwriting mgr., 1981-84; with Worcester (Mass.) Ins. Co. subs. HMIC, 1984-92, asst. v.p., 1987-89, v.p., 1989-92, asst. v.p. comml. underwriting group, 1992—. Mem. adv. bd. Mechs. Hall, Worcester, 1987-92; bd. dirs., mem. fin. com. Worcester Community Action Coun., 1991-92. Mem. Soc. CPCUs (dir. cand. devel. 1985-87), Greater Valley Forge Soc. CPCUs (founder, bd. dirs. 1983-94), Cen. Mass. Soc. CPCUs, Pa. Assn. Mut. Ins. Cos. (edn. com. chmn. 1980-82, mem. consumer and edn. com. 1994—), Ins. Soc. Phila. (mem. faculty 1980-84), Ins. Inst. Am. (mem. grading bd. Malvern, Pa. 1981—), Mensa. Republican. Methodist. Office: A 3 Harleysville Ins 355 Maple Ave Harleysville PA 19438-2200

RANKIN, CAROL HARRIS, economics educator, consultant; b. St. Louis, Dec. 17, 1952; d. Robert Lowell and Laverne Marie (Jasper) Harris; m. John Stephen Rankin, May 25, 1974; children: Timothy, Daniel. BA, U. Dallas, 1974; MA, U. Houston, 1976, PhD, 1980. Asst. prof. econs. Ctrl. Mich. U., Mt. Pleasant, 1980-83; asst. prof. econs. Xavier U., Cin., 1984-88, assoc. prof., chair dept. econs., 1988-92, dir. Xavier Ctr. for Econ. Rsch., 1992-94; assoc. acad. v.p. Xavier U., 1994—. Contbr. articles to profl. jours. Mem. econ. adv. com. Greater Cin. C. of C., 1992—; mem. bd. econs. Cin. Enquirer, 1992-94; mem. econs. sub-com. Ohio-Ky.-Ind. Regional Coun. of Govts., 1993-94; mem. Com. on the Status of Women in the Econs. Profession. Mem. Am. Econs. Assn., Midwest Bus. Econs. Assn. (mem. bd. dirs. 1994—), Miami Valley Bus. Economists, Omicron Delta Epsilon. Office: Xavier U 3800 Victory Pkwy Cincinnati OH 45207

RANKIN, DEBORAH MARIE, journalist; b. N.Y.C., Aug. 17, 1943; d. Ruth Rankin; m. Lawrence A. Heald, Feb. 10, 1974; children: David Heald, Michael Heald. BA, Mundelein Coll., 1968. Bus. writer, fgn. desk editor, reporter AP, N.Y.C. and Chgo., 1968-74; econs. editor Consumer Reports, N.Y.C., 1974-76; fin. reporter, columnist N.Y. Times, N.Y.C., 1977-81; freelance journalist N.Y. Times, others, 1982—. Author: Investing on Your Own, 1994, also article series on fin. impact of divorce, 1986 (award N.Y. State Soc. CPAs 1986). Treas. Bronxville (N.Y.) PTA, 1987-89; 1st v.p. Lincoln H.S. PTA, Portland, Oreg., 1994; bd. dirs. Friends of the Library, Bronxville, 1991-92. Walter Bagehot fellow Columbia U., 1976-77. Mem. City Club of Portland. Home: 2894 NW Ariel Ter Portland OR 97210

RANKIN, DIANNE MARY, financial planner; b. Mineola, N.Y.; d. David Jay and Rose Mary (Ruggerio) Keller.; m. Eric Lynn Rankin, Nov. 18, 1972; 1 child, Derek. BA, U. Louisville, 1969. CPA, N.J.; cert. fin. planner; registered investment adviser; cert. tax. profl. Stewardess Pan Am. Airways, 1969-72; material contr. RCA, Somerville, N.J., 1972-75; pvt. practice acctg., Flemington, N.J., 1975—; investment adviser SEC, 1982; instr. tax preparation, Flemington, 1976-78. Mem. Delaware Twp. Mcpl. Utilities Authority, 1979—. Dean's scholar U. Louisville, 1969. Author: Financial Planning, 1984, Tax Reform, 1987, Personal Financial Planning and Tax Guide, 1990. Mem. Nat. Soc. Pub. Accts., Nat. Tax Tng. Inst. Address: 174 Ferry Rd Flemington NJ 08822-2740

RANKIN, DONNA WEATHERLY, school counselor; b. Baxley, Ga., June 9, 1939; d. Totten Hughes and Lillie Bess (Johnson) Weatherly; m. June 19, 1960; children: Renee Jones, LeAnn Matthews, Terri Turner. BS in Elem. Edn. and Psychology, Wesleyan and LaGrange Colls., 1961; MS in Sch. Counseling and Guidance, West Ga. Coll., 1990, Ednl. Specialist, 1991. Lic. real estate salesperson, Ga. Tchr. 4th grade Glynn County Bd. Edn., Brunswick, Ga., 1961; tchr. 3d grade DeKalb County Bd. Edn., Decatur, Ga., 1962-66, Oak Mountain Acad., Carrollton, Ga., 1977-84; tchr. 5th and 8th grades Carrollton City Bd. Edn., 1985-90; sch. counselor K-5 Carroll County Bd. Edn., Carrollton, 1990—; therapist West Ga. Ctr. for Behavioral Medicine, P.C., Carrollton; real estate agt. First Realty Real Estate Co., Carrollton, 1984-91; ptnr. Weatherly Land Ownership, Baxley, 1989—; cons. in counseling; parent edn. tchr. Carroll County Vocat. High Sch., Carrollton, 1993—; instr. grief workshop "Windows," RESA of West Ga., Grantville, 1991—; instr. "Super I" Carroll County Juvenile Ct./RESA, Carrollton, 1992—; facilitator Ga. Child Abuse Coun., Atlanta, 1993—. Contbr. articles to profl. jours. Chair comty. awareness com. Carroll County Child Abuse Coun., 1991—, pres., 1993-94; adult survivor support group facilitator Ga. Child Abuse Coun.; membership co-chair Advocate Exec. Com., 1991—; active Sand Hill PTO; co-chair devel. Carroll County Emergency Foster Care Hospice Com.; mem. adv. bd. Carroll Assn. for Prevention of Sexual Abuse, 1993—; Sunday sch. tchr. Carrollton First United Meth. Ch., mem. adminstrv. bd., 1991—, mem. Altar Guild, 1978—; mem. bd. dirs. Carroll County Literary Task Force, 1991—, Carroll County Parenting Assn., 1994—, Cmty. Care Home, 1995—; apptd. by superior justice Dewey Smith Task Force on Family Violence, Coweta Judicial Cir., 1994. Mem. ACA, Profl. Assn. Ga. Educators, Carroll County Sch. Counselors Assn., Ga. Sch. Counselors Assn. (legis. rep. 1991-92, 6th dist. chair 1993-94, region 1 chair-elect 1994—), Am. Sch. Counselors Assn., Kiwanis (bd. dirs.), Sunset Hills Country Club, Phi Delta Kappa. Home: 109 Briarwood Dr Carrollton GA 30117-4104 Office: Carroll County Sch Counsel Sand Hill Sch 45 Sandhill School Rd Carrollton GA 30116-9736

RANKIN, ELIZABETH ANNE DESALVO, nurse, psychotherapist, educator, consultant; b. Wurtzburg, Germany, Sept. 30, 1948; d. William Joseph and Elizabeth Agnes (Faraci) DeSalvo; m. Richard Forrest Rankin, June 5, 1971; children: William Alvin, David Michael. BSN, U. Md., Balt., 1970, MS, 1972; PhD., U. Md., College Park, 1979. Cert. health edn. specialist, specialist stress mgmt. edn., master hypnotherapist, master practitioner neurolinguistic programming, cert. Nat. Bd. Cert. Clin. Hypnotherapists. Mem. dept. psychiat. mental health/community health nursing U. Md. at Balt. Sch. Nursing, dir. div. bus. and industry; cns. Ctr. for Alternative Medicine, Pain Rsch. and Evaluation; cons. various publs. Co-author of books; contbr. chpts. to books, articles to profl. jours.; mem. editorial bd. Md. Nurse, Delmarva Found. Newsletter. Advisor U. Md. chpt. Nat. Student Nurses Assn. Recipient Twila Stinecker Leadership award, 1987, Leadership Excellence award Md. Assn. Nursing Students, 1990-92. Mem. ANA, Md. Nursing Assn. (bd. dirs., exec. com., 2d v.p., appointments mgr.), U. Md. Assn. Nursing Students (chpt. Nat. Student Nurses Assn. advisor), Nat. Coun. Family Rels., Coun. Nurse Researchers, Nat. Assn. Cert. Health Educators (charter), Am. Assn. Profl. Hypnotherapists, Milton H. Erickson Found., Washington Soc. Clin. Hypnosis, Sigma Theta Tau, Phi Epsilon Alpha, Phi Kappa Phi, Alpha Xi Delta.

RANKIN, HELEN CROSS, cattle rancher, guest ranch executive; b. Mojave, Calif; d. John Whisman and Cleo Rebecca (Tilley) Cross; m. Leroy Rankin, Jan. 4, 1936 (dec. 1954); children—Julia Jane King Sharr, Patricia Helen Denvir, William John. A.B., Calif. State U.-Fresno, 1935. Owner, operator Rankin Cattle Ranch, Caliente, Calif., 1954—; founder, pres. Rankin Ranch, Inc., Guest Ranch, 1965—; mem. sect. 15, U.S. Bur. Land Mgmt.; mem. U.S. Food and Agrl. Leaders Tour China, 1983, Australia and N.Z., 1985; dir. U.S. Bur. Land Mgmt. sect. 15. Pres., Children's Home Soc. Calif., 1945; mem. adv. bd. Camp Ronald McDonald. Recipient award Calif. Hist. Soc., 1983, Kern River Valley Hist. Soc., 1983. Mem. Am. Nat. Cattlemen's Assn., Calif. Cattlemen's Assn., Kern County Cattlemen's Assn., Kern County Cowbelles (pres. 1949, Cattlewoman of Yr. 1988), Calif. Cowbelles, Nat. Cowbelles, Bakersfield Country Club, Bakersfield Raquet Club. Republican. Baptist. Office: Rankin Ranch Caliente CA 93518

RANKIN, JACQUELINE ANNETTE, communications expert, educator; b. Omaha, Nebr., May 19, 1925; d. Arthur C. and Virdie (Gillispie) R. BA, Calif. State U., L.A., 1964, MA, 1966; MS in Mgmt., Calif. State U., Fullerton, 1977; EdD, U. LaVerne, Calif., 1981. Tchr. Rowland High Sch., La Habra, Calif., 1964-66, Lowell High Sch., La Habra, Calif., 1966-69, Pomona (Calif.) High Sch., 1969-75; program asst. Pomona Adult Sch., 1975-82; dir. Child Abuse Prevention Program, 1985-86; faculty evening div. Mt. San Antonio C.C., 1966-72, Calif. State U., L.A., 1972-73; asst. prof. speech Ball State U., Muncie, Ind., 1993; assoc. faculty dept. comm. and theatre Ind. U./Purdue U., Indpls., 1993; trainer internat. convs., sales groups, staffs of hosps., others; lectr. in field; cons. in field. Columnist, Jackie's World, Topics Newspapers, Indpls.; author: Body Language: First Impressions; contbr. articles to profl. jours. Chair pers. com. YWCA; v.p. Pomona Valley Dem. Women's Club; alt. County Ctrl. Com., L.A. County; Cramer Key woman 62d Assembly Dist.; sec. Braswell Ent. for Convalescent Care and Child Care. Mem. Pi Lambda Theta, Phi Delta Kappa. Home and Office: 7006 Elkton Dr Springfield VA 22152

RANKIN, SALLY WHITTINGTON, personnel director; b. Crisfield, Md., Sept. 11, 1956; d. Norman Thomas and Wanda Lou (Beer) Whittington; m. John Perry Rankin, Feb. 25, 1989. BA in Sociology, Coll. of William and Mary, 1978. Pers. officer U. Md., College Park, 1978-83, employment mgr., 1983-85; mgr. staff rels. Nat. Assn. Securities Dealers, Inc., Rockville, Md., 1985-88; dir. human resources Neurology Ctr., P.A., Chevy Chase, Md., 1988-91; dir. pers. Adminstrv. Office of Cts., Annapolis, Md., 1991—. Mem. AAUW, Soc. Human Resources, Chesapeake Human Resources Assn., Kappa Alpha Theta Alumnae. Office: Adminstrv Office of Cts Cts of Appeal Bldg Annapolis MD 21401

RANKIN, TERESA P. FRONCEK, former state agency administrator; b. Camp Lejeune, N.C., May 5, 1952; d. Richard A. and Carol Ann (Leverenz) Froncek; m. Robert W. Rankin, Dec. 22, 1978. BA, Ariz. State U., 1974; JD, U. Ariz., 1979. Chartered property casualty underwriter. Atty. Smith & Gamble, Carson City, Nev., 1979-80; dep. legis. counsel Legis. Counsel Bur., Carson City, 1981-83; chief ins. asst. Nev. Ins. Divsn., Carson City, 1984-91, commr. ins., 1991-95. Recipient Recognition award U. Nev. Las Vegas-Inst. Ins. & Risk Mgmt., 1993. Mem. Nat. Assn. Ins. Commrs., Reno Jaquar Club (bd. dirs. 1986-95). Home: 4221 Tara Carson City NV 89706

RANKS, ANNE ELIZABETH, retired elementary and secondary education educator; b. Omaha, June 10, 1916; d. Salvatore and Concetta (Turco) Scolla; m. Harold Eugene Ranks, Aug. 20, 1955 (dec.). B in Philosophy, Duchesne Coll., Omaha, 1937; MA, Creighton U., 1947. Tchr. Good Shepherd Parochial HighSch., Omaha, 1937-38, St. Benedicts High Sch., Omaha, 1938-39, Omaha Pub. Schs., 1939-81. Pres. women's divsn. Dem. Cen. Com., Nebr.; chmn. Gov.'s Profl. Practices Commn. Nebr., 1938-39; vol. Bergan-Mercy Hosp., Omaha, 1980-86, hosp. mem. aux. bd. dirs., 1985-86; vol. Saddleback Hosp., Laguna Hills, Calif., 1989-91; bd. dirs. Sylvia Tischhauser CRTA divsn. Scholarship Found., 1989-94; mem. bd. dirs. Saddleback Valley Edn. Found., 1990-92. Mem. AAUW (v.p. Laguna Hills br. 1988-90), Calif. Ret. Tchrs. Assn. (corr. sec. divsn. 42, 1988-89, v.p. 1989-92), Coun. Cath. Women Club (v.p. Laguna Hills chpt. 1988-91), Womens Club, Cath. Daus. Regent Omaha Ct. (rec. sec. Lake Forest, Calif. Ct. 1988-90), Orange Diocesan Coun. Cath. Women Calif. (bd. dirs. 1989-90, 2d v.p. 1990-94), Coll. Club of Leisure World (v.p. 1990—).

RANNEY, HELEN MARGARET, physician, educator; b. Summer Hill, N.Y., Apr. 12, 1920; d. Arthur C. and Alesia (Toolan) R. AB, Barnard Coll., 1941; MD, Columbia U., 1947; ScD, U. S.C., 1979. Diplomate: Am. Bd. Internal Medicine. Intern Presbyn. Hosp., N.Y.C., 1947-48, resident, 1948-50, asst. physician, 1954-60; practice medicine specializing in internal medicine, hematology N.Y.C., 1954-70; instr. Coll. Phys. and Surg. Columbia, N.Y.C., 1954-60; assoc. prof. medicine Albert Einstein Coll. Medicine, N.Y.C., 1960-64, prof. medicine, 1965-70; prof. medicine SUNY, Buffalo, 1970-73; prof. medicine U. Calif., San Diego, 1973-90, chmn. dept. medicine, 1973-86, Disting. physician vet. adminstr., 1986-91; mem. staff Alliance Pharm. Corp., San Diego, 1991—. Master ACP; fellow AAAS; mem. NAS, Inst. Medicine, Am. Soc. for Clin. Investigation, Am. Soc. Hematology, Harvey Soc., Am. Assn. Physicians, Am. Acad. Arts and Scis., Phi Beta Kappa, Sigma Xi, Alpha Omega Alpha. Office: Alliance Pharm Corp 3040 Science Park Rd San Diego CA 92121-1102

RANSOM, EVELYN NAILL, language educator; b. Memphis, Apr. 20, 1938; d. Charles Rhea and Evelyn (Goodlander) Naill Ransom; m. Gunter Heinz Hiller, June 7, 1960 (div. Mar. 1964). AA, Mt. Vernon Jr. Coll., 1958; BA, Newcomb Coll., 1960; MA, N.Mex. Highlands U., 1965; PhD, U. Ill., 1974. Cert. secondary tchr. N.Mex. Instr. Berlitz Sch. Langs., New Orleans, 1961; tchr. MillerWall Elem. Sch., Harvey, L.A., 1961-62; teaching asst. N.Mex. Highlands U., Las Vegas, 1963-64; instr. U. Wyo., Laramie, 1965-66; teaching asst. U. Ill., Urbana, 1966-70; prof. English lang. Ea. Ill. U., Charleston, 1970-93; vis. prof. in linguistics No. Ariz. U., Flagstaff, 1990-91, adj. faculty mem., 1993—; referee Pretext: Jour. of Lang. and Lit., Ill., 1981; co-chair roundtable Internat. Congress of Linguistics, 1987; linguistics del. People to People, Moscow, St. Petersburg, Prague, 1993; dissertation reader SUNY, Buffalo, 1982; vis. scholar UCLA, 1977; conductor workshop in field. Author: Complementation: Its Meanings and Forms, 1986; contbr. articles to profl. publs. Organizer Prairie Women's Ctr., Champaign, 1981-83; mem. Women's Ctr., Yavapai County, Ariz., 1993. Nat. Def. Fgn. Lang. fellow, 1969; grantee Ea. Ill. U., 1982, 87, 88, NSF, 1988. Mem. Linguistic Soc. Am., Linguistic Assn. S.W., Assn. for Computers and Humanities. Home: 201 E Southern Ave # 135 Apache Junction AZ 85219

RANSOM, NANCY ALDERMAN, sociology and women's studies educator, university administrator; b. New Haven, Feb. 25, 1929; d. Samuel Bennett and Florence (Opper) Alderman; m. Harry Howe Ransom, July 6, 1951; children—Jenny Alderman, Katherine Marie, William Henry Howe. B.A., Vassar Coll., 1950; postgrad. Columbia U., 1951, U. Leeds (Eng.), 1977-78; M.A., Vanderbilt U., 1971; EdD, Vanderbilt U., 1988. Lectr. sociology U. Tenn.-Nashville, 1971-76; grant writer Vanderbilt U., Nashville, 1976-77, dir. Women's Ctr., 1978—, instr. sociology, 1972, 74, lectr. sociology and women's studies, 1983, 90—; speaker profl. meetings. Vol. counselor family planning Planned Parenthood Assn. of Nashville, 1973-77, bd. dirs., 1978—, v.p., 1981—, pres., 1987-89. Columbia U. residential fellow, 1951; Vanderbilt U. fellow, 1971, Mem. Am. Sociol. Assn., Nat. Women's Studies Assn., Southeastern Women's Studies Assn., AAUW, Women in Higher Edn. Tenn. (planning com. ACE/ACE nat. identification program), NOW, Nat. Women's Polit. Caucus, LWV, Phi Beta Kappa. Club: Cable. Office: Vanderbilt U PO Box 1513 Nashville TN 37235

RANTA AHO, MARTHA HELEN, retired elementary education educator; b. Poplar, Wis., July 12, 1923; d. John and Aurora (Aho) Ranta; m. Wayne August Aho, Dec. 19, 1942 (dec. June 1978); children: Dennis Wayne, Marla Jane Thibodeau. BS in Elem. Edn. with honors, U. Wis., Superior, 1968, MS in Teaching, Elem. Edn., 1977, postgrad., 1979-86; postgrad., U. Minn., Superior, 1980-91, Coll. of St. Scholastica, 1978, Coll. St. Scholastica, Duluth, Minn, 1991. Cert. elem. tchr., Minn. Tchr. kindergarten Ind. Sch. Dist. #709, Duluth, 1968-75; tchr. first grade ISD #709, Duluth, 1975-89, master tchr., 1978-89, ret., 1989. Mentor tchr. Kenwood Elem. Sch., 1987-89, vol. storyteller, 1989-93, Chester Park Elem. Sch., 1993-95; vol. Family Svc. St. Luke's Hosp., 1991—; mem. St. Luke's Vol. Svc. Guild; tchr. leader insvc. sessions, 1972-80; docent St. Louis County Hist. Soc.-Depot Mus., Duluth, 1989—. Recipient trophy and award Wis. Indianhead Dist. of Garden Club, Superior, 1959. Mem. AAUW, Minn. Reading Assn., Arrowhead Reading Coun., Duluth Area Ret. Educators Assn., Am. Assn. Ret. Persons, Minn. Hist. Soc, Univ. for Srs. (vol. tchr. leader 1991), Parent Tchr. Student Assn. (hon. life), Finnish Am. Hist. Soc., Nat. Storytelling Assn., Minn. Gen. Fedn. Women's Clubs, Twentieth Century Club, Delta Kappa Gamma. Democrat. Lutheran. Home: 2722 E 1st St Duluth MN 55812-1907

RANTS, CAROLYN JEAN, college official; b. Hastings, Nebr., Oct. 3, 1936; d. John Leon and Christine (Helzer) Halloran; m. Marvin L. Rants, June 1, 1957 (div. July 1984); children: Christopher Charles, Douglas John. Student, Hastings Coll., 1954-56; BS, U. Omaha, 1960; MEd, U. Nebr., 1968; EdD, U. S.D., 1982. Tchr. elem. Ogallala (Nebr.) Community Sch., 1956-58, Omaha Pub. Schs., 1958-60, Hastings Pub. Schs., 1960-64, Grosse Pointe (Mich.) Community Schs., 1964-67; asst. prof., instr. Morningside Coll., Sioux City, Iowa, 1974-82, dean for student devel., 1982-84, v.p. for student affairs, 1984-94, interim v.p. for acad. affairs, 1992-94; v.p. enrollment and student svcs., 1994—. Mem. new agy. com., chmn. fund distbn. and resource deployment com. United Way, Sioux City, 1987-94; mem. Iowa Civil Rights Commn., 1989—; bd. dirs. Leadership Sioux City, 1988—, pres., 1992-93; bd. dirs. Siouxland Y, Sioux City, 1985-90, pres., 1988; mem. Vision 2020 Community Planning Task Force, 1990-92. Mem. Iowa Women in Ednl. Leadership (pres. Sioux City chpt. 1986), Nat. Assn. Student Pers. Adminstrs.(region IV-E adv. bd.), Nat. Assn. for Women Deans, Adminstrs. and Counselors, Iowa Student Pers. Adminstr. (chmn. profl. devel. Iowa chpt. 1988-89, pres. 1991-92), AAUW (corp. rep.), P.E.O. (pres. Sioux City chpt. 1994—, Tri-State Women's Bus. Conf. (treas., planning com. Sioux City chpt. 1987-89), Quota Club (com. chmn. Sioux City 1987-89, v.p. 1992-94, pres. 1994—, Siouxland Woman of Yr. award 1988), Sertoma (officer, bd. govs., regional dir.), Omicron Delta Kappa, Delta Kappa Gamma (state 1st v.p. 1993—). Republican. Methodist. Home: 2904 S Cedar St # 4 Sioux City IA 51106-4246 Office: Morningside Coll 1501 Morningside Ave Sioux City IA 51106-1751

RANUM, JANE BARNHARDT, lawyer; b. Charlotte, N.C., Aug. 21, 1947; d. John Robert and Gladys Rose (Swift) B.; m. James Harry Ranum, Mar. 29, 1972; 1 child, Elizabeth McBride. B.S., East Carolina U., 1969; J.D., Hamline U., 1979. Bar: Minn. 1979, U.S. Dist. Ct. Minn. 1979. Tchr. elem. sch. Durham County, Durham, N.C., 1969-70; tchr. Dept. Def., Baumholder, W.Ger., 1970-72, Dist. 196, Rosemount, Minn., 1972-76; law clk. Hennepin County Dist. Ct., Mpls., 1982; asst. county atty. Hennepin County, Mpls., 1982—. Mem. exec. com., lobbying coordinator DFL Feminist Caucus, St. Paul, 1980-84; bd. dirs. Project 13 for Reproductive Rights, Mpls., 1981-82; state del. Minn. Democratic Farmer Labor Party Conv., 1982, 84, precinct del., 1974—; mem. Minn. Sen., 1991—, chair legislature commn. on children, youth and their families, 1993—; senate rep. chemical abuse and prevention resource coun., 1993. Named Feminist of the Yr. Minn. NOW, 1994, Legis. of the Yr. Minn. Assn. for Retarded Citizens, 1994. Mem. Minn. Women's Lawyers, Minn. Family Support and Recovery Council, Hennepin County Bar Assn., Minn. Bar Assn. Democrat. Home: 5045 Aldrich Ave S Minneapolis MN 58419-1207 Office: County Govt Ctr A-2000 Hennepin Minneapolis MN 55487

RAPHAEL, LOUISE ARAKELIAN, mathematician, educator; b. N.Y.C., Oct. 24, 1937; d. Aristakes and Antionette (Sudbeaz) Arakelian; m. Robert Barnett Raphael, June 12, 1966 (div. 1985); children: Therese Denise, Marc Philippe. BS in Math., St. John's U., 1959; MS in Math., Cath. U., Washington, 1962; PhD in Math, Cath. U., 1967. Asst. prof. math. Howard U., Washington, 1966-70, vis. prof., 1981-82, assoc. prof., 1982-86, prof., 1986—; assoc. prof. Clark Coll., Atlanta, 1971-79, prof., 1979-82; vis. assoc. prof. MIT, Cambridge, 1977-78, vis. prof., 1989-90. Contbr. over 30 rsch. articles to profl. jours. Program dir. NSF, Washington, 1986-88; acting adminstrv. officer Conf. Bd. Math. Scis., 1985-86. Grantee NSF, 1975-76, 79-81, 89-91, Army Rsch. Office, 1981-89, Air Force Sci. Rsch., 1981-82, 91—. Mem. AAAS, Am. Math. Soc. (com. mem.), Math. Assn. Am. (chmn. minorities in math. task force 1988), Soc. Indsl. and Applied Math., Sigma Xi. Democrat. Roman Catholic. Office: Howard U Dept Math Washington DC 20059

RAPHAEL, SALLY JESSY, talk-show host; b. Easton, Pa., Feb. 25, 1943; children: Allison (dec.), Andrea; m. Karl Soderlund; 2 step-daughters, 1 adopted son, also foster children. BFA, Columbia U. Anchored radio program Jr. High Sch. News Sta. WFAS-AM, White Plains, N.Y., 1955; host of cooking program WAPA-TV, San Juan, P.R., 1965-67; radio and television broadcaster Miami and Ft. Lauderdale, Fla., 1969-74; host Sta. WMCA-Radio, N.Y.C., 1976-81; talk show host NBC Talk-net, N.Y.C., 1982-88, ABC Talkradio, N.Y.C., 1988-91; syndicated TV talk-show host N.Y.C., 1983—; part-time owner of a perfume factory, 1964-68; owner of an art gallery, 1964-69; owner, The Wine Press, N.Y.C., 1979-83; ind. producer TV films, 1991;. Author: (with M.J. Boyer) Finding Love, 1984, (with Pam Proctor) Sally: Unconventional Success, 1990; film appearances include: Resident Alien, 1990, The Addams Family, 1991; TV appearences include: Murphy Brown, Dave's World, The Nanny, The Tonight Show, Nightline. Recipient Bronze medal, Internat. Film & Television Festival of NY, 1985; Emmy award as outstanding talk-show host, daytime, 1988, 89. Office: Multimedia Entertainment 515 W 57th St New York NY 10019-2902

RAPHEL, ROBIN, federal official; b. Vancouver, Wash., Sept. 16, 1947; m. Leonard Arthur Ashton; 2 children. BA, U. Wash.; Diploma in Hist. Studies, Cambridge U., Eng.; MA, U. Md. Econ. analyst CIA; lectr. history Damavand Coll., Tehran, Iran; with Fgn. Svc., 1977, Islamabad, Pakistan, 1977-78; with office investment affairs bur. econs. Dept. of State, 1978-80, staff asst. to asst. sec. Near East and South Asian affairs, 1980-81, econ. officer Israel desk, 1981-82, spl. asst. to under sec. polit. affairs, 1982-84; 1st sec. polit. affairs London, 1984-88; polit. counselor Pretoria, South Africa, 1988-91, New Delhi, 1991-93; asst. sec. South Asian affairs Dept. of State, Washington, 1993—. Mem. Am. Econ. Assn., Am. Fgn. Svc. Assn., Pres.'s Estate Polo Club (New Delhi), Phi Beta Kappa. Office: S Asian Affairs 2201 C St NW Washington DC 20520-6243

RAPIN, ISABELLE, physician; b. Lausanne, Switzerland, Dec. 4, 1927; d. Rene and Mary Coe (Reeves) R.; m. Harold Oaklander, Apr. 5, 1959; children: Anne Louise, Christine, Stephen, Peter. Physician's Diploma. Faculte de Medicine, U. Lausanne, 1952, Doctorate in Medicine, 1955. Diplomate Am. Bd. Psychiatry and Neurology. Intern in pediatrics N.Y. U. Bellevue Med. Center, 1953-54; resident in neurology Neurol. Inst. of N.Y., Columbia-Presbyn. Med. Center, 1954-57, fellow in child neurology, 1957-58; mem. faculty Albert Einstein Coll. Medicine, Bronx, N.Y., 1958—; prof. neurology and pediatrics Albert Einstein Coll. Medicine, 1972—; attending neurologist and child neurologist Einstein Affiliated Hosps., Bronx.; Mem. Nat. Adv. Neurol. and Communicative Disorders and Stroke Coun., NIH, 1984-88. Contbr. chpts. to books, articles to med. jours. Recipient award Conf. Ednl. Adminstrs. Serving the Deaf, 1988. Fellow Am. Acad. Neurology; mem. Internat. Child Neurology Assn. (sec.-gen. 1979-82, v.p. 1982-86, Frank R. Ford lectr. 1990), Am. Neurol. Assn. (v.p. 1982-83), Child Neurology Soc. (Hower award 1987), Internat. Neuropsychology Soc., AAAS, N.Y. Acad. Scis., Assn. Research in Nervous and Mental Diseases (v.p. 1986). Office: Albert Einstein Coll Medicine 1410 Pelham Pky S Bronx NY 10461-1101

RAPOPORT, JUDITH, psychiatrist; b. N.Y.C., July 12, 1933; d. Louis and Minna (Enteen) Livant; m. Stanley Rapoport, June 25, 1961; children: Stuart, Erik. BA, Swarthmore Coll., 1955; MD, Harvard U., 1959. Lic. psychiatrist. Cons., child psychiatrist NIMH/St. Elizabeth's Hosp., Washington, 1969-72; clin. asst. prof. Georgetown U. Med. Sch., Washington, 1972-82, clin. assoc. prof., 1982-85, clin. prof. psychiat., 1985—; med. officer biol. psychiatry br. NIMH, Bethesda, Md., 1976-78, chief, child mental illness unit, biol. psychiat. br., 1979-82, chief, child psychiatry lab. of clin. scis., 1982-84, chief, child psychiatry div. intramural rsch. programs, 1984—; prof. psychiatry George Washington U. Sch. Med., Washington, 1979—; prof. pediatrics Georgetown U., Washington, 1985—; cons. in field. Author: (non-fiction) The Boy Who Couldn't Stop Washing, 1989 (best seller literary guild selection 1989), Childhood Obsessive Compulsive Disorder, 1989. Fellow Am. Psychiat. Assn., Am. Acad. Child Psychiat.; mem. D.C. Psychiat. Assn., Inst. Medicine. Home: 3010 44th Pl NW Washington DC 20016-3557 Office: NIMH Bldg 10 Rm 6N240 Bethesda MD 20892

RAPOPORT, SONYA, artist; b. Boston; d. Louis Aaron and Ida Tina (Axelrod) Goldberg; m. Henry Rapoport; children—Hava Rapoport de Feres, David, Robert. Student Mass. Coll. Art, 1941-42; B.A., NYU, 1945; M.A., U. Calif.-Berkeley, 1949. One woman shows N.Y.C. Pub. Library, 1979, New Sch. Social Research, N.Y.C., 1981, NYU Grad. Sch. Bus. Adminstrn., 1982, Sarah Lawrence Coll., Bronxville, N.Y., 1984, Kuopio Mus., Finland, 1992; group shows include Union Gallery San Jose State U., Calif., 1979, Ctr. for Visual Arts, Oakland, Calif., 1979, Walker Art Ctr., Mpls., 1981, Nat. Library, Madrid, 1982, SUNY Library, Purchase, 1983, Otis Art Inst. of Parsons Sch. of Design, Los Angeles, 1984, Cleve. Inst. Art, 1984, FISEA93 4th Internat. Symposium on Electronic Art, Mpls.also others; represented in permanent collections Stedelijk Mus., Amsterdam, Indpls. Mus. Art, Grey Art Gallery, NYU, San Francisco Mus. Modern Art, San Jose State U. Found.-Union Gallery, Crocker Art Mus., Sacramento, Hall of Justice, Hayward, Calif.; book artist Shoe-Field, Chinese Connections, About Me, Objects on My Dresser, (interactive books) Gateway to Your Ka, Your Fate is in Your Feet, Digital Mudra2; producer A Shoe-In, Biorhythm, Coping with Sexual Jealousy, (computer assisted interactive installations) The Animated Soul, Digital Mudra, Transgenic Bagel; contbr. to profl. publs. Home: 6 Hillcrest Ct Berkeley CA 94705-2805

RAPP, JOANNA A., geriatrics, mental health nurse; b. Youngsville, Pa., Nov. 22, 1920; d. Wade Hampton and Edith (Hodges) Brazee; m. Ellsworth G. Rapp, Nov. 6, 1976; children: Sallie Angel, Suzanne Herzing. Diploma, Meadville (Pa.) City Hosp., 1941; BS in Nursing Edn., Western Res. U., 1947. Field team nurse Bur. Occupational Health; staff nurse USPHS Hosp., Anchorage; supr. Hale-Makua, Mauia, Hawaii; instr. John Howard Forensic Psychiat. Hosp., Washington (D.C.); DON Twinbrooke So. Nursing Facility; quality assurance specialist Nueva Vista Devel. Ctr. 1st. Lt. ANC, 1944-46. Named Dist. Nurse of Yr. Mem. ANA, TNA (past. dist. v.p., pres.). Home: 2104 John Ave Edinburg TX 78539-6903 Office: Nueva Vista Devel Ctr PO Box 3245 Edinburg TX 78540-3245

RAPS, MAUREEN JOY, occupational health nurse; b. Newark, Aug. 2, 1961; d. John and Lillian (Raffa) McBride; m. Eric Corey Raps, July 19, 1992; 1 child, Daniel Alan. BS, Trenton State Coll., 1983; MS, U. Pa., 1993. RN, Pa.; cert. adult nurse practitioner. RN Hosp. U. Pa., Phila., 1983-92; rsch. asst. Grad. Sch. Nursing U. Pa., Phila., 1992-93; nurse practitioner occupl. medicine dept. Phila. Naval Shipyard, 1993—. Mem. Am. Assn. Occupl. Health Nurses, Am. Acad. Nurse Practitioners, Sigma Theta Tau. Home: 41 Sorrel Run Mount Laurel NJ 08054

RAREWALA, KATHLEEN AGNES BERTI, educational director; b. Bronx, N.Y., Sept. 30, 1949; d. John Woodrow and Josephine May (Calzerano) Berti; m. Jasjit Singh Rarewala, Aug. 13, 1973; 1 child, Kahikisha. Cert, Art Instr. Schs., 1967; BFA, Pratt Inst., 1970, MFA, 1973. Cert. tchr., N.Y. Jewelry designer Design Studio 444, N.Y.C., 1970-78; artist in residence Dakota House-Novak, N.Y.C., 1970-71; sculptor Bellardo's Ltd., N.Y.C., 1974-75; chmn. art Community Sch. P932K, Bklyn., 1970-75; display designer Maimonides Hosp., Bklyn., 1975-76; jewelry designer AIX, L.A., 1978-79; owner, clothing designer Haute Chocolate, Torrance, Calif., 1980-84; sec., treas. Lamborghini of N.Am., Carson, Calif., 1983-87; tchr. gifted Gifted Student Program/Soleado, Palos Verde Estates, Calif., 1987-88; dir., tchr. Children's Acad. of Art, Rolling Hill Estates, Calif., 1988—; chair, cons. Art at Your Fingertips, Palos Verde, Calif., 1986-88; judge art show PTSA Reflections, Rolling Hills Estates, 1987-90; coord. art show Ridgecrest Sch., Palos Verde, 1989-91, P.V.P. High Schs., Rolling Hills Estates, 1992, coord. PTSA reflections contest, 1993-94, parliamentarian music boosters, 1993-94; chmn. nominating com., 1993-94, directory coord., editor, chmn. art show, 1993-94; 33d dist. coord. Reflections art show PTSA, 1993-94; 5th v.p. PTSA Palos Verdes Peninsula High Sch., 1993-94. Contbg. artist: Designs from Nature: Debrie Taylor, 1971; exhibited in group shows at Soc. Arts and Crafts, 1976, N.Y. Mus. Natural History, 1968, N.Y. Women's Interart Gallery, 1975, N.E. Craftfair Rhinebeck, 1976; one-woman shows include Art Gallery Pratt Inst., 1973. Chair-at-large Athletic Boosters, Rolling Hills Estates, 1991; 3rd v.p. Music Boosters, Rolling Hills Estates, 1992; 4th v.p. PTA, 1986-87, 5th v.p., 1987—, editor newspaper, 1992. Recipient 1st place award for jewelry design Bklyn. Mus. Art Show, 1975, HSA Silver Bar award PTA Calif., 1988, HSA Gold Bar award PTA Calif., 1990, Music Boosters award for continuing svc. Palos Verdes Peninsula H.S., 1994; Pratt fellow, 1971-73. Mem. Nat. Art Edn. Assn. (chair art show 1988—). Home: 43 Aspen Way Rolling Hills Estates CA 90274-3407

RASCH, ELLEN MYRBERG, cell biology educator; b. Chicago Heights, Ill., Jan. 31, 1927; d. Arthur August and Helen Catherine (Stelle) Myrberg; m. Robert W. E. Rasch, June 17, 1950; 1 son, Martin Karl. PhB with honors, U. Chgo., 1945, BS in Biol. Sci., 1947, MS in Botany, 1948, PhD, 1950. Asst. histologist Am. Meat Inst. Found., Chgo., 1950-51; USPHS postdoctoral fellow U. Chgo., 1951-53, rsch. assoc. dept. zoology, 1954-59; rsch. assoc. Marquette U., Milw., 1962-65, assoc. prof. biology, 1965-68, prof. biology, 1968-75, Wehr Disting. prof. biophysics, 1975-78; rsch. prof. biophysics East Tenn. State U., James H. Quillen Coll. Medicine, Johnson City, 1978-94, interim chmn. dept. cellular biophysics, 1986-94, prof. anatomy and cell biology, 1994—. Mem. Wis. Bd. Basic Sci. Examiners, 1971-75, sec. bd., 1973-75. Recipient Post-doctoral fellowship USPHS, 1951-53, Research Career Devel. award, 1967-72; Teaching Excellence and Disting. award Marquette U., 1975; Kreeger-Wolf vis. disting. prof. in biol. sci. Northwestern U., 1979. Mem. Royal Microscopic Soc., Am. Soc. Cell Biology, Am. Soc. Zoologists, Am. Soc. Ichthyologists and Herpetologists, The Histochem. Soc., Phi Beta Kappa, Sigma Xi. Contbr. articles to various publs. Home: 1504 Chickees St Johnson City TN 37604-7103 Office: East Tenn State U Dept Anatomy & Cell Biology PO Box 70, 421 Johnson City TN 37614-0421

RASCH, MARCIA ANN, mental health services professional, psychologist; b. Cin., July 16, 1963; d. Charles Frederick and Terese Marie (Bockelman) R. BA in Psychology, U. Dayton, 1985; MA in Counseling Psychology, U. Akron, 1988, PhD in Counseling Psychology, 1993. Lic. psychologist, Ohio. Child and family therapist Child and Adolescent Svc. Ctr., Canton, Ohio, 1989-93, Barbara Fordyce and Assocs., Canton, Ohio, 1992-93; dir. Butler County Children's Treatment program Middletown (Ohio) Area Mental Health, 1993—; presenter acad. rsch. Soc. Personality Assessment, New Orleans, 1991, Chgo., 1994, Soc. Multiple Personality/Dissociative States, Chgo. and Akron, 1988; guest lectr. psychology U. Akron, 1991, 92, 93; workshop presenter Cmty. Mental Health Ctr., 1994. Co-author: (test manual) The Hand Test: Interpretations of Child and Adolescent Responses, 1991; contbr. articles to profl. jours. Mem. APA (student affiliate divsn. counseling psychology 1988-90, assoc.), Am. Assn. Partial Hospitalization, Ohio Assn. Family-Based Svcs. Roman Catholic. Office: Butler County Childrens Treatment Ctr 1020 Manchester Ave Middletown OH 45042-1928

RASCO, CAROL HAMPTON, federal official; b. Columbia, S.C., Jan. 13, 1948; d. Frank Barnes and Mary Ruby (Dallas) Hampton; children: Howard Hampton, Mary-Margaret. Student, Hendrix Coll., 1965-66; BSE, U. Ark., 1969; MS, U. Ctrl. Ark., 1972. Elem. sch. tchr. Springdale and Fayetteville (Ark.) Pub. Schs., 1969-71; counselor Bryant (Ark.) Middle Sch., 1972-73; liaison to human svcs. and health agys. Gov. Bill Clinton, Little Rock, Ark., 1983-85; exec. asst. for govtl. ops. Gov. Bill Clinton, Little Rock, 1985-91, sr. exec. asst., 1991-92; liaison to Nat. Govs. Assn., 1985-92; asst. to President U.S. for domestic policy White House, Washington, 1993—. V.p., pres. Ark. Symphony Orch. Soc. Guild Bd., 1975-78, mem. exec. com., 1976-78; pres. Fullbright Elem. Sch. PTA, 1982-83; child advocate coord. Little Rock Conf. United Meth. Women's Bd., 1979-80; family life coord. Little Rock Conf. United Meth. Ch. Coun. Ministries, 1980-82; active Friends of Ark. Repertory Theatre Bd., 1977-79, First United Meth. Ch., 1973—, chmn. bd. stewards, 1981, chmn.coun. on ministries, 1980, lay leader, 1982, chmn. child devel. ctr. bd., 1982, bd. trustees, 1988-90, Ark. Devel. Disabilities Svcs. Bd., 1979-82; vol. Ark. Coalition for Handicapped, 1974-77, Little Rock Mcpl. Ct. Vols. in Probation, 1975-78, Gov. Task Force on Coordination of Svcs. Sch.-Aged Children, 1979, Little Rock Pub. Sch. Spl. Edn. Adv. Com., 1981-91, Pulaski County Coord. for Bill Clinton for Gov., 1982. Recipient Germaine Menteil Vol. Activist award, 1976, Community Svc. award Channel 4-GOVCP, 1979. Spl. Friend of Children award Ark. Advocates for Children and Families, 1985. Democrat. Office: The White House 1600 Pennsylvania Ave NW Washington DC 20500-0001

RASKIN, SARAH BLOOM, lawyer; b. Medford, Mass., Apr. 15, 1961; d. Herbert and Arlene (Perlis) Bloom; m. Jamin B. Raskin, Aug. 11, 1990; 1 child, Hannah Grace. BA in Econs., Amherst Coll., 1983; JD, Harvard U., 1986. Bar: N.Y. 1987, D.C. 1989, U.S. Dist. Ct. Md. Assoc. Mayer, Brown & Platt, N.Y.C., 1986-88, Arnold & Porter, N.Y.C. and Washington, 1989-93; counsel U.S. Senate Banking Com., Washington, 1993—. John Woodruff Simpson fellow Amherst Coll., 1983. Mem. Women Housing and Fin., Phi Beta Kappa. Home: 7209 Holly Ave Takoma Park MD 20912 Office: US Senate Banking Com 534 Dirksen Senate Office Bldg Washington DC 20510

RASMUSSEN, GAIL MAUREEN, critical care nurse; b. Can., Feb. 22, 1941; d. Thomas Alfred and Bernice Hilda (Sayler) Salisbury; m. Byron Karl Rasmussen, June 28, 1964; children: Stephen, Carla, Wade, Gregory. AS, Riverside City Coll., 1961; BSN, U. Phoenix, 1987; MS in Health Professions Edn., Osteo. Coll. the Pacific, 1991. RN, Calif.; CCRN. Staff nurse Meml. Med. Ctr., Long Beach, Calif., 1961-63, UCLA Med. Ctr., 1963-64; clin. nurse ICU, critical care unit Intercommunity Med. Ctr., Covina, Calif., 1964-71, 78—; instr. advanced cardiac life support L.A. Counties, 1991—. Mem. AACN.

RASMUSSEN, JANE ELLIOTT, endocrinologist; b. Madison, Wis., Oct. 13, 1963; d. Howard and Jane Claire (Spence) R.; m. Thomas Jude Christopher, May 23, 1992. BA, Smith Coll., 1985; MD, Yale U., 1990. Intern internal medicine Yale-New Haven (Conn.) Hosp., 1990, resident internal medicine, 1990-91; resident internal medicine Barnes Hosp., St. Louis, 1991-92, fellow endocrinology, 1992—. Contbr. articles to profl. jours. Recipient Undergrad. award for excellence in analytical chemistry ACS, Smith Coll., 1984. Mem. AAAS, AMA, Am. Med. Women's Assn. Home: 5124 Bischoff Ave Saint Louis MO 63110-3104 Office: Barnes Hosp One Barnes Hosp Plaza St Louis MO 63110

RASMUSSEN, JESSIE K., state legislator; b. Chgo., Apr. 1, 1945; m. Dean F. Rasmussen, 1967; children: Jennifer, Janine. BS, U. Nebr., 1967, MS, 1984. Mem. Nebr. Legislaturefrom 20th dist., 1990—. Mem. Nebr. Task Force Early Childhood Edn,. Mem. Nebr. Assn Edn. Young Children, Nat. Coun. Exceptional Children. Democrat. Office: Nebr Legislature State Capitol Lincoln NE 68509*

RASMUSSEN, MAXINE KONIG, therapist, counselor, educator; b. Grand Forks, N.D., May 29, 1930; d. Maximillian and Frances (Ellis) Konig; children: Michael John Rasmussen, Lori Anne Swinney, Mari Beth Rasmussen, Eric Thomas Rasmussen. BS in Home Econs., U. N.D., 1965, MEd in Counseling and Edn., 1968, PhD in Counseling and Psychology, 1973. Lic. profl. counselor, N.D.; cert. tchr., N.D.; cert. clin. mental health counselor. Dir. counseling dept. GFAFB, 1969-73; dept. counseling instr. U. N.D., Grand Forks, 1969-73, prof. continuing edn., 1986—; dir. outreach program Mental Health Ctr., Grand Forks, 1973-76; prof. psychology U. Minn., Crookston, 1990—; pvt. practice Grand Forks, 1976—; host interview program Sta. KTHI-TV, Grand Forks, 1964-66; tchr. St. Michael' Sch., Grand Forks, 1963-64; counselor, chair St. James H.S., Grand Forks, 1966-69, psychology instr., 1966-69; elem. and secondary sch. cons., Grand Forks, Walsh Pembina Counties, N.D., 1976-83; psychiat. cons. psych. unit United Hosp., Grand Forks, 1976-89; presenter Gov.'s Commn. Children and Adolescence at Risk, Bismarck, N.D., 1986. Contbr. articles to profl. jours. Bd. dirs. Pine to Prairie Girl Scouts, Grand Forks, 1991—; pres. Greater Grand Forks Symphony Assn., 1991—; mem. task force on chem. dependency Meth. Ch., N.D., Minn., and S.D., 1984-89. Mem. APA, Nat. Assn. Counselors, Mortar Bd. (pres., dir. 1965-73). Republican. Roman Catholic. Office: 667 Demers Ave Ste 2003 Grand Forks ND 58201

RASMUSSEN, ROBERTA A., state legislator; m. Curtis Rasmussen; 4 children. Student, Dakota Wesleyan U. Acct. and pork prodr.; mem. S. D. State Senate from 9th dist. Democrat. Methodist. Home: RR 2 Box 23 Hurley SD 57036 Office: Senate House State Capitol Pierre SD 57501*

RASMUSSSEN, TINA MARIE, management consultant; b. Chgo., Oct. 17, 1963; d. William and Barbara (Meyer) R. BA cum laude, No. Ill. U., 1985; MA, Fielding Inst., 1994. Program developer Gandalf Techs., Wheeling, Ill., 1985-89; trainer Citizen Watch Co., L.A., 1989-90; v.p. Santa Barbara (Calif.) Bank, 1990-93; mgr.- orgn. devel. Nestle, San Francisco, 1993—; cons. Advantage Consulting, Moraga, Calif., 1994—. Author: (with others) Leadership in A New Era, 1994. Bd. dirs. Am. Red Cross, Santa Barbara, 1992-93, active pub. rels., 1992-93. Alumni scholar No. Ill. U., 1984-85. Mem. ASTD (speaker), OD Network, Greenleaf Ctr. Office: Advantage Consulting 1947 Filbert St San Francisco CA 94123

RASO, MARGARET MILDRED, educator; b. Yonkers, N.Y., Aug. 22, 1933; d. Michael and Josephine Rose (Pisco) Trotta; m. Anthony Joseph Raso, Oct. 31, 1964; children: Joanne Marie, Michael Anthony. BS in Elementary Edn., Fordham U., 1955; MA in Edn., Fairfield U., 1961. Cert. elementary tchr., high sch. English, N.Y. Tchr. Yonkers (N.Y.) Pub. Schs., 1955-65; substitute tchr. Rockland County Schs., 1966-68, 75-87; real estate salesperson Trilling, Century 21 Assocs., Sufferin, New City, N.Y., 1985-87; juvenile justice chmn. Cen. Hudson PTA Dist., N.Y., 1977-79; family ct. monitor, 1978-79; del. Leadership Conv. NEA, West Point, N.Y., 1968. Inventor: hosiery donning and removing appliance, 1984. Auditor 12th Ward Rep. Club, Yonkers, 1962; mem. legal com. Pine Creek Area Assn., Fairfield Conn., 1974-80. Named Hon. Life Mem. Yonkers (N.Y.) PTA, 1962; recipient Spl. Olympics award, 1985. Mem. Columbiettes (major degree), Cath. Alumni Club (social com. chmn.). Home: 2 Dutch Ct West Nyack NY 10994-1701

RASOR, DINA LYNN, investigator, journalist; b. Downey, Calif., Mar. 21, 1956; d. Ned Shaurer and Genevieve Mercia (Eads) R.; m. Thomas Taylor Lawson, Oct. 4, 1980. BA in Polit. Sci., U. Calif., Berkeley, 1978. Editorial asst. ABC News, Washington, 1978-79; researcher Pres.'s Commn. on Coal, Washington, 1979; legis. asst. Nat. Taxpayers Union, Washington, 1979-81; founder, dir. Project on Mil. Procurement, Washington, 1981-89; investigative reporter Lawson-Rasor Assocs., El Cerrito, Calif., 1990-92; pres., CEO, investigator Bauman & Rasor Group, El Cerrito, Calif., 1993—. Author: The Pentagon Underground, 1985; editor: More Bucks, Less Bang, 1983; contbr. articles to profl. jours. Recipient Sigma Delta Chi Outstanding Leadership award Soc. Profl. Journalists, 1986; named to register Esquire Mag., 1986, Nat. Jour., 1986. Mem. United Ch. Christ.

RASOR, DORIS LEE, secondary education educator; b. Gonzales, Tex., June 25, 1929; d. Leroy and Ora (Power) DuBose; m. Jimmie E. Rasor, Dec. 27, 1947; children: Jimmy Lewis, Roy Lynn. BS, Abilene (Tex.) Christian U., 1949. Part-time sec. Abilene Christian Coll., 1946-50; sec. Radford Wholesale Grocery, Abilene, 1950-52; tchr. Odessa (Tex.) High Sch., 1967—. Author play: The Lost Pearl, 1946. Recipient Am. Legion award, 1946. Mem. AAUW, Classroom Tchrs. Assn., Tex. Tchrs. Assn., NEA, Tex. Bus. Educators Assn., Alpha Delta Kappa (pres. 1976-78). Ch. of Christ. Home: 3882 Kenwood Dr Odessa TX 79762-7018 Office: Odessa High School 1301 Dotsy Ave Odessa TX 79763-3597

RASP, LISA PATRICIA, bank executive; b. Ridgewood, N.J., Dec. 15, 1964; d. Robert and Rita (Mafull) R. BA in Econs., Rutgers Coll., 1986. Sr. loan reviewer UJB Fin., Princeton, N.J., 1986-89; asst. v.p. credit rev. Republican Nat. Bank of N.Y., N.Y.C., 1989-91; v.p. credit rev. Republic NH Bank of N.Y., N.Y.C., 1991-93; v.p. comml. lending Safra Republic Bank, Miami, Fla., 1993-94; asst. v.p. loan rev. Union Chelsea NH Bank, N.Y.C., 1994—. Vol. Big Sisters of Passaic County, N.J., 1986-89, Big Sisters of Middlesex County, N.J., 1989-91, Evas Kitchen, Paterson , N.J., 1986—, Habitat for Humanity. Democrat. Home: 323 N Fullerton Ave Montclair NJ 07042 Office: Union Chelsea NH Bank 609 Fifth Ave New York NY 10022

RASSULO, DONNA MARIE, nurse, poet, writer, TV producer; b. Boston, Jan. 18, 1951; d. Donald and Eleanor (Kadish) Guay; m. John A. Rassulo, June 20, 1981; children: Garret John, Nicole Darcy. Diploma, Shepard-Gill Sch. Practical Nursing, 1978; cert., Inst. Children's Lit., 1990. LPN, Mass. Model, cons. Reflections Unlimited, Amherst, Mass., 1974; med. sec. Mass. Gen. Hosp., Boston, 1969-78; staff nurse, acute medicine Mass. Gen. Hosp., 1978-1990, staff nurse, pediatric intermediate care, 1990—; mem. Long Ridge Writers Group, West Redding, Conn., 1991—. Author numerous poems and articles; co-producer (with Marjorie Harrison) Clay Pit Pond Prodns., 1991—, Parent 2 Parent Show. Mem. Neonatal ICU Parent Support Inc., Newton, Mass., 1989—, Parent Care, Inc., Alexandria, Va., 1990—. Recipient Disting. Poet award Sparrowgrass Poetry Forum, 1990, Golden Poet award World of Poetry Press, 1990. Mem. Lic. Practical Nurses Mass., Nat. Fedn. Lic. Practical Nurses. Democrat. Roman Catholic. Home: 65A Trowbridge St Belmont MA 02178-4001

RAST, VICKI JEAN, air force officer; b. New Orleans, May 3, 1966; d. Charles Harry and Marlene Ross (Barrett) Besecker; m. Marcus Caldwell, Nov. 18, 1989; 1 child, Brandon. BS in History, USAF Acad., 1988; MPA, Troy State U., Sumter, S.C., 1992; postgrad., U. Ala., Montgomery, 1993—. Commd. 2d lt. USAF, 1988, advanced through grades to capt., 1992; officer-in-charge munitions br. 363D Fighter Wing, Sumter, 1989-90; officer-in-charge munitions br. Operation Desert Storm 363D Fighter Wing, United Arab Emirates, 1990-91; asst. maintenance officer 363D Fighter Wing, Sumter, 1991-92, Sumter and, Dharan, Saudi Arabia, 1992-93; flight comdr. maintenance ops. 363D Fighter Wing, Sumter, 1993; chief future sys. and tech. Air Command and Staff Coll., Montgomery, 1993-94, academic instr. war theory and campaign studies directorate, 1994—. Decorated SWA Svc. medal, Kuwaiti Liberation medal. Mem. VFW, Air Force Assn., Assn. Grad. USAF Acad., Pi Sigma Alpha. Home: 6721 Sansone Ct Montgomery AL 36116 Office: Air Command and Staff Coll Maxwell A F B 225 Chennault Cir Montgomery AL 36112

RATAJ, ELIZABETH ANN, artist; b. Flint, Mich., Oct. 3, 1943; d. Lloyd Milton Clem and Mildred (Lamrock) Clem-Taylor; m. David Henry Rataj, Oct. 17, 1970. BA, Bob Jones U., 1966; BFA, U. Iowa, 1987. Educator Oscoda (Mich.) Area Schs., 1966-71, 73-83, Ft. Wayne (Ind.) Pub. Schs., 1971-72, St. Louis Pub. Schs., 1983-85. Represented in permanent collections Mich. Edn. Assn., Lansing, 1978, Munson Williams Proctor Mus., Utica, N.Y., 1989, Jesse Besser Mus., Alpena, Mich., 1993; exhibited in group show Mus. Modern Art Miami. Mem. Delta Kappa Gamma (1978-82, 86-87, 76-87), Nat. Mus. of Women in the Arts (charter).

RATAJSKI, MAGDA ANNE, public relations executive; b. Farnborough, Eng., Dec. 20, 1950; came to U.S., 1957; d. James May and Halina K. (Podlewski) R. BA, Marquette U., 1972; MA, Georgetown U., 1979; grad. Advanced Mgmt. Program, Harvard U., 1992. Asst. to v.p. pub. affairs Norfolk and Western Ry. Co., Washington, 1976-77, rep. pub. affairs, 1977-80, asst. v.p. pub. affairs, 1980-82; asst. v.p. pub. affairs Norfolk So. Corp., Washington, 1982-84; v.p. pub. rels. Norfolk (Va.) So. Corp., 1984—; bd. dirs. Sta. WHRO Pub. TV and Radio, Norfolk. Mem. exec. adv. coun. Coll. Bus. and Pub. Adminstrn., Old Dominion U., Norfolk, 1986—; chmn. Norfolk Area Mktg. Adv. Commn.; mem. Bus. Com. Arts, Inc., N.Y. Mem. Assn. Am. R.R. (chmn. pub. rels. exec. com., mem. legal affairs com.), R.R. Pub. Rels. Assn., Assn. R.R. Advt. and Mktg., Pub. Rels. Soc. Am., Hampton Roads C. of C. (bd. dirs. 1985, pub. info. com.), Am. Coun. R.R. Women, Nat. Dem. Club (Washington), The Harbor Club, 116 Club (Washington. Office: Norfolk So Corp 3 Commercial Pl Norfolk VA 23510-2191

RATH, MARY LOU, state senator; b. Buffalo, June 17; d. George Lewis and Margaret M. Whetzle; m. Edward A. Rath, Jan. 10, 1959; children—Allison, Melinda, Edward A., III. B.S., Buffalo State U., 1956; Ins. Broker's lic., U. Buffalo, 1965. Home service rep. Nat. Fuel Gas, Buffalo, 1958-61; communications affiliate Communications Affiliates of N.Y.C., 1961-67; legislator, Erie County, N.Y., 1978—, mem. N.Y. State Senate, chmn. Community Sentencing Task Force, 1982, Buffalo Better Bus. Found. Bur., 1983—, Adminstrv. Regulations Rev. Commn., mem. Alcohol & Drug Abuse, Children & Families, Civl Svc. & Pensions, Edn., Higher Edn. & Taxation, Investigations & Govt. Ops. Coms., various other legis. coms. 1979—. Vice pres. Research and Planning Council, Buffalo and Erie County, 1973-74; pres. Jr. League, 1973-74, mem. admissions com., 1974-78; chmn. Theodore Roosevelt Inaugural Site Restoration com., 1974-78; vol. WBEN "Call for Action", 1974-78; moderator candidates night Coalition for Better Edn., community adv. council SUNY-Buffalo, 1974—, arts adviser, 1981—; mem. Regan Dinner com., 1975; appointed Republican com. woman 8th Dist., Town of Amherst, N.Y., 1979—; trustee Buffalo Sem., 1975-79; bd. dirs. United Way of Buffalo and Erie County, 1977-78; pres. Landmark Soc. of Niagara Frontier, 1977-78; trustee, mem. vestry Calvary Episcopal Ch., Williamsville, N.Y., 1975-78; founding mem. Amherst "Lunch and Issues" program, 1980; bd. dirs. Daemen Coll. Assocs., 1980-81, Buffalo Better Bus. Bur., 1981—, Buffalo Soc. Natural Scis, 1984—; mem. commn. adv. com. State U. of N.Y. at Buffalo, 1985. Recipient Disting. Community Service award Crisis Services, 1984; named Pub. Servant of Yr., Erie County Fedn. Sportsmen's Clubs, 1981, Outstanding Women in Western N.Y., SUNY, 1984; Participant Am. Gas Assn. Lab. Tour, Cleve., 1982 (one of 8 persons invited-nationwide). Mem. Buffalo Philharm. Orchestra Soc., Buffalo Zool. Soc., Erie County Hist. Soc., Landmark Soc. Niagara Frontier, Williamsville Hist. Soc., Amherst C. of C., Buffalo C. of C., Alpha Hon. Soc. Home: 125 S Cayuga Rd Buffalo NY 14221-6732 Office: NY State Senate State Capitol Albany NY 12247

RATHER, LUCIA PORCHER JOHNSON, library administrator; b. Durham, N.C., Sept. 12, 1934; d. Cecil Slayton and Lucia Lockwood (Porcher) Johnson; m. John Carson Rather, July 11, 1964; children: Susan Wright, Bruce Carson. Student, Westhampton Coll., 1951-53; A.B. in History, U. N.C., 1955, M.S. in Library Sci., 1957; PhD in History, George Washington U., 1994. Cataloger Library of Congress, Washington, 1957-64; bibliographer Library of Congress, 1964-66, systems analyst, 1966-70; group head MARC Devel. Office, 1970-73, asst. chief, 1973-76, acting chief, 1976-77, dir. for cataloging, 1976-91; Chmn. standing com. on cataloguing Internat. Fedn. Library Assns., 1976-81; sec. Working Group on Content Designators, 1972-77; chmn. Working Group on Corp. Headings, 1978-79, Internat. ISBD Rev. Com., 1981-87. Co-author: the MARC II Format, 1968. Recipient Libr. Congress Disting. Svc. award, 1991, Disting. Alumnus award U. N.C. Sch. Libr. and Info. Sci., 1992. Mem. ALA (Margaret Mann award 1985, Melvil Dewey award 1991), Phi Beta Kappa. Democrat. Presbyterian. Home: 10308 Montgomery Ave Kensington MD 20895-3327

RATHKE, SHEILA WELLS, advertising and public relations executive; b. Columbia, S.C., Aug. 9, 1943; d. Walter John and Betty Marie (McLaughlin) Wells; m. David Bray Rathke, Sept. 1966 (div. Apr. 1977); 1 child, Erinn Michele. BA summa cum laude, U. Pitts., 1976, postgrad., 1976-77. Loan coord. Equibank, Pitts., 1961-65; office mgr. U.S. Steel Corp., Pitts., 1966-70; various account and mgmt. positions Burson-Marsteller, Pitts., 1977-87, exec. v.p., gen. mgr., 1987-94; CEO Can. ops. Burson-Marsteller, Toronto, Montreal, Ottawa, Vancouver, 1994—; also bd. dirs. Burson-Marsteller Americas; bd. dirs. Y & R Group of Cos., Can.; instr. Slippery Rock Coll., Pitts., 1984-85; adviser Exec. Report Mag., Pitts., 1986-88. Trustee U. Pitts., 1976-80; mem. alumni bd. dirs., trustee Robert Morris Coll., 1992—; bd. dirs. Vocat. Rehab. Ctr., 1987-93, Freewheeelers, 1989-92, Pitts. Hist. Soc., River City Brass Band. Named Disting. Alumnus, U. Pitts., 1992. Mem. Female Execs. Am., Am. Assn. Advt. Agys. (chair ea. region 1994-95), Pitts. Advt. Club (bd. dirs. 1988-91, pres. 1990), Alpha Sigma Lambda (charter). Home: 15 Marquette Rd Pittsburgh PA 15229-1766 Office: Burson-Marsteller, 80 Bloor St W, Toronto, ON Canada M5S 2V1 office: Burson-Marsteller One Gateway Center #2000 Pittsburgh PA 15222

RATHMELL, SANDRA LEE, women's health nurse; b. St. Louis, Apr. 3, 1944; d. Charles Chester and Estelle Lucille (Simon) Dunham; m. Thomas S. Rathmell, Sept. 17, 1965 (div. May 1990); children: John Thomas, Tamara Lynn. Diploma, St. Luke's Hosp., 1965. RN, Ariz., Mo., Del. Staff nurse Dover (Del.) AFB Hosp., 1966-68, Luth. Med. Ctr., St. Louis, 1975-82, Maricopa Med. Ctr., Phoenix, 1982-84, Chandler (Ariz.) Regional Hosp., 1984—; instr. hosp. postpartum classes, St. Louis, Phoenix. Mem. St. Luke's Alumni Assn.

RATHORE, UMA PANDEY, utilities executive; b. Unnao, India, Mar. 5, 1950; came to U.S., 1978; d. O Nath and R Devi Pandey; m. Ram N.S. Rathore, Dec. 18, 1978; children: Dinesh, Rana. BS, Kanpur U., 1967, MS, 1969. Adviser, Consul Gen. of Iceland to India, 1976-85; v.p. Nevaid Cons., 1974-82; with North Jersey Utilities, Mount Freedom, N.J., 1983—, pres.; sr. ptnr. Translantic Cons.; founder Maxim Imports, 1994—; ind. mgmt. cons. Mem. ethics bd. Randolph Twp., N.J., 1986-91, county and state rep. Shongrum Sch. PTA, 1989—, mem. multicultural com., 1993-94; membership chmn. LWV, 1979-81, com. person Dem. dist. 3 Randolph Twp., 1990, 92, 94, mem. ethics com., 1994, mem. com., 1994; mem. drug action com. Randolph Twp., 1994, 95; mem. Dem. task force N.J. Women's Polit. Caucus, 1994; ; county and state rep. Randolph Intermediate Sch. PTA, 1993-94. Mem. Dau. Brit. Empire (supporting mem.). Democrat. Avocations: reading, jogging, hiking, mountaineering. Home and Office: 3 Hickory Pl Randolph NJ 07869-4528

RATLIFF, JANICE KAY, legal administrator; b. Odessa, Tex., Aug. 11, 1949; d. Boyce Emery and Fay LaNell (Russell) Albert; m. Richard Wayne Ratliff, May 4, 1974; children: Ryan, Courtney, Ashlee. BS in Secondary Edn., Tex. Tech U., 1971. Cert. secondary tchr., Tex. Recreation counselor Wichita Falls (Tex.) Parks and Recreation Dept., 1967, Austin (Tex.) Parks and Recreation Dept., 1969; rehab. technician Tex. Rehab. Commn., Austin, 1971-76; co-owner, mgr. Locker Room, sporting goods store, Monahans, Tex., 1984-88; contract worker Calame, Linebarger & Graham, Odessa, Tex., 1983-88; area mgr., paralegal Calame, Linebarger, Graham & Peña, Odessa, Tex., 1988—. Pres. Gifted and Talented Parents Orgn., Monahans, 1986; mem. local parent/tchr. orgn. Tatom Life; v.p. Band Booster Club; Sunday sch. tchr. Ch. of Christ. Recipient dist. 1st place award for poetry Tex. Fedn. Women's Clubs, 1987. Mem. Tex. Assn. Assessing Officers (v.p. Permian Basin chpt. 1994-96), Rotary Internat. (bd. dirs. 1994-95, program chmn. 1994-95), Wednesday Study Club (pres. 1986-88). Republican. Home: 1309 S Murray St Monahans TX 79756-6305

RATLIFF, KRISS ALENE, human resources executive; b. Pawnee, Okla., Mar. 27, 1965; d. Jerry M. and Judy C. (Jesse) Elwood; m. Matt D. Ratliff, July 25, 1987. BS in Pub. Affairs, Okla. State U., 1987. Adminstrv. coord. Instructional TV Network, U. So. Calif., L.A., 1988-90; human resources generalist Halliburton Energy Svcs., Duncan, Okla., 1990—. Mem. Soc. for Human Resources Mgmt. (cert.), Oklahoma City Human Resource Soc. Republican. Office: Halliburton Energy Svcs 2600 S 2nd St Duncan OK 73536

RATLIFF, LEIGH ANN, pharmacist; b. Long Beach, Calif., May 20, 1961; d. Harry Warren and Verna Lee (Zwink) R. D in Pharmacy, U. Pacific, 1984. Registered pharmacist, Calif., Nev. Pharmacist intern Green Bros. Inc., Stockton, Calif., 1982-84, staff pharmacist Thrifty Corp., Long Beach, Calif., 1984-85, head pharmacist, 1986-87, pharm. buyer, 1987-92; pharmacy. mgr. Kmart Pharmacy, Long Beach, Calif., 1992—; mem. joint mktg. com. Calif. Pharmicist's Assn. Mem. Pacific Alumni Assocs., Nat. Trust for Hist. Preservation, Friends of Rancho Los Cerritos; treas. Bixby Knolls Ter. Homeowners Assn., 1988-92, pres. 1992—; vol. Docent Rancho Los Cerritos Hist. Site, 1988—; vol. preceptor U. So. Calif. Sch. Pharmacy; vol. Fairfield YMCA, Long Beach. Mem. Am. Pharm. Assn., Am. Inst. History Pharmacy, Calif. Pharmacist Assn., Lambda Kappa Sigma. Republican. Methodist. Avocations: creative writing, raising aquarium fish, house plants, collecting Lladro pieces. Home: 3913 N Virginia Rd Unit 301 Long Beach CA 90807-2670 Office: Kmart Pharmacy 5450 Cherry Ave Long Beach CA 90805-5502

RATLIFF, LOIS L., secondary education educator; b. Anson County, N.C., May 8, 1951; d. Walter A. and Corine S. Ratliff. BS, Bennett Coll., Greensboro, N.C., 1971; MS, N.C. A&T State U., 1974. Cert. tchr., N.C., S.C. Instr. biology Paine Coll., Augusta, Ga., 1976-78, Livingston Coll., Salisbury, N.C., 1979-80; tchr. chemistry Florence (S.C.) Sch. Dist. 1, 1980-85; tchr. phys. sci. Union County Schs., Monroe, N.C., 1985-86; tchr. chemistry Myers Park High Sch., Charlotte, N.C., 1986-89; tchr. phys. sci. Darlington (S.C.) Schs., 1989—; advisor Jr. Acad. Sci.; mem. evaluation team Nat. Assn. State Dept. Tchr. Edn. Evaluation Com. Mem. NEA, ASCD, NSTA.

RATLIFF, MARY JEAN DOUGHERTY, fine arts educator; b. Wichita Falls, Tex., July 25, 1933; d. Robert Byron and Thelma Irene (Dickson) Dougherty; m. Charles Richard Ratliff, Aug. 28, 1953; children: David Charles, Richard Byron, Melany Elaine, James Brett. Student, Tex. Tech. U., 1952-53; AAS, Richland U., 1975; BFA, U. North Tex., 1978. Instr. Art Brookhaven Coll., Dallas, 1982—. Com. mem. Tex. Bicentennial Com., Farmers Branch, Tex., 1975-76, Imagination Celebration, 1990-91. Mem. Farmers Br. Carrollton Art Assn. (sec. 1993—, founder), Tex. Visual Arts Assn. (signature mem. status), Southwestern Watercolor Soc. Republican. Baptist. Home: 1202 Mackie Dr Carrollton TX 75007-4835

RATNER, LILLIAN GROSS, psychiatrist; b. N.Y.C., Aug. 18, 1932; d. Herman and Sarah (Widelitz) Gross. BA, Barnard Coll., 1953; postgrad. U. Lausanne (Switzerland), 1954-56; MD, Duke U., 1959. Diplomate Bd. Pediatrics, Am. Bd. Psychiatry and Neurology, Am. Bd. Child Psychiatry; m. Harold Ratner, Feb. 4, 1961; children: Sanford Miles, Marcia Ellen. Intern Kings County Hosp., Bklyn., 1959-60, resident, 1967-70, fellow in child psychiatry, 1969-70, psychiatrist devel. evaluation clinic, 1970-72; resident Jewish Hosp. Bklyn., 1960-62, fellow in pediatric psychiatry, 1962-63; physician in charge pediatric psychiat. clinic Greenpoint (N.Y.) Hosp., 1964-67; pvt. practice psychiatry, Great Neck, N.Y., 1970—; clin. instr. psychiatry Downstate Med. Ctr., Bklyn., 1970-74, clin. asst. prof., 1974—; lectr. in psychiatry Columbia U., 1974—; psychiat. cons. N.Y.C. Bd. Edn., 1972-75, Queens Children's Hosp., 1975—; mem. med. bd. Camp Sussex (N.J.), 1963—, Saras Ctr., Great Neck, N.Y., 1977—. Fellow Am. Acad. Pediatrics, Am. Acad. Psychiatry, Am. Acad. Child Psychiatry, Am. Soc. Clin. and Exptl. Hypnosis, N.Y. Soc. Clinical Hypnosis (past pres.); mem. AMA, Am. Psychiat. Assn., Nassau Psychiat. Assn., Bklyn. Psychiat. Assn., Bklyn. Pediatric Soc. (sr. mem.), Nassau Pediatric Socs., Soc. Adolescent Psychiatry, N.Y. Coun. Child Psychiatry, Soc. Clin. and Exptl. Hypnosis, Am. Med. Women's Assn. (Nassau, pres. 1955-56, past pres.), N.Y., Kings County med. socs., N.Y. Soc. Clin. Hypnosis (past pres.), Internat. Soc. for Study of Multiple Personality and Dissociation (founder, pres. L.I. component study group). Home and Office: 55 Blue Bird Dr Great Neck NY 11023-1001

RATNER, RHODA SUE, librarian; b. Bklyn., Apr. 25, 1935; d. Leon Elias and Anne Ella (Nissenbaum) Mitteldorf; m. Fredric Beryl Ratner, Dec. 25, 1954 (div. 1983); children—Jessica, Deborah, Judith. A.A., Montgomery Coll., 1974; B.A., U. Md., 1976; M.L.S., 1978. Chief librarian mus. reference ctr. Smithsonian Instn., Washington, 1978-82, chief librarian Nat. Mus. Am. History, 1982—. Editor proceedings panels on libraries in mus.', 1980-83. Leader Montgomery County council Girl Scouts Am., 1968-72. Mem. Am. Libraries Assn., Am. Assn. Mus.' (chmn. ad hoc com. 1979—). Democrat. Jewish. Clubs: NAAMAT U.S.A. (council pres.), Jewish Community Council (exec. bd.). (Washington). Office: Smithsonian Instn Nat Museum Am History 10th and Constitution Ave NW Washington DC 20560*

RATNER-GANTSHAR, BARBARA GRACE, religious organization administrator; b. Phila.; d. Jules and Samuella (Isadora) Ratner; m. Martin Gantshar, June 1961 (div. 1984); children: Judith Susan Claire, Lois Nichole Merraine, David Joseph. MS, Simmons Coll., 1985. Project dir. Boston Family Inst., Brookline, Mass., 1982-84; exec. dir. Summer's World Ctr. for the Arts, Worcester, Mass., 1985-87; assoc. dir. of devel. Am. U., Washington, 1987-88; dir. devel. Harford Day Sch., Bel Air, Md., 1988-90, Balch Inst. for Ethnic Studies, Phila., 1991-92; exec. dir. Temple Beth Hillel/Beth El, Wynnewood, Pa., 1993—; fair coord. Mass. and R.I. Antiquarian Booksellrs Assn., 1978-79; cons. Alzheimer's Disease Ctr., Falls Ch., Va., 1988, The Galleries, Wellesley, Mass., 1984-85, The Etz Chaim Ctr., Balt., 1990. Author: A Beacon Was Hoisted in Boston, 1975, Philadelphia: The City and the Bell, 1976. Mem. women's div. cabinet Fedn. Allied Jewish Appeal. Mem. N.Am. Assn. Synagogue Execs., Delaware Valley Assn. Synagogue Adminstrs., Antiquarian Booksellers Assn. Am. (emeritus), Nat. Soc. Fundraising Execs. Democrat. Home: 409 Society Hill Blvd Cherry Hill NJ 08003-2412 Office: Temple Beth Hillel/Beth El Lancaster Ave And Remi Rd Wynnewood PA 19096

RATTAZZI, SERENA, art museum and association administrator; b. Taranto, Italy, Aug. 20, 1935; came to U.S., 1969; d. Umberto and Ligetta (Maresca) Bardelli; m. Mario Cristiano Rattazzi, Jan. 15, 1962; 1 child, Claudia. BA, Liceo Umberto I, Naples. Italy, 1953; MSW, U. Naples, 1958; postgrad. in legal problems of mus. adminstrn., Am. Legal Inst., ABA, 1985, 86, 87, 89. Pub. rels., publs. asst. Albright-Knox Art Gallery, Buffalo, 1974-76, coord. pub. rels., 1976-82, asst. dir. for adminstrn., 1982-84; asst. dir. for adminstrn. The Bklyn. Mus., 1984-85, vice dir. for adminstrn., 1985-89, assoc. dir., 1989-90; dir. Am. Fedn. Arts, N.Y.C., 1990—; adv. bd. The Pitts. Ctr. for Arts, 1989-92, A.I.R. Gallery, N.Y.C., 1990-93; field reviewer Inst. Mus. Svcs., Washington, 1990; adv. coun. dept. art history and archaeology Columbia Univ., 1992—. Mem. ArtTable Inc. (bd. dirs. 1986-88, pres. 1986-88), Am. Assn. Museums (standing profl. com. on pub. rels. mgmt. 1978-82, bd. 1990—). Office: Am Fedn Arts 41 E 65th St New York NY 10021-6594

RATTLEY, JESSIE MENIFIELD, former mayor, educator; b. Birmingham, Ala., May 4, 1929; d. Alonzo and Altona (Cochran) Menifield; m. Robert L. Rattley; children: Florence, Robin. BS in Bus. Edn.with hons., Hampton U., 1951; postgrad., Hampton Inst., 1962, IBM Data Processing Sch., 1960, LaSalle Extension U., 1955. Tchr. Huntington High Sch., Newport News, Va., 1951-52; owner, operator Peninsula Bus. Coll., Newport News, 1952-85; hosp. adminstr. Newport News Gen. Hosp., from 1986; fellow Inst. Politics John F. Kennedy Sch. Govt. Harvard U., 1990; sr. lectr. polit. sci. Hampton U.; elected mayor of Newport News, 1986-90. Mem. Nat. League Cities, bd. dirs., 1975, 2d v.p., 1977, 1st v.p., 1978, pres., 1979-90, active various coms. and task forces; active on adv. bds. and coms. State Dem. Party; mem. exec. com. Va. Mcpl. League, 1974, 2d v.p., 1976, 1st v.p., 1977, pres., 1979; chair state adv. com. U.S. Civil Rights Commn.; apptd. trustee Va. Vet. Care Facility. Recipient Cert. of Merit Daus. of Isis, 2d annual Martin Luther King, Jr. Meml. award Old Dominion U., Sojourner Truth award Nat. Assn. of Negro Bus. and Profl. Women's Clubs, Cert. of Appreciation NAACP, Hampton Inst. Presdl. award for Outstanding Citizenship.

RATTY, TESS MCBRIDE, media executive; b. Billings, Mont., July 20, 1944; d. Murray Wallace and Patricia Jean (Franzen) McBride; m. Raymond W. Nunn, Apr. 24, 1964 (div. 1969); children: Shannon McBride Waibel, Amy McBride Nunn; m. Brian Dudley Ratty, Dec. 4, 1971. Student, Calif. Coll. Arts and Crafts, Oakland, 1962-65; BS, Portland (Oreg.) State U., 1988. Mgr. advt. prodn. Meier & Frank, Portland, 1967-69; asst. mgr. advt. Pendleton Woolen Mills, Portland, 1969-74; corp. v.p. Media West, Inc., Beaverton, Oreg., 1974—. Exec. producer spl. interest videos, 1986, 87 (Double 5-Star award Video Choice Mag. 1988). Bd. dirs. Northwest Pilot Project, Portland, 1984-86; pres. bd. dirs. Beaverton Arts Commn., 1988-89; chmn. Art in the Marketplace, Beaverton, 1987; trustee Parry Ctr. for Children, Portland, 1987—; judge Oreg. Jr. Miss Scholarship, Eugene, 1986; adv. Metro Pub. Art Adv. Panel, 1987—; active in Edn. Svc. Dist. County of Washington, Oreg., 1987—. Recipient Vol. award Beaverton Arts Commn., 1987, 88. Mem. NAFE, Oreg. Media Producers Assn., Portland Advt. Fedn. (Nat. Addy award nat. fedn. 1972), Portland State Alumni Assn., Portland C. of C., Washington County Hist. Soc., Nat. Mus. Women in the Arts (charter Beaverton sister cities chpt.). Republican. Office: Media West Inc PO Box 1563 Lake Oswego OR 97035-0558

RATZER, MARY BOYD, secondary education educator, librarian; b. Troy, N.Y., Sept. 6, 1945; d. John Leo and Katherine M. (Van Derpool) Boyd; m. Philip J. Ratzer, July 30, 1972; children: Joseph, David. BA cum laude, Coll. of St. Rose, Albany, N.Y., 1967; MA, SUNY, Albany, 1968, MLS, 1981. Cert. secondary tchr., sch. libr. media specialist, N.Y. Secondary tchr. English, Shenendehowa Cen. Sch., Clifton Park, N.Y., 1968-85; sch. libr. media specialist Shendehowa Cen. Sch., Clifton Park, N.Y., 1985—; coord., mentor tchr. intern program; lectr. SUNY Grad. Sch. Info. Sci. and Policy, Albany; frequent speaker at state-level confs., 1986—. Contbr. articles to profl. jours. Recipient grants. Mem. ALA, N.Y. Libr. Assn., Nat. Coun. Tchrs. English, N.Y. Assn. for Supervision and Curriculum Devel., LIRT, LUERT (past pres.). Home: 433 County Rd 68 Saratoga Springs NY 12866

RAUCH, IRMENGARD, linguist, educator; b. Dayton, Ohio, Apr. 17, 1933; d. Konrad and Elsa (Knott) R.; m. Gerald F. Carr, June 12, 1965; children: Christopher, Gregory. Student, Nat. U. Mex., summer 1954; B.S. with honors, U. Dayton, 1955; M.A., Ohio State U., 1957; postgrad. (Fulbright fellow), U. Munich, Fed. Republic Germany, 1957-58; Ph.D., U. Mich., 1962. Instr., German and linguistics U. Wis., Madison, 1962-63, asst. prof., 1963-66; assoc. prof. German U. Pitts., 1966-68; assoc. prof. German and linguistics U. Ill., Urbana, 1968-72, prof., 1972-79; prof. U. Calif., Berkeley, 1979—. Author: The Old High German Diphthongization: A Description of a Phonemic Change, 1967, The Old Saxon Language: Grammar, Epic Narrative, Linguistic Interference, 1992; editor: (with others) Approaches in Linguistic Methodology, 1967, Spanish edit., 1974, Der Heliand, 1974, Linguistic Method: Essays in Honor of Herbert Penzl, 1979, The Signifying Animal: The Grammar of Language and Experience, 1980, Language Change, 1983, The Semiotic Bridge: Trends from California, 1989, On Germanic Linguistics: Issues and Methods, 1992, editor of two series: Berkeley Insights in Linguistics and Semiotics, Berkeley Models of Grammars; contbr. articles to profl. jours. Named outstanding woman on campus U. Ill. Sta. WILL, 1975; recipient Disting. Alumnus award U. Dayton, 1985; research grantee U. Wis., summer 1966, U. Ill., 1975-79, Eastern Ill. U., 1976, Nat. Endowment Humanities, 1978, U. Calif., Berkeley, 1979—; travel grantee NSF, Linguistics Soc. Am., 1972; Guggenheim fellow, 1982-83; IBM Distributed Acad. Computing Environment, 1986; NEH grantee, 1988. Mem. Linguistics Soc. Am., MLA, Am. Assn. Tchrs. German, Society for Germanic Philogy, Philogical Assn. of the West Coast, Phonetics Assn., Semiotic Soc. Am. (pres. 1982-83), Semiotic Circle of Calif. (founder), Internat. Assn. for Semiotic Studies (pres., dir. 5th congress 1994), Alpha Sigma Tau, Delta Phi Alpha. Home: 862 Camden Ct Benicia CA 94510-3633 Office: U Calif Dept German Berkeley CA 94720

RAUCH, KATHLEEN, computer executive; b. Franklin Square, N.Y., Oct. 30, 1951; d. William C. and Marian (Shull) R.; B.A., U. Rochester, 1973; M.A. in L.S., U. Mich., 1974; postgrad. N.Y. U., 1981-82. Media specialist Sutton (Mass.) Sch., 1974-76; program cons. Advanced Mgmt. Rsch. Internat., N.Y.C., 1976-79; pub. rels. cons., N.Y.C., 1979; pres. N.Y. chpt. NOW, N.Y.C., 1979-80; computer programmer Blue Cross/Blue Shield of Greater N.Y., N.Y.C., 1981-82; computer programmer analyst Fed. Res. Bank of N.Y., 1983-84; systems officer Citibank, N.A., 1984-85; systems analyst Fed. Res. Bank of N.Y., 1986-89; computer and children's libr. East Meadow (N.Y.) Pub. Libr., 1989-91; pres. Panorama Children's Videos, Inc., 1988-93; microcomputer specialist N.C. State U., 1992-93; prin., v.p. The Computer Lab., Inc., 1993—. Mem. ALA, NOW (dir. pub. rels. N.Y.C. chpt. 1978, v.p. programs 1978, chmn. bd. 1981, founding mem., sec. svc. fund NOW, N.Y.C. chpt. 1981), Assn. for Women in Computing (v.p. membership 1984, exec. v.p. 1985, treas. 1986, mem.-at-large 1987, pres. 1988), N.C. Libr. Assn., Capital Area Libr. Assn., Triangle Bus. and Profl.

Guild, Our Own Place (Durham N.C.). Home and Office: The Computer Labs Inc 8711 Six Forks Rd Ste 160 Raleigh NC 27615-2968

RAULERSON, PHOEBE HODGES, high school principal; b. Cin., Mar. 16, 1939; d. LeRoy Allen and Thelma A. (Stewart) Hodges; m. David Earl Raulerson, Dec. 26, 1959; children: Julie, Lynn, David Earl, Jr., Roy Allen. BA in Edn., U. Fla., 1963, MEd, 1964. Tchr. several schs., Okeechobee, Fla., 1964-79; asst. prin. Okeechobee Jr. H.S., 1979-81, prin., 1983-84; asst. prin. South Elem. Sch., Okeechobee, 1981-82; asst. prin. Okeechobee H.S., 1982-83, prin., 1984—; mem. Dept. Edn. Commr.'s Task Force on H.S. Preparation, 1993-94. Mem. Okeechobee Exchange Club. Recipient Outstanding Citizen award Okeechobee Rotary Club, 1986; week named in her honor, Okeechobee County Commrs., 1990. Mem. Am. Bus. Women's Assn., Fla. Assn. Secondary Sch. Prins. (pres. 1993-94, Fla. Prin. of Yr. award 1990), Fla. Assn. Sch. Adminstrs. (bd. dirs. 1992—), Okeechobee Cattlewomen's Assn. Democrat. Episcopalian. Home: 3898 NW 144th Dr Okeechobee FL 34972-0930 Office: Okeechobee HS 2800 Hwy 441 N Okeechobee FL 34972-0930

RAUSCH, JOAN MARY, art historian; b. Calmar, Iowa, Dec. 25, 1937; d. Bernard Joseph and Irene Sophia (Wieling) Menne; m. Gerald William Rausch, Sept. 3, 1960; children: John Thomas, Jennifer Nicole Rausch Goodhart. BS, Coll. St. Teresa, Winona, Minn., 1959; postgrad., U. Wis., LaCrosse, 1974-79; MA, U. Wis., Milw., 1982. Instr. nursing Mercy Hosp., Iowa City, Iowa, 1960-63, St. Francis Hosp./Viterbo Coll., LaCrosse, 1966-71; rsch. asst. dept. art U. Wis., LaCrosse, 1977-79; asst. dept. art history U. Wis., Milw., 1979-81; historic planner Southwest Regional Planning Commn., Platteville, Wis., 1982-83; pres. Archtl. Researches, Inc., LaCrosse, 1983—; cons. historic preservation divsn. State Hist. Soc. Wis., 1983—, Wis. Dept. of Transp., Dist. 5, 1991—. Author: A Catalog of the Oyen Collection, 1979, Historic LaCrosse Architectural and Historic Record, 1984, Chippewa Falls, 1985, Watertown, A Guide to Its Historic Architecture, 1987; (with Joyce McKay) Richland Center Wiconsin, Architectural and Historical Survey Report, 1988; (with Carol Cartwright) City of Mineral Point, Architectural and Historic Survey Report, 1992. Pres. Women's Polit. Caucus, LaCrosse, 1972-73. Recipienc Scholarship award Victorian Soc. in Am., 1981, Workshop award Ctr. for Art Criticism, Mpls., 1986. Mem. Soc. Archtl. Historians (pres. Wis. chpt. 1982-84), Nat. Trust Hist. Preservation (Preservation Forum(, Wis. Trust Hist. Preservation (charter, task force mem. 1986), Preservation Alliance of LaCrosse (bd. dirs. 1982-88, Heritage award 1989), LaCrosse County Hist. Soc. (hist. preservation com. 1992—, bd. dirs. 1994—). Home and Office: Archtl Researches Inc 5722 W Sherwood Dr La Crosse WI 54601

RAUSCHER, DIANE MARILYN, information center manager; b. Newark, May 11, 1953; d. Edward Albert and Elaine Lucille (Engel) Cattle; m. Robert Thomas Rauscher, Dec. 13, 1980. BA in Psychology, Montclair State U., 1975. Methods analyst Prentice-Hall, Englewood Cliffs, N.J., 1975-77; procedures analyst Klopman Mills divsn. Burlington Industries, Rockleigh, N.J., 1977-79; orgnl. analyst Mercedes-Benz of N.A., Montvale, N.J., 1979-89, mgr. info. ctr., 1989-93, bus. sys. analyst, 1994—; quality coun. mem. Mercedes-Benz of N.Am., Inc., Montvale, 1988-89. Recipient Tribute to Women in Industry award YWCA, Ridgewood, N.J., 1992. Mem. N.J. Assn. Women Bus. Owners. Office: Mercedes-Benz of NA Inc One Mercedes Dr Montvale NJ 07645

RAVEN-RIEMANN, CAROLYN SUE, actress, model, small business owner; b. Evergreen Park, Ill., Dec. 7, 1945; d. Eugene Alexander and Eloise Irene (McGhee) Raven; m. Herbert Friedrich Riemann, Aug. 1, 1981. BA, Northwestern U., 1967. Model, actress Mannequin Models, N.Y.C., 1969-86, several talent agts., 1969—; model Les Girls Ltd., N.Y.C., 1986-92, Johnston Models, Norwalk, Conn., 1986—; owner, pres. The OrchidPhile, Stamford, Conn., 1984—; sec., treas. GearGrip, Inc., Stamford, 1983—; author, pub., owner OrchidPhile Log. Mem. SAG, AFTRA, Am. Orchid Soc. (edn. com., vice chair 1994—), Greater N.Y. Orchid Soc. (trustee 1993—), Internat. Phalaenopsis Alliance, Inc. (co-founder, sec. 1990—), Greater Westchester Orchid Soc., Northwestern U. Alumni Assn., Tri Delta Sorority Alumnae Soc. Republican. Congregationalist.

RAVICCHIO, GRACE VENETA, home health nurse; b. Spokane, Wash., Jan. 30, 1967; d. Russell Dean and Claudia Sue (Cook) Beaver; m. Steven Richard Ravicchio, Sept. 19, 1987; 1 child, Stephanie Lynn. BSN, U. Ariz., 1989. RN, Ariz.; cert. instr. BLS and pediat. BLS, ARC. Nurse extern Tucson Med. Ctr., 1989; staff nurse St. Mary's Hosp., Tucson, 1990-91; field nurse Kimberly Quality Care, Tucson, 1991-93; Medicare case mgr. Nursefinders, Tucson, 1992-94, clin. dir. pvt. svcs., 1994—.

RAVITCH, DIANE SILVERS, historian, educator, author, government official; b. Houston, July 1, 1938; d. Walter Cracker and Ann Celia (Katz) Silvers; m. Richard Ravitch, June 26, 1960 (div. 1986); children: Joseph, Steven (dec.), Michael. BA, Wellesley Coll., 1960; PhD, Columbia U., 1975; LHD (hon.), Williams Coll., 1984, Reed Coll., 1985, Amherst Coll., 1986, SUNY, 1988, Ramapo Coll., 1990, St. Joseph's Coll., N.Y., 1991. Adj. asst. prof. Tchrs. Coll., Columbia U., N.Y.C., 1975-78, assoc. prof., 1978-83, adj. prof., 1983-91; asst. sec. office ednl. rsch. and improvement U.S. Dept. Edn., Washington, 1991-93, counselor to the sec. edn., 1991-93; vis. fellow Brookings Instn., Washington, 1993-94; sr. rsch. scholar NYU, 1994—; bd. dirs. Ency. Britannica Corp. Author: The Great School Wars, 1974, The Revisionists Revised, 1977, The troubled Crusade, 1983, The Schools We Deserve, 1985, National Standards in American Education, A Citizens Guide, 1995, (with other) Educating an Urban People, 1981, The School and the City, 1983, Against Mediocrity, 1984, Challenges to the Humanities, 1985, What Do Our 17 Year Olds Know?, 1987, The American Reader, 1990; co-editor: The Democracy Reader, 1992; editor: Learning from the Past, 1995. Chair Ednl. Excellence Network, 1988-91; trustee N.Y. Pub. Libr., N.Y.C., 1981-87, hon. life trustee, 1988—; bd. dirs. Woodrow Wilson Nat. Fellowship Found., 1987-91, Coun. Basic Edn., 1989-91. Recipient Award for Disting. Svc., N.Y. Acad. Pub. Edn., 1994; Guggenheim fellow, 1977-78; Phi Beta Kappa vis. scholar. Mem. Nat. Acad. Edn., Am. Acad. Arts and Scis., Soc. Am. Historians, N.Y. Hist. Soc. (trustee 1995—). Office: NYU 32 Press Bldg Washington Place New York NY 10003-6644

RAVIV, SHEILA, public relations executive. Degree, Ind. U., U. Wis. Faculty mem. Sch. Medicine and Health Sci. George Washington U.; dir. rsch. Ministry Social Welfare, Israel; dir. Nat. Vol. Orgns. for Ind. Living for the Aging; asst. dir. Nat. Coun. on the Aging; sr. v.p., dir. of constituency rels. Burson-Marsteller, 1988-91, mem. Am. bd. dirs., 1993, exec. v.p., dir. constituency rels., 1991—. Office: Burson-Marsteller 1850 M St NW Washington DC 20036*

RAWLEY, ANN KEYSER, small business owner, picture framer; b. N.Y.C., July 11, 1923; d. Ernest Wise and Beatrice (Oberndorf) Keyser; m. James Albert Rawley, Apr. 7, 1945; children: John Franklin, James Albert. BA, Smith Coll., 1944. Owner Ann Rawley Custom Framing, Lincoln, Nebr., 1969—. Pres. Friends of Fairview, Lincoln, 1976, Lincoln City Ballet Co., 1983-84; bd. dirs. Lincoln Community Playhouse; mem. adv. bd. Nebr. Repertory Theatre. Mem. Nebr. Art Assn. (sec. 1976-77, life trustee). Republican. Episcopalian. Home and Office: 2300 Bretigne Dr Lincoln NE 68512-1910

RAWLINSON, HELEN ANN, librarian; b. Columbia, S.C., Mar. 30, 1948; d. Alfred Harris and Mary Taylor (Moon) R. BA, U. S.C., 1970; MLS, Emory U., 1972. Asst. children's librarian Greenville (S.C.) County Library, 1972-74, br. supr., 1974-76, asst. head extension div., 1976-78; children's room librarian Richland County Pub. Library, Columbia, 1978-81; sr. adult services librarian Richland County Pub. Library, 1981-82, chief adult services, 1982-85, dep. dir., 1985—; mem. adv. com. S.C. Pre-White House Conf. on Libr. and Info. Svcs., chmn. program com. Mem. ALA, S.E. Libr. Assn., S.C. Libr. Assn. (2d v.p. 1987-88, 88-93, editorial com.). Baptist. Home: 1316 Guignard Ave West Columbia SC 29169-6137 Office: Richland County Pub Libr 1431 Assembly St Columbia SC 29201-3101

RAWLS, EUGENIA, actress; b. Macon, Ga.; d. Hubert Fields and Louise (Roberts) R.; m. Donald Ray Seawell, Apr. 5, 1941; children: Brook Ashley, Donald Brockman. Grad., Wesleyan Conservatory, Macon, 1932; student, U. N.C., 1933; L.H.D., U. No. Colo., Greeley, 1978; D.F.A., Wesleyan Coll., Macon, Ga., 1982. Participant 25th Anniversary of Lillian Smith Book Awards, Atlanta, 1993. Author: Tallulah—A Memory, 1979; Broadway appearances include The Children's Hour, 1934, Pride and Prejudice, 1936, The Little Foxes, 1939, 41, Guest in the House, 1942, Rebecca, 1945, The Second Mrs. Tanqueray, 1940, The Shrike, 1952, Private Lives, 1949, The Great Sebastians, 1956, First Love, 1961, The Glass Menagerie, 1964, 67, Our Town, 1967, Tallulah: A Memory; appeared at Lincoln Ctr., 1971, London, 1974, U.S. tour, 1979, Denver Ctr. Performing Arts, 1980, Theatre of Mus., N.Y.C., 1980, Four Arts Soc., Palm Beach, Fla., 1981, Herbst Theater, San Francisco, 1981, Kennedy Ctr. (cable TV), 1981, Nat. Theatre Great Britain, 1984, Queen Elizabeth II, 1984-86; one-woman show Affectionately Yours Fanny Kemble, London, 1974, U.S. tour, 1979, Nat. Portrait Gallery, Washington, 1983, Grolier Club Exhbn., N.Y.C., 1988; appeared in The Enchanted, 1973, Sweet Bird of Youth, 1975, 76, Daughter of the Regiment, 1978, Just the Immediate Family, 1978, Women of the West, U.S. tour, 1979, Am. Mus. in Britain, Bath, Eng., 1981, Kennedy Ctr. and Denver Ctr. Performing Arts, 1980; one-woman show Fanny Kemble, Arts Theatre, London, 1969, Queen's Hall, Edinburgh, 1980, St. Peter's Ch., N.Y.C., 1980, Internat. Theater Festival, Denver, 1982, also Kennedy Center; appeared as Emily, Denver, 1976; with Abbey Theatre, Dublin, Ireland, 1972; one-woman show tour of Europe, 1972; appeared as: Fanny Kemble, Shakespeare World Congress, Washington, 1976; TV appearances, U.S. Steel Hour, Love of Life, Women of the West; (for ednl. TV) Tallulah: A Memory (performed for presdl. inauguration), 1977; Memory of a Large Christmas, Folger Shakespeare Library, 1977; mem., Sarah Caldwell Opera Co., Boston, 1978; rec. talking books for blind; mem. com.: Plays for Living, 1964-67; Rockefeller Found. artist-in-residence, Denver U., 1967, 68, U. Tampa, Fla., 1970, artist-in-residence, U. No. Colo., 1971, 72, 73; artist Annenberg Theatre, Desert Art Mus., Palm Springs, Calif., 1988, 89, "Our Town" Pitts. Pub. Theatre, 1990; author: (poems) A Moment Ago, 1984; participant Edwin Forrest Day Celebrating Shakespeare's 427th Birthday The Actors' Fund of Am.'s Nursing and Retirement Home Lucille Lortel Theatre, 1991; appeared in Our Town, Pitts. Pub. Theater, 1990-91, Three Sisters, 1991—. Mem. Internat. Women's Forum, Vail, Colo., 1989. Recipient Alumna award U. N.C., 1969; Disting. Achievement award Wesleyan Coll., 1969; Gold Chair award Central City (Colo.) Opera House Assn., 1973; (with husband) Frederick H. Koch Drama award U. N.C., 1974; citation Smithsonian Instn., 1977. Address: care Donald Seawell 1050 13th St Denver CO 80204

RAWLS, LETA ANNETTE BOYD, educational administrator; b. Star City, Ark., Jan. 2, 1940; d. Howard Theodore and Leta Ozell (McDougald) Boyd; m. Joe Ray Rawls, June 10, 1960; children: Melissa Anne Rawls Green, Marian Ruth Rawls Peters. AS in Home Econs., Ark. A&M, 1960, BS in Edn., 1967; MEd, U. Ark., 1978, EdD, 1993. Cert. elem. tchr. and prin., reading specialist, ednl. adminstr., Ark. Tchr. Rison (Ark.) Elem. Sch., 1960-80, Headstart tchr., 1967-68, tchr. adult edn., 1967, prin., 1980—; instr. program for effective teaching Ark. Dept. Edn., Little Rock, 1981—; mem. mktg. com. Ark. Reading Recovery Adv. Coun., Little Rock, 1990—. Mem. adv. coun. Cleveland County Health Dept., Rison, 1985-86; v.p. Rison Devel. Club, 1986-87; com. mem. Rison Centennial Celebration, 1990. Grantee Ark. Dept. Edn. and Fed. Programs, 1986-93. Mem. NASEP, ASCD, Ark. Assn. Elem. Sch. Prins. (presenter 1989, bd. dirs. 1985-90, membership awards 1987, 88, Ark. Zone 5 Prin. of Yr. award 1989), Ark. ASCD, Internat. Reading Assn., Ark. Reading Assn., AAUW, Am. Bus. Women's Assn., Ark. Genealogy Soc., Cleveland County Genealogy Soc., Shrine Aux., Phi Delta Kappa. Methodist. Home: Rt 2 Box 3 Rison AR 71665 Office: Rison Elem Sch PO Box 600 Rison AR 71665-0600

RAWSKI, EVELYN SAKAKIDA, history educator; b. Honolulu, Feb. 2, 1939; d. Evan T. and Teruko (Watase) Sakakida; m. Thomas G. Rawski, Dec. 16, 1967. B.A., Cornell U., 1961; M.A., Radcliffe Coll., 1962; Ph.D., Harvard U., 1968. Asst. prof. history U. Pitts., 1967-72, assoc. prof., 1973-79, prof. history, 1980—. Author: Agricultural Change and the Peasant Economy of South China, 1972, Education and Popular Literacy in Ch'ing China, 1979; co-author: Chinese Society in the Eighteenth Century, 1987; co-editor: Popular Culture in Late Imperial China, 1985; Death Ritual in Late Imperial and Modern China, 1988. Am. Coun. Learned Soc. grantee, 1973-74; NEH fellow, 1979-80, Chinese Studies fellow Am. Coun. Learned Soc./Sci. Rsch. Coun., 1989; Guggenheim Meml. Found. fellow, 1990, Woodrow Wilson Internat. Ctr. fellow 1992-93. Mem. Assn. Asian Studies (China-Inner Asia coun., bd. dirs. 1976-79, v.p. 1994-95, pres. 1995—). Home: 5317 Westminster Pl Pittsburgh PA 15232-2120 Office: U Pitts Dept History Pittsburgh PA 15260

RAWSON, ELEANOR S., publishing company executive; m. Kennett Longley Rawson (dec.); children—Linda, Kennett Longley. V.p., exec. editor David McKay Co.; exec. v.p., editor-in-chief Rawson, Wade Publishers, Inc.; v.p. Scribner Book Cos.; pub. Rawson Assocs. divsn. Macmillan; v.p., chmn. Rawson Assocs. (divsn. Macmillan Pub. Co.); teaching staff Columbia U., 1956-58; lectr. NYU, New Sch., N.Y.; organizer, panelist various writers' confs.; mem. exec. coun., nominating chair Am. Assn. Pubs., 1970-74. Former editorial staff writer Am. mag.; free-lance writer radio and mags., newspaper syndicates; fiction editor Collier's mag., Today's Woman. Trustee, past v.p. Museums at Stony Brook. Mem. Assn. Women's Nat. Book Assn., P.E.N., Am. Assn. Museums, Yale Club, Cosmopolitan Club, Old Field Club, Women's Forum, Women In Media, Women in Comms. Office: 866 3rd Ave New York NY 10022-6221

RAY, ANNETTE D., corporate secretary; b. Decatur, Ind., Mar. 24, 1950; d. Gilbert O. and Florence L. Hoffman; m. Richard M. Ray, Nov. 28, 1975; children: Michelle Ann, Ellen Marie, Laura Leigh, David Richard, Ruth Anne. AA, Concordia Jr. Coll., Ann Arbor, Mich., 1970; BS, Concordia Tchrs. Coll., Seward, Nebr., 1972; attended, Ctrl. Fla. C.C., Ocala, 1974. Lic. real estate, Ind.; lic. tchr., Ind., Fla. Elem. tchr. St. John's Luth., Ocala, 1972-74; mgr. apt. complex Victoria Sq. Apts., Ft. Wayne, Ind., 1974-75; substitute tchr. East Allen County Schs., Allen County, Ind., 1976-79, Circut A Luth. Schs., Adams and Allen County, Ind., 1977-81; corp. sec., office manager Heritage Wire Die, Monroeville, Ind., 1987—. Co-author, co-editor: 1928-1988 A Rememberance, 1988. Vol. Monroeville C. of C., 1987—, Concerned Area Residents Quality Edn., Allen County, 1990—, Am. Cancer Soc., Allen County, 1991—; bd. dirs. Hoagland (Ind.) Hist. Soc., 1985—. Lutheran. Home: 16901 Berning Rd Hoagland IN 46745-9753 Office: Heritage Wire Die Inc 19819 Monroeville Rd Monroeville IN 46773-0416

RAY, EULA ZOLINE, broadcast executive. Motivational and directional speaker various cities, 1958-78; host, producer KHVN Radio, Anchorage, 1978-80; mgr. trainee Peck & Peck, Las Vegas, 1980-81; studio mgr. CPI Corp., 1981-82; station mgr. Roughrider Broadcasting, KPAH Radio, Tonopah, Nev., 1982—; guest lectr. Clark County C.C., Las Vegas, Nev., Miss Nev. Teen-USA, Official Preliminaries for Miss Universe 1992; pub. rels. com. Easy Living in Las Vegas, 1992. Bd. dirs. Pioneer Ter. for NYE County, State Job Tng., 1986—, Econ. Devel. and Tourism for Tonopah, Tonopah Conv. Ctr., 1985, Cen. Nev. Devel. Authority, 1987; mem. Town Bd. for Tonopah, 1991—; chmn. Jim Butler Celebration, Tonopah. Named Woman of Yr. for Tonopah, 1986. Mem. Tonopah C. of C. (pres. 1985). Home: 4437 Greenhill Dr Las Vegas NV 89121-6211

RAY, GAYLE ELROD, sheriff; b. Murfreesboro, Tenn., Oct. 22, 1945; d. Jesse Smith and Jennie Hare (McElroy) Elrod; m. Roy Norman Ray, Dec. 27, 1970; children: Molly Elizabeth, Austin Elrod. BA, Mid. Tenn. State U., 1967; MA, U. Ark., 1969; MBA, Belmont U., 1989. Instr. English La. State U., Baton Rouge, 1969-72, Tenn. State U., Nashville, 1972-76; program coord. Vanderbilt U., Nashville, 1992-94; sheriff Davidson County, Nashville, 1994—. Pres. LWV, Nashville, 1987-89; mem. Women's Polit. Caucus, Nashville, 1987—; mem. alumni bd. Leadership Nashville, 1993. Recipient Polit. Star award Davidson County Dem. Women, 1993.

RAY, JANE ZIMRUDE, retired machine shop executive; b. Strawn, Tex., May 9, 1937; d. M.A. and Susie Matilda (Kitchens) Wooton; m. Earl Vernon Ray, Oct. 19, 1956; children: Marcus Vernon, Martha Ruth Ray O'Grady, Douglas Wayne, Patricia Ann. Grad., Stephenville (Tex.) High Sch., 1955. Bookkeeper Ray's Texaco Svc. Ctr., Ft. Worth, Tex., 1967-74; bookkeeper Ray's Repair & Mfg., Ft. Worth, Tex., 1974-79, pres., 1979-80; pres. Ray's Repair & Mfg., Cisco, Tex., 1980-92. Sunday sch. tchr., Cisco, Tex., 1983-92, sub. tchr., 1992—; mem. Civic League of Cisco, 1990—; instr. Community Svc. course Cisco Jr. Coll., 1991.

RAY, JENNY, artist; b. Ontario, Oreg.; d. Thompson and Othela Jean Towell Carper; m. Gary Wayne Limbaugh, Apr. 14, 1971; children: Cindy Sue, Tina Marie, Kay Jean, Tamara Rae, Cody Wayne. Cosmetologist, Pendleton (Oreg.) Coll. Beauty, 1972; student, Blue Mountain C.C., 1979-80, Ea. Oreg. State Coll., 1991-92. Mem. Lakota Sioux Tribe. Owner Butter Creek Beauty Salon, Hermiston, Oreg., 1977-80, Pretty Quick Constrn. Co., Hermiston, Oreg., 1978-93, McCord's Corner Art Gallery, Baker City, Oreg., 1986-88, Creations, Inc., Baker City, 1984-85, Western Mountain Art, Inc., Joseph, Oreg., 1982—, Age of Bronze Art Foundry, Joseph, 1992—. Author: Self Esteem Repair in Recovery, 1992; artist oil portraits of famous native Americans, 1985—; one woman shows at McCords Corner Art Gallery, 1986, Klondikes of Baker City, 1987, Baker County Chamber Office, 1988, Sumpter Valley R.R. Baker, 1988. Asst. dir. Ch. of Christ Christian Sch., Hermiston, 1980, Wallowa Valley Players, Joseph, 1990-92; econ. devel. com. Wallowa Valley Arts Coun., Enterprise, Oreg., 1993—; exec. dir. Wallowa Valley Mktg. Assn., Joseph, 1994; chair Jane Jefferson Club, Pendleton, Oreg., 1975; del. Umatilla County Dem. Com., Pendleton, 1976; campaign chair Jimmy Carter Campaign, Umatilla County, 1976. Recipient Cert. of Merit Pendleton Coll. Beauty, 1980; Western Art Prodns. scholar, 1988. Mem. Lakota Sioux Tribe, Nat. Mus. of the Am. Indian (charter), Nat. Mus. of Women in the Arts, Smithsonian Assocs., Grant County Art Assn., Union County Art Guild, The Cross Roads Art Ctr. Home: PO Box 320 Joseph OR 97846-0320 Office: Western Mountain Art Inc 84587 Walker Ln Joseph OR 97846-8228

RAY, JOYCE MARIE, archivist, historian; b. Mobile, Ala., Dec. 29, 1948; d. Jack W. and Juliet (Craddock) Butler; m. Dennis A. Ray, Apr. 1, 1972 (div. 1980); 1 child, Nathan C.; m. F. G. Gosling, Aug. 13, 1982. BA, U. Houston, 1970; MLS, U. Tex., 1974, PhD, 1992. Tech. svcs. libr., archivist Tusculum Coll., Greeneville, Tenn., 1974-76; head hist. collections U. Tex. Health Sci. Ctr., San Antonio, 1977-87; archivist Office Nat. Archives Nat. Archives and Records Adminstrn., Washington, 1988, appraisal archivist Office Records Adminstrn., 1989, archives specialist Office Mgmt. and Adminstrn., 1989-93, spl. asst. to the Archivist, 1993—; tchr. Georgetown U., 1992, 93; presenter in field. Contbr. articles to profl. jours. Rsch. fellow Med. Coll. Pa., 1989. Mem. Soc. Am. Archivists (mem. acquisitions and appraisal sect., sect. chair 1987-88, chair nominating com. 1989, cons. SAA basic archival conservation program 1989), Soc. S.W. Archives (exec. bd. 1986-87, chair profl. devel. com. 1984-85, local arrangements com. 1984-85), Mid-Atlantic Regional Archives Conf., Orgn. Am. Historians. Democrat. Home: # 502 3930 Connecticut Ave NW Washington DC 20008 Office: Nat Archives Rm 111 7th and Pennsylvania Aves Washington DC 20408

RAY, MARILYN CLAIRE, dermatologist; b. New Orleans, Nov. 11, 1951; d. C. Thorpe and Lillian Ray; m. Leonard Edward Gatsby, Oct. 8, 1984. BA, Stephens Coll., 1973; MD, Tulane U., 1977. Intern Ochsner Found., 1977-78; resident Tulane U. Sch. of Medicine, 1978-81; fellow Southwestern Med. Ctr., Dallas, 1981-84; asst. prof. U. Tex. Health Sci. Ctr., Dallas, 1983-84; mem. staff Ochsner Clinic, New Orleans, 1984—. Editor: Applied Immunodermatology, 1991. Recipient Rsch. award Dermatology Found., 1983. Office: Ochsner Clinic 1514 Jefferson Hwy New Orleans LA 70121

RAY, MARY-ANN, architect, educator; b. Seattle, July 19, 1958; d. Norman Gene and Barbara Ann (Wechsler) R. BFA, U. Wash., 1981; MArch, Princeton U., 1987. Designer Michael Graves, Architect, Princeton, N.J., 1984, Richard Meier and Ptnrs., L.A. and N.Y.C., 1987-88; prin., designer Studio Works, L.A., 1988—; grad. faculty So. Calif. Inst. Architecture, L.A., 1988—; mem. adv. bd. L.A. Mcpl. Art Gallery, 1992—. Prin. works include (master plans) Progressive Architecture, 1990-91 (Urban Design award 1992), Inland Architect, 1990-91, Lotus Internat., 1990-91. Recipient Lili Auchincloss fellowship Am. Acad. Rome, 1987-88, Norton prize Princeton U., 1987, Max Beckmann Meml. fellowship Bklyn. Mus., 1981-82, Ford Found. grant in fine arts U. Wash. and Ford Found., 1978, 80, 81. Home and Office: Studio Works Bldg # 3 6775 S Centinela Ave Culver City CA 90230-6303

RAY, REBECCA LEA, communication consultant, educator; b. Yokohama, Japan, Nov. 19, 1955; (parents Am. citizens); d. Gerald C. and Beverly (Lindstrom) R. BA in Theatre, Speech and English, U. Fla., 1976; MA in English Lit., Fla. Atlanta U., 1978; cert., Shakespeare Inst., Stratford-upon-Avon, Eng., 1979; PhD in Comm. Arts and Scis., NYU, 1985. Tchr., dir. speech and drama program Palm Beach Gardens (Fla.) High Sch., 1978-81; tchr., co-dir. drama program Southside High Sch., Rockville Centre, N.Y., 1982-86; assoc. prof. Stroudsburg U., East Stroudsburg, Pa., 1986-92; prin. Rebecca Ray & Assocs., Long Valley, N.J., 1986—; adj. asst. prof. NYU, 1988—; instr. Oxford (Eng.) U., summer 1992; corp. trainee for Fortune 500 cos. in the areas of presentation skills, interviewing strategies, sexual harassment, and comm. skills; presenter at nat. convs.; chmn. numerous profl. panels. Author: (one-act plays) Reflections on Loss, 1982, Brat, 1991; editor: Bridging Both Worlds: The Communication Consultant in Corporate America, 1993. Mem. ASTD, Speech Comm. Assn., Ea. Comm. Assn., Dramatists Guild-Author's League Am., Phi Delta Kappa, Kappa Delta Sorority.

RAY, SUZANNE JUDY, writer; b. Petworth, Sussex, Eng., Aug. 20, 1939; came to U.S., 1969; d. Wilfrid Tom Huxtable and Doris Ella (Bird) Morrish; m. Donald Anthony James, July 8, 1961 (div. 1969); 1 child, Sapphina; m. David Eugene Ray, Feb. 21, 1970. BA with honours, Southampton U., Eng., 1960. Sec. registrar's office Makerere U., Kampala, Uganda, 1961-64; sec., editorial asst. Transition Mag., Kampala, 1965-67; assoc. editor New Letters Mag., Kansas City, Mo., 1971-85; radio producer New Letters On the Air, Kansas City, 1982-86; exec. dir. The Writers Pl., Kansas City, 1992—. Author: The Jaipur Sketchbook, 1991, (poetry books) Pebble Rings, 1980, Pigeons in the Chandeliers, 1993; co-editor: New Asian Writing, 1979. Mem. Poetry Soc. Am. Mem. Soc. of Friends.

RAYBURN, MARGARET S., state legislator; b. North Powder, Oreg., Apr. 5, 1927; d. John Alexander and Pearl Laurel (Wicks) Shaw; m. Glenn Albert Rayburn, July 19, 1946; children: Jeffrey John, Mary Jane Victoria Rayburn Ahlbeck. BA, Eastern Wash. U., 1949. Elem. tchr. Harriett Thompson Elem. Sch., Grandview, Wash., 1949-63; jr. high tchr. Grandview Jr. High, 1963-76, counselor, 1976-83; mem. Wash. Legislature, 1985—; chair Agr. Comm., Olympia, Wash., 1987—, Edn. Commn., Olympia, 1985-89, Local Gov. Comm., Olympia, 1985—, Energy and Utilities Commn., 1991-92, Higher Edn. Commn., 1993—. Bd. dirs. Crisis Ctr., Sunnyside, Wash., 1979-89, Wash. State Policy Inst., 1989—; vice chair agr. and timber com. Nat. Conf. State Legis.; mem. nat. task force on wine. Named Outstanding Elected Official Grandview C. of C., 1985. Mem. AAUW, Dem. Club, Fedn. Women's Club, Grandview Grange, Delta Kappa Gamma (pres. 1974-76). Home: 1610 S Euclid Rd Grandview WA 98930-9494 Office: PO Box 40629 301 John L O'Brien Bldg Olympia WA 98504-0629

RAYGOZA, LYNETTE ROSALIND, educational administrator; b. Hanford, Calif., Sept. 16, 1953; d. King and Lupe (Vasquez) R. BA in History, St. Mary's Coll., Moraga, Calif., 1976. Adminstrv. asst. fin. aid office U. Calif., Davis, 1980-83, systems coord. fin. aid office, 1983-87; asst. dir. fin. aid office Santa Clara (Calif.) U., 1987-90, mgr. student systems and registration svcs., 1990—. Precinct capt. Dem. Party, Santa Clara, 1988; precinct worker Vasconcillos Campaign, Santa Clara, 1992; vol. Green Initiative, Palo Alto, 1990, United Farm Workers Inst., 1978. Mem. Nat. Assn. Student Fin. Aid Adminstrs., Western Assn. Student Fin. Aid Adminstrs., Calif. Assn. Student Fin. Aid Adminstrs., Nat. Assn. SIGMA Users, Am. Coun. on Edn., Nat. Idenfication Program. Roman Catholic. Home: # 279 151 Buckingham Dr Santa Clara CA 95051

RAYHILL, MARY MORGAN, business executive, educator; b. Princeton, N.J., Dec. 4, 1946; d. Burton Davis and Margaret Louise (Clark) Morgan; m. Mark Delano Robeson Jr., (div. 1973); 1 child, Mark Delano III; m. William Rayhill; children: Keith Morgan, Brooke Morgan. AA, Stephens Coll., 1966; BA, U. Mo., 1968; MPA, U. So. Calif., 1974; PhD, Claremont Grad. Sch., 1977. High sch. tchr. McKemy Jr. High Sch., Tempe, Ariz., 1968-73; adminstrv. asst. City of L.A., 1974-76; mgr. bus. programs Inst. for

Profl. Devel., Irvine, Calif., 1977-79; dir. tng. Xerox Learning Systems, Irvine, 1979-81; ptnr., founder Morgan Rsch. and Innovation, Inc., Santa Rosa, Calif., 1981-93; lectr. Portland (Oreg.) State U., 1990—; with The Alignment Group, Santa Rosa, Calif., 1994—; counselor MRI, Portland, 1991, cons., Santa Rosa, Calif., 1981-91. Author: Corporate Healing, 1990. Planning commr. City of San Juan Capistrano, Calif., 1979-81; youth group leader Community Ch., Sebastapol, 1984-88; bd. dirs. United Way, 1988—. Mem. Am. Soc. Quality Control, Am. Compensation Assn. (speaker). Republican. Church of Religious Science. Home: 11001 Falstaff Rd Sebastopol CA 95472 Office: The Alignment Group 4527 Montgomery Rd Ste E Santa Rosa CA 95401

RAYL, INDIA, marketing executive; b. Chateauroux, France, May 1, 1956; d. Rommie Clarence and Peggeanne (Moore) Walker; m. Robert Richard Rayl, Jr., June 19, 1982; children: Brandon Joseph, Nelia Ashley. Student, Mesa Coll., San Diego, 1982-85, U. San Diego, 1988-89; cert. in direct mktg., San Diego State Univ., Univ. San Diego, 1990. Brand mgr. Undergear Catalog, San Diego, 1983; dir. customr relations Internat. Male, San Diego, 1977-86; catalog dir. ACA Joe, San Diego, 1986-87; media mgr. Internat. Male-Hanover House Ind., San Diego, 1988; gen. mgr. Petco-Animal City, San Diego, 1988-89; mktg. mgr. More Direct Health Products, 1989-90; dir. sales and mktg. Healy and Clark, San Diego, 1991-92; mktg. promotions mgr. Road Runner Sports, San Diego, 1992-93, dir. new bus., 1993-95; dir. product devel. Entrepreneur Mag. Group, 1995—; new bus. cons. Gift Baskets, Inc., San Diego, 1988. Editor various catalogs. Mem. Nat. Assn. Female Execs., Nat. Assn. Mil. Spouses, San Diego Direct Mktg. Club. Office: Road Runner Sports 6150 Nancy Ridge Rd San Diego CA 92121

RAYMOND, BETTY JEAN, critical care nurse; b. Harriman, Tenn., Feb. 28, 1955; d. Charles E. and Elizabeth Jane (Crump) R. Student, State Vo-Tech, Harriman, 1982, Roane State Community Coll., Harriman. Staff nurse ICU, CCU, cardiac rehab. Chamberlain Meml. Hosp., Rockwood, Tenn.; charge nurse Spring City (Tenn.) Health Care; staff nurse intensive care-coronary care unit Loudon (Tenn.) County Meml. Hosp.; charge nurse Marshall Voss Health Care, Harriman, Tenn.; staff nurse Roane County Ambulance Svc., staff nurse with pediat. nursing specialists, Nashville, 1992, Elk Valley Health Svcs., Fayetteville, Tenn., 1994. Home: PO Box 483 Harriman TN 37748-0483

RAYMOND, DIANE MARIE, marketing professional; b. Sudbury, Ont., Can., Dec. 28, 1962; came to U.S., 1981; AA in Fashion Merchandising & Comm., Internat. Fine Arts Coll., Miami, Fla., 1983. Buyer Cache Inc., Miami, 1983-84, advt. and promotion dir., 1984-86; fashion dir. Saks Fifth Ave, Boca Raton, Fla., 1986-89; promotion mgr. Hallmark Cards Inc., Kansas City, Mo., 1989-90, advt. and promotion mgr., 1990-91, drive period mgr., 1992-93, bus. and mktg. mgr., 1993—. Home: 617 West 70th Terr Kansas City MO 64113 Office: Hallmark Cards Inc 2501 McGee Kansas City MO 64111

RAYMOND, DOROTHY GILL, lawyer; b. Greeley, Colo., June 2, 1954; d. Robert Marshall and Roberta (McClure) Gill; m. Peter J. Raymond, June 8, 1974. BA summa cum laude, U. Denver, 1975; JD, U. Colo., 1978. Bar: Conn. 1978, Colo. 1981. Assoc. Dworkin, Minogue & Bucci, Bridgeport, Conn., 1978-80; counsel Tele-Communications, Inc., Englewood, Colo., 1981-88; v.p., gen. counsel WestMarc Communications, Inc., Denver, 1988-91, Cable Television Labs., Inc., Boulder, Colo., 1991—. Mem. Am. Corp. Counsel Assn. (pres. 1990-91, Colo. chpt. dir. 1988-94), Colo. Assn. Corp. Counsel (pres. 1987), Sports Car Club Am. (nat. champion ladies stock competition 1981, 85, 86, 88). Office: Cable Television Labs Inc 400 Centennial Pky Louisville CO 80027-1266

RAZ, HILDA, editor-in-chief periodical, educator; b. Rochester, N.Y., May 4, 1938; d. Franklyn Emmanuel and Dolly (Horwich) R.; m. Frederick M. Link, June 9, 1957 (div. 1969); children: John Franklin Link, Sarah Link; m. Dale Nordyke, Oct. 4, 1980. BA, Boston U., 1960. Asst. dir. Planned Parenthood League of Mass., Boston, 1960-62; edit. asst. Prairie Schooner, Lincoln, Nebr., 1970-74; contbg. editor Prairie Schooner, 1974-77, assoc. editor, 1977-87, acting editor, 1981-83, 85, poetry editor, 1980-87, editor-in-chief, 1987—; assoc. prof. dept Eng. U. Nebr., Lincoln, 1990—; lectr., reader, panelist in field; participant many workshops, symposia, confs.; panelist arts com. NEA, 1994; judge Kenyon Rev., 1990, Soc. Midland Authors Best Book of 1987 award, 198, Ill. Art Coun./NEA fellowships, 1987; bd. govs. Ctr. for Great Plains Studies, U. Nebr., 1989-95. Author numerour poems, essays; editor Nebr. Humanist, 1990. Pres. Assoc. Writing Programs, bd. dirs., 1988-89, ex-officio pres., 1989-90, v.p., 1987-88; mem. program com. Friends of Librs. U. Nebr., 1989-90; bd. dirs. Nebr. Libr. Heritage Assn., 1988-91; mem. Mayor's Blue Ribbon Com. on Arts, 1985-88; bd. dirs. Planned Parenthood League Nebr., 1978-83, sec. bd. dirs., 1979-80, chairperson long-term planning com., 1980-81, 81-82. Recipient Literary Heritage award Mayor's Art Awards, Lincoln, 1988; Bread Loaf scholar editors, 1974, poetry, 1985; Robert Frost fellow, 1988, 89, Mag. Panel fellow, 1993, 94. Home: 960 S Cotner Blvd Lincoln NE 68510 Office: Univ of Nebraska Lincoln Prairie Schooner 201 Andrews Hall Lincoln NE 68588-0334

RAZANI, SARA SHIRIN, lawyer; b. Cleve., Feb. 20, 1964; d. Reza and Sally Gertrude (Henn) R. BA in History with high honors, U. Hawaii Manoa, Honolulu, 1988, BA in Internat. Rels. with distinction, 1988; JD, Notre Dame Law Sch., 1992. Bar: Hawaii 1992. Parole officer Hawaii Paroling Authority, Honolulu, 1988-89; law intern Paul W. Ferrell, Atty. at Law, London, 1991, Law Offices of Gary M. Ferman, London, 1991; assoc. Goodsill Anderson Quinn & Stifel, Honolulu, 1992-94; ind. model, Honolulu, 1988-89. Illustrator: Smack the Little Savage, 1980. Vol. atty. Hawaii Lawyers Care, Honolulu, 1993; guest spkr. No Hope in Dope Program, Honolulu Police Dept. Capt. Hawaii Army N.G., 1982—. Mem. ABA, Hawaii State Bar Assn., Nat. Guard Officer's Assn., Women in Mil. Svc. in Am. Meml. Found. (charter mem.), Soc. Profls. in Dispute Resolution (Chgo. chpt.), Amnesty Internat., So. Party Law Ctr., Phi Alpha Theta. Home: 5116 S Woodlawn Ave # 2R Chicago IL 60615

RAZE-GRENIER, TARA LYNN, product applications engineer; b. Polson, Mont., Mar. 29, 1966; d. Franklin Junior and Beverly Ann (Hendricks) Raze; m. Ed Michael Grenier, Oct. 23, 1993. AS, Treasure Valley C.C., 1986; AS in Elecs. Engring. Tech., Oreg. Inst. Tech., 1989, BS in Laser Electro-Optics Tech., 1990. With printed circuit bd. imaging dept. Hewlett-Packard, Boise, 1988, printed circuit bd. testing, 1989; product applications engr. Met One, Inc., Grants Pass, Oreg., 1991—. Republican. Home: 540 E Park St Grants Pass OR 97527 Office: Met One Inc 481 California Ave Grants Pass OR 97526

REA, ANN HADLEY KUEHN, social organization marketing administrator; b. Arlington, Va., Oct. 14, 1962; d. Alvin Henry Kuehn and Barbara Ann (Schmall) Schanzenbach; m. Burt Richard Rea, June 30, 1990; 1 child. BA in Communications, Va. Poly. Inst. & State U., Blacksburg, 1984; MA in Liberal Studies, Georgetown U., Washington, 1993. Desk asst., prodn. asst. ABC News, Washington, 1986-88; media/info. officer Embassy of Australia, Washington, 1988-90; mktg. and membership dir. YWCA, Summit, N.J., 1992—. Mem. LWV. Episcopalian. Home: 38 Minton Ave Chatham NJ 07928 Office: Summit YWCA 79 Maple St Summit NJ 07901-2586

READ, ELEANOR MAY, financial analyst; b. Arcadia, N.Y., July 4, 1942; d. Henry and Lena May (Fagner) Van Koevering; 1 child, Robin Jo. Typist, clk., sec., credit corr. Sarah Coventry, Inc., Newark, N.Y., 1957-61; exec. sec. Mobil Chem. Co., Macedon, N.Y., 1961-68; bus. mgr. Henry's Hardware, Newark, 1968-72; with Xerox Corp., Fremont, Calif., 1973—, internat. clk. analyst, personnel adminstrv. asst., employment coordinator, exec. sec., cycle count analyst., acctg. specialist, tax preparer H&R Block, 1985-92. Mem. Xerox/Diablo Mgmt. Assn., Am. Mgmt. Assn., Profl. Businesswomen's Assn., NAFE. Office: Xerox 5724 W Los Positas Blvd Pleasanton CA 94588

READ, SISTER JOEL, college administrator. BS in Edn., Alverno Coll., 1948; MA in History, Fordham U., 1951; hon. degrees, Lakeland Coll., 1972, Wittenburg U., 1976, Marymount Manhattan Coll., 1978, DePaul U., 1985, Northland Coll., 1986, SUNY, 1986. Former prof., dept. chmn. history dept. Alverno Coll., Milw., pres., 1968—; pres. Am. Assn. for Higher Edn., 1976-77; mem. coun. NEH, 1977-83; bd. dirs. Ednl. Testing Svc., 1987-93, Neylan Commn., 1985-90; past pres. Wis. Assn. Ind. Colls. and Univs.; mem. Commn. on Status of Edn. for Women, 1971-76, Am. Assn. Colls., 1971-77; mem. exec. com. Greater Milw. com. GMC Edn. Trust. Mem. exec. bd. Milw. YMCA. First recipient Anne Roe award Harvard U. Grad. Sch. Edn., 1980. Fellow Am. Acad. Arts and Scis.; mem. Found. for Higher Edn. Office: Alverno Coll Office of the President PO Box 343922 Milwaukee WI 53234-3922

READY, ELIZABETH M., state legislator; b. Burlington, Vt., Oct. 7, 1953; m. John H. McLain; 3 children. BA, U. Vt. Selectman Town of Lincoln, Vt.; state senator Vt. Senate, Montpelier, 1989—; regional planning commr.; educator. Home: Box 2018 RR 1 Bristol VT 05443-8857 Office: Vt State Senate State Capitol Montpelier VT 05602*

REAGAN, GERTI, management consultant; b. Weyer, Austria, Oct. 22, 1951; arrived in U.S., 1956; d. Johann and Eva (Mack) Goetz; m. Michael James Reagan, July 4, 1970; 1 child, Rebecca Susan. BSBA, Calif. State U., L.A., 1978. CPA, Calif.; cert. profl. cons. to mgmt. Various claims and adminstrv. positions Occidental Life Ins., L.A., 1971-77; sr. acct. Coopers & Lybrand, L.A., 1978-81; contr. Maxicare, Hawthorne, Calif., 1981-82; sr. fin. cons. HealthWest Assocs., Chatsworth, Calif., 1982-84; contr. Santa Teresita Hosp., Duarte, Calif., 1984-86; v.p. KH Cons., L.A., 1986-90, Garner Cons., Pasadena, Calif., 1990—; treas. bd. dirs. Transformations Family Svcs., Arcadia, Calif., 1987—. Chmn. audit com. All Saints Ch., Pasadena, 1991-93, mem. fin. com., 1993—, treas., 1994—. Fellow Life Mgmt. Inst.; mem. AICPA, Healthcare Fin. Mgmt. Assn. (bd. dirs. 1991-93, parliamentarian 1993-94, Outstanding Mem. of Yr. award So. Calif. chpt. 1992, Follmer bronze merit award 1992), Western Claim Conf. (program chmn. 1993-94). Office: Garner Cons Ste 560 199 S Los Robles Ave Pasadena CA 91101

REAGAN, NANCY DAVIS (ANNE FRANCIS ROBBINS), volunteer, wife of former President of United States; b. N.Y.C., July 6, 1923; d. Kenneth and Edith (Luckett) Robbins; step dau. Loyal Davis; m. Ronald Reagan, Mar. 4, 1952; children: Patricia Ann, Ronald Prescott; stepchildren: Maureen, Michael. BA, Smith Coll.; LLD (hon.), Pepperdine U., 1983; LHD (hon.), Georgetown U., 1987. Contract actress, MGM, 1949-56; films include The Next Voice You Hear, 1950, Donovan's Brain, 1953, Hellcats of the Navy, 1957; Author: Nancy, 1980; formerly author syndicated column on prisoner-of-war and missing-in-action soldiers and their families; author: (with Jane Wilkie) To Love a Child, (with William Novak) My Turn: The Memoirs of Nancy Reagan, 1989. Civic worker, visited wounded Viet Nam vets., sr. citizens, hosps. and schs. for physically and emotionally handicapped children, active in furthering foster grandparents for handicapped children program; hon. nat. chmn. Aid to Adoption of Spl. Kids, 1977; spl. interest in fighting alcohol and drug abuse among youth: hosted first ladies from around the world for 2d Internat. Drug Conf., 1985; hon. chmn. Just Say No Found., Nat. Fedn. of Parents for Drug-Free Youth, Nat. Child Watch Campaign, President's Com. on the Arts and Humanities, Wolf Trap Found. bd. of trustees, Nat. Trust for Historic Preservation, Cystic Fibrosis Found., Nat. Republican Women's Club; hon. pres. Girl Scouts of Am. Named one of Ten Most Admired Am. Women, Good Housekeeping mag., ranking #1 in poll, 1984, 85, 86; Woman of Yr. Los Angeles Times, 1977; permanent mem. Hall of Fame of Ten Best Dressed Women in U.S.; recipient humanitarian awards from Am. Camping Assn., Nat. Council on Alcoholism, United Cerebral Palsy Assn., Internat. Ctr. for Disabled; Boys Town Father Flanagan award; 1986 Kiwanis World Service medal; Variety Clubs Internat. Lifeline award; numerous awards for her role in fight against drug abuse. Address: Century City Fox Plaza Tower 34th Fl Los Angeles CA 90024

REAGAN, RENEE GABRIELLE, upholstery textile designer; b. Dedham, Mass., Aug. 23, 1964; d. Bernard Michael and Brooke Ann (Trudell) R. AA in Art/Studio, Lasell Jr. Coll., 1984; BFA in Weaving & Textile Design, Rochester Inst. Technol., 1987. Art leader Camp Tara, Mallets Bay, Vt., 1983-84; painting supr. Rochester Inst. Tech. Phys. Plant, 1985-86; asst. to designer Harrisville (N.H.) Designs, 1986-87; sign artist Rochester Inst. Technol. Coll. Union Cafeteria, 1984-87; costumer Nat. Tech. Inst. of Deaf Performing Arts Theatre, Rochester, 1986-87, Hope Summer Repertory Theatre, Holland, Mich., 1987; dressmaker alterations Marge's Bridal Shop, Wyoming, Pa., 1990-91; design technician Chromatex, Inc., Hazleton, Pa., 1987-92, designer, 1992—. Exhibited in group shows including The Show, 1987, Rochester Inst. Technol., 1987, Lasell Jr. Coll., 1984. Named to Dean's List, Lasell Jr. Coll., 1982-84. Home: RR 1 Box 1818 Waymart PA 18472

REAMER, SHIRLEY JEAN, minister; b. South Bend, Ind., Aug. 15, 1935; d. John Lewis and Vivian Leora (Hammer) Helvey; m. Thomas Charles Reamer, June 22, 1956; children: Thomas Darwin, Trent Alan, Terry Michael, Traci Sue, Tricia Ann. Grad. high sch., South Bend, 1953; ThD, Shalom Bible Coll. and Sem., West Des Moines, Iowa, 1992. Ordained to ministry Full Gospel Fellowship, 1974. Dir. children's ministry Calvary Temple, South Bend, 1972-73; evangelist Full Gospel Fellowship, 1976—; founder, pastor Maranatha Temple, South Bend, 1981-83; founder, pres. Women's Aglow Fellowship, Michiana, Ind., 1976-79; founder, dir. Prison Ministry-Aglow, Westville, Ind., 1976-77; founder, dir. Soup Kitchen/Care Ctr., Maranatha Temple, 1982—, Supplied Facilities for Ctr. for Homeless, 1984-87, dir. City March, 1989; mem. United Religious Community Task Force, South Bend, 1985. Author: Ministerial Ethics, 1984, Teaching Syllabus, 1985, Recruits for Christ, 1987, Teaching Syllabus, Genesis, The Beginning, 1994. Recipient Spirit of Am. Women award J.C. Penneys, South Bend, 1988; named one of 16 Best Pastors, Charisma Mag., 1988.

REAMS, RACHEL YVONNE, veterinarian, pathologist; b. Kokomo, Ind., Mar. 11, 1961; d. Albert L. and Elizabeth Ann (Beaver) R. BS in Biology, Purdue U., 1983, DVM, 1986, MS in Pathology, 1992. Dir. P.R. Dept. Agr. Diagnostic Lab., Dorado, 1986-89; owner Unicorn Vet. Clinic, Vega Alta, P.R., 1988-89; grad. staff Purdue U., West Lafayette, Ind., 1989—. Contbr. articles to profl. jours. Mem. Phi Zeta, Phi Kappa Phi. Home: 1124 Happy Hollow Rd West Lafayette IN 47906-2761 Office: Purdue Univ Addl West Lafayette IN 47907

REAP, KATHERINE KISSANE, brokerage executive; b. Chgo., Dec. 27, 1954; d. Elmer Charles and Jeanne (O'Toole) Kissane; m. Thomas Leo Reap, July 19, 1980. BA, John Carroll U., 1976; AM in English, U. Chgo., 1982. Tchr. St. Mary's Sch., Lake Forest, Ill., 1976-77, Willows Acad., Glencoe, Ill., 1978-81; asst. syndicate mgr. Chgo. Corp., 1986-94, sr. v.p., 1994—. Mem. Bond Club of Chgo., Women's Syndicate Assn. (regional rep. 1987-90). Office: Chicago Corp 208 S LaSalle St Chicago IL 60604

REAP, SISTER MARY MARGARET, college administrator; b. Carbondale, Pa., Sept. 8, 1941; d. Charles Vincent and Anna Rose (Ahern) R. BA, Marywood Coll., Scranton, Pa., 1965; MA, Assumption Coll., Worcester, Mass., 1972; PhD, Pa. State U., 1979. Elem. tchr. St. Ephrem's, Bklyn., 1966-67; secondary tchr. South Catholic High, Scranton, Pa., 1967-69, Maria Regina High Sch., Uniondale, N.Y., 1969-72; mem. faculty Marywood Coll., Scranton, Pa., 1972-86, dean, 1986-88, pres., 1988—; tchr. Mainland China, Wuhan, 1982, Marygrove Coll., Detroit, 1979; bd. dirs. Moses Taylor Hops., Scranton Prep. Sch.; bd. dirs., exec. com. Lourdesmont Sch. Contbr. articles to profl. jours. Recipient bilingual fellowship Pa. State U., 1976-79, Local Chpt. Svc. award UN, 1984, Woman of Yr. awrd Boy Scouts Am., 1993; named Northeast Woman, Scranton Times, 1986, Outstanding Alumna, Pa. State Coll. Edn., 1989. Mem. Pa. Assn. for Colls. and Univs. (exec. com.), Coun. for Ind. Colls. and Univs., Am. Assn. Cath. Colls., Phi Delta Kappa (Educator of Yr. award 1990). Office: Marywood Coll Office of the President Scranton PA 18509-1598

REARDEN, CAROLE ANN, clinical pathologist, educator; b. Belleville, Ont., Can., June 11, 1946; d. Joseph Brady and Honora Patricia (O'Halloran) R. BSc, McGill U., 1969, MSc, MDCM, 1971. Diplomate Am. Bd. Pathology, Am. Bd. Immunohematology and Blood Banking. Resident and fellow Children's Meml. Hosp., Chgo., 1971-73; resident in pediatrics U. Calif., San Diego, 1974, resident then fellow, 1975-79, dir. histocompatability and immunogenetics lab., asst. prof. pathology, 1979-86, assoc. prof., 1986-92, prof., 1992—, head div. lab. medicine, 1989—; dir. med. ctr. U. Calif. and Thorton Hosp. Clin. Labs., San Diego, 1993—; prin. investigator devel. monoclonal antibodies to erythroid antigens, recombinant autoantigens; dir. lab. exam. com. Am. Bd. Histocompatibility and Immunogenetics. Contbr. articles to profl. jours. Mem. Mayor's Task Force on AIDS, San Diego, 1983. Recipient Young Investigator Rsch. award NIH, 1979; grantee U. Calif. Cancer Rsch. Coordinating Com., 1982, NIH, 1983. Mem. Am. Soc. Investigative Pathology, Acad. Clin. Lab. Physicians and Scientists, Am. Soc. Hematology, Am. Assn. Blood Banks (com. organ transplantation and tissue typing 1982-87), Am. Soc. Histocompatibility and Immunogenetics. Office: U Calif San Diego Dept Pathology 0612 9500 Gilman Dr La Jolla CA 92093-0612

REARDON, BEA, social worker; b. Queens, N.Y., July 10, 1955; d. James Joseph and Evelyn May (Meyerricks) R. BS in Social Work, Salem (Mass.) State Coll., 1979; MSW, Smith Coll., 1984. Bd. cert. diplomate in clin. social work. Clin. social worker Valley Adult Counseling Svc., Milford, Mass., 1984-86; clin. social worker, outpatient psychiatry Univ. Hosp., Boston, 1986-88; clin. social worker Tri City Mental Health Ctr., Medford, Mass., 1986-88, dir. children's outpatient program, 1988-90; pvt. practice social work Cambridge, Mass., 1987—. Mem. Mass. Acad. Clin. Social Work (pres. 1993-95). Office: 2557 Massachusetts Ave Cambridge MA 02140

REARDON, JACQUELYN MILLER, communications executive; b. Northampton, Mass., Apr. 16, 1947; d. Everett Russell and Alma Margaret (Montgomery) Miller; m. Thomas Joseph Reardon, May 3, 1974 (seperated); 1 child, Heather Lynn. BFA, Miami U., 1970; M of Liberal Arts, Harvard U., 1983. Printmaking tchr. The Newport (R.I.) Sch., 1972-73; art exhibit dir. Harvard Chamber Music Soiree Series, Cambridge, 1974; advt. artist Cambridge Pub. Libr., 1975—; course asst. Harvard U., 1988-89. Mem. Miami U. Alumni Assn., Harvard Grad. Soc., Harvard Alumni Assn. Democrat. Home: 5 Waldo Ave Somerville MA 02143 Office: Cambridge Pub Libr 449 Broadway Cambridge MA 02139

REARDON, LOUISE ARLEEN, medical school administrator; b. Fall River, Mass., June 21, 1923; d. John Brackett and Catherine (Ironside) Bartlett; m. Malcolm B. Reardon, Oct. 25, 1940 (dec. 1953); children: John B., David W. (dec.). BA, Boston U., 1976. Stenographer USAF, Rapid City, S.D., 1951-54; stenographer, asst. to contr. USAF, Falmouth, Mass., 1955-73; adminstr. Harvard Med. Sch., Boston, 1976—. Bd. dirs. Old South Ch., Boston; mem. Women's State-Wide Legis. Network, Boston, 1985—. Mem. AAUW (Boston br., pres. 1983-85), Falmouth Bus. and Profl. Women (pres. 1968-70), Coll. Club of Boston (bd. dirs.), Order of Ea. Star. Home: 59 Bay State Rd Boston MA 02215-1813 Office: Harvard Med Sch Resource Devel Office 25 Shattuck St Boston MA 02115

REASONER, MACEY HODGES, employment and training consultant; b. Dec. 2, 1940; m. Harry M. Reasoner, Apr. 15, 1963; children: Barrett Hodges, Elizabeth Macey. BA magna cum laude, U. Tex., 1962, postgrad., 1962-63; postgrad., U. Houston, 1963, Rice U., 1965-66. Adminstrv. asst. admissions office Yale U., New Haven, 1963-64; grad. teaching asst. sociology dept. Rice U., Houston, 1965-66; rsch. asst. Rice U. Urban Studies Ctr., Houston, 1966-67; project assoc. Ctr. for Human Resources U. Houston, 1969-70, rsch. assoc. Inst. Labor & Indsl. Rels., 1977-81, project assoc. feasability study on degree programs in apprenticeship and labor studies, 1978-81; project assoc. apprenticeship rsch. program Ctr. for Study of Human Resources U. Tex., 1979-81; project dir. CETA-Vocat. Edn. Linkage program Tex. Dept. Community Affairs, 1980-81; pvt. cons. employment & tng. Meyer & Assocs., Houston, 1981—; cons. Tex. Employment Commn., 1979-81, State Apprenticeship Adv. Coun., 1979-81; asst. editor Manpower Briefs nat. newsletter, 1979-80, editor, 1981. Chmn. monitoring & evaluation com. City of Houston Labor Market Adv. Coun., 1970-72; chmn. monitoring & evaluation com. City of Houston Manpower Adv. Planning Coun., 1972-81, chmn. proposal rev. com., chmn. full coun., 1976-77; chmn. City of Houston Employment Coun., 1980-81; mem. Harris County Flood Control Task Force, 1973-85, vice-chmn., 1974-75, chmn., 1975-76; bd. dirs. Rice Design Alliance, 1977-85, v.p., 1979, chair urban affairs symposia; Houston panelist Vice-Pres. Mondale's Task Force on Youth Employment, 1979-80; alt. del. Mayor's Urban Policy Adv. Bd., 1978-79; mem. state adv. coun. Tex. Employment Commn., 1980-81, 87-91; bd. dirs. Houston Coun. Human Rels., 1980-84, Children's Resource Info. Svc., 1982-84, Girl's Club of Houston, 1984-86, Houston Proud, 1986-88, Vocat. Guidance Svc., 1987-90, Houston Grand Opera, 1989—, Houston Mus. Fine Arts, 1991—, Tex. Dept. Commerce, 1991—; mem. Legis. Oversight Com. on Job Tng., 1984-86, 1989—; chair planning, mem. exec. com. State Job Tng. Coordinating Coun., 1983-87, chmn., 1991—; Tex. rep. Nat. Conf. State Job Tng. Couns., 1985-86; mem. State Apprenticeship & Tng. Adv. Coun., 1985-90, chair planning, 1986-87; mem. exec. com. U. Tex. Liberal Arts Found. Bd., 1986—; mem. Legis. Task Force on Work and Welfare, 1986-87; Tex. 1990 roundtable mem. Anti-Defamation League, 1987—; bd. dirs., exec. com. Houston Architecture Found., 1988—; treas., exec. com. Houston Job Tng. Partnership Coun., 1988-90. Home: 2312 Rice Blvd Houston TX 77005-2622

REAVES, DORA ANN WOOLFREY, reporter, newspaper; b. Conway, S.C., Sept. 1, 1946; d. Frederick Wilson and Ruth (Paterson) Woolfrey; m. James Joseph Reaves Jr., Jan. 11, 1969; 1 child, James Joseph III. BA in English, Winthrop Coll., 1968. Reporter Evening Post Pub. Co., Charleston, S.C., 1968-81, copy desk chief, 1981, asst. chief copy editor The Evening Post, 1981-91. Recipient 2d Place Spot Reporting award S.C. AP, 1972, Sch. Bell award S.C. Ednl. Assn., 1973, Order of the Flying Orchid award Delta Airlines, 1978. Mem. Charleston Press Club (v.p. 1971, pres. 1972), Soc. Profl. Journalists. Lutheran. Home: 9 Dunvegan Dr Charleston SC 29414-6939 Office: Evening Post Pub Co 134 Columbus St Charleston SC 29403-4809

REAVIS, LIZA ANNE, telecommunications executive; b. N.Y.C., July 27, 1959; d. William Ralph and Juliette (Bustillo y Zelaya) Bartlett; m. Paul H. Reavis, May 25, 1985. BA in Internat. Rels., Rice U., 1981; MBA, Georgetown U., 1988. Project asst. Latham, Watkins & Hills, Washington, 1982-83; assoc. mgr. countertrade Sears World Trade, Washington, 1983-85; export asst. Weadon, Dibble & Rehm, Washington, 1985-86; assoc. cons. Vanguard Communications Corp., Palo Alto, Calif., 1988-90; bus. mgr. Teleport Communications Corp., San Francisco, 1990—. Contbr. Project Open Hand, San Francisco, Calif. Wheelchair Vets. Assn., Am. Assn. for AIDS Rsch., San Francisco, 1990—; mem. Golden Gate Nat. Recreation Area, San Francisco, 1990—. Mem. NAFE, Women in Telecomm., Acad. Polit. Sci. Club des Hiboux (sec. 1979-80), Commonwealth Club, Sierra Club, Cousteau Soc., Beta Gamma Sigma (TCG Annual Hero), Phi Beta Kappa, Pi Delta Phi (Presdl. scholar). Home: 6931 Geary Blvd San Francisco CA 94121 Office: Teleport Communications 1 Bush St Ste 510 San Francisco CA 94104

REBACK, JOYCE ELLEN, lawyer; b. Phila., July 11, 1948; d. William and Sue (Goldstein) R.; m. Itzhak Brook, Aug. 2, 1981; children: Jonathan Zev, Sara Jennie. BA magna cum laude, Brown U., 1970; JD with honors, George Washington U., 1976. Bar: D.C. 1976, U.S. Dist. Ct. D.C. 1976, U.S. Ct. Appeals (D.C. cir.) 1976, U.S. Ct. Appeals (3d cir.) 1983, U.S. Ct. Appeals (Fed. cir.) 1985. Assoc. Fulbright & Jaworski, Washington, 1976-84, ptnr., 1984-87; legal cons. IMF, Washington, 1987—. Contbr. articles to profl. jours. Mem. ABA, D.C. Bar Assn., Phi Beta Kappa. Jewish. Office: Internat Monetary Fund 700 19th St NW Washington DC 20431-0001

REBAGAY, TEOFILA VELASCO, chemist, chemical engineer; b. Pangasinan, Philippines, Feb. 5, 1928; came to U.S., 1965; d. Dionisio Opiniano and Antonia (Flora) Velasco; m. Guillermo Rabadam Rebagay, Apr. 4, 1956; children: Guillermo V., Teofilo V. BS in Chemistry, U. Philippines, Quezon City, 1951; BS in Chem. Engring., Nat. U., Manila, 1954; PhD in Chemistry, U. Ky., 1969. Postdoctoral fellow U. Ky., Lexington, 1969-71, U. Va., Charlottesville, 1971-72; rsch. assoc. U. Ky., Lexington, 1973-76; sr. chemist Ky. Ctr. Energy Rsch., Lexington, 1976-78; radiochemist Allied-Gen. Nuclear Svcs., Barnwell, S.C., 1978-83; sr. chemist Rockwell Hanford Ops., Richland, Wash., 1983-87; prin. scientist Westinghouse Hanford Co., Richland, 1987—. Contbr. articles to profl. publs. IAEA fellow UN, Tokyo, 1963; grantee Rockefeller Found., 1965. Mem. ASTM, Soc. Applied Spectroscopy. Office: Westinghouse Hanford Co Richland WA 99352

REBBER, RUTH ANN, fundraiser, non-profit agency administrator; b. Seymour, Ind., Dec. 28, 1946; d. Gayle F. and Joyce (Glasson) Marley; m. James W. Rebber, Aug. 12, 1967; children: J. Andrew, David M., Rebecca A. BS, Ind. State U., Terre Haute, 1969; MS, Ind. U., 1978. Exec. dir. Jackson County United Fund, Seymour, 1980—. Sec., Seymour Area Day Care, 1993-94; sec. Jackson County Day Care Network, Inc., 1993-95; mem. Leadership Jackson County. Office: Jackson County United Fund 121 N Chestnut St Seymour IN 47274-2101

REBELSKY, FREDA ETHEL GOULD, psychologist; b. N.Y.C., Mar. 11, 1931; d. William and Sarah (Kaplan) Gould; BA, U. Chgo., 1950, MA, 1954; PhD, Radcliffe Coll., 1961; m. William Rebelsky, Jan. 1, 1956 (dec. 1979); 1 son, Samuel; m. Nicholas Camp, Aug. 14, 1988 (div. Oct. 1993). Counselor, U. Chgo. Orthogenic Sch., 1952-55; research asst. Kenyon & Eckhart, Inc., 1956-58; research asst. lab. human devel. Harvard U., 1959-60, teaching asst. psychology, then instr. edn., 1960-61; research asso. Speech research lab. Children's Hosp., Boston, 1960-61, M.I.T., 1961-62; mem. faculty Boston U., 1962—, prof. psychology, 1972—, dir. doctoral program in devel. psychology, 1969-74; vis. lectr. U. Utrecht (Netherlands), 1965-67; Froman prof. Russell Sage Coll., Troy, N.Y., 1972. Grantee U.S. Office Edn., 1964-65, Boston U. Grad. Sch., 1967-70, OEO, 1967-69. NIMH, 1974-76; Bunting fellow Radcliffe Coll., 1985-86; recipient Distinguished Tchr. Psychology award Am. Psychol. Found., 1970; Harbison award excellence teaching Danforth Found., 1971; Metcalf award Boston U., 1978; Disting. Career in Psychology award Mass. Psychol. Assn., 1982; Community Svc. award Boston U. Faculty, 1993. Mem. AAAS, Soc. Research Child Devel. (sec. Boston 1963-65), AAUP (sec. Boston U. 1964-65, pres. 1984-85, 86-88, 91—), Am., Eastern, Mass. (chmn. program com. 1962-64) Psychol. Assns., Sigma Xi, Psi Chi. Author: Child Behavior and Development: A Reader, 1969; Child Behavior and Development, 2d edit., 1973: Life: The Continuous Process, 1975; Growing Children, 1976. Address: 1 Billings Park Newton MA 02158 Office: 64 Cummington St Boston MA 02215-2407

REBER, CHERYL ANN, social worker; b. Cin., Feb. 7, 1956; d. Randland John and Marcella Catherine (Hollstegge) R. AA, Xavier U., 1976, BA, 1980. Lic. social worker. Social worker Altercrest, Cin., 1977-79; social worker Hamilton County Dept. Human Svcs., Cin., 1979-85, adoption specialist, social worker, 1985-92; social worker, AIDS specialist Hospice of the Miami Valley, 1992—; trainer, program developer Hamilton County Dept. Human Svcs., Cin., 1988-92. Mem. Community Task Force on Adoption, Cin., 1989-91. Mem. S.W. Ohio Adoption Resource Exch. (pres. 1990-91, treas. 1991-92), Beechmont Players, Inc. (v.p. 1982-86, pres. 1990-92). Democrat. Roman Catholic.

REBOY, DIANE L., medical/surgical and community health nurse; b. Buffalo, Apr. 24, 1953; d. Herbert R. and Mary E. (Mallon) Osterman; m. Louis R. Reboy Jr., May 17, 1975; children: Louis R. III, Mark William. BSN, D'Youville Coll., Buffalo, 1976; cert. in mid. mgmt., SUNY at Buffalo, 1992. Cert. in acute care nursing. CCU staff nurse Buffalo Gen. Hosp.; critical care staff nurse Sheehan Emergency Hosp., Buffalo, per diem staff nurse; patient care coord. Vis. Nurse Assn. Western N.Y., Depew; RN Staff Builders, Niagara Falls, N.Y.; asst. DON Williamsville (N.Y.) View Manor; supr. community health nurse, Episcopal Gen. Home Care, Buffalo. Mem. Community Blue Advisory Group.

RECCHIA, SUSAN MARGARET, artist, author; b. Hyde Park, N.Y., July 11, 1955; d. Gerard and Grace (Spaulding) R. Sculptress Blackbird Mold Co., Trenton, N.J., 1976; portrait artist Great Adventure Park, Trenton, N.J., 1976; photographer/bus. cons. Olan Mills, Inc., various locations, 1977-79; photographer I.B.M., Fishkill, N.Y., 1982; art tchr. Hyde Park (N.Y.) Sch. Dist., 1983-86, Dutchess County Sr. Citizens of United Way, Poughkeepsie, N.Y., 1992—; dir. Masque Gallery, Hyde Park, 1992—; creator Masque Gallery of Entertainers; works included with the Libr. of Congress, Washington, Fla., Dutchess County Arts Coun. Ref. File, Poughkeepsie, N.Y. Portrait artist, Kaydeross Park, Saratoga, N.Y., 1983; muralist, scenic designer Bardavon Theatre, Poughkeepsie, 1977, Children's Community Theatre, 1985, Dutchess Tourism, Dutchess County Fair, Rhineback, N.Y., 1993; one woman exhbn. Northbound Ent., 1980-87; exhbn. artist Fasia Tipton Yearling Sales, 1980-82; author: Our Western Worlds Greatest Poems, 1983, Who's Who in Poetry, 1986, Bible Series, from the Book of Revelation, Endangered Wildlife, 1976—, The Fantasy Collection, 1974—, Bicentennial Tribute, 1976, others; cover artist Albany Dist Directory, 1994. Recipient Freddy award for sculpture, Mid-Hudson Ceramic League of N.Y., 1974, Peggy award for best of show, 1975, Golden Poet award World of Poetry, Calif., 1982, Silver Poet award, 1983, Grand Marshall award Town of Hyde Park, N.Y., 1986. Mem. Hyde Park C. of C., Dutchess County Arts Coun., Nat. Mus. of Women in the Arts. Roman Catholic. Office: Masque Gallery 9350 Yellow Lake Dr New Port Richey FL 34654-4236

RECHTSCHAFFEN, JOYCE A., legislative staff member, lawyer; b. Bklyn., Jan. 21, 1955; d. Bernard and Florence Rechtschaffen. AB, Princeton U., 1975; JD, Harvard U., 1978. Bar: D.C. 1978. Atty. Fried, Frank, Harris, Shriver & Jacobson, 1978-83; sr. atty. environ. enforcement sect. land and natural resources divsn. Dept. of Justice, 1983-89; legis. asst., counsel to Senator Joseph I. Lieberman, counsel state com. on environment and pub. works, 1989—. Mem. Phi Beta Kappa. Office: Environ & Pub Works 505 Senate Hart Office Bldg Washington DC 20510*

RECHTZIGEL, SUE MARIE (SUZANNE RECHTZIGEL), child care center executive; b. St. Paul, May 27, 1947; d. Carl Stinson and Muriel Agnes (Oestrich) Miller; m. Gary Elmer Rechtzigel, Aug. 20, 1968 (div. Feb. 1982); children: Brian Carl, Lori Ann. BA in Psychology, Sociology, Mankato (Minn.) State U., 1969. Lic. in child care, Minn. Rep. ins. State Farm Ins. Co., Albert Lea, Minn., 1969-73; free-lance child caretaker Albert Lea, Minn., 1973-78; owner, dir. Lakeside Day Care, Albert Lea, Minn., 1983—; asst. Hawthorne Sch. Learning Ctr., Albert Lea, 1978-83. Mem. New Residents and Newcomers Orgn., Albert Lea, 1970—, past. pres.; asst. pre-sch. United Meth. Ch., Albert Lea, 1975-78, tchr. Sunday sch., 1976-80, tchr. Bible sch., 1980-85; active Ascension Luth. Ch., 1976-80. Mem. Freeborn Lic. Day Care Assn. (v.p. 1986, pres. 1987), AAUW (home tour 1977, treas. 1980-81), Bus. and Profl. Women, YMCA, Albert Lea Art Ctr. Republican. Club: 3M Families. Home and Office: 1919 Brookside Dr Albert Lea MN 56007-2142

RECKITT, LOIS GALGAY, social welfare administrator; b. Cambridge, Mass., Dec. 31, 1944; d. George Alphonsus and Marjorie Lois (Wright) G. BA, Brandeis Univ., 1966; MA, Boston U., 1968. Exec. dir. Family Crisis Shelter, Portland, Maine, 1979-84, 90—; exec. v.p. NOW, Washington, 1984-87; dep. dir. Human Rights Campaign Fund, Washington, 1987-88; presenter workshops in field. Co-founder Maine NOW, 1973, Maine Right to Choose, 1975, Maine Coalition for Human Rights, 1976; co-founder, bd. dirs. Maine Women's Lobby, 1979-83; mem. Portland's Task Force on the Homeless, 1983-84; bd. dirs. Southern Regional Alcohol and Drug Abuse Coun., 1982-84; chair Maine Coalition for Family Crisis Svcs., 1982-83; sec. Maine Coalition for the Homeless, 1990-91; legis. chair Maine Coalition for Family Crisis Svcs., 1990-91; mem. Maine Commn. on Domestic Abuse, 1990—, chair, 1994—. Named Woman of Yr. Maine Commn. for Women, 1991. Mem. NOW (nat. com. to end violence against women, chair com. on pornography, 1990-92, lesbian rights com. 1988-92, coord. nat. resource kit on violence against women 1986-87, N.E. regional dir. 1976-84, nat. bd. dirs. 1994—), Matlovich Soc., Nat. Coalition of Domestic Violence (Maine rep. to nat. steering com. 1983-84). Office: Family Crisis Shelter PO Box 704 Portland ME 04104

RECKLEIN, LINDA SUE, library administrator; b. St. Louis, Feb. 19; d. Clifford H. and Billie M. (Bader) Lincks; m. Dan S. Recklein, Sept. 4 1993; 1 stepchild, Allison Faith. BA in Psychology cum laude, U. Mo., St. Louis, 1972; MLS, U. Mo., 1977. Supr., para-profl. St. Louis County Libr., 1972-80; mgr. info. ctr., info. specialist Ralston Purina Co., St. Louis, 1980—; mem. bus. adv. bd. cons. group Gale Rsch., Detroit, 1990—. Distbr. campaign lit. for Dem. and Rep. parties; vol. phone support at campaign hdqs.; vol. solicitor ARC Corp. Asscs. Ann. Fund, 1994. Recipient Cert. of Leadership, YWCA, 1991; named Outstanding Young Woman of Am., 1981. Mem. NAFE, AAUW, Soc. Competitive Intelligence Profls., Spl. Librs. Assn. (chpt. bd. dirs. 1983-84), Women in Bus. NEtwork (treas. 1982-83), Am. Mgmt. Assn. Roman Catholic. Home: 637 Laven Del Ln Saint Louis MO 63122-1115 Office: Ralston Purina Co Checkerboard Sq Saint Louis MO 63164

RECTOR, MARGARET HAYDEN, writer; b. Azusa, Calif., May 23, 1916; d. Floyd Smith and Anna Martha (Miller) Hayden; m. Robert Wayman Rector, Aug. 25, 1940; children: Cleone Rector Grabowski Black, Robin Rector Krupp, Bruce Hayden. AA, Citrus Jr. Coll., 1936; BA, Pomona Coll., 1938; postgrad., Stanford U., 1938-40, Columbia U., 1942-46, St. John's Coll., Annapolis, Md., 1946-56, U. So. Calif., 1959-65, UCLA, 1959-66. Mem. advt. staff Curt Wagner, Redondo Beach, Calif., 1957-67; writer Am. Home Mag., N.Y.C., 1942-46, House Beautiful Mag., N.Y.C., 1942-46; author children's books Grossmont Press, San Diego, 1974-76. Author: Norton and Gus, 1976; Alva, That Vanderbilt-Belmont Woman, 1992; editor: History of Citrus, 1994; playwright, screenwriter. Dem. organizer, Annapolis, Md., 1946-56; mem. UCLA affiliates; bd. dirs. Friends of Rsch. Libr. Mem. AAUW (life), PEN, Women in Film, Women in Theatre, UCLA Faculty Wives Writers Group, Surfwriters Palos Verdes Peninsula, First Stage, The Audrey Skirball-Kenis Theatre, Dramatists Guild, Authors Guild, Womens Internat. Ctr. in San Diego, Pomona Coll. Alumni, Stanford U. Alumni. Home: 10700 Stradella Ct Los Angeles CA 90077-2604

REDD, J. DIANE, professional fund raiser and grants management executive; b. Beckley, W.Va., Apr. 10, 1945; d. Robert Fountain and Lillian (Fitts) Redd. B.S., W.Va. State Coll., 1967. Instr. bus. subjects Paterson (N.J.) Bus. Edn., 1967-68; with U. Medicine and Dentistry N.J., Newark, 1968-89, adminstrv. asst. research and sponsored programs, 1968-73, asst. dir. health edn., 1973-76, sr. devel. officer, 1976-79, asst. dir. devel., 1979-83, chief devel. and alumni affairs, 1983-89; dir. devel. Planned Parenthood Fedn. Am., Inc, N.Y.C., 1989—. Mem. priorities com., devel. com. United Way of Essex and West Hudson, Newark, 1983-85; chmn. human resources com. Community Adv. Bd., U. Medicine and Dentistry N.J., Newark, 1978-82; mem. rsch. bd. advisors Am. Biographical Inst., 1992—. Recipient Recognition of Achievement award Young Women of America, Inc., Montgomery, Ala., 1979, Black Achiever award YMWCA, 1986. Mem. Council Advancement and Support of Edn., Nat. Soc. Fund Raising Execs. Inc. (cert., trustee, v.p., parliamentarian, sec.), Assn. Am. Med. Colls., Exec. Women N.J. (trustee, chmn. scholarship com.), Women in Fin. Devel., Consortium of Devel. and Alumni Profls. of Greater N.Y. Democrat. Office: Planned Parenthood Fedn of Am 810 7th Ave New York NY 10019-5818

REDENBACH, SANDRA IRENE, educational consultant; b. Boston, Nov. 18, 1940; d. David and Celia (Wish) Goldstein; m. Gunter L. Redenbach, Mar. 16, 1963 (div. 1980); 1 child, Cori-Lin; m. Kenneth L. Gelatt, June 25, 1989. BA, U. Calif., Davis, 1972; postgrad. in Ednl. Leadership, St. Mary's Coll., Moraga, Calif., 1988, 93-95. Cert. tchr., Calif. Tchr. Solano County Juvenile Hall, Fairfield, Calif., 1968-70, St. Basil's Sch., Vallejo, Calif., 1970-73, St. Philomenes Sch., Sacramento, 1973; tchr., assoc. dean Vet.'s Spl. Edn. Program, U. Calif., Davis, 1973-75, Woodland (Calif.) Jr. High Sch., 1973-76, Lee Jr. High Sch., Woodland, 1976-79, Woodland High Sch., 1979-89; founder, coord., tchr. Ind. Learning Ctr., Woodland, 1989-94; dir. instrn. Dixon Unified Sch. Dist., 1994—; teaching asst., lectr. U. Calif., Davis, 1985-86; pres., cons. Esteem Seminar Programs and Pubs., Davis, 1983—; cons., leader workshop. Author: Self-Esteem: The Necessary Ingredient for Success, 1991; author tng. manual: Self-Esteem: A Training Manual, 1990-91, Innovative Discipline: Managing Your Own Flight Plan. Active Dem. Club of Davis, 1976-79; human rights chair Capitol Svc. Ctr., Sacramento, 1987-92. Martin Luther King scholar, 1986; Nat. Found. for Improvement of Edn. grantee, 1987-88. Mem. ACSA, Woodland Edn. Assn. (pres. 1980-83, Outstanding Educator 1992, 93), Phi Delta Kappa (pres. 1992-93). Jewish. Home: 313 Del Oro Ave Davis CA 95616-0416 Office: Esteem Seminar Programs & Publs 313 Del Oro Ave Davis CA 95616-0416

REDGRAVE, LYNN, actress; b. London, Eng., Mar. 8, 1943; d. Michael Scudemore and Rachel (Kempson) R.; m. John Clark, Apr. 2, 1967; children: Benjamin, Kelly, Annabel. Ed., Queensgate Sch., London, Central Sch. Speech and Drama, London. Stage debut as Helena in Midsummer Night's Dream, 1962; theatrical appearances include The Tulip Tree, Andorra, Hayfever, Much Ado About Nothing, Mother Courage, Love for Love, Zoo, Zoo, Widdershins Zoo, Edinburgh Festival, 1969, The Two of Us, London, 1970, Slag, London, 1971, A Better Place, Dublin, 1972, Born Yesterday, Greenwich, 1973, Hellzapoppin, N.Y., 1976, California Suite, 1977, Twelfth Night, Stratford Conn. Shakespeare Festival, 1978, The King and I, St. Louis, 1983, Les Liaisons Dangereuses, L.A., 1989, The Cherry Orchard, L.A., 1990, Three Sisters, London, 1990; Broadway appearances include Black Comedy, 1967, My Fat Friend, 1974, Mrs. Warren's Profession (Tony award nomination), 1975, Knock, Knock, 1976, St. Joan, 1977, Sister Mary Ignatius Explains It All, 1985, Aren't We All?, 1985, Sweet Sue, 1987, A Little Hotel on the Side, 1992, The Masterbuilder, 1992, Shakespeare For My Father (Tony and Drama Desk nominations, Elliot award 1993), 1993, also nat. tour, 1993; film appearances include Tom Jones, Girl With Green Eyes, Georgy Girl (Recipient N.Y. Film Critics award, Golden Globe award, Oscar nomination for best actress 1967), The Deadly Affair, Smashing Time, The Virgin Soldiers, Last of the Mobile Hotshots, Don't Turn the Other Cheek, Every Little Crook and Nanny, Everything You Always Wanted to Know About Sex, The National Health, The Happy Hooker, The Big Bus, Sunday Lovers, Morgan Stuart's Coming Home, Getting It Right; TV appearances include: The Turn of the Screw, Centennial, 1978, The Muppets, Gauguin the Savage, Beggarman Thief, The Seduction of Miss Leona, Rehearsal for Murder, 1982, Walking On Air, The Fainthearted Feminist (BBC-TV), 1984, My Two Loves, 1986, The Old Reliable, 1988, Jury Duty 1989, Whatever Happened to Baby Jane, 1990, Fighting Back (BBC-TV), 1992, Calling the Shots (Masterpiece Theatre), 1993; guest appearances include Carol Burnett Show, Evening at the Improv and Steve Martin's Best show Ever, Circus of the Stars; co-host nat. TV syndication Not for Women Only, 1977—; nat., TV spokesperson Weightwatchers, 1984-92; TV series include House Calls, 1981, Teachers Only, 1982, Chicken Soup, 1989; albums: Make Mine Manhattan, 1978, Cole Porter Revisited, 1979; video: (for children) Meet Your Animal Friends, Off We Go, Off We Go Again: audio book readings include, Pride and Prejudice, The Shell Seekers, The Blue Bedroom, The Anastasia Syndrome, The Women in His Life, Snow In April, Gone With The Wind, 1994; author: This is Living, 1990. Named Runner-up Actress, All Am. Favorites, Box Office Barometer 1975; recipient Sarah Siddons award as Chgo.'s best stage actress of 1976, 94. Mem. The Players (pres. 1994). Office: care John Clark PO Box 1207 Topanga CA 90290-1207

REDGRAVE, VANESSA, actress; b. London, Jan. 30, 1937; d. Michael and Rachel (Kempson) R.; m. Tony Richardson, Apr. 28, 1962 (div.); children: Natasha Jane, Joely Kim, Carlo. Student, Central Sch. Speech and Drama, London, 1955-57. Prin. theatrical roles include Helena in Midsummer Night's Dream, 1959, Stella in Tiger and the Horse, 1960, Katerina in The Taming of the Shrew, 1961, Rosalind in As You Like It, 1961, Imogene in Cymbeline, 1962, Nina in The Seagull, 1964, Miss Brodie in The Prime of Miss Jean Brodie, 1966; other plays include Cato Street, 1971, Threepenny Opera, 1972, Twelfth Night, 1972, Antony and Cleopatra, 1973, Design for Living, 1973, Macbeth, 1975, Lady from the Sea, 1976, 78, 79, The Aspern Papers, 1984, The Seagull, 1985, Chekhov's Women, 1985, The Taming of the Shrew, Ghosts, 1986, Touch of the Poet, 1988, Orpheus Descending, 1989, A Madhouse in Goa, 1989, Three Sisters, 1990, When She Danced, 1991, Heartbreak House, 1991, Maybe, 1993, Brecht in Hollywood, 1994, Vita and Virginia, 1994—; film roles include Leonie in Morgan-A Suitable Case for Treatment, 1965 (Best Actress award Cannes Film Festival 1966), Sheila in Sailor from Gibraltar, 1965, Anne-Marie in La Musica, 1965, Jane in Blow-Up, 1967, Guinevere in Camelot, 1967, Isadora in Isadora Duncan, 1968 (Best Actress award Cannes Film Festival); other films include The Charge of the Light Brigade, 1968, The Seagull, 1968, A Quiet Place in the Country, 1968, Daniel Deronda, 1969, Dropout, 1969, The Trojan Women, 1970, The Devils, 1970, The Holiday, 1971, Mary, Queen of Scots, 1971, Murder on the Orient Express, 1974, Winter Rates, 1974, 7 per cent solution, 1975, Julia, 1977 (Academy award Best Supporting Actress, Golden Globe award), Agatha, 1978, Yanks, 1978, Bear Island, 1979, Playing for Time, 1980, My Body My Child, 1981, Wagner, 1982, The Bostonians, 1984 (Oscar nomination Best Actress, Golden Globe nomination), Wetherby, 1985, Steaming, 1985, Prick Up Your Ears, 1987, Comrades, 1987, Consuming Passions, 1988, Diceria dell'Untore, 1989, The Ballad of the Sad Café, 1990, Howard's End, 1992 (Oscar nomination Best Supporting Actress), Great Moments in Aviation, 1993, Crime and Punishment, 1993, The House of the Spirits, 1994, Mother's Boys, 1994, A Month by the Lake, 1994; TV film and miniseries appearances include Snow White and the Seven Dwarfs, 1985, Three Sovereigns for Sarah, 1985, Peter the Great, 1986, Second Serve, 1986 (Emmy award, Golden Globe award), A Man for All Seasons, 1988, Young Catherine, 1990, Whatever Happened to Baby Jane, 1991, Playing for Time (Emmy award), The Wall, 1992, Down Came A Blackbird, 1994; Author: Pussies and Tigers, 1964, (autobiography) Vanessa, 1991, Vanessa Redgrave: An Autobiography, 1994. Bd. govs. Central Sch. Speech and Drama, 1963—. Decorated comdr. Order Brit. Empire; recipient 4 times Drama award Evening Standard, 1961-91, Best Actress award Variety Club Gt. Brit., 1961, 66, Best Actress award Brit. Guild TV Producers and Dirs., 1966, Laurence Olivier award Best Actress for The Aspern Papers, 1984, London Standard Drama award Best Actress for The Seagull, 1985, New York Film Critics Circle award Best Supporting Actress for Prick Up Your Ears, 1988, Evening Standard award Best Actress for When She Danced, 1991, Ace award Best Supporting Actress movie/mini-series for Young Catherine, 1992, Variety Club of Great Britain award, 1992, Best Actress Nat. Film Critics (USA) New Delhi Internat. Film Festival for The Bostonians, Laurence Olivier award Actress of the Yr. in a Revival for A Touch of the Poet; fellow Brit. Film Inst., 1988.

REDICK, EVA JANE, piano educator; b. Grand Island, Nebr., Jan. 14, 1901; d. Hans Peter and Blanche (Crocker) Johnson; divorced; 1 child, Victoria. Student, U. Wash., 1918-19, U. So. Calif., 1932, 37, UCLA, 1939; studied with T. Bennett, 1933-37. Pvt. tchr. piano L.A. and Beverly Hills, Calif., 1927-89; ret., 1989; mem. faculty Sherwood Sch. Music, Chgo., 1954-89. Author: Eva Redick Piano Improvising Book I, 1962, Book II, 1982, Piano Playtime; patentee piano practice glove; recitalist Bel Air Hotel, Beverly Hills, 1961-89. Eva Redick Day proclaimed City of Beverly Hills, 1988; recipient Cert. of Appreciation Commendation L.A. County, 1988. Mem. Nat. Music Tchrs. Assn., Nat. Guild Piano Tchrs., Music Tchrs. Assn. Calif. (pres. West Los Angeles County br. 1960-62). Republican. Home and Office: 9933 Young Dr Beverly Hills CA 90212-3611

REDLER, SHERRY PRESS, audiologist; b. N.Y.C.; d. Martin M. and Elsie (Opin) Press; B.A., Adelphi U., 1954; M.S., So. Conn. State Coll., 1971, postgrad., 1976-79; children—Michael, Steven, Lynda. Speech pathologist Roslyn (N.Y.) Public Schs., 1954-56; tchr. drama Rollins Coll., Winter Park, Fla., 1961-63; personnel counselor Internat. Bus. Assn., Pitts., 1965; speech pathologist Fairfield (Conn.) Public Schs., 1968-75, ednl. audiologist, 1977-92; clin. audiologist Rehab. Center, Bridgeport, Conn., 1975-76, supr. audiology, 1992-94, dir. audiology, 1994—; sign lang. instr. Bridgeport Rehab. Center, 1976-78, Staples High Sch., Westport, Conn.; instr. So. Conn. State Coll., New Haven, 1976—; lectr., cons. in field; ind. evaluator of programs for hearing impaired; author, project dir. Title IV Fed. Grant, Conn., 1976-80; mem. Conn. State Task Force to assess services provided to mentally retarded, 1981—; author, project dir. sch. audiology program, Conn., 1981. Trustee Congregation B'Nai Israel, 1985—, chmn. older adult com., music com.; mem. com. to revise hearing screening guidelines, Conn., 1987, State Conn. com. to establish guidelines for services to hearing impaired children, 1988—; mem. commn. on community rels., urban issues com., 1989—; mem. commn. on the elderly; mem. Dem. Town Com. Town of Fairfield, 1992—. Mem. Am. Acad. Audiology, Conn. Speech and Hearing Assn. (co-chmn. com. on edn. hearing impaired 1976—), NEA, Conn. Edn. Assn., Fairfield Edn. Assn., Am. Speech and Hearing Assn. (legis. counsellor 1994), Am. Ednl. Audiology Assn. (1st v.p. 1986—, pres. 1987-88), Conn. Audiology Assn. (v.p. 1991). Home: 28 Lockwood Cir Fairfield CT 06432-2645 Office: 60 Thompson St Fairfield CT 06432-4349

REDMOND, PATRICIA, radiologist, educator; b. N.Y.C., May 10, 1946; d. William Patrick and Mary (Boland) R.; m. Leonard Berliner, Aug. 13, 1982; children: Alanna, Ryan. BA cum laude, Fordham U., 1968; student, SUNY, Bklyn., 1968-70; MD, NYU, 1972. Diplomate Am. Bd. Radiology. Resident diagnostic radiology NYU-Bellevue Med. Ctr., 1972-76, fellow in abdominal imaging, 1976; asst. attending in radiology NYU Med. Ctr. and Bellevue Hosp., N.Y.C., 1976-81; chief gastrointestinal radiology NYU Hosp., N.Y.C., 1977-81; attending radiologist, asst. dir. radiology S.I. (N.Y.) Hosp., 1981-84, dir. radiology, 1984—; pres. Seaview Radiology, 1987—, S.I. Radiol. Assocs., P.C., 1985—; pvt. practice, S.I., 1985—; instr. NYU Med. Ctr., 1976-77, asst. prof., 1977-81, clin. asst. prof., 1981—; med. dir. The Women's Health Exch., S.I. U. Hosp., 1992—; presenter in field. Contbr. articles to med. jours. Mem. N.Y. Med. Polit. Action Com., Albany, 1985—; advisor, mem. sci. coun. S.I. chpt. Nat. Found. for Ileitis and Colitis. Mem. AMA, Am. Med. Women's Assn., Radiol. Soc. N.Am., Am. Profl. Practice Assn., Am. Assn. Women Radiologists, Am. Coll. Phys. Execs., Women's Med. Assn. N.Y.C., N.Y. C. of C., N.Y. Postgrad. and Univ. Hosp. Alumni Assn., Bellevue Hosp. Alumni Assn., NAFE, Phi Beta Kappa. Office: SI U Hosp 475 Seaview Ave Staten Island NY 10305-3498

REDO, MARIA ELAINE, gerontologist, educator; b. N.Y.C., Jan. 12, 1925; d. Ernest and Mary C. Lappano; B.S. in Edn., Fordham U., 1945; cert. in gerontology, Brookdale Sch. Social Sci., 1979; m. S. Frank Redo, June 27, 1948; children—Philip L., Martha Maria. Tchr. pvt. sch., N.Y.C., 1946-56; dir. Child Service League, Queens, N.Y., 1949-57; founder, dir. Community Concern for Sr. Citizens, Inc., N.Y.C. Dept. for the Aging, 1971-85; dir. N.Y.C. Silver Pages Directory, Silver Savers' Passport. Bd. dirs. Escort Service of Yorkville (N.Y.), 1977—, Sr. Citizen Outreach Program for Elderly, N.Y.C., 1970—; mem. Community Planning Bd., N.Y.C., 1970-77; del. Nat. Republican Conv., N.Y.C., 1976, N.Y. State White House Conf. on Aging, 1981, Nat. White House Conf. on Aging, N.Y.C., 1981; del. N.Y. State Conf. on Mid-Life and Older Women, 1983. Recipient Mayor's Cert. of Appreciation N.Y.C., 1975; Hon. Sec. of State of Mont., 1975; Franny award WPIX-TV, 1974. Mem. LWV, Roman Catholic. Club: Met. Rep. (pres. 1975-77). Contbr. tng. manuals, brochures for dept. on aging., 1973-85. Home: 435 E 70th St New York NY 10021-5342 Office: 91 Fifth Ave 5th fl New York NY 10003

REDRUELLO, ROSA INCHAUSTEGUI, municipal department executive; b. Havana, Cuba, Dec. 6, 1951; came to U.S., 1961, naturalized, 1971; d. Julio Lorenzo and Laudelina (Vazquez) Inchaustegui; m. John Robert Redruello, Dec. 14, 1972; 1 child, Michelle. AA, Miami-Dade Community Coll., 1972; BS, Fla. Internat. U., 1974. Cert. systems profl. With Fla. Power & Light Co., Miami, 1975-81, records analyst, 1981-84, sr. records analyst, 1984-87, office mgr. Miami Beach Sanitation Dept., 1987—; exec. Mcpl. Dept., 1986-89; police officer patrol divsn. Miami Police Dept., 1989-91, narcotics divsn., 1991—; mem. spl. task force Drug Enforcement Adminstrn. HDTA Group 1, 1994-95; cons. United Bus. Records, Miami, 1985—. Editor South Fla. Record newsletter, 1983-86; editor, producer Files Mgmt. video tape, 1984-85. Rotary Club scholar, 1970. Mem. Assn. Records Mgrs. and Adminstrs. (chpt. chmn. bd. 1985—, chpt. mem. of yr. 1985), Assn. for Info. and Image Mgmt., Exec. Female, Nuclear Info. and Records Mgmt. Assn. (Appreciation award 1985). Republican. Roman Catholic. Avocations: swimming, jazzercise, reading. Office: Miami Beach Police Dept 1100 Washington Ave Miami FL 33139-4665

REDSTON-ISELIN, AUDREY, child psychiatric clinical specialist; b. N.Y.C., Apr. 29, 1948; d. Robert Donald and Leona (Bell) Redston; m. David Robert Iselin, May 28, 1978; children: Joshua, Alexander. BS, Boston U., 1970; MA, NYU, 1973. RN, N.Y., Mass. Nurses aide, LPN L.I. Jewish Hosp., Glen Oaks, N.Y., 1968, 69; staff, charge nurse in-patient psychiat. unit Mass. Mental Health Ctr., Brookline, 1970; gen. med.-surg. staff nurse N.Y. Hosp.-Cornell Med. Ctr., N.Y.C., 1970-71, 1971-73; child psychiat. nurse clin. specialist Developmental Evaluation Clin, Kings County Hosp., 1973; child psychiat. nurse therapist Sound View Throgs Neck CMHC Albert Einstein Coll. Medicine, Bronx, N.Y., 1974—; instr. div. continuing edn. N.Y.C. C.C., Bklyn., 1974-77; pvt. practice child, adolescent, adult and family psychotherapy, 1975—. Author: (with others) Principles & Practice of Psychiatric Nursing, 1979, 5th edit., 1994. Mem. ANA (cert. clin. specialist in child and adolescent psychiat. and mental health nursing), Assn. Child and Adolescent Psychiat. Nurses, Coun. Specialists in Psychiat./Mental Health Nursing, Network N.Y. Clin. Specialists in Psychiat. Mental Health Nursing. Home: 6 Vermont Ave White Plains NY 10606-3508 Office: Soundview Throgs Neck CMHC 2527 Glebe Ave Bronx NY 10461-3109 also: 90 Bryant Ave White Plains NY 10605

REEB, SUE ELLEN, biochemist; b. Balt., Feb. 7, 1959; d. Thomas John and Catherine Jacqueline (Insley) R.; m. George Wesley Lee, Jr., July 16, 1976 (div. Nov. 1985). AA summa cum laude, Catonsville C.C., Balt., 1987; BS, Towson State U., 1993. Area supr. Pizza Hut of Md., Inc., Balt., 1979-81; regional mgr. Godfathers Pizza, Inc., Omaha, Nebr., 1981-83; credit analyst Citicorp Fin. Inc., Towson, Md., 1983-84; fine wine cons. Kronheim Co., Inc., Balt., 1984-86; asst. sch. adminstr. O'Conor, Piper & Flynn, Inc., Timonium, Md., 1986-88; analyt. chemist Analyte Labs., Balt., 1988-89; rsch. chemist E.I. DuPont de Nemours & Co., Inc., Newark, Del., 1989; rsch. biochemist Martek Bioscis., Inc., Columbia, Md., 1989-94; biochem. engr. Cephalon, Inc., Beltsville, Md., 1993-94; rsch. scientist Human Genome Scis., Inc., Rockville, Md., 1994—. Author: (with others) Lipids, 1992; contbr. articles to profl. jours.; patentee in field. Md. Indsl. Partnership grantee, 1990-92. Mem. Am. Oil Chemists Soc., Am. Diabetes Assn., Soc. Indsl. Microbiologists, Walters Art Gallery, Towson State Alumni Assn., Sierra Club, Upsilon Eta.

REECE, BETH PAULEY, commodities broker; b. Warsaw, Ind., June 4, 1945; d. Lester Elden and Genevene (Walter) Pifer; m. Gyle Barry Reece, June 20, 1987. BA, Grace Coll., 1967; student, Harrington Inst. Design, Chgo., 1993—. Grain trader, hedger Cen. Soya Inc., Ft. Wayne, Ind., 1973-82; account exec. ACLI Internat. Inc., Chgo., 1982-83; account exec., hedger Cen. States Enterprises, Ft.Wayne, 1983-84; account exec. Stotler & Co., Chgo., 1984-89, LaSalle Brokerage Inc., Chgo., 1989—. Mem. Nat. Futures Assn., Art Inst. of Chgo., Met. Club. Republican. Presbyterian. Home: 227 E Delaware Pl Apt 5C Chicago IL 60611-1743 Office: LaSalle Div Refco 200 W Adams St Bldg 1500 Chicago IL 60606-5227

REECE, GERALDINE MAXINE, elementary education educator; b. L.A., May 13, 1917; d. Charles Kenneth and Bertha (Austin) Ballou; m. Thomas Charles Bauman, Aug. 16, 1942 (div. Oct. 1971); children: Thomas Charles Bauman, Jr., Kathleen Marie Bauman Messenger, Stephen Kenneth Bauman; m. Wilbert Wallingford Reece, Nov. 3, 1973 (dec. 1988). AA, L.A. City Coll., 1942; BA, U. So. Calif., L.A., 1966. Specialist tchr. in reading, elem. edn. Tchr. Archdiocese of L.A., Altadena, Calif., 1962-66; master tchr. Alhambra (Calif.) City and High Sch., 1966-79, writer multicultural component early childhood edn. program. Author poetry. Mem. San Gabriel Child Care Task Force, 1984-86; mem. steering com. West San Gabriel Valley Cmty. Awareness Forum, 1985-87; past pres. Women's Divsn. San Gabriel (Calif.) C. of C., 1989-90, bd. dirs. 1989-90; mem. sch. site and facilities com. Sch. Dist. Unification, San Gabriel, 1992-93; task force mem. Episcopal Parish/Healing Our Cities, San Gabriel, 1992-93. Recipient Exceptional Svc. awards Am. Heart Assn., West San Gabriel Valley, 1990, 91, 93, 94, Dedicated Svc. award San Gabriel C. of C., 1989, Outstanding and Dedicated Cmty. Svc. award Fedn. Cmty. Coord. Couns., San Gabriel, 1986, 87, others, Women of Yr. award City of San Gabriel, 1994. Mem. Calif. Retired Tchrs. Assn. (past pres. 1989-91, Outstanding Svc. plaque 1994), AAUW (Money Talks sect. chair 1981, 82, corr. sec./treas. Alhambra-San Gabriel 1983-85, 82-83), Nat. Soc. DAR (3rd vice-regent 1994), Pasadena Women's City Club, St. Francis Guild, San Gabriel Retired Tchrs. (past pres. 1985-89), San Gabriel Hist. Assn., San Gabriel Community Coord. Coun. (past pres. 1986). Democrat. Episcopalian.

REECE, JULIETTE M. STOLPER, community health and mental health nurse; b. Muskogee, Okla., Oct. 4, 1926; d. Joseph Harry and Marie (Duquesne) Stolper; m. Warren Crane, Apr. 12, 1947; children: Warren Crane, Judith Gayle Crane Cox Fitzpatrick, Janice M. Crane Sharp, Cathy L. Crane Hubble; m. Roy M. Reece Jr., July 16, 1970 (dec.). Diploma, Muskogee Gen. Hosp., 1947; BS in Psychology, Cameron Coll., Lawton, Okla., 1993, postgrad., 1993; student, U. Okla. Cert. pub. health nurse. ICU nurse Southwestern Hosp., Lawton, 1976-77; psychiat. nurse Taliaferro Community Mental Health Ctr., 1977-86; cons. nurse Cedar Crest Manor, Lawton, 1985-86, dir. nursing svc., 1986-87; asst. head nurse Reynolds Family Practice Clinic, Ft. Sill, Okla., 1987-91, head nurse, 1991—, also diabetes educator, 1991—; vis. mem. Pub. Health Nursing Study Group, USSR, 1979. Vol. for Am. Cancer Soc., Am. Heart Assn., Am. Diabetes Assn., Am. Lung Assn., ARC, Easter Seal Programs; tchr. classes for home health care aides, ARC; tchr. med. terminology to hosp. receptionists. Recipient nursing grants. Home: 1601 NW Pollard Ave Lawton OK 73507-9930 Office: Reynolds Family Practice Clinic # 4 Thomas St Bldg # 4300 Fort Sill OK 73503

REECE, KARYN LYNN, financial consultant; b. Niagara Falls, N.Y., Apr. 14, 1967; d. George John and Eleanor Roberta (O'Donnell) R. student, Niagara County Coll., 1987-88, Buffalo State Coll., 1992. Lic. stockbroker and fin. cons., N.Y. Stockbroker B.C. Fin., Buffalo, 1989; ins. agt. Mutual of Omaha, Buffalo, 1989-90; fin. cons. Cook Fin. Group, Buffalo, 1990—. Mem. Women Everywhere. Republican.

REECE, SANDRA BLAZE, non-commissioned officer; b. Coral Gables, Fla., Jan. 25, 1950; d. William Clayton and Pauline (Hill) Meyers; m. Virgil Clinton Reece, May 13, 1972; 1 stepchild, Richard David; 1 child, Laquita Dawn. Student, Ohio State U., 1968-70, U. Md., 1982, 88, Park Coll., 1985-87; AS in Constrn. Mgmt., Park Coll., 1987. With U.S. Army Corp. Engrs., 1992—, advanced through grades to 1st sgt., 1992. Mem. Women in Mil. Svc. to Am., NOW, NAFE, Non-Commd. Officers Assn., Asns. U.S. Army, Army Engrs. Assn. Home: 25 Dogwood Old Farm Estates Waynesville MO 65583

REECE, SHARON ANN, adult education educator; b. Cin., Nov. 28, 1953; d. Edward and Claudia (Ownes) Reece; divorced, 1981; children: Erika Lynn, Melanie Joyce. BS in Consumer Sci., Xavier Edgecliff U., 1975; cert. clerical computer, So. Ohio Coll., 1984; MEd in Gen. Edn., SUNY, Buffalo, 1994; DEd in Adult Edn., Nova U., 1994—. Cert. tchr., Ohio. Dept. supr., asst. buyer Mabley & Carew, Cin., 1975-76; claims adjuster Allstate Ins. Co., Cin., 1976-78; sales merchandiser Ekco Houseware, Cin., 1979-80; sales rep. Met. Life Inc., Cin., 1981-83; info. processing specialist GPA/Robert Half/Word Source, Cin., Dallas, 1985-87; tchr. adult edn. Princeton City Schs., Cin., 1984-90; with Rainbow Internat. Non-Profit Adult Ednl. Rsch. Ctr., Buffalo, 1990—; edn. specialist rsch. found. SUNY, Buffalo, 1993; prof. computer sci. So. Ohio Tech. and Bus. Coll., Cin., 1986-90; computer software tng. cons., 1987-89. Tutor U.S. div. Internat. Laubach Literacy, Clermont County, Ohio, 1984. Mem. NAFE, ASTD, Internat. DOS Users Group, Am. Ednl. Rsch. Assn., World Assn. Women Entrepreneurs, Boston Computer Soc., Cin. Orgn. Data Processing Educators and Trainers, Internat. Platform Assn., Cin. C. of C. (cert. minority supplier devel. coun.), Nat. Assn. Women Bus. Owners. Baha'i. Home: 173 Palmdale Dr Buffalo NY 14221-4006 Office: Rainbow Internat Adult Ednl Rsch and Consulting 7954 Transit Rd Ste 253 Buffalo NY 14221-4100

REECE MYRON, MONIQUE ELIZABETH, marketing, advertising and sales consultant; b. Eldora, Iowa, Jan. 12, 1960; d. Barry Lynne and Vera Marie (Powell) R.; m. Gordon Duane Myron, Mar. 14, 1992; 1 child, Morgan Reece. BSBA, Regis U., 1991. Mgr. regional advt. Silo, Inc., Denver, 1979-86; dir. mktg. LaserLand Corp., U.S.A., Denver, 1986-87; advt. mgr. King Soopers, Denver, 1987-90; supr. brand devel. Garrison-Lontine Advt., Denver, 1991; pres. Monique Myron and Assocs., Denver and La Jolla, Calif., 1991-94, MarketSmarter, Denver and San Diego, 1994—; chmn. bus. partnership com. Colo. Mktg. Tech. Advt. Com., Denver, 1987-91. Mem. publ. rels. com. Make-A-Wish Found., Denver, 1989. Recipient 1st Place Advt. award Nat. Frozen Food Assn., 1988, 89, 90, award Retail Advt. Coun., 1990. Mem. NAFE, Am. Soc. Tng. Devel., Nat. Assn. Women Bus. Owners, Nat. Assn. Profl. Saleswomen, Colo. Women's C. of C., Toastmasters, La Jolla C. of C. (bus., profl. com. 1992-93), Denver Metro. C. of C. Home: 430 S Garfield St Denver CO 80209-3505 Office: MarketSmarter 430 S Garfield Denver CO 80209

REED, AMELIA MATZ, customer service professional; b. Corpus Christi, Tex., Mar. 22, 1963; d. Joseph John and Grace Rosalie (Dalzell) Matz; m. David Henry Reed, Feb. 14, 1990; children: Bryan Matz, Jacob Daniel. Student, San Antonio Coll., 1983-84, Our Lady of the Lake U., 1985-86. Sales adminstr. Stainless Ice-Tainer Co., San Antonio, 1981-88; mgr. customer svc. Lancer Corp., San Antonio, 1988—. Vol. fund raiser Cystic Fibrosis, San Antonio, 1984, Am. Heart Assn., San Antonio, 1986, United Way, San Antoinio, 1988—; pub. safety sponsor Tex. State Troopers. Mem. NAFE, Nat. Humane Soc., Animal Def. League, Greenpeace. Office: Lancer Corp 235 W Turbo San Antonio TX 78216

REED, CAROL LOUISE, designer; b. Pontiac, Ill., Apr. 16, 1938; d. Rollin Kenneth and Lucille Hortence (Myer) Snethen; m. Richard Willis Reed, Feb. 13, 1960; children: Rena Louise Davis, Ronda Lee Howle. BBA in Mktg. and Advt., Tex. Tech. U., 1959. Office mgr. Sappington Devel., Inc., Rociada, N.Mex., 1990-91; owner Designs by Carol, Rociada, 1988—. Elected state officer Tierra y Montes Soil and Water Conservation Dist., Las Vegas, 1990—; mem. Mora-San Miguel Water Planning Bd., 1991—; treas. First Meth. Ch., Las Vegas, 1989-90; sec. Calvary Bapt. Ch., Las Vegas, 1991-92. Recipient award of merit Goodyear Tire and Rubber Co., 1991; named Outstanding Supr. of Tierra y Montes Soil and Conservation Dist., 1992, 95. Mem. N.Mex. Assn. Soil and Water Conservation Dists. (chair region IV 1994), Phi Kappa Phi. Republican. Home: PO Box 853 Rociada NM 87742 Office: Designs by Carol PO Box 853 Rociada NM 87742

REED, CINDY LEA, neonatal nurse practitioner; b. Hickory, N.C., Jan. 15, 1960; d. Jones Carroll and Eunice Lea (Rhoney) R. ADN, Western Piedmont Community, Morganton, N.C., 1980; BSN, U. N.C., Charlotte, 1983; cert. neonatal nurse practitioner, W.Va. U., 1986. Cert. neonatal nurse practitioner; cert. neonatal CCRN, neonatal resuscitation instr., BCLS instr., pediatric ACLS. RN float pool Frye Regional Med. Ctr., Hickory, 1980-81, RN pediatrics, 1981-82, RN newborn nursery and neonatal ICU, 1982-86, RN neonatal nurse practitioner, 1986—. Mem. AACN, Nat. Assn. Neonatal Nurse, Carolinas Assn. Neonatal Nurse Practitioners, Northwestern N.C. Regional Perinatal Coun., Sigma Theta Tau. Methodist. Home: 1021 6th Avenue Dr NW Hickory NC 28601-3405 Office: Frye Regional Med Ctr 420 N Center St Hickory NC 28601-5033

REED, CONSTANCE LOUISE, materials management and purchasing consultant; b. Point Pleasant, W.Va.; d. John Melvin Supple and Garnet L. Tooley; m. James Wesley Reed Jr., Sept. 20, 1985. Student, Ohio State U., 1974-76, Capital U., 1984-85. Buyer Abex Corp., Columbus, Ohio, 1971-79; maj. component buyer Grumman Corp., Delaware, Ohio, 1979-81; purchasing mgr. Atlantic Richfield (ANATEC), Dublin, Ohio, 1981-85; purchasing agt. Columbus Lodging, Inc., 1986-87, Monitronix Corp., Westerville, Ohio, 1988-89; contracts adminstr. Cellular Communications Inc., Worthington, Ohio, 1989-90; dir. materials mgmt. Fibrebond Corp., Minden, La., 1991-92; v.p. C&P Mgmt. Cons., Powell, Ohio, 1985—. Mem. NAFE, Am. Mgmt. Assn., Nat. Assn. Purchasing Mgmt., Bus. and Profl. Women's Club. Republican. Roman Catholic. Home: 1166 Highland Dr Columbus OH 43220-4940 Office: C&P Mgmt PO Box 158 Powell OH 43065-0158

REED, CYNTHIA KAY, minister; b. Amarillo, Tex., July 10, 1952; d. Carlos Eugene and Marjorie Marie (Daughetee) R. B of Music Edn., McMurry Coll., Abilene, Tex., 1976; MDiv, Perkins Sch. Theol., Dallas, 1991. Ordained to ministry Meth. Ch., 1989; cert. dir. music. Dir. music and Christian edn. Oakwood United Meth. Ch., Lubbock, Tex., 1978-84; dir. music and Christian edn. 1st United Meth. Ch., Childress, Tex., 1976-78, Littlefield, Tex., 1984-86; intern min. 1st United Meth. Ch., Lubbock, 1989-90, assoc. min., 1990-91; min. Meadow and Ropesville United Meth. Chs., 1991-93, Earth (Tex.) United Meth. Ch., 1993—; extern chaplain Meth. Hosp., Lubbock, 1989—, Walk to Emmaus Renewal Movement, Lubbock, 1990—. Com. mem. Life Gift-Organ Donation, Lubbock, 1991; mem. Arthritis Found., Lubbock, 1991. Georgia Harkness scholar Div. Ordained Ministry, 1989. Mem. Christian Educators & Musicians Fellowship, Am. Guild Organists.

REED, DIANE GRAY, business information service company executive; b. Trion, Ga., Sept. 5, 1945; d. Harold and Frances (Parker) Gray; m. Harry Reed, Oct. 2, 1982. Student, Jacksonville U., 1963-64, Augusta Coll., 1972-74; BS, Ga. State U., 1981. Various mgmt. positions Equifax Svcs., Inc., Atlanta, 1964-72, field rep., 1972-74, tech. rep., 1974-79, mgr. systems and programs, 1979-84, dir. tech., 1984-86, asst. v.p., 1986—; v.p. info. tech. sector Equifax Svcs., Inc., 1989—; presdl. adv. council Equifax Svcs., Inc., Atlanta, 1984—; cons. Ga. Computer Programmer Project, Atlanta, 1984-86, spkr. Oglethorpe U. Career Workshop, Atlanta, 1986. Bd. dirs. Atlanta Mental Health Assn., 1985-89; bd dirs., pres. Atlanta Women's Network, 1990; bd. dirs. United Way Bd. Bank, Atlanta, 1984-86; chairperson EquiFax United Way Campaign, 1988-89; vol. Cobb County Spl. Olympics, Marietta, Ga., 1984-87; mem. adv. coun. Coll. Bus. Adminstrn. Ga. State U. mgmt. info. systems industry adv. bd. U. Ga.; mem. Leadership Atlanta Class of '92, Girl Scouts Friendship Circle, Friends of Spelman Coll.; vol. coord. Atlanta Partnership Bus. and Edn.; co-chair salute to women of achievement YWCA, 1992; mem. Leadership Am. Class 1994; tech. steering com. 1996 Olympic Games. Named Woman of Achievement, Atlanta YWCA, 1987; recipient Decca award as one of top 10 bus. women in Atlanta, 1992; named to Leadership Am. Class 1994. Mem. Women in Info. Processing, Inst. Computer Profls. (cert.), Soc. Info. Mgmt., Internat. Women's Alliance, Ga. State Alumni, LWV, Atlanta Yacht Club, Kiwanis Internat. (bd. dirs. Atlanta Buckhead chpt.). Office: Equifax Svcs Inc 1600 Peachtree St NW Atlanta GA 30309-2403

REED, DIANE MARIE, psychologist; b. Joplin, Mo., Jan. 11, 1934; d. William Marion and Olive Francis (Smith) Kinney; married; children: Wendy Robison, Douglas Funkhouser. Student, Art Ctr. Col., L.A., 1951-54; BS, U. Oreg., 1976, MS, 1977, PhD, 1981. Lic. psychologist. Illustrator J.L. Hudson Co., Detroit, 1954-56; designer, stylist N.Y.C., 1960-70; designer, owner Decor To You, Inc., Stamford, Conn., 1970-76; founder, exec. dir. Alcohol Counseling and Edn. Svcs., Inc., Eugene, Oreg., 1981-86, clin. supr., 1986; clin. supr. Christian Family Svcs., Eugene, 1986-87; pvt. practice Eugene, 1985-94; founder Reed Consulting, Bend, Oreg., 1995—, 1995—. Evaluator Vocat. Rehab. Div., Eugene, 1982—; alcohol and drug evaluator and commitment examiner Oreg. Mental Health Div., 1981-86; life mem. Rep. Presdle. Task Force. Mem. APA, Oreg. Psychol. Assn., Lane County Psychol. Assn. (pres. 1989-90), Lane Mental Health Providers Assn., C2 Investors (treas. 1987-88), Altair Ski and Sport, Oreg. Track. Office: 990 NW Brook St Bend OR 97701

REED, ELIZABETH MAY MILLARD, mathematics and computer science educator, publisher; b. Shippensburg, Pa., July 1, 1919; d. Jacob Franklin and Isabelle Bernadine (Dorn) Millard; m. Jesse Floyd Reed, Aug. 5, 1961; 1 child, David Millard. BA, Shepherd Coll., 1941; MA, Columbia U., 1948; postgrad., W.Va. U., U. Hawaii, Columbia U., NSF Summer Insts., Oakland U., 1974-85. Cert. assoc. in tchr. edn., W.Va. Math. tchr. Hedgesville (W.Va.) High Sch., 1941-47, Martinsburg (W.Va.) High Sch., 1948-51, George Washington High Sch. and Territorial Coll. Guam, Agana, 1952-54, Valley Stream (N.Y.) Meml. Jr. High Sch., 1954-55, Rye (N.Y.) High Sch., 1955-57, Elkins (W.Va.) Jr. High Sch., 1971-87; dir. admissions Davis and Elkins Coll., 1957-67, asst. prof. math., 1968-71, adj. prof., 1987—, lectr. geography, 1971-73; pres. Three Reeds Studios, Elkins, 1989—; statis. clk. Lord, Abbett & Co., N.Y.C., 1947-48; customer rep. Kay, Richards & Co., Winchester, Va., 1951-52; mem. adj. grad. faculty W.Va. U., Morgantown, 1984-91; mem. adj. faculty Evans Coll. U. Charleston, W.Va., 1989-90; presenter regional and state computer workshops, W.Va. Author: Computer Literacy at Elkins Junior High School, 1983; project dir. (video) Women: Professionally Speaking, 1988. Dir. pilot project Project Bus., Jr. Achievement, Elkins, 1972-78; organizer Randolph County Math. Field Day, Elkins, 1977; initiator Comprehensive Achievement Monitoring, Elkins, 1980; treas. Humanities Found. W.Va., Charleston, 1983-85, pres., 1985-87; vice-moderator quadrant II Presbytery of W.Va. Recipient Presdl. award for Excellence in Tchg. Math. in W.Va., NSF, 1985. Mem. AAUW (pres. W.Va. divsn. 1977-79, editor 1983—, pres. Elkins br. 1988-94), W.Va. Coun. Tchrs. of Math., Nat. Coun. Tchrs. of Math., W.Va. Item Writing Workshop-Math. 9-12 (writer 1985-86). Home: 4 Lincoln Ave Elkins WV 26241-3669 Office: Davis & Elkins Coll 100 Campus Dr Elkins WV 26241-3996

REED, HELEN I., medical/surgical nurse; b. Radford, Va., Aug. 3, 1967; d. Billy Wayne and Beverly Gayle (Sparks) R. Cert. Practical Nursing, Radford City Sch. Nursing, 1986; BSN, Radford U., 1990. RN, Va.; med., surg. cert. Student nurse intern Radford Community Hosp., 1989-90, staff nurse, 1990—. Jr. vol. Radford Community Hosp., 1981-85; provider Adv. Cardiac Life Support, 1994; CPR instr. AM. Heart Assn.; substitute instr. Radford City Sch. of Practical Nursing, med. unit continuing edn. coord., preceptor to new staff. Recipient Nette Whitehead Nursing scholarship, John Nye scholarship, Jr. Vol. scholarship, U.S. Achievement Acad. award, 1984. Mem. ANA, NSNA. Methodist. Office: Radford Community Hosp Acute Care Ctr 700 Randolph St Radford VA 24141-9988

REED, IRENE, management consultant; b. San Francisco, Nov. 28, 1962; d. Erik Bjorn and Erna Ellen (Evje) Werner; m. George Franklin Reed Jr., June 1, 1991. BS in Bus., San Diego State U., 1985. Inside sales account mgr. Computer Assoc. Internat., San Jose, Calif., 1988-89; field sales account mgr. Computer Assoc. Internat., Dallas, 1989-90, dist. sales mgr., 1990-91, account mgr. nat. accounts, 1991; account mgr. nat. accounts Micrografx, Richardson, Tex., 1992-93, nat. accounts sales mgr., 1993-94, bus. planning mgr., 1994; mgr. strategic svcs. consulting KPMG Peat Marwick, Palo Alto, Calif., 1994—; fashion cons. Doncaster, Dallas, 1993-94. Republican. Presbyterian.

REED, JACQUELINE KEMP, educational researcher; b. Newark, June 12, 1947; d. Thomas and Jessie (Bullock) R.; 1 child, Cecil Bernard Brown Jr. BA, U. Ill., Chgo., 1970; MA, Northeastern Ill. U., 1976; PhD, U. Wis., 1978. Rsch. asst. U. Ill., Chgo., 1970-72; zonal coord. Model Cities-Chgo. Com. on Urban Opportunities, Chgo., 1972-73; vocat. specialist Model Cities-CCUO, Chgo., 1973-74, child care tng. coord., 1974-76; program coord. U. Wis., Madison, 1977-79; post-doctoral rsch. fellow Mich. State U., East Lansing, 1979-80; acting asst. dean U. Md., College Park, 1980-81; rsch. assoc. D.C. Pub. Schs., Washington, 1983-85; spl. asst. U. Md., College park, 1985-89; rsch. policy specialist Prince George's County Pub. Schs., Upper Marlboro, Md., 1989—; resource colleague Human Rels. Commn., Evanston, Ill., 1971; reviewer U.S. Dept. Edn., Washington, 1979-81; cons. NEA, Washington, 1982; adv. com. P.G. County Correctional Ctr., Upper Marlboro, 1990—; presenter in field. Contbr. chpt. to book and articles to profl. jours. Exec. bd. Eleanor Roosevelt High Sch. PTSA, Greenbelt, Md., 1980-84; vol. United Communities Against Poverty, Capitol Heights, Md., 1987-89, Md. Higher Edn. Commn., Prince George's County, 1990; bd. dirs. Town of Kettering, Upper Marlboro, 1992. Recipient Vol. award United Communities Against Poverty, Capitol Heights, 1989. Mem. AAUW, Nat. Assn. Multi-Cultural Edn. (exec. bd. mem. 1990—, editorial bd. mem. 1990—), Am. Ednl. Rsch. Assn., Nat. Coun. Negro Women, Inc., U. Ill. Alumni Assn., U. Wis. Alumni Assn., Md. Choral Soc., Phi Delta Kappa, Pi Lambda Theta (eligibility co-chair 1977-78). Democrat. Office: Prince Georges Pub Sch Office Rsch & Evaluation 14201 School Ln Rm 138 Upper Marlboro MD 20772

REED, JANE GARSON, accounting educator, consultant; b. Cleve., Jan. 11, 1948; d. Joseph John Guzowski and Irene Sophie (Dominic) Garson; m. Wayne Ellis Reed, May 17, 1969; children: Craig Michael, Kevin Matthew. BBA magna cum laude, Baldwin Wallace Coll., 1977; MBA in Mgmt., Case Western Res. U., 1983; postgrad., Cleve. State U., 1991—. CPA, Ohio. Letter carrier U.S. Postal Svc., Brecksville, Ohio, 1966-76; sr. asst. acct. Deloitte, Haskins & Sells, Cleve., 1977-78; sr. corp. auditor White Motor Corp., Beachwood, Ohio, 1979-81; instr. acctg. Cuyahoga C.C., Parma, Ohio, 1981-82; ind. contractor State of Wash., Olympia, 1982-84; dir. fin. The Montefiore Home, Cleveland Heights, Ohio, 1985-86; contr., bus. mgr. Western Res. Human Svcs., Inc., Akron, Ohio, 1986-87; lectr. mgmt. acctg. U. Akron, 1987-88; asst. prof. Baldwin-Wallace Coll., Berea, Ohio, 1989-94. Chairperson Trinity (Marymount) High Sch. Reunion Com., 1990-91; mem. acctg. curriculum adv. com. Lorain County C.C. Mem. AICPA, AAUP, Am. Women's Soc. CPAs, Ohio Soc. CPAs (mem. editorial bd. Ohio CPA Jour. com. 1992—, mem. task force on implementing quality edn. 1992-94), Inst. Mgmt. Accts. (faculty advisor to Baldwin-Wallace student chpt. 1990-94), Am. Soc. Women Accts. (pres. 1993-94), Am. Acctg. Assn. Methodist. Home: 1254 Hadcock Rd Brunswick OH 44212-3018 Office: Jaane Garson Reed CPA Div Bus 1254 Hadcock Rd Brunswick OH 44212

REED, JOAN-MARIE, special education educator; b. St. Paul, Sept. 8, 1960; d. William Martin Reed and Diana-Marie (Miller) Reed Moss. BA, U. Minn., 1982, BS, 1983; MEd, Tex. Woman's U., 1986. Cert. tchr., Tex. Tchr. emotionally disturbed Birdville Ind. Sch. Dist., Ft. Worth, 1984-86; tchr. emotionally disturbed Goose Creek Ind. Sch. Dist., Baytown, Tex., 1986-92, ctr. leader, 1992-93, dept. chairperson, 1987-91; tchr. emotionally disturbed Conroe (Tex.) Ind. Sch. Dist., 1993-94, Willis (Tex.) Ind. Sch. Dist., 1994—; Co-editor: New Teacher Handbook, 1986-87, Behavior Improvement Program Handbook, 1987-88. Mem. NEA, Coun. for Exceptional Children. Congregationalist. Home: Apt 513 2200 Montgomery Park Blvd Conroe TX 77304

REED, KIMBERLY DAWN, lawyer; b. Winchester, Va., Oct. 22, 1965; d. Wayne Gill and Patricia (Parker) R.; m. Christopher Joseph Feeley, July 4, 1993. BA, Duke U., 1986; JD, U. Va., 1989. Bar: Calif. 1989, Md. 1993, D.C. 1994. Atty. Gibson, Dunn & Crutcher, L.A., 1990-92, Howrey & Simon, Washington, 1992—. Contbr. articles to profl. jours. Chair civil rights com. Women's Nat. Dem. Club, Washington, 1993—; mem. alumni admissions com. Duke U.; mem. People for the Am. Way; bd. dirs. Coalition to Prevent Handgun Violence, 1993—, Gifts for Homeless, Washington, 1992—; vol. Whitman Walker Legal Clinic, Washington, 1992—. Mem. Bar Assn. Dist. of Columbia (exec. com., chair career devel. com. 1993—). Home: 8402 Irvington Ave Bethesda MD 20817 Office: Howrey & Simon 1299 Pennsylvania Ave NW Washington DC 20004

REED, MARY LOU, state legislator; m. Scott Reed; children: Tara, Bruce. BA, Mills Coll. Mem. Idaho State Senate, 1985—; Senate Minority Leader; coord. Com. for Fair Rates. Democrat. Office: 10 Giesa Rd Coeur D Alene ID 83814-9489

REED, PAMELA, actress; b. Tacoma, Wash., Apr. 2, 1949; d. Vernie Reed; m. Sandy Smolar. BA in Drama, U. Wash. Prin. stage roles include Getting Through the Night, Ensemble Studio Theatre, N.Y.C., 1976, Curse of the Starving Class, N.Y. Shakespeare Festival, Pub. Theatre, 1978, The November People (Broadway debut), Billy Rose Theatre, 1978, All's Well That Ends Well, N.Y. Shakespeare Festival, Delacorte Theatre, 1978, Getting Out, Phoenix Theatre, Marymount Manhattan Theatre, N.Y.C., 1978, Seduced, Am. Place Theatre, N.Y.C., 1979, Sorrows of Stephen, N.Y. Shakespeare Festival, Pub. Theatre, 1979, Fools, Eugene O'Neill Theatre, N.Y.C., 1981, Criminal Minds, Theatre Guinevere, N.Y.C., 1984, Fen, N.Y. Shakespeare Festival, Pub. Theatre, 1984, Aunt Dan and Lemon, N.Y. Shakespeare Festival, Pub. Theatre, 1985, Mrs. Warren's Profession, Roundabout Theatre, N.Y.C., 1985, Haft Theatre, 1986; film appearances include The Long Riders, 1980, Melvin and Howard, 1980, Eyewitness, 1981, Young Doctors in Love, 1982, The Right Stuff, 1983, The Goodbye People, 1984, The Best of Times, 1986, The Clan of the Cave Bear, 1986, Rachel River, 1989, Chattahoochee, 1990, Cadillac Man, 1990, Kindergarten Cop, 1990, Passed Away, 1992, Junior, 1994; TV series appearances include The Andros Targets, 1977, Tanner, 1988, The Dark Horse (HBO), 1988, Grand, 1990; TV films include Inmates: A Love Story, 1981, I Want to Live, 1983, Heart of Steel, 1983, Scandal Sheet, 1985, Born Too Soon, 1993, Mary Hemingway miniseries, 1988, Caroline? (Hallmark Hall of Fame), 1989. Office: ICM 8942 Wilshire Blvd Beverly Hills CA 90211*

REED, PAMELA LYNN, adolescent counselor; b. Independence, Kans., Nov. 19, 1963; d, Billy Eugene and Mary Sue (Younger) Reed; (div.); 1 child, Tanner Keith . BS, U. Tex., Arlington, 1987. Cert. alcohol and drug abuse counselor, compulsive gambling counselor; lic. chem. dependency counselor. Phys. therapy asst. Dr. James Elbaor, Arlington, 1980-83; supr. cashiers Target, Arlington, 1983-84; unit sec. Mansfield (Tex.) Community Hosp., 1984-85; sec. Willow Creek Hosp., Arlington, 1986-87, ednl. tester, 1987-89, student assistance counselor, 1989-90; case mgr., counselor Oak Grove Treatment Ctr., Burleson, Tex., 1990-91; coord. student assistance program Dist. Wide S.A. Program, I.S.D., Mansfield, 1991-94; juvenile detention officer Tarrant County, Ft. Worth, 1994-95; adolescent case mgr. All Saints Episc. Hosp., Hurst, Tex., 1995—; cons. ednl. tester Carpenter & Assocs., Arlington, 1988-90, Mind Time, Arlington, 1989, Willow Creek Hosp., Arlington, 1989-90, Oak Grove Treatment Ctr., Burleson, 1990. Coach Mansfield Pee-Wee Cheerleading, 1986-90, coach adult volleyball; vol. Dallas Intertribal Ctr., 1990, Project Charlie, Kids Safe Saturday, 1990-91, AIDS Outreach Ctr., 1994, Horizons Tng. Mem. NAFE, Nat. Orgn. Student Asst. pevention Profls., Tex. Assn. Alcohol and Drug Abuse Counselors, North Ctrl. Tex. Assn. Counselors, Tarrants County Assn. Alcohol and Drug Abuse Counselors, Tex. Intelligence Tng. Assn., Tex. Assn. Studetn Asst.

Profls., Assn. Tex. Profl. Educators. Republican. Home: 326 Baldwin Grand Prairie TX 75052 Office: All Saints Hosp 720 Harwood Rd Ste 300 Hurst TX 76054

REED, ROSALIE, horse trainer; b. San Diego, May 5, 1954; d. Lester Woodrow Reed and Pearl (Peterson) Hampton. Trainer Fletcher Hills Ranch, San Diego, 1970-74, Willow Glen Farm, El Cajon, Calif., 1974-77, Moreno Valley Ranch, Lakeside, Calif., 1978-80, Mill Creek Farm, Malibu, Calif., 1980-81, L.A. Equestrian Ctr., 1981—; Judge Appaloosa Horse Club Nat. Show, Syracuse, N.Y., Appaloosa Horse Club. Can. Author: Handbook of Hunter Seat Equitation, 1977, Handbook of Saddle Seat Equitation, 1977; contbr. to profl. publs. Inducted San Diego Hall of Champions, 1978; winner 8 world championships, Appaloosa Horse Club, 1972-76, 7 nat. championships, 1972-76; demonstrator 1984 Summer Olympics, L.A. Mem. ASCAP, Am. Horse Show Assn. (judge), Internat. Arabian Horse Assn. (judge), Pacific Coast Horse Show Assn., Calif. Profl. Horsemen's Assn., Equestrian Trails Internat. Office: LA Equestrian Ctr 480 Riverside Dr Burbank CA 91506

REED, SHEILA KAYE, program coordinator; b. East Prairie, Mo., Apr. 9, 1950; d. George Allen and Corine Laverne (Tyner) Turner; m. Scott Earl Reed, Oct. 18, 1975; 1 child, Scott Allen Hamilton. BS in Edn., S.E. Mo. State U., 1972; postgrad., N.E. Mo. State U., 1979; MBA, Lindenwood Coll., 1986; cert. adult edn., Ctrl. Mo. State U., 1991. Cert. coord. adult edn., cert. tchr. Tchr. Potosi (Mo.) Elem. Sch., 1972-74, Hazelwood (Mo.) Armstrong Sch., 1974-80; foster care worker Div. Family Svcs., St. Charles, Mo., 1987-89; coord. adult edn. Washington (Mo.) Sch. Dist., 1989-93; coord. admissions and fin. aid Sch. Nursing Mo. Bapt. Med. Ctr., St. Louis, 1993—; mem. adv. bd. Non-Traditional Careers, Union, Mo., 1991-93; mem. Franklin County Svc. Providers, 1992-93, Practical Nursing Program Adv. Bd., Washington, 1989-93. Bd. mem. Acad. Sacred Heart, St. Charles, Mo., 1989-91; chair Mktg. Com. for centennial celebration Mo. Bapt. Med. Ctr. Sch. Nursing, 1994-95. Recipient Certs. of Appreciation Enactment Com., Washington Sch. Dist./East Ctrl. Coll., 1991, Speaker for Todays Women Seminar, East Ctrl. Coll., 1991. Mem. Am. Vocat. Assn., Mo. Assn. Cmty. and Continuing Educators (bd. mem. for bus. and industry 1991-94, planning com.), Mo. Assn. Customized Trainers, Mo. Vocat. Assn. Office: Mo Bapt Med Ctr Sch Nursing 3015 N Ballas Rd Saint Louis MO 63131

REED, VASTINA KATHRYN (TINA REED), child psychotherapist; b. Chgo., Mar. 5, 1960; d. Alvin Hillard and Ruth Gwendolyn (Thomas) R.; 1 child, Alvin J. BA in Human Svcs. magna cum laude, Nat.-Louis U., Chgo., 1988; MA, Ill. Sch. Profl. Psychology, 1991. Tchr. early childhood edn. Kendall Coll. Lab. Sch., Evanston, Ill., 1983-85, Rogers Park Children's Learning Ctr., Chgo., 1983-85; child life therapist Mt. Sinai Hosp., Chgo., 1988; child psychotherapist Nicholas Barnes Therapeutic Day Sch., Chgo., 1989-90. Den leader Boy Scouts Am., Chgo., 1989-92, scoutmaster troop 267, 1992—. Recipient Cub Scouter award Boy Scouts Am., 1990, Scoutmaster Award of Merit, 1993, 94, Okpik winter camping cert., 1994, 95, Presdl. Sports award in backpacking, 1993, 94. Mem. APA, Nat. Orgn. for Human Svc. Edn., Order of the Arrow, Phi Theta Kappa, Kappa Delta Pi. Democrat. Roman Catholic. Home: 1872 S Millard Ave Chicago IL 60623-2542

REED-GROSS, PATRICIA ELAINE, special education educator; b. Charleston, S.C., Dec. 17, 1952; d. David and Theodocia (Kennedy) Reed. BS, Winthrop Coll., 1974, MEd, 1976; postgrad., Columbia Coll., S.C., 1978—; Masters, U. S.C., 1988, postgrad. Head spl. edn. Chester (S.C.) County Pub. Schs., 1976-77; spl. edn. cons. Winthrop Coll., Rock Hill, S.C., 1977-78; tchr. aphasic children S.C. Sch. for Deaf and Blind, Spartanburg, 1978-79; tchr. juvenile delinquents Spartanburg Boys' Home, 1979-80; tchr. learning disabled Springdale Sch., Camden, S.C., 1981-84; tchr. emotionally handicapped Hillcrest High Sch., Sumter, S.C., 1984-85; head tchr. autistic adults Pine Grove Sch., Elgin, S.C., 1985—; tchr. severely and profoundly retarded Dept. Mental Retardation, Columbia, 1986—; tchr. learning disabled and emotionally handicapped children Maryville Elem. Sch., Georgetown, S.C., 1987-91; tchr. learning disabled children Sangaree Intermediate Sch., Summerville, S.C., 1991—; tchr. adult edn. Manning Correctional Instn., Columbia, 1981-87; community companion Columbia Area Mental Health, 1981-84. Mem. NEA, ASCD, S.C. Reading Assn., Internat. Platform Assn. Home: PO Box 2656 Summerville SC 29484-2656 Office: Sangaree Intermediate Sch 303 Live Oak Ave Moncks Corner SC 29461

REED-ROGERS, NOREEN ANN, nurse; b. Chgo., Apr. 16, 1958; d. Charlotte Lillian (Comptou) Ronayne; m. David Alan Reed, May 30, 1981 (dec. Dec. 1986); children: Michael David, Megan; m. James Rogers, May 12, 1990; 1 stepchild, James Michael. BSN, Creighton U., 1980. RN, Nebr. Staff nruse Meth. Hosp., Omaha, 1981—; life and health agt., dist. mgr. Primerica Fin. Svcs., Atlanta, 1988—; registered rep. Primerica & 1st Am. Nat. Securities, Atlanta, 1989—; sec.-treas. J & N Investments, Inc., Omaha, 1992—. Vol. ARC, Omaha, 1979, 84. Roman Catholic. Home: 10330 Z St Omaha NE 68127 Office: Meth Hosp 80th and Dodge St Omaha NE 68134

REEDY, CATHERINE IRENE, science and health educator, library/media specialist; b. Suffolk County, N.Y., Dec. 27, 1953; d. Edward and Catherine (Spindler) Grafenstein. A.A., Suffolk Community Coll., Selden, N.Y., 1980; B.A. in Social Sci., summa cum laude, Dowling Coll., Oakdale, N.Y., 1983, M.S. in Edn., 1986. Media specialist, tchr. coord. for sci. and health St. Ignatius Sch., Hicksville, N.Y., 1983—, dir. sci. lab. and media ctr., also sci. mentor. Mem. N.Y. Acad. Scis., Long Island Social Studies Council, N.Y. Sci. Tchrs. Assn., Assn. for Supervision and Curriculum Devel., Alpha Zeta Nu (1st sec.), Phi Theta Kappa, Phi Alpha Sigma, Kappa Delta Pi (pres. Xi Chi chpt. 1985-87). Home: 15 Nikia Dr Islip NY 11751-2630 Office: St Ignatius Sch 30 E Cherry St Hicksville NY 11801-4396

REEDY, PATRICIA M., playwright, actress; b. Mt. Vernon, N.Y., May 1, 1940; d. William Valentine Reedy and Gertrude E (Mongarell) Reedy Zaffino. Grad., Berkeley Sch. Bus., 1960; advt. cert., Y&R Sch. Advtg., 1961; student, Hunter Coll., Arts Students League, SUNY, Purchase, Fairfield U. Actress: Promises, Promises, 1973-74, Black Mountain, 1974, Paranoia Pretty, 1975, Sisters & Brothers, 1976, It's Only Temporary, 1976, Bagging It, 1981, Cordelia Tynside, Ever Wake Up, 1987; soloist: Var Restaurants; singer: SUNY, Purchase; TV appearances Dick Lamb Show, 1973, Another World, 1976, Stage Struck, 1977, Hotline, 1976, Joe Franklin, 1979, Go For It, 1982; dir. performances incl.: A Bundle for Brunch, 1979, American Theatre of Actors, 1981, The Stop Over, 1981, A Step Beyond, The Pond, NYU, 1987, Terror Brokers, Theater at Ams., Inc., 1988, Trapped in the Basement, Am. Theater Actors Play Fest, 1983; playwright Off Off Broadway It's Only Temporary, A Bundle for Brunch, The Stop Over, A Step Beyond, Bagging It. Mem. NOW, SAG, AFTRA, Actors Equity Assn., Dramatists Guild, Smithsonian Instn. Home: PO Box 77 West Mystic CT 06388

REEMELIN, ANGELA NORVILLE, dietitian consultant; b. Pitts., Apr. 28, 1945; d. Richard Gerow and Kathleen Taylor (Brannen) Norville; m. Philip Barrows Reemelin, Nov. 17, 1973; children: Richard Barrows, Kathleen Easson. BS, U. Tenn., 1967; dietetic intern, Emory U., 1968. Registered lic. dietitian. Adminstr. dietitian Servomation of Atlanta, 1968-70; food svc. dir. ARA Food Svcs., Norfolk, Va., 1970-80; cons. Jacksonville, Fla., 1980—; cons. William T. Hall Convalescent Home, Portsmouth, Va., 1975-79. Mem. ARC (30 yr. Vol. award), Jr. Womans Club Orange Park (pres. 1986-87, v.p., fundraiser, membership chair, Outstanding Dist. Pres. 1987), U. Tenn. Alumni Assn. (pres. 1982-84, bd. govs. 1984-85), Omricon Nu. Roman Catholic. Home: 601 Lorn Ct Orange Park FL 32073-4228

REENTS, SUE, state legislator. Mem. Idaho State Senate from dist. 19, 1989—. Home: 908 N 18th St Boise ID 83702-3317 Office: Idaho State Senate State Capitol Boise ID 83720*

REES, EDITH STEVENS, retired association executive; b. Kent County, Md., Jan. 5, 1911; d. Howard Dale and Ella Gertrude (Stevens) R. BA, Washington Coll., Chestertown, Md., 1931. Tchr. history and math. Easton (Md.) High Sch., 1931-35; dir. young adult program YWCA, Canton, Ohio, 1935-37, Cleve., 1937-42, Cin., 1942-46; dir. mid city ctr. YWCA, Phila., 1946-50; dir. loop ctr. YWCA, Chgo., 1950-55; rsch. assoc. Coun. Social Agys., Chgo., 1955-57; mem. pers. and field staff Nat. Bd. YWCA of U.S.A., N.Y.C., 1957-60; co-owner New Canaan (Conn.) Book Shop, 1960-72; realtor Chatham (Mass.) Real Estate, 1976-86. Mem. NASW (gold card). Home: 719 Maiden Choice Ln Apt Br438 Baltimore MD 21228-6124

REES, NORMA S., university president, educator; b. N.Y.C., Dec. 27, 1929; d. Benjamin and Lottie (Schwartz) D.; m. Raymond R. Rees, Mar. 19, 1960; children—Evan Lloyd, Raymond Arthur. B.A., Queens Coll., 1952; M.A., Bklyn. Coll., 1954; Ph.D., NYU, 1959. Cert. speech-language pathology, audiology. Prof. communicative disorders Hunter Coll., N.Y.C., 1967-72; exec. officer, speech and hearing scis. grad. sch. CUNY, N.Y.C., 1972-74, assoc. dean for grad. studies, 1974-76, dean grad. studies, 1976-82; vice chancellor for acad. affairs U. Wis., Milw., 1982-85, from 1986, acting chancellor, 1985-86; vice chancellor for acad. policy and planning Mass. Bd. Regent for Higher Edn., Boston, 1987-90; pres. Calif. State U., Hayward, 1990—; bd. dirs. Coun. of Postsecondary Accreditation, Washington, 1985-94; chmn. Comm. Recognition of Postsecondary Accreditation, 1994—. Contbr. articles to profl. jours. Trustee Citizens Govtl. Rsch. Bur., Milw., 1985-87; active Task Force on Wis. World Trade Ctr., 1985-87; bd. dirs. Greater Boston UWCA; mem. Mayor's Cabinet Ednl. Excellence, Oakland, Calif. Fellow Am. Speech-Lang-Hearing Assn. (honors); mem. Am. Coun. Edn. (com. internat. edn. 1991-93), Am. Assn. Colls. and Univs. (chair task force on quality assessment 1991-92, mem. steering com. of coun. of urban met. colls. & univs. 1992—), Nat. Assn. State Univs. and Land Grant Colls. (exec. com. divsn. urban affairs 1985-87, com. accreditation 1987-90). Office: Calif State Univ 25800 Carlos Bee Blvd Hayward CA 94542

REESE, ANN N., financial executive. Formerly tres. Mobil Europe; asst. treas. ITT Corp., 1987-89, v.p., 1989-92, sr. v.p., treas., 1992—. Office: ITT Corp 1330 Avenue Of The Americas New York NY 10019-5422

REESE, ELLEN PULFORD, psychologist, writer; b. Hartford, Conn., Aug. 30, 1926; d. Alfred Ely and Katherine Cary (Cook) P.; m. Thomas Whelan Reese, Dec. 17, 1949. B.A., Mt. Holyoke Coll., South Hadley, Mass., 1948, M.A., 1954. Lic. psychologist, Mass. Research asst. Mt. Holyoke Coll., 1948-56, asst. dir. psychol. labs., 1956-64, dir. psychol. labs., 1964-69, lectr. psychology, 1970-80, assoc. prof., 1980-85, prof., 1986-88; Norma Cutts Dafoe prof. psychology, 1989—; adj. prof. U. Kans., 1988—; v.p. Hampshire Communications, Amherst, Mass., 1969-76. Author books including: Human Behavior, 1978; (with Beth Sulzer-Azaroff) Applying Behavior Analysis, 1982; author, dir. ednl. films including: Behavior Theory in Practice, 1965, Imprinting, 1968; mem. editorial bd. Behavior Modification, 1977-82, Behavior Therapy, 1976-78, The Behavior Analyst, 1980-82. Trustee Cambridge Ctr. Behavioral Studies, Cambridge, Mass., 1981-88, 89-93, exec. com., 1982-88, adv. bd., 1988-89, 94—; trustee Loomis Chaffee Sch., Windsor, Conn., 1972-87. Recipient award for disting. contbn. to edn. in psychology Am. Psychol. Found., 1986, award Loomis Chaffee Sch., 1987; Mt. Holyoke Coll. grantee, 1970, 71, 75, 77, 81, 83, 84, 87, 88. Fellow Am. Psychol. Assn. (mem. exec. com. Div. 25 1973-75 77-79, 90-92, pres. 1991), Assn. for Behavior Analysis (mem. council 1981-86, pres. 1984), Animal Behavior Soc., N.Y. Acad. Scis., Sigma Xi. Office: Mount Holyoke Coll South Hadley MA 01075

REESE, NORMA CAROL, psychologist; b. Biloxi, Miss., Oct. 26, 1946; d. Virgil Stephen and Lila Mae (Shelton) Tatom; m. John Jay Reese, June 5, 1965 (div. Mar. 1983); children: Cher LeAnne, James Steven. AA in Psychology, Dade County Jr. Coll., Kendall, Fla., 1971; BS in Psychology, U. Miami, 1973; MS and PhD in Psychology, U. So. Miss., 1976. Lic. cons. psychologist, Minn., N.D. Rsch. asst. NASA Lang. Rsch. Lab., Coral Gables, Fla., 1971-73; psychology instr. U. So. Miss., Hattiesburg, 1975-76, Grambling (La.) State U., 1976-78; clin. psychologist II Lake Charles (La.) Mental Health Ctr., 1979-83; tng. cons. Human Rels. Cons., Lake Charles, 1983-86; clin. dir. Grafton (N.D.) State Sch., 1986-89; dir. psychol. svcs. State Devel. Ctr., Grafton, 1989—; ind. contractor, cons. psychol. svcs. Harley Residential Svcs. (name changed to Applied Behavioral Cons., Inc. 1990), Roseville, Minn., 1990-91; pvt. practice MYNDAK Moblie Cons., Minn. and N.D., 1990—; dir. sexual health project for devel. disabled and mentally retarded N.D. Dept. Human Svcs., Grafton, 1989—, dir. sex offender and treatment program developmentally disabled offenders, 1986-87; mem. adj. faculty grad. clin. psychology dept. U. N.D., Grand Forks, 1994—; presenter in field. Author: The Bulletin of the Psychonomic Soc., 1975-76; author/cartoonist The Worm Runner's Digest, 1975-80. Freedom writer Amnesty Internat., Midwest, 1989; founding mem. Sexual Health Coalition Steel of N.D., 1990; nat. disaster mental health technician, chpt. family svc. worker Red River Valley chpt. ARC, 1993—; mentor Am. Assn. Mental Retardation, 1992—; vol. Red Cross Nat. Disaster Mental Health Team, 1993, Emilys List, 1993. Named Silver Knight candidate, art, Miami (Fla.) Herald News, 1965; nominated Profl. of the Yr., La. Assn. Retarded Citizens, Lake Charles, 1983. Mem. N.D. Psychol. Assn. (legis. action com. 1990-91, mem. disaster action com. 1993-94, mem. women in psychology 1995), Am. Assn. Mental Retardation (sec.-treas. N.D. chpt. 1991), Women in Networking, Assn. for Advancement of Psychology, Century Club. Republican. Methodist. Office: The Developmental Ctr W 6th St Grafton ND 58237

REESE, PATRICIA ANN, retired editor, columnist; b. Superior, Nebr., Mar. 14, 1954; d. Robert John and Billie Jo (Gooch) R. BS in Wildlife Ecology, Communications, Okla. State U., 1976. Proofreader Ada (Okla.) Evening News, 1976-77, reporter, 1977-81, wire editor, 1981-85, city editor, 1985-92, sects. editor, 1992, ret., 1992. Bd. dirs. Ada Arts and Humanities Coun., 1981-85, 92—, historian, 1982-83, sec., 1983-85, 92—; charter mem. Seekers dept. Tanti Study Club, Ada, 1982. Recipient Carl Rogan News Excellence award Associated Press/Okla. News Execs., 1986, 90, 91, 92, Best Column award Okla. Natural Gas, 1991. Mem. Am. Mus. Natural History, Archaeology Inst. Am., Okla. Lupus Assn., Ada Cmty. Theater II, Okla. Press Assn., Internat. Ceramic Inst., Soc. Environ. Jounalists. Democrat. Home: RR 4 Box 118 Ada OK 74820-9407

REESE, SARA FOWLER, accounting educator; b. Danville, Va., Aug. 19, 1952; d. Eugene Arnold and Lenora Willis (Perkins) Fowler; m. Charles Womble Reese, May 23, 1986. BBA, U. Miss., 1979, M of Accountancy, 1980. CPA, Miss. Asst. prof. acctng. Va. Union U., Richmond, 1987—; treas. Interfaith Housing Corp., Richmond, 1993-94. Treas. Bon Air Christian Ch., Richmond, 1992—. Mem. Am. Acctng. Assn., Inst. Mgmt. Accts. Office: Va Union U 1500 N Lombardy St Richmond VA 23220

REESE, WINA HARNER, speech pathologist, consultant; b. Greensburg, Pa., Jan. 27, 1940; d. Clarence N. Harner and Gladys (Kell) Jaros; m. Richard F. Reese, Aug. 3, 1989; 1 child, Brian Olmsted. BS in Edn., Bowling Green (Ohio) State U., 1961. Speech pathologist La Grange (Ill.) Highlands, 1961-69, Richland Co., Mansfield, Ohio, 1970, Rehab. Svcs. N.C. Ohio, Mansfield, 1970-77; pvt. practice Lexington, Ohio, 1977-89; speech pathologist Mansfield City Schs., 1977—; cons., tutor Bur. Vocat. Rehab., Mansfield, 1980—. Mem. Learning Disabilities Assn., Ohio Speech-Lang.-Hearing Assn. (dist. rep. 1975-76), N.C. Ohio Speech-Hearing Assn. (pres. 1975-76), Orton Dyslexia Soc. Home: 95 Otterbein Dr Mansfield OH 44904-9341 Office: Mansfield City/St Peters 67 Mulberry St S Mansfield OH 44902-1909

REESE-BROWN, BRENDA, primary educator, mathematics specialist; b. Tampa, Fla., Mar. 22, 1948; d. James T. and Mary Reese; m. Willie L. Brown. AA, Hillsborough C.C., Tampa, 1976; BA, U. South Fla., 1979; M in Early Childhood, Nova U., 1993. Cert. elem. and early childhood tchr., Fla. Tchr. kindergarten Town n County Elem. Sch., Tampa, 1979-80; primary tchr. Temple Terrace Elem. Sch., Tampa, 1980-91, tchr. kindergarten, 1991—, mem. sch. improvement team, 1992—, math. specialist, 1992—. Mem. Zeta Phi Beta, Inc. (grammateus Nu Upsilon Zeta chpt. 1990-92). Office: Temple Terrace Elem Sch 124 Flotto Ave Tampa FL 33617-5524

REESER, RACHEL ANNE EVERSON, graphic designer; b. Shreveport, La., Nov. 16, 1964; d. Robert Higgins and Marian Louise (Wimberly) Everson; m. Kirk Allen "Korky" Reeser, Feb. 1, 1994. BS, Okla. State U., 1986. Mgr. Fabric, Floors & Such, Oklahoma City, Okla., 1986-87; advt. dir. Pipkin Cameras & Video, Oklahoma City, 1987-88; asst. nat. advt. mgr. Morgan Bldgs. & Spas, Dallas, 1988-89; sr. art dir. Avrea/Pugliese, Coconut Grove, Dallas, 1989-91; pres., creative dir. Freestyle Studio, Inc., Dallas, 1991—. Mem. Dallas Soc. Illustrators (bd. dirs. 1992-94, Merit award 1993), Dallas Soc. Visual Comms. Office: Freestyle Studio Ste 1000 8150 N Ctrl Expy Dallas TX 75206 Address: PO Box 823554 Dallas TX 75382

REEVES, ALEXIS SCOTT, journalist; b. Atlanta, Feb. 4, 1949; d. William Alexander and Marian (Willis) Scott; m. Marc Anthony Lewis, Sept. 14, 1968 (div. 1973); m. David Leslie Reeves, Mar. 16, 1974; children: Cinque Scott, David Leslie, Jr. Student Barnard Coll., 1966-68; student Spellman Coll., 1989-90, Regional Leadership Inst., 1992. Reporter, asst. city editor, cable TV editor, mgr. video edit., v.p. community affairs Atlanta Jour. & Constn., Atlanta, 1974-93; dir. Diversity and Community Rels. for Cox Enterprises Inc., 1993—; vis. instr. summer program for minority journalists, Berkeley, Calif., 1980, 81, 84, 85, 87 Grady High Sch., Atlanta, 1982-83; journalist-in-residence Clark Coll., Atlanta, 1983. Researcher, writer: The History of Atlanta NAACP, 1983 (NAACP award, 1984). Recipient Disting. Urban Journalism award Nat. Urban Coalition, 1980. Michele Clark fellow Columbia U. Sch. Journalism, 1974. Named one of 100 Top Black Bus. & Profl. Women, 1986; recipient Acad. Achievement award YWCA, 1989. Mem. Nat. Assn. Media Women (Media Woman of Yr. award, 1983, Media Woman of Yr. nat. award 1983, pres. Atlanta chpt. 1985-87), Atlanta Assn. Black Journalists (Commentary Print award 1983), Nat. Assn. Black Journalists, Sigma Delta Chi (bd. dirs. 1980-84, treas. 1985-88). Moderator, First Congl. Ch., 1982-92. Office: Cox Enterprises Inc PO Box 105357 1400 Lake Hearne Dr NE Atlanta GA 30348

REEVES, BARBARA ANN, lawyer; b. Buffalo, Mar. 29, 1949; d. Prentice W. and Doris Reeves; m. Richard C. Neal; children: Timothy R. Neal, Stephen S. Neal (dec.), Robert S. Neal, Richard R. Neal. Student, Wellesley Coll., 1967-68; B.A. (NSF fellow, Lehman fellow), New Coll., Sarasota, Fla., 1970; J.D. cum laude, Harvard U., 1973. Bar: Calif. 1973, D.C. 1977. Law clk. U.S. Ct. Appeals, 9th Circuit, Portland, Oreg., 1973-74; assoc. firm Munger, Tolles and Rickershauser, L.A., 1977-78; trial atty. spl. trial sect. Dept. Justice (Antitrust div.), 1974-75; spl. asst. to asst. atty. gen. Antitrust div. Dept. Justice, Washington, 1976-77; chief antitrust div. L.A. field office, 1978-81; ptnr. Morrison & Foerster, L.A., 1981-94, Fried, Frank, Harris, Shriver & Jacobson, L.A., 1995—; mem. exec. com. state bar conf. of dels. L.A. Delegation, 1982-91; del. 9th Cir. Jud. Conf., 1984-88; mem. Fed. Ct. Magistrate Selection Com., 1989; bd. dirs. Pub. Counsel, 1988-92, Western Ctr. Law and Poverty, 1992—; lectr. in field. Editor: Federal Criminal Litigation, 1994; contbr. articles to profl. jours. Mem. ABA (litigation sect., antitrust sect.), Am. Arbitration Assn. (arbitrator, mediator, mem. adv. panel large complex case program), L.A. County Bar Assn. (antitrust sect. officer 1980-81, litigation sect. officer 1988-93 trustee 1990-92, chair alternative dispute resolution sec. 1992—, L.A. County Ct. ADR com.). Home: 1410 Hillcrest Ave Pasadena CA 91106-4503 Office: Fried Frank Harris Shriver & Jacobson 725 S Figueroa St # 3890 Los Angeles CA 90017

REEVES, CATHERINE GRENDA, accountant; b. Riverside, N.J., July 21, 1960; d. Joseph Andrew and Patricia Ann (Pettit) Grenda; m. Kevin Joseph Reeves, May 3, 1986. AS, Burlington C.C., Pemberton, N.J., 1985; BS in Bus. Adminstrn., Rider U., 1992. Acctg. clk. U.S. Pipe & Foundry Co., Burlington, N.J., 1979-87, pers. asst., 1987-92, sr. acct., 1992—. Mem. Inst. Mgmt. Accts. Roman Catholic. Home: 911 Mooney Rd Burlington NJ 08016 Office: US Pipe & Foundry Co 1101 E Pearl St Burlington NJ 08016

REEVES, CONNIE LYNN, retired army officer, writer; b. Ellington AFB, Tex., Oct. 12, 1954; d. Calvin Arthur and Ineva Dorthene (Wilkinson) R.; m. Clifton Willey Lewis, Jr., May 19, 1979; children: Derek Alexander, Jessica Megan. BA in Sociology, U. Tex., 1975; MA in History, George Washington U., 1987. Commd. 2d lt. U.S. Army, 1976, advanced through grades to lt. col., ret., 1994; ops. officer Davison Army Airfield, Ft. Belvoir, Va., 1985; instr. and course mgr. Def. Intelligence Coll., Washington, 1985-86; indications and warning intelligence analyst, polit./mil. intelligence analyst for Western Europe; div. chief Joint Intelligence Ctr., Directorate of Intelligence U.S. European Command, Stuttgart, Germany, 1988-91; defense fgn. lang. program U.S. Army, Washington, 1992-93; staff officer U.S. Army Counter Drug Program, 1993-94. Author: French Women During World War I: Their Contribution to the National Defense, 1987. Mem AAUW, Ret. Officer Assn., Women Mil. Aviators, Ninety-Nines, Whirly-Girls, Internat. Women Helicopter Pilots. Republican. Office: PO Box 117 Dowell MD 20629

REEVES, DIANNE L., artist; b. Milw., Apr. 8, 1948; d. John J. and Bernice M. (Hendricksen) Kleczka; m. Robert A. McCoy, Oct. 15, 1983 (div. June 1988). BFA, U. Wis., Milw., 1968; student, Mus. Fine Arts, Houston, 1974-77, 83, Glassell Sch. Art, Houston, 1980-83. Instr. papermaking Glassell Sch. Art, 1984-85. Exhibitee in solo shows at Women and Their Work Gallery, Austin, Tex., 1988, Moreau Galleries/Hamms Gallery, Notre Dame, Ind., 1991; internat. exhibns. include Leopold-Hoesch Mus., Duren, Germany, 1991, 92, 93, galleries in Netherlands and Basel, Switzerland; exhibited in numerous group exhbns.; author: (ltd. edit.) From Fiber to Paper, 1991. Bd. dirs., sec. Friends of Dard Hunter, Inc., 1993-94. NEA/Tex. fellow Mid-Am. Arts Alliance/NEA, 1986; recipient awards for art work. Mem. Internat. Assn. Hand Papermakers and Paper Artists (co-chair nominating com. 1993-94), Women and Their Work, Inc., Sierra Club, Tex. Fine Arts Assn., Austin Visual Arts Assn. Home and Studio: 1615 W 9 1/2 St Austin TX 78703-4711

REEVES, DONNA ANDREWS, golfer; b. Boston, Apr. 12, 1967; d. James Barclay and Helen Louise (Munsey) Andrews; m. John A. Reeves, Nov. 13, 1993. BBA, U. N.C., 1989. Qualified golfer LPGA Tour, Fla., 1990; winner Ping-Cellular One Golf Tounament, Portland, Oreg., 1993, Ping-Welch's Golf Tournament, Tucson, Ariz., 1994, Dinah Shore Major Golf Tournament, Palm Springs, Calif., 1994. Office: LPGA 2570 Volusia Ave Daytona Beach FL 32114-1119

REEVES, JOY BENNETT, sociology educator; b. Evanston, Ill., Apr. 17, 1938; d. Christy Michael Delmas and Dorothy Hertha (Abel) Tinnell; m. Hershel C. Reeves, Feb. 1, 1964; children: Karen, John. BA, Long Beach State Coll., 1964; MA, La. State U., 1966, PhD, 1972. Asst. prof. part-time Stephen F. Austin State U., Nacogdoches, Tex., 1971-74, asst. prof. dept. sociology, 1975-80, chairperson, prof. dept. sociology, 1976—; cons. in field. Conrbr. chpts. to books and articles to profl. jours. Travel grant Fulbright Hays Found., 1986, 89, 93. Mem. Mid-Smith Sociol. Assn. (pres. 1991-92, v.p. 1983-84), Am. Sociol. Assn., Profl. Women's Assn. (v.p. 1984-85). Democrat. Episcopalian. Office: Stephen F Austin State U PO Box 13047 Nacogdoches TX 75962

REEVES, NANCY ALICE, critical care nurse; b. Manhasset, N.Y., Aug. 19, 1965; d. Kenneth George and Jean Adele (Reineke) Leib; m. Gregory Douglas Reeves, Sept. 29, 1990. BSN, Hartwick Coll., 1988. RN, N.Y. Staff nurse intermediate care unit Mercy Med. Ctr., Rockville Center, N.Y., 1988-92, staff nurse CCU, 1992—; office nurse Gary Friedman, MD, Rockville Center, 1993—. Mem. AACN, N.Y. State Nurses Assn., Alpha Omicron Pi.

REEVES, PATRICIA RUTH, heavy machinery manufacturing company executive; b. Bklyn., Mar. 26, 1931; d. Maurice G. and Ethel Helen (Kessler) Der Brucke m. Cedric E. Reeves, June 22, 1952. BA, Adelphi U., 1952. Chief of records sect. Hydrocarbon Rsch., Inc., N.Y.C., 1952-65; lead sec. C.F. Braun & Co., Murray Hill, N.J., 1965-69; exec. sec. Wilputte Corp., Murray Hill, N.J., 1969-75, adminstrv. asst., 1975-79, sales coord., 1979-81, pers. adminstr., 1981-82; sales coord. Krupp Wilputte Corp., Murray Hill, N.J., 1982-84; pers. adminstr. Somerset Techs., Inc., N.J., 1984-85, pers. mgr., 1985—. Pres. Mountain Jewish Community Ctr., Warren, N.J., 1976-77, bd. dirs., 1972-81. Mem. NAFE, AAUW, Women's NetWork Ctrl. N.J. (v.p., editor newsletter 1981-83, coord. career assistance 1984-85, membership chair 1986-89), Am. Soc. Pers. Adminstrs. (membership chair 1986-88, sec. 1986-88), Soc. Human Resources Mgmt. (sec. Ctrl. N.J. chpt. 1986-88, v.p. 1988-89, pres. 1989-90, sec.-treas. N.J. State Coun. 1990-92, sec.-treas. Area I bd. 1993—, co-chair N.J. Conf., 1994—). Home: 89 Knollwood Dr Watchung NJ 07060-6245 Office: Somerset Tech Inc 15 Campus Dr Somerset NJ 08873-9999

REEVES, PAULETTE SMITH, counselor; b. McRae, Ga., Apr. 20, 1947; d. Marion Mallette and Quinelle (Hargrove) Smith; m. Joseph Wiley Reeves, May 16, 1968; children: Nathan Patrick, Jason Eric. BA, Mercer U., 1972, MEd, 1980; M in Sch. Counseling, Ga. So. U., 1993. Tchr. elem. Bibb County Pub. Schs., Macon, Ga., 1972-92, counselor, 1992—. Vol. outreach program Mulberry Meth. Ch., Macon, 1988—. Mem. Am. Sch. Counseling Assn., Ga. Sch. Counseling Assn., Profl. Assn. Ga. Educators, Mid. Ga. Sch. Counselors Assn. (dir. profl. resl. 1993—), Ctr. High Sch. PTA, Parents for Pub. Schs., Phi Kappa Phi. Democrat.

REEVES, PEGGY LOIS ZEIGLER, accountant; b. Orangeburg, S.C., May 12, 1940; d. Joseph Harold and Lois Vivian (Stroman) Zeigler; m. Donald Preston Reeves, Sept. 9, 1961. Degree in Secretarial Sci., Coker Coll., 1960. Sec. Ladson Beach, CPA, Orangeburg, 1960-61; acctg. clk. Milliken & Co., Laurens, S.C., 1962-67, sec., 1967-73, mgmt. trainee, 1973, plant contr., 1973-74, 76-81; cost acctg. supr. Milliken & Co., Spartanburg, S.C., 1974-76, 81—. Chair bd. dirs. Enoree (S.C.)-Lanford Fire Dist., 1982—, treas., 1988—. H.L. Jones scholar Coker Coll., 1959-60. Mem. Inst. Mgmt. Accts. (sec. 1991-94, v.p. membership 1994-95), Profl. Secs. Internat. (v.p., rec. sec., Sec. of Yr. 1973). Baptist.

REEVES-DUDLEY, BEVERLY JAYNE, nurse anesthetist; b. New Orleans, Nov. 26, 1956; d. Clarence Thomas and Roberta Lilian (Preston) Reeves; m. Thomas Harris Dudley, Aug. 23, 1986. BSN, U. Iowa, 1979; MA in Biology, U. Mo., Kansas City, 1984. Cert. RN anesthetist, Kans., ACLS. Staff nurse neurology U. Iowa Hosp., Iowa City, 1979-80; staff nurse ICU and CCU Broadlawns Med. Ctr., Des Moines, 1980-82; instr. anesthesia U. Kans., Kansas City, 1985; free-lance anesthetist Anesthesia Svc., Inc., Leavenworth, Kans., 1986; staff nurse anesthetist Humana Hosp., Overland Park, Kans., 1987-94; self-employed Overland Park, 1994—; del. People to People Citizen Ambassador, People's Rep. of China, 1989. Contbr. articles to profl. jours. County del. Jimmy Carter Re-Election, Iowa City, 1980; vol. Com. for State ERA Amendment, Des Moines, 1980. Des Moines Women's Club scholar, 1982. Mem. ANA, Am. Assn. Nurse Anesthetists, Sigma Theta Tau, Phi Eta Sigma.

REEVES-HOCHÉ, MARY KATHRYN, pulmonary medicine nurse; b. Travis AFB, Calif., Mar. 14, 1956; d. George I. and Kathryn Ann (Randall) Reeves; m. Georges A. Hoché, June 24, 1981. BSN, Jamestown Coll., 1977; MA, Cen. Mich. U., 1980; MS, U. Del., 1987. RN, Calif., Pa. Pub. health nurse Migrant Health Svcs., Whapeton, N.D., 1977; staff nurse St. Jude's Hosp., Fullerton, Calif., 1977-78; commd. 2d lt. USAF, 1978, advanced through grades to maj., 1990—; staff nurse, head nurse Malcolm Grow USAF Hosp., Washington, 1978-84; charge nurse ICU Erhling Bergquist Regional Hosp., Omaha, 1984-85; instr. Reading (Pa.) Area C.C., 1986; night shift supr. Med. Base Am. USAF, Saudi Arabia, 1991; pulmonary nurse specialist Pa. State U. Hosp., Hershey, 1987—; cons. VA Med. Ctr., Lebanon, Pa., 1989—. Editor, reviewer Critical Care Nurse, 1988—; contbr. to profl. jours. Mem. AACN, ANA (cert. advanced med.-surg. nurse), Am. Thoracic Soc. (chmn. nominating com. for assembly on nursing 1993-95), Pa. Thoracic Soc. (chmn. com. on nursing), Pa. Nurses' Assn. (dist. sec. 1989-91, chmn. nursing edn. com. 1988-92), Sigma Theta Tau. Office: Pa State U Hosp PO Box 850 Hershey PA 17033-0850

REGALMUTO, NANCY MARIE, small business owner, psychic consultant, therapist; b. Bay Shore, N.Y., Aug. 24, 1956; d. Antonio J. Jr. and Agnes C. (Dietz) R. Student, SUNY, Stony Brook. Sales mgr. Fire, Inc., Hempstead, N.Y.; sports handicapper Red Hot Sport, J. Dime Sports, Diamond Sports, Hicksville, N.Y.; small bus. owner, pres. Synergy (vitamin/nutritional product mfr. and distributor), Bellport, N.Y., 1989—; cons. on medicine, fin., past life, bus. readings, hypnosis, substance abuse, archeology, law enforcement investigations, family, counseling, inter-species comm., animal therapy, psychic surgery, healing; lectr. in field, specializing in holistic remedies and therapies. Columnist Daily Racing Form; appeared on numerous TV programs, worldwide radio, mags., newspapers. Lectr., seminar leader, written about in several books. Mem. NAFE, Horse Protection Assn., Am. Biog. Inst. (named Woman of Yr. 1994). Home and Office: 18 Woodland Park Dr Bellport NY 11713-2315 also: 200 Leslie Dr Ste 806 Hallandale FL 33009

REGAN, ELLEN FRANCES (MRS. WALSTON SHEPARD BROWN), ophthalmologist; b. Boston, Feb. 1, 1919; d. Edward Francis and Margaret (Moynihan) R.; A.B., Wellesley Coll., 1940; M.D., Yale U., 1943; m. Walston Shepard Brown, Aug. 13, 1955. Intern, Boston City Hosp., 1944; asst. resident, resident Inst. Ophthalmology, Presbyn. Hosp., N.Y.C., 1944-47, asst. ophthalmologist, 1947-56, asst. attending ophthalmologist, 1956-84; instr. ophthalmology Columbia Coll. Physicians and Surgeons, 1947-55, asso. ophthalmology, 1955-67, asst. clin. prof., 1967-84. Mem. Am. Ophthal. Soc., AMA, Am. Acad. Ophthalmology, N.Y. Acad. Medicine, N.Y. State Med. Soc., Mass. Med. Soc., River Club. Office: PO Box 632 Tuxedo Park NY 10987-0632

REGAN, JUDITH THERESA, publishing executive; b. Leominster, Mass., Aug. 17, 1953; d. Leo James and Rita Ann (Imprescia) R.; children: Patrick, Lara. BA, Vassar Coll., 1975. Sr. editor, v.p. Simon & Schuster, N.Y.C., 1989-94; pres., pub. Regan Books, N.Y.C., 1994—; TV prodr. Entertainment Tonight, N.Y.C., Geraldo, N.Y.C.; prodr. 20th Century Fox Films, Fox TV; corr. Full Disclosure, Fox TV; pub. Regan Books, Harper Collins. Author: The Art of War for Women; editor numerous books including And the Beat Goes On (Sonny Bono), 1991, The Way Things Ought to Be (Rush Limbaugh), 1992, Shampoo Planet and Life After God (Douglas Coupland), 1992, She's Come Undone (Wally Lamb), 1992, Rogue Warrior (Richard Marcinko), 1992, Feminine Force: Release the Power Within You to Create the Life You Deserve (Georgette Mosbacher), 1993, Private Parts (Howard Stern), 1993, I Can't Believe I Said That (Kathie Lee Gifford), 1994. Office: Regan Books 1211 Ave of the Americas New York NY 10036

REGAN, LINDA ANNE, insurance agent; b. Summitt, N.J., Jan. 9, 1957; d. Steven George and Anne M. (Vivian) Fasold; m. Kevin M. Regan, Dec. 7, 1985; children: Anne M., Evan M. Student, Eckerd Coll., 1980. Claims rep. Ohio Casualty Ins. Co., St. Petersburg, Fla., 1973-74; comml. rep. Nat. Ins. Assoc., St. Petersburg, 1974-82, Baynard Bros. Ins., St. Petersburg, 1982-83; comml. underwriter Hull and Co. Inc., Gainesville, Fla., 1983-84; sr. underwriter Harvey, Percy & Jones Inc., Tampa, Fla., 1984-85; office mgr. Aanco Underwriters Inc., St. Petersburg, 1985-86; comml. rep. Wittner, Klutts & Co., St. Petersburg, 1986-88; office mgr. Italiano Ins. Svcs., Englewood, Fla., 1988-90; ins. agt. James T. Blalock Agy., Venice, Fla., 1991-93, Gifford-Heiden Ins. Agy., Venice, 1993—; v.p. Insurors Allied Svc. Corp., Englewood, 1991—; instr. individual devel. program. Editor (newsletter) The Bull., 1989-91. Volunteer Englewood Community Hosp., 1990, Adopt A Hwy. Program, Englewood, 1990, 91, Vineland Elem. Sch., Englewood, 1991. Mem. Fla. West Coast Ins. Women (pres. Pt. Charlotte chpt. 1992-93, Ins. Woman of Yr. 1991), Fla. Assn. Ins. Agts., Profl. Inst. Agts. Assn., Nat. Assn. Ins. Women (Fla. coun. sec. 1988-90), Ins. Women of St. Petersburg (bd. dirs. 1988, v.p. 1989-90), Bus. and Profl. Women's Club (bd. dirs. Englewood chpt. 1989—). Republican. Episcopalian. Home: 7410 Cape Girardeau St Englewood FL 34224-8004

REGAN, MURIEL, small business owner; b. N.Y.C., July 15, 1930; d. William and Matilda (Riebel) Blome; m. Robert Regan, 1966 (div. 1976); 1 child, Jeanne Booth. BA, Hunter Coll., N.Y.C., 1950; MLS, Columbia U., 1952; MBA, Pace U., N.Y.C., 1982. Post libr. US Army, Okinawa, 1952-53; researcher P.F. Collier, N.Y.C., 1953-57; asst. libr. to libr. Rockefeller Found., N.Y.C., 1957-67; dep. chief libr. Manhattan Community Coll., N.Y.C., 1967-68; libr. Booz Allen & Hamilton, N.Y.C., 1968-69, Rockefeller Found., N.Y.C., 1969-82; prin. Gossage Regan Assocs., Inc., N.Y.C., 1980—; dir. NY Met. Reference and Rsch. Libr. Agy., 1988—, Coun. of Nat. Libr. and Info. Assns., 1991—; cons. Librs., Info. ctrs. Mem. SLA (pres. 1989-90), Archons of Colophon, N.Y. Libr. Club. Home: 792 Columbus Ave New York NY 10025-5150 Office: Gossage Regan Assocs Inc 25 W 43rd St New York NY 10036-7406

REGAN, SYLVIA, playwright; b. N.Y.C., Apr. 15, 1908; d. Louis and Esther (Albert) Hoffenberg; m. James J. Regan, Feb. 11, 1931 (div. June 1936); m. 2d Abraham Ellstein, Nov. 7, 1940 (dec. Mar. 1963). Student pub. schs. Broadway actress N.Y.C., 1927-31; with pub. relations and promotion dept. Theatre Union and Orson Welles Mercury Theatre, N.Y.C., 1932-39; playwright, 1940—. Author: Morning Star, 1940, The Golden Door, 1951; musical Great to be Alive, 1951; The Fifth Season, 1953; libretto for grand opera The Golem, N.Y.C., 1962; Zelda, 1969. Sec. Sydney Epstein Meml. Fund for Strang Cancer Clinic, N.Y.C., 1948-68. Recipient citition Fedn. Women Zionists of Gt. Britain and Ireland, 1953. Mem. Dramatists Guild, Authors League of Am., Am. Jewish Hist. Soc., Nat. Council Jewish Women (citation of merit 1953). Democrat. Home: 55 E 9th St New York NY 10003

REGENAUER, CAROL MCCURDY, elementary education educator, consultant; b. Providence, Oct. 1, 1935; d. Russell Joseph and Margaret Mary (Bresnahan) McCurdy; m. Bernard John Regenauer, Sept. 20, 1958 (dec. Aug. 1988); children: Bernard John Jr., Russell McCurdy, Michael Edward. BA, Newton Coll. Sacred Heart, 1957; MS, Lesley Coll., 1991. Cert. tchr. grades 1-8, Mass. Elem. tchr. R.I. Pub. Schs., Providence, 1957-58, Boston (Mass.) Pub. Schs., 1958-60, Hudson (Mass.) Pub. Schs., 1969—; ednl. cons. Sci. Rsch. Assocs., Chgo., 1980-88, IBM, Boca Raton, Fla., 1989-90, CTB Macmillan-McGraw Hill, Monterey, Calif., 1993. Recipient Tchr. of Yr., Local Area Women's Club, Boston, 1985, Grant to Fund Purchase of Books for Cross-Age Program, Digital Corp., Maynard, Mass., 1994. Mem. NEA, Mass. Tchrs. Assn., Hudson Edn. Assn.

REGES, MARIANNA ALICE, marketing executive; b. Budapest, Hungary, Mar. 23, 1947; came to U.S., 1956, naturalized, 1963; d. Otto H. and Alice M. R.; m. Charles P. Green, Feb. 15, 1975; children: Rebecca, Charles III. AAS with honors, Fashion Inst. Tech., N.Y.C., 1967; BBA magna cum laude, Baruch Coll., 1971, MBA in Stats., 1978. Media rsch. analyst Doyle, Dane, Bernbach Advt., N.Y.C., 1967-70; rsch. supr. Sta. WCBS-TV, N.Y.C., 1970-71; rsch. mgr. Woman's Day mag., N.Y.C., 1971-72; asst. media dir. Benton & Bowles Advt., N.Y.C., 1972-75; mgr. rsch. and sales devel. NBC Radio, N.Y.C., 1975-77; sr. rsch. mgr. Ziff-Davis Pub. Co., N.Y.C., 1977-84; media mgr. Bristol-Myers Squibb Co., 1984—; mem. Spanish Radio Adv. Coun., N.Y.C., 1986-88; mem. Pan-European TV Audience Rsch. Mgmt. Com., 1988—. Mem. Vt. Natural Resources Council, 1977—; advisor Baruch Coll. Advt. Soc., 1975—. Mem. Am. Mktg. Assn., Am. Advt. Fedn., Media Rsch. Dirs. Assn., Radio and TV Rsch. Coun., Advt. Rsch. Found., Nature Conservancy, Vt. Natural Resources Coun., World Future Soc., Beta Gamma Sigma. Home: 626 E 20th St New York NY 10009 Office: Bristol-Myers Squibb Co 345 Park Ave New York NY 10154-0004

REGISTER, MARY CARNEY, human resource executive; b. Denver, Nov. 20, 1953; d. Edward A. and Mary Florence (Duncan) Carney; m. Dennis L. Register, Sept. 9, 1972; 1 child, Dena Mary. Human resource mgr. Tri-Eagle Distbg. Ltd., Tallahassee, Fla., 1981—. Vice chair Keep Tallahassee/Leon Co. Beautiful, 1993; co-chair E.A.P. Consortium Tallahassee, 1992-93; bd. dirs. N. Fla. Safety Coun., 1994. Mem. Human Resources Assn. Tallahassee, Soc. Human Resource Mgrs. Democrat. Roman Catholic. Office: 3420 W Tharpe St Tallahassee FL 32303-1138

REGISTER, PAMELA LEARNED, corporate communications consultant; b. Wilmington, N.C., Dec. 27, 1958; d. Daniel Charles and Polly Ann (Vliet) Learned; m. Robert Bruce Register, July 29, 1978; children: Michelle Nicole, Mark Robert. BA in English, Smith Coll., 1982. Copy editor French dept. U. Mass., Amherst, 1980; libr. aide Med. Sch. Libr. U. Mass., Worcester, 1980-81; staff writer The Reporter, Lansdale, Pa., 1988-92; prin. Word Work, Lansdale, 1992—. Editor book on family med. practice, 1981-82; contbr. articles to retail mag. Dir. Pa. Citizens for Better Librs. 1991-92; mem. com. The Reporter Literacy Fair; pres. Friends of North Penn Librs., 1992; named to Pub. Libr. Project, 1992. Recipient 1st pl. award AP Mng. Editors of Pa., 1989, 92. Office: Word Work 664 Park Rd Lansdale PA 19446-5610

REGN, BONNIE MARIE, construction company executive; b. Neptune, N.J., Mar. 29, 1957; d. Alfred Wesley and Jennie Jeanette (Osinga) R.; m. William Cook, Mar. 7, 1987. BA, U. Calif., Santa Cruz, 1978; EdS, Rutgers U., 1983, MA, 1983. Cert. tchr. of the handicapped. Tchr. Search Day Program, Wanamassa, N.J., 1978-87; v.p. Fin-Addict Charters, Wall, N.J., 1987-93, Archtl. Woodworking, Bradley Beach, N.J., 1994—; v.p., dir. fin. William Cook Custom Homes, Wall, 1987—; v.p. Archtl. Woodworking, 1993—. Mem. sisterhood Temple Beth Torah. Mem. Autism Soc. Am., Long Branch Ski Club. Office: Archtl Woodworking 42 A Main St Bradley Beach NJ 07720

REGNELL, BARBARA CARAMELLA, media educator; b. Paterson, N.J., May 5, 1935; d. William Joseph and Mafalda Erminia (Benedetto) Caramella; m. Joseph C. Tirre, July 12, 1958 (div. June 1977); children: Conrad J., William C.; m. John Albin Regnell, Apr. 2, 1983. BS, Syracuse U., 1957, MA, 1966; postgrad., Washington U., St. Louis, 1972. Editor, continuity dir. Sta. WWBZ-AM, Vineland, N.J., 1958; dir. publicity Conti Adv., Ridgewood, N.J., 1958; copywriter Sta. KCNY, San Marcos, Tex., 1959; tchr. Henninger High Sch., Syracuse, N.Y., 1966-67; instr. Belleville (Ill.) Area Jr. Coll., 1968; from instr. to assoc. prof. So. Ill. U., Edwardsville, 1967—, chmn. mass communications, 1985—; trainer Nat. Iranian Radio, TV, Tehran, Iran, 1974-75. Mem. NATAS (mem. bd. govs. St. Louis chpt. Syracuse unit regional coun.), BEA, Internat. Radio and TV Soc., Delta Sigma Rho, Alpha Chi Omega. Republican. Home: 6 Hawthorne Ct Saint Louis MO 63122-4512 Office: So Ill U Dept Mass Communications PO Box 1775 Edwardsville IL 62026

REHDER, JENNIFER JO, microbiologist; b. Des Moines, Apr. 20, 1965; d. Dennis Lloyd and Patricia Ann (O'Brien) R. BA, Drake U., 1987, MA, 1989. Rsch. microbiologist Ambico, Inc., Dallas Center, Iowa, 1989—; intern Iowa State U., Ames, 1988. Sec., mem. soc. com. Grace Luth. Ch., Des Moines; vol. salesperson Global Gifts, Des Moines, 1993—. Mem. Nat. Wildlife Fedn., Nat. Parks and Conservation Assn., Nature Conservancy, Mid Iowa Cactus and Succulent Soc. Democrat. Office: Ambico Inc PO Box 522 Dallas Center IA 50063-0522

REHL, JANE FRANCES, history of art educator; b. Salem, N.J., Jan. 1, 1947; d. Harold Francis and Esther Teresa (MacMaster) Walenta; m. Richard A. Rehl, July 7, 1967 (div. 1974); m. James K. Kettlewell, Sept. 5, 1987. BA, U. Va., 1968; MA, Rutgers U., 1973. Rsch. asst. Libr. of Congress, Washington, 1968-70; asst. libr. Marquand Libr., Princeton (N.J.) U., 1970-71; libr. asst., teaching asst. Rutgers U., New Brunswick, N.J., 1971-72, 73-75, asst. mus. curator Jane Zimmerli Mus., 1972-73; curator slide/photo coll. Tyler Sch. Art Temple U., Phila., 1975-77; adj. prof. art history Skidmore Coll., Saratoga Springs, N.Y., 1978—, curator Art Coll., 1979-82; curator, asst. dir. mus. Hist. Soc. Saratoga Springs, 1986-90, cons., 1990—, bd. dirs., 1994—, project dir., 1989-93; mus. cons. Saratoga County History Ctr., Brookside Ballston Spa, N.Y., 1990—;. Editor: Saratoga: An Architectural History, 1991; co-author, editor mus. catalogues, 1987, 92. Mem. AAUW, NAACP, Am. Assn. Mus., Coll. Art Assn. Home: 19 Lafayette St Saratoga Springs NY 12866-3210 Office: Skidmore Coll Dept Art and Art History Saratoga Springs NY 12866

REHNS, MARSHA LEE, magazine editor; b. Balt., Dec. 23, 1946; d. Fred and Ruth (Lieber) R.; m. Walter Richard Arnheim, Sept. 5, 1971; children: Ethan, Phillip. BS, U. Pitts., 1967; MPhil, Yale, 1970. editor Sci. Med. Pub., N.Y.C., 1972-75; editor Haymarket Pub., London, 1975-76; mng. editor Harcourt Brace Jovanovich, N.Y.C., 1977-79; editor Sta. WGBH-TV, Boston, 1979-80; columnist Weightwatchers Mag., N.Y.C., 1979-81; editor Cahners Pub., N.Y.C., 1981—; cons. Cradle Pub., N.Y.C., 1990—; writer Kids Discover, N.Y.C., 1991—, Nat. Mus. Natural History, 1994—. Publicity chmn. Potomac Elem. Sch., Md., 1990-92; docent Nat. Mus. Natural History, Washington, 1990—. Home: 10712 Barn Wood Ln Potomac MD 20854-1326

REHRAUER, ANN FRANCES, academic administrator; b. Norway, Mich., Apr. 24, 1948; d. Mark Joseph and Frances June (Schunk) R. BA in Edn., St. Norbert Coll., 1971; MA in Liturgical Studies, St. John's U., Collegeville, Minn., 1982; JCL, Cath. U. Am., 1985. Lic. canon law. Tchr. St. Matthew Sch., Green Bay, Wis., 1970-73, St. Jude Sch., Green Bay, 1973-76; vice-prin., tchr. Holy Family Sch., Marinette, Wis., 1976-79; prin., tchr. St. Mary Sch., Bear Creek, Wis., 1979-81; cons. worship Cath. Diocese Green Bay, 1981-83, asst. chancellor, 1985-86, acting chancellor, 1986, chancellor, 1987—, judge tribunal, 1988—; mem. gen. coun. Sisters of St. Francis, Green Bay, 1985-93; canonical cons. Sisters of Our Lady of Charity, N.Am. Union, Wisconsin Dells, Wis., 1987-90. Mem. Canon Law Soc. Am. (cons. bd. govs. 1990-92), Am. Mgmt. Assn. Roman Catholic. Home: 3025 Bay Settlement Rd Green Bay WI 54311-7301 Office: Cath Diocese Green Bay PO Box 23066 Green Bay WI 54305-3066

REIBMAN, JEANETTE FICHMAN, retired state senator; b. Ft. Wayne, Ind., Aug. 18, 1915; d. Meir and Pearl (Schwartz) Fichman; m. Nathan L. Reibman, June 20, 1943; children: Joseph M. Edward D., James E. AB, Hunter Coll., 1937; LLB, U. Ind., 1940; LLD, Lafayette Coll., 1969; hon. degree, Lehigh U., 1986, Wilson Coll., 1974, Cedar Crest Coll., 1977, Moravian Coll., 1990. Bar: Ind., 1940, U.S. Supreme Ct. 1944. Pvt. practice law Ft. Wayne, 1940; atty. U.S. War Dept., Washington, 1940-42, U.S. War Prodn. Bd., Washington, 1942-44; mem. Pa. Ho. of Reps., 1956-66, Pa. State Senate, Harrisburg, 1966-94; chmn. com. on edn. Pa. State Senate, 1971-81, minority chmn., 1981-90, majority caucus adminstr., 1992—; mem. Edn. Commn. of the States. Trustee emeritus Lafayette Coll.; bd. mem. Pa. Higher Edn. Assistance Agy., Pa. Coun. on Arts, Camphill Schs. Recipient Disting. Dau. of Pa. award and medal Gov. Pa., 1968, citation on naming of Jeanette F. Reibman Adminstrn. Bldg., East Stroudsburg State Coll., 1972, Early Childhood Learning Ctr. Northampton Community Coll., 1992, Pub. Svc. award Pa. Psychol. Assn., 1977, Jerusalem City of Peace award Govt. Israel, 1977; named to Hunter Coll. Alumni Hall of Fame, 1974; U. Ind. Law Alumni fellow, 1993. Mem. Hadassah (Myrtle Wreath award 1976), Sigma Delta Tau, Delta Kappa Gamma, Phi Delta Kappa, Order Ea. Star. Democrat. Jewish. Office: 711 Lehigh St Easton PA 18042-4325

REICE, SYLVIE, columnist, editor, author; b. N.Y.C.; d. Samuel and Dora (Weinstock) Wolshine; m. Albert Reice, July 15, 1962; children: Milo, Naomi, Seth, Andrew, Richard. BA cum laude, CUNY, 1939; postgrad., New Sch. for Social Rsch., N.Y.C., 1940. Mng. editor Co-ed mag. Scholastic Publs., N.Y.C., 1955-59; editor-in-chief Ingenue mag. Dell Pub. Co., N.Y.C., 1959-67; sr. editor McCalls mag., N.Y.C., 1967-71; editor-in-chief Family Health mag., N.Y.C., 1971-74; exec. editor Newspaper books Chgo. Tribune-N.Y. News Syndicate, N.Y.C., 1975-76; sr. editor Grosset & Dunlap Books, N.Y.C., 1976-79; columnist United Features Syndicate, N.Y.C., 1980—; freelance writer, 1946—; adj. prof. mag. journalism SUNY-Stony Brook. Author: (short story collections) For Girls Only, 1957, Season of Love, 1962, (novel) Now or Never, 1994; contbr. articles to various publs., including McCalls, Health, Seventeen, Ladies Home Jour. Guest editor Taproot mag. for elder citizens, L.I., N.Y., 1986-87. Recipient Penney Missouri award for best article of yr., 1970, award for best short story Bur. of Intercultural Edn., 1952. Mem. PEN, Newswomens Club N.Y. (v.p. 1984—, pres. 1983-84), Phi Beta Kappa. Home: 401 E 81st St New York NY 10028

REICH, KATHLEEN JOHANNA, librarian, educator; b. Mannheim, Germany, May 1, 1927; came to U.S., 1955, naturalized, 1958; d. Robert and Luise Charlotte Helene (Kurowsky) Weichel; 1 child, Robert Weichel. MAT in English, Rollins Coll., 1976, EdS, 1981, postgrad., U. Leipzig, 1948-50, U. Mainz, 1950-54. With Orlando (Fla.) Pub. Library, 1955-57; cataloguer, instr. U. Detroit, 1957-60, Trinity U., San Antonio, 1960-61; adminstr. Fla. Book Processing Ctr., Orlando, 1961-68; bur. chief, div. libr. svcs. Fla. State Dept., Winter Park, 1968-71; assoc. prof. libr. sci. Rollins Coll., Winter Park, 1971—, asst. dean faculty, 1981-83, dir. overseas studies, 1983-84; head archives and spl. collections Rollins Coll., 1983—; acad. dean Prew Prep. Sch., Sarasota, Fla., 1983-85. Mem. AAUP, African Lit. Assn., Am. Water Ski Assn., Soc. Am. Archivists, Soc. Fla. Archivists, Fla. Hist. Assn., Winter Park Hist. Soc. (bd. dirs.), Kappa Delta Pi. Home: 211 Fawsett Rd Winter Park FL 32789-6014 Office: Rollins Coll Winter Park FL 32789

REICH, ROSE MARIE, retired art educator; b. Milw., Dec. 24, 1937; d. Valentine John and Mary Jane (Grochowski) Kosmatka; m. Kenneth Pierce Reich, July 13, 1968; 1 stepson, Lance Pierce. BA, Milw. Downer Coll., 1959; MA, U. Wyo., 1967. Art tchr. Oconomowoc (Wis.) Area Schs., 1959-93, ret., 1993. Mem. Oconomowoc Edn. Assn., NEA (life), Wis. Edn. Assn., AAUW (v.p. membership 1989—), Delta Kappa Gamma (past pres.). Roman Catholic. Home: 3717 N Golden Lake Rd Oconomowoc WI 53066-4104

REICHBLUM, AUDREY ROSENTHAL, public relations executive; b. Pitts., June 28, 1935; d. Emanuel Nathan and Willa (Handmacher) Rosenthal; m. M. Charles Reichblum, Jan. 25, 1956; children: Robert Nathan, William Mark. Student, Bennington Coll., 1952-53; BS, Carnegie Mellon U., 1956. Accredited Pub. Rels. Soc. Pitts. Founder, creator, chmn. Pitts. Children's Mus., 1970-73; mag. writer Pitts. Mag., 1978; dir. pub. rels. Pitts. Pub. Theater, 1978-79; pres. arPR audrey reichblum PUB. RELS. inc., Pitts., 1980—; pub. rels. cons., bd. mem. Pitts. Planned Parenthood, 1980—, United Jewish Fedn., Bus. and Profl. Women, Pitts., 1980—, Pitts. City Theater, 1985—. Recipient Gold Cindy award Info. Film Producers Am., 1982, award of excellence Internat. Assn. Bus. Communicators, Pitts., 1986. Mem. Publ. Rels. Soc. Am. (award of merit 1983, G. Victor Barkman award for excellence 1984, pst place award Race For The Cure), Women in Comm. (Matrix-sales promotion award 1987), Nat. Assn. Women Bus. Owners, Exec. Women's Coun., Am. Women in Radio and TV, Am. Mktg. Assn., Rotary. Office: 1420 Centre Ave Ste 2216 Pittsburgh PA 15219-3528

REICHENBACH, M. J. GERTRUDE, retired university program director, consultant; b. Heerlen, Limburg, The Netherlands, Aug. 18, 1912; came to U.S., 1946; d. Jan Hubert Emile and M.J. Gertruda (Cardaun) Consten; m. Joseph Winfield, May 7, 1946; children: Paul Joseph, Peter David, Miriam Johanna, Eric Emile, Ingrid Gertrude. MA in English, U. Utrecht, The Netherlands, 1936; postgrad., Post Grad. Sch., The Netherlands, 1942-43; MA in German, U. Pa., 1971. English tchr. St. Clara Coll., Heerlen, The Netherlands, 1940-46; coord., originator Dutch studies U. Pa., Phila., 1969-87, cons. Dutch programs, 1987—; cons. Dutch programs Syracuse (N.Y.) U., 1987—. Co-editor presentations and lectures, 1985. Recipient John Adams medal The Netherlands Govt., 1976; named Officer in the Order of Orange Nassou, The Netherlands Govt., 1986, Officer in the Crown Order of Belgium, Belgian Govt., 1987. Mem. Internat. Assn. Netherlandic Studies, Am. Assn. Netherlandic Studies, Netherlands Soc. Phila. (chmn. lectures, mem. exec. bd. 1988—), Netherland Am. Assn. Delaware Valley (exec. bd. 1988—), Assn. for Advancement Dutch Studies, Can. Assn. English Netherlandic Studies, Am. Translators Assn., Germantown Cricket Club, AAUW. Republican. Roman Catholic. Home: 3031 W Coulter St Philadelphia PA 19129-1021

REICHER, JOANNE LOUISE, oncological nurse, clinical research coordinator; b. Pitts., Mar. 30, 1946; d. Eli and Mae (Slone) Reich; m. John Andrew Reicher, Nov. 29, 1970; children: Leslie Elizabeth, Jennifer Eileen. BA, Ga. State U., 1967; AS, Dekalb Coll., 1985. oncology cert. nurse. Staff nurse I med./surg. St. Joseph's Hosp., Atlanta, 1985-90, staff nurse I oncology, 1990-92, staff nurse II oncology, 1992-93; clin. rsch. nurse Winship Cancer Ctr. Emory U., Atlanta, 1993—. Mem. Oncology Nursing Soc. Home: 1472 Mile Post Dr Atlanta GA 30338 Office: Winship Cancer Ctr Emory U 1327 Clifton Rd Atlanta GA 30322

REICHERT, CHERYL MCBROOM, pathologist, research consultant; b. Great Falls, Mont., Sept. 4, 1946; d. Harold and Arlyne (Cohn) R.; m. Sherwood McBroom Jr., 1964 (div. 1971); children: Scott, Cari. BS, Coll. of Great Falls, 1969; MS, U. Mich., 1971, PhD, 1974, MD, 1976. Diplomate Am. Bd. of Med. Examiners. Tchr. fellow dept. biochemistry U. Mich., Ann Arbor, 1969-74; resident in anatomic pathology Nat. Cancer Inst., Bethesda, Md., 1977-79; resident in clin. pathology NIH, Bethesda, 1979-80, surgical pathologist, chief autopsy service, 1981-85; pathologist Sibley Meml. Hosp., Washington, 1985-86; cons. Digene Corp., College Park, Md., 1985-90, Nat. Cancer Inst., Bethesda, 1985—; pathologist Columbus Hosp., Great Falls, 1987—, dir. labs., 1990-91, 94—; assoc. rsch. scientist McLaughlin Research Inst., Great Falls, 1987—; clin. assoc. prof. Uniformed Svcs. U. Health Scis., Bethesda, 1983-86; presenter President's Nat. Cancer Adv. Bd., Washington, 1983. Contbr. 50 articles to profl. jours. Trustee Coll. of Gt. Falls, 1991-94; mem. profl. edn. com. Am. Cancer Soc.; bd. dirs. Ann Arbor Child Care and Devel.; charter mem., bd. dir. Project Heal Montana, 1993—. Lt. comdr. USPHS, 1977-80. Named Outstanding Young Women of Yr., State of Mich., 1983, Great Falls Profl. Women of Yr., YMCA, 1991. Mem. U.S.

Acad. Pathologists, Mont. Pathologists Soc. (pres. 1989-90, sec.-treas. 1990-91), Galens Med. Soc., Alpha Omega Alpha. Home: 51 Prospect Dr Great Falls MT 59405-4123

REICHERT, MARLENE JOY, secondary education educator; b. Davao City, Philippines, Nov. 29, 1957; d. Jacob and Lois Marie Bouw; m. David Julius Reichert, June 13, 1981 (June 23, 1991). BA in English, Nyack Coll., 1980; postgrad., St. Thomas Aquinas, 1987-88. Cert. tchr., N.Y., N.J. Tchr. St. Anne's Sch., Yonkers, N.Y., 1988-89; substitute tchr. Nyack (N.Y.) Pub. Schs., 1989-91, E. Ramapo Schs., Spring Valley, N.Y., 1989-91, Ramapo Ctrl. Schs., Hillburn, N.Y., 1989-91; tchr. BOCES Night High Schs., West Nyack, N.Y., 1989—, John Peter Tetard Intermediate Sch. 143, Bronx, N.Y., 1991—; instr. after sch. program Achieving Success, 1992-94. Contbr. poetry to Nat. Libr. of Poetry anthology. Democrat. Episcopalian. Home: 114 Depot Pl S Nyack NY 10960 Office: John Peter Tetard Ind Sch 120 W 231st St Bronx NY 10468

REICHGOTT JUNGE, EMBER D., lawyer, state senator; b. Detroit, Aug. 22, 1953; d. Norbert Arnold and Diane (Pincich) R.; m. Michael Junge. BA summa cum laude, St. Olaf Coll., Minn., 1974; JD, Duke U., 1977; MBA, U. of St. Thomas, 1991. Bar: Minn. 1977, D.C. 1978. Assoc., Larkin, Hoffman, Daly & Lindgren, Bloomington, Minn., 1977-84; counsel Control Data Corp., Bloomington, Minn., 1984-86; atty. The Gen. Counsel, Ltd., 1987—; mem. Minn. State Senate, 1983—, chmn. legis. com. on econ. status of women, 1984-86, senate majority whip, 1990-94, chmn. property tax div. senate tax com., 1991-92, chmn. senate judiciary com., 1993-94; senate asst. majority leader, 1995—, chmn. legis. com. on econ. status of women, 1984-86, vice chairman senate edn. com., 1987-88; instr. polit. sci. St. Olaf. Coll., Northfield, Minn., 1993; dir. Citizens Ind. Bank, St. Louis Park, Minn., 1993—. Host (cable TV monthly series) Legis. Report, 1985-92. Trustee, bd. dirs. N.W. YMCA, New Hope, Minn., 1983-88; Greater Mpls. Red Cross, 1988—, United Way Mpls., 1989—. Youngest woman ever elected to Minn. State Senate, 1983; recipient Woman of Yr. award North Hennepin Bus. and Prof. Women, 1983, Award for Contbn. to Human Svcs., Minn. Social Svcs. Assn., 1983, Clean Air award Minn. Lung Assn., 1988, Disting. Svc. award Mpls. Jaycees, 1984, Minn. Dept. Human Rights award, 1989, Myra Bradwell award Minn. Women Lawyers, 1993, Disting. Alumnae award Lake Conf. Schs., 1993; named One of Ten Outstanding Young Minnesotans, Minn. Jaycees, 1984, Policy Advocate of Yr. NAWBO, 1988, Woman of Achievement Twin West C. of C., 1989, Marvelous Minn. Woman, 1993. Mem. Minn. Bar Assn. (bd. govs. 1992—, Pro Bono Publico Atty. award 1990), Hennepin County Bar Assn., Corporate Counsel Assn. (v.p. 1989—), Minn. Dem. Farmer-Labor Party (state co-chair Clinton/Gore Presdl. Campaign 1992, del. nat. Dem. conv. 1984, 92, state exec. com. 1980-82). Home: 7701 48th Ave N Minneapolis MN 55428-4515

REICHMAN, DAWN LESLIE, lawyer, educator, deputy sheriff; b. Portsmouth, Va., Feb. 15, 1951; d. Stanley J. and Ernestine Enid (Kaiserman) Greif; m. James Richard Smith, Apr. 27, 1975 (div. July 1978); m. Victor I. Reichman, Nov. 24, 1979; children: Mark Heath, Margo Ilene, Shelley Renee. BA, U. Calif., L.A., 1972; cert. dep. sheriff, Sheriff Acad., 1974; JD, Whittier Coll., 1988. Bar: Calif. 1988, U.S. Dist. Ct. (ea. and cen. dists.) Calif. 1988. Dep. sheriff L.A. County Sheriff's Dept., 1973-81; substitute tchr. Palmdale (Calif.) Sch. Dist., 1988-90; pvt. practice law Palmdale, 1988—; alt. def. counsel, 1990-91. Spokesperson Ana Verde Homeowners Assn., Palmdale, 1989-94; assoc. Alpha Charter Guild of Antelope Valley Hosp.; former bd. dirs. Palmdale Cmty. Assn.; bd. dirs. Families Caring for Families, Desert Haven Enterprises; mem. strategic planning task force Antelope Valley Hosp. Med. Ctr.; mem. prin. adv. com. Highland H.S.; mem. dist. law and govt. career prep com. A.V. Union H.S. Mem. AAUW, Antelope Valley Bar Assn. (pres.), Calif. Women Lawyers, High Desert Criminal Def. Bar Assn. (former v.p., former sec.), Antelope Valley Bar Citizens Law Sch. (chmn.), Encouraging Potential in Children (co-chmn.), Palmdale & Quartz Hill C. of C., Phi Alpha Delta. Office: 1305 E Palmdale Blvd Ste 4 Palmdale CA 93550-4853

REICHMAN, NANCI SATIN, oil company owner; b. Tulsa, July 7, 1939; d. Jack Harold and Tybie Mary (Davis) Satin; m. Louis Reichman, Dec. 25, 1960 (dec. Feb. 1972); children: David Michael, Jill Satin; life ptnr. Phillip M. Citrin. Student, Sarah Lawrence Coll., Bronxville, N.Y., 1957-59; cert. Jungian psychology, C.G. Jung Inst., Evanston, Ill., 1988. Fashion model Miss Jackson's, Tulsa, 1969-70; pres. LIR Investments, Tulsa, 1972-78; pres., dir. devel. Tymar Oil Co., Tulsa and Santa Fe, N.Mex., 1990—; owner ind. oil prodn. Chgo., 1972—; audio tape lectr for various workshops. Pres. C.G. Jung Inst., Evanston, Ill., 1980-81, 81-82, 84-85, also mem. adv. bd.; v.p. Tulsa Jr. Philharm., 1968; sec. Tulsa Ballet, 1968. Home: 399 W Fullerton Pky Apt 8-e Chicago IL 60614-2810

REID, CAROLYN ANNE, medical librarian; b. Vincennes, Ind., Dec. 23, 1944; d. Charles MacArthur and Josephine Angeline (Boulet) Cummins; m. David Albert Reid, Aug. 7, 1967 (div. July 1980). BA in Libr. Sci. and Theatre, U. Mo., 1970, MA in Libr. Sci. and Computer, 1971. Cert. med. libr. Clin. med. libr. U. Mo.-Kansas City Med. Libr., 1971-75, sr. cin. med. libr., head online svcs., instr. medicine, 1975-80; online svcs. coord., asst. prof. Midcontinental Regional Med. Libr. Program U. Nebr. Med. Ctr, Omaha, 1980-83, assoc. dir., asst. prof., 1983-86, interim dir., assoc. prof., 1986-87; asst. prof. Sch. Libr. and Info. Sci. Pratt Inst., Bklyn., 1989—; assoc. dir., assoc. libr. Cornell U. Med. Coll. Libr., N.Y.C., 1987-93; assoc. dir., libr. Cornell U. Med. Libr., N.Y.C., 1993—; cons. Medline Database-Westchester County, White Plains, N.Y., 1991; cons./developer Med. Libr. Assn.-CE course-MESH for Online Searchers, Chgo., 1991-92; Vail vis. prof. Ottawa Regional Cancer Ctr., Ont., Can., 1985; parliamentarian U. Nebr. Med. Ctr. Faculty Svc., 1982-87, com. to rev. by-laws, 1986-87; automation advc. coun. N.Y. Met. Reference and Rsch. Libr. Agy., 1987-90; union catalog med. periodicals subcom. Med. Libr. Ctr. N.Y., 1987-93; presentations various meetings throughout U.S. Author, compiler numerous teaching workbooks on online searching, 1980—; contbr. articles to profl. jours. Vol. Planned Parenthood, Kansas City, Mo., 1978-80; organizer, coord. TAoismDiscussion Group, N.Y.C., 1990-93. Fellow in health sci. libr. Nat. Libr. Medicine, U. Mo., Columbia, 1970-71. Mem. ALA, Med. Libr. Assn. (bd. dirs. 1990-93, chmn. Midcontinental chpt. 1984-85, parliamentarian N.Y.-N.J. chpt. 1988-91, Rsch. Devel. and Project award 1986, Libr. of Yr. 1992), Spl. Librs. Assn. (chpt. archivist 1984-87), Libr. Adminstrn. and Mgmt. Assn., Assn. Coll. and Rsch. Librs., Acad. Health Info. Profls. (disting.), M.Y. Libr. Assn., Beta Phi Mu. Office: Cornell Med Libr 1300 York Ave New York NY 10021-4896

REID, DONNA JOYCE, small business owner; b. Springfield, Tenn., June 25, 1954; d. Leonard Earl Reid and Joyce (Robertson) Kirby; m. Kenneth Bruce Sadler, June 26, 1976 (div. Apr. 1980); m. John Christopher Moulton, Oct. 18, 1987 (div. Dec. 1992); m. Peter Leatherland, Apr. 3, 1993. Student, Austin Peay State U., Clarksville, Tenn., 1972-75. Show writer, producer WTVF-TV (CBS affiliate), Nashville, 1977-83, promotion producer, 1983-85, on-air promotion mgr., 1985-86; gen. mgr. Steadi-Film Corp., Nashville, 1986-90; co-owner Options Internat., Nashville, 1990—. Big sister Buddies of Nashville, 1981-87. Named to Honorable Order of Ky. Cols. John Y. Brown, Gov., 1980; recipient Significant Svc. award ARC, 1982, Clara Barton Communications award, 1983. Mem. NAFE, Nat. Assn. TV Arts and Scis., Nat. Film Inst., Nat. Assn. Broadcasters. Methodist. Office: Options Internat Inc 913 18th Ave S Nashville TN 37212

REID, FRANCES EVELYN KROLL, cinematographer, director, film company executive; b. Oakland, Calif., Mar. 25, 1944; d. William Farnham and Marion Storm (Teller) Kroll. BA, U. Oreg., 1966. Tchr. secondary sch., Los Angeles, 1968-69; sound recordist Churchill Films, Los Angeles, 1971; freelance sound recordist Los Angeles, 1972-75, freelance producer, dir., 1975-78; freelance cinematographer Berkeley, Calif., 1978—; pres. Iris Films, Berkeley, 1977—; vol. Peace Corps, Malawi, Africa, 1969-70. Dir. (film) In The Best Interests of the Children, 1977 (Blue Ribbon Am. Film Festival 1978), The Changer: A Record of the Times, 1991, Skin Deep, 1995, Talking About Race, 1994, Straight from the Heart, 1994; cinematographer: (film) The Times of Harvey Milk, 1984 (Oscar 1985), Living with AIDS, 1986 (Student Acad. award 1987), Common Threads: Stories from the Quilt, 1989 (Oscar award 1990). Mem. Film Arts Found., Assn. Ind. Video and Filmmakers, No. Calif. Women in Film and TV. Office: Iris Films PO Box 5353 Berkeley CA 94705-0353*

REID, GERALDINE WOLD (GERALDINE REID SKJERVOLD), artist; b. Portland, Oreg., Apr. 11, 1944; d. Alden Elroy and Verna (Kocinski) Wold; B.A. in Fine Art, Calif. State U., Sacramento, 1972, M.F.A., 1975; postgrad. Ind. U.-Purdue U. Instr. dental aux. edn. U. Minn., 1966-70; anthrop. research asst., 1975-76; asst. prof. dental aux. edn. Ind. U.-Purdue U., 1976-78; mng. editor Nat. Arts Guide, Chgo., 1978-80; freelance artist, Chgo., 1981-94; pres. Chgo. Art Emerging Inc., 1983-85; graphic artist Reid Design & Illustration, Chgo., 1981-94; dir. show coordination Circle Fine Art, Chgo., 1981; instr. comm. art and design Alexandria Tech. Coll., Minn., 1994—; seminar lectr., 1977, 86; lectr. art and math. Dept. Math. U. Ill., 1987-88. One-woman shows include Artists' Coop. Gallery, Santa Fe, 1976, Artlink, Ft. Wayne, Ind., 1979, 84—, D.E.O. Fine Arts, Inc., Chgo., 1982-83, Union League Gallery, Chgo., 1989, Brodsky Gallery, 1993; group exhbns. include Crocker Art Mus., Sacramento, 1975, Ft. Wayne Mus. Art, 1978, Artists Guild Chgo., 1981, Charles A. Wustum Mus., Racine, Wis., 1983, Limelight, Chgo., 1986, 87, 88, Neville-Sargent Gallery, 1986, 87, Beacon Street Hull House Gallery, 1988, McDonalds Corp., Chgo., 1988, Prairie Ave. Gallery, Chgo., 1990, Peace Mus., Chgo., 1990, Hyde Park Art Ctr., Chgo., 1990, Lettuce Entertain You Enterprises, Inc., 1990. Olive Tree Gallery, Daley Coll., Chgo., 1991, Crown Ctr. Gallery, Loyola U., Chgo., 1992, Agora Syndicate, Inc., 1992, Kieffer-Nolde/TIC, 1992, Flora '92, 1992, Chgo. Botanic Garden, 1992, Open Spectrum, David Adler Cultural Ctr., 1994, Upper West Gallery, Alexandria Tech. Coll., Min., 1995; contbr. artwork to 2 ann. 1994 calendars. Mem. Artists Guild Chgo., Chgo. Artists' Coalition.

REID, JOAN EVANGELINE, lawyer, stockbroker; b. Mich., Apr. 22, 1932; d. August W. and Evangeline R. (Brozeau) Rogers; m. Belmont M. Reid. AA in Bus., San Jose State U., 1951; JD, McGeorge Sch. Law, 1989. Bar: Nev.; lic. realtor, life, disability and annuity ins. Officer, dir. Lifetime Fin. Planning Corp., San Jose, Calif., 1967-77, Lifetime Realty Corp., San Jose, 1967-77; co-founder, officer, dir. Belmont Reid & Co., San Jose, 1960-77; officer, corp. counsel, dir. JOBEL Fin. Inc., Carson City, Nev., 1980—. Past sec., treas. Nev. Fedn. Rep. Women; charter pres. Santa Clara Valley Rep. Women Federated; past v.p. Carson City Rep. Women's Club. Paul Harris fellow Rotary. Mem. ABA, First Jud. Dist. Bar Assn., Washoe County Bar Assn., State Bar Nev., No. Nev. Women Lawyers Assn., Carson City C. of C., Soroptomist (past pres. Carson City club). Address: PO Box 3676 Carson City NV 89702-3676

REID, KATHLEEN MARIE, advertising and marketing executive; b. N.Y.C., May 20, 1947; d. James Robert and Mildred E. (Hattling) Flannery; m. Gary L. Reid, July 31, 1965 (div. Dec. 1968); 1 child, Lisa A.; m. Douglas E. Lund, Mar. 21, 1981. Key accounts mgr. Coty Cosmetics, N.Y.C., 1969-74; account supr. The Bloom Agy., Dallas, 1974-79; pres. KNR & Co., Mktg. and Advt., Dallas, 1979—; v.p. Mary Kay Cosmetics, 1979-94, Immudyne, Inc., Houston, 1994—. Recipient Echo award Direct Mktg. Assn., Dallas, 1984. Am. Assn. Advt. Agys., Am. Mktg. Assn. (chmn., Marketer of Yr. award 1985-86), Am. Advt. Fedn., Southwest Assn. Advertisers, Dallas Advt. League (bd. dirs. 1983-85, 2nd v.p. 1985-86, dir. Dallas comm., Tops award 1984, 85). Office: Immudyne Inc 11200 Welcrest Green Dr Houston TX 77042

REID, L. DIANNE, association executive; b. Asheboro, N.C., Mar. 27, 1950; d. Charlie Theodore and Frances and Willard (Wingate) R.; m. Peter Thomas Stroup, Nov. 15, 1975 (div. Aug. 1984); 1 child, Katherine Reid Stroup. BA in Sociology and Urban and Regional Studies with highest honors, U. N.C., 1973, M of Regional Planning, 1978. Coord. ops. and rsch. Puerto Rican Unity for Progress, Camden, N.J., 1980-81; dir. ops. Camden Econ. Devel. Corp., 1981-91; exec. dir. YWCA Germantown, Phila., 1991—; instr. Rutgers U., Camden, 1979-91; dir. career and bus. svcs. Women's Assn. for Women's Alternatives, Wawa, Pa., 1987-88. Bd. dirs. Del. Valley Community Reinvestment Fund, Phila., 1987-90, Germantown Fed. Credit Union, 1990-92; pres. bd. dirs. YWCA Germantown, 1989-91. Mem. Phi Beta Kappa. Office: YWCA Germantown 5820 Germantown Ave Philadelphia PA 19144-2139

REID, LYNNE MCARTHUR, pathologist; b. Melbourne, Australia, Nov. 12, 1923; d. Robert Muir and Violet Annie (McArthur) R. M.D., U. Melbourne, 1946; M.D. (hon.), Harvard U., 1976. Reader in exptl. pathology London U., 1964-67, prof. exptl. pathology, 1967-76; dean Cardiothoracic Inst., 1973-76; pathologist-in-chief Children's Hosp., Boston, 1976-89, pathologist-in-chief emeritus, 1990—; S. Burt Wolbach prof. pathology Harvard Med. Sch., Boston, 1976—. Fellow Royal Coll. Physicians (U.K.), Royal Australian Coll. Physicians, Royal Coll. Pathologists, Royal Soc. Medicine, Royal Inst. Gt. Britain, Pathol. Soc. Gt. Britain and Ireland, Thoracic Soc., Assn. Clin. Pathologists, Brit. Thoracic/Soc., Fleischner Soc., Can. Thoracic Soc., Neonatal Soc., Am. Thoracic Soc., Am. Soc. Pathologists, Fleischner Soc., Fedn. Am. Socs. Exptl. Biology. Office: 300 Longwood Ave Boston MA 02115-5737

REID, MARGARET FRIEDERIKE, political scientist, educator; b. Fulda, Hesse, Germany, June 15, 1951; d. Richard A. and Liesel M. (Vorwerk) Bohning; m. Jack J. Reid. Degree in Polit. Sci., U. Bonn, West Germany, 1977; MPA, U. Okla., 1979; MBA, Central State U., 1984; PhD in Polit. Sci., U. Okla., 1986. Rsch. asst. Bur. Govt. Rsch. U. Okla., 1980-81, instr. dept. polit. sci., 1986, vis. asst. prof., 1986-87; asst. prof. dept. polit. sci. U. North Tex., 1987-91, U. Louisville, 1991-93; asst. prof. dept. polit. sci. U. Ark., Fayetteville, 1993—, dir. MPA program. Contbr. chpts. to books, articles to profl. jours. Chmn. mcpl. waste com. Edmond (Okla.) Energy Com., 1981-83. Recipient various profl. awards. Mem. Internta. Soc. for Strategic Mgmt. and Planning (mem. Planning Forum), Louisville Com. on Fgn. Rels., Urban Affairs Assn., Am. Soc. Pub. Adminstrn. (sect. on govt. and bus.), Middle East Studies Assn., Assn. for Rsch. on Nonprofit Orgns. and Voluntary Action, Policy Studies Assn. (and Devel. Studies Consortium), Internat. Pers. Mgmt. Assn. Office: U Ark 428 Old Main Fayetteville AR 72701

REID, MARILYN JOANNE, lawyer, state representative; b. Chgo., Aug. 14, 1941; d. Kermit and Newell Azile (Hahn) N.; m. M. David Reid, Nov. 26, 1966 (div. Mar. 1983); children: David, Nelson. Student, Miami U., 1959-61; BA, U. Ill, 1963; JD, Ohio No. U., 1966. Bar: Ohio 1966, Ark. 1967, U.S. Dist. Ct. 1967. Trust adminstr. First Nat. Bank, Dayton, Ohio, 1966-67; assoc. Sloan & Ragsdale, Little Rock, Ohio, 1967-69; ptnr. Reid and Reid, Dayton, 1969-76, Reid & Buckwalter, Dayton, 1975—; mem. Ohio Ho. of Reps. 76th Dist., 1993—; mem. Judiciary and Criminal Justice com., vice chmn. ins. com., Vets. com., Pub. utilities com. Mem. Ohio adv. bd. U.S. Commn. Civil Rights; chmn., treas. various polit. campaigns, 1975—; trustee Friends Libr. Beavercreek (Ohio); bd. dirs. Beavercreek YMCA, 1985-88; active Mt. Zion United Ch. of Christ. Mem. ABA, Ohio Bar Assn., Greene County Bar Assn., Beavercreek C. of C. (pres. 1986-87), Dayton Panhellenic Assn. (pres. 1982), Altrusa (v.p. Greene County 1978-79, pres. 1979-80), Lioness (pres. Beavercreek 1975), Rotary, Kappa Beta Pi, Gamma Phi Beta (v.p. 1974-75). Republican. Mem. Ch. Christ. Office: Reid & Buckwalter 3866 Indian Ripple Rd Dayton OH 45440-3448

REID, MARION L., lieutenant governor, educator; b. North Rustico, P.E.I., Can., Jan. 4, 1929; d. Michael Doyle and Loretta Whelan; m. Lea P. Reid, June 29, 1949; children: Maureen and Colleen (twins), Kevin, Bethany, Marylea, David, Andrew, Tracy. Tchr.'s lic., Prince Wales Coll., P.E.I., 1947. Tchr. elem. schs. P.E.I., from 1947; prin. St. Ann's Elem. Sch., Hope River, 1964-68; mem., dep. speaker Legis. Assembly of P.E.I., Charlottetown, 1974-84, speaker, 1984-86, opposition house leader; lt. gov. P.E.I., Charlottetown, 1990—; past bd. govs., sec., mem. various coms. P.E.I. Tchrs. Fedn. Pres. Sterling Women's Inst.; charter mem. Queen Elizabeth Hosp. Found. Named Dame of Grace, Order of Hosp. of St. John of Jerusalem, 1990. Mem. Cath. Women's League, Zonta Club. Address: Govt House, PO Box 846, Charlottetown, PE Canada C1A 7L9

REID, NANCI GLICK, health care professional; b. Brookline, Mass., Sept. 22, 1941; d. Robert Louis and Esther (Shostack) Green; m. Ronald Jay Coleman, July 5, 1962 (div. Sept. 1969); 1 child, Lori Sue; m. Alan Marshall Glick, Jan. 12, 1976 (div. Oct. 1978); 1 child, Staci Alison; m. Raymond Augustus Reid, Feb. 15, 1985. AS, Garland Jr. Coll., Boston, 1960; student, Harvard U. Extension, 1961, 64, 65; BS, Northeastern U., 1983, postgrad., 1989—; postgrad., Ecole Superieure de Commerce, Reims, France, 1990-91; MBA, Northeastern U., 1991. Cert. clin. lab. sci., clin. lab. specialist in cytogenetics. Rsch. technician Children's Hosp., Boston, 1961-63; sr. rsch. technician, med. technician New England Med. Ctr., Boston, 1963-65, 67-69; cytogeneticist supr. Carney Hosp., Boston, 1969-84; instr. medicine Med. Sch. Tufts U., Boston, 1969-86; systems analyst Cognos/Coulter Corp., Waltham, Mass., 1976-77; med. technologist Milton (Mass.) Hosp, 1978-83, Mass. Eye and Ear, Boston, 1983-84; lab. mgr. Harvard Cmty. Health Plan, Braintree, Mass., 1985-88; chairperson com. continuing edn. Harvard Cmty. Health Plan, Boston, 1986-88; quality control mgr. Oncolab Inc., Boston, 1988-90; supr. Park Med. Lab., Inc., 1990-91; clin. lab. adminstrn. Dept. Health and Hosp. Mattapan, Boston, 1991—; labo. coord. New England regional newborn screening program State Lab. Inst., Jamaica Plain, Mass., 1993—; presenter abstracts at 12th and 13th Internat. Hematology Soc. confs. Contbr. articles to profl. jours. Vol. human body discovery space program Mus. Sci., 1990; adv. bd. trustees Jordan Hosp., 1993—. Mem. Assn. Cytogenetic Technologists (pres. 1976-78), Am. Soc. Med. Tech. (lectr.), Mass. Ski Club (supr. 1989—), Plymouth Yacht Club, Pythian Sisters Club (sec., editor 1966-67), Sigma Epsilon Rho (pres. 1994-96, v.p. 1987-88, former treas.). Republican. Jewish. Home: 10 Woodbine Dr Plymouth MA 02360-3525

REID, ROSALIND, magazine editor; b. Iowa City, Nov. 16, 1954; d. Isaac Errett and Eleanor Mary Reid; children: Sarah C. Herndon, Kathryn A. Herndon. AB in Journalism, Polit Sci., Syracuse U., 1975; MA in Pub. Policy Scis., Duke U., 1981. Reporter and columnist Lewiston (Maine) Daily Sun, 1975-77; staff writer The News and Observer, Raleigh, N.C., 1979-80, The Cary (N.C.) News, 1981-84; asst. news dir. N.C. State U., Raleigh, 1984-90; assoc. editor Am. Scientist, Research Triangle Park, N.C., 1990-91, mng. editor, 1991-92, editor, 1992—. Recipient Best Local Column award Maine Press Assn., 1977, HEW Pub. Svc. fellowship, Duke U., 1977-78. Mem. Nat. Assn. Sci. Writers, Phi Beta Kappa. Office: Am Scientist 99 Alexander Dr Research Triangle Park NC 27709

REID, SARAH LAYFIELD, lawyer; b. Kansas City, Mo., Sept. 22, 1952; d. Jim Tom and Sarah Pauline (Clark) R.; m. David Harris Gikow, June 12, 1983; children: Stephen Nathaniel, Emily Pauline. AB, Bryn Mawr Coll., 1974; JD, Harvard U., 1977. Bar: N.Y. 1978, U.S. Dist. Ct. (so. and ea. dists.) N.Y. 1978, U.S. Ct. Appeals (11th cir.) 1981, U.S. Ct. Appeals (2d cir.) 1982, U.S. Supreme Ct. 1988, U.S. Ct. Appeals (3d cir.) 1990. Assoc. Kelley Drye & Warren, N.Y.C., 1977-85, ptnr., 1986—. Mem. ABA, N.Y. State Bar Assn., Fed. Bar Coun., Assn. of Bar of City of N.Y. Office: Kelley Drye & Warren 101 Park Ave New York NY 10178-0062

REID, SUE TITUS, law educator; b. Bryan, Tex., Nov. 13, 1939; d. Andrew Jackson Jr. and Loraine (Wylie) Titus. BS with honors, Tex. Woman's U., 1960; MA, U. Mo., 1962, PhD, 1965; JD, U. Iowa, 1972. Bar: Iowa 1972, U.S. Ct. Appeals (D.C. cir.) 1978, U.S. Supreme Ct. 1978. From instr. to assoc. prof. sociology Cornell Coll., Mt. Vernon, Iowa, 1963-72; assoc. prof., chmn. dept. sociology Coe Coll., Cedar Rapids, Iowa, 1972-74; assoc. prof. law. U. Wash., Seattle, 1974-76; exec. assoc. Am. Sociol. Assn., Washington, 1976-77; prof. law U. Tulsa, 1978-88; dean, prof. Sch. Criminology, Fla. State U., Tallahassee, 1988-90; prof. pub. adminstrn. Fla. State U., 1990—; acting chmn. dept. sociology Cornell Coll., 1965-66; vis. assoc. prof. sociology U. Nebr., Lincoln, 1970; vis. disting. prof. law and sociology U. Tulsa, 1977-78, assoc. dean 1979-81; vis. prof. law U. San Diego, 1981-82; mem. People-to-People Crime Prevention Del. to People's Republic of China, 1982; George Beto Vis. Prof. criminal justice Sam Houston U., Huntsville, Tex., 1984-85; lecture/study tour of Criminal Justice systems of 10 European countries, 1985; cons. Evaluation Policy Rsch. Assocs., Inc., Milw., 1976-77, Nat. Inst. Corrections, Idaho Dept. Corrections, 1984, Am. Correctional Inst., Price-Waterhouse. Author: (with others) Bibliographies on Role Methodology and Propositions Volume D - Studies in the Role of the Public School Teacher, 1962, the Correctional System: An Introduction, 1981, Crime and Criminology, 7th edit., 1994, Criminal Justice, 1987, 3d edit., 1993, Criminal Law, 1989, 3d edit., 1995; editor: (with David Lyon) Population Crisis: An Interdisciplinary Perspective, 1972; contbr. articles to profl. jours. Recipient Disting. Alumni award Tex. Woman's U., 1979; named One of Okla. Young Leaders of 80's Oklahoma Monthly, 1980. Mem. Am. Correctional Assn., Am. Soc. Criminology, Acad. Criminal Justice Scis. Office: Fla State Univ Dept Pub Adminstrn Tallahassee FL 32306

REID, WILMA KATHLEEN, direct marketing agency owner; b. Victory, N.Y., Aug. 24, 1940; d. Sewell Webster and Loretto Margaret (Maroney) R. AB, LeMoyne Coll., 1962; MA, Catholic U., 1964. Instr. Immaculata Coll. Women, Washington, 1963-64; fund raiser Nat. Coun. Catholic Men, Washington, 1965-68; promotion mgr. Herder & Herder Publ. Co., N.Y.C., 1968-70; circulation dir. Scholastic Mags., Inc., N.Y.C., 1970-83; owner Reid Resources, N.Y.C., 1983—; seminar speaker Direct Mktg. to Schs., N.Y., 1984, N.Y. Venture Group, N.Y., 1990. Democrat. Office: Reid Resources 454 W 23rd St New York NY 10011-2138

REIDA-ALLEN, PAMELA ANNE, healthcare consultant; b. Fitchburg, Mass., June 8, 1944; d. Alvah Michael Reida and Sirkka Margaret (Anttila) Kao; m. Dennis Alan Joaquin, 1967 (div. 1973); children: Joshua, Amy, Sebastian; m. Yahya Radazar, Oct. 1983 (dec. Sept. 1987); m. Loyall C. Allen. BA in English, Philosophy, Calif. State U., Los Angeles, 1966; RN diploma with honors, Leominster (Mass.) Hosp., 1976; BS in Nursing cum laude, Fitchburg (Mass.) State Coll., 1982; MS magna cum laude, Lesley Coll., 1986. Substitute tchr. Fitchburg Pub. Schs., 1966-67; social worker N.Y.C. Dept. Social Services, N.Y.C., 1967-68; news correspondent The Lowell (Mass.) Sun, 1969-71; nurse lab., delivery Leominster Hosp., 1976-77A; inservice coordinator Birchwood Manor Nursing Home, Fitchburg, 1977, asst. dir. nursing, 1977-78, dir. nursing, 1978-80; dir. nursing Naukeag Hosp., Ashburnham, Mass., 1980-84; asst. dir. nursing Beech Hill Hosp., Dublin, N.H., 1984-87, dir nursing, 1987-90, chair utilization rev. com., 1985—; mem. adv. council allied health majors Mass. Regional Vocat. Sch., Fitchburg, Mass., 1977-84; with Area Speakers Bur., Fitchburg, 1980-84, vice chair Quality Assurance Program, 1988; cons. Quality Healthcare Resources, Inc. subs. Joint Commn. on Accreditation of Hosps., 1988—. Vol. Family Planning, Fitchburg, 1981-82; del. Intercity Mgmt. Council, Fitchburg, 1980-84. Mem. NAFE, Tri-City Nursing Home Assn. (pres. 1978-80), Nat. Nurses Assn., N.H. Nurses Assn. (program com. 1985—), Greater Fitchburg C. of C., N.H. Orgn. Exec. Nurses, N.H. Quality Assurance Assn. Office: RR 1 Box 976 Dublin NH 03444

REID-BILLS, MAE, editor, historian; b. Shreveport, La.; d. Dayton Taylor and Bessie Oline (Boles) Reid; m. Frederick Gurdon Bills (div.); children: Marjorie Reid, Nancy Hawkins, Frederick Taylor, Virginia Thomas, Elizabeth Sharples. AB, Stanford U., 1942, MA, 1965; PhD, U. Denver, 1977. Mng. editor Am. West mag., Tucson, Ariz., 1979-89; cons. editor, 1989—. Gen. Electric fellow, 1963, William Robertson Coe fellow, 1964. Mem. Orgn. Am. Historians, Am. Hist. Assn., Phi Beta Kappa, Phi Alpha Theta.

REID-POLLARD, CHERYL ANN, early childhood education specialist; b. Chgo., Mar. 24, 1948; d. Isiah Akins and Annie Pearl Reid-Akins; m. Renwick Darrell Pollard; 1 child, Donna Luctricia. BS in Elem. Edn., Ga. State U.; MA in Early Childhood Edn., Mercer U.; cert. edn. specialist, West Ga. Coll., 1992. Cert. tchr., Ga. Tchr. East Thomaston (Ga.) Elem. Sch., 1973, Yatesville (Ga.) Elem. Sch., 1973-80; tchr. kindergarten Barnesville (Ga.) Elem. Sch., 1980-87, North Side Elem. Sch., Griffin, Ga., 1987-94; remedial tchr. Jordan Hill Elem. Sch., Griffin, 1994; adult edn., homework tutorial Griffin Tech. Jordan Hill Elem. Sch.; tutor at-risk students; vol. tutor Elbow Learning Lab.; homework tutorial Griffin Tech. Vocat., 1993; lead tchr. Latchkey Program; sch. rep. Am. 2000 Edn. Showcase, Griffin, 1992; participant ednl. workshops, seminars; Remedial Edn. Program Jordan Hill Elem. Sch., Grinnin, Ga., 1994-95; adult edn. Griffin Tech.; cons. in field. vis. com. mem. for Dekalb County Sch. Sys. So. Assn. Colls. and Schs.; mem. Pres.'s com. Employment of People with Disabilities. Mem. NEA, Ga. Edn. Assn., Ga. Conf. Ministers' Wives, United Meth. Women, Alpha Kappa Alpha. Democrat. Home: 612 E Broad St Griffin GA 30223-3623

REID-ROBERTS, DAYL HELEN, mental health counselor; b. Rochester, N.Y., Oct. 15, 1941; d. Russell Harrison and Elizabeth Spencer (Page) Ferrey; m. David Alan Reid, July 16, 1960 (div. 1982); children: Deborah

Elizabeth, Patricia Anne, David Alan Jr., Matthew Stephen; m. David Gillies Roberts, Aug. 9, 1985. BA, Salisbury (Md.) State U., 1988, MEd, 1990. Lic. profl. counselor. Clinician Community Svcs. Bd., Eastern Shore, Nassawadox, Va., 1990—; clinician substance abuse svc. Community Svcs. Bd., Eastern Shore, Onancock, Va., 1990—; clinican, mental social worker, psychiat. Northampton Accomack Meml. Hosp., Nassawadox, 1992-93; v.p. Humanitec, Inc., Accomac, Va., 1993—; asst. dir. Literacy Coun. of No. Va., Annandale, 1980-85. Contbr. articles to profl. jours. Treas., co-founder Ea. Shore Literacy Coun., 1986. Mem. Am. Counseling Assn., Am. Psychologists Assn. (student), Phi Sigma Tau, Kappa Delta Phi. Republican. Presbyterian. Home: The Oliver House Onancock VA 23417 Office: Humanitec Inc Front St PO Box 580 Accomac VA 23301-0580

REIFF, DOVIE KATE, urban planner; b. Birmingham, Ala., Nov. 5, 1931; d. Roy Humes and Lou Ada (Erwin) Petty; married, Dec. 25, 1956 (div. Dec. 1977); children: Donna Lynn Reiff Jayanathan, Benjamin Lyle, Johanna Carol Davis. BArch, U. Pa., 1954, M in City Planning, 1969, postgrad. in city and regional planning, 1975. Registered architect, Pa. Architect Oskar Stonorov Architect, Phila., 1954-57; research asst. Inst. Environ. Studies, Phila., 1967-68; sr. planner Montgomery County Planning Commn., Norristown, Pa., 1969-71; urban planner Wallace McHarg Roberts & Todd, Phila., 1971-74; research analyst Del. Valley Regional Planning Commn., Phila., 1974-77; recreation planner U.S. Heritage Conservation and Recreation Service, Phila., 1977-80; community planner U.S. Gen. Services Adminstrn., Phila., 1980-85; vol., urban planner U.S. Peace Corps, Kathmandu, Nepal, 1986-87; program devel. planner Chattanooga Neighborhood Enterprise Inc., 1987-88; environ. planner dept. urban planning City of Birmingham, 1989-92; planning cons. Monteagle, Tenn., 1992—; mem. exec. com. Phila. chpt. Am. Inst. Planners, 1970-75; bd. dirs. Phila. chpt. AIA, 1978-79, mem. architects in govt. com., Washington, 1984-85. Participant nat. conf. Pres.'s Com. on Employment of Handicapped, Washington, 1974-76; regional del. Gov.'s Coun. on Handicapped, Harrisburg, Pa., 1975, Birmingham Urban Forestry & Tree Commn., 1990-92, Tenn. Urban Forestry Coun., 1993—; vol. Laurel House Women's Shelter, Norristown, Pa., 1985, GSA Adopt-a-Sch. Program, Phila., 1985, Birmingham Ptnrs. in Edn., 1990; VISTA vol. East Tenn. Comty. Design Ctr., 1994—. Brunner grantee AIA, N.Y.C., 1974. Mem. Am. Inst. Cert. Planners, Am. Planning Assn., Nat. Trust for Hist. Preservation, The Nature Conservancy. Republican. Home: 1211 Red Oak Dr Monteagle TN 37356

REIGSTAD, RUTH ELAINE, lay worker, retired physical therapy consultant; b. Mpls., Apr. 26, 1923; d. Olin Spencer and Amanda Sophia (Fjelstad) R. BA, St. Olaf Coll., Northfield, Minn., 1945; cert., U. Minn., 1947. Lic. phys. therapist, Wash. Phys. therapist Crippled Childrens's Sch., Jamestown, N.D., 1948-52; phys. therapist, clin. instr. Shriners Hosp., U. Minn., Mpls., 1955-58; phys. therapist Rehab. Center, Albuquerque, N.M., 1958-60, Brit. Nat. Health Svc., London; phys. therapy cons. Wash. State Health Dept., Olympia, 1961-73, cons., 1961-74; lay worker Good Shepherd Luth. Ch., Olympia, 1972-75; mem. various coms. Christ Luth. Ch., Tacoma, 1980—; Vol. Children Health Svcs. and Pub. Health of Wash. 1974—; bd. dirs. Morningside Rehab. Orgn., Olympia, Wash., PAVE rehab. orgn. Bd. dirs. Wash. State Phys. Therapy Assn., 1965-68; mem. communiversity planning com. Pierce County Assoc. Ministries. With USCG, 1943-45. Recipient Fellowship award Nat. Easter Seal Soc. Chgo. 1949; Scholarship award US Pub. Health Service Wash. 1962-64. Mem. Am. Phys. Therapy Assn. (life), Am. Pub. Health Assn., Am. Acad. Religion, Luth. Brotherhood Fraternity and Benevolent Orgn. (bd. dirs. Pierce County), Air Force Assn. (exec. coun. Pierce County, 1985—). Mem. Evang. Luth. Ch. Am. Home: Point Defiance Village 6613 N 52d St Bldg 6613 # 4 Tacoma WA 98407

REILLEY, KATHLEEN PATRICIA, lawyer; b. Pitts., Oct. 31, 1948; d. Edward Michael and Mary Elizabeth (Davidson) R. BA, U. Calif., Berkeley, 1976; JD, Golden Gate U., 1979. Bar: Calif. Staff atty. Fresno County Legal Svcs., Calif., 1979-85, Santa Monica (Calif.) Rent Control Bd., 1985-89; asst. city atty. City of Berkeley, 1990-91; atty. Linda DeBene Inc., Danville, Calif., 1991—. Co-founder Calif. Housing Action & Info. Network, 1976. Mem. Calif. State Bar Assn. (real property sect.), Contra Costa County Bar Assn. (real property sect.). Democrat. Episcopalian. Office: 1563 Solano Ave #528 Berkeley CA 94707

REILLY, ANNE HUEDEPOHL, university educator, researcher; b. Chgo., Sept. 16, 1957; d. E. Bradley and Lynne (Swanson) Huedepohl; m. John J. Reilly, Aug. 12, 1978; children: Kristine Anne, Meghan Lynne. BA in Econs. and Bus. Adminstrn. summa cum laude, Knox Coll., 1978; MBA in Finance, U. Iowa, 1980; PhD in Organizational Behavior, Northwestern U., 1989. Banking officer spl. industries Cont. Ill. Nat. Bank, Chgo., 1980-82; asst. v.p. corp. banking Lloyds Bank Internat., Chgo., 1983-84; lectr. bus. adminstrn. U. Iowa, 1979-80; teaching asst. Northwestern U., Evanston, 1987; asst. prof. mgmt. Loyola U., Chgo., 1988—. Presented numerous papers in field; contbr. articles to profl. jours; ad hoc reviewer Jour. of Orgnl. Behavior, 1993, 94, Acad. Mgmt. Jour., 1992, Sloan Mgmt. Rev., 1991, Orgn. Sci., 1990, Indsl. Crisis Quar., 1990, Jour. Mgmt. Studies, 1987, Jour. Vocat. Behavior, 1994; reviewer Smart Growth: Critical Choices for Business Continuity and Prosperity, 1989, Organization Development and Change 5th edit., 1987. Trustee CARE Found., Atlanta, 1990—; active Knox Coll. Alumni, Galesburg, Ill., 1978—. Rsch. grantee Northwestern U. Banking Rsch. Ctr., 1987, 88, Nat. Ctr. for Mgmt. R&D, Can., 1989-90, Employee Relocation Coun., 1989-90, Loyola U. Summer Rsch., 1990. Mem. Acad. Mgmt., Strategic Mgmt. Soc., Rsch. Com. on Disasters, Phi Beta Kappa. Democrat. Lutheran. Office: Loyola U Chgo 820 N Michigan Ave Chicago IL 60611-2103

REILLY, JEANETTE P., clinical psychologist; b. Denver, Oct. 19, 1908; d. George L. and Marie (Bloedorn) Parker; A.B., U. Colo., 1929; M.A., Columbia U., 1951, Ed.D., 1959; m. Peter C. Reilly, Sept. 15, 1932; children: Marie Reilly Heed, Sara Jean Reilly Wilhelm, Patricia Reilly Davis. Lectr. psychology Butler U., Indpls., 1957-58, 60-65; cons. child psychologist Mental Hygiene Clinic, Episcopal Community Services, Indpls., 1959-65; cons. clin. psychologist VA Hosp., Indpls., 1965-66; Christian Theol. Sem., 1968-70; pvt. practice clin. psychology, Indpls., 1967-89; cons. clin. psychologist St. Vincent's Hosp., 1973-86; adv. cons. middle mgmt. group Indpls. City Council, 1980-81. Mem. women's aux. council U. Notre Dame, 1953-65; trustee Hanover (Ind.) Coll., 1975-91; bd. dirs. Community Hosp. Found., Indpls., 1978-92, Regional Cancer Hosp. Bd., 1988-90, Indpls. Mus. Art, 1987-93; mem. Ind. Bd. Examiners in Psychology, 1969-73; mem. Com. for Future of Butler U., 1985-86. Mem. Am. Psychol. Assn., Am. Personnel and Guidance Assn., Am. Vocat. Assn., Ind. Psychol. Assn., Central Ind. Psychol. Assn., Ind. Personnel and Guidance Assn., Nat. Registry Psychologists in U.S.A. Office: 3777 Bay Rd North Dr Indianapolis IN 46240-2973

REILLY, JEANNE ELISE, accountant, educator; b. Orange, Calif., May 16, 1944; d. Edward Barclay and Jean Elizabeth (Altman) Cosad; m. Timothy Weaver Reilly, July 25, 1986. BA in English, Calif. State U., 1966; MA in English, Holy Names Coll., 1974; MS in Library Sci., Catholic U., 1976; MBA, J.F. Kennedy U., 1991. Tchr. English Oak Valley Union Elem. Sch., Tulare, Calif., 1970-73; libr. Cremona Violin, San Francisco, 1976-80; plant contr. Schlage Lock Co., San Jose, Calif., 1980-92; contr., CFO Productivity Technologies, Sunnyvale, Calif., 1992—; dir. Advanced Cybernetics Group, Sunnyvale, 1992-93. Mem. Inst. Mgmt. Accountants, Beta Phi Mu. Democrat. Roman Catholic. Home: 2023 Morrill Ave San Jose CA 95132

REILLY, JOY HARRIMAN, theatre educator, playwright, actress/director; b. Dublin, Ireland, May 17, 1942; came to U.S., 1969; d. Rene William and Sybil Mary (MacGowan) Harriman; m. Lawrence W. Kieffer, Dec. 29, 1965 (div. Sept. 1974); m. Richard Reilly, June 23, 1978; 1 child, Patrick Harriman. BFA, Ohio State U., 1977, MA, 1979, PhD, 1984. Intern The Times, London, 1961-62; asst. radio-TV prodn. J. Walter Thompson Advt., Frankfurt and London, 1962-67; copy editor, journalist The Newark (Ohio) Adv., 1970-83, part-time, 1973-80; assoc. prof. Ohio State U., Columbus, 1985—; artistic dir. Grandparents Living Theatre, Columbus, 1984; theatre critic Sta. WOSU Radio, Columbus, 1979—; presenter papers Internat. Found. for Theatre Rsch., Stockholm, 1989, Dublin Eire, 1992, Assn. for Theater in Higher Edn., N.Y.C., 1989, Chgo., 1990, Seattle, 1991, Atlanta, 1992, Phila., 1993; presenter 1st Internat. Festival Sr. Adult Theater, Cologne, Germany, 1991, 1st Nat. Festival Sr. Theatre, 1993, numerous others. Author: (plays) A Grandparent's Scrapbook, 1986, Golden Age is All the Rage, 1989, I Was Young, Now I'm Wonderful!, 1991, A Picket Fence, Two Kids and a Dog Named Spot, 1993, (chpt.) Olga Nethersole's Sapho, 1989. Commr. Upper Arlington (Ohio) Arts Coun., 1987. Recipient Ohioana citation Ohioana Libr. Assn., 1989, Columbus Mayor's award for Vol. Svcs. in Arts, 1986, Woman of Achievement award YWCA, 1991, Outstanding Achievement in Theatre award Ohio Theatre Alliance, 1991, Living Faith awards Columbus Met. Area Ch. Coun., 1992, Disting. Teaching award Ohio State U., 1994; Battelle Endowment for Tech. and Human Affairs grantee, 1994. Mem. Am. Theatre Assn., Am. Soc. for Theatre Rsch., Internat. Fedn. for Theatre Rsch., Assn. for Theatre in Higher Edn., Ohio Theatre Alliance. Roman Catholic. Office: Ohio State U Dept Theatre Columbus OH 43210

REILLY, KAREN POWERS, marketing professional; b. Pittsfield, Mass., Apr. 25, 1953; d. Donald Edward and Sally Helen (Zajac) Powers; m. Edward Martin Reilly, Jan. 18, 1985; children: Karenanne Kelly, Sara Erin. Student, North Adams State Coll., 1986, Berkshire C.C., Pittsfield, Mass., 1988—. Mktg. mgr. Greylock Credit Union, Pittsfield, Mass., 1983—, cmty. reinvestment act (CRA) officer, 1992—. Editor: Money Talks newsletter, 1981—. Bd. dirs. Jr. Achievement, Pittsfield, 1985-89, Credit Union League Mass., Waltham, 1986-87, Elder Svcs. Berkshire County, Pittsfield, 1991—, YMCA, Pittsfield, 1995—; mem. com. Cen. Berkshire Campaign to Elect Ed Reilly Mayor, Pittsfield, 1991—; chmn. City of Pittsfield's 1st Night Com., 1992—; mem. Williams Sch. Coun., 1993—. Mem. Am. Mktg. Assn., New Eng. Bank Mktg. Assn., Finl. Instns. Mktg. Assn. (medal of honor 1988), Fin. Mktg. Assn., Credit Union Execs. Soc. (1st pl. award 1985), Consumer Bankers Assn., Nat. Assn. Desktop Pubs. Roman Catholic. Home: 96 E Housatonic St Pittsfield MA 01201-6453 Office: Greylock Credit Union 75 Kellogg St Pittsfield MA 01201-4336

REILLY, LAURA J., lawyer; b. Ames, Iowa; d. Lawrence J. and Dorothy J. (Waller) R.; m. James L. Abrams, 1975; children: Reilly Katherine, Merrill Elizabeth, Jacqueline Lee. BS, U. Iowa, 1969; MS, U. Calif., San Francisco, 1970; JD, Rutgers U., 1975; LLM, U. Denver, 1983. Bar: Colo. 1975, Tex. 1978. Rsch. asst. Baker, Baker & Wilson, Oklahoma City, 1975-77; atty. Office of Gen. Counsel, U. Tex., Austin, 1977-79; asst. atty. gen. Colo., Denver, 1979-81; atty. U.S. West Communications, Denver, 1981-89; chief counsel U.S. West Svc. Link, 1989-91; sr. atty. U.S. West Inc., 1992—; bd. dirs. Vis. Nurses Support Svcs., Inc., 1985—, chmn., 1987-91. Mem. ABA, Colo. Bar Assn., Colo. Women's Bar Assn. Roman Catholic. Office: U S West Inc 7800 East Orchard Rd Englewood CO 80111

REILLY, LOIS ANN PELCARSKY, eductor, consultant; b. Cleve., Feb. 25, 1941; d. William Paul and Eleanor (Mikulski) Pelcarsky; m. Anthony Eugene Reilly, June 19, 1980; stepchildren: Michael, Diane, David. BS in Edn., Baldwin-Wallace Coll., Berea, Ohio, 1962; MEd, Kent State U., 1970. Cert. reading specialist, permanent tchr., Ohio. Elem.-jr. high sch. tchr., reading specialist South Euclid-Lyndhurst (Ohio) Schs., 1962-74; ednl. cons. Scott, Foresman & Co., Glenview, Ill., 1974-75, Laidlaw Bros. Pubs., River Forest, Ill., 1978-80; reading cons. Pub. Schs. Cleveland Heights and University Heights, Ohio, 1975-76, Solon (Ohio) Schs., 1976-77; ednl. cons. Chgo. Sun-Times, 1981-84; elem. tchr. Solomon Schechter Day Sch., South Euclid, Ohio, 1984-87; jr. high sch. tchr. St. Joseph-Collinwood Sch., Cleve. Cath. Diocese, Cleve., 1988—; seminar presenter, 1974—; bd. dirs. South Euclid-Lyndhurst Tchrs. Credit Union, 1969-74. Contbr. articles to various publs. Pres. Women's Christian Fellowship League, Forest Hill Presbyn. Ch., Cleveland Heights, 1987-89, v.p., 1990-91. Mem. AAUW (v.p. 1976-78, sec. 1980-81, newsletter editor 1981-82, v.p 1988-90), Cleve. Coll. Club, Irish Am. Club East. Home: 343 Royal Oak Blvd Richmond Heights OH 44143-1709

REILLY, MARGARET MARY, therapist; b. N.Y.C.; d. Thomas Michael and Margaret Mary (Lane) R. AB, Coll. of New Rochelle, 1933; MSW, Fordham U., 1966. Case worker, case supr., sr. case supr., dir. N.Y.C. Dept. Social Svc., 1947-77; therapist Cath. Charities Counselling Svc., N.Y.C., 1980-94. Mem. NASW, Acad. Cert. Social Workers. Roman Catholic. Home: 309 E Mosholu Pky N Bronx NY 10467

REILLY, THERESE CECELIA, management consultant; b. Algoma, Iowa, July 14, 1956; d. Louis Henry and Bernadette (Zook) R. BS, Briar Cliff Coll., 1978; BFA, Pitts. State U., 1981. Instr. art Aims C.C., Greeley, Colo., 1985-87; instr. elem. Greeley Catholic Sch., Colo., 1985-86; product info. dir. The Wright Group, San Diego, 1987-92; mgr. tng. rsch. and devel. The Wright Group, Bothell, Wash., 1992-93, mgr. projects in reading, 1993-94; v.p. Visionary Learning Co., Inc., Puyallup, Wash., 1994—; dir. high sch. and collegiate journalism awards Washington Press Assn., 1992-93; trainee for vol. tutors Eastside Literacy Coun., Bellevue, Wash., 1991-94. Mem. Internat. Reading Assn., Nat. Coun. of Techrs. of English, Assn. Supervision and Curriculum Devel. Democrat. Roman Catholic. Office: Visionary Learning Co Inc 629 2nd St SE Ste B Puyallup WA 98371

REIMER, LUREE DEASON, women's health nurse; b. Pontiac, Mich., Oct. 5, 1956; d. George Veachel and Johnnie Marie (Miller) Deason. BS in Nursing, Oakland U., 1978; MS in Adminstrn., Ctrl. Mich. U., 1994. RN, Mich. Nurse North Oakland Med. Ctr., Pontiac, Mich., 1978-94; nurse coord. ob/gyn The Wellness Plan, Detroit, 1994—. Office: The Wellness Plan 6500 John E Lodge Detroit MI 48202

REIN, CATHERINE AMELIA, financial services executive, lawyer; b. Lebanon, Pa., Feb. 7, 1943; d. John and Esther (Scott) Shultz. BA summa cum laude, Pa. State U., 1965; JD magna cum laude, NYU , 1968. Bar: N.Y. 1968, U.S. Supreme Ct. 1971. Assoc. Dewey, Ballantine, Bushby, Palmer & Wood, N.Y.C., 1968-74; with Continental Group, Stamford, Conn., 1974-85, sec., sr. atty., 1976-77, v.p., gen. counsel, 1980-85; sec., asst. gen. counsel Continental Diversified Ops., 1978-80; v.p. human resources Met. Life Ins. Co., N.Y.C., 1985-88, sr. v.p. human resources, 1988-89, exec. v.p. corp. and profl. svcs. dept., 1989—; bd. dirs Bank of NY., Gen. Pub. Utilities, Corning Inc., Nat. Urban League, Inroads, N.Y.C. Trustee Nat. Urban League, NYU Sch. Law Found. Mem. ABA, Assn. of Bar of City of N.Y. Episcopalian. Home: 21 E 22nd St Apt 8B New York NY 10010-5335 Office: Met Life Ins Co 1 Madison Ave New York NY 10010

REINER, CELIANE LEVY, technical data analyst; b. Rio de Janeiro, Apr. 13, 1953; came to U.S., 1956; d. Samuel and Paulette (Schinazi) Levy; m. Jay Evan Reiner, Sept. 1, 1990 (div. 1994). BA, Queens Coll., 1979. Registered rep. Tech. data analyst Morgan Stanley, N.Y.C., 1976—. Actress: Critic, A Musical, 1987. N.Y. State Regents scholar, 1971. Mem. Mensa (pres. Greater N.Y. chpt. 1990-91). Democrat. Jewish. Home: 82 Schrade Rd Briarcliff Manor NY 10510 Office: Morgan Stanley & Co 1251 Ave of the Americas New York NY 10020

REINER, MARY ELISABETH, public relations specialist; b. N.Y.C., Apr. 19, 1931; d. Francis Drake and Ethel B. (Pleis) Wells; m. John Paul Reiner, July 27, 1961; children: Mary E., Clark B. B.A., Middlebury Coll., 1953; M.A. in Anthropology, NYU, 1955; diploma Russian Inst., Columbia U., 1960, M.A. in Pub. Law and Govt., 1960. Prof. govt. Notre Dame campus St. John's U., N.Y.C., 1960-62; editor UNICEF, N.Y.C., 1973-77; info. officer U.S. Com. for UNICEF, N.Y.C., 1977-79; dir. pub. info. Internat. Human Assistance Programs, N.Y.C., 1979-81; devel. dir. Nat. Child Labor Com., N.Y.C., 1981-83; dir. resource devel. Internat. Inst. Rural Reconstrn., N.Y.C., 1984-86; dir. devel. N.Y.C. Mission Soc., 1986-89. Editor newsletter News of the World's Children, 1977-79, NGO-UNICEF Newsletter, 1973-77. Nat. bd. dirs. Girl Scouts U.S.A., 1975-81; chmn. devel. World Leisure and Recreation Assn., 1980-83; del. Care, Inc., 1979-81; mem., head team of reps. at UN, World Assn. Girl Guides and Girl Scouts, 1969-78, hon. assoc. world com., London, 1978—, mem. world conf. Finland, 1969, Can., 1972, London, 1975, bd. dirs., 1987-90, World Found. Girl Guide and Girl Scouts; mem. adv. coun., bd. dirs.The Rogosin Inst. of N.Y. Hosp. Cornell U. Med. Coll., 1992—. Mem. Women Execs. in Pub. Relations, Pub. Relations Soc. Am. (chpt. pub. service council 1979-84), Nat. Soc. Fund-Raising Execs., Women in Communications, N.Y. Jr. League (dir. 1969-70, chmn. sustaining mems. com. 1973-74). Republican. Roman Catholic. Home: 340 E 72d St New York NY 10021 Office: The Rogosin Inst 505 E 70th St New York NY 10021

REINHARD, SISTER MARY MARTHE, educational organization administrator; b. McKeesport, Pa., Aug. 29, 1929; d. Regis C. and Leona (Reese) R. AB, Notre Dame Coll.; MA, U. Notre Dame. Asst. prin. Regina High Sch., Cleve., 1960-62, prin., 1963-64; prin. Notre Dame Acad., Chardon, Ohio, 1965-72; pres. Notre Dame Coll. of Ohio, Cleve., 1973-88; dir. devel. Sisters of Notre Dame Ednl. Ctr., Chardon, 1989—. Trustee, mem. exec. com. NCCJ, Cleve., 1987; bd. dirs. Centerior Energy; mem. coun. Geauga United Way Svcs., 1990—, vice chair fund raising, 1991; mem. adv. bd. Kent State U., Geauga campus, 1991-94. Recipient Fidelia award Notre Dame Coll., 1989, Woman of Yr. award 1990; Humanitarian award Cleve. chpt. NCCJ, 1990; named one of 100 most influential women in Cleve. Women's City Club, 1983, one of 79 most interesting people in Cleve. The Cleve. mag., 1979. Roman Catholic. Home and Office: 13000 Auburn Rd Chardon OH 44024-9331

REINHART, MARY ANN, medical board executive; b. Jackson, Mich., Aug. 14, 1942; d. Herbert Martin and Josephine Marie (Keyes) Conway; m. David Lee Reinhart, Dec. 28, 1963; children: Stephen Paul, Michael David. MA, Mich. State U., 1983, PhD, 1985. Rsch. asst. Mich. State U., East Lansing, 1979-82, 85, teaching asst. dept psychology, 1982-84, asst. prof. Office Med. Edn. R&D, Coll. Human Medicine, 1985-88; assoc. exec. dir. Am. Bd. Emergency Medicine, East Lansing, 1988—; cons. Am. Bd. Emergency Medicine, 1985-88; chairperson collegewide evaluation com. Coll. Human Medicine, Mich. State U., East Lansing, 1985-88; adj. asst. prof. Office Med. Edn. Rsch. and Devel., Coll. Human Medicine, 1988—. Reviewer Annals of Emergency Medicine, 1987—. Bd. dirs. Neahtawanta Rsch. and Edn. Ctr., Traverse City, Mich., 1991—. Mem. APA (divsn. indsl./orgnl. psychology, health psychology), AAAS, Phi Kappa Phi. Office: Am Bd Emergency Medicine 3000 Coolidge Rd East Lansing MI 48823-6319

REINING, BETH LAVERNE (BETTY REINING), public relations consultant, journalist; b. Fargo, N.D.; d. George and Grace (Twiford) Reimche; student N.D. State Coll., U. Minn., Glendale Community Coll., Calif. State Coll., Carson; 1 dau., Carolyn Ray Toohey Hiett; m. Jack Warren Reining, Oct. 3, 1976 (div. 1984). Originated self-worth seminars in Phoenix, 1970-76; owner Janzik Pub. Relations, 1971-76; talk show reporter-hostess What's Happening in Ariz., Sta. KPAZ-TV, 1970-73; writer syndicated column People Want to Know, Today newspaper, Phoenix, 1973; owner JB Communications, Phoenix, 1976-84; owner, pres. Media Communications, 1984—; freelance writer; tchr. How to Weigh Your Self-Worth courses Phoenix Coll., Rio Solado Community Coll., Phoenix, 1976-84; instr. pub. rels. Scottsdale (Ariz.) Community Coll., 1987; muralist, works include 25 figures in med. office. Founder Ariz. Call-A-Teen Youth Resources, Inc., pres., 1975-76, v.p., 1976-77, now bd. dirs. Recipient awards including 1st pl. in TV writing Nat. Fedn. Press Women, 1971-88, numerous state awards in journalism Ariz. Press Women, 1971-76, Good Citizen award Builders of Greater Ariz., 1961. Mem. Ariz. Press Women (1st place award 1988), No. Ariz. Press Women (pres. 1983), Nat. Fedn. Am. Press Women, Pub. Relations Soc. Am., Phoenix Pub. Relations Soc., Nat. Acad. TV Arts and Scis., Phoenix Valley of Sun Convention Bur., Verde Valley C. of C. (bd. dirs., tourism chmn. 1986-87, Best Chair of Yr. award 1986), Phoenix Metro C. of C. Cottonwood C. of C. (chmn. of Yr. award, 1986). Inventor stocking-tension twist footlet, 1962. Club: Phoenix Press. Office: PO Box 10509 Phoenix AZ 85064-0509

REINING, PRISCILLA COPELAND, anthropologist; b. Chgo., Mar. 11, 1923; d. Kenneth Bayard and Mary Elsie (Weser) Copeland; m. Conrad Copeland Reining, June 26, 1944 (dec. Oct. 1984); children: Robert Cushman, Anne Elizabeth, Conrad Copeland Schilling. AB, U. Chgo., 1945, AM, 1949, PhD, 1967. Lectr. U. Minn., Mpls., 1956-60, Howard U., Washington, 1960-65; rsch. assoc. Cath. U. Am., Washington, 1966-68; assoc. Smithsonian Instn., Washington, 1966, 68, 70; cons. The World Bank, 1972, USAID, 1973; cons. AAAS, Washington, 1971-73, project dir., 1974-81, program dir., 1982-90; vis. prof. African Studies U. Fla., Gainesville, 1994—; mem. bd. on sci. and tech. for internat. devel. NAS, Washington, 1976-80; mem. arid ecosys. interation Internat. Geosphere/Biosphere Program, Boulder, 1989—; mem. adv. bd. Population and Environ., N.Y.C., 1990—; bd. dirs. Renewable Natural Resources Found., Bethesda, Md., 1991—; mem. U.S. del. UN Conf. on Desertification, Nairobi, Kenya, 1977; mem. Com. for Rsch. and Exploration, 1993. Author: Challenging Desertification, 1980; author, editor: Village Women, 1977; editor: Village Viability, 1980, Resource Inventory, 1984. Mem. Peace Commn. Washington Cathedral, 1986-91. Grantee NIMH, 1966, NSF, 1967, Nat. Geographic Soc. Com. for Rsch. and Exploration, 1994. Fellow AAAS (sec. 1978-89), Am. Anthrop. Assn. (task force on AIDS, task force on environ., Disting. Svc. award 1990), African Studies Assn. (bd. dirs. 1978-80); mem. Anthrop. Soc. Washington (pres. 1976-77). Home: 3601 Rittenhouse St NW Washington DC 20015-2413

REININGHAUS, RUTH, artist; b. N.Y.C., Oct. 4, 1922; d. Emil William and Pauline Rosa (Lazarik) R.; m. George H. Morales, Feb. 20, 1944; children: George James, Robert Charles; m. Allan Joseph Smith, May 28, 1960. Student, Hunter Coll., NYU, Nat. Acad. Sch. of Design, 1960-61, Frank Reilly Sch. of Art, 1963, Art Students League, 1968. Instr. art Banker's Trust, N.Y.C., 1971-77, 79—, Kittredge Club for Women, N.Y.C. Exhibited in group shows at Berkshire Art Mus., 1970s, Hammer Galleries, Inc., N.Y.C., 1974, Far Gallery, N.Y.C., 1974, Mufalli Gallery, N.Y. and Fla., 1983-90, Pen and Brush Club, 1985—, Petrucci Gallery, Saugerties, N.Y., 1988-94, Pastel Soc. Am., 1988—, John Lane Gallery, Rhinebeck, N.Y., 1992—, Regianni Gallery, N.Y.C., 1994, Catherine Lorillard Wolfe Club, Salmagundi Club, Allied Arts Am., Heidi Newhoff Gallery, N.Y.C., Hudson Valley Art Assn., Knickerbocker Artists, N.Y.C., others. Recipient Robert Lehman award, 1960s, 3d prize in oils Murray Hill Art Show, 1968, Coun. Am. Artists award, 1985, Internat. award Oil Pastel Assn., 1987; scholar Nat. Acad., 1962, Frank Reilly Sch. Art, 1963, NYU, 1968; subject NBC TV show You Are an Artist, 1950s. Fellow Am. Artists Profl. League (Claude Parsons Meml. award 1974), Hudson Valley Art Assn.; mem. Pastel Soc. Am. (bd. dirs. 1988-90, J. Giffuni purchase award 1988, Flora B. Giffuni pres.' award 1990), Allied Artists Am. (assoc.), Soc. Illustrators (hon. 1983-87), Nat. Arts Club, Reciprocal, Artists Fellowship, Washington Sq. Outdoor Art Assn. (bd. dirs. 1983-90, Talens award 1963, Richtone Artists award 1968), Salmagundi Club N.Y. (pres. 1983-87, curator 1989—, Baker Brush award 1969, scholar 1969, Philip Isenberg award 1974, 89, 90, 92, 95, hon. mention 1983, 84, Salmagundi Club prize 1985, Franklin B. Williams Fund prize 1987, Tom Picard award 1987, Mortimer E. Freehof award 1988, John N. Lewis award 1988, Salmagundi Club medal of honor 1989, John N. Lewis award 1989, Samuel T. Shaw award 1990, Thomas Moran award 1990, Helen S. Coes award 1990, hon. mention 1991, Alice B. McReynolds award 1991, Salmagundi award 1991, Alphaeus Cole Meml. award 1991), Catharine Lorillard Wolfe Art Club (bd. dirs. 1987—, Anna Hyatt Huntington award 1978), Coun. Am. Artists (award 1985, hon. mention 1991, Catharine Lorillard Wolfe award for pastel 1992, cash award 1993), Pen and Brush Club (Helen Slotman award 1986, OPA Internat. award 1987, Gene Alden Walker award 1988, Pen and Brush Solo award 1992), hon. mention 1991, Knickerbocker Artists (Flora B. Giffuni PSA Pres.' award 1990), Oil Pastel Assn. (Pen and Brush award 1987, Strathmore award 1989, Salmagundi Club award 1991), Am. Artists Profl. League (Claude Parson's Meml. award 1974, 2nd prize in oils 1992, 3d prize oils 1993, Pres. award 1994), Alpha Delta Pi. Lutheran. Home: 222 E 93d St Apt 26A New York NY 10128

REINISCH, NANCY RAE, therapist, consultant; b. Chgo., Mar. 31, 1953; d. Charles Richard and Marianne (Gross) R.; m. Paul A. Salmen, June 14, 1980; children: Chas, Marcus. BA in Sociology cum laude, Colo. Coll., 1975; cert. drug and alcohol counseling, U. Minn., 1980; MSW, U. Denver, 1982. Cert. relationship therapist; lic. clin. social worker. Counselor Rampart Boys' Home, Colorado Springs, Colo., 1975; advocate bilinqual community Migrants in Action, St. Paul, 1976; therapist Chrysalis Ctr. for Women, Mpls., 1979; team leader and prevention specialist Project Charlie, Edina, Minn., 1977-80, also trainer, cons., 1985—; mental health worker Bethesda Mental Health Ctr. and Hosp., Denver, 1980-83; therapist Gateway Alcohol Recovery Ctr., Aurora, Colo., 1983-84; pvt. practice therapy, also dir. Family Practice Counseling Service, Glenwood Springs, Colo., 1984—; co-dir. Valley Sexual Abuse Ctr.; bd. dirs. Adv./Safehouse Project, Glenwood Springs; mem. Valley View Hosp. Ethics com., Glenwood Springs, 1986—. Mem. sch. accountability com. Glenwood Springs, Human Svcs.

Commn., Garfield County. Mem. Nat. Assn. Social Workers, NOW, Nat. Abortion Rights Action League, ACLU, Colo. Pub. Interest Research Group. Democrat. Office: Family Practice Counseling Svc 1905 Blake Ave Glenwood Springs CO 81601-4250

REINITZ, JANE ANN, counselor, secondary education educator; b. Evansville, Ind., July 31, 1945. BA in Latin, Ind. State U., 1967, MAT in Latin, 1969, MS in Counseling Psychology, 1973. Nat. cert. counselor; nat. cert. sch. counselor. Tchr. Boonville (Ind.) H.S., 1967-73, tchr., counselor, 1973—; adj. instr., counseling practicum U. Evansville, Ind., 1974-75. Mem. NEA, Ind. State Tchrs. Assn., Warrick County Teachrs. Assn., Am. Counseling Assn., Ind. Counseling Assn., Am. Classical League, Classical Assn. Middle, West & South, Delta Kappa Gamma (treas. 1988—), Alpha Sigma Alpha (alumni). Roman Catholic. Office: Boonville High Sch 300 N 1st St Boonville IN 47601

REINKE, DARLENE SUSAN, management executive; b. Cook County, Ill., Sept. 29, 1965; d. Robert Charles and Darlene Carol (Strom) Reinke; m. Jeffrey P. Arndt, July 29, 1988. Student, Mt. Mary Coll., 1983-85; BBA, U. Milw., 1988. V.p. Classic Med. Products, Muskego, Wis., 1986-94; pres. Bouqhets of Lake Geneva, Wis., 1994—; corp. sec. Classic Med. Group, Muskego, 1991—. Mem. NAFE, Assn. System Mgmt. Home: 8325 Eagle Ln Waterford WI 53185-1183

REINKE, DORIS MARIE, retired elementary education educator; b. Racine, Wis., Jan. 12, 1922; d. Otto William Reinke and Louise Amelia Goehring. BS, U. Wis., Milw., 1943; MS, U. Wis., Whitewater, 1967. Tchr. kindergarten Elkhorn (Wis.) Area Sch. System, 1943-69, bldg. prin., 1968-70, summer sch. dir., 1974-75, grade 2 tchr., 1970-84, primary dept. chmn., 1971-84, administrv. asst., supervising tchr., 1957-83, student tchr., 1984, ret., 1984; oriented experience tchr. Program Area Sch. System, Elkhorn, 1966; pres. Elkhorn Edn. Assn., 1949-50; rep. dist. State Kindergarten Conf., Oshkosh, Wis., 1966; participant early edn. conf. State Early Edn. Conf., Eagle River, Wis., 1968. Monthly columnist Beacon, 1994—; contbr. weekly newspaper column Webster Notes, 1989; Walworth County Diary monthly coljn in The Week, 1991—; author Doris' Corner newsletter Walworth County Geneal. Soc., 1992—. Bd. dirs. Food Pantry, Elkhorn, 1985-88, RSVP Vol. Food Pantry, Elkhorn, 1985-95; del. dist. constn. conv. Evang. Luth. Ch. Am., Beloit, Wis., 1987; com. mem. Luth. Ch., Elkhorn, 1987; chm. sch. centennial, Elkhorn, 1987; mem. Elkhorn Hist. Preservation Com., 1991—; archivist Sugar Creek Luth. Ch., 1992—. Recipient Wis. Edn. Research, West Bend, Wis., 1966, Outstanding Elem. Tchrs., Wash., 1973, Wis. Dept. Edn., Madison, 1980, Local History award State Hist. Soc. Wis., 1993. Mem. Nat. Ret. Tchrs. Assn., Walworth County Ret. Tchrs. Assn. (v.p. 1988, pres. 1991), Walworth County Hist. Soc. (treas. 1985-89, v.p. 1990-91, pres. 1991-95), Walworth County Geneal Soc. (bd. dirs. 1991-92), Alpha Delta Kappa (state pres. 1968-70, 76-78). Home: 516 N Wisconsin St Elkhorn WI 53121-1119

REINKER, NANCY CLAYTON COOKE, artist; b. Owensboro, Ky., July 6, 1936; d. Billie Clayton and Barbara Jane (Mitchell) Cooke; m. Dale Bruce Reinker, Sept. 29, 1956; children: Shahn Elizabeth, Laura Beth, Karen Christian. Student, Kent State U., 1954-55, Cleve. Art Inst., 1956-57; studied sculpture with, Stanley Bleifeld, 1979-80; student, Silvermine Sch. of Art, 1988-89; 1979-80. Owner Nettle Creek Shops of Westport and Cos Cob, Conn., 1974-86, Cross River Design Studio, 1986-89. One woman shows at Hayes Gallery, 1992 Silvermine Guild Arts Ctr., 1992, Art Place, 1993, Westport Art Ctr., 1994, also in numerous nat. and internat. exhbns. Vice chmn. Cultural Events Commn., Weston, Conn., 1993-94; pres. Inst. for Visual Artists, New Canaan, Conn., 1992-93; v.p., pres. Art Place Gallery, Southport, Conn., 1991-92, 94. Named to 1992 Cir. of Excellence, Soc. Nat. Art Patrons, 1992; recipient 1st prize Spectrum, 1992, 93, 94. Mem. ASID, Silvermine Guild of Artists (trustee 1994—), New Haven Paint and Clay (Merit award 1993), Nat. Assn. Women Artists, Conn. Women Artists (Painting award 1991), Greenwich Art Soc. (Randolph Chitwood award 1994), Women's Caucus for Art, Chi Omega. Home and Studio: 87 Valley Forge Rd Weston CT 06883-1913

REINSCHMIEDT, ANNE TIERNEY, nurse, lawyer, rancher; b. Washington, Mar. 6, 1932; d. Edward F. and Frances (Palmer) Tierney; m. Edwin Ruben Reinschmiedt, Sept. 20, 1959 (div. 1961); 1 child, Kathleen Frances Tierney. BS, Cen. State U., Edmond, Okla., 1975; JD, Oklahoma City U. Sch. Law, 1991. RN, Calif., Okla.; lic. residential care facility adminstr., nursing home adminstr. Nurse San Jose (Calif.) Hosp., 1952-55; owner, operator Hominy Studio, 1960-62; dir. nurses, lab and x-ray, technician, adminstr. Hominy (Okla.) City Hosp., 1961-63; nurse Jackson County Dept. Health, Altus, Okla., 1963-65; adminstr. Propp's Inc., Oklahoma City, 1965-80; nursing homes cons. Propps & Self, Oklahoma City, 1965—; pres. Shamrock Health Care Ctr., Bethany, Okla., 1981—; operator Lakeview Lodging Residential Care Facility, 1981—; adult edn. instr., med. aide technicians East Central U., Ada, Okla., 1987-89; cons. residential care facilities, 1985—. Author: Recovery Room Procedures, 1958. Mem. Jackson County (Okla.) Draft Bd., 1965-70. Lt. USN, 1955-60. Mem. ANA, Nat. Assn. Residential Care Facilities (sec., bd. dirs. 1983-85), Okla. Bar Assn., Okla. Assn. Residential Care Facilities (founding pres. 1981-87, bd. dirs. 1981—), Beta Sigma Phi, Phi Alpha Delta (vice justice, exec. bd. 1988-90). Republican. Roman Catholic. Office: Shamrock Health Care PO Box 848 Bethany OK 73008-0848

REIS, CATHERINE JANE, academic counselor; b. Marshalltown, Iowa, Mar. 10, 1950; d. Harold Emmet and Lois Virginia (Valentine) Sauer; div.; children: Jay, Erin, Jody. BA, U. Iowa, 1973; MEd, Coll. Idaho, 1991. Cert. tchr., Idaho; lic. profl. counselor. Tchr. Sch. Dist. 411, Twin Falls, Idaho, 1973-76, 91-92, counselor, 1992—. Mem. ACA, Am. Specialists Group Work, Nat. Assn. Student Activity Advisors, Idaho Sch. Counselor Assn., Idaho Soc. Individual Psychology. Home: 1187 Skyline Dr Twin Falls ID 83301

REIS, JEAN STEVENSON, administrative secretary; b. Wilburton, Okla., Nov. 30, 1914; d. Robert Emory and Ada (Ross) Stevenson; m. George William Reis, June 24, 1939 (dec. 1980). BA, U. Tex., El Paso, 1934; MA, So. Meth. U., 1935; postgrad., U. Chgo., summers 1937-38, U. Wash., 1948-49. Tchr. El Paso High Sch., 1935-39; safety engr., trainer Safety and Security Div., Office of Chief Ordnance, Chgo., 1942-45; tchr. Lovenberg Jr. High Sch., Galveston, Tex., 1946; parish sec. Trinity Parish Episcopal Ch., Seattle, 1950-65; adminstrv. sec., asst. Office Resident Bishop, United Meth. Ch., Seattle, 1965-94. Mem. AAUW, Beta Beta Beta. Home: 9310 42nd Ave NE Seattle WA 98115-3814

REIS, JOSEPHINE GOODALE MILLS, retired association executive; b. Upper Montclair, N.J., Jan. 15, 1908; d. Irving Parker and Sophia (Goodale) Mills; m. L. Sanford Reis, Jan. 15, 1932; children: Curtis, Barbara G. Reis Johnson. BA, Cornell U., 1929. With trust dept. City Bank Farmers Trust Co., N.Y.C., 1929-34; pres. YWCA, Ridgewood, N.J., 1960-63; nat. bd. dirs., chair teen adv. com. YWCA U.S.A., 1964-76, mem. world svc. coun. Contbr. poetry to the Saturday Rev. Lit. Asst. dir. vol. svcs. ARC, Bklyn., 1942-45; hon. mem. YWCA, Ridgewood, N.J.; past mem. trustee nominating com. Cornell U. Recipient Army-Navy E award Armed Forces, 1945. Mem. AAUW, LWV, NOW, Coll. Club (hon., pres. 1957-59), Mortar Bd., Penthama. Democrat. Home: 4200 Shell Rd Sarasota FL 34242

REISCHMAN, SHIRLEY ANN, systems designer; b. Kansas City, Mo., Feb. 4, 1944; d. Louis and Yetta (Swartz) Agronin; m. Henry Joseph Coopersmith, Sept. 3, 1969 (div. Nov. 1979); children: Marc Daniel Coopersmith, Stacy Janine Coopersmith; m. James Edward Reischman, Apr. 16, 1988. Cons. Tustin, Calif., 1972-78, 88-89; mktg. analyst Basic Four Corp., Tustin, 1978-80; regional mgr. Data Solutions, Inc., Santa Ana, Calif., 1980-82; mgr. info. resources PNIC Ins. Co., Fullerton, Calif., 1982-88; asst. v.p. Splty. Ins. Svc., Orange, Calif., 1989-92; systems designer GRE Ins. Group, Cin., 1993—. Pres. bd. dirs. Tustin Village HOA, 1982-85; steering com. Ohions for Health Care Access, Columbus, Ohio, 1993. Mem. DPMA (Data Processing Mgmt. Assn.).

REISER, THERESE ANNE, medical/surgical nurse; b. Bklyn., Nov. 13, 1952; d. Ralph W. and Margaret T. (Cleary) R. BSN, Adelphi U., 1986. Cert. med./surgical nurse. Staff nurse Doctor's Hosp., N.Y.C., 1986-89; primary staff nurse Massapequa Gen. Hosp., Seaford, N.Y., 1989—, asst. nursing care coord., 1993—. Mem. ANA, N.Y. State Nurses Assn. Home: 33 Primrose Ln North Babylon NY 11703-3244

REISLER, HELEN BARBARA, product promotion and human resources development executive, consultant ; b. N.Y.C., June 21; d. George and Elizabeth Lois (Schultz) Gottesman; BS, in Edn., N.Y. U., 1954; MS in Edn. and Reading, L.I. U., 1978; m. Melvin Reisler, June 5, 1955; children: Susan O'Brien, Karen Reisler, Keith James. Elem. tchr., N.Y.C., 1954-78; instr. grad. sch., adj. lectr. L.I. U., Bklyn., 1978; account exec. N.Y. Yellow Pages, Inc., N.Y.C., 1979, personnel mgr., 1979, adminstrv. dir., 1980-83, v.p. personnel, 1983-84, v.p. adminstrn./personnel, 1984-85, also dir.; staff specialist sales and market support Southwestern Bell Publs., 1985-88, NY. mgr. pub. relations and recruitment N.Y. Yellow Pages/Mast Advt. and Publs., Inc. of Southwestern Bell, 1988; cons. human resources devel. and product promotion, 1989—; recruiter N.E. Region, N.Y. area community rels. rep.; moderator weekly cable TV show New York Business Forum, N.Y.C., 1983-85. Named Ptnr. in Edn., N.Y.C. Bd. Edn., 1984. Mem. Internat. Assn. Sales Profls. (bd. dirs. 1993, 94), UN Assn., Sales Execs. Club N.Y. (bd. dirs., reception, membership and mem. rels. coms., chmn. youth edn., v.p. 1987-88, chmn. internal communications 1989), Execs. Assn. Greater N.Y. (chmn. com. Sec. Day), Heritage Hills Country Club Westchester, Sales Execs. Club (v.p.), Rotary (chmn. environ. com. N.Y. chpt. 1991—, bd. liaison to pub. rels. and membership coms. 1994—, mem. interviewing com. to select ambassadorial scholarship candidates 1993, 94, mentor to Japanese ambassadorial scholars, 1992, 93, divsn. chmn. community svcs., 1st woman elected to bd. dirs. N.Y. chpt., Paul Harris fellow 1992). Profiled in various bus. publs. Home and Office: 47 Plaza St Park Slope Brooklyn NY 11217

REISMAN, ELAINE, writer, poet, nurse; b. Queens, N.Y., Jan. 3, 1948; d. Alfred William and Ann (Adams) Holle; m. Barry Michael Reisman, May 29, 1980; children: Michael Blaine, Geoffrey Blake. Grad., Lenox Hill Hosp. Sch. Nursing, N.Y.C., 1968; BFA in Sculpture, Parsons Sch. Design, 1989; postgrad., NYU, 1992—. RN, N.Y. Head nurse, asst. supr. insvc. edn. Lenox Hill Hosp., N.Y.C., 1968-79; vol., asst. to dir. Artists Choice Mus., N.Y.C., 1984-85; intern, vol. to edn. dir. Whitney Mus. of Am. Art, N.Y.C., summer 1986, 87. Groups shows include Parsons Sch. Design; one-woman show of drawing, sculpture, and painting, Passaic, N.J., 1987. Mem. MLA, Poetry Soc. Am., Coll. Art Assn.

REISNER, ELENA MACKAY, educational administrator; b. Inverness, Scotland, June 1, 1922; came to U.S., 1932; d. John Alexander and Jane Logan (Wells) Mackay; m. Sherwood Hartman Reisner, June 1, 1946 (dec. 1990); children: Ruth Reisner Brock, James Sherwood. BA, Wellesley Coll., 1944; MA, Columbia U., 1945. Tchr. St. Margaret's Sch., Waterbury, Conn., 1945-46; missionary tchr. Presbyn. Ch. U.S.A., Mexico City, 1946-50; instr. Tex. A&I U., Kingsville, 1960-65; tchr. Presbyn. Pan Am. Sch., Kingsville, 1957-80, interim pres., 1990-91, asst. to pres., 1991—. Founder Amistad Vol. Coun., Kingsville, 1984; past pres. Laurel Home Extension Club; mem. Kleberg County Resource Coun.; chmn. Mission Presbytery's Hispanic Ministries Coun., Presbyn. Ch. U.S.A., 1993, 94, 95; elder Presbyn. Ch., 1976—. Named One of 10 Outstanding Women in Kingsville History, Zonta Club, 1975; recipient lifetime svc. award Kingsville C. of C., Bell-MacKay prize for mission Presbyns. for Renewal-Presbyn. Gen. Assembly, 1994. Mem. AAUW (pres. 1977-79), Downtown Mchts. Assn., Presbyn. Women (hon. life, pres. 1985-87), Phi Beta Kappa, Delta Kappa Gamma (hon.). Democrat. Home: 332 University Blvd Kingsville TX 78363 Office: Presbyn Pan Am Sch PO Box 1578 Kingsville TX 78363

REISNER, SUSAN L., public defender; b. Dec. 1, 1953; m. Paul H. Schneider. BA, Princeton U., 1975; JD, Rutgers U., Newark, 1978. Chief pub. utilities and civil rights sect. N.J. Dept. Law and Pub. Safety, Newark, 1988-91; chief environ. sect. N.J. Dept. Law and Pub. Safety, Trenton, 1991-92, dep. atty. gen. in charge of agy. advise, 1992-93; dir. divsn. rate counsel N.J. Dept. Pub. Advocate, Newark, 1993-94; acting commr. N.J. Dept. Pub. Advocate, Trenton, 1994; pub. defender N.J. Office Pub. Defender, Trenton, 1994—; commr. gov.'s study commn. on discrimination in pub. works, procurement and contrn. contracts, Trenton, 1992. Contbr. articles to profl. jours. Mem. N.J. Bar Assn. Office: Office Pub Defender Justice Complex CN 850 Trenton NJ 08625

REISSENWEBER, BETH RANDERSON, controller, small business owner; b. Berwyn, Ill., June 14, 1961; d. Robert M. and Gloria (Dallner) Randerson; m. Klaus Wolfgang Reissenweber, Feb. 14, 1991. BS, Elmhurst (Ill.) Coll., 1981; MBA, Ind. U., 1983. CPA, cert. mgmt. acct. Fin. analyst The Christian Sci. Monitor, Boston, 1984-85; assoc. prof. Massasoit Community Coll., Canton, Mass., 1985-86; sr. fin. analyst The 1st Ch. of Christ, Scientist, Boston, 1986-88, payroll mgr., 1988-89, income acctg. mgr., 1989; chief fin. officer Chgo. Jr. Sch., Elgin, Ill., 1990; controller Legal Assistance Found. Chgo., 1990—; owner Acctg. Info. Systems, Chgo., 1990—. Mem. Rep. Nat. Com., Washington, 1984. With USN, 1985. Mem. Nat. Assn. Accts., Ind. U. Alumni Assn., Omicron Delta Kappa, Sigma Kappa (1st v.p. 1979). Office: Legal Assistance Found Chgo 343 S Dearborn St Ste 700 Chicago IL 60604-3807

REISSMAN, ROSE CHERIE, elementary education educator; b. N.Y.C., Nov. 4, 1951; d. Seymour Frank and Sidonia (Blank) R.; m. Steven Feld. Cert. tchr., N.Y. Classroom tchr. various schs., N.Y.C., from 1972; now tchr. specialist for curriculum design Sch. Dist. 25, N.Y.C.; founder, mgr. Writing Inst. Peer Teaching, Forum, and Oral History, 1983—; grant writer, curriculum writer N.Y.C. Bd. Edn.; adj. prof. edn. Manhattanville (N.Y.) Coll., Fordham U., N.Y.C.; mem. tchr. network Cradle Ctr. for Law-Related Edn., Writing Notebook; mem. adv. bd. Giraffe Educator, N.Y. Newsday; v.p. edn. Wedgewood Brandeis Community Group; mem. tchr. adv. coun. Impact II; presenter workshops on grant writing. Author: Newday's 1988 Elections, 1989, Mayoral Curriculum, 1990, Gubernatorial Curriculum, N.Y. Board of Education Infusing Critical Thinking in the Middle Schools with Word Processing Software and Picture Disc, Entrepreneurial Empowerment 6-12 Curriculum Workbook, Rights and Responsibilities, 1992, Mayoral Campaign, 1993, The Evolving Multicultural Classroom; field editor Learning Mag., 1991—. Christa McAuliffe fellow, 1988; grantee Dupont Found., Am. Cancer Heart Assn., 1992; recipient Judy Blume Ctr. award, 1988, Valley Forge Bill of Rights medal, 1992; named NYSEC Tchr. of Excellence, 1993; recipient numerous other awards and grants. Mem. N.Y.C. Assn. Tchrs. English (v.p. 1993, pres. 1994), Nat. Found. Teaching Entrepreneurships (cons., bd. dirs.), Assn. Computers in Edn. (v.p.). Office: Writing Inst 110 Seaman Ave Apt 5C New York NY 10034-2808

REISTER, RUTH ALKEMA, lawyer, business executive; b. Grand Rapids, Mich., May 30, 1936; d. Henry and Lena (Land) Alkema; m. Raymond A. Reister, Oct. 7, 1967. B.A., U. Mich., 1958, J.D., 1964; grad. Program in Bus. Adminstrn., Harvard U., 1959, postgrad. Program in Mgmt. Devel., 1976. Bar: Minn., Mich. 1964, U.S. Supreme Ct. 1976. Trust officer Northwestern Nat. Bank, Mpls., 1964-70; asst. counsel, asst. v.p., sec. Fed. Res. Bank, Mpls., 1970-81; asst. sec., bd. govs. Fed. Res. System, 1977; dep. under sec. U.S. Dept. Agr., Washington, 1981-83; pres. First Bank Systems Agrl. Credit Corp., Mpls., 1983-84; pres. Groveland Corp., Mpls., 1986—; dir. Herman Miller, Inc., Zealand, Mich., 1984—. Bd. dirs. United Way, ARC, Jones Harrison Home, Mpls.; chmn. Jones-Harrison Found. Mem. Harvard Bus. Sch. Club Minn., Minn. Women's Econ. Round Table (pres. 1980-81). Republican. *

REITANO, MARGARET ANN, neonatal nurse; b. Poughkeepsie, N.Y., July 16, 1951; d. Paul B. and Rose I. (Crevino) Pulichene; m. Bruce W. Reitano, Aug. 5, 1973 (div. Apr. 1981); 1 child, Anthony P. Diploma, Vassar Bros. Hosp. Sch. Nursing, 1971; BSN, Mount Saint Mary Coll., 1995. Cert. in neonatal intensive care, NAACOG. Staff nurse newborn care Vassar Bros. Hosp., Poughkeepsie, N.Y., 1971-79, staff nurse newborn nursery, 1980-82, staff nurse postpartum, 1982-84, nurse mgr., non-regional level III NICU, 1984—. Mem. Nat. Assn. Neonatal Nurses, Assn. Women's Health, Obstetric and Neonatal Nursing, Sigma Theta Tau. Roman Catholic. Office: Vassar Bros Hosp Reade Pl Poughkeepsie NY 12601

REITER, DAISY K., elementary education educator; b. Lewisburg, Pa., Aug. 25, 1936; d. Clark B. and Maude E. (Bensinger) Zimmerman; m. Edward P. Reiter, June 3, 1978; children: Edward, Amy, Russ, Elizabeth Sieber White, Katheryn Sieber Ellis, Ann Sieber Myers. BS in Elem. Edn., Pa. State U., 1957; postgrad., U. No. Colo., Greeley, Pa. State U. Cert. permanent elem. tchr., Pa.; lic. real estate agt. Tchr. grade 4 Hershey (Pa.) Sch. Dist., 1957-58; tchr. grades 4 and 5 Red Land Sch. Dist., New Cumberland, Pa., 1959-61; kindergarten tchr. Topeka City Schs., 1958-59; tchr. grade 5 Wallaceton-Boggs Elem. Sch. Philipsburg (Pa.)-Osceola Area Sch. Dist., 1975—; inservice leader transactional analysis and arts in edn.; researcher Civil War, newspapers, animals and habitats, body systems. Mem. choir 1st Luth Ch. Recipient Arts in Edn. grants (4 yrs.). Mem. NEA, Pa. State Edn. Assn., Philipsburg-Osceola Edn. Assn, Toughlove Chpt. (founder). Home: PO Box 704 Philipsburg PA 16866-0704

REITMAN, JOYCE BUCKNER, psychologist, educator; b. Benton, Ark., Sept. 25, 1937; d. Waymond Floyd Pannell and Willie Evelyn (Wright) Kaufman; m. John W. Buckner, Aug. 29, 1958 (div. 1970); children: Cheryl, John, Chris. BA, Ouachita Bapt. Coll., 1959; MS in Edn., Henderson State U., 1964; PhD, North Tex. State U., 1970. Lic. psychologist, Tex.; cert. Coun. of Nat. Registry Health Svc. Providers n Psychology; master trainer in imago relationship therapy. Assoc. prof. U. Tex., Arlington, 1970-80, chmn. dept. edn., 1976-78; pvt. practice psychology, Arlington, 1974—; author, profl. speaker; appeared on internat. TV shows, including Oprah Winfrey Show. Mem. APA, Nat. Assn. for Imago Relationship Therapy (pres.). Home: 1509 Millbrook Dr Arlington TX 76012-2120

REITZ, BARBARA MAURER, poet, freelance writer; b. Teaneck, N.J., Dec. 26, 1931; d. William Ritschy and Ruth Gunhill (Noren) Maurer; m. William Stanley Reitz, Jr., Sept. 15, 1956; children: William Stanley III, David Stewart. BA in English, Bucknell U., 1953. Sec. UN, N.Y.C., 1953-54; sec. to pres. Charles Scribner's Sons, N.Y.C., 1954-56; freelance writer Chillicothe, Ohio, 1987—, poet, 1949—. Contbr. articles to local newspapers. Campaign mgr., creative dir. William S. Reitz, Jr. , Chillicothe City Coun. pres.; patron Bucknell Assn. for Arts, Columbus Symphony, Area Artist Series, Majestic Theatre; mem. Friends of WOSU-PBS, Pump House Art Gallery, Civic Theatre. Mem. AAUW (Chillicothe br. 1988-90, v.p. Rockville, Md. bd. 1961-62, pres.), Bucknell Alumni Assn. (class reporter 1968-83), Chillicothe Tennis Assn. (sec.-treas. 1973-82), Sigma Tau Delta (pres. 1952-53), Pi Delta Epsilon, Alpha Lambda Delta Pi Beta Phi (treas. 1952-53). Republican. Presbyterian (elder 1981—).

REITZ, STEPHANIE KAREN, journalist; b. Grosse Pointe, Mich., July 22, 1968; d. Robert Elwin Reitz and Pamela (Granger) Boone. BA in Journalism, Mich. State U., 1991. Staff reporter Lake Orion (Mich.) Rev., 1983-86; newspaper intern, 1986-90; copy editor Detroit News, 1990; bureau chief Fla. Today, Melbourne, 1991-93; govt. and politics reporter Waterbury (Conn.) Rep.-Am., 1993—. Recipient Golf Writer's Excellence award Golf Writers Assn. Am., 1988, 89, Commentary award Detroit Press Club, 1990. Mem. Soc. Profl. Journalists (chpt. pres. 1987-89), Investigative Reporters and Editors. Home: 440 Meriden Rd #418 Waterbury CT 06705

REJENT, MARIAN MAGDALEN, pediatrician; b. Toledo, Aug. 12, 1920; d. Casimir Stanley and Magdalen (Szymanowski) R. BS, Mary Manse Coll., 1943; MD, Marquette U., 1946; MPH, U. Mich., 1960. Diplomate Am. Bd. Pediatrics. Intern St. Vincent Med. Ctr., Toledo, 1946-47; resident communicable diseases City Hosp., Cleve., 1947-48; resident pediatrics Childrens Hosp., Akron, Ohio, 1948-50; pvt. practice Toledo, 1950-54; chief div. maternal child health Toledo Bd. Health, 1953-64; dir. pediatrics Maumee Valley Hosp., Toledo, 1964-69; assoc. prof. pediatrics Med. Coll. Ohio, Toledo, 1969-76; med. dir. State Crippled Childrens Program, Columbus, Ohio, 1976-78; attendant pediatrician St. Vincent Med. Ctr., Toledo, 1978-80, 87—; chief pediatric svcs. Wake County Health Dept., Raleigh, N.C., 1980-87; clin. prof. pediatrics Med. Coll. Ohio, 1987—. Exec. com. March of Dimes, 1988-92. Mem. AMA, APHA, Am. Acad. Pediatrics, Am. Med. Women's Assn., Ohio PHA, Ohio State Med. Assn., NW Ohio Pediatric Assn., Acad. Medicine Toledo, Alpha Omega Alpha. Republican. Roman Catholic. Home: 2902 Evergreen Rd Toledo OH 43606-2724

REJMAN, DIANE LOUISE, systems analyst; b. Hartford, Conn., Jan. 14, 1956; d. Louis P. and Genevieve (Walukevich) R. BS in Aviation Adminstrn., Embry Riddle Aero. U., 1980; M in Internat. Mgmt., Am. Grad. Sch. Internat. Mgmt., 1991; cert. in cross cultural negotiation, Western Internat. Univ., 1994. Indsl. engr./planner Hamilton Aviation, Tucson, 1980-82; indsl. engr. assoc. Gates Learjet, Tucson, 1984; tech. writer, FAA coord. Dee Howard Co., San Antonio, 1984-86; indsl. engr. McDonnell Douglas Helicopter Systems, Mesa, Ariz., 1986-88; systems analyst McDonnell Douglas Helicopter Co., Mesa, Ariz., 1988—; bd. dirs. McDonnell Douglas Helicopter Co. Employee Community Fund., adminstr. 1993—. With U.S. Army, 1977-80. Home: 7532 E Drummer Ave Mesa AZ 85208-2041

RELIFORD, CAROL ANNETTE, nurse; b. Jasper, Tex., Sept. 5, 1948; d. Tommy and Willie R.; 1 child, Kimberly. BSN, Prairie View A&M Univ., 1971. Asst. charge nurse St. Joseph Hosp., Houston, 1971-74; staff nurse Jefferson Davis Hosp., Houston, 1974-80, Westbury Hosp., Houston, 1980-82; asst. head nurse Thomas St. Clinic, Houston, 1988-89, nurse mgr., 1989—; HIV clin. trainer, Houston, 1992, test counseling, 1993. Mem. Coun. Nurse Mgrs., Assn. Nurses in AIDS Care. Baptist. Home: 3322 Trail Lake Dr Houston TX 77045

RELL, M. JODI, state official; b. Norfolk, Va.. Grad., Old Dominion U., Conn. State U. Mem., dep. minority leader Conn. Ho. Reps., 1984-94; lt. gov. State of Conn., 1995—. Past vice chmn. Brookfield Rep. Town Com.; trustee YMCA Western Conn. Mem. Nat. Order Women Legislators (immed. past nat. pres., former v.p., treas., corr. sec.), Brookfield Polit. Women's Club (past pres.), Brookfield Bus. and Profl. Womens Club. Address: 125 Long Meadow Hill Rd Brookfield CT 06804 Office: Office Lt Governor State Capitol Rm 304 Hartford CT 06106*

REMAK, JEANNETTE ELIZABETH, quality control executive; b. Queens, N.Y., Nov. 23, 1952; d. Bela Alexander and Helen (Almassy) R. Student, N.Y. Inst. Photography, 1971-72; student, Sch. Visual Arts, N.Y.C., 1972-73, CUNY, 1973-76. Cert. photo finishing engr. Photo Mktg. Assn. Prodn. mgr. Rembrandt Color Labs., Jamaica, N.Y., 1976-80; builder, operator Fast Photo, N.Y.C., 1980-83; prodn. mgr. Jackson Photo, N.Y.C., 1983-86; quality control and prodn. mgr. Universal Photo, N.Y.C., 1986—. Paintings exhibited at Internat. Art Challenge Art Show, Calif., 1987; paintings included in (book) American Artists an Illustrated Survey, 1990, USAF Mus., Wright-Patterson AFB, Ohio, the Pentagon, Washington. Contbg. mem. USAF Art Program. Mem. Soc. Photofinishing Engrs., Am. Soc. Aviation Artists, Am. Soc. Sci. Fiction Fantasy Artists, Challenger Ctr. for Edn. (sponsor).

REMBE, TONI, lawyer; b. Seattle, Apr. 23, 1936; d. Armin and Doris (McVay) R.; m. Arthur Rock, July 19, 1975. Cert. in French Studies, U. Geneva, 1956; LL.B., U. Wash., 1960; LLM in Taxation, NYU, 1961. Bar: N.Y., Wash., Calif. Assoc. Chadbourne, Parke, Whiteside & Wolff, N.Y.C., 1961-63; assoc. Pillsbury, Madison & Sutro, San Francisco, 1964-71, ptnr., 1971—; dir. Potlatch Corp., San Francisco, Pacific Telesis, San Francisco, Am. Pres. Cos., Ltd., Oakland, Calif., Transamerica Corp., San Francisco. Pres. Van Loben Sels Charitable Found., San Francisco; trustee Am. Conservatory Theatre, San Francisco. Fellow Am. Bar Found.; mem. ABA, Am. Judicature Soc., State Bar Calif., Bar Assn. San Francisco, Commonwealth Club of Calif. (govs. of the club). Office: Pillsbury Madison & Sutro 225 Bush St San Francisco CA 94104-4207

REMBRANDT, MELANIE MARIE, actress, word processor; b. Toledo, Ohio, July 15, 1968; d. John Joseph IV and Donna Jean (Ganson) Jacobs. BA in Theater, Film, TV magna cum laude, UCLA, 1990. Sec., receptionist Western Temp. Svc., 1986; saleswoman, model Lion Dept. Store, 1986; comml. sales rschr. L.A. Rsch., Inc., 1986-87; ticket saleswoman, usher Westwood Playhouse, 1987; performing arts counselor Bruin Kids UCLA, 1988-89, patient affairs asst. cardiology dept. Med. Ctr., 1989, legal clk., receptionist student legal svcs., 1987-90; sr. word processor Applied Risk Mgmt., Inc., L.A., 1990—; instr. children's dance workshops, Ohio, Calif.;

asst. performance tchr. Children's Theater Workshop; student dir. Young Rep Prodns. Theatre performances include 42d Street, Long Beach CLO, You Can't Take It with You, Start Theatre, Curse You, Jack Dalton!, Ohio Players, A Chorus Line, Lourdes Theater, The Music Man, Rep Theater, Mr. Scrooge, Rep Theater, others; dinner theater performances include Charlie Brown, Southend Theater, Bride of Tomorrow, Westgate Theater, Little Mary Sunshine, St. Pat's Theater; appeared on TV programs Good Morning America, ABC, Entertainment Tonight, NBC, Two on the Town, CBS, Beverly Hills 90210, Fox, Miss Teenage America, CBS; film appearances include Gypsy, Kaileen's Gift, Cast a Deadly Spell, Malibu Beach Vampires, others. Vol. ARC, children's safe Halloween program UNICEF, Brentwood Ch., Mardi Gras sales for Spl. Olympics, UCLA, sales for Toledo Rep Theater; numerous vol. performances for charity. Mem. SAG, AFTRA, Gold Key, Kappa Delta.

REMEN, JANET MARION, computer science educator; b. London, 1941; came to U.S., 1967; d. Robert Henry and Lorna Helen (Lee) Kerlogue; m. Seymour Remen, 1965. BSc, Durham (Eng.) U., 1962; MS, U. Mich., 1979. Tchr. Math. London Edn. Authority, London, 1962-64, Colo. Rocky Mtn. Sch., Carbondale, 1964-65, Hornsey High Sch., London, 1966-67; instr. Computer Sci. U. Mich., Ann Arbor, 1978-80; instr. Math. and Computer Sci. Washtenaw C.C., Ann Arbor, 1980—, chair dept. computer info. sys. and computer sci., 1986—; reviewer computer sci. curriculum for 2-yr. colls., Washington, 1992. Mem. Assn. Computing Machinery, Computer Profls. for Social Responsibility, Math. Assn. Am. Office: Washtenaw C C 4800 E Huron River Dr Ann Arbor MI 48106-0978

REMETTA, JANET, pharmaceutical company executive, veterinarian; b. Camden, N.J., July 11, 1952; d. John Matthew and Marie Stella (Klemaszewski) R.; m. Neal Robert Frank, Oct. 19, 1974. BA, Trenton State Coll., 1974; MSW, Rutgers U., 1975; postgrad., Delaware Valley Coll., 1977-79; VMD, U. Pa., 1985. Lic. vet. medicine, Pa., N.J. Program specialist N.J. Dept. Health, Trenton, 1975-77, labor/mgmt. cons., 1977-79, supervising program specialist, 1979-81; clin. vet. Emerson Vet. Clinic, Buckingham, Pa., 1985-86, Ewing Vet. Hosp., Trenton, 1986-88; mgr. issues mgmt. Sandoz Pharm. Corp., East Hanover, N.J., 1988-90, assoc. dir. issues mgmt., 1990-91, dir. issues mgmt., 1992, interim dept. head sci. and external affairs, 1992-93; exec. dir. site ops., 1993—. Mem. policy and legis. com. N.J. Chem. Industry Coun., Trenton, 1988-92, chairperson-biotech. com., 1989-91; legis. com. N.J. Bus. and Industry Assn., Trenton, 1988-92; apptd. mem. N.J. Commn. on Smoking & Health, 1991-92; exec. chairperson N.J. Lung Assn., 1994; mem. bus. adv. bd. Women in Govt., 1994—; mem. steering com. Ctr. for the Am. Woman, 1995; bd. dirs. YWCA, 1994—. Recipient Tribute to Women in Industry award, 1992. Mem. NAFE, AVMA, Pa. Vet. Med. Assn. (legis. com. 1990—), Am. Mgmt. Assn., Am. Lung Assn. (exec. chairperson 1994), Pa. Assn. Indsl. Vets., Healthcare Businesswomen's Assn., N.J. Health Products Coun. (chairperson elect 1989-91, chairperson 1991-93), Nat. Pharm. Coun. (pub. affairs com. 1988-91, sci. affairs com. 1989-90), Pharm. Mfrs. Assn. (govt. affairs com. 1989-93), Greater Valley Forge Rhodesian Ridge Back Club (founding mem.). Home: 379 Sweet Briar Rd Perkasie PA 18944-3868 Office: Sandoz Pharms Corp 59 State Route 10 East Hanover NJ 07936-1011

REMICK, DIANE MARIE, artist; b. L.A., Oct. 16, 1944; d. Leon F. and Ruth Marie (Virgo) Driggs; m. Norman F. Remick, July 11, 1964; children: Frederick A., Matthew L. BA in Art, Calif. State U., Northridge, 1990, MA in Art, 1992. Artist Northridge, 1991—; Mem. L.A. Ctr. for Photog. Studies, 1992—, L.A. Contemporary Exhbns., 1992—, So. Calif. Women's Caucus for Art, 1994—. One-woman shows include Creative Art Ctr., Burbank, Calif., 1994, Las Vegas Mus. Art, 1994, Acanthus Gallery, Portland, Oreg., 1994, Cerro Coso C.C., Ridgecrest, Calif., 1995; exhibited in group shows at Brea (Calif.) Civic and Cultural Ctr. Gallery, 1991, 92, Allstate Plz. Gallery, Glendale, Calif., 1991, Gallery Concord, Calif., 1991, West L.A. City Hall Gallery, 1992, Berkeley (Calif.) Art Ctr. Assn., 1992, Parkersburg (W.Va.) Art Ctr., 1992, 93, 94, 95, Downtown Gallery, San Jose, Calif., 1992, The Carlson Gallery, Bridgeport, Conn., 1993, Brand Art Gallery, Glendale, 1993, L.R.C. Gallery Sinclair C.C., Dayton, Ohio, 1993, Creative Art Ctr., Chico, Calif., 1994, Merging One Gallery, Santa Monica, 1994, Artspace Gallery, Woodland Hills, Calif., 1994, Palm Springs (Calif.) Desert Mus., 1994, Muse Gallery, Kansas City, Mo., 1995, Artlink, Inc., Ft. Wayne, Ind., 1995, Pence Gallery, Davis, Calif., 1995; contbr. articles to profl. jours. Mem. Southern Calif. Women's Caucus for Art, L.A. Ctr. for Photography Studies. Recipient Hon. mention award San Jose Art League, 1992, First place award Bridgeport Area Arts Coun., 1993.

REMLEY, AUDREY WRIGHT, educational administrator, psychologist; b. Warrenton, Mo., Dec. 26, 1931; d. Leslie Frank and Irene Lesetta (Graue) Wright; m. Alvin Remley, Mar. 25, 1951 (dec. Mar. 1986); children: Steven Leslie, David Mark. AA, Hannibal-LaGrange Coll., 1951; BS in Edn. cum laude, U. Mo., 1963, MA, 1969, PhD, 1974. Lic. psychologist, Mo; cert. health svc. provider, Mo. Asst. prof. psychology Westminster Coll., Fulton, Mo., 1969-74, assoc. prof., 1975-88, prof., 1988—, prof., assoc. dean faculty, 1989—, chmn. dept. psychology, 1975-78, dir. counseling svcs., 1975-79, dir. student devel., 1979-80, dir. acad. advising and counseling svcs., 1980-88; cons. OVID Bell Press, 1988-89; mem. adv. bd. Callaway Community Hosp., 1988—, pres. 1992-95; bd. dirs. Serve, Inc., Fulton, 1989-95, pres. 1991-93; mem. adv. bd. social learning program Fulton State Hosp., chair, 1992-94. Recipient Outstanding Young Woman of Am. award Jaycettes, 1965, Athena award, 1991; NDEA fellow, 1968. Mem. APA, AACD, Am. Coll. Pers. Assn. (exec. council 1982-85, co-editor ACPA Developments, 1984-87, v.p. state divs., 1987-89, treas.-elect 1990-91, treas., 1991-93, treas. ednl. found. bd., 1994-95, Outstanding State Div. Leader 1982, profl. svc. award 1991, Annuit Coeptis awrd 1994), Mo. Coll. Pers. Assn. (pres. 1981-82, profl. svc. award 1987), Mo. Psychol. Assn. (lic.), Kiwanis (exec. bd. 1989-92, v.p. 1992, pres.-elect 1992-93, pres. 1993-94). Presbyterian. Avocations: singing; antique collecting; knitting. Office: Westminster Coll 501 Westminster Ave Fulton MO 65251-1299

RENDELL, MARJORIE O., judge; m. Edward G. Rendell. BA, U. Pa., 1969; postgrad., Georgetown U., 1970-71; JD, Villanova U., 1973; LLD (hon.), Phila. Coll. Textile and Sci., 1992. Ptnr. Duane, Morris & Heckscher, Phila., 1972-93; judge U.S. Dist. Ct. (ea. dist.) Pa., 1994—; asst. to dir. annual giving Dept. Devel., U. Pa., 1973-78; mem. adv. bd. Chestnut Hill Nat. Bank/East Falls Adv. Bd.; mem. alternative dispute resolution com. mediation divsn. Ea. Dist. Pa. Bankruptcy Conf. Active Acad. Vocal Arts, Market St. East Improvement Assn., Pa.'s Campaign for Choice, Phila. Friends Outward Bound; vice chair Ave. of Arts, Inc.; vice chair bd. trustees Vis. Nurse Assn. Greater Phila. Mem. ABA, Am. Bankruptcy Inst., Pa. Bar Assn., Phila. Bar Assn. (bd. dirs. young lawyers sect. 1973-78), Phila. Bar Found. (bd. dirs.), Forum Exec. Women, Internat. Women's Forum, Phi Beta Kappa. Office: US Courthouse 601 Market St Rm 3114 Philadelphia PA 19106*

RENDER, ARLENE, ambassador. Joined Fgn. Svc., Dept. State, 1970; consular officer Fgn. Svc., Dept. State, Abidjan, Cote D'Ivoire, 1971-73, Tehran, Iran, 1973-76, Genoa, Italy, 1976-78; polit. officer Fgn. Svc., Dept. State, 1978-79, internat. rels. officer AF/C, 1979-81; dep. chief of mission Fgn. Svc., Dept. State, Brazzaville, Republic of the Congo, 1981-84; consul-gen. Fgn. Svc., Dept. State, Kingston, Jamaica, 1984-86; dep. chief of mission Fgn. Svc., Dept. State, Accra, Ghana, 1986-89; mem. sr. seminar Fgn. Svc., Dept. State, 1989-90, amb. to The Gambia, 1990-93; dir. Office of Ctrl. African Affairs Fgn. Svc., Dept. State, Washington, 1993—. Office: State Dept Office Ctrl African Affairs Washington DC 20520

RENDL-MARCUS, MILDRED, artist, economist; b. N.Y.C., May 30, 1928; d. Julius and Agnes (Hokr) Rendl. BS, NYU, 1948, MBA, 1950; PhD (Dean Bernice Brown Cronkhite fellow 1950-51), Radcliffe Coll., 1954; m. Edward Marcus, Aug. 10, 1956. Economist, GE, 1953-56, Bigelow-Sanford Carpet Co., Inc., 1956-58; lectr. econs. evening sessions CCNY, 1953-58; rsch. investment problems in tropical Africa, 1958-59; instr. econs. Hunter Coll. CUNY, 1959-60; lectr. econs. Columbia U., 1960-61; rsch. econ. devel. Nigeria, West Africa, 1961-63; sr. economist Internat. div. Nat. Indsl. Conf. Bd., 1963-66; asst. prof. Grad. Sch. Bus. Adminstrn., Pace Coll., 1964-66; assoc. prof. Borough of Manhattan Community Coll., CUNY, 1966-71, prof., 1972-85; vis. prof. Fla. Internat. U., 1986; prin. MRM Assocs., Rendl Fine Art; corp. art econ. and contemporary art cons.; fine arts appraiser; artist Allied Social Sci. Assn. Conf., Boston, 1994; participant Internat. Econ. Meeting, Amsterdam, 1968, Prague, Czech Republic, 1993, Brussels, 1994, Econs. of Fine Arts in Age of Tech., 1984, Internat. Economic Assn. N.Am., Laredo, Tex., 1987-88, London, 1994, Soc. Southwestern Economists, San Antonio, 1988, New Orleans, 1989, Dallas, 1989, Houston, 1991, Dallas, 1994, S.W. Soc. Economists, San Antonio, 1992, Dallas, 1994, San Diego, 1990, 92, Reno, 1991, Western Econ. Assn. Internat., 1990, Ind. U. Pa., 1990, London, 1992, 93. Exhibited New Canaan Art Show, 1982, 83, 84, 85, New Canaan Soc. for Arts Ann., 1983, 85, New Canaan Arts, 1985, Silvermine Galleries, 1986, Stamford Art Assn., 1987, Women in the Arts at Phoenix Gallery, Group Show, N.Y.C., 1988, Parkview Point Gallery, Miami Beach, Fla., 1982-89, Art Complex, New Canaan, 1988-89; group shows include Lever House, N.Y.C., 1990, Cork Gallery, Lincoln Ctr., N.Y.C., 1990, Women's Caucus for Art, San Antonio, 1990, Artist's Equity, Broome St. Gallery, N.Y.C., 1991, Greater Hartford Architecture Conservancy, 1991; symposium participant Sienna, Italy, 1988, South Fla. Art Ctr., Miami Beach, 1990, 92, 93; contbr. articles to Women in the Arts newsletter, 1986-87, Coalition Womens Art Orgns., 1986-87. Bd. dirs. N.Y.C. Coun. on Econ. Edn., 1970—; mem. program planning com. Women's Econ. Roundtable, N.Y.C.; participant Eastern Econ. Assn., Boston, 1988, Art and Personal Property Appraisal, NYU, 1986-88. Recipient Disting. Svc. award CUNY, 1985. Fellow Gerontol. Assn.; mem. Internat. Schumpeter Econs. Soc. (founding), Am. (vice chmn. ann. meeting 1973), Met. (sec. 1954-56) econ. assns., Indsl. Rels. Rsch. Assn., Audubon Artists and Nat. Soc. Painters in Casein (assoc. 1987-88) Allied Social Sci. Assn. (vice chmn. conv. 1973, artist Boston nat. conv. 1994), AAUW, N.Y.C. Women in Arts, Allied Social Sci. Assn. (artist 1994), Women's Econ. Roundtable, Greater Hartford Architecture Conservancy, NYU Grad. Sch. Bus. Adminstrn. Alumni (sec. 1956-58), Radcliffe Club, Women's City Club (art and landmarks com.). Author: (with husband) Investment and Development of Tropical Africa, 1959, International Trade and Finance, 1965, Monetary and Banking Theory, 1965; Economics, 1969; (with husband) Principles of Economics, 1969; Economic Progress and the Developing World, 1970; Economics, 1978; also monographs and articles in field. Econ. and internat. rsch. on industrialization less developed areas, internat. debtor nations and workability of buffer stock schemes, pricing fine art; columnist economics of art, Art As An Investment, Money Substitute, or Consumer Durable Good Art Valuation; Prices and Varied Appraisals, Women in the Arts Found. Newsletter, other profl. publs. Home: PO Box 814 New Canaan CT 06840-0814 Office: Art Complex PO Box 814 New Canaan CT 06840-0814 also: 7441 Wayne Ave Miami Beach FL 33141

RENDON-PELLERANO, MARTA INES, dermatologist; b. Sept. 19, 1957; d. Uriel and Rosa Rendon. BA and Scis., U. P.R., Mayaquez, 1977; postgrad., Autonoma U., Santo Domingo, Dominican Republic, 1977-79; MD, U. P.R., San Juan, 1982. Diplomate Am. Bd. Internal Medicine, Am. Bd. Dermatology; lic. physician, Fla., Tex., Pa., ACLS, Drug Enforcement Adminstrn. Intern and resident in internal medicine Albert Einstein Med. Ctr., Phila., 1982-85; resident in dermatology Parkland Meml. Hosp., Southwestern Med. Sch., Dallas, 1985-88; emergency rm. physician Pottsborough (Tex.) Med. Clinic, 1985-86; coord. dermatology clinic Kayser Permanente Med. Assn. Tex., Dallas, 1986-88; dermatology assoc. Dermatology Ctr., Dallas, 1988-89; staff physician Southwestern Med. Sch., Vets. Hosp., Dallas, 1988-89; clin. asst. prof. dept. deramtology U. Miami (Fla.) Sch. Medicine, 1989—; chief dept. dermatology Cleveland Clinic Fla., Ft. Lauderdale, 1989—; mem. adv. bd. South Fla. Vis. Lectureship Series, 1991-92; mem. rsch. bd. advisors Medecis Corp. Contbr. articles to profl. jours., chpts. to books. Recipient Radio Klaridad award for best sci. work, Miami, 1990. Fellow Am. Acad. Dermatology; mem. ACP (assoc.), AAUW, Womens Med. Assn., Womens Dermatol. Soc., Cuban-Interam. Dermatol. Soc., Women of Spanish Origin, Tex. Med. Assn., Miami Dermatology Soc., Fla. Med. Assn., Broward Dermatology Soc., Broward County Med. Assn., Etta Gamma Delta. Roman Catholic. Office: Cleveland Clinic Fla 3000 W Cypress Creek Rd Fort Lauderdale FL 33309

RENEE, LISABETH MARY, secondary school educator, artist; b. Bklyn., July 28, 1952; d. Lino P. and Elizabeth M. (Dines) Rivano; m. John S. Witanowski, May 15, 1982. Student, U. Puget Sound, 1972-74; BA in Art, SUNY, Buffalo, 1977; MFA, L.I. U., 1982; postgrad., U. Cen. Fla., 1989—. Cert. art tchr., Fla. Adj. faculty L.I. U., Greenvale, N.Y., 1980-82, Rollins Coll., Winter Park, Fla., 1982; art tchr. Phyllis Wheatley Elem. Sch., Apopka, Fla., 1983-85, McCoy Elem. Sch., Orlando, Fla., 1985-86, Lake Howell High Sch., Winter Park, Fla., 1986—; adj. faculty mem. U. Cen. Fla., 1994—; dir. So. Artists' Registry, Winter Park, 1984-87; cons. Fla. Dept. Edn., 1989-90, mem. curriculum writing team for arts edn. program; com. Fla. Bd. Edn. Task Force for Subject Area Subtest of Fla. Tchr. Cert. Exam; visual arts dir. Very Spl. Arts Ctrl. Fla. Fest., 1995; presenter at profl. confs. Editor: Children and the Arts in Florida, 1990. Visual arts dir. Very Spl. Arts Ctrl. Fla. Festival, 1995; mem. local Sch. Adv. Coun., Winter Park, 1992. Recipient Tchr. Merit award Walt Disney World Co., 1990; grantee Found. for Advancement of Community Through Schs., 1991; ACE scholar Arts Leadership Inst., 1993. Mem. NEA, ASCD, Fla. Art Edn. Assn. (regional rep. 1989—), Seminole County Art Edn. Assn., Coll. Art Assn., Caucus on Social Theory and Art Edn., Womens Caucus for Art, Phi Kappa Phi, Kappa Delta Pi. Home: 20 Cobblestone Way Casselberry FL 32707 Office: Lake Howell High Sch 4200 Dike Rd Winter Park FL 32792

RENEKER, MAXINE HOHMAN, librarian; b. Chgo., Dec. 2, 1942; d. Roy Max and Helen Anna Christina (Anacker) Hohman; m. David Lee Reneker, June 20, 1964 (dec. Dec. 1979); children: Sarah Roeder, Amy Johannah, Benjamin Congdon. BA, Carleton Coll., 1964; MA, U. Chgo., 1970; DLS, Columbia U., 1992. Asst. reference libr. U. Chgo. Libraries, 1965-66; classics libr. U. Chgo. Libr., 1967-70, asst. head acquisitions, 1970-71, personnel libr., 1971-73; personnel/bus. libr. U. Colo. Libr., Boulder, 1978-80; asst. dir. sci. and engring. div. Columbia U., N.Y.C., 1981-85; assoc. dean of univ. librs. for pub. svcs. Ariz. State U. Libr., Tempe, 1985-89; dir. instrnl. and rsch. svcs. Stanford (Calif.) Univ. Librs., 1989-90; dir. info. svcs., dir. Dudley Knox Libr. Naval Postgrad. Sch., Monterey, Calif., 1993—; acad. libr. mgmt. intern Coun. on Libr. Resources, 1980-81; chmn. univ. librs. sect. Assn. Coll. and Rsch. Librs., 1989-90. Contbr. articles to profl. jours. Rsch. grantee Coun. on Library Resources, Columbia U., 1970-71, fellow, 1990-92. Mem. ALA, Am. Soc. Info. Sci., Sherlockian Scion Soc., Phi Beta Kappa, Beta Phi Mu. Home: 437 College Ave Palo Alto CA 94306-1525 Office: Naval Postgrad Sch Dudley Knox Libr 411 Dyer Rd Monterey CA 93943

RÉNI See BROWN, ARLENE PATRICIA THERESA

RENICK, CAROL BISHOP, insurance planning company executive, consultant; b. Arlington, Mass., June 5, 1956; d. Francis Joseph and Mary Ruth (Robinson) Bishop; m. Lawrence A. Balboni, May 5, 1979 (div. 1982); m. Gary L. Renick, Jan. 31, 1986. Grad., Harvard U., 1991. Mgr. Larson Ins., Arlington, Mass., 1979-85; v.p. Larson Ins., Arlington, 1987-88; mgr. Merrill Lynch Realty Ins. Svcs., Boca Raton, Fla., 1985-87; pres. Essex Ins. Planners, Haverhill, Mass., 1988—; v.p. United Internat. Ins. Agy., Inc., Braintree, Mass., 1992-94. Vol. Mus. Sci., Boston, 1988, Mus. Sci., 1988—; vol., cultural cons., advisor Free Romania Found., Cambridge, Mass., 1990—; tutor Mass. Campaign for Literacy, 1988—. Mem. Profl. Ins. Agts., Inc. Democrat.

RENK, CAROL ANN, secondary education educator; b. Elizabeth, Pa., May 19, 1937; d. Benjamin Franklin and Anna Jeannette (Carnahan) Smart; m. Ralph Charles Renk, Oct. 5, 1961 (dec. May 1965); 1 child, Tracy Renk Caldwell. BS in Biol. Scis., U. Pitts., 1959, MEd, 1970. Cert. secondary edn. biol. and social scis. Tchr. Quaker Valley Schs., Leetsdale, Pa., 1959-60, Pitts. City Schs., 1960-94; liaison tchr. South Hills H.S., Pitts., 1984-86. Coach Pleasant Hills (Pa.) Area Recreation Assn., 1970-73. NSF grantee, 1965. Mem. Pitts. Fedn. Tchrs., Am. Legion, Allegheny Club, Alpha Delta Kappa (state, local office 1969-73), Beta Beta Beta, Alpha Psi Omega, Delta Zeta (sec. 1958-59). Republican. Methodist. Home: 349 Tara Dr Pittsburgh PA 15236-4318

RENNE, JANICE LYNN, interior designer; b. Los Angeles, July 16, 1952; d. George Joseph and Dolly Minni (Neubaurer) R.; m. William Lee Kile, Dec. 6, 1975 (div. Sept. 1983). BA, Sweet Briar Coll., 1974; AA, Interior Designers Inst., 1985. Lic. gen. contractor, Calif.; cert. interior designer, Calif. Coun. for Interior Design Certification. Exec. trainee Bullock's, Santa Ana, Calif., 1974, Pub. Fin., Inc., Huntington Beach, Calif., 1975; bookkeeper William L. Kile DDS, Inc., Santa Barbara, Calif., 1979-81, Nelson & Hamilton, Inc., Santa Barbara, 1981-82; interior designer Ultimate Designs, Irvine, Calif., 1984-85, sr. designer, 1985-86; draftsperson JBI Inc., Long Beach, Calif., 1984-85; prin. designer Janice Renne Interior Designs, Newport Beach, Calif., 1986—; space planner Design Pak II, Newport Beach, 1987-88; State of Calif. rep. task force for developing self-cert. process for Calif. interior designers, Internat. Soc. Interior Design, 1991. Created utility room design for Easter Seals Design House, 1985; weekly radio show host on restaurant design, 1986; work published in Orange County mag. and L.A. Times., 1988. Recipient scholarship Calif. Inst. Applied Design, Newport Beach, 1984. Mem. Internat. Soc. Interior Designers (grad. assoc. designer butler's pantry, assoc. designer Design House powder rm. 1988, Orange County chpt. 1988-89, asst. editor Orange County chpt. Quar. Newsletter, Orange County chpt. gen. bd. 1991-92, chair licensing com. 1991-92, bd. dirs. 1991-92), Color Assn. of U.S., Constrn. Specifier Inst., Nat. Exec. Women in Hospitality, Calif. Legis. Conf. in Interior Design (gen. bd. 1991-92, v.p. communications 1992-93), Orange County and Newport Beach, Letip Internat. (sec. 1987, 89, 90, treas. 1991, pres. 1993), Internat. Interior Design Assn., Tall Club Orange County (Miss Congeniality 1994, exec. v.p. 1995, co-editor High Life 1994-95). Republican. Lutheran. Office: 2915 Redhill Ave Ste E100 Costa Mesa CA 92626

RENNE, LOUISE HORNBECK, city attorney; b. Pitts., Aug. 26, 1937; d. Lewis Alvin and Anne (Bartrem) Hornbeck; m. Paul A. Renne, July 11, 1959; Christine, Anne. BA, Mich. State U., 1958; postgrad. law, Harvard U., 1958-59, U. Pa., 1959-60; JD, Columbia U., 1961. Bar: Calif. 1964, D.C. 1961, U.S. Supreme Ct. 1969. With broadcast bur., office gen. counsel FCC, 1961-64; assoc. Peterson & Barr, San Francisco, 1964-66; dep. atty. gen. State of Calif., San Francisco, 1966-77; pres. Calif. Women Lawyers, San Francisco, 1977-78; mem. Bd. Suprs., San Francisco, 1978-86; city atty. San Francisco, 1986—. Office: Office of City Atty Room 206 City Hall San Francisco CA 94102

RENNER, DEBRA A., state official; b. Phila., Dec. 18, 1954; d. Robert R. and Helaine G. (Mogel) R. BA in Econs., Colgate U., 1977; MPA, Syracuse U., 1979. Budget examiner N.Y. State Div. Budget, Albany, 1979-82, sr. budget examiner, 1982-84, assoc. budget examiner, 1984-88, prin. budget examiner, 1988—; mentor N.Y. State Pub. Mgmt. Internship Program, Albany, 1988—. Trustee Renner Found., 1978—, also sec.; sec. bd. mems. Albany YMCA, 1991—. N.Y. State Regents' scholar, 1973-77. Mem. Maxwell Sch. Alumni Assn. (bd. dirs. 1992—).

RENNER, KYAN STOUDER, mental health therapist, musician; b. Huntington, Ind., July 27, 1953; d. Charles Arthur and Mary Elizabeth (Props) Stouder; m. Kent Allen Young, June 2, 1973 (div.); m. Larry Russell Renner, Oct. 9, 1987. BA, Huntington Coll., 1976; MS, U. Dayton, 1993. Cert. tchr., sch. counselor, Ohio; lic. profl. counselor, Ohio; cert. foster parent, Ind. Interim tchr. Harrisburg (Pa.) Christian Acad., 1979-80; substitute tchr. Huntington County Schs., 1984-85; educateur II Starr Commonwealth Schs., Van Wert, Ohio, 1988; SBH aide, substitute tchr. Van Wert County Schs., 1989-91; music tchr. Parkway local schs., Willshire-Rockford, Ohio, 1991; therapist Van Wert Comprehensive Mental Health Svcs., 1992—, Tri-County Mental Health Emergency Line Svcs., 1993—; pvt. music tchr. Hoverman Music Ctr., Van Wert, 1988-92; freelance musician, 1971—; resident counselor The Marsh Found., Van Wert, 1994—; cmty. speaker in mental health issues, 1992—. Vocalist TRinity Quartet, Van Wert, 1988-94; mem. Trinity Friends Ch., 1988—, Wassenburg Art Ctr., 1989—; charter mem. Leadership Van Wert County Program, 1994-95. Office: Van Wert Comp Mental Health Svcs 118 N Walnut St Van Wert OH 45891

RENNICK, KYME ELIZABETH WALL, lawyer; b. Columbus, Ohio, Dec. 27, 1953; d. Robert Leroy and Julie (Allison) Wall; m. Ian Alexander Rennick, Oct. 15, 1983; children: Daniel Alexander, Julie Ellen. BA, Centre Coll., 1975; MA, Ohio State U., 1978; JD, Capital U., 1982. Bar: Ohio 1982, U.S. Dist. Ct. (no. and so. dists.) Ohio 1983. Legal intern Ohio Dept. Natural Resources, Columbus, 1981-83, gen. counsel, 1983-86, chief counsel, 1986—. Editor: Baldwin's Ohio Revised Code Annotated, Title 15 Conservation of Natural Resources, 1984. Presbyterian. Office: Ohio Dept Natural Resources Fountain Sq Fountain Sq Bldg 3D Columbus OH 43224

RENNIE, MILBREY TOWER, television news producer; b. Milw., Aug. 19, 1946; d. William Roxburgh and Jean (Tower) R.; m. David Hendrickson Taylor, Jr., Sept. 15, 1973; children: Rennie, Milbrey. BA, Vassar Coll., 1968. Caseworker Sen. Charles Percy, Washington, 1968-69; campaign asst. to Re-elect Mayor John Lindsay, N.Y.C., 1969; rschr. ABC News, Washington, 1970-71; reporter, prodr. NPACT (PBS), Washington, 1971-75; exec. prodr. CBS News, N.Y.C., 1976—. Trustee Vassar Coll., Poughkeepsie, N.Y., 1989—, Miss Porter's Sch., Farmington, Conn., 1976-81, 93—, Nightingale Bamford Sch., 1994—; dir. OTR Lecture Series, FPA, N.Y.C., 1990—; mem. Counkilon Fgn. Rels. Luce scholar Henry Luce Found., Manila, 1975-76. Office: CBS News Weekend News/Sunday News 524 W 57th St New York NY 10019-2902

RENNINGER, MARY KAREN, librarian; b. Pitts., Apr. 30, 1945; d. Jack Burnell and Jane (Hammerly) Gunderman; m. Norman Christian Renninger, Sept. 3, 1965 (div. 1980); 1 child, David Christian. B.A., U. Md., 1969, M.A., 1972, M.L.S., 1975. Tchr. English West Carteret High Sch., Morehead City, N.C., 1969-70; instr. in English U. Md., College Park, 1970-72; head network services Nat. Libr. Svc., Libr. of Congress, Washington, 1974-78, asst. for network support, 1978-80; mem. fed. women's program com. Libr. of Congress, Washington, 1978-80; chief libr. divsn. Dept. Vets. Affairs, Washington, 1980-90; chief serial and govt. publs. divsn. Libr. of Congress, Washington, 1991—, mem. fed. libr. com., 1980-90, mem. exec. adv. bd., 1985-90; mem. USBE pers. subcom., 1982-84; bd. regents Nat. Libr. of Medicine, 1986-90, mem. outreach panel, 1988-89; fed. libr. task force for 1990 White House Conf. on Librs., 1986-90; liaison to The White House Conf. Med. Libr. Assn., 1989-90. Recipient Meritorious Svc. award Libr. of Congress, 1974, Spl. Achievement award, 1976, Performance award VA, ann. 1982-89, Adminstr.'s Commendation, 1985, Spl. Contbn. award, 1986. Mem. ALA (Govt. Documents Roundtable), Libr. Tech. Assn., Med. Libr. Assn. (govt. rels. com. 1985—), D.c. Libr. Assn., Soc. Applied Learning Tech., Med. Interactive Videodisc Consortium, Govt. Documents Roundtable, Knowledge Utilization Soc., U.S. Tennis Assn., Phi Beta Kappa, Alpha Lambda Delta, Beta Phi Mu. Home: 840 College Pky Rockville MD 20850-1931 Office: Libr of Congress Ser and Govt Pub Divsn LM 133 Washington DC 20540

RENO, ELIZABETH LEE, bank executive; b. Concord, Calif., Feb. 15, 1961; d. James Thomas and Patricia Lee (Atkins) R.; m. Roy G. Wuchitech, Aug. 26, 1994. BA, Loyola Marymount U., L.A., 1983. Asst. v.p. Bank of Am., San Diego, 1980-88; v.p. Security Pacific Bank, San Diego, 1988-92; v.p., bus. devel. officer Sanwa Bank Calif., L.A., 1992-94; v.p. bus. devel. officer Sumitomo Bank of Calif., 1994—. Chmn. speaker bur. Am. Diabetes Assn., San Diego, 1992-94; corp. campaign mem. United Way/CHAD, San Diego, 1993-94. Republican. Home: 121 S Hope St Apt 606 Los Angeles CA 90012-5014 Office: Sumitomo Bank of Calif 611 W 6th St #3900 Los Angeles CA 90017

RENO, JANET, U.S. attorney general; b. Miami, Fla., July 21, 1938; d. Henry and Jane (Wood) R. A.B. in Chemistry, Cornell U., 1960; LL.B., Harvard U., 1963. Bar: Fla. 1963. Assoc. Brigham & Brigham, 1963-67; ptnr. Lewis & Reno, 1967-71; staff dir. judiciary com. Fla. Ho. of Reps., Tallahassee, 1971-72; cons. Fla. Senate Criminal Justice Com. for Revision Fla.'s Criminal Code, spring 1973; adminstrv. asst. state atty. 11th Jud. Circuit Fla., Miami, 1973-76, state atty., 1978-93; ptnr. Steel Hector and Davis, Miami, 1976-78; atty. gen. Dept. Justice, Washington, 1993—; mem. jud. nominating commn. 11th Jud. Circuit Fla., 1976-78; chmn. Fla. Gov.'s Council for Prosecution Organized Crime, 1979-80. Recipient Women First award YWCA, 1993. Mem. ABA (Inst. Jud. Adminstrn. Juvenile Justice Standards Commn. 1973-76), Am. Law Inst., Am. Judicature Soc. (Herbert Harley award 1981), Dade County Bar Assn., Fla. Pros. Atty.'s Assn. (pres. 1984-86). Democrat. Office: Dept Justice 10th & Constitution Ave NW Washington DC 20530*

RENO, ROSEMARY, marketing professional, real estate agent; b. Chillicothe, Ohio, Jan. 15, 1934; d. James Cullen Varney and Mary Melba (Harlow) Tanner; m. Chester M. Reno, May 18, 1956 (div. 1961); children: Denyce Dianne, Todd Blake Wilson; m. Donald D. Williamson, Mar. 10, 1989. Student, Marin Coll., 1952-53, Santa Rosa Jr. Coll., 1957-58, Glendale Coll., 1975-77, L.A. City Coll., 1977-78. Personal sec. Adj. Gen., Oklahoma City, 1966-70; project coord. Am./West, Glendale, Calif., 1970-76; asst. to pres. United Recording, Hollywood, Calif., 1976-82; dir. mktg. Desarralladora Los Gatos, Rosarito Beach, Mex., 1982-92, Century 21 Coastal, Rosarito Beach, Mex., Mex., 1993—. Mem. Red Cross, Rosarito Beach, 1991; guardian counsel Jobs Daus., Glendale, 1973-76; troop leader Campfire Girls, Oklahoma City, 1968-69. Address: PO Box 439030 San Diego CA 92143-9030

RENSE, PAIGE, editor, publishing company executive; b. Iowa, May 4, 1929; m. Kenneth Noland, Apr. 10, 1994. Student, Calif. State U., Los Angeles. Editor-in-chief Architectural Digest, Los Angeles, 1970—; sr. v.p., also bd. dirs. Knapp Communications Corp. Recipient Nat. Headliner Women in Communications award, 1983, Pacifica award So. Calif. Resources Coun., 1978, Editorial award Dallas Mkt. Ctr., 1978, Golden award Chgo. Design Resources Svc., 1982, Agora award, 1982, Outstanding Profls. in Communications award, 1982, Trailblazers award, 1983, ; named Woman of Yr. Los Angeles Times, 1976, Woman of Yr. Muses, 1986; named to Interior Design Hall of Fame. Office: Architectural Digest 6300 Wilshire Blvd 11th Fl Los Angeles CA 90048

RENSHAW, AMANDA FRANCES, physicist, nuclear engineer; b. Wheelwright, Ky., Dec. 10, 1934; d. Taft and Mamie Nell (Russell) Wilson; divorced; children: Linda, Michael, Billy. BS in Physics, Antioch Coll., 1972; MS in Physics, U. Tenn., 1982, MS in Nuclear Engring., 1991. Rsch. asst. U. Mich., Ann Arbor, 1970-71; teaching asst. Antioch Coll., Yellow Springs, Ohio, 1971-72; physicist GE, Schenectady, N.Y., 1972-74, Union Carbide Corp., Oak Ridge, Tenn., 1974-79; rsch. assoc. Oak Ridge Nat. Lab., 1979-91, mgr. strategic planning, 1991-92, liaison for environ. scis., 1993—; asst. to counselor for sci. and tech. Am. Embassy, Moscow, 1990; asst. to dir. nat. acid precipitation assessment program Office of Pres. U.S., 1993-94. Contbr. articles to profl. jours. Mem. AAUW, Am. Assn. Artificial Intelligence, Am. Nuclear Soc. (Oak Ridge chpt.), Soc. Black Physicists. Home: 1850 Cherokee Bluff Dr Knoxville TN 37920-2215 Office: Oak Ridge Nat Lab Bldg 1505 PO Box 2008 Oak Ridge TN 37831-6038

RENT, CLYDA STOKES, university president; b. Jacksonville, Fla., Mar. 1, 1942; d. Clyde Parker Stokes Sr. and Edna Mae (Edwards) Shuemake; m. George Seymour Rent, Aug. 12, 1966; 1 child, Cason Lynley Rent Helms. BA, Fla. State U., 1964, MA, 1966, PhD, 1968; LHD (hon.), Judson Coll., 1993. Asst. prof. Western Carolina U., Cullowhee, N.C., 1968-70; asst. prof. Queens Coll., Charlotte, N.C., 1972-74, dept. chair, 1974-78, dean Grad. Sch. and New Coll., 1979-84, v.p. for Grad. Sch. and New Coll., 1984-85, v.p. acad. affairs, 1985-87, v.p. community affairs, 1987-89; pres. Miss. U. for Women, Columbus, 1989—; bd. dirs. Trustmark Nat. Bank, Trustmark Corp; cons. Coll. Bd., N.Y.C., 1983-89; sci. cons. N.C. Alcohol Rsch. Authority, Chapel Hill, 1976-89; mem. adv. bd. Nat. Women's Hall of Fame; rotating chair Miss. Instns. Higher Edn. Learning Pres.' Coun., 1990-91; commn. govtl. rels. Am. Coun. Edn., 1990-93; adv. bd. Miss. Power and Light, 1994—. Author rsch. articles in acad. jours.; speeches pub. in Vital Speeches; mem. editorial bds. acad. jours. Trustee N.C. Performing Arts Ctr., Charlotte, 1988-89, Charlotte County Day Sch., 1987-89; bd. visitors Johnson C. Smith U., Charlotte, 1985-89; exec. com. bd. dirs. United Way Allocations and Rev., Charlotte, 1982-88; bd. advisors Charlotte Mecklenburg Hosp. Authority, 1985-89; bd. dirs. Jr. Achievement, Charlotte, 1983-89, Miss. Humanities Coun., Miss. Inst. Arts and Letters, Miss. Symphony, Miss. Econ. Coun.; chair Leadership Miss. and Collegiate Miss.; chmn. bd. dirs. Charlotte/Mecklenburg Arts and Sci. Coun., 1987-88; Danforth assoc. Danforth Found., St. Louis, 1976-88, Leadership Am., 1989; golden triangle adv. bd. Bapt. Meml. Hosp.; pres. So. Univ. Conf., 1994-95; mem. commn. govt. rels. Am. Coun. Edn., 1990-93. Recipient Grad. Made Good award Fla. State U., 1990; named Prof. of Yr., Queens Coll., 1979, One of 10 Most Admired Women Mgrs. in Am., Working Women mag., 1993, one of 1000 Women of the 90's, Mirabella mag., 1994; grantee Ford Found., 1981; Paul Harris follow, 1992. Mem. Am. Assn. State Colls. and Univs. (bd. dirs. 1994—), Sociol. Soc., N.C. Assn. Colls. and Univs. (exec. com. 1988-89), N.C. Assn. Acad. Officers (sec.-treas. 1987-88), Soc. Internat. Bus. Fellows, Miss. Assn. Colls. (pres. 1992), Newcomen Soc. U.S., Internat. Women's Forum, Univ. Club, Rotary. Office: Miss U Women Presidents Office Box W 1600 Columbus MS 39701

RENTER, LOIS IRENE HUTSON, librarian; b. Lowden, Iowa, Oct. 23, 1929; d. Thomas E. and Lulu Mae (Barlean) Hutson; m. Karl A. Renter, Jan. 3, 1948; children: Susan Elizabeth, Rebecca Jean, Karl Geoffrey. BA cum laude, Cornell Coll., 1965; MA, U. Iowa, 1968. Tchr. Spanish Mt. Vernon High Sch., 1965-67; head libr. Am. Coll. Testing Program, Iowa City, Iowa, 1968-89, ret., 1989; vis. instr. U. Iowa Sch. Library Sci., 1972-82. Mem. Phi Beta Kappa. Methodist. Home: 1125 29th St Marion IA 52302-1529

RENTERIA, CHERYL CHRISTINA, retired federal agency administrator; b. Corpus Christi, Tex., May 11, 1944; d. C.J. and Nazelle (Smart) Casey; m. Carlos Raymundo Renteria, Oct. 17, 1975; children: Crissa Cybele, Cori Renee. Grad. Inst. U.S. & World Affairs, Am. U., 1965; BA, Tex. Christian U., 1966. Inventory mgmt. specialist Tinker AFB, Oklahoma City, 1966-67; with U.S. Dept. HUD, 1967-94; resident initiatives coord., program mgr. region VI U.S. Dept. HUD, Ft. Worth, 1988-92; mgr. Office of Pub. Housing, 1993-94; ret., 1994. Pres. Dallas Office Orgn. Women, 1974-75; treas. Fed. Woman's Program Coun., Dallas, 1977-78; bd. dirs. Ballet Guild, Ft. Worth, 1984—, treas., 1985, v.p., 1986-88, programs chmn., 1990, 91, 92, 93, 94; bd. dirs. lectr. series U. Tex., Arlington, 1987-91, Dance Theatre, Arlington, 1987-91; bd. dirs. Planned Parenthood North Tex., 1986-90, Coun. Advisors, 1990—; vol. Tex. Christian U. LINKS, Campfire; treas. Arlington Speech/Debate Booster Club, 1994; rec. sec. Ft. Worth Panhellenic Coun., 1994-95. Smith scholar, 1966. Mem. Women in Govt., (pres. 1989-90), Fed. Bus. Assn., Theater Arlington Guild, Internat. Sister Cities, Opera Guild Ft. Worth, Friends Univ. Tex. Libr., Symphony Soc. Tarrant County (editor newsletter 1984), Jr. Woman's Club Decortique (v.p. 1977), Woman's Club Ft. Worth, Delta Gamma (pres. house corp. 1985, 86, bd. dirs. 1987—, chair Province leadership seminar 1987, corr. 1984). Home: 1115 Montreau Ct Arlington TX 76012-2737 Office: US Dept HUD PO Box 2905 Fort Worth TX 76113-2905

RENTZ, DORENE MAY, neuropsychologist, educator; b. Flushing, N.Y., Feb. 27, 1951; d. John Allen and Mary Ann (Matusiak) R. BA, St. Xavier, 1972; PsyD, Ill. Sch. Profl. Psychology, 1987. Registered psychologist. Tchr., psychotherapist Tolentine Ctr., Olympia Fields, Ill., 1976-87; psychologist Northwestern U., Chgo., 1987-90; neuropsychologist, instr. Harvard Med. Sch., Boston, 1990—. Contbr. chpts. to books and articles to profl. jours. Named Outstanding Alumni, Ill. Sch. Profl. Psychology, Chgo., 1993. Mem. APA, Mass. Neuropsychol. Assn. (bd. dirs. 1991—), Internat. Neuropsychol. Soc. Democrat. Roman Catholic. Office: Beth Israel Hosp K-2 330 Brookline Ave Boston MA 02215-5400

RENTZ, TAMARA HOLMES, software consultant; b. Austin, Tex., Nov. 23, 1964; d. Thomas Michael and Elizabeth Dianne (Ames) Holmes; m. Christopher Michael Rentz, Sept. 21, 1991. BS in Speech/Orgnl. Comm., U. Tex., 1987. Cert. meeting facilitator; notary public State of Tex. Mgr. PC Sta., Inc., Austin, 1985-86; telecom. advisor Internat. Talent Network, Austin, 1986-87; mktg. rep. Wm. Ross & Co., Austin, 1987; life ins. rep. A.L. Williams, Austin, 1987-88; exec. sec. Adia Temporaries/SEMATECH, Austin, 1988; tng. adminstr. SEMATECH, Austin, 1988-89, data coord. equipment improvement program, 1989-90, user group program mgr., 1992-93; pres. Innovative Bus. Solutions, Austin, 1994—. Mem. NAFE, Tech. Transfer Soc., Austin Software Coun., Sofware Quality Inst. U. Tex. Austin. Home and Office: 4004 Lovebird Ln Austin TX 78730

RENUART, JANET ANDREE, school psychologist; b. Miami, Jan. 25, 1945; d. Amedee E. and Rose Blanche (Roy) R. BA, Jacksonville U., 1973; MA, U. North Fla., 1982; EdS, U. Fla., 1984, PhD, 1986. Nat. cert. sch. psychologist; cert. sch. psychologist, Fla. Tchr. Christ the King Sch., Jacksonville, Fla., 1967-68, Assumption Sch., Jacksonville, Fla., 1969-73, Macclenny (Fla.) Elem. Sch., 1973-83; sch. psychologist Clay County Sch. Bd., Green Cove Springs, Fla., 1984—. Author: (manual) Suicide Intervention, 1987, Intervention with Sexually Abused Children, 1990, Crisis Intervention, 1st edit., 1988, 2d edit., 94, Child Study Team, 1st edit., 1990, 2d edit., 1994. Mem. Suicide Intervention Team, Jacksonville, 1989-92, First Coast AIDS Coalition, Jacksonville, 1994. Deans scholar U. North Fla., 1980-82; recipient Excell award Clay County Sch. Bd., 1988, 94. Mem. Fla. Assn. Sch. Psychologists, Nat. Assn. Sch. Psychologists, Clay County Crisis Intervention Team, Delta Kappa Gamma Soc. Internat., Pi Lambda Theta, Kappa Delta Pi. Office: Clay County Sch Bd 900 Walnut St Green Cove Springs FL 32043

REPASS, ANDREA NINA, marketing professional; b. Middletown, Conn., Oct. 6, 1962; d. Richard Roger and Edna (Cunha Rego) R. BS in Econs., U. Mass., 1984; MBA in Mktg., Pepperdine U., 1989. Promotion coord. Pubs. Mktg. Enterprises, N.Y.C., 1987-88; asst. project dir. J.D. Power and Assocs., Agoura Hills, Calif., 1990-91; product rsch. specialist Mazda Motor Am., Irvine, Calif., 1992-93; project dir. Allison-Fisher, Inc., Gardena, Calif., 1993—. Mem. Advt. Rsch. Found. Home: 2142 Miramar Dr Balboa CA 92661-1519

REPOVICH, WENDY E. ST. JOHN, exercise science educator; b. Cin., Feb. 17, 1950; d. Robert Campbell and Mildred Harriet (Burnett) St. John; m. Jerald Leland Sparks, June 1, 1971 (div. Feb. 1976); m. Mike N. Repovich, May 20, 1983; 1 child, Sheri Elizabeth. BA with honors, U. Puget Sound, 1972; MEd, U. Cin., 1978; PhD, U. So. Calif., 1990. Vol. U.S. Peace Corps, Dominican Republic, 1976-77; grad. asst. U. Cin., 1977-78; cardiac rehab. dir. Jewish Community Ctr., Cin., 1978-80; grad. asst. U. So. Calif., L.A., 1981-84; instr. Calif. State U., Fullerton, 1982-83; asst. prof. So. Calif. Coll. Chiropractic, Pico Rivera, 1985-89, Ea. Wash. U., Cheney, 1991—; cons. Pediat. Heart Found., Spokane, Wash., 1993—; dir. human performance lab. Ea. Wash. U., Cheney, 1991—. Author: Laboratory Manual for PHED 250, 1993; contbg. author Exercise in Pregnancy, 1986. CPR instr. Am. Heart Assn., Spokane, 1991—; youth soccer coach Spokane Youth Sports Assn., 1990—. Grantee Stairmaster, 1993, Sea First Bank, 1994. Mem. AAHPERD, Am. Coll. Sports Medicine, Assn. Worksite Health Promotion (edn. chair 1991—), Nat. Wellness Assn., Delta Delta Delta (pres. Spokane). Republican. Unitarian. Office: Eastern Washington Univ MS 66 Hpera Complex Cheney WA 99004

REPPERT, NANCY LUE, former county official, consultant; b. Kansas City, Mo., June 17, 1933; d. James Everett and Iris R. (Moomey) Moore; m. James E. Cassidy, 1952 (div.); children: James E., II, Tracy C. Student Cen. Mo. State U., 1951-52, U. Mo., Kansas City, 1971-75; cert. legal asst., Rockhurst Coll., Kansas City, Mo., 1980; cert. risk mgr., 1979. With Kansas City (Mo.) chpt. ARC, 1952-54, N. Cen. region Boy Scouts Am., 1963-66, Clay County Health Dept., Liberty, Mo., 1966-71, City of Liberty, 1971-80; risk mgr. City of Ames (Iowa), 1980-82; risk mgr. City of Dallas, 1982-83; dir. Dept. Risk Mgmt., Pinellas County, Fla., 1984-94; ind. cons., Cedar Rapids, Iowa, 1994—; mem. faculty William Jewell Coll., Liberty, 1975-80; vis. prof. U. Kans., 1981; adj. prof. dept. polit. sci. masters program U. So. Fla., 1990; seminar leader, cons. in field. Lay min.r United Meth. Ch., 1965—; dir. youth devel. Hillside United Meth. Ch., Liberty; co-chmn. youth dir. Collegiate United Meth. Ch. scouting coord. Palm Lake Christian Ch., Exec. Fellow U. South Fla., mem. Coun. of Ministries; advancement chmn. Mid-Iowa Coun. Boy Scouts Am., membership chmn. White Rock Dist. coun., health and safety chmn. West Cen. Fla. coun., 1985—; scouting coord., chmn. youth dept., bd. dirs., pastor's cabinet, diaconate Palm Lake Christian Ch., 1987—; skipper Sea Explorer ship, 1986—; bd. dirs. Neighborly Sr. Svcs., Inc. Recipient Order of Merit, Boy Scouts Am., 1979, Living Sculpture award, 1978,79; Svc. award Rotary Internat., 1979; Internat. Award of Merit/Leadership Excellence, IBA, 1992; Exec. fellow U. South Fla., 1988. Mem. NAFE, Am. Mgmt. Assns., Internat Platform Assn., Risk Mgrs. Soc., Pub. Risk & Ins. Mgmt. Assn., Am. Soc. Profl. & Exec. Women, Am. Film Inst., U.S. Naval Inst., Nat. Inst. Mcpl. Law Officers. Author: Kids Are People, Too, 1975. Pearls of Potentiality, 1980; also articles. Home: 257 38th St # 8 Cedar Rapids IA 52403

RERES, MARY EPIPHANY, health care and administration consultant; b. Kansas City, Mo., Jan. 31, 1941; d. Mathew and Mary Ellen (Connelly) R. B.S. in Nursing, Creighton U., Omaha, 1963; M.Psychiat. Nursing, U. Nebr., 1965; Ed.D in Adminstrn., Columbia U., 1970. Staff nurse Nebr. Psychiat. Inst., 1963-65; clin. specialist Norfolk (Nebr.) State Hosp., 1965-66; instr. Creighton U. Sch. Nursing, 1966-68; prof. nursing, medicine and edn. U. Va., 1970-77; prof., dean Sch. Nursing, UCLA, 1977-85, prof.-at-large Med. Sch., 1977-85; pres. Human Services Tng. and Research Corp., 1974-85; co-chmn. Gov.'s Mental Health and Mental Retardation Adv. Bd., 1973-76; rsch. review com. VA, 1992—; cons. in field. Co-author: Your Future in Nursing Careers, 1972; editor Am. Psychiat. Nurses Assn. Newsletter, 1989; mem. editorial bd. JAPNA, 1994—; book rev. editor: Jour. Psychosocial Nursing, 1980-94. Bd. dirs. Kaiser Permanente Health Plan and Hosps., 1980—, Med. Media Group, 1989—; mem. adv. bd. hosp. adminstrn. program Charles A. Drew Med. Ctr., 1992—. Recipient Outstanding Alumni award Creighton U. Sch. Nursing, 1972; named Disting. Vis. Scholar U. Tex., Arlington, 1986. Mem. Am. Acad. Nursing (pres. 1974), Am. Nurses Assn., Am. Assn. Colls. Nursing, Western Interstat Am. Hosp Higher Edn., Am. Psychosocial Nursing Assn. (bd. dirs., sec. 1986-90), Am. Hosp. Assn. (alt. Calif. del. 1992, trustee rep. regional policy bd. 1993—, regional policy bd. 1994—), Calif. Assn. Hosps. and Health Systems (Gov.'s Forum 1989—, nominating com. 1992. pub. affairs com. 1991—, vice chmn. program com. 1992), Governance Forum (chmn. 1993—, CAHHS trustee 1993—, trustee 1993-94), Am. Psychiat. Nurses Assn. (Disting. Leadership and Meritorious Svc. award 1989, vice chmn. progs. 1991-93, mem. pub. policy com. 1991—), Delta Sigma Rho, Alpha Sigma Nu, Sigma Theta Tau. Democrat. Roman Catholic. Office: Human Resource Assocs 6410 Surfside Way Malibu CA 90265-3628

RESCH, CYNTHIA FORTES, secondary education educator; b. Providence, Dec. 9, 1951; d. Alfred Antone and Mabel (Duarte) F.; m. Joseph Bernard Resch III, June 26, 1982; children: Jeffrey, Jason, Steven, Kayla. BA, R.I. Coll., 1974; postgrad., U. Sorbonne, Paris, 1975, U. Valencia, Spain, 1979, Providence Coll., 1981. Cert. secondary edn. tchr., R.I. Tchr. French and Spanish North Kingstown (R.I.) High Sch., 1977—. Active Women for a Non-Nuclear Future, Providence, 1982—; advisor N. Kingstown High Sch. Internat. Club. Mem. NEA, R.I. Fgn. Lang. Assn. Office: N Kingstown HS 150 Fairway Dr North Kingstown RI 02852-6207

RESCHKE, KATHRYN LOUISE, school counselor; b. Salina, Kans., Apr. 7, 1958; d. William Leo and Peggy Sue (Haynes) McLaughlin; m. Edward Robert Reschke, Aug. 13, 1983; children: Ryan Lee, Sharla Michelle. BS in Edn., Emporia (Kans.) State U., 1980, MS in Edn., 1985. Cert. sch. counselor, elem. tchr., English tchr., Kans.; advanced catechist cert. Head tchr. Logan Avenue Day Care Ctr., Emporia, 1978-80; kindergarten tchr. Unified Sch. Dist. 490, El Dorado, Kans., 1980-85; tchr. 2d grade El Dorado, 1985-87; substitute tchr. Spring Hill (Kans.) Elem. Sch., 1987-90; guidance counselor St. Pauls Sch., Olathe, Kans., 1990-92; guidance counselor, K-8 cons. Holy Trinity Sch., Lenexa, Kans., 1992-94; K-5 elem. sch. counselor Spring Hill Dist. #230, 1994—. Tchr. religion St. Paul's Ch., Olathe, 1987—, vacation Bible sch. tchr., 1988-90; coord. parenting edn. St. Paul's Parish, 1990-91, initiator, coord. Rainbows for All God's Children, 1990-92; project leader Rustlers 4-H Club, Spring Hill, 1992—; mem. archdiocese Kansas City Spkr.'s Bur., 1993—. Mem. ACA, Am. Sch. Counselor Assn. Office: Spring Hill Elem 300 N Madison Spring Hill KS 66083

RESKA-HADDEN, MARCIA ANN, special education educator; b. LacKawanna, N.Y., Mar. 16, 1952; d. Edward Walter and Harriet Theresa (Kozlowski) Reska; m. Dennis Lynn Hadden, June 29, 1985; 1 child, Dennis Edward. BA in History, Canisius Coll., 1974, MS in Edn., 1979; MAT in History, Niagara U., 1974-76; mentally impaired student, Eastern Mich. U., 1988-90. Tchr. Spl. Edn., N.Y., Mich. Jr. high sch. tchr. St. Barbara's Sch., Lackawanna, N.Y., 1974-75; 5th grade tchr. St. Ambrose Sch., Buffalo, N.Y., 1975-76; jr. high sch. tchr. The Cathedral Sch., Buffalo, N.Y., 1976-79, St. Mary's of the Lake Sch., Hamburg, N.Y., 1979-83, Our Lady of Victory Sch., Lackawanna, N.Y., 1983-85; substitute tchr. Lakeville (Mich.) Sch. Dist., 1986-87; substitute tchr. Genesee Intermediate Sch. Dist., Flint, Mich., 1986-88, spl. edn. tchr., 1988—; mem. Coun. for Exceptional Children, Reston, Va., 1988—; speaker, presentor Functional Curriculum for a SMI Student, 1991. Co-author: Functional Curriculum GISD Secondary Functional Curriculum, 1989-90. Mem. Polish Union Am., Canisus Coll. Alumnae Assn., Genesee County Hist. Soc., Mich. Edn. Assn., Genesee Intermediate Ednl. Assn., Beta Sigma Phi. Home: 7211 Timberwood Dr Davison MI 48423-9522 Office: Genesee Intermediate Sch Dist 2413 W Maple Ave Flint MI 48507-3429

RESNECK-FISCH, SUSAN ELIZABETH, dietitian; b. Marion, Ind., Dec. 30, 1952; d. Daniel Herman and Barbara Helen (Morrison) Resneck; m. Bruce J. Fisch, July 31, 1977; children: Ian Lawrence Fisch, Paul Jeffrey Fisch. BA in Psychology, Ind. U., 1975; MS in Nutrition, Purdue U., 1978. Lic. dietitian, La., registered dietitian. Clin. dietitian Meth. Hosp., Indpls., 1981-82; nutrition cons. Holy Name Hosp., Teaneck, N.J., 1985-89; pvt. practice Diet Yes, Tenafly, N.J., 1989-90; chief clin. dietitian New Orleans Adolescent Hosp., 1990—; cons. dietitian health care facilities, 1985—; spkr. in field. Mem. Am. Dietetic Assn., No. Dist. N.J. Dietetic Assn. (co-chmn. publicity com. 1989-90), New Orleans Dietetic Assn. (chmn. decorations and publicity com. culinary hearts cook-off 1991, 92, 93). Office: New Orleans Adolescent Hosp 210 State St New Orleans LA 70118

RESNICK, ALICE ROBIE, state supreme court justice; b. Erie, Pa., Aug. 21, 1939; d. Adam Joseph and Alice Suzanne (Spizarny) Robie; m. Melvin L. Resnick, Mar. 20, 1970. PhB, Siena Heights Coll., 1961; JD, U. Detroit, 1964. Bar: Ohio 1964, Mich. 1965, U.S. Supreme Ct. 1970. Asst. county prosecutor Lucas County Prosecutor's Office, Toledo, 1964-75, trial atty., 1965-75; judge Toledo Mcpl. Ct., 1976-83, 6th Dist. Ct. Appeals, State of Ohio, Toledo, 1983-88; instr. U. Toledo, 1968-69; justice Ohio Supreme Ct., 1989—; co-chairperson Ohio State Gender Fairness Task Force. Trustee Siena Heights Coll., Adrian, Mich., 1982—; organizer Crime Stopper Inc., Toledo, 1981—; mem. Mayor's Drug Coun.; bd. dirs. Guest House Inc. Mem. ABA, Toledo Bar Assn., Lucas County Bar Assn., Nat. Assn. Women Judges, Am. Judicature Soc., Toledo Women's Bar Assn., Ohio State Women's Bar Assn. (organizer), Toledo Mus. Art, Internat. Inst. Toledo. Roman Catholic. Home: 2407 Edgehill Rd Toledo OH 43615-2321 Office: Supreme Ct Office 30 E Broad St 3rd Fl Columbus OH 43266-0419

RESNICK, CINDY, state legislator; b. Three Rivers, Mich., July 31, 1949; married; 4 children. Former mem. Ariz. Ho. of Reps., dist. 14; mem. Ariz. State Senate. Mem. Am. Assn. Bus. and Profl. Women, Orgn. Women Legis., Tucson Assn. Child Care, B'nai B'rith Women. Democrat. Jewish. Office: Ariz State Sen State Capitol Phoenix AZ 85007*

RESNICK, LAUREN B., psychology educator. EdD in Rsch. in Instrn., Harvard U., 1962; doctorate (hon.), U. Geneva, 1991. With dept. psychology U. Pitts., 1966—; dir. Learning Rsch. & Devel. Ctr., U. Pitts., 1977—. Author, editor chpts. to books; contbr. articles to profl. jours. Trustee Nat. Ctn. Edn. and the Economy, Harvard U. Bd. of Overseers, Ednl. Testing Svc., Carnegie Found. for the Advancement of Teaching. Recipient Disting. Svc. medal Teacher's Coll., Columbia U.; fellow Ctr. Advanced Study in the Behavioral Scis., 1976-77; vis. fellow Nat. Inst. Edn., 1974-75. Fellow AAAS, Am. Psychol. Assn. (divsn. exptl. psychology, devel. psychology, ednl. psychology, exptl. analysis of behavior, past pres. divsn. ednl. psychology); mem. Am. Ednl. Rsch. Assn. (past v.p. divsn. learning and instrn., pres. 1986—, Disting. Contbns. in Edn. award), Nat. Acad. Edn. Office: U Pitts Learning Rsch Devel Ctr 3939 O'Hara St Pittsburgh PA 15260

RESNICK, STEPHANIE, lawyer; b. N.Y.C., Nov. 12, 1959; d. Diane Gross. AB, Kenyon Coll., 1981; JD, Villanova U., 1984. Bar: Pa. 1984, N.J. 1984, U.S. Dist. Ct. (ea. dist.) Pa. 1984, U.S. Dist. Ct. N.J. 1984, N.Y. 1990. Assoc. Cozen and O'Connor, Phila., 1984-87; assoc. Fox, Rothschild, O'Brien & Frankel, Phila., 1987-92, ptnr., 1992—. Mem. Vols. for Indigent Program, Phila., 1987-92. Mem. ABA, Pa. Bar Assn. (disciplinary bd. study com. 1989-91, profl. liability com. 1991-92), Phila. Bar Assn. (profl. responsibility com. 1992—, prof. guidance com. 1992—, mem. investigative divsn. Commn. on Jud. Selection and Retention 1988-94, mem. subcom. on investigative divsn. tng. and commn. guidelines 1992, women's rights com. 1993—, co-chair 1995, mem. Commn. on Jud. Selection and Retention 1995), N.J. Bar Assn., N.Y. Bar Assn. Home: 233 S 6th St Apt 2306 Philadelphia PA 19106 Office: Fox Rothschild O'Brien & Frankel 2000 Market St 10th Fl Philadelphia PA 19103-3291

RESNIK, LINDA ILENE, marketing and information executive, consultant; b. Dallas, Oct. 26, 1950; d. Harold and Reatha (Gordon) R. BJ in Broadcast Journalism, U. Mo., 1971; MA in Journalism, U. North Tex., 1977, MBA in Mktg., 1980. News and documentary producer Sta. KDFW-TV, Dallas, 1971-73; mktg.-info. officer Dallas County Community Coll. Dist., 1973-79; dir. mktg. The Learning Channel, Washington, 1980-82; dir. Nat. Narrowcast Service, Pub. Broadcasting Service, Washington, 1982-85; exec. dir. Am. Soc. Info. Sci., Washington, 1985-89, White House Conf. on Libr. and Info. Svcs., Washington, 1990—; mem. adv. com. ALA Library/Book Fellows Project; fellow Ctr. for Info. and Communication Scis., Ball State U.; mem. U.S. exec. com. U. of the World; mktg., tng. and telecommunications cons. to ednl. assns., others. Writer and editor college-level study guides; scriptwriter college credit TV courses. Youth activities coordinator YMCA, Dallas, 1975-78; spl. event organizer Am. Cancer Soc., Dallas, 1976-77; com. leader Goals for Dallas, 1978-80. Recipient Best TV Feature Story award AP, Tex., 1973. Mem. Am. Soc. Assn. Execs., Am. Soc. Info. Sci. (pub. bull. 1985-89), Women in Cable, Info. Inst., Am. Mktg. Assn., Washington Met. Cable Club. Office: 3533 Piedmont Dr Plano TX 75075-6254

RESOR, PAMELA P., state legislator; b. Lincoln, Nebr., Feb. 26, 1942; d. Roland B. and Margaret L. (Flynn) Phillips; m. Griffith L. Resor III, July 6, 1963; children: Karen E. Resor Savage, Philip G., Kristen M. BA, Smith Coll., 1964. Exec. dir. Mass. Assn. Conservation Com., Belmont, 1986-88; mem. Mass. Ho. Reps., Boston, 1990—. Selectman Town of Acton, Mass., 1981-87. Mem. LWV (pres. 1978-80). Office: State Ho Reps State Ho 33 Boston MA 02133

RESTANI, JANE A., federal judge; b. San Francisco, Feb. 27, 1948; d. Roy J. and Emilia C. Restani. BA, U. Calif., Berkeley, 1969; JD, U. Calif., Davis, 1973. Bar: Calif., 1973. Trial atty. U.S. Dept. Justice, Washington, 1973-76, asst. chief comml. litigation sect., 1976-80, dir. comml. litigation sect., 1980-83; judge U.S. Ct. Internat. Trade, N.Y.C., 1983—. Mem. Order of Coif. Office: US Ct Internat Trade 1 Federal Plz New York NY 10278-0001*

RETTENBERG, ANNE ELIZABETH, social worker; b. Alexandria, Va., Mar. 22, 1964; d. Frank and Sharon Lee (Kalass) R. BA, Earlham Coll., 1985; MSW, NYU, 1991. Cert. social worker, N.Y. Reporter Md. Ind., Waldorf, 1986-87, Potomac News, Woodbridge, Va., 1987-89; reporter, Washington corr. Pace Pubs., N.Y.C., 1989; social worker Samaritan Village, Inc., N.Y.C., 1991-92, Ednl. Alliance, N.Y.C., 1992—; pvt. practice psychotherapy, N.Y.C., 1991—. NYU scholar, 1990. Mem. NASW, Nat. Women's Polit. Caucus, Amnesty Internat. Democrat.

RETTIG, CAROLYN FAITH, educator; b. Tarentum, Pa., June 30, 1951; d. William and Jennie Annetta (Lear) Ambrose; m. Gary Alan Rettig, July 10, 1985. BS in Edn., Ind. U. Pa., 1973; MA in Student Pers., Slippery Rock U., 1988. Cert. secondary English tchr., Pa. Jr. high tchr. Saxonburg and Butler, Pa., 1974-75; English tchr. Butler Area High Sch., 1975-76; assessor cmty. needs Butler County C.C., Pa., 1977-78; tchr. English Butler Area Sch. Dist., 1978—, speech and debate coach, 1979-84, curriculum writing coord., 1986-87; chmn. English dept. Butler Intermediate High Sch., 1986-88; coord. fin. aid counselor practicum Butler County C.C., 1988. Pub. high sch. student art and lit. mag., 1988-91. Mem. Butler Edn. Assn., Pa. State Edn. Assn., NEA. Democrat. Lutheran. Home: 421 Fisher Rd Cabot PA 16023 Office: Butler Intermediate HS 151 Fairground Hill Rd Butler PA 16001-5627

REUDER, MARY E(ILEEN), retired psychology and statistics educator; b. Mpls., Mar. 12, 1923; d. Leo Aloysius and Mary Agnes (McGuire) R.; m. Marvin Alvin Iverson, July 11, 1953 (dec. Dec. 1979); children: Carol Mary,

Kent Gery. BA, Coll. St. Catherine, St. Paul, 1944; MA, Brown U., 1945; PhD, U. Pa., 1951. Lic. psychologist, N.Y. Asst. instr. psychology U. Pa., Phila., 1946-51; work mgmt. specialist U.S. Naval Ammunition Depot, Ft. Mifflin, Pa., 1951-52; rsch. psychologist pers. br. Adj. Gen.'s Office, Dept. Army, Washington, 1952-54; instr. psychology Queens Coll., CUNY, Flushing, 1957-62, asst. prof., 1962-66, assoc. prof., 1966-71, prof., 1971-86, chmn. dept., 1984-85, chmn. acad. senate, 1982-85, prof. emerita, 1986—; mem. grad. faculty CUNY, 1977-86; mem. adv. bd. Dushkin Press, Guilford, Conn., 1975-84; cons. NATO postdoctoral fellowships NSF, Washington, 1978; cons., manuscript peer reviewer Acad. Psychology Bull., 1980-85, Jour. Profl. Psychology, 1986-88, Am. Psychologist, 1987-88. Contbr. articles to profl. jours. and encys., also monographs, chpt. to book. Cons. com. on rsch. and evaluation Nassau coun. Girl Scouts U.S., 1971-74; bd. dirs. Walker Lake Community Assn., 1993—. Grantee NSF, 1964, Sigma Xi, 1962. Fellow APA (pres. divs. 1 and 36 1987-88, exec. com. div. 1 1981-87, div. 36 1979—, coun. reps. div. 36 1980-83, 91—, award for exceptional svc. to div. gen. psychology), Am. Psychol. Soc., N.Y. Acad. Scis., Am. Assn. Applied and Preventive Psychology (charter); mem. AAAS, Ea. Psychol. Assn. (adminstrv. coord. 1961-67, 70), Psychometric Soc., Biometric Soc., Am. Statis. Assn., Queens Coll. Faculty Club (past bd. dirs., v.p.), U. Pa. Club L.I. (bd. govs. 1980—, Jack White award), Brown U. Club L.I., N.Am. Lake Mgmt. Soc., Pa. Lake Mgmt. Soc., Sigma Xi (grantee 1962, regional lectr. 1977-86, nat. bd. dirs. 1972-75, 77), Alpha Sigma Lambda, Pi Gamma Mu, Delta Phi Lambda, Kappa Gamma Pi, Alpha Pi Epsilon, Psi Chi. Democrat. Roman Catholic. Home: PO Box C Shohola PA 18458-0080 Office: CUNY Queens Coll Dept Psychology Flushing NY 11367

REUTER, CAROL JOAN, insurance company executive; b. Bklyn., June 1, 1941; d. Michael John and Elizabeth Lucille (Garmer) R. BA, St. John's U., 1962. Exec. dir. N.Y. Life Found., N.Y.C., 1979-89, sec., 1989-90, pres., 1990—, bd. dirs., 1992—; asst. v.p. N.Y. Life Ins. Co., N.Y.C., 1984-89, corp. v.p., 1990—. Mem., former chmn. contbns. coun. Conf. Bd., N.Y. Contbns. Adv. Group; mem. corp. adv. coun. ARC; chmn. nat. corp. adv. com. Found. Ind. Higher Edn.; mem. corp. adv. com. United Negro Coll Fund; mem. corp. assocs. United Way of Am. Named Acad. of Women's Achievers, YWCA, 1987. Republican. Roman Catholic. Office: NY Life Ins Co 51 Madison Ave New York NY 10010-1603

REUTHER, ROSANN WHITE, advertising agency executive; b. Nashville, Nov. 24, 1943; d. Wiley Butler and Mildred Elizabeth (Little) White; student George Peabody Coll., 1961-64; m. Peter Martin Reuther, Oct. 3, 1964. Advt. copywriter WHMA Radio, Anniston, Ala., 1964-65, Bapt. Sunday Sch. Bd., Nashville, 1965-72, Thomas Nelson Pubs., Nashville, 1972-73; account exec. Holder-Kennedy Pub. Relations, Nashville, 1973-74; pub. relations dir. T. Nelson, Nashville, 1974-75; pension adminstr. Wood, Bateman, Nord, Assos., Nashville, 1975-76; owner, pres. In-Vision Advt. and Pub. Relations, Nashville, 1976—; lectr. Tenn. State U., 1978-79; part-time instr. Nashville State Tech. Inst.; faculty Tenn. Entrepreneur Forum, 1984. Worker, Carter for Pres. campaign, Tenn., 1976; bd. dirs. Nat. Neighborhood Alliance, 1992. Recipient Paul M. Hinkhous award of excellence in advt., 1974. Mem. Nashville Advt. Fedn. (bd. dirs. 1986-88), Am. Women in Radio and TV (pres. Nashville chpt. 1981-82, dir. dist. B, 1982-83), Hist. Waverly Place Neighborhood Assn. (pres. 1988-89). Baptist. Home: 1908 Elliott Ave Nashville TN 37204-2004 Office: PO Box 41161 Nashville TN 37204-1161

REVEAL, ARLENE HADFIELD, librarian, consultant; b. Riverside, Utah, May 21, 1916; d. Job Oliver and Mabel Olive (Smith) Hadfield; children: James L., Jon A. BS with hons., Utah State U., 1938; grad. in librarianship San Diego State U., 1968; M in Libr. and Info. Sci., Brigham Young U., 1976. Social case worker Boxelder County Welfare, Brigham City, Utah, 1938-40; office mgr. Dodge Ridge Ski Corp., Long Barn, Calif., 1948-65, Strawberry Inn, Strawberry, Calif., 1950-65, Pinecrest Permittees Assn., 1955-66; adminstrv. asst. Mono County Office of Edn., Bridgeport, Calif., 1961-67; catalog libr. La Mesa-Spring Valley Sch. Dist., La Mesa, Calif., 1968-71; libr. Mono County Libr., Bridgeport, Calif., 1971—; chmn. Mountain Valley Library System, 1987-89. Author: Mono County Courthouse, 1980. Chmn. Devel. Disabilities Area Bd. # 12, 1974—, chmn., 1990-92. Recipient John Cotton Dana award H.W. Wilson Co., 1974; named Bridgeport Citizen of Yr., Devel. Disabilities Area Bd., 1993. Mem. Delta Kappa Gamma (pres. Epsilon Alpha chpt. 1984-88), Beta Sigma Phi (treas. Xi Omicron Epsilon chpt. 1981, 83-85, 91—, pres. 1982, 85, 89), Beta Phi Mu. Lodge: Rebekah (treas. 1973-90). Home: PO Box 532 Bridgeport CA 93517-0532 Office: Mono County Free Libr PO Box 398 Bridgeport CA 93517-0398

REVELL, DOROTHY EVANGELINE TOMPKINS, dietitian; b. Rugby, N.D., Dec. 22, 1911; d. Clarence Herbert and Regina Andrea (Bergh) Tompkins; m. Eugene Allen Revell, Sept 17, 1935; children: Eugene Allen II, Dorothy Ann. BS in Food and Nutrition, U. N.D., Grand Forks, 1933. Lic. registered dietician. Dietetic intern Harper Hosp., Detroit, 1933-34, staff dietitian, 1934-35; nutrition instr. student nurses Mercy Hosp., Valley City, N.D., 1958; dietitian Dakota Clinic, Fargo, N.D., 1958-76; pvt. practice Revell's Diet Svc., Fargo, 1977—; home nursing chmn. ARC, Fargo, 1952-54; participant at internat. dietetic meetings. Author 8 books; contbr. articles to profl. jours. Invitee Dietetic Assn. South Africa, Cape Town, 1974, Nutrition and Health Care Study, China, 1984; del. People to People, China, 1987; mem. nutrition study to former USSR, 1974. Recipient Sioux Award to Alumni U. of N.D., named Outstanding Alumni of U. N.D. Mem. Am. Dietetic Assn. (registered dietician), N.D. Affiliate of Am. Diabetic Assn. (pres. 1950-59), Daughters Am. Colonists, Pi Beta Phi. Republican. Episcopalian. Home: 2407 E Country Club Dr Fargo ND 58103-5730 Office: Revell's Diet Svc 2407 E Country Club Dr Fargo ND 58103-5730

REVERE, VIRGINIA LEHR, clinical psychologist; b. Long Branch, N.J.; d. Joseph and Essie Lehr; m. Robert B. Revere; children: Elspeth, Andrew, Lisa, Robert Jr. PhB, U. Chgo., 1949, MA, 1959, PhD, 1971. Lic. cons. clin. psychologist, Va. Intern, staff psychologist Ea. Mental Health Reception Ctr., Phila., 1959-61; instr. Trenton (N.J.) State Coll., 1962-63; staff psychologist Trenton State Hosp., 1964-65, Bucks County Psychiat. Ctr., Phila., 1965-67; assoc. prof. Mansfield (Pa.) State U., 1967-77; clin. rsch. psychologist St. Elizabeth Hosp., Washington, 1977-81, tng. psychology coord., 1981-83, staff psychologist, 1985-91; child psychologist Community Mental Health Ctr., Washington, 1983-85; pvt. practice Alexandria, Va., 1980—; cons., lectr. in field. Author: Applied Psychology for Criminal Justice Professionals, 1982; contbr. articles to profl. jours. Recipient Group Merit award St. Elizabeth's Hosp., 1983, Community Svc. award D.C. Psychol. Assn., 1978, Outstanding Educator award, 1972; traineeship NIH, USPHS, Chgo., 1963-65; fellow Family Svcs. Assn., 1958-59. Mem. APA, No. Va. Soc. Clin. Psychologists, Va. Acad. Clin. Psychologists. Home: 9012 Linton Ln Alexandria VA 22308-2733 Office: 5021 Seminary Rd Ste 110 Alexandria VA 22311-1923

REVOR, BARBARA KAY, secondary education educator; b. Mt. Vernon, Ill., June 16, 1948; d. Russell Harold and Mary Alice (Byars) Page; m. Bryan J. Revor, Dec. 19, 1981; children: Rachel, Joshua, Jacob. BA, Okla. Bapt. U., 1971; MS in Edn., Nat. Louis U., 1991. Tchr. North Palos Sch. Dist. 117, Hickory Hills, Ill., 1971—. Mem. Nat. Coun. Tchrs. of English, Ill. Assn. Tchrs. of English, Nat. Writing Project.

REY, CARMEN ROSELLO, food product researcher; b. Santiago, Cuba, Feb. 14, 1923; came to U.S., 1961, naturalized, 1968; m. Alfredo Rey, May 16, 1948 (div. 1969); children—Lauri, Roberto. B.A. in Agrl. Engring., Havana U., 1945, B.S. in Sugar Chemistry, 1946; M.S., Iowa State U., 1968, Ph.D., 1975. Head quality control Alto Songo Sugar Co., Cuba, 1947-60; lab. technician dept. food sci. Iowa State U., Ames, 1963-65, research grad. asst., 1965-68, research assoc., 1968-70, assoc., 1970-75; chem. engr. Stokely-Van Camp, Inc., Indpls., 1975-76, sr. microbiologist, 1976-79, supr. microbiology labs., 1979-81, mgr. microbiology lab. svcs., 1981-83, mgr. research and devel., 1983-84; scientist Quaker Oats Co., Inc., Chgo., 1984-85, rsch. scientist, 1984-87, group mgr. R & D, 1987-92, prin. scientist of thermal processing, 1992—. Contbr. articles to profl. jours. Past bd. v.p., mem. at large bd. dirs. Hispano Am. Multi Service Ctr.; bd. dirs., personnel com. Indpls. Settlements, Inc.; past sec. Indpls. Employment and Tng. Adv. Council. Recipient Profl. Achievement award Ctr. for Leadership and Devel., Inc., 1983. Mem. Inst. Food Technologists (mem. at large exec., com. microbiology div. 1979-81, chmn. nominating com. microbiology div. 1981), Am. Frozen Food Inst. (microbiology and food safety com.), Nat. Assn. Agronomic and Sugar Engrs. of Cuba in Exile, Inc., Cuban Assn. Ind., Toastmasters (chpt. pres.), Sigma Xi, Phi Kappa Phi, Gamma Sigma Delta. Office: Quaker Oats Co Inc 617 W Main St Barrington IL 60010-4113

REY, MARGRET ELIZABETH, writer; b. Hamburg, Germany, May 16, 1906; came to U.S., 1940; d. Felix and Gertrude (Rosenfeld) Waldstein; m. Hans A. Rey (dec. 1977). Art degree, Art Acad., Hamburg, Germany, 1929, Bauhaus, Dessau, Germany, 1931, Acad. Art, Dusseldorf, Germany, 1932. Children's author Houghton Mifflin Co., Boston, 1941—, Harper & Row, N.Y.C., 1945—; script cons. Curgeo, Montreal, Quebec, Can., 1977-83; adj. prof. Brandeis U., Waltham, Mass., 1978-84. Author: Pretzel, 1944, Spotty, 1945, Billy's Picture, 1948; co-author: Curious George, 1941, Curious George Takes a Job, 1947, Curious George Rides a Bike, 1952, Curious George Gets a Medal, 1957, Curious George Flies a Kite, 1958, Curious George Learns the Alphabet, 1963, Curious George Goes to the Hospital, 1966. Founder, trustee The Curious George Found., Cambridge, Mass., 1991—; bd. dirs. Phillips Brooks House, Harvard U., Cambridge, Mass., 1989—. Mem. World Wildlife, Smithsonian, Mus. Fine Arts, Audobon Soc., Defenders of Wildlife. Democrat. Home: 14 Hilliard St Cambridge MA 02138-4922

REYES, MARCIA STYGLES, medical technologist; b. Winchester, Mass., July 15, 1950; d. Bernard Francis and Eleanore Cecilia (Nicgorska) Stygles; B.S. in Med. Tech., Merrimack Coll., North Andover, Mass., 1972; M.S. in Health Scis. (Kellogg Found. grantee), SUNY, Buffalo, 1977; m. Carlos Reyes, Aug. 5, 1978. Sr. med. technologist Symmes Hosp., Arlington, Mass., 1970-73; sr. microbiologist and serologist Mt. Auburn Hosp., Cambridge, Mass., 1973-75; asst. prof., clin. coordinator Quinnipiac Coll., Hamden, Conn., 1976-81; lab. supr. Canberra Clin. Labs., Meriden, Conn., 1981-86; lab. supr. Hill Health Ctr, New Haven, Conn., 1984—; cons. in med. tech. mgmt., allied health edn. Mem. Am. Soc. Clin. Pathologists, Am. Soc. Med. Tech., Conn. Soc. Med. Tech. (Speaker awards), Am. Soc. Microbiology, Am. Soc. Allied Health Profls. Home: 199 Dover St New Haven CT 06513-4818

REYES, SHIRLEY NORFLIN, computer learning center educator; b. New Orleans, Aug. 5, 1949; d. William Jr. and Annie (Stephens) Norflin; m. Vide Manuel Reyes, Oct. 2, 1972 (div. 1979); 1 child, Drew Haynes Reyes. BS, U. New Orleans, 1975, MA, 1990. Elem. tchr. Caddo Parish Pub. Sch. System, Shreveport, La., 1975-78; 4th grade tchr. St. Charles Parish Sch. System, Luling, La., 1979-80; elem. tchr. Jefferson Parish Sch. System, Gretna, La., 1980—; GED tchr. St. Bernard Community Bapt. Ch., New Orleans, 1991—; ranking tchr. Live Oak Manor Elem. Sch., Westwego, La., 1991—, dir. child care site, 1992-94, coord. testing and La. Edn. Assessment Program, 1992-94, La. Assessor for Intern Tchrs.: Field Test and Pilot, 1993-94; chmn. drug free schs. Jefferson Parish Pub. Sch. Sys., also instrnl. TV chmn.; pres. Edn. Network Agy., Inc. Writer/storyteller children's books and songs; writer gospel songs; producer, writer learning aids for children. Edn. program writer The Reading Literacy Project, 1991—; coord. reading literacy project St. Bernard Community Bapt. Ch., 1991—; den mother Boy Scouts Am., 1991—. Recipient Parent Adv. award Waggaman Kindergarten Ctr., 1985-86, New Music writer Gospel Music Workshop of Am., 1989. Mem. AAUW (chmn. community interest), Jefferson Fedn. of Tchrs., La. Edn. Assn., U. New Orleans Alumni Assn. Democrat. Home and Office: 131 Prairieview Ct Westwego LA 70094-2541

REYNARD, MURIEL JOYCE, lawyer; b. Miami Beach, Fla., May 20, 1945; d. Hyman and Faye (Feinstein) Friedkin; m. Brian Patrick Delaney, Nov. 27, 1983; children: Kelly, Charlotte. BA, SUNY, Stony Brook, 1967, MS, 1973; JD cum laude, Yeshiva U., 1983. Bar: N.Y. 1984, U.S. Dist. Ct. (so. and ea. dists.) N.Y. 1984. Health planner Nassau-Suffolk RMP/CHP, Centereach, N.Y., 1972-74; adminstr. N.Y.C. Health and Hosps. Corp., 1974-75; health planner AFSCME Dist. Coun. 37, N.Y.C., 1975-76; adminstr. Inst. Emergency Medicine Albert Einstein Coll. Medicine, N.Y.C., 1977-80; asst. atty. U.S. Atty.'s Office (so. dist.) N.Y., N.Y.C., summer 1982; assoc. Skadden, Arps, Slate, Meagher & Flom, N.Y.C., 1983-85, Paskus, Gordon & Mandel, N.Y.C., 1985-86; v.p., sr. assoc. counsel The Chase Manhattan Bank, N.A., N.Y.C., 1986—. Notes and comments editor Cardozo Law Rev.; contbr. numerous articles to law jours. Mem. ABA, N.Y.C. Bar Assn., N.Y. State Bar Assn. Home: 607 Colonial Ave Pelham NY 10803 Office: Chase Manhattan Bank NA 1 Chase Manhattan Plz 25th Fl New York NY 10005-1402

REYNOLDS, ALBERTA E., fundraiser; b. Braintree, Mass.; d. Albert E. and Emma Julia (Schupbach) Roberts; widowed. AB, Stoneleigh Coll., 1942. Mgr. Plymouth Shops, N.Y.C., 1956-60; assoc. buyer Gimbels, N.Y.C., 1960-64; buyer Goldsmiths, N.Y.C., 1964-66; sales mgr. Avon Products, N.Y.C., 1966-70; dir. charities RKO Gen., N.Y.C., 1970-88; promotional planner United Way, Conn., 1989—. Bd. dirs., co-founder Tournament of Champions for disabled children, N.J., 1973—, fundraiser, 1988—; bd. dirs. Myopia Internat. Rsch. Found. Inc., N.Y.C., 1985—. Recipient Emmy award NATAS, 1981. Republican. Episcopalian. Home: 142 W End Ave New York NY 10023-6103

REYNOLDS, BEVERLY MAY, public relations executive; b. Calgary, Alberta, Can., Mar. 20, 1948; d. Roy George and Irene Muriel (Gilliham) R. Grad., Mt. Royal Coll., 1974. Accredited pub. rels. Communications asst. TransCan. Pipelines, Calgary, 1975-77; v.p., sr. counsel McKim, Baker, Lovick, Calgary, 1977-92; CEO, pres. BRPR, Inc., 1992—. Bd. govs. Mt. Royal Coll., 1990—; campaign cabinet YWCA, Calgary, 1992-93; media advisor Alta Progressive Conservatives, Alberta, 1977-92; bd. dirs. 1st Night Festival, 1993—; judge Alta Internat. Edn. awards 1994—, Oilweek Ann. Report awards 1990—, CPRS Nat. campaign awards 1994—. Mem. Can. Pub. Rels. Soc. (bd. dirs. 1982-84, town crier 1991). Office: BRPR Inc, 3520-14A St SW, Calgary, AB Canada T2T 3X9

REYNOLDS, BILLIE ILES, financial representative and counselor, former association executive; b. Oakland, Calif., Mar. 26, 1929; d. Walter F. and Frances Olive (Blakesley) Iles; m. William V. Reynolds, June 23, 1950; children: Gilbert, Wendy Lee Bryant, Cynthia Lea Waple, Christy Dirren. Registered fin. rep.; registered fin. counselor; registered pension and retirement specialist. Ptnr. Reynolds Advt. Agy., 1963-70; asst. to exec. dir. Nat. Sch. Transp. Assn., Springfield, Va., 1964-76; exec. dir. Nat. Sch. Transp. Assn., 1976-83, Ariz. Landscape Contractors Assn., 1984-86; Registered life and health ins. agt. Freelance writer scripts for radio, TV, newspapers, nat. mags., 1953-70; author: Planning is the Key: Basics of Financial Understanding for Beginners, 1984. Methodist.

REYNOLDS, CAROLYN MARY, elementary educator; b. Bklyn., May 17, 1936; d. Wesley and Christine (Cardieri) Russo; m. Richard Martin Reynolds, Apr. 12, 1958; children: Donna Marie Reynolds Dewey, Richard Edward. BS, Adelphi U., 1968; MA, SUNY, Stony Brook, 1971. Cert. tchr., N.Y. Tchr. Rocky Point (N.Y.) Sch., 1956-57, Little Flower Sch., Wading River, N.Y., 1957-59, Shoreham (N.Y.)-Wading River Sch. Dist., 1969—; supervising tchr. St. Joseph Coll., 1991, Dowling Coll., Oakdale, N.Y., 1992, S.W. Post Coll., Southampton, N.Y.; coord. constructivist course, Shoreham, N.Y., 1990—; active Sch. Consolidation Task Force, 1992-93. Editor tchr. union publ. VOX, 1989-90 (award 1990). Leader Girl Scouts U.S.A., Rocky Point, N.Y., 1956; mem. Sch. Consolidation Task Force, 1993-94. Noyes Found. fellow; NSF grantee. Mem. ASCD, Nat. Coun. Tchrs. English, N.Y. State United Tchrs., Shoreham-Wading River Tchrs. Assn. (co-pres., sec., negotiator tchrs. contract), United Fedn. Tchrs. (10 Yr. pin for leadership), Internat. Reading Assn. (coun. pres. 1980—). Home: 50 Highland Down Shoreham NY 11786

REYNOLDS, CONSTANCE MARY, clinical psychologist; b. Utica, N.Y., May 5, 1955; d. H. Ray Reynolds and Phyllis (Earl) Lowry; children: Zachary D. Frantz, Joshua R. Frantz. BA in Psychology and Biology, Washington U., St. Louis, 1977; MA in Clin. Psychology, Fordham U., 1982, PhD in Clin. Psychology, 1988. Lic. psychologist, Mont. Group therapist Daytop Village, N.Y.C., 1981-84; therapist Albany (N.Y.) Internship Consortium, 1984-85, Bronx (N.Y.) Ctr. for Community Svc., 1986-87, Treasure Coast Rehab. Hosp., Vero Beach, Fla., 1987-89; rsch. asst. high sch., Bronx, 1985-86; developer psychol. svc. Palmview Hosp., Lakeland, Fla., 1989; pvt. practice Ralph Mora, PhD, Vero Beach, Fla., 1990; psychotherapist Rivendell of Billings, Mont., 1990-92; pvt. practice, 1991—. Mem. APA, Yellowstone County Psychol. Assn., Sigma Xi, Phi Kappa Phi. Office: Ste 111 2110 Overland Ave Billings MT 59102

REYNOLDS, DANNIE HARRIS, executive assistant and office manager; b. Augusta, Ga., Nov. 20, 1949; d. Alfred Joseph and Mildred Elizabeth (Carr) Zeller; m. Michael J. Harris, Aug. 9, 1969 (div. 1988); 1 child, Christopher Neil; m. David John Reynolds, July 18, 1988. Student, Augusta Coll., 1967-69, 89-91. Cert. profl. sec. Asst. to civil engr. Ga. ANG, 1970-71; office mgr. Iain Jones Internat., Ltd., 1971-73; asst. to athletic dir./chmn. phys. edn. Augusta Coll. Athletic Assn., 1974-76, asst. to athletic dir./head basketball coach, 1988-91; adminstrv. asst. Jones Intercable, Inc., 1985-88; asst. to gen. mgr. Radisson Hotel Augusta and Conf. Ctr., 1991-92; office mgr./exec. asst. Davidson Retirement Properties, Inc., 1992—; tchr. Aiken Tech. Coll., 1993—; owner, operator Word for Word; speaker to local civic groups and corps. on cert. profl. secs. Charter mem. Arthritis Found. Mem. Cert. Profl. Sec. Inst. for Certification, Profl. Secs. Internat. (Sec. of Yr. 1991-92, editor newsletter for Fairways chpt., bd. dirs. Fairways chpt., image counselor Ga. divsn., bd. contact Ga. divsn.), C. of C. Women in Bus. (steering com.), Augusta Coll. Jaguar Club. Episcopalian. Home: 2421 Camelot Dr Augusta GA 30904-3381 Office: Davidson Retirement Propert 119 Davis Rd Ste 1A Augusta GA 30907-2399

REYNOLDS, DEBBIE (MARY FRANCES REYNOLDS), actress; b. El Paso, Tex., Apr. 1, 1932; m. Eddie Fisher, Sept. 26, 1955 (div. 1959); children—Carrie, Todd; m. Harry Karl, Nov., 1960 (div. 1973); m. Richard Hamlett (separated). Active high sch. plays; screen debut Daughter of Rosie O'Grady; motion pictures include: June Bride, 1948, The Daughter of Rosie O'Grady, 1950, Three Little Words, 1950, Two Weeks With Love, 1950, Mr. Imperium, 1951, Singin' in the Rain, 1952, Skirts Ahoy!, 1952, I Love Melvin, 1953, The Affairs of Dobie Gillis, 1953, Give a Girl a Break, 1953, Susan Slept Here, 1954, Athena, 1954, Hit the Deck, 1955, The Tender Trap, 1955, The Catered Affair, 1956, Bundle of Joy, 1956, Tammy and the Bachelor, 1957, This Happy Feeling, 1958, The Mating Game, 1959, Say One for Me, 1959, It Started With a Kiss, 1959, The Gazebo, 1959, The Rat Race, 1960, Pepe, 1960, The Pleasure of His Company, 1961, The Second Time Around, 1961, How the West Was Won, 1962, My Six Loves, 1963, Mary, Mary, 1963, The Unsinkable Molly Brown, 1964, Goodbye Charlie, 1964, The Singing Nun, 1966, Divorce American Style, 1967, How Sweet It Is!, 1968, What's the Matter with Helen?, 1971, Charlotte's Web, (voice only) 1973, That's Entertainment!, 1974, The Bodyguard, 1992, Heaven and Earth, 1993; star TV program The Debbie Reynolds Show, 1969; star Broadway show Irene, 1973-74, Annie Get Your Gun, Los Angeles, San Francisco, 1977, Woman of the Year, 1984, The Unsinkable Molly Brown, 1989-90 (nat. tour); author: If I Knew Then, 1963, Debbie-My Life, 1988; creator exercise video Do It Debbie's Way, 1984. Prin. Debbie Reynolds's Hotel/Casino and Hollywood Motion Picture Mus., Las Vegas, 1993—. Named Miss Burbank, 1948. Office: Debbie Reynolds Studios care Margie Duncan 6514 Lankershim Blvd North Hollywood CA 91606-2496

REYNOLDS, GINGER FAY, healthcare company executive; b. Jackson, Miss., July 14, 1950; d. Neville Scott and Mabel Fay (Covington) R. Diploma, Miss. Gulf Coast Jr. Coll. (formerly Perkinston (Miss.) Jr. Coll.), 1969, Bates Bus. Coll., 1970; BSBA in Acctg., U. So. Miss., 1973. With Stallworth Furniture Co., Pascagoula, Miss., 1969-71; asst. sec. U. So. Miss., Hattiesburg, 1972-73; office acct. South Miss. Home Health Inc. (formerly South Miss. Home Health and Reahb. Agy. Inc.), Hattiesburg, 1973, comptr., 1973—, sec., 1976—, comptr., sec.-treas., 1987—; sec.-treas. Health Care Enterprises Inc., Hattiesburg, 1985—. Vol. Am. Cancer Soc., Hattiesburg, 1984, South Miss. Home Health Found., Inc., 1987-91. Mem. U. So. Miss. Alumni Assn., Internat. Platform Assn., Miss. Gulf Coast Jr. Coll. Alumni Assn. Republican. Baptist. Office: South Miss Home Health Inc PO Box 16929 Hattiesburg MS 39404-6929

REYNOLDS, HELEN ELIZABETH, service executive; b. Minerva, N.Y., Aug. 30, 1925; d. Henry James and Margurite Catherine (Gallagher) McNally; m. Theodore Laurence Reynolds, Feb. 27, 1948; children: Laurence McBride, David Scott, William Herbert. BA, SUNY, Albany, 1967; MA, Union Coll., Schenectady, N.Y., 1971. Grad. Realtors Inst., N.Y. Owner, mgr. Schafer Studio, Schenectady, 1970-73; co-owner, v.p. Reynolds Chalmers Inc., Schenectady, 1971—; pres. HR Mgmt. Cons., Schenectady, 1994—; program coord. Schenectady County, 1980-81; adminstr. Wellspring House of Albany, N.Y., 1981-94; pres. HR Mgmt. Cons., 1994—; cons., examiner N.Y. State Civil Service, Albany, 1971-81; mem. adv. council SBA, Washington, 1978-80. Mem. planning bd. Town of Niskayuna, N.Y., 1977-81, town councilwoman, 1986-94; co-chair Gt. N.E. Festival on the Mohawk River, 1989, 90; bd. dirs. HAVEN, Schenectady YWCA; mem. Schenectady Indsl. Devel. Agy., N.Y. State Commn. on The Capital Region, 1994—, Acad. of Women of Achievement, Schenectady, 1994, Libr. of Congress. Named Woman Vision, 1986, 87, Today's Woman, 1987, Schenectady YWCA. Mem. Antique and Classic Boat Soc. (bd. dirs. 1974-89, Disting. Svc. award 1979, Founders award 1989), Assn. Adminstrs. Ind. Housing (pres. 1986-88, 92-94), Zonta (pres. 1981-82), Nat. Trust for Historic Preservation, Adirondack Mus., Antique Boat Mus., Schenectady Mus., League of Schenectady Symphony Orch., Union Coll. Alumni Assn. Home: Apt J104 1365 Van Antwerp Rd Niskayuna NY 12309-4441

REYNOLDS, JENNIFER C., public relations executive. BA, Denison U. Asst. acct. exec. J. Walter Thompson; acct. exec. Kalish & Rice; pub. rels. dir. Vaden Comms. & Mkts., 1983-86, v.p. pub. rels., 1987; prin. Reynolds Ink. Office: Walter Thompson 84 N Landsdowne Ave Lansdowne PA 19050*

REYNOLDS, JUDY MAXINE, property manager; b. Jackson, Mich., Dec. 3, 1938; d. Max Everett and Iva May (Frarey) Donovan; m. William Henry Reynolds, Jan. 29, 1977; children: Danny, Michael, Cindy, Troy, Michele. Cert. property mgr. Saleswoman, property mgr. McDevitt Mgmt. Co., Jackson, 1966-86; owner Reynolds Mgmt. Inc. (formerly McDevitt Mgmt. Co.), Jackson, 1986—. Mem. Foote Hosp. Aux., 1973—, Moral Majority, 1984—, Nat. Right to Life, 1985—; mothers' marcher Muscular Dystrophy, 1971-75; vol. Meals on Wheels, 1971-75; city co-chmn. March of Dimes, 1973, twp. chmn., 1974; Jackson County vol. probation officer, 1979-80; vol. United Way, 1980; mem. City of Jackson Com., 1985-90, All Am. City Com. and Spkrs. Bur., 1986, prison liaison com., 1988-95, Jackson Image com., 1989-95; amb. to C. of C., 1989-95; chmn. Ducky Derby, Am. Cancer Soc., 1990-95; mem. Berean Adv. Bd., 1994-95. Named Realtor Assoc. of Yr. 1972, Jackson County, Realtor of the Yr. 1981, Jackson Bd. Realtors, Disting. Citizen of Yr., City of Jackson, 1994; recipient pres.'s award Am. Cancer Soc., 1992. Mem. ACRE (life), Inst. Real Estate Mgmt. (sec. 1982, v.p. 1983, pres.-elect 1984, pres. 1985, exec. bd. 1986-87, nat. pub. rels. com. 1988-93), Women's Coun. Realtors (charter pres. 1971-72, state co-chmn. budget & fin. com. 1973, state nominating com. 1973-74, state dist. v.p. 1974, R-Pac chmn. 1975, col. editor 1976, state treas, 1977, state v.p. 1978, Jackson chpt. pres. 1978, state pres. 1979, nat. gov. 1980, nat. regional v.p. 1981, Jackson chpt. v.p. 1982, 86, woman of yr. com. 1992), Real Estate Alumni Mich. (state pres. 1994), Exch. Club (dir. 1994-95). Office: Reynolds Mgmt Inc PO Box 273 501 W Franklin St Jackson MI 49201-2023

REYNOLDS, KATHLEEN DIANE FOY (KDF REYNOLDS), transportation executive; b. Chgo., Dec. 9, 1946; d. David Chancy Foy and Vivian Anne (Schwartz) R. Student, San Francisco State U., 1964-68. Studio coord. KTVU-TV, Oakland, Calif., 1968-70; assoc. prodr. KPIX-TV, San Francisco, 1970-72; music publicist Oakland, 1966-78; writer PLEXUS, West Coast Women's Press, Oakland, 1974-82, gen. mgr., 1984-86; screen writer Oakland, 1970—; gen. ptnr. Designated Driver Group, Oakland, 1990—; coun. mem. West Coast Women's Press, Oakland, 1975-86; founding assoc. Women's Inst. for Freedom of the Press, Washington, 1977—. Author of periodical news, reviews, features, 1974-82; author of six documentaries for comml. and PBS-TV, 1968-73. Mem. Soc. Mayflower Descendants, Casper, Wyo., 1967—. Mem. Profl. Businesswomen's Conf., Ind. Feature Project, San Francisco Film Soc. Home: PO Box 2742 Oakland CA 94602

REYNOLDS, LOUISE K., retired school nurse; b. Waynesboro, Va., May 28, 1935; d. Emil Herman and Cora Lee (Hammer) Kruse; m. Elbert B. Reynolds Jr., June 13, 1964; children: David Emil, Jane Marie. Diploma,

Rockingham Meml. Hosp., 1956; student, Madison Coll., Tex. Tech U. RN, Tex., Va, cert. sch. nurse. Head nurse surg. flr. Waynesboro Hosp., Va., 1962-64; head nurse orthopedic, opthalmology dept. surgery Duke U., Durham, N.C., 1961-62; head nurse surg. fl. Waynesboro (Va.) Hosp., 1962-64; sch. nurse Lubbock (Tex.) Ind. Sch. Dist., 1974, ret., 1994. Mem. Va. Nurses Assn. (dist. sec., chair), Tex. Assn. Sch. Nurses (sec., treas. dist. 17, program chair 1989 state conv.).

REYNOLDS, MARGARET JENSEN, quality assurance professional; b. Miami, Fla., Nov. 15, 1950; d. Arden Edward Jensen and Elizabeth Emma (Stevenson) Galliher; m. Lawrence S. Stewart, Jr., June 2, 1969 (div. Aug. 1990); 1 child, Lawrence S. Stewart, Jr.; m. Thomas L. Reynolds, June 17, 1993. BS, Auburn U., 1972; MS, U. So. Miss., 1991. Chemist Am. So. Dyeing & Finishing Corp., Opa Locka, Fla., 1972-74; sr. chemist Morton Internat., Moss Point, Miss., 1976-91, quality cert. coord., TQM facilitator, 1991—; treas. Dog River Fed. Credit Union, Moss Point, 1981-83. Vestry St. John's Episcopal Ch., Ocean Springs, Miss., 1989-91; mem. City/County Taxation Commn., Miss. Econ. Coun., Jackson, 1985-86. Mem. Am. Soc. Quality Control (cert., treas. 1994—, auditor 1993-94), AAUW (br. v.p. 1980-82, br. pres. 1984-87, Miss. state Edn. Found. chair 1984-86, crisis in higher edn. forum chair 1986). Home: 10805 Eagle Nest Rd Ocean Springs MS 39564-8339 Office: Morton Internat 5724 Elder Ferry Rd Moss Point MS 39563-9500

REYNOLDS, MARILYN DIANE, educational administrator; b. Moscow, Idaho, Apr. 1, 1949; d. Guy Elmer and Karen Alice (Larsen) R.; m. Robert Duane Edwards, Mar. 18, 1972 (div. Dec. 1988); m. Verne Lyman Gallup, Dec. 16, 1989. BS in Bus. Edn., Oreg. State U., 1971, MEd, 1975; EdS, U. Idaho, 1993. Cert. bus. edn. tchr., secondary schs. adminstr., Idaho. Tchr. Sweet Home (Oreg.) Sch. Dist., 1971-73, Eugene (Oreg.) Sch. Dist., 1973-78; substitute tchr. Boise (Idaho) Sch. Dist., 1978-83; tchr. Meridian (Idaho) Sch. Dist., 1984-92, prin., 1992—. Mem. Nat. Assn. Secondary Sch. Prins., Nat. Bus. Edn. Assn., Idaho Bus. Edn. Assn. (treas. 1988-90), Idaho Assn. Sch. Adminstrs., Meridian Assn. Sch. Adminstrs., Meridian Edn. Assn. (treas. 1984-92), N.W. Women for Ednl. Action, Soroptimist. Republican. Methodist.

REYNOLDS, MARY RUTH, educator, psychologist, researcher; b. Stuart, Va., June 8, 1944; d. Jesse Fay and Ruth Staples (Shockley) Reynolds; children: Richard Franklin Hawkins III, Mary Ellen Hawkins, James Hawkins. BS in Elem. Edn., Longwood Coll., Farmville, Va., 1966; MS in Psychology, Radford U., 1983, EdS. in Sch. Psych., 1986; PhD in Child Devel., Va. Polytechnic Inst. & State U., 1994. Cert. sch. psychologist, tchr., Va. Elem. tchr. Patrick County Schs., Stuart, Va., 1967-68; elem. tchr. Henrico County Schs., Richmond, Va., 1968-71; pvt. tutor for learning disabled students U. Richmond, Richmond, 1974-75, Carlisle Sch., Martinsville, Va., 1977-78; sch. psych. practicum Wythe County Schs., Wytheville, Va., 1984; lectr. Wytheville Community Coll., 1984-89, 93-94; sch. psychologist Smyth County Pub. Schs., Marion, Va., 1984-90; cons. Va. State Dept. of Social Svcs., 1993-94; founder Lifetime Cons., 1994—; Del. and mem. State Adv. Com for Gifted Edn., 1982-84; participant Va. Assembly on Policy for Elem. & Sec. Edn., Wintergreen, Va., 1984; presenter Preschooler Assessment Va. State Dept. of Edn. Conf., 1989, Cross-sex Friendship Mid-South Ednl. Rsch. Assn., 1991, Communication Between Caregivers and Children Va. Tech. Parenting Seminars, 1991, Retirees and Child Care Grad. Student Symposium, 1991; rsch. collaborator Improving Svcs. for Battered Women, 1992. Presenter: research, Creativity in Young Children, Va. Conf. 1985, Playfulness in Children, Va. Tech. Grad. Student Forum, 1987, Children's Play Human Devel. Conf. U. of Fla. 1988; workshop, Enhancing Playfulness, Va. Assn. for Early Childhood Edn. Conf. 1988, others. Co-founder Supporters Enriched Edn. and Knowledge, Support Group for Enriched Edn. for Gifted, Smyth County, Va., 1981; vol. coach Olympics of Mind Team, Marion (Va.) Mid. Sch., 1984; mentor Edn. for Ministry, Abingdon, Va., 1989; del. 9th dist. Va. Dem. Conv., 1992; mem. Cmty. Chorus, Smyth County, 1994. Mem. AAUW (Wythe County br.), Va. Assn. of Sch. Psychologists, Nat. Assn. of Sch. Psychologists, Smyth County Mental Health Assn. (bd. dirs. 1985-91, 85-92), Smyth County C. of C., Appalachian Peace Edn Ctr., Va. Assn. for Edn. of the Gifted (treas. 1981-82), Va. Assn. Early Childhood Edn. (mem. 38th ann. conf. com. 1994). Democrat. Episcopalian. Home and Office: Rte 58 PO Box 769 Meadows Of Dan VA 24120

REYNOLDS, MARY TRACKETT, political scientist; b. Milw., Jan. 11, 1913; d. James P. and Mary (Nachtwey) Trackett; m. Lloyd G. Reynolds, June 12, 1937; children: Anne Reynolds Skinner, Priscilla Reynolds Roosevelt, Bruce; m. Yoke San Lee. BA, U. Wis., 1935, MA, 1935; postgrad. (Rebecca Green fellow), Radcliffe Coll., 1935-36; PhD (U. fellow, Barnard fellow), Columbia U., 1939. Rsch. asst. Littauer Sch. Harvard U., 1938-39; instr. Queens Coll., 1939-40; instr. Hunter Coll., 1941-42, lectr., 1945-47; assoc. in polit. sci. Johns Hopkins U., 1942-43; lectr. Conn. Coll., 1947-48, asst. prof., 1948-50; rsch. assoc. in econs. Yale U., 1961-67, vis. lectr. in English, 1973-82; assoc. fellow Berkeley Coll., 1982—; meml. lectr. Joyce Centennial, 1982; assoc. fellow Berkeley Coll., 1982—. Author: Interdepartmental Committees in the National Administration, 1940, Joyce and Nora, 1964, Source Documents in Economic Development, 1966, Joyce and D'Annunzio, 1976, Joyce and Dante: The Shaping Imagination, 1982, Mr. Bloom and the Lost Vermeer, 1989, James Joyce: New Century Views, 1993; bd. editors James Joyce Quar., 1985—, James Joyce Studies Ann., 1990—. Rsch. asst. Pres.'s Com. Adminstrn. Mgmt., 1936; sr. economist Nat. Econ. Com., 1940; adminstrn. asst. Glenn L. Martin Aircraft Co., Balt., 1942-43; editorial asst. pub. adminstrn. com. Social Sci. Rsch. Coun., 1944-45; cons. Nat. Def. Adv. Commn., 1949, Nat. Mcpl. Assn., 1956, Orgn. Econ. Cooperation and Devel., Paris, 1964, U.S. State Dept.-AID 1965. Mem. MLA, AAUP, LWV, Am. Polit. Sci. Assn., Dante Soc. Am., Internat. James Joyce Found. (bd. trustees 1995—), Conn. Acad. Arts and Scis. (coun. 1988-89), Elizabethan Club (sec.-treas. 1984-89, bd. incorporators 1986-89), Sulgrave Club (Washington), Grolier Club, Appalachian Mountain Club, Phi Beta Kappa. Home: 4000 Cathedral Ave NW Apt 147B Washington DC 20016-5249 Office: Yale Sta PO Box 604 New Haven CT 06520

REYNOLDS, NANCY BRADFORD DUPONT (MRS. WILLIAM GLASGOW REYNOLDS), sculptor; b. Greenville, Del., Dec. 28, 1919; d. Eugene Eleuthere and Catherine Dulcinea (Moxham) duPont; m. William Glasgow Reynolds, May 18, 1940; children: Kathrine Glasgow Reynolds, William Bradford, Mary Parminter Reynolds Savage, Cynthia duPont Reynolds Farris. Student, Goldey-Beacom Coll., Wilmington, Del., 1938. One-woman shows include Rehoboth (Del.) Art League, 1963, Del. Art Mus., Wilmington, Caldwell, Inc., 1975, Wilmington Art Mus., 1976; exhibited group shows Corcoran Gallery, Washington, 1943, Soc. Fine Arts, Wilmington, 1937, 38, 40, 41, 48, 50, 62, 65, NAD, N.Y.C., 1964, Pa. Mil. Coll., Chester, 1966, Del. Art Ctr., 1967, Met. Mus. Art, N.Y.C., 1977, Lever House, N.Y.C., 1979; sculpture work Brookgreen Gardens, S.C.; represented in permanent collections Wilmington Trust Co., E.I. duPont de Nemours & Co., Children's Home, Inc., Claymont, Del., Children's Bur., Wilmington, Stephenson Sci. Ctr., Nashville, Lutheran Towers Bldg., Travelers Aid and Family Soc. Bldg., Wilmington, bronze fountain head Longwood Gardens, Kennett Square, Pa., bronze statue Brookgreen Gardens, Murrells Inlet, S.C.; contbr. articles to profl. jours. Organizer vol. svc. Del. chpt. ARC, 1938-39; chmn. Com. for Revision Del. Child Adoption Law, 1950-52; pres. bd. dirs. Children Bur. Del.; pres., trustee Children's Home, Inc.; del. regent Gunston Hall Plantation, Lorton, Va.; mem. adv. com. Longwood Gardens, Kennett Sq., Pa.; garden and grounds com. Winterthur (Del.) Mus.; mem. rsch. staff Henry Francis DuPont Winterthur Mus., 1955-63. Recipient Confrerie des Chevaliers du Tastevin Clos de Vougeot-Bourgogne France, 1960; Hort. award Garden Club Am., 1964, medal of Merit, 1976; Dorothy Platt award Garden Club of Phila., 1980; Alumni medal of merit Westover Sch., Middlebury, Conn. Mem. Pa. Hort. Soc., Wilmington Soc. Fine Arts, Mayflower Descs., Del. Hist. Soc., Colonial Dames, League Am. Pen Women, Nat. Trust Hist. Preservation. Garden Club of Wilmington (past pres.), Garden Club of Am. (past asst. zone 4 chmn.), Vicmead Hunt Club, Greenville Country Club, Chevy Chase Club (Washington), Colony Club (N.Y.C.). Episcopalian. Address: PO Box 3919 Greenville DE 19807

REYNOLDS, NANCY HUBBARD, sociology educator; b. Norfolk, Va., Aug. 1, 1923; d. Francis Marion and Nancy Augustine (Bell) Jones; m. Lawrence James Hubbard, May 16, 1955 (dec. Nov. 1968); m. George Allen Reynolds, Feb. 19, 1970 (dec. Feb. 1971). AA, Longview Community Coll., 1974; BA, U. Mo., 1976, MA, 1979; PhD, Kans. State U., 1985. Clerical asst. U.S. Govt., 1942-67; rsch. asst., lectr. U. Mo., Kansas City, 1978-79; aging cons. North Cen.. Flint Hills Area Agy. on Aging, Manhattan, Kans., 1982-84; instr. Kans. State U., Manhattan, 1979-86, Emporia (Kans.) State U., 1986-92. Author: Older Volunteer Leaders in a Rural Community; contbr. articles to profl. jours. Mem. Hospice, bd. dirs., 1989. Mem. Mental Health Assn. (bd. dirs. 1989), Am. Sociol. Assn., Midwest Sociol. Soc., Midwest Coun. for Social Rsch. in Aging, Phi Kappa Phi, Mortar Bd.

REYNOLDS, NANCY REMICK, editor, writer; b. San Antonio, July 15, 1938; d. Donald Worthington and Edith (Remick) R.; m. Brian Rushton, June 25, 1983; 1 child, Ehren T. Park. Student, Sch. Am. Ballet, 1951, 53-61, Juilliard Sch. Music, 1957, Martha Graham Sch. Contemporary Dance, N.Y.C., 1959, U. Sorbonne, Paris, 1962; BA in Art History, Columbia U., 1965; postgrad., Goethe Inst., Prien, 1972, U. Chgo. and Sarah Lawrence Coll., 1974-77. Dancer N.Y.C. Ballet, 1956-61; editor Praeger Pubs., N.Y.C., 1965-71; dir. rsch. book Choreography by George Balanchine: A Catalogue of Works, N.Y., 1979-82 (pub. 1983); dir. rsch. pub. TV spl. pub. TV spl. Balanchine, N.Y.C, N.Y., 1983-84; assoc. editor Internat. Ency. of Dance, 1991—; dir. rsch. The George Balanchine Found., N.Y.C., 1994—; co-pub. Twentieth-Century Dance in Slides, 1978—. Author: Repertory in Review: Forty Years of the New York City Ballet, 1977 (De la Torre Bueno prize 1977), The Dance Catalog: A Complete Guide to Today's World of Dance, 1979, co-author: In Performance,1980, Dance Classics, 1991 (rec. for teen age N.Y. Pub Libr.); editor: Movement and Metaphor: Four Centuries of Ballet (Lincoln Kirstein), 1970, Dance as a Theatre Art: Source Readings in Dance History from 1581 to the Present (Selma Jeanne Cohen), 1974, School of Classical Dance (V. Kostrovitskaya and A. Pisarev), 1978; contbr. (book) Ballet: Bias and Belief, "Three Pamphlets Collected" and Other Dance Writings of Lincoln Kirstein, 1983, also numerous articles and revs. to Dancing Times, Ballet News, Playbill, ArtsLine, Dancemag., Town & Country, Connoisseur, N.Y. Times, Ency. Britannica., others. Ford Found. Travel and Study grantee, 1974; Mary Duke Biddle Found. grantee, 1990. Mem. Dance Critics Assn. (pres. 1986-87), Soc. Dance History Scholars, Soc. for Dance Rsch., Am. Soc. for Theatre Rsch., European Assn. Dance Historians, Internat. Fedn. for Theatre Rsch. in affiliation with Societe Internat. des Bibliotheques et Musees des Arts du Spectacle. Home: 9 Prospect Park W Brooklyn NY 11215-5902

REYNOLDS, SALLIE BLACKBURN, civic volunteer, retired career federal employee; b. Kansas City, Mo., Feb. 9, 1940; d. Anton and Sallie Churchill (Blackburn) Zajic; m. Jeffrey Calhoun Loker, Mar. 25, 1959 (div. May 1965); children: Toni Lynne, Michael David, Kathryn Lee Loker Simpson; m. Everett Lee Reynolds, Mar. 29, 1969 (dec. Sept. 1992). Student, William Jewell Coll., 1959, BA magna cum laude, 1977; student, U. Mo., Kansas City, 1966-67, Kansas City Art Inst., 1966-70; Cert., Famous Artists Sch., 1965. Cert. tchr., Mo. From clk. to sec. Hdqrs. Strategic Air Command, Offutt AFB, Omaha, 1960-62; sec., wage and hr. law enforcement asst. wage hr. div. U.S. Dept. of Labor, Kansas City, 1963-68, exec. sec. to regional manpower adminstr., 1968-71, spl. asst. to regional exec. com., 1971-72, mgmt. asst. Office of Regional Dir., 1972-73; from. clk. to sec. air carrier dist. office FAA, Kansas City, 1978-81; from clk. typist to sec. regional personnel officer Bur. of Reclamation, U.S. Dept. of Interior, Boulder City, Nev., 1982-84; editorial asst. div. of planning Bur. of Reclamation, Boulder City, 1984-86; owner, operator B-Bar-L Angus Farms, 1990—. Editor newsletter Laurie Fine Art, 1989-90. Ofcl. commr., sec., corr. Clay County (Mo.) Bicentennial Commn., 1974-76; mem. Ozark Brush and Palette, Inc., Camdenton, Mo., 1987—, editor newsletter, 1988-89; v.p., sec. Clay County Hist. Soc., 1972—, active Nat. Wildlife Fedn. Recipient 1st Pl. award Nat. Soc. DAR Am. Heritage Contest in oil/acrylic painting, 1990, 3d pl., 1991, 1st pl. gold award 1992, 1st pl. award profl. photography Laurie Fine Art Show, 1991, miscellaneous local art show awards, 1988—. Mem. DAR (pub. rels. chmn., rec. sec., archives chmn., corr. sec. Niangua chpt. Camdenton 1987—), Nat. Oil and Acrylic Painters Soc., Phi Epsilon of Phi Beta Kappa, Versailles Saddle Club. Presbyterian. Home and Office: RR 1 Box 95A Versailles MO 65084-9724

REYNOLDS, SIDNEY RAE, marketing communications executive; b. Alliance, Nebr., June 27, 1956; d. Harold Edward and Dolores Jean (Bestol) James; m. Eddie Ellis Reynolds, May 27, 1975; children: Ashley Dawn, Tyler John. BAgr, Kans. State U., 1977. Asst. editor Harvest Pub. Co., Lansing, Mich., 1977-78, assoc. editor, 1978-80; assoc. editor Harvest Pub. Co., Topeka, 1980-82; editor Specialized Agrl. Publs., Raleigh, N.C., 1982-88, editorial dir., 1984-88; rep. NCH Corp., Raleigh, N.C., 1988-89; pres. Wordcraft, Inc., The Signature Agy., Raleigh, 1987—. Contbr. articles to profl. jours.; developed models for integrated mktg. agys. and pub. rels. measurement, 1987—. Advisor Episcopal Youth Group, Wake Forest, N.C., 1986-89, Raleigh, N.C., 1987—. Named Writer of Yr., Harvest Pub. Co., 1978. Mem. Am. Agrl. Editors Assn., Women in Comms. (bd. dirs. 1978-79), Soc. Profl. Journalists (reorgnl. chairperson 1985-88), Spurs Club (nat. v.p. 1976-78), Agrl. Communicators Club (pres. Manhattan Kans. chpt. 1976), Rotary (treas. Raleigh-Millbrook chpt. 1992-94, v.p. 1994—), Am. Mktg. Assn., Sigma Delta Chi, Gamma Sigma Delta, Alpha Zeta. Home: 512 Brookfield Rd Raleigh NC 27615-1510 Office: 6608 Six Forks Rd Ste 201 Raleigh NC 27615-6522

REYNOLDS, SUSAN, public relations executive. Spokesperson Frank Sinatra; exec. Solters/Roskin/Friedman, Inc., 1981-87; v.p., mgr. entertainment mktg. and publicity Burson-Marsteller, 1988; acct. exec. Thomas Mahon & Assocs., 1989-90; prin. Scoop Mktg., 1991—. Office: Scoop Marketing 3701 Wilshire Blvd Los Angeles CA 90010*

REYNOLDS, SUSAN ELIZABETH, computer scientist; b. Pasadena, Calif., Apr. 17, 1950; d. Clayton Howard and Elsie Mae (Schermerhorn) Minkley; m. James William Reynolds, June 23, 1973. BA in Music Performance, U. Calif., Santa Barbara, 1972; MA in Psychology, Calif. State U., Arcata, 1976; MS in Computer Sci., Pacific Lutheran U., 1985. Cert. info. systems auditor, systems profl. Psychologist Ferndale (Calif.) Sch. Dist., 1976-79, North Mason Sch. Dist., Belfair, Wash., 1979-83; scientific programmer Honeywell Inc., Seattle, 1983-84; EDP auditor Puget Sound Bank, Tacoma, Wash., 1985-87; sr. staff mem. BDM Internat., Inc., Tacoma, 1987-88; sr. rsch. scientist Battelle Pacific N.W. Labs., Tacoma, 1988-91; mgr. cons. Knight, Vale & Gregory, Inc., Tacoma, 1991-94; owner Reynolds Cons. Group, Tacoma, 1994—; speaker, cons. Tacoma Ch. of Community Sem., 1994. Mem. Info. Sys. Security Assn., EDP Auditors Assn., Contingency Planning Group (exec. com. 1986-87), Rotary #8 Tacoma. Home and Office: 2914 N 29th St Tacoma WA 98407

REYNOLDS, SUSAN FOSTER, emergency physician; b. Phila., Feb. 12, 1949; d. William Rothermel and Wilhelmina Foster Reynolds; m. Henry William Root, Oct. 12, 1985 (div.); 1 child, Christopher William Root. AB in Chemistry magna cum laude, Vassar Coll., 1970; PhD in Biochemistry, UCLA, 1974, MD, 1976. Diplomate Am. Bd. Internal Medicine; lic. ACLS instr. and provider. Intern in internal medicine med. ctr. UCLA, 1976-77, resident in internal medicine, 1977-79, fellow in cardiology, 1979-81; emergency physician Janzen, Johnston, and Rockwell, 1977-82; dir. critical care svcs. Century City Hosp., Nat. Med. Enterprises, 1980-81; founder, med. dir. Cmty. Emergency Svcs. Malibu, 1982-85; owner, dir., key physician Malibu Emergency Rm. and Family Med. Ctr., 1982-94; contract physician Hughes Rsch. Labs., 1985-93; founder, pres. Health Care Reform Cons., 1993—; v.p., utilization mgr. Associated Physicians St. John's, 1994; dir. ambulatory care and women's health Prairie Med. Group, 1994—; co-prodr. Malibu emergency rm. benefit concerts Cmty. Emergency Svcs. Malibu, 1982-85; with St. John's Hosp. and Health Ctr., Santa Monica, 1982—; asst. clin. prof. dept. internal medicine, divsn. emergency medicine, sch. medicine UCLA; nat. spkr. health care reform Nationwide Spkrs.' Bur., 1993—; mem. White House health profls. rev. group Clinton Health Care Task Force, 1993; mem. transition team task group health care delivery White House; Calif. co-chair steering com. Nat. Health Policy Coun.; regional co-coord. Nat. Health Leadership Coun.; chair bd. dirs. Fractal Med. Solutions, 1994; spkr. in field. Author: (with others) Advances in Coronary Care, 1982; contbr. articles to profl. jours. Mem. Nat. Women's Adv. Coun. Clinton/Gore Campaign; statewide chair Calif. Physicians Clinton/Gore. Recipient Disting. Citizen award County of L.A., 1982, L.A. County Disting. Svc. award, 1991; named Citizen of Yr., Malibu Times, 1991, Disting. Alumna, Springside Sch., 1992, Woman of Yr., Calif.'s 44th Assembly Dist., 1992. Mem. Am. Coll. Emergency Physicians (councillor 1991—, chair health policy sect. 1994—, bd. dirs. Calif. chpt. 1991—, mem. govt. affairs com. 1992—), Am. Assn. Women Emergency Physicians (pres. 1991-93), Am. Med. Women's Assn. (del. 1992—, Calif. state dir. 1993—, Cmty. Svc. award 1992), Calif. Med. Assn. (del. ho. dels. 1990—, mem. fed. health issues ref. com. 1990-93, mem. tech. adv. coun. violence prevention 1993—), L.A. County Med. Assn. (mem. bay dist. exec. bd. 1989-91, co-chair legis. com. 1991—), Phi Beta Kappa. Office: Prairie Med Group 2825 Santa Monica Blvd Santa Monica CA 90404

REYNOLDS, W(YNETKA) ANN, university system administrator, educator; b. Coffeyville, Kans., Nov. 3, 1937; d. John Ethelbert and Glennie (Beanland) King; m. Thomas H. Kirschbaum; children—Rachel Rebecca, Rex King. BS in Biology-Chemistry, Kans. State Tchrs. Coll., Emporia, 1958; MS in Zoology, U. Iowa, Iowa City, 1960, PhD, 1962; DSc (hon.), Ind. State U., Evansville, 1980; LHD (hon.), McKendree Coll., 1984, U. N.C., Charlotte, 1988, U. Judaism, L.A., 1989, U. Nebr., Kearney, 1992; DSc (hon.), Ball State U., Muncie, Ind., 1985, Emporia (Kans.) State U., 1987; PhD (hon.), Fu Jen Cath. U., Republic of China, 1987; LHD (hon.), U. Nebr., Kearney, 1992, Colgate U., 1993. Asst. prof. biology Ball State U., Muncie, Ind., 1962-65; asst. prof. anatomy U. Ill. Coll. Medicine, Chgo., 1965-68, assoc. prof. anatomy, 1968-73, research prof. ob-gyn, from 1973, prof. anatomy, from 1973, acting assoc. dean acad. affairs Coll. Medicine, 1977, assoc. vice chancellor, dean grad. coll., 1977-79; provost, v.p. for acad. affairs, prof. ob-gyn. and anatomy Ohio State U., Columbus, 1979-82; chancellor Calif. State Univ. system, Long Beach, 1982-90, prof. biology, 1982-90; bd. dirs. Abbott Labs., Maytag, Owens-Corning, Humana, Inc.; clin. prof. ob/gyn. UCLA, 1985-90; chancellor CUNY, 1990—; mem. Nat. Rsch. Coun. Com. Undergrad. Sci. Edn., 1993—; co-chair Fed. Task Force on Women, Minorities and Handicapped in Sci. and Tech., 1987-90, Pacesetter Program Reform for Secondary Sch. Coll. Bd., 1992—; adv. bd. Congl. Black Caucus Inst. Sci., Space and Tech., 1987-91; Calif. Labor Employment and Tng. Corp., 1993—;. Contbr. chpts. to books, articles to profl. jours; assoc. editor Am. Biology Tchr., 1964-67. Active numerous civic activities involving edn. and the arts; mem. nat. adv. bd. Inst. Am. Indian Arts, 1992—; bd. dirs. Calif. Econ. Devel. Corp., 1984-90; trustee Internat. Life Scis. Inst.-Nutrition Found., 1987—, Southwest Mus., L.A. County High Sch. for Arts Found., 1985-90; bd. dirs. UAW Calif. Recipient Disting. Alumni award Kans. State Tchrs. Coll., 1972, Calif. Gov.'s Award for the Arts for an Outstanding Individual in Arts in Edn., 1989, Prize award Cen. Assn. Obstetricians and Gynecologists, 1968; NSF Predoctoral fellow, 1958-62, Woodrow Wilson Hon. fellow, 1958. Fellow ACOG; mem. AAAS, Perinatal Rsch. Soc., Soc. Gynecol. Investigation (sec./treas. 1980-83, pres. 1992-93), Nat. Assn. Systems Heads (pres. 1987-88), Sigma Xi. Office: CUNY Office of the Chancellor 535 E 80th St New York NY 10021-0795

RHAMY, JENNIFER FRANCES, marketing professional; b. Swindon, Eng., Nov. 14, 1954; d. Robert Keith and Evelyn Imel Rhamy. BS in Med. Tech., U. Ariz., 1977; postgrad., Vanderbilt U., 1979, U. Tex., Galveston, 1985; MBA, Colo. State U., 1994. Registered med. technologist. Med. technologist blood bank Vanderbilt U. Hosp., Nashville, 1979-84; tech. dir. United Blood Svcs., Tucson, 1985-87; supr. blood bank Park Plaza Hosp., Houston, 1987-88; mgr. transfusion svc. St. Luke's Episcopal Hosp., Houston, 1988-90; clin. application specialist blood component tech. COBE BCT, Inc., Lakewood, Colo., 1990—; presenter in field; rotation faculty blood bank U. Ariz., 1986-87; faculty, adminstr., specialist in blood banking program St. Luke's Episcopal Hosp., 1988-90. Scholar Gulf Coast Regional Blood Ctr., Houston, 1985. Mem. Am. Soc. Clin. Pathology, South Cen. Assn. Blood Banks, Am. Assn. Blood Banks, Am. Soc. for Apheresis. Democrat. Office: COBE BCT Inc 1201 Oak St Lakewood CO 80215-4409

RHEA, MARCIA CHANDLER, accountant; b. Columbia, S.C., Apr. 27, 1956; d. Foster Frazier and Virginia Elizabeth (Goude) Chandler; m. Randall W. Rhea, Aug. 23, 1980. AA, Bauder Coll., Atlanta, 1975; BA magna cum laude, Coll. of Charleston, S.C., 1981; postgrad., CPA studies. Cert. tax practice ptnr., notary pub., S.C. Acct. Foster F. Chandler, Acctg., St. John's Island, S.C.; writer, producer U.S. Army C.E., Charleston, 1984; mng. ptnr. Care/Share Prodns., Charleston; agt. Greg Merhige Merdon Mktg.; media cons., roving reporter Worldfest-Charleston Internat. Film Festival. Author: (books) Does It Have to Happen Again?, From Hell's Angel to Heaven's Saint, (screenplay) The Carolina Storyteller; contbr. articles to mags. and profl. jours.; producer various films; prodr. films. Adult tchr. Ashley Rivers Bapt. Ch.; mem. Tri-County Advocates for Women on Bds. and Commns. for S.C. Recipient Outstanding Acad. Achievement award Coll. of Charleston. Mem. Am. Soc. Notaries, S.C. Assn. CPA's, S.C. Motion Picture TV Assn., Script Writers of S.C., Inc., Acctg. Assn., Coll. of Charleston Alumni, Film Soc. Coll. Charleston (bd. dirs.), Phi Kappa Phi, Phi Mu. Republican. Baptist. Office: 3226 Maybank Hwy Ste 1 PO Box 508 Johns Island SC 29455

RHEA, MARY ELIZABETH, financial planner; b. Warren, Pa., Nov. 26, 1924; d. Francis H. and Wilma (Burkett) Nelson; m. Charles Otis Rhea, June 2, 1984; children by previous marriage: Susan, Judy, Milt, Betsy. Student, Westmar Coll., 1951-52, Coll. of Desert, 1963, Cypress Coll., 1968-69. CFP. Fin. planner Am. Pacific Securities, San Diego, 1970-89, co-owner, mgr., sec., 1984-88; fin. planner Fin. Network, San Diego, 1989—; mgr. Fin. Network, 1988—; gen. securities prin., 1973-89. Recipient Big Eagle award Am. Pacific Securities, 1983, 84, 86, 87. Mem. Internat. Assn. Fin. Planning, Inst. Cert. Fin. Planners, C. of C., Soroptomists. Office: Fin Network 3131 Camino Del Rio N #780 San Diego CA 92108-5708

RHEA, MILDRED LOUISE, author, poet; b. Cleburne, Tex., Nov. 2, 1911; d. Henry Clay and Bettie (Miller) Bedinger; m. Roy H. Rhea, Nov. 2, 1929 (dec. 1956); children: Allure, Vivian, Marlene, Dale, Howard, Glenda, Karen, Henry. BEd, Humboldt State Coll., Arcata, Calif., 1960. Tchr. Shasta County (Calif.) pub. schs., 1949-53, Mendocino County Pub. Schs., 1953-54, Colusa County (Calif.) pub. schs., 1955-59, Contra Costa County (Calif.) pub. schs., 1959-68, Santa Cruz County (Calif.) pub. schs., 1968-77; ret. Author: Henry and Bettie Book I, 1990, Henry and Bettie Book II, 1991; author published poetry. Mem. Am. Assn. Retired Persons. Methodist. Home: 2408 Tracy St Baker City OR 97814-4142

RHEDIN, JUDITH A., state government administrator; b. San Marcos, Tex., July 19, 1948; d. James Porter and Ethel Louise (Belcher) Washington; m. Peter Bjorn V. Rhedin, May 19, 1971 (dec. 1976). B Profl. Studies, Pace U., N.Y.C., 1985; JD/MSc. in Judicial Admin, U. Denver, 1987. Asst. passage adminstr. Interair Luftfahrt Service Duesseldorf Internat. Airport, W. Germany, 1973-77; profl. actress TV Stage, U.S.A., Europe, 1977-82; asst. to Mrs. Lee Hart 1988 Campaign, Denver, 1987; research asst. U. Denver Coll. Law; law clerk, judge Colo. Court of Appeals, Denver, 1988; asst. dir. narcotics control unit N.Y.C. Dept. Housing Preservation and Devel., 1988-92; dir. housing trust fund Tex. Dept. Housing and Community Affairs, Austin, 1992—. Co-Author: Denver Journal of Internat. Law and Policy; contbr. articles to law jours. Mem. Coalition of 100 Black Women, N.Y.C. 1989. Recipient Commencement award Pace U., 1985, Distinguished Service award Sam Cary Bar Assn., Denver 1985. Mem. Nat. Acad. TV Arts and Sci., Am. Assn. U. Women, U. Denver Coll. Law, Nat. Bar Assn., Alpha Kappa Alpha, Phi Gamma Mu. Democrat. Episcopal. Office: Tex Dept Housing and Cmty Affairs 811 Barton Springs Rd Austin TX 78704-1162

RHOADES, MARYE FRANCES, paralegal; b. Ft. Defiance, Va., Jan. 29, 1937; d. Silas Caswell Sr. and Mary Ann Frances (James) Rhodes; m. Minter James Rowe, May 1964 (div. 1968); children: Margaret Frances Omar, James Robert; m. Robert Charles Rhoades Jr., July 25, 1980. Student, Coll. W.Va., 1956-58, 68, U. Charleston, 1962-63, 74, 89, Antioch U., 1972-73; grad., Mike Tyree Sch. Real Estate, 1984, Evans Coll. Legal Studies, 1990. Educator Nicholas County Sch. System, Summersville, W.Va., 1958-61; edit. staff, columnist, staff writer, reporter, photographer Beckley Newspapers Corp., 1962-76; Educator Raleigh County Bd. Edn., Beckley, W.Va., 1967-68; exec. editor, columnist Local News Jour., Whitesville, W.Va., 1976-77; libr. bookmobile, asst. ref. libr., outreach coord. Raleigh County Pub. Libr., Beckley, 1977-78; agt. Combined Ins. Co., Chgo., 1978-79; legal sec., paralegal W.Va. Legal Svcs. Inc., Beckley, 1979-82; parpalegal Applachian Rsch. adn Defense Fund Inc., Beckley, 1982-83; exec. dir., owner Rhoades and Rowe, Beckley, 1983-85; paralegal, patinet advocate Cmty. Health Sys. Inc., Beckley, 1986—. Contbr. articles to mags. State bd. dirs., pub. resl. LWV, Beckley; pub. rels., various coms. Raleigh County Dem. Women, Beckley; sec., pub. rels. Orchard Valley Women's Club, Crab Orchard, W.Va.; trustee Fraternal Order Ealges; pub. rels., various coms. Loyal Order Moose, Beckley, Beckley Profl. Bus. Women; com. mem. Nat. Coalition to Save the New River; sales rep. So. U.S. Rep. to U.S. Mil. Acad., West Point, N.Y.; mem. Am. Legion Aux., Mullens, W.Va. Mem. NEA, Classroom Tchrs. Assn., Nat. Paralegal Assn., Nat. Fedn. Paralegals Assn., Nat. Ind. Paralegals Assn., Nat. Com. Save Soc., Sec. Medicare, Nat. Legal Aid and Def. Assn., Nat. Orgn. Social Security Claimants Reps., State Soc. Sec. Task Force, Nat. Vets. Legal Svcs. Project Inc., W.Va. U. Alumni Assn., Community AIDS Edn. Com., W.Va. Edn. Assn. Democrat. Pentacostal Holiness. Home: PO Box 416 Mac Arthur WV 25873-0416 Office: Cmty Health Sys 252 Rural Acres Dr Beckley WV 25801

RHOADS, PATRICIA MARY (GRUENEWALD), securities consultant; b. St. Louis, Mar. 17, 1953; m. Harvey D. Rhoads; children: Kevin G. Gruenewald, Grant A. BSBA, U. Mo., St. Louis, 1975; MA in Computer Data Mgmt., Webster U., 1985. Mgr. estates and legal securities Edward D. Jones & Co., St. Louis, 1978-80, mgr. money market fund processing, 1980-84, mgr. mut. fund processing, 1983-84, mgr., gen. prin. funds processing and daily passport cash trust, 1984-88, mgr. trade processing, 1989-93; mem. broker/dealer adv. com. Investment Co. Inst., Washington, 1987-88; mem. retail adv. bd. Chgo. Stock Exch., 1990-93; ind. contractor Coopers & Lybrand Internat., 1994. Bd. dirs. CORO, St. Louis, 1990-91; mem. day care svcs. panel United Way, 1990-94, mem. admissions com., 1993—; candidate for City Coun., 1995. Mem. NAFE.

RHODES, ALICE GRAHAM, lawyer; b. Phila., June 15, 1941; d. Peter Graham III and Fannie Isadora (Bennett) Graham; m. Charles Milton Rhodes, Oct. 14, 1971; children: Helen, Carla, Shauna. BS, East Stroudsburg U. Pa., 1962; MS, U. Pa., 1966, LLB, 1969, JD, 1970. Bar: N.Y. 1970, U.S. Dist. Ct. (so. and ea. dists.) N.Y. 1971, U.S. Ct. Appeals (2d cir.) 1971, Ky. 1983, U.S. Dist. Ct. (ea. dist.) Ky. 1985, 69-72. Staff atty. Office of Econ. Opportunity OEO, N.Y.C., 1969-70; coord. Cmty. Action Legal Svcs., N.Y.C., 1970-72; assoc. dir. HUD Model Cities Community Law Offices, N.Y.C., 1972-73; resource assoc. Commn. on Women, N.C. Dept. Adminstrn., Raleigh, 1975-76; mgr. policies and procedures Div. for Youth, N.C. Dept. Human Resources, Raleigh, 1976; petroleum atty. Ashland (Ky.) Oil, Inc., 1980-82, corp. atty., 1985-87, 88-91; Ashland City Commn. Human Rights, 1993—; bd. regents Ea. Ky. U., 1994; mem. task force on sex discrimination ins. N.C. Dept. Ins., 1976; mem. bd. regents Ea. Ky. U., 1994—; mem. Ashland City Commn. on Human Rights, 1993—; mem. Property Valuation Appeals Commn., 1994—. Mem. usher bd. New Hope Bapt. Ch., Ashland, 1980-94; bd. dirs. YWCA Ashland, 1983-84; bd. dirs. Ashland Heritage Park Commn., 1983-85; bd. dirs. United Way, Greenup County, Ashland, 1988-92; driver Meals on Wheels, Ashland, 1983-91; vol. Am. Heart Assn., 1982-91. Recipient Community Svc. award Queens Community Corp., N.Y.C., 1972, Ashland Community Coll., 1986; NSF fellow, 1964, 65, Reginald Heber Smith fellow 1969; faculty friends of Pa. scholar U. Pa., 1966-69; named to Hon. Order of Ky. Cols. Fellow Ky. bar found., 1994—; mem. N.Y. Bar, Ky. Bar Assn., Boyd County Bar Assn., Nat. Bar Assn., AAUW (bd. dirs. Phila. 1963-65), Pilot Club (exec. bd. Ashland 1983), Links, Paramount Women's Assn., Penn Club, Auxually OLBH Hosp. Democrat. Home: 507 Country Club Dr Ashland KY 41101

RHODES, ANN L(OUISE), theatrical producer, invester; b. Ft. Worth, Oct. 17, 1941; d. Jon Knox and Carol Jane (Greene) R.; student Tex. Christian U., 1960-63. V.p. Rhodes Enterprises Inc., Ft. Worth, 1963-77; owner-mgr. Lucky R Ranch, Ft. Worth, 1969—, Ann L. Rhodes Investments, Ft. Worth, 1976—; pres., chmn. bd. ALR Enterprises, Inc., Ft. Worth, 1977-93; pres. ALR Prodns., Inc., 1993—. Bd. dirs. Tarrant Coun. Alcoholism, 1973-78, hon. bd. dirs., 1978—; bd. dirs. N.W. Tex. coun. Arthritis Found., 1977-84; adv. bd. Stage West, 1987—, Hip Pocket Theatre, 1994—; bd. dirs. Circle Theater, 1987-94, Arts Coun. of Ft. Worth and Tarrant County, 1991-94; bd. govs. Ft. Worth Theatre, 1989—; mem. proarts bd. TCU Coll. Fine Arts & Communications, 1994; exec. com. Tarrant County Rep. Party, 1964-69; bd. dirs. Live Theatre League Tarrant County, 1993—. Recipient various svc. awards, including Patron of Yr. award Live Theatre League Tarrant County, 1992-93. Mem. Jr. League Ft. Worth, Addison and Randolph Clark Soc. Tex. Christian U., Alpha Psi Omega, Kappa Kappa Gamma. Episcopalian. Office: Ste 908 Ridglea Bank Bldg Fort Worth TX 76116

RHODES, ELIZABETH FLEMING, writer, association executive; b. Pitts., July 11, 1915; d. Thomas and Margaret (Brown) Fleming; m. Kenneth O. Rhodes, Nov. 19, 1938; children: Richard, Margaret, Thomas, Edgar. Student, Scripps Coll., 1933-35; BA, Wellesley Coll., 1937. Author: Call Me Margaret, 1984, On the Fringe of Fame. Bd. dirs. Calif. Inst. Tech. YWCA, Pasadena (Calif.) Jr. League, Hospice Pasadena, Pasadena Settlement, Westridge Sch.; pres. bd. dirs. Pasadena Child Health Found., Pasadena YWCA; mem. Pacific Clinics Adv. Coun., YWCA World Svc. Coun. Recipient Pres.'s medal Claremont Grad. Sch., 1985. Mem. Soc. Values in Higher Edn., YWCA World Svc. Coun., Caltech Assocs., Hist. Soc. So. Calif., Sierra Club, Phi Beta Kappa. Democrat. Episcopalian. Home: 880 Chula Vista Ave Pasadena CA 91103

RHODES, HELEN MARY, real estate broker, educator; b. Ft. Branch, Ind., Jan. 12, 1921; d. Henry A. and Anna J. (Herr) Wirth; m. David A. I, May 3, 1952; children: David A. II and Brooke Anthony. Grad., Lockyear Coll., 1939, Real Estate Inst., 1981. Grad. Realtors Inst. Clk. War Dept., Washington, 1942-44; stenographer OSS, Washington (D.C.), 1944-45; clk. Dept. of Fgn. Svc., London, 1945-46; asst. sales mgr. printing and advt. Keller Crescent Co., Evansville, Ind., 1946-52; stenographer Indpls. Air Procurement, Evansville, 1952-53; asst. media dir. Grant Advt., 1953-56; freelance writer, 1955-70; prin. real estate Columbus, Ohio, 1970—; real estate instr. Columbus State Community Coll., 1977—. Author: Josie's Bedtime Stories, 1966; writer Chicago Heights Star, Ill., 1961-61; contbr. articles to profl. jours. Pub. rels. officer Sauk Village, Ill., 1962. Mem. Nat. Assn. Realtors, Ohio Assn. Realtors, Columbus Bd. Realtors, Nat. Real Estate Educators Assn. (charter), Ohio Real Estate Educators Assn.

RHODES, IDA ELIZABETH, human services professional; b. Ansonia, Conn., May 26, 1942; d. Samuel Lee and Beersheba Queen (London) R. AS in Human Svcs., South Ctrl. C.C., 1977; BS in Human Svcs., N.H. Coll., 1982. Asst. housing dir., counselor Urban League Greater New Haven (Conn.), 1978-83; mental health worker Conn. Mental Health Ctr., New Haven, 1984-86; social worker trainee Bridgeport (Conn.) Community Mental Health, 1986-87; psychiatric social worker asst. Bridgeport (Conn.) Community Mental Health, New Haven, 1987-88, Conn. State Mental HEalth Ctr., New Haven, 1988-89; resident advocate, social worker Conn. AIDS Residence Program, New Haven, 1989-90; social worker NIH AIDS Rsch. Program, Hill Health Ctr., New Haven, 1990; corrections psychiatric treatment worker State of Conn. Dept. Corrections, Bridgeport, 1990—; membership coord. Community Housing Resource Bd., Dept. Housing & Urban Devel. & New Haven Bd. Realtors, 1979-80; asst. coord. N.H. Coll. Student Community Svc. Group, 1980-82. Author of poems. Mem. East Coast Affirmative Action Com., 1978-79; v.p. Urban League Guild-Urban League Greater New Haven, Inc., 1979-83; mem. Mayor's Task Force on AIDS, New Haven, 1989-90; sec., bd. dirs. Afro-Am. Hist. Soc., New Haven, 1979; nominated honoree Women in Leadership-YWCA, New Haven, 1983. Home: PO Box 7733 New Haven CT 06519-0733

RHODES, JACQUELINE YVONNE, marketing executive; b. Fairfield, Ala., Mar. 3, 1949; d. Lee Oliver and Jimmye Lucille (Warren) Rhodes. Student pub. schs., Cleve. Bus. services rep. Ohio Bell Telephone Co., Cleve., 1969-73, bus. officer instr., 1973-74, spl. communications cons., 1974-76, account exec. II, 1976-80, personnel mgr., 1980-82; account exec. American Bell, Cleve., 1983; dir. sales and mktg. Psychassess, Inc., Cleve., 1983-84 ; telecommunications analyst Clev. Clinic Found., 1985—; sec. Turner & Knight, Inc., Cleve., 1981-83. Vice pres. Harambee: Services to Black Families, Cleve., 1983. Mem. Nat. Assn. Female Execs., Citizens' League, Women's City Club. Baptist. Home: 17722 Tarkington Ave Cleveland OH 44128-3961

RHODES, LINDA JANE, psychiatrist; b. San Antonio, May 23, 1950; d. George Vernon and Lucy Agnes (O'Dowd) R.; m. Timothy Robin Stacey, Dec. 29, 1972 (div. Apr. 1975). BA, Trinity U.; MD, U. Tex. Diplomate Am. Bd. Pediat. Resident in pediat. U. Tex. Med. Br., Galveston, 1975-78; fellow in ambulatory pediat. U. Tex. HSC, Houston, 1978-80; pediatrician Kelsey Seybold Clinic, P.A., Houston, 1980, on leave; resident in psychiatry U. Tex. HSC, San Antonio, 1990-92, child and adolescent psychiatrist, fellow in biology, 1992—; pediat. rep. Tex. Lay Midwifery Bd. Tex. Dept. Health, Austin, 1994—. Active San Antonio Conservation Soc., San Antonio Zool. Soc., San Antonio Mus. Assn. Fellow Am. Acad. Pediat.; Am. Psychiat. Assn. Ambulatory Pediat. Assn. Tex. Pediat. Soc., Tex. Soc. Psychiat. Physicians, Tex. Acad. Child and Adolescent Psychiat., Am. Med. Women's Assn. Office: UTHSC-SA Dept Psychiatry/Divsn Biol 7703 Floyd Carl Dr San Antonio TX 78284

RHODES, MARLENE RUTHERFORD, counseling educator, educational consultant; b. St. Louis; d. Odie Douglas and Helen (Ward) Rutherford; m. David L. Rhodes, Nob. 18, 1961; children: Jay David, Michael Stanford, John David, Mark Stanford. BS in Psychology cum laude, Washington U., St. Louis, 1973, MA in Counseling Edn., 1975; postgrad., St. Louis U., 1987—. Registered med. record libr. Caseworker I and II, Mo. Div. Family Svcs., St. Louis, 1961-65, supr. caseworker II's, 1965-70; personal effectiveness trainer women's program U. Mo., St. Louis, 1974-77; assoc. prof. counseling, chair counseling St. Louis C.C. at Forest Park, 1975—, chmn. dept., 1993—, dir. step up coll. program, 1990-93; developer, coord. crisis intervention facilitation tng. St. Louis Pub. Schs., 1987-88; ednl. project cons. Project Achievement, Ralston Purina Co., 1993-94; developer, presenter over 80 ednl. project consultations for area colls., profl. orgns. and bus. groups, 1975—. Author: Crisis Intervention Facilitation Training Manual, 1988. Chmn. Ft. Louis Friends of Arts, 1984—; com. co-chmn. for black dance and unity ball Better Family Inc., St. Louis, 1990—; panelist for counseling support svcs. for families United Way Greater St. Louis, 1993—. Recipient Disting. Svc. as Am. Educator award Alpha Zeta chpt. Iota Phi Lambda, 1990, role model award St. Louis Pub. Schs., 1993, cert. of achievement Nat. Orgn. for Victim Assistance, 1993. Mem. NEA (co-coord. polit. action com. St. Louis, 1985-90, bargaining negotiator 1987—), ACA (nat. chair orgn., adminstrn. and mgmt. com. 1994-95), Assn. Multicultural Counseling and Devel. (Presdl award 1993-94), Nat. Assn. for Multicultural Counseling and Devel. (AMCD rep. for 13 states 1990-92, pres. 1994-95, Exemplary Svc. award 1992, 94), Mo. Assn. Multicultural Counseling and Devel. (chpt. pres. 1977-78). Democrat. Roman Catholic. Home: 5935 Pershing Ave Saint Louis MO 63112 Office: St Louis CC at Forest Park 5600 Oakland Ave Saint Louis MO 63110

RHODES, MARY, mayor; m. Donald A. Rhodes; children: Bryan, Randy. Grad., Youngstown Hosp. Assn. Mem. council. City of Corpus Christi, Tex., mayor, 1991—. Mem. LWV, Bus. and Profl. Womens Assn. Presbyterian. Office: Office of the Mayor PO Box 9277 1201 Leopard St Corpus Christi TX 78401-2162

RHODES, ROBERTA ANN, dietitian; b. Red Bank, N.J., Apr. 11; d. Franklin Galloway and Frances (Kieswetter) DuBuy; m. Albert Lewis Rhodes, Feb. 10, 1978; 1 child, Juliet. BS, Fla. State U., 1977, MS, 1988. Registered dietitian, Fla. Clin. dietitian Archbold Hosp., Thomasville, Ga., 1988-90; nutritionist Women, Infant and Children program, Tallahassee, 1990-91; sr. mgmt. clin. and adminstrv. dietitian Sunrise Community, Inc., Tallahassee, 1991-93; clin. svcs. specialist Heritage Health Care Ctr., Tallahassee, 1993-94; clin. dietitian Arbors, Tallahassee, 1994-95; clin. dietitian cons. Southwestern State Hosp., Thomasville, Ga.; clin. dietitian Fla. State Hosp., Chattahoochie. Mem. Am. Dietetic Assn., Fla. Dietetic Assn., Sigma Xi, Omicron Nu. Home: 4112 Alpine Way Tallahassee FL 32303-2244

RHUDY, HELEN MAE, waste management administrator; b. Corpus Christi, Tex., Nov. 16, 1942; d. John Calvin and Clara Mae (Preston) Smith; m. Walter D. Rhudy, May 27, 1961 (div. May 15, 1986); children: Joel, Rana, Rhonda (adopted) Shandi, Joshua, Kelly, David. AS, Tex. State Tech. Inst., 1978; postgrad., U. Phoenix, Tucson, 1993-95. Cert. grade IV wastewater, grade III water. From operator to supr. maps and records Pima County Wastewater Dept., Tucson, 1979-91, asst. supt., 1991—. Mem. Water Environment Fedn. (sec.-treas. 1991-94, Hatfield award 1993), Am. Waterworks Assn. (chair, sec.-treas. 1991-94), Ariz. Water Pollution Assn. (sec. treas. 1991-94, v.p. 1994-95, com. chairs 1991-97), Ariz. Safety Assn. (Outstanding Achievement award 1987). Republican.

RHYAN, RENITA PORTER, nurse; b. Memphis, Nov. 22, 1956; d. Irvin Porter and Ada Mae (Cherry) McNeal; divorced; 1 child, James Hilbert Rhyan Jr. AS, Shelby State U., Memphis, 1988; student, Memphis State U., 1974-75, 93. Cert. oper. rm. technician. Oper. rm. technician City of Memphis Hosp., 1977-79; sr. nursing asst. Shelby County Health Care Ctr., Memphis, 1979-80; phlebotomist The Med, Memphis, 1980-88, ICU nurse, 1989-92, nurse, woundcare ctr., 1992, nurse mgr. woundcare ctr., 1992—. Mem. AACCN. Baptist. Home: 1370 N Merton Memphis TN 38108

RIBACK, ESTELLE POSNER, art dealer; b. Bklyn., June 8, 1934; d. Max Jacob and Rose (Rosen) Posner; m. Arnold O. Riback, June 17, 1956; children: Phillip Scott, Stephen Craig, Debra Lyn. BS in Psychology, Tufts U., 1956; MS in Elem. Edn., Hofstra U., 1964; MA in Art History, NYU, 1981, cert. art appraiser, 1993. Cert. elem. tchr., N.Y. Tchr. reading improvement Glen Cove (N.Y.) Pub. Schs., from 1964; ptnr., v.p. Artlego, N.Y.C., 1980-83; devel. officer East Harlem Tutorial Program, N.Y.C., 1985-86; asst. to dir. devel. Ams. Soc., N.Y.C., 1986-89; pres., ptnr. Manley-Riback, Inc., N.Y.C., 1989—. Pres., bd. dirs. Azzizz Theatre, Inc., Bklyn., 1993—, chmn. benefit com., 1993-94, chmn. fundraising, 1993—; former mem. Hebrew Sch. of Congregation Tifereth Israel Bd. Edn., Glen Cove; former chmn. major gifts Suffolk region Hadassah Med. Orgn., former v.p. for fundraising Huntington chpt. Mem. Soc. for Advanced Judaism, Westhampton Yacht Squadron, Psi Chi, Alpha Xi Delta. Democrat. Home and Office: 201 E 79th St Apt 19D New York NY 10021-0846

RIBAR, DIXIE LEE, nursing administrator; b. Albia, Iowa, June 22, 1938; d. Eugene Guy Clark and Margaret Ellen (Edwards) De Joode; m. John David Ribar, Aug. 22, 1959 (div. 1981); children: Michael, Christopher, Patrick. Diploma, St. Joseph Hosp. Sch. Nursing, Ottumwa, Iowa, 1959; BSN, U. Dubuque, 1987, MSN, 1991. RN, Iowa; cert. emergency room nurse; cert. emergency med. technician, Iowa. Staff nurse Ottumwa Hosp., 1959-60; surg. staff nurse Jane Lamb Hosp., Clinton, Iowa, 1960-67; dir. nursing ICU-CCU Jane Lamb Health Ctr., Clinton, Iowa, 1967-79, dir. cardiac rehab., 1980-86; instr. edn. Samaritan Health Ctr., Clinton, 1986-91; nurse mgr. Asbury-Salina (Kans.) Regional Med. Ctr., 1991-92; assoc. chief nursing svc. ambulatory care VA Med. Ctr., Knoxville, Iowa, 1992-93, chief ambulatory care svcs., 1993—; internat. edn. cons. Am.-Mideast Ednl. and Tng. Svcs., 1989-90; contractual instr. med. svcs. Emergency Learning Resources Ctr., Univ. Iowa Hosp., Iowa City, 1976-90, Ea. Iowa Community Coll., Davenport, Iowa, 1978-90, Marycrest Coll., Davenport, 1986-90; parmedic River Cities Ambulance Co., Clinton, 1987-90; presenter in field. Contbr. articles to profl. jours. Bd. dirs. Clinton County Heart Assn., 1976-90; coord. emergency med. tech. program Clinton Fire Dept., 1980-88; med. missionary 1st Congl. Ch. Clinton, Ghana, 1983. Mem. ANA, Emergency Nurses Assn., Kans. Emergency Nurses Assn., Iowa Nurses Assn. Republican. Roman Catholic. Home: 502 N Roche St Knoxville IA 50138-1623 Office: VA Med Ctr 1515 W Pleasant St Knoxville IA 50138-3399

RIBBLE, ANNE HOERNER, communications representative; b. Balt., Oct. 30, 1932; BA, Smith Coll., 1954; M.A., Harvard U., 1955; m. John C. Ribble, July 26, 1974; tech. asst. IBM, N.Y.C., 1958-63, editor, Armonk and White Plains, N.Y., 1969-75, mgr. editorial services data processing div., White Plains, 1976-77, program adminstr. systems communications div., N.Y.C., 1977-78, staff tech. edn., fed. systems div., Houston, 1978-80, info. rep., 1980-87, staff info. IBM Federal Systems Co., 1988-93; prin. Creative Commn., 1993—. Bd. dirs. Stanley Isaacs Community Center, N.Y.C., 1968-72; mem. United Way allocations com., Houston, 1989-94. Mem. Pub. Rels. Soc. Am., Internat. Assn. Bus. Communicators (pres. Houston chpt. 1982, community rels. dir. 1989-92), Internat. TV Assn. (sec. bd. 1992-93), Women In Communications Inc. (program v.p. 1993—). Home: 6200 Willers Way Houston TX 77057-2808 Office: Creative Commn 6355 Westheimer Rd #171 Houston TX 77057-2808

RIBBY, ALICE MARIE, nurse; b. Lowell, Mich., Oct. 16, 1943; d. Merle Levi and Merleen Maude (Gooden) Bickford; children: Bobette Morgan, Mylie Wasylewski, Joseph R. Ribby, Barbara A. Cupp. AD in Gen. Edn. cum laude, Lansing (Mich.) Community Coll., 1975, AS in Nursing cum laude, 1976; BA in Family Life Edn., Spring Arbor Coll., 1992. co-founder, co-owner nurse therapist, workshops and seminars on childhood sexual abuse Ptnrs. Psychol. Svcs., Lansing, 1994—; dialysis cons. Foote Hosp., Jackson, 1985; lectr. in field. Nurse ICU Ingham Med. Ctr., Lansing, Mich., 1976-81; nurse acute and chronic hemo and peritoneal dialysis Sparrow Hosp., Lansing, Mich., 1983-84; head nurse, alternate CEO Community Dialysis Ctr., Jackson, Mich., 1984-87, dir. Continuous Ambulatory Peritoneal Dialysis Program; nurse adolescent in-patient psychiatry unit and geriatric psychiatry St. Lawrence Hosp., Diamondale and Lansing, Mich., 1990; nurse therapist Inst. Attitude and Behavior Modification, Lansing, 1990-94; co-founder, co-owner, nurse therapist Ptnrs. Psychol. Svcs., Lansing, 1994—; dailysis cons. Foote Hosp., Jackson, 1985; lectr. in field. Founder One Another's Support Group. Mem. Am. Assn. Christian Counselors. Republican.

RIBLET, ROBIN L., judge; b. 1949. BA cum laude, Univ. of Fla., 1971; JD cum laude, Univ. of San Diego, 1975; LLM, N.Y.U., 1979. With Stutman, Treister & Glatt, 1979-88; bankruptcy judge U.S. Bankruptcy Ct. (Calif. ctrl. dist.), 9th circuit, Santa Barbara, 1988—. Mem. L.A. Bar Assn., L.A. County Bar Assn., San Diego Bar Assn. Office: US Courthouse 222 E Carrillo St Rm 104 Santa Barbara CA 93101*

RICARDO-CAMPBELL, RITA, economist, educator; b. Boston, Mar. 16, 1920; d. David and Elizabeth (Jones) Ricardo; m. Wesley Glenn Campbell, Sept. 15, 1946; children: Barbara Lee, Diane Rita, Nancy Elizabeth. BS, Simmons Coll., 1941; MA, Harvard U., 1945, PhD, 1946. Instr. Harvard U., Cambridge, Mass., 1946-48; asst. prof. Tufts U., Medford, Mass., 1948-51; labor economist U.S. Wage Stabilization Bd., 1951-53; economist Ways and Means Com. U.S. Ho. of Reps., 1953; cons. economist, 1957-60; vis. prof. San Jose State Coll., 1960-61; sr. fellow Hoover Instn. on War, Revolution, and Peace, Stanford, Calif., 1968—; lectr. health svc. adminstrn. Stanford U. Med. Sch., 1973-78; bd. dirs. Watkins-Johnson Co., Palo Alto, Calif., Gillette Co., Boston; mgmt. bd. Samaritan Med. Ctr., San Jose, Calif. Author: Voluntary Health Insurance in the U.S., 1960, Economics of Health and Public Policy, 1971, Food Safety Regulation: Use and Limitations of Cost-Benefit Analysis, 1974, Drug Lag: Federal Government Decision Making, 1976, Social Security: Promise and Reality, 1977, The Economics and Politics of Health, 1982, 2d edit., 1985; co-editor: Below-Replacement Fertility in Industrial Societies, 1987, Issues in Contemporary Retirement, 1988; contbr. articles to profl. jours. Commr. Western Interstate Commn. for Higher Edn. Calif., 1967-75, chmn., 1970-71; mem. Pres. Nixon's Adv. Coun. on Status Women, 1969-76; mem. task force on taxation Pres.'s Coun. on Environ. Quality, 1970-72; mem. Pres.'s Com. Health Services Industry, 1971-73, FDA Nat. Adv. Drug Com., 1972-75; mem. Econ. Policy Adv. Bd., 1981-90, Pres. Reagan's Nat. Coun. on Humanities, 1982-89, Pres. Nat. Medal of Sci. com., 1988-94; bd. dirs. Ind. Colls. No. Calif., 1971-87; mem. com. assessment of safety, benefits, risks Citizens Commn. Sci., Law and Food Supply, Rockefeller U., 1973-75; mem. adv. com. Ctr. Health Policy Rsch., Am. Enterprise Inst. Pub. Policy Rsch., Washington, 1974-80; mem. adv. coun. on social security Social Security Adminstrn., 1974-75; bd. dirs. Simmons Coll. Corp., Boston, 1975-80; mem. adv. coun. bd. assocs. Stanford Librs., 1975-78; mem. coun. SRI Internat., Menlo Park, Calif., 1977-90. Mem. Am. Econ. Assn., Mont Pelerin Soc. (bd. dirs. 1988-92, v.p. 1992—), Harvard Grad. Soc. (coun. 1991), Phi Beta Kappa. Home: 26915 Alejandro Dr Los Altos CA 94022-1932 Office: Stanford U Hoover Instn Stanford CA 94305-6010

RICCARDI, DEBORAH, artist, educator; b. Lansdale, Pa., Dec. 6, 1965; d. Pasquele James Riccardi and Susan Ann Gilbert. Student, Pa. Acad. Fine Arts, 1982-84, 86; BFA, Temple U., 1987; MFA, U. Pa., 1990; postgrad., Barnes Found., 1990—. Teaching fellow U. Pa., Phila., 1987-89; tchr. Montco Votech, Lansdale, Pa., 1992; with Acts, Actors Cmty. Theatre, Montgomery County, Pa., 1993; mem. faculty Ohio U., Belmont, 1994, Recent U., Virginia Beach, Va., 1995. One woman show North Penn Sr. Ctr., Lansdale, 1986; exhibited in group shows at Montgomery County C.C., 1983, Walnut Street Gallery, Phila., 1987, U. Pa., Phila., 1988, 89, 90, U. Pa. Faculty Club, 1988, Bonwit Teller, Phila., 1989, Cheltenham (Pa.) Ctr. for the Arts, 1989, Gutman Ctr., New Hope, Pa., 1990, Geiger Farm, Perkasie, Pa., 1990, Dutch County Players Theatre, Telford, Pa., 1991, Red Barn Antiques, Montgomeryville, Pa., 1991-92, North Penn C. of C., Montgomeryville, 1991-92, Blackburn & Yates Gallery, Frenchtown, N.J., 1991-92, DeVirgilis Designs, North Wales, Pa., 1991-94, Michelyn Galleries, New Britain, Pa., 1991-94, Race Street Cafe, Frenchtown, 1992, Grand Opera House, Wilmington, Del., 1992, Internat. Design Ctr., Long Island City, N.Y., 1992, Isospin Gallery, Balt., 1992, 93, Phillips Mill, New Hope, 1993, Agora Gallery, N.Y.C., 1993-94, Matrix Gallery, Sacramento, Calif., 1994. Waldo F. Bates Meml. scholar, 1983, Summer scholar Phila. Sch. Textiles, 1983, Tyler Sch. of Art, 1983, Dept. scholar U. Pa., 1987-88; recipient Promising Young Artist award Nat. Found. Advancement of the Arts, 1983, Paul Mazza, Jr. Meml. award Cheltenham Art Ctr., 1989. Mem. Coll. Art Assn.

RICCI, PAMELA ANN, city planner; b. Sacramento, Oct. 13, 1956; d. Lawrence D. and Charlotte E. (Scully) R. AA, Am. River Coll., 1976; BA in Geography, U. Calif., Davis, 1978; postgrad., Calif. State U./Cal Poly, 1980, 85, 86; mgmt. devel. cert., Cal Poly, 1990. Student asst. Caltrans, Sacramento, 1977; cartographic tech. Bur. of Land Mgmt., Sacramento, 1978; rschr., intern People for Open Space, San Francisco, 1979; planner I Shasta Co. Office Gen. Planning, Redding, Calif., 1979-80; planner II Econ. Advancement for Rural Tribal Habitats, Redding, 1980-81; city planner City of Dinuba, Calif., 1981-83; asst. planner City of San Luis Obispo, Calif., 1983-85; planner II City of Visalia, Calif., 1985-86; assoc. planner City of San Luis Obispo, Calif., 1986—; rschr. in field. Participant internat. planning exch. program City of Redditch, Eng., 1995. Mem. Am. Inst. Cert. Planners (cert. planner), Am. Planning Assn. Office: City of San Luis Obispo 990 Palm St San Luis Obispo CA 93401-3249

RICCIO, JANET MARIE, advertising executive; b. Bridgeport, Conn., Oct. 1, 1957; d. Victor Salvatore and Joyce (Reichert) R. BA, Boston U., 1979. Traffic mgr. Shailer Davidoff Rogers, Inc., Fairfield, Conn., 1980-81; account exec. Savitt Tobias Balk, Inc., N.Y.C., 1981-83; v.p., account supr. Rosenfeld Sirowitz & Lawson, Inc., N.Y.C., 1983-86; sr. v.p., mgmt. supr. Laurence, Charles, Free & Lawson, Inc., N.Y.C., 1986-87; v.p. new bus. devel. Corinthian Communications, Inc., 1987-88; v.p., gen. mgr. Della Femina McNamee WCRS, Hartford, Conn., 1988-89; sr. v.p. regional dir. Arnold Fortuna Lawner & Cabot, Hartford, 1989—. Active Hartford Stage, Conn. Forum, Jr. Achievement. Mem. AAUW, NAFE. Roman Catholic. Avocations: travel, music, cooking, movies, reading. Office: Arnold Fortuna Lawner & Cabot 241 Main St Hartford CT 06106

RICCIO-SAUER, JOYCE, art educator; b. Jersey City, Nov. 19, 1950; d. Frank and Jennie (Giuliano) Riccio; children: Jessica, Joshua; m. Peter Edmund Sauer, Aug. 8, 1992. BA, William Paterson Coll., 1972, MA, 1981. Cert. elem. tchr., art tchr., N.J. Elem. art tchr. West Milford (N.J.) Bd. Edn., 1972-74; art tchr. Bridgewater Raritan Bd. of Edn., Raritan, N.J., 1974-81, tchr. 4th grade, 1975-76, tchr. 6th grade, 1981-82; tchr. reading, social studies 7th and 8th grade Wood-Ridge (N.J.) Bd. Edn., 1985-86; secondary tchr. visual arts Ridgewood (N.J.) High Sch., 1986—; Cons. Grove Pubs., Teaneck, N.J., 1992. Mem. NEA, NJEA, Nat. Art Edn. Assn., Art Educators of N.J. (conference speaker), Ridgewood Edn. Assn. (rep. 1991—). Office: Ridgewood High Sch 627 E Ridgewood Ave Ridgewood NJ 07451

RICCO, BERNADETTE MARIE, elementary educator; b. New Rochelle, N.Y., Sept. 25, 1958; d. Robert Frances and Mary Therese (Nora) Deierlein; m. Maurice P. Ricco III, Oct. 15, 1983 (div. Mar. 1994); children: Kevin, David. BA in Elem./Spl. Edn. summa cum laude, Felician Coll., 1980; MSEd in Gifted Edn., Coll. of New Rochelle, 1989. Cert. tchr., N.J. Coord. gifted programs Norwood (N.J.) Pub. Sch. Dist., 1980—; insvc. instr. No. Valley Regional Sch. Dist., Demarest, N.J., 1982; tchr. Gifted Child Soc., Glen Rock, N.J., 1983-89, curriculum coord., 1985-86; enrichment tchr. Tenafly (N.J.) Pub. Sch. Dist., 1993—; adj. faculty grad. edn. Coll. of New Rochelle, 1989-90; master tchr./trainer Fairleigh Dickinson U., Teaneck,

N.J., 1993—; presenter in field; curriculum coord., workshop developer Gifted Child Soc., 1987. Co-author grant proposals in field, curriculum materials. Mem. ASCD, Coun. for Exceptional Children, Nat. Assn. for Gifted Children, Bergen County Consortium of Tchrs. of Gifted (libr., historian 1993—). Home: 96 Blauvelt Ave Bergenfield NJ 07621

RICE, (ETHEL) ANN, publishing executive, editor; b. South Bend, Ind., July 3, 1933; d. Walter A. and Ethylan Maude (Worden) R. A.B., Nazareth Coll., Kalamazoo, 1955. Editorial asst. Ave Maria mag., Notre Dame, Ind., 1955-63, asst. editor, 1963-64; asst. editor Today mag., Notre Dame, 1963-64, Scott, Foresman & Co., Chgo., 1964-67; editor U. Notre Dame Press, 1967-74, exec. editor, 1974—. Democrat. Roman Catholic. Office: U Notre Dame Press Notre Dame IN 46556

RICE, ANNE, author; b. New Orleans, Oct. 14, 1941; d. Howard and Katherine (Allen) O'Brien; m. Stan Rice, Oct. 14, 1961; children: Michele (dec.), Christopher. Student, Tex. Woman's U., 1959-60; BA, San Francisco State Coll., 1964, MA, 1971. Author: Interview with the Vampire, 1976, The Feast of all Saints, 1980, Cry to Heaven, 1982, The Vampire Lestat, 1985, The Queen of the Damned, 1988, The Mummy or Ramses the Damned, 1989, The Witching Hour, 1990, Tale of the Body Thief, 1992, Lasher, 1993, Taltos, 1994; (as A.N. Roquelaure) The Claiming of Sleeping Beauty, 1983, Beauty's Punishment, 1984, Beauty's Release: The Continued Erotic Adventures of Sleeping Beauty, 1985, (as Anne Rampling) Exit to Eden, 1985, Belinda, 1986; screenwriter: Interview with a Vampire, 1994. Office: care Alfred A Knopf Inc 201 E 50th St New York NY 10022-7703*

RICE, ANNIE L. KEMPTON, medical/surgical and rehabilitation nurse; b. West Fairlee, Vt., Oct. 26, 1932; d. James Warren and Lena May (Bower); m. Abbott Eames Rice, Aug. 29, 1959; children: James W., Beverly A., Abbott Jr., David K. Diploma, Mary Hitchcock Sch. Nursing, Hanover, N.H., 1955; student, U. R.I., 1956-57; BSN, Boston U., 1959; postgrad., St. Anthlems Coll., Manchester, N.H. RN. Staff nurse spl. care unit R.I. Hosp., 1955; staff nurse New Eng. Deaconess Hosp., Boston, 1957; head nurse Jordan Hosp, Plymouth, Mass., 1960; staff nurse ICU/emergency Lakes Region Hosp., Laconia, N.H., 1968; staff nurse Pine Hill Nurses Registry, Nashua, N.H., 1976; charge nurse Greenbriar Terr., Nashua, 1985—. Past mem. Arthritis Found.; active ARC, Hist. Soc. Mem. Mary Hitchcock Sch. Nursing Alumae, Boston U. Alumnae, Ea. Star, Grange Women's Club. Home: 28 Sunland Dr Hudson NH 03051-3209

RICE, ARGYLL PRYOR, Hispanic studies and Spanish language educator; b. Va.; d. Theodorick Pryor and Argyll (Campbell) R. BA, Smith Coll., 1952; MA, Yale U., 1956, PhD, 1961. Spanish instr. Yale U., New Haven, 1959-60, 61-63; asst. prof. Spanish, Conn. Coll., New London, 1964-67, assoc. prof., 1967-72, prof., 1972—, chair dept. Hispanic Studies, 1971-74, 77-84. Author: Emilio Ballagas: poeta o poesia, 1967, Emilio Ballagas, Latin American Writers II; editor in chief Carlos A. Sole, Charles Scribner's Sons, 1989. Mem. MLA, Am. Assn. Tchrs. of Spanish and Portuguese, New Eng. Coun. Latin Am. Studies, U.S. Tennis Assn. (New England hall of fame), Phi Beta Kappa. Avocations: music, tennis. Home: 292 Pequot Ave 2L New London CT 06320

RICE, BARBARA LOUISE, secondary education educator; b. Detroit, Sept. 15, 1949; d. Frederick J. and Ellen G. (Cox) R. BA, Nazareth Coll., 1971; M in Reading, Oakland U., 1985; postgrad., Madonna U., 1992-94. Cert. writing cons. Tchr. Hampton Middle Sch. Detroit Bd. Edn., 1972—; exch. tchr., Japan, 1985, Toyota, 1990-93, Shiga, Japan; tchr. ESL, Berkley, Mich., 1988-89; tchr. Mercy Coll., Detroit, 1988-89. Mem. Internat. Reading Assn., Mich. Reading Coun., Mich. Japanese Lang. Improvement, Detroit Reading Coun. Home: 2859 E Maple # 4 Birmingham MI 48009

RICE, BARBARA LYNN, stage manager; b. Hartford, Conn., Nov. 9, 1955; d. Joe Roger and Betty Barbara (Baxter) R. BA in Theatre and French, Ind. U., 1978; MFA in Directing, U. Cin., 1982. Freelance stage mgr. N.Y.C.; dir. The Open Eye: New Stagings, N.Y.C., 1989; prodn. stage mgr. Belmont Italian-Am. Playhouse, N.Y.C., 1994. Dir. The Open Eye: New Stagings, N.Y.C., 1989; stage mgr. 20 Years Ago Today, Cin., 1989, Fourscore & 7 Years Ago, Paramus, N.J., 1989-90, Hanging the President, N.Y.C., 1990; prodn. asst. Kiss of the Spiderwoman, Purchase, N.Y., 1990, (off-Broadway) Beau Jest, N.Y.C., 1992, Belmont Italian-Am. Playhouse, N.Y.C., 1994. Mem. Actors' Equity Assn., Stage Mgrs. Assn. Presbyterian. Home: 412 W 56th St Apt 10 New York NY 10019-3647

RICE, BARBARA POLLAK, advertising and marketing executive; b. Ft. Scott, Kans., Nov. 11, 1937; d. Olin N. and Jeanette E. (Essen) Brigman; m. Stanley Rice, Apr. 28, 1978; 1 child, Beverly Johnson. Student N. Central Coll., 1955, Elmhurst Coll., 1956; BA in Communications, Calif. State U., Fullerton, 1982. Art dir. Gonterman & Assos., St. Louis, 1968-71; advt. mgr. Passpoint Corp., St. Louis, 1971-73; advt., pub. relations mgr. Permaneer Corp., St. Louis, 1973-74; advt. cons., advt. mgr. Hydro-Air Engring., Inc., St. Louis, 1974-76; mgr. mktg. services Hollytex Carpet Mills subs. U.S. Gypsum Co., City of Industry, Calif., 1976-79; pres. B.P. Rice & Co., Inc., Cerittos, Calif., 1979—; press affiliate Inst. Bus. Designers. Recipient Designer Best Exhibit award Nat. Farm Builders Trade Show, Creative Challenge Mead Top 60 award L.A. Bus. Profl. Advt. Assn. Mem. Am. Advt. Fedn. (past nat. bd. dirs., region chmn., Silver medal), L.A. Advt. Women (pres., dir., LULU award), Bus. Profl. Advt. Assn., Calif. State U.-Fullerton Sch. Comm. Alumni Assn., Beta Sigma Phi (past pres., outstanding mem.). Author: Truss Construction Manual, 1975. Home: 1721 N Redwillow Rd Fullerton CA 92633-1433 Office: 16330 Marquardt St Cerritos CA 90703-2104

RICE, DOROTHY PECHMAN (MRS. JOHN DONALD RICE), medical economist; b. Bklyn., June 11, 1922; d. Gershon and Lena (Schiff) Pechman; m. John Donald Rice, Apr. 3, 1943; children: Kenneth D., Donald B., Thomas H. Student, Bklyn. Coll., 1938-39; BA, U. Wis., 1941; DSc (hon.), Coll. Medicine and Dentistry N.J., 1979. With hosp., and med. facilities USPHS, Washington, 1960-61; med. econs. studies Social Security Adminstrn., 1962-63; health econs. br. Community Health Svc., USPHS, 1964-65; chief health ins. rsch. br. Social Security Adminstrn., 1966-72, dep. asst. commr. for rsch. and statistics, 1972-75; dir. Nat. Ctr. for Health Stats., Rockville, Md., 1976-82; prof. Inst. Health & Aging U. Calif., San Francisco, 1982-94, prof. emeritus, 1994—; developer, mgr. nationwide health info. svcs.; expert on aging, health care costs, disability, and cost-of-illness. Contbr. articles to profl. jours. Recipient Social Security Adminstrn. citation, 1968, Disting. Service medal HEW, 1974, Jack C. Massey Found. award, 1978. Fellow Am. Public Health Assn. (domestic award for excellence 1978, Sedgwick Meml. medal, 1988), Am. Statis. Assn.; mem. Inst. Medicine, Assn. Health Scvs. Rsch. (President's award 1988), Am. Econ. Assn., Population Assn. Am., LWV. Home: 13895 Campus Dr Oakland CA 94605-3831 Office: U Calif Sch Nursing Calif # N631 San Francisco CA 94143

RICE, FERILL JEANE, writer, civic worker; b. Hemingford, Nebr., July 4, 1926; d. Derrick and Helen Agnes (Moffatt) Dalton; m. Otis LaVerne Rice, Mar. 7, 1946; children: LaVeria June McMichael, Larry L. Student, U. Omaha, 1961. Dir. jr. and sr. choir Congl. Ch., Tabor, Iowa, 1952-66; tchr. Fox Valley Tech. Inst., Appleton, Wis., 1970-77; activity dir. Family Heritage Nursing Home, Appleton, Wis., 1972-75; dir. activity Peabody Manor, Appleton, Wis., 1975-76. Editor: Moffatt and Related Families, 1981; asst. editor (mag.) Yester-Year, 1975-76; contbr. articles to profl jours. Chmn. edn. Am. Cancer Soc., Fremont County, 1962, 63, 64; founder Mothers Club Nishna; 1st pres. valley chpt. Demolay Boys. Mem. DAR, Internat. Carnival Glass Assn., Heart Am. Carnival Glass Assn., Nat. Cambridge Collectors, Heisey Collectors Am., Iowa Fedn. Women's Clubs (Fremont county chmn. 1964, 65, 66, 67, 7th dist. chmn. libr. svcs. 1966-67), Tabor Women's Club (pres. 1962, 63, 64), Jr. Legion Aux. (founder, 1st dir. 1951-52), Fenton Art Glass Collectors Am. (co-founder 1977, sec., editor newsletter 1976-86, editor/sec. 1988-93, pres./editor 1993—), Mayflower Soc., John Howland Soc., Ross County Ohio Geneal. Soc., Iowa Geneal. Soc., Dallas County Mo. Geneal. Soc., Imperial Collectors Am., Clay County (Ind.) Geneal. Soc., Owen County (Ind.) Geneal. Soc., Fenton Finders of Wis. (chpt. #1, pres. 1988-90). Republican. Methodist. Lodge: Order of Eastern Star (worthy matron 1959, 64), Rainbow for Girls (bd. dirs. 1964), Internat. Order Jobs Daughters (honored queen 1945). Home: 302 Pheasant Run Kaukauna WI 54130-1802 Office: Rice Enterprises & Rice & Rice 1665 Lamers Dr # 305 Little Chute WI 54140-2519

RICE, JEAN ANN, marketing professional; b. Scranton, Pa., Dec. 1, 1932; d. William Gerard and Loretta Anastasia (Horan) Mattern; m. Philip J. Rice, Apr. 7, 1956 (wid. 1989); children: Monica, Adrienne. AA, Canada Coll., Redwood City, Calif., 1972; BA, San Jose State U., 1975; MBA, U. Santa Clara, 1983. Cert. pub. rels. profl. Tech. report editor SRI Internat., Menlo Park, Calif., 1956-57; publicity coord. Lockheed Missiles & Space Co., Sunnyvale, Calif., 1974-84; account exec. Hill & Knowlton, Santa Clara, Calif., 1984-86; account supr. Smith & Shows, Menlo Park, 1986-88; pres. Jean Rice & Assocs., Atherton, Calif., 1988—. Contbr. articles to profl. jours. Bd. govs. Com. for Art at Stanford U., 1991—; v.p. Stanford Singles, 1992-93; bd. dirs. Inst. for Med. Rsch., San Jose, 1983-84, Menlo Park C. of C., 1989-90; adv. bd. Jr. League of Palo Alto, Calif., 1989-90; active Peninsula Vols., 1960-70. Mem. Pub. Rels. Soc. Am. (accredited, pres. Peninsula chpt. 1985, Cmty. Rels. award, Market Support award, Fund Devel. award), Inst. Mgmt. Cons., Nat. Investor Rels. Inst. (v.p., sec. 1986-89), Phi Kappa Phi. Home: 118 Heather Dr Atherton CA 94027-2120 Office: Jean Rice & Assocs 118 Heather Dr Atherton CA 94027-2120

RICE, KAREN A., industrial engineer; b. Seattle, Apr. 18, 1964; d. Keith R. and Joyce I. (McLachlan) R.; m. Alireza Sadigh, May 1, 1993; 1 child, Alexander. BA, Mills Coll., 1986. Pers. computer specialist Golden Grain/Quaker Oats, Seattle, 1986-90, assoc. indsl. engr., 1990—. Mem. Inst. Indsl. Engrs., Mills Coll. Alumni Assn. Office: Golden Grain/Quaker Oats 4100 4th Ave S Seattle WA 98134

RICE, KAY DIANE, elementary education educator, consultant; b. Redding, Calif., Mar. 21, 1952; d. Ray H. and Patricia Barton (Stabler) Quibell; m. 1976 (div. 1982); 1 child, Brooke Elise; m. F. Scott Rice, June 29, 1985. AA in Gen. Edn., Shasta Coll., Redding, 1972; BA in Liberal Studies, Calif. State U., Chico, 1975; EdM in Policy and Govt., U. Wash., 1991. Cert. tchr., Calif., Wash., cert. prin., Wash. Tchr. Anderson (Calif.) Schs., 1976-79; chpt. 1 resource coord. Redding (Calif.) Elem. Sch., 1979-81; tchr. grade 1 Redding (Calif.) Elem. Schs., 1984-86; tchr. grade 2 Bellevue (Wash.) Pub. Schs., 1987-88; tchr. grade 4 Lake Wash. Sch. Dist., Kirkland, Wash., 1988-89; tchr. grades 3-4 Bellevue (Wash.) Pub. Schs., 1989-90; prin. intern Bellevue (Wash.) and Mercer Island (Wash.) Schs., 1990-91; tchr. grades K-1 Bellevue (Wash.) Pub. Schs., 1991-93, tchr. grades 1-2, 1993—; co-presenter North State Reading Conf., Redding, 1985; mem. adv. com. Supts. Edn. Program Com. Bellevue (Wash.) Pub. Schs., 1992-94; with Early Childhood Assessment Project, 1993-95. Vol. ZEST-Sch. Dist. Vol. Program, Bellevue, 1991-93; vol. asst. children's choir, First Presbyn. Ch., Bellevue, 1992-93, vol. asst. youth handbells, 1993-95. Recipient Pres.'s Merit award, Parent Student Tchr. Assn., 1988, U.S. Presdl. EPA award, 1987; Bellevue Schs. Found. grantee, 1987, Danforth Edn. Leadership grantee Bellevue Pub. Schs., 1990-91, Ednl. Travel Study grantee Shunju Club, Japanese Bus. People Wash., 1994. Mem. ASCD, NEA, AAUW (hospitality com. 1982), North State Reading Assn., Wash. Orgn. Reading Devel., Ea. Star (adult advisor to Rainbow for Girls 1978-80, Grand Cross of Color 1981), PEO. Republican. Home: 6818 205th Ave NE Redmond WA 98053-4721 Office: Bellevue Pub Schs PO Box 90010 Bellevue WA 98009-9010

RICE, LOIS DICKSON, former computer company executive; b. Portland, Maine, Feb. 28, 1933; d. David A. and Mary D. Dickson; m. Alfred B. Fitt, Jan. 7, 1978 (dec. 1992); children: Susan, John Rice. A.B. magna cum laude, Radcliffe Coll., 1954; postgrad. (Woodrow Wilson fellow), Columbia U., 1954-55; LL.D. (hon.), Brown U., 1981, Bowdoin Coll., 1984. Dir. counseling services Nat. Scholarship Service and Fund for Negro Students, N.Y.C., 1955-59; with The Coll. Bd., N.Y.C. and Washington, 1959-81; v.p. The Coll. Bd., Washington, 1973-81; sr. v.p. govt. affairs, bd. dirs. Control Data Corp., 1981-91; guest scholar The Brookings Inst., Washington, 1991—; bd. dirs. McGraw Hill Inc., Bell Atlantic, Washington, Hartford Steam Boiler Inspection and Ins. Co., Internat. Multifoods, Shawmut Nat. Corp., UNUM Corp.; overseer Tuck Sch. Mgmt. Dartmouth Coll., 1990-94; mem. Pres. Fgn. Intelligence adv. bd., 1993—; trustee George Washington U., 1992-94. Contbr. articles on edn. to profl. publs.; editor: Student Loans: Problems and Policy Alternatives, 1977. Mem. Gov.'s Commn. on Future of Postsecondary Edn. in N.Y. State, 1976-77; mem. Carnegie Coun. on Higher Edn., 1975-80; bd. dirs. Potomac Inst., 1977-92, German Marshall Fund, 1984-94, Joint Ctr. Polit. and Econ. Studies, 1991-94, Harry Frank Guggenheim Found., 1990—, Reading is Fundamental, 1991—; trustee Radcliffe Coll., 1969-75, Stephens Coll., Mo., 1976-78, Beauvoir Sch., Washington, 1970-76, Children's TV Workshop, 1970-73; chmn. adv. bd. to dir. NSF, 1981-89, chair 1986-89. Recipient Disting. Service award HEW, 1977. Mem. Cosmos Club, Phi Beta Kappa. Episcopalian. Home: 2332 Massachusetts Ave NW Washington DC 20008-2801 Office: The Brookings Instn 1775 Massachussetts Ave NW Washington DC 20036

RICE, LOUISE ALLEN, reading educator; b. Augusta, Ga.; m. Wilson L. Rice, Apr. 4, 1965; children: Wilson L. Rice, Jr., Robert Christopher Rice. BS, Tuskegee U., 1963; MA, Columbia Univ., 1969; PhD, U. Ga., 1979; postgrad., Augusta Coll., 1982-83, U. Ga. Instr. English Washington High Sch., Cairo, Ga., 1963-66; instr. reading and English Lucy Laney High Sch., Augusta, Ga., 1966-68; instr. of reading and English Paine Coll., Augusta, 1968-70, reading specialist, instr., 1972-73, asst. prof. of reading, 1973-77, 79-80, assoc. prof. reading and coord. reading dept., 1980-81; instrnl. lead tchr. Joseph Lamar Elem. Sch., Augusta, 1981-84; assoc. dir. admissions and minority recruitment officer Augusta Coll., 1984-87, asst prof. edn., 1988, asst. prof. of reading in devel. studies, 1988-93, assoc. prof. reading in devel. studies, 1993—; chair dept. English Washington High. Sch., Cairo, 1964-66; instr. reading Upward Bound Program, Paine Coll., Augusta, 1968-70, instr. reading EPDA Summer Lang. Arts Workshop for Elem. Sch. Tchrs., summer 1971; reading cons. Everett High Sch. Lansing, spring 1972; co-dir., co-organizer Creative Dramatics Workshop for Pre-Schoolers, Paine Coll., 1971; dir. acad. skills clinic, 1973-74, curriculum coord. freshman studies, 1974-77; asst. dean of instrn. and dir. Paine Coll.-Fort Gordon Resident Ctr., 1979-80. Adv. bd. Richmond County Bd. Edn., Augusta, 1987—, chair edn. com. of the adv. bd., 1988-89, SAT study com., 1989-90; career day cons. Lucy Laney High Sch., 1988-92; coll. rep., bd. dirs. CSRA Econ. Opporutnity Authority, Inc., 1984—; mem. Augusta Coll. Speakers bus., 1987—; edn. com. Richmond County Human Rels. Commns., Augusta, 1989-90; bd. dirs. United Way of the CSRA, 1987-88; United Way Alvin W. Vogtle Vol. of the Yr. Selection Com., 1988; mem. Bethlehem Community Ctr. Study Com., 1987. Recipient Disting. Leadership award United Negro Coll. Fund, Inc., 1990, Educator of Yr. award Augusta Lincoln Leagues, 1988, Urban Builders award Augusta Black History Coms., 1985, Disting. Svc. award Augusta Alumni Pan-Hellenic coun., 1984; named Hon. Sgt.-at-arms Tenn. Ho. of Reps. in Recognition of Outstanding Svc. to the State, 1989. Mem. Nat. Assn. of Univ. Women, Nat. Coun. of Negro Women (life), Coll. Reading and Learning Assn., Nat. Assn. for Devel. Edn., Ga. Assn. for Devel.Edn., Internat. Reading Assn., Ga. Coun. of the Internat. Reading Assn., CSRA Coun. of the Internat. Reading Assn., Delta Sigma Theta (advisor Mu Xi chpt., 1984—, Svc. award 1993, Woman of Yr. 1991, Proclamation of Svc. Valdosta Alumnae chpt., 1989, regional dir. southern region 1986-91, nat. sec. 1992—). Office: Augusta Coll 2500 Walton Way Augusta GA 30904-2200

RICE, MARY ESTHER, biologist; b. Washington, Aug. 3, 1926; d. Daniel Gibbons and Florence Catharine (Pyles) R. AB, Drew U., 1947; MA, Oberlin Coll., 1949; PhD, U. Wash., 1966. Instr. biology Drew U., Madison, N.J., 1949-50; rsch. assoc. Columbia U., N.Y.C., 1950-53; rsch. asst. NIH, Bethesda, Md., 1953-61; curator invertebrate zoology and dir. Smithsonian Marine Sta., Smithsonian Instn., Washington, 1966—; mem. adv. panel on systematic biology NSF, Washington, 1977-78; mem. com. on marine invertebrates Nat. Acad. Sci., 1976-81; mem. overseers com. on biology Harvard U., Cambridge, Mass., 1982-88. Assoc. editor Jour. Morphology, Ann Arbor, Mich., 1985-91; editor: (with M. Todorovic) Biology of Sipuncula and Echiura, 1975, 2nd vol., 1976; (with F.S. Chia) Settlement and Metamorphosis of Marine Invertebrate Larvae, 1978; contbr. articles to profl. jours. Recipient Drew U. Alumni Achievement award in sci., 1980. Fellow AAAS; mem. Am. Soc. Zoologists (pres. 1979), Phi Beta Kappa. Office: Smithsonian Marine Sta 5612 Old Dixie Hwy Fort Pierce FL 34946-7303

RICE, MELVA GENE, education educator, elementary school educator; b. Celeste, Tex., July 24, 1918; d. Lilbum Miller and Mary Ruth (Green) Powell; m. Clarence Prather Rice, Feb. 6, 1944; 1 child, Anna Rice Cleary. BS, East Tex. U., 1955, MEd, 1958. Cert. elem. tchr. Elem. tchr. Tidwell Ind. Sch., Greenville, Tex., 1938-39; prin. Merrick Ind. Sch., Greenville, 1942-44, Ctr. Pt. Ind. Sch., Greenville, 1944-45; office mgr. S.H. Kress and Co., Greenville, 1945-55; tchr. Greenville Ind. Schs., 1955-84; adj. prof. East Tex. State U., Commerce, 1985—; dir., instr. summer enrichment Greenville Ind. Sch., 1961-63; supr. student tchrs. East Tex. State U., 1985—. Soliciter silent auction Hunt County Mus., Greenville, 1991; bd. dirs. YMCA, Greenville, 1987-88; bell ringer, register Salvation Army, Greenville, 1980—; fund collector Am. Heart Assn., 1987-89; lifetime mem. Travis Elem. Sch. PTA, Greenville, 1983—. Fellow Ret. Tchrs. Assn., Tex. State Tchrs. Assn., Nat. Educators; mem. Delta Kappa Gamma (pres. 1964-66, auditor). Democrat. Baptist. Home: 14 Mullaney Rd Greenville TX 75402-7143

RICE, NANCY MARIE, nursing consultant; b. Murphy, N.C., Aug. 3, 1940; d. Berlon and Elizabeth Beryl (Ammons) Lovingood; m. Lewis T. Rice, Jan. 23, 1976; 1 child, Elizabeth Robertson Flowers. Diploma, Grady Meml. Hosp., Atlanta, 1961; BA, U. West Fla., Pensacola, 1973; MS, Fla. State U., Tallahassee, 1979. Cert. cmty. health nurse, nursing administr.; diplomate Am. Bd. Quality Assurance and Utilization Review Physicians. Staff nurse Riegel Community Hosp., Trion, Ga., 1961; pub. health nurse Escambia County Health Unit, Pensacola, 1962-63, Santa Rosa County Health Unit, Milton, Fla., 1963-73; pub. health nursing supr. I Leon County Health Unit, Tallahassee, Fla., 1973-77; pub. health nurse Broward County Health Unit, Ft. Lauderdale, Fla., 1977-78; nursing cons. social and econ. svcs. Tallahassee, 1978-79; HMO program specialist social and econ. scvs. program office DHRS Dist. X, Ft. Lauderdale, 1979; pub. health nurse, supr. II Sarasota (Fla.) County Health Unit, 1979-81; health program specialist health program office DHRS Dist X, Ft. Lauderdale, Fla., 1981-83; nursing cons. Dept. Labor, Div. Workers' Compensation, Tallahassee, 1983—. Recipient Cert. of Svc. State of Fla., 10 yr., 20 yr., 25 yrs., 30 yrs., Cert. of Appreciation, 1976, Leon County-Tallahassee Community Action Program. Mem. Am. Nurses Assn., Fla. Nurses Assn., Eta Sigma Gamma. Home: PO Box 13731 Tallahassee FL 32317-3731

RICE, REGINA KELLY, marketing executive; b. Yonkers, N.Y., July 11, 1955; d. Howard Adrian and Lucy Virginia (Butler) Kelly; m. Mark Christopher Rice, Sept. 11, 1981; children: Amanda Kelly, Jaime Brannen. BS in Community Nutrition, Cornell U., 1948. Account exec. J. Walter Thompson Co., N.Y.C., 1978-79; sr. account exec. Ketchum, MacLeod & Grove, N.Y.C., 1979-80; supr. Burson Marstellar, Hong Kong, 1981-83; v.p., dep. dir. food and beverage unit, creative dir. N.Y. office Hill and Knowlton, N.Y.C., 1983-91; mktg. cons. Rice & Rohr, N.Y.C., 1991-93; sr. v.p., dir. consumer mktg. practice Manning, Selvage & Lee, N.Y.C., 1993—. Writer Fast and Healthy Mag., 1991. Mem. Pub. Rels. Soc. Am., Women Execs. in Pub. Rels. Roman Catholic. Home: 18 Westminster Dr Croton On Hudson NY 10520 Office: Manning Selvage & Lee 79 Madison Ave New York NY 10017

RICE, SANDRA DIANE, publicist; b. Eugene, Oreg., May 16, 1964; d. James Robert and Judith Ann (Allen) R. BA, U. Oreg., 1986. Publicist Rogers & Cowan, L.A., 1987-92, PMK, Inc., L.A., 1992—. Alumni Assn. scholar/grantee U. Oreg., 1982, scholar State of Oreg., 1982. Mem. Pub. Rels. Soc. of Am. (L.A. young profls. sect. profl. outreach chair 1989, pres. sect. 1990), Publicist's Guild Am. Office: PMK Inc 955 Carrillo Dr # 200 Los Angeles CA 90048-5400

RICE, SHARON MARGARET, clinical psychologist; b. Detroit, Sept. 4, 1943; d. William Christopher and Sylvia Lucille (Lawecki) R.; m. John Robert Speer, Aug. 14, 1977. AB, Oberlin Coll., 1965; MA, Boston U., 1968, PhD, 1977. Clin. psychologist Los Angeles County Juvenile Probation, L.A., 1969-75, Las Vegas (Nev.) Mental Health Ctr., 1976-81, Foothills Psychol. Assn., Upland, Calif., 1981—; pvt. cons., Claremont, Calif., 1984—. NIMH grantee, 1967-69; recipient Good Apple award Las Vegas Tchrs. Ctr., 1978-80. Mem. APA, Calif. Psychol. Assn., Internat. Soc. for Study of Dissociation, Inst. Noetic Scis., Sigma Xi. Office: Foothills Psychol Assn 715 N Mountain Ave # G Upland CA 91786-4364

RICE, SUE ANN, dean, industrial and organizational psychologist; b. Ponca City, Okla., Sept. 17, 1934; d. Alfred and Helen (Revard) R. BS in Edn., U. Okla., 1956; MA, Cath. U., 1979, PhD, 1988. Ensign USN, 1956, advanced through grades to comdr., 1973; ednl. svcs. officer 9th Naval Dist., Great Lakes, Ill., 1956-58; adminstr., asst. staff, comdr. in-chief Pacific Fleet, Honolulu, 1958-61; head edn. div. Naval Air Sta., Lemoore, Calif., 1961-63; instr., acad. dir. Women Officers' Sch., Newport, R.I., 1963-66; head. tng. div. Naval Command Systems Support Activity, Washington, 1966-70; head, ops. support sec., comdr.-in-chief Lant, Norfolk, Va., 1970-74; sr. U.S. rep. NATO, subgroup 5 orgn. JCS, Washington, 1974-77; ret. USN, 1977; head vocation office Archdiocese of Washington, 1977-78; con. Notre Dame Inst., Arlington, Va., 1989—, dean of students, 1990—; lectr. Cath. U. Am., Washington, 1983-84; bd. dirs. Villa Cortona Apostolic Ctr., Bethesda, 1984-94. Tech. reviewer Personnel Administration, 1964; editor (newsletter) Vocation News, 1978. Conoco scholarship Continental Oil Co., 1952-56; recipient Meritorious Svc. medal Pres. of U.S., 1977, rsch. grant Cath. U., Sigma Xi, 1986. Mem. Washington Acad. Scis., Cath. War Vets. (nat. dir., chmn. nat. security com., nat. youth act subcom., combined Nat. Vets. Assn. rep., post comdr.), Lay Women's Assn. (nat. pres.), Potomac Ch. Human Factors Soc. (assoc.), Kappa Delta Pi, Gamma Phi Beta. Roman Catholic. Office: PO Box 1035 Falls Church VA 22041-0035

RICE-RITCHIE, SHARON MARIE, accountant; b. Sisseton, S.D., May 24, 1953; d. Howard Wendell and Delores Loretta (Janisch) Rice; m. Stephen Christian Ritchie, Apr. 26. 1975; 1 child, Adriane Terese. Grad., Watertown Bus. U., 1972. Mgr. payroll dept. accounts payable Car Tapes Inc., Chatsworth, Calif., 1973-76; supr. acctg. Dynamic Scis. Inc., Chatsworth, 1977-89; supr. accounts payable, asst. to CFO Ambulatory Med. Mgmt., Van Nuys, Calif., 1989-90; owner Woodland Hills Garage, North Hollywood, Calif., 1979—; negotiator fin. Hewlett Packard, Thousand Oaks, Calif., 1981-89. Contbr. Northridge (Calif.) Hosp., 1985, San Sum Med. Ctr., Santa Barbara, Calif., 1990, Henry Mayo Newhall Meml. Hosp., Valencia, 1993. Mem. ASCettes Calif. (pres. 1984-85, author articles 1984-85), San Fernando Valley Quilt Assn. (pres. 1986-87, author newsletter articles 1986-87), Santa Clarita Valley Quilt Guild, Woodland Hills Optimists, Automotive Svcs. Coun. #11, Universal City-North Hollywood C. of C. Democrat. Roman Catholic. Home: 20560 Romar Ln Santa Clarita CA 91350-3801 Office: Woodland Hills Garage 11553 Sherman Way North Hollywood CA 91605-5829

RICH, ADRIENNE, writer; b. Balt., May 16, 1929; d. Arnold Rice and Helen Elizabeth (Jones) R.; m. Alfred H. Conrad (dec. 1970); children: David, Paul, Jacob. AB, Radcliffe Coll., 1951; LittD (hon.), Wheaton Coll., 1967, Smith Coll., 1979, Brandeis U., 1987, Coll. Wooster, Ohio, 1988, CCNY, Harvard U., 1990, Swarthmore Coll., 1992. Tchr. workshop YM-WHA Poetry Ctr., N.Y.C., 1966-67; vis. lectr. Swarthmore Coll., 1967-69; adj. prof. writing divsn. Columbia U., 1967-69; lectr. CCNY, 1968-70, instr., 1970-71, asst. prof. English, 1971-72, 74-75; Fannie Hurst vis. prof. creative lit. Brandeis U., 1972-73; prof. English Douglass Coll., Rutgers U., 1976-79; Clark lectr., disting. vis. prof. Scripps Coll., 1983-84; A.D. White prof.-at-large Cornell U., 1981-87; disting. vis. prof. San Jose State U., 1984-85; prof. English and feminist studies Stanford U., 1986-93; Marjorie Kovler vis. lectr. U. Chgo., 1989. Author: A Change of World, 1951, The Diamond Cutters and Other Poems, 1955, Snapshots of a Daughter-in-Law, 1963, Necessities of Life: Poems, 1962-65, 1966, Leaflets, Poems, 1965-68, Necessities of Life: Poems, 1965-68, 1969, The Will to Change, 1971, Diving into the Wreck, 1973, Poems Selected and New, 1950-74, 1975, Of Woman Born: Motherhood as Experience and Institution, 1976, 10th anniversary ed., 1986, The Dream of a Common Language: Poems, 1974-1977, 1978, others. Mem. nat. adv. bd. Bridges, Boston Women's Fund, Sisterhood in Support of Sisters in South Africa. Recipient Yales Series of Young Poets award, 1951, Ridgely Torrence Meml. award Poetry Soc. Am., 1955, Nat. Inst. Arts and Letters award poetry, 1961, Bess Hokin prize Poetry mag., 1963, Eunice Tietjens Meml. prize, 1968, Shelley Meml. award, 1971, Nat. Book award, 1974, Fund for Human Dignity award Nat. Gay Task Force, 1981, Ruth

Lylly Poetry prize, 1986, Brandeis U. Creative Arts medal for Poetry, 1987, Nat. Poetry Assn. award, 1989, Elmer Holmes Bobst award arts and letters NYU, 1989, others. Mem. PEN, Am. Acad. Arts and Letters (dept. of lit. 1990—), Nat. Writers Union, The Authors Guild, Am. Acad. Arts and Scis. Office: care W W Norton Co 500 Fifth Ave New York NY 10110-0002

RICH, ELIZABETH MARIE, nursing educator; b. Bklyn., Nov. 20, 1949; d. Oren Edward and Catherine (Raffaele) R. ADN, Grossmont Coll., El Cajon, Calif., 1983; BSN, U. Phoenix, 1988; MS, Nat. U., San Diego, 1991. Cert. pub. health nurse, gerontol. nurse. ICU-CCU staff nurse Villa View, San Diego, 1983-85, AMI Valley Hosp., El Cajon, 1985-86; nurse Nursing Registries, 1986-87; charge nurse, supr. nights Beverly Manor Convalescent Home, Escondido, Calif., 1987-88; dir. staff devel. Beverly Manor Convalescent Home, Escondido, 1988-90; DON, nurse educator cons. Vista Del Mar Care Ctr., San Diego, 1990; instr. vocat. nursing Maric Coll. Med. Careers, San Marcos, Calif., 1991-94, curriculum coord., placement coord., 1994—. Mem. Calif. Vocat. Nurse Educators. Home: 872 Venice Gln Escondido CA 92026-3165

RICH, FRANCES LUTHER, sculptor; b. Spokane, Wash., Jan. 8, 1910; d. Elvo Elcourt Deffenbaugh and Irene (Luther Deffenbaugh) Rich. BA, Smith Coll., 1931; art student, Paris studios, 1933-35, Boston Mus. Sch. Art, 1935-36, Cranbrook Acad. Art, Bloomfield Hills, Mich., 1937-40, Claremont (Calif.) Coll., 1946-47, Columbia U., 1946-47; pupil of, Malvina Hoffman, Carl Milles, Alexandre Iacovleff. Dir. pub. relations Smith Coll., 1947-50; with pvt. studios Rome, 1950-52, Paris, 1960-62. Pub. and pvt. marble sculpture include Army-Navy-Air Force Nurses Arlington Nat. Cemetery, Washington, 1938, Terra Cotta, Benedictine Abbey Chapel, Mt. Angel, Oreg., 1954, Bronze Pelican, Earle C. Anthony Bldg., U. Berkeley, Calif., 1958, St. Joseph, Guadelupe Coll., Los Gatos, Calif., 1966; Bronze series St. Francis of Assisi, 4' St. Francis, Little Austria Terrace, Millesgården, Lidingö, Sweden, 1960; 6'7" St. Francis, St. Margaret's Episcopal Ch., Palm Desert, Calif., 1970, 7'6" Pierce-Deree Coll., Mt. Hymettus, Athens, Greece, 1970, 7'6" St. Francis, Pres.'s Garden Smith Coll., Northampton, Mass., 1978, 4'4" bronze Cranbrook Acad. Art Mus., Bloomfield Hills, Mich., 1983, 10' bronze "Our Lady of Combermere" grounds, The Madonna House Lay Apolstolate Tng. Ctr., Combermere, Ont., Can., 1960, 19" bronze "Our Lady of Combermere", Madonna House Chapel, Edmonton, Can., medals of Our Lady of Combermere at Combermere Madonna House Tng. Ctr., and 22" bronze "St. Catherine of Siena" (Santa Catalina Sch., Monterey, Calif.), 1968, 89, " Crucifix, The Madonna Chapel, Grace Cathedral, San Francisco, 1972, 30" bronze crucifix St. Margaret's Episcopal Ch., Palm Desert, Calif., 1990, bronze "The Healer", David L. Reeves Meml. Libr., Cottage Hosp., Santa Barbara, Calif., 1973, 15 bronze "Birds in Flight", Living Desert Reserve, Palm Desert, Calif., 1978; reliefs include: 6 nine ' stone panels Union Bldg., Purdue U., Lafayette, Ind., 1939; bronze 4'x 6' panel "Nunc Dimittis", St. Peter's Episcopal Ch., Redwood City, Calif., 1957; 8' "Our Lady Seat of Wisdom", St. Cecelia Ch., Stanwood, Wash., 1965; 8' bronze "Christ of the Sacred Heart", St. Sebastian's Ch., West Los Angeles, Calif. 1972; portraits include: Margaret Sanger, 1957 and Pres. Herbert Davis, 1950, Nielson Libr., Smith Coll., Northampton, Mass., Prof. Henry Russel Hitchcock, marble bust Alice Stone Blackwell, Boston Pub. Library, 1961; 3'6" terra cotta figure Katharine Hepburn, Shakespeare Mus., 1962 and bronze bust of Hepburn, 1961, both as Cleopatra, at Am. Shakespeare Theatre, Stratford, Conn.; also bronze head Lawrence Langner, Shakespeare Theater Foyer, 1963; bronze head Virgil Thomson, Virgil Thomson Room, NYU, 1977; Smith Coll. Mus. Art collection includes bronze portraits of Katharine Hepburn as Cleopatra, Lotte Lehman, Diego Rivera, 1978, terra cotta portrait of Margaret Sanger, cotta portrait of Lotte Lehman; bronze portrait of Pres. Herbert Davis and bronze bas relief of Laura Scales; marble bust of Alice Stone Blackwell; further sculpture collections Smith Coll. Mus. Art and Cranbrook Acad. Art, 1981; one man shows: Art Ctr., Phoenix, 1954, Santa Barbara Mus. Art, 1955, Calif. Palace Legion of Honor, San Francisco, 1955, Laguna Blanca Sch., Santa Barbara, 1955, Palm Springs Desert Mus., 1969, 77, Smith Coll Mus. Art, 1981, Cranbrook Acad. Art Mus., 1983; group exhbns.: Am. Art Exhibit, World's Fair, N.Y., 1939, First Nat. Biennale Contemporary Religious Art, Set Hall Coll., Pa., 1953, Denver Liturgical Art Show, 1952, De Young Mus., Calif Liturgical Artists, 1952, Grace Cathedral, San Francisco, 1957, Knoedler's Gallery, N.Y.C., 1962, Members Exhibit, Archtl. League, N.Y.C., 1962, Boston Pub. Libr.; 10 bronzes Nat. Liturgical Art Week, Seattle World's Fair, 1962; 8 bronzes "Students of Carl Milles" Exhibit, Millesgården, Lidingö, summer 1986; Milles as Mentor: The Work of Cranbrook Sculptors, 1931-51, 5 bronzes Cranbrook Acad. Art, Bloomfield Hills, Mich., summer, 1990;12 1/2" bronzes of Our Lady of Combermere in each of 27 Madonna House Chapels Lay Apostolates Worldwide, 1989, 4'5" bronze St. Francis of Assisi, Botanic Garden Ctr., Fort Worth. 1990; 15" bronze of St. Margaret of Scotland St. Margaret's Episcopal Ch., Palm Desert, 1990, Canongate Kirk, Edinburgh, 1991; 18" bronze crucifix Canongate Kirk Manse; life size bronze bust Dr. George Bass, underwater archaeologist, 1993; numerous portraits, fountains, small bronzes and silvers for pvt. collectors. Served to lt. comdr. USNR, 1942-46. Mem. Archtl. League N.Y.C., Smith Coll. Alumnae Assn., Cosmopolitan Club (N.Y.C.). Home and Studio: 1208 E Bolivar St Payson AZ 85541 also: 4385 Marina Dr Santa Barbara CA 93110*

RICH, PHYLLIS JEANNE, elementary educator; b. Livermore, Iowa, Dec. 18, 1935; d. John George and Violet Goldie (Smith) Sykes; m. Fred H. Struthers, Feb. 7, 1953 (div. 1962); children: Fred H., Phillip E., Felicia D, Starr, Sheila R.; m. John Edward Rich, May 27, 1972 (dec.). AA, Emmetsburg (Iowa) Jr. Coll., 1970; BA, Buena Vista Coll., 1972; student, various colls., 1975-91. Mail clerk Bunche Store, Ft. Smith, Ark., 1954-55; waitress Chrome Cafe, Algona, Iowa, 1957-61; intermediate sci. and fifth grade tchr. Dunlap (Iowa) Community Sch., 1972—; tchr. Harrison County Poster Context, Dunlap, Iowa, 1984-91, Drug Abuse on local tv, Dunlap, 1991; judge Hawkeye Sci. Fair, West Des Moines, 1987-89. Com. mem. Human Growth & Devel., Dunlap, 1990—; active Fist Meth. Ch., Dunlap, 1972, Am. Legion Auxiliary, Dunlap, 1980, DAV Auxiliary, 1987. Recipient Dist. Tchr. award Harrison County Soil and Water Conservation, Logan, Iowa, 1991, Gov.'s Vol. award State of Iowa, Denison, 1991, cert. of completion Resource Enhancement and Protection, Denison, 1991. Mem. AAYW, Internat. Reading Assn., Profl. Educators of Iowa, Dunlap Tchrs. Orgn. Republican. Methodist. Home: 702 Court St Dunlap IA 51529-1316 Office: Dunlap Community Sch 1101 Iowa St Dunlap IA 51529-1557

RICH, ROSAN, manufacturing executive; b. Sebastopol, Calif., June 1, 1946; d. Emil John and Betty Ceclia (Garcia) Duckhorn; 1 child, Eric. Student, Calif. State U., Sonoma, Rohnert Park, 1964-67. Claims supr. Blue Cross No. Calif., Oakland, 1971-76; treas. Bridge Pubs., L.A., 1980-82; plant mgr. EZ Sportswear, Chatsworth, Calif., 1985-88, v.p. mfg., 1988-90, v.p. distbn. facilities, 1991; shipping mgr. and spl. items prodn. mgr. Jem Sportswear, San Fernando, Calif., 1991-93; spl. items supr. Chorus Line, Vernon, Calif., 1993-94; purchasing mgr. SoftPoint, Inc., Reno, Nev., 1994—. Mem. NAFE, NRA. Democrat. Roman Catholic. Office: SoftPoint Inc # 202 4750 Longley Ln Reno NV 89502-5982

RICH, S. JUDITH, public relations executive; b. Chgo., Apr. 14; d. Irwin M. and Sarah I. (Sandock) R. BA, U. Ill., 1960. Staff writer, reporter Economist Newspapers, Chgo., 1960-61; asst. dir. pub. rels. and communications Coun. Profit Sharing Industries, Chgo., 1961-62; dir. advt. and pub. rels. Chgo. Indsl. Dist., 1962-63; account exec., account supr., v.p., sr. v.p., exec. v.p. and nat. creative dir. Daniel J. Edelman Inc., Chgo., 1963-85; exec. v.p., dir. Ketchum Pub. Rels., Chgo., 1985-89, exec. v.p., exec. creative dir. USA, 1990—; frequent spkr. on creativity and brainstorming. workshop facilitator, spkr. in field. Mem. pub. rels. adv. bd. U. Chgo. Grad Sch. Bus., Roosevelt U., Chgo., DePaul U., Chgo., Gov.'s State U. Mem. Pub. Rels. Soc. Am. (Silver Anvil award, judge Silver Anvil awards), Counselors Acad. of Pub. Rels. Soc. Am. (exec. bd.), Chgo. Publicity Club (8 Golden Trumpet awards). Home: 2500 N Lakeview Ave Chicago IL 60614-1836 Office: Ketchum Pub Rels 142 E Ontario St Chicago IL 60611-2818

RICH, SHARON LEE, financial planner; b. Houston, Sept. 7, 1956; d. Hershel Maurice and Hilda R.; children: Mariah, Sophie. BA, Cornell U., 1977; MAT, U. Chgo., 1978; diploma in fin. planning, Boston U., 1985; EdD, Harvard U., 1986. High sch. tchr. Clear Lake High Sch., Houston, 1978-80; rschr. Harvard U., Cambridge, Mass., 1981-86; fin. planner, pres. Womoney, Belmont, Mass., 1984—; instr. Cambridge Ctr. for Adult Edn. Co-author: The Challenges of Wealth, 1988; co-editor: Women's Experience and Education, 1985. Conf. organizer Haymarket People's Fund, Jamaica Plain, Mass., 1988—; bd. dirs. Boston Women's Fund, 1988-90; speaker Pub. Edn. Svcs., Boston, 1984—; organizer, mem. The Consortium, Boston, 1991—; referral for battered women B'nai Brith Women's Connection Card, Boston, 1991—. Named One of Ams. Top 60 Fin. Advisors, Worth Mag., 1994. Mem. Internat. Assn. Fin. Planners, U.S. Security and Exch. Commn. (registered investment advisor), Inst. CFPs (assoc. mem.), Nat. Assn. Personal Fin. Advisors, Social Investment Forum, Coop. Am. (bus. mem.). Office: Womoney 76 Townsend Rd Belmont MA 02178

RICHARD, ELAINE, educational therapist; b. N.Y.C., Apr. 24, 1930; d. Jacob Michael and Mildred (Levenstein) Simon; m. Jack Richard, Apr. 11, 1954; children: Mark Steven, Susan Richard Weiller. BA, St. Lawrence U., 1950; MA, Columbia U., 1981. Cert. spl. edn. tchr., N.Y. Psychiat. social worker Ralph S. Banay, M.D., N.Y.C., 1950-54, 61-66; asst. to headmaster Dalton Sch., N.Y.C., 1967-70; asst. to prin. Horace Mann Elem. Sch., N.Y.C., 1970-72; dir. admissions Calhoun Sch., N.Y.C., 1972-80; ednl. cons. Ethical Culture Schs., N.Y.C., 1980-81; pvt. practice as ednl. therapist N.Y.C., 1981—; bd. dirs. Ind. Schs. Admissions Assn. Greater N.Y., 1974-80. Mem. Nat. Coun. Tchrs. Math., Assn. for Children with Learning Disabilities, N.Y. Orton-Dyslexia Soc. Home and Office: 501 E 79th St New York NY 10021-0735

RICHARD, MARGRET BULL, accountant and writer; b. Norfolk, Va., Apr. 7, 1930; d. Charles Russell and Margret Worthington (Davis) Bull; m. Lawrence J. Richard Jr., Oct. 4, 1952; children: Margret Leigh, Allan, Steven, Brian. Student, Mary Washington Coll., 1947-48; BA, Nathaniel Hawthorne Coll., 1979; MA in Liberal Studies, Dartmouth Coll., 1985. RN, Va. Pvt. duty nurse St. Luke's Hosp.-Med. Coll. Va., Richmond, 1951-52; postgrad. surg. nurse Polyclinic Hosp., N.Y.C., 1952; operating rm. nurse Polyclinic Hosp.-Kerbs Hosp., N.Y.C. and St. Albans, Vt., 1952-55; gen. duty nurse Mary Hitchcock Hosp., Hanover, N.H., 1957-58, Alice Peck Day Hosp., Lebanon, N.H., 1957-58; corp. clk., acct. Richard Electric, Inc., White River Junction, Vt., 1963—, also bd. dirs.; guest reader, writer elem. schs., Hartford, Vt. and Hanover, 1989—. Pub. co. newsletter, 1993—. Proposal writer Community Betterment Soc., Hartford, 1973-79; writer, dir. League Vt. Writer's Playwrights, Woodstock, Vt., 1993. Mem. Nat. Coun. Tchrs. English, Am. Forestry Assn., League Vt. Writer's Assn., Dartmouth Alumni Assn., Poetry Soc. Vt. (dir. poetry contest 1988, 89, 90), Dartmouth Outing Club (life). Office: Richard Electric Inc PO Box 700 20 A St Wilder VT 05088

RICHARDS, ALETA WILLIAMS, marketing professional; b. Pitts., Nov. 16, 1965; d. John Quincy and Sara Ann (Dorman) Williams; m. Frank D. Richards III, Nov. 16, 1982; 1 chidl, Cassandra Nicolle. BSBA, U. Pitts., 1990. Asst. to exec. directory Allegheny County Pvt. Industry Coun., Pitts., 1984-90; mktg. rep. composite spltys. Miles Corp., Pitts., 1990-93; co-owner Richards Properties, Pitts., 1991-93; tech. mktg. rep. II Miles, Inc., Pitts., 1994—, bus. champion Miles re-engring. project, 1995; cons. AWR Comm., Pitts., 1994—; speaker employment Salem (W.Va.)-Teikyo U., 1991-92; communications graphic designer The Way, The Truth and Life Ministries, Pitts., 1989-91; mentor Mobay Corp. program Reizenstein Mid. Sch., 1990-91. Author, editor: (reference book) Funding Resources Guide, 1989. Speaker Pitts. in Partnership with Parents, 1988-90; bd. dirs. Ptnrs. in Self-Sufficiency, Pitts., 1986-90. Recipient Mayor's Recognition award City of Pitts., 1990. Mem. NAFE, Nat. Assn. Desktop Pubs., Steel Structures Paint Coun., Nat. Assn. Corrosion Engrs., River City Elite Track Club (treas. 1995). Home: PO Box 2816 Pittsburgh PA 15230-2816

RICHARDS, ANN WILLIS, former governor; b. Lakeview, Tex., Sept. 1, 1933; d. Cecil and Ona Willis; children: Cecile, Daniel, Clark, Ellen. B.A., Baylor U., 1954; postgrad., U. Tex., 1954-55. Cert. tchr. Tex. Tchr. Austin Ind. Sch. Dist., Tex.; mgr. Sarah Weddington Campaign, Austin, Tex., 1972, adminstrv. asst., 1973-74; county commr. Travis County, Austin, 1976-82; treas. State of Tex., Austin, 1983-91; gov. State of Tex., until 1994; chair Dem. Nat. Conv. 1992; Austin Transp. Study, Tex., 1977-82, Capital Indsl. Devel. Corp., Austin, Tex., 1980-81, Spl. Commn. Delivery Human Services in Tex., 1979-81; Dem. com. Southern Governor's Assn. Travis County Dem. com. Author (with Peter Knobler): Straight From the Heart, 1989. Mem. com. strategic planning Dem. Nat. Com., 1983; keynote speaker Dem. Nat. Conv., 1988. Named Woman of Yr. Tex. Women's Polit. Caucus, 1981, 83. Mem. Nat. Govs.' Assn. Office: care Office of the Governor State Capitol PO Box 12428 Austin TX 78711

RICHARDS, BARBARA ANNE, community education director; b. Scottsville, Ky., Dec. 15, 1955; d. James E. and Mary Ann (Cooksey) Ogles; m. Nathan Edward Richards, Aug. 28, 1973; children: Dustin Erik, Rebekah Christianne. AA, Western Ky. U., 1993. Cert. profl. sec. V.p. human resources and loans Farmers Nat. Bank, Scottsville, 1973-92; cmty. edn. dir. Allen County Schs., Scottsville, 1992—; sec., treas. Scottsville Allen County Pub. Properties Corp., 1982—, bd. dirs. Cons. Youth and Bus. in Partnership, 1989—, Jr. Achievement, 1991. Mem. Am. Banking Inst. (sec. So. chpt. 1984—), Ky. Banking Assn. (founding bd. young bankers div. 1987—, named Outstanding Personal Econs. Prog. Coord. 1991-92), Profl. Secs. Inst., Nat. Assn. Bank Women (chmn. awards and scholarships com. 1987—). Methodist. Home: 155 Lakeside Dr Scottsville KY 42164-9200

RICHARDS, CARMELEETE A., computer training executive; b. Springport, Ind., Feb. 8, 1948; d. Gordon K. and Virginia Christine (New) Brown; 1 child, Annasheril. AA in Elem. Edn., No. Okla. Coll., 1969; BS in Edn., Southwestern State Coll., Weatherford, Okla., 1971; postgrad., Ashland (Ohio) Coll., 1981—; postgrad. in Edn., U. Phoenix, 1994—. Cert. tchr., Ohio. 6th grade tchr. Scott City, Kans., 1971; salesperson, customer svc. Jafra Cosmetics, 1979-81; br. asst. mgr. Barclays Am. Fin., Columbus, 1981-84; tng. mgr., ednl. dir. Computer Depot, Columbus, Ohio, 1984-85; corp. trainer, exec. sales Litel Telecommunications, Worthington, Ohio, 1985-87; communications cons. Telemarketing Communications of Columbus, Ohio, 1988-89; corp. computer tng. O/E Learning, Troy, Mich., 1989-94; corp. computer trainer ETOP Cols., Ohio, 1989-94. Pres. PTA, 1981-82. Recipient Outstanding Participation award Dorothy Carnegie Pub. Speaking. Mem. NAFE, Am. Soc. for Tng. and Devel., Columbus Computer Soc., Kappa Delta Pi. Baptist.

RICHARDS, CHARLENE ANNA, computer manufacturing company executive; b. Muncie, Ind., May 10, 1963; d. Delmar Gene and Mary Catherine (O'Bryant) Coffman; m. Bruce Richards, Aug. 26, 1983; children: Shaun Michael, Shannon Michelle. Grad. high sch., Albuquerque. Dispatcher asst. Morgan Drive Agy., Albuquerque, 1979-80; account asst. Sta. KOB-TV, Albuquerque, 1980-81, TV copywriter, 1982-83; display advt. cons. Albuquerque Jour.-Tribune, 1981-82; mgr. TLC Svcs., Albuquerque, 1983-87; owner, mgr. The Computer Man, Beaufort, S.C., 1988-91; pres. Computer Techs. Systems, Inc., Beaufort, 1991—, East Coast Holdings, Ltd., Beaufort, 1994—; instr. Tech. Coll. Low Country, Beaufort, 1989. Designer mfg. computer systems. Mem. NAFE, Nat. Fedn. Ind. Bus., U.S. C. of C., Nat. Platform Assn. Republican. Baptist. Home: 8 Wiggins Rd Beaufort SC 29902-9283 Office: 2850 Boundary St Beaufort SC 29902

RICHARDS, DIANA LYN, psychologist; b. Baton Rouge, Dec. 8, 1944; d. William Allen Richards and Julia Viola (Hamilton) Richards Hamilton. AA, Stephens Coll., 1964; BA, U. Colo., 1966; MA, Miami U., Oxford, Ohio, 1969, PhD, 1974. Lic. psychologist, Mo. Dir. community psychol. svcs. Malcolm Bliss Mental Health Ctr., St. Louis, 1975-77; mem. staff Women's Counseling Ctr., St. Louis, 1976-78; mem. faculty Gestalt Inst., St. Louis, 1977-80; instr. Washington U., St. Louis, 1977; dir. psychology Lindenwood Coll. for Individualized Edn., St. Louis, 1978-80, core faculty in psychology, 1984-94; psychologist in pvt. practice St. Louis, 1977—; career cons. Stephens Coll., Columbia, Mo., 1994—; mem. Psychoanalytic Study Group, St. Louis, 1980—; supr. psychology clinic, clin. doctoral program U. Mo., St. Louis, 1994—. Contbr. articles to profl. jours. Mem. Operation Food Search, Defenders of Wildlife, Human Soc., People for Ethical Treatment of Animals, Arts and Edn. Fund, Mo. Bot. Garden, Digit Fund, Earth Island Inst., World Wildlife Fund, Nature Conservancy, Audubon Soc., Human Farming Assn.; mem. A Course in Miracles study group; founding mem. The Pleiades; vol. food ministry Trinity Episcopal Ch. Mem. Am. Psychol. Assn., Mo. Psychol. Assn., St. Louis Psychol. Assn. (program chair 1988-89), Network of Women Psychologists (program chair 1986), St. Louis Psychoanalytic Inst. Democrat. Home: 2014 S Mason Rd Saint Louis MO 63131-1619 Office: 7396 Pershing Ave Saint Louis MO 63130-4206

RICHARDS, ELEANOR GORDON, auditor, accountant; b. Washington, Apr. 30, 1955; d. Gordon Stuart and Virginia May (Whithed) R. BSN, Duke U., 1977; MBA, Vanderbilt U., 1986. RN, Va., Tex.; CPA, Va. Staff nurse Nat. Naval Med. Ctr., Bethesda, Md., 1978-79, clin. nurse specialist, 1980-82; staff nurse Walter Reed Army Med. Ctr., Washington, 1978-80, N.E. Bapt. Hosp., San Antonio, 1982-83, U. Tex. Med. Ctr., San Antonio, 1983-84; auditor Fed. Election Com., Washington, 1986-90; fin. auditor Group Hospitalization and Med. Svcs., Inc., Washington, 1990—. Treas. St. Georges Episcopal Ch., Arlington, Va., 1992—. Mem. D.C. Inst. CPAs. Office: Blue Cross Blue Shield Nat Cap Area 550 12th St SW Washington DC 20065

RICHARDS, ELISABETH MUIR, retired small business owner; b. Worcester, Mass., Nov. 9, 1913; d. Joseph Napoleon and Mabel Elizabeth (Robinson) Muir; m. Mervyn E. Richards, June 10, 1939 (dec.); children: Elisabeth, David, John, William (dec.). BA, Wellesley Coll.; postgrad., Clark U., Assumption Coll., 1993-94. Pres., treas. Muir's Laundry and Drycleaning, Inc., Worcester, 1936-80. Pres. Worcester Better Bus. Bur.; mem. Rep. Exec. Com., Mass. Rep. State Com., Boston, 1970; mem. altar guild All Saints Episcopal Ch.; asst. treas. Washburn Home Aged Women, 1986—; pres. Worcester YWCA, bd dirs. nat. YWCA of USA. Home: 205 Pleasant St Paxton MA 01612-1409

RICHARDS, JANE AILEEN, rehabilitation nursing consultant; b. Oakland, Calif., Oct. 19, 1948; d. John Donald and Mary Dolores (Peters) R. BS in Nursing, U. San Francisco, 1970; MS in Nursing, San Jose State U., 1976. RN; cert. ins. rehab. specialist, cert. case mgr. Staff nurse ICU Mills Meml. Hosp., San Mateo, Calif., 1970-73; asst. head nurse ICU, 1973-76, edn. specialist, 1976-80, mgr. acute rehab. ctr., 1980-83; case mgr. J.R. Assocs., San Mateo, 1983—; nurse cons. Calif. State Dept. Corps., 1989—. Pres. United Cerebral Palsy Assn., Mt. View, Calif., 1983-85, 79-82, 93—, bd. dirs. N.Y.C. chpt., 1983-91, vice chmn. vol. devel. com., N.Y.C., 1989-91. Mem. Rehab. Ins. Nurse Group (pres. 1987-89), Sigma Theta Tau (Alpha Gamma chpt.), PEO (chpt. GR-Calif.). Republican. Avocations: golf, camping. Home and Office: JR Assocs Ste 210 456 Mariner's Island Blvd San Mateo CA 94404

RICHARDS, JETTA JORGENSEN, paralegal; b. Gonzales, Tex., Nov. 8, 1951; d. Elmer Andrew and N. Murl (DuBose) Jorgensen; m. James Ross Richards, July 3, 1976 (div. Mar. 1990); 1 child, Murchinson Ross. BA, U. Tex.-Dallas, Richardson, 1976, postgrad., 1978-81; postgrad., North Tex. State U., 1978; paralegal cert., Inst. Paralegal Studies, 1989. Tchr. Dallas, 1979-81, small bus. owner, 1986-88, contract paralegal, 1989—. Mem. Am. Assn. of U. Women, 1997-79, Dallas Symphony Orch. League, 1997-79, colors bd. mem. Hickory Creek Hunt, 1978, 79, Susan G. Komen Found., 1980; vol. Jim Richards City Coun., Dallas, 1983-88, Steve Bartlett Congress, Dallas, Bill Clements Gov., Dallas. Home: 13730 Spring Grove Ave Dallas TX 75240

RICHARDS, KATHRYN HERBERHOLZ, speech/language pathologist; b. Chicago, Aug. 18, 1941; d. Martin P. and Ella L. (Lindstrom) Herberholz; m. James S. Richards, Dec. 23, 1962 (dec. Mar. 1992); children: Kira Lennon, Eric. BA, Capital U., Columbus, Ohio, 1963; MS, Purdue U., 1965. Speech pathologist Ashland (Ohio) City Schs., 1965-66, 2nd Saratoga Bd. Coop. Ednl. Svcs., South Glens Falls, N.Y., 1966-67, Groton (Conn.) Pub. Schs., 1967, Charleston (S.C.) Speech and Hearing Clinic, 1967-68; pvt. practice Rochester, N.Y., 1970-77; speech pathologist Monroe #2/Orleans Bd. Coop. Ednl. Svcs., Spencerport, N.Y., 1980—, assistive tech. cons./trainer, 1989—, augmentative comm. cons./trainer, 1989—. Mem. Genesee Valley Speech/Lang. Hearing Assn. (membership chair 1992-93), N.Y. State Speech/Lang. Hearing Assn. Home: 53 Hogan Point Rd Hilton NY 14468-8945 Office: Monroe #2/Orleans Bd Coop Ednl Svcs 3599 Big Ridge Rd Spencerport NY 14559-1799

RICHARDS, LACLAIRE LISSETTA JONES (MRS. GEORGE A. RICHARDS), social worker; b. Pine Bluff, Ark.; d. Artie William and Geraldine (Adams) Jones; m. George Alvarez Richards, July 26, 1958; children: Leslie Rosario, Lia Mercedes, Jorge Ferguson. BA, Nat. Coll. Christian Workers, 1953; MSW, U. Kans., 1956; postgrad. Columbia U., 1960. Diplomate Clin. Social Work, Am. Bd. of Examiners in Clin. Social Work, Nat. Assn. Social Workers; cert. gerontologist. Psychiat. supervisory, teaching, community orgn., adminstrv. and consultative duties Hastings Regional Ctr., Ingleside, Nebr., 1956-60; supervisory, consultative and adminstrv. responsibilities for psychiat. and geriatric patients VA Hosp., Knoxville, Iowa, 1960-74, field instr. for grad. students from U. Mo., EEO counselor, 1969-74, 78-90, com. chmn., 1969-70, Fed. women's program coordinator, 1972-74; sr. social worker Mental Health Inst., Cherokee, Iowa, 1974-77; adj. asst. prof. dept. social behavior U. S.D.; instr. Dept. of Psychiatry U. S.D Sch. of Medicine, 1988—, Augustana Coll., 1981-86; outpatient social worker VA Med. and Regional Office Center, Sioux Falls, S.D., 1978-90; med., surg. & intensive care social worker, 1990-92, surg. & intermediate care social worker, 1992—; EEO counselor. Mem. Knoxville Juvenile Adv. Com., 1963-65, 68-70, sec., 1965-66, chmn., 1966-68; sec. Urban Renewal Citizens' Adv. Com., Knoxville, 1966-68; mem. United Methodist Ch. Task Force Exptl. Styles Ministry and Leadership, 1973-74, mem. adult choir, mem. ch. and society com.; counselor Knoxville Youth Line program; sec. exec. com. Vis. Nurse Assn., 1979-80; canvasser community fund drs., Knoxville; mem. Cherokee Civil Rights Commn.; bd. dirs., pub. relations, membership devel. and program devel. cons. YWCA, 1983-85; bd. dirs. Family Svc. Agy., 1989-90, Food Svcs. Ctr. Inc., 1992—; mem. S.D. Symphonic Choir, 1991—. Named S.D. Social Worker of Yr., 1983. Mem. NAACP (chmn. edn. com. 1983-85), AAUW (sec. Hastings chpt. 1958-60), Nat. Assn. Social Workers (co-chmn. Nebr. chpt. profl. standards com. 1958-59), Acad. Cert. Social Workers, S.D. Assn. Social Workers (chmn. minority affairs com., v.p. S.E. region 1980, pres. 1980-82 exec. com. 1982-84, mem. social policy and action com.), Nebr. Assn. Social Workers (chmn. 1958-59), Seventh Dist. S.D. Med. Soc. Aux., Coalition on Aging., Nat. Assn. Social Workers (qualified clin. social worker 1991—), Methodist (Sunday sch. tchr. adult div.; mem. commn. on edn.; mem. Core com. for adult edn.; mem. Adult Choir; mem. Social Concerns Work Area). Home: 1701 E Ponderosa Dr Sioux Falls SD 57103-5019

RICHARDS, LINDA SUE, medical nurse; b. Anderson, Ind., Sept. 4, 1947; d. Hubert Charles Priser and Kathleen (Fisher) Callender; m. Jeffrey Lynn Richards, May 5, 1968; children: Laura Lynn, Stacey Lynn. Student, Porter Coll., 1965-66; LPN, Kokomo Sch. Practical Nursing, Ind., 1986; Kidney Dialysis tech., Ind. U., Indpls.; office lab. tech., Doppler Tech. Head nurse Don J. Wagoner MD, Burlington, Ind., 1986—; EMTD Sharpsville (Ind.) Ambulance Svc., 1976—; kidney dialysis tech. Ind. U. Med. Ctr., Indpls., 1983-86; Liberty Twp. Trustee, Sharpsville, 1983—. Founder and treas. Melanie Boyer Liver Transplant Found., 1985-87; bd. dirs. Kokomo Sch. Practical Nursing, 1989-92. Mem. Nat. Assn. Clin. Lab. Tech., Nat. Assn. LPN. Republican. Methodist. Home: 1777 W 500 N Sharpsville IN 46068-9005 Office: Don J Wagoner MD 601 State Rd 22 E Box 38 Burlington IN 46915

RICHARDS, LYNN, company training executive, consultant; b. Kansas City, Mo., Sept. 2, 1949; d. Robert A. and Betty (Arnold) Nelson. BS in Edn., U. Kans., 1971; MA in Edn., San Diego State U., 1979. Prin. staff ORI, Inc., Silver Spring, Md.; sr. corp. trainer Amerada Hess Corp., Woodbridge, N.J.; tng. and devel. mgr. Kimberly-Clark Corp., Beech Island, S.C.; orgn. devel. mgr. M&M Mars, Hackettstown, N.J.; corp. tng. and devel. mgr. Rohr, Inc., Chula Vista, Calif.; customer edn. mgr. ComputerVision, Corp., San Diego, Calif.; dir. devel. cons. Children's Hosp., San Diego; cons. pvt. practice, San Diego. Contbr. articles to profl. mags. Mem. NSPI (awards com. chmn. 1988, presidential citations, Achievement award).

RICHARDS, MARTA ALISON, lawyer; b. Memphis, Mar. 15, 1952; d. Howard Jay and Mary Dean (Nix) Richards; m. Jon Michael Hobson, May 5, 1973 (div. Jan. 1976); m. 2d, Richard Peter Massony, June 16, 1979 (div. Apr. 1988); 1 child, Richard Peter Massony, Jr. Student Vassar Coll., 1969-

70; AB cum laude, Princeton U., 1973; JD, George Washington U., 1976. Bar: La. 1976, U.S. Dist. Ct. (ea. dist.) La. 1976, U.S. Ct. of Appeals (5th cir.) 1981, U.S. Supreme Ct. 1988, U.S. Dist. Ct. (mid. dist.) La., 1991. Assoc. Phelps, Dunbar, Marks, Claverie & Sims, New Orleans, 1976-77; assoc. counsel Hibernia Nat. Bank, New Orleans, 1978; assoc. Singer, Hutner, Levine, Seeman & Stuart, New Orleans, 1978-80, Jones, Walker, Waechter, Poitevent, Carrere & Denegre, New Orleans, 1980-84; ptnr. Mmahat, Duffy, & Richards, 1984, Montgomery, Barnett, Brown, Read, Hammond & Mintz, 1984-86, Montgomery, Richards & Ballin, 1986-89, Gelpi, Sullivan, Carroll and Laborde, 1989; gen. counsel Maison Blanche Inc., Baton Rouge, 1990-92; gen. counsel La. State Bond Commn., 1992—; lectr. paralegal inst. U. New Orleans, 1984-89, adj. prof., 1989. Contbr. articles to legal jours. Treas. alumni coun. Princeton U., 1979-81. Mem. ABA, La. State Bar Assn., Fed. Bar Assn., New Orleans Bar Assn., Baton Rouge Bar Assn., Nat. Assn. Bond Lawyers, Princeton Alumni Assn. New Orleans (pres. 1982-86). Episcopalian. Home: 7813A Jefferson Place Blvd Baton Rouge LA 70809-7631 Office: La Dept Treasury State Capitol Bldg 3d Fl PO Box 44154 Baton Rouge LA 70804

RICHARDS, PAMELA SPENCE, library and information studies educator; b. N.Y.C., June 2, 1941; d. Guy and Mary Frances (Lavine) R.; m. Jacobus W. Smit, June 6, 1969; children: Guy, Marijke. BA magna cum laude, Harvard U., 1963; MA, Columbia U., 1966, MLS, 1971, DLS, 1979. Adminstrv. asst. German dept. Columbia U., N.Y.C., 1963-69, rsch. assoc. Grad. Sch. Bus., 1972-76; reference libr. Westchester Community Coll., Valhalla, N.Y., 1976, 77; instr. Grad. Sch. Libr. Svc. Rutgers U., New Brunswick, N.J., 1977-79, asst. prof. Grad. Sch. Libr. and Info. Studies, 1979-84, assoc. prof. Sch. Communication, Info. and Libr. Studies, 1984-91, prof., 1991—. Author: Scholars and Gentlemen, 1984, Marketing Books and Journals to Europe and the United Kingdom, 1986; Scientific Information in Wartime: The German and Allied Rivalry 1939-45, 1994; editor-in-chief Jour. of Rutgers U. Librs., 1980-94; assoc. editor Libr. Quar., 1985—, Internat. Libr. Rev., 1989—. Mem. Fedn. Support Act Fellowship Selection Com., 1994. Summer fellow NEH, 1982, Am. Philos. Soc., 1983; IREX fellow, 1994; Martinus Nijoff Found. grantee, 1990; recipient Acad. Specialist award U.S. Info. Agy., 1987, Libr. Edn. Specialist, USSR Coun. Librs. and Am. Coun. Learned Studies, 1991. Mem. ALA, Am. Soc. Info. Sci. (chmn. internat. rels. com. 1988-91), Assn. for Libr. and Info. Sci. Edn. (leader Citizen Am. Delegation to Russia, Lithuania and Czechoslovakia 1992). Home: 90 Morningside Dr New York NY 10027-7124 Office: Rutgers U Sch Info & Libr Studies 4 Huntington St New Brunswick NJ 08901-1071

RICHARDS, RHODA ROOT WAGNER, civic worker; b. Phila., Oct. 2, 1917; d. Edward Stephen and Rhoda Earley (Root) Wagner; student U. Pa., 1937-39; A.A., Wildcliff Jr. Coll., 1938; m. J. Permar Richards, Jr., May 18, 1940; children: Patricia A.V. Richards Cosgrave, J. Permar III. Profl. artist; founder, chmn. Hosp. Corps, Navy League Service, 1941-43; chmn. ARC Nurses Aide Corps, Jacksonville, Fla., 1944-45, Long Beach, Calif., 1945-46; founder, chmn. Fiesta Benefits, Hahnemann Hosp., 1950-57; former chmn. jr. com. Met. Opera; bd. dirs. Phila. Lyric Opera Co.; chmn. Ring for Freedom Republican Campaign of S.E. Pa., 1960; pres. Emergency Aid of Pa., 1961-64; v.p. bd. dirs. Inglis House, Phila., 1977-82; pres. women's bd. Phila. div. Am. Cancer Soc., 1978-81, hon. life mem.; gen. chmn. 1st Ann. Washington Crossing Assembly, 1978; trustee Baldwin Sch.; co-chmn. fundraising com. Ambulatory Service Pavilion, Presbyn.-U. Pa. Med. Center; vice chmn. Women's Commn. for Bicentennial, 1976; bd. dirs., mem. Appleford Commn. Parsons-Banks Arboretum. Vol., chmn. women's bd. Phila. div. Am. Cancer Soc., 1978-86; vol. Phila. chpt. Lupus Found., 1980-81; mem. Delaware Valley women's bd. Freedoms Found. at Valley Forge; past v.p. women's assn., past chmn. fin. com., chmn. centennial spl. event and gen. com. for the celebration Bryn Mawr Presbyn. Ch.; hon. col. corps of cadets Valley Forge Mil. Acad. and Jr. Coll.; founder, chmn. Rittenhouse Preservation Coalition, 1982—; founder, v.p., asst. treas. Preservation Coalition of Greater Phila., 1984—; mem. Hospitality, Phila. Style; chmn. bd. dirs. Emergency Aid of Pa. Found., chmn. 75th anniversary celebration, fin., long range planning, investment coms.; liaison Fairmont Park Waterworks Com. Recipient Crusade award Am. Cancer Soc., 1976; spl. award for community service St. John's Settlement House, 1977; Florence A. Sanson award for patriotism, 1986; named Disting. Dau. of Pa., 1985. Mem. Phila. Mus. Art, Pa. Acad. Fine Arts, Hahnemann Hosp. Women's Assn. (Phila. chpt.), DAR, Daus. of the Cincinnati, Dames of Loyal Legion, Nat. Soc. Colonial Dames of XVII Centuary, Dames Sovereign Mil. Order Temple of Jerusalem, Honolulu Mus. Art, Geneal. Soc. Pa., Am. Hist. Soc., Nat. Trust for Historic Preservation, Smithsonian Instn., Friends of Independence Hall, Friends of Hist. Cliveden, Andalusia Friends. Clubs: Sedgeley, Cosmopolitan, Bald Peak Colony. Home: 1250 Lafayette Rd PO Box 608 Bryn Mawr PA 19010-0608

RICHARDS, RUTH, graphic artist; b. Longmont, Colo., Dec. 29, 1920; d. Fredrick and Mildred Heinley Sullivan; m. Dean A. Richards, July 28, 1937; 1 child, R. Jean. Grad. h.s., Denver. Fashion artist Denver Day Goods; occupational therapist Ft. Logan Mental Health Ctr. One man shows include Denver Vogue Theatre; represented in exhbns. at Denver Art Mus., Gilpim County Arts, 1st Nat. Space Exhibit. Vol. Painting Potting and Piddling, 1962-72. Mem. Englewood Arts Assn. (publicist newspaper 1960-70). Home: 3241 S Ogden Englewood CO 80110

RICHARDS, SHIRLEY MASTIN, public housing executive; b. Osceola, Ark., Jan. 16, 1927; d. Gilbert Edward and Florence Wilma (Sangster) Mastin; m. Robert Herman Richards, Dec. 28, 1930; children: Roberta, Gilbert, Mary. Grad. high sch., Osceola. Cert. public housing mgr. Bank teller Mississippi County Bank, Osceola, 1945-53; mgmt. aide, dir. Osceola Housing Authority, 1961-78, asst. exec. dir., 1978—. Charter mem., sec.-treas. Mississippi County (Ark.) Hist. and Geneal. Soc., 1988—. Republican. Baptist. Home: 515 W Ford Ave Osceola AR 72370-2401 Office: Osceola Housing Authority 501 Coston Ave Osceola AR 72370-3119

RICHARDS, SUE BAKER, insurance representative; b. Biloxi, Miss., Aug. 24, 1954; d. John Luther and Margaret (Ross) Baker; m. Neil Thomas Richards, Nov. 17, 1979; 1 child, Gregory Thomas. BA in Comm., U. Ala., 1977. Cert. ins. counselor; accredited advisor in insurance; cert. profl. ins. woman. Sr. rater Aetna Casualty & Surety, Birmingham, Ala., 1981-85, Mktg. Mgmt., Inc., Pelham, Ala., 1985-87; account coord. Molton, Allen & Williams, Birmingham, 1990-91; sr. account svc. rep. McGriff, Seibels & Williams, Birmingham, 1987-89, 91—. Recipient Edn. Achievement award Order of Blue Goose, 1990, Acad. Excellence award Am. Inst. Chartered Property & Casualty Underwriters, 1994. Mem. Birmingham Assn. Ins. Women (membership chair 1992-93, dir. 1993-94, treas. 1994—, budget com. 1994—, Rookie of Yr. award 1993). Republican. Methodist. Home: 1725 Murray Hill Rd Birmingham AL 35216 Office: McGriff Seibels & Williams Inc 2211 7th Ave S Birmingham AL 35233

RICHARDS, WANDA JAMIE, education educator; b. Brownwood, Tex., Jan. 11, 1930; d. William Steven and Mary (Effie) Rodgers; m. Kenneth E. Graham, Mar. 29, 1949 (div. Jan. 3, 1963); 1 child, Kenneth Jr.; m. Neill Richards, Mar. 15, 1972 (dec. Dec. 2, 1982). BA, Eastern N.Mex. U., 1962; MA, Colo. State Coll., 1964; EdD, U. No. Colo., 1966. Tchr. spl. edn. Pub. Sch., Roswell, N.Mex., 1961-63; dept. head spl. edn. Eastern N.Mex. U., Portales, 1965-69; curriculum researcher N.Mex. State U., Las Cruces, 1969-71; dir. edn. Inst. of Logopedics, Wichita, Kans., 1971-72; owner W. J. Enterprises, Kans., 1973-89; pres., treas. W.J.G. Enterprise Corp., Sedona, Ariz., 1990—; pres.'s coun. on spl. edn. Fed. Govt., Washington, 1967-69; planning cons. in field. Contbr. articles to profl. jours. Mem. Citizens for Quality Edn., Sedona, 1991, C. of C., Sedona, 1990-91, Humane Soc., Sedona, 1991. Recipient Fellowship in Spl. Edn., Fed. Govt. Pub. Law 85962, 1963-65; named Faculty Woman of Yr., Eastern New Mex. U., 1967. Republican. Home: 30 Senora St Sedona AZ 86336-7752

RICHARDS-KORTUM, REBECCA RAE, biomedical engineering educator; b. Grand Island, Nebr., Apr. 14, 1964; d. Larry Alan and Linda Mae (Hohnstein) Richards; m. Philip Ted Kortum, May 12, 1985; children: Alexander Scott, Maxwell James. BS, U. Nebr., 1985; MS, MIT, 1987, PhD, 1990. Asst. prof. biomed. engring. U. Tex., Austin, 1990—. Named Presdl. Young Investigator NSF, Washington, 1991; NSF presdl. faculty fellow, Washington, 1992; recipient Career Achievement award Assn. Advancement Med. Instrumentation, 1992, Dow Outstanding Young Faculty awd., Am. Soc. for Engineering Education, 1992. Mem. AAAS, Am. Soc. Engring. Edn. (Outstanding Young Faculty award 1992), Optical Soc. Am., Am. Soc. Photobiology. Office: U Tex Dept Elec & Computer Engring Austin TX 78712

RICHARDSON, ARLINE ANNETTE, accountant, comptroller; b. N.Y.C., Aug. 20, 1939; d. Charles Sidney and Kathleen Gertrude (Sinclair) Hunt; m. David Edward Richardson, Sept. 13, 1958; children: Valerie-Jayne, LaVerne; stepchildren: James, David, Carl. AA, Bronx (N.Y.) C.C., 1976; BBA, CUNY, 1979, MPA, 1984. Mgr. patient accounts Jewish Home and Hosp. for Aged, N.Y.C., 1960-80; chief bookkeeper Edwin Gould Svcs. for Children, N.Y.C., 1980-81; staff acct. N.Y. Hosp., N.Y.C., 1981-84; mgr. Met. Transp. Authority, N.Y.C., 1984-92; compt. The Computer Lab., Morrisville, N.C., 1993—. Vol. community tax aide, N.Y.C., 1979-83; tutor Henderson (N.C.) Mid. Sch., 1993—. Mem. Am. Assn. Ret. Persons (assoc. dist. coord., instr. tax-aide program North Ctrl. N.C. 1993—), Henderson Bus. and Profl. Women's Club, Beta Gamma Sigma, Phi Theta Kappa. Home: 1614 Peace St Henderson NC 27536-3549 Office: The Computer Lab 2700 Gateway Centre Ste 300 Morrisville NC 27560-9137

RICHARDSON, BARBARA HULL, state legislator, social worker; b. Danville, Pa., Sept. 30, 1922; d. Robert Alonzo and Clara Lucille (Woodruff) H.; widowed; children: Barbara Follansbee, Lawrence, Christine, Lovel Pratt. BA, Bryn Mawr Coll., 1944; MSW, Smith Coll., 1973. Social worker child and family svcs. divsn. children and youth svcs. HHS, Keene, N.H., 1969-71; adminstr. child and family svcs. HHS, Concord, N.H., 1975-88, supr., policy writer, 1988-91; mem. N.H. Ho. Reps., Concord, 1992—. Trustee Meeting Sch., 1980—; bd. dirs. Cheshire Housing Trust, 1986-93, pres., 1993—; adv. bd. Casey Family Svcs. N.H., 1990—; vol. Hospice Monadnock Region, 1991—; mem. community coun. Luth. Social Svcs. New England, 1993—. Democrat. Home: 101 Morgan Rd Richmond NH 03470-4909 Office: NH Ho of Reps State Capitol Concord NH 03301

RICHARDSON, BETH ANN, magazine editor, diaconal minister, consultant; b. Norman, Okla., Apr. 4, 1957; d. Charles H. and Margaret E. (Wilson) R. BA, Oklahoma City U., 1979; MDiv, Vanderbilt U., 1984. Ordained diaconal min. United Meth. Ch., 1984. Group coord. Appalachia Svc. Project, Nashville, 1979-81; asst. editor Alive Now mag. The Upper Room, Nashville, 1986—; co-coord., founder Reconciling Congregation Program, Nashville, 1984-87; cons. Ctr. for Prevention Sexual and Domestic Violence, Seattle, 1992-93; trainer on clergy misconduct Tenn. Conf., United Meth. Ch., 1993. Author: Storyteller's Companion to the Bible, 1991, 94; compiler, editor: Seasons of Peace, 1986; contbr. articles to profl. publs. Mem. Clergy and Laity Concerned, Nashville, 1979-83; bd. dirs. Penuel Ridge Retreat Ctr., Ashland City, Tenn., 1985-92. Recipient Degree of Light award Kappa Phi, 1990, 93; Harold S. Vanderbilt scholar, 1981-84. Mem. Fellowship United Meths. in Worship, Music and Other Arts, Kappa Phi Alumnae. Office: The Upper Room 1908 Grand Ave Nashville TN 37212-2129

RICHARDSON, BETTY KEHL, nursing administrator, counselor, researcher; b. Jacksonville, Ill., Mar. 24, 1938; d. Alfred Jason and Hilda (Emmons) Kehl; m. Joseph Richardson, June 27, 1959 (div. 1980); children: Mark Joseph, Stephanie Elaine. BA in Nursing, Sangamon State U., 1975, MA in Adminstrn., 1977; MSN, Med. Coll. Ga., 1980; PhD in Nursing, U. Tex., 1985. Cert. advanced nursing adminstrn., clin. specialist child and adolescent psychiat. nursing ANCC; lic. profl. counselor, marriage and family counselor. Instr. nursing Lincoln Land Community Coll., Springfield, Ill., 1978-79; acting dir. nursing MacMurray Coll., Jacksonville, Ill., 1979-81; asst. prof. Sangamon State U., Springfield, 1981-82; adminstr. children and adolescent programs Shoal Creek Hosp., Austin, 1989-90; nursing dir. Austin State Hosp., 1983-89; therapist San Marcos (Tex.) Treatment Ctr., 1989-90; instr. Austin C.C., 1990—; pvt. practice psychotherapy, Austin, 1990—. Advising editor: Parenting in the 90s jour.; contbr. articles to profl. jours. Pres. PTA, 1968. Named Outstanding Nurse, Passavant Hosp., 1958, Fabulous 5 Nurse of the Yr. TNA, 1994-95; recipient Plaque for Outstanding Leadership, Austin State Hosp., 1989. Mem. ANA, Ill. State Geneal. Soc. (corr. sec. 1970-73), Assn. Play Therapy, Rotary, Sigma Theta Tau, Phi Kappa Phi. Methodist. Home: 5207 Doe Valley Ln Austin TX 78759-7103 Office: Austin C C 1020 Grove Blvd Austin TX 78741-3300

RICHARDSON, CAROL ANN, electrical engineer, educator; b. Bismark, N.D., Dec. 4, 1944; d. Harold A. and Virginia E. (Kroeber) Foltz; m. Holbrook Mann Richardson, Nov. 29, 1969; children: Gunnar, Margery. BSEE, U. Wyo., 1967; MSEE, Union Coll., 1975. Elect. engr. Collins Radio Co., Cedar Rapids, Iowa, 1967-72, GE, Schnectady, N.Y., 1972-77; from asst. to assoc. prof. Rochester (N.Y.) Inst. Tech., 1978-89, prof., 1990—; dept. chmn., 1994—; grant author NSF, 1989. Mem. IEEE (chair 1990), Am. Soc. for Engring. Educators, Soc. Women Engrs. (sr. mem., pres. 1989), Rochester Engring. Soc. (pres. 1991). Office: Rochester Inst Tech 78 Lomb Memorial Dr Rochester NY 14623

RICHARDSON, CYNTHIA SUE, music educator; b. N.J., July 21, 1959; d. William Alfred and Joan Carol (DeMar) R. BA, Monmouth Coll., 1981, MA in Edn., 1988, MS in Edn., 1992. Pianist First Ch. of Christ Scientist, Red Bank, N.J., 1972—; tchr. Freehold (N.J.) Twp. Bd. Edn., 1981-82; asst. mgr. Abraham and Straus Pianos, Eatontown, N.J., 1988-89, musician, pianist, 1989-91; mgr. Tustings Piano Co., Asbury Park, N.J., 1989-90; tchr. Sea Girt (N.J.) Bd. Edn., 1982—, tchr.-in-charge, chairperson music dept., 1991—, dir. theater group, 1984—; chairperson selection com. N.J. Tchr. Recognition Program, Monmouth County, 1988-89. Author: A Pre-High Approach to Music History, 1987, Interdisciplinary Approach to Music Appreciation, 1992. Corr. sec. Sea Girt PTO, 1992. Recipient Jr. Artist award Piano Tchrs. Congress of N.Y., 1981; named Tchr. of Yr. Gov.'s Convocation on Excellence in Teaching, 1990. Mem. Music Educators Nat. Conf. (pres. 1982), All Shore Music Conf. (sec. 1983-85), People for the Ethical Treatment of Animals, Principia Club Coastal N.J. (sec. 1984—), Kappa Delta Pi (Jr. Tchr. award 1981), Phi Alpha Theta. Democrat. Christian Scientist. Home: 71 Cooper Blvd Red Bank NJ 07701 Office: Sea Girt Bd Edn Bell Pl Sea Girt NJ 08750

RICHARDSON, DEANNA RUTH, microbiologist; b. Columbus, Ohio, Jan. 7, 1956; d. Raymond and Anna Mary (Underwood) R. BS, Ohio State U., 1978. Lab tech. Ohio Dept. Agr., Reynoldsburg, Ohio, 1978-81, lab technologist, 1981-86, microbiologist, 1986—. Active East Columbus Christian Ch.; mem. Neighborhood Civic Assn., 1983-87. Mem. Ohio Valley Inst. Food Technologists, Vet. Microbiologists Assn., Ohio State U. Alumni Assn., Franklin County Alumni Club, Smithsonian Instn., Nat. Wildlife Fedn., Internat. Wildlife Fedn., World Wildlife Fund, African Wildlife Found., Columbus Zoo, Ohio State U. Century Club, Ohio State U. Friend of the Wexner Art Ctr. Home: 6267 Barberry Holw Columbus OH 43213-3308 Office: Ohio Dept Agr Labs 8995 E Main St Reynoldsburg OH 43068-3398

RICHARDSON, DOROTHY HOOD, minister; b. Clayton, N.C., Aug. 2, 1943; d. Gillis Jr. and Malissie (Sanders) Hood; m. James Richardson, Aug. 19, 1961; children: Linda Faye Richardson-Jones (Mrs. Jay Jones), Beverly Ann Richardson-Ham (Mrs. Jerry Ham), Geraldine Richardson-Royal (Mrs. Ronnie Royal), Debra J. BTh, United Christian Coll., 1983; cert. of leadership in pers. rels., N.C. State U.; postgrad. Sch. Divinity, Duke U. Ordained to ministry AME Ch. as elder, 1983. Pastor St. Peter AME Ch., Warsaw, N.C., 1984-86, St. Paul AME Ch., Kenly, N.C., 1986—, Lee's Chapel AME Ch., Selma, N.C., 1986—. Founder, treas. Clayton Ministerial Alliance, v.p., 1989—; mem. exec. bd., co-coord. Kenly Area Ministry, 1987—; mem. Johnson County Ministerial Alliance; founder Inspirational Singers, Clayton, Richardson Singers, Clayton, W.M. Cooper Heritage Alumni. Recipient plaque Natvar, Inc., Clayton, 1982, pin, 1987, cert. of recognition Missionary Soc., Smithfield, N.C., 1988, plaque Inspirational Gospel Singers, cert. Sallie Richardson Missionary Soc. Mem. N.C. Conf. AME Ch. (asst. supt., head resolution com.), Order Ea. Star (chaplain Star of Hope chpt. 70). Home: 4434 Peele Rd Clayton NC 27520-9082

RICHARDSON, ELSIE HELEN, retired elementary education educator; b. Vancouver, Wash., Feb. 1, 1918; d. Anthony William and Marie Julia (Dusek) Podhora-Clark; m. Clyde Stanley Richardson, Oct. 16, 1944 (dec. 1989). BA, Cen. Washington Coll. Edn., 1939. Cert. jr. high sch. prin.; cert. life elem. tchr., Calif., life spl. secondary to teach mentally retarded; cert. psychometrist, Calif. Tchr. 2d and 3d grades Randle (Wash.) Sch. Dist., 1939-40; remedial tchr. Randle, 1940-41; 2d grade tchr. Seattle Sch. Dist., 1941-44; remedial tchr., child guidance, mental tester Vancouver, Wash., 1944-45; child guidance, mental tester 3d grade Lancaster (Calif) Sch. Dist., 1946-48; tchr. spl. edn. Bakersfield (Calif.) Sch. Dist., 1948-49; tchr. 2d grade Norco (Calif.) Sch. Dist., 1950-51; tchr. 4th grade Chino (Calif.) Sch. Dist., 1951-55, tchr. spl. edn., 1955-79, ret., 1979. Leader Girl Res., Camp Rimrock, Wash., summer 1939; leader Bluebird Club, 1939. Recipient Cert. of Appreciaiton, State Assembly of Calif., 1979. Mem. NEA, AAUW, Am. Assn. Ret. Persons, Calif. Tchrs. Assn. (rep.), Calif. Ret. Tchrs. Assn., Vancouver Edn. Assn., Chino Tchrs. Assn. (past v.p., sec.), Calif. Tchrs. Assn.), PTA (life), Fun After Fifty Club, Delta Kappa Gamma.

RICHARDSON, EMILIE WHITE, manufacturing company executive, investment company executive, lecturer; b. Chattanooga, July 8; d. Emmett and Mildred Evelyn (Harbin) White; B.A., Wheaton Coll., 1951; 1 dau., Julie Richardson Morphis. With Christy Mfg. Co., Inc., Fayetteville, N.C., 1952—, sec. 1956-66, v.p., 1967-74, exec. v.p., 1975-79, pres., chief exec. officer, 1980—; v.p. E. White Investment Co., 1968-83, pres., 1983—; cons. Aerostatic Industries, 1979—; v.p. Gannon Corp., 1981—; cons. govt. contacts and offshore mfg., 1981—; lectr., speaker in field. Vice pres. public relations Ft. Lauderdale Symphony Soc., 1974-76, v.p. membership, 1976-77, adv. bd., 1978—; active Atlantic Found., Ft. Lauderdale Mus. Art, Beaux Arts, Freedoms Found.; mem. East Broward Women's Republican Club, 1968—, Americanism chmn., 1971-72. Mem. Internat. Platform Assn., Nat. Speakers Assn., Fla. Speakers Assn. Presbyterian. Clubs: Toastmasters, Coral Ridge Yacht Club. Home: 1531 NE 51st St Fort Lauderdale FL 33334-5709 Office: 3311 Fort Bragg Rd Fayetteville NC 28303-4763

RICHARDSON, GAIL MARGUERITE, community services agency executive; b. Brattleboro, Vt., Oct. 15, 1955; d. Guilford Elwin and Verna Marie (Buckey) Richardson; m. Eric Paul Johnson, Oct. 16, 1982. BS in Bus. Adminstrn., U. Vt., 1978. CPA, Vt. In-charge auditor P.F. Jurgs & Co., Burlington, Vt., 1978-81; assoc. R.F. Lavigne Co., Burlington, 1981-82; supr. fin. reporting C & S Wholesale Grocers, Inc., Brattleboro, Vt., 1982-86; audit supt., non-profit specialist Joseph Pieciak & Co., Brattleboro, 1986-89; comptroller, chief fin. officer Marlboro (Vt.) Coll., 1990-92; contr. Seventh Generation, Colchester, Vt., 1992-93; primary caregiver V. Buffum, Shelburne, Vt., 1993-94; tng. specialist Howard Cmty. Svcs., Burlington, Vt., 1994—; dir. Vt. Student Assistance Corp., Winooski, 1991—; prof. Cmty. Coll. Vt., Brattleboro, 1987-90; fin. cons. Assist, Inc., Wilder, Vt., 1982-86, 94—. Treas. Vt.-N.H. Belfast Kids, Inc., Brattleboro, 1987-91, Brattleboro Child Devel. Corp., 1989-90; active Big Bro. and Big Sister Program, Brattleboro, 1983-85; asst. basketball coach Vt. Spl. Olympics, Burlington. Office: Howard Community Services Burlington VT 05401

RICHARDSON, GRACE ELIZABETH, consumer products company executive; b. Salem, Mass., Nov. 22, 1938; d. George and Julia (Sheridan) R.; m. Ralph B. Henderson, Mar. 3, 1979. B.S., Simmons Coll., 1960; M.S., Cornell U., 1962; M.B.A., NYU, 1981. Textile technologist Harris Research Lab., Washington, 1962-65; instr. Simmons Coll., Boston, 1965-66; dir. consumer edn. materials J.C. Penney, N.Y.C., 1966-73; dir. residential conservation Con Edison, N.Y.C., 1974-81; dir. consumer affairs Chesebrough-Ponds, Greenwich, Conn., 1981-85; v.p. consumer affairs Colgate Palmolive, N.Y.C., 1985—. Named Nat. Bus. Home Economist of Yr., Home Economists in Bus., 1979; recipient Consumer Edn. award Major Appliance Consumer Action Panel, 1977. Mem. Am. Home Econs. Assn. (v.p. external affairs 1983-85), Cornell U. Council, 1981-88. Nat. Coalition Consumer Edn. (bd. dirs. 1983—). Home: 531 Main St New York NY 10044-0105 Office: Colgate Palmolive Co 300 Park Ave New York NY 10022-7402

RICHARDSON, IRENE M., company executive; b. Columbia, Tenn., Oct. 22, 1938; d. John Frank and Beatrice (Hill) Murphy; m. Joseph Richardson, Dec. 27, 1960; children: Pamela, Joseph, John, Karen. BS, Ramapo Coll., Mahwah, N.J., 1981; MBA, Farleigh Dickinson U., 1987; nursing diploma summa cum laude, St. Thomas Sch. of Nursing, Nashville, 1959. RN, N.J.; cert. sr. profl. in human resources. Clin. instr. St. Thomas Hosp., Nashville; coord. edn., staff nurse St. Clare's Hosp., Denville, N.J.; dir. edn. St. Clares Riverside Med. Ctr., Denville; pres. Cygnus Assocs., Inc., Kinnelon, N.J., 1986—. Author: RN Job Satisfaction. Recipient U.S. Pub. Health Svc. scholarship. Mem. Am. Soc. for Health Care Edn. and Tng., Soc. for Health Care Edn. and Tng. N.J. (bd. dirs.), Women's Svc. Orgn. Home: 65 Fayson Lake Rd Kinnelon NJ 07405-3129

RICHARDSON, JUDITH VAS, naval administrator; b. Budapest, Hungary; m. John B. Richardson, Apr. 9, 1983; children: Kevin M., Emily I., Natalie G. BS magna cum laude, U. Md., 1974; MBA summa cum laude, George Washington U., 1981. Cert. Supervisory Excellence Program, Consolidated Civilian Pers. Office; cert. acquisition profl. Contract specialist Naval Air Systems Command, Arlington, Va., 1974-82, procuring contracting officer, 1982-84, procurement analyst spl. projects, 1986-91, supervisory procurement analyst, 1991—; procurement analyst Asst. Sec. of Navy, Arlington, 1984-86. Author: Naval Air Systems Command Handbook for Contract Specialists, 1990, 94 (Acquisition Improvement award and Blanche Witte Meml. award 1991). SECNAV fellow Sec. Navy, 1980; recipient Outstanding Acad. Achievement award Nat. Contracts Mgmt. Assn., 1981. Mem. Beta Gamma Sigma.

RICHARDSON, JULIEANNA LYNN, cable television executive; b. Pitts., June 10, 1954; d. Julius Laconia and Margaret (Barfield) R. BA, Brandeis U., 1976; JD, Harvard U., 1980. Bar: Ill. 1980. Corp. lawyer Jenner & Block, Chgo., 1980-82; asst. cable adminstr., chmn. Chgo. Cable Commn., 1985; pres. Richardson & Assocs., Chgo., 1985-86; pres., chief exec. officer Shop Chgo., Inc., 1986—. Bd. dirs. Kuumba Theatre, Chgo., 1980-88, Chgo. Reporter, 1986-88. Mem. ABA, Ill. Bar Assn., Nat. Assn. Telecommunications Officers and Adminstrs., Lawyers for Creative Arts (bd. dirs. 1983—). Club: Harvard (Chgo.). Home: 2635 N Talman Ave # 1so Chicago IL 60647-1821

RICHARDSON, KATHLEEN, microbiologist, educator; b. Balt., Aug. 24, 1950; d. Wilbur Andeen and Elouise (Bidwell) R. BA, UCLA, 1972, PhD, 1981; MS, Calif. State U., San Diego, 1976. Teaching asst. dept. microbiology Calif. State U., 1973-76; predoctoral fellowship UCLA, 1976-81; postdoctoral fellowship dept. microbiology/immunology U. Mo., Columbia, 1981-83; postdoctoral fellow Ctr. for Vaccine Devel. U. Md., Balt., 1983-85; asst. prof. dept. microbiology and immunology Oreg. Health Scis. U., Portland, 1985-93; staff scientist Gen. Atomics, San Diego, Calif., 1993—. Author rsch. publs. in bacterial pathogenesis of Vibrio cholerae. Rsch. grantee Oreg. Med. Rsch. Found., 1985-86, 89-90, NIH-NIAID, 1986-89, 91-96. Mem. Am. Soc. Microbiology, AAAS, Iota Sigma Pi. Office: Gen Atomics Biosciences 3550 General Atomics Ct San Diego CA 92121-1122

RICHARDSON, LAUREL WALUM, sociology educator; b. Chgo., July 15, 1938; d. Tyrrell Alexander and Rose (Foreman) R.; m. Herb Walum, Dec. 27, 1959 (div. 1972); children: Benjamin, Joshua; m. Ernest Lockridge, Dec. 12, 1981. AB, U. Chgo., 1955, BA, 1956; PhD, U. Colo., 1963. Asst. prof. Calif. State U., Los Angeles, 1962-64; postdoctoral fellow Sch. Medicine Ohio State U., Columbus, 1964-65, asst. prof. sociology, 1970-75, assoc. prof., 1975-79, prof. sociology, 1979—; asst. prof. sociology Denison U., Granville, Ohio, 1965-69; mem. editorial bd. Jour. Contemporary Ethnography, Symbolic Interaction, Gender & Soc., Qualitative Sociology, Sociol. Quar. Author: Dynamics of Sex and Gender, 1977, 3d edit. 1988, The New Other Woman, 1985, Die Neve Andere, 1987, A Nova Outra Mulher, 1987, Writing Strategies: Reaching Diverse Audiences, 1990, Gender and University Teaching: A Negotiated Difference, 1991n; editor: Feminist Frontiers, 1983, 2d edit., 1989, 3rd. edit., 1992; contbr. over 100 research articles and papers. Ford Found. fellow, 1954-56; NSF dissertation fellow, 1960-62; post doctoral fellow Vocat. Rehab., Columbus, 1964; grantee Ohio Dept. Health, 1986-87, Nat. Inst. Edn., 1981-82, NIMH, 1972-74, NSF, 1963-64, NEH, 1992; recipient Disting. Affirmative Action award Ohio State U., 1983. Mem. Am. Sociol. Assn. (com. on coms. 1980-81, com. on pub. info. 1987—), North Ctrl. Sociol. Assn. (pres. 1986-87), Sociologists for Women in Soc. (coun. mem. 1978-80), Ctrl. Ohio Sociologists for Women in Soc. (past pres.), Women's Poetry Workshop, Soc. for Study of Symbolic

Interaction (publs. com.). Democrat. Office: Ohio State Univ Dept of Sociology 190 N Oval Mall Columbus OH 43210-1321

RICHARDSON, LILY PENDARVIS, occupational health nurse; b. Columbia, N.C., Feb. 23, 1939; d. Theophilus Pendarvis and Comeller (Bowser) Johnson; m. Napoleon Richardson, Apr. 4, 1959; children: Donald Felton, Napoleon Jr. BS cum laude, N.C. A&T U., 1961. RN, D.C. Charge nurse L. Richardson Hosp., Greensboro, N.C., 1961-63; charge nurse medicine Georgetown U. Med. Ctr., Washington, 1963-64; charge nurse of nursery D.C. Gen. Hosp., Washington, 1964-67; occupational health nurse, occupational health adminstr. FBI, Washington, 1967—; part time instr. practical nurses Dudley High Sch., Greensboro, 1962; cons. Establishing Health Units, 1990-94, Med. Standard Task Force, Washington, 1993, Bloodborne Pathogen Task Force, 1993. Active cmty. svc. Rosemary Hills Sch., Silver Spring, Md., 1992-94, sch. bd., 1993; blood pressure screener, counselor at several cmty. chs. and cmty. health ctrs.; mail worker Health Reform Com., Washington, 1993-94. Mem. NAACP, Nat. Black Nurses Assn., Black Nurses Greater Washington D.C. ARea (rec. sec. 1985—), Met. Washington Assn. Occupational Health Nurses, Teloca Nursing Alumni (parliamentarian 1970—), A&T Alumni, Sigma Theta Tau (Mutau chpt. internat. charter, Gamma Beta chpt. 1 of 100 Extraordinary Nurses 1994). Home: 2212 Ross Rd Silver Spring MD 20910-2336

RICHARDSON, MARGARET MILNER, federal agency administrator, lawyer; b. Waco, Tex., May 14, 1943; d. James W. and Margaret Wiebusch Milner; m. John L. Richardson, July 22, 1967; 1 child, Margaret Lawrence. AB in Polit. Sci., Vassar Coll., 1965; JD with honors, George Washington U., 1968. Bar: Va. 1968, D.C. 1968, U.S. Dist. Ct. D.C. 1968, U.S. Ct. Appeals (4th, 5th, D.C. and Fed. cirs.) 1968, U.S. Claims Ct. 1969, U.S. Tax Ct. 1970, U.S. Supreme Ct. 1971. Clk. U.S. Ct. Claims, Washington; with Office Chief Counsel IRS, Washington, 1969-77; with Sutherland, Asbill and Brennan, Washington, 1977-80, ptnr., 1980-93; commr. IRS, Washington, 1993—; mem. commr.'s adv. group IRS, 1988-90, chair, 1990; mem. fed. tax adv. group Prentice Hall. Contbr. articles to profl. jours. Assisted Clinton 1992 gen. election campaign; served as team leader Justice Dept./Civil Rights Cluster during Presdl. Transition. Mem. ABA, D.C. Bar Assn. (tax sect.), Va. State Bar Assn., Fed. Bar Assn. (coun. taxation), Fin. Women's Assn. N.Y. Office: IRS 1111 Constitution Ave NW Washington DC 20224-0001

RICHARDSON, MARTHA, nutrition analyst; b. Noble, La., Apr. 22, 1917; d. Alexander M. and Olive (Barlow) R.; A.B., U. Mo., 1938, Ph.D., 1953; M.S., Kans. State U., 1939. Dietitian, William Newton Meml. Hosp., Winfield, Kans., 1940-42, Molly Stark Sanatorium, Canton, Ohio, 1942-47; asst. dir. residence halls, instr. home econs. U. Mo., 1947-50, instr. home econs., 1951-53; head of foods and nutrition U. Utah, 1953-55; nutrition analyst Agrl. Research Service, Washington, 1955-80. Named Disting. Alumna, U. Mo., 1968. Fellow AAAS; mem. Am. Dietetic Assn., Am. Home Econs. Assn., Am. Med. Writers Assn., Am. Inst. Food Techologists, Am. Chem. Soc. Am. Assn. Cereal Chemists, Am. Forestry Assn., AAUW, N.Y. Acad. Scis., Sigma Xi, Gamma Sigma Delta, Phi Upsilon Omicron, Sigma Delta Epsilon. Contbr. articles to profl. jours. Home: 18700 Walkers Choice Rd Apt 302 Gaithersburg MD 20879-2552

RICHARDSON, MARY LOU, psychotherapist; b. Topeka, Oct. 4, 1953; d. Darrell and Beverly Nutter; m. Kenneth T Richardson Jr. children: Shad Martin, Cheralyn Pasbrig, Kenneth T Richardson III, Russ Richardson. Cert. addictions counselor, Ariz.; cert. Nat. Assn. of Alcolism and Drug Abuse Counselors. Counselor Compcare Alcoholism Ctr. The Meadows Treatment Ctr., Phoenix, 1986-88; co-dir. Phoenix Cons. & Counseling Assocs., Ariz., 1989—; founder and adminstr. The Orion Found., Ariz.; project mem. The Hutoomkhum Com. and Support Program, Hopi Reservation, Ariz.; cons. Baywood Hosp., 1988-89; faculty instr. The Recovery Source, 1989-90; chair Nat. Conv. Women, 1992. Author: Women's Acts of Power, 1991-93, Relationship Recovery, 1992, Women's Empowerment, 1992-94, Body, Mind & Spirit, 1994. Mem. Am. Mental Health Counselors, Am. Counseling Assn., Nat. Assn. Alcoholism & Drug Abuse Counselors, Nat. Reciprocity Consortium. Office: Phoenix Cons & Counseling Assocs 5333 N 7th St Ste A202 Phoenix AZ 85014-2803 also: PO Box 3045 Sedona AZ 86340

RICHARDSON, MIRANDA, actress; b. Lancashire, England, 1958. Studied, Drama Program Bristol. Stage performances London: Moving, All My Sons, Who's Afraid of Virginia Woolf, The Life of Einstein, A Lie of the Mind; others include The Changling, Mountain Language; TV appearances: The Hard World, Sorrel and Son, A Woman of Substance, Underworld, Death of the Heart, (series) Black Adder II, Sweet as You Are, (miniseries) Die Kinder; films: Dance with a Stranger, 1985, The Innocent, 1986, Empire of the Sun, 1987, Eat the Rich, 1987, Twisted Obsession, 1990, The Bachelor, 1991, Enchanted April, 1992, Damage, 1992, The Crying Game, 1992 (Acad. award nominee for best supporting actress), Fatherland, HBO, 1994 (Golden Globe award), Tom & Viv, 1994 (Acad. award nominee for best actress 1995). Office: care Susan Smith & Assocs 192 Lexington Ave New York NY 10016*

RICHARDSON, NATASHA JANE, actress; b. May 11, 1963; d. Tony Richardson and Vanessa Redgrave; m. Liam Neeson, July 3, 1994. Acting debut on stage at Leeds (England) Playhouse, 1983; appearences include (plays) A Midsummer's Night Dream, Hamlet, 1985, The Seagull, 1985, High Society, 1987, Anna Christie, 1993 (Tony award nominee 1993, Drama Desk award), (films) Every Picture Tells a Story, 1984, Gothic, 1987, A Month in the Country, 1987, Patty Hearst, 1988, Fat Man and Little Boy, 1989, The Handmaid's Tale, 1990, The Comfort of Strangers, 1991, The Favor, The Watch and the Very Big Fish, 1992, Past Midnight, Widows' Peak, 1994, Nell, 1994, (TV) In a Secret State, 1984, The Copper Beaches, 1984, Ghosts, 1986, Suddenly Last Summer, 1992, Hostages, 1993, Zelda, 1993. Recipient Most Promising Newcomer award Plays & Players, 1986; named Best Actress by London Theatre Critics, Plays & Players, 1990, Evening Standard Best Actress, 1990.

RICHARDSON, PATRICIA, actress; b. Bethesda, Md., Feb. 23, 1951; d. Laurence Baxter and Elizabeth (Howard) R.; m. Raymond Baker, June 20, 1982; children: Henry, Roxanne, Joseph. BFA, So. Meth. U., 1972. Appearences include (Broadway) Gypsy, Loose Ends, The Wake of Jamie Foster; (off-Broadway) The Collected Works of Billy the Kid, The Frequency, Vanities, The Coroner's Plot, Hooters, Company, Fables for Friends, The Miss Firecracker Contest, Cruise Control; (regional theatre) King Lear, The Killing of Sister George, Relatively Speaking, The Importance of Being Earnest, Of Mice and Men, The Philadelphia Story, Room Service, Fifth of July, About Face; (nat. tours) Gypsy, Vanities; (films) Gas, 1972, You Better Watch Out, Lost Angels, 1988, In Country, 1988; (TV) Double Trouble, 1984, Eisenhower & Lutz, 1988, FM, 1989-90, Home Improvement, 1991— (Lead Actress in a Comedy Series Emmy award nominee, 1994, Golden Globe award nominee, 1993, 94). Office: William Morris Agy 151 El Camino Beverly Hills CA 90210

RICHARDSON, RHONDA JEAN, principal; b. Ashland, Ky., Mar. 21, 1949; d. Ralph Edward and Juanita (Ferguson) Smitley; m. Delphis Coleman Richardson, June 12, 1970; children: Shoshone Alleina, Arianna Wauneka, Adam Doren. BS, Ohio State U., 1971, MA, 1974. Cert. ednl. specialist, ednl. adminstr. Sch. liaison Balt. City Schs., 1974-75; tchr. Chinle (Ariz.) Pub. Schs., 1975-76, project dir., 1976-78; curriculum coord. Franklin County Dept. Edn., Columbus, Ohio, 1981-82; tchr. Hamilton Local Schs., 1982-89; asst. prin. Hamilton Local Schs., Columbus, 1986-89; asst. prin. Del. (Ohio) City Schs., 1989-90, prin., 1990-93; prin. Chandler (Ariz.) Unified Schs., 1994—; com. mem. Sch. Study Coun. Ohio Mid. Sch. Commn., Columbus, 1990-93. Recipient Dan H. Eikenberry award Ohio State U., 1989; named mentor Ohio Leadership Acad., 1991-93. Mem. Nat. Multi-Cultural Assn., Nat. Assn. Elem. Prins., Ariz. Mid. Level Assn., Nat. Mid. Sch. Assn., Phi Kappa Phi. Home: 316 E Caroline Ln Tempe AZ 85284-3115 Office: Anderson Jr HS 1255 N Dobson Rd Chandler AZ 85224

RICHARDSON, RUTH GREENE, social worker; b. Washington, Mar. 30, 1926; d. Arthur Alonzo and Ruth Naomi (Conway) Greene; m. Frederick D. Richardson, June 7, 1968; 1 child, Arthur William Boler. BS, St. Louis U., 1948; MSW, Washington U., St. Louis, 1950. Exec. dir. Anna B. Heldman Community Center, Pitts., 1962-64; assoc. dir. Hillhouse Assn., Pitts., 1964-67; assoc. dir. Dixwell House, also supr. group work services in community schs., New Haven, 1967-69; exec. dir. Three Rivers Youth Inc., Pitts., 1969-91; adv. bd. Sch. Social Work, U. Pitts., 1979-80; pres. Assn. Residential Youth Care Agys., 1973-77; artist, photographer, social work cons. Peoples Art Show Carnegie, 1991; pres., bd. dirs. Pa. Council Vol. Child Care Agys., 1973-78; asst. v.p. Allegheny Children and Youth Services Council, 1974-76, Ward Program Svcs. Participated in juried nat. art shows: Westmoreland County Mus., 1992, Three Rivers Art, 1992. Bd. dirs. Children's Council Western Pa.; adv. council Booth Home; bd. dirs. Nat. Assn. Homes for Children, Campfire Boys and Girls, 1988, South Arts, YWCA Greater Pitts. Recipient Social Assistance award Pitts. region Women's Am. ORT, 1975, Internat. Yr. of Child award region III, HEW, 1979; Jurors award, 1991, Images Show, 1991, Pitts. Black Artists William Pitt Union Gallery U. Pitts. 1986, Purchase prize Images III Waterworks, 1st prize in water color South Arts Sr. Citizen Show, Purchase prize Community Coll. Show, Ann. Svc. award Children's Coun. Western Pa., 1990, Best Of The Show award Carnegie Ethnic Art Show, 1993, Merit award South Hills Art League, 1993, Best Floral award Pitts. Garden Ctr., 1993, Real Pittsburgher award Pitts. Mag., 1993, First Place award Native Am. Heritage Com., 1993, Best Overall Artistic Achievement award Cranberry Area Coun. for the Arts, 1993, Community Svc. award Pitts. Club, Nat. Assn. Negro Bus. and Profl. Women's Club, Inc, 1993, Best of the Show award West Hills Art League, 1993, Outstanding Artistic Achievement award Cranberry Twp. Juried Art Exhibit, 3rd Prize award Pitts. Progressive Artist Annual Show, 1995, 3rd Prize award Native Am. Art Compition, 1995. Mem. Child Welfare League Am., Nat. Assn. Social Workers, Pitts. Watercolor Soc., Pa. Soc. Watercolor Painters, Pitts. Soc. Artist, Black Adminstrs. in Child Welfare, Creative Lens, Visions (v.p.), South Hills Art League (bd. dirs.). Presbyterian. Paintings exhbited in Pitts. region. Home and Office: 23 Stratford Ct Carnegie PA 15106-1575

RICHARDSON, SHARON NALBONE, school system administrator, educator, lawyer; b. Trenton, N.J., July 22, 1952. BA in English cum laude, U. Hartford, 1973, MEd, 1974; MA in English LIt., Wroxton Coll., Banbury, Eng., 1977; EdD, Temple U., 1980, JD, 1986. Bar: Pa. 1986, N.J. 1985; cert. reading and English tchr., prin., sch. adminstr., N.J., English and reading tchr., supr., prin., supt., Pa. Reading tchr., homebound tutor Highland Regional High Sch., Blackwood, N.J., 1974-77; adminstrv. asst. to asst. supt. curriculum and instrn. Gloucester Twp. Pub. Sch., Blackwood, 1977-78; reading coord. Haddon Twp. (N.J.) Sch. Dist., 1978-79, curriculum coord., 1979-81; acting prin. Lower Moreland Twp. Sch. Dist., Huntingdon Valley, Pa., 1982-83, asst. supt., 1981-83, 84-85, acting supt., 1983-84, 85-86; asst. supt. Sch. Dist. Springfield Twp., Oreland, Pa., 1986-93; supt. Pottsgrove Sch. Dist., Pottstown, Pa., 1993—; adj. prof. ednl. adminstrn. Temple U., 1985—; presenter, speaker in field; ednl. cons. Scott Foresman Co., 1984; mem. evaluation com. Mid. States Assn., 1980. Contbr. articles to profl. publs.; editor Origins of Haddon Twp.; author tchrs.' manual Haddon Twp. Elementary Writing Curriculum. Mem. Montgomery County Commrs. Task Force on Women, 1986-87; bd. dirs. Northwestern unit Am. Cancer Soc. Leadership scholar. Mem. ABA, Pa. Bar Assn., Am. Assn. Sch. Adminstrs., Nat. Sch. Bds. Assn., Nat. Orgn. for Legal Problems in Edn., Pa. Sch. Bd. Assn., Ea. Pa. Assn. Sch. Pers. Adminstrs., Pa. Assn. Sch. Pers. Adminstrs. (exec. bd. 1987-91), Temple U. Ednl. Adminstrs. Alumni Assn. (exec. bd., pres. 1988—), Phi Delta Kappa. Home: 407 Hedgerow Ln Malvern PA 19355

RICHARDSON, SHIRLEY MAXINE, public relations director; b. Rising Sun, Ind., May 3, 1931; d. William Fenton and Mary (Phillips) Keith; m. Arthur Lee Richardson, Feb. 11, 1950; children—Mary Jane Hamm, JoDee Mayfield, Steven Lee Richardson. Personnel mgr. Mayhill Pubs., Knightstown, Ind., 1967-87, prodn. mgr., 1975-87, editor, 1967-87; info. staff, assoc. editor Ind. Farm Bur., Inc., 1987-89, dir. info. and pub. rels., 1989-94, ret., 1994; part time real estate agent Century 21, 1994—. Mem. Newspaper Farm Editors of Am., Am. Agrl. Editors' Assn., Profl. Journalists of Am. Republican. Avocations: traveling; reading; boating; quilting. Home: 366 E Carey St Knightstown IN 46148-1208 Office: 225 S East St Indianapolis IN 46202

RICHARDSON, TINA, psychologist; b. Cheverly, Md., Sept. 22, 1963; d. Raymond and Ruby Mae (Broadus) R. BA, U. Md., 1985, MA, 1988, PhD, 1991. Psychology intern Towson (Md.) State U., 1989-90; staff psychologist Kans. State U., Manhattan, 1990-91; asst. prof. Lehigh U., Bethlehem, Pa., 1991—; affil. staff psychologist U. Counseling Svc., Bethlehem, 1991—; fashion designer, Esi's Corner, Bethelehem, 1993—; adj. faculty African Studies, Lafayette Coll., Easton, Pa., 1993—. Mem. conf. planning comm. OBSIDIAN, Bethlehem, 1993—. Fulbright-Hayes fellow U.S. Dept. Edn., Ghana, W. Africa, 1992, svc. grantee, 1993. Mem. APA, Assn. Black Psychologists. African Methodist Episcopalian. Office: Lehigh U Mountaintop Campus 111 Research Dr Bethlehem PA 18015-4732

RICHARDSON, WANDA LOUISE GIBSON, family practice nurse; b. Dallas, Jan. 6, 1931; d. Ralph Harrison and Letha Lee (McKiddy) Gibson; children: James L. (dec.), Bruce S., Judith Richardson Holt, Janai Richardson Buentello. Lic. vocat. nurse, Dallas Vocat. Sch., 1960; ADN, Dallas/El Centro Coll., 1981; student, U. Dallas, Irving, 1978. RN, Tex. Staff nurse RHD Hosp., Dallas, 1981; sr. nurse physicians office, Irving, 1960-80; head nurse family practice residency program St. Paul Hosp./U. Tex. Southwestern Med. Sch., Dallas, 1984—. Contbg. columnist Lake Cities Sun News; contbr. poems to anthologies. Vol. tutor Literacy Program, Denton, Tex.; founding mem., mem. choir Cornerstone Bapt. Ch., Plano, 1990; mem. Friends of Libr. of Denton; vol. Big Sisters/Big Bros., Denton. Named one of Notable Women Tex., 1984; recipient Golden Poet award World Poetry, 1991, 92. Mem. Am. Med. Surg. Nurses (charter), Lic. Vocat. Nurses Assn. (v.p. 1974), Cercle Internat. le Recherches Culturelles et Spirituelles Inc. (charter, officer local chpt.), Nurse Healers Profl. Assn., Dallas Archeol. Soc., Denton J.S. Bach Soc. Office: St Paul Hosp 5959 Harry Hines Blvd Dallas TX 75235

RICHARDSON-BONCZYK, LORI ANN, finance manager; b. Worcester, Mass., Mar. 27, 1968; d. Frank R. and Dorothy A. (Hagan) Bonczyk; m. Jeffrey N. Richardson. BS summa cum laude, Southeastern Mass. U., 1989; MBA, Nichols Coll., 1992. Staff acct. Harvey Industries Inc., Waltham, Mass., 1989-91; cons. Genica Pharm., Worcester, Mass., 1991-92; fin. acct. Hybridon, Worcester, 1992; conversion technician FDIC, Westboro, Mass., 1992-93; fin. mgr. HMA Behavioral Health Inc., Worcester, 1994—; cons. Worcester Minority Newspaper, 1992-93. Campaign coord. United Way; mem. campaign staff Brian J. Buckley for Dist. Atty. Worcester County. Mem. Delta Mu Delta. Roman Catholic.

RICHBART, CAROLYN MAE, mathematics educator; b. Catskill, N.Y., Aug. 12, 1945; d. George R. and Frances (Reynolds) Eden; m. Lynn A. Richbart, Aug. 15, 1987. BS, SUNY, Geneseo, 1967, MEd, 1982; PhD, U. Albany, 1992. Cert. math. tchr., elem. tchr., N.Y. Tchr. Wolcott St. Sch., Le Roy, N.Y., 1967; math. tchr. Le Roy Cen. High Sch., 1969-72, Attica (N.Y.) Mid. Sch., 1978-84; assoc. prof. Genesee C.C., Batavia, N.Y., 1984-87; grad. asst. U. Albany, 1987-90; asst. prof. Russell Sage Coll., Troy, N.Y., 1990-92, SUNY, New Paltz, 1992—; project dir. grades kindergarten through 6, N.Y. State Math Mentor Network. Contbr. articles to profl. jours. Mem. Nat. Coun. Tchrs. Math. (speaker), Assn. Math. Tchrs. N.Y. State (pres. 1995-96, pres.-elect 1994-95, corr. sec. 1991-92, rec. sec. 1988-89, dir. workshop 1992, chairperson workshop program 1989, chairperson Wyo. County sect. 1985-88), N.Y. State Assn. Two-Yr. Colls. (exec. bd. 1986-90, legis. chairperson 1986-89, chairperson 1989-90, project dir. N.Y. State K-6 Math Mentor Network). Home: 25 Martha's Ct Saugerties NY 12477 Office: SUNY at New Paltz Old Main New Paltz NY 12561-2499

RICHBURG, KATHRYN SCHALLER, nurse, educator; b. Picayune, Miss., Nov. 29, 1949; m. Edward Richburg Sr., June 24, 1972; children: William II, Kathryn. Diploma, Gilfoy Sch. Nursing, 1970; BSN, U. Miss. Med. Ctr., 1972. Cert. in nursing adminstrn., nursing continuing edn., infection control; cert. healthcare quality profl. Oper. rm. nurse, instr. ARC, 1970-82; infection control nurse U.S. Naval Hosp., Guam, 1982-83; nurse epidemiologist, utilization review coord. Nemours Children's Hosp., Jacksonville, Fla., 1983-86; utilization review coord. SunCare HMO, Jacksonville, Fla., 1986-87; program mgr. Trident Tech. Coll. Dept. Continuing Edn., Charleston, S.C., 1987-89; program mgr., acting dir. dept. continuing edn. Med. U. S.C., Charleston, 1989-90; edn. coord. quality mgmt. VA Med. Ctr., Charleston, 1990-93; quality assurance risk mgr. U.S. Naval Hosp., Yokosuka, Japan, 1993—. Mem. S.C. Nurses Assn. (chmn. conv. com. 1992, mem. continuing edn. provider unit 1990-92), Trident Nurses Assn. (del. 1990-92, mem. planning com. Rsch. Day 1991, 92), Nat. Assn. Healthcare Quality.

RICHEIMER, MARY JANE, retired educator; b. Massillon, Ohio, Oct. 20, 1913; d. Thomas Carl and Nellie (Bea) R. AB, Lake Erie Coll., 1936; MA, Kent State U., 1951; postgrad., Northwestern U., 1960, U. London, 1968-69. Asst. libr. Lake Erie Coll., Painesville, Ohio, 1936-37; tchr. Edmund Jones Jr. High Sch., Massillon, 1937-45, Washington High Sch., Massillon, 1945-51; libr. New Trier High Sch., Winnetka, Ill., 1951-53; tchr., chmn. dept. English Evanston (Ill.) Twp. High Sch., 1953-74; mem. classified advt. staff Pioneer Press, Wilmette, Ill., 1975-82; now ret.; summer sch. instr. lit. for adolescents, Northwestern U., Evanston, 1960; mem. nat. bd. tchrs. of English, Scholastic mags., N.Y.C., 1960—; vol. libr. Evanston Hosp. Med. Libr., 1989—. Author: A Century of Education, 1947; co-author: Planning My Future, 1961; contbr. poetry, articles to various publs. Vol. tutor Walker Sch., Evanston, 1990—; editor The Chimes newsletter Presbyn. Homes, Evanston, 1990—; mem. vestry St. Augustine's Episcopal Ch., Wilmette. Mem. AAUW, Evanston Hosp. Women's Aux., Nat. Ret. Tchrs. Assn., North Shore Ret. Tchrs. Assn., Viewers for Quality Television. Republican. Episcopalian. Home: 601 Trinity Ct Evanston IL 60201-1909

RICHENS, KIMBERLEE MARIE, real estate property manager, appraiser; b. Marion, Ohio, May 12, 1957; d. Rudolph Richard and Margaret Charlott (Carroll) Mucheck; m. Tim Richens, Dec. 10, 1978; 1 child, Jessica Elizabeth. Residential mgr. cert., IREM, 1984; cert., Am. Schs., Anaheim, Calif., 1992. Licensed Real Estate Appraiser. Property mgr. Forest City Mgmt. Inc., Cleveland, 1979—; real estate appraiser Grand Terrace, Calif., 1992—. Inventor sun enhancer, 1993; contbr. articles to profl. jours. Mem. Inst. Real Estate Mgmt., Nat. Assn. Real Estate Appraiser, San Bernardino Ch. of C., Grand Terrace C. of C. Democrat. Roman Catholic. Home: 22636 Lark St Grand Terrace CA 92313 Office: Forest City Mgmt Inc 11750 Mt Vernon Ave Grand Terrace CA 92324

RICHENS, MURIEL WHITTAKER, therapist, counselor, educator; b. Prineville, Oreg.; d. John Reginald and Victoria Cecilia (Pascale) Whittaker; children: Karen, John, Candice, Stephanie, Rebecca. BS, Oreg. State U.; MA, San Francisco State U., 1962; postgrad., U. Calif., Berkeley, 1967-69, U. Birmingham, Eng., 1973, U. Soria, Spain, 1981. Lic. sch. adminstr., tchr. 7-12, pupil personnel specialist, Calif., marriage, child and family counselor, Calif. Instr. Springfield (Oreg.) High Sch., San Francisco State U.; instr., counselor Coll. San Mateo, Calif., San Mateo High Sch. Dist., 1963-86; therapist AIDS health project AIDS Health Project, U. Calif., San Francisco, 1988—; pvt. practice MFCC San Mateo; guest West German-European Acad. seminar, Berlin, 1975. Lifeguard, ARC. postgrad. student Ctr. for Human Communications, Los Gatos, Calif., 1974, U. P.R., 1977, U. Guadalajara (Mex.), 1978, U. Durango (Mex.), 1980, U. Guanajuato (Mex.) 1982. Mem. U. Calif. Berkeley Alumni Assn., Am. Contract Bridge League (Diamond Life Master, cert. instr., tournament dir.), Women in Comm., Computer-Using Educators, Commonwealth Club, Pi Lambda Theta, Delta Pi Epsilon. Republican. Roman Catholic. Home and Office: 847 N Humboldt St Condo 309 San Mateo CA 94401-1451

RICHEY, NORMA JEAN, English language educator; b. Wetumka, Okla., Feb. 14, 1937; d. Melvin Levi and Jewell Ova (Hill) Smith; m. David M. Richey, Nov. 5, 1965 (div. 1974); children: Thomas William, Julie Melissa. BA, U. Okla., 1965, MA, 1968, PhD, 1986. Teaching assoc. U. Okla., Norman, 1980-83; mem. English faculty La. State U., Baton Rouge, 1983-87; lectr. Okla. State U., Stillwater, 1994; panelist Assn. Study of Australian Lit., Launceston, Tasmania, 1987, South Ctrl. Modern Lang. Assn., Arlington, Tex., 1988; exec. dir. Australian-Am. Fiction/Film Fedn., Austin, Tex., 1988; vis. asst. prof. U. Okla., Norman, 1995; speaker in field. Mem. editl. staff Henry James Rev., 1983-87; contbr. book revs., articles to profl. jours. U. Okla. Press fellow, 1965; Fulbright Rsch. scholar Coun. Internat. Exch. of Scholars, 1987. Mem. Am. Assn. Study Australian Lit. (founding mem., mem. exec. bd. 1986-88). Democrat. Office: PO Box 5113 Shawnee OK 74801

RICHMAN, BETH, marketing consultant; b. Stamford, Conn., May 18, 1964; d. Irving and Myrna (Robinson) R. BA in Psychology and Studio Art, Ithaca Coll., 1986. Assoc. editor MacLean Hunter Media, Stamford, 1986-88; mng. dir. Sono Gallery, Norwalk, Conn., 1988-93; mktg. specialist Wood Logan Assocs., Greenwich, Conn., 1991—; freelance writer Stamford, 1986—. Editor: Lit. Rev., 1980-82. Vol. state Dem. campaigns, 1978-82; attendant Bruce Mus., Greenwich, 1990-91. White House fellowship nominee, 1993. Mem. Norwalk Mchts. Assn., Soroptomists' Club (v.p. 1980-81), Entrepreneurial Women's Network, Conn. Press Club. Home: 158 Seaside Ave # B Stamford CT 06902-5333

RICHMAN, GERTRUDE GROSS (MRS. BERNARD RICHMAN), civic worker; b. N.Y.C., May 16, 1908; d. Samuel and Sarah Yetta (Seltzer) Gross; B.S., Tchrs. Coll. Columbia U., 1948, M.A., 1949; m. Bernard Richman, Apr. 5, 1930; children—David, Susan. Vol. worker Hackensack Hosp., 1948-70; mem. bd. dirs. YM-YWHA, Bergen County, N.J., 1950-75, bd. mem. emeritus, 1975—; chmn. Leonia Friends of Bergen County Mental Health Consultation Center, 1959; founder, hon. pres. Bergen County Serv-A-Com., affiliated with women orgns. Div. Nat. Jewish Welfare Bd.; v.p. N.J. sect. Nat. Jewish Welfare Bd., 1964-71; hon. trustee women's div. Bergen County United Jewish Community; mem. adv. council Bergen County Office on Aging, 1968-83, reappointed, 1984—; mem. Hackensack Bd. Edn., 1946-51; mem. pub. relations com. Leonia Pub. Schs., 1957-58; N.J. del. White House Conf. on Aging, 1971; trustee Mary McLeod Bethune Scholarship Fund; v.p. Bergen County nat. women's com. Brandeis U., 1966-67. Recipient citation Nat. Council Jewish Women and YWCA in Bergen County, 1962; citation Nat. Jewish Welfare Bd., 1964, Harry S. Feller award N.J. Region, 1965; 14th Ann. Good Scout award Bergen council Boy Scouts Am., 1977; Woman Vol. of Distinction, Bergen County council Girl Scouts, 1979; Human Relations award Bergen County sect. Nat. Council Negro Women, 1982; recipient Gov.'s award, 1988, Cert. of Commendation County Exec. and the Bergen County Bd. of Chosen Freeholders, 1989; honored at testimonial United Jewish Community Bergen County, 1987; Senior Advocate award Divsn. on Aging, 1993. Mem. Kappa Delta Pi.

RICHMAN, JOAN F., television consultant; b. St. Louis, Apr. 10, 1939; d. Stanley M. and Barbara (Friedman) R. B.A., Wellesley (Mass.) Coll., 1961. Asst. producer Sta. WNDT, N.Y.C., 1964-65; researcher CBS News, N.Y.C., 1961-64, researcher spl. events unit, 1965-67; mgr. rsch. CBS News (Rep. and Dem. nat. convs.), N.Y.C., 1968; assoc. producer CBS News, N.Y.C., 1968, producer spl. events, 1969-72; sr. producer The Reasoner Report, ABC News, N.Y.C., 1972-75; exec. producer Sports Spectacular CBS, N.Y.C., 1975-76; exec. producer weekend broadcasts CBS News, N.Y.C., 1976-81, v.p., dir. spl. events, 1982-87, v.p. news coverage, 1987-89; fellow Inst. Politics, John F. Kennedy Sch. Govt., Harvard U., 1990. Mem. nat. patrons coun. Opera Theatre St. Louis. Recipient Emmy award for CBS News space coverage Nat. TV Acad. Arts and Scis.; Alumnae Achievement award Wellesley Coll., 1973. Mem. Coun. on Fgn. Rels., Wellesley Coll. Alumnae Assn. (pres. class of 1961, 1966-70). Home: 14 Tinicum Creek Rd Erwinna PA 18920-9246

RICHMAN, PHYLLIS CHASANOW, newspaper critic; b. Washington, Mar. 21, 1939; d. Abraham and Helen (Lieberman) C.; m. Alvin Richman, June 5, 1960 (div. 1984); children—Joseph, Matthew, Libby. B.A., Brandeis U., 1961; postgrad., U. Pa., 1961-63, Purdue U., 1966-70. Restaurant critic Washington Post, 1976—, exec. food editor, 1980-88, food critic, 1988—. Author: Barter, 1976, Best Restaurants, 1980, 82, 85, 89. Mem. Washington Ind. Writers (adv. bd.). Home: 2118 O St NW Washington DC 20037-1007 Office: Washington Post 1150 15th St NW Washington DC 20071-0002

RICHMOND, ALICE ELENOR, lawyer; b. N.Y.C.; d. Louis A. and Estelle (Muraskin) R.; m. David L. Rosenbloom, July 26, 1981; 1 child, Elizabeth Lara. BA magna cum laude, Cornell U., 1968; JD, Harvard U., 1972; DLH (hon.), North Adams State U., 1987. Bar: Mass. 1973, U.S. Dist. Ct. Mass. 1975, U.S. Ct. Appeals (1st cir.) 1982, U.S. Supreme Ct.

1985. Law clk. to justices Superior Ct., Boston, 1972-73; asst. dist. atty. Office of Dist. Atty., Boston, 1973-76; spl. asst. atty. gen. Office of Atty. Gen., Boston, 1975-77; asst. prof. New Eng. Sch. of Law, Boston, 1976-78; assoc. Lappin, Rosen, Boston, 1978-81; ptnr. Hemenway & Barnes, Boston, 1982-92, Deutsch, Williams, Boston, 1993—; asst. team leader, faculty Trial Advocacy Course, Boston, 1978-82; examiner Mass. Bd. Bar Examiners, Boston, 1983—; trustee Mass. Continuing Legal Edn., Inc., Boston, 1985—. Author (2 chpts.) Rape Crisis Intervention Handbook, 1976; contbr. articles to profl. jours. Bd. of overseers Handel & Haydn Soc., Boston, 1985-94, mem. bd. govs. Handel & Haydn Soc., 1994—. Named one of Outstanding Young Leaders Boston Jaycees, 1982; Sloan Found. Urban fellow, N.Y.C., 1969. Fellow Am. Coll. Trial Lawyers: mem. ABA (ho. of dels. 1980—, vice chmn. com. on rules and calendar 1986-88), Mass. Bar Assn. (pres. 1986-87), Mass. Bar Found. (pres. 1988-91), Bay Club. Office: Deutsch Williams 99 Summer St 13th Fl Boston MA 02110

RICHMOND, KIMBERLY KAREN, marketing professional; d. Walter G. and Shirley May (Bayers) Kazragis; m. Phillip J. Richmond, Dec. 2, 1984. BS in Journalism and Advt., No. Ill. U., 1976; MBA, Loyola U., 1982. Various positions Sears, Roebuck & Co., Chgo., 1976-82, store of the future coord. home fashions, 1982-83, asst. group retail mktg. mgr. home appliances and electronic, 1983-84, nat. retail mktg. mgr. home appliances, 1984-88, dir. the Sears Advantage, 1987-88, catalog media mgr. promotional and splty. media, 1988-90, dir. strategic planning, 1991-94; mktg. mgr. Kraft Foodservice, Inc., Deerfield, Ill., 1991-95, dir. brand devel., 1995—. Home: 1616 N Hudson Ave Chicago IL 60614-5658

RICHMOND, LEE JOYCE, psychologist, educator; b. Balt., May 31, 1934; d. Alexander J. and Anne (Morganstern) Blank; m. Aug. 9, 1953 (div. 1983); children: Roth, Stephen, Sharon, Jessica. BS, Loyola Coll., 1961; MEd, Johns Hopkins U., 1968; PhD, U. Md., 1972. Licensed psychologist. Prof. psychology Dundalk Community Coll., Balt., 1971-75; prof. edn. Johns Hopkins U., Balt., 1975-86, Loyola Coll., Balt., 1986—; psychologist Counseling and Psychol. Svcs., Balt., 1975—; cons. in field; pres. Counseling & Psychol. Svcs., Balt., 1987—; speaker in field. Co-author: (monograph) Stress in Clergy, 1988; contbr. articles to profl. jours. Recipient Outstanding Contbn. to Psychology award Md. Psychol. Assn., 1986, Disting. Svc. award Nat. Vocat. Guidance Assn., 1984. Mem. ACA (gov.'s coun. 1988-90, pres. 1992, mem. ins. trust 1994—, Appreciation cert. 1990), Nat. Career Devel. Assn. (pres. 1988-89, Past Pres. award 1990). Home: 8907 Greylock Rd Baltimore MD 21208-1004 Office: Loyola Coll 105 Beatty Hall 4501 N Charles St Baltimore MD 21210

RICHMOND, MARILYN SUSAN, lawyer; b. Bethesda, Md., Oct. 19, 1949; d. Carl Hutchins Jr. and Elizabeth Adeline (Saeger) R. BA with honors, U. Fla., 1971; JD, Georgetown U., 1974. Bar: Md. 1974, D.C. 1975. Atty. Office of Gen. Counsel, FTC, Washington, 1974-77, antitrust atty. Bur. of Competition, 1977-81; counsel, consumer subcom. of com. on commerce, sci. and transp. U.S. Senate, Washington, 1981-85; assoc. Heron, Burchette, Ruckert & Rothwell, Washington, 1985-87, ptnr., 1987-90; dep. asst. sec. for govtl. affairs U.S. Dept. Transp., Washington, 1990-91, acting asst. sec. for govtl. affairs, 1991-92; cons. Raffaelli, Spees, Springer & Smith, Washington, 1993-94; asst. exec. dir. govt. rels. APA Practice Directorate, 1995—; lectr. Brookings Instn. Ctr. for Pub. Policy Edn., Washington, 1985-88. Active Lawyers for Bush-Quayle, Washington, 1988. Mem. ABA (antitrust, adminstrv. law sect., vice chair transp. industry com. antitrust sect. 1992-95). Republican. Methodist. Home: Apt 503 I 2725 Connecticut Ave NW Washington DC 20008-5305

RICHMOND, ROCSAN, television/video producer, publicist, inventor, interior designer; b. Chgo., Jan. 30; d. Alphonso and Annie Lou (Combest) R.; divorced; 1 child, Tina S. Student, Wilson Jr. Coll., 1963, 2d City Theatre, Chgo., 1969, Alice Liddel Theatre, Chgo., 1970. Lic. 3d class radio/tel. operator FCC. Vegetarian editor Aware mag., Chgo., 1977-78; investigative reporter, film critic Chgo. Metro News, 1975-81; producer, talk show host Sta. WSSD Radio, Chgo., 1980-81; dir. pub. rels. IRMCO Corp., Chgo., 1981-82; pub. rels. agt., newsletter editor Hollywood (Calif.) Reporter newspaper, 1985-86; exec. producer Donald Descendent's Prodns., Hollywood, 1983—, (TV show) Future News, 1983-86; pres. Richmond Estates. Inventor invisible drapery tieback. Jehovah's Witness. Office: PO Box 665 Los Angeles CA 90078-0665

RICHSTONE, BEVERLY JUNE, psychologist; b. N.Y.C., June 8, 1952; d. Max and Rosalyn Richstone. BA summa cum laude, Queens Coll., 1975; MEd, U. Miami, 1978; PsyD, Nova U., 1982. Lic. clin. psychologist. Staff psychologist Met. State Hosp., Waltham, Mass., 1983-85; asst. attending psychologist McLean Hosp., Belmont, Mass., 1983; asst. psychologist North Charles Mental Heath Ctr. Cambridge (Mass.) Hosp., 1984; assoc. dir. Coastal Geriatric Svcs., Hingham, Mass., 1985-86, Alpha Geriatric Svcs., Hingham, 1986-87; rsch. assoc. Harvard Sch. Pub. Health, Boston, 1992-94; instr. psychology Harvard U., Boston, 1983-84; consulting psychologist Coastal Geriatric Svcs, Hingham, 1985. Contbg. author: The New Our Bodies, Ourselves, 1992. Cmty. advisor Mass. Office Disability, Boston, 1992—. Clin. fellow Harvard U., 1982-83. Mem. APA, Phi Beta Kappa.

RICHTER, CAROL DEAN, sales representative; b. Cummings, Ga., May 14, 1940; d. William Ralph and Mildred Mae (Heard) Bottoms; m. Cary James Simmons, July 5, 1959 (div.); children: Joel Perry, Carlton Wesley, Rebecca Lynn; m. Robert Warren Richter Sr., July, 1970 (div.); 1 child, Robert Warren Jr. Student, Unity Sch. of Christianity, Unity Village, Mo., 1974—; AS in Mental Sci., First Ch. of Religious Sci., 1979; Degree in Aesthesiology, Derma-Clinic, 1990. Transcriptionist Med. Coll. Hosp., Charleston, S.C., 1960-64, St. Joseph's Infirmary, Atlanta, 1965-70; med. sec. Coal Mountain Clinic, Cummings, 1971-74; sales rep. Amway Distbrs. Assn., Ada, Mich., 1970—; transcriptionist Northside Hosp., Atlanta, 1974-89, Gwinnett Med. Ctr., Lawrenceville, Ga., 1989-93; cert. image cons., 1986-90; esthetician Classy You Salon, Duluth, Ga., 1991-92, You-Nique Salon, Buford, Ga., 1990-92; distbr. Amway Distbrs. Assn., Ada, Mich., 1970—; owner, pres. Richter Rallies, LAwrenceville, 1970—. Member John Birch Soc., Chamblee, Ga., 1964-70, North Ga. Mountain Planning and Devel. Commn., Gainesville, 1970-74; bd. dirs. Breakthru House, Decatur, Ga., 1975-81. Nominated Woman of Yr., Am. Biog. Inst. Bd. Internat. Rsch., 1993, Most Admired Woman of the Decade, 1994; named Miss Derma Clinic 1990 Acad. Skin Care and make-up, Derma Clinic, Atlanta, Acad. Richmond County, Augusta, Ga., 1959. Mem. NAFE, Nat. Trust for Historic Preservation, Ga. Trust for Historic Preservation, Internat. Platform Assn. Home and Office: 943 Terrace Trace Lawrenceville GA 30244-2717

RICHTER, DEBBIE KAY, artist; b. Riverside, Calif., Feb. 15, 1952; d. Charles Ray and Normajeane (Nicodemus) Dickey; m. Kurt E. Richter, Apr. 14, 1984; 1 child, Christopher Michael. AA, Riverside City Coll., 1971; BA, U. Calif., Riverside, 1975; culinary degree, Williams Sonoma, 1977. Ops. mgr. Brown Interpacific, Tustin, Calif., 1977-80; purchasing mgr. Anderson Winn, Burbank, Calif., 1980-84; artist DKR Inc., Kent, Wash., 1984—. Works exhibited in Manahatten Arts, 1993, Ency. Living Artists, 1993, 94, 95; publisher Gango Editions, Portland, Oreg. Republican. Lutheran.

RICHTER, ELIZABETH LEE, artist; b. Mount Vernon, N.Y., Feb. 1, 1927; d. Frank George and Edna Marguerite (Heese) Lee; m. Edwin Walter Richter, Apr. 10, 1948; children: Marilyn E. Tuma, Barbara J. Grover-Ordahl. BA summa cum laude, U. Bridgeport, 1986. Freelance needlework designer, tchr., 1973-87, freelance artist, 1987—; restoration asst. New Canaan (Conn.) Hist. Soc. Costume Mus., 1976-81. Mem. Rowayton Arts Ctr., Inc. (bd. dirs. 1992—), Silvermine Guild Artists, Phi Kappa Phi, Alpha Sigma Lambda. Home: 15 Winthrop Woods Rd Huntington CT 06484-5025

RICHTER, JUDITH ANNE, pharmacology educator; b. Wilmington, Del., Mar. 4, 1942; d. Henry John and Dorothy Madelyn (Schroeder) R. BA, U. Colo., 1964; PhD, Stanford U., 1969. Postdoctoral fellow Cambridge (Eng.) U., 1969-70, U. London, 1970-71; asst. prof. pharmacology Sch. Medicine Ind. U., Indpls., 1971-78, assoc. prof. pharmacology and neurobiology, 1978-84, prof., 1984—; vis. assoc. prof. U. Ariz. Health Sci. Ctr., Tucson, 1983; mem. biomed. rsch. rev. com. Nat. Inst. on Drug Abuse, 1983-87. Mem. editorial bd. Jour. Neurochemistry, 1982-87; contbr. numerous articles to sci. jours. Scholar Boettcher Found., 1960-64; fellow Wellcome Trust, 1969-71. Mem. AAAS, Am. Soc. for Pharmacology and Exptl. Therapeutics (exec. com. neuropharmacology div. 1989-91), Am. Soc. for Neurochemistry, Internat. Soc. for Neurochemistry, Soc. for Neurosci., Women in Neurosci., Assn. Women in Sci., Phi Beta Kappa, Sigma Xi. Office: Ind U Sch Medicine 791 Union Dr Indianapolis IN 46202-4887

RICHTER, KIM ANNE, accountant; b. Darby, Pa., July 7, 1955; d. John George and Darleen Joan (Hoff) Keidel; m. Randall Thomas Richter, May 27, 1978; children: Jacqueline Anne, Christopher Randall. BS in Acctg., U. Del., 1977; MBA, Pa. State U., 1981. Cert. mgmt. acct. Cost acct. Hercules, Inc., Wilmington, Del., 1977-78; sr. rsch. tech. Pa. State U., University Park, 1978-81; sr. fin. analyst Johnson & Johnson Corp. Hdqs., New Brunswick, N.J., 1981-85; sr. fin. analyst Johnson & Johnson/McNeil Pharm., Springhouse, Pa., 1985-87, rsch. acctg. mgr., 1987-88, ops. acctg. mgr., 1988-90, fin. acctg. mgr., 1990-93; plant contr. Johnson & Johnson/Ortho McNeil Pharm., Springhouse, 1993; process reengring. contr. Johnson & Johnson/Ortho McNeil Pharm., Raritan, N.J., 1994—. Trustee Calvary Presbyn. Ch., Wyncote, Pa., 1988-91, mem. chancel choir 1991—; mem. adv. bd. Math Options 92 & 93, Pa. State U., 1992-93. Mem. Inst. Mgmt. Accts. (chair publicity 1984-86), Beta Alpha Psi. Home: 8114 Washington Ln Wyncote PA 19095

RICHTER, MARCIA FRANCES, art educator; b. Chgo., Jan. 16, 1934; d. Thurlow King and Magdoline Elizabeth (Zinn) R. BA, Ball State Tchrs. Coll., 1956; MEd, Miami U., Oxford, Ohio, 1959. Cert. art educator, Ind., Ohio. Elem. art tchr. Tipp City (Ohio) Schs., 1956-58, Greenhills (Ohio) Schs., 1959-61, Franklin (Ohio) City Schs., 1961-64; jr. high art tchr. Findlay (Ohio) City Schs., 1964-71; art cons. Binney & Smith, Inc., Easton, Pa., 1971-75; mid. sch. art tchr. Bremen (Ind.) Pub. Schs., 1976—. Vol. Hotline-Cmty. Resource, South Bend, Ind., 1977—, Canco, South Bend, 1985-88. Mem. NEA, Nat. Art Edn. Assn., Art Educators Ind., Ind. State Tchrs. Assn., Bremen Edn. Assn. (pres. 1992). Roman Catholic. Home: 321 E North St Bremen IN 46506-1231

RICHTER, NAOMI BERNICE, mental health nurse; b. Chgo., Mar. 26, 1936; d. Otto Paul and Bernice Katherine (Plumbeck) R. BSN, U. Ill., Chgo., 1958; M of Religious Edn., No. Bapt. Sem., 1963; MS, No. Ill. U., 1977. Staff, H.N., instr. Cook County Hosp., Chgo., 1958-63; asst. dir. staff edn. Sherman Hosp., Elgin, Ill., 1963-64; instr. Bacone Coll., Muskogee, Okla., 1964-66; teaching asst. U. Ill. Coll. Nursing, Chgo., 1967; instr. South Chgo. Community Hosp., 1969-76; asst. prof. Nazareth Coll., Kalamazoo, Mich., 1977-80; asst. dir. South Chgo. Community Hosp. Sch. Nursing, 1980-82; dir., staff, patient edn. Borgess Med. Ctr., Kalamazoo, 1982-87; asst. prof. Nazareth Coll., Kalamazoo, 1987-92; psychiat. home health nurse Allegan (Mich.) Gen. Hosp. and Allegan County Health Dept., 1992—; adjunct faculty Grand Valley State Univ., 1992-94. Bd. dirs. Allegan County Prevention of Child Abuse/Neglect Coun. Mem. ANA, Sigma Theta Tau. Baptist. Home: 254 East D Ave # 57 Kalamazoo MI 49004

RICHTER, SUSAN MARY, medical/surgical nurse; b. Breese, Ill., Aug. 17, 1959; d. Jerome J. and Emilia C. (Robke) Albers; m. Michael Richter, Nov. 14, 1980; children: David, Timothy, Alicia. ADN, Kaskaskia Coll., 1979. Nurse aide St. Joseph's Hosp., Breese, Ill., 1977-79; staff nurse ICU/telemetry unit St. Joseph's Hosp., Breese, 1979—; instr. BCLS, ACLS; provider ACLS. Com. chmn. pack 273 Boy Scouts Am., Germantown, 1993. Recipient ARC Nurse Vol. award; named Outstanding Young Women in Am., 1989.

RICKARD, LISA ANN, lawyer; b. Englewood, N.J., Oct. 22, 1955; d. Joseph Mitchell and Ann Marie (Samen) Moore; m. J. Scott Rickard, June 18, 1977; children: Jack Taylor, Justin Moore. BA in Govt. and French, Lafayette Coll., 1977; JD, Am. U., 1982. Legis. asst. Bank of Am., Washington, 1977-78; spl. asst. and press asst. to Sen. Richard Stone, Washington, 1978-80; legis. asst. to Sen. Frank Murkowski, Washington, 1981; assoc. and ptnr. Akin, Gump, Strauss, Haver & Feld, Washington, 1982-93; v.p. federal affairs Ryder System, Inc., Washington, 1993—; mem., corp. adv. coun. Women's Rsch. and Edn. Inst., Washington, 1991—. Polit. fundraiser various fed. dem. candidates. Diplome D'Etudes Francaises Cours Moyen, Deuxieme Degres, U. Strasbourg, France, 1976. Mem. D.C. Bar Assn. Episcopalian. Home: 10112 Darmuid Green Dr Potomac MD 20854 Office: Ryder System Inc Ste 580 1100 New York Ave NW Washington DC 20005

RICKARD, RUTH DAVID, retired history and political science educator; b. Fed. Republic Germany, Feb. 20, 1926; came to U.S., 1940; d. Carl and Alice (Koch) David; m. Robert M. Yaffe, Oct. 1949 (dec. 1959); children: David, Steven; m. Norman G. Rickard, June 1968 (dec. 1988); 1 stepson, Douglas. BS cum laude, Northwestern U., 1947, MA, 1948. Law editor Commerce Clearing House, Chgo., 1948; instr. history U. Ill., Chgo., 1949-51; instr. extension program U. Ill., Waukegan, 1960-67; instr. history Waukegan (Ill.) Schs., 1960-69; original faculty, prof. western civilization, polit. sci. Coll. of Lake County, Grayslake, Ill., 1969-92; mem. Inter-Univ. Seminar on Armed Forces and Soc. Author: History of College of Lake County, 1987 (honored by city of Waukegan 1987), (poem) I Lost My Wings, 1989, Au Revoir from Emeritusdom, 1993, Where are the Safety Zones, 1994; spkr. on various ind. radio and TV programs; contbr. articles to profl. jours. Mem. Econ. Devel. Commn., Waukegan, 1992-93. Scholar Freedoms Found. Am. Legion, Valley Forge, Pa., 1967. Mem. AAUW (pres. Waukegan chpt. 1955-57, scholarship named for her 1985; mem. McLean chpt. 1993—), LWV (charter, v.p.), Nat. Press Club (D.C.), Phi Beta Kappa.

RICKEL, ANNETTE URSO, psychology educator; b. Phila.; d. Ralph Francis and Marguerite (Calcaterra) Urso; m. Peter Rupert Fink, July 21, 1989; 1 child, John Ralph. BA, Mich. State U., 1963; MA, U. Mich., 1965, PhD, 1972. Lic. psychologist, Mich. Faculty early childhood edn. Merrill-Palmer Inst., Detroit, 1967-69; adj. faculty U. Mich., Ann Arbor, 1969-75; asst. dir. N.E. Guidance Ctr., Detroit, 1972-75; asst. prof. psychology Wayne State U., Detroit, 1975-81; vis. assoc. prof. Columbia U., N.Y.C., 1982-83; assoc. prof. psychology Wayne State U., 1981-87, asst. provost, 1989-91, prof. psychology, 1987—; Am. Coun. on Edn. fellow Princeton and Rutgers Univs., 1990-91; AAAS and APA Congl. Sci. fellow on Senate Fin. Subcom. on Health and Pres. Nat. Health Care Reform Task Force, 1992-93. Cons. editor Am. Jour. of Community Psychology; co-author: Social and Psychological Problems of Women, 1984, Preventing Maladjustment..., 1987; author: Teenage Pregnancy and Parenting, 1989; contbr. articles to profl. jours. Mem. Pres.'s Task Force on Nat. Health Care Reform, 1993; bd. dirs. Children's Ctr. of Wayne County, Mich., The Epilepsy Ctr. of Mich., Planned Parenthood League, Inc. Grantee NIMH, 1976-86, Eloise and Richard Webber Found., 1977-80, McGregor Fund, 1977-78, 82, David M. Whitney Fund, 1982, Katherine Tuck Fund, 1985-90; recipient Career Devel. Chair award, 1985-86; Congl. Sci. fellow AAAS, 1992-93. Fellow APA (div. pres. 1984-85); mem. Midwestern Psychol. Assn., Mich. Psychol. Assn., Soc. for Rsch. in Child Devel., Soc. for Rsch. in Child and Adolescent Psychopathology, Internat. Assn. of Applied Psychologists, Sigma Xi, Psi Chi. Roman Catholic. Office: 3614 Prospect St NW Washington DC 20007

RICKERSON, JEAN MARIE, video producer, journalist, photographer; b. Takoma Park, Md., Dec. 29, 1956; d. Charles Marvin and Rita Ann (Smith) Blackburn; m. Ronald Wayne Rickerson, Oct. 18, 1989; 1 child, Drew. BS, U. Md., 1978. Pres. Videofax Inc., Bethesda, Md., 1982-90; founder, dir. Found. for Acad. Excellence Inc., Bethesda, 1985-90; video prodr. Applied Measurement Systems Inc., Bremerton, Wash., 1990—; pres. Photo Graphics Inc., Bremerton, 1992—. Contbr. articles and photographs to profl. jours.; writer, prodr., dir. videotape SEAFAC, 1992, USNS Hayes, 1993, High Gain Array Test Module, 1993, Advanced Mine Detection Sonar, 1995. Office: Applied Measurement Sys Inc 645 4th St Ste 202 Bremerton WA 98337

RICKETSON, HELEN MIXON, school psychologist, consultant; b. Perry, Fla., July 13, 1944; d. William Lonnie and Jessie Pearl (Knight) M.; m. Edward Irvin Ricketson, Jr., Oct. 9, 1962; children: Michael Edward, William Adam. BA, U. Fla., 1981, MEd, 1984, EdS, 1984. Cert. sch. psychologist; lic. sch. psychologist. Sch. psychologist Levy County Dist. Schs., Bronson, Fla., 1984-87; psychology specialist Dept. Corrections, Trenton, Fla., 1987-88; pvt. practice Chiefland, Fla., 1988—. Little king and queen contest emcee Chiefland Activities, 1992, 93. Mem. Nat. Assn. Sch. Psychologists, Fla. Assn. Sch. Psychologists, Kappa Delta Pi, Pi Lambda Theta, Phi Kappa Phi. Episcopal. Home: PO Box 489 Chiefland FL 32626

RICKETTS, FRANCES B., psychologist, marriage and family therapist; b. Oskaloosa, Iowa, Jan. 29, 1947; d. Raymond E. and Ada F. (Patten) Horn; m. Dennis R. Ricketts, Aug. 11, 1973; children: Sara I., Douglas R. BA, U. Iowa, 1969, MA, 1971, PhD, 1989. Lic. clin. psychologist, Ill., marriage and family therapist, Iowa. Jr./sr. h.s. counselor Lisbon (Iowa) Cmty. Schs., 1970-71; sr. h.s. counselor Pleasant Valley (Iowa) Cmty. Schs., 1971-86; counselor Family Resources, Bettendorf, Iowa, 1986-88; marriage and family therapist Southpark Psychology, Moline, Ill., 1988-89; psychologist Child & Family Psychology Ctr., Moline, 1989—. Pres. Pleasant Valley Edn. Assn., 1976-77; mem. Quad Citians Affirming Diversity, Davenport, Iowa, Scott County Master Gardener, Bettendorf. Mem. PEO, Am. Assn. Marriage and Family Therapy (clin.), Internat. Network Personal Relationships, Internat. Soc. Study of Personal Relationships, Delta Zeta. Office: Child & Family Psychology Ctr 3919 16th St Moline IL 61265

RICKIN, SHEILA ANNE, personnel professional; b. N.Y.C., Oct. 13, 1945; d. Louis and Ethel (Schmukler) Bernstein; BA, CCNY, 1966; postgrad. NYU; MBA, Pace U., 1988. Rsch. asst. pre-baccalureate program CCNY, 1966-68; placement counselor Elaine Revell, Inc., N.Y.C., 1968; adminstr. assoc. to CEO Parenthood Fedn. of Am., N.Y.C., 1969-74; pers. mgr. Family Circle Mag./N.Y. Times Mag. Group, 1974-87; sr. human resources rep., Drexel Burnham Lambert, 1987-88; asst. v.p., dir. pers. and adminstrn. Oppenheimer Mgmt. Corp. div. Mass Mut. Ins. Co., 1989-93; assoc. human resources mgr. AVSC Internat., N.Y.C., 1994—; cons. human resources, 1993—. Mem. Am. Compensation Assn., Human Resources Soc., Soc. Human Resources Mgmt., Internat. Found. Benefits, Am. Mgmt. Assn., Am. Soc. Tng. and Devel. (securities industry group), N.Y. Human Resources Planners, N.Y. Pers. Mgrs. Assn. (program com.), Mag. Pubs. Assn. (pers. com. 1978-87). Office: AVSC Internat 79 Madison Ave New York NY 10016

RICKS, JOYCE REGINA, educator; b. West Newton, Mass., Sept. 6, 1948; d. Oscar and Sletha (Winfield) Carter; m. Raynor J. Ricks Jr., Aug. 30, 1969; children: Bryan A., Raynor J. III. BA, Coll. St. Francis, Joliet, Ill., 1985; MEd, Nat.-Louis U., 1992. Tchr. Emmanuel Christian Sch., Chgo., 1975-81; master tchr. Kennedy-King Coll., Chgo., 1981-87, asst. dir., 1988—; ednl. specialist Children's Home & Aid Soc., Chgo., 1987-88; lectr. Kennedy-King Coll., Chgo., 1992—. Mem. Alpha Kappa Alpha, Xi Nu Omega. Home: 1914 W 83rd St Chicago IL 60620-6013

RICKS, JOYCIA CAMILLA, enforcement supervisor, lawyer; b. Atlanta, Feb. 17, 1949; d. George Palmer and Johnnie Mae (Ricks) Redd. BBA, Albany State Coll., 1971; MS, Ga. State U., 1977; JD, Woodrow Wilson Coll. Law, Atlanta, 1979, LLM, 1987. Bar: Ga. 1979, U.S. Dist. Ct. (no. dist.) Ga. 1979, U.S. Ct. Appeals (5th cir.) 1979, Acctg. clk. Gulf Oil Corp., Atlanta, 1971; clk. EEOC, Atlanta, 1971-73, paralegal specialist, 1973-79, investigator, 1979-91; gen. counsel Albany State Coll. Alumni Assn. 1986-90. Mem. NAACP, Atlanta, 1983—. Recipient Presdl. citation award Equal Opportunity in Higher Edn., Washington, 1981, Spl. Achievement award EEOC, Atlanta, 1982-84, 86-89. Mem. ABA, Atlanta Bar Assn., Ga. Assn. Black Women Attys., Albany State Coll. Alunmi Assn. (pres. Atlanta chpt. 1983-85, gen. counsel 1986-90), Assn. Trial Lawyers Am., Ga. State U. Alumni Assn., Woodrow Wilson Coll. Law Alumni Assn., Women of the Ch. Presbyn. (hon. life), Am. Bus. Women's Assn. (Woman of Yr., Tara chpt. 1985, 91). Democrat. Presbyterian. Club: Spreading Oak Community. Office: EEOC 75 Piedmont Ave NE Ste 1100 Atlanta GA 30303-2507

RIDDIFORD, LYNN MOORHEAD, zoologist, educator; b. Knoxville, Tenn., Oct. 18, 1936; d. James Eli and Virginia Amalia (Berry) Moorhead; m. Alan Wistar Riddiford, June 20, 1959 (div. 1966); m. James William Truman, July 28, 1970. AB magna cum laude, Radcliffe Coll., 1958; PhD, Cornell U., 1961. Rsch. fellow in biology Harvard U., Cambridge, Mass., 1961-63, 65-66, asst. prof. biology, 1966-71, assoc. prof., 1971-73; instr. biology Wellesley (Mass.) Coll., 1963-65; assoc. prof. zoology, U. Wash., Seattle, 1973-75, prof., 1975—; mem. study sect. tropical medicine and parasitology NIH, Bethesda, Md., 1974-78; mem. Competitive Grants panel USDA, Arlington, Va., 1979, 89; mem. regulatory biology panel NSF, Washington, 1984-88; mem. governing coun. Internat. Ctr. for Insect Physiology and Ecology, 1985-91, chmn. program com., 1989-91; chmn. adv. com. SeriBiotech, Bangalore, India, 1989; mem. bio. adv. com. NSF, 1992—. Contbr. articles to profl. jours. Mem. editorial bd. profl. jours. NSF fellow, 1958-60, 61-63; grantee NSF, 1964—, NIH, 1975—, Rockefeller Found., 1970-79, USDA, 1978-82, 89—; fellow John S. Guggenheim, 1979-80, NIH, 1986-87. Fellow AAAS, Am. Acad. Arts and Scis., Royal Entomol. Soc.; mem. Am. Soc. Zoologists (pres. 1991), Am. Soc. Biochem. and Molecular Biology, Entomol. Soc. Am., Am. Soc. Cell Biology, Soc. Devel. Biology. Methodist. Home: 16324 51st Ave SE Bothell WA 98012-6138 Office: U Wash Dept Zoology Seattle WA 98195

RIDDLE, CAROL ANN, counselor; b. Houston, Jan. 29, 1936; d. Caddell Eugene and Alma (Abernathy) Scruggs; m. Arol Sumner Riddle, Aug. 15, 1958 (div. 1980); children: Prentiss A.S., Suzanne Elizabeth. MusB, Tex. Christian U., 1957; MS in Elem. Edn., Okla. State U., 1972, EdD in Counseling, 1978. Lic. profl. counselor, lic. chem. dependency counselor. Vis. asst. prof. U. Tex., Dallas, 1977; tng. dir. City of Ft. Worth, Tex., 1981-83, U. Tex., Arlington, 1983-85; pvt. practice Dallas, 1985-88; asst. prof. psychology Lamar U., Orange, Tex., 1988-89; counselor Pvt. Hosps., Webster, Tex., 1990-91, Pearland (Tex.) Ind. Sch. Dist., 1990-92; with Lewisville (Tex.) Ind. Sch. Dist., 1992—; cons. Dallas City Credit Union, Standard Meat Co. Author: (with Debra Julian) Students Helping Students, 1979. Mem. AACD (Nat. Disting. Svc. Registry 1990), Tex. Assn. Counseling and Devel., Nat. Assn. Alcoholism and Drug Abuse Counselors, Tex. Assn. Alcoholism and Drug Abuse Counselors, Phi Delta Kappa, Kappa Delta Pi. Unitarian. Home: 713 Mack Dr Denton TX 76201-6347

RIDDLE, CLARINE NARDI, housing association administrator, former attorney general; b. Apr. 23, 1949; m. Mark A. Riddle; children: Carl, Julia. AB in Math. with honors, Ind. U., 1971, JD, 1974; LHD (hon.), St. Joseph Coll., 1991. Bar: Ind. 1974, U.S. Dist. Ct. (so. dist.) Ind. 1974, Conn. 1979, U.S. Dist. Ct. Conn. 1980, U.S. Supreme Ct. 1980, U.S. Ct. Appeals (2d cir.) 1986, D.C. Ct. Appeals 1994. Staff atty. Ind. Legis. Svcs. Agy., 1974-78; legal counsel com. law revision local planning laws Ind. State Bar Assn., 1979; asst. counsel Senate majority Conn. Gen. Assembly, 1979; dep. corp. counsel City of New Haven, 1980-82; counsel to atty. gen. State of Conn., 1983-85, dep. atty. gen., 1986-88, atty. gen., 1989-90; judge Conn. Superior Ct., 1991-93; staff asst. U.S. Senator Joseph I. Lieberman, 1994—; sr. v.p. govt. affairs Nat. Multi Housing Coun./Nat. Apt. Assn., 1995—; co-organizer Ind. Continuing Legal Edn. Forum Inst. Legal Drafting Legislature and Pvt. Practice; Internat. Women's Yr. panelist Credit Laws and Their Enforcement; mem. Atty. Gen.'s Blue Ribbon Commn., Chief Justice's Com. Study Publs. Policy Conn. Law. Jour., Law Revision Commn. Adminstrv. Law Study, Chief Justice's Task Force Gender, Justice and Cts., Gov.'s Task Force Fed. Revenue Enhancements; mem. exec. com. Jud. Dept.; mem. panel arbitrators Am. Arbitration Assn., 1994; gen. counsel Nat. Multi Housing Coun.; lectr in field. Author: (with F.R. Rembusch) Drafting Manual for the Indiana General Assembly, 1976; sr. editor Ind. U. Law Sch. Interdisciplinary Law Jour.; contbr. articles to profl. jours. Mem. bd. visitors sch. law Ind. U.-Bloomington; mem. Mayor's City of New Haven Task Force Reorganization Corp. Counsel's Office, Gov.'s Child Support Commn., Gov.'s Missing Children Commn., Conn. Child Support Guidelines Commn., Gov.'s Task Force Justice Abused Children, Mayor of New Haven's Blue Ribbon Commn.; former bd. dirs. New Haven Neighborhood Music Sch.; bd. dirs., mem. youth adv. com. Gov.'s Partnership Prevent Substance Abuse Workforce-Drugs Don't Work. Recipient Women in Leadership Recognition award Hartford Region YWCA, 1986, Award of Merit, Women & Law Sect. Conn. Bar Assn., 1989, Fellowship award South End Ladies Dem. Club, 1989, Woman of Yr. award Greater Hartford Fedn. of Bus. & Profl. Women's Clubs, 1990, Conn. Original award Somers-Mabelle B. Avery Sch., 1990, Cert. of Recognition, Consortium Law-Related Edn., 1990, Citizen award Conn. Task Force Children's Constl. Rights, 1991, Ann. award Hartford Assn. Women Attys., 1993; named Conn. History Maker, U.S. Dept. Labor, Women's Bur. & Permanent Commn. Status Women, 1989, Impact Player, The Conn. Law Tribune, 1992. Mem. ABA, Nat. Assn. Attys. Gen. (rep. adv. bd. ABA Ctr. Children And Law, chair charitable trusts and solicitations subcom., rep. nat. com. ethics and values ind. sector), Ind. Bar Assn., Conn. Bar Assn. (chair com. gender bias legal profession), Indpls. Bar Assn., Ind. Civil Liberties Union (bd. dirs., mem. exec. com., chair long range planning com., mem. women's rights project, membership v.p., Disting. Svc. award), Conn. Consortium Law and Citizenship Edn., Inc. (bd. dirs.), Conn. Judges Assn. (mem. legislation com.), Ind. U. Law Sch. Alumni Assn. (bd. dirs.), Enomene Hon. Soc., Pleiades Hon. Soc., Mortar Bd. (nat. fellow), Alpha Lambda Delta. Address: 10607 Millet Seed Hill Columbia MD 21044

RIDDLE, JUDITH LEE, lawyer; b. Princeton, N.J., Nov. 27, 1950; d. Donald Husted and Leah Dunlap (Gallagher) R.; m. James Melvin Kohler, Aug. 20, 1976 (div. Dec. 1987). BS, West Chester U., 1973; MEd, Colo. State U., 1976; ABD, Temple U., 1982; JD cum laude, Villanova U. Sch. Law, 1986. Bar: Pa. 1986, U.S. Dist. Ct. (ea. dist.) Pa. 1988. Atty., assoc. Ballard Spahr Andrews & Ingersoll, Phila., 1986-87; law clk., hon. Robert S. Gawthrop III U.S. Dist. Ct. (ea. dist.) Pa., Phila., 1987-88; assoc. Dechert Price & Rhoads, Phila., 1988-91; asst. dist. atty. Dist. Atty. Office, Phila., 1992—; cons. in field. Assoc. editor: Villanova Law Review, 1985-86. Vol. atty. Support Ctr. Child Advocates, Phila., 1988-92, Phila. Vol. Lawyers for Arts, 1986-90, Women's Law Project, Phila., 1991-92; bd. mem. Young Women's Cmty. Ctr., 1993—. Fulbright exchange tchr., 1978-79. Mem. Fed. Bar Assn. (chmn. young lawyers 1986-88, sec. 1988-90, 3d v.p. 1990-92, 2d v.p. 1992-93. 1st v.p. 1993—), Phila. Bar Assn., Order of Coif, Phi Delta Kappa. Democrat. Office: Dist Atty's Office 1421 Arch St Philadelphia PA 19102

RIDDLE, KATHARINE PARKER, nutrition educator; b. Mussoorie, Uttar Pradesh, India, May 21, 1919; (parents Am. citizens); d. Allen Ellsworth and Irene (Glasgow) Parker; m. Charles W. Riddle, Sept. 2, 1941 (div. Oct. 1976); children: Dorothy Irene, William Parker, Patricia Karen. BA with honors, Park Coll., 1940; MSc in Nutrition, U. Chgo., 1942; cert. Chinese lang. and culture, Yale U., 1946; PhD, Union Grad. Sch., Yellow Springs, Ohio, 1974. Nutritionist Elizabeth McCormick Meml. Fund, Chgo., 1942-44; missionary United Presbyn. Ch., Peiping, China and Punjab, India, 1944-65; assoc. dir., home economist Agrl. Missions Div. Overseas Ministry Nat. Coun. Chs., N.Y.C., 1965-69; rsch. cons. Morehead (Ky.) State U., 1970-74; asst. prof. nutrition Pa. State. U., State Coll., 1974-76; dir. Nourishing Space for Women, Vail, Ariz., 1976-78; adj. prof., researcher Dept. Family and Community Medicine, Coll. Medicine U. Ariz., Tucson, 1978-81; nutrition specialist, officer women in devel. Coop. Extension Internat. Programs U. Nebr., Lincoln, 1981-86, prof. emerita, 1986—; cons. Ch. Women United, N.Y.C., 1966-69, others; vis. scholar Coll. Bus. Adminstrn., U. Nebr., 1988. Author: Food with Dignity, 1977, Women and the Development of the World, 1983, (with C.M. Taylor) International Bibliography of Nutrition Education, 1971; editor: The Landour Book of International Recipes, 1965. Mem. Task Force on Voluntary Action by Women, White House Conf. Food, Nutrition, and Health, Washington, 1970, Gov.'s Commn. on Elderly, Ky., 1972; pres. bd. dirs. Internat. Ctr., Lincoln, 1986-88; researcher, program dir. Papago Breast Feeding Project, Sells, Ariz., 1979-81; project dir. Nebr. in the World, Lincoln, 1983-88; bd. dirs. Doté Found., San Antonio, Tex., 1989—; founder (with USDA, USAID, UNICEF, World Hunger Orgn., Food and Agrl. Orgn.) Task Force on Women's Participation in Rural Devel. Recipient Svc. award Agrl. Missions Inc., 1969, Disting. Alumna award Park Coll., 1977, Tribute to Women award YWCA, 1987. Mem. Am. Home Econs. Assn., Internat. Fedn. Home Econs., Soc. Nutrition Edn., Assn. Women in Devel. (founder 1982). Democrat. Home and Office: 13603 Forest Walk San Antonio TX 78231-1810

RIDDLE, LYNNE, judge; b. L.A., Sept. 9, 1938; d. James Edgar and Lois Elaine (Martin) R. BA, Calif. State Univ., L.A., 1960, MA, 1963; EdD, Syracuse Univ., 1966; JD, Hastings Coll. of Law, Univ. of Calif., 1977. Bar: Calif. 1978. Asst. prof. Calif. State Univ., Long Beach, 1966-68, Univ. of Iowa, 1968-69, Univ. of Calif., Santa Barbara, 1970-71, Dalhousie Univ., Halifax, Nova Scotia, 1971-73; atty. Santa Ana, 1978-88; bankruptcy judge U.S. Bankruptcy Ct. (cen. dist.) Calif., San Bernardino, 1988—; dir. Orange County Bankruptcy Forum; mem. Inland Empire Bankruptcy Forum. Mem. Orange County Women Bankruptcy Lawyers. Office: US Dist Cst 699 N Arrowhead Ave San Bernardino CA 92401*

RIDDLE, STACIE ANNE SCHWARTZ, special education educator; b. San Angelo, Tex., July 28, 1965; d. Erwin Frank and Gloria Mae (Debus) Schwartz; m. Thomas Clay Riddle, June 21, 1986; children: Megan Louise, Seth Thomas. BS, Angelo State U., San Angelo, Tex., 1987. Cert. tchr., Tex. Bug scout San Angelo, 1985—; sec. Wall (Tex.) Coop Gin, 1985-87; cake decorator Miles, Tex., 1980—; tchr. spl. edn. Miles Ind. Sch. Dist., 1987—. Mem. Assoc. Tex. Profl. Educators, St. Theresa Altar Soc., Miles PTA, Miles Booster Club. Roman Catholic. Home: PO Box 577 Miles TX 76861-0577 Office: Miles Ind Sch Dist PO Box 308 Miles TX 76861-0308

RIDDOCH, HILDA JOHNSON, accountant; b. Salt Lake City, July 25, 1923; d. John and Ivy Alma (Wallis) Johnson; m. Leland Asa Riddoch, Nov. 22, 1942; children: Ivy Lee, Leland Mark. Vocal student, Ben Henry Smith, Seattle; student, Art Instrn. Schs. Sales clk, marking room and dist. office Sears, Roebuck & Co., Seattle, 1940-42; with billing dept., receptionist C.M. Lovsted & Co., Inc., Seattle, 1942-51; acct., exec. sec. Viking Equipment Co., Inc., Seattle, 1951-54; acct., office mgr. Charles Waynor Collection Agy., Seattle, 1955-57; pvt. practice, 1957—; acct., office mgr. Argus Mag., Seattle, 1962-67; acct. Law Offices Krutch, Lindell, Donnelly, Dempsey & Lageschulte, Seattle, 1967-72, Law Offices Sindell, Haley, Estep, et al, Seattle, 1972-77; co-founder, acct. Bus. Svc., Inc. and Diversified Design and Mktg., Federal Way and Auburn, Wash., 1975—; co-founder L & H Advt. and Distbg. Co., Orting, Wash., 1992—; sec.-treas., dir. Jim Evans Realty, Inc., Seattle, 1973-87; agt. Wise Island Water Co., P.U.D., Victoria, B.C., 1973-88, Estate Executrix, Seattle, 1987—. Author: Ticking Time on a Metronome, 1989-90; writer, dir. hist. play Presidents of Relief Society Thru Ages; writer, dir. teenager activation video, 1984; pub., editor Extended Family Newsletter, 1983—. Dir. speech and drama LDS Ch., 1938-88, ward pres. young women's orgn., mem. ward and stake choirs, 1963-85, stake genealogy libr., Federal Way, 1983-85, ward and stake newsletter editors various areas, West Seattle, Seattle, Renton, Auburn, 1950-90, 1st counselor in presidency, tchr. various courses Ladies' Relief Soc. Orgn., 1965—; co-dir., organizer 1st Silver Saints Group, 1990-92; interviewer LDS Ch. Employee Svcs., 1992-93; founder WE CARE, 1993. Recipient Letter of Recognition Howard W. Hunter, Pres. LDS Ch. Home: PO Box 1300 Orting WA 98360-1300

RIDE, SALLY KRISTEN, physics educator, scientist, former astronaut; b. Los Angeles, May 26, 1951; d. Dale Burdell and Carol Joyce (Anderson) R.; m. Steven Alan Hawley, July 26, 1982 (div.). B.A. in English, Stanford U., 1973, B.S. in Physics, 1973, Ph.D. in Physics, 1978. Teaching asst. Stanford U., Palo Alto, Calif.; researcher dept. physics Stanford U.; astronaut candidate, trainee NASA, 1978-79, astronaut, 1979-87; on-orbit capsule communicator STS-2 mission Johnson Space Ctr. NASA, Houston; on-orbit capsule communicator STS-3 mission NASA, mission specialist STS-7, 1983, mission specialist STS-41G, 1984; sci. fellow Stanford (Calif.) U., 1987-89; dir. Calif. Space Inst. of U. Calif. San Diego, La Jolla, 1989—; prof. Physics U. Calif. San Diego, La Jolla, 1989—; mem. Presdl. Commn. on Space Shuttle, 1986, Presdl. Com. of Advisors on Sci. and Tech., 1994—. Author: (with Susan Okie) To Space and Back, 1986, (with T.O'Shaughnessy) Voyager: An Adventure to the Edge of the Solar System, 1992, The Third Planet: Exploring the Earth From Space, 1994. Office: Calif Space Inst 0221 Univ Calif San Diego La Jolla CA 92093-0221

RIDEOUT, EDNA BAKER, artist; b. Billings, Mont., Sept. 29, 1918; d. Frederick Hubbard and Edna Beers (Baker) Ballou; m. Horton Burbank Rideout, May 26, 1951; children: Douglas Burbank Rideout, Nancy Penelope Rideout, Thomas Ballou Rideout. BA, U. Wash., 1940, MA, 1949. Cert. secondary tchr., Wash. Art editor Croftonian Crofton House Sch., Vancouver, B.C., Can., 1935-36; art tchr. Neah Bay (Wash.) High Sch., 1940-41, Winlock (Wash.) High Sch., 1942-44, Seattle Pub. Schs., 1945-47, 49-51, Fish and Wildlife Svc. Pribilof Islands, St. George Island, Alaska, 1951-53; dir. Visual Art Sch., Edmonds, Wash., 1972-74; sec. Gallery North, Edmonds, 1974-76; artist, 1953—. Watercolors included in 5 nat. juried exhbns., 8 juried mem. and regional exhbns., 1992-93, 25 nat. juried shows in 5 yrs., invitational exhbns. sponsored by Bellevue, Wash. Art Mus., North West Water Color Soc.; works included in In Harmony with Nature, 1990; 1 ink drawings used as cover designs for Alaska Timber Econ. Studies texts. Recipient Masterfield award Fla. Soc. Exptl. Artists, 2 purchase awards Watercolor U.S.A., Ajomari/Arches/Rives award Watermedia Mont., 1st pl. award Artstravaganza Nat., 3rd pl. award Navarro Coun. of Arts, Judge's Spl. award North Coast Collage Soc. Mem. Women Painters of Wash. (program dir. 1992-93), North West Watercolor Soc. asst. program dir. 1989-91), Soc. Exptl. Artists Fla., Pa. Watercolor Soc., north Coast Collage Soc. (sec. 1993—), East Side Assn. Fine Arts, Gallery North (hon.), Planetary Soc. Home: 18616 92d Ave NE Bothell WA 98011-2207

RIDEOUT, PHYLLIS MCCAIN, university official, educator; b. Macon, Ga., Sept. 15, 1938; d. Wayne Eugene and Lois Stone (Rollins) McC.; m. William Milford Rideout, Jr., Mar. 10, 1961; children: Christina Lynn, William Milford III, Julie Linda. AB in Modern European Lit., Stanford U., 1961; MA in English, Fla. State U., 1973, PhD in Humanities, 1981. Cert. community coll. life teaching credential, Calif. Teaching asst. Fla. State U., Tallahassee, 1974-75; program coord. humanities U. So. Calif., L.A., 1981-82, program adminstr. Norris Comprehensive Cancer Ctr., 1983-86, adminstrv. dir. Norris Comprehensive Cancer Ctr., 1986-89, assoc. dir. for adminstrn. and edn. Norris Comprehensive Cancer Ctr., 1989—, clin. instr. preventive medicine Sch. Medicine, Norris Comprehensive Cancer Ctr., 1989—. Leader, trainer Girl Scouts U.S.a., Tallahassee and Los Alamitos, Calif., 1975-81; bd. dirs. jr. and sr. high schs. PTA's, Los Alamitos, 1977-81; bd. dirs. Cancer Coalition Calif., 1986-91; bd. dirs., vice chair AIDS Healthcare Found., 1992—; treas. So. Calif. Cancer Pain Initiative. Mem. Nat. Assn. Women in Edn., Cancer Ctr. Adminstrs. Forum (exec. com. 1987-91), U. So. Calif. Women in Mgmt. (bd. dirs. 1986-89, 90—, pres. 1993-95), Stanford U. Alumni Assn. (life), Stanford Profl. Women (pres., bd. dirs. 1982-85), Stanford Club Los Angeles County (bd. dirs. 1985-88). Office: U So Calif Norris Comprehensive Cancer Ctr 1441 Eastlake Ave Los Angeles CA 90033-0800

RIDER, FAE B., educational consultant; b. Summit Point, Utah, Mar. 1, 1932; d. Lee Collingwood and Jessie (Hammond) Blackett; m. David N. Rider, Jan. 26, 1952; children: David Lee, Lawrence Eugene. BS, No. Ariz. U., 1971, MA, 1974; postgrad., U. Nev., Las Vegas, 1985-88. Lic. tchr. in elem., reading, spl. edn. Learning specialist Las Vegas, summers 1974-76; tchr. kindergarten Indian Springs (Nev.) Pub. Schs., 1971-76; reading tchr. Las Vegas Pub. Schs., 1976-80; curriculum coord. Indian Springs Pub. Schs., 1980-91; tchr. 1st grade Las Vegas Pub. Schs., 1991-92, reading specialist, 1992-93; pvt. edn./reading cons. Las Vegas, 1993—. Author booklet: Door to Learning - A Non-Graded Approach, 1978. Bd. dirs. Jade Park, Las Vegas, 1988. Mem. Internat. Reading Assn., Ret. Tchrs. Assn., Am. Legion Aux., Delta Kappa Gamma (pres., Rose of Recognition), Kappa Delta Phi.

RIDER, JANE LOUISE, artist, educator; b. Brownfield, Tex., Sept. 11, 1919; d. Oscar Thomas and Florence Myrtle (Bliss) Halley; m. Rolla Wilson Rider Jr., Mar. 26, 1944 (dec. July 1992); 1 child, Dorothy Jo Neil. BA, UCLA, Westwood, 1943, tchg. diploma in secondary art; postgrad., Chgo. Art Inst., 1945, Chouinards, L.A., U. Oreg., Scripps, Claremont, Calif. Art supr., elem. and jr. high art tchr. Tulare (Calif.) City Schs. Dist., 1943-44, 44-45; art tchr. Beverly Hills (Calif.) High Sch., 1946-47; art tchr. jr. high gen. art and ceramics Santa Barbara City Schs., Goleta, Calif., 1964-66; head art dept., tchr. Morro Bay (Calif.) Jr.-Sr. High Sch. Dist., 1967-70; pvt. practice studio potter Cambria, Calif., 1961-85; artist, Santa Rosa, Calif., 1985—; founder, dir., tchr. La Canada (Calif.) Youth House, 1953-60; dir. Pinedorado Art Show, Allied Arts Assn., Cambria, 1970-80. Exhibited in group shows Wine Country Artist's Spring Show, 1991, 92, 93, 94, Gualala Art in Redwoods, 1986, 87, 88, Rodney Strong Vineyards Art Guild, 1994; revolving exhibits Berger Ctr. and Chalais-Oakmont, Santa Rosa, 1985-94. Mem. Nat. League Am. Pen Woman, Inc. (artist 1994), Santa Rosa Art Guild (rec. sec. 1989, statewide art show 1986-94, Spring Palettes Mumm Cuvee Winery, Napa, Calif. 1994), Ctrl. Coast Watercolor Soc. (charter 1977), Oakmont Art Assn. (Women Creating Luther Burbank Ctr., Santa Rosa 1994). Republican. Home: 7019 Overlook Dr Santa Rosa CA 95409-6376

RIDGLEY, SHERRY E., lawyer; b. Klamath Falls, Oreg., Apr. 21, 1952; d. William Wesley and Iva Lee (Redi) R. BA, U. So. Calif., 1975; JD, Loyola Law Sch., 1978. Bar: Calif. 1978, Fed. Tax Ct. 1980. Ptnr. Nagata, Conn & Ridgley, L.A., 1983-87, Musick, Peeler & Garrett, L.A., 1987-89, 92—; of counsel Jones, Day, Reavis & Pogue, L.A., 1989-91. Mem. ABA, L.A. County Bar Assn., Women Lawyers Assn. Office: Musick Peeler & Garrett One Wilshire Blvd Ste 2000 Los Angeles CA 90017

RIDGWAY, DIANE MARIE, government official, tax specialist; b. Puyallup, Wash., June 13, 1951; d. William Jr. and Lorinda Louise (Kenoyer) R. AAS, Ft. Steilacoom C.C., Tacoma, 1972. Acct. Money Savers, Inc., 1972-75, Liberty U., 1975-78, Occoquan-Woodbridge and Dumfries-Triangle Sanitary Dist., Woodbridge, Va., 1975-78, Marvac, Inc., 1979; tax technician IRS, Seattle, 1981-87, supervisory tax technician, 1987-90, dir. coop. adminstrv. support unit, 1990—, career counselor, 1984-86, mentor, 1985-89, instr. tax law, 1985-90, mediator, 1994—. Loaned exec. Combined Fed. Campaign, Seattle, 1989, Former Loaned Exec. Mentor mem., 1992; bd. dirs. Life Choices King County, Seattle, 1994; mem. planning com. Wash. Student Leadership, Seattle, 1991-94. Recipient quality performance award President's Coun. for Mgmt. Improvement, 1992, outstanding leadership award, 1993. Mem. ASAP, Profl. Women's Fellowship, Bible Study Fellowship. Republican. Home: 407 5th St NE Puyallup WA 98371 Office: Coop Adminstrn Support Unit 915 2d Ave Rm 302 Seattle WA 98174

RIDGWAY, HELEN JANE, chemist, consultant; b. Ft. Worth, Aug. 10, 1937; d. Ralph Pope and Virginia Leah (Link) R. AS, Arlington (Tex.) State Coll., 1957; BA, North Tex. State Coll., Denton, 1959; MS, Baylor U., Waco, Tex., 1963, PhD, 1968. Rsch. asst. Wadley Rsch. Inst., Dallas, 1960-68; sr. investigator Wadley Insts. Molecular Medicine, Dallas, 1968-86, chmn. chemistry, 1986-92; R & D hemostasis mgr. Helena Labs., Beaumont, Tex., 1993—; cons. Helena Labs., Beaumont, 1986-92. Contbr. articles to sci. jours. AAUW scholar, 1955, 56. Fellow Internat. Soc. Hematology; mem. Am. Chem. Soc., Am. Heart Assn. (coun. on thrombosis).

RIDGWAY, MARCELLA DAVIES, veterinarian; b. Sewickley, Pa., Dec. 24, 1957; d. Willis Eugene and Martha Ann (Davies) R. BS, Pa. State U., 1979; VMD, U. Pa., 1983. Intern Univ. Ill., Urbana, 1983-84, resident in small animal internal medicine, 1984-87; small animal vet. Vet. Cons. Svcs., Savoy, Ill., 1987—. Contbr. articles to profl. jours. Mem. Am. Vet. Med. Assn., Am. Animal Hosp. Assn., Acad. Vet. Clinicians, Ednl. Resources in Environ. Sci. (bd. dirs.), Savoy Prairie Soc. (pres. 1989—), Grand Prairie Friends (bd. dirs. 1993-96). Home and Office: Vet Cons Svcs 194 Paddock Dr E Savoy IL 61874-9663

RIDGWAY, PRISCILLA, association executive; b. Schenectady, N.Y.; d. Whitman and Priscilla (Hawley) R. BS in Bus. and Edn., Russell Sage Coll., 1970. Exec. dir. Mystery Writers Am., N.Y.C., 1987—. Mem. Crime Writers Assn., John Buchan Soc., Coffee House. Office: Mystery Writers Am 17 E 47th St Fl 6 New York NY 10017-1920

RIDGWAY, ROZANNE LEJEANNE, government executive, former diplomat; b. St. Paul, Aug. 22, 1935; d. H. Clay and Ethel Rozanne (Cote) R.; m. Theodore E. Deming. BA, Hamline U., 1957, LLD (hon.), 1978; LLD (hon.), George Washington U., 1986; hon. degree, U. Helsinki, Elizabethtown Coll., Albright Coll., Coll. of William and Mary, Hood Coll. Career diplomat U.S. Fgn. Svc., 1957-89, amb. at large for oceans and fisheries, 1975-77; amb. to Finland, 1977-80; counselor of the Dept. State, Washington, 1980-81; spl. asst. to sec. state, 1981; amb. to German Dem. Republic, 1982-85; asst. sec. state Europe and Can., 1985-89; pres. The Atlantic Coun. U.S., Washington, 1989-92, co-chair, 1993—; chair Baltic-Am. Enterprise Fund, 1994—; bd. dirs. 3M Corp., RJR Nabisco, Union Carbide Corp., Bell Atlantic, Citicorp, Citibank, Emerson Electric Co., The Boeing Corp., Sara Lee Corp., Nat. Geog. Soc., Internat. Bd. Advisors, New Perspective Fund. Trustee Hamline U.; bd. dirs. Am. Acad. Diplomacy, Coun. on Ocean Law, Ptnrs. for Democratic Change, Catalyst, Aspen Inst., Bookings Instn. Recipient Profl. awards Dept. State, Presdl. Disting. Performance award, Joseph C. Wilson internat. rels. achievement award, 1982, Sharansky award Union Couns. Soviet Jewry, 1989, Grand Cross of the Order of the Lion, Finland, 1989; named Person of Yr., Nat. Fisheries Inst., 1977, Knight Comdr. of the Order of Merit, Fed. Republic Germany, 1989, U.S. Presdl. Citizens Achievement medal, 1989. Fellow Nat. Acad. Pub. Adminstrn.; mem. Met. Club, Army-Navy Country Club. Office: The Atlantic Coun of The US 910 17th St NW Ste 1000 Washington DC 20006

RIDINGS, DOROTHY SATTES, communications executive, newspaper publisher; b. Charleston, W.Va., Sept. 26, 1939; d. Frederick L. and Katharine E. (Backus) Sattes; m. Donald Jerome Ridings, Sept. 8, 1962; children: Donald Jerome Jr., Matthew Lyle. Student, Randolph-Macon Woman's Coll., 1957-59; BSJ, Northwestern U., 1961; MA, U. N.C.-Chapel Hill, 1968; D.Pub. Svc. (hon.), U. Louisville, 1985; LHD (hon.), Spalding U., 1986. Reporter Charlotte Observer, N.C., 1961-66; instr. U. N.C. Sch. Journalism, 1966-68; freelance writer Louisville, 1968-77; news editor Ky. Bus. Ledger, Louisville, 1977-80, editor, 1980-83; communications cons., editor, 1983-86; mgmt. assoc. Knight-Ridder Inc., Charlotte, N.C., 1986-88; pres., publisher The Bradenton (Fla.) Herald, 1988—; adj. prof. U. Louisville, 1982-83; v.p. Nat. Mcpl. League, 1985-86; bd. dirs. com. on Constl. System, Nat. Com. Against Discrimination in Housing, 1982-87, Com. for Study of Am. Electorate, 1982-89; bd. dirs. Ind. Sector, 1983-88, 92—; mem. exec. com. Leadership Conf. Civil Rights, 1982-86. Pres. LWV U.S., 1982-86, 1st v.p. 1980-82, human resources dir., 1976-80, chair edn. fund, 1982-86, 1st vice chair, 1980-82, trustee, 1976-80, pres. Louisville/Jefferson County, 1974-76, bd. dirs. 1969-76; trustee Louisville Presbyn. Theol. Sem., 1992—, Ford Found., 1990—, Manatee Community Coll., 1992—; bd. dirs. Benton Found., 1987—, Fla. Press Assn., 1994—; mem. ABA Accreditation Com., 1987-93, Gov.'s Council Ednl. Reform, 1984-85; chair Prichard Com. Acad. Excellence, 1985-86; bd. dirs. Leadership Ky., 1984-87, Leadership Louisville, 1983-86, Louisville YWCA, 1978-80, Jr. League Louisville, 1972-74; mem. Gov.'s Comm. Full Equality, 1982-83; mem. state adv. council U.S. Commn. Civil Rights, 1975-79; mem. steering com. Task Force for Peaceful Desegregation, 1974-75; elder 2d Presbyn. Ch., 1972-75, 78-81; mem. adv. council on ch. and soc. United Presbyn. Ch. in USA, 1978-84; mem. bd. visitors U. N.C., 1992—. Recipient Northwestern U. Alumni Merit award, 1994, Leadership award Nat. Assn. Cmty. Leadership Orgns., 1986, Alumnae Achievement award Randolph-Macon Woman's Coll., 1985, Disting. Citizens award Nat. Mcpl. League, 1983. Mem. Fla. Press Assn. (bd. dirs.). Home: 3412 Avenida Madera Bradenton FL 34210 Office: The Bradenton Herald PO Box 921 Bradenton FL 34206-0921

RIDLEN, LILLIAN MAY HEIGLE, public relations, sales and marketing executive, writer, inventor; b. New Orleans, Nov. 15, 1946; d. Joseph Manuel and Lillian Mae (Theriot) H.; m. Larry Vinson Ridlen, Dec. 28, 1968; children: Larry V. Jr., Kenneth C., Jennifer C. Degree in Nursing, Orleans Parish Sch. Practical Nursing, 1969. Nurse So. Bapt. Hosp., New Orleans, 1970-72; pres. Sunshine & Co., LaPlace, La., 1983-86, The Gift Gallery, LaPlace, 1984-85; v.p. La. Bartending Inst., Kenner, Baton Rouge and New Orleans, 1986-87; dir. La. Bartending Inst., 1987-89; pub. rels. officer, sales and mktg. dir. Universal Fast Foods of LaPlace, Chalmette and Marrero, 1989—; nurse St. Charles Manor Nursing Ctr., 1989—; owner, pres. Ton-Lil Pub. Co., LaPlace, 1990—. Author: A Sampling of Southern Cooking, 1985, A Home Study Course in Bartending, 1989; composer, lyricist songs; lyricist Tony's Song for artist Wayne Presley; inventor Santa's Snack Pack; author poetry pub. in anthologies. Organizer Mothers for Safe Edn. St. John the Bapt. Parish, La., 1984. Poetry selected for inclusion in world record effort by Internat. Soc. of Poets, 1994. Mem. NAFE, Internat. Soc. Poets. Democrat. Roman Catholic.

RIDLEY, BETTY ANN, educator, church worker; b. St. Louis, Oct. 19, 1926; d. Rupert Alexis and Virginia Regina (Weikel) Steber; m. Fred A. Ridley, Jr., Sept. 8, 1948; children: Linda Drue Ridley Archer, Clay Kent. BA, Scripps Coll., Claremont, Calif., 1948. Christian sci. practitioner, Oklahoma City, 1973—; tchr. Christian sci., 1983—; mem. Christian Sci. Bd. Lectureship, 1980-85. Trustee Daystar Found.; mem. The First Ch. of Christ Scientist, Boston, Fifth Ch. of Christ Scientist, Oklahoma City. Mem. Jr. League Am. Home: 7908 Lakehurst Dr Oklahoma City OK 73120-4324 Office: Suite 100-G 3000 United Founders Blvd Oklahoma City OK 73112

RIDLEY, DENISE MICHELLE, city official; b. Ky., Dec. 21, 1958; d. Lawrence Wayne and Georgia R. (Wright) Wagner; m. Kenneth D. Ridley, June 9, 1979. Cert. mcpl. clk. Legal sec. Franklin, Hobgood, Hibbs & Troop, Madisonville, Ky., 1979-82; clk.-treas. City of Dawson Springs, Ky., 1982—. Treas. Dawson Springs Main St. Program, 1988—. Mem. Acad. for Advanced Edn., Ky. Mcpl. Clks. Assn. (bd. dirs.), Pennyrile Clks. Assn. (pres.), Inst. Inst. Mcpl. Clks., Dawson Springs C. of C. (treas. 1986—). Office: City of Dawson Springs PO Box 345 200 W Arcadia Ave Dawson Springs KY 42408-0345

RIEBEL, JOAN STROM, social services administrator; b. Madelia, Minn., Oct. 30, 1942; d. Percy Carroll and Marcella Theresa (Rohe) Strom; m. Leland John Riebel, June 12, 1965; children: John, Andrew. BA, Coll. of St. Benedict, 1964; MSW, U. Minn., 1978. Tchr. Our Lady of Peace High Sch., St. Paul, 1964-65; social worker Cath. Charities, Rockford, Ill., 1965-68, Ramsey County Human Svcs., St. Paul, 1968-78; adminstr. of HHS grant U. Minn., Mpls., 1978-80; pvt. practice cons. and psychotherapist Mpls., 1980-84; exec. dir. Family Alternatives, Inc., Mpls., 1985—; mem. Legis. Task Force on Foster Care, St. Paul, 1990—; mem. Gov.'s Commn. on Children's Mental Health, St. Paul, 1988-90; chair social work adv. com. Coll. St. Benedict, St. Joseph, Minn., 1989-92; pres. N.Am. Foster Family-based Treatment Assn., Mpls., 1988-90; co-chair subcom. Nat. Commn. on Foster Care/Child Welfare League Am., Washington, 1990-92. Author: (chpt.) Sexual Abuse of Children: A Prevention Strategy, 1980. Mem. 4th Ward, Dist. 65A Caucus, St. Paul, 1978-90; pres. St. Joan of Arc Ch. Coun., Mpls., 1990—. Recipient Recognition award Nat. Foster Parent Assn., 1989, Benedictan Svc. award Coll. St Benedict, 1989, Outstanding Alumna award U. Minn., 1992. Mem. NASW, Am. Group Psychotherapy Assn., Nat. Assn. Foster Parents, Orthopsychiat. Assn. Office: Family Alternatives Inc 416 E Hennepin Ave # 218 Minneapolis MN 55414-1071

RIECK, JANET RAE, special education educator; b. Atchison, Kans., Oct. 24, 1948; d. Clinton Everett and Bernice Marie (Schreurs) Wendland; m. Arthur Wyman Hand, Mar. 1970 (div. Feb. 1977); m. Doyle Elmer Rieck, Sept. 21, 1986. B in Music Edn., Otterbein Coll., 1970; MA, U. No. Colo., 1980; MS, No. Ill. U., 1989. Cert. tchr. Nebr. Music tchr. Blanchester (Ohio) Schs., 1970-74; tchr. aide N.Mex. Sch. for Visually Handicapped, Alamogordo, 1976-78; tchr. visually impaired Edn. Svc. Unit 7, Columbus, Nebr., 1979—; piano tchr., Cin., 1975-76, Alamogordo, 1976-78. Mem. NEA, Coun. Exceptional Children, Assn. for Edn. and Rehab. of Blind and Visually Impaired (Nebr. pres. elect 1990-92, pres. 1992-94, cert. orientation and mobility specialist). Lutheran. Home: RR 2 Box 148 Albion NE 68620-9323 Office: Ednl Svc Unit 7 2657 44th Ave Columbus NE 68601-8537

RIEDEL, DELLA JUDITH, software project manager; b. Prichard, W.Va., July 31, 1941; d. Percy and Blanche (McCoy) Roberts; m. Larry Dean Riedel, Dec. 31, 1965; children: Michael Loring, Monica Lucille. AB in Math. and Phys. Sci., Marshall U., 1961; postgrad., East Ctrl. Okla. U., 1984, U. Tex., Dallas, 1992. Tchr. math. Ky. Bd. Edn., 1961-64; cartographer USAF, Mo., 1965-66; programmer USN, Calif. and Iowa, 1966-70, USAF, Colorado Springs, Colo., 1973-77, E Systems, Blue Cross, Dallas, 1977-79; data processing cons. JC Penney, Mobil, Collin Co., others, Tex. and Okla., 1980-87; project mgr. data processing Blue Cross/Blue Shield, Dallas, 1987—; mem. Carroll Ind. Sch. Dist. Tech. Com., Southlake, Tex., 1993. Mem. Am. Bus. Women's Assn. Republican. Roman Catholic. Home: 1342 Meadow Gln Southlake TX 76092-8552

RIEDEL, JUANITA MAXINE, writing educator; b. Overbrook, Kans., Nov. 17, 1918; d. Albert Ernest and Gladys Jennie (Hadsell) Smith; m. Richard Joseph Riedel, May 16, 1943 (dec. Aug. 1888); children: Nancy Riedel Basford, Linda Riedal Haynes. BE, U. Kans., 1944. Instr. creative writing Jackson (Mich.) C.C., 1979-86; instr. Creative Writers Workshop, Jackson, 1982—. Author: Words--Power and the Pattern, 1981, Church on Main Street, Jackson, MI, 1984, Wahroonga, 1994, Sidewalks, 1995; editor numerous books. Mem. AAUW (pres. 1976-78, grantee 1980), Beta Sigma Phi (various offices 1949—), 1st United Meth. Ch. Republican. Home: 3149 Halstead Blvd Jackson MI 49203-2553

RIEDENER, KAREN, photographer, painter; b. Manhattan, N.Y., Aug. 12, 1946; d. Oscar and Katherine (Jackson) R.; m. Arthur Gerard Piacentino. Student, Art Students League, N.Y.C., 1964-68; studied with various profl., photographers. Career fine arts photographer and painter Croton-on-Hudson, N.Y.; tchr. painting and photography Rye (N.Y.) Arts Ctr., 1988-89; lectr. Renaissance Humanities Festival, Byram Hills High Sch., Armonk, N.Y., others; asst. Charlotte Brooks, staff photographer for Look Mag., 1976-77; fine arts painter, Europe, 1968-75. Exhbns. include The Bklyn. Mus., 1983, The Israel Mus., Jerusalem, 1982, The Hudson River Mus., Yonkers, N.Y., 1979-81, 83, 86, The Albright-Knox Mus., Buffalo, N.Y., 1982, The Aldrich Mus. of Contemporary Art, Ridgefield, Conn., 1978, Bertha Urdang Gallery, N.Y.C., 1982, 84, 87, The Katonah (N.Y.) Gallery, 1977, 79, 80, 81, 83, 85, 87, 89, De Pree Gallery/Hope Coll., Holland, Mich., 1983 and numerous others; permanent collections in The Bklyn. Mus., The Israel Mus. and De Pree Art Gallery. Bd. dirs. The Hudson River Contemporary Artists in Westchester, 1985-87. Office: 15 Furnace Dock Rd Croton-on-Hudson NY 10520

RIEDESEL, LAUREEN FALK, librarian; b. Wakefield, Nebr., June 1, 1951; d. Arlyn Dale and Glaura Milly (Harry) Falk; m. Charles Paul Riedesel, May 25, 1973; children: Aprilla Florentine Lynnae, Amerilla Maye Falk. BA, Wheaton Coll., 1973; MA in Libr. Sci., U. Mo., 1974. Cert. pub. libr., Nebr. Youth svcs. libr. Dunklin County Libr., Kennett, Mo., 1974-77; dir. Beatrice (Nebr.) Pub. Libr., 1977—; speaker Nebr. Humanities Coun. Speakers Bur., 1993—; instr. Nebr. Libr. Commn., Lincoln, 1988-92. Contbr. articles to profl. jours. Incorporator, mem. exec. bd. Gage county Heritage Preservation, Inc., Beatrice, 1987—; alt. del. White House Conf. on Librs., Washington, 1991; hist. preservation rep. City Plan Coordinating Com., Beatrice, 1991-92; mem. Gov.'s Task Force on Hist. Preservation, 1992-94. Named Excalibur Outstanding Librarian, Pub. Libr. Sect., Nebr. Libr. Assn., 1991, Outstanding genealogist Nebr. State Geneal. Soc., 1992, Woman of Yr., Beatrice Bus. and Profl. Women, 1993, Outstanding Cmty. leader Jaycees, 1993. Mem. ALA, Nebr. Libr. Assn. (pres. 1989), S.E. Nebr. Geneal. Soc., S.E. Nebr. Coords. for Literacy (v.p. 1994-95), Nat. Mgmt. Assn. (exec.bd. 1993, chmn. of bd. 1994-95), Nebr. Ctr. for the Book (exec. bd. 1992—). Democrat. Ch. of the Brethren.

RIEFER, GLORIA JOYCE, educational consultant; b. Canton, Ohio, Dec. 8, 1940; d. Alexander and Mary Anne Sollie; children: Lisa Leigh, Mark Turner. BS in Edn., Malone Coll., 1971; MS in Edn. Adminstrn., U. Akron, 1975. Cert. elem. tchr., elem. prin. Elem. tchr. North Canton (Ohio) Schs., 1971-75, prin., 1975-94; cons. grants and spl. projects Summit County Office Edn., Cuyahoga Falls, Ohio, 1994—; owner Joy's Flower Shop. Recipient Adminstrv. Leadership award Martha Holden Jennings Found., 1980-81. Mem. Nat. Assn. Elem. Adminstrs., Ohio Assn. Elem. Adminstrs. (zone dir. 1983-87, Red Feather awards 1983-87), North Canton Adminstrs. Assn. (pres. 1981, sec. 1985), Coll. Club Canton (chmn. Mature Women's grant com. 1975), Order Eastern Star (Canton chpt. star point 1968, 91), Phi Delta Kappa (scholarship com. 1983). Republican. Home: 6111 Pilotview Cir NE Louisville OH 44641 Office: Summit County Office Edn 420 Washington Ave Cuyahoga Falls OH 44221

RIEGER, ANNA LORRAINE, management consultant, fashion designer; b. Vancouver, B.C., Can., Oct. 15, 1959; came to U.S., 1990; d. Harry Anthony and Ann Irwin (Johnston) R. Diploma in Design Arts, Seneca Coll. of Applied Arts, Toronto, Ont., Can., 1981; diploma in Bus./Mktg., B.C. Inst. of Tech., Vancouver, 1986. Property mgr. Bucci Investment Corp., Vancouver, 1986-87; v.p. mktg., co-founder Unitrol Am. Computer Corp., Vancouver, 1987-90; pres. Spirit West Mgmt., Seattle, 1990—; v.p. mktg. Project Mgmt. Inst., Seattle, 1992—, bd. dirs.; designer clothing line Spirit Wear, 1994—. Office: Spirit West Mgmt 7348 12th Ave NW Seattle WA 98117

RIEGER, DONNA MARIE, critical care nurse, educator, consultant; b. St. Louis, May 5, 1957; d. Elvern E. and Eleanore E. (Zimmerer) R. BSN, St. Louis U., 1979. Cert. BLS affiliate faculty, Mo., ACLS affiliate faculty, Mo., BLS, ACLS Am. Heart Assn. Critical care nurse St. Anthony's Med. Ctr., St. Louis, 1979-86; critical care nurse Barnes Hosp., St. Louis, 1986-88, nursing edn. specialist, 1988—; mem. ACLS regional com., BCLS regional com. Am. Heart Assn., St. Louis, 1988—, chair ACLS regional com., 1991—, mem. ACLS state com., 1993—, del. to bd., 1991—; adj. faculty Barnes Coll. Mem. AACN, Greater St. Louis Chpt. of Critical Care Nurses (mem. edn. com. 1991—), Barnes Coll. Nursing Honor Soc. Roman Catholic. Home: 418 Autumn Peak Dr Saint Louis MO 63026 Office: Barnes Hosp One Barnes Hosp Plz Saint Louis MO 63110

RIEGER, ELAINE JUNE, nursing consultant; b. Lebanon, Pa., June 7, 1937; d. Frank and Florence (Hitz) Plasterer; m. Jere LeFever Longenecker, Sept. 13, 1958 (div. 1968); children: Julie Lynn Porto, Jere Lee Longenecker; m. Bernhard Rieger, Oct. 12, 1971. Nursing diploma, Coatesville (Pa.) Hosp. Sch. of Nursing, 1958; BA, U. Redlands, 1976; MS in Healthcare Mgmt., Calif. State U., L.A., 1984. Cert. nursing adminstr., gerontol. nurse. From staff nurse to clin. supr. to dir. of nurses St. Johns Regional Med. Ctr., Oxnard, Calif., 1966-86; dir. of nurses Motion Picture and TV Hosp., Woodland Hills, Calif., 1987-89; with Care West, Nothridge-Reseda, Calif., 1989-90; dist. nurse mgr. Hillhaven Corp., Newbury Park, Calif., 1990-91; quality assurance nursing cons. Beverly Enterprises, Rancho Cordova, Calif., 1991—. Home: 1817 Shady Brook Dr Thousand Oaks CA 91362-1335 Office: Beverly Enterprises 10969 Trade Center Dr Ste 106 Rancho Cordova CA 95670

RIEGLE, LINDA B., federal judge; b. 1948. BS, Shepherd Coll., Shepherdstown, W.Va.; JD, Union U., Albany, N.Y. Admitted to bar, 1978. Bankruptcy judge U.S. Dist. Ct. Nev., Las Vegas, 1988-94, chief bankruptcy judge, 1994—. Office: US Dist Ct 300 Las Vegas Blvd S Las Vegas NV 89101-5812*

RIEHECKY, JANET ELLEN, writer; b. Waukegan, Ill., Mar. 5, 1953; d. Roland Wayne and Patricia Helen (Anderson) Polsgrove; m. John Jay Riehecky, Aug. 2, 1975; 1 child, Patrick William. BA summa cum laude, Ill. Wesleyan U., 1975; MA in Communication, Ill. State U., 1978; MA in English, Northwestern U., 1983. Tchr. English Blue Mound (Ill.) High Sch., 1977-80, West Chicago (Ill.) High Sch., 1984-86; editor The Child's World Pub. Co., Elgin, Ill., 1987-90; freelance writer Elgin, 1990—. Author: Dinosaur series, 24 vols., 1988, UFOs, 1989, Saving the Forests, 1990, The Mystery of the Missing Money, 1995, The Mystery of the UFO, 1995, Irish Americans, 1995, others. Recipient Summit award for best children's nonfiction Soc. Midland Authors, 1988. Mem. Soc. Am. Magicians, Children's Reading Round Table, Soc. Children's Book Writers and Illustrators, Mystery Writers of Am., Phi Kappa Phi. Democrat. Baptist.

RIEHL, MAUREEN BRIGID, lawyer, lobbyist; b. Detroit, Nov. 6, 1965; d. Leonard John and Mary Theresa (McMahon) Malinowski; m. Scott Lawrence Riehl, Sept. 22, 1990. BA in Comm., Mich. State U., 1987, BS in Polit. Sci., 1987, JD, 1992. Bar: Va. 1993. Legis. aide Mich. Ho. of Reps., Lansing, 1988-89; constituent, legis. asst. to senate majority flr. leader Mich. Senate, Lansing, 1989-93; dir. State Advt. Coalition, Washington, 1993—. Mem. Fairfax County Reps., Falls Church, Va., 1994—; bd. dirs. Washington Area State Rels. Group, 1993—; mem. State Govt. Affairs Coun., 1993—. Mem. ABA, Va. State Bar Assn. Republican. Roman Catholic. Office: State Advt Coalition 1899 L St NW Ste 700 Washington DC 20036

RIEKE, ELIZABETH ANN, federal agency administrator; b. Buffalo, July 10, 1943; divorced; children: Frederick Martin, Eowyn Ann. BA in Polit. Sci. summa cum laude, Oberlin Coll., 1965; JD with highest distinction, U. Ariz., 1981. Rsch. asst. S.W. Environ. Svc., Tuscon, 1976-79; law clk. Snell & Wilmer (formerly Bilby, Shoenhari, Warnock & Dolph), Tuscon, 1979; law clk. Office of Solicitor Divsn. Conservation and Wildlife, Dept. Interior, Washington, 1980; law clk. to Hon. William C. Canby Jr. U.S. Ct. Appeals (9th cir.), 1981-82; dep. legal counsel Ariz. Dept. Water Resources, 1982-85, chief legal counsel, 1985-87, dir., 1991-93; assoc. Jennings, Strouss & Salmon, Phoenix, 1987-89, ptnr., 1989-91; asst. sec. for water and sci. Dept. Interior, Washington, 1993—; adj. prof. Ariz. State U., Phoenix, 1989; speaker in field. Recipient Disting. Alumnus award U. Ariz., 1986. Office: Dept Interior 1849 C St NW Washington DC 20240-0001*

RIELS, NANCY BRICKELL, general contractor; b. Birmingham, Ala., Jan. 30, 1950; d. Manuel Cook and Elvada (Willcutt) Brickell; m. James A. Riels, Sept. 30, 1972 (div. July 1992); children: Patrick Thomas, Brandon Cook. BS in Consumer Affairs, Auburn U., 1974. Lic. gen. contractor, N.C. Tchr. remedial reading Ala. State Tng. Sch., Birmingham, 1971-72; pvt. reading tutor Birmingham and Montgomery, Ala., 1971-75; restaurant co-owner/operator Springside Assocs., Asheville, N.C., 1981-83; designer/constrn. coord. Process Svcs., Inc., Asheville, 1983-88; pres. High Country Homes, Inc., Asheville, 1989—. Leader cub scouts, coun. officer Boy Scouts Am., Asheville, 1979-81, 84-86; mem., officer PTA Asheville Country Day Sch., 1984-89; vol. cmty. svc. Jr. League Asheville, 1987-89; adminstr. '75 boy's soccer N.C. Olympic Devel. Program, Chapel Hill, 1990-93. Recipient Gov.'s Recognition for Voluntarism award Glen Arden Sch., 1980-82; named Builder of Month, Builder/Architect Mag., 1993. Mem. Nat. Assn. Women Constrn. (Asheville chpt., judge block kids contest 1992-95, dir./treas. 1993-95), Nat. Assn. Home Builders (alt. nat. dir. 1995), N.C. Home Builders Assn. (alt. state dir. 1995), Home Builders Assn. Greater Asheville (dir./treas. 1993-95, Award for Outstanding Achievement in Home Bldg. Industry 1991, parade of homes judge 1992, Award for Outstanding Svc. as Treas. and Audit Com. Chairperson 1994, Asheville Builder of Yr. 1994), Racquet Club Village Assn. (bd. dirs., treas. 1993-95). Methodist. Office: High Country Homes Inc 32 Village Dr Asheville NC 28803

RIELY, CAROLINE ARMISTEAD, physician, medical educator; b. Washington, Feb. 1, 1944; d. John William and Jean Roy (Jones) Riely. AB, Mt. Holyoke Coll., 1966; MD, Columbia U., 1970. Diplomate Am. Bd. Internal Medicine. Med. intern Presbyn. Hosp., N.Y.C., 1970-71, resident in medicine, 1971-73; fellow in liver disease Yale U., New Haven, 1973-75, asst. prof., 1975-80, assoc. prof., 1980-88; prof. medicine U. Tenn., Memphis, 1988—. Fellow ACP, Am. Coll. Gastroenterology; mem. Am. Assn. Study Liver Disease, Internat. Assn. Study Liver, N.Am. Soc. for Pediatric Gastroenterology and Nutrition. Home: 1756 Central Ave Memphis TN 38104-5116 Office: U Tenn 951 Court Ave Rm 555D Memphis TN 38103-2813

RIEMERSMA, MARY JO, association director; b. Phoenix, Oct. 3, 1950; d. Joseph and Mary Jane (Wadsworth) Detta; m. Kenneth Jerry Riemersma, May 23, 1970; 1 child, Cristopher Nowell. BA, Ariz. State U., 1975, MS, 1979, MBA, 1983. Cert. assn. exec. Tchr. North Phoenix and Cen. High Schs., Phoenix, 1976-77; asst. to exec. dir. and various positions Sheetmetal and Air Condition Trades Industry Program, Phoenix, 1968-76, asst. exec. dir., 1978-82, exec. dir., 1982-85; exec. dir. Calif. Assn. Marriage and Family Therapists, San Diego, 1985—. Fellow Am. Soc. Assn. Execs. (bd. dirs. 1991-94), San Diego Soc. Assn. Execs. (pres., other offices 1985-93), Calif. Fedn. Assn. Execs. (chmn., other 1987-90), Ariz. Soc. Assn. Exec. (pres.-elect and others 1977-85). Office: Calif Assn Marriage and Family Therapists 7901 Raytheon Rd San Diego CA 92111-1606

RIES, BARBARA ELLEN, alcohol and drug abuse services professional; b. Chgo., Oct. 27, 1952; d. Laurence B. and Genieveve (Wasiek) R. AAS in Human Svcs., Coll. of DuPage, Glen Ellyn, Ill., 1973; BA in Social Work, Sangamon State U., Springfield, Ill., 1978; postgrad., U. Mo., 1987-88, U. Tex., Arlington, 1991—. Cert. social therapist; nat. cert. alcohol and drug counselor; qualified chem. dependency counselor. Counselor Ray Graham Assn. for Handicapped, Addison, Ill., 1975-76; child abuse counselor Ill. Dept. Children and Family Svcs., Springfield, 1977-78; alcoholism counselor non-med. detoxification program S.H.A.R.E., Villa Park, Ill., 1978-80; outpatient therapist Ingalls Meml. Hosp., Harvey, Ill., 1980-83; dir. aftercare Lifeline Program, Chgo., 1984-85; case mgr. Lifecenter Program, Kansas City, Mo., 1985-87; counselor, acting clin. coord. Lakeside Hosp., Kansas City, 1988-89; program mgr., dir. chem. recovery programs Two Rivers Psychiat. Hosp., Kansas City, 1989-90; dir. day program and chem. dependency program SW Hosp./Citadel, Dallas, 1990—; dir. Flexcare program Dallas Meml. Hosp., 1990-91; pvt. practice Federal Way, Wash., 1991—; program coord. Advanced Clin. Svcs., Federal Way, 1992-94; exec. dir. Spokane Care, 1994—. Recipient commendation Ingalls Hosp., 1983. Mem. Nat. Assn. Drug and Alcohol Counselors (cert.), Nat. Assn. for Relapse Prevention Counselors, Learning Disabilities Assn. Wash., Wash. Assocs. Alcoholism & Addictions Programs, Wash. Advs. Mentally Ill, Employee Assistance Profls. Am., Coalition Drug and Alcohol Leaders, Wash. Assn. Alcoholism and Drug Abuse Counselors, Nat. Assn. of Alcoholism and Drug Counselors (NCAC II), Am. Mktg. Assn., Dual Diagnosis Com.

RIESEN, LOU RITA, educator; b. Muskogee, Okla., Oct. 7, 1952; d. Roy Edward and Wauniece (Cariker) Satterfield; m. John Meyer Riesen, Mar. 12, 1984. AS in Speech Drama, Ea. Okla. State Coll., 1971; BSEd in Speech Drama, U. Okla., 1974, MEd in Reading Specialist, 1977. 4th grade element St. John's Acad., Yukon, Okla., 1979; GED tchr. adult edn. Oklahoma City C.C., 1980-84; reading specialist Okla. Pub. Sch. Emerson High Sch., Oklahoma City, 1992—; reading specialist Moore Pub. Sch. Sky Ranch, state spelling bee coach, 1974-78, 1980-84, Norman Pub. Sch., N. H.S., 1987-90, spl. olympics coach, 1987; dir. acad. decathlon Emerson High Sch., coach of team 1993, sponsor student coun., 1992. Del. grand assembly state Okla. Rainbow Girls Order, worthy advisor, 1969; mem. PTA, 1974-90. Spl. edn. arts grant Okla. Art Humanities, State of Okla., 1989-90, Lew Wentz grant EOSC, 1970-74. Mem. Am. Fedn. of Tchrs., State Reading Assn., PTSA, Kappa Delta. Episcopalian. Home: 3305 Walnut Rd Norman OK 73072-7514

RIESER-DANNER, LORETTA ANN, psychology educator; b. Phila., Jan. 29, 1958; d. David Paul and Loretta Ann (Purcell) Rieser; m. James M. Danner Jr., June 27, 1981; children: James M. Danner III, Joshua M. Danner, Jeremy M. Danner. BS, Pa. State U., 1981; PhD, U. Tex., 1989. Teaching/rsch. asst. U. Tex., Austin, 1981-87; asst. prof. psychology Villanova (Pa.) U., 1987-91, Pa. State U.-Ogontz campus, Abington, 1991—; instr. child psychology U. Tex., 1985-87. Contbr. articles to profl. jours. reviewer Internat. Jour. Behavioral Devel., Developmental Psychology, Jour. of Exptl. Child Psychology. Recipient Edith Pitt Chase award Coll. of Human Devel., Pa. State U., 1980, Francis Hoffman award, 1981, Ogontz Scholars award, 1993; Abby A. Sutherland scholar, 1978; Pa. State U. grantee, 1991-92, 92-93, 93, 93-94. Mem. APA, Am. Psychol. Soc., Jean Piaget Soc., Internat. Soc. for Infant Studies, Soc. for Rsch. in Child Devel. Office: Pa State U 1600 Woodland Rd Abington PA 19001-3990

RIESS, SUSAN ELIZABETH, lawyer; b. Chgo., Oct. 21, 1956; d. Robert John and Helen Elizabeth (Hughson) Riess; m. Lloyd Perry Korn, June 21, 1986. B in Gen. Studies, U. Miami, Fla., 1978, JD, 1982. Bar: Fla., 1983, Tex., 1984, Calif., 1987. Gen. counsel Roma Corp., Dallas, 1982-86; assoc. McCutchen, Black, Verleger & Shea, L.A., 1987-89; pvt. practice L.A., 1989-91; sr. counsel Nissan Motor Corp., Carson, Calif., 1991-93, Nissan N. Am., Inc., Torrance, Calif., 1994—. Mem. Law Review U. Miami. 1980-82. U. Miami Honor scholar, 1976, 77, 79, Harvey T. Reid scholar, 1979, 80, 81. Mem. ABA, L.A. County Bar Assn., Fla. Bar Assn., Calif. Bar Assn., Am. Corp. Counsel Assn. Home: 4616 Glencoe Ave # 2 Marina Del Rey CA 90292 Office: Nissan N Am Inc PO Box 2814 Torrance CA 90509-2814

RIETH, CHRISTA ELISABETH, psychologist, anthropologist, researcher; b. Hamburg, Germany, Sept. 28, 1946; came to U.S., 1982; d. Hans Heinrich and Inge Erika (Bruns) Rieth; m. Joseph Charles Rieth, July 1, 1988; 3 stepchildren. MSc, U. Hamburg, 1972, MA, 1982, PhD, 1986. Lic. psychologist, Federal Republic of Germany. Exam. officer UN Tng. and Exam. Svc., N.Y.C., 1982-89; pers. officer UN Econ. and Social Commn. for Asia and Pacific, Bangkok, 1989-92; internat. civil servant, ops. officer UN Dept. Peace Keeping Ops., N.Y.C., 1992—; psychologist German Soc. Selection of Personnel for Govt. Positions, Hannover, Germany, 1974-81. Recipient Peter Zenger prize U.S. Embassy, Hamburg, 1966, Silver Band award European Culture Exch. Instn., Bonn, Germany, 1968. Mem. APA, N.Y. Acad. Sci. Home: 10630 Canyon Lake Dr San Diego CA 92131 Office: United Nations UN Plz Room S-2200E New York NY 10017

RIETH, LORI KAY, nursing administrator; b. Sheboygan, Wis., Oct. 6, 1954; d. Felix and Rosalind (Wettstein) R. BSN, Marian Coll., 1977; MS, U. Wis., Milw., 1985. Cert. occupl. health nurse, case mgr. Staff nurse St. Mary's Hosp., Milw., 1977-79; supr. health svcs. Johnson Controls Inc., Milw., 1980-86, Bristol-Myers Squibb, Wallingford, Conn., 1986-88; mgr. corp. med. strategies Owens-Corning, Toledo, 1988-94; mgr. health mgmt. programs Abbott Labs., Abbott Park, Ill., 1994—. Mem. ANA, APHA, Am. Assn. Occupl. Health Nurses (dir. 1991-93, treas. 1993—), Coun. Nurse Leaders Bus. and Health (steering com. 1993—), Sigma Theta Tau. Home: 738 Waterview Dr Round Lake IL 60073 Office: Abbott Labs 200 Abbott Park Rd Abbott Park IL 60064

RIFAS, KAREN ANNABETH, artist, educator; b. Chgo., Mar. 29, 1942; d. William S. Kline and Lucille L. (Wellins) Kligerman; m. Harold M. Rifas, Nov. 22, 1962; children: William Mark, Sheryl Lynn. BEd, U. Miami, 1964, BFA in Sculpture, 1985, MFA in Art and Sculpture, 1988. Instr. U. Miami, Fla., 1988—, Miami-Dade C.C., 1988—, New World Sch. Arts, Miami, 1988—. One-woman show includes Museo De Arte Comtemporaneo, Panama City, 1993; represented in permanent collections Metro-Dade Art in Pub. Places Trust, Miami, Fla., Valencia C.C., Orlando, Fla., Fairchild Tropical Gardens, Miami; exhibited in group shows at North Miami Ctr. of Contemporary Art, 1991. Home: 9603 SW 93d Ave Miami FL 33176

RIFKIND, ARLEEN B., physician, researcher; b. N.Y.C., June 29, 1938; d. Michael C. and Regina (Gottlieb) Brenner; m. Robert S. Rifkind, Dec. 24, 1961; children: Amy, Nina. BA, Bryn Mawr Coll., 1960; MD, NYU, 1964. Intern Bellevue Hosp., N.Y.C., 1964-65, resident, 1965; clin. assoc. Endocrine br. Nat. Cancer Inst., 1965-68; research assoc., asst. resident physician Rockefeller U., 1968-71; asst. prof. medicine Cornell U. Med. Coll., N.Y.C., 1971-82, assoc. prof. medicine, 1983—, asst. prof. pharmacology, 1973-78, assoc. prof., 1978-82, prof., 1983—; chmn. Gen. Faculty Council Cornell U. Med. Coll., 1984-86; mem. Nat. Inst. Environ. Health Scis. Rev. Com., 1981-85, chmn., 1985-86; mem. toxicology study sect. Nat. Inst. Health, 1989-91, chmn. 1991-93; bd. sci. counselors USPHS Agy. for Toxic Substances and Disease Registry, 1991—. Mem. editorial bd. Drug Metabolism and Disposition, 1994—; contbr. articles to profl. jours. Chmn. Friends of the Library, Jewish Theol. Sem. Am., 1984-86; trustee Dalton Sch., 1986-92; mem. Environ. Health and Safety Coun. Am. Health Found., 1990—. Recipient Andrew W. Mellon Tchr.-Scientist award, 1976-78; USPHS spl. fellow, 1968-70, 71-72. Mem. Endocrine Soc., Am. Soc. Clin. Investigation, Am. Soc. Pharmacology and Exptl. Therapeutics, AAAS, Internat. Soc. Study Xenobiotics, Soc. Toxicology. Office: Cornell U Med Coll Dept Pharmacology 1300 York Ave New York NY 10021-4805

RIFMAN, EILEEN NISSENBAUM, music educator; b. Bklyn., June 10, 1944; d. Jack and Sarah (Bednarsh) Nissenbaum; m. Samuel Sholom Rifman, Aug. 12, 1972; children: Edward, Aimee. MusB, Manhattan Sch. Music, 1966, M Music Edn., 1967; MusM, Ind. U., 1970; cert., Fontainebleau, France, 1967. Music specialist N.Y.C. Pub. Sch. System, 1966-67; instr. Long Beach (Calif.) City Coll., 1970-72, Immaculate Heart Coll., Hollywood, Calif., 1971-74, U. Judaism, Hollywood, 1973-74; co-coord. Community Sch. Performing Arts, L.A., 1974-82, instr., 1973-83; pvt. piano tchr. Manhattan Beach, Calif., 1963—; tchr. gifted and talented edn. program GATE, Manhattan Beach, Calif., 1990-91; tchr. Etz Jacob Hebrew Acad., L.A., 1991-94. Performer Pratt Inst., Clinton Hill Symphony, N.Y.C., 1962, Sta. WNYC-FM, 1964. Chair Cultural Arts Com., Manhattan Beach, 1985-86; bd. dirs. Hermosa Beach (Calif.) Community Ctr., 1990-91. Mem. AAUW, Music Tchrs. Assn., Nat. Fedn. Music Clubs (adjudicator 1970). Home: 1700 Lynngrove Dr Manhattan Beach CA 90266-4242

RIGAL, DEBORAH LYNN, insurance claim manager; b. Richland, Wash., Oct. 12, 1952; d. Manfred Altman and Lillian Ruth (Menkes) Bockris; m. Roberto E. Rigal, June 2, 1973 (div. July 1989); children: Robert Thomas, Rachel Paige. BA in Econs., U. Pa., 1974; AA in Legal Assisting, Hillsborough C.C., 1993. Assoc. producer CBS Television/WCAU-TV, Phila., 1970-73; mktg. & acct. exec. Spanish Mktg. & Advt., Phila., 1973-78; claim rep. Cigna Corp., Tampa, Fla., 1978-87, sr. claim rep., 1987-88, claim supr., 1988-92, casualty claim team leader, 1992-94, shared svcs. team leader, 1994—; claim team leader Md. Casualty Ins. Co., 1994—. Mem. ins. adv. com. Hillsborough County Sch. Bd., Tampa, 1990—; vol. March of Dimes, Tampa, 1990-93. Mem. West Coast Claims Assn. (pres. 1991-92). Home: 4309 Shadberry Dr Tampa FL 33624 Office: The Md Ins Group PO Box 25317 Tampa FL 33622-5317

RIGGS, JANET MARIE, cardiovascular nurse. BSN, U. Ky., 1972; MSN, U. Ala. in Birmingham, 1988. CCRN; cert. BCLS. Staff nurse U. Ky. Med. Ctr., 1972-83, team leader, primary nurse neonatal ICU, 1983-86; relief charge nurse, primary nurse cardiac ICU BMC Montclair Hosp., 1986-88; pediatric cardiothoracic clin. nurse specialist St. Christopher's Hosp. for Children, 1988-89; home nurse for adults and children on ventilators Newborn Nurses and Bayada Nurses, 1990—; mem. critical care, pediatric faculty Episc. Hosp. Sch. Nursing affiliate Pa. State U., Phila., 1991—. Mem. ANA, AACN (past bd. dirs. S.E. Pa. chpt., mem. nomination com.), Pa. State Nurses Assn., Am. Heart Assn., Sigma Theta Tau. Home: 13 Battery Hill Dr Voorhees NJ 08043

RIGGS, LINDA KAY, veterinarian; b. Dallas, July 23, 1959; d. Karl Alton Jr. and Patricia Ann (Hartrick) R. BS in Med. Tech., Miss. State U., 1981, DVM, 1990. Registered med. tech.; lic. veterinarian. Staff med. tech. Bapt. Meml. Hosp., Memphis, 1981-86; veterinary med. officer USDA, Jackson, Miss., 1990-91; supervisory veterinary med. officer USDA, Canton, Miss., 1991—. Salsbury Alt. Career scholar Miss. State U., 1990. Mem. AVMA, Miss. Veterinary Med. Assn. Home: 303 Feather Glen Ridgeland MS 39157

RIGGS, MARY LOU, investment executive; b. Ashland, Ky., June 16, 1927; d. John Russell and Elizabeth (Prichard) Fields; m. James Webster, June 16, 1951 (dec. 1969); children: Mary Elizabeth Cohen, Martha Ann Lowry, Marjorie Louise Pike. BA, U. Ky., 1949. Pres. Clothier Corp., Huntington, W.Va., 1981, MLR, Inc., Huntington, 1982, Clothier Investment, Huntington, 1985—. trustee Huntington Mus. Art, 1972-90, Marshall Univ. Artists Series, 1975-76, Salem Acad. and Coll., Winston-Salem, 1984-89; elder Presbyn. ch. Mem. Jr. League Huntington (exec. bd.), Jr. League Garden Club (v.p. Huntington chpt.). Presbyterian. Home: 2109 Holswade Dr Huntington WV 25701-5335

RIGGS, ROBERTA BELL, storage facility owner; b. N.Y.C., Sept. 3, 1930; d. Conrad Jr. and Roberta (Burbridge) Bell; widowed, 1988; children: Margot, Roberta, Isobel Meacham, John Riggs, Elizabeth Riggs. Grad. high sch., Albany, N.Y. Owner, mgr. Mex. House, Inc., La Jolla, Calif., 1970-80, Container Storage, Inc., St. Croix, V.I., 1983—. Mem. St. Croix Yacht Club (rear commodore 1986-88, fleet capt. 1988-90). Democrat. Roman Catholic. Home: # 97 Estate Solitude Christiansted VI 00822 Office: Container Storage Inc PO Box 3945 Christiansted VI 00822

RIGGSBY, DUTCHIE SELLERS, education educator; b. Montgomery, Ala., Oct. 26, 1940; d. Cleveland Malcolm and Marcelia (Bedsole) Sellers; m. Ernest Duward Riggsby, Aug. 25, 1962; 1 child, Lyn. BS, Troy (Ala.) State Coll., 1962, MS, 1965; postgrad., George Peabody Coll., 1963; EdD, Auburn U., 1972. Cert. tchr., Ala., Ga.; cert. libr., Ga. Tchr. Montgomery Pub. Sch.s, 1962-63, Troy City Schs., 1963-67; instr. Auburn (Ala.) U., 1968-69; asst. prof. Columbus (Ga.) Coll., 1972-77, assoc. prof., 1978-83, prof., 1983—; vis. prof. U. P.R., Rio Piedras, 1972, 73; cons. schs. Columbus and Ft. Benning, Ga., 1980; leader various workshops, 1989; software reviewer Nat. Sci. Tchrs. Assn. Photographer: (book) Families, Professionals and Exceptionality, 1986, (textbook) Counseling Parents of Exceptional Children, 1986; contbr. more than 75 articles to profl. jours., 1968—; reviewer instrnl. materials. Educator internal aerospace CAP, Maxwell AFB, 1980-90. Recipient STAR Tchr. award Nat. Sci. Tchrs. Assn., Washington, 1968. Mem. Assn. for Ednl. Comms. and Tech. (non-periodical publs. com. 1994-96, awards com. 1994-96), Nat. Congress on Aviation and Space Edn. (dir. spl. promotions 1986-90), World Aerospace Edn. Orgn., Ga. Assn. Instrnl. Tech. (bd. dirs. 1982-84), Phi Delta Kappa (pres. Chattahochee Valley chpt. 1986-87, Svc. award 1989, Svc. Key award 1993). Baptist. Home: 1709 Ashwood Ct Columbus GA 31904-3009 Office: Columbus Coll Sch Edn 4225 University Ave Columbus GA 31907-5645

RIGSBY, CAROLYN ERWIN, music educator; b. Franklinton, La., Apr. 11, 1936; d. Sheldon Aubrey and Edna Marie (Fussell) Erwin; m. Michael Hall Rigsby, May 30, 1959; 1 child, Laura Elaine Rigsby Boyd. B in Music Edn., Northwestern State U., La., 1958; MEd, Nicholls State U., 1970. Cert. vocal music tchr. k-12. Music tchr. Terrebonne Parish Sch., Houma, La., 1958-81, 81-83; music coord. Terrebonne Parish Sch., Houma, 1983-84;

music tchr. Pasadena (Tex.) Ind. Sch. Dist., 1988—. Mem. Tex. Music Educators Assn., Packard Autombile Classics, Lone Star Packard Club, Delta Kappa Gamma (pres. 1988-90). Republican. Methodist. Home: 16014 Mill Point Dr Houston TX 77059-5216

RIGSBY, LINDA FLORY, lawyer; b. Topeka, Kans., Dec. 16, 1946; d. Alden E. and Lolita M. Flory; m. Michael L. Rigsby, Aug. 14, 1963; children: Michael L. Jr., Elisabeth A. MusB, Va. Commonwealth U., 1969; JD, U. Richmond, 1981. Bar: Va. 1981, D.C. 1988. Assoc. McGuire, Woods, Battle & Boothe, Richmond, Va., 1981-85; dep. gen. counsel Crestar Fin. Corp., Richmond, 1985—. Bd. dirs. Foxchapel Civic Assn., Richmond, 1987-89. Recipient Disting. Svc. award U. Richmond, 1987; named Vol. of Yr. U. Richmond, 1986. Mem. Va. Bar Assn. (exec. com. 1993—), Richmond Bar Assn. (bd. dirs. 1992—), Va. Bankers Assn. (chair legal affairs 1992—), U. Richmond Estate Planning Coun. (chmn. 1990-92). Roman Catholic. Home: 10005 Ashbridge Pl Richmond VA 23233-5402 Office: Crestar Fin Corp 919 E Main St Richmond VA 23219-4625

RIGSBY, SHEILA GOREE, accounting firm executive; b. Macon, Ga., June 13, 1955; d. David Wendell and Carolyn (Canington) Goree; children: Jason, Ryan. Student, Macon Coll., 1979. cert. tax preparer. Tax preparer Better Income Tax Svc., Macon; acct. Bass Tool and Indsl. Supply, Macon, Padgett Bus. Svc., Macon; owner Ind. Acctg. Svcs., Macon. Mem. NAFE, Nat. Fedn. Ind. Businessmen, Nat. Soc. Tax Profls., Nat. Assn. Tax Preparers, Nat. Assn. Tax Practitioners, Ga. Assn. Pub. Accts. Office: 4000 Mercer University Dr Macon GA 31204-5702

RIKE, SUSAN, public relations executive; b. N.Y.C., Aug. 29, 1952; d. George Carson and Mildred Eleanor (Geehr) R. BA cum laude, Bklyn. Coll., 1975. Editorial asst. Artforum Mag., N.Y.C., 1975-77; co-owner Say Cheese, Bklyn., 1977-80; editorial asst. The Star, N.Y.C., 1980-82; acct. sec. Robert Marston and Assocs., N.Y.C., 1983-84; asst. acct. exec. Marketshare, N.Y.C., 1984; acct. exec. Doremus Pub. Rels. BBDO Internat., N.Y.C., 1984-86; pres. Susan Rike Pub. Rels., Bklyn., 1986—. Democrat. Office: Susan Rike Pub Rels 335 State St Ste 3C Brooklyn NY 11217-1719

RILEY, ANN J., state legislator, technology specialist; b. Memphis, Oct. 27, 1940; m. Ray T. Riley, Apr. 28, 1962. BSBA, U. Albuquerque, 1985; MBA, Webster U., 1988; cert. in pub. policy, Harvard U., 1994. Loan officer Ravenswood Bank, Chgo., 1970-74; mgr. dist. sales Security Lockout, Chgo., 1974-77; owner AR Fasteners, Albuquerque, 1977-82; tech. transfer agt. Sandia Nat. Labs., Albuquerque, 1983—; mem. N.Mex. Senate, Santa Fe, 1993—; resolutions chair energy com. Nat. Order of Women Legil. Nat. Conf. State Legislators. Bd. dirs. All Faiths Receiving Home. Albuquerque, 1989-92, Law Enforcement Acad., Santa Fe, 1991-92. Democrat. Home: 10201 Karen NE Albuquerque NM 87111-3635

RILEY, ANN PEOPLES, marketing professional; b. Mooreland, Okla., Dec. 31, 1947; d. Estel Paul and Mary Jane (Munkres) Peoples; m. Michael Edward Riley, June 6, 1970 (div. Nov. 1985); children: Timothy, Andrea. BA, U. Okla., 1970, MA, 1973; JD, Temple U., 1979. Mgmt. cons. Software Inc., Norman, Okla., 1971-72; adj. prof. law Burlington Community Coll., Cinnaminson, N.J., 1979-81, Camden County Coll., Blackwood, N.J., 1981-82; with mktg. support IBM Office Products Div., Phila., 1981-82; program adminstr. nat. mktg. div. IBM, Phila., 1981-83; product mktg. mgr. nat. distbn. div. IBM, Princeton, N.J., 1983-86; program mgr. IBM-Asia Pacific Group, Tokyo, 1986-89; prof. law Newport U., Tokyo, 1988-89; investment cons. IBM-U.S., Somers, N.Y., 1989-92; mem. faculty, IBM exec. Cons. Inst., Palisades, N.Y., 1991; program mgr. human resources IBM Corp., Armonk, N.Y., 1992—. Mem. Fgn. Exec. Women Tokyo, Soc. Human Resource Mgrs. Republican. Roman Catholic. Home: 20 Zygmont Ln Greenwich CT 06831-2706

RILEY, CAROLYN J., critical care, medical, surgical nurse; b. Aledo, Ill., Feb. 1, 1956; d. Alan Gene and Shirley Jean (Sutton) Garmer; m. John P. Riley, June 27, 1982; children: Britney, Shannon, Sean. Student, Black Hawk Coll., Moline, Ill., 1974; diploma in nursing, Meth. Med. Ctr., Peoria, Ill., 1977; student, Ill. Cen. Coll., 1982, Southwestern Bapt. U., Bolivar, Mo., 1985. RN, Ill., Mo., La.; cert. advanced cardicac life support, oncology nurse. Staff nurse Meth. Med. Ctr.; charge nurse Mo. State Chest Hosp., Mt. Vernon; staff nurse St. John's Regional Health Ctr., Springfield, Mo.; charge nurse Beauregard Meml. Hosp., Deridder, La.; staff Nurse Zale Lipshy U., U. Tex., Dallas. Vol. tng. bone marrow transplant Am. Cancer Soc. Zale Lipshy U. Mem. AACCN.

RILEY, DAWN C., educational philosopher, special education educator, researcher; b. Rochester, N.Y., Mar. 18, 1954; d. John Joseph Jr. and June Carol (Cleveland) R. BA in Edn., Polit. Sci., SUNY, 1976; MEd, in Special Edn., summa cum laude, U. Ariz., 1980; PhD, Univ. Calif., Berkeley, 1994. Cert. multiple subject credential (K-Coll.), specialist credential (K-12), Calif., coun. of educators for deaf; elem. permanent credential, N.Y. Elem. sch. tchr., 4th grade Escola Americana do Rio de Janeiro, Brazil, 1975; pvt. practice, commercial artist Rochester, 1972-80; elem. tchr. Rochester City Sch. Dist., 1976-78; rsch. asst., summer vestibule program The Nat. Tech. Inst. for the Deaf, 1976-79; tchr. English, 7th-12th grades The Calif. Sch. for the Deaf-Fremont, 1980-94; rsch. asst. to Dr. Richard J. Morris, dept. special edn. and ednl. psychol. The Univ. Ariz., 1978-80; rsch. asst., Calif. new tchr. support project The Far West Lab. for Ednl. Rsch. & Devel., San Francisco, 1989; chair high sch. English dept. The Calif. Sch. for the Deaf-Fremont, 1990—; coord. & devel., Practical Lang. in Applied Settings Program, 1981-82; chair, Computer Curriculum Com., 1982-84, Critical and Creative Thinking Skills Com., 1983-84; coord. Gifted and Talented Program, 1983—. Recipient Kate Navin O'Neill Grad. scholar Univ. of Calif., Berkeley, 1989; University fellow, 1978-80, Evelyn Lois Corey fellow, 1990; Recipient Sustained Superior Accomplishment award Calif. Dept. Edn., 1991. Mem. AAUW, Nat.Coun. Tchrs. of English, Am. Ednl. Rsch. Assn., Am. Assn. Colls. for Tchr. Edn., Philosophy of Edn. Soc., John Dewey Soc., Phi Beta Kappa. Home: 3015 58th Ave Oakland CA 94605-1123 Office: Calif Sch for the Deaf 39350 Gallaudet Dr Fremont CA 94538-2308

RILEY, DEBORAH ANN, marketing executive; b. Pitts., June 30, 1953; d. Lionel Glen and Ethel Louise (Alexander) Davidson; m. Richard Earl Riley, May 27, 1977 (div. Dec. 1983); children: Steven Earl, Michael Glen. BA, W.Va. Wesleyan Coll., 1975. Sec., treas. Anniston Joint Venture, Inc., Dallas, 1982-85; exec. v.p. Insignia Corp., Dallas, 1985—, bd. dirs.; pres. Sports Concepts, Dallas, 1986-88. Mem. Glenshaw (Pa.) Players, 1975-76. Capt. U.S. Army, 1976-77, with Res. 1981—. Mem. Res. Officers Assn., Nat. Assn. Female Execs., Am. Mgmt. Assn. Republican. Presbyterian. Home: 3526 Highway 66 # B-181 Rowlett TX 75088-4090

RILEY, DOROTHY COMSTOCK, state supreme court justice; b. Detroit, Dec. 6, 1924; d. Charles Austin and Josephine (Grima) Comstock; m. Wallace Don Riley, Sept. 13, 1963; 1 child, Peter Comstock. B.A. in Polit. Sci., Wayne State U., 1946, LL.B., 1949; LLD (hon.), Alma Coll., 1988, U. Detroit, 1990. Bar: Mich. 1950, U.S. Dist. Court (ea. dist.) Mich. 1950, U.S. Supreme Court 1957. Atty. Wayne County Friend of Court, Detroit, 1956-68; ptnr. Riley & Roumell, Detroit, 1968-72, 73-76; judge Wayne County Circuit, Detroit, 1972, Mich. Ct. Appeals, Detroit, 1976-82; assoc. justice Mich. Supreme Court, Detroit, 1982-83, 85—; chief justice Mich. Supreme Court, Lansing, 1987-91; mem. U.S. Jud. Conf. Commn. on State-Fed. Ct. Rels.; chmn. tort reform com. Conf. of Chief Justices; bd. dirs. Nat. Ctr. for State Cts., Thomas J. Cooley Law Sch. Co-author manuals, articles in field. Mem. steering com. Mich. Children Skillman Found., 1992; mem. multistate profl. responsibility exam. com. Nat. Conf. Bar Examiners, 1992. Recipient Disting. Alumni award Wayne U., 1990; Headliner award Women of Wayne, 1977; Donnelly award, 1946; Law Enforcement Commendation medal Nat. Soc. Sons of Am. Revolution, 1991; inducted in Mich. Women's Hall of Fame, 1991. Mem. ABA (family law sect. 1965—, vice chmn. gen. practice sect. com. on juvenile justice 1975-80, mem. jud. adminstrn. sect. 1973—, standing com. on fed. ct. improvements, mem. judges adv. com. of standing com. on ethics and profl. responsibility 1992), Am. Judicature Soc., Fellows Am. Bar Found., Mich. State Bar Found., State Bar Mich. (civil liberties com. 1954-58), Detroit Bar Assn. (pub. rels. com. 1955-56, author Com. in Action column, Detroit Lawyers 1955, chmn. friend of ct. and family law com. 1974-75), Nat. Women Judges Assn., Nat. Women Lawyers Assn., Women Lawyers Assn. Mich. (pres. 1957-58), Mich. Sup. Ct. Hist. Soc., Karyatides, Pi Sigma Alpha. Republican. Roman Catholic. Office: Mich Supreme Ct 500 Woodward Ave 20th Fl Detroit MI 48226

RILEY, GEORGIANNE MARIE, lawyer; b. Chgo., Feb. 5, 1953. BA in Psychology, Drake U., 1974, JD, 1978. Bar: Ill., 1978. Chief counsel Ill. Indsl. Commn., Chgo., 1979-83; dep. chief counsel Ill. Dept. Transp., Chgo., 1983-89; counsel Chem. Waste Mgmt., Oakbrook, Ill., 1989-91, sr. counsel, 1991-92; gen. counsel, v.p., sec. Rust Indsl. Svcs., Westchester, Ill., 1993—. Office: Waste Mgmt Inc 3003 Butterfield Rd Oak Brook IL 60521

RILEY, HELENE MARIA KASTINGER, Germanist; b. Vienna, Austria, Mar. 11, 1939; came to U.S., 1959; d. Josef and Helene (Friedl) Kastinger; m. Edward R. Riley, Nov. 6, 1957 (div. May 1970); children: India Helene, John Edward, Jesse Dale, Michael Rutledge; m. Darius G. Ornston, May 11, 1983. Grad., bus. coll., Vienna, 1955; BA in Music, North Tex. State U., 1970; MA in Germanics, Rice U., 1973, PhD in Germanics, 1975. Teaching asst. Rice U., Houston, 1971-75; asst. prof. German Yale U., New Haven, Conn., 1975-78, head summer lang. inst., 1979-81, assoc. prof., 1979-85; chmn. Dept. Fgn. Langs. Wash. State U., Pullman, 1981-82; head Dept. Langs. Clemson (S.C.) U., 1985-86, prof., 1985—; guest prof. Middlebury (Vt.) Coll., 1976; speaker in field. Author: Achim von Arnim, 1979, Virginia Woolf, 1983, Clemens Brentano, 1985, Die Weibliche Muse, 1986, Max Weber, 1991, others; contbr. numerous articles to profl. jours. Grantee Griswold Found., 1975-76, 78, S.C. Dept. Edn., 1986, NEH, 1986, Provost's award, Clemson U., 1989, Hilles Fund, 1976, 79, 82; NDEA fellow, 1972, 73; Rice fellow, 1971, 74; Morse fellow, 1977-78; Deutscher Akademischer Austausch-Dienst, 1979; sr. faculty fellow Yale U., 1981-82; Holland Fund, 1982; Deutsche Forschungsgemeinschaft, 1982; recipient German-Am. Friendship award Consul Gen. of the German Fed. Republic, 1989; Mesda fellow, 1993. Fellow Davenport Coll., Yale U.; mem. AAUP (v.p. 1987-88, pres. 1988-89), MLA, Am. Assn. Tchrs. German, So. Comparative Lit. Assn., others. Democrat. Office: Clemson U Dept Langs 717 Strode Twr Clemson SC 29634-1515

RILEY, KATHLEEN ANN, pharmaceuticals consultant; b. Norfolk, Va., Jan. 30, 1945; d. Edward Miles and Ruth Annette (Powers) R.; m. Wendell Earl Dunn III, Mar. 29, 1981; 1 child, Elissa Brooks Dunn. Student, Tulane U., 1962-64; BS in Chemistry, Coll. William & Mary, 1967; MS, U. Ill., 1970; MBA, Northwestern U., 1977. Pharm. chemist Abbott Labs., North Chicago, Ill., 1970-73; clinical research assoc. Abbott Labs., North Chicago, 1973-75; cons. Mgmt. Analysis Ctr., Northbrook, Ill., 1975-76; mgr. strategic planning agrl. chemicals FMC Corp., Phila., 1977-81, mgr. strategic planning phosphorus chemicals, 1981-82; mgr. new compound opportunities Smith Kline French Internat. Labs., Phila., 1982-86, market planning mgr., 1986-88; assoc. dir. new product evaluation Smith, Kline & French, Phila., 1988-89; assoc. dir. new compound evaluation Smith Kline Beecham Pharms., Phila., 1989-91, dir. product evaluation and analysis, 1991-94, dir. portfolio planning, 1994; prin. The Gladstone Group, Haddonfield, N.J., 1995—. Patentee in field; contbr. articles to profl. jours. Bd. dirs. Community Arts Alliance, Phila., 1982-87; cons., counselor Girl Scouts Am., Haddonfield, N.J., 1986-87. Mem. World Future Soc. (profl.), Internat. Health Futures Network, Phila. Women's Network (bd. dirs. 1980-84, treas. 1983-84, chmn. strategic planning com. 1982-87), Haddon Fortnightly Club (program speaker 1991, 93, bd. dirs. 1987-93, chmn. internat. rels. com. 1987-89, chmn. conservation and gardening com. 1987-91, internat. affairs com. 1991-93), Sigma Xi, Iota Sigma Pi. Lutheran. Office: 443 Gladstone Ave Haddonfield NJ 08033-4005

RILEY, LYNNE JOYCE, veterinarian; b. N.J., Mar. 28, 1953; d. Joseph Carroll and Barbara (Joyce) R. Student, Mary Wash. Coll., 1971-72; BS in Wildlife Conservation, N.C. State U., 1975, DVM, 1990. Asst. curator Cohanzick Zoo, Bridgeton, N.J., 1976-78; curator Cape May County Park Zoo, Cape May Court House, N.J., 1978-79; zookeeper Phila. Zool. Park, 1979; conservation officer N.J. Divsn. Fish, Game and Wildlife, Williamstown, 1979; vegetation wildlife specialist N.J. Pinelands Commn., New Lisbon, 1979-84; technician Coll. Vet. Medicine N.C. State U., Raleigh, 1984-86; vet. med. officer USDA/Animal Plant Health Inspection Svc., Lumberton, N.C., 1990—; coord. N.C. and Southeast Regional exercise program USDA/Animal Plant Health Inspection Svcs., Lumberton, 1993—; fgn. animal disease diagnostician USDA/APHIS Vet. Svcs., Lumberton, 1991—, recruiter animal/plant svc. coord. vol. flock cert. program, 1992—; chairperson N.C. Vet. Svc. Equal Opportunity and Civil Rights com., 1992—. Lay min., CCD tchr., parish coun. St. Francis de Sales Parish, Lumberton, 1991-93; mem. Woodhaven Nursing Home Pet Therapy, 1991-93. Mem. Nat. Assn. Fed. Vets., Optimists (sec.-treas. Lumberton chpt. 1992, v.p. 1993—), Robeson County Vet. Assn., Twin State Vet. Med. Assn., Phi Zeta. Roman Catholic. Office: USDA/APHIS Vet Svcs PO Box 27048 Raleigh NC 27611-7048

RILEY, MARILYN GLEDHILL, communications executive; b. Pitts., Pa., July 17, 1954; d. John Edward and Mary Elizabeth (Ogden) Gledhill; m. John F. Riley Jr. AS with high honors, Community Coll. of Allegheny County, 1981; BS in Bus. Adminstrn. cum laude, Robert Morris Coll., 1985. Sec. MODCOM Assocs., Pitts., 1977-79, asst. account exec., 1979-82, account exec., 1982-84; gen. mgr. MODCOM Advt., Pitts., 1984-90, v.p., gen. mgr., 1989-90; dir. comms. Allegheny County Med. Soc., Pitts., 1990-93; advt. mgr. Intergroup Healthcare Corp., Phoenix, Ariz., 1994—; guest speaker Pa. State U., Robert Morris Coll., Allegheny C.C., 1987; mem. pub. issues and info. com. adolescent resource network adv. bd. Hosp. Coun. of West Pa., 1990-93. Mem. editorial bd. Nursing News, 1991. Communications vol. North Hills Art Festival, McCandless, Pa., 1986-87; judge Jefferson (Pa.) Hosp. Poster Contest, 1987; bd. mgrs. YMCA North Boroughs; reading tutor Greater Pitts. Literacy Coun., 1988-89; bd. dirs. Rachel Carson Homestead Assn. Recipient Communications Mgmt. Honors award Robert Morris Coll. Mem. Bus. and Profl. Advt. Assn. (bd. dirs., v.p. edn.), North Hills C. of C., SMC Pa. Small Bus. Coun., Pitts. Advt. Club, Phoenix Advt. Club, Alpha Tau Sigma. Office: Intergroup Healthcare Corp 2800 N 44th St 10th Fl Phoenix AZ 85008

RILEY, MATILDA WHITE (MRS. JOHN W. RILEY, JR.), sociology educator; b. Boston, Apr. 19, 1911; d. Percival and Mary (Cliff) White; m. John Winchell Riley, Jr., June 19, 1931; children: John Winchell III, Lucy Ellen Riley Sallick. BA, Radcliffe Coll., 1931, MA, 1937, DSc (hon.), 1994; DSc, Bowdoin Coll., 1972; LHD (hon.), Rutgers U., 1983. Rsch. asst. Harvard U., Cambridge, Mass., 1932; v.p. Market Rsch. Co. Am., 1938-49; chief cons. economist WPB, 1941; rsch. specialist Rutgers U., 1950, prof., 1951-73, dir. sociology lab., chmn. dept. sociology and anthropology, 1959-73, emeritus prof., 1973—; Daniel B. Fayerweather prof. polit. econ. and sociology Bowdoin Coll., 1974-78, prof. emeritus, 1978—; assoc. dir. Nat. Inst. on Aging, 1979-91, sr. social scientist, 1991—; mem. faculty Harvard U., summer 1955; staff assoc., dir. aging and society Russell Sage Found., 1964-73, staff sociologist, 1974-77; chmn. com. on life course Social Sci. Rsch. Coun., 1977-80; sr. rsch. assoc. Ctr. for Social Scis., Columbia U., 1978-80; adv. bd. Carnegie Aging Soc. Project, 1985-87; mem. Commn. on Coll. Retirement, 1982-86; vis. prof. NYU, 1954-61; cons. Nat. Coun. on Aging, Acad. Ednl. Devel.; mem. study group NIH, 1971-79, Social Sci. Rsch. Coun. Com. on Middle Years, 1973-77; chmn. NIH Task Force on Health and Behavior, 1986-91; cons. WHO, 1987—; Winkelman lectr. U. Mich., 1984, Selo lectr. U. No. Calif., 1987, Boettner lectr. Am. Coll., 1990, Claude Pepper lectr. Fla. State U., 1993, Disting. lectr. Southwestern Social Scis. Assn., 1990, Standing lectr. SUNY, 1992, Inaugural lectr. Cornell U., 1992; lectr. Internat. Inst. of Sociology, Plenary, 1993, Inter-Univ. Consortium Pol. and Social Rsch., U. Mich., 1993, Duke U., 1993. Author: (with P. White) Gliding and Soaring, (with Riley and Toby) Sociological Studies in Scale Analysis, 1954, Sociological Research, vols. I, II, 1964, (with others) Aging and Society, vol. I, 1968, vol. II, 1969, vol. III, 1972, (with Nelson) Sociological Observation, 1974, Aging from Birth to Death: Interdisciplinary Perspectives, 1979, (with Merton) Sociological Traditions from Generation to Generation, 1980, (with Abeles and Teitelbaum) Aging from Birth to Death: Sociotemporal Perspectives, 1982, (with Hess and Bond) Aging in Society, 1983; editor: (with M. Ory and D. Zablotsky) AIDS in an Aging Society: What We Need to Know, 1989; co-editor: Perspectives in Behavioral Medicine: The Aging Dimension, 1987, (with J. W. Riley) The Quality of Aging, 1989, The Annuals, 1989; sr. editor: Structural Lag, 1994; editorial com.: Ann. Rev. Sociology, 1978-81, Social Change and the Life Course, vol. 1, Social Structures and Human Lives, (with B. Huber and B. Hess) Sociological Lives, vol. II, 1988; contbr. chpts. to books, articles to profl. jours. Former trustee The Big Sisters Assn. Recipient Lindback Rsch. award Rutgers U., 1970, Social Sci. award Andrus Gerontology Ctr., U. So. Calif., 1972, Radcliffe Alumnae award, 1982, Commonwealth award 1984, Kesten Lecture award U. So. Calif., 1987, Sci. Achievement award Washington Acad. Scis., 1989, Disting. Sci. award, 1989, Disting. Creative award Gerontol. Soc. Am., 1990, Presdl. Meritorious award, 1990, Stuart Rice award Columbia Sociol. Soc., 1992, Kent award Gerontol. Soc. Am., 1992; fellow Advanced Study in Behavioral Scis., 1978-79; Matilda White Riley award in rsch. and methodology established in her honor Rutgers U., 1977; Matilda White Riley prize established Bowdoin Coll., 1987. Fellow AAAS (chmn. sect. on social and econ. scis. 1977-78); mem. NAS, Inst. Medicine of NAS (sr.), Acad. Behavioral Medicine Rsch., Am. Sociol. Assn. (exec. officer 1949-60, v.p. 1973-74, pres. 1986, 91, chmn. sect. on sociology of aging 1989, Disting. Scholar in Aging 1988, Career award 1992), Am. Assn. Public Opinion Rsch. (sec.-treas. 1949-51, Disting. Svc. award 1983), Eastern Sociol. Soc. (v.p. 1968-69, pres. 1977-78, Disting. Career award 1986), Soc. for Study Social Biology (bd. dirs. 1986-92), Am. Acad. Arts and Scis., D.C. Sl. Soc. (co-pres. 1983-84), Sociol. Rsch. Assn., Internat. Orgn. Study Human Devel., Am. Philos. Soc. (membership lectr. 1987), Phi Beta Kappa, Phi Beta Kappa Assocs. Home: 4701 Willard Ave Apt 1607 Chevy Chase MD 20815-4630 Office: NIH Nat Inst on Aging 7201 Wisconsin Ave Bethesda MD 20814-4808

RILEY, MONICA, microbiologist, educator; b. New Orleans, Oct. 4, 1926; d. Chauncey Wesley and Maude (Kemper) R.; children: Adam, Christine (dec.), Katherine. BA, Smith Coll., 1947; PhD, U. Calif.-Berkeley, 1960. Asst. prof. U. Calif., Davis, 1960-66; assoc. prof. SUNY-Stony Brook, 1966-75, prof. and provost, 1975-78, prof. biochemistry, 1975-89, acting chmn., 1984-85, emeritus prof., 1989—; sr. scientist Marine Biol. Lab., Mass., 1989—; vis. prof. U. Paris-Sud-Orsay, 1991—; mem. program com. for meeting Engineered Organisms in the Environment, 1985; mem. rev. panel NSF; organizer Conf. on Orgn. Bacterial Chromosome, 1988; chair Gordon Rsch. Conf. on Population Biology of Microorganisms, 1989; mem. Recombinant DNA Adv. Com. NIH, 1988-91; lectr. Found. for Microbiology, 1987-88; co-organizer 1st Internat. Conf. on E coli Genome, 1992, coord. 3d conf., 1993-94. Editor: The Bacterial Chromosome, 1990; co-editor: Escherichia coli and Salmonella typhimurium, 2d edit.; contbr. articles to profl. jours., chpts. to books. Bd. dirs. Brookhaven chpt. LWV, N.Y., 1982-87, Falmouth chpt., Mass., 1990—. Grantee NIH, 1960—, NSF, 1960—. Mem. Am. Soc. Microbiology (chmn. com. genetic and molecular microbiology of pub. and sci. affairs bd. 1984-90, chmn. com. genomics 1991-94), Genetics Soc. Am., Am. Soc. Biol. Chemists, Phi Beta Kappa, Sigma Xi. Office: Marine Biol Lab Woods Hole MA 02543

RILEY-DAVIS, SHIRLEY MERLE, advertising agency executive, marketing consultant, writer; b. Pitts., Feb. 4, 1935; d. William Riley and Beatrice Estelle (Whittaker) Byrd; m. Louis Davis; 1 child, Terri Judith. Student U. Pitts., 1952. Copywriter, Pitts. Mercantile Co., 1954-60; exec. sec. U. Mich., Ann Arbor, 1962-67; copy supr. N.W. Ayer, N.Y.C., 1968-76, assoc. creative dir., Chgo., 1977-81; copy supr. Leo Burnett, Chgo., 1981-86; freelance advt. and mktg. cons., 1986—; advt. and mktg. dir. Child and Family Svc., Ypsilanti, Mich., 1992—; vis. prof. Urban League Black Exec. Exch. Program; print, radio, and TV commercials. Recipient Grand and First prize N.Y. Film Festival, 1973, Gold and Silver medal Atlanta Film Festival, 1973, Gold medal V.I. Film Festival, 1974, 50 Best Creatives award Am. Inst. Graphic Arts, 1972, Clio award, 1973, 74, 75, Andy Award of Merit, 1981, Silver medal Internat. Film Festival, 1982, Corp. Mgmt. Assistance Program award, 1986, Good Sam award 1981, Svc. Advt. Creativity of Distinction cert., 1981; Senatorial scholar. Mem. Women in Film, Facets Multimedia Film Theatre Orgn. (past bd. dirs.), Greater Chgo. Coun. for Prevention of Child Abuse (past bd. dirs.), Internat. Platform Assn. Democrat. Roman Catholic. Avocations: dance, poetry, design, writing, volunteering. Office: 118 S Washington Ypsilanti MI 48197

RILEY-SCOTT, BARBARA POLK, librarian; b. Roselle, N.J., Nov. 21, 1928; d. Charles Carrington and Olive Bond P.; AB, Howard U., 1950; BS, N.J. Coll. Women, 1951; MS, Columbia U., 1955; m. George Emerson Riley, Feb. 23, 1957 (dec.); children: George E., Glenn C., Karen O.; m. William I. Scott, Oct. 6, 1990. Asst. librarian, Fla. A&M U., 1951-53; with Morgan State Coll., 1955; with Dept. Def., 1955-57, S.C. State Coll., 1957-59, U.Wis., 1958-59; asst. librarian Atlanta U., 1960-68; asst. dir. Union County Anti Poverty Council, 1968; librarian Union County Tech. Inst., Scotch Plains, N.J., 1968-82, Plainfield campus Union County Coll., 1982—. Mem. Roselle Bd. Edn., 1976-78; bd. dirs. Union County Anti Poverty Council, 1969-72; mem. Roselle Human Relations Commn., 1971-73, Plainfield Sci. Center, 1974-76, Union County Psychiat. Clinic, 1980-83, Pinewood Sr. Citizens Council, 1981-85; bd. dirs. Project, Women of N.J, 1985-93, Pinewood Sr. Citizen Housing, 1981-85, Black Women's History Conf., 1985—, pres., 1989-91. Mem. N.J. Library Assn., Council Library Tech., ALA (Black caucas), N.J. Coalition of 100 Black Women, African Am. Women's Polit. Caucus, N.J. Black Librarians Network (bd. dirs.), Links, Inc. (North Jersey chpt.), Black Women's History Conf., Alpha Kappa Alpha. Mem. A.M.E. Ch. Club: Just-A-Mere Lit. Home: 114 E 7th Ave Roselle NJ 07203-2028 Office: 232 E 2d St Plainfield NJ 07060-1308

RILL, BARBARA JEAN, family counselor; b. Long Beach, Calif., Nov. 13, 1946; d. Frank and Dorothy (Hudsbeth) Perkins; m. Robert E. Rill Jr., Aug. 18, 1967; children: Brigette Anne, Brent Allen. BA, Biola U., 1968; MA, Ctrl. Mich. U., 1989. Lic. profl. counselor. Dir. women's ministries Good News Camp, Gladwin, Mich., 1974-89; chem. dependency specialist Bay Haven Outpatient Clinic, Bay City, Mich., 1989-91; dir. Today's Family Life Counseling & Ednl. Ctr., Midland, Mich., 1991—; mem. external adv. bd. dept. counseling and spl. edn. Ctrl. Mich. U., Mt. Pleasant, 1992—. Mem. Am. Counseling Assn., Am. Assn. Christian Counselors. Republican. Home: PO Box 372 Gladwin MI 48624 Office: Today's Family Life Ctr PO Box 366 510 E Isabella Midland MI 48640

RILL, LYNDA REILLY, elementary education educator; b. New Haven, Sept. 24, 1945; d. Matthew Joseph and Margaret (Mulcreevy) Reilly; m. Thomas Albert Rill, Aug. 10, 1968; children: Christopher Collin, Scott Sargent. BA, Albertus Magnus Coll., 1967; postgrad., Syracuse U., 1987. Cert. tchr., grades N-6, English tchr. grades 7-9, N.Y. Tchr. Amity Jr. High Sch., Bethany, Conn., 1967-68, Ensworth Sch., Nashville, 1968-70; tchr. grades 8-9 Waterville (N.Y.) High Sch., 1970-71; diet and nutrition counselor The Diet Ctr., Fayetteville, N.Y., 1982-85; tchr. grade 6 St. Ann's Sch., Syracuse, N.Y., 1985-94; tchg. grade 6 Donlin Dr. Elem., Liverpool, N.Y., 1994—; tchr. rep. St. Ann's PTA, Syracuse, 1989-90; sci. mentor St. Ann's Sch., Syracuse, 1988-94, coord. sci. fair; rep. tchrs. coun. Diocese of Syracuse, N.Y., 1985-86. Pres. Dewittshire Cmty. Club, Dewitt, N.Y., 1977-78; girl scout leader, Dewitt, 1977-78; v.p. Moses Dewitt PTA, 1979-80, pres., 1980-81; bd. dirs. Jr. League, Syracuse, N.Y., 1978-79. Mem. Nat. Assn. Sci. Tchrs., Nat. Cath. Ednl. Assn., Nat. Coun. Tchrs. English. Roman Catholic. Home: 201 Wellington Rd De Witt NY 13214-2225 Office: Donlin Dr Elem Sch Donlin Dr Liverpool NY 13088

RIMA, INGRID HAHNE, economics educator; d. Max F. and Hertha G. (Grunsfeld) Hahne; m. Philip W. Rima; children: David, Eric. BA with honors, CUNY, 1945; MA, U. Pa., 1946, PhD, 1951. Prof. econs. Temple U., Phila., 1967—. Author: Development of Economic Analysis, 1967, 5th edit., 1991, Labor Markets Wages and Employment, 1981, The Joan Robinson Legacy, 1991, The Political Economy of Global Restructuring, Vol. I, Production and Organization, Vol. II, Trade and Finance, 1993, Measurement, Quantification and Economic Analysis, 1994. Fellow Ea. Econ. Assn.; mem. Am. Econ. Assn., History of Econs. Soc. (pres. 1993-4), Phi Beta Kappa. Office: Temple U Broad & Montgomery Ave Philadelphia PA 19122

RIMBACH, EVANGELINE LOIS, music educator; b. Portland, Oreg., June 28, 1932; d. Raymond Walter and Viola Clara (Gaebler) Rimbach. BA, Valparaiso (Ind.) U., 1954; MMus, Eastman Sch. Music, Rochester, N.Y., 1956; PhD, Eastman Sch. Music, 1967; student, Pacific Luth. U., Parkland, Wash., 1950-52. Vocal music instr. Goodwin Jr. High Sch., Redwood City, Calif., 1956-57; music instr. Calif. Concordia Coll., Oakland, Calif., 1957-62; prof. music Concordia U., River Forest, Ill.,

1964—, chmn. dept., 1989—. Contbg. editor: Church Music, 1965-80; editor book: Johann Kuhnau: Magnificat, 1980; editor cantata: Johann Kuhnau: Lobe den Herrn, 1993; contbr. articles to profl. jours. Bd. dirs. Civic Symphony of Oak Park-River Forest, 1974-80, concert com. chmn., 1976-78, prog. annotator, 1976-80; mem. choir Grace Luth. Ch., River Forest, 1964—. AAUW postdoctoral fellow, 1969-70; DAAD grantee, Munich, 1980; recipient Rose of Honor award, Sigma Alpha Iota, 1987. Mem. Am. Musicol. Soc., Am. Recorder Soc., Luth. Edn. Assn., Sigma Alpha Iota. Republican. Lutheran. Home: 1115 Bonnie Brae Pl River Forest IL 60305-1515 Office: Concordia U 7400 Augusta St River Forest IL 60305-1402

RIMEL, REBECCA WEBSTER, foundation executive. BS, U. Va., 1973; MBA, James Madison U., 1983. RN, Va. Head nurse, emergency dept. U. Va. Hosp., Charlottesville, 1973-74, coord. med. out-patient dept., 1974-75, nurse practitioner dept. neurosurgery, 1975-77, instr. in neurosurgery, 1975-80, asst. prof., 1981-83; program mgr. health Pew Charitable Trusts, Phila., 1983-84; asst. v.p. Glenmede Trust Co., Pew Charitable Trusts, Phila., 1984-85; v.p. for programs Pew Charitable Trusts, Phila., 1985-88, exec. dir., 1988-94; pres., 1994—; mem. Coun. on Founds., Washington; prin. investigator dept. neurosurgery U. Va., 1981-85; adv. com. for U.S. Olympics on Boxing, 1983-86; adv. coun. Nat. Inst. of Neurol. Disorders & Strokes, 1988-91, also bd. dirs.; bd. dirs. Nat. Environ. Edn. and Tng. Found., Inc., Washington, Thomas Jefferson Meml. Found., Ind. Sector, Washington. Contbr. articles and abstracts to profl. jours., chpts. in books. Recipient Disting. Nursing Alumni award U. Va., 1988; Kellogg Nat. fellow, 1982. Mem. APHA, ANA, Va. State Nurses Assn. (membership and credentials com. 1982-86), Am. Acad. Nursing, Am. Assn. Neurosurg. Nurses, Emergency Dept. Nurses Assn.

RIMLAND, LISA PHILLIP, writer, composer, lyricist, artist; b. Stamford, Conn., Mar. 27, 1954; d. Maurice Louis and Eva (Kreiz) R. BA, U. Conn., 1978. Owner Ph Rimland Press, Storrs, Conn., 1991—. Composer numerous songs, including Your Heart or Mine, 1990, Drive Me Crazy, 1991, Send Me an Angel, 1992; contbr. articles, essays to profl. jours. Vol. dairy barn U. Conn., 1992—, vol. photographer Morgan horse facility, 1982-91. Recipient DAR award, 1969, Soc. Women Engrs. award, 1971; Nat. Merit scholar, 1972. Mem. ASCAP. Home: PO Box 408 Storrs Mansfield CT 06268-0408

RIMSKY-CLARKE, LAURENCE TATIANA, molecular biologist; b. Paris, Aug. 4, 1957; came to U.S., 1987; d. Alexandre and Yveline Mauricette (Renault) Rimsky; m. Peter Leonard Clarke, Dec. 4, 1989; children: Maxin Alexandre Hasche, Herve Yves Penfield, Rémy Pierre Bushnell. PhD in Biochemistry, U. Pierre and Marie Curie, Paris, 1984. Postdoctoral fellow Institut de la Recherche sur le Cancer, Villejuif, France, 1984-87; rsch. assoc. Howard Hughes Med. Inst., Durham, N.C., 1987-89; rsch. investigator Rhone Poulenc Rorer, Paris, 1989-90; rsch. assoc. Ctr. for AIDS Rsch., Duke U., Durham, 1990—; rsch. assoc. prof. Pasteur Inst., Paris, 1989-90. Contbr. articles to profl. jours.; patentee in field. Mem. Am. Soc. Microbiology, Mothers of Multiples Club. Home: 3822 Hillgrand Dr Durham NC 27705 Office: Duke U Med Ctr Ctr for AIDS Rsch SORF-118 Box 2926 Durham NC 27710

RINCK, ELIZABETH APPEL, editor; b. Indpls., Apr. 14, 1961; d. Wilbur Lewis and Myrna Jeanne (Pipes) Appel; m. Jeffrey Bliss Rinck, May 11, 1985. BS, Butler U., 1983. Asst. editor Internat. Computer Programs, Indpls., 1982; coord. community rels. John County Meml. Hosp., Franklin, Ind., 1983-85; editor Children's Playmate Children's Digest Mag., Indpls., 1985-94; editl. dir. Children's Better Health Inst., 1994—; editor Turtle Mag. for Presch. Kids, 1994—; speaker Reader's Digest/ U. S.C. Mag. Writing Workshop, 1993. Guest editor Pacific N.W. Writer's Conf., 1994; contbg. editor Children's Mag. Mkt., 1992. Bd. advisors Young Writer's Contest Found., McLean, Va., 1985-91. Recipient Edn. Press Disting. Achievement award for Excellence in Ednl. Journalism, 1991. Mem. Soc. Profl. Journalists, Ednl. Press Assn. Am. (Ednl. Journalism Disting. Achievment award 1991). Office: Children's Better Health Inst PO Box 567 1100 Waterway Blvd Indianapolis IN 46206

RINDSKOPF, ELIZABETH R., general counsel; b. Detroit, Dec. 2, 1943; d. Arthur C. and Kathryn G. (Rodgers) Roediger; m. Peter E. Rindskopf, May 25, 1968. BA in Philosophy cum laude, U. Mich., 1964, JD, 1968. Bar: Ga. 1968, U.S. Dist. Ct. (no. dist.) Ga. 1969, U.S. Ct. Appeals (5th cir.) 1970, U.S. Supreme Ct. 1971, U.S. Ct. Appeals (6th cir.) 1972, U.S. Ct. Appeals (3rd cir.) 1974, U.S. Ct. Appeals (4th cir.) 1977, U.S. Ct. Appeals (9th cir.) 1978, D.C. 1979. Reginald Heber Smith fellow, mng. atty. Emory Legal Svcs., Atlanta, 1968-71; ptnr. Moore, Alexander & Rindskopf, Atlanta, 1971-74; dir. New Haven Legal Assistance Assn., Inc., 1974-76; dep. dir. Lawyers Com. Civil Rights Under Law, Washington, 1978-78; ptnr. Cohen, Vitt & Annand, Alexandria, Va., 1978-79; acting asst. dir. mergers and joint ventures, dep. asst. dir. health care Bur. of Competition, Fed. Trade Commn., 1979-81; of counsel Surrey & Morse, Washington, 1981-84; gen. counsel Nat. Security Agy., Dept. of Def., 1984-89; prin. dep. office of the legal adviser Dept. of State, 1989-90; gen. counsel CIA, Washington, 1990—; co-operating atty. NAACP Legal Def. and Edn. Fund, Inc., 1971-74. Contbr. articles to profl. jours. Mem. ABA (standing com. law and nat. security), Coun. Fgn. Rels. Office: US Dept Def Nat Security Agy The Pentagon Washington DC 20301 also: CIA Office Of Gen Counsel Washington DC 20505*

RINEHART, NITA, state senator; b. Tex. BA, So. Meth. U.; JD. U. Wash. Mem. Wash. State Ho. of Reps., 1979-82; mem. Wash. State Senate, 1983—, vice chmn. edn. com., mem. rules, ways and means, govtl. ops. coms. Bd. dirs. Planned Parenthood of Seattle. Mem. LWV, Bus. and Profl. Women. Democrat. Office: State Senate State Capitol Olympia WA 98504 Home: 4515 51st Ave NE Seattle WA 98105-3830*

RING, RENEE E., lawyer; b. Frankfurt, Germany, May 29, 1950; arrived in U.S., 1950; d. Vincent Martin and Etheline Bergetta (Schoolmeesters) R.; m. Paul J. Zofnass, June 24, 1982; Jessica Renee, Rebecca Anne. BA, Catholic U. Am., 1972; JD, U. Va., 1976. Bar: N.Y. 1977. Assoc. Whitman & Ransom, N.Y.C., 1976-83; assoc. Carro, Spanbock, Fass, Geller, Kaster & Cuiffo, N.Y.C., 1983-86, ptnr., 1986; ptnr. Finley Kumble Wagner et. al., N.Y.C., 1987; of counsel Kaye, Scholer, Fierman, Hays & Handler, N.Y.C., 1988; ptnr. Kaye Scholer Fierman Hays & Handler, N.Y.C., 1989—. Mem. exec. com. Lawyers for Clinton, Washington, 1991-92; team capt. Clinton Transition Team, Washington, 1992-93; mem. Nat. Lawyers Coun. Dem. Nat. Com., 1993—. Mem. ABA (chmn. programs subcom. for partnerships com., sect. bus. law), N.Y. Women's Bar Assn. Democrat. Roman Catholic. Office: Kaye Scholer Fierman Hays & Handler 425 Park Ave New York NY 10022-3506

RINGEL, ELEANOR, film critic; b. Atlanta, Nov. 3, 1950; d. Herbert Arthur and Sara (Finklestein) R.; m. John Gillespie, Nov. 18, 1989. BA magna cum laude, Brown U., 1972. With Alliance Theatre, 1974, S.C. Open Road Ensemble, 1974-75, N.Y. Shakespeare Festival, 1975-78, Children's TV Workshop, 1975-77; obituary writer Atlanta Jour., 1978; critic, editor Atlanta Jour.-Constitution Film, 1978—. Named Best Local Critic Atlanta Mag., 1990, Best of Cox Newspapers Critisims, 1987, Finalist Citations Critisims, 1984-85, Merit award, 1981. Mem. Nat. Soc. Film Critics (elected). Home: 235 1/2 East Wesley Rd Atlanta GA 30305 Office: Atlanta Journal Constitution Entertainment Desk 72 Marietta St NW Atlanta GA 30303-2804

RINGGENBERG, CHRISTINE MARIE, radiologic technologist, sonographer; b. Great Lakes, Ill., Feb. 2, 1964; d. Verl Albert and Betty Jane (Buddenhagen) R. AAS, SUNY Health Sci. Ctr., Syracuse, 1984; postgrad., Ultrasound Diagnostic Sch., 1991-93, Med. Tech. Mgmt. Inst., 1994. Radiologic technologist St. Anthonys Hosp., Warwick, N.Y., 1984-85, Horton Meml. Hosp., Middletown, N.Y., 1984-85, Cornwall (N.Y.) Hosp., 1985-88, Health Med., New Windsor, N.Y., 1985-88; radiologic technologist, sonographer CAT scan technologist VA Med. Ctr., Castle Point, N.Y., 1988—. Dept. coord. Savings Bond Campaign, Castle Point, 1988, 94, United Way/ Combined Fed. Campaign, Castle Point, 1988, 89. Mem. Am. Registry Diagnostic Sonographers, Am. Registry Radiologic Technologists, Soc. Diagnostic Med. Sonographers. Independent. Presbyterian. Home: 297 Quassaick Ave New Windsor NY 12553 Office: VMAC Castle Point Castle Point Rd Castle Point NY 12511

RINGGOLD, FAITH, artist; b. N.Y.C., Oct. 8, 1930. B.S., CCNY, 1955; M.A., 1959; DFA (hon.), Moore Coll. Art, Phila., 1986, Coll. Wooster, Ohio, 1987, Mass. Coll. Art, Boston, 1991, CCNY of CUNY, 1991, DSc (hon.), Brockport (N.Y.) State U., 1992, Calif. Coll. Arts. and Crafts, Oakland, Calif., 1993, RISD, 1994. Art tchr. N.Y. Pub. Schs., 1955-73; lectr. Bank St. Coll. Grad. Sch., N.Y.C., 1970-80; prof. art U. Calif., San Diego, 1984—. Solo exhbns. include Spectrum Gallery, N.Y.C., 1967, 70, 10 year retrospective, Voorhees Gallery, Rutgers U., 1973, Summit Gallery, N.Y.C., 1979, 20 year Retrospective, Studio Mus. in Harlem, N.Y.C., 1984, Bernice Steinbaum Gallery, N.Y.C., 1987-88, Balt. Mus., Deland (Fla.) Mus., Faith Ruggold 25 Yr. Survey Fine Arts Museum L.I., Hempstead, 1990-93; exhibited in group shows at Meml. Exhibit for MLK, Mus. Modern Art, N.Y.C., 1968, Chase Manhattan Bank Collection, Martha Jackson Gallery, N.Y.C., 1970, Am. Women Artists, Gedok, Kunstalle, Hamburg, Ger., 1972, Jubilee, Boston Mus. Fine Arts, 1975, Major Contemporary Women Artists, Suzanne Gross Gallery, Phila., 1984, Committed to Print Mus. Modern Art, N.Y.C., 1988, The Art of Black Am. in Japan, Terada Warehouse, Tokyo, Made in the USA, Art in the 50s and 60s U. Calif. Berkeley Art Mus., Craft Today Poetry of the Physical, Am. Craft Mus., N.Y.C., Portraits and Homage to Mothers Hecksher Mus. Huntington, 1987; works in collections at Chase Manhattan Bank, N.Y.C., Philip Morris Collection, N.Y.C., Children's Mus., Bklyn., Newark Mus., The Women's House of Detention, Rikers Island, N.Y., The Studio Mus., N.Y.C., High Mus., Atlanta, Guggenheim Mus., Met. Mus. Art, Boston Mus. Fine Arts, MOMA. Author: Tar Beach, 1991, Aunt Harriet's Underground Railroad in the Sky, 1992; contbr. articles to profl. jours. Recipient AAUW travel award to Africa, 1976, Caldecott honor award, Coretta Scott King award best illustrated children's books Tar Beach, 1991; John Simon Guggenheim Meml. Found. Fellowship (painting), 1987, N.Y. Found. for Arts award (painting), 1988, Nat. Endowment Arts award (sculpture) 1978, (painting) 1989, La Napoule Found. award (painting in So. of France) 1990, Arts Internat. award (travel to Morocco) 1992. Office: Marie Brown Assocs 625 Broadway New York NY 10012-2611

RINGQUIST, LYNN ANNE, micrographics company executive; b. Panama City, Fla., June 12, 1952; d. George Willard and Juanita Anne (Vinson) Thomas; m. Ronald Scott Nelson, Sept. 5, 1970 (div. Mar. 1978); children: Faith Nichole, Jason Jay; m. Eric James Ringquist, Sept. 19, 1993. Student, Fullerton (Calif.) Jr. Coll., 1970-71, Mpls. Coll. Art & Design, 1987-93. Microfilm technician Microfilming Services, Corona, Calif., 1970-71; microfilm technician Blue Cross/Blue Shield, Eagan, Minn., 1972-73, customer service rep., 1973-76; regional sales rep. MicroD Internat., Burnsville, Minn., 1974-83, gen. sales mgr., 1983-85, v.p., 1985—; bd. dirs. Neoteric Arts, Inc., Burnsville, 1983—. Mem. Am. Soc. for Non-Destructive Testing, Assn. Info. and Image Mgmt. Home: 14901 Judicial Rd Burnsville MN 55306-4866 Office: MicroD Internat 15000 County Road 5 Burnsville MN 55306-5318

RINGWALD, LYDIA ELAINE, artist, poet; b. L.A., Oct. 8, 1949; d. Siegfried Carl Ringwald and Eva M. (Macksoud) Mack; m. Hal von Hofe, July 31, 1972 (div. 1978). BA, Scripps Coll., 1970; student, Ruprecht-Karl Univ., Heidelberg, Germany, 1971; MA in Comparative Lit., U. Calif., Irvine, 1972; studied with William Bailey, Yale Art Sch., 1972-74; postgrad., U. Conn., 1976. Instr. English and German Cerritos (Calif.) Coll., 1975-83; instr. German Golden West Coll., Huntington Beach, Calif., 1976-83; instr. English Saddleback Coll., Mission Viejo, Calif., 1976-81, Long Beach (Calif.) City Coll., 1976-83; curator exhbns. Cultural Affairs Satellite Dept., L.A., 1994; cons., lectr. in field. Solo exhbns. include Great Western Bank, 1989, Atlantis Gallery, 1992, L.A. Pub. Libr., Sherman Oaks, Calif., 1993, Sumitomo Bank, 1993, Phoenix Gallery, 1994; group exhbns. include Long Beach (Calif.) Arts, 1988-89, Installations One, 1989, 90, Heidelberger Kunstverein, Heidelberg, Germany, 1990, Barbara Mendes Gallery, L.A., 1991, Folktree Gallery, 1991-92, Armand Hammer Mus., 1992, Jansen-Perez Gallery, L.A., 1993; author: Blessings in Disguise: Life is a Gift; Accept it with Both Hands, 1990, Blau: Kaleidescope einer Farbe, 1992. Mem. Internat. Friends Transformative Arts, Humanistic Arts Alliance, Nat. Mus. Women in Arts, L.A. Mcpl. Art Gallery, Mus. Contemporary Art, L.A. County Mus., U. Calif. Irvine Alumni Assn., Scripps Coll. Alumni Assn., Inst. Noetic Scis., Philosophical Rsch. Soc. Home and Office: Creative Realities 2801 Coldwater Canyon Dr Beverly Hills CA 90210-1305

RINN, COLETTE LEE, art educator and consultant; b. DeKalb, Ill., Aug. 2, 1954; d. Rodney James and Helen Lillian (Thurm) Latimer; m. James Edward Rinn, Nov. 18, 1978. BS in Art Edn., Ill. State U., 1976; MS in Ednl. Adminstrn., No. Ill. U., 1988. Cert. art chr. K-12, cert. in ednl. adminstrn. K-12. Tchr. art Gibson City (Ill.) High Sch., 1976-77; art dept. chair, tchr. and pub. sponsor Lincoln-Way High Sch., New Lenox, Ill., 1977—; pub. design cons. Walsworth Pub. Co., Kansas City, Mo., 1990—, various univs. Author slide program: Walsworth Educational Materials, 1993. Recipient Excellence in Design award Printing Industries of Am., 1991. Mem. Ill. Art Edn. Assn., Nat. Scholastic Press Assn. (judge, Pacemaker award 1991), Journalism Edn. Assn., Columbia Scholastic Press Assn., No. Ill. Scholastic Press Assn. Home: 4119 Franklin Ave Western Springs IL 60558-1403 Office: Lincoln-Way High Sch 1801 E Lincoln Hwy New Lenox IL 60451-2098

RINSCH, MARYANN ELIZABETH, occupational therapist; b. L.A., Aug. 8, 1939; d. Harry William and Thora Analine (Langlie) Hitchcock; m. Charles Emil Rinsch, June 18, 1964; children: Christopher, Daniel, Carl. BS, U. Minn., 1961. Registered occupational therapist, Calif. Staff occupational therapist Hastings (Minn.) State Hosp., 1961-62, Neuropsychiat. Inst., L.A., 1962-64; staff and sr. occupational therapist Calif. Children's Svcs., L.A., 1964-66, head occupational therapist, 1966-68; researcher A. Jean Ayres, U. So. Calif., L.A., 1968-69; pvt. practice neurodevel. and sensory integraton Tarzana, Calif., 1969-74; pediat. occupational therapist neurodevel. & sensory integration St. Johns Hosp., Santa Monica, Calif., 1991—; pvt. practice, cons. Santa Monica-Malibu Unified Sch. Dist., 1994—. Mem. alliance bd. Natural History Mus., L.A. County, 1983—; cub scouts den mother Boy Souts Am., Sherman Oaks, Calif., 1986-88, advancement chair Boy Scout Troop 474, 1989—; bd. dirs. Valley League San Fernando Valley, Van Nuys, Calif., 1987-90. Mem. Am. Occupational Therapy Assn., Calif. Occupational Therapy Assn. Home: 19849 Greenbriar Dr Tarzana CA 91356-5428

RINSKY, JUDITH LYNN, foundation administrator, educator consultant; b. Sept. 12, 1941; d. Allen A. and Sophie (Schwartz) Lynn; m. Joel C. Rinsky, Jan. 29, 1963; children: Heidi Mae Schnapp, Heather Star Maxon. Jason Wayne. BA in Home Econs., Montclair State U., 1963. Notary pub., N.J. Tchr. home econs. Florence Ave. Sch., Irvington, N.J., 1963-66; substitute tchr. Millburn-Short Hills Sch. System, 1978-82, 90—, sr. citizen coord., 1982-87; respite care coord. Essex County Respite Care, East Orange, N.J., 1988-90; pvt. practice educator Short Hills, N.J., 1990—; bd. mem. adv. com. gerontology Seton Hall U., 1984-90; coord. Mayor's Adv. Bd. Sr. Citizens, Millburn-Short Hills, 1982-87. Pres. Deerfield Sch. PTA, 1979-80, Millburn H.S. PTA, 1983-85; co-chmn. dinner dance Charles T. King Student Loan Fund, 1981; mem. Handicapped Access Study Com., 1983-85; bd. dirs. Coun. on Health and Human Svcs., 1985-90, mem., 1985-94; acting dir. B'nai Israel Nursery Sch., 1994. Mem. Lake Naomi Assn. (chmn. sailing com. 1981), N.J. Home Econs. Assn., Am. Home Econs. Assn., Rotary (pres. Millburn chpt. 1992-93, bd. dirs. 1992-95, advisor Millburn Interact club 1987-92, chairperson Internat. Interact dist. 7470 1993-95). Home and Office: 23 Winthrop Rd Short Hills NJ 07078-1411

RINTA, CHRISTINE EVELYN, nurse, air force officer; b. Geneva, Ohio, Oct. 4, 1952; d. Arvi Alexander and Catharina Maria (Steenbergen) R. BSN, Kent State U., 1974; MSN, Case Western Res. U., 1979. CNOR. Staff nurse in oper. rm. Euclid (Ohio) Gen. Hosp., 1974-76, oper. rm. charge nurse, 1977-79; commd. 1st lt. USAF, 1979, advanced through grades to lt. col.; staff nurse oper. rm. Air Force Regional Hosp., Sheppard AFB, Tex., 1979-82; staff nurse oper. rm., asst. oper. rm. supr. Regional Med. Ctr. Clark, Clark Air Base, Philippines, 1982-83; chief, nurse recruiting br. 3513th Air Force Recruiting Squadron, North Syracuse, N.Y., 1983-87; nurse supr. surg. svcs. 432d Med. Group, Misawa Air Base, Japan, 1987-89; course supr./instr. oper. rm. nursing courses 3793d Nursing Tng. Squadron, Keesler Med. Ctr., Keesler AFB, Miss., 1989-92; asst. dir., then dir. oper. rm. and ctrl. sterile supply Keesler Med. Ctr., Keesler AFB, Miss., 1992-93; comdr., enlisted clin. courses flight 383d Tng. Squadron, Sheppard AFB, Tex., 1993-94; comdr., officer clin. courses flight 383rd Tng. Squadron, Sheppard AFB, Tex., 1994—. Decorated Air Force Commendation medal, Air Force Achievement medal, Meritorious Svc. medal. Mem. ANA, Ohio Nurses Assn., Assn. Operating Rm. Nurses, Air Force Assn., Sigma Theta Tau. Home: 14 Pilot Point Dr Wichita Falls TX 76306-1000 Office: 383d Tng Squadron 939 Missile Rd Ste 3 Sheppard AFB TX 76311-2262

RIOS, EVELYN DEERWESTER, columnist, musician, artist, writer; b. Payne, Ohio, June 25, 1916; d. Jay Russell and Flossie Edith (Fell) Deerwester; m. Edwin Tietjen Rios, Sept. 19, 1942 (dec. Feb. 1987); children: Jane Evelyn, Linda Sue Rios Stahlman. BA with honors, San Jose State U., 1964, MA, 1968. Cert. elem., secondary tchr., Calif. Lectr. in music San Jose State U., 1969-75; bilingual cons., then assoc. editor Ednl. Factors, Inc., San Jose, 1969-76, mgr. field research, 1977-78; writer, editor Calif. MediCorps Program, 1978-85; contbg. editor, illustrator The Community Family Mag., Wimberly, Tex., 1983-85; columnist The Springer, Dripping Springs, Tex., 1985-90; author, illustrator, health instr. textbooks elem. schs., 1980-82. Choir dir. Bethel Luth. Ch., Cupertino, Calif., 1965-83; organist Holy Spirit Episc. Ch., Dripping Springs, Tex., 1987-94; music dir. Cambrian Park (Calif.) Meth. Ch., 1961-64; chmn. planning and zoning commn. City of Dripping Springs, 1991-93. Mem. AAUW, Am. Guild Organists (dean 1963-64), Phi Kappa Phi (pres. San Jose chpt. 1973-74). Episcopalian. Home and Office: 23400 FM 150 Dripping Springs TX 78620

RIPLEY, ALEXANDRA BRAID, author; b. Charleston, S.C., Jan. 8, 1934; m. Leonard Ripley, 1958 (div. 1963); m. John Graham, 1981; children Elizabeth, Merrill. BA in Russian, Vassar Coll., 1955. Former tour guide, travel agent, underwear buyer; former manuscript reader, publicity director N.Y.C. Author: Charleston, 1981, On Leaving Charleston, 1984, The Time Returns: A Novel of Friends and Mortal Enemies in Fifteenth Century Florence, 1985, New Orleans Legacy, 1987, Scarlett: The Sequel to Margaret Mitchell's Gone With the Wind, 1991, From Fields of Gold, 1994. Office: care Janklow-Nesbit Assoc 598 Madison Ave New York NY 10022

RIPLEY, KATHRYN JANE, art gallery director, docent; b. Leamington, Ont., Can.. Student, U. Pa., George Mason U. Coord. docent programs Greater Reston (Va.) Arts Ctr., 1976-80; docent Corcoran Gallery Art, Washington, 1983-89, chair of docent body, 1989-90, tour dir, 1990-92, sr. docent, 1992-94; coord. of docent Kreeger Mus., Washington, 1994—. Office: Kreeger Mus 2401 Foxhall Rd NW Washington DC 20007 also: Corcoran Gallery Art 17th & E Sts NW Washington DC 20006-4899

RIPPER, RITA JO (JODY RIPPER), strategic planner, researcher; b. Goldfield, Iowa, May 8, 1950; d. Carl Phillip and Lucille Mae (Stewart) Ripper; BA, U. Iowa, 1972; MBA, NYU, 1978. Contracts and fin. staff Control Data Corp., Mpls., 1974-78; regional mgr. Raytheon Corp., Irvine, Calif., 1978-83; v.p. Caljo Corp., Des Moines, Iowa, 1980-84; asst. v.p. Bank of Am., San Francisco, 1984-88; pres. The Northhaven Co., 1988—, The Boardroom Adv. Group, 1990—. Vol. and alt. del. Rep. Party, Edina, Minn., N.Y.C., 1974—; vol. Cancer, Heart, Lung Assns., Edina, N.Y.C., Calif., 1974-78, 84—, Lita, 1986-90. Mem. Amnesty Internat., Internat. Mktg. Assn., World Trade Ctr. Assn., Acctg. Soc. (pres. 1975-76), World Trade Club, Intertel, Mensa, Beta Alpha Psi (chmn. 1977-78), Phi Gamma Nu (v.p. 1971-72) Presbyterian. Clubs: Corinthian Yacht, Mt. Tamalpais Racquet. Home and Office: 501 Oak Lane Dr West Des Moines IA 50265-5146 also: The Northhaven Co PO Box 25145 West Des Moines IA 50265 also: The Boardroom Adv Group 537 Newport Center Dr # 277 Newport Beach CA 92660-6900

RIPPY, FRANCES MARGUERITE MAYHEW, English educator; b. Ft. Worth, Sept. 16, 1929; d. Henry Grady and Marguerite Christine (O'Neill) Mayhew; m. Noble Merrill Rippy, Aug. 29, 1955 (dec. Sept. 1980); children: Felix O'Neill, Conrad Mayhew, Marguerite Hailey. BA, Tex. Christian U., 1949; MA, Vanderbilt U., 1951, PhD, 1957; postgrad., U. London, 1952-53. Instr. Tex. Christian U., 1953-55; instr. to asst. prof. Lamar State U., 1955-59; asst. prof. English Ball State U., Muncie, Ind., 1959-64; assoc. prof. English, Ball State U., 1964-68, prof., 1968—, dir. grad. studies in English, 1966-87; editor Ball State U. Forum, 1960-89; vis. asst. prof. Sam Houston State U., 1957; vis. lectr., prof. U. P.R., summers 1959, 60, 61; exch. prof. Westminster Coll., Oxford, Eng., 1988; cons.-evaluator North Cen. Assn. Colls. and Schs., 1973—, commn.-at-large, 1987-91; cons.-evaluator New Eng. Assn. Schs. and Colls., 1983. Author: Matthew Prior, 1986; contbr. articles to profl. jours., encys., ref. guides, chpts. to anthology; contbr. to Dictionary of Literary Biography. Recipient McClintock award, 1966; Danforth grantee 1964, Ball State U. Rsch. grantee, 1960, 62, 70, 73, 76, 87, 88, 89, 90, 92, 93, Lilly Libr. Rsch. 1978; Fulbright scholar U. London, 1952-53; recipient Outstanding Faculty award Ball State U., 1992. Mem. MLA, AAUP, Coll. English Assn., Nat. Coun. Tchrs. English, Am. Soc. 18th Century Studies, Am. Fedn. Tchrs., Ind. Coll. English Assn. (pres. 1984-85, Ind. Tchr./Scholar of 1994), Johnson Soc. Midwest (sec. 1961-62). Home: 4709 W Jackson St Muncie IN 47304-3514

RISELEY, MARTHA SUZANNAH HEATER (MRS. CHARLES RISELEY), psychologist, educator; b. Middletown, Ohio, Apr. 25, 1916; d. Elsor and Mary (Henderson) Heater; BEd, U. Toledo, 1943, MA, 1958; PhD, Toledo Bible Coll., 1977; student Columbia U., summers 1943, 57; m. Lester Seiple, Aug. 27, 1944 (div. Feb. 1953); 1 child, L. Rolland, III; m. Charles Riseley, July 30, 1960. Tchr. kindergarten Maumee Valley Country Day Sch., Maumee, Ohio, 1942-44; dir. recreation Toledo Soc. for Crippled Children, 1950-51; tchr. trainable children Lott Day Sch., Toledo, 1951-57; psychologist, asst. dir. Sheltered Workshop Found., Lucas County, Ohio, 1957-62; psychologist Lucas County Child Welfare Bd., Toledo, 1956-62; tchr. educable retarded, head dept. spl. edn. Maumee City Schs., 1962-69; pvt. practice clin. psychology, 1956—; instr. spl. edn. Bowling Green State U., 1962-65; instr. Owens Tech. Coll., 1973-78; interim dir. rehab. services Toledo Goodwill Industries, summer 1967, clin. psychologist Rehab. Center, 1967—; staff psychologist Toledo Mental Health Center, 1979-84. Dir. camping activities for retarded girls and women Camp Libbey, Defiance, Ohio, summers 1951-62; group worker for retarded women Toledo YWCA, 1957-62; guest lectr. Ohio State U., 1957. Health care profl. mem. Nat. Osteoporosis Found., 1988—. Mem. Ohio Assn. Tchrs. Trainable Youth (pres. 1956-57), NW Ohio Rehab. Assn. (pres. 1961-62), Toledo Council for Exceptional Children (pres. 1965), Greater Toledo Assn. Mental Health, Nat. Assn. for Retarded Children, Ohio Assn. Tchrs. Slow Learners, Am. Assn. Mental Deficiency, Am. Soc. Psychologists in Marital and Family Counseling, Psychology and Law Soc. Am. (assoc.), Ohio, NW Ohio (sec.-treas. 1974-77, pres. 1978-79), Am. Theater Orgn. Soc., Ohio Psychol. Assn. (continuing edn. com. 1978—), NEA, AAUW, Am. Soc. Psychologists in Pvt. Practice (nat. dir. 1976—), State Assn. Psychologists and Psychol. Assts., Bus. and Profl. Women's Club, (pres. 1970-72), Ohio Fedn. Bus. and Profl. Women's Clubs (dist. sec. 1970-71, dist. legis. chmn. 1972-74), Toledo Art Mus., Women's Aux. Toledo Bar Assn., League Women Voters (pres. Toledo Lucas County 1991-93), Y Matrons (pres. 1993—), Toledo Area Theater Orgn. Soc. (sec. 1991—), Zonta Internat. (local pres. 1973-74, 78-79, area dir. 1976-78, Maumee River Valley Woman of Yr. for svc. to community and Zonta, 1992), Maumee Valley Hist. Soc., MBLS PEO (chpt. pres. 1950-51), Toledo Council on World Affairs, Internat. Platform Assn. Baptist. Home and Office: 2816 Wicklow Rd Toledo OH 43606-2833

RISER, VIRGINIA MARIE, principal, consultant; b. La Crosse, Wis., Jan. 3, 1942; d. Frank A. and Cornelia Marie (Hurm) R. BA, State U. Iowa, 1964; MLS, Rosary Coll., 1971; PhD, U. Minn., 1981. Tchr. Oelwein (Iowa) Community Sch., 1964-66, Eastern Community Schs., Lansing, Iowa, 1966-69; library dir. Fox Lake City (Ill.) Library, 1971-72; instructional media ctr. dir., tchr. Derham Hall High Sch., St. Paul, 1972-81; instrl. developer U. Medial Sch., St. Paul and Mpls., 1976-81; prin. Assumption Sch., Richfield, Minn., 1981-84; lectr. St. Thomas Coll., Archdiocese St. Paul, U. Minn., St. Pauls and Mpls., 1973—; prin. St. Odilia Sch., St. Paul, 1984-90; vice prin. South Jr. High Sch., St. Cloud, Minn., 1990-94; prin. McKinley Sch., St. Cloud, 1994—; instrnl. developer U. Minn., 1990—, Archdiocese St. Paul, Mpls., 1976, IMC designer, 1978—, tchr., supr., 1981—; speaker, cons. parent groups and sch. facilities in upper midwest, 1981—; Minn. rep. to

Coun. on Am. Pvt. Edn., 1987—; assoc. prof. St. Mary's Coll. Minn., 1987—, Winona and Grad. Ctr., Mpls., 1987—; mem. METONIA Cons. Co.; chmn. internat. edn. Minn. Gov.s' Task Force on Math., Sci., Internat. Edn., and Tech., 1990. Contbr. articles to profl. jours. Chair Deaney Elem. Archdiocesan Sch. Community St. Pauls; mem. Edn. Bd. Archdiocese St. Paul; human rights commr. City of St. Cloud, Minn. Mem. NAESP, ASCD, AAUW, Archdiocesan Cath. Sch. Prins. Assn. (exec. bd. 1984—), Minn. Assn. Pvt. Sch. Adminstrs. (pres. 1987—), Deanery Prins. (chmn.), Coun. Am. Pvt. Edn., Minn. Elem. Sch. Prins. Assn. Home: 2108 Kileen Ct Saint Cloud MN 56301-4794 Office: McKinley Elem Sch Waite Park MN 56387

RISQUEZ, ANNE MARIE, software engineer; b. Caracas, Venezuela, June 10, 1955; came to U.S., 1974; d. John A. and Anne Marie (deFeriet) Obregon; 1 child, Anne Marie. Student, U. Simón Bolivar, Caracas, 1972-74; BA in Math., Chapman U., 1977; MA in Math. Stats., U. Calif., Irvine, 1979. Tutor Chapman U., Orange, Calif., 1975-77; interpreter World Linguistics, Glendale, Calif., 1976-77; tchr. asst. U. Calif., Irvine, Calif., 1977-79; tech. staff Space Applications Corp., Santa Ana, Calif., 1979-83; from software engr. to sr. staff engr. Logicon-Ultrasystems, El Segundo, Calif., 1983—; software engrng. cons., 1992—. Team mother, uniform coord., snack bar coord. Bobby Sox/Am. Girls Softball, Irvine, 1983-88; team mother Am. Youth Soccer Orgn. Soccer, Irvine, 1983-85; team coord. Nightmare Soccer Team, Irvine, 1985-88; tennis, softball, soccer supporter Woodbridge High Sch., Irvine, 1989-93. Roman Catholic. Home: 14 Birdsong Irvine CA 92714-4500 Office: Logicon 222 W 6th St San Pedro CA 90731

RISS, TONI PALLETT, telecommunications executive; b. Kans. City, Mo., Dec. 4, 1952; d. Richard Roland Riss and Freda Gale (Hunt) Middaugh. B in Humanities summa cum laude, New Coll. Calif., 1978; postgrad. Loretto Heights Coll., 1971-73, U. Colo., 1973-74, Columbia U., 1980; cert. telecomm. mgmt. Golden Gate U., 1984. Network comm. specialist Network, San Francisco, 1979-81; telecomm. operator Bechtel, San Francisco, 1981-83, network customer service coordinator 1983-84; tech. specialist I MCI Network Svc. Ctr., San Francisco, 1985-90, team leader, 1990-91; tech. specialist II MCI Nat. INSC Svc. Ctr., Sacramento, 1991-93; telecomm. engr. MCI PLP Engring., Richardson, Tex., 1993—; cons. Home Office Corp., San Francisco, 1983-84. Henry J. Kaiser fellow, 1988; ADA grantee. Author: (poetry) Seasons of Myself, 1978; composer, singer, musician albums Fire and Wind, 1994, the Earth's Wound, 1994. Activist Bay Area Com. Against Briggs Initiative, San Francisco, 1978; organizer Crimewatch, Dallas, 1994, the Beat, Dallas, 1994; active Abalone Alliance, San Francisco, 1981—, ARC, San Francisco, 1981-83, Nat. Wildlife, 1984—, PETA, 1990—, Wilderness Soc., 1990—, Nat. Resources Def. Coun., 1992—. Lt. USN, 1978-80. Mem. Women in Telecomm., Rosicrucian Order Club (San Francisco, Humanitarian award 1994). Democrat. Jewish. Avocations: astronomy, autograph collecting. Home: PO Box 852378 Richardson TX 75085-2378

RISSLER, PATRICIA F., legislative staff director; b. Charles Town, W.Va., May 22, 1944; d. Lewis Shaull and Barbara Kathleen (Johnson) R.; m. James A. Rogers. Staff asst. to Rep. Neil Staebler Mo., 1963-65; staff asst. to Senator Patrick McNamara Mich., 1965-67, staff asst. to Senator Philip A. Hart, 1967-73; clk. subcom. on agri. labor House Com. on Edn. and Labor, 1973-77, dep. staff dir. subcom. on postsecondary edn., 1977-81; dep. staff dir. House Com. on Post Office and Civil Svc., 1981-89, staff dir., 1989-91; staff dir. House Com. on Edn. and Labor, 1991—. Office: Edn & Labor 2181 Rayburn House Office Bldg Washington DC 20515*

RISTOW, GAIL ROSS, educator, paralegal, children's rights advocate; b. Carmel, Calif., Oct. 18, 1949; d. Kenneth E. and Lula Mae (Craft) Ross; m. Steven Craig Ristow, Sept. 15, 1971. BS in Biochemistry, Calif. Polytech State U., San Luis Obispo, 1972; MEd, Ariz. State U., 1980. Cert. tchr., Calif. Asst. instr. Calif. State Polytech U., Pomona, 1972; grad. asst. Calif. Polytech State U., 1973-74; tchr. Mt. Carmel High Sch., L.A., 1974-76, Cartwright Sch. Dist., Phoenix, 1976-80; pres., owner Handmade With Love, Bay City, Tex., 1984-88; tchr. art Aiken, S.C., 1989—; tchr. Community Edn., Bay City, 1986-88, Palacios, Tex., 1987. Sec. Chukker Creek Homeowners, Aiken, S.C., 1989—; mem. S.C. Foster Care Rev. Bd., 1991—. Mem. AAUW, Am. Chem. Soc., Nat. Soc. Tole and Decorative Painters, Aiken Newcomer's Club (sec. 1989-91), Aiken Lioness Club (pres. 1991-94), Alpha Delta Kappa (v.p. 1986-87). Home: 2944 Oak Brook Dr Aiken SC 29803-9287

RITCH, KATHLEEN, diversified company executive; Harbor Beach, Mich., Jan. 23, 1943; d. Eunice (Spry) R.; B.A., Mich. State U., 1965: student Katharine Gibbs Sch., 1965-66. Exec. sec., adminstrv. asst. to pres. Katy Industries, Inc., N.Y.C., 1969-70; exec. sec., adminstrv. asst. to chmn. Kobrand Corp., N.Y.C., 1970-72; adminstrv. asst. to chmn. and pres. Ogden Corp., N.Y.C., 1972-74; asst. sec., adminstr. office services, asst. to chmn. Ogden Corp., N.Y.C., 1974-81, corporate sec., adminstr. office services, 1981-84, v.p., corporate sec., adminstr. office services, 1984-92, v.p. corp. sec., 1992—; part-owner Unell Mfg. Co., Port Hope, Mich., 1966-87. Bd. dir. Young Concert Artists, Inc., 1991—. Mem. Am. Soc. Corporate Secs. Home: 500 E 77th St New York NY 10162-0025 Office: Ogden Corp Two Pennsylvania Pla New York NY 10121

RITCHIE, CATHERINE DLORAH, correctional officer, deputy constable; b. Lynwood, Calif., Aug. 22, 1954; d. Harold Francis and Betty J. (Matlock) R.; m. Walter B. Ritchie Jr., July 21, 1977; children: Jeffrey, Bradley. Bookkeeper, sec. Severy Dental Labs., Orange, Calif., 1972-74, Shell Oil Co., Santa Ana, Calif., 1974-77; owner, ptnr. Vista (Calif.) Chevron Co., 1977-78; sec.-treas. Am. Battery Corp., Escondido, Calif., 1978-85; owner, operator Sophisticated 2ds, Vista, 1983-85, Bridal Elegance, Escondido, 1984-87; sr. correctional officer Humboldt County Sheriff's Dept., Eureka, Calif., 1988—; dep. constable North Humboldt Jud. Dist., Arcata, Calif., 1991—; sgt. correction divsn. Humboldt County Sheriff's Dept., Arcata, 1991—; Co-pub. How to Avoid Auto Repair Rip-offs, 1981. Mem. Nat. Bridal Service (cert., cons.), Nat. Assn. Female Execs., Escondido C. of C., Calif. Farm Bur. Republican.

RITCHIE, KAREN, advertising agency executive. Former sr. v.p. Campbell-Ewald Co. (formerly Lintas: Campbell Ewald), Warren, Mich.; sr. v.p. McCann-Erickson/Detroit, Troy, Mich., 1989-94; exec. v.p., mng. dir. GM Mediaworks, Warren, Mich., 1994—. Office: PO Box 6001 12200 Thirteen Mile Rd Warren MI 48090-6001

RITCHIE, KATHERINE ANNETTE, publishing company executive; b. Rapid City, S.D., June 2, 1956; d. Robert Jay Hungerford and Patricia Ann (Trew) Fessler; m. Gary Lee, Nov. 7, 1981 (div. Aug. 1984); 1 child; m. Lee R. Ritchie, Jan. 1, 1995. Student, Elec Computer Programming Inst, Kansas City, Mo., 1980. Programmer, technician Townley Sentery Hardware, Lenexa, Kans., 1981-83; programmer analyst Kansas City Star and Times, 1983-86; systems analyst Olathe (Kans.) Med. Ctr., 1986-88; MIS site mgr. Vance Pub. Corp., Overland Park, Kans., 1988-93; sys. analyst Mid-West Conveyor, Kansas City, Kans., 1993-95, SPRNT project mgr., 1995—. Office: Sprint 1200 Main St Kansas City MO 64105

RITCHIN, BARBARA SUE, educational administrator, consultant; b. N.Y.C., Mar. 7, 1940; d. Harry and Miriam Rosalyn (Schoenberg) R. BS in Spl. Edn., SUNY, Buffalo, 1961; MS in Ednl. Guidance, CCNY, 1969; PhD in Urban Edn., Fordham U., 1990, postdoctoral student, 1991. Cert. tchr., spl. edn. tchr., counselor, adminstr., N.Y. Tchr. spl. edn. East Elem. Sch., Long Beach, N.Y., 1962-68; asst. prof. N.Y.C. Community Coll., Bklyn., 1970-76; ednl. cons. N.Y.C., 1976-92; dir. bus. programs N.Y.C. Tech. Coll., Bklyn., 1981-87; dir. continuing edn. Queens Coll. CUNY, Flushing, N.Y., 1988—; bd. dirs. Foresight Sch., S.I., N.Y., 1986-92; cons. N.Y. Telephone Co., N.Y.C., 1988-92; chair subcom. on community outreach Queens Coll. Presdl. Com. on Multiculturalism. Co-author: Teachers Learn Metrics, 1981. Pres. bd. dirs. Greenwich Village Orchestra, 1991; admissions and rules com. mem. 401 E. 74 Corp., N.Y.C., 1990-92. Named Disting. Woman of Yr. Queens Women's Ctr., 1989. Mem. Continuing Edn. Assn. N.Y. (regional chair 1990-91, membership chair 1988-90), UN Assn. N.Y. (bd. dirs.), Assn. Continuing Higher Edn. (sec.-treas. 1991-92), Phi Delta Kappa, Kappa Delta Pi. Office: Queens Coll CUNY 65-30 Kissena Blvd Flushing NY 11367

RITTENHOUSE, CAROL HARDISON, manager, community health nurse; b. Macon, Ga., Sept. 25, 1943; d. John Wesley and Helen Elizabeth (Branam) Hardison; m. Oliver Charles Rittenhouse, Aug. 29, 1964; children: Todd Wesley, Lisa Cheryl. BSN, Fla. State U., 1964. RN., Ga., Ind. Psychiat. nurse Madison (Ind.) State Hosp., 1964; pub. health nurse Fulton County Health Dept., Atlanta, 1965-70; dir. nursing and health svcs. ARC, Atlanta, 1973-78, dir. tng. and devel., 1978-84, asst. mgr., 1984-92, mgr. ops., 1992-94, gen. mgr., 1994—; sec. of bd., exec. com. AID Atlanta, 1986-91; steering com. Atlanta Wellness Coun., 1985-91; nat. AIDS/HIV adv. com. ARC, Washington, 1991-93; nat. faculty Nat. Inst. Tng. Conf./ARC Washington, 1978-94. Mem. Young Reps., Atlanta, 1965-67, Moorings Homeowners Assn., Lithonia, Ga., 1976—, East Point (Ga.) Jr. Women's Club, 1965-73; mem. Atlanta Regional Commn. Health, 1994—. Recipient Jane Delano award Am. Nat. Red Cross, 1992, Outstanding Young Women of Am. award, 1975. Mem. ANA (bd. dirs. 1982-85), Am. Nurses Found. (bd. dirs. 1982-87), Ga. Nurses Assn. (v.p. 1975-79, pres. 1979-81, Spl. Recognition award 1982), Ga. Nurses Found. (v.p. 1983-85, 92-95, pres. 1980-83), Ga. Soc. Assn. Execs., Brookwood Rotary, Sigma Theta Tau. Republican. Baptist. Home: 2987 Moorings Pky Lithonia GA 30058-7013 Office: Am Red Cross 1955 Monroe Dr NE Atlanta GA 30324-4828

RITTER, ANN L., lawyer; b. N.Y.C., May 20, 1933; d. Joseph and Grace (Goodman) R. B.A., Hunter Coll., 1954; J.D., N.Y. Law Sch., 1970; postgrad. Law Sch., NYU, 1971-72. Bar: N.Y. 1971, U.S. Ct. Appeals (2d cir.) 1975, U.S. Supreme Ct. 1975. Writer, 1954-70; editor, 1955-66; tchr., 1966-70; atty. Am. Soc. Composers, Authors and Pubs., N.Y.C., 1971-72, Greater N.Y. Ins. Co., N.Y.C., 1973-74; sr. ptnr. Brenhouse & Ritter, N.Y.C., 1974-78; sole practice, N.Y.C., 1978—. Editor N.Y. Immigration News, 1975-76. Mem. ABA, Am. Immigration Lawyers Assn. (treas. 1983-84, sec. 1984-85, vice chair 1985-86, chair 1986-87, chair program com. 1989-90, chair speakers bur. 1989-90, chair media liaison 1989-90), N.Y. State Bar Assn., N.Y. County Lawyers Assn., Assn. Trial Lawyers Am., N.Y. State Trial Lawyers Assn., N.Y.C. Bar Assn., Watergate East Assn. (v.p., asst. treas. 1990—). Democrat. Jewish. Home: 47 E 87th St New York NY 10128-1005 Office: 420 Madison Ave New York NY 10017-1107

RITTER, BEVERLY LOEBLEIN, writer, publisher; b. Balt., July 21, 1942; d. Henry John and Eleanor Strieb (May) Loeblein; m. Charles Davis Ritter, Nov. 29, 1983; stepchildren: Jeannie, Charsy, Chuck. BA, U. Md., 1965. English tchr. Montgomery County Pub. Schs., Rockville, Md., 1965-71; editor Dissley Systems, Reston, Va., 1971-73; v.p. Stentran Systems, Inc., Vienna, Va., 1973-79; founder, pres. Stenotype Ednl. Products, Inc., Melrose, Fla., 1979—. Author: Real-Time Machine Shorthand Theory, 1991, 10 Steps to Real-Time Writing, 1993; co-author: Medical Terminology for Stenotypists, 1992, Proper Noun Speller, 1994; author, editor various textbooks for ct. reporting and med. transcription tng. Mem. Nat. Ct. Reporters Assn. Office: Stenotype Ednl Products Inc PO Box 959 Melrose FL 32666-0959

RITTER, DEBORAH ELIZABETH, anesthesiologist, educator; b. Phila., May 16, 1947; d. Charles William and Elizabeth Angeline (Coffman) R. BA, Susquehanna U., 1968; MS, U. Pa., 1969; MD, Med. Coll. Pa., 1973. Diplomate Am. Bd. Anesthesiology (assoc. examiner oral bds. 1990, 92). Intern Thomas Jefferson Univ. Hosp., Phila., 1973-74, resident in anesthesia, 1974-76, clin. fellow in anesthesiology, 1976-77; affiliate resident in anesthesia Children's Hosp. Pa., Phila., 1975; assoc. in anesthesiology Frankford Hosp., Phila., 1977-78; clin. instr. anesthesiology Med. Coll. Pa., Phila., 1977-78; clin. instr. anesthesiology Thomas Jefferson U., 1978-80, clin. assoc. prof., 1980-86, clin. asst. prof., 1986—, vice chmn. dept. anesthesiology, 1985—. Contbr. articles to profl. jours. Named Top Doc, Phila. Mag., 1994. Mem. AMA, Am. Women's Med. Assn., Am. Soc. Anesthesiologists, Internat. Anesthesia Rsch. Soc., Soc. Edn. Anesthesia, Assn. Anesthesia Clin. Dirs. Lutheran. Office: Thomas Jefferson U Dept Anesthesiology 111 S 11th St Ste 6460G Philadelphia PA 19107

RITTER, KAREN A(NNE), state legislator; b. Shirley, Mass., Feb. 28, 1953; d. James P(ierce) and Faye E(ileen) (Morrissey) R. Cert. legal asst., Northampton County Area Community Coll., 1978. Legal sec. Brennen and Gross, Allentown, Pa., 1971-75, Gross and Brown, Allentown, 1975-76; exec. sec. The Goodman Co., Allentown, 1976-77, legal asst., 1977-78; mgr., co-owner Allen Abstract Inc., Allentown, 1978-81; br. mgr. Indsl. Valley Title Ins. Co., Allentown, 1981-83; mgr. Associated Abstract Inc., Allentown, 1983-84, Realty Abstract Inc., Allentown, 1984-86; mem. Pa. Ho. of Reps., Harrisburg, 1986—. Alt. del. Dem. Nat. Conv., N.Y.C., 1980, del., San Francisco, 1984, Atlanta, 1988; local coord. Ted Kennedy for Pres. com., Allentown, 1980; mem. Allentown City Council, 1982-86, v.p., 1982; mem. Allentown Art Mus., 1982—; bd. dirs. Lehigh Valley Dem. Assn., 1985—, pres. 1988—; bd. dirs. The Program for Female Offenders, Allentown, 1985-86, Girls Club of Allentown, 1985—; lector Trinity Meml. Luth. Ch., Allentown, 1987—. Mem. Pa. Elected Women's Assn., Pa. Fedn. Dem. Women, LWV. Lodge: Altrusa (pres. local chpt. 1983-85). Office: 425 Allentown Dr Allentown PA 18103-9121*

RITTER-CLOUGH, ELISE DAWN, publishing company executive, consultant; b. Balt., Aug. 14, 1952; d. Nelson Fred and Marjorie Jean (Corke) Ritter; m. Philip Anthony Gibson, Apr. 7, 1979 (div. Feb. 1990); 1 child, Christopher Ritter Gibson; m. Victor Wayne Clough, Jr., Mar. 3, 1990; stepchildren: Wesley T., Lindsay, Sharon. Student, Austro-Am. Inst., Vienna, Austria, 1973; BS, U. Kans., 1974. Researcher, Impeachment Inquiry Staff U.S. Ho. of Reps., Washington, 1974; researcher APA, Washington, 1975; editor prodn. The New Republic Mag., Washington, 1976-77; copy editor Time-Life Books, Alexandria, Va., 1977-79, assoc. editor, 1979-83; series adminstr. Time-Life Books, Alexandria, 1983-87, asst. dir. editorial resources, 1988-90; dir. editorial resources Time Warner, Time-Life Books, Alexandria, 1990-94. Active Donaldson Run Civic Assn., Mt. Olivet Meth. Ch., Arlington, 1989—.

RITTERHOUSE, KATHY LEE, librarian; b. Hutchinson, Kans., May 24, 1952; d. Fayne Lee and Elizabeth Rose (Tener) R.; m. Michael Raymond Demmitt, July 8, 1972 (div. Apr. 1990). BA in English, Kans. State U., 1974; MLS, U. Okla., 1979. Circulation libr. Grand Prairie (Tex.) Meml. Libr., 1979-80, libr. dir., 1980—. Bd. dirs. Grand Prairie Arts Coun., 1980-95, pres., 1989. Named Pub. Svc. Employee of Yr. Grand Prairie C. of C., 1989. Mem. ALA, Tex. Libr. Assn. (Tex./SIRS Intellectual Freedom award 1993), Metro Rotary Club (bd. dirs. 1992-95), Beta Phi Mu. Office: Grand Prairie Meml Libr 901 Conover Dr Grand Prairie TX 75051-1521

RITTERSPACHER, KATHERINE FRANCES, educational administrator; b. Portland, Oreg., May 31, 1943; d. Phillip Carl and Lavelle Kathleen (Fox) R. BA in Edn., Ctrl. Wash. U., 1965, MEd in Curriculum and Supervision, 1980. Tchr. West Valley Sch. Dist., Yakima, Wash., 1965-86, adminstr., 1977-84; asst. prin. Snoqualmie Valley Sch. Dist., 1986-88, adminstr. curriculum and instrn., 1988—; presenter in field. Mem. AAUW, Nat. Staff Devel. Coun., Nat. Assn. Supervision and Curriculum Devel., Wash. Assn. Sch. Adminstrs., Wash. State Staff Devel. Coun., Wash. State Assn. Supervision and Curriculum Devel., Wash. State Assn. Mid Level Edn., Wash. Ednl. Rsch. Assn., King County Alcoholism and Substance Abuse Adminstrv. Bd. Office: PO Box 400 Snoqualmie WA 98065-0400

RITTMER, CYNTHIA KAY, accountant; b. Dexter, Mo., Mar. 12, 1959; d. Leo Herman and Joyce Evelyn (Hyten) Lowery; m. David Ronald Rittmer, July 21, 1984; children: Daniel Robert, Michael Keith, Ryan Douglas. BBA, U. Iowa, 1986. CPA, Iowa; NASD registered rep. Adminstrv. asst. Johnson County Emergency Ambulance, Iowa City, Iowa, 1981-85; staff acct. II SCI Fin. Group, Inc., Cedar Rapids, Iowa, 1986-88, asst. acctg. mgr., 1988-89, acctg. mgr., 1992—; v.p. and contr. Securities Corp. of Iowa, Cedar Rapids, 1989-92. Mem. AICPAs, Securities Industry Assn., Iowa Soc. CPAs, Profl. Women's Network. Office: SCI Financial Group Inc R2 78 Joel Lane Mount Vernon IA 52314

RITTMER, ELAINE HENEKE, library media specialist; b. Maquoketa, Iowa, Feb. 4, 1931; d. Herman John and Clara (Luett) Heneke; m. Sheldon Lowell Rittmer, June 11, 1950; children: Kenneth, Lynnette, Robyn (dec.), infant son (dec.). BA, Marycrest Coll., 1973; MS, Western Ill. U., 1980. Permanent teaching cert. K-14, Iowa; cert. libr. media specialist K-14, Iowa. Sch. libr. Calamus-Wheatland (Iowa) Community Schs., 1970-74; high sch. libr. media specialist, libr. coord. Camanche (Iowa) Community Sch., 1974—; ind. tech. cons., 1988—. Mem. Iowa Edn. Media Assn., Iowa State Edn. Assn., Camanche Edn. Assn., Camanche Cmty. Schs. Tech. Com., Media Tech. Cons. Republican. Home: 3539 230th St De Witt IA 52742-9208 Office: Camanche High Sch PO Box 160 937 9th St Camanche IA 52730

RITZ, ESTHER LEAH, civic worker, volunteer, investor; b. Buhl, Minn., May 16, 1918; d. Matthew Abram and Jeanette Florence (Lewis) Medalie; m. Maurice Ritz, Apr. 8, 1945 (dec. 1977); children—David Lewis, Peter Bruce. B.A. summa cum laude, U. Minn, 1940, postgrad., 1940-41; postgrad., Duke U., 1941-42. Adminstrv. analyst, economist Office of Price Adminstrn., N.Y., Washington and Chgo., 1942-46. Pres., Nat. Jewish Welfare Bd., 1982-86; v.p. Council of Jewish Fedns., 1981-84; pres. World Conf. Jewish Community Ctrs., 1981-86; bd. dirs. Am. Jewish Joint Distbn. Com., 1977-93, bd. dirs. (hon. life mem.) Joint Distbn. Com., 1994; trustee United Jewish Appeal, 1982-87; vice-chmn. bd. dirs. Jerusalem Ctr. Pub. Affairs, 1984—; bd. dirs. Wurzweiler Sch. Social Work Yeshiva U., 1984-89, HIAS, 1983-86; mem. Jewish Agy. Com. on Jewish Edn., 1984-90, bd. govs., 1988-92; bd. dirs. Legal Aid Soc., Milw. County, 1983-85; mem. Community Issues Forum, Milw.; vice chmn. bd. United Way Greater Milw., 1977-81; pres. Florence G. Heller Jewish Welfare Bd. Research Ctr., 1979-83; pres. Mental Health Planning Council of Milw. County, 1976-79; vice chmn Large City Budgeting Conf., 1976-82; pres. Jewish Community Ctr. Milw., 1966-71; pres. Milw. Jewish Fedn., 1978-81; bd. dirs. Shalom Hartman Inst., 1989—; bd. dirs.; mem. exec. com., policy com. Nat. Jewish Dem. Coun., 1991—, vice-chmn. bd. dirs., 1994—; bd. dirs. Nat. Jewish Ctr. for Learning and Leadership, 1988-92, Ams. Peace Now, 1989—, vice-chmn. bd. dirs., 1995—, Coun. Initiatives Jewish Edn., 1990—, Friends of Labor Israel (steering com. 1988—, chair 1988-90); bd. vis. Ctr. for Jewish Studies U. Wis., Madison, 1994—. Named to Women's Hall of Fame YWCA, 1979; recipient Cmty. Svc. award Wis. Region NCCJ, 1977, William C. Frye award Milw. Found., 1984, Telesis award Alverno Coll., Milw., 1984, Hannah G. Solomon award. Nat. Coun. Jewish Women, ProUrbe award Mt. Mary Coll., Evan P. Helfer award Milw. chpt. Nat. Soc. of Fund Raising Execs., 1994, Margaret Miller award Planned Parenthood of Wis., 1994. Mem. LWV, NAACP, NOW, Hadassah, Na'amat, Common Cause, Nat. Women's Polit. Caucus, Nat. Coun. Jewish Women, Planned Parenthood. Democrat. Home: 626 E Kilbourn Ave Milwaukee WI 53202

RITZER, KAREN RAE, executive secretary, office administrator; b. Sioux City, Iowa, Nov. 26, 1946; d. Robert Leland and Wanda Lily (Kirby) Taylor; m. Thomas Arthur Ritzer, Nov. 23, 1963; children: Robert Arthur, Kristina Marie, Teresa Lynn Ritzer Jones, Carl Robert White. Grad., Arnolds Park (Iowa) High Sch., 1968. Office mgr., sec. Tom's Plumbing and Heating, Arnolds Park, 1964-93; sec./treas., bd. dirs. Ritz Closet Seat Corp., Arnolds Park, 1985—. Sec./treas. Concerned Citizens Com., Arnolds Park, 1985, 86, 87. Mem. Nat. Trust for Hist. Preservation, The Smithsonian Assn., Am. Mus. Natural History (assoc.), United We Stand Am. (founding), Friends of Iowa Pub. TV, Ladies Aus. VFW. Address: Box 585 Arnolds Park IA 51331

RIVAS, PAULITA, municipal official; b. N.Y.C., Feb. 28, 1956; d. Jose and Maria (Pastrana) R.; m. Derrick Berrios, Mar. 25, 1975 (div. Oct. 1982). Student, City Coll., N.Y., 1994—. Claims clk. Social Security Adminstrn., N.Y.C., 1974-75, data review technician, 1975-80; claims rep. Social Security Adminstrn., Jamaica, N.Y., 1980-87; claims examiner Office of Worker's Compensation Programs, U.S. Dept. Labor, N.Y.C., 1987-89, sr. claims examiner, 1989-90, supervisory claims examiner, 1990—, mgr. Hispanic employement, 1992—. Home: 18834 87th Dr Apt 6B Jamaica NY 11423

RIVERA, CHITA (CONCHITA DEL RIVERO), actress, singer, dancer; b. Washington, Jan. 23, 1933; d. Pedro Julio Figuerva del Rivero; m. Anthony Mordente. Student, Am. Sch. Ballet, N.Y.C. Broadway debut: Call Me Madam, 1952; appeared on stage in: Guys and Dolls, Can-Can, Seventh Heaven, Mister Wonderful, West Side Story, Father's Day, Bye Bye Birdie, Three Penny Opera, Flower Drum Song, Zorba, Sweet Charity, Born Yesterday, Jacques Brel is Alive and Well and Living in Paris, Sondheim-A Musical Tribute, Kiss Me Kate, Ivanhoe, Chicago, Bring Back Birdie, Merlin, Jerry's Girls, 1985, The Rink, 1984 (Tony award 1984), Can-Can, 1988, Kiss of the Spider Woman (Tony award, Best Actress in a musical), 1993; performs in cabarets and nightclubs around world; starred in: film Sweet Charity, 1969; numerous TV appearances include Kojak and the Marcus Nelson Murders, 1973, The New Dick Van Dyke Show, 1973-74, Kennedy Ctr. Tonight-Broadway to Washington!, Pippin, 1982, The Mayflower Madam, 1987, Sammy Davis Jr.'s 60th Birthday Celebration, 1990. Mem. AFTRA, SAG, Actors Equity Assn. Office: William Morris Agy 1350 Ave Americas New York NY 10019*

RIVERA, DOLORES, elementary education educator; b. Bklyn., Apr. 2, 1955; d. Gregorio and Carmen Lydia (Mercado) R.; 1 child, Carmen Christina Bissessar. AA in Liberal Arts, N.Y.C. C.C., 1976; BS, Bklyn. Coll., 1981, MS, 1994. Bilingual asst., bilingual pupil svcs. Pub. Sch. 189, Bklyn., 1978-81; tchr. Spanish as second lang. Pub. Sch. 149, Bklyn., 1981-84; bilingual tchr. Pub. Sch. 72, Bklyn., 1984—; condr. numerous tchr. tng. workshops, N.Y.C., 1991. Mem. Puerto Rican Educators Assn., Hispanic Educators Rsch. and Enrichment (active 1984—).

RIVERA-RAMIREZ, ANA ROSA, English educator; b. Bronx, Sept. 5, 1950; d. Marcelino and Ana Maria (Reyes) Rivera; m. Jose Antonio Ramirez, July 11, 1986; 1 child, Marisol Helena Feijoo. Bachelors, Hunter Coll., 1973, Masters, 1986; postgrad., NYU, 1990—. Cert. ESL tchr., N.Y. Tchr. bilingual Bethel Bapt. Day Care Ctr., Bklyn., 1974-75, Pequeños Souls Day Care Ctr., N.Y.C., 1975-76; tchr. Sacred Heart Sch., Carvin Sch., Santurce, P.R., 1977-79; tchr. adult edn. Mobicentrics Bus. Inst., Bronx, 1979-85; tchr. spl. edn. CJ High Sch. 145, Bronx, 1986-88, tchr. English, 1988—; tchr. ESL Clinton High Sch., Bronx, 1989-90; con. ESL curriculum Clinton High Sch., Bronx, 1988-89, cons., writer ESL curriculum Mobicentrics Bus. Inst., Bronx, 1984-85. Participant Constitution Works Program, N.Y.C., 1992. Recipient Bronx Rookie Tchr. award Bd. Edn., 1987. Mem. ASCD, AAUW, Phi Delta Kappa (NYU chpt.).

RIVERA-URRUTIA, BEATRIZ DALILA, psychology and rehabilitation counseling educator; b. Bayamón, P.R., Jan. 16, 1951; d. José and Carmen B. (Urrutia) Rivera; m. Julio C. Ribera, July 1, 1978; 1 child, Alejandra B. BA, U. P.R., 1972, MA, 1975; PhD, Temple U., 1982. Staff psychologist Learning Plus, Inc., Phila., 1979-80; cons. Hispanic Mental Health Inst., Phila., 1981-82; staff psychologist J.F. Kennedy Community Mental Health Ctr., Phila., 1982-83; assoc. prof. U. P.R., Rio Piedras, 1983—; cons. Jewish Employment & Vocat. Svcs., Phila., 1980; staff psychologist San Juan VA Hosp., Rio Piedras, 1990—. Contbr. articles to profl. jours. Vol. Parroquia San Juan Apóstol y Evangelista, Caguas, P.R., 1988-90, ARC, San Juan, 1990. Faculty U. P.R. instnl. rsch. grantee, 1986-87. Mem. P.R. Psychol. Assn. (bd. editors jour. 1984-89, bd. dirs. 1989-91), P.R. Lic. Bd. Psychologists (pres. ethics com. 1991-92). Home: Roble D 23 Alborada Caguas PR 00725 Office: PO Box 22724 San Juan PR 00931-2724

RIVERS, CHERYL P., state legislator; b. Rutland, Vt.; m. Richard H. Rivers; 1 child. Student, U. Vt., Burlington; BS, Castleton State Coll., 1978. Mem. Vt. State Senate, 1991—; owner River Echo Morgans. Office: Vt State House State Capitol Montpelier VT 05602*

RIVERS, JESSIE MAE, writer; b. Chgo., Aug. 31, 1933; d. Charlie Hill and Eula (White) Cunningham; m. Willie Rivers,. Student, Palmer Writers Sch., 1974. Writer Palmer Writers Sch., Mpls., 1972-74; mgr. Jackson Pk. Hotel, Chgo., 1957-62, Herman Roberts Motel, Chgo., 1962-68; private duty Chgo., 1984-88. Home: 640 W Briar Pl Chicago IL 60657-4545

RIVERS, JOAN, entertainer; b. N.Y.C., June 8, 1937; d. Meyer C. Molinsky; m. Edgar Rosenberg (dec.), July 15, 1965; 1 child, Melissa. BA, Barnard Coll., 1958. Formerly fashion coordinator Bond Clothing Stores. Debut entertaining, 1960; mem. From Second City, 1961-62; TV debut Tonight Show, 1965; Las Vegas debut, 1969; nat. syndicated columnist Chgo. Tribune, 1973-76; creator: CBS TV series Husbands and Wives, 1976-

77; host: Emmy Awards, 1983; guest hostess: Tonight Show, 1983-86; hostess The Late Show Starring Joan Rivers, 1986-87, Hollywood Squares, 1987—, (morning talk show) Joan Rivers (Daytime Emmy award 1990), 1989—; originator, screenwriter TV movie The Girl Most Likely To, ABC, 1973; other TV movies include: How to Murder A Millionaire, 1990; cable TV spl. Joan Rivers and Friends Salute Heidi Abromowitz, 1985; film appearances include The Swimmer, 1968, Uncle Sam, The Muppets Take Manhattan, 1984; co-author, dir.: (films) Rabbit Test, 1978 (also acted), Spaceballs, 1987; actress: theatre prodn. Broadway Bound, 1988; recs. include: comedy album What Becomes a Semi-Legend Most, 1983; author: Having a Baby Can be a Scream, 1974, The Life and Hard Times of Heidi Abromowitz, 1984, (autobiography with Richard Meryman) Enter Talking, 1986, (with Richard Meryman) Still Talking, 1991; debuted on Broadway (play) Broadway Bound, 1988. Nat. chmn. Cystic Fibrosis, 1982—, benefit performer for AIDS, 1984. Recipient Cleo awards for commls., 1976, 82, Jimmy award for best comedian, 1981; named Hadassah Woman of Yr., 1983, Harvard Hasty Pudding Soc. Woman of Yr., 1984. Mem. Phi Beta Kappa. Office: care Dorothy Melvin DTM Mgmt 145 S Fairfax Ave Ste 201A Los Angeles CA 90036-2166*

RIVERS, JOAN NADIA, graphics designer; b. Santa Ana, Calif., Nov. 1, 1944; d. Hubert Murray and Alix (Bredé) Brown; m. David Allen Rivers, Sept. 3, 1965; 1 child, Kristan David. BFA, U. Tex., 1978. Staff artist Sta. KLRN/KLRU TV, Austin, Tex., 1975-78; art dir. J. Walter Thompson Co., N.Y.C., 1979-81; designer Steck-Vaughn Pub. Co., Austin, 1982-83, Tex. Instruments, Austin, 1984-85; designer, owner Rivers Graphic Design, Austin, 1985—. Author, illustrator cartoon: Word Processing and Info. Systems mag., 1980-83. Recipient Cert. Recognition Nat. Assn. Ednl. Broadcasters, 1977-78, Best of Show award Internat. Assn. Bus. Communicators, 1986, Cert. Merit Printing Industries Am., 1986. Mem. Am. Inst. Graphic Arts, Austin Graphic Arts Soc. (award of Excellence 1986), Soc. Tech. Communication (Achievement award 1986). Democrat.

RIVERS, LYNN N., congresswoman; b. Augres, Mich., Dec. 19, 1956. BA, U. Mich., 1987; JD, Wayne State U., 1992. Mem. sch. bd. City of Ann Arbor, Mich., 1984-92; mem. Mich. House of Reps., 1992-94. married; 2 children. Office: US House Reps 2107 Rayburn House Office Bldg Washington DC 20515-0513*

RIVERS, MARIE BIE, broadcasting executive; b. Tampa, Fla., July 12, 1928; d. Norman Albion and Rita Marie (Monrose) Bie; m. Eurith Dickinson Rivers, May 3, 1952; children—Eurith Dickinson, III, Rex B., M. Kells, Lucy L., Georgia. Student, George Washington U., 1946. Engaged in real estate bus., 1944-51, radio broadcasting, 1951—; pres., CEO, part owner Sta. WGUN, Atlanta, 1951—, Stas. KWAM and KJMS, Memphis, Sta. WEAS-AM-FM, Savannah, Ga., Stas. WGOV and WAAC, Valdosta, Ga., Sta. WSWN and Sta. WBGF, Belle Glade, Fla.; owner, chairperson Sta. WCTH, Islamorado, Fla.; pres. The Gram Corp., real estate com. Creative Christian Concepts Corp., 1985, Ocala, 1986; owner Suncoast Broadcasting Inc. Author: A Woman Alone, 1986; contbr. articles to profl. jours. Mem. Fla. Assn. Broadcasters (bd. dirs.), Coral Reef Yacht (Coconut Grove, Fla.), Palm Beach Polo and Country Club, Kappa Delta. Roman Catholic. Office: 11924 W Forest Hill Blvd Ste 1 West Palm Beach FL 33414-6257

RIVERS, WILGA MARIE, foreign language educator; b. Melbourne, Australia, Apr. 13, 1919; came to U.S., 1970; d. Harry and Nina Diamond (Burston) R. Diploma in edn, U. Melbourne, 1940, BA with honours, 1939, MA, 1948; License es L., U. Montpellier, France, 1952; PhD, U. Ill., 1962; MA (hon.), Harvard U., 1974; D Langs. (hon.), Middlebury Coll., 1989. High sch. tchr. Victoria, Australia, 1940-48; asst. in English lang. France, 1949-52; tchr. prep. schs., 1953-58; asst. prof. French No. Ill. U., DeKalb, 1963-64; assoc. prof. Monash U., Australia, 1964-69; vis. prof. Columbia U., 1970-71; prof. French U. Ill., Urbana-Champaign, 1971-74; prof. Romance langs. and lit., coord. lang. instrn. Harvard U., 1974-89, prof. emerita, 1989—; cons. NEH, Ford Found., Rockefeller Found., others; lectr 38 countries and throughout U.S.; adv. coun. Modern Lang. Ctr., Ont. Inst. for Studies in Edn., Nat. Fgn. Lang. Ctr., Lang. Acquire Rsch. Ctr., San Diego. Author: The Psychologist and the Foreign-Language Teacher, 1964, Teaching Foreign-Language Skills, 1968, 2d edit., 1981, A Practical Guide to the Teaching of French, 1975, 2d edit., 1988; co-author: A Practical Guide to the Teaching of German, 1975, 2d edit., 1988, A Practical Guide to the Teaching of Spanish, 1976, 2d edit., 1988, A Practical Guide to the Teaching of English as a Second or Foreign Language, 1978, Speaking in Many Tongues, 1972, 3d edit., 1983, Communicating Naturally in a Second Language, 1983, Teaching Hebrew: A Practical Guide, 1989, Opportunities for Careers in Foreign Languages, 1993, others; editor and contbr.: Interactive Language Teaching, 1987, Teaching Languages in Coll.: Curriculum and Content, 1992, writing translated into 9 languages; editorial bd. Studies in Second Language Acquisition, Applied Linguistics, Language Learning, System; mem. adv. com. Can. Modern Lang. Rev.; contbr. articles to profl. jours. Recipient Nat. Disting. Fgn. Lang. Leadership award N.Y. State Assn. Fgn. Lang. Tchrs., 1974. Mem. MLA, Am. Assn. Applied Linguistics (charter pres.), Am. Coun. on Teaching Fgn. Langs. (Florence Steiner award 1977, Anthony Papalia award 1988), Mass. Fgn. Lang. Assn. (Disting. Svc. award 1983), Tchrs. of English to Speakers of other Langs., Am. Assn. Tchrs. French, Linguistic Soc. Am., Am. Assn. Univ. Suprs. and Coords. Fgn. Lang. Programs Northeast Conf. (Nelson Brooks award 1983), Internat. Assn. Applied Psycholinguistics (v.p. 1983-89), Japan Assn. Coll. English Tchrs. (hon.), Am. Assn. Tchrs. German (hon.), Internat. Assn. Lang. Labs. (hon.). Episcopalian. Home and Office: 84 Garfield St Watertown MA 02172-4916

RIVEST, ANNE-MARIE THERESE, post anesthesia nurse; b. Springfield, Mass., Dec. 25, 1959; d. Robert Frances and Marguerite Marie (Dupuis) R. BSN, Fitchburg State Coll., 1982. Cert. post anesthesia nurse; cert. in pediat. advanced life support. Staff nurse med./surg. fl. Baystate Med. Ctr., Springfield, Mass., 1982-86, staff nurse post anesthesia care unit, 1986—; annual conf. program dir. post anesthesia care unit Baystate Med. Ctr., Springfield, 1989-93, co-unit educator, 1992—; rep., sec. Intensive Peer Rev. Bd., 1992-94. Solicitor Local United Way, Baystate Med. Ctr., Springfield, 1986—; mem. Nat. Wildlife Fedn., Washington, 1994, Nat. Arbor Day Found., Nebraska City, Nebr., 1994. Mem. Am. Soc. Post Anesthesia Nurses, Mass. Soc. Post Anesthesia Nurses. Roman Catholic. Home: 166 Line St Easthampton MA 01027 Office: Baystate Med Ctr 759 Chestnut St Springfield MA 01199

RIVET, DIANA WITTMER, lawyer, developer; b. Auburn, N.Y., Apr. 28, 1931; d. George Wittmer and Anne (Jenkins) Wittmer Hauswirth; m. Paul Henry Rivet, Oct. 24, 1952; children: Gail, Robin, Leslie, Heather, Clayton, Eric. BA, Keuka Coll., 1951; JD, Bklyn. Law Sch., 1956. Bar: N.Y. 1956, U.S. Dist. Ct. (ea. and so. dists.) N.Y. 1975. Sole practice, Orangeburg, N.Y., 1957—; county atty. Rockland County (N.Y.), 1974-77; asst. to legis. chmn. Rockland County, 1978-79; counsel, adminstr. Indsl. Devel. Agy., Rockland County, 1980-91, Rockland Econ. Devel. Corp., 1981-90; counsel, exec. dir. Pvt. Industry Coun. Rockland County, 1980-90; pres., chief exec. officer Environ. Mgmt. Ltd., Orangeburg, 1980—; mem. air mgmt. adv. com. N.Y. State Dept. Environ. Conservation 1984-92, Orangetown Planning Bd., 1993—; pres. Indoor Enviroment Ltd. Pres. Rockland County coun. Girl Scouts U.S., 1981-84; chmn. Rockland County United Way campaign, 1983-84, 88-89, 93—; bd. dirs. 1988-94, Rockland Bus. Assn., West Nyack, 1981—, Leadership Rockland. Recipient Community Svc. award Keuka Coll., 1965, Disting. Svc. award Town of Orangetown, 1970, Disting. Svc. award Rockland County, 1989, Econ. Devel. award Rockland Econ. Devel. Corp., 1990; named Businessperson of Yr., Jour. News, Rockland County, 1982. Mem. ABA, N.Y. State Bar Assn. (mcpl. law sect. exec. com. 1976-83, environ. law sect. exec. com. 1974-86), Rockland County Bar Assn. (chair environ. law com. 1994—). Democrat. Mem. Religious Soc. of Friends. Home: 1 Lester Dr Orangeburg NY 10962-2316

RIVIN, NANCY, public relations executive. Newspaper reporter; with news dept. Sta. WNEW-TV; account exec. G.S. Schwartz, 1982-84, group supr., 1984-85, v.p., 1985-87; mng. dir. Koteret Internat., 1988; prin. New Venture Mktg., 1989—. Office: New Venture Marketing 545 W 111th St New York NY 10025*

RIVLIN, ALICE MITCHELL, economist; b. Phila., Mar. 4, 1931; d. Allan C. G. and Georgianna (Fales) Mitchell; m. Lewis Allen Rivlin, 1955 (div. 1977); children: Catherine Amy, Allan Mitchell, Douglas Gray; m. Sidney Graham Winter, 1989. B.A., Bryn Mawr Coll., 1952; Ph.D., Radcliffe Coll., 1958. Mem. staff Brookings Instn., Washington, 1957-66, 69-75, 83-93; dir. econ. studies Brookings Inst., 1983-87; dir. Congl. Budget Office, 1975-83; prof. pub. policy George Mason U., 1992; dep. dir. U.S. Office Mgmt. and Budget, 1993-94, dir., 1994—; dep. asst. sec. program coordination HEW, Washington, 1966-68, asst. sec. planning and evaluation, 1968-69; mem. Staff Adv. Commn. on Intergovtl. Rels., 1961-62. Author: The Role of the Federal Governemnt in Financing Higher Education, 1961, (with others) Microanalysis of Socioeconomic Systems, 1961, Systematic Thinking for Social Action, 1971, (with others) Economic Choices 1987, 1986, (with others The Swedish Economy, 1987, (with others) Caring for the Disabled Elderly: Who Will Pay?, 1988, Reviving the American Dream, 1992. MacArthur fellow, 1983-88. Mem. Am. Econ. Assn. (nat. pres. 1986). Office: U S Office Mgmt and Budget Office of the Director Old Exec Office Bldg Washington DC 20503*

RIVLIN, RACHEL, lawyer; b. Bangor, Maine, Sept. 1, 1945; d. Lawrence and A. Sara (Rich) Lait. BA, U. Maine, 1965; MA, U. Louisville, 1968; JD, Boston Coll., 1977. Bar: Mass. 1977, U.S. Dist. Ct. Mass. 1978, U.S. Ct. Appeals (1st cir.) 1983, U.S. Supreme Ct. 1985. Audiologist Boston City Hosp., 1969-72; dir. audiology Beth Israel Hosp., Boston, 1972-74; atty. Legal Systems Devel., Boston, 1977-78, Liberty Mutual Ins., Boston, 1978-82; counsel, sec. Lexington Ins. Co., Boston, 1982-85, v.p., assoc. gen. counsel, 1985—. Mem. Civil Rights Com. Anti-Defamation League, Boston, 1982—; bd. dirs. DanceArt, Inc., Boston, 1985-92. Mem. ABA (vice chmn. com. on pub. regulation of ins. 1981-84, chmn. elect 1984-85, chmn. 1985-86, chmn. pub. relations 1981-84, excess surplus lines and reins. com. 1982—, vice chmn. 1986-87, chair-elect 1987-88, chmn. 1988-89, internat. ins. law com. 1982—, 1988 ann. arrangements for TIPS, nat. inst. insurer involvency 1986, 89, nat. inst. reins. collections and involvency 1988), Boston Bar Assn. (chmn. corp. counsel com., 1987, chmn. membership com. 1978-83, subcom. on ABA model rules of profl. conduct 1980-81, council 1983-86, chmn. ins. law com. 1987-90, chmn. profl. liability ins. com. 1990—, steering com. corp. bus. law and fin. sect. 1987-89, edn. com. 1987-89, 90-91), Boston Coll. Law Sch. Alumni Assn. (ann. fund com. 1981-89, coun. 1983-87, chmn. telethon com. 1989-94, nominating com. 1990, leadership gift exec. com. 1994—). Home: 122 Lincoln St Newton MA 02161 Office: Lexington Ins Co 200 State St Boston MA 02109-2694

RIVLIN-BARTHOLOMEW, SUSANNA BAHAAR, art educator; b. N.Y.C., Apr. 10, 1957; d. Stanley and Evelyn (Yesky) Rivlin; m. Juan Manuel Cerdan, June 22, 1978 (div. 1984); m. Raymond C. Bartholomew, May 1, 1993. BA, Alfred (N.Y.) U., 1982, BFA, 1982; M in Art Edn., SOSC, 1992. Cert. art tchr., instr. K-12 C.C. Spanish instr. Medford (Oreg.) Sch. Dist., 1992-93, art instr., 1993—; artist handpainted clothing originals Susanna, 1987-91. Regents scholarship N.Y. State Bd. Regents, 1975. Mem. NEA, Nat. Art Edn. Assn. Sufi. Home: 645 W Valley View Rd Ashland OR 97520-9638

RIZZETTA, CAROLYN TERESA, musical instrument, sound recording entrepreneur; b. Chgo., June 22, 1942; d. Frank Thomas and Teresa Margaret (Sylvester) Peter; m. Samuel Charles Rizzetta, Apr. 23, 1966. Student, Art Inst. Chgo., 1961-63; BA, Rosary Coll., 1964, MLS, 1965. Reference librarian Art Dept. Chgo. Pub. Library, 1965; freelance illustrator Macmillan Pub. Co., N.Y.C., 1966; registrar, cataloger Kalamazoo (Mich.) Pub. Mus., 1967; asst. librarian Def. Nuclear Agy., Washington, 1968-69; serials cataloger Library of Congress, Washington, 1970-73, with intern, 1971-72; head of serials U. Va., Charlottesville, 1974-77; musical instrument maker Valley Head, W.Va., 1978-83; bus. mgr. Rizetta Music, Inwood, W.Va., 1984—. Illustrator Invertabrate Zoology, 1969. Mem. Am. Craft Council, Guild of Am. Luthiers. Home and Office: Rizzetta Music PO Box 510 Inwood WV 25428-0510

RIZZI, DEBORAH L., public relations professional; b. Jersey City, N.J., Feb. 26, 1955; d. Edwin Joseph and Beulah Marie (Ardoin) R. BA, Rutgers U., 1977. Program dir. Am. Cancer Soc., Jersey City, 1977-79; internat. program asst. Stevens Inst. Tech., Hoboken, N.J., 1980; dir. pub. rels. United Hosps. Med. Ctr., Newark, 1981-90; dir. practice devel. Stryker Tams & Dill, Newark, 1990-92; corp. comm. mgr. Hackensack Water Co., Harrington Pk., N.J., 1992—; adv. bd. Nat. Boxing Safety Ctr., Newark, 1984-88; sr. producer Children's Miracle Network Telethon, N.J., 1985-90. Contbg. author: (book) Children With HIV Source Book, 1990, (booklet) Guide for Victims of Sexual Assualt, 1985, Child With AIDS . . . Guide for the Family, 1986; co-producer: (video) Diagnosing Sexual Assault in Children, 1990. Recipient Mercury award Internat. Acad. Comm. Arts and Scis., 1993, 94, Galaxy award, 1993, 94, Ace award N.Y. Internat. Assn. Bus. Communicators, 1993, 94, EPIC award Phila. Internat. Assn. Bus. Communicators, 1994, Silver Quill award U.S. Dist. I Internat. Assn. Bus. Communicators, 1994, Iris award N.J. Internat. Assn. Bus. Communicators, 1994, Jaspar award Jersey Shore Pub. Rels. and Advt. Assn., 1994. Mem. Am. Hosp. Assn. (Nat. Touch Stone award 1987), Pub. Rels. Soc. Am., Nat. Assn. Law Firm Marketers, N.J. Hosp. Assn. (Percy award, 1986, 88, 90). Office: Hackensack Water Co 200 Old Hook Rd Harrington Park NJ 07640-1799

RIZZI, TERESA MARIE, bilingual speech and language pathologist; b. Denver, Aug. 8, 1964; d. Theophilus Marcus and Maudie Marie (Pitts) R. BA in Speech Pathology, U. Denver, 1986, BA in Spanish, 1986; MS in Speech Pathology, Vanderbilt U., 1988. Pediatric speech-lang. pathologist Rose Med. Ctr., Denver, 1988-90; pvt. practice Denver, 1990—; Spanish tchr. Temple Emanuel, Denver, 1992—; owner, operator Niños De Colo., Denver; Spanish tutor and interpreter, Denver, 1988—; bilingual pediatric speech-lang. pathologist The Children's Hosp., Denver, 1994—; presenter in field. G'arin grantee Ctrl. Agy. Jewish Edn., 1993, grantee U. No. Colo. Grad. Sch., 1994. Mem. Am. Speech-Lang.-Hearing Assn. (Continuing Edn. award 1991), Colo. Speech-Lang.-Hearing Assn., Internat. Assn. Orofacial Myology, Phi Sigma Iota. Office: Teresa M Rizzi MS CCC 695 S Colorado Blvd Ste 410 Denver CO 80222

RIZZO, JOANNE T., family nurse practitioner; b. Boston, Feb. 20, 1950; d. Anthony M. and Barbara R. BS, Northeastern U., 1972; MS, U. Colo., Denver, 1976. ACLS; cert. family nurse practitioner. RN pediatrics Mass. Gen. Hosp., Boston, 1972-75; family nurse practitioner Frontier Nursing Svc., Hyden, Ky., 1976-78, Family Health Svc., Worcester, Mass., 1982-89; nurse practitioner migrant health program U. Colo., Alamosa, 1978-79; family nurse practitioner, clinic mgr. Plan de Salud del Valle, Ft. Lupton, Colo., 1979-82; fgn. svc. nurse practitioner State Dept., Washington, 1989—; fgn. svc. nurse practitioner Am. Embassy, Bucharest, Romania, 1989-91, Lima, Peru, 1991—; nurse practitioner preceptor U. Lowell, Worcester, 1984-88. Recipient Cert. of Appreciation, Agy. Internat. Devel., Romania, 1990, Meritorious Honor award & Group Valor award, Romania, 1990; Robert Wood Johnson fellow, 1980-81. Mem. Sigma Theta Tau. Home: Am Embassy Lima Unit 3755 APO AA 34031

RIZZO, MARY ANN FRANCES, international trade executive, former educator; b. Bryn Mawr, Pa., Jan. 11, 1942; d. Joseph Franklyn and Armella Louise (Grubenhoff) R. BA magna cum laude (N.Y. State scholar), Marymount-Manhattan Coll., 1963; MA (fellow), Yale U., 1965, PhD (Lounsbury-Cross fellow), 1969; postgrad. Harvard U. Bus. Sch., 1979. Instr. Romance langs. and lit. Yale U., New Haven, 1966-70; asst. prof. Finch Coll., N.Y.C., 1971-73; v.p. Joseph F. Rizzo Co., Fla., 1969-87; owner, pres., 1987—; minister of the Word coordinator Our Lady of Perpetual Help Ch., Scottsdale, Ariz., 1986—, eucharistic min.; mem. bd. adv. Assn. Internat. des Etudiants en Sciences Economiques et Commerciales, Ariz. State U. Vice chmn., charter mem. bd. regents Cath. U. Am.; mem., coord. export counseling svc. Ariz. Dist. Export Coun.; 2d v.p. bd. advisors sch. bus. mgmt. Ariz. State U., Phoenix; bd. advisors bus. studies Paradise Valley (Ariz.) C.C. Mem. Il Circolo Italian Cultural Club (Palm Beach, Fla.), Fgn. Trade Coun. Palm Beach County (charter mem.), World Affairs Coun. of Ariz., Scottsdale C. of C. (internat. bus. devel. com.), World Trade Ctr., Alpha Chi. Republican. Roman Catholic (community coun. 1972-74). Clubs: Harvard Bus. Sch. Greater N.Y., Yale (N.Y.C. and Phoenix), Alliance Francaise (Phoenix), Ariz., Yale of Palm Beaches, Cercle Français de Palm Beach (Fla.), Ariz. Harvard Bus. Sch. Translator: From Time to Eternity, 1967; bibliographer: Italian Literature-Roots and Branches, 1976. Home: Villa Serein 2170 Ibis Isle Rd Palm Beach FL 33480-5323 also: 5665 N 74th Pl Scottsdale AZ 85250-6416 Office: 7436 E Stetson Dr Ste 180 Scottsdale AZ 85251

RIZZOTTO-MOORE, PATRICIA, educational administrator; b. Allentown, Pa., Oct. 4, 1950; d. Warren R. and Helen (Heidsh) R.; 1 child, Matthew R. Moore. BS in Edn., Ohio State U., 1972; MEd, Lehigh U., 1978; EdM in Ednl. Adminstrn., Columbia U., D of Ednl Adminstrn., 1984. Office mgr., dlk. John B. Rizzotto & Sons, Inc., Jerome Builders, Pa., 1967-81; Tchr. Southwestern City Schs., Grove City (Ohio) High sch., 1972-73, Beaver Coll., Am. Lang. Acad., Pa., 1981-82, Louis E. Dieruff High Sch., Allentown, Pa., 1973-83; supr. ESOL City of Allentown Sch. Dist., 1983-86; asst. prin. Northampton (Pa.) Area Sr. High Sch., 1986-90, Northampton Area Jr. High Sch., 1990-93; dir. support svcs. Northampton Area Sch. Dist., 1993—; presenter in field. Golf classic vol., ladies lite tournament chair Am. Heart Assn., 1990, 91, devel. com., 1992; pub. rels. com. Lehigh Valley Pride, pub. rels. com. co-chair, exec. bd., Keystone games vol., 1988-91; active Lehigh Valley Red Cross, (Communications Excellence award in Pubs. 1987); team mem. intermediate unit evaluation Big Spring High Sch., 1984. Mem. Am. Assn. Sch. Adminstrs., Nat. Assn. Secondary Sch. Prins., Pa. Assn. Sch. Adminstrs., Pa. Assn. Secondary Sch. Prins., Pa. Sch. Bds. Assn., Kappa Delta Pi, Phi Delta Kappa.

RIZZUTO, CARMELA RITA, nursing administrator; b. Waterbury, Conn., Aug. 26, 1942; d. Joseph Anthony and Carmella Rosa R.; m. Thomas Lee Chernesky, Aug. 28, 1982. BS, St. Joseph Coll., 1965; MS, Boston Coll., 1971; EdD, Sch. Edn., UCLA, 1983. RN, Calif. Nursing instr. Samaritan Hosp. Sch. Nursing, Troy, N.Y., 1969; med. nursing coord., clin. specialist Harvard Community Health Plan, Boston, 1971-72; instr. inservice edn. Tufts-New Eng. Med. Ctr., Boston, 1972-73; instr. inservice edn. St. John's Hosp. and Health Ctr., Santa Monica, Calif., 1974-76; asst. clin. prof. Sch. Nursing, UCLA, 1976-79; assoc. dir. nursing edn. St. Francis Hosp. of Santa Barbara, 1981-83; asst. dir. nursing edn. and rsch. Stanford U. Hosp., 1983-90, dir. geriatric patient care grant, 1990-93; rsch. coord. sch. medicine Stanford U., 1994—. Grantee USPHS, NIH, DHHS, USPHS nurse trainee, 1969-71; recipient Chancellor's Patent Fund, UCLA, 1972-73. Contbr. articles to profl. publs. Home: 925 Cascade Dr Sunnyvale CA 94087-4043

ROACH, ELEANOR MARIE, elementary education educator; b. Indpls., Nov. 30, 1932; d. Armand Dunnington and Ruth (Holman) R. BS in Art Edn., Ind. U., 1954; MS in Elem. Edn., Butler U., 1966. Cert. life K-12 art tchr., K-8 gen. elem. tchr., Ind. Tchr. art Wayne Twp. Pub. Schs., Indpls., 1954-57; freelance artist, 1957-60; artist, libr. designer Remington Rand, Indpls., 1960-61; elem. tchr. Indpls. Pub. Schs., 1962-70, tchr. academically talented, 1970-92, upper elem. tchr., 1992-94; content cons. Macmillan-McGraw Hill, N.Y.C., 1989-90; cons. Ind. State Mus., Indpls., 1988, 92. Photographer textbook Indiana, 1990. Former set designer Footlite Mus., Indpls.; stage mgr. Christian Theol. Sem. Repetory Theatre, Indpls., 1979-75. Recipient 1st place for ceramics Ind. State Fair, 1953, 2d place, 1954. Mem. NEA, Ind. Tchrs. Assn., Indpls. Edn. Assn., Ind. Coun. for Social Studies, Washington County Ind. Hist. Soc., Rush County Heritage, Inc., Nature Conservancy, Ind. Audubon Soc., Ind. Hist. Soc. Democrat. Roman Catholic. Home and Office: PO Box 635 Mooresville IN 46158

ROACH, JOYCE GIBSON, English language educator, author; b. Cleburne, Tex., Dec. 18, 1935; d. David Henry and Ann (Hartman) Gibson; m. Claude D. Roach, June 15, 1957; children: Darrell, Delight Hardee. BFA, Tex. Christian U., 1958, MA in English, 1965. Tchr. Ft. Worth Pub. Schs., 1958-63, Rabyor Pvt. Sch., Ft. Worth, 1972, Keller (Tex.) Ind. Sch. Dist., 1976-85; adj. English faculty mem. Tex. Christian U., Ft. Worth, 1984—. Author: The Cowgirls, 1977 (Best Non-fiction Book award Western Writers Am. 1978, (with Ernestine Sewell Linck) Eats: A Folk History of Texas Foods, 1990 (Best Non-fiction Book award Tex. Inst. Letters 1990); author: (with others) Hoein' the Short Rows, 1988 (Best Short Non-fiction award Western Writers Am. 1988), Women of the West, 1991 (Best Short Fiction award Western Writers Am. 1991). Mem. Tex. Inst. Letters, Tex. Folklore Soc. (pres. 1976), Western Writers Am. (bd. dirs. 1994—), German Assn. for Study the Western, Western Lit. Assn. Methodist. Home: PO Box 143 Keller TX 76244

ROACH, NANCY KATHRYN, health facility administrator; b. Lexington, N.C., Feb. 25, 1954; d. Henry Herman Jr. and Evelyn Frances (Cline) R. BA in Speech Comm. Edn., U. N.C., 1977; postgrad., Ea. Ill. U., 1982-83. cert. dir. vol. svcs. Form art resource tchr. to learning lab coord. Davidson County Schs., Lexington, N.C., 1977-79; dir. Arts Coun. for Davidson County, Lexington, N.C., 1979-82; grad. asst. Ea. Ill. U., Charleston, 1982-83; asst. mgr. Gingerbread House Toy Store, Lexington, 1983-86; dir. vol. svcs. Lexington Meml. Hosp., 1986-89, Wesley Long Community Hosp., Greensboro, N.C., 1989-93, Cape Fear Valley Med. Ctr., Fayetteville, N.C., 1993—. Charter bd. dirs. Lexington Friends the Theater, 1980-82, Actor's Chairty Theatre, Lexington, 1984-89; loaned exec. United Way Guilford County, Greensboro, 1990-91. Mem. Am. Soc. Dir. Vol. Svcs. (state membership rep. 1991-92, affiliate group leader 1992-93), N.C. Soc. Dir. Vol. Svcs. (bylaws chair 1988-89, pub. rels. chair 1989-90, recording sec. 1990-91, pres.-elect 1991-92, pres., bd. dirs. 1992-93, workshop leader 1993), Phi Alpha Theta. Methodist. Office: Cape Fear Valley Med Ctr 1638 Owen Dr Fayetteville NC 28302-2000

ROARK, MARY LOU, educator, counselor; b. Greene, Iowa, Oct. 25, 1938; d. Alfred H. and Anna M. (Voigts) Heuer; m. Eldridge W. Roark, Jr., June 20, 1964; children Lisa K., Michael E. BA, Wartburg Coll., 1961; MA, Syracuse U., 1964; EdD, Va. Poytech. Inst. & State U., 1978. Nat, cert, counselor. (Nat. Bd. for Cert. Counselors). Tchr. Madison (Wis.) City Schs., 1961-62, Iowa City (Iowa) Schs., 1964-65, Syracuse (N.Y.) City Schs., 1965-67; coop. edn. coord. Va. Polytech. and State U., Blacksburg, Va., 1977-78; from assoc. prof. to prof. edn. dept. SUNY, Plattsburgh, 1980-93, counseling programs coord., 1989—, prof., 1993—; bd. dirs. Campus Violence Prevention Ctr., Towson, Md., 1989—; cons., counselor, pvt. practice, Plattsburgh, 1980—. Author: (handbook) Guide to Preventing Campus Violence, 1988; contbr. articles to profl. jours., chpts. to books. Pres. LWV, Plattsburgh, 1983-85; chair Community Svcs. Bd., Plattsburgh, 1985-89; moderator Dist. Atty.'s Child Sex Abuse Coun., Plattsburgh, 1991-92. Mem. Northeastern N.Y. Counselors Assn. (pres. 1992-93), Am. Coll. Pers. Assn. (chair task force 1985-90), Phi Kappa Phi (pres. 1992-94), Omicron Delta Kappa, Phi Delta Kappa. Office: SUNY at Plattsburgh Ward Hall # 106C Plattsburgh NY 12901

ROATH-ALGERA, KATHLEEN MARIE, massage therapist; b. Binghamton, N.Y., Feb. 7, 1952; d. Stephen James and Virginia Mary (Purdy) Roath; m. Parker Newcomb Wheeler Jr., Sept. 18, 1971 (div. June 1976); 1 child, Colleen Marie Wheeler; m. John M. Algera, Feb. 14, 1981. AS in Phys. Edn., Dean Jr. Coll., Franklin, Mass., 1971; BS in Edn., Boston U., 1977; postgrad., U. Ctrl. Fla., Orlando, 1981-82; grad., Reese Inst. Massage Therapy, Oviedo, Fla., 1988. Lic. massage therapist; master practitioner in myofascial release. Counselor Dept. Def., Orlando, 1979-84; tchr. Divine Mercy Cath. Sch., Merritt Island, Fla., 1984-85; courier Emery Worldwide, Orlando, 1985-89; massage therapist, dir., owner Massage Therapy Clinic of Titusville, Fla., 1989—; instr., supr. clin. internship Reese Inst., 1992—. Mem. Am. Massage Therapy Assn., Fla. State Massage Therapy Assn. (pres. Brevard County 1992—, Therapist of Yr. 1991-92), Nat. Cert. Bd. Therapeutic Massage and Bodywork (recert. chair 1994—). Home: 1660 Saratoga Dr Titusville FL 32796-4206 Office: Massage Therapy Clinic Titusville 3410 S Park Ave Titusville FL 32780-5139

ROBAK, KIM M., state official; b. Columbus, Nebr., Oct. 4, 1955; m. William J. Mueller; children: Katherine, Claire. BA with distinction, U. Nebr., 1977, JD with high distinction, 1985. Tchr. Lincoln (Nebr.) Pub. Schs., 1978-82; clerk Cline Williams Wright Johnson & Oldfather, Lincoln, 1983; summer assoc. Cooley Godward castro Huddleson & Tatum, San Francisco, 1984, Steptoe & Johnson, Washington, 1985; ptnr. Rembolt Ludtke Parker & Berger, Lincoln, 1985-91; legal counsel Gov. E. Benjamin Nelson/State of Nebr., Lincoln, 1991-92, chief of staff, 1992-93; lt. gov. State of Nebr., Lincoln, 1993—; chair Prairie Fire Internat. Symposium on Edn., 1986. Fellow Leadership Lincoln, 1986-87, program com., 1987-90; chair program com. Leadership Lincoln Alumni Assn., 1987, selection com., 1990; chair Landfill Alternatives and Ops. Task Force, 1986-87; chair Gladys Forsyth award subcom. YWCA Tribute! to Women, 1987, chair nominations, 1991; mem. adv. com. U.S. Constitution Bicentennial Competition, 1987; gen. Dem. Counsel, Nebr., 1985-93; bd. women's ministries First Plymouth Congl. Ch., 1988-91, bd. trustees, 1991-94. Mem. Nat. Conf. Lt. Govs. (fed. practice com. 1989-92), Nat. Inst. Trial Attys., Nebr. State Bar Assn. (ethics com. 1987-92, vice chair com. on pub. rels. 1988-92, chair com. on yellow page advt. 1988, ho. dels. 1989—, ways and means com. 1991-94), Lincoln Bar Assn., U. Nebr. Coll. Law Alumni Assn. (bd. dirs. 1986-89), Order of Coif, Updowntowners. Office: Lt Gov's Office PO Box 94863 Lincoln NE 68509-4848*

ROBARDS, BROOKS, mass communication educator; b. Mt. Kisco, N.Y., Aug. 21, 1942; d. Sidney Marshall and Claire Louise (Sherman) R.; m. Jonathan Josef Von Ranson, Mar. 13, 1965 (div. Dec. 1975); children: Erik Josef, Kristin Brooks, Joel Robert; m. James Lamport Kaplan, June 21, 1988. AB in English Lit., Bryn Mawr Coll., 1964; MA in English Lit., U. Hartford, 1970; PhD in Comm., U. Mass., 1982. Reporter Life Mag., N.Y.C., 1964-65; editor women's page Presque Isle (Maine) Star-Herald, 1965-67; editor/pub. Newington (Conn.) Town Crier, 1973-75; asst. prof. mass comm. Westfield (Mass.) State Coll., 1979-85, assoc. prof. mass comm., 1985-88, prof. mass comm., 1988—; corp. mem. Nathan Mayhew Seminars, Vineyard Haven, Mass., 1988-91, trustee, 1991—. Author: Arnold Schwarzenegger, 1992; contbr. articles, poem to profl. publs. Mem. Northampton (Mass.) Cable TV Bd., 1983-92. Fulbright Commn. teaching fellow, Beijing, 1993-94. Mem. Internat. Comm. Assn., Speech Comm. Assn. Popular Culture Assn., N.E. Popular Culture Assn. (pres. 1991-92). Democrat. Episcopalian. Office: Westfield State Coll Dept Mass Comm Westfield MA 01086

ROBB, KAREN, counsel; b. Pitts., July 17, 1953. BA, U. Pitts., 1953; JD, Duquesne U., 1977. Assoc. Royston, Robb, Leonard, Edgecomb & Miller, 1977-78; law clerk U.S. Judge Herbert Sorg (we. dist.) Pa., 1978-79; atty. adv. justice mgmt. divsn. U.S. Dept. Justice, 1979-86; spl. asst. to comptroller and office congl. affairs U.S. Customs Svc., 1986-89; majority chief counsel, staff dir. subcom. on patents, copyrights & trademarks, sen. judiciary com., 1990—. Office: Subcom on Patents Copyrights & Trademarks 327 Senate Hart Office Bldg Washington DC 20510*

ROBB, KIMBERLY KAY, critical care nurse, medical, surgical nurse, infant immunization nurse; b. Princeton, Ind., Nov. 18, 1963; d. Carl Eugene and Cherry Johnetta (Lewis) R. AD, Ind. Vocat. Tech. Sch., 1990. Cert. IV and Tb nurse; cert. CPR; cert. ACLS. Staff nurse Holiday Manor Nursing Home, Princeton, Ind., 1990-91, Gibson Gen. Hosp., Princeton, 1991—, Gibson County Health Dept., 1994—. Mem. Nat. League for Nursing, Am. Assn. Critical Care Nurses. Baptist. Home: 611 N Hart St Princeton IN 47670-1449

ROBB, LYNDA JOHNSON, writer; b. Washington, Mar. 19, 1944; d. Lyndon Baines and Claudia Alta (Taylor) Johnson; m. Charles Spittal Robb, Dec. 9, 1967; children: Lucinda Desha, Catherine Lewis, Jennifer Wickliffe. BA with honors, U. Tex., 1966. Writer, McCall's mag., 1966-68; contbg. editor Ladies Home Jour., 1968-80; lectr. bd. dirs. Reading Is Fundamental, 1968—, Lyndon B. Johnson Family Found., 1969—. Mem. Va. State Coun. on Infant Mortality, Va. Maternal & Child Health Coun., Nat. Commn. to Prevent Infant Mortality, 1987-93; chmn. Pres.'s Adv. Com. for Women, 1979-81; bd. dirs. Nat. Home Libr. Found., Ford Theatre; chmn. Va. Women's Cultural History Project, 1982-85; mem. adv. bd. Commn. Presdl. Debates. Mem. Nat. Wildflower Rsch. Ctr., Zeta Tau Alpha. Democrat. Episcopalian.

ROBBEN, MARY MARGARET, portrait artist; b. Bethesda, Md., Oct. 30, 1948; d. John Otto and Mary Margaret (McConnaughy) R. Student, Ohio U., 1967-71; B.Visual Art, Ga. State U., 1984. Visual merchandising staff Macy's Dept. Store, Union City, Ga., 1985-86; embroidery designer So. Promotions, Peachtree City, Ga., 1987-90; portrait artist Personal Touch Portraits, Peachtree City, Ga., 1991—. Mortar Bd. scholar, 1984. Mem. AAUW, Ga. State U. Alumni Assn., Golden Key, Leads Club. Home and Office: 207 Battery Way Peachtree Cty GA 30269-2126

ROBBINS, ANNE FRANCIS See REAGAN, NANCY DAVIS

ROBBINS, CHRISTINE BLACK, principal; b. McKeesport, Pa., Apr. 24, 1952; d. Anthony Joseph and Anna M. (Hlad) Merda; m. Donald C. Robbins, Nov. 21, 1990; children: Melissa, Heather. BS, Pa. State U., 1974; MS, Va. Tech., 1979; EdD, U. Va., 1987; postgrad., Harvard U., 1994—. Tchr., coord. Chesapeake (Va.) Pub. Schs., 1974-84; grad. asst. U. Va., Charlottesville, 1984-86; asst. prin. Northampton County Pub. Schs., Eastville, VA., 1986-87; adminstrv. asst. Hewlett (N.Y.)-Woodmere Union Free Sch. Dist., 1987-89; asst. prin. North Rockland Ctrl. Sch. Dist., Garnerville, N.Y., 1989-91; prin. Freeport (N.Y.) Pub. Schs., 1991-92; prin. Piscataway (N.J.) Twp. Schs., 1992-93, prin.-at-large, 1993-94; ind. cons. for spl. projects, 1994—; advisor 1981 jr. class and 1982 sr. class Deep Creek High Sch.; mem. Va. Secondary Sch. Prins.' Inst. for Effective Instrn., 1987-88; chairperson Dist. Drug Free Schs. and Communities Adv. Coun., 1988-89, Dist. AIDS Adv. Coun., 1988-89; chairperson vis. com., sch. staff and adminsntrn. com. Syosset High Sch., 1990; advisor Piscataway (N.J.) Bd. Edn. Coms. Contbr. articles to profl. jours. Active LWV, Chesapeake, 1978-84. Mem. ASCD, Nat. Assn. Secondary Sch. Prins., N.J. Pub. Sch. Adminstrs., Pa. State Alumni Assn. (chairperson scholarship com. 1986-87), U. Va. Alumni Assn., Va. Tech. Alumni Assn., Omicron Nu, Phi Delta Kappa, Phi Upsilon Omicron, Pi Lambda Theta. Home: 50 Wilbar Dr Stratford CT 06497

ROBBINS, HULDA DORNBLATT, artist, printmaker; b. Atlanta, Oct. 19, 1910; d. Adolph Benno and Lina (Rosenthal) Dornblatt. Student, Phila. Mus's. Sch. Indsl. Art, 1928-29, Prussian Acad., Berlin, 1929-31, Barnes Found., Merion, Pa., 1939. Poster designer and maker ITE Circuit Breaker Co. Inc., Phila., 1944; instr. serigraphy Nat. Serigraph Soc. Sch., N.Y.C., 1953-60; instr. creative painting Atlantic County Jewish Community Centers, Margate and Atlantic City, N.J., 1960-67. One-man shows, Lehigh U. Art Galleries, 1933, ACA Galleries, Phila., 1939, 8th St. Gallery, N.Y.C., 1941, Serigraph Gallery, N.Y.C., 1947, Atlantic City Art Center, 1961, 71, numerous group shows, 2d Nat. Print ann. Bklyn. Mus., Carnegie Inst., Library of Congress, LaNapoule Art Found., Am. Graphic Contemporary Art; represented in permanent collections, including, Met. Mus. Art, N.Y.C., Mus. Modern Art, N.Y.C., Bibliotheque Nationale, Smithsonian Instn., Art Mus. Ont., Can., Victoria and Albert Mus., London, U.S. embassies abroad, Lehigh U., Princeton (N.J.) Print Club. Recipient Purchase prize Prints for Children, Mus. Modern Art, N.Y.C., 1941; prize 2d Portrait of Am. Competition, 1945; 2d prize Paintings by Printmakers, 1948. Mem. Am. Color Print Soc., Print Club, Graphics Soc., Serigraph Soc. (mem. founding group, charter sec., Ninth Ann. prize 1948, 49). Home and Office: 16 S Buffalo Ave Ventnor City NJ 08406-2635

ROBBINS, JANE BORSCH, library science educator, information science educator; b. Chgo., Sept. 13, 1939; d. Reuben August and Pearl Irene (Houk) Borsch; 1 child, Molly Warren Robbins. B.A., Wells Coll., 1961; M.L.S., Western Mich. U., 1966; Ph.D., U. Md., 1972. Asst. prof. library and info. sci. U. Pitts., 1972-73; asso. prof. Emory U., Atlanta, 1973-74; cons. to the bd. Wyo. State Library, 1974-77; asso. prof. La. State U., Baton Rouge, 1977-79; dean La. State U. (Sch. Library and Info. Sci.), 1979-81; prof., dir. Sch. Library and Info. Studies U. Wis., Madison, 1981-94; dean, prof. Sch. Libr. and Info. Studies Fla. State U., Tallahassee, 1994—. Author: Public Library Policy and Citizen Participation, 1975, Public Librarianship: A Reader, 1982, Are We There Yet?, 1988, Libraries: Partners in Adult Literacy, 1990, Keeping the Books: Public Library Financial Practices, 1992, Balancing the Books: Financing American Public Library Services, 1993, Evaluating Library Programs and Services: A Manual and Sourcebook, 1994; editor Libr. and Info. Sci. Rsch., 1982-92; contbr. articles to profl. jours. Mem. ALA (councilor 1976-80, 91—), Am. Soc. Info. Sci., Assn. for Library and Info. Sci. Edn. (dir. 1979-81, pres. 1984), Wis. Library Assn. (pres. 1986). Democrat. Episcopalian. Office: Fla State U Sch Libr and Info Studies Louis Shores Bldg Tallahassee FL 32306

ROBBINS, JANET EDITH, social work administrator; b. Detroit, Jan. 15, 1955; Lyon Herbert and Lois Mildred (Burton) R.; m. Richard Andrew Hopkins, De. 31, 1977. BS with distinction, U. N.Mex., 1978; M in Social Work Adminstrn., Rutgers U., 1989. Program asst. Las Vegas (N.Mex.) Campus Community Ministry, 1975-76; asst. dir. Project Hold State of Fla., Jacksonville, pub. assistance eligibility specialist, social rehab. specialist, child support investigator, vocat. rehab. specialist, 1979-84; coord. of tng. Prairie Freedom Ctr., Sioux Falls, S.D., 1984-85; personnel supr. Kelly Svcs., Inc., Somerville, N.J., 1985-86; account exec. Pitney Bowes, Inc., Lawrenceville, N.J., 1986-88; community problem solving specialist Somerset United Ways, Somerville, 1988-89; dir. social work and discharge planning Hunterdon Med. Ctr., Flemington, N.J., 1989—; chairperson Suffrage Anniversary Celebration Event, Albuquerque, 1978, Somerset County Child Care Alliance, Somerville, 1988—, Teen Esteem Curriculum Com., Somerville, 1988—, planner, Human Svcs. Mgmt. Inst., New Brunswick, N.J., 1988—; mem. consumer adv. coun. United Telephone Co. N.J., Inc., 1990—. Founder, Pres. U. N.Mex. Women's Studies Student Assn., 1977-78; founder, Women Who Love Too Much Support Group, Bridgewater, N.J., 1987—; pres. Southwestern Right to Choose, Albuquerque, 1977-79. Fellow Nat. Assn. Social Workers, Inst. on Rsch. for Women, Union for Concerned Scientists, Physicians for Social Responsibility; mem. NOW, Soc. for Hosp. Social Work Dirs., N.J. Chpt. Soc. Social Work Dirs. Democrat. Unitarian Universalist. Home: 2 Wythe Cir Neshanic Station NJ 08853-1101

ROBBINS, JANET SUE, graphic artist; b. Bangor, Maine, May 4, 1961; d. Wallace Clifton and Beverly Lillian (Daggett) R. BA in Journalism, U. Maine, 1983. Prodn. coord. Farmstead Press, Freedom, Maine, 1983-86; graphic artist Jiffy Print, Bangor, Maine, 1986-87; asst. dir. art and prodn. Internat. Maine/McGraw-Hill, Camden, Maine, 1987—. Mem. Mid-Coast Graphic Arts Network (treas. 1992—), Down East Singers (bd. dirs. 1992-94, graphic artist). Republican. Baptist. Home: 24 Pearl St Apt B Camden ME 04843-1957 Office: Internat Maine/McGraw-Hill 633 Rte 1 Rockport ME 04856

ROBBINS, JUDITH HOFFMAN, mayor; b. L.A., Feb. 24, 1937; d. Richard John and Ruth Janet (Lofthouse) Hoffman; m. Marcus Page Robbins, Jr., June 25, 1961; children: Andrew Page, Janet Elizabeth. BA, Stanford U., 1958; MPA, Suffolk U., 1982. Mem. Attleboro (Mass.) Charter Commn., 1971-73; councilman-at-large City of Attleboro, 1974-89, coun. pres., 1984-89; dir. Massachusetts Bay Transp. Authority, Boston, 1983-91; mayor City of Attleboro, 1992—; coord. spl. com. on pay equity Mass. Ho. of Reps., Boston, 1985-89. Pres. Celebrity Nights of Attleboro; bd. dirs. Plymouth Bay coun. Girl Scouts USA, Sturdy Meml. Hosp., Attleboro, 1980-89, 92—; pres. Little Folks Coop. Nursery Sch., Attleboro, 1970-71. Mem. AAUW, LWV, ASPA (treas. 1991—), Am. Pub. Transit Assn., Mass. Mcpl. Assn. (bd. dirs. 1981-84, 92—), Mass. Mcpl. Councillors Assn. (pres. 1984), Women's Transp. Seminar, Stanford U. Alumni Assn., Phi Beta Kappa, Pi Alpha Alpha. Congregationalist. Home: 20 Ashton Rd Attleboro MA 02703-1604

ROBBINS, LILLIAN CUKIER, psychology educator; b. Nancy, France, Sept. 6, 1933; came to U.S., 1943; BA, CCNY, 1954; MA, U. Ill., 1956; PhD, NYU, 1961. Cert. psychologist, N.Y. Research psychologist NYU Med. Ctr., 1962-67; asst. prof. Hunter Coll., N.Y.C., 1967-70, CCNY, 1970-71; assoc. prof. Rutgers U., Newark, 1971-76, prof., 1976—; prin. investigator Citizen's Com. for Children, N.Y.C., 1973-75; dir. coll. honors program Rutgers U., Newark, 1980—. Contbr. articles to profl. jours. Chair women's issues Am. Jewish Com., N.Y.C., 1984-86. Mem. AAAS (life), AAUP (exec. council), Am. Psychol. Assn., Phi Beta Kappa. Democrat. Jewish. Home: 49 E 96th St New York NY 10128-0782 Office: Rutgers U Newark NJ 07102

ROBBINS, LISA STUEDLE, management and human resources consultant; b. Louisville, July 12, 1965; d. Joseph Anthony and Mary (Falvey) Stuedle; m. Todd Barrett Robbins, June 15, 1984; children: Amber Nicole Robbins, Elizabeth Michael Robbins. BA, Bellarmine Coll., 1987; MA, Webster U., 1992. From customer svc. rep. to tng. specialist Humana, Inc., Louisville, 1987-92; regional customer svc. mgr. Circuit City Stores, Inc., Louisville, 1992-94; pers. mgr. Walmart Stores, Inc., Louisville, 1994—. Mem. ASTD. Home: 10700 Bruners Way Louisville KY 40299

ROBBINS, MARJORIE JEAN GILMARTIN, educator; b. Newton, Mass., Sept. 19, 1940; d. John and Helen (Arbuckle) Gilmartin; m. Maurice Edward Robbins, Aug. 1, 1962; children: John Scott, Gregory Dale, Kris Eric. BS in Edn., Gordon Coll., 1962; postgrad., U. Maine, Augusta, 1976, U. Maine, Orono, 1986, U. Maine, Portland, 1987. Cert. tchr. Tchr. Ctr. St. Sch., Hampton, N.H., 1962-64, Claflin Sch., Newton, 1965-66, Israel Loring Sch., Sudbury, Mass., 1966-67, Cheney Sch., Orange, Mass., 1967-69, Palermo (Maine) Consolidated Sch., 1975—; founder, tchr. Primary Edn. Program, Palmero, 1990—; dir., author Child Sexual Abuse Program, Palmero, 1994—. Mem. 2d Bapt. Ch., Newton, 1949-90; bd. Christian Edn. Winter St. Bapt. Ch., Gardiner, Maine, 1993—, bd. Missions, 1993-94; bd. dirs. Hillside Christian Nursery Sch., 1994—; coord. student assistance team Maine Sch. Unit #51, 1993—, United Team bd. dirs., 1993—; publicity com. mem., 1991-92; coord. Nursing Home Ministry, Gardiner, 1990—. Mem. NEA, Maine Tchrs. Assn., Palermo Tchrs. Assn. (pres. 1984-86), Maine Educators of the Gifted and Talented, Maine Sch. Union 51 (sec. certification steering com. 1990—, rep. gifted-talented com. 1976—), Palermo Sch. Club (exec. bd. 1985-88, the United Team 1993—, student assistance team coord. 1993—). Home: 204 Dresden Ave Gardiner ME 04345-2618 Office: Palermo Consolidated Sch RR 3 Palermo ME 04354

ROBBINS, NANCY LOUISE See MANN, NANCY LOUISE

ROBBINS, WENDY, television and cable director; b. L.A., Jan. 12, 1960; d. Robert and Elaine (Abrams) Hoffman. Grad., Julliard Sch., 1984. Tchr. UCLA, 1989-93, Art Ctr., Pasadena, Calif., 1993—. Dir. TV series for PBS, 1986-90, Fox, 1991, CBS, 1990-91, NBC, 1991-92, also TV documentaries for PBS, 1986-90, ABC, 1991-92, cable documentary for Discovery Channel, 1988, film for Lifetime, 1992, also cable series, commls., music videos for MTV, 1992-93, cable pilot for HBO, 1993; dir. Kids Saving Kids (Emmy award), Mysteries of the Mind, Ozone Danger Zone (Emmy award), Hollywood: A Town Remembered (Emmy nomination), Ode to a Bit Player, Grasping the Last Branch, It's A Big Country; dir. (with Steven Spielberg and Kate Capshaw) Shattered Lullabies; (series) Celebrations, Fantastic Facts, Best of the Worst, Encounters, Take 5, The Big Picture; segment prodr. Trauma Center; co-developer Mickey Mouse Club; author: Folk Tales From Outer Space, 1993; contbr. articles to profl. jours. Active NARAL, Washington, 1993, Amnesty Internat., San Francisco, 1981-93, Didget Fund, Gorilla's Diane Fossey, Colo., 1989-93, Reading is Fundamental, N.Y., 1990-93. Recipient 2 Emmy awards Acad. TV Arts & Scis., 1989, 90, Nat. Endowment Arts award NEA, 1991, Gold award Houston Film Festival, 1988. Mem. SAG, AFTRA, Dirs. Guild Am., Internat. Documentary Assn. (v.p. 1988-91), Women in Film, Ind. Filmmakers Assn. Home: 10628 Whipple St North Hollywood CA 91602-2760

ROBBINS-WILF, MARCIA, English language educator; b. Newark, Mar. 22, 1949; d. Saul and Ruth (Fern) Robbins; m. Leonard A. Wilf, June 21, 1970; 1 child, Orin. Student, Emerson Coll., 1967-69, Seton Hall U., 1969, Fairleigh Dickinson U., 1970; BA, George Washington U., 1971; MA, NYU, 1975; postgrad., St. Peter's Coll., Jersey City, 1979, Fordham U., 1980; MS, Yeshiva U., 1981, EdD, 1986; postgrad., Monmouth Coll., 1986. Cert. elem. tchr., N.Y., N.J., reading specialist, N.J., prin., supr., N.J., adminstr., supr., N.Y. Tchr. Sleepy Hollow Elem. Sch., Falls Church, Va., 1971-72, Yeshiva Konvitz, N.Y.C., 1972-73; intern Wee Folk Nursery Sch., Short Hills, N.J., 1978-81, dir. day camp, 1980-81, tchr., dir., owner, 1980-81; adj. prof. reading Seton Hall U., South Orange, N.J., 1987, Middlesex County Coll., Edison, N.J., 1987-88; asst. adj. prof. L.I. U., Bklyn., 1988, Pace U., N.Y.C., 1988—; ednl. cons. Cranford High Sch., 1988; presenter numerous workshops; founding bd. dirs. Stern Coll. Women Yeshiva U., N.Y.C., 1987; adj. vis. lectr. Rutgers U., New Brunswick, N.J., 1988. Chairperson Jewish Book Festival, YM-YWHA, West Orange, N.J., 1986-87. mem. early childhood com., 1986—, bd. dirs., 1986—; vice chairperson dinner com. Nat. Leadership Conf. Christians and Jews, 1986; mem. Hadassah, Valerie Children's Fund, Women's League Conservative Judaism, City of Hope, assoc. bd. bus. and women's profl. div. United Jewish Appeal, 1979; vol. reader Goddard Riverside Day Care Ctr., N.Y.C., 1973; friend N.Y.C. Pub. Libr., 1980—; life friend Millburn (N.J.) Pub. Libr.; pres. Seton-Essex Reading Coun., 1991-92. Co-recipient Am. Heritage award, Essex County, 1985; recipient Award Appreciation City of Hope, 1984, Profl. Improvement awards Seton-Essex Reading Council, 1984-86, Cert. Attendance award Seton-Essex Reading Council, 1987. Mem. N.Y. Acad. Scis. (life), N.J. Council Tchrs. English, Nat. Council Tchrs. English, Am. Ednl. Research Assn., Coll. Reading Assn. (life), Assn. Supervision and Curriculun Devel., N.Y. State Reading Assn. (council Manhattan), N.J. Reading Assn. (council Seton-Essex), Internat. Reading Assn., Nat. Assn. for Edn. of Young Children (life N.J. chpt., Kenyon group), Nat. Council Jewish Women (vice chairperson membership com. evening br. N.Y. sect. 1974-75), George Washington U. Alumni Club, Emerson Coll. Alumni Club, NYU Alumni Club, Phi Delta Kappa (life), Kappa Gamma Chi (historian). Club: Greenbrook Country (Caldwell, N.J.); George Washington Univ. Home: 242 Hartshorn Dr Short Hills NJ 07078-1914 also: 820 Morris Tpke Short Hills NJ 07078-2619

ROBE, LUCY BARRY, editor, educator; b. Boston, Jan. 15, 1934; d. Herbert Jr. and Lucy (Brown) Barry; m. Robert S. Robe Jr., Feb. 6, 1971; 1 child, Parrish C. BA, Harvard U., 1955; MA in Med. Writing, Pacific Western U., 1992. Writer Alcoholism Update Biomed. Info. Corp., N.Y.C., 1979-85; editor newsletter Am. Soc. of Addiction Medicine News, Washington, 1985—; v.p. L.I. Coun. on Alcoholism, Mineola, N.Y., 1978-92. Author: Just So It's Healthy, 1978, Haunted Inheritance, 1982, Co-Starring: Famous Women & Alcohol, 1986; editor numerous books. Mem. Authors Guild of Am., Am. Med. Writer's Assn., Fla. Soc. Addiction Medicine (conf. mgr. 1992-95). Office: 303D Sea Oats Dr Juno Beach FL 33408-1422

ROBECK, LINDA SOPHIE, aerospace engineer; b. Vero Beach, Fla., Jan. 24, 1964; d. Peter Hermann and Gisela (Schiebeling) R. BS, MIT, 1986; MS, Stanford U., 1987. Rsch. asst. Man-Vehicle Lab, MIT, Cambridge, Mass., 1982, 86; systems analyst General Electric, Houston, 1984; cons. engr. Payload Systems, Inc., Wellesley, Mass., 1986; aerospace engr. Jet Propulsion Lab., Pasadena, Calif., 1987—. Contbr. articles to profl. jours. Recipient Group Achievement award NASA, 1984, 91. Mem. AIAA, U.S. Metric Assn., Tau Beta Pi, Sigma Gamma Tau. Office: Jet Propulsion Lab 171-300 4800 Oak Grove Dr Pasadena CA 91109

ROBECK, MILDRED COEN, academic affairs executive; b. Walum, N.D., July 29, 1915; d. Archie Blane and Mary Henrietta (Hoffman) Coen; m. Martin Julius Robeck, Jr., June 2, 1936; children: Martin Jay Robeck, Donna Jayne Robeck Thompson, Bruce Wayne Robeck. BS, U. Wash., 1950, MEd, 1954, PhD, 1958. Ordnance foreman Sherman Williams, U.S. Navy, Bremerton, Wash., 1942-45; demonstration tchr. Seattle Pub. Schs., 1946-57; reading clinic dir. U. Calif., Santa Barbara, 1957-64; vis. prof. Victoria Coll., B.C., Can., summer 1958, Dalhousie U., Halifax, summer 1964; rsch. cons. State Dept. Edn., Sacramento, Calif., 1964-67; prof., head early childhood edn. U. Oreg., Eugene, Oreg., 1967-86; vis. scholar West Australia Inst. Tech., Perth, 1985; v.p. academic affairs U. Santa Barbara, Calif., 1987—; trainer, evaluator U.S. Office of Edn. Head Start, Follow Thru, 1967-72; cons., evaluator Native Am. Edn. Programs, Sioux, Navajo, 1967-81; cons. on gifted Oreg. Task Force on Talented and Gifted, Salem, 1974-76; evaluator Early Childhood Edn., Bi-Ling Petroleum and Minerology, Dhahran, Saudi Arabia, 1985. Author: Materials KELP: Kgn. Evaluation Learning Pot, 1967, Infants and Children, 1978, Psychology of Reading, 1990; contbr. articles to profl. jours. Evaluation cons. Rosenburg Found. Project, Santa Barbara, 1966-67; faculty advisor Pi Lambda Theta, Eugene, Oreg, 1969-74; guest columnist Oreg. Assn. Gifted and Talented, Salem, Oreg., 1979-81; editorial review bd. ERQ, U.S. Calif., L.A., 1981-91. Recipient Nat. Dairy award 4-H Clubs, Wis., 1934, scholarships NYA and U. Wis., Madison, 1934-35, faculty rsch. grants U. Calif., Santa barbara, 1958-64, NDEA Fellowship Retraining U.S. Office Edn., U. Oreg., 1967-70. Mem. APA, Am. Ednl. Rsch. Assn., Internat. Reading Assn., Phi Beta Kappa, Pi Lambda Theta. Democrat. Home: 452 Venado Dr Santa Barbara CA 93111 Office: U Santa Barbara 4050 Calle Real Santa Barbara CA 93110

ROBERGE, JILL QUIGLEY, editorial director; b. Englewood, N.J., Feb. 7, 1955; d. Charles Joseph and Constance (Osberg) Quigley; m. John Philip Roberge, Sept. 25, 1982; 1 child, Kelly Richard. BA, Franklin Pierce Coll., 1977. With Globetech Pub., Wilton, Conn., 1985—. Editl. dir. Med. Imaging Internat., Critical Care Internat., Chirurgia Internat., Lab. Medica Internat., 1989—. Asst. coach little league and basketball, Monroe, Conn., 1988-90. Mem. Am. Med. Writer's Assn. Home: 182 Jockey Hollow Rd Monroe CT 06468-1235 Office: Globetech Pubs 30 Cannon Rd Wilton CT 06897-2625

ROBERGE, M. SHEILA, state legislator; b. Manchester, N.H.; m. A. Roland Roberge; 2 children. Ed. St. Anselm's Coll. Mem. N.H. Senate, 1985—; chmn. Manchester, N.H., Rep. com., 1979-80; del., Rep. Nat. Conv., 1980, 84; Rep. nat. committeewoman from N.H.; vice-chmn., Rep. Nat. Com., 1980-88. Roman Catholic. Office: Rep Nat Com 310 1st St SE Washington DC 20003-1801 also: Senate House State House Concord NH 03301*

ROBERSON, CARLA SHAW, public relations executive; b. Gadsden, Ala., Mar. 13, 1953; d. James Lonnie and Irene (West) Shaw; m. Loyd Whitfield Roberson Jr., May 18, 1985; children: Anna Catherine, Mary Elizabeth, Emily Barton. BS in Home Econs. and Consumer Scis., U. Ala., Tuscaloosa, 1975. Tchr. home econs. Bessemer (Ala.) City Schs., 1975-83; in mktg. Ala. Power Co., Birmingham, 1983-86, in human resources, 1986-93, in community devel., 1993—. Exec. bd. dirs. Ala. Symphony Orch., Birmingham, 1992-93. Recipient Leadership award Nat. Mgmt. Assn., 1994. Mem. Leadership Devel. Assn. (bd. dirs. 1991-94, pres. 1992-93), Women's Com. of Ala. Symphony Assn. (sec., v.p., pres. 1985-94), Nat. Mgmt. Assn. (nat. bd. dirs.), Svc. Guild of Birmingham. Methodist. Home: 123 Lorena Ln Birmingham AL 35213 Office: Ala Power Co 600 N 18th St Birmingham AL 35291

ROBERSON, JANET WHITE, management analyst, consultant; b. Alexandria, Va., June 22, 1950; d. Bruce G. and Dolores M. (White) Styers; m. Joseph O. Roberson III, May 18, 1984; 1 child, Megan Welsh. BA, Dickinson Coll., 1972; MS in Libr. Sci., Cath. U., 1976; MPA, Am. U., 1980. Libr. Montgomery County Pub. Libr., Rockville, Md., 1973-78; personnel mgmt. specialist U.S. Navy, Arlington, Va., 1978-79; mgmt. analyst, labor rels. specialist U.S. Dept. Labor, Washington, 1979-80; presdl. mgmt. intern U.S. Dept. HUD, Washington, 1980-83; sr. mgmt. analyst U.S. Dept. HUD, Navy, Office Mgmt. & Budget, Nat. Oceanic Atmospheric Adminstrn., Washington, 1983-90; dir., adminstrn. ctr. coord. staff U.S. Nat. Oceanic Atmospheric Adminstrn., Washington, 1990-91; dir. office of orgn. and resource mgmt. U.S. Resolution Trust Corp., Washington, 1991—. Methodist. Office: Resolution Trust Corp 801 17th St NW Washington DC 20434

ROBERSON, LINDA, lawyer; b. Omaha, July 15, 1947; d. Harlan Oliver and Elizabeth Aileen (Good) R.; m. Gary M. Young, Aug. 20, 1970; children: Elizabeth, Katherine, Christopher. BA, Oberlin Coll., 1969; MS, U. Wis., 1970, JD, 1974. Bar: Wis. 1974, U.S. Dist. Ct. (we. dist.) Wis. 1974. Legis. atty. Wis. Legis. Reference Bur., Madison, 1974-76, sr. legis. atty., 1976-78; assoc. Rikkers, Koritzinsky & Rikkers, Madison, 1978-79; ptnr. Koritzinsky, Neider, Langer & Roberson, Madison, 1979-85, Stolper, Koritzinsky, Brewster & Neider, Madison, 1985-93, Balisle & Roberson, Madison, 1993—; lectr. U. Wis. Law Sch., Madison, 1978—. Co-author: Real Women, Real Lives, 1981, Wisconsin's Marital Property Reform Act, 1984, Understanding Wisconsin's Marital Property Law, 1985, A Guide to Property Classification Under Wisconsin's Marital Property Act, 1986, Workbook for Wisconsin Estate Planners, 2d edit., 1993. Fellow Am. Acad. Matrimonial Lawyers; mem. ABA, Wis. Bar Assn., Dane County Bar Assn., Legal Assn. Women, Nat. Assn. Elder Law Attys. Office: Balisle and Roberson 217 S Hamilton # 302 PO Box 870 Madison WI 53701-0870

ROBERSON, RUTH MARIE, middle school educator; b. Clifton Forge, Va., Dec. 7, 1944; d. John Burton and Nina Lee (Barger) Tidwell; m. Arthur Clayton Roberson, Aug. 21, 1965 (dec. July 1987); children: Deborah Ann, Patrick John, Matthew Clay. Student, Concord Coll., 1966, Ohio State U., 1975; BEd, No. Ky. U., 1979, MEd, 1986, postgrad., 1991—. Cert. tchr., Ky. 8th grade math. tchr. Twenhofel Mid. Sch., Independence, Ky., 1981—; leader math cluster Kenton County Sch. Dist., 1992-94, KIRIS assessment fellow, 1993, mem. curriculum devel. com., 1992-93, staff devel. leader, 1993; leader Nat. Jr. Honor Soc., Independence, 1987—; mem. curriculum devel. com. Curriculum Frameworks, 1991. Mem. Nat. Coun. Tchrs. Math., Nat. Writing Inst., Nat. Assn. Student Activity Advisors, Phi Delta Kappa. Methodist. Home: 784 Kingston Dr Edgewood KY 41017-9619 Office: Twenhofel Mid Sch 11800 Taylor Mill Rd Independence KY 41055

ROBERT, MARY, opera company executive. MFA, Ariz. State Univ. Resident stage dir. Ariz. State Univ. Music Dept.; artistic dir., gen. mgr. Opera/Omaha, 1980—. Office: Opera Omaha Inc PO Box 807 Omaha NE 68101-0807*

ROBERTI, MARY TERESA, English language educator; b. St. Mary's, Pa., Oct. 21, 1933; d. Alfonso and Antonietta (Irace) R.; m. Milan Anton Bradac, Aug. 29, 1977 (dec. Sept. 25, 1991). BA magna cum laude, Marygrove Coll., Detroit, 1958; cert., U. Rome, 1961; MA, U. Mich., 1964, PhD, 1972. English tchr. Cantrick Jr. High Sch., Monroe, Mich., 1958-70, Monroe High Sch., 1970-88; humanities chair Monroe County Community Coll., 1988-92, English prof., 1992—; Italian tchr. Italian/Am. Soc., Monroe. Mem. St. Mary Acad. Alumnae, Marygrove Coll. Alumnae, U. Mich. Alumni. Republican. Roman Catholic. Home: 5710 W Dunbar Rd Monroe MI 48161 Office: Monroe County Community Col 1555 S Raisinville Rd Monroe MI 48161

ROBERTO, KATHY ANNE JACOBS, software consultant; b. Berlin, N.H., Apr. 24, 1953; d. John and Doris Marie (Jung) Jacobs; m. Thomas Allan Roberto, May 29, 1982 (div. 1994); children: Melissa Jacobs, Jessica Jacobs, Jason Jacobs. BS in Spl. Edn., U. Conn., 1976. Spl. edn. tchr. West Hartford (Conn.) Elem. Schs., 1976-78; programmer, analyst Keane Inc., Boston, 1978-80, sys. analyst, 1986-88; tech. support mgr. McCormack & Dodge, Natick, Mass., 1980-82; sys. analyst Mut. Data Inc., Boston, 1982-84; project mgr. AT&T Am. Transtech., Boston, 1988-91, EOS, Boston, 1991-92; software cons. Bonitech & Adept, Boston, 1992—. Chmn. Bellingham (Mass.) Zoning Bds. and Appeals, 1984-85; co-dir. Pilgrim Choir First Parish, East Derry, N.H., 1990-94; cookie mgr. Troop 862, Girl Scouts USA, Londonderry, N.H., 1990-94. Home: 2 King John Dr Londonderry NH 03053-2813 Office: TSSG/First Data Corp 53 State St Boston MA 02109

ROBERTS, ALIDA JAYNE, elementary school educator; b. Bristol, Conn., Aug. 11, 1967; d. James and Barbara Mae (Carlson) R. BA in Elem. Edn., Anna Maria Coll., Paxton, Mass., 1990; MS in Reading and Lang. Arts, Calif. State U., Fullerton, 1992. Cert. tchr., Conn., Mass., Calif. Elem. tchr. Rowland Unified Sch. Dist., Rowland Heights, Calif., 1990-94, Edgewood Elem. Sch., Bristol, Conn., 1994—; tchr. Gifted and Talented Edn. After Sch. Program, West Covina, Calif., 1993-94, Chpt. 1 After Sch. Program, West Covina, 1993-94; intramural coach Edgewood Elem. Sch., 1994-95. Tchr. advisor PTA, La Puente, 1991-92. Scholar Bristol Fedn. Tchrs., 1986; grantee Anna Maria Coll., 1986-90. Mem. NEA, ASCD, Internat. Reading Assn., Calif. Reading Assn., Calif. Tchrs. Assn., Orange County Reading Assn. Home: 291 Morris Ave Bristol CT 06010

ROBERTS, ANN R., public relations executive; b. Weehawken, N.J.. BA in Bus., Montclair Coll.; MA in Comm., NYU. Pub. rels specialist Nat. Found. of March of Dimes, 1969-72; editor in chief McGraw-Hill, 1972-75; asst. prof. comm. County Coll. Morris, 1976-79; sr. acct. exec. Robert Marston & Assocs., 1979-81; pub. rels. programs mgr. J.C. Penney Co., 1981-88; asst. v.p. corp. affairs Citicorp./Citibank, 1988-92; mgr. consumer and pub. affairs Whitehall-Robins divsn. of Am. Home Products, Madison, N.J., 1993—. Recipient JC Penney Comm. Achievement award, 1987. Mem. Fin. Women's Assn., Pub. Rels. Soc. Am. (Big Apple award). Office: Whitehall-Robins Div Am Home Products 5 Giralda Farms Madison NJ 07940*

ROBERTS, ANNA RUTH, financial consultant; b. Sweetwater, Tex., Apr. 10, 1942; d. Charles Heddington and Ethel Dorothy (Harris) Elliott; m. David Ira Roberts, Apr. 10, 1960; children: Craig Spencer, Edward Aaron. BA in Edn., Ariz. State U., 1976. CFP. Acct. Miller-Wagner & Co. Ltd., Phoenix, 1982-87; asst. v.p., sr. fin. cons. Merrill Lynch, Sun City, Ariz., 1987—; organizer, presenter seminars Pres.'s Club. Recipient Dist. Merit award Boy Scouts Am., Flagstaff, Ariz., 1975. Mem. Am. Bus. Women Assn., B'nai B'rith Women (Edith K. Baum chpt., Woman of Yr. 1976), Kiwanis (sec.-treas. 1987—, Disting. Svc. award 1991). Home: 6090 W Lone Cactus Dr Glendale AZ 85308-6280 Office: Merrill Lynch 9744 W Bell Rd Sun City AZ 85351-1399

ROBERTS, BETTY JO, retired librarian, speech therapist; b. Ft. Worth, Tex., Nov. 11, 1927; d. Harry Pulliam and Mamie Josephine (Parker) Easton; m. Robert Lester Roberts, Jr.; children: Jo Lu, Lee Ann. Student, Tex. State Coll. Women, Denton, 1945-47, Tex. Wesleyan Coll.; postgrad., Tex. Wesleyan Coll.; BS, SW Tex. State U., 1952. Tchr. Milton H. Barry Sch. for Physical Rehab., Houston, United Cerebral Palsy Ctr., Ft. Worth, Tex., San Marcos Pub. Schs., Tex., 1952-53; supr. practice tchrs. SW Tex. State Tchrs. Coll., 1952-53; tchr. Waco (Tex.) Ind. Schs., 1953-54; speech therapist Providence Crippled Children's Hosp., Waco; tchr. phonics, creative art Latin Am. Ctr., Waco, 1961-69; ch. librarian Trinity United Methodist Ch., Waco, 1979-88; ch. lib. Cen. United Methodist Ch., Waco, Tex., 1988-91. Compilor, Editor: Swedishes and More 1984. Mem. YWCA Waco, Tex. 1954, Assn. Childhood Assn. Waco, Tex. 1954, Tex. Mem. Ch. and Synagogue Libr. Assn., Internat. Browning Soc., Browning Library, Baylor U. Waco Tex., Am. Speech and Hearing Assn., Gem & Mineral Soc. Club Waco Tex., Cokebury Libr. Assn., United Meth. Women. Democrat. Methodist. Home: 3248 Village Park Dr Waco TX 76708

ROBERTS, CAROLYN C., hospital administrator; b. Parkersburg, W.Va., Dec. 4, 1938; married. M, Northeastern U., 1981. Various positions, 1962-75; dir. clin. adminstrn. svcs. Sidney Farber Cancer Inst., Boston, 1975-82; pres., CEO Copley Health Sys., Morrisville, Vt., 1982—. Author books; contbr. articles to profl. jours. Recipient cmty. svc. awards. Fellow Am. Acad. Med. Administrs.; mem. Am. Hosp. Assn. (bd. dirs., chmn., del., trustee), Am. Soc. Healthcare Risk Mgmt. (coms.), Vt. Hosp. Assn. (coms., trustee). Home: RR # 2 Box 290 Morrisville VT 05661 Office: Copley Health Sys Box 760 RR # 3 Morrisville VT 05661*

ROBERTS, CAROLYN JUNE, medical school department manager; b. Reading, Mass., June 10, 1938; d. Frank Hiram and Blanche Laura (Robertson) Gifford; m. Roy Dale Roberts, Apr. 4, 1956; children: Kathleen, Charles, Cindy. BS in Microbiology, San Diego State U., 1973, MBA, 1982. Lic. med. tech.; real estate broker, Calif. Microbiologist Kaiser Permanente, San Diego, 1973-74; mgr. anesthesiology U. Calif., San Diego, 1975-81; dir. ambulatory care Merced (Calif.) Community Med. Ctr., 1983-84; mgr. medicine U. Calif., San Francisco, 1984-89; mgr. surgery U. Calif., San Diego, 1989-94; pres. Acad. Bus. Officers San Francisco (Calif.) Gen. Hosp., 1986-87. Mem. Am. Assn. Med. Colls. on Bus. Affairs (program com. 1991-92), Soc. Rsch. Adminstrn. (western sect. pres. elect 1993-94), Sigma Iota Epsilon. Home: 3174 Sandra Valley Way Spring Valley CA 91977

ROBERTS, CASSANDRA FENDLEY, investment company executive; b. Port St. Joe, Fla., Sept. 24, 1951; d. Pope and Sophie Virginia (McGee) Fendley; m. Charles Stanton Roberts, Aug. 7, 1971; 1 child, Davis McGee. BSBA, Edison State Coll., 1983. Sales assoc., v.p. Cooper Corp., Atlanta, 1979-85; sales assoc., broker WTM Investments, Atlanta, 1985-92, v.p., 1992—. Mem. Nat. Bd. Realtors, Ga. Bd. Realtors, Atlanta Bd. Realtors. Office: WTM Investments Inc PO Box 13256 Atlanta GA 30324

ROBERTS, CHERYL DORNITA LYNN, medical administrator; b. Martinsburg, W.Va., July 31, 1958; d. Shelby Louis and Dorothy Juanita (Davenport) R. BS, Shepherd Coll., 1980; MA, U. D.C., 1984. Recreation specialist Edgemeade of Md., Upper Marlboro, 1980-81; basketball coach U. D.C., Washington, 1981-85; recreation therapist Vet. Affairs Med. Ctr., Martinsburg, W.Va., 1985-87; vocat. rehab. specialist Vet. Affairs Med. Ctr., Boston, 1987-88; domiciliary officer Vet. Affairs Med. Ctr., Martinsburg, 1988—. Bd. dirs. FOCUS, Charles Town, W.Va., 1990—; bd. dirs., vol. basketball coach Martinsburg-Berkeley County Boys and Girls Club, 1994—; basketball coach Jefferson County Schs., Shepherdstown, W.Va., 1989—. Named to Outstanding Young Women of Am. Mem. Delta Sigma Theta. Democrat. Methodist.

ROBERTS, CHERYL JEAN, lawyer; b. Wichita, Kans., Jan. 25, 1958; d. Henry H. Jr. and Emogene (Freeman) R. BA, S.E. Okla. State U., 1980; JD, Washburn U., 1985. Bar: Kans. 1985, U.S. Dist. Ct. Kans. 1985. Pub. defender County of Sedgwick, Wichita, 1986-90; atty., prosecutor City of Wichita, 1990-91; pvt. practice Wichita, 1991—. Mem. ABA, Kans. Bar Assn., Wichita Bar Assn. Episcopalian. Office: 301 W Central Wichita KS 67226

ROBERTS, CORINNE BOGGS (COKIE ROBERTS), correspondent, news analyst; b. New Orleans, Dec. 27, 1943; d. Thomas Hale and Corinne Morrison (Claiborne) Boggs; m. Steven V. Roberts, Sept. 10, 1966; children: Lee Harriss, Rebecca Boggs. BA with distinction in Polit. Sci., Wellesley Coll., 1964; hon. degrees, Amherst Coll., Columbia Coll., Loyola U. of the South. Assoc. prodr., host Altman Prodns., Washington, 1964-66; prodr. Altman Prodns., L.A., 1969-72; reporter, editor Cowles Communications, N.Y.C., 1967; prodr. Sta. WNEW-TV, N.Y.C., 1968, Sta. KNBC-TV, L.A., Greece, 1972-74; reporter CBS News, Athens, Greece, 1974-77; corr. Nat. Pub. Radio, Washington, 1977—, MacNeil/Lehrer Newshour, Washington, 1984-88; spl. Washington corr. ABC News, Washington, 1988—; interviewer, commentator This Week With David Brinkley, Washington, 1992—; lectr. in field. Co-host weekly pub. TV program on Congress, The Lawmakers, 1981-84; producer, host pub. affairs program Sta. WRC-TV, Washington; producer Sta. KNBC-TV Serendipity, L.A. (award for excellence in local programming, Emmy nomination for children's programming); contbr. articles to newspapers, mags. Bd. dirs. Dirksen Ctr., Pekin, Ill., 1988—, Everett Dirksen award, 1987; bd. dirs. Fgn. Students Svc. Ctr., Washington, 1990—, Manhattenville Coll., Purchase, N.Y., 1991—, Children's Inn at NIH, Bethesda, Md., 1992—. Recipient Broadcast award Nat. Orgn. Working Women, 1984, Everett McKinley Dirksen disting. reporting of Congress, 1987, Weintal award Georgetown U., 1988, Corp. Pub. Broadcasting award, 1988, Edward R. Murrow award Corp. Pub. Broadcasting, 1990, Broadcast award Nat. Women's Polit. Caucus, 1990, David Brinkley Comm. award, 1992, Mother of Yr. award Nat. Mothers' Day Com., 1992. Mem. Radio-TV Corrs. Assn. (pres. 1981-82, bd. dir. 1980—), U.S. Capitol Hist. Soc. Roman Catholic. Office: ABC News 1717 DeSales St NW Washington DC 20036 also: Nat Pub Radio 2025 M St NW Washington DC 20036*

ROBERTS, DEBORAH LEE, electrical engineer; b. Regensburg, Germany, May 6, 1958; came to U.S., 1960; d. Therodore Irwin and Janet L. (Vert) R. BS, U. Louisville, 1981, M of Engring., 1981. Assoc. engr. South Ctrl. Bell, Louisville, 1980-81; engr. Martin Marietta, Balt., 1981-83; prin. engr. Fairchild Space & Defense Corp., Germantown, Md., 1983-94, Orbital Sci. Corp., Germantown, 1994—. Author: (book) Software Development of Land Based Navigational Systems, 1981. Outstanding Achievement award NASA, Calif., 1992. Mem. Toastmasers Internat. (local club monitor, sponsor, 1992-94, v.p. of edn., 1992-93, pres. 1993-94, area gov., 1993-94, div. gov. 1994—, nat. facilitator 1993—). Nat. Mgmt. Assn. Republican. Home: 1475 A2 W Key Pky Frederick MD 21702 Office: Orbital Sci Corp 20301 Century Blvd Germantown MD 20874

ROBERTS, DONNA JOYCE, chemical company executive; b. Detroit, Jan. 5, 1935; d. Clarence and Marcella (Just) Hawke; m. Raymond Roberts, May 22, 1954 (div.); children: Michael J., Christopher J.; m. Donald R. Petersen, Nov. 1, 1979. JD, U. Detroit, 1964. Bar: Mich. 1965, U.S. Dist. Ct. (ea. dist.) Mich., 1965, U.S. Dist. Ct. (ea. dist.) Wis. 1974, U.S. Supreme Ct. 1980. Atty., investigator Wayne County Friend Ct., Detroit, 1965-67, 69-70; atty. adminstrv. law Dow Chem. Co., Midland, Mich., 1973-76, dir. product stewardship, 1976-79, sr. staff counsel, mgr. environ. law sect., 1979-81, asst. gen. counsel, mgr. bus. law sect., 1981-86, corp. sec., asst. gen. counsel, 1986—; bd. dirs. Dow Chem. Employees' Credit Union, Midland, 1974-92, pres. 1977, 82, 89; local dir. Comerica Inc., 1992—. Mem. corp. adv. com. LWV, Washington, 1986—; mem. bd. edn. Midland Pub. Schs., 1975-79; mem. bd. fellows Saginaw Valley State Univ. (pres. 1991-92), University Center, Mich., 1984—; mem. Midland Art Council; trustee Midland Community Ctr., 1986-92, Saginaw Valley State Univ. bd. control, 1992—; bd. dirs. United Way Midland County, 1979-85, mem. jud. selection com. Congress of the U.S., 1991—. Named to Acad. Women Achievers, N.Y.C. YWCA, 1985. Fellow Mich. Bar Found.; mem. ABA, Mich. Bar Assn., Midland County Bar Assn. (pres. 1985-86, v.p. 1984-85, sec. 1983-84, treas. 1982-83), Nat. Womens' Econ. Alliance. Republican. Roman Catholic. Clubs: Midland Country; Birchwood Farms Estate (Traverse City, Mich.). Office: Dow Chem Co 2030 Dow Ctr Midland MI 48674*

ROBERTS, DORIS, actress; b. St. Louis, Nov. 4, 1930; d. Larry and Ann (Meltzer) R.; m. William Goyen, Nov. 10, 1963 (dec.); m. Michael R. Cannata, June 21, 1950. Student, NYU, 1950-51; studies with, Sanford Meisner, Neighborhood Playhouse, N.Y.C., 1952-53, Lee Strasberg, Actors' Studio, N.Y.C., 1956. Ind. stage, screen and TV actress, 1953—. Profl. stage debut, Ann Arbor, Mich., 1953; appeared in summer stock Chatham, Mass., 1955; Broadway debut in The Time of Your Life, 1955; other Broadway and off-Broadway appearances include The Desk Set, 1955, The American Dream, 1961, The Death of Bessie Smith, 1961, The Office, 1965, The Color of Darkness, 1963, Marathon 33, 1963, Secret Affair of Mildred Wilde, 1972, Last of the Red Hot Lovers, 1969-71, Bad Habits, 1973 (Outer Circle Critics award 1974), Cheaters, 1976, Fairie Tale Theatre, 1985, The Fig Tree, 1987, It's Only a Play, 1992; movie debut Something Wild, 1961, movies include Barefoot in the Park, 1968, No Way to Treat a Lady, 1973, A Lovely Way to Die, 1969, Honeymoon Killers, 1969, A New Leaf, 1970, Such Good Friends, 1971, Little Murders, 1971, Heartbreak Kid, 1972, Hester Street, 1975, The Taking of Pelham, One, Two, Three, 1974, The Rose, 1979, Good Luck, Miss Wyckoff, 1979, Rabbit Test, 1979, Ordinary Hero, 1986, #1 with a Bullet, 1987, For Better or for Worse-Street Law, 1988, National Lampoon's Xmas Vacation, 1989, Used People, 1992, The Night We Never Met, Momma Mia, 1994; TV debut on Studio One, 1958, Mary Hartman, Mary Hartman, 1975, Mary Tyler Moore Hour, 1976, Soap, 1978-79, Angie, 1979-80, Remington Steele, 1984-88, Lily Tomlin Comedy Hour, Barney Miller, Alice, Full House, Perfect Strangers, Sunday Dinner, A Family Man, The Fig Tree (Pub. Broadcasting System), 1987, (TV films) The Story Teller, 1979, Ruby and Oswald, 1978, It Happened One Christmas, 1978, Jennifer: A Woman's Story, 1979, The Diary of Anne Frank, 1982, A Letter to Three Wives, Blind Faith, 1989, The Sunset Gang, 1990, Crossroads, 1993, Dream On, 1993, The Boys, 1993, A Time To Heal, 1994, Murder She Wrote, Step By Step, Burk's Law Walker, Texas Ranger, 1994. Recipient Emmy award Nat. Acad. TV Arts and Scis., 1984, 85, Emmy nominations, 1986, 88, 91. Mem. Screen Actors Guild, AFTRA, Actors Equity Assn., Dirs. Guild Am.

ROBERTS, DORIS EMMA, epidemiologist, consultant; b. Toledo, Dec. 28, 1915; d. Frederic Constable and Emma Selina (Reader) R. Diploma, Peter Bent Brigham Sch. Nursing, Boston, 1938; BS, Geneva Coll., Beaver Falls, Pa., 1944; MPH, U. Minn., 1958; PhD, U. N.C., 1967. RN, Mass. Staff nurse Vis. Nurse Assn., New Haven, 1938-40; sr. nurse Neighborhood House, Millburn, N.J., 1942-45; supr. Tb Baltimore County Dept. Health, Towson, Md., 1945-46; Tb cons. Md. State Dept. Health, Balt., 1946-50; cons., chief nurse Tb program USPHS, Washington, 1950-57; cons. divsn. nursing USPHS, 1958-63; chief nursing practice br. Health Resources Adminstrn., HEW, Bethesda, Md., 1966-75; adj. prof. U. N.C. Sch. Pub. Health, 1975-92; cons. WHO, 1961-82. Contbr. articles to profl. jours. With USPHS, 1945-75. Recipient Disting. Alumna award Geneva Coll., 1971, Disting. Svc. award USPHS, 1971, Outstanding Achievement award U. Minn., 1983. Fellow APHA (v.p. 1978-79, Disting. Svc. award Pub. Health Nursing sect. 1975, Sedgwick Meml. medal 1979), Am. Acad. Nursing (hon. fellow); mem. Inst. Medicine of NAS, Common Cause, LWV, Delta Omega. Democrat. Episcopalian. Home: 6111 Kennedy Dr Bethesda MD 20815-6509

ROBERTS, GERRY REA, elementary school educator, organist; b. Brady, Tex., Nov. 13, 1940; d. Willie Melvin and Mary Catherine (Brown) Howard; m. Leslie Wayne Templeton, July 28, 1961 (div. Feb. 1977); children: Todd Wayne, Gwen Marie; m. Harold James Roberts Jr., Sept. 24, 1977. Student, Sam Houston State U., 1959-60; MusB, U. Houston, 1962, postgrad., 1964-65; grad., North Tex. State U., 1966, Stephen F. Austin U., 1983; postgrad., East Tex. State U., 1984, Memphis State U., 1984-85, Las Vegas U., 1985. Cert. music tchr., 1-12, Tex., elem. tchr., 1-6, Tex., cert. music tchr., elem.-sec. (K-12), elem. edn. (K-8), Okla.; cert. Orff-Schulwerk levels I, II, III. Music tchr. Deer Park (Tex.) Ind. Sch. Dist., 1962-63, Dallas Ind. Sch. Dist., 1963, Richardson (Tex.) Ind. Sch. Dist., 1964-68; kindergarten tchr. Houston Ind. Sch. Dist., 1971, tchr. 1st grade, 1974-78; tchr. music Klein (Tex.) Ind. Sch. Dist., 1978-90; music tchr. grades 1-6 Choctaw (Okla.)-Nicoma Park Sch. Dist., Okla., 1993—. Pianist, mus. dir. 1960 Playhouse, 1979; pianist prodns. Klein Forest High Sch., 1984-86, Klein High Sch., 1987-90; singer Houston Symphony Chorale, 1960-62, Richardson Choral Club, 1963-64, Jeffrey Ross Chorale, 1988-89, Tomball (Tex. Community Ch., 1988-90. Organist St. Paul's Ch., Houston, 1975-77, Lakewood United Methodist Ch., Tex., 1978-80, Windwood Presbyn. Ch., Cypress, Tex., 1981-90; Music dir. 1st United Meth. Ch., Choctaw, 1990-93; handbell dir., organist St. Matthews United Meth. Ch., 1994—. Recipient Tex. Pianist 2nd Pl. award Tex. Music Tchrs. Assn, 1959; Jesse Jones Foundation scholar, 1959, Houston 1st Pl. award-piano Houston Music Tchrs. Assn., 1959; Sam Houston State U. scholar, 1959, U. Houston scholar, 1960. Mem. NEA, Okla. Educators Assn., Music Educators Nat. Conf., Nat. Music Tchrs. Assn., Am. Guild Organists, Am. Guild of English Handbell Ringers, Inc., The Choristers Guild, Tex. Music Educators Assn., Tex. Tchrs. Assn., Klein Educators Assn., Okla. Music Tchrs. Assn., Okla. Kodály Educators, Kodály Educator Am., Am. choral Dirs.' Assn., Okla. Choral Dirs.' Assn., Okla. Orff-Schulwerk Assn., Am. Orff-Schulwerk Assn. (cert. levels I-III), Gulf Coast Orff-Schulwerk Assn., Sigma Alpha Iota (v.p. Houston alumni chpt. 1971-72, Sword of Honor 1972). Republican. Home and Office: RR 1 Box 799 Harrah OK 73045-7401

ROBERTS, JACQUELINE, state legislator, political consultant; m. Curley Roberts; children: Lisa LaVon, Curlee LaFayette, Dwyane Keith. BS in Instl. Dietetics, U. Ark., Pine Bluff, 1967, cert. teaching, 1968, cert. libr. sci., 1970. Sales rep. Brown & Williamson Tobacco Co., 1976-83; shipping and receiving supt. U. Ark., Pine Bluff, 1975-86; office mgr. numerous bus. Pine Bluff, 1983-85; housing complex mgr. Mays Property Mgmt., North Little Rock, 1986-90; polit. cons. Little Rock, 1991—; state rep. Dist. 73 Ark. Legis., Little Rock, 1991—, sec. legis. black caucus, city county and local affairs com., jud. com., legis. coun., house mgmt. com., chair subcom. on hate-motivated crime. Mem. affirmative action com. Ark. Dem. State Party, state exec. com., black caucus; chmn. Jefferson County Ctrl. Dem. Com., mem. pub. rels. subcom.; vol. dep. vote registrar, organizer; vol. Neighborhood Clean-up; bd. dirs. Parents as Tchrs., Cornerstone, Pine Bluff Literacy Coun., Pine Bluff Hippy Bd., St. John Apts./Alexander Town, U.S. Postal Svc., Coalition for Diversity in Edn.; mem. Ark. steering com. Minority Recruitment in Edn; founder Young Enhancement Svcs., Inc.; mem. performing arts com. Pine Bluf Arts Ctr.; active St. John A.M.E. Ch., Assn. for Communities Organized for Reform Now, Pine Bluff Downtown Devel., Ptnrs. for a Better Pine Bluff, Ark. Cancer Coalition/Breast Cervical Control, Top Ladies of Distinction, Pine Bluff Black Caucus. Recipient Recognition award Pine Bluff Frat. Order of Police, 1992, Assn. of Communities Organized for Reform Now (ACORN), 1990, Ark. Polit. Survivor citation, 1991, Capital citation, 1991, St. John A.M.E. Bible Sch., 1991, Order of Distinction Social Club, 1992, Blacks in Govt., 1992, M.L.K. Planning Commn. Ft. Smith, 1994, Pine Bluff Arsenal-Dr. Martin Luther King, 1994, Nat. Assn. Equal Opportunity in Higher Edn., among others. Mem. NAACP, Nat. Conf. State Legislators, Nat. Conf. Black State Legislators (com. on law and justice, com. on youth), Ark. Dem. Black Caucus, Ark. Women's Polit. Caucus (Uppity Woman award 1991), Women in Govt. (state dir. Ark.), Urban League of Ark., Pine Bluff C. of C. (chairmans club), Ctr. for Women in Am. Politics, Elks Daus. Office: Ark House of Reps State Capitol Little Rock AR 72201*

ROBERTS, JAN M., school system administrator, psychologist; b. Dallas, Aug. 6, 1932; d. Samuel Hayden Carnes and Janice (Smith) Buckow; m. Thomas Oliver Blackmon, Apr. 3, 1953 (div. June 1966); children: Terry, Shari, Lorrie; m. William Francis Roberts, June 10, 1967. BA in English/Spanish with honors, U. Houston, 1965, MA in Psychology, 1966. Cert. tchr., Tex.; cert. assoc. sch. psychologist, profl. counselor, ednl. supr. Sec. Farmers Ins., Houston, Acorn Oil Co., Houston; psychologist Max A. Mertz, Houston; psychol. assoc. Harris County Dept. of Edn., Houston, coord. psychol. svcs.; dir. psychol. svcs. Alief (Tex.) Ind. Sch. Dist.; coord. psychol. svcs. Conroe (Tex.) Ind. Sch. Dist. Vol., donor SPCA, Houston, Conroe. Mem. Tex. Psychol. Assn., Tex. State Bd. of Examiners of Psychologists, Hou-Met, T Case. Republican. Home: 11511 Walden Rd Montgomery TX 77356

ROBERTS, JEAN REED, lawyer; b. Washington, Dec. 19, 1939; d. Paul Allen and Esther (Kishter) Reed; m. Thomas Gene Roberts, Nov. 26, 1958; children: Amy, Rebecca, Nathanial. AB in Journalism, U. N.C., 1966; JD, Ariz. State U., 1973. Bar: Ariz. 1974. Sole practice, Scottsdale, Ariz., 1975—; pvt. practice Jean Reed Roberts, P.C., 1994—; legal dir., advisor to gov. Ariz.-Mex. Commn., 1980-89; judge pro tem Superior Ct., Maricopa County, Ariz., 1979-92; chmn. Bd. of Adjustment, Town of Paradise Valley, 1984-91; bd. dirs. YWCA, Maricopa County. Mem. ABA, Charter 100 of Phoenix, Nat. Acad. Elder Law, Scottsdale Bar Assn., Ariz. Bar Assn., Ariz. Women's Town Hall. Democrat. Jewish. Office: 8283 N Hayden Rd Ste 250 Scottsdale AZ 85258

ROBERTS, JEANNE ADDISON, English language educator; b. Washington; d. John West and Sue Fisher (Nichols) Addison; m. Markley Roberts, Feb. 19, 1966; children: Addison Cary Steed Masengill, Ellen Carraway Masengill Coster. A.B., Agnes Scott Coll., 1946; M.A., U. Pa., 1947; Ph.D., U. Va., 1964. Instr. Mary Washington Coll., 1947-48; instr., chmn. English Fairfax Hall Jr. Coll., 1950-51; tchr. Am. U. Assn. Lang. Center, Bangkok, Thailand, 1952-56; instr. Beirut (Lebanon) Coll. for Women, 1956-57, asst. prof., 1957-60, chmn. English dept., 1957-60; instr. lit. Am. U., Washington, 1960-62; asst. prof. Am. U., 1962-65, asso. prof., 1965-68, prof., 1968-93; dean faculties Am. U., 1974; lectr. Howard U., 1971-72; seminar prof. Folger Shakespeare Library Inst. for Renaissance and 18th Century Studies, 1974; dir. NEH Summer Inst. for High Sch. Tchrs. on Teaching Shakespeare, Folger Shakespeare Library, 1984, 85, 86. Author: Shakespeare's English Comedy: The Merry Wives of Windsor in Context, 1979, The Shakespearean Wild: Geography, Genus and Gender, 1991; editor: (with James G. McManaway) A Selective Bibliography of Shakespeare: Editions, Textual Studies, Commentary, 1975; (with Peggy O'Brien) Shakespeare Set Free, vol. 1, 1993, vol. 2, 1994, vol. 3, 1995; contbr. articles to scholarly jours. Danforth Tchr. grantee, 1962-63; Folger Sr. fellow, 1969-70, 88. Mem. MLA (chmn. Shakespeare div. 1981-82), Renaissance Soc. Am., Milton Soc., Shakespeare Assn. Am. (trustee 1978-81, 87-89, pres. 1986-87), AAUP (pres. Am. U. chpt. 1966-67), Southeastern Renaissance Conf. (pres. 1981-82), Phi Beta Kappa, Mortar Board, Phi Kappa Phi. Episcopalian. Home: 4931 Albemarle St NW Washington DC 20016-4359 Office: Am U Dept Lit Washington DC 20016

ROBERTS, JO ANN WOODEN, school system administrator; b. Chgo., June 24, 1948; d. Tilmon and Annie Mae (Wardlaw) Wooden; m. Edward Allen Roberts Sr. (div.); children: Edward Allen Jr., Hillary Ann. BS, Wayne State U., 1970, MS, 1971; PhD, Northwestern U., 1977. Speech, lang. pathologist Chgo. Bd. Edn., 1971-78, adminstr., 1978-88; dir. spl. svcs. Rock Island (Ill.) Pub. Schs., 1988-90; supt. Muskegon Hts. (Mich.) Pub. Schs., 1990-93; deputy supr. Chgo. Pub. Schs., 1993—; instr. Chgo City Community Coll., 1976-77; project dir. Ednl. Testing Svc., Evanston, Ill., 1976-77; exec. dir. Nat. Speech, Lang. and Hearing Assn., Chgo., 1984-86; hon. guest lectr. Govs. State U., University Park, Ill., 1983-86; cons. in field. Author: Learning to Talk, 1974. Trustee Muskegon County Libr. Bd., 1990, Mercy Hosp. Bd., Muskegon, 1990, St. Mark's Sch. Bd. Dirs., Southborough, Mass., 1989, United Way Bd., Muskegon, 1990; mem. Mich. State Bd. Edn. Systematic Initiative in Math and Sci., 1991, Gov. John Engler Mich. 2000 Task Force, 1991, Chpt. II Adv. Commn., 1991. Recipient Leadership award Boy Scouts Am., 1990; named finalist Outstanding Young Working Women, Glamour Mag., 1984, Outstanding Educator, Blacks in Govt., 1990. Mem. Am. Assn. Sch. Adminstrs., Nat. Alliance Black Sch. Educators, Mich. Assn. Sch. Adminstrs., Assn. Supervision & Curriculum Devel., Phi Delta Kappa. Office: Chgo Pub Schs 1819 W Pershing Rd Chicago IL 60001

ROBERTS, JUDITH MARIE, librarian, educator; b. Bluefield, W.Va., Aug. 5, 1939; d. Charles Bowen Lowder and Frances Marie (Bourne)

Lowder Alberts; m. Craig Currence Jackson, July 1, 1957 (div. 1962); 1 child, Craig, Jr.; m. Milton Rinehart Roberts, Aug. 13, 1966 (div. 1987). BS, Concord State Tchrs. Coll., 1965. Libr., Cape Henlopen Sch. Dist., Lewes, Del., 1965-91; with Lily's Gift Shop, St. Petersburg, Fla., 1991—. Pres. Friends of Lewes Pub. Libr., 1986-90; chmn. exhibits Govs. Conf. Librs. and Info. Svcs., Dover, Del., 1978; mem. Gov.'s State Library Adv. Coun., 1987-91. Mem. ALA, NEA, Del. State Edn. Assn., Sussex Help Orgn. for Resources Exchange (pres. 1984-85), Del. Library Assn. (pres. 1982-83), Del. Learning Resources Assn. (pres. 1976-77). Methodist.

ROBERTS, JUDITH VIRGINIA, social worker; b. Phoenix, Mar. 31, 1940; d. George Merle and Edith Virginia (Sevitz) Nycum; m. Kenneth Richard Dragoo, Dec. 28, 1958 (div. 1976); children: Kathryn Virginia Dragoo Lewis, Charles Allen, Kenson Michael; m. Ronald William Roberts, July 12, 1979; stepchildren: Shane Kugler, Noelle Brooke. AA, Mid Plains Community Coll., 1983; BSW, Kearney State Coll., 1986. Cert. social worker, Nebr. Bookkeeping, payroll clk. Dragon Enterprise, North Platte, Nebr., 1972-76, City of North Platte, 1976-83; social worker Nebr. Dept. Social Svcs., North Platte, 1987—. Bassist, Omaha Symphony Orch., 1965-72, Lincoln (Nebr.) Symphony Orch., 1965-72; Lincoln County Republican del., North Platte, 1988. Mem. Nat. Assn. Social Workers, Nebr. Assn. Social Workers, Nebr. Musicians Union, Nebr. Cattlewomen (publicity chair 1980-88). Office: Nebr Dept Social Svcs Craft State Office Bldg 200 S Silber St North Platte NE 69101-4200

ROBERTS, JULIA B., banker; b. Great Falls, Mont., May 25, 1953; d. George Clyde and Florence Ethelyn (Snyder) Baldwin; m. William Geoffrey Roberts, Mar. 31, 1973 (div. 1989); children: W. Jay, Zachary W.; m. Bronson B. Smith, Aug. 14, 1992 (div. Dec. 1993). BA cum laude, U. Mont., 1977. Teller Valley Bank Kalispell, Mont., 1977-78, note window supr., 1978-81, money desk mgr., 1981-84, investment officer, 1984-87, investment and security officer, 1987—. Scorekeeper Pee Wee Baseball, Kalispell, 1989-91; vol. sect. chair United Way Flathead County, Kalispell, 1990-91. Mem. Fin. Women Internat. (v.p. Flathead Valley group 1987-88, pres. 1988-89, state awards and scholarship chmn. 1989-90, group pub. affairs chmn., 1990-91, group pres. 1992-93, state v.p. 1993-94, state pres. 1994—). Office: Valley Bank Kalispell 41 3d St W Kalispell MT 59901

ROBERTS, JULIA FIONA, actress; b. Smyrna, Ga., Oct. 28, 1967; d. Betty and Walter Motes; m. Lyle Lovett, Jun. 27, 1993. Film appearances include Blood Red, 1986, Satisfaction, 1987, Mystic Pizza, 1988, Steel Magnolias, 1989 (Acad. Award nominee, Golden Globe award), Pretty Woman,1990 (Acad. Award nominee, Golden Globe Award), Flatliners, 1990, Sleeping With the Enemy, 1991, Hook, 1991, Dying Young, 1991, The Player, 1992, The Pelican Brief, 1993, I Love Trouble, 1994, Ready to Wear (Prêt-à-Porter), 1994; TV movies include Baja Oklahoma, 1988. Named Female Star of the Yr., Nat. Assn. Theatre Owners, 1991. also: PMK Pub Rels Inc 955 Carrillo Dr Los Angeles CA 90048-5400*

ROBERTS, KAREN BARBARA, art educator; b. Bklyn., May 20, 1953; d. Sol and Adele (Barnett) R.; m. Donald F. Baret, Jr. BA, U. Miami, 1971; MA, Mich. State U., 1972; PhD, SUNY, Binghamton, 1985. Sr. prof. art Broward C.C., Pompano Beach, Fla., 1973—, chmn. dept., 1973-82, dir. Honors Inst. north campus, 1993—; lectr., cons. Fakes and Forgeries Assn., 1985—; lectr. Ft. Lauderdale (Fla.) Mus. Art, 1989—, Hollywood (Fla.) Art and Culture Ctr., 1989-90, Friends of Mus., Ft. Lauderdale, 1978—, community librs., Broward County, Fla., 1975—, Caucus Women Artists, 1975—. One-woman show Broward Coll. Art Gallery, 1995; exhibited in group show Ft. Lauderdale Mus. Art, 1990; presented in permanent collection Ft. Lauderdale Mus. Art. Mem. Broward Theatre Performing Arts, Ft. Lauderdale, 1990—. Recipient Prof. of Yr. Broward C.C., 1991, Endowed chair award, 1992-95. Mem. Coll. Art Assn., Gold Coast Watercolor Soc. (pres. 1994-95), Broward Art Guild, Ft. Lauderdale Mus. Art. Office: Broward Community Coll 1000 Coconut Creek Blvd Pompano Beach FL 33066-1697

ROBERTS, KAREN MARIE, counselor, educator; b. Des Moines, Oct. 20, 1951; d. John Wallace and Pauline Marie (Hansen) Crowell; m. Paul L. Roberts Jr., Aug. 25, 1973; B. Scott, Douglas P., John P. AA, Grand View Coll., Des Moines, 1971; BS in Secondary Edn., Graceland Coll., 1973; MA in Secondary Sch. Counseling, Ctrl. Mo. State U., 1992. Social studies tchr. Independence (Mo.) Sch. Dist., 1974-78, 88-92, substitute tchr., 1983-84, in-sch. suspension supr., 1984-88, h.s. counselor, 1992—; part-time travel agt. Four Seasons Travel, Independence, 1993—. Mem. ACA, Am. Sch. Counselor Assn., Mo. Sch. Counselor Assn., Greater Kansas City Sch. Counselor Assn., Epsilon Sigma Alpha (Delta Iota chpt. past state pres., past chpt. pres.), Child Abuse Prevention Assn. (bd. dirs.). Mem. LDS Ch. Office: William Chrisman HS 1223 N Noland Rd Independence MO 64050

ROBERTS, KATHLEEN ANNE, judge. BA in English summa cum laude, U. Mass., Boston, 1971; PhD program in English Lit., Yale U., 1971-72, JD, 1977. Bar: N.Y., U.S. Dist. Ct. (so. dist.) N.Y., U.S. Ct. Appeals (2nd cir.). Rsch. dir. Conn. Citizen Rsch. Group, 1972-73; investigator, monitor, evaluator grants, cons. Fund for City of N.Y., 1973-77; law clk. U.S. Dist. Ct. (so. dist.) N.Y., 1977-79; asst. U.S. atty. criminal div. So. Dist. N.Y., N.Y.C., 1979-83, asst. U.S. atty. civil div., 1983-85, U.S. magistrate, 1985—; law clk. San Francisco Neighborhood Legal Assistance Found., summer 1975, U.S. Attys. Office, So. Dist. N.Y., criminal div., summer 1976; adj. prof. law, trial advocacy instr. Bklyn. Law Sch., 1983—. Office: US Dist Ct US Courthouse Foley Square New York NY 10007*

ROBERTS, KATHLEEN JOY DOTY, school administrator, educator; b. Jamaica, N.Y., Apr. 19, 1951; d. Alfred Arthur and Helen Caroline (Sohl) Doty; m. Robert Louis Roberts, Nov. 24, 1974; children: Robert Louis, Michael Sean, Kathleen Meagan. BA in Edn., Queens Coll., 1972, MS in Spl. Edn., 1974; cert. of advanced study in ednl. adminstrn. Hofstra U., 1982. Cert. N.Y. State Dept. Mental Hygiene; cert. sch. adminstr., math tchr., N.Y.; lic. spl. edn. supr., ednl. adminstr. Health conservation tchr. Woodside Jr. High Sch., Woodside, N.Y., 1973-77; coord. spl. edn. dept., Ridgewood (N.Y.) Jr. High Sch., 1977-81; adminstrv. asst., health coord., compliance coord., resource tchr. mentor Grover Cleveland High Sch., Ridgewood, N.Y., 1981—. Author: Closed Circuit Television and Other Devices for the Partially Sighted, 1971. Legis. chmn. Fairfield Jr./Sr. PTA and Massapequa Coun., 1987-92. Mem. AAUW, DAR, NEA, N.Y. State Tchrs. Assn., Coun. for Exceptional Children, Soc. Mayflower Descendants, Colonial Daus. of 17th Century (pres. 1985-91, registrar, historian founders' chpt. 1991-94, nat. chmn. hist. activities com. 1988-91, nat. councillor, publicity chmn. 1991-94, centennial com. 1994—, historian gen. nat. soc. 1994—), Pilgrim Edward Doty Soc. Republican. Home: 52 Hicksville Rd Massapequa NY 11758-5843 Office: Grover Cleveland HS 2127 Himrod St Flushing NY 11385-1299

ROBERTS, KIMBERLY SUZETTE, marketing and sales professional; b. Kingsport, Tenn., Sept. 24, 1960; d. James Paul Roberts and Wilma Joyce (Osborne) O. Palmer. BS in Bus. Adminstrn., Tenn. Technol. U., 1984. Acct. exec. Sta. WKPT-TV Holston Valley Broadcasting, Kingsport, 1985; sales rep. Looney Chevrolet-Cadillac-Subaru, Kingsport, 1985; mktg. rep. Office Machines and Supply Co., Bristol, Tenn., 1985-87; sales rep. Sprint Cellular, Kingsport, 1987-94; authorized agt., owner United Cellular, Kingsport, 1994—. Mem. Kingsport Bus. and Profl. Women's Club, C. of C., Nat. Audubon Soc. Democrat. Mem. Baptist/Bible Ch.

ROBERTS, LYNNE JEANINE, physician; b. St. Louis, Apr. 19, 1952; d. H. Clarke and Dorothy June (Cockrum) R.; m. Richard Allen Beadle Jr., July 18, 1981; children: Richard Andrew, Erica Roberts. BA with distinction, Ind. U., 1974, MD, 1978. Diplomate Am. Bd. Dermatology, Am. Bd. Pediatrics, Am. Bd. Laser Surgery. Intern in pediats. Children's Med. Ctr., Dallas, 1978-79, resident in pediats., 1979-80; resident in dermatology U. Tex. Southwestern Med. Ctr., Dallas, 1980-83, chief resident in dermatology, 1982-83, asst. instr. dermatology and pediatrics, 1983-84, asst. prof., 1984-90, assoc. prof., 1990—; physician Cons. Dermatol. Specialists, Dallas, 1990-93; pres. Lynne J. Roberts, MD, PA, Dallas, 1993—; dir. dermatology Children's Med. Ctr., Dallas, 1986—; dermatology sect. chief Med. City Dallas Hosp., 1994-95. Contbr. articles to profl. jours., chpts. to books. Recipient Scholastic Achievement Citation Am. Med. Women's Assn., 1978. Fellow Am. Acad. Dermatology, Am. Acad. Pediatrics, Am. Soc. Laser Medicine and Surgery (bd. dirs. 1994—); mem. Soc. Pediatric Dermatology, Am. Soc. Dermatologic Surgery, Tex. Med. Assn., Dallas Zool. Soc., Dallas Arboretum, Kappa Alpha Theta, Alpha Omega Alpha. Office: 7777 Forest Ln Ste C737 Dallas TX 75230

ROBERTS, MARGARET HAROLD, editor, publisher; b. Aug. 18, 1928. A.B., U. Chattanooga, 1950. Editor, pub. series Award Winning Art, 1960-70, New Woman mag., Palm Beach, Fla., 1971-84; editor, pub. Going Bonkers mag., 1992—. Author: juvenile book series Daddy is a Doctor, 1965. Office: PO Box 189 Palm Beach FL 33480-0189

ROBERTS, MARGOT MARKELS, business executive; b. Springfield, Mass., Jan. 20, 1945; d. Reuben and Marion (Markels) R.; children: Lauren B. Phillips, Debrah C. Herman. B.A., Boston U. Interior designer Louis Legum Furniture Co., Norfolk, Va., 1965-70; buyer, mgr. Danker Furniture, Rockville, Md., 1970-72; buyer W & J Sloane, Washington, 1972-74; pres. Bus. & Fin. Cons., Palm Beach, Fla., 1976-80, Margot M. Roberts & Assocs., Inc., Palm Beach, 1976—; dealer 20th century Am. art and wholesale antiques Margot M. Roberts, Inc., Palm Beach, 1989—; v.p., dir. So. Textile Svcs. Inc., Palm Beach. Pres. Brittany Condominium Assn., Palm Beach, 1983-87; v.p. South Palm Beach Civic Assn., 1983-88, South Palm Beach Pres.'s Assn., 1984-88; vice chmn. South Palm Beach Planning Bd., 1983-88, 90-91; elected town commr. Town South Palm Beach, Fla., 1991-92, elected vice mayor, 1992-93, mayor, 1993—; apptd. Commn. on Status of Women of Palm Beach County, 1992—; voting mem. Palm Beach County Mcpl. League, 1992—; vice chair Commn. Status of Women of Palm Beach County, 1994—. Mem. Nat. Assn. Women in Bus., Palm Beach C. of C. Republican. Office: Town Hall South Palm Beach 3577 S Ocean Blvd Palm Beach FL 33480-5706

ROBERTS, MARIANNE, realtor; b. Columbus, Ohio, May 27, 1930; d. George W. and Alice L. (Scott) Hunt; m. L.R. Foreman, Sept. 19, 1948 (dec. Aug. 1957); children—Georgia Foreman Masselli, L. Scott, Jeffrey W. (dec.), Alyce Foreman Heminger; m. Knute Roberts, Apr. 5, 1962; children—Ruthie Roberts McCloud, L. Charlie L. Student Ohio State U., 1980-82; grad. Impact Drug and Alcohol Abuse Tng. Lic. real estate saleswoman, Ohio; Grad. Realtors Inst., Ohio; critique commn. tchr. cert., Ohio. Saleswoman, sec. Hunt Milling Co., Richwood, Ohio, 1947-64; reporter, feature writer Marion Star, Ohio and Marysville Jour., Ohio, 1974-80; saleswoman, appraiser Nelson Blue Agy., Richwood, 1972—. Soloist Ohio OES White Shrine and First Bapt. Ch., supr. Sunday Sch., 1971-74, chmn. fin. com., 1982-85, dir. jr. choir, 1975-80, fin. sec., 1988—; pres. North Union Local Sch. Bd., Richwood, 1984-85, 1988-89, legis. liaison, 1980—; elected All Region Ohio Bd., 1991, Tri Rivers JVS Bd., 1993—; treas. First Baptist Ch., Richwood, 1979—; coordinator Fed./State Relations Network, Washington, 1983—; dir. Richwood Showboat Serenaders, 1980-82; sec. Union County Bd. Mental Retardation, 1971-79; emeritus bd. dirs. Lewis Sch. for Retarded, Marysville, 1983; impact drug and alchohol conselor Hospice, 1991—. Recipient numerous civic awards, Ohio Sch. Bd. award, 1992. Mem. Ohio Sch. Bds. Assn. (exec. com. 1983-84, pres. cen. region 1986, com. ploicy and legis. 1985, 86-88), Internat. Platform Assn., Speakers Unltd. Republican. Clubs: Carpe Diem (sec. and v.p. 1982-84, pres. 1988), Mother's Study (Richwood) (pres. 1952-54), Matrons (pres. 1986, Worthy Matron Mt. Carmel chpt. 1962-82); Christian Women (chmn. 1987—), Union County Rep. Women's Club. Lodge: Order Ea. Star. Avocations: music, reading, embroidery, writing. Home: 28 George St Richwood OH 43344-1274 Office: Blue Agy E Blagrove St Richwood OH 43344

ROBERTS, MARIE DYER, computer systems specialist; b. Statesboro, Ga., Feb. 19, 1943; d. Byron and Martha (Evans) Dyer; BS, U. Ga., 1966; student Am. U., 1972; cert. systems profl., cert. in data processing; m. Hugh V. Roberts, Jr., Oct. 6, 1973. Mathematician, computer specialist U.S. Naval Oceanographic Office, Washington, 1966-73; systems analyst, programmer Sperry Microwave Electronics, Clearwater, Fla., 1973-75; data processing mgr., asst. bus. mgr. Trenam, Simmons, Kemker et al, Tampa, Fla., 1975-77; mathematician, computer specialist U.S. Army C.E., Savannah, Ga., 1977-81, 83-85, Frankfurt, W. Ger., 1981-83; ops. rsch. analyst U.S. Army Contrn. Rsch. Lab., Champaign, Ill., 1985-87; data base adminstr., computer systems programmer, chief info. integration and implementation div. U.S. Army Corps of Engrs., South Pacific div., San Francisco, 1987-93; computer specialist, IDEF repository coord., Functional Process Improvement Expertise , Defense Info. Systems Agy., Arlington, Va., 1993—. instr. computer scis. City Coll. of Chgo. in Franfurt, 1982-83. Recipient Sustained Superior Performance award Dept. Army, 1983. Mem. Am. Soc. Hist. Preservation, Data Processing Mgmt. Assn., Assn. of Inst. for Cert. Computer Profls., Assn. Women in Computing, Assn. Women in Sci., NAFE, Am. Film Inst., U. Ga. Alumni Assn., Sigma Kappa, Soc. Am. Mil. Engrs. Author: Harris Computer Users Manual, 1983.

ROBERTS, MARILYN BUSTEED, university administrator, financial advisor; b. Lewellen, Nebr., July 23, 1937; d. Andrew Guy and Merlie Elise (Mardis) R.; m. Richard Busteed, Aug. 15, 1956 (div. 1983); children: Patrick, Mitchell, Scott. B, Colo. State U., 1975, M, 1985. Adminstr. computer ctr. Colo. State U., Ft. Collins; CFO Nat. Technol. U., Ft. Collins. Author: Phases of the Moon, 1973. Home: 231 Jefferson Fort Collins CO 80526 Office: Nat Technol U 700 Centre Fort Collins CO 80526

ROBERTS, MARJORIE HELEN, editor; b. Port Chester, N.Y., Feb. 23, 1938; d. George and Blanche (Mulwitz) Goldowitz; m. Arthur W. Roberts, Aug. 23, 1959 (div. Aug. 1967); children: Scott Eric, Allison. BA in Journalism, U. Mich., 1959. Lic. real estate broker, N.Y. Reporter and editor Gannett Westchester Newspapers, Port Chester, N.Y., 1955-60; fin. adminstr. Investors Diversified Svcs., White Plains, N.Y., 1969-73; real estate adminstr. Schulman Realty Group, White Plains, 1973-78; exec. v.p. R.S. Silver & Co., Greenwich, Conn., 1978-89; freelance writer, editor. med. columnist Women's News, Westchester, N.Y., 1981-93; dir. mktg. pub. rels. Matthew J. Warshauer Architects, PC, Hawthorne, NY, 1989-90; editor Women's News, Westchester, N.Y., 1990-92; asst. dir. pub. rels. New York Med. Coll., Valhalla, N.Y., 1992—. Contbr. articles to mags. and newspapers. Mem. Harrison Archtl. Rev. Bd., N.Y., 1979-87, Harrison Com. Cable TV, 1977-79; bd. dirs. Home for Mentally Retarded, Harrison, 1982-87, Westchester Symphony, 1983-86. Home: 101 River W Greenwich CT 06831-4100

ROBERTS, MARY LOU, school psychologist; b. Green Bay, Wis., Sept. 28, 1950; d. Elmer David and Leona Theodora (Puyleart) DeGrand. BA in Elem. Edn. and English, U. Wis., Oshkosh, 1972, student, 1977; MS in Counseling Psychology, U. Cen. Tex., 1989; student, U. Hawaii, 1988. Lic. sch. counselor, Tex.; lic. profl. counselor, Tex.; lic. marriage and family therapist, Tex.; cert. tchr., Tex., Wis., Hawaii. Kindergarten tchr. Howard-Suamico ISD, Green Bay, 1972-78; elem. tchr. St. Anthony's Sch., Kalihi, Hawaii, 1978-80, Ave. E. Copperas Cove (Tex.) ISD, 1983-85; elem. tchr. Killeen (Tex.) ISD, 1985-89, sch. psychologist, 1989—; parent teaching cons. Chpt. I Killeen ISD, 1989—, tchr. inservice training, 1989—, child psychologist, 1989—, cons. family and community counselor, 1989—, community speaker, 1988—. Author: (handbook) Counseling Sessions for Small Groups, 1990; editor, reviewer: Let's Learn More About Responsibility, 1991. Vol. Families In Crisi Inc., Killeen, 1987-89; presenter Family Fair Killeen Ind. Sch. dist., 1989; mentor for two at-risk children in Killeen; sch. bd. mem. St. Joseph Sch., Killeen. Mem. AACD, Am. Bus. Women of Am. (scholarship 1985, ways and means com. chmn. Globe chpt. 1986), Tex. Fedn. Tchrs. U. Cen. Tex. Alumni Assn., Tex. Assn. Counseling Devel., Tex. Sch. Counselor Assn., Mid-Tex. Assn. for Counseling Devel. (sec. 1990—). Democrat. Roman Catholic. Office: Killeen Ind Sch Dist 200 WS Young Dr Killeen TX 76541

ROBERTS, MARY MARGARET, retired speech communication educator; b. Independence, Iowa, Mar. 30, 1923; d. Thomas Robert and Bertha Belle (Beal) R.. BA, Luther Coll., Decorah, Iowa, 1944, LittD (hon.), 1984; MA, Northwestern U., 1949; PhD, La. State U., 1959. Tchr. speech and debate Red Wing (Minn.) H.S., 1944-46, Jefferson High Sch., Council Bluffs, Iowa, 1946-49; vis. asst. prof. Luther Coll., 1949-50; tchr. grad. asst. in speech La. State U., Baton Rouge, 1956-57; instr., asst. prof. speech U. Pitts., 1957-61; instr. speech and debate Pittsburg (Kans.) State U., 1950-54, assoc. prof., then prof. speech comm., 1961-90, dir. comm. grad. studies, 1961-90, prof. emerita, 1990—; vis. instr. speech Appalachian State U., Boone, N.C., summer 1955; adj. prof. Mo. Southern Coll., 1994—. Contbg. author: Pamphlets and the American Revolution, 1977, Women Public Speakers in the U.S.: 1800-1925, 1993; mem. editl. bd. Mentoring Internat., 1987-91, Jour. Comm. and Religion, 1992-94, Women Communicating: Studies of Women's Talk, 1988; editor Commn. Edn., 1973-75; contbr. articles to profl. jours. Vol. tutor Beaver Lake Literacy Coun., Bentonville, Ark., 1993—. Recipient award for outstanding contbns. to speech comm. Zeta Phi Eta, 1979, Alumni Disting. Svc. award Luther Coll., 1966; rsch. and mentoring grantee U.S Office Edn. Title III, 1986-89. Mem. Speech Comm. Assn. (legis. coun. 1973-75, 78-80, convener nominating com. 1981, award for outstanding contbns. to speech comm. edn. 1979), Ctrl. States Comm. Assn. (pres. 1983-84), Kans. Speech Comm. Assn. (pres. 1969-70), AAUW (bd. dirs. Kans. 1967-69, 75-76), NOW, Phi Beta Kappa, Delta Kappa Gamma (past chpt. pres.).

ROBERTS, MARY WENDY, state official; b. Champaign, Ill., Dec. 19, 1944; d. Frank and Mary Roberts; m. Richard P. Bullock, Nov. 27, 1976 (div. 1984); 1 child, Alexandra Louise McKay Prentice Bullock. Student Chinese-Japanese Inst., U. Colo., 1964; B.A. in Polit. Sci., U. Oreg., 1965; M.A. in Polit. Sci., U. Wis.-Madison, 1971. Social worker Children's Services Div., Portland, Oreg., 1967-71; counselor Juvenile Ct., Portland, 1971; mem. Oreg. Ho. of Reps., Salem, 1973-75; mem. Oreg. State Senate, Salem, 1975-79; commr. Oreg. Bur. Labor and Industries, Portland, 1979-94; mem. Oreg. adv. com. U.S. Civil Rights Commn.; chmn. Oreg. Apprenticeship and Tng. Council; mem. State Workforce Quality Council; exec. sec. Oreg. Wage and Hour Commn. Oreg. del. democratic Nat. Conv., 1980, 84, co-chmn. Oreg. del., 1984. Mem. Oreg. Women's Polit. Caucus (Mary Riekeway award 1978), Am. Council Young Polit. Leaders, Oreg. Hist. Soc., Portland Art Assn., Nat. Assn. Govt. Labor Ofcls. (nat. bd. dirs.), Women Execs. in State Govt. (founder). Office: Bur Labor and Industries 800 NE Oregon Ste 1045 Portland OR 97232

ROBERTS, MAVIS KIST, steel company executive; b. Latrobe, Pa., Aug. 10, 1929; d. Raymond Eugene and Annabelle (Miller) Kist; children: Cyndi, Linda, George, Sonya, Robert. BA, Pa. State U., 1967; postgrad., Boise State U., 1977-82. Lab. asst. Pa. State U., 1945-49; elem. tchr. Pa. schs., 1968-69; iron worker, estimator, mgr., co-owner R&M Steel, Boise, Idaho, 1970-85; mgr., CEO Outland Steel, Boise, 1985—. Mem. Am. Welding Soc., Am. Women in Constrn., Assoc. Gen. Contractors, Intermountain Contractors. Office: Outland Steel Co 19047 Franklin Rd Nampa ID 83687

ROBERTS, NANCY, computer educator; b. Boston, Jan. 25, 1938; d. Harold and Annette (Zion) Rosenthal; m. Edward B. Roberts, June 14, 1959; children: Valerie Friedman, Mitchell, Andrea. AB, Boston U., 1959, MEd, 1961, EdD, 1975. Elem. tchr. Sharon (Mass.) Pub. Schs., 1959-63; asst. prof. Lesley Coll., Cambridge, Mass., 1975-79, assoc. prof., 1980-83; prof., 1983—; dir. grad. programs in computers in edn. Lesley Coll., Cambridge, Mass., 1980—, dir. Project Bridge,, 1987-92; dir. Ctr. for Math., Sci. and Tech. in Edn., Cambridge, Mass., 1990-91; rsch. assoc. MIT, Cambridge, 1976-79; mem. nat. steering com. Nat. Edn. Computing Conf., Eugene, Oreg., 1979—, co-chmn. nat. conf., 1989, vice chmn. steering com., 1991—. Author: Dynamics of Human Service Delivery, 1976, Practical Guide to Computers in Education, 1982, Computers in Teaching Mathematics, 1983, Introduction to Computer Simulation, 1983 (J.W. Forrester award 1983), Integrating Computers into the Elementary and Middle School, 1987, Computers and the Social Studies, 1988, Integrating Telecommunications into Education, 1990; mem. editorial bd. Jour. Ednl. Computing, 1983—, Jour. Rsch. in Sci. Teaching; editor Computers in Edn. book series, 1984-89. Mem. Computer Policy Com., Boston, 1982-84, mem. adv. bd. Electronic Learning, 1989-91; bd. dirs. Computers for kids, Cambridge, 1983-85; mem. State Ednl. Tech. Adv. Coun., 1990—. NSF grantee, 1985—. Mem. System Dynamics Soc. (bd. dirs. policy com. 1987-89). Republican. Jewish. Home: 300 Boylston St # 1102 Boston MA 02116-3923 Office: Lesley Coll 29 Everett St Cambridge MA 02138-2790

ROBERTS, NICOLA TERESA, school district administrator; b. Fort Walton Beach, Fla., Nov. 6, 1958; d. William Byrd and Nicola Teresa (Chine) Harbeson; m. John Michael Roberts, Dec. 17, 1982; children: Megan Teresa, Shannon Elizabeth. BA in Acctg., U. West Fla., 1979; MS in Pub. Adminstrn., Troy State U., 1982. Acct. fin. Sch. Dist. of Okaloosa County, Fort Walton Beach, 1980-85, specialist fin., 1985-87, program dir. fin., 1987-93, dir. fin. and bus., 1993—; appointed mem. Fla. Sch. Fin. Coun., Commr. of Edn. State of Fla. Adv. Bd., 1992—. Mem. AAUW (treas. 1990-92), Okalosa county Adminstrs. and Suprs. Assn., Fla. Ednl. Negotiators, Fla. Sch. Fin. Officer's Assn. (bd. dirs. 1992-94). Democrat. Roman Catholic.

ROBERTS, PRISCILLA WARREN, artist; b. Montclair, N.J., June 13, 1916; d. Charles Asaph and Florence (Berry) R. Student, Art Students League, 1937-39, Nat. Acad., 1939-43. Represented in permanent collections Met. Mus., Cin. Art Mus., Canton Art Inst., Westmoreland County Mus. Art, Pa., IBM, Dallaas Mus., Walker Art Ctr., Mpls., Butler Inst., Youngstown, Ohio, Nat. Mus. Am. Art, Washington. Recipient Proctor prize, 1947, popular prize Corcoran Biennial, 1947, prize Westmoreland County Mus., 3d prize Carnegie Internat., Pitts., 1950, Nat. Mus. Women in Arts, Washington, Snite Mus., U. Notre Dame, Ind. Mem. NAD (Hallgarten prize 1945), Allied Artists Am. (Zabriskie prize 1944, 46), Catherine Lorillard Wolfe Assn. (hon.). Address: PO Box 716 Georgetown CT 06829

ROBERTS, RITA FRANCES, librarian, educator; b. Manchester, N.H., Mar. 27, 1929; d. Gustave N. and Alice Marie-Louise (Hamel) Poirier; m. Horace L. Roberts, Nov. 20, 1982; children: Sylvia, Melody, Mark. B in Edn., Cath. Tchrs. Coll., 1961; MLS, St. John's U., 1969. Tchr. various Cath. schs., Fall River, Mass., 1954-57, Woonsocket, R.I., 1957-61; tchr.-libr. Villa Augustina Acad., Goffstown, N.H., 1961-70, St. Clare High Sch., Woonsocket, 1970-73; libr. Franklin (N.H.) High Sch., 1973-83; libr., cataloger St. Paul's Sch., Concord, N.H., 1983-85; part-time libr. mgr. Magdalen Coll., Warner, N.H., 1985—, Grantham (N.H.) Village Sch., 1985-89; part-time prof. libr. ref. Sch. Life Long Learning, U. N.H., summer 1991; owner, mgr. Pine Cone Media, Warner, 1985—. Roman Catholic.

ROBERTS, ROSALEE ANN, public relations executive; b. Omaha, Dec. 17, 1943; d. Leo Joseph and Madeline (Elder) Ohlinger; m. Robert Wesley Roberts, Oct. 21, 1967; 1 child, Catherine Ann Martin. BA cum laude, Duchesne Coll. of Sacred Heart, 1965. Writer, producer Nat. Agys. Corp., Omaha, 1965-66; account exec. J. Lipsey & Assocs., Omaha, 1968; freelance writer and producer Omaha, 1969, 74; promotion mgr. pub. affairs Sta. KETV, Omaha, 1969-73; copywriter, producer Bozell & Jacobs, Omaha, 1966-67; dir. pub. rels. Bozell, Jacobs, Kenyon & Eckhardt, Omaha, 1974-88; v.p. pub. rels. Bozell, Inc., Omaha, 1988-94; ptnr. Bozell Worldwide, 1994—. past bd. dir. Omaha Community Playhouse, Arthritis Found., Nebr.; bd. dirs. ARC, Heartland, Nebr., Omaha Food Bank, Omaha Literacy Coun. and Child Saving Inst., 1993—; past bd. dirs. YWCA, Western Heritage Mus.; bd. dirs. Arthritis Found.; nat. communications adv. coun. ARC. Mem. Pub. Rels. Soc. Am. (bd. dirs.-at-large 1988-89, nat. sec. 1990, pres.-elect 1991, nat. pres. 1992, Midwest dist. chair 1987, pres. Nebr. chpt. 1981, Profl. of Yr. award 1988, 5 Nat. Presdl. Citations 1985-90). Republican. Roman Catholic. Office: Bozell Inc 302 S 36th St Ste 800 Omaha NE 68131-2453

ROBERTS, RUBY ALTIZER, poet, author, fiction; b. Floyd Co., Vt., Apr. 22, 1907; d. Waddy William and Dana Adeline (Cummings) Altizer; m. Laurence Luther Roberts, July 23, 1927; 1 child, Heidi. Grad., Christianburg (Va.) High Sch.; nursing course, Norfolk (Va.) Protestant Hosp.; DHL, Coll. William and Mary, 1961. Freelance writer, 1939—, newspaper corr.; rep. of Spirit of Va., 1993. Author (with Rosa Altizer Bray) Emera Altizer and His Descendants, 1937, 2 vols. poetry, Forever is Too Long, command the Stars, (biography) The Way It Was, 1979, The Way It Is, 1992; editor juvenile verse dept. Embers Mag., Batavia, N.Y., 1944—; owner, editor, pub. The Lyric Mag.; poetry columnist Va. newspaper; contbr. over 120 poems to anthologies, newspapers, mags, numerous articles to jours. Recipient First Poetry prize Sanctuary Mag., Ballaman award Disting. Svc. to Poetry, 1956, citation Disting. Svc. Poetry Khalsa Coll.; named poet laureate Va. Gen. Assembly, 1950, poet laureate Va. emeritus Gen. Assembly Va., 1992. Home: 301 Roanoke St Christiansburg VA 24073

ROBERTS, SANDRA, editor; b. Humboldt, Tenn., July 22, 1951; d. Harold and Margaret (Headrick) R.; m. Parker W. Duncan Jr., Aug. 11, 1990. Student, Tex. Christian U., 1969-70; BS, U. Tenn., 1972; MLS, Peabody Coll. Libr. The Tennessean, Nashville, 1975-82, editorial writer, 1982-87, editorial editor, 1987—. Pres. Women's Polit. Caucus, Nashville, 1982. Recipient John Hancock award John Hancock Co., 1983, Freedom award Tenn. Trial Laywers Assn., 1988. Mem. Am. Soc. Newspaper Editors, Nat. Conf. Editorial Writers, Sigma Delta Chi (Nat. Headliner award 1982). Mem. Christian Ch. Office: The Tennessean 1100 Broadway Nashville TN 37203-3116

ROBERTS, SANDRA BROWN, realty company executive; b. Boston, May 26, 1939; d. Frederick Thomas and Christine (Peyton) Brown; m. Joseph Peter Roberts, Aug. 26, 1962 (div. May 1984); children: Christine, Joseph, Paul. B.A., Boston Coll., 1981. Lic. real estate broker, Mass. Owner, mgr. real estate, Wellesley, Mass., 1963—; pres. Riverview Realty, Wellesley, 1970—; comml. realtor, Boston, 1974—; cons. Berkshire Hathaway, New Bedford, Mass., 1983—; asst. to pres. BHR, Inc., New Bedford, 1988—. Founder, pres., bd. dirs. Friends of Ft. Washington, Inc.; active Friends of Boston Ballet, 1983—. Mem. DAR (Boston Tea Party chpt. regent 1983-84, 84-85). Navy League of U.S., New Eng. Hist. Geneal. Soc. Republican. Roman Catholic. Club: College (Boston). Lodge: Order of Crown of Charlemagne (life mem.), Order of Lafayette (bd. dirs.). Home: 52 Kenilworth Rd Wellesley MA 02181-7428 Office: Friends Ft Washington Inc 1 Post Office Sq Ste 310 Boston MA 02109-2103

ROBERTS, SHARON S., secondary school educator; b. Louisville, Oct. 30, 1944; d. William E. and Hazel Marie (Funk) R. BA, Nazareth Coll., 1968; MA, Spalding U., 1973; postgrad., Ea. Ky. U., 1989. Tchr. Presentation Acad., Louisville, 1968-70, Holy Rosary Acad., Louisville, 1970-85; chemistry tchr. St. Xavier High Sch., Louisville, 1985—. Educator rep. Radon Action Coalition, Ky., 1992—. Recipient Chemistry Tchr. award Rohm and Haas Ky., 1992. Mem. Nat. Sci. Tchrs. Assn., Ky. Sci. Tchrs. Assn., Louisville Area Chemistry Alliance (Cath. sch. liaison 1992—). Democrat. Roman Catholic. Home: 3008 Tremont Dr Louisville KY 40205-2946 Office: St Xavier High Sch 1609 Poplar Level Rd Louisville KY 40217-1359

ROBERTS, SUZANNE, artist; b. N.Y.C., July 28, 1955; d. James Rose and Laura (Forman) Lauer; m. William Scott Roberts, May 30, 1982; children: Alexandra, Zara. BA in Psychology, U. Miami, 1977. Cover photograph Archtl. Digest, 1994. Mem. Stencil Artisan League. Home: 43 Cedar Rd Wilton CT 06897

ROBERTS, THOMASENE BLOUNT, entrepreneur; b. Americus, Ga., Sept. 5, 1943; d. Thomas Watson and Mary Elizabeth (Smith) Blount; m. Henry Lee Roberts, Apr. 24, 1970 (div. 1991); 1 child, Asha Maia. Student, Fisk U., 1960-63; BA, Morris Brown Coll., 1965; MA, Atlanta U., 1970, postgrad., 1979-82; postgrad., Clark Atlanta U. Social worker Gate City Day Nursery Assn., Atlanta, 1965-66; ticket agt. Delta Air Lines, Inc., Atlanta, 1966-68; clk. accounts payable Kraft Foods, Inc., Decatur, Ga., 1967-68; cons. family svcs. Atlanta Housing Authority, 1970-72, supr. family svcs., 1972-73, mgr. family relocation, 1974-79; grad. rsch. asst. Sch. Edn. Atlanta U., 1979-82; city coun. asst. City of Atlanta, 1984-88, rsch. asst. Dept. Pub. Safety, 1987-88; dir. govtl. rels. Morris Brown Coll., Atlanta, 1988-93; owner TBR Ent., Atlanta, 1993—; researcher/intern Project Focus Teen Mother Program, Atlanta, 1981-82; moderator Nat. Black Women's Health Project, Atlanta, 1985; workshop leader Assn. Human Resources Mgrs., Atlanta, 1989; pres.'s rep. U. Ctr. Devel. Corp., Inc., 1989-93; cons. entrepreneur devel. workshop Morris Brown Coll. Chairperson Ida Prather YWCA Cmty. Bd., Atlanta, 1985-90; bd. dirs. YWCA Met. Atlanta, 1986-90, Met. Atlanta Coalition 100 Black Women, 1988-90, 94—, Hammonds House Mus., 1995—; active fund dr. com. Jomandi Prodn., 1988-89; v.p. maj. gifts com. Camp Best Friends, City of Atlanta, 1989; mem. Multi-Cultural Leadership Group, Gov.'s Coun. on Developmental Disabilities. Mem. Atlanta-Trinidad/Tobago Exch. (sec., treas. 1983-89, Pt. of Spain cert. 1986), Nat. Polit. Congress Black Women (corr. sec. 1989-90), Nat. Assn. for Equal Opportunity Higher Edn. (coll. liaison 1988-93), Coun. for Advancement-Support of Edn., Info. Forum, Atlanta Urban League, Inc., Nat. Assn. for Equal Opportunity in Higher Edn. (Disting. Alumni award 1991), Nat. Soc. Fund-Raising Execs. (cert. 1992), Friends of Morehouse Sch. Medicine, Delta Sigma Theta (pub. rels. asst. 1986-89). Home: 1817 King Charles Rd SW Atlanta GA 30331-4909 Office: TBR Enterprises Ste A-3165 2740 Greenbriar Pky SW Atlanta GA 30331

ROBERTS, VICTORIA LYNN PARMER, antique expert; b. N.Y.C., Sept. 15, 1953; d. Edgar Alan Parmer and Nina Joyce (Ash) Gross; m. George E. Roberts, Dec. 1, 1978 (div. 1985); 1 child, Joshua Henry. Student, Yale U. Pres. High Gear Creative Svcs., Savannah, Ga., 1979-81; v.p. Rossignol Modeling Agy., N.Y.C., 1981-82; mgr., dir. Parc Monceau Antiques, Westport, Conn., 1982-85; pres., owner Victoria & Cie, Norwalk, Conn., 1985—; antiques tchr. Sacred Heart U., Fairfield, Conn., 1988, 89, Norwalk Community Coll., 1989; antique lectr. various hist. socs., Conn., 1989-90; speaker in antiques field; antique expert seminars to interior designers, Norwalk, 1989; creator, sole contbr. spls. on antiques CNBC TV, 1989, 90. Antiques editor Brooks Community Newspaper, Westport, 1989-91; contbr. Antiques Mag., 1991—. Mem. Entrepreneurial Woman's NEtwork, Appraisers Assn. Am. (sr.), Coll. Arts Assn., Alpha Sigma Lambda. Office: Victoria & Cie 3 Nelson Ave Norwalk CT 06851-3910

ROBERTS, WANDA COMER, secondary education educator; b. Montgomery, W.Va., Oct. 5, 1928; d. Clyde Lundy and Anna Laura (Myers) Gray; m. James Gemala Comer, Dec. 27, 1947 (dec. July 14, 1972); children: Sharon Ann, James Robert; m. George Herman Roberts, July 31, 1972 (div. Jan. 19, 1983). AB in Speech and Art, W.Va. U., 1956; Cert. Secondary Edn./Speech/Art/English, Morris Harvey Coll., 1959; MA in Edn., W.Va. U., 1968. Pub. sch. tchr. Van High Sch./Boone County Bd. Edn., Madison, W.Va., 1957-59, McKinley Jr. High Sch., Nitro High Sch., 1960-70; tchr. St. Albans Jr. High Sch., 1971-72; tchr. East Bank High Sch. Kanawha County Bd. Edn., Charleston, W.Va., 1973-89; ret., 1989—; high sch. debate club sponsor Nitro (W.Va.) High Sch., 1963-71, sponsor Nat. Forensic League, 1965-71. Exhibited in art shows including in W.Va. and Ky. Mem. Nat. Dem. Com, 1993-95. Mem. AAUW (chair art com. 1961-66), NEA, ACLU, NOW, W.Va. Edn. Assn., Delta Kappa Gamma. Democrat. Home: 194 Manor Dr Beckley WV 25801-2537

ROBERTSON, DAWNA LEA, advertising executive; b. Oklahoma City, Apr. 22, 1956; d. J.C. and Joyce (Neal) R. BA in Advt., U. Okla., 1978. Copywriter Oklahoma Jour., Oklahoma City, 1977-78, GKD Advt., Oklahoma City, 1978-80, Margo Wood Advt., Honolulu, 1980-82; advt. mgr. Blackfield Hawaii Corp., Honolulu, 1982-85; copywriter Gib Black Advt., Honolulu, 1985-86; copy dir. Beals Advt., Oklahoma City, 1986-87; advt. dir. Hawaiiana Resorts, Honolulu, 1987—. Recipient Honor award Honolulu Pele Awards, 1980, 81, 82, 86. Mem. Honolulu Ad Club II (copywriter pub. svcs. 1980-82), Oklahoma City Ad Fedn. (Addy Awards coms. 1978-79). Republican. Office: Hawaiiana Resorts 1270 Ala Moana Blvd Honolulu HI 96814-4217

ROBERTSON, FLORENCE WINKLER, advertising and public relations agency executive; b. Hampton, Va., Sept. 11, 1945; d. Fred Felty Jr. and Florence Bernice (Shamo) Schnopp; m. John Park Winkler Jr., June 24, 1967 (div. 1977); m. James Milton Robertson, Oct. 21, 1982. AA, Palm Beach Jr. Coll., 1965; BA, U. South Fla., 1967. Reporter, Lexington (Ky.) Leader, 1967-70; freelance writer, 1971-76; TV and radio news reporter Sta. KCRG, Cedar Rapids, Iowa, 1972-73; asst. dir. pub. relations Coe Coll., Cedar Rapids, 1973-78; info. specialist Cedar Rapids (Iowa) Pub. Schs., 1979-83; adv. mgr. Smulekoff's Fine Home Furnishings, 1984-93; owner Fox Ridge Adv., Cedar Rapids, 1993—; mem. bd. dirs. Linn County Farm Bur., 1994—. Pres. Home Fire Safety Task Force of Ea. Iowa, 1983-86; chmn. Cedar Rapids Promotion Com., 1986-87; bd. dirs. Grant Wood Area chpt. ARC; organizer, bd. dirs., Cedar Rapids Christmas Parade, 1985—. Recipient Regional award Council Advancement and Support Edn., 1975, 77, 78, nat. award CASE, 1977; Gov.'s award for Volunteerism, 1986; Pub. Service awards Nat. Police Officers Assn., City of Shively (Ky.) and Am. Legion, 1970; Nat. award Nat. Sch. Pub. Relations Assn., 1981, 83, Gov.'s Award for Volunteerism, 1987. Mem. Nat. Mgnt. Assn. (v.p. 1993-94). Home: 3794 Toddville Rd Toddville IA 52341-9773 Office: Fox Ridge Adv PO Box 134 Hiawatha IA 52233

ROBERTSON, JANE RYDING, marketing executive; b. Dallas, Apr. 11, 1953; d. Ronald and Olive Stacey (Hodgkinson) Pearce; m. James Randall Robertson, May 25, 1974; children: James Andrew, Jessica Ryding. Assoc. degree, Tyler Jr. Coll., 1972; BS, Tex. Tech U., 1974. Store mgr. trainee Montgomery Ward, Dallas, Lubbock, Tex., 1974-75; dist. sales rep. Max Factor & Co., Dallas, 1975-78; sr. asst. buyer cosmetics Sanger Harris, Dallas, 1978-88, also cosmetic mktg.-divisional mktg. account exec., 1978-88; v.p. mktg. Dallas Market Ctr., 1988-90; dir. mktg.-pub. rels. Galleria/Hines Interests Dallas, 1990—. Bd. dirs. Ctr. for Profl. Selling, Baylor U., Waco, Tex., 1989—; mem. nat. bd. Susan G. Komen Found. for Breast Cancer, Dallas, 1990—; charter bd. mem. Nat. Kidney Found. of Tex., Dallas chpt., 1991—. Mem. Internat. Coun. Shopping Ctrs., Fashion Group Internat., Univ. Club (bd. dirs. profl. women's com. 1990-92). Methodist. Office: Hines Interests Ltd Ptnr 13355 Noel Rd Ste 250 Dallas TX 75240-6603

ROBERTSON, JEANNE BENNETT, interior designer and artist; b. San Francisco, May 21, 1916; d. Willard Winslow and Mary Louise (Weymann) Bennett; m. Charles Bennett Robertson, July 5, 1941; children: David Bennett, Philip Bennett, Anne Louise Robertson Thomas. AB, U. Calif., 1938. Playground dir. San Francisco Recreation Dept., 1939-41, Washington D.C. Recreation Dept., 1941-42; pilot WASP, Sweetwater, Tex., 1943-44, Long Beach, Calif., 1943-44; pvt. practice interior design San Francisco & Honolulu, 1967—; artist Art a la Carte Gallery, Honolulu, 1987—. Mem. AAUW (pres. 1983-85), Hawaii Watercolor Soc. (leader workshops 1975—, pres. 1979), Assn. Hawaiian Artists, Gen. Fedn. Women (pres. 1988), Nat. League Am. Pen Women (pres. 1992—). Republican.

ROBERTSON, JEWELL LEWIS, investment company executive; b. Lelia Lake, Tex., Mar. 17, 1911; d. Earnest Luther and Margaret Mae (Reeves) Lewis; m. Charles Andrew Robertson, Dec. 31, 1950 (dec. May 1976). Student, Clarendon (Tex.) Jr. Coll., 1929; grad., Amarillo (Tex.) Bus. Coll., 1930; student, Amarillo Coll., 1978. Sec., bookkeeper Rolla V. Cartwright Ins., Amarillo, 1930-36; sec. to gen. mgr. Farm Security Adminstrn., Amarillo, 1936-42; paymaster, banker Pantex Ordnance Plant, Amarillo, 1942-45; sec. to pres. Oil Devel. Co. Tex., Amarillo, 1945-48, Maynard Sash and Door Co., Amarillo, 1948-50; sec. to sales mgr. Graham Plow Co., Amarillo, 1950-59; exec. dir. Tex. Panhandle Home Builders Assn., Amarillo, 1959-70; adminstrv. asst. Tex. State Tech. Inst., Amarillo, 1970-72; br. office adminstr. Edward D. Jones & Co., Amarillo, 1972—. Recipient Mem. Devel. awards Nat. Assn. Home Builders, Washington, 1963, 64, 65. Mem. Nat. Asns. Female Execs., Fin. Planners Assn., Amarillo Fedn. Women's Clubs(v.p. 1955-56), Amarillo Coun. Garden Clubs (sec. 1960), Amarillo C. of C. (program chmn. women's div. 1963), Daus. of the Nile, Order Eastern Star. Home: 2803B W 27th Ave Amarillo TX 79109-1713 Office: Edward D Jones & Co 2414-4 Lakeview Dr Amarillo TX 79109-1713

ROBERTSON, KAREN LEE, county official, acoustical consultant; b. Whittier, Calif., Mar. 21, 1955; d. Lethal Greenhaw Robertson and Lloydine Ann (Pierce) Robertson-Reese; children: Kimberlee Ann Kubski, Krista Linn Robertson. Student Calif. State U. Acoustical technician Hilliard & Bricken, Santa Ana, Calif., 1977-79, John J. Van Houten, Anaheim, Calif., 1979; prin. Robertson & Assocs., Boulder, Colo., 1980; acoustical technician David Adams & Assocs., Denver, 1980; v.p. engring. John Hilliard & Assocs., Tustin, Calif., 1985—; acoustical specialist County of Orange, Santa Ana, 1980-87; airline access, noise officer John Wayne Airport Adminstrn. of Orange County, 1987-92; chair Noise Abatement Com., 1987-92; chair DFW Noise Forum, 1992—; sr. noise compatibility planner Dallas/Ft. Worth Internat. Airport, 1992—; mem. advanced subsonic transport noise reduction steering com. NASA/FAA, 1993—; mem. airports coun. Internat.-N.Am. Environ. Affairs Com. Co-author Land Use/Noise Compatibility Manual, 1984; editor Noise Element of General Plan, 1984. Speaker in field. Mem. acoustical adv. bd. Orange County, 1985-92; mem. Calif. Noise Officers Forum, 1987—. Recipient Achievement award Nat. Assn. Counties, 1986, 90, 91, Orange County Achievement award, 1990, Woman Achievement award, 1991. Mem. Acoustical Soc. Am. (bd. dirs. 1985-86), Transp. Research Bd. (tech. mem. 1985—), Nat. Assn. Noise Control Ofcls., Community/Indsl. Noise Control Assn., Inst. Noise Control Engring. (affiliate), Calif. Assn. Window Mfrs. (STC Task Group 1985). Republican. Home: 1804 Sandalwood Ln Grapevine TX 76051-7344 Office: Dallas/Ft Worth Internat Airport PO Drawer DFW Dallas TX 75261

ROBERTSON, LAURIE LUISSA, computer scientist; b. Dallas, Feb. 19, 1960; d. Jack Weldon and Gretchen Luissa (Roeschlaub) R. BA, Rice U., 1982; MLS, U. Pitts., 1983; cert. procurement and contracting, U. Va., 1993. Programmer/statistician Galveston (Tex.) Dist. Atty., 1980-82; programmer/analyst Def. Systems Inc., McLean, Va., 1983-85; computer scientist Computer Scis. Corp., Falls Church, Va., 1985-94, Sci. Applications Internat. Corp., Arlington, Va., 1994—. Mem. Computer Soc. of IEEE, Assn. for Computing Machinery, Beta Phi Mu. Office: Sci Applications Internat Ste 910 200 N Glebe Rd Arlington VA 22203

ROBERTSON, LUCRETIA SPEZIALE, interior designer, author; b. Pitts., Feb. 23, 1944; d. Louis Albert and Irene (Lavenka) Speziale; m. Ronald Paul Parlato, Aug. 21, 1965 (div. Dec. 1967); m. William Sterling Robertson III, Feb. 3, 1973; children: Evan Alexander, Ian Stewart. BFA in Art History, Fine Arts and Archtl. Design, Smith Coll., 1965. Asst. art dept. Condé Nast-Mademoiselle, N.Y.C., 1965-66; dir. fashion M. Lowenstein and Sons, N.Y.C., 1966-67; fashion coordinator Vogue/Butterick Pattern Co., N.Y.C., 1967-70, creative dir. advt./promotions, 1970-73; prin. Lang/Robertson, Ltd., N.Y.C. and Montclair, N.J., 1975—; cons., designer Boussac of France, N.Y.C., 1975—; cons. Burlington Industries, N.Y.C., 1976-79, Levolor/Lorentzen, Parsippany, N.J., 1980—; designer McCalls Patterns, N.Y.C., 1979-81, AABE Fabrieken, Tillburg, Holland, 1983-85. Author: (ghost-writer) Body and Beauty Secrets of the Superbeauties, 1978, Decorating with Fabric, 1986; contbr. to Am. Psychiat. Press, Inc.; presenter paper on vol. work to 5th Nat. Conv. on Pediatric AIDS, L.A., 1989. Vol. St. Luke's Ch. Outreach program, Montclair, 1978—, Whole Theatre Co., Montclair, 1980—, AIDS Resource Found. for Children, Newark; singer N.J. Oratorio Soc.; vol. pediatric AIDS, Albert Einstein Coll. Medicine, Bronx, N.Y.; devel. bd. Hyacinth Found. AIDS Resources, N.J.; mem. Montclair AIDS Task Force; organizing com. St. Luke's Episcopal Ch. AIDS Task Force. Mem. Smith Club. Democrat. Episcopalian. Office: 36 Eagle Rock Way Montclair NJ 07042-2017

ROBERTSON, MARIAN ELLA (MARIAN ELLA HALL), small business owner, handwriting analyst; b. Edmonton, Alta., Can., Mar. 3, 1920; d. Orville Arthur and Lucy Hon (Osborn) Hall; m. Howard Chester Robertson, Feb. 7, 1942; children: Elaine, Richard. Student, Willamette U., 1937-39; BS, Western Oreg. State U., 1955. Cert. elem., jr. high. tchr., supt. (life) Oreg.; cert. graphoanalyst. Tchr. pub. schs. Mill City, Albany, Scio and Hillsboro, Oreg., 1940-72; cons. Zaner-Bloser Inc., Columbus, Ohio, 1972-85, assoc. cons., 1985-89; pres. Write-Keys, Scio, 1980-90; owner Lifelines, Jefferson, Oreg., 1991—; tchr. Internat. Graphoanalysis Soc., Chgo., 1979; instr. Linn-Benton Community Coll., 1985-89. Sr. intern 5th Congl. Dist. Oreg., Washington, 1984, mem. sr. adv. coun.; precinct com. mem. Rep. Cen. Com., Linn County, 1986, alt. vice-chair, 1986, parliamentarian, 1988—; candidate Oreg. State Legis., Salem, 1986; del. Northwest Friends Yearly Meeting, Newberg, Oreg., 1990, 91, 92; master gardener vol. Marion County, Oreg. State U. Extension Svc., 1992; floriculture judge Marion County Fair, 1992; master gardener clinic Oreg. State Fair, 1992; clerk Marion Friends Monthly Meeting, 1992-93. Mem. Altrusa Internat. (internat. chmn. 1985-86, chmn. pub. rels. 1989—, corr. sec. 1990-91), Internat. Platform Assn. Republican. Mem. Soc. of Friends. Home: 2757 Pheasant Ave SE Salem OR 97302-3710 Office: Lifelines PO Box 54 Jefferson OR 97352-0054

ROBERTSON, MARTHA RAPPAPORT, state senator, consultant; b. Boston, Sept. 14, 1952; d. Jerome Lyle and Nancy (Vahey) Rappaport; m. T.L. Robertson, Nov. 22, 1980; 1 child, Colby. BA, Franklin & Marshall Coll., 1974; MBA, U. Pa., 1976. Mktg. and new bus. devel. exec. Gen. Mills, Inc., Mpls., 1976-91; state senator State of Minn., 1993—. Republican. Office: State of Minn 125 State Office Building Bldg Saint Paul MN 55155-1201*

ROBERTSON, MARY LOUISE, archivist, historian; b. L.A., May 19, 1945; d. Snell and Dorothy (Tregoning) R. BA, UCLA, 1966, MA, 1968, PhD, 1975. Teaching asst. dept. history UCLA, 1967-70; acting instr. UCLA Extension, 1973-74; acting instr. dept. history Pepperdine U., L.A., 1970, Calif. State U., Northridge, 1972-73; asst. curator manuscripts Huntington Libr., San Marino, Calif., 1975, assoc. curator, 1977, chief curator, 1979—; adj. prof. English Claremont Grad. Sch., 1994. Author: Guide to British Historical Manuscripts in the Huntington Library, 1982; co-author, editor: Guide to American Historical Manuscripts in the Huntington Library, 1979; contbr. articles on Tudor history to profl. jours. Mabel Wilson Richards dissertation fellow, 1970-72. Mem. Am. Hist. Assn., Soc. Am. Archivists, Soc. Calif. Archivists, N.Am. Conf. on Brit. Studies, Pacific Coast Conf. on Brit. Studies (treas. 1986-88, pres. 1988-90), Phi Beta Kappa. Office: Huntington Libr 1151 Oxford Rd San Marino CA 91108-1218

ROBERTSON, MARY VIRGINIA, retired elementary educator; b. Lincoln, Nebr., Oct. 1, 1925; d. Dean Leroy and Anna Charlotte (Boge) R. AB in Philosophy and Psychology, U. Nebr., Lincoln, 1949, BS in Elem. Edn., 1953; postgrad., U. Toronto, Ont., Can., 1949. Cert. elem. tchr., Nebr. Country sch. tchr. Lancaster County schs., Nebr., 1943-44, Otoe County schs., Palmyra, Nebr., 1944-45; 3d-5th grade tchr. Palmyra Schs., 1945-46; 3d grade tchr. Valley (Nebr.) Schs., 1953-57, Lincoln Pub. Schs., 1957-81; ret.; leader workshop in field; math. coord. Riley Elem. Sch., Lincoln, 1970-71. Author pamphlet A Letter for You, 1954. Mem. NEA, AAUW, Nebr. State Edn. Assn., Nat. Coun. Math. Tchrs., Am. Child Edn. Internat., Belmont PTA (life), Eastern Star, Lincoln Women's Club. Methodist.

ROBERTSON, MELVINA, construction company executive; b. Guilford, Mo., June 3, 1934; d. Charlie Gale and Christina Gertrude (Nelson) Turner; m. Ponnie Leonard Robertson, June 3, 1955; children: Raymond Edward, Richard Leonard. Student, Cen. Mo. State Coll., 1966. Mgr. Knowles Restaurant, Kansas City, Mo., 1954-55; v.p. P.L. Robertson Concrete Found. Co., Inc., Ozark, Mo., 1972-90; pres. P.L. Robertson Concrete Found. Co., Inc., 1990—. Mem. Rose Soc. of Ozark, Nat. Audubon Soc. Mem. Reorganized LDS Ch.

ROBERTSON, PAMELA N., public relations executive; b. Newton, Mass., July 14, 1958. BA in Journalism, Boston U. Dir. pub. rels. Hotel Inter-Continental, Miami, 1987-88; dir. comm. Hotel Macklowe, 1988-90; dir. pub. rels. Mktg. Support Inc., 1990-91; pres. NRS Comm., Chgo., 1991—. Mem. Pub. Rels. Soc. Am., Women in Comm. Inc. Office: NRS Communications 200 N Racine #2230 Chicago IL 60614*

ROBERTSON, SANDRA KAYE, school counselor, psychotherapist; b. Spartanburg, S.C., Mar. 1, 1961; d. William Perry and Eula Virginia (Riddings) Foster; m. Michael Dean Robertson, Nov. 24, 1993. BA, Converse Coll., 1983; MEd, U. S.C., 1993. Cert. elem. tchr.; cert. sch. counselor; lic. counselor, S.C. Tchr. Sunny View Elem. Sch., Mill Springs, N.C., 1984-88, Polk Ctrl. H.S., Mill Springs, N.C., 1988-91; counselor Green Creek, Mill Springs, N.C., 1991, Polk Ctrl. Elem. Sch., Mill Spring, 1992-94; pvt. practice Anchoring Place Therapy Group, Spartanburg, 1994—; counselor Spartanburg Sch. Dist. 7, S.C., 1994—. Mem. NEA, N.C. Edn. Assn., Am. Counseling Assn., Am. Sch. Counselors Assn., Internat. Assn. for Marriage and Families. Republican. Home: 5 Drayton Ct Spartanburg SC 29301 Office: Raintree Office Park One 347 E Blackstock Rd Spartanburg SC 29301

ROBERTSON, SARA STEWART, investment company executive; b. N.Y.C., Feb. 4, 1940; d. John Elliott and Mary Terry (Schlamp) Stewart; m. James Young Robertson, Nov. 29, 1975 (dec. Mar. 1988). BA, Conn. Coll., 1961; MBA, Am. U., 1969. From trainee to officer First Nat. Bank/First Chgo. Corp., 1969-75, v.p., 1975-92; prin. Royall Enterprises, Chgo., 1992—; bd. dirs. Youth Guidance, Chgo., 1982-85, 92—, chair individuals fundraising, mem. exec. com., 1993—. Bd. dirs. Harbor House Condominium Assn. Chgo., 1990-92; bd. trustees Sherwood Conservatory Music, 1993—, chair bd. devel., 1993—; mem. allocations com. and family life priority grants com. United Way-Chgo., 1992—. Home and Office: Ground Level Ste 1243 W Barry Ave Chicago IL 60657-4209 Winter Address: 470 S Ocean Blvd Apt 5 Palm Beach FL 33480

ROBERTSON, SUSAN CAROLYN, occupational therapy educator. BA in Psychology and Anthropology, Pitzer Coll., 1969; cert. occupational therapy, San Jose State U., 1973, MS in Occupational Therapy, 1977; postgrad., Va. Commonwealth U., 1977-79, U. Md., 1989—. Nurse's aide Lindenhof Spital, Bern, Switzerland, 1969-70; psychiat. aide Waldau Spital, Ostermundigen, Switzerland, 1970; in-home aide pvt. family San Jose, 1971-72; dir. handicapped recreation Los Gatos (Calif.) Saratoga Recreation Dept., 1972; psychiat. aide Belmont (Calif.) Hills Psychiat. Hosp., 1972-73; occupational therapy intern gen. med. and surg. units Ventura (Calif.) Gen. Hosp., 1973; occupational therapy intern psychiat. unit Mt. Zion Hosp., San Francisco, 1973; program asst. Phys. Fitness for Fun Jewish Community Ctr., San Francisco, 1974; dir. occupational therapy Psychiatric Day Ctrs., Inc., San Francisco, 1974-77; asst. prof. occupational therapy Med. Coll. Va., Richmond, 1977-80; continuing edn. specialist, liaison to spl. interest sects. Am. Occupational Therapy Assn., Rockville, Md., 1981-82, internat. coord., 1985-88, mental health program mgr., 1986-90, asst. dir. continuing edn. divsn., 1982-88, program mgr. post-profl. program devel., 1990-92, program mgr. continuing edn. program devel., 1988-92; project mgr. leadership project TriAlliance of Health and Rehab. Professions, Rockville, Md., 1992—; asst. prof. occupational therapy dept. Towson (Md.) State U., 1992-94; sr. occupational therapist NIH, 1994—; cons. Shady Grove Med. Ctr., Rockville, Md., 1992-93; grant reviewer Dept. Edn., Divsn. Student Svcs., 1991; designer for accessibility continuing edn. design Washington, 1990; mem. profl. adv. com. Long-term Care Conf. Program, Hillhaven Found., Washington, 1985; designer continuing edn. occupational therapy dept. U. N.D., Grand Forks, 1985, Howard U., Washington, 1985; designer competency-based curriculum Bur. Health Professions, Rockville, Md., 1984; rsch. asst. edn. U. Md., 1992, Chesapeake Inst., Wheaton, Md., 1988-90; presenter in field. Author: Study Guide to Occupational Therapy Treatment Goals for Physically and Cognitively Disabled, 1993, Find a Mentor or Be One, 1992, Effective Programming: Blueprint for Success, Faculty Guide, 1989, Managing in an Environment of Change, 1989, Mental Health Focus: Skills for Assessment and Treatment, 1988, Mental Health Scope: Strategies, Concepts, and Opportunities for Program Development and Evaluation, 1986, Planning and Implementing Vocational Readiness in Occupational Therapy, 1985, Vocational Readiness Assessment in Occupational Therapy, 1984, The Prospective Payment System and Its Implications for Occupational Therapy, 1983, Re-Entry Packet, 1982; contbr. articles to profl. jours. Recipient Good Citizen award DAR, 1966, Excellence award Am. Soc. Assn. Execs., 1986, 88. 89; named Disting. Alumna, San Jose State U., 1993; Adminstrn. Aging Grantee, 1982; Office Spl. Edn. and Rehab. Svcs. grantee, 1982. Fellow Am. Occupational Therapy Assn.; mem. World Fedn. Occupational Therapists, Me. Occupational Therapy Assn., Nat. Coun. for Internat. Health. Home: 5618 Greentree Rd Bethesda MD 20817 Office: NIH Bldg 10 Rm 6S235 10 Center Dr MSC 1604 Bethesda MD 20892-1604

ROBERTSON, SUSAN JOYCE COE, educational behavior intervention specialist, consultant; b. Pinedale, Wyo., May 22, 1954; d. Cecil James and Geraldine Ada (Greene) Coe; children: Jamie Michelle, Mark David. BS in Edn., Chadron (Nebr.) State Coll., 1976, MS in Counseling and Guidance, 1977; specialist in emotionally disturbed, U. No. Colo., 1982. Cert. crisis prevention intervention master trainer, peer mediation facilitator. Elem. tchr. pub. schs., Alliance, Nebr., 1976-77; social worker Community Action, Cheyenne, Wyo., 1978-79; Chpt. 1 tchr. Laramie County Sch. Dist. 1, Cheyenne, 1979-81, elem. tchr., 1981-84, tchr. severely emotionally disturbed, 1984-89, cons., specialist for severely emotionally disturbed, 1989-92, behavior intervention team specialist, 1992—; mem. Dist. Placement Com., 1981-92. Mem. Community Commn., Cheyenne, 1981-92; basketball coach YMCA, 1994. Mem. NEA, Am. Guidance and Counseling Assn., Coun. for Exceptional Children (faculty adviser 1991), Wyo. Edn. Assn., Cheyenne Tchr. Edn. Assn., Trailblazer Parent Assn., PEO. Presbyterian. Home: 5425 Gateway Dr Cheyenne WY 82009-4035 Office: Laramie County Sch Dist 1 2810 House Ave Cheyenne WY 82001-2860

ROBERTSON, SUZANNE MARIE, primary education educator; b. Canton, Ohio, Nov. 21, 1944; d. Jules Michael and Emma Louise (Olmar)

Franzen; m. William K. Robertson, June 30, 1973 (dec. 1979). BS in Early Childhood Edn., Kent State U., 1966; M in Early Childhood Edn., Southern Conn. U., 1976; postgrad., Fairfield U. and U. Bridgeport, 1981-82. Kindergarten tchr. Ridgefield (Conn.) Bd. Edn., 1966—, Internat. Sch. Basel, Switzerland, 1993-94; children's gymnastics instr. Ridgefield (Conn.) YMCA, 1982-83, Sherman Parks & Recreation, Conn., 1983-85. Toy designer; mem. nat. adv. bd. Learning Mag. Campaign vol. Cancer Fund of Am., Sherman, 1980-81. Awarded Honorable Mention Learning Mag., 1989; recipient Profl. Best Teaching awards. Mem. NEA, Tchrs. Assn. Supporting Children (chmn. 1986-89, Fairfield County pub. rels. com. 1986-89), Conn. Edn. Assn., Internat. Platform Assn., Sherman Hist. Soc., Phi Delta Kappa (historian 1989-90, rsch. rep. 1990-91). Office: Farmingville Elem Sch 324 Farmingville Rd Ridgefield CT 06877

ROBERTSON, SYLVIA DOUGLAS, middle school educator; b. Lynchburg, Va., June 25, 1952; d. Alfred Lynch and Rena (Irvin) Douglas; m. Lawrence Edward Robertson, Apr. 26, 1975 (div. May 1985); 1 child, Lawrence Edward Jr. BA, Cedar Crest Coll., 1974; MEd, Lynchburg Coll., 1990. Cert. tchr., Va. Tchr. 7th grade Big Island (Va.) Elem. Sch., 1974-89; tchr., team leader 7th grade Bedford (Va.) Mid. Sch., 1989-93, tchr., grade level chairperson 7th grade, 1993—. Facilitator Police, Pub. Educators and Peer Counselors Utilizing the Leadership of Students at Risk, Bedford, Va., 1991-92; vol. Free Clinic Ctrl. Va., Inc., Lynchburg, Va., 1993. Mem. Nat. Coun. Tchrs. Math., Nat. Sci. Tchrs. Assn., Nat. Energy Edn. Devel. Project, Bedford County Edn. Assn., Va. State Reading Assn., Va. Mid. Sch. Assn., Piedmont Area Reading Coun., Kappa Delta Pi, Phi Delta Kappa, Alpha Delta Kappa (corr. sec. 1993—), Alpha Kappa Alpha. Home: Rte 7 Box 122 Arbor Ct Madison Heights VA 24572 Office: Bedford Mid Sch 503 Longwood Ave Bedford VA 24523

ROBERTSON, VESTA-NADINE (SEVERS), secretary, writer; b. Racine, Mo., May 28, 1935; d. Delmer William and Anna Marie (Hiebert) Severs; m. Edward Luellen Robertson, Dec. 11, 1960 (dec.); children: Jonathan E.D., Felicia D., Nathan C., Vincent S., Diana R. Cert., Draughon's Sch. Bus., 1954. Sec. Earl L. Hogard, CPA, Tulsa, 1954-56; comm. operator Rocketdyne divsn. NAA, Inc., Neosho, Mo., 1956-60; sec.-bookkeeper Barton Constrn. Co., Tulsa, 1965-67; sec. Okla. Mil. Dept., Oklahoma City, 1984—; writer in residence Prague (Okla.) Pub. Schs., 1979; active creative writing summer program Shawnee (Okla.) Parks & Recreation, 1981; writer in residence 4th-5th grades Neosho Pub. Schs., 1989. Author: Lucinda, 1978, Nation's Oldest Fish Hatchery, 1982, God Love Your Hearts!, 1992; editor: Man's Six Hearts, 1992; contbr. articles to newspapers and mags. Vol. cook/laundry Golden Rule Nursing Home, Shawnee, Okla., 1980-83; active Don Nickles for U.S. Senate, Oklahoma City, 1992. Mem. Soc. Children's Book Writers, Okla. Soc. Children's Book Writers, Okla. Hist. Soc. Republican. Mem. Ch. of God. Home: PO Box 1554 Guthrie OK 73044

ROBEY, BRENDA J. HALL, elementary school counselor; b. Winchester, Va., May 20, 1950; d. James Edward and Laura Jeanne (Crabb) Hall; m. Ronald Kirk Robey, June 27, 1971; children: Jennifer, Jason, Jeffrey. BS, George Mason U., 1972; MEd, James Madison U., 1987. 0. Elem. sch. tchr. Fairfax (Va.) County Schs., 1972-78; elem. sch. counselor Page County Schs., Luray, Va., 1986-89, Rockingham County Schs., Harrisonburg, Va., 1989—; mem. counseling psychology adv. com. James Madison U., Harrisonburg, 1992—; camp counselor, resource leader Highroad Program Ctr., Middleburg, Va., 1970, 72-73, 77, 78; vol. James Madison U. Human Devel. Ctr., 1987; facilitator Systematic Tng. Effective Parenting, 1986—; camp resource cons., staff trainer Camp Overlook, Keezletown, Va., 1979—; summer playground leader Fairfax County Dept. Recreation; bus driver Fairfax County Pub. Schs., 1970-71. Jr. high youth counselor St. Georges United Meth. Ch., Fairfax, 1970-73; Sunday sch. tchr. Mountain Valley United Meth. Ch., Harrisburg, 1979—; hotline aide tng. Concern Hotline, Inc., Luray. Mem. AACD, Va. Sch. Counselors Assn. (membership chmn. 1991-93, workshop presenter, elem. sch. counselor of yr. 1990), Page County Health Assn. (bd. dirs. 1988-89), Harrisonburg-Rockingham County Mental Health Assn. (bd. dirs. 1990-92). Home: RR 1 Box 203 Keezletown VA 22832-9725 Office: Lacey Spring Elem PO Box 228 Lacey Spring VA 22833-0228

ROBEY, KATHLEEN MORAN (MRS. RALPH WEST ROBEY), civic worker; b. Boston, Aug. 9, 1909; d. John Joseph and Katherine (Berrigan) Moran; B.A., Trinity Coll., Washington, 1933; m. Ralph West Robey, Jan. 28, 1941. Actress appearing in Pride and Prejudice, Broadway, 1935, Tomorrow is a Holiday, road co., 1935, Death Takes a Holiday, road co., 1936, Left Turn, Broadway, 1936 Come Home to Roost, Boston, 1936; pub. relations N.Y. Fashion Industry, N.Y.C., 1938-43. Mem. Florence Crittenton Home and Hosp., Women's Aux. Salvation Army, Gray Lady, ARC; mem. Seton Guild St. Ann's Infant Home. Mem. Christ Child Soc., Fedn. Republican Women of D.C. English-Speaking Union. Republican. Roman Catholic. Clubs: City Tavern, Cosmos (Washington), Nat. Woman's Republican. Home: 4000 Cathedral Ave NW Washington DC 20016-5249

ROBEY, SHERIE GAY SOUTHALL GORDON, secondary education educator, consultant; b. Washington, July 7, 1954; d. James Edward and Gene Elizabeth (Gray) Southall; children: m. Robert Jean Claude Robey; children: Michael Aaron Gordon, Robert Eugene Robey, Jamie Lea Robey. BS, U. Md., 1976; MA in Edn. and Human Devel., George Washington U., 1988. Tchr. Esperanza Mid. Sch., Hollywood, Md., 1980-84, Chopticon High Sch., Morganza, Md., 1984—; coach Odyssey of Mind, Waldorf, Md., 1985—; sponsor Future Tchrs. Am., Morganza, 1990—, S.H.O.P./S.A.D.D., Morganza, 1990—; cons. Ednl. Cons., Waldorf, 1980—. Mem. Ednl. Rep. Assn. St. Mary's County, Lighthouse Hist. Soc. Methodist. Home: 2615 Ferguson Ct Waldorf MD 20602-1700 Office: Chopticon High Sch Rt 242 Morganza MD 20660

ROBFOGEL, SUSAN SALITAN, lawyer; b. Rochester, N.Y., Apr. 4, 1943; d. Victor and Janet (Rosenthal) Salitan; m. Nathan Joshua Robfogel, July 12, 1965; children: Jacob Morris, Samuel Salitan. BA cum laude, Smith Coll., 1964; JD, Cornell U., 1967. Bar: N.Y.1967, U.S. Dist. Ct. (we. dist.) 1968, U.S. Ct. Appeals (2d cir.) 1971, U.S. Supreme Ct. 1971, U.S. Dist. Ct. (no. dist.) 1974, D.C. 1982. Asst. corp. counsel, then sr. asst. corp. counsel City of Rochester, N.Y., 1967-70; assoc. Harris, Beach & Wilcox, Rochester, 1970-75; ptnr. Harris, Beach, Wilcox, Rubin & Levey, Rochester, 1975-85; ptnr., chair health svcs. practice Nixon, Hargrave, Devans & Doyle, Rochester, 1985—; panel mem., Fed. Svc. Impasses Panel, Washington, 1983-94; mem., past chair Data Protection Rev. Bd., Albany, N.Y., 1984—. Mem. trustees vis. com. U. Rochester Med. Sch., 1990; mem. mgmt. adv. panel SUNY, 1990. Recipient Brockport Coll. Found. Community award, 1989. Fellow Am. Bar Found., N.Y. State Bar Found.; mem. ABA, N.Y. State Bar Assn., Washington D.C. Bar Assn., Monroe County Bar Assn. (Rodenbeck award 1988). Home: 1090 Park Ave Rochester NY 14610 Office: Nixon Hargrave Devans & Doyle Clinton Sq PO Box 1051 Rochester NY 14603-1051

ROBICHAUD, LAURA JEAN, social worker, educator; b. Worcester, Mass., Sept. 23, 1963; d. Gerald James Robichaud and Jean Susan (Harris) Partridge. AA, Cazenovia Coll., 1983; BA, Assumption Coll., Worcester, 1985; MA, Anna Maria Coll., Paxton, Mass., 1987; MSW, Boston Coll., Chestnut Hill, Mass., 1990. Lic. ind. clin. social worker, Mass. Dir. emergency svcs. Human Resource Ctr., Athol, Mass., 1986-89; behavioral specialist North Ctrl. Human Svcs., Gardner, Mass., 1989-93, coord. mental health svcs., 1991-93; sattelite dir. North Ctrl. Human Svcs., Athol, 1993—; adj. prof. Mt. Wachasett C.C., Gardner, 1992—. Mem. Rotary. Roman Catholic. Home: 157 High Knob Rd Athol MA 01331 Office: North Ctrl Human Svcs 491 Main St Athol MA 01331-1846

ROBICHAUD, PHYLLIS IVY ISABEL, artist, educator; b. Jamaica, West Indies, May 16, 1915; came to U.S., 1969, naturalized, 1977; d. Peter C. and Rose Matilda (Rickman) Burnett; grad. Tutorial Coll., 1933, Kingston, Jamaica, Munro Coll., St. Elizabeth, Jamaica, 1946; student Central Tech. Sch., Toronto, Ont., Can., 1960-63, Anderson Coll., Can., 1968-69; m. Roger Robichaud, July 22, 1961; children by previous marriage—George Wilmot Graham, William Henry Heron Graham, Mary Elizabeth Graham Watson, Peter Robert Burnett Graham. Sec. to supr. of Agr., St. Elizabeth, 1940-50; loans officer and cashier Confederation Life Assn., Kingston, 1950-53; tchr. art Jamaica Welfare Ltd., 1963; tchr. art recreation dept. New Port Richey, Fla., 1969-77; tchr. art Pasco Hernando Community Coll., New Port Richey, 1977—; demonstrator various organizations including West Pasco Art Guild, New Port Richey, Ace Artists, New Port Richey; propr., mgr. Band Box Dress Shop, Kingston, Jamaica, 1954-57; numerous one-woman shows of paintings including various banks, libraries, Kingston, 1963-64, 67, Toronto, 1968, New Port Richey, 1969, 70, 73, 76, Tampa, Fla., 1974, 75, 76, Omaha Cattle Company restaurant, Clearwater Fla., 1982, Mus. Pasco Hernando Community Coll., New Port Richey, Fla., 1989, 92, Alric C.T. Pottberg Libr. of the PHCC, 1992; numerous group shows, latest being: Sweden House, Tampa, 1977-78, Chasco Fiesta, New Port Richey, 1977, Magnolia Valley Golf and Country Club, New Port Richey, 1978, West Pasco Art Guild, New Port Richey, 1978, 79, 92, Indian Rocks Beach, 1985, Hernando Community Coll. at the Mus. of the Coll., 1989, other cities in Fla.; executed murals, New Port Richey and Kingston; decorated New Port Richey C. of C., also pvt. collections. Patron, St. Alban's 4H Club, 1942; sec. Sunday sch. Ch. of Eng., Kingston, 1937-39. Recipient award T. Eaton Co. of Can., 1961, cert. of merit, Mayor of New Port Richey, 1976, appreciation award New Port Richey Recreation Dept., 1977; award Fla. Heart Fund. Mem. Nat. League Am. Pen Women (v.p. Tampa br. 1978-80, dir. 1969—), West Pasco Art Guild (Blue ribbons 1978, 79, 2d Pl. Mixed Media award 1991), Fla. Fine Arts Guild. Republican. Roman Catholic. Address: 7032 Lenox Dr New Port Richey FL 34653-1920

ROBIN, NANCY SCHNEIDER, nurse, educator; b. Loreauville, La., Oct. 12, 1955; d. Raymond Francis and Elaine (Harbin) Schneider; m. John Timothy Robin, Dec. 18, 1976; children: Emily Annette, Timothy Patrick. BSN, U. Southwestern La., 1977; MSN with honors, U. Tex., Houston, 1991. Cert. Ob-gyn. nurse; RN, La. Prenatal coord. Lafayette (La.) Health Unit, 1984-90; staff nurse U. Med. Ctr., Lafayette, 1989-92; nursing instr. La. State U., Eunice, 1993—; faculty instr. La. State U. Med. Sch., Lafayette, 1992—; mem. speaker's bur. Ciba/Geigy Pharm. Co. Leader Girl Scouts Am.; mem. Lafayette Parish Tenneage Pregnancy Task Force; vol. Acadiana chpt. ARC, City of Lafayette Summer Day Camp; coach Lafayette Parish Youth Soccer Assn. Team. Mem. Assn. Women's Health, Obstetrics and Neonatal Nurses, (chair 1992-93), Am. Assn. Nurse Practitioners, La. Assn. Nurse Practitioners, Sigma Theta Tau. Office: La State U Med Sch 2390 W Congress St Lafayette LA 70506-4205

ROBINETTE, BETSYE HUNTER, school psychologist; b. Nashville, Sept. 30, 1960; d. Gerald Sylvan and Eleanor Louise (Felts) Hunter; m. Michael David Robinette, Aug. 13, 1988; 1 child, David. 030PhD, U. Tenn., 1993; MA cum laude, Wheaton (Ill.) Coll., 1984; postgrad., U. Tenn. Lic. psychol. examiner, cert. sch. psychologist, Tenn.; cert. psychologist, Ky. Adolescent counselor Mercy Ctr., Aurora, Ill., 1983-84; mental health technician Glendale Heights (Ill.) Community Hosp., 1984; staff psychologist Cumberland River Comprehensive Care Ctr., Harlan, Ky., 1985-86; psychotherapist Family Svc. Ctr., Asheville, N.C., 1987; psychol. examiner Overlook Mental Health Ctr., Knoxville, Tenn., 1987-88; sch. psychology intern Cherokee Mental Health Ctr., Morristown, Tenn., 1989-90; sch. psychologist Knox County Schs., Knoxville, Tenn., 1990-94, Christian Acad. of Knoxville; crisis intervention worker RAFT, Inc. Crisis Intervention, Blacksburg, Va., 1981-82; grad. asst. Wheaton Coll., 1984, U. Tenn., Knoxville, 1988-89; clinic coord. U. Tenn., 1989. Missionary Campus Crusade for Christ, Tokyo, 1982. Mem. Am. Psychol. Assn., Nat. Assn. Sch. Psychologists, Tenn. Assn. Sch. Psychologists, Christian Assn. Psychol. Studies, Phi Kappa Phi, Pi Lambda Theta, Psi Chi (v.p. 1981-82). Presbyterian. Home: 1624 Summerhill Dr Knoxville TN 37922-6257

ROBINETTE, SHEREE, construction executive; b. Tampa, Fla., Mar. 12, 1957; d. William J. and Patricia Ann (Gearhart) R. BA in Acctg. U. South Fla., 1980. Mgr. Fontaine Supply, Tampa, 1977-80; owner, mgr. Tampa Accessory Corp., 1980—. Mem. Constrn. Trade Assn., Nat. Assn. Women in Constrn., Nat. Assn. Profl. Estimators, Tampa Builders Exch., Am. Subcontractor Assn., Builder's Exch. Constn. Trade Assn. Republican. Office: Tampa Accessory Corp 7219F Benjamin Rd Ste F Tampa FL 33634-3037

ROBINOVITZ, DORIS JEAN HOLMES, psychologist; b. Glen Ridge, N.J.; d. Harold Henry and Doris Anita (Smith) Holmes; m. Edward Robinovitz, Apr. 8, 1993. AB, Allegheny Coll., 1963; PhD, Temple U., 1989. Lic. psychologist, Pa. Med. editor W.B. Saunders Co., Phila., 1967-81; psychologist Community Coun. for Mental Health-Mental Retardation, Phila., 1986-91, Crozer-Chester Med. Ctr., Upland, Pa., 1991—. Mem. APA, Pa. Psychol. Assn., Phila. Soc. Clin. Psychologists. Office: Crozer-Chester Med Ctr 1 Medical Center Blvd Upland PA 19013

ROBINS, LEE NELKEN, medical educator; b. New Orleans, Aug. 29, 1922; d. Abe and Leona (Reiman) Nelken; m. Eli Robins, Feb. 22, 1946 (dec. Dec. 1994); children: Paul, James, Thomas, Nicholas. Student, Newcomb Coll., 1938-40; BA, Radcliffe Coll., 1942, MA, 1943; PhD, Harvard U., 1951. Mem. faculty Washington U., St. Louis, 1954—, prof. sociology in psychiatry, 1968-91, prof. sociology, 1969-91, univ. prof. social sci., prof. social sci. in psychiatry, 1991—; past mem. Nat. Adv. Coun. on Drug Abuse; past mem. task panels Pres.'s Commn. on Mental Health; mem. expert adv. panel on mental health WHO; Salmon lectr. N.Y. Acad. Medicine, 1983. Author: Deviant Children Grown Up, 1966; editor 11 books; N.Am. Assoc. editor Internat. Jour. Methods in Psychiat. Rsch.; mem. editl. bd. Psychol. Medicine, Jour. Child Psychology and Psychiatry, Devel. and Psychopathology, Jour. Studies on Alcohol, Epidemiol. e Psychiat. Sociale, Criminal Behavior and Mental Health; contbr. articles to profl. jours. Recipient Rsch. Scientist award USPHS, 1970-90, Pacesetter Rsch. award Nat. Inst. Drug Abuse, 1978, Radcliffe Coll. Grad. Soc. medal, 1979, Sutherland award Soc. Criminology, 1991, Nathan B. Eddy award Com. on Problems of Drug Dependence, 1993; rsch. grantee NIMH, Nat. Inst. on Drug Abuse, Nat. Inst. on Alcohol Abuse and Alcoholism. Fellow Am. Coll. Epidemiology, Royal Coll. Psychiatrists (hon.); mem. APHA (Rema Lapouse award 1979, Lifetime Achievement award sect. on alcohol and drug abuse 1994), World Psychiat. Assn. (mem. sect. com. on epidemiology and cmty. psychiatry, treas.), Soc. Life History Rsch. in Psychopathology, Am. Coll. Neuropsychopharmacology, Am. Sociol. Assn., Internat. Sociol. Assn., Inst. Medicine, Internat. Epidemiol. Assn., Am. Psychopahtol. Assn. (Paul Hoch award 1978, pres. 1987-88). Office: Washington U Dept Psychiatry Med Sch Saint Louis MO 63110

ROBINS, MARJORIE MCCARTHY (MRS. GEORGE KENNETH ROBINS), civic worker; b. St. Louis, Oct. 4, 1914; d. Eugene Ross and Louise (Roblee) McCarthy; AB, Vassar Coll., 1936; diploma St. Louis Sch. Occupational Therapy, 1940; m. George Kenneth Robins, Nov. 9, 1940; children: Carol Robins Von Arx, G. Stephen, Barbara A. Robins Foorman. Mem. Mo. Libr. Commn., 1937-38; mem. bd. St. Louis Jr. League, 1945, 46; mem. bd. Occupational Therapy Workshop of St. Louis, 1941-46, pres., 1945, 46; mem. bd. Ladue Chapel Nursery Sch., 1957-60, 61-64, pres. bd., 1963, 64; past regional chmn. United Fund; past mem. St. Louis Met. Youth Commn., St. Louis Health and Welfare Coun.; bd. dirs. Internat. Inst. of St. Louis, 1966-72, 76-82, 83-92, sec., 1968, v.p., 1981; bd. dirs. Mental Health Assn. St. Louis, 1963-70, Washington U. Child Guidance and Evaluation Clinic, 1968-78; bd. dirs. Cen. Inst. for Deaf, 1970—, v.p., 1975-76, pres., 1976-78; bd. dirs. Met. St. Louis YWCA, 1954-63, 64-74, pres. bd., 1960-63, trustee, 1977—; mem. nat. bd. YWCA, 1967-79, nat. v.p., 1973-76; vol. tchr. remedial reading clinic St. Louis City Schs., 1968-71; trustee John Burroughs Sch., 1960-63, John Burroughs Found., 1965-80, Roblee Found., 1972—, Nat. YWCA Retirement Fund, 1979-88; bd. dirs. Gambrill Gardens United Meth. Retirement Home, 1979-85, Thompson Retreat and Conf. Center, 1981-87; bd. dirs. Springboard to Learning Inc., 1980—, v.p., 1980-90. Mem. Archeol. Inst. Am. (bd. dirs. 1993—, treas. St. Louis chpt. 1985-87), Vassar Club (sec. and pres. 1939-40), Wednesday Club (dir. 1968-70, 77-79, 80-81, 93— St. Louis. Home: 45 Loren Woods Saint Louis MO 63124-1903

ROBINSON, ALICE JEAN MCDONNELL, drama and speech educator; b. St. Joseph, Mo., Nov. 17, 1922; d. John Francis and Della M. (Mavity) McDonnell; m. James Eugene Robinson, Apr. 21, 1956 (dec. 1983). BA, U. Kans., 1944, MA, 1947; PhD, Stanford U., 1965. Tchr. Garden City (Kans.) High Sch., 1944-46; asst. prof. Emporia (Kans.) State U., 1947-52; dir. live programs Sta. KTVH-TV, Hutchinson-Wichita, Kans., 1953-55; assoc. prof. drama and speech U. Md. Baltimore County, Balt., 1966—, rsch. theatre history. Author: The American Theatre: A History in Slides, 1992, Betty Comden and Adolph Green: A Bio-Bibliography, 1993; co-editor: Notable Women in the American Theatre, 1989; appeared in plays, including Landscape, 1983, Tartuffe, 1985, Rockaby, 1990. Mem. Am. Soc. Theatre Rsch., Assn. Theatre Higher Edn., East Central Theatre Conf., Phi Beta Kappa. Republican. Home: 606 Edgevale Rd Baltimore MD 21210-1904 Office: U Md Baltimore County Wilkens Ave Baltimore MD 21228

ROBINSON, AMY, film producer. Films include: Chilly Scenes of Winter, 1979, Baby It's You, 1983, After Hours, 1985, Running On Empty, 1987, White Palace, 1990, Once Around, 1991, With Honors, 1994. Office: Double Play Prodns 1501 Broadway Ste 2600 New York NY 10036*

ROBINSON, ANN MCK., federal agency administrator; b. Norristown, Pa., Feb. 27, 1937; d. John J. and Anna (Sedor) McKernan; m. Armand I. Robinson, June 25, 1970. BS in Edn., Temple U., 1958; degree in bus. adminstrn., U. Pa., 1962; postgrad., U. Va., 1977; MS in Mgmt., MIT, 1983. Instr. Chestnut Hill Coll., 1958-59, U. Pa., 1959-63; asst. to dir. indsl. rels. McCall Corp., 1963-64; asst. to dir. employee benefits Lever Bros. Co., 1964-66; mgmt. internbur. of pers. U.S. Postal Svc., Washington, 1966-69, systems analyst, 1969-73, sr. systems analyst office of mgmt. systems, 1973, gen. mgr. internat. divsn. office of mail classification, 1973-77, gen. mgr. distbn. procedures divsn. office of distbn. systems, 1977-79, gen. mgr. employee and placement divsn. office of human resources, 1979-82, exec. asst. to postmaster gen., 1983-85, consumer adv., v.p., 1985—. With U.S. Army, 1979. Sloan fellow Postal Svc., 1982-83. Mem. Alpha Sigma Alpha, Delta Psi Kappa. Office: US Postal Service 475 L'Enfant Plz SW Rm 5821 Washington DC 20260*

ROBINSON, ANNETTMARIE, entrepreneur; b. Fayetteville, Ark., Jan. 31, 1940; d. Christopher Jacy and Lorena (Johnson) Simmons; m. Roy Robinson, June 17, 1966; children: Steven, Sammy, Doug, Pamela, Olen. BA, Edison Tech. U., 1958; BA in Bus., Seattle Community Coll., 1959. Dir. perss. Country Kitchen Restaurants, Inc., Anchorage, 1966-71; investor Anchorage, 1971—; cons. Pioneer Investments, Anchorage, 1983—, M'RAL, Inc. Retail Dry Goods, Anchorage, 1985. Mem. Rep. Presdl. Task Force, Washington, 1984—, Reps. of Alaska, Anchorage, 1987; mem. chmn. round table YMCA, Anchorage, 1986—; active Sta. KWN2, KQLO, Reno, Nev.; active in child abuse issues and prosecution. Named Woman of Yr. Lions, Anchorage, 1989, marksman first class Nat. Rifle Assn., 1953. Mem. NAFE, Spenard Lion's Aux. (past pres.).

ROBINSON, BARBARA MABBS, marketing executive; b. Evanston, Ill., Mar. 6, 1949; d. Ralph Renner and Barbara Ann (Birge) Mabbs. BA, Northwestern U., 1971; MA Emerson Coll., 1992; CSS Harvard U., 1992. With Sears Roebuck and Co., 1971-75; mgr. merchandising svcs. Samsonite Corp., Denver, 1976-78; v.p. mktg. Chidco Microsystems Corp., Denver, 1979-83; dir. mktg. Cen. City Opera House Assn., Denver, 1981; dir. mktg. svcs. Nat. Demographics, Denver, 1982; prin./pres. BMC Mktg., Denver, 1982-85, Portland, Maine, 1985-87; dir. advt. comm. and mktg. svcs. Gerber Children's Wear, Inc., Boston, 1987-90; sr. dir. mktg. cons. Blue Cross & Blue Shield, Maine, 1992-94; mktg. comm. mgr. Cole Haan, Portland, Maine, 1994—. Office: Mktg Comm Cole Haan Yarmouth ME 04096

ROBINSON, BARBARA PAUL, lawyer; b. Oct. 19, 1941; d. Leo and Pauline G. Paul; m. Charles Raskob Robinson, June 11, 1965; children: Charles Paul, Torrance Webster. AB magna cum laude, Bryn Mawr Coll., 1962; LLB, Yale U., 1965. Bar: N.Y. 1966, U.S. Dist. Ct. (so. and ea. dists.) N.Y. 1975, U.S. Tax Ct. 1972, U.S. Ct. Appeals (2d cir.) 1974. Assoc. Debevoise & Plimpton (formerly Debevoise, Plimpton, Lyons & Gates), N.Y.C., 1966-75, ptnr., 1976—; mem. adv. bd., lectr. Practising Law Inst.; arbitrator Am. Arbitration Assn., 1987—, Am. Judicature Soc. Contbr. articles to profl. jours. Mem. adv. coun., bd. visitors CUNY Law Sch., Queens, 1984-90; trustee Trinity Sch., 1982-86, pres., 1986-88; bd. dirs. Found. for Child Devel., 1989—, chmn., 1991—; bd. dirs. Catalyst, 1993—; trustee The William Nelson Cromwell Found., 1993—. Fellow Am. Coll. Trust and Estate Counsel, Am. Bar Found., N.Y. Bar Found.; mem. ABA, N.Y. State Bar Assn. (vice chmn. com. on trust adminstrn., trusts and estates law sect. 1977-81, ho. of dels. 1984-87, 90-92, mem. com. ann. award 1993—), Assn. of Bar of City of N.Y. (chmn. com. on trusts, estates and surrogates cts. 1981-84, judiciary com. 1981-84, coun. on jud. adminstrn. 1982-84, chair nominating com. 1984-85, mem. exec. com. 1986-91, chair 1989-90, v.p. 1990-91, pres. 1994—, chair com. on honors 1993-94, mem. com. on long-range planning 1991-94), Assn. of Bar of City of N.Y. Fund, Inc. (bd. dirs., pres.), Yale Coun., Yale Law Sch. Assn. N.Y. (mem. devel. bd., exec. com. 1981-85, pres. 1988-93), Yale Club, Washington Club. Office: Debevoise & Plimpton 875 3rd Ave New York NY 10022-6225

ROBINSON, CARI SUZANNE, library director; b. Nashville, Nov. 21, 1956; d. William Allen and Nan (Fussell) Robinson. BA, David Lipscomb Coll., 1979; M of Library Sci, Vanderbilt U., 1981. Conservation clk. Am. Gen. Life Ins. Co., Nashville, 1982-83; library dir. Dickson (Tenn.) County Pub. Library, 1983--. Bd. dirs. Dickson County Lit. Coun., Dickson County Interagy. Coun. Mem. Tenn. Libr. Assn., Southeastern Libr. Assn., Tenn. Archivists, Beta Phi Mu. Office: Dickson County Pub Library 305 E Hunt St Dickson TN 37055-2098

ROBINSON, CAROL A., usability analyst; b. Seattle, Aug. 4, 1963; d. Mischa Elman and Betty Anne (Slater) R. BS, U. Wash., 1985, MS, 1992. Usability specialist Asymetrix, Bellevue, Wash., 1992-93, Microsoft, Redmond, Wash., 1993-94; usability analyst McGraw-Hill, Monterey, Calif., 1994—. Fellow Keck Found., 1991-92; scholar Alcoa Co., 1982-83. Mem. Computer-Human Interaction, Usability Profls. Assn. Office: McGraw-Hill 20 Ryan Ranch Rd Monterey CA 93940

ROBINSON, CAROLE ANN, insurance executive, retired; b. Omaha, Dec. 21, 1935; d. Harry B. and Mildred (Daley) Baker; widowed Mar. 1989; 1 child, Pamela Fleming. Clk. Blue Cross/Blue Shield Colo., Denver, 1969-70; mgr. Blue Cross/Blue Shield Colo., 1970-72, asst. to treas., 1972-74, dir., 1974-79, treas., 1980-86, sr. v.p., treas., 1986-90; v.p., treas., chief investment officer Rocky Mountain Health Care (Holding Co.), Denver, 1991-93, sr. v.p., chief investment officer, CFO, 1986-93; ret., 1993; bd. dirs. Denver, Colo. Compensation Ins. Authority, Denver, Combined Health Appeal, Denver. Mem. investment com. City and County of Denver, 1988. Mem. Colo. Cash. Mgmt. Assn., Nat. Cash Mgmt. Assn., Life Office Mgmt. Assn. (treasury ops. com. 1985-93). Republican. Office: Rocky Mountain Health Care 700 Broadway Ste 990 Denver CO 80203-3443

ROBINSON, CATHY, retail manager; b. Denison, Iowa, June 1, 1951; d. Teddy Junior and Ruth F. (Paulsen) Cornelius; m. Billy Don Turner, July 3, 1975 (div. Dec. 1979); 1 child, Michelle Suzanne; m. Gary L. Robinson, June 24, 1989; 1 child, Brittany Sue. BA, U. Iowa, 1973. Asst. store mgr. Casual Corner, Houston, 1975-77, store mgr., 1977-80, dist. mgr., Tampa, Fla., 1980-81, regional mgr., Tampa, 1981—; bd. dirs., sec. Galleria Mall, Houston, 1979-80. Mem. Nat. Assn. Female Execs., Gamma Phi Beta. Lutheran. Avocations: water skiing, skiing, snorkeling, softball. Office: Casual Corner 3302 W Buffalo Ave Ste 1022 Tampa FL 33607-6213

ROBINSON, CHARLENE G., mental health nurse; b. Mt. Union, Pa., Jan. 10, 1932; d. Lester and Clarabelle (Parsons) Garman; m. John W. Robinson, Dec. 21, 1951 (dec.); children: John W. Jr., Susan, Cheryl, Lester, Nancy. Diploma, Temple U., 1954; BSN, U. Louisville, 1983, MSN, 1986; MEd, Western Ky. U., 1984. Asst. prof. nursing Elizabethtown (Ky.) Community Coll.; staff nurse Ireland Army Hosp., Ft. Knox, Ky.; asst. mgr. psychiatry J.C. Blair Meml. Hosp., Huntingdon, Pa.; nursing instr. Kauai Community Coll., Lihue, Hawaii; asst. mgr. psychiatry J.C. Blair Meml. Hosp., Huntingdon. Mem. Am. Psychiat. Nurses Assn. Home: 306 4th St Huntingdon PA 16652-1422

ROBINSON, CONNIE MORRISON, counselor, consultant; b. Seneca, Pa., June 24, 1937; d. Glade Emery and Jane Lucille (Rankin) Morrison; m. Erven Cecil Robinson, Aug. 17, 1957; children: Rick Emery, Alexa McConnell Robinson O'Neill. BS in Edn., Youngstown State U., 1970, MEd, 1977; PhD, Kent State U., 1991. Tchr. Canfield (Ohio) Local Schs., 1970-78; counselor Poland (Ohio) Local Schs., 1978—; career cons. Youngstown, 1993—. Mem. Greater Youngstown Civic Leader Commn., 1990-91, Am. Cancer Soc. Women's Meml. Golf Tournament, Youngstown, 1992-93.

Mem. ASCD, Am. Counseling Assn., Ea. Ohio Counselor's Assn., Ohio Counselor's Assn., Ohio Assn. Coll. ADmissions Counselors. Home: 5657 Colgate Dr Youngstown OH 44515-4141 Office: Poland Sem High Sch 3199 Dobbins Rd Poland OH 44514-2327

ROBINSON, CUMMIE ADAMS, librarian; b. Mansfield, La., Sept. 27, 1945; d. Roosevelt and Annie B. Adams; m. Johnnie Robinson Jr.; children: Jared, Cynara, Cynecia. BS, So. U., Baton Rouge, 1967; MSLS, U. So. Calif., 1972; PhD, Walden U., 1992. Cert. tchr., La. Tchr. Compton (Calif.) Unified Schs., 1970-73; libr. Xavier U., New Orleans, 1973-75, Nicholls H.S., New Orleans, 1989—; tchr. Delgado C.C., 1992; adj. faculty So. U., New Orleans, 1994—. Block coord. Nat. Leukemia Soc., New Orleans, 1992—, March of Dimes, New Orleans, 1992—, Muscular Dystrophy Assn., New Orleans, 1988—. Mem. Nat. Coun. Negro Women, Delta Sigma Theta. United Methodist. Home: 5800 Kensington Blvd New Orleans LA 70127 Office: 3820 Saint Claude Ave New Orleans LA 70117-5736

ROBINSON, DEBORAH A., judge; b. 1953. BA, Morgan State Univ.; JD, Emory Univ. Law Sch., 1978. Law clk. to chief judge Superior Ct. of D.C., 1978-79; asst. U.S. atty. D.C., 1979-87; magistrate judge U.S. Dist. Ct., D.C. circuit, 1988—. Office: US Courthouse 333 Constitution Ave NW Rm 1205 Washington DC 20001*

ROBINSON, DOROTHY K., lawyer; b. New Haven, Feb. 18, 1951; m. Philip Hancock Bouwsma; children—Julia Robinson, Alexandra Toby. BA in Econs. with honors, Swarthmore Coll., 1972; JD, U. Calif.-Berkeley, 1975, MA (hon.) Yale U., 1987. Bar: Conn. 1981, N.Y. 1976, Calif. 1975, U.S. Ct. Appeals (2d cir.) 1975, U.S. Dist. Ct. (so. dist.) N.Y. 1978, U.S. Dist. Ct. Conn. 1981, U.S. Tax Ct. 1981. Assoc. Hughes Hubbard & Reed, N.Y.C., 1975-78; asst. gen. counsel Yale U., New Haven, 1978-79, assoc. gen. counsel, 1979-84, dep. gen. counsel, 1984-86, gen. counsel, 1986—, dir. fed. relations, 1986-88, acting sec., 1993. Trustee Hopkins Grammar Day Prospect Hill Sch., New Haven, 1983-88, sec., 1986-88; trustee Wenner-Gren Found. Anthrop. Rsch.,1991—; bd. dirs. Cold Spring Sch., New Haven, 1990—; mem. adv. bd. Conn. Mental Health Ctr., New Haven, 1979-89; bd. dirs. Nat. Assn. Coll. and U. Attys., 1987-90, Nat. Assn. Indep. Coll. and U., 1994—. Editor articles and book revs. Calif. Law Rev. Fellow Ezra Stiles Coll. Yale U. Fellow Am. Bar Found.; mem. Nat. Assn. Coll. and Univ. Attys., Conn. Bar Assn., Calif. Bar Assn., Assn. of Bar of City of N.Y., New Eng. Assn. Schs. and Colls. Commn. on Instns. Higher Edn., Phi Beta Kappa. Office: Yale U Office of Gen Counsel PO Box 208255 Yale Sta New Haven CT 06520-8255

ROBINSON, FLORINE SAMANTHA, marketing executive; b. Massies Mill, Va., Feb. 4, 1935; d. John Daniel and Fannie Belle (Smith) Jackson; m. Frederick Robinson (div. 1973); children: Katherine, Theresa, Freda. BS, Morgan State U., 1976; postgrad., U. Balt., 1977-81, Liberty U., 1987. Writer, reporter Phila. Independent News, 1961-63; freelance writer, editor Balt., 1963-71; asst. mng. editor Williams & Wilkins Pubs. Inc., Balt, 1971-76; mktg. rep., then mktg. mgr. NCR Corp., Balt., 1977-93; assoc. minister, trustee Christian Unity Temple, Balt., 1976—; pres. ABCOM, Inc., Balt., 1993—; bd. dirs. Armstrong & Bratcher, Inc., Balt. Editor: Stedman's Medical Dictionary, 1972; contbr. articles to profl. jours. Active PTA, Balt., 1963-65; bd. dirs. Howard Pk. Civic Assn., Balt., 1967—, pres. 1991—; leader, cons. Girl Scouts USA, 1970-73. Recipient Excellence in Rsch. award Psi Chi, 1976, Citizen citation Mayor of Balt. Mem. NAFE, Mid-Atlantic Food Dealers Assn., Am. Soc. Notaries, Internat. Platform Assn., Edelweiss Club, Order of Eastern Star. Democrat. Home: 3126 Howard Park Ave Baltimore MD 21207-6715

ROBINSON, GAIL E., artist; b. San Antonio, July 16, 1949; d. Eugene Aaron and Phyllis Leone (Wolfe) Englert. BFA, U. Okla., 1970. Exhibited paintings in numerous shows including Shapiro Gallery N.H. Coll., 1993, Nature N.H. Statewide Traveling Exhbn., 1992, Faber Birren Color show, Stamford, Conn., 1992, 88, League of N.H. Craftsmen Gallery, 1992, Belknap Mills Soc. Visual Arts Coalition Statewide Exhbn., Laconia, N.H., 1991, Sharon (N.H.) Gallery, 1989, Newport (R.I.) Art Mus., 1987, others; paintings represented in numerous corp. collections including Salomon Bros. Investments, Chubb Life Am., Browning Ferris Industries. Art colony fellow Va. Ctr. for Creative Arts, 1991, 92, Vt. Studio Colony, 1991. Mem. Pastel Soc. Am. (master), Copley Soc. (Copley artist), League N.H. Craftsmen, Women's Caucus for Art, N.H. Art Assn. Home: 9 Government St Kittery ME 03904

ROBINSON, IDA LAFOSSE, minister, broadcaster; b. Phila., July 27, 1934; d. Charles and Alma Elizabeth (Johnson) B.; m. Benjamin H. LaFosse; children: Andre, Marcel, Benita, Tania. DD, Trinity Hall Coll. & Sem., Denver, 1985. Ordained to ministry Pentacostal Ch., 1963. Min. Ch. of God in Christ, Phila., 1959-63; evangelist Ch. of the Open Door, Phila., 1963-66; pastor Miracle Tabernacle, Camden, N.J., 1966-67, Salvation Tabernacle, Phila., 1967—; broadcaster Move of God Inc., Phila., 1967-73, overseer, 1985—; pastor Move of God Cathedral, N.Y.C., 1968—, broadcaster, 1985—; pres. Move of God Crusade Team and Radio Prayer Line. Editor Amb. mag., 1973. Office: Move of God Cathedral 501503 W 152nd St New York NY 10031-1435

ROBINSON, JOAN, education educator; b. White Plains, N.Y., Aug. 28, 1963; d. Joseph Franklin and Mattie Ann (Chapman) R.; children: Jovan R., Derrick C., Gian D. BS, Mercy Coll., 1987. Respite counselor Westchester Ass. for Retarded Citizens, White Plains, 1986-87; educ. cons. sales Early Learning Ctr., White Plains, 1987; crisis counselor Children's Village, Dobbs Ferry, N.Y., 1986-87, sociotherapist; psych. counselor Med. Ctr. of Cen. Ga., Macon, 1987-88; career agt. Prudential Co., Ryebrook, N.Y.; dir. KIDS daycare and afterschool enrichment program WMJ; edn. cons. Discovery Toys, White Plains, 1985-87; proprietor Heavens Little Creations, White Plains, Juana Prodns., Scarsdale; cons. Mary Kay Beauty; dir. WMJ's Kids Daycare and Afterschool. Mem. Mt. Vernon Community Choir, Calvary Bapt. Ch.; vol. Union Child Day Care Ctr., Victim Info. Bur.'s Children's Village Program, Exch. Club Child Abuse Prevention Program. Mem. NAFE, Entrepreneurs Am., Cen. Westchester Audubon Soc., Westchester Assn. Women Bus. Owners. Republican. Home: 60 Gibson Ave White Plains NY 10607-2003

ROBINSON, JULIE ANN, judge; b. Omaha, Jan. 14, 1957; d. Marvin Harold and Charlene Helen (Womack) Robinson. B.S. in Journalism, U. Kans., 1978; J.D., 1981 Bar: Kans. 1981, Mo. 1983. Law clk. Schnider, Shamberg & May, Fairway, Kans., 1981; law clk. to chief judge U.S. Bankruptcy Ct., Kansas City, Kans., 1981-83, asst. atty., Kansas City, 1983-94; judge U.S. Bankruptcy Ct., Topeka, Kans., 1994—. Reporter, writer U. Kans. Daily Kansas newspaper, 1977-78; bd. govs. U. Kans., 1987—. Recipient Black Woman of Distinction award Yates br. YWCA, Kansas City, 1982. Fellow ABA (Kans.); mem. Kans. Bar. Assn., Am. Judicature Soc. (student leader award 1980), Am. Inn of Ct., Phi Delta Phi, Delta Sigma Theta. Methodist. Office: US Bankruptcy Ct 444 SE Quincy Rm 225 Topeka KS 66683

ROBINSON, JULIENELL NAPIER, military public health officer; b. Eugene, Oreg., July 13, 1950; d. Jules Verne and Connell Priestley (Napier) Napier; m. George Robinson, Dec. 21, 1977; 1 child, Chad Fitzgerald. BSN, U. Portland, Oreg., 1974; MPH, U. Tex. Health Sci. Ctr., Houston, 1983. RN, Oreg.; cert. Occupational Health Nurse. Commd. USAF, advanced through grades to lt. col., 1977—; mental health nurse USAF, Travis AFB, Calif., 1977-80, chief evening and night suprs. David Grant Med. Ctr., 1980-82, supr. inpatient mental health and alcohol rehab., 1982; chief environ. health Regional Med. Ctr. USAF, Wiesbaden, Fed. Republic Germany, 1983-87; cons. Occupational Environ. Health Lab. USAF, Brooks AFB, Tex., 1987-88; dep. chmn. mil. pub. health and occupational medicine, master instr. USAFSAM, Brooks AFB, Tex., 1988-93; chief Dept. Pub. Health, Kelly AFB, Tex., 1993—; Cons. TB Outbreak USAF, 1983, Automated Occupational Health System, 1987-88. Cubmaster Pack 485 Boy Scouts Am., San Antonio, 1988-90, sec. Troop 484, 1990-93. NIOSH fellow, 1993-94. Mem. APHA, Am. Orgn. Occupational Health Nurses, Nat. Environ. Health Assn., Soc. Environ. Health Profls. (editor newsletter 1990-92, sec./treas. 1990-92). Republican. Presbyterian. Office: 651 MEDSQD/SGE Kelly AFB TX 78241

ROBINSON, JUNE K., dermatologist, educator; b. Phila., Jan. 26, 1950; d. George and Helen S. (Kerswell) R.; m. William T. Barker, Jan. 31, 1981. BA cum laude, U. Pa., 1970; MD, U. Md., 1974. Diplomate Am. Bd. Dermatology, Nat. Bd. Med. Examiners, Am. Bd. Mohs Micrographic Surgery and Cutaneous Oncology. Intern Greater Balt. Med. Ctr., Hanover, N.H., 1974; resident in medicine Greater Balt. Med. Ctr., 1974-75; resident in dermatology Dartmouth-Hitchcock Med. Ctr., Hanover, N.H., 1975-78, chief resident, clin. instr., 1977-78; instr. in dermatology Dartmouth-Hitchcock Med. Ctr., Hanover, 1978; fellow Mohs; chemosurgery and dermatologic surgery NYU Skin and Cancer Clinic, N.Y.C., 1978-79; instr. in dermatology NYU, N.Y.C., 1979; asst. prof. dermatology Northwestern U. Med. Sch., Chgo., 1979, asst. prof. surgery, 1980-85, assoc. prof. dermatology and surgery, 1985-91, prof. dermatology and surgery, 1991—; mem. consensus devel. conf. NIH, 1992; lectr. in field. Author: Fundamentals of Skin Biopsy, 1985, also audiovisual materials; mem. editl. bd. Archives of Dermatology, 1988—; sect. editor The Cutting Edge: Challenges in Med. and Surg. Therapeutics, 1989—; contbg. editor Jour. of Dermatol. Surgery and Oncology, 1985-88; editl. com. 18th World Congress of Dermatology, 1982; contbr. numerous articles, abstracts to profl. publs., chpts. to books. Bd. dirs. Northwestern Med. Faculty Found., 1982-84, chmn. com. on benefits and leaves, 1984, nominating com. 1988. Grantee Nat. Cancer Inst., 1985-91, Am. Cancer Soc., 1986-89, Skin Cancer Found., 1984-85, Dermatology Found., 1981-83, Northwestern U. Biomed. Rsch., 1981, Syntex, 1984. Fellow Am. Coll. Chemosurgery (chmn. sci. program ann. meeting 1983, chmn. publs. com. 1986-87, chmn. task force on ednl. needs 1989-90, co-editor bull. 1984-87; mem. AMA, Am. Dermatol. Assn., Am. Acad. Dermatology (Stephen Rothman Lect. award 1992, Presdl. citation 1992), Dermatology Found., Am. Coll. Chemosurgery, Internat. Soc. Dermatol. Surgery, Am. Soc. Dermatol. Surgery, Soc. Investigative Dermatology, Ill. Cancer Coun., Women's Dermatol. Soc., Chgo. Dermatol. Soc., Am. Fedn. Clin. Rsch. Home: 910 N Lake Shore Dr # 1419 Chicago IL 60611 Office: Northwestern U Med Sch Dept Dermatology 303 E Chicago Ave # 767 Chicago IL 60611

ROBINSON, KAREN ANN, educator; b. N.Y.C., May 30, 1959; d. Olen Wesley and Barbara Ann (Simmons) R. BS, Syracuse U., 1981; MA, George Washington U., 1984. Cert. advanced profl. in spl. edn., Md. Tchr. Shield of David, Bronx, N.Y., 1981, Cerebral Palsy Sch., Syracuse, N.Y., 1982, United Cerebral Palsy, Bronx, 1982-83, Low Meml. Day Care, Bklyn., 1983; program support tchr. specialist Montgomery County Pub. Schs., Rockville, Md., 1994—, insvc. tchr., 1986-89; instr. Johns Hopkins U. Continuing Studies, 1994—; com. mem. Supts. Com. on Evaluation, Rockville, 1988-89; guest lectr. Bowie (Md.) State U., 1990-91. Mem. NEA, Md. Tchrs. Assn. (del. 1985—, del. leadership conf. 1989), Montgomery County Edn. Assn. (organizer, assoc. rep. 1985—), Montgomery County Assn. Black Sch. Educators (newsletter editor), Nat. Assn. Black Sch. Educators.

ROBINSON, LAURA BOST, insurance company executive; b. Winnsboro, S.C., June 20, 1966; d. Dewey Tate and Gloria Jean (Coiner) Bost; m. Patrick Andrew Robinson, Apr. 5, 1991. BA in Acctg., Furman U., 1988. CMA; assoc. in ins. acctg. and fin. Acct. Blue Cross/Blue Shield of S.C., Columbia, 1988-89, supr. fin. svcs., 1989-91, mgr. fin. svcs., 1991—. Mem. Inst. Mgmt. Accts. Home: 101 Lakeview Dr Winnsboro SC 29180 Office: Blue Cross/Blue Shield of SC PO Box 100165 Columbia SC 29202

ROBINSON, LISA G., public relations executive; b. Norristown, Pa., Mar. 28, 1959. BS in Comm. and Journalism, Millersville U., 1981. News reporter WGAL-TV, 1980-84; pub. info. rep. Three Mile Island, Gen. Pub. Utilities Corp., 1984-88; mgr. nuclear info. Consolidated Edison, 1988-90; dir. corp. comm. N.Y. Daily News, 1990-91; mgr. corp. comm. Ciba-Geigy Corp., 1992-93; dir. media rels. McGraw-Hill Inc., N.Y.C., 1993—. Mem. Women in Comm. Inc. Office: McGraw-Hill Inc 1221 Ave of the Americas New York NY 10020*

ROBINSON, LOIS HART, retired public relations executive; b. Freeport, Ill., Aug. 9, 1927; d. Seril N. and Cora (Stabenow) Hart; m. Noel M. Henze, Nov. 15, 1947 (div. 1964); m. Jack Fay Robinson, July 16, 1968; children: Susan Henze Bentley, Cynthia Henze Berkeley, Charles Henze. Student Oakton Community Coll., 1976-77, Northwestern U., 1977-81. Med. sec. Freeport Meml. Hosp., 1945-47; sec. No. Ill. Corp., 1947-49; adminstrv. asst. to supt. schs. Community Sch. Dist. 303, St. Charles, Ill., 1962-68; exec. sec. Bell & Howell Co., Chgo., 1969-73, supr. corp. rels., 1973-79, mgr. corp. communications, 1979-85, mgr. corp. communication svcs., 1985-88; pres., dir. Bell & Howell Found., 1983-88; free-lance writer, Evanston, Ill., 1989-91. Recipient Effie award Am. Mktg. Assn., 1983. Bd. dirs. Evanston Ecumenical Action Coun., 1991-93. Congregationalist. Home: 321 E Morse Ave Bartlett IL 60103

ROBINSON, LORNA JANE, marketing executive; b. N. Tonawanda, N.Y., Jan. 28, 1957; d. Lawrence Esdras and Irene Nancy (Sachuk) Cyr. AS in Bus. Methods, SUNY, Buffalo, 1983, BS in Bus. Adminstrn., 1987. Credit clk. Nat. Assn. Credit Mgmt., Buffalo, 1975-77; sec. to v.p. The Sample, Inc., Buffalo, 1977-78; credit rep. Liberty Nat. Bank and Trust, Buffalo, 1978-79, Spencer Kellogg Div. Textron, Buffalo, 1979-82; sr. customer svc. rep. Spencer Kellogg/NL Chems., Buffalo, 1982-86; account exec. WYRK-FM, Buffalo, 1986, Genigraphics Corp., Phila., 1986-90; mgr. advt. Trade Show Pubs., Morrisville, Pa., 1991—. Roman Catholic. Home: 5153 Judson Dr Bensalem PA 19020-3850 Office: Trade Show Pubs 20 N Pennsylvania Ave Morrisville PA 19067-1110

ROBINSON, LOUISE EVETTE, marriage family child counselor; b. San Francisco, May 8, 1952; d. Ellis Hart and Doris Sonia (Morris) R.; stepmother Anita Robinson. BA in Psychology, U. Calif., Berkeley, 1973; MA in Psychology, Sonoma State U., 1976. Lic. marriage, family and child counselor. Co-therapist John Champlin M.D., Berkeley, 1976, Jonothon Gross M.D., Napa, Calif., 1976; counselor Buckelew House, Kentfield, Calif., 1975-77, Petaluma (Calif.) Peoples Svcs. Ctr., 1977; intake counselor Youth Advocates C.C. Riders Clinic, Novato, Calif., 1978-80, clin. supr., 1980-82; psychotherapist Robert Cohen M.D., Santa Rosa, Calif., 1984-85; dir., founder Sonoma County Assocs. in Drug Edn., Rohnert Park, Calif., 1982-90; pvt. practice marriage, family and child counseling Kentfield, Rohnert Park and Petaluma, Calif.; speaker Marin Gen. Hosp. Pediatricians, 1981, Chope Hosp. Psychiatry Residents, San Mateo, Calif., 1984; guest speaker Marin County Grand Jury Edn. Com., 1981; instr. Sonoma State U., 1984. Contbr. articles to profl. jours. Mem. Internat. Platform Assn. Democrat. Office: 100 Avram Ave Ste 105 Rohnert Park CA 94928-3100

ROBINSON, MARILYN L. O'BRYANT, small business owner; b. Pine Bluff, Ark., June 11, 1944; d. Edward and Geraldine (Henderson) O'Bryant; m. John H. Robinson, July 18, 1964; children: LaJuana Robinson-Brown, John H. II. BA, U. Ark., Pine Bluff, 1974; MSW, U. Ark., Little Rock, 1976; postgrad., Webster U., 1988, Washington U., 1991-92. Lic. clin. social worker, Mo. Psychiat. social worker Ark. State Hosp., Little Rock, 1976-78; sch. social worker Ferguson-Florrisant (Mo.) Sch. Dist., 1979-80; from psychotherapist II to psychotherapist III Provident Counseling, Inc., St. Louis, 1981-84, dist. dir. Crestwood and North County offices, 1984-86, v.p. core svcs., 1986-87, COO, sr. v.p., 1987-89; CEO, exec. dir. YWCA of Met. St. Louis, 1989-94; pres., owner Urban Solutions, Inc., St. Louis, 1994—; bd. dirs. People's Health Ctrs., Inc.; participant various leadership programs including Leadership St. Louis, 1990-91, Greater Mo.: Focus on Leadership, 1992, Leadership Am., 1993, Fordyce II Summit Racial Polarization/Diversity; presenter numerous seminars. Contbr. articles to profl. jours. Bd. pres. Ctrl. Cath. Community Sch., 1987-89; with St. Louis County Housing Resources Commn., 1991—, chair, 1992—; adv. coun. Salvation Army Adult Rehab. Ctr., 1991-93; editor's adv. coun. minority issues St. Louis Post-Distpatch, 1991-93 ; bd. dirs. Confluence St. Louis, 1992-93; adv. bd. Dropout Prevention Program St. Louis Pub. Schs.' Community Initiatives, 1992-93; active Success By Six Initiatives United Way, 1993; mem. project respond planning com. Vision of Children-At-Risk; v.p. Fair Minority Rels. Com.; mem. Marian Oldham scholarship com., U. Mo., St. Louis, adv. com. proposed relocation of MSW program; adv. group, early childhood devel./sch. readiness task force, social agy. team captain United Way. Mem. NAFE, NASW, Acad. Cert. Social Workers (cert.), Am. Mgmt. Assn., Mo. Assn. Social Workers, Downtown St. Louis (bd. dirs. 1991-93, govt. affairs com.), North County, Inc. (bd. dirs. 1991-93), Regional Commerce and Growth Assn., St. Louis Black Leadership Roundtable (econ. devel. com.), YWCA Met. Group for Exec. Dirs. U.S.A. Home: 12595 Tremblewood Dr Florissant MO 63033-4727 Office: Urban Solutions Inc Ste 204 7544 W Florissant Ave Saint Louis MO 63136

ROBINSON, MARY E. GOFF, retired historian, researcher; b. East Providence, R.I., Jan. 3, 1925; d. Newell Darius and Eva Agnes (Crane) Goff; m. Charles Albert Robinson, July 30, 1954; 1 child, Thomas Goff (dec.). BA, Wheaton Coll., Norton, Mass., 1947. Cataloger, fine arts Chester County Hist. Soc., West Chester, Pa., 1973-76; cataloger artifacts Chadds Ford (Pa.) Hist. Soc., 1992, 93. Co-author: (monograph) Ada Clendenin Williamson, 1983; author: (monograph) The Life of a Young Entrepreneur at the Turn of the Twentieth Century, 1992; editor: A Quiet Man from West Chester, 1974. Mem. Jr. League, Providence, 1957-62, Providence Athenaeum, 1955-63, Providence Preservation Soc., 1959-63, Brandywine Conservancy, Kennett Symphony Orch., Del. Symphony Orch., Winterthur Mus. Mem. AAUW, Chester County Hist. Soc. (bd. dirs. 1974-80), R.I. Hist. Soc. (trustee), Chester County Art Assn., Danville (Vt.) Hist. Soc., Hershey's Mill Country Club.

ROBINSON, MARY JO, pathologist; b. Spokane, Wash., May 26, 1954; d. Jerry Lee and Ann (Brodie) R. BS in Biology, Gonzaga U., 1976; DO, Coll. Osteo. Medicine and Surgery, U. Med. Health Scis., 1987. Diplomate Nat. Bd. Osteo. Med. Examiners, Am. Osteo. Bd. Pathology. Med. technologist Whitman Comty. Hosp., Colfax, Wash., 1977-81, Madigan Army Med. Ctr., Ft. Lewis, Wash., 1981-83; intern Des Moines Gen. Hosp., 1987-88; resident in pathology Kennedy Meml. Hosp., Stratford, N.J., 1988-92; asst. prof. pathology Sch. Medicine U. Medicine and Dentistry of N.J., Stratford, 1995—; staff pathologist Kennedy Meml. Hosp., Cherry Hill, N.J., 1995—; fellow in dermatopathology Jefferson Med. Coll., Phila., 1994. Fellow Coll. Am. Pathologists; mem. AMA, Am. Osteo. Coll. Pathologists (1st prize resident paper 1992), Am. Osteo. Assn., Am. Soc. Clin. Pathologists, N.J. Assn. Osteo. Physicians and Surgeons. Office: Kennedy Meml Hosp U Med Ctr 2201 Chapel Ave Cherry Hill NJ 08002

ROBINSON, MARY LOU, federal judge; b. Dodge City, Kans., Aug. 25, 1926; d. Gerald J. and Frances (Pierce) Strueber; m. A.J. Robinson, Aug. 28, 1949; children: Rebecca Aynn Gruhlkey, Diana Ceil, Matthew Douglas. B.A., U. Tex., 1948, LL.B., 1950. Bar: Tex. 1949. Ptnr. Robinson & Robinson, Amarillo, 1950-55; judge County Ct. County Ct. at Law, Potter County, Tex., 1955-59; judge (108th Dist. Ct.), Amarillo, 1961-73; assoc. justice Ct. of Civil Appeals for 7th Supreme Jud. Dist. of Tex., Amarillo, 1973-77; chief justice Ct. of Civil Appeals for 7th Supreme Jud. Dist. of Tex., 1977-79; U.S. dist. judge No. Dist. Tex., Amarillo, 1979—. Named Woman of Year Tex. Fedn. Bus. and Profl. Women, 1973. Mem. Nat. Assn. Women Lawyers, ABA, Tex. Bar Assn., Amarillo Bar Assn., Delta Kappa Gamma. Presbyterian. Office: US Dist Ct 205 E 5th Ave Rm 13248 Amarillo TX 79101-1563

ROBINSON, NAN SENIOR, not-for-profit organization consultant; b. Salt Lake City, Jan. 11, 1932; d. Clair Marcil Senior and Lillian (Worlton) Senior Davis; m. David Zav Robinson; Sept. 6, 1954; children: Marc S. Robinson, Eric S. Robinson. BA with hons., Mills Coll., 1952; MA, Harvard U., 1953. Spl. asst. to undersec. Dept. Housing and Urban Devel., Washington, 1966-69; asst. to the pres. U. Mass. Statewide System, Boston, 1970-73, v.p. for planning, 1973-78; dep. commr. Conn. Bd. Higher Edn., Hartford, 1978-81; v.p. adminstrn. The Rockefeller Found., N.Y.C., 1981-90; mem. governing coun. Rockefeller Archive Ctr., Pocantico Hills, N.Y., 1986-89; com. mem. Coun. on Founds. N.Y. Regional Assn. Grantmakers, 1985-89; mem. nat. advisory panel on governance Carnegie Found. for the Advancement of Teaching, Princeton, N.J., 1980-82. Trustee, chmn. fin. com. Inst. for Current World Affairs, Hanover, N.H., 1987-90; trustee Calif. Sch. Profl. Psychology, San Francisco, 1985—. Recipient Centennial award Am. Assn. U. Women Hartford Br., 1981; named Woman of Yr. Hartford YWCA, 1980; named to Centennial Honor List of 100 Women Barnard Coll., 1989. Mem. Soc. for Coll. and U. Planning (com. chmn. 1985-86, nominating com. 1980-85, regional rep. 1975-77), Harvard Club, Phi Beta Kappa. Home: 622 Greenwich St Apt 5B New York NY 10014

ROBINSON, NELL BRYANT, nutrition educator; b. Kopperl, Tex., Oct. 15, 1925; d. Basil Howell and Lelia Abiah (Duke) Bryant; m. Frank Edward Robinson, July 14, 1945 (dec.); 1 child, John Howell Robinson. B.S., N. Tex. State U., 1945; M.S., Tex. Woman's U., 1958, Ph.D., 1967. Registered dietitian, Tex. Tchr. Comanche High Sch., Tex., 1945-46, Kopperl High Sch., Tex., 1946-48; county extension agt. Agrl. Extension Service, Tex., 1948-56; prof. nutrition Tex. Christian U., Fort Worth, 1957-92, chmn. dept. nutrition and dietetics, 1985-91, ret., 1992. Pres., bd. dirs. Sr. Citizens Svcs. of Greater Tarrant County, 1990-91. Contbr. chpt. to book. Named Top Prof., Tex. Christian U. Mortar Bd., 1978. Mem. Am. Dietetic Assn. (del. 1983-88, ethics com. 1985-88, coun. edn. 1988-90, chmn. coun. on edn. divsn. edn. accreditation/approval 1989-90, medallion award 1990), Am. Home Econs. Assn., Tex. Dietetic Assn. (pres., 1972-73, Disting. Dietitian 1981), Tex. Home Econs. Assn. (pres. 1978-80, Home Economist of Yr. 1975). Club: Fort Worth Women's. Lodge: Order Eastern Star. Home: 5729 Wimbleton Way Fort Worth TX 76133-3651

ROBINSON, NELLIE MAE, land surveyor, county official; b. Louisville, July 14, 1945; d. Paul Edward and Mary Ellen (Flannary) De Rossett); m. William George, Dec. 19, 1965 (div. Aug. 1985). Student, St. Petersburg Jr. Coll., 1963-64, Clearwater Tech. Inst., 1964-65, 69, Sawyer Bus. Coll., Tampa, Fla., 1970; AA in Liberal Arts, Hillsborough C.C., 1975, A in Sci., 1977; postgrad., U. S. Fla., 1978. Cert. engring. technician, profl. land surveyor, Fla., cadastrist, Fla. Drafting technician Chesapeake & Potomac Tel. Co., Washington, 1965-66; engring. technician Reynolds, Smith & Hills, Jacksonville, Fla., 1966-68, Heidt & Assocs., Tampa, 1968-74; field supr. Cumbey & Fair, Clearwater, Fla., 1975-78; office mgr. Morris Land SurveyingLutz, Lutz, Fla., 1978-80; drafting supr. Office Property Appraiser Pasco County, Dade City, Fla., 1980-81; land surveyor Deltona Corp., Spring Hill, Fla., 1980-83; county surveyor, mgr. G.I.S., Geographic Info. Sys., New Port Richey, 1981—. Worker local polit. campaigns, Tampa, 1984, New Port Richey, 1990. Mem. Am. Congress on Surveying and Mapping, Fla. Soc. Profl. Land Surveyors, Surveyors in Local Govt. (founder, pres. 1992-93). Republican. Methodist. Home: 11150 Knotty Pine Dr New Port Richey FL 34654-1916 Office: Pasco County Survey Div 7432 Little Rd New Port Richey FL 34654-5520

ROBINSON, PATRICIA ANN, marketing educator; b. Tallulah, La., Sept. 30, 1952; d. Roosevelt Martin and Lorene Robinson. BA, Tarkio (Mo.) Coll., 1973; MBA, Prairie View (Tex.) A&M U., 1978; MS, Tex. So. U., 1980; PhD, Okla. State U., 1986. Cert. elem. tchr.; cert. home economist. Catalogue inventory specialist Montgomery Ward & Co., Kansas City, Mo., 1974-77; fiscal affairs asst. Prairie View (Tex.) A&M U., 1977-78; adminstrv. asst., instr. Tex. So. U., 1978-82; grad. asst. Okla. State U., Stillwater, 1980-84; cons. Kate's McGehee (Ark.) Tng. Ctr., 1985-86; assoc. prof. mktg. U. Ark., Fayetteville, 1984-87; asst. prof. mktg. U. Akron, Ohio, 1987-88, Tenn. Tech. U., 1988-90; chancellor scholar Fayetteville State U., 1990-91, chmn. dept. acctg., mktg. and mgmt., assoc. prof. mktg., 1990-91, chmn. dept. mgmt. and mktg., 1991-92; cons. Kate's McGehee (Ark.) Tng. Ctr., 1975-76. Recipient Acad. Advising Svc. award U. Ark., 1986. Mem. Am. Collegiate Retailing Assn., Am. Home Econs. Assn., Am. Mktg. Assn., Consumer Rsch. Assn., So. Mktg. Assn., Internat. Assn. Black Bus. Educators, Acad. Internat. Bus., Midsouth Mktg. Assn., Midwest Mktg. Assn., Tenn. Home Econs. Assn., Southwestern Mktg. Assn., Pi Sigma Epsilon, Durcury Hon. Soc., Beta Gamma Sigma (first v.p.), Delta Mu Delta, Durcury Hon. Soc. Democrat. Baptist. Home: 1501 Londonderry Pl Fayetteville NC 28301-2886 Office: Fayetteville State U Sch Bus And Econs Rm 233-234 Fayetteville NC 28301

ROBINSON, PATRICIA EILEEN, grain company executive; b. Odessa, Wash., Aug. 12, 1950; d. Herbert Harry and Montana Rose (Schorzman) Hardung; widowed; children: Matt, Jake, Nick. Grad. high sch., Harrington, Wash. Pres. Hardung, Inc., 1990—; asst. mgr. Women World Shops, 1994—; real estate agt., Wash. and Calif., 1983-87. Home: 659 W Brooks Rd Medical Lake WA 99022

ROBINSON, PATRICIA ELAINE, women's health nurse; b. St. Louis, June 30, 1955; d. Harold Winford and Robbie LaVeal (Ferguson) Hammett;

m. Kenneth M. Robinson, Nov. 18, 1978 (div.); children: Barry Christopher, Emily Vanessa; m. C. gilbert, Nov. 20, 1990. ADN, St. Louis Community Coll., 1987; student, Webster U., 1990—; cert. in forensic pathology, St. Louis U., 1975; cert. in pharmacology, St. Louis Coll. Health, 1984. Per diem float nurse St. Louis U. Hosp.; coord. ob-gyn. unit Group Health Plan, St. Louis; staff nurse Barnes Hosp., St. Louis; staff nurse dept. ob-gyn. Washington U. Sch. Medicine, St. Louis, 1990—; chief exec. study coord. women's health rsch. Obstetric & Gynecologic Diagnosis & Consultation, Florissant, Mo., 1992—; acting dir. Nurses for Reproductive Health Svcs., St. Louis, 1990—. Mem. NAFE, Nurse Assn. Am. Coll. Obstetrics and Gynecologists, Med. Group Mgmt. Assn., Nat. Assn. Nurse Practitioners Reproductive Health, Phi Theta Kappa. Office: Obstet & Gynecol Diagnosis & Consultation 1150 Graham Rd Ste 105 Florissant MO 63031

ROBINSON, SALLY WINSTON, artist; b. Detroit, Nov. 2, 1924; d. Harry Lewis and Lydia (Kahn) Winston; m. Eliot F. Robinson, June 28, 1949; children: Peter Eliot, Lydia Winston, Sarah Mitchell, Suzanne Finley. BA, Bennington Coll., 1947; postgrad. Cranbrook Acad. Art, 1949; grad. Sch. Social Work, Wayne U., 1948, MA, 1972; MFA, Wayne State U., 1973. Psychol. tester Detroit Bd. Edn., 1944; pyschol. counselor and tester YMCA, N.Y.C., 1946; social caseworker Family Service, Pontiac, Mich., 1947; instr. printmaking Wayne State U., Detroit, 1973—. One person shows U. Mich., 1973, Wayne State U., 1974, Klein-Vogol Gallery, 1974, Rina Gallery, 1976, Park McCullough House, Vt., 1976, Williams Coll., 1976, Arnold Klein Gallery, 1977; exhibited group shows Bennington Coll., Cranbrook Mus., Detroit Inst. Art, Detroit Artists Market, Soc. Women Painters, Soc. Arts and Crafts, Bloomfield Art Assn., Flint Left Bank Gallery, Balough Gallery, Detroit Soc. Women Painters, U. Mich., U. Ind., U. Wis., U. Pittsburg, Toledo Mus., Krannert Mus.; represented in permanent collections, Detroit, N.Y.C., Birmingham, Bloomfield Hills; tchr. children's art Detroit Inst. Art, 1949-50, now artistic advisor, bd. dirs. drawing and print orgn. Bd. dirs. Planned Parenthood, 1951—, mem. exec. bd., 1963—; bd. dirs. PTA, 1956-60, Roeper City and Country Sch., U. Mich. Mus. Art, 1978; trustee Putnam Hosp. Med. Research Inst., 1978; mem. Gov.'s Commn. Art in State Bldgs., 1978-79; mem. art and devel. coms. So. Vt. Art Ctr., 1987-88; mem. vol. com. Marie Selby Gardens. Mem. Detroit Artists Market (dir. 1956—), Bennington Coll. Alumnae Assn. (regional co-chmn. 1954), Detroit Soc. Women Painters, Birmingham Soc. Women Painters (pres. 1974-76), Bloomfield Art Assn. (program co-chmn. 1956), Founders Soc. Detroit Inst. Art., Village Women's Club (Birmingham, Mich.), Women's City Club (co-ordinator art shows Detroit 1950), Garden Club, Am. Club (Bennington, Vt., Sarasota, Fla.), Cosmopolitan (N.Y.C.). Unitarian. Home: 7 Monument Cir Bennington VT 05201-2134 also: 840 N Casey Key Rd Osprey FL 34229

ROBINSON, SANDRA LYNN, educator; b. Halifax, Can., Nov. 11, 1963; came to U.S., 1988; d. Graham Roland and Joyce Mary (Logan) R.; m. Navin Mithel, Aug. 13, 1993; 1 child, Alexandra Mithel. BA in Psychology, U. B.C., 1985, MS in Bus. Adminstrn., 1988; PhD in Bus. Adminstrn., Northwestern U., 1992. Lectr. Northwestern U., Evanston, Ill., 1989-92; asst. prof. mgmt. NYU, N.Y.C., 1992—. Contbr.a rticles to profl. jours. Northwestern U. fellow, 1988-92. Mem. Am. Psychol. Assn. (award 1991), Acad. Mgmt., Adminstrv. Sci. Assn. Can. (award 1993). Office: NYU Stern Sch Bus Mgmt Dept 44 W 4th St New York NY 10012

ROBINSON, SHARON E. MITCHELL, chemical engineer, researcher; b. Fayetteville, Tenn., Sept. 6, 1958; d. Lyndal and Wanda Ree (Storey) Mitchell; m. David Nicols Robinson, Mar. 24, 1979. BS in Chem. Engring., Tenn. Technol. U., Cookeville, 1980; MS, U. Tenn., Knoxville, 1985, PhD, 1992. Registered profl. engr., Tenn. Devel. engr. Oak Ridge Nat. Lab., 1980—. Contbr. chpt. to book, articles to profl. jours. Recipient Martin Marietta Energy System award, 1992, Tribute to Women award YWCA, Knoxville, 1990; named to Outstanding Young Women of Am., 1989. Mem. Am. Inst. Chem. Engrs. (pub. rels. chair, dir.), Soc. Women Engrs. (treas.), Soc. Profl. Engrs., Tenn. Soc. Profl. Engrs. (Young Engr. of Yr. 1990), Tau Beta Pi. Office: Oak Ridge Nat Lab PO Box 2007-6044 Oak Ridge TN 37830

ROBINSON, SUE LEWIS, federal judge; b. 1952. BA with highest honors, U. Del., 1974; JD, U. Pa., 1978. Assoc. Potter, Anderson & Corron, Wilmington, Del., 1978-83; asst. U.S. atty. U.S. Attys. Office, 1983-88; U.S. magistrate judge U.S. Dist. Ct. (Del. dist.), 1988-91, dist. judge, 1991—. Mem. Del. State Bar Assn. (sec. 1986-87). Office: US Dist Ct J Caleb Boggs Fed Bldg 844 King Street Rm 6124 Wilmington DE 19801*

ROBINSON, SUSAN MITTLEMAN, data processing executive; b. Bklyn., Nov. 18, 1941; d. Samuel and Ida (Priest) Mittleman; m. Sheldon N. Robinson, June 5, 1962; children: Edward Bruce, Nancy Michelle, Jonathan Scott, Karen Barbara, Judith Lynn. AAS in Computer Sci., BCC, Lincroft, N.J., 1981; BBA, CUNY, 1962; MS in Computer Sci., Fairleigh Dickinson U., 1983; postgrad., Seton Hall U., 1983-85. Engr. asst. United Technologies, East Hartford, Conn., 1962-64; programmer, systems analyst Litton Industries (Sweda), Pine Brook, N.J., 1981-83; asst. prof. data processing Mercer Coll., West Windsor, N.J., 1983-85; adj. instr. data processing Brookdale Community Coll., Lincroft, N.J., 1983—; coord. MIS N.J. Dept. Health, Trenton, N.J., 1985—, Novell Lan administr., 1994—; outsource cons. Medicare/Medicaid, Trenton, 1989—; cons. Health Care Fin. Authority, Balt., 1995—. Author (reference material) Info-Henco, 1987, Automated Survey Processing Environment Users Training Manual, 1993; developer computerized sys. to help patients and their family select a nursing home. Exec. bd. Temple Beth Am, Parsippany, N.J., 1972-80. Mem. SAS Users Group, N.J. DOH Prime Users Group. Office: NJ Dept Health CN 367 Trenton NJ 08625

ROBINSON, TERI LYNN, city official; b. Denver, Nov. 28, 1958; d. Lenwood and Jeanette M. Robinson. BS in Bus., Calif. State U., L.A., 1981; MPA, Calif. State U., Hayward, 1992. Adminstrv. analyst City of Berkeley, Calif., 1988-89, sr. mgmt. analyst, 1989-90, asst. to city mgr., 1990-93; adminstrv. svcs. mgr. II City of Oakland, Calif., 1993—. Mem. Nat. Forum for Black Pub. Adminstrs. (bd. dirs. 1991—, Outstanding Young Black Pub. Adminstr. 1992). Office: City of Oakland Office Planning & Bldg 1330 Broadway 2nd Fl Oakland CA 94612

ROBISON, BARBARA ANN, retired newspaper editor; b. Portland, Oreg., July 15, 1933; d. Louis Keith and Marjorie (Work) R.; 1 child, Nancy. Student, Coll. Idaho, 1951-54, U. Utah, 1968-70. Reporter Caldwell (Idaho) News Tribune, 1951-54; sports editor LaGrande (Oreg.) Evening-Observer, 1954-55; reporter Idaho Daily Statesman, Boise, 1955-57; asst. women's editor Tacoma (Wash.) News Tribune, 1958-59; lifestyle editor Salt Lake Tribune, 1967-93. Episcopalian. Home: 4210 Caroleen Way Salt Lake City UT 84124-2507

ROBISON, BARBARA JANE, tax accountant; b. Bkln., Oct. 17, 1924; d. Matthews and Sara (Birnbaum) Brilliant; m. Morris Moses Robison, Aug. 30, 1945; 1 child, Susan Kay. BS, Ohio State U., 1945; MBA, Xavier U., 1976. CPA. Acct. Antenna Research Lab. Inc., Columbus, Ohio, 1948-51; office mgr. Master Distributors, Inc., Columbus, 1951-57; treas. Antlab Inc., Columbus, 1957-69; tax acct. AccuRay Corp., Columbus, 1969-76, tax mgr., 1976-92; pvt. practice Powell, Ohio, 1992—. Mem. AICPA, Ohio Soc. CPA's, Am. soc. Women Accts. (pres. 1978-79). Home: 1888 Jewett Rd Powell OH 43065-8988 Office: Ohio 04-1-16510 1888 Jewett Rd Powell OH 43065

ROBISON, PAULA JUDITH, flutist; b. Nashville, June 8, 1941; d. David Victor and Naomi Florence R.; m. Scott Nickrenz, Dec. 29, 1971; 1 child, Elizabeth Hadley Amadea Nickrenz. Student, U. So. Calif., 1958-60; B.S., Juilliard Sch. Music, 1963. Founding artist, player Chamber Music Soc., N.Y.C., 1970-90, N.Y. Côro Band, 1994; co-dir. chamber music Spoleto Festival, Charleston, S.C., 1978-88; Filene artist-in-residence Skidmore Coll., Saratoga Springs, N.Y., 1988-89; mem. faculty New Eng. Conservatory Music, 1991—. Soloist with various major orchs., including N.Y. Philharm.; player, presenter Concerti di Mezzogiorno, Spoleto (Italy) Festival, 1978—; commd. flute concertos by Leon Kirchner, Toru Takemitsu, Oliver Knussen, Robert Beaser, Kenneth Frazelle; author: The Paula Robison Flute Warmups Book, 1989, The Andersen Collection, 1994, Paula Robison Masterclass: Paul Hindemith, 1995; recs. on CBS Masterworks, Music Masters, Vanguard Classics, New World Records, Omega, Arabesque, Sony Classical. Recipient First prize Geneva Internat. Competition, 1966, Adelaide Ristori prize, 1987; named Musician of Month, Musical Am., 1979, House Musician for Isamu Noguchi Garden Mus., N.Y.C., 1988; Martha Baird Rockefeller grantee, 1966; Nat. Endowment for Arts grantee, 1978, 86; Fromm Found. grantee, 1980; Housewright Eminent scholar Fla. State U., 1990-91. Mem. Sigma Alpha Iota (hon.). Office: care Shaw Concerts 1900 Broadway New York NY 10023-7004

ROBISON, SUSAN MILLER, psychologist, educator, consultant; b. Chgo., Nov. 15, 1945; d. William Louis and Constance Mary (Maloney) Miller; m. Philip Dean Robison, Dec. 27, 1969; 1 child, Christine Alyssa. BS, Loyola U., Chgo., 1967; MS, Ohio U., 1969, PhD, 1971. Lic. psychologist, Md. Asst. prof. psychology Ohio U., Lancaster, 1970-72; prof. psychology Coll. Notre Dame, Balt., 1972—; pvt. practice Ellicott City, Md., 1982—; leadership cons. Nat. Coun. Cath. Women, Washington, 1987—. Author: Sharing Our Gifts, 1987, 2d edit., 1992, Discovering Our Gifts, 1989, Thinking and Writing in College, 1991. Troop leader Girl Scouts U.S.A., Ellicott City, 1982-85, mem. adv. bd. Girl Scouts Central Md., 1987-88; mem. adv. bd. Archdiocese of Balt., 1986. Mem. Am. Psychol. Assn., Am. Assn. Sex Educators, Counselors and Therapists, Assn. for Advancement Behavior Therapy. Home: 3725 Font Hill Dr Ellicott City MD 21042-4932

ROBISON, WILMA N., building products company professional; b. Noblesville, Ind., Aug. 22, 1943; d. Wilson Reeves and Mary Elizabeth (Dixon) Phillips; m. William Austin Robison, Apr. 25, 1965 (div. Dec. 1975); 1 child, Andrew. Sales sec. Liberty Mut. Ins., Indpls., 1961-64; prodn. sec. Firestone Indsl. Products, Noblesville, 1964-68; fin. sec. J.I. Case Co., Indpls., 1969-80; various positions in sales, tech., customer svc., fin. svc. Firestone Bldg. Products, Carmel, Ind., 1981-94, sr. analyst. Facilitator Prevail, Inc., Noblesville, 1989—; dir. Christian edn. 1st Ch. of God, Noblesville. Named Vol. of Yr., Prevail, Inc., 1990. Democrat.

ROBLE, CAROLE MARCIA, accountant; b. Bklyn., Aug. 22, 1938; d. Carl and Edith (Brown) Dusowitz; m. Richard F. Roble, Nov. 30, 1969. MBA with distinction, N.Y. Inst. Tech., 1984. CPA, Calif., N.Y. Compt. various orgns. various orgns., 1956-66; staff acct. ZTBG CPA'S, L.A., 1966-67; sr. acct. J.H. Cohn & Co., Newark, 1967-71; prin. Carole M. Roble, CPA, South Hempstead, N.Y., 1971-90; ptnr. Roble & Libman, CPAs, Baldwin, N.Y., 1990-93; prin. Carole M. Roble, CPA, Baldwin, N.Y., 1993—; speaker, moderator Found. for Acctg. Edn., N.Y., 1971—; lectr. acctg. various schs. including New Sch., Queens Coll., Empire State Coll., Touro Coll., N.Y. Inst. Tech., N.Y.C., Parsons Sch., 1971—. Guest various N.Y. radio and TV stas. Treas. Builders Devel. Corp. of L.I., Westbury, N.Y., 1985; dir. Women Econ. Devels. of L.I., 1985-87. Recipient Sisterhood citation Nat. Orgn. Women, 1984, 85, cert. of Appreciation Women Life Underwriters, 1988, Women in Sales, 1982, 84; named top Tax Practitioner Money Mag., 1987. Mem. AICPA, Am. Acct. Assn. (auditing sect.), Am. Soc. Women Accts. (pres. N.Y. chpt. 1980-81), Am. Woman's Soc. CPAs, Nat. Conf. CPA Practitioners (trustee L.I. chpt. 1981-82, sec. 1982-83, treas. 1983-84, v.p. 1984-85, 1st v.p. 1985-86, pres. 1986-87, nat. nominating com. 1983-84, 88-89, nat. continuing profl. edn. chmn. 1988-90, nat. treas. 1991-94, nat. v.p. 1994—), Calif. Soc. CPAs, N.Y. State Soc. CPAs (bd. dirs. Nassau chpt. 1981-86, 91-93, bd. dirs. profl. devel., 1982-86, sec., mem. fin. acctg. standards com. 1990—), Kiwanis (program chmn. County Seat chpt. 1989-90, sec. 1990-91, pres. 1991-92), Baldwin C. of C. (treas. 1990-93). Home: 626 Willis St Hempstead NY 11550-8000

ROBLEE, MARTHA ANN, librarian; b. Noblesville, Ind., July 9, 1949; d. Muret Eads and Elsie Fern (Bucklew) Nugent; m. Thomas Allen Roblee, May 27, 1972. BA, Ind. U., 1971, MLS, 1972. Cert. libr., Ind. Asst. Ind. State Libr., Indpls., 1972-73, adminstrv. libr., 1973-76, libr. cons., 1976-86, head ext. divsn., 1986-89, assoc. dir. ext. svcs., 1989-91, assoc. dir. network coord., 1991—. Neighborhood chair Am. Sewing Guild, Indpls., 1993, 94. Mem. ALA, Ind. Libr. Fedn. (chair archives task force 1984-89, chair conf. local arrangements 1986, Spl. Svcs. award 1990). Office: Ind State Libr 140 N Senate Ave Indianapolis IN 46204-2296

ROBOHM, PEGGY ADLER (PEGGY ADLER), researcher, consultant, writer, illustrator; b. N.Y.C., Feb. 10, 1942; d. Irving and Ruth (Relis) Adler; m. Jeremy Abbott Walsh, June 1, 1962 (div. Dec. 1968); children: Tenney Whedon, Avery Denison (Mrs. Adam Lapidus); m. Richard A. Robohm, Dec. 24, 1976 (div. May 1993). Student, Bennington Coll., 1959-60, Columbia U., 1962. Illustrator, author childrens books, 1958—; agt. Jan J. Agy., Inc., N.Y.C., 1981-82; freelance talent scout Cuzzins Mgmt., N.Y.C., 1982-83; personal mgmt. and pub. rels. cons. Madison, Conn., 1983-93; logistics ticket sales and mgmt. the world premiere "Butch Cassidy and the Sundance Kid", 1969; rsch. assoc. SIG Steve Fredericksen, Pvt. Investigator, Conn. and N.Y., 1990—; investigative researcher, writer, lit. cons., 1986—, pub. speaker, 1991—; asst. investigator Ho. of Reps. October Surprise Task Force, Washington, 1992. Author, illustrator: The Adler Book of Puzzles and Riddles, 1962, The 2nd Adler Book of Puzzles and Riddles, 1963, Metric Puzzles, 1977, Math Puzzles, 1978, Geography Puzzles, 1979; author: Hakim's Connection, 1988; co-author: Skull and Bones: The Skeleton in Bush's Closet?, 1988; illustrator numerous books including (Humane Soc. of U.S. pubs.) Pet Care, 1974, Caring for Your Cat, 1974, Hot and Cold, 1959, Numbers New and Old, 1960, Do a Zoomdo, 1975, Reading Fundamentals for Teen-Agers, 1973; graphic designer various book covers, posters, co. logos: PR, Sweetie, Baby, Cookie, Honey (Freddie Gershon), 1986; researcher Passion and Prejudice: A Family Memoir (Sallie Bingham), 1989, The Village Voice, 1991, 92, numerous others; cons. The President's Private Eye: The Journey of Detective Tony U. From N.Y.P.D. to the Nixon White House (Anthony Ulasewicz with Stuart McKeever), 1990; cons., researcher Bush's Boys Club: Skull and Bones, 1990; cons. Spy Saga (Philip H. Melanson), 1990; contbr. Lies of Our Times; licensee/story cons. 60 Minutes, 1991; cons., researcher London Sunday Times, 1991; rsch. asst. The Connecticut Cowboy, 1992; rsch. and document retrieval CNN, Kroll Assocs., 1992; contbr. The Independent, London, 1994. Founder Shoreline Youth Theatre, Inc., 1979, mem. adv. bd., 1981-86; bd. dirs. The Greens Condominium Assn. of Branford, Conn., 1975-78, Arts Coun. Greater New Haven, 1971-73, Planned Parenthood of Greater New Haven, 1972-73, Assassination Archives and Rsch. Ctr., Washington, 1990—; v.p., bd. dirs. Pub. Info. Rsch., Washington, 1989; hon. mem. Forgotten Families. Mem. Shoreline Sailing Club (bd. dirs., mem. chmn. 1994, 95), Assassination Archives and Rsch. Ctr. (Washington bd. dirs. 1990—), Conn. Soc. Genealogists Inc., Yale Club of New Haven, AFIO. Home and Office: 32 Founders Vlg Clinton CT 06413-1837

ROBOLD, ALICE ILENE, mathematician, educator; b. Delaware County, Ind., Feb. 7, 1928; d. Earl G. and Margaret Rebecca (Summers) Hensley; m. Virgil G. Robold, Aug. 21, 1955; 1 son, Edward Lynn. B.S., Ball State U., 1955, M.A., 1960, Ed.D., 1965. Substitute elem. tchr. Am. Elem. Sch., Augsburg, Germany, 1955-56; instr. Ball State U., Muncie, Ind., 1960-61; teaching fellow Ball State U., 1961-64, asst. prof. math. scis., 1964-69, assoc. prof., 1969-76, prof., 1976—. Mem. Nat. Coun. Tchrs. Math., Ind. Coun. Tchrs. Math., Sch. Sci. and Math. Assn., Pi Lambda Theta. Mem. Ch. of God. Office: Ball State U Dept Math Scis Muncie IN 47306

ROBY, CHRISTINA YEN, data processing specialist, educator; b. Shanghai, China; came to U.S., 1980; d. Hai Zhou and Yun Qui (Zhang) Yen; m: Ronald L. Roby; 1 child, Colin H. BS, Jiao-Tung U., Shanghai, 1957; MS, U. Balt., 1986. Lic. engr., Peoples Republic of China. Chief mech. engr. Shenyang Valve Rsch. Inst., China, 1958-1980; computer system operator U. Balt., 1984, rsch. asst., 1984-86; sales assoc. V. F. Assocs., Inc., Balt., 1986-88; system analyst Computer Data Systems, Inc., Rockville, Md., 1988-89; data processing specialist Dept. of Health and Mental Hygiene, Balt., 1989—; instr. Community Coll. of Balt., 1986, 88; cons. Nat. Ins. Agency, Balt., 1988. Author: Guide to Using MS-DOS, 1988; contbr. author Japanese-Chinese Electrical Mechanical Industry Dictionary, 1980; transl., editor Analysis of Gas, Impurities and Carbide in Steel, 1961; contbr. articles to profl. jours. Vol. tutor U. Balt., 1983; vol. tchr. Chinese Lang. Sch., Balt., 1985-86, 90—; lectr. Internat. Festival Exhbn., 1986. Recipient cert. of appreciation Chinese Lang. Sch., 1986. Mem. NAFE, Sci. and Tech. Assn., Beta Gamma Sigma, Delta Mu Delta.

ROCHA, OSBELIA MARIA JUAREZ, librarian; b. Odessa, Tex., Aug. 3, 1950; d. Tomas R. and Maria Socorro (Garcia) Juarez; m. Ricardo Rocha, July 8, 1972; children: Nidia Selina, René Ricardo. AA, Odessa Coll., 1970; BA, Sul Ross State U., 1972; MA, Tex. A & I U., 1977; MLS, Tex. Woman's U., 1991. Cert. tchr., reading specialist, Tex. Math. tchr. Del Rio (Tex.) Jr. High Sch., 1972-78; reading tchr. Del Rio High Sch., 1978-79; math. tchr. Ector High Sch., Odessa, 1979-81, Permian High Sch., Odessa, 1981-88; libr. Blackshear Elem. Magnet Sch., Odessa, 1988-93, Bowie Jr. High Sch., Odessa, 1993—. Reviewer of children's and adolescents' books for MultiCultural Rev.; author articles. Mem. NEA, Internat. Reading Assn., Nat. Coun. Tchrs. Math., Tex. State Tchrs. Assn., Tex. Reading Assn., Tex. Libr. Assn., Tex. Coun. Tchrs. Math., West Tex. Assn. Bilingual Edn., Ector County Ind. Sch. Dist. Media Specialists (sec. 1990-91), Permian Basin Reading Assn., Delta Kappa Gamma, Beta Phi Mu. Roman Catholic. Home: 1717 W 24th St Odessa TX 79763 Office: Bowie Jr High Sch 500 W 21st St Odessa TX 79761

ROCHA-WEAVER, BETSY, pharmaceutical sales executive; b. Decatur, Ala., Aug. 21, 1960; d. Manuel Medrios and Betty Jean (Dale) R.; m. Jere H. Weaver, Jan. 12, 1991. Attended, Auburn U., 1978-81; BSN, U. Ala., 1984. RN. RN coord. Decatur Med. Surg. Ctr., 1984-89; RN hypertension specialist Dr. John A. Hollifield, Nashville, 1989-90; RN coord. Centennial Heart Ctr., Nashville, 1990-92; sales rep. Lederle Labs., Wayne, N.J., 1992—. Recipient Gold Cup Am. Cyanamid, 1992, 93. Republican. Roman Catholic. Home: 4406 Murray Dr Decatur AL 35603

ROCHE, RUTH ANNE, artistic director; b. San Francisco, Aug. 14, 1964; d. Robert Francis and Donald Geraldine (McIsaac) R. Student, U. Calif., Santa Barbara. Cert. cosmetologist, Calif., N.Y. Hairdresser, educator Apace Hair Design, Santa Barbara, 1985-88; advanced dept. educator Pivot Point Internat., Chgo., 1988-90; mem. nat. artistic team Trevor Sorbie Internat., L.A. and London, 1988—, mem. nat. artistic team trainer, 1991—, nat. artistic dir., 1993—. Recipient Industry Leader award Internat. Beauty Show, 1994; named Top Rising Star, I.B.S. Beauty Press, 1994. Home: 94 Finch Ln # 2B Islip NY 11751

ROCHELEAU, BARBARA SCHWARTZ, library media specialist; b. Washington, Feb. 10, 1944; d. Jerome and Frances (Greenbaum) Schwartz; m. Dennis William Rocheleau, Apr. 12, 1968; children: Shana Renée, Lauren Michele. BS in Elem. Edn., U. Md., 1965; MLS, So. Conn. State U., 1989. Cert. sch. libr. media specialist, Conn. Tchr. North Chevy Chase (Md.) Elem. Sch., Montgomery County Pub. Schs., 1965-68; tchr. devel. reading Van Antwerp Mid. Sch., Niskayuna (N.Y.) Pub. Schs., 1968-72; reference libr. Fairfield (Conn.) Pub. Libr., 1989-91; sch. libr. media specialist Fairfield Pub. Schs., 1990—; critical reviewer The Book Report, Linworth Pub., Inc., Worthington, Ohio, 1991—. Mem. Rep. Town Meeting, Fairfield, 1987-91; dist. leader Fairfield Dem. Town Com., 1988-89; pres. Fairfield High Sch. PTA, 1989-90. Mem. ALA, Conn. Libr. Assn., Conn. Ednl. Media Assn., AAUW, Conn. Audubon Soc., Nat. Coun. Jewish Women (pres. 1981-82), Beta Phi Mu. Home: 460 Papurah Rd Fairfield CT 06432

ROCHELEAU, BETH ANN, printing company representative; b. Ft. Rucker, Ala., Mar. 24, 1963; d. David Bernard and Pamela Jane (Steele) Bradley. BA in English, U. N.H., 1985. Sales rep. Dartmouth Printing Co., Hanover, N.H., 1986—; speaker at pub. seminars. Contbr. articles to profl. publs.; inventor printing implement. Mem. Nat. Abortion Rights Action League; fundraiser Westmonte Recreation Ctr., Altamonte Springs, Fla., 1987-89; mem. Literacy Vols. of Am. Mem. NOW, NAFE, Am. Mgmt. Assn., Am. Soc. Assn. Execs., Fla. Mag. Assn. (bd. dirs., Charlie awards 1990), Soc. Nat. Assn. Pubs., Toastmasters. Democrat. Address: 1153 Davidson Rd Lexington SC 29072

ROCK, ANGELA, volleyball player; b. Carlsbad, Calif., Oct. 15, 1963. BA in Psychology, San Diego State U., 1994. Fire-fighter San Diego; profl. volleyball tour player; mem. U.S.A. Nat. Team, 1987-90. Winner bronze medal Pan Am. Games, 1987; named USVBA Most Valuable Player, 1987, WPVA Best Hitter, 1991, Winner of the Miller Lite Ice Cup. Mem. Assn. Volleyball Profls., Women's Profl. Volleyball Assn. Office: care Assn Volleyball Profls 15260 Ventura Blvd Ste 2250 Sherman Oaks CA 91003

ROCK, GAIL ANN, obstetrics/gynecology nurse; b. Maquokela, Iowa, Mar. 24, 1960; d. Robert William and Mary Anne (Franzen) Scheckel; m. William Beale Rock III, June 6, 1981; 1 child, William Beale IV. Chiropractic Asst., Palmer Coll. Chiropractic, Davenport, Iowa, 1979; AAS in Nursing, North County Community Coll., Saranac Lake, N.Y., 1987; student, SUNY, Plattsburg, 1992—. Cert. resolve thru sharing counselor, inpatient obstet. nurse; cert. childbirth educator. Staff nurse ob-gyn. Adriondack Med. Ctr., Saranac Lake, N.Y., 1987-90, nurse mgr. ob-gyn., 1990—; group educator sibling and new parent classes, Saranac Lake, 1991—. Mem. NAACOG, AWHONN, NAFE. Home: RD 1 Box 252 Lake Clear NY 12945 Office: Adirondack Med Ctr Old Lake Colby Rd Saranac Lake NY 12983

ROCKAFELLOW, DEBORAH S., career planning administrator; b. Red Bank, N.J., Dec. 17, 1954; d. Louis S. and Shirley M. (Krapf) Van Zandt; m. Phillip E. Rockafellow. BS, Monmouth Coll., 1976; MEd, Rutgers U., 1983, EdD, 1992. Bus. educator high schs., adult schs., community colls., N.J., 1977-89; edn. program specialist N.J. State Dept. Edn., Trenton, 1989-91; supr. career devel. Paterson (N.J.) Pub. Schs., 1993—; teaching asst. Rutgers U., 1987-88. Editor Bus. Edn. Forum, 1993, 94. With USCGR, 1973-94. Mem. ASCD, AAUW, Am. Vocat. Assn., N.J. Bus. Edn. Assn. (exec. bd. 1986-90, pres. 1994-95, first v.p. 1992-93, pres.-elect 1993-94), Res. Officers Assn., Phi Delta Kappa. Home: 18 Timber Rd Edison NJ 08820-3221 Office: Paterson Pub Schs 33-35 Church St Paterson NJ 07505

ROCKBURNE, DOROTHEA G., artist; b. Montreal, Que., Can. Student, Black Mountain Coll. Milton and Sally Avery Disting. prof. Bard Coll., 1986; trustee Ind. Curators Inc., N.Y., Art in Gen.; artist in residence Am. Acad. in Rome, 1991; vis. artist Skowhegan Sch. Printing and Sculpture, 1984. One-person shows include Sonnabend Gallery, Paris, 1971, New Gallery, Cleve., 1972, Bykert Gallery, N.Y.C., 1970, 72, 73, Galleria Toselli, Milan, Italy, 1972, 73, 74, Galleria D'Arte, Bari, Italy, 1972, Lisson Gallery, London, 1973, Daniel Weinberg Gallery, San Francisco, 1973, Galerie Charles Kriwin, Brussels, 1975, Galleria Schema, Florence, Italy, 1973, 75, 92, John Weber Gallery, N.Y.C., 1976, 78, Galleria la Polena, Geona, Italy, 1977, Tex. Gallery, Houston, 1979, 80, 81, Xavier Fourcade Gallery, N.Y.C., 1980, 82, 83, 85, 86, David Bellman, Toronto, 1980, 81, Margo Leavin, Calif., 1982, Arts Club of Chgo., 1987, André Emmerich Gallery, N.Y.C., 1988, 89, 91, 92, 94, 95, 10 yr. retrospective Rose Art Mus., 1989, P. Fong & Spratt Galleries, San Jose, Calif., 1991, Sony Music Hdqs., N.Y.C., 1993, Frederick Spratt Gallery, San Jose, 1994; group shows include Whitney Mus. Am. Art, 1970, 73, 77, 79, 82, Mus. Modern Art, Buenos Aires, 1971, Kolner Kunst Market, Cologne, Germany, 1971, Stedelijk Mus., Holland, 1971, Spoleto (Italy) Festival, 1972, Palazzo Taverna, Rome, 1973, Nat. Gallery Victoria, Melbourne, Australia, 1973, Art Gallery NSW, Sydney, 1973, Auckland (New Zealand) City Art Gallery, 1973, Inst. Contemporary Art, London, 1974, Mus. d'Arte de la Ville, Paris, 1975, Galerie Aronowitsch, Stockholm, 1975, Stadtiches Mus., Manchengladbach, Germany, 1975, Galleria D'Arte Moderna, Bologna, Italy, 1975, Art Gallery Ont., Toronto, Can., 1975, Mus. Fine Art, Houston, 1975, Contemporary Arts Ctr., Cin., 1973, 75, 81, Mus. Contemporary Art, Chgo., 1971, 77, 86, Corcoran Gallery of Art, Washington, 1975, 87, Städtisches Mus., Leverkusen, Germany, 1975, Cannaviella Studio d'Arte Rome, 1976, Phila. Coll. Art, 1976, 83, Balt. Mus. Art, 1976, New Mus., N.Y.C., 1977, 80, 84, 83, Renaissance Soc. of U. Chgo., 1976, Lowe Art Mus., U. Miami, Fla., 1976, Inst. Contemporary Art, Boston, 1976, Seibu Mus. Art, Tokyo, 1976, N.Y. State Mus., Albany, 1977, Drawing Ctr., 1977, Kansas City (Mo.) Art Inst., 1977, Smithsonian Inst., Washington, 1977, Kassel, Fed. Republic Germany, 1972, 77, Ackland Art Ctr., Chapel Hill, N.C., 1979, 84, Milw. Art Ctr., 1978, 81, Biblioteca Nacional, Madrid, 1980, Gulbenkian Mus., Lisbon, Portugal, 1980, Bklyn. Mus., 1981, 89, Guggenheim Mus., 1982, 88, 89, Albright Knox Art Gallery, Buffalo, 1979, 80, 88, 89, Kuustforeningen Mus., Copenhagen, 1980, Venice Biennale, 1980, Cranbrook (Mich.) Acad. Art, 1981, Mus. Fine Arts, Boston, 1983, Contemporary Arts Mus., Houston, 1983, Norman Mackenzie Art Gallery, U. Regina, Sask., Can., 1983, Galleriet, Sweden, 1983-84, Seattle Art Mus., 1979-84, Nat. Mus. Art, Osaka, Japan, 1984, Fogg Art Mus., Cambridge, Mass., 1984, Am. Acad. and Inst. Arts and Letters, N.Y.C., 1984, 87, L.A. County Mus. Art, 1984, 86, Wadsworth Atheneum, Hartford, Conn., 1981, 84, Evehart Mus., Pa.,

1984, Grey Art Gallery, NYU, 1977, 84, 87, Avery Ctr. Arts, Bard Coll., N.Y., 1985, 87-88, Stamford (Conn.) Mus., 1985, Aldrich Mus., Conn., 1979, 82, Bronx Mus. Arts, N.Y.C., 1985, High Mus., Atlanta, 1975, 81, Phila. Mus. Art, 1986, Nat. Gallery Art, Washington, 1984, Mus. Art, Ft. Lauderdale, Fla., 1986, Nat. Mus. Women in Art, Washington, 1987, Xavier Fourcade Gallery, 1983, 87, L.A. County Mus. Modern Art, 1986-87, The Hague, The Netherlands, 1986, Carnegie-Mellon Art Gallery, Pitts., 1979, 87, Balt. Mus. Art, 1975, 76, 88, Ctr. for Fine Arts, Miami, 1989, Milw. Art Mus., 1989, Cin. Art Mus., 1989, New Orleans Mus., 1989, Denver Art Mus., 1989, Parrish Art Mus., South Hampton, N.Y., 1990, 91, Margo Leavin Gallery, L.A., 1991, Mus. of Modern Art, N.Y.C., 1991, Guild Hall Mus., East Hampton, N.Y., 1991, Am. Acad., Rome, 1991, Mus. Contemporary Art, L.A., 1991, Hunter Coll., N.Y., 1991, Centro Cultural/Arte Contemporanea, Mexico City, 1991, Hilton, San Jose, Calif., 1992, Hillwood Art Mus., L.I., N.Y., 1992, Am. Acad. and Inst. Arts and Letters, 1992, Neuberger Mus., 1992, Statue of Liberty Group, 1993, Foster Harmans Galliers of Am. Art, Sarasota, Fla., 1993, Kohn-Abrams Gallerie, L.A., 1993, The Gallery at Bristol Myers Squibb, N.J., 1993, Friends of Art and Preservation in Embassies, N.Y.C., 1993, Just Art, N.Y.C., 1993, Mus. Modern Art, N.Y.C., 1994, TZ Art and Co., N.Y.C., Andre Emmerich Gallery, N.Y.C., 1993, Nat. Gallery of Art, Washington, 1994, Fred Spratt Gallery, San José, Calif., 1994, RAAB Galarie, Berlin, 1994, Gallary at Bristol Myer Squibb, N.J., 1994, Moma, N.Y.C., 1994, N.Y. Studio Sch., N.Y.C., 1995, Aldrich Mus., Conn., 1995; represented in permanent collections Milw. Art Ctr., Mus. Modern Art N.Y.C., Fogg Mus., Cambridge, Mass., Phila. Mus. Art, High Mus. Art, Atlanta, Houston Mus. Fine Arts, Corcoran Gallery, Washington, Phila. Art Inst., Mpls. Art Mus., Met. Mus. Art, N.Y.C., Guggenheim Mus., N.Y.C., Ludwig Mus., Aachen, Fed. Republic Germany, Holladay, Washington, Saatchi, London, Bard, Albright-Knox Art Gallery, Buffalo, Whitney Mus. Am. Art, N.Y.C., U. Mich., Ann Arbor, Ohio State U., Columbus, Gilman Paper Co., N.Y., Auckland (New Zealand) City Art Mus., Portland (Oreg.) Art Mus., Aaken Art Mus., Oberlin, Ohio, Highhold Internat., S. Africa, U. Ohio Art Gallery, Columbus, HHK Charitable Found., Milw., Art Gallery Ont., Toronto, Can., Nat. Mus. Women in Art, Washington, Chase Manhattan Bank, N.Y.C., Hilton Hotel, San Jose, Calif., Sony Music Hdqs. Mem. artists adv. bd. New Mus. of Contemporary Art, N.Y.C.; trustee Ind. Curators, N.Y.C. Recipient Witowsky prize 72d Am. Exhbn., Art Inst., Chgo., 1976, Creative Arts award Brandeis U., 1985, Bard Coll., 1986; Guggenheim fellow, 1972; Nat. Endowment Arts grantee, 1974, Am. Acad., Rome, 1991.

ROCKEFELLER, MARGARETTA FITLER MURPHY (HAPPY ROCKEFELLER), widow of former vice president of U.S.; m. Nelson Aldrich Rockefeller (dec.); children: James B. Murphy, Margaretta H. Bickford, Carol Murphy Lyden, Malinda Murphy Menotti, Nelson A. Rockefeller, Jr., Mark F. Rockefeller. Dir. Archer-Daniels-Midland Co., Decatur, Ill.; alt. rep. of U.S. to 46th Session of UN Gen. Assembly, 1991, 47th Session, 1992.

ROCKEFELLER, MARY FRENCH (MRS. LAURANCE S. ROCKEFELLER), association executive; b. N.Y.C., May 1, 1910; d. John and Mary Montague (Billings) French; m. Laurance Spelman Rockefeller, Aug. 15, 1934; children—Laura Rockefeller Chasin, Marion Rockefeller Weber, Lucy Rockefeller Waletzky, Laurance. Student, Vassar Coll., 1927-29, Art Students League N.Y.C., 1929-34. Mem. nat. bd. YWCA, 1951-88, trustee, 1988—; chmn. Am. Centennial Observance and Celebration, 1955, co-chmn. nat. convocation on racial justice, 1972; chmn. World Service Council, 1958-64, chmn. world relations com., 1964-73. Mem. coun. Found. Child Devel.; trustee Spelman Coll., Atlanta, 1946-70, hon. trustee, 1970—, mem. exec. com.; trustee Whitney Mus. of Am. Art, 1965-89, Gordon-Conwell Theol. Sem., 1976—, United Bd. For Christian Higher Edn. in Asia, 1989—, Woodstock Hist. Soc., Calvin Coolidge Found.; trustee YWCA of City N.Y., 1971-84, hon. bd. dirs., 1984—; trustee Fgn. Policy Assn., 1977-86, hon. trustee, 1986—; mem. distbn. com. N.Y. Community Trust, 1969—; bd. dirs. N.Y. Community Fund, Inc., 1969—; mem. adminstrv. bd. Meml. Sloan-Kettering Cancer Center, 1976—. Recipient Gold medal Nat. Inst. Social Scis., 1972, Ambassador award YWCA of the U.S.A., 1993. Mem. N.Y. Zool. Soc., Hort. Soc. N.Y., Met. Mus. Art, Mus. Modern Art, Philharmonic Symphony, Park Assn. N.Y.C., Women's Nat. Republican Club. Clubs: Women's City (N.Y.C.), Cosmopolitan (N.Y.C.), Colony (N.Y.C.). Home: 30 Rockefeller Pla Rm 5600 New York NY 10112

ROCKEFELLER, SHARON PERCY, broadcast executive; b. Oakland, Calif., Dec. 10, 1944; d. Charles H. and Jeanne Dickerson Percy; m. John D. Rockefeller IV; children: John, Valerie, Charles, Justin. BA cum laude, Stanford U.; LLD (hon.), U. Charleston, 1977, Beloit Coll., 1978; LHD (hon.), West Liberty State Coll., 1980, Hamilton Coll., 1982, Wheeling Coll., 1984. Founder, chmn. Mountain Artisans, 1968-78; chmn. Corp. Pub. Broadcasting, Washington, 1981-84; bd. dirs. Stas. WETA-TV-FM, Washington, 1987-89, pres., 1989—; bd. dirs. State. WETA-TV-FM, Washington, 1987-89, pres., 1989—; bd. dirs. Pub. Broadcasting Svc., W.Va. Edn. Broadcasting Authority. Mem.-at-large Dem. Nat. Conv., del., 1976, 80, 84; bd. dirs. Rockefeller Bros. Fund. Office: Sta WETA-FM 3700 S Four Mile Run Dr Arlington VA 22206-2304

ROCKELMAN, GEORGIA F(OWLER) BENZ, retail furniture executive; b. Jefferson City, Mo., June 7, 1920; d. Charles Herman and Marinda Julia (Fowler) Benz; m. Elvin John Henry Rockelman, Nov. 9, 1940; 1 child, Barbara Jean. BBA, Lincoln U., 1964, MBA, 1977. Sec./acct. Harry Benz Enterprises, Jefferson City, 1932-52; ptnr. Benz Furniture Co., Jefferson City, 1952-59, Benz-Rockelman Furniture Co., Jefferson City, 1961-82; v.p., sec. Benz-Rockelman Ltd., Jefferson City, 1982-93, pres., sec., 1993-94. Pres. Trinity-Luth. PTA, Jefferson City, 1952-54; pres. Jefferson City Council Nat. Congress PTA, 1954-56; mem. City Water Flouridation com., 1956; candidate Jefferson City Council, 1983; bd. dirs. Southside Bus. League, Jefferson City, 1981-82, v.p., 1983-84; Rep. com. women Cole County, 1984, 86. Mem. AAUW (sec. 1990-94), DAR, Am. Legion, Cole County Hist. Soc., Hist. City of Jefferson City, Cole County Rep. Women's Club. Lutheran. Home: 216 W Ashley St Jefferson City MO 65101-1606 Office: 121 and 129 W Dunklin St Jefferson City MO 65101

ROCKETT-BOLDUC, AGNES MARY, nurse; b. Medford, Mass., Jan. 19, 1930; d. John Francis and Agnes Mary (Connor) R.; m. Richard Joseph Bolduc, Mar. 23, 1928. Diploma, Lawrence Meml. Hosp., 1951; BSN, Boston Coll., 1958; MEd, Tufts U., 1962. RN; cert. nurse oper. rm. Staff nurse Mass. Gen. Hosp., Boston, 1951-56; instr. nursing Lawrence Meml. Hosp., Medford, Mass., 1958-61; asst. dir. Boston Lying-In Hosp., 1962-67; asst. dean admissions Tufts Med. Sch., Boston, 1967-71; chmn. dept. oper. rm. nursing svcs. Mass. Gen. Hosp., 1971-86; nurse mgr. oper. rm. Portsmouth (N.H.) Regional Hosp., 1987-92; pres. Rover Sky Corp., Hampton, N.H., 1992—; part-time staff nurse Phillips Exeter (N.H.) Acad., 1992—. Author: The Roving Reporter, 1969; mem. editorial bd. Today's Oper. Rm. Nurse, 1978-86. Trustee St. Elizabeth's Hosp., Boston, 1969-72, St. Margaret's Hosp., Boston, 1972-74; bd. dirs. Lifewise, N.H., 1992—; vol. Spl. Olympics, N.H., 1991-92, Hampton C. of C., 1993; chmn. Seacoast Heart Assn., 1989-90; mem. State N.H. Health Ins. Adv. Com., 1981-88. Mem. Am. Assn. Oper. Rm. Nurses, Sigma Theta Tau. Roman Catholic. Home and office: 15 Penniman Ln Hampton NH 03842

ROCKEY, DAWN E., state treasurer; b. Des Moines, Nov. 12, 1961; m. Brian Rockey. BA, U. Nebr. Formerly rsch. technician MX Missile Planning Project Gov.'s Policy Rsch. Office; legis. aide to sen. Jerry Miller, adminstrv. asst. to sen. Ron Withem; state treas. State of Nebr., 1991—. Mem. Nat. Mgmt. Assn., nat. Assn. State Treas. (Midwest regional v.p. 1993—), Assn. Govt. Accts., Nebr. Assn. Pub. Employees, Women Execs. in State Govt., Nat. Assn. Auditors, Comptrollers and Treas. Office: State Treas PO Box 94788 Lincoln NE 68509-4788*

ROCKLEN, KATHY HELLENBRAND, lawyer, banker; b. N.Y.C., June 30, 1951. BA, Barnard Coll., 1973; JD magna cum laude, New England Sch. Law, 1977. Bar: N.Y. 1978, U.S. Dist. Ct. (so. and ea. dists.) N.Y. 1982, U.S. Dist. Ct. (no. dist.) Calif. 1985. Interpretive counsel N.Y. Stock Exchange, N.Y.C.; 1st v.p. E.F. Hutton & Co. Inc., N.Y.C.; v.p., gen. counsel and sec. S.G Warburg (U.S.A.) Inc., N.Y.C.; counsel Rogers & Wells, N.Y.C; pvt. practice N.Y.C. Office mgr. Com. to elect Charles D. Breitel Chief Judge, N.Y. Named one of Outstanding Young Women in Am. Mem. ABA, N.Y. State Bar Assn., N.Y. Women's Bar Assn., Assn. of Bar of City of N.Y. (2d century com., sec., sex, and law com., young lawyers com., corp. law com., spl. com. drugs and legis. com., chair fed. legis. com., securities law com.), Athletic and Swim Club. Office: Law Office 515 Madison Ave New York NY 10022

ROCKRISE, SALLY SCOTT, real estate broker; b. Mpls., Oct. 28, 1929; d. Harold Francis Scott and Mabel Vivien (Verdolyack) Alexander; m. George T. Rockrise, Dec. 18, 1959 (div. Jan. 1965); 1 child, Celia Rockrise Porch. BS, Francis Shimer Coll., 1950. Pres./CEO Verdolyack Paper Specialties, 1952-57; mgr. ROMA, Inc., San Francisco, 1959-65; real estate agt. various cos., Palm Beach, Fla., 1965-82; mgr. Cutler Gardens, Inc., Miami, Fla., 1989-91; pres. S.E. Savs. Realty, Inc., West Palm Beach, 1982—; cons. to homeowner assns., 1991—. Mem. Community Assn. Inst., Million Dollar Club. Office: SE Savs Realty Inc 707 S Chillingworth Dr West Palm Beach FL 33409-4128

ROCKWELL, ELIZABETH DENNIS, retirement specialist, financial planner; b. Houston; d. Robert Richard and Nezzell Alderton (Christie) Dennis. Student Rice U., 1939-40, U. Houston, 1938-39, 40-42. Purchasing agt. Standard Oil Co., Houston, 1942-66; v.p. mktg. Heights Savs. Assn., Houston, 1967-82; sr. fin. planner Oppenheimer & Co., Inc., Houston, 1982—; 2d v.p. Desk and Derrick Club Am., 1960-61. Contbr. articles on retirement planning, tax planning and tax options, monthly article 50 Plus sect. for Houston Chronicle newspaper. Bd. dirs. ARC, 1985-91, Houston Heights Assn., 1973-77; named sr. v.p. Oppenheimer, 1986—; mem. Coll. Bus. U. found. bd. Houston, 1990, mem. million dollar roundtable, 1991—, mem. ct. of the table, 1991—, mem. sys. planned giving coun., 1992—, mem. coll. bus. adv. bd., 1992—, mem. alumni bd., 1987—; appointed trustee U. Houston Sys. Found., Inc., 1992. Named Disting. Alumnae Coll. Bus. Alumn. Assn. U. Houston, 1992; named YWCA Outstanding Woman of Yr., 1978. Mem. Am. Savs. and Loan League (state dir. 1973-76, chpt. pres. 1971-72; pres. S.W. regional conf. 1972-73; Leaders award 1972), Savs. Inst. Mktg. Soc. Am. (Key Person award 1974), Inst. Fin. Edn., Fin. Mgrs., Soc. Savs. Instns., U.S. Savs. and Loan League (com. on deposit acquisitions and adminstrn.), Houston Heights Assn. (charter, dir. 1973-77), Houston North Assn., Friends of Bayou Bend, Harris County Heritage Soc., U. Houston Alumni Orgn. (life), Rice U. Bus. and Profl. Women, River Oaks Bus. Womens Exchange Club, U. Houston Bus. Womens Assn. (pres. 1985), Forum Club, Greater Houston Women's Found. (charter). Office: Oppenheimer & Co Inc 333 Clay St Ste 4700 Houston TX 77002-4103

ROCKWELL, ELIZABETH GOODE, dance company director, consultant, educator; b. Portland, Oreg., Sept. 10, 1920; d. Henry Walton and Elizabeth (Harmon) Goode; m. William Hearne Rockwell, Feb. 3, 1948; children: Enid, Karen, William. BA, Mills Coll., 1941; MA, NYU, 1946. Instr. dance Monticello Jr. Coll., Alton, Ill., 1941-42; dir. masters program in dance Smith Coll., Northampton, Mass., 1946-48; 1st dir. dance dept. High Sch. of Performing Arts, N.Y.C., 1948-51, 53-54; dir. Elizabeth Rockwell Sch. Dance, Bedford, N.Y., 1956-86, Rondo Dance Theater, Bedford, 1971-93; mem. adv. ednl. com. Calif. Ctr. for Arts, Escondido, Calif., 1993-95, dir. dance workshops, 1994—. Choreographer (suite of dances) Jazz Suite, 1966, (50-minute dances) Catch the Wind, 1969, Genesis, 1972 (narrative modern ballet) The Executioner, 1974, Decathalon, 1982; dir. (subscription series) Dance-Art-Poetry-Jazz, 1978-79, (dance/music 1600-1900) Stages in Ages, 1981, (Am. dance revivals) Masterpieces of American Dance, 1982-84, Dances of the Decades, 1985-90, (revival & new choreography) Dances of Our Times, 1991. Bd. dirs. Coun. for Arts in Westchester, White Plains, N.Y., 1978-79, affiliate, 1978—. Recipient Medal for Performance Israeli Army, 1966, Award for Excellence in Arts Edn. Alumnae of High Sch. of Performing Arts, 1990, various grants N.Y. State Coun. on Arts, 1971-93, Coun. Arts in Westchester, 1973-92, dance touring program grant Nat. Endowment for Arts, 1976-79. Mem. Am. Dance Guild, Westchester Dance Coun. (program dir. 1965-69), Assn. Am. Dance Cos., San Diego Area Dance Alliance. Home: 205 Tampico Glen Escondido CA 92025

ROCKWELL, JO ANNE LAUGHLIN, mental health counselor; b. Mobile, Ala., Dec. 4, 1947; d. Oma Howard and Annie Frances (Larkins) Laughlin; m. Gary Lamar Rockwell, Aug. 30, 1969; 1 child, Ashley Mariah. Bachelor's Degree, Auburn (Ala.) U., 1987, Master's Degree, 1990. Lic. profl. counselor. Asst. to geography dept. head Miss. State Coll. for Women, Columbus, 1967-69; supr., teller First Fed. Savs. & Loan, Mobile, Ala., 1971-72; sec., treas. Rockwell Design, Birmingham, Ala., 1972-79; supr., tutor athletic dept. Auburn U., 1987-89; dir. Profl. Counseling Svc., Opelika, Ala., 1990—. Officer, tchr., youth advisor, coms., chairperson Presbyn. Ch., Birmingham and Auburn, 1973—; vol., tutor, tchrs. asst. Auburn Pub. Schs. Sys., 1984-89; vol. Crisis Ctr. East Ala., Auburn, 1984-89, trainer vols., 1986-89; advisor Parents Without Partners, Auburn, 1991—; dir. Presbyn. Cmty. Ministry, Auburn, 1992—. Recipient Cert. of Recognition Crisis Ctr. of East Ala., Auburn, 1989, Recognition Task Force of Northside Ministry, Birmingham, 1975; cert. Nat. Crisis Prevention Inst. in Nonviolent Crisis Intervention, 1990. Mem. ACA, Am. Mental Health Counselors Assn., Ala. Mental Health Counselors Assn. (chairperson publicity, historian exec. coun. 1991—), Ala. Counseling Assn. Democrat. Presbyterian. Home: 1152 Knollwood Ct Auburn AL 36830 Office: Profl Counseling Svc 2807 Lee Rd 166 Opelika AL 36801

ROCKWELL, VIRGINIA CONSIDINE, school counselor; b. Fall River, Mass., Dec. 27, 1940; d. John F. and Lucy (Graham) Considine; m. Ralph Edwin Rockwell Jr., Aug. 28, 1965; children: Richard, Katherine. BS in Edn., Bridgewater (Mass.) State U., 1962; MEd, U. Mass., 1965. English tchr. Arcturus Jr. High Sch., Ft. Richardson, Ala., 1962-64; sch. counselor Hopkins Acad., Hadley, Mass., 1964-65; sch. counselor, dept. chair High Point High Sch., Beltsville, Md., 1965-67; employment counselor State of Oreg., Eugene, 1967-69; libr. asst. UCLA, L.A., 1969-70; placement asst. Northwestern U., Evanston, Ill., 1970-71; counselor Swink (Colo.) Sch. Dist., 1982—. Mem. AACD, Am. Sch. Counselor Assn. (recipient Multi Level Sch. Counselor of Yr. Honorable Mention 1991), Colo. Assn. Counseling and Devel., Colo. Sch. Counselor Assn. (recipient Region I Counselor of Yr. Honorable Mention 1986, named Multi Level Sch. Counselor of Yr. 1990), Delta Kappa Gamma. Home: 30 Sierra Dr La Junta CO 81050-3335 Office: Swink Sch 610 Columbia Ave Swink CO 81077-9999

RODDA, DONNA S., media specialist, library coordinator; b. Cleve., Apr. 30, 1945; d. O. Richard and Margaret Marilyn (Jones) Slater. BA in English, Baldwin Wallace Coll., 1967; MS in Libr. Sci., Case Western Reserve, 1970. Cert. in libr. sci. and ednl. media, Ohio, 1970. Children's asst. Cuyahoga County Pub. Libr., Cleve., 1967-70; sch. libr. Euclid Pub. Libr., Ohio, 1970-71; media specialist Solon City Schs., Ohio, 1971—, libr. coord., 1977—; lectr. John Carroll Univ., Cleve., 1970-74, Case Western Res. U., Cleve., 1974-77; cons. Lake Erie Ednl. Media Consortium, Cleve., 1980-81. Contbr. articles to profl. jours. Mem. Am. Libr. Assn., Am. Assn. Sch. Librs., Ohio Ednl. Libr. Media Assn., Phi Delta Kappa, Kappa Delta Gamma. Office: Orchard Mid Sch 6800 SOM Center Rd Solon OH 44139

RODELL, ANGELA MARIE, financial analyst; b. West Bend, Wis., Sept. 21, 1967; d. Richard Allan and Suzanne Carol (Nielsen) R. BA, Marquette U., Milw., 1989; MPA, U. Ky., 1992. Sales rep. Clinique, Eau Claire, Wis., 1989-90; intern Coun. of State Govt., Lexington, Ky., 1990-91, Congl. Budget Office, Washington, 1991; intern Ky. Housing Corp., Frankfort, 1991-92, fin. analyst, 1992—. Issues coord. Ellinger for Congress Campaign, Lexington, 1992; vol. U. Ky. Med. Ctr., Lexington, 1991; troop leader Girl Scouts U.S.A., Lexington, 1993. HUD fellow, 1990-92. Mem. Am. Soc. Pub. Adminstrs., Toastmasters (v.p. 1993). Republican. Lutheran. Home: 3820 Nicholasville Dr #613 Lexington KY 40503 Office: Kentucky Housing Corp 1231 Louisville Rd Frankfort KY 40601

RODERICK, DOROTHY PAETEL, retired educator; b. Portland, Oreg., Feb. 16, 1935; d. Henry William and Mildred (Wenzlaff) Paetel; m. William Rodney Roderick, Oct. 21, 1965. AB, Wheaton Coll., 1956. Libr.'s asst. Armour Rsch. Found., Chgo., 1956-59; chaplain's asst. Episcopal ch. Northwestern U., Evanston, Ill., 1959-63; trainer Stouffer Restaurants, Skokie, Ill., 1963-65; tchr. jr. high sch. English Kildeer Countryside Consol. Community Sch. Dist. 96, Buffalo Grove, Ill., 1967-94; ret., 1994. Dep. voter registrar Lake County, Waukegan, Ill., 1983—. Mem. AAUW (br. pres. 1985-87, Gift Honoree 1976), Ill. Edn. Assn. (local pres. 1983-85), Delta Kappa Gamma (mem. Lambda state com. on women and the arts 1989-92, chpt. pres. 1994—). Home: 15193 W Redwood Ln Libertyville IL 60048-1447

RODES, BARBARA KNAUFT, library director, environmental researcher; b. Cin., Aug. 6, 1938; d. Robert Wesley and Mary Elizabeth (DeBus) Knauft; m. Thomas M. Rodes, June 18, 1960; children: Lindsay DeBus, Peter Bakewell, Thomas Owsley. BA, Wellesley (Mass.) Coll., 1960; MSLS, Marywood Coll., 1973. Libr. Johnson Sch. Tech., Scranton, Pa., 1973-75; libr. dir. The Environ. Law Inst., Washington, 1975-80, The Conservation Found., Washington, 1980-85, U.S. World Wildlife Fund, Washington, 1985—. Author/compiler: A Dictionary of Environmental Quotations, 1992; joint editor: A Locater/Directory (ea. Europe), 1994. Grantee for collection devel. in environ. law Andrew Mellon Found., Washington, 1978. Mem. Spl. Librs. Assn. (chair natural resource div. 1986-87). Office: World Wildlife Fund 1250 24th St NW Washington DC 20037-1124

RODGER, LINDA JOAN MACINTOSH, librarian; b. Hartford, Conn., Nov. 29, 1940; d. Malcolm and Lois Audrey (Palmer) Macintosh; married, Dec. 15, 1973; 1 child, Jessica. BA in English, Tufts U., 1963; MLS, SUNY, Albany, 1971. Underwriter Travelers, Aetna, Hartford, 1963-68; libr. U. Conn. Health Ctr., Hartford, 1968-69, Springfield (Mass.) Tech. Community Coll., 1970-72; libr. The Futures Group, Glastonbury, Conn., 1973-75, researcher, 1976-79; libr. Springfield Acad. Medicine, 1987-89, Holyoke (Mass.) Hosp., 1989-92; rschr. Am. Inventors Corp., Westfield, Mass., 1994—; ptnr. Info-Edge, Northampton, Mass., 1990-92. Editor: Reflections of Longmeadow, 1983; publisher The Rodger Rev., 1988—. Mem. Med. Libr. Assn. (co-editor Tech. Notes 1991), Western Mass. Health Info. (sec. 1988-91, v.p. 1991-92). Republican. Episcopalian. Home: 61 Chatham Rd Longmeadow MA 01106-1203

RODGERS, AGGIE GUERARD, costume designer; m. Peter Laxton; children: James, Thomas. Grad., Fresno State Coll., 1967; MA in Theatre Arts, Calif. State U., Long Beach. Former wardrobe supr. Am. Conservatory Theatre, San Francisco. Films include American Graffiti, 1973, The Conversation, 1974, One Flew Over the Cuckoo's Nest, 1975, Corvette Summer, 1978, More American Graffiti, 1979, Return of the Jedi, 1983, The Adventures of Buckaroo Banzai: Across the 8th Dimension, 1983, Pee Wee's Big Adventure, 1985, Warning Sign, 1985, Cocoon, 1985, The Color Purple, 1985 (Academy Award nomination best costume design 1985), Fatal Beauty, 1987, Leonard Part VI, 1987, The Witches of Eastwick, 1987, Batteries Not Included, 1987, My Stepmother is an Alien, 1988, Beetlejuice, 1988, I Love You to Death, 1989, In Country, 1989, Forever Young, 1992, Grand Canyon, 1992, Benny and Joon, 1993, The Fugitive, 1993. Office: care Lawrence Mirisch The Mirisch Agency 10100 Santa Monica Blvd Ste 700a Los Angeles CA 90067*

RODGERS, AUDREY PENN, public information officer, public relations consultant; b. Berkeley, Calif., Aug. 8, 1923; d. Lewis August and Edith Harriet (Siler) Penn; m. David Leigh Rodgers, June 13, 1943 (div. Mar. 1982); children: Timothy Leigh, Janice Leigh Rodgers Bracken. AB, U. Calif., Berkeley, 1944. Designer Landscape Design, San Francisco, 1960-70; pres. Campaign Date Svc., Inc., San Francisco, 1970-80; pub. info. dir. East Bay Infiltration Study, Oakland, Calif., 1980-85; pub. info. officer wastewater dept. East Bay Mcpl. Utility Dist., Oakland, 1985—. V.p. devel. Greenbelt Alliance, San Francisco, 1990—; bd. dirs. San Francisco Planning Urban Rsch. Assn., 1970, action chair LWV, San Francisco, 1967. Mem. Pub. Rels. Soc. Am. (chmn. accreditation com. 1984-86, bd. dirs.), Water Polution Control Fedn., Acad. Polit. Sci., Women in Landscape, Calif. Native Plant Soc. (v.p. 1984-85), Sierra Club, Met. Club, Alpha Xi Delta. Democrat. Avocations: swimming, gardening, landscape design, travel, photography. Office: PO Box 24055 Oakland CA 94623-1055 also: 3732 21st St San Francisco CA 94114

RODGERS, BRENDA LYNN, accounting manager; b. Niles, Mich., Mar. 1, 1961; d. Charles Edward and Evelyn Laurie (Dolph) Bolton; m. James Edward Rodgers, June 6, 1992; step-son; James Edward Jr. AA in Liberal Arts with Pres.'s honors, Southwestern Mich. Coll., 1981; BS in Bus. Adminstrn. with distinction, Ferris State U., 1985. Sales rep. First Investors Corp., Mishawaka, Ind., 1985-86; Can. acct. Nat.-Standard, Niles, 1986-90; acctg. mgr. Lindberg/MPH A Gen. Signal Co., Riverside, Mich., 1990—. Mem. Inst. Mgmt. Accts. (v.p. adminstrn. 1993-94, pres. 1994—). Republican. Methodist. Home: 2620 Old # 31 Niles MI 49120 Office: Lindberg/MPH PO Box 131 3827 Riverside Rd Riverside MI 49120

RODGERS, DIANNA SUE, private school educator; b. Mineral Wells, Tex., Feb. 18, 1953; d. William Floyd and Nellie Rose (Frazier) R. Student, Glassboro State Coll., 1971-73; BA, Southeastern Coll. Assemblies of God, 1975; postgrad., Rollins Coll., 1976-77. Cert. tchr., N.J. 6th grade tchr. First Christian Assembly Acad., Memphis, 1975-81; kindergarten tchr. Ambassador Christian Acad., Glassboro, N.J., 1981-85; dir. Children's Edn. Ctr., Upland, Pa., 1985-86; 7th and 8th grade tchr. Ambassador Christian Acad., Glassboro, 1986-87, presch. tchr., 1987-88; 3d-6th grade tchr. Cen. Jersey Christian Sch., Asbury Park, N.J., 1988-94, elem. prin., 1990-93; tchr. 2d grade Calvary Acad., Lakewood, N.J., 1994—. Asst. Brownie leader Girl Scouts Am., Glassboro, 1971-72; dir., organizer Vacation Bible Sch., Calvary Hill Assembly of God, Glassboro, 1988, Children's Ch. leader, 1981-88; tchr. Vacation Bible Sch., First Assembly of God, Shrewsbury, N.J., 1991, 92, 93, sec. bd. dirs., 1991-94, toddler ch. tchr., 1989—; Sunday sch. tchr. First Christian Assembly, Memphis, 1975-81. Mem. Delta Kappa Gamma (Mu chpt.), Alpha Zeta. Home: 96 Wallace St Red Bank NJ 07701 Office: Calvary Acad 1133 E County Line Rd Lakewood NJ 08701

RODGERS, EMILY SAMPSON, field superintendent; b. Mpls., July 19, 1965; d. Wayne Emmet and Helen M. (Skufca) Sampson; m. Gregory Rodgers. BS in Finance, U. Minn., 1988. Inventory/pricing mgr. Miles Homes, Plymouth, Minn., 1988-89, fin. analyst, 1989-90; fin. analyst Milestar Corp., Plymouth, 1990-91; fin. analyst Del Webb Corp., Phoenix, 1991-93, contract adminstr., 1993-94, field supt., 1994—. Active Jr. League, Phoenix, 1994. Mem. Inst. Cert. Mgmt. Accts. Lutheran. Office: Del Webb Terravita Corp 14901 N Scottsdale Rd Ste 200 Scottsdale AZ 85254

RODGERS, IMOGENE SEVIN, occupational and environmental health sciences consultant; b. Rochester, Pa., Nov. 13, 1945; d. Irvin Edward and Hester Pearl (Barto) Sevin; m. John W. Horm (div. 1974); m. James Earl Rodgers, July 4, 1982; 1 child, Kimberly. BS, U. Pitts., 1967; PhD, Duquesne U., 1975; MS in Bus., Johns Hopkins U., 1994. Rsch. asst. U. Pitts., 1968-71; postdoctoral assoc. Allegheny Gen. Hosp., Pitts., 1975-76; chemist Dept. Health Human Svcs. Nat. Inst. Occupational Safety and Health, Rockville, Md., 1976-80; health scientist U.S. Dept. Labor/OSHA, Washington, 1980-89; sci. coord. EPA, Washington, 1989-93; cons. occupational and environ. health scis., 1993—; guest lectr. OSHA Tng. Inst., Chgo., 1989. Author: (with others) Handbook of Radiation Measurement and Protection, 1979, Alpha-2u-Globulin: Association with Chemically Induced Renal Toxicity and Neoplasia in the Male Rat, 1991; contbr. articles to profl. jours. Mem. APHA, Soc. for Risk Analysis, N.Y. Acad. Sci., Rho Chi. Home and Office: 2302 Eagle Rock Pl Silver Spring MD 20906-3248

RODGERS, JAN CAROL, import and export company executive; b. Big Springs, Tex., Feb. 22, 1941; d. Louis Pike Sr. and Bertha Lee (Cook) McCasland; widowed; children: Tamara Laurene, James David, Charles Gordon. Student, Tri-State Cosmetology, Durham's Bus Coll. Radio operator Tex. Hwy. Dept., Van Horn, 1956-57; sec., typist Culberson County, Van Horn, 1957-58; pres. Kut & Kurl, Inc., Alpine, Tex., 1958-65, Eye Catchers, Inc., Oklahoma City, 1965-77, Jan Rodgers Ltd., Inc., North Palm Beach, Fla., 1977—; speaker in field. Advisor Women in Prison, Okla., 1965-72; pres. PTA, Oklahoma City, 1966-67; bd.dirs. Parent Tchr. Soc., Oklahoma City, 1968; sec. United Meth. Ministers Wives, Oklahoma City, 1966-68. Named Model of Yr., El Paso, Tex., 1963, Showmanship award State 4-H, Tex., 1957. Mem. Ports O' Call Assn., Internat. C. of C. Democrat.

RODGERS, LYNNE SAUNDERS, women's health nurse; b. Winchester, Va., May 11, 1956; d. Ronald Otho and Anne Coleman (Grille) Saunders; m. Joseph Rodgers, Dec. 21, 1985; children: Joseph Anthony, John Robert, Stephanie Lynne. BSN, George Mason U., 1978. Cert. inpatient obstetric nursing, prenatal childbirth educator, Resolve Through Sharing counselor, perinatal grief counselor. Clin. nurse specialist in labor and delivery Bethesda (Md.) Naval Hosp., 1978-87; labor and delivery staff nurse clinician Fairfax Hosp. Assn., Falls Church, Va., 1987—; clinician, staff nurse in obstetrics Fauquier Hosp., Warrenton, Va., 1990—. Mem. Assn. Women's Health Obstetric and Neonatal Nurses. Office: Fauquier Hosp 500 Hospital Dr Warrenton VA 22186-3099

RODGERS, NANCY LUCILLE, corporate executive; b. Denver, Aug. 22, 1934; d. Francis Randolph and Irma Lucille (Budy) Baker; student public schs.; m. George J. Rodgers, Feb. 18, 1968; children by previous marriage: Kellie Rae, Joy Lynn, Timothy Francis, Thomas Francis. Mgr., Western Telearm, Inc., San Diego, 1973-93; ind. rep. Nat. Telephone Comm.; pres. Rodgers Police Patrol, Inc., San Diego, 1973-80; br. mgr. Honeywell Inc., Protection Services div., San Diego, 1977-80; pres. Image, Inc., Image Travel Agy., Cairo, Egypt, 1981-83, Western Solar Specialties, 1979-80; founder, pres. Internat. Metaphysicians Associated for Growth through Edn., San Diego, 1979; founder, dir. Point Loma Sanctuary, 1983-86; co-founder, producer Zerciee Prodns. Unltd., 1986—, co-founder, producer, dir. mktg., 1986—. Bd. dirs. Cen. City Assn. Named Woman of Achievement Cen. City Assn., 1979. Mem. Nat. Assn. for Holistic Health, Am. Bus. Women's Assn. (Woman of Yr. 1980), Am. Union Metaphysicians. Republican.

RODGERS, ROSEMARY, property manager, real estate agent; b. Grafton, N.D., Oct. 14, 1946; d. Edward Max and Ruth Lavonne (Kline) Ebertowski; m. William James Rodgers, Oct. 31, 1964; children: William James II, Brenda Lynn, Rebecca Marie. Grad. high sch., Grafton, 1964. Cert. occupancy specialist. Buyer, mgr. Fashion Shoppe, Grafton, 1970-76, Reylecks, Grafton, 1976-78; apt. mgr. GO Devel., Grafton, 1979-88; real estate agt. Country Realty, Inc., Grafton, 1979-89, Town & Country Real Estate, Grand Forks, N.D., 1988-90, R&R Properties, 1988-90; sales agt. Realty Unltd., Shorewood, Minn., 1992—, Westminster Corp. Property Mgmt., St. Paul, 1993-95; property mgr. MIG Mortgage Svcs., Plymouth, Minn., 1995—; real estate agt. NCHP Property Mgmt., 1989-93. Chmn. Mchts. Com., Grafton, 1976; advisor Distbn. Edn. Club of Am., Grafton, 1985-89. Mem. NAFE, Nat. Bd. Realtors, Nat. Ctr. Housing Mgmt., Minn. Bd. Realtors, Mpls. Bd. REaltors, Multi Housing Assn. Roman Catholic. Clubs: Grafton Heathers, Grafton Golf. Home: 235 Nathan Ln N Apt 140 Minneapolis MN 55441-6330 Office: MIG Mortgage Svcs Willow Creek Apts 135 Nathan Ln Minneapolis MN 55441

RODI, CATHERINE FATH, business administrator; b. Chgo., Dec. 1, 1950; d. Andrew Carl and Eva Rose (Honiges) Fath; m. Ernest Anthony Rodi, Aug. 17, 1974; children: Joanna Marie, Ernest Anthony Jr., Keri Lynn. BSBA, Our Lady Holy Cross Coll., New Orleans, 1994. Sec. West Jefferson Hosp., Marrero, La., 1982-84; mgr. Westbank Home Health Care, Gretna, La., 1984-85; adminstrv. dir. Am. Recovery Assn., Inc., New Orleans, 1985—. Democrat. Roman Catholic. Office: Am Recovery Assn Inc Ste 1122 4450 General Degaulle Dr New Orleans LA 70131-6954

RODICH-HODGES, NANCY ANN, librarian; b. Fresno, Calif., Aug. 15, 1931; d. Clyde Burgner and Marjorie Elizabeth (Fairgrieve) Gentle; m. Grover William Rodich, June 13, 1951 (div. Dec. 1976); children—Susan, Lorraine, Donald, Bruce, Scott; m. William M. Hodges, Sept. 26, 1987. B.A. in Math., U. Oreg., 1953, M.L.S., 1968. Tchr. math. Hughson, Calif. pub. schs., 1955-57; libr. asst. San Joaquin County Libr., Tracy, Calif., 1959-64, Oreg. System Higher Edn., Corvallis and Portland, 1963-67; catalog libr. U. Oreg. Med. Ctr., Portland, 1968-73; tech. services libr. Georgetown Med. Ctr., Washington, 1974-76; tech. services libr. Mid-Miss. Regional Libr., Kosciusko, 1976—; instr. cataloging U. Md.-College Park, 1974-76. U. Oreg. Med. Ctr. Nat. Libr. Medicine grantee, 1971-73. Mem. ALA, Miss. Libr. Assn., Kosciusko Bus. and Profl. Women (past pres.), NOW. Democrat. Presbyterian. Home: RR 4 Box 415 Kosciusko MS 39090-9061

RODIN, JUDITH SEITZ, academic administrator, educator; b. Phila., Sept. 9, 1944; d. Morris and Sally R. (Winson) Seitz. A.B., U. Pa., 1966; Ph.D., U. Columbia, 1970. Asst. prof. psychology NYU, 1970-72; assoc. prof. Yale U., 1975-79, prof., dir. grad. studies, 1982-89, Philip R. Allen prof. psychology, medicine and psychiatry, 1984-94, chmn. dept. psychology, 1989-91, dean Grad. Sch., 1991-92, provost, 1992-94; pres. U. Pa., Phila., 1993—, prof. psychology, medicine & psychiatry, 1994—; chmn. John D. and Catherine T. MacArthur Found. Rsch. Network on Determinants and Consequences of Health-Promoting and Health-Damaging Behavior, 1983-93. Author: (with S. Schachter) Obese Humans and Rats, 1978, Exploding the Weight Myths, 1982, Body Traps, 1992; chief editor: Appetite Jour., 1979-92; contbr. articles to profl. jours. Vice-chair coun. of pres. Univs. Rsch. Assn., 1994—; mem. Pa. Gov.'s keystone commn., 1994-95, White House Security Rev., 1994-95, Pa. task force on higher edn. funding, 1994. Fellow Woodrow Wilson Found., 1966-67, John Simon Guggenheim Found., 1986-87; grantee NSF, 1973-82, NIH, 1981—. Fellow AAAS, Am. Acad. Arts and Scis., Am. Psychol. Assn. (bd. sci. affairs 1979-82), Soc. Behavioral Medicine; mem. Inst. Medicine of NAS, Acad. Behavioral Medicine Rsch., Ea. Psychol. Assn. (exec. bd. 1980-83, pres. div. 38 health psychology 1982-83, Outstanding Contbn. award 1977), Disting. Sci. award 1977), Phi Beta Kappa, Sigma Xi (pres. Yale chpt. 1986-87). Office: U Pa 121 College Hall Philadelphia PA 19104-6380

RODITTI, ESTHER C., lawyer, author, publisher; b. Los Angeles, Feb. 7, 1933; d. David and Lucy Roditti; m. Oscar H. Schachter, Aug. 8, 1957 (div. Oct. 1992); children—Charles David, Susan Dayana. B.A., UCLA, 1954; J.D., Harvard U., 1957. Bar: N.Y. 1959. Assoc. Stickles, Hayden and Kennedy, N.Y.C., 1957-62; asst. dir. Legis. Drafting Fund Columbia U., N.Y.C., 1962-65, cons., 1965-67; cons. N.Y.C. Air Pollution Control Dept., 1965-67; instr. and cons. New Sch. for Social Research, N.Y.C., 1968-70; cons. Internat. League for Rights of Man, N.Y.C., 1969, Rand Inst., N.Y.C., 1969, U.S.-Soviet Environ. Studies Program, UN Assn., N.Y.C., 1969; sr. research assoc. Ctr. for Policy Research Columbia U., 1970-73; sr. program officer Ford Found., N.Y.C., 1972-78; pres. Esther Roditti Schachter, P.C., N.Y.C., 1978-83; ptnr. Schachter & Froling, N.Y.C., 1983-85, Schachter, Courter, Purcell & Kobert, N.Y.C., 1985-92; pres. Esther C. Roditti, P.C., 1992—; speaker, lectr., panelist profl. assn. confs., forums, workshops, U.S., Can., Tokyo, London. Author: N.Y.C. Air Pollution Control Code Annotated, 1965, Enforcing Air Pollution Controls, 1979, Financial Support of Women's Programs in the 1970's, 1979, Computer Contracts Reference Directory, 1979-83, Hiring and Firing Knowledge Workers, 1995; co-author: Charities and Charitable Foundations, 1974; author, co-author articles in field; legal editor: Computer Economics, 1983-89; editor Computer Law & Tax Report, 1984-86, pub., editor, 1986—; author, editor Computer Contracts-Negotiating Drafting, 1992—. Nat. governing bd. Common Cause, 1979-82, mem. state governing bd., N.Y., 1982-84; mem. com. on urban environ. Citizens Union, N.Y.C., 1969-73; mem. West Side Democratic Club, 1958-63. Ford Found. grantee, 1970; NSF grantee, 1971; recipient Award for Outstanding Service Brandeis U., Nat. Women's Com., 1973. Mem. ABA (lectr. 1987), Assn. Bar City N.Y. (founder, chmn. com. on computer law 1980—), N.Y. State Bar Assn., Computer Law Assn. (lectr. 1985), Am. Arbitration Assn. (chair com. for computer disputes 1985—), Phi Beta Kappa.

RODMAN, JANET E., rehabilitation nurse manager; b. Buffalo; d. Oliver James and Dorthea (Voelker) Sullivan; m. Harold Murray Rodman; children: Harold, Jr., Michael, Timothy, Mark, Janet Mary. Student, Sisters of Charity Hosp., Buffalo, Canisius Coll., Buffalo, D'Youville Coll., Buffalo. RN, CCM, CIRS. Staff RN, relief head RN Our Lady of Victory Hosp., Lackawawa, N.Y., 1955-65; head nurse emergency room Galion (Ohio) Cmty. Hosp., 1965-74; asst. head nurse emergency room Westview Hosp., Indpls., 1974-76; mktg. rep. Intracorp, Kansas City, Mo., 1976-78; owner, cons. Rehab Inc., Blue Springs, Mo., 1978-85; rehab. mgr. Dodson Ins. Group, Kansas City, 1985—; nurse cons. Federated Rural Exec., Lenexa, Mo., 1983-84. Mem. ins. adv. bd. Kansas City Rehab. Network, 1993-94, Spine Ctr., Kansas City, 1993. Mem. Med. Care Mgmt. Assn. (adv. bd. 1992-94), Ins. Rehab. Study Group (guidelines com. 1987-94), Rehab. Nurses Group (chairperson 1985-94). Home: 1008 Brave Circle Blue Springs MO 64015 Office: Dodson Ins Group Blue Springs MO 64015

RODMAN, SUE ARLENE, wholesale Indian crafts company executive, artist; b. Fort Collins, Colo., Oct. 1, 1951; d. Marvin F. and Barbara I. (Miller) Lawson; m. Alpine C. Rodman, Dec. 13, 1970; 1 child, Connie Lynn. Student Colo. State U., 1970-73. Silversmith Pinel Silver Shop, Loveland, Colo., 1970-71; asst. mgr. Traveling Traders, Phoenix, 1974-75; co-owner, co-mgr. Deer Track Traders, Ltd., Loveland, 1975-85, exec. v.p., 1985—. Author: The Book of Contemporary Indian Arts and Crafts, 1985. Mem. U.S. Senatorial Club, 1982-87, Rep. Presdl. Task Force, 1984-90; mem. Civil Air Patrol, 1969-73, 87-90, pers. officer, 1988-90. Mem. Internat. Platform Assn., Indian Arts and Crafts Assn., Native Am. Art Studies Assn., Inc., Western and English Sales Assn., Crazy Horse Grass Roots Club. Baptist. Avocations: museums, piano, recreation research, fashion design, reading, flying. Office: Deer Track Traders Ltd PO Box 448 Loveland CO 80539-0448

RODRIGUEZ, BEATRIZ, ballerina; b. Ponce, P.R.. Attended, Newark Acad. Ballet, N.J. Sch. of Ballet; scholarship student, Joffrey Ballet Sch. Former dancer N.J. Ballet; dancer Richard Englund's Dance Repertory Co., 1970; mem. Joffrey II Dancers, 1971-72; mem., sr. dancer Joffrey Ballet, N.Y.C., 1972—. Repertory includes: Cakewalk, Dream Dances, Illuminations, Love Songs, Offenbach in the Underworld, Petrouchka, Return to the Strange Land, Rodeo, and The Green Table, Moves, Interplay, Deuce Coupe, As Time Goes By, Billy the Kid, The Dream, Taming of the Shrew, Wedding Bouquet, Force Field, Concerto Grosso, Valentine, Trinty, Kettentans, Fanfarita, The Rite of Spring, Cotillion, Romeo and Juliet, Forgotten Land, Le Sacre du Printemps, The Green Table. Recipient Dance Mag. award, 1993. Office: The Joffrey Ballet 130 W 56th St New York NY 10019-3818

RODRIGUEZ, BELGICA, museum director; b. Venezuela, July 25, 1941; came to U.S., 1988; m. Vidal Rodriquez-Lemoine; children: Samuel, Gabriel. BA in Lit., Cen. U., Caracas, Venezuela, 1969; MA, Courtauld Inst., London, 1976; doctorate, U. Sorbonne, Paris, 1979. Supr. art gallery, gen. sec. Ateneo de Caracas, 1964-71, cons., 1984—; prof. Cen. U., 1967—, mem. permanent staff, 1982—; dir. Art Mus. Ams., OAS, Washington, 1988—; dir. visual arts Found. for Arts and Culture, Venezuela, 1980-86; dir. Nat. Gallery Caracas, 1984-86; dir. Found. Mus. Fine Arts Caracas, 1986—; mem. editl. adv. bd. Latin Am. Art mag., 1989-91; mem. adv. bd. Fine Art Collector mag., 1990—. Author: La Pintura Abstracta en Venezuela 1945-65, 1980, Indagacion de la imagen, 1982, Ramon Vasques Brito, El Hombre el Artista, 1986, Jose Sancho, Sculptor from Costa Rica, et al, 1990, Enrique Grau, Colombian Painter, 1991, Rafa Fernandez from Costa Rica, 1992; contbr. numerous articles to profl. jours., criticisms and exhbn. catalogues. Decorated Order of Andres Bello (Venezuela). Mem. Internat. Assn. Art Critics (pres. 1987-90). Office: Art Museum of the Americas OAS 1889 F St NW Washington DC 20006

RODRIGUEZ, CASSANDRA JEAN, paralegal, legal researcher, social worker; b. Rochester, N.Y., July 17, 1957; d. Raymond Howard Belyea and Corinne Frances (O'Kelley) Lee; m. Raul Rodriguez, June 2, 1980 (div. 1989); children: Anastasia, Tatiana, Raul II. Student, U. Md., Germany, 1979-80, U.S. Army Tng. Support Ctr., 1981-83, St. Mary of Woods, 1989-95; BSW, U. Indpls., 1991. Cert. legal asst., med. records clk., social svc. designee. Vol. activist VISTA, Kansas City, Mo., 1976-77; counselor Shares, Shelbyville, Ind., 1977; self employed paralegal San Antonio, 1982-85, Orlando, Fla., 1985-88; adminstrv. asst. Orlando Airport Marriott, 1985-88; paralegal Forgey & Forgey Attys. at Law, Shelbyville, 1988-90; dir. med. records/quality assurance Sheffield Manor, Franklin, Ind., 1990-92; with social svcs. Coburn Pl., Indpls., 1992-93; br. mgr. Work Force, Indpls., 1993-94; with social svcs. Parkview Pl., Indpls., 1994—; tchr. Headstart, Kansas City, 1976-77, Shelbyville, 1988-89. Pres. parent coun. Headstart, Shelbyville, 1988-89; vol. Habitat for Humanity, Orlando, 1988. With U.S. Army, 1979-85. Decorated Good Conduct medal, Overseas medal; Cert. recipient Headstart, 1989, Ind. Sports Games, 1990. Mem. NAFE, Am. Legion, Young Reps., Ind. Assn. Paralegals (bankruptcy div.), Ind. Legal Assts., Inds. Assn. Quality Assurance Profls. Republican. Methodist. Home: 1105 Brandywine Ct Apt G Shelbyville IN 46176-2890 Office: Parkview Pl Apts 2372 Beckwith Dr Indianapolis IN 46218

RODRIGUEZ, DEBRA KAY NALL, nurse practitioner; b. Hebron, Nebr., Jan. 17, 1955; d. Lloyd H. and Shirley A. (Bruski) Nall; m. Ernest R. Rodriguez Jr., Jan. 25, 1980; 1 child, Nina. ADN, Madison (Wis.) Area Tech., 1977; BSN, Corpus Christi State U., 1987, MSN, 1991; cert. PNP, U. Wis., 1994. Cert. adult nurse practitioner; cert. emergency nurse; cert. instr. ACLS, Am. Heart Assn. Dir. nurse ARC, Rockford, Ill., 1980-81; staff nurse Meml. Med. Ctr., Corpus Christi, Tex., 1981-88, Coastal Bend Women's Ctr., Corpus Christi, 1988-90; with patient edn. Humana Hosp., Corpus Christi, 1990-92; adult nurse practitioner, clin. mgr. East Towne Clinic, U. Wis., Madison, 1992-93; adult nurse practitioner East Clinic, U. Wis., Madison, 1992-94; pediatric/adult nurse practitioner, clinic mgr. Westfield Family Med. Ctr., 1994—; adj. faculty Del Mar Coll., Corpus Christi, 1983-91. Named Outstanding Young Women Am., 1984. Mem. Am. Diabetic Assn. (bd. dirs. Corpus Christi Bay area chpt. 1991-92), Wis. Nurses Assn., Tex. Nurses Assn., Nueces County Med. Edn. Found. (ACLS support com. 1984-92), Sigma Theta Tau. Home: S3730 Bent Tree Dr Baraboo WI 53913

RODRIGUEZ, GILDA ENA, lawyer; b. Santurce, P.R., Feb. 20, 1952; d. Ismael and Ena (Perez) R. BA, Fordham U., 1973; JD, NYU, 1979. Bar: D.C. 1980, N.Y. 1981, U.S. Dist. Ct. D.C. 1981, U.S. Ct. Appeals (D.C. cir.) 1981, U.S. Dist. Ct. (so. and ea. dist.) N.Y. 1982. Atty. FTC, Washington, 1979-82; asst. atty. gen. State of N.Y., N.Y.C., 1982-83; atty. AT&T, Basking Ridge, N.J., 1983-86; atty. advisor FERC, Washington, 1987, legal advisor to commr., 1990-93, atty. advisor, 1993—. Mem. NYU Rev. of Law and Social Change, 1977-78. Helena Rubenstein Found. scholar 1977-79. Mem. ABA, D.C. Bar Assn., N.Y. State Bar Assn. Home: 2727 29th St NW Apt 320 Washington DC 20008-5540 Office: FERC 825 N Capitol St NE Washington DC 20002-4232

RODRIGUEZ, GRACIELA PILAR, psychotherapist; b. Buenos Aires; came to U.S., 1978; d. Benedicta Vasquez. M. Psychology, U. Buenos Aires, 1977; MSW, Calif. State U., San Jose, 1985. Psychol. asst. El Centro Human Svcs. Corp., L.A., 1978-83, San Gabriel Family Svcs., San Gabriel Valley, Calif., 1981-83; clin. social worker, clin. supr. Hathaway Children's Svcs., Lake View Terrace, Calif., 1985—; pvt. practice psychotherapy Torrance, Calif., 1988—; clin. cons. Jewish Family Svcs., Santa Monica, Calif., 1987-89; counselor cons. Personal Performance Cons., L.A., 1989—; clin. cons. Child Abuse Ctr., Harbor UCLA Med. Ctr., Torrance, 1989—. Fellow Nat. Assn. Social Workers, Soc. Clin. Social Work, Calif. Hispanic Psychol. Assn., Marriage, Family and Child Counselors Assn. Democrat. Office: 23706 Crenshaw Blvd Ste 101B Torrance CA 90505-5231

RODRIGUEZ, LINDA TAKAHASHI, secondary education educator; b. L.A., June 22, 1941; d. Edward S. and Mary Yoneko Takahashi; divorced; children: Regina Marie Rodriguez, maria Sari Rodriguez. AA, Trinidad (Colo.) Jr. Coll., 1961; BA, We. State Coll., Gunnison, Colo., 1963; MA, U. Colo., Denver, 1991. Cert. tchr., adminstr., Colo. Tchr. Stratton (Colo.) Jr./Sr. High Sch., 1964-65, Pikes Peak Elem. Sch., Colorado Springs, 1966-68, Prince Sch., Tucson, 1968-70, Ipava (Ill.) Grade Sch., 1970-72, Macomb (Ill.) Schs., 1972-74, Colchester (Ill.) Jr./Sr. High Schs., 1979-83, Hazel Park (Mich.) Alternative Sch., 1984-85; tchr. 8th grade lang. arts and social studies Denver Pub. Schs., 1986-95, chair lang. dept., 1987-95, tchr. reading resource, 1987-92; creator, dir. Reading Summer Sch., 1987-91; presenter insvcs. Denver Pub. Schs., 1987-94; mentor Alternative Tchr. Cert. Program; mem. bd. dirs. Asian Cultural Ctr. Advisor Asian Edn. Adv. Bd., Denver, 1989-95; bd. dirs. Colo. Youth-at-Risk, Denver, 1992-93. Mem. Landmark Edn. Forum, Delta Kappa Gamma. Home: 1617 Daphne Broomfield CO 80020

RODRIGUEZ, LORRAINE DITZLER, biologist, consultant; b. Ava, Ill., July 4, 1920; d. Peter Emil and Marie Antoinette (Mileur) D.; m. Juan G. Rodriguez, Apr. 17, 1948; children: Carmen, Teresa, Carla, Rosa, Andrea. BEd, So. Ill. U., 1943; MS, Ohio State U., 1944; PhD, U. Ky., 1973. Asst. nutritionist OARDC, Wooster, Ohio, 1944-49; postdoctoral fellow U. Ky., Lexington, 1973-74, pesticide edn. specialist, 1978-89; pvt. cons. Lexington, 1974-79, 89—. Author ext. publs. in field; co-author rsch. publs. and book chpts. in field. Leader 4-H, Lexington, 1962-68. Named Outstanding 4-H Alumni Woman, Ky., 1969. Mem. Vegetation Mgmt. Assn. Ky. (chmn. adv. bd. 1985-89), Am. Chem. Soc. Democrat. Roman Catholic. Home: 1550 Beacon Hill Rd Lexington KY 40504-2304

RODRIGUEZ, LOURDES DE LOS ANGELES, lawyer; b. Havana, Cuba, Mar. 1, 1957; came to U.S., 1960; d. Oscar Armando and Romana Irene (Orfila) R.; m. R. Izquierdo, Feb. 19, 1993. BA, U. Miami, 1976, JD, 1988. Bar: Fla. 1990, U.S. Dist. Ct. (so. dist.) Fla. 1990. Appeals officer IRS, N.Y.C., 1982-85, Miami, Fla., 1985-87; legal intern to Hon. Kenneth L. Ryskamp, So. Dist. Fla., Miami, 1987; legal intern to Hon. Charlene Sorrentino U.S. Dist. Ct. (so. dist.) Fla., Miami, 1987; various law clerkships Miami, 1988-91; assoc. Law Office Miguel A. Suarez, Miami, 1990-91, Castro, Ramirez & Netsch, P.A., Miami, 1991; atty. Am. Immigration Lawyer's Assn. pro bono project Legal Svcs. Greater Miami, Inc., 1991—; vol. guardian ad litem 11th Jud. Cir., Miami, 1987-91. Mem. Cath. Hispanic Ctr., Miami, 1985—; bd. dirs. Task Force Cuban Civic Orgns., Miami, 1990—; cons., instr. to families Cuban prisoners/detainees, Miami, 1990—. Recipient Recognition award IRS, 1985, 11th Jud. Cir., 1989. Mem. Fla. Assn. Women Lawyers, Latinas Ptnrs. for Health, Amnesty Internat. Office: Legal Svcs Greater Miami AILA Pro Bono Project 3000 Biscayne Blvd Miami FL 33137

RODRIGUEZ, MARIA, social worker, counselor; b. Mayaguez, P.R., Jan. 2, 1953; d. Pablo Velez and Genara Valle; m. Carlos A. Rodriguez (div. 1990); children: Carlos A. Jr., Leslie A. Student, Passaic C.C., Patterson, N.J. Cert. HIV specialist. Case mgr. Mayaquez (P.R.) Med. Ctr., 1970-71, Hispanic Multi-Purpose Ctr., Patterson, N.J., 1989-90, Cure AIDS Now, Miami, Fla., 1991-93; adminstrv. asst. Carles Imports & Exports, Patterson, 1975-80; tchg. asst. St. John's Sch., Patterson, 1981-87; counselor Passaic (N.J.) City Hall, 1987-89; hot line counselor Health Crisis Network, Miami, 1990-91; job placement coord. Alternatives Svcs., Hialeah, Fla., 1993-94; social worker Beckham Hall for Homeless, Miami, 1994, Metro Dade Human Resouces, Miami, 1994—. Dep. registrar Metro Dade Elections Dept., Miami, 1991; chairperson L.Am. Com., North Miami Beach, Fla., 1993; advocate people with disabilities Archdiocese of Miami, 1994; active Voters Coun. North Miami Beach, 1993; active LWV of Dade County, Policemen's Benevolent Assn. Recipient Appreciation cert. Coalition of Homeless, 1993, City Hall of North Miami Beach for svcs. in cmty., 1993, State of Fla., 1993. Mem. NAFE. Democrat. Roman Catholic. Home: 1301 NE 181 St North Miami Beach FL 33162

RODRIGUEZ, MARIA ESTELA, art gallery director, owner; b. Stamford, Conn., Dec. 10, 1966; d. Francisco José and Estela Maria (Monjo) R.; m. John Paul Comes, July 24, 1993. BBA, Loyola U., 1989. Mgr. Imperial Cathay, Chgo., 1988-90; freelance artist, commd. painter, designer, 1989-91; art dir. Am. Grains, Chgo., 1991-93; owner, dir. Zeus Gallery, Chgo., 1992—. Illustrator: (med. book) La Vos Normal, 1992. Mem. Beta Gamma Sigma, Alpha Sigma Nu. Roman Catholic. Office: Zeus Gallery 1844 N Wood St Chicago IL 60622-1129

RODRIGUEZ, TERESA IDA, elementary education educator, educational consultant; b. Levittown, N.Y., Oct. 10, 1951; d. George Arthur and Frieda (Diaz) R. BA in Secondary Edn., Hofstra U., 1973, MA in Bilingual Edn., 1978; profl. diploma in multicultural leadership, L.I. U., 1990. Cert. permanent nursery, kindergarten, elem., Spanish, ESL tchr., sch. dist. adminstr., sch. adminstr., supr., N.Y. Bilingual elem. tchr. Long Beach (N.Y.) Pub. Schs., 1973-76, Hempstead (N.Y.) Pub. Schs., 1976-79; account exec. Adelante Advt., N.Y.C., 1979-81; adminstrv. asst. Assocs. and Nadel, N.Y.C., 1981-84; freelance outside prop and set decorator for TV commls., N.Y.C., 1984-88; tchr. ESL Central Islip (N.Y.) Pub. Schs., 1988-92; ednl. cons. Houghton Mifflin, Princeton, N.J., 1992—; cons. on tchr. tng. Staff Devel. Ctr. Islips, Central Islip, 1989—; cons. on stff devel. Nassau Bd. Coop. Ednl. Svcs., Westbury, N.Y., 1990—, edn. instrn. specialist IBM, 1991; presenter confs., workshops, seminars. Grantee N.Y. State Div. Bilingual Edn., 1988-90, Staff Devel. Ctr. Islips, 1988, Suffolk Bd. Coop. Ednl. Svcs., 1989; WLIW Pub. TV mini grantee; Pres.'s fellow L.I.U., 1989-90. Mem. ASCD, Nat. Assn. Bilingual Educators, State Assn. Bilingual Educators, Internat. Reading Assn. (presenter nat. conf. 1992, 93), N.Y. State ASCD, Suffolk Reading Coun. Home: 30 Wheelwright Ln Levittown NY 11756-5233 Office: 103 Campus Dr Princeton NJ 08540

RODRIGUEZ, VIRGINA, public relations executive; b. N.Y.C., July 31, 1939. Student, No. Va. C.C., Am. U., Boston Coll. With Doyle Dane Bernbach, 1962-64; confidential sec. The Washington Post, 1967-72, pub. rels rep., 1972-74, pub. rels. supr., 1974-76, asst. pub. rels. mgr., 1976-78, pub. rels. mgr., 1978-85, pub. rels. dir., 1978-85, 1985—. Mem. Pub. Rels. Soc. Am., Internat. Assn. Bus. Communicators. Office: Washington Post 1150 15th St NW Washington DC 20071*

RODRIGUEZ-MENDOZA, AMALIA, administrator; b. Del Rio, Tex., Feb. 17, 1946; d. Jesus M. and Guadalupe (Soto) R.; m. Val Mendoza, July 14, 1973 (div. Jan. 1986); 1 child, Melyssa. BA in Sociology, U. Tex., 1972; MEd, Antioch Coll., 1974. Project coord. Mex.-Am. Cath. Alliance, Austin, Tex., 1972-75; dir. Tex. Ser Job Bank, Austin, 1975-81; dir., voter registration Travis County Tax Office, Austin, 1982-89; dist. clk. Travis County, Austin, 1991—. Chair Gov.'s Commn. Women, Austin, 1991-93; chair bd. dirs. Travis County Adult Literacy Coun., 1983-94, La Pena Arts Orgn., 1993-94. Recipient Mary McCloud Bethune award Sojourner Trust Orgn., Austin, 1992, Good Gal award Tex. Women's Polit. Caucus, Houston, 1993. Mem. Mex.-Am. Bus. & Profl. Women (pres. 1976-78, Outstanding Woman 1976), Hispanic Women's Network Tex. (v.p. 1989-90), Nat. Network Hispanic Women (bd. dirs. 1983-93, Outstanding Woman 1985). Democrat. Roman Catholic. Home: 2710 Addison Ave Austin TX 78757-2317 Office: Travis County 1000 Guadalupe St Austin TX 78701-2336

RODRIGUEZ-MOJICA, WILMA, radiologist, educator; b. Mayaguez, P.R., Mar. 23, 1946; d. Manuel and Rosa (Mojica) Rodriguez; divorced; 1 child, Rebecca Rodriguez-Rodriguez. BS, U. P.R., Mayaguez, 1966; MD, U. P.R., San Juan, 1970. Diplomate Am. Bd. Radiology. Intern U. P.R. Dist. Hosp., 1970-71, resident in diagnostic radiology, 1971-75; radiologist Auxilio Mutuo Hosp., Rio Piedras, P.R., 1976-79; radiologist ptnr. Advanced Radiology Group, Hato Rey, P.R., 1979—; assoc. prof. radiology dept. radiol. scis. U. P.R. Sch. Medicine, Rio Piedras, 1986—; dir. ultrasound Univ. Hosp. Med. Scis. Campus U. P.R., 1980—, proctor radiology electives for med. students, 1975—. Recipient Disting. Citizen award Jaycees Club, 1979, Lions Club, 1987, Mcp. Assembly Women's Week, 1993. Mem. Am. Coll. Radiology (P.R. chpt., treas. 1982-84, counselor 1992, 94), Radiol. Soc. N.Am., Am. Inst. Ultrasound in Medicine, Am. Assn. Women Radiologists, Soc. Radiologists in Ultrasound. Democrat. Roman Catholic. Home: Parque de las Fuentes Apt 2403 Hato Rey PR 00918

ROE, ALLIE JONES, technical writer; b. Greenville, S.C., Dec. 3, 1950; d. James Richard and Allie McGreg (Singletary) Jones; m. Eugene Bartlett Roe, Aug. 29, 1970 (div. 1986); 1 child, David Michael. AB in English, Valdosta State Coll., 1972; MA in Journalism, Ohio State U., 1982. Instr. II State of Ga. Health Svcs., Valdosta, 1972-74; prodn. asst. Easton (Md.) Publ. Co., 1974-75; sec. office of radiation safety Emory U., Atlanta, 1977-79; asst. mgr. classified The Booster Newspaper, Columbus, Ohio, 1980-81; editorial aide Battelle Columbus Labs., 1983-84; publs. coord. specialist Battelle Project Mgmt. Div., Columbus, 1984-85, adminstv. coord., 1985-87; free-lance editor Am. Ceramic soc., Westerville, Ohio, 1988; tech. writer, editor Resource Internat., Westerville, 1988-89; tech. writer Cons. & Designers, Winter Park, Fla., 1989-91, Westinghouse, Orlando, Fla., 1991—. Vol. Am. Heart Assn., Columbus, 1984-88, Am. Cancer Soc., Columbus, 1986-88. Mem. Women in Comm. Inc. (v.p. projects 1986-87, chair job placement com. 1987-89), Nat. Mus. for Women in the Arts (charter 1988—), Internat. Platform Assn., Altrusa Internat. (v.p. Orlando chpt. 1994), Phi Kappa Phi. Methodist. Home: 3732 E Grant St Orlando FL 32812-8417

ROE, ENID ADRIAN TALTON, retired elementary and special education educator; b. Eldorado, Ark., Dec. 11, 1921; d. Adolphus Wiltz and Ileta Dennett (Frank) Talton; m. Joseph Benjamin Roe Sr., Aug. 31, 1942; children: Joseph Benjamin Jr., Phyllis C., Rebecca Louise (dec.), Deborah Elizabeth. AA, Hendrix Coll., 1941; BSEd, Northwestern U., 1946; MEd, U. Nebr., 1973. Cert. elem. tchr., Nebr., Kans.; cert. spl. edn. tchr., learning disabilities and educable mentally handicapped tchr., Kans. Tchr. Pooler

Sch. Dist. #273, Sheridan, Ill., 1943-44; tchr., dir. student svcs. Hawthorne Pub. Sch., Lincoln, Nebr., 1975-76; tchr. Shelton (Nebr.) Pub. Sch., 1976-79; resource tchr. Cambridge Pub. Sch. K-12, Cambridge, Nebr., 1980-81; spl. edn. resource tchr., learning disabled and handicapped Norton (Kans.) Pub. Sch., 1981-91; diaconal minister United Meth. Ch., Nebr., Ks., 1983-91; cert. lay speaker United Meth. Ch., 1988. Sec. First United Meth. Ch., Ainsworth, Nebr., 1959, vacation ch. tchr., 1958-64, ch. libr., 1964-66, vacation ch. sch. tchr., Big Springs, Nebr., 1955-56, Elmwood, Nebr., 1966-70, St. Marks-Lincoln, Nebr., 1964-68, tchr. trainer lab. schs., Elmwood, 1964-68, tchr. study sessions with jr. choir, 1966-70, jr. high youth camp counelor, Fremont, Nebr., 1966, mem. United Meth. women and circle 4, Norton, Kans., 1985—, worship commn., 1988-91, tchr. after sch. program, 1991—; cub scout den mother Boy Scouts Am., 1956-58; asst. scout leader Girl Scouts Am., 1967-79; dialysis nurse trainee Mayo Clinic, 1973; tchr. Laubach Literacy Tutor in Reading, 1974-75; pres. Mother's Club Internat. Order Job's Daughters of Lincoln, 1974-75; mem. Norton Arts Coun., 1989—. Consecrated diaconal minister United Meth. Ch., 1983; presented monetary gift in honor of Enid, Kans. to Spl Olympics Program, 1983; recipient bronze trophy for dedication Spl. Olympics, 1985, coach's cert., 1986. Mem. AAUW, NEA, Kans. Nat. Edn. Assn., Norton Tchrs. Assn., Philanthropic Ednl. Orgn. Sisterhood (chpt. CE 1983-85, chpt. AA 1985—), Delta Kappa Gamma, Kappa Kappa Iota (Alpha conclave 1974-76). Democrat. Methodist. Home: 502 N 1st Ave Norton KS 67654-1304

ROE, RADIE LYNN, educational services manager; b. Stuart, Fla., Nov. 14, 1962; d. Albert R. III and Martha Katherine (Brooks) Krueger; 1 child, Travis; m. Dan C. Roe, May 24, 1990. AB, Ga. Wesleyan Coll., 1984; postgrad., U. Cen. Fla. Tchr. English Brevard County Sch. System, Melbourne, Fla., 1984-86; bank officer, tng. dir. First Nat. Bank and Trust, Stuart, 1987-90; dir. Christian edn. 1st Presbyn. Ch., Stuart, 1990-91; prof. English, Indian River Community Coll., Ft. Pierce, Fla., 1990-91; employment comm. cons. Curtis and Assocs., Grand Island, Nebr., 1992-93; exec. dir. Community HelpCenter, Grand Island, 1993-94, Martin County Literacy Coun., Stuart, Fla., 1993-94; mgr. ednl. svcs. The Palm Beach Post subs. Cox Enterprises, Inc., West Palm Beach, Fla., 1994—. Active Treasure Coast Literacy Coalition, Inter-Agy. Coalition, Laubach Literacy in Action. Mem. AAUW, NAFE, Toastmasters, Habitat for Humanity, Audubon Soc. Republican. Lutheran. Home: 4119 SE Jacaranda St Stuart FL 34997

ROEBUCK, JUDITH LYNN, secondary school educator; b. Huntington, W.Va., Jan. 1, 1946; d. Russell Vance and Janice Lee (Adams) Dickey; m. William Benjamine Roebuck Jr., Mar. 28, 1970; children: Lisa, Paul. AB, Marshall U., 1968; MA, W.Va. U., 1973; postgrad., Marshall U., W.Va. U., 1973—. Cert. tchr., adminstr., W.Va. Tchr. art, English Vinson High Sch., Huntington, 1967-68; tchr. art Wayne (W.Va.) and Crockett Elem. Sch., 1968-69; tchr. art, speech Ona (W.Va.) Jr. High/Mid. Sch., 1969-91; tchr. speech, debate Huntington High Sch., 1991-92; tchr. art Barboursville (W.Va.) High Sch., 1992-94, Midland H.S., Ona, W.Va., 1994—; chair related arts team Ona Mid. Sch., 1988-91; mem. adv. bd. Teen Inst., Huntington, 1990-94, Drama/Debate program Huntington, 1991-92; mem. Invitationalism Coun., Huntington, 1990—, Sch. Improvement Team, Ona, 1990-91, Cabell County Curriculum Coun., Huntington, 1991-92, Cabell County Reading Coun., 1991-92, Cabel County Tchr.'s Acad., Tchr. Expectancy Student Achievement, W.Va. Healthy Schs. program; mediator, trainer Helping Improve Peace, 1994; mentor Impact; counselor Coll. Scouts Program 1994—. Contbr. articles to endl. jours. Counselor, Coll. Scouts Program, 1994—. Mem. NEA, DAR (sec. 1988—), Nat. Art Edn. Assn. (curriculum coun., art chairperson 1993-94, county del. 1994), W.Va. edn. Assn., Cabell Edn. Assn. (membership chair 1989-91), Horizons, Phi Delta Kappa (Mu chpt.). Home: 30 Chris Ln Rt 2 Milton WV 25541 Office: Midland High Sch Rt 60 East Ona WV 25545

ROEDER, GLORIA JEAN, civil rights specialist, private investigator; b. Des Moines, Iowa, Dec. 4, 1945; d. Gerald Arthur and Dorothy Jean (Pardekooper) R. BA, Simpson Coll., 1970; postgrad., Iowa State U., 1990. Examiner disability determination divsn. Disability Determination Div. State of Iowa, Des Moines, 1970-75; owner, pres. Aaron Investigations, Des Moines, 1975—; pvt. investigator Des Moines; cons. All Area Detective Agy., Des Moines, 1965-78. Civil rights specialist Iowa Civil Rights Commn., Des Moines, 1978—, primary liaison; mem. ctrl. com. Iowa Dem. Com. Polk County, Des Moines, 1991—; vol. Luth. Social Svcs., 1988—. Mem. Nat. Assn. Human Rights Workers, Nat. Assn. Prevention Child Abuse (bd. dirs. 1988-91), Iowa Assn. Pvt. Investigators, White Shrine Iowa, Order Ea. Star (officer). Democrat. Office: Iowa Civil Rights Commn 211 Maple St Des Moines IA 50309-1858

ROEDER, REBECCA EMILY, software engineer; b. Findlay, Ohio, Nov. 2, 1959; d. Brian Eldon and Barbara Lee (Melton) R.; m. Stephen William Bigley, May 28, 1983. BS in Edn. and Computer Sci., Bowling Green State U., 1983, MS in Computer Sci., 1993. Systems analyst NCR Corp., Dayton, Ohio, 1983-84; sr. systems analyst Unisys (Burroughs) Corp., Detroit, 1984-88; asst. dir. St. Vincent Med. Ctr., Toledo, 1988—. Active Sta. WGTE/WGLE Pub. Radio, Toledo, 1984—, Toledo Mus. Art, 1988—, Toledo Zoo, 1993—; presenter Women in Sci. Career Day, Lourde's Coll., 1992. Marathon scholar Marathon Oil Co., Findlay, 1978, Hancock scholar Findlay Area C. of C., 1978. Mem. AAUW, Assn. for Computing Machinery. Republican. Episcopalian. Home: 1029 Hugo St Maumee OH 43537 Office: St Vincent Med Ctr 2213 Cherry St Toledo OH 43608

ROEDIGER, JANICE ANNE, artist, educator; b. Trenton, N.J.; d. John and Anne Balint; m. Paul Margerum Roediger; children: Pamela Anne, Matthew Paul, Joan Margaret. Student, Beaver Coll., 1975-78; grad. cert., Pa. Acad. Fine Arts, 1988. Instr. multi-media Jane Law Long Beach Island Gallery, Surf City, N.J., 1992-94; instr. drawing Long Beach Island Found., Loveladies, N.J., 1994; docent Mus. Am. Art, Pa. Acad. Fine Arts, Phila., 1992-94. Exhibited in group shows at Rittenhouse Galleries, Phila., 1988-94, Phila. Mus. Art, ASR Gallery, 1992-94. Mem. vestry, rector's warden St. Anne's Episcopal Ch., Abington, Pa., 1970-73; chair med. staff aux. Abington Meml. Hosp., 1973-7, chair scholarship com., 1974; coord. student com. Pa. Acad. Fine Arts, Phila., 1986-88; active Phila. Mus. Art, 1972—. Recipient Rohm & Haas Outstanding Achievement award Pa. Acad. Fine Arts, 1987, Pearl Van Sciver award Woodmere Mus., 1991, Blumenthal award Cheltenham Ctr. for Arts, 1991, Lance Lauffler award for visionary painting Pa. Acad. Fine Arts, 1988. Mem. Nat. Mus. Women in Arts, Phila. Art Alliance, Artists Cultural Exch. (bd. dirs. 1989—). Episcopalian. Home: 1244 Rydal Rd Rydal PA 19046 Studio: 1010 Arch St Philadelphia PA 19107

ROEFER, PEGGY ANNE, microbiologist; b. East St. Louis, Ill., Aug. 28, 1957; d. Donald Richard and Anne Janet (Menken) R. BA in Microbiology cum laude, U. Tex., 1979. Rsch. lab. asst. U. Tex., Austin, 1979; pub. health microbiologist State of Tenn., Nashville, 1980-81; clin. microbiologist Greater Bakersfield (Calif.) Meml. Hosp., 1982-85; clin. virologist Humana Hosp. Sunrise, Las Vegas, 1985; microbiologist II Las Vegas Valley Water Dist., 1985-88, supr. microbiology, 1988—. Contbr. articles to profl. jours. Vol. Clark County Election Dept., Las Vegas, 1992, 93. Mem. Am. Water Works Assn. adminstr. water quality exam 1990—), Am. Soc. Microbiology, Am. Soc. Clin. Pathologists. Office: Las Vegas Valley Water Dist 243 Lakeshore Rd Boulder City NV 89005-1201

ROEHL, KATHLEEN ANN, financial executive; b. Chgo., June 1, 1948; d. Walter Steven and Catherine (Puss) Kalchbrenner; m. Eric C. Roehl, June 28, 1969; children: Aaron C., Marc E. BA with honors, U. Ill., 1969. Registered investment advisor. Tchr. Ft. Huachuca (Ariz.) Accomodation Schs., 1969-70; interior designer Key Kitchens, Dearborn Heights, Mich., 1979-80; stockbroker, fin. cons. Merrill Lynch, Dearborn, Mich., 1980-81; v.p., registered investment advisor Merrill Lynch, Northbrook, Ill., 1982—; bd. dirs. ATA Info. Systems. Mem. Ill. Govt. Fin. Officers Assn., Internat. Assn. for Fin. Planning (bd. dirs. 1987-88), Northbrook C. of C. (bd. dirs. 1991-93), Northbrook Early Risers Rotary (charter mem.). Office: Merrill Lynch 400 Skokie Blvd Northbrook IL 60062-2816

ROEHM, CAROLYNE JANE, fashion designer; b. Jefferson City, Mo., May 7, 1951; d. Kenneth Smith and Elaine C. (Beaty) Bresee; m. Axel Roehm, June 3, 1978 (div. 1981); m. Henry Raymond Kravis, Nov. 23, 1985. BFA, Washington U., St. Louis, Mo., 1973. Designer Kellwood Co., N.Y.C., 1974-75; asst. designer Oscar de la Renta Ltd., N.Y.C., 1975-84; designer, owner Carolyne Roehm, Inc., N.Y.C., 1984—; design critic Fashion Inst. of Tech., N.Y.C., 1986, Parsons Inst., N.Y.C., 1988; mem. Fashion Group, 1988. Mem. of assn. Met. Opera, N.Y.C., 1988—; chairperson N.Y.C. Ballet Gala, Met. Opera Gala, 1987-88, Winter Antiques Fair for Eastside Settlement House, 1988; co-chair Fête de Famille (Aids), 1988-89, Sta. WNET TV Silver Anniversary Ball, 1988; patron Lions of Performing Arts Dinner N.Y. Pub. Libr., 1989; co-sponsor embassy benefit ball French Am. Found. for Med. Rsch., 1987. Recipient Key to City St. Louis C. of C., 1988, Dallas C. of C., 1988, New Orleans C. of C., 1988, Chgo. Fashion awards, 1988; named Woman of Achievement Girl Scouts U.S., 1988, The Girls' Club, 1988. Mem. Coun. Fashion Designers (pres. 1989-90), N.Y. Pub. Libr. (bd. trustees), Carnegie Hall (steering com.), Kappa Kappa Gamma. Republican. Office: Carolyne Roehm Inc 257 West 39th St 4th Fl New York NY 10018-3203*

ROEHR, KATHLEEN MARIE, nursing administrator; b. San Francisco, June 24, 1950; d. Robert E and Patricia L. (Lawler) Tupa; 1 child, Michael Scott. BSN, U. San Francisco, 1972; MS, U. S.C., 1986. RN, Calif., S.C., CNAA, CHE. Commd. officer U.S. Army, 1971, advanced through grades to col., 1994; staff nurse surg. ICU U.S. Army MEDDAC, Ft. Polk, 1972-73; staff nurse surg. ICU 2d Gen. Hosp., Landstuhl APO, N.Y., 1973-76, asst. chief, 1976-77, head nurse emergency room, 1977-78; clin. staff nurse emergency room Walter Reed Army Med. Ctr., Washington, 1978-79, head nurse emergency room, 1979-81; head nurse emergency room Irwin Army Community Hosp., Ft. Riley, Kans., 1981-82; chief nurse 16th MASH U.S. Army, Ft. Riley, 1982-84; head nurse emergency room Moncrief Army Community Hosp., Ft. Jackson, S.C., 1986-89; chief, clin. ops. analysis br. Health Facilities, 7th MEDCOM, Heidelberg, Fed. Republic Germany, 1989-90; chief health facilities planning div. 7th MEDCOM, Heidelberg, Germany, 1990-91; chief, nursing adminstrn. 67th EVAC Hosp., Wuerzburg, Germany, 1991-92; chief, dept. of nursing 67th EVAC Hosp., 1993—; dep. comdr. nursing 67th Combat Support Hosp., Wuerzburg, 1993-94; chief dept. nursing Reynold Army Cmty. Hosp., Ft. Sill, Okla., 1994—; presenter numerous confs. Decorated Legion of Merit, Meritorious Svc. medal with 4 oak leaf clusters. Mem. ANA, Am. Orgn. Nurse Execs., Am. Coll. Healthcare Execs., Nat. League Nursing, Okla. Nurses Assn., Sigma Theta Tau. Office: 537 Batson Ave Fort Sill OK 73503

ROELKE, ADA (KNOCK-LEVEEN), psychotherapist; b. Cumberland, Md., Aug. 24, 1928; d. George William Knock and Mary Emma (Roelke) Eichelberger; children: Karen Bahnsen, Steven Leveen. BA, Syracuse U., 1950; MSW, San Diego State U., 1967; PhD, Profl. Sch. of Psychol. Studies, 1986. Diplomate Am. Bd. Psychotherapy; bd. cert. social worker; lic. clin. social worker, Calif. Tchr. pub. schs., Syracuse, N.Y., 1960-61; social worker Dept. Pub. Welfare, San Diego, 1964-66; psychiat. social worker State of Calif., Bakersfield, 1967-68; child protection worker Dept. Social Svc., San Diego, 1968-77; pvt. practice psychotherapy La Mesa, Calif., 1969-93; coord., psychotherapist chronic program Grantville Day Treatment Ctr., San Diego, 1977-81; chief social svcs. Edgemoor Geriatric Hosp., Santee, Calif., 1981-88; field supr. Grad. Sch. U. Nev., Reno. Coord. Sr. Help Line Carson City Sr. Ctr. Felow NASW. Unitarian. Home: 919 Arrowhead Carson City NV 89706

ROEMER, ELIZABETH, astronomer, educator; b. Oakland, Calif., Sept. 4, 1929; d. Richard Quirin and Elsie (Barlow) R. B.A. with honors (Bertha Dolbeer scholar), U. Calif., Berkeley, 1950, Ph.D. (Lick Obs. fellow), 1955. Tchr. adult class Oakland pub. schs., 1950-52; lab technician U. Calif. at Mt. Hamilton, 1954-55; grad. research astronomer U. Calif. at Berkeley, 1955-56; research asso. Yerkes Obs. U. Chgo., 1956; astronomer U.S. Naval Obs., Flagstaff, Ariz., 1957-66; asso. prof. dept. astronomy, also in lunar and planetary lab. U. Ariz., Tucson, 1966-69; prof. U. Ariz., 1969—; astronomer Steward Obs., 1980—; Chmn. working group on orbits and ephemerides of comets comm. 20 Internat. Astron. Union, 1964-79, 85-88, v.p. comm. 20, 1979-82, pres., 1982-85, v.p. commn. 6, 1973-76, 85-88, pres., 1976-79, 88-91; mem. adv. panels Office Naval Research, Nat. Acad. Scis.-NRC, NASA; researcher and author numerous publs. on astrometry and astrophysics of comets and minor planets including 79 recoveries of returning periodic comets, visual and spectroscopic binary stars, computation of orbits of comets and minor planets. Recipient Dorothea Klumpke Roberts prize U. Calif. at Berkeley, 1950, Mademoiselle Merit award, 1959; asteroid (1657) named Roemera, 1965; Benjamin Apthorp Gould prize Nat. Acad. Scis., 1971; NASA Spl. award, 1986. Fellow AAAS (council 1966-69, 72-73), Royal Astron. Soc. (London); mem. Am. Astron. Soc. (program vis. profs. astronomy 1960-75, council 1967-70, chmn. div. dynamical astronomy 1974), Astron. Soc. Pacific (publs. com. 1962-73, Comet medal com. 1968-74, Donohoe lectr. 1962), Internat. Astron. Union, Am. Geophys. Union, Brit. Astron. Assn., Phi Beta Kappa, Sigma Xi. Office: U Ariz Lunar and Planetary Lab Tucson AZ 85721

ROEMER, ELIZABETH K., lawyer; b. South Bend, Ind., Sept. 29, 1952; d. Thomas Joseph and Shirley Marie (Shoemaker) R. BA, Ind. U., 1974; MA, Princeton U., 1978; JD, Stanford U., 1981. Bar: Calif., 1981. Atty. Shartsis, Friese & Ginsburg, San Francisco, 1981-83; sr. counsel, asst. sec. Pacific Telesis Group, San Francisco, 1983—. Office: Pacific Telesis Group 130 Kearny St Ste 3609 San Francisco CA 94108

ROEPKE, NANCY JEAN, investment company executive; b. Arlington, Va., Jan. 16, 1955; d. Duane Henry and Helen (Smeltzer) R. Student, Radford (Va.) Coll., 1973-77. Staff asst. Capitol Investors, Ltd., Alexandria, Va., 1979-82; adminstr. DeRand Corp. Am., Arlington, 1982-88; sec. Bankwest Corp., Denver, 1977—; pres., bd. dirs. Pace Investments, Inc., Washington, 1988-90; bd. dirs. Unocam, Inc., Washington; gen. securities prin. Washington Investment Corp., 1990—. Mem. chancel choir, deacon Columbia Bapt. Ch., Falls Church, Va. Home: 2205 Hunters Run Dr Reston VA 22091 Office: NV Comml Inc Ste 500 8230 Leesburg Pike Vienna VA 22182

ROERDEN, CHRIS (CLAIRE ROERDEN), editor, business owner, consultant; b. N.Y.C., Aug. 28, 1935; d. Marion Smolin; m. Harold H. Roerden (div. 1985); children: Ken, Doug. BA in English summa cum laude, U. Maine, 1969, MA in English cum laude, 1971. Mem. pub. rels. staff Shell Oil Co., N.Y.C., 1952-55; asst. to pub. rels. dir. Interchem. Corp., N.Y.C., 1956-59; staff editor Newkirk Assocs., Albany, N.Y., 1960-62; instr. in English U. Maine, Portland, 1969-71; mentor Empire State Coll., SUNY, Rochester and Syracuse, N.Y., 1973-74; mng. editor CPA Digest, Brookfield, Wis., 1983; owner Edit It, Brookfield, 1984—; lectr. U. Wis., Milw., 1991—; speaker and trainer in field. Author: Collections from Cape Elizabeth, 1965, Oops 'n Options Game, 1982, Open Gate: Teaching in a Foreign Country, 1990; editor: The Thoughtful Art of Discipline (Dale Olen, PhD), 1994, Mrs. Wheeler Goes to Washington (Elizabeth Wheeler Colman), 1989, Give This Man a Hand (Earl Harrell), 1990, Education: A Dream Deferred (Emma L. York), 1992. Pres. Brookfield Civic Chorus, 1986-88; v.p. Brookfield Civic Music Assn., 1989-91. Recipient cert. of honor Korean Nat. Commn. for UNESCO, 1989, Kate Mooney Vol. Svc. award Counseling Ctr. Milw., 1991. Mem. Soc. for Tech. Comm. (bd. dirs. 1991—), Women in Comm. (bd. dirs. 1988), Am. Soc. Quality Control, Mid-Am. Pubs. Assn. (bd. dirs. 1993—, v.p. 1994-95), Women Bus. Owners Wis., Wis. Bus. Women's Coalition (bd. dirs. 1988—), Wis. Women's Network (founding), Feminist Bus. and Profl. Women's Forum (coord. 1990—), Wis. Regl. Writers Assn., Brookfield C. of C., NOW (Wis. pres. 1978-81, Positive Action award for leadership 1977), Mensa Internat., Phi Kappa Phi. Office: Edit It 3225 Hillcrest Dr Brookfield WI 53045-1529

ROERIG, DADJA ANN, mobile teleproduction company engineer; b. Landstühl, Rhineland, Germany, Apr. 23, 1963; d. Richard Newton and Margaret Ellen (Bert) R. BA, U. North Tex., 1985. Prodn. coord. Medallion Video Prodns., Dallas, 1985-87; prodn. coord. Unitel Mobile Video, Inc., Pitts., 1987-88, remote engr., 1988—. Mem. Human Rights Campaign Fund - Fed. Advocacy Network. Taoist. Office: Unitel Mobile Video Inc 4100 Steubenville Pike Pittsburgh PA 15205

ROESSER, JEAN WOLBERG, state legislator; b. Washington, May 8, 1930; d. Solomon Harry Wolberg and Mary Frances Brown; m. Eugene Francis Roesser, Aug. 3, 1957; children: Eugene Francis, Mary Roessler Calderon, Anne. BA, Trinity Coll., Washington, 1951; postgrad. in econs., Cath. U. of Am., 1951-53. Congl. relations asst. U.S. Info. Agy., Washington, 1954-58; news reporter for Montgomery County Council Suburban Record, 1983-86; del. Md. Gen. Assembly, Annapolis, 1986-94; mem. State Senate, Md. Gen. Assembly, Annapolis, 1994—, mem. fin. com., ethics con., 1994—. Contbr. articles to polit. jours. Mem. Md. Gov.'s Task Force on Energy; former pres. Montgomery County Fedn. Rep. Women, Potomac Women's Rep. Club; former 3d v.p. Md. Fedn. Rep. Women; founding mem. Montgomery County Arts Coun.; alt. del. Rep. Nat. Convention, 1992. Recipient Cmty. Achievement awrd Washington Psychiat. Soc., 1994, Trinity Coll. Leadership award, 1994, Common Cause Md. award, 1993, Md. Underage Drinking Preventio Coalition award, 1994. Mem. Women Legislators Md., also area citizens assns. and chambers commerce. Republican. Roman Catholic. Home: 10830 Fox Hunt Ln Rockville MD 20854-1553 Office: James Senate Office Bldg State Capitol Annapolis MD 21401*

ROESSLER, P. DEE, lawyer, former municipal judge, educator; b. McKinney, Tex., Nov. 4, 1941; d. W.D. and Eunice Marie (Medcalf) Powell; m. George L. Roessler, Jr., Nov. 16, 1963; (div. Dec. 1977); children: Laura Diane, Trey. Student Austin Coll., 1960-61, 62-64, Wayland Bapt. Coll., 1961-62; BA, U. West Fla., 1968; postgrad. East Tex. State U., 1975, U. Tex.-Dallas, 1977; JD, So. Meth. U., 1982. Bar: Tex. 1982, U.S. Dist. Ct. (ea. dist.) Tex. 1983, U.S. Dist. Ct. (no. dist.) Tex. 1983. Tchr., Van Alstyne Ind. Sch. Dist., Tex., 1968-69; social worker Dept. Social Services, Fayetteville, N.C., 1971-73, Dept. Human Services, Sherman and McKinney, Tex., 1973-79, 81; assoc. atty. Abernathy & Roeder, McKinney, Tex., 1982-85, Ronald W. Uselton, Sherman, 1985-86; prof., program coord. for legal asst. and criminal justice programs Collin County C.C., McKinney, 1986—; judge City of McKinney Mcpl. Ct., 1986-89; mem. Tex. State Bar Com. on Legal Assts., 1990-94. Mem. Collin County Shelter for Battered Women, 1984-86, chmn., 1984-85; v.p. Collin County Child Welfare Bd., 1986, pres. 1987-88, treas. 1989, mem., 1994—; Rep. jud. candidate Collin County, 1986; chmn. bd. Tri County Consortium Mental Health Mental Retardation, 1984-85; mem. Tex. Area 5 Health System Agy., 1979, Collin County Mental Health Adv. Bd., 1978-79; trustee Willow Park Hosp., HCA, 1987-88; chair Collin County Criminal Justice Sub-com., 1987-88; mem. Collin County Pub. Responsibility Com., 1991—, chair, 1994—; bd. dirs. Ct. Apptd. Spl. Advocates, 1991-95. Mem. Collin County Bar Assn., Plano Bar Assn. Baptist. Avocations: gardening, reading, writing, traveling. Home: 2118 Chippendale Dr Mc Kinney TX 75070-2850 Office: Collin County Community Coll 2200 W University Dr Mc Kinney TX 75070-2999

ROESSNER, BARBARA, journalist; b. Elizabeth, N.J., Sept. 16, 1953; d. Gilbert George and Dorothy Anne (Hector) R.; m. Craig William Baggott, Jan. 20, 1982; children: Craig, Taylor, Liam, Katherine, Elizabeth. BA, Wesleyan U., 1975. Reporter, editor Meriden (Conn.) Record-Jour., 1975-78; reporter The Hartford (Conn.) Courant, 1978-81, chief polit. writer, 1981-86, columnist, 1986—; column distributed worldwide by L.A. Times-Washington Post News Svc. Recipient Best Mag. Column award Soc. Profl. Journalists, 1993, Best Mag. Feature award, 1993. Home: 22 Vanderbilt Rd West Hartford CT 06119 Office: Hartford Courant Co 285 Broad St Hartford CT 06115-2510

ROETS, LORI DAWN, systems development professional; b. Charleston, W.Va., Aug. 12, 1962; d. Paul E. Jr. and Carol A. (Baker) Smith; m. Thomas G. Roets Jr., Sept. 20, 1986; children: Ryan, Joshua. AS, Roane State Community Coll., 1980; BA in Am. History, U. Tenn., 1982, BS in Fin., 1985; MS in Bus. Mgmt., LaSalle U., 1994. Cert. in data processing Inst. Cert. Computer Profls. Programmer analyst U. Tenn., Knoxville, 1982-85; v.p. CompuStock Ltd., Knoxville, 1984-85; programmer analyst Blue Cross/Blue Shield, Jacksonville, Fla., 1985-86; systems analyst Provider Automated Services, Jacksonville, 1986-87; v.p. Concepts: Matrix Inc., Jacksonville, 1987-88; applications cons. CSX Technology, Jacksonville, 1987—. Mem. NAFE, Am. Coun. R.R. women, Order Eastern Star, Civitan, Delta Zeta. Democrat. Roman Catholic. Home: 826 Brookmont Ave E Jacksonville FL 32211-6314

ROFFE-STEINROTTER, DIANN, Olympic athlete. Silver medalist, Giant Slalom Albertville Olympic Games, 1992. Silver medalist Giant Slalom, Albertville Olympic Games, 1992, Gold medalist Super-G, Lillehammar Olympic Games, 1994. Address: PO Box 611 Potsdam NY 13676

ROFHEART, ELEANOR FRANCES, financial planner; b. N.Y.C., June 13, 1928; d. Harry Manuel and Ada Veronica (Allen) Gomez-Franco; children: Debba, Douglas. BS in Social Studies, Fordham U., 1950; MS in Elem. Edn., Hofstra U., 1965, profl. diploma in ednl. adminstrn., 1975, EdD, 1984. Tchr. Rockville Centre (N.Y.) Sch. Dist., 1964-76; prin. North Merrick (N.Y.) Sch. Dist., 1976-84; supt. schs. Woodbridge (Conn.) Pub. Sch. Dist., 1984-85, edn. cons., 1985-87; silver team fin. planner IDS Fin. Svcs. Inc., Glendale, Calif., 1989—; speaker in field. Bd. dirs. L.A. Regional Coun. Family Planning, 1991—, Comision Femenil de L.A., 1987-90, Comision Femenil Mexicana Nacional, L.A., 1991—. Recipient citation for gifted edn. program N.Y. State Senate, 1983. Mem. NAFE, NOW, Nat. Women's Polit. Caucus, Glendale C. of C., Phi Delta Kappa (pres. 1979-80, Disting. Svc. Key 1983). Home: 412 N Kenwood St Apt 204 Glendale CA 91206-3272 Office: IDS Fin Svcs Inc 100 W Broadway Ste 100 Glendale CA 91210

ROGALSKI, CAROL JEAN, clinical psychologist; b. Chgo., Sept. 25, 1937; d. Casimir Joseph and Lillian Valentine (Wachowski) R. BS, Loyola U., Chgo., 1961; PhD, NYU, 1968; cert. in psychoanalysis, Postgrad. Ctr. Mental Health, 1973. Lic. clin. psychologist, N.Y., Ill. Rsch. assoc. William Alanson White Inst., N.Y.C., 1961-66; rsch. asst., intern Hillside Hosp., Glen Oaks, N.Y., 1966-68; cons. Mt. Sinai Hosp., N.Y.C., 1968-73; staff psychologist Westside VA Hosp., Chgo., 1974—. Mem. editorial bd. Internat. Jour. Addictions, 1994—; contbr. articles to profl. publs. Mem. APA, Communal Studies Assn., Chgo. Soc. for Psychotherapy Rsch. (Chair 1988-91). Office: Westside VA Hosp 820 S Damen Ave Chicago IL 60612-3740

ROGALSKI, LOIS ANN, speech and language pathologist; b. Bklyn.; d. Louis J. and Filomena Evelyn (Maro) Giordano; m. Stephen James Rogalski, Jun e 27, 1970; children: Keri Anne, Stefan Louis, Christopher James, Rebecca Blair, Gregory Alexander. BA, Bklyn. Coll., 1968; MA, U. Mass., 1969; PhD., NYU, 1975. Lic. speech and lang. pathologist, N.Y. Speech, lang. and voice pathologist Rehab. Ctr. of So. Fairfield County, Stamford, Conn., 1969, Sch. Health Program-P.A. 481, Stamford, 1969-72; pvt. practice speech, lang. and voice pathology Sch. Health Program-P.A. 481, Scarsdale, N.Y., 1972—; cons. Bd. Coop. Ednl. Svcs., 1976-79, Handicapped Program for Preschoolers for Alcott Montessori Sch., Ardsley, N.Y., 1978—; rsch. methodologist Burke Rehab. Ctr., 1977. Mem. profl. adv. bd. Found. for Children with Learning Disabilities, 1978—; bd. dirs. United Way of Scarsdale-Edgemont, 1988-89. Fellow Rehab. Svcs. Adminstrn., 1968-69; N.Y. Med. Coll., 1972-75. Mem. N.Y. Speech & Hearing Assn., Westchester Speech & Hearing Assn., Am. Speech, Hearing & Lang. Assn. (cert. clin. competence), Coun. for Exceptional Children, Assn. on Mental Deficiency, Am. Acad. Pvt. Practice in Speech Pathology & Audiology (bd. dirs., treas. 1983-87, pres. 1987-89), Internat. Assn. Logopedics & Phoniatrics, Sigma Alpha Eta. Office: PO Box 1242 Scarsdale NY 10583-9242

ROGAN, ELEANOR GROENIGER, cancer researcher, educator; b. Cin., Nov. 25, 1942; d. Louis Martin and Esther (Levinson) G.; m. William John Robert Rogan, June 12, 1965 (div. 1970); 1 child, Elizabeth Rebecca. AB, Mt. Holyoke Coll., 1963; PhD, Johns Hopkins, 1968. Lectr. Goucher Coll., Towson, Md., 1968-69; rsch. assoc. U. Tenn., Knoxville, 1969-73; rsch. assoc. U. Nebr. Med. Ctr., Omaha, 1973-76, asst. prof., 1976-80, assoc. prof. Eppley Inst., dept. pharm. scis., U. Nebr., 1980-90, prof., 1990—. Contbr. articles to profl. jours. Predoctoral fellow USPHS, Johns Hopkins U., 1965-68. Mem. AAAS, AAUP, Am. Assn. Cancer Rsch., Am. Soc. Biochem. Molecular Biology. Democrat. Roman Catholic. Home: 8210 Bowie Dr Omaha NE 68114-1526 Office: U Nebr Med Ctr Eppley Inst 600 S 42d St Omaha NE 68198-6805

ROGAT, DOROTHY SHIFF, marketing firm executive, researcher; b. Columbus, Ohio, Nov. 18, 1913; d. Samuel Shiff and Hannah Rochelle Zobin; m. Louis Jack Rotman, June 21, 1936 (dec. Aug. 1966); children: Richard Michael, Hannah Rochelle Rotman Kuhn, Beverly Sue Rotman Praver, Joseph Bruce; m. Morris Edward Rogat, June 4, 1978 (dec. Sept.

1990). BS, Ohio State U., 1935; MB, Western Reserve, 1955; student, Rollins Coll., 1972. Substitute tchr. Euclid (Ohio) Bd. Edn., 1946-56; tchr. Willoughby Eastlake (Ohio) Bd. Edn., 1956-66; rsch. salesperson Kemp Rsch., Rochester, N.Y., 1956-66; owner Doro-Lou Inc., Willowick, Ohio, 1956-66; mktg. rsch. person Harvey Rsch., Rochester, 1964-66; rsch. analyst Nat. Opinion Rsch., Chgo., 1960—; owner Am. Sales and Mktg., Hendersonville, N.C., 1972—, Cert.Reports, Hendersonville, 1979—; rsch. analyst Starch NRA Hooper, Marmoneck, N.Y., 1984—, Shop 'n Check, Atlanta, 1980—. Pres. Ft. Pierce-Port St. Lucie Haddassan Fla., 1982-84, Willoughby-East Lake PTA, 1965-66; vol. Fgn. Student Placement, N.C., 1991, Fish Orgn., women's aux. Temple Agudas Israel. Mem. AARP (sec. 1978, bd. dirs.), AAUW (v.p. 1974), Women's Am. Orgn. Rehab. Tng. (sec. 1972), Bus. and Profl. Women (v.p. 1972), Port St. Lucie Women's Club (membership chmn. 1978), Quota Club (v.p. 1960), Am. Bus. Women (pres. 1961), Hendersonville Women's Club (chmn. fund raising 1991, community svc. coord. 1991), Port St. Lucie Lioness Club (pres. 1982-84), Hendersonville Lions Club, Hendersonville Assn. Ret. Persons Club. Jewish. Home and Office: 216 Vance St Hendersonville NC 28739-5958

ROGENESS, MARY SPEER, state legislator; b. Kansas City, Kans., May 18, 1941; d. Frederic A. and Jeannette (Hybskmann) Speer; m. Dean Rogeness, Aug. 31, 1964; children: Emily, James, Paul. BA, Carleton Coll., 1963. Computer analyst Dept. Def., Ft. Meade, Md., 1963-66; freelance writer, editor Longmeadow, Mass., 1982-91; mem. Mass. Ho. of Reps., Boston, 1991—. Editor: Reflections of Longmeadow, 1983. Mem. Longmeadow Rep. Town Com., 1983—; Mass. alt. del. Rep. Nat. Conv., Houston, 1992. Mem. Jr. League Springfield, World Affairs Coun. of Western Mass. (bd. dirs. 1990—). Office: Mass House of Reps State House Boston MA 02133

ROGERS, AMY, management consultant; b. Wilmington, Del.; d. Samuel and Dorothy (Chassen) R. BA in Govt., Am. U., 1969; MSW, Yeshiva U., 1975. Cert. social worker, N.Y. Social worker psychiat. Kings Psychiat. Ctr., N.Y.C., 1975; exec. asst. city council mem. Henry Berger, N.Y.C., 1977; dir. home healthcare services People Care, N.Y.C., 1978-79; exec. asst. Nat. Jewish Archives Broadcasting, N.Y.C., 1982-84, dir. tng. and devel. dept. fin., 1984-91, sr. tng. cons., 1991—; owner, pres. Portraits of Your Home and Bus.; cons. Amy Rogers Assocs., N.Y.C., 1980-83; trainer sales Bloomingdales, N.Y.C., 1983-84; dir. tng. and devel., N.Y. City. Dept. Fin., 1984—. Mem. People for Am. Way, N.Y.C., 1985-87, Nat. Abortion Rights Action League, N.Y.C., 1985-87. Named Hon. Citizen Md., Gov. Tawes, 1964; recipient Americanism medal, Am. Legion, 1964. Mem. Am. Soc. Tng. and Devel. (Chat. award 1987). Democrat.

ROGERS, BETTY GRAVITT, research company executive; b. Valdosta, Ga., June 24, 1945; d. Jim Aldine and Ruby Romell (Mann) Gravitt; m. Ennis Odean Rogers, May 8, 1967; children: Catheryne, Charles, Elizabeth, Susanne. Student, Fla. Community Coll., Jacksonville, 1988. Chief exec. officer Info. Rsch. Ctr., Inc., Jacksonville, 1982—; co-mgr. Sizes Unltd., The Ltd., Tampa, Fla., 1984-85. Mem. Plan and City Bus. and Profl. Women's Club, Phi Theta Kappa, Beta Phi Gamma. Democrat. Methodist. Home: 17443 Eagle Bend Blvd Jacksonville FL 32226-9500

ROGERS, BRENDA GAYLE, educational administrator, educator, consultant; b. Atlanta, July 27, 1949; d. Claude Thomas and Louise (Williams) Todd; m. Emanuel Julius Jones, Jr., Dec. 17, 1978; children: Lavelle, Brandon. BA, Spelman Coll., 1970; MA, Atlanta U., 1971, EdS, 1972; PhD, Ohio State U., 1975; postgrad. Howard U., 1980, Emory U., 1986. Program devel. specialist HEW, Atlanta, 1972; research assoc. Ohio State U., Columbus, 1973-75; asst. prof. spl. edn. Atlanta U., 1975-78, program adminstr., 1978—, CIT project dir., 1977-91, exec. dir. Impact project, 1992—; tech. cons. Dept. Edn., Washington, 1978-93, cons. head start, 1990-91; due process regional hearing officer Ga. State Dept Edn., Atlanta, 1978-84, adv. bd., 1980-84; mem. parent adv. coun. APS, 1988—; cons. program devel. Ga. Respite Care, Inc., 1988-89; mem. exec. bd., pres. PTA Stone Mountain Elem. Sch., 1989-91. Mem. Ga. Assessment Project com., Atlanta Pub. Schs. Adv. Council, 1986—; bd. dirs. Mountain Pines Civic Assn., 1988—; mem. Grady Meml. Hosp. Community Action Network, Atlanta, 1982-83; exec. bd. PTA Shadow Rock Elem. Sch., 1992-94. Recipient disting. service award Atlanta Bur. Pub. Safety, 1982, award Atlanta Pub. Sch. System, 1980, 82, 83, 89-90; fellow Ohio State U., 1972-74, Howard U., 1980; mem. Assn. for Retarded Citizens, Council for Exceptional Children, NAFE, Phi Delta Kappa, Phi Lambda Theta. Democrat. Roman Catholic. Avocation: gourmet cooking. Office: Atlanta U 233 James P Brawley Atlanta GA 30314-3913

ROGERS, CANDACE MARIE, nursing educator; b. Mt. Pleasant, N.Y., June 24, 1948; d. Arthur Trice and Kathryn Marie (Bartow) Marrow; widowed; m. Samantha Lynn, Joseph Micheal, Aimee Louise. AAS, Thomas Nelson Community Coll., 1973; BSN, Hampton Inst., 1983; MS in Nursing, Hampton U., 1986; postgrad., U. Ala., Birmingham, 1993—. LPN, RN, Va., CNA. Med. nurse Riverside Regional Med. Ctr., Newport News, Va., 1969-70, critical care nurse, 1970-71, charge nurse, 1971-73, primary nurse, 1973-77, acting head nurse, 1977, head nurse, 1977-79, staff nurse, 1979-80, IV nurse, 1980-86; nurse mgr. Riverside Rehab. Inst., Newport News, 1986-89; asst. prof. Norfolk (Va.) State U., 1989—; curriculum coord., 1993-94, AD program coord., 1994—. Contbr. articles to profl. publs. Leader Colonial Coast coun. Girl Scouts U.S.A., Newport News, 1989-93, products coord. svc. team, 1990-93; CPR instr. Peninsula chpt. ARC, 1989-91. 1st lt. USAR, 1990—. Mem. ANA, Va. Nurses Assn. (chair conv. planning com. 1990—), Dist. 10 Nurses Assn., Sigma Theta Tau (treas. 1991-93, sec. 1993—), Chi Eta Phi. Democrat. Baptist. Home: 937 Sherry Cir Newport News VA 23602-2624 Office: Norfolk State U 2401 Corprew Ave Norfolk VA 23504

ROGERS, DALENE CAROLE, clergy member; b. Malden, Mass., June 7, 1950; d. Warren Bonner and Doris Alma (Nickerson) Fuller; m. Brian Joseph Rogers, June 12, 1976 (dec. Feb. 22, 1986); children: Carolyn Fuller, Kristen Lanelle. AAS, Grahm Jr. Coll., Boston, 1970; MDiv, Episcopal Divinity Sch., Cambridge, Mass., 1990. Cert. nuclear medicine technician; ordained Anglican priest, 1990; received privilege of call with United Ch. of Christ, 1994. Staff nuclear medicine tech. Cape Ann Med. Ctr., Gloucester, Mass., 1970-71, Cardinal Cushing Gen. Hosp., Brockton, Mass., 1971-75; nuclear medicine supr. tech. Choate Meml. Hosp., Woburn, Mass., 1975-78; chief nuclear medicine tech. Marlboro (Mass.) Hosp., 1982-87; asst. priest St. John the Evangelist Anglican Ch., Kitchener, Ont., Can., 1990-92; supply priest Episcopal Diocese of Vt., 1992-93; interim priest St. Paul's Episcopal Ch., Windsor, Vt., 1993; pastor Timothy Frost United Meth. Ch., Thetford Ctr., Vt., 1993-94; interim pastor First Congl. Ch. of Haverhill, N.H., 1994; pastor North Pomfret Congl. Ch., 1994—; Adv. Survivors of Childhood Abuse Kitchener-Waterloo Support Group, 1991-92; bd. dirs. Kitchener-Waterloo Sexual Assault Support Ctr., pastoral counsel to staff 1991; presch. instr. Ch. of the Good Shepherd, Acton, Mass., 1982-86, mem. adult Christian Edn. Com., 1986-88, mem. Lay Pastoral Visitors Team, 1986-88. Mem. Vt. Coun. Family Violence, 1993—; mem. Violence Prevention Task Force, Vt., 1993, Task Force on Clergy Misconduct, 1993-94; chairperson Littleton (Mass.) Bd. Health, 1985; bd. dirs. Sexual Assault Support Ctr., Kitchener, Waterloo, Ont., 1991. Mem. LVW, Soc. Nuclear Med. (scientific program com. 1972-74). Home: RR1 Box 750A Woodstock VT 05091

ROGERS, DEBRA MAE AMIDON, international consulting executive; b. Boston, Oct. 20, 1946; d. Frederick E. and Mildred (MacDonald) Amidon; 1 child, Kendra Mae Rogers. BS, Boston U., 1968; MA, Columbia U., 1972; MS, MIT, 1989. Cert. elem. edn. tchr. Tchr. Marshfield, Hanover, Natick Pub. Schs., Mass., 1968-70; asst. dean women Rider Coll., Trenton, N.J., 1971-73; assoc. dean women Babson Coll., Babson Park, Mass., 1973-78; dir. student support services U. Mass., Boston, 1978-79; asst. sec., exec. officer ednl. affairs Commonwealth of Mass., Boston, 1979-80; mgr. strategic planning Digital Equipment Corp., Hudson, Mass., mgr. U.S. sponsored rsch. and ednl. mktg., 1981-93; pres., chief strategist Entovation Internat., Lexington, Mass., 1993—; exec. dir. NE Consortium Colls. and Univs., Salem, Mass., 1980-81; cons. Mass. Bd. Edn., Boston, 1978, Boston Coll., 1977; mem. innovation coun. Women's World Banking; mem. bd dirs. Nat. Conf. Advancement Rsch.; mem. bd. trustees Middlesex C.C.; mem. bd. engring. rsch. coun. Am. Soc. Engring. Edn.; mem. exec. com. Gov's. Commn. on Status of Women. Author: Managing the Knowledge Asset into the 21st Century; Global Innovation Strategy; contbr. articles to profl. jours, presentations in field. Alfred P. Sloan fellow MIT, IC2 Sr. Rsch. fellow; named Outstanding Young Profl. Nat. Assn. Student Personnel Adminstrn., Pi Lambda Theta scholar Boston U. Mem. Technol. Transfer Soc. (Presidents award 1987). Roman Catholic. Clubs: Boston U. (Boston); Bus. and Profl. Women (Wellesly, Mass.). Office: Entovation Internat 2233 Lexington Ridge Dr Lexington MA 02173

ROGERS, DESIREE GLAPION, state official; b. New Orleans, June 16, 1959; d. Roy and Joyce Glapion; m. John Rogers, Jr.; 1 child, Victoria. B in Polit. Sci., Wellesley Coll., 1981; MBA, Harvard U., 1985. Customer svc. mktg. mgr. AT&T, N.J., 1985-87; dir. devel. Levy Orgn., Chgo., 1987-89; founder, pres. Mus. Ops. Consulting Assocs., Chgo., 1989-91; dir. Ill. State Lottery, Chgo., 1991—. Bd. dirs. Sta. WTTW-Pub. TV, Chgo., The Marwen Found.; mem. The Chgo. Children's Mus., Old St. Patrick's Sch., Chgo. Mem. The Econ. Club, Harvard Bus. Sch. Club, Wellesley Club. Office: Ill State Lottery 676 St Clair Chicago IL 60611

ROGERS, DOLORES MCMANUS, training company executive; b. Bellflower, Calif., Mar. 31, 1936; d. Joseph John and Thelma Joanne (Hinds) McManus Miller; m. Michael Creighton Rogers, Nov. 26, 1971; children—Michael Creighton II, Eric Grinnell, Blake Lawrence. m. Clinton Lewis Byers, Jr., Aug. 2, 1958 (div. Mar. 1971). B.S., UCLA, 1957. Sales promotion staff Georgia Bullock, Inc., Los Angeles, 1957-62, v.p. sales promotion, 1962-66; dir. sales promotion Travilla, Los Angeles, 1966-71; owner, mgr. Exec. Assocs., Sherman Oaks, Calif., 1975—. Bd. dirs. Coldwater Counseling Ctr., Studio City, Calif., 1974-76; rec. sec. Las Donas, Los Angeles, 1979—. Mem. Am. Soc. Tng. and Devel., Fashion Group, AAUW. Republican. Episcopalian. Clubs: Sherman Oaks C. of C., UCLA Alumni Assn., Kappa Kappa Gamma. Avocations: cooking; reading; travel; golf; needlework. Home: 3906 Stone Canyon Ave Sherman Oaks CA 91403-4538 Office: Exec Assocs 14755 Ventura Blvd Sherman Oaks CA 91403-3641

ROGERS, DORIETA GWEN, school counselor; b. Levelland, Tex., Oct. 21, 1940; d. Alvin A. and Wanda Laurice (Kirby) Y.; m. Jimmie J. Roger, July 10, 1957; children: Johnna Gay Rogers Kenney, Delana Kay Rogers Grant. AA, South Plains Jr. Coll., 1967; BS in Secondary Edn., Tex. Tech. U., 1971. Cert. elem. educator. Tchr. Levelland (Tex.) Ind. Sch. Dist., 1971-83; real estate sales rep. Century 21, Lubbock, Tex., 1985-89; case worker Buckners Childrens Home, Lubbock, 1991-92; pvt. counselor Lubbock, 1992—; sch. counselor Post (Tex.) Ind. Sch. Dist., 1993—. Vol. Rape Crisis Ctr., Lubbock, 1990-92; steering com. Court Apptd. Spl. Advocate, Lubbock, 1993; vol. counselor Buckner, Lubbock, 1992-93. Mem. ACA, LWV, AAUW. Democrat. Mem. Ch. of Christ. Home: 9709 Memphis Ave Lubbock TX 79423-3807

ROGERS, DOTTIE LOVELADY, counselor, educator; b. Birmingham, Ala., Feb. 14, 1953; d. William Grady and Dorothy Nell (Grant) Lovelady; m. Kenneth Weldon Rogers, Nov. 11, 1983. BA, Huntingdon Coll., 1975; MA, Scarritt Coll., 1977; MS, U. South Ala., 1991. Ordained to Diaconal ministry Meth. Ch., 1980; lic. counselor, Ala. Dir. Christian edn. 1st United Meth. Ch., Enterprise, Ala., 1977, Forest Hill United Meth. Ch., Mobile, Ala., 1978-88; campus min., dir. Wesley Found. U. South Ala., Mobile, 1988-92, victim advocate for crisis intervention, 1989-92; contracted ednl. specialist Charter Acad., Mobile, 1992-93; counselor Crossway Counseling Ctr., Daphne, Ala., 1992-94; clin. therapist TriCare, Mobile, Ala., 1994—; ch. cons., workshop leader S.E. region, United Meth. Ch., 1977—; bd. dirs. higher edn. Ala.-West Fla. Conf., United Meth. Ch., 1988—. Contbr. articles to profl. jours. Singer Mobile Choral Soc., 1979-80; actor Mobile Theater Guild, 1989, Mobile Family Counseling Ctr., 1978-85. Mem. Am. Counseling Assn., Am. Assn. Christian Counselors, Mobile Lic. Profl. Counselor Assn., Christian Educator's Fellowship (past pres.), Acad. Family Mediators. Home: 9151 Valley Ct Mobile AL 36695 Office: 1110 Hillcrest Rd Ste 2-D Mobile FL 34695

ROGERS, FERNE MARY, educator; b. Scranton, Kans., Oct. 5, 1936; d.Leal Alden and Hazel Marie (Phillips) Isaacs; m. Donald Lee Rogers, June 26, 1954; children: Debra Dawn, Michelle Maureen, Jennifer Jill, Amy Annette. BS in Zoology, Ea. Ill. U., 1974, MS in Zoology, 1977, MA in Speech Comm., 1980. Lab. technician Dr. S.T. Schlamowitz, Syracuse, N.Y., 1958-59, Dr. Russell Frink, Lawrence, Kans., 1960-63; rsch. asst. Cell Rsch. Lab., Lincoln, Nebr., 1968-70; educator Wen Tzao Acad., Kaohsiung, Taiwan, 1977-78, Ea. Ill. U., Charleston, 1980—. Contbr. articles to profl. jours. Advisor Girl Scouts Am., Charleston, 1971-74; officer, mem. Coun. for the Aged, Charleston, 1970-77; mem. Charleston Sch. Bd., 1974-77; adv. bd. Am. Cancer Soc., Charleston, 1983-85. Mem. PEO, NOW, AAUW, Audubon Soc., Sierra Club, Beta Beta Beta, Phi Sigma. Home: 2720 Whippoorwill Dr Charleston IL 61920-4144 Office: Ea Ill U 600 Lincoln Ave Charleston IL 61920-3011

ROGERS, FRANCES EVELYN, author, retired educator and librarian; b. Mobile, Ala., Aug. 30, 1935; d. James Richard Graves and Jessie Reynolds (Butler) Lay; m. Jay Dee Rogers, Mar. 22, 1957; children: Laura, Larry. BA, North Tex. State U., 1957; MSLS, Our Lady of the Lake U., San Antonio, 1975. Cert. tchr., libr., Tex. Tchr. Ector County Ind. Sch. Dist., Odessa, Tex., 1958-59; social dir. svc. club Lackland AFB, San Antonio, 1960-61; tchr. San Antonio Ind. Sch. Dist., 1965-70; tchr., libr. Northside Ind. Sch. Dist., San Antonio, 1970-90, ret. Author: (hist. novels) Midnight Sins, 1989, Texas Kiss, 1989, Wanton Slave, 1990, Surrender to the Night, 1991, A Love So Wild, 1991, Sweet Texas Magic, 1992, Desert Fire, 1992, Desert Heat, 1993, Flame, 1994, Raven, 1995, Angel, 1995, (hist. novels under name Keller Graves) Brazen Embrace, 1987, Rapture's Gamble, 1987, Desire's Fury, 1988, Velvet Vixen, 1988, Lawman's Lady, 1988. Sec., vol. Opera Guild San Antonio, 1980—. Home: 2722 Belvoir Dr San Antonio TX 78230-4507

ROGERS, GINGER (VIRGINIA KATHERINE MCMATH), dancer, actress; b. Independence, Mo., July 16, 1911; d. William Eddins and Lela Emogene (Owens) McMath; m. Edward Jackson Culpepper, 1929 (div. 1931); m. Lew Ayres, 1934 (div. 1941); m. Jack Briggs, 1943 (div. 1949); m. Jacques Bergerac, 1953 (div. 1957); m. G. William Marshall, 1961 (div. 1972). Ed. pub. schs. Began as a child dancer, 1926; stage debut in Ginger and Her Redheads, 1925; vaudeville appearances include The Original John Held Jr. Girl, 1926, Ginger and Pepper, 1928-31; stage appearances include Top Speed, 1929, Girl Crazy, 1930, Love and Let Love, 1951, The Pink Jungle, 1959, More Perfect Union, 1963, Hello, Dolly!, 1965, Our Town, 1972; appeared in motion pictures, 1930—; starred in Young Man of Manhattan, 1930, Queen High, 1930, The Sap From Syracuse, 1930, Follow the Leader, 1930, Honor Among Lovers, 1931, The Tip-Off, 1931, Suicide Fleet, 1931, Carnival Boat, 1932, The Tenderfoot, 1932, The Thirteenth Guest, 1932, Hat Check Girl, 1932, You Said a Mouthful, 1932, Forty Second Street, 1933, Broadway Bad, 1933, Gold Diggers of 1933, 1933, Professional Sweetheart, 1933, A Shreik in the Night, 1933, Don't Bet on love, 1933, Sitting Pretty, 1933, Flying Down to Rio, 1933, Chance at Heaven, 1933, Rafter Romance, 1934, Finishing School, 1934, Twenty Million Sweethearts, 1934, Change of Heart, 1934, Upperworld, 1934, The Gay Divorcee, 1934, Romance in Manhattan, 1934, Roberta, 1935, Star of Midnight, 1935, Top Hat, 1935, In Person, 1935, Follow the Fleet, 1936, Swing Time, 1936, Shall We Dance, 1937, Stage Door, 1937, Having a Wonderful Time, 1938, Vivacious Lady, 1938, Carefree, 1938, The Story of Vernon and Irene Castle, 1939, Bachelor Mother, 1939, Fifth Avenue Girl, 1939, Primrose Path, 1940, Lucky Partners, 1940, Kitty Foyle, 1940 (Academy award best actress 1940), Tom, Dick and Harry, 1941, Roxie Hart, 1942, Tales of Manhattan, 1942, The Major and the Minor, 1942, Once Upon a Honeymoon, 1942, Tender Comrade, 1943, Lady in the Dark, 1944, I'll Be Seeing You, 1944, Weekend at the Waldorf, 1945, Heartbeat, 1946, Magnificent Doll, 1946, It Had to Be You, 1947, The Barkleys of Broadway, 1949, Perfect Strangers, 1950, Storm Warning, 1950, The Groom Wore Spurs, 1951, We're Not Married, 1952, Monkey Business, 1952, Dreamboat, 1952, Forever Female, 1953, Black Widow, 1954, Beautiful Stranger, 1954, Tight Spot, 1955, The First Travelling Saleslady, 1956, Teenage Rebel, 1956, Oh, Men! Oh, Women!, 1957, The Confession, 1964, Harlow, 1965, That's Entertainment!, 1974, That's Dancing!, 1984; TV appearances include (episodic) Dick Powell's Zane Gray Theatre, 1958, The DuPont Show with June Allyson, 1960, Ginger Rogers Show, 1961, The Red Skelton Show, 1962, Ed Sullivan Show, Perry Como Show, Bob Hope Show; (specials) The Ginger Rogers Special, 1958, Carissima, 1959, Bob Hope's Potomac Madness, 1960, The Songs of Irving Berlin, 1962, Rodgers and Hammerstein's Cinderella, 1965; dir. play Babes in Arms, 1987; author: Ginger, 1991. Recipient Kennedy Ctr. Honors, 1992. *

ROGERS, GINGER LOU, educator; b. Sheridan, Ark., July 5, 1947; d. James Roscoe Lane and Willie Mae (Sites) Brewer; m. Bruce Ferguson Schlegel, Nov. 3, 1968 (div. Mar. 1987); children: Jenny Lane Schlegel Bartley, Ray Benjamin; m. Donald Karl Rogers, Oct. 26, 1991. BA, U. Ark., 1971; MEd, Southwestern Okla. State U., 1981. Cert. tchr. in art K-12, reading K-12, adminstrn. Elem. art cons. Chanute (Kans.) Pub. Schs., 1972-74; title IV-C art tchr. Custer City (Okla.) Pub. Schs., 1979-81; jr. high art tchr. Clinton (Okla.) Pub. Schs., 1982-83; ednl. cons. Boston Mountain Migrant Coop., Prairie Grove, Ark., 1984-86; parent involvement specialist Region XVI Ednl. Svc. Ctr., Amarillo, Tex., 1986-88; ednl. cons. N.E. Ark. Migrant Coop., Bald Knob, Ark., 1988-92; dir. Migrant Even Start Project, Bald Knob, 1993—. Artist painting stained glass, 1972-93; photographer cover Okla. English Jour., 1982. Vol. tutor White County Lit. Coun., Searcy, Ark., 1993; pub. HUGS, Searcy, Ark., 1988-91. Mem. ASCD, Internat. Reading Assn., Phi Delta Kappa. Democrat. Methodist. Office: Migrant Even Start Project 103 W Park Ave Bald Knob AR 72010-3154

ROGERS, IRENE, retired librarian; b. Yonkers, N.Y., Oct. 12, 1932; d. Franklyn Harold and Mary Margaret (Nealy) R.; BS in Edn., New Paltz State Tchrs. Coll., 1954; MLS (N.Y. State Tng. grantee), Columbia U., 1959. Tchr., West Babylon (N.Y.) Sch. System, 1954-57, Yonkers Sch. System, 1957-58; reference librarian Yonkers Pub. Library, 1959-67, adult services coordinator, 1967-73, asst. library dir., 1973-92, ret., 1993. Mem. Mayor's Adv. Com. Consumer Edn., Yonkers, 1970—; active United Way of Yonkers; mem. curriculum adv. com., report card revision com. Office Supt. Schs., 1982; mem. Yonkers unit Am. Cancer Soc. West Library System grantee, 1966. Mem. ALA, Westchester, N.Y. library assns., Soroptimists (pres. 1978-79, 80-81, sec. dist. I North Atlantic region), Bus. and Profl. Women's Club (pres. Yonkers chpt. 1989-90). Home: 41 Amackassin Ter Yonkers NY 10703-2213

ROGERS, J. SUSAN, English language educator; b. Albertville, Ala., Aug. 7, 1964; d. David Keith Rogers and Judy Carol (Waits) Blackaby. BA in English, Lee Coll., 1986; MA in English, U. Ala., Tuscaloosa, 1988, postgrad. Grad. teaching asst. U. Ala., 1986-88, part-time instr., 1989; instr. English Lee Coll., Cleveland, Tenn., 1989—. Mellon fellow Appalachian Coll. Assn., 1994—. Mem. South Atlantic Modern Lang. Assn., Tenn. Tchrs. English. Mem. Ch. of God. Office: Lee Coll Dept Language Arts Cleveland TN 37312

ROGERS, JANE PALIKAN, school projects coordinator; b. East Chicago, Ind., Jan. 1, 1951; d. John Michael and Gloria Lou (Simpson) Palikan; m. John Liebermann, June 23, 1973 (div. sept. 1978); m. Raymon E. Rogers, Nov. 17, 1990; stepchildren: Brian, Laurie. BS in Edn., George Mason U., 1973, MS in Reading, 1977. Cert. elem. and secondary tchr., Fla. Tchr. elem. Fairfax (Va.) County Sch. Bd., 1973-74, Prince William County Sch. Bd., Woodbridge, Va., 1974-77; tchr. reading Cocoa (Fla.) High Sch., 1977-82, reading specialist, 1982-85; coord. state and fed. projects Brevard (Fla.) County Sch. Bd., 1985—; tchr. adult edn. Brevard C.C., Cocoa, 1977-85. Grantee Sr. Mentor, 1985, Critical Thinking Skills, 1986, Multi-Agy., 1988, PRIME, 1988, BluePrint for Career Edn., 1990, State of Art Automotive Ctr., 1990, Fgn. Lang. Assistance Program, 1993, Bus. Partnership, 1993, Summer Math., Sci., Computer Camps, 1993, 353 Disceretionary, 1993, Magnet Schs., 1993. Mem. Internat. Reading Assn., Zonta Profl. Leaders, Phi Delta Kappa, Kappa Delta Phi. Office: Sch Bd Brevard County 2700 St Johns St Melbourne FL 32940

ROGERS, JEANNE VALERIE, art educator, artist; b. Islip, N.Y., Dec. 1, 1935; d. Joseph Oliver and Louise Valerie (Bayer) Fields; m. James Aubrey Rogers, Jan. 1, 1956; children: Bradley, Tyler, Lisa, Todd. BFA in Ceramics Design, Alfred U., 1957; MS in Art Edn., SUNY, New Paltz, 1962; postgrad., L.I. U., 1986-90, Parsons Sch. Design, 1988-90. Cert. art edn. tchr. K-12, elem. tchr., N.Y. Elem. art tchr. Sayville (N.Y.) Sch. Dist., 1957-61, high sch. art tchr., 1987-90; art tchr. Bayport (N.Y.)/Bluepoint Sch. Dist., 1980; art dir., art tchr. The Hewlett Sch., East Islip, N.Y., 1984-87; field supr. of student tchrs. Dowling Coll., Oakdale, N.Y., 1990—; high sch. art tchr. Torah Acad., Commack, N.Y., 1991—; instr. oil painting adult edn. East Islip High Sch., 1961-62; dir. children's art Summer Outdoor Art Workshops, East Islip, 1967-78; adj. prof. Dowling Coll., 1991-92, art cons., 1990—. Co-author/illustrator: Suffolk Scribes Calligraphic Poetry, 1980 (Libr. award East Islip, 1980); exhibited in group show at Babylon (N.Y.) Citizens Coun. Arts, 1994 (Best in Show award), Invitational Exhibit of Women Artists, Patchogue, N.Y., 1995; reader children's poetry Women in the Arts cable TV show, 1974; contbr. painting as cover design Suffolk Woman Watch Newspaper (premier issues), 1994. Instr. life saving and water safety ARC, Islip, 1955-61; tchr. Sunday sch. Presbyn. Ch., Islip, 1957-63; instr., dir. lifesaving and water safety Shoreham Beach Club, Sayville, 1965-70; instr. preschool, youth and adult swimming Bayshore YMCA, Lasalle Acad., Oakdale, 1971-88, instr., swim dir., 1983-88; art judge C. of C. Summerfest, Sayville, 1990. Recipient award of merit in painting, Nat. League Am. PEN Women, Vanderbilt Mus., Centerport, N.Y., 1993, 94, Cash award for painting Chem. Bank, Arts Coun., 1992, East Islip Pub. Libr., 1992, HTAL winners show Hutchins Gallery, CW Post Campus/L.I. U., 1991, others. Mem. AAUW (implementation chair soc.'s reflection in arts study 1972-74, legis. chair Islip area br. 1972-74, cultural interests chair 1973-75), Suffolk Scribes (charter mem.), Nat. League Am. PEN Women, South Shore Watercolor Soc., N.Y. State Tchrs. Assn., L.I. Art Tchrs. Assn. Republican. Presbyterian. Home: 274 Marilynn Ct East Islip NY 11730-3315

ROGERS, JOAN ANN, community research and development executive; b. Riverhead, N.Y., Oct. 16, 1957; d. Frank B. and Helen (Zimnoski) R.; 1 child, Robert Laurent Wells-Rogers. BSED, Ship State Coll.; M Urban & Regional Devel. Fin., Johns Hopkins U.; postgrad., Boston U. Cert. pub. housing mgr. Asst. planning dir. Fox & Assoc., Hagerstown, Md., 1980-83; pres. Rogers Community Rsch., Harpers Ferry, W.Va., 1983-87; owner Chianti's Restaurant, Harper's Ferry, 1983-87; exec. dir. N.H. Housing Coop., North Conway, 1987-91; pres. Community R & D, Burlington, Vt., 1991—. Author: Housing Development Manual, 1993, Low Income Housing Tax Credit Manual, 1993. Chairperson 1st planning dept. City of Hagerstown, 1988; pres. City Ctr. Found., Hagerstown, 1988; bd. dirs. Granite State Econ. Devel. Corp., Portsmouth, N.H., 1991; mem. gov.'s round table Gov. John H. Sununu, Jackson, N.H., 1992. Recipient Fannie Mae Found. award, 1992, 93. Mem. Ethan Allen Club, Gamma Theta Epsilon. Home: 30 Poor Farm Rd Colchester VT 05446

ROGERS, JUDITH W., federal judge. AB cum laude, Radcliffe Coll., 1961; LLB, Harvard U., 1964; LLM, U. Va., 1988; LLD (hon.), D.C. Sch. Law, 1992. Bar: D.C. 1965. Law clk. Juvenile Ct. D.C., 1964-65; asst. U.S. atty. D.C., 1965-68; trial atty. San Francisco Neighborhood Legal Assistance Found., 1968-69; atty. assoc. atty. gen.'s office U.S. Dept. Justice, 1969-71, atty. criminal divsn., 1969-71; gen. counsel Congl. Commn. on Organization of D.C. Govt., 1971-72; coordinator legis. program Office of Dep. Mayor D.C., 1972-74, spl. asst. to mayor for legis., 1974-79, corp. counsel, 1979-83; assoc. judge D.C. Ct. Appeals, 1983-88, chief judge, 1988-94; cir. judge U.S. Ct. Appeals-D.C. Cir., 1994—; mem. D.C. Law Revision Commn., 1979-83, Mayor's Commn. on Crime and Justice, 1982, grievance com. U.S. Dist. Ct. for D.C., 1982-83, exec. com. Conf. Chief Justices, 1993-94. Bd. dirs. Wider Opportunities for Women, 1972-74, Friends of the D.C. Superior Ct., 1972-74; mem. vis. com. Harvard U. Sch. Law, 1984-90; trustee Radcliffe Coll., 1982-88. Named Woman Lawyer of Yr., Women's Bar Assn. D.C., 1990; recipient citation for work on D.C. Self-Govt. Act, 1973, Disting. Pub. Svc. award D.C. Govt., 1983, award Greater Washington Area Women Lawyers divsn. Nat. Bar Assn., 1989, award Nat. Bar Assn., 1989. Fellow ABA; mem. D.C. Bar Assn., Nat. Assn. Women Judges, Conf. Chief Justices (bd. dirs. 1993-94). Office: US Ct Appeals 333 Constitution Ave NW Washington DC 20001-2866

ROGERS, KATE ELLEN, educator; b. Nashville, Dec. 13, 1920; d. Raymond Lewis and Louise (Gruver) R.; diploma Ward-Belmont Jr. Coll., 1940; BA in Fine Arts, George Peabody Coll., 1946, MA in Fine Arts, 1947; EdD in Fine Arts and Fine Arts Edn., Columbia U., 1956. Instr., Tex. Tech.

Coll., Lubbock, 1947-53; co-owner, v.p. Design Today, Inc., Lubbock, 1951-54; student asst. Am. House, N.Y.C., 1953-54; asst. prof. housing and interior design U. Mo., Columbia, 1954-56, assoc. prof., 1956-66, prof., 1966-85,. emeritus, 1985—, chmn. dept. housing and interior design, 1973-85; mem. accreditation com. Found. for Interior Design Edn. Research, 1975-76, chmn. standards com., 1976-82, chmn. research, 1982-85. Mem. 1st Bapt. Ch., Columbia, Mo.; bd. dirs. Meals on Wheels, 1989-91. Nat. Endowment for Arts research grantee, 1981-82. Fellow Interior Design Educators Council (pres. 1971-73, chmn. bd. 1974-76, chmn. research com. 1977-78); mem. Am. Soc. Interior Designers, (hon., medal of honor 1975), Am. Home Econs. Assn., Columbia Art League (adv. bd. 1988-93), Pi Lambda Theta, Kappa Delta Pi, Phi Kappa Phi (hon.), Gamma Sigma Delta, Delta Delta Delta (Phi Eta chpt.), Phi Upsilon Omicron, Omicron Nu (hon.). Democrat. Author: The Modern House, USA, 1962; editor Jour. Interior Design Edn. and Research, 1975-78.

ROGERS, KATHERINE, association executive; b. Lihue, Hawaii, May 14, 1949; d. Benjamin and Juanita (Escalante) Querubin; m. Charles H. Rogers, June 5, 1971; children: Sara Elizabeth, Jon Michael. BA, Summit Christian Coll., 1971; MA, Calif. State Polytechnic, 1983. Tchr. Ft. Wayne (Ind.) Community Schs., 1971-72, Big Hollow Sch., Ingleside, Ill., 1973-75; dir. Family World Preschool, Pomona, Calif., 1977-79; prin. Little People & Co., Alta Loma, Calif., 1980-89; adminstrv. asst. World Vision-Ea. Europe, Bonn, Germany, 1990-92; exec. dir. YWCA of West End, Pomona, 1991—; instr. Chaffey C.C., Alta Loma, 1984-89. Mem. Nat. Assn. for Edn. of Young Children, YWCA. Presbyterian. Office: YWCA of West End 600 N Park Ave Pomona CA 91768

ROGERS, KATHERINE DIANE, political consultant, state legislator; b. Concord, N.H., Mar. 7, 1955; d. Albert A. and Alta (Whittier) R. BA, Clark U., Worcester, Mass., 1977. Mem. N.H. Ho. of Reps., Concord, 1992—; bd. dirs. N.H. Bus. Fin. Authority. Mem. City Coun., Concord, 1991—. Democrat. Lutheran. Home: 4 Jay Dr Concord NH 03301-7831

ROGERS, LISA, artist; b. Valdez, Alaska, July 24, 1951. BFA, U. Alaska, 1988. artist in residence Koyukuk, Bettles, Thorne Bay, Naknek, Nulato, Alaska, 1990-91. One-woman shows include U. Alaska Gallery, Fairbanks, 1986, Wood Ctr. U. Alaska, 1987, Kenai Peninsula Coll. Gallery, Soldotna, Alaska, 1989, 94, Plate & Palete, Fairbanks, 1994, others; exhibited in group shows at Civic Ctr. Gallery, Fairbanks, 1987, 88, 89, 90, 93, 94, Anchorage Mus. History & Art, 1991, Statewide Touring Exhibit, Alaska, 1991-92, Internat. Ice Sculpture, 1993, Visual Arts Ctr., Anchorage, 1992, New Horizons Gallery, Fairbanks, 1992, 93, 94, Main St. Gallery, Ketchikan, Alaska, 1993, Site 250 Gallery, Fairbanks, 1993, Artworks Gallery, Fairbanks, 1993, 94, many others; represented in permanent collections U. Alaska Mus., Fairbanks, First Nat. Bank Alaska. Home: PO Box 83843 Fairbanks AK 99708

ROGERS, LISA HENNING, training consultant; b. Jersey City, Aug. 22, 1959; d. George Frank and June Phyllis (Fegely) Henning; m. Leo Paul Rogers Jr., May 27, 1984. BA, Coll. of William and Mary, 1981, EdS in Higher Edn., 1986; MSW in Adminstrn., Rutgers U., 1983. Asst. coordinator Rutgers U., New Brunswick, N.J., 1981-83; ednl. rep. March of Dimes, Fairfield, N.J., 1983-84; dir. facilities Coll. William and Mary, Williamsburg, Va., 1984-86; tng. cons. Child Devel. Resources, Lightfoot, Va., 1986—. Vol. Colonial Prevention Coalition, 1988—, Big Sisters, Williamsburg, 1985—; coord. Interagy. Coun. for Young Children, 1990—; mem. Tidewater Regional Interagy. Coordinating Coun., 1990—; edn. chmn. Jr. Women's Club, 1992—. Named Outstanding Young Woman of Yr., Jr. Women's Club, 1992; Garden State scholar State of N.J., 1977-81, George Anderson Meml. scholar Coll. William and Mary, 1977-78, Chubb Found. scholar Chubb & Son, Inc., 1977-81. Mem. Am. Coll. Pers. Assn. (bd. dirs. 1980-81), Assn. of Coll. Unions Internat., Coun. for Exceptional Children (divsn. early childhood 1990), Rural Network, Jr. Women's Club, Psi Chi, Kappa Delta Pi. Home: 110 Links Of Leith Williamsburg VA 23188-7461 Office: Child Devel Resources PO Box 299 Lightfoot VA 23090-0299

ROGERS, LORENE LANE, university president emeritus; b. Prosper, Tex., Apr. 3, 1914; d. Mort M. and Jessie L. (Luster) Lane; m. Burl Gordon Rogers, Aug. 23, 1935 (dec. June, 1941). B.A., N. Tex. State Coll., 1934; M.A. (Parke, Davis fellow), U. Tex., 1946, Ph.D., 1948; D.Sc. (hon.), Oakland U., 1972; LL.D. (hon.), Austin Coll., 1977. Prof. chemistry Sam Houston State Coll., Huntsville, Tex., 1947-49; research scientist Clayton Found. Biochem. Inst. U. Tex., Austin, 1950-64, asst. dir., 1957-64, prof. nutrition, 1962-80, assoc. dean Grad. Sch., 1964-71, v.p. univ., 1971-74, pres., 1974-79, mem. exec. com. African grad. fellowship program, 1966-71; research cons. Clayton Found. for Research, Houston, 1979-81; Vis. scientist, lectr., cons. NSF, 1959-62; cons. S.W. Research Inst., San Antonio, 1959-62; mem. Grad. Record Exams Bd., 1972-76, chmn., 1974-75; adv. com. ITT Internat. Fellowship, 1973-83; dir. Texaco, Inc., Gulf States Utilities, Republic Bank, Austin. Bd. dirs. Tex. Opera Theatre, Austin Lyric Opera; chmn. bd. trustees Texaco Philanthropic Found.; chmn. council of presidents Nat. Assn. State Univs. and Land-Grant Colls., 1976-77, mem. exec. com., 1976-79; mem. com. on identification of profl. women Am. Council on Edn., 1975-79, mem. com. on govt. relations, 1978-79; mem. target 2000 project com. Tex. A&M U. System; mem. ednl. adv. bd. John E. Gray Inst., Lamar U., Beaumont, Tex. Eli Lilly fellow, 1949-50; Recipient U. Tex. Students Assn. Teaching Excellence award, 1963; Disting. Alumnus award N. Tex. State U., 1972; Outstanding Woman of Austin award, 1950, 60, 71, 80; Disting. Alumnus award U. Tex., 1976; Honor Scroll award Tex. Inst. Chemists, 1980. Fellow Am. Inst. Chemists; mem. AAAS, Am. Chem. Soc. (sec. 1954-56), Am. Inst. Nutrition, Am. Soc. Human Genetics, Nat. Soc. Arts and Letters, Assn. Grad. Schs. (internat. edn. com. 1967-71), Sigma Xi, Phi Kappa Phi, Iota Sigma Pi, Omicron Delta Kappa. Home: 4 Nob Hill Cir Austin TX 78746-3650

ROGERS, LORI DIANNE, comparative literature educator; b. San Antonio, Feb. 27, 1965; d. Jimmy Eldon and Irene Martha (Soos) R. BA, Creighton U., 1987; MA, Purdue U., 1989; PhD, SUNY, Stony Brook, 1994. Grad. instr. Purdue U., West Lafayette, Ind., 1987-89, SUNY, Stony Brook, 1990—. Mem. AAUW, MLA, Am. Comparative Lit. Assn., Am. Conf. for Irish Studies, N.E. Modern Lang. Assn. Office: SUNY Dept Comparative Lit Stony Brook NY 11794

ROGERS, MARGARET ELLEN JONSSON, civic worker; b. Dallas, Aug. 7, 1938, d. John Erik and Margaret Elizabeth (Fonde) Jonsson; m. Robert D. Rogers; children: Emily, Erik, Laura. Student Skidmore Coll., 1956-57, So. Methodist U., 1957-60. Civic worker, Dallas; dir. Sta. KRLD radio, Dallas, 1970-74; dir. 1st Nat. Bank, Dallas, 1976-85, vice-chmn. dirs. trust com.; trustee Meth. Hosps., 1972-82, mem. exec. com., 1977-82, corp. bd. mem., 1990-94, mem. fin. com., 1990-93. Bd. dirs. Lamplighter Sch., 1967—; past mem. vis. com. dept. psychology MIT; mem. vis. com. Stanford U. Librs., 1984—; bd. dirs. Callier Ctr. Communication Disorders, 1967-90, Winston Sch., 1973-85; bd. dirs., mem. exec. com. Episc. Sch., 1976-83; chmn. Crystal Charity Ball; co-chmn. nat. major gifts com. Stanford Centennial Campaign; bd. dirs. Children's Med. Center, Hope Cottage Childrens' Bur., Baylor Dental Sch., Dallas Health and Sci. Mus., Dallas YWCA, Day Nursery Assn.; mem. devel. bd. U. Tex., Dallas, 1988-90; bd. govs. The Dallas Found., 1988—, chmn. investment com. 1991-92; trustee So. Meth. U., mem. investment com., 1988—, chmn. investment com., 1992—; mem. visiting com. Dedman Coll., 1989-90; life trustee Dallas Mus. Art, mem. investment com.; mem. collectors com. Nat. Gallery Art; bd. dirs. Dallas Arboretum, 1991-92. Margaret Jonsson Charlton Hosp. of Dallas named in her honor, 1973. Mem. Internat. Coun. Mus. of Modern Art., Ctr. for Strategic and Internat. Studies. (mem. steering com.), MJR Fund (pres.), Jonsson Found., Susan G. Komen Found. (mem. steering com.).

ROGERS, MONICA LEE, lawyer; b. Penang, Malaysia, Dec. 25, 1963; d. Weldon Guy and Lisa (Ng) R. BBA with highest honors, U. Tex., 1986; JD cum laude, Baylor U., 1989. Bar: Tex. 1989. Atty. Haynes and Boone LLP, Dallas, 1989-92, J.C. Penney Co., Inc., Dallas, 1992—. Bd. dirs. Plano (Tex.) Internat. Pre-sch., 1994. Recipient Am. Jurisprudence award for real estate finance Am. Jurisprudence Pub., 1989. Mem. ABA, Tex. Bar Assn., Nat. Asian Pacific ABA (v.p. for membership 1992-93), Dallas Asian ABA (sec. 1991-92). Home: 2028 Maitland Ln Plano TX 75025 Office: JC Penney & Co PO Box 10001 Dallas TX 75301-1103

ROGERS, PATRICIA JUNE, clinical social worker; b. Cordele, Ga., June 15, 1930; d. Culma and Sara Van (Tison) Harris; m. William Judson Rogers, Apr. 30, 1961. BA, Tift Coll., 1951; MSW, Tulane U., 1963. Diplomate Am. Bd. Examiners in Clin. Social Work; lic. clin. social worker, Fla. Pub. welfare worker State of Ga., Tifton, 1951-56; sr. child welfare worker State of Ga., Savannah, 1957-60; dist. child welfare supr. State of Fla., Jacksonville, 1963-65; caseworker Family Counseling Svc., 1965-68; sr. clin. social worker Guidance Ctr., Inc., Daytona Beach, Fla., 1968-73; sr. clin. social worker Human Resources Ctr., Daytona Beach, 1973-79, outpatient team leader, 1974-81, component dir., 1981; program dir. Act Corp., Daytona Beach, 1981—; child and family therapist Counselling Assocs., Ormond Beach, Fla., 1985—. Dep. registrar County of Volusia, Fla., 1990—. Mem. AAUW (mem.-at-large), NASW (cert., Social Worker of Yr. 1981), Am. Assn. Marriage and Family Therapists (clin. mem.). Democrat. Home: 918 Pineapple Rd South Daytona FL 32119 Office: Act Corp 1220 Willis Ave Daytona Beach FL 32114

ROGERS, PAULA ANN, secondary education educator; b. Springfield, Ill., July 21, 1954; d. Paul I. and Pearl L. (Montgomery) R. BS in Math. Edn., Ill. State U., 1976; postgrad., Murray State, 1977; MS in Animal Sci., U. Ill., 1981. Cert. math. tchr., Ill. Math. tchr. Griffin High Sch., Springfield, Ill., 1976-78; adult educator Urbana, Ill., 1981-83; math. tchr. Danville (Ill.) High Sch., 1983-85, Urbana High Sch., 1985—; tutor Urbana Sch. Dist., 1985-93; Job Tng. Partnership Act summer youth worksite coord. Urbana Adult Edn., 1983—; coach math. team competitions Urbana H.S., 1985—, booster pal participant, 1992-93. Contbr. articles to profl. jours. Mem. Math. Assn. of Am., Ill. Coun. Tchrs. Math. Methodist. Office: Urbana High Sch 1002 S Race St Urbana IL 61801-4998

ROGERS, ROSEMARY, author; b. Panadura, Ceylon, Dec. 7, 1932; came to U.S., 1962; naturalized citizen.; d. Cyril Allan and Barbara (Jansze); m. Summa Navaratnam (div.); children: Rosanne, Sharon; m. Leroy Rogers (div.); children: Michael, Adam; m. Christopher Kadison. B.A., U. Ceylon. Writer features and pub. affairs info. Associated Newspapers Ceylon, Colombo, 1959-62; sec. billeting office Travis AFB, Calif., 1964-69; sec. Solano County (Calif.) Parks Dept., Fairfield, 1969-74; part-time reporter Fairfield Daily Republic. Author: (novels) Sweet Savage Love, 1974, The Wildest Heart, 1974, Dark Fires, 1975, Wicked Loving Lies, 1976, The Crowd Pleasers, 1978, The Insiders, 1979, Lost Love, Last Love, 1980, Love Play, 1981, Surrender to Love, 1982, The Wanton, 1985, Bound by Desire, 1988; (with Sean Kelly) Saints Preserve Us!: Everything You Need to Know About Every Saint You'll Ever Need, 1993. Mem. Authors Guild of Authors League Am., Writers Guild Am. *

ROGERS, ROXANNE SUE, management consultant; b. Norton, Kans., Apr. 26, 1951; d. Leslie and Betty G. (Burger) R.; m. Leslie D. Lippincott. BS, N.E. Mo. State U., 1973; postgrad., Drake U., 1988. Secondary sch. tchr. Mo. pub. schs., Lathrop, Gallatin,, 1972-77; svc. corr. Equitable Life Assurance Soc. of U.S., West Des Moines, Iowa, 1977-78; exec. v.p. Mid Am. Search, Inc., West Des Moines, 1977-86; exec. v.p., cons. Mid Am. Rsch. Svc., West Des Moines, 1986-90; cons., owner Rogers Resource, Inc., West Des Moines, 1991—. Author: The Successful Job Search: A Step By Step Guide for a Successful Job Search in the 1990's, 1993; prodr., talk show host WHO Radio, Des Moines, 1989—. Mem. NAFE. Office: Rogers Resource Inc 3737 Woodland Ave # 410 West Des Moines IA 50266

ROGERS, SALLY ANN, artist; b. Traverse City, Mich., Aug. 30, 1960; d. Joseph H. and Ann M. (Doran) R. A. of Liberal Arts, Northwestern Mich. Coll., 1981; BFA, Coll. Art and Design, 1984; MFA, Kent State U., 1989. Grad. teachng asst. Kent (Ohio) State U., 1987-89; artist-in-residence Penland (N.C.) Sch. Crafts, 1989-92, instr., 1991, 92. Prin. works featured in books: Twentyfive Years: Glass as an Art Medium, 1987, Glass: State of the Arts, 1984, Glass: State of the Art II, 1989, La Verre Contemporain--Florilege, 1991. Bd. dirs. Mitchell County (N.C.) Animal Rescue, 1993-94. David B. Smith fellow, Kent State U., 1987. Mem. Nat. Mus. Women in Arts (charter). Office: PO Box 48 Penland NC 28765-0048

ROGERS, SARAH JEANNE, curator; b. Buffalo, Aug. 8, 1956; 1 child, Molly Katherine. BA, Wells Coll., 1978; MA, Northwestern U., 1980. NEA intern, Abby Grey fellow Walker Art Ctr., Mpls., 1980-81; asst. dir. The New Gallery Contemporary Art, Cleve., 1981-82; curator The Contemporary Arts Ctr., Cin., 1982-89; curator exhbns. Wexner Ctr. for the Arts, Columbus, Ohio, 1989-91, sr. curator, 1991-92; dir. exhbns., 1992—; panelist Ohio Arts Coun., Columbus, 1985; juror Columbus Met. Libr. Sculpture Project, 1990, Ohio State U. Cancer Hosp. Sculpture Project, 1990; mem. Ohio State Arts & Memls. com., 1993-95, Dublin Pub. Art com., 1994; panelist Colo. Coun. on Arts, 1995. Curated exhbns. include Maya Lin, Terry Allen, Amy Hamilton. Office: Wexner Ctr for the Arts 30 W 15th Ave Columbus OH 43210-1305

ROGERS, SHARON J., university administrator; b. Grantsburg, Wis., Sept. 24, 1941; d. Clifford M. and Dorothy L. (Beckman) Dickau; m. Evan D. Rogers, June 15, 1962 (div. Dec. 1980). BA summa cum laude, Bethel Coll., St. Paul, 1963; MA in Libr. Sci., U. Minn., 1967; PhD in Sociology, Wash. State U., Pullman, 1976. Lectr., instr. Alfred (N.Y.) U., 1972-76; assoc. prof. U. Toledo, 1977-80; assoc. dean Bowling Green (Ohio) State U. Librs., 1980-84; univ. libr. George Washington U., Washington, 1984-92, asst. v.p. acad. affairs, 1989-92, assoc. v.p. acad. affairs, 1992—, co-dir. Univ. Teaching Ctr., 1990—; mem. Online Computer Libr.Ctr. Users Coun., 1985-92, pres., 1989-90, mem. rsch. adv. com., 1990-92, trustee, 1992—. Contbr. articles to profl. jours. Bd. dirs. ACLU, Toledo, 1978-84, Cap Access, 1993—, treas., 1993. Jackson fellow U. Minn., 1964-65; NSF trainee Wash. State U., 1969-72. Mem. ALA (exec. coun. 1987-91, pub. com. 1989-93, chair 1990-93), Assn. Coll. and Rsch. Librs. (pres. 1984-85), Am. Sociol. Assn., Washington Rsch. Libr. Consortium (bd. dirs 1987-90), Universal Serials and Book Exch. (bd. dirs., treas. 1987). Office: George Washington Univ Rice Hall Ste 602 2121 Eye St NW Washington DC 20052

ROGERS, SUSAN (SUE ROGERS), data processing consultant; b. Jonesboro, Ark., Aug. 22, 1949; d. Eric J. Jr. and Suzanne (Payne) Rogers; m. Joseph Edward Aldrich, July 3, 1974 (div. Mar. 1985); m. Walter J. Wakefield, Oct. 1, 1994; 2 stepchildren. BS in Math, U. Ark., 1975. Cert. computer programmer. Chief programmer State Ark. Dept. Fin. and Adminstrn., Little Rock, 1973-76; programmer, analyst Dillards Dept. Stores, Little Rock, 1976-77; mem. profl. staff Cutler-Williams Inc., Dallas, 1977-79; sr. tech. cons. Sterling Software (formerly Informatics Gen.), Dallas, 1979-86; pvt. practice cons. Dallas, 1986-87; programmer, analyst Fed. Res. Bank, Dallas, 1988-89; pvt. practice Dallas, 1989—; tchr. disabled students Dallas County Community Coll., 1990-92; tchr. jewelry making Dallas Community Coll., 1988-91. Exhibitions at State Fair of Tex., 1985-87, Plano Art Assn., 1985, Arlington Art Assn., 1986, North Lake Coll., 1987. Vol. arts and crafts program Dallas County Juvenile Detention Ctr., 1985-89. Mem. Craft Guild of Dallas, Soc. Creative Anachronism, North Tex. Herb Club, Mensa. Home and Office: 2925 Seymour Dr Dallas TX 75229-4932

ROGERS, SUSAN JANE, engineer, marketing professional; b. Kaduna, Nigeria, Oct. 4, 1963; came to U.S., 1984; d. Brian Anthony and Beryl Margery (Monday) Rogers; m. Thomas Adams Lutz, Aug. 1988. MEng with distinction, Leeds (Eng.) U., 1986; MCE, Villanova U., 1991. Registered profl. engr., Pa. Project mgr., engr. John C. Haas & Assocs., State College, Pa., 1986-88; project engr., project mgr. Vitetta Group, Phila., 1988-92; dir. mktg. T.A.L. Enterprises, Phila., 1992—. Recipient Muasher prize, U.K., 1986, Design award Armitage Corp., U.K., 1986, others. Office: TAL Enterprises 2027 Wallace St Philadelphia PA 19130

ROGERS, SUSAN JANET, public relations specialist; b. N.Y.C., Feb. 17, 1956; d. Michael A. and Lotte (Weil) R. BA in Psychology, Kent State U., 1978, MA in Journalism, 1986. Holds supr. Kent (Ohio) State U. Librs., 1979-84; journalism intern comms. svcs. Kent State U., 1984-85, editorial specialist in rsch. News and Info., 1986-92, interim dir. News and Info., 1992-93, asst. dir. univ. comms. News and Info., 1993—. Editor newsletter: Animal Protective League, Portage County, 1985—. Mem. comms. com. United Way, Portage County, Ohio, 1990—. Named to Outstanding Young Women of Am., 1989, 91; recipient Spl. Recognition award United Way of Portage, Ohio, 1990. Mem. NASW, Pub. Rels. Soc. Am. Home: 548 E Summit St #207 Kent OH 44240 Office: Kent State Univ News & Info 201 Auditorium Bldg Kent OH 44240

ROGERS, TERESA, broadcast executive; b. Oklahoma City, May 26, 1956; d. William Guy and Virginia D. (Hicks) R.; m. Michael E. Worrall, Sept. 27, 1980. BS in Broadcasting, Ariz. State U., 1974-78. News anchor Sta. KRUX-AM, Phoenix, 1978-79, Sta. KARZ-AM, Phoenix, 1979-80; asst. news dir. Sta. KMJJ-AM, Las Vegas, Nev., 1980-84; news dir. Sta. KNPR-FM, Las Vegas, Nev., 1984-88; owner/mgr. Sta. KCMT-FM, Chester, Calif., 1988-90; news dir. Sta. KXBS-FM, Ventura, Calif., 1991; gen. mgr. Sta. KCSN-FM, Northridge, Calif., 1991—. Vol. publicist Sunset Symphony Orch., Las Vegas, Nev., 1986-88; cons. Am. String Tchrs. Assn., Athens, Ga.; bd. dirs. Plumas County Arts Commn., 1988-90, San Fernando Valley Arts Coun., 1992-93; vol. Ventura Arts Coun., 1990; dir. Fine Arts for Youth, Camarillo, Calif., 1991.

ROGET, CRISTIANE, producer; b. L.A., July 12, 1955; d. Richard and Beverlie Yvonne (Roget) Peterson. AA, U. Calif., Berkeley, 1974; student, UCLA, 1977-79. Dir., founder Third World Film Fest, L.A., 1978, 79; sr. editor Movie Goers Mag., Miami, Fla., 1980-83; pres. Producer's Resource, Miami, 1988—; corr. Backstage, Billboard, Shoot, Variety, N.Y.C., 1980-90; prodr. photog. promotion for Andy Garcia, Sony Discos; founder Discop Latina, internat. TV distbn. market, Miami, 1994—; line prodr. Safari Kids, Davis Panzer Prodns., News Segments for Am. Jour., King World Prodns.; unit publicist The Girl with the Hungry Eyes, Hard Evidence. Prodr. music video Chayanne-Dance This Dance Like This, 1989 (MTV Best Internat.); co-prodr. NBC News Inside Cuba Series, 1989; prodn. mgr. nat. campaign Cadillac, 1990-91, Best of Fla., St. Lauderdale Film Festival; lind. prodr. Jane Connolly Show, 1995. Mem. film aquisition program Nat. Endowment Arts Rep. U. Calif., grantee, 1979. Mem. Interam. Co-Producer Market (bd. dirs., coord. 1989-90), Fla. Motion Picture and TV Assn., Miami Beach Film Soc. (bd. dirs.). Democrat. Roman Catholic. Office: Penthouse 460 Ocean Dr Miami Beach FL 33139

ROGNE, CAROL JEAN, school psychologist, therapist, educator; b. Mankato, Minn., Feb. 10, 1941; d. James Arnold and Evelyn Francis (Nelson) Gisvold; m. Duane John Rogne, May 11, 1960 (div. Apr. 1991); children: Jay Louis, Dustin Boe. BA in Psychology, Moorhead State U., 1978-80, MS in Sch. Psychology Level II, 1980-82; postgrad., Clayton U., 1989-90. Lic. psychologist, N.D., Minn.; diplomate Nat. Bd. Cert. Counselors. Supr. sch. psychology grad. students Moorhead State U., Fargo, N.D., 1981; dir. ednl. counseling ctr. Concordia (Minn.) Coll., 1982-84; founder and dir. Discovery Counseling and Ednl. Ctr., Fargo, 1984—; sch. psychologist, 1981—; supr./liaison practicum placements and instr. Moorhead State U.; instr. grad. counseling program N.D. State U., 1988-94; supr. counseling grad. studies, 1991—; instr. Moorhead Tech. Coll., 1988—; co-founder, dir. Discovery Ednl. Workshops, 1991—; mem. grant task force Dilworth-Glyndon-Felton Cmty. Sch., Dilworth, Minn., 1993—; spkr. in field, 1984—. Author: Understanding and Enhancing Self-Esteem, 1992, Dealing With Guilt, Control and Power in Relationships, 1992. Active Stop the Violence, Moorhead, Dilworth, 1993—, Rape and Abuse Crisis Ctr., Fargo. Recipient Women of Distinction award Soroptimist Club, 1994. Mem. Am. Counseling and Devel. Assn. Democrat. Lutheran. Office: Discovery Counseling and Ednl Ctr 115 N University Dr Fargo ND 58102-4667

ROGNLIEN-EVENSON, KARI LYNN, county treasurer, recorder; b. Williston, N.D., July 19, 1963; d. Erik Kristoffer and Linda Rae (Braaten) Rognlien; m. Mark Oscar Evenson, Oct. 23, 1993; 1 child, Kjersti Rae. AA, U. N.D., Williston, 1983. Surveyor's helper, engring. asst. Williams County Hwy. Dept., Williston, 1981-87; dep. treas. Williams County Treas.'s Office, Williston, 1987-91, county treas., 1991-95, county treas., recorder, 1995—. Mem. Nat. Assn. of County Treas. and Fin. Officers, N.D. Assn. County Treas., Am. Legion Aux., Nat. Assn. County Recorders, Election Officials and Clks., N.D. Register of Deeds Assn. Lutheran. Home: 1619 11th Ave W Williston ND 58801-3834 Office: Williams County 205 E Broadway Williston ND 58801

ROGO, KATHLEEN, safety engineer; b. Carrollton, Ohio, Sept. 28, 1952; d. Silvio and Mary (Siragusano) R. Grad. high sch., Carrollton; PhD in Med. Sci. (hon.), Ohio Valley Pathologists, Inc., 1992. Cert. histotechnologist, emergency med. technologist, safety engr. Rsch. pathology trainee Aultman Hosp., Canton, Ohio, 1970-75, supr. anatomic pathology, 1974-75; lab. mgr. W. Morgan Lab., Canton, 1973-74; supr. anatomic pathology Dr.'s Hosp., Massillon, Ohio, 1975-78; emergency med. technician Canton Fire Dept., 1976-81; safety engr. Ashland Oil Co., Canton, 1980-82; rsch. pathologist assoc., med. cons, v.p. Ohio Valley Pathologists, Inc., Wheeling, W.Va., 1990—. Mem. Am. Soc. Clin. Pathology (cert. histotechnician), Am. Soc. Safety Engrs. (cert.), Am. Soc. Emergency Med. Technicians (cert.), Ohio State Med. Soc., Internat. Platform Assn. Democrat. Roman Catholic.

ROGOFF, MAI-LAN ALICIA, psychiatrist; b. Paris, Apr. 1, 1946; came to U.S. 1947; d. Joseph Bernard and Nguyen Thi (Trung) Rogoff. AB, Columbia U., 1967; MD, N.Y. Med. Coll., 1971. Diploamte Nat. Bd. Med. Examiners, Am. Bd. Psychiatry and Neurology. Intern N.E. Deaconess Hosp., Boston, 1971-72; resident in adult psychiatry Dartmouth-Hitchcock Affiliated Hosps., Hanover, N.H., 1972-75; asst. prof. psychiatry Dartmouth Coll., Hanover, N.H., 1975-80; resident in child psychiatry Children's Hosp. Med. Ctr., Boston, 1979-81; instr. psychiatry Harvard Med. Sch., Boston, 1981-84; assoc. prof. psychiatry U. Mass. Med. Sch., Worcester, 1983—. Laughlin fellow, Am. Coll. Psychiatrists. Mem. Am. Psychiatric Assn., Am. Acad. Child and Adolescent Psychiatrists, New Eng. Coun. Child and Adolescent Psychiatrists. Office: 55 Lake Ave N Worcester MA 01655-0001

ROHDE, BARBARA JO, consultant, public affairs researcher; b. Jamestown, N.D., July 9, 1952; d. Lorenz and Opal Irene (Sandvik) R. BA, U. N.D., 1973; MPA, U. Denver, 1980. Asst. press sec. Office Lt. Gov., St. Paul, 1975-76; program dir. Office of Gov., St. Paul, 1976-78; chief of staff Cong. Byron Dorgan, Washington, 1981-86; dir. State of Minn., Washington, 1987-91; rsch. fellow Hubert H. Humphery Inst. Pub. Affairs, U. Minn., 1991—; cons. Sagamore Assocs., Washington, 1994—. Mem. Leadership Am., Women Execs. in State Govt. (nat. bd. 1990—), Women in Trnasp., Women in Internat. Trade, Women in Govt. Rels., Orgn. Lic. Women Pilots (chmn. 1984), Jr. League of Washington (bd. dirs. 1987—). Democrat. Lutheran. Home: 2700 Virginia Ave NW Washington DC 20037-2626

ROHDE, GAYLE LYNETTE, municipal official; b. St. Paul, May 29, 1940; d. William Adolph and Carley Delilah (Pickle) Baumgardt; m. Robert Vincent Rohde, Feb. 16, 1963; childen: Dana Lynn, Darcye Ann. Student, U. Minn., 1959-60, Dixie Coll., 1977-92, So. Utah U., 1981-82. Cert. mcpl. clk. Pub. rels. specialist Softness Group, N.Y.C., 1960-61, Teen Screen Publs., L.A., 1961-62; office mgr. Discout Merchandise, Las Vegas, 1969-71, Bilt-Rite Constrn., Las Vegas, 1963-68; city recorder, adminstr. City of Enterprise, Utah, 1982—. Pres. North Las Vegas (Nev.) Women's Club, 1969-85; vice chair Enterprise Rep. Ctrl. Com., 1980's; mem. Enterprise Valley Med. Ctr., 1981-85, chair bd. dirs., 1983-85; pres. PTA Enterprise; bd. dirs. Rural Arts Co., Enterprise, 1978; mem. home econs. adv. com. Dixie Coll., St. George, Utah, 1978-85, mem. theatre coun., 1980's. Mem. Internat. Inst. Mcpl. Clks. (U.S.A. membership com. 1989-90), Utah Mcpl. Clks (bd. dirs., pres. 1983-94, state bd. 1985-90, state pres. 1988-89), Utah Mcpl. Fin. Officers. Mem. LDS Ch. Office: City of Enterprise 375 S 200 E PO Box 340 Enterprise UT 84725

ROHLOFF, LORI LUANNE, special education educator; b. Calgary, Alberta, Can., June 23, 1961; came to U.S., 1977; d. Robert John and Catherine Anne (Sled) R.; m. Leon A. Peek, 1993. BS in Psychology, U. N. Tex., 1984; BA in Edn., Tex. Women's U., 1991. Cert. tchr. spl. edn., Tex. Mental health counselor Brookaven Psychiat. Pavilion, Farmer's Br., Tex., 1984-86; spl. edn. art educator Jane Marshall Elem., Middle Sch., Denton, Tex., 199-91; spl. edn. educator high sch. Sanger (Tex.) Ind. Sch. Dist., 1991—; tchr. secondary art Sanger High Sch., 1994—. One-woman shows include Connectivity, 1992; exhibited in group shows at North Tex. Area Arts League, 1993 (Best of Show). Mem. NEA, Tex. State Tchrs. Assn., Coun. for Exceptional Childen, Nat. Mus. for Women in the Arts, Nat. Art Edn. Assn., Mortarboard. Democrat. Episcopalian. Office: Sanger High Sch 105 N Berry Sanger TX 76266

ROHRBACH, HEIDI A., lawyer; b. Buffalo, N.Y., Jan. 25, 1953; d. William R. and A.T. R.; divorced; 1 child, Peter R. Frank. BA, Northwestern U., Evanston, Ill., 1974; JD, Vanderbilt U., Nashville, 1977. Bar: N.Y., 1978. V.p. asst. gen. counsel Chemical Bank, N.Y.C., 1985—. Office: Chemical Bank 270 Park Ave 40th Fl New York NY 10017

ROHRBAUGH, JOANNA BUNKER, psychotherapist, educator; b. Washington, Sept. 1, 1943; d. Lewis H. and Ruth (Bunker) R.; m. Nathan E. Clark, June, 1964 (div. 1970); m. Melody L. Brazo; children: Emma Bunker Brazo, Jordan Bunker Brazo. BA, Brown U., 1964; PhD, Harvard U., 1976. Cert. Nat. Register Health Svc. Providers in Psychology; lic. psychologist, Mass. Instr. psychology of women Boston Ctr. for Adult Edn., 1975-77, Boston U. Summer Sch., 1976; NIMH postdoctoral fellow, intern Mass. Gen. Hosp./Erich Lindemann Mental Health Ctr., 1976-78; from clin. fellow to clin. assoc. in psychology dept. psych. Mass. Gen. Hosp., 1976-86; rsch. fellow dept. psychiatry Harvard Med. Sch., 1976-78, clin. instr. psychology, 1978-86, 88—; clin. instr. psychology dept. psychiatry Cambridge (Mass.) Hosp., 1988—; asst. prof. dept. psychology Wellesley (Mass.) Coll., 1980; pvt. practice Boston, 1978-89; dir. Rohrbaugh Assocs., Cambridge, M, 1989—; lectr. psychology dept. U. Mass., Boston, 1979. Author: Women: Psychology's Puzzle, 1979; contbr. articles to profl. jours. Elisha Benjamin Andrews scholar Brown U., 1960-61; NSF predoctoral fellow Harvard U., 1971-74, Danforth Found. predoctoral fellow Harvard U., 1971-76. Mem. APA, Am. Bd. Forensic Examiners, Assn. for Women in Psychology, Assn. for Lesbian and Gay Psychologists, Nat. Women's Studies Assn., Soc. for Psychol. Study of Social Issues, Mass. Psychol. Assn., Phi Beta Kappa. Office: Rohrbaugh Assocs 192R Upland Rd Cambridge MA 02140

ROHRBAUGH, LISA ANNE, librarian; b. Girard, Ohio, Sept. 17, 1956; d. John Michael and Josephine Antoinette (Oliva) Sultan; m. Paul Hugh Rohrbaugh Jr., July 28, 1979. BA, Youngstown State U., 1978; MLS, Kent State U., 1979. Libr.. readers assistance dept. Youngstown (Ohio) Pub. Libr., 1979-86; libr., researcher Ajax Magnethermic Corp., Warren, Ohio, 1986-90; asst. reference libr. Youngstown State U., 1990-93; dir. East Palestine (Ohio) Meml. Pub. Libr., 1993—; helped edit articles for Ency. Libr. Sci., 1978-79; translator articles dealing with electronics and induction heating/melting tech. from Spanish, German and French into English. Reviewer childrens books State Libr. of Ohio. Recipient Quest '91 Creative Scholarship award Youngstown State U., 1991. Office: East Palestine Meml Pub Libr 309 N Market St East Palestine OH 44413-2153

ROHRBECK, CYNTHIA ANN, psychology educator; b. Phila., Jan. 6, 1958; d. Charles Wesley and Annette (Searson) R.; m. Philip William Wirtz, May 19, 1991. BA, Cornell U., 1980; MA, U. Rochester, 1983, PhD, 1986. Lic. clin. psychologist, Md., D.C. Asst. prof. George Washington U., Washington, 1985-91, assoc. prof., 1991—; part-time pvt. practice Devel. and Psychol. Svcs., Inc., Ft. Washington, Md., 1989—. Contbr. book chpt.: Advances in Child Clinical Psychology, 1993; contbr. articles to profl. jours. Grantee Soc. for Psychol. Study of Social Issues, 1992, Murney Rsch. Ctr., Radcliffe Coll., 1993. Mem. APA, Assn. for Advancement of Behavior Therapy, Soc. for Rsch. in Child Devel. Office: George Washington U Dept Psychology 2125 G St NW Washington DC 20052

ROHRBOUGH, ELSA CLAIRE HARTMAN, artist; b. Shreveport, La., Sept. 26, 1915; d. Adolph Emil and Camille Claire (Francis) Hartman; m. Leonard M. Rohrbough, June 19, 1937 (dec. Jan. 1977); children: Stephen, Frank, Leonard. Juried exhbns. Massur Mus. Art, Monroe, La., Mobile (Ala.) Art Gallery, Gulf Coast Juried Exhibit, Mobile, La., Juried Arts Nat., Tyler, Tex., Greater New Orleans Nat., La. Watercolor Soc. Nat., Ky. Watermedia Nat., So. Watercolor Ann., La. Women Artist, many others. One-woman shows include Le Petit Theatre du Vieux Carre, New Orleans World Trade Ctr.'s Internat. House, Singing River Art Assn., Pascagoula, Miss., La. Font Inn, Pascagoula, Mandeville (La.) City Hall, St. Tammany Art Assn., Covington, La., others; exhibited in groups shows at 1st Guaranty Bank, Hammond, La., St. Tammany Art Assn., Ft. Isabel Gallery, Covington. Mem. Nat. League Am. Pen Women (v.p. S.E. La. br. 1986-87, pres. 1987-92, 94—), St. Tammany Art Assn. (bd. dirs. 1985-86, 87, instr. 1977-78, classes chmn. 1986-88). Republican. Roman Catholic. Home: 2525 Lakeshore Dr Mandeville LA 70448-5627

ROHRBOUGH, LINDA JANDECKA, computer center administrator; b. Akron, Ohio, Dec. 7, 1947; d. Clyde William and Dorothy Jean (Nine) Jandecka; m. Gene L. Rohrbough; 1 child, Zachary William. AAS, U. Akron, 1967, BSBA, 1971. With info. svcs. U. Akron (Ohio) Computer Ctr., 1970-72, sec. to dir., 1972-75, computer svcs. coord., 1975—. Bd. dirs. Firestone Pk. Citizens Council, Akron, 1980—, newsletter editor Akron, 1984-87. Mem. NOW. Republican. Baptist. Home: 217 N Firestone Blvd Akron OH 44301-2060 Office: U Akron Computer Ctr 185 Carroll St Akron OH 44325-3501

ROHREN, BRENDA MARIE ANDERSON, therapist; b. Kansas City, Mo., Apr. 18, 1959; d. Wilbur Dean and Katheryn Elizabeth (Albright) Anderson; m. Lathan Edward Rohren, May 10, 1985; 1 child, Amanda Jessica. BS in Psychology, Colo. State U., 1983; MA in Psychology, Cath. U. Am., 1986. Mental health therapist, sr. case mgr. Rappahannock Area Community Svcs. Bd., Fredericksburg, Va., 1986-88; mental health therapist, case mgmt. supr. Rappahannock Area Community Svcs. Bd., 1988; rsch. assoc. Inst. Medicine, NAS, Washington, 1988-89; supr. adult psychiat. program Lincoln (Nebr.) Gen. Hosp., 1989, program supr. mental health svcs., 1989-91; adj. instr. S.E. Community Coll., Lincoln, 1990—; assessment & referral specialist Rivendell Psychiat. Ctr., Seward, Nebr., 1993-95; therapist Lincoln Day Treatment Ctr., Lincoln, Nebr., 1993—; adj. instr. Coll. of St. Mary, 1994—; computer cons. Syscon Corp., Washington, 1983-84. Author: (report) Bottom Line Benefits: Building Economic Success Through Stronger Families; editor: (newsletter) Alliance for Mentally Ill, Lincoln. Active Cmty. Child Abuse Prevention Coun., Lincoln Alliance for the Mentally Ill, Nebr. Domestic Violence/Sexual Assault Coalition. Mem. NOW, APA (assoc.), Nat. Alliance for Mentally Ill, Nebr. Psychol. Assn. (assoc.). Democrat. Roman Catholic. Home: 3821 S 33rd St Lincoln NE 68506-3806 Office: SE Community Coll 8800 O St Lincoln NE 68520-1299 also: Lincoln Day Treatment Ctr 6020 S 58th St Lincoln NE 68516

ROHRER, CHRISTINA MARiE, artist; b. Washington, June 18, 1940; d. Andrew F. and Mary C. (Scanlon) Scheele; m. Dean C. Rohrer, Dec. 20, 1969; children: Jonathan W., M. Kirstin, Jay A. AB, Randolph-Macon Woman's Coll., 1962; PhD, Harvard U., 1970; studied with Robert Reed, Eve Ingalls, Carolyn Ginsberg, Lorina Naylor. Biol. rsch. asst. NIH, Bethesda, Md., 1962-65; Damon Runyon Meml. Postdoctoral fellow Pub. Health Rsch. Inst., N.Y.C., 1970-72, Leukemia Soc. Am. Spl. fellow, 1972-74. One-woman shows Landmark Lobby Gallery, Stamford, Conn., 1989, Art/Ex Gallery, Stamford, 1993; group exhbns. Stamford Mus. and Nature Ctr., 1985, 87, 88, 90, 92, 93, Hurlbutt Gallery, Greenwich, Conn., 1991; contbr. articles to profl. jours. and mags. Mem. Stamford Art Assn. (exhbn. co-chair), Loft Artists Assn. (mem. publicity, signage, bd. dirs.), Women's Caucus for Art-Conn. (mem. nominating com., sec.), Inst. Visual Artists (mem. steering com.). Home: 37 Woodland Rd Pound Ridge NY 10576 Office: 190 Henry St Bldg 18 Stamford CT 06902

ROIGNANT, SARA ALICE, secondary school educator, small business owner; b. Joliet, Ill., Aug. 3, 1939; d. Ernest Richard and Mary Claire (Steffen) Blondis; m. Germain Herve Roignant, Nov. 27, 1965; children: Marie Claire Louise, Jane Noelle, Jeremiah John. BA, Barat Coll., 1961; postgrad., Alliance Francaise,, Paris, 1963; postgrad. studies French, U. Calif., San Francisco, 1968-70; contg. edn. in edn., De Paul, Loyola Univs., Chgo., 1970—. Cert. tchr., Ill., Calif. Tchr. Wilshire Sch., Fullerton, Calif., 1961-63, Berlitz Sch., Paris, 1963; Berlitz Sch., N.Y.C., 1964; tchr. San Francisco City Schs., 1965-70; tchr., tutor, substitute tchr. St. Sebastian's Elem. Sch., Chgo., 1975-79; tchr. Films, TV, Commercials, Chgo., 1979—; restaurateur La Creperie, Chgo., 1972—. Producer, writer, dir.: several plays including Savon at La Creperies Cafe Theatre, 1972-82. Bd. dirs. Our Lady of Mt. Carmel Sch., 1987-90. Mem. Lakeview E. C. of C. (bd. dirs. 1990—, sec. 1992-93). Roman Catholic. Home: 2845 1/2 N Clark St Chicago IL 60657-5207 Office: 2845 N Clark St Chicago IL 60657-5207

ROISMAN, HANNA MASLOVSKI, classics educator; b. Wroclaw, Poland; d. Leon and Eugenia (Shlager-Katz) Maslovski; m. Joseph Roisman, Aug. 5, 1971; children: Elad L., Shalev G. BA in Classics, MA in Classics, Tel Aviv U., Ramat Aviv, Israel, 1977; PhD in Classics, U. Wash., 1981. Lectr. classics Tel Aviv U., 1981-87, sr. lectr. classics, 1987-90; assoc. prof. classics Colby Coll., Waterville, Maine, 1990-94, prof., 1994—; jr. fellow Ctr. Hellenic Studies, Washington, 1985-86; vis. scholar U. Wash. Seattle, 1983, Cornell U., Ithaca, N.Y., 1989; sec. Israel Soc. for Promotion of Classical Studies, 1987-89; vis. assoc. prof. Cornell U., 1986-94. Author: Loyalty in Early Greek Epic and Tragedy, 1984; contbr. articles to profl. jours. AAUW fellow, 1980-81. Office: Colby Coll Mayflower Hill Waterville ME 04901

ROITMAN, JUDITH, mathematics educator; b. N.Y.C., Nov. 12, 1945; d. Leo and Ethel (Gottesman) R.; m. Stanley Lombardo, Sept. 26, 1978; 1 child, Ben Lombardo. BA in English, Sarah Lawrence Coll., 1966; MA in Math., U. Calif., Berkeley, 1971, PhD in Math., 1974. Asst. prof. math. Wellesley (Mass.) Coll., 1974-77; from asst. prof. to prof. math. U. Kans., Lawrence, 1977—. Author: Introduction to Modern Set Theory, 1990; contbr. articles to profl. jours. Grantee NSF, 1975-87, 92-95. Mem. Assn. Symbolic Logic, Am. Math. Soc., Assn. Women in Math. (pres. 1979-81), Kans. Assn. Tchrs. of Math., Nat. Assn. Tchrs. Math.

ROIZ, MYRIAM, foreign trade executive; b. Managua, Nicaragua, Jan. 21, 1938; came to U.S., 1949; d. Francisco Octavio and Maria Herminia (Briones) R.; m. Nicholas M. Orphanopoulos, Jan. 21, 1957 (div.); children: Jacqueline Doggwiler, Gene E. Orphanopoulos, George A. Orphanopoulos. BA in Interdisciplinary Social Sci. cum laude, San Francisco State U., 1980. Lic. ins. agt. Sales rep. Met. Life Ins. Co., San Francisco, 1977-79; mktg. dir. Europe/Latin Am., Allied Canners & Packers, San Francisco, 1979-83, M-C Internat., San Francisco, 1983-88; v.p. mktg. Atlantic Brokers, Inc., Bayamon, P.R., 1988-92; owner Aquarius Enterprises Internat., San Ramon, Calif., 1992—. Coord. Robert F. Kennedy Presdl. campaign, Millbrae, San Mateo County, local mayoral campaign, Millbrae, 1975; bd. dir., organizer fund-raising campaign for earthquake-devastated Nicaragua; active World Hunger Program Brown U., Children Internat., World Vision, Childhelp USA. Named Outstanding Employee of Yr. Hillsborough City Sch. Dist., 1973; recipient Sales award Met. Life Ins. Co., 1977. Mem. Nat. Assn. Female Execs., World Affairs Coun. Republican. Roman Catholic.

ROJAK, REBECCA LEE, realtor; b. State College, Pa., Apr. 6, 1957; d. George Alan Lee and Alberta May (Junkin) Lee; m. Ronald Lee Rojak, Mar. 18, 1984. BA in Interdisciplinary Studies, Maharishi Internat. U., 1979. Grad. Realtors Inst. Realtor Coldwell Banker Real Estate, Silver Spring, Md., 1987-89; property mgr., realtor Heartland Real Estate, Fairfield, Iowa, 1989—; v.p. mktg. The VCR Maniac, Fairfield, 1991—. V.p. bd. dirs. Chevy Chase Condo Assn., Silver Spring, 1989. Mem. NAFE, Nat. Fedn. Profl. and Bus. Women, Nat. Assn. Realtors, Golden Speakers Toastmasters Club, Toastmasters Internat. (Competent Toastmaster 1982), Golden Speakers Toastmasters Club (pres., Able Toastmaster 1992).

ROJAS, KRISTINE BRIGGS, insurance underwriter; b. Pocatello, Idaho, July 25, 1947; d. Fergus Jr. and Shirley (Tanner) Briggs; divorced; children: Anthony Ted, Nancy Kristine. Student, Idaho State U., 1965-66. Tech. coord. Farmers Ins. Group, Pocatello, 1971-81; svc. rep. All Seasons Ins. Agy., Ventura, Calif., 1982; sr. comml. underwriting asst. Royal Ins. Co., Ventura, 1982-85; sr. comml. lines underwriter Andreini & Co., Ventura, 1985-88; large comml. account unit coord. Frank B. Hall, Inc., Oxnard, Calif., 1988-93; account exec. Fox Ins. Agy. Inc., Camarillo, Calif., 1993—. Editor (bulletin) News Waves, 1985-87; artist various works specializing in charcoal portraits. Mem. NAFE, Ins. Women Ventura County (treas. 1987-88, v.p. 1988-90, pres. 1990-91, corr. sec. 1991-92, bd. dirs. 1986-87, Woman of Yr. 1989-90), Nat. Assn. Ins.Women. Republican. Baptist. Home: 2197 Brookhill Dr Camarillo CA 93010-2107 Office: Fox Ins Agy Inc 2301 Daily Dr Ste 200 Camarillo CA 93010-6618

ROKOS, MEG DAVIDSON, management consultant; b. Waterbury, Conn., June 17, 1953; d. Robert Key and Jeanne Margaret (Smith) Davidson; m. Paul E. Rokos, June 24, 1988; children: Kate, Zachary. AA, Am. Coll. in Paris, 1974; BS, U. N.H., 1976, MBA, 1978. Corp. devel. specialist Nashua (N.H.) Corp., 1978-79; mktg. analyst Xerox Corp., Rochester, N.Y., 1979-81; account mgr. Xerox Corp., Rochester, 1981-84; sales mgr. Xerox Corp., Lexington, Mass., 1985-87; mgr. of hiring Xerox Corp., Boston, 1988-90, dist. mgr., 1990-92; ind. total quality mgmt. cons. North Andover, Mass., 1992—; instr. total quality mgmt., 1993. Vol. Cystic Fibrosis Found., Natick, Mass. Mem. Am. Mgmt. Assn., Am. Soc. for Quality Control. Office: 981 Johnson St North Andover MA 01845-5527

ROKOSZ, GRACE L., actuary; b. Denver, Nov. 8, 1959; d. John Francis Jr. and Janet Margaret (Green) Malloy; m. Vaughn Rokosz, June 11, 1994. BS, Mass. Inst. of Tech., Cambridge, 1982. Actuary asst. John Hancock Mut. Life Ins. Co., Boston, 1982-85, assoc. actuary, 1989—. Mem. Natick (Mass.) Town Meeting, 1990-92; trustee, former chmn. bd. trustees Natick Village Condominium, 1991—. Fellow Soc. Actuaries (edn. and exam. com. 1989-93); mem. Am. Acad. Actuaries, Boston Actuaries Club.

ROLAND, BRENDA, medical, surgical and mental health nurse; b. Gainesville, Tex., Nov. 1, 1950; d. George W. Jr. and Joyce (Moore) R. Diploma, Cameron U., Lawton, Okla., 1978, BS, 1978; student, North Tex. State U., Denton. RN. Charge nurse, mental health and med.-surg. Med. Plaza Hosp., Sherman, Tex.; staff nurse in mental health Brookhaven Hosp., Dallas; med.-surg. staff nurse Texoma Med. Ctr., Denison, Tex. Mem. Nat. Profl. Psychiat. Nurses Am. Home: RR 4 Box 103 Whitesboro TX 76273-9446

ROLAND, MARYA FRANCES, artist, educator; b. Berkeley, Calif., Sept. 27, 1949; d. Vern Jacob and Winnifred Patricia (Price) R.; m. David Freeman, 1974 (div. 1980). BA in Art History, U. Calif., Berkeley, 1971; MFA in Sculpture, U. Wash., 1988; postgrad, Video-Editing Workshop, Johnson, Vt., 1991, Virtual Reality and Interactive Arts Workshop, Normal, Ill., 1992. Asst. prof. art Johnson (Vt.) State Coll., 1989-91, Ill. State U., Normal, 1991—; arts specialist, adminstr., designer summer arts program King County Park Dept., 1982; mgr. pub. rels. Marymoor Arts Ctr. Gallery, Kirkland, Wash., 1982; artist-in-residence Washington State U., 1983-85. One woman shows include Pelican Bay Gallery, Seattle, 1979, Loaded Brush Gallery, Seattle, 1984, King County Arts Commn. Gallery, Seattle, 1990, Tough Gallery, Chgo., 1993, Moreau Gallery, South Bend, Ind., 1993, St. Xavier U. Gallery, Chgo., 1993, Contemporary Art Ctr. of Arlington, Arlington Heights, Ill., 1993, Gallery N.W., Gary, Ind., 1994, Parkland Coll., Champaign, Ill., 1994; exhibited in group shows at Whatcom County Art Mus., Bellingham, Wash., 1979, Bellevue (Wash.) Art Mus., 1980, Hoffman Gallery, Portland, Oreg., 1980, Traver Sutton Gallery, Seattle, 1983, Pioneer Sq. Auction Invitational, Seattle, 1982, 83, Bumbershoot Arts Festival, Seattle, 1982, 83, Henry Gallery, Seattle, 1988, AFLN Gallery, Seattle, 1989, Dibden Ctr. for the Arts, Johnson, Vt., 1991, Art Guild Gallery, Peoria, Ill., 1992, Univ. Galleries, Normal, 1991, 93, Tough Gallery, Chgo., 1993, Artemesia Gallery, Chgo., 1993, U. Hawaii Art Gallery, Honolulu, 1994, Indpls. Art League, 1994, Tough Gallery, Chgo., 1994, Merwin Gallery Ill. Wesleyan U., Bloomingtonm 1994. Grantee Seattle Arts Commn., 1980, King County Arts Commn., 1990; Faculty Devel. grantee Johnson State Coll., 1991, Small grantee Ill. State U., 1993-94, Rsch. grantee, 1993-94; Regional Artists' Projects grantee, 1993-94; Artist fellow State of Ill. Arts Coun., 1993. Mem. NOW, Internat. Sculpture Ctr., Women's Caucus for the Arts (nat. and Chgo. chpts.), Chgo. Artists Coalition, Coll. Art Assn., Mus. Contemporary Art, Chgo. Office: Ill State U Dept of Art CVA 119 Normal IL 61761

ROLAND, MELISSA MONTGOMERY, accountant; b. Houston, Mar. 6, 1961; d. John Edgar and Mariann (Guggino) Montgomery; m. Larry Dean Roland, Sept. 20, 1984. BBA, Tex. A&M U., 1983. CPA, Tex., cert. fraud examiner, Tex. Audit sr. Arthur Andersen & Co., Houston, 1983-87; cons. mgr.-performance improvement group Ernst & Young, San Antonio, 1988-91; COO Roy Smith Shoes, Inc. d/b/a Accenté, Houston, 1991—. Bd. dirs., treas. Grandparents Outreach, San Antonio, 1989—. Mem. AICPA, Tex. Accts. and Lawyers for the Arts (adv. bd.), Tex. Soc. CPAs, Young Reps., Jr. League Houston, S.W. Found. Forum. Presbyterian. Home: 5523 Boyce Springs Dr Houston TX 77066-2401 Office: 3120 Rogerdale Rd Ste 190 Houston TX 77042-4125

ROLFE, JUDITH LEWIS, special education educator; b. Chgo., Dec. 1, 1939; d. Earl A. and Eileen (Karlin) Lewis; m. Michael Rolfe, June 16, 1959; children: Andrew Jay, Lisa Kay, James Lewis. BA summa cum laude, Barat Coll., 1982; MEd, Nat. Coll. Edn., 1988. Cert. spl. edn. tchr., elem. edn., LD/BD, Ill. Learning disabilities specialist Barat Coll., Lake Forest, Ill., 1981-82; learning disabilites specialist/diagnostician Highland Park (Ill.) High Sch., 1982—. Mem. Coun. for Exceptional Children (mem. publs. com. 1988-90), Learning Disabilities Assn., Profls. in Learning Disabilities.

ROLFES, REBECCA THOMASON, journalist and communications consultant; b. Morganfield, Ky., Dec. 15, 1948; d. Ben Thomas and Lucy Agnes (Spalding) Thomason; m. Edward John Rolfes, Mar. 25, 1942; children: Charles Edward, Lea Spalding. BA in English and French, U. Ky., 1970; postgrad., Am. Sch. Classical Studies, Athens, Greece, 1976-77; U. Libre, Brussels, Belgium, Belgium, 1992. Editor Eason Pubs., Atlanta, 1981-83; columnist and editor Ackroyd Pubs., Brussels, 1985-92; comms. assoc. The Conf. Bd. Europe, Brussels, 1989-92; conf. program dir. The Conf. Bd., N.Y.C., 1992-93; v.p. external rels. IEG, Chgo., 1993-94; exec. editor Imagination Pub., Chgo., 1994—. Author: (monograph) The Glass Ceiling in Europe, 1990. Pub. rels. dir. Rainbow House, Chgo., 1994. Mem. Internat. Assn. Bus. Communicators, Women Employed, FOCUS (Brussels).

ROLLBERG, JEANNE NORTON, educator; b. Jacksonville, Fla., Oct. 31, 1957; d. James Thomas and Joan Wade (Jennings) N.; m. Charles Anthony Rollberg, Aug. 4, 1956. BA, Wesleyan Coll., Macon, Ga., 1979; MA in Journalism, U. Mo., 1980. Stringer Dayton (Ohio) Daily News, 1981; asst. news dir. KAMU-TV/FM, Tex. A&M U., College Station, 1981-82, news dir., 1983; asst. prof. U. Ark., Little rock, 1983—; pub. affairs show producer KLRE-KUAR/FM, Little rock, 1987—; gen. asst. rep. part time KTHV-TV, Little Rock, 1984, 89—. Recipient 1st place pub. affairs award Ark. AP, 1989-93, award for talk show Am. Women in Radio and TV, Inc., 1989, 92. Mem. Assn. Edn. Journalism and Mass Communications, Soc. Profl. Journalists, Broadcast Edn. Assn., Ark. Press Women, Internat. Communication Assn. Office: U Ark 2801 S University Ave Little Rock AR 72204-1000

ROLLE, ESTHER, actress; b. Pompano Beach, Fla., Nov. 8; d. Jonathan Rolle. Student, Spellman Coll., Hunter Coll., New Sch. for Social Research. Dancer, Shogola Obola Dance Co., then mem., Negro Ensemble Co.; off-Broadway debut: The Blacks, 1962; London stage debut: God is a (Guess What?), 1969; numerous stage appearances include Macbeth, Amen Corner, Blues for Mister Charlie, Don't Play Us Cheap; toured Scandinavia in stage prdn. The Skin of Our Teeth; toured Australia, New Zealand in stage prdns. Black Nativity; other stage prdns. The Member of the Wedding, 1988, Nothing But a Man, 1964, Cleopatra Jones, 1973, Don't Play Us Cheap, 1973, P.K. and the Kid, 1982, Driving Miss Daisy, 1989, The Mighty Quinn, 1989, Color Adjustment, 1991, House of Cards, 1993, Nobody's Girls, 1994; TV series include Maude, 1972-74, One Life to Live, 1972-74, Good Times, 1974-77, 78-79, Singer and Sons, 1990; TV appearances include Summer of My German Soldier, 1979 (Emmy award 1979), I Know Why the Caged Bird Sings, 1979, Age Old Friends, 1989, The Kid Who Loved Christmas, 1990, Dinah's Place, N.Y.P.D., Like It Is, East Side, West Side, To Dance with a White Dog, 1993, Message From Nam, 1993, Scarlet, 1994. Hon. chmn. Pres.'s Com. on Employment of Handicapped.; Grand Marshall Cherry Blossom Festival, Washington, 1975. Named Woman of Yr. 3d World Sisterhood, 1976; recipient Image awards, NAACP, 1973, 74, 79, Leadership award, 1990, Hall of Fame, 1987; guest Bahamian gov. dedication Nat. Bank, 1993. Office: William Morris Agy 152 El Camino Dr Beverly Hills CA 90212*

ROLLENCE, MICHELE LYNETTE, molecular biologist; b. Takoma Park, Md., Nov. 23, 1955; d. John Francis and Martha Jo (Jackson) R.; m. David H. Specht, June 3, 1978 (div. Sept. 1982). AA, Montgomery Coll., 1976; BS, U. Md., 1978. Lab. technician Dairy and Food Labs., San Francisco, 1979-81; rsch. asst. Genex Corp., Gaithersburg, Md., 1981-82, rsch. assoc., 1982-86, sr. rsch. assoc., 1986-88, rsch. scientist, 1989-93; rsch. assoc. Genetic Therapy, Inc., Gaithersburg, Md., 1993—. Contbr. articles to profl. publs.; patentee in field. Pres. Explorer Post div. Boy Scouts Am., Gaithersburg, 1973; youth advisor Neelsville Presbyn. Ch., Germantown, Md., 1990. Recipient Nat. Exploration award TRW/Explorers Club, 1973. Mem. AAAS, Am. Soc. Microbiology, DAR, Pleasant Plains of Damascus. Republican. Presbyterian. Office: Genetic Therapy Inc 19 Firstfield Rd Gaithersburg MD 20878

ROLLIN, BETTY, author, television journalist; b. N.Y.C., Jan. 3, 1936; d. Leon and Ida R.; m. Harold M. Edwards, Jan. 21, 1979. BA, Sarah Lawrence Coll., 1957. Assoc. features editor Vogue mag., 1964; sr. editor Look mag., 1965-71; network corr. NBC News, N.Y.C., 1971-80, contbg. corr., 1985—; network corr. ABC News Nightline, 1982-84; lectr. in field. Profl. actress on stage and television, 1958-64; Author: I Thee Wed, 1958, Mothers Are Funnier Than Children, 1964, The Non-Drinkers' Drink Book, 1966, First, You Cry, 1976, reissue, 1993, Am I Getting Paid for This?, 1982, Last Wish, 1985; columnist Hers, N.Y. Times; Contbr. articles to popular mags. Office: care NS Bienstock Inc 1740 Broadway New York NY 10019-4315

ROLLINS, DONNA LEE, art educator, photographer; b. Portland, Oreg., May 3, 1951; d. Edgar Lynn and Stephanie Marcel (Charlet) R. BFA magna cum laude, U. Maine, Gorham, 1978; MFA, Rochester Inst. Tech., 1987. Chairperson divsn. fine art Fox Sch. Photography, Portland, Maine, 1980-83, assoc. dir., 1981-83; pres. Photog. Artists of Maine, Portland, 1983-84; exhbn. coord. RIT Photo Gallery, Rochester, N.Y., 1986-87; photo preservationist Just B&W Custom Photo Lab., Portland, 1987-88; grad. tchg. asst. Coll. Photo Art and Scis., Rochester Inst. Tech., 1986-87; instr. photography U. So. Maine, Gorham, 1987, Maine Coll. Art, Portland, 1987—; ptnr., illustrator Off-Season Pub. Co., South Portland, Maine, 1992—; photography curator Danforth Gallery, Portland, Maine, 1994—. Artist/photographer ltd. edit. portfolios, 1987, 88, 90, 91; exhibitor Fight That AIDS Thang benefit auction, Portland, 1991-92, Women's Resource Ctr. benefit auction, Portland, 1992. Mem. ACLU, Soc. for Photog. Edn., Coll. Art Assn., Photog. Resource Ctr. Home: 111 Pine St South Portland ME 04106

ROLLINS, DOROTHY GENEVIEVE, quality management professional; b. Mobridge, S.D., May 12, 1946; d. Roscoe Henry and Dorothy Ardith (Carsten) R. BSN, U. Washington, 1972; ThM, Aquinas Inst., 1978; M of Religious Studies, Gonzaga U., 1984. RN, Wash., Oreg.; cert. Zenger-Miller tng. facilitator. Staff nurse Group Health Hosp., Seattle, 1972-74; dir. pastoral care dept. Holy Family Hosp., Spokane, Wash., 1978-81; campus ministry intern Gonzaga U., Spokane, Wash., 1982-84; from assoc. campus min. to dir. campus ministry Coll. St. Benedict, St. Joseph, Minn., 1984-87, coord. student vol. program to needy and homeless, 1984-87; HIV program coord., psychiat. staff nurse VA Med. Ctr., St. Cloud, Minn., 1987-89; quality mgmt. coord. and quality improvement coord. Providence Med. Ctr., Portland, Oreg., 1989—; AIDS cmty. edn. VA Med. Ctr., St. Cloud, 1988-89. Contbr. articles to profl. jours. Chair 1st ann. womens week Gonzaga U., Spokane, 1984; coord. student vol. program to needy and homeless Coll. St. Benedict, St. Joseph, Minn., 1984-87. Gonzaga U. fellow in campus ministry, 1982-84; nursing scholar U. Wash., 1970-72. Mem. Am. Soc. Quality Control, Oreg. League for Nursing, Sigma Theta Tau. Democrat. Roman Catholic. Home: 4405 SE 48th Ave Portland OR 97206

ROLLINS, JUDITH ANN, sociologist, educator, researcher, writer; b. Boston; d. Edward Bryant and Edith Frances (Wade) R. BA, Howard U., 1970, MA, 1972; PhD, Brandeis U., 1983. Instr. Sociology Fed. City Coll., Washington, 1972-77; asst. prof. Sociology N.E. U., Boston, 1983-84; asst. prof. Sociology Simmons Coll., Boston, 1984-89, assoc. prof. Sociology, 1989-92; assoc. prof. Africana Studies and Sociology Wellesley (Mass.) Coll., 1992—. Author: Between Women, 1985 (Am. Sociol. Assn. award 1987). Office: Wellesley Coll Dept Africana Studies Wellesley MA 02181

ROLLINS, SHERRIE SANDY, television executive; b. Roanoke, Va., June 11, 1958; d. William Gresham and Charlotte (Weeks) Sandy; m. Edward John Rollins, Jr., May 2, 1987. BA, U. Va., 1980. Sr. v.p. ABC TV Network, Washington, 1980; advt. dir. Georgetown mag., Alexandria, Va., 1980-81; exec. dir. Bus. and Profl. Assn. Georgetown, Washington, 1981-84;

v.p. communications The Oliver Carr Co., Washington, 1985-89; asst. sec. for pub. affairs HUD, Washington, 1989-90; dir. news info. ABC News, N.Y.C., 1990-92; asst. to Pres. of U.S. for pub. liason and intergovtl. affairs The White House, Washington, 1992; sr. v.p. U.S. News and World Report, Washington, 1992-94; sr. v.p. Network Comms. ABC TV Network, N.Y.C., 1994—; bd. dirs. Am. Coun. Young Pol. Leaders, Cities in Schs. Mem. U. Va. Alumni Assn. (bd. mgrs.). Home: 7732 Southdown Rd Alexandria VA 22308-1341 Office: Capital Cities/ABC 77 West 66th St New York NY 10023

ROLNICK, JOAN JACOBS, psychotherapist, retired; b. N.Y.C., Jan. 17, 1925; d. Irving Louis and Frances (Tarakoff) Jacobs; m. Gerald Rolnick, Dec. 27, 1945; children: Neil Burton, Kyle, Peter Owen, Brian Jacobs. BS in Home Econs., Syracuse U., 1945; MEd, Western Conn. State U., 1966; AA in Mental Health, U. Bridgeport, 1973; MA in Counseling, So. Conn. State U., 1985. Elem. sch. tchr. Burr Farms Sch., Westport, Conn., 1966-73; counselor Info. & Referral Svc., Westport, 1973-74; psychotherapist Catholic Family Svcs., Danbury, Conn., 1974-75; counselor State Conn. Labor Dept., Danbury, 1976-78; social worker Dept. Children & Youth Svcs., Danbury, 1978-88; psychotherapist Options Counseling, Danbury, 1988-91; staff U. Bridgeport (Conn.), 1973-74; counselor United Hosp. Portchester (N.Y.), 1973-74; dir. Community House, Norwalk, Conn., 1976-80; co-dir. Open Door Day Care Ctr., Westport, 1976-78; dir. P-FLAG of S.W. Conn., Norwalk, 1979—. Editor: (newsletter) Voice of P-Flag of S.W. Conn., 1979—. Bd. dirs. A World of Difference, Danbury, 1990—; advisor to lesbian and gay community, S.W. Conn., 1979—; active Parents & Family & Friends of Lesbians and Gays. Recipient mayoral citation, 1992, community citation, 1992. Democrat. Jewish.

ROMAGNUOLO, AMY BETH, elementary educator; b. Syracuse, N.Y., May 25, 1968; d. Gary Allen and Patricia Ann (Owens) David; m. Andrew Frank Romagnuolo, July 7, 1990. BS, SUNY, Brockport, 1990; MEd, Nat. Louis U., Heidelberg, Germany, 1992. 3d grade tchr. Vogelwen Elem. Sch., Dept. Def. Dependent Schs., Kaiserlautern, Germany, 1990-92; adult GED tchr. Onondaya, Cortland Madison McEvoy Edn. Campus, BOCES, Cortland, N.Y., 1992-94, ESL tchr. for adults; 4th grade tchr. St. Mary's Elem. Sch., Cortland, 1992-94; 6th grade sci. tchr. Tulley Elem. Sch., 1994—; ESL tutor Lansing (N.Y.) Mid. Sch. Mem. NAFE. Roman Catholic. Home: 54 Miller St Cortland NY 13045

ROMAIN, BELLA MARY, graphic designer; b. Oakland, Calif., June 16, 1949; d. John Thomas Kondrup and Anna (Rabinowitz) Friedman; m. Stewart Jay Romain, Mar. 19, 1972. Student, SUNY, Stony Brook, 1967-68, Sch. Visual Arts, 1973-75; BFA magna cum laude, West Ga. Coll., 1989. Asst. to editor Dell Pub. Co., N.Y.C., 1968-72; reporter, proofreader Local News, Long Island, N.Y., 1973-76; graphic designer, editor Yellow Book Corp., N.Y.C., 1976-78; freelance graphic designer, editor N.Y.C., 1978-82; owner, graphic designer, editor designplus, Carrollton, Ga., 1982—; publs. cons. West Ga. Coll., Carrollton, 1985—. Paintings exhibited in numerous juried shows, including Alexandria Mus. Art, 1992. Speaker to civic groups, Carrollton, 1993; vol. Amateur Radio Emergency Svcs., Carrollton, 1985—; vol. designer Carroll County Humane Soc., Carrollton, 1993—. Recipient Fine Arts Achievement award Binney & Smith, 1989. Mem. Nat. Mus. Women in Arts, Toastmasters (chair membership local chpt. 1993), Carroll County C. of C., Phi Kappa Phi. Home: 285 Timber Ridge Trail Carrollton GA 30117 Office: designplus 104 Corporate Dr Carrollton GA 30117

ROMAINE, CATHERINE, writer; b. Johnson City, Tenn., Oct. 31, 1959; d. Joseph David and Helene (Storie) R. BS in Criminal Justice, East Tenn. State U., 1981, BS in English, 1983, MA, 1985. Cert. pool and spa operator. Editor Elizabethton (Tenn.) Newspapers Inc., 1986-88; comm. specialist N.Am. Rayon Corp., Elizabethton, 1988-92; sr. editorial specialist Sonoco Products Co., Hartsville, S.C., 1992—; pub. rels. cons. Sycamore Shoals Hosp., Elizabethton, 1989-91; writer East Tenn. Cath., Knoxville, 1990-92, Cath. Miscellany, Charleston, S.C., 1993—. Author of poems. Chmn. publicity Elizabethton/Carter County Chamber Tourism, 1990-92; mem. Keep Am. Beautiful, Darlington County, S.C., 1993—. Named Vol. of Yr., United Way, Elizabethton, 1990; recipient Honorarium for Women in Bus., Altrusa, Kingsport, Tenn., 1990, Comm. award Kingsport (Tenn.) Times News, 1991, 93. Mem. Carolina Assn. Bus. Communicators (1st place Best Magapaper 1993). Roman Catholic. Office: Sonoco Products Co 1 N Second St Hartsville SC 29550

ROMAN, CECELIA FLORENCE, cardiologist; b. Phila., June 12, 1956; d. Stanley Jeremiah and Doris (Manus) Romanowski. BA magna cum laude, Boston U., 1977; DO, Phila. Coll. Osteo. Medicine, 1981. Intern, internal medicine resident Del. Valley Med. Ctr., Langhorne, Pa., 1981-84; cardiology fellow Deborah Heart and Lung Ctr., Browns Mills, N.J., 1984-86, cardiology attending dir. med. intensive care unit, 1986-90; clin. instr. dept. medicine Robert Wood Johnson Med. Sch., U. Medicine, Dentistry N.J.; cardiology attending physician Clin. Cardiology Group, Langhorne, Pa., 1990-93; pvt. practice Clin. Cardiology Group, Bristol, Pa., 1993—; staff cardiologist Albert Einstein Med. Ctr., Med. Coll. Pa., Del. Valley Med. Ctr., Lower Bucks Hosp., St. Mary's Hosp. Author med. videos; lectr. in field; contbr. articles to profl. jours. Recipient Physicians Recognition award, 1987—. Fellow Am. Coll. Angiology, Am. Coll. Osteo. Internists; mem. Am. Osteo. Assn., Pa. Osteo. Med. Assn., Am. Coll. Osteo. Internists-cardiology and geriatric divs. Home: 12 Duffield Dr West Trenton NJ 08628-2006

ROMAN, KAREN JANE, systems executive; b. Cleve., Sept. 15, 1946; d. John G. and Jean R. (Koval) R. BA, Wheeling Jesuit Coll., 1968; MA, Bowling Green State U., 1970. Instr. Bowling Green (Ohio) State U., 1972-77, Cen. Mich. U., Mt. Pleasant, 1977-81; adminstr. U. Mass. Med. Sch., Worcester, 1981-85; mgr. Digital Equipment Corp., Bedford, Mass., 1985-90; dir. Agora Resources, Lexington, Mass., 1990-91; officer, v.p. Index Tech., Cambridge, Mass., 1986-91; v.p. Banyan Systems, Inc., Westboro, Mass., 1991—. Counselor Rape Crisis Ctr., Worcester, 1981-85. Fellowship Bowling Green State U., 1972. Mem. ADAPSO. Office: Banyan Systems Inc 115 Flanders Rd Westborough MA 01581-1027

ROMANANSKY, MARCIA CANZONERI, book company executive; b. Bklyn., Apr. 22, 1941; d. Nicholas C. and Ellen (Zukas) Canzoneri. BA in History, Coll. of Misericordia, Dallas, Pa., 1962; MLS, Pratt Inst., 1969; MA in Edn., Seton Hall U., 1973; postgrad. Fairleigh Dickinson U., 1980—. Acquisitions libr. St. Peter's Coll., Jersey City, 1963-68; sch. libr. Roselle (N.J.) High Sch., 1968-72; selection libr. Baker & Taylor, Somerville, N.J., 1972-74, chief libr., 1974-80, asst. mgr. program services, 1980-81, mgr. program svcs., 1981-87, dir. pub. libr. mktg., 1987-88; v.p. Yankee Book Peddler, Contoocook, N.H., 1988-89; dir. collection devel. svcs. Blackwell N.Am., Blackwood, N.J., 1989-90, v.p. purchasing and ops., 1990—. Contbr. articles to profl. jours. Mem. publicity com. Showhouse, Aux. Muhlenberg Hosp., Plainfield, N.J., 1982, 84. Mem. ALA (tech. svcs. com. 1982-84), Beta Phi Mu. Home and Office: Blackwell NAm Inc 100 University Ct Blackwood NJ 08012

ROMAN-BARBER, HELEN, corporate executive; b. Dec. 20, 1946. LLB, U. Paris, 1971, M of Internat. Law, 1972. Chmn., chief exec. officer Roman Corp. Ltd., Toronto, Ont., Can. Office: Roman Corp Ltd, 200 King St W Box 82, Toronto, ON Canada M5H 3T4

ROMANELLO, MARGUERITE MARIE, librarian; b. San Francisco, Feb. 14, 1939; d. Antonio Joseph and Josephine Remilda (Magliano) R. BA cum laude, Lone Mountain Coll., 1960, MA, 1961. Cert. secondary tchr. and librarian, Calif. Instr. Portola Jr. High Sch., San Francisco, 1961-74, Abraham Lincoln High Sch., San Francisco, 1978-81; libr. Francisco Jr. High Sch., San Francisco, 1974-75, instr., 1975-78; libr., media specialist Raoul Wallenberg Traditional High Sch., San Francisco, 1981—; judge U.S. Acad. Decathalon, San Francisco, 1988, 89. Author: MOSAIC, 1975, (play) Scenes from Sense and Sensibility, 1986; editor San Francisco Guitar Soc. Newsletter, 1975-76; exhibitor Festival of Needlework, San Francisco, 1979. Founder, curator Raoul Wallenberg Mus., San Francisco, 1981—; active in Community Adv. Coun., San Francisco, 1968-70, KRON Community Adv. Com., San Francisco, 1985—, Adopt-A-Sch. Program, San Francisco, 1988—, San Francisco Opera Guild; vol. Humanities West, 1993—. Grantee Office of Supt., San Francisco, 1972, Calif. State Assembly, Sacramento, 1988; hist. Dickens Fellowship of San Francisco, 1992. Mem. Jane Austen Soc. North Am. (chmn. mem. 1986-89), Assoc. Alumni of Sacred Heart, Alpha Psi (treas. Alpha Delta Kappa chpt. 1978-80, corr. sec. 1976-78, 92-94, recording sec. 1994-96). Roman Catholic. Home: 15 Red Rock Way # 301N San Francisco CA 94131-1758 Office: Wallenberg High Sch 40 Vega St San Francisco CA 94115-3826

ROMANO, DEE IRENE, medical administrator, medical consultant; b. S.I., N.Y., June 26, 1950; d. Joseph Anthony and Rose (Losco) R.; m. Michael E. Smilowitz, May 2, 1972 (div. June 1980); m. Mark M. Kitzman, Mar. 31, 1994. Grad., UCLA, 1987. Administr. Posner, Stenson, MD's, L.A., 1980-91, Providence Ambulatory Surg. Ctr., Orange, Calif., 1993-94; ind. cons. in med. mgmt.; cons. L.A. Urology Med. Ctr., 1991—, White Meml. Hosp., L.A., 1991—. Mem. Concord Coalition, L.A., 1993. Mem. NAFE, Med. Group Mgrs. Assn. (affiliate), UCLA Alumni Assn. Democrat. Jewish.

ROMANOFF, MARJORIE REINWALD, education educator; b. Chgo., Sept. 29, 1923; d. David Edward and Gertrude (Rosenfield) Reinwald; m. Milford M. Romanoff, Nov. 6, 1945; children: Bennett Sanford, Lawrence Michael, Janet Beth (dec.). Student, Northwestern U., 1941-42, 43-45, Chgo. Coll. Jewish Studies, 1942-43; BEd, U. Toledo, 1947, MEd, 1968, EdD, 1976. Tchr., Old Orchard Elem. Sch., Toledo, 1946-47, McKinley Sch., Toledo, 1964-65; substitute tchr., Toledo, 1964-68; instr. Mary Manse Coll., Toledo, 1974; instr. children's lit. Sylvania (Ohio) Bd. Edn., 1977; supr. student tchrs. U. Toledo, 1968-73, 85—, instr. advanced communications, 1977, researcher, 1973-74, instr. Am. Lang. Inst., 1978—; part-time asst. prof. elem. edn. Bowling Green (Ohio) State U., 1978-88; presenter numerous workshops and demonstrations in children lit. and analysis of tchr. behavior, 1976—; chairperson rsch. com. Am. Language Inst. U. Toledo, 1985-94, asst. prof. elem. edn. in lang. arts 1985-87; part time asst. prof. Elem. Edn., instr. U. Toledo, Am. Lang. Inst. 1994—. Author: Language and Study Skills: For Learners of English, Prentice Hall Regents, 1991. Trustee Children's Svcs. Bd., 1974-76; pres. bd. Cummings Treatment Ctr. for Adolescents, 1978-80; mem. Crosby Gardens Adv. Bd., 1976-82, Community Planning Coun., 1980-84, Citizens Rev. Bd. of Juvenile Ct., 1979—; mem. allocations com. Mental Health and Retardation Bd., 1980-81; mem. Bd. Jewish Edn., 1976—, pres., 1982-84; mem. Jewish Family Svc., 1978-85, v.p., 1980-85; mem. allocations com. Jewish Welfare Fedn., 1980, 89-91; bd. dirs. Family Life Edn. Coun., 1984-90, sec., 1988-90; mem. budget and allocations com. Jewish Fedn., 1989-93; bd. dirs. Friends Toledo-Lucas County Librs., 1991-93, bd. pres., 1991-93; program chair U. Toledo Women's Commn., 1991-93; bd. dirs. Ohio Friends of Pub. Librs., 1992-94; presenter ann. conf. N.W. Ohio Libr. Assn., 1993. Named One of Ten Women of Yr., St. Vincent's Hosp. Guild, 1985, Outstanding Instructional Staff Woman, U. Toledo, 1990. Mem. ASCD, Tchrs. English to Speakers Other Langs. (presenter 1986, presenter Internat. TESOL Atlanta 1993), Nat. Soc. for Study Edn., Toledo Libr. Legacy Found., Orgn. Rehab. and Tng. (named Outstanding Woman in Community Svc. 1987), Hadassah (chpt. pres. regional bd. 1961-64), Northwestern U. Alumni Assn., Phi Kappa Phi, Phi Delta Kappa, Kappa Delta Pi (pres./faculty adv. 1971-75, Point of Excellence award 1992), Pi Lambda Theta (chpt. pres. 1978-80, nat. com. 1979-84). Democrat. Home: 2514 Bexford Pl Toledo OH 43606-2414 Office: U Toledo SSac # 2006B Toledo OH 43614

ROMANOV, ELISABETH LOUISE, technical writer; b. New Haven, Conn., Aug. 19, 1957; d. Peter L. and Louise M. (Baraniak) R.; m. David Charles Laurance, June 24, 1983 (div. Oct. 1991); 1 child, Peter Andrew. BA cum laude, Yale U., 1978. Writer/editor Cognetics Corp., Princeton Junction, N.J., 1983-85; documentation specialist Standard Data Corp., N.Y.C., 1985-86; writer, trainer Syncsort, Inc., Woodcliff Lake, N.J., 1986-88; mem. tech. staff Bell Comms. Rsch., Piscataway, N.J., 1990—; freelance cons., 1988-90. Roman Catholic. Home: 68 Lawrence Ave Highland Park NJ 08904-1834 Office: Bellcore 444 Hoes Ln Piscataway NJ 08854-4104

ROMEO, EILEEN VIRGINIA, nurse; b. Peckville, Pa., July 16, 1959; d. Anthony Charles and Patricia Ellen (McGee) R. A Acctg., Lackawanna Jr. Coll., Scranton, Pa., 1979; diploma in nursing, Mercy Hosp. Sch. Nursing, Scranton, 1985; BSN, U. Scranton, 1992; postgrad., SUNY, Binghamton, 1992—. RN, Pa.; cert. ACLS instr. Am. Heart Assn., instr. Basic Life Support Am. Heart Assn.; cert. emergency nursing. Nurse mgr. emergency dept. Mid-Valley Hosp., Peckville, Pa., 1985-94, dir. home health svcs., 1994—; nurse emergency rm. Mid Valley Hosp., Peckville, Pa, 1986-93; nurse mgr. emergency dept., 1993-94; dir. dept. home health svcs. Mid-Valley Hosp., 1994—. Recipient Nat. Collegiate Nursing award, 1991. Mem. ANA, Pa. Nurses Assn., Emergency Nurses Assn. Home: 129 Main St Blakely PA 18447

ROMERO, ELIZABETH RIVERA, public health nurse; b. Manila, Jan. 10, 1958; d. Vivencio Delapaz and Erlinda (Magalona) Rivera; m. Oscar Dedios Romero; 1 child, Sherilynn R. B.S. in Nursing cum laude, San Francisco State U., 1980. R.N., Calif. Staff nurse St. Lukes Hosp., San Francisco, 1980-85; pub. health nurse St. Mary's Hosp., San Francisco, 1984-85, Kimberly Home Patient Care, Pinole, Calif., 1984-87, utilization rev. case mgr. Brookside Hosp., San Pablo, Calif, 1987-90; head nurse, utilization mgmt. case mgr. San Francisco General Hosp., 1990—; Mem. ANA, Calif. Nurses Assn., Golden Gate Nurses Assn., Am. Heart Assn. (Contra Costa chpt.), Calif. Scholarship Fedn. Roman Catholic. Avocations: dancing; travel; camping; photography.

ROMINE, JOAN MARIE WINTERS, comptroller; b. Teacneck, N.J., July 13, 1951; d. Robert Grant and Joan Clare (Mooney) Winters; m. Mario Alejandro Romine, Oct. 31, 1972 (div. Dec. 1985); children: Jeremy Patrick, Kelly Marie, Christopher Grant. BS in Acctg., Kean Coll., 1988; postgrad. in Fine Arts, Coll. of New Rochelle, 1969-72. Staff acct. Shader & Co. CPA's, Westfield, N.J., 1988; CFO, sec. to bd. dirs., co. sec.-treas. Hanita Cutting Tools, Inc., Montainside, N.J., 1988—; CFO, sec., treas., 1992—, also bd. dirs. Republican. Home: 925 Harding St Westfield NJ 07090 Office: Hanita Cutting Tools Inc 1167 Globe Ave Mountainside NJ 07092

ROMM, JESSICA BETH, policy research/project implementation executive; b. San Francisco, Mar. 17, 1944; d. Arthur and Esther (Orloff) R. BA in Social Welfare, U. Calif., Berkeley, 1965; MA in Urban Planning, CUNY, 1970; PhD in Pub. Policy and Adminstrn., NYU, 1976. Vol. Peace Corps, San Cruz, Bolivia, 1965-67; rsch. asst. Hunter Coll. Urban Rsch. Ctr., N.Y.C., 1968-70; planning process cons. Model Cities and Office of Econ. Opportunity, N.Y.C., 1968-70; project dir. Environ. Resource Assocs., N.Y.C., 1970-72; family ct. cons. N.Y.C. Family Ct. and N.Y. State Jud. Conf., 1972-74; asst. dir. edn. fund Dist. Coun. 37, N.Y.C., 1976-79; mng. of programs Planning Assistance and U.S. Agy. Devel., Cen. Am., 1979; sr. planner Bechtel Civil Corp., Caracas, Venezuela, 1980; labor rels. coord. to stragegic planning and mktg. profl. Bechtel Civil Corp., San Francisco, 1980-91; cons. J.B. Romm Bechtel Corp., various, 1991—, Baytrade Cons., 1994, San Francisco Redevel. Agy., 1994; cmty. econ. devel. cons. for base closure Hunters Point Shipyard, San Francisco, 1994—; jazz preservation dist. cons. San Francisco, 1994—; adj. prof. Golden Gate U., San Francisco, 1993—, UN Devel. Program, 1989, 93; presenter in field. Producer/dir.: ednl. TV programs, 1977. Vol. Am. Cancer Soc., Marin County, Calif., 1993—, Big Bros./Big Sisters, Marin County, 1992—, Christmas in April, San Francisco, 1991—; bd. dirs. Alumnae Resources, San Francisco, 1990-94, Soc. for Internat. Devel., 1994—, Am. Jewish Congress, 1994—. Recipient recognition from Gov. Bellon, Okla., 1986, Gov. Dukaksis, Mass., 1986, ILO award, 1990; Fulbright fellow, Buenos Aires, 1974-75. Mem. ASPA, Soc. Internat. Devel. (bd. dirs. 1994), Women Constrn. Owners and Execs., Pan Am. Soc. (bd. dirs. 1981), Women in Internat. Trade, Indsl. Rels. Assn., U. Calif.-Berkeley Alumnae Assn., NYU Alumnae Assn. Home: 504 Seaver Dr Mill Valley CA 54941

ROMO, SYLVIA, state legislator, accountant; b. San Antonio, Dec. 27; d. Alfred B. and Josephine (Jimenez) Sepulveda; children: David, Samuel, Randall, Daniel. BBA in Acctg., U. Tex., San Antonio, 1976, postgrad., 11981. CPA, Tex., Ill. Acting fiscal dir. Bexar County Mental Health and Mental Retardation, San Antonio, 1979-81; pres. Romo and Co., CPA's, San Antonio, 1981-93, Sylvia Romo & Assocs., Ltd., San Antonio, 1994—; mem. Tex. Ho. of Reps., Austin, 1993—; acct. adv. SBA, 1989; advisor Pres.'s Adv. Com. on Women's Bus. Ownership; seminar leader on instrn. minority bus. women Nat. Assn. Banking Women. Mem. adv. bd. U. Tex. Coll. Bus.; commr. Housing Authority Bexar County; mem. adv. coun. U. Tex. Health Sci. Ctr. Med. Sch.; chmn. San Antonio Mayor's Task Force on Small, Minority and Women's Bus. Devel.; mem. San Antonio Bd. Rev. for Hist. Dists.; commr., vice chmn. Bexar County Women's Ctr.; bd. dirs. AMC Cancer Rsch. Ctr., Epilepsy Found. Bluebonnet Region; mem. allocation com. United Way; chmn. Bexar County Dem. Com., 1990; grad. Leadership San Antonio, 1986, mem. steering com., 1986-88. Tarrant C.C. scholar, Bus. and Profl. Found. scholar U. Tex.; named One of Top 10 Women of Decade in U.S., Bus. and Profl. Women's Found., Outstanding Woman of South Tex. in bus. San Antonio Express-News, 1989, Legislator of Yr., League United L.Am. Citizens, 1993, Woman of Yr., Mexican Am. Bus. and Profl. Women San Antonio, 1993, Small Bus. Adv. of Yr., San Antonio Hispanic C. of C., 1994. Mem. Am. Women's Soc. CPA's, Am. Soc. Women Accts., Tex. Soc. CPA's, Ill. CPA Soc., San Antonio Assn. Hispanic CPA's, Phi Theta Kappa. Office: 4606 Centerview Ste 206 San Antonio TX 78228

ROMZEK, BARBARA S(UE), public administration educator; b. Mt. Clemens, Mich., Aug. 3, 1948; d. Lawrence John and Theresa Agnes (Kociba) R.; m. David Alan Greenamyre, May 19, 1984; children: Wallis Greenamyre Romzek, Spencer Romzek Greenamyre. BA, Oakland U., 1970; MA, Western Mich. U., 1972; PhD, U. Tex., Austin, 1979. Asst. instr. U. Tex., Austin, 1977-79; asst. prof. polit. sci. U. Kans., Lawrence, 1979-85, rsch. assoc. Ctr. for Pub. Affairs, 1981-84, assoc. prof. pub. adminstrn., 1985-95, chairperson Dept. Pub. Adminstrn., 1988-93, prof. pub. adminstrn., 1995—; cons. pub. affairs various local, state, nat. and internat. orgns., 1980—; interim dir. human resources Bd. Pub. Utilities, Kansas City, Kans., 1986. Co-author: American Public Administration: Politics and the Management of Expectations, 1991; co-editor: New Paradigms for Government: Issues for the Changing Public Service, 1994; mem. editorial bd. Pub. Adminstrn. Rev., 1987-90, Adminstrn. and Soc., 1990—, Jour. Pub. Adminstrn. Rsch. and Theory, 1990-93, Am. Jour. Polit. Sci., 1994—; contbr. articles to profl. jours. Recipient Mosher award ASPA, 1988; dissertation fellow AAUW, Washington, 1978-79. Mem. Am. Polit. Sci. Assn. (pub. adminstrn. sect. chairperson 1988-89, mem. pub. adminstrn. sect. exec. coun. 1986-91, mem. Gaus award com. 1989, nat. coun. 1992-94, chair com. organized sects. 1993—), Am. Soc. Pub. Adminstrn. (governing bd. Kans. chpt. 1983-84, Brownlow award com. 1987, Moshers award com. 1989, chair Levine award com. 1993-95, vice chair task force confs. 1994-95), Acad. Mgmt. (Levine award com. 1989, exec. com. pub. sector div. 1989—), Nat. Assn. Schs. of Pub. Affairs and Adminstrn. (exec. coun. 1990-93, dissertation award com. 1988-89, com. chair 1989, commn. on peer rev. and accreditation 1989-92, rsch. com. 1987-90, joint task force on local govt. edn. with Internat. City Mgmt. Assn. 1987-90, task force on edn. for state and local pub. svc. 1991-93, chair Staats award com. 1994-95), Internat. City Mgmt. Assn. (task force on continuing edn. and profl. devel. 1991-93), League Kans. Mcpls. (spl. com. on future 1989), Pi Alpha Alpha (nat. coun. 1989-93). Office: U Kans Dept Pub Adminstrn 318 Blake Lawrence KS 66045

RONALD, PAULINE CAROL, school system administrator; b. York, Yorkshire, Eng., Feb. 28, 1945; came to U.S., 1966; d. Peter Vincent Leonard and Doris Annie (Clark) Hume-Shotton; m. James Douglas Ronald, July 16, 1966 (div. 1986); 1 child, Alexia Denise; m. James Donald Wadsworth, Feb. 15, 1991 (div. July 1994). Diploma, Harrogate Sch. Art, Yorkshire, 1965, U. New Castle, Upon Tyne, 1966; MA, Ball State U., 1977. Cert. art tchr., Ind. Art tchr. Knightstown (Ind.) Schs., 1966-67, Dunkirk (Ind.) Schs., 1967-68, Richmond (Ind.) High Sch., 1968—; part time tchr. Ind. U., East Richmond 1974-84; set painter Richmond Civic Theatre. Exhibited in numerous group shows; illustrator History of Wayne County, History of Centerville. Coach State Acad. Fine Arts Team Champions for 1988, 2d Pl. for the state, 1989; bd. dirs., mem. permanent collection com. Richmond Art Mus. Recipient Best Set awards, also numerous awards for drawing and painting. Mem. NEA, Ind. State Tchrs. Assn., Art Assn. Richmond. Home: 417 S 20th St Richmond IN 47374-5729

RONDEAU-BASSETT, CHERYL MARYANN, publisher, editor; b. Ortonville, Minn., Oct. 21, 1952; d. Walter T. and Martha Evelyn (King) Quade; m. Mark J. Rondeau, Oct. 21, 1971 (div. 1985); children: Christopher, Samuel, Daniel, Sally, Joseph, Patrick; m. Scott D. Bassett, Feb. 26, 1994. BA, Mount Marty Coll., Yankton, S.D., 1988; postgrad., S.D. State U., 1992. Proprietor Wilmot (S.D.) Cafe, 1972-73; from salesperson to dist. mgr. Beeline Fashions Inc., Wilmot, 1973-79; salesperson Century 21 - Accent Realty, Lebanon, Oreg., 1978-79; sales and mktg. dir. Hercules Metal, Corona, S.D., 1983-86; sales cons. Mary Kay Cosmetics, Wilmot, 1986-87; pub., editor Wilmot Enterprise, 1988—; Internat. Soc. Weekly Newspaper Editors grad. asst., dept. journalism S.D. State U., 1992-94; presenter in field. Dir., producer: Welcome Home Jennifer, 1990; dir., creator: After the Storm, 1991; dir. Just A Little Bit Country, 1995. Organizer Citizens for Edn., Wilmot, 1986-89; organizer, 1st pres. student body orgn. Harmony Hill Ctr., Watertown, S.D., 1986-88; chmn. Wilmot Summer Recreation, 1989-91; vice chmn. Roberts County Dems., Sisseton, 1989-93; cons., advisor Roberts County Econ. Devel. Com., 1991-93; dir. Ground Hog Day in Branson, 1994. Recipient Community Svc. award Mount Marty Coll., 1988, scholar. Mem. NAFE, AAUW, Soc. Profl. Journalists, Nat. Fedn. Press Women, Nat. Newspaper Assn., S.D. Newspaper Assn., S.D. Press Women's Assn., Mo. Valley Adult Edn. Assn. Nat. Fedn. Ind. Bus., Am. Legion Aux., Wilmot Alumni Assn. (pres., com. chair), Wilmot Community Club, Kappa Delta Pi. Lutheran. Home: PO Box 296 Wilmot SD 57279-0296 Office: The Wilmot Enterprise PO Box 37 Wilmot SD 57279-0037

RONEN, CAROL, state legislator. BS, Bradley U.; MA, Roosevelt U. Dir. legis. and cmty. affairs Chgo. Dept. Human Svcs., 1985-89; exec. dir. Chgo. Commn. on Women, 1989-90; dir. planning and rsch. Chgo.-Cook County Criminal Justice Commn.; asst. commn. Chgo. Dept. Planning, 1991, Chgo. Dept. Housing; mem. Ill. Ho. of Reps., 1993—. Former pres. Ill. Task Force on Child Support; bd. dirs. Cook County Dem. Women, St. Martin De Porres Shelter for Women and Children. Democrat. Home: 6033 N Sheridan Chicago IL 60660 Office: Ill Ho of Reps State Capitol Springfield IL 62706*

RONEY, LOIS, English language educator, medievalist; Children: Deirdre Anne, Patrick Daniel. BA in English, Stanford U., 1961; MA, U. Chgo., 1965; PhD, U. Wis., 1978. Asst. prof. U. Tex., Dallas, 1982-87; from asst. to assoc. prof. St. Cloud (Minn.) State U., 1987-92, prof. English, 1992—; panelist NEH, Washington, 1987; participant Coun. for Philos. Studies and NEH Summer Inst. in Medieval Philosophy, Cornell U., 1980. Author: Chaucer's Knight's Tale and Theories of Scholastic Psychology, 1990; co-editor: Sign, Sentence, Discourse: Language in Medieval Thought and Literature, 1989; contbr. articles to profl. jours. Recipient Outstanding Contbn. award St. Cloud State U., 1990. Mem. MLA (del. Great Lakes region 1993—), Medieval Assn. Midwest (councillor 1990—, v.p. 1994—), Medieval Acad. Am., New Chaucer Soc., Phi Beta Kappa. Home: 300 State St #5 Albany NY 12210 Office: St Cloud State U Dept English Saint Cloud MN 56301

RONNINGSTAM, ELSA FRIDEBORG, psychologist; b. Boden, Sweden, Oct. 17, 1950; came to U.S., 1985; d. Yngue Fritjof and Frideborg (Rönnberg) Karlsson. BA, U. Umeå, Sweden, 1971; MSc, U. Stockholm, 1976, PhD, 1988. Clin. psychologist dept. psychiatry Huddinge Hosp., Stockholm, 1980-85, 87-88; rsch. fellow in clin. psychology, psychosocial rsch. program McLean Hosp., Harvard Med. Sch., Belmont, Mass., 1985-87, rsch. and clin. fellow, 1989-90; instr. in psychology Harvard Med. Sch., 1990—; asst. psychologist McLean Hosp., 1990—. Author: (in Swedish) Bereavement in Childhood, 1978. Swedish Am. Found. scholar, 1989-91. Office: McLean Hosp Psychol Rsch Pr 115 Mill St Belmont MA 02178-1048

RONQUILLO, ANNA MARIA DOMINGO, programmer, analyst; b. Manila, Philippines, Feb. 10, 1967; came to U.S., 1992; d. Arsenio Aricayos and Aurora (Domingo) R. BS in Computer Sci., De LaSalle U., Manila, 1988. Sr. systems analyst Fareast Bank and Trust Co., Manila, 1989-92; systems engr. Info. Industries, Kansas City, Mo., 1992—. Roman Catholic. Office: Info Industries Inc 8880 Ward Pkwy Kansas City MO 64114

RONSON, SUSAN, administrative assistant; b. N.Y.C., June 30, 1940; d. Solomon Blondheim and Harriet (Lustbader) Kohn; m. Raoul Ronson, July

22, 1962; 1 child, Paul. Student, Miami U., Oxford, Ohio, 1958-60; cert., Katharine Gibbs, N.Y.C., 1960-61, Emergency Mgmt. Inst., Emmitsburg, Md., 1983, Nat. Def. U., Washington, 1988. Sec. Doubleday & Co., N.Y.C., 1961-65; freelance editor N.Y.C., 1965-73; exec. sec. Howard Needles Tammen & Bergendoff, N.Y.C., 1974-87; adminstrv. asst., office mgr. The Capital Group Cos., Inc., N.Y.C., 1987—; exec. sec., dir. Seesaw Music Corp., N.Y.C., 1988—; adminstrv. officer, Fed. Emergency Mgmt. Agy., N.Y.C. Mem. Nat. Def. Exec. Res., Assn. of Nat. Def. Exec. Reserve (exec. v.p. and dir. N.Y. met. chpt. 1988—). Republican. Home: 825 W End Ave New York NY 10025-5349 Office: The Capital Group Cos Inc 630 5th Ave Fl 36 New York NY 10111

RONSTADT, LINDA MARIE, singer; b. Tucson, July 15, 1946; d. Gilbert and Ruthmary (Copeman) R. Rec. artist numerous albums including Evergreen, 1967, Evergreen Vol. 2, 1967, Linda Ronstadt, The Stone Poneys and Friends, Vol. 3, 1968, Hand Sown, Home Grown, 1969, Silk Purse, 1970, Linda Ronstadt, 1972, Don't Cry Now, 1973, Heart Like a Wheel, 1974, Different Drum, 1974, Prisoner In Disguise, 1975, Hasten Down the Wind, 1976, Greatest Hits, 1976, Simple Dreams, Blue Bayou, 1977, Living in the U.S.A, 1978, Mad Love, Greatest Hits Vol. II, 1980, Get Closer, 1982, What's New, 1983, Lush Life, 1984, For Sentimental Reasons, 1986, Trio (with Dolly Parton, Emmylou Harris), 1986, 'Round Midnight, 1987, Canciones de Mi Padre, 1987, Cry Like a Rainstorm-Howl Like the Wind, 1989, Mas Canciones, 1991, Frenesi, 1992, Winter Light, 1993; starred in Broadway prodn. of Pirates of Penzance, 1981, also in film, 1983, off Broadway as Mimi in La Boheme, 1984. Recipient Am. Music awards, 1978, 1979, Grammy awards, 1975, 76, 87, 88 (with Emmylou Harris and Dolly Parton), 1989 (with Aaron Neville), 1990 (with Aaron Neville), Emmy award, 1988-89, Acad. Country Music awards, 1987, 88. Office: care Peter Asher Mgmt Inc 644 N Doheny Dr West Hollywood CA 90069-5526

ROOFNER, MARILYN ALBRIGHT, physical therapist; b. Jefferson City, Tenn., Feb. 7, 1950; d. William Wallace and Jane (Austin) Albright; m. Larry C. Roofner, Aug. 18, 1979. BS in Phys. Therapy, U. Tenn., 1972. Registered phys. therapist. With Montgomery County Orthopaedic Assn., Blacksburg, Va., 1973-75; staff therapist to chief therapist South Lake Meml. Hosp., Clermont, Fla., 1975-78; staff therapist to dir. phys. therapy Kissimmee (Fla.) Hosp., 1977-78; with Walt Disney World Phys. Therapy and Rehab., Fla., 1986—; Winter Park Phys. Therapy; pres., owner Buena Vista Phys. Therapy, Orlando, Fla., 1991—, Orange Phys. Therapy and Sports Rehab., Orlando, 1980—, Seminole Sports, 1993. Contbr. articles to profl. jours. State med. chair Sunshine State Games, 1988—; chmn. med. com. Pan Am. Jr. Championships, 1986; mem., vice chair Gov.'s Coun. on Phys. Fitness and Sports, 1984—. Mem. Am. Phys. Therapy Assn. (orthopaedic sect., sports medicine sect., pvt. practice sect.), Fla. Phys. Therapy Assn. (bd. dirs. 1989-93, legis. panel 1989-93, fed. legis. chmn. 1989-93, state ethics com. 1982-87, chmn. 1985-87, state nomination com. 1984-87), Am. Coll. Sports Medicine, Orlando Amateur Athletic Assn. Methodist. Office: Winter Park Phys Therapy 2711 W Fairbanks Winter Park FL 32789

ROOK, JUDITH RAWIE, producer, writer; b. Long Beach, Calif., Jan. 25, 1942; d. Wilmer Ernest and Margaret Jane (Towle) Rawie; children: Daryn Kirsten, Dawn Malia; m. Timothy Daniel Rook. BBA, Loyola-Marymount Coll., 1964; BA in Visual Arts and Communication, U. Calif., San Diego, 1978. Producer/writer PBS series Achieving (Emmy award 1982, ACE nominee), asst. dir. rsch. and video/producer IABC, San Francisco, 1982; dir. programming Group W Cable, Westinghouse Co., 1983-85; devel. mgr. Nelson/Embassy Home Entertainment, 1986-87; ptnr. Real Magic, 1988-89; ind. prodr.- screenwriter R2 Prodns., 1989—. Mem. Am. Film Inst., Women in Film, Ind. Features Assn. Democrat. Episcopalian.

ROOMBERG, SUSAN KELLY, city administrator; b. Corpus Christi, Tex., May 22, 1961; d. Oscar Olie and Barbara Ann (Hodson) Sjerven. BA in English, Psychology, Austin Coll., 1983; M in Pub. Affairs, U. Tex., 1986. Adminstrv. intern Austin (Tex.) Fire Dept., 1983-84; intern to congressman Washington, summer 1984; adminstrv. intern Asst. City Mgrs. Office, Austin, 1984-85, adminstrv. asst., 1985-86; acting adminstrv. asst. Transp. and Pub. Services Dept., Austin, 1986-87, coordinator adminstrv. services, 1987-89; budget analyst Fin. Svcs. Dept., Austin, 1989-90; budget and mgmt. analyst Office Mgmt. and Budget, City of Alexandria, Va., 1990-94. Trustee merit scholar Austin Coll., 1979-83, Clarence E. Ridley scholar, 1985-86. Mem. Lyndon Baines Johnson Sch. Alumni Assn. (sec. nat. bd. dirs. 1987-88, pres. 1989-90, bd. dirs., pres. Austin chpt. 1988-90, bd. dirs. Washington chpt. 1991, 93-94), Austin Soc. Pub. Adminstrn., Tex. City Mgmt. Assn. (edn. com. 1986-89, conf. com. 1989-90), Internat. City Mgmt. Assn., Alpha Phi Omega, Delta Phi Nu. Presbyterian. Home: 1905 Huntington Midland TX 79705

ROOMSBURG, JUDY DENNIS, industrial and organizational psychologist; b. Seoul, Korea, June 2, 1954; came to U.S., 1957; children: Michael Scott, Christopher Thomas. MA, Chapman Coll., Orange, Calif., 1983, U. Tex., 1988; PhD, U. Tex., 1989. Enlisted USAF, 1973, commd., 1979, advanced through grades to maj., 1990; human factors engr. Aero. Systems Div., Wright-Patterson AFB, Ohio, 1984-85; behavioral scientist Armstrong Lab., Brooks AFB, Tex., 1985-86; chief behavioral analysis Hdqrs. USAF, Washington, 1989-93; mgr. organizational devel. and tng. Allied Signal Inc., Columbia, Md., 1993—. Mem. APA, ASTD, Am. Psychol. Soc., Soc. Indsl./Orgnl. Psychology, Acad. Mgmt., Am. Statis. Assn., Soc. Human Resource Mgmt. Office: AlliedSignal Inc One Bendix Rd Columbia MD 21045-1897

ROONEY, CAROL BRUNS, dietitian; b. Milw., Dec. 20, 1940; d. Edward G. and Elizabeth C. (Lemke) Bruns; m. George Eugene Rooney Jr., July 1, 1967; children: Steven, Sean. BS, U. Wis., 1962; MS, U. Iowa, 1965. Cert. nutrition specialist. Intern VA Med. Ctr., Hines, Ill., 1962-63; resident in dietetics VA Med. Ctr., Iowa City, 1963-65; dietitian nutrition clinic VA Med. Ctr., Hines, 1965-67, 69-70, chief clin. dietetics, 1970-71, chief adminstrv. dietetics, 1971-73; clin. dietitian VA Med. Ctr., Memphis, 1967-68; asst. chief dietetic service Zablocki VA Med. Ctr., Milw., 1974-85, chief dietetic service, 1985—; adj. lectr. Loyola U. Coll. Dentistry, Maywood, Ill., 1969-72; investigator nutrition VA/Med. Coll. Wis., Milw., 1975—, co-dir. ann. clin. nutrition symposium, Milw., 1979—; chmn. task force on ration allowance VA, Washington, 1977-84, mem. dietetic svc. spl. interest users group, Washington, 1983-85, chmn. tech. adv. group region IV, 1986: mem. Dept. Vets. Affairs Mktg. Ctr. Subsistence Task Force, 1991—, dietetic internship adv. bd. St. Luke's Hosp., Milw., 1983-87; lectr. in field, 1965—; mem. Dept. Vets. Affairs Dietetic Svc. Policy Manual Revision Task Force, 1992—, Dept. Vets. Chiefs, Dietetic Svc. Mentor Group, 1992—. Author videocassette, 1976; editor: Nutrition Principles and Dietary Guidelines for Patients Receiving Chemotherapy and Radiation Therapy, 1980; contbr. articles to profl. jours., 1978—. Mem. profl. edn. com. Milw. South unit Am. Cancer Soc., 1976-86, bd. dirs. Milw. South unit, 1984-86, Milw. div., 1986-87, Wis. div., 1987-91, media spokesperson, 1983-91, del. to Milw. div., 1984-85, mem. organizational and expansion com. Milw. div., 1986-87, profl. edn. com. Milw. div., 1986-87, Wis. div., 1987-91, mem. taking control Wis. div., 1987-91, chmn. nutrition Wis. div., 1989-91; mem. med. adv. com. YMCA Met. Milw., 1985—; mem. Marquette U. High Sch. Mothers Guild, 1990-94. Recipient Disting. Svc. award Am. Cancer Soc. Milw. South unit, 1980, Women of Achievement award Girl Scouts Milw. Area, 1987, Leadership award VA, 1989, Dept. Vets. Affairs Fed. Women's Program cert. merit for outstanding profl. leadership, 1994; Paralyzed Vets. Am. rsch. grantee, 1981-83. Mem. Am. Soc. for Hosp. and Food Svc. Adminstrs., Am. Soc. Hosp. Food Svc. Adminstrs. (dir.-at-large Wis. chpt. 1993-95), Am. Dietetic Assn. (registered, practice groups in mgmt. responsibilities in health care delivery, gerontology nutrition 1980—, dietetics in phys. medicine and rehab. 1983—, clin. nutrition mgmt. 1987—, amb., nat. media spokesperson 1983-89, Resource Amb. 1991—, Outstanding Svc. award 1983-89), Wis. Dietetic Assn. (co-chmn. div. mgmt. practice 1976-77, chmn. 1977-78, bd. dirs. 1981-83, 87-91, coun. on practice 1982-83, coordinating cabinet 1984-91, pres. 1988-89, chmn. nominating com. 1989-90, chmn. long-range planning com. 1989-90, mem. legis. com. 1988—, Wis. Medallion award 1986), Milw. Dietetic Assn. (community nutrition and clin. dietetics & rsch. coms. 1975-76, chair ad hoc com. for nutrition and oncology patients 1976-79, clin. dietetics & rsch. study group 1981-90, chair 1983-85, pres. 1982-83, by-laws com. 1983-84, chair policies & procedures com. 1983-87, pub. rels. com. 1983-87, chair nominating com. 1984-85), Fed. Execs. Assn., Leadership Vet. Affairs Alumni Assn. (charter, life). Home: 18230 Le Chateau Dr Brookfield WI 53045-4922 Office: Zablocki VA Med Ctr 5000 W National Ave Milwaukee WI 53295-0001

ROONEY, GAIL SCHIELDS, college administrator; b. St. Francis, Kans., Feb. 15, 1947; d. Fred Harlan and Darlene Mary (Saint) Schields; m. Thomas Michael Rooney, June 27, 1970; children: Shane Michael, Shauna Meghan. BA, U. Colo., 1969; MS, George Williams Coll., 1974; PhD, U. Ill., 1982. Asst. dir. Spl. Svcs. Program Cleve. State U., 1970-71; admissions counselor George Williams Coll., Downers Grove, Ill., 1972-73; coord. of career exploration ctr. Women's Programs Cuyahoga Community Coll., Cleve., 1973-76; vis. asst. prof. Sch. Clin. Medicine U. Ill., Champaign, 1981-82; counselor, instr. Cuyahoga Community Coll., Cleve., 1982-84, dir. counseling, career and psychol. svcs., 1984-85; dir. career, counseling and health svcs. Briar Cliff Coll., Sioux City, Iowa, 1985-88, v.p. for student devel., 1988—; adj. instr. counselor edn. Wayne (Nebr.) State Coll., 1988; program presenter Myers Briggs Type Indicator, Sioux City, 1986—. Bd. dirs. Gordon Chem. Dependency Ctr., Sioux City, 1986-89, St. Luke's Gordon Recovery Ctr., Sioux City, 1991—. Mem. ACA, Am. Coll. Pers. Assn., Nat. Assn. Student Pers. Adminstrs. Home: 52 Red Bridge Dr Sioux City IA 51104-1061 Office: Briar Cliff Coll 3303 Rebecca St Sioux City IA 51104-2340

ROONEY, SUSAN KAY, financial services manager; b. Fargo, N.D., Aug. 22, 1946; d. Glenn William and Phyllis Elaine (Ellingson) Heaton; m. Carl A. Moreno, May 28, 1976 (div. 1980); m. R. Timothy Rooney. Student, N.D. State U., 1964-68. Acct. asst. Bank of Am., San Francisco, 1969-75; credit analyst Central Bank of Colo., Colorado Springs, 1975-77; ops. mgr. Transamerica Comml. Fin. Corp., Palatine, Ill., 1978—. Republican. Home: 328 Woodbury Ct Schaumburg IL 60193-2238

ROONEY, THERESA PATRICIA, budget administrator; b. Phila., Nov. 2, 1957; d. John Patrick and Theresa Alberta (Yheaulon) R. BS in Sociology, Northeastern U., Boston, 1980, MBA, 1985. Cost acct. Blue Cross Blue Shield of Mass., Boston, 1985-86, price adminstr., 1987-89, mgr. budget and reporting, 1989-91; cons. Blue Cross Blue Shield Assn., Washington, 1986-87; acct., budget coord. Keystone Health Plan East, Phila., 1991-92; mgr. adminstrv. budget Independence Blue Cross, Phila., 1992—. Alumni recruiter Northeastern U., Phila., 1991—. Mem. Inst. Cert. Mgmt. Accts. Office: Independence Blue Cross 1901 Market St Philadelphia PA 19103-1400

ROOS, KATHLEEN SUSAN, environmental scientist; b. Norwalk, Conn., Mar. 27, 1949; d. Ralph Roos and Mary Mathilda (Mahoney) Morgan. BA, Hartwick Coll., 1971; MS, L.I. U., 1975; postgrad., NYU, 1990—. Registered environ. assessor, Calif. Asst. dir. biol. sci. Environ. Analysis, Inc., Woodbury, N.Y., 1973-79; tech. scientist Rockwell Internat.-EMSI, Newbury Park, Calif., 1980-83; instr. Naval Energy and Environ. Support Activity, 1983-84; dir. hazardous waste environ. program McClelland Engrs., Inc., Ventura, Calif., 1984-87; environ. advisor Royal Govt. Thailand, Bangkok, 1985-86; program mgr. CH2M Hill, Santa Ana, Calif., 1987-89; dir. environ. div. Naval Air Sta. Miramar, San Diego, 1989-92; envrion. tech. advisor naval facilities engring. command Pub. Works Ctr., La Mesa, Calif., 1992-94; dir. environ. tng. Naval Facilities Engring. Command Naval Civil Engr. Corps Offices Sch., Port Hueneme, Calif., 1994—; tech. advisor USSR Ambassador Program, 1991; program mgr. Love Canal Gt. Lakes Environ. Analysis, Niagara Falls, N.Y., 1977-79. Author: American Petroleum Institute, 1975, Jour. Environmental Regulation, 1991, Jour. Environmental Technology, 1991, ; contbr. articles to profl. jours. and newsletters. Recipient Tribute to Women award Calif. Women in Govt., 1989. Mem. ASTM, Water Pollution Control Fedn., Cert. Profl. Mgrs., Nat. Environ. Def. Coun. Office: Naval Sch Civil Engr Corps Offices 3502 Goodspeed St Ste 1 Port Hueneme CA 93043

ROOS, SYBIL FRIEDENTHAL, secondary school educator; b. L.A., Jan. 29, 1924; d. Charles G. and Besse (Weixel) Friedenthal; m. Henry Kahn Roos, May 8, 1949 (dec. Dec. 1989); children: Catherine Alane Cook, Elizabeth Anne Garlinger, Virginia Ann Bertrand. BA in Music, Centenary Coll., 1948; MEd, Northwestern State U., 1973. Cert. elem. edn. tchr., spl. edn. tchr. Tchr. Caddo Parish Schs., Shreveport, 1968-75, Spring Branch Ind. Schs., Houston, 1975-85; vol. Houston Grand Opera/Guild, 1979—, Houston Mus. of Fine Arts/Guild, 1990—. Author tchrs. guides. Pres. Nat. Coun. Jewish Women, Shreveport, 1958, Houston Grand Opera Guild, 1989-91; bd. dirs. Mus. Fine Arts; area coord. Spl. Olympics, Shreveport, 1974-75; mem. Houston Symphony League, Houston Ballet Guild. With USN, 1944-46. Mem. AAUW (pres. Spring Valley Houston chpt. 1985-87), Houston Grand Opera Guild (bd. dirs.), Houston Symphony League, Houston Ballet Guild, Mus. of Fine Arts Guild (bd. dirs.), Am. Needlepoint Guild (bd. dirs. Lone Star chpt.), Shepherd Soc. Rice U., Delta Kappa Gamma (treas. 1987-89), Phi Mu. Republican. Home: 10220 Memorial Dr Apt 78 Houston TX 77024-3227

ROOT, DORIS SMILEY, artist; b. Ann Arbor, Mich., June 28, 1924; d. George O. and Hazel (Smith) Smiley. Student, Art Inst. of Chgo., 1943-45, N.Y. Sch. Design, 1976-77, Calif. Art Inst., 1984-85. Creative dir. All May Co.'s, L.A., 1962-63; advt. sales pro. dir. Seibu, L.A., 1963-64; v.p. Walgers & Assoc., L.A., 1964-70; owner, designer At The Root of Things, L.A., 1970-73; adv. sales pro. dir. Hs. of Nine, L.A., 1973-74; asst. designer MGM Grand, Reno, Nev., 1974-76; designer, office mgr. Von Hausen Studio, L.A., 1976-82; ABC libr. ABC/Cap Cities, L.A., 1982-89; portrait artist (also known as Dorian), AKA Dorian, art studio, L.A., 1982—. One-man shows include Cookeville, Tenn., 1989, Beverly Hills, Calif., 1991; artist in residence, Cookeville, 1989-90. Republican. Presbyterian.

ROOT, KATHLEEN, interior designer, secretary; b. Long Beach, Calif., Dec. 4, 1962; d. David Allen Root and Margaret (Heran) Harvey. BSc in Interior Design, Drexel U., 1985; MAT in Teaching Art, U. Arts, 1993. Cert. art tchr., Pa., N.J. Receptionist Saul Lampert Optical, Phila., 1980-83; interior designer Laverne Design Assocs., Phila., 1986-93; sec. The Women's Group, Phila., 1993—; interior designer Katie's Designs, Phila., 1993—; cons. interior design Laverne Design Assocs., 1992—; jewelry maker Katie's Designs, 1993—. Mem. Nat. Art Edn. Assn. Home and Office: Katie's Designs 2027 S 20th St Philadelphia PA 19145

ROOT, M. BELINDA, chemist; b. Port Arthur, Tex., May 2, 1957; d. Robert A. and Charlene (Whitehead) Lee; m. Miles J. Root, Nov. 8, 1980; children: Jason Matthew, Ashley Erin. BS in Biology, Lamar U., 1979; MBA, U. Houston, 1994. Asst. chemist Merichem Co., Houston, 1979-81, project chemist, 1982-84, instrument chemist, 1984-85, quality assurance coord., 1986-89, product lab. supr., 1989-91; quality control supr. mfg. Welchem Inc. subs. Amoco, 1991—; mgr. Quality Control Petrolite Corp., 1993; mgr. quality control Akzo-Nobel Chems., Pasadena, Tex., 1994—. Editor (newsletter) Merichemer, 1989-91. Mem. MADD, 1989—, PTA, 1988—. Recipient Gulf Shore Regional award Cat Fanciers Assn., 1981, Disting. Merit award, 1990. Mem. NAFE, Am. Soc. for Quality Control (cert. quality auditor, quality engr.), United Silver Fancier (sec. 1980-82), Lamar U. Alumni Assn., Am. Chem. Soc., Beta Beta Beta (sec. 1978-79). Office: Akzo-Nobel Chem Inc Akzo Chems 13000 Bay Park Dr Pasadena TX 77507

ROOT, NINA J., librarian; b. N.Y.C., Dec. 22; d. Jacob J. and Fannie (Slivinsky) Root; BA, Hunter Coll.; MSLS, Pratt Inst.; postgrad. U.S. Dept. Agr. Grad. Sch., 1964-65, City U. N.Y., 1970-75. Reference and serials libr. Albert Einstein Coll. Medicine Libr., Bronx, N.Y., 1958-59; asst. chief libr. Am. Cancer Soc., N.Y.C., 1959-62; chief libr. Am. Inst. Aeros. and Astronautics, N.Y.C., 1962-64; head ref. and libr. svcs. sci. and tech. div. Libr. of Congress, Washington, 1964-66; mgmt. cons. Nelson Assocs., Inc., N.Y.C., 1966-70; dir. libr. svcs. Am. Mus. Natural History, N.Y.C., 1970—; free-lance mgmt. cons. and libr. planning, 1970—. Trustee Barnard Found., 1984-91; mem. libr. adv. coun. N.Y. State Bd. Regents, 1984-89, trustee Metro, 1987-92; bd. dirs. Hampden/Booth Libr., Players, 1990—; trustee Mercantile Libr. N.Y., 1993—. Recipient Meritorious Svc. award Libr. of Congress, 1965. Mem. ALA (preservation com. 1977-79, chmn. library/binders com. 1978-80, chmn. preservation sect. 1980-81, mem. coun. 1983-86), Spl. Librs. Assn. (sec. documentation group N.Y. chpt. 1972-73, 2d v.p. N.Y. 1975-76, treas. sci. and tech. group N.Y. 1975-76, mus. arts and humanities div. program planning chairperson-conf. 1977), Archons of Colophon (convener 1978-79), Soc. Natural History (N.Am. rep. 1977-85), N.Y. Acad. Scis. (mem. publs. com. 1975-80, 89-91, archives com. 1976-78, search com. 1976). Home: 400 E 59th St New York NY 10022-2342 Office: Am Mus Natural Hist Library Central Park St W New York NY 10026-4355

ROOZEN, MARY LOUISE, public relations executive; b. Milw., Mar. 31, 1921; d. Edward E. and Margaret (May) Silverman; m. Edwin Cramer Roozen, Sept. 18, 1943; children: Mary Katrina Roozen Hass, Joanna Roozen Satorius, Margaret Roozen Monahan. BA in Speech, U. Wis., 1942. With Met. Milw. Assn. Commerce, 1942-43; adminstrv. asst. Curative Workshop of Milw., 1968-69; adminstrv. asst. mktg. Marine Corp., Milw., 1969-70, mktg. officer, 1970-73, asst. v.p., 1973-76, v.p. pub. relations, 1976-84, v.p. pvt. banking, 1984-87; v.p. Marine Bank, N.A., Milw., 1977-87, cons. corp. pub. relations, 1987-93; devel. dir. VNA Milw., 1989-90; curator Marine Collection of Wis. Art, 1969-87, v.p. Marine Found., 1980-87; bd. dirs. Plaza Bldg. Mgmt., 1980-87. Bd. dirs. Neighborhood House, Milw., 1963-78, co-chair capital fund drive, 1984; pres. Tempo, 1980-81; chair 440th Tactical Air Wing Community Council, USAFR, 1988, dir. 1985-90; bd. dirs. Curative Workshop, Milw., 1970-78, Wis. Humane Soc., 1976-85, Friends of Art, Milw., 1980-84, Ozaukee Humane Soc., 1983-86, Vol. Ctr. Greater Milw., Friends of PBS Channel 10/36, bd. dirs. Red Bus. Corp., 1993—, docent Milw. Art Mus., 1992—. Recipient Recognition award Nat. Ctr. for Voluntary Action, 1977. Mem. Pub. Relations Soc. Am. (chair fin. insts. sect. 1983-85, exec. com. 1980-84), Wis. Sr. Pub. Relations Forum, Nat. Assn. Bank Women (chmn. Milw. group 1976-77), Women's Club of Wis. (mem. fin. com. 1983-85, mem. art com., 1993-94, mem. house com., 1994—), River Tennis Club (Milw.). Episcopalian. Home and Office: 7716 N Boyd Way Milwaukee WI 53217-3209

ROPELEWSKI, DEBORAH KAY VANDER WAAL, reinsurance intermediary; b. Ft. Meade, Md., Dec. 26, 1952; d. James Dewey and Frances Harding (Kidd) Vander Waal; m. Richard V. Ropelewski, May 26, 1991; 1 child, Frances L. BS in Gen. Bus., Va. Poly. Inst. and State U., 1974. CPCU; assoc. in underwriting; assoc. in risk mgmt.; assoc. in reins.; cert. profl. ins. woman. All lines rater Aetna Ins. Co., Camp Hill, Pa., 1974-77; underwriter trainee Md. Casualty Ins. Co., Camp Hill, 1977-78; sr. personal lines underwriter Gt. Am. Ins. Co., Lancaster, Pa., 1978-82; malpractice underwriter Phico Ins. Co., Mechanicsburg, Pa., 1983-87; sr. comml. underwriter Va. Profl. Underwriters, Richmond, Va., 1987-88; v.p. Willis Faber N.Am., Nashville, 1988—. Recipient award for acad. excellence Conf. Spl. Risk Underwriters, 1987. Mem. Soc. CPCU (edn. com.), Nat. Assn. Ins. Women, Profl. Liability Underwriting Soc. (acad. subcom. chmn. 1994-95), Am. Bus. Women's Assn. (Chpt. Woman of Yr. award 1981, 92). Democrat. Methodist. Office: Willis Faber NAm PO Box 290307 Nashville TN 37229-0307

ROPER, BERYL CAIN, library director; b. Long Beach, Calif., Mar. 1, 1931; d. Albert Verne and Ollie Fern (Collins) Cain; m. Max H. Young, Aug. 22, 1947 (div. 1958); children: Howard, Wade, Debra, Kevin, John R., Christopher; m. George Albert Roper, Mar. 24, 1962 (dec. July 1978); children: Ellen, Georgianne; m. Jack T. Hughes, Sept. 21, 1993. BA, West Tex. State U., 1986; MA, Tex. Womans U., 1989. Libr. clk. Cornette Libr., West Tex. State U., Canyon, 1981-87; dir. Clarendon (Tex.) Coll. Libr., 1988—; lectr. in history and archaeology; co-owner Aquamarine Publs. Editor, pub.: In the Light of Past Experience, 1989, Transactions of the Southwest Federation of Archeological Societies, 1993; author, pub.: Trementina, 1990, Trementina Revisited, 1994; author articles on women and history. Mem. Clarendon Archaeol. Soc. (charter mem., v.p. 1990-91), Tex. Libr. Assn., Tex. Jr. Coll. Tchrs. Assn., Am. Soc. Indexers, Tex. Intertribal Indian Orgn. (charter mem.), Saints Roost Scribes, Pi Gamma Mu, Beta Phi Mu, Alpha Chi, Phi Alpha Theta. Republican. Mem. LDS Ch. Office: Clarendon Coll Libr PO Box 968 Clarendon TX 79226-0968

ROPER, DONNA LOUISE, director ambulatory services; b. Lebanon, Mo., Dec. 17, 1946; d. William James and Elsie Lois (Magee) Morgan; m. H. James Roper, June 18, 1970; 1 child, Patrick Neil. Diploma, Burge Sch. of Nursing, 1967; BSN, Drury Coll., 1973, MEd, 1982. Staff nurse Cox Med. Ctr., Springfield, Mo., 1967-69, head nurse med.-surg., 1969-71, head nurse recovery, 1971-74; faculty Burge Sch. of Nursing, Springfield, Mo., 1974-85; nurse mgr. post anesthesia care unit, same day surg., endoscopy, and pre admission Cox Med. Ctr., Springfield, Mo., 1985-94; dir. ambulatory svcs. Cox Health Systems, Springfield, Mo., 1994—; item writer AORN Cert. Exam, Denver, 1986, 87; nurse mgr. rep. exec. coun. nursing Cox Med. Ctr., Springfield, 1990-92. Com. mem. Boy Scouts Am., Springfield, 1982—, mem. explorer team, 1993—. Mem. Am. Soc. Post Anesthesia Nurses (cert.), Soc. Gastrointestinal Nurses and Assts., Mo. Coun. Nurse Mgrs. (bd. dirs. 1991-92), Burge Sch. of Nursing Alumni, Kappa Delta Pi. Methodist. Office: Cox Med Ctr South 3801 S National Ave Springfield MO 65807-5297

ROPER, KATHERINE RUTH ARCHER, retired occupational health nurse; b. Cantonment, Okla., Sept. 28, 1925; d. James Henderson and Martha Katherine (Osborn) Archer; m. Ozon Albert Colwell (dec.); 1 child, Kenneth Gerald; m. Clay Mitchell Roper, Sept. 6, 1956; children: Norman Frank, Martha Grace, Fred Dwight. Diploma in nursing, U. Okla., Oklahoma City, 1948; student, U. Okla., Norman, 1969-70, Rockhurst Coll., 1978. RN, Okla. Staff nurse Presbyn. Hosp., Oklahoma City, 1968-77; nurse Medox, Oklahoma City, 1977-79; occupational health nurse U.S. Postal Svc., Oklahoma City, 1979-89; ret., 1989. Mem. celebration choir So. Bapt. Ch., Del. City, Okla. Recipient numerous awards of appreciation. Mem. ANA, Am. Assn. Occupational Health Nurses, Nat. Postal Profl. Nurses Assn. (nat. v.p. 1983-89), Okla. Hist. Soc., Okla. Geneal. Soc., Spencer Hist. Soc., Nat. Assn. Ret. Fed. Employees (pres.), Archer Reunion Assn. (pres.). Home: 8309 NE 28th St Spencer OK 73084-3617

ROPER, SALLY ANN, health facility coordinator; b. Hazelton, Pa., Aug. 24, 1950; d. Robert H. and Margaret F. (Baskin) Walk; m. John D. Roper, Dec. 1, 1984; children: Julia Kane, Laurie Kane, Karen. Diploma in nursing, Kings County Hosp., 1972; student, Wilkes U., Bklyn. Coll., Luzerne County C.C.; BA in Mgmt. Health svcs., Ottawa U., 1992. RN, Pa.; cert. ACLS instr., BLS instr. Nurse Kings Highway Hosp., Bklyn.; staff nurse ICU, CCU Kings County Hosp., Bklyn.; staff nurse progressive care Nesbitt Meml. Hosp., Kingston, Pa., nursing quality improvement coord. Mem. Nat. Assn. for Healthcare Quality.

ROPER, SUSAN BETH, writer; b. Lincoln, Nebr., Mar. 6, 1956; d. Lloyd Glenn and Evelyn Ruth (Ohlson) Neyhart; m. Federico Fragnada, July 31, 1980 (div. Nov. 1984); 1 child, Teresa; m. Craig Roper, Dec. 16, 1986; 1 child, Miles. BA in Art, U. Nebr., 1990; MA in Performance Studies, NYU, 1992. Asst. prodr. Dick Richards Prodns., N.Y.C., 1980-84; owner, mgr. Stunning Entertainment, N.Y.C., 1984-88; editorial asst. U. Nebr. Press, Lincoln, 1993-94; supr. AmeriCorps., Lincoln, 1993—; writer Wagon Train Project, Lincoln, 1993—. Scholar NYU, 1990-92. Mem. Internat. Dance and Exercise Assn. Home: 1234 S 25th St Lincoln NE 68502-1813 Office: NRCS 5930 So 58th St Lincoln NE 68516

RORER, MARY ABIGAIL, artist; b. Norristown, Pa., May 9, 1949; d. Thomas Rogers III and Anne (Wilkinson) R.; m. Charles William Buell, July 7, 1976; children: Katherine Anne Buell, Andrew Charles Buell. BFA in Printmaking, R.I. Sch. of Design, Providence, 1971. Art tchr. Brandon Sch., Petersham, Mass., 1971-75; freelance artist Petersham, 1975—; pub. Lone Oak Press, Petersham, 1989—. Work includes illustrations for numerous books including Saving Graces, 1991, Crickets and Katydids: Concerts and Solos, 1992 (John Burroughs award for best nature book 1992), Faith in a Seed, 1993, Maybe I Will Do Something, 1993. Lectr. in printmaking. Exhbns. include one-woman show B. Beamesderfer Gallery, 1993, Four Illustrators, R. Michelson Galleries, 1993, Miniature Print Biennial John Szoke Gallery, N.Y.C., 1989. Collections in several librs., mus. Wood engravings notable. Home: 16 Oliver St Petersham MA 01366-0175

RORIE, NANCY KATHERYN, elementary and secondary school educator; b. Union County, N.C., May 31, 1940; d. Carl Van and Mary Mildred (Pressley) R. BA, Woman's Coll. U. N.C., 1962; MEd, U. N.C., 1967; EdD, Duke U., 1977. Cert. curriculum and instrnl. specialist, social studies tchr. for middle and secondary levels, English tchr., N.C. Social studies and

English tchr. Guilford County Schs., Greensboro, N.C., 1962-67; social studies instr. Lees-McRae Coll., Banner Elk, N.C., 1967-76; social studies tchr. Monroe (N.C.) City Schs., 1977-93; curriculum instrnl. specialist, social studies tchr. Union County Schs., Monroe, N.C., 1993—. Democrat. Baptist. Home: 2401 Old Pageland-Monroe Rd Monroe NC 28112

RORISON, MARGARET LIPPITT, reading consultant; b. Wilmington, N.C., Feb. 6, 1925; d. Harmon Chadbourn and Margaret Devereux (Lippitt) R. AB, Hollins Coll., 1946; MA, Columbia U., 1956; Diplôme de langue, L'Alliance Française, Paris, 1966; postgrad. U. S.C., 1967-70, 81—. Market and editorial researcher Time, Inc., N.Y.C., 1949-55; classroom and corrective reading tchr. N.Y.C. public schs., 1956-65; TV instr. ETV-WNDT, Channel 13, N.Y.C., 1962-63; grad. asst., TV instr. U. S.C., Columbia, 1967-70; instrnl. specialist in reading S.C. Office Instrnl. TV and Radio, S.C. Dept. Edn., Columbia, 1971-81; reading cons. S.C. Office Instructional Tech., 1982—. Active Common Cause. Mem. Internat. Reading Assn., Am. Ednl. Rsch. Assn., Assn. Supervision and Curriculum Devel., Nat. Soc. Study of Edn., Phi Delta Kappa . Episcopalian. Author instrnl. TV series: Getting the Word (So. Ednl. Communications Assn. award 1972, Ohio State award 1973, S.C. Scholastic Broadcasters award 1973), Getting the Message, 1981. Home: 460 S 23rd St Wilmington NC 28403-0200

RORKE, LUCY BALIAN, neuropathologist; b. St. Paul, June 22, 1929; d. Aram Haji and Karzouhy (Ousdigian) Balian; m. Robert Radcliffe Rorke, June 4, 1960. A.B., U. Minn., 1951, M.A., 1952, B.S., 1955, M.D., 1957. Diplomate Am. Bd. Pathology. Intern Phila. Gen. Hosp., 1957-58, resident anat. pathology and neuropathology, 1958-62, asst. neuropathologist, 1963-67, chief pediatric pathologist, 1967-68, chief neuropathologist, 1968-69, chmn. dept. anat. pathology and chief neuropathologist, 1969-73, chmn. dept. pathology, 1973-77, pres. med. staff, 1973-75; practice medicine specializing in neuropathology Phila., 1962—; neuropathologist Children's Hosp., Phila., 1965—, pres. med. staff, 1986-88; cons. neuropathologist Wyeth Rsch. Labs., Radnor, Pa., 1961-87, Wistar Inst. Anatomy and Biology, Phila., 1967-93; assoc. prof. pathology U. Pa. Sch. Medicine, Phila., 1970-73, prof., 1973—, clin. prof. neurology, 1979—; forensic neuropathologist Office of Med. Examiner, Phila., 1977—. Author: Myelinization of the Brain in the Newborn, 1969, Pathology of Perinatal Brain Injury, 1982; mem. editorial bd. Jours. Neuropathology Exptl. Neurology, 1980-85, 93—, Pediatric Neurosurgery, 1984—, Child's Nervous System, 1984-88, Brain Pathology, 1990—; contbr. articles to profl. jours. NIH fellow in neuropathology, 1961-62; NIH grantee for study of neonatal brain, 1963-68. Fellow Coll. Am. Pathologists; mem. Phila. Gen. Hosp. Med. Staff (pres. 1973-75), Phila. Neurol. Soc. (v.p. 1971-72, editor Transactions 1973, pres. 1975-76), Am. Assn. Neuropathologists (exec. council 1976-85, v.p. 1979-80, pres. 1981-82), Am. Neurol. Assn., AMA, Burlington County Med. Soc., Phila. Coll. Physicians. Home: 120 Chestnut St Moorestown NJ 08057-2937 Office: Children's Hosp of Philadelphia 324 S 34th St Philadelphia PA 19104-4303

ROSA, MARGARITA, lawyer, state agency official; b. Bklyn., Jan. 5, 1953; d. Jose and Julia (Mojica) R.; 1 child, Marisol Kimberly Rosa-Shapiro. BA in History cum laude, Princeton U., 1974; JD, Harvard U., 1977. Bar: N.Y. Assoc. Rosenman & Colin, N.Y.C., 1977-79, Rabinowitz & Boudin, N.Y.C., 1981-84; staff atty. Puerto Rican Legal Def. Edn. Fund, N.Y.C., 1979-81; teaching fellow Urban Legal Studies program CUNY, 1984-85; gen. counsel N.Y. State Div. Human Rights, N.Y.C., 1985-88, exec. dep. commr., 1988-90, commr., 1990—; vice chmn. N.Y. State Task force on ADA Implementation, 1991—; mem. N.Y. Gov.'s Task Force on Sexual Harassment, 1992; bd. dirs. Pub. Interest Law Found., NYU Law Sch., 1982-84. Bd. dirs. N.Y. Civil Liberties Union, 1981-86, Lower East Side Family Union, N.Y.C., 1982-84. Recipient Hispanic Women Achievers award N.Y. State Gov.'s Office Hispanic Affairs, 1990, Woman of Excellence award CUNY, 1992; Lombard Assn. fellow Office of U.S. Atty., So. Dist. N.Y., 1975; Revson Teaching fellow Charles Revson Found., 1984-85. Office: NY State Div Human Rights 55 W 125th St New York NY 10027-4512

ROSADO, ELIZABETH SCHAAR, elementary education educator; b. Mpls., Aug. 5, 1961; d. Merton Arnold and Mardelle Anne (Lindborg) Schaar; m. Pablo Augusto Rosado, Aug. 19, 1983; children: Kristina, Alexander. BA, U. Minn., 1985; MEd, Houston Bapt. U., 1990; postgrad., U. Houston, 1993—. Cert. bilingual, ESL, reading recovery, kindergarten tchr., Tex. Tchr. Harlandale Ind. Sch. Dist., San Antonio, 1986-87, Spring Branch Ind. Sch. Dist., Houston, 1987—. Title VII scholar Houston Bapt. U., 1988-90, U. Houston, 1992; Title 7 fellow, 1994. Mem. ASCD, Kappa Delta Pi. Roman Catholic. Office: Shadow Oaks Elem 1335 Shadowdale Dr Houston TX 77043-4298

ROSALES, SUZANNE MARIE, hospital coordinator; b. Merced, Calif., July 23, 1946; d. Walter Marshall and Ellen Marie (Earl) Potter; children: Anita Carol, Michelle Suzanne. AA, City Coll., San Francisco, 1966. Diplomate Am. Coll. Utilization Review Physicians. Utilization review coord. San Francisco Gen. Hosp., 1967-74; mgr. utilization review/discharge planning UCLA Hosp. and Clinics, 1974-79; nurse III Hawaii State Hosp., Kaneohe, 1979-80; review coord. Pacific Profl. Std. Review Orgn., Honolulu, 1980-81; coord. admission and utilization reviewq The Rehab. Hosp. of the Pacific, Honolulu, 1981-85; coord. Pacific Med. Referral Project, Honolulu, 1985-87; dir. profl. svcs. The Queen's Healthcare Plan, Honolulu, 1987-88; utilization mgmt. coord. Vista Psychiat. Physician Assocs., San Diego, 1989; admission coord. utilization review San Francisco Gen. Hosp., 1989-91, quality improvement coordinator, 1991—; cons. Am. Med. Records Assn. Contbr. articles to profl. jours. Mem. Nat. Assn. Utilization Review Profls. Home: 505 Hanover St Daly City CA 94014-1351 Office: San Francisco Gen Hosp 1001 Potrero Ave San Francisco CA 94110-3518

ROSALES, TERESA O., pediatric ophthalmologist; b. Oakland, Calif., Aug. 21, 1950; d. Martin C. and Beverly Francis (Becker) Olavarri; m. Carlos A. Rosales, Aug. 18, 1973; children: Christina, Stephanie. BS in Biology, Stanford U., 1972; MD, UCLA, 1976. Intern Harbor-UCLA, Torrance, Calif., 1977-80, ophthalmology resident, 1980-81; fellow in pediat. ophthalmology Jules Stein Eye Inst., L.A., 1981; pvt. practice Family Eye Med. Group, Long Beach, Calif., 1981—; clin. instr. UCLA, 1981—; clin. prof. U. Calif., Irvine, 1987—. Fellow Am. Acad. Ophthalmology; mem. Am. Assn. Pediat. Ophthalmology and Strabisnews. Office: Family Eye Med Group 2840 Long Beach Blvd # 408 Long Beach CA 90806

ROSALES-SAID, MARTA MILAGROS, elementary educator; b. Bilbao, Bizkaia, Spain, Aug. 5, 1959; d. Elias and Milagros (Franco) Rosales; m. Haroon Said, Sept. 8, 1984; 1 child, Iskander. BEd, Escuela de Magisterio, Spain, 1980; Spanish Final Diploma, London Inst. Linguistics, 1986. Spl. edn. tchr. Colegio INTXA Verondo, Durango, Spain, 1981-83; tchr. Pasadena (Calif.) Unified Sch. Dist., 1988—, mentor tchr., 1991—. Prodr., editor, dir.: Bilingual Education (video), 1991. Pasadena Ednl. Found. grantee, 1989-90. Mem. London Inst. Linguists, Nature Conservancy.

ROSAN, SHIRA JUDITH, architect, writer; b. N.Y.C., Feb. 23, 1950; d. Howard J. and Menorah J. (Wagman) R. AB in Communications, Oberlin (Ohio) Coll., 1972; MArch, SUNY, Buffalo, 1980. Staff architect Zachary Rosenfield Ptnrs., N.Y.C., 1979; staff architect The Stein Partnership, N.Y.C., 1980-83, assoc., 1983—; vis. artist Sch. Dist. 30, N.Y.C., 1986; cons. Hudson Guild Settlement House, N.Y.C., 1986—, Spuyten Duyvil Pre-Sch., Bronx, N.Y., 1981. Exhibited in group shows at Women in Arch., 1981; with Environ. Design and Rsch. Assn., 1985; author: (as S.J. Rozan) China Trade, 1994, Concourse, 1995. Active Save the Village, N.Y.C., Amnesty Internat., N.Y.C. Recipient 1st prize Strycker's Bay Neighborhood Assn., 1985, citation Consultation Internationale pour l'Amenagement du Quartier des Halles, Paris, 1980, design citation Ethnic Heritage Festival, 1980. Mem. AIA, Greenwich Village Soc. for Hist. Preservation, Nat. Trust for Hist. Preservation. Democrat. Jewish. Home: 344 W 12th St New York NY 10014-1707 Office: The Stein Partnership 20 W 20th St New York NY 10011-4213

ROSCHE, LORETTA G., medical/surgical nurse; b. New Philadelphia, Ohio, Sept. 16, 1934; d. Seldon E. and Margaret (Murphy) Donohue; m. Thomas R. Rosche, Sept. 6, 1954; children: Melanie Rosche Smith, Cynthia Rosche Geeker, Lori Rosche Davis, Julia Rosche Sivyer. Diploma, Lafayette Sch. Nursing, 1984; cert., Jewish Hosp., 1985; student, Am. Healthcare Inst. RN, Va. Office mgr., nurse, surg. asst. to pvt. physician Williamsburg, Va., 1979—; advanced tng. in laparoscopic surgery Abbott Northwestern Hosp., Mpls., 1990; surg. nurse vol. surg. team Esperanza, Amazon region of Brazil, 1988, 91; lectr. various groups including Med. Soc., Rotary, Hand Soc. Named Speaker of Yr. Psi Beta, 1990. Mem. Assn. Hand Care Profls. (co-founder, treas.), Am. Assn. Med. Assts. (cert.), Soc. Laparoendoscopic Surgeons. Home: 128 Country Club Dr Williamsburg VA 23188-1516

ROSCHER, NINA MATHENY, chemistry educator; b. Uniontown, Pa., Dec. 8, 1938; d. Charles Kenneth and Wilma Pauline (Solomon) Matheny; m. David Roscher, Dec. 27, 1964. BS in Chemistry, U. Del., 1960; PhD in Chemistry, Purdue U., 1964. Phys. chemist Nat. Bur. of Standards, 1958-61; rsch. and teaching asst. Purdue U., West Lafayette, Ind., 1960-64, fellow in chemistry, instr. chemistry, 1964-65; instr. U. Tex., Austin, 1965-67; sr. staff chemist Coca-Cola Export Corp., 1967-68; asst. prof. Douglass Coll., Rutgers U., The State U., 1968-74, asst. dean, 1971-74; dir. acad. adminstrn. Am. U., Washington, 1974-76, assoc. prof. chemistry, 1974-79, prof., 1979—, assoc. dean grad. affairs Coll. Arts and Scis., 1976-79, vice-provost acad. svcs., 1979-82, vice provost for acad. affairs, 1982-85, dean faculty affairs, 1981-85, chair chemistry dept., 1991—; program dir. sci. edn., NSF, 1986—; lectr. in field. Contbr. articles to profl. jours. Standard Oil fellow, 1961-62, David Ross fellow, 1963-64, Rutgers U. Rsch. Fund, Biomed. Support grantee. Fellow AAAS, Am. Inst. Chemists (profl. opportunities for women com., pres. dist. inst. chemists 1978-79, sec. 1976-77, fin. com. 1983-87, exec. com., bd. dirs. 1986); mem. Am. Chem. Soc. (treas. Monmouth County sect. 1970-72, chmn. 1974, pres. Washington sect. 1995, profl. programs planning and coord. com. 1976-78, admissions com. 1981-89, 91—, GM scholar 1956-60, Virgil F. Payne award, numerous others), N.Y. Acad. Scis., AAUA, Assn. Women in Sci., Soc. Applied Spectroscopy, Sci. Manpower Commn. Profls. in Sci. Home: 10400 Hunter Ridge Dr Oakton VA 22124-1616 Office: Am Univ Dept Chemistry Washington DC 20016-8014

ROSE, ANITA CARROLL, retired educator; b. New Bedford, Mass., Oct. 14, 1922; d. Louis Arthur and Aline (Chicoine) Carroll; m. Anthony E. Rose, Sept. 24, 1955 (dec.); children: Anthony David, Stephen Arthur. BA, U. Mass., Dartmouth, 1971; MAT, R.I. Coll., 1975. Exec. sec. Berkshire-Hathaway, Inc., New Bedford, 1941-55, New Bedford Cancer Soc., 1956-59; tchr. French and English New Bedford Pub. Schs., 1971-88; ret., 1988; clk. Friends of Coastline Elderly Svcs., Inc., 1991-93. Pres. New Bedford Jr. Women's Club, 1950-51; v.p. Cath. Women's Club, 1957-59, del. Coun. of Women's Orgns., 1989-91; pres. Fairhaven Mothers' Club, 1967-69, book chmn., 1989-91, sunshine chmn., 1991-93, nominating com. chmn., 1993—; mem. Fairhaven Town Mtg., Mass., 1965—; trustee Millicent Libr., Fairhaven, 1980—; rec. sec. Fairhaven Improvement Assn., 1982—; sec. Fairhaven Rep. Town Com., 1980—; bd. dirs. St. Anne Credit Union, New Bedford, 1988—, asst. treas., mem. investment com. 1991-93, pres., chmn. bd., 1993—; mem. adv. coun. Coastline Elderly Svc. Inc., 1988-92; del. Mass. Rep. Conv., 1974, 82, 86, 90, 94; mem. YWCA, Old Dartmouth Hist. Assn., Friends of the Zeiterion Theatre. Mem. AAUW (pres. Coll. Club New Bedford Inc. 1983-85, 1st v.p. 1989-91, del. nat. conv. 1981, 83, 84, 93, chmn. nominating com. Mass. divsn. 1988-90), Tri-County Music Assn. (pres. 1992—, bd. dirs. 1988—), R.I. Coll. Alumni Assn., U. Mass.-Dartmouth Alumni Assn., Southeastern Mass. Assn. Social Studies, Mil. Order of the World Wars, Am. Ex-Prisoners of War, St. Jospeh's Couples' Club (pres. 1987-88), Fairhaven Colonial Club (2d v.p. 1988-89). Home: 49 Laurel St Fairhaven MA 02719-2817

ROSE, BEVERLY ANNE, pharmacist; b. Lewiston, Idaho, June 11, 1950; d. Burton Roswell and Nell Dora (Greenburg) Stein; m. Fred Joseph Rose, July 21, 1973 (div. Aug. 1980). BS in Pharmacy, Ohio No. U., 1973; MBA, Cleve. State U., 1987. Registered pharmacist, Ohio, N.Y. Staff pharmacist Lorain (Ohio) Community Hosp., 1973-79, dir. pharmacy, 1979-91; dir. dept. pharmacy svcs. The House of the Good Samaritan Health Care Complex, Watertown, N.Y., 1991-93; adj. faculty, clin. tng. specialist U. Toledo Coll. Pharmacy, 1980-91; computer cons. Hosp. Pharmacy Network; mem. State Bd. Legis. Rule Rev., Ohio State Bd. Pharmacy, 1987, 88; mem. pres. adv. bd. Ohio No. U., Ada, 1990—. Mem. editl. bd. Aspen Publs., 1992—. Mem. Am. Soc. Health Sys. Pharmacists (apptd. coun. legal and pub. affairs 1988-89, 89-90, state del. ho. of dels. Ohio 1984, 85, 86, 87, 88, 89, mem. psychotherapeutics-spl. practice group 1990—), Adminstrs. Practice Mgmt. Group, Am. Pharm. Assn., Ohio Soc. Hosp. Pharmacists (pres. 1985-89, Squibb Leadership award 1988, Ciba-Geigy Svc. award 1988, Evlyn Gray Scott award 1987), N.Y. State Coun. Hosp. Pharmacists, Am. Soc. Parenteral and Enteral Nutrition, Fedn. Internat. Pharmaceutique, N.Y. Chpt. Am. Coll. Clin. Pharmacy, others. Home: 20 Cambridge Dr Apt 4 Georgetown OH 45121

ROSE, BONNIE LOU, state official; b. Philipsburg, Pa., Feb. 24, 1951; d. Wasil and Ethel Louise (Crain) Harsomchuck; m. James Edward Rose, Aug. 31, 1975 (sept. 1981). Student, Harrisburg Area Community Coll, 1969-70; diploma, Harrisburg Hosp. Sch. Nursing, 1972; postgrad., Pa. State U., 1987. RN, Pa. Charge nurse Plasmapheresis Ctr., Harrisburg, Pa., 1973-75, Longterm Care Facility, Harrisburg, Pa., 1975; nurse Oral Surgery Practice, Harrisburg, Pa., 1975; nurse, utilization review Pa. Dept. Pub. Welfare, Harrisburg, 1975-79; chief planning, implementation Pa. Dept. Pub. Welfare, Office Med. Assistance, Harrisburg, 1979-83, dir. provider inquiry, 1983-87, dir. provider rels., 1987, dir. long term care provider svcs., 1989—; cons. in field; instr. Pa. Dept. Pub. Welfare, 1985—, coping with difficult behavior, 1985—, coping with difficult behavior, 1985—, stress mgmt., 1985—, burnout, 1986—, team bldg., facilitator-organizational devel., 1987—, team building, 1992—. Mem. Harrisburg Hosp. Alumni Assn. Home: 1704 Creek Vista Dr New Cumberland PA 17070-2212

ROSE, CAROL ANN, air transportation executive; b. Toledo, Jan. 4, 1942; d. Donald Lucien and Dorothy Josephine (Maus) Edmunds; m. Saul Rose, Feb. 3, 1971 (div. 1976). BA, Kent State U., 1963. Entertainer, restaurant supr. S.S. Aquarama Cruiseship, Cleve., 1961-63; airline reservation agt. United Airlines, Cleve., 1963-68; internat. passenger svc. rep. United Airlines, Miami, Fla., 1969-70; V.I.P. customer svc. receptionist-expediter United Airlines, Phila., 1971-79, account exec., 1980-84; spl. events mgr. United Airlines, Chgo., 1984-87, red carpet club coord., 1987-88, corp. meeting planner, 1988-90; comml. aircraft weight and balance planner United Airlines, Seattle, 1991—; speaker Am. Mktg. Assn., Chgo., 1989. Author: Red Carpet Club Procedure Manual-O'Hare, 1987, Corporate Meeting Planners Manual, 1989; editor: Sky Lines Seattle Station Newsletter, 1992. Recipient Oustanding Svc. award Airline Passengers Assn., Phila., 1981, Outstanding Contbn. award Muscular Dystrophy Assn.-Jerry Lewis Telethon, Las Vegas, 1985, 86, 89, Leadership award United Way Campaign, Chgo., 1988. Mem. Meeting Planners Assn., Mgmt. Club (v.p. 1983, pres. 1984), Women United (exec. bd. 1982-83), Delta Zeta. Home: 609 S 222nd St Apt 202 Des Moines WA 98198-6277 Office: United Airlines Seattle-Tacoma Airport Seattle WA 98158

ROSE, CAROL DENISE, orthopedic unit nurse administrator, educator; b. Las Vegas, Nev., July 31, 1960; d. Howard Elden and Sarah (Haley) Heckethorn; m. Michael Shaun Rose, June 19, 1982; 1 child, Carissa Denise. ADN, U. Nev., Las Vegas, 1981, BSN, 1985. Staff nurse orthopedic unit Univ. Med. Ctr. So. Nev., Las Vegas, 1981-84, acting head nurse, then head nurse orthopedic unit, 1984-88, asst. mgr. orthopedic unit, 1988, orthopedic unit mgr., 1988—; adj. faculty health scis. dept. Clark County C.C., North Las Vegas, Nev.; speaker at profl. confs. Mem. ANA, Nat. Assn. Orthopaedic Nurses (pres. So. Nev. chpt.), Sigma Theta Tau, Phi Kappa Phi. Democrat. Roman Catholic. Office: Univ Med Ctr So Nev 1800 W Charleston Blvd Las Vegas NV 89102-2386

ROSE, DEMETA JO, underwriter; b. Vivian, La., July 13, 1958; d. Willie Hodge and Lela Bell (Stroy) Player; m. Michael Rose, June, 1976; children: Michael, Marquis. AA in Acctg., Pa. Valley C.C., 1988; BS in Acctg. and Mgmt., Park Coll., 1990. Adminstrv. asst. Commerce Bank, Kansas City, Mo., 1983-85; acctg. technician Gen. Svc. Adminstrn., Kansas City, Mo., 1987-90; investment acctg. analyst Bus. Men's Assurance, Kansas City, Mo., 1990-93, underwriter trainee, 1993—. Mem. Inst. Mgmt. Accts. Baptist. Home: 10608 Wenzel Ave Kansas City MO 64137-1858 Office: Bus Mens Assurance PO Box 419458 Kansas City MO 64141-6458

ROSE, ELIZABETH, author, satirist; b. N.Y.C., Sept. 18, 1941; children: Kimberly, Dana. Nurse, Lenox Hill Hosp. Sch. Nursing, 1962; BA summa cum laude, U. Redlands, 1976. Asst. head nurse emergency room N.Y.C., 1963-66; head nurse San Pedro (Calif.) Hosp., 1968-69; pub. Butterfly Pub. Co., Santa Monica, 1985; radio and TV personality L.A., 1985—; founder Candida Anonymous, Santa Monica, 1985; cons. health profls. Author: Lady of Gray: Healing Candida-The Nightmare Chemical Epidemic, 1985, 2d edit. 1987, 3d edit. 1989, Sainthood and Single Motherhood, 1990. Recipient Internat. World Leader award Better Worlds Soc., Cambridge, Eng., 1989; N.Y. State Regents scholar, 1959. Mem. UCLA Alumni Assn. (life), Women's Nat. Book Assn., Pubs. Mktg. Assn., Cousteau Soc., Abortion Rights League, Coalition Against Malathion Spraying, Tesla Soc., L.A. Blue Book Club, Sierra Club. Office: Butterfly Publishing Co PO Box 893 Chanhassen MN 55317-0893

ROSE, LEATRICE, artist, educator; b. N.Y.C., June 22, 1924; d. Louis Rose and Edna Ades; m. Sol Greenberg (div.); children: Damon, Ethan; m. Joseph Stefanelli, Oct. 10, 1975. Student, Cooper Union, 1941-45, Arts Students League, 1946, Hans Hoffman Sch., 1947. Solo exhbns. include Hansa Gallery, N.Y.C., 1954, Zabriskie Gallery, N.Y.C., 1965, Landmark Gallery, N.Y.C., 1974, Tibor de Nagy Gallery, N.Y.C., 1975, 78, 81, 82, Elaine Benson Gallery, Bridgehampton, N.Y., 1980, Armstrong Gallery, N.Y.C., 1985, Benton Gallery, Southampton, N.Y., 1987, Cyrus Gallery, N.Y.C., 1989; group exhbns. include Sam Kootz Gallery, N.Y.C., 1950, Peridot Gallery, N.Y.C., 1952, Poindexter Gallery, N.Y.C., 1959, Tanager Gallery, N.Y.C., 1960, 62, Riverside Mus., N.Y.C., 1964, Frumkin Gallery, N.Y.C., 1964, Pa. Acad. Fine Arts, Phila., 1966, N.Y. Cultural Ctr., 1973, The Queens (N.Y.) Mus., 1974, 83, Nat. Acad. Design, N.Y.C., 1974, 75, 76, 92, 93, Weatherspoon Art Gallery, Greensboro, N.C., 78, 81, Whitney Mus. Am. Art, N.Y.C., 1978, Albright-Knox Gallery, Buffalo, 1978, 81, Met. Mus. Art, 1979, Vanderwoude Tananbaum Gallery, N.Y.C., 1982, Benton Gallery, 1986, 87.; public collections include Albrect Gallery, St. Joseph, Mo., Guild Hall Mus., East Hampton, N.Y., Tibor de Nagy, Met. Mus. Art. Grantee N.Y. State Coun. Arts, 1974, The Ingram Merrill Found., 1974, AAUW, 1975, NEA, 1977, Esther and Aldolph Gottlieb Found., 1980, 88; recipient Altman prize NAD, 1974, Phillips prize NAD, 1992, award AAAL, 1992, Am. Inst. Art award. Mem. NAD. Office: 463 West St New York NY 10014

ROSE, LOUISE, realtor; b. Pitts., Sept. 3, 1941; d. Louis B. Rose and Saralouise Hirshberg; children: Andrew Morrison, Justin Bailey. BS, U. Pitts., 1963. Stockbroker Newburger & Co., Phila., 1966-69, Shearson Hammill, Denver, 1970-73; realtor, owner ERA Taos, Realtors, Taos, N.Mex., 1981-91, Realty World, Taos formerly Louise Rose, Inc., Taos, N.Mex., 1991—. Office: Realty World Taos 413B Paseo Del Pueblo Norte Taos NM 87571-5907

ROSE, MARGARETE ERIKA, pathologist; b. Esslingen, Germany, Feb. 12, 1945; came to U.S., 1967; d. Wilhelm Ernst and Lina (Schurr) Pfisterer; m. Arthur Caughey Rose, Feb. 3, 1967; children: Victoria Anne, Alexandra Julia, Frederica Isabella. MD, U. So. Calif., L.A., 1972. Diplomate Am. Bd. Anatomic and Clin. Pathology. Pathologist St. Joseph Med. Ctr., Burbank, Calif., 1977-78, Glenview Pathology Med. Ctr., Culver City, Calif., 1979—; dir. anatomic pathology Glenview Mem. Pathology, Culver City, 1988—; dir. Life Chem. Lab., Woodland Hills, Calif., 1992—, Clin. Sci. Labs., North Hollywood, Calif.; co-dir. lab. Holy Cross Med. Ctr., Mission Hills, Calif., 1994—. Mem. Because I Love You, L.A., 1994. Fellow Am. Soc. Pathology, Coll. Am. Pathology. Office: Brotman Med Ctr Dept Pathology 3828 Hughes Ave Culver City CA 90231

ROSE, MARIANNE HUNT, business educator; b. Portsmouth, Ohio, Nov. 6, 1940; d. Harry Duke and B. Marie (Craycraft) Hunt; m. W. Craig Rose, Aug. 9, 1958 (dec. 1988); children: W. Stuart, Deirdre Anne. BS in Edn., Ohio U., 1962; postgrad., U. Va., James Madison U., George Mason U. Cert. tchr., Va., Ohio. Asst. editor Morehead (Ky.) News, 1962-63; mgr. Birthday Calendar Co., Morehead, 1963-64; bus. tchr. Clay Twp. Schs., Portsmouth, 1964-65, Prince William County Adult Edn., Woodbridge, Va., 1977-80, Prince William County Schs., Woodbridge, 1973—; co-sponsor Future Bus. Leaders Am., Gar-Field Sr. High Sch., Woodbridge, mentor TLC program, 1990—; team mem. Tech-Prep Consortiu, No. Va. C.C., Woodbridge, 1992—. Mem. Dale City Civic Assn., Woodbridge; elder, sec. 1st United Presbyn. Ch., Woodbridge, 1972—. Recipient Professionalism award Tchr. Recognition Com./Gar-Field, 1993. Mem. NEA, AAUW, Va. Edn. Assn., Va. Bus. Edn. Assn., Prince William Edn. Assn. (bldg. rep.). Home: 14415 Fairview Ln Woodbridge VA 22193 Office: Gar Field Sr High Sch 14000 Smoketown Rd Woodbridge VA 22192

ROSE, MELISSA EVA ANDERSON, small business owner; b. Grayson, Ky., Sept. 24, 1959; d. thomas Erwin and Betty Jane (Mauk) Hall; m. William David Rose, JUne 19, 1992. Student, Araphoe Bus. Coll., Denver, 1976-78; BA, Morehead State U., 1979-84. Sales clk. Cases Hardware and Antiques, Olive Hill, Ky., 1970-72; waitress Los Gringitos, Morehead, Ky., 1975; tele-mktg. operator Citi-Corp Fin. Svcs., Denver, 1977-78; model, spokeswoman Ford Agy. NY, N.Y.C., 1979-81; counselor Christian Social Svcs., 1979-81; activities coord. Dept. Corrections, Denver, 1979; pres. ops. Dimensions Unltd. Inc., Denver, 1981—; owner, pres. Dimensions Unltd. Inc., Huntington, W.Va., 1985—; cons. Home Interior Designs, Inc., Denver, 1985-86; sec. Denver County Real Estate Commn., 1987-88; bd. dirs. Found. for Human Concerns, Morehead, Ky., 1987-88, Excalibur Fin. Svc., Olive Hill, Ky., Melissa E. Rose Inc.; cons. Ky. c. of Comml., Glasgow, 1988—; founder, pres. Unified Fortress Group, Inc., 1989; founder, pres. Gold Link Publs., 1991—; contr. Alpha Mktg. Corp., 1992—. Author: Business Ethics 2nd Moral Values, 1987, Life After Death 2 Cultural Explorations, 1987, Business Marketing-Sales for the 90s, 1992. Spokesperson Nat. Rep. Group, Morehead, 1981; chairperson Tiffany's Gold Charity Soc., Denver 1986; sec. Bus. Devel. Soc., Las Vegas, 1987; charter sponsor NATO Culture Exch. in W.Va., NY, 1989. Mem. NAFE, Dunn V. Bradstree, Inc., Nat. Assn. Mchts., Encore Gold Purchasing Club, League Human Rights, Nat. Assn. Euroeoan Bus. Cmtys., Met. Mus. Art, Smithsonian Instn., Citizens for a Better Govt. (chair), Olive Hill C. of C. Office: Dimensions Unltd Inc 3845 Bluestone Bratton Br Rd Morehead KY 40351-9788 also: Golden Link Publs PO Box 869 Olive Hill KY 41164-0869

ROSE, MERRILL, public relations counselor; b. Beaufort, N.C., Apr. 20, 1955; d. Robert Lloyd Rose and Betty Lou (Merrill) Ellis. Student, U. N.C., 1977. Reporter, editor Consumer News, Washington, 1978-79; v.p. Fraser/Assocs., Washington, 1979-82; sr. assoc. Porter/Novelli, Washington, 1982-85, v.p., 1985-87; sr. v.p., food practice leader Porter/Novelli, N.Y.C., 1989-91, exec. v.p., 1990—; gen. mgr. Chgo. Porter/Novelli, 1991—. Bd. dirs. CARE, N.Y.C., 1991—; bd. visitors U. N.C. Sch. Journalism, Chapel Hill, 1992—; bd. dirs. Friends of Prentiss affiliate Northwestern Meml. Hosp., 1993—. Mem. Am. Inst. of Wine and Food, Pub. Rels. Soc. Am. Office: Porter/Novelli 303 E Wacker Dr 12th Fl Chicago IL 60601

ROSE, PHYLLIS, English language professional, author; b. N.Y.C., Oct. 26, 1942; d. Eli and Minnie (Selesko) Davidoff; m. Mark Rose, (div. 1975); 1 son, Ted.; m. Laurent de Brunhoff, 1990. BA summa cum laude, Radcliffe Coll., 1964; M.A., Yale U., 1965; Ph.D., Harvard U., 1970. Teaching fellow Harvard U., Cambridge, Mass., 1966-67; acting instr. Yale U., New Haven, 1969; asst. prof. Wesleyan U., Middletown, Conn., 1969-76, assoc. prof., 1976-81, prof. English, 1981—; vis. prof. U. Calif., Berkeley, 1981-82; chmn. fiction jury Nat. Book Awards, 1993; bd. dirs. Wesleyan Writers Conf. Key West Literary Seminar. Author: Woman of Letters: A Life of Virginia Woolf, 1978, Parallel Lives: Five Victorian Marriages, 1983, Writing of Women, 1985, Jazz Cleopatra: Josephine Baker in Her Time, 1989, Never Say Goodbye: Essays, 1991; editor: The Norton Book of Women's Lives, 1993; book reviewer N.Y. Times Book Rev., The Atlantic; essayist. Nat. Endowment for Humanities fellow, 1973-74; Rockefeller Found. fellow, 1984-85; Guggenheim fellow, 1985. Mem. PEN, Nat. Book Critics Circle, Authors Guild. Home: 74 Wyllys Ave Middletown CT 06457-3243 Office: Wesleyan U Dept English Middletown CT 06457

ROSE, PHYLLIS KAY, sales executive; b. Vernon, Tex., Dec. 15, 1955; d. Wilbert Arnold and Mildred Ruth (Forster) Kieschnick; m. Evertte Neal Johnson, Feb. 23, 1980 (div. 1987); m. Michael Lynn Rose, Aug. 29, 1992. BBA, Tex. Tech. U., 1978. Sales rep. R.J. Reynolds Tobacco,

Wichita Falls, Tex., 1978-79, area sales rep., 1979-84; asst. div. mgr. R.J. Reynolds Tobacco, Ft. Worth, 1984-85, tng. and devel. mgr., 1985-86, spl. accounts mgr., 1986-87; div. sales mgr. R.J. R. Nabisco, Memphis, 1987—. Republican. Home: 251 Summerfield Ln Cordova TN 38018-7421

ROSE, ROSLYN, artist; b. Irvington, N.J., May 28, 1929; d. Mark and Anne Sarah (Green) R.; m. Franklin Blou, Nov. 26, 1950; 1 child, Mark Gordon Blue (dec.). Student, Rutgers U., 1949-51, Pratt Ctr. for Contemporary, Printmaking, N.Y.C., 1967; BS, Skidmore Coll., 1976. Artist. One-person shows include Midday Gallery, Caldwell, N.J., 1972, Caldwell Coll., 1972, Kean Coll., Union, N.J., 1973, Art Corner Gallery, Millburn, N.J., 1974, Brandeis U., Mass., 1974, Newark (N.J.) Mus., 1974, George Frederick Gallery, Rochester, N.Y.,1 981, Robbins Gallery, Washington, 1981, Signatures Gallery, Washington, 1981, Arnot Art Mus., Elmira, N.Y., 1982, Douglas Coll./Rutgers Univ., New Brunswick, 1987, Nathans Gallery, West Paterson, N.J., 1984, 86, 89; exhibited in group shows at Seattle Art Mus., Portland (Oreg.) Mus., NYU U. Small Works Show, Montclair Art Mus., N.J., Middlesex County Mus., Piscataway, N.J., and others; permanent collections include N.J. State Mus., Trenton, Citibank of N.Y., Russia, N.J. State Libr., Trenton, Roddenbery Meml. Libr., Cairo, Ga., Rosenberg Libr., Galveston, Tex., Newark Mus., Newark Pub. Libr., AT&T, BASF Wyandotte Corp., Canon Calculator Systems, N.Y.C., First Fed. Bank, Rochester, Gulf & Western Industries, Irving Trust Co., N.Y., Kidder, Peabody & Co., N.Y., McAllen Internat. Mus., Tex., Nabisco Brands Corp., East Hanover, N.J., N.J. Bell, Readers Digest Collection, Voorhees-Zimmerli Mus., Rutgers U., New Brunswick, N.J., others; creator UNCIF cards, 1979-80. Recipient graphic award Westchester (N.Y.) Art Soc., 1973, Best-in-Show award Livingston (N.J.) Art Assn., 1971, N.J. Ctr. for Visual Arts, Summit, 1969; numerous others. Mem. Nat. Assn. Women Artists (Innovative Painting award 1990), N.Y. Artists Equity, Hoboken (N.J.) Creative Alliance, Pen and Brush Club (N.Y.C.). Office: Atelier Rose PO Box 5095 Hoboken NJ 07030-1501

ROSE, SHARON MARIE, critical care nurse; b. Big Spring, Tex., Feb. 16, 1958; d. William Coleman Smith and Grace Marie (Arnett) Karns; m. Christopher Robin Rose, Jan. 21, 984; 1 child, Crystal Alyss. AAS, Odessa Coll., 1981; BS in Occupational Edn., Wayland Bapt., 1987. Critical care RN Lubbock (Tex.) Gen. Hosp., 1981-88, med-surg. instr., 1988-89; dialysis RN St. Mary of the Plains Hosp., 1989-91; asst. CCU mgr. St. Mary of the Plains Hosp., Lubbock, 1990-91; health occupations instr. Lubbock Ind. Sch. Dist., 1991-94; in-svc. coord. Dialysis Ctr. Lubbock, Tex., 1994—; tchr. summer session Asst. for Med. Terminology course, 1993; mem. Health Occupations Adv. Com., Lubbock, 1988. Mem. Tex. Health Occupations Assn. (v.p. 1993-94), Health Occupation Students Am. (advisor 1991—). Baptist. Home: 2802 N Quaker Ave Apt 57 Lubbock TX 79415-2707 Office: Dialysis Ctr Lubbock 4110 22nd Pl Lubbock TX 79410

ROSE, SUSAN A. SCHULTZ, retired theological librarian; b. Mountain Lake, Minn., Dec. 22, 1911; d. David D. and Anna (Eitzen) Schultz; m. Delbert R. Rose, Dec. 27, 1986. BA, John Fletcher Coll., 1940; BSLS, U. Ill., 1946, MLS, 1949; LittD (hon.), Houghton Coll., 1974. Dean women John Fletcher-Kletzing Coll., University Park, Iowa, 1940-45; asst. libr. Bethany (Okla.) Coll., 1946-47; dir. libr. svcs. Asbury Theol. Sem., Wilmore, Ky., 1949-78, ret., 1978; cons. grad. schs. theology librs. The Philippines, 1978-80, 85-86, Nairobi, Kenya, 1983-84, Zagreb, Yugoslavia, 1984, Taiwan, Korea, Japan, 1987, Allahabad, India, 1989, Kericho, Kenya, 1989, Manila, 1990; cons. grad. schs. theology librs. Wesly Bible Seminary, Jackson, Miss., 1987-93, Kaohsiung, Taiwan, 1992, Owerri, Nigeria, 1993; mem. exec. com. 1st Alliance Ch., Lexington, Ky., 1958-61, 66-73; del. to nat. Congress Christian and Missionary Alliance, Columbus, Ohio, 1964, to Nat. Congress on Edn., St. Paul, 1970. Contbr. articles to profl. jours. Sunday sch. tchr. 1st Alliance Ch., Lexington, 1951-70; mem. libr. bd. Withers-Jessamine County Libr., Nicholasville, Ky., 1966-77. Recipient Outstanding Spl. Libr. of Yr. award Ky. Trustees Assn., 1967, Disting. Svc. award Asbury Theol. Sem., 1974, Emily Russell award Assn. Christian Librs. , 1974, Disting. Alumnus award Vennard Coll. (successor to John Fletcher-Kletzing Coll.), 1982. Mem. Am. Theol. Libr. Assn. (ret., exec. sec. 1967-71, dir. 1974-77), Wesley Theol. Soc. (ret.), Christian Holiness Assn., Ky. Libr. Assn. (bd. dirs. 1960—, sect. chair 1966-67). Mem. Christian and Missionary Alliance. Home: Shell Point Village 3905 Lucina Fort Myers FL 33908-1671

ROSE, SUSAN ANN, psychology educator, developmental psychologist; b. Brockton, Mass., June 27, 1939; d. George and Pessie (Task) Lazarus; m. Israel H. Rose, Mar. 26, 1961. BA, U. Mass., 1961; PhD, NYU, 1969. Lic. psychologist, N.Y. NIMH predoctoral fellow NYU, N.Y.C., 1963-67; NIH postdoctoral fellow Albert Einstein Coll. Medicine, Yeshiva U., Bronx, N.Y., 1969-72, instr. psychiatry, 1972-74, asst. prof., 1974-77, assoc. prof., 1978-83, prof. psychiatry, 1983—, prof. pediatrics, 1985—; mem. rev. com. NIMH, 1987-91; invited prof. Sorbonne, U. Paris, 1983; vis. scientist B.J. Wadia Hosp. for Children, Bombay, 1984; Flora Stone Mather Disting. Vis. prof. Case Western Res. U., Cleve., 1990. Co-author: The Language of Learning, 1978, (tests) Preschool Language Assessment Instrument, 1978, Spanish version, 1983; mem. editorial bd. Infant Behavior and Devel., 1980—, Child Devel., 1982-83, Devel. Psychology, 1986-93; contbr. over 60 articles to profl. jours., chpts. to books. Indo-Am. fellow Coun. for Internat. Exch. of Scholars, 1984; grantee NIH and Nat. Found. March of Dimes, 1974—. Fellow APA; mem. Soc. for Behavioral Pediatrics (exec. coun. 1988-91), Internat. Conf. on Infant Studies (steering com. 1986-91). Home: 18 Floral Dr Hastings-on-Hudson NY 10706 Office: Albert Einstein Coll Medicine Dept Pediatrics 1300 Morris Park Ave Bronx NY 10461

ROSE, SUSAN CAROL, restaurant executive, chef, consultant; b. Rochester, N.Y., Jan. 29, 1942; d. Frederick Raymond Smith and Grace Eunice (Read) Smith Drum; m. Larry Anthony Rose, Jan. 5, 1963 (div. Jan. 1976); children: John David, Karen Michelle Haines, Patricia Anne. Student, Monroe Community Coll., Rochester, 1959-60; cert. exec. steward, Innisbrook Resort, 1976; student, St. Petersburg Jr. Coll., Tarpon Springs, Fla., 1978-80, Pinellas Voc. Tech., 1987—. With Blue Cross-Blue Shield, Rochester, 1959-67; from coffee service mgr. to exec. steward Innisbrook Resort, Tarpon Springs, 1974-84; catering team supr. Bon Appetit Restaurant, Dunedin, Fla., 1984, Bounty Caterers, Dunedin, 1984; asst. mgr. trainee Wendy's Internat., Largo, Fla., 1984; store mgr. Long John Silver's, Largo, 1984-85; exec. steward, banquet chef, room service mgr., cons. Sandestin Beach Hilton, Destin, Fla., 1985; day mgr. Shells Restaurant, Clearwater, Fla., 1986-87; sous chef, kitchen mgr. Saltwaters Seafood Grille, Palm Harbor, Fla., 1987; exec. steward Adam's Mark Caribbean Gulf Resort, Clearwater Beach, 1987—; chef/kitchen mgr. Seafood Broiler, 1990-91; chef Hwy. Ribbery Restaurant, 1991, Boomerangs Cafe, 1992; galley supr., cook Empress Cruise Lines, 1992-94; chef Wards Seafood, 1994—; garde manger 94th Aero Squadron Restaurant, Las Fontanas Restaurant; cons. restaurant mgmt. Mem. Nat. Assn. Female Execs., Hospitality Industry Assn., Smithsonian Inst. Assocs., Holiday Inn Priority Club, Internat. Travel Club, Encore Travel Club, Clearwater Jaycees. Democrat. Roman Catholic. Home: 1162 Jackson Rd Clearwater FL 34615-4605 Office: Adam's Mark Caribbean Gulf Resort Gulfview Blvd Clearwater Beach FL 34616

ROSE, SUSAN PORTER, federal commission administrator; b. Cin., Sept. 20, 1941; d. Elmer Johnson and Dorothy (Wurst) Porter; m. Jonathan Chapman Rose, Jan. 26, 1980; 1 child, Benjamin Chapman. BA, Earlham Coll., 1963; MS, Ind. State U., Terre Haute, 1970. Staff asst. Congressman Richard L. Roudebush, Washington, 1963-64; asst. dean George Sch., Bucks County, Pa., 1964-66; asst. dir. admissions Mt. Holyoke Coll., South Hadley, Mass., 1966-71; asst. dir. correspondence First Lady (Mrs. Nixon) The White House, 1971-72, appointments sec. to First Lady (Mrs. Nixon), 1972-74, to First Lady (Mrs. Ford), 1974-77; spl. asst. to asst. atty. gen. Office Improvements in Adminstrn. Justice, Washington, 1977-79, Justice Mgmt. div. U.S. Dept. Justice, 1979-81; chief of staff to Mrs. Bush, asst. to v.p. Office of V.P. of U.S. Washington, 1981-89; dep. asst. to Pres. of U.S., chief of staff to First Lady (Mrs. Bush) The White House, 1989-93; commr. U.S. Commn. Fine Arts, 1993—. Bd. dirs. Barbara Bush Found. for Family Literacy; bd. trustees Bush Presdl. Libr. and Ctr. Recipient Dist. Alumni award Earlham Coll., 1992, Ind. State U., 1991. Mem. Ind. Acad. Home: 501 Slaters Ln # 1001 Alexandria VA 22314

ROSE, VIRGINIA ROGERS, executive relocator, consultant; b. Cleve., Feb. 15, 1942; d. Walter M. and Ruth E. (Rittberger) Rogers; m. Stanley Timothy Rose, Sept. 12, 1964; children: Catherine, Thomas, James. BS, Ohio State U., 1964; MBA, U. Wisc., Oshkosh, 1986. Mgmt. trainee First Interstate Trust Co., Green Bay, Wisc., 1986-87; fin. adminstr. Valley Periodontics, Appleton, Wisc., 1987—; pres. Transition, Inc., Appleton, 1989—; bd. dirs. Appleton Med. Ctr. Found., bd. dirs., vols. in Svc. to Appleton; co-chmn. Leadership Fox Cities Devel. Com., Appleton, 1991—. Pres. United Way of Appleton and Heart of the Valley, 1986; chmn. Appleton Recycling Task Force, 1990; alderman City of Appleton, 1988—. Mem. Kappa Kappa Gamma Alumni Assn. (pres., 1979-82); Beta Gamma Sigma, Kiwanis, C. of C. Presbyterian. Office: Transition Inc 1136 E Moorpark Ave Appleton WI 54911-3462

ROSE, VIRGINIA SHOTTENHAMER, secondary school educator; b. San Jose, Calif., Feb. 3, 1924; d. Leo E. and Mae E. (Slavich) Shottenhamer; m. Paul V. Rose, June 21, 1947; children: Paul V. Jr., David P., Alan P. AB, W. Calif., San Jose, 1945, MA, 1972. Tchr. grades 5-6 Evergreen Sch. Dist., San Jose, 1945-47; 6th grade tchr. Washington Sch., San Jose, 1947-57; elem. tchr. San Jose Unified Sch. Dist., 1967-82, reading specialist, 1982-93; ret., 1993; cons. in field; mem. project literacy San Jose Unified Schs., 1987-91; mem. instrnl. materials evaluation panel Calif. State Edpt. Edn., Sacramento, 1988; master tchr. U. Calif., San Jose, 1991. Co-author: Handbook for Teachers' Aides, 1967. Active Alexian Bros. Hosp. League, San Jose, 1965, bd. dirs., chair libr. cart, 1966-76. Mem. AAUW (com. chair 1978-81), Internat. Reading Assn., Calif. Reading Assn., Santa Clara County Reading Coun. (pres. 1986-87, Asilomar conf. chair 1991, IRA honor coun. pres. club 1987, bd. dirs.), Soroptimist Internat. (sec. 1993-94), Pi Epsilon Tau (pres. 1944-45), Kappa Delta Pi (pres. 1943-45), Pi Lambda Theta (pres. San Jose chpt. 1987-89, auditor 1980, sec. 1985-86, Biennium award 1987). Office: Willow Glen Ed Park S 2001 Cottle Ave San Jose CA 95125-3588

ROSE-ACKERMAN, SUSAN, law and political economy educator; b. Mineola, N.Y., Apr. 23, 1942; d. R. William and Rosalie (Gould) Rose; m. Bruce A. Ackerman, May 29, 1967; children: Sybil, John. B.A., Wellesley Coll, 1964; Ph.D., Yale U., 1970. Asst. prof. U. Pa., Phila, 1970-74; lectr. Yale U., New Haven, Conn., 1974-75, asst. prof., 1975-78, assoc. prof., 1978-82; prof. law and polit. economy Columbia U., N.Y.C., 1982-87, dir. Ctr. for Law and Econ. Studies, 1983-87; Ely prof. of law and polit. econ. Yale U., New Haven, 1987-92, Luce prof. jurisprudence (law and polit. sci.), 1992—; Mem. rev. panel Program on Regulation and Policy Analysis, NSF, Washington, 1982-84, rev. panel Am. studies program Am. Coun. Learned Socs., 1987-90; vis. prof. U. Rome, 1984. Author: (with Ackerman, Sawyer and Henderson) Uncertain Search for Environmental Quality, 1974 (Henderson prize 1982); Corruption: A Study in Political Economy, 1978; (with E. James) The Nonprofit Enterprise in Market Economies, 1986; editor: The Economics of Nonprofit Institutions, 1986; (with J. Coffee and L. Lowenstein) Knights, Raiders, and Targets: The Impact of the Hostile Takeover, 1988, Rethinking the Progressive Agenda: The Reform of the American Regulatory State, 1992, Controlling Environmental Policy: The Limits of Public Law in Germany and the United States, 1995; contbr. articles to profl. jours.; bd. editors: Jour. Law, Econs. and Orgn., 1984—, Internat. Rev. Law and Econs., 1986—, Jour. Policy Analysis and Mgmt., 1989—, Polit. Sci. Quar., 1988—. Guggenheim fellow 1991-92, Fulbright fellow, Free U. Berlin, 1991-92. Mem. Am. Land and Econs. Assn. (bd. dirs. 1993—), Am. Econ. Assn. (mem. exec. com. 1990-93), Am. Polit. Sci. Assn., Assn. Am. Law Schs., Assn. Pub. Policy and Mgmt. (mem. policy coun. 1984-88). Democrat. Office: Yale U Law Sch 401A Yale Ave New Haven CT 06515

ROSEANNE, actress, comedienne; b. Salt Lake City, Nov. 3, 1952; d. Jerry and Helen Barr; m. Bill Pentland, 1974 (div.1989); children: Jessica ,Jennifer, Jake; m. Tom Arnold, 1990 (div. 1994); m. Ben Thomas, 1994. Former window dresser, cocktail waitress; owner Roseanne and Tom's Big Food Diner, Eldon, Iowa, 1993—. As comic, worked in bars, church coffeehouse, Denver; produced showcase for women performers Take Back the Mike, U. Boulder (Colo.); performer The Comedy Store, L.A.; showcased on TV special Funny, 1986, also The Tonight Show; featured in HBO-TV spl. On Location: The Roseanne Barr Show, 1987 (Am. comedy award Funniest female performer in TV spl., 1987, Ace award funniest female in comedy, 1987, Ace award Best Comedy Spl. 1987); star of TV series Roseanne ABC, 1988— (U.S. Mag. 2d Ann. Readers Poll Best Actress Comedy series, 1989, Golden Globe nomination Outstanding lead actress comedy series 1988, Emmy award Outstanding Lead Actress in a Comedy Series, 1993); actress: (motion picture) She-Devil, 1989, Look Who's Talking Too (voice), 1990, Freddy's Dead, 1991, Even Cowgirls Get the Blues, 1994; TV movies: Backfield in Motion, The Woman Who Loved Elvis, 1993; author: Roseanne: My Life as a Woman, 1989, My Lives, 1994. Office: 14755 Ventura Blvd 1-170 Sherman Oaks CA 91403*

ROSEBERRY, FRANCES JANET, secondary mathematics educator; b. Easton, Pa., Apr. 10, 1937; d. Anna Lisetski; m. Charles Abert Roseberry, Oct. 15, 1960; children: Ann M., C. Richard, Keith M., Craig S. BSEd, West Chester U., 1959; MSEd, Wilkes U., 1990. Cert. profl. instr., Pa. Tchr. high sch. Allentown (Pa.) Sch. Dist., 1959-64, tchr. mid. sch., 1984—; bookkeeper, acct. Applied Equipment Co., Easton, 1969—; coach Mathcounts, Allentown, 1987-92; contest judge Pa. Commn. for Women, Harrisburg, 1989—. Author: History of Easton, PA, 1985. Asst. leader Girl Scouts U.S.A., Palmer Twp., Pa., 1974-76; treas. PTA, Palmer Twp., 1977-79; asst. coord. Adv. Com. on Edn., Easton, 1977-84; pres. West Point Parents Club, Lehigh Valley, Pa., 1989-92. Grantee Palmer Twp. PTA, Easton, 1979. Mem. AAUW (v.p. 1981-83, grantee 1987), Nat. Coun. Tchrs. Math.

ROSEBROUGH, CAROL BELVILLE, cable television company executive; b. Ironton, Ohio, June 5, 1940; d. Lindsey and Bessie (Reed) Belville; m. John R. Rosebrough, Mar. 4, 1960 (dec. Nov. 1974); children: G. Suzanne, John R., Rebecca J. Student, Columbia (Mo.) Coll., 1958-59; BSBA, Franklin U., 1985. Cons. CBR and Assocs., Columbus, 1978-82; dir. adminstrn. United Cerebral Palsy Columbus and Franklin County, 1972-82; bus. mgr. Times Mirror, Newark, Ohio, 1982-83; ops. mgr. Times Mirror, Newark, 1983-85; gen. mgr. Times Mirror, Logan/Waverly/Greenfield, Ohio, 1985-86, Times Mirror doing bus. as Dimension Cable Svcs., Marion, Ohio, 1986-88; gen. mgr. Cable TV div. Times Mirror doing bus. as Dimension Cable Svcs., Williamsport, Pa., 1988—. Bd. dirs United Way, Marion County, 1987-88, Lycoming County, 1989—; exec. com. comm. task force Pa. Rural Devel. Coun., 1992—. Mem. Ohio Cable TV Assn. (bd. dirs. 1986-88), Pa. Cable TV Assn. (bd. dirs. 1990—), Pa. Edn. Communications Systems (bd. dirs. 1990—), Pa. Rural Devel. Coun. (exec. com., telecommunications task force 1992—), Mid-Ohio Regional Planning Commn. (transp. com. 1980-82). Office: Dimension Cable Svcs 330 Basin St Williamsport PA 17701-5216

ROSEHNAL, MARY ANN, educational administrator; b. Bklyn., July 25, 1943; d. Frank Joseph and Mary Anna (Corso) R.; 1 child, Scott Stoddart. BA in Sociology, San Francisco State U., 1968; M in Sch. Bus. Adminstrn., No. Ariz. U., 1985. Lic. substitute tchr., Ariz.; lic. vocat. nurse, Calif.; cert. sch. bus. mgr., Ariz. Deliquency counselor, Calif., 1969-73; office mgr. Nurses Central Registry, Sun City, Ariz., 1973-75; bus. mgr. Nadaburg sch. dist., Wittmann, Ariz., 1975-78, Morristown (Ariz.) sch. dist., 1978—; served on 1st Assessment Handbook editing task force, Fair Employment Practices Handbook task force, 1979-80; mem. tech. adv. com. Ariz. Dept. Edn., 1993-94. Columnist Wickenburg Sun, 1975—. Clk. Morristown sch. bd., 1974-76; pres. Morristown PTA, 1977-78; sec. Wickenburg area bd., 1979; bd. dirs. Future Frontiers, 1979-81; rep. HUD block grant adv. com., 1979-85; active Wickenburg Friends of Music, 1984—, sec. of bd. dirs., 1986-92; sec. Wickenburg Regional Health Care Found., 1989-92, trustee, 1988—. Named to Ariz. Sch. Bd. Assn. Honor Roll, 1976; named Morristown Area Vol. of Yr., 1988. Mem. Assn. Govt. Accts., Ariz. Assn. Sch. Bus. Ofcls. (fin. dir., bd. dirs. 1985-91, v.p. 1991, pres. elect 1992-93, pres. 1993-94, immediate past pres. 1994-95, Gold awards 1986, 87, 88, 90, 91, 92, 93, 94, Silver award 1989), Assn. Sch. Bus. Ofcls. Internat. (mem. pres.'s adv. coun. 1993-94, election com. 1994—), Morristown Federated Women's Club (edn. chair 1990-94, Wickenburg scenic corridor com. 1990-92), Ariz. Theatre Guild, Wickenberg C. of C. (assoc.). Roman Catholic. Office: PO Box 98 Morristown AZ 85342-0098

ROSEL, CAROL ANN, artist; b. Dodge City, Kans., June 12, 1944; d. John Elbert and Mary Claire (Wetmore) Frazier; m. Herbert Carey Zortman, Aug. 21, 1960 (div. Jan. 1989); children: Elaine Marie, Anita Louise, Stanley Dale; m. George D. Rosel, Sept. 22, 1990. Student, Ctrl. Coll., McPherson, Kans., 1961; BFA cum laude, Ft. Hays State U., 1994. Cert. machine embroidery instr. Dress designer Ms. Cosmo Ltd., Wichita, Kans., 1975-76; designer artistic embroidery garments, 1977-80; owner Carol Ann's Gallery, Liberal, Kans.; piano, vocal soloist, accompanist for various singing groups, church and civic functions. One-woman show Ft. Hays Libr., 1993. Mem. Baker Art Ctr., Liberal, 1989—, Hays (Kans.) Arts Coun., 1993; tchr. Sunday sch.; counselor girls ch. camp. Recipient All Am. Scholar Collegiate award, 1994, Grand Champion award State Fair, 1989, 90, Purple Champion award, 1990, among others. Mem. Mid. Am. Arts and Crafts Assn., Pinnacle Honor Soc., Art Club. Republican. Home and Office: 406 Harvard Ave Liberal KS 67901

ROSELL, SHARON LYNN, physics and chemistry educator, researcher; b. Wichita, Kans., Jan. 6, 1948; d. John E. and Mildred C. (Binder) R. BA, Loretto Heights Coll., 1970; postgrad., Marshall U., 1973; MS in Edn., Ind. U., 1977; MS, U. Wash., 1988. Cert. profl. educator, Wash. Assoc. instr. Ind. U., Bloomington, 1973-74; instr. Pierce Coll. (name formerly Ft. Steilacoom (Wash.) Community Coll.), 1976-79, 82, Olympic Coll., Bremerton, Wash., 1977-78; instr. physics, math. and chemistry Tacoma (Wash.) Community Coll., 1979-89; instr. physics and chemistry Green River Community Coll., Auburn, Wash., 1983-86; researcher Nuclear Physics Lab., U. Wash., Seattle, 1986-88; asst. prof. physics Cen. Wash. U., Ellensburg, 1989—. Lector and dir. Rite of Christian Initiation of Adults, St. Andrew's Ch., Ellensburg, Wash., 1993—. Mem. Am. Assn. Physics Tchrs. (rep. com. on physics for 2-yr. colls. Wash. chpt. 1986-87, v.p. 1987-88, 94-95, pres. 1988-89, 95-96), Am. Chem. Soc., Math. Assn. Am., Internat. Union Pure and Applied Chemistry (affiliate). Democrat. Roman Catholic. Home: 1100 North B St Apt 2 Ellensburg WA 98926 Office: Cen Wash U Physics Dept Ellensburg WA 98926

ROSEME, SHARON DAY, lawyer; b. Sacramento, Aug. 6, 1953; d. George Roseme and Alice Diane Day; m. Daniel George Glenn, June 26, 1982 (div. Nov. 1989); 1 child, Hilary. Student, San Francisco State U., 1971-72; BA, U. Calif., Santa Cruz, 1975; JD, Boalt Hall Sch. of Law, 1978. Jud. staff atty. Calif. State Ct. of Appeal, San Francisco, 1978-80; assoc. Feldman, Waldman & Kline, San Francisco, 1980-82, McDonough, Holland & Allen, Sacramento, 1982—. Contbr. articles to profl. jours. Mem. ABA, State Bar Calif., County Bar Sacramento, County Bar Placer, County Bar San Francisco, Comml. Real Estate Woman Sacramento, Order of Coif. Office: McDonough Holland & Allen 555 Capitol Mall Ste 950 Sacramento CA 95814-4692

ROSEN, ANA BEATRIZ, electronics executive; b. Guayaquil, Ecuador, May 16, 1950; came to U.S., 1962; d. Luis A. and Luz Aurora (Rodriguez) Moreira; m. Manuel Jose Farina, Dec. 15, 1979 (dec. Apr. 1990); children: Kevin, Mark; m. Michael G. Rosen, June 6, 1992. AA, Latin-Am. Inst., 1971. Adminstr. asst. M&T Chem. Inc., N.Y.C., 1971-75; mgr. sales Singer Products Co., N.Y.C., 1975-78; v.p. Argil Internat. Ltd., N.Y.C., 1978-83; pres. KMA Enterprises Inc., Bklyn., 1983-94, KMA Industries Inc., Palm Beach Gardens, Fla., 1994—. Mem. NAFE, World Trade Coun. (Palm Beach County). Roman Catholic.

ROSEN, BETH DEE, travel agency executive; b. N.Y.C., June 27, 1945; d. Walter and Anne (Goodman) Werfel; m. Martin H. Rosen, June 9, 1968. BA, Queens Coll., 1967, MA, 1970; cert. adminstrn. and supervision, CUNY, 1982. mem. reader adv. panel Conde Nast Traveler, 1991. Tchr. N.Y.C. Bd. Edn., 1967—; lectr. City U. N.Y., 1971-73; pres. Uniglobe Rainbow Travel Inc., Middletown, N.J., 1982-94; dir. Uniglobe Rainbow Travel Sch., 1983-87; with Excel Travel, Middletown, N.J. Columnist "The Courier" newspaper, Middletown, N.J. Office: Uniglobe Rainbow Travel 500 Hwy 35 Union Sq Mall Red Bank NJ 07701

ROSEN, CAROL MENDES, artist; b. N.Y.C., Jan. 15, 1933; d. Bram de Sola and Mildred (Bertuch) Mendes; m. Elliot A. Rosen, June 30, 1957. BA, Hunter Coll., 1954; MA, CUNY, 1962. Tchr. art West Orange (N.J.) Pub. Schs., 1959-85; co-curator exhibit Printmaking Coun. N.J., Somerville, 1981; exhibit curator 14 Sculptors Gallery, N.Y.C., 1988, Collection: NCFA, Smithsonian Instn., Newark Mus., N.J. State Mus., Bristol-Myers Squibb. Contbr. articles to arts mags. Fellow N.J. State Coun. on Arts, 1980, 83; recipient Hudson River Mus. award, Yonkers, 1983. Jewish. Home: 10 Beavers Rd Califon NJ 07830-3433

ROSEN, ESTHER YOVITS, artist; b. Schenectady, N.Y., June 3, 1916; d. Albert and Goldie (Goldsmith) Yovits; m. Myor Rosen; children: Linda, David. Painted constructions art form done in collaboration with husband, Myor Rosen. One-woman shows Bodley Gallery, N.Y.C., 1983, John Harms Ctr. for Arts, Englewood, N.J., 1986, Musicorda, Mt. Holyoke (Mass.) Coll., 1988, Palm Beach (Fla.) Internat. Airport, 1991, Bryant Galleries, Fla., 1993; one-woman and group shows Pa. Acad., Phila., 1938, Am. Fedn. Arts, 1938-39, N.Y. Philharm. Hall, 1969, Nabisco Co., East Hanover, N.J., 1981-83, Women's Caucus for Art, N.Y.C., 1982, numerous others; murals executed Amherst, Mass., 1981, Japan, 1984; executed mural on ceramic tile by commission of Arlene and Alan Alda, 1992, mural of musicians for shirley and Arnold Schreiber, Fla., 1993, painting on cover of playbill Kravis Ctr. For the Performing Arts, West Palm Beach, Fla., 1994; presented in permanent pub. and pvt. collections including Jane Voorhees-Zimmerli Mus., Princeton, N.J., Bergen Community Mus., Ridgewood, N.J. Tchr. Teaneck (N.J.) Jewish Community Ctr., 1953-72, Young Men, Young Women Hebrew Orgn, Hackensack, N.J., 1965-80. Recipient award Prentice Hall, 1963, B'nai B'rith Women, 1963, Halsey & Griffith award, 1991. Mem. Nat. Assn. Women Artists (Llewelyn award 1960, Feist-Mason award 1978, Grumbacher award 1990, 1st v.p. Fla. br. 1995), Artists Guild of Norton Gallery, Art Ctr. No. N.J., LWV. Home and Studio: 1649 Flagler Manor Cir West Palm Beach FL 33411

ROSEN, LORI, public relations executive; b. Phila., Dec. 9, 1955. BA in Comm., George Washington U., 1978. Acct. exec. John Adams Assocs., 1981-83; pres. Rosen Group, 1984—. Office: Rosen Group Puck Bldg 295 Lafayette St #802 New York NY 10012*

ROSEN, RHODA, obstetrician-gynecologist; b. Trenton, N.J., Jan. 17, 1933; d. Max and Gussie (Thierman) R.; m. Seymour Kanter, Aug. 19, 1956; children: Cynthia, Gregg, Larry, Brad. BA, U. Pa., 1954, MD, 1958. Diplomate Am. Bd. Obstetrics and Gynecology. Intern Albert Einstein Phila. Med. Ctr., 1958-59, resident, 1959-62; clin. prof. ob-gyn. Temple U. Med. Sch., Phila.; assoc. staff gyn. exec. com. Albert Einstein Med. Ctr., Phila.; attending physician Rolling Hill Hosp., Elkins Park, Pa.; pvt. practice obs/gyn Phila., 1962—; chmn. gynpathology com. Albert Einstein Med. Ctr., Phila. Bd. dirs. Joseph J. Peters Inst. Fellow ACOG, ACS; mem. AMA, Pa. Med. Soc., Phila. Colposcopy Soc. (past pres.), Ex-Residents Assn. (past pres. Albert Einstein Med. Ctr.), Philadelphia County Med. Soc. (com.), Phila. Bar Assn. (com.). Jewish. Home: 1011 Valley Rd Philadelphia PA 19126-1814

ROSENAU, BLANCHE GOTTARDO, secondary education educator; b. Chgo., Oct. 21, 1918; d. William James and Marie Josephine (Oplt) Hubeny; m. Paul Gottardo Jr., Oct. 24, 1942 (div. Aug. 1957); children: Laura Jane Gottardo Denault, Gail Ann Gottardo Fagan, Paul Gottardo III; m. Milton Joseph Rosenau, Dec. 27, 1967 (dec.). BS, Northwestern U., Evanston, Ill., 1940; MEd, U. fla., 1963. Cert. elem. and art edn. supervision, jr. coll. tchr., Fla. Instr. in art progressive edn. workshop Northwestern Ill., summer 1940, tchr. art lab. sch., 1940-41; tchr. elem., art coord. Fairlawn Sch., Ft. Pierce, Fla., 1958-68; tchr. elem. Chester A. Moore Sch., Ft. Pierce, 1968-69; tchr. art, dept. chmn. Ft. Pierce Cen. High Sch., 1970-81; reviser elem. art sect. curriculum guide St. Lucie County Schs., Ft. Pierce, 1976. Woman's chmn. St. Lucie County Farm Bur., Ft. Pierce, 1966; chmn. Ft. Pierce Opera Guild, 1980—; bd. dirs. St. Lucie County Humane Soc., Ft. Pierce, 1965; bd. dirs., sec. Treasure Coast Opera Soc., Ft. Pierce, 1979—. Mem. AAUW (bd. dirs. 1983-84), St. Lucie County Ret. Educators, Pelican Yacht Club (bd. dirs. 1992—, bd. dirs. women's aux. 1982—, pres. women's aux. 1989—), Woman's Club of Ft. Pierce (bd. dirs. 1984—, 1st v.p. 1989-90, corr. sec. 1993-94, 94-95), Nobel-ettes (1st v.p. 1986-89), Kappa Delta Pi. Democrat.

Presbyterian. Home: 510 Hartman Rd Fort Pierce FL 34947-3404 Office: Treasure Coast Opera Soc 1309 Indiana Ave Fort Pierce FL 34950-4954

ROSENBACH, KATHRYN BETH KAYNE-SERIO, pianist, educator, choral director, organist; b. Buffalo, Aug. 14, 1957; d. Daniel Walter and Carole Ann (Rosenbach) Kayne; m. Michael Thomas Serio, June 25, 1982 (div. May 30, 1991); 1 child, Anthony Michael. BFA magna cum laude, SUNY, Buffalo, 1979, MFA, 1981; postgrad., Eastman Sch. Music, 1982-86; artist diploma, Accademia Musicale di Chigiana, Siena, Italy, 1984. Choir dir., organist Stephen's-Bethlehem United Ch. Christ, Williamsville, N.Y., 1978-80, North Presbyn. Ch., North Tonawanda, N.Y., 1981-83, Leroy (N.Y.) Bapt. Ch., 1983-85, 1st Congl. Ch., Stoughton, Mass., 1988—; lectr. piano Genesee Community Coll., Batavia, N.Y., 1985-86; instr. piano Eastman Sch. of Music, SUNY, Buffalo, 1978-80, Community Music Sch., Buffalo, 1981-83; music dir. Community Choir Sharon, Mass., 1988-90; mem. faculty Longy Sch. Music, Cambridge, Mass., 1989-91. Composer (choral works) Gloria Alleluia, 1978, I Wonder What Child This Is, 1990, Christ the Lord Is Risen, 1991, Alleluia, Jesus Christ is Coming, 1991, A Hymn of Celebration, 1993, Christmas Cameos, 1995. Eastman Sch. Music grantee, Italy, 1984. Mem. Am. Guild of Organists, Music Tchrs. Nat. Assn., Coll. Music Soc.

ROSENBAUM, PATRICIA JEANNE, nurse, educator; b. Mobile, Ala., May 7, 1943; d. Alvin Monroe Pitt and Betty Jeanne (Brown) Russell; m. James Steven, May, 1961 (div. 1963); 1 child, James Randall Rosenbaum. BS, Okla. Bapt. U., 1983; MEd, U. Ctrl. Okla., 1993; postgrad., U. Okla. Registered critical care nurse, registered med. surg. clinician. Staff nurse oper. rm. Bapt. Meml. Hosp., Oklahoma City, 1966-67; perfusionist Drs. Greer, Carey, Zuhdi, Hawley, Hartsuck, Inc., Oklahoma City, 1967-78; med.-surg. charge nurse Shawnee (Okla.) Med. Ctr., 1979-81; asst. head nurse Presbyn. Hosp., Oklahoma City, 1981-89; staff nurse coronary care Bapt. Med. Ctr., Oklahoma City, 1989-90, critical care instr., 1990-93; comty. nurse educator S.W. Med. Ctr., Oklahoma City, 1993, dir. emergency svcs., 1993—; guest lectr. So. Nazarene U., Bethany, Okla., 1993—; guest lectr. cardiac related topics various civic, comty. and religious orgns., Oklahoma City, 1993—; adj. faculty critical care Okla. State U., Oklahoma City, 1989-90. Contbr. Okla. Polit. Action Com., Oklahoma City, 1993—; vol. nurse Good Shepherd Clinic, Oklahoma City, 1992—, various city sponsored runs, walks, bikathons for Am. Heart Assn., March of Dimes, Oklahoma City, 1986—. Fellow Am. Soc. Extracorporeal Circulation; mem. AACN (chair recognition com. 1987-89), Okla. Orgn. Nurse Execs., Sigma Theta Tau. Democrat. Evangelical. Home: 6601 Edgewater Dr Oklahoma City OK 73116 Office: S W Med Ctr 4401 S Western Oklahoma City OK 73109

ROSENBAUM, POLLY, state legislator; b. Ollie, Iowa; widowed. BA, U. Colo.; MEd, U. So. Calif. Former tchr., stenographer, gen. office worker copper and asbestos industrys, law, real estate appraisal, savings and loan, dental receptionist, former county clk. and recs. offices; mem. Ariz. Ho. of Reps., mem. appropriations com., edn. com., rules com., human resources and aging com., rules com.; mem. Gila County Tuberc Control Bd. Mem. Globe Bus. and Profl. Women's Club, Zonta Internat., Eastern Star (Winkleman chpt., past matron). Democrat. Address: PO Box 609 Globe AZ 85502*

ROSENBERG, ALISON P., public policy official; b. Miami, Fla., Sept. 5, 1945; d. Mortimer I. and Gail (Sklar) Podell; m. Jeffrey Alan Rosenberg, May 4, 1969; 1 child, Robert Aaron. BS in Econs., Smith Coll., 1967. Mng. officer Citibank, N.Y.C., 1967-69; legis. aide Senator Charles Percy, Washington, 1969-80; profl. staff mem. Senate Fgn. Rels. Com., Washington, 1981-85; assoc. asst. adminstr. Agy. for Internat. Devel., Washington, 1985-87; dir. African affairs Nat. Security Coun., Washington, 1987-88; dep. asst. sec. for Africa State Dept., Washington, 1988-92; asst. admnstr. for Africa Agy. for Internat. Devel., Washington, 1992-93; co-financing advisor to the v.p. for Africa The World Bank, Washington, 1993—.

ROSENBERG, DIANE LYNNE, law librarian, consultant; b. Pitts., May 19, 1945; d. A. Maurice and Rhea (Klein) R. BA, Pa. State U., 1966; MLS, U. Pitts., 1968; postgrad., Columbia U., 1974. Asst. and rsch. libr. Law Ctr. Georgetown U., Washington, 1968-72, Antioch Sch. Law, Washington, 1972-73; corp. law libr. Paul, Weiss, Rifkind, Wharton & Garrison, N.Y.C., 1973-93; corp. database adminstr. Paul, Weiss, Rifkind, Wharton & Garrison, 1993—. Mem. Spl. Librs. Assn., Am. Assn. Law Librs., Phi Sigma Sigma. Office: Paul Weiss Rifkind Wharton & Garrison 1285 Ave Of The Americas New York NY 10019-6064

ROSENBERG, ELLEN SMALL, clinical psychologist; b. Chgo., June 27, 1950; d. Raymond Leo and Rose (Small) Small; m. Marc L. Rosenberg, Aug. 30, 1970; children: Douglas Jeremy, Lauren Rebecca. BS magna cum laude, U. Ill., 1971; PhD, Northwestern U., 1975. Lic. clin. psychologist, Ill. Staff psychologist Inst. Psychiatry, Northwestern Meml. Hosp., Chgo., 1975-78; assoc. dept. psychiatry and behavioral scis. div. psychology Northwestern U. Med. Sch., Chgo., 1975—; pvt. practice clin. psychology Chgo., Evanston, Ill., 1976—; staff psychologist Counseling and Psychol. Svcs., Northwestern U., Evanston, 1983—; mem. med. staff, affiliated profl. staff Northwestern Meml. Hosp., Chgo., 1977-93. Mentor Midwest talent search Northwestern U., Evanston, 1989-90; mem. McKenzie Sch. PTA, Wilmette, Ill., 1988-90, mem. PTA bd., 1990-91, 92-93; benefit com. mental health profl. divsn. Jewish United Fund, Chgo., 1990. Ill. State scholar Ill. State Scholarship Com., 1968, James scholar U. Ill., 1968-71; Northwestern U. fellow, 1971-72; named Woodrow Wilson Fellowship finalist, 1971. Mem. APA, Chgo. Assn. Psychoanalytic Psychology (founding mem., coun. 1988—, treas. 1985-88, pres.-elect 1990, pres. 1991, past pres. 1992-93, local chpt. rep. 1993—), Ill. Psychol. Assn., Assn. for Advancement of Psychology, Nat. Register Health Svc. Providers in Psychology, Phi Beta Kappa. Office: 333 N Michigan Ave Ste 3400 Chicago IL 60601-4106

ROSENBERG, JANET SUE, retail supervisor; b. Cin., Sept. 10, 1960; d. Philip and Barbara Ann (Perry) R. BS in Elem. Edn., U. Cin., 1982; Legal Sec. Cert., Fla. Internat. U., 1993, postgrad., 1993—. Head counselor Cin. Community Ctr., 1976-78, Russell Community Ctr., Miami, 1979-81; retail supr. Burdine's Dept. Store, Miami, Fla., 1982-83, Macy's Dept. Store, Miami, 1983—. Editor: (newsletter) The Star, 1993; concert pianist, Coll. Conservatory of Music, U. Cin., 1978-82. Vol. Contemporaries Art Mus. of Ft. Lauderdale, 1991-93; bd. dirs. South Broward Am. Cancer Soc., 1990-91; mem. Women's Internat. Zionist Ogn., Miami, 1991—, Cin. Social Svc. Orgn., 1980-82. Mem. Miami Young Leadership Coun. Devel., Diabetes Inst. of Miami, Ft. Lauderdale Leadership Coun., Ft. Lauderdale Bus. and Profl. Women, Women's Div. Miami Jewish Fedn., Coconut Grove Jaycees, Kappa Delta Pi. Democrat. Jewish. Home: 917 NE 24th Ave Hallandale FL 33009-2865 Office: Macys Dept Store 19535 Biscayne Blvd N Miami Bch FL 33180-2314

ROSENBERG, JILL, realtor, civic leader; b. Shreveport, La., Feb. 17, 1940; d. Morris H. and Sallye (Abramson) Schuster; m. Lewis Rosenberg, Dec. 23, 1962; children: Craig, Paige. BA in Philosophy, Tulane U., 1961, MSW, 1965. Cert. residential specialist Residential Sales Coun.; grad. Realtor Inst. Social worker La. Dept. Pub. Welfare, 1961-62, 63-64; genetics counselor Sinai Hosp., Balt., 1967-69; ptnr. Parties Extraordinaire, cons., 1973-77; realtor assoc. Robert Weil Assocs., Long Beach, Calif., 1982—. Pres. western region Brandeis U. Nat. Women's Com., 1972-73; bd. dirs. Long Beach Symphony Assn., 1984-85; v.p. Jewish Community Fedn. Long Beach and West Orange County, 1983-86, bd. dirs., 1982-86; pres. Long Beach Cancer League, 1987-88, exec. bd. dirs., 1984—; pres. Long Beach Jewish Community Sr. Housing Corp., 1989-91; v.p. fundraising S.E. unit Long Beach Harbor chpt. Am. Cancer Soc., 1989-90; fund chair St. Mary Med. Ctr., 1992-94; pres. nat. conf. NCCJ, 1994-95; pres. Leadership Long Beach, 1994-95, numerous others. Recipient Young Leadership award Jewish Community Fedn. Long Beach and West Orange County, 1981, Jerusalem award State of Israel, 1989, Hannah G. Solomon award Nat. Coun. Jewish Women, 1992; scholar La. Dept. Pub. Welfare, 1962, NIMH, 1964. Office: Robert Weil Assocs 5220 Los Altos Plz E Long Beach CA 90815-4251

ROSENBERG, JUDITH LYNNE, middle school educator; b. Bklyn., Nov. 1, 1944; d. Benjamin and Rose (Delbaum) Jackler; m. Joel Barry Rosenberg, Aug. 26, 1965; children: Jeffrey Alan, Marc David. BA in Edn., Queens Coll., Flushing, N.Y., 1966, MS in Edn., 1972. Lic. advanced profl. elem. and mid. sch. math., Md., elem. edn., N.Y. Elem. tchr. N.Y.C. and Cranston, R.I., 1966-68; tchr. math. Earl B. Wood Mid. Sch., Rockville, Md., 1981-82, Walt Whitman High Sch., Bethesda, Md., 1982-83, Robert Frost Mid. Sch., Rockville, Md., 1983-89; math. and interdisciplinary resource Julius West Mid. Sch., Rockville, 1989—. Mem. NEA, Nat. Coun. Tchrs. Math., Md. State Tchrs. Assn. Home: 16 Flameleaf Ct Gaithersburg MD 20878-5216 Office: Julius West Mid Sch Great Falls Rd Rockville MD 20850

ROSENBERG, JUDITH META, brokerage executive; b. N.Y.C., Sept. 17, 1964. BS in Fin., Lehigh U., 1986. With Morgan Stanley, N.Y.C., 1986; broker Bear Stearns & Co., N.Y.C., 1987, v.p., 1988, assoc. dir., 1989; mng. dir., 1990. Bd. dirs. Henry Kaufmann Campgrounds. Mem. N.Y. Jr. League, Lehigh Alumni Assn., Women's Nat. Rep. Club. Republican. Office: 245 Park Ave Fl 9 New York NY 10167-0002

ROSENBERG, LESLIE KAREN, media director; b. Camden, N.J., Mar. 3, 1949; d. Lorimer and Doris Selma (Kohn) R. BS in Radio, TV, Film, U. Tex., 1971. Continuity dir. WEAT-TV/AM/FM, West Palm Beach, Fla., 1971-74; media buyer Wm. F. Haselmire Advt., West Palm Beach, 1974-75, media dir., 1982-85; program and pub. svc. dir. WTBS-TV, Atlanta, 1975-78; nat. traffic coord. WXIA-TV, Atlanta, 1978-80; sr. sales asst. CBS Radio Spot Sales, Atlanta, 1980-82; acct. exec. WRMF-FM, West Palm Beach, 1985; media dir., acct. exec. Merlin Masters & Nomes Advt., West Palm Beach, 1985-88; pres., media dir. Media Magic Plus, Inc., West Palm Beach, 1988—; communications adv. bd. Palm Beach Jr. Coll., Lake Worth, 1972-74. Talent, author various radio commercials (Addy award 1973, 74), talent various TV commercials (Addy award 1974). Bd. dirs. Lake Worth (Fla.) Playhouse, 1989-92, program co-chmn., 1989-91; producer LWP Internat. Cultural Exch. for 1994 to Eng. Mem. Advt. Club of the Palm Beaches (bd. dirs. 1983-85), NAFE, Nat. Acad. Arts & Sciences, Fireside Theatre, U.S. Racquetball Assn. (dir. tournament control 1976-80). Office: Media Magic Plus Inc PO Box 19962 West Palm Beach FL 33416-4962

ROSENBERG, MARILYN ROSENTHAL, artist, visual poet; b. Phila., Oct. 11, 1934; m. Robert Rosenberg, June 12, 1955; 2 children. B in Profl. Studies in Studio Arts, SUNY, Empire State Coll., 1978; MA in Liberal Studies, NYU, 1993. Solo exhbns. include Irvine Gallery, State U. Calif., Irvine, 1981, The Sandor Tezsler Libr. Gallery, Spartanberg, S.C., 1983, U. Wis., River Falls, 1984, 361 Degrees Gallery, Greenfield, Mass., 1987; two-person exhbns. include SUNY Purchase Libr., 1982, The Hudson River Mus., Yonkers, N.Y., 1984, Women's Studio Workshop Inskirts Gallery, Rosendale, N.Y., 1986, Brownson Art Gallery, Purchase, N.Y., 1988, (with collaborator) Westchester County Gallery, White Plains, N.Y., 1989, Marymount Coll., Tarrytown, N.Y., 1993; group exhbns. include Long Beach (Calif.) Mus. Art, 1977, Kathryn Markel Fine Arts Gallery, N.Y.C., 1978, Pratt Graphic Ctr. Gallery, N.Y.C., 1978, Polytechnic State U. Gallery, San Luis Obispo, Calif., 1979, Phila. Art Alliance, Glassboro State Coll., Pa., 1979, Ridotte del Treatro Comunale, Italy, 1980, SUNY Purchase Gallery, 1982, Galerie Caroline Corre, Paris, 1983, Thorpe Intermedia Gallery, Sparkhill, N.J., 1983, U. Rochester Gallery, Rochester, N.Y., 1984, 14 Sculptors Gallery, N.Y.C., 1984, Georgetown U., Washington, 1984, Franklin Furnace, N.Y.C., 1986, Douglas & Cook Colleges, New Brunswick, N.J., 1985, City Without Walls, Newark, 1986, Galleri T.V., Malmo, Sweden, Post Machina Group and Am. Consulate, Bologna, Italy, 1986, Technical U. of Nova Scotia, Halifax, 1986, Museu Municipal, Figuira Da Foz, Portugal, 1987, King Stephen Mus., Szekesfehrvar, Hungary, 1987, Allen Meml. Art Mus., Oberlin, Ohio, 1987, Cultural Centre of San Paulo, Brazil, 1988, Centro Cultural de la Caja de Ahorros de Valencia, Spain, 1988, Cooper Union Art, N.Y.C., 1989, San Francisco Craft and Folk Art Mus., 1990, Alternatives Gallery, San Luis Obispo, Calif., 1990-91, San Antonio Art Inst., 1991, Sazama Gallery, Chgo., 1992, SUNY Oneonta, 1992, Ralston Fine Arts, Johnson City, Tenn., 1993, Va. Ctr. for Craft Arts, 1993, Libr. Can., 1993, Muée de la Post, Paris, 1993, Pratt Inst., N.Y.C., 1993, Musée de la Poste, Paris, 1993-94, Papertrail, Ottawa, Can., 1993-94, Nexus Found. for Arts, Phila., 1994, Va. Ctr. for Craft Arts, Richmond, 1994, Ormond Meml. Art Mus., Fla., 1994, Libr. Nat. Mus. Women, Washington, 1994-95, Spirit Sq. Ctr. Arts, Charlotte, N.C., 1994, Ellipse Arts Ctr., Arlington, Va., 1995, Monterserrat Coll. Art Gallery, Beverly, Mass., 1995, Yale U. Art Gallery Sculpture Hall, New Haven, Conn., 1995, Harper Collins, N.Y.C., 1995, Brookfield Craft Ctr., Conn., 1995, Muscatine Art Ctr., Iowa, 1995, Sangre de Cristo Art Ctr., Pueblo, Colo., 1995, ; public collections and archives include Art Gallery New South Wales, Sydney, Australia, Artpool Art Rsch. Ctr., Budapest, Hungary, Bibliotheque Nationale, Paris, Canadian Postal Mus. Archive, Ottawa, Electrografia Museo Internacional, La Mancha, Cuenca, Spain, Fogg Art Mus., Cambridge, Mass., Mus. of Modern Art Libr., N.Y.C., The Ruth and Marvin Sackner Archive, Miami Beach, Fla., Tate Gallery Libr., London, Victoria and Albert Mus., London, Yale U. Libr., New Haven, Ct., Canberra Sch. Art Gallery, Australia, Cleve. Inst. Art Libr., Harvard U. Fogg Mus. and Houghton Libr., Cambridge, Mass., Rochester (N.Y.) Inst. Tech., Sch. Art Inst. Chgo. Libr., Amherst (Mass.) Coll. Library, Atlanta Coll. of Art Library, Brown U. Library, Cleve. Inst. of Art Library, Dartmouth Coll., Sherman Art Library, Georgetown U. Library, The N.Y. Pub. Library, Rhode Island Sch. of Design, Stanford U. Library, Temple U. Library, Phila., U. Calif. at Davis, Santa Barbara Libraries, U. Chgo. Libr., U. Utah, Mariott Library, U. Va. Library, Va. Commonwealth U. Library, Wellesley Coll. Library, Libr. Mus. Fine Arts, Boston, Sch. Mus. of Fine Art Libr., Boston; works included in various publs. and periodicals. Studio: 67 Lakeview Ave W Peekskill NY 10566-6415

ROSENBERG, SARAH ZACHER, institute arts administration executive, humanities administration consultant; b. Kelem, Lithuania, Jan. 10, 1931; came to U.S., 1938; d. David Meir Zacher and Rachel Korbman; m. Norman J. Rosenberg, Dec. 30, 1950; children: Daniel, Alyssa. BA in History, U. Nebr., 1970, MA in Am. History, 1973. Rsch. historian U. Mid-Am., Lincoln, Nebr., 1974-78, program developer dept. humanities, 1978-79, asst. dir. div. acad. planning, 1980-81, dir. program devel., 1981-82; exec. dir. Nebr. Humanities Coun., Lincoln, 1982-87, Nebr. Found. for Humanities, Lincoln, 1984-87; exec. dir. Am. Inst. for Conservation Hist. and Artistic Works, Washington, 1987—, exec. dir. found., 1991—; program officer, spl. cons. mus. div. NEH, Washington, 1987, external reviewer, 1981, 89; lay participant long-range planning conf. Nebr. Bar Assn., Hastings, 1986. Co-editor: The Great Plains Experience: Readings in the History of a Region, 1978; contbr. articles to profl. jours. Action mem. Haddasah, Lincoln, 1961-87, Tifereth Israel Synagogue, 1961-87, Beth El Congregation, Bethesda, Md., 1988—; bd. dirs. Sta. KUCV, affiliate Nat. Pub. Radio, Lincoln, 1986-87, Lincoln Community Playhouse, 1986-87. NEH grantee, 1981, 86, merit awards, 1983, 87; Humanities Resource Ctr. grantee, Peter Kiewit Found., 1984. Mem. Am. Hist. Assn., Western Hist. Assn., Alpha Theta. Democrat. Home: 8102 Appalachian Terr Potomac MD 20854 Office: Am Inst for Conservation Ste 301 1717 K St NW Washington DC 20006

ROSENBERG, SHELI ZYSMAN, lawyer, financial management executive; b. N.Y.C., Feb. 2, 1942; d. Stephen B. and Charlotte (Laufer) Zysman; m. Burton X. Rosenberg, Aug. 30, 1964; children: Leonard, Marcy. BA, Tufts U., 1963; JD, Northwestern U., 1966. Bar: Ill. 1966. Ptnr. Schiff, Hardin & Waite, Chgo., 1973-80; exec. v.p., gen. counsel Equity Fin. Mgmt., Chgo., 1980—; exec. v.p., gen. counsel Equity Group Investments, Inc., Chgo., 1988-95, pres., CEO, 1995—; pres., CEO Equity Fin. and Mgmt. Co., Chgo., 1995—; prin. Rosenberg & Liebentritt, P.C., Chgo., 1995—; bd. dirs. Gt. Am. Mgmt. & Investment, Chgo., 1984—, v.p., gen. counsel, 1985—, sec., 1983-90; bd. dirs. CFI Industries, Inc., Am. Classic Voyages Co., Revco, D.S., Inc., Jacor Comm., Inc., The Vigoro Corp., Itel Corp., Capsure Holdings Corp., Eagle Industries, Inc., Falcon Bldg. Products, Inc.; bd. trustees Equity Residential Properties Trust. Bd. dirs., pres. Chgo. Network.

ROSENBERG, SHIRLEY SIROTA, publications and public relations executive, editor; b. Bklyn.; d. Charles and Donia (Rudoy) Sirota; m. Jerome D. Rosenberg; children: Jonathan, Hindy. BA, Bklyn. Coll. Freelance writer, 1968—; contract writer-editor Dept. HEW, Washington, 1968-72; editor Smithsonian Instn., Washington, 1972-77; instr. George Washington U., 1979—, Georgetown U., Washington, 1992; editor-in-chief, pres. SSR, Inc., Washington, 1977—; Washington corr. Parent's Mag.; cons., bd. dirs. NSF, Nat. Task Force on Minorities, Women and the Handicapped in Sci. and Engring., Joseph P. Kennedy Inst., Office of Comm., U.S. Holocaust Meml. Coun., Humanities mag. NEH, George Washington U. Pubs. specialist program, Washington Edpress, ARC Blood Svcs., Georgetown U. Author: The First Oil Rush, 1967, Code of Ethics and Professional Standards for Print Media Professionals; contbr. articles to trade and profl. jours. Recipient 1st place award Soc. Tech. Communicators, 1983, Achievement award, 1990, Merit award Art Dirs. Club, 1984, Silver award Excellence in Print, 1993. Mem. Am. Soc. Journalists and Authors (past v.p.), Assn. Edit. Businesses (past v.p., bd. dirs.), Am. Med. Writers Assn., EdPress (bd. dirs.), Fed. Pubs. Com., Nat. Assn. Govt. Communicators (1st pl. award 1981, 2d pl. award 1990), Womens Nat. Book Assn., Washington Women in Pub. Rels. (past bd. dirs.).

ROSENBERG, SUSAN BROWNE, laboratory director; b. Rahway, N.J., Dec. 13, 1957; d. Frank Patrick and Eva June (Huneke) Browne; m. Jess William Rosenberg, June 17, 1979. BA in Biology, Douglass Coll., 1979. Cert. indsl. hygienist. Lab. technician John Brown Assocs., Berkeley Heights, N.J., 1979-82; rsch. assoc. City of Hope, Beckman Rsch. Inst., Duarte, Calif., 1982-85; chemist Health Sci. Assocs., Inc., Los Alamitos, Calif., 1985-88, organic supr., 1988-90, lab. mgr., 1990-91, lab. dir., 1991—. Mem. NOW, ASTM, Am. Indsl. Hygiene Assn. (sec. Orange County sect. 1992-94, Edward Baier Tech. Achievement award 1993, chair environ. lead lab. accreditation com. 1994-95), Air and Waste Mgmt. Assn. Democrat. Office: Health Sci Assn Inc 10771 Noel St Los Alamitos CA 90720-2547

ROSENBLATT, JOAN RAUP, mathematical statistician; b. N.Y.C., Apr. 15, 1926; d. Robert Bruce and Clara (Eliot) Raup; m. David Rosenblatt, June 10, 1950. AB, Barnard Coll., 1946; PhD, U. N.C., 1956. Intern Nat. Inst. Pub. Affairs, Washington, 1946-47; statis. analyst U.S. Bur. of Budget, 1947-48; rsch. asst. U. N.C., 1953-54; mathematician Nat. Inst. Standards and Tech. (formerly Nat. Bur. Standards), Washington, 1955—, asst. chief statis. engring., 1963-68, chief statis. engring. lab., 1969-78, dep. dir. Ctr. for Applied Math., 1978-88; dep. dir. Computing and Applied Math. Lab., Gaithersburg, 1988-93, dir., 1993—; mem. com. on indsl. rels. Dept. Stats. Ohio State U.; mem. adv. com. in math. and stats. USDA Grad. Sch., 1971—; mem. Com. Applied and Theoretical Stats., Nat. Rsch. Coun., 1985-88. Mem. editorial bd. Communications in Stats., 1971-79, Jour. Soc. for Indsl. and Applied Math., 1965-75, Nat. Inst. Stds. and Tech. Jour. Rsch., 1991-93; contbr. articles to profl. jours. Chmn. Com. on Women in Sci., Joint Bd. on Sci. Edn., 1963-64. Rice fellow, 1946, Gen. Edn. Bd. fellow, 1948-50; recipient Fed. Woman's award, 1971, Gold medal Dept. Commerce, 1976, Presdl. Meritorious Exec. Rank award, 1982. Fellow AAAS (chmn. stats. sect. 1982, sec. 1987-91), Inst. Math. Stats. (coun. 1975-77), Am. Statis. Assn. (v.p. 1981-83, dir. 1979-80, Founders award 1991), Washington Acad. Scis. (achievement award math. 1965); mem. AAUW, IEEE Reliability Soc., Am. Math. Soc., Royal Statis. Soc. London, Philos. Soc. Washington, Internat. Statis. Inst., Bernouilli Soc. Probability and Math. Stats., Caucus Women Stats. (pres. 1976), Assn. Women Math., Exec. Women Govt., Phi Beta Kappa, Sigma Xi (treas. Nat. Bur. Standards chpt. 1982-84). Home: 2939 Van Ness St NW Apt 702 Washington DC 20008-4628 Office: Nat Inst Stds and Tech Rm B118 Technology Bldg Gaithersburg MD 20899-0001

ROSENBLATT, JULIA CARLSON, journalist, psychology educator; b. Orange, N.J., Dec. 26, 1940; d. Harold S. and Anabel (Alberts) Carlson; m. Albert M. Rosenblatt, Aug. 23, 1970; 1 child, Betsy L. BA, Upsala Coll., East Orange, N.J., 1962; MA, U. Iowa, 1964, PhD, 1965. Postdoctoral fellow Ednl. Testing Svc., Princeton, N.J., 1965-67; asst. prof. psychology Vassar Coll., Poughkeepsie, N.Y., 1967-73; freelance journalist Pleasant Valley, N.Y., 1973—; instr. Mohawk Mountain Ski Sch., Cornwall, Conn., 1983-93; bd. dirs. Poughkeepsie Savs. Bank, 1979-88; vis. asst. prof. Victorian studies Vassar Coll., 1993. Co-author: Dining with Sherlock Holmes, 1976, rev., 1990; also articles. Bd. dirs. Dutchess County Assn. Sr. Citizens, Poughkeepsie, 1980-86, Mid-Hudson Civic Ctr., Poughkeepsie, 1982-91, Dorothy Albertson Fund for Little People, Pleasant Valley, 1984-92; treas. Ret. Sr. Vol. Program, Poughkeepsie, 1980-81; mem. adv. bd. Wartburg Luth. Svcs., 1993—. USPHS fellow, 1962-65. Mem. APA, Eastern Ski Writers Assn., N.Am. Ski Journalists Assn., Profl. Ski Instrs. Am. Avocations: photography, skiing. Home and Office: Freedom Rd Pleasant Valley NY 12569

ROSENBLATT, PHYLLIS G., artist, educator; b. Washington, Aug. 26, 1942. BFA, Cooper Union, 1963; MFA, Yale Sch. Art, 1965. Dir. edn. Walker Art Ctr., Mpls., 1967-68; instr. art Normandale State Jr. Coll., Bloomington, Minn., 1968-69; asst. prof. art Mpls. Coll. Art and Design, 1970-74; adj. asst. prof. York Coll., CUNY, 1974, N.Y. Inst. Tech., Old Westbury, 1974-76, Pratt Inst., Bklyn., 1976-77; vis. artist Mpls. Coun. of Art and Design, summer 1984; assoc. prof. art Hampshire Coll., Amherst, Mass., 1983-86; adj. prof. Parsons Sch. Art, N.Y.C., 1988-89; vis. lectr. painting East Carolina U., Greenville, N.C., 1992-93; vis. artist/lectr. Mpls. Coll. Art and Design, 1982, Empire State Coll., SUNY, N.Y.C., 1988, San Jose State U., 1993, others. One-person shows include Peter Cooper Gallery, N.Y.C., 1966, The Little Gallery, Mpls. Inst. Art, 1970, West Lake Gallery, Mpls., 1971, Honeywell, Inc., Mpls., 1971, 83, Hampshire Coll., 1983, Gray Gallery, East Carolina U., 1993; group exhbns. include Gallery 118, Mpls., 1972, Webb & Parsons Gallery, Bedford, N.Y., 1973, Hansen Gallery, N.Y.C., 1980, AIR Gallery, N.Y.C., 1981-82, Wisteriahurst Mus., Holyoke, Mass., 1984, Manhattan Ctr. Gallery, 1988, Frank Bernarducci Gallery, N.Y.C., 1988, Margulies/Taplin Gallery, Boca Raton, Fla., 1991-92, Fla. State U. Mus. and Gallery, 1993; works in permanent collections at Norry Bros. Co., Arco Oil, Chase Manhattan Bank, First Nat. Bank, Gen. Mills, Inc., Atlantic Richfield, many others. Nat. Adv. Coun. grantee, 1985, Assn. Ind. Colls. of Art grantee, 1972; Yale Sch. Art scholar, 1963-65, Provincetown Workshop scholar, 1965. Mem. Coll. Art Assn. Home: 486 Broadway New York NY 10013

ROSENBLITH, JUDY FRANCIS, psychology educator; b. Salt Lake City, Mar. 20, 1921; d. John Edward and Mary Louise (Slack) Francis; m. Walter A. Rosenblith, Sept. 27, 1941; children—Sandra Y., Ronald F. Student Occidental Coll., 1938-40; A.B., UCLA, 1942; M.A., Radcliffe Coll., 1950, Ph.D., 1958. Asst. prof. psychology Simmons Coll., 1951-52; New Eng. supr. Nat. Opinion Research Center, 1953-57; teaching fellow social relations Harvard U., 1948-50, Grad. Sch. Edn., 1953-56, instr., 1956-57, lectr., 1962-63; asst. prof. psychology Brown U., 1957-61, asst. mem. to mem. Inst. Life Scis., 1961-75, sr. research investigator div. biol. and med. scis., 1975-77; assoc. psychology dept. psychiatry Harvard Med. Sch., 1961-64, clin. assoc., 1965-67; assoc. prof. Wheaton Coll., Norton, Mass., 1965-68, prof. psychology, 1968-84, prof. emerita, 1984—; vis. prof. Fla. Internat. U., 1992; mem. maternal and child health research adv. com. Nat. Inst. Child Health and Human Devel., 1974-78. Author: (with Judith Sims-Knight) In the Beginning: Development in the First Two Years, 1985, In the Beginning: Development from Conception at Age Two, 2d edit., 1992, (with M. Rands and B. Myers) Student Manual for In the Beginning, 1992. Adv. editor Contemporary Psychology, 1979-80; sr. editor: The Causes of Behavior: Readings in Child Development and Educational Psychology, 3 edits., 1962, 66, 72. Named Meneely Prof., Wheaton Coll., 1972-74; N.Y. Acad. Scis. fellow, 1976; grantee NIMH, 1958-60, Neurol. Diseases and Blindness, 1961-64, Child Health and Human Devel., 1966-70, Grant Found., 1971-77. Fellow Am. Psychol. Assn. (mem. bd. social and ethical responsibility for psychology 1977-81, mem. pub. info. com. 1981-84) mem. Soc. for Research in Child Devel. (sec. 1965-69, chmn. conv. arrangements 1979-81, chmn. history com. 1993—), Am. Psychol. Soc., Internat. Conf. Infant Studies, Internat. Assn. Cross-Cultural Psychology, Internat. Assn. Applied Psychology, Internat. Soc. Study of Behavioral Devel., Psychonomic Soc., New Eng. Psychol. Assn., Eastern Psychol. Assn., Sigma Xi. Home: 100 Memorial Dr Apt 11-1A Cambridge MA 02142 also (winter): 4000 Towerside Ter Apt 2309 Miami FL 33138

ROSENBLOOM, NORMA FRISCH, lawyer; b. N.Y.C., Dec. 2, 1925; d. Jacob Frisch and Anna (Fox) Frisch Schwartz; BA, New Sch. Social Rsch., 1951; m. Philip Rosenbloom, Oct. 31, 1946; children: David, James, Eric. JD, Rutgers U., Newark, 1979. Bar: N.J., 1979, N.Y. 1980. Mem. faculty, head dept. music Ranney Sch., Tinton Falls, N.J., 1962-74; chief law clk. Monmouth County (N.J.) Prosecutor's Office, 1979-80; assoc. Karasic & Karasic, P.C., Oakhurst, N.J., 1980-82; ptnr. Abrams, Gatta, Rosen & Rosenbloom, Ocean Twp., N.J., 1982-90, Abrams, Gatta, Rosen, Rosenbloom & Sevrin, P.C., 1990-92; of counsel, Abrams, Gatta, Falvo & Sevrin,

P.C., 1992— asst. county counsel Monmouth County, 1987-88. Sec., mem. exec. bd. Temple Beth Miriam, Elberon, N.J., 1969-74; mcpl. leader Monmouth Beach (N.J.) Dem. Com., 1973—; del. Dem. Nat. Conv., 1976; freeholder rep. to Monmouth County Community Action Program, poverty program, 1975-76; bd. dirs. Cen. Jersey Regional Health Planning Bd., 1973-75; trustee search com. Brookdale Community Coll., Lincroft, N.J., 1984-85; trustee, Planned Parenthood Monmouth County, 1981-88. Recipient award for community involvement Asbury Park-Neptune Youth Coun., 1970. Fellow Am. Acad. Matrimonial Lawyers; mem. ABA, N.J. Women Lawyers Assn. (pres.), Monmouth County Bar Assn., N.J. State Bar Assn. (dispute resolution sec.), N.J. Supreme Ct. Family Part Practice Com., Women Lawyers Monmouth County. Democrat. Jewish. Avocation: classical pianist. Home: Channel Club Towers Monmouth Beach NJ 07750 Office: Abrams Gatta Falvo & Servin 1127 Highway 35 Asbury Park NJ 07712

ROSENBLUM, JUDITH BARBARA, psychologist; b. Bklyn., July 18, 1951; d. Barnett and Bette (Bromberg) R.; m. Alan Scott Goldberg, Dec. 27, 1986. BA magna cum laude, Adelphi U., 1973; PhD, Yeshiva U., 1983; cert. analytic psychotherapy, Advanced Inst. Analytic Psychotherapy, Jamaica, N.Y., 1991. Cert. sch. psychologist. Psychotherapist Advanced Ctr. for Psychotherapy, Jamaica, 1977-86; police psychologist N.Y.C. Police Dept., Rego Park, N.Y., 1986-87; sch. psychologist N.Y.C. Bd. Edn., Bklyn., 1987-88, Glen Cove (N.Y.) City Schs., 1988-93; pvt. practice Deer Park, N.Y., 1993—; with Pederson-Krug Ctr., 1993—. Mem. APA, Nat. Assn. Sch. Psychologists, Nassau County Psychol. Assn., Suffolk County Psychol. Assn., Employee Assistance Program Assn. Home: 28 W 11th St Deer Park NY 11729-4010

ROSENBLUM, MINDY FLEISCHER, pediatrician; b. Bronxville, N.Y., June 5, 1951; d. Herman and Muriel (Gold) Fleischer; m. Jay S. Rosenblum, June 22, 1971; children: Meira, Tamar, Rafi, Rachel. BA, Yeshiva U., 1972; MD, Albert Einstein Coll., 1976. Diplomate Am. Bd. Pediatrics, Am. Bd. Pediatrics Endocrinology. Intern in pediatrics Bronx Mcpl. Hosp. Ctr., 1976-77, residency in pediatrics, 1977-79; fellow in pediatric endocrinology Children's Hosp. of Phila., 1981; asst. prof. U. Pa., Phila., 1981—; attending physician Bryn Mawr (Pa.) Hosp., 1981—, Lankenau Hosp., Wynnewood, Pa., 1983—. Fellow Am. Acad. Pediatrics; mem. Phila. Pediatrics Soc. (bd. dirs. 1988-92), Am. Diabetes Assn., Lawson Wilkins Pediatric Endocrine Soc.

ROSENBLUM, SANDRA PLETMAN, music educator; b. Yonkers, N.Y., May 13, 1928; d. Max and Rose (Lissauer) Pletman; m. Louis Rosenblum; children: Laurie Beth, Bruce David. BA, Wellesley Coll., 1949; MA, Harvard U., 1953. Instr. music, choral dir. Tenacre Sch., Wellesley, Mass., 1949-50; instr. music theory and piano, choral dir. South End Music Ctr., Boston, 1953-55; instr. music history Wellesley Coll., 1949-50, 52-53, 55-56; tchr. music theory and piano Concord (Mass.) Acad., 1956-73, chair dept. music, tchr. piano, 1973-85, chair dept. performing arts, tchr. piano, 1985—; with exec. com. Powers Music Sch., Belmont, Mass., 1964-75; adjudicator New England Conservatory and nat. piano tchrs.' assns., 1970—; chair com. to rev. music program Belmont Pub. Schs., 1976-77; liaison between Powers Music Sch. and Belmont Sch. Adminstrn., 1970-72; lectr. on performance styles at colls., conservatories, and musicol. confs., 1965—. Author: Performance Practices in Classic Piano Music, 1988 (Choice award 1989), Introduction to Facs. of Muzio Clementi's Introduction to the Art of Playing the Pianoforte, 1974, editions of keyboard music ty Scarlatti and Clementi; contbr. numerous articles to profl. jours. Recipient Billings Music prize Wellesley Coll., 1949; grantee Ballatine Fund Concord Acad., 1970-71, NEH, 1992; fellow Bunting Inst. Radcliffe Coll., 1970-71, 72-73, Am. Coun. Learned Socs., 1991-92. Mem. Am. Musicol. Soc., Music Tchrs. Nat. Assn., New England Pianoforte Tchrs. Assn. (chair editions com. 1984—), Phi Beta Kappa. Home: 24 Cedar Rd Belmont MA 02178-2905

ROSENBLUTH, LUCILLE MAXINE, health research facility administrator; b. N.Y.C., Sept. 18, 1931; d. David and Rhea (Farber) Moses; m. Sol Rosenbluth, June 8, 1952; children: Shelly Kratzer, Martin. BA in Polit. Sci., Bklyn. Coll., 1952; M in Pub. Adminstrn., NYU, 1953. Intern N.Y. State Adminstrn. Internship Program, 1953-54; rsch. aide N.Y. State Workmen's Compensation Bd., 1954-55; personnel asst. Dept. Personnel, N.Y.C., 1955-57; lectr. Bklyn. Coll., 1958, 59; rsch. asst. Temporary State Commn. on Operation N.Y.C. Govt., 1959-60; cons. Dept. Health, N.Y.C., 1960-61; rschr. study of profl., tech. and managerial manpower needs City of N.Y. Brookings Instn., 1961-63; cons. personnel utilization Dept. Health, N.Y.C., 1963-64; chief rschr. Med. and Health Rsch. Assn. N.Y.C., Inc., 1964-67, project coord., work com. chmn. systems study of sch. health records, 1967-70, project dir., policy com. chmn. N.Y.C. infant day care study, 1970-75, exec. v.p., 1975-86, pres., 1986—; cons. Commonwealth of Mass., 1982; mem. adj. faculty grad. sch. program in pub. health, dept. environ. and community medicine Rutger Med. Sch. U. Medicine and Dentistry N.J., 1984-86; mem. maternal and child health steering com. Sch. Pub. Health Columbia U., 1983—, lectr. pub. health, 1986—. Author: (with others) Caring Prescriptions: Comprehensive Health Care Strategies for Young Children in Poverty, 1993; contbr. articles to profl. jours. Fellow N.Y. Acad. Medicine (assoc., exec. com. on pub. health); mem. APHA (chair breastfeeding com. 1985, 86, 87), Family Planning Couns. Am. (chair grantee adv. com. Region II 1987, 88), N.Y. State Family Planning Advocates, N.Y. State Pub. Health Assn. (co-chmn. legis. com., bd. dirs. 1986—), Pub. Health Assn. N.Y.C., Soc. Rsch. Adminstrs., Health Care Execs. Forum (pres. 1988, 89), Hermann Biggs Soc., Women's City Club N.Y. (chair com. pub. health 1982-84). Office: Medical Health Rsch Assn of NYC 40 Worth St # 720 New York NY 10013-2904

ROSENBLUTH, MARION HELEN, educator, consultant, psychotherapist; b. Chgo., Apr. 4, 1928; d. Edwin William and Louise (Sulzberger) Eisendrath; m. Paul Richard Rosenbluth, June 16, 1950 (dec. Nov. 1972); children: Daniel, Jane Baldwin, Thomas, James, Catherine Rothschild. BA, Harvard U., 1949; MSW, Cath. U. of Am., 1951; PhD, U. Ill., 1986. Lic. clin. social worker, Ill. Clin. therapist Chgo. Dept. of Health, 1973-80; pvt. practice Chgo., 1980—; prof. Loyola U., Chgo., 1986—; cons. Inst. for Clin. Social Work, Chgo., 1988—; cons. student health Loyola U., 1978-80. Bd. dirs. Chgo. Area Project, 1978—, Rec. for the Blind, Chgo., 1980—, Inst. Psychiatry Northwestern U. Mem. NASW, Coun. on Social Work Edn., Bd. Examiners Clin. Social Work (diplomate), Ill. Soc. Clin. Social Work, Arts Club of Chgo., Cliff Dwellers, Friday Club. Office: 676 N St Clair St Chicago IL 60611-2927

ROSENE, LINDA ROBERTS, organizational consultant, researcher; b. Miami, Fla., Nov. 1, 1938; d. Wilbur David and Dorothy Claire (Baker) Roberts; m. Ralph W. Rosene, Aug. 3, 1957; children: Leigh, Russ, Tim. MA, Fielding Inst., 1981, PhD in Clin. Psychology, 1983. Lic. clin. psychologist. Counselor Rapid City (S.D.) Regional Hosp., 1978-81, Luth. Social Svcs., Rapid City, 1978-82; exec. v.p. Target Systems Inc., Dallas and Irving, Tex., 1983-85, cons., 1985—; cons. S.W. Home Furnishing Assn., Dallas, 1984, Northwestern Bell, Omaha, 1985; presenter, developer seminars gest-Accor Retail Assn. of Can., So. Home Furnishings Convs., 1989, Am. Assn. Med. Assts. Pub. Convenience Store News, Nat. Petroleum News, Nat. Home Furnishing Assn.-West news mag., Profl. Furniture Merchants mag.; mem. nat. adv. group Nat. Assn. Convenience Stores; presenter Internat. Sleep Products Assocs., 1990, Profit Mgmt. Systems, 1990, S.E. Buying Assocs., 1990, Nat. Assn. Casual Furn. Retailers, Petroleum Mktg. Edn. Found., 1991, Nat. Petroleum Mktg. & Edn. Found., 1991, Nat. Adv. Group, 1993, Tex. Mini Storage Retailers Assn., 1992, Workforce 2000, 1992, Nat. Adv. Group, 1993, ann. conf. Gen. Elec. Retail Systems, 1993, 94, Va. Petroleum Jobbers Assn., 1993, Ft. Worth, Tex. Pers. Assn., 1994, N.Y. chpt. Young Pres. Orgn., 1994—, Next Generation, Waco, Tex., 1994, Internat. Conf. Shopping Ctrs., 1994, Bank North Tex., 1994, Ky. Grocers Assn., Can. Retailers Contrex, Spring Air Dealers Assn., Mortgage Loan Industry, Weiner & Assocs. Nat. Seminars, 1995—; developer copyrighted hiring system, 1985, rev., 1989, copyrighted recruitment tng. system for retail mgmt., 1988, rev., 1989; speaker in field. Pub. Mini Storage Messenger Mag., Recovery, Bed Times; contbr. articles to newspapers and mags. Bd. dirs. Assn. Children with Learning Disabilities, S.D., 1983-84, West River (S.D.) Alcoholism Svcs., 1983-84, Health Adv. Com. of Head Start, S.D., 1980-84, St. Martins Acad., S.D., 1971-75; mem. Rapid City Mayor's Commn. on Racial Conciliation, 1971-73, Nat. Trust for Hist. Preservation; charter mem. Nat. Mus. Women in the Arts; presenter parenting seminar Westminster Presbyn. Ch., Dallas. Rsch. grantee Nat. Luth. Ch., 1981. Mem. APA, Am. Group Psychotherapist Assn., Dallas Group Psychotherapist Assn., N.C. Psychol. Assn., Assn. Marriage and Family Therapists, S.W. Home Furnishing Assn. Internat. Avocations: aviation, bicycling, racquetball, music, birdwatching. Home: 7005 Deloache Ave Dallas TX 75225-2422

ROSENFELD, ROBYN GAIL, food broker; b. Washington, July 1, 1953; d. Hans and Sondra (Rosenberg) R.; divorced. BS, Am. U., 1975. Terr. salesperson Quaker Oats, Elizabeth, N.J., 1977-83; sales mgr. Universal Foods, Milw., 1983-90; exec. v.p. Hn'm Assocs, Laurel, Md., 1990-94; pres. Hn'm Assocs., Laurel, Md., 1994—. Home: 406 Suffield Dr North Potomac MD 20878-2642 Office: Hn'm Assocs 9811 Mallard Dr Laurel MD 20708-3143

ROSENFELD, SARENA MARGARET, artist; b. Elmira, N.Y., Oct. 17, 1940; d. Thomas Edward and Rosalie Ereny (Fedor) Rooney; m. Robert Steven Bach, June 1958 (div. 1963); children: Robert Steven, Daniel Thomas; m. Samson Rosenfeld III, June 5, 1976. Student, Otis/Parson Art Inst., L.A., 1994—, Idyllwild Sch. Music and Arts, 1994—. One-woman shows and group exhbns. include Robert Dana Gallery, San Francisco, Gordon Gallery, Santa Monica, Calif., Art Expressions, San Diego, Ergane Gallery, N.Y.C., Nat. Mus. of Women in the Arts, Washington, also in L.A., La Jolla, Calif., Aspen, Colo., New Orleans, Soho, N.Y.C., Santa Barbara, Calif., Tanglewood, Mass., Honolulu, Johannesburg, South Africa, La Sierra U., Riverside, Calif. Recipient Best of Show award Glendale Regional Arts Coun., 1984-85, 1st pl. awards Santa Monica Art Festival, 1982, 83, 84, 85, 86, Sweepstakes award and 1st pl., 1986, Purchase prize awards L.A. West C. of C., 1986-87, Tapestry in Talent Invitational San Jose Arts Coun., 1986, 1st pl. awards Studio City and Century City Arts Couns., 1976-84. Mem. Nat. Mus. of Women in the Arts. Republican. Home: 6570 Kelvin Ave Canoga Park CA 91306-4021

ROSENHEIM, CHRISTINE LABODA, health management consultant; b. N.Y.C., June 22, 1952; d. Henry Oliver and Olga Caroline (Chupurdy) Laboda; m. Thomas Rosenheim, May 19, 1973; children: Brad Erik, Randy Thomas. AA in Nursing, Queensborough Community Coll., 1972; BS in Health Care Adminstrn., Stockton State Coll., 1976. RN., N.J., N.Y. Staff nurse N. Shore Med. Ctr., Manhassett, N.Y., 1972-73, W. Jersey Hosp., Voorhees, N.J., 1973-79; nurse Everrett R. Curran Jr. M.D., Cherry Hill, N.J., 1979-83, Valley Rehab. Co., Hammonton, N.J., 1983-85; nurse auditor Consolidated Rehab. Co., Haddon Heights, N.J., 1986-87; pres. Medi Fax Cons., Atco, N.J., 1987—; presenter case mgmt. tng. Nursing Spectrum, 1994-95. Editor: Pediatric Press, 1982. Chairperson Cub Scouts Am., Atco 1986-87; v.p. Waterford Twp. Home and Sch. Assn., Atco 1985-87. Mem. NAFE, Emergency Dept. Nurses Assn., South Jersey Claims Assn., Profl. Rehab. Network (pres. elect 1992-94, pres. 1994-96), Nat. Assn. Rehab. Profls. Home: 807 Linden Ave Atco NJ 08004-1210 Office: Medi-Fax Cons 556 Jackson Rd Atco NJ 08004-1100

ROSENHEIM, MARGARET KEENEY, social welfare policy education educator; b. Grand Rapids, Mich., Sept. 5, 1926; d. Morton and Nancy (Billings) Keeney; m. Edward W. Rosenheim, June 20, 1947; children: Daniel, James, Andrew. Student, Wellesley Coll., 1943-45; J.D., U. Chgo., 1949. Bar: Ill. 1949. Mem. faculty Sch. Social Service Adminstrn., U. Chgo., 1950—, assoc. prof., 1961-66, prof., 1966—, Helen Ross prof. social welfare policy, 1975—, dean, 1978-83; vis. prof. U. Wash., 1965, Duke U., 1984; lectr. in law; acad. visitor London Sch. Econs., 1973; cons. Pres.'s Commn. Law Enforcement and Adminstrn. Justice, 1966-67, Nat. Adv. Commn. Criminal Justice Standards and Goals, 1972; mem. Juvenile Justice Standards Commn., 1973-76; trustee Carnegie Corp. N.Y., 1979-87, Children's Home and Aid Soc. of Ill., 1981—; dir. Nat. Inst. Dispute Resolution, 1981-89, Nuveen Bond Funds, 1982—. Editor, contbr.: Justice for the Child, 1962, reprinted, 1977, Pursuing Justice for the Child, 1976, Early Parenthood and Coming of Age in the 1990s, 1992; contbr. articles and book revs. to profl. jours. Home: 5805 S Dorchester Ave Chicago IL 60637-1730 Office: 969 E 60th St Chicago IL 60637-2640

ROSENKRANTZ, LINDA, writer; b. N.Y.C., May 26, 1934; d. Samuel H. and Frances (Sillman) R.; m. Christopher Finch, Feb. 2, 1973; 1 child, Chloe. BA, U. Mich., 1955. Founding editor Auction Mag., N.Y.C., 1967-72; columnist Copley News Svc., San Diego, 1986--. Author: Talk, 1968; co-author: Gone Hollywood, 1979, SoHo, 1981, Beyond Jennifer and Jason, 1988, Beyond Charles and Diana, 1992, Beyond Shannon and Sean, 1992, Beyond Sarah and Sam, 1992, The Last Word on First Names, 1995.

ROSENOW, DORIS JANE, critical care nurse, nursing consultant; b. Sharon, Pa., Sept. 13, 1935; d. John J. and Mary F. (Koss) Skertic; m. Galen J. Rosenow, Dec. 14, 1957; children: Mary K. Gage, Gail E. Logan. Diploma in Nursing, St. Anthony de Padua Hosp., Chgo., 1955; BSN and BA in Psychology, Incarnate Word Coll., San Antonio, 1980; MSN, U. Tex. Health Sci. Ctr., San Antonio, 1984; PhD, U. Tex., 1990. RN, Tex.; cert. critical care RN. Critical care nurse Good Shephard Hosp., Longview, Tex., 1977, Brooke Army Med. Ctr., San Antonio, 1978-85; instr. Health Scis. Ctr. Tex. Tech. U., Odessa, 1985-88; asst. prof. Incarnate Word Coll., San Antonio, 1990-91, U. Tex., Galveston, 1991—; researcher in field. Contbr. articles to profl. jours. Served to 1st lt. USAF, 1957-60. Mem. ANA, Tex. Nurses Assn., Sigma Theta Tau (Nat. Honor Soc. 1984), Phi Kappa Phi (Nat. Honor Soc. 1990). Home: 15615 Boulder Creek St San Antonio TX 78247-2936

ROSENSTEIN, AMY LEE, psychotherapist; b. N.Y.C., Dec. 24, 1952; d. Milton and Rebecca (Yarenberg) R.; m. Aleksander Horecki, May 13, 1990. BA cum laude, CUNY, 1975; MSW, NYU, 1980. Cert. social worker, N.Y.; diplomate Am. Bd. Examiners in Clin. Social Work. Dir. activities Williamsbridge Manor Nursing Home, Bronx, N.Y., 1975-77, Rego Park Nursing Home, Flushing, N.Y., 1977-79; dir. social work The Lawson Life Extension Inst., Bklyn., 1979-80, Manhasset Hosp., New Hyde Park, N.Y., 1981-82; program dir. SW Queens Sr. Svcs., Woodhaven, N.Y., 1982-87; psychotherapist County Counseling Ctr., Bayside, N.Y., 1984-88; dir. Archer Avenue Sr. Ctr., Jamaica, N.Y., 1987-90; pvt. practice psychotherapist, Roslyn, N.Y., 1980—; adj. prof. N.Y. Inst. Tech., Old Westbury, 1981; social work cons. Forest Hills (N.Y.) Nursing Home, 1982-86; MSW field instr. Cath Charities and Jamaica Svc. Program for Older Adults, Queens, N.Y., 1982-90. Mem. Acad. Cert. Social Workers. Home and Office: 250 Locust Ln Roslyn Heights NY 11577-1413

ROSEN-SUPNICK, ELAINE RENEE, physical therapist; b. N.Y.C., May 7, 1951; d. Oscar Arthur and Sydell (Zimmerman) R.;m. Jed Supnick, Apr. 21, 1985. BS, Hunter Coll., 1973; MS, L.I. U., Bklyn., 1977. Cert. orthopedic specialist. Phys. therapy cons. Lenox Hill Hosp. Home Care, N.Y.C., 1977-83, GHI, Queens, N.Y., 1977-83, Vis. Nurse Assn., Bklyn., 1977-83; sr. phys. therapist Bird S. Coler Hosp., Roosevelt Island, N.Y., 1973-77; assoc. prof. Hunter Coll. CUNY, 1977—; ptnr. Queens Phys. Therapy Assocs., Forest Hills, N.Y., 1982—. Mem. Am. Phys. Therapy Assn. (dist. dir. Greater N.Y. dist. 1984-88, Merit award 1985, Outstanding Svc. award 1986, Dist. Svc. award 1988), Am. Acad. Orthopaedic Manual Therapists, Am. Assn. Orthopaedic Medicine, N.Y. State Acad. Coords. Clin. Edn. (treas. 1985-88). Democrat. Jewish. Office: Queens Phys Therapy Assocs 6940 108th St Flushing NY 11375-3851

ROSENTHAL, ELLY, financial director; b. Bklyn., Dec. 20, 1953; d. Allan Abraham and Theda (Bram) Kogon; m. Mark Alan Rosenthal, June 17, 1976; children: Joshua, Lindsay. BS in Acctg., Bklyn. Coll., 1975. CPA, N.Y. Auditor Peat Marwick Mitchell & Co., N.Y.C., 1975-82; contr. Finley Kumble Wagner, N.Y.C., 1982-85; dir. fin. and adminstrn. Morrison, Cohen & Singer, N.Y.C., 1985-87; dir. fin. Stroock & Stroock & Lavan, N.Y.C., 1987-92, Proskauer Rose Goetz, N.Y.C., 1992—. Jewish. Office: Proskauer Rose Goetz 1585 Broadway New York NY 10036-8200

ROSENTHAL, HELEN NAGELBERG, county official, advocate; b. N.Y.C., June 6, 1926; d. Alfred and Esther (Teichholz) Nagelberg; m. Albert S. Rosenthal, Apr. 10, 1949; children: Lisa Rosenthal Michaels, Apryl Meredith Rosenthal Stuppler. BS, Bklyn. Coll., 1948; MA, NYU, 1950; postgrad., Adelphia U., L.I. U., Lehman Coll., 1975. Cert. early childhood and gifted edn. tchr., N.Y., N.J., elem. and secondary tchr., Fla. Tchr. gifted students N.Y. Bd Edn., Bklyn., 1949-77, 79-87, Baldwin (N.Y.) Pub. Schs., 1977-79; rep. community affairs County of Dade, Fla., 1988-92; ret., 1992. Author: Criteria for Selection and Curriculum for the Gifted, 1977, Science Experiments for Young Children, 1982. Dir. Condominium, 1989-91. Recipient Departmental award, 1948. Mem. CCEGT (officer), AGATE, AICR.

ROSENTHAL, LEE H., federal judge; b. Nov. 30, 1952; m. Gary L. Rosenthal; children: Rebecca, Hannah, Jessica, Rachel. BA in Philosophy with honors, U. Chgo., 1974, JD with honors, 1977. Bar: Tex. 1979. Law clk. to Hon. John R. Brown U.S. Ct. Appeals (5th cir.), 1977-78; assoc. Baker & Botts, 1978-86, ptnr., 1986-92; judge U.S. Dist. Ct. (so. dist.) Tex., 1992—. Editor topics and comments Law Rev. U. Chgo., 1977-78. Active vis. com. Law Sch. U. Chgo., 1983-86, 94—; mem. devel. coun. Tex. Children's Hosp., 1988-92; pres. Epilepsy Assn. Houston/Gulf Coast, 1989-91; trustee Briarwood Sch. Endowment Found., 1991-92; bd. dirs. Epilepsy Found. Am., 1993—. Fellow Tex. Bar Found.; mem. ABA, Am. Law Inst., Texas Bar Assn., Houston Bar Assn. Office: US Dist Ct US Courthouse Rm 8631 515 Rusk Ave Houston TX 77002

ROSENTHAL, NAN, curator, author; b. N.Y.C., Aug. 27, 1937; d. Alan Herman and Lenore (Fry) R.; m. Otto Piene (div.); m. Henry Benning Cortesi, Sept. 5, 1990. BA, Sarah Lawrence Coll., 1959; MA, Harvard U., 1970, PhD, 1976. Asst. prof. art history U. Calif., Santa Cruz, 1971-77, assoc. prof., 1977-84, prof., 1985-86, chair dept. art history, 1976-80; curator 20th-century art Nat. Gallery Art, Washington, 1985-92; cons. Dept. of 20th Century Art, Metro. Mus. of Art, N.Y.C., 1993—; vis. prof. art history Fordham U., Lincoln Ctr., 1981, 85; vis. scholar N.Y. Inst. for Humanities, NYU, 1982-83; vis. lectr. visual arts Princeton U., 1985, 88, 92. Author: George Rickey, 1977; also exhbn. catalogues, catalogue essays and articles; art editor Show, 1963-64; assoc. editor, then editor at large and contbg. editor Art in Am., 1964-70. Radcliffe Inst. fellow, 1968-69, scholar, 1970-71; travelling fellow Harvard U., 1973-74, rsch. fellow U. Calif., 1978, Ailsa Mellon Bruce curatorial fellow Nat. Gallery of Art, 1988-89; rsch. and travel grantee U. Calif., Santa Cruz, 1974, 77-80, 82-85. Office: Met Mus of Art 20th Century Art 1000 Fifth Ave New York NY 10028-0113

ROSENTHAL, ROSALIE, sales and marketing professional; b. Bklyn., Apr. 26, 1943; d. Joseph and Esther (Cohen) Strassner; m. Jerrold Rosenthal, Nov. 24, 1962 (div. 1984); children: Shari, Jeffrey, Jay. Student, C.W. Post Coll., 1961; cert. in bus., Berkeley Bus. Sch., Hicksville, N.Y., 1962. Adminstrv. asst. H.J. Heinz Co., Lake Success, N.Y., 1972-78; sales rep. Tura Co., Great Neck, N.Y., 1978-79; sales mgr. U.S. Bus. Corp., Hicksville, 1979-82, Dataline Co., Hicksville, 1982-87; dir. sales and mktg. Sandata Inc., Port Washington, N.Y., 1987-88; dir. sales Softpoint Systems, Carle Place, 1988-91; mktg. specialist Med-Fin Inc., Mineola, N.Y., 1991; sales mgr. Creative Socio Medics, Islip, N.Y., 1991-92; dir. sales and mktg. Accumedic, Boca Raton, Fla., 1992-93; adminstr. Integrated Billing Alternatives, Deerfield, Fla., 1993—. Pres. Park Ridge Condominium Assn. Mem. NAFE, Homecare Assn. N.Y. State, Healthcare Fin. Mgmt. Assn., Nat. Coun. Jewish Women, N.Y. State Med. Bus. Assn., Hadassah (life). Democrat. Office: Integrated Billing Alternatives 1239 Newport Center E Ste 110 Deerfield FL 33442

ROSENTHAL, SUSAN BARBARA, retired librarian; b. Elberon Park, N.J., Apr. 7, 1946; d. Joseph and Anna (Warar) Rosenthal. B.A., Montclair State Coll., 1967; M.Ed. in L.S., U. Miami, 1973. Cert. media specialist, tchr., Fla., N.J. Tchr., Manasquan Bd. Edn. (N.J.), 1967-71; tech. services librarian Oakland Park Library (Fla.), 1978-92, asst. dir., 1992-93, acting dir., 1993, ret. Author: (mag.) Galumph, 1965-67; contbr. A Micro Handbook for Small Libraries and Media Centers, 1983, 2nd edit., 1986, 3d edit., 1991. Mem. Humane Soc., Broward County, Fla., 1981, WPBT-TV PBS sta., 1975—; charter mem. Mus. of Discovery and Sci., 1989—, U.S. Holocaust Meml. Mus., 1994-95. Recipient St. Cloud Teaching award Société d'Enseignement, St. Cloud, France, 1966, 2 awards Libr. Pub. Rels. Coun., winner, 1983, honorable mention, 1985. Mem. ALA, Fla. Library Assn. (continuing edn. com. 1980), Fla. Pub. Library Assn., Broward County Library Assn. (treas. 1981-83), Apple Libr. Users Group, Apple Computer Enjoyment Soc. (chpt. sec. 1984-87, corp. sec. 1985-89), Consumers Union, Wilderness Soc., World Wildlife Fund, Environ. Def. Fund, People for Ethical Treatment Animals, Nature Conservancy, Mensa, Procrastinators Club Am., Pi Delta Phi. Office: Bibliothéque Lamienne 1522 NE 34th Ct Oakland Park FL 33334-5305

ROSENTHAL, SUSAN LESLIE, psychologist; b. Washington, Sept. 27, 1956; d. Alan Sayre and Helen (Miller) R. BA, Wellesley Coll., 1978; PhD, U. N.C., 1986. Postdoctoral fellow Yale Child Study Ctr., New Haven, 1986-88; asst. prof. clin. pediatrics U. Cin., 1988-93, dir. psychology div. adolescent medicine, 1988—, assoc. prof. clin. pediatrics, 1993—; adj. faculty dept. psychology Miami U., Oxford, Ohio, 1992—. Contbr. articles to profl. jours. Grantee NIH, 1994—. Mem. APA (program chair divsn. 37 1992), Cin. Soc. Clin. Child Psychologists (treas. 1992-94, pres. 1994—), Ohio Psychol. Assn., Soc. Behavioral Pediatrics, Soc. Rsch. on Adolescence, Cin. Acad. Profl. Psychology. Office: Children's Hosp Med Ctr Div Adolescent Medicine 3333 Burnet Ave Cincinnati OH 45229-3026

ROSER, ROBERTA LOUISE, marketing professional; b. Newark, Jan. 30, 1957; d. John Arthur and Edith Anna (Friedrich) R. Diploma, Stafford Hall Bus. Sch., 1976; student, Fairleigh Dickinson U., 1977-82; BSBA, Thomas Edison State Coll., 1994. Sec. Allied Chem.- Specialty Chems., Morristown, N.J., 1976-77; sr. stenographer AT&T Gen. Depts., Basking Ridge, N.J., 1977-81, staff asst., 1981-82; svcs. staff mgr. AT&T Info. Systems, Parsippany, N.J., 1982-85; staff mgr. AT&T Bus. Comms. Systems, Bridgewater, N.J., 1985-91; staff supr. AT&T Consumer Market Mgmt., Basking Ridge, 1991-93; staff supr., product mgr. AT&T Mobile Comms. Svcs., Basking Ridge, 1993-94; staff mgr. AT&T Network Sys.-Network Cable Sys., Morristown, N.J., 1994—. Vol./Essex bd. dirs. Orgn., Gladstone, N.J., 1992-94; hostess Mansion in May '94, mem. Woman's Assn. Morristown (N.J.) Meml. Hosp., 1994—. Republican. Methodist. Home: 289 Potomac Dr Basking Ridge NJ 07920-3171 Office: Rm 4N24A 111 Madison Ave Morristown NJ 07960

ROSETT, ANN DOYLE, librarian; b. Valdosta, Ga., Jan. 9, 1955; d. David Spencer Doyle and Lois Annette Gray; m. Robert Allen Richardson, Aug. 1, 1976 (div. June 1981); children: Caitlin Ann, Brendan Wesley; m. John David Rosett, Aug. 6, 1983. Student, Kenyon Coll., 1972-75, U. Dayton, 1974, U. Ala., Birmingham, 1978; BA, Shepherd Coll., 1982; MLS, U. Wash., 1988. Cert. profl. libr., Wash. College libr. Northwest Coll., Kirkland, Wash., 1988—. Mem. ALA, Assn. Christian Librs. (dir.-at-large 1992-93), Assn. Coll. and Rsch. Librs., Am. Theol. Lib. Assn., N.W. Assn. Christian Librs. (treas. 1989-91, pres. 1991-93). Democrat. Office: NW Coll DV Hurst Libr PO Box 579 5520 108th Ave NE Kirkland WA 98033-7523

ROSHONG, DEE ANN DANIELS, dean, educator; b. Kansas City, Mo., Nov. 22, 1936; d. Vernon Edmund and Doradell (Kellogg) Daniels; m. Richard Lee Roshong, Aug. 27, 1960 (div.). BMusEd., U. Kans., 1958; MA in Counseling and Guidance, Stanford U., 1960; postgrad. Fresno State U., U. Calif.; EdD, U. San Francisco, 1980. Counselor, psychometrist Fresno City Coll., 1961-65; counselor, instr. psychology Chabot Coll., Hayward, Calif., 1965-75; coord. counseling services Chabot Coll., Valley Campus, Livermore, Calif., 1975-81, asst. dir. student pers. svcs., 1981-89, Las Positas Coll., Livermore, Calif., 1989-91, assoc. dean student svcs., 1991-94, dean student svcs., 1994—; writer, coord. I, A Woman Symposium, 1974, Feeling Free to Be You and Me Symposium, 1975, All for the Family Symposium, 1976, I Celebrate Myself Symposium, 1977, Person to Person in Love and Work Symposium, 1978; The Healthy Person in Body, Mind and Spirit Symposium, 1979, Feelin' Good Symposium, 1980, Change Symposium, 1981, Sources of Strength Symposium, 1982, Love and Friendship Symposium, 1983, Self Esteem Symposium, 1984, Trust Symposium, 1985, Prime Time: Making the Most of This Time in Your Life Symposium, 1986, Symposium on Healing, 1987, How to Live in the World and Still Be Happy Symposium, 1988, Student Success is a Team Effort, Sound Mind, Sound Body Symposium, 1989, Creating Life's Best Symposium, 1990, Choices Symposium, 1991, Minding the Body, Mending the Mind Symposium, 1992, Healing through Love and Laughter Symposium, 1993, Healing Ourselves

Changing the World Symposium, 1994, Finding Your Path Symposium, 1995; mem. cast TV prodns. Eve and Co., Best of Our Times, Cowboy; chmn. Calif. Community Coll. Chancellor's Task Force on Counseling, Statewide Conf. on Emotionally Disturbed Students in Calif. Community Colls., 1982—, Conf. on the Under Represented Student in California Community Colleges, 1986, Conf. on High Risk Students, 1989. Mem. Assn. Humanistic Psychologists, Western Psychol. Assn., Nat. Assn. Women Deans and Counselors, Assn. for Counseling and Devel., Calif. Assn. Community Colls. (chmn. commn. on student services 1979-84), Calif. Community Colls. Counselors Assn. (Svc. award 1986, 87, award for Outstanding and Disting. Service, 1986, 87, Spl. Svc. award for outstanding svc Calif. advocated for re-entry edn., 1991), Alpha Phi. Author: Counseling Needs of Community Coll. Students, 1980. Home: 1856 Harvest Rd Pleasanton CA 94566 Office: 3033 Collier Canyon Rd Livermore CA 94550

ROSIGNOLO, BEVERLY ANN, information specialist, consultant; b. N.Y.C., Sept. 12, 1950; d. Alexander George and Gunhild Marie (Berg) Sgourdos; m. Steve Francesco Rosignolo, Oct. 14, 1972; 1 child, Adam Nicholas. BA, Queens Coll., 1974, MLS, 1975. Cataloger H.W. Wilson Co., N.Y.C., 1975-77; cataloger The Coll. of Ins., N.Y.C., 1977-81, assoc. libr., 1981-84, chief libr., 1984-90; info. specialist Rosignolo Assocs., Teaneck, N.J., 1990—. Editor: (periodical) Ins. and Employee Benefits Lit., 1980-84; joint editor: 1975 Supplement to Children's Catalog, 1975. Mem. Spl. Librs. Assn. (indexer: Ins. Periodicals Index, Ins. and Employee Benefits Div. 1978—, chairperson 1989-90, treas. N.Y. chpt. 1984-86), Beta Phi Mu. Home and Office: Rosignolo Assocs 264 Grayson Pl Teaneck NJ 07666-3406

ROSITA, ALMA See DAVIES, ALMA

ROSLANOWICK, JEANNE M., legislative staff director; b. Erie, Pa., Aug. 31, 1948. BA magna cum laude, Marquette U., 1970; MPA, U. Mass., 1972; JD, Yale Coll., 1979. Mem. Dept. Pub. Welfare, Boston, 1972-76; assoc. Patton, Boggs & Blow, Washington, 1980-83; counsel subcom. on econ. stabilization, 1983-87; sr. counsel house small bus. com., 1987-93, staff dir., 1993—. Office: Com on Small Business 2361 Rayburn House Ofc Bldg Washington DC 20515*

ROS-LEHTINEN, ILEANA, congresswoman; b. Havana, Cuba, July 15, 1952; d. Enrique Emilio and Amanda (Adato) Ros; m. Dexter Lehtinen. AA, Miami (Fla.)-Dade C.C., 1972; BA, Fla. Internat. U., 1975, MS, 1987. Prin. Ea. Acad., from 1978; mem. Fla. Ho. of Reps., Tallahassee, 1982-86, Fla. Senate, 1986-89, 101st-104th Congresses from 18th Fla. Dist., 1989—; mem. govt. ops. com., subcom. employment, housing, commerce, consumer monetary affairs., govt. info., justice agrl., fgn. affairs. com. Roman Catholic. Office: 127 Cannon House Office Bldg Washington DC 20515-0918

ROSLUND, CAROL L., lawyer; b. Ark., Sept. 5, 1943; d. Oliver Sidney and Lois (Stratton) R.; 1 child, Kari Ann Roslund-Mercurio. Student, Stockholm (Sweden) U., 1963-64; BA, Colo. Women's Coll., 1965; PhD, Syracuse (N.Y.) U., 1972; JD, Denver U., 1981. Bar: Colo. 1982. Dir. Pretrial Release Svcs., Arapahoe County, Colo., 1974-83; counsel, sr. project adminstr. U. Denver, 1983-84; div. counsel Honeywell Inc., Denver, 1984-88; assoc. counsel Olin Corp., East Alton, Ill., 1988-90; sr. counsel Olin Ordnance, St. Petersburg, Fla., 1990—; sec. Olin Pantex Inc., Tex., 1990-93; bd. dirs. Nat. Assn. Pretrial Svc. Agys., Washington, 1973-85. Am. Scandinavian Found. fellow, 1971, Lithgow Osborne fellow, 1976. Mem. ABA, Am. Corp. Counsel Assn., Colo. Bar Assn. Office: Olin Ordnance 10101 9th St N Saint Petersburg FL 33716-3807

ROSOFF, JEANNIE I., association administrator; b. Clamart, France, Nov. 8, 1924; came to U.S., 1948; d. Georges Auguste Marie and Suzenne (Philomene) Martin; m. Morton Rosoff, Dec. 8, 1945 (div. 1958); 1 child, Ann Susan. BA in Law cum laude, U. Paris, 1946. Cmty. organizer East Harlem Project, N.Y.C., 1953-56; assoc. dir. N.Y. Com. for Dem. Voters, N.Y.C., 1960-64; spl. projects coord. Planned Parenthood Fedn. Am., N.Y.C., 1964-74, assoc. dir., 1968-74, assoc. dir. Ctr. for Family Planning Program Devel., 1968-74; v.p. govt. affairs Planned Parenthood Fedn. Am., Washington, 1974-77, dir. Washington office, 1976-81; sr. v.p. Alan Guttmacher Inst., Washington, 1974-78, pres., 1978—; participant in UN Population Conf., Bucharest, 1974, UN Conf. on Internat. Women's Yr., Mexico City, 1975; ofcl. U.S. del. UN Conf. on Population and Devel., Cairo, 1994; del.-at-large Internat. Women's Yr. Conf., Houston, 1977. Author: Teenage Pregnancy in Industrialized Countries, 1986, Health Care Reform: A Unique Opportunity, 1993, (govt. publs.) Family Planning: An Analysis of Laws, 1974, Family Planning: Contraception, 1979. Recipient merit award Nat. Family Planning and Repro. Health Assn., 1980, Ten for Ten award Ctr. for Population Options, 1990. Mem. APHA (pres., chair population sect. 1976, Carl S. Schultz award 1980; maternal and child health sec. 1973-76), Nat. Health Lawyers Assn., Population Assn. Am., Nat. Inst. Child Health and Human Devel., Pathfinder Internat. (bd. dirs. 1993—). Office: Alan Guttmacher Inst 120 Wall St Fl 21 New York NY 10005-3901

ROSS, ADDIE MARIE, special education educator, consultant; b. Calvert, Tex.; d. Will A. and Jessie May (Diggs) Stephens; m. John Alvin Waits, Dec. 11, 1950 (div. 1960); children: Nedra, Ronald, Donald; m. Thomas A. Ross, Aug. 10, 1970. BA, Huston-Tillotson Coll., Austin, Tex., 1950; postgrad., San Francisco State U., 1955-68, 89-91. Tchr. San Francisco Unified Sch. Dist., 1956-62, resource cons. Title I program, 1963-71, resource coord., 1973-82, cons., 1984-88; tchr. U.S. Ind. Sch., Heidelberg, Germany, 1971-73, English Speaking Sch., Bander Sri Begawan, Brunei, 1982-83; learning disabled specialist Ravenswood Sch. Dist., East Palo Alto, Calif., 1988—; cons. Calif. Bd. Edn., Sacramento, 1979-81; cons. in field. Bd. trustees Third Bapt. Ch., San Francisco Aid to Retarded Children. Recipient Disting. Alumna award Huston-Tillotson Coll., 1982. Mem. NEA, Calif. Tchrs. Assn., San Francisco Black Leadership Caucus, Nat. Coun. Negro Women, San Francisco Commonwealth Club. Baptist. Home: 2455 14th Ave San Francisco CA 94116

ROSS, ALLYNE R., federal judge; b. 1946. BA, Wellesley Coll., 1967; JD cum laude, Harvard Law Sch., 1970. Assoc. Paul, Weiss, Rifkind, Wharton & Garrison, 1971-76; asst. U.S. atty. U.S. Dist. Ct. (N.Y. ea. dist.), 2nd circuit, Brooklyn, 1976-83, chief, appeals div., 1983-86, magistrate judge, 1986-94, dist. judge, 1994—. Mem. Federal Bar Coun., New York City Bar Assn. Office: US District Court 225 Cadman Plz E Rm 619 Brooklyn NY 11201-1876*

ROSS, BELLA MARY, nurse; b. Leeds, Yorkshire, Eng., Apr. 23, 1942; came to U.S., 1986; d. Patrick M. and Anne K. (Gormley) Ferguson; m. John P. Ross, Sept. 26, 1964; children: Gerard, Vincent, Siobhan. Degree in Nursing, St. James' Hosp., Leeds, 1963, midwifery diploma, 1964. RN. Staff nurse, oper. rm. St. James' Hosp., Leeds, 1964-65, occupational health nurse, 1965-66; indsl. nurse Turner Engring., Leeds, 1966-67; ward sister St. James' Hosp., Leeds, 1967-73; staff nurse, head pub. health nurse Leeds Area Health Authority, 1973-76; staff nurse St. Joseph's Hosp., Longford, Ireland, 1976-86; staff nurse ob-gyn unit Mountainside Hosp., Montclair, N.J., 1988—. Mem. Irish Nurses Orgn. (sec. Longford 1976-86), Irish-Am. Orgn./CCE (treas. N.J. 1991-93), Irish CCE (auditor Garden State br. 1993—). Roman Catholic. Home: 263 Bloomfield Ave Bloomfield NJ 07003-4867

ROSS, CHARLOTTE PACK, suicidologist; b. Oklahoma City, Oct. 21, 1932; d. Joseph and Rose P. (Traibich) Pack; m. Roland S. Ross, May 6, 1951 (div. July 1964); children: Beverly Jo, Sandra Gail; m. Stanley Fisher, Mar. 17, 1991. Student U. Okla., 1949-52, New Sch. Social Rsch., 1953. Cert. tchr. Exec. dir. Suicide Prevention and Crisis Ctr. San Mateo County, Burlingame, Calif., 1966-88; pres., exec. dir. Youth Suicide Nat. Ctr., Washington, 1985-93; exec. dir. Death with Dignity Edn. Ctr., San Mateo, Calif., 1994—; pres. Calif. Senate Adv. Com. Youth Suicide Prevention, 1982-84; speaker Menninger Found., 1983, 84; instr. San Francisco State U., 1981-83; conf. coord. U. Calif., San Francisco, 1971—; cons. univs. and health svcs. throughout world. Contbg. author: Group Counseling for Suicidal Adolescents, 1984, Teaching Children the Facts of Life and Death, 1985; mem. editorial bd. Suicide and Life Threatening Behavior, 1976-89. Mem. regional selection panel Pres.'s Commn. on White House Fellows, 1975-78; mem. CIRCLON Svc. Club, 1979—, Com. on Child Abuse, 1981-85; founding mem. Women for Responsible Govt., co-chmn., 1974-79. Recipient Outstanding Exec. award San Mateo County Coordinating Com., 1971, Koshland award San Francisco Found., 1984. Fellow Wash. Acad. Scis.; mem. Internat. Assn. Suicide Prevention (v.p. 1985—), Am. Assn. Suicidology (sec. 1972-74, svc. award 1990), bd. govs. 1976-78, accreditation com. 1975—, chair region IX, 1975-82), Assn. United Way Agy. Execs. (pres. 1974), Assn. County Contract Agys. (pres. 1982), Peninsula Press Club.

ROSS, DEBRA BENITA, marketing executive; b. Carbondale, Ill., May 1, 1956; d. Bernard Harris and Marian (Frager) R. BS, U. Ill., 1978; MS, U. Wis., 1979. Dir. mktg. Ambion Devel., Inc., Northbrook, Ill., 1983-89; dir. mktg. Fitness Horizons, Inc., Northbrook, 1989-91, v.p. mktg., 1991—; owner Benita Ross Designs, Northbrook, 1992—. Mem. Am. Mktg. Assn., Chgo. Advt. Club, Chgo. CitiWomen. Home: 1853 Mission Hills Ln Northbrook IL 60062-5760

ROSS, DIANA, singer, actress, entertainer, fashion designer; b. Detroit, Mar. 26, 1944; d. Fred and Ernestine R.; m. Robert Ellis Silberstein, Jan. 1971 (div. 1976); children: Rhonda, Tracee, Chudney; m. Arne Naess, Oct. 23, 1985; 1 son: Ross Arne. Grad. high sch. Pres. Diana Ross Enterprises, Inc., fashion and merchandising, Anaid Film Prodns., Inc., RTC Mgmt. Corp., artists mgmt., Chondee Inc., Rosstown, Rossville, music pub. Started in Detroit as mem. the Primettes; lead singer until 1969, Diana Ross and the Supremes; solo artist, 1969—; albums include Diana Ross, 1970, 76, Everything Is Everything, 1971, I'm Still Waiting, 1971, Lady Sings The Blues, 1972, Touch Me In The Morning, 1973, Original Soundtrack of Mahogany, 1975, Baby It's Me, 1977, The Wiz, 1978, Ross, 1978, 83, The Boss, 1979, Diana, 1981, To Love Again, 1981, Why Do Fools Fall In Love?, 1981, Silk Electric, 1982, Swept Away, 1984, Eaten Alive, 1985, Chain Reaction, 1986, Workin' Overtime, 1989, Red Hot Rhythm and Blues, 1987, Surrender, 1989, Ain't No Mountain High Enough, 1989, The Force Behind the Power, 1991, The Remixes, 1994; films include Lady Sings the Blues, 1972, Mahogany, 1975, The Wiz, 1978; NBC-TV spl., An Evening With Diana Ross, 1977, Diana, 1981, numerous others; TV movie Out of Darkness, 1994; album Endless Love, 1982; author: Secrets of a Sparrow, 1993. Recipient citation Vice Pres. Humphrey for efforts on behalf Pres. Johnson's Youth Opportunity Program, citation Mrs. Martin Luther King and Rev. Abernathy for contbn. to SCLC cause, awards Billboard, Cash Box and Record World as worlds outstanding singer, Grammy award, 1970, Female Entertainer of Year NAACP, 1970, Cue award as Entertainer of year, 1972, Golden Apple award, 1972, Gold medal award Photoplay, 1972, Antoinette Perry award, 1977, nominee as best actress of year for Lady Sings the Blues Motion Picture Acad. Arts and Scis., 1972, Golden Globe award, 1972; named to Rock and Roll Hall of Fame, 1988. Office: RTC Mgmt PO Box 1683 New York NY 10185-1683 also: care Shelly Berger 6255 W Sunset Blvd Los Angeles CA 90028-7403*

ROSS, DONNA LEE, auditor; b. San Francisco, Dec. 1, 1956; d. Arthur J. and Myrtle Joan (Haynes) Lee; m. Eugene Ross Sr., Mar. 31, 1990. BS in Acctg., U. San Francisco, 1983. CPA, Calif. Sales supr. Macy's Calif., San Francisco, 1974-84; acctg. clk. 3/33 Ins. Co., San Francisco, 1979-80; advt. acct. San Francisco Newspaper Agy., 1980-83; supervising sr. auditor Arthur Young & Co., San Francisco, 1984-87; corp. auditor Hewlett-Packard Co., Palo Alto, Calif., 1987-90; ea. region audit mgr. Hewlett-Packard Co., Paramus, N.J., 1990-92, sr. internal auditor, 1992—. Author: (classroom tng. material) Understanding Basic Business Controls in a Changing Environment, 1992. Active Hist. Preservation Soc. Mem. Nat. Assn. Black Accts., State Soc. CPAs, Inst. Internal Auditors (mem. N.J. chpt.). Democrat. Roman Catholic.

ROSS, ELGENIA RUTH SNIPES, art educator; b. Winston-Salem, N.C., July 3, 1940; d. Carl Homer and Elsie Beatrice (Berry) Snipes; m. James Asbury Ross, Jr., Oct. 10, 1965; children: Kimberly McCall, Molly Shannon. BA, Furman U., 1962; MS, Parson's Sch. Design/Bank St. Coll., 1991. Cert. art specialist, art supr. Tchr. North Charleston (S.C.) High Sch., 1963-65, Monticello (Ark.) High Sch., 1979-94; regional bd. dirs. Mus. Women in Arts, 1991; adj. instr. U. Ark., Monticello, 1993; mem. panel tchr. licensure task force Ark. Dept. Edn., Little Rock, 1994, fine arts framework com., 1994. Exhibited in group shows including Pine Art Show, Monticello, 1989-94, Mus. Women in Arts, 1990, U. Ark., Monticello, 1993. Bd. dirs. Ark. Endowment Humanities, 1980-83; founding mem., bd. dirs. Ark. Women's History Inst., Little Rock, 1983-86. Mem. Nat. Art Educators Assn., Ark. Art Educators Assn. (sec. exec. bd. coun. 1992-94, Secondary Educator of Yr. 1994), S.E. Ark. Concert Assn. (bd. dirs. 1973-76, 89-94), Monticello Women's Investment Club (sec. 1992-94), Monticello Art League (founder, pres. 1989), Delta Kappa Gamma. Home: PO Box 209 Monticello AR 71655

ROSS, ELINOR, soprano; b. Tampa, Fla., Aug. 1, 1932; d. Joe D. and Lillian Rosenthal; m. Aaron M. Diamond; 1 son, Ross. Student, Syracuse U. Debuts include: Turandot, Met. Opera, N.Y.C., Il Trovatore, Cin. Opera, Cavalleria Rusticana, La Scala, Milan, Tosca, Bolshoi, Moscow; leading soprano roles with, Met. Opera, LaScala, Bolshoi, Chgo. Lyric Opera, San Francisco Opera, Tulsa Opera, Cin. Opera, Staatsoper, Vienna, LaFenice, Venice, Teatro Colon, Buenes Aires, Argentina, Arena de Verona, Massimo de Palermo; inaugurated Rossini Festival in Pesaro; televised concert tour in Peoples Republic of China, Taiwan; appeared in concerts, opera, symphony in Hong Kong, Japan, Thailand, Korea; appeared with symphony orchs. throughout world. Recipient medal of honor Novosibiresk, Siberia. Jewish. *

ROSS, EUNICE LATSHAW, judge; b. Bellevue, Pa., Oct. 13, 1923; d. Richard Kelly and Eunice (Weidner) Latshaw; m. John Anthony Ross, May 29, 1943 (dec. Jan. 1978); 1 child, Geraldine Ross Coleman. BS, U. Pitts., 1945, LLB, 1951. Bar: Pa. 1952. Atty., Pub. Health Law Research Project, Pitts., 1951-52; atty. jud. asst., law clk. Ct. Common Pleas, Pitts., 1952-70; adjunct law prof. U. Pitts., 1967-73; dir. family div. Ct. Common Pleas, Pitts., 1970-72; judge Ct. Common Pleas of Allegheny County, Pitts., 1972—; mem. Bd. Jud. Inquiry and Rev., Commonwealth of Pa., 1984-89, Gov's Justice Commn., 1972-78. Author: (with others) Survey of Pa. Public Health Laws, 1952. Co-author: Will Contests, 1992; contbr. articles to legal publs. Com. person for 14th ward, vice chmn. Democratic Com., Pitts., 1972; exec. com. bd. trustees U. Pitts., 1980-86, bd. visitors law sch., 1985—, bd. visitors sch. health, 1986—; adv. bd. Animal Friends, Pitts., 1973—; bd. mem. The Program, Pitts., 1983-87, Pitts. History and Landmarks FDTN., West Pa. Hist. Soc., West Pa. Conservancy. Recipient Disting. Amumna award U. Pitts., 1973, Medal of Recognition, 1987, Susan B. Anthony award Womens' Bar Assn. Western Pa., 1993, Probate and Trusts award, 1994; named Girl Scout Woman of Yr., Pitts. coun. Girl Scouts U.S., 1975; cert. of Achievement Pa. Fedn. Women's Clubs, 1975, 77. Mem. Allegheny County Bar Assn. (vice chmn., exec. com. young lawyers sect. 1956-59), Pa. State Trial Judges Conf., Order of Coif. Home: 1204 Denniston Ave Pittsburgh PA 15217-1329 Office: Frick Bldg 3d Fl Pittsburgh PA 15219

ROSS, HOLLY RAE, systems engineer; b. Scranton, Pa., Feb. 11, 1966; d. James Adrian and Gloria Ray (Ammer) R.; m. Paul Stanton Sipes, Sept. 6, 1992. BS in Elec. Engring., Bucknell U., 1988; MS in Systems Mgmt., U. Denver, 1992; MS in Elec. Engring., Drexel U., 1994. Computer intern Tie Comm., Shelton, Conn., 1987; database mgr. Sprague & Henwood, Scranton, Pa., 1988-89; elec. engr. Naval Air Warfare Ctr., Lakehurst, N.J., 1989-92, systems engr., 1992—. Participant Women's Exec. Leadership Program, 1994. Mem. IEEE, Soc. Women Engrs.

ROSS, IRMA MYERS, clinical therapist; b. New Haven, July 22, 1954; d. Paul A. and Margaret Myers (Strauss) R. BA cum laude, Boston U., 1976; MS in Counseling, So. Conn. State U., 1977, cert. gestalt therapist, 1980, cert. advanced grad. study, 1981. Substance abuse counselor Lower Naugatuck Valley Svc. Ctr., Ansonia, Conn., 1977-79; psychiat. therapist Waterbury (Conn.) Hosp., 1979-90, sr. clin. therapist and supr., 1990—; cofounder, pres. Creative Awareness Ctr., Cheshire, Conn., 1982—; cons. AIDS Project Waterbury, Waterbury, 1990—, ethics com. Waterbury Hosp., 1993. Contbr. articles to profl. jours. Active Hadassah. Jewish.

ROSS, JEAN LOUISE, physical education educator; b. Lebanon, Pa., June 20, 1951; d. Jonas John and Eloise Mary (Miller) Walmer; m. Edward Richard Ross, Nov. 10, 1978; 1 child, Aaron Edward. BS in Health and Physical Edn., West Chester U., 1973; MS in Physical Edn., Pa. State U., 1979; MSEd in Counseling Psychology, St. Bonaventure U., 1992. Health and physical edn. tchr. Lower Dauphin Sch. dist., Hummelstown, Pa., 1973-78; health and physical edn. tchr. Bradford Area Sch. Dist., Pa., 1978-80, 1986—; in-home edn. specialist SCAN/PEP Program, The Guidance Ctr., Bradford, 1985-86. Recipient mini-grants Rotary Club of Bradford, 1984,86-88. Mem. Am. Alliance Health, Physical Edn., Recreation and Dance, Pa. State Alliance Health, Physical Edn., Recreation and Dance. Democrat. Office: Fretz Jr High Sch 140 Lorana Ave Bradford PA 16701

ROSS, JOYCE ADAMS, gerontological clinical specialist; b. Phila., June 29, 1944; d. Thomas Grandville and Dorothy (Anglea) Adams; m. Jerome Samuel Ross, June 8, 1963; children: Mary Teresa, Dorothy, Jerome Jr., Michael, Erin. ADN, Gwynedd Mercy Coll., 1987, BSN cum laude, 1988, MSN, 1992. RN, Md., Pa.; cert. gerontol. nurse. Gerontol. nurse clinician Franklin Sq. Hosp. Ctr., Balt., 1988-89; instr. Fair Acres Geriatric Ctr., Lima, Pa., 1989; dir. staff devel., cert. gerontol. clin. specialist Dunwoody Village Continuing Care Retirement Community, Newtown Square, Pa., 1989—, mem. speakers bur., 1989-94; nursing home adminstr., mem. speakers bur.; mem. long term care consortium Main Line, Inc.; evaluator continuing care accreditation Am. Assn. Homes for the Aged, 1993—. Nurst of Hope Am. Cancer Soc., Media, Pa., 1981, mem. edn. com., 1990-92. Mem. Delaware Valley Geriatric Soc., Sigma Theta Tau (Iota Kappa chpt.). Roman Catholic. Home: 347 Sussex Blvd Broomall PA 19008 Office: Dunwoody Village Continuing Care Retirement Cmty 3500 W Chester Pike Newtown Square PA 19073-4101

ROSS, JULIA ANN, advertising executive; b. Austin, Tex., Sept. 9, 1966; d. William John and Janetta Ann (Witten) Sewall; m. Patrick Edward Ross, Sept. 15, 1990; 1 child, Cameron Patrick Ross. Attended, U. Tex., 1985-89. Pres., owner Lake Travis Sch. of Dance, Austin, Tex., 1988-91; advt. exec. KHFI Radio Rusk Corp., Austin, 1992-93, KHFI Radio/Clear Channel Comm., Austin, 1993—; founder Ross Agency, Inc. (Ross Norton Agency, Media Tech., Ads Unltd., Carousel Design), Austin, 1994—; mem. Dance Repretory Theatre, Austin, 1986-89; dancer 50th Anniversary Fine Arts Performance U. Tex., 1988. Advt. exec. Teen Summer, Austin, 1993. Recipient fine arts scholarship U. Tex., 1987; mem. Top 10 Finalists for Student of Yr. scholarship, Tex. Ex-Student Assn., Austin, 1987; named to All-State Dance Team and All Am. Dance Teams, Tex., 1984-85. Mem. Advt. Fedn., Better Bus. Bur., Am. Women in Radio and TV, Am. Mktg. Assn. Episcopalian. Office: 11615 Angus Rd 216 Austin TX 78759

ROSS, JUNE ROSA PITT, biologist; b. Taree, May 2, 1931; came to U.S., 1957; d. Bernard and Adeline Phillips; m. Charles Alexander, June 27, 1959. BS with honors, U. Sydney, New S. Wales, Australia, 1953, PhD, 1959, DSc, 1974. Research assoc. Yale U., New Haven, 1959-60, U. Ill., Urbana, 1960-65; research assoc. Western Wash. U., Bellingham, 1965-67, assoc. prof., 1967-70, prof. biology, 1970—, chair dept. biology, 1989-90; pres. Western Wash. U. Faculty Senate, Bellingham, 1984-85; conf. host Internat. Bryozoology Assn., 1986. Author: (with others) A Textbook of Entomology, 1982, Geology of Coal, 1984; editor (assoc.) Palaios, 1985-89; contbr. articles to profl. jours. Grantee NSF; recipient Western Wash. U. Outstanding Educator award, 1973, Western Wash. U. Research award, 1986. Mem. Australian Marine Scis. Assn., The Paleontol. Soc. (councillor 1984-86, treas. 1987-93), U.K. Marine Biol. Assn. (life), Microscopy Soc. of Am., Internat. Bryozoology Assn. (pres. 1992—). Office: Western Wash U Dept Biology Bellingham WA 98255-9060

ROSS, KATHLEEN ANNE, college president; b. Palo Alto, Calif., July 1, 1941; d. William Andrew and Mary Alberta (Wilburn) R. BA, Ft. Wright Coll., 1964; MA, Georgetown U., 1971; PhD, Claremont Grad. Sch., 1979; LLD (hon.) Alverno Coll. Milw., 1990, Dartmouth Coll., 1991, Seattle U., 1992; LHD (hon.) Whitworth Coll., 1992, LLD (hon.) Pomona Coll., 1993. Cert. tchr., Wash. Secondary tchr. Holy Names Acad., Spokane, Wash., 1964-70; dir. rsch. and planning Province Holy Names, Wash. State, 1972-73; v.p. acads. Ft. Wright Coll., Spokane, 1973-81; rsch. asst. to dean Claremont Grad. Sch., Calif., 1977-78; assoc. faculty mem. Harvard U., Cambridge, Mass., 1981; pres. Heritage Coll., Toppenish, Wash., 1981—; cons. Wash. State Holy Names Schs., 1971-73; coll. accrediting assn. evaluator N.W. Assn. Schs. and Colls., Seattle, 1975—; dir. Holy Names Coll., Oakland, Calif., 1979—; cons. Yakima Indian Nation, Toppenish, 1975—; speaker, cons. in field. Author: (with others) Multicultural Pre-School Curriculum, 1977, A Crucial Agenda: Improving Minority Student Success, 1989; Cultural Factors in Success of American Indian Students in Higher Education, 1978. Chmn. Internat. 5-Yr. Convocation of Sisters of Holy Names, Montreal, Que., Can., 1981; TV Talk show host Spokane Council of Chs., 1974-76. Recipient E.K. and Lillian F. Bishop Founds. Youth Leader of Yr. award, 1986, Golden Aztez award Washington Human Devel., 1989, Harold W. McGraw Edn. prize, 1989, John Carroll award Georgetown U., 1991, Holy Names medal Ft. Wright Coll., 1981, Pres. medal Eastern Washington U., 1994, Disting. Citizenship Alumna award Claremont Grad. Sch., 1986; named Yakima Herald Rep. Person of Yr. 1987, First Annual Leadership award Region VIII Coun. Advancement and Support Edn., 1993; numerous grants for projects in multicultural higher edn., 1974—. Mem. Nat. Assn. Ind. Colls. and Univs., Am. Assn. Higher Edn., Soc. Intercultural Edn., Tng. and Research, Sisters of Holy Names of Jesus and Mary. Roman Catholic. Office: Heritage Coll Office of Pres 3240 Fort Rd Toppenish WA 98948-9599

ROSS, LESA MOORE, quality assurance engineer; b. New Orleans, Jan. 25, 1959; d. William Frank and Carolyn West Moore; m. Mark Neal Ross, Nov. 30, 1985; children: Sarah Ann, Jacquelyne Caroline. BS in Engring., U. N.C., Charlotte, 1981; MBA in Quality and Reliability Mgmt., U. North Tex., 1991. Seismic qualification engr. Duke Power Co., Charlotte, N.C., 1981-82; quality assurance engr. Tex. Instruments Inc., Lewisville, Tex., 1982-91; compliance mgr. Am. Med. Electronics, Inc., 1992-93; owner Ross Quality Cons., 1993—. Recipient Nat. Sci. Found. Rsch. Grant, U. N.C., Charlotte, 1980. Mem. Am. Soc. Quality Control (cert. quality engr., quality auditor, reliability engr., cert. quality technician, sec. Dallas sect. 1994-95), Zeta Tau Alpha (pres. 1984-85). Home: 4925 Wolf Creek Trl Lewisville TX 75028-1955

ROSS, MADELYN ANN, newspaper editor; b. Pitts., June 26, 1949; d. Mario Charles and Rose Marie (Mangieri) R. B.A., Indiana U. of Pa., 1971; M.A., SUNY-Albany, 1972. Reporter Pitts. Press, 1972-78, asst. city editor, 1978-82, spl. assignment editor, 1982-83, mng. editor, 1983-93; mng. editor Pitts. Post-Gazette, 1993—; instr. Community Coll. Allegheny County, 1974-81; Pulitzer Prize juror, 1989, 90. Mem. Task Force Leadership Pitts., 1985-92; v.p. Old Newsboys Charity Fund; bd. dirs. Dapper Dan Charity. Mem. Associated Press Mng. Editors (bd. dirs.), Am. Soc. Newspaper Editors, Women's Press Club (bd. dirs.). Democrat. Roman Catholic. Office: Pitts Press 34 Blvd Of The Allies Pittsburgh PA 15222

ROSS, MARIE HEISE, retired librarian; b. N.Y.C., June 19, 1930; d. Henry Albert and Sophie Elizabeth (Stoever) Heise; m. Leon T. Stark, Aug. 9, 1952 (div. 1977); children: Antony A. Stark, Kathy T. Stark, Leslie Stark Wolff; m. David H. Ross, May 2, 1982; 1 stepchild, Randolph E. BA, CUNY, 1952, MLS, 1969. Cert. libr., N.Y. Sr. libr. Queens Borough Pub. Libr., Jamaica, N.Y., 1969-82, 83-85; libr., indexer H.W. Wilson Co., Bronx, N.Y., 1986-92, ret., 1992. Home: 14304 Stalgren Ct NE Albuquerque NM 87123

ROSS, MARY RIEPMA COWELL (MRS. JOHN O. ROSS), retired lawyer; b. Oklahoma City, Okla., Oct. 1, 1910; d. Sears F. and Elizabeth (Van Zwaluwenburg) Riepma; AB, Vassar Coll., 1932; LLB, Memphis State U., 1938; LLD, U. Nebr., 1973; m. Richard N. Cowell, Mar. 1, 1946 (dec. Jan. 1953); m. 2d, John O. Ross, Mar. 31, 1962 (dec. June 1966). Bar: Tenn. 1938, D.C. 1944, N.Y. 1947. Atty. U.S. Govt., Washington, 1940-44; pvt. practice Cromelin & Townsend, Washington, 1944-46. Royall, Koegel & Rogers and predecessors, N.Y.C., 1946-61; individual practice law, 1961-88; dir. 39 E. 79th St. Corp., 1966-73; dir. 795 Fifth Ave. Corp., 1977-90; mem. adv. com. N.Y. Commn. on Estates, 1965-67. Bd. dirs. Silver Cross Day Nursery, N.Y.C., 1963-70, Cunningham Dance Found., 1969-72, Central Park Community Fund, 1977-81, Mary Riepma Ross Film Theatre, 1988—; trustee U. Nebr. Found., 1966—, bd. dirs., 1974-79; hon. trustee Nebr. Art

Assn. Mem. Am. Bar Assn., N.Y. Women's Bar Assn. (pres. 1955-57, dir. 1957-63, 74-80, adv. coun. 1963—), Bar Assn. City N.Y. (surrogate cts. com. 1961-65, library com. 1965-78, com. on profl. responsibility 1972-75), Nat. Assn. Women Lawyers (assembly del. 1962-64, 73-74, UN observer 1965-67, v.p. 1967, chmn. 1971 ann. conv., distinguished service award 1973), Vassar Coll. Alumnae Assn., Phi Alpha Delta, Delta Gamma, Dinner Dances, Inc. (bd. govs. 1979-93). Address: 2 E 61st St Apt 2404 New York NY 10021-8402

ROSS, MOLLY OWINGS, gold and silversmith, jewelry designer, small business owner; b. Ft. Worth, Feb. 5, 1954; d. James Robertson and Lucy (Owings) R. BFA, Colo. State U., 1976; postgrad., U. Denver, 1978-79. Graphic designer Amber Sky Illustrators and Sta. KCNC TV-Channel 4, Denver, 1977-79; art dir. Mercy Med. Ctr., Denver, 1979-83, Molly Ross Design, Denver, 1983-84; co-owner Deltex Royalty Co., Inc., Colorado Springs, Colo., 1981—, LMA Royalties, Ltd., Colorado Springs, 1993—; art dir., account mgr. Schwing/Walsh Advt., Mktg. and Pub. Rels., Denver, 1984-87, prodn. mgr., 1987-88; jewelry designer Molly O. Ross, Gold and Silversmith, Denver, 1988—. Pres. Four Mile Hist. Park Vol. Bd., Denver 1985-87; bd. dirs. Four Mile Hist. Park Assn., 1985-86, Hist. Denver, Inc., 1986-87, Denver Emergency Housing Coalition, 1989-90; coun. mem. feminization of poverty critical needs area coun. Jr. League Denver, 1989-90, chmn. children in crisis/edn. critical needs area, 1990-91, project devel., 1991-92, co-chmn. Done in a Day Cmty. Project 75th Anniversary Celebration, 1991-93, mem. bd. dirs., 1993-94, v.p. cmty. projects, 1993-94; co-chmn. Project IMPACT, 1994-95; exec. v.p. external affairs Jr. League of Denver, 1995—; mem. bd. dirs. Denver Area Prep., 1994—. Named Vol. of Month (March), Jr. League Denver, 1990, Vol. of Yr., Four Mile Hist. Pk., 1988; recipient Gold Peak Mktg. award-team design Am. Mktg. Assn., 1986, Silver Peak Mktg. award-team design Am. Mktg. Assn., 1986, Gold Pick award-art dir. Pub. Rels. Soc. Am., 1980-81. Mem. Natural Resources Def. Coun., Physicians for Social Responsibility, Am. Farmland Trust, Nat. Trust for Hist. Preservation, Sierra Club, Environ. Def. Fund.

ROSS, NANCY KATHRYN, management consultant; b. July 21, 1945; d. Eugene Goldstein; m. Alan Jay Ross, Feb. 5, 1984; children: Julie Shapiro, Brian Ross, Brittany. BA, U. Wis., 1967. Head Start sch. tchr. Washington, 1970-73; owner Once is Not Enough, Columbia, Md., 1976-81; cons., mgr. Geneological Pub. Co., Balt., 1980-81; image cons. Balt., 1981-85; mgmt. cons. Charlie Smith Assocs., 1985-87; ptnr. Ross & Ross, Rockville, Md., 1987—; leader over 2000 people in pub. programs in cmty. and personal effectiveness. Vol. Landmark Edn., Alexandria, Va., 1978-94, Hands Across Am., Alexandria, Hunger Project, Alexandria, Holiday Project, Alexandria, 1978-94. Jewish. Home and Office: 9501 Mary Knoll Dr Rockville MD 20850

ROSS, NELL TRIPLETT, financial consultant, educator, corporate secretary; b. Winterville, Miss., Feb. 14, 1922; d. Ethel Earl and Myrtie (Harrison) Triplett; m. William Dee Ross, Jr., July 25, 1944; 1 child, William Dee III. BA, Millsaps Coll., 1942. Tchr., Consol. Sch. of Chatham (Miss.), 1942-43, Glen Allan (Miss.) Consol. Sch., 1943-46; sec. econs. dept. Duke U., Durham, N.C., 1946; tchr. Durham High Sch., 1947, E.K. Powe Sch., Durham, 1947-48, Lakewood Elem. Sch., Durham, 1948-49; with purchasing dept. La. State U., Baton Rouge, 1949-50; enrollment officer La. Hosp. Service, Inc., Baton Rouge, 1950-51; owner Mentone Plantation, Erwin and Chatham, Miss., 1961—; owner, dir., v.p., corp. sec. Fin. Cons. Svcs., Inc., 1970—. Methodist. Clubs: Baton Rouge Country, Camelot. Home: 2738 Mcconnell Dr Baton Rouge LA 70809-1113 also: 2763 E Bocage Ct Baton Rouge LA 70809-1143

ROSS, PATTI JAYNE, obstetrics and gynecology educator; b. Nov. 17, 1946; d. James J. and Mary N. Ross; B.S., DePauw U., 1968; M.D., Tulane, U., 1972; m. Allan Robert Katz, May 23, 1976. Asst. prof. U. Tex. Med. Sch., Houston, 1976-82, assoc. prof., 1982—, dir. adolescent ob-gyn., 1976—, also dir. phys. diagnosis, dir. devel. dept. ob-gyn.; speaker in field. Bd. dirs. Am. Diabetes Assn., 1982—; mem. Rape Coun. Diplomate Am. Bd. Ob-Gyn. Mem. Tex. Med. Assn., Harris County Med. Soc., Houston Ob-Gyn. Soc., Assn. Profs. Ob-Gyn., Soc. Adolescent Medicine, AAAS, Am. Women's Med. Assn., Orgn. Women in Sci., Sigma Xi. Roman Catholic. Clubs: River Oak Breakfast, Profl. Women Execs. Contbr. articles to profl. jours. Office: 6431 Fannin St Houston TX 77030

ROSS, RHODA, artist; b. Boston, Dec. 24, 1941. Student, Carnegie Mellon U., 1960-62; BFA, RISD, 1964; MFA, Yale U., 1966. tchr. NYU, 1994—, Chautauqua (N.Y.) Sch. Art, 1991; participant Art in Embassies Program Dept of State, Havana, Cuba, 1991-93. One-woman shows include Frick Gallery, Belfast, Maine, Yale U., New Haven, Convent of the Sacred Heart, Mcpl. Art Soc., L.I. U., Emma Willard Sch. Dietal Gallery, Marymount Manhattan Coll., N.Y.C., N.Y.C. Landmarks Preservation Commns. 25th Silver Anniversary, numerous others; permanent collections include The White House, Gracie Mansion, N.Y.C., The Juilliard Sch., N.Y.C., Bankers Trust, Mus. City of N.Y., Chem. Bank Nat. Hqrs., Lehman Coll., Waldorf Astoria Hotel, N.Y.C., Russian Tea Rm., Rose Assocs., numerous other pvt. and public collections. Treas. R.I. Sch. Design Alumni Exec. com., 1986-90. Fellow Va. Ctr. for Creative Arts. Mem. RISD Alumni Assn. (treas. 1986, mem. alumni exec. com.), Phi Tau Gamma. Home and Studio: 473 W End Ave New York NY 10024-4934

ROSS, ROBINETTE DAVIS, publisher; b. London, May 16, 1952; d. Raymond Lawrence and Pearl A. (Robinette) D.; m. William Bradford Ross III, Mar. 16, 1979; children: Nellie Tayloe, William Bradford IV. Student, Am. U., 1977-78. Asst. to editor The Chronicle of Higher Edn., Washington, 1978, advt. mgr., 1978-82, advt. dir., 1986-94, assoc. pub., 1988-94; assoc. pub. The Chronicle of Philanthropy, 1988-94; publ. The Chronicle of Higher Edn., Washington, 1994—; pub. The Chronicle of Philanthropy, Washington, 1994—. Mem. Newspaper Assn. Am., Am. News Women's Club, City Tavern Club. Episcopalian. Home: 3908 Virgilia St Chevy Chase MD 20815-5026 Office: The Chronicle of Higher Edn 1255 23rd St NW Washington DC 20037-1125

ROSS, SALLY PRICE, artist, mural painter; b. Cleve., Oct. 25, 1949; d. Philip E. and Mimi (Einhorn) Price; m. Howard D. Ross, Mar. 3, 1979; children: Sasha, Emily. BFA, Kent State U., 1971; MA, U. Iowa, 1974, MFA, 1975; student, Art Students League, N.Y.C., 1976-78. art cons. Art Options, Cleve., 1990—; 1st and only woman artist to paint murals in the U.S. Capital/Ho. of Reps. corridors, 1978-79. Art exhbns. include Cain Park Art Gallery, Cleve., 1967, Jewish Cmty. Ctr. Cleve., 1967, 86, Canton (Ohio) Art Inst., 1969, Studio Theatre, Iowa City, 1973; designed and executed murals Montefiore Nursing Home, Cleve. Edwin Abbey scholar, 1975-77, Fresco scholar Skowhegan Sch. Painting and Sculpture, 1977. Home: 25 Mill Creek Ln Chagrin Falls OH 44022

ROSS, SHIRLEY MAE, industrial psychologist; b. St. Louis, Dec. 12, 1949; d. Jackson Jerry and Beatrice (Ward) Claunch; m. Douglas E. Ross, Apr. 25, 1970 (div. 1982); 1 child, Shannon Maureen; m. John C. Lovell, Apr. 4, 1985. BA, U. Mo., St. Louis, 1975; MPhil, George Washington U., 1988, PhD, 1990. Lic. psychologist, Va. Command intelligence briefer, maj. Hdqs. Pacific Air Force, Honlulu, 1982-83, exec. officer to chief of intelligence, 1983-85; asst. prof. dept. behavioral scis. USAF Acad., Colorado Springs, 1987-90; chief survey policy, Air Force rep. for joint testing Hdqs. Air Force, The Pentagon, 1990-92; internal cons. Anheuser Busch Cos., St. Louis, 1993-94, human resources mgr., 1994—; adj. lectr., grad. instr. Grad. Sch. Arts & Scis. George Washington U., Washington, 1991-92. Contbr. articles to profl. jours. Designer, deliverer tng. program Literacy Vols. of Am., Colorado Springs, 1990. Named Disting. Grad. officer Tng. Sch. USAF, 1980; grantee F.J. Seiler Labs., 1988, 89. Mem. APA, Soc. for Indsl./Orgnl. Psychology, Gateway Indsl./Orgnl. Psychologists, Pers. Testing Coun. Office: Anheuser-Busch Cos One Busch Pl 202-7 Saint Louis MO 63118-1852

ROSS, SHIRLEY MARIE, educational program director; b. Hammond, Ind., Nov. 28, 1952; d. W. Orville and Velma Marie (Owens) Gilliam; m. Donald L. Ross, Dec. 23, 1977; 1 child, James Gilliam. BA in English, Ind. U., 1975; MS in Secondary Edn., Purdue U., 1978. Cert. tchr. reading, gifted and talented students; cert. in adminstrn. Tchr. of English Lake Ctrl. Sch. Corp., St. John, Ind., 1975-78; tchr. of English Sch. City of Mishawaka, Ind., 1978-88, dir. gifted and talented programs, 1988—; mem. Effective Schs. Improvement Team, Mishawaka, 1987—, Gifted/Talented Coun., South Bend, Ind., 1991—; chairperson Sch. Partnership Com., Mishawaka, 1990-92; cons. Time Out for Parents, Mishawaka, 1994. Author: (program brochures) DEEP, PAAL, FOCUS, 1992—, (corp. brochure) Children First, 1993—; editor (newsletter) Gifted/Talented Currents, 1989—, (newsletters) CLASS Notes and CLASS Views, 1992—. Legis. host Ind. U., Bloomington, 1987—; active Mishawaka Rep. Women, 1988—; group leader Congress on Ethics, Indpls., 1990; scholarship chairperson Panhellenic Assn., South Bend/Mishawaka, 1991—. Recipient Outstanding Teaching award U. Chgo., 1989, letter of commendation Advance Coll. Project, 1990; named Significant Tchr., Anderson U., 1990; named for Excellence and Achievement, Ind. Pub. Rels. Assn., 1992, 93. Mem. ASCD, Nat. Assn. Gifted Children, Ind. Assn. for Gifted, Ind. U. Alumni Assn. (mem. exec. coun. 1995—), Hoosiers for Higher Edn., Delta Kappa Gamma. Home: 420 Miami Club Dr Mishawaka IN 46544 Office: Sch City of Mishawaka 1402 S Main St Mishawaka IN 46544

ROSS, SUE, entrepreneur, author; b. Chgo., Feb. 2, 1948; d. Irving and Rose (Stein) R. BA in Speech, Western Mich. U., 1971; postgrad., Northwestern U., Chgo. State U., U. Ill., 1971-75. Dir. youth employment Ill. Youth Svcs. Bur., Maywood, Ill., 1978-79; exec. dir. Edn. Resource Ctr., Chgo., 1979-82; asst. dir. devel. Art Inst. Chgo., 1982-83, mgr. govt. affairs, 1983-84, dir. govt. affairs, 1984-85; v.p. devel. Spertus Coll. Judaica, Chgo., 1985-90; mgmt. and fundraising counsel Sue Ross Enterprises, San Francisco, 1990—; founder, pres. Kid Angels Internat., San Francisco, 1993-94; lectr. Sch. Art Inst., Chgo., 1982-85, Episcopalian Archdiocese, Chgo., 1984, Nat. Soc. Fund Raising Execs. and Donor's Forum, Chgo., 1987; instr. DePaul U. Sch. for New Learning, 1987-88, Columbia Coll., Chgo., 1980-91. Resident counsel for devel. The Joffrey Ballet, 1990-91; adv. panelist Chgo. Office Fine Arts, 1981-82; mem. adv. coun. Greater Chgo. Food Depository, 1984-85; exec. com. Chgo. Coalition Arts in Edn., 1981-82; mem. info. svcs. com. Donors' Forum Chgo., 1986-88, mem. internationally renowned Gospel Choir of Glide Meml., 1991-93, San Francisco City Chorus, 1994—; active Congregation Sherith Israel, San Francisco Angel Club, 1994—, Angel Collector's Club of Am., 1994—, Angels of World, 1994—. Mem. Nat. Soc. Fund Raising Execs. (mem. svcs. com. Golden Gate chpt. 1993). Democrat. Jewish. Avocations: community service, singing. Home and Office: 1807 Octavia St San Francisco CA 94109-4328

ROSS, VONIA PEARL, insurance agent, small business owner; b. Taylorville, Ill., Dec. 4, 1942; d. Alvin Clyde and Lois Eva (Weller) Brown; m. Wyatt Gene Ross, Nov. 11, 1962 (Div. Nov. 1986); children: Craig Allen Ross, Cayle Allen Ross. Student, So. Ill. U., 1962-64, Palomar Coll., 1986-88, San Diego State U., 1988-90. Real estate agt. Joe Foster Agy., Collinsville, Ill., 1964-69; office mgr. real estate Bank of St. Louis, 1969-73; real estate agt. Palmer-Stelman, San Diego, 1986-89; office mgr. real estate McMillin Realty, San Diego, 1989-90; mgr., ins. agt. Calif. Plus Ins., San Diego, 1990-93; prin. Vonia Ross Ins. Agy., 1993—, Bernardo Flooring, 1993—; mem. Calif. Assn. Real Estate, Sacramento, 1986—, San Diego Bd. Realtors, 1986—, Health Underwriters, 1991—. Mem. adv. com. Rancho Bernardo Libr. Campaign, 1994—; active NOW, San Diego, 1988; mem. activist Barbara Boxer Campaign, San Diego, 1992, Susan Golding Campaign, San Diego, 1992, Barbara Warden Campaign for San Diego City Councilwoman. Recipient Ill. State Assembly scholarship, 1962. Mem. Soroptimist Rancho Bernardo (pres. 1993-94), Rancho Bernardo C. of C. (v.p. bd. dirs. 1993—). Methodist. Home: 18284 Fernando Way San Diego CA 92128-1213

ROSS, WENDY CLUCAS, newspaper editor, journalist; b. Balt., Apr. 15, 1942; d. Charles Max and Jean (Talbot) Clucas; m. David N. Ross, Sept. 5, 1964 (div. 1979). BA, Bradley U., 1964. Women's editor DeKalb (Ill.) Daily Chronicle, 1968-69; reporter Chgo. Tribune, 1969-70; copy editor, mag. editor Mpls. Tribune, 1970-72; copy editor Peoria (Ill.) Jour. Star, 1973-75, Miami (Fla.) Herald, 1975-77; asst. news editor Washington Post, 1977-83, dep. news editor, 1983-87, news editor, 1987-93; asst. mng. editor news desk, 1993—. Recipient award of excellence Soc. Newspaper Design, 1985, 87-91, Disting. Alumnae award Bradley U. Centurion Soc., 1994; Nieman fellow Harvard U., 1983-84. Office: The Washington Post 1150 15th St NW Washington DC 20071-0002

ROSSBACHER, LISA ANN, dean, geology educator, writer; b. Fredericksburg, Va., Oct. 10, 1952; d. Richard Irwin and Jean Mary (Dearing) R.; m. Dallas D. Rhodes, Aug. 4, 1978. BS, Dickinson Coll., 1975; MA, SUNY, Binghamton, 1978, Princeton U., 1979; PhD, Princeton U., 1983. Cons. Republic Geothermal, Santa Fe Springs, Calif., 1979-81; asst. prof. geology Whittier (Calif.) Coll., 1982-84; asst. prof. geology Calif. State Poly. U., Pomona, 1984-86, assoc. prof. geol. sci., 1986-91, assoc. v.p. acad. affairs, 1987-93, prof. geol. sci., 1991-95; v.p. acad. affairs, dean faculty Whittier (Calif.) Coll., 1993-95; dean of coll. Dickinson Coll., Carlisle, Pa., 1995—; vis. researcher U. Uppsala, Sweden, 1984. Author: Career Opportunities in Geology and the Earth Sciences, 1983, Recent Revolutions in Geology, 1986; (with Rex Buchanan) Geomedia, 1988; columnist Geotimes, 1988—; contbr. articles to profl. jours. Recipient scholarship Ministry Edn. of Finland, Helsinki, 1984; grantee NASA, 1983-94. Mem. AAAS (geol. nominating com. 1984-87), Geol. Soc. Am., Coun. on Undergrad. Rsch., 1990—, Sigma Xi (grantee 1976). Office: Whittier Coll V P Academic Affairs Whittier CA 90608

ROSS-BLUMER, BETTIE LOUISE, musician, composer, songwriter; b. L.A., May 12, 1948; d. Jack Wayland Ross and Margaret Cregar (Stryker) McCartney; m. Franklin P. Blumer; children: Noelle Bezart Simeon, Margaux Andrea Simeon; stepchildren: Leslie Syniec, Omer Theodore Simeon III, Eric Albert Simeon. Student, Trinity Coll., London, L.A., 1953-60, Calif. State U., Northridge, 1966-68, 69-71, Jamie Faunt Sch. Creative Music, 1979-81, 86-87; studies with Dr. Philip Springer, Eddy L. Manson, L.A., 1973-74; studies with Mario Feninger, 1990. Keyboardist various bands, musicals, and plays; tchr. piano, pipe organ, organ, synthesizers, music theory; accompanist various sch. orchestras, choral groups; keyboardist Melissa Manchester U.S. Tour, 1980, Bellamy Bros. U.S. Tour, 1976; conductor Bellamy Bros. Fifth Ann. Tokyo Music Festival, 1976; pipe organist various So. Calif. chs., 1963—; organist Encino (Calif.) Cmty. Ch., 1990-94, Pacific Palisades Cmty. United Meth. Ch., Woodland Hills, Calif., 1994-95, Our Lady of Grace, Encino, 1995—. Composed, played, recorded, performed music for Vogue 2000, 1986-87, (films) Have a Banana, 1985, Galaxy Express 999, 1985, Closing Night, 1984, (plays) Neon (A Vaudeville of Obsession), 1983, The Melville Boys, 1988; composed original score for In Search of Fellini, 1992, for reading of classic fiction works by L. Ron Hubbard, 1993-94; commd. to compose music for Fanfare for Celebrity Ctr. Grand Opening Anniversary, 1993; music dir. John Travolta's Christmas Stories with Isaac Hayes, Edgar Winter, Kelly Preston, Nancy Cartwright, Juliette Lewis, 1993, 94; music dir. charities, shows with Raven Kane, 1994—. Vol. 1st and 2nd ann. Baby Golf Classic for newborn intensive care unit Cedars-Sinai Med. Ctr., L.A., 1984, 85. Named Donna Delle Fave Meml. scholar, 1970-71; recipient Frederick Chopin Piano award, 1966, Bank of Am. Music award, 1966, Grand Prize and 3 awards Music City Song Festival, 1988. Mem. ASCAP, NARAS, Songwriters and Composers Assn. (pres. 1986-91), Am. Guild Organists, Musicians Union, Nat. Acad. Songwriters, L.A. Women in Music (bd. dirs. 1991-93). Democrat.

ROSSEL, CAROL ELAINE LEENERTS, nursing educator and consultant in informatics and statistical analysis; b. Golden, Ill., July 2, 1936; d. Clarence Frederick and Lillian Louise Maxine (Aden) Leenerts; m. Allan John Rossel, Sept. 13, 1959; children: Janet Louise, Joyce Linda. BS in Nursing, Washington U., St. Louis, 1960; MS in Nursing, U. Ill., Chgo., 1975; EdD in Adult Continuing Edn., No. Ill. U., 1984; postgrad., Lewis U., 1994—. With Barnes Hosp., St. Louis, 1957-58; supr. Phelps Hosp., Macomb, Ill., 1958-59; instr. DePaul Hosp. Sch. Nursing, St. Louis, 1960, Hines (Ill.) VA Hosp., 1961-63; supr. Riveredge Hosp., Forest Park, Ill., 1963-65; ICU/CCU nurse MacNeal Hosp., Berwyn, Ill., 1971-73; nursing faculty Triton Community Coll., River Grove, Ill., 1975-84; assoc. prof. nursing Lewis U., Romeoville, Ill., 1985-88, prof., coord. learning resources and data mgmt., 1988—; cons. in field. Chairwoman High Sch. Caucus Nominating Bd., Riverside, Ill., 1985, adviser, 1987; mem. Women's Morning Forum, Riverside, 1988; blood drive interviewer Presby. Ch., Riverside, 1980—. USPHS grantee, 1957-60; rsch. grantee U. Md., 1986, div. Nursing Health and Human Svcs., 1988; scholar Nurse Scholar Program, Altlanta, 1991. Mem. Am. Nursing Assn. (cert., mem. council on computers 1987 , Ill. Nurses Assn. (chairwoman rsch. com. dist. 19, mem. CE rev. panel, mem. interdivisional council on nursing diagnosis), North Am. Nursing Diagnosis Assn., AAUW (sec. 1985-86), Swim and Tennis Club, Sigma Theta Tau, Kappa Delta Pi. Republican. Presbyterian. Home: 375 Bartram Rd Riverside IL 60546-1826 Office: Lewis U Rte 53 Romeoville IL 60441

ROSSELLINI, ISABELLA, actress, model; b. Rome, June 18, 1952; d. Roberto Rossellini and Ingrid Bergman; m. Martin Scorsese, Sept. 1979 (div. Nov. 1982); m. Jonathan Wiedemann (div.); 1 child, Elettra Ingrid. Student, Finch Coll., 1972, New Sch. for Social Research, N.Y.C. Became model for Lancôme, 1982. Appeared in films A Matter of Time, 1976, Il Pap'occhio, 1980, The Meadow, 1982, White Nights, 1985, Blue Velvet, 1986, Siesta, 1987, Red Riding Hood, 1987, Tough Guys Don't Dance, 1987, Zelly and Me, 1988, Cousins, 1989, Wild at Heart, 1990, Les Dames Galantes, 1990, Death Becomes Her, 1992, The Pickle, 1992, Fearless, 1993, Wyatt Earp, 1994, The Innocent, 1994, Immortal Beloved, 1994; TV films: The Last Elephant, 1990, Lies of the Twins, 1991. also: Ford Modeling Agency 344 E 59th St New York NY 10022-1570*

ROSSER, ANDREA JEANETTE, naval officer; b. Flint, Mich., Aug. 17, 1963; d. Averon James and Ellen Ruth (Robison) R. BA, U. Mich., 1985. Commd. ensign USN, 1989, advanced through grades to lt.; quality assurance officer USN, Barbers Pt., Hawaii, 1989-90, aircraft divsn. officer, 1990-91, material control officer, 1991-92, maintenance/material control officer, 1992-93, maintenance adminstrn./tng. officer, 1993-94, asst. editor, 1994—. Decorated Navy Achievement medal (3). Mem. Gamma Phi Beta Alumnae (v.p. Hawaii chpt. 1990).

ROSSER, ANNETTA HAMILTON, composer; b. Jasper, Fla., Aug. 28, 1913; d. Carlos Calvin and Jermai Reuben (Gilbert) Hamilton; m. John Barkley Rosser, Sept. 7, 1935 (dec. Sept. 1989); children: Edwenna Merryday, John Barkley Jr. BM, Fla. State U., 1932. Cert. tchr., Fla. Tchr. music Kirby-Smith Jr. High Sch., Jacksonville, Fla., 1932-35; 1st violinist Santa Monica (Calif.) Symphony, 1949-50; concertmaster Ithaca (N.Y.) Chamber Orch., 1948-56; concertmaster Cornell Univ. Orch., Ithaca, 1948-56, soloist, 1957; 1st violinist Princeton (N.J.) Symphony, 1959-61; concertmaster Madison (Wis.) Symphony Orch., 1963-66, 1st violinist, 1967-82. Composer of over 100 vocal and instrumental compositions including Meditations on Cross, song cycle for 2 voices, flute and piano, 1976, An Offering of Song, book of 48 songs, 1977, Songs of a Nomad Flute, song cycle for soprano, flute and piano, 1978, Six Songs of the T'ang Dynasty for soprano and violin, 1983, Nocturne for violin and piano, 1989, Trio for flute, violin and piano, 1991, Scherzo for flute ensemble, 1991. Bd. dirs. Madison Opera Guild, 1972-86, Madison Civic Music Assn., 1983-85; past pres. Madison Symphony Orch. League, Ithaca Federated Music Club, Ithaca Composers Club; trustee Madison Art Ctr., 1979-83, Madison Civics Club, 1976-79, Madison Woman of Distinction, 1980. Recipient Sr. Svc. award Rotary Club, 1994. Mem. AAUW, Univ. League, Univ. League Bird Study Group, Madison Club, Madison Federated Music Club, PEO, Phi Kappa Phi, Pi Kappa Lambda, Sigma Alpha Iota. Republican. Presbyterian. Home: 4209 Manitou Way Madison WI 53711-3703

ROSSER, GWENDOLYN DORIS, nurse, educator; b. Allentown, Pa., Mar. 19, 1944; d. David Evan and Doris Gwendolyn (Berresford) R. Student, Pa. State U., 1962-63; BS, Pa. Coll., 1970; MA, Ea. Bapt. Theol. Sem., 1972; MS, U. Scranton, 1985. RN, Pa.; cert. instr. CPR. Nurse Allentown (Pa.) Hosp., 1965—; instr. Allentown Hosp. Sch. Nursing, 1972-88, Allentown Hosp. Sch. Nursing-Lehigh Valley Hosp. Ctr., 1987-92; program coord. Lehigh Valley Hosp. (formerly Lehigh Valley Hosp. Ctr.), Allentown, 1992—. Supt. Sunday sch. 1st Bapt. Ch., Allentown, 1978—, chair Christian edn. com., 1980—. Mem. ASTD, Am. Heart Assn. (CPR instr.), Devel. Dimensions Internat. (instr.), Delta Epsilon Chi. Republican. Baptist. Office: Lehigh Valley Hosp 17th And Chew St Allentown PA 18102

ROSSER, RHONDA LANAE, psychotherapist; b. Champaign, Ill., Aug. 29, 1953; d. Neill Albert and Grace Lee (Byers) R.; (div. June 1, 1993); children: Anthony Neill Williams, Joseph Neill Jackson Hogan. BS in Psychology, Guilford Coll., 1975; MEd in Edn., U. N.C., Greensboro, 1979, PhD in Counseling, 1991. Instr. U. N.C., Greensboro, 1985-88; dir. Montagnard Program Luth. Famnily Svcs., Greensboro, 1985-88; psychotherapist pvt. practice, Greensboro, 1989—. Contbr. articles to profl. jours. Recipient Presdl. citation U.S. Govt., 1987. Mem. Am. Counseling Assn. (Outstanding Rsch. award 1991), Chi Sigma Iota. Democrat. Roman Catholic. Home and Office: 2318 W Cornwallis Dr Greensboro NC 27408-6802

ROSSET, LISA KRUG, editor; b. N.Y.C., Nov. 11, 1952; d. George William and Rita (Earle) Krug; m. Barney Rosset, Nov. 5, 1980 (div. Dec. 1990); 1 child, Chantal. B.A. magna cum laude, Smith Coll., 1974; M.A., Columbia U., 1976. Editor Latin Am. Series, N.Y.C., 1976-86; gen. editor Grove Press, N.Y.C., 1976-86; mng. editor Aperture, N.Y.C., 1987-90; pvt. practice N.Y.C., 1990—. Author: James Baldwin, 1989, Thurgood Marshall, 1993. Mem. Phi Beta Kappa. Office: 106 Perry St New York NY 10014

ROSSI, CYNTHIA ANN, advertising and public relations executive; b. Latrobe, Pa., Jan. 2, 1954; d. Gerald T. and Edith Mary (Condi) R. BA cum laude, Washington and Jefferson Coll., 1976. Coord. pub. rels. Washington (Pa.) Sch. Dist., 1976-77; account exec. Washington (Pa.) Broadcasting Co., 1978-79; dir. advt. pub. rels. Reed and Cameron Hardware, Inc., Washington, Pa., 1979-80; prin. C.A. Rossi and Assocs., Washington, Pa., 1980—; lectr. mktg. and advt. various community and bus. groups, 1980—. Editor The Marginal Rev., 1978-80; author various poems, 1975-81; contbr. articles to profl jours. Trustee Washington and Jefferson Coll., 1991—, Washington County Found., 1993—; bd. dirs. Washington and Jefferson Coll. Aux., 1986—, v.p., 1989, co-pres., 1990; active many other community svcs.; active Washington and Jefferson Devel. Coun., 1986-91, exec. com., 1990-91; life mem. Friends of Citizens Libr.; founder, coord. People United to Save Homes, 1994—. Recipient numerous graphic design awards; named Bus. Woman of Yr., Bus. & Profl. Women's Club, 1993. Mem. AAUW, Am. Quarter Horse Assn., Greater Pitts. MG Club. Home and Office: 99 Zediker Station Rd Washington PA 15301

ROSSING, CATHERINE BARRETT SCHWAB, dental hygienist; b. San Francisco, Apr. 8, 1932; d. Richard James and Mary Ann (McAuliff) and Richard Thomas Barrett; m. Donald Theodore Schwab, Aug. 8, 1954 (div. 1965); 1 child, Carla Diane; m. Alan Robert Rossing, Mar. 31, 1989. AA, U. Calif., Berkeley, 1952, BS, 1954; MPA, Calif. State U., 1983. Registered dental hygienist, Calif. Preventive specialist Dr. Thomas Evans Office, Anaheim, Calif., 1968-72, 90; mem. T.E.A.M. program U. So. Calif., L.A., 1972-73; staff hygienist Dr. Joseph Berger Dental Office, Fountain Valley, Calif., 1974-88; pub. Rossing Enterprises, Pebble Beach, Calif., 1991—; co-founder Preventive Dental Care, L.A., 1985-90; co-owner Schwab/Flora Meeting Organizers, Anaheim, 1981-90. Mem. Calif. Dental Hygienists' Assn. (editor jour. 1974-76, 81-84, 89—, Golden Pen award 1976), Am. Dental Hygienists' Assn. (trustee 1977-81, Recognition award 1981). Home: 1060 The Old Drive Pebble Beach CA 93953

ROSSITER, PHYLLIS J., author; b. Carthage, Mo., Dec. 22, 1938; d. Howard Levi and Pauline (Crawford) Anderson; m. Dennis L. Rossiter, Mar. 30, 1968 (dec. Apr. 1992); 1 child, Eric Shawn. Head libr. Trs. Regional Libr. Br., Odessa, Mo., 1979-83; editor, gen. mgr. Ozark County Times Newspaper, Gainesville, Mo., 1989; freelance writer, tchr., editor, lectr., photographer. Author: On the Scent of Danger, 1989, Moxie, 1990, A Living History of the Ozarks, 1992; contbr. articles to profl. jours., periodicals, short story anthologies. Mem. Soc. Children's Book Writers, Authors Guild, Western Writers of Am., Mo. Writers Guild (Best Column 1989, Best Book 1991, Best Major Work 1992), Ozark Writers League (v.p. 1990, Dan Saults award 1988, 93), OzarksWatch Soc. Home: 1075 S Raleigh St Denver CO 80219

ROSS-JACOBS, RUTH ANN, investment company executive, retired golf and country club executive; b. Milw., Mar. 10, 1934; d. Arthur Theodore and

Mary Marilyn (Digert) Kamman; m. Warren Ross, Aug. 9, 1957 (div. Sept. 1972); 1 child, Michael Edward; m. Albert Jacobs, June 28, 1973 (dec. Apr. 1978). BS, U. Miami, Coral Gables, Fla., 1958; MS, Wayne State U., 1961; postgrad. U. Wis., 1967-69. R.N., Fla., Wis., Mich. Staff nurse Lafayette Clinic, Detroit, 1958-59; instr. Milw. Inst. Tech., 1962-67; dir. inservice edn. St. Mary's Hosp., Milw., 1963-69; cons. Hearthside Rehab., Milw., 1968-69; owner Peddler Stores, Milw., 1969-72; pres. Jacobs & Densmore Ltd., Toronto, Ont., Can., 1978-83; v.p. Vaughn Ltd., Toronto, 1978-87; pres. Glen Road Leasing Ltd., Toronto, 1978-79, Evnor Apts. Ltd., Toronto, 1978-79, Norman Lathing Ltd., Toronto, 1978-79, Allied Capital Enterprises, Inc., 1989—; v.p. Elgin Mills Investments Ltd., Toronto, 1978-80. Author: Inservice Education, 1967; Nursing Procedures, 1969. Pres. PTO, Boca Raton, Fla., 1973-76; mem. Republican Nat. Com., Washington, 1984—; mem. Inner Circle, Washington, 1984—, Security and Intelligence Found., 1986—, Second Amendment Found., Washington, 1989—, Presdl. Roundtable, Washington, 1987—, Presdl. Task Force, Washington, 1986—, U.S. Com. for Battle of Normandy, Washington, 1987—, Heritage Found., 1990—, The Pres.'s Club. Recipient stipend NIH, Bethesda, Md., 1959. Mem. Pres. Club USO, Wayne State Univ. Deans Club, Internat. Platform Assn., NRA, Madisons Eagles, Boca Raton Club, Sigma Theta Tau. Republican. Lutheran. Avocations: real estate investments, travel, charity. Home: Penthouse K 2000 S Ocean Blvd Boca Raton FL 33432

ROSSMAN, JANET KAY, architectural interior designer; b. Lansing, Mich., Feb. 13, 1954; d. Elmer Chris and Jean Elizabeth (Schell) R.; m. Farzad Moazed; children: Alexander, Christina. BA with High Honors, Mich. State U., 1976. Designer Tilton & Lewis Assocs., Inc., Chgo., 1977-79, Swanke Hayden Connell & Ptnrs., N.Y.C., 1979-81, Bonsignore Brignati & Mazzotta Architects, N.Y.C., 1982-84; dir. design, assoc. SPGA Group, Inc., N.Y.C., 1984—; instr. Design Edn. Ctr., Lansing, 1975-76. Fellow Mus. Modern Art, N.Y.C., 1977—. Mem. Am. Soc. of Interior Designers (chair. 1973-76, editor Collage 1973-76), Inst. Bus. Designers, Nat. Assn. for Female Execs., Omicron Nu. Republican. Club: Atrium, Landmark. Home: 367 W Hill Rd Stamford CT 06902

ROSSMAN, TOBY GALE, genetic toxicology educator, researcher; b. Weehawken, N.J., June 3, 1942; d. Norman N. and Sylvia Betty (May) Natowitz; m. Neil I. Rossman, Sept. 16, 1962 (div. Sept. 1980); m. Gordon Rauer, Aug. 19, 1990. AB, NYU, 1964, PhD, 1968; postgrad., Brandeis U., 1964-65. Instr. Polytech. Inst. of N.Y., N.Y.C., 1968-69; postdoctoral dept. pathology NYU, N.Y.C., 1969-71; from asst. to assoc. prof. Inst. for Environ. Medicine Nelson Inst. of Environ. Medicine, N.Y.C., 1974-85; prof. Inst. for Environ. Medicine, 1985—. Mem. editorial bd. Molecular Toxicology, 1989-91, Teratogenesis, Carcinogenesis, Mutagenesis, 1990-91, Environmental and Molecular Mutagenesis, 1994—, Mutation Research, 1994—; contbr. numerous articles to profl. jours. EPA grantee, NIH grantee. Mem. AAAS, Assn. for Women in Sci., Am. Assn. for Cancer Rsch., Am. Soc. for Microbiology, Environ. Mutagen Soc. (councilor 1990-93). Office: NYU Inst Environ Medicine Long Meadow Rd Tuxedo Park NY 10987

ROSSMAN-MCKINNEY, KELLY, public relations counselor; b. Aberdeen, Wash., Oct. 21, 1954; d. Charles Kirk and Melva Marie (Anderson) Hanna; m. Roger Owen Rossman, Sept. 4, 1976 (div. 1981); 1 child, Alexander Charles; m. Kevin Anders McKinney, Aug. 17, 1991; 1 child, Connor Max. BA in Radio/TV/Film Psychology, Wayne State U., 1977; AA, Macomb County C.C., 1975. Prodn. asst. Sta. WKBD and WWJ-TV, Detroit, 1976-78; legis. asst. Mich. Ho. of Reps. and Senate, Lansing, 1979-82; pub. affairs officer Mich. Twp. Assn., Lansing, 1982; press sec. Mich. Youth Corps, Lansing, 1983, dir., 1984; specialist pub. affairs Mich. Dept. Commerce, Lansing, 1983; dir. Office Mich. Products Dept. Commerce, Lansing, 1984-86; outreach advisor Gov.'s office State of Mich., Lansing, 1986-88; CEO K. Rossman Comm., Lansing, 1988—. Bd. dirs. Mich. Children, Lansing, 1993. Recipient awards PACE, 1990, 91, 92, 93, named Pace Maker of Yr., 1993. Mem. Pub. Rels. Soc. Am. (accredited), Pub. Rels. Student Soc. Am. (profl. advisor), Lansing Regional C. of C., Small Bus. Assn. Mich., Pub. Rels. Soc. Am. Counselors Acad., Rotary Club Lansing (bd. dirs. 1989—). Home: 6950 Eaton Hwy Lansing MI 48906-9006 Office: K Rossman Comm Inc dba Rossman Martin & Assocs 119 Pere Marquette Dr Lansing MI 48912-1270

ROSSNER, JUDITH, novelist; b. N.Y.C., Mar. 31, 1935; d. Joseph George and Dorothy (Shapiro) Perelman; m. Robert Rossner (div.); children: Jean, Daniel; m. Mort Persky (div.). Student, City Coll. N.Y., 1952-55. Author: novels To the Precipice, 1966, Nine Months in the Life of an Old Maid, 1969, Any Minute I Can Split, 1972, Looking for Mr. Goodbar, 1975, Attachments, 1977, Emmeline, 1980, August, 1983, His Little Women, 1990, Olivia, or the Weight of the Past, 1994; also short stories. Address: care Wendy Weil Agency 232 Madison Ave New York NY 10016

ROSSO, CHRISTINE HEHMEYER, lawyer; b. N.Y.C., Apr. 7, 1947; d. Alexander and Florence I. (Millar) Hehmeyer; m. David John Rosso, Mar. 18, 1978; children—Christine, Mark. BA, Pitzer Coll., 1969; JD, Northwestern U., 1972. Bar: Ill. 1972. Assoc., Isham, Lincoln & Beale, Chgo., 1972-78; participating ptnr. Chapman and Cutler, Chgo., 1978-83; chief charitable trusts and solicitations div. Office of Ill. Atty. Gen., Chgo., 1983-87; chief Consumer Protection Div., 1986; sr. asst. Atty. Gen., 1987—, chief antitrust div., 1989—. Pres. bd. dirs. Chgo. Hearing Soc., 1991-93, sec. 1994—; v.p. women's bd. Goodman Theatre, Chgo. Mem. ABA, Ill. State Bar Assn. (vice trust antitrust sect. coun.), Chgo. Bar Assn. (vice chmn. pub. utility law com. 1979, chmn. 1980), Nat. Assn. State Charity Ofcls. (pres. 1987-88). Episcopalian. Club: Econ. (Chgo.). Home: 520 W Fullerton Pky Chicago IL 60614-5919 Office: Atty Gen Ill 100 W Randolph St Fl 12 Chicago IL 60601-3220

ROSSO DE IRIZARRY, CARMEN (TUTTY ROSSO DE IRIZARRY), finance executive; b. Ponce, P.R., Feb. 9, 1947; d. Jorge Ignacio and Carmen Teresa (Descartes) Rosso Castain; m. Alfredo R. Irizarry Sile, Aug. 29, 1967. BBA, U. P.R., Rio Piedras. Vice pres. Alcay Inc., San Juan, P.R., 1972—, also bd. dirs.; v.p. J.I.C. Corp., M.I.C. Corp.; bd. dirs., now pres. bd. Construcciones Urbanas Inc., Internat. Fin. Corp. Troop leader Girl Scouts U.S.A., 1977-80; bd. dirs. PTA, San Juan, 1978-81, 86-88; activities coord. Colegio Puertorriqueño Niñas, San Juan, 1987-88; judge Miss P.R. Pageant, San Juan 1987-88, 94, Miss World P.R. Pageant, San Juan, 1987-88, Miss World of P.R., 1990; pres. fundacion dept. Oncologia Pediatrica Hosp. Universitario Dr. Antonio Ortiz, 1990; organizer Best of Saks Fifth Avenue Benefit, 1991, 92, 93, 94, pres. 1992, 94; com. mem. Make a Wish Found. Coleccion Alta Moda, 1994; mem. com. Muceo Ponce Gala, 1994; mem. com. Museo Ponce Coala, 1994; luminaria J.C. Penney, 1994; destellos de la Moda, 1994; pres. Best of Saks 5th Avenue Benefit, 1993, 94. Named to Ten Best Dressed List, San Juan Star, 1986-87, Hall of Fame of Ten Best Dressed, 1989; recipient luminaria J.C. Penney, 1994. Fellow Assn. Porcelanas; mem. Club de Leones (Garden Hills, P.R., Lady of Yr. award 1978), Caparra Country Club (pres. 1985-86), Club Civicos Damas (judge hat how 1989, in charge spl. events 1992), Mu Alpha Phi. Republican. Roman Catholic. Office: Internat Fin Corp PO Box 8486 Santurce San Juan PR 00910-0486

ROSSON, PEGGY, state legislator; b. Apr. 11, 1935. Mem. Tex. State Senate from 29th dist., 1991—. Democrat. Office: Tex State Senate State Capitol Austin TX 78711

ROSSOTTI, BARBARA JILL MARGULIES, lawyer; b. Englewood, N.J., Feb. 28, 1940; d. Albert and Loretta (Jill) Margulies; m. Charles Ossola Rossotti; children: Allegra Jill, Edward Charles. BA magna cum laude, Mount Holyoke Coll., 1961; LLB, Harvard U., 1964. Bar: D.C. 1966. Assoc. Nutter McClennen & Fish, Boston, 1964-65, Covington & Burling, Washington, 1965-72; assoc. Shaw, Pittman, Potts & Trowbridge, Washington, 1972-73, ptnr., 1973—. Trustee Mt. Holyoke Coll., South Hadley, Mass., 1984, vice chmn., 1989-94, chmn., 1994—; chmn. exec. com. Campaign for Mt. Holyoke Coll.. 1986-91; trustee Legal Aid Soc., D.C., 1979-92, pres. 1985-89., mem. pres. coun., 1992—; trustee Choral Arts Soc., Washington, 1989—, chair, 1993—, bd. dirs. Washington Home, 1989—. Fellow Am. Bar Found.; mem. ABA (sect. on taxation 1978—), Am. Soc. Internat. Law, Internat. Law Assn., D.C. Bar Assn., 1925 F Street Club. Office: Shaw Pittman Potts & Trowbridge 2300 N St NW Washington DC 20037-1122

ROSTOW, ELSPETH DAVIES, political science educator; b. N.Y.C.; d. Milton Judson and Harriet Elspeth (Vaughan) Davies; m. Walt Whitman Rostow, June 26, 1947; children: Peter Vaughan, Ann Larner. AB, Barnard Coll., 1938; AM, Radcliffe Coll., 1939; MA, Cambridge (Eng.) U., 1949; LHD (hon.), Lebanon Valley Coll.; LLD (hon.), Austin Coll., 1982, Southwestern U., 1988. Mem. faculty various instns. Barnard Coll., N.Y.C. and MIT, Boston, 1939-69; mem. faculty U. Tex., Austin, 1969—, dean div. gen. and comparative studies, 1975-77, prof. govt., 1976—, dean Lyndon B. Johnson Sch. Pub. Affairs, 1977-83, Stiles prof. Am. studies, 1985-88, Stiles prof. emerita, 1988—; mem. Pres.'s Adv. Com. for Trade Negotiations, 1978-82, Pres.'s Commn. for a Nat. Agenda for the Eighties, 1979-81; rsch. assoc. OSS, Washington, 1943-45; Geneva corr. London Economist, 1947-49; lectr. Air War Coll., 1963-81, Army War Coll., 1965, 68, 69, 78, 79, 81, Nat. War Coll., 1962, 68, 74, 75, Indsl. Coll. Armed Forces, 1961-65, Naval War Coll., 1971, Fgn. Svc. Inst., 1974-77, Dept. of State, Europe, 1973; bd. dirs. U.S. Inst. of Peace, vice chmn., 1991, chmn. 1991-92; co-founder The Austin Project, 1991; mem. Gov.'s Task Force on Revenue, Tex., 1991. Author: Europe's Economy After the War, 1948, (with others) American Now, 1968, The Coattailless Landslide, 1974; editor (with Barbara Jordan) The Great Society: A Twenty-Year Critique, 1986; columnist Austin Am. Statesman, 1985-92; contbr. articles to revs., poems to scholarly jours., newspapers, and mags. Trustee Sarah Lawrence Coll., 1952-59, Nat. Acad. Pub. Adminstrn., 1989—, So. Ctr. for Internat. Studies, 1990—; bd. visitors and govs. St. John's Coll., 1986-89; bd. dirs. Barnard Coll., 1962-66, Lyndon Baines Johnson Found., 1977-83, Salzburg Seminar, 1981-89; vis. scholar Phi Beta Kappa, 1984-85. Recipient award Air U., ; Fulbright lectr., USIA participant, 1983-84, 90. Mem. Tex. Philos. Soc. (trustee 1989—), Phi Beta Kappa, Phi Nu Epsilon (hon.), Mortar Bd. (hon.), Omicron Delta Kappa. Club: Headliners (Austin). Home: One Wild Wind Point Austin TX 78746 Office: Drawer Y University Station Austin TX 78713

ROTCHFORD, PATRICIA KATHLEEN, lawyer; b. Chgo., Nov. 17, 1945; d. Charles E. Sr. and Mary (Rodde) R.; 1 child, John. BA with honors, Rosary Coll., River Forest, Ill., 1966; JD, No. Ill. U., 1979. Bar: Ill. 1979. Tchr. pub. schs. Schiller Park, Ill., 1966-76; sole practice Elmhurst, Ill., 1977-79; assoc. Shand, Morahan, Evanston, Ill., 1979-83; corp. counsel CNA Fin., Chgo., 1983-86; gen. counsel, v.p. and corp. sec. MMI Cos., Bannockburn, Ill., 1986-87; gen. counsel, v.p., corp. sec. Inland Group, Northbrook, Ill., 1987-90; pvt. practice fin. and ins. legal counsel Northbrook, 1990—; bd. dirs. Notre Dame Corp., Chgo.; mem. nat. bd. dirs. NAFWIC; U.S. rep. ins. claims Lloyds of London. Author: (pamphlet) Handle Your Own Claims, 1983, (book) Women's Resource Guide, 1988, Women's Insurance and Financial Resource Guide, 1988. Counselor for battered women. Mem. Mich. Bar, Womens Bar Assn. Ill. (active coms. and activities), Corp. Councils Am., Womens Exec. Network, Nat. Assn. Women in Careers. Office: PO Box 4422 Northbrook IL 60065-4422

ROTE, NELLE FAIRCHILD, business management consultant; b. Watsontown, Pa., May 23, 1930; d. Edwin Dunkel and Phebe Hill (Fisher) Fairchild; m. John Austin Hefty, Mar. 20, 1948 (div. June, 1970); children: Harry Edwin, John Bradford, Susan Elizabeth; m. Keith Maynard Rote, Dec. 16, 1983 (dec. Aug., 1985). Student, Bucknell U., 1961, Williamsport Sch. of Commerce, 1968-69, Pa. State U., 1971-72, 83, Susquehanna U., 1986. Typesetter, page designer Colonial Printing House, Inc., Lewisburg, Pa., 1970-76; account exec. Sta. WTGC Radio, Lewisburg, 1976-78; co-owner Colonial Printing Co., Lewisburg, 1978-83; sec., adminstrv. asst. HATS-Temps, Lewisburg, 1980-89; artist, editor Create-A-Book, Inc., Milton, Fla., 1980-92; census crew leader, spl. svc. Dept. Commerce, Washington, 1990; ind. living skills instr. Ctr. for Ind. Living, Lewisburg, Pa., 1989—; cons. Presto Personalized Books; bus. cons. John B. Hefty Pub. Co., Inc., Gulf Breeze, Fla., 1991—. Artist: Children's Playmate Mag., 1942, Christmas Wish, Big Parade, 1989-90. Vol. proofreader Lewisburg Bicentennial Commn., 1976; editor-poet Holiday Newspaper Bus. Assn., Lewisburg, 1987; donor of flagpole, Am. flags to Hufnagle Meml. Park, Lewisburg, 1987; charter sponsor Women in Mil. Svc. Meml., Washington, 1991; chmn. Rooftop Garden Project Evangelical Hosp., Pa., 1995—. Recipient Humanitarian award Union County Fedn. Women's Clubs, Pa., 1965, Grand Prize in Cooking, Milton Std., 1966, Most Profl. Photo award, Lewisburg Festival of Arts, 1980, Hon. Mention award Women in Arts, Harrisburg, Pa., 1981, Photo Contest award Congressman Allen Ertel, Washington, 1981, Photo awards 2nd and 3rd Place Union County Fair, Laurelton, Pa., 1981; Hon. Mention Photo award Susquehanna Art Soc., Pa., 1981. Mem. DAR (nat. def. reporter Shikelimo chpt. 1989-95, sec. 1992-95, regent 1995—), Civic Club of Lewisburg (v.p. 1994-96), Orgn. United for Environment, Nat. Wildlife Fedn. Assn. (cert.), Inst. for Lifelong Learning Susquehanna U. Republican. Home: 1015 Saint Paul St Lewisburg PA 17837-1213

ROTERT, DENISE ANNE, occupational therapist, army officer, educator; b. Sioux Falls, S.D., Nov. 18, 1949; d. Leonard Joseph and Irene Winnifred (Jennings) R. BS, U. Puget Sound, 1971; MA, U. No. Colo., 1975. Commd. 2d lt. Med. Specialist Corps, U.S. Army, 1970, advanced through grades to lt. col. , 1990; staff occupational therapist Tripler Army Med. Center, Honolulu, 1973-76, officer in charge occupational therapy sect. Ireland Army Hosp., Fort Knox, Ky., 1976-77; clin. supr. occupational therapy sect. Letterman Army Med. Center, Presidio of San Francisco, 1977-79; chief instr. occupational therapy asst. course Acad. Health Scis., Ft. Sam Houston, Tex., 1979-84; chief occupational therapy Tri-Service Alcohol Recovery Dept., Naval Hosp., Bethesda, Md., 1984-89, Womack Army Hosp., Ft. Bragg, N.C., 1989-90, ret., 1990; mem. faculty U. S.D., 1991—. Recipient Myra McDaniel Writer's award, 1989. Mem. Am. Occupational Therapy Assn., D.C. Occupational Therapy Assn., World Fedn. Occupational Therapists, S.D. Occupational Therapy Assn. Roman Catholic. Home: 2609 S Prairie Sioux Falls SD 57105 Office: USDSM OT Dept 414 E Clark Vermillion SD 57069

ROTH, ANN, costume designer. Student, Carnegie-Mellon U. Designer costumes for theatre and film prodns., 1958—; Broadway shows include Maybe Tuesday, Make a Million, Gay Divorcee, A Far Country, Purlie Victorious, This Side of Paradise, A Case of Libel, The Last Analysis, The Odd Couple, The Impossible Years, Play It Again Sam, They're Playing Our Song, Tiny Alice, What the Butler Saw, Fun City, 6 Rms Riv Vu, The Best Little Whorehouse in Texas, Lunch Hour, Present Laughter, The Misanthrope, Open Admissions, Arms and the Man, Hurlyburly, Design for Living, Biloxi Blues, Juno's Swans, 1985, The House of Blue Leures, numerous others; films Midnight Cowboy, 1969, The Day of the Locust, 1975, Independence, 1976, Burnt Offerings, 1976, The Goodbye Girl, 1977, Nunzio, 1978, Coming Home, 1978, Hair, 1979, Promises in the Dark, 1979, The Island, 1980, Nine to Five, 1980, Dressed to Kill, 1980, Honky Tonk Freeway, 1981, Only When I Laugh, 1981, Rollover, 1981, The World According to Garp, 1982, The Man Who Loved Women, 1983, Silkwood, 1983, The Survivors, 1983, Places in the Heart, 1984 (Academy Award nomination for best costume design 1984), Jagged Edge, 1985, Maxie, 1985, The Slugger's Wife, 1985, Sweet Dreams, 1985, Heartburn, 1986, The Morning After, 1986, Biloxi Blues, 1988, Funny Farm, 1988, Stars and Bars, 1988, The Unbearable Lightness of Being, 1988, Working Girl, 1988, Family Business, 1989, Her Alibi, 1989, The January Man, 1989, The Bonfire of the Vanities, 1990, Pacific Heights, 1990, Postcards From the Edge, 1990, Q & A, 1990, Everybody Wins, 1990, The Mambo Kings, 1992, School Ties, 1992, Dave, 1992, Dennis the Menace, 1993, Wolf, 1994; also designed costumes for various regional repertory theatres including costumes Am. Conservatory Theatre, Am. Ballet Theatre, Am. Shakespeare Festival, Kennedy Center, Mpls. Opera, San Francisco Opera. Office: care United Scenic Artists 575 Fifth Ave New York NY 10017-2422*

ROTH, CAROLYN LOUISE, art educator; b. Buffalo, June 17, 1944; d. Charles Mack and Elizabeth Mary (Hassel) R.; m. Charles Turner Barber, Aug. 4, 1991. Student, Art Student's League N.Y., 1965, Instituto Allende, San Miguel de Allende, Mex., 1966; BFA, Herron Sch. Art, 1967; MFA, Fla. State U., 1969. Asst. prof. art U. Tenn., Chattanooga, 1969-72; lectr. art So. Ill. U., Carbondale, 1973-75; asst. prof. art U. Evansville, Ind., 1975-80; lectr. art U. So. Ind., Evansville, 1984—; exhbn. coord., gallery dir. Krannert Gallery, U. Evansville, 1977-79; exhbn. coord., conf. advisor Ind. Women in Arts Conf., Ind. Arts Commn., Evansville, 1978. One woman shows include Wabash Valley Coll., Mt. Carmel, Ill., 1994; exhibited in group shows at Liberty Gallery, Louisville, 1992, Artlink Contemporary Art Gallery, Ft. Wayne, Ind., 1994, S.E. Mo. Coun. on Arts, Cape Girardeau, 1994; works appeared in: Contemporary Batik and Tie-Dye, 1973, Kalliope, A Journal of Women's Art, vol. XIV, no. 1, 1992, Jour. Am. Vet. Med. Assn., vol. 203, no. 3, 1993. Mem. Nat. Mus. Women in Arts, Met. Mus. Art, J. B. Speed Mus., Evansville Mus. Arts and Sci., New Harmony Gallery of Contemporary Art. Democrat. Mem. Unity Ch. Home: 10801 S Woodside Dr Evansville IN 47712 Office: U So Ind 8600 University Blvd Evansville IN 47712

ROTH, EVELYN AUSTIN, elementary school educator; b. Coronado, Calif., May 31, 1942; d. Robert Emmett and Marjorie Eastman (Rice) Austin; m. John King Roth, June 25, 1964; children: Andrew Lee, Sarah Austin. BA, San Diego State U., 1964; MA, U. of LaVerne, Calif., 1984; postgrad., U. Calif., Riverside, 1985. Cert. elem. tchr., Calif. Elem. tchr. Poway (Calif.) Unified Schs., 1964, Wallingford (Conn.) Unified Schs., 1964-66, Ontario (Calif.) Montclair Sch. Dist., 1982-88, Claremont (Calif.) Unified Schs., 1966-67, 83-93, Foothill Country Day Sch., Claremont, 1993—. Pres., bd. trustees Friends of Stone Libr., Claremont, 1993-94. Mem. AAUW, NEA, Calif. Tchrs. Assn., Internat. Reading Assn. (treas. Foothill Reading Coun. 1985-86), Delta Kappa Gamma (v.p. 1991-92). Republican. Presbyterian.

ROTH, JANE RICHARDS, federal judge; b. Philadelphia, Pa., June 16, 1935; d. Robert Henry Jr. and Harriett (Kellond) Richards; m. William V. Roth Jr., Oct. 9, 1965; children: William V. III, Katharine K. BA, Smith Coll., 1956; LLB, Harvard U., 1965; LLD (hon.), Widener U., 1986, U. Del., 1994. Bar: Del. 1965, U.S. Dist. Ct. Del. 1966, U.S. Ct. Appeals (3d cir.) 1974. Adminstrv. asst. various fgn. service posts U.S. State Dept., 1956-62; assoc. Richards, Layton & Finger, Wilmington, Del., 1965-73, ptnr., 1973-85; judge U.S. Dist. Ct. Del., Wilmington, 1985-91, U.S. Ct. Appeals (3d cir.), Wilmington, 1991—; adj. faculty Villanova U. Sch. Law. Mem. Chesapeake Bay coun. Girl Scouts U.S.; hon. chmn. Del. chpt. Arthritis Found., Wilmington; bd. overseers Widener U. Sch. Law; trustee Hist. Soc. Del. Recipient Nat. Vol. Service citation Athritis Found., 1982. Mem. Fed. Judges Assn., Del. State Bar Assn. Republican. Episcopalian. Office: US Ct House J Caleb Boggs Fed Bldg 844 King St Rm 5100 Wilmington DE 19801-3519*

ROTH, JUDITH SHULMAN, lawyer; b. N.Y.C., Apr. 25, 1952; d. Mark Alan and Margaret Ann (Podell) Shulman; m. William Hartley Roth, May 30, 1976; children: Andrew Henry, Caroline Shulman. AB, Cornell U., 1974; JD, Columbia U., 1977. Bar: N.Y. 1978, U.S. Dist. Ct. (ea. dist.) N.Y. 1978, U.S. Dist. Ct. (so. dist.) N.Y. 1993, U.S. Ct. Appeals (2d cir.) 1993. Assoc. Phillips Nizer Benjamin Krim & Ballon, N.Y.C., 1978-87, ptnr., 1988—; lectr. CLE Fordham Law Sch., N.Y.C., 1990. Mem. Cosmopolitan Club. Jewish. Office: Phillips Nizer Benjamin Krim & Ballon 31 W 52nd St New York NY 10019

ROTH, KATHRYN GAIE, foundation executive; b. Torreson, Spain, Mar. 19, 1964; came to U.S., 1964; d. Edwin Isaac and Deborah (Weissman) R. BA, Bryn Mawr Coll., 1987; MPA, Princeton U., 1991. Founder, editor-in-chief Jour. for Pub. and Internat. Affairs, Princeton, N.J., 1989-91; asst. sec. to bd., dir. spl. projects Nathan Cummings Found., N.Y.C., 1991-92; assoc. dir. presdl. advance White House, Washington, 1993-95; v.p. Revlon Found. MacAndrews & Forbes Holding, Inc., N.Y.C., 1995—; bd. dirs. Fillmore Mercantile, Inc.; polit. cons. Mondale Campaign, Dukakis Campaign, Simon Campaign, Clinton for Pres. Campaign and Transition. Contbg. author: Public Opinion in U.S. Foreign Policy: The Controversy Over Contra Aid, 1994; contbr. articles to profl. publs. Recipient Conf. Paper award Assn. Profl. Schs. of Internat. Affairs, 1991; Woodrow Wilson fellow, 1989-91. Mem. Women in Philanthropy, Coun. Fgn. Rels. Democrat. Jewish. Home: 525 E 86th St Apt 10B New York NY 10028 Office: McAndrews and Forbes Inc 38 E 63d St New York City NY 10021

ROTH, SISTER M. AUGUSTINE, nun, educator; b. Mpls., Jan. 16, 1926; d. J.A., and Anne A. (Boies) R. BA, U. Minn., 1947, MA, 1948; PhD, Cath. U. Am., 1961. Joined Sisters of Mercy, Roman Catholic Ch., 1949. Faculty Mt. Mercy Coll., Cedar Rapids, Iowa, 1948—, prof. dept. English; v.p. bd. dirs. Mercy Med. Ctr. Endowment Found., exec. dir., 1987—, chmn. bd. trustees of med. ctr., 1987—. Author: Written in His Hands, 1976; With Mercy Toward All, 1979; Courage and Change, 1980, One Life, 1987. Home: 1125 Prairie Dr NE Cedar Rapids IA 52402-4730

ROTH, MARJORY JOAN JARBOE, special education educator; b. Ranger, Tex., May 24, 1934; d. James Aloysius and Dorothy Knight (Taggart) Jarboe; m. Thomas Mosser Roth, Jr., Dec. 22, 1959; children: Thomas Mosser III, James Jarboe. BA in English, Rice U., 1957; MEd in Ednl. Adminstrn., U. N.C., Greensboro, 1981. Cert. tchr.-specific learning disabilities, middle grades lang. arts and social studies, intermediate grades, adminstr.-prin., N.C. Tchr. 4th grade Houston Ind. Sch. Dist., 1957-60; specific lang. disabilities instr. Forsyth Tech. C.C., Winston-Salem, N.C., 1976-77; specific learning disabilities tchr. Forsyth Country Day Sch., Winston-Salem, 1977-80; tchr. 5th grade Winston-Salem/Forsyth County Schs., 1982-83, specific learning disabilities tchr. Mt. Tabor High Sch., 1983-86; part time instr. English and Learning Disabilities Forsyth Tech. C.C., 1986-90; founding pres., prin. Greenhills Sch., Winston-Salem, 1990—. Co-author, co-editor booklets. Sunday Sch. dir., tchr. Galloway Meml. Episcopal Ch., 1960-70, pres., treas., sec. Churchwomen, 1963-74; treas. Elkin Jr. Woman's Club, 1962; chmn. Elkin Heart Fund Drive, 1968; bd. dirs. Hugh Chatham Hosp. Auxillary, 1968, Friends of the Elkin Pub. Libr., 1968-74, chmn., 1970-72, chmn., exhibits chmn. summer reading program; pres. South Surry Heart Assn., 1969; mem. Churchwomen of St. Paul's Episcopal Ch., Winston-Salem, 1982—, Fiddle and Bow Folk Music Soc., Winston-Salem, 1992—. Forsyth fellow NEH, 1985; grantee in field. Mem. ASCD, AAUW, Nat. Coun. Tchrs. English, Children with Attention Deficit Disorder (profl. adv. bd. N.C. Triad chpt. 1990—), Learning Disability Assn. N.C. (sec., bd. dirs. 1981-86), Orton Dyslexia Soc. (sec., bd. dirs. Carolinas br. 1981-85, founding pres. N.C. br. 1987-91, bd. dirs. 1987—, nat. nominating com. 1992-94). Republican. Home: 940 Foxhall Dr Winston Salem NC 27106 Office: Greenhills Sch 1360 Lyndale Dr Winston Salem NC 27106

ROTH, NANCY LOUISE, former nurse, veterinarian; b. Cin., June 24, 1955; d. Jack Leopold Jr. and Elsie Harriet (Shemin) R. BS in Agr., U. Mo., 1977, DVM, 1989; BSN, Avila Coll., 1980. Critical care RN. Staff nurse St. Louis Univ. Hosp., 1980-81, Barnes Hosp., St. Louis, 1981-85, U. Mo. Hosp. and Clinic, Columbia, 1985-89; assoc. veterinarian Ill. Equine Field Svc., North Aurora, 1989-95; proprietor Cedar Ln. Equine Clinic, New Haven, Mo., 1995—. Contbr. articles to profl. jours. Vol. instr. U.S. Pony Club, Wayne, Ill., 1991—, 4-H Club, Wheaton, Ill., 1991—; bd. dirs. Ill. Dressage and Combined Tng. Assn. Mem. AVMA, Am. Assn. Equine Practitioners (trails and events com.), Sigma Theta Tau, Phi Zeta. Home: 34w856 Country Club Rd Saint Charles IL 60174-1380 Office: Cedar Ln Equine Clinic PO Box 108 New Haven MO 63068

ROTH, PAMELA JEANNE, marketing professional; b. Huntington, N.Y., Sept. 9, 1955; d. Julius Leo and Constance Abby (Gettenberg) R. BA with honors, New Coll. Hofstra U., 1975; MS, Rensselaer Inst. Tech., 1977; JD, New England Sch. Law, 1983. Assoc. editor Functional Photography, Hempstead, N.Y., 1976; documentation specialist Allendale Ins., Johnston, R.I., 1977-78; systems analyst Comml. Union Ins., Boston, 1978-79; sr. software writer NEC Info. Systems, Lexington, Mass., 1979-82; pres. TEKDOC Tech. Communications, North Andover, Mass., 1978-86; sr. tech. writer Software Internat., Andover, Mass., 1983; pres., CEO SPIRAL Communications, Inc., SPIRAL Group, SPIRAL Books, Bedford, N.H., 1986—; presenter in field. Author: The First Book of Adam, 1984, The Second Book of Adam, 1984, Using the PFS Family, 1985, The Standard Catalog of Client/Server Computing, 1993, Data Warehousing and Decision Support-The State of the Art, 1994, Customer or Employer? Vendor or Employee?, 1995; contbr. articles to profl. jours. Gen. mgr. ImprovBoston, 1986. Mem. Boston Computer Soc. (founder legal interests group 1984), NRA (life). Office: SPIRAL Communications Inc 7 Colby Ct Ste 4-104 Bedford NH 03110-6427

ROTH, PATRICIA ANN, mental health nurse; b. Dallas, Aug. 19, 1932; d. James Vernon and Stella Frances (Skiles) Stone; divorced; children: James Roth, Carol Roth Christensen, Charles. BSN, Tex. Christian U., 1954; primary cert., Inst. Rational Emotive Therapy, N.Y. RN. Instr. pediatrics and med./surg. nursing Ind. Vocat. Tech. Coll., Columbus; instr. pediatrics nursing and basic nursing skills Kellogg Community Coll., Battle Creek, Mich.; pub. health nurse Calhoun County Health Dept., Battle Creek; head nurse blind rehab. clinic VA Med. Ctr., Waco, Tex.; mem. psychiat. nursing del. Citizen Amb. program People to People Internat., People's Republic of China, 1990, mem. post trauma stress del. Citizen Amb. program, 1992. Mem. ANA, Nurses Orgn. of VA, Soc. Trauma Stress Studies. Home: 1308 Chapel Downs Rd Waco TX 76712-8115

ROTH, SUSAN KING, design educator; b. Millville, N.J., Nov. 13, 1945; d. Frank N. and Ruth (Ludlam) King; m. Richard L. Roth, Sept. 17, 1973; 1 child, Justin King Roth. BFA, Cooper Union, 1968; MA, Ohio State U., 1988. With advt. prodn. Mayer/Martin, Inc., N.Y.C., 1968-70; dir. graphics N.Y.C. Parks, Recreation and Cultural Affairs Adminstrn., 1970-73; designer Whole Earth Epilog, Sausalito, Calif., 1974-75; asst. art dir. TV Guide mag., Radnor, Pa., 1975-77; design cons. various orgns., Chgo., 1978-80; instr., tchg. assoc. Ohio State U., Columbus, 1985-88, assoc. prof., 1988—; vis. designer Sch. Art Inst., Chgo., 1980-81, Ohio Wesleyan U., Delaware, 1982-84; co-founder, co-dir. Ctr. for Interdisciplinary Studies, Columbus, Ohio, 1992—; evaluator Nat. Assn. Schs. Art and Design, Reston, Va., 1994—; cons. Ohio Sec. of State, Columbus, 1993-94. Consulting editor Jour. Visual Literacy, 1992—; contbr. articles to profl. jours. Battelle grantee Battelle Endowment for Tech. & Human Affairs, 1993-94. Mem. Am. Ctr. Design, Assn. Computing Machinery, Graphic Design Edn. Assn., Internat. Visual Literacy Assn., Indsl. Designers Soc. Am. (mem. edn. bd. 1993-95). Home: 3158 Glenrich Pkwy Columbus OH 43221 Office: Ohio State U 380 Hopkins Hall Columbus OH 43210

ROTH, SUZANNE ALLEN, financial services agent; b. Santa Monica, Calif., May 31, 1963; d. Raymond A. and Ethel Allen; m. Steve Milstein Roth, Dec. 27, 1992. BA, U. Calif., Santa Cruz, 1986; student, Calif. State U., L.A., 1987-93, Art Ctr. Sch. Design, Pasadena, Calif., 1994—. Cert. tchr., Calif.; lic. real estate agt., Calif. Interviewer L.A. Times Newspaper, 1986-88; educator L.A. Unified Sch. Dist., 1987-90; educator Burbank (Calif.) Unified Sch. Dist., 1990-94, vol., 1994—; ptnr. fin. svcs. Roth & Assocs./N.Y. Life, L.A., 1993—. Mem. NEA, Burbank Tchrs. Union.

ROTHENBERG, GLORIA SUSAN, psychologist; b. N.Y.C., May 26, 1952; d. Joseph Louis and Yetta (Shevlinsky) Joldoff; m. Howard Rothenberg, Oct. 10, 1971; 1 daughter. BA in Psychology summa cum laude, CCNY, 1974; MA, SUNY, Stony Brook, 1980, PhD in Clin. Psychology, 1983. Lic. psychologist, sch. psychologist, N.Y. Pvt. practice Merrick, N.Y., 1984—; cons. supr. Transitional Svcs. N.Y., Far Rockaway, 1991—; sch. psychologist Farmingdale (N.Y.) Sch. Dist., 1989-91, Syosset (N.Y.) Ctrl. Sch. Dist., 1988-89; staff psychologist Schneider Children's Hosp., New Hyde Park, N.Y., 1986-87, Ctrl. Nassau Guidance and Counseling Svcs., Hicksville, N.Y., 1985-86, dept. child and adolescent psychiatru Gouveneur Hosp., N.Y.C., 1984-85; sch. psychologist Flushing (N.Y.) High Sch., 1983-84; psychology intern, trainee VA Med. Ctr., Northport, N.Y., 1977-82. Contbr. articles to profl. jours. Vol. Nassau Psychol. Svcs. Inst., 1985—. Mem. Am. Psychol. Assn., Nassau County Psychol. Assn. (pres.-elect 1993-94, pres. 1994-95, co-chair com. 1987—), N.Y. State Psychol. Assn. (regional rep. to task force on managed care, regional coord. grassroots network 1992—), Nat. Register Health Svc. Providers in Psychology. Office: 1674 Meadowbrook Rd Merrick NY 11566-2505

ROTHENBERG, MIRA KOWARSKI, clinical psychologist and psychotherapist; b. Wilno, Poland; came to U.S., 1938; d. Jacob and Rosa (Joffe) Kowarski; m. Tev Goldsman, Dec. 7, 1960 (div. June 1974); 1 child, Akiva. BA, Bklyn. Coll., 1943; MA, Columbia U., 1957, Yeshiva U., 1959; ABD, Yeshiva U., 1962. Lic. psychologist, N.Y. Therapist, tchr.ir. Hawthorne (N.Y.) Cedar Knolls, 1952-53, League Sch., Bklyn., 1953-58; founder, clin. dir. Blueberry Treatment Ctrs., Bklyn., 1958-90; staff psychologist L.I. Coll. Hosp., Bklyn., 1970—; cons. Beachbrook Nursery, Bkyn., 1969-70, San Felipe Del Rio, Santa Fe, 1980—, Children's House Montessori Nursery, Bklyn., 1982-89, Austrlia Dept. Edn., Carynia, New South Wales; adj. prof. L.I. U., Bklyn., 1976-78; internat. speaker in field. Author: Children with Emerald Eyes, 1977, (with others) Pet Oriented Psychotherapy, 1980, The Outsiders, 1989; contbr. to books and articles to profl. jours. Mem. World Fedn. Mental Health, Am. Psychol. Assn., N.Y. State Psychol. Assn., Inter. Soc. Child Abuse and Neglect (Hamburg, Germany), Physicians for Social Responsibility, N.Y. Acad. Scis., Amnest Internat., ACLU, NOW, Anti Defamation League, Yivo, Nat. Register Svc. Providers in Psychology. Home and Office: 160 State St Brooklyn NY 11201-5610

ROTHENBERG, SUSAN, artist; b. Buffalo, Jan. 20, 1945; d. Leonard M. and Adele (Cohen) R.; m. George Trakas, May 1, 1971-1976; 1 dau., Maggie. B.F.A., Cornell U., 1966. One-woman shows of paintings include Willard Gallery, N.Y.C., 1976, 77, 79, 81, 83, Univ. Art Mus., Berkeley, Calif., 1978, Walker Art Center, Mpls., 1978, Greenberg Gallery, St. Louis, 1978, Mayor Gallery, London, 1980, Akron (Ohio) Art Mus., 1981-82, Stedelijk Mus., Amsterdam, 1982, Los Angeles County Mus., 1983, San Francisco Mus. Art, 1983, Carnegie Inst. Mus. Art, Pitts., 1984, Baltimore Museum of Art, 1988, Albright-Knox, Buffalo, NY, 1992-94; numerous group shows, 1974—, including Mus. of Modern Art, N.Y.C., 1980, Padiglione d'Arte Contemporanea di Milano, Italy, 1980, Clarke-Benton Gallery, Santa-Fe, 1980, Indpls. Mus. Art, 1980, Yarlow/Salzman Gallery, Toronto, 1980, Tex. Gallery, Houston, 1981, Young Hoffman Gallery, Chgo., 1981, Inst. Contemporary Art, Richmond, Va., 1981, Kunsthalle, Basel (Switzerland), 1981, Willard Gallery, N.Y., 1983, Los Angeles County Mus. Art, 1983, Inst. Contemporary Art, Boston, 1983, Barbara Krakow Gallery, Boston, 1984, Des Moines Art Ctr., 1985, A.P. Giannini Gallery, San Francisco; group exhbns. include A.M. Sachs Gallery, N.Y.C., 1974, Willard Gallery, 1975, 76, Inst. for Art and Urban Resources, Long Island City, N.Y., 1977, Mus. Modern Art, N.Y., 1977, Cleve. Mus. Art, 1978, Inst. Contemporary Art, Philadelphia, 1991-92, Museum of Modern Art, NY, 1992. N.Y., 1978, Whitney Mus. Am. Art, 1979, Renaissance Soc. of U. Chgo., 1979, Clarke-Benton Gallery, Santa Fe, 1980, Audrey Stohl Gallery, 1980, Tex. Gallery, Houston, 1981, Univ. Art Mus., Santa Barbara, 1981, Akron Art Mus., 1981, Art Inst. Chgo., 1982, Sidney Janis Gallery, 1982,Paula Cooper Gallery, N.Y., 1983, Fogg Art Mus., Harvard U., 1984, CDS Gallery, 1984, N.Y. Pub. Library, 1985, Seattle Art Mus., 1985, Daniel Weinberg Gallery, 1985,Barbara Mathes Gallery, 1986, Butlre Inst. Am. Art, Youngstown, Ohio, 1986, 1st Bank of Mpls., 1986-87, Mus. Fine Arts, Boston, 1986-87; represented in permanent collections, Mus. Modern Art, N.Y.C., Mus. Fine Arts, Houston, Whitney Mus. Am. Art, N.Y.C., Albright-Knox Art Gallery, Buffalo, Walker Art Center, Des Moines, Iowa., Akron Art Mus., Stedelijk Mus., Carnegie Inst. Mus. Art, Dallas Mus. Fine Art. Guggenheim fellow, 1980. mem. Am. Acad and Inst. of Arts and Letters, 1990. Office: care Sperone Westwater 142 Greene St New York NY 10012-3236*

ROTHENBERGER, BRENDA JOYCE, academic coordinator; b. Tuscola, Ill., Mar. 11, 1943; d. Harry Lloyd and Mary Ferne (Myers) Ingrum; m. Harry J. Rothenberger, June 17, 1962; children: Denise M. Rothenberger Oakley, Daryn M., Dyke M. AA, Parkland Coll., 1971; BS in Elem. Edn., U. Ill., 1973; M in Elem. Edn., Ea. Ill. U., 1981, specialist in edn., 1984. Cert. tchr., gen. adminstr. and supt., Ill. Tchr. Paris (Ill). Union Sch. Dist. 95, 1973-88; elem. sch. prin. Paris (Ill.) Union Sch. Dist., 1988-94; curriculum coord. Paris (Ill.) Union Sch. Dist. 95, 1994—. Bd. dirs. Human Resources, Paris, 1989—. Mem. ASCD, Phi Delta Kappa. Office: Paris Sch Dist # 95 414 S Main St Paris IL 61944

ROTHFIELD, NAOMI FOX, physician; b. Bklyn., Apr. 5, 1929; d. Morris and Violet (Bloomgarden) Fox; m. Lawrence Rothfield, Sept. 18, 1954; children—Susan, Lawrence, John, Jane. B.A., Bard Coll., 1950; M.D., N.Y. U., 1955. Intern Lenox Hill Hosp., N.Y.C., 1955-56; instr. N.Y. U. Sch. Medicine, 1956-62, asst. prof., 1962-68; assoc. prof. U. Conn. Sch. Medicine, Farmington, 1968-72; prof., chief div. rheumatic diseases U. Conn. Sch. Medicine, 1972—. Contbr. chpts. to books; contbr. articles to med. jours. Mem. Am. Soc. Clin. Investigation, Am. Rheumatism Assn., Assn. Am. Physics. Jewish. Home: 540 Deercliff Rd Avon CT 06001-2859 Office: U Conn Sch Medicine Div of Rheumatic Diseases Farmington CT 06030

ROTHMAN, ARLENE BARBARA, producer; b. Bklyn., Apr. 1, 1954; d. Elliot and Clara (Sternklar) R. BA magna cum laude, UCLA, 1976, cert. pub. rels., 1978. Cert. elem., secondary and adult edn. tchr., Calif. Assoc. dir. mktg., acquisition and distbn. Motivational Media; coord. prodn. VSI; publicist Shefrin Co.; ptnr., acct. exec. Executive Sport Promoters; assoc. dir. promotion and publicity Brasch & Brasch; acct. exec. Fanorama, Pub. Info. Network; v.p. acquisitions Robert Schnitzer Prodns.; coord. talent Playgirl Mag.; co-producer Per Diem Prodns.; assoc. producer cable show Playboy Prodns.; prodr. commls., cons. media mktg. Luna & Assocs.; ind. prodr. L.A. Asst. prodn. mgr., location scout Rocky II; co-prodr.: (video) The Time Machine VCR GAme, World's Greatest Movie Challenge, NFL Trivia Game, Person to Person Magazine, Lilly's Looking Glass, Art and Anatomy, Distaster in Space, Space Music; prodn. coord. (TV comml.) Leodus & Arbusto Prodns., (cable TV show) And If I'm Elected; assoc. prodr. (feature film) Lobodamy; prodr. (video) L.A.'s Best; segment prodr.: (series) Hit Squad, (pilot) America's Funniest Home Videos; coordinating prodr.: James Brown Special. Participant, donator Concern II Cancer Fundraiser, 1984-85. Mem. Young Exec. Singles, Jewish Assn. Single Profs., Phi Beta Kappa, Alpha Kappa Delta, Phi Gamma Mu. Democrat. Home: 550 S Barrington Ave 4103 Los Angeles CA 90049

ROTHMAN, CLAIRE LYNDA, arena executive; b. Phila., Aug. 8, 1928; d. Paul and Anna (Schwartz) Polakoff; div.; children: Barry S., Karen Rothman Weinryt. Grad. high sch., Phila. Bus. mgr. The Spectrum, Phila., 1967-71; v.p. Wild Kingdom, Orlando, Fla., 1971-73; gen. mgr. Richfield (Ohio) Coliseum, 1973-75; dir. booking Calif. Sports, Inglewood, 1975-78, v.p., 1979-88; pres., gen. mgr. Calif. Forum, Inglewood, 1988—; bd. dirs. Music Ctr. Operating Co. Bd. dirs. Am. Collegiate Talent Showcase, 1985-88, L.A. Sports Coun., Beckman Rsch. Inst., Women's Trusteeship/Internat. Women's Forum, mem., 1984, pres., 1993—, City of Hope, Duarte, Calif., Women Yr. Benefactor's award, 1986, mem. resources bd., former mem. conv. cabinet; mem. adv. bd. Centinela Hosp., Inglewood, 1980-91; active Women in Bus.; speaker numerous civic orgns.; commr. L.A. Conv. Ctr., 1993—, pres. commn., 1994—. Named Facility Mgr. Yr. Billboard mag., 1976, 79-82, One of Ten Women of the Decade Women in Bus., 1984; recipient Diamond Superwoman award Harper's Bazaar mag., 1980, Portfolio award Bullock's 1985, Sports and the Law award Constitutional Rights Found. 1988, Silver Achievement award YMCA, 1990, Outstanding Bus. Woman award Am. Bus. Women's Assn., 1991. Mem. Internat. Assn. Auditorium Mgrs. (past bd. dirs., speaker). Office: Forum 3900 W Manchester Blvd Inglewood CA 90306

ROTHMAN, DEANNA, electroplating company executive; b. Bklyn., Sept. 20, 1938; d. Frank Philip and Elsie (Goldstein) Dukofsky; m. Edward Rothman, Dec. 8, 1956 (div. July 1984); children: Jeffrey Scott, Michele Dawn, Robert Jay; m. Ronald Friedman, Aug. 17, 1986. B.A., Bklyn. Coll., 1968. Exec. Bronzemaster Co., Bklyn., 1969-80, Perma Plating Co. Inc., Bklyn., 1980-84; pres. Duratron Finishing Corp., Bklyn., 1984—, Skillman Metal Corp., Bklyn., 1987—. Sec. Tenants Assn., S.I., 1973-77; v.p. Orgn. Rehab. and Tng., Woodmere, N.Y., 1978-80; sponsor Spl. Olympics; mem. East N.Y. Local Devel. Corp. Mem. Masters Electroplating Assn., Am. Metal Finishers, NAFE, NOW. Republican. Avocations: painting, collecing art deco, dance, theatre. Office: Duratron Finishing Corp PO Box 789 East NY Sta Brooklyn NY 11207

ROTHMAN, GAIL ANN, counseling services administrator; b. Rochester, N.Y., June 25, 1944; d. Herman Tony and Grace Helen (Fortuna) Giancola; m. Michael Frederick Rothman, Feb. 6, 1967 (div. 1977); m. Gerald Francis Marshall, Feb. 26, 1995. BA, SUNY, Albany, 1970; MS, SUNY, Brockport, 1976; PhD, SUNY, Buffalo, 1989. Cert. clin. mental health counselor, cert. fitness profl. Dance and drama instr. Baden St. Settlement, Rochester, N.Y., 1968-69; day care ctr. instr. Action for a Better Community, Rochester, N.Y., 1968-70; sr. residential counselor Rochester Sch. for the Deaf, 1970-74; interpreter Rochester Inst. of Tech., 1974-75, counselor, 1975-79, chairperson of counseling svcs., 1979—, diagnostician learning assessment team, 1987-90; sign and content expert Nat. Tech. Inst. for the Deaf, Rochester, 1983; part-time adj. prof. psychology Coll. Liberal Arts Rochester Inst. Tech., 1990-93, 94—, part-time adj. prof. aerobics dept. phys. edn. and recreation, 1992—; mem. activity faculty Am. Jour. Health Promotion Conf., 1994. Contbr. articles to profl. jours. Vol. Drug and Alcohol Coun., Rochester, 1987-89; program com. co-chmn. Niagara Assn. for Psychol. Type, Rochester, 1986-88; chaperone, vol. Spl. Olympics, Rochester, 1989, 90, tenure com. chmn., 1991-94. Sch. of Visual Comms. grantee, 1986, 89, 93, Ctr. for Student Resources grantee, 1994. Mem. Am. Counseling Assn., Assn. for Psychol. Type, Am. Coll. Pers. Assn., Assn. for Counselor Edn. and Supervision, Am. Mental Health Counselors Assn., Nat. Career Devel. Assn., Monroe County Assn. for the Hearing Impaired, Aerobic Fitness Assn. Am. Home: 61 Marquette Dr Rochester NY 14618-5613 Office: Rochester Inst of Tech Johnson Bldg 52 Lomb Memorial Dr Rochester NY 14623

ROTHMAN, JUDITH LEE, publisher; b. N.Y.C., Nov. 17, 1940; d. William and Beatrice (Schwartz) R. BA, CUNY, Queens, 1962; student, CBS Sch. Mgmt., N.Y.C. and Boston, 1979-80, Hennig/Jardim Mgmt. Sch. for Women, N.Y.C., 1979-81. Legal sec. Kaufman, Taylor & Kimmel, N.Y.C., 1962-64; editor Fairchild Publs., N.Y.C., 1964-71; prodn. asst. Paramount Pictures, N.Y.C., 1971; editor coll. div. Appleton Century Crofts, N.Y.C., 1971-73, Prentice-Hall, Inc., Englewood Cliffs, N.J., 1973-78; pub. humanities div., Holt Rinehart & Winston Publs., N.Y.C., 1978-80; editorial dir. CBS Edn. Pub., N.Y.C., 1980-81; sr. editor Random House, Inc., N.Y.C., 1981-84; editor in chief Harper & Row, Inc., N.Y.C., 1984-90; pub. Grolier Press, N.Y.C., 1990-92; v.p., dir. Sage Publs., Inc., Newbury Park, Calif., 1992—; cons. Assn. Am. Publishers, N.Y.C., 1981-82. Mem. Nat. Women's Book Assn. (Women Who Make A Difference award 1987). Office: Sage Publs Inc 2455 Teller Rd Thousand Oaks CA 91320-2218

ROTHMAN, LYNN, writer, editor; b. Phila., Nov. 24, 1951; d. Sidney and Sylvia (Katz) R.; 1 child, Michelle. BS in Comm., Temple U., 1973. Cert. tchr., Fla. Newswriter KTTV-Channel 13, L.A., 1974; mag. editor On Location Pub., L.A., 1976-78; sr. writer Miles Communication Group, L.A., 1978-84; retail copywriter United Merchandise Corp., L.A., 1984-90; mktg. rsch. Elec. Conventions Mgmt., L.A., 1990-91; copywriter Sch. Book Fairs, St. Petersburg, Fla., 1994; editor USF mag. U. South Fla., Tampa, 1994—. Author: (book) Disco The Book, 1979; editor: (trade mag.) On Location Magazine, 1976-77, (alumni mag.) USF, 1994; writer: (trade mag.) Action Magazine, Millimeter Magazine, 1979. Mem. NAFE, Dramatist Guild. Office: U South Fla 4202 E Fowler Ave Tampa FL 33620

ROTHMAN-BERNSTEIN, LISA J., nursing and health care recruiter; b. Toledo, Dec. 29, 1949; 1 child, Daniel Karvinen. Diploma, Mercy Hosp. Sch. Nursing, Toledo, 1974; B Individualized Studies magna cum laude, Lourdes Coll., Sylvania, Ohio, 1989; AS in Bus., U. Toledo, 1970; student, U. Florence, Italy, 1972. Buyer Lamson's of Toledo; owner/designer FUNKtional Art, Inc.; owner/baker Tres Bon Cheesecakes, Inc., Margate, Fla.; cruise ship nurse Costa Cruise Line, Miami, Fla.; home health nurse Upjohn, Ft. Lauderdale, Fla.; patient svcs. coord. Fla. Med. Ctr., Lauderdale Lakes; vol. nurse in ob-gyn. Yoseftal Hosp., Eilat, Israel; staff nurse in ob-gyn. Mt. Sinai Med. Ctr., Miami Beach, Fla.; staff nurse on eye svc., operating room St. Vincent Med. Ctr., Toledo, oper. rm. nurse. Co-chmn. Lourdes Coll. Red Cross Blood Drive, 1988-89; publicity chairperson St. Vincent Med. Ctr. 1993 Nurses' Week. Mem. Assn. Operating Room Nurses, NAHCR, Kappa Gamma Pi.

ROTHMAN-DENES, LUCIA BEATRIZ, biology educator; b. Buenos Aires, Feb. 17, 1943; came to U.S., 1967; d. Boris and Carmen (Couto) Rothman; m. Pablo Denes, May 24, 1968; children: Christian Andrew, Anne Elizabeth. Lic. in Chemistry, Sch. Scis., U. Buenos Aires, 1964, PhD in Biochemistry, 1967. Vis. fellow NIH, Bethesda, Md., 1967-70; postdoctoral fellow biophysics U. Chgo., 1970-73, rsch. assoc., 1973-74, asst. prof., 1974-79, assoc. prof., 1980-83, prof. molecular genetics and cell biology, 1983—; mem. microbial genetics study sect. NIH, 1980-83, 93—, chair, 1994—, genetic basis of disease study sect., 1985-89; mem. Damon Runyon and Walter Winchell Sci. Adv. Com., N.Y.C., 1989-93; mem. biochemistry panel NSF, 1990-92. Contbr. numerous articles to profl. publs. Fellow Am. Acad. Microbiology; mem. AAAS, Am. Soc. Microbiology (divsn. chair 1985, divsn. group II rep. 1990-92, vice chair GMPC 1995—), Am. Soc. Virology (councilor 1987-90), Am. Soc. Biochemistry and Molecular Biology. Office: Univ Chgo 920 E 58th St Chicago IL 60637-1432

ROTHOLZ, ELIZABETH BRUCH, fitness director; b. Cleve., July 29, 1958; d. Frank Osborne and Sally Ann (Rounds) Bruch; m. Stephen Samuel Rotholz, June 29, 1986; 1 child, Joshua Gabriel. BA, Middlebury (Vt.) Coll., 1980; MA, U. Ariz., 1988. Fitness specialist Canyon Ranch, Tucson, 1987-89; fitness dir. U.S. Dept. of Vet. Affairs, Washington, 1989—; cons. People Karch Internat., Chantilly, Va., 1989—; personal trainer, Fairfax, Va., 1990—. Co-author: The Circuit, 1990. Mem. Am. Coll. Sports Medicine, Am. Coun. on Exercise, Internat. Dance Exercise Assn., Nat. Strength and Conditioning Assn., Assn. Worksite Health Promotions. Democrat. Presbyterian.

ROTHROCK, JANE CLAIRE, nursing educator; b. Abington, Pa., Mar. 20, 1948; d. John Richard and Dorothea Ethel (Leser) Lynch; m. Joseph Rothrock, III, Apr. 17, 1977. BSN, U. Pa., 1974, MSN, 1978; DNSc, Widener U., 1987. Staff nurse Hosp. U. Pa., Phila., 1969-71, staff developer, 1971-74; dir. operating room Grad. Hosp., Phila., 1974-76; clin. instr. U. Pa., Phila., 1976-77; dir. operating room, Bryn Mawr Hosp., Pa., 1978-79; prof. Delaware County Community Coll., Media, Pa., 1979-87, prof., 1987—; pres. Quest RN Inc., Wallingford, Pa., 1985—; mem. adv. bd. Sch. of Nursing, U. Pa., 1990—. Bd. dirs. Community Mental Health Ctr., Chester, Pa., 1980-90. Author: Chesapeake Odysseys, 1984, Perioperative Care Planning, 1990; editor: The RN First Assistant, 1986, 93, Core Curriculum for RN First Assistants, 1990, 94, Alexanders Care of the Patient in Surgery, 1991, 95; editor, pub. newsletter First Hand; contbr. articles to profl. jours. Assn. Operating Rm. Nurses scholar, 1974, 85-86, 86-87. Mem. Am. Nurses Assn., Pa. Council Operating Rm. Nurses (pres. 1984-86), Assn. Operating Rm. Nurses (bd. dirs. 1987-91, treas 1991-93, pres. 1994-95, edit. bd. 1983-86, research com. 1986-87, pres.-elect 1993-94), Soc. Research in Nursing Edn. Republican. Methodist. Clubs: Pine Ridge Garden, Jr. Womens. Avocations: sailing, skiing, needlework. Office: Del County Community Coll Rte 252 Media PA 19063

ROTHS, SISTER TARCISIA, academic administrator; b. Ransom, Kans., Apr. 11, 1930. BS in Edn., Sacred Heart Coll., 1954; PhD in Modern European Hist., St. Louis U., 1959. Joined Adorers of the Blood of Christ, Roman Cath. Ch., 1948. Registrar Kans. Newman Coll., Wichita, 1959-62, acad. dean, 1962-67, 69-73, prof hist., 1967-69, 73-79, 80-82, pres., 1991—; provincial coord. Adorers of the Blood of Christ, 1982-90; vis. prof. Kaohsiung U., Taiwan, 1979-80; bd. dirs. St. Joseph Regional Med. Ctr., Wichita. Active Nat. Conf. of Christians and Jews, Wichita, Kans. Ind. Coll. Fund. NEH grantee Stanford U., 1976. Mem. Assn. Catholic Colls. and Univs., Kans. Ind. Coll. Assn., Rotary. Office: Kans Newman Coll Office of the President 3100 McCormick Wichita KS 67213-2097

ROTHSCHILD, AMALIE RANDOLPH, filmmaker, producer, director; b. Balt., June 3, 1945; d. Randolph Schamberg and Amalie Getta (Rosenfeld) R. BFA, R.I. Sch. Design, 1967; MFA in Motion Picture Production, NYU, 1969. Spl. effects staff in film and photography Joshua Light Show, Fillmore E. Theatre, NYC, 1969-71; still photographer TWA Airlines Pub. Relations Dept., Village Voice newspaper Rolling Stone magazine, Newsweek magazine, After Dark, N.Y. Daily News, numerous others, 1968-72; co-founder, partner New Day Films, distbn. coop., 1971—; owner, operator Anomaly Films Co., NYC, 1971—; mem., co-founder Assn. of Independent Video and Filmmakers, Inc., NYC, 1974, bd. dirs., 1974-78; instr. in film and TV, N.Y. U. Inst. of Film and TV, 1976-78; cons. in field to various organizations including Youthgrant Program of Nat. Endowment for Humanities, Washington, 1973-76; motion pictures include: Woo Who? May Wilson, 1969; It Happens to Us, 1972; Nana, Mom and Me, 1974; Radioimmunoassay of Renin, Radioimmunoassay of Aldosterone, 1973; Conversations with Willard Van Dyke, 1981; Richard Haas: Work in Progress, 1984; Painting the Town: The Illusionistic Murals of Richard Haas, 1990 (Emily award Am. Film and Video Festival 1990); editor: Doing It Yourself, Handbook on Independent Film Distribution, 1977. Mem. Community Planning Bd. 1, Borough of Manhattan, N.Y.C., 1974-86. Recipient spl. achievement award Mademoiselle mag., 1972; independent filmmaker grant, Am. Film Inst., 1973; film grantee N.Y. State Coun. on the Arts, 1977, 85, 87, Nat. Endowment Arts, 1978, 85, 87, Md. Arts Coun., 1977, Ohio Arts and Humanities Couns., 1985. Mem. Assn. Ind. Video Filmmakers (bd. dirs. 1974-78) Univ. Film and Video Assn., N.Y. Women in Film, Ind. Documentary Assn., Laboratorio Immagine Donna. Democrat. Address: 135 Hudson St New York NY 10013 also: Via delle Mantellate 19, Rome 00165, Italy

ROTHSCHILD, BERYL ELAINE, mayor; m. Edmund W. Rothschild; children: Margaret, Dan. BS in Journalism, Ohio U., 1951. Councilman City of University Heights, Ohio, 1968-78, mayor, 1979—; sec. Regional Coun. of Govts. Former mem. legis. policy com. Ohio Mcpl. League; past mem. exec. bd. N.E. Ohio Areawide Coord. Agy.; trustee Citizens League Greater Cleve. and Citizens League Rsch. Inst., YWCA (Metro) Cleve., Meridia Suburban Hosp., 1987-90, chmn., Meridia Health System, 1987-90; bd. dirs. Cuyahoga County Nursing Home; mem. community adv. bd. Coop. Human Tissue Network, Case Western Res. U.; mem. adv. bd. Adult Basic and Literacy Edn.; charter mem., v.p. Ind. Living Experience Achievement Program; mem. adv. com. John Carroll U. Edn. Dept., 1988-90; past mem. com. on svcs. to the disabled Jewish Community Fedn. of Cleve., special needs adv. com. Jewish Community Ctr., advanced program employer adv. coun. Jewish Vocat. Svcs.; active mem. Learning Disabilities Assn. of Greater Cleve., Frends of the Cleveland Heights-Univ. Heights Libr. System, Hadassah, Pioneer Women, Coun. of Jewish Women, Heights Y, Univ. Heights Club 100, Fairmount Temple, Women's Com. of The Cleve. Orchestra, Cleve. Mus. Art. Recipient Career Woman of Achievement award Cleve. YWCA, 1986, Woman of Achievement Recognition award Greater Cleve. chpt. Hadassah, Recognition cert. Cleveland Heights-University Heights Bd. Edn., 1980-81, City of Peace award State of Israel Bonds, 1984, Kenneth R. Oldman Meml. award (with husband) Cleve. Assn. for Children and Adults with Learning Disabilities, 1988; named one of Outstanding Women of Yr. Greater Cleve. State of Israel Bonds, 1988. Mem. Nat. League of Cities and U.S. Conf. of Mayors, Cuyahoga County Mayors and Mgrs. Assn. (exec. bd., waste mgmt. com., legis. com., cable TV com.), Women in Comms., Inc., Alpha Sigma Nu (hon.). Office: City of University Heights 2300 Warrensville Center Rd University Heights OH 44118

ROTHSTEIN, BARBARA JACOBS, federal judge; b. Bklyn., Feb. 3, 1939; d. Solomon and Pauline Jacobs; m. Ted L. Rothstein, Dec. 28, 1968; 1 child, Daniel. B.A., Cornell U., 1960; LL.B., Harvard U., 1966. Bar: Mass. 1966, Wash. 1969, U.S. Ct. Appeals (9th cir.) 1977, U.S. Dist. Ct. (we. dist.) Wash. 1971, U.S. Supreme Ct. 1975. Pvt. practice law Boston, 1966-68; asst. atty. gen. State of Wash., 1968-77; judge Superior Ct., Seattle, 1977-80; judge Fed. Dist. Ct. Western Wash., Seattle, 1980—, chief judge, 1987-94; faculty Law Sch. U. Wash., 1975-77, Hastings Inst. Trial Advocacy, 1977, N.W. Inst. Trial Advocacy, 1979—; mem. state-fed. com. U.S. Jud. Conf., chair subcom. on health reform. Recipient Matrix Table Women of Yr. award Women in Communication, Judge of the Yr. award Fed. Bar Assn., 1989. Mem. ABA (jud. sect.), Am. Judicature Soc., Nat. Assn. Women Judges, Fellows of the Am. Bar, Wash. State Bar Assn., U.S. Jud. Conf. (state-fed. com., health reform subcom.), Phi Beta Kappa, Phi Kappa Phi. Office: US Dist Ct 705 US Courthouse 1010 5th Ave Seattle WA 98104-1130

ROTHSTEIN, RUTH M., hospital adminstrator. Dir. Cook County Hosp., Chgo.; chief Cook County Bur. of Health Svcs. Mailing: Cook County Hosp 1835 W Harrison St Chicago IL 60612

ROTHSTEIN, SUSAN PETSCHAFT, financial analyst; b. Newton, Mass., Aug. 29, 1966; d. Hans and Jane Imogene (Brown) Petschaft; m. Ned Rothstein, Oct. 2, 1993. BA in Anthropology & Sociology cum laude, Wellesley Coll., 1988; postgrad., Northeastern U., 1994—. Disc jockey WZLY-FM, Wellesley, Mass., 1984-88, rec. libr., 1984-86, program dir., 1986-87, gen. mgr., 1987-88; paralegal, legal sec. Atty. Dennis R. Brown, Wellesley, Mass., 1984-89; fin. analyst, exec. sec. Burr, Egan, Deleage & Co., Boston, 1989-94; assoc. bus. assurance group Coopers & Lybrand, Boston, 1994—. Mem. Boston U. Ctr. Archeol. Studies, 1983—, Boston U. Nikopolis Project, 1991—. Wellesley Town scholar, 1984-88; recipient Scholastic All-Am. Collegiate award, 1988. Mem. NOW, N.Am. Fishing Club, Alpha Kappa Delta (scholar 1988). Avocations: piano, photography, reading, travel, freshwater fishing.

ROTHWELL, LISA JANINE, sales engineer; b. Sparta, Wis., Feb. 7, 1959; d. Harry Gordon and Laurel M. R.; m. Timothy J. O'Loughlin, Jun. 22, 1982 (div. 1990); 1 child, Ian J. O'Loughlin. AA in Math., Marian Coll., Wis., 1982; BS in Indsl. Tech. cum laude, So. Ill. U., 1986. Sales engr. M.J. Foley, Roseville, Mich. Asst. cub scout leadership Boy Scouts Am. Pack #96, Harrison Twp., Mich., 1993-94. Mem. Soc. Mfg. Engrs. (sec. mem. chmn. chpt. 45 1990-93, mem. chmn. chpt. 1 Detroit 1994), Soc. Auto Engrs. Home: 27900 Coleridge Rd 105-X Harrison Township MI 48045 Office: MJ Foley 16580 Eastland Roseville MI 48066

ROTTENBUCHER, JO ANN, parole-probation officer; b. Monroe, Mich., Dec. 3, 1951; d. Donald George and Dorothy Mae Rottenbucher; m. James Eugene Abercrombie, June 23, 1978 (div. 1990); 1 child, James Jonathan Abercrombie. AS, Monroe (Mich.) C.C., 1972; AA, Mercy Coll. Detroit, 1973, BA, 1974. Parole-probation officer Mich. Dept. Corrections, Lansing, Mich., 1978—. Pres. Elmhurst Park Neighborhood Assn., Dearborn, Mich., 1980-85. Mem. UAW (local 6000, trustee, mem. exec. bd. 1986-89, chief steward 1991—), Macomb County Detective Assn., Fraternal Order of Police. Democrat. Office: Mich Dept Corrections Cir Ct Probation Dept County Bldg 9th Fl Mount Clemens MI 48043

ROTUNNO, PHYLLIS DI BUONO, accounting educator, researcher; b. Phila., Mar. 22, 1929; d. Salvatore and Rose (Pontolillo) di Buono; m. Rocco Michael Rotunno, Apr. 18, 1948; children: Roxane Rotunno Tise, Philip Anthony, Diane Rotunno Ellertsen. BS magna cum laude, N.Y. Inst. Tech., 1979; M in Acct., U. No. Fla., 1983. CPA, Fla. Mgr. acct. controls ITT Community Devel. Corp., Palm Coast, Fla., 1978-88; asst. prof. acct. Bethune-Cookman Coll., Daytona Beach, Fla., 1989—; dir. bd. Trustees ACT Corp., 1990-92; dir. student activities Inst. Mgmt. Accts., Daytona Beach, 1990-92; area coord. Acct. Bethune Cookman Coll., 1990—. Study rschr. A Comparative Analysis of Test Scores in Principles of Acct. II, 1989; prin. rschr. Tchr. Effectiveness Evaluation; co-founder North Shore Sci. Mus., Manhasset, N.Y. Mem. AICPA, Fla. Inst. CPAs (mem. industry, govt. and edn. com. 1992-93). Office: Bethune-Cookman Coll 640 Mary McLeod Bethune Blvd Daytona Beach FL 32114-3099

ROUCH-CHRISTIANSON, LIBBY KATHLEEN, elementary school counselor; b. Bremen, Ind., Dec. 9, 1952; d. Clarence Ernald and Mary Jane (McDonald) Rouch; m. Thomas Edwin Christianson, Dec. 27, 1981; children: Abram Thomas, Matthew Elias, Taylor Isaac. BA, U. Utah, 1977; M in Counseling, Gallaudett U., 1979; cert. in sch. counseling, Ind. U., 1993. Lic. sch. counselor, Ind.; cert. clin. social worker, Ind.; cert. interpreter for the deaf, Utah; nat. cert. counselor. Coun. for the deaf, counselor/rehab. Ind. State Dept. of Human Svcs., Divsn. Vocat. Rehab., South Bend, 1981-86; coord., case worker Marshall County Single Parents Program, Plymouth, Ind., 1986-89; sign lang. instr. div. continuing edn. Ind. U., State Bend, 1991-92, coord. of disabled student svcs., 1990-91; sign lang. instr. St. Mary's Coll., Notre Dame, Ind., 1991-92; therapist, ind. living coord. The Children's Campus of the Family and Children's Ctr., Mishawaka, Ind., 1991-92; sch. counselor Baugo Sch. Corp., Elkhart, Ind., 1992—; therapist deaf families Albion, Ind., 1994-95; sign lang. instr. WaNee Pub. Sch. Corp.-Adult Edn. Program, Nappanee, Ind., 1993—, Wakaruse Pub. Libr., Wakarusa, 1993; interpreter for the deaf, No. and Ctrl. Ind. Grand writing cons. Urban League of South Bend and St. Joseph County, 1993. Mem. ACA, Midwest Regional Network for Intervention with Sex Offenders, Ind. Sch. Counseling Assn., Ind. Counseling Assn., Ind. Registry of Interpreters for the Deaf. Republican. Mem. Brethren. Home: 605 S Locke St Nappanee IN 46550-2521 Office: Baugo Sch Corp Jimtown Elem 58901 County Road 3 Elkhart IN 46517-9303

ROUDEBUSH, COLLEEN GOODILL, industrial designer; b. Erie, Pa., Nov. 22, 1958; d. John J. and Joan (Gibbons) Goodill; m. Gary Mason Roudebush, June 4, 1994. BA in English, Art, and Theatre Art, Hollins Coll., 1980; AAS in Fashion Design, Fashion Inst. Tech., N.Y.C., 1982, AAS in Surface/Textile, Design, 1987; MA in English Lit., Hunter Coll., 1994. Designer Ford Motor Co., Dearborn, Mich., 1989-90; sr. designer Mazda R&D of N.Am., Irvine, Calif., 1990—. Office: Mazda R&D of N Am 1421 Reynolds Ave Irvine CA 92714

ROUDYBUSH, ALEXANDRA, novelist; b. Hyres, Cote d'Azur, France, Mar. 14, 1911; d. Constantine and Ethel (Wheeler) Brown; m. Franklin Roudybush, 1942. Student, St. Paul's Sch. for Girls, London, London Sch. Econs., 1930. Journalist London Eve. Standard, 1931, Time mag., 1933, French News Agy., 1935, CBS, 1936, MBS, 1940; White House corr. MBC Radio, 1940-48. Author: Before the Ball Was Over, 1965; Death of a Moral Person, 1967; Capital Crime, 1969; House of the Cat, 1970; A Sybaritic Death, 1972; Suddenly in Paris, 1975; The Female of the Species, 1977; Blood Ties, 1981. Mem. Crime Writers Am. and Brit., Am. Woman's Club (Paris), Miramar Golf Club (Porto, Portugal). Democrat. Episcopalian.

ROUGHGARDEN, TRUDY ANNETTE, piano teacher; b. Mpls., Jan. 31, 1947; d. James Wesley and Dorothy Jean (Eaton) Shean; m. Jonathan David Roughgarden, May 31, 1969; 1 child, Timothy Avelin. BA, U. Rochester, 1968. Pvt. piano tchr., composer Palo Alto, Calif., 1973—. Mem. Fortnightly Music Club (piano chmn. 1988-90). Home: 1822 Hamilton Ave Palo Alto CA 94303-3007

ROUKEMA, MARGARET SCAFATI, congresswoman; b. Newark, N.J., Sept. 19, 1929; d. Claude Thomas and Margaret (D'Alessio) Scafati; m. Richard W. Roukema, Aug. 23, 1951; children—Margaret, Todd (dec.), Gregory. B.A. with honors in History and Polit. Sci, Montclair State Coll., 1951, postgrad. in history and guidance, 1951-53; postgrad. program in city and regional planning, Rutgers U., 1975. Tchr. history, govt., public schs. Livingston and Ridgewood, N.J., 1951-55; mem. 97th-103rd Congresses from 5th N.J. dist., Washington, D.C., 1981—; mem. Banking, Fin. Urban Affairs com., subcom. Housing, Community devel., Internat. devel., Fin., Trade, Monetary Policy, Econ. Growth on; mem. Credit formation, Edn. Labor com., subcom. labor mgmt. rels., elementary, sec., vocat. edn., post-secondary edn. tng.; vice pres. Ridgewood Bd. Edn., 1970-73; bd. dirs., co-founder Ridgewood Sr. Citizens Housing Corp. Trustee Spring House, Paramus, N.J.; trustee Leukemia Soc. No. N.J., Family Counseling Service for Ridgewood and Vicinity; mem. Bergen County (N.J.) Republican Com.; NW Bergen County campaign mgr. for gubernatorial candidate Tom Kean, 1977. Mem. Bus. and Profl. Women's Orgn. Clubs: Coll. of Ridgewood, Ridgewood Rep. Office: US Ho of Reps 2244 Rayburn Washington DC 20515

ROULET, TRINA MARIE, financial executive, accountant; b. Colfax, Wash., June 12, 1946. BSBA with high honors, Mich. Tech. U., 1984. CPA, Mich. Sr. acct. Richard C. Woodbury, CPA, Hancock, Mich., 1984-87; mem. inventory support group and tax dept. Accountants One, Southfield, Mich., 1987-88; fin. reporting officer, mgr. fin. analysis, asst. v.p. D & N Bank, Hancock, 1988—; mem. ad hoc com. acctg. programs Mich. Tech. U., fall 1986. Bd. dirs. Copper Country Community Arts Coun.; bd. dirs. Portage Lake Libr. Bd., 1986-87. Mem. AICPA, AAUW (treas. Copper Country 1991-93), Mich. Assn. CPAs, Buellwood Weavers Guild. Office: D & N Bank 400 Quincy St Hancock MI 49930-1829

ROUMELL, LISA, venture capitalist; b. Grosse Pointe, Mich., Feb. 6, 1959; d. George Theodore and Aphrodite (Doukas) R. BA, Harvard U., 1981, MBA, 1985. Fin. analyst corp. fin. Smith Barney Harris Upham, N.Y.C., 1981-83; assoc. Gen. Electric Venture Co., Fairfield, Conn., 1984; v.p., gen. ptnr. First Century Ptnrs., N.Y.C., 1985—. Vol. Mus. Modern Art Contemporary Art Coun., Harvard Coll. Fund Leadership Coun. Elizabeth Aguissey scholar Harvard U., 1981. Mem. Nat. Venture Capital Assn., N.Y. Venture Forum, Harvard Bus. Sch. Club. Democrat. Episcopalian.

ROUMM, PHYLLIS EVELYN GENSBIGLER, English language educator, writer; b. New Alexandria, Pa., Jan. 1, 1927; d. Theodore Roosevelt and Daisy Isabelle (Patterson) Gensbigler; m. Milton Leonard Roumm, Nov. 23, 1946; children: David Lynn, Nikolyn, Dennis Eric, Janna Leigh. BS in English Edn., Indiana U. of Pa., 1945, MEd, 1963; postgrad., Ohio U., 1964, 65; PhD, Kent State U., 1977. Tchr. English Elders Ridge (Pa.) Joint High Sch., 1945-46, Apollo (Pa.) High Sch., 1946-47; tchr. English, speech Indiana Area Jr.-Sr. High Sch., 1959-67; teaching fellow Kent (Ohio) State U., 1970-71; prof. English Indiana U. of Pa., 1967-85, prof. emeritus, 1985—; freelance writer, 1985—. Bd. dirs. Hist. and Geneal. Soc. of Indiana County, 1984, Indiana Free Libr., 1988-91. Mem. AAUW, Coll. English Assn., Ligonier Valley Writers Assn., So. Humanities Conf., Pa. Ret. State Employees, Am. Assn. Ret. People, Assn. Pa. State Coll. and Univ. Ret. Faculty, Ind. (Pa.) Wordsmiths, Alpha Delta Kappa (pres. 1968-70, Silver Sister award 1991), Phi Delta Kappa. Home: 310 Poplar Ave Indiana PA 15701-3024

ROUND, ALICE FAYE BRUCE, school psychologist; b. Ironton, Ohio, July 19, 1934; d. Wade Hamilton and Martha Matilda (Toops) Bruce; m. Leonard Paul Round, June 21, 1958; children: Leonard Bruce, Christopher Frederick. BA, Asbury Coll., 1956; MS in Sch. Psychology, Miami U., Oxford, Ohio, 1975. Cert. tchr., sch. psychologist, supr., Ohio; cert. tchr., Calif. Tchr. Madison County (Ohio) Schs., 1956-58, Columbus (Ohio) Pub. Schs., 1958, San Diego Pub. Schs., 1958-60, Poway (Calif.) Unified Sch. Dist., 1960-64; substitute tchr. Princeton City Schs., Cin., 1969-75; sch. psychologist, intern Greenhills/Forest Park City Schs., Cin., 1975-76; sch. psychologist Fulton County Schs., Wauseon, Ohio, 1976-77, Sandusky (Ohio) pub. and Cath. schs., 1977—; tchr. art cmty. group and pvt. lessons, Sandusky, 1962, Springdale, Ohio, 1962-69; mem. Youth Svcs. Bd., Sandusky, 1978-88; bd. dirs., cons. Sandusky Sch. Practical Nursing, 1983-91; presenter suicide prevention seminars for mental health orgns.; speaker at ch., civic and youth orgns., local radio and TV programs; cons. on teen pregnancy to various schs., health depts. Mem. Huron (Ohio) Boosters Club, 1978-92, Vols. in Action, Sandusky, 1987—. Mem. NAACP, NEA, Nat. Sch. Psychologist Assn., Ohio Sch. Psychologist Assn., Maumee Valley Sch. Psychologist Assn., Coun. Exceptional Children, Ohio Edn. Assn., Sandusky Edn. Assn., Phi Delta Kappa (historian 1984-88, Most Innovative Preservation of History award 1988). Home: 821 Seneca Ave Huron OH 44839-1842 Office: Sandusky Bd Edn 407 Decatur St Sandusky OH 44870-2442

ROUNDS, BARBARA LYNN, psychiatrist; b. L.A., Mar. 17, 1934; d. Ralph Arthur and Florene V. (Heyer) Behrend; divorced 1962; children: Steve, Mike, Pamela, Ronald, Thomas. BA, Stanford U., 1964, MD, 1966; postgrad., San Francisco Psychoanalytic, 1973-81. Diplomate Am. Bd. Psychiatry and Neurology; cert. psychoanalyst. Intern New Orleans Pub. Health Svc., 1966-67; resident psychiat. Mendocino State Hosp., 1967-69, U. Calif. Davis, 1969-70; staff psychiatrist U. Calif. Davis Med. Sch., Sacramento, 1970-77, clin. instr., 1970-76; psychiatrist pvt. practice, Sacramento, 1971—; asst. clin. prof. U. Calif. Davis, Sacramento, 1976-84, assoc. clin. prof., 1984—. Mem. Am. Psychiat. Assn., Am. Psychoanalytic Assn., AMA, Cen. Calif. Psychiat. Soc. (pres.-elect 1990-91, pres. 1991-92). Democrat. Home: 8910 Leatham Ave Fair Oaks CA 95628-6506 Office: 1317 H St Sacramento CA 95814-1906

ROUP, BRENDA JACOBS, nurse, army officer; b. Petersburg, Va., July 8, 1948; d. Eugene Thurman and Sarah Ann (Williams) Jacobs; m. Clarence James Roup, May 8, 1976. B.S.N., Med. Coll. Va., Richmond, 1970; M.S.N., Cath. U. Am., 1977; postgrad. U. Md., 1989—. Commd. 2d lt. U.S. Army, 1970, advanced through grades to lt. col., 1986; infection control cons. 7th MEDCOM, Fed. Republic Germany, 1982-83; chief infection control Brooke Army MEDCEN, San Antonio, 1983-86; chief infection control Walter Reed MEDCEN, Washington, 1986-92, ret., 1992; nurse cons. in infection control to U.S. Army Surgeon Gen., 1986-92. Contbr. articles to profl. jours. Mem. Nat. League for Nurses, Assn. Practitioners in Infection Control, Am. Assn. Mil. Surgeons, Sigma Theta Tau. Avocations: reading, swimming, cooking.

ROUSE, SHARON NEVIN, art specialist; b. Grand Island, Nebr., June 13, 1940; d. Merle F. and Luella S. (Plummer) Nevin; m. Terrance S. Rouse. BA, U. Colo., 1962; student, Met. State Coll., Denver, 1987; M in Visual Arts, U. No. Colo., 1994. Art specialist grades 7-10 Littleton, Colo., 1962-64; art specialist grades 9-12 Midland, Tex., 1964-65; art specialist grades 4-8 Savanna, Ill., 1966-68; art specialist grades 1-9 Graland Country Day Sch., Denver, 1988—; docent, cons. Denver Art Mus., 1981—, co-chair Art of Crafts show, 1986-88. Mem. com. All About Art, Denver, 1993. Mem. Nat. Art Edn. Assn., Colo. Art Edn. Assn. (coun. 1988-94, Marion Quin Dix Leadership award 1994).

ROUSH, DOROTHY EVELYN, medical laboratory educator, consultant; b. Flatwoods, Ky., July 16, 1930; d. William Arch and Mary Jane (Frasure) Salyers; m. Gilbert Riley Dush, Aug. 26, 1951 (div. 1972); m. Virgil Bernard Roush, Nov. 18, 1972. Med. tech. degree, Clin. Lab., Mt. Vernon, Ohio, 1953; student, Ohio State U., 1967-72. Registered med. tech. Med. tech. Hosp. & Tb Hosp., Newark, Ohio, 1953-60; office nurse various physicians, Newark and Columbus, Ohio and Seattle, 1960-93; nursing home coord. Med. Lab., Seattle, 1980-89; sr. phlebotomist Roche BioMed. Lab., Burlington, N.C., 1990—; nurse, phlebotomist ARC Blood Program, Columbus, Ohio, 1961-72; instr. in field; cons. in field. Contbr. articles to profl. jours. Vol. ARC, 1957-72, Boulder (Colo.) County Foster Parents, 1976, Cath. Shared Missions, Seattle, 1987. Recipient Appreciation award Gt. Brit. Red Cross Nursing Svc., 1969, Internat. Cancer Congress, 1982. Mem. Am. Assn. Med. Assts., Am. Med. Techs. (chairperson com., Disting. Achievement award 1991), Wash. State Soc. Am. Tech. (sec., v.p., Tech. of Yr. 1989, 90), Am. Legion Aux. Roman Catholic. Home and Office: 18002 Hyacinth Dr Sun City West AZ 85375

ROUSH, JEANNE, association administrator. Exec. dir. People for the Ethical Treatment of Animals, D.C. Office: PETA Box 42516 Washington DC 20015*

ROUSON, VIVIAN REISSLAND, alcohol/drug abuse services professional; b. New Orleans, July 18, 1929; d. Albert Isaac and Ophelia (Scott) Reissland; m. W. Ervin Rouson, June 22, 1953 (dec. May 1979); children: Lizette Hélène, Darryl Ervin, Brigette Maria, Janine Patrice, Damian William. BA, Xavier U., 1951; MS, Nova U., 1979; postgrad., U. Ky., 1965, U. South Fla., 1970. Tchr., cons. Gibbs Jr. Coll., St. Petersburg, Fla., 1958-60; tchr., cons. Pinellas County Schs., St. Petersburg,, Clearwater, Fla., 1960-78; freelance opinion editorial columnist U.S. newspaper, 1976-82; columnist Evening Independent, Pinellas County, Fla., 1976-78, Palm Beach (County, Fla.) Post, 1979-82; tchr., cons. Palm Beach County Sch., Lake Worth, W. Palm Beach, Fla., 1978-82; editorial writer St. Petersburg Times, 1979; program coord. Women's Resource Ctr., Normandale Community Coll., Bloomington, Minn., 1986-89, interim dir., 1989; vol., intern program coord. Inst. on Black Chem. Abuse, Mpls., 1989-90; assoc. editor Nat. Black Media Coalition, Washington, 1991—; V.I.P. coord. Inst. on Black Chem. Abuse, Mpls., 1989-90; writing and fgn. lang. cons. Pinellas County and Palm Beach County, fla., 1960-82; bd. dirs. Carroll Pub. Co. Author: The Hummingbird Within Us, 1980, Like a Mighty Banyan, 1982, Alcohol and Drug Abuse in Black America, 1988; editor conf. proceedings; editorial writer-columnist; editorial bd. St. Petersburg Times, 1979. Bd. dirs. St. Petersburg Cath. High Sch., 1976, Minn. divsn. Am. Cancer Soc., Mpls., 1983-90, Ind. Sch. Dist. 191, Burnsville, Eagan, Savage, Minn., 1984-87, Minn. Valley YMCA, Dakota County, Minn., 1987-90; pres. D.C. chpt. Hook-Up Black Women, 1992—; sec., bd. dirs. Ionia Whipper Home, Inc., 1992—; mem. D.C. chpt. Nat. Urban League. Named Outstanding Journalist south Atlantic region Alpha Kappa Alpha, 1978, 79, 80; recipient Appreciation Pub. Svc. cert. Nat. Assn. Black Accts., 1992. Mem. AAUW, Twin Cities Black Journalists (co-chair 1985-86, v.p. 1989-90), Minn. Polit. Congress Black Women (charter), Nat. Urban League (subscribing life, Washington chpt.), Minn. Elected Women Ofcls., Dakota County Soc. Black Women (founder, v.p. 1983-84), Pinellas County Fgn. Lang. Tchrs. (treas., pres.), The Links (sec. Capital City chpt.), Alpha Kappa Alpha (life). Roman Catholic. Home: 2311 N Capitol St NE Washington DC 20002-1105 Office: One Church One Addict 1146 19th St NW Washington DC 20036

ROUSSEL, LEE DENNISON, diplomat; b. N.Y.C., May 15, 1944; d. Ethan Allen and Frances Isabel (Ferry) Dennison; m. Andre Homo Roussel, Sept. 6, 1980; children: Cecilia Frances, Stephanie Anne. AB, Wellesley Coll., 1966; MA, Northeastern U., 1973. Mgmt. intern U.S. Dept. HEW, 1966-68; with Planning Office Commonwealth of Mass., 1968-70; exec. dir. Gov.'s Commn. Citizen Participation, Boston, 1973; with Boston Area Office U.S. Dept. HUD, 1970-78; fgn. svc. officer USAID, 1978—; with Housing and Urban Devel. Office USAID, Washington and Tunis, 1978-82; chief Housing and Urban Devel. Office for C.Am. USAID, Honduras, 1982-87; asst. dir. Office Housing and Urban Programs USAID, Washington, 1987-91; country rep. for Czech and Slovak Fed. Rep. USAID, 1991-92, country rep. for Czech Rep., 1993-94; min. counselor, U.S. rep. to Devel. Assistance Com. OECD, Paris, 1995—. Episcopalian. Office: USOECD, 19 rue de Franqueville, 75016 Paris France also: OECD PSC 116 APO AE 09777

ROUTSON JARRELL, JANET LOUISE, nursing administrator; b. Durand, Mich., Oct. 20, 1943; d. Earl F. and Eva Christiana (Krueger) R.; m. James C. Jarrell; children: Andrew, Anthony. ADN, Mott Coll., 1972; BSN, Mich. State U., 1978; MSN, U. Mich., 1982; postgrad. studies, Med. Coll. of Va., 1993—. RN; cert. nursing adminstr. Staff nurse Owosso (Mich.) Meml. Hosp., 1972-80; shift supr. Saginaw (Mich.F) Osteo. Hosp., 1978; floor supr. Genessee Meml. Hosp., Flint, Mich., 1978-82; dir. critical care McLaren Hosp., Flint, 1982-89; staff nurse Providence Hosp., Anchorage, Alaska, 1989; program dir. Dept. of Vet. Affairs, Anchorage, 1989-92; svc. line mgr. U. Va. Med. Ctr., Charlottesville, 1992—; cons., pvt. practice, Flint, Mich., 1990-92. Editor (newsletters) Va. Health, 1990-92, Picu W&R, 1992—. Mem. support staff Alaska Naval Militia, 1989-92. Mem. AACN, Emergency Nurses Assn., Naval Reserve Assn., Am. Heart Assn. Home: 326 Whispering Oaks Dr Charlottesville VA 22902-7246 Office: Children's Med Ctr /HSC 7 East Charlottesville VA 22905

ROUTT, KAREN ELIZABETH, real estate consultant; b. Detroit, May 3, 1955; d. Robert Fletcher and Catherine (Weiss) R. Student, Denison U., 1973-75; BA, U. Mich., 1977; MBA, Stanford U., 1983. Cons. Arthur Andersen & Co., Detroit, 1977-79, sr. cons., 1979-81; project mgr. Bank One Columbus, N.Am., Ohio, 1983-84, project mgr., officer, 1984, mgr. on-line support, 1984-85, mgr. interest rate swap portfolio, 1985-86, mgr. check capture, 1986-87; sr. assoc. Index Group Inc., Cambridge, Mass., 1988-89; assoc. dir. Prism, 1989-92; chief of staff to the mayor Cambridge, Mass., 1992-93; pres., real estate cons. K. Routt & Assocs., Cambridge, 1993—. Active Big Sister, 1986-89; chmn. Commn. to Promote and Enhance Cen. Square Now!, 1992-93; bd. dirs. Shelter, Inc., 1992-94; mem. Devel. Commn., 1992-93, Property Mgmt. Commn., 1994, R&H Investments, 1989—, pres. 1990-91; charter mem. Coalition of 100 Black Women, Boston chpt. 1991—, chmn. nominating com., 1992-93. Mem. Zonta (bd. dirs. Columbus club 1987-88, chair girls group home 1986-88), Am. Soc. on Aging. Mem. United Ch. Christ.

ROUX, MILDRED ANNA, retired secondary education educator; b. New Castle, Pa., June 1, 1914; d. Louis Henri and Frances Amanda (Gillespie) R. BA, Westminster Coll., 1936, MS in Edn., 1951. Tchr. Farrell (Pa.) Sch. Dist., 1939-55; tchr. Latin, English New Castle (Pa.) Sch. Dist., 1956-76; ret., 1976; chmn. sr. high sch. fgn. lang. dept. New Castle Sch. Dist., 1968-76, faculty sponsor sch. fgn. lang. newspapers, 1960-76, 71-76, Jr. Classical League, 1958-76. Mem. Lawrence County Hist. Soc., Am. Classical League, 1958-76. Mem. AAUW (chmn. publicity, chmn. program com. Lawrence County chpt. 1992-94), AARP, Nat. Ret. Tchrs. Assn., Pa. Assn. Sch. Retirees (chmn. cmty. participation com. Lawrence County br. 1976-81), Coll. Club New Castle (chmn. sunshine com. 1989-91, mem. social com. 1991-92), Woman's Club New Castle (chmn. pub. affairs com. 1988-90, mem. internat. affairs com. 1990-92, mem. program com. 1990-92, telephone com. 1992-94). Republican. Roman Catholic. Home: 6 E Moody Ave New Castle PA 16101-2356

ROVELSTAD, MATHILDE VERNER, library science educator; b. Kempten, Germany, Aug. 12, 1920; came to U.S., 1951, naturalized, 1953; d. George and Therese (Hohl) Hotter; m. Howard Rovelstad, Nov. 23, 1970. Ph.D., U. Tubingen, 1953; M.S. in L.S, Catholic U. Am., 1960. Cataloger Mt. St. Mary's Coll., Los Angeles, 1953; sch. librarian Yoyogi Elem. Sch., Tokyo, 1954-56; mem. faculty Cath. U. Am., 1960-90, prof. library sci., 1975-90, prof. emeritus, 1990—; vis. prof. U. Montreal, 1969. Author: Bibliotheken in den Vereinigten Staaten, 1974; translator Bibliographia, an Inquiry into its Definition and Designations (R. Blum), 1980, Bibliotheken in den Vereinigten Staaten von Amerika und in Kanada, 1988; contbr. articles to profl. jours. Research grantee German Acad. Exch. Svc., 1969, Herzog August Bibliothek Wolfenbüttel, Germany, 1995. Mem. ALA (internat. relations com. 1977-80), Internat. Fedn. Library Assns. and Instns. (standing adv. com. on library schs. 1975-81), Assn. for Library and Info. Sci. Edn. Home: PO Box 111 Gibson Island MD 21056 Office: Cath U Am Sch Libr & Info Sci Washington DC 20064

ROVERUD, ELEANOR, pathologist, neuropathologist; b. Spring Grove, Minn., Oct. 24, 1912; d. Henry S. and Sigrid (Bakken) R.; m. Stuart Henry Nam (dec. Nov. 1986); children: Sue, Kay, Becky, Howard, Signe, Sonia, Tom, Ted, Kurt. Diploma, Kahler Sch. Nursing, Rochester, Minn., 1934; BS in Nursing Edn., U. Minn., 1940; MD, Med. Coll. Pa., 1947. Intern Swedish Hosp., Mpls., 1947-48; resident in pathology, resident instr. Sch. of Tropical Medicine U. P.R., San Juan, 1949-52; fellow in Neuropathology Columbia U., Presbyn. Hosp., N.Y.C., 1952-54; neuropathologist Wayne County Gen. Hosp., Eloise, Mich., 1954-59; assoc. prof. Woman's Med. Coll./Med. Coll. Pa., Phila., 1959-61; pathologist Women's Hosp., Phila., 1961-62, St. Anthony Regional Hosp., Carroll, Iowa, 1962-77; cons. in pathology Carroll, Iowa, 1977-87, Spring Grove, 1987—; expert witness forensic cases Carroll County, Iowa, 1962-77. Chmn., v.p., sec. Carroll chpt. ARC, 1968-75. Mem. AMA, Am. Assn. Neuropathologists, Iowa Med. Soc. (life), Carroll County Med. Assn. (sec. 1968-74), Am. Med. Women's Assn., Zumbro Valley Med. Soc., Minn. Med. Assn. Democrat. Lutheran. Office: PO Box 706 Spring Grove MN 55974-0706

ROVIROSA, DOLORES GONZALEZ-QUEVEDO, librarian; b. Matanzas, Cuba, Dec. 6, 1926; came to U.S., 1962; d. Jose and Dolores (Gonzalez-Quevedo) R. DPhil, U. Havana, 1955, degree in librarianship, 1956; MEd, U. Miami, 1975. Cert. tchr. Fla. Asst. libr. Pre-Univ Sch., Havana, Cuba, 1951-60; head catalog dept. Nat. Libr., Havana, Cuba, 1959-61; prof. cataloging U. Havana, 1961; asst. catalog libr. U. Nev., Reno, 1962-63; instr. So. Ill. U., Carbondale, 1963-64; catalog libr. U. Tex., Austin, 1964-70; media specialist Lourdes Acad., Miami, 1971-74; clk. of cts. County and Circuit Cts., Miami, 1977-90; media specialist Miami Sr. Adult Edn. Ctr., 1994—; libr. Hilda Perera, Miami, 1994—; libr. specialist Brigada 2506's Libr., Miami, 1987-88, Dr. Modesto Maidique's Libr., Miami, 1985-86. Author of bibliographies. Founder, 1st pres. Colegio Nat. Bibliotecarios, Miami, 1987—; rec. sec., treas., Cuban Women's Club, Miami, 1984-92 (Floridana award 1983); founder Assn. Cubana Mujeres Univs., 1989; rec. sec. Circulo de Cultura Panamericano, Miami, 1993. Recipient Juan J. Remos award Cruzasa Educative Cubana, 1982; Gran Orden Martiana del merit, 1983. Mem. AAUW, Cuban Assn. Univ. Women, Centro Hispano Catolico., Epsilon Tau Lambda. Roman Catholic. Home: 1809 Brickell Ave Apt 1012 Miami FL 33129

ROVNER, ILANA KARA DIAMOND, federal judge; b. Aug. 21, 1938; came to U.S., 1939; d. Stanley and Ronny (Medalje) Diamond; m. Richard Nyles Rovner, Mar. 9, 1963; 1 child, Maxwell Rabson. AB, Bryn Mawr Coll., 1960; postgrad., U. London King's Coll., 1961, Georgetown U., 1961-63; JD, Ill. Inst. Tech., 1966; LittD (hon.), Rosary Coll., 1989, Mundelein Coll., 1989; DHL (hon.), Spertus Coll. of Judaica, 1992. Bar: Ill. 1972, U.S. Dist. Ct. (no. dist.) Ill. 1972, U.S. Ct. Appeals (7th cir.) 1977, U.S. Supreme Ct. 1982. Jud. clk. U.S. Dist. Ct. (no. dist.) Ill., Chgo., 1972-73; asst. U.S. atty. U.S. Atty.'s Office, Chgo., 1973-77; dep. chief of pub. protection, 1975-76, chief pub. protection, 1976-77; dep. gov., legal counsel Gov. James R. Thompson, Chgo., 1977-84; dist. judge U.S. Dist. Ct. (no. dist.) Ill., Chgo., 1984-92; cir. judge U.S. Ct. Appeals (7th cir.), Chgo., 1992—. Trustee Bryn Mawr Coll., Pa., 1983-89; mem. bd. overseers Ill. Inst. Tech./Kent Coll. of Law, 1983—; trustee Ill. Inst. Tech., 1989—; adv. coun. Rush Ctr. for Sports Medicine, Chgo., 1991—; civil justice reform act adv. com. for the 7th cir., Chgo., 1991-92; bd. visitors No. Ill. U. Coll. of Law, 1992-94; vis. com. Northwestern U. Sch. of Law, 1993—; vis. com. U. Chgo. Law Sch., 1993—. Recipient Spl. Commendation award U.S. Dept. of Justice, 1975, Spl. Achievement award 1976, Ann. Nat. Law and Social Justice Leadership award League to Improve the Community, 1975, Ann. Guardian Police award, 1977, Profl. Achievement award Ill. Inst. Tech., 1986, Louis Dembitz Brandeis medal for Disting. Legal Svc., Brandeis U., 1993, First Woman award Valparaiso U. Sch. of Law, 1993, ORT Women's Am. Community Svc. award, 1987-88, Judaica Svc. award Spertus Coll., 1987, Ann. award Chgo. Found. for Women, 1990; named Today's Chgo. Woman of Yr., 1985, Woman of Achievement Chgo. Women's Club, 1986, more. Mem. ABA, Ill. Bar Assn., Chgo. Bar Assn. (commendation def. of prisoners com. 1987),

Women's Bar Assn. Ill (ann. award 1989, 1st Myra Bradwell Woman of Achievement award 1994), Fed. Bar Assn. (jud. selection com. Chgo. chpt. 1977-80, treas. 1978-79, sec. 1979-80, 2d v.p. 1980-81, 1st v.p. 1981-82, pres. 1982-83, nat. 2d v.p. 7th cir. 1983-84, v.p. 1984-85), Fed. Judges Assn., Nat. Assn. Women Judges, Chgo. Coun. Lawyers, Decalogue Soc. (citation of honor 1991), Kappa Beta Pi, Phi Alpha Delta (hon.). Republican. Jewish. Office: 219 S Dearborn St Rm 2774 Chicago IL 60604-1803

ROWAN, PATRICIA ANN, credit union executive; b. Chgo., Aug. 11, 1964; d. Leroy and Elsie (Young) Toles; m. Ernest Rowan III, Apr. 5, 1985; children: Charles A., Kiana A. Student, Florissant Valley Coll., 1983-84; student, Palomar Coll., 1993—. Teller supr. MCWFCU, Camp Pendleton, Calif., 1985-88, EE Credit Union, St. Louis, 1988-90; br. mgr. USAF Credit Union, San Diego, 1990—. Democrat. Baptist. Office: USA Fed Credit Union 9889 Erma Rd San Diego CA 92131-2487

ROWAN, RENA JUNG, apparel company design executive; b. Lida, Poland, Jan. 4, 1928; came to U.S., 1945; d. Henryk and Maria (Gryiel) Jung; children: Nina, Jimmy, David, Lisa. Student, Mus. Sch. Art, Phila. Model, designer Gustave Tassell, 1953-54; sleepwear designer Youtheme Lingerie, Wilmington, Del., 1958-60; children's fashion designer Cinderella Dresses, Phila., 1960-66; sportswear fashion designer Villager, Phila., 1966-70; fashion designer Jones Apparel Group, N.Y.C., 1970-77, v.p. design, 1977—; designer Christian Dior div., 1981-83, Rena Rowan blouse line, 1984; pres. Christian Dior div., 1989—. Bd. dirs. Phila. Coll. Textile Sci., 1993—. Mem. Artists Equity Club (Phila.). Democrat. Roman Catholic. Home (winter): 200 Via Bellaria Palm Beach FL 33480 Office: Jones New York 1411 Broadway New York NY 10018-3404*

ROWARK, MAUREEN, fine arts photographer; b. Edinburgh, Midlothian, Scotland, Feb. 28, 1933; came to U.S., 1960, naturalized, 1970; d. Alexander Pennycook and Margaret (Gorman) Prezdpelski; m. Robert Rowark, May 3, 1952 (div. July 1965). 1 child, Mark Steven. Student, Warmington Bus. Coll., Royal Leamington Spa, Eng., 1950-51, Royal Leamington Spa Art Sch.; diploma, Speedwriting Inst., N.Y.C., 1961; AS in Edn., St. Clair County Community Coll., Port Huron, Mich., 1977, AA, 1978. Supr. proof reading Nevin D. Hirst Advt., Ltd., Leeds, Eng., 1952-55; publicity asst. Alvis Aero Engines, Ltd., Coventry, Eng., 1955-57; adminstrv. asst. Port Huron Motor Inn, 1964-66; adminstrv. asst. pub. rels. dept. Geophysics and Computer Svcs., Inc., New Orleans, 1966-68; sales mgr. Holiday Inn, Port Huron, 1968-70; adminstrv. asst. Howard Corp., Port Huron, 1971-73; sales and systems coord. Am. Wood Products, Ann Arbor, Mich., 1973-74; systems coord. Daniels & Zermack Architects, Ann Arbor, 1974; systems coord., cataloger fine arts dept. St. Clair County Community Coll., Port Huron, 1976-79; freelance fine arts photographer Port Huron, 1978—; photographer Patterns mag. front cover, 1978, Erie Sq. Gazette, 1979, Bluewater Area Tourism Bur. brochure, 1989, Port Huron, Can. Legion, Wyo., Ont. Br., 1987, 88—, Grace Episcopal Ch. Mariner's Day, Port Huron, 1987, 92, 93, 94, Homes mag., 1989. Exhibited in internat. shows at Ann. Ea. Mich. Internat. Exhbn., 1982, 83, 84 (awards of excellence 1982, 83), St. Clair County C.C., 1983, 86 (award of excellence), Sarnia (Ont.) Gallery, 1983-92, 94, Bluewater Bridge Exhibit, 1988, Kaskilaaksontie exhibit, Finland, 1991 (Par Excellence award), others; contbr. short stories to mags. Cons., buyer interior decor Grace Episcopal Ch., 1994; active Mus. of Arts and History, Port Huron, 1985—. Recipient Hon. Mention award Sarnia Art Gallery, 1981; named Best Photographer, Sarnia Art Gallery, 1988; winner 2d and 3d Pl. awards Times Herald Newspaper, 1988. Mem. St. Clair County C.C. Alumni Assn., Camaraderie Club, Phi Theta Kappa, Lambda Mu. Democrat. Episcopalian. Home and Office: # 15 2005 Riverside Dr Port Huron MI 48060-2677

ROWE, ALISON REBECCA, investment broker; b. Cin., June 22, 1956; d. Joseph and Sara Lee (Rogers) R.; m. Stephen Iglehart, Aug. 25, 1984; 1 child, Laura Iglehart. BA, Catawba Coll., 1978. Commodity broker E.F. Hutton, N.Y.C., 1981-83; investment broker Prudential Secs., Danbury, Conn., 1983-90; assoc. v.p. investments Prudential Secs., Charlotte, N.C., 1990-94, Legg Mason Wood Walker, Charlotte, 1994—. Co-founder Women for Personal & Profl. Devel., Danbury, 1987-90. Mem. NAFE (v.p. Charlotte chpt. 1993, pres. 1995). Office: Legg Mason Wood Walker 3750 Nationsbank Plz Charlotte NC 28280

ROWE, AUDREY, postal service administrator; b. Albuquerque, June 26, 1958; d. James Franklin Ringold and Geneva Doris (Jennings) Robinson. ASB in Acctg., ICS Ctr. for Degrees, Scranton, Pa., 1988, ASB in Fin., 1989; BSBA, Century U., 1991, postgrad., 1993—. Svc. rep. Mountain and Southwestern Bell Telephone Co., Albuquerque, Houston, 1978-83; clk., carrier U.S. Postal Svc. PS05, Bellaire, Sugar Land, Tex., 1983-86; supr. mails U.S. Postal Svc. EAS15, Sugar Land, 1986-87; officer-in-charge U.S. Postal Svc. EAS 18, Rosharon, Tex., 1987; from supr. mails EAS 15 to gen. supr. mails EAS 17 U.S. Postal Svc., Houston, 1987-89; relief tour supt. U.S. Postal Svc. EAS 21 (Detail Assignment), Houston, 1989; mgr. gen. mail facility U.S. Postal Svc. EAS22 (Detail Assignment), Capitol Heights, Md., 1989-90; mgr. mail processing U.S. Postal Svc. EAS21, Charlottesville, Va., 1990-91; MSC dir. city ops. U.S. Postal Svc. EAS23 (Detail Assignment), Roanoke, Va., 1991; mgr. gen. mail facility U.S. Postal Svc. EAS24, Washington, 1991—; plant mgr. U.S. Postal Svc. EAS25, Dulles, Va., 1992; chairperson women's program U.S. Postal Svc., Houston, 1986-87, ex-officio women's program, 1988. Mem. Am. Soc. Profl. and Exec. Woman, 1988, NAFE, 1989, CDS-Student Assn., 1989. Mem. NAFE, Am. Soc. Notaries. Home: PO Box 220411 Chantilly VA 22022-0411

ROWE, BETTE SUE, real estate broker; b. Indpls., June 26, 1937; d. George Harold and Sarah Amanda Carpenter; m. Robert Rowe, Aug. 20, 1966. Flight attendant Am. Airlines, Learning Ctr., Ft. Worth, 1958, supr. stewards, 1962; stewardess's tng. instr., 1962; lic. real estate, Troyer Real Estate Sch., 1987. Broker Master Real Estate, Ft. Wayne, Ind., 1989-92, Roth Wehthy Real Estate Sch., Ft. Wayne, 1993—; mem. edn. com., events com., legis. com. Bd. Realtors, Ft. Wayne, 1989-93. Com. chair Rep. Party, Ft. Wayne, 1989-93; chair Dan Quayle for Congress and Senate, Huntington, Ind., 1976-78, 86—; active Rep. Women, Ft. Wayne, 1993; pres. Humane Soc., 1985-86. Mem. Ind. Sotosis (pres. 1987-88), Am. Lung Assn. (bd. dirs.), Ind. Sotosis (pres. 1987-88), Tri Kappa. Home: 9711 Covington Rd Fort Wayne IN 46804

ROWE, DEVONA POWELL, guidance counselor; b. Bethesda, Md., Jan. 28, 1951; d. Julius Devon and Martha Ann (Molnar) Powell; m. Ralph Leon Rowe, June 11, 1971; children: Adam Powell, Reagan Powell. BA in History and Libr. Sci. magna cum laude, Fla. State U., 1971; MA in Edn. summa cum laude, U. North Fla., 1982; EdS in Counselor Edn., U. Fla., 1990. Cert. counselor, Nat. Bd. Cert. Counselors; cert. media specialist and guidance and adminstrn. tchr., Fla. Sch. libr. Most Holy Redeemer Sch., Tampa, Fla., 1972-74; asst. dir. N.E. Fla./S.E. Ga. divsn. Nat. Health Svcs., Palatka, Fla., 1981-83; guidance counselor St. Joseph Acad., St. Augustine, Fla., 1983-85; tchr. 8th grade social studies Putnam County Sch. System, 1985-86; county svcs. coord. Child Abuse Prevention Project, Palatka, 1986-92; guidance counselor E.H. Miller/Dist. Opportunity Ctr., Palatka, 1992-94; social worker Palatka H.S., 1994—; mem. Health Edn. Coun., 1986—, v.p., 1986, pres., 1987; workshop presenter in field. Crucillo coord. St. Mark's Episcopal Ch., 1977-80; mem. Putnam Children's Task force, Children's Home Soc.; rep. Dist. Juvenile Justice Bd. Dept. Health and Rehab. Svcs. Dist. III; mem. Local Juvenile Justice Bd., Putnam County, 1993. Named Women Involved Today winner Palatka Daily News, 1988; grantee in field; Fla. Regent scholar. Mem. Am. Assn. Counseling and Devel., Nat. Com. Prevent Child Abuse, Fla. Ctr. Children and Youth, Fla. Com. Prevent Child Abuse, Child Welfare League, Adv. Network Severely Emotionally Disturbed Children, Jr. Woman's Club Palatka (hon., state jr. project chair 1975, leadership chair 1976, 1st v.p. 1977, pres. 1979, Outstanding Clubwoman 1978), Woman's Club Palatka (edn. chair 1988), Beta Sigma Phi (program chair 1987, cultural chair 1988), Chi Sigma Iota, Kappa Delta Pi. Democrat. Office: E H Miller Sch RR 5 Box 500 Palatka FL 32177-9307

ROWE, ELIZABETH WEBB, paralegal administrator; b. Canton, Ohio, Dec. 2, 1957; d. Thomas Dudley Webb and Verity Elizabeth (Voight) O'Brien; m. David Lee Rowe, June 21, 1986; children: Schuyler Jourdan, Thomas Prentiss. AB in History, Mt. Holyoke Coll., 1979. Legal asst. Willkie Farr & Gallagher, N.Y.C., 1979-82, legal asst. supr., 1983-88, adminstrv. asst., 1988-89; outreach dir. St. Bartholomew's Ch., 1989-93, dir. comm., 1991-93; legal asst. Community Law Offices, N.Y.C., 1980-82; clerical asst. 17th Precinct Police Detective, N.Y.C., 1981-82; paralegal mgr. Patterson, Belknap, Webb & Tyler, N.Y.C., 1993—. Chair homeless shelter St. Bartholomew's Ch., N.Y.C., 1984-85; vol. Breakfast Feeding Program, 1983-92, mem. Community Ministry Coun., 1986-88, 93—; mem. N.Y. Jr. League, 1979-94, Pres.'s Coun., 1988-91; rep. Mt. Holyoke Coll. Alumnae Fund, 1986-89, class officer, 1989-94; bd. dirs. 509 E 83d St Corp., E 67th St. Owners, Inc. Recipient Mary Lyon award Mt. Holyoke Coll., 1994. Home: 167 E 67th St Apt 6E New York NY 10021-5916 Office: Patterson Belknap Webb & Tyler 1133 Ave of the Americas New York NY 10036

ROWE, MAE IRENE, investment company executive; b. Gardner, Mass., Dec. 6, 1927; d. Clifford Wesley and Mertie (Moore) Mann; m. Willard Chase Rowe, June 18, 1951 (div. 1979); children: Gail B. Rowe Simons, Bruce C. B.A. with high honor, Am. Internat. Coll., 1949. Cert. real property adminstr. Social worker City of Montague, Turners Falls, Mass., 1949-51; mgr. Park Investment Co., Cleve., 1979-94; ret. 1994. Pres., v.p., bd. dirs. Park Ridge Counseling Service, Ill., 1972-76; clk. Village of Kildeer, Ill., 1977; bd. dirs. Maine Township Mental Health Service, Park Ridge, 1975-76; trustee Heathermore Condominium Assn., 1987, 93, pres. 1988, 93-94, sec.-treas., 1989. Mem. Cleve. Bldg. Owners Mgrs. Assn. (mem. edn. com. 1983—), Bldg. Owners Mgrs. Assn. Internat., Soc. Real Property Adminstrs. (cert.), LWV (v.p., mem. city adv. com. 1973-76), Am. Mensa Soc. Republican. Unitarian. Club: Cleve. Racquet. Lodge: Kiwanis (bd. dirs., pres., trustee Kiwanis Found. Cleve.). Avocations: tennis. Home: 34108 Chagrin Blvd Apt 5103 Chagrin Falls OH 44022-1042

ROWE, MARIELI DOROTHY, media literacy education consultant, organization executive; b. Bonn, Germany, Aug. 13; came to U.S., 1939; m. John Westel Rowe; children: Peter Willoughby, William Westel, Michael Delano. BA, Swarthmore Coll.; postgrad., U. Colo., 1990; MA, Edgewood Coll., 1990. Interim exec. dir. Friends of Sta. WHA-TV, Madison, Wis., 1976; exec. dir. Nat. Telemedia Coun., Madison, 1978—; project assoc. Loyola U., Chgo., 1989-92; bd. dirs. Sta. WYOU, Madison. Co-prodr., author TV documentary Kids Meet Across Space, 1983; editor Telemedium, Jour. of Media Literacy, 1980—. Co-founder, bd. dirs., pres. Friends of Pub. Stas. WHA-TV, radio, Madison, 1968-78; v.p. bd. Nat. Friends of Pub. Broadcasting, N.Y. and Washington, 1970-76; pres., v.p. bd. Wis. Coun. and Am. Coun. for Better Broadcasts, Madison, 1963-75; commr. Gov.'s Blue Ribbon Commn. on Cable Communications, Wis., 1971-73; bd. dirs. Broadband Telecommunications Regulatory Bd., Madison, 1978-81. Recipient Spl. Recognition award, Am. Coun. Better Broadcasts, 1981. Mem. Soc. Satellite Profls. Internat. (charter), Internat. Visual Literacy Assn., Zeta Phi Eta (1st v.p. 1992, pres. 1993, Marguerite Garden Jones award 1989). Unitarian. Home: 1001 Tumalo Trl Madison WI 53711-3024

ROWE, MARY SUE, accounting executive; b. Melrose, Kans., Aug. 31, 1940; d. Gene and Carmen (Glidewell) Woffard; m. Edward Rowe, Nov. 27, 1985; children from previous marriage: Denise, Dynell, Dalene, Denette. Student, MTI Bus. Coll., 1968, Calif. State U., Fullerton, 1969, Broome (N.Y.) Community Coll., 1974-76; cert. sch. Bus. Mgmt., Calif. State U., San Bernardino, 1986; student, Calif. Coast U., 1991—. Variou bookkeeping and secretarial, 1968-76; asst. mgr., acct. RM Dean Contracting, Chenango Forks, N.Y., 1976-80; acctg. asst. Hemet (Calif.) Unified Sch. Dist., 1981-86; dir. acctg. Desert Sands Unified Sch. Dist., Indio, Calif., 1986-91; bus. svcs. cons. ednl. div. Vicenti, Lloyd & Stutzman, CPA, La Verne, Calif., 1991—. Bd. dirs. Family Svcs. Assn., Hemet, 1982-83, PTA Officer, 1993—. Mem. NAFE, Calif. Assn. Bus. Ofcls. (acctg. com., R*D com., vice chmn. 1988-90, chmn. 1990-91, state acctg. adv. com. 1990-92), Riverside Assn. Chief Accts. (co-chmn. 1986-88), Coalition for Adequate Sch. Housing. Republican. Home: 2668 Grand Teton Ave Hemet CA 92544-3200 Office: Vicenti Lloyd & Stutzman 2100A Foothill Blvd La Verne CA 91750-2947

ROWE, SANDRA MIMS, newspaper editor; b. Charlotte, N.C., May 26, 1948; d. David Lathan and Shirley (Stovall) Mims; m. Gerald Paul Rowe, June 5, 1971; children—Mims Elizabeth, Sarah Stovall. BA, East Carolina U., Greenville, N.C., 1970; postgrad., Harvard U., 1991. Reporter to asst. mng. editor The Ledger-Star, Norfolk, Va., 1971-80, mng. editor, 1980-82; mng. editor The Virginian-Pilot and The Ledger Star, Norfolk, Va., 1982-84, exec. editor, 1984-86, v.p., exec. editor, 1986-93; editor The Oregonian, Portland, 1993, 1994—; mem. nominating jury for Pulitzer Prize in Journalism, 1986, 87, mem. Pulitzer Prize Bd., 1994—. Bd. visitors James Madison U., Harrisonburg, Va., 1991—. Named Woman of Yr. Outstanding Profl. Women of Hampton Rds., 1987. Mem. Am. Soc. Newspaper Editors (bd. dirs. 1992—, treas. 1995), Va. Press Assn. (bd. dirs. 1985-93). Episcopalian. Office: The Oregonian 1320 SW Broadway Portland OR 97201-3469

ROWEN, RUTH HALLE, musicologist, educator; b. N.Y.C., Apr. 5, 1918; d. Louis and Ethel (Fried) Halle; m. Seymour M. Rowen, Oct. 13, 1940; children: Mary Helen Rowen, Louis Halle Rowen. B.A., Barnard Coll., 1939; M.A., Columbia U., 1941, Ph.D., 1948. Mgmt. ednl. dept. Carl Fischer, Inc., N.Y.C., 1954-63; assoc. prof. musicology CUNY, 1967-72, prof., 1972—, mem. doctoral faculty in musicology, 1967—. Author: Early Chamber Music, 1948, reprinted, 1974; (with Adele T. Katz) Hearing-Gateway to Music, 1959, (with William Simon) Jolly Come Sing and Play, 1956, Music Through Sources and Documents, 1979, (with Mary Rowen) Instant Piano, 1979, 80, 83; contbr. articles to profl. jours. Mem. ASCAP, Am. Musicol. Soc., Music Library Assn., Coll. Music Soc., Nat. Fedn. Music Clubs (nat. musicianship chmn. 1962-74, nat. young artist auditions com. 1964-74, N.Y. state chmn. Young Artist Auditions 1981, dist. coord. 1983, nat. bd. dirs. 1989—, rep. UN 1991—), N.Y. Fedn. Music Clubs (pres.), Phi Beta Kappa. Home: 115 Central Park W New York NY 10023-4153

ROWINSKI, JILL, artist; b. Nanticoke, Pa., Aug. 14, 1956; d. Walter John and Ruth (Price) R.; m. John J. Mulhern, Jr., Aug. 1979 (div. May 1984); m. Robert Dean Johnson, July 1987. BFA, Art Acad. Cin., 1991. Office mgr. Moon Lake County Park, Hunlock Creek, Pa., 1974-78; adminstrv. asst. Red Rock Job Corps Ctr., Lopez, Pa., 1979, placement coord., 1980-84; office mgr. Congressman Paul Kanjorski, Washington, 1984-87. Exhibit curator: Beyond the Quilt, 1993; artist: Metro Art, Empty Vessels of Anticipation, 1994; selected exhbns. Textile Arts Ctr., Chgo., 1993. Co-pres. Ohio Women's Caucus for Art, 1993-95; chpt. rep. Nat. Women's Caucus for Art, 1994-95. Recipient performance scholarship Anderson Ranch Arts Ctr., Snowmass, Colo., 1993; Bench Project grantee Cin. Fine Arts Fund., 1993, Individual Artist grantee Cin. Arts Allocation, 1992, Wilder Travel grantee, Art Acad. Cin., 1991. Mem. Ohio Women's Caucus for Art (co-pres. 1993-95), Art Force (bd. dirs. 1993-94, v.p.), Gallery 99 Coop. (bd. dirs. 1990-93, treas. 1991-93). Home: 1109 Fuller St Cincinnati OH 45202 Studio: 3205 Enyart St Cincinnati OH 45205

ROWLAND, CECILIA STUDLEY, information systems specialist; b. Cin., Dec. 1, 1953; d. George David and Dorothy Mae (Fehder) Studley; m. Earl Lester, Aug. 27, 1984 (div. 1993). AS in Ornamental Horticulture, Cin. Tech. Coll., 1977; BS, U. Toledo, 1986. Acctg. coord. Burke Mktg. Svcs., Inc., Cin., 1978-81, programmer/analyst, 1981-83, personal computer specialist, 1983-84; CATI systems supr. NFO Rsch., Inc., Toledo, Ohio, 1984-88, microcomputer systems specialist, 1988-89, systems/ops. supr., 1989-93; mem. LUG steering com. Digital Equipment Corp., 1989—. Republican. Roman Catholic.

ROWLAND, DOROTHY ESTHER, library science educator retired; b. Waterbury, Conn., Jan. 25, 1914; d. Clifford Frank and Esther Emaranth (Gothberg) Rowland. BS, U. Conn., 1937; MS in Libr. Sci., Syracuse U., 1950. Chief of art, music room, head of films and recordings Hartford (Conn.) Pub. Libr., 1937-50; asst. prof., librarian, head of pub. svcs. Westfield (Mass.) State Coll., 1952-69; part time lectr. to groups, 1941—. Mem. Women's Fellowship, Prospect Sr. Citizens, Amaranth (historian 1981—), Order of the Eastern Star, Beta Phi Mu. Republican. Congregationalist. Home: 6 Terry Rd Prospect CT 06712-1125

ROWLAND, ESTHER E(DELMAN), college dean; b. N.Y.C., Apr. 12, 1926; d. Abraham Simon and Ida Sarah (Shifrin) Edelman; m. Lewis P. Rowland, Aug. 31, 1952; children: Andrew, Steven, Judith. B.A., U. Wis., 1946; M.A., Columbia U., 1948, M.Phil., 1984. Instr. in polit. sci. CCNY, 1947-51, Mt. Holyoke Coll., South Hadley, Mass., 1948-49; dir. health professions adv. bd. U. Pa., Phila., 1971-73; adviser to pre-profl. students Barnard Coll., N.Y.C., 1974-79, dean for pre-profl. students, 1980-93, assoc. dean studies, 1989—. Mem. exec. com. Nat. Emergency Civil Liberties Com., N.Y.C., 1975-90; mem. exec. com. Women's Counseling Project, 1981-86. Mem. N.E. Assn. Health Professions Advisers (exec. com. 1973-74), N.E. Assn. Pre Law Advisors (exec. com. 1981-83, 85-86), Neurol. Inst. Aux. Home: 404 Riverside Dr New York NY 10025-1861 Office: Barnard Coll New York NY 10027

ROWLAND, JANIE OGBURN, post-anesthesia nurse, obstetrics nurse; b. Raleigh, N.C., Dec. 8, 1953; d. William Robert and Geraldine (Moore) Ogburn; m. Reggie Lynn Southerland, Nov. 8, 1981 (dec. Dec. 1985); m. Archie Lee Rowland, Oct. 30, 1987. ADN, W.W. Holding Tech. Sch., Raleigh, N.C., 1975. Cert. BLS. Pvt. labor nurse, prenatal educator Ruark Clinic P.A., Raleigh, 1978-79; staff nurse labor and delivery Wake Med. Ctr., Raleigh, 1975-78, 79-80, staff nurse post-anesthesia care unit, 1980-85, supr. labor and delivery, 1985-86, staff nurse III post-anesthesia care unit, 1986-92, supr. post anesthesia care unit, 1992—. Editor newsletters. Vol. United Way, Raleigh, 1989, Jim Hunt for Gov. Campaign, Raleigh, 1985, 92. Mem. NAACOG, Am. Soc. Post Anesthesia Nurses (govtl. affairs com. 1990-91), N.C. Assn. Post Anesthesia Nurses (newsletter editor 1989-91, chair nominations com. 1990-91, chair membership com. 1991-92, v.p. 1991-92, pres. 1992—), Triangle Area Post Anesthesia Nurses (charter mem., pres. 1988), N.C. Nurses Assn. Democrat. Baptist. Home: 7821 Maude Stewart Rd Fuquay Varina NC 27526-7848 Office: Wake Med Ctr 3000 New Bern Ave Raleigh NC 27610-1295

ROWLAND, JOAN CHARLOTTE, pianist, educator; b. Toronto, Ont., Can., May 7, 1930; came to U.S., 1951; d. Walter Mills and Kathryn Meengs (Bowman) R.; m. John M. Thornton, May 5, 1976; children: Christopher, Fenella, Hugh, Robert. BA in English Lit., Columbia U., 1970. Pianist Columbia Can. Trio, 1951-53, Reginald Kell Players, 1953-55, The Piano Duo Schnabel, 1980—; tchr. piano Manhattan Sch. Music, 1990—. Solo debut with Toronto Symphony, 1942; solo recital, London, 1994; recordings for Town Hall Records. Mem. Internat. Soc. Contemporary Music (bd. dirs. 1993—). Home: 285 Riverside Dr New York NY 10025

ROWLAND, NOREEN, elementary education educator, music educator; b. Wilmington, Del., Oct. 20, 1967; d. Fred William and Jewel (Zaleski) R. BS in Music Edn., West Chester U., 1990, postgrad., 1990—. Cert. elem. tchr., Md., Pa. Student tchr. Kennett Consol. Schs., Kennett Square, Pa., 1989; pre-sch. music specialist Darlington Ctr. Performing Arts, Media, Pa., 1989-90, Suburban Music Sch., Chester, Pa., 1990; elem. music specialist Prince George's County Schs., East Marlboro, Md., 1990-91, Gen. Music Programs, Wilmington, 1991-92, Coatesville (Pa.) Area Schs., 1992—; accompanist Kennett Symphony Children's Choir, Kennett Square, 1992—; pvt. piano tchr., 1990-93. Editor Pa. Collegiate Music Educators Assn. Newsletter, 1989-90. Cherub choir dir. Westminster Presbyn. Ch., West Chester, 1989-90, music dir. vacation Bible sch., 1990; music dir. Hockessin (Del.) United Meth. Ch., 1991-93,. Swope Found. scholar, 1989, Hewlett-Packard scholar, 1986. Mem. Nat. Edn. Assn., Pa. Music Educators Assn. (collegiate state sec. 1985-86), Music Educators Nat. Conf., Am. Orff-Schulwerk Assn., Phila. Area Orff-Schulwerk Assn. (corres. sec. 1988—), Pi Kappa Lambda. Home: 1324 Bridge Rd West Chester PA 19382-2033

ROWLEY, CHARLENE MARIE, educational administrator; b. Chgo., May 27, 1943; d. Edward Joseph Flis and Mary Irene (Radosevic) Hoyt; m. Douglas Allen Rowley, Nov. 6, 1987; children: Tammy, Shannon, Chris, Kevin, Jon, Rebecca. AA, Glen Oaks Community Coll., 1978; BS, We. Mich. U., 1980, M in Edl. Leadership, 1984, EdS, 1988. cert. adminstr., tchr, vocat. Bus. educator Burr Oak (Mich.) Pub. Schs., 1981-83, Constantine (Mich.) Pub. Schs., 1983-84; asst. supt. Watervliet (Mich.) Pub. Schs., 1984-87, Comstock Park (Mich.) Pub. Schs., 1987—; trustee Rist Mgmt. Trust, Grand Rapids, Mich., 1990—, Comstock Park Ednl. Found., 1988—; dir. North Kent Community Edn. Consortium, Comstock Park, 1987—; chmn. leg. com. Kent County Community Edn. Assn., Grand Rapids, 1989-91. Co-author: A Typing Simulation, 1984, Document Processing, 1989; author, speaker, presentor in field. Chmn. Watervliet Econ. Devel. Corp., 1987; trustee Berrien County Econ. Commn., Bridgeport, Mich., 1987; mem. allocations com. Kent County United Way, Grand Rapids, 1989. Mem. Mich. Sch. Bus. Ofcls., Mich. Assn. Sch. Adminstrs., Kent Negotiators Assn. (v.p.), Kent Regional Community Edn. Assn. (exec. bd. 1987), Grand Valley Sch. Bus. Ofcls., West Mich. Risk Mgmt. Trust, West Mich. Workers Compensation Fund (v.p.), Watervliet C. of C. (pres., svc. recognition award 1989). Republican. Home: 2833 Central Park Way NE Grand Rapids MI 49505-3482

ROWLEY, JANET DAVISON, physician; b. N.Y.C., Apr. 5, 1925; d. Hurford Henry and Ethel Mary (Ballantyne) Davison; m. Donald A. Rowley, Dec. 18, 1948; children: Donald, David, Robert, Roger. PhB, U. Chgo., 1944, BS, 1946, MD, 1948; DSc (hon.), U. Ariz., 1989, U. Pa., 1989, Knox Coll., 1991, U. So. Calif., 1992. Cert. Am. Bd. Med. Genetics. Rsch. asst. U. Chgo., 1949-50; intern Marine Hosp., USPHS, Chgo., 1950-51; attending physician Infant Welfare and Prenatal Clinics Dept. Pub. Health, Montgomery County, Md., 1953-54; rsch. fellow Levinson Found., Cook County Hosp., Chgo., 1955-61; clin. instr. neurology U. Ill., Chgo., 1957-61; USPHS spl. trainee Radiobiology Lab. The Churchill Hosp., Oxford, Eng., 1961-62; rsch. assoc. dept. medicine and Argonne Cancer Rsch. Hosp. U. Chgo., 1962-69, assoc. prof. dept. medicine and Argonne Cancer Rsch. Hosp., 1969-77, prof. dept. medicine and Franklin McLean Meml. Rsch. Inst., 1977-84, Blum-Riese Disting. Svc. prof., dept. medicine and dept. molecular genetics and cell biology, Franklin McLean Meml. Rsch. Inst., 1984—; mem. Nat. Cancer Adv. Bd., 1979-84; bd. scientific counsellors Nat. Ctr. for Human Genome Rsch. NIH, 1994—, chmn., 1994—; mem. scientific adv. bd. Dana Farber Cancer Ctr., 1994—. Co-founder, co-editor Genes, Chromosomes and Cancer; mem. editl. bds. Oncology Rsch., Cancer Genetics and Cytogenetics, Internat. Jour. Hematology, Genomics, Internat. Jour. Cancer, Leukemia; past mem. editorial bd. Blood, Cancer Rsch., Hematol. Oncology, Leukemia Rsch.; contbr. chpts. to books, articles to profl. jours. Mem. Bd. Sci. Counsellors, Nat. Inst. Dental Rsch., NIH, 1972-76, chmn. 1974-76, Nat. Cancer Adv. Bd. Nat. Cancer Inst., 1979-84, Frederick Cancer Rsch. Facility adv.com., 1983-85, med. adv. bd. Leukemia Soc. Am., 1979-84, MIT Corp. vis. com., Dept. Applied Biol. Scis., 1983-86, selection com., scholar awards in Biomed. Sci., Lucille P. Markey Charitable Trust, 1984-87; trustee Adler Planetarium, Chgo., 1978—; bd. dirs. Am. Bd. Med. Genetics, 1982-83, Am. Bd. Human Genetics, 1985-88; bd. sci. cons. Meml. Sloan-Kettering Cancer Ctr., 1988-90; nat. adv. com. McDonnell Found. Program for Molecular Medicine in Cancer Rsch., 1988—; adv. com. Ency. Britannica, U. Chgo., 1988—; med. adv. bd. Howard Hughes Med. Inst., 1989—. Served with USPHS, 1950-51. Recipient First Kuwait Cancer prize, 1984, Esther Langer award Ann Langer Cancer Rsch. Found., 1983, A. Cressy Morrison award in natural scis. N.Y. Acad. Scis., 1985, Past State Pres.' award Tex. Fedn. Bus. and Profl. Women's Clubs, 1986, Karnofsky award and lecture Am. Soc. Clin. Oncology, 1987, prix Antoine Lacassagne Lique Nationale Francaise Contre le Cancer, 1987, King Faisal Internat. prize in medicine (co-recipient), 1988, Katherine Berkan Judd award Meml. Sloan-Kettering Cancer Ctr., 1989, (co-recipient) Charles Mott Prize Gen. Motors Cancer Rsch. Found., 1989, Steven C. Beering award U. Ind. Med. Sch., 1992, Robert de Villiers award Leukemia Soc. Am., 1993. Mem. NAS, Am. Acad. Arts and Scis., Am. Philos. Soc., Am. Soc. Human Genetics (pres.-elect 1992, pres. 1993, Allen award and lectr. 1991), Genetical Soc. (Gt. Britain), Am. Soc. Hematology (Presdl. Symposium 1982, Dameshek prize 1982), Am. Assn. Cancer Rsch. (G.H.A. Clowes Meml. award 1989), Inst. Medicine (coun. 1988-90), Sigma Xi (William Proctor prize for sci. achievement 1989). Episcopalian. Home: 5310 S University Ave Chicago IL 60615-5106 Office: U Chgo 5841 Maryland Ave NC 2115 Chicago NM 60637-1470

ROWLEY, SUSAN MARIE, psychiatrist; b. Iowa Falls, Iowa, Dec. 16, 1947; d. Wendell Harrison and Maxine Marie Peet; m. James Edwin Rowley, June 20, 1970; children: Ann Marie, Christine Regina. BS in Zoology with honors, Iowa State U., 1970; MS in Biology, Purdue U., 1971; M of Med. Sci., Rutgers U., 1975, MD, 1977. Diplomate Am. Bd. Psychiatry and Neurology. Lab. asst. in helminthology Iowa State U., Ames, 1967, rschr. in helminthology, 1968, lab. technician, rschr. dept. dairy nutrition, 1969-70; grad. teaching asst. Purdue U., West Lafayette, Ind., 1970-71, rschr. in endocrinology, 1971; biochemistry lectr. Coll. of Medicine and Dentistry of N.J., Rutgers Med. Sch., Piscataway, N.J., 1973-77; resident in psychiatry Inst. Mental Health Scis. Coll. of Medicine and Dentistry of N.J., Rutgers Med. Sch., Piscataway, 1977-81; psychiat. cons. Ea. Star Home for Aged, Bridgewater, N.J., 1987; pvt. practice Somerville, N.J., 1982—; clin. asst. prof. dept. psychiatry Univ. Medicine and Dentistry of N.J.-Robert Wood Johnson, 1982—. Recipient Sci. fellowship NSF, 1968. Mem. AMA, Somerset County Med. Soc., Med. Soc. N.J., N.J. Psychiat. Assn., Am. Psychiat. Assn., Am. Soc. Addiction Medicine (cert.), Alpha Omega Alpha, Alpha Lambda Delta, Gamma Sigma Delta, Phi Kappa Phi, Med. Honor Soc. Office: 10 N Gaston Ave Somerville NJ 08876

ROY, CATHERINE ELIZABETH, physical therapist; b. Tucson, Jan. 16, 1948; d. Francis Albert and Dorothy Orme (Thomas) R.; m. Richard M. Johnson, Aug. 31, 1968 (div. 1978); children: Kimberly Anne, Troy Michael. BA in Social Sci. magna cum laude, San Diego State U., 1980; MS in Phys. Therapy, U. So. Calif., 1984. Staff therapist Sharp Meml. Hosp., San Diego, 1984-89, chairperson patient and family edn. com., 1986-87, chairperson sex edn. and counselling com., 1987-89, chairperson adv. bd. for phys. therapy, asst. for edn. program, 1987-89; mgr. rehab. phys. therapy San Diego Rehab. Inst., Alvarado Hosp., 1989-91; dir. therapeutic svcs. VA Med. Ctr., San Diego, 1991—; lectr. patient edn., family edn., peer edn.; mem. curriculum rev. com. U. So. Calif. Phys. Therapy Dept., 1982; bd. dirs. Ctr. for Edn. in Health; writer, reviewer licensure examination items for phys. therapy Profl. Examination Services.. Tennis coach at clinics Rancho Penasquitos Swim and Tennis Club, San Diego, 1980-81; active Polit. Activities Network, 1985; counselor EEO, 1992-95. Mem. Am. Phys. Therapy Assn. (rsch. presenter nat. conf. 1985, del. nat. conf. 1986-94, rep. state conf. 1987-89, 92-94, Mary McMillan student award 1984, mem. exec. bd. San Diego dist. 1985-88, 92-94), AAUW, NAFE, Am. Congress Rehab. Medicine, Phi Beta Kappa, Phi Kappa Phi, Chi Omega. Home: 5067 Park West Ave San Diego CA 92117-1048 Office: San Diego VA Med Ctr Spinal Cord Injury Svc 3350 La Jolla Village Dr San Diego CA 92161

ROY, ELSIJANE TRIMBLE, federal judge; b. Lonoke, Ark., Apr. 2, 1916; d. Thomas Clark and Elsie Jane (Walls) Trimble; m. James M. Roy, Nov. 23, 1943; 1 son, James Morrison. JD, U. Ark., Fayetteville, 1939; LLD (hon.), U. Ark., Little Rock, 1978. Bar: Ark. 1939. Atty. Rose, Loughborough, Dobyns & House, Little Rock, 1940-41, Ark. Revenue Dept., Little Rock, 1941-42; mem. firm Reid, Evrard & Roy, Blytheville, Ark., 1945-54, Roy & Roy, Blytheville, 1954-63; law clk. Ark. Supreme Ct., Little Rock, 1963-65; assoc. justice Ark. Supreme Ct., 1975-77; U.S. dist. judge then sr. judge Ea. and We. Dists. Ark., Little Rock, 1977—; judge Pulaski County (Ark.) Cir. Ct., Little Rock, 1966; asst. atty. gen. Ark., Little Rock, 1967; sr. law clk. U.S. Dist. Ct., Little Rock and Ft. Smith, 1967-75; Mem. med. adv. com. U. Ark. Med. Center, 1952-54; Committeewoman Democratic Party 16th Jud. Dist., 1940-42; vice chmn. Ark. Dem. State Com., 1946-48; mem. chmn. com. Ark. Constnl. Commn., 1967-68. Recipient disting. alumnae citation U. Ark., 1978, Gayle Pettus Pontz award, 1986, Brooks Hays Meml. Christian Citizenship award, 1994; named Ark. woman of yr., Bus. and Profl. Women's Club, 1969, 76, outstanding appellate judge, Ark. Trial Lawyers Assn., 1976-77, Delta Theta Phi mem. of yr. 1989; named among top 100 women in Ark. bus., 1995; Paul Harris fellow Rotary Club Little Rock, 1992. Mem. ABA, Nat. Assn. Women Lawyers, Ark. Bar Assn., Ark. Women Lawyers (pres. 1940-41), Little Rock Women Lawyers, Mortar Bd., PEO, Altrusa Club, Chi Omega. Office: US Dist Ct 600 West Capitol Rm 423 Little Rock AR 72201-3325

ROY, JENNIFER COMES, journalist; b. Ft. Dix, N.J., May 1, 1955; d. John Edward Comes and Peggy Joyce (Cummings) Ipson; m. Rex Allyn Roy, May 30, 1992. Student, U. Colo., 1980-82; BA, Wichita State U., 1987; studying fellow, Atlantik Brukke/Bosch Found., Berlin, 1989. Editorial writer The Wichita (Kans.) Eagle, 1986-89, staff writer, 1989—. Mem. Nat. Conf. Editorial Writers, Soc. Profl. Journalists, Women in Communications (v.p. Wichita chpt. 1987—). Office: The Wichita Eagle 825 E Douglas Ave Wichita KS 67202-3512

ROY, MELINDA, dancer; b. Lafayette, La.. Student, Sch. Am. Ballet. Mem. corps de ballet N.Y.C. Ballet, 1978—, soloist, 1984, prin., 1989—. Dancer in ballets including The Nutcracker, Symphont in C (third movement), Symphony in Three Movements, Apollo (polyhymnia), Brahms-Schoenberg Quartet (first movement), Who Cares, the rubies sect. of Jewels, Divertimento no. 15, Serenade, Western Symphony (first movement), Chaconne (fast pas de deux), Tschaikovsky suite no. 3 (Scherzo), Stars and Stripes, Tschaikovsky pas de Deux, Walpurgisnacht ballet, Golberg Variations, The Concert, Gershwin Concerto, Fanfare, Interplay, The Four Seasons (spring), The Unanswered Questions, Behind the China Dogs, The Waltz Project, Seven by Five, N.Y.C. Ballet's Balanchine Celebration, 1993; performed in Spain, Italy, Denmark, Eng., France, Germany, China, Japan. Office: NYC Ballet Inc NY State Theater Lincoln Ctr Plz New York NY 10023 also: 133 W 71st St New York NY 10023-3834*

ROYBAL-ALLARD, LUCILLE, congresswoman; b. Boyle Heights, Calif., June 12, 1941; d. Edward Roybal; m. Edward T. Allard; 4 children. BA, Calif. State U., L.A. Former mem. Calif. State Assembly; mem. 103rd Congress from 33rd Calif. dist., 1993—. Office: House of Reps Washington DC 20515

ROYCE, GLORIA, legislative staff director; b. Berlin, N.H., July 19, 1951. AS, Champlain Coll., 1971. Sec., French interpreter Vt. law firm, 1971-73; staff asst. Rep. Richard Mallory, 1973-74; personal sec., office mgr. Rep. Ray Roberts, 1975-83, staff asst., 1983—; staff dir. subcom. on housing and meml. affairs, house com. on vet. affairs, 1983—. Office: Subcom on Housing & Meml Affairs 337 Cannon House Office Bldg Washington DC 20515*

ROYCE, MARY WELLER SA'ID, artist, poet; b. Tupper Lake, N.Y., July 9, 1933; d. Gerard Charles and Mary Weller (McCarthy) de Grandpré; m. Majed Farhan Sa'id, Nov. 19, 1960 (dec. 1966); children: Mary Weller Richardson, Emily Ann Bacon; m. William Ronald Royce, Sept. 2, 1974. AA with honors, Georgetown Visitation Jr. Coll., 1953; BS cum laude, Georgetown U., 1960; MA in Italian, Middlebury Coll., 1968. Writer, artist, 1954—; translator, adminstrv. asst. U.S. Army, Orleans, France, 1956-58; tchg. asst. dept. Italian Rutgers U., New Brunswick, N.J., 1968-70; translator N.J., Ariz., 1971-84; owner, designer The Stamp Act, Rockville, Md., 1990-93. Groups shows include Rockville (Md.) Arts Place, 1992—, Rockville Art League, 1993—, Montpelier Cultural Arts Ctr., Laurel, Md., 1994, Strathmore Hall Arts Ctr., North Bethesda, Md., 1994—; poetry collected in anthologies. Coord. Equal Rights Coalition, Utah, 1975; ACLU rep. So. Ariz. Coalition for ERA, Tuscon, 1975-78; mem. steering com. Ariz. ERA, 1976-78; Md. state activist Catholics for a Free Choice, 1991-93. Fulbright grantee, 1960. Mem. Acad. Am. Poets (assoc.), Nat. Mus. Women in Arts (charter), Washington Project for Arts, Rockville Art League, Strathmore Hall Arts Ctr., Rockville Arts Place. Avocations: photography, jazz, swimming.

ROYER, KATHLEEN ROSE, pilot; b. Pitts., Nov. 4, 1949; d. Victor Cedric and Lisetta Emma (Smith) Salway; m. Michael Lee Royer, June 6, 1971 (div. Aug. 1975). Student, Newbold Coll., 1968-69; BS, Columbia Union Coll., 1971; MEd, Shippensburg U., 1974; student, Lehigh U., 1974-75. Cert. tchr. Pa. Music tchr. Harrisburg (Pa.) Sch. Dist., 1971-77; flight instr. Penn-Air, Inc., Altoona, Pa., 1977; capt., asst. chief pilot Air Atlantic Airlines, Centre Hall, Pa., 1977-80; capt., chief pilot Lycoming Air Svc., Williamsport, Pa., 1980-81; govs. pilot Commonwealth of Pa., Harrisburg, 1981-87; flight engr. Pan-Am, N.Y.C., 1987-91; pilot, 1st officer B737 United Airlines, Chgo., 1992—; first woman pilot/engr. crew mem. on 747, 1989-91, chief pilot, cons. Mem. Internat. Soc. Women Airline Pilots, Flight Engrs. Internat. Assn. (scheduling rep. 1989, scheduling dir. 1990, 1st vice chmn., mem. bd. adjustments 1989, v.p., dir. scheduling, 1991-92), Airline Pilots Assn., 99's (local chair Cen. Pa. chpt. 1987-92), Whirley-Girls (Washington). Republican. Home: 2047 Raleigh Rd Apt D Hummelstown PA 17036-8709 Office: United Airlines PO Box 66140 O'Hare Internat Airport Chicago IL 60666

ROYSE, MARY KAY, judge; b. Hutchinson, Kans., Oct. 3, 1949; d. J.R. and Patricia Ann (Lamont) R. BS in Edn., Emporia State U., 1970, MA, 1972; JD, Kans. U., 1978. Instr. Miami U., Hamilton, Ohio, 1972-75; assoc. atty. Foulston & Siefkin, Wichita, 1978-82, Law Offices Bryson E. Mills, Wichita, 1982-86; judge Dist. Ct. (18th dist.) Kans., Wichita, 1986-93, Kans. Ct. Appeals, Topeka, 1993—; mem. Kans. Jud. Coun. Com. Pattern Instructions Kans., 1989—. Bd. dirs. Work Option Women, Wichita, 1980, Emporia State U. Alumni Assn., 1982-85, Kans. Dialysis Assn., Wichita, 1986—. Named Woman Achievement, Women in Communications, Wichita, 1988, Disting. Alumni, Emporia State U., 1990. Mem. ABA, Kans. Bar Assn., Kans. Commn. Bicentenial U.S. Constitution, Kans. Bar Assn. Commn. Status of Women in Profession, Wichita Bar Assn.

ROZEN, DIANE MARIE LAUGHRUN, psychoanalyst, psychologist; b. Artesia, Calif., Oct. 15, 1958; d. James Odell and Winona Dean (Stokes) Laughrun; m. Roland Rozen, July 29, 1989; 1 child, Max Ariel. BA in Psychology, San Diego State U., 1980; MA in Psychology, Calif. Grad. Inst., 1983, PhD in Psychology, 1987, psychoanalytic cert., 1989. Drug rehab. counselor South Bay Human Svc. Ctr., Torrance, Calif., 1982; psychol. intern Calif. Grad. Inst., Westwood, 1983-89; asst. clin. dir. Calif. Grad. Inst. Counseling Ctr., Westwood, 1988-89; tchr., supr. Pasadena (Calif.) Mental Health, 1989; sr. faculty psychoanalytic dept. Calif. Grad. Inst., Westwood, 1989—; tng. and supr. analyst, 1994; pvt. practice Beverly Hills, Calif., 1989—; group supr. Valley Community Clinic, North Hollywood, Calif., 1990-92; staff therapist The Linden Ctr. Sch., L.A., 1990—; postdoctoral intern La Canada (Calif.) Counseling Ctr., 1987-90; adj. faculty Ryocan Coll., L.A., 1991—. Office: 462 N Linden Dr Ste 430 Beverly Hills CA 90212-2200

ROZIER, KAREN PICKETT, elementary teacher; b. Greenwood, Miss., Feb. 7, 1953; d. William Eugene and Barbara Faye (Grantham) Pickett; m. Robert Edward Rozier, Jr., June 12, 1971 (div. Mar. 1994); children: Beth, Ashley. BA, Delta State U., 1974. Cert. elem./primary tchr. Tchr. seventh grade sci. Leflore County High Sch., Itta Bena, Miss., 1974-75; tchr. second grade Carver Elem. Sch., Indianola, Miss., 1975-79; tchr. fourth grade DeSoto County, Southaven, Miss., 1979-80; tchr. fourth/sixth grade Ross Rd. Elem., Memphis, Tenn., 1980-84; kindergarten tchr. R.L. Brown/Neptune Elem., Jacksonville, Fla., 1984-90; tchr. third grade Sabal Palm Elem., Jacksonville, 1990-94. Republican. Baptist. Home: 1800 The Greens Way # 802 Jacksonville FL 32250 Office: Sabal Palm Elem Sch 1201 Kernan Blvd N Jacksonville FL 32225-5005

ROZIN, ELISABETH, author, lecturer, consultant; b. N.Y.C., May 19, 1936; d. Caesar J. and Lillian (Solomon) Briefer; m. Paul Rozin, June 9, 1957 (div. Dec. 1991); children: Lillian, Seth, Alexander. BA, Hunter Coll., 1957; MA, Brandeis U., 1961. Author: Flavor Principle Cookbook, 1973, Ethnic Cuisine, 1983, Blue Corn and Chocolate, 1992, The Primal Cheeseburger, 1994. Mem. Am. Inst. Wine and Food, Internat. Assn. Culinary Profls., Phila. Women's Culinary Guild, Dames d'Escoffier, Authors Guild. Home: HC 60 Box 7 Pagosa Springs CO 81147-8601

ROZOVSKY, FAY ADRIENNE, lawyer, risk manager; b. Providence, Dec. 10, 1950; d. Maurice and Beatrice (Sandperil) Frank; m. Lorne Elkin Rozovsky, Dec. 16, 1979; children: Joshua I., Aaron A. AB summa cum laude, Providence Coll., 1973; JD, Boston Coll., 1976; MPH, Harvard U., 1977. Asst. prof. law, medicine Wright State U. Sch. Medicine, Dayton, Ohio, 1978-79; cons. health law pvt. practice, Hailfax, Nova Scotia, 1979-84; asst. prof. health adminstrn. Dalhouse U., Hailfax, Nova Scotia, 1984-85; asst. prof. gerontology Mt. St. Vincent U., Hailfax, Nova Scotia, 1986-87; pres. LEAFR Health, Hailfax, Nova Scotia, 1986-93; assoc. dir. risk mgmt., legal counsel Franciscian Health System, Aston, Pa., 1993; dir. risk mgmt. and legal affairs AIG Cons., Inc., Phila., 1993—; adj. asst. prof. gerontology Mt. St. Vincent U., 1985-86, adj. prof. law & medicine Dalhouse Sch. Law and Medicine, 1988-93; sec. Franciscian Elder Care Corp., Aston, 1993—. Author: Consent to Treatment: A Practical Guide, 1984, Credential Health Facilities Law Guide, 1984, Credential Law Patiant Records, 1984, Credential Law of Consent to Treatment, 1990, Home Health Care Law, 1993, Medical Staff Credentialing: A Practical Guide, 1994. Mem. Am. Soc. Health Risk Mgmt. (diplomate). Home: 245 Wiltshire Rd Wynnewood PA 19096-3332

ROZZELLE, ARLENE A., plastic surgeon; b. Hempstead, N.Y., Jan. 3, 1957; d. Charles William and Lois Cheryl (Ott) R. BA, Wellesley (Mass.) Coll., 1982; MD, U. Mass., 1987. Diplomate Nat. Bd. Med. Examiners. Gen. and plastic surgery residencies Brown U.-R.I. Hosp.; craniogacial/pediat. plastic surgery fellow St. Louis Children's Hosp. Recipient Janey M. Glasgow Meml. award Am. Med. Women's Assn., 1987; Sarah Perry Wood Med. fellowship Wellesley Coll., 1983, Durant scholar, 1982. Mem. Am. Soc. Plastic and Reconstructive Surgeons (candidate), Am. Cleft Palate-Craniofacial Assn., Am. Soc. Aesthetic Plastic Surgery (candidate), Phi Beta Kappa. Episcopalian.

ROZZI, SANTA CAPUTO, county official; b. Brklyn., Aug. 4, 1950; d. Frank Vincent and Mary (LaCava) Caputo; m. Samuel J. Rozzi, Mar. 7, 1981 (dec. July 1992). BA, Marymount Coll., N.Y., 1971; JD, St. John U. Law Sch, Jamaica, N.Y., 1981. Admission Bar of N.Y., 1982. Sec. Office of Town Atty., Town of Oyster Bay, N.Y., 1972-73, Office of County Comptroller, County Nassau, Mineola, N.Y., 1973-81; insp. Office of Compt. County of Nassau, Mineola, N.Y., 1981-82, dep. county atty., 1982-84, deputy county treas., 1984-86, bur. chief BREI, Office of County Atty., 1986-88, deputy county exec., 1988-93, treas., 1993—. Mem. Bar Assn. of Nassau County, Columbian Lawyers Assn. of N.C. Republican. Roman Catholic. Office: Office County Treas 240 Old Country Rd Mineola NY 11501

RUANE, MAUREEN MURIEL, labor union official; b. Oceanside, N.Y., June 8, 1945; d. Joseph William and Muriel Helen (Bennett) Murphy; m. Martin Conrad Ruane, July 15, 1967 (div. May 1992). Grad. high sch., Valley Stream, L.I., N.Y. Sec. Local 854 IBT, H&W Benefits Plan, Valley Stream, N.Y., 1971-81; fund mgr. Local 854 Pension Fund Health & Welfare Benefits Plan, Valley Stream, N.Y., 1981-89; bus. agt. Local 854 I.B. of T., Valley Stream, N.Y., 1989, pres., 1990—; dir. Labor Edn. and Community Svc. Agy. Inc., Westbury, N.Y., 1988—; trustee Local 854 Health and Welfare and Pension Fund, Valley Stream, 1990—; del. Eastern Conf. Teamsters, Bethesda, Md., 1990—, Joint Coun. #16, N.Y.C., 1990—, indsl. trade divsn. Internat. Brotherhood of Teamsters, 1992—; area v.p. Internat. Teamsters' Women's Caucus, 1992—; adv. bd. Nat. Conf. Unions and Employees Benefit Funds, 1992—; commr. Teamsters Human Rights Com. and Joint Coun. 16 (rep. women's issues). Mem. Internat. Found. of Employee Benefits Plans, Assn. Benefit Adminstrs., N.Y. Inst. Technol., Indsl. Rels. Rsch. Assn., Ednl. Conf. Health and Welfare and Pension Plans. Lutheran.

RUBEN, BARBARA LOUISE, magazine editor; b. Cleve., Apr. 26, 1960; d. Joseph M. and Ardys A. (Klann) R. BA, Miami U., Oxford, Ohio, 1982; MA in Journalism, Ind. U., 1988. Editorial intern Nat. Geographic WORLD Mag., Washington, 1982; pub. info. assoc. Defenders of Wildlife, Washington, 1983-87; reporter Almanac Newspapers, Potomac, Md., 1988-90; staff writer Occupational Therapy Week, Rockville, Md., 1990; editor Environ. Action Mag., Takoma Park, Md., 1990—. Contbr. articles to mags. and newspapers. Recipient 1st place award Ind. chpt. Soc. Profl. Journalists/Sigma Delta Chi, 1987; scholar Ind. U., 1988. Mem. Soc. Environ. Journalists, Environ. Editors Network. Office: Environ Action 6930 Carroll Ave Ste 600 Takoma Park MD 20912

RUBEN, IDA GASS, state senator; b. Washington, Jan. 7, 1929; d. Sol and Sonia E. (Darman) Gass; m. L. Leonard Ruben, Aug. 29, 1948; children: Garry, Michael, Scott, Stephen. Del. Md. Ho. of Dels., Annapolis, 1974-86; mem. Md. Senate, Annapolis, 1986—, majority whip, 1995—; chair Montgomery County House Delegation, 1981-86, Montgomery County Senate Delegation, 1987—; mem. house econ. matters com., 1974-85, house ways and means com., 1985-86, legis. policy com., 1991—, senate budget and taxation com., joint budget and audit com., 1991—, exec. nominations com., 1991—, joint protocol com., 1991—, chair subcom. on pub. safety, transp., econ. devel. and natural resources, 1995—, mem. joint com. on spending affordability, 1995—, mem. capital budget subcom., 1995—; mem. Gov.'s Motor Carrier Task Force, 1989—; conv. chair Nat. Order Women Legislators, 1980. Chair Women Legislators Caucus Md., 1982-84; trustee Washington Adventist Hosp., Takoma Park, Md.; bd. dirs. Ctrs. for Handicapped, Silver Spring, Md.; former internat. v.p. B'nai Brith Women. Recipient Cert. of Appreciation Ctrs. for Handicapped, 1987, Meritorious Svc. award Safety and Survival, 1989, Cover Those Trucks award AAA Potomac, 1989, Leadership Laurel award Safety First Club Md., 1989, Woman of Valor award B'nai B'rith Women, 1991, Pub. Affairs award Planned Parenthood Md., 1992, ESOL support recognition Montgomery County Pub. Schs., 1992, Appreciation award Fraternal Order Police, 1992, John Dewey award Montgomery County Fedn. Tchrs., 1992, Appreciation award ARC of Md., 1992, Safety Leader award Advocates for Hwy. and Auto Safety, 1993, Disting. Svc. award Gov.'s Commn. Employment of People with Disabilities, 1993, award Faculty Guild U. Md. for support of faculty and univ., 1993, Sincere Appreciation award for commitment to Md.'s youth Md. Underage Drinking Prevention Coalition, 1994, Faithful Svc. to citizens of Montgomery County award Montgomery County Assn. of Realtors, 1994; named Most Effective Pub. Ofcl. by residents of Silver Spring, 1990, One of 100 Most Powerful Women in Washington Metro Area by Washingtonian Mag., 1994. Mem. Coun. State Govts. (com. on suggested legislation), Hadassah. Democrat. Jewish. Home: 11 Schindler Ct Silver Spring MD 20903-1329 Office: Md State Senate 204 James Senate Off Bldg 110 College Ave Annapolis MD 21401-1676

RUBENS, LINDA MARCIA, nursing administrator; d. Harry and Ruth Slutzah; m. Robert A. Rubens; children: Scott, Mark. AS, Fla. Jr. Coll., Jacksonville. Lic. nursing home adminstr. RN U. Hosp. of Jacksonville, 1976-82; dir. nursing Mandarin Manor Nursing Home and Retirement Village, 1982-85, asst. adminstr., 1985-87; dir. nursing P.H.E.O. Med. Ctr., 1987-88; dir. clin. and profl. svcs. Kimberly Quality Care, 1988-90, br. mgr., 1990-93; healthcare mgmt. cons. Health Care Mgmt. Cons., Jacksonville, 1993-94; govt. compliance specialist Atkinsons Home Health Care, Jacksonville, 1994-95, Ind. Home Health Svcs., 1994—; part-time Dept. Labor, Office of Worker's Compensation, 1992—; vice chairperson Statewide Human Rights Advocacy Com. Past mem. Gerontol. Search Team for Cathedral Found.; past treas. Mayor's Orgn. for Vol. Effort, past bd. dirs.; vice chairperson State-Wide Human Rights Adv. Com., chairperson consumer rels. subcom., 1990—; apptd. to Dist. IV Ombudsman Com., 1982-90, Dist. IV Human Rights Adv. Com., 1989-90; bd. dirs. Mt. Carmel Retirement Cmty. Mem. Rehab. Nurses Assn., Dirs. of Nursing Assn. (sec. long term care). Home: 13116 Mandarin Rd Jacksonville FL 32223-1748

RUBENSTEIN, BONNIE SUE, fraternal organization executive; b. Shreveport, La., Feb. 7, 1961; d. David Ochs and Marilyn Sue (Goldstein)R. BBA, Emory U., Atlanta, 1983. Office adminstr. Sanger-Harris, Dallas, 1983-85; asst. buyer Sanger-Harris, 1985-87, Foley's, Houston, 1987-88; exec. dir. Alpha Epsilon Phi Sorority, Columbus, Ohio, 1988—; province dir., pledge programming chmn. Alpha Epsilon Phi Sorority, 1985-87, nat. v.p. collegiate chpts., 1987-88; dir. devel. Alpha Epsilon Phi Found., 1992—; mem. Fraternity Ins. Purchasing Group, 1991—, bd. dirs., 1994—. Contbr. articles to profl. jours. Tchr. religious sch. Temple Israel, Columbus, 1989—, pres. young adults congregation, 1991-93, bd. dirs., 1990-93, bd. dirs. sisterhood, 1991—, also mem. dues revision com. and recruitment com., search com., ritual com. Mem. Assn. Frat. Advisors, Ctrl. Office Execs. Assn. (sec. 1993-94), Frat. Execs. Assn. (bus. mgr. 1993-94), Order of Omega, Women's Am. ORT (activities chmn. 1986-87). Republican. Jewish. Home: 5616B Hibernia Dr Columbus OH 43232-8502 Office: Alpha Epsilon Phi 6100 Channingway Blvd # 302 Columbus OH 43232-2910

RUBERG, CYNTHIA LIEF, counselor; b. N.Y.C., Feb. 12, 1946; d. Frederick Paul and Florence Hope (Suskind) Lief; m. Robert Lionel Ruberg, June 26, 1966; children: Frederick Lief, Mark Lewis, Joshua Laurence. BA Sociology, Boston U., 1967; MEd in Counseling, U. Dayton, 1987. Diplomate Am. Bd. Sexology; lic. profl. counselor; nat. cert. counselor. Relationship and sex counselor Beechwold Family Counseling Assocs., Columbus, Ohio, 1988—; counselor Ohio Profl. Counseling Svcs., Columbus, Ohio, 1993—; clin. sexologist, educator Masters & Johnson Sex Edn. Inf. Line, Columbus, 1993-94; instr. Ohio State U. Coll. Medicine, 1992—. Columnist Today's Columbus Woman, 1992—; media reviewer Jour. Sex Edn. and Therapy, 1992—. Hotline vol.; parent visitor at Ohio state hosps. League Against Child Abuse, 1984-87. Assoc. fellow Am. Acad. Clin. Sexologists; mem. Am. Assn. Sex Educators, Counselors and Therapists (cert. sex counselor), Am. Counseling Assn., Ohio Counseling Assn., Soc. Sci. Study of Sexuality, Sex Info. and Edn. Coun. U.S., Assn. Women Therapists, Nat. Coun. Jewish Women, Hadassah, Temple Israel Sisterhood, Ohio Assn. Counseling and Devel., Ohio Mental Health Counselors Assn., Internat. Assn. Marriage and Family Counselors, Boston U. Alumni Assn. Office: 28 W Henderson Rd Columbus OH 43214-2628

RUBIN, BONNIE MILLER, journalist; b. Chgo., Aug. 17, 1951; d. George and Florence Ila (Rubin) Miller; m. David Rubin, June 30, 1974; children: Michael, Alyssa. BA, Drake U., 1973. Sports reporter Quad City Times, Davenport, Iowa, 1973-75; community rels. asst. dir. Metropolitan Med. Ctr., Minn., 1975-77; reporter Minneapolis Star Tribune, 1977-85; features editor Post Tribune, Gary, Ind., 1985-90; home editor Chgo. Tribune, 1990-93, met. reporter, 1993—. Author Time Out, 1987, Great Escapes from Chicago, 1992. Mem. Am. Assn. Sunday and Feature Editors. Office: Chgo Tribune Co 435 N Michigan Ave Chicago IL 60611-4001

RUBIN, DEBORAH ANN, artist; b. Chgo., Apr. 17, 1948; d. Harry Marshall and Hazel Etta (Glick) Rubin; m. Norman Howard Sims, Mar. 9, 1971; 1 child, Gordon Burnside. BFA, U. Ill., 1970. Contbr. articles to profl. jours. Solo exhbns. include Capricorn Galleries, Bethesda, Md., 1985, 87, 90, 93, R. Michelson Gallery, Amherst, Mass., 1991, 92, 93, Mus. Fine Arts, Springfield, Mass., 1985, 92, Sync Gallery, Northampton, Mass., 1989, Zimmerman-Saturn Gallery, Nashville, 1987, Quadrum Gallery, Chestnut Hill, Mass., 1982, W.P.A. Gallery, N.Y.C., 1981, Bibo's Gallery, Peoria, Ill., 1978; group shows include Milw. Art Mus., 1979, Butler Inst. Am. Art, 1981, 83, 84, 85, 89, Nat. Acad. of Design, N.Y.C., 1982, Nat. Soc. Painters in Casein and Acrylic, N.Y., 1983, Boston U. Art Gallery, U. Mass., 1983, (traveling show) U. Fla., Deland Mus. Art, Tampa Mus. Art, 1991-92; represented in permanent collections Capricorn Galleries, R. Michelson Galleries; represented in corp. collections Fidelity Investments Mgmt. Corp., Mass Mut. Life Ins. Co., Employers Mut. Wausau, Wis., Cabot Corp., Bridgestone U.S.A., Cooper & Lybrand, Merrill, Lynch, Pierce, Fenner & Smith, Farm Credit Bank New Eng., Marriott Hotel Corp. Hdqs. Recipient Grumbacher Gold Medallion, Springfield Art League, 1985, Works on paper award Berkshire Mus., Pittsfield, Mass., 1982, Audubon Artist Anniversary award, 1982. Mem. Watercolor USA Honor Soc., New Eng. Watercolor Soc. (Merit award 1988). Democrat. Jewish. Home: 143 Flat Hills Rd Amherst MA 01002-1213

RUBIN, DEBRA, editor, journalist; b. Bklyn., Sept. 20, 1958; d. Seymour and Maxine (Abel) R. BA, Rutgers Coll., 1980. Mng. editor Metrowest Jewish News, Whippany, N.J., 1989—. Mem. N.J. Press Women, Am. Jewish Press Assn. (3d v.p.).

RUBIN, JANE LOCKHART GREGORY, lawyer; b. Richmond, Va., May 27, 1944; d. Phillip Henry and Jane Ball (Lockhart) Gregory; m. Reed Rubin, Jan. 22, 1966; children: Lara Ross, Maia Ayers, Peter Lyon. BA, Vassar Coll., 1965; JD, Columbia U., 1975; LLM, NYU, 1984. Bar: N.Y. 1976. Of counsel Lankenau Kovner and Kurtz, N.Y.C., 1985—; bd. dirs., treas. Reed Found., N.Y.C., 1985—; adv. bd. Vt. Studio Ctr., 1985—, Assn. of the Bar of the City of N.Y. Fund, Inc.; mem. Mcpl. Archives Reference and Rsch. Adv. Bd., 1991-94, N.Y.C. Commn. for Cultural Affairs, 1992—; dir. InterAmericas, 1992—. Author intro. and catalog for exhibit Temple of Justice: The Appellate Division Courthouse, (with others) The Art World and the Law, 1987. Bd. dirs., vice chair Vol. Lawyers for the Arts. Harlan Fiske Stone scholar Columbia U. Sch. Law. Mem. ABA (sect. real property and probate law, sect. internat. law and practice), N.Y. Bar Assn., Union Internationale des Avocats (mem. permanent commn. on tax law and intellectual property working group), Assn. of Bar of City of N.Y. (adj., com. on non-profit orgns. 1984—), Copyright Soc. of the U.S.A. Office: Lankenau Kovner & Kurtz 1740 Broadway Fl 25 New York NY 10019-4315

RUBIN, KAREN BETH, publishing, marketing and representation executive; b. N.Y.C., Aug. 30, 1951; d. Samuel M. and Eleanor (Spiegel) Rubin; m. Neil Leiberman, Dec. 29, 1983; children: David, Eric. BA magna cum laude, SUNY, Binghamton, 1972. Sr. editor Travel Agt. mag., N.Y.C.,

1973-86, Tour & Travel News, Manhasset, N.Y., 1986-89; pres. Travel Exec. Search, Great Neck, N.Y., 1989—; founder, pub., editor Making It!, Great Neck, 1981—; pres. Workstyles, Inc., Great Neck, 1989—; adj. prof. NYU, 1992—. Author: Flying High in Travel, 1986, 92; contbr. thousands of articles to newspapers and profl. jours. Recipient Neal Cert. of Merit, Am. Bus. Press, 1984. Office: Workstyles Inc 5 Rose Ave Great Neck NY 11021-1530

RUBIN, NANCY RUTH ZIMMAN, journalist, author; b. Boston, Nov. 25, 1944; d. Stuart Wendell and Ethel Charlotte (Rabinovitz) Simman; m. Peter H. Rubin, July 9, 1967; children: Elisabeth, Jessica. BA, Tufts U., 1966; MA in Teaching, Brown U., 1967. English tchr. Rochester, N.Y., 1967-70; playwright, dir. Equity Library Theatre, Roundabout, Joseph Jefferson and St. Clement's theaters, N.Y.C., 1971-74; writer Westchester-Gannett newspapers and mags., 1975-77; free-lance reporter N.Y. Times, N.Y.C., 1977—; mem. faculty Purchase Coll., SUNY, 1994—; faculty affiliate Bush Ctr. in Child Devel., Yale U., New Haven, 1981—; mem. Westchester County Women's Adv. Bd., chair, 1988. Author: The New Suburban Women: Beyond Myth and Motherhood, 1982, The Mother Mirror: How a Generation of Women is Changing Motherhood in America, 1984, Isabella of Castile: The First Renaissance Queen, 1991; American Empress: The Life and Times of Marjorie Merriweather Post, 1995. contbg. editor Parents mag., 1987-91, Time, Inc.-Bread Loaf Writers' Colony scholar, 1979, McCalls, Savvy, Travel & Leisure, Ladies Home Journal, 1980-92; theater critic Stamford Advocate, 1994—. Recipient Washington Irving award Westchester Libr. Assn., 1993; Time, Inc.-Bread Loaf Writers' Colony scholar, 1979. Fellow MacDowell Colony; mem. Author's Guild, Am. Soc. Journalists and Authors (Author of Yr. award 1992), PEN, NOW. Office: care Elaine Markson Agy 44 Greenwich Ave New York NY 10011

RUBIN, ROSALYN AARON, psychology educator; b. Mpls., Sept. 29, 1933; d. Meyer and Mary (Resnick) Aaron; m. Edmond Harvey Rubin, Dec. 18, 1960; children: Ellen Rubin Rosen, Beth. BA magna cum laude, U. Minn., 1954, BS, 1955, MA, 1957, PhD, 1961. Lic. cons. psychologist, sch. psychologist, supr. of sch. psychology. Sch. psychologist Robbinsdale (Minn.) Pub. Schs., 1960-63, dir. rsch., 1961-63; asst. prof. psychology Macalester Coll., St. Paul, 1964-66; rsch. assoc. U. Minn., Mpls., 1966-82, interim dir. R & D Ctr. in edn. of handicapped children, 1971, dir. study of edn. and behavioral sequelae of prenatal and perinatal conditions, 1971-80, assoc. prof., 1971-82; mem. community faculty Met. State U., Mpls., 1983-91, assoc. prof. psychology, 1991—; pvt. practice St. Paul, 1983-91; cons. Wayzata (Minn.) Pub. Schs., 1980-83, Hennepin Tech. Ctrs., Mpls., 1981-86, Ind. Sch. Dist. 287, Robbinsdale, 1983-90. Author: (with others) Annual Progress in Child Psychology and Child Development, 1979, Advances in Child Clinical Psychology, 1977; contbr. articles to profl. jours. Mem. APA, Am. Ednl. Rsch. Assn., Coun. for Exceptional Children, U. Minn. Edn. Assn. (v.p. 1980-82). Home: 681 Woodlawn Ave Saint Paul MN 55116-1052

RUBIN, ROSEMARY ANN, school counselor, consultant; b. L.A., Apr. 1, 1949; d. Arnold and Judith Rubin. BA, UCLA, 1971; MS, Mt. St. Mary's Coll., 1974. Credential in pupil pers. svcs., reading specialist and standard secondary tchr. Tchr. L.A. (Calif.) Unified Sch. Dist., 1972-80, sch. counselor, 1981-92, sch. counselor, cons., 1992—, sch. counselor, cons. suicide prevention unit; cons., participant Dist. Crisis Teams, L.A. (Calif.) Unified Sch. Dist. Active L.A. Unified Sch. Dist. Suicide Prevention Unit. Recipient Crisis Intervention Suicide Prevention pin Am. Sch. Counselor Assn., 1994. Mem. Calif. Sch. Counselors Assn. (area 6A rep. 1990—, crisis intervention chair 1993—), L.A. Sch. Counselors Assn. (pres. 1988-90). Office: LA Unified Sch Dist Suicide Prevention Unit 11301 Bellagio Rd Rm 4 Los Angeles CA 90049

RUBIN, SANDRA MENDELSOHN, artist; b. Santa Monica, Calif., Nov. 7, 1947; d. Murry and Freda (Atliss) Mendelsohn; m. Stephen Edward Rubin, Aug. 6, 1966. BA, UCLA, 1976, MFA, 1979. Instr. Art Ctr. Coll. Design, Pasadena, Calif., 1980, UCLA, 1981. One-woman exhbns. include L.A. County Mus. Art, 1985, Fischer Fine Arts, London, 1985, Claude Bernard Gallery, N.Y.C., 1987, L.A. Louver Gallery, L.A., 1992; group exhbns. include L.A. County Mus. Artm 1977, 82, 83, L.A. Mcpl. Art Gallery, 1977, 83, 93, L.A. Contemporary Exhbns., 1978, L.A. Inst. Contemporary Arts, 1978, Newport Harbor Art Mus., Newport Beach, Calif., 1981, Odyssia Gallery, N.Y.C., 1981, Nagoya (Japan) City Mus., 1982, Long Beach (Calif.) Mus. Art, 1982, Brooke Alexander Gallery, N.Y.C., 1982, Laguna Beach (Calif.) Mus. Art, 1982, Jan Baum Gallery, L.A., 1984, San Francisco Mus. Art, 1986, Claude Bernard Gallery, 1986, Struve Gallery, Chgo., 1987, Boise (Idaho) Mus., 1988, Judy Youen's Gallery, London, 1988, Tatistscheff Gallery, Inc., Santa Monica, Calif., 1989, Tortue Gallery, Santa Monica, 1990, Contemporary Arts Forum, Santa Barbara, Calif., 1990, San Diego Mus. Art, 1991, Fresno (Calif.) Met. Mus., 1992, Jack Rutberg Fine Arts, L.A., 1993. Recipient Young Talent Purchase award L.A. County Mus. Art, 1980; Artist's Fellowship grant NEA, 1981, 91.

RUBIN, VERA COOPER, research astronomer; b. Phila., July 23, 1928; d. Philip and Rose (Applebaum) Cooper; m. Robert J. Rubin, June 25, 1948; children: David M., Judith S. Young, Karl C., Allan M. BA, Vassar Coll., 1948; MA, Cornell U., 1951; PhD, Georgetown U., 1954; DSc (hon.), Creighton U., 1978, Harvard U., 1988, Yale U., 1990, Williams Coll., 1993. Research assoc. to asst. prof. Georgetown U., Washington, 1955-65; physicist U. Calif.-LaJolla, 1963-64; astronomer Carnegie Inst., Washington, 1965—; Chancellor's Disting. prof. U. Calif., Berkeley, 1981; vis. com. Harvard Coll. Obs., Cambridge, Mass., 1976-82, 92—, Space Telescope Sci. Inst., 1990-92; Beatrice Tinsley vis. prof. U. Tex., 1988; Commonwealth lectr. U. Mass. 1991, Yunker Lectr. Oregon state U., 1991, Bernhard vis. fellow Williams Coll., 1993, numerous lectures US, Chile, Russia, Armenia, India, Japan, China, Europe; trustee Associated Univs., Inc., 1993—. Assoc. editor: Astrophys. Jour. Letters, 1977-82; editorial bd.: Sci. Mag., 1979-87; contbr. numerous articles sci. jours.; assoc. editor: Astron. Jour., 1972-77. Pres.'s Disting. Visitor, Vassar Coll., 1987. Mem. Smithsonian Instn. Coun., 1979-85; Phi Beta Kappa scholar, 1982-83; recipient Pres.'s Nat. Medal of Sci., 1993, Dickson prize in sci. Carnegie-Mellon U. Mem. NAS (Space Sci. Bd. 1974-77, chmn. sect. on astronomy 1992—), Am. Astron. Soc. (coun. 1977-80, Russell prize lectr.), Internat. Astron. Union (pres. Commn. on Galaxies 1982-85), Assn. Univ. Rsch. in Astronomy (divs. 1973-76, 94—), Astron. Soc. Pacific (bd. dirs. 1991—), Am. Acad. Arts and Scis., Phi Beta Kappa. Democrat. Jewish.

RUBINSTEIN, EVA (ANNA), photographer; b. Buenos Aires, Argentina, 1933; d. Arthur and Aniela (Mlynarska) R.; m. William Sloane Coffin Jr., 1956 (div. 1968); children: Amy, Alexander (dec.), David. Ballet tng., Paris, N.Y.C., Calif., 1938-53; student, Scripps Coll., 1950-51, UCLA, 1952-53; student in photography, Lisette Model, 1969, Jim Hughes, 1971, Ken Heyman, 1970, Diane Arbus, 1971. lectr. numerous workshops, seminars, confs.; photo seminars Lodz Film Sch., Poland, 1986, 86-87. Dancer, actress: off-Broadway and Broadway, including original prodn. The Diary of Anne Frank, 1955-56; European dance tour, 1955; one-person shows of photographs include Underground Gallery, N.Y.C., 1972, Dayton Art Inst., Ohio, 1973, Arles Festival, France, 1975, Canon Photo Gallery, Amsterdam, 1975, Neikrug Gallery, N.Y.C., 1975, 79, 81, 82, 85, La Photogalerie, Paris, 1975, Friends of Photography, Carmel, Calif., 1975, Galerie 5.6, Ghent, Belgium, 1976, Gallery Trochenpresse, Berlin, 1977, Frumkin Gallery, Chgo., 1977, Galeria Sinisca, Rome, 1979, Hermitage Found. Mus., Norfolk, Va., 1982, Photographers Gallery, London, 1983, Galerie Forum Labo, Arles, France, 1983, Galerie Nicephore, Lyon, France, 1983, Image Gallery, Madrid, 1984, Muzeum Sztuki, Lodz, Poland, 1984, Il Diaframma/Canon Gallery, Milan, 1984, A.R.P.A. Gallery, Bordeaux, 1984, Chateau d'Eau, Toulouse, France, 1985, Galerie Demi-Teinte, Paris, 1985, Associated Artist Photographers galleries in Warsaw, Krakow, Lodz, Katowice and Gdansk, Poland, 1985-86, Foto/Medium/Art Gallery, Wroclaw, Poland, 1986, Visions Gallery, San Francisco, 1986, Canon Galerie, Paris, 1986, Salone Internat. SICOF, Milan, 1987, St. Krzysztof Gallery, Lodz, 1987, L'Image Fixe, Lyon, 1988, Artotheque, Grenoble, 1988, Neikrug Gallery, N.Y.C., 1988-89, Neikrug Photographica Elegies, N.Y.C., 1984-88, Heuser Art Ctr. Gallery, Bradley U., Peoria, Ill., 1989, 3-os Encontros da Imagem, Braga, Portugal, 1989, Bibliotheque Nat. Galerie Colbert, Paris, 1989, Galerie Picto-Bastille, Paris, 1989-90, Portfolio Gallery, London, 1990, Vaison-La-Romaine, France, 1990, Hist. Mus. of City of Lodz, 1990, Galerie Artem, Quimper, France, 1993, Galerie F.N.A.C. Etoile, Paris, 1994, other F.N.A.C. galleries (France, Belgium, Spain), 1994—, Galerie Augustus, Berlin, 1995, L'Imagerie, Lannion, France, 1995; group shows include, Internat. Salon, Krakow, Poland, 1971, Delgado Mus., New Orleans, 1972, Neikrug Gallery, 1972, 73, 75, Salone Internationale, Milan, Italy, 1973, Photo-OVO, Montreal, Que., Can., 1974, Nat. Portrait Gallery, London, 1976, Hera Gallery, R.I., 1977, Musee National d'Art Moderne Georges Pompidou, Paris, 1977, Centre Culturel de l'ouest Aquitain, Bordeaux, France, 1978, Fotografiska Museet, Stockholm, 1978, Nat. Arts Club, N.Y.C., 1979, Chrysler Mus., Norfolk, 1979, Maine Photog. Gallery, 1981, Floating Found. Photography, N.Y.C., 1970, 71, 72, 73, 79, 82, Ffoto Gallery, Cardiff, Wales, 1983, Musée d'Art Moderne de la Ville de Paris, 1987-88, Boca Raton (Fla.) Mus., 1989, Galerie PICTO Bastille, Paris, 1989, Galerie Arena, Arles, 1989-90, Settimana della Fotografia, Palermo, 1990, Festival de l'Image, Le Mans, France, 1993; represented: in permanent collections Library of Congress, Washington, Met. Mus. Art, N.Y.C., Bibliotheque Nationale, Paris, Musee Reattu, Arles, France, Kalamazoo Inst. Arts, Israel Mus., Jerusalem, Fotografiska Museet, Stockholm, Muzeum Sztuki, Lodz, Poland, Histo Mus. of City of Lodz, others; author 2 monographs, 2 ltd. edit. portfolios with introductions by John Vachon and André Kertész; contbr. photographs in various books, mags., profl. jours.

RUBLE, ANN, minister; b. Seattle, Oct. 26, 1953; d. Monte Rahe and Stella (Terefinko) R.; m. Francis Michael Trotter, Aug. 29, 1984. Cert. sec., Met. Bus. Coll., Seattle, 1972. Ordained to ministry Ch. of Scientology, 1980. Minister Ch. of Scientology, Seattle, 1980—, dir. pub. affairs, 1983; pres. Ch. of Scientology of Wash. State, Seattle, 1984-88, dir., 1989—. Bur. chief Jour. Freedom News, 1984-88. Mem. Citizen's Commn. Human Rights, Seattle, 1984—, Com. on Religious Liberties, Seattle, 1985—; bd. dirs. Denny Regrade Crime Prevention Coun., 1994—. Office: Ch Scientology Washington State 2226 3d Ave Seattle WA 98121

RUBLEY, CAROLE A., state legislator; b. Bethel, Conn., Jan. 18, 1939; d. George B. and Evelyn M. (Maloney) Drumm; m. C. Ronald Rubley, Aug. 25, 1962; children: Lauren M. Rubley Simpson, Stephen R., Kristin A. BA in Biology, Albertus Magnus Coll., 1960; MS in Environ. Health, West Chester U., 1988. Tchr. biology Danbury (Conn.) High Sch., 1960-62, Waltham (Mass.) High Sch., 1962-63; real estate salesperson Henderson-Dewey, Wayne, Pa., 1976-81; solid waste coord. Chester County Health Dept., West Chester, Pa., 1981-88; environ. cons. Environ. Resources Mgmt., Exton, Pa., 1988-92; mem. Pa. Ho. Reps., Valley Forge, 1992—. Author: (with others) Leading Pennsylvania into 21st Century, 1990. Chmn. Ea. Chester County Regional Planning Commn., 1976-85; vice chmn. planning commn. Tredyffrin Twp., Berwyn, Pa., 1976-86, mem. bd. suprs., 1987-92; bd. dirs. Pa. Resources Coun., exec. v.p., 1988-92. Mem. LWV (pres. Upper Main Line chpt. 1976-78, Involved Voter of Yr. award 1993), Pa. Environ. Coun., Green Valleys Assn., Open Land Conservancy. Republican. Roman Catholic. Home: 621 Vassar Rd Wayne PA 19087

RUBY, GLORIA, health policy analyst consultant; b. N.Y.C., Jan. 15, 1926; d. Max and Helen (Dinaburg) Gross; m. Stanley Ruby, Nov. 24, 1920; children: Jonathon, Joseph, Allen. BA in Biology, Hunter Coll., 1946; MS in Zoology, Columbia U., 1948. Tech. info. specialist Nat. Libr. Medicine, Bethesda, Md., 1968-72; rsch. assoc. Inst. Medicine, Nat. Acad. Sci., Washington, 1972-79; project dir., sr. policy analyst Office of Tech. Assessment, U.S. Congress, Washington, 1981-91; cons. health policy Gloria Ruby & Assocs., Garrett Park, Md., 1991—. Pres. nat. capital area chpt. Hunter Coll., Washington, 1991—; mem. State Md. Podiatric Bd., Balt., 1992—; exec. v.p. Nat. Coun. Jewish Women, Montgomery County, Md., 1994—; pres. LWV, Reading, Mass., 1960-62. Sci. fellow Nat. Ctr. Health Svcs. Rsch., Hyattsville, Md., 1979-81; Columbia U. scholar, 1948; elected to Hunter Coll. Hall of Fame, 1992. Home and office: 10913 Kenilworth Ave Garrett Park MD 20896

RUBY, PEGGY MARIE, social worker; b. Mt. Clemens, Mich., June 12, 1962; d. Kenneth William and Bonnie Marie (DuCharme) R. Student, Macomb C.C., Mt. Clemens, Mich., 1980-82; BS, Cen. Mich. U., 1984, MS in Adminstrn., 1991. Crisis counselor Macomb County Community Mental Health, Mt. Clemens, 1984-85; vocat. evaluator Rehab. Resources, Southfield, Mich., 1985-86; children's svc. worker St. Clair County Dept. Social Svcs. State of Mich., Port Huron, 1986—. Mem. St. Clair County Critical Incident Stress Debriefing Team, 1994—, Macomb Players & Studio M Players. Recipient Svc. Merit award Foster Parent Assn., 1994. Mem. St. Clair County Child Abuse and Neglect Coun. (Child Advocate award 1987).

RUCKER, DELLA LEE (BOBBI RUCKER), broadcasting company executive; b. Servilla, Tenn., June 9, 1921; d. William L. and Donnie C. (Forrester) Lee; m. Arthur C. Rucker, Sept. 1, 1940 (dec. Dec. 1988); children: Rita Jean, James William. Student, Massey Bus. Coll., Atlanta, 1951. With Copper Basin Broadcasting, Copperhill, Tenn., 1964-82; sta. mgr. Mountain Broadcasting, Jasper, Ga., 1981-93; pres., owner Lee Broadcasting Co., Inc., Ellijay, Ga., 1985—; bd. dirs. Pinnacle Ins. Co., Carrollton, Ga. Talk show host, Let the Peeple Speak, Sta. WLJA AM/FM. Mem. LWV. Home: PO Box 613 Copperhill TN 37317 Office: Lee Broadcasting Co Inc PO Box 545 Ellijay GA 30540-0545

RUCKI, JUDITH ANN, public relations executive; b. Buffalo, N.Y., Oct. 7, 1950; d. Alphonse Steven and Harriet Josephine (Kuzniarek) R. BSBA, SUNY, Buffalo, 1983. Adminstrv. asst. to market analyst Westinghouse Electric Corp., Buffalo, 1969-82; market analyst Sierra Research div. LTV Missiles and Electronics Group, Buffalo, 1984-85; mgr. pub. relations, advt. Sierra Research div. LTV Corp., Buffalo, 1985—. Counselor Crisis Intervention Ctr., Buffalo, 1975-76; mem. Buffalo Philharmonic Women's Com., Buffalo Fine Arts Acad. Mem. AAUW, Pub. Relations Soc. Am. (bd. dirs. 1987-88), Internat. Assn. Bus. Communicators, Women in Communication Inc., SUNY at Buffalo Alumni Assn., Mgmt. Alumni Assn. Home: 182 Eastland Pky Buffalo NY 14225-3113 Office: LTV Missiles & Electronics Group Sierra Rsch Div 247 Cayuga Rd Buffalo NY 14225-1911

RUDD, HYNDA L., city official; b. Salt Lake City, May 20, 1936; d. Morris and Irene (Feldman) Aronovich; m. Eugene B. Chernick, Nov. 26, 1954 (div. Aug. 1955); 1 child, Jeffrey Allen; m. Hyman Z. Rudd, Mar. 7, 1956 (div.); 1 child, Melinda Renee Rudd Feldman. BS, U. Utah, 1974, MS, 1978; MLS, U. So. Calif., L.A., 1981. Co-owner Salt Lake Sanitation Co., Salt Lake City, 1961-73; librarian Marriott Library, U. Utah, Salt Lake City, 1970-74; records mgmt. specialist U. Utah, Salt Lake City, 1974-78; archivist City of L.A., 1980-85, records mgmt. officer, 1985—; established Jewish archives U. Utah, 1976; speaker records program City of L.A., So. Calif., 1980—; cons. Info. Mgmt., Glendale, Calif., 1986—. Author: Mountain West Pioneer Jewry: An Historical and Genealogical Source Book, 1980; project dir., compiler: Los Angeles and its Environs in the Twentieth Century: A Bibliography of a Metropolis--Part II, 1970-1990. Pres. Homeowner's Assn., Glendale, 1983-90; campaigner polit. offices, L.A. and Glendale, 1985—. Mem. L.A. City Hist. Soc. (bd. dirs. 1984—, pres. 1986-87), So. Calif. Jewish Hist. Soc. (bd. dirs. 1981—, v.p. 1985-87, 91—), Assn. Records Mgmt. and Adminstrs. (edn. chair 1988-90), Soc. Am. Archivists (cert. archivist 1989), Soc. Calif. Archivists, Great Books and Reading Discussion Group. Home: Unit E 103 W Mountain Glendale CA 91202-1927 Office: City of LA 555 Ramirez St # 320 Los Angeles CA 90012-2974

RUDDER, CATHERINE ESTELLE, political science association administrator; b. Atlanta, Dec. 16; d. James M. and Virginia Rudder. BA, Emory U., 1969; MA, Ohio State U., 1972, PhD, 1973. Asst. prof. U. Ga., Athens, 1973-77; chief staff to Rep. W. Fowler, Jr. U.S. House Reps., Washington, 1978-81, assoc. dir., 1983-87; exec. dir. Am. Polit. Sci. Assn., Washington, 1987—. Office: Am Polit Scis Assn 1527 New Hampshire Ave NW Washington DC 20036-1206

RUDDICK, BONNIE LOU KNEEBONE, writer, lecturer; b. Bethlehem, Pa., Aug. 29, 1946; d. George John Gregory Sysko and Shirley (Smith) Kale; children by previous marriage: Kimberly Anne, Mark David; m. Douglas Hampton Ruddick, July 12, 1980; stepchildren: Debbi, Daniel. Student, l'Univ. Laval, Que., Can., summer 1967; BA, East Stroudsburg U., 1977, MA, 1985. Pub. speaker to sales and civic orgns., 1979—; communications specialist Easton Area Sch. Dist., Pa., 1979-80; free-lance writer North Am. Moravian, Bethlehem, 1979—; owner Markim Assocs. Pub. Relations and Writing Cons., Brodheadsville, Pa., 1986-89; presenter living history The Moravians-From Herrnhut to Bethlehem, 1980-86; guest speaker City of Bethlehem Advent Breakfast, 1981; guest lectr., 1984—; faculty Am. history dept. Northampton County Area Community Coll., parttime 1985-86; dir. community relations LaBar Village, Pa., 1985; writer, producer children's programs with religious themes; writer, moderator religious book discussion groups Inspirational Exchanges, 1980—. Committeewoman Rep. Party, Bethlehem, 1978-79; co-founder Moravian Hall Sq. Mus. and Gift Shop, Nazareth, Pa., 1980; founder Speakers Bur., 1987, Parents for Students Against Drunk Drivers, 1987; founder Srs.' Info. Day; co-founder First Ann. all Night Chem. Free Graduation Party, 1988; bd. dirs. Single Parent Outreach and Housing Devel. Assn., 1987-88, Monroe County Com. Housing and Homelessness, 1987-88. Mem. Pleasant Valley Citizens' Adv. Com., Monroe County Sesquicentennial Pub. Relations Com. Mem. AAUW, Ohio Hist. Soc., Moravian Hist. Soc., Pocono Mountains C. of C. Women's Exec. Council, West End Bus. Assn., LWV, Burnley Workshop of the Poconos, Phi Alpha Theta. Avocations: designer needlepoint canvases, oil painting, sewing, other crafts. Home: PO Box 9067 Bethlehem PA 18018-9067

RUDERT, CYNTHIA SUE, gastroenterologist; b. Cin., Mar. 17, 1955; d. John Wayne and Hilda Wanda (Loftus) R.; children: Ronald Lamar Hilley II, Henry Byron Hilley. BS with honors, U. Ky., 1975; MD, U. Louisville, 1979. Diplomate Am. Bd. Internal Medicine, Am. Bd. Gastroenterology. Intern internal medicine Emory U., Atlanta, 1979-80, resident, 1980-82, fellow gastroenterology, 1982-84, asst. prof. medicine, Emory U., Atlanta, 1984-91; guest speaker Alcoholism Conf., Kanasawa, Japan, 1987; nat. and internat. speaker in gastroenterology; author: Medicine for the Practicing Physician, 3rd rev. edition, 1991, (chpts.) Acute Pancreatitis, Chronic Pancreatitis, Ischaemic Hepatitis, Rudert, C.S. Alcohol Related Symptons. Recipient Newburg award U. Louisville, 1979. Fellow ACP; mem. AMA, Am. Med. Women's Assn., Am. Assn. for Study Liver Disease, Am. Gastroent. Assn., Am. Assn. for Study Liver Diseases, So. Med. Assn., Am. Liver Found., Am. Acad. Scis., Ga. Gastroent. Soc., Med. Assn. Ga., Med. Assn. Atlanta, Atlanta Women's Med. Alliance (founder). Office: 2500 Hospital Blvd Ste 210 Roswell GA 30076

RUDGE, NANCY KIM, critical care nurse; b. Woodbury, N.J., June 3, 1958; d. Richard Raymond and Margery Arline (Brush) R. BSN, U. Tenn., 1980. CCRN, BLS. Staff RN Meth. Hosp., Memphis, 1980-84; nurse clinician II Bapt. Meml. Hosp., Memphis, 1984-89, nurse clinician III, 1989-90, nurse clinician IV, 1990-91, unit supr., 1991—; BLS instr. Am. Heart Assn., Memphis, 1991—. Choir officer Bellevue Bapt. Ch., Memphis, 1988—. Named one of top 100 nurses in Shelby and Fayette counties Celebrate Nursing, 1991. Mem. AACN. Baptist. Office: Bapt Meml Hosp 899 Madison Ave Memphis TN 38146

RUDIBAUGH, MELINDA CAMPBELL, mathematics educator; b. Indiana, Pa., Feb. 25, 1948; d. Steele Evans and Kathryn Norine (Grater) C.; m. Jerry Rudibaugh, Dec. 5, 1970; children: Amy, Evan. BS in Edn., Indiana (Pa.) U., 1970; M Natural Sci., Arizona State U., 1981; postgrad., No. Arizona U. Tchr. sci., math. Western Christian High, Phoenix, Ariz., 1979-80, Phoenix Hebrew Sch., 1980-81; instr. math. Arizona State U., Tempe, 1980-84, Maricopa C.C., Phoenix, 1981-89, Chandler-Gilbert C.C., Chandler, Ariz., 1989—. Vol. March of Dimes, 1988—, Am. Cancer Soc., 1989—; advisor Phi Theta Kappa, Chandler-Gilbert C.C., 1993. 2d lt. USAF, 1970-71. Mem. ASCD, Nat. Coun. Tchrs. Math., Math. Assn. Am., Am. Assn. Univ. Women, Am. Math. Assn. Two-Yr. Colls., Am. Assn. Higher Edn., Nat. State Devel. Coun., Nat. Coun. Staff, Program and Organizational Devel., Ariz. Assn. Supervision and Curriculum Devel., World Future Soc. Republican. Home: 10417 S 46th Way Phoenix AZ 85044 Office: Chandler Gilbert C C 2626 E Pecos Rd Chandler AZ 85225

RUDIN, ANNE NOTO, former mayor, nurse; b. Passaic, N.J., Jan. 27, 1924; m. Edward Rudin, June 6, 1948; 4 children. BS in Edn., Temple U., 1945, RN, 1946; MPA, U. So. Calif., 1983; LLD (hon.), Golden Gate U., 1990. RN, Calif. Mem. faculty Temple U. Sch. Nursing, Phila., 1946-48; mem. nursing faculty Mt. Zion Hosp., San Francisco, 1948-49; mem. Sacramento City Council, 1971-83; mayor City of Sacramento, 1983-92. Pres. LWV, Riverside, 1957, Sacramento, 1961, Calif. Elected Women's Assn., 1973—; mem. Calif. bd. dirs. Common Cause; bd. trustees Golden Gate U.; adv. bd. U. So. Calif., Army Depot Reuse Commn.; bd. dirs. Sacramento Theatre Co. Recipient Women in Govt. award U.S. Jaycee Women, 1984, Woman of Distinction award Sacramento Area Soroptimist Clubs, 1985, Civic Contbn. award LWV Sacramento, 1989, Woman of Courage award Sacramento History Ctr., 1989, Peacemaker of Yr. award Sacramento Mediation Ctr., 1992, Regional Pride award Sacramento Mag., 1993, Humanitarian award Japanese Am. Citizen's League, 1993, Outstanding Pub. Svc. award Am. Soc. Pub. Adminstrn., 1994; named Girl Scouts Am. Role model, 1989.

RUDNER, SARA, dancer, choreographer; b. Bklyn., Feb. 16, 1944; d. Henry Nathaniel and Jeannette (Smolensky) R.; m. Edward C. Marschner ; 1 child, Edward Eli. A.B. in Russian Studies, Barnard Coll., 1964. Dancer Sansardo Dance Co., N.Y.C., 1964-65, Am. Dance Co. at Lincoln Ctr., N.Y.C., 1965, Shakespeare Festival Touring Children's Show, N.Y.C., 1966; featured dancer Twyla Tharp Dance Found., N.Y.C., 1966-85; artistic dir., dancer 18th St. Dance Found., N.Y.C., 1977—; guest dancer Joffrey Ballet, N.Y.C., 1973, Pilobolus Dance Theatre, N.Y.C., 1975, Lar Lubovitch Dance Co., N.Y.C., 1975-76; guest lectr., choreographer grad. dance dept. UCLA, 1975; tchr. master workshop NYU Theater Program, 1988, 89, 90. Choreographer: Palm Trees and Flamingoes, 1980, Dancing for an Hour or So, 1981, Minute by Minute, 1982, Eight Solos, 1991, Heartbeats, Inside Out, 1993 (with Jennifer Tipton and Dana Reitz) Necessary Weather, 1994. Grantee Creative Artists Pub. Svc. Program, N.Y., 1975-76, N.Y. State Coun. on Arts, 1975-78, Nat. Endowment for Arts, 1979-81, 91-92, 94-97; Guggenheim fellow, 1981-82; recipient N.Y. Dance and Performance award, 1984.

RUDNICK, ELLEN AVA, health care executive; b. New Haven; d. Harold and C. Vivian (Soybel) R.; children from previous marriage: Sarah, Noah; m. Paul W. Earle. BA, Vassar Coll., 1972; MBA, U. Chgo., 1973. Sr. fin. analyst Quaker Oats, Chgo., 1973-75; various positions Baxter Internat., Deerfield, Ill., 1975-80, dir. planning, 1980-83, corp. v.p., 1985-1990; pres. Baxter Mgmt. Svcs., Deerfield, 1983-1990, HCIA, Northbrook, Ill., 1990-92, CEO Advs., Northbrook, Ill., 1992—; prin. BioQuant, Northbrook, 1993—. Chief crusader Met. Chgo. United Way, 1982-85; pres. coun. Nat. Coll. Edn., Evanston, Ill., 1983—; circle of friends Chgo. YWCA, 1985-89; bd. dirs. Highland Park Hosp., 1990—. Mem. Chgo. Network, Econs. Club Chgo. (officer, bd. dirs.). Office: CEO Advs 255 Revere Dr Ste 111 Northbrook IL 60062-1595

RUDNICK, IRENE KRUGMAN, lawyer, state legislator, educator; b. Columbia, S.C., Dec. 27, 1929; d. Jack and Jean (Getter) Krugman; AB cum laude, U. S.C., 1949, JD, 1952; m. Harold Rudnick, Nov. 7, 1954; children: Morris, Helen Gail. Admitted to S.C. bar, 1952; individual practice law, Aiken, S.C., 1952—, now ptnr. Rudnick & Rudnick; instr. bus. law, criminal law U. S.C., Aiken, 1962—; tchr. Warrenville Elem. Sch., 1965-70; supt. edn. Aiken County, 1970-72; mem. S.C. Ho. of Reps., 1972-78, 80-84, 86—; pres. Adath Yeshurun Synagogue; active Aiken County Dem. Party, S.C. Dem. Party, Network Aiken; hon. mem. Aiken Able-Disabled. Recipient Citizen of Yr. award, 1976-77, Bus. and Profl. Women's Career Woman of Yr., 1978, 94, Aiken County Friend of Edn. award, 1985, 93, Outstanding Legis. award Disabled Vets., 1991, Citizen of the Yr. award Planned Parenthood, 1994. Mem. NEA, S.C. Tchrs. Assn., Aiken County Tchrs. Assn., Am. Bar Assn., Aiken County Bar Assn., Nat. Order Women Legislators, AAUW, Network Aiken, Aiken Able-Disabled (hon.), Alpha Delta Kappa. Jewish. Clubs: Order Eastern Star, Hadassah, Am. Legion Aux., Lioness. Office: PO Box 544 407 Hayne Ave SW Aiken SC 29802

RUDNICK, JUDITH RENEE, medical epidemiologist; b. Bklyn., Nov. 19, 1962; d. Alvin Joel and Helene Nancy (Brown) R. BA, Johns Hopkins U., 1984; MD, Washington U., 1988. Diplomate Am. Bd. Internal Medicine. Resident in internal medicine Michael Reese Hosp., Chgo., 1988-91; med. epidemiologist CDC, Atlanta, 1991—. Mem. AMA, ACP. Office: CDC Mailstop E10 1600 Clifton Rd Atlanta GA 30333

RUDNICK, REBECCA SOPHIE, lawyer, educator; b. Bakersfield, Calif., Nov. 26, 1952; d. Oscar and Sophie Mary (Loven) R.; m. Robert Anthoine, Dec. 2, 1990. BA, Willamette U., Salem, Oreg., 1974; JD, U. Tex., 1978; LLM, NYU, 1984. Bar: Tex. 1978, La. 1979, N.Y. 1980, Calif. 1980. Law clk. to Hon. Charles Schwartz, Jr. U.S. Dist. Ct., New Orleans, 1978-79; assoc. Winthrop, Stimson, Putnam & Roberts, N.Y.C., 1979-85; spl. counsel N.Y. Legis. Tax Study Commn., N.Y.C., 1983-84; vis. assoc. prof. of law U. Conn., Hartford, 1984-85; asst. prof. law Ind. U., Bloomington, 1985-90; assoc. prof. of law Ind. U. Sch. of Law, Bloomington, 1990-94; assoc. prof. law London Law Consortium, Eng., 1994; vis. asst. prof. law U. Tex., Austin, 1988; vis. assoc. prof. law U. N.C., Chapel Hill, 1991, Boston U., 1994-95, U. Pa., 1995—; prof.-in-residence, IRS, 1991-92; vis. scholar NSW, Australia, 1994, U. Sydney, Australia, 1994. Contbr. articles to various profl. jours. and publs. Dir., gen. counsel Project GreenHope: Svcs. for Women, N.Y.C., 1980-83; advisor, tech. asst. Internat. Monetary Fund, Washington, 1994. Mem. ABA (tax sect. 1982—, sec. tax sect. passthrough entities task force 1986-88, subcom. chairs for incorps. and CLE/important devel. tax sect. corp. tax com. 1989—, corp. tax com. 1989—, tax sect. task force on integration 1990—), Am. Assn. Law Schs. (editor tax sect. newsletter 1987—), Assn. Bar of City of N.Y. (admiralty com. 1982-85), Internat. Fiscal Assn., Internat. Bar Assn. Office: U Pa Sch Law 3400 Chestnut St Philadelphia PA 19104

RUDOFF, JACQUELINE ANN, interior designer, consultant; b. Milford, Conn., Aug. 7, 1932; d. John Albert and Bertha Elizabeth (Hamm) Rifkin; m. Alex Rudoff, Dec. 28, 1960; children: John A., Alexandra S. BA, Marymount Coll., 1954; postgrad., Valley Coll., San Bernardino, Calif., 1976. Fashion coord. Ed W. Malley Dept. Store, New Haven, Conn., 1954-57; mdse. and promotion asst editor Harper's Bazaar Mag., N.Y.C., 1957-59; sales promotion copywriter Allied Stores, N.Y.C., 1959-61; dir. spl. events May Co., L.A., 1961-64; fashion stylist Bullocks Dept. Store, L.A., 1968-72; interior designer Richardson Interiors, Apple Valley, Calif., 1976-78; prof. interior design Victor Valley Coll., Victorville, Calif., 1977-87; owner Interiors by Jacqueline, Apple Valley, 1978—; cons. Apple Valley Country Club, 1994. Fund raiser Am. Cancer Soc., Victorville, 1990-93, United Way, Victorville, 1976-90. Office: Interiors by Jacqueline 14065 Seminole Rd Apple Valley CA 92307-5769

RUDOLPH, SUSANNE HOEBER, political and social science educator; b. Mannheim, Fed. Republic of Germany, Germany, Apr. 3, 1930; (parents Am. citizens); d. Johannes and Elfriede (Fischer) H.; m. Lloyd I. Rudolph, July 19, 1952; children: Jenny W., Amelia C., Matthew C. J. AB, Sarah Lawrence Coll., 1951; MA, Radcliffe Coll., 1953; PhD in Polit. Sci., Harvard U., 1955. Instr., lectr. govt. Harvard U., Cambridge, Mass., 1957-64; assoc. prof. polit. and social scis. U. Chgo., 1964-72, prof., 1972—, master social scis. collegiate div., 1973-75, chair dept. polit. sci., 1976-79, 89, dir. South Asia Ctr., 1980—; bd. dir. Rockefeller Residency Inst., 1990-94; lectr. Phi Beta Kappa, 1977-79, 86-90; mem. Bd. Fgn. Scholarships, 1979-82; chmn. com. on problems and policy, Social Sci. Rsch. Coun., 1987-89. Author: (with Lloyd I. Rudolph) The Modernity of Tradition: Political Development in India, 1967, Education and Politics in India, 1972, The Regional Imperative: Foreign Policy in South Asia, 1980, Gandhi, 1983, Essays on Rajputana, 1984, In Pursuit of Lakshmi, 1987. Bd. dirs. Sarah Lawrence Coll., 1984-90, Kodaikanal-Woodstock Found., 1988—. Ford Found. fgn. area tng. fellow, India, 1956-57, Fulbright sr. fellow, India, 1962-63, 87-88, Am. Inst. Indian Studies faculty fellow, India, 1966-67, 83-84, 91-92, Guggenheim fellow, 1970-71; grantee NSF, 1973-75, NEH, 1977-79, 95. Mem. Am. Polit. Sci. Assn. (v.p. 1973-74), Assn. Asian Studies (bd. dirs. 1973-75, v.p. 1985-86, pres. 1986-87), Asia Soc. (bd. dirs. 1991—). Office: U Chgo Dept Polit Sci 5828 S University Ave Chicago IL 60637-1515

RUDY, LINDA MAE, secondary education educator; b. York, Maine, Mar. 26, 1948; d. Maynard Everett and Frances Irene (Cross) Fuller; m. Jacob William Rudy, Sept. 27, 1980. BS, U. So. Maine, 1971, postgrad., 1978-81; postgrad., George Washington U., 1983-86. Cert. tchr., Md. Math tchr. Cape Elizabeth (Maine) Middle Sch., 1971-78, Meml. Jr. High Sch., South Portland, Maine, 1978-79, York (Maine) High Sch., 1979-81; math tchr. LaPlata (Md.) High Sch., 1983—, chmn. Md. student assistance program, 1988-94; math tchr. Md. Tomorrow Program, LaPlata, 1988, Certificate of Appreciation, 1988. Co-author: (teaching program) Challenging Choices, 1989. Mem. Cobb Island Citizens Assn., 1983—; treas. Cobb Island Bapt. Ch., 1989-94. Recipient Certificate of Recognition, Charles County Bd. Edn., LaPlata, 1988, Certificate of Appreciation, 1990, Certificate of Instructional Leadership, Md. State Dept. of Edn., Annapolis, Md., 1989. Mem. NEA, Nat. Coun. Tchrs. Math., Edn. Assn. Charles County (bldg. rep. 1988-89), Md. State Tchrs. Assn., Md. Coun. Tchrs. Math. Baptist. Home: 12048 Neale Sound Dr Cobb Island MD 20625

RUDY, RUTH CORMAN, state legislator; b. Millheim, Pa., Jan. 3, 1938; d. Orvis E. and Mabel Jan (Stover) Corman; m. C. Guy Rudy, Nov. 21, 1956; children: Douglas G., Donita Rudy Koval, Dianna F. Degree in x-ray tech. Carnegie Inst., 1956; student Pa. State U., 1968-71. Clk. of cts. County of Centre (Pa.), Bellefonte, 1976-82; rep. Pa. Gen. Assembly, Harrisburg, 1982—. Mem. Dem. Nat. Com., 1980—, chair women's caucus, 1989-91; past pres. Pa. Fedn. Dem. Women, Harrisburg; pres. Nat. Fedn. Dem. Women, 1987-89; mem. exec. com. Dem. Nat. Com., 1987-89, chmn. women's caucus, 1989-91. Named Woman of Yr., Pa. Fedn. Dem. Women, 1982. Methodist. Office: Pa Ho Reps PO Box 115 Harrisburg PA 17108-0115

RUEDY, LYNNE RUSSELL, elementary education educator; b. Green Bay, Wis., Aug. 27, 1942; d. Rollin Marsh and Mary Ellen (Lindsay) Russell; m. Kenneth Glenden Ruedy, June 15, 1963; children: Jill Ruedy Welch, Richard Marsh. BA, Calif. State U., Northridge, 1963. Cert. tchr. elem., secondary, mentally retarded, learning handicaped education, community coll. Resource specialist Irvine (Calif.) Unified Sch. Dist., 1972-76; tchr. 5th grade Shiraz (Iran) Internat. Community Sch.-Pahlavi U., 1976-78; curriculum specialist, cons. Lady Sarah Sch., Shiraz, 1978-79; resource specialist Fairfax County Schs., Springfield, Va., 1979-81; instr. Rancho Santiago C.C., Santa Ana, Calif., 1988-89; resource specialist Irvine Unified Sch. Dist., 1983-87, tchr. 5th grade., 1987—; cons. Fairfax County Schs., 1982-83. Mem. exec. com. Susan G. Komen Breast Cancer Found. Race for the Cure, San Clemente, Calif., 1992-93; vice-chmn. adv. bd. Irvine Residents with Disabilities. Mem. Zeta Tau Alpha (province pres. 1983-87, alumnae-collegiate chmn. 1983—, Cert. of Merit 1984, Honor Ring 1987, nat. officer 1985—). Republican. Episcopalian. Office: Springbrook Sch 655 Springbrook N Irvine CA 92714-7568

RUEGG, ROSALIE TRIPP, economist; b. Washington, N.C., Sept. 30, 1942; d. William Earl and Ida Wooten (Mewborn) Tripp; m. F. Churchill Ruegg, July 11, 1964 (div. Nov. 1977); 1 child, F. William II. BA in Econs., U. N.C., Greensboro, 1964; MA in Econs., U. Md., 1966; MBA in Fin., Am. U., 1985; cert. trainer, Georgetown U., 1988. Fin. economist, bd. govs. Fed. Res. Sys., Washington, 1966-68; instr. econs. Montgomery Coll., Rockville, Md., 1969-74; economist Nat. Bur. Standards, Gaithersburg, Md., 1969-80, staff asst. to dep. dir. Nat. Engring. Lab, 1981-82, analyst, dir.'s office, 1982-83, industry economist Ctr. Bldg. Tech., 1984-89; chief economist Advanced Tech. Program, 1990—; instr. short courses U. Calif., U. Wis., MIT, Presdl. Press. Author: (book) Building Economics: Theory and Practice, 1990; mem. editorial bd. Jour. Constrn. and Mgmt., 1989-94; contbr. over 50 publs. Fellow Woodrow Wilson Found., 1965-66. Mem. NAFE, Am. Econ. Assn., Phi Beta Kappa. Home: 18810 River Rd Poolesville MD 20837-9162

RUEHL, MERCEDES, actress; b. Queens, N.Y.. BA in English, Coll. of New Rochelle; studied acting with Uta Hagen, Tad Danielewski. Appearances include (theatre) Vanities, 1977-78, Billy Irish, 1980, Much Ado About Nothing, Misalliance, Androcles and the Lion, Tartuffe, Medea, 1980-82, Three Sisters, 1982-83, The Day They Shot John Lennon, 1982-83, Flirtation, 1983, June Moon, 1983-84, Monday After the Miracle, 1983-84, Coming of Age in Soho, 1985, The Marriage of Bette and Boo, 1985, I'm Not Rappaport, 1985 (Obie Award), American Notes, 1988, Other People's Money, 1989, Lost in Yonkers, 1991 (Tony award, 1991, Drama Desk award, 1991, Outer Critics Circle award 1991), The Shadow Box, 1994, (film) The Warriors, 1979, Four Friends, 1981, Heartburn, 1986, 84 Charing Cross Road, 1987, Leader of the Band, 1987, The Secret of My Success, 1987, Radio Days, 1987, Big, 1988, Married to the Mob, 1988, Slaves of New York, 1989, Crazy People, 1990, Another You, 1991, The Fisher King, 1991 (Acad. Best Supporting Actress award), Lost in Yonkers, 1993, Last Action Hero, 1993. Recipient Nat. Film Critics Circle award, 1988, Clarence Derwent award, 1989. Office: UTA 9560 Wilshire Blvd 5th Fl Beverly Hills CA 90212*

RUEHLE, DIANNE MARIE, elementary education educator; b. Detroit, Aug. 14, 1943; d. Richard Francis and Luella Mary (Kopp) R. BS, Ea. Mich. U., 1966, MA, 1971, adminstrv. cert., 1990. Cert. tchr., adminstr., Mich. Tchr. Cherry Hill Sch. Dist., Inkster, Mich., 1966-85; tchr. elem. sch. Wayne-Westland (Mich.) Community Schs., 1985—; dist. com. Pub. Act 25 for State of Mich., Westland, 1990-93, chair bldg., 1991-95. Improvement Instrn. grantee Wayne Westland Found., 1992-94. Mem. ASCD, NEA, Mich. Edn. Assn., Wayne-Westland Edn. Assn. Home: 26117 LaSalle Ct Roseville MI 48066 Office: David Hicks Elem Sch 100 Helen St Inkster MI 48141

RUE-POTTER, JOYCE, nurse, actress, talk show host, columnist; b. Chgo., July 20, 1942; d. John West and Bertha L. (Delopez) Rue; m. Robert Irwin Potter, Mar. 31, 1990. BA in Advt., U. Wash., 1966; grad., Grant Hosp Sch. Nursing, Chgo., 1963. Nurse multiple hosps., 1964-77; social dir. R&B Enterprises, Inc., L.A., 1977-80; founder, dir. Abundantly Yours, Inc., San Diego, 1979—; ind. counselor, publicist, educator, speaker; founder Enthusyattituditiks Social Support Group, Fletcher, N.C. Appeared in plays Our Town, 1986, Shadow Box, 1987, Sea Horse, 1988 (Best Actress award), Amadeus, 1988; on TV shows Oprah, Donahue, Geraldo, Joan Rivers, Groups; radio talk show host Sta. KMJC, 1988-89, Joyce Rue (Hyphen) Potter Show, WISE/WTZQ; author: Waist Size Isn't About Self Worth, Enthusiologist Handbook; columnist for 3 publs. Mem. Performing Arts Theatre Handicapped (Svc. award 1985, bd. dirs. 1986-89), Actors Network San Diego County (pres., bd. dirs. 1985-89). Office: Enthusyattituditiks PO Box 907 Fletcher NC 28732-0907

RUESCH, JANET CAROL, federal magistrate judge; b. New Brunswick, N.J., May 9, 1943. AB in Polit. Sci., Gettysburg Coll., 1965; JD, Ind. U., 1970. Bar: Tex. 1971, U.S. Dist. Ct. (we. dist.) Tex. 1973, U.S. Ct. Appeals (5th cir.) 1975, U.S. Dist. Ct. (so. dist.) Tex. 1977, U.S. Supreme Ct. 1979. Law clk. Malcolm McGregor and Mark Howell, El Paso, Tex., 1970-71; ptnr. Malcolm McGregor, Inc., El Paso, 1971-78; substitute mcpl. ct. judge City of El Paso, 1977-78; asst. U.S atty. Western Dist. Tex., El Paso, 1978-79; U.S. magistrate judge El Paso divsn. U.S. Dist. Ct. (we. dist.) Tex., 1979—. Bd. dirs. El Paso County Gen. Assistance Agy., 1977-79; past mem. profl. adv. bd. El Paso Mental Health Assn.; v.p. El Paso Women's Pol. Caucus, 1977, program chair, 1976, pub. chair, 1975. Mem. Tex. Bar Assn., El Paso Bar Assn. (pres. 1984), El Paso Women's Bar Assn. (pres. 1975). Office: 206 US Courthouse 511 E San Antonio El Paso TX 79901

RUFF, CAROLYN M., art gallery owner, director; b. Mpls., Apr. 18, 1947; d. Alfred Henry and Marion Lucille (Pearson) Cheese; m. Stephen McAlpin Ruff, Aug. 16, 1968; children: Veronika Lis, Per Jordan. BS, U. Minn., 1968, MA, 1976. Elem. tchr. Mounds View Pub. Sch., St. Paul, 1968-70; tchg. asst. U. Minn., Mpls., 1975-76; dir. Art Dealers Assocs., Mpls., 1984-87; owner, dir. Carolyn Ruff Gallery, Mpls., 1989—; contemporary arts guide Walker Art Ctr., Mpls., 1986—; assoc. Mpls. Coll. Art, 1993—; cons. Dept. Def. Sch., Tokyo, 1970-73, Fulda, Germany, 1973-75, Minnetonka (Minn.) Pub. Sch., 1976-84. Mem. Mpls. Inst. Art, Walker Art Ctr. (dirs. cir. 1976—, collector's cir. 1993—). Democrat. Office: Carolyn Ruff Gallery 400 1st Ave N Ste 134 Minneapolis MN 55401-1700

RUFF, DUREEN ANNE, small business owner, operater; b. Grand Forks, N.D., Feb. 27, 1931; d. Conrad and Margaret (Johnson) A.; m. R. William Ruff, June 23, 1956; children: Susan Lynne, Kristine Louise, Steven W., Anne Marie. BS, U. N.D., 1953. Cert. tchr., N.D., Minn., Calif. Tchr. Roosevelt Elem. Sch., Grand Forks, 1953-56, San Miguel Elem. Sch., Sunny Vale, Calif., 1956-57, Regent Jr. High Sch., Robbinsdale, Minn., 1957-59, Carl Sandburg Jr. High Sch., Golden Valley, Minn., 1959-60; designer, mfr. d. Anne Ruff Miniatures, Plymouth, Minn., 1970—. Mem. Abbott Hosp. Aux., Mpls., 1968-78, Abbott Northwestern Aux., 1978—; elder Westminister Presbyn. Ch., 1981-87. Mem. Nat. Assn. Miniature Enthusists (Acad. Honor 1986—), Miniatures Industry Assn. Am., Cottage Industry Miniatures Trade Assn., Miniature Guild of Minn, Internat. Guild of Miniature Artisans (artisan status 1989—). Republican. Home and Office: 1100 Vagabond Ln N Minneapolis MN 55447-2560

RUFF, ELIZABETH HARVEY, social work educator; b. Hartford, Conn., Oct. 17, 1934; d. Thomas Gray and Olga Evelyn (Aldrin) Harvey; m. William John Ruff, Aug. 17, 1957; children: Julianne, David, Melissa. BA, U. Maine, 1956; MSW, U. Conn., 1983. Tchr. City of New Britain (Conn.), 1956-57, Anne Arundel County, Odenton, Md., 1957-59; tchr. pre-sch. Concordia Luth. Ch., Concord, N.H., 1959-60; substitute tchr. City of Concord, 1960-63; dir. Keene (N.H.) Day Care Ctr., 1973-76, Freeport (Maine) Cmty. Svcs., 1978-85; coord. field placement & classes U. Conn. Sch. Social Work, West Hartford, 1985-86, instr., 1986-87; faculty mem U. New England Sch. Social Work, Biddeford, Maine, 1987—. Town councilor Town of Freeport, 1978-81, 92—; cons. to bd. Freeport Cmty. Svcs., 1988—; bd. dirs. Planned Parenthood No. New Eng., Burlington, Vt., 1991-94. Named Citizen of Yr. Concord Assn. Retarded People, 1969. Mem. NAS (br. rep. 1985—, pers. com. chair 1988-90), Coun. Social Work Edn. Home: 55 Durham Rd Freeport ME 04032 Office: U New England Sch Social Work Hills Beach Rd Biddeford ME 04005

RUFF, LORRAINE MARIE, public relations executive; b. Washington, Feb. 13, 1947; d. William Stanley and Jeanne Ann (Murray) Charlton; m. R. Eugene Ruff, July 17, 1968; 1 child, David Michael. BS in Liberal Arts, Oreg. State U., 1976. Reporter The Oregonian, Corvallis, Oreg., 1976-79, Union-Bull., Walla Walla, Wash., 1979-80; dir. pub. rels. Strategic Mktg., Corvallis, 1980-82; gen. mgr. Campaigns Northwest, Corvallis, 1982-84; account supr. Arthur D. Little, Inc., Cambridge, Mass., 1985-87, mgr. corp. ID, 1988-89; dir. biotechnology New Eng. Hill and Knowlton, Waltham, Mass., 1989, v.p., dir. biotechnology, 1990, sr. v.p., mng. dir. internat. biotechnology practice, 1990-91, sr. v.p., gen. mgr., 1991-93; sr. v.p., mng. dir. divsn. biosci. comm. Stoorza, Ziegaus & Metzger, San Diego, 1993-94, dir. life scis. practice, 1993-94; owner Charlton Ruff Comm., Puyallup, Wash., 1994—. Chmn. mktg. think tank U. Calif.-San Diego Cancer Ctr. Found., 1993-94; bd. dirs. San Diego chpt. Am. Lung Assn. Mem. Pub. Rels. Soc. Am. (treas. Boston chpt. 1990-92), Nat. Investor Rels. Inst., Oreg. Biotech. Assn., Wash. State Biotech. Assn., San Diego Biomed. Industry Coun. (exec. dir. 1994, mem. biotech. edn. program for students and tchrs. 1993-94), San Diego Investor Rels. Group. Republican. Office: Charlton Ruff Comm 12124 138th Ave E Puyallup WA 98374

RUFFALO, MARIA THERESE, mechanical engineer; b. Seattle, Feb. 26, 1963; d. Patrick and Helen (Eckhardt) R.; m. Joseph Patrick Otterbine, May 5, 1987. BS in Mech. Engring., U. Rochester, 1985. Proj. engr. Polycast Tech. Corp., Hackensack, N.J., 1985-86, sr. project engr., 1986-87; cons. Polycast Tech. Corp., Hackensack, 1987; project engr. Ink div. J.M. Huber Corp., Edison, N.J., 1987-89; sr. engr. Himont USA, Inc., East Brunswick, N.J., 1990-93; engring. team leader Anchor Glass Container, Cliffwood, N.J., 1993—. Mem. ASME, Nat. Assn. Female Execs. Home: 342 Woodbine Dr Cliffwood Beach NJ 07735-5528

RUFFIN, SHIRLEY ANN, federal financial director; b. Tokyo, Japan, Sept. 1, 1955; (parents Am. citizens); d. Alfred Lewis and Linda Eiko (Yokomura) R. BSBA in Acctg., George Mason U., 1977; MBA in Fin., Am. U., 1982. Cert. in Procurement Mgmt. Staff acct., auditor EPA, Def. Contract Audit Agy., Dept. Agriculture, Dept. Navy, Washington, 1973-86; chief accounts payable, travel mgmt. sect. EPA, 1986-87, chief quality assurance staff, 1987-89; assoc. dir. acctg. ops. Comptroller of the Currency, Washington, 1989-91; acting dir. sys. and acctg. standards divsn. IRS, Washington, 1991-93; dir. fin. mgmt. policy Dept. Health and Human Svcs., Washington, 1993—; adj. faculty U.Va., Falls Ch., 1985-87. Sec./v.p. Lyongate Owners Assn., Arlington, Va., 1993—; mem. fin. com. Arlington Village Condo Assn., 1985-86. Mem. Assn. Govt. Accts. (Appreciation award 1988), Annandale Bus. & Profl. Women (corr. sec. 1990-91, Young Careerist award 1990).

RUFFING, JANET KATHRYN, spirituality educator; b. Spokane, Wash., July 17, 1945; d. George Benjamin and Dorothy Edith (Folsom) R. BA, Russell Coll., 1968; M of Applied Spirituality, U. San Francisco, 1978; lic. in Sacred Theology, Jesuit Sch. Theology, 1984; PhD in Christian Spirituality, Grad. Theol. Union, 1986. Joined Sisters of Mercy Congregation, Roman Cath. Ch., 1963. Tchr. reading and English Mercy High Sch., Burlingame, Calif., 1968-72, 75-77, San Francisco, 1972-75; tchr., dept. head Marian High Sch., San Diego, 1978-80; faculty and originating team mem. Fully Alive, Burlingame, 1980-86; faculty, facilitator Permanent Diaconate Formation Program, Oakland, Calif., 1984-86; faculty Internship in Art of Spiritual Direction, Burlingame, 1984, 85, 87; assoc. prof. spirituality and spiritual direction Fordham U., Bronx, N.Y., 1986—; spiritual dir., supr. of dirs., Calif., N.Y., 1975-91; speaker Roger Williams Symposium, Pullman, Wash., 1985; vis. faculty Australian Cath. U., Brisbane, summer 1994, San Francisco Theol. Sem., summer 1993, U. San Francisco, summer 1991, St. Michael's Coll., Vt., summer 1990. Author: Uncovering Stories of Faith, 1989; contbr. articles to profl. jours. Mem. Cath. Theol. Soc. Am. (seminar moderator 1987-90), Am. Acad. Religion (chairperson mysticism group 1994—), Mercy Assn. in Scripture and Theology (treas. 1987—, mem. editorial bd. MAST jour.), Spiritual Dirs. Internat. (founding coord. com. mem. 1990-93, coord. of regions 1990-93), Women's Ordination Conf. Democrat. Office: Fordham U Grad Sch Religion and Religious Bronx NY 10458

RUFFNER, MYRNA SMART, opera company executive. Exec. dir. Tulsa Opera, Tulsa, Okla. Office: Tulsa Opera Chapman Music Hall 1610 S Boulder Ave Tulsa OK 74119-4408*

RUGGIERI, ELAINE, public relations administrator; b. Kennett Square, Pa., Nov. 20, 1933; d. Arcangelo and Angelina (Leo) R.; m. William S. Satterthwaite Jr., Aug. 13, 1959 (div. 1982); children: Amy Nelson Satterthwaite, Jane Clifford Satterthwaite. AB, Bucknell U., 1955; postgrad., U. Va., 1973-75, 1973-75, NYU, 1983-88. Dir. pub. rels. Darden Grad. Sch. Bus. Adminstrn. U. Va., Charlottesville, 1979—, instr., 1982-85, 88, instr. written communications dept. tng. and devel., 1988—; various writing, editorial and pub. rels. positions, 1955—. Editor mag. The Darden Report, 1979-86, 89—, jour. Fin. Analysts Rsch. Assn., 1981-82; TV show host FOCUS, 1982-86. Recipient George Washington medal Freedoms Found. Valley Forge, 1958, 1st pl. graphics communications award Printing Industries Va., 1984, APEX award of excellence Comm. Concepts Inc., 1993, 94; named one of 100 Top Pub. Rels. Profls., Sch. Mass. Comm., Va. Commonwealth U., 1993. Mem. Pub. Rels. Soc. Am. (accredited, dir. Old Dominion chpt. 1991). Office: U Va Darden Grad Sch Bus Adminstrn PO Box 6550 Charlottesville VA 22906-6550

RUGGIERO, MARY GRACE, real estate broker; b. L.A., Oct. 25, 1952; d. Ralph John and Mary Theresa (Gulli) R.; m. Kenneth Ray LeMar, Aug. 25, 1984 (div. June 1991); m. Steven Dale Hethcoat, Aug. 10, 1991; 1 child, Amethyst Hope. BA in Psychology, Calif. State U., Fullerton, 1974, MA in Psychology, 1977; PhD in Social Ecology, U. Calif., Irvine, 1984. Pvt. piano tchr., 1972-77; rsch. dir. U. Calif., Irvine, 1980-83; real estate licensing instr. Real Estate Trainers, Santa Ana, Calif., 1985-87; real estate office tng. dir., mgr. Century 21 Emery, Anaheim, Calif., 1986-91, real estate salesperson, 1984-91; real estate salesperson Re/Max of Ctrl. Orange County, Anaheim, 1992-93; real estate broker Amethyst Real Estate, Anaheim, 1994—. Contbr. articles to profl. jours. Recipient award for best dissertation APA, 1984. Mem. Anaheim Assn. Realtors. Democrat. Roman Catholic. Home: 2229 S Loara St Anaheim CA 92802-3913

RUGGIERO-KARP, NANCY ELIZABETH, advertising executive, graphics consultant; b. Wallkill, N.Y., June 20, 1953; d. Angelo Salvatore and Irene Katherine (McLinden) R.; m. Steven Brooks Karp, Sept. 3, 1989. AA, Harriman Coll., 1973; postgrad., Parsons Sch. Design, 1978, Advance Graphic Design Sch. of Visual Arts, N.Y., 1982. Graphic artist Walden (N.Y.) printing Co., 1975-76; advt. design Cornwall (N.Y.) Local, 1976-77; art dir. Devito Assocs., Goshen, N.Y., 1977-81; advt. mgr. Conklin Lumber Co., Warwick, N.Y., 1981-82; owner Ad Crafters and Co., Goshen, N.Y., 1982-85; creative dir., computer artist Slide Presentations, Inc., Monroe, N.Y., 1985-87; ptr., v.p. Brooks Advt. and Design, Goshen, N.Y., 1986-92; logo designer Town of Shawangunk Bicentennial Com., Wallkill, N.Y., 1988, speaker advt. Inst. Bus. and Industry, Middletown, N.Y. 1985-88; advt. design cons. Conklin Lumber LMC Buying Coop.; desktop pub./graphics cons. Nynex Corp., White Plains, N.Y., 1992—. Artist, mem. Goshen Hist. Track Aux., 1982. Recipient Outstanding Graphic Design award Dynamic Graphics, Inc., 1978. Mem. Harriman Coll. Alumni Assn., Warwick Valley Chorale, Phi Theta Kappa. Republican. Roman Catholic. Office: RR 1 Box 498 Westtown NY 10998

RUHE, SHIRLEY LOUISE, government official; b. Des Moines, Mar. 20, 1943; d. Merritt Elton and Grace Alberta (Crabtree) Bailey; B.S., Iowa State U., 1965, M.S., 1969; m. Jonathan Mills Ruhe, Feb. 28, 1970; children—Alix-Nicole, Jonathan G. B. Wire editor, photographer Ames (Iowa) Daily Tribune, 1968-69; legis. asst. Congressman John Culver, 1969-72; staff asst. Congressman John Blatnik, 1973-75; dep. dir. budget process and ops. Ho. of Reps., Washington, 1978-82, assoc. dir., 1983-86, dir. budget policy, 1987-94; co-staff dir. Reconciliation Task Force, 1981—; adviser Spl. Rules Com. Task Force on Budget Process, 1982-83; mem. bd. dirs. Le Neon French-Am. Theatre, Christian Edn. Bd. Rock Spring Congl. Ch., Resource Coun. Inst. Ednl. Policy. Ford Found. grantee, 1969. Mem. Delta Sigma Phi, Phi Kappa Phi. Democrat. Home: 3915 N Woodstock St Arlington VA 22207-2941 Office: Budget 203 O'Neill House Office Bldg Washington DC 20515

RUHLIN, PEGGY MILLER, investment adviser, financial planner; b. Dayton, Ohio, May 20, 1949; d. Charles Raymond and Shirlee E. (Menke) Miller; m. John B. Ruhlin Jr., June 19, 1982; 1 child, Megan Falla. BA magna cum laude, Otterbein Coll., 1979. CPA, Ohio; Cert. fin. planner. Acct. Borden, Inc., Columbus, Ohio, 1971-72; mgr. Intraspace Planning Group, Inc., Columbus, Ohio, 1972-74; v.p. Mgmt. Media, Inc., Columbus, Ohio, 1974-80, pres., 1980-87; prin. Budros & Ruhlin, Inc., Columbus, Ohio, 1987—; adj. prof. Capital U., Columbus, 1992—; mem. nat. adv. bd./coun. Schwab Instl., 1994—. Columnist Bus. First of Greater Columbus, 1986; commentator Sta. WCBE-FM, 1989-91; contbr. articles to profl. jours. Mem. AICPA, Assn. for Investment Mgmt. and Rsch., Internat. Assn. Fin. Planning (chpt. pres. 1989-91, nat. bd. dirs. 1992—), Nat. Assn. Personal Fin. Advisers (Fin. Planner of Yr. award 1988), Inst. Cert. Fin. Planners, Internat. Women's Forum. Office: Budros & Ruhlin Inc 1650 Lake Shore Dr Ste 150 Columbus OH 43204-4895

RUIZ-VALERA, PHOEBE LUCILE, law librarian; b. Barranquilla, Colombia, Jan. 27, 1950; d. Ramon and Marion (Mehlman) Ruiz-Valera; m. Thomas Patrick Winkler, Mar. 27, 1981. BA cum laude, Westminster Coll., 1971; MLS, Rutgers U., 1974; MA, NYU, 1978. Libr. trainee Passaic (N.J.) Pub. Libr., 1973-74, reference libr., 1974; libr. assoc., cataloger NYU Law Libr., N.Y.C., 1974-79, asst. curator, cataloger, 1979-81; libr. III, cataloger Rutgers U. Library, New Brunswick, N.J., 1981-82; chief cataloger Assn. Bar City N.Y., 1982-85, head tech. svcs., 1985—. Mem. ALA, Am. Assn. Law Librs., Am. Translators Assn. (cert. translator English to Spanish), Law Libr. Assn. Greater N.Y., Reforma, Salalm. Democrat. Presbyterian. Office: Assn Bar City NY 42 W 44th St New York NY 10036-6686

RULE, ANN, author; 4 children. Degree in English, U. Washington, 1958, postgrad. in police sci. Former policewoman, Seattle; speaker on subject of serial killers. Author (non-fiction books): The Stranger Beside Me, 1980, The I-5 Killer, Want-Ad Killer, Lust Killer, Beautiful Seattle, 1984, Small Sacrifices, 1987, If You Really Loved Me, 1991, Everything She Ever Wanted, 1992, (novel): Possession, 1983, A Rose for Her Grave, 1993, You Belong to Me, 1994, Dead by Sunset, 1995, A Fever in the Heart, 1995; contbr. over 1400 articles to newspapers and mags. including True Detective, Cosmopolitan, and others. Vol. Seattle Crisis Clinic. Address: PO Box 98846 Seattle WA 98198

RULLKOETTER, JILL E., museum education administrator; b. St. Louis, Oct. 2, 1953; d. Robert Carl Rullkoetter and Evelyn K. (Herrman) Stacy; m. William L. Hurley, Jr., Sept. 1, 1985; 1 child, Nicholas Rullkoetter Hurley. BA in Art History, U. Mo., 1976; MA, U. Wash., 1984. Rsch. asst. Mus. Art & Archaeology U. Mo., Columbia, 1975-76; curatorial asst.

Henry Art Gallery U. Wash., Seattle, 1978-79, teaching asst. dept. art history, 1979-80; coord. edn. program Seattle Art Mus., 1982-85, head edn., 1986—; staff liason architect selection com. Seattle Mus. Art; speaker and panelist in field. Author (guide booklet) Treasures from the National Museum of American Art: A Family Guide, 1986. Trustee Seattle Archtl. Found., 1990-92. Mem. Am. Assn. Mus. (chmn. edn. com. western region 1985-87, bd. dirs. 1994—), Wash. Mus. Assn., Western Mus. Assn. (bd. dirs., sec. 1988-92, 2d v.p. 1992-94, pres. 1994—), N.W. Inst. Architecture and Urban Studies in Italy (bd. dirs. 1981-91, 2d v.p. 1987-88). Office: Seattle Art Mus PO Box 22000 Seattle WA 98122-9700

RULLO-COONEY, DIANE, psychotherapist; b. Newark, Sept. 2, 1955; d. Jerome Peter and Rosina Joan (Bongo) Rullo; m. John Michael Cooney, Apr. 8, 1978. BA, Mount Clair State Coll., 1981; MA, Montclair State Coll., 1984; M of Social Work, Fordham U., 1993, postgrad., 1994—. Cert. social worker, N.Y.; internat. cert. alcohol and drug counselor; lic. clin. social worker, N.J.; cert. alcohol and drug counselor, N.J. Program dir. Main St. Counseling Ctr., West Orange, N.J., 1981-86; clinician Elizabeth (N.J.) Gen. Med. Ctr., 1986-87; clin. supr. Ctr. for Drug & Alcohol Prrevention & Treatment, Woodbridge, N.J., 1987-92; supr. family preservation svcs. Bayshore Youth and Family Svcs., Matawan, N.J., 1992-94; psychotherapist pvt. practice, Aberdeen and Hazlet, N.J., 1992—; cons. ExtraCare Health Svcs., Old Bridge, N.J., 1993-95; lectr. in field; adj. prof. Rutgers U., New Brunswick, N.J., 1994, 95. Mem. Nat. Assn. Social Workers. Home: 55 11th St Keansburg NJ 07734-3013 Office: Rullo Psychotherapy Assocs 1 Bethany Rd Bldg 6 Ste 78B Hazlet NJ 07730-1630 also: Youdin Counseling Ctr Ste L 1070 Hwy 34 Matawan NJ 07747

RUMBERGER, REGINA, retired English language educator; b. Pitts., Aug. 6, 1921; d. Edward T. and Margaret (Berry) Flynn; m. Wilson A. Rumberger, July 31, 1943 (div. 1974); children: Edward, Wilson J., Susan A., Gerard, Paul, Nancy, Joe. BEd, Duquesne U., 1942; MEd, U. Pitts., 1950; grad., State Office Div. Blind Svcs., Ft. Myers, Fla., 1984. Professed Lay Carmelite, 1990. Primary tchr. Allegheny County Pub. Sch., Pa., 1942-43, Sharpsburg (Pa.) Schs., 1943-50; instr. English, Edison C.C., Ft. Myers, 1964-78; ret., 1978; media cons., Lee County and Ft. Myers, 1956; cons., evaluator State of Fla. and Lee County, 1987-88; cons., evaluator Lee County Dept. Transp., Ft. Myers, 1988-90. Chmn. water and safety ARC, Ft. Myers, 1960-65, first aid adminstr., 1965-68; pres. Lee County Med. Aux., 1965-66; consumer rep. Lee County Dept. Transp.; bd. dirs. Met. Planning Orgn., Ft. Myers, 1990—; v.p. S.W. Fla. Curia, 1988—; asst. tour guide to Fr. Stanislaw Pierog, tour dir. Andrew's Pilgrimages, Stockbridge, Mass., 1990—; cons. on accessibility for handicapped Mayor's Alliance, mem. Coun. Disabled, 1991-92; cons., citizen adv. Divsn. Blind Svcs., State of Fla., 1990-91; vol. Lee Mem. Hosp., 1992; mem. coun. Lee County Bd. Parks and Recreation, 1994—. Recipient award Boy Scouts Am., Ft. Myers, 1967, State of Fla., 1984, Ft. Myers Care Ctr./Lee Convalescence, 1990, Vol. of Yr., State of Fla., 1994. Mem. AAUW (pub. rels. com. Ft. Myers 1987-90). Roman Catholic. Home: 2140 Cottage St Apt 109 Fort Myers FL 33901-3666

RUMBLEY, ROSE-MARY, speaker, actress; b. Dallas, Sept. 14, 1932; d. Philip and Amy (Hass) Brau; m. Jack Rumbley, May 30, 1953; children: Jill Rumbley Beam, Phil. BA, U. North Tex., 1952, MEd, 1953, PhD, 1970. Actress Dallas Summer Musicals; prof. edn. Dallas Bapt. U., 1965-77; lectr., speaker various cities, 1965—. Author: Century of Class, 1986, Unauthorized History of Dallas, Texas, 1991. Named Disting. Alumna U. North Tex., 1986; recipient Nat. P.R. award. Mem. SAG-AFTRA, Actors Equity. Home: 5438 Vanderbilt Ave Dallas TX 75206-6024

RUNGE, KAY KRETSCHMAR, library director; b. Davenport, Iowa, Dec. 9, 1946; d. Alfred Edwin and Ina (Paul) Kretschmar; m. Peter S. Runge Sr., Aug. 17, 1968; children: Peter Jr., Katherine. BS in History Edn., Iowa State U., 1969; MLS, U. Iowa, 1970. Pub. service librarian Anoka County Library, Blaine, Minn., 1971-72; cataloger Augustana Coll., Rock Island, Ill., 1972-74; dir. Scott County Library System, Eldridge, Iowa, 1974-85, Davenport (Iowa) Pub. Libr., 1985—. Bd. dirs. River Ctr. for Performing Arts, Davenport, 1983—, Am. Inst. Commerce, 1989—, Quad-Cities Conv. and Visitors Bur., 1991—, Quad-Cities Grad. Study Ctr., 1992—, Downtown Davenport Devel. Corp., 1992—, Hall of Honor Bd. Davenport Ctrl. High Sch., 1992—; mem. steering com. Quad-Cities Visions for the Future, 1987-91; bd. govs. Iowa State U. Found., 1991—. Recipient Svc. Key award Iowa State U. Alumni Assn., 1979. Mem. ALA (chmn. library adminstrs. and mgrs. div., fundraising section 1988), Iowa Library Assn. (pres. 1983), Pub. Library Assn. (bd. dirs. 1990—), Iowa Edn. Media Assn. (Intellectual Freedom award 1984), Alpha Delta Pi (alumni state pres. 1978). Lutheran. Office: Davenport Pub Libr 321 N Main St Davenport IA 52801-1409

RUNTE, ROSEANN, academic administrator; b. Kingston, N.Y., Jan. 31, 1948; arrived in Can., 1971, naturalized, 1983; d. Robert B. and Anna Loretta (Schorkopf) O'Reilly; m. Hans-Rainer Runte, Aug. 9, 1969. BA summa cum laude, SUNY-New Paltz, 1968; MA, U. Kans., 1969, PhD, 1974, DLitt (hon.), Acadia U., 1989, Meml. U., 1990. Lectr. Bethany Coll., W.Va., 1970-71; lectr. adult studies St. Mary's U., Halifax, N.S., Can., 1971-72; from lectr. to assoc. prof. Dalhousie U., Halifax, 1972-83, asst. dean, 1980-82, chmn. dept. French, 1980-83; pres. Universite Sainte-Anne, Pointe-de-l'Eglise, N.S., Can., 1983-88; prin. Glendon Coll., Toronto, 1988-94; pres., vice chancellor Victoria U., 1994—. Author: Brumes bleues, 1982; Faux-Soleils, 1984, Birmanie Blues, 1993; editor: Studies in 18th Century Culture, vols. VII, VIII, IX, 1977, 78, 79; co-editor: Man and Nature, 1982, Le Développement régional, 1986, 87, From Orality to Literature/de L'Oralite la littérature, 1991, Lectures canadiennes, 1993, Visions of Beauty, 1994; rev. editor French Rev., 1988-94; co-translator Local Development, 1987. Bd. dirs. Assn. Med. Svcs., 1989-92; adv. bd. Nat. Libr., 1984-91; v.p. Can. Commn. for UNESCO, 1991-92, pres., 1992—; vice chair exec. bd. Found. for Internat. Tng., 1994—, chair Gottschalk Prize Com., 1994; chairwoman publs. com. Hannah Found, 1989-92. Decorated Ordre du Mérite; recipient Prix Fr. Coppée French Acad., 1989; regents scholar SUNY-New Paltz, 1965; NDEA Title IV grantee U. Kans., Lawrence, 1968; Acad. Palmes, 1986. Mem. Internat. Soc. 18th Century Studies (assoc. treas. 1983-87), Internat. Assn. of Comparative Lit. (treas. 1985-91, sec. 1991-94), Can. Fedn. Humanities (pres. 1982-84), Atlantic Soc. 18th Century Studies (pres. 1972-76), Canadian Soc. 18th Century Studies (pres. 1975-76), Soc. for Study Higher Edn. (bd. dirs. 1988-90), Found. Internat. Tng. (bd. dirs. 1992), Knights of Malta (grande dame 1991—), Delta Kappa Gamma, Phi Delta Kappa, Club of Rome. Home: 44 Charles St W # 3803, Toronto, ON Canada M4Y 1R8 Office: 73 Queen's Park Crescent, Toronto, ON Canada M5S 1K7

RUNYON, MARY LUCILLE, banker; b. Mt. Sterling, Ky., Aug. 17, 1927; d. Jess and Mary (Martin) Gilbert; married; children: Joy Lynette Ramirez, Pamela Lea Perez, Dreama Carol. Student, U. Ky. Lic. in real estate. V.p. 1st Nat. Bank, Palm Beach, Fla., 1969-85, Bankers Trust of Fla., West Palm Beach, 1987—. Founder, v.p. Adopt-A-Family of Palm Beach, Inc., West Palm Beach, 1984—; bd. dirs. Vol. Ctr. of Palm Beach, 1983—, League of Charities, Palm Beach, 1987—; com. mem. Am. Heart Auction, West Palm Beach, 1985—; v.p. Good Samaritan Hosp. Aux., West Palm Beach, 1987—, mem. assoc. bd. Good Samaritan Hosp. Recipient Congrl. award for volunteerism Pres. Reagan, 1984, Jefferson award Channel 12, 1985-86, Vol. award Bankers Trust Co., 1988. Fellow Nat. Am. Bank Women. Republican. Baptist. Lodge: Shriners. Home: 12062 Basin St S West Palm Beach FL 33414-5718

RUOFF, CYNTHIA OSOWIEC, foreign language educator; b. Chgo., Mar. 1, 1943; d. Stephen R. and Estelle (Wozniak) O.; m. Gary Edward Ruoff, June 5, 1965; children: Gary S., Laura A. AB, Loyola U., 1965; MA, Western Mich. U., 1973; PhD in French Lang. and Lit., Mich. State U., 1992. Tchr. Kalamazoo (Mic.) Pub. Schs., 1965-68; instr. Western Mich. U., Kalamazoo, 1980—; nat. and internat. spkr. in field. Contbr. articles to profl. jours. Mem. MLA, N.Am. Soc. Seventeenth-Century French Lit., Am. Assn. Tchrs. of French, Mich. Fgn. Lang. Assn., Internat. Soc. Phenomenology and Lit., L'Alliance Française, Southeast Am. Soc. French Seventeenth-Century Studies, Phi Sigma Iota, Pi Delta Phi. Office: Dept Fgn Langs & Lit Western Mich Univ Kalamazoo MI 49008

RUPKE, BONNIE JO, nurse; b. Hays, Kans., Mar. 19, 1958; d. Lloyd John and Maxiline Deloris (Huser) Kisner; m. Robert James Rupke, Sept. 17, 1977; children: Dustin James, Daisha Marie, Nichole Ann. AAS, Pratt C.C., 1990; AAS, ADN, Barton County C.C., 1992; student, Ft. Hays State U. LPN, Kans. Nursing asst. Medicine Lodge (Kans.) Meml. Hosp., 1989-90; RN charge skilled care unit, rehab. unit Hays (Kans.) Med. Ctr., 1990-93; dir. nursing Hays (Kans.) Good Samaritan Hosp., 1993-94; tchr., trainer Medstaff Temp Personal, 1995—; adminstr. blood pressure clinics area health fairs. Office: Hays Good Samaritan Ctr 27th and Canal Hays KS 67601

RUPP, JEAN LOUISE, communications executive, author; b. Portland, Oreg., Aug. 29, 1943; d. Edward Howard and Dorothy Eugenia (Ross) Brown; m. Herbert Gustav Rupp, July 4, 1987. BA in English, Portland State U., 1965. Cert. tchr., Oreg. Tchr., dept. head Beaverton (Oreg.) Sch. Dist., 1967-88; pres., founder Write Communications, Portland, 1988—; adj. faculty Portland C.C., Clackamas C.C., Concordia Coll.; nat. trainer, cons. State of Oreg., City of Portland, Nike, Inc., Oreg. Health Scis. U., Oreg. Mil. Acad., Oreg. Fin. Instns. Assn., Freightliner, Automated Data Processing, others, 1988—; speaker Tektronix, Fred Meyer, Pacific Power, Am. Inst. of Banking, Utah Power, Pacific Telecom, Inc., other; writing dir. U.S. Army Corp of Engrs., USDA Forest Svcs., PacifiCare, others, 1988-90. Author: Grammar Gremlin: An Instant Guide to Perfect Grammar for Everybody in Business, 1994; TV appearances include Stas. KATU-TV and KGW-TV. Vol. Dove Lewis Emergency Veterinary Clinic, Portland, 1989—, Doerbecher Childrens Hosp. Mem. ASTD, Oreg. Speakers Assn. (membership chair, bd. dirs. 1991—), Nat. Speakers Assn., Ctr. for Marine Conservation. Republican. Office: Write Comm 8885 SW Canyon Rd # 201 Portland OR 97225-3455

RUPPE, LORET MILLER, former ambassador; b. Milw., Jan. 3, 1936; d. Frederick C. Miller and Adele (Kanaley) O'Shaughnessy; m. Philip E. Ruppe, Nov. 30, 1957; children: Antoinette B., Adele E., Loret M., Katherine T., Mary Speed. D Pub. Svc. (hon.), No. Mich. U., 1981; LHD (hon.), Marymount Coll., 1981, Luther Coll., 1990; HHD (hon.), Wheeling Coll., 1982, Loyola U., 1987; DCL (hon.), Marquette U., 1983, Marquette U., 1986; hon. degree, Nebr. Wesleyan U., Augustana Coll., Concordia Coll., 1994, St. Bonaventure, 1994, Pace U., Concordia Coll., St. Bonaventure U. Chair Bush Campaign Com., Mich., 1980; co-chair Reagan-Bush Com., Mich., 1980; dir. Peace Corps, Washington, 1981-89; amb. to Norway U.S. Embassy, Oslo, 1989-93. Chair Vice Presdl. Inaugural Reception, 1981; trustee U. Notre Dame, 1988—; bd. dirs. Nat. Peace Garden, Save the Children, The Hewlett Found., Winrock Internat. Decorated Grand Cross Royal Norwegian Order of Merit, Dame of Sovereign Mil. Order Malta. Mem. LWV, Internat. Neighbor's Club IV, Overseas Edn. Fund (hon.), Coun. Am. Ambs., The Explorer's Club, Sons of Norway. Roman Catholic. Office: 1 Darby Ct Bethesda MD 20817-2910

RUPPERT, MARY FRANCES, school counselor, management consultant; b. Flushing, N.Y., May 14; d. Raymond Edward and Mary Josephine (Reilly) R.; m. Donald Francis O'Brien (div.); children: Donald Francis O'Brien III, Kevin Raymond O'Brien; m. Patrick J. Falzone, July 31, 1993. BA in English, Loyola Coll.; MS in Psychology, Counseling, Queens Coll., 1965. Counselor Plainview (N.Y.)-Old Bethpage Schs., 1965—; trainer, cons. stress mgmt., time mgmt., comm., pres. Productivity Programs, Huntington, N.Y., 1975—. Contbr. articles in field; author audiotapes on stress mgmt., 1975—; appearances radio and TV. Mem. ASTD (pres. 1988, chmn. bd. 1989—), AAUW, N.Y. State Counselors Assn., Nassau Counselors Assn. Office: 20 Richard Ln Huntington NY 11743

RUPPERT, SUSAN DONNA, nursing educator; b. LaSalle, Ill., Aug. 17, 1953; d. Joseph J. and Phyllis A. (Koontz) Stachowicz; m. Robert M. Ruppert; children: Sarah E., Michael R. AAS in Nursing, Ill. Valley C.C., Oglesby, 1974, AS in Sci., 1975; BSN, No. Ill. U., 1976; MSN, U. Tex. Health Sci. Ctr., San Antonio, 1979; PhD in Nursing, Tex. Woman's U., 1992. Evening supr. Met. Gen. Hosp., San Antonio, 1978-79; instr. U. Iowa Coll. Nursing, Iowa City, 1979-81; program coord. continuing edn. Meth. Hosp., Houston, 1981-89; assoc. prof. U. Tex. Health Sci. Ctr., Houston, 1989—. Contbr. articles to profl. jours. and books. Mem. AACN (past bd. dirs.), ANA, Tex. Nurses Assn., Am. Bus. Women's Assn., So. Nursing Rsch. Soc., Soc. Critical Care Medicine, Sigma Theta Tau. Home: 4602 Springfield Lakes St Sugar Land TX 77479 Office: U Tex Health Sci Ctr Sch Nursing Ste 6.250 1100 Holcombe Blvd Houston TX 77030-3907

RUPPRECHT, CAROL SCHREIER, comparative literature educator, dream researcher; b. Stafford Springs, Conn., June 30, 1939; d. William Joseph and Caroline Brown (Comstock) Schreier; divorced; children: Jody Francine, Whitney Glenn; m. Richard P. Suttmeier, May 8, 1987. BS, U. Va., 1962; MA, Yale U., 1963, M in Philosophy, 1973, PhD, 1977. Teaching fellow Yale U., 1973; asst. prof. Kirkland Coll., Clinton, N.Y., 1974-78; asst. prof. Hamilton, Coll., Clinton, 1978-81, assoc. dean, 1981-82, assoc. prof. comparative lit., 1982-89; prof., 1989—, chmn. dept., 1984-89; lectr. Switzerland, Israel, The Netherlands, Ireland, People's Republic China, Eng., Japan. Author, editor: The Dream and the Text: Essays on Literature and Language, 1993; co-editor and author: Feminist Archetypal Theory, 1985; cons. editor Dreaming; contbr. articles to profl. jours., chpts. to books. NEH fellow Dartmouth Dante Inst., 1986. Founding mem. Assn. for Study Dreams, 1983, Conn. Assn. Jungian Psychology, 1981. Merrill fellow Bunting Inst., 1970-72. Mem. MLA, Am. Comparative Lit. Assn., Shakespeare Soc., Assn. Study of Dreams (pres., v.p. bd. dirs., mem. editorial bd.), Conn. Assn. for Jungian Psychology (bd. dirs.). Avocations: sports; wilderness activities. Office: Hamilton Coll Clinton NY 13323

RUPPRECHT, NANCY ELLEN, historian, educator; b. Coeur d'Alene, Idaho, Sept. 23, 1948; d. George John and Nancy Berneeda (Baird) R. BA with honors, U. Mo., 1967, MA, 1969; PhD, U. Mich., 1982. Acad. dir. pilot program U. Mich., Ann Arbor, 1971-73, lectr. in women studies, 1973-75; vis. lectr. history U. Mo., St. Louis, 1976-77; vis. instr. of history Wash. U., St. Louis, 1977-79, Grinnell (Iowa) Coll., 1979-81; asst. prof. Oakland U., Rochester, Mich., 1981-83; asst. prof. of history Mid. Tenn. State U., Murfreesboro, 1985-91, assoc. prof., 1991—; dir., women's studies program Middle Tenn. State U., 1989—, publicity dir. women's history month, 1988-92, mem. faculty senate, 1992—. Contbr. articles to profl. jours. Mem. AAUP (chpt. v.p. 1988-89, pres. 1989-93), AAUW, NOW, Am. Hist. Assn., S.E. Women's Studies Assn., So. Hist. Assn., So. Humanities Assn., Holocaust Studies Assn., Mid. Tenn. Women's Studies Assn., German Studies Assn., Women in Higher Edn. in Tenn., Concerned Faculty and Adminstrv. Women (chpt. v.p. 1993-95, chpt. pres. 1995—), Phi Kappa Phi, Phi Alpha Theta (sponsor 1986-89), Tri-Penta. Home: 1106 Jones Blvd Murfreesboro TN 37129-2310 Office: Middle Tenn State U 275 Peck Hall Murfreesboro TN 37132-0001

RUSAK, HALINA RODKO, librarian, artist; b. Navahradak, Belarus; came to U.S., 1949; d. Filaret and Vera Rodko; m. Vasil Rusak, July 21, 1951; children: Ludmila Rusak Grant, Natalia. BA, Rutgers U., 1954, MLS, 1956, MA, 1976. Art bibliographer, reference librarian Douglass Coll. Rutgers U., New Brunswick, N.J., 1956-83, slide libr., 1970-83; art librarian Rutgers U., New Brunswick, 1983-85, dir. art libr., 1985—; art cons. Belarusan Inst. Art and Sci., Rutherford, N.J., 1978—; mem. steering com. art and architecture program RLG, Mountain View, Calif., 1988-90. Contbr. articles to profl. jours.; exhibited in solo and group shows; cons. editor Art Reference Svcs. Quar., 1990—. Mem. planning bd. N.J. Dept. State Ethnic Ctr., Trenton, 1978-81; mem. heritage com. Garden State Arts Ctr., Holmdel, 1978-83. Rutgers U. grantee, 1981, 84, 85, 94, N.J. Com. for Humanities grantee, 1983, NEH grantee, 1986. Mem. Art Libr. Soc. N.Am. (v.p. N.J. chpt. 1984-85, pres. 1985-86, co-chmn. architecture sect. 1989-90), Coll. Art Assn., Women's Caucus for Art, Belarusan-Am. Assn. (v.p. N.J. chpt. 1982—), Belarusan-Am. Cultural and Ednl. Soc. (pres. 1994—), Nature Conservancy, Nat. Resources Def. Coun., Sierra Club. Eastern Orthodox. Home: 40 Deerfield Rd Somerset NJ 08873-1603 Office: Rutgers U Art Libr Voorhees Hall Cac New Brunswick NJ 08903

RUSCH, JODI ANN, sales manager; b. Shawano, Wis., Aug. 29, 1962; d. Dennis Auther and Rita Ann (Doran) R. BA, U. Wis., Green Bay, 1984. Asst. mgr. Cross Contry of Wis., Green Bay, 1985; sales rep. Kellogg Sales Co., Green Bay, 1985-86, territory mgr. I, 1987-88, territory mgr. II, 1989-91, sr. acct. mgr., 1991—. Mem. Green Bay Optimist Club. Roman Catholic. Home: 2433 Deer Trail Green Bay WI 54302

RUSCH, VALERIE WILLIAMS, thoracic surgeon; b. N.Y.C., Oct. 16, 1951. AB in Biochemistry, Vassar Coll., 1971; MD, Columbia U., 1975. Diplomate Nat. Bd. Med. Examiners, Am. Bd. Surgery, Am. Bd. Thoracic Surgery. Intern in gen. surgery U. Wash., Seattle, 1975-76, resident in gen. surgery, 1975-80, resident in cardiothoracic surgery, 1980-82; faculty assoc. dept. of thoracic surgery M.D. Anderson Cancer Ctr., Houston, 1982-83; thoracic surgeon Harborview Med. Ctr., Seattle, 1983-86, assoc. staff mem., 1986-89; thoracic surgeon Group Health Coop. of Puget Sound, Seattle, 1983-84; chief cardiothoracic surgery VA Hosp., Seattle, 1986-87; thoracic surgeon Univ. Hosp., Seattle, 1983-89; mem. courtesy med. staff Pacific Med. Ctr., Seattle, 1987-89; assoc. attending surgeon thoracic svc. Meml. Hosp. for Cancer and Allied Diseases, N.Y.C., 1989-94, attending surgeon, 1994—; faculty assoc. dept. thoracic surgery M.D. Anderson Cancer Ctr., 1982-83; asst. prof. div. cardiothoracic surgery U. Wash., 1983-88, assoc. prof., 1988-89; asst. mem. divsn. clin. rsch. Fred Hutchinson Cancer Rsch. Ctr., Seattle, 1985-89; assoc. mem. Meml. Hosp., Meml. Sloan-Kettering Cancer Ctr., N.Y.C., 1989-94, mem., 1994—; assoc. prof. surgery Cornell U. Med. Coll., N.Y.C., 1989—; mem. cancer clin. investigations rev. com. Nat. Cancer Inst., 1991—. Mem. editorial bd. Jour. Thoracic and Cardiovascular Surgery, 1992—; guest reviewer The Annals of Thoracic Surgery, Cancer Rsch., Chest, Gastrointestinal Endoscopy Thorax; contbr. articles to profl. publs.; author abstracts in field. Grantee NIH, 1985-89, Deknatel Corp., 1986-87, Bard Electro Med. Systems, 1989, NeoRx Corp., 1989-90. Fellow ACS (Henry Harkins award Wash. state chpt. 1979), Am. Coll. Cardiology, Am. Coll. Chest Physicians; mem. Am. Assn. Thoracic Surgery (mem. program com. 1994, 95), Soc. Thoracic Surgeons, Assn. Acad. Surgery, Soc. Surg. Oncology (mem. com. tng. 1993—, mem. edn. com.), Am. Soc. Clin. Oncology, (mem. program com. 1993), Am. Thoracic Soc., N.Y. Soc. Thoracic Surgery, N.Y. Cancer Soc., Internat. Assn. for Study of Lung Cancer, North Pacific Surg. Assn., Am. Med. Women's Assn., Seattle Surg. Soc., Henry Harkins' Surg. Soc., M.D. Anderson Assocs., Gen. Thoracic Surg. Club, Alpha Omega Alpha. Office: Meml Sloan-Kettering Cancer Thoracic Surgery Svc 1275 York Ave New York NY 10021

RUSCHE, MARGIT FRANCES CHIRIACO, secretary, treasurer; b. Indio, Calif., Mar. 14, 1938; d. Joseph L. and Ruth Elvine (Bergseid) Chiriaco; m. Jerome A. Rusche, June 15, 1987; children: Heather Lynne, Christoffer Sean Baldivid. BA, UCLA, 1959. Mem. mcpl. adv. coun. City of Bloomington, Calif., 1982-86; mem. Calif. desert adv. bd. Dept. of Interior, Washington, 1981-86; sec.-treas. Joseph L. Chriaco, Inc., Chiriaco Summit, Calif., 1986—; also bd. dirs. Gen. Patton Mus., Chiriaco Summit, Calif. Numerous one-woman art shows. Founder, pres. HOW Found., 1979—; founder, bd. dirs. Gen. Patton Mus., Chiriaco Summit, 1988—, chmn. Veterans Day com., 1988-93. Mem. Women in Arts, R.A.A. Republican. Roman Catholic. Home: 11110 Laurel Ave Bloomington CA 92316-3015

RUSH, CHARLOTTE LOUISE, public affairs executive; b. Coshocton, Ohio, May 12, 1951; d. Donald William and Barbara Ruth (Putnam) R. BS in Edn., Bowling Green State U., 1973; MBA, U. Pitts., 1980. Legis. asst. Gulf Oil Corp., Washington, 1974-75; mgr. policy analysis Gulf Oil Corp., Pitts., 1976-80, dir. policy analysis, 1980-81; dir. fed. regulations Gulf Oil Corp., Washington, 1981-85; pres. Rush & Assocs., Washington, 1985-86; group mgr. comm. Ducks Unlimited, Chgo., 1987-92; v.p. pub. affairs MasterCard Internat., Washington, 1992—; bd. dirs., mem. exec. com. Pub. Affairs Coun., Washington; mem. coun. Nat. Policy Forum, Washington, 1994. Mem. editl. bd. Privacy & Am. Bus., 1993—. Recipient Leadership award Nat. Womens Econ. Alliance, 1985. Mem. Internat. Credit Assn. (mem. various coms.). Office: MasterCard Internat 1401 I St NW # 240 Washington DC 20005

RUSH, DOMENICA MARIE, health facilities administrator; b. Gallup, N.Mex., Apr. 10, 1937; d. Bernardo G. and Guadalupe (Milan) Iorio; m. W. E. Rush, Jan. 5, 1967. Diploma, Regina Sch. Nursing, Albuquerque, 1958. RN N.Mex.; lic. nursing home adminstr. Charge nurse, house supr. St. Joseph Hosp., Albuquerque, 1958-63; dir. nursing Cibola Hosp., Grants, 1960-64; supr. operating room, dir. med. seminars Carrie Tingley Crippled Children's Hosp., Truth or Consequences, N.Mex., 1964-73; adminstr. Sierra Vista Hosp., Truth or Consequences, 1974-88, pres., 1980-89; clin. nursing mgr. U. N.Mex. Hosp., 1989-90; adminstr. Nor-Lea Hosp., Lovington, N.Mex., 1990—; with Presbyn. Healthcare Svcs., Albuquerque, 1990-94, regional ops., 1994—; bd. dirs. N.Mex. Blue Cross/Blue Shield, 1977-88, chmn. hosp. relations com., 1983-85, exec. com. 1983—; bd. dirs. Region II Emergency Med. Svcs. Originating bd. SW Mental Health Ctr., Sierra County, N.Mex., 1975; chmn. Sierra County Personnel Bd., 1983—. Named Lea County Outstanding Woman, N.Mex. Commn. on Status of Women; Woman of Yr. for Lea County, N.Mex., 1993. Mem. Am. Coll. Health Care Adminstrs., Sierra County C. of C. (bd. dirs. 1972, 75-76, svc. award 1973, Businesswoman of the Yr. 1973-74), N.Mex. Hosp. Assn. (bd. dirs., sec.-treas., pres.-elect, com. chmn., 1977-88, pres. 1980-81, exec. com., 1980-83, 84-85, recipient meritorius svc. award 1988), N.Mex. So. Hosp. Coun. (sec. 1980-81, pres. 1981-82), Am. Hosp. Assn. (N.Mex. del. 1984-88, regional adv. bd. 1984-88). Republican. Roman Catholic. Home: 1100 N Riverside Truth or Consequence NM 87901

RUSH, ELIZABETH IRENE (LIZ RUSH), production director; b. York, Pa., Dec. 23, 1959; d. Ronald and Thelma Mae (Blevins) R. Student, No. Va. C.C., 1980, U. Calif., Berkeley, 1983; BFA, Acad. of Art, San Francisco, 1987; cert., Graphic Arts Tech. Found., 1993. Prodn. mgr. Arone Publs., Arlington, Va., 1980-82; art asst. Profl. Pilot Mag., Washington, 1980-82; designer, typesetter L.C. Litho & Graphics, San Francisco, 1982-88; designer Hunt Weber Clark, San Francisco, 1988-89; sr. designer Elan Graphics, San Francisco, 1989-90; designer Jewish Times, Balt., 1990-91; sr. graphic designer USF&G Ins., Balt., 1992-93, Guild, Inc., Hyattsville, Md., 1993-94; prodn. dir. Hunt Weber Clark, San Francisco, 1994—. With U.S. Army, 1977-80. Mem. Am. Inst. Graphic Arts. Democrat. Home: 2269 Chestnut St # 171 San Francisco CA 94123 Office: Hunt Weber Clark Ste 302 525 Brannan St San Francisco CA 94107

RUSH, NAOMI DEAN, tax administrator; b. Sewickley, Pa., Oct. 5, 1953; d. George William and Lillian Dean (Henry) Baugher. AS, Robert Morris Coll., Coraopolis, Pa., 1986, BS in Bus. Mgmt., 1991, postgrad., 1991—. Clk. typist Pa. Gov.'s Justice Commn., Pitts., 1972-76; N/C programmer Miller Printing Equipment Co., Pitts., 1976-80; sec. CSR/Contraves Corp., Pitts., 1980-81; corrd. taxes Allegheny Internat. Inc., Pitts., 1981-89; mgr. divsn. state and local tax Roadway Package Sys., Inc., Coraopolis, 1989—. Mem. Inst. Property Taxation. Republican. Presbyterian. Office: Roadway Package System Inc 410 Rouser Rd Coraopolis PA 15108-2767

RUSHFORD, ELOISE JOHNSON, land manager; b. Elmwood, Ill.; d. Albert Earl and Edna Merle (Dixon) Johnson; (div. June 1967); children: Gregory Gene, Barbara Merle Rushford Grimes. BA, Bradley U., 1936. Cert. tchr., Ill. Tchr. English Manual High Sch. Dist. 150, Peoria, 1955-56; ptnr. Johnson Devel. Co., 1956-76; v.p. Johnson's Men's Store, 1972-74; land mgr. Peoria, 1974—. Bd. dirs. Crippled Children's Found., Peoria, organized vols., 1974-76; bd. dirs. Women's Civic Fedn.; pres. Women's Assn. 1st Federated Ch., Mothers' Club; mem. women's adv. bd. Internat. Christian U., Tokyo; mem. chpt. AH PEO; chmn. Cottey Coll., 1993-95; spearheaded teaching of French in 4th grade, Peoria, 1959; chmn. Symphony Guild student concerts, organized Peoria Symphony student concerts that included all grade sch. students in Peoria County. Mem. AAUW (pres. 1958-60, chmn. bd. dirs. Peoria br., award 1977), Univ. Women's Investment Club (founder, past pres.), Lasertoma (pres. Peoria chpt. 1961-63), Pi Beta Phi (pres. Peoria chpt. 1960-61), Lambda Phi. Republican. Congregationalist. Home: 220 W Merle Ln Peoria IL 61604-1617

RUSHIN, LINDA JEAN, insurance agent, vocalist; b. Sandersville, Ga., May 13, 1957; d. Isadore and Willie Mae (Roberts) Jordan; m. Larry Stephens, Jan. 1975 (div.); children: Taurus D., Keila L.; m. Arthur L. Rushin, Sept. 10, 1985 (div. 1994); children: Carlethia S., Shemica S., Ibrihim Jibril, Takarthur. Cert. data entry, Atlanta Urban League, Inc., 1979; cert. word processing, IBM Word Processing Ctr., Atlanta, 1984. Lic. ins. agt., Ga. Tchr.'s aide, counselor asst. Washington County High Sch., Sandersville, 1972-75; beauty cons. Mary Kay Cosmetics, 1977-78; vocalist, songwriter, prodr., 1980-84; exec. producer Haywood's Studio, Atlanta, 1982; songwriter, publisher ASCAP, 1990; ins. agt. Primerica, Sandersville, 1982—; bus. mgr., co-owner Rushin Income Tax Svc., Sandersville, 1985—. Producer, writer, vocalist song: Believe in Yourself. Mem. Bldg. for Equal Equality, Atlanta Urban League, 1979-80; sec. Ideal Chpt. 101, 1978-93. Mem. NAFE, ASCAP, Order Ea. Star. Democrat. Baptist.

RUSHING, DOROTHY MARIE, historian; b. Bonham, Tex., Aug. 28, 1925; d. Van Bain and Ada Belle (Price) Hawkins; m. J. E. Rushing, Aug. 6, 1960 (dec. 1985); children: Charles Maret, Bill Maret, Bob Maret, Charles Rushing, Martha Rushing Sosebee. BA, Tex. Woman's U., 1972; MA, East Tex. State U., 1974; PhD, U. North Tex., 1981. Cert. history, lang. arts. secondary tchr., Tex. Tchr. pub. schs., 1972-86; instr. East Tex. State U., Commerce, 1972-74, 80-81; teaching fellow U. North Tex., Denton, 1975-76; prof. Richland Coll., Dallas, 1975—, Collin County Community Coll., McKinney, Tex., 1985-88; historian-archivist J.C. Penney, Inc., Dallas, 1988-93; owner Corp. Heritage Rsch., 1993—; lectr., Dallas, 1972—; vis. prof. Johns Hopkins U., 1985, U. Va., 1989; statis. analyst Dallas County C.C., 1982; lay rep. N.E. Tex. Libr. System, 1984-89. Editor, author: Texas: The Lone Star State, 1984; contbg. author: Beyond Sundown, 1975, Handbook of Texas, 1994. Chmn. Garland (Tex.) Sesquicentennial Com., 1985-86; trustee Garland Pub. Libr., 1980-90. Decorated Honorary Cross of Lorraine (France); named Outstanding Instr., Richland Coll., 1987; postdoctoral fellow NEH, 1985, 89; grantee Dallas County C.C. Dist., 1984. Mem. Phi Kappa Phi, Sigma Tau Delta, Phi Alpha Theta. Home: 1214 Patricia Ln Garland TX 75042-8041

RUSHING, SUSAN DEERING, protective services official; b. Hazelton, Pa., July 3, 1954; d. Richard R. and Mary A. (Gasper) Deering; m. Thomas J. Rushing, Nov. 24, 1979 (div. 1989). Student, Loyola U., New Orleans, 1993—. Detective JPSO, Harvey, La., 1980-84, sgt., 1984-87, lt. comdr., 1987—, lt., asst. comdr. criminal investigation bur., 1990—, expert in stalking and workplace violence, 1992—, negotiator, 1994—. Served USN, 1972-76. Mem. Am. Soc. Indsl. Security, Am. Legion, Hostage Negotiators Am., Fraternal Order of Police, Daystar (bd. dirs.), Alpha Sigma Nu. Republican. Roman Catholic. Home: 1300 Mississippi St Kenner LA 70062

RUSHINSKY, LAURA KATHLEEN, critical care nurse; b. Michigan City, Ind., Aug. 20, 1969; d. Clois Jean and Allie Ophelia (Howard) Blalack; m. Michael Rushinsky, July 11, 1992. Grad., Purdue U., Westville, Ind., 1990; BS, Purdue U., West Lafayette, Ind., 1991. RN, Tex., CCRN. Nurse extern St. Anthony Hosp., Michigan City, 1988-90; staff nurse St. Elizabeth Hosp., Lafayette, 1990-92; resident in critical care nursing Meth. Hosp., Houston, 1992, staff nurse cardiovascular ICU, 1992—, patient care coord., staff nurse, 1994—. Mem. Sigma Theta Tau. Baptist. Home: 18515 Sondleford Dr Katy TX 77449

RUSHO, KAREN G., critical care and community health nurse, educator; b. Albany, N.Y., Sept. 18, 1955; d. Joseph R. and Ann E. (Cline) Gabriels; m. Michael E. Rusho, Dec. 18, 1976; 1 child, Elizabeth Ann. BSN, Mt. St. Mary Coll., Newburgh, N.Y., 1977; MS in Nursing, Boston U., 1984. Cert. emergency nurse. Staff and charge nurse, emergency dept. Jennie Stuart Med. Ctr., Hopkinsville, Ky., 1977-80, Commanche County Hosp., Lawton, Okla., 1980; staff and charge nurse ICU 97th Gen. Army Hosp., Frankfurt Am Main, West Germany, 1981-82; sch. nurse Enterprise (Ala.) City Sch. System, 1989-91; clin. instr. Quinnipiac Coll., Hamden, Conn., 1991-94; client care coord. Vis. Nurse Assn. Hospice, Inc., Waterbury, Conn., 1993-94; dir. nursing Brian Ctr., Concord, N.C., 1994—. Active Girl Scouts Am. Mem. ANA. Home: 1023 Reverdy Ln Matthews NC 28105

RUSHWORTH, BETSY, psychologist; b. Jamestown, N.Y., Mar. 3, 1940; d. Elverton Crissey and Joan (Isbell). R. BA, Lake Erie Coll., 1962; MA, U. Ariz., 1965; PhD, U. Portland, 1972. Lic. psychologist. Psychology trainee Winnebago (Wis.) State Hosp., 1963, VA Hosp., Tucson, 1963-65; staff psychologist Marianne Frosting Ctr. Ednl. Therapy, L.A., 1965-68; psychol. asst. Ctr. for Behavior Therapy, Beverly Hills, Calif., 1966-69; staff psychologist, co-dir. Larri E. Welty Sch. Ednl. Therapy, Glendale, Calif., 1968-69; psychology trainee Clark County Mental Health Ctr., Vancouver, Wash., 1970-71; seminar leader Clark County Mental Health Ctr., Vancouver, 1971-72; mem. splty. exam. grading com. PhD candidates dept. psychology U. Portland, 1973; unit psychologist, ednl. cons. Fairview Hosp. and Tng. Ctr., Salem, Oreg., 1972-74; clin. psychologist Northcentral Mont. Community Mental Health Ctr., Great Falls, 1974-75; pvt. practice Great Falls, 1975—; presenter, workshops, lectr. in visual perception, lang., various psychol. topics, Calif., N.Y., Mont., 1996—. Bd. dirs. Community Concerts Assn., 1987-93, Cascade County Mental Health Assn., 1979-86. Mem. APA, Wash. State Psychol. Assn., Mont. Psychol. Assn. (mem.-at-large 1982-86, pres.-elect 1986-88, pres. 1988-90, past pres. 1990-92), Psi Chi. Democrat and Republican. Roman Catholic. Office: 2300 12th Ave S #117 Great Falls MT 59405

RUSK, HELEN MARIE, critical care nurse; b. Portsmouth, Va., June 4, 1966; d. Charles M. Rusk and Joyce Lee (Spell) Grant; m. Rudolph W. Steiger, Aug. 29, 1992; 1 child, Katelyn Marie Steiger. AS, San Jacinto Coll., 1986; BSN, U. Tex., 1990. RN Tex.; Cert. Pediatric advanced life support. Unit tchr. Tex. Children's Hosp., Houston, 1986-89, head charge nurse, 1989—, staff nurse, emergency pediatric nurse, preceptor, 1990—; sr. renal transplant coord. Tex. Childrens's Hosp., Houston. Mem. AACN, N.Am. Transplant Coords. Orgn., Am. Organ Transplant Orgn. (v.p.), Tex. Nurses Assn., Tex. Nurses Soc. Am. Home: 15826 Camino Del Sol Dr Houston TX 77083-3923

RUSKAI, MARY BETH, mathematics researcher, educator; b. Cleve., Feb. 26, 1944; d. Michael J. and Evelyn (Gortz) R. BS, Notre Dame Coll., Cleve., 1965; MA, PhD, U. Wis., 1969. Battelle fellow in theoretical physics U. Geneva, 1969-71; rsch. assoc. in math. MIT, Cambridge, Mass., 1971-72; rsch. assoc. in physics U. Alta., Edmonton, Can., 1972-73; asst. prof. math. U. Oreg., Eugene, 1973-76; asst. prof. U. Lowell, Mass., 1977-82, assoc. prof., 1982-86, prof. dept. math., 1986—, pres. faculty senate, 1990-91; sci. scholar Bunting Inst., Cambridge, Mass., 1983-85; vis. prof. Rockefeller U., N.Y.C., 1980-81, U. Vienna, Austria, 1981, Rome, 1988; faculty rsch. assoc. Naval Surface Warfare Ctr., Silver Springs, Md., 1986; vis. prof. math. U. Mich., Ann Arbor, 1991-92; vis. mem. Courant Inst. Math. Sci., NYU, 1988-89; cons. Bell Labs., Murray Hill, N.J., 1972, 83, 88-89; conf. dir. NSF/CBMS Conf. on Wavelets, 1990; Flora Stone Mather vis. prof. Case Western Res. U., Cleve., 1995. Mem. editorial bd. Wavelets and Their Applications, 1990-92; contbr. articles to profl. jours. NSF predoctoral fellow, 1965-69; recipient NSF Career Advancement award, 1988-89. Fellow AAAS (symposium organizer, 1991, nominating com. math. sect. 1991—); mem. Internat. Assn. Math. Physicists, Am. Math. Soc. (reviewer, session chmn.-com. 1987—, com. chmn.), Math. Assn. Am. (com.), Am. Phys. Soc. (reviewer), Assn. Women in Math., Assn. Women in Sci. (pres. New Eng. chpt. 1986-87), Appalachian Mountain Club (Boston, winter leader 1979—), Sigma Xi. Club: Appalachian Mountain (Boston) (winter leader 1979—). Office: U Lowell Dept Math 1 University Ave Lowell MA 01854-2881

RUSKAUFF, CATHERINE, advertising executive; b. Ogden, Utah, May 13, 1967; d. Ronald and Joyce (Fischer) R. BS, Weber State U., 1990. Mktg. asst. Utah State Dept. Agriculture, Salt Lake City, 1988-89; acct. exec. R&R Advt., Salt Lake City, 1989—. Mem. Utah Advt. Fedn. Democrat. Home: 850 N Hwy 89 # 4C North Salt Lake UT 84054 Office: R&R Advertising 837 E South Temple Salt Lake City UT 84102-1341

RUSKELL, VIRGINIA ANN, librarian, educator; b. Nashville, June 4, 1948; d. George Channing Ruskell and Douglass (McFerrin) Rudkoff. AA, Reinhardt Coll., 1967; BA in history, Emory U., 1969; MLS, George Peabody Coll., 1970; MA in English, West Ga. U., 1975. Libr. asst. George Peabody Coll. Libr. Sch., 1969-70; interlibr. loan libr. West Ga. Coll., Carrollton, 1970-76, bibliog. instrn. libr., 1977-80, reference coord., 1980-83, head of reference, 1983—, assoc. prof., 1980-88, prof., 1988—. Treas. LWV, Carrollton, 1975-77; chmn., bd. dirs. Wesley Found., 1985; chmn. social concerns St. Andrew United Meth. Ch., Carrollton, 1981-82, fin. sec., 1980-81, chmn. fin. com., 1982, Carrollton First United Meth. Ch., 1988—; pres. Carrollton League Women Voters, 1991-92. Council Libr. Resources Libr. Svcs. Enhancement grantee, 1976-77. Mem. Southeastern Libr. Assn., AAUP (sec. 1974-75, v.p. 1975-76), AAUW (v.p. programs 1982-83, v.p. membership 1986-87, pres. 1987-89), Beta Phi Mu, Phi Kappa Phi (pres. elect 1986-87, pres. 1987-88). Democrat. Home: PO Box 844 Carrollton GA 30117-0844 Office: West Ga Coll Libr Carrollton GA 30118

RUSLING, BARBARA N(EUBERT), real estate executive, state legislator; b. St. Louis, Nov. 27, 1945; d. Ralph L. and Rosemary (Stroot) Neubert; m. Randolph H. Wieser, Apr. 23, 1966 (div. Nov. 1983); children: Keith, Steve, Eric; m. Robert Best Rusling, Aug. 2, 1985. BA, Vanderbilt U., 1966; postgrad., Baylor U., 1975. Lic. real estate broker. Appraisal intern Smith Real Estate, Waco, Tex., 1975; resident real estate broker Sanger Suburban Realty, Waco, 1975-81, sales mgr., 1981-83; pres., gen. mgr. Coldwell Banker Hallmark Realty, Waco, 1983—; mem. Tex. Ho. of Reps., Austin, 1995—; mem. from dist. 57 Tex. State Ho. Reps., 1995—. Chmn. bd. dirs. YWCA, Waco, 1976-79; dir. Leadership Waco Program, 1986-87; various positions Hist. Waco Found.; bd. dirs. Waco Civic Theatre, Family Counseling Ctr., 1991—, United Way, 1992—, Family Abuse Ctr., 1993—, Waco Better Bus. Bur., 1994—. Mem. Tex. Assn. Realtors (edn. com., strategic planning com. 1983—, realtor lawyer com. 1985-93), Realtors Nat. Mktg. Inst. (cert.), Waco Bd. Realtors (past bd. dirs., salesman of yr. 1979), Waco C. of C. (bd. dirs. 1990-93), Waco Sailing Club, Kappa Delta. Home: 1635 Meandering Way China Spring TX 76633-2905 Office: Coldwell Banker Hallmark Realty 7101 Bosque Blvd Waco TX 76710-4018

RUSS, JOANNA, writer, English language educator; b. N.Y.C., Feb. 22, 1937; d. Evarett and Bertha (Zinner) R. B.A. in English with high honors, Cornell, U., 1957; M.F.A. in Playwriting and Dramatic Lit, Yale U., 1960. Lectr. in English Cornell U., 1967-70, asst. prof., 1970-72; asst. prof. English, Harpur Coll., State U. N.Y. at Binghamton, 1972-75, U. Colo., 1975-77; asso. prof. English, U. Wash., 1977-90, prof., 1984-90. Author: Picnic on Paradise, 1968, And Chaos Died, 1970, The Female Man, 1975, We Who Are About To, 1977, Kittatinny: A Tale of Magic, 1978, The Two of Them, 1978, On Strike Against God, 1980, The Adventures of Alyx, 1983, The Zanzibar Cat, 1983, How To Suppress Women's Writing, 1983, Extra (Ordinary) People, 1984, Magic Mommas, Trembling Sisters, Puritans and Perverts: Feminist Essays, 1985, The Hidden Side of the Moon, 1987; also numerous short stories. Mem. Sci. Fiction Writers Am. (Nebula award for best short story 1972, Hugo award for best novella 1983). Address: 8961 E Lester St Tucson AZ 85715-5568

RUSSELL, ANGELA VETA, state legislator, social worker; b. Crow Agency, Mont., Aug. 25, 1943; d. William A. and Josephine (Pease) R. BA, U. Mont., 1965; MSW, Tulane U., 1974. Lic. social worker, Mont. Field rep. United Scholar Svc., Denver, 1965-67; child welfare worker Yellowstone County Pub. Welfare, Billings, Mont., 1968-72; counselor Rocky Mt. Coll., Billings, Mont., 1972-73; com. organizer Crow Tribe Office of Coal Rsch., Crow Agency, Mont., 1975-76; cons. pvt. practice, Lodge Grass, Mont., 1976-77; project dir. Denver U. Social Rsch., 1977-78; med. social wroker USPHS, Crow Agy., Brow Agency, 1978-85; psychotherapist, cons. pvt. practice, Billings, 1985—; bd. mem. Rocky Mountain Coll., Billings. Editor Hist. Crow Calender, 1978—. State adv. com. U.S. Civil Rights Commn. Rocky Mt. Region, Denver, 1976-83; trustee Lodge Grass Schs., 1981-84; rep. Mont. Ho. of Reps., Helena, 1987—; chmn. Mt. Rhodes Scholar Com., Missoula, Mont., 1990—, Nat. Assn. Native Am. Legis., Denver, 1991—; mem. adv. bd. Mont. Initiative for Abatement of Mortality in Infants, Helena, Mont., 1991—; cmty. organizer Crow Healthy Mothers/Healthy Babies, Apsaalooke Com. for the Arts. Named to Salute to Women, YWCA, Billings, 1990; named Mont. Social Worker of Yr., 1993. Mem. NASW, Nat. Assn. Indian Social Workers (treas. 1986-88), Indian Law Resource Ctr. (bd. dirs. 1992—). Democrat. Baptist. Home: PO Box 333 Lodge Grass MT 59050-0333 Office: 1236 N 28th #103 Billings MT 59101

RUSSELL, ATTIE YVONNE, academic administrator, dean, pediatrics educator; b. Washington, Aug. 10, 1923; d. George and Kathleen L. (Milliner) Werner; m. Rex Hillier, Apr. 19, 1954 (dec.); m. Henry J. Russell, 1960 (div. 1971); children: Richard Russell, Margaret Jane Russell-Harde; m. Harry F. Camper, Sept. 2, 1984. BS, Am. U., 1944; PhD, State U. Iowa, 1952; MD, U. Chgo., 1958. Intern Phila. Gen. Hosp., 1958-59; resident in pediatrics Bronx (N.Y.) Mcpl. Hosp., 1960-61, Del. Hosp., Wilmington, 1962-63; dir. maternal and child health, crippled children's svcs. Del. State Bd. Health, Dover, 1963-68; asst. dean community health affairs, assoc. prof. pediatrics U. Cin. Coll. Medicine, 1968-71; clin. assoc. prof. pediatrics Med. Coll. Pa., Phila., 1966-68, 71-74; dep. dir. div. pub. health State of Del., Dover, 1971-74; dir. Santa Clara Valley Med. Ctr., San Jose, Calif., 1974-79; assoc. dean, clin. prof. pediatrics, family medicine Stanford (Calif.) U. Sch. Medicine, 1974-79; dir. USPHS Hosp., Boston, 1979-81, Balt. City Hosps., 1981-82; asst. v.p. community affairs, prof. pediatrics U. Tex. Med. Br., Galveston, 1982-87, asst. v.p. student affairs, dean students, prof. pediatrics, 1987-92, clin. prof. pediatrics, 1992—; reviewer Coun. for Internat. Exchange of Scholars, Washington, 1987-94; dir. III Symposium on Health and Human Svcs. in the U.S.-Mex., Brownsville, 1988; mem. sci. coun. Am. Fedn. for Aging Rsch., Inc., 1983-86. Contbr. articles and abstracts to profl. jours. Mem. budget com. United Way, Galveston, 1982-84; mem. Mayor's Adv. Com. for Sr. Citizens and Handicapped Persons for the City of Galveston, 1983-85; bd. dirs. Galveston County Coordinated Community Clinics, 1983-87; bd. advisors Galveston Hist. Found., 1983-88; mem. Com. for Coop. Action Planning, 1983-88, Houston-Galveston Health Promotion Consortium, 1983-88, Injury Control Prevention (Houston), 1984-89, aging programs adv. com. Houston-Galveston Area Coun., 1985-92. Recipient Disting. Alumni award Am. U., 1984. Fellow Am. Acad. Pediatrics, Am. Pub. Health Assn.; mem. AMA, Am. Coll. Preventive Medicine, Soc. for Adolescent Medicine, Am. Physiol. Soc., Am. Fedn. for Aging Rsch., Am. Geriatrics Soc., Mass. State Med. Soc., Galveston Med. Soc., Tex. Med. Assn., Tex. Pediatric Soc., Galveston C. of C. (legis. com. 1983-88), Order of Eastern Star, Sigma Xi, Alpha Omega Alpha. Office: U Tex Med Branch Ashbel Smith Rm 1.208 Galveston TX 77550

RUSSELL, CAROL ANN, personnel service company executive; b. Detroit, Dec. 14, 1943; d. Billy and Iris (Driver) Koud; m. Victor Rojas (div.). BA in English, Hunter Coll., 1993. Registered employment cons. Various positions in temp. help cos. N.Y.C., 1964-74; v.p. Wollborg-Michelson, San Francisco, 1974-82; co-owner, pres. Russell Staffing Resources, Inc., San Francisco and Sonoma, 1983—; media guest, speaker, workshop and seminar leader in field. Pub. Checkpoint Newsletter; contbr. articles to profl. publs. Named to the Inc. 500, 1989, 90. Mem. Soc. to Preserve and Encourage Radio Drama Variety and Comedy, Internat. Platform Assn., No. Calif. Human Resources Coun., Soc. Human Resource Mgmt., Calif. Assn. Pers. Cons. (pres. Golden State chpt. 1984-85), Calif. Assn. Temp. Svcs., Bay Area Pers. Assn. (pres. 1983-84), Pers. Assn. Sonoma County. Office: Russell Pers Svcs Inc 120 Montgomery St San Francisco CA 94104-4303

RUSSELL, CATHERINE F., legislative staff director; b. Silver Spring, Md., May 16, 1963; d. Thomas M. and Mary Jane (Doane) R. BS in Journalism, U. Md., 1986. Assoc. dir. assns. coun. Nat. Assn. Mfrs., 1987-90, assoc. dir. energy and natural resources, 1990-92; legis. asst. to Senator Robert C. Smith, 1992—. Author: Manufacturing Trade Associations: Their Changing Focus and Management, 1989. Methodist. Office: Com on the Judiciary 224 Senate Dirksen Office Bldg Washington DC 20510*

RUSSELL, CHARLOTTE SANANES, biochemistry educator, researcher; b. N.Y.C., Jan. 4, 1927; d. Joseph and Marguerite (Saltiel) Sananes; m. Joseph Brooke Russell, Dec. 20, 1947; children: James Robert, Joshua Sananes. BA, Bklyn. Coll., 1946; MA, Columbia U., 1947, PhD, 1951. Asst. prof. biochemistry CCNY, N.Y.C., 1958-68, assoc. prof., 1968-72, prof., 1972—; peer reviewer NSF, NIH; ad hoc reviewer sci. jours. including Jour. Bacteriology, Biochemistry. Contbr. articles to profl. jours. Mem. AAAS, AAUP, AAUW (internat. fellowship panel 1986-89), Am. Soc. Biochemistry and Molecular Biology, Am. Chem. Soc., Amnesty Internat., Urgent Action Network, Sigma Xi. Office: CCNY Dept Chemistry 138th St & Convent Ave New York NY 10031

RUSSELL, CLAIRE WARREN, nurse, home health agency administrator; b. Atlanta, Dec. 28, 1960; d. James Furman and Claire Eleanor (Hastings) Warren; m. George David Russell Jr., Jan. 12, 1985; children: George David III, Jamie Claire. Student, U. Ga., 1979-81; BSN cum laude, Med. Coll. Ga., 1983. RN, Ga. Staff level I nurse Henrietta Engleston Hosp., Atlanta, 1983-84, staff level II nurse, 1984; staff nurse Comprehensive Home Health Care, Thomson, Ga., 1985-88; dir. nursing Ctrl. Savannah River Area Home Health Agy., Inc., Washington, Ga., 1989-90; sec., treas. Ctrl. Savannah River Assn. Nonprofit Home Care Agy., Washington, Ga., 1990—; mem. bd. State Tech. Adv. Com. for Gov., Atlanta, 1993. Grad. Leadership McDuffie, Thomson, Ga., 1993. Mem. Nat. Assn. Home Care, Ga. Assn. Home Health (region dir. 1993-95), Ga. Gerontology Soc., Jr. Woman's Club, Sigma Theat Tau. Roman Catholic. Home: 358 Ridge Rd NW Thomson GA 30824 Office: CSRA Home Health Agency Inc 127 Gordon St Washington GA 30673

RUSSELL, CLARA B., systems analyst; b. Washington, Mar. 20; d. Gilbert Lee Sr. and Emma Lucile (Howard) Bullock; m. William A. Russell. BA, Howard U., D.C., 1971. Cert. arbitrator. Computer programmer U.S. Gen. Svcs. Adminstrn., Washington, 1971-76; system analyst U.S. Dept. Defense, Atlanta, 1976-79; data processing contract officer, sr. systems analyst U.S. Dept. Health and Human Svcs., Atlanta, 1979—. Vol. arbitrator Better Bus. Bur., Atlanta, 1988—. Mem. Am. Pub. Welfare Assn., Am. Arbitration Assn., Order of Ky. Colonels. Office: US Dept Health and Human Svcs PO Box 826 Atlanta GA 30307

RUSSELL, CRISTINE ELAINE, petroleum company official; b. Ogallala, Nebr., Aug. 20, 1953; d. Donald Eugene and Elaine Marie (Geisert) R.; 1 child, Sanger Anne. BS in Edn., U. Colo., 1976; MBA in Mktg. with high honors, Oklahoma City U., 1989. Independent landman Bill Maddox Oil Properties, Denver, 1979, Baker Oil/Aeon Energy, Denver, 1980-82; field landman Exxon Co. U.S.A., Denver, 1980-81; cons. landman Phoenix Resources Co., Oklahoma City, 1982; staff asst. Anadarko Petroleum Corp., Oklahoma City, 1982-89; sr. gas contract analyst Anadarko Petroleum Corp., Houston, 1989-91, adminstr. gas sales adminstrn., 1991—. Vol. for charity benefits Metro Denver March of Dimes Found., 1976-79, Children's Diabetes Found., Denver, 1976-79, Sickle Cell Anemia Found., Denver, 1976-79. Scholastic scholar Metro Denver March of Dimes, 1971; recipient Scholastic Achievement award Brith Benet Found., Denver, 1971. Mem. NAFE, Denver Assn. Petroleum Landmen, Rocky Mountain Inst. Petroleum Landmen, Colo. Bd. Realtors (assoc.), Okla. Bd. Realtors (assoc.), Natural Gas Assn. Houston, Natural Gas Assn. Okla., N.Mex. Oil and Gas Assn., Internat. Toastmasters. Republican. Lutheran. Office: Anadarko Petroleum Corp 16855 Northchase PO Box 1330 Houston TX 77251-1330

RUSSELL, DEBORAH ELIZABETH, artist, educator; b. Lewes, Del., Jan. 15, 1951; d. Norman Linwood and Jacqueline Elizabeth (Beauchamp) Short; children: Dawn Elizabeth, Sandra Lee, Rachel Ann. Grad. high sch., Seaford, Del. Founder, dir. Kidzart, 1987-94; artist, instr. kids kollege Del. Tech. C.C.; edn. chair, instr., ednl. liaison Art Inst. and Gallery, Salisbury, Md.; also bd. dirs. Art Inst. and Gallery; lectr., tchr. in field. One-woman shows include Losonczy-Russell, Parallels Studio, Salisbury, Md., Downtown Plz., Salisbury, Berlin Libr., 1984, 86, Ocean City Libr., 1989, Wicomico County Libr., 1990; exhibited in group shows at Howard Johnson's, Salisbury, 1977, Ocean City (Md.) Art League, 1983, 85, Hooper's, Ocean City, 1987; developer Md. State PTA Cultural Arts Project Planning Guide, other classroom instrnl. materials. Active PTA, 1975-94; vol. pub. schs., 1975-94; vol. aide Career Employment Tng. Act, 1978; mem. Worcester County Art Coun., 1985; in-svc. vol. Buckingham Elem., 1987-90; sec. Internat. Art Galleries Assn., 1986-90; fund-raising chair Berlin-Ocean City Pop Warner Football, 1990; artist chair Berlin Pk. Renovation Com., 1990-91; cultural art chair Worcester County PTA, 1988-92, Md. Congress Parents and Tchrs., 1990-92. Recipient Outstanding Artistic Instrn. award Buckingham Elem. Sch., Leadership certs. Md. Congress Parents & Tchrs., Cert. of Svc., Worcester County Boy Scouts Am.; named Outstanding Vol., Md. State Bd. Edn. Home and Office: 1305 Middle Neck Dr Salisbury MD 21801

RUSSELL, DEBORAH GAYLE, realtor; b. East Chicago, Ind., Dec. 7, 1955; d. George Pelter and Patricia Gayle Russell; children: Lisa Ann, Anthony James. Student, Ind. U., Northwest, Napa Valley Coll. Editor Herald News Group, 1982-87; mng. editor The News, 1987; photo journalist The Times, 1987-89; mktg. and edn. dir. Vis. Nurse Assn., 1987-89; advt. sales person San Francisco Bus. Times, 1989-91; realtor Prudential Calif. Realty, Napa, 1991—. Mem. Napa County Dem. Cen. Com., 1990—; pres. Napa County Dem. Caucus, 1991, 92; dir. Open Space Dist. Appointee, Napa County, 1992; mem. DARE Found., 1993—; bd. dirs. Boys & Girls Clubs, 1993—. Recipient writing awards Women's Press Club Ind., 1982-87. Mem. Nat. Assn. Realtors, Napa County Assn. Realtors. Mem. Ch. of Religious Sci. Home: PO Box 238 Napa CA 94559 Office: Prudential Calif Realty 1957 Sierra Ave Napa CA 94558

RUSSELL, ELIZABETH G., defense and arms control researcher; b. Chgo., Apr. 15, 1958; d. Charles Wilbur and Patricia Ann (Lincoln) R. BA in Internat. Rels., Mount Holyoke Coll., 1980; postgrad., Dartmouth U., 1980-81, Harvard U., 1983-85, U. Md., 1987—. Aide Sen. Charles H. Percy, Washington, 1979-80; legal historian Nat. Vets. Law Ctr., Washington, 1980-83; researcher Resource Policy Ctr., Hanover, N.H., 1980-81; exec. interviewer Temple, Barker & Sloane, Lexington, Mass., 1987; MacArthur fellow Ctr. Internat. Security Studies U. Md., College Park, 1987-88; rsch. fellow in def. & arms control Ctr. Internat. Security MIT, 1989-91; rsch. assoc. Inst. for Nat. Strategic Studies, Nat. Defense U., Fort McNair, Washington, 1991—. Fundraiser Mass. Abortion Coalition, Boston, 1986; legal aide Nat. Vets. Task Force on Agt. Orange, Washington, 1979-83. Thayer Sch. Engring fellow Dartmouth Coll., 1980-81. Democrat. Club: Yankee Rescue (Andover, Mass.). Home: 710 1/2 A St SE Washington DC 20003-1338

RUSSELL, FRANCIA, ballet director, educator; b. Los Angeles, Jan. 10, 1938; d. W. Frank and Marion (Whitney) R.; m. Kent Stowell, Nov. 19, 1965; children: Christopher, Darren, Ethan. Studies with, George Balanchine, Vera Volkova, Felia Doubrouska, Antonina Tumkovsky, Benjamin Harkarvy; student, NYU, Columbia U. Dancer, soloist N.Y.C. Ballet, 1956-62, ballet mistress, 1965-70; dancer Ballets USA/Jerome Robbins, N.Y.C., 1962; tchr. ballet Sch. Am. Ballet, N.Y.C., 1963-64; co-dir. Frankfurt (Fed. Republic Germany) Opera Ballet, 1976-77; dir., co-artistic dir. Pacific N.W. Ballet, Seattle, 1977—; affiliate prof. of dance U. Wash. Dir. staging over 100 George Balanchine ballet prodns. throughout world, including the Soviet Union and People's Republic of China, 1964—. Named Woman of Achievement, Matrix Table, Women in Communications, Seattle, 1987, Gov.'s Arts award, 1989. Mem. Internat. Women's Forum. Home: 2833 Broadway E Seattle WA 98102-3935 Office: Pacific NW Ballet 301 Mercer St Seattle WA 98109

RUSSELL, HARRIET SHAW, social worker; b. Detroit, Apr. 12, 1952; d. Louis Thomas and Lureleen (Hughes) Shaw; m. Donald Edward Russell, June 25, 1980; children: Lachante Tyree, Krystal Lanae. BS, Mich. State U., 1974; AB, Detroit Bus. Inst., 1976; BA in Pub. Adminstrn., Mercy Coll. Detroit, 1988; MSW, Wayne State U., 1992. Factory employee Gen. Motors Corp., Lansing, Mich., 1973; student supr. tour guides State of Mich., Lansing, 1974; mgr. Ky. Fried Chicken, Detroit, 1974-75; unemployment claims examiner State of Mich. Dept. Labor, Detroit, 1975-77; asst. payment worker, 1977-84, social svcs. specialist, 1984-90; ind. contractor Detroit Compact pres. Victory Enterprises, 1991; sch. social worker Detroit Bd. of Edn., 1992—; moderator Michigan Opportunity Skills and Tng. Program, 1985-86. Vol. Mich. Cancer Soc., East Lansing, 1970-72, Big Sisters/Big Bros., Lansing, 1972-73; elected rep. Mich. Coun. Social Svcs. Workers; speaker Triumphant Bapt. Ch., Detroit, 1976-80; chief union steward Mich. Employees Assn., Lincoln Park, 1982-83; leader Girl Scouts U.S.; area capt. Life Worker Project Program. Recipient Outstanding Work Performance Merit award Mich. Dept. Social Services, 1979; grad. profl. scholar, 1990-91, Dean's scholar, 1991-92; elected to Wayne State Sch. Social Work Bd., 1992—. Mem. NAFE, Am. Soc. Profl. and Exec. Women, Assn. Internat. Platform Speakers, Mich. Coun. Social Svcs. Workers, Nat. Fedn. Bus. and Profl. Women's Clubs, Inc. U.S.A. (elected del. to China), Nat. Assn. Black Social Workers, Wayne State U. Social Work Alumni Assn. (bd. dirs. 1992—), Delta Sigma Theta. Democrat. Baptist. Office: PO Box 361 Lincoln Park MI 48146-0361

RUSSELL, HELEN SITZES (DEE RUSSELL), retired telecommunications administrator; b. Palestine, Ark., Jan. 14, 1943; d. Willard Lyvern and Helen Kathleen (Moor) Sitzes; m. Donald Lloyd Smith, Oct. 4, 1959 (dec.

Mar. 1972); children: Lisa Dee Smith Manka, Wendy Elizabeth Smith May; m. William Beecher Russell, Apr. 26, 1975. Grad. high sch., Memphis. With South Cen. Bell Tel. Co., Memphis, 1962-91, mgr. tng., 1972-75, mgr. customer svc., 1975-85, mgr. toll dept., 1985-91, ret., 1991. Mem. Civitan (pres. Memphis club 1990, sec. 1987-88, honor key 1988). Republican.

RUSSELL, JOYCE ANNE ROGERS, librarian; b. Chgo., Nov. 6, 1920; d. Truman Allen and Mary Louise (Hoelzle) Rogers; m. John VanCleve Russell, Dec. 24, 1942; children: Malcolm David, John VanCleve. Student, Adelphi Coll., 1937; B.S. in Chemistry, U. Ky., 1942; M.L.S., Rosary Coll., 1967; postgrad., Rutgers U., 1970-71. Research chemist Sherwin Williams Paint Co., Chgo., 1942-45; reference librarian Chicago Heights (Ill.) Pub. Library, 1959-61; librarian Victor Chem. Works, Chicago Heights, 1961-62; lit. chemist Velsicol Chem. Corp., Chgo., 1964-67; chemistry librarian U. Fla., Gainesville, 1967-69; interim assoc. prof. U. Fla., 1967-69; librarian Thiokol Chem. Corp., Trenton, N.J., 1969-73; supr. library operations E.R. Squibb Co., Princeton, N.J., 1973-80, sr. research info scientist, 1980-91; mem. library adv. commn. Mercer Community Coll., 1979—; adv. asso. Rutgers U. Grad. Sch. Library and Info. Scis., 1978—. Editor: Bibliofile, 1967-69; contbr. articles to profl. jours. Mem. PTA, 1950-66; den mother Cub Scouts, 1952-59. Mem. Spl. Libraries Assn. (sec., dir., v.p., pres. Princeton-Trenton 1971, 75-80), Am. Chem. Soc. (bus. mgr., sec., dir. Trenton sect. 1969-78), AAUW, Mortar Board, Beta Phi Mu, Sigma Pi Sigma, Chi Delta Phi, Pi Sigma Alpha. Home: 1189 Parkside Ave Trenton NJ 08618-2625

RUSSELL, JOYCE M., lawyer, apparel executive; b. Green County, Ky., Oct. 23, 1946; d. Woodson and Sybil (Milby) R.; m. Arnold H. Haberkorn, Apr. 7, 1977. BA, Western Ky. U., 1968; JD, U. Ky., 1972. Bar: Ky. Supreme Ct. 1972. Assoc. Harlin, Parker, Lucas and English, Bowling Green, Ky., 1972-74; ptnr. Cole, Harned & Broderick, Bowling Green, 1974-75; corp. counsel Fruit of the Loom, Bowling Green, 1975-80, v.p., gen. counsel, 1980-93, sr. v.p., gen. counsel, 1993—. Mem. ABA, Am. Corp. Counsel, Internat. Trademark Assn., Ky. Bar Assn., Bowling Green Bar Assn. Republican. Office: Fruit of the Loom PO Box 90015 1 Fruit of the Loom Dr Bowling Green KY 42102

RUSSELL, LOUISE, educator, folklorist; b. Stratford, Okla., Aug. 9, 1931; d. Virgel Wylie and Louise J. (Hayden) R. BA magna cum laude, Oklahoma City U., 1953; MA, Northwestern U., 1955; PhD, Ind. U., 1977; postgrad. Ea. N.Mex. U., Ruidoso, 1992-93. Sterling, Colo., 1958-59, Washington-Lee High Sch., Arlington, Va., 1959-62, John Handley High Sch., Winchester, Va., 1962-63, Weld Sch. Dist. No. 6, Greeley, Colo., 1963-68, 72-87, Colegio Internacional, Valencia, Venezuela, 1968-69, Holmdel Schs., N.J., 1971-72; chmn. staff devel. team, English and basic skills, subject specialist Northland Pioneer Coll., Holbrook, Ariz., 1987-91; instr. English humanities Ea. N.Mex. U., 1992-93; with Dulce (Ind. Sch. Dist., 1994—. Author: Understanding Folklore, 1975, Understanding Folk Music, 1977; also articles. Named Tchr. of Yr. Masons; Grant dir. Title V Indian Edn., 1994—. Mem. MLA, Am. Anthrop. Assn., Am. Folklore Soc., Nat. Coun. Tchrs. English, Apache County Hist. Soc. (mus. bd.), Kiwanis, Phi Delta Kappa. Office: Dulce Ind Sch Dist PO Box 547 Dulce NM 87528-0547

RUSSELL, MARIANNE, human resources manager; b. Kansas City, Mo., Oct. 9, 1963; d. William Howard and Linda Lee (Chinn) Chenault; m. Michael Robert Ludy, Nov. 30, 1985 (div. Feb. 1991); 1 child, Elliott Tyler Ludy; m. Gary William Russell, Sept. 5, 1992; 1 child, Shannon Kathleen. BA, Park Coll., 1991; postgrad., Ottawa U., 1993—. Cert. profl. human resources mgr. Benefits adminstr. Borden, Inc., Liberty, Mo., 1983-84; mktg. svcs. adminstr. Western Water Mgmt., North Kansas City, Mo., 1984-87, mktg. svcs. mgr., 1988—; human resources mgr. Western Water Mgmt., North Kansas City, 1992—. Mem. siltation control com. Weatherby Lake (Mo.) Improvement Co., 1993; vol. Platte County (Mo.) 4-H, 1992—; recreation chmn. Renner Elem. PTA, Kansas City, Mo., 1993—. Mem. Am. mgmt. Assn., Soc. Human Resource Mgmt., Human Resource Mgmt. Assn. of Kansas City, Job Svc. Employer's Com. (hospitality com. 1992—), NAFE. Republican. Roman Catholic. Home: 8111 NW Miami Weatherby Lake MD 64152-1507 Office: Western Water Mgmt 1345 Taney St North Kansas City MO 64116

RUSSELL, MARJORIE ROSE, manufacturing company executive; b. Welcome, Minn., Sept. 3, 1925; d. Emil Frederick and Ella Magdalene (Sothman) Wohlenhaus; m. Kenneth Kollmann Russell, Sept. 15, 1947 (div. May 1973); children: Jennie Rose, Richard Lowell, Laura Eloise, James Wesley. Student, Northwestern Sch., Mpls., 1944-45, St. Paul Bible Inst., 1946-47. Cook U. Minn., Mpls., 1943-45; maintenance person U. Farm Campus/N.W. Schs., St. Paul, 1945-46; clk. Kresge Corp., Mpls., 1945; cook, waitress, mgr. Union City Mission Bible Camp, Mpls., 1944-47; caterer for v.p. Gt. No. R.R., St. Paul, 1947; custodian Old Soldiers Home, St. Paul, 1946; nurse Sister Elizabeth Kenney Polio Hosp., St. Paul, 1946; seamstress Hirsch, Weis, White Stag, Pendleton, Mayfair, Portland, Oreg., 1960-72; owner, operator, contract mgr., creative designer The Brass Needle, Portland, 1972—; contractor Forrester's Sanderson Safety, Scotsco, Nero & Assocs., Gara Gear, Portland, 1972—, Columbia Sportswear; tchr. Indo Chinese Cultural Ctr., Portland, 1982. Designer, producer Kisn Bridal Fair, 1969; composer: He Liveth in Me, 1968; prodr. Safety Chaps for Loggers. Sec. Model Cities Com., Portland, 1969; com. mem. Neighborhood Black Christmas Parade, Portland, 1970; custume designer Local Miss Jr. Black Beauty Contest, Portland, 1973; nominating com. Nat. Contract Mgmt. Assn., Portland, 1978; mem. nominating com. Multi-Cultural Sr. Adv. Com., 1988-91. Mem. NAFE, Urban League, Urban League Guild (historian 1991-92), Am. Assn. Ret. Persons, Nat. Contract Mgmt. Assn. Democrat. Mem. United Ch. of Christ. Home and Office: The Brass Needle 2809 NE 12th Ave Portland OR 97212

RUSSELL, MARLOU, psychologist; b. Tucson, June 2, 1956; d. William Herman and Carole Eleanor (Musgrove) McBratney; m. Jan Christopher Russell, Sept. 9, 1989. BA U. Ariz., 1981; MA Calif. Grad. Inst., 1983, PhD, 1987. Lic. psychologist, marriage, family and child counselor. Asst. to pres. Western Psychol. Svcs., L.A., 1978-81; crisis counselor Cedars-Sinai Med. Ctr., L.A., 1980-84; counselor South Bay Therapeutic Clinic, Hawthorne, Calif., 1982-84; psychotherapist PMC Treatment Systems, L.A., 1984-85, Beverly Hills Counseling Ctr., 1984-85, Comprehensive Care Corp., L.A., 1985-86; pvt. practice, L.A., 1986—; counselor Brotman Med. Ctr., L.A., 1982-83, Julia Ann Singer Ctr., L.A., 1984; bd. dirs. Los Angeles Commn. Assualts Against Women, 1987-89. Mem. Internat. Assn. Eating Disorders Profls, Women in Health, Women's Referral Svc., Calif. State Psychol. Assn., Calif. Assn. Marriage & Family Therapists (bd. dirs. 1993-94), Am. Adoption Congress, Westside Bus. Womens Assn. (bd. dirs. 1993-94). Democrat. Office: 1452 26th St Ste 103 Santa Monica CA 90404-3042

RUSSELL, SUSAN FIELDS, sales executive; b. Wilmington, N.C., July 9, 1967; d. Parks Cadman and Linda Faye (Sutton) Fields; m. Donald Craig Russell, Sept. 12, 1992. BA in Apparel Arts and Design, U. N.C., Greensboro, 1989. Sales exec. Bus. Digest Mag., Greensboro, 1989-90; sales cons. Watkins Interiors, Greensboro, 1990-91; acct. mgr. Alfred Williams and Co., Greensboro, 1992—. Chmn. triad bus. adv. coun. United Cerebral Palsy, Greensboro, 1991-93. Brenda Kaye Shaw Meml. scholar Sales and Mktg. Exec. Greensboro, 1989. Greensboro Area Incentives Network (v.p. 1992—), Greensboro C. of C. (ambassador 1993—), Small Bus. Week-Chamber (chmn. 1993—). Office: Alfred Williams and Co Ste 200 7815 National Service Rd Greensboro NC 27409-9403

RUSSELL, SUSAN WEBB, elementary and middle school education educator; b. Richmond, Va., Feb. 18, 1948; d. William Camper and Isabel McLeod (Smith) Webb; m. Russell Christian Proctor, III, Dec. 30, 1972 (div. 1981); 1 child, Alexander Christian Proctor; m. Walter William Russell, III, July 16, 1988; stepchildren: Walter William IV, Brian Earl. AB in English, Fine Arts, and Edn., Randolph-Macon Woman's Coll., 1970. Cert. tchr., Va. Customer svc. rep. Xerox Corp., Richmond, 1970-72; tchr. English grades 7, 8, 9 Am. Internat. Sch., Lagos, Nigeria, West Africa, 1973-75; group travel counselor Dynasty World Travel, Richmond, 1980-81; sec. to dir. athletics and receptionist The Collegiate Schs., Richmond, 1982-84, tchr. English and reading grades 6, 7, 9, 1984-88, tchr. word processing grade 5, 1984-86; tchr. social studies Norfolk (Va.) Acad., 1988-91, tchr. English and reading, 1991-94; forensics coach Norfolk Acad., 1991-94. Editor Bulldog News, 1988-90; advisor Bullpup News, 1990-94. Methodist. Office: Norfolk Acad 1585 Wesleyan Dr Norfolk VA 23502

RUSSELL, TARA D., food technologist; b. Manitowoc, Wis., June 16, 1960; d. Robert Carl and Gloria Doris (Zwalsh) R.; m. Gregory Jon Muske, Oct. 17, 1981. BS in Agrl. Engring., U. Wis., 1982; MBA, Keller Grad. Sch., 1992. Prodn. asst. Archer Daniels Midland, Decatur, Ill., 1982-84; project mgr., food technologist Beatrice Cheese Inc., Waukesha, Wis., 1987—. Mem. Inst. Food Technologists. Home: S108 W37103 Draper Eagle WI 53119 Office: Beatrice Cheese Inc 770 N Springdale Rd Waukesha WI 53186

RUSSELL, THERESA LYNN, actress; b. San Diego, Mar. 20, 1957; d. Jerry Russell Paup and Carole (Mall) Platt; m. Nicholas Jack Roeg, Feb. 12, 1986; children: Statten Jack, Maximilian Nicolas Sextus. Appeared in films including The Last Tycoon, 1976, Straight Time, 1977, Blind Ambition, 1978, Bad Timing, 1980, Eureka, 1981, Razor's Edge, 1983, Insignificance, 1984, Aria, 1984, Black Widow, 1985 (Nat. Assn. Theater Owners award 1985), Track 29, 1986 (Newcomer of Yr. award), Physical Evidence, 1987, Impulse, 1988, Cold Heaven, 1989 (Best Actress award Viareggio Film Festival 1991), Whore, 1990, Kafka, 1990, Thicker Than Water, 1992, Flight of the Dove, 1994, The Trade Off, 1994, (narrator) Being Human, 1994; TV movies Blind Ambition, 1979, Women's Guide to Adultery, 1993; BBC radio play Double Indemnity, 1993.

RUSSELL, VALERIE EILEEN, social service executive; b. Winchester, Mass., Apr. 28, 1941; d. John Randolph Russell and Carrie Belle (Finley) Jones. BA in Sociology, Suffolk U., 1967; postgrad., Columbia U.; D in Theology (hon.), LaFayette Coll., 1985. Program dir. Blue Hill Christian Ctr., Roxbury, Mass., 1965-67; racial justicestaff mem. Nat. Bd. YWCA, N.Y.C., 1967-72; cons. Riverside Ch., N.Y.C., 1972-73, nat. conf. organizer, 1980-81; asst. to pres. United Ch. of Christ, N.Y.C., 1973-79; pres., exec. dir. City Mission Soc., Boston, 1981-90; adj. prof. Union Theol. Sch., N.Y.C., 1976, Harvard U. Div. Sch., Cambridge, Mass., 1983—; bd. dirs. Ctr. Ministry of the Laity, Newton, Mass. Author: Laity in the Church, 1987; inventor simulation game on pluralism, 1973; regular panelist weekly TV program A Show of Faith, Boston; lectr. in field. Bd. dirs. United Way Mass. Bay, Boston, 1984-88, Women and Poverty Network, Boston, 1984—; co-founder Christians for Justice Action, United Ch. of Christ, 1980—. Named Outstanding Young Women in N.Y., 1969; Recipient Outstanding Alumni award Suffolk U., 1981, Outstanding Social Work award The Girl Friends, Boston, 1985, Outstanding Human Services award Delta Sigma Phi, Boston, 1986. Uniter Ch. of Christ. Office: Office for Ch in Soc United Ch of Christ 700 Prospect Ave Cleveland OH 44115

RUSSELL, VIRGINIA LOUISE, corporate executive, social worker; b. Clintonville, Pa., Aug. 20, 1909; d. Edward Budd and Louisa McKean (Dewoody) Gordon; m. Lester Tibbits Russell, Jan. 1, 1942; children: Richard Gordon, Judith Louise Russell Davidson. BA, U. Pitts., 1931. Tchr. langs. Saltsburg (Pa.) High Sch., 1931-32; social worker Irene Kaufmann Settlement, Pitts., 1931-33; tchr. Pitts. Pub. Schs., 1932-37; social worker Soho Settlement House, Pitts., 1934-37; dir. Franklin Ave. Settlement, Youngstown, Ohio, 1937-41; tchr. Put-in-Bay (Ohio) High Sch., 1941; sec.-treas. Taconic Plastics, Inc., Petersburgh, N.Y., 1961-75; dir. Taconic Internat. Ltd., Mullingar, Ireland, 1975-94; sec. bd. dirs. Taconic Plastics, Inc., 1961-75, Taconic Properties, Inc., 1965-77. Author: Dewoody Families of Venango County, 1981, Gordons of Western Pennsylvania, 1981, Derrick of Destiny, 1995; contbr. articles to profl. jours. Mem. Newark (Ohio) Bd. Edn., 1947-48. Honor scholar U. Pitts., 1928-31; Panhellenic scholar, 1929-31. Mem. AAUW (treas. Newark chpt. 1942-48, chmn. scholarships 1944-48, chmn. children's theatre 1944-48, sec. Newburgh chpt. 1950-53). Democrat.

RUSSELL-RADER, KATHLEEN, secondary education educator; b. Dayton, Ohio, Jan. 23, 1954; d. Reid Jerome and Margie (Miller) Russell; m. Donald Mark Rader, July 9, 1977. BS, Bowling Green (Ohio) State U., 1975; MS, U. Dayton, 1987. Cert. tchr., Ohio. English tchr. Fairborn (Ohio) City Schs., 1976—, Sinclair C. C., Dayton, 1991—; dir., choreographer Fairborn High Sch. Flyerette Dance Corps, 1976-81; adv. Nat. Jr. Honor Soc., Fairborn, 1985—, student leadership, 1990—, mem. acad. coun., 1988—; adv./dir. Drama Club, Fairborn, 1991—; coach Power of the Pen Writing Team, Fairborn, 1987—. Named Tchr. of Yr. Fairborn City Schs., 1989-90, Tchr. Honor Roll, Ohio Interscholastic Writing League, Cleve., 1990; Vera Schneider Teaching grantee Fairborn City Schs., 1988-92. Mem. Nat. Coun. Tchrs. English (judge Promising Young Writers Program 1991-93), Western Ohio Coun. Tchrs. English, Ohio Coun. Tchrs. English, Ohio Coun. English and Lang. Arts (judge writing contest 1989-93), Dayton Area Coun. Internat. Reading Assn. (pres. 1991-92), Ohio Coun. Internat. Reading Assn., Internat. Reading Assn., Nat. Assn. Student Activity Advisers, Phi Delta Kappa. Republican. Roman Catholic. Home: 7667 Turtle Creek Dayton OH 45414 Office: Fairborn City Schs 200 Lincoln Dr Fairborn OH 45324

RUSSO, BARBARA JANE, business professional; b. Ozone Park, N.Y., Dec. 4, 1955; d. Emil and Mary Jane Russo. BS in Gen. Studies, N.Y. Inst. Technology, 1982. Registered dental hygienist. Dental hygienist Great Neck, New Hyde and, N.Y.C., 1975-85; sales rep. Oral B Labs., Redwood City, Calif., 1984-92; br. mgr. Henry Schein, Inc., Woodbury, N.Y., 1993—; dental hygienist Zurich, Switzerland, 1978-79, Kibutz/Israel, 1984. Mem. Am. Dental Hygiene Assn. Home: 2756 Woods Ave Oceanside NY 11572 Office: Henry Schein Inc 135 Duryea Rd Melville NY 11747

RUSSO, IRMA HAYDEE ALVAREZ DE, pathologist; b. San Rafael, Mendoza, Argentina, Feb. 28, 1942; came to U. S., 1972; d. Jose Maria and Maria Carmen (Martinez) de Alvarez; m. Jose Russo, Feb. 8, 1969; 1 child, Patricia Alexandra. BA, Escuela Normal MTSM de Balcarce, 1959; MD, U. Nat. of Cuyo, Mendoza, 1970. Diplomate Am. Bd. Pathology. Intern Sch. of Medicine Hosps., Argentina, 1969-70; resident in pathology Wayne State U. Sch. Medicine, Detroit, 1976-80; rsch. asst. and instr. Inst. of Histology and Embryology Sch. Medicine U. Nat. of Cuyo, 1963-71, assoc. prof. histology Faculty of Phys., Chem. and Math. Scis., 1970-72; rsch. assoc. Inst. for Molecular and Cellular Evolution, U. Miami, Fla., 1972-73; rsch. assoc. exptl. pathology lab. div. biol. scis., Mich. Cancer Found., Detroit, 1973-75, rsch. scientist, 1975-76, vis. rsch. scientist, 1976-82, asst. mem., pathologist, 1982-89, assoc. rsch. mem., 1989-91, co-dir. pathology reference lab., 1982-86, chief exptl. pathology lab., 1989-91; co-dir. Mich. Cancer Found. Lab. Svcs., 1986-91; mem. Dept. Pathology Fox Chase Cancer Ctr., 1991—, dir. anatomic pathology, 1991-92; dir. Lab. Svcs., 1992—; mem. dept. pathology Fox Chase Cancer Ctr., Phila., 1992—; chief resident physician dept. pathology Wayne State U. Sch. Medicine, 1978-80, asst. prof., 1980-82; mem. staff Harper-Grace Hosps., Detroit, 1980-82; adj. prof. Pathology and Cell Biology Jefferson Sch. of Medicine/Thomas Jefferson Univ., 1992—. Rockefeller grantee, 1972-73; Nat. Cancer Inst. grantee, 1978-81, 84-87, 1994—; Am. Cancer Soc. grantee 1988-89, 91—; Recipient Shannon award Nat. Cancer Inst./NHHSS, 1992-94. guest lectr. dept. obstetrics Sch. Medicine U. Nat. of Cuyo, 1965-71. Mem. AAAS, Nat. Cancer Inst. (breast cancer working group, breast cancer program 1984-88), Nat. Alliance Breast Cancer Orgns. (med. adv. bd. N.Y.C. chpt. 1986—), Eastern Coop. Oncology Group, 1992—, Coll. Am. Pathologists, Am. Soc. Clin. Pathologists, Am. Assn. for Cancer Research, Mich. Soc. Pathologists, Am. Assn. Clin. Chemistry, Electron Microscopy Soc. Am., The Endocrine Soc, Internat. Assn. Against Cancer, Mich. Electron Microscopy Forum, Sigma Xi. Roman Catholic. Contbr. numerous articles on pathology to profl. jours. Office: Fox Chase Cancer Ctr 7701 Burholme Ave Philadelphia PA 19111-2497 also: PO Box 549 Abington PA 19001-0549

RUSSO, JOSEPHINE MARIE, company executive, interior designer; b. Lawrence, Mass., Aug. 21, 1948; d. Alfio and Ida (Cavallaro) R.; m. Gary G. Prunier, Apr. 4, 1971 (div. 1985); children: Kathryn, Matthew, Elizabeth; m. Fred J. Dobelbowed, Mar. 20, 1986; 1 child, Alexandra. BA in English, Merrimack Coll., 1969; MEd, Salem State Tchrs. Coll., 1971; Assocs. Diploma, Am. Sch. Interior Design, Mesa, Ariz., 1987. Tchr. Methven Pub. Sch., Mass., 1969-77; dir. Mary Moppetts Sch., Phoenix, 1978-79; owner, dir. Rocking Horse Pre-Sch., Phoenix, 1979-84; CEO K.M.E. Enterprises, Scottsdale, Ariz., 1984-91; interior designer Laura's Home Fashions, Phoenix, 1991-92; CEO Jo Maue Creators, Scottsdale, Ariz., 1992—. Author: Doorknobs, 1981; contbr. articles to popular mags. Treas. Ariz. Assn. Child Care Devel. and Edn., Phoenix, 1979-80. Mem. ASTD (assoc.), Longridge Writers Group.

RUSSO, KIMBERLY KING, financial consultant. Advt. sales exec., 1980, claim payments approver for major ins. co., 1982; ptnr. Joseph P. King & Assocs. CLU, ChFC, 1983—; acct. exec. Cadaret, Grant & Co., Inc.; owner, founder Tifkim Fin. Svcs., Inc., Longwood, Fla.; tchr. fin. awareness classes at accredit bus. sch., 1990-93; presenter at workshops and seminars in field; mem. product panel Equitable Life Assurance of U.S., 1985-86. Chair membership Ctrl. Fla. chpt. Mercedes Benz Club Am., 1987-91, sec., 1990-91; bd. govs. Timacuan Golf & Country Club, 1987-91; membership com. Home Bldrs. Assn., 1985-86; charitable planning and fin. dir. Jr. Golf Assn. Ctrl. Fla., 1990-91. Mem. Internat. Assn. Fin. Planners, Nat. Leaders Corps, Nat. Assn. Life Underwriters, Seminole County C. of C., CPS/Internat. Comprehensive Planners, Am. Horse Shows Assn., Am. Quarter Horse Assn., U.S. Dressage Fedn. Office: 2170 W Hwy 434 Ste 318 Longwood FL 32779

RUSSO, NANCY FELIPE, psychologist, educator; b. Oroville, Calif., May 3, 1943; d. Joseph and Ruby Helena (Gould) Felipe; m. Thomas Anthony Russo, June 18, 1966 (div.); m. D. Allen Meyer. AA, Yuba Coll., 1963; BA, U. Calif., Davis, 1965; PhD, Cornell U., 1970. Asst. prof. psychology Am. U., Washington, 1970-71, 73-74; asst. prof. social scis. Richmond Coll., CUNY, S.I., N.Y., 1971-73; staff assoc. APA, Washington, 1974-76, adminstrv. officer women's programs, 1977-85; health scientist adminstr. Nat. Inst. Child Health and Human Devel., Washington, 1976-77; prof. psychology and women's studies Ariz. State U., Tempe, 1985—; vis. scholar U. Mich., Ann Arbor, 1994. Author: A Women's Mental Health Agenda, 1985; co-author: Models of Achievement: Eminent Women in Psychology, Vol. I and II, 1983, 88, Women in Psychology, 1990, No Safe Haven: Male Violence Against Women, 1994; editor Psychology of Women Quar., 1994—; contbr. articles to profl. publs. Fellow APA (coun. rep. 1992—, divsn. 35 pres. 1989-90, divsn. 34 pres. 1978, Cert. of Recognition 1983, 93, Cert. of Appreciation 1985, Disting. Leadership citation 1986, Carolyn Wood Sherif award 1993, Heritage award 1992, Disting. Svc. award 1990, Recognition award 1985), Soc. for Ethnic Minority and Cross-Cultural Psychology (fellows chair); mem. Assn. for Women in Psychology (Disting. Career award 1991, Publ. award), Rocky Mountain Psychology Assn. (pres. 1990-92), Assn. Women in Psychology. Home: 4230 E Mountain View Phoenix AZ 85028-4511 Office: Ariz State U Box 871104 Tempe AZ 85287-1104

RUSSO DEMETRICK, MARY MARGARET, publications director; b. Syracuse, N.Y., Aug. 4, 1942; d. Nicholas Philip and Theresa Maria Dolores (Gelfuso) Russo; children: Brian, Christopher, Gregory, Katrina. BA in Speech Comm. magna cum laude, Syracuse U., 1993. With Syracuse (N.Y.) U. Publs. Office, 1986—, asst. dir. publs., 1992—; owner Hale Mary Press. Author (poems) First Pressing, 1994. Mem. Am. Italian Hist. Assn., Italian Am. Writer's Assn., Nat. League Am. Penwomen, Nat. Women's Studies Assn., Nat. Orgn. Italian Students and Educators, Alpha Sigma Lambda. Office: Syracuse U Publs Office 820 Comstock Ave Rm 308 Syracuse NY 13244

RUSTIN, FAYE E., employment agency executive; b. Lyons, Ga., Feb. 20, 1950; d. Charlie Hugh and Lillian Jeanette (Rollins) R.; m. John Logan, Aug. 8, 1975. Grad., Swainsboro (Ga.) Area Vo-Tech., 1969. Office mgr. Kaiser Agrl. Chemicals, Lyons, 1969-79, United Groves, Ft. Pierce, Fla., 1980-82; constrn. office mgr. ITT-Grimmell, Oswego, N.Y., 1982-85; office mgr. Fibermart Designs, Jacksonville, Fla., 1985-87; acct. placement specialist Career Opportunity, Inc., Jacksonville, 1987-88; permanent placement specialist Adia Pers., Jacksonville, 1988; owner, founder Active Profls., Jacksonville, 1989—. Vol. cons. Prisoners of Christ; fundraising chmn. Harden's Chapel Cemetery, Toombs County, Ga.; chmn. 25th H.S. Class Reunion; program resource cons. North Fla. Coun. Girl Scouts U.S.A.; child sponsor, active program and project resource cons. Children's Home Soc. Fla., 1992—; charter, founding mem., program chmn., liaison to C. of C., sec. EDEN-Econ. Devel. and Enhancement of North Jacksonville Group; cochmn. town meeting for Rep. Tillie Fowler; mem. Write Your Congressman; active campaigner local judge. Mem. Mandarin Bus. Assn., Jacksonville C. of C. (pres. 1994, small bus. bd., small bus. issues task force, Small Bus. Leader of Yr./Northside award 1993, pres.-elect north coun., bd. dirs. north coun., chmn. north journey, other coms.), Northside Businessman Club. Office: Active Profls 2572-1 Atlantic Blvd Jacksonville FL 32207

RUSZKIEWICZ, CAROLYN MAE, newspaper editor; b. Tucson, Nov. 10, 1946; d. Robert Frank and Charlotte Ruth (Hadley) Knapton; m. Joseph Charles Ruszkiewicz, July 11, 1969. BA, Calif. State U., Long Beach, 1971, MA, 1973. Reporter Long Beach (Calif.) Press-Telegram, 1968-85, consumer editor, 1985-86, lifestyle editor, 1986-89, regional news editor, 1989-91, city editor, 1991-95, asst. mng. editor, 1995—. Office: Long Beach Press-Telegram 604 Pine Ave Long Beach CA 90844-0003

RUTENBERG, BRIGITTE SUSANNE, artist; b. Tegernsee, Bavaria, Germany, Feb. 28, 1939; came to U.S., 1961; d. Hans and Henny (Lorenz) Woithe; m. Michael J. Rutenberg, Aug. 6, 1963; children: Claudia L., Richard J. Student, U. Paris, Sorbonne, 1959-60; cert., Pa. Acad. of Fine Arts, 1976-80. Translator Becker & Van Hulien, Krefeld, 1960-61; tchr. Berlitz Sch. of Lang., Phila., 1963-64; acquisitions of rare books U. Pa., 1961-63; artist Phila., 1981—; pres. Fellowship Pa. Acad., Phila., 1990-91; rep. Old City Arts Orgn., Phila., 1992—. One woman shows include Zone One, 1993—, Moravian Coll., 1993, Phila. Art Alliance; exhibited in group shows at Center Square Gallery, Phila., Internat. Sculpture Conf., Pa. State U., Port of History Mus., Gross-McCleaf Gallery, Rodger Lapelle Gallery, Allentown Mus., Marion Locks Gallery. Active Art in Embassies Program, Washington, 1994—. Recipient P. Puzinas Prize Nat. Acad. of Design, 1980, Eingorn Meml. award, 1990, May Audubon Post prize; fellowship to Rome Creative Artists Network, 1985; William Emlen Cresson European Traveling scholar. Mem. Old City Arts Orgn. (pres.), Zone One Gallery. Home: 531 New Gulph Rd Haverford PA 19041 Office: Zone One Gallery 139 N 2nd St Philadelphia PA 19106

RUTENBERG-ROSENBERG, SHARON LESLIE, journalist; b. Chgo., May 23, 1951; d. Arthur and Bernice (Berman) Rutenberg; m. Michael J. Rosenberg, Feb. 3, 1980; children: David Kaifel and Jonathan Reuben (twins), Emily Mara. Student, Harvard U., 1972; B.A., Northwestern U., 1973, M.S.J., 1975; cert. student pilot. Reporter-photographer Lerner Home Newspapers, Chgo., 1973-74; corr. Medill News Service, Washington, 1975; reporter-newsperson, sci. writer UPI, Chgo., 1975-84. Interviewer: exclusives White House chief of staff, nation's only mother and son on death row; others. Vol. Chgo.-Read Mental Health Ctr. Recipient Peter Lisagor award for exemplary journalism in features category, 1980, 81; Golden Key Nat. Adv. Bd. of Children's Oncology Service Inc., 1981; Media awards for wire service feature stories, 1983, 84, wire service news stories, 1983, 84, all from Chgo. Hosp. Pub. Relations Soc. Mem. Profl. Assn. Diving Instrs., Nat. Assn. Underwater Instrs., Hon. Order Ky. Cols., Hadassah, Sigma Delta Chi, Sigma Delta Tau. Home: 745 Marion Ave Highland Park IL 60035-5123

RUTGERS, KATHARINE PHILLIPS (MRS. FREDERIK LODEWIJK RUTGERS), dancer; b. Butler, Pa., Sept. 2, 1910; d. Thomas Wharton and Alma (Sherman) Phillips; m. Frederik Lodewijk Rutgers, Feb. 2, 1942; children: Alma, Corinne Tolles. Diploma Briarcliff Coll., 1928; student L'Hermiage, Versailles, France, 1929-30; pupil ballet Vera Trefilova, Paris, Carl Raimund, Vienna, Varga Troyanoff, Budapest; pupil modern dance with Iris Barbura, Bucharest Ballet, Vincenzo Celli, N.Y.C., Igor Schwezoff, N.Y.C., Jean Yazvinsky, N.Y.C. Performed dance concerts Bucharest, 1937-40, U.S., 1941—; repertoire includes patriotic, dramatic, poetical dances, religious interpretations; dance therapist St. Barnabas Hosp., N.Y.C., 1965-70; author numerous pamphlets on dance, verses for choreographies. Chmn. ethnol. dance dept. Bruce Mus. Assocs., Greenwich, Conn., 1970—. Bd. dirs. Bruce Mus. Recipient citation for promoting culture with dance programs Nat. Fedn. Music Clubs, 1973. Mem. DAR, Conn. Fedn. Music Clubs (chmn. dance dept. 1965-66), Nat. League Am. Pen Women (local pres. 1973-78), Alliance Francaise, Mayflower Soc., Colonial Dames Am., Federated Music Club N.Y.C. (dir., dance chmn.), Met. Farm and Garden Club (dir.), Indian Harbor Club. Home: 51 La Cova Pecks Land Rd Greenwich CT 06830

RUTH, CAROL A., public relations executive; b. N.Y.C., June 19, 1942; d. Edward McDonald and Dorothea (Beauman) Smith. BBA, CUNY, 1979. Sr. v.p. Hill and Knowlton, Inc., N.Y.C., 1968-86; pres., chief exec. officer Dewe Rogerson, Inc., N.Y.C., 1986—, also bd. dirs.; Dewe Rogerson Group, London; exec. dir. Dewe Rogerson Asia. Recipient Woman Achievers award YWCA of N.Y. 1985, bd. dirs. 1991—. Mem. Nat. Investors Rels. Inst. (bd. dirs. 1981-85, chmn. bd. 1984-85). Office: Dewe Rogerson Inc 850 3rd Ave New York NY 10022-6222

RUTH, LOIS-JEAN, social welfare company administrator, statistical analyst; b. Abbottstown, Pa., Aug. 24, 1931; d. Stewart Philip and Florence Kathryn (Mummert) Ruth. BA, Pa. State U., 1953. Engring. expeditor AMP Inc., Harrisburg, Pa., 1953-56, statis. analyst, 1956-59, head statis. analysis, 1959-73, systems procedures coord., 1957-73, mem. divisional cost improvement com., 1966-73, sales stats. tng. coord., 1963-73; v.p., asst. sec. Mobile Home Brokers Inc., Hanover, Pa., 1973-83; co-owner Suburban Developers, Gettysburg, Pa.; office mgr., loan processor Shelter Am. Corp, Aurora, Colo., 1984; v.p., treas. GTP Enterprises, Inc., Gettysburg; supr. caseworkers. Domestic Rels. Office Adams County, Pa., 1986-88; with Harry Ness & Co., 1988; v.p. fin. and adminstrn. Adams County United Way, 1988—. Chmn. legis. task force Pa. Mfg. Housing Assn., Harrisburg, Pa., 1979-80. Mem. Gov.'s Com. for Constl. Rev., State of Pa., 1963-66; chmn. Parks and Recreation Commn., 1966-72; sec. Zoning Hearing Bd., 1972-79; mem. Zoning Revision Com., Boro of New Cumberland, Pa., 1977-79; mem. exec. bd., chmn. personnel YWCA, Gettysburg, 1980-83; mem. Indoor Sports Complex Fund Commn., 1978-81; active Coll. Liberal Arts Endowment Fund; mem. alumni coun. Pa. State U., 1984—, bd. advisers, Mont Alto. Mem. AAUW (bd. dirs. 1954-56), Coll. of Liberal Arts Alumni Soc. (pres. 1982-88, Alumni award 1988), Dwight Eisenhower Soc., Pa. Fedn. Women's Clubs (pres., chmn. legis. com. New Cumberland, Pa. chpt.), Lions, Phi Mu. Republican. Presbyterian. Home: 70 Hunters Trl Gettysburg PA 17325-8472

RUTHCHILD, GERALDINE QUIETLAKE, training and development consultant, writer, poet; d. Nathan and Ruth (Feldman) Stein; m. Neil Wolinsky, Dec. 31, 1993. BA summa cum laude, Queens Coll., 1977; MA in Am. Lit., Johns Hopkins U., 1980, PhD in Am. Lit., 1983. Asst. prof. Albion (Mich.) Coll., 1982-84; assoc. Investor Access Corp., N.Y.C., 1984-85; program dir. Exec. Enterprises, Inc., N.Y.C., 1985-86; pres. Ruthchild Assocs., N.Y.C., 1987-90, Exemplar, N.Y.C., 1991—; cons. J.P. Morgan & Co., Inc., Chase Manhattan Bank N.A., Merrill Lynch, Nat. Westminster Bank, U.S.A., Citibank N.A., Robert Morris Assocs., Goldman, Sachs & Co., Dean Witter Reynolds, Inc., also others, 1987—. Contbr. articles, poems to profl. and lit. jours. Vol. handicapped children N.Y. Foundling Hosp., N.Y.C., 1988-90, Fgn. Visitors Desk, Met. Mus. Art, N.Y.C., 1989—. Hopkins fellow Johns Hopkins U., 1979-80, Andrew Mellon Found. fellow, 1980-81, 81-82. Mem. ASTD, Assn. Bank Trainers and Cons., Internat. Soc. Philos. Enquiry, Phi Beta Kappa. Office: Exemplar 501 E 87th St Fl 12 New York NY 10128-7601

RUTHERFORD, LINDA MARIE, hospital official; b. Chgo., Sept. 13, 1947; d. Allen A. and Marie (Romano) Gregory; children: Jason Alan Hunt, Lisa Marie Hunt; m. John H. Rutherford; stepchildren: Maury, Helena. BS, U. Phoenix, 1987. Adminstrv. asst. Old Tucson/Old Vegas, 1975-78; asst. mgr. W & W Mktg. Corp., Houston, 1978-83; adminstr. profl. rels. Tucson Gen. Hosp., 1983-84; mgr. Romero Road Med. Clinic, Tucson, 1984-89; mgr. physician svcs. El Dorado Hosp. and Med. Ctr., Tucson, 1989—; with N.W. Hosp., Tucson, 1994—. Bd. dirs. Flowing Wells Community Effort Coun., 1988; mem. Concerned Women for Am., 1986—. Mem. NAFE, Med. Group Mgmt. Assn. Baptist. Office: NW Hosp 6200 N La Cholla Tucson AZ 85741

RUTHERFORD, MEGAN JANE, psychologist; b. Dunedin, South Isld, New Zealand, May 27, 1960; came to U.S., 1968; d. Barry Douglas Rutherford and Judith Katherine (McKenzie) Church; m. James Ross MacRae, May 2, 1992. BS in Zoology, Oreg. State U., 1983, BS in Psychology, 1983; PhD in Clin. Psychology, Hahnemann Med. Coll., 1990. Lic. clin. psychologist, Pa. Practicum counselor Harcum Jr. Coll., Phila., 1984-85; practicum drug counselor J.F.K. Methadone Clinic, Phila., 1985; practicum, psychologist Ea. State Sch. and Hosp., Trevose, Pa., 1985; pracitum/counselor Segaloff Methadone Clinic, Camden, N.J., 1985-88; rsch. asst. Robert Wood Johnson Sch. U. Medicine and Dentistry, 1988-89; substance abuse evaluator for juveniles Camden County Ct., 1987-88; psychologist intern Devereaux Found.-Hall Manor, Devon, Pa., 1988-89; rsch. specialist, lectr. U. Pa., Phila., 1989—, rsch. asst., prof. psychology, 1993—; lectr. to fellows, residents, U. Pa., 1992—; tchng. asst. Ctr. for Substance Abuse Treatment, Washington, 1992—. Contbr. articles to profl. jours., chpt. to Psychopathy and the Criminal Justice System, 1992. Grantee Nat. Inst. Drug Addiction, Mt. Sinai Hosp., Phila., 1993-97. Mem. APA, No. Ohio Assn. Herpatologists. Office: U Pa Treatment Rsch Ctr 3900 Chestnut St Philadelphia PA 19104-3109

RUTLAND-AMAGLIANI, CAROL ELAINE, music director, educator; b. Memphis, Aug. 11, 1952; d. Charles Wesson and Evelyn (Matthew) Rutland; m. Malcolm Brown Futhey (div. Mar. 1986); children: Malcolm Brown III, Meredith Elaine; m. Michael Lewis Amagliani, July 1993; 1 child, Christopher Ian Amagliani. Cert. in theory teaching/piano pedagogy, St. Louis Inst. Music, 1970, 71; BS in Edn., Memphis State U., 1989. Cert. in theory and piano, Tenn. Pvt. tchr. piano, voice and keyboard Memphis, 1970—; lower sch. music coord. Evangelical Christian Sch., Memphis, 1983—; judge piano competitions, drama tchr. and choreographer; fgn. study culture and music and missions trip, Papua, New Guinea, 1990. Keyboard accompanist, voice tchr. various chs., Memphis; mem. King's Daughter Women's Fellowship. Mem. Tenn. Counseling Assn., Women's Fellowship, Kings Daus., Pi Mu Beta.

RUTLEDGE, GLORIA JUDITH, property manager; b. Jackson, Tenn., Nov. 22, 1961; d. Rustico Dizon and Kathryn Lillian (Crump) Garcia; m. Corey Neal Rutledge, Oct. 28, 1983. Student, Okla. A&M Coll., 1979-80; AAS, San Jacinto Coll., 1986; AA, Austin C.C., 1991; postgrad., St. Edwards U., 1994—. Asst. mgr. Southland Corp., Norman, Okla., 1980-81; hydrologic rsch. asst. U.S. Geol. Survey, Oklahoma City, 1982-83; service adminstr. Berkey Mktg. Co., N.Y.C., 1983; exec. adminstr. First Computer Corp., Houston, 1984; mktg. support asst. IBM/NYNEX, Houston, 1984-86; exec. adminstr. Coulson and Assocs. Engrs., Houston, 1987-89; pres. Quality, Time & Money, Austin, 1988—. Author: (short story) Inverted Origins, 1980. Asst., Rep. Campaign, Houston, 1984; vol. Hospice Austin, Muscular Dystrophy Assn., Am. Cancer Soc., United Jewish Appeal, 1979—; pres. Camp Fire, 1976-80, Horizon Rep., 1977, congress rep. 1979-80. Named Mgr. of Yr., Austin Apt. Assn., 1994. Mem. B'nai Brith, Alpha Sigma Epsilon (named Outstanding Pledge 1982). Home and Office: Lindy's Landing Apts 121 Woodward Ste 114 Austin TX 78704 Office: Quality Time & Money PO Box 218586 Houston TX 77218-8586

RUTSKY, LYN, home health agency administrator; b. Portsmouth, Va., Nov. 27, 1951; d. Charles Albert and Mildred (Berschneider) Stahl; m. Richard Rutsky, July 3, 1971; children: Megan, Erin. Diploma nursing, Presbyn. U. Hosp. Sch. Nursing, Pitts., 1972; BS in Health Care Adminstrn., St. Joseph's Coll., Windham, Maine, 1989. Case mgr. various nursing agys., Md., 1984-87; acting dir. social svc. discharge planning dept. So. Md. Hosp. Ctr., Clinton, 1987; continuing care coord. Group Health Assn., Washington, 1987-89; adminstr., dir. So. Md. Home Health Svcs. Inc., Clinton, 1989—; cons. utilization reviewer, 1987—; co-founder, bd. dirs. Family Maternity Care Assocs., Inc.; pvt. cons. Bd. dirs. So. Md. Home Health Svcs., Inc.; adv. bd. Charles County C.C. Health and Tech. Ctr. Mem. Group Health Assn. (svc. excellence trainer, chmn. svc. excellence com.), Md. Assn. for Home Care (bd. dirs.).

RUTTER, ELIZABETH JANE, secretary; b. Doylestown, Pa., Oct. 11, 1937; s. Walter Norman and Helen Loretta (Fryday) Lawrence; m. Thomas Dale, Oct. 12, 1957; children—Alan Dale, Jeffrey Scott. Grad. exec. secretarial course Pierce Jr. Coll., 1956; student Coll. Ins. and Temple U., 1971, Albright Coll., 1972-77. Sec. U.S. Gauge div. Am. Machine Corp., Sellersville, Pa., 1956-58; sec. engring. Met-Ed. Co., Reading, Pa., 1966-68, exec. sec. to gen. counsel Gilbert Assocs., Inc., Reading, 1968-70, adminstrv. asst. to gen. counsel, 1970-74, asst. corp. sec., 1974-77, corp. sec., 1977-89; asst. corp. sec., 1989—, corp. sec. engring. subs., Gilbert/Commonwealth Inc., 1977—. Republican. Lutheran. Office: Gilbert Assocs Inc PO Box 1498 Reading PA 19603-1498

RUTTMAN, MARGARET LORETTA, secondary school educator; b. Borger, Tex., Mar. 20, 1940; d. Allen C. and Edith L. Womble; children: Rashell Lemmons, Rhett Ruttman. BBA, West Tex. State U., 1962. Cert. tchr., Tex.; cert. vocat. office edn. Tchr. Springlake-Earth (Tex.) High Sch., 1962-66, Spearman (Tex.) High Sch., 1966-68, Crosbyton (Tex.) High Sch., 1968-69, Ralls (Tex.) High Sch., 1970-81, Follett (Tex.) High Sch., 1981—. Author: Points and Pica, 1993. Mem. Am. Assn. Retired Persons, Assn. Tex. Profl. Educators. Methodist. Home: 401 N Main Follett TX 79034 Office: Follett Pub Schs PO Box 28 Follett TX 79034-0028

RUZICKA, MARY HELEN, voice educator; b. Balt., Sept. 1, 1945; d. William John and Helen Mary (Hladky) R.; m. Edward Dickerson Crook, Dec. 22, 1973. BA, Notre Dame of Md., 1967; MA, Columbia U., 1970. Music tchr. Balt. Pub. Schs., 1967-77; ind. voice tchr. Balt., 1977—; voice tchr. Balt. Symphony, 1978—; lectr. Balt. Symphony Chorus, 1985-88, Handel Choir, Balt., Choral Arts Soc.; music tchr. Loyola Coll., Balt., 1984-86, Notre Dame Md., Balt., 1987. Dir. Three Arts Women's Chorale. Mem. Am. Guild Mus. Artists (contralto soloists), Nat. Assn. Tchrs. Singing (v.p. local chpt. 1993—), Concert Artists of Balt., Balt. Choral Arts Soc. Profl. Chorus. Democrat. Home and Studio: 2210 Midridge Rd Timonium MD 21093

RYALL, JO-ELLYN M., psychiatrist; b. Newark, May 25, 1949; d. Joseph P. and Tekla (Paraszczuk) R.; BA in Chemistry with gen. honors, Douglass Coll., Rutgers U., 1971; MD, Washington U., St. Louis, 1975. Diplomate Am. Bd. Psychiatry and Neurology. Resident in psychiatry Washington U., 1975-78, psychiatrist Student Health, 1980-84, clin. instr. psychiatry, 1978-83, clin. asst. prof. psychiatry, 1983—; inpatient supr. Malcolm Bliss Mental Health Center, St. Louis, 1978-80, psychiatrist outpatient clinic, 1980-82; pvt. practice medicine specializing in psychiatry, St. Louis, 1980—. Bd. dirs. Women's Self Help Ctr., St. Louis, 1980-83. Fellow APA, Soc. (pres. Ea. Mo. Dist. Br. 1983-85, sect. coun. Am. Med. Assn. 1986—); mem. AMA (alt. del. Mo. 1988-90, 93-94, del. 1995—), Am. Med. Women's Assn. (pres. St. Louis Dist. br. 1981-82, 92, regional gov. VIII 1986-89, spkr. house of dels., 1993—), St. Louis Met. Med. Soc. (del. to state conv. 1981-86, 93—, councilor 1985-87, v.p. 1989), Mo. State Med. Assn. (vice speaker ho. of dels. 1986-89, speaker 1989-92), Manic Depressive Assn. St. Louis (chmn. bd. dirs. 1985-89), Washington U. Faculty Club. Office: 9216 Clayton Rd Saint Louis MO 63124-1560

RYALS, CONNIE, state government department administrator; b. Nampa, Idaho, June 6, 1952; d. Samuel Wesley and Elaine Louise (Pace) Beeson; m. Steven Elden Ryals, April 20, 1969. Audit clerk Albertson's Inc., Boise, Idaho, 1970-73, adminstrv. sec., 1973-75, staff acct., 1975, coord. accts. payable, 1975-78, acctg. supr. pvt. label, 1978-82, mgr. sales audit dept., 1982-87; adminstr. internal ops. Idaho Dept. Adminstrn., Boise, Idaho, 1987-91; dir. Idaho Dept. of Employment, Boise, Idaho, 1991—; mem. bd. dirs. Idaho Total Quality Inst., 1991—, Interstate Conf. of Employment Security Adminstrs., Washington, 1993—; mem. strategic planning com. Boise State U., 1993; mem. steering com. State Employee Compensation Com., Boise, 1993—. Chmn. Govt. Andrus/Robert Redford Fund Raiser, Boise, 1989. Mem. Idaho Total Quality Inst. (dir. 1991—). Home: 2773 Haven Dr Eagle ID 83616 Office: Employment Dept 317 Main St Boise ID 83735

RYAN, BARBARA DIANE, management information systems director; b. Phila., Nov. 3, 1950; d. Joseph Wayne and Elsie Elaine (Schafer) Hart; m. Dennis M. Ryan, Mar. 20, 1976; 1 child, Christine Susan. BA in Math., Eastern Coll., St. Davids, Pa., 1972. Computer programmer H. F. Michel, King of Prussia, Pa., 1972-73, L. P. Muller, King of Prussia, 1973-77, Hajoca Corp., Ardmore, Pa., 1977-78; MIS dir. Hajoca Corp., Ardmore, 1978—; pvt. practice installing, setting up and tng. for home personal computers, 1991—. Vol. chmn. publicity com. Trinity Luth. Ch., 1985-87, supt. Sunday sch., 1986-88, vol. Sunday sch. tchr., 1988-91, chmn. staff support Cong. Coun. 1988-91, v.p. Congl. Coun., 1991-92, sec. Congl. Coun., 1992-94, chmn. Evangelism, 1992-94, co-chmn. fall holiday bazaar, 1994, fin. rec. sec., 1995—; mem. Haverford Band & Orch. Parents, 1994—, treas., 1994—. Mem. Llanerch Civic Assn., Ea. Coll. Alumni Assn. Republican. Office: Hajoca Corp 127 Coulter Ave Ardmore PA 19003

RYAN, BEVERLY KLEINFELDER, real estate broker; b. Phila., Dec. 23, 1925; d. William F. and Anna Marie (Klein) Kleinfelder; m. Jack H. Milne, May 20, 1950 (dec.); children: Barbara Jo Milne Luurtsema, Robin Milne Terral, Jack H. Jr., Terianna, Scott; m. Joseph J. Ryan, May 26, 1989. A.A., Penn Hall Jr. Coll., Chambersburg, Pa., 1945; student, Pa. State U., 1965; grad., Real Estate Inst., 1982. Lic. real estate broker, Pa.; cert. residential specialist, residential broker. Assoc. broker Century 21 Einhorn-Adler, Inc., Elkins Park, Pa. Vol. Abington (Pa.) Hosp., Holy Redeemer Hosp.; past pres. Abington Newcomer's Club, Lower Moreland Mid. Sch. PTA, Lower Moreland High Sch. PTA, Lower Moreland Gen. PTA, Women's Club Huntingdon Valley, Pa.; com. mem. Miss American Pageant; program presenter Shriners Children's Hosp.; established health fair Lower Moreland Twp. Community; marshall LPGA Classic, Somers Point, N.J.; mem. women's group St. John's Episcopal Ch., Huntingdon Valley; numerous others. Mem. Pa. Assn. Realtors (bd. dirs. 1983-91, exec. com. 1986, chmn. multiple listing com. 1991, Par Excellence award 1980-82, Par Excellence Life award 1983-91, Realtor Active in Politics award 1985), East Montgomery County Bd. Realtors (bd. dirs. 1983-93, 2d v.p. 1989, 1st v.p. 1990, pres. 1991, Realtor Assoc. of Yr. award 1983, 94, Presdl. Svc. award 1986, Realtor of Yr. award 1992), USCG Aux., Ocean City Colony Club. Home: 7 Gilbert Ln Ocean City NJ 08226 Office: Century 21 Einhorn Adler 8039 Old York Rd Elkins Park PA 19117

RYAN, CATHRINE SMITH, publisher; b. Calif.; d. Owen W. and Margarette D. Griffin; A.A., Bellevue Jr. Coll., Denver, 1948; grad. Barnes Sch. Commerce, Denver, 1950; student N.Y. Ballet Acad., 1954. Dir. Ballet Workshop, Enumclaw, Wash., 1958-64; dir. confs. and seminars San Francisco Theol. Sem., 1977-80; pres., dir. Cathi, Ltd., pub. and cons. office orgn. and mgmt., San Francisco, 1980—; freelance travel photographer, 1968-80; guest instr. in field; guest lectr. on German rsch. Recipient various certs. of recognition. Republican. Mormon. Author: Face Lifting Exercises, 1980, Sullivan's Chain, 1986; contbr. articles to procedure and policy manuals, geneal. rsch., family histories; translator old German script. Avocation: scuba diving.

RYAN, CHARLOTTE MURIEL, oncology nurse; b. Beedeville, Ark., Sept. 2, 1939; d. Eugene Sanford and Edith Elizabeth (Goforth) Breckenridge; children: Russell Kent, Cary Randall, Molly Renee. BSN cum laude, Calif. State U., Fresno, 1991, postgrad., 1991—. Cert. oncology nurse. Psychiat. technician Porterville (Calif.) State Hosp., 1959-67; tchr. developmentally disabled Ariz. Tng. Ctr., Coolidge, 1967-71; Montessori tchr. Tucson, 1972-77; tchr. developmentally disabled Heartland Opportunity Ctr., Madera, Calif., 1977-79; med. office mgr. office of orthopedic surgeon, Madera, 1979-83, office mgr., x-ray technician, 1983-87; staff nurse in oncology St. Agnes Med. Ctr., Fresno, 1991—; instr. nursing dept. Calif. State U., Fresno, 1992, 93. Treas. Hospice of Madera County, 1990-92, bd. dirs., 1992; peer counselor Calif. State U., Fresno, 1989-91; pres. bd. dirs. Easter Seals Soc., Madera, 1981. Mem. No. Calif. Cancer Pain Inst. (editor newsletter 1994-95), Oncology Nursing Soc., Nightingale Soc., Golden Key Nat. Honor Soc., Sigma Theta Tau (chair pub. com., editor Mu newsletter 1994-95). Republican. Mormon. Home: 8060 N Glenn # 108 Fresno CA 93711 Office: St Agnes Med Ctr 1303 E Herndon Ave Fresno CA 93720-3309

RYAN, DIANE PHYLLIS, nurse; b. Buffalo, June 19, 1954; d. Edward John and Helen (Pasko) Vnuk; m. Terrance Patrick Ryan, May 14, 1977; children: Kevin Daniel, Jaclyn Nicole, Amanda Leigh, Scott Michael. BSN, D'Youville Coll., 1976; MS in Nursing, SUNY, 1980. Cert. adult nurse practitioner. Staff nurse Buffalo VA Med. Ctr., 1976-79, nurse practitioner, 1980-83, community referral nurse coordinator, 1983-92, nurse practitioner, 1992—. Contbr. articles to profl. jours. Recipient continuing edn. award Homemaker's Upjohn, Buffalo, 1976, Carol Sinicki manuscript award Am. Diabetes Educators, 1984, 1st place award 11th Ann. Discharge Planning Symposium, Soc. Hosp. Social Work Dirs., Am. Hosp. Assn. Mem. Western N.Y. Nurse Practitioners, Sigma Theta Tau. Office: Buffalo VA Med Ctr 3495 Bailey Ave Buffalo NY 14215-1129

RYAN, ELEANORE A., clinical psychologist; b. Chgo.; children: Robert, James, Mark, John, Christopher, Marynel. BS with honors in Chemistry, Mundelein Coll.; PhD in Clin. Psychology, Northwestern U., 1978. Cert. psychologist, Ill., Ind. Staff psychologist Porter-Starke Svcs., Valparaiso, Ind., 1978-80; psychol. cons. Gary (Ind.) Community Mental Health Center, 1980-81; pvt. practice clin. and cons. psychology, Clarendon Hills, Ill., 1981—; cons. Francenter, Darien, Ill., 1988—; dir. Assocs. in Clin. Therapy, 1987—; psychologist Hines VA Hosp. (Ill.), 1983-88, Oak Park (Ill.) Vet. Ctr., 1988—. Mem. APA, Ill. Psychol. Assn. (chmn. Disaster Response Network), Assn. DuPage Psychologists (pres. 1993), Soc. for Clin. and Exptl. Hypnosis, Soc. for Traumatic Stress Studies, Health Services Adv. Bd., Chgo. Psychologists in Addictive Behavior, Consortium Vietnam Vet. Svc. Providers. Roman Catholic. Home and Office: 215 Coe Rd Clarendon Hills IL 60514-1001

RYAN, HOLLY ANNE, nurse, civic worker; b. Oak Park, Ill., Dec. 25, 1945; d. Bernard Lawrence and Ethel Eleanor (Kropf) Daleske; m. Patrick Michael Ryan, Aug. 31, 1968; children: Rebecca, Brendan, Abigail, Lucas. Student, Coll. St. Teresa, 1963-65; diploma in nursing, Oak Park Hosp., 1968. R.N., Wis. Staff nurse Misericordia Hosp., Milw., 1968-69, Dean Clinic, Madison, Wis., 1969-70, Marina View Manor, Milw., 1970-76. Co-chair gen. gifts United Performing Arts Fund, Milw., 1976-77; mem. panel United Way Ozaukee County, Milw., 1978-84; pres. Cedarburg (Wis.) Presch., 1980-81; chair Citizen Rev. Bd. Milw. County, 1981-84; bd. dirs. Cedarburg Youth Ctr., 1987-92, Cedarburg Athetic Booster Club, 1994—, Applaud Cedarburg, 1992—; mem., treas. Cedarburg Sch. Dist. Bd. Edn., 1988-94; active Ctr. for Integrated Living, 1989-93; mem. Ozaukee County NAACP, 1990—. Mem. Jr. League Milw. (chair 1981-84), Cedarburg Soccer Club (sec. 1987-89). Home: 363 Huntington Dr Cedarburg WI 53012-9507

RYAN, IONE JEAN ALOHILANI, retired educator, counselor; b. Honolulu, Oct. 18, 1926; d. William Alexander and Lilia (Nainoa) Rathburn; m. Edward Parsons Ryan, June 23, 1962 (dec.); children: Ralph M., Lilia K. BEd, U. Hawaii, 1948; MS in Pub. Health, U. Minn., 1950; EdD, Stanford U., 1960. Cert. marital and family therapist, N.C. Tchr. W.R. Farrington High Sch., Honolulu, 1948; instr. to asst. prof. U. Hawaii, Honolulu, 1950-66; assoc. prof. to prof. East Carolina U., Greenville, 1966-90; prof. emerita East Carolina U., Greenville, N.C., 1990—; adv. com. Eastern Regional Tng. Program, Greenville, N.C., 1975-80; cons. Title III Grant, Lenoir Community Coll., Kinston, N.C., 1981; adult svcs. adv. com. Pitt County Mental Health, Greenville, N.C., 1976-78. Contbr. articles to profl. publs. Recipient scholarship Honolulu C. of C., 1948-50. Mem. APA.

RYAN, SISTER JANICE E., college administrator. BA in English, Trinity Coll., 1965; MEd in Spl. Edn., Boston U., 1967; postgrad., U. Minn., 1968, U. Lund, Sweden, 1971, Harvard U., 1974-76, 80. Joined Sisters of Mercy, Roman Cath. Ch., 1954. Dir. pub. relations Trinity Coll., Burlington, Vt., 1967-71, asst. prof. spl. edn., 1967-74; lobbyist Vt. Legis., 1974-79; chair spl. edn. div., pres. Trinity Coll., Burlington, Vt., 1979—; mem. Am. Council on Edn.'s Govtl. Relations Commn. on Nat. Challenges in Higher Edn.; corporator, dir. Bank of Vt., trustee Vt. Law Sch.; task force on econ. devel. infrastructure, edn. and tng. NE-Midwest Leadership Council. Exec. com. Campus Compact, chair fed. initiatives task force; active Vt. Higher Edn. Coun.; lobbyist Vt. Legislature (chmn. spl. edn. div.), 1974-79. Mem. NACIU (bd. dirs. 1990), Am. Assn. Higher Edn. (participant Spring Hill Conf. 1987), Gov.'s Econ. Coun. Office: Trinity Coll Office of the President 208 Colchester Ave Burlington VT 05401-1496

RYAN, JULIA ANN, environmental specialist, artist; b. Bartlesville, Okla., Mar. 12, 1952; d. Howard Allen and Mary Ardis (Reed) R. BA, U. Calif., Berkeley, 1975, MA, 1977, MFA, 1979; student, Las Positas, Livermore, Calif. Cert. in hazardous materials mgmt., environ. auditing. Art reference libr., dept.art U. Calif., Berkeley, 1974-75, lab. asst. depts. entomology and botany, 1975-85, pest mgmt. specialist environ. health and safety, 1985-88; lectr. Delphi U., Berkeley, 1988-89; founder Delphi U. Ch. of the Divine Man, Berkeley, 1988-89, women's counselor, 1989—; environ. specialist environ. health and safety U. Calif., Berkeley, 1988—; mem. Calif. Radioactive Materials Forum, Orangeville, 1988—; mem. Internat. Sculpture Ctr., Washington, 1979, Nat. Mus. Women in the Arts, Washington, 1993—; founder Delphi U. Ch. of Divine Man, Berkeley, 1988-89; lectr. Delphi U., 1988-89; women's counselor Ch. of Divine Man, 1989—. Author: Consideration, 1979, Talking at My Boundaries, 1979, Location/Dislocation, 1979. Sec. Peralta Neighborhood Assn., Oakland, Calif., 1994. Home: 1051 5th Ave Oakland CA 94606 Office: Environment Health & Safety University Hall 3d Fl Berkeley CA 94720

RYAN, KATHRYN E., accountant; b. Canton, Ohio, May 9, 1965; d. Herbert Ralph and Elizabeth Ann (Klein) R. B in Fin., Bowling Green State U., 1987. Accounts payable clk. Hendrickson Turner, Canton, 1988, accounts payable adminstr., 1988-89, payroll adminstr., 1989-91, Can. acct., 1991-94, cost acct., 1994—. Mem. Inst. Mgmt. Accts. (assoc. dir. pub. rels. 1993-94, dir. cert. mgmt. acct. program 1994—). Office: Hendrickson Trailer Suspension Sys 2070 Industrial Pl SE Canton OH 44707

RYAN, MARLEIGH GRAYER, Japanese language educator; b. N.Y.C., May 1, 1930; d. Harry and Betty (Hurwick) Grayer; m. Edward Ryan, June 4, 1950; 1 child, David Patrick. B.A., NYU, 1951; M.A., Columbia U., 1956, Ph.D., 1965; Cert., East Asian Inst., 1956; postgrad., Kyoto U., 1958-59. Research assoc. Columbia U., N.Y.C., 1960-61, lectr. Japanese, 1961-65, asst. prof., 1965-70, assoc. prof., 1970-72; vis. asst. prof. Yale U., New Haven, 1966-67; assoc. prof. U. Iowa, Iowa City, 1972-75, prof., 1975-81, chmn. dept., 1972-81; prof. Japanese SUNY, New Paltz, 1981—, dean liberal arts and scis., 1981-90; vice chmn. seminar on modern Japan, Columbia U., 1984-85, chmn., 1985-86; co-chmn. N.Y. State Conf. on Asian Studies, 1986, editor, 1993—, mem. exec. com., 1993-96, sec., 1993—. Co-author: (with Herschel Webb) Research in Japanese Sources, 1965; author: Japan's First Modern Novel, 1967, The Development of Realism in the Fiction of Tsubouchi Shoyo, 1975; assoc. editor: Jour. Assn. Tchrs. Japanese, 1962-71, editor, 1971-75. East Asian Inst. fellow Columbia U., 1955; Ford Found. fellow, 1958-60; Japan Found. fellow, 1973, Woodrow Wilson Ctr. Internat. Scholars fellow, 1988-89; recipient Van. Am. Disting. Book award Columbia, 1968. Mem. MLA (sec. com. on teaching Japanese Lang. 1962-68, mem. del. assembly 1979-87, mem. exec. com. div. Asian lit. 1981-86), Assn. Tchrs. Japanese (exec. com. 1969-72, 74-77), Assn. Asian Studies (bd. dirs. 1975-78, coun. of confs., 1993—), Midwest Conf. Asian Studies (pres. 1980-81). Office: SUNY Ft # 414 New Paltz NY 12561

RYAN, MARY A., diplomat; b. New York, N.Y., Oct. 1, 1940. B.A., St. John's Univ., 1963, M.A., 1965. With Foreign Service, Dept. of State, 1966—; consular and adminstrv. officer Naples, Italy, 1966-69; personnel officer Am. Embassy, Tegucigalpa, Honduras, 1970-71; consular officer Am. Consulate Gen., Monterrey, Mexico, 1971-73; adminstrv. officer Bur. of African Affairs, Dept. of State, Washington, 1973-75, post mgmt. officer, 1975-77; career devel. officer Bur. of Personnel, Dept. of State, 1977-80; adminstrv. counselor Abidjan, Ivory Coast, 1980-81, Khartoum, Sudan, 1981-82; inspector, Office of Insp. Gen. Dept. of State, Washington, 1982-83, exec. dir. Bur. of European and Can. Affairs, 1983-85, exec. asst. to Under Sec. of State for Mgmt., 1985-88; ambassador to Swaziland, 1988-90; dep. asst. sec. Bur. of Consular Affairs, Washington, 1990; dir. Kuwait task force, 1990-91, ops. dir. UN spl. commn. on elimination of Iraqi weapons, 1991; dep. asst. sec. Bur. European & Can. Affairs, Washington, 1991-93; asst. sec. Bur. of Consular Affairs, Washington, 1993—. Office: Dept State Bureau of Consular Affairs 2201 C St NW Washington DC 20520

RYAN, MARY CATHERINE, pediatrician; b. N.Y.C., Mar. 22, 1938; d. Thomas Michael and Catherine (Scullin) McLaughlin; m. Enda Kieran Ryan, Feb. 8, 1969; children: Denise Marie, Kathleen May. BS in Chemistry, St. John's U., Bklyn., 1959; MD, NYU, 1963. Diplomate Am. Bd. Pediatrics. Cons. Hampton health dept. Va. State Dept. Health, 1969-71; med. coord. N.Y.C. Bur. Handicapped, 1971-72; asst. prof. pediatrics L.I. Hosp., Bklyn., 1972-73; pub. health clinician Fairfax County Health Dept., Fairfax, Va., 1973—; pvt. contractor pediatrics PHP Healthcare Corp., Fairfax, 1987-93. Tchr. religious edn. St. Thomas al Becket Ch.,

Reston, Va., 1978-81. Maj. M.C., U.S. Army, 1969. Fellow Am. Acad. Pediatrics; mem. AMA, Med. Soc. Va., No. Va. Pediatric Soc., Fairfax County Med. Soc., Soc. Devel. Pediatrics. Home: 1423 Aldenbam Ln Reston VA 22090 Office: Fairfax County Health Dept 1850 Cameron Glen Dr Ste 100 Reston VA 22090

RYAN, MARY NELL H., training consultant; b. Milw., Oct. 17, 1956; d. Robert Healey and Elizabeth Anne (Schulte) R. BA, Marquette U., 1979; MS, U. Wis., Milw., 1991. Tchr. St. Francis Borgia Sch., Cedarburg, Wis., 1979-81; dir. pub. rels. Aerobics West Club, N.Y.C., 1981; unit head, team leader Northwestern Mut. Life Ins. Co., Milw., 1982-84, asst. supr., 1984-86, tng. coord., 1986-87, mgr. tng., 1987-92; tng. cons. for ins. industry Workplace Learning, Inc., Milw., 1992—; cons. Aetna Life and Casualty Co., Hartford, Conn., 1988, Robertson-Ryan & Co., Milw., 1989, Blue Cross/Blue Shield United of Wis., Northwestern Mut. Life Ins. Co., CMI Group, Inc., Homes for Ind. Living, Inc., Aurora Health Care, Literacy Svcs. Wis., Executrain, Inc., Milw. First in Quality, Wis. Quality Network, United Wis. Svcs., Inc., Ameritech, Milw. Art Mus., Blood Ctr. Southeastern Wis., Meretz, Inc., Radiology Assocs. Wis., Deluxe Data, Inc., Portable Solutions, Inc., Hewlett-Packard Users Group of Wis.; guest lectr. U. Wis., Milw., 1989, Milw. Area Tech. Coll., 1990, Marquette U., 1990; speaker confs., devloper/trainer workshops. Mem. exec. com. Lakefront Festival Arts, Milw., 1985—, vol. com. chair, silent auction chair; exec. fundraiser United Performing Arts Fund, Milw., 1986; com. chmn. Jr. League Milw., 1983-87; fundraiser YMCA Ptnr. Youth, Milw. 1987-88; tutorHead Start Read with Me program, 1993—. Recipient gold medal Life Communicators Assn., 1987. Mem. ASTD (bd. dirs. Wis. chpt., membership com. 1989-90, chmn. Train Am.'s Workforce and community svcs. 1992-94), Milw. Mgmt. Support Orgn. (bd. dirs. 1988), Wis. Ins. Club (speaker), InRoads (bd. dirs. Wis. chpt.). Office: Workplace Learning Inc 1426 W Westport Cir Mequon WI 53092-5753

RYAN, MEG, actress; b. Fairfield, Conn., Nov. 19, 1961; m. Dennis Quaid, 1991; 1 child, Jack Henry. Student, NYU. Appearences include (TV) One of the Boys, 1982, As The World Turns, 1982-84, Wild Side, 1985, (films) Rich and Famous, 1981, Amityville 3-D, 1983, Top Gun, 1986, Armed and Dangerous, 1986, Innerspace, 1987, Promised Land, 1987, D.O.A., 1988, The Presidio, 1988, When Harry Met Sally, 1989, Joe Versus the Volcano, 1990, The Doors, 1991, Prelude to a Kiss, 1992, Sleepless in Seattle, 1993, Flesh and Bone, 1993, When a Man Loves a Woman, 1994, Restoration, 1994, I.Q., 1994. Recipient Golden Apple award Hollywood Women's Press Club, 1989. *

RYAN, SHEILA BARBARA, legal secretary; b. Long Branch, N.J., Aug. 15, 1956; d. William Wallace and Mary Barbara (Grager) Ryan; m. John D. Jones, Sept. 23, 1994. Grad., Asbury Park H.S. Legal sec. Law Offices Philip G. Auerbach, Red Bank, N.J., 1976—. Recipient Berkeley Bus. award Berkeley Sch. Bus., 1973. Office: Law Offices of Philip & Auerbach 231 Maple Ave Red Bank NJ 07701

RYAN, SUZANNE IRENE, nursing educator; b. Yonkers, N.Y., Mar. 13, 1939; d. Edward Vincent and Winifred E. (Goemann) R. BA in Biology, Mt. St. Agnes Coll., Balt., 1962; BSN, Columbia U., 1967, MA in Nursing Svc., 1973, MEd in Nursing Edn., 1975; MS in Oncology, San Jose (Calif.) State Coll. U., 1982. RN, N.Y.; cert. AIDS educator, N.Y. Prof. nursing Molloy Coll., Rockville Centre, N.Y., 1970—, co-dir. health svcs., dir. ednl. programs, 1987-94, dir. health svcs., 1994—, health educator, 1992—, co-dir. mobile health van, adminstr. health edn., 1992—; pres., CEO SIR Enterprises, Inc., 1982—; photographer Molloy Coll. Pubs., 1991—; photographic dir. Bale Art, N.H., 1992—; mem. N.Y. State AIDS Coun., 1987—, L.I. Alcohol Consortium, 1987—; educator Nassau County Dept. Sr. Citizens Health, 1991—; photographer-in-residence Molloy Coll., 1992—; lectr. on landscape, wildlife and flower photography, L.I., N.H., Can., 1993—. Represented in permanent collections in photographic galleries in Carmel, Calif., Laconia, Wolfboro and Moultonboro, N.H., 1963—; photographer 4 books on Monterey Peninulsa, New Eng. and N.H.; writer, editor Health News Letter Molloy Coll., 1990—. Health educator Nassau County Dept. of Sr. Citizens Outreach Program, Molloy Coll., AIDS educator, 1991—; adminstr., chief AIDS counselor Interaction AIDS Counseling, Babylon, N.Y., 1992. USPHS fellow, 1962, Nat. Cancer Inst. fellow, 1981-82. Mem. AAUP, AAUW, Nat. Congress Oncology Nurses, N.Y. State Fedn. Health Educators, Inc., Nurses Assn. Counties L.I. Dist. 14, N.Y. State Nurses Assn., World Wildlife Orgn., Audubon Soc., Internat. Ctr. Photography, Nature Conservancy, Sierra Club, Sigma Theta Tau (Epsilon Kappa chpt., rsch. grantee 1985, 87). Roman Catholic. Home: 16 Walker St Malverne NY 11565-1829

RYAN, TERESA WEAVER, obstetrical nurse; b. Dallas, July 18, 1956; d. J.E. and Mary (Davis) Weaver; m. Patrick Hallaron Ryan, Apr. 7, 1991. BS, Troy State U., 1983; BSN, Tex. Christian U., 1987; MSN, U. South Ala., 1994. RN; cert. maternal newborn nurse. Intelligence analyst USN, Dallas, 1983-87; enlisted USAF, 1987, advanced through grades to capt. (obstetrical nurse), 1987—; childbirth educator USAF, 1988—. Mem. NOW, Assn. Women's Health, Obstetrical and Neonatal Nurses, Nat. Humane Soc. Educators, People for the Ethical Treatment of Animals, Sigma Theta Tau (sec. 1987—, rsch. grant 1987). Roman Catholic. Home: 101 Hampton Ct W Niceville FL 32578-3935

RYAN, THERESA ANN JULIA, accountant; b. N.Y.C., Mar. 1, 1962; d. John Patrick and Diane Elizabeth (Duggan) R. BA in Math. and Econs., Fordham U., 1984, MBA in Profl. Acctg., 1989. CPA, N.Y. With sales dept. Abraham & Straus, White Plains, N.Y., 1980-84; adminstrv. asst. Companion of N.Y., Rye, 1984-86, asst. fin. analyst, 1986-87; with tech. ctr. Fordham U., N.Y.C., 1987-88; staff acct. Konigsberg Wolf & Co., N.Y.C., 1989-91; sr. audit assoc. Coopers & Lybrand, L.L.P., N.Y.C., 1992—. Mem. Beta Gamma Sigma. Republican. Roman Catholic. Home: 5 Clare Ter Yonkers NY 10707-3201 Office: Coopers & Lybrand 1301 Avenue Of The Americas New York NY 10019-6053

RYBERG, BETTY ANN, process engineer, lawyer; b. West Palm Beach, Fla., July 27, 1963. BChemE, Auburn U., 1984; JD, Quinnipiac Coll., 1994. Process engr. Minn. Mining & Mfg., Decatur, Ala., 1984-87; program mgr. Pitney Bowes, Stamford, Conn., 1987—. Patentee in field. Mem. IEEE (chair edn. 1993-94, program com. 1993—), Am. Electronics Assn. (DFE task force 1991-93), Am. Chem. Soc., Soc. Plastics Engrs., Soc. Environ. Toxicology & Chemistry, Omega Chi Epsilon. Office: Pitney Bowes Inc MS 63-65 1 Elmcroft Rd Stamford CT 06926

RYCOMBEL, JUDITH THERESA, librarian, information specialist, consultant; b. Chgo., Mar. 13, 1947; d. Edward Titus and Theresa Rita (Karac) Labash; m. John I. Rycombel, June 18, 1977. MusB, De Paul U., 1969; MLS, Rosary Coll., 1978. Tchr. music Komarek Schs., North Riverside, Ill., 1969-71; circulation and ref. asst. libr. De Paul U., Chgo., 1971-77, ref. libr., 1977-85, head ref. libr., 1985-93; info. specialist Motorola, Schaumburg, Ill., 1993—; cons. Am. Assn. Individual Investors, Chgo., 1984; mem. libr. bd. Probus Pub., Chgo., 1993—. Literacy vol. High Sch. Dist. 214, Arlington Heights, Ill., 1993—. Mem. Spl. Librs. Assn. Lutheran. Office: Motorola 1303 E Algonquin Rd Schaumburg IL 60196

RYDELL, CLAIRE JEAN, photographer; b. Long Beach, Calif., Mar. 3, 1955; d. Donald Russell and Gloria Marie (Sasso) R.; m. Paul Vincent Reale, Dec. 16, 1989. AA, L.A. Pierce Coll., 1984; BA, UCLA, 1977; MA, Calif. State U., Northridge, 1981. Freelance photographer UCLA Ethnomusicology, 1986-87, Interpress Agy., Quebec, Can., 1988-89, World Book Encyclopedia, Chgo., 1988, Delta Sky, Am. West, 1989-92, L'Express Mag., Paris, 1992, Corel Corp., Toronto, Can., 1993-95. One woman shows include L.A. Photography Ctr., 1984, El Camino Coll., 1987, Union Gallery, Tucson, 1990, White Gallery, Portland, Oreg., 1990, L.A. Mcpl. Galleries, 1991, Rotunda Gallery, Tucson, 1994, Casa de la Cultura Oaxaca, Mexico City, 1994; exhibited in group shows at William Grant Still Art Ctr., 1986, 89, Cleve. Photog. Workshop, 1990, Larson Gallery, Yakima, Wash., 1994, Rachele Lozzi Gallery, L.A., 1994. Music dir. Sherman Oaks Meth. Ch., 1979-94, 1st Luth. Ch. Northridge, 1995—; photographer Free Arts for Abused Children, L.A., 1993—. Mem. Nat. Press Photographers Assn., Women in Photography. Home: 22125 Gault St Canoga Park CA 91303-1806

RYDER, GEORGIA ATKINS, university dean, educator; b. Newport News, Va., Jan. 30, 1924; d. Benjamin Franklin and Mary Lou (Carter) Atkins; m. Noah Francis Ryder, Sept. 16, 1947; children: Olive Diana, Malcolm Eliot, Aleta Renee. B.S., Hampton (Va.) Inst., 1944; Mus.M., U. Mich., 1946; Ph.D., NYU, 1970. Resource music tchr., Alexandria, Va., 1945-48; faculty music dept. Norfolk State U., 1948—, prof., 1970—, head dept., 1969-79, dean Sch. Arts and Letters, 1979-86. Contbr. articles to profl. jours, contbr. chpts. to books. Trustee Va. Symphony, Va. Wesleyan Coll.; bd. dirs. Black Music Rsch. Ctr., Columbia Coll., Chgo., Nat. Assn. Negro Musicians, Southeastern Va. Arts Assn.; mem. advisory com. Norfolk chpt. Young Audiences, Va. Coalition for Mus. Edn., Gordon Inst. Music Learning, Temple U. Grantee So. Fellowship Fund, 1967-69, Consortium Rsch. Tng., 1973; recipient Norfolk Com. Improvement Edn. award, 1974, People's Acad. of Arts award, 1985, City of Norfolk award, 1989, Nat. Assn. Negro Musicians award, 1989, Nat. Conf. Christians and Jews award, 1990, Va. Laureate in Music award, 1992, Cultural Alliance award Greater Hampton Roads, 1992, Disting Alumni award Hampton U., 1993, Norfolk State U. Alumni. award, 1994. Mem. Music Educators Nat. Conf., Coll. Music Soc., Intercoll. Music Assn., Va. Music Educators Assn., Delta Sigma Theta.

RYDER, LOIS IRENE, artist; b. Pittsfield, Mass., Dec. 5, 1932; d. George Iver and Marion Irene (Allen) Kisselbrock; married, Jan. 19, 1952; children: Sharon, Karen, Charlene, Shawn, Scott. instr. Westenhook Art Gallery, 1983. Exhibited in group shows at Redwood Arts, Gualala, Calif., Allentown Arts Festival, Buffalo, Trinity Ch., Lime Rock, Conn., Art in the Yard, Norman Rockwell Mus., Stockbridge, Mass., Crafts Expo, Hartford (Conn.) Civic Ctr., Marietta (Ga.) Mus. Art, Valley Forge (Pa.) Conv. Ctr., Kent (Conn.) Art Assn., Berkshire Mus., Pittsfield, Mass., Albany (N.Y.) Profl. Crafts, New Eng. Profl. Show, Northampton, Mass., St. Timothy's Ch., West Hartford, Conn., Welles Gallery, Lenox, Mass., others. Active Sheffield (Mass.) Art League, 1973-91, chair juried art show, 1982-83, chair country arts and crafts show, 1984-86, chair art league membership show, 1991, mem. adv. bd., 1991, chair scholarship com., 1987-88, Pittsfield Art League, 1976—, com. bd. mem. league coop., 1991, Springfield Art League, 1981-91, Kent Art Assn., 1986—, bd. dirs., active artist status, v.p. Copley Soc., Boston, 1992—. Recipient Award for Excellence, Sheffield Art League (2) 1987, (2) 1989, First pl. award in grapics, 1988, Best in Fine Arts award Westfest, 1990, Art award Sheffield Art League, 1993, Cert. of Merit, Kent Art Assn., 1993, Graphics award Sheffield Art League, 1993, Graphics award Kent Art Assn., 1993, First in Oil award Pittsfield Art League, 1994. Mem. Nat. Mus. Women in Arts (charter), Acad. Artists Assn., Miniature Art Soc. Mont., Miniature Art Soc. Fla., Miniature art Soc. N.J., Miniature Art Soc., Miniature Painters, Sculptors and Gravers Soc. of Washington. Republican. Home and Studio: Creative Artworks Star Rte 62 Box 35A Great Barrington MA 01230-8405

RYDER, WINONA (WINONA LAURA HOROWITZ), actress; b. Winona, Minn., Oct. 29, 1971; d. Michael and Cynthia (Istas) Horowitz. Films include: Lucas, 1986, Square Dance, 1987, 1969, 1988, Beetlejuice, 1988, Great Balls of Fire, 1989, Heathers, 1989, Edward Scissorhands, 1990, Mermaids, 1990, Welcome Home, Roxy Carmichael, 1990, Night On Earth, 1992, Bram Stoker's Dracula, 1992, Age of Innocence, 1993 (Golden Globe for Best Supporting Actress, 1994, Academy award nominee, Best Supporting Actress, 1993), The House of the Spirits, 1994, Reality Bites, 1994, Little Women, 1994 (Acad. Awd. nom., Best Actress). Office: CAA 9830 Wilshire Blvd Beverly Hills CA 90212*

RYLANT, CYNTHIA, author; b. Hopewell, Va., June 6, 1954; d. John Tune and Leatrel (Rylant) Smith; 1 child, Nathaniel. BA, Morris Harvey Coll., 1975; MA, Marshall U., 1976; MLS, Kent State U., 1982. English instr. Marshall U., Huntington, W.Va., 1979-80, U. Akron, Ohio, 1983-84; children's libr. Akron (Ohio) Pub. Libr., 1983; part-time lectr. Northeast Ohio Univs. Coll. Medicine, Rootstown, Ohio, 1991—. Author: (picture books) When I Was Young in the Mountains, 1982 (Caldecott Honor book 1983, English Speaking Union Book-Across-the-Sea Amb. of Honor award 1984, Am. Book award nomination 1983), Miss Maggie, 1983, This Year's Garden, 1984, The Relatives Came, 1985 (Horn Book Honor book 1985, Children's Book of Yr. Child Study Assn. Am. 1985, Caldecott Honor Book 1986), Night in the Country, 1986, Birthday Presents, 1987, All I See, 1988, Mr. Grigg's Work, 1989, An Angel for Solomon Singer, 1992, The Everyday Town, 1993, The Everyday School, 1993, The Everyday House, 1993, The Everyday Garden, 1993, The Everyday Children, 1993, The Everyday Pets, 1993, Mr. Putter and Tabby Pour the Tea, 1994, Mr. Putter and Tabby Walk the Dog, 1994, The Old Woman Who Named Things, 1994, The Blue Hill Meadows and the Much Loved Dog, 1994, Gooseberry Park, 1995; (Henry and Mudge series) Henry and Mudge: The First Book of Their Adventures, 1987, Henry and Mudge in Puddle Trouble, 1987, Henry and Mudge in the Green Time, 1987, Henry and Mudge Under the Yellow Moon, 1987, Henry and Mudge in the Sparkle Days, 1988, Henry and Mudge and the Forever Sea, 1989, Henry and Mudge Get the Cold Shivers, 1989, Henry and Mudge and the Happy Cat, 1990, Henry and Mudge and the Bedtime Thumps, 1991, Henry and Mudge Take the Big Test, 1991, Henry and Mudge and the Long Weekend, 1992, Henry and Mudge and the Wild Wind, 1993, Henry and Mudge and the Careful Cousin, 1994, Henry and Mudge and the Best Day Ever, 1995; (poetry) Waiting to Waltz ... a Childhood, 1984 (Nat. Coun. for Social Studies Best Book 1984), Soda Jerk, 1990, Something Permanent, 1994; (novels) A Blue-Eyed Daisy, 1985 (Children's Book of Yr. Child Study Assn. Am. 1985), A Fine White Dust, 1986 (Newbery Honor Book 1987), A Kindness, 1988; (stories) Every Living Thing, 1985, Children of Christmas: Stories for the Season, 1987, A Couple of Kooks: And Other Stories About Love, 1990; (autobiography) But I'll Be Back Again: An Album, 1989, Best Wishes, 1992; (other) Appalachia: The Voices of Sleeping Birds, 1991 (Boston Globe/Horn Book Honor book for nonfiction 1991), Missing May, 1992 (John Newbery medal 1992), I Have Seen Castles, 1993, The Dreamer, 1993. Office: PO Box 368 Kent OH 44240*

RYMER, PAMELA ANN, federal judge; b. Knoxville, Tenn., Jan. 6, 1941. AB, Vassar Coll., 1961; LLB, Stanford U., 1964; LLD (hon.), Pepperdine U., 1988. Bar: Calif. 1966, U.S. Ct. Appeals (9th cir.) 1966, U.S. Ct. Appeals (10th cir.), U.S. Supreme Ct. V.p. Rus Walton & Assoc., Los Altos, Calif., 1965-66; Assoc. Lillick McHose & Charles, L.A., 1966-72, ptnr., 1973-75; ptnr. Toy and Rymer, L.A., 1975-83; judge U.S. Dist. Ct. (cen. dist.) Calif., L.A., 1983-89, U.S. Ct. Appeals (9th cir.), L.A., 1989—; faculty The Nat. Jud. Coll., 1986-88; mem. com. summer ednl. programs Fed. Jud. Ctr., 1987-88; chair exec. com. 9th Cir. Jud. Conf., 1990; mem. com. criminal law Jud. Conf. U.S., 1988-93, Ad Hoc com. gender-based violence, 1991-94, fed.-state jurisdiction com., 1993—. Mem. editorial bd. The Judges' jour., 1989-91; contbr. articles to profl. jours. and newsletters. Mem. Calif. Post-secondary Edn. Commn., 1974—, chmn., 1980-84; mem. L.A. Olympic Citizens Adv. Commn.; bd. visitors Stanford U. Law Sch., 1986—, chair, 1993-94, exec. com. Pepperdine U. Law Sch., 1987—; mem. Edn. Commn. of States Task Force on State Policy and Ind. Higher Edn., 1987; bd. dirs. Constl. Rights Found., 1985; Judicial Conf. U.S. Com. Federal-State Jurisdiction, 1993, Com. Criminal Law, 1988-93, ad hoc comm. gender based violence, 1991—; chair exec. com. 9th cir. judicial conf., 1990-94. Recipient Outstanding Trial Jurist award L.A. County Bar Assn., 1988. Mem. ABA (task force on civil justice reform 1991—), State Bar Calif. (antitrust and trade regulation sect., exec. com. 1990-92), L.A. County Bar Assn. (chmn. antitrust sect. 1981-82), Assn. of Bus. Trial Lawyers (bd. govs. 1990-92), Stanford Alumni Assn., Stanford Law Soc. Soc. Calif., Vassar Club So. Calif. (past pres.). Office: US Ct Appeals 9th Cir Ste 600 125 S Grand Ave Pasadena CA 91105-1652

RYMER, THÉRÈSE ELIZABETH, family practice nurse practitioner; b. New London, Conn., Dec. 5, 1947; d. Kenneth Frank and Ursula Kathleen (O'Reilly) Gmeiner; m. Timothy Charles Rymer, Dec. 29, 1973; children: Gerard, Andrew, Deirdre. Diploma, St. Joseph's Coll. Nursing, 1969; cert. nurse practitioner, U. Calif., San Diego, 1976, cert. occupational health nurse, 1990. RN, Calif.; cert. Am. Bd. Occupational Health Nurses. Staff nurse ICU Marin Gen. Hosp., San Rafael, Calif., 1969-70, Pacific Med. Ctr., San Francisco, 1970-71; staff nurse, charge nurse Mercy Hosp., San Diego, 1972-75; family practice nurse practitioner U. Calif. San Diego Med. Ctr., 1976-83, employee health nurse, coord., then dir. employee health, 1983-91; dir. clin. svc. U. Calif. San Diego Ctr. Occupational and Environ. Medicine, 1991—; Exec. steering com., mem. med. planning bd. St. Vincent de Paul/Joan Kroc Med. Clinic, San Diego. Mem. editorial bd. Jour. Hosp. Occupational Health, 1993—; contbr. articles to profl. jours. Mem. disaster med. assistance team Nat. Disaster Med. System. Mem. Calif. State Assn. Occupational Health Nurses (bd. dirs. 1992-94, membership chair San Diego chpt. 1991-92), Assn. Hosp. Employee Health Profls. (pres. San Diego chpt. 1988-89). Roman Catholic. Office: U Calif San Diego Ctr Occupational & Environ Med 3500 5th Ave Ste 102 San Diego CA 92103-5020

RYNEAR, NINA COX, retired registered nurse, author, artist; b. Cochranville, Pa., July 11, 1916; d. Fredrick Allen and Nina Natalie (Drane) Cox; m. Charles Spencer Rynear, Aug. 22, 1934 (dec. May 1941); children: Charles Joseph, Stanley Spencer. RN, Coatesville Hosp. Sch. Nursing, 1945; BS in Nursing Edn., U. Pa., 1954. Interviewer Nat. Opinion Rsch. Ctr., U. Denver, Colo., 1942-47; sch. nurse West Goshen Elem. Sch., West Chester, Pa., 1946-47; pub. health nurse Pa. Dept. Health Bur. Pub. Health Nursing, Harrisburg, 1947-51; staff nurse V.A. Hosp., Coatesville, Pa., 1951-54; staff nurse, asst. head nurse V.A. Hosp., Menlo Park, Calif., 1954-56; asst. chief nursing svc. Palo Alto and Menlo Park VA Hosps., Palo Alto, Menlo Park, Calif., 1956-76; self employed Reno, Nev., 1976—. Author: (poems, musical compositions) Old Glory and the U.S.A., 1989, Mister Snowman, 1988, Dawn Shadow of Lenape, 1988, (poem and song compilation) This Side of Forever, 1990; (musical compositions) Blessed Are Those Who Listen, What Can I Leave, The Hobo's Promise; contbr. sonnets to Newsletter of N.Am. Acad. Esoteric Studies; monthly contbr. N.Am. Acad. Esoteric Studies; paintings represented in numerous pvt. collections. Pres. Chester County Pub. Health Nurses Assn., 1950. Staff nurse Cadet Corps, 1944-45. Mem. VFW Aux. (patriotic instr. 1989-90, chmn. safety div. Silver State #3396 chpt. 1990-91), New Century Rebekah Lodge #244. Methodist. Home and Office: 7655 Hillview Dr Reno NV 89506-8670

RYPCZYK, CANDICE LEIGH, employee relations executive; b. Norman, Okla., Apr. 24, 1949; d. John Anthony and Lee (Brunswick) Wirth; m. Peter Charles Rypczyk, Nov. 27, 1976. BA, Kalamazoo Coll., 1971; cert. labor studies extension program, Cornell U., N.Y. Sch. Indsl., Labor Relations, Middletown, 1985. Personnel asst. PFW divsn. Hercules Inc., Middletown, N.Y., 1973-77, asst. personnel mgr., 1977-79, mgr. employee relations, 1979-92; mgr. human resources Huck Internat., Kingston, N.Y., 1992—. Mem. Am. Soc. for Pers. Adminstrn. (v.p. Mid-Hudson Valley chpt. 1985, pres. 1986, treas. N.Y. State coun. 1986, dist. bd. dirs. 1988-90, cert.), Orange County C. of C. (Vol. of the Yr. 1986, program com., treas., exec. com.). Office: Huck Internat 85 Grand St Kingston NY 12401

RYSDAHL, DOLORES MAE, psychologist; b. Faribault, Minn., Apr. 18, 1929; d. Albert Otto and Ruby Mae (Jones) Spitzack; m. Alton Cyrus Rysdahl, May 9, 1929; children: Renee, Dennis, Ellen, Diane, Paul, Joyce, Wayne. BA, S.W. State U., Marshall, Minn., 1971; MS, S.D. State U., 1989. Lic. psychologist, Minn. Founder, ptnr. Decor Designs, Inc., Madison, Minn., 1972—; area dir. S.W. Minn. Pvt. Industry Coun., Marshall, 1985-87; counselor S.W. State U., Marshall, 1989, Psychol. Resources, Marshall, 1989-90; psychologist, interim dir. Western Humen Devel. Ctr., Marshall, 1990—. Bd. dirs., chair S.W. State U. Found., Marshall, 1976-82, S.W. Minn. Pvt. Ind. Coun., Marshall, 1983-84. Mem. ACA, Am. Mental Health Counselors Assn. Republican. Lutheran. Home: RR 2 Box 108 Clarkfield MN 56223 Office: Western Human Devel Ctr 1106 E College Marshall MN 56258

RYSER, PAMELA HORTON, small business owner; b. Grove Hill, Ala., June 13, 1952; d. Glover Wade and Gwendolyn (Finch) Horton; m. William Edward Ryser; children: William Joseph, Edward Wade. Student, Ala. So. Coll. Cert. accomplishment H&R Block. Head teller Merchants Bank, Jackson, Ala., 1972-79; sec., bookkeeper McLain Constrn. Co., Jackson, 1978-80, Melton DuBose, P.A., Jackson, 1982-84; pres., owner McLain Hardware, Inc., Jackson, 1984—. Den leader Cub Scouts Am., Jackson, 1988-89; Sunday Sch. tchr. Goodsprings Bapt. Ch. Mem. NAFE, Jackson C. of C. (vice chair Christmas Parade 1993, chair 1994), Downtown Merchants Assn., Phi Theta Kappa. Home: Rte 1 Box 52-F Jackson AL 36545 Office: McLain Hardware Inc 108 Carrol St Jackson AL 36545

RZEWNICKI, JANET C., state official; b. Akron, Ohio, May 21, 1953; d. Robert Myers; m. Victor Rzewnicki, June 3, 1972. B.S. in Acctg. and Fin. with distinction, U. Del. CPA. Sr. acct. KPMG Peat Marwick, Wilmington, Del., 1978-80; corp. acct. internat. sect. Hercules Inc., Wilmington, 1980-81; acctg. instr. U. Del., Newark, 1980-82; pvt. practice acctg., Wilmington, 1981-82; state treas. State of Del., Dover, 1983—; mem. Del. Econ. Adv. Coun. Leader People to People Del., People's Republic of China, 1985; treas., bd. dirs. March of Dimes, Newark, 1979—; bd. dirs. United Way of Del., Wilmington, 1980-82; active Gov.'s Coun. on Devel. Fin., 1982—. Mem. Nat. Assn. State Treas., AICPA, Del. Soc. CPAs, Pa. Inst. CPAs, Am. Soc. Women Accts. (bd. dirs. 1981), Beta Gamma Sigma. Republican. Office: Office of State Treas Thomas Collins Bldg PO Box 1401 Dover DE 19903-1401

SAAB, DEANNE KELTUM, real estate appraiser, broker; b. Allentown, Pa., Jan. 27, 1945; d. James A. and Agnes G. (Hanzlik) S. BA, Cedar Crest Coll., 1966; MS, U. Calif., Santa Barbara, 1973; realtors cert., Pa. State U., 1978. Cert. appraiser, Pa.; state accredited affiliate Appraisal Inst. Tchr. Ojai (Calif.) Unified Sch. Dist., 1966-74; pvt. practice Allentown, Pa., 1978—; pres./treas. DeAnne & Assoc., Inc., Allentown, Pa., 1987—; owner Heritage Gardens, Allentown, Pa., 1981—. Mem. AAUW (various offices), Nat. Assn. Realtors, Pa. Assn. Realtors, Allentown Lehigh County Bd. Realtors (various offices), Cedar Crest Coll. Alumnae Assn. (various offices), Lehigh Valley Guild Craftsmen (various offices). Home and Office: 1360 Dorney Ave Allentown PA 18103-9731

SAAR, MARY-EM CORNISH, banker; b. Newark, Dec. 11, 1944; d. Paul Cowles and Bertice Mary (Andrews) Cornish; m. Fredrick A. Saar, Sept. 10, 1995. BA, U. Vt., 1967; postgrad., Union Theol. Sem., 1967-68, Ga. State U., 1977-79. Personal banker Security Savs. and Loan, Milw., 1979-81; ops. officer, product mgr. 1st Interstate Bank Utah, Salt Lake City, 1982-89; asst. v.p., mgr. 1st Interstate Bank, Ltd., L.A., 1989-91; asst. v.p., project leader mgmt. svcs. group 1st Interstate Bank, Portland, Oreg., 1991—. Office: 1st Interstate Bank 1300 SW 5th Ave # T9 Portland OR 97201-5616

SAARI, JOY A., geriatrics and medical/surgical nurse; b. Chippewa Falls, Wis., July 14, 1953; d. Harry R. and Hilda R. (Christianson) Harwood; m. Allan A. Saari, Dec. 31, 1973 (dec.); children: Christopher, Erik. BSN summa cum laude, U. Wis., Eau Claire, 1978; postgrad., Blue Ridge Community Coll., Verona, Va., 1987, George Mason U., 1993-95. RN, Mich., Wis., Va.; cert. BLS instr., ACLS. Staff nurse Portage View Hosp., Hancock, Mich., 1979-80; evening supr., asst. dir. nursing Chippewa Manor, Chippewa Falls, 1980-86; staff nurse Bridgewater (Va.) Home, Inc., 1986-90; p.m. charge nurse Medicalodge Leavenworth, Kans., 1990-91; outdoor edn. nurse Montgomery County Med. Schs., 1991-93. Capt. USAR Nurse Corps. Mem. Nat. League of Nursing, No. Va. Nurse Practitioner Assn., Res. Officer Assn., Am. Legion Aux., Phi Kappa Phi.

SAARI, KATHRYN CELESTE, public health nurse; b. Chgo., Sept. 3, 1948; d. H. Thaine and Margaret F. (Sauntry) Lyman; m. Charles T. Saari, Feb. 2, 1974; children: Matthew, Julia. BS in Nursing, Coll. St. Teresa, Winona, Minn., 1970. RN, Minn.; cert. pub. health nurse. Asst. head nurse St. Mary's Hosp., Rochester, Minn., 1970-73; instr. Coll. St. Teresa, Winona, 1973-74, St. Cloud (Minn.) Hosp. Sch. Nursing, 1974-76; staff nurse St. Cloud Hosp., 1976-78; instr. Minn. Area Vocat. Tech. Inst. System, St. Cloud, Alexandria, 1974-80; charge nurse Long Prairie (Minn.) Meml. Hosp., 1980-86; pub. health nurse Polk County Nursing Svc., Crookston, Minn., 1986-94, Cen. for American Indian Resources, 1994—; mem. Minn. Perinatal Guidelines Task Force, Mpls., 1988-90; dir. Improved Pregnancy Outcome Program, Crookston, Minn., 1986-94; sexuality educator, workshop presenter, 1986—; mem. adv. bd. dirs. Early Childhood Family Edn.; mem. Polk County Child Protection Team, Family Resource Group; coord. Ptnrs. in Parenting; mem. Polk County HIV Task Force; co-founded Polk County Alliance for Youth and Families, 1991-94. Chmn. Cathedral Sch. Bd., Crookston, 1987-90; mem. Diocesan Sch. Bd., Crookston, 1988-90, Jr. High Action Bd., Crookston, 1988-90, 91-94, Sr. High Action Bd., 1990-94; co-chmn. Nurses Fun Night Scholarship, Crookston, 1989-90; cert. nurse ARC; mem. Diocesan Respect Life Commn., 1987-90, Diocesan Sexuality Task Force; mem. adv. com. March Dimes Health Profl., 1992-94. Named Nurse of Yr., Polk County Nursing Svc., 1993. Mem. Minn. Perinatal Orgn., Parents Active in Cath. Edn., Minn. Pub. Health Assn. Roman Catholic. Home: 1702 Fern Ave Duluth MN 55811-2107 Office: Ctr for Am Indian Resources 211 W 4th St Duluth MN 55806

SABA, BETTYE MILLER, librarian; b. Evansville, Ind., Oct. 3, 1917; d. James Monroe and Helene Wilhelmina (Thiele) Miller; m. Ralph Francis Saba, Jan. 17, 1976. AB, U. Evansville, 1939; BLS, Simmons Coll., 1947; MLS, Ind. U., 1962. Cert. libr., Ind. Children's libr. Evansville (Ind.) Pub. Libr., 1939-44, order libr., 1946, east br. libr., 1947-69, adult program supr., 1969-72; head libr. Willard Libr., Evansville, 1972-75; ret. Adv. mem. Evansville Arts and Edn. Coun., 1969. Petty officer USN, 1944-46. Mem. ALA (life), AAUW (life), Ind. Libr. Assn. (life). Home: 19 Dreier Blvd Evansville IN 47712-5034

SABANAS-WELLS, ALVINA OLGA, orthopedic surgeon; b. Riga, Latvia, Lithuania, July 30, 1914; d. Adomas and Olga (Dagilyte) Pipyne; m. Juozas Sabanas, Aug. 20, 1939 (dec. Mar. 1968); 1 child, Algis (dec.); m. Alfonse F. Wells, Dec. 31, 1977 (dec. 1990). MD, U. Vytautas The Great, Kaunas, Lithuania, 1939; MS in Orthopaedic Surgery, U. Minn., 1955. Diplomate Am. Bd. Orthopaedic Surgery. Intern Univ. Clinics, Kaunas, 1939-40; resident orthopaedic surgery and trauma Red Cross Trauma Hosp., Kaunas, 1940-44; orthopaedic and trauma fellow Unfall Krankenhous, Vienna, Austria, 1943-44; intern Jackson Park Hosp., Chgo., 1947-48; fellow in orthopaedic surgery Mayo Clinic, Rochester, Minn., 1952-55; assoc. orthopaedic surgery Northwestern U., 1956-72; asst. prof. orthopaedic surgery Rush Med. Sch., 1973-76; pvt. practice orthopaedic surgery Sun City, Ariz., 1976-89; pres. cattle ranch corp. Contbr. articles to profl. jours. Fellow ACS; mem. Am. Acad. Orthopaedic Surgery, Physicians Club Sun City, Mayo Alumni Assn. Mem. U. Minn. Alumni Assn., Ruth Jackson Orthopedic Soc. Republican. Mem. Evang. Reformed Ch. Home: 3101 Skipworth Dr Las Vegas NV 89107

SABAROFF, ROSE EPSTEIN, retired education educator; b. Cleve., Sept. 4, 1918; d. Hyman Israel and Bertha (Glaser) Epstein; m. Bernard Joseph Sabaroff, Dec. 28, 1940; children: Ronald Asher, Nina Katya. B.A., U. Ariz., 1941; M.A., San Francisco State U., 1954; Ed.D., Stanford U., 1957. Tchr. Presidio Hill Elem. Sch., San Francisco, 1951-55; asst. prof. edn. Oreg. State U., Corvallis, 1958-61; asst. dir., then dir. elem. edn. Harvard Grad. Sch. Edn., Cambridge, Mass., 1961-66; prof. edn. Va. Poly. Inst. and State U., Blacksburg, 1967-82; dir. Grad. Edn. Ctr. Calif. Luth. Coll., North Hollywood, 1982-84; reading specialist How to Learn, Inc., West Los Angeles, Calif., 1983-88. Author: (with Hanna, Davies, Farrar) Geography in the Teaching of Social Studies, 1966, (with Mary Ann Hanna) The Open Classroom, 1974, Teaching Reading with a Linguistic Approach, 1980, Developing Linguistic Awareness, 1981; contbr. articles to profl. jours. Recipient Disting. Research award Va. Edn. Research Assn., 1977; Phi Delta Kappa grantee, 1980. Mem. AAUP, Internat. Reading Assn., NEA, Va. Edn. Assn., Va. Coll. Reading Educators (pres. 1976-77), Va. Reading Assn., Phi Delta Kappa, Pi Lambda Theta, Gamma Theta Upsilon. Democrat. Jewish. Home: 23826 Villena Mission Viejo CA 92692

SABAT, ROSEMARY ANN, elementary education educator; b. Oakmont, Pa., Jan. 30, 1944; d. Frank and Rose (Mikos) Stangl; m. Peter Ludwig Sabat, June 2, 1973; 1 child, Peter. BA magna cum laude, Duquesne U., 1965, MA, 1968, MEd, 1989. Cert. elem. tchr., Pa. Elem. tchr. St. Irenaeus Sch., Oakmont, Pa., 1965-66, St. Catherine Sch., Allentown, Pa., 1973-74; grad. teaching asst. Duquesne U., Pitts., 1966-68; counselor Cath. Social Svc., Pitts., 1968-71, Transitional Svcs., Pitts., 1971-73; elem. tchr. Nativity Sch., Pitts., 1981—. Co-author: Energizing Strategies for the Future, 1991. Pres. Nativity Parish Coun., 1987-90. Mem. Nat. Cath. Ednl. Assn., Nat. Wildlife Fedn., Nat. Arbor Day Found., Internat. Platform Assn., Western Pa. Coun. Tchrs. English, Western Pa. Conservancy, Cousteau Soc. Republican. Home: 2988 Amy Dr Library PA 15129-9348 Office: Navitity Sch 5811 Curry Rd Pittsburgh PA 15236-3521

SABATINI, GABRIELA, tennis player; b. Buenos Aires, May 16, 1970; d. Osvaldo and Beatriz S. Office: care Womens Tennis Assn 500 Ave Of The Champions Palm Beach Gardens FL 33410*

SABATINI, SANDRA, physician; b. N.Y.C., Dec. 1, 1940. BS in Chemistry, Millsaps Coll., 1962; MS in Pharmacology, Marquette U., 1966; PhD in Pharmacology, U. Miss., 1968; MD in Internal Medicine, Tex. Med. Sch., 1974. Lic. physician, Ill., Tex. Intern in medicine U. Ill. Hosp., Chgo., 1974-75; asst. prof. U. Tex. Med. Sch., San Antonio, 1968-70; assoc. dir. U. Ill. Hosp., Chgo., 1977-78; asst. prof. U. Ill. Coll. of Medicine, Chgo., 1977-83, assoc. prof. medicine and physiology, 1983-84; attending physician in nephrology VA, Chgo., 1977-84; med. dir. Dialysis Unit U. Ill., Chgo., 1978-84; prof. internal medicine and physiology Tex. Tech. U. Health Sci. Ctr., Lubbock, 1985—, chmn. dept. physiology, 1993—; attending physician in nephrology U. Med. Ctr., Lubbock, 1985—; lab. instr. Millsaps Coll., Jackson, Miss., 1961-62; instr. in pharmacology, Bapt. Hosp. Sch. Nursing, Jackson, 1966-68; merit rev. mem. NSF, 1987, 91, 92; rev. mem. several orgns. including Chgo. Heart Assn., 1984, NIH, 1982, 86, 89-93, Nat. Kidney Found., 1987, 89—, Am. Heart Assn., 1981-84, others. Editorial referee Am. Jour. Kidney Disease, Am. Jour. Physiology, Am. Jour. Nephrology, Annals of Internal Medicine, others; editorial bd. Am. Jour. Nephrology, 1989-93, Seminars in Nephrology, 1984—; ; author numerous publs. and abstracts in field; contbr. articles to profl. jours. Recipient predoctoral fellowship tng. grant, Marquette U., 1963-66, pub. health predoctoral fellow U. Miss. Med. Sch., 1967-69, gen. medicine sci. rsch. grant U. Tex. Med. Sch., 1968-70, post-grad. fellowship award Karolinska Inst., Swedish Med. Coun., 1971, 73, NIH grants, 1979-82, 1984—, Chgo. Heart Assn. grant-in-aid, 1979-85, Nat. Eye Inst. grant, 1979-80, Banes Charitable Trust award U. Ill.,1984-85, U.S. Olympic Com. Rsch. Found. Clin. Study, 1986-87, numerous others awards in field. Fellow Am. Coll. Physicians; mem. AAAS, AAUP, Am. Fedn. Clin. Rsch., Am. Heart Assn., Am. Physiol. Soc., Am. Soc. Nephrology, Am. Soc. Pharmacology and Exptl. Therapeutics, Am. Soc. Renal Biochemistry and Metabolism (pres. elect 1994), Cen. Soc. Clin. Rsch., Ill. Kidney Found., Internat. Soc. Nephrology, Italian-Am. Nephrologists, Inc., Nat. Kidney Found. (numerous offices including chmn. several coms.), Nat. Kidney Found. of West Tex. (bd. dirs. 1993—), Alpha Omega Alpha, numerous others. Office: Tex Tech U Health Sci Ctr 3601 4th St Lubbock TX 79430-0002

SABAU, CARMEN SYBILE, chemist; b. Cluj, Romania, Apr. 24, 1933; naturalized U.S. citizen; d. George and Antoinette Marie (Chiriac) Grigorescu; m. Mircea Nicolae Sabau, July 11, 1956; 1 child, Isabelle Carmen. MS in Inorganic and Analytical Chemistry, U. C.I. Parhon, Bucharest, Romania, 1955; PhD in Radiochemistry, U. Fridericiana, Karlsruhe, Fed. Republic of Germany, 1972. Chemist, Argonne (Ill.) Nat. Lab., 1976—. Internat. Atomic Energy Agy. fellow, 1967-68, Humboldt fellow, 1970-72. Mem. Am. Chem. Soc., Am. Nuclear Soc., Am. Romanian Acad. Arts and Sci., Assn. for Women in Sci., N.Y. Acad. Sci., Sigma Xi. Author: Ion-exchange Theory and Applications in Analytical Chemistry, 1967; contbr. articles to profl. jours. Home: 689 Banbury Way Bolingbrook IL 60440-1057 Office: Argonne Nat Lab 9700 Cass Ave Bldg 205 Argonne IL 60439-4803

SABBAGH, SHERAINE KAY, textile designer; b. Springfield, Ill., Mar. 2, 1959; d. Russ B. and Beverly Jane (McCarthy) Dhondy; m. John Peter Sabbagh, July 26, 1986; 1 child, Elliott Cyrus. BFA in Textile Design, Sophia Polytechnic, Bombay, India, 1981; AOS, Pratt Inst., N.Y.C., 1983. Cert. CPR and first aid, ARC. Trainee designer Laxmi-Vishnu Textile Mills, Ltd., Bombay, 1981; lectr. history of textiles Sophia Polytechnic, Bombay, 1981-82, assoc. of occupational studies in textile design, 1981-82; textile designer Piramal Spinning and Weaving Mills, Ltd., Bombay, 1981-82; colorist Quaker Fabric Corp., N.Y.C., 1984; spl. asst. designer Spectrum Fabrics Corp., N.Y.C., 1984-85; pres., owner, designer Sheraine Kay Designs, 1983—; computer aided stylist West Point Stevens, 1991—; clients include Greeff Fabrics Inc., Walt Disney Prodns., Western Textile, Henry Glass & Co.; cons. The Master Weavers India show, Smithsonian Instn., Washington, 1986; guest lectr., film producer Mus. Natural History, N.Y.C., 1988, 90, N.Y. Pub. Libr., N.Y.C., 1988, Great Neck (N.Y.) Libr., 1987. Producer, art dir. documentary film Journey to Arhikkal, 1988; set designer play The Elephant Man, Bombay, 1981; exhibited textile designs Sophia Poly., Bombay, 1979, 80, 81, Internat. House, N.Y.C., 1983, Pratt Inst., N.Y.C., 1983. Active Friends and Advs. the Mentally Ill, N.Y.C., 1989—; mem. W.P.P. Recycling Task Force, 1991—. Scholar Maharashtra State Directorate, 1979; recipient 1st prize woven divsn. 11th ann. competition Home Fashion Products Assn., 1983. Democrat. Office: West Point Stevens 1185 Avenue of the Americas New York NY 10036

SABIDO, ALMEDA ALICE, mental health facility administrator; b. Blairsville, Pa., Sept. 24, 1928; d. George Jackson and Dora Irene (Byrd) McClellen; m. Frederick Lionel Harrison, Feb. 1, 1963; children: Frederick L.H., Derek M. BS in Secondary Edn., Indiana U. of Pa., 1950; MSW cum laude, U. Pitts., 1958. Staff psychiat. social worker S.I. Mental Health Soc., 1958-63, supr. psychiat. social worker, 1963-66, asst. dir. psychiat. social work, 1967-69, dir. psychiat. social work, 1969-81, acting dir. Children's Community Mental Health Ctr., 1981, dir. Children's Community Mental Health Ctr., 1982—. Mem. NAACP, NASW, N.Y. Urban League, Nat. Coun. Negro Women, S.I. Com. on Child and Adolescent Mental Health (pres. 1984-86), S.I. Mental Health Coun. (sec. 1982-84), S.I. Mental Health Soc. (Richard M. Silberstein award 1991). Presbyterian. Home: 142 Benedict Ave Staten Island NY 10314-2315 Office: SI Mental Health Soc 669 Castleton Ave Staten Island NY 10301-2028

SABIN, MARTHA CLAIRE, rehabilitation administrator; b. Buenos Aires, Jan. 22, 1936; came to U.S., 1937; d. Dewey James and Clarie Marie (Gilday) S.; m. Thomas L. Poppelbaum, 1955 (div. 1976); 1 child, Claire Anne. BA, Okla. U., 1957; MA, Colgate U., 1969; PhD in Rehab., So. Ill. U., 1987. Cert. rehab. counselor, gen. counselor. Employment counselor N.Y. State Dept. Labor, Utica, 1964-72; rehab. counselor, coord. Office of Vocat. Rehab., Marcy and Rome, N.Y., 1972-77; rehab. counselor Smyrna (Tenn.) Rehab. Ctr., 1977-83; program and fiscal evaluator Evaluation and Devel. Ctr., So. Ill. U., Carbondale, 1984-87; dir. spl. projects Beaumont (Tex.) State Ctr., 1987—; part-time rehab. and alcoholism counselor Oneida County Mental Agy., Rome, 1973-77; part-time rsch./evaluation Jackson County Cmty. Mental Health Agy., Carbondale, 1984-87; presenter in field. Contbr. articles to profl. jours. Past pres. N.Y. State Rehab. Counselor Assn.; past pres., conf. coord. N.Y. State Employment Counselor Assn.; past bd. dirs. Ill. Rehab. Counselors, N.Y. State Rehab. Counselors. Mem. Am. Assn. Mental Retardation, Am. Evaluation Assn., Am. Rehab. Assn. (counselor), Golden Triangle Rehab. Assn. (past pres.), Tex. Rehab. Adminstrn. Assn. (ppres.-elect, subchpt. pres.). Office: Beaumont State Ctr 655 S 8th St Beaumont TX 77701

SABLE, BARBARA KINSEY, former music educator; b. Astoria, L.I., N.Y., Oct. 6, 1927; d. Albert and Verna Rowe Kinsey; B.A., Coll. Wooster, 1949; M.A., Tchrs. Coll. Columbia U., N.Y.C., 1950; D.Mus., U. Ind., 1966; m. Arthur J. Sable, Nov. 3, 1973. Office mgr., music dir. sta. WCAX, Burlington, Vt., 1954; instr. Cottey Coll., 1959-60; asst. prof. N.E. Mo. State U., Kirksville, 1962-64; asst. prof. U. Calif., Santa Barbara, 1964-69; prof. music U. Colo., Boulder, 1969—. Author: The Vocal Sound, 1982; contbr. poetry to literary jours. Mem. Nat. Assn. Tchrs. Singing (past state gov., asso. editor bull.), AAUP, Colo. State Music Tchrs. Assn. Democrat. Avocation: poetry. Home: 3430 Ash Ave Boulder CO 80303-3432 Office: U Colo Coll Music Campus Box 301 Boulder CO 80309

SABLOSKY, JILL, sculptor; b. Phila., Oct. 14, 1954; d. Norman Wilson and Maxine Sharpe (Goldenberg) S. BA, U. Md., 1976; MFA, U. Pa., 1979. Exhibited at Huntington Art Gallery, U. Tex., Austin, 1989-90; commd. by GSA for permanent outdoor sculpture for Fed. Bldg., San Antonio, 1994-95, Redevelopment Authority Phila. for permanent outdoor sculpture, 1994; represented in collections at El Paso Mus. Art, Ursinus Coll., Collegeville, Pa., Beaver Coll., Wyncote, Pa., Barrett Collection, Dallas, Berman Collection, Allentown, Pa., also pvt. commns. and collections U.S. and Italy. Home: PO Box 1552 Glen Rose TX 76043

SABOSIK, PATRICIA ELIZABETH, publisher, editor; b. Newark, Aug. 25, 1949; d. George Aloysius and Elizabeth Ann (Simko) S.; m. Kenneth Donald Gursky, Apr. 21, 1972 (div. 1980). BA in English, Kean Coll. N.J., 1976; MBA in Mktg., Seton Hall U., 1984; cert. advanced study in fin., Fairfield U., 1989. Proofreader Baker & Taylor, Somerville, N.J., 1969-71, database coordinator, 1971-74, prodn. editor, 1974-77, publs. mgr., editor, 1977-82; dir. mktg. services H.W. Wilson Pub. Co., Bronx, N.Y., 1982-84; editor, pub. Choice mag. Am. Library Assn., Middletown, Conn., 1984-94; v.p. electronic text Booklink Technologies, Wilmington, Mass., 1994; v.p. Linked Media, Navi Soft Divsn. Am. Online, Inc., Needham, Mass., 1994—; project dir. Books for Coll. Librs., Middletown, 1985-88, Guide to Reference Books, 1988-94; membership chmn. Serials Industry Systems Adv. Com., 1983-89, vice chmn., 1985-86, newsletter editor, 1986-87. Contbr. articles to profl. jours. Party rep. Twp. Com. Cranford, N.J., 1977-79; hon. bd. advisors U. Conn. Women's Ctr., 1989-91; mem. Conn. Women's Edn. and Legal Fund; nat. bd. dirs. Literacy Vols. of Am., 1992-94, also chair pub. and mktg. com. Mem. ALA (coms., editorial bd. Choice), AAUW, Assn. Coll. and Rsch. Librs. (publs. com.), Soc. for Scholarly Pub. (membership com., editor newsletter 1988-91, budget and fin. com. 1990-92, sec.-treas. 1994—, bd. dirs. 1994—), Appalachian Mountain Club, Women's Outdoors Club (newsletter editor 1984-86, regional rep. 1986-87). Republican. Roman Catholic. Office: Navi Soft Inc An Am Online Co 75 2d Ave Ste # 710 Needham MA 02194

SABOTA, CATHERINE MARIE, horticulturist, educator; b. Bridgeton, N.J., Sept. 9, 1949; d. John Robert Sabota and Colleen Catherine Moran Schultz. BS, Tex. Tech. U., 1973, MS, 1975; PhD, U. Ill., 1983. Rsch. asst. Tex. Tech. U., Lubbock, 1973-75, rsch. assoc., 1975-76; asst. horticulturist U. Ill., Dixon Springs, 1978-80; rsch. assoc. U. Ill., Champaign, 1980-83; horticulturist, asst. prof. Ala. A&M, Normal, 1983-88, horticulturist, assoc. prof., 1988—; advisor Ala-Tenn Fruit & Vegetable Assn., Elora, Tenn., 1985-90. Contbr. articles to profl. jours. Recipient award of excellence Coop. Extension program Ala. A&M U., 1989, 93; Tex. State scholar, 1971-73; grantee CSRS-USDA, 1986—, Soil Conservation Svc., 1986, Ala. U./TVA Consortium, 1987. Mem. Am. Soc. Hort. Sci. (Continuing Edn. Aids award 1994), Ala. Fruit & Vegetable Growers, So. Region Soc. Hort. Sci. (chmn. awards com. 1990, ext. divsn. chair 1994). Office: Ala A&M Univ PO Box 69 Normal AL 35762-0069

SACCA, HARRIET WANDS, music educator; b. Pittsfield, Mass; d. Harry J. and Anna F. (Mara) Wands; BS, Coll. St. Rose, 1939, MA, 1962; student SUNY, Albany, Oneonta. Tchr. pub. schs., Albany, N.Y., 1942-66; instr. Coll. St. Rose, 1962-63; dir. music edn. Albany (N.Y.) Bd. Edn., 1966—; bur. assoc. examiner personnel N.Y. State Dept. Edn. Past pres. Soroptimist Internat., 1969-70, City Club Albany, Inc., 1974-75; active Albany County Dem. Com., 1962—; jud. del. 3d Jud. Dist. N.Y. State, 1975-93; mem. Albany Local Devel. Corp.; bd. dirs. St. Joseph's Housing Corp., Albany Tulip Festival; mem. adv. bd. capital Region Ctr. Arts in Edn., 1983—, Albany County Alteratives to Incarceration, 1983-94, chair sub com., 1985—; bd. dirs. Coop. Extension Community Resources Devel., 7 County Youth Symphony Orch., 1970-84; project dir. N.Y. Council on Arts; chair festival N.Y. Sch. Music, 1988; mem. com. of 5 appointed select name for 16, 000 seat Civic Arena. Recipient Citizen of Yr. award Ford Motor Co., 1971; Women Helping Women award Soroptimist, 1975; Disting. Service award N.Y. State PTA, 1985. Fellow Harry Truman Library; mem. Nat. Coun. Music Adminstrs., Music Educators Nat. Conf., N.Y. State Sch, Music Assn., Capitol Hill Choral Soc. (dir.), N.Y. St. Council Arts Award Childrens Opera (dir. project), Albany Adminstrs. Assn., Albany Civic Auditorium (dir.), Delta Kappa Gamma, Delta Epsilon. Democrat. Roman Catholic. Clubs: Bus. and Profl. Women's, Soroptimist, Club of Albany, Cath. Women's Service League, Coll. St. Rose Alumni, Pres.'s Soc. Home: 226 Morris St Albany NY 12208-3525 Office: Albany Bd Edn Acad Park Albany NY 12207

SACHS, LORRAINE PHYLLIS, professional society administrator; b. Jersey City, Feb. 25, 1936; d. Abe and Ann (Beitel) S. BA, U. Mich., 1956; MA, Columbia U., 1958. Cert. assn. exec. Asst. dir. evaluation Nat. League for Nursing, N.Y.C., 1959-69, dir. evaluation, 1969-73, dir. test svc., 1973-83; exec. v.p., COO Nat. Assn. State Bds. Accountancy, N.Y.C., 1984—. Author: Measurement and Evaluation in Nursing Education, 1980; contbr. articles to Nursing Outlook, 1975-82. Scholar U. Mich. Alumni Assn., 1987-90. Mem. Am. Assn. for Counseling & Devel., Am. Psychol. Assn., Am. Psychol. Soc., Am. Soc. Assn. Execs., Nat. Coun. on Measurement in Edn., N.Y. Assn. for Applied Psychology, N.Y. Soc. Assn. Execs. Home: 420 E 55th St Apt 6C New York NY 10022-5141 Office: NASBA 380 Lexington Ave New York NY 10168-0002

SACHS, MARILYN STICKLE, author, lecturer, editor; b. N.Y.C., Dec. 18, 1927; d. Samuel and Anna (Smith) Stickle; m. Morris Sachs, Jan. 26, 1947; children: Anne, Paul. BA, Hunter Coll., 1949; MSLS, Columbia U., 1953. Children's libr. Bklyn. Pub. Libr., 1949-60, San Francisco Pub. Libr., 1961-67. Author: Amy Moves In, 1964, Laura's Luck, 1965, Amy and Laura, 1966, Veronica Ganz, 1968, Peter and Veronica, 1969, Marv, 1970, The Bears' House, 1971 (Austrian Children's Book prize 1977, Recognition of Merit award George C. Stone Ctr. for Children's Books 1989)), The Truth About Mary Rose, 1973 (Silver Slate Pencil award 1974), A Pocket Full of Seeds, 1973 (Jane Addams Children's Book Honor award 1974), Matt's Mitt, 1975, Dorrie's Book, 1975 (Silver State Pencil award 1977, Garden State Children's Book award 1978), A December Tale, 1976, A Secret Friend, 1978, A Summer's Lease, 1979, Bus Ride, 1980, Class Pictures, 1980, Fleet Footed Florence, 1981, Hello...Wrong Number, 1981, Call Me Ruth, 1982 (Assn. Jewish Librs. award 1983), Beach Towels, 1982, Fourteen, 1983, The Fat Girl, 1984, Thunderbird, 1985, Underdog, 1985 (Christopher 1986), Baby Sister, 1986, Almost Fifteen, 1987, Fran Ellen's House, 1987 (award Bay Area Book Reviewers Assn. 1988, Recognition of Merit award George C. Stone Ctr. for Children's Books 1989), Just Like A Friend, 1989, At the Sound of the Beep, 1990, Circles, 1991, What my Sister Remembered, 1992, Thirteen, 1993; co-editor: (with Ann Durell) Big Book for Peace, 1990 (Calif. Children's Book award 1991, Jane Addams Children's Book prize 1991); reviewer books N.Y. Times, San Francisco Chronicle, 1970—. Mem. PEN, ACLU, SANE-Freeze, Sierra Club, Authors' Guild, Soc. Children's Book-writers. Democrat. Jewish. Home: 733 31st Ave San Francisco CA 94121-3523

SACKETT, DIANNE MARIE, city treasurer, accountant; b. Oil City, Pa., Dec. 29, 1956; d. Clarence Benjamin and Donna Jean (Grosteffon) Knight; m. Mark Douglas Sackett, May 26, 1984; children: Jason Michael, Cory James. BBA, Ea. Mich. U., 1979, MBA, 1986. Accounts payable supr. Sarns, Inc., Ann Arbor, Mich., 1979-81; cost acct. Simplex Products Divsn., Adrian, Mich., 1981-83, gen. acctg. supr., 1983-88; city treas. City of Tecumseh, Mich., 1991—. Mem. Mich. Mcpl. Treas.' Assn., Mich. Mcpl. Fin. Officers Assn., Mcpl. Treas.' Assn. of the U.S. and Can. Pentecostal. Office: 309 E Chicago Blvd Tecumseh MI 49286

SACKETT, SUSAN DEANNA, film and television production associate, writer; b. N.Y.C., Dec. 18, 1943; d. Maxwell and Gertrude Selma (Kugel) S. B.A. in Edn., U. Fla., 1964, M.Ed., 1965. Tchr. Dade County Schs., Miami, Fla., 1966-68, L.A. City Schs., 1968-69; asst. publicist, comml. coordinator NBC-TV, Burbank, Calif., 1970-73; asst. to creator of Star Trek Gene Roddenberry, 1974-91; prodn. assoc. Star Trek: The Next Generation TV Series, 1987-91; writer Star Trek: the Next Generation, 1990-94; lectr. and guest speaker STAR TREK convs. in U.S., Eng., Australia, 1974—. Author and editor: Letters to Star Trek, 1977; co-author: Star Trek Speaks, 1979; The Making of Star Trek-The Motion Picture, 1979; You Can Be a Game Show Contestant and Win, 1982, Say Goodnight Gracie, 1986, The Hollywood Reporter Book of Box Office Hits, 1990, Prime Time Hits, 1993, Oscar Sings, 1995. Mem. ACLU, Writers Guild Am., Am. Humanist Assn., Mensa, Sierra Club. Democrat.

SACKLEY, MARTHA V., lawyer; b. Chgo., May 23, 1959. BBA, U. Iowa, 1981, JD, 1984. Bar: Ill. 1984. Ptnr. McDermott, Will & Emery, Chgo., 1984—. Note and comment editor Iowa Law Rev., 1983-84. Mem. Fed. Bar Assn., Ill. Bar Assn., Chgo Bar Assn. (litigation sect.). Office: McDermott Will & Emery 227 W Monroe St Chicago IL 60606-5016

SACKLOW, HARRIETTE LYNN, advertising agency executive; b. Bklyn., Apr. 12, 1944; d. Sidney and Mildred (Myers) Cooperman; m. Stewart Irwin, July 2, 1967; 1 child, Ian Marc. BA, SUNY, Albany, 1965, postgrad., 1967-69; postgrad., Union Coll., 1969-70, Telmar Media Sch., N.Y.C., 1981. Tchr. math. Guilderland (N.Y.) Cen. Schs., 1967-76; v.p. Wolkcas Advt., Inc., Albany, N.Y., 1975—; supr. internship programs Coll. St. Rose, Albany, 1981; lectr. to area colls., Albany, 1981-83. V.p. Sisterhood Congregation Ohav Sholom, Albany, 1983-86; bd. dirs. Northeastern N.Y. chpt. Arthritis Found.; key market coord. Partnership for a Drug Free Am., 1994—; advisor Ronald McDonald House; bd. dirs. Takundewide Homeowners Assn. Mem. NAFE, Am. Women in Radio and TV (pres. 1982-84, chmn. task force for new mem. acquisition, v.p. N.E. area 1987-89, chmn. area conf. 1987, pres. 1982-84, speaker, dist. dir.), N.Am. Advt. Agy. Network (bd. dirs. 1992—), Advt. of the Capital Dist., Albany (N.Y.) Yacht Club. Office: Wolkcas Advt Inc 435 New Karner Rd Albany NY 12205-3833

SACKS, PATRICIA ANN, librarian, consultant; b. Allentown, Pa., Nov. 6, 1939; d. Lloyd Alva and Dorothy Estelle (Stoneback) Stahl; m. Kenneth LeRoy Sacks, June 27, 1959. A.B., Cedar Crest Coll., 1959; M.S. in L.S., Drexel U., 1965. News reporter Call-Chronicle, Allentown, 1956-59, 1961-63; reference librarian Cedar Crest Coll., Allentown, 1964-66, head librarian, 1966-73; dir. libraries Muhlenberg and Cedar Crest Colls., Allentown, 1973-94; dir. libr. svcs. Cedar Crest Coll., 1994; sr. fellow Lehigh Valley Assn. Ind. Colls., 1994—. del. On Line Computer Library Ctr. Users Council, Columbus, Ohio, 1977-84; cons. colls./health care orgns., libr. bldgs. 1981-84. Author: (with Whildin Sara Lou) Preparing for Accreditation: A Handbook for Academic Librarians, 1993; mem. editorial bd. Jour. Acad. Librarianship, 1982-84, Coll. and Undergrad. Libr., 1993—. Trustee Cedar Crest Coll., 1985-89. Mem. United Way Lehigh Valley Coms., 1993—; bd. dirs. John and Dorothy Morgan Cancer Ctr., 1994—. Named Outstanding Acad. Woman, Lehigh Valley Assn. for Acad. Women, 1984, Muhlenberg Coll. Outstanding Adminstr., 1987, Alumni Tricorn award Muhlenberg Coll., 1989, Alumnae Achievement award Cedar Crest Coll., 1994. Mem. ALA (chmn. copyright com. 1985-87), Assn. Coll. and Research Libraries (chmn. standards and accreditation com. 1976-78, 81-84), Lehigh Valley Assn. Ind. Colls. (chmn. librarians sect. 1967-81, 88-92), AAUW, LWV Lehigh Valley Conservancy, Appalachian Mountain Club, Phi Alpha Theta, Phi Kappa Phi, Beta Phi Mu. Democrat. Home: 2997 Fairfield Dr Allentown PA 18103-5413 Office: Lehigh Valley Assn Ind Colls care Moravian Coll 1200 Main St Bethlehem PA 18018-6650

SACKS, TEMI J., public relations executive; b. Phila.; d. Jule and Adeline (Levin) S. BA, Temple U. Pubs. editor Del. Valley Regional Planning Commn., Phila.; communications assoc. Fedn. Jewish Agys., Phila.; pres. T. J. Sacks Pub. Relations, Phila.; exec. v.p., mng. dir. healthcare div. Lobsenz-Stevens Inc., N.Y.C.; guest lectr. Temple U. Sch. Communications. Mem. Healthcare Businesswomen's Assn., Pharm. Advt. Coun., Women Execs. in Pub. Rels. Home: 142 West End Ave New York NY 10023-6103 Office: Lobsenz-Stevens Inc 460 Park Ave S New York NY 10016-7315

SADDLEMYER, ANN (ELEANOR SADDLEMYER), English educator, critic, theater historian; b. Prince Albert, Sask., Can., Nov. 28, 1932; d. Orrin Angus and Elsie Sarah (Ellis) S. BA, U. Sask., 1953, DLitt, 1991; MA, Queen's U., 1956, LLD (hon.), 1977; PhD, U. London, 1961; DLitt (hon.), U. Victoria, 1989, McGill U., 1989, Windsor U., 1990. Lectr. Victoria (B.C.) Coll., 1956-57, instr., 1960-62, asst. prof., 1962-65; assoc. prof. U. Victoria, 1965-68, prof. English, 1968-71; prof. English Victoria Coll. U. Toronto, 1971-95; prof., dir. grad. ctr. for study of drama Grad. Ctr. Study of Drama, U. Toronto, 1972-77, 85-86; sr. fellow Massey Coll., 1975-88, master, 1988-95; Berg prof. NYU, 1975. Dir. Theatre Plus, 1972-84; dir. Colin Smythe Pubs.; author: The World of W.B. Yeats, 1965, In Defence of Lady Gregory, Playwright, 1966, Synge and Modern Comedy, 1968, J.M. Synge Plays Books One and Two, 1968, Lady Gregory Plays, 4 vols, 1970, Letters to Molly: Synge to Maire O'Neill, 1971, Letters from Synge to W.B. Yeats and Lady Gregory, 1971, Collected Letters of John Millington Synge, Vol. 1, 1983, vol. II, 1984, Theatre Business, The Correspondence of the First Abbey Theatre Directors, 1982, (with Colin Smythe) Lady Gregory Fifty Years After, 1987, Early Stages: Theatre in Ontario, 1800-1914, 1990; co-editor Theatre History in Canada, 1980-86; editorial bds. Modern Drama, 1972-82, English Studies in Can., 1973-83, Themes in Drama, 1974—, Shaw Rev, 1977—, Research in the Humanities, 1976-90; Irish Univ. Rev, 1970—, Yeats Ann., 1982-86, Studies in Contemporary Irish Lit., 1986—; contbr.

articles to profl. jours. Recipient Brit. Acad. Rose Mary Crawshay award, 1986, Disting. Svc. award Province of Ont., 1985, U. Toronto Alumni award of excellence, 1991; named Disting. Dau. of Pa., 1992, Women of Distinction in Letters, Toronto, YWCA, 1994; Can. Coun. scholar, 1958-59, fellow, 1968, Guggenheim fellow, 1968, 77, sr. rsch. fellow Connaught, 1985. Fellow Royal Soc. Can., Royal Soc. Arts; mem. Internat. Assn. Study Anglo-Irish Lit. (chmn. 1973-76), Assn. Can. Theatre History (pres. 1976-77), Can. Assn. Irish Studies, Assn. Can. Univ. Tchrs. English, Can. Assn. Univ. Tchrs., Assn. Can. and Que. Lit. Home: 100 Lakeshore Rd E Apt 803, Oakville, ON Canada L6J 6M9 Office: Massey Coll, 4 Devonshire Pl, Toronto, ON Canada M5S 2E1

SADER, CAROL HOPE, former state legislator; b. Bklyn., July 19, 1935; d. Nathan and Mollie (Farkas) Shimkin; m. Harold M. Sader, June 9, 1957; children: Neil, Randi Sader Friedlander, Elisa. BA, Barnard Coll., Columbia U., 1957. Sch. tchr. Bd. Edn., Morris, Conn., 1957-58; legal editor W. H. Anderson Co., Cin., 1974-78; freelance legal editor Shawnee Mission, Kans., 1978-87; mem. Kans. Ho. of Reps., 1987-94; chair Ho. Pub. Health and Welfare Com., 1991-92; chair Joint Ho. and Senate Com. on Health Care Decisions for the 90's, 1992; vice chair Ho. Econ. Devel. Com., 1991-92; policy chair Ho. of Dem. Caucus, 1993-94. Dem. candidate for Kans. Lt. Gov., 1994; chmn. bd. trustees Johns County C.C., Overland Park, Kans., 1984-86, trustee, 1981-86; pres. LWV Johnson County, 1983-85; bd. dirs. United Cmty. Svcs. of Johnson County Shawnee Mission, 1984-92, Jewish Vocat. Svc. Bd., 1983-92; chmn. Kans. State Holocaust Commn., Johnson County C.C. Found.; bd. dirs. Jewish cmty. rels. Johnson County Para-transit Coun., founding pres., 1994—, adv. bd., arts Coun.; bd. dirs. Johnson County Found on Aging; mem. mainstream coalition, sec. bd. Coalition for Positive Family Relationships. Recipient Trustee award Assn. of Women in Jr. and C.C., 1985, awards Kans. Pub. Transit Assn., 1990, AARP, 1992, Assn. Kans. Theater, 1992, Nat. Coun. Jewish Women, 1992, Kans. Assn. Osteo. Medicine, 1992, Kans. Chiropractic Assn., 1992, United Com. Svcs. Johnson County, 1992, Disting. Pub. Svcs. award Johnson County, 1993, Hallpac Kans. Pub. Svc. award Hallmark Cards, Inc., 1993. Mem. Coun. Women Legislators, LWV (pres. Johnson County chpt. 1983-85, mem. state bd. 1986-87), Phi Delta Kappa. Democrat. Home: 8612 Linden Dr Shawnee Mission KS 66207-1807

SADLER, BARBARA ANN, quality assurance professional; b. Bklyn., Nov. 27, 1955; d. Raymond Theodore Jr. and Elaine Mary (Bortscheller) S. Student, Suffolk C.C., 1978-79, 84, N.H. Coll., 1991-93, N.H. Tech. Coll., 1994. Various positions CEAG Electric Corp., Hauppauge, N.Y., 1981-87; indsl. engr., aide Hazeltine Corp., Greenlawn, N.Y., 1987-88; rep. quality assurance Def. Logistics Agy., Boston, 1988—; com. chmn. Hazeltine Corp., 1987-88, bldg. rep. Hazeltine Corp., Riverhead, N.Y., 1987-88, com. mem. Ceag Electric Corp., 1985-86. Author: Workmanship Manual STD Practices and Procedures, 1986, various process specification procedure manuals, 1985-88. Fellow NAFE; mem. Lions Club Internat. Republican. Roman Catholic. Home: Wells St RR 2 Box 19 Enfield NH 03748 Office: SBB DCMDN-GFQNF Highway 4 Lebanon NH 03766

SADLER, DOLORES ANN (DEE SADLER), retired clinical social worker, psychotherapist; b. N.Y.C., Feb. 18, 1943; d. Gerard R. and Helen C. (Moran) Endres; m. Charles L. Sadler, May 1962 (div. 1975); children: Lynn, Robert, Kristine; m. John K. Hobbins, Aug., 1976 (div. 1978). AAS, County Coll. of Morris, Randolph, N.J., 1981; BA, Rutgers U., 1983, MSW, 1984. Lic. clin. social worker, N.J. Adminstrv. asst. Morristown (N.J.) Rehab. Ctr., 1972-82; social worker Lyons (N.J.) VA Med. Ctr., 1982-84, Americare Rehab., Englewood, Fla., 1984-85; psychotherapist, clin. social worker Med. Ctr. Hosp. psychiat. ctr., Punta Gorda, Fla., 1985-93; pvt. practice psychotherapy Punta Gorda, 1993-95; supr. grad. students U. South Fla., 1987-93, Barry U., 1987-90, Nova U., 1991-93. Bd. dirs. Heart and Lung Assn. of Charlotte County, 1985-86; bd. trustees Mt. Olive Assn. Tenants, 1983-84; developer Swim, Inc (for handicapped), 1975-79; organizer Orgn. Handicapped Students, 1979-81; vol. Morris County Hotline, 1982-83; advocate Arts & Culture Assn. Charlotte County, Fla. Mem. NASW, ACLU, NOW, Acad. Cert. Social Workers (cert.), Amnesty Internat., Alumni Assn. Rutgers U. Democrat.

SADLER, RUTH E., journalist; b. Phila., Apr. 20, 1950; d. Alvin J. and Frances (Lubar) S.; m. Robert P. Byrnes, Feb. 15, 1980. BA, Syracuse (N.Y.) U., 1972; MA, Towson (Md.) State U., 1987. Reporter Buffalo Evening News, 1972; sports reporter Watertown (N.Y.) Daily Times, 1972-73; asst. sports editor Titusville (Fla.) Star-Advocate, 1973-74; sports reporter Port Huron (Mich.) Times Herald, 1974-75, Camden Courier-Post, Cherry Hill, N.J., 1975-78; sports copy editor Balt. Sun, 1978—. Mem. Assn. Women in Sports Media, Phila. Sports Writers Assn., Syracuse U. Varsity Club, Soc. Profl. Journalists. Home: 5615 Greenspring Ave Baltimore MD 21209 Office: Balt Sun 501 N Calvert St Baltimore MD 21278

SADLER, SALLIE INGLIS, social worker; b. Phila., Nov. 16, 1941; d. H. Barton Off and Janet (Miller) Nelson; m. William A. Sadler, Jr., Apr. 23, 1977; children: Bill, Lisa, Nelson, Ashley, Kirsten. BA, Rollins Coll., Winter Park, Fla., 1964; MSW with high acad. achievement, Rutgers U., 1979; postgrad., Pa. State U., 1986-89. Cert. social worker. Caseworker II, dir. group work Family and Children's Svc. West Essex, Caldwell, N.J., 1979-81; dir. Single Parent Ctr. West Essex, Montclair, N.J., 1981-85; pvt. practice Upper Montclair, N.J., 1981-85; chief clin. svcs. Family Svc. Ctr., U.S. Naval Air Base, Alameda, Calif., 1990-95; sr. psychiat. social worker dept. psychiatry Kaiser Permanente Med. Ctr., San Francisco, 1995—; adj. instr. div. social scis. Bloomfield (N.J.) Coll., 1979-81, N.J. Inst. Tech., 1984-85; instr. psychology dept. Lock Haven (Pa.) U., 1985-90. Mem. NASW, APA, Assn. Women Faculty in Higher Edn.

SADOFF, MICKY, organization administrator; b. Chgo., Apr. 30, 1944; m. Ronald B. Sadoff, June 12, 1965; children: Bryan D., Michael A. BA in Edn., Cardinal Stritch Coll., Milw., 1981. On-air producer, interviewer Sta.-WUWM-FM, Milw., 1977-82; founder, pres., southeastern Wis. chpt. MADD, Milw., 1982-87; nat. bd. MADD, 1984-88, pres., 1988-90, currently mem. nat. bd. dirs.; mem. nat. MADD bd. fin., legis.; chmn. victim issues and exec. coms.; organized two state confs. with nat. speakers, 1983, 85; supervised and marketed all activities for MADD regarding pub. rels., media, speakers bur.'s, legislation, vol. tng., fund raising, edn. and monitoring justice system, 1982-87; apptd. Gov.'s ADv. Coun. Hwy. Safety, Wis., 1984-89, Nat. Safety Coun. Hwy. Safety Com., 1985—, Milw. County Safety Commn., 1986-89, Sta. WUWM-FM Community Adv. Bd., 1983-89; speaker in field. Mem. Harvard Alcohol Com., 1988; bd. dirs. Nat. Safety Coun., 1989. Recipient J.C. Penney Golden Rule award, 1983, Voluntary Action Ctr. award, 1985, Wis. Drivers Edn. Vol. award, 1986, Dept. Transp. Citizen Activist award, 1986, Nat. Hwy. Traffic Safety Adminstrn. Citizen award, 1986, Award of Excellence for Vol. Leadership Assn. for Vol. Adminstrs., 1987, Ione Quinby Griggs award Vis. Nurses Assn., 1987, Cardinal Stritch Coll. Alumni award, 1989. Office: MADD Ste 700 511 E John W Carpenter Fwy W Irving TX 75062

SAENGER, ELIZABETH ANN, psychologist, educator; b. Northampton, Mass., Apr. 20, 1956; d. Rudolph Alfred and Virginia Ellen (Roth) S. BA in Psychology, Columbia U., 1976; MA in Social Psychology, Harvard U., 1979, PhD in Social Psychology, 1981; postgrad., U. Calif., Berkeley, 1981. Ptnr. Gentlepeople of N.Y., Ltd., N.Y.C., 1985-86; resident, staff psychologist Care Ctr. for Mental Health, Key West, Fla., 1988-93; cons., psychologist Key West, 1992—; cons. Harvard U. Police, Cambridge, Mass., 1978-79; teaching fellow Harvard U., Cambridge, 1977-81; adj. asst. prof. Columbia U., N.Y.C., 1982-87; v.p. Inter-Agy. Coun., Key West, 1989-90, pres., 1990-91, 91-92. Sec. Monroe County Coalition for a Woman's Right to Choose, Key West, 1989; bd. dirs. Mood Disorder Support Group, Inc., N.Y.C., 1984-89; 1st v.p. Unitarian Universalist Fellowship, Key West, 1992, 94. Grace Potter Rice fellow Barnard Coll., 1976, fellow Harvard U., 1976, NSF, 1977, U. Calif., Berkeley, 1981. Mem. APA, AAUW (sec. 1989-90), Fla. Psychol. Assn., Inter-Agy. Coun. Home: 1900 B Patterson Ave Key West FL 33040 Office: 422 Fleming St Key West FL 33040

SAFARS, BERTA See FISZER-SZAFARZ, BERTA

SAFERITE, LINDA LEE, library director; b. Santa Barbara, Calif., Mar. 25, 1947; d. Elwyn C. and Polly (Frazer) S.; m. Andre Doyon, July 16, 1985. BA, Calif. State U., Chico, 1969; MS in Library Sci., U. So. Calif., 1970; cert. in Indsl. Relations, UCLA, 1976; MBA, Pepperdine U., 1979. Librarian-in-charge, reference librarian Los Angeles County Pub. Libr. System, 1970-73, regional reference librarian, 1973-75, sr. librarian-in-charge, 1975-78, regional adminstr., 1978-80; libr. dir. Scottsdale (Ariz.) Pub. Libr. System, 1980-93, Fort Collins (Colo.) Pub. Libr., 1993—; task force del. White House Conf. on Libr. and Info. Svcs., 1992—, rep. Region V, 1982-94. Bd. dirs. Scottsdale-Paradise Valley YMCA, 1981-86, Ariz. Libr. Friends, 1990-92; bd. dirs. AMIGOS, 1990, chmn., 1992-93; mem. Class 5, Scottsdale Leavership, 1991. Recipient Cert. Recognition for efforts in civil rights Ariz. Atty. Gen.'s Office, 1985, Libr. award Ariz. Libr. Friends, 1988, Women of Distinction award for Edn., 1989; named State Libr. of Yr., 1990. Mem. ALA, Ariz. State Libr. Assn. (pres. 1987-88), Ariz. Women's Town Hall AlumniAssn., Met. Bus. and Profl. Women (Scottsdale, pres. 1986-87), Soroptimist (pres. 1981-83). Republican. Office: Fort Collins Pub Libr 201 Peterson St Fort Collins CO 80524

SAFFER, AMY BETH, foreign language educator; b. N.Y.C., Apr. 19, 1950; d. William and Evelyn (Yankowitz) S. BA, Fairleigh Dickinson U., 1972, MA, 1983; postgrad., Jersey City State Coll., 1983-84. Cert. tchr. Spanish K-12, N.J. Tchr. Madison (N.J.) High Sch., 1973, Livingston (N.J.) High Sch., 1973—; mem. faculty and dist. coms. Livingston Sch. Dist., 1975—; advisor to class of 1977, Livingston High Sch., 1975-77, chair mid. states subcom., 1990. Inducted Livingston H.S. Alumni Hall of Fame, 1993. Mem. NEA, Am. Assn. Tchrs. of Spanish and Portuguese, N.J. Edn. Assn., Fgn. Lang. Educators of N.J., Livingston Edn. Assn. (negotiations rep. 1980—), Essex County Edn. Assn. Jewish. Office: Livingston High Sch Livingston NJ 07039

SAFFIR, CYNTHIA RUTH, lawyer; b. N.Y.C., Oct. 13, 1954; d. Richard Benjamin and Leona (Rostov) S. BA with honors, U. Calif., Santa Cruz, 1976; JD, Loyola U., L.A., 1980. Bar: Calif. 1980, U.S. Dist. Ct. (ctrl. dist.) Calif. Assoc. Kahn, Stern, Blaney & Kittrell, L.A., 1981-82, Silver Kreisler Goldwasser and Shaeffer, Santa Monica, Calif., 1982-86; assoc. counsel Writers Guild of Am., West Inc., L.A., 1987-91, dir. legal svcs., 1991—. Activist, rschr., paralegal United Farmworkers Union, L.A., 1964, Salinas, Calif., 1974-75. Mem. L.A. County Bar Assn. (exec. com. labor and employment sect. 1993—, mem. planning com. entertainment law and employment conf. 1990), Beverly Hills Bar Assn. Democrat. Office: Writers Guild of Am W Inc 8955 Beverly Blvd Los Angeles CA 90048

SAFIAN, GAIL ROBYN, public relations executive; b. Bklyn., Dec. 12, 1947; d. Jack I. and Harriet S.; m. Jay Mark Eisenberg, Jan. 6, 1979; children: Julia, Eric. BA, SUNY, Albany, 1968; MBA, NYU, 1982. Reporter Albany (N.Y.)-Knickerbocker News/Times-Union, 1969, Athens (Ohio) Messenger, 1969-71; pub. relations asst. Mountainside Hosp., Montclair, N.J., 1971-74; dir. pub. relations Riverside Hosp., Boonton, N.J., 1974-78; consumer affairs coordinator Johnson & Johnson Personal Products Div., Milltown, N.J., 1978-79; v.p., group mgr. Harshe Rotman & Druck, N.Y.C., 1979-82; exec. v.p., dir. Health Care Div. Ruder Finn & Rotman, N.Y.C., 1982-84; v.p., mgr. client services Burson-Marsteller, N.Y.C., 1984-86; v.p., group mgr. health care Cohn & Wolfe, N.Y.C., 1986-90; exec. v.p., gen. mgr. MCS, Summit, N.J., 1990-94; pres. Safian Comm. Inc., Maplewood, N.J., 1994—. Mem. devel. com. Cancer Care, N.Y.C., 1985—. Recipient MacEachern award Am. Hosp. Assn., 1974, Communications Award Internat. Assn. Bus. Communicators, 1976, Creativity in Pub. Rels. award Inside PR, 1992, 93. Mem. N.Y. Acad. Scis., Drug Info. Assn., Women in Communications (Clarion award 1974), Healthcare Businesswomen's Assn. Jewish. Home: 31 Hickory Dr Maplewood NJ 07040-2107 Office: Safian Comm Inc 31 Hickory Dr Maplewood NJ 07040

SAFIAN, SHELLEY CAROLE, advertising agency executive; b. Bklyn., May 29, 1954; d. Jack Israel and Harriet Sara (Cohen) S. BFA, Parsons Sch. Design/New Sch. for Social Rsch., 1975. Asst. art dir. Axelrod and Assocs., N.Y.C., 1975-77; art dir. Sta. WDBO-TV-AM/FM, Orlando, Fla., 1978-80; owner, pres. Safian Comm. Svcs., Inc., Winter Park, 1981—, Bonté Sportswear, Inc., Winter Park, 1993—; mem. adv. com. Career Edn., Orange County, Fla., 1981-88, chmn., 1982-83. Exec. producer/dir. March of Dimes Telethon, Orlando, 1984; bd. dirs. Boy Scouts Am., 1987-91; exec. dir. United Cerebral Palsy Telethon, Orlando, 1982-83; pub. rels. liaison United Cerebral Palsy, Orlando, 1983-84; founder Career Dir. for the Deaf, Orlando, 1985; trustee, pub. rels. chair Nat. Multiple Sclerosis Soc., 1991-92, bd. dirs., 1990, 91. Recipient 1st pl. Addy awards Orlando Advt. Fedn., 1981, 87, 88, 89, 1st pl. Addy award, 2d pl. awards, merit awards, 1982, 84, 85, 87, 88, Nat. Telly award Bronze Statue, 1988, Up and Coming award Price Waterhouse/Orlando Bus. Jour., 1988, Pro-Mark 1st pl. awards Fla. Coun. Shopping Ctrs., 1989, 90, merit award, 1990, Telly awrad Bronze finalist, 1989, 91. Mem. Broadcast Promotion and Mktg. Execs. Assn. (Silver Medallion 1983, nat. finalist 2 Silver Microphone awards 1986, 87), Broadcast Designer's Assn. (bd. dirs. 1980-82), Am. Women in Radio and TV (bd. dirs. 1980-81). Republican. Avocation: horseback riding. Office: Safian Communications Svcs PO Box 1016 Winter Park FL 32790-1016

SAGAMI, KIM, dancer; b. Inglewood, Calif.. Scholarship student, The Joffrey Ballet Sch. Dancer Am. Ballet Theatre II, N.Y.C., 1981-82, Garden State Ballet, 1982, The Joffrey Ballet, N.Y.C., 1983—. Office: The Joffrey Ballet 130 W 56th St New York NY 10019-3818*

SAGAWA, SHIRLEY SACHI, lawyer; b. Rochester, N.Y., Aug. 25, 1961; d. Hidetaka H. and Patricia (Ford) S.; m. Gregory A. Baer; 1 child, Jackson Ford Baer. AB, Smith Coll., 1983; MSc, London Sch. Econs., 1984; JD, Harvard U., 1987. Bar: Md. 1988. Chief counsel youth policy, labor and human resources com. U.S. Senate, Washington, 1987-91; sr. counsel and dir. family and youth policy Nat. Women's Law Ctr., Washington, 1991-93; spl. asst. to Pres. Clinton for domestic policy, 1993; mng. dir., exec. v.p. Corp. for Nat. and Community Svc., Alexandria, 1993—. Mem. exec. bd. Orgn. for Pan-Asian Am. Women, Washington, 1987-89; mem. Women of Color Leadership Coun., 1991-92; vice chair, bd. dirs. Nat. Community Svc. Commn., 1991-93. Recipient Philip V. McGance award Coun. for Advancement of Citizenship, 1991, cert. of recognition Nat. Coun. Jewish Women, 1989; Harry S Truman scholar, 1981; Smith Coll. Alumnae Assn. fellow, 1983; AAUW fellow, 1986. Mem. Md. Bar Assn. Democrat. Episcopalian. Office: Corp for Nat and Community Svc 1201 New York Ave NW Washington DC 20525-0001

SAGE, AMY SUZANNE, public relations executive; b. Omaha, Nebr., July 1958; d. Bernard and Lucille Gregg; m. Jay C. Sage. BS in Journalism, U. Kans., 1980; postgrad., Denver U. News intern Sta. WDAF-TV, Kansas City, Mo., 1979, Sta. WOW-TV, Omaha, 1979; news anchor, reporter Sta. KCNA-TV, Norfolk, Nebr., 1980; news reporter, anchor Sta. KWCH-TV, Wichita, Kans., 1980-88; pub. info. officer City of Wichita, 1988-89; dir. pub. rels. Colo. Dept. Health, 1989—; media rels. trainer Nat. Assn. Govt. Comm., other local and nat. groups. Columnist health and environ. 30 Colo. newspapers. Vol. Samaritan Ho. Homeless Shelter Denver Jr. League, 1989-92;. Recipient Nat. Clarion award, 1988. Mem. Colo. Pub. Health Assn. (newsletter editor 1990-91), Nat. Pub. Health Info. Coalition (Excellence in Pub. Health Comm. award, profl. devel. com. chair), Kans. Univ. Alumni Assn. (news sec. 1982-88). Office: Colo Dept of Health 4300 Cherry Creek Dr S Denver CO 80222

SAGE, GLORIA ARLINE WELT, chemist; b. Bklyn., Mar. 7, 1936; d. Harold L. and Syd (Colin) Welt; m. Martin L. Sage, June 15, 1958; 1 child, Daniel S. AB, Cornell U., 1957; AM in Chemistry, Radcliffe Coll., 1958; PhD in Phys. Chemistry, Harvard U., 1963. Teaching fellow Harvard U., Cambridge, Mass., 1957-61; jr. chemist Avco Corp., Wilmington, Mass., 1957, 58; instr. U. Oreg., Eugene, 1961-67; rsch. assoc. Syracuse (N.Y.) U., 1967-70, 78-79; asst. prof., rsch. assoc. SUNY Health Sci. Ctr., Syracuse, 1970-77; vis. scientist Tel Aviv (Israel) U., 1977-78, Oxford (Eng.) U., 1985-86; sr. scientist Syracuse Rsch. Corp., 1980—. Assoc. editor, author: (book) Handbook of Environmental Fate and Exposure Data, Vol. I, 1989, Vol. 2, 1990, Vol. 3, 1991, Vol. 4, 1993. Exec. com. mem. Sierra Club, Iroquois Group, Syracuse, 1970-85; bd. dirs. Syracuse U. Women's Club, 1980-83; mem. Cmty. Devel. Adv. Com., Syracuse, 1980-90; pres. Outer Comstock Neighborhood Assn., Syracuse, 1990—. Mem. AAAS, Am. Chem. Soc., Assn. Harvard Chemists. Home: 1217 Jamesville Ave New York NY 13210 Office: Syracuse Rsch Corp Merrill Ln Syracuse NY 13210

SAGER, CAROLE BAYER, lyricist, singer; b. N.Y.C., Mar. 8, 1947; d. Elias and Anita (Nathan) Bayer; m. Burt Bacharach, 1982 (div.); 1 son, Cristopher Elton. B.S. in Speech and Dramatic Art, N.Y. U., 1967. Lyricist numerous songs including Midnight Blue, A Groovy Kind of Love, Don't Cry Out Loud, You're Moving Out Today, Nobody Does It Better, When I Need You, Come In From the Rain, I'm Coming Home Again, I'd Rather Leave While I'm In Love, Heartbreaker, You're the Only One, If You Remember Me, 1979, It's My Turn, 1981, Arthur's Theme (Best that You Can Do) (Academy award 1982) That's What Friends Are For, 1986 (Grammy award 1987; recorded by Dionne Warwick, Elton John, Stevie Wonder, Gladys Knight), On My Own (Patti La Belle and Michael Mac Donald), Love Power, (Dionne Warwick and Jeffrey Osborne), Heartlight (Neil Diamond); Love is My Decision (Chris De Burgh), The Day I Fall in Love (from Beethoven's 2nd, 1993, Academy award nominee, Best Original Song, 1993); lyricist in collaboration with Marvin Hamlisch (Broadway play) They're Playing Our Song, 1979, Dancin', 1978; also movies The Spy Who Loved Me, 1977, Ice Castles, 1979, Arthur, 1981, Continental Divide, 1981, The Devil and Max Devlin, 1981, I Ought to Be in Pictures, 1982, Night Shift, 1982, Making Love, 1983, Tough Guys, 1986, Baby Boom, 1987, Three Men and A Baby, 1987, Arthur 2: On the Rocks, 1988; rec. artist, 1977—; albums include: Carole Bayer Sager, 1977, Carole Bayer Sager, Too, 1979, Carole Bayer Sager/Sometimes Late at Night, 1981 (Voted Best New Artist in France and Germany, German Record Acad. 1977); collaborated with numerous composers including Peter Allen, Marvin Hamlisch, Alice Cooper, Mike MacDonald, Melissa Manchester, Bette Midler, Bruce Roberts, Neil Sedaka, Burt Bacharach; author: (novel) Extravagant Gestures, 1986. Recipient Academy award for best song (Arthur's Theme), 1982; Acad. award nom. Best Original Song ("Look What Love Has Done" from Junior, 1994); Grammy award for song of the yr., (That's What Friends Are For), 1986. Office: care Guttman & Pam 118 S Beverly Dr Ste 201 Beverly Hills CA 90212-3016*

SAGER, RUTH, geneticist; b. Chgo., Feb. 7, 1918; married, 1973. BS, U. Chgo., 1938; MS, Rutgers U., 1944; PhD, Columbia U., 1948. Merck fellow Nat. Research Council, 1949-51; asst. in biochemistry Rockefeller Inst., 1951-55; research assoc. in zoology Columbia U., N.Y.C., 1955-60, sr. research assoc. in zoology, 1961-65; prof. biology Hunter Coll., CUNY, 1966-75; prof. cellular genetics Harvard Med. Sch., 1975-88, prof. emeritus, 1988—; chief cancer genetics div. Dana-Farber Cancer Inst., from 1975; mem. sci. adv. bd. Friedrich Miescher Inst., Basle, 1990—; mem. coun. Nat. Inst. Aging NIH, 1993—. Author: (with F.J. Ryan) Cell Heredity, 1961, Cytoplasmic Genes and Organelles, 1972. Recipient Gilbert Morgan Smith medal Nat. Acad. Scis., 1988, Alumni medal U. Chgo. Alumni Assn., 1994; Guggenheim fellow, 1972-73. Fellow AAAS; mem. Am. Acad. Arts and Sci., Nat. Acad. Scis., Inst. of Medicine, Am. Soc. Cell Biologists, Genetics Soc. Am., Am. Assn. Cancer Rsch., Am. Soc. Biol. Chem., Sigma Xi, Phi Beta Kappa. Office: Dana-Farber Cancer Inst 44 Binney St Boston MA 02115-6084

SAHATJIAN, MANIK, nurse, psychologist; b. Tabris, Iran, July 24, 1921; came to U.S., 1951; d. Dicran and Shushanig (Der-Galustian) Mnatzaganian; m. George Sahatjian, Jan. 21, 1954; children: Robert, Edwin. Nursing Cert., Am. Mission Hosps.-Boston U., 1954; BA in Psychology, San Jose State U., 1974, MA in Psychology, 1979. RN, Calif., Mass. Head nurse Am. Mission Hosp., Tabris, 1945-46; charge nurse Banke-Melli Hosp., Tehran, 1946-51; vis. nurse Vis. Nurse Assn., Oakland, Calif., 1956-57; NASA Ames Rsch. Ctr.; research asst. Stanford U., 1979-81, Palo Alto (Calif.) Med. Research Found., 1981-84; documentation supr. Bethesda Convalescent Ctr., Los Gatos, Calif., 1985-86; sr. outreach worker City of Fremont (Calif.) Human Svcs., 1987-90, case mgr., 1990—; guest rsch. asst. NASA Ames Lab., Mountain View, Calif., summers 1978, 79. Author (with others) psychol. research reports. Fulbright scholar, 1951; Iran Found. scholar, 1953. Mem. AAUW, Western Psychol. Assn. Democrat. Mem. St. Andrew Armenian Church. Home: 339 Starlite Way Fremont CA 94539-7642

SAHNI, JULIE, culinary educator; b. Poona, Maharamtra, India, Oct. 16, 1945; d. Venkata Raman and Padma (Iyer) Ranganathan; m. Virant Sahni, Dec. 31, 1968 (div. Apr. 1983); 1 child, Vishal. BSc in Architecture, Delhi Sch. Architecture, New Delhi, India, 1967; MS in Urban Planning, Columbia U., N.Y.C., 1970. City planner, architect N.Y.C. Planning Commn., 1970-79; founder/dir. Julie Sahni's Cooking Sch., Bklyn., 1973—; mem. faculty culinary arts program New Sch. Social Rsch., 1976-80, Boston U., 1989-91, De Gustibus at Macy's, Culinary Guilds, cooking schs. in U.S. and Can.; adj. prof. NYU, 1985-90; cons. Time-Life Books, Gen. Foods; guest chef Hawaii-Cusines of the Sun, City of Phila. Food and Wine Gala, Festival of India, 1986, Citymeals-on-Wheels, March of Dimes, Table of Contents-N.Y. Pub. Libr.; exec. chef/cons. Nirvana Penthouse and Nirvana Club One Restaurants, N.Y.C., 1983-86; spkr. in field. Author: Classic Indian Cooking, 1980 (Andre Simon commendation award 1986), Classic Indian Vegetarian Cooking, 1985 (Glenfiddich Best Cookbook award 1985), Moghul Microwave, 1990; contbr. articles to profl. jours.; featured in major newspapers, appearances on radio and TV talk shows. Mem. Internat. Assn. Cooking Profls., Newspaper Food Editors and Writers Assn., Am. Hist. Preservation Soc., Les Dames D'Escoffier. Home and Office: Julie Sahnis Cooking Sch 101 Clark St Brooklyn NY 11201

SAHS, MAJORIE JANE, art educator; b. Altadena, Calif., Aug. 27, 1926; d. Grayson Michael and Janie Belle (Aaron) McCarty; m. Eugene Otto Sahs, July 21, 1949; children: Victoria, Stephen, Jeffry. Student, Emerson Coll., Boston, 1945; BA, Sacramento State U., 1970; MA in Art Edn., Calif. State U., Sacramento, 1972, postgrad., 1973-79. Cert. secondary tchr., Calif. Tchr. art Sacramento County Schs., 1971-80; cons. Whole Brain Learning Modes, Sacramento, 1980-84; tng. specialist Art Media, Sacramento, Calif., 1983—; instr. Found. for Continuing Med. Edn., Calif., 1985; presenter Nat. Art Edn. Conf., Chgo., 1993, Internat. Conf., Montreal, Can., 1993; cons. and lectr. in field; judge U.S. Treas.' Dept. of Calif. Student Art. Prodr., writer guide and video Gesture Painting Through T'ai Chi, 1992; editor, pub. Calif.'s state newspaper for art edn., 1987-90; editor: Crocker Museum Docent Guide, 1990; mem. editl. bd. Jour. for Nat. Art Edn. Assn., 1990—; editor (newsletter) U.S. Soc. for Edn. Through Art, 1994; designer of ltd. edits. scarves and cards for Nat. Breast Cancer Rsch. Fund, Exploration Inspiration '95. Del. Calif. Arts Leadership Symposium for Arts Edn., 1979, Legis. Coalition Through The Arts, Calif., 1989; judge Calif. State Fair Art Show, 1989, Fed. Treasury Poster Contest; organizer and host art show and fundraiser for women candidates, 1992. Recipient State award of Merit. Mem. Internat. Assn. Edn. through Art, U.S. Soc. Edn. through Art (editor newsletter 1994), Nat. Art Edn. Assn. (mem. editl. bd. jour. 1990—, Nat. Outstanding Newspaper Editor award 1988, 89), Calif. Art Edn. Assn. (mem. state coun., mem. area coun., editor state paper, State Award of Merit), Calif. Children's Homes Soc. (pres. Camellia chpt. 1990-91), Asian Pacific Arts Educators Assn., Art Ctr. L.A. Alumni. Home and Office: 1836 Walnut Ave Carmichael CA 95608

SAIKI, PATRICIA (MRS. STANLEY MITSUO SAIKI), former federal agency administrator, former congresswoman; b. Hilo, Hawaii, May 28, 1930; d. Kazuo and Shizue (Inoue) Fukuda; m. Stanley Mitsuo Saiki, June 19, 1954; children: Stanley Mitsuo, Sandra Saiki Williams, Margaret C., Stuart K., Laura H. BA, U. Hawaii, 1952. Tchr. U.S. history Punahou Sch., Kaimuki Intermediate Sch., Kalani High Sch., Honolulu, 1952-64; sec. Rep. Party Hawaii, Honolulu, 1964-66, vice chmn., 1966-68, 82-83, chmn., 1983-85; rsch. asst. Hawaii State Senate, 1966-68; mem. Hawaii Ho. of Reps., 1968-74, Hawaii State Senate, 1974-82, 100th-101st Congresses from 1st Hawaii dist., Washington, 1987-91; adminstr. SBA, Washington, 1991-93; mem. Pres.'s Adv. Coun. on Status of Women, 1969-76; mem. Nat. Commn. Internat. Women's Yr., 1969-70; commr. We. Interstate Commn. on Higher Edn.; fellow Eagleton Inst., Rutgers U., 1970; fellow Inst. of Politics, Kennedy Sch. Govt., Harvard U., 1993; bd. dirs. Bank of Am.-Hawaii, Landmark Systems Corp., Internat. Asset Recovery Corp. Mem. Kapiolani Hosp. Aux.; sec. Hawaii Rep. Com., 1964-66, vice chmn., 1966-68, chmn., 1983-85; del. Hawaii Constl. Conv., 1968; alt. del. Rep. Nat. Conv., 1968, del., 1984; Rep. nominee for lt. gov. Hawaii, 1982; mem. Fedn. Rep. Women.; trustee Hawaii Pacific Coll.; past bd. govs. Boys and Girls Clubs Hawaii; mem. adv. coun. ARC; bd. dirs. Nat. Fund for Improvement of Post-Secondary Edn., 1982-85 ; past bd. dirs. Straub Med. Rsch. Found., Honolulu, Hawaii's Visitors Bur., Honolulu, Edn. Commn. of States, Honolulu, Hawaii Visitors Bur., 1983-85; trustee U. Hawaii Found., 1984-86,

Hawaii Pacific Coll., Honolulu; Rep. nominee for Gov. of Hawaii, 1994. Episcopalian. Home: 784 Elepaio St Honolulu HI 96816-4710

SAILER, KATHARINE GROVE, artist, educator; b. Balt., Nov. 20, 1921; d. John Robert and Catherine (Nicols) Grove; m. John R. Sailer; children: John Hampton, Katharine Wright. Student, Corcoran Sch. Fine Arts, 1940-42, Pa. Acad. Fine Arts, 1943-48. Instr. Moravian Prep. Sch. Sch., Bethlehem, Pa., 1942-45; instr. Summit (N.J.) Art Ctr., 1952-80, pres., 1954-56; instr. Acad. of Arts, Easton, Md., 1980—; art show judge. Exhibited in 23 one-person shows; group shows include N.J. State Mus., Trenton, 1968, Lehigh U., 1945, U. N.J., Art Inst., Dayton, Ohio, Inst. of Art, Mpls., Currier Gallery of Art, Inst. of Design, Chgo., Leon House, N.Y.C., Union League Club, N.Y.C.; portrait commns. in Md., Va., N.Y., N.J., Calif., Vt., N.H.; represented in Time and Life Mag., 1948. Mem., trustee, past pres. Summit Art Ctr.; panelist Federated Art Assn. N.J., 1973; advisor Jr. League of Summit, Inc., 1967; past mem. vestry St. Lukes Episcopal Ch., Church Hill, Md.; trustee Acad. of Arts, Easton; past cuator Wrights Chance, Centreville, Md., Historic Mus. House of Queen Anne's County Hist. Soc., Md. Recipient Cecelia Baux portrait prize Pa. Acad. Fine Arts, 1947, Toppin prize, 1947, others; Cresson European Meml. scholar, 1947. Mem. Working Artists Forum, Nat. Soc. Colonial Dames in Am. (regent of Gunston Hall 1993—), Nat. Assn. Women Artists (Mildred T. Atkins portrait prize 1951), Harbor Club (Easton, Md.). Home: 1711 Ruthsburg Rd Queen Anne MD 21657

SAILER, RUTH LUCKENBILL, retired women's health nurse; b. Port Carbon, Pa., Jan. 28, 1925; d. Oscar I. and Kathryn (Sanders) Luckenbill; m. Donald Stanley Sailer, June 21, 1952. Diploma, Reading Hosp. Sch. Nursing, West Reading, Pa., 1946. Asst. head nurse newborn nursery Reading Hosp., 1946-52; obstet. staff nurse Chambersburg (Pa.) Hosp., 1952-61, head nurse labor and delivery, 1961-73, charge nurse labor and delivery, 1973-87. Mem. Alumni Assn. of Reading Hosp. Sch. Nursing (life), Am. Assn. Ret. Persons.

SAIN, KAREN GAIL, army officer; b. Pawtucket, R.I., Feb. 22, 1955; d. Thomas and Delores Ann (Jarjoura) Kando; m. James Andrew Connell, May 19, 1979 (div. Oct. 1985); m. Robert Chaderton Sain, June 21, 1986; children: Nicolas Andrew, Brett Thomas. BS in Biology, Providence Coll., 1977; postgrad., Naval Postgrad. Sch., 1984-85; MS in Ednl. Leadership, Troy State U., Dothan, Ala., 1992. Commd. 2d lt. U.S. Army, 1977, advanced through grades to lt. col., 1994; exec. officer A Co., 3rd Bn., Engr. Ctr. Brigade U.S. Army, Ft. Belvoir, Va., 1978-79; co. comdr. HHC, 18th Engr. Brigade U.S. Army, Karlsruhe, Germany, 1981-82, brigade exec. officer 18th Engr. Brigade, 1983-84; project mgr. Combat Devel. Experimentation Ctr. U.S. Army, Ft. Ord, Calif., 1985-86; staff engr. U.S. Army Pacific Command, Ft. Shafter, Hawaii, 1989-90, ops. officer 29th Topographic Bn., 1990-91, chief 5th engr. detachment, 1992; chief topography divsn. Def. Mapping Sch., Ft. Belvoir, 1993—; mem. total quality coun. Def. Mapping Agy., Merrifield, Va., 1993-94. Contbr. to Am. Poetry Anthology, Vol. VIII, 1988, Love's Greatest Treasures: Today's Poets Speak From the Heart, Vol. II, 1989. Chmn. Ptnrs. in Edn., Ft. Belvoir, 1993-95. Decorated Army Commendation medal, Meritorious Svc. medals (3), Armed Forces Res. medal, Nat. Def. Svc. medal. Mem. Soc. Am. Engrs. (treas. Ft. Belvoir chpt. 1994), Kappa Delta Pi, Ft. Belvoir Officers Club (adv. coun. 1992-94). Orthodox Ch. Office: Defense Mapping Sch 21st St Fort Belvoir VA 22060-5921

SAINE, BETTY BOSTON, elementary school educator; b. Newton, N.C., Dec. 1, 1932; d. Glenn and Carrie Queen Boston; m. Thomas Paul Saine, Aug. 3, 1968; 1 child, Carrie Ann. BA, Lenoir Rhyne Coll., 1956. Tchr. grade 4 High Point (N.C.) City Schs., 1956-59, Charlotte City Schs./Charlotte-Mecklenburg Schs., 1959-66; art tchr. grades 1-8 Newton-Conover City Schs., 1966-67; tchr. grade 4 Charlotte-Mecklenburg Schs., 1967-68; tchr. grade 6 Lincolnton (N.C.) City Schs., 1968-70; tchr. grades 5 and 6 Lincolnton City Schs./Lincoln County Schs., 1972-90; ret. Historian, publicity chair beautification com. Sunflower Garden Club, Lincolnton, 1976-87. Mem. Alpha Delta Kappa (various offices and coms.). Methodist. Home: 2492 Pickwick Pl Lincolnton NC 28092-7748

SAINT, EVA MARIE, actress; b. Newark, July 4, 1924; d. John Merle and Eva Marie (Rice) S.; m. Jeffrey Hayden, Oct. 28, 1951; children: Darrell, Laurette. BA, DFA, Bowling Green State U., 1946; student, Actors Studio, after 1950. Appeared in various radio and TV dramatic shows, N.Y.C., 1947—; theater roles include The Trip to Bountiful, 1953 (Outer Circle Critics award, N.Y. Drama Critics award, 1953), The Rainmaker, 1953, Winesburg, Ohio, 1970, The Lincoln Mask, 1972, Summer and Smoke, 1973, Desire Under the Elms, 1974, The Fatal Weakness, 1976, Candida, 1977, Mr. Roberts, First Monday in October, 1979, Duet for One, 1982-83, The Country Girl, 1986 (L.A. Dramalogue award 1986), Death of a Salesman, 1994, Love Letters, 1994; appeared in films On the Waterfront, 1954 (Acad. Award for best supporting actress, 1955), Raintree County, 1957, That Certain Feeling, 1956, A Hatful of Rain, 1957, North by Northwest, 1959, Exodus, 1961, All Fall Down, 1962, 36 Hours, 1963, The Sandpiper, 1964, The Russians Are Coming, The Russians Are Coming!, 1965, Grand Prix, 1966, The Stalking Moon, 1969, Loving, 1970, Cancel My Reservation, 1972, Nothing in Common, 1986; TV dramas The Macahans , 1976 (Emmy nom.), The Fatal Weakness, 1976, Taxi!!, 1978 (Emmy nom.), A Christmas to Remember, 1978, When Hell Was in Session, 1980, The Curse of King Tut's Tomb, The Best Little Girl in the World, 1981, Splendor in the Grass, 1981, Love Leads the Way, 1983, Jane Doe, 1983, Fatal Vision, 1984, The Last Days of Patton, 1986, A Year in the Life, 1986, Breaking Home Ties, 1987, I'll Be Home for Christmas, 1988, Voyage of Terror: The Achille Lauro Affair, 1990, People Like Us, 1990 (Emmy award, 1990), Palomino, 1991, Kiss of the Killer, ABC, 1992, documentary Primary Colors: The Story of Corita, 1991, My Antonia, 1994; also appeared in TV series Moonlighting, 1986-89.

ST. ANDREWS, BARBARA (FITTERER TROMBLEY), Episcopal priest. AB in English magna cum laude, U. Rochester, 1966, MA in English Lit., 1967; MDiv magna cum laude, Wesley Theol. Sem., 1979; postgrad. Princeton Theol. Sem., 1983, Grad. Theol. Union, Berkeley, 1986-88. Ordained to ministry Episcopal Ch. as deacon, 1979, as priest, 1979. Tchr. English, Pittsford High Sch., N.Y., 1967-68; instr. English, U. Rochester, N.Y., 1967-68; editor, nat. cons. Houghton Mifflin Pub. Co., 1968-75, mgr. Washington office, 1976-79; Presidential fellow President's Exec. Exch. Program, Washington, 1975-76; assigned U.S. Travel Svc. Dept of Commerce; curate Parish of St. John the Evangelist, Hingham, Mass., 1979-80; with Bishop's staff Episcopal Diocese Calif., 1980-83; assoc. rector St. Stephen's Episcopal Ch., Belvedere, Calif., 1983-84, St. John's Episcopal Ch., Ross, Calif., 1984-86; host Mosaic program Sta. KPIX-CBS/TV, San Francisco, 1989; exec. dir. medicine and philosophy Calif. Pacific Med. Ctr., San Francisco, 1990-93; exec. prodr. New Dimensions Radio Series The Roots of Healing, 1994—; bd. dirs. ecumenical ministry First Bapt. Ch. Washington, 1976-78; liturgist U.S. Naval Chapel, Washington, 1977-79; clin. pastoral Sibley Hosp., Washington, 1978; offered opening prayers U.S. Ho. of Reps. and U.S. Senate, 1982-83, 85, 87-91 (first ordained woman to do so); guest chaplain State of Union Address, visit of Queen Elizabeth II to Joint Houses of Congress. Mem. coun. U. Rochester, 1975-85; mem. standing com. Diocese of Calif., 1983-84. With Chaplain's Res. Corps, USN, 1978-80. Reading fellow Coll. Preachers, Washington, 1983. Mem. Am. Bus. Women's Assn. (hon.), Rockefeller Found. (Bellagio 1987). Office: Calif Pacific Med Ctr 2485 Clay St San Francisco CA 94115-1808

ST. CLAIR, JANE ELIZABETH, management executive; b. Concord, Mass., Aug. 15, 1944; d. James F. and Mary E. (Clyne) Connell. BA, Salem State Coll., 1969; MPH, Columbia U., N.Y.C., 1990. Field rep., safety program Am. Red Cross of Greater N.Y., 1971-72; program dir. Bronx Community Coll., N.Y., 1973-75; dir. edn. Council N.Y.C., Inc., 1975-77, asst. exec. dir., 1978; exec. dir. Regional Emergency Med. Services, N.Y., 1979-91; dir. Peace Corps, Kenya, 1991-94; adjunt asst. prof., Hunter Coll. N.Y., 1973-91. Contbr. articles to profl. jours. Mem. Emergency Cardic Care Com. N.Y., Heart Assn., Am. Soc. Safety Engrs., Profl. Edn. Com., Am. Red Cross, First Aid Com. Address: 1749 Highland Ave Apt 12A Clearwater FL 34616

ST. GEORGE, JUDITH ALEXANDER, author; b. Westfield, N.J., Feb. 26, 1931; d. John Heald and Edna (Perkins) Alexander; m. David St. George, June 5, 1954; children: Peter, James, Philip, Sarah Anne. BA, Smith Coll., 1952. Author: Turncoat Winter, Rebel Spring, 1970, The Girl with Spunk, 1975, By George, Bloomers!, 1976, The Chinese Puzzle of Shag Island, 1976, The Shad Are Running, 1977, The Shadow of the Shaman, 1977, The Halo Wind, 1978, The Halloween Pumpkin Smasher, 1978, Mystery at St. Martin's, 1979, The Amazing Voyage of the New Orleans, 1980, Haunted, 1980, Call Me Margo, 1981, The Mysterious Girl in the Garden, 1981, The Brooklyn Bridge: They Said It Couldn't Be Built, 1982 (Am. Book award), Do You See What I See?, 1982, In The Shadow of the Bear, 1983, What's Happening to My Junior Year?, 1983, Who's Scared? Not Me!, 1984, The Mount Rushmore, 1985 (Christopher award), Panama Canal: Gateway to the World, 1989 (Golden Kite award), The White House, 1990, Mason and Dixon's Line of Fire, 1991, Dear Dr. Bell...Your Friend Helen Keller, 1992, Crazy Horse, 1994; (from filmscript) A View to a Kill, 1985; (from screenscript) Tales of the Gold Monkey, 1983. Mem. adv. coun. on children's lit. Rutgers U., 1977—; chmn. ednl. com. Bklyn. Bridge Centennial Commn., 1981-83. Mem. Soc. Children's Book Writers, Author's Guild. Episcopalian. Home: 8 Binney Rd Old Lyme CT 06371

ST. GERMAIN, JEAN MARY, medical physicist; b. N.Y.C.; d. Herbert and Mary J. (Newman) S.; BS, Marymount Manhattan Coll., 1966; MS, Rutgers U., 1967. Diplomate Am. Bd. Med. Physics, Am. Bd. Health Physics. Fellow radiol. health USPHS, Rutgers U., New Brunswick, N.J., 1967; fellow dept. med. physics Meml. Hosp., N.Y.C., Cornell U. Med. Coll., 1967-68, asst. physicist, 1968-71, instr. radiology (physics), 1971-78, clin. assoc. prof., 1979-94, assoc. prof. clin. radiology, 1994—; assoc. attending physicist Meml. Sloan-Kettering Cancer Ctr., 1993—; cons. in field. Fellow Am. Assn. Physicists in Medicine (sec., bd. dirs.); mem. Am. Inst. Physics (gov. bd.), Am. Bd. Health Physics, Health Physics Soc. (pres. N.Y. chpt., pres. med. health physics sect.), N.Y. Acad. Scis., Radiol. & Med. Physics Soc. N.Y. (past pres.), Nat. Soc. Arts and Letters (regional dir., pres. N.Y. chpt.). Iota Sigma Pi (treas., pres. V chpt.). Author: The Nurse and Radiotherapy, 1978; contbr. articles, chpts. to med. jours., texts. Office: 1275 York Ave New York NY 10021-6007

ST GERMAINE, JACQUELYN, psychologist; b. Kansas City, Mo., Sept. 8, 1951; d. Dale Dwight and Elizabeth Louise (Rose) Warnock; m. James Rosenberger. BS, Old Dominion U., 1975, MS in Edn., 1977; MA, Pepperdine U., 1981; PhD, U. Ariz., 1993. Exec. dir. Flynn Home, Poretsmouth, Va., 1978-81; supr. Cohise County Cousneling, Bisbee, Ariz., 1982; dir. Westcenter Inst., Tucson, 1982-87; rschr., cons. St. Germaine & Assoc., Tucson, 1987—; dir. S.W. Inst., Tucson, 1991—. Pres. Ariz. Bd. for cert. of Addiction Counselors, Phoenix, 1991-93; bd. dirs. Internat. Cert. Reciprocity Consortium, Raleigh, N.C., 1991—. Mem. Ariz. Group Psychotherapy Soc. (bd. dirs. 1991-93).

ST. JAMES, LYN, business owner, professional race car driver; b. Cleve., Mar. 13, 1947; d. Alfred W. and Maxine W. (Rawson) Cornwall; m. John Raymond Carusso, Dec. 7, 1970 (div. 1979); m. Roger Lessman, Feb. 27, 1993; 1 stepchild, Lindsay. Cert. in piano, St. Louis Inst. Music, 1967. Sec. Cleve. dist. sales office U.S. Steel Corp., 1967-69, Mike Roth Sales Corp., Euclid, Ohio, 1969-70; co-owner, v.p. Dynasales Fla., Hollywood, 1970-79; owner, pres. Autodyne, Ft. Lauderdale, Fla., 1974—, Creative Images, Inc., 1979—; professional race car driver, 1979—; ranked 11th Indpls. 500, 1992; race car driver Ford Motor Co., Dearborn, Mich., 1981—, spokesperson, cons., 1981—; media spokesperson 3M Co., Mpls., 1987. Author: Lyn St. James Car Owner's Manual, 1989; contbg. editor automotive articles Seventeen mag., 1987—, Cosmopolitan mag., 1989-90. Bd. trustees Women's Sports Found., N.Y.C., 1988—. Recipient Rookie of the Year, AutoWeek Magazine, 1984, Woman of Yr. award McCalls mag., 1986, Leadership award Girl Scouts U.S., 1988, Rookie of the Year at the Victory Banquet, 1992; first woman since Janet Evans to qualify for the Indpls. 500. Mem. Internat. Motorsports Assn., Sports Car Club of Am. Republican. Office: U.S. Auto Club PO Box 660460 Dallas TX 75266-0460*

ST. LAURENT, MICHELE ANN, quality analyst; b. Columbus, Ohio, Sept. 1, 1962; d. Paul Rosario and Catherine Maureen (Glencross) St. L. Student, Salem (Mass.) State Coll., 1989-91. Sr. sales asst. Copy Quik, Everett, Mass., 1985-87; office mgr. Jordan Dairy, Lynnfield, Mass., 1987-88; sr. exec. sec. Semiconductor Equipment Bus. Customer Support, Gloucester, Mass., 1988-91; quality analyst Varian SEB-CS, Palo Alto, Calif., 1991—. Bd. examiners Calif. Gov.'s Golden State Quality Award, 1994. Mem. Semiconductor Equipment and Materials Internat. Edn. Bd., Coun. for Continuous Improvement, Varian Quality Excellence Action Team. Office: Varian SEB-CS 3100 Hansen Way Palo Alto CA 94304-1030

ST.MARIE, SATENIG, writer; b. Brockton, Mass., June 2, 1927; d. Harry and Mary K. Sahjian; m. Gerald L. St. Marie, Dec. 26, 1959. B.S., Simmons Coll., Boston, 1949; M.A., Columbia U., 1959; LL.D. (hon.), N.D. State U., 1976. Extension home economist U. Mass. Extension Service, 1949-52, U. Conn. Extension Service, 1953-56; with J.C. Penney Co., Inc., 1959-87, mgr. endl. and consumer relations, 1967-73, dir. consumer affairs, 1973-87, div. v.p., 1974-87; dir. Nat. Reins. Co.; mem. U.S. Metric Bd. Author: Homes Are For People, 1973, Romantic Victorian Weddings: Then and Now, 1992; pub. J.C. Penney Consumer Edn. Services, 1981-87; lifestyles editor Victorian Homes Mag., 1987—. Mem. Am. Home Econs. Assn. (past pres.), Antiques Dealers Assn. Am. (exec. dir. 1987—). Office: PO Box 335 Greens Farms CT 06436

ST. PIERRE, CATHY M., family nurse practitioner; b. Manchester, N.H., Mar. 23, 1954; d. Roland J. and Beatrice A. (Devine) St. P. BS in Nursing, Northeastern U., Boston, 1977; MS in Nursing, U. Pa., Phila., 1981; PhD, Boston Coll., 1994. Cert. family nurse practitioner. Staff nurse St. Elizabeth's Hosp., Brighton, Mass., 1977-78, VA Med. Ctr., Manchester, N.H., 1978-79, Boston Vis. Nurse Assn., 1979-80, Grad. Hosp., Phila., 1980-82; family nurse practitioner Dorchester (Mass.) House Health Ctr., 1982-85; instr., lectr. U. Lowell (Mass.), 1985-88; adolescent nurse practitioner Child Health Svcs., Manchester, 1988-89; family nurse practitioner Valley Med. Assocs. HMO, Methuen, Mass., 1989-94; asst. prof. Rivier Coll., Nashua, N.H., 1994—; instr., lectr. U. Pa., Phila., 1981-82; clin. instr. Northeastern U., Boston, 1984-85, U. Mass., Boston, 1982-84; mem. nurse practitioner liaison com. Bd. Nursing in N.H., 1986-88; asst. prof. master's program Rivier Coll., Nashua, N.H. Bd. mem. Family Svcs. Greater Lowell, 1987-88. Mem. ANA, N.J. Nurses Assn., N.H. Nurse Practitioner Assn. (co-pres. 1986-88, v.p. 1992-94).

ST. THOMAS, LINDA, museum director; b. Cambridge, Mass., May 24, 1949; d. Leo and Violet (Peardon) S.; m. James McDonald, 1975; 2 children. BA, Cath U. of Am., 1971. Asst. editor Modern Brewery Age Mag., Stamford, Conn.; news bur. mgr. pub. rels. office Cath. U. of Am., Washington; pub. affairs specialist, assoc. dir., then acting dir. office pub. affairs Smithsonian Instn., Washington. Recipient Pub. Rels. Soc. of Am. award. Roman Catholic. Office: Smithsonian Instn Office Pub Affairs 900 Jefferson Dr SW Rm 2410 Washington DC 20560*

SAITO, KATHLEEN KEIKO, architect, interior design; b. Honolulu, May 4, 1955; d. Raymond Mitsuyoshi and Midlred Tomiko (Kuromoto) Kawano; m. Sanford Sadamu Saito, July 31, 1982. BArch, U. Hawaii. Registered architect, Hawaii. Intern architect Group 70, Honolulu, 1979-81, assoc. architect, interior design, 1982-87; interior designer, draftsperson Paul Kamada and Assocs., Honolulu, 1981-82; archtl. draftsperson Zephyr Archtl. Ptnrship, Honolulu, 1981-82; owner Saito Design Assocs., 1987—. Recipient Lishman award Bldg. Industry Assn. and Am. Soc. Interior Designers, 1984, Renaissance award Bldg. Industry Assn. and Honolulu mag., 1990, 91. Mem. AIA.

SAITO, KIYOMI, investment banking executive; b. Tokyo, Japan, Dec. 1, 1950; d. Genichiro and Kimiko Saito; m. Tsuguo Tadakawa, Aug. 20, 1974 (div. Aug. 1975); m. Kenji Takei, Dec. 3, 1994. BA, Keio U., Tokyo, 1973; MBA, Harvard Bus. Sch., 1981. Staff Nihon Econ. Jour., Tokyo, 1973-74; asst. Sony Corp., Tokyo, 1975-79; account officer, product specialist Bank of Am., Tokyo, 1981-82; mktg. mgr. Elizabeth Arden, Tokyo, 1982-84; v.p. Morgan Stanley Internat., Tokyo, 1984-88, N.Y.C., 1988-89, Morgan Stanley Realty, 1989-91; prin. Rep. Office Morgan Stanley Realty Inc., Tokyo, 1991-92; pres. Pont du Gard Co. Ltd., 1992—. Author: A Woman's New Start, 1984, Women's Era, 1986, Kiyomi's Challenge, 1994. Home: 4-35-13 Nishiogi-Kita, Suginamiku Tokyo 167, Japan

SAIZAN, PAULA THERESA, oil company executive; b. New Orleans, Sept. 12, 1947; d. Paul Morine and Hattie Mae (Hayes) Saizan; m. George H. Smith, May 26, 1973 (div. July 1976). BS in Acctg. summa cum laude, Xavier U., 1969. CPA, Tex.; notary pub. Systems engr. IBM, New Orleans, 1969-71; acct., then sr. acct. Shell Oil Co., Houston, Tex., 1971-76, sr. fin. analyst, 1976-77, fin. rep., 1977-79, corp. auditor, 1979-81, treasury rep., 1981-82, sr. treasury rep., 1982-86; asst. treas. Shell Credit Inc., Shell Leasing Co., Shell Fin. Co. 1986-88, sr. pub. affairs rep., 1988-89, sr. staff pub. affairs rep., 1990-91, program mgr., 1991—. Bd. dirs. Houston Downtown Mgmt. Corp., Greater Houston Conv. and Visitors Bur., St. Joseph Hosp. Found., Children at Risk; mem. adv. coun. U.S. SBA region VI, Houston; acctg. dept. adv. bd. Tex. So. U. Mem. AICPA, NAACP, Tex. Soc. CPAs (bd. dirs. Houston chpt.), Leadership Houston, Greater Inwood Partnership, LWV of Houston, Xavier U. Alumni Assn., Nat. Assn. Black Accts., Nat. Coun. Negro Women, Inc., Nat. Political Congress Black Women, Alpha Kappa Alpha, Phi Gamma Nu, Kappa Gamma Pi. Roman Catholic. Home: 5426 Long Creek Ln Houston TX 77088-4407 Office: Shell Oil Co PO Box 2463 Houston TX 77252-2463

SAKAI, HIROKO, trading company executive; b. Nishiharu, Aichi-ken, Japan, Jan. 9, 1939; came to U.S., 1956; d. Kichiya and Saki (Shiraishi) S. BA, Wellesley Coll., 1963; MA, Columbia U., 1967, PhD, 1972. Journalist Asahi Evening News, Tokyo, 1963-65; escort interpreter Dept. State, Washington, 1967-68; econ. analyst Port Authority N.Y. and N.J., N.Y.C., 1968-69; sr. cons. Harbridge House, Inc., Boston, 1970-84, Quantum Sci. Corp., White Plains, N.Y., 1984-87; corp. planner ITOCHU Internat. Inc., N.Y.C., N.Y., 1988-92; dir. bus. devel. ITOCHU Internat. Inc., N.Y.C., 1993—. Interpreter Govt. Mass., Boston, 1974. Wellesley Coll. fellow, 1960-63, Columbia U. fellow, 1965-68; Columbia U. grantee, 1969. Mem. Regional Sci. Assn., Assn. Am. Geographers. Buddist. Home: 235 E 51st St Apt 5C New York NY 10022-6523 Office: ITOCHU Internat Inc 335 Madison Ave New York NY 10017-4605

SAKANO, BARBARA UNGER, educator, poet; b. N.Y.C., Oct. 2, 1932; d. David and Florence (Schuchalter) Frankel; m. Bernard Unger, 1954 (div. 1976); m. Theodore Sakano, 1987. B.A., CCNY, 1955, M.A., 1957; advanced cert. NYU, 1970; children: Deborah, Suzanne. Grad. asst. Yeshiva U., 1962-63; edn. editor County Citizen, Rockland County, N.Y., 1960-63; tchr. English, N.Y.C. Pub. Schs., 1955-58, Nyack (N.Y.) High Sch., 1963-67; guidance counselor Ardsley (N.Y.) High Sch., 1967-69; prof. English, Rockland Community Coll., Suffern, N.Y., 1969—; poetry fellow Squaw Valley Community of Writers, 1980; writer-in-residence Rockland Ctr. for Arts, 1986. Author: (poetry) Basement, 1975, Learning to Fox Trot, 1989, The Man Who Burned Money, 1980, Inside the Wind, 1986, Blue Depression Glass in Troika One, 1991; (fiction) Dying for Uncle Ray, 1990; contbr. poetry to over 50 lit. mags., including: Kans. Quar., Carolina Quar., Beloit Poetry Jour., Minn. Rev., Poet and Critic, The Nation, Poetry Now, Invisible City, Thirteenth Moon, So. Poetry Rev., Mass. Rev., Nebr. Rev., Wis. Rev., So. Humanities Rev., Denver Quarterly, Mississippi Valley REv., The G.W. Rev. Wordsmith; contbr. to Anthology Mag. Verse, Yearbook Am. Poetry, 1984, 89; contbr. poetry (anthologies) Two Worlds Walking, Life on the Line, Looking for Home, 80 on the Eighties, Disenchantments, Women and Work, If I Had a Hammer, Sexual Harassment: Women Speak Out; contbr. fiction to True to Life Adventure Stories, Midstream, Esprit, Beloit Fiction Jour., Am. Fiction '89 and numerous others; poetry reading in colls. and libraries throught N.Y. and elsewhere; critical reviewer Contact II. Ragdale Found. fellow, 1985, 86, 89, SUNY Creative Writing fellow, 1981-82, Edna St. Vincent Millay Colony fellow, 1984, Djerassi Found. fellow, 1991, Hambidge Ctr. for Creative Arts and Scis. fellow, 1988; NEH grantee, 1975. Recipient Goodman Poetry award, 1989, Anna Davidson Rosenberg award Judah Magnes Mus., 1989, Roberts Writing award, 1990, New Letters Literary awards, 1990; finalist Am. Fiction Competition, 1989, W.Va. Writing Competition, 1982, John Williams Narrative Poetry Competition, 1992; honorable mention Chester Jones Nat. Poetry Contest. Mem. Poets and Writers, Poetry Soc. Am., Writers' Community. Office: Rockland Community Coll 145 College Rd Suffern NY 10901-3611

SAKASH, LANA CAROL, county official; b. Ermine, Ky., Dec. 10, 1948; d. William and Sarah Evelyn (Hall) Cook; m. George John Sakash, Mar. 13, 1982; children: Jennifer, Jeffrey, Teresa, Susan. BA cum laude, Carson-Newman Coll., Jefferson City, Tenn., 1971. Lic. social worker, Ohio. Supr. Dept. Human Resources, Whitesburg, Ky., 1972-73; social worker Seneca County Dept. Human Svcs., Tiffin, Ohio, 1974-80; supr. Wyandot County Dept. Human Svcs., Upper Sandusky, Ohio, 1980-85, dir., 1985—. Pres. Community Coun. of Upper Sandusky, 1988-90; chmn. Wyandot County Substance Abuse Task Force, Upper Sandusky, 1988—; sec. Salvation Army, Upper Sandusky, 1988—; asst. leader Girl Scouts U.S.A., McCuthchenville, Ohio, 1988—; CCD and confirmation tchr. Our Lady of consolations, Carey, Ohio, 1983-92; sec. Wyandot County Sesquincentennial com., 1994-95. Mem. Am. Pub. Welfare League of Am., Pub. children's Svcs. Assn. of Ohio (trustee 1984-88), Ohio Human Svcs. Dirs. Assn. (workshop chmn. 1992-93), N.W. Ohio Dirs. Assn. (pres. 1988-89), Ohio Human Svcs. Dirs. Assn. (sec. 1994). Roman Catholic. Office: Wyandot County Human Svcs 137 S Sandusky Ave Upper Sandusky OH 43351-1489

SAKELLARIOS, GERTRUDE EDITH, retired office nurse; b. Lowell, Mass., Mar. 14, 1929; d. William V. and Eileen E. (Hale) Yoachimciuk; m. Angelos D. Sakellarios, Dec. 30, 1966. Diploma, Lowell Gen. Hosp., 1949; student, Boston U., 1949-53, Boston Coll./St. Josephs Hosp., Lowell, 1951. Gen. duty med.-surg. nurse Lowell Gen. Hosp., 1949-50, operating room nurse, 1950-52; office nurse gen. practitioner's office, Lowell, 1952-83. Home: 124 Cashin St Lowell MA 01851-2004

SAKS, JUDITH-ANN, artist; b. Anniston, Ala., Dec. 20, 1943; d. Julien David and Lucy-Jane (Watson) S.; student Tex. Acad. Art, 1957-58, Mus. Fine Arts, Houston, 1962, Rice U., 1962; BFA, Tulane U., 1966; postgrad. U. Houston, 1967; m. Haskell Irvin Rosenthal, Dec. 22, 1974; 1 child, Brian Julien. One-man shows include: Alley Gallery, Houston, 1969, 2131 Gallery, Houston, 1969; group shows include: Birmingham (Ala.) Mus., 1967, Meinhard Galleries, Houston, 1977; Galerie Barbizon, Houston, 1980, Park Crest Gallery, Austin, 1981; represented in permanent collections including: L.B. Johnson Manned Space Mus., Clear Lake City, Tex., Harris County Heritage Mus., Windsor Castle, London, Smithsonian Instn., Washington: commns. include: Pin Oak Charity Horse Show Assn., Roberts S.S. Agy., New Orleans, Cruiser Houston Meml. Rm., U. Houston; curator student art collection U. Houston, 1968-72; artist Am. Revolution Bicentennial project Port of Houston Authority, 1975-76. Recipient art awards including: 1st prize for water color Art League Houston, 1969, 1st prize for graphics, 1969, 1st prize for sculpture, 1968, 1st place award for original print, DAR, Am. Heritage Com., 1987. Mem. Art League Houston, Houston Mus. Fine Arts, DAR (curator 1983-85, 93—, contbr. Tex. sesquicentennial drawing for DAR mag.), Daus. Republic Tex. Home: 2215 Briar Br Houston TX 77042-2959

SAKSON, SHARON R(OSE), journalist, writer, educator; b. Trenton, N.J., June 6, 1952; d. John Andrew and Helen Hope (Haggerty) S. BA, Georgetown U., 1974. Desk asst. ABC News, Washington, 1972-73, prodn. asst., 1973-74; TV news field prodr. ABC-TV News, London and Miami, Fla., 1979-85; news producer Sta. WBAL-TV, Balt., 1974-75; news prodr. Stas. ABC-TV/CBS-TV, Chgo., 1976-77; exec. producer Sta. KPIX-TV (Westinghouse), San Francisco, 1977-79; freelance writer Lawrenceville, N.J., 1985—; tchr. Oxbridge Acads., Paris, 1990-94; exec. dir. Oxbridge Academics, 1994—. Author: (short stories) 2d Gazette Fiction Collection, 1987, Streetsongs, 1990, (book) Miami, 1990, Florida, 1991. Recipient Katherine Ann Porter prize for fiction, 1989, Nimrod Lit. prize, 1989; grantee Commonwealth of Pa., 1989. Mem. Am. Whippet Club, Dog Writers Assn. Am., Trenton Kennel Club. Roman Catholic. Home: #273 3375 Brunswick Pike Lawrenceville NJ 08648

SALAGI, DORIS, educator; b. Perth Amboy, N.J., July 30, 1947; d. Joseph William and Anna Salagi. BA, Trenton State Coll., 1969, MA, 1973. Cert. elem. sch. tchr., supr., tchr. of the handicapped. 3d grade tchr. Willingboro

(N.J.) Bd. Edn., 1969-79, basic skills math. tchr., 1979-83, resource rm. tchr., 1983-87, tchr. of the handicapped, 1987-92, individualized ednl. plan facilitator, 1992—; curriculum writer Willingboro Bd. Edn., 1973, 77, 79-83. Co-author: (composition curriculum) The Care and Handling of Compositions, 1973. Vol. Rancocas Hosp., Willingboro, 1978—. Named for Outstanding Achievement in Edn., Trenton State Coll. Alumni Assn., 1991. Mem. Willingboro Edn. Assn. (rep. 1974-76), Twin Hills PTA, Rancocas Hosp. Aux. (pres. 1987-89, rec. sec. 1983-87, bazaar chair 1981-85, scholarship chair 1978-81), Delta Kappa Gamma (rec. sec. Alpha Zeta state 1995—, Eta chpt., treas. 1992—, pres. 1990-92, 1st v.p. 1988-90, fundraising 1985-88). Office: Willingboro Bd Edn Levitt Bldg 50 Salem Rd Rm A8 Willingboro NJ 08046-2847

SALAKA, KATHLEEN A., health system administrator; b. Youngstown, Ohio, Aug. 16, 1954; d. Andrew Joseph and Josephine Agnes (Bizub) S. BA in Liberal Arts, Youngstown State U., 1976, MS, 1981, AAS, 1991. Asst. dir. pub. rels. Hillside Rehab. Hosp., Warren, Ohio, 1979-84; dir. vol. svcs. Western Res. Care Sys., Youngstown, 1984—. Dir: video prodn. United Way, 1991, We Can Make a Difference, 1993, Hero-Volunteers, 1994. Advisor Rayen H.S., Youngstown, 1991—, Option IV Choffin Career. Youngstown, 1991—, Vol. Svcs., Youngstown, 1993—; chair award com. Youngstown area YMCA, 1993—; United Way Loaned Exec., 1994—. Recipient Profl. Achievement award Am. Hosp. Assn., 1994. Mem. Am. Soc. Dir. Vol. Svcs., Ohio State Dir. Vol. Svcs. (membership chair 1986-87, editor newsletter, 1993-94), Youngstown State U. Alumni Assn. Democrat. Home: 641 Bedford Rd Lowellville OH 44436 Office: Western Res Care Sys 345 Oak Hill Ave Youngstown OH 44501

SALAMON, LINDA BRADLEY, university dean, English literature educator; b. Elmira, N.Y., Nov. 20, 1941; d. Grant Ellsworth and Evelyn E. (Ward) Bradley; divorced; children: Michael Lawrence, Timothy Martin. B.A., Radcliffe Coll., 1963; M.A., Bryn Mawr Coll., 1964, Ph.D., 1971; Advanced Mgmt. Cert., Harvard U. Bus. Sch., 1978; D.H.L., St. Louis Coll. Pharmacy, 1993. Lectr., adj. asst. prof. Eng. Dartmouth Coll., Hanover, N.H., 1967-72; mem. faculty lit. Bennington Coll., Vt., 1974-75; dean students Wells Coll., Aurora, N.Y., 1975-77; exec. asst. to pres. U. Pa., Phila., 1977-79; assoc. prof. English Washington U., St. Louis, 1979-88, prof., 1988-92, dean Coll. Arts and Scis., 1979-92; prof. English, dean Columbia Sch. Arts and Scis. George Washington U., Washington, 1992—; mem. faculty Bryn Mawr Summer Inst. for Women, 1979—. Author, coeditor: Nicholas Hilliard's Art of Limning, 1983; co-author: Integrity in the College Curriculum, 1985; contbr. numerous articles to literary and ednl. jours. Bd. dirs. Assn. Am. Colls., vice chmn., 1985, chmn., 1986; bd. dirs. Greater St. Louis council Girl Scouts U.S.A.; trustee Coll. Bd., St. Louis Coll. Pharmacy. Fellow Radcliffe Coll. Bunting Inst., 1973-74; Am. Philos. Soc. Penrose grantee, 1974; fellow Folger Shakespeare Library, 1986, NEH Montaigne Inst., 1988. Mem. MLA, Renaissance Soc., Cosmos Club, Phi Beta Kappa. Office: George Washington U Washington DC 20052

SALAMON, RENAY, real estate broker; b. N.Y.C., May 13, 1948; d. Solomon and Mollie (Friedman) Langman; m. Maier Salamon, Aug. 10, 1968; children: Mollie, Jean, Leah, Sharon, Eugene. BA, Hunter Coll., 1969. Licensed real estate borker, N.J. Mgr. office Customode Designs Inc., N.Y.C., 1966-68; co-owner Salamon Dairy Farms, Three Bridges, N.J., 1968-86; assoc. realtor Max. D. Shuman Realty Inc., Flemington, N.J., 1983-85; pres., chief exec. officer Liberty Hill Realty Inc., Flemington, N.J., 1985—; cons. Illva Saronna Inc. (Illva Group), Edison, N.J. 1985—; real estate devel. joint venture with M.R.F.S. Realty Inc. (Illva Group), 1986—. Mem. Readington Twp. Environ. Commn., Whitehouse Sta., N.J., 1978-87, N.J. Assn. Environ. Commrs., Trenton, 1978—; fundraiser Rutgers Prep. Sch., Somerset, N.J., 1984—; bd. dirs. Hunterdon County YMCA, 1987—. Named N.J. Broker Record, Forbes Inc., N.Y.C. 1987. Mem. Nat. Assn. Realtors, N.J. Assn. Realtors, Hunterdon County Bd. Realtors (mem. chair 1986), Realtor's Land Inst. Republican. Jewish. Office: Liberty Hill Realty Inc 415 US Hwy 202 Flemington NJ 08822-9465

SALAMONE-KOCHOWICZ, JEAN GLORIA, banker; b. White Deer, Pa., Dec. 28, 1929; d. Dewey and Pearl Viola (Bastian) Smith; m. Daniel W. Salamone, Nov. 2, 1946 (div. 1977); children: Daryl Joseph, John Daniel; m. John T. Kochowicz, Feb. 10, 1990. Student, Bloomsburg State Coll., 1946, Am. Inst. Banking, 1974-85. Sec. Chef Boy-ar-Dee Foods, Milton, Pa., 1946-48, Arthur Andersen & Co., Washington, 1948-58; exec. sec. Citizens Bank and Trust Co., Riverdale, Md., 1970-74, asst. treas., 1974-77, asst. v.p., 1977-84; v.p. Citizens Bank and Trust Co. (name now Citizens Bank Md.), Riverdale, Laurel, Md., 1984—; also corp. sec. Citizens Bancorp (holding co. for Citizens Bank Md.), Laurel. Trustee Prince George's Arts Coun., Riverdale, 1983—, treas., 1983-89, pres. 1990-91. Mem. Fin. Women Internat. (pres. met. Md. group 1977-78). Roman Catholic.

SALAND, LINDA CAROL, anatomy educator, researcher; b. N.Y.C., Oct. 24, 1942; d. Charles and Esther (Weingarten) Gewirtz; m. Joel S. Saland, Aug. 16, 1964; children—Kenneth, Jeffrey. B.S., CCNY, 1963, Ph.D. in Biology, 1968; M.A. in Zoology, Columbia U., 1965. Research assoc. dept. anatomy Columbia U. Coll. Physicians and Surgeons, N.Y.C., 1968-69; sr. research assoc. dept. anatomy Sch. Medicine, U. N.Mex., Albuquerque, 1971-78, asst. prof., 1978-83, assoc. prof., 1983-89, prof., 1989—. Mem. editorial bd. Anat. Record, 1980—; contbr. articles to profl. jours. Predoctoral fellow NDEA, 1966-68; research grantee Nat. Inst. on Drug Abuse, 1979-83, NIH Minority Biomed. Research Support Program, 1980—; NIH research grantee, 1986—. Mem. AAAS, Am. Assn. Anatomists, Soc. for Neurosci., Women in Neuroscience (chair steering comm. 1991-93), Am. Soc. Cell Biology, Sigma Xi. Office: U NMex Sch Medicine Dept Anatomy Basic Med Sci Bldg Albuquerque NM 87131

SALANTRO, MARIA VOGEL, retired art educator; b. N.Y.C., Jan. 25, 1918; d. Salvatore and Marie (Mondello) S.; children: Michele Jolly, Linda Vogel Kelley. Student, Art Students League, N.Y.C., Salmugundi Club, N.Y.C. Art tchr. Mission Hills Mus. Am. Folk Art, N.Y.C., 1979-85, Forest Hills (N.Y.) Sr. Ctr., 1984-87; tchr. art Mission Hills; artist Miniature Art Soc. Fla., 1987-93, O.T.O.W. Art Guild, Clearwater, Fla., 1991-93. Recipient many awards for paintings. Mem. Nat. Mus. Women in Arts. Democrat. Roman Catholic. Home: 1439 Mission Dr W Clearwater FL 34619

SALAS-DARK, ANGELINA TELLEZ, city official; b. Anthony, N.Mex., Apr. 12, 1948; d. Jose P. and Alicia C. (Chavez) Tellez; m. David J. Dark, Dec. 15, 1990; children: Manuel Joseph, Jaime Christopher. AA, Chaffey Jr. Coll., Alta Loma, 1990. Receptionist Fire Dept. City of Ontario, Calif., 1975-79, sec. housing and bldg. dept., 1979-84, housing and code enforcement specialist, 1984-93, downtown devel. coord., 1993—; supervisory chmn. Ontario Pub. Employees Fed. Credit Union, 1990-94, bd. dirs., 1994—; notary pub., Calif., 1981—. Campaign sub-chair City of Ontario County Seat, 1992; den. mother Boy Scouts Am., Ontario, 1980; newsletter chair City of Ontario Firebelles, 1976-80; mem. adv. bd. Salvation Army,1993—. Recipient Recognition award D.A.R.E., Ontario, 1992. Mem. Nat. Mgmt. Assn. (cert., newsletter editor 1986-90), Downtown Ontario Bus. and Profl. Assn. (bd. dirs. 1993—), Kiwanis (v.p. 1993-94, Kiwanian of the Yr. 1992-93), Nat. Women in Constrn. (membership com. 1989-91). Democrat. Roman Catholic. Home: 1388 E Bonnie Brae St Ontario CA 91764-2118 Office: City of Ontario 303 E B St Ontario CA 91764-4196

SALAVERRIA, HELENA CLARA, educator; b. San Francisco, May 19, 1923; d. Blas Saturnino and Eugenia Irene (Loyarte) S. AB, U. Calif., Berkeley, 1945, secondary teaching cert., 1946; MA, Stanford U., 1962. High sch. tchr., 1946-57; asst. prof. Luther Coll., Decorah, Iowa, 1959-60; prof. Spanish, Bakersfield (Calif.) Coll., 1961-84, chmn. dept., 1973-80. Vol., Hearst Castle; mem. srs. adv. group edn. Cuesta Coll. Community Svcs. Mem. AAUW (edn. com.), NEA, Calif. Fgn. Lang. Tchrs. Assn. (dir. 1976-77), Kern County Fgn. Lang. Tchrs. Assn. (pres. 1975-77), Union Concerned Scientists, Natural Resources Def. Coun., Calif. Tchrs. Assn. (chpt. sec. 1951-52), Yolo County Coun. Retarded, Soc. Basque Studies in Am., RSVP, Amnesty Internat., Common Cause, Sierra Club, Prytanean Alumnae, U. Women of Cambria, U. Calif. Alumni Assn., Stanford U. Alumni Assn. Democrat. Presbyterian. Address: PO Box 63 Cambria CA 93428-0063

SALAY, CINDY ROLSTON, systems analyst, nurse; b. Roanoke, Va., July 18, 1955; d. Gilbert Wilson and Elinor Patterson (Sandridge) Rolston; m. John Matthew, July 7, 1988; 1 child, David. AAS, Va. Western Community Coll., 1976; AS, J. Sargeant Reynolds Community Coll., 1982; BS, Va. Commonwealth U., 1984. RN. Operating room RN Henrico Doctors Hosp., Richmond, Va., 1979-80; nursing supr. Johnston Willis Hosp., Richmond, 1980-87; systems analyst, coord. Health Corp Va., Richmond, 1983-87, sr. project leader, 1987-88; sr. systems analyst Hosp. Corp. Am., Nashville, 1987; sr. systems cons. IBAX Healthcare Systems, Reston, Va., 1988-94; systems analyst MCV Hosps. Info. Sys., Richmond, Va., 1994—. Presbyterian. Home: 5307 Chestnut Bluff Terr Midlothian VA 23112

SALAZAR, LUCY LINA, psychologist; b. Las Vegas, N.Mex., Apr. 21, 1961; d. Joe C. and Louise E. (Berniger) S.; m. Charles B. Heath, Apr. 13, 1981 (div. Oct. 1981). BA, N.Mex. H. Univ., 1986, MA, 1987. Clin. specialist Sangre de Cristo Community Mental Health Svcs., Inc., Santa Fe, N.Mex., 1988-89; dep. ctr. dir. Mental Health Resources, Inc., Clovis, N.Mex., 1989-90; psychologist San Miguel More Community Mental Health Svcs., Las Vegas, 1990-91, N.Mex. Boys Sch., Springer, N.Mex., 1991—; lab. asst. NIH/Minorities Biomed. Rsch., Las Vegas, 1984-86. Home visitations Mental Health Resources, Mora, N.Mex., 1988, SM-MCMHS, 1989. Mem. ACA. Republican. LDS.

SALDIVAR-GARZA, SYLVIA, social worker; b. San Benito, Tex., Aug. 17, 1957; d. Samuel and M. Dora (Balli) Saldivar; m. Gustavo Ch. Garza, Aug. 17, 1988; children: Maritza, Josejulian, Karla, Kayla. BSW, U. Tex. Pan Am., 1980. Child protective svcs. specialist II Child Protective Unit, Tex. Dept. of Human Svcs., Harlingen, Tex., 1980-87; counselor, ednl. social worker Communities in Schs., Harlingen, 1987-90; ednl. social worker Out Reach: Harligen CISD, 1990; social worker Pregnancy Edn. and Parenting Lyford (Tex.) Sch. Dist., 1993—. Chairperson Women's Group, Rio Hondo, Tex., 1983-84, Youth Orgn. Group, Rio Hondo, 1984-86; vol., tchr. Rio Hondo, 1983-86, Our Lady of Guadalupe Ch., Raymondville, 1992—; treas. Write in Candidate, Raymondville, 1992. Roman Catholic. Home: PO Box 305 Raymondville TX 78580 Office: Pregancy Edn and Parenting Lyford High Sch PO Box 220 Lyford TX 78569

SALEEBY-GARDNER, DIANE LYNN, mental health counselor; b. Binghamton, N.Y., Oct. 29, 1947; d. Edward and Alice (Haick) Saleeby; m. James Molinaro, May 5, 1969 (div. Mar. 1973); children: David, Joseph.; m. Christopher Gardner, Oct. 2, 1990. AA, Broome Tech. C.C., Binghamton, 1967; BA, MS, Fla. Internat. U., 1993; postgrad., Fla. Inst. Religious Studies, 1993—, pastoral degree, 1994. Ct. reporter Pro Reporting, Inc., Long Island, N.Y., 1974-88; counselor Domestic Abuse Shelter, Tavernier, Fla., 1988-91; co-counselor Domestic Safety Program, Tavernier, 1991—; delinquency counselor Health & Rehab. Svcs., Tavernier, 1991-93; clinician Bertha Abess Children's Ctr./Key Largo (Fla.) Sch., 1993—; mem. Family Svc. Planning Team, Tavernier, 1993—; pastor/counselor Universal Ch., 1994. Coun. mem. Interagy. Coun., Tavernier, 1991—; mem. Friends of Islamorada (Fla.) State Parks, 1991—. Mem. Am. Mental Health Counselors' Assn., Fla. Assn. for Counseling & Devel. (scholarship grant 1992), Bus. & Profl. Women's Club (scholarship bd.). Home: PO Box 264 Tavernier FL 33070 Office: Bertha Abess Children's Ctr 10800 Biscayne Blvd Ste 200 Miami FL 33161

SALEM, SUSANNE FRANCES, consulting executive; b. San Francisco, Mar. 25, 1945; d. Edward L. and Mary F. (Adams) Ledinski; m. Lee C. Salem, July 14, 1979. B.S., Ariz. State U., 1979. Ins. agt. Atlantic Mut. Ins. Co. and Harris & Assocs., Los Angeles, 1964-73; ptnr. Acero Enterprises, Sierra Vista, Ariz., 1973-77; lease account mgr. Truck Leasing, Phoenix, 1979-80; sales and cons. Internat. Transp., Phoenix, 1980; owner Corp. Directions Cons. & Recruiting, Phoenix, 1980-86; v.p., bd. dirs. The Prism Group, Inc., Cons., Tempe, Ariz., 1987-94; human resource leader W.L. Gore & Assocs., 1994—; guest speaker. Bd. dirs. Southeastern Ariz. Drug Abuse Coun., 1975-77, The Ariz. Partnership, 1989—, adv. bd. dirs. Maricopa Skill Ctr., 1989—. Mem. Am. Trucking Assns. (bd. dirs., scholar 1977-79, outstanding transp. grad. 1979), Ariz. C. of C. Contbr. articles to profl. jours. Office: W.L. Gore & Assocs, Inc 4747 E Beautiful Lane #2 Phoenix AZ 85044

SALEMBIER, VALERIE BIRNBAUM, publishing executive; b. Teaneck, N.J., July 2, 1945; d. Jack and Sara (Gordon) Birnbaum; m. David J. Salembier, June 23, 1968 (div. 1980); m. Paul J. Block, Dec. 9, 1990. B.A., Coll. of New Rochelle, 1973. Merchandising mgr. Life Internat., Time, Inc., N.Y.C., 1964-69; merchandising copywriter Newsweek, Inc., N.Y.C., 1970; promotion prodn. mgr. Newsweek, Inc., 1971, adv. sales rep., 1972-76; advt. dir. Ms. Mag., N.Y.C., 1976-79, assoc. pub., 1979-81; pub. Inside Sports Mag., N.Y.C., 1982; v.p., pub. 13-30 Corp., N.Y.C., 1983; sr. v.p. advt. USA Today, 1983-88; pub. TV Guide, Radnor, PA, 1988-89; pres. N.Y. Post, N.Y.C., 1989-90; pub. Family Circle Mag., N.Y.C., 1991-93; v.p. advt. The N.Y. Times, 1993—; lectr. in field. Trustee Coll. New Rochelle, N.Y.C. Police Found.; mem. exec. com. Women of Distinction, United Jewish Appeal; v.p., bd. dirs. Supportive Children's Advocacy Network; bd. dirs. Nat. Alliance Breast Cancer Orgns., N.Y. Road Runners Club, BOX (Beneficial Orgn. to Aid Ex-Fighters). Mem. C200, Women in Comm., Internat. Womens Forum, Orgn. for Rehab. Through Tng., Women's City Club, Nat. Coun. Jewish Women, Hadassah (bd. dirs.), N.Y. Rd. Runners Club. Home: 1075 Park Ave New York NY 10128-1003 Office: The NY Times 229 W 43rd St New York NY 10036-3913

SALEM-MURDOCK, MUNEERA, anthropologist; b. Amman, Jordan, May 15, 1947; d. Yahya Salem and Zahra (Shapsugh) Abzach; m. Paul Irving Murdock, Apr. 14, 1973 (div. Apr. 1983); 1 child, Tamara. MA in English Lit., Ill. State U., 1973; MA in Anthropology, SUNY, Binghamton, 1977, PhD in Anthropology, 1984. Mem. Pakistan Forestry Planning and Devel. Project, 1983; project mgr. Evaluation of Potable Water Projects in Rural Tunisia, 1983; dir. Liberia: Social Institutional Profile of Agrl. Sector, 1984; dir. rsch. devel. Ctrl. Tunisia Devel. Authority, 1985-87, 86-88; co-dir. African River Basin Devel. Project, 1984-85, 85-89; dir. Regional Range Mgmt. Project, UN Food and Agriculture Orgn., 1986-88; dir. long term rsch. Senegal River Basin Monitoring Activity I, 1988-90, Senegal River Basin Monitoring Activity II, 1990—; socioeconomist Maroc/MIAC Dryland Rsch. Ctr.: Socioeconomic Monitoring and Evalution USAID/Rabat and U. Nebr., 1989, Island of Socotra, People's Dem. Republic of Yemen, 1989; environ. and resettlement expert The World Bank, 1987; sr. rschr. USAID/Tunis and Tunisian Govt., 1985; community devel. specialist Rural Community Deve. Project, 1984; rschr. Socio-institutional Profile of Niger, 1982-83, rschr. numerous other projects; conference presenter. Contbr. numerous articles to profl. jours. Scholarship Ministry of Edn., Govt. of Jordan, 1965-69, Am. Friends of the Middle East, 1971-73, Lang. scholarship Goethe Inst., 1969; grad. rsch. fellowship SUNY, Binghamton, 1975-80, 82, Inst. for Devel. Anthropology, 1979-80; grantee Social Sci. Rsch. Coun., 1982, Wenner-Gren Found. for Anthropol. Rsch., 1981. Democrat. Islam. Home: 15 Beethoven St Binghamton NY 13905-4245 Office: PO Box 2207 Binghamton NY 13902-2207

SALENGER, LUCY LEE, producer, consultant; b. St. Louis, Sept. 12, 1938; d. Leo and Lucille (Mier) Berner; m. Marvin Zonis, Jan. 4, 1976; children: Laura, Nadia, Leah. BA with honors, UCLA, 1961. Press asst. Kennedy for Pres., L.A., 1968; field producer, reporter, researcher 60 Minutes, CBS News, L.A., 1970-72; reporter, producer Sta. WLS-TV, Chgo., 1972-74; field producer CBS News, Chgo., 1974-75; dir. Ill. Film Office, Chgo., 1975-83; gen. ptnr. The Odeon Group, Chgo., 1986—; sr. cons. Harpo Studios, Chgo., 1988-89; assoc. prodr. Brewster Place, Chgo., 1989-90; cons. to gov. on culture State of Ill., Chgo., 1988; v.p. Marvin Qonis and Assoc., Internat. Cons., 1990—; bd. dirs. Radio Sta. WBEZ. Bd. advisors Ill. State Fair, Chgo., 1980-83; bd. dirs. Chgo. Film Festival, 1978-82, Rehab. Inst. Chgo., 1981-83, Mus. Broadcasting, Chgo., 1984-89, Chgo. Coalition, 1980-83. Recipient 1st achievement award Facets Multimedia, 1980, ann. award Chgo. Coalition, 1983, Woman of Yr. award Sta. WBBM, Chgo., 1985, 1st ann. achievement award Women in Film 1987; urban fellow Northeastern U., 1985. Mem. Chgo. Network (bd. dirs. 1989—), Women in Film (Chgo. adv. bd. 1990), Nat. Assn. Film Communicators (bd. dirs. 1984—). Jewish. Home: 4942 S Ellis Ave Chicago IL 60615-2708

SALERNO, SISTER MARIA, nursing educator, adult and gerontological nurse; b. Syracuse, N.Y.; d. Joseph and Josephine (Ostrowski) S. Diploma in nursing, St. Joseph's Hosp., Syracuse, 1962; BSN summa cum laude, Cath. U. Am., 1974, MS in Nursing, 1976, D of Nursing Sci., 1981; cert. nurse practitioner, U. Rochester, 1983. RN, N.Y., D.C.; joined Sisters of Third Franciscan Order, Roman Cath. Ch., 1963. Staff nurse St. Joseph Hosp. Health Ctr., Syracuse, 1962-63; sr. charge nurse ICU, gen. med. and surg. units St. Elizabeth Hosp., Utica, N.Y., 1965-66, head nurse pediatrics unit, 1966-69; head nurse ECF Loretto Geriatric Ctr., Syracuse, 1969-72; asst. prof. Cath. U. Am., Washington, 1978-79, 81-92, assoc. prof. nursing, 1992—, dir. primary care adult nurse practitioner program, 1984—. Contbr. chpts. to books; contbr. articles to profl. jours. Vol. nurse practitioner Community of Hope, Washington. Grantee NIH, 1984-89, Cath. U. Am., 1989-90. mem. ANA (cert. adult nurse practitioner, mem. coun. nurse researchers), AAUP, Am. Acad. Nurse practitioners, Nat. Gerontol. Nurses Assn., Nat. Orgn. Nurse Practititoner Faculties, Nat. League Nursing, Nat. Italian Am. Found., N.Y. Acad. Scis., Cath. U. Am. Nursing Alumni Assn. (mem. chpt. exec. bd. 1992—, pres. 1986-87), DCNP Assoc., Sigma Theta Tau (grad. counselor Kappa chpt. 1985-87, 91—, mem. awards com. 1987-89, mem. eligibility com. 1985-87, 91—).

SALERNO-MCCARTHY, LAURA L. MARIA CATHERINE, cooking instructor and consultant; b. New Britain, Conn., Dec. 8, 1958; d. Salvatore Sebastion and Lillian Genieve (Drozd) Salerno; m. Frank James McCarthy II, Nov. 26, 1993; children: Grace Theodora Kalif Salerno, Faith Celeste McCarthy. Dance Diploma, Conservatory Music and Dance, Hartford, Conn., 1985. Macrobiotic cook Macrobiotic Assocs. of Conn., Middletown, 1982-84, It's Only Natural Restaurant, Middletown, 1984-92, Kushi Inst., Becket, Mass., 1988; freelance pvt. cons., cooking instr. Hartford and Middlesex Counties, Conn., 1980—. Bd. dirs. Middlesex Postal Adv. Com., Middletown, 1993-94. Democrat. Christian. Home: 24 Neanda St New Britain CT 06053

SALERNO-SONNENBERG, NADJA, violinist; b. Rome, Jan. 10, 1961; came to U.S., 1969; d. Josephine Salerno-Sonnenberg. Grad., Curtis Inst. Music, 1975, Juilliard Sch., 1982. Profl. debut Phila. Orch., Phila., 1971; appearances include Am. Symphony Orch., Balt. Symphony, Chgo. Symphony, Cin. Symphony, Cleve. Orch., Detroit Symphony, Houston Symphony, Indpls. Symphony, Los Angeles Chamber Orch., Milw. Symphony, Montreal Symphony, New Orleans Philharm., N.J. Symphony, N.Y. Philharm., Phila. Orch., Pitts. Symphony, L.A. Philharmonic, Minn. Orch.; guest appearances include Mostly Mozart Festival, Ravinia, Blossom, Meadow Brook, Great Woods, Caramoor, Aspen, Hollywood Bowl; internat. appearances in Vienna, Munich, Stuttgart, Frankfurt, Geneva, Rotterdam, Lisbon, Tokyo; featured on CBS' 60 Minutes, CBS Sunday Morning, NBC Nat. News, PBS' Live From Lincoln Ctr., Charlie Rose Show; numerous appearances on The Tonight Show with Johnny Carson; rec. artist Angel, 1987. Recipient 1st prize Naumburg Violin Competition, N.Y.C., 1981; Avery Fisher Career grantee., N.Y.C., 1983. Mem. AFTRA, Screen Actors Guild. Office: care M L Falcone Pub Rels 155 W 68th St New York NY 10023-5808

SALGADO, LISSETTE, dancer; b. Hialeah, Fla.. Dancer Miami (Fla.) Dance Theater Co., 1980-86, Joffrey II Dancers, N.Y.C., 1986-88, The Joffrey Ballet, N.Y.C., 1988—. Office: The Joffrey Ballet 130 W 56th St New York NY 10019-3818*

SALHANICK, BRENDA CRANE, lawyer; b. Keene, N.H., Aug. 2, 1951; d. Clayton Howard and Anita (Barry) Crane; BA cum laude, St. Anselm Coll., 1974; CLU Northeastern U. 1978; JD cum laude Suffolk U. Law Sch. 1987; m. Joel A. Salhanick, Sept. 16, 1978; children: Marc Allan, Scott Joseph. With Jules Meyers Assocs., Chestnut Hill, Mass. 1975-83, dir. pension dept. 1977-83, v.p. Employee Benefit Plan Services 1979-83; assoc. Jenkens & Gilchrist, P.C., Dallas, 1987-92, Settle and Pou P.C., Dallas, 1992—. Instr. first aid ARC 1972-81; bd. dir. Our Friends Place, 1993—; cub scout den leader, 1993—; adj. prof. U. Dallas.

SALHANY, LUCILLE S., broadcast executive. Formerly with Paramount Pictures; pres. Paramount Domestic Television, from 1985; chmn. Twentieth Television, a unit of Fox Inc., 1991-92, Fox Broadcasting Co., Beverly Hills, Calif., 1993-94; pres. United ParamountNetwork, 1994—.

SALICE, LICIA A., telecommunications executive; b. Milan, Italy, July 28, 1958; came to U.S., 1984; d. Antonio and Dafne (Domenighetti) S.; m. Martin D. Chrisney, Apr. 5, 1986 (div. 1995); children: Sylvia, Ian. BA with honors, Kingston U., Surrey, Eng., 1982; MSc in Econs., London Sch. Econs., 1984. CFA. Cons. World Bank, Washington, 1985-86; fin. analyst Intelsat, Washington, 1986-90, sr. fin. and planning analyst, 1991-93, sr. exec. corp. strategies, 1993—, chmn. investment adv. com., 1991—. Recipient award Social Sci. Rsch. Coun., London, 1983. Mem. Assn. Investment Mgmt. and Rsch., Soc. Satellite Profl. Internat., Global Telecommunications Soc. (founding). Office: Intelsat 3400 International Dr NW Washington DC 20008-3098

SALINAS, SONIA, elementary school educator; b. Corpus Christi, Tex., Nov. 20, 1955. BA, St. Mary's U., 1978; postgrad., Incarnate Word Coll., 1983-87, Tex. A & I U., 1983-87; bilingual edn. certificate, Corpus Christi State U., 1993. Provisional teaching cert., Tex. Tchr. migrant program grades 1,2,3,4,5 Ind. Sch. Dist., Corpus Christi, 1978-79, tchr. grade 1, 1979-90, after-sch. tutorial program grades 1 and 2, 1983-86, tchr. grade 2, 1990-92, tchr. grade 3, 1992—; sect. leader Garcia Elem. Primary Module I, Corpus Christi, 1986-88, Garcia Elem. Bldg. Leadership Team, 1988-92, Garcia Elem. Primary Module II, 1990-92, Garcia Elem. Site Base Mgmt. Decision Making Team, 1990-92; tchr. young readers summertime reading program Lulac Ednl. Svc. Ctr., Corpus Christi, 1991; chmn. Garciafest Coronation Pageant, Corpus Christi, 1991-92; officer standing com. PTA, Corpus Christi, 1992-93. Roman Catholic. Home: 2925 Morris St Corpus Christi TX 78405-2235

SALIOLA, FRANCES, retired corporate administrator; b. Westfield, N.J., Oct. 27, 1921; d. Antonio and Maria (Chironna) Ponturo; m. Peter Saliola, Aug. 25, 1945; 1 child, George. Grad. high sch., Westfield, N.J., 1939. Sec., bookkeeper Pearsall & Frankenbach, Inc., Westfield, 1939-45; legal sec. Dughi & Johnstone, Westfield, 1945-51; exec. sec. Arthur Venneri Co., Westfield, 1951-65; office mgr. Torcon, Inc., Westfield, 1965-77, dir. mgmt. risk and finance, 1977-86, dir. adminstrv. mgmt., 1983-86, corp. sec., dir., 1965-90. Sec. Sodality of the Blessed Virgin, Westfield, 1938, Civic Club Westfield, 1944; mem. Union County Boys' Town of Italy, 1951-63, Rosary Soc., 1993—. Mem. Rosary Soc. Roman Catholic.

SALISBURY, ALICIA LAING, state senator; b. N.Y.C., Sept. 20, 1939; d. Herbert Farnsworth and Augusta Belle (Marshall) Laing; m. John Eagan Salisbury, June 23, 1962; children: John Eagan Jr., Margaret Laing La Rue. Student Sweet Briar Coll., 1957-60; BA, Kans. U., 1961. Mem. Kans. Senate, 1985—, chmn. commerce com., legis. post audit com., telecomm. strategic planning com.; vice chmn. ways and means com., mem. pub. health and welfare com., mem. joint com. on econ. devel.(mem. orgn. and calendar rules comm.). Elected mem. State Bd. Edn., Topeka, 1981-85, Kans.,; past pres. Jr. League of Topeka; trustee Leadership Kans., 1982-89; bd. dirs. Topeka Community Found., 1983—, Topeka Pub. Sch. Found., 1985-89, Capitol Area Pla. Authority, 1989—, Mid-Am. Mfg. Tech. Ctr., mem. workers' compensation fund oversight com., mem. Kids Count steering com., mem. Stormont-Vail Hosp. Aux.; mem. adv. commn. Juvenile Offenders Program, Kans., 1985-89; mem. adv. bd. Kans. Action for Children, 1982—, Kans. Ins. Edn. Found., 1984—, Youth Center at Topeka, 1987—; mem. Nat. Fedn. Rep. Women; United Way Greater Topeka, ARC, Family Service and Guidance, Topeka, Shawnee County Mental Health Assn., Florence Crittenton Services, Topeka, Topeka City Commn. Govtl. Adv. Com. Mem. Nat. Conf. State Legislators (chmn. state and fed. assembly's commerce, labor and regulation com., chmn. blue ribbon adv. panel on workers' compensation, chmn. task force on workers' compensation), Nat. Rep. Legislators' Assn. (Nat. Rep. Legislator of Yr. 1993, Bus. Guardian award 1990, Outstanding Individual Legis. Achievement award 1989), Shawnee County Rep. Women, Kappa Kappa Gamma. Episcopalian. Avocations: tennis; downhill skiing; water sports; horseback riding; gardening. Office: Kans State Senate State Capital Topeka KS 66612

SALISBURY, JENNY OLIVIA, marketing company executive; b. Berea, Ohio, May 15, 1959; d. Donald Edward and Dorothy Olivia (Theurer) S. Student, Bowling Green U., 1977-81, Cleve. State U., 1981—. Collection supr., computer operator, sales rep. Preview Subscription TV, Cleve., 1981-83; account exec. US Sprint Communications, Independence, Ohio, 1983-87; real estate agt. Ohio Savs. Realty, North Olmstead, Ohio, 1987-88, Hunter Realty, 1987-88; pres., owner NorthCoast Telemktg., Cleve., 1987—; telemarketing tng. cons., Ohio. Fellow Soc. Telecommunication Profls.; mem. Sales and Mktg. Execs. Internat., Direct Mktg. Assn. (N.E. Ohio chpt.), Am. Mktg. Assn. Republican. Episcopalian. Club: Sixth Day (pres. 1987—). Home and Office: 7009 Franklin Blvd # 2 Cleveland OH 44102-2964

SALISBURY, MARGARET MARY, educator; b. LaGrange, Tex., Oct. 23, 1932; d. Charles Frederick and Hedwig Mary (Fajkus) Meyer; m. Harrison Bryan Salisbury, Jan. 8, 1955; children: Elaine, Kathleen, David, Stephen, Mark, Margaret II. BA, Our Lady of the Lake, San Antonio, 1954; MA, U. Tex., San Antonio, 1975. Lic. elem., secondary edn., English and sch. adminstrn. High sch. tchr. St. Joseph's Sch. for Girls, El Paso, Tex., 1954-55; tchr. 1st grade St. Patricks Cathedral Sch., El Paso, 1954; tchr. 2d grade S.W. Ind. Sch. Dist., San Antonio, 1971, tchr. 6th grade, 1974-75, supr. testing, reading, 1975-81, 82-86, jr. high sch. prin., 1981-82, dir. alternative sch., 1986-87, tchr. 3d grade, 1987—; pres. Cooperating Tchr./Student Tchr. U. at Tex., San Antonio, 1986-87. Mem. AAUW, Internat. Reading Assn., Alamo Reading Coun., Reading Improvement, Tex. State Reading Assn., Pres. Club. Republican. Roman Catholic. Home: 126 Meadow Trail Dr San Antonio TX 78227-1639 Office: Big Country Elem 11914 Dragon Ln San Antonio TX 78252-2612

SALISBURY, TAMARA PAULA, foundation executive; b. N.Y.C., Dec. 14, 1927; d. Paul Terrance and Nadine (Korolkova) Voloshin; m. Franklin Cary Salisbury, Jan. 22, 1955; children: Franklin Jr., John, Elizabeth, Elaine, Claire. BA, Coll. Notre Dame, 1948; postgrad., Am. U., George Washington U. Chemist depts. pathology and chemotherapy NIH Cancer Inst., Bethesda, Md., 1946-52; asst. to chief of Chemistry Br. Office of Naval Rsch., Bethesda, 1953-55; v.p., COO Nat. Found. Cancer Rsch., Bethesda, 1973—. Mem. Krebsforschung Internat., Assn. Internat. Cancer Rsch. Decorated d'Officier De L'Ordre De Leopold II; outstanding contbns. award Internat. Soc. Quantum Biology, 1983, award of appreciation Beth Israel Hosp., Harvard Med. Sch., Brigham & Women's Hosp., 1993. Mem. AAAS, Am. Chem. Soc., N.Y. Acad. Scis., Inst. Phys. and Chem. Biology (fgn.), Assn. Internat. Cancer Rsch., Krebsforschung Internat., Nat. Liberal Club. Home: 10811 Alloway Dr Potomac MD 20854 Office: Nat Found Cancer Rsch 7315 Wisconsin Ave Ste 500W Bethesda MD 20814-3206

SALMERI, FRANCES JEANETTE, critical care nurse; b. Bklyn., Apr. 4, 1939; d. Francis Rosario and Gertrude (Hamburger) Freddoso; m. Carlo S. Salmeri, June 30, 1956; children: Carlo A., Donna Salmeri Vizaro, Theresa Salmeri Craig, Barbara, Gary F. ADN, St. Petersburg Jr. Coll., 1975; BA in Psychology, St. Leo's Coll., Dade, Fla., 1977. Staff nurse St. Anthony's Hosp., St. Petersburg, 1975-77; critical care nurse Ed White Hosp., St. Petersburg, Fla., 1978; staff and charge nurse ICU-CCU, relief supr. Pinellas Cmty. Hosp., Pinellas Park, Fla., 1980—; relief supr. Pinellas Community Hosp. (name changed from Met. Gen. Hosp.), 1994—. Mem. AACN.

SALMON, KATHLEEN A., insurance company executive; b. 1945. With Commonwealth of Penn., Harrisburg, 1967-79, Penn. Blue Shield, Camp Hill, Penn., 1979-83; sr. v.p.-adminstrn. Capital Blue Cross, Harrisburg, Penn., 1983—. Office: Capital Blue Cross 2500 Elmerton Ave Harrisburg PA 17110

SALMON, PHYLLIS WARD, early education educator; b. Dallas, Aug. 10, 1948; d. Clinton David and Reba (Gilbert) Ward; m. James Y. Barbo, Dec. 12, 1970 (div. Jan. 1975); m. William Wellington Salmon, Jan. 21, 1977; 1 child, Megan Alyssa. A. in Acctg., Richland Coll., 1977; B.S. in Edn., Stephen F. Austin U., 1971. Cert. tchr. secondary edn., Tex. Cost acct. Jackson-Shaw, Dallas, 1975-79, Dal-Mac Devel., Dallas, 1979-81; store mgr. Shepard & Vick, Dallas, 1983-84; mktg. coordinator Tex. Instruments, Dallas, 1984-85; pres. Computer Expertise, Richardson, Tex., 1985-91; pres. TI's Only, 1986-91, pres. TechnaServe, 1987-91; early edn. tchr. The da Vinci Sch., Dallas, 1992-94; mgr. Kids Town, 1994—. Mem. NAFE, Tex. Computer Dealers Assn. (organizing mem.), Dallas Needlework and Textile Guild. Republican. Episcopalian. Club: St. Clare's Guild (bd. dirs. 1980-81, Dallas). Avocations: needlepoint, photography, travel. Office: Kids Town 751 S Central Expy Richardson TX 75080

SALONGA, LEA, actress, singer; b. Manila, Feb. 22, 1971; d. Feliciano Genuino and Maria Ligaya (Imutan) S. Attended, Ateneo De Manila U., 1988-89. Actress, singer The King and I, Manila, 1978, Annie, Manila, 1980, The Rose Tattoo, Manila, 1980, The Bad Seed, Manila, 1981, The Goodbye Girl, Manila, 1982, Paper Moon, Manila, 1983, The Fantasticks, Manila, 1988, Miss Saigon, London, 1989-90 (Outstanding Performance by Actress in Musical Olivier award 1990), Broadway, 1991-92 (Best Actress in Musical Tony award 1991, Best Actress in Musical Drama Desk award 1991, Best Actress in Musical Outer Critics Circle award 1991, Outstanding Debut Theatre World award 1991), Les Miserables, Broadway, 1993, My Fair Lady, Manila, 1994, Into the Woods, Singapore, 1994, also The Sound of Music, Manila, Fiddler on the Roof, Manila, Cat on a Hot Tin Roof; Philippine films include Bakit Labis Kitang Mahal?, Dear Diary, Pik Pak Boom, Captain Barbell, Ninja Kids, Like Father, Like Son, Tropang Bulilit; Philippine TV: (host) Kulit Bulilit, Love Lea, Naku, Ha!, Sunday Special, Iba Ito!, That's Entertainment!, This is It!, (co-host) Patok Na Patok!; opening act for Stevie Wonder, Menudo; concerts: The Filipinos of Miss Saigon, A Miss Called Lea, Lea Salonga in Concert, L.A., San Francisco; recs. include Small Voice, 1981 (gold record), Lea, Happy Children's Club, Christmas Album, We are the World, (debut album) Lea Salonga, 1993, Miss Saigon original London cast rec. (gold record), The King and I, Aladdin, 1992 (singing voice Princess Jasmine, motion picture soundtrack), The Little Tramp. Recipient AWIT award outstanding svc. Philippings Recording Industry, 1993, ASEAN Industry award performing arts, 1992, Ten Outstanding Young Men award outstanding debut, 1991, AWIT award outstanding performer, 1990, Presdl. Award of Merit Pres. Aquino, 1990, Laurence Olivier award best actress musical, 1990, Cecil award best recording by a child, 1984, Tining award one of 10 outstanding singers, 1983, 94, 92, ALIW award best child performer, 1980, 81, 82; named Outstanding Manilan by Govt. City of Manila, 1990. Mem. AFTRA, Actor's Equity Assn. Roman Catholic. Office: C Winston Simone Mgmt 1790 Broadway Fl 10 New York NY 10019-1412*

SALTER, LANORA JEANETTE, corporate financial officer; b. Omaha, Nebr., June 7, 1964; d. Phillip Ray Sr. and Charlene (Sanford) H.; m. Howard Douglas Salter, March 26, 1964; children: Ryan Douglas, Erin Jeanette. AS, Chattohochee Valley C.C., 1988; diploma, Am. Inst. Banking, 1988. Office mgr. Zales, Mobile, Ala., 1983-85; customer svc. rep. Columbus (Ga.) Bank & Trust, 1985-88; adminstrv. asst. First Atlanta Bank, Augusta, Ga., 1988-90; customer svc. specialist Am. South Bank, Mobile, 1990-92; v.p. finance adminstrn. Performance Rehab. Assocs., Inc., Fairhope, Ala., 1992—; treas. bd. dirs. AIB, 1989-90. tutor Am. Literacy Coun., 1994. Republican. Episcopalian. Office: Performance Rehab Assoc Inc 8075 Spring Run Rd Fairhope AL 36532

SALTER, MERLE MEYERS, oncologist; b. Cleve., Sept. 25, 1937; m. Paul P. Salter; children: Susan P., Scott M., Sally P. BS in Biology, U. Ala., 1959, MD, 1962. Intern Lloyd Noland Hosp., Fairfield, Ala., 1963; resident U. Ala. Hosp., Birmingham, 1966, instr. dept. radiology, 1967-69, instr. dept. radiation, 1969-70, prof. dept. radiation, 1981—, chair dept. radiation, 1986—; mem. cons. staff Lloyd Noland Hosp., Shelby Med. Ctr., Alabaster, Ala., 1970—, Children's Hosp., Birmingham, Ala., 1978—, Eye Found. Hosp., 1990—; mem. bd. dirs. Am. Cancer Soc., Birmingham and Jefferson County, 1994—. Contbr. articles to medical jours. Fellow Am. Coll. Radiology. Office: U Ala Birmingham Hosp 619 S 19th St Birmingham AL 35233-6832

SALTUS, PHYLLIS BORZELLIERE, music educator; b. Rochester, N.Y., Jan. 17, 1931; d. Nicholas and Sadie Veronica (Leone) Borzelliere; m. William Thomas Saltus, Aug. 21, 1965 (div. Apr. 1991); children: Julie Marie Nicole, William Nicholas. AA, Burlington County Coll., Pemberton, N.J., 1987; MEd in Measurement and Guidance, U. Maine, Orono, 1963; BS in Music Edn., SUNY, 1953, MS, 1957. Cert. student personnel svcs., music and guidance, N.J., N.Y. Music tchr., choral dir. Rochester Pub. Schs., 1953-56, 62-63, 1969-70, high sch. guidance counselor, 1963-65; asst. prof. music edn. SUNY, Geneseo and Fredonia, 1956-62; music tchr, choral dir. Concord (Mass.) Pub. Schs., 1965-66; owner, dir. Saltus Music Studio, Medford, N.J., 1982—; music tchr., choral dir. Delanco (N.J.) Pub. Schs., 1984-86; music tchr., choral dir. Delanco (N.J.) Pub. Schs., 1984-86; tchr. voice N.J.Dept. Edn. Sch. Arts, Glassboro (N.J.) State Coll., 1987-89; sr. adj. prof. Burlington County Coll., Pemberton, N.J. and Ft. Dix Mil. Post and McGuire AFB, 1989—, Addition Power Package Accelerated Program, 1995—; music coord., dist. tchr. for gifted and talented program Mt. Laurel (N.J.) Pub. Schs., 1989—; music dir. Triple Threat Prodns., Cherry Hill, N.J., 1991—, Kosciusko Boys Choir, Rochester, 1959-60, Young Adults Cath. Youth Orgn. Choir, Dunkirk, N.Y., 1960-62; lectr., researcher in field. Artist: The Fredonia Main Street Diner, 1952-53, Clarence Welcome Wagon Gourmet Cook Book, N.Y., 1973; contbr. poems to various publs.; soloist Rochester Philharm. Orch. Concert Series, Songsters, Inc., 1953-59. Choir dir., organist, soloist St. Philip Neri R.C. Ch., Rochester, 1949-65, St. Peter's Episc. Ch., Medford, 1989-90; vocal dir., accompanist Pineland Players of South Jersey Community Theatre, Medford, 1987-89, Cherry Hill East High Sch., N.J., 1991—; team capt. United Way, Rochester, 1953-56; membership chair Rochester Community Theater, 1955; founding mem. Sta. WCVF, 1952-58; bd. dirs., founding mem. Rochester Chamber Orch., 1964-65, Medford (N.J.) Newcomers Club, 1977—; vol. Medford PTO, 1976-85; judge preliminary Miss Am. contest Jr. C. of C., Jamestown, N.Y., 1962, vocal dir., accompanist Miss Dunkirk (N.Y.) pageant, 1962, vocal coach Miss Burlington County Pageant, Jr. C. of C., 1989; active Welcome Wagon, Inc., Clarence, N.Y., pres., 1974, historian, 1981; chair Medford (N.J.) Evening Book Review Group, 1978-80; mem. Medford Morning Book Review Group, 1980—; active Meml. Health Alliance, Burlington County Women's Health Network. NDEA grantee, 1964; EEOC scholar, 1986-87; recipient Jr. County Rifle Championship award Monroe County Dept. Health and Recreation, 1948, Womens Student Table Tennis Championship award SUNY, 1952, Outstanding Scholarship award Charlotte Putnam Landers award SUNY, 1953. Mem. AAUP (treas. 1960-62, state del. 1961), Music Educators Nat. Conf., Am. Personnel and Guidance Assn., South Jersey Music Tchrs. Assn., Meml. Health Alliance, Women's Health Network, Order Sons of Italy in Am., Kappa Delta Pi. Roman Catholic. Home: 112 Pine Valley Dr Medford NJ 08055-9214

SALTZ, CAROLE POGREBIN, publisher; b. N.Y.C., Feb. 23, 1949; d. Isidore Lee and Dorothy (Greene) Pogrebin; children: Sam Isaiah, Katherine Emma. BA, Bard Coll., 1970. Editorial asst. Praeger Spl. Studies, N.Y.C., 1970-72; from asst. mng. editor to mng. editor Appleton-Century-Crofts, N.Y.C., 1972-74; editorial cons. Carole Saltz Pub., N.Y.C., 1974-76; v.p. Springer Pub., N.Y.C., 1976-84; pub. Tchrs. Coll. Press-Columbia U., N.Y.C., 1984—. Rep. New Lincoln Parents Assn., N.Y.C., 1986—. Mem. Book Industry Study Group (statistics com. 1986—), Assn. Am. Pub., Assn. Am. Univ. Presses, Women in Production, Women's Nat. Book Assn. Home: 175 W 79th St New York NY 10024-6450 Office: Columbia U Tchrs Coll Press 1234 Amsterdam Ave New York NY 10027-6602

SALTZBERG, JUDITH ANN, psychologist; b. Boston, Nov. 25, 1963; d. Edwin F. and Edith H. (Herman) S. BA in Psychology, U. Pa., 1985; MA in Psychology, SUNY, Stony Brook, 1988, PhD in Psychology, 1991. Psychology intern McLean Hosp., Belmont, Mass., 1989-90; postdoctoral fellow Ctr. for Cognitive Therapy, Phila., 1990-91, mem. psychology staff, 1991-92; mem. behavior therapy svc. Inst. of Pa. Hosp., Phila., 1992—; presenter in field. Contbr. articles to profl. jours. Mem. Student Assn. for Advancement of Behavior Therapy, Sigma Xi (student chpt., rsch. grantee 1989). Office: Inst of Pa Hosp Dept of Psychology 111 N 49th St Philadelphia PA 19139

SALTZMAN, ELLEN S., lawyer; b. Bklyn., Apr. 6, 1946; d. Joseph and Hilda (Lazar) Estrin; m. Stuart Saltzman, June 25, 1966; children: Todd, Michael. BA in Sociology, L.I. U., 1967; JD, CUNY, 1993. Bar: Pa. 1993, N.J. 1994. Fin. cons. Cigna Fin. Svcs., Syosset, N.Y., 1983-84; pension cons. Pension Svcs. Corp., Port Washington, N.Y., 1984-86, Consulting Actuaries Internat., Inc., N.Y.C., 1986-89; mktg. mgr. New Eng. Life Ins. Co., N.Y.C., 1986-89; atty. Vaccaro & Prisco, Hauppauge, N.Y., 1993-95. Mem. task force Women on the Job, Port Washington, N.Y., 1989—, bd. dirs., 1994—; bd. dirs., chair pub. affairs com. L.I. region March of Dimes, 1994—; mem. N.Y. State legis. com. March of Dimes. Mem. ABA, Pa. Bar Assn., N.Y. State Bar Assn., Nassau County Women's Bar Assn., Nat. Women's Polit. Caucus, L.I. Ctr. for Bus. and Profl. Women (pres. 1992-94). Home: 28 Driftwood Dr Port Washington NY 11050-1717

SALVESEN, B(ONNIE) FORBES, artist; b. Elgin, Ill., Nov. 6, 1944; d. Donald Behan and Helen Elaine (Krajacik) Forbes; m. Bruce Michael Salvesen, Sept. 3, 1966. Studied with Elvira Spivey, Barrington, Ill., 1972-74; studied with Peter Schoelch, Cary, Ill., 1975-82; student, Am. Acad. Art, 1976, Sch. Art Inst. Chgo., 1980-82, Kulick-Startk Byzantine Jewelry Sch., 1983. Asst. to purchasing agt. Harnischfeger, Crystal Lake, Ill., 1962-64; rec. sec. Electric Mfrs. Credit Bur., Cary, Ill., 1964-66; student and practicing artist, 1968—. Illustrator: (book) There were Reasons, 1983. Recipient numerous awards of excellence in art, most recent being award for photography AAUW, Elgin, 1988, 89, award for art Randhurst (Ill.) Art Fair, 1988, J. Hindley hon. award Kenosha Pub. Mus., 1989, 1st place award Itasca Jr. Woman's Club, 1989, Kenosha Lake Arts Coun., 1990, Award of Excellence Barrington Area Arts Coun., 1990, Outstanding Fine Arts award Haymarket Guild of Artists, 1990, Arts Alliance of Ogle County award, 1990, best of show, Portage Pauquette Art Fair, Wis., 1991, Best of Show award Art Fair on the Fox, Ill., 1991, Merit award Arts Alliance of Ogle County, 1991, 1st pl. photography award Tallman Mus. Art Show, 1991, award of excellence in photography Festival of Arts, 1991, Wis. Judge award Wilhelm Tell Art, 1991, 1st pl. fine arts Rockford Area Artists, 1991, 1st pl. Freeport (Ill.) Art Mus., 1992, award of Excellence, Hinsdale (Ill.) Art Fair, 1992, Mayor's award, Skokie (Ill.) Art Guild Fair, 1992, award of Excellence-Art, Friends of Kenosha (Wis.) Pub. Mus., 1992, award of Excellence Glen Ellyn, Ill. Art Show, 1992, Merit award Oshkosh Pub. Mus., Wis. 1993, Judges Choice award 29th Annual Sauk County Art Festival, Wis., 1993, Best of Show award Tallman Arts Festival, Wis., 1993, award of Hon. 24th Annual Glen Ellyn Festival of the Arts, Ill., 1993, 37th Winnebagoland Art Fair award, 1994, Excellence award Spring Green Arts and Crafts Fair, 1994, Judges Choice award 30th Ann. Sauk County Assn. Fair, 1994, Best of Show award Janesville Art League at Rock County Mus., 1994. Democratic. Roman Catholic. Home and Office: 1312 Whippoorwill Dr Crystal Lake IL 60014-2614

SALVO, DONNA JEAN, artist, educator; b. Fort Knox, Ky., Apr. 21, 1954; d. Carl Jr. and Jacqueline A. (Capone) S. BS in Art Edn., U. Wis., 1976. Dancer, actress La Mama Theatre, N.Y.C., 1976-79; studio mgr. Joel Baldwin Photography, N.Y.C., 1979-81; artist in residence State Coun. on the Arts, R.I., 1980-83; tchr. art Providence (R.I.) Sch. Dept., 1981—; dancer, singer Harlem Performance Ctr., N.Y.C., 1977-80; choreographer Mus. Natural History, Providence, 1982-84. One woman show Brown U., 1988. Singer R.I. Coll. Chorus, Providence, 1982-92. Mem. Nat. Mus. Women in the Arts (charter), Nat. Mus. Am. Indian (charter), Hope Tunnel String Band. Democrat. Roman Catholic. Home: 37 E Manning St Providence RI 02906

SALVO, GINGER CALHOUN, horse trainer, sculptor; b. Columbia, S.C., June 20, 1947; d. George Clifton Salvo and Eugenia Calhoun (Gerald) Landon; divorced; 1 child, Tiffany Ann. Student, Rollins Coll., 1965. Horse trainer Mountain Home, Idaho, 1965—; designer Mountain Home, 1975—; instr. Wyo. Barrel Racing Club, Jackson, 1980, Idaho High Sch. Rodeo Assn., 1985. Leader 4-H Club, Mountain Home, 1975; founder, pres. Idaho High Sch. Rodeo Club, Mountain Home High Sch.; chmn. Idaho Barrel Racing Futurity Horse Sale, 1991, 93; founder Wilderness Barrel Racing Futurities Award, Idaho, Nev., Utah, 1991. Recipient several awards for sculptures Nat. Cowgirl Hall of Fame, numerous championships Idaho Cowboys Assn., Idaho Barrel Racing Futurity Assn. (including All-Around champion 1992, Res. All Around champion 1993), Am. Quarter Horse Assn., Utah Barrel Racing Futurity, Ea. Idaho Barrel Racing Futurity, Golden Spike Barrel Racing Futurity, Sweetwater Barrel Futurity, Idaho Quarter Horse Breeders Assn. Mem. NW Barrel Futurities Assn., Idaho Barrel Racing Futurity Assn. (bd. dirs. 1981-83, champion 1979, 83), Idaho Cowboys Assn. (bd. dirs. 1974-75, res. champion 1984), Ea. Idaho Rodeo Assn. (clinic instr. horsemanship, judge open house shows 1993), United Daus. of the Confederacy (Charleston, S.C.). Home and Office: RR 1 Box 756A Mountain Home ID 83647-9732

SALZMAN, MARILYN B. WOLFSON, service company executive; b. Chgo., Dec. 25, 1943; d. Joseph and Sera (Krol) Wolfson; 1 son, Lawrence Todd. Student, U. Ill., Barat Coll., Lake Forest, Ill., 1961-64. Adminstrv. project asst. Sci. Research Assocs., Chgo., 1964-70; reporter Suburban Trib of Chgo. Tribune, 1979-80; pres. MWS Assocs., Los Angeles and Fullerton, Calif., 1980—; exec. adminstrv. dir. Crystal Tips of No. Ill., Inc., 1980-83; dir. adminstrn. Ice Dispensers, Inc., 1981-83, Sani-Serv of Ill., Inc., 1981-83; adminstrv. and organizational cons. 1140 Corp., 1980-83; adminstrv. dir. Iceman's Ico Co., Inc., 1980-83; founder, moderator DWC Workshops, 1984; dir. data processing Florence Crittenton Svs., Orange County, 1984-86, dir. MIS, 1986-88, dir. support svcs., 1988-92, bd. dirs. ways and means com., 1991—, dir. adminstrn. & contract compliance, 1992-94, dir. devel. & cmty. svcs., 1994—; pres. MWS Prodns., L.A. and Fullerton, Calif., 1990—; exec. producer (TV series) The State of the Child, 1990-91; panelist computers in residential treatment Child Welfare League Am. Biennial Conf. Workshop, 1986; presenter outcomes and svc. evaluation North Am. Out-of-Home Care Conf., 1991, families & children in residential treatment Calif. State U. Child Devel. Conf., Fullerton, 1994, advancing your message Child Welfare League of Am. Nat. Conf., 1995. Active Friends of Fullerton Library, Boy Scouts Am.; panelist Child Welfare League Am., Bienniel Conf. Workshop; chmn. govtl., pub. affairs coms. Orange County Assn. of Children's Svcs.; mem. steering com. Orange County UN Assn. Yr. of Family, 1993—; mem. com. Internat. Yr. of the Family Exhibit & Celebration, Bowers Mus., 1994; mem. planning com. Orange County Summit for Children, 1994—; mem. exec. com. Anne Frank Orange County Organizing Com., 1994—; mem. adv. com. Child Devel. & Family Life Dept., Fullerton Coll., 1994; facilitator Orange County Together, 1994—. Mem. Calif. Assn. Svcs. for Children (rsch. and evaluation com. 1993—), Mgmt. Forum, Women's Am. ORT, Fullerton C. of C. (indsl. com. 1994—). Contbr. articles to newspapers and indsl. jours.

SALZMAN, SHARON MARIE, administrator; b. Chgo., Aug. 8, 1962; d. John J. and Marilyn Ann (Wilson) S. Grad. high sch., Villa Park, Ill. Asst. import mgr., inventory analyst Florsheim Shoe Co., Inc., Chgo., 1980-86; dir. spl. markets N.Am. Bear Co., Inc., Chgo., 1986-92; dir. merchandising Ty, Inc., Oak Brook, Ill., 1992-93, gen. mgr., 1993—. Founder, vol. Friends of Maryville, Des Plaines, Ill., 1989; com. mem. Women's Bd. Maryville, Des Plaines, 1989. Mem. NAFE. Office: PO Box 5377 Oak Brook IL 60522

SAMA, VICTORIA E., television broadcast executive; b. Bellville, N.J., Nov. 19, 1962; d. Frank Lincoln and Jennie (Bonoccorso) S. BA in Journalism, Montclair (N.J.) State Coll., 1984. Prodn. asst. ABC Wide World of Sports, N.Y.C., 1982-84, Cable News Network, N.Y.C., 1984-85; writer CNN Headline News, Atlanta, 1985-88; producer CNN Spanish News, Atlanta, 1988-92, CNN Internat., Atlanta, 1992—; n.e. regional coord., Alpha Epsilon Rho, N.Y.C., 1984-85. Alumni Award scholar Montclair State Alumni Com., 1983; Spanish Lang. fellow Nat. Press Found., Washington, 1990. Mem. Handgun Control, Nature Conservancy. Office: Cable News Network 1 CNN Center Plz Atlanta GA 30335-4201

SAMANIEGO, PAMELA SUSAN, executive producer; b. San Mateo, Calif., Nov. 29, 1952; d. Armando C. and Harriott Susan (Croot) S. Student, UCLA, 1972, Los Angeles Valley Coll., 1970-72. Asst. new accts. supr. Beverly Hills Fed. Savings, 1970-72; asst. controller Bio-Science Enterprises, Van Nuys, Calif., 1972-74; adminstr. asst. Avery/Tirce Prodns., Hollywood, Calif., 1974-78; sr. estimator N. Lee Lacy and Assocs., Hollywood, 1978-81; head of prodn. Film Consortium, Hollywood, 1981-82; exec. producer EUE/Screen Gems Ltd., Burbank, Calif., 1982-88; advt. agency dir. Barrett & Assocs., Las Vegas, Nev., 1988-90; exec. producer Laguna/Take One, Las Vegas, 1990-93; dir. Sta. KXLY-4 ABC, Spokane, Wash., 1993—. Author: Millimeter & Backstage, 1982-88. Emergency room vol. San Mateo (Calif.) County Hosp., 1968-70; Sunday sch. tchr. Hillsdale Meth. Ch., San Mateo, 1968-70; vol. worker Hillsdale Meth. Ch. Outreach, San Francisco, 1967-70. Recipient CLIO award CLIO Awards, Inc., 1985, ADDY award Las Vegas Advt. Fedn., 1988. Mem. Dirs. Guild Am. (2nd asst. dir. 1987-88), Assn. Ind. Comml. Producers, Am. Horse Show Assn., Internat. Arabian Horse Assn., AHASFV (sec. 1978-79), AHASC (sec. 1978-88). Democrat. Methodist. Home: 803 Osprey Dr Post Falls ID 83854 Office: Sta KXLY-4 500 W Boone Ave Spokane WA 99201

SAMBORN, JANET SUE, secondary education educator; b. Bay City, Mich., Apr. 2, 1948; d. Wesley Warren and Donna June (Gardner) S. AB in Spanish and Secondary Edn., Asbury Coll., 1970; MA in Teaching Sr. H.S., Ctrl. Mich. U., 1974, MA in Ednl. Adminstrn., 1986. Cert. tchr. secondary edn., Mich. Tchr. Midland (Mich.) Pub. Schs., 1971—, Internat. Lang. Sch., Midland, 1987-88; instr. Ctrl. Mich. U., Mt. Pleasant, 1992-93; adj. faculty Saginaw (Mich.) Valley State U., 1989-92; area profl. Delta Coll., Saginaw, 1991—; owner The Tin Roof Ice Cream Shop, Auburn, Mich., summers 1980-84. Mem. NEA, Am. Assn. Tchrs. of Spanish and Portuguese, Am. Coun. Teaching Fgn. Langs., Ctrl. States Conf., Mich. Edn. Assn., Midland City Edn. Assn. United Methodist. Office: H H Dow H S 3901 N Saginaw Rd Midland MI 48640-5670

SAMMARONE, PAULA GWEN, athletic training educator; b. Pitts., Apr. 10, 1960; d. Dino G. and Angelina (Christiano) S. BS, West Chester State Coll., 1982; MA, Mich. State U., 1984; postgrad., U. Pitts., 1987-88, 89-90; EdD, U. Va., 1994. Cert. tchr. K-12, Pa.;. Head athletic trainer East Lansing (Mich.) High Sch., 1983-84; instr., student trainer edn. workshop Cramer Products, Inc., Gardner, Kans., 1985-86; cons. for sports medicine product devel. Cramer Products, Inc., Gardner, 1988-89; mem. U.S. Olympic Com., Colorado Springs, 1985-87, 92—; instr., athletic trainer Ea. Ky. Univ., Richmond, 1984-86, U. Pitts., 1986-89; corp. health educator Health Am., Inc., Pitts., 1989-90; Sport First Aid nat. faculty Am. Coaching Effectiveness Program, Champagne, Ill., 1991—; adminstrv. asst. to assoc. dean of edn. U. Va., Charlottesville, Va., 1990-92; dept. chair, asst. prof. Rangos Sch. of Health Scis. Duquesne Univ., Pitts., 1992—; adj. faculty Pa. State U., Scranton, 1991; lectr. in field. Contbr. articles to profl. jours. Std. first aid instr., CPR instr. ARC. Mem. AAHPERD, ASCD, Pa. Athletic Trainers Soc. (long range planning com. 1988-90, parliamentarian 1992, pres.-elec 1995), Mid-Atlantic Trainers Assn., Inc., Ea. Athletic Trainers Assn. (chair 1989-90, David G. Moyer award), Nat. Athletic Trainers Assn. (cert.). Office: Duquesne Univ Dept Athletic Tng 119 Health Scis Bldg Pittsburgh PA 15282

SAMMET, JEAN E., computer scientist; b. N.Y.C.; d. Harry and Ruth S. B.A., Mt. Holyoke Coll., Sc.D. (hon.), 1978; M.A., U. Ill. Group leader programming Sperry Gyroscope, Great Neck, N.Y., 1955-58; sect. head, staff cons. programming Sylvania Electric Products, Needham, Mass., 1958-61; with IBM, 1961-88; adv. program mgr. Boston, 1961-65; program lang. tech. mgr. IBM, 1965-68; programming tech. planning mgr. Fed. Systems div., 1968-74, programming lang. tech. mgr., 1974-79, software tech. mgr., 1979-81, div. software tech. mgr., 1981-82, programming lang. tech. mgr., 1983-88; programming lang. cons. Bethesda, Md., 1989—; chmn. history of computing com. Am. Fedn. Info. Processing Socs., 1977-79; mem. exec. com. Software Patent Inst., 1991—, edn. com., 1992—, chair edn. com., 1992-93; bd. dirs. Computer Mus., 1983-93. Author: Programming Languages: History and Fundamentals, 1969; editor-in-chief: Assn. Computing Machinery Computing Revs, 1979-87; contbr. articles to profl. jours. Fellow Assn. for Computing Machinery, 1994, (charter, pres. 1974-76, Disting. Svc. award 1985); mem. NAE, Upsilon Pi Epsilon. Office: PO Box 30038 Bethesda MD 20824-0038

SAMOSZUK, MARY LENA, non-profit organization administrator; b. St. Paul, Jan. 7, 1956; d. Michael Eliah and Gennowefa (Borodenko) S.; 1 child, Zolly Ben Becker. BA, Carleton Coll., 1978; MA, U. Minn., 1983. Asst. to dir. Minn. Higher Edn. Bd., St. Paul, 1978-81; v.p. pub. affairs Coun. Hosp. Corps., Mpls., 1983-86; cons. Perspectives, Inc., Minnetonka, Minn., 1986-92, adminstr., 1992—; vice chair, bd. dirs. Medica Self-Insured, Minnetonka; bd. dirs. Allina. Active Citizen's League, Mpls., 1983-87, NOW, Planned

Parenthood, Sustainable Resources, Minn. Coalition for Homeless. McKinney Supportive Housing grantee HUD, 1992. Home: 697 Brookside Ln Mendota Heights MN 55118 Office: Perspectives Inc 17717 Hwy 7 Minnetonka MN 55345

SAMPAS, DOROTHY M., government official; b. Washington, Aug. 24, 1933; d. Lawrence and Anna Cornelia (Henkel) Myers; m. James George Sampas, Dec. 8, 1962; children: George, Lawrence James. AB, U. Mich., 1955; postgrad., U. Paris, 1955-56; PhD, Georgetown U., 1970; cert., Nat. War Coll., Washington, 1987, Naval Post Grad. Sch., 1993. With Bur. Pub. Affairs Dept. State, Washington, 1958-60, analyst Bur. of Adminstrn., 1973-75, div. chief, dep. chief Office of Position and Pay Mgmt., 1979-83, div. chief Office of Mgmt., 1983-84, dir. Office of Mgmt., 1984-86; vice consul Am. Consulate Gen., Hamburg, Fed. Republic Germany, 1960-62; cons. Trans Century Corp., Washington, 1972; gen. svcs. officer Am. Embassy, Brussels, 1975-79; embassy minister-counselor Am. Embassy, Beijing, 1987-90; minister-counselor U.S. Mission to UN, N.Y.C., 1991-94; Am. ambassador to Mauritania, 1994—. Presbyterian. Home: 4715 Trent Ct Chevy Chase MD 20815-5516 Office: Am Embassy Nouakchott Dept State Washington DC 20521-2430 also: Am Embassy, Boite Postale 22, Nouakchott Mauritania

SAMPLE, ALTHEA MERRITT, secondary education educator, conductor; b. Miami, Fla., Apr. 6, 1937; d. Otis and Alma (Carter) S. BS in Music Edn., Fla. A&M, 1960; Master in Music Edn., U. Miami, 1971. Tchr. elem. music edn. Dade County, Miami, Fla., 1960-65, dir. jr. h.s. orch., 1965-84, dir. orch. sr. h.s., 1984—; dir. orch. Miami Northwestern Performing Arts Ctr., 1984—; clin. tchr. internship program U. Miami, 1988-90; clinician Broward County Orch. Evaluation, 1986, 87; participant workshops in field, 1965—. Coord. North Area Festival, 1988; conducted Supt.'s Honors Orch., 1988, 92, South Area Festival Orch., 1989, tribute Dr. George Bornoff Concert, 1994, Gov. Fla. Inaugural Concert, 1993; performed Nat. Educator Reception, 1993; sponsor Miami Herald Silver Knight Award winners, 1988, 90, 92. Recipient Black Music Achievement award, 1992, Outstanding Educator award U.S. Rep. Dante Fussell, 1992, Area III Tchr. of Yr., Dade County, 1992. Mem. United Tchrs. Dade, Fla. Orch. Assn., Fla. Music Educators, Dade Music Educators, Nat. Alliance Educators, Eta Phi Beta. Democrat. Episcopalian. Home: 15720 E Bunche Park Dr Opa Locka FL 33054

SAMPLE, CLARE ELISABETH, biochemist, researcher; b. Felixstowe, Suffolk, Eng., June 25, 1957; d. Ivan Edward and Christine P. Phillips; m. Jeffery Thomas Sample, Apr. 27, 1985. BA summa cum laude, Temple U., 1980; M degree, U. Calif., Berkeley, 1981; PhD, U. So. Fla., 1985. came to U.S., 1975;. Postdoctoral fellow U. Chgo., 1985-87, Harvard Med. Sch., Boston, 1987-90; asst. mem. St. Jude Children's Rsch. Hosp., Memphis, 1990—; asst. prof. U. Tenn., Memphis, 1993—. Contbr. articles to profl. jours. Recipient Nat. Rsch. Svc. award NIH, 1987-88, Pub. Health Svc. Award grant Nat. Cancer Inst., 1992—. Mem. Am. Soc. Virology, Am. Soc. Biochemists and Molecular Biologists, Internat. Assn. for Rsch. on Epstein-Barr Virus and Associated Diseases, Phi Kappa Phi. Office: St Jude Childrens Rsch Hosp 332 N Lauderdale Memphis TN 38101

SAMPLES, IRIS LYNETTE, elementary school educator; b. Ravenna, Ohio, July 28, 1948; d. Enzo Joseph and Iris Lynette (Wiley) Lanari; m. Charles Victor Samples, Aug. 24, 1968. BS in Edn., Kent State U., 1973; postgrad. in Reading Instruction, U. Akron, 1977-79; student, Gesell Inst. Human Devel., 1989. Cert. tchr., Ohio. Tchr. first grade Highland Local Schs., Medina County, Ohio, 1968-72; tchr. first grade Barberton (Ohio) City Schs., 1973-77, reading tchr., 1977—; mem. faculty adv. com. Woodford Sch., 1982-89, Right to Read activities coord., 1983—, Buckeye Book activities coord., 1990—, young authors coord., 1991—, tchr. kindergarten pilot program chpt. one students, 1987-88; sch. levy com. Barberton City Schs., 1982, 93, mem. reading curriculum com., 1987-88, mem. Right to Read dist. com., 1987—, reading textbook selection com., 1987-89. Tchr. Bible Sch., Sunday Sch. 1st Luth. Ch., 1978-82, coord. Christmas program, 1979-80; active Woodford PTA, past program chair; vol. various health founds., 1975—. Named Woodford Tchr. of Yr., Woodford PTA, 1994; Jennings scholar, 1984—. Lutheran. Home: 670 E Paige Ave Barberton OH 44203-3439 Office: Woodford Elem Sch 315 E State St Barberton OH 44203-2964

SAMPSON, CAROL ANN, interior design firm executive, writer; b. Wabash, Ind., Dec. 5, 1942; d. John Roland Bennett and Virginia Ann (Garthwait) Mulholland; student Bradley U., 1961-62; AA, Riverside City Coll., 1971; BS cum laude, Woodbury U., 1975; children: Tracy Lee, John Russell IV (Arrison). Interior designer Imperial Co., Riverside, Calif., 1971-72; asso. interior designer Booth & Assos., Riverside, 1972-74; owner, prin., project designer Carol Sampson's Interior Designs, Riverside, 1974-88; tchr. interior design bus. procedures San Bernardino Valley Coll., 1978-84; house and home editor Inland Empire mag., 1978-90; interior design staff writer Inland Empire Bus. Quar., 1978-81; home interiors editor for Inland News on cable TV for Falcon, Liberty and Group P-W stas.; interior design cons. radio program Sta. KPRO, Riverside, 1978-81. Author: Estimating for Interior Designers, 1991. Recipient Gold Key award (2), Nat. Home Fashions League, 1975, Proclamation award City of Riverside Mayor's Office, 1983. Mem. Internat. Soc. Interior Designers (profl.). Episcopalian. Office: Carol Sampson Interior Designs 2441 E Granite View Dr Phoenix AZ 85044-9060

SAMPSON, DAPHNE RAE, library director; b. Milw., Aug. 11, 1943; d. Gerald Joseph and Helene Virginia Babbitt; m. Charles Sargent Sampson, Oct. 23, 1971. BA, U. Wis., 1965, MLS, 1966. Reference libr. Def. Intelligence Agy., Washington, 1966-68; sr. reference libr. U.S. Dept. of State, Washington, 1968-78, Exec. Office of the Pres., Washington, 1978-80; chief readers' svcs. Fed. Trade Commn., Washington, 1980-81; chief readers' svcs. U.S. Dept. of Justice, Washington, 1981-84, asst. dir. libr. staff, 1984-86, dep. dir. libr. staff, 1986, acting dir. libr. staff, 1986-87, dir. libr. staff, 1987—, sr. exec. svc., 1995—. Active Berkshire Civic Assn., Alexandria, Va., 1976—. Mem. Am. Assn. Law Librs., Law Librs. Soc. of Washington, Fed. Libr. and Info. Ctr. Com. (bd. mem. 1992). Home: 5838 Wyomissing Ct Alexandria VA 22303 Office: US Dept of Justice Libr Rm 5317 10th & Pennsylvania Ave NW Washington DC 20530

SAMPSON, EARLDINE ROBISON, education educator; b. Russell, Iowa, June 18, 1923; d. Lawrence Earl and Mildred Mona (Judy) Robison; m. Wesley Claude Sampson, Nov. 25, 1953; children: Ann Elizabeth, Lisa Ellen. Diploma, Iowa State Tchrs. Coll., 1943, BA, 1950; MS in Edn., Drake U., 1954; postgrad., No. Ill. U., Iowa State U., 1965-66, 74. Cert. tchr., guidance counselor, Iowa. Tchr. elem. sch. various pub. sch. sys., 1943-48; cons. speech and hearing Iowa Dept. Pub. Instrn., Des Moines, 1950-52; speech therapist Des Moines Pub. Schs., 1952-54, 55; lectr. spl. edn. No. Ill. U., DeKalb, 1964-65; tchr. of homebound Cedar Falls (Iowa) Pub. Schs., 1967-68; asst. prof. edn. U. No. Iowa, Cedar Falls, 1968; asst. prof., counselor Wartburg Coll., Waverly, Iowa, 1968-70; instr. elem. edn., then head of advising elem. edn. Iowa State U., Ames, 1972-82; field supr. elem. edn. U. Toledo, 1988, 89; ind. cons. Sylvania, Ohio, 1989—; cons. Des Moines Speech and Hearing Ctr., 1958-59, bd. dirs., 1962, 63; cons. Sartori Hosp., Cedar Falls, 1967-69; bd. dirs. Story County Mental Health Ctr., Ames, 1972-74. NDEA fellow, 1965. Mem. AAUW, Univ. Women's Club, Zeta Phi Eta. Methodist. Home: 4047 Newcastle Dr Sylvania OH 43560-3450

SAMPSON, PATSY HALLOCK, college president; b. Picher, Okla., July 9, 1932; d. Daniel Webster and Mary Gladys (Whitehead) Hallock; children: Catherine, Jacquelyn, Rebecca. B.A. with spl. distinction, U. Okla., 1961; Ph.D. in Psychology, Cornell U., 1966. Asst. prof. SUNY, Binghamton, 1965-66; NIMH postdoctoral fellow Cornell U., 1966-67; asst. prof. Wellesley (Mass.) Coll., 1967-70; prof., chmn. dept. psychology Calif. State Coll., Bakersfield, 1970-73; adminstr. Nat. Inst. Child Health and Human Devel., Bethesda, Md., 1973-75; psychologist Nat. Inst. Alcohol Abuse and Alcoholism, Washington, 1975-77; dean faculty, prof. psychology Pitzer Coll., Claremont, Calif., 1977-80; dean Coll. Liberal Arts, Drake U., Des Moines, 1980-83; pres. Stephens Coll., Columbia, Mo., 1983—. Bd. dirs. Commn. on Women in Higher Edn., 1984-87, Coun. for Adult and Experiential Learning, 1986-92; mem. Pres.'s Commn. of Nat. Collegiate Athletic Assn., 1984-86; trustee The Fielding Inst., 1986-92, chmn., 1988-90; trustee Totts Gap Med. Rsch. Found., 1988—; mem. nat. adv. bd. Outward Bound U.S.A., 1987-90, Drake U. bd. govs., 1992—. Mem. AAUP, Am. Coun. Edn. (bd. dirs. 1985-88), North Ctrl. Assn. Colls. and Schs. (v.p. 1992, pres. 1993, commr. commn. on instns. of higher edn. 1988-92), Phi Beta Kappa, Sigma Xi. Office: Stephens Coll Office of the President Columbia MO 65215-0001

SAMPSON, THYRA ANN, mediator; b. Oakland, Calif., Apr. 22, 1948; d. Harold Joseph and Velma Louise (Robinson) S.; 1 child, Leon Broussard III. BA, U. Calif., 1970; JD, Hastings Coll of Law, 1978. Project dir. Univ. Calif. Medical Sch., L.A., 1980-81; legislative staff Calif. State Assembly, Sacramento, 1981-85; adminstr. support for dir. Toward Utility Rate Normalization, San Francisco, 1985-86; program devel. rep. Network Solutions Inc., Sacramento, 1988-89; mediator Sacramento Mediation Ctr., 1990—; founder Realistic Solutions, Inc., Sacramento, 1991; staff cons. Calif. Legislative Black Caucus, Sacramento, 1982, Angel City Dental Soc., L.A., 1978-79. Campaign cons., precinct leader Jessie Jackson for Pres., 1988.

SAMS, DORIS LAVERNE, college counselor; b. Youngwood, Pa., Apr. 26; d. Benjamin F. and Lucinda (Myers) S. BA, Seton Hill Coll., 1950; MEd, postgrad., U. Pitts., 1959. Lic. mental health counselor, Fla.; pet grief therapist. Psychiat. aide Inst. of Living, Hartford, Conn., 1950-51; employment interviewer Conn. State Employment Service, Thompsonville, 1951-53; tchr. Hempfield Area Schs., Greensburg, Pa., 1953-58, sch. psychologist, 1958-66; sr. prof., counselor Broward Community Coll., Ft. Lauderdale, Fla., 1966—; human potential seminar leader Rational Behavior Therapist. Mem. Gov.'s Com. on Handicapped. Frick scholar. Mem. Am. Psychol. Assn. (assoc.), Nat. Acad. Cert. Clin. Mental Health Counselors, Nat. Bd. Cert. Counselors, Am. Counseling Assn., Am. Mental Health Counselors Assn., Humane Soc. Republican. Home: 1400 SW 19th St Fort Lauderdale FL 33315-1963 Office: Broward Community Coll Hollywood FL 33024

SAMS, JUDITH ANN, counselor, mental health nurse; b. Akron, Ohio, May 18, 1943; d. Clifford and Virginia (Slider) Starcher; m. Robert E. Sams, Dec. 15, 1963; children: Robert Steven, Patricia Ann, Erik Jason. RN, St. Joseph's Nursing Sch., Parkersburg, W.Va., 1963; BSN cum laude, Ohio U., 1980, MEd, 1991. Cert. counselor. Staff nurse W.Va. U. Med. Ctr. Cancer Rsch., Morgantown, 1963-65; sch. nurse Ea. Sch. Dist., Meigs County, Ohio, 1976-78; psychiat. nurse Worthington Ctr. Inc., Parkersburg, 1990-93, dir. adult mental health, 1993—. Pres. Acad. Parkersburg Med. Aux., 1976. Mem. Ohio Counselors Assn., Chi Sigma Iota. Democrat. Methodist. Home: 49200 Hickory Hills Rd Reedsville OH 45772-9774 Office: Worthington Ctr Inc 3199 Core Rd Parkersburg WV 26104

SAMUELS, CYNTHIA KALISH, communications executive; b. Pitts., May 21, 1946; d. Emerson and Jeanne (Kalish) S.; m. Richard Norman Atkins, Sept. 12, 1971; children: Joshua Whitney Samuels Atkins, Daniel Jonathan Samuels Atkins. BA, Smith Coll., 1968. Press aide McCarthy for Pres. Campaign, Washington, 1968; assoc. producer Newsroom program Sta. KQED, San Francisco, 1972-73; with CBS News, 1973-80, researcher, Washington, 1969-71, documentary researcher, N.Y.C., 1973-74, asst. fgn. editor, 1974-76, asst. N.Y. bur. chief, 1976-80; writer, field producer Today program NBC News, N.Y.C., 1980-84, polit. producer Today program, 1984-89; planning producer, 1988-89; sr. producer Main Street program NBC News, N.Y.C., 1987; founding exec. producer Channel One Program, 1989-92; exec. v.p. Whittle Communications, N.Y.C., 1989-94; now interactive TV and multi-media cons., 1994—. Author: It's A Free Country!: A Young Person's Guide to Politics and Elections, 1988; contbr. book revs. to N.Y. Times Book Rev., Washington Post Book World. Recipient Emmy award No. Calif. Acad. TV Arts and Scis., 1974, Columbia DuPont citation, 1975, Media Access award Calif. Office of Handicapped, 1991, Silver award Nat. Mental Health Assn., 2 Bronze awards Nat. Assn. Edn. in Film and TV, 1993.

SAMUELS, JANET LEE, lawyer; b. Pitts., July 18, 1953; d. Emerson and Jeanne (Kalish) S.; m. David Arthur Kalow, June 18, 1978; children: Margaret Emily Samuels-Kalow, Jacob Richard Samuels-Kalow, Benjamin Charles Samuels-Kalow. BA with honors, Beloit Coll., 1974; JD, NYU, 1977. Bar: N.Y. 1978, D.C. 1980. Staff atty. SCM Corp., N.Y.C., 1977-80, corp. atty., 1980-83, sr. corp. atty., 1983-85, assoc. gen. counsel Allied Paper div., 1983-86, corp. counsel, 1986, Holtzmann, Wise & Shepard, 1986—. Mem. ABA, N.Y. State Bar Assn., Mortar Board, Phi Beta Kappa.

SAMUELSON, BARBARA SHALITA, financial consultant; b. N.Y.C., Apr. 8, 1943; d. Harry and Celia Shalita; m. John Samuelson, Feb. 27, 1966; children: Charles Aaron, Richard Adam. AB, Wheaton Coll., 1964; MBA, NYU, 1967. Feature editor Investment Dealers' Digest, N.Y.C., 1965-67; fin. writer Barron's, 1967-77; sr. editor Merrill Lynch, Pierce, Fenner & Smith, Inc., N.Y.C., 1977-79, dir. investor rels. Merrill Lynch & Co., Inc., 1979-87, dir. corp. and fin. svcs., 1987—. Mem. N.Y. Soc. Security Analysts, Fin. Women's Assn., Nat. Investor Rels. Inst. Office: 717 Fifth Ave New York NY 10022-8101

SAMUELSON, BILLIE MARGARET, artist; b. Long Beach, Calif., Apr. 11, 1927; d. William Christian and Gladys Margaret (Caffrey) Newendorp; m. Fritz Eric Samuelson, Aug. 12, 1950 (div. 1985); children: Craig Eric, Clark Alan, Dana Scott. Student, Long Beach City Coll., 1945-46. Pvt. art tchr. Wycokoff/Allendale, N.J., 1985—; workshop instr. Jane Law Studio, Long Beach Island, N.J., 1990—. Exhibited in solo show at Ridgewood (N.J.) Art Inst., 1985, West Wing Gallery, 1991; group shows include Craig Gallery, Ridgewood, 1979, Charisma Gallery, Englewood, N.J., 1981-83, Custom Gallery, Waldwick, N.J., 1985, Wyckoff (N.J.) Gallery, 1987-90, West Wing Gallery, Ringwood State Park, N.J., 1991, Union Camp Corp., 1992. Recipient 1st in State N.J. Womens Clubs, 1978-80, Watercolor award N.J. Painters and Sculptors, 1981. Mem. DAR, Community Arts Assn. (pres. 1978-79), Am. Artists Profl. League (bd. dirs. 1985-87, watercolor prize 1992), Ringwood Manor Arts Assn. (sr. profl.), Catherine Lorillard Wolfe Art Club (cash award 1993), Salute to Women in the Arts, Art Ctr. Watercolor Affiliates, Nat. Mus. of Women in the Arts. Home: 1-3 Chestnut Pl Waldwick NJ 07463

SAMUELSON, ELLEN BANMAN, state legislator; b. Mathiston, Miss., Dec. 11, 1930; d. Alvin Kornelius and Florence Ellen (True) Banman; m. Armin Otto Samuelson, June 22, 1952; children: Alida Jayne, Ronald Ramin, Eric Carl, Mark Alan. BS, Kans. State U., 1952, MS, 1974. Tchr. elem. sch. Newton (Kans.) Pub. Schs., 1952-53, tchr. home econs., 1957-58; tchr. home econs. Hesston (Kans.) Unified Sch. Dist. 460, 1965-79; prof. home econs. Bethel/Hesston Coll., North Newton, Hesston, Kans., 1979-82, Bethel Coll., North Newton, 1982-87; cons., 1987-88; legislator ho. of reps. State of Kans., Topeka, 1989—. Precinct committeewoman Rep. Ctrl. Com., Harvey County, Kans., 1956-68, 88—; mem., sec. Harvey County Extension Coun., 1960-64; mem. Family Life Adv. Coun. for Community Mental Health, Kans., 1967-71, Ct. Appointed Spl. Advocate Adv. Bd., Harvey County, 1991—; mem. Hertzler Rsch. Found. Bd., 1993—. Mem. Am. Home Econs. Assn. (speaker ann. meeting student sect. 1989), Am. Vocat. Home Econs. Assn., Kans. Home Econs. Assn. (past sec., past pres. bd. dirs.), Kans. Vocat. Home Econs. Assn. (past pres. bd. dirs. 1971-80), Kans. State U. Alumni Assn., Kans. State U. Coll. Human Ecology Alumni (bd. dirs. 1991-94), Harvey County Rural Life, Soroptimists, Delta Kappa Gamma (pres. 1984-86), Kappa Omicron Phi. Methodist. Office: House Reps State House Topeka KS 66612*

SAN AGUSTIN, MARIA THERESA BORROMEO, research physician; b. Manila, Oct. 4, 1957; d. Oscar D. and Amelia R. (Borromeo) San A. BS, Creighton U., 1980; MD, Virgen Milagrosa Inst. Medicine, The Philippines, 1987. IRTA fellow NIH, Nat. Inst. Deafness and Other Comm. Disorders, Bethesda, Md., 1990-91, staff fellow, 1991-94; spl. asst. to dir. for med. policy and program devel. Nat. Inst. Disability and Rehab. Rsch., Washington, 1994—; assoc. investigator NIH, Nat. Inst. Deafness and Other Comm. Disorders, Bethesda, 1994—, mem. deafness and other comm. disorders interagency coordinating com., 1994; mem. fed. working group on bone diseases NIH, Nat. Inst. Arthritis and Musculoskeletal and Skin Diseases, Bethesda, 1994; mem. adv. bd. Paralyzed Vets. Am. Mem. NAFE, AAAS, Am. Auditory Soc., Am. Soc. Human Genetics (interagy. com. disability rsch. subcom. med. rehab. 1995). Roman Catholic. Office: Nat Inst Disability & Rehab Rsch MES # 3430 600 Independence Ave SW Washington DC 20202-2572

SANBORN, ANNA LUCILLE, pension and insurance consultant; b. Bklyn., Mar. 29, 1924; d. Peter Francis and Matilda M. (Stumpp) Galligen; B.A., Bklyn. Coll., 1945; 1 son, Dean Sanborn. Head dept. benefit and estate planning Union Central Life Ins. Co., N.Y.C., 1949-51; adminstr. employee benefits Seaboard Oil Co., N.Y.C., 1952-56; with Frank J. Walters Assocs., Inc., N.Y.C., 1957—, pres., 1970—. Bd. dirs. Archdiocesan Service Corp. Mem. Am. Acad. Actuaries, Republican. Roman Catholic. Home: 58-11 Seabury St Elmhurst NY 11373 Office: Frank J Walters Assocs 58-13 Seabury St Flushing NY 11373-4825

SANBORN, DOROTHY CHAPPELL, librarian; b. Nashville, Apr. 26, 1920; d. William S. and Sammie Maude (Drake) Chappell. BA, U. Tex., 1941; MA, George Peabody Coll., 1947; MPA, Golden Gate U., 1982; m. Richard Donald Sanborn, Dec. 1, 1943; children: Richard Donald, William Chappell. Asst. cataloger El Paso (Tex.) Pub. Libr., 1947-52, Libr. of Hawaii, Honolulu, 1953; cataloger Redwood (Calif.) City Pub. Libr., 1954-55, 57-59, Stanford Rsch. Inst., Menlo Park, Calif., 1955-57; libr. Auburn (Calif.) Pub. Libr., 1959-62; cataloger Sierra Coll., Rocklin, Calif., 1962-64; reference libr. Sacramento City Libr., 1964-66; county libr. Placer County (Calif.), Auburn, 1966-89, ret., 1989; chmn. Mountain Valley Libr.System, 1970-71, 75-76, 1984-85; cons. county libr. Alpine County Libr., Markleeville, Calif., 1973-80. Peace corps vol., Thailand, 1991-93. With WAVES, 1944-46. Mem. AAUW (pres. chpt. 1982-84), Calif. Libr. Assn., Soroptimists. Democrat. Mem. United Ch. Christ. Home: 135 Midway Ave Auburn CA 95603-5415

SANCETTA, CONSTANCE ANTONINA, oceanographer; b. Richmond, Va., Apr. 17, 1949; d. Anthony Louis and Joyce Louise (Kellogg) S. BA, Brown U., 1971, MSc, 1973; PhD, Oreg. State U., 1976. Rsch. assoc. Stanford (Calif.) U., 1977-78; assoc. rsch. scientist Columbia U., N.Y.C., 1979-84, rsch. scientist, 1985-87, sr. rsch. scientist, 1988-94; assoc. program mgr. divsn. ocean sci. NSF, Washington, 1992—; mem. adv. com. divsn. ocean sci. NSF, 1981-86, 89-92. Editl. bd. Marine Micropaleontology, Oceanography, 1983—; contbr. articles to profl. jours. Fellow AAAS, Geol. Soc. Am.; mem. Am. Quarternary Soc. (councilor 1988-90), Am. Geophys. Union (sec. ocean sci. sect. 1988-90), Oceanography Soc. (councilor 1989-93), Paleontol. Rsch. Instn. (trustee 1991-92). Home: 1637 Irvin St Vienna VA 22182 Office: NSF Rm 725 4201 Wilson Blvd Arlington VA 22203

SANCHEZ, JANICE PATTERSON, psychotherapist, educator; b. Indpls., Nov. 5, 1948; d. Jack Downey and Elizabeth (Evard) Patterson; m. Adel Sanchez, Sept. 20, 1972; children: Christina, Alison. BS in Edn., Ind. U., 1970; MSW, Cath. U. Am., 1983; grad. adv. psychotherapy tng. prog., Washington Sch. Psychiatry, 1988-91. Lic. clin. social worker, Va., Washington. Tchr. Fairfax County Pub. Schs., McLean, Va., 1970-76; psychotherapist D.C. Inst. Mental Hygiene, Washington, 1984-89; pvt. practice Arlington, Va., 1989—. Vol. tchr. Jr. Gt. Books, Taylor Elem. Sch., Arlington, Va., 1987-89; active Columbia Bapt. Ch. Mem. NASW, Greater Washington Soc. for Clin. Social Workers, Jr. League No. Va. Office: 3801 Fairfax Dr Ste 14 Arlington VA 22203-1762

SANCHEZ, MARLA RENA, finance director; b. Espanola, N.Mex., Mar. 3, 1956; d. Tomas Guillermo and Rose (Trujillo) S.; m. Bradley D. Gaiser, Mar. 5, 1979. BS, Stanford U., 1979, MS, 1979; MBA, Santa Clara U., 1983. Rsch. biologist Syntex, Palo Alto, Calif., 1980-81; fin. analyst Advanced Micro Devices, Sunnyvale, Calif., 1983-85; fin. mgr. ultrasound divsn. Diasonics, Inc., Milpitas, Calif., 1985-86, contr. therapeutic products divsn., 1989-93, contr. internat. divsn., 1992-93; contr. Ridge Computers, Santa Clara, Calif., 1986-88; dir. fin. VLSI Tech., Inc., San Jose, Calif., 1993—. Home: 1234 Russell Ave Los Altos CA 94024-5541

SANCHEZ, SUSAN WALTMAN, secondary school educator; b. Appleton, Wis., Aug. 15, 1951; d. Robert George and Janice Mae (Wickesberg) Waltman; children: Jeanette Cristina, Maria Fernanda, Ana Catalina. BA in Interam. and Border Studies, U. Tex., El Paso, 1981; MA in Applied English Linguistics, U. Tex., 1986. Cert. tchr. TESOL, lang. arts, Spanish, social studies, N.Mex., Tex. Spanish and English tchr. Am. Sch., Tuxtla Gutierrez, Chiapas, Mexico, 1977-78; English tchr. Univ. Autonoma de Chiapas, Tuxtla Gutierrez, 1978-88; lang. arts and reading tchr. Instituto Bicultural, Tuxtla Gutierrez, 1987-91; subdir. Instituto Bicultural, 1990-91; ofcl. interpreter for the press for Pope Paul II's visit to Chiapas, Mexico, 1990; trainer of tchrs., 1993—; mem. task force for high sch. ESOL curriculum writing for El Paso Ind. Sch. Dist., 1993—; trainer of tchrs. in reading curriculum. Vol. Habitat for the Humanities, Project Bravo; co-sponsor Close Up for New Americans Club, Burges High Sch., mem. comm. com. Mem. El Paso County Coun. Internat. Reading Assn., Tex. Tchrs. of English to Speakers of Other Langs. Assn., Tex. Assn. Whole Langs., AFT and Support Personnel (area coord 1993—). Home: 1353 Backus El Paso TX 79925 Office: Burges High Sch 7800 Edgemere El Paso TX 79925

SAND, PHYLLIS SUE NEWNAM, retired special education educator; b. Epworth, N.D., Feb. 12, 1931; d. Zelnoe Jackson and Susie Ella (Lindley) Newnam; m. Shirley Sylvester Sand, Aug. 24, 1952; children: Thomas Richard, James Waldow, Catherine Roberta, Constance Renae. AA, Minot State Tchrs. Coll., 1952; BS in Edn., U. N.D., 1970, MEd, 1971. Cert. profl. educator, N.D., tchr., Minn. Tchr. various rural schs. in Ward and Cavalier Counties, Ward County and Cavalier County, N.D., 1950-53; cons., tchr. Griggs, Steele, & Trail Spl. Edn. Unit, N.D., 1976-78; diagnostician, tchr. learning disabled Larimore (N.D.) Elem., 1978-92. Mem. NEA (life), N.D. Edn. Assn. (life), Coun. for Exceptional Children, N.D. Ret. Tchrs. Assn., Greater Grand Forks Ret. Tchrs. Assn., Delta Kappa Gamma (v.p. 1988-90, pres. 1990-92, program chmn.). United Methodist. Home: 418 Conklin Ave Grand Forks ND 58203-1669

SANDAGE, ELIZABETH ANTHEA, market research executive; b. Larned, Kans., Oct. 13, 1930; d. Curtis Carl and Beulah Pauline (Knupp) Smith; student Okla. State U., 1963-65; BS, U. Colo., 1967; MA, 1970; PhD in Communications U. Ill., 1983; m. Charles Harold Sandage, July 18, 1971; children by previous marriage: Diana Louise Danner Wilson, David Alan Danner. Pub. rels. rep., editor Martin News, Martin Marietta Corp., Denver, 1960-63, 65-67; retail advt. salesperson Denver Post, 1967-70; instr. advt. U. Ill., 1970-71, vis. lectr. advt., 1977-84; v.p., corp. sec., dir. Farm Rsch. Inst., Urbana, 1984—. Bd. dirs. U. Ill. Libr. Friends, 1991—. Exec. dir. Sandage Charitable Trust, 1986—. Mem. U. Ill. Alumni Assn. (pres.'s coun.), Champaign Social Sci. Club., The Book Club, , Moneymakers Investment Club, Kappa Tau Alpha. Editor: Occasional Papers in Advertising, 1971; The Sandage Family Cookbook, 1976, 2d edit., 1986; The Inkling, Carle Hosp. Aux. Newsletter, 1975-76. Home: 106 The Meadows Urbana IL 61801

SANDAHL, BONNIE BEARDSLEY, pediatric nurse practitioner, nurse manager; b. Washington, Jan. 17, 1939; d. Erwin Leonard and Carol Myrtle (Collis) B.; m. Glen Emil Sandahl, Aug 17, 1963; children: Cara Lynne, Cory Glen. BSN, U. Wash., 1962, MN, 1974, cert. pediatric nurse practitioner, 1972. Dir. Wash. State Joint Practice Commn., Seattle, 1974-76; instr. pediatric nurse practitioner program U. Wash., Seattle, 1976, course coordinator quality assurance, 1977-78; pediatric nurse practitioner/health coordinator Snohomish County Head Start, Everett, Wash., 1975-77; clin. nurse educator (specialist), nurse manager Harborview Med. Ctr., Seattle, 1978—, dir. child abuse prevention project, 1986—; speaker legis. focus on children, 1987; clin. assoc. Dept. of Pediatrics, U. Wash. Sch. medicine, 1987—, clin. faculty Sch. Nursing. Mem. Task Force on Pharmacotherapeutic Courses, Wash. State Bd. Nursing, 1985-86; Puget Sound Health Systems Agy., 1975-88, pres., 1980-82; mem. child devel. project adv. bd. Mukilteo Sch. Dist., 1984-85; mem. parenting adv. com. Edmonds Sch. Dist., 1985—; chmn. hospice-home health task force Snohomish County Hospice Program, Everett, 1984-85, bd. dirs. hospice, 1985-87, adv. com. 1986-88; mem. Wash. State Health Coordinating, Council, 1977-82, chmn. nursing home bed projection methodology task force, 1986-87; mem., interim chair Nat. Council Health Planning and Devel., HHS, 1980-87; mem. adv. com. on uncompensated care Wash. State Legislature, 1983-84; mem. Joint Select Com., Tech. Adv. Com. on Managed Health Care Systems, 1984-85. Pres., Alderwood Manor Community Council, 1983-85; treas. Wash. St. Women's Polit. Caucus, 1983-84; mem. com. to examine changes in Wash. State Criminal Sex Law, 1987; appointee county needs assessment com. Snohomish County Govt. United Way, 1989; chair human svcs. adv. coun. Snohomish County Human Svcs. Dept., chair adv. com., 1992—. Recipient Golden Acorn award Seattle-King County

PTA, 1973, Katherine Rickey Vol. Participation award, 1987. Mem. Am. Nurses Assn. (chmn. pediatric nurse practitioner subcom. Com. Examiners Maternal-Child Nursing Practice, 1986-92, chair Com. Examiners Maternal-Child Nursing Practice 1988-90), Wash. State Nurses Assn. (hon. leadership award 1981, chair healthcare reform task force 1992—), King County Nurses Assn. (1st v.p. 1992—, Nurse of Yr. 1985), Wash. State Soc. Pediatrics, Sigma Theta Tau. Democrat. Methodist. Home: 1814 201st Pl SW Alderwood Manor WA 98036 Office: Harborview Med Ctr 325 9th Ave # ZA-53 Seattle WA 98104-2499

SANDE, BARBARA, interior decorating consultant; b. Twin Falls, Idaho, May 5, 1939; d. Einar and Pearl M. (Olson) Sande; m. Ernest Reinhardt Hohener, Sept. 3, 1961 (div. Sept. 1971); children: Heidi Catherine, Eric Christian; m. Peter H. Forsham, Apr. 1990. BA, U. Idaho, 1961. Lic. designer, Calif. Asst. mgr., buyer Home Yardage Inc., Oakland, Calif., 1972-76; cons. in antiques and antique valuation, Lafayette, Calif., 1977-78; interior designer Neighborhood Antiques and Interiors, Oakland, Calif., 1978-86; owner, Claremont Antiques and Interiors, Lafayette, Calif., 1987-94; assoc. Neiman-Marcus, San Francisco, 1994—; cons. Benefit Boutique Inc., Lafayette; cons., participant antique and art fair exhibits, Orinda and Piedmont, Calif., 1977—. Decorator Piedmont Christmas House Tour, 1983, 88, 89, Oakland Mus. Table Setting, 1984, 85, 86, Piedmont Showcase Family Room, 1986, Piedmont Showcase Music Room, 1986, Piedmont Kitchen House Tour, 1985, Santa Rosa Symphony Holiday Walk Benefit, 1986, Piedmont Benefit Guild Showcase Young Persons Room, 1987, Piedmont Showcase Library, 1988, Peidmont Showcase Solarium, 1989, Jr. League Table Setting, Oakland-East Bay, 1989, 90. Bd. dirs. San Leandro Coop. Nursery Sch., 1967; health coord. parent-faculty bd., Miramonte High Sch., Orinda, 1978, Acalanes Sch. Dist., Lafayette, Calif., 1978; bd. dirs. Orinda Community Ctr. Vols., 1979; originator Concerts in the Park, Orinda, 1979; cons. not-for-profit Benefit Boutique, Inc., Lafayette, Calif, 1991. Mem. Am. Soc. Interior Design (assoc.), Am. Soc. Appraisers (assoc.), Am. Decorative Arts Forum, De Young Mus., Nat. Trust Historic Preservation, San Francisco Opera Guild, San Francisco Symphony Guild. Democrat. Avocations: travel, hiking.

SANDELS, LINDA RYAN, musical education speaker; b. Hackensack, N.J., Dec. 7, 1940; d. Harry Alfred and Ruth Mildred (Minto) R.; m. Theodore E. Leverenz, June 13, 1964 (div. Aug. 1983); children: Tracy Leigh Massih, Kevin Theodore Leverenz; m. Stephen C. Sandels, Mar. 15, 1985. BS, Northwestern U., 1988. Legal sec. various law firms, Chgo., 1958-73, 80-85; dist. sales mgr. Avon Products, Inc., Morton Grove, Ill., 1973-80; docent lecture corps Lyric Opera of Chgo., 1986-94, chmn. lecture corps, 1990-93; tour dir. Ronald McDonald House, Chgo., 1991-93; bd. dirs., chpt. exec. bd. Lyric Opera of Chgo., 1991-93. Performer: One Person Live Biography of W.A. Mozart, 1986—. Active Near North Assn. Condominium Pres., Chgo., 1991-94; pres. Park Astor Concominium Assn. Bd., 1989-94. Named one of 100 Women Making a Difference, Today's Chgo. Woman, 1992. Mem. AAUW (bd. dirs. 1988-92, Outstanding Svc. award 1991), Northwestern U. Alumni Assn. (bd. dirs. 1989-93), Alpha Sigma Lambda (mem. membership com. Alpha chpt. 1988). Home: PO Box 6546 554 Sinclair Rd Snowmass Village CO 81615-6546

SANDEMAN, SONJA ELINOR, lawyer; b. San Francisco, Nov. 25, 1938; d. William Henry and Georgia Barbara (Jones) S.; divorced; children: Dinah Elka Malkin, Aaron Sandeman Malkin. BA, Coll. of Notre Dame, Belmont, Calif., 1960; JD, U. Calif., San Francisco, 1964. Bar: Calif. 1966. Pvt. practice, San Francisco, 1966—. Legis. chmn., v.p. San Francisco sect. Nat. Coun. Jewish Women, 1974-87; chmn. ct.-appointed spl. advs.. governing bd. Juvenile Hall, San Francisco, 1984-85. Office: 656 Post St Ste 1 San Francisco CA 94109

SANDER, SUSAN BERRY, environmental planning engineering corporation executive; b. Walla Walla, Wash., Aug. 26, 1953; d. Alan Robert and Elizabeth Ann (Davenport) Berry; m. Dean Edward Sander, June 3, 1978. BS in Biology with honors, Western Wash. U., 1975; MBA with honors, U. Puget Sound, 1984. Biologist, graphic artist Shapiro & Assocs., Inc., Seattle, 1975-77, office mgr., 1977-79, v.p., 1979-84, pres., owner 1984—, also bd. dirs. Merit scholar Overlake Service League, Bellevue, Wash., 1971, Western Wash. U. scholar, Bellingham, 1974-75, U. Puget Sound scholar, 1984; named Employer of Yr. Soc. Mktg. Profl. Svcs. 1988, Small Bus. of Yr. City of Seattle, Environ. Cons. of Yr., King County, Entrepreneur of Yr., Inc. Mag. Mem. UN U.S.A. Mem. Seattle C. of C., Soroptimist Internat. (bd. dirs.), Exec. Officers Club. Avocations: swimming, hiking, traveling, painting. Office: Shapiro & Assocs Inc 1201 3rd Ave Ste 1700 Seattle WA 98101-3027

SANDERS, AUGUSTA SWANN, retired nurse; b. Alexandria, La., July 22, 1932; d. James and Elizabeth (Thompson) Swann; m. James Robert Sanders, Jan. 12, 1962 (div. 1969). Student, Morgan State U., 1956. Pub. health nurse USPHS, Washington, 1963-64; mental health counselor Los Angeles County Sheriff's Dept., 1972-79; program coordinator Los Angeles County Dept. Mental Health, 1979-88; program dir. L.A. County Dept. Health Svcs., 1989-92; ret., 1992; appointee by Calif. Gov. Jerry Brown to 11th Dist. Bd. Med. Quality Assurance, 1979-85; health cons., legal, 1994-95. Mem. Assemblyman Mike Roo's Commn. on Women's Issues, 1981—, Senator Diane Watson's Commn. on Health Issues, 1979—; chmn. Commn. Sex. Equity Los Angeles Unified Sch. Dist., 1984-90. Mem. NAFE, L.A. County Employees Assn. (v.p. 1971-72), So. Calif. Black Nurses Assn. (founding mem.), Internat. Fedn. Bus. and Profl. Women (pres. L.A. Sunset dist. 1988-89, dist. officer 1982-89), Internat. Assn. Chemical Dependency Nurses (treas. 1990-92), Chi Eta Phi. Democrat. Methodist.

SANDERS, EMILY CHALEF, treasurer; b. N.Y.C., Apr. 29, 1954; d. Morton N. and Rita (Mendelson) Chalef; m. Joaquim D. Sanders, Aug. 7, 1983; children: Shawn, Ashley. BA in Internat. Rels., U. Pa., 1975; MBA in Acctg., NYU, 1978. CPA, Ga.; registered investment adviser, Ga., Fla.; cert. cash mgr. Internat. acct. Tambrands, Inc., Lake Success, N.Y., 1975-77; mgr. profit planning Charter Pub. Co., N.Y.C., 1977-79; corp. budget mgr. Coca-Cola Co., Atlanta, 1979-83, mgr. organization planning, 1983-85; mgr. internat. fin. BellSouth Corp., Atlanta, 1985-90, asst. treas., 1990-94; pres. Sanders Internat., Inc., Atlanta, 1994—. Participant Leadership Atlanta, 1993-94; fundraiser Atlanta History Mus., 1991; bd. dirs. Planned Parenthood Atlanta, 1981-87. Mem. AICPA, Ga. Soc. CPAs, Treasury Mgrs. Assn. Home: 1336 Wyntercreek Rd Atlanta GA 30338-3819

SANDERS, GEORGIA ELIZABETH, secondary school educator; b. Holmwood, La., July 14, 1933; d. Frederick Rudolph and Susie W. (Hackett) S. Student, La. Coll., 1951-53, La. State U., 1959-60; BS, then MS in Microbiology, U. Southwestern La., 1970; MS in Math., U. So. Miss., 1983. Instr. dept. biology U. New Orleans, 1976-79, instr. dept. math., 1983-86; tchr. East Baton Rouge Parish Schs., 1988-89; tchr. math. St. Tammany Parish, La., 1990—. Mem. NEA, Am. Math. Soc., Math. Assn. Am., Nat. Coun. Tchrs. Math. Home: PO Box 968 Slidell LA 70459-0968

SANDERS, JACQUELYN SEEVAK, psychologist, educator; b. Boston, Apr. 26, 1931; d. Edward Ezral and Dora (Zoken) Seevak; 1 son, Seth. BA, Radcliffe Coll., 1952; MA, U. Chgo., 1964; PhD, UCLA, 1972. Counselor, asst. prin. Orthogenic Sch., Chgo., 1952-65; research assoc. UCLA, 1965-68; cons. Osawatomie State Hosp. (Kans.), 1965-68; asst. prof. Ctr. for Early Edn., L.A., 1969-72; assoc. dir. Sonia Shankman Orthogenic Sch., U. Chgo., 1972-73, dir., 1973-93, dir. emeritus, 1993—; curriculum cons. day care ctrs. L.A. Dept. Social Welfare, 1970-72; instr. Calif. State Coll., L.A., 1972; lectr. dept. edn. U. Chgo., 1972-80, sr. lectr., 1980-93, clin. assoc. prof. dept. psychiatry, 1990-93, emeritus, 1993—; instr. edn. program Inst. Psychoanalysis, Chgo., 1979-82. Author: Greenhouse for the Mind, 1989; editor: (with Barry L. Childress) Psychoanalytic Approaches to the Very Troubled Child: Therapeutic Practice Innovations in Residential & Educational Settings, 1989, Severly Disturbed Children and the Parental Alliance, 1992, (with Jerome M. Goldsmith) Milieu Therapy: Significant Issues and Innovative Applications, 1993; contbr. articles to profl. jours. UCLA Univ. fellow, 1966-68; Radcliffe Coll. Scholar, 1948-52. Mem. Am. Orthopsychiat. Soc., Am. Psychol. Assn., Am. Assn. Children's Residential Ctrs. (pres.). Clubs: Quadrangle, Radcliffe of Chgo. (sec/treas. 1986-87, pres. 1987-89); Harvard of Chgo. (bd. dirs. 1986—). Home: 5842 S Stony Island Ave Apt 2G Chicago IL 60637-2023

SANDERS, JUDITH BROWN, nursing administrator; b. York, Pa., Sept. 27, 1940; d. Robert Lawrence and Melvine Louise (Schroeder) Brown; children: Jonathan, Robert. Diploma, Del. Hosp. Sch. Nursing, Wilmington, 1964; BS, U. Del., 1964; MS in Nursing, U. Md., 1967. Psychiat.-mental health nursing cons. Dept. Mental Health State of Mo., Jefferson City, 1978-80; asst. prof. U. Mo. Sch. Nursing, Columbia, 1976-83; dir. dept. nursing Fulton (Mo.) State Hosp., 1980-83; nurse exec. The Brattleboro (Vt.) Retreat, 1983—. Contbr. articles to profl. jours. Mem. AAUW, Am. Nurses Assn., Vt. Nurses Assn., Vt. Orgn. Nurse Execs., Am. Orgn. Nurse Execs., Am. Coll. Mental Health Adminstrn., Am. Coll. Health Care Execs., Sigma Theta Tau. Home: 29 Arbor Hill Ln Brattleboro VT 05301-2697 Office: Brattleboro Retreat 75 Linden St PO Box 803 Brattleboro VT 05301

SANDERS, MARLENE, academic administrator, educator, freelance broadcast journalist; b. Cleve., Jan. 10, 1931; d. Mac and Evelyn (Menitoff) Sanders; m. Jerome Toobin, May 27, 1958 (dec. Jan. 1984); children: Jeff, Mark. Student, Ohio State U., 1948-49. Writer, prodr. Sta. WNEW-TV, N.Y.C., 1955-60, P.M. program Westinghouse Broadcasting Co., N.Y.C., 1961-62; asst. dir. news and public affairs Sta. WNEW, N.Y.C., 1962-64; anchor, news program ABC News, N.Y.C., 1964-68, corr., 1968-72, documentary prodr., writer, anchor, 1972-76, v.p., dir. TV documentaries, 1976-78; corr. CBS News, N.Y.C., 1978-87; host Currents Sta. WNET-TV, N.Y.C., 1987-88; host Met. Week in Review, 1988-90; host Thirteen Live Sta. WNET-TV, 1990-91; prof. depth journalism NYU, 1991-93; adj. prof. journalism, adminstr. Columbia U. Grad. Sch. Journalism, N.Y.C., 1994—. Co-author: Waiting for Prime Time: The Women of Television News, 1988. Recipient award N.Y. State Broadcasters Assn., 1976, award Nat. Press Club, 1976, Emmy awards, 1980, 81, others. Mem. Am. Women in Radio and TV (Woman of Yr. award 1975, Silver Satellite award 1977), Women in Comm. (past pres.), Soc. Profl. Journalists.

SANDERS, ONA CAROL, librarian; b. Houston, Jan. 20, 1939; d. Perry Blackmer and Ona Gertrude (Felker) Hall; m. Richard F. Sanders, Sept. 28, 1954; children: Susan, Kenneth, Margaret, Elizabeth. BS in Libr. Sci., Slippery Rock U., 1972; MLS, U. Pitts., 1973. Cert. sch. libr., Pa. Libr. Shaler Area Jr. High Sch., Pitts., 1973-86, Shaler Area Sr. H.S., Pitts., 1986—. Vol. Sheldon Jackson Coll., Sitka, Alaska, 1994. Mem. NEA, AAUW, NOW, Pa. Sch. Librs. Assn. (conf. com. 1988-92), Nat. Abortions Rights Action League, So. Poverty Law Ctr., Amyotrophic Lateral Sclerosis Assn., Beta Phi Mu. Home: 10470 Meinert Rd Wexford PA 15090-9544

SANDERS, PHYLLIS ADEN, retired radio and television broadcaster; b. Buenos Aires, June 27, 1919; d. Fred and Anna Almeda (Pettit) Aden; BA, Occidental Coll., 1941; MA, Scarritt Coll., 1943; m. Olcutt Sanders, Apr. 8, 1947; children: Lynn Edwin, Marta Almeda, Jay Olcutt, Fred Aden, R. Elizabeth. Formerly tchr., lectr., workshop leader on changing roles of women, 1973-75; producer, host weekly radio interview show Changing World of Women, Sta. WNYC, N.Y.C., 1972-79; TV reporter, host, commentator on women's issues Sta. WNYC-TV, N.Y.C., 1975-78; regular weekly commentator Prime of Your Life, NBC-TV, N.Y.C., 1979-83; reporter Age Whys, AM Phila., Sta. WPVI-TV, 1981-83; producer, host weekly series Growing Older with Style, WCAU-TV, Phila., 1983-84, feature reporter Noonbreak, 1984, senior reporter NEWS, 1987—; producer, host series on aging WHYY-TV, 1984-85; reporter, interviewer Modern Maturity TV series on aging, nat. PBS-TV, 1986-88; host weekly talk show Over 50 Sta. WCAU-TV, 1989—. Community relations dir. Town of New Castle (N.Y.), 1972-73, originator, coordinator Community Day, New Castle, 1971; coordinator N.Y.C. women's adv. com. on meeting with network mgmt., 1976-77. Recipient award N.Y. chpt. NOW, 1973, N.J. Women, 1976; named to Phila. Mayor's Sr. Citizen Honor Roll, 1984. Mem. AFTRA, Nat. Acad. TV Arts and Scis., Women's Inst. for Freedom of Press, ACLU, Friends Com. on Nat. Legis., NOW, Older Women's League, Occidental Coll. Alumni (award 1985). Mem. Soc. of Friends. Home: 142 Medford Leas Medford NJ 08055

SANDERS, REVA ISABEL, elementary education educator; b. Bklyn., July 30, 1935; d. Isidore and Estelle (Silber) Minkin; m. Gilbert E. Sanders, Dec. 19, 1954; children: Diana, Jill Sanders-DeMott. Student, Bard Coll., 1952-54; BS, Bklyn. Coll., 1957, MS, 1965. Lic. elementary educator in social studies and English, N.Y.C. Substitute tchr. (per diem) N.Y.C. Bd. Edn., 1957-77; tchr. Queens (N.Y.) Sch. Dist. 24, 1978—. Home: 1641 3rd Ave Apt 28H New York NY 10128-3632 Office: PS 128Q 69-26 65th Dr Middle Village NY 11379

SANDERS, RUTH ANN NOMATHEMBA SIDZUMO, social services administrator; b. Johannesburg, South Africa, Feb. 2, 1941; came to U.S., 1969; d. Robert Bantubonke and Miriam Nozipho (Mkhosana) Sidzumo; m. Ferrell Lee Sanders, Sept. 3, 1970 (div. 1978); children: Muzill Lumkile, Valrie Nozipho Vuyo. BA in Social Work, San Francisco State U., 1970; MA in Guidance and Counseling, Wayne State U., 1976, EdS in Adminstrn. and Supervision, 1981, PhD, 1989. Social case worker Quaker Svc. Fund, Johannesburg, 1967; social worker London Borough of Hounslow, 1968-69, San Francisco Housing Authority, 1970; study skills counselor Wayne State U., Detroit, 1973-74; asst. dir. Todd-Phillips Children's Home, Detroit, 1975-84; program dir. Barat Human Svcs., Detroit, 1984-87; project dir. Transformations in Employment, Detroit, 1987-88; contractual family worker Family and Neighborhood Svcs., Detroit, 1988; program dir. Boysville of Mich., Detroit, 1989—; family reunication specialist private consultation lectr. Eastern Mich. U., Ypsilanti, 1989-91; instr. African history Roeper City and County Sch., Birmingham, Mich., 1994—; assoc. prof. sch. social work U. Transkei, South Africa, 1995. Bd. dirs. E.W. Daniel Episcopal Credit Union, Detroit, 1988; fellow mem. Episcopalian Coun. of Women, Detroit, 1980. Recipient Families 1st Program award Mich. Dept. Social Svc. Family Preservation, 1994, Program Mgr. of Yr. award, 1994, various fed. and county grants. Mem. Internat. Assn. Black Social Workers, Nat. Assn. Black Social Workers, Mich. Fedn. Pvt. Agys., Wayne State Alumni Assn., Mich. Assn. Sch. Adminstrs., Child Care Coordinating Coun., NAACP. Home: 800 W Boston Blvd Detroit MI 48202-1408 Office: Boysville of Mich 19403 W Chicago St Detroit MI 48228-1741

SANDERS, SUMMER, Olympic athlete; b. 1972; d. Bob and Barbara S. Gold medalist, 200m Butterfly Barcelona Olympic Games, 1992, Silver medalist, 200m Individual Medley, 1992, Bronze medalist, 400m Individual Medley, 1992. Address: US Olympic Com 1750 E Boulder St Colorado Springs CO 80909*

SANDERS-CHILDEARS, LINDA, banker; b. Council Bluffs, Iowa, Jan. 25, 1950; d. Nolan Glen and Mary Lucile (Dunken) Jackson. Grad., U. Wis., Am. Inst. Banking; student, U. Colo., U. Denver. Various positions First Nat. Bank Bear Valley (name changed to United Bank Bea, Colo., 1969-79; v.p. adminstrn. First Nat. Bancorp., 1979-83; pres., CEO, Equitable Bank of Littleton, 1983—; founder The Fin. Consortium; pres., CEO, Young Ams. Bank, Denver, 1987—, also vice-chmn. bd. dirs.; chmn. bd., pres. Young Ams. Edn. Found. Contbr. articles to Time and Newsweek. Bd. dirs. Cherry Creek Art Festival, Denver 1989—, now chmn.-elect, Grad. Sch. Banking, Colorado Student Loan Program, Denver; vice chmn. Nat. Assembly; past dir. Jr. Achievement, Panorama Products and Svcs., Mile High United Way; mem. adv. bd. Campfire Coun. Colo., nat. past pres. Named hon. life mem. Nat. CampFire, past chmn., numerous other awards Camp Fire Inc. Mem. Am. Bankers Assn. (past chmn. Edn. Found., edn. coun.), Found. Tchg. Econs. (trustee), Colo. Bankers Assn. Republican. Office: Young Ams Bank 311 Steele St Denver CO 80206-4453

SANDERSON, MARY LOUISE, medical association administrator; b. Fairmont, W. Va., Oct. 29, 1942; d. Lawrence Oliver and Frances Evelyn (Shuttleworth) Shingleton; m. William W. Olmstead III, Dec. 1966 (div. June 1974); children: William W. IV, Happy; m. Lester F. Davis, III, Oct. 1979 (div. Dec. 1986); m. David S. Sanderson, Sept. 1992. Student, Vassar Coll., 1960-62, Carnegie Mellon, 1962-63. Real estate broker, N.C. Exec. sec. Creative Dining, Raleigh, N.C., 1980-83, Sea Pines Plantation Co., Hilton Head, S.C., 1973-79; adminstr. Am. Bd. Neurological Surgery, Houston, 1983—. Vol. Interact, Raleigh, 1984-86, M.D. Anderson Career Hosp./Camp Star Trails, 1994—; docent Mordicai House Hist. Preservation, Raleigh, 1981-83. Recipient Vol. award N.C. State Gov., 1986. Mem. Am. Soc. Assn. Execs. Democrat. Episcopalian. Office: Am Bd Neurol Surgery 6550 Fannin St Ste 2139 Houston TX 77030-2722

SANDERSON, SUSAN GAIL, city planner; b. Poughkeepsie, N.Y., June 29, 1951; d. Isadore and Ruth (Smith) Cooperman; m. Robert W. Sanderson, Aug. 25, 1979. BA, Rider Coll., 1973. Planner trainee City of Poughkeepsie, 1976-78, planner, 1979, sr. planner, 1980—; liaison to zoning bd. appeals, waterfront adv. com., planning bd., shade tree commn., and common coun. City of Poughkeepsie, 1976—. Office: City of Poughkeepsie Box 300 Poughkeepsie NY 12602

SANDIDGE, KANITA DURICE, communications company executive; b. Cleve., Dec. 2, 1947; d. John Robert Jr. and Virginia Louise (Caldwell) S. AB, Cornell U., 1970; MBA, Case Western Res. U., 1979. Supr. assignments service ctrs. and installation AT&T, Cleve., 1970-78, chief dept. data processing and acctg., 1979-80; adminstrn. mgr. exec. v.p. staff AT&T, N.Y.C., 1980-83; sales forecasting and analysis mgr. resources planning AT&T, Newark, 1983-86; planning and devel. mgr. material planning and mgmt. AT&T Network Systems, Morristown, N.J., 1986-87; dir. adminstrv. services AT&T Network Systems, Lisle, Ill., 1987-89; dir. divsn. staff customer support and ops. AT&T Network Systems, Morristown, 1990-94; dir. global procurement minority and women bus. enterprises AT&T, Basking Ridge, N.J., 1994—. Mem black exchange program Nat. Urban League, N.Y.C., 1986—. Named Black Achiever in Industry, Harlem YMCA, 1981; recipient Tribute to Women and Industry Achievement award YWCA, 1985. Mem. Nat. Black MBA's, Alliance Black AT&T Mgrs., Am. Mgmt. Assn., Nat. Assn. for Female Execs., NAACP, Beta Alpha Psi. Mem. African Meth. Episcopal Ch. Home: 10 Trade Winds Dr Randolph NJ 07869-1238 Office: AT&T 295 N Maple Ave Basking Ridge NJ 07920-1002

SAND LEE, INGER, artist; b. Sauda, Norway, Apr. 8, 1938; came to U.S., 1960; d. Inge Sigvald and Johanne Elise (Hamre) Sand; m. Charles Allen Lee, Aug. 28, 1981. Cert. in decorative art, N.Y. Sch. Interior Design, 1968; BFA, Marymount Manhattan Coll./N.Y. Sch. Interior Design, 1980; cert. completion, Art Students League, 1993; postgrad., Nat. Acad. Design, 1993-94. One-woman shows include Art 54, N.Y.C., 1988, Pyramid Gallery, N.Y.C., 1990, Exhbn. Space, N.Y.C., 1991, Denise Bibro Fine Art, N.Y.C., 1993, 95; selected exhbns. include Lincoln Ctr., N.Y.C., 1988, Avery Fisher Hall, N.Y.C., 1988, Mus. Atheism and Realism, Lviv, USSR, 1990, Lever House, N.Y.C., 1991, Nat. Acad. Mus., N.Y.C., 1994; group exhbns. include Pyramid Gallery, N.Y.C., 1989, 90, 91, Ariel Gallery, N.Y.C., 1991, Broome Street Gallery, N.Y.C., 1992, 93, Ward-Nasse Gallery, N.Y.C., 1992, Hudson Guild Art Gallery, N.Y.C., 1992, Denise Bibro Fine Art, N.Y.C., 1992, 94, 95, Frank Bustamante Gallery, N.Y.C., 1993, Southern Alleghenies Mus. Art, Loretto, Pa., 1994; represented in numerous permanent pvt. and pub. collections. Recipient Alumni award N.Y. Sch. Interior Design, 1979; merit scholar Art Student's League, 1991. Mem. Archtl. League N.Y.

SANDLER, BERNICE RESNICK, women's rights specialist; b. N.Y.C., Mar. 3, 1928; d. Abraham Hyman and Ivy (Ernst) Resnick; children: Deborah Jo, Emily Maud. BA cum laude, Bklyn. Coll., 1948; MA, CCNY, 1950; EdD, U. Md., 1969; LLD (hon.), Bloomfield Coll., 1973, Hood Coll., 1974, R.I. Coll., 1980, Colby-Sawyer Coll., 1984; LHD (hon.), Grand Valley State Coll., 1974; Dr. Pub. Service (hon.), North Adams State Coll., 1985; LLD (hon.), Goucher Coll., 1991; LHD (hon.), Plymouth State Coll., 1992, Wittenberg U., 1993. Research asst., nursery sch. tchr., employment counselor, adult edn. instr., sec.; psychologist HEW, 1970; tchr. psychology Mt. Vernon Coll., 1970; head Action Com. for Fed. Contract Compliance, Women's Equity Action League, 1970-71; edn. specialist U.S. Ho. Reps., Washington, 1970; dep. dir. Womens Action program, HEW, Washington, 1971; dir. project on status and edn. of women Assn. Am. Colls., Washington, 1971-91; sr. assoc. Ctr. for Women Policy Studies, 1991-94; sr. scholar in residence Nat. Assn. Women in Edn., Washington, 1994—; vis. lectr. U. Md., 1968-69; adv. bd. Women's Equity Action League Ednl. and Legal Def. Fund, 1980—, trustee, 1974-80, Women's Equity Action League, 1971-78; adv. com. Math/Sci. Network, 1979—, Wider Opportunities for Women, 1978-85, Women's Legal Def. Fund, 1978-84; adv. bd. N.J. project Inst. for Rsch. on Women Rutgers U., New Brunswick, 1987—, Nat. Coun. for Alternative Work Patterns Inc., 1978-85, Women's Hdqrs. State Nat. Bank for Women's Appointments, 1977-78, and others. Mem. adv. bd. Jour. Reprints Documents Affecting Women, 1976-78, Women's Rights Law Reporter, 1970-80; editor: About Women On Campus (newsletter), 1991—; contbr. articles to profl. jours. Mem. bd. overseers Wellesley Coll. Ctr. for Research on Women, 1975-87; bd. dirs. Ctr. for Women's Policy Studies, 1972—; mem. exec. com. Inst. for Ednl. Leadership, 1982-87, mem. program adv. com., 1987—, chair bd. dirs., 1981, chair adv. com., 1975-81; mem. affirmative action com., task force on family, nat. affairs commn. Am. Jewish Com., 1978—, bd. dirs. D.C. chpt.; tech. adv. com. Nat. Jewish Family Ctr., 1980-89; adv. council Ednl. Devel. Ctr., 1980-85; adv. bd. Urban Inst., 1981-85, Women Employed Inst., 1981-84, Ex-New Yorkers for N.Y., 1978-79; mem. adv. com. Arthur and Elizabeth Schlesinger Library History of Women in Am., 1981-85, Ctr. for Women Scholars, 1979-83; nat. adv. com. Shelter Research Inst., Calif., 1980-82; chair adv. panel project on self-evaluation Am. Insts. for Research, 1980-82; bd. dirs. Equality Ctr., 1983—, Evaluation and Tng. Inst., Calif., 1980—, Inst. for Studies in Equality, 1975-77. Recipient Athena award Intercollegiate Assn. Women Students, 1974, Elizabeth Boyer award Women's Equity Action League, 1976, Rockefeller Pub. Svc. award Princeton U., 1976, Women Educators award for activism, 1987, Anna Roe award Harvard U., 1988, Readers Choice honors Washington Woman Mag., 1987, Woman of Distinction award Nat. Assn. Women in Edn.., 1991, Georgina Smith award AAUP, 1992, Woman of Achievement Turner Broadcasting System, 1994; named one of 100 Most Powerful Women Washingtonian Mag., 1982, one of the nation's 100 Most Important Women, Ladies Home Jour., 1988. Mem. Am. Psychol. Assn., Assn. for Women in Sci. Found. (bd. dirs. 1977—), Am. Soc. Profl. and Exec. Women (adv. bd. 1980—). Office: Nat Assn Women in Edn Ste 850 1350 Connecticut Ave NW Washington DC 20036

SANDLER, JENNY, dancer; b. N.Y.C.. Scholarship student, The Joffrey Ballet Sch. Dancer Joffrey II Dancers, N.Y.C., 1988-90, The Joffrey Ballet, N.Y.C., 1990—. Featured in mag. Mirabella, 1994. Office: The Joffrey Ballet 130 W 56th St New York NY 10019-3818*

SANDLER, LUCY FREEMAN, art history educator; b. N.Y.C., June 7, 1930; d. Otto and Frances (Glass) Freeman; m. Irving Sandler, Sept. 4, 1958; 1 child, Catherine Harriet. B.A., Queens Coll., 1951; M.A., Columbia U., 1957; Ph.D., NYU, 1964. Asst. prof. NYU, 1964-70, assoc. prof., 1970-75, prof. fine arts, 1975-86, Helen Gould Sheppard prof. art history, 1986—, chmn. dept., 1975-89; editorial cons. Viator, UCLA, 1983—. Author: The Peterborough Psalter in Brussels, 1974, The Psalter of Robert De Lisle in the British Library, 1983, Gothic Manuscripts 1285-1385, 1986, 'Omne Bonum': A Fourteenth-Century Encyclopedia of Universal Knowlege, 1995; editor: Essays in Memory of Karl Lehmann, 1964, Art the Ape of Nature: Studies in Honor of H.W. Janson, 1981, Monograph Series, 1970-75, 86-89, Gesta, 1991-94; asst. editor Art Bull., 1964-67, mem. editl. bd., 1994; mem. editl. bd. Jour. Jewish Art, 1978, Speculum, 1994. Trustee Godwin-Ternbach Mus., Queens Coll., 1982-94. NEH fellow, 1967-68, 77; fellow Pierpont Morgan Library; Guggenheim fellow, 1988-89. Fellow Soc. Antiquaries (London); mem. AAUP, Coll. Art Assn. (pres. 1981-84), Medieval Acad. Am., Internat. Ctr. Medieval Art (adv. bd., bd. dirs. 1976-80, 84-87, 89-92, 95—). Home: 100 Bleecker St Apt 30A New York NY 10012-2207 Office: NYU Dept Fine Arts New York NY 10003

SANDLER, MARION OSHER, savings and loan association executive; b. Biddeford, Maine, Oct. 17, 1930; d. Samuel and Leah (Lowe) Osher; m. Herbert M. Sandler, Mar. 26, 1961. BA, Wellesley Coll., 1952; postgrad., Harvard U.-Radcliffe Coll., 1953; MBA, NYU, 1958; LLD (hon.), Golden Gate U., 1987. Asst. buyer Bloomingdale's (dept. store), N.Y.C., 1953-55; security analyst Dominick & Dominick, N.Y.C., 1955-61; sr. fin. analyst Oppenheimer & Co., N.Y.C., 1961-63; sr. v.p., dir. Golden West Fin. Corp. and World Savs. & Loan Assn., Oakland, Calif., 1963-75, vice chmn. bd. dirs., CEO, mem. exec. com., dir., 1975-80, pres., co- chief exec. officer, dir., mem. exec. com., 1980-93, chmn. bd. dirs., CEO, mem. exec. com., 1993—; pres., chmn. bd. dirs., CEO Atlas Assets, Inc., Oakland, 1987—, Atlas Advisers, Inc., Oakland, 1987—, Atlas Securities, Inc., Oakland, 1987—; mem. adv. com. Fed. Nat. Mortgage Assn., 1983-84. Mem. Pres.'s Mgmt. Improvement Coun., 1980, Thrift Insts. Adv. Coun. to Fed. Res. Bd., 1989-91, v.p., 1990, pres., 1991; mem. policy adv. bd. Ctr. for Real Estate and Urban Econs. U. Calif., Berkeley, 1981—, mem. exec. com. policy adv. bd.,

1985—; mem. ad hoc com. to rev. Schs. Bus. Adminstrn. U. Calif., 1984-85; vice chmn. industry adv. com. Fed. Savs. and Loan Ins. Corp., 1987-88, Ins. Corp., 1987-88; bd. overseers NYU Schs. Bus., 1987-89; mem. Glass Ceiling Commn., 1992-93. Mem. Phi Beta Kappa, Beta Gamma Sigma. Office: Golden W Fin Corp 1901 Harrison St Oakland CA 94612-3588

SANDLIN, DEBBIE CROWE, critical care nurse; b. Columbia, Tenn., Oct. 1, 1953; d. William Taylor and Jean (Burns) Crowe; divorced; 1 child, Ashley Taylor. AS cum laude, Columbia State Coll., 1973; student, U. Tenn., Nashville, 1974-76. RN, Tenn.; cert. ACLS, BCLS. Charge nurse surg. unit Maury Regional Med. Ctr., Columbia, 1973-74; charge nurse surg. ICU HCA Pk. View Med. Ctr., Nashville, 1974-76; staff nurse post anesthesia care unit HCA Westside Hosp., Nashville, 1976-79; head nurse Parkside Surgery Ctr., Nashville, 1979-85; head nurse HCA So. Hills Med. Ctr., Nashville, 1985—, post anesthesia care unit nurse, 1985—. Maury Regional Med. Ctr. Auxillary scholar, 1971. Mem. Mid. Tenn. Soc. Post Anesthesia Nurses (founder, pres. 1986, bd. dirs. 1986-88, Outstanding Svc. award 1986-87, pub. newsletter, editor 1986-87, mem. various coms.), Tenn. Soc. Post Anesthesia Nurses (v.p. 1986-87, pres. 1987-88, bd. dirs. 1986-93, state seminar com. chairperson 1993-94, congl. rep. Point Systems Winner 1987, 88, chair edn. com. 1994-95, various coms.), Am. Soc. Post Anesthesia Nures (Tenn. dir. 1990-93, membership com., 1993—, ethics com. 1993-94, new products com., exec. com. 1992-93, chair bylaws com. 1992-93, nat. conf. com. 1991-92, amb. to Nat. Assn. Orthopaedic Nurses 1994, Pres. Appreciation award 1992, 93, 94). Home: 508 Michele Dr Antioch TN 37013-4109

SANDO, CAROL RENEE, medical/surgical nurse; b. Seattle, Apr. 11, 1949; d. Frank A. and Nancy N. (Embree) S.; children: Renee Coddington, Marilu Coddington. BSN, Widener Coll., 1978; MS in Edn., St. Joseph's U., 1987; MSN, Widener U., 1990, postgrad., 1992. RN, Pa., N.J.; cert. nurse educator. Emergency dept. staff nurse West Park Hosp., Phila., 1978-80, emergency dept. nurse mgr., 1980-81, critical care coord., 1981-82, staff devel. instr., 1983-84; surg. nurse Drs. Davis and Fox, Phila., 1984-87, Scheie Eye Inst., Phila., 1988-89; instr. Meth. Hosp. Sch. Nursing, Phila., 1987—, curriculum chair, 1990—; adj. faculty dept. nursing Neuman Coll., Aston, Pa., 1987-88; CPR instr. Am. Heart Assn., Phila., 1980-92; collagen therapist Collagen Corp., N.Y.C., 1986; edn. cons. Jefferson-Park Hosp., Phila., 1984-86; guest lectr. Widener U., Chester, Pa., 1990, cons., 1993-94. Author: (copyright) Critical Care Clinical Nurse Specialist Model, 1990. Keynote speaker Meth. Hosp. Nurse's Week, Phila., 1991. Recipient Excellence in Nursing Edn. award Nat. CoAlliance for Teaching Excellence, Shawnee Mission, Kans., 1992, 93; named NCLEX-RN Item Writer nominee Pa. State Bd. of Nursing, Harrisburg, 1991, 92. Mem. Nat. League for Nursing, Southeastern Pa. Assn. for Health Edn. and Tng., Sigma Theta Tau. Office: Meth Hosp Sch of Nursing 2301 S Broad St Philadelphia PA 19148-3542

SANDO, NORMA JEAN PATRICK, county assessor; b. Lebanon, Pa., Feb. 2, 1954; d. Richard Tilden and Martha Rank (Miller) Patrick; m. Barry W. Stickler, July 7, 1973 (div. Dec. 1978); m. John Randolph Sando, Oct. 6, 1984; children: Lori Lyn, Karin Leigh. AAS, Reading Area C.C., 1975. Cert. evaluator, Pa., person property evaluator, Pa. Photogammatrist Lebanon County Commr., 1974-81, chief county assessor, 1981—; colorguard instr. No. Lebanon Sch. Dist., Fredericksburg, Pa., 1984—. Mem., Sunday sch. tchr. Little Swatara Ch. of Brethren, Rehrepsburg, Pa., 1963—; mem. Lebanon County Rep. Women, 1978—; leader Girl Scouts Daisy Troop #1409, Annville, 1993; leader, mem. Girl Scouts Brownie Troop # 362, Annville, 1993—. Mem. Assessor's Assn. Pa. (bd. govs. 1986-89, pres., pres.-elect, v.p., sec., treas. 1981—, Trailblazer award 1994), N.E. Regional Assn. Assessing Officers (bd. govs. 1990—, pres. 1994-95, Shirley Vermil award 1994), Internat. Assn. Assessing Officers, No. Lebanon Women's Club (sec., 1992, v.p. 1994—). Office: Lebanon County Commrs 400 S 8th St Lebanon PA 17042-6794

SANDOWSKI, NORMA JEWELL, insurance executive; b. Tulsa, Dec. 30, 1940; d. Norman Jesse Sandusky and Gulia Ida (Poynor) Foster; divorced; children: Sheila Jewell Lester, Sheryl Lee Sanders, Michael Lance Sandowski. AS in Welding Tech., Tulsa Jr. Coll., 1970; BS in Indsl. Safety, Cen. State U., 1983; MS in Environ. Sci., Nova U., 1987; cert. in hazardous materials mgmt., U. Calif., Davis, 1988. Cert. assoc. risk mgmt.; cert. assoc. loss control mgmt. Safety and personnel dir. Utility Contractors, Tulsa, 1976-77; safety officer City of Tulsa Water and Sewer Dept., 1977-78; risk control rep. Comml. Union Ins., Dallas, Oklahoma City, 1978-81; cons. Parallel Resources, Oklahoma City,, San Francisco, 1981-86; mgr. environ. and occupational health Linde div. Union Carbide, Santa Rosa, Calif., 1987; mgr. tech. svcs., asst. v.p. risk engring. dept. Zurich-Am. Ins., Schaumburg, Ill., 1987—. Author: Right to Know in Educational Institutions, 1986, Environmental Auditing and Recordkeeping, 1987, Chemical Industry and its Accidents, 1991, Future of Ammonia, 1992. Mem. Adult Literacy Coun., Make Today Count-Am. Cancer Soc. Pres.' scholar Tulsa Jr. Coll., 1969, Flint Steel scholar, Tulsa, 1970; recipient Danforth award Cities Svc. Oil, Bartlesville, Okla., 1958, Silver Trefoil Woman of Achievement award Ill. Crossroads coun. Girl Scouts U.S.A., 1994. Mem. Am. Soc. Safety Engrs. (profl.). Jewish. Office: Zurich Am Ins 1400 American Ln Schaumburg IL 60196-1063

SANDRY, KARLA KAY FOREMAN, industrial engineering educator; b. Davenport, Iowa, Apr. 2, 1961; d. Donald Glen and Greta Geniveve (VanderMaten) Foreman; m. William James Sandry, Oct. 12, 1985; children: Zachary Quinn, Skyler David. BS in Indsl. Engring., Iowa State U., 1983; MBA, U. Iowa, 1992. Quality control supr., indsl. engr. Baxter Travenol Labs, Hays, Kans., 1983-84; indsl. engr. HQ Amccom, Rock Island, Ill., 1984-86; mgmt. engr. St. Lukes Hosp., Davenport, 1986-90; adj. instr. engring. St. Ambrose U., Davenport, 1990—; chair space allocations St. Luke's Hosp., Davenport, 1987-90; pres. employee rels. coun. HQ Amccom, Rock Island, 1986, chair savings bonds, 1985; speaker in field. Vol., past counselor Fellowship Christian Athletes Cen. High Sch., Davenport, 1984-87, vol., adult chpt., 1988—; counselor Explorer Scout Troop, Davenport, 1984-85; leader, counselor ch. youth group, 1985-89. Mem. Inst. Indsl. Engrs. (sr. mem.), Healthcare Info. & Mgmt. Systems Soc. (recognition & comms. com. 1988), Soc. for Health Systems (founding mem.), Found. for Christian Living, Iowa State U. Alumni Assn., U. Iowa Alumni Assn.; Positive Thinkers Club. Office: St Ambrose U 518 W Locust St Davenport IA 52803-2829

SANDS, MARY KAREN, critical care nurse; b. Lumberton, N.C., Jan. 26, 1966; d. Lilbia Thomas and Mary Foy (Blackburn) Singletary; m. Alvin Thomas Sands, Aug. 26, 1989. BSN, U. N.C., Wilmington, 1988. RN, N.C.; cert. ACLS. Cardiac operating rm. nurse N.C. Bapt. Hosp., Winston-Salem, 1988-89, staff nurse ICU trauma, 1989-90; staff nurse ICU Forsyth Meml. Hosp., Winston-Salem, 1990-93; preceptor for new nurses Forsyth Meml. Hosp., 1990-93, ICU clinician 1994—. Sun. sch. group leader Calvary Bapt. Ch., Winston-Salem, 1990—, choir mem., 1990—. Mem. AACN (visions ptnr. 1994, Old Salem chpt. pres.-elect 1994). Republican. Home: 1545 Trinity Garden Cir Clemmons NC 27012

SANDS, ROBERTA ALYSE, real estate investor; b. N.Y.C., Oct. 7, 1937; d. Harry and Irene (Mytelka) S. BEd, U. Miami, 1960; postgrad., U. Oslo, 1960. Cert. secondary educator biology, Mass. Phys. edn. instr. Key Biscayne and Ludlam Elem. Sch., Miami, 1961-63; sci. tchr. Plantation (Fla.) Mid. Sch., 1969-71, Rickards Middle Sch., Ft. Lauderdale, Fla., 1972-76; founder U. Miami Diabetes Rsch. Inst., 1989. Author: Biology on the Secondary Level, 1970. Vol. Douglas Garden Retirement Home, Miami, 1988-92, Mus. of Art, Ft. Lauderdale, 1988-92, Imperial Point Hosp., Ft. Lauderdale, 1981-83. Mem. AAUW (rec. sec. 1988-92, cultural chair 1993-94, legis. chair Ft. Lauderdale br. 1994-95, Recognition of Significant Svc. award 1983). Home: 4250 Galt Ocean Dr Fort Lauderdale FL 33308-6100

SANDS, SHARON LOUISE, graphic design executive, art publisher, artist; b. Jacksonville, Fla., July 4, 1944; d. Clifford Harding Sands and Ruby May (Ray) MacDonald; m. Jonathan Michael Langford, Feb. 14, 1988. BFA, Cen. Washington U., 1968; postgrad, UCLA, 1968. Art dir. East West Network, Inc., L.A., 1973-78, Daisy Pub., L.A., 1978; prodn. dir. L.A. mag., 1979-80; owner, creative dir. Carmel Graphic Design, Carmel Valley, Calif., 1981-85; creative dir., v.p. The Video Sch. House, Monterey, Calif., 1985-88; graphic designer ConAgra, ConAgra, Nebr., 1988; owner, creative dir. Esprit de Fleurs, Ltd., Carmel, Calif., 1988—; lectr. Pub. Expo, L.A., 1979, panelist Women in Mgmt., L.A., 1979; redesign of local newspaper, Carmel, Calif., 1982. Contbr. articles to profl. mags. Designer corp. ID for Carmel Valley C. of C., 1981, 90, redesign local newspaper, Carmel, Calif., 1982. Recipient 7 design awards Soc. Pub. Designers, 1977, 78, Maggie award, L.A., 1977, 5 design awards The Ad Club of Monterey Peninsula, 1983, 85, 87, Design awards Print Mag. N.Y., 1986, Desi awards, N.Y., 1986, 88. Mem. NAFE, Soc. for Prevention of Cruelty to Animals, Greenpeace. Democrat. Home and Office: 15489 Via La Gitana Carmel Valley CA 93924-9669

SANDSTROM, ALICE WILHELMINA, accountant; b. Seattle, Jan. 6, 1914; d. Andrew William and Agatha Mathilda (Sundius) S. BA, U. Wash., 1934. CPA, Wash. Mgr. office Star Machinery Co., Seattle, 1935-43, Howe & Co., Seattle, 1943-46; pvt. practice acctg., Seattle, 1945-85; controller Children's Orthopedic Hosp. and Med. Ctr., Seattle, 1948-75, assoc. adminstr. fin., 1975-81; lectr. U. Wash., Seattle, 1957-72. Mem. Wash. State Title XIX Adv. Com., 1975-82, Wash. State Vendors Rate Adv. Com., 1980-87, Mayor's Task Force for Small Bus., 1981-83; bd. dirs. Seattle YWCA, 1981—, pres., 1986-88; bd. dirs. Sr. Services Seattle/King County, 1985, treas., 1986, pres. 1988-90; bd. dirs. Children's Orthopedic Hosp. Found., 1982-90. Fellow Hosp. Fin. Mgmt. Assn. (charter, state pres. 1956-57, nat. treas. 1963-65, Robert H. Reeves Merit award 1970, Frederick T. Muncie award 1985), Wash. State Hosp. Assn. (treas. 1956-70), Am. Soc. Women Accts. (pres. Seattle chpt. 1946-48), Am. Soc. Women CPAs, Wash. Soc. CPAs, Women's Univ. Club (Seattle), City Club (Seattle, charter mem.). Home and Office: 5725 NE 77th St Seattle WA 98115-6345

SANDSTROM, DEBORAH SNAPP, sales executive; b. Bethesda, Md., June 24, 1946; d. Roy Baker and Dorothy (Loftis) Snapp; m. Roy Sandstrom, Oct. 1, 1983. BA, Wake Forest U., 1968; MA, Tulane U., 1970. Educator Old Lyme (Conn.) Pub. Schs., 1974-80; fed. account mgr. NBI, Arlington, Va., 1981-88; nat. account mgr. Apple Computer, Reston, Va., 1988—. Mem. Columbia Country Club (Washington), Mortar Board. Presbyterian. Home: 9724 Brimfield Ct Potomac MD 20854-4338 Office: Apple Computer 1892 Preston White Dr Reston VA 22091-4325

SANDWEISS, MARTHA A., museum director, author, American studies educator; b. St. Louis, Mar. 29, 1954; d. Jerome Wesley and Marilyn Joy (Glik) S. BA magna cum laude, Radcliffe Coll., 1975; MA in History, Yale U., 1977, MPhil in History, 1981, PhD, 1985. Smithsonian-Nat. Endowment Humanities fellow, Nat. Portrait Gallery, Washington, 1975-76; curator photographs Amon Carter Mus., Ft. Worth, 1979-86, adj. curator photographs, 1987-89; dir. Mead Art Mus. Amherst Coll., 1989—, adj. assoc. prof. of fine arts and Am. studies, 1989-94, assoc. prof. Am. studies, 1994—. Author: Carlotta Corpron: Designer with Light, 1980, Masterworks of American Photography, 1982, Laura Gilpin: An Enduring Grace, 1986, (catalogue) Pictures from an Expedition: Early Views of the American West, 1979; co-author: Eyewitness to War: Prints and Daguerreotypes of th Mexican War, 1989; editor: Historic Texas: A Photographic Portrait, 1986, Contemporary Texas: A Photographic Portrait, 1986, Denizens of the Desert, 1988, Photography in Nineteenth Century America, 1991; co-editor: Oxford History of the American West, 1994. Fellow Ctr. for Am. Art and Material Culture, Yale U., 1977-79, NEH, 1988. Office: Amherst Coll Mead Art Mus Amherst MA 01002

SANERA, MARGE See KRASCHNESKE, MARGARETHE REGINA

SANFORD, JULIE ROSE TANNER, nursing consultant, nursing educator; b. Lucedale, Miss., Aug. 7, 1962; d. Eugene Joseph and Lena Marie (Eubanks) Tanner; m. Robert Roy Sanford Jr., Feb. 21, 1987; children: Joseph Robert, Brannan Terrell. BSN, U. Ala., Tuscaloosa, 1984; MSN, U. South Ala., 1990. RN, Ala.; cert. ACLS instr., Am. Heart Assn.; cert. BCLS instr., Am. Heart Assn.; cert. CCRN. Nurse in ICU Mercy Hosp., New Orleans, 1984-85; office nurse Pulmonary Assocs., Mobile, Ala., 1987-88; staff nurse in emergency dept. U. So. Ala. Med. Ctr., Mobile, 1985-87, 1987-88, critical care cons., 1988-90, staff nurse in emergency dept., 1990-91; staff develop. inservice specialist, patient edn. U. So. Ala. Knollwood Pk. Hosp., Mobile, 1991-92; staff nurse emergency dept. U. So. Ala. Med. Ctr., Mobile, 1992-93; clin. asst. prof., 1993—; lectr. numerous presentations in field. Mem. AACN (Mobile Bay area pres. 1990), Am. Heart Assn., Sigma Theta Tau. Republican. Baptist. Home: 6871 Walter Tanner Rd Wilmer AL 36587

SANFORD, KATHERINE KOONTZ, cancer researcher; b. Chgo., July 19, 1915; d. William James and Alta Rachel (Koontz) S.; m. Charles Fleming Richards Mifflin, Dec. 11, 1971. BA, Wellesley Coll., 1937; MA, Brown U., 1939, PhD, 1942; DSc (hon.), Med. Coll. Pa., 1974, Cath. U. Am., 1988. Teaching asst. Brown U., Providence, 1937-39, rsch. asst., 1939-41; instr. biology Western coll., Oxford, Ohio, 1941-42, Allegheny Coll., Meadville, Pa., 1942-43; asst. dir. Johns Hopkins Nursing Sch., Balt., 1943-47; rsch. biologist Nat. Cancer Inst. NIH, Bethesda, Md., 1947-74; head cell physiology and oncogenesis sect. Lab. Biochemistry, Bethesda, 1974-77; chief in vitro carcinogenesis sect. Nat. Cancer Inst. NIH, Bethesda, 1979—. Contbr. 150 articles to profl. jours. Ross Harrison fellow, 1954. Mem. Phi Beta Kappa, Sigma Xi. Home: 101 Stuart Dr Dover DE 19901-5817 Office: Nat Cancer Inst In Vitro Carcinogenesis Bethesda MD 20892

SANFORD, RUTH EILEEN, data processing company administrator; b. Two Harbors, Minn., Mar. 15, 1925; d. John Arvid and Helene (Lind) Bostrom; m. Keith N. Sanford, Sept. 21 1950 (div. Sept. 1960); m. Michael R. Notaro, Mar. 10, 1984. Degree in bus., Cable's Secretarial Coll., 1944; student, Northwestern U., 1966. Exec. sec. 1st Am. Nat. Bank, Duluth, Minn., 1944-48; pvt. sec. Adam Thomson, Duluth, Minn., 1948-52; exec. sec. and administrv. asst. Res. Mining Co., Silver Bay, Minn., 1952-62, United Calif. Bank, San Francisco, 1963-64; office mgr. Poly-Tech, Mpls., 1964-66; corp. sec. and administrv. asst. to pres. Statis. Tabulating Corp., Chgo., 1966-90. Mem. NAES. Roman Catholic. Club: Butterfield Country (Hinsdale, Ill.). Lodge: Women of Moose. Home: 500 Linden Ave Oak Park IL 60302-1659

SANGIULIANO, BARBARA ANN, tax manager, accountant; b. Bronx, N.Y., Dec. 28, 1959; d. Patrick John and Mildred (Soell) Gallo; m. John Warren Sangiuliano, Aug. 28, 1982. BA, Muhlenberg Coll., 1982; MST, Seton Hall U., 1989. CPA, N.J.; cert. mgmt. acct. Sr. tax mgr. KPMG Peat Marwick, Short Hills, N.J., 1988-92; sr. tax analyst Allied Signal, Morristown, N.J., 1992-93; tax mgr. AT&T, Morristown, 1993—. Fellow N.J. Soc. CPAs; mem. AICPA, Inst. Mgmt. Accts., Mensa, Omicron Delta Epsilon, Phi Sigma Iota. Republican. Roman Catholic. Home: 340 William St Scotch Plains NJ 07076 Office: AT&T 412 Mt Kemble Ave Morristown NJ 07962

SANKEY, SANDRA ROCHELLE, elementary school educator; b. Pottstown, Pa., June 24, 1949; d. Herman and Esther Lenora (Strom) S. BS in Elem. Edn., Kutztown (Pa.) U., 1971, MEd in Reading, 1974. Elem. tchr. Srping-Ford Sch. Dist., Collegeville, Pa., 1971—. Past pres. Towne and Country Coun. Rep. Women, Limerick, Pa.; sec. congregation Mercy and Truth Synagogue, Pottstown, pres. 1994—; pres. Jewish Women's League, Pottstown, 1984-88, 93-94. Mem. NEA, Pa. Edn. Assn., Spring-Ford Edn. Assn., Limerick Elem. Sch. Home-Sch. League, AAUW, B'nai B'rith (Person of Yr. award). Home: 47 Swamp Pike Limerick PA 19468-1405

SAN MIGUEL, SANDRA BONILLA, social worker; b. Santurce, P.R., May 23, 1944; d. Isidoro and Flora (Carrero) Bonilla; m. Manuel San Miguel, July 12, 1969. BA, St. Joseph's Coll., 1966; MS in Social Work, Columbia U., 1970. Case worker Dept. Labor, Migration Div., N.Y.C., 1966-68; clin. social worker N.Y.C. Housing Authority, N.Y.C., 1968-69, Children's Aid Soc., N.Y.C., 1969-71; sr. social worker Traveler's Aid Soc., San Juan, P.R., 1971-74; coord., supr. Dept. Addiction Control Svcs., San Juan, P.R., 1974-77; substance abuse div. dir. Seminole County Mental Health Ctr., Altamonte Springs, Fla., 1978-81; cons. pvt. practice Hispanic Cons. Svcs., Winter Springs, Fla., 1982—; adj. prof. Seminole Community Coll., Lake Mary, Fla., 1986-90; sch. social worker I Seminole County Pub. Schs., Sanford, Fla., 1986-91, lead sch. social worker, 1991—; mem. pres.'s minority adv. coun. U. Ctrl. Fla., 1982—, vice chair, 1982-86, chair, 1986-90; mem. bd. regents EEO adv. com. State Univ. System Fla., 1985-89; bd. dirs. Seminole Community Mental Health Ctr., 1986—, v.p., 1988-90, pres., 1990-91; mem. Fla. Consortium on Tchr. Edn. for Am. Minorities, 1990—; mem. local com. Hispanic Info. and Telecomms. Network, 1990; mem. Seminole County (Fla.) Juvenile Justice Coun., 1993—; mem. statewide student svcs. adv. com. Dept. Edn., Fla., 1993—. Mem. NASW, Fla. Assn. Sch. Social Workers (co-founder minority caucus 1988, columnist quar. newsletter Minority Corner 1988-92, bd. dirs. 1989—, sec. 1990-92, v.p. 1992-93, pres. 1993-94), Collegiate Social Workers P.R., Columbia U. Alumni Assn., St. Joseph's Coll. Alumni Assn. Home: 1214 Howell Creek Dr Winter Springs FL 32708-4516 Office: Seminole County Pub Schs 1401 Magnolia Ave Sanford FL 32771-2999

SANQUIST, NANCY JOHNSON, international facility management professional; b. Muncie, Ind., Aug. 31, 1947; d. Charles Elof and Pauline Lydia (Murphy) S.; m. James M. Johnson, Dec. 1988. BA, UCLA, 1970; MA, Bryn Mawr Coll., 1973; MS, Columbia U., 1978. Instr. Lafayette Coll., Easton, Pa., 1973-74, Muhlenberg Coll., Bethlehem, Pa., 1974-75, Northampton Area Community Coll., Bethlehem, 1974-75; dir. Preservation Office City of Easton, 1977-78; cons. El Pueblo de Los Angeles State Historic Park, 1978-79; dir. restoration Bixby Ranch Co., Long Beach, Calif., 1979-82; mgr. computer applications Cannel-Heumann & Assoc., Los Angeles, 1982-84; dir. Computer-Aided Design Group, Marina del Rey, Calif., 1984-93, Strategic Asset Mgmt. PAE Inc., L.A., 1993—; adj. instr. UCLA, 1979-86, Grad Sch. Calif. State U., Dominguez Hills, 1981. Author numerous tech. articles and manuals. Bd. dirs. Historic Easton, Inc., 1977-78, Simon Rodia's Towers in Watts, Los Angeles, 1979-81, Los Angeles Conservancy, 1982-86, Friends of Schindler House, West Hollywood, Calif., 1978—, pres., 1982-85. Recipient Outstanding Contbn. award Nat. Computer Graphics Assn., 1987. Mem. Internat. Facility Mgmt. Assn. (seminar leader, lectr. N.Am., Asia, Australia, Europe and Mid. East 1987—).

SANSEIGNE, MARY JOSEPHINE, certified registered nurse anesthetist; b. Kearny, N.J., Aug. 29, 1931; d. Joseph A. and Catherine E. (Ward) Mac Neill; m. Alain Sanseigne, Nov. 1, 1952 (div. 1958); 1 child, Katherine; m. James C. Candy, June 18, 1983. Student, Jersey State Coll., 1950-53; RN, Jersey City Med. Ctr., 1953; cert. RN anesthetist, Jersey Shore Med. Ctr., Neptune, N.J., 1966; Jersey State Coll., Monmouth Coll., 1977-78. RN Army Hosp., Ft. Monmouth, N.J., 1957-64; chief cert. RN anesthetist Plainfield, N.J., 1968-82; staff cert. RN anesthetist Univ. Hosp., Newark, 1984-88; chief cert. RN anesthetist Centra State Med. Ctr., Freehold, N.J., 1988-92. Mem. Property Owner's Assn., Neptune, 1990-91. Mem. N.J. Assn. Nurse Anesthetists (bd. trustees 1972-74, pub. rels. 1970-72, legal adv. 1971-72), Am. Assn. Nurse Anesthetists (McGaw award 1968), N.J. Hosp. Assn. Republican. Roman Catholic. Home: 308 Hillside Dr Neptune NJ 07753

SANT, BARBARA HARDING, artist, educator; b. Emporia, Va., July 6, 1935; d. Bland Tisdale and Lucille Virginia (Paschall) Harding; m. Martin Francis Sant, June 21, 1956 (div. 1970); children: Martin Francis III, Paul Wesley; m. Brian Michael Donahue, Dec. 7, 1984. BFA, Va. Commonwealth U., 1957; postgrad., Norfolk State, Old Dominion U., 1981-82. Art tchr. Hopewell (Va.) City Schs., 1957-58, Greensville County Schs., Emporia, Va., 1969-79; 3d grade tchr. Charlottesville (Va.) Pub. Schs., 1959-60; mus. aide Portsmouth (Va.) Cmty. Arts Ctr., 1981-84; art instr. Chowan Art Coun., Edenton, N.C., 1994—. One-person shows Richmond (Va.) Profl. Inst., 1962, Yeatts Gallery, Roanoke, Va., 1974, Richardson Meml. Libr., Emporia, Va., 1979, 89, Options Gallery, Nashua, N.H., 1986, Caswell County Civic Ctr., Yanceyville, N.C., 1992, Chowan Arts Coun., 1993; group shows include Massilon (Ohio) Mus. Regional, 1969, Walter Cecil Rawls Libr. & Mus., Courtland, Va., 1973, Kill Devil Hills (N.C.) Gallery, 1975-77, Eric Schindler Gallery, Richmond, Va., 1975-78, Ghent Art Festival, Norfolk, Va., 1984, McKowan-Knipe Fine Arts, Concord, N.H., 1986, 87, 88, Portland (Maine) Art Festival, 1986, Currier Gallery Art, Manchester, N.H., 1987, 88, Whistler House Mus., 1989, Durham (N.C.) Art Guild, 1989, 90, Firehouse Fine Art Galleries, 1992, numerous others; permanent collections include Peterborough (N.H.) Bank, Indian Head Bank, Nashua, N.H., Bank of N.H., Vance-Granville C.C., Henderson, N.C., Walter C. Richardson Meml. Libr., Dominion Nat. Bank, Virginia Beach, Va., numerous others. Recipient 1st Place award Albemarle Art Assn., 1964, Greely Park Art Show, 1986, Whistler House Mus. Art, 1989, Firehouse Galleries, 1991, Kerr Lake Spring Show, 1990, Caswell Coun. for Arts & Scis., 1990, Merit award Ann. Juried Seawall Art Show, 1980, Purchase award Henley Southeastern Spectrum Nat. Juried Show, 1991, 2nd prize Landmark Competition, Elizabeth City, N.C., 1994, Crestar Bank award Suffolk Art League, 1994, Art Excellence award Frank Stick Meml. Art Show, 1995; named Best of Show, Mansfield Fine Arts Guild Ann. Juried Art Show, 1967. Mem. Chowan Arts Coun. (bd. dirs. 1992-93). Methodist. Home: 406 N Broad St Edenton NC 27932

SANTAELLA, IRMA VIDAL, state supreme court justice; b. N.Y.C., Oct. 4, 1924; d. Rafael and Sixta (Thillet) Vidal; children: Anthony, Ivette. Acctg. degree, Modern Bus. Coll., 1942; BA, Hunter Coll., 1959; LLB, Bklyn. Law Sch., 1961, JD, 1967; LLD, Sacred Heart U., Conn., 1990. Bar: N.Y. 1961. Sole practice N.Y.C., 1961-63, with ptnr., 1966-68; dep. commr. N.Y.C. Dept Correction, 1963-66; mem. N.Y. State Human Rights Appeal Bd., N.Y.C., 1968-83, chmn., 1975-83; justice N.Y. State Supreme Ct., N.Y.C., 1983-94; mem. N.Y.C. Adv. Council on Minority Affairs, 1982—, N.Y.C. Commn. on Status of Women, 1975-77. Founder, chmn. Legion of Voters, 1962-68; nat. del. Presdl. Democratic Convs., 1968, 72, 76, 80; vice chmn. N.Y. State del. 1976 Conv.; founder Nat. Assn. for Puerto Rican Civil Rights, 1962, Hispanic Community Chest Am., 1972; chmn. bd. dirs. Puerto Rican Parade, 1962-67; bd. dirs. Catholic Interracial Council, 1968-81; nat. co-chmn. Coalition Hispanic People, 1970; fund raiser Boy Scouts Am., 1962-63; chmn. Children's Camp, South Bronx (N.Y.) 41st Police Precinct, 1967; active City-Wide Steering Com. for Quality Edn., 1962-64, Community Service Soc., 1972-74, Talbott Perkins Children's Services, 1973-75, Planned Parenthood Assn., 1968-69, Puerto Rican Crippled Children's Fund, 1965-69; founder N.Y. chpt. Clinica Grillasca, P.R. Cancer Assn., 1974—. Recipient citations for civic work Gov. Rockefeller, 1972, Gov. Carey, 1982, First Puerto Rican woman to be elected to the N.Y. State Supreme Ct., County of Bronx, 1983; recipient Recognition award Gov. Mario M. Cuomo, 1990, Nat. Puerto Rican Coalition Life Achievement award, 1990, Life Achievement award Pres. of Dominican Republic, 1991, Life Achievement award Nat. Coun. Hispanic Women, 1991, others. Mem. Am. Judicature Soc. Roman Catholic. Home: 853 7th Ave New York NY 10019 Office: Supreme Ct State NY 60 Centre St New York NY 10007-1402

SANTANGELO, BETTY J., lawyer; b. N.Y.C., Sept. 5, 1950; d. Alfred E. and Betty L. Santangelo; m. Thomas Egan, Oct. 11, 1981. BA, Trinity Coll., 1971; JD, Fordham U., 1974. Bar: N.Y. 1975, Fla. 1975, U.S. Dist. Ct. (so. and ea. dists.) N.Y. 1975, U.S. Ct. Appeals (2d cir.) 1975. Assoc. Martin, Obermaier & Morvillo, N.Y.C., 1974-76; law clk. to presiding justice U.S. Dist. Ct. (so. dist.) N.Y., N.Y.C., 1976-77; asst. U.S. atty. So. Dist. N.Y., N.Y.C., 1977-83; 1st v.p., asst. gen. counsel Merrill Lynch, Pierce, Fenner & Smith, N.Y.C., 1983—; adj. prof. law Fordham U., N.Y.C., 1982-84. Mem. ABA (div. dir. litigation com. 1991-92), N.Y. Women's Bar Assn., Assn. of Bar of City of N.Y. Office: Merrill Lynch 2 Broadway Fl 21 New York NY 10004-2207*

SANTHUFF, CAROL JEAN, librarian; b. Springfield, Mo., Jan. 7, 1946; d. Ludwig Wilhelm and Meta Beata (Nobe) Knaust; m. Charles Lewis Santhuff, Sept. 24, 1966; children: Joanna, Emily. BS in Edn., U. Mo., 1970. Cert. tchr., sch. libr., Mo. 1st grade tchr. Summersville (Mo.) Sch. Dist., 1968-69, jr. high tchr., 1971-73, math. tchr. grades 7-8, 1975-77; math. tchr. grades 7-8 New Madrid (Mo.) County Schs., 1969-71; jr. high tchr. Eminence (Mo.) R-1 Sch. Dist., 1973-75, libr., 1977-83; libr. Mountain View (Mo.) Birch Tree R-3, 1983—. Grantee Mo. Dept. Elem. and Secondary Edn., 1986. Mem. Mo. Assn. Sch. Librs., Pi Lambda Theta. Lutheran. Home: PO Box 458 Eminence MO 65466-0458 Office: Liberty High Sch PO Box 464 Mountain View MO 65548-0464

SANTI, ELLYN E., mathematics educator. BS, No. Ariz. U., 1971, MA, 1974; postgrad., George Mason U., 1980-82. Cert. tchr., Va. Tchr. math. Flagstaff (Ariz.) Pub. Schs., 1972-76, head math. dept., 1974-76; asst. prof. math. No. Va. C.C., Annandale, Va., 1976—; participant Writing Across the Curriculum Workshops, Annandale, 1992-93. Recipient recognition for outstanding contbns. to edn. No. Va. C.C. Alumni Fedn., 1993. Mem. Am.

Math. Assn. Two-Yr. Colls., Va. Math. Assn. Two-Yr. Colls. (regional v.p. 1989-91, coord. spring conf. 1992), Phi Kappa Phi. Office: No Va C C 8333 Little River TP Annandale VA 22003-3743

SANTIAGO, NELLIE, state legislator; m. Ben Fernandez. BA, Hunter Coll., 1970; MA, Columbia U., 1972; PhD, U. Mass., 1977. Dir. chronic mental health svcs. Jefferson County Health Dept., Birmingham, Ala., 1978-84; adminstr. Bklyn. Manor Home for Adults, 1987-92; asst. bur. dir. N.Y. State Health, Albany, 1984-87; mem. N.Y. State Senate, Albany, 1992—; health care adminstrn. cons.; mem. adj. faculty U. Ala., Birmingham, 1978-84; mem. White House Conf. on Families, 1980. Recipient Pub. Health award Kings County Dist. Atty., 1992, also awards from Johns Hopkins U. Sch. Hygiene and Pub. Health, SUNY Ctr. for Women in Govt.. Office: NY State Senate Legis Office Bldg Rm 513 Albany NY 12247

SANTILLO, JOSEPHINE, social worker, psychotherapist; b. Passaic, N.J., June 11, 1943; d. Richard Lorenzo and Minnie (Cannizzaro) S. BA, Fairleigh Dickinson U., 1965; MSW, Va. Commonwealth U., 1977. Interviewer N.J. Employment Svc., Hackensack, 1965-66; rehab. counselor N.J. Rehab. Svc., Newark, 1967; social worker N.J. Dept. Instns. And Agys., Wayne, 1968-74; fair hearing officer N.J. Bd. Adminstrv. Rev. and Appeals, Trenton, 1974-81; social work supr., spl. asst. to Essex County mgr. N.J. Div. Youth and Family Svcs., Newark, 1981—; pvt. practice psychotherapy, Pompton Plains, N.J., 1977—. Mem. Nat. Assn. Social Workers, Am. Legion, Nat. Paralegal Assn. Home: PO Box 14 Pompton Plains NJ 07444-0014 Office: NJ Div Youth and Family Svc 153 Halsey St Newark NJ 07102-2825

SANTIN, JEAN, cosmetic company executive, consultant; b. Trenton, N.J., May 31, 1938; d. Joseph and Angeline (Parziale) Inverso; m. Louis Santin, Apr. 12, 1958; children: Renee, Scott. Grad. high sch., Trenton. Self employed jewelry bus. Hamilton Square, N.J., 1967-71; credit mgr. Lenape Products, Inc., Pennington, N.J., 1971-80; sales dir. Mary Kay Cosmetics, Ringoes, N.J., 1979—; fashion, beauty and color analysis cons. Mary Kay Cosmetics, Ringoes, 1980-91. Beauty cons. for drug and alcohol rehab. area hosps., 1980-91; organizer of Christmas gifts for the underpriviledged, Hunterdon County, 1989, 90. Mem. Hunterdon County C. of C. Home and Office: Mary Kay Cosmetics 23 Runyon Mill Rd Ringoes NJ 08551-1514

SANTOMASSIMO, CYNTHIA LEA, association executive; b. Lawrence, Mass., Nov. 29, 1954; d. Alphonse Anthony and Madeleine Marie (Pelletier) S. BA in Politics, Framingham (Mass.) State Coll., 1987; MA in Polit. Sci., U. R.I., 1989. Program coord. Reclaim Our Community, Woburn, Mass., 1990-91; co-founder, dir. Woburn Coalition Against Substance Abuse, 1991—; owner Cmty. Prevention Specialists, Woburn, 1993—; pres. 12 Step Ednl. Programs of New Eng., Woburn, 1993—; mem. exec. bd. Mass. Communities in Partnership, 1992—; founder Cmty. Edn. and Prevention, Inc. Named Drug Fighter of Yr., Gov.'s Alliance Against Drugs, Boston, 1993. Mem. NAACP, NAFE, Assn. Prevention Profls. Roman Catholic. Office: Woburn Coalition Against Substance Abuse 33 Plympton St Woburn MA 01801

SANTONA, GLORIA, lawyer; b. Gary, Ind., June 10, 1950; d. Ray and Elvira (Cambeses) S.; m. Douglas Lee Frazier, Apr. 12, 1980. BS in Biochemistry, Mich. State U., 1971; JD, U. Mich., 1977. Bar: Ill. 1977. Atty. McDonald's Corp., Oak Brook, Ill., 1977-82, dir. staff, 1982-86, dir. home office, 1986-87, dir. dept., 1987-89, sr. corp. atty., 1982-87, asst. gen. counsel, v.p., 1987—, asst. v.p., 1989—. Mem. ABA, Ill. Bar Assn., Chgo. Assn., Am. Corp. Counsel Assn., Am. Soc. Corp. Secs. (securities law com.). Office: McDonalds Corp 1 Mcdonalds Plz Hinsdale IL 60521*

SANTORE, CARRIE-BETH, computer training professional; b. Torrington, Conn., July 28, 1953; d. Michael and Dolores Leonard S. BA History and Am. Studies cum laude, Conn. Coll., 1975; MA History, U. Conn., 1977; MBA Mktg., Va. Polytechnic Inst., 1988. Analyst CIA, Washington, 1980-90; dep. dir. ops. programs Quality Systems, Inc., Fairfax, Va., 1990—; Lotus cert. cons., 1994. Bd. dirs., sec. Seminary Walk Condo Assn., Alexandria, Va., 1987-88, editor newsletter, 1986-87; vol. Alexandria Waterfront ARC, 1989-90; mem. com. to devel. internat. studies program Conn. Coll., New London, 1988-89. Mem. ASTD, Balt.-Washington Info. Systems Educators, Phi Alpha theta. Office: Quality Systems Inc 4000 Legato Rd Ste 1100 Fairfax VA 22033-4055

SANTORO, YVONNE MICHELE, English educator; b. Paterson, N.J., Dec. 21, 1958; d. Edward Patrick and Rose Barbara (Rinaldi) Migliaccio; m. Joseph Anthony Santoro, Feb. 8, 1992; 1 child, Jeannine Marie. BA in English cum laude, Montclair State U., 1981, MA in Counseling, 1992. English tchr. Nutley (N.J.) Sch. Dist., 1981-88; English tchr. Cedar Grove (N.J.) Sch. Dist., 1988—, substance abuse coord., 1990-94; tutor, SAT preparation Cedar Grove Sch. Dist., 1990—; parenting for prevention, facilitator Veronia Twp., 1992; forensic adviser, coach Cedar Grove Sch. Dist., 1990—; drama dir. Nutley and Cedar Grove Sch. Dist., 1983-94. Mcpl. Alliance mem. Cedar Grove Mcpl. Alliance Against Substance Abuse, 1990-93. Mem. NEA, N.J. Edn. Assn., Cedar Grove Edn. Assn., N.J. Coun. Tchrs. of English, Nat. Coun. Tchr. of English, Assn. of Substance Abuse Profls. Roman Catholic. Office: Cedar Grove Sch Dist Rugby Rd Cedar Grove NJ 07009

SANTOS, ADELE NAUDE, architect, educator; b. Cape Town, South Africa, Oct. 14, 1938; came to U.S., 1973; d. David Francois Hugo and Aletta Adèle Naudé. Student, U. Cape Town, South Africa, 1956-58; Diploma, Archtl. Assn., 1961; MArch in Urban Design, Harvard U., 1963; M in City Planning, U. Pa., 1968, MArch, 1968. Pvt. practice architecture with Antonio de Souza Santos, 1966-73; ptnr. Interstudio, Houston, 1973-79; assoc. prof. architecture Rice U., Houston, 1973-78, prof., 1979; prof. architecture and urban design, dept. architecture U. Pa., Phila., 1981-90; founding dean Sch. Architecture U. Calif., San Diego, 1990—; pvt. practice architecture and urban design Adele Naude Santos, Architect, Phila., 1979-90, Adele Naude Santos and Assocs., San Diego and Phila., 1991—; founding dean Sch. of Architecture, U. Calif., San Diego, 1990—. Project dir., co-filmmaker for 5 part series, 1979-80. Wheelwright Travelling fellow, Harvard U., 1968; NEA grantee, 1976, Tex. Com. for Humanities grantee, 1979; recipient (with Hugo Naudé) Bronze medal for House Naudé Capt. Inst. South African Architects, 1967, award for public TV program So. Ednl. Communications Assn., 1980, 3d place award Inner city Infill Competition, 1986; winner Internat. Design Competition, Hawaii Loa Coll., hon. mention Cin. Hillside Housing Competition and City Visions, Phila., 1986; winner competition for Franklin/La Brea Affordable Housing Project Mus. Contemporary Art and Community Redevel. Agy. City L.A., 1988, Pa. Soc. Architects design award for Franklin/La Brea Multi-Family Housing, 1988; winning entry collaborative competition for amphitheater, restaurant and natural history mus., Arts Pk., La., 1989; winner competition for 24-unit residential devel., City of Camden, N.J., 1989, for New Civic Ctr., City of Perris, Calif., 1991. Office: 2527 South St Philadelphia PA 19146-1037 also: 2947 1st Ave San Diego CA 92103-5906

SANTOS, LISA WELLS, critical care nurse; b. Richardson, Tex., Oct. 25, 1963; d. Malcolm R.N. and Maitland Anne (MacIntyre) Wells; m. Ignacio Santos, Jr., Dec. 17, 1988. Cert. med. asst., x-ray-lab. technician, Tex. Coll. Osteopathy, 1983; AS in Nursing, El Centro Coll., Dallas, 1988; student, U. North Tex.; BS in Bus. Mgmt., Le Tourneau U., Longview, Tex., 1993. RN, Tex.; cert. in CPR; cert. case mgr., cert. profl. in health care quality; advanced cert. in continuity of care; assoc. cert. mgr. Med. technologist Family Med. Ctr., 1984-85, Beltline Med. Clinic, 1985-86; nurse, lab. technician Primacare, 1986-88; charge nurse telemetry unit NME Hosp.-RHD Meml. Hosp., Dallas, 1988-89; nurse ICU, Denton (Tex.) Regional Med. Ctr.; nurse Angel Touch, 1989; nursing cons. Travelers Ins., 1990-91; med. rev. specialist Nat. Group Life, 1991-94; mgr. case mgmt. Nat. Group Life/Nat. Health Svcs. Contbr. articles to profl. jour. Mem. AACCN, NAFE, Nat. Assn. Health Care Quality, Nat. Assn. Quality Assurance Profls., Assn. of Nurses in AIDS Care, Case Mgmt. Soc. Am., Am. Assn. for Continuity of Care, Alpha Epsilon Delta, Alpha Beta Kappa, Gamma Beta Phi.

SANUA, MARIANNE RACHEL, historian, educator; b. Boston, Mar. 1, 1960; d. Victor D. and Stella (Sardell) S. BA, Princeton U., 1982; postgrad., Hebrew Univ. Jerusalem, 1982-84, Jewish Theol. Seminary, 1985-87; MA, Columbia U., 1988, PhD, 1994. Editorial asst. Congress Monthly mag. Am. Jewish Congress, 1984-86; tchr. high sch. history program Jewish Theol. Seminary, 1986-91; intern dept. Jewish life Jewish Home and Hosp. Aged, 1987—; instr. U. Wash., Seattle, 1993-94; lectr. Sephardic Ho. Speaker's Bur., 1991-92; adj. asst. prof. Queens Coll., 1991-92, 94, Touro Coll., 1995. Contbr. articles to profl. jours. Recipient Leo Wasserman prize Am. Jewish Hist. Soc., 1987, award Lucius N. Littauer Found., Meml. Found. Jewish Culture, Nat. Found. Jewish Culture; Rabbi Benjamin Plotkin fellow Jewish Theol. Seminary, 1986-87, Revson fellow, 1987-88; Presdl. fellow Columbia U., 1987-90; Rabbi Theodore S. Levy Tribute fellow Am. Jewish Archives, 1989-90; scholar German Acad. Student Exchange, 1990; grantee Jewish Hist. Soc. N.Y., 1991-93; Hazel D. Cole fellow in Jewish Studies U. Wash., 1993-94. Home: 2416 Quentin Rd Brooklyn NY 11229

SANZ, KATHLEEN MARIE, management consultant; b. L.A., Sept. 29, 1955; d. Jess Quevedo and Rosemary Helen (Debley) S. Student, Chabot Coll., 1975-76, City of Costa Mesa (Calif.), 1985. Lic. tax preparer, Calif. Admistrv. positions, 1973-80; office mgr. The Printery, Laguna Hills, Calif., 1980-83, Astro Vista, Inc., Irvine, Calif., 1983-85; adminstrv. dir. Orange County Pacific Symphony, Santa Ana, Calif., 1985-86, Image Printing, Irvine, 1986-88; adminstr. Conant Constrn. Corp., Corona Del Mar, Calif., 1988-90; owner, cons. KMS & Assocs., Mission Viejo, Calif., 1990—; nat. coord. PED Inc., Reno, Nev., 1985-86; cons. Forms Mgmt. Co., Reno, 1987-89. Author: (collection of poetry) In the Twighlight of Life, 1978; author acctg. system; contbr. articles to profl. jours. Mem. Santa Ana City Renovation Com., 1985, Environ. Def. Fund, Washington, 1989—; team capt. San Clemente (Calif.) Triathlon, 1988; vol. Orange County Rep. Orgn., Santa Ana, 1989-90; mem. coun. South County Region, 1990—, officer, sec., 1991-93, logistics coord. Cmty. Expo, 1993; vol. Orange County United Way, logistics chmn. campaign kick-off, 1994; cmty. rels. chmn., liaison to corp. mktg. dept. South County, 1994; mem. Saddleback Valley Cmty. Task Force. Named Outstanding Vol., Lake Forest Showboaters, 1988, South Orange County region United Way, 1993, Shining Star award United Way. Mem. NAFE, Lake Forest Showboaters (bd. govs. 1987-88), Nat. Conservatory, World Wildlife Found., Amnesty Internat., United We Stand Am., Saddleback C. of C., Greenpeace, Cousteau Soc., Soc. Poets, Internat. Platform Assn. Presbyterian. Home and Office: KMS & Assocs 26196B Sanz Mission Viejo CA 92691-6822

SANZONE, DONNA S., editor-in-chief; b. Bklyn., Apr. 4, 1949; d. Joseph J. Seitz and Faye (Brooks) Rossman; m. Charles F. Sanzone, Jan. 2, 1972; children: Danielle, Gregory. BA magna cum laude, Boston U., 1970; MA, Northeastern U., 1979. Grad. placement specialist Inst. Internat. Edn., N.Y.C., 1970-72; adminstr. AFS Internat. Scholarships, Brussels, 1972-74; editor Internat. Ency. Higher Edn., Boston, 1974-76; editor G.K. Hall & Co., Pubs., Boston, 1977-81, exec. editor, 1981-91, editor-in-chief, 1991—. Contbg. author: Access to Power, 1981. Mem. ALA, Assn. Am. Pubs., Assn. Coll. and Rsch. Librs., Libr. and Info. Tech. Assn. Office: G K Hall & Co 18 Pine St Weston MA 02193-1804

SAPADIN, LINDA ALICE, psychologist, writer; b. N.Y.C., Mar. 20, 1940; d. Samuel Miles and Helen Leah (Bogen) Fink; m. Seymour Sapadin, Nov. 10, 1962 (div. 1980); children: Brian, Glenn, Daniel; m. Ronald J. Goodrich, May 15, 1983. BA, Bklyn. Coll., 1960; MA, Temple U., 1961, CUNY, 1986; PhD, CUNY, 1986. Lic. psychologist, N.Y. Sch. psychologist N.Y.C. Bd. Edn., 1962-66, rsch. cons., 1985-87; tchr. Hewlett-Woodmere (N.Y.) Adult Edn., 1975-84; devel. dir. Ctr. for Women and Achievement, Island Park, N.Y., 1984-89; dir. Biofeedback and Stress Reduction Ctr., Valley Stream, N.Y., 1990—; pvt. practice Valley Stream, 1987—; forum leader, adj. prof. Hofstra U., N.Y. Inst. Tech., Five Towns Coll., Nassau Community Coll., L.I., 1974-90; cons. Nassau County Town of Hempstead, N.Y., 1986; adj. prof. continuing edn. Hofstra U., Uniondale, N.Y., 1985—; talk show host Sta. WGBB Radio, Merrick, N.Y., 1987. Columnist Chanry Communications, 1987-90, Richner Publs., 1992; contbr. articles to profl. jours. Chmn. psychology com. Nassau County NOW, Uniondale, 1983; speaker L.I. Assn. Planned Parenthood, Econ. Opportunities Coun., L.I. Libr. System, B'nai Brith, Women's Forum, Nat. Coun. Jewish Women, 1984—. Recipient Outstanding Community Svc. award State Senator Carol Berman, 1984. Mem. APA (media div., psychology of women div.), Nassau County Psychol. Assn. (women's studies com.). Home and Office: Biofeedback and Stress 19 Cloverfield Rd Valley Stream NY 11581-2421

SAPHIRE, NAOMI CARROL, bookkeeper; b. Cleve., Mar. 22, 1938; d. Ben F. and Marian (Lackritz) S.; m. Sanford M. Goldstein (div. 1979); children: Jodi Hayes, Jonathan Goldstein, Daniel Goldstein. BS, CSU, Fullerton, 1980; postgrad. cert., U. Calif., Irvine, 1991-93. Tax svc. coord. ADP, LaPalma, Calif., 1980-87; conversion analyst Bank of Am., Anaheim, Calif., 1987-91; account exec. Systems Tax Svc., Fountain Valley, Calif., 1992—; bookkeeper constrn. notebook Dickinson Printers, Las Vegas, Nev., 1994—. Home: 3304 Ewa Beach Dr Las Vegas NV 89122-3936 Office: Tax Svc Systems 2551 Santa Barbara # 102 Costa Mesa CA 92626

SAPINSLEY, LILA MANFIELD, state official; b. Chgo., Sept. 9, 1922; d. Jacob and Doris (Silverman) Manfield; BA, Wellesley Coll., 1944; D. Pub. Service, U. R.I., 1971; D. Pedagogy, R.I. Coll., 1973, LHD, Brown U., 1993; m. John M. Sapinsley, Dec. 23, 1942; children—Jill Sapinsley Mooney, Carol Sapinsley Rubenstein, Joan Sapinsley Lewis, Patricia Sapinsley Levy. Mem. R.I. Senate, 1972-84, minority leader, 1974-84; dir. R.I. Dept. Community Affairs, 1985; chmn. R.I. Housing and Mortgage Fin. Corp., 1985-87; Commr. R.I. Pub. Utilities Commn., 1987-93. Mem. R.I. Gov.'s Commn. on Women; commr. Edn. Commn. of States; pres. bd. trustees Butler Hosp., 1978-84; trustee R.I. State Colls., 1965-70, chmn., 1967-70; trustee U. R.I., R.I. Coll. Found.; bd. dirs. Miriam Hosp., Hamilton House, Trinity Repertory Co., Lincoln Sch., Wellesley Center for Research on Women, 1980, Providence Pub. Libr. Recipient Alumnae Achievement award Wellesley Coll., 1974; Outstanding Legislator of Yr. award Republican Nat. Legislators Assn., 1984. Republican. Jewish. Home: 25 Cooke St Providence RI 02906-2022

SAPOS, MARY ANN, advertising agency executive. Formerly with Al Paul Lefton, Inc.; pres., CEO, Hutchins/Young & Rubicam, Rochester, N.Y. Office: Hutchins/Young & Rubicam 400 Midtown Tower Rochester NY 14604-2069

SAPP, MARY ELLEN, state official, educator; b. Bethesda, Md., Aug. 6, 1945; d. Richard Friend and Anne Carr (Garges) S. BA in Math., Incarnate Word Coll., 1968; MS in Health Care Adminstrn., Trinity U., 1972; M in Theol. Studies, Oblate Sch. Theology, San Antonio, 1984. Tchr. Archdiocese of San Antonio, 1965-71; adminstrv. resident Spohn Hosp., Corpus Christi, 1971, Morningside Manor, San Antonio, 1972; exec. dir. St. Benedict Health Care Ctr., San Antonio, 1972-85, Benedictine Health Resource Ctr., Austin/San Antonio, 1985-89, Tex. Dept. Aging, Austin, 1992—; town meeting specialist Alamo Area Coun. of Govts., San Antonio, 1990-91; pres. Tex. Conf. Cath. Health Facilities, Austin, 1980-81; cmty. advisor San Antonio Light Newspaper, 1989-91; mem. adj. faculty Inst. on Aging Incarnate Word Coll., San Antonio, 1991-93; active Tex. Indigent Health Care Task Force, Austin, 1983-84. Recipient Headliners award for pub. endeavors Women in Comm., 1990; named Regional Citizen, Alamo Area Coun. Govts., 1987. Office: Tex Dept Aging 1949 IH 35 South Austin TX 78711

SAPP, SUE DUFFIELD, accountant; b. Sycamore, Ill., Dec. 25, 1956; d. Dale James and N. Elizabeth (Gothard) Duffield; m. Jerry Carl Sapp, May 29, 1988; children: James Duffield, Michael Glen. BS in Math., Bradley U., 1978; MBA, No. Ill. U., 1981. Cert. mgmt. acct. Actuarial asst. D.F. Campbell Consulting Actuaries, Chgo., 1979-80; rsch. analyst Allied Van Lines, Broadview, Ill., 1981-82, forecast analyst, 1982-84, supr., mgr. profit planning, 1984-89; forecast mgr. ACCO USA, Wheeling, Ill., 1989-94; contr. Polyblend (divsn. ACCO USA), St. Charles, Ill., 1994—. Grad. fellow No. Ill. U., 1980-81. Mem. Inst. Mgmt. Accts. Methodist. Home: 345 Windsor Dr Bartlett IL 60103

SARAH, AIDA TERESA, administrator; b. L.A., Jan. 5, 1958; d. Luis Richard and Stella (Chavez) Castillejos; m. John Sarah, Aug. 1, 1987; 1 child, Anthony Ray. BA, Long Beach State U., 1982; MBA, U. LaVerne, 1991. Customer svc. asst. supr. Bank of Am., Long Beach, Calif., 1974-84; adminstr. plans, schedule mgmt. Rockwell Internat., Downey, Calif., 1984—. Author: Success of Business Women in the 90s', 1994. Mem. Nat. Mgmt. Assn., Toastmasters Internat. (pub. speaking trophies). Home: 2116 Beechwood Ave Fullerton CA 92635

SARANDON, SUSAN ABIGAIL, actress; b. N.Y.C., Oct. 4, 1946; d. Phillip Leslie and Lenora Marie (Criscione) Tomalin; m. Chris Sarandon, Sept. 16, 1967 (div. 1979); children: Eva Maria Livia Amurri, Jack Henry Robbins, Miles Guthrie Robbins. B.A. in Drama and English, Cath. U. Am., 1968. Actress: (plays) include An Evening with Richard Nixon, 1972, A Coupla White Chicks Sittin' Around Talkin', 1980-81, A Stroll in the Air, Albert's Bridge, Private Ear, Public Eye, Extremities, 1982, (films) Joe, 1970, Lady Liberty, 1972, The Rocky Horror Picture Show, 1975, Lovin' Molly, 1974, The Front Page, 1974, The Great Waldo Pepper, 1975, Dragon Fly, 1976, Crash, 1976, The Other Side of Midnight, 1977, The Last of the Cowboys, 1978, Checkered Flag or Crash, 1978, Pretty Baby, 1978, King of the Gypsies, 1978, Something Short of Paradise, 1979, Loving Couples, 1980, Atlantic City, 1980 (Prix Genie Best Fgn. Actress award 1981, Acad. award nominee 1981), Tempest, 1982 (Venice Film Festival Best Actress 1982), The Hunger, 1983, Buddy System, 1984, Compromising Positions, 1985, The Witches of Eastwick, 1987, Bull Durham, 1988, Sweet Hearts Dance, 1988, A Dry White Season, 1989, The January Man, 1989, White Palace, 1990, Thelma and Louise, 1991 (Acad. award nominee 1992, Golden Globe award nominee 1992), The Player, 1992, Light Sleeper, 1992, Bob Roberts, 1992, Lorenzo's Oil, 1992 (Acad. award nominee 1993), The Client, 1994 (Acad. Awd. nom., Best Actress), Little Women, 1994, Safe Passage, 1994; TV appearances The Haunting of Rosalind, 1973, F. Scott Fitzgerald and The Last of the Belles, 1974, Who Am I This Time, 1982, A.D., 1985. Mussolini: The Deline and Fall of Il Duce, 1985, (TV series) A World Apart, 1970-71, Search for Tomorrow, 1972-73. Mem. AFTRA, Screen Actors Guild, Actors Equity, Acad. Motion Picture Arts and Scis., NOW, MADRE, Amnesty Internat., ACLU. Office: Internat Creative Mgmt Martha Luttrell 8899 Beverly Blvd Los Angeles CA 90048-2412*

SARASON, BARBARA RYRHOLM, psychology educator; b. Chgo., June 13, 1929; d. John Oswald and Esther Katherine (Lohse) Ryrholm; m. Irwin Gerald Sarason, Sept. 19, 1953; children: Suzanne, Jane, Donald. BA, DePauw U., 1951; MS, U. Iowa, 1954; PhD, Ind. U., 1956. Sr. rsch. assoc. U. Wash., Seattle, 1976-86, rsch. assoc. prof., 1986-89, rsch. prof., 1989—; vis. scholar Netherlands Inst. Advanced Studies, 1975-76; prof. Fred Hutchinson Cancer Rsch. Ctr., Seattle, 1990—. Mem. King County, Wash. Charter Review Com., 1975-76. Nat. Heart, Lung & Blood Inst. grantee, 1985—; Nat. Cancer Inst. grantee, 1988-93. Fellow APA, Soc. Behavioral Medicine, Western Psychol. Assn.; mem. LVW, Soc. Exptl. Soc. Psychology, Delta Gamma, Sigma Xi. Office: U Wash Psychology NI-25 Seattle WA 98195

SARAVO, ANNE COBBLE, clinical psychologist, mental health administrator; b. Atlanta, Feb. 23, 1938; d. William Edwin and Iris Benny (Norman) Cobble; m. James Vincent Saravo, June 13, 1958; children: Stacy Anne, Lisa Ames Furmanek. BA, Tex. Tech. U., 1959; MS, U. Mass., 1964, PhD, 1965; postgrad., Regional Health Authority, London, 1978-79, U. So. Calif., 1980-81. Lic. psychologist, Calif. Assoc. prof. psychology Antioch Coll., Yellow Springs, Ohio, 1966-69; cons. Winchester (Eng.) Day Treatment Nursery Sch., 1971-73; sch. psychologist Muroc Unified Sch. Dist., Edwards AFB, Calif., 1974-75; clinical psychologist Antelope Valley Hosp., Lancaster, Calif., 1975-76, Farnborough Hosp., Kent, Eng., 1978-80, Orange County (Calif.) Mental Health Svc., 1981-84; pvt. practice clin. psychology Seal Beach, Calif., 1981—; chief adult out-patient svc. Orange County (Calif.) Mental Health Svc., 1984-87, chief adult inpatient svcs., 1987—; bd. dirs. High Hopes Neurol. Recover Group, Costa Mesa, Calif., chair profl. adv. bd., 1988—; oral examination commr. Calif. Bd. Psychology, 1989—; geriatric coord. Orange County Mental Health Svcs., 1985-87; profl. adv. bd. Orange County Caregiver Resource Ctr., 1989—; mem. Alzheimers Disease rev. panel Calif. Dept. Mental Health, 1990—. Contbr. articles to profl. jours. Chairperson Conf. Geriatric Mental Health, Asilomar, Calif., 1986, So. Calif. Geriatric Mental Health Coordinators, 1985-87. U.S. Pub. Health fellow Fels Research Inst., 1966-67. Mem. APA, Calif. Psychol. Assn. (chair medicare/pub. sector subcom. 1990—), Nat. Acad. Neuropsychology (grad.), Brit. Psychol. Soc. Office: Orange County Mental Health Svc 515 N Sycamore St Santa Ana CA 92701-4637 also: # 203 550 Pacific Coast Hwy Seal Beach CA 90740

SARDISCO, KAREN A., artist, educator; b. Rochester, N.Y., July 18, 1955; d. Samuel Peter and Florence Rose (Montrose) Sardisco; m. Norman A. Williams, Oct. 28, 1990; 1 child, Ian Andrew Williams. BS in Art Edn., SUNY, Buffalo, 1977; MFA in Painting, Rochester Inst. Tech., 1985. Tchr. art, chari dept. art Bishop Kearney High Sch., Rochester, 1979-82; prof. Sch. of Art and Design, Rochester Inst. Tech., 1984—. One-woman shows include Cell Gallery, Rochester, 1989, So. Vt. Coll. Gallery, Bennington, 1990, Geva Theatre, Rochester, 1992, ARC Gallery, Chgo.; group exhbns. include G.A.L. Gallery, Greensboro, N.C., 1988, Bevier Gallery, Rochester, 1988, 89, 90, Dawson Gallery, Rochester, 1988, Mercer Gallery, 1989, Artspace Gallery, New Haven, 1990, Berkshire Mus., Pittsfield, Mass., 1990, Everson Mus., Syracuse, 1990, Meml. Art Gallery, Rochester, 1991, Adams Art Gallery, Dunkirk, N.Y., 1991, Angel Fire Gallery, Rochester, 1992, many others; permanent collections include Westinghouse Corp., Pitts., Chase Lincoln Bank, Buffalo, Westwood Pharms., Buffalo, others. Recipient Merit award Cheekwood Nat. Contemporary Painting Competition, 1992, Purchase award Three Rivers Arts Festival '87, Pitts. by Westinghouse Corp., Light Impressions award for excellence in two-dimensional artwork Rochester Finger Lakes Exhbn., 1984. Mem. Coll. Art Assn.

SARFATY, SUZANNE, internist and researcher; b. Irvington, N.Y., Apr. 11, 1962; d. Sam and Pat (Petrovich) S. BS, Boston U., 1984, MD, 1988, MPH, 1994. Diplomate Am. Bd. Internal Medicine. Intern and resident Boston City Hosp., 1988-91; attending/clin. instr. Boston U., 1991-93, asst. prof. medicare and pub. health, 1995—. Mem. prof. com. Am. Cancer Soc., Boston, 1991—; mentor Boston Ptnrs. for Edn., 1991—. Recipient Cmty. Svc. award CIBA Geigy, 1986; Dana Farber cancer prevention fellow, 1993-94. Fellow ACP. Home: 11 Verndale St Brookline MA 02146-2423

SARGEANT, DIANE MARIE, human resources specialist; b. York, Pa., Nov. 15, 1956; m. Thomas R. Sargeant. BS in Secondary Edn., Millersville U., 1978. Mgr. pers. adminstrn. Danskin Inc., York, 1978-84; pers. rep. AMP, Inc., Harrisburg, Pa., 1984-87; mgr. human resources devel. York Hosp., 1987—. Vol., com. rep. United Way York County, 1988-92. Mem. ASTD, Am. Mgmt. Assn., Am. Soc. for Human Resources Mgmt. (cert. profl.). Office: York Hospital 1001 S George St York PA 17403-3676

SARGENT, CONSTANCE ANNE, community educator; b. Middlebury, Vt., Apr. 15, 1949; d. Rudolph Morgan and Helen Doris (Cook) S.; m. Stephen Leigh Paquette, Jan. 9, 1971 (div. July 1981). BS in Home Econs. Edn., U. Vt., 1973; MA in Cmty./Clin. Psychology, Mansfield U., 1993. Tchr. Middlebury Union High Sch., 1973-74; home econs. asst. Addison County Extension Svc., Middlebury, 1975; tchr. St. Johnsbury Jr. High Sch., 1975-80; cmty. educator U. Vt. Extension, Chelsea, Vt., 1980-85, Cornell Coop. Extension, Bath, N.Y., 1986—; mem. nat. adv. panel Parent-Caregiver Partnership Program, Ithaca, N.Y., 1989; mem. adv. coun. N.Y. State Region II Health Edn. and Svcs. Network, Mt. Morris, N.Y., 1990-92; tutor Empire State Coll., Corning, N.Y., 1992. Mem. Steuben County Task Force for Prevention of Child Abuse, Bath, 1986—, chair, 1994; mem. adv. coun. Steuben Office for Aging, Bath, 1990-92, 94; mem. Steuben Child Care Coord. Coun., Bath, 1990—; chair Women's Alliance for Family Peace, Corning, 1990-91. Mem. APA (psychology of women div.), NOW, Nat. Assn. for Poetry Therapy. Office: Cornell Coop Extension Steuben County 3 E Pulteney Sq Bath NY 14810

SARGENT, DIANA RHEA, corporate executive; b. Cheyenne, Wyo., Feb. 20, 1939; d. Clarence and Edith (de Castro) Hayes; grad. high sch.; m. Charles Sargent, Apr. 17, 1975 (div. 1991); children: Rene A. Coburn, Rochelle A. Rollins, Clayton R. Weldy, Christopher J. IBM proof operator Bank Am., Stockton, Calif., 1956-58, gen. ledger bookkeeper, Modesto, Calif., 1963-66; office mgr., head bookkeeper Cen. Drug Store, Modesto, 1966-76; pres. Sargent & Coburn, Inc., Modesto, 1976—; ptnr. R.C.D. Farms (almond ranch), Just a Little Something (antique dolls and miniatures). Mem. Stanislaus Women's Ctr. Mem. NOW, San Francisco Mus. Soc., Modesto Women's Network. Office: 915 14th St Modesto CA 95354-1010

SARGENT, LIZ ELAINE (ELIZABETH SARGENT), safety consulting executive; b. Meadville, Pa., Apr. 17, 1942; d. Melvin Ellsworth and Roberta Jean (Beach) Taylor; m. Lawrence Sargent, Sept. 6, 1969; 1 child, Kathy-Dawn. Student, Allegheny Coll., 1964; AA cum laude, Cuyahoga C.C., Cleve., 1987, Assoc. in Transp. cum laude, 1989; BA, Ithaca Coll., 1993. Student, 1964; car distbr. Norfolk and Western R.R., Cleve., 1963-69; account mgr. Ill. Cen. R.R., Cleve., 1970-73; traffic coord. Carlon Pipe, Mantua, Ohio, 1973-75; chief dispatcher X.L. Trucking, Coshocton, Ohio, 1975-77; corp. log auditor Anchor Motor Freight, Beachwood, Ohio, 1977-78; cons. Saf-T, Parma, Ohio, 1978-84; v.p. safety Saf-T, Shaker Heights, Ohio, 1987-91; dir. safety Sherwin Williams, Cleve., 1984-87; pres. Safety Advisors for Transp., Inc., Beachwood, Ohio, 1991—; speaker Coshocton (Ohio) Traffic Club, 1984, Am. Indsl. Hygiene, Cleve., 1985. Author: Hall Chemical-Safety Procedures, 1983-84, Progressive Insurance, 1987, RL Lipton Co. manual, 1994; contbr. articles to profl. jours. Chairperson intergenerational com. Ch. in Aurora, Ohio, 1984-86; bd. dirs. Shaker Heights Teen Recreational Com., 1984-87. Delta Nu Alpha scholar, 1977. Mem. Ohio Trucking Assn. (nat. safety coun.), Cleve. Bd. Realtors, Motor Fleet Safety Suprs. (nat. com.), Fleet Maintenance Coun., Phi Theta Kappa. Republican. Office: Saf-T 14716 Rockside Rd Maple Heights OH 44137-4016

SARGENT, PAMELA, writer; b. Ithaca, N.Y., Mar. 20, 1948. BA, SUNY, Binghamton, N.Y., 1968, MA, 1970. Am. editor: The Bull. of the Sci. Fiction Writers Am., Johnson City, N.Y., 1983-91; mng. editor Binghamton, 1970-73, asst. editor, 1973-75; editor (anthology) Women of Wonder, 1975, Bio-Futures, 1976, More Women of Wonder, 1976, The New Women of Wonder, 1978, (with Ian Watson) Afterlives, 1986, Women of Wonder, The Classic Years, 1995, Women of Wonder, The Contemporary Years, 1995, Nebula Awards 29, 1995; author: Starshadows, 1977, The Best of Pamela Sargent, 1987, Cloned Lives, 1976, The Sudden Star, 1979, Watchstar, 1980, The Golden Space, 1982, The Alien Upstairs, 1983, Earthseed, 1983, Eye of the Comet, 1984, Homesmind, 1984, Venus of Dreams, 1986, The Shore of Women, 1986, The Best of Pamela Sargent, 1987, Alien Child, 1988, Venus of Shadows, 1988, Ruler of the Sky, 1993, (Nebula Best Novelette award 1992, Locus Best Novelette award 1993). Office: PO Box 486 Johnson City NY 13790-0486 also: care Richard Curtis Assocs Inc 171 E 74th St New York NY 10021

SARGUT, SUSAN H., pharmacist; b. Gardner, Mass., Feb. 19, 1954; d. John J. and Helen T. (Macionis) S.; B.S. in Pharmacy, U. R.I., 1977; MBA U. Pitts., 1990. Pharmacist, Adams Drug Co., North Kingstown, R.I., 1977-78, Brooks Drug Co., Augusta, Maine, 1978-80, Sun Drug Co., North Versailles, Pa., 1980-81, Eckerd Drug, Uniontown, Pa., 1981-82; pharmacist mgr. Revco Drug, Waynesburg, Pa., 1982-87; staff pharmacist Children's Hosp. Pitts., 1987-92; dir. of pharmacy Potomac Valley Hosp., Kegser, W.Va., 1992—; ptnr. Rufff's Double S Farm, Prosperity, Pa., 1981—. mem. Am. Soc. Hosp. Pharmacists. Office: 425 Apple Hill Rd Waynesburg PA 15370-9341

SARICKS, JOYCE GOERING, librarian; b. Nov. 8, 1948; d. Joe W. and Lovella Goering; m. Christopher L. Saricks, Aug. 21, 1971; children: Brendan James, Margaret Katherine. BA with highest distinction in Eng.& Ger, U. Kans., 1970; MA in Comparative Lit., U. Wis., 1971; MA/MAT in Library Sci., U. Chgo., 1977. Reference librarian Downers Grove (Ill.) Pub. Library, 1977-80, head tech. svcs., 1980-83, coord. lit. and audio svcs., 1983—; presenter workshops in field. Author: (with Nancy Brown) Readers' Advisory Service in the Public Library, 1989. Mem. Read Ill. adv. com., 1990-91. Woodrow Wilson fellow, 1970; recipient Allie Beth Martin award Pub. Library Assn., 1989. Mem. ALA, Ill. Library Assn., Adult Reading Round Table (founder), Phi Beta Kappa, Delta Phi Alpha, Pi Lambda Theta, Beta Phi Mu. Home: 1116 61st St Downers Grove IL 60516-1819 Office: Downers Grove Pub Library 1050 Curtiss St Downers Grove IL 60515-4606

SARIS, PATTI B., federal judge; b. 1951. BA magna cum laude, Radcliffe Coll., 1973; JD cum laude, Harvard U., 1976. Law clerk to Hon. Robert Braucher Mass. Supreme Judicial Ct., 1976-77; atty. Foley Hoag & Eliot, Boston, 1977-79; staff counsel U.S. Senate Judiciary Com., 1979-81; atty. Berman Dittmar & Engel, Boston, 1981-82; chief civil divsn. U.S. Atty.'s Office, 1984-86; U.S. magistrate judge U.S. Dist. Ct. Mass., 1986-89; assoc. justice Mass. Superior Ct., 1989-94; dist. judge U.S. Dist. Ct. Mass., 1994—; mem. com. on civil rules Supreme Judicial Ct. Comments editor civil rights Civil Liberties Law Rev. Bd. trustees Beth Israel Hosp.; active Wexner Heritage Found. Nat. Merit scholar, 1969; recipient award Mothers of Murdered Children, 1993. Mem. Nat. Assn. Women Judges, Am. Jewish Com., Women's Bar Assn. (bd. dirs. 1982-86), Mass. Bar Assn., Mass. Assn. Women Judges, Boston Bar Assn., Boston Inns Ct., Phi Beta Kappa. Office: John W McCormack Courthouse 90 Devonshire St Rm 707 Boston MA 02109-4583*

SARKISIAN, CHERILYN See CHER

SARKISIAN, PAMELA OUTLAW, artist; b. Spokane, Sept. 26, 1941; d. Willard Clinton and Frances (Montieth) Outlaw; m. Ronald Edward Sarkisian, Nov. 11, 1960; children: Ronald Abraham, Michelle Suzanne. Grad. high sch., Stockton, Calif. Art student Oceanside, Calif., 1972-80; founder Palette 'N Easel Studio, Oceanside, Calif., 1980—, operator, mgr., 1980-85; art tchr. in residence Palette 'N Easel Studio, Oceanside, 1985-91. Designer floral collector plate series Danbury Mint/MBI, Inc.; represented in Laura Larkin Gallery, Del Mar, Calif., 1993-94, Charles Hecht Galleries, Tarzana and Palm Desert, Calif., 1993-94, Lou Martin Gallery, Laguna Beach, Calif., 1994. Pres. Zonta Internat., Oceanside, 1980-81; mem. Emblem Club #177, Oceanside, 1971-91; princess Daughters of the Nile, San Diego, 1974; bd. dirs. Oceanside Girls Club, 1980. Recipient 1st Pl. award San Dieguito Art Guild, 1978, 85, 2nd Pl. award, 1983, 89, 3rd Pl. award, 1983, 1990. Mem. North County Art Assn. (founder), Carlsbad Oceanside Art League, 1978, San Dieguito Art Guild, Fallbrook Art Assn., San Diego Art Inst., Assn. pour Promotion Artiste Français, ARTISPHERE. Office: Palette 'N Easel Studio 1021 S Hill St Oceanside CA 92054-5004

SARNO, PATRICIA ANN, biology educator; b. Ashland, Pa.; d. John Thomas and Anna (Harvest) S. BS, Pa. State U., 1966, MEd, 1971; postgrad. Bucknell U., 1967, Bloomsburg U., 1970. Programmer planetarium, tchr. sci. Pottsville (Pa.) High Sch., 1967; tchr. biology Schuylkill Haven (Pa.) Area High Sch., 1967-91, sci. chmn., coord. dist., 1973-91; lead tchr. sci. Pa. Acad. Suprs. and Curriculum Devel. Dist. Pa. Sch., 1991—; cons. Contbr. to profl. jours. Pa. Edn. Dept., career program Pottsville Hosp. Dow Chem. Co. grantee, 1971. Mem. AAAS, AAUW, NEA, Pa. Edn. Assn. (exec. bd.), Nat. Assn. Biology Tchrs., Nat. Tchrs. Assn., Pa. Assn. Supervision and Curriculum Devel., N.Y. Acad. Scis., Pa. Tchrs. Assn., Am. Inst. Biol. Scis., Pa. Acad. Scis., Pa. State U. Alumni Assn., Schuylkill Haven Edn. Assn., Phi Sigma, Delta Kappa Gamma. Discoverer spider species Atypus snetzingeri, 1973. Home: 49 S Balliet St Frackville PA 17931-1703 Office: Schuylkill Haven HS Schuylkill Haven PA 17972

SARNOFF, LILI-CHARLOTTE DREYFUS (LOLO SARNOFF), artist, business executive; b. Frankfurt, Germany (Swiss citizen), Jan. 9, 1916; came to U.S., 1941, naturalized, 1941; d. Willy and Martha (Koch von Hirsch) Dreyfus; m. Stanley Jay Saronff, Sept. 11, 1948; children: Daniela Martha Bargezi, Robert L. Grad. Reimann Art Sch. (Germany), 1934, U. Berlin, 1935; student U. Florence (Italy), 1948-54. Rsch. asst. Harvard Sch. Pub. Health, 1955-89; rsch. assoc. cardiac physiology Nat. Heart Inst., Bethesda, Md., 1954-59; pres. Rodana Rsch. Corp., Bethesda, 1959; v.p. Catrix Corp., Bethesda, 1958-61; inventor FloLite light sculptures under name Lolo Sarnoff, 1968; one-woman shows include Agra Gallery, Washington, 1969, Corning Glass Ctr. Mus., Corning, N.Y., 1970, Gallery Two, Woodstock, Vt., 1970, Gallery Marc, Washington, 1971, 72, Franz Bader Gallery, Washington, 1976, Gallery K, Washington, 1978, 81, Alwin Gallery, London, 1981, Galerie von Bartha, Basel, Switzerland, 1982, Gallery K, Washington, 1982, 83, 84, 85, 87, 88, 89, 90, 91, La Galerie L'Hotel de Ville, Geneva, Switzerland, 1982, Pfalzgalerie, Kaiserlautern, Fed. Republic of Germany, 1985, Gallery K, Washington, 1987-91, Galerie Les Hirondelles, Geneva, 1988, Rockville (Md.) Civic Ctr., 1988, Washington Square Sculpture Group, 1989, Internat. Sculpture Congress, Washington, 1990; represented in collections: Fed. Nat. Mortgage Assn., Washington, Brookings Inst., Washington, Corning Glass Ctr. Mus., Nat. Air and Space Museum, Washington, Kennedy Ctr., Washington, Nat. Acad. Sci., Chase Manhattan Bank, N.Y.C., Israel Mus., Jerusalem, Nat. Mus. Women in the Arts, Washington, others. Past trustee Nat. Ballet, Mt. Vernon Coll.; founder, pres. Arts for the Aging, Inc., Bethesda, Md., 1988—; active Washington Opera Soc., Washington Ballet Soc.; bd. overseers Corcoran Gallery Art, 1991. Recipient Gold medal Accademia Italia delle Arti e del Lavoro, 1980. Mem. City Tavern Club (Washington), Cosmos Club. Democrat. Co-inventor electrophrenic respirator; inventor flowmeter. Home: 7507 Hampden Ln Bethesda MD 20814-1331

SAROSY, ANNE ZVARA, educational association administrator; b. Campbell, Ohio, July 14, 1923; d. Joseph and Dorothy (Sarvas) Zvara; m. John J. Sarosy, May 10, 1941 (dec. Aug. 1981); children: Sandra Duve, Martha Zetts. BS in Edn. (cum laude), Youngstown State U., 1964; MEd, Westminster Coll., 1969. Tchr. Youngstown (Ohio) Cath. Diocese, 1958-62, Campbell Bd. Edn., 1962-87; pres. Slovak Cath. Sokol, Youngstown, 1977-81; supreme ladies v.p. Slovak Cath. Sokol, Passaic, N.J., 1979-87; nat. v.p. Slovak League Am., Passaic, 1983—; scholarship dir. Slovak League Am., Campbell, 1987—. Dir. Slovak Cath. Sokol Chorus, Youngstown, 1967-76, Slovak Cath. Sokol Youth Chorus, Campbell, 1976—; v.p. Am. Slovak Cultural Assn., Mahoning County, Youngstown, 1936-48; dir. Slovak Cath. Sokol Mus., Passaic, 1983-87. Mem. Mahoning and Ohio Ret. Tchrs. Assn. (life), Youngstown Bus. and Profl. Women's Club, Slovak League Am. (v.p. 1980—), Slovak World Congress (internat. chmn. women's com. 1993—), Slovak Cath. Fedn. Sokol # 26 (pres. 1981—). Republican. Home: 183 Struthers Liberty Rd Campbell OH 44405-1965 Office: Slovak League Am Scholarship Campbell OH 44405

SARRAF, ROBERTA JEAN, planning consultant; b. Pitts., Nov. 9, 1945; d. Walter H. and Margaret E. (Ondof) S. BA, U. Pitts., 1967, M in Urban and Regional Planning, 1969. Intern Rep. James G. Fulton, Washington, 1965; planner Pa. Dept. Community Affairs, Pitts., 1970-76; dir. community devel. Twp. of Upper St. Clair, Pitts., 1976-82; cons. planning Pitts., 1982—; instr. Pa. Dept. Community Affairs, 1976—; del. Environ. Planning to People's Republic of China. Creator and performer (musical program), History of Am. Popular Music. Sec., bd. dirs. Chartiers Mental Health Ctr., Bridgeville, Pa., 1986-90; vol. U. Pitts. Ann. Giving Fund, 1973—; dem. committeewomen, Mt. Lebanon, Pa., 1965-68, 82-88; speaker civic and svc. clubs; mem. long range planning com. and choir Bower Hill Community Ch., elder, 1990-92; mem. devel. com. South Hills Family Hospice. Mem. Am. Planning Assn. (pres. Pitts. chpt. 1982-83), Nat. Assn. Housing and Redevel. Ofcls. (v.p. Pitts. chpt. 1980-81), Pa. Planning Assn. (bd. dirs. 1975-76, state conf. chmn. 1981), Women in Community Devel. (charter), Am. Fedn. Musicians, Grad. Sch. Alumni Assn. (chmn. com. 1987-88), Am. Inst. Cert. Planners, Three Rivers Corvette Club (activities com. 1987), Lions Club (pres. 1990-91, zone chmn. 1991-92, region chmn. 1992-93). Democrat. Presbyterian. Home and Office: 1316 Bower Hill Rd Pittsburgh PA 15243-1308

SARRY, CHRISTINE, ballerina; b. Long Beach, Calif., May 25, 1946; d. John and Beatrice (Thomas) S.; m. Jim Varriale, Sept. 12, 1984; 1 child, Maximilian Sarry Varriale. With Joffrey Ballet, 1963-64; With Am. Ballet Theatre, 1964-68, prin. dancer, 1971-74; leading dancer Am. Ballet Co., 1969-71; ballerina Eliot Feld Ballet, 1974-81; mem. faculty New Ballet Sch., also freelance guest tchr. Performed ballets for Agnes DeMille, Antony Tudor, Jerome Robbins, Eliot Feld; appeared at White House, 1963, 67; U.S. Dept. State tours include, Russia, 1963, 66, S.Am., 1964, 76, various tours of N.Am., Orient, Europe, various appearances U.S. nat. TV; partnered by Mikhail Baryshnikov.

SARTON, MAY, author, poet; b. Wondelgem, Belgium, May 3, 1912; came to U.S., 1916, naturalized, 1924; d. George Alfred Leon and Eleanor Mabel (Elwes) Sarton. Grad., Cambridge High and Latin Sch., Brussels, 1929; Litt.D. (hon.), Russell Sage Coll., Troy, N.Y., 1959, Clark U., 1975, U. N.H., 1976, Bates Coll., 1976, Colby Coll., 1976, Thomas Starr King Sch. Ministry, 1976, U. Maine, 1981, Bowdoin Coll., 1983, Bucknell U., 1985, Providence (R.I.) Coll., 1989, Centenary Coll., 1990. Lectr. poetry U. Chgo., Harvard U., U. Iowa, Colo. Coll., Wellesley Coll., Beloit Coll., U. Kans., Denison U., others; Briggs-Copeland instr. composition Harvard U., 1950-52. Author: The Single Hound, 1938, The Bridge of Years, 1946, Shadow of a Man, 1950, A Shower of Summer Days, 1952, Faithful Are the Wounds, 1955, The Birth of a Grandfather, 1957, The Fur Person (fiction), 1957, The Small Room, 1961, Joanna and Ulysses, 1963, Mrs. Stevens Hears the Mermaids Singing, 1965, Miss Pickthorn and Mr. Hare, 1966, The Poet and the Donkey, 1969, Kinds of Love, 1970, Journal of a Solitude, 1973, As We Are Now, 1973, Punch's Secret, 1974, Crucial Conversations, 1975, A Walk Through the Woods, 1976, A Reckoning, 1978, Anger, 1982, The Magnificent Spinster, 1985, The Education of Harriet Hatfield, 1989; (poems) Encounter in April, 1937, Inner Landscape, 1939, The Lion and The Rose, 1948, The Leaves of the Tree, 1950, The Land of Silence, 1953, In Time Like Air, 1957, Cloud, Stone, Sun, Vine, 1961, A Private Mythology, 1966, As Does New Hampshire, 1967, A Grain of Mustard Seed, 1971, A Durable Fire, 1972, Collected Poems, 1974, Selected Poems of May Sarton, 1978, Halfway to Silence, 1980, A Winter Garland, 1982, Letters from Maine, 1984, The Phoenix Again, 1988, The Silence Now, 1988, Collected Poems, 1993, Coming Into Eighty, 1994; (autobiographies) I Knew a Phoenix, 1959, Plant Dreaming Deep, 1968, A World of Light, 1976, May Sarton: a Self Portrait, 1986, Honey in the Hive, 1988; (jours.) The House by the Sea, 1977, Recovering, 1980, After the Stroke, 1988, Endgame, 1992; (essays) Writings on Writing, 1981; (play) The Underground River: A Play in Three Acts, 1947; (anthology) Sarton Selected: An Anthology of Novels, Journals and Poetry, 1991; editor: Letters to May, 1986. Recipient Golden Rose award for poetry, 1945, Edward Bland Meml. prize Poetry Mag., 1945, Alexandrine medal Coll. St. Catherine, 1975, Deborah Morton award, Westbrook, 1981, Ministry to Women award Unitarian Universalist Women's Fedn., 1982, Avon/COCOA Pioneer Woman award, 1983, Fund for Human Dignity award, 1984, Human Rights award, 1985, Am. Book award, 1985, Maryann Hartman award U. Maine, 1986, N.E. Author award N.E. Booksellers Assn., 1990; Bryn Mawr fellow in poetry, 1953-54, Guggenheim Found. fellow, 1954-55; Nat. Found. Arts and Humanities grantee, 1967. Fellow Am. Acad. Arts and Scis.; mem. N.E. Poetry Soc., Poetry Soc. Am. (Reynolds lyric award 1953).

SARTORY, WENDY DIANE, lawyer; b. Boynton Beach, Fla., Aug. 25, 1964; d. John Lawrence Sartory and Priscilla M. (Moorhouse) Poitras. BS, U. N.C., 1986; JD, Duke U., 1989. Assoc. Sheppard, Mullin, et al., L.A., 1989-92, Shearman & Sterling, L.A., 1992-94, Gunster, Yoakley & Stewart, West Palm Beach, Fla., 1994—. Republican. Roman Catholic.

SARUBBI, JUDITH ALICE CLEARWATER, guidance counselor; b. Englewood, N.J., Oct. 5, 1956; d. Jasper and Mary (Fadden) Clearwater; m. Edward J. Sarubbi, July 7, 1979; children: Brian, Alyssa, Christopher. BA, William Paterson Coll., 1978; MA, Kean Coll. N.J., 1983. Cert. tchr., spl. edn. tchr., reading specialist, guidance and counseling, N.J. Tchr. Bergen County Bd. Spl. Svcs., Paramus, N.J., 1978-82; asst. dir. Day Camp Oratam, Harriman State Park, N.Y., 1980-82; co-dir. Skyland Learning and Guidance Assocs., Ringwood, N.J., 1985--89; guidance counselor Wharton (N.J.) Borough Pub. Schs., 1992—; cons. Embossography, Paramus, 1979-81. Steering com. Alliance of Wanaque (N.J.) and Ringwood for Edn. and Substance Abuse Prevention, 1989-92. Mem. ASCD, ACA, Pi Lambda Theta. Roman Catholic. Office: Alfred C MacKinnon Mid Sch 137 E Central Ave Wharton NJ 07885

SARVER, CATHERINE JO, executive recruiting company executive; b. Enid, Okla., Dec. 7, 1949; d. Mel Henry Harth and Marysue (Anderson) Ward; m. Charles Eugene Sarver, May 22, 1982; children: Catherine E., Steven E., Alexandria K. BA, U. Calif., Santa Barbara, 1973; profl. designation in pers. mgmt., UCLA, 1982. Various positions to asst. pers. adminstr. Joslyn Electronic Systems, Goleta, Calif., 1971-78; various positions to employment mgr. Hughes Aircraft, Goleta, 1978-89; corp. employment mgr. Applied Magnetics Corp., Goleta, 1989-91; prin. ptnr. Sarver & Carruth Assocs., Buellton, Calif., 1991—. Mem. Santa Barbara Women's Polit. Com. Mem. Soc. for Human Resource Mgmt., NAFE, Santa Barbara Human Resources Assn., Nat. Assn. Women Bus. Owners, Nat. Assn. Exec. Recruiters, Santa Barbara C. of C., SBRC Mgmt. Club (bd. control). Republican. Office: 286 E Highway 246 Ste 20 Buellton CA 93427-1967 also: PO Box 1967 Buellton CA 93427-1967

SARWAR, BARBARA DUCE, school system administrator; b. Mpls., Aug. 9, 1938; d. Harold Taylor and Barbara (Thayer) Duce; m. Mohammad Sarwar, Dec. 28, 1972; children: Barbara, Sarah, Franklin. BS, U. Colo., 1972; M Spl. Edn., Ea. N.Mex. U., 1975, Edn. Specialist, 1979. Cert. tchr., adminstr., N.Mex. Tchr. 2d grade, English as 2d lang. Lake Arthur (N.Mex.) Mcpl. Schs., 1972-74; tchr. spl. edn. Artesia (N.Mex.) Pub. Schs., 1974-79, ednl. diagnostician, 1979-88, dir. spl. edn., 1988—. Contbr. to profl. publs. Pres. Altrusa Club Artesia, 1981-82, 86-87, The Arc of Artesia, 1990-92. Mem. NEA, Artesia Edn. Assn. (pres. 1978-79), Internat. Reading Assn. (pres. Pecos Valley chpt. 1975-76, sec. N.Mex. unit 1977-78), Nat. Assn. Sch. Psychologists, N.Mex. Sch. Adminstrs. Assn., Phi Kappa Phi, Phi Delta Kappa. Home: PO Box 1493 Artesia NM 88211-1493 Office: Artesia Pub Schs 1106 W Quay Ave Artesia NM 88210-1857

SASEK, GLORIA BURNS, English language and literature educator; b. Springfield, Mass., Jan. 20, 1926; d. Frederick Charles and Minnie Delia (White) Burns; B.A., Mary Washington Coll. of U. Va., 1947; Ed.M., Springfield Coll., 1955; postgrad. Sorbonne, summer 1953; M.A., Radcliffe Coll., 1954; postgrad. Universita per Stranieri, Perugia, Italy, summer 1955; m. Lawrence Anton Sasek, Sept. 5, 1960. Tchr., head dept. jr. and sr. high sch. English, Somers, Conn., 1947-51, 52-59; tchr. English, Winchester (Mass.) pub. schs., 1959-60; faculty La. State U., Baton Rouge, 1961—, asst. prof. English, 1971—, chmn. freshman English, 1969-70. Recipient George H. Deer Disting. Tchr. award La. State U., 1977, Gumbo Favorite Prof., 1978, Disting. Undergrad. Teaching award Amoco Found., 1994. Mem. MLA, South Central Modern Lang. Assn., South Central Renaissance Soc., AAUP (chpt. v.p. 1981-84). Address: 1458 Kenilworth Pky Baton Rouge LA 70808-5737

SASSEN, GEORGIA, psychologist, educator; b. N.Y.C., July 27, 1949; d. Bernard Nicholas Sassen and Rose Ellen Joseph Benjamin; m. L.S. Laing, Aug. 27, 1983; 1 child, Tai. BA, Wesleyan U., 1971; EdM, Harvard U., 1977; MS, U. Mass., 1981, PhD, 1985. Lic. psychologist, Mass. Program assoc. Am. Friends Svc. Com., Cambridge, Mass., 1971-76; field faculty Goddard-Cambridge Grad. Program, 1974-76; dir. field study Hampshire Coll., Amherst, Mass., 1977-80; asst. prof. U. Mass. Med. Sch., Worcester, 1985-88, asst. clin. prof., 1988-91, assoc. in psychiatry, 1991-94; affiliate asst. prof. psychology Clark U., Worcester, 1989—; pvt. practice Shrewsbury, Mass., 1988—; active staff Med. Ctr. Ctrl. Mass., Shrewsbury, 1993—; summer faculty Smith Coll. Sch. Social Work, Northampton, Mass., 1985-90; cons. Mass. Sch. Profl. Psychology, Dedham, 1991, Syndicate Nat. des Psychologues, Paris, 1985, Mass. Dept. Elder Affairs and Other Mental Health Agys., 1981—; dir. Women's Relational Devel. Group, Boston, 1990-93. Co-author: Corporations and Child Care, 1974, The Abortion Business, 1975; contbr. articles to profl. jours. Vice pres. Women's Rsch. Action Project, Boston/Cambridge, 1975—. U. Mass. fellow in gerontology, 1986-87; Joseph P. Healey Found. grantee, 1986, AARP/Andrus Found. grantee, 1985, Sigma Xi grantee, 1985; NIMH and Harvard U. traineeship. Mem. APA, Assn. for Women in Psychology, Am. Group Psychotherapy Assn. Office: 48 Maple Ave Shrewsbury MA 01545

SASSER, ELLIS A., gifted and talented education educator; b. Norfolk, Va., June 14, 1946; d. Haywood Ellis and Jessie (Johnson) S.; m. R. Wayne Kitsteiner, June 11, 1983. BA, Emory and Henry Coll., 1968; MA, Va. Commonwealth U., 1976; cert. creative problem solving, Ctr. for Creative Learning, Honeoye, N.Y., 1990, cert. advanced creative problem solving, 1990. Primary tchr. Henrico County Pub. Schs., Richmond, Va., 1968-76; tchr. gifted Henrico County Pub. Schs., Richmond, 1976—; tchr. humanities Three Chopt Gifted Ctr. Henrico County Pub. Schs.; gifted adv. bd. Henrico County Programs for the Gifted, Richmond, 1990—. Recipient R.E.B. award for teaching excellence Greater Richmond Community Found., 1989. Mem. AAUW, NEA, Va. Edn. Assn., Henrico Edn. Assn., Coun. for Exceptional Children, Va. Assn. for Gifted Edn., Va. Hist. Soc., Richmond Area Friends of the Gifted, Richmond Symphony Chorus, West of the Blvd. Civic Assn., Delta Kappa Gamma Soc. Internat. (pres. Gamma Chi chpt. 1994—). Home: 3223 Floyd Ave Richmond VA 23221

SASSO, ELEANOR CATHERINE, state senator; b. Fall River, Mass., Dec. 9, 1934; d. Robert Charles and Ellen (O'Hare) Ashworth; m. Louis Anthony Sasso, 1957; children—Ellen Marie, Ann Marie, Robert. B.S., Immaculata Coll., Pa., 1957. Mem. R.I. State Senate, 1979—; researcher Bur. Nat. Affairs, from 1978. Chmn. Cranston Recycling Commn., 1972-73; mem. Cranston Transvan Com., from 1973; mem. Spl. Gov.'s Commn. To Study Entire Election Process, 1977-78. Mem. LWV, Met. Nursing and Health Assn. (bd.), Common Cause, Save the Bay. Democrat. Roman Catholic. Office: 60 Glenmere Dr Cranston RI 02920 also: Senate House State House Providence RI 02903*

SATCHELL, DONNA ROCHELLE, sales executive, consultant; b. Bklyn., Dec. 20, 1951; d. Jay Horton and Jennie (Richardson) Campbell; divorced. AAS in Bus. and Mktg., Westchester C.C., Valhalla, N.Y., 1987; BSBA summa cum laude, Mercy Coll., 1989. Market rsch. intern The Telephone Ctr. Decision Ctr. Corp., New Rochelle, N.Y., summer 1988; adminstrv. asst. Clairol, Inc., N.Y.C., 1984-89, mktg. asst., 1989-91, asst. product mgr., 1991-92; divsnl. sales analyst Clairol, Inc., Atlanta, 1992-94, sales analyst nat. accounts, 1994—; owner Cultural Art Works. Creator (board game) Human Body Game. Recipient scholarships Westchester C.C., 1987, Mercy Coll., 1987. Mem. NAFE, Nat. Black MBAs Inc., Black Newcomers Network Inc. (treas., mem. exec. bd.). Home: 6304 Southland Forest Dr Stone Mountain GA 30087-4941 Office: Clairol Inc 100 Hartsfield Center Pky Atlanta GA 30354-1347

SATIN, KAREN W., university publications director; b. Chgo., Apr. 12, 1938; d. Harry E. and Gertrude (Plotkin) Weiss; m. Lawrence Z. Satin, Sept. 11, 1960 (div. 1980); children: Wendy, Scott, Kimberly. BA in English and Sociology, U. Conn., 1958; MA in Journalism, U. Md., 1984. Prodn. editor Encyclopedia Britannica, Chgo., 1960-64; freelance editor Washington, 1977-81; program editor Nat. Sci. Tchrs. Assn., Washington, 1981-83; sr. tech. writer Computer Scis. Corp., Arlington, Va., 1983-84; publs. mgr. Sci. Applications Rsch., Lanham, Md., 1984-89; dir. publs., adj. faculty comm. studies U. Md. Univ. Coll., College Park, 1989—. Mem. Capitol Assn. for Women in Edn. Office: U Md Univ Coll University Blvd at Adelphi Rd College Park MD 20740

SATTERFIELD-HARRIS, RITA, workers compensation representative; b. Bklyn., Oct. 14, 1949; d. Wilton Anthony and Hattie Eva (Tunstall) Satterfield; m. Sidney Harris, Jan. 5, 1973; 1 child, Marcial A.H. BA in Psychology, Bernard Baruch Coll., N.Y.C., 1983; student, CCNY, 1971-74; Cert. in Paralegal Studies, L.I. U., Bklyn., 1982; cert. unemployment ins. benefits law, Cornell U., 1984. Lic. claimant's workers compensation rep. N.Y.; registered agt. N.Y. State Unemployment Ins. Dir. social svcs. Lincoln Sq. Neighborhood Ctr., N.Y.C., 1979-88; pvt. practice N.Y.C., 1988—; writer proposals funded by N.Y.C. Dept. for Aging Inc., 1980-82, and N.Y.C. Cmty. Devel. Agy., 1984-88. Recipient Cert. of Appreciation for participation in vol. income tax assistance program Dept. Treasury, IRS, 1985, 86, Ptnrs. in Change award Nat. Displaced Homemakers Network, 1991. Mem. Workers' Def. League, Nat. Orgn. Social Security Claimant's Reps. Office: 141 Livingston St Brooklyn NY 11201

SATTLER, NANCY JOAN, math and physical science educator; b. Toledo, July 14, 1950; d. Thomas Joseph and Margaret Mary (Linenkugel) Ainsworth; m. Rudolph Henry Sattler, June 17, 1972; children: Cortlund, Clinton, Corinne. BS, U. Toledo, 1972, MEd, 1988. Office worker/bookkeeper Gilbert Mail Svc., 1967-71; computer typesetter Quality Composition, Toledo, 1971-89; instr. Terra Tech. Coll. (now Terra C.C.), Fremont, Ohio, 1988-89; dept. head Terra Tech. Coll., Fremont, Ohio, 1989-95, curriculum chair bus., assoc. studies, math. and arts, 1995—; adj. instr. Terra Tech. Coll., Fremont, 1982-88, U. Toledo, 1988, Lucas County Bd. Edn. Gifted Program, Toledo, 1988-92; computer coord. St. Joseph Elem. Sch., Fremont, 1987-94, quiz bowl, 1993; externship quality control Atlas Crankshaft, Fostoria, Ohio, 1990; instr. devel. math. A.O. Smith, Bellvue, Ohio, 1991, 93, 94; adult edn. computer instr. St. Joseph Cen. Cath., Fremont, 1990—; instr. developmental math and sci. Whirlpool Corp., Findlay, Ohio, 1992; presenter Am. Math Assn. of Two-Yr. Colls., 1991, 92, 93, 94, Nat. Coun. Tchrs. Math Conf., 1993; co-presenter Continuous Improvements through Faculty Externship, League for Innovation, 1992; co-chmn. Ohio Great Tchrs. Seminar, 1993, 94, 95; chmn. Kids Coll., Fremont, 1993-95; facilitator Mo. Great Tchrs. Seminar, 1993, 94, Ohio Gt. Tchrs. Retreat, 1994, N.Y. Gt. Tchrs. Seminar, 1994; co-chair, presenter Ohiomatyc Winter Inst., 1994; TOM trainer Terra C.C., 1994. Author: The Implication of Math Placement Testing in the Two Year College, 1988, Applied Math for Industrial Technology, 1989; co-author: Math and Science Made Easy, 1992, The Metric System, Preparing for the Future, 1992, Workplace Literacy, 1994. Sec. St. Joseph Ctrl. Cath. Sch. Bd., 1989-94, pres., 1991-94; Sunday sch. dir. St. Joseph Ch., Fremont, 1977-87; pres. Plant 'N Bloom Garden Club, Fremont, 1977-79; clk. Sandusky County Fair, 1977—, St. Joe Ctrl. Cath. Music Boosters, 1991-93; rep. for deanery Early Childhood Devel., 1982-84; parliamentarian Welcome Wagon, 1980; Eucharistic min., 1991—. Mem. Ohio Assn. Garden Clubs, Ohio Math. Assn. of 2-Yr. Colls. (pres. 1992, 93, 94, NSF grant com. mem. 1992), Am. Math. Assn. of 2-Yr. Colls. (assessment com. 1990—, chmn. 1993—, program com. 1993), Nat. Coun. Tchrs. Math., Ohio Coun. Tchrs. Math. Democrat. Roman Catholic. Home: 712 Hayes Ave Fremont OH 43420-2914 Office: Terra C C 2830 Napoleon Rd Fremont OH 43420-9670

SATUR, NANCY MARLENE, dermatologist; b. Philipsburg, Pa., Apr. 12, 1953; d. Nicholas and Mary (Kutzer) S.; m. John David Lortscher, Oct. 20, 1979; children: David Nicholas, Glenn William, Stephen John. BS magna cum laude, Pa. State U., 1974; MD, Thomas Jefferson U., 1976. Diplomate Am. Bd. Dermatology. Intern Allentown (Pa.) Gen. Hosp., 1976-77; resident in pathology U. Ill. Hosp., Chgo., 1978-79; resident in dermatology Case Western Res. U. Hosp., Cleve., 1979-82; dermatologist Dermatology Assocs. of San Diego County, Encinitas, Calif., 1985—; sr. instr. dermatology Case Western Res. U. Hosp., 1982-83, sr. clin. instr. dermatology, 1983-84. Fellow Am. Acad. Dermatology; mem. Am. Soc. Dermatologic Surgery, Am. Soc. Laser Medicine and Surgery, N.Am. Soc. Phlebology, San Diego Dermatologic Soc., Pacific Dermatologic Assn. Office: Dermatology Assocs San Diego County 477 N El Camino Real B303 Encinitas CA 92024

SATURNELLI, ANNETTE MIELE, school system administrator; b. Newburgh, N.Y., Dec. 1, 1937; d. William Vito and Anna (Marso) M.; m. Carlo F. Saturnelli, Oct. 15, 1960; children: Anne, Karen, Carla. BA, Vassar Coll., 1959; MS, SUNY, New Platz, 1978; EdD, NYU, N.Y.C., 1993. Rsch. chemist Lederle Labs/Am. Cyanamid, Pearl River, N.Y., 1959-64; sci. coord. Marlboro (N.Y.) Cen. Sch. Dist., 1974-84; state sci. supr. N.Y. State Dept. Edn., Albany, 1984-86; dir. sci. edn. Newburgh (N.Y.) City Sch. Dist., 1986—; proposal reviewer NSF, Washington, 1984—; state coord. N.Y. State Sci. Olympiad, 1985-86; mem. Gov. Cuomo's Task Force on Improving Sci. Edn., Albany, N.Y., 1989—. Author: Focus on Physical Science, 1981, 87; editor: Transforming Testing in New York State--A Collection of Past, Present and Future Assessment Practices, 1994. Recipient Presidential award-Excellence in Sci. Teaching, Washington, 1983. Mem. ASCD, Nat. Sci. Tchrs. Assn. (exemplary sci. tchrs. award 1982), Sch. Adminstrs. Assn. N.Y. State, N.Y. State Sci. Suprs. (bd. dirs., pres. 1991), Sci. Tchrs. Assn. N.Y. State (outstanding sci. tchrs. award 1983, fellows award 1990, pres. 1993), Phi Delta Kappa. Home: 3 Taft Pl Cornwall On Hudson NY 12520-1713 Office: Newburgh Free Acad 201 Fullerton Ave Newburgh NY 12550-3798

SAUCIER, MARIE E. Z., accountant; b. Adams, Mass., Aug. 6, 1961; d. John Henry and Mary Alice (Brackett) Ziemba; m. William Joseph Saucier, July 9, 1983; children: John A., Stacey R., Amber M. BS in Acctg., Husson Coll., 1983, postgrad., 1992—. Computer asst. Haverlock, Estey & Curran, Bangor, Maine, 1980-81; mgr. Fudge Factory Confectionary Delights, Woburn, Mass., 1981-83; salesperson, asst. mgr. Radio Shack, Bangor, 1983-84; internal auditor, staff acct., mgr. gen. acctg. Webber Oil Co., Bangor, 1985—; mem. Penobscot County Budget Com., 1992-94; panelist State Growth Mgmt. Conf., 1991. Elected mem. Glenburn Town Coun., 1991-94; coord. Glenburn Comprehensive Plan Com., 1989-91; foreman Bangor Creative Playground, 1988. Mem. Bus. and Profl. Women U.S. (v.p. UPtown Bangor 1987-89, chair young careerist 1990-91, del. to nat. conv., young careerist mentor 1992, dir. dist. IV 1991-93), Inst. Mgmt. Accts. (Bangor-Waterville chpt.), Bangor Internal Audit Club. Democrat. Roman Catholic. Office: Webber Oil Co 700 Main St Bangor ME 04401-6800

SAUER, GEORGIA BOORAS, newspaper writer; b. Kalamata, Greece, May 9, 1946; came to U.S., 1946; d. Peter P. and Angela (Dimopoulos) Booras; m. Mark Sauer, Jan. 4, 1969; children: Peter, Alexander. BS, U. Ill., 1968. Obituary and feature writer Champaign (Ill.)-Urbana Courier, 1966-68; reporter Times-Democrat, Davenport, Iowa, 1968; reporter, travel writer, copy editor Chgo. Tribune, 1969-70, fashion and feature writer, asst. Lifestyle editor, 1971-75; reporter Home Furnishings Daily, Fairchild Publs., N.Y.C., 1970-71; fashion reporter, Sunday women's editor N.Y. Daily News, N.Y.C., 1975-76; fashion editor St. Louis mag., 1981-86; became feature writer St. Louis Post-Dispatch, 1986-91; fashion editor Pitts. Post Gazette, 1993—. Pres. bd. dirs. Ladue Chapel Nursery Sch.; bd. dirs. Martha's Shelter, St. Louis, 1985-91, DG Found. for Visually Impaired Children, St. Louis, 1985-91, St. Louis Pub. Libr., 1987-91, Payback, St. Louis, 1987-91; mem. Jr. League St. Louis and Pitts.; bd. dirs. Three Rivers South, Pitts., Ozanam Cultural Ctr., mem. bd. parents coun. Shadyside acad., mem. devel. com. Greek Orthodox. Office: Pittsburgh Post-Gazette 34 Blvd of the Allies Pittsburgh PA 15222*

SAUERBREY, ELLEN ELAINE RICHMOND, radio talk show host; b. Balt., Sept. 9, 1937; d. Edgar Arthur and Ethel Frederika (Landgraf) Richmond; m. Wilmer John Emil Sauerbrey, June 27, 1959. AB summa cum laude in Biology and English, Western Md. Coll., 1959. Biology instr., chmn. sci. dept. Baltimore County Sch. System, 1959-64; dist. mgr. Baltimore County U.S. Census, 1970; Md. Ho. of Dels., Annapolis, 1978-95, minority leader, 1986-95; radio talk show host Sta. WBAL; Rep. candidate for Gov., 1994. Del. Rep. Nat. Convs., 1968, 76, 84, 88, 92, mem. credentials com., 1984, platform com., chmn. subcom. on economy, 1977; vice chmn. Rep. State Ctrl. Com. of Balt. County, 1966-71; trustee Md. Coun. Econ. Edn., Franklin Sq. Hosp.; nat. chmn. Am. Legis. Exec. Coun., 1990-91; Rep. candidate Gov. Md., 1994. Named Legislator of Yr., Md. Assn. Bldrs. and Contrs., 1982, Am. Legis. Exec. Coun., 1986, Western Md. Coll. Alumni of Yr., 1988, Outstanding Legis. Leader, Am. Legis. Exec. Coun., 1992; recipient Pvt. Property award Greater Balt. Bd. Realtors, 1984. Mem. DAR, Md. Fedn. Rep. Women, Am. Legis. Exch. Coun. Found. (chmn. emeritus, legislator of yr. 1986), Nat. Taxpayers Union, Md. Farm Bur., Women Legislators of Md., Md. Conservation Union, Beta Beta Beta. Presbyterian.

SAUKERSON, ELEANOR, state legislator; m. Wilbur Saukerson; 6 children. Register of deeds Brule County, S.D.; mem. S.D. Senate. Home: 406 S Courtland St Chamberlain SD 57325-1510 Office: SD Senate House State Capitol Pierre SD 57501*

SAUL, ANN, public relations executive; b. Columbia, Miss.; d. Otto and Ruth (Stamps) Saul. BS in Edn., Miss. Coll., 1961; postgrad., U. Louisville. Staff writer, circulation mgr. Louisville Mag. and Louisville Area C. of C., 1971-77; employee communications staff Brown & Williamson Tobacco Corp., 1977-79; media rels. staff NKC Hosps., 1979-80; pub. rels. and sales promotion staff Am. Temp. Svcs., 1980-82; sr. account supr. Daniel J. Edelman Pub. Rels., Chgo., 1982-87; dr. communication svcs. Nat. Easter Seal Soc., Chgo., 1987-89; v.p. Sam Huff & Assocs., Pub. Rels., Chgo., 1989-91; founder Ann Saul Pub. Rels,, 1991—. Mem. Pub. Rels. Soc. Am., Publicity Club of Chgo. (Silver Trumpet 1985, bd. dir.), Midwest Healthcare Mktg. Assn.

SAUL, BARBARA ANN, securities representative; b. Vincennes, Ind., Feb. 20, 1940; d. Charles Dudley and Essie Faye (York) Green; children: Beth Suzanne, Becca Lynn, Brian William. BA with honors, So. Ill. U., Carbondale, 1961; MS, So. Ill. U., Edwardsville, 1988. Cert. secondary English tchr., spl. reading K-12 tchr., Mo.; cert. lang. arts specialist, K-12, English 6-12, Ill.; registered securities rep. English tchr. James Island High Sch., Charleston, S.C., 1961-63, Waterloo (Ill.) High Sch., 1963-65; instr. rhetoric and composition Belleville Area Coll., 1966-67; homebound tchr. Belleville Twp. High Sch., 1966-73; Title I reading tchr. Freeburg (Ill.) Community High Sch., 1973-80; grad. asst. So. Ill. U., Edwardsville, 1986-87; reading specialist Hazelwood Schs., St. Louis, 1987-92; instr. Lion's Quest, 1988-91; team mem. Write-On project Highland (Ill.) Community Schs., 1980-83; clinician Edwardsville Adult Literacy Prescription Project, 1986-88; presenter Mo/IRA State Conv., 1991; coordinating tchr. Intergenerational Oral History Gateway Writing Project, 1991-92. Bd. dirs. presch. 1st Presbyn. Ch., Belleville, 1969-73; mem. coun., conf. del. Evang. United Ch. of Christ, Highland, 1979-85, mem. choir, 1985-87; mem. Jr. High Reading Curriculum Revision Com. Mem. Phi Kappa Phi, Kappa Delta Pi, Sigma Kappa. Home and Office: 1209 N Morgan Olney IL 62450

SAULNIER, KAREN LOIS, education researcher; b. Berwyn, Ill., Sept. 28, 1940; d. Edward Stanley and Martha Veronica (Kwiatkowski) Luczak; m. Francis Edward Saulnier, Apr. 8, 1972; children: Aimee Danielle, Jeremy Edward. BA, Merrimack Coll., 1962; MEd, Boston U., 1963. Cert. tchr. for the deaf. Tchr. elem. level Clarke Sch. Deaf, Northampton, Mass., 1963-65; instr. grad. program Gallaudet U., Washington, 1965-68, asst. prof., 1968-75, supervising tchr. preschool level, 1969-70, rsch. assoc. psychology dept., 1975-84, rsch. assoc. ctr. studies edn. and human devel., 1984—; cons. Blue Ridge Hearing and Speech Ctr., Leesburg, Va., 1965-68, Ctr. Effective Learning, Virginia Beach, Va., 1972-74, Sch. Contemporary Edn., McLean, Va., 1973-74, Phila. Pub. Sch. System, 1983-86. Co-developer: (teaching aids) The Signed English Series, 1972—. Mem. Am. Ednl. Rsch. Assn., Conv. Am. Instrs. Deaf, Alexander Graham Bell Soc. Office: Gallaudet U 800 Florida Ave NE Washington DC 20002

SAULSBURY, HELEN BURNS, tax preparer; b. Kingsburg, Calif., Aug. 24, 1945; d. Cecil Morris and Thelma Louise (Poole) Burns; m. John Albert Saulsbury, Mar. 21, 1964 (div. Sept. 1991); children: Yvonne La Fleur, Elaine Mello, Jennifer Ferrario. BBA, Fresno State U., 1982. Owner Saulsbury's Tax Svc., Exeter, Calif.; tax preparer svc. rep. IRS, Visolia, Calif., Bakersfield, Calif.; property mgr. LIST, Exeter; owner Financially Smart Sems., Exeter, 1990-93; fin. coord. Saulsbury's Tap Svc., Exeter, 1990-93; speaker in field. Author of short stories. Active Exeter Garden Club, 1990; trustee Lemoncove (Calif.) Sch. Bd., 1979-87. SPCA award. Democrat. Home and office: 22536 Carson Exeter CA 93221

SAUM, ELIZABETH PAPE, community volunteer; b. Evanston, Ill., Aug. 7, 1930; d. Karl James and Catherine (Schwall) Pape; m. William Joseph Saum, Dec. 31, 1960; children: JeanMarie, Katherine Anne, Mary Elizabeth. BA in English cum laude, Fontbonne Coll., 1952; MA in English, Northwestern U., 1958. Cert. tchr., Ill. Tchr. Our Lady of Perpetual Help, Glenview, Ill., 1952-55, Wilmette (Ill.) Jr. High Sch., 1955-61; dir. religion edn. St. Paul's Ch., Valparaiso, Ind., 1972-76; activities dir. Heritage Manor Nursing Home, Plano, Tex., 1982-84; exec. dir. Jessamine County Assn. Exceptional Citizens, Nicholasville, Ky., 1985-89; ret., 1989. Pres. bd. dirs. Women's Neighborly Orgn., Lexington, 1977-81; mem. Bluegrass Long-Term Care Ombudsman, Lexington, 1984-89, pres., 1986-88; bd. dirs. Women's History Coalition Ky., Midway, 1985-90; bd. dirs. Sr. Citizens East, Louisville, 1991-93, treas., 1992-93; creator, pres. Ky. Women's Heritage Mus., Lexington, 1986-90; adminstrn. coord. Transfiguration Ch., Goshen, Ky., 1991-93. Mem. AAUW (bd. dirs. Ky. br. 1977-81, 85—, named gift 1988, v.p. Ednl. Found. 1988-94, co-pres. 1994—, named gift honoree Lexington br. 1987, pres. 1984-86, 88-90, Louisville br. editor newsletter 1990-93, treas. 1991-93, chmn. ednl. found. 1991-93), Lexington Newcomers (editor newsletter 1976-78). Democrat. Roman Catholic. Home: PO Box 1510 Cadiz KY 42211-1510

SAUNDERS, ARLENE, opera singer; b. Cleve., Oct. 5, 1935. MusB, Baldwin-Wallace Coll., 1957. Tchr. voice Rutgers U., New Brunswick, N.J., 1987-88; tchr. classical vocal repertoire Abraham Goodman Sch., N.Y.C., 1987-88; advisor, tchr. vocal dept. NYU, 1990—, tchr. master classes, head opera dept., 1993; tchr. master classes Baldwin Wallace Coll., Santa Fe Opera Co., etc.; founder, dir. Opera Mobilé, Inc., N.Y.C., 1991—; adjudicator Met. Opera Regional Auditions, Liederkranz Voice Auditions, etc. Debut Milan Opera, 1961; Met. Opera debut in Die Meistersinger, 1976; specializes in Strauss and Wagner; performer with Phila. Opera, Lyric Opera, Houston Opera, Covent Garden, London, Teatro Colon, Buenos Aires, San Francisco Opera, Vienna Staatsoper, Paris Opera, Australian Opera, Sydney, Berlin Deutsche Opera, Munich Staatsoper, Hamburg State Opera, 1963-86, Rome Opera, Brussels Opera, Maggio Musicale, Florence, Italy, Geneva (Switzerland) Opera, Berlin Festival, Lisbon Opera, Glyndebourne Festival Opera, Eng., English Opera North, Boston Opera, N.Y.C. Opera; performed world premieres of Beatrix Cenci, 1971, Jakobowsky und der Oberst, 1965, Help, Help, The Globolinks, 1968, Ein Stern Geht Auf Aus Jaakob, 1970 (Gold medal Vercelli (Italy) voice competition); appeared in opera films including Arabella (title role), Meistersaenger (Eva), Marriage of Figaro (Countess), Help, Help the Globolinks (Mme. Euterpova), Der Freischuetz (Agathe), Gasparone (Carlotta); recs. for Philips and Victor. N.Y.C. Mayor's award, 1962; Kammersängerin Hamburg, 1967. Mem. Pi Kappa Lambda (Epsilon Phi chpt.). Address: 535 E 86th St New York NY 10028-7533

SAUNDERS, DORIS EVANS, editor, educator, business executive; b. Chgo., Aug. 8, 1921; d. Alvesta Stewart and Thelma (Rice) Evans; m. Vincent E. Saunders Jr., Oct. 28, 1950 (div. 1963); children: Ann Camille, Vincent E. III. B.A., Roosevelt U., 1951; M.S., M.A., Boston U., 1977; postgrad., Vanderbilt U., 1984. Sr. library asst. Chgo. Pub. Library, 1942-46, prin. reference librarian, 1946-49; librarian Johnson Pub. Co., 1949-66, dir. book div., 1961-66, 73-77; prof., coord. print journalism Jackson (Miss.) State U., 1977—, acting chair dept. mass communication, 1990—, chair, 1991—; Disting. minority lectr. U. Miss., Oxford, 1986; pres. Ancestor Hunting, Inc., Chgo., 1982—; dir. community rels. Chgo. State Coll., 1968-70; acting dir. instnl. devel. and community rels Chgo. State Coll., 1969-70; columnist Chgo. Daily Defender, 1966-70, Chgo. Courier, 1970-73; staff assoc. Office of Chancellor, U. Ill. at Chgo. Circle, 1970-73. Host: radio program The Think Tank, 1971-72; writer, producer: (TV) Our People, 1968-70; producer, host: Faculty Review Forum, Sta. WJSU, 1987—; author: Black Society, 1976; assoc. editor: Negro Digest mag, 1962-66; editor: The Day They Marched, 1963, The Kennedy Years and the Negro, 1964, DuBois: A Pictorial Biography, 1979, Wouldn't Take Nothin' for My Journey (L. Berry), 1981; compiler, editor: The Negro Handbook, 1966, The Ebony Handbook, 1974; pub. Kith and Kin; contbr. to profl. jours., mags. Bd. dirs. Arts Alliance, Jackson-Hinds County, Miss., 1993; mem. com. on ministry and commn. on racism Diocese of Miss. Mem. NAACP, Nat. Assn. Black Journalists, Assn. for Edn. in Journalsim and Mass Comms., Black Coll. Comms. Assn. (v.p., pres. elect). Democrat. Episcopalian. Office: Jackson State U Dept Mass Communication PO Box 18067 Jackson MS 39217 also: PO Box 2413 Chicago IL 60690

SAUNDERS, IRIS ELAINE, social work administrator; b. N.Y.C.; d. Sidney Denison and Viola (Francis) Simon. BA, CUNY, 1946, MSW with honors, 1993. Cert. social worker N.Y. Case mgr. Dept. Social Svcs., N.Y.C., 1949-51, supr., 1952-60; case supr. Div. Employment and Rehab., N.Y.C., 1960-70; dir. Human Resources Adminstrn., N.Y.C., 1970-92; ret., 1993; notary public N.Y. Bd. dirs. Tioga Carver Found., N.Y.C., 1989—, mem. dem. club; active M.L. Wilson Boys and Girls Club, N.Y.C., 1986, The Schomberg Ctr. for Rsch. in Black Culture, 1993. Recipient cert. of achievement Am. Soc. Profl. and Exec. Women, 1987, Vol. Leadership award United Negro Coll. Fund, 1987, Vol. Recognition cert., 1988, 89, 90, Outstanding Fund Raising award M.L. Wilson Boys and Girls Club Harlem, 1991, Recognition for Cmty. Svc., N.Y. Newsday, 1992, cert. of merit Tioga Carver Cmty. Found., 1993, Recognition award CUNY Alumni Assn., 1994. Mem. NASW, NAACP, AAUW, Assn. Black Social Workers, Hunter Coll. Alumni Assn., Nat. Caucus and Ctr. on Black Aged, Coalition 100 Black Women, Smithsonian Instn., Studio Mus. in Harlem. Democrat. Baptist.

SAUNDERS, KATHRYN A., retired data processing administrator; b. Elgin, Minn., Apr. 12, 1920; d. William P. and Mathilda M. (Mielke) Hagner; m. James L. Saunders, June 14, 1952; children: Gary, Wade, Brian. BA, U. Calif., Berkeley, 1941; cert., Coll. of Marin, Kentfield, Calif., 1948. Mem. gen. staff Fed. Res. Bank, San Francisco; with civilian pers./payroll dept. USAF, Hamilton AFB, Calif.; coord. data processing Sir Francis Drake High Sch., San Anselmo, Calif. Sec. program resource Untied Meth. Women, 1988—, treas., 1994—; active First United Meth. Ch. Mem. AAUW, Calif. Sch. Employees Assn., Calif. Scholarship Fedn. (life), Nat. Assn. Ret. Fed. Employees, Coll. of Environ. Design Alumni Assn. of U. Calif. Berkeley, Order of Golden Rose of Delta Zeta. Address: 118 Tamal Vista Dr San Rafael CA 94901

SAUNDERS, PATRICIA GENE, book editor; b. Tulsa, Okla., Nov. 29, 1946; d. Eugene Merritt and Patricia May (Hough) Knight; m. Joseph Eugene Saunders, June 24, 1989. BA, Baylor U., 1969. Nat. advt. sec. KTVT-TV, Ft. Worth, 1969-71; tchr. Arlington (Tex.) Ind. Sch. Dist., 1971-77, Garland (Tex.) Ind. Sch. Dist., 1977-79; spl. projects assoc. Electronic Data Systems, Dallas, 1979-81; adminstrv. asst. Diversifield Innovators, Dallas, 1981-82; system ops. mgr. Span Instruments, Plano, Tex., 1982-86; data processing mgr. Claire Mfg., Addison, Ill., 1986-87, Everpure, Inc., Westmont, Ill., 1987-88; software cons. Software Alternatives, Inc., Downers Grove, Ill., 1988-89; data processing asst., cons. J&J Maintenance, Inc., Austin, Tex., 1989-90; pres., computer cons. Cardinal Software Solutions, Inc., Austin, 1990-93; assoc. editor Holt, Rinehart & Winston, Inc., Austin, 1993—. Contbr. articles to Tex. Hwy. Patrol Assn. Mag., Hill Country Sun, South Austin News, Police Vet. Mem. Smithsonian Instn., N.Y. Met. Mus. Fine Art, Austin Writers' League, Baylor Alumni Assn. Republican. Baptist. Home: 410 Teal Ln Kyle TX 78640-8888 Office: Holt Rinehart & Winston 1120 Capital Of Tex Hwy S Austin TX 78746

SAUNDERS, PHYLLIS S., business and financial broker, consultant; b. N.Y.C., May 2, 1942; d. Jack and Bella (Bader) Bloom; widowed; children: Todd B., Dean B. Founder, pres. P.S. Export Co., Inc., consulting service, bus. cons., fin. cons., money mgmt. for Cen. and S.Am., Bahamas, Caribbean, and third world countries, 1971—; pres. Burnett Enterprises Ltd. Mem. Am. Bus. Women's Assn., Nat. Assn. Women Bus. Owners, Am. Liver Found., Am. Jewish Com., Nat. Home Asthmatic Children, Hope Ctr. Mentally Retarded Children, U. Miami Booster Club, U. Miami Ctr. for Liver Diseases, U. Miami AIDS Research Ctr., Fla., Miami Childrens Hosp., Jewish Home for the Aged, Ctr. Fine Arts, Concert Assn. Fla., Fla. Grand Opera, Miami Ballet, Greater Miami Opera Guild, Fla. Philharm., Lowe Art Gallery, New World Symphony, Miami Chamber Symphony, PBS, Muscular Dystrophy, Multiple Sclerosis, Cerebal Palsy, Am. Cancer Soc., Am. Heart Assn. Republican. Avocations: golf, tennis, aerobics, fishing, boating. Home: 2 Grove Isle Dr Apt 205 Coconut Grove FL 33133-4102

SAUNDERS, SUSAN PRESLEY, real estate executive; b. South Bend, Ind., Feb. 27, 1956; d. William Presley Jr. and Anne Summers (Winburn) S. Student, Converse Coll., 1974-77, Sandhills Community Coll., Southern Pines, N.C., 1978-86. Lic. real estate broker, N.C.; ins. lic., N.C.; notary pub.; accredited Relo coord. With Gouger, O'Neal & Saunders, Southern Pines, 1973-74, 75, Ceralon Mfg., Aberdeen, N.C., 1976; bank teller The Carolina Bank, Aberdeen, 1977-78; from clk. to v.p. fin. G.O.S., Inc., Southern Pines, 1978—. Mem. NAFE, Am. Soc. Profl. and Exec. Women, Am. Inst. Profl. Bookkeepers, Sandhills Area C. of C. (membership com. So. Pines chpt. 1989-94), Moore County Leadership Inst. Democrat. Presbyterian. Home: 130 Pebble Bch Southern Pines NC 28387-2345 Office: GOS Inc 177 W Pennsylvania Ave Southern Pines NC 28387-5428

SAUNDERS, TERRY ROSE, lawyer; b. Phila., July 13, 1942; d. Morton M. and Esther (Hauptman) Rose; m. George Lawton Saunders Jr., Sept. 21, 1975. BA, Barnard Coll., 1964; JD, NYU, 1973. Bar: D.C. 1973, Ill. 1976, U.S. Dist. Ct. (no. dist.) Ill. 1976, U.S. Ct. Appeals (7th cir.) 1976, U.S. Supreme Ct. 1983. Assoc. Williams & Connolly, Washington, 1973-75; assoc. Jenner & Block, Chgo., 1975-80, ptnr., 1981-86; ptnr. Susman, Saunders & Buehler, Chgo., 1987-94; pvt. practice Law Offices of Terry Rose Saunders, Chgo., 1995—. Author: (with others) Securities Fraud: Litigating Under Rule 10b-5, 1989. Mem. ABA (co-chair class actions and derivative suits com. sect. litigation), Ill. State Bar Assn., Chgo. Bar Assn., NYU Alumni Assn. (bd. dirs. 1985—). Office: 30 N LaSalle St Chicago IL 60602

SAUNTRY, SUSAN SCHAEFER, lawyer; b. Bangor, Maine, May 7, 1943; d. William Joseph and Emily Joan (Guenter) Schaefer; m. John Philip Sauntry, Jr., Aug. 18, 1968; 1 child, Mary Katherine. BS in Foreign Service, Georgetown U., 1965, JD, 1975. Bar: D.C. 1975, U.S. Dist. Ct. D.C. 1975, U.S. Ct. Appeals (D.C. cir.) 1975, (4th cir.) 1977, (6th cir.) 1978, (10th cir.) 1983, U.S. Supreme Ct. 1983. Congl. relations asst. OEO, Washington, 1966-68; program analyst EEO Com., Washington, 1968-70, U.S. Dept. Army, Okinawa, 1970-72; assoc. Morgan, Lewis & Bockius, Washington, 1975-83, ptnr., 1983-94; pvt. practice, 1994. Co-author: Employee Dismissal Law: Forms and Procedures, 1986; contbr. articles to profl. jours. Mem. ABA, D.C. Bar Assn., D.C. Women's Bar Assn., Am. Assn. Univ. Women, USA, Phi Beta Kappa, Pi Sigma Alpha. Democrat. Office: 1747 Pennsylvania Ave NW Ste 1050 Washington DC 20006

SAUSE, KAREN DIANE, executive; b. Framingham, Mass., Aug. 28, 1935; d. Ernest A. and Helen L. (Connolly) Thorsell; m. Don Cornelius, Jan. 1967 (div. 1971); 1 child, Adam Jacob; m. George L. Sause (dec. Feb. 1992); 1 child, Ian Matthew. BS, Skidmore Coll., 1957. Tchr, N.Y.C. Schs., 1970-71; owner VR Bus. Brokers, Wilmington, N.C., 1982-92, Check X-Change, Wilmington, N.C., 1992—. Actress, singer on Broadway and television. V.p. Wilmington C. of C., 1989-92; legis. chair LWV, Cohasset, Mass., 1972-78; choir St. James Ch., Wilmington, 1979-93. Recipient Spl. Bus. award Small Bus. Coalition, Wilmington, 1992. Mem. U.S. Tennis, Assn., Cape Fear Garden Club, Cape Fear Country Club. Democrat. Epsicopalian. Office: Check X-Change 4402 Market St Wilmington NC 28403

SAUSMAN, KAREN, zoological park administrator; b. Chgo., Nov. 26, 1945; d. William and Annabell (Lofaso) S. BS, Loyola U., 1966; student, Redlands U., 1968. Keeper Lincoln Park Zoo, Chgo., 1964-66; tchr. Palm Springs (Calif.) Unified Sch., 1968-70; ranger Nat. Park Svc., Joshua Tree, Calif., 1968-70; zoo dir. The Living Desert, Palm Desert, Calif., 1970—; natural history study tour leader internat., 1974—; part-time instr. Coll. Desert Natural History Calif. Desert, 1975-78; field reviewer conservation grants Inst. Mus. Svcs., 1987—, MAP cons., 1987—, panelist, 1992—; internat. studbook keeper for Sand Cats, 1988—, for Cuvier's Gazelle, Mhorr Gazelle, 1990—; co-chair Arabian Oryx species survival plan propogation group, 1986—; spkr. in field. Author Survival Captive Bighorn Sheep, 1982, Small Facilities- Opportunities and Obligations, 1983; wildlife illustrator books, mags, 1970—; editor Fox Paws newsletter Living Desert, 1970—, ann. reports, 1976—; natural sci. editor Desert Mag., 1979-82; compiler Conservation and Management Plan for Antelope, 1992; contbr. articles to profl. jours. Past bd. dirs., sec. Desert Protective Coun.; adv. coun. Desert Bighorn Rsch. Inst., 1981-85; bd. dirs. Palm Springs Desert Resorts Convention and Visitors Bur., 1988-94; bd. dirs., treas. Coachella Valley Mountain Trust, 1989-92. Named Woman Making a Difference Soroptomist Internat., 1989, 93. Fellow Am. Assn. Zool. Parks and Aquariums (bd. dirs., accredation field reviewer, desert antelope taxon adv. group, caprid taxon adv. group, felid taxon adv. group, small population mgmt. adv. group, wildlife conservation and mgmt. com., chmn. ethics com. 1987, mem. com., internat. rels. com., ethics task force, pres'. award 1972-77, outstanding svc. award 1983, 88, editor newsletter, Zool. Parks and Aquarium Fundamentals 1982); mem. Internat. Species Inventory System (mgmt. com., policy adv. group 1980-88), Calif. Assn. Mus., Calif. Assn. Zoos and Aquariums, Internat. Union Dirs. Zool. Gardens, Western Interpretive Assn. (so. Calif. chpt.), Am. Assn. Mus., Arboreta and Botanical Gardens So. Calif. (coun. dirs.), Soc. Conservation Biology, Nat. Audubon. Soc., Jersey Wildlife Preservation Trust Internat., Nature Conservancy, East African Wildlife Soc., African Wildlife Found., Kennel Club Palm Springs (past bd. dirs., treas. 1978-80), Scottish Deerhound Club Am. (editor SCottish Deerhounds in N.A., 1983, life mem. U.K. chpt.). Office: The Living Desert 47 900 Portola Ave Palm Desert CA 92260

SAUTTER-SUTHERLAND, CATHERINE, video/film production manager; b. Fullerton, Calif., Oct. 20, 1963; d. Herbert and Dorothy Joan (Morrissey) Sautter; m. George Ronald Sutherland Jr., Sept. 17, 1988. AA, Saddleback C.C., 1984; BA, Calif. State U., Northridge, 1986. Asst. mgr. Edwards Cinemas, Mission Viejo, Calif., 1980-83; med. asst. Dr. Wayne Landry, Tustin, Calif., 1983-86; adminstrv. asst. Barrage Inc., L.A., 1985-86; office mgr. Dr. Liz Ashley, Newport Beach, Calif., 1986-88; various prodn.

positions, 1986-92; owner, operator Cat Sautter Prodn. Svcs., Carlsbad, Calif., 1992-94, prodn. mgmt. and prodn. coord. svcs., 1994—. Prodr.: (music video) Let's Bop, 1983; co-prodr.: (ednl. program) Hispanic Gangs, 1993. Mem. San Diego Prodn. Assn. (co-dir. directory com. 1991). Office: PO Box 360 Carlsbad CA 92018

SAVACOOL, MILDRED L., association executive; b. Pottstown, Pa., July 9, 1916; d. Jacob S. and Anna Ruth (Long) S. AB, Wilson Coll., 1936; AM, Columbia U., 1940, MSW, 1950. Program dir. YWCA Pitts., 1940-49, exec. dir., 1960-69; exec. dir. YWCA Worcester, Mass., 1950-55, YWCA Nat. Capital Area, Washington, 1969-81; exec. cmty. divsn. YWCA of U.S.A., N.Y.C., 1955-60. Democrat. Lutheran. Home: 2601 Woodley Pl NW Apt 304 Washington DC 20008-1533

SAVAGE, ELLEN L., surgeon; b. Appleton, Wis., Aug. 11, 1956. BA, St. Olaf Coll., 1978; MD, Med. Coll. Wis., 1983. Diplomate Am. Bd. Gen. Surgery. Resident William Beaumont Meml. Hosp., Royal Oak, Mich., 1983-88; gen. surgeon USAF, Ellsworth AFB, S.D., Incurlek AFB, Turkey.

SAVAGE, GRETCHEN SUSAN, information management consulant; b. Seattle, Jan. 15, 1934; d. Lester W. and Gretchen M. (Percy) Wood; m. Terry R. Savage, Sept. 26, 1964; children: Terry, Christopher, Richard. BA, UCLA, 1955. Life librarianship credential, Calif. Head libr. Douglas Missiles & Space Co., Santa Monica, Calif., 1957-63; dept. mgr. sci. and tech. info. NASA, Washington, 1963-65; cons. on info. systems, Washington and, Calif., 1965-77; sch. libr. Goleta (Calif.) Union Schs., 1970-73; project mgr. Documentation Assocs., L.A., 1974-77; pres. Savage Info. Svcs., Torrance, Calif., 1977—; presenter to profl. orgns. Contbr. numerous articles to profl. jours. Pres. Chorusliners, Palos Verdes Peninsula, 1988-90; mem. bus. coun. Arts Assn., Palos Verdes Peninsula, 1989—; bd. dirs. New Place Theatre Co., Palos Verdes Peninsula, 1989-91, South Bay Infant Ctr., Redondo Beach, Calif., 1988-91. Recipient Community Achievement award Panhellenic, Palos Verdes, 1985, 90. Mem. Spl. Librs. Assn. (chmn. cons. sect. 1983-84, info. tech. div. 1985-86, mem. profl. devel. com. 1988-91), Am. Soc. for Info. Sci. (professionalism com. 1989-91), Assn. Records Mgrs. and Adminstrn., So. Calif. Online Users Group, Soroptimists (bd. dirs.), Alpha Phi. Home: 30000 Cachan Pl Palos Verdes Peninsula CA 90274-5412 Office: 2510 W 237th St Ste 200 Torrance CA 90505-5234

SAVAGE, KAY WEBB, lawyer, health center administrator, accountant; b. Piedmont, Ala., Mar. 30, 1942; d. Robert Benjamin and Ellon Marie (Posey) Webb; m. Perry Lauren Savage, Nov. 18, 1961; children: Perry Lauren Jr., Shannon Hunter. BS in Secondary Edn., Jacksonville State Coll., Ala., 1963, AB, 1964; BS, Birmingham-So. Coll., 1987; JD, U. Ala., 1989. Bar: Ala. 1989; CPA, Ala.; cert. secondary tchr., Ala. Tchr. English, Hokes Bluff High Sch., Gadsden, Ala., 1963-64; tchr. sci. and math. McArthur Sch., Birmingham, Ala., 1964-68; tchr. sci. Mountain Brook Jr. High Sch., Birmingham, 1968-69; acct. Robert Resha, CPA, Birmingham, 1984-86; pvt. practice acctg. Birmingham, 1986—, pvt. practice law, 1989—; adminstr. Ala. Orthopaedic and Spine Ctr., Birmingham, 1987—; pres. Aleco, Inc., Birmingham, 1990—, Savage Enterprises, Birmingham, 1985—; bd. dirs. Assoc. Agys. Am., Coastal Bend Oil & Gas Co., Piedmont Ednl. Trust. Pres., sec. Snowcrest Condominium Assn., Snowshoe, W.Va., 1984-88; mem. exec. bd. Rep. Congl. Leadership Coun., Washington, 1988—; mem. Senatorial Trust, Washington, 1989, Presdl. Roundtable, Washington, 1989—, Piedmont Schs. Found., Birmingham Olympic Com., 1990—, Birmingham So. Coll. Arts Coun., 1992—; v.p. United Cerebral Palsy; sponsor U.S. Olympic Team; bd. dis. Piedmont Schs. Found., mem. scholarship com.; del. 1st Moscow Conf. on Law and Econ. Coop.; mem. exec. com. Com. for Fair Cts., 1994—; legis. chmn. Jefferson County Med. Alliance, 1994—. Fulbright fellow, 1964; recipient (5) Am. Jurisprudence awards. Mem. AAUW, Ala. Bar Assn., Ala. Soc. CPAs, Birmingham Bar Assn., Med. Group Mgmt. Assn., Bones Orthopedic Mng. Group, Attys. at Law and CPA U.S.A., Am. Soc. Law and Medicine, Pilot Lawyers Assn., Assn. Agys. Am. (bd. advisors), Coastal Ben Oil and Gas (bd. dirs.), Exec. Women Internat., C. of C. (bd. dirs. 1994—), Ninety Nines, Rotary Club Internat. (dir.), Sigma Delta Kappa (svc. award 1989), Sigma Kappa Delta, Sigma Tau Delta, Pi Gamma Mu. Home: 3815 River View Cir Birmingham AL 35243-4801 Office: 52 Med Park East Dr Ste 115 Birmingham AL 35243

SAVAGE, M. SUSAN, mayor. Student, U. Aix-Marseilles, Aix-en-Provence, France, 1969, City of London Poly., Eng., 1972; BA in Sociology with honors, Beaver Coll., 1974. Pre-trial rep. Phila. Ct. Common Pleas, 1974-75; criminal justice planner Montgomery County Criminal Justice Unit, 1975-77; exec. dir. Met. Tulsa Citizens Crime Com., 1977-87; vol. coord. Vote Yes For Tulsa, 1987; chief of staff to mayor City of Tulsa, 1988-92, mayor, 1992—. Active Lee Elementary Sch. PTA; bd. dirs., treas. Okla. Crime Prevention Assn.; bd. dirs. Youth Svcs. of Tulsa County, 1984-88, pres., 1986-87; co-chair Safe Streets/Enhanced 911 Steering Com., 1987; mem. C. of C. Task Force/Community Edn. Network, 1983. Office: Office of Mayor City Hall Rm 1115 200 Civic Ctr Tulsa OK 74103-3827*

SAVAGE, MARGOT GREEN, clinical psychologist; b. Washington, Feb. 15, 1960; d. Gary S. and Shia Toby (Riner) Green; m. Walter T. Savage, June 7, 1987; 1 child, Max Griffin. BA in Psychology cum laude/high honors, Smith Coll., 1981; MA, Temple U., 1983, PhD, 1988. Lic. psychologist, Calif. Staff clinician Temple U. Psychol. Svcs. Ctr., Phila., 1982-86; group leader Temple U. Stress Mgmt. Ctr., Phila., 1984-86; rsch. assoc. Temple Psychology Dept., Phila., 1982-85; psychology intern Phila. Psychiat. Ctr., 1986-87; counselor Pacific Presbyn. Med. Ctr., San Francisco, 1987-88; staff psychologist Palo Alto (Calif.) VA Med. ctr., 1988-91, asst. chief drug and alcohol rehab. unit, 1991-93; pvt. practice, 1993—; presenter in field; teaching asst. Temple U., 1982, instr., 1985; lectr. Thomas Jefferson U., Phila., 1984. Named to Dean's list Smith Coll., 1978-81; First Group scholar Smith Coll., 1979-80; recipient NIMH Clin. Svc. Tng. grant Temple U., 1981-82, Grad. Fellowship Merit award Temple U., 1984, HIV/AIDS Edn. Demonstration Project VA Nat. Edn. Plan award, 1989, VA HSR & D Field Program Rsch. grant, 1991. Mem. APA, Soc. Behavioral Medicine, Phi Beta Kappa, Sigma Xi, Psi Chi. Office: East County Mental Health 3720 Sunset Ln Ste D Antioch CA 94509-6124

SAVAGE, MARSHA KAY, education educator; b. Linden, Tex., Mar. 22, 1947; d. William Travis and Jewel Marie (Craver) Bowden; m. Tom Verner Savage, May 28, 1988; stepchildren: Greg, Steve. BS, Sam Houston State U., 1968; MEd, Tex. A&M U., 1985, PhD, 1989. Cert. tchr. secondary schs., Tex. Tchr. English A&M Consolidated High Sch., College Station, Tex., 1968-85; lectr. Tex. A&M U., College Station, 1985-88; chmn. dept edn. Calif. Bapt. Coll., Riverside, 1989-91, chmn. div. profl. svcs., 1991—. Contbr. articles to profl. jours. Mem. ASCD, Nat. Coun. Tchrs. of English, Am. Ednl. Rsch. Assn., Internat. Reading Assn., Phi Delta Kappa, Phi Kappa Phi, Kappa Delta Pi. Office: Calif Bapt Coll 8432 Magnolia Ave Riverside CA 92504

SAVAGE, OPAL EUDY, risk management company executive, nurse; b. Oakboro, N.C., Aug. 5, 1937; d. Mary Arzelia (Whitley) Eudy; m. Jack Savage, July 12, 1959; children: David Jack, Ronald Ashley. Diploma, Presbyn. Hosp. Sch. Nursing, 1958; BSN, U. N.C., Charlotte, 1977. Lic. life, health and accident ins. agt.; cert. gen. ins.; assoc. designation in risk mgmt.; RN, N.C. Staff nurse Stanly Meml. Hosp., Albemarle, N.C., 1958-59; staff nurse supervision Union Meml. Hosp., Monroe, N.C., 1959-64, pharmacy coord., 1968-74; physician nurse Dr. E. F. Hamel, Monroe, 1964-68; critical care nurse, staffing coord. Mercy Hosp., Charlotte, 1974-79; instr. Ctrl. Piedmont C.C., Charlotte, 1975-79; adminstr. Holy Angels Nursery, Belmont, N.C., 1979; cons. St. Paul Fire and Marine Ins., Charlotte, 1979-92; pres. Risk Mgmt. Contracting Inc., Charlotte, 1993—; speaker in field, 1984-92. Mem. Am. Nurses Assn., N.C. Assn. Hosp. Risk Mgmt., Monroe Jr. Women's Club (sec. 1966), Nat. Assn. Hosp. Risk Mgmt. Office: Risk Mgmt Contracting 8910 St Pierre Ln Charlotte NC 28277

SAVAGE, RUTHANN, human factors specialist; b. McKeesport, Pa., Sept. 3, 1956; d. John Donald and Roberta Marie (Palus) S. BA in Psychology, Calif. State U., Northridge, 1987, MA in Exptl. Psychology/Human Factors. Missionary, actor Covenant Players Repertory Theater Co., Woodland Hills, Calif., 1980-85; clerical supr. Comml. Union Ins. Co., Encino, Calif., 1985-89; human factors specialist USAF, Edwards AFB, Calif., 1989-92, lead for life support/chem. def. test team, 1992—. Author tech. reports. Served with U.S. Army, 1976-80, Germany. Mem. Human Factors and Ergonomics Soc. Home: 45800 Challenger Way # 79 Lancaster CA 93535

SAVAGE, SANDRA HOPE SKEEN, mathematics educator, curriculum writer; b. Charleston, W.Va., Apr. 4, 1938; d. Raymond and Freda (Burgess) Skeen; m. Steven William Savage, Aug. 17, 1963; 1 child, Samantha. BS in Secondary Edn. Math and English, Bob Jones U., 1960; MS in Math., Ill. Inst. Tech., 1966; EdD in Math. Edn., Columbia U., 1976. Cert. tchr., Calif., N.Y., Ill., Fla., W.Va., Minn. Math. tchr. S. Charleston Jr. High Sch., 1960-61, Citrus Grove Jr. High Sch., Miami, Fla., 1961-62, Skiles Jr. High Sch., Evanston, Ill., 1962-65, Evanston Twp. High Sch., 1965-67, White Plains (N.Y.) High Sch., 1967-68; chmn. math. dept. The Scarborough Sch., Scarborough-on-Hudson, N.Y., 1968-71; math. tchr. Alexander Ramsey High Sch., Roseville, Minn., 1971-72, Minnehaha Acad., Mnpls., 1971-72; lectr. math. Pace U., Westchester County, N.Y., 1972-73; team leader, math. tchr. Fox Lane Mid. Sch., Bedford, N.Y., 1973-74; prof. math. Orange Coast Coll., Costa Mesa, Calif., 1977—; lectr. math. edn. North Park Coll., Chgo., 1965; judge Odyssey of the Mind Competition, 1995; math. media cons. Annenberg Found., Washington, 1991; cons Business Link, Costa Mesa, 1990—. Speaker Expanding Your Horizons Women's Conf., Irvine, Calif., 1984-87; guild mem. Orange County Performing Arts Ctr., Costa Mesa, 1985-87; asst. troop leader Girl Scouts Am., Laguna Niguel, Calif., 1985-87; active Geneva Presbyn. Ch., Laguna Hills, Calif., 1983—. Recipient Cert. Merit, Nat. Merit Scholarship Corp., 1956, Tchr. of Yr. award Orange County Tchrs., 1994, Nat. Inst. for Staff and Orgn. Devel. awrd U. Tex., 1993, U.S.A. Today Teaching Excellence award, 1993; Dept. Edn. Nat. Workplace Literacy Program grantee, 1995. Fellow NSF (grantee 1983); mem. AAUW, Am. Math. Assn. Two Yr. Colls., Math. Assn. Am., Assn. for Women in Sci., Calif. Math. Coun., Orange County Math. Assn. (sec. 1982-83), Phi Delta Kappa (pres. Trabuco chpt. 1986-87). Democrat. Home: 12 Novilla Laguna Beach CA 92677-8915 Office: Orange Coast Coll PO Box 5005 2701 Fairview Rd Costa Mesa CA 92626-5561

SAVAGE-SUPERNAW, PHYLLIS JEAN, marketing consultant; b. Dayton, Ohio, Nov. 13, 1946; d. William Kenneth and Jannie Ione (Weatherly) Savage; m. Muhammad Hakeem, June 27, 1978 (div.); children: Majeeda, Naimah, Nasser, Ameerah; m. William Michael Supernaw, Mar. 16, 1990. BS in Child Devel., Home Econs., Psyc., U. Houston, 1970; degree in early childhood edn., Calif. State U., Hayward, 1976; degree in early childhood/spl. edn., Columbia U., 1980. Cert. tchr., Calif., N.Y. Dir. devel., grantwriter Self Advancement through Edn. (SATE), Oakland, Calif., 1966-77; cons. real estate Suzzanne Pathy Speak Up Inst., other orgns., N.Y.C., 1978-88; comedienne, actress Sadie Hogwaller Show, N.Y.C., 1981-92, L.A., 1992—; dir. family ctr. Odyssey House of N.Y., Wards Island, 1988-90; pres. Savage-Supernaw Cons., various locations, 1990—; educator, advocate, spokesperson Houston PBS, Channel 8-TV, Houston, L.A. and San Diego; advocate, cons. Mayor's Com. for Persons with Disabilities, N.Y.C., 1980-92; tech. advisor Women Alcohol & Drugs, Drug Addicted Infants, Early Intervention, 1979-91; advocate, pub. speaker Harriet Cornell for Senate, Rockland County, N.Y., 1990. Spokesperson, activist Civil Rights, Student Non-Violent Coord. Com., Houston, 1960-69; fundraiser pub. rels. Bosnian Relief, Redwood City, Calif., 1993; spokesperson N.Y. State Gov.'s Task Force on Drug Abuse, 1989-90. SNAPP Neighborhood grantee N.Y.C. Neighborhood Watch, 1979, fed. edn. grantee Columbia U., 1980. Mem. SAG (advocate performers with disability com. 1983-92), Kappa Delta Phi (hon.). Democrat. Muslim. Office: Savage Supernaw Cons Ste 237 3100 Riverside Dr Los Angeles CA 90027

SAVEDGE, ANNE CREERY, artist, photographer; b. Richmond, Va., Jan. 29, 1947; d. Leslie Roy Jr. and Dorothy (Rakes) C.; m. Edwin Clement Savedge Jr., Aug. 11, 1967; 1 child, Ross Alan. BS, James Madison U., 1969; M in Art Edn., Va. Commonwealth U., 1977. Art instr. Colonial Heights (Va.) High Sch., 1969-78; instr. Va. Mus. Robinson House, Richmond, 1983-86; vis. artist Office of Youth and Community Svcs., Dinwiddie, Va., 1986-87; artist-in-residence Richmond Children's Mus., 1987-88; instr. Shenandoah Photographic Workshops, 1988; adj. faculty U. Richmond, 1978—; artist-in-residence Va. Mus. of Fine Arts, Richmond, 1984-86, Richmond Children's Mus., 1987—; curator Bedford Gallery Photoshow Longwood Coll., Farmville, Va., 1985, Light Images Gallery Photoshow James Madison U., Harrisonburg, Va., 1985, 1708 East Main Gallery Photoshow, Richmond, 1987, 90; artist Fay Gold Gallery, Atlanta, 1985-87, Nat. Copier Art Show; artist-in-edn. gifted program, Dinwiddie, Va., 1988; instr. Chesterfield Tech. Ctr., 1989—. Solo shows include Marsh Gallery, U. Richmond, 1986, Pleiades Gallery, N.Y.C., 1989, Martin Gallery, Washington, 1989, 1708 Gallery, 1994, Baton Rouge, 1991; exhibited in group shows Pleiades Gallery, N.Y.C., 1989, Martin Gallery, Washington, 1989, Midwest Invitational, 1993-94, Mars Gallery, Ariz., 1994; represented in permanent collections Polaroid Internat. Collection, Fed. Res. Bank. Adv. coun. Richmond Arts Coun.; evaluation com. Partners-in-Arts; master educator for U.S. Skill Olympics Edn. Team. Mem. Richmond Artists Assn. (pres. 1978-80, cert. distinction 1980), Soc. for Photographic Edn., Va. Soc. for Photographic Arts (steering com. 1976—, fundraising chmn. 1978—, mem. chmn. 1980-86). Methodist. Home and Office: 5318 Verlinda Dr Richmond VA 23237-3307

SAVITRIPRIYA, SWAMI, religious leader, author; b. Apr. 1, 1930; divorced; three children. Ordained Hindu nun, Holy Order of Sannyas, 1975. Psychotherapist, 1970-75; founder, spiritual dir. Shiva-Shakti Kashmir Shaivite Hindu Ch., Ashram, Marin County, Calif., 1975-77, Shiva-Shakti Ashram, Oakland, Calif., 1978, Convent of the Divine Mother, Kona, Hawaii, 1979-80, Holy Mountain Monastery and Retreat Ctr., Groveland, Calif., 1984-92, Holy Mountain U., Groveland, Calif., 1985-92; founder, spiritual dir. Inst. for New Life, Groveland, Calif., 1990-92, Santa Cruz, Calif., 1992-95; founder, spiritual dir. Shiva-Shukti Ashram, Lake Chapala, Jalisco, Mex., 1995—. Author (books) Kundalini-Shakti: From Awakening to Enlightenment, 1980, The Psychology of Mystical Awakening: The Yoga Sutras, 1991, The Cloud of the Universe, 1986, The Worlds of the Chakras, 1987, Arising Woman, 1988, Arising Man, 1988, Tantras of Personal and Spiritual Unfoldment, 1989, New World Hinduism, 1990, others; translator: Bhagavad Gita, 1974, Narada Bhakti Sutras, 1976, Upanishads, 1981, Shiva Sutras, 1984, Pratyabhijnahridayam, 1987, Vijnana Bhairava, 1989, others. Home and Office: Shiva-Shakti Inst for New Life PO Box 2067 Santa Cruz CA 95063-2067

SAVITZ, MAXINE LAZARUS, aerospace company executive; b. Balt., Feb. 13, 1937; d. Samuel and Harriette (Miller) Lazarus; m. Sumner Alan Savitz, Jan. 1, 1961; children: Adam Jonathan, Alison Carrie. BA in Chemistry magna cum laude, Bryn Mawr Coll., 1958; PhD in Organic Chemistry, MIT, 1961. Instr. chemistry Hunter Coll., N.Y.C., 1962-63; sr. electrochemist Mobility Equipment Rsch. and Devel. Ctr., Ft. Belvoir, Va., 1963-68; prof. chemistry Federal City Coll., Washington, 1968-72; program mgr. NSF, Washington, 1972-74; dir. FEA Office Bldgs. Policy Rshc. U.S. Dept. Energy, Washington, 1974-75, dir. div. indsl. conservation, 1975-76, from dir. div. bldgs. and community systems to dep asst sec., 1975-83; pres. Lighting Rsch. Inst., 1983-85; asst. to v.p. engring. Ceramic Components div. The Garrett Corp., 1985-87; gen mgr. Ceramic Components div. AlliedSignal Aerospace Co., Torrance, Calif., 1987—; lectr. in field; bd. dirs. Am. Coun. for Energy Efficient Economy, 1984—, Internat. Inst. Energy Conservation, 1984—, Energy Found., 1991—; cons. State Mich. Dept. Commerce, 1983, N.C. Alternative Energy Corp., 1983, Garrett Corp., 1983, Energy Engring. Bd., Nat. Rsch. Bd., 1986-93, Office Tech. Assessment, U.S. Congress Energy Demand Panel, 1987-91, nat. materials adv. bd. NRC, 1989-94; bd. dirs. U.S. Advanced Ceramic Assn., 1989—, chmn., 1992; mem. adv. com. div. ceramics/materials ORNL, 1989-92, mem. adv. com. dir., 1992—; mem. adv. bd. Sec. of Energy, 1992—; mem. Def. Sci. Bd., 1993—; mem. visiting com. adv. tech. Nat. Inst. Stds. & Tech., 1993—. Editor Energy and Bldgs.; contbr. articles to profl. jours. Policy com. mem. NAE, 1994—. NSF postdoctoral fellow, 1961, 62, NIH predoctoral fellow, 1960, 61. Mem. Nat. Acad. Engring. Office: AlliedSignal Ceramic Components Divsn 2525 W 190th St Torrance CA 90504-6002

SAVOCCHIO, JOYCE A., mayor; b. Erie, Pa.; d. Daniel and Esther S. BA in History, Mercyhurst Coll., 1965; MEd, U. Pitts., 1969; cert. secondary sch. adminstrn., Edinboro U., 1975; DHL (hon.), Gannon U., 1990. Tchr. social studies Erie Sch. Dist., 1965-85, asst. prin. Strong Vincent High Sch., 1985-89, tchr. coord. high sch. task force, 1971-75; pres. Erie Edn. Assn., 1975-76; mem. coun. City of Erie, 1981-90, pres. coun., 1983, mayor, 1990—; bd. dirs., co-chair legis. com. Pa. League of Cities and Municipalities; mem. subcoms. on transp. and communications U.S. Conf. of Mayors; bd. dirs. State Job Tng. Partnership Bd.; mem., sec. Electoral Coll. for Commonwealth of Pa.; mem. various coms. Erie Sch. Dist. Past pres. Erie Hist. Mus.; past mem. editorial bd. Erie Hist. Soc.; mem. Pa. Gov.'s Flagship Commn., Community Task Force on Drug and Alcohol Abuse; bd. dirs. Pa. League Cities and Mcpls., co-chair legis. com.; mem. subcoms. Transp. and Communications U.S. Conf. Mayors; mem., sec. Electoral Coll. Commonwealth Pa.; bd. dirs. State Job Tng. Partnership Bd. Named Woman of Yr., Dem. Women Erie, 1981, Italian Am. Women's Assn., 1987; recipient Disting. Alumna award Mercyhurst Coll., 1990, Community Svc. award Roosevelt Mid. Sch., 1990, Disting. Citizen award French Creek coun. Boy Scouts Am., 1991. Mem. Delta Kappa Gamma. Roman Catholic. Office: Office of Mayor Mcpl Bldg 626 State St Erie PA 16501-1128

SAVOY, SUZANNE MARIE, critical care nurse; b. N.Y.C., Oct. 18, 1946; d. William Joseph and Mary Patricia (Moclair) S. BS, Columbia U., 1970; M in Nursing, UCLA, 1978. RN. Staff nurse MICU, transplant Jackson Meml. Hosp., Miami, Fla., 1970-72; staff nurse MICU Boston U. Hosp. (Mass.), 1972-74; staff nurse MICU VA Hosp., Long Beach, Calif., 1974-75; staff nurse MIRU Cedars-Sinai Med. Ctr., L.A., 1975-77; critical care clin. nursing specialist Anaheim (Calif.) Meml. Hosp., 1978-81; practitioner, instr. Rush-Presbyn.-St. Luke's Med. Ctr. Coll. Nursing, Chgo., 1982-88; rsch. assoc. dept. neurosurgery, Rush U., 1984-88; clin. rsch. assoc. Medtronic, Inc. Drug Adminstrn. Systems, Mpls., 1988-91; staff nurse critical care Harper Hosp., Detroit, 1992-93; clinical nurse specialist, surgical/trauma critical care, Detroit Recieving Hosp., 1993—; lectr. Wayne State U. Coll. of Nursing, Detroit, 1991—; program coord. Critical Care MSN, Wayne State U., 1993—; neurosci. clinician acute stroke unit Harper Hosp., Detroit, 1989; edn. cons. Critical Care Svcs., Inc., Orange, Calif., 1979-81. Co-author articles for profl. jours. Mem. Am. Assn. Neurosci. Nurses (treas. Ill. chpt. 1983-85, pres. 1986-87), Am. Assn. Critical Care Nurses (bd. dirs. Long Beach chpt. 1981-82), No. Am. Nursing Diagnosis Assn., Gamma Phi (bd. dirs.), Sigma Theta Tau. Roman Catholic. Office: Wayne State Univ Coll of Nursing 5557 Cass Ave Detroit MI 48202-3615

SAWDEY, SHERRY N., real estate broker; b. Boulder, Colo., July 21; d. William L. and Evelyn Fae Sheets; m. Robert I. Sawdey, Aug. 31, 1962; children: Richard, LeeRoy. Grad., Realtors Inst. Utah, 1991. Cert. residential specialist. Broker assoc. Wardley Better Home & Gardens Corp., Heber City, Utah, 1990—. Mem. Utah Assn. Realtors (conv. com.), Wasatch County Bd. Realtors (v.p. 1985, pres. 1986, sec.-treas. 1987-89, chmn. membership 1988-91). Home: 126 W 500 N Heber City UT 84032 Office: Wardley Better Homes & Gdns 76 E Center St Heber City UT 84032-1941

SAWYER, (L.) DIANE, television journalist; b. Glasgow, Ky., Dec. 22, 1945; d. E.P. and Jean W. (Dunagan) S.; m. Mike Nichols, Apr. 29, 1988. BA, Wellesley Coll., 1967. Reporter Sta. WLKY-TV, Louisville, 1967-70; adminstr. press office White House, 1970-74; rschr. Richard Nixon's memoirs, 1974-78; gen. assignment reporter, then Dept. State corr. CBS News, 1978-81; co-anchor Morning News CBS, from 1981, co-anchor Early Morning News, 1982-84; corr., co-editor 60 Minutes CBS-TV, 1984-89; co-anchor Prime Time Live ABC News, 1989—; co-anchor Day One, 1995—; co-anchor Day One ABC News. Recipient Peabody award for Pub. Svc., 1988, Robert F. Kennedy award, 8 Emmy awards, Spl. Dupont award. Mem. Coun. Fgn. Rels. Office: PrimeTime Live 147 Columbus Ave 3rd Fl New York NY 10023-5900*

SAWYER, HELEN ALTON, artist; b. Washington; d. Wells Moses and Kathleen Alton (Bailey) S.; m. Jerry Farnsworth, Aug. 26, 1925. Student, Master's Sch., Dobbs Ferry, 1914-18; studied art with Johansen and Hawthorne. Painter, artist in oil and water color, lithographer; exhibited at principal galleries and museums of U.S.; represented permanent collections numerous museums,including Whitney Mus. Am. Art, Pa. Acad., Toledo Mus., Syracuse U. Mus., John Herron Mus., Indpls., Atlanta Mus., Amherst Coll. Mus., Williams Coll. Mus. Art, Chrysler Mus., U. Fla. Mus. Collection, others; IBM collection, Libr. of Congress, C. & O. R.R. collections, Norfolk Mus., Samuel P. Harm Mus. of Art, Gainesville, Fla., Holyoke Pub. Mus.; contbr. articles and verse to jours. Recipient numerous awards, honors. Mem. N.A.D., Nat. Arts Club, Provincetown, Yonkers, Sarasota art assns., Audubon Artists, Nat. Assn. Women Artists. Home: 3482 Flamingo Ave Sarasota FL 34242-1004 also: Corbina Galleries 1472 Main St Sarasota FL 34236*

SAWYERS, CLAIRE ELYCE, arboretum administrator; b. Maryville, Mo., May 30, 1957; d. Scott Kirkir and Betty Jane (Alexander) S. BS with distinction, Purdue U., 1978, MAg., 1981; MS, U. Del., 1984. Adminstrv. asst. Mt. Cuba Ctr. Study of Piedmont Flora, Queenville, Del., 1983-90; dir. Scott Arboretum of Swarthmore (Pa.) Coll., Greenville, 1990—. Office: Scott Arboretum 500 College Ave Swarthmore PA 19081-1306

SAWYERS, ELIZABETH JOAN, librarian, administrator; b. San Diego, Dec. 2, 1936; d. William Henry and Elizabeth Georgiana (Price) S. A.A., Glendale Jr. Coll., 1957; B.A. in Bacteriology, UCLA, 1959, M.L.S., 1961. Asst. head acquisition sect. Nat. Library Medicine, Bethesda, Md., 1962-63, head acquisition sect., 1963-66, spl. asst. to chief tech. services div., 1966-69, spl. asst. to assoc. dir. for library ops., 1969-73; asst. dir. libraries for tech. services SUNY-Stony Brook, 1973-75; dir. Health Scis. Library Ohio State U., Columbus, 1975-90, spl. asst. to dir. Univ. librs., 1990—. Mem. Assn. Acad. Health Scis. Library Dirs. (sec./treas. 1981-83, pres. 1983-84), Med. Library Assn., Am. Soc. for Info. Sci., Spl. Libraries Assn., ALA. Office: Ohio State Univ Librs 1858 Neil Ave Columbus OH 43210-1225

SAX, MARY RANDOLPH, speech pathologist; b. Pontiac, Mich., July 13, 1925; d. Bernard Angus and Ada Lucile (Thurman) TePoorten; m. William Martin Sax, Feb. 7, 1948. BA magna cum laude, Mich. State U., 1947; MA, U. Mich., 1949; Cert. clin. competence in speech and language pathology. Supr. speech correction dept. Waterford Twp. Schs., Pontiac, 1949-69; lectr. Marygrove Coll., Detroit, 1971-72; pvt. practice speech and lang. rehab., Wayne, Oakland Counties, Mich., 1973—; adj. speech pathologist Southfield, Mich.; lectr. on stroke Mich. Speakers Bur., Am. Heart Assn., 1990—; pub. speaking coach, 1989—; adj. faculty SS. Cyril and Methodius Sem., Orchard Lake, Mich., 1989-90, St. Mary's Preparatory Sch., Orchard Lake, Mich., 1990—; founder, mem. Stroke Project Task Force for Detroit, 1993—; com. mem. Charrette, study Architecture and Design for physical restructuring Franklin, Mich., 1993. Mem. sci. coun. stroke Am. Heart Assn. Grantee Inst. Articulation and Learning, 1969, others, project choices and funding Meadow Lake Community Coun., Birmingham, Mich., 1989—; christian svc. commn. St. Owen, Birmingham co-chmn. blood drive Red Cross, Franklin, Mich., 1991—. Mem. Am. Speech-Lang.-Hearing Assn. (clin. competence cert.), Mich. Speech-Lang.-Hearing Assn. (com. community and hosp. svcs.), Am. Heart Assn. of Mich. (mem. stroke awareness seminar, planning and operation ednl.), Stroke Com. of Am., Internat. Assn. Logopedics and Phoniatrics (Switzerland), Pvt. Practitioners in Speech-Lang. Pathology (founder, profl. liaison with Mich. Speech-Lang.-Hearing Assn. 1991—), Franklin Found. (mem. natural resources adv. coun. 1991—, bd. dirs. 1994—), Founders Soc. of Detroit Inst. Arts, Mich. Humane Soc., Theta Alpha Phi, Phi Kappa Phi, Kappa Delta Pi, Gamma Phi Beta. Contbr. articles to profl. jours. including Language and Language Behavior Abstracts, Language Speech & Hearing Services, Speech Language Hearing Jour. Achievements include research in language and speech acquisition in children in reference to the development of and prediction of biological speech change; research interests in adult acquisition of language and speech relative to central and autonomic nervous systems. Home and Office: 31320 Woodside Dr Franklin MI 48025-2027

SAXE, LINDA, psychiatric nurse, psychiatric social worker; b. San Antonio; d. Manuel and Beulah M. (Pope) Flores; m. Henry Irving Saxe, Feb. 22, 1961; 1 child, Susan. BSN, Tex. Women's U., 1988; MA in Social Work, U. Chgo., 1968. Cert. clin. nurse specialist, Va.; lic. prof. counselor, Tex.; adv. clin. practitioner, Tex.; lic. ind. clin. social worker, D.C. Forensic social worker Cook County Cts./Social Svcs., Chgo., 1969-74; clin. social worker Killgore Children's Psychiat. Hosp., Amarillo, Tex., 1975-77; cons. social worker Tex. Bd. Day Nurseries, Amarillo, Tex., 1975-77; program dir.

Adolescent Ctr.-Houston Internat. Hosp., Houston, 1980-83, West Br. Ctr., Houston, 1984-86; psychiat. review specialist Am. Psychiat. Assn., Washington, 1987-90; intensive care mgmt. specialist Value Behavioral Health, Falls Church, Va., 1990—; clin. nurse specialist Multiple Personality Disorders Program, Psychiat. Inst. D.C., Washington, 1990—, Inpsych, Inc., 1994—. Mem. Sigma Theta Tau. Republican. Home: 1006 Salisbury Ct Sterling VA 20164-4807

SAXE, THELMA RICHARDS, educator; b. Ogdensburg, N.J., Apr. 21, 1941; d. George Francis and Evelyn May (Howell) Richards; m. Kenneth Elwood Meeker, Jr., June 22, 1957 (div. 1965); children: Sylvia Lorraine Meeker Hill, Michelle Louise Meeker Aromando, David Sean (dec.); m. Frederick Ely Saxe, Feb. 18, 1983; stepchildren: Jonathan Kent, Holly Harding Schenker. BA, William Paterson Coll., Wayne, N.J., 1972, MEd, 1975, postgrad., 1983-84; Dyslexia cert., Fairleigh Dickinson U., 1994. Cert. paralegal, dyslexia specialist Fairleigh Dickonson U. Tchr. handicapped Sussex (N.J.)-Wantage Regional Sch. Dist., 1972-75; resource rm. tchr. Sussex County Vo-Tech Sch., Sparta, N.J., 1975-77; learning cons. Sussex County Vo-Tech Sch., 1977-83; learning specialist Bennington-Rutland Supervisory Union, Manchester, Vt., 1986-87; learning cons. Stillwater (N.J.) Twp. Sch., 1987-88, Independence Twp. Cen. Sch., Great Meadows, N.J., 1989; learning cons., tutor in pvt. practice specializing dyslexia Sparta, 1986—; asst. prin. Harmony Twp. Sch., Harmony, N.J., 1989-92; coordinator gifted/talented Sussex Vo-Tech, 1980-83; coordinator child study team Stillwater Twp. Sch., 1987-88. Mem. Coun. for Exceptional Children, Learning Disabilities Assn., Orton Dyslexia Soc., N.J. Assn. Learning Cos., LD Network, Kappa Delta Pi. Republican. Presbyterian. Home and Office: 17 Park Rd Sparta NJ 07871-2002

SAXL, JANE WILHELM, state legislator; b. N.Y.C., Aug. 26, 1939; d. Seymour F. and Doris (Fuld) Wilhelm; m. Joseph Saxl, Nov. 17, 1957; children: Susan S., Ruth L., Mary-Anne, Michael V. BA, Sangamon State U., 1973, MA, 1974. City councilor City of Bangor, Maine, 1987-93; mem. Maine Ho. Reps., Augusta, 1992—. sec./treas. Penobscot Valley Coun. Govts., 1988-91. Mem. Bangor Sch. Bd., 1984-87; bd. dirs. Bangor Beautiful, Bangor Conv. and Visitors Bur.; past chmn. Bangor Recycling; mem. Family Planning Maine, Natural Resources Coun., Penobscot River and Bay Inst., Jewish Cmty. Coun.; mem. Penobscot Dem. Com. Mem. LWV (pres. Maine chpt. 1987-93), Nat. League State Legislators, Nat. Women's Polit. Caucus, Maine Women's Lobby, Friends of Bangor Pub. Libr., Spruce Run Assocs., Maine Audubon Soc., Tuesday Forum, Women's Legis. Lobby, Intown Arts Ctr., N.Y. Pub. Libr. Democrat. Jewish. Home: 37 Pond St Bangor ME 04401 Office: Maine Legislature State House Sta # 3 Augusta ME 04330*

SAXTON, CAROLYN VIRGINIA, fund raising executive; b. Charleston, W.Va., June 24, 1948; d. Robert Everett and Jo Ann (Rader) S.; children: Jon Hamilton Rickey Jr., Leigh Ann Rickey; m. Harlow William Gregory Jr., May 27, 1989. BA, W.Va. Wesleyan Coll., 1971; postgrad., Loma Linda U., 1989-91. Cert. Fund Raising Exec. Counselor Open Door, Annapolis, Md., 1971-73; social worker Salvation Army, Charleston, 1977-79; patient educator Womens Health Ctr., Charleston, 1979-83; community edn. specialist Shawnee Hills Mental Health, Charleston, 1983; exec. dir. W.Va. Nat. Abortion Rights Action League, Charleston, 1983-86; lobbyist Charleston, 1986; exec. dir. Community Hospice, Ashland, Ky., 1986-89; dir. home hospice Home Hospice VNA North, Evanston, Ill., 1989-90; exec. dir. Community Chest Oak Park/River Forest, Ill., 1990—, Oak Park/River Forest Cmty. Found., 1993—. Active Ky. Cancer Program Network, Ashland, 1986-89, Ky. Religious Coalition for Abortion Rights, Frankfort, 1987-88; mem. Citizens Coun. Oak Park/River Forest H.S., 1991-93; mem. W.Va. Task Force on Adolescent Residential Treatment Ctr./Drug Abuse, 1983; mem. Nat. Abortions Rights Task Force on Minor's Access, 1986-87; mem. com. on minor's access W.Va. Dept. Health, 1986-87; mem. Jr. League Charleston, 1982-86; chmn. usher com. Paramount Womens Assn., Ashland, 1988-89; mem. choir 1st Presbyn. Ch., Ashland, 1986-89, Sunday sch. tchr., 1988-89; choir mem. Fair Oaks Presbyn. Ch., 1990-92, bd. deacons; mem. task force linkage cmty. svcs. for high risk adolescents, 1995. Mem. NAFE, Nat. Soc. Fundraising Execs. (programming com. 1991-93, internat. conf. com. 1994-95, scholarship com. 1994-95, bd. dirs. 1995—), Nat. Hospice Orgn. (award of excellence 1988), Ky. Assn. Hospice (bd. dirs., mem.-at-large 1989, chmn. nominating com. 1988-89), Coun. for Non-Profits (vol. action com. 1988-89, co-chmn. cmty. support com. 1989), Zonta (status of women com., program com.), Women in Mgmt. (treas. 1993—), Rotary (program co-chair, bd. dirs. 1993-95, co-chair spl. events 1994-95). Democrat. Home: 851 Fair Oaks Ave Oak Park IL 60302-1546 Office: Community Chest Oak Park/River Forest 1042 Pleasant St Oak Park IL 60302-3002

SAXTON, CATHERINE PATRICIA, public relations executive; b. Sheffield, Eng., July 5, 1944; d. Clifford and Kate Ann (Ruane) S. B.A. cum laude, Fordham U., 1978. Account supr. The Rowland Co., N.Y.C., 1980; Mgr. corporate communications Westinghouse Broadcasting & Cable Co., N.Y.C., 1981-82; prin., pres. Saxton & Assocs., N.Y.C., 1983—; chief exec. officer Potter/Saxton Assocs., Inc., 1985—; prof. pub. speaking Katharine Gibbs Coll., N.Y.C., 1977—. Mem. exec. com. Mayor's Commn. for a Vietnam Vet's Meml., 1982—; bd. dirs. Vets. Ensemble Theatre Co. Mem. Internat. Radio and TV Soc. Roman Catholic. Home: 325 E 90th St New York NY 10128-5260

SAXTON, ELIZABETH GWYN, educator, researcher; b. Indpls., Apr. 21, 1947; d. Richard Eugene and Dorothy Elizabeth (Brannan) Gwyn; m. William Robert Delameter, Dec. 21,1968 (div. Dec., 1982); children: Jonathan W., Gregory Gwyn; m. Harry James Saxton, Aug. 20, 1983. BA, U. Calif., Santa Barbara, 1969; MA in Edn., Coll. of Santa Fe, 1994. Owner Wall Graphics Bus., Albuquerque, New Mex., 1984-92; educator, rschr. New Futures Sch., Albuquerque, 1986—. Bd. dirs. New Mex. Teen Pregnancy Coalition, Albuquerque, 1990—, pres. 1993-94; bd. dirs. New Futures Sch., Albuquerque, 1991-93. Mem. Jr. League of Albuquerque (sustaining), Phi Delta Kappa. Home: 65 Arroyo Venada Placitas NM 87043

SAXTON, MARY JANE, management educator; b. Syracuse, N.Y., Mar. 3, 1953; d. John Cook and Florence (Cooper) S.; m. Paul Hood. BA, SUNY, Cortland, 1975; MBA, U. Pitts., 1979, PhD, 1987. Counselor Methadone Mgmt. Svcs., Inc., N.Y.C., 1975-76; resident mgr. Crossroads Svcs., Inc., Jackson, Miss., 1976; outreach worker Jackson Mental Health Ctr., 1977-78; cons. Organizational Design Cons., Inc., Pitts., 1982-83, mktg. dir., 1984-86; asst. prof. mgmt. U. Houston, 1988-93; lectr. mgmt. U. Colo., Denver, 1994—, U. Denver, 1994—; part-time lectr. Sch. Indsl. Adminstrn., Carnegie Mellon U., Pitts., 1986, U. Pitts., 1983-87; cons. Wessex, Ctr. for Creative Comm., Children's Hosp., Pullman Swindell, Westinghouse Elec. Corp. Co-editor: Gaining Control of the Corporate Culture, 1985; co-author: The Kilmann-Saxton Culture-Gap Survery, 1983; contbr. articles to profl. jours. Mem. Greater Houston Women's Found., 1991-93. U.S.-Soviet Joint Ventures grantee U. Houston, 1990. Mem. Acad. of Mgmt., Am. Soc. Tng. and Devel., Colo.-Wyo. Assn. Psychologists, Inst. Ops. Rsch. and Mgmt. Svcs.

SAYLOR, BEVERLY EDDE, accountant; b. Shelbyville, Tenn., Apr. 10, 1962; d. Hershel Wilson and Mary Jane (Walker) Edde; m. Roy Louis Saylor, Apr. 9, 1989; children: Kelsey Marie, Kyle Lucas. BBA, Mid. Tenn. State U., 1984; postgrad., U. North Fla., 1992—. CPA, Tenn., Fla. Auditor Ernst & Young, CPA, Chattanooga, 1984-87, audit mgr., 1988-89; audit mgr. Ernst & Young, CPA, Jacksonville, Fla., 1989-90; controller HealthCorp., Inc., Chattanooga, 1987-88; bus. analyst Small Bus. Devel., Jacksonville, 1994; acctg. mgr. Fla. Rock Industries, Jacksonville, 1994—. Treas., Christian Coalition, Nassau County, Fla., 1994. Mem. AICPA, Tenn. Soc. CPAs, Inst. Mgmt. Accts., Beta Gamma Sigma. Republican. Home: 2217 Wesley Rd Yulee FL 32097-9795 Office: Fla Rock Industries 155 E 21st St Jacksonville FL 32201

SAYLOR, KATHLEEN MARIE, pediatrics nurse; b. Suffern, N.Y., Dec. 4, 1956; d. Hans J. and Margaret M. (Brown) Wend; m. Robert A. Mohan, 1980 (dec. 1991); m. Richard Gary Saylor, Apr. 8, 1995. BS in Nursing, Duquesne U., 1978; MS in Nursing, U. Pa., 1988. Nurse adult surg. staff Fitzgerald Mercy Hosp., Lansdown, Pa., 1978-80; nurse med. staff Children's Hosp. Phila., 1980-82, with short stay unit, 1982-83, primary nurse pediatric ICU, 1983-88; rehab. clin. nurse specialist Children's Rehab. Hosp., 1988-89; pediatric nursing instr. Roxborough Meml. Hosp., 1992—; instr. basic cardiac life support Am. Heart Assn., Phila., 1987-90. Mem. Child Passenger Safety Project, Pa., 1986-88. Mem. AACN (workshop com. S.E. Pa. chpt. 1986-88, exec. bd. dirs. 1986), Am. Trauma Soc., Nurses Assn. Tchr. Edn. (mem. exec. com. 1994—), Keystone Safety Belt Network, Sigma Theta Tau. Home: 3068 Bowers Mill Rd Pennsburg PA 18073-1904

SAYSETTE, JANICE ELAINE, vertebrate paleontologist, zoo archaeologist; b. San Francisco, Feb. 27, 1949; d. James Monroe and Isabel Christine (Saysette) Heffern; m. Thomas Arthur Haygood, Aug. 6, 1978 (div. June 1991); children: Grant Thomas, Ian James. AA in Nursing, Ohlone Coll., 1974; BSN, Metro State, 1981; MS in Nursing, U. Colo., 1982; MA in Anthropology, Colo. State U., 1990, postgrad., 1991—. Staff nurse Palo Alto (Calif.) VA Hosp., 1974-75, San Jose (Calif.) Hosp., 1975-78, O'Connor Hosp., San Jose, 1978-80; clin. nursing instr. U. No. Colo., Greeley, 1982-87; nursing supr. Poudre Valley Hosp., Ft. Collins, Colo., 1988-89; grad. teaching asst. Colo. State U., Ft. Collins, 1988-90, ind. contractor-zooarchaeology, 1990—; crew mem. U. Wyo. Lookingbill Archaeological Site, 1991; crew chief Denver Mus. Natural History Porqupine Cave Paleontological Site, 1993; lectr., presenter in field. Mem. Am. Soc. Mammologists, Internat. Coun. Archaeozoology, Soc. Am. Archaeology, Soc. Vertebrate Paleontology, Plains Anthrop. Soc. Democrat. Office: Colo State U Dept of Biology Colorado State University CO 80523

SAZAMA, KATHLEEN, pathologist, lawyer; b. Sutherland, Nebr., May 8, 1941; d. Roger William and Esther Mary (Reitz) Paulman; m. Franklin Jed Sazama, Aug. 26, 1962; children: Clare Ann, Jill Patrice. BS, U. Nebr., 1962; MS, Am. U., 1969; MD, Georgetown U., 1976; JD, Cath. U. Am., 1990. Diplomate Am. Bd. Pathology; lic. pathologist Mich., Va., Md., D.C., Calif., Pa.; bar: Md. Chief lab. of blood bank practices FDA Ctr. for Biologics Evaluation and Rsch., Bethesda, Md., 1986-89; cons. Ober, Kaler, Grimes & Shriver, Balt., 1989-90; assoc. med. dir. Sacramento (Calif.) Med. Found. Blood Ctr., 1990-92; intern and resident Georgetown U. Med. Ctr., Washington, 1976-78; resident NIH, Bethesda, Md., 1978-79; asst. clin. prof. pathology U. Calif., Davis, 1990-92, assoc. prof., dir. clin. pathology, 1992-93; prof. pathology and lab. medicine Med. Coll. Pa.-Hahnemann U., Phila., 1994—; clin. asst. prof. pathology Uniformed Svcs. U. of Health Scis., Bethesda, 1981-89; clin. affiliate Ferris State Coll., Big Rapids, 1985-86; v.p. Bd. Met. Washington Blood Banks, Inc., 1981-84; speaker in field. Author: (with others) Stat: The Laboratory's Role, 1986; contbr. numerous articles to profl. jours. Comdr. USPHS, 1986-89. Fellow Coll. Am. Pathologists, Am. Soc. Clin. Pathologists; mem. AMA, ABA, Pa. Med. Soc., Am. Assn. Blood Banks, Pa. Blood Bank Assn., Nat. Health Lawyers Assn., Phi Kappa Phi, Beta Beta Beta. Office: Med Coll Pa Hahnemann U 3300 Henry Ave Philadelphia PA 19129-1121

SCAFFIDI, JUDITH ANN, school volunteer program administrator; b. Bklyn., Aug. 2, 1950; d. Anthony William and Rose Virginia (Nocera) S. BA, SUNY, Plattsburg, 1972, MS, 1973; postgrad. Kennedy Learning Ctr., Einstein Coll. Medicine, 1983; PhD (hon.), Internat. U. Bombay, 1993; HHD (hon.), London Inst. Applied Rsch., 1993. Cert. secondary edn. English. VISTA mem. ACTION, N.Y.C., 1976-77; coord. cultural resources N.Y.C. Sch. Vol. Program, N.Y.C., 1977-80; dist. coord. in Bklyn. N.Y.C. Sch. Vol. Program, 1980—; field supr., adj. faculty Coll. for Human Svcs., N.Y.C., 1984-86; adv. coun. chairperson Ret. Sr. Vol. Program in Bklyn., 1983-86; adv. bd. Ret. Sr. Vol. Program in N.Y.C., 1983-86. Mem. Am. Friends Svc. Com., 1994—. Recipient award for svcs. in promotion literacy Internat. Reading Assn. and Bklyn. Reading Coun., 1986, award for outstanding leadership Ret. Sr. Vol. Program, 1986, cert. of appreciation Mayor City of N.Y., 1991,. Mem. NAFE, Nat. Sch. Vol. Program Ptnrs. in Edn., Cath. Tchrs. Assn. Bklyn. (del. sch. dist. 18, 1982-91), Am. Mus. Natural History, Internat. Platform Assn., World Found. Successful Women, Am. Biog. Inst. (rsch. bd. advisors 1992-93), Am. Biog. Inst. Rsch. Assn. (bd. govs. 1992—), Internat. Parliament for Safety and Peace (dep. mem. and diplomatic passport), Maisson Internat. de Intellectuels (Acad. MIDI), Cath. Alumni Club N.Y., Amnesty Internat. Roman Catholic. Home: 2330 Ocean Ave Apt 3H Brooklyn NY 11229-3036 Office: NYC Sch Vol Program 443 Park Ave S 9th Fl New York NY 10016

SCAFFIDI-WILHELM, GLORIA ANGELAMARIE, elementary education educator; b. Vineland, N.J., June 3, 1960; d. Joseph J. and Gloria (Izzi) Scaffidi; m. Andrew H. Wilhelm, Nov. 7, 1992. BA summa cum laude, Glassboro State Coll., 1982. Cert. tchr. elem. edn., N.J. Tchr. 3rd grade St. Nicholas Sch., Egg Harbor City, N.J., 1982-85; 4th grade tchr. Charles L. Spragg Sch., Egg Harbor City, N.J., 1986—; advisor cheerleading club Egg Harbor City Schs., 1988-91, journalism club, 1989-93, staff mem. yearbook com., 1990-94, editor sch. newspaper, 1989-94, advisor pub. rels. sch. activities, 1989-94. Named Tchr. of Yr., Egg Harbor City Schs., 1989-90. Mem. N.J. Edn. Assn., Kappa Delta Pi. Roman Catholic.

SCALES, DIANN ROYLETTE, librarian; b. Birmingham, Ala., Aug. 15, 1945; d. Alphonso Monroe and Ella (Allen) Scales. BA in Am. History, Miles Coll., Birmingham, Ala., 1966; MA in European History, Atlanta U., 1969, MSLS, 1973. Substitute tchr. C.W. Hayes High Sch., Birmingham, 1967-68; reserve librarian Atlanta U., 1969-73, ref. librarian, 1973-81; ref. librarian Miles Coll., Birmingham, 1981-82, U. Montevallo, Ala., 1984—. Mem. Coalition of 100 Black Women, Birmingham, 1990—. Mem. ALA, Nat. Librs. Assn. (exec. bd. mem.-at-lg. 1989-92), Ala. Libr. Assn. (reference and adult svcs. round table mem.-at-lg. 1990-91), Assn. Social and Behavioral Scientists, So. Hist. Assn., Delta Sigma Theta Sorority, Inc. (corr. sec. 1987-89). Democrat. Baptist. Home: 616 6th St N Birmingham AL 35203-1403 Office: U Montevallo Station 6101 Carmichael Libr Montevallo AL 35115

SCALETTA, HELEN MARGUERITE, volunteer; b. Sioux City, Iowa, Apr. 13, 1927; d. Ralph J. and Ruth Cora (Coyle) Beedle; m. Phillip Jasper Scaletta, May 21, 1946; children: Phillip Ralph, Cheryl Diane Kesler. AA in Bus., Edwards Coll. Bus., Sioux City, 1946. Acct. Towners Dept. Store, Iowa City, 1947-48; legal sec. Phillip Scaletta, Sioux City, 1950-74; service chmn. Easter Seal Soc., Lafayette, Ind., 1970-88; recording sec. Home Hosp. Aux., Lafayette, 1989; danced in Civic Theatre Follies, 1962. Orch. mem. June's All-Girl Ensemble, 1943-50. Pres. Newcomers club YWCA, Lafayette, 1967-68, mem. chmn., bd. dirs., 1979; leader Girl Scouts Am., Ft. Wayne, Ind., 1960-63; chmn. Mental Health Inc., Ft. Wayne, 1960-61, Cancer Crusade, West Lafayette, 1973-74; precinct worker Rep. Cen. Com., West Lafayette, 1974-76; Nat. Missions sec. 1st Presbyn. Ch., 1957. Recipient Citation Easter Seal Soc., 1981. Mem. Purdue U. Women's Club (pres. 1973-74), Lafayette Country Club (golf chmn. 1971, 90, bowling pres. 1992-93), Purdue Women's Bowling League (treas. 1978-79), Cosmopolitan Club, Sigma Kappa (corp. bd., sec., treas. 1971—), Kappa Kappa Sigma (pres. 1972), Sigma Kappa Lafayette Alumnae (pres. 1970, 1988-93). Home: One Via Verde Lafayette IN 47906

SCALFANO, JENNIE LOU, real estate executive; b. Beaumont, Tex., Nov. 4, 1956; d. Willie Slaton and Pauline (Leight) Spears; m. Dennis Allen Knapp, Dec. 23, 1973 (div. 1984); 1 child, Myron Allen; m. Thomas Charles Scalfano, Nov. 1, 1986; children: Rachael Michelle, Thomas Charles Jr. Student, Lamar U., Beaumont, 1981-85. Bookkeeper Heufelder Masonry & Sons, Beaumont, 1976-78; accounts payable staff M&I Ind., Beaumont, 1979-80, acctg. clk. supr., 1980-81, credit/collections supr., staff acct., 1981-82; acctg. supr., staff acct. Jefferson Ind. Inc., Port Arthur, Tex., 1982, corp. controller, 1982-84; v.p., sec., treas., gen. mgr. B.M. Odom Estate, R.E. Odom, Odom Bldg., Inc., Duphil, Inc., Orange, Tex., 1984—; dir. Ta-Lo Co., Orange, Odom Bldg. Co., Orange, Duphil, Inc., Orange. Roman Catholic. Home: 3326 Pheasant St Orange TX 77630-2042 Office: Estate of BM Odom PO Box 458 Orange TX 77631-0458

SCANLON, DOROTHY THERESE, history educator; b. Bridgeport, Conn., Oct. 7, 1928; d. George F. and Mazie (Reardon) S.; A.B., U. Pa., 1948, M.A., 1949; M.A., Boston Coll., 1953; Ph.D., Boston U., 1956; postdoctoral scholar Harvard U., 1962-64, 72. Tchr. history and Latin Marycliff Acad., Winchester, Mass., 1950-52; tchr. history Girls Latin Sch., Boston, 1952-57; prof. Boston State Coll., 1957-82, Mass. Coll. Art, 1982—. Recipient Disting. Service award Boston State Coll., 1979, Faculty Award of Excellence, Mass. Coll. Art, 1985, Faculty Disting. Service award, Mass. Coll. Art, 1987. Mem. Pan-Am. Soc., Latin Am. Studies Assn., Am. Hist. Assn., Orgn. Am. Historians, Am. Studies Assn., Am. Assn. History of Medicine, History of Sci. Soc., AAUP, AAUW, Phi Alpha Theta, Delta Kappa Gamma. Author: Instructor's Manual to Accompany Lewis Hanke, Latin America: A Historical Reader, 1974; contbr. Biographical Dictionary of Social Welfare, 1986. Home: 140 Thornton Rd Chestnut Hill MA 02167-3638 Office: Mass Coll Art Dept History 621 Huntington Ave Boston MA 02115-5878

SCANLON SPENCE, MARY EVALINA MARTIN See SPENCE, MARTY

SCANNELL, NANCY JOAN, economics educator; b. Detroit, Aug. 27, 1956; d. John Thomas and Norma Ann (Brenda) S. BA in Econs., Mich. State U., 1978; AA in Data Processing, Lansing Community Coll., 1981; PhD in Pub. Policy/Econs., U. Ill., Chgo., 1992. Teaching/rsch. asst. U. Ill., Chgo., 1985-89, lectr. econs., 1989-92; instr. ESL Wright Community Coll., Chgo., 1989-91; lectr. econs. Northwestern U., Chgo., 1992-94; vis. asst. prof. econs. North South U., Dhaka, Bangladesh, spring 1993; vis. asst. prof. fin. U. Ill., Chgo., 1994—. Recipient Traveling Scholar award U. Chgo., 1985. Office: U Ill at Chgo Dept Fin M/C 168 601 S Morgan St Chicago IL 60607-7124

SCARF, MARGARET (MAGGI SCARF), author; b. Phila., May 13, 1932; d. Benjamin and Helen (Rotbin) Klein; m. Herbert Eli Scarf, June, 1953; children: Martha Samuelson, Elizabeth Stone, Susan Merrell. BA, South Conn. State U., 1989. Writer in residence Jonathan Edwards Coll., Yale U.; contbg. editor New Republic, Washington, DC, 1978—, Self Mag., N.Y.C., 1991—; assoc. fellow Jonathan Edwards Coll. Yale U., New Haven, 1979, 81, 83; sr. fellow Bush Ctr. in Child Devel. and Social Policy, Yale U., 1991—; mem. adv. bd. Am. Psychiat. Press. Author: Meet Benjamin Franklin, 1968, Antarctica: Exploring the Frozen Continent, 1970, Body, Mind, Behavior, 1976 (Nat. Media award Am. Psychological Assn. 1977), Unfinished Business: Pressure Points in the Lives of Women, 1981, Intimate Partners: Patterns in Love and Marriage, 1987; contbr. numerous articles to jours. including N.Y. Times mag. and book rev., Psychology Today. Recipient Nat. Media award Am. Psychol. Found., 1971, 74, Conn. UN award Outstanding Conn. Women, 1987; Ford Found. fellow, 1973-74, Neiman fellow Harvard U., 1975-76, Ctr. Advanced Study in Behavioral Scis. fellow, 1977-78, 85-86, Alicia Patterson Found. fellow, 1978-79. Mem. Conn. Soc. Psychoanalytic Psychologists, Am. Psychiat. Press (mem. adv. bd. 1992), Lawn Club, Elizabethans. *

SCARFF, HOPE DYALL, photographer; b. Mt. Pleasant, Iowa, Oct. 25, 1952; d. Charles and Marjorie (Hope) Dyall; m. David L. Scarff, Oct. 20, 1972; children: Misty Michelle, Shasta Shannon. Student, Southeastern Community Coll., Burlington, Iowa, 1973. Receptionist Dyall Photography, Mt. Pleasant, 1974-78, photographer, 1978—, mgr., 1978-80, owner, 1980—. Exhibited in group shows Epcot Ctr., Disneyworld, nat. convs. for Profl. Photographers Am., 1987—; portrait pub. in Eastman Kodak book The Portrait. Mem. Profl. Photographers Am., Am. Soc. Photographers, Profl. Photographers Iowa (One of Top 10 Photographers awards 1984, 90, Profl. Photographer of Yr. award 1988, 99, highest scoring portrait from Iowa for 1989 conv., M. Photography degree, 1990, Iowa Masters Silver Cup 1992), S.E. Iowa Assn. Photographers (pres. 1984), Mt. Pleasant C. of C., Mt. Pleasant Athletic Boosters Club. Republican. Methodist. Home: RR 3 Mount Pleasant IA 52641-9803 Office: Dyall Photography 123 N Main St Mount Pleasant IA 52641-2027

SCARPATO, KIM ANN, insurance claims supervisor; b. West Islip, N.Y., Oct. 3, 1960; d. Richard Xavier and Lorraine (Jerome) Egloff; m. James Edward Scarpato, Sept. 30, 1994. BS in Acctg., N.Y. Inst. Tech., 1984. Project acct. Morse/Diesel, N.Y.C., 1984-85, Tishman Constrn., N.Y.C., 1985-86; acctg. supr. Timko Contracting, N.Y.C., 1986-87; casualty supr. Crawford & Co., Uniondale, N.Y., 1992—. Scholar Delta Mu Delta, 1982. Republican. Office: Crawford & Co 333 Earle Ovington Blvd Uniondale NY 11553

SCARPONE, JANET MARIE, adult education educator, speech consultant; b. N.Y.C., Dec. 15, 1953; d. Daniel and Jean Gloria (Liscio) S. BA in Speech Comm. magna cum laude, U. Bridgeport, 1975; MS in Speech Comm., So. Ill. U., 1976. Cert. tchr., Calif. Speech comm. instr. So. Ill. U., Carbondale, 1975-76, Montclair (N.J.) State Coll., 1977-81, CCNY, 1977-81, Manhattan C.C., N.Y.C., 1978-79, Rutgers U., Newark, 1980; tng. specialist Mfrs. Hanover Trust Co., N.Y.C., 1981-83; speech comm. instr. San Diego C.C., 1983-88; ESL/GED and writing instr. Sweetwater Adult Sch., National City, Calif., 1987—; speech cons., N.Y.C., 1978-81, San Diego, 1985—. Author: (ednl. videotape) ASCD Directory, 1994. Mem., sec. Upas Park Homeowners Assn., San Diego, 1992-93; pres. U. Bridgeport Forensic Forum, 1974-75, v.p., 1973-74. Recipient scholarship N.Y. State Regents, 1971, U. Bridgeport, 1975. Mem. Profls. in Adult Continuing Edn., Calif. Coun. for Adult Edn., Calif. Tchrs. ESL. Office: Sweetwater Adult Sch 2800 Highland Ave National City CA 91950

SCARROTT, MARIE ELAINE, elementary education educator; b. Seneca Falls, N.Y., Aug. 8, 1953; d. Albert F. and Janice E. (Clark) S. MusB, Ithaca Coll., 1975, M of Music Edn., 1981; postgrad., SUNY, Brockport, 1982-83. Cert. music tchr., N.Y. Tchr. Pioneer High Sch., Yorkshire, N.Y., 1975-76, Keshequa Elem. Sch., Dalton, N.Y., 1976—; coach divsn. I Odyssey of the Mind teams, 1989, 90, 92, 93, 94. Mem. Nunda Ambulance, 1979—; sec. Genessee Valley Sch. Music Assn., Livingston City, 1987; pres. Local Tchr.'s Assn., Nunda, N.Y., 1988-90; treas. Nunda Ambulance Corp., 1991-93, capt., 1995—; ch. organist Holy Angels Ch., Nunda, 1976—, United Meth. Ch., Nunda, 1980—; performer Hornell (N.Y.) Area Wind Ensemble, 1989—; music dir. Nunda Theater Guild, 1987; cert. lab. instr. N.Y. State EMT Program. Named Vol. of Yr., ARC, 1991. Republican. Roman Catholic. Home: 2645 Rt 436 Nunda NY 14517 Office: Keshequa Ctrl Sch Church St Dalton NY 14836

SCARROW, PAMELA KAY, health care manager; b. Washington, Nov. 4, 1949; d. Edward Charles and Elsie Lorine (Kay) Scarrow; m. Antonio Joseph Franz, Sept. 4, 1979; 1 child, Vanessa Motil Franz. AA, Navarro Coll., Tex., 1981; BS, Golden Gate U., 1983. Cert. med. staff coordinator, 1986. Adminstrv. asst. Trust Ter. of the Pacific Islands, Saipan, Mariana Islands, 1976-79; adminstrv. asst. Navarro Coll., Corsicana, Tex., 1979-81; staff asst. San Francisco Symphony, 1981-82; med. staff liaison Calif. Med. Assn., San Francisco, 1982-87; provider, practitioner cons. Calif. Med. Rev., Inc., San Francisco, 1987-90; med. rev. specialist Am. Med. Peer Rev. Assn., Washington, 1990-93; adminstr. quality assurance Am. Coll. Ob-gyn., 1993—. Editor: Contracting Resource and Assistance Dept., Inc., Economic Resource Guide, 1986, Medical Staff Resources Manual, 1987. Democrat. Roman Catholic. Office: Am Coll Ob-gyn 409 12th St SW Washington DC 20024

SCARRY, MARY, financial executive; b. Pitts., Apr. 1, 1934. BS in Edn., Slippery Rock U., 1956, MEd, 1970; cert., Coll. Fin. Planning, 1982. Tchr. McGuffy Sch., Claysville, Pa., 1956-58; tchr., chmn. dept. Elizabeth (Pa.) Forward Sch., 1958-62; dir. student activities Allegheny Gen. Hosp., 1962-66; tchr. econs. Ringgold Sch. Dist., Monongahela, Pa., 1966-67; registrar, counselor U. Pitts., 1967-77; registered rep., fin. planner Shoal P. Berer Assocs., Pa., 1977-87; fin. services mgr. United Resources, Inc., Pitts., 1987-88; with Hackett Assocs. Inc., Pitts., 1988-90; cons. Berer Fin. Mgmt., Monroeville, Pa., 1990—; pension mgr. Lincoln Nat. Life Ins., Pitts., 1991-93; owner Rushmore Fin. Cons., 1993—. Mem. Inst. Cert. Fin. Planning (chief exec. officer Pitts. chpt., pres. 1984-87, founder), Internat. Assn. Fin. Planning (Pitts. chpt., v.p. programs 1980-84, v.p. ethics com. 1984-86). Home: 218 Rock Run Rd Elizabeth PA 15037-2429 Office: Berer Fin Mgmt Monroeville PA 15146 also: Lincoln Nat Life Ins Koppers Bldg 436 7th Ave Ste 600 Pittsburgh PA 15219

SCARSE, OLIVIA MARIE, cardiologist, consultant; b. Chgo., Nov. 10, 1950; d. Oliver Marcus and Marjorie Ardis (Olsen) S. BS, North Park Coll., 1970; MD, Loyola U., Maywood, Ill., 1973. Diplomate Am. Bd. Internal Medicine, Am. Bd. Cardiovascular Diseases. Surg. intern Resurrection Hosp., Chgo., 1974; resident in internal medicine Northwestern U., Chgo., 1974-77; cardiovascular disease fellow U. Ill., Chgo., 1977-80; dir. cardiac lab. Cook County Hosp., Chgo., 1981; dir. heart sta. MacNeal Hosp., Berwyn, Ill., 1983; dir. electrophysiology Hines VA Hosp., Maywood, Ill., 1984-85; dir. progressive care Columbus Hosp., Chgo., 1985-88, pvt. practice, 1984—; pvt. practice Ill. Masonic Hosp., Chgo., 1989—. Pillsbury fellow Pillsbury Fund, 1980. Fellow Am. Coll. Cardiology; mem. AMA, ACP, Chgo. Med. Assn., Ill. State Med. Assn., Am. Heart Assn. Home and Office: 2650 N Lakeview # 4109 Chicago IL 60614

SCATENA, LORRAINE BORBA, rancher, women's rights advocate; b. San Rafael, Calif., Feb. 18, 1924; d. Joseph and Eugenia (Simas) de Borba; m. Louis G. Scatena, Feb. 14, 1960; children: Louis Vincent, Eugenia Gayle. BA, Dominican Coll., San Rafael, 1945; postgrad., Calif. Sch. Fine Arts, 1948, U. Calif., Berkeley, 1956-57. Cert. elem. tchr., Calif. Tchr. Dominican Coll., 1946; tchr. of mentally handicapped San Anselmo (Calif.) Sch. Dist., 1946; tchr. Fairfax (Calif.) Pub. Elem. Sch., 1946-53; asst. to mayor Fairfax City Recreation, 1948-53; tchr., libr. U.S. Dependent Schs., Mainz am Rhine, Fed. Republic Germany, 1953-56; translator Portugal Travel Tours, Lisbon, 1954; bonding sec. Am. Fore Ins. Group, San Francisco, 1958-60; rancher, farmer Yerington, Nev., 1960—; hostess com. Caldecott and Newbury Authors' Awards, San Francisco, 1959; mem. Nev. State Legis. Commn., 1975; coord. Nevadans for Equal Rights Amendment, 1975-78, rural areas rep., 1976-78; testifier Nev. State Senate and Assembly, 1975, 77; mem. adv. com. Fleischmann Coll. Agr. U. Nev., 1977-80, 81-84; speaker Grants and Rsch. Projects, Bishop, Calif., 1977, Choices for Tomorrow's Women, Fallon, Nev., 1989. Trustee Wassuk Coll., Hawthorne, Nev., 1984-87; mem. Lyon County Friends of Libr., Yerington, 1971—, Lyon County Mus. Soc., 1978; sec., pub. info. chmn. Lyon County Rep. Women, 1968-73, v.p. programs, 1973-75; mem. Lyon County Rep. Cen. Com., 1973-74; mem. Marin County Soc. Artists, San Anselmo, Calif., 1948-53; charter mem. Eleanor Roosevelt Fund Women and Girls, 1990, sustaining mem., 1991—; Nev. rep. 1st White House Conf. Rural Am. Women, Washington, 1980; participant internat. reception, Washington, 1980; mem. pub. panel individual presentation Shakespeare's Treatment of Women Characters, Nev. Theatre for the Arts, Ashland, Oreg. Shakespearean Actors local performance, 1977. Recipient Outstanding Conservation Farmer award Mason Valley Conservation Dist., 1992, Soroptimist Internat. Women Helping women award 1983, invitation to first all-women delegation to U.S.A. from People's Republic china, U.S. House Reps., 1979; Public Forum Travel grantee Edn. Title IX, Oakland, Calif., 1977; fellow World Lit. Acad., 1993. Mem. Lyon County Ret. Tchrs. Assn. (unit pres. 1979-80, 84-86, v.p. 1986-88, Nev. div. Outstanding Svc. award 1981, state conv. gen. chmn. 1985), Rural Am. Women Inc., AAUW (br. pres. 1972-74, 74-76, edn. found. programs, 1983—, state convention gen. chmn. 1976, 87, state div. sec. 1970-72, state div. legis. program chmn. 1976-77, state div. chmn. internat. rels. 1979-81, state div. pres. 1981-83, br. travelship, discovering women in U.S. history Radcliffe Coll. Div. Humanities award 1975, Future Fund Nat. award 1983), Mason Valley Country Club, Italian Cath. Fedn. Club (pres. 1986-88), Uniao Portuguesa Estado da Calif. Roman Catholic. Home: PO Box 247 Yerington NV 89447

SCEARSE, PATRICIA DOTSON, nurse educator, college dean; b. Wabash, Ind., Sept. 4, 1931; d. Claude Richard and Lilly Etta (Colvill) D.; m. Vernon Quinton Scearse, June 26, 1955 (dec. Mar. 1990); 1 child, Victoria Lynn Lenderman. BS, Earlham Coll., 1955; MS, U. Colo., 1968; D in Nursing Sci., U. Calif., San Francisco, 1974. RN. Staff nurse Reid Meml. Hosp., Richmond, Ind., 1954-55; head nurse, instr. Hillcrest Bapt. Hosp., Waco, Tex., 1955-56; instr. Sch. Nursing Candler Hosp., Savannah, Ga., 1956-60; adminstrv. asst., edn. cons. Wyo. State Bd. Nursing, Cheyenne, 1964-68; asst. prof. San Diego State U., 1969, Ball State U., Muncie, Ind., 1969-71; assoc. prof., area chairperson U. Mich., Ann Arbor, 1974-80; prof., dean Coll. Nursing Tex. Christian U., Ft. Worth, 1980—. Pub. policy editor Jour. Profl. Nursing, Phila., 1986-89; editorial cons. Jour. Pub. Health Nursing, New Haven, 1984-89; contbr. articles to profl. jours. Recipient Outstanding Nurse award Sigma Theat Tau, Beta Alpha, Ft. Worth, 1986; Kennedy Inst. Ethics postdoctoral fellow, Georgetown U., 1978. Mem. ANA, APHA (bd. govs. 1976), Am. Assn. Colls. of Nursing (bd. dirs. 1982-84, 85-87), Nat. League for Nursing, Coun. Baccalaureate and Higher Degree Programs (bd. rev.), Assn. Community Health Nurse Educators (named Great 100 Nurses 1992). Home: 5511 Ledgestone Dr Fort Worth TX 76132-2342 Office: Tex Christian U Harris Coll Nursing PO Box 32899 TCU Sta Fort Worth TX 76129

SCEERY, BEVERLY DAVIS, realtor, writer, educator; b. Hartford, Conn.; d. Howard Coe and Gladys (Cotton) Davis; m. Walter Raymond Sceery; children: Nancy Bazar, Edward Sceery, Walter Sceery Jr., Martha Creed, Mary Heaton. BS magna cum laude, U. Md., 1975, MS, 1977, postgrad., 1977-82. Fin. counselor U. Md., College Park, 1975-77, lectr., 1977-82; realtor Jack Lawlor Realty, Washington, 1982—; dir. handicapped program U. Md., College Park, 1975-77. Editor Capital Gardener mag., 1980-84; contbr. articles to profl. jours. Leader Girl Scouts Am., Potomac, Md., 1963-73, chmn., 1970-73, dir., Bethesda, Md., 1973. Mem. AAUW (chmn. nomination com. 1991), DAR (state registrar 1994—), chmn. Am. History 1991-94, nat. vice chmn. vo. geneaologists, mus. docent, speakers staff, organizing regent Potomac hundred chpt. 1992—), Nat. Capital Area Fedn. Garden Clubs (chmn. 1992—, flower show sch. 1989-91, master judge flower shows, landscape design 1972—), Nat. Assn. Realtors, Md. Assn. Realtors, Phi Kappa Phi, Alpha Lambda Delta, Omicron Nu. Home: 10307 Riverwood Dr Potomac MD 20854-1539

SCEPPAGUERCIO, MARIA ANN, food company executive; b. Newark, Jan. 29, 1962; d. Angelo Frank and Ann Barbara (La Rezza) S.; m. Alan Shaw Gever, June 15, 1986. BS, Montclair State Coll., 1984; MBA, Seton Hall U., 1990. Fin. intern, then fin. analyst Nabisco Biscuit Co., East Hanover, N.J., 1983-86; sr. fin. analyst Nabisco Brands, Inc., East Hanover, 1986-88; mgr. fin. ops. Nabisco Brands, Inc., Parsippany, N.J., 1989; mgr. bus. planning Nabisco Brands, Inc., East Hanover, 1989-90, sr. mgr. bus. planning, 1990-91; dir. bus. planning Nabisco Brands, Inc., Parsippany, 1991-93; dir. fin. and bus. analysis Splty. Products Co., Parsippany, 1993—; instr., adj. prof. Grad. Sch. Seton Hall U., South Orange, N.J., 1990. Mem. Planning Forum. Office: Nabisco Brands Inc PO Box 311 Parsippany NJ 07054-0311

SCHAAF, BARBARA CAROL, writer, consultant, educator; b. Chgo.; d. William and Mary (Krutilla) S. BS cum laude, Roosevelt U., 1971; MBA, U. Chgo. Exec. Program, 1976. Free-lance writer, Harvey, Ill., 1977—; cons. transp., housing, taxation, labor and econs., bus.; lectr. urban, labor, mil. and ethnic history, English medieval history, writing; lectr. on urban and ethnic history USIA, 1978-81; mem. adv. com. Artists in Residence Program, Chgo. Coun. Fine Arts, 1979-83; bd. dirs. Chgo. Ctr. Hosp., 1982-87; treas., bd. dirs. Chgo. Ctr. Health System, 1985-87; instr. Richard J. Dale Coll., 1988—. Author: Mr. Dooley's Chicago, 1977 (Carl Sandburg award 1978, also nominee Am. Hist. Assn. Gershoy award and Pulitzer prize), Mr. Dooley, We Need Him Now, 1988, Shattered Hopes, 1991; contbr. articles to newspapers, mags. Press sec. Eleanor McGovern, 1971-72, Richard M. Daley, 1979-80J. F. and Robert F. Kennedy presdl. campaigns and other polit. campaigns; treas. Harvey Pub. Libr. Bd. Trustees, 1977—. Nat. Found. for Humanities fellow Writing in Chgo. Program, 1978; Ind. scholar urban history and mil. history. Mem. ALA, Nat. Book Critics Circle, PEN, Soc. Midland Authors, Mystery Writers of Am., Ill. Libr. Assn., Richard III Soc., South Downers, Jane Austen Soc. Home and Office: 400 Streamside Dr Harvey IL 60426-1260

SCHAAF, MARTHA ECKERT, author, library director, musician; b. Madison, Ind., Sept. 21, 1911; d. Frederick William and Julia (Richert) Eckert; m. Clarence William Schaaf, Dec. 27, 1941 (dec. 1987); 1 child, Susan Elizabeth Lee. AB with distinction, Ind. U., 1933; MLS, Columbia U., 1945; postgrad., Butler U., Ind. U. Lic. tchr. Music tchr., libr. dir. Twp. System, Crothersville, Ind., 1936-38; libr. music instr. Angola, Ind., 1938-39, Howe High Sch., Indpls., 1939-42; libr. dir. Reitz High Sch., Evansville, Ind., 1942; county libr. organizer County Brs. Libr., Columbus, Ga., 1943; hosp. libr. dir. Camp Van Dorn, Woodville, Miss., 1943-44; organized libr. Bulova Sch. for Disabled Vets., L.I., N.Y., 1944-45; organized bus. rsch. libr. Eli Lilly & Co., Indpls., 1946-50; rsch. libr. Wallace Collection Ind. Hist. Soc. Libr., 1958-61; dir. Pub. Libr., Pompano Beach, Fla., 1967-72; pres. Ind. Spl. Libr. Assn., 1948. Author: Lew Wallace: Boy Writer, 1961, Duke Ellington: Music Master, 1975; contbg.author: War Paint and Wagon Wheels, 1968, Reading Incentive Series, 1969; contbr. articles to profl. jours. Named Valedictorian, Madison (Ind.) High Sch., 1929; recipient History award Daughters Am. Revolution, 1930, C. of C. award Pompano Beach, Fla., 1970, Disting. Alumni award Ind. U., Bloomington, 1983. Mem. Nat. League Am. Pen Women, Mortar Board, Ind. U. Alumni Assn., Columbia U. Alumni Assn., Phi Beta Kappa, Pi Lambda Theta, Chi Omega. Home: 6065 S Verde Trl Apt G119 Boca Raton FL 33433-4410

SCHAAR, SUSAN CLARKE, state legislative staff member; b. Lawrenceville, Va., Dec. 21, 1949; d. Garland Lewis and Frances Virginia (Matthews) Clarke; m. William Berkley Schaar Jr., Nov. 24, 1990. BA, U. Richmond, 1972. Engrossing clk. Senate Va., Richmond, 1974, legis. rsch. analyst, 1974-77; asst. to the clk. Senate of Va., Richmond, 1977-83; asst. clk. Senate Va., Richmond, 1983-90, clk. of the Senate, 1990—. mem. YMCA Model Gen. Assembly Adv. com., Richmond, 1990—; trustee U. Richmond, 1990—; pres. Richmond Club of Westhampton, 1988-90; mem. Spider Club Athletic Bd., Richmond, 1988-90; co-chair Arts Around the Lake, Richmond, 1990-91. Mem. Am. Soc. Legis. Clks. and Secs., Omicron Delta Kappa, Pi Sigma Alpha. Baptist. Office: Senate of Va PO Box 396 Richmond VA 23203-0396

SCHACHTEL, BARBARA HARRIET LEVIN, epidemiologist, educator; b. Rochester, N.Y., May 27, 1921; d. Lester and Ethel (Neiman) Levin; m. Hyman Judah Schachtel, Oct. 15, 1941; children: Bernard, Ann.Mollie. Student Wellesley Coll., 1939-41; BS, U. Houston, 1951, MA in Psychology, 1967; PhD, U. Tex.-Houston, 1979. Psychol. examiner Meyer Ctr. for Devel. Pediatrics, Tex. Children's Hosp., Houston, 1967-81; instr. dept. pediatrics Baylor Coll. Medicine, Houston, 1967-81, asst. prof. dept. medicine, 1982—; asst. dir. biometry and epidemiology Sid W. Richardson Inst. for Preventive Medicine, Meth. Hosp., Houston, 1981-88, dir. quality assurance, 1988-93; retired 1993; mem. instl. rev. bd. for human rsch. Baylor Coll. Medicine, Houston, 1981-87; mem. devel. bd. U. Tex. Health Sci. Ctr., Houston, 1987—; mem. dean's adv. bd. Sch. Architecture U. Houston, 1987; bd. dirs. Tex. Medical Ctr, 1990-93. Contbr. articles to profl. jours. Vice pres., bd. dirs. Houston-Harris County Mental Health Assn., 1966-67; vice-chmn. bd. mgrs. Harris County Hosp. Dist., Houston, 1974-90, chmn. 1990-92, bd. dirs., 1970-93; trustee Inst. Religion in Tex. Med. Ctr., 1990— bd. mem. Planned Parenthood of Houston, Inc., 1994—, Houston Ind. Sch. Dist. Found., 1993—; sec. Bo Harris County Hosp. Dist. Found. Bd., 1993—. Named Great Texan of Yr., Nat. Found. for Ilietis and Colitis, Houston, 1982, Outstanding Citizen, Houston-Harris County Mental Health Assn., 1985; recipient Good Heart award B'nai Brith Women, 1984, Women of Prominence award Am. Jewish Com., 1991, Mayor's award for outstanding vol. svc., 1994. Mem. APA, APHA, Wellesley Club of Houston (pres. 1968-70). Avocations: golf, tennis, books. Home: 2527 Glen Haven Blvd Houston TX 77030-3511

SCHACK, MARY LOU, clinical psychologist, educator; b. New Brunswick, N.J., June 28, 1941; d. John Alexander and Mary Grace (Rooney) S. BA, Trenton State Coll., 1963; MA, Temple U., 1969, PhD, 1972. Lic. psychologist, Pa. English tchr. Woodbridge (N.J.) Twp. Pub. Schs., 1963-67; teaching asst. psychology Temple U., Phila., 1968-72; postdoctoral intern Community Guidance Ctr., Trenton and Princeton, N.J., 1972-73; supervising psychologist Ill. Masonic Med. Ctr., Chgo., 1974-77; asst. clin. prof. Abraham Lincoln Med. U., Chgo., 1975-77; chief psychologist Phila. Psychol. Ctr., 1977-81; clin. asst. prof. psychology U. Pa., Phila., 1979-82; founder, dir. faculty Gestalt Therapy Inst. Phila., Bryn Mawr, 1982—; prs. PsychSolutions, Bala Cynwyd, Pa., 1992—. Dir. Eromin, Inc., Phila., 1978-82. Recipient scholarship N.J., 1959-63; fellow Temple U., 1969-72. Fellow Pa. Psychol. Assn., Phila. Soc. Clin. Psychologists (exec. bd. dirs. 1978-82); mem. APA, Assn. for Advancement of Gestalt Therapy. Home: 1315 Arrowmink Rd Villanova PA 19085 Office: PsychSolutions 111 Presidential Blvd # 229 Bala Cynwyd PA 19004

SCHACTMAN, MARYLIN, clinical nurse specialist; b. N.Y.C., Sept. 11, 1943; d. William and Doris (Shron) Cohen; m. Morrie Schactman, Sept. 8, 1963; children: Mark, Brian, Eric. B Commerce, McGill U., 1964; AS, Miami Dade Community Coll., 1976; BSN, SUNY, 1983; MSN, U. Miami, 1985. CCRN, BCLS, ACLS. Staff nurse ICU Doctor's Hosp., Coral Gables, Fla., 1976-79; instr. nursing Dade County Schs., Miami, Fla., 1979-83; staff nurse CCU Bapt. Hosp., Miami, Fla., 1984-85, clin. specialist, 1985-87; clin. specialist St. Francis Hosp., Roslyn, N.Y., 1987-89, asst. v.p., 1989-93; clin. nurse specialist L.I. Jewish Med. Ctr., New Hyde Park, N.Y., 1993—. Contbr. articles to profl. jours. Mem. AACN (appeals com. 1984, 85), Am. Heart Assn. (coronary care com. nursing edn. com., continuing edn. com.). Home: 19 Beverly Rd Port Washington NY 11050

SCHADE, CHARLENE JOANNE, adult and early childhood education educator; b. San Bernardino, Calif., June 26, 1935; d. Clarence George Linde and Helen Anita (Sunny) Hardesty; m. William Joseph Jr., Apr. 12, 1958 (div., 1978); children: Sabrina, Eric, Camela, Cynthia; m. Thomas Byron Killens, Sept. 25, 1983. BS, UCLA, 1959. Tchr. dance & pe L.A. Unified Secondary Schs., Calif., 1959-63; dir., instr. (Kindergym) La Jolla YMCA, Calif., 1972-76; instr. older adult San Diego Community Colls., 1977—; artist in residence Wolf Trap/Headstart, 1984-85; workshop leader S.W. Dance, Movement and Acro-Sports, prime-time adult activities coord., 1988—, Am. Heart Assn., Arthritis Found., Am. Lung Assn.; cons. to Calif. Gov.'s Coun. of Phys. Fitness, 1993; workshop leader AAHPERD, Calif. Assn. HPERD, Head Start, San Diego Assn. Young Child, Calif. Assn. Edn. Young Child, Calif. Kindergarten Assn., Assn. Childhood Edn. Internat., San Diego C.C., Internat. Assn. Fitness Profls., Am. Soc. Aging, 1977—; guest KFMB and KPBS TV Shows, San Diego, 1980-88. Author: Move With Me From A to Z, 1982, Move With Me, One, Two, Three, 1988; co-author: Prime Time Aerobics, 1982, Muevete Conmigo, uno, dos, tres, 1990; co-writer: Guide for Physical Fitness Instructors of Older Adults, Grant Project, 1990, The Empowering Teacher, 1990, Handbook for Instructors of Older Adults, 1994. Dir. We Care Found., San Diego, 1977-79, Meet the Author programs San Diego County Schs., 1988—; founder SOLO, San Diego, 1981-83; adminstr., v.p. ODEM chpt. Toastmasters, San Diego, 1982; chmn. People with Arthritis Can Exercise com. San Diego chpt. Arthritis Found., 1994-95; workshop leader Am. Heart Assn., Arthritis Found., Am. Lung Assn. Grantee Video Showcase of Exercises for Older Adults, 1992-93. Mem. AAHPERD, Calif. AAHPERD. Office: Exer Fun/Prime Time Aerobic 3089C Clairemont Dr Ste 130 San Diego CA 92117-6767

SCHAEDIG, CYNTHIA SUE, county planner; b. Rogers City, Mich., Dec. 22, 1953; d. Willard Ray and Virginia Ruth (Brown) S. BS, Ctrl. Mich. U., 1976, MPA, 1988. Keyliner McKay Press, Midland, Mich., 1977-80; engring. aide City of Midland, 1980-86; mgmt. analyst Ramsey County, St. Paul, 1986-88; planner Dakota County, Hastings, Minn., 1988—. Mem. study com. Citizens League, Mpls., 1993-94. Mem. Minn. chpt. Am. Soc. Pub. Adminstrn. (pres.-elect 1993-94, bd. dirs. 1991-92, 93-94, pres. 1994-95), Minn. Ctr. for Women in Govt. (program com., spkr. breakfast series, leadership com.), Minn. chpt. Am. Planning Assn. (facility chair ann. conf. 1989-90). Office: Dakota County 1590 Highway 55 Hastings MN 55033

SCHAEFER, HELENE G(ERALDINE), social services professional; b. Chgo., Apr. 4, 1948; d. Jerry and Helen (Hruska) Souta; m. Kenneth Schaefer (div.) June 4, 1972; children: Rebecca, Benjamin. BA, Valparaiso U., 1970; MA, Govs. State U., 1984. Registered social worker, Ill. Social worker Ill. Dept. of Children & Family Svcs., Chgo., 1970-76, Bodimetric Health Svcs., Hillside, Ill., 1984-86; counselor svc. dir. Crisis Ctr. For So. Suburbia, Worth, Ill., 1979-82; child protection investigator Ill. Dept. Children and Family Svcs., Chgo., 1987-93, supr., 1993—. Bd. dirs. Rainbow House Shelter for Battered Women; leader Girl Scouts of So. Cook County, Palos Heights, 1982-87; active No. Ill. Hockey League. Mem. AAUW, Parent Faculty Assn., Chgo. Met. Battered, Women's Movement, Ill. Juvenile Officers Assn. Office: Ill Dept Children & Family Svcs 2033 S Indiana Ave Chicago IL 60616-1312

SCHAEFER, MARILYN LOUISE, artist, writer, educator; b. Cedar Rapids, Iowa, Apr. 22, 1933; d. Henry Richard and Maria Augusta (Dickel) S. AA, Monticello Coll. for Women, 1953; BFA, Cranbrook Acad. Art, 1956, MFA, 1960; MA cum laude, U. Chgo., 1958; MA, St. John's Coll., Santa Fe, 1979. Rsch. asst. editor Encyclopaedia Britannica, Chgo., 1960-63; humanities editor Encyclopedia Americana, N.Y., 1964-68; acquisitions editor Litton Ednl. Pub., N.Y., 1968-70; from instr. to prof. art and advt. design dept. N.Y.C. Tech. Coll. CUNY, 1970—; contbg. editor Encyclopedia Americana, 1979—, Coll. Teaching jour., 1979. Contbr. articles to profl. publs. including Art and Auction mag., Art and Antiques mag., Am. Artist mag., Encyclopedia Americana, 1970—. Luce Found. postgrad. study fellow St. John's Coll., 1976-79; Ingram Merrill Found. grantee, 1983-84. Mem. AAUW, CUNY Acad. Arts and Scis. Home: 306 W 76th St New York NY 10023-8065 Office: NYC Tech Coll CUNY 300 Jay St Brooklyn NY 11201-2902

SCHAEFER, PATRICIA, librarian; b. Ft. Wayne, Ind., Apr. 23, 1930; d. Edward John and Hildegarde Hartman (Hormel) S. MusB, Northwestern U., 1951; MusM, U. Ill., 1958; MLS, U. Mich., 1963. With U.S. Rubber Co., Ft. Wayne, 1951-52; sec. to promotion mgr. Sta. WOWO, Ft. Wayne, Ind., 1952, sec. to program mgr., 1953-55; coord. publicity and promotion Home Telephone Co., Ft. Wayne, 1955-56; sec. Fine Arts Found., Ft. Wayne, 1956-57; libr. asst. Columbus (Ohio) Pub. Libr., 1958-59; audio-visual librarian Muncie (Ind.) Pub. Libr., 1959-86, asst. libr. dir., 1981-86; libr. dir., 1986—; chmn. Ind. Libr. Film Cir., 1962-63; treas. Ind. Libr. Film Svc. 1969-70, 83-85; mem. trustee adv. coun. Milton S. Eisenhower Libr., Johns Hopkins U.; bd. dirs. Franklin Electric Co., Inc.; cons. in field. Weekly columnist Libr. Lines, Muncie Evening Press, 1981-83; program annotator Muncie Symphony Orch. and Masterworks Chorale; contbr. articles to profl. jours. Bd. dirs. Muncie Symphony Assn., 1964-74, 85-91; trustee Masterworks Chorale; bd. dirs. Cen. City Bus. Assn., 1986-92, Ind. Inst. Tech., United Way of Delaware County, Ind.; adv. coun. Coll. Fine Arts, Ball State U.; mem. adv. bd. dirs. Sta. WIPB-TV; mem. adv. com., bookshop dir. Midwest Writers Workshop, 1976-77; sec. Del. County Coun. for the Arts, 1978-79, pres., 1979-81, bd. dirs., 1985-86; mem. pres.'s coun. Berea Coll.; bd. dirs. Muncie YWCA, 1977-82, 85-89, treas., 1981-82, 88-89; gen. chmn. Ind. Renaissance Fair, 1978-79; pres. Muncie Matinee Musicale, 1965-67; past pres. Ind. Film and Video Coun.; mem. adv. bd. Community Found. Muncie and Delaware County; bd. dirs. Wapehani coun. Girl Scouts U.S., 1989—. Named Woman Achievement Pub. Svcs., 1986. Mem. ALA, Ind. Libr. Assn. (pres. 1987-88), Nat. League Am. Pen Women (pres. Muncie br. 1974-78), Altrusa (pres. 1986-87), Riley-Jones Club, Delta Zeta, Mu Phi Epsilon. Republican. Roman Catholic. Home: 5400 W Deer Run Ct Muncie IN 47304-5775 Office: 301 E Jackson St Muncie IN 47305-1808

SCHAEFER, PATRICIA ANN, retired librarian; b. Lebanon, Ohio, Jan. 22, 1933; d. Riley Ray and Louise Collette (Fraher) Freeze; BS, Miami U., Oxford, Ohio, 1954; m. William H. Schaefer, Aug. 11, 1956; children: Susan P., Nancy A., William H. III (dec.). Med. technologist Mercy Hosp., Hamilton, Ohio, 1954-58, Middletown (Ohio) Hosp., 1958-62; libr. Middletown City Schs., 1979—, intermediate libr. McKinley Sch., 1982-93, retired 1993. Active YMCA, pres., 1977-79; bd. dirs. Middletown Symphony, 1974-78, Arts in Middletown, 1983—, Middletown Symphony Women, 1992—; hon. bd. dirs. Am. Cancer Soc., 1961—; chmn. legis. City Charter Rev. Com., 1970, charter revision com. 1989; residential chmn. United Way, 1976, residential-retiree chmn., 1990; chmn. Sch. Tax Levy, 1978; mem. Middletown City Commn., 1983-88; mem. exec. com. Ohio-Ky.-Ind. Regional Coun., 1986-88; mem. Bicentennial Com. of Middletown; mem. Citizen's Adv. Com. for Miami U.; v.p. Middletown Needy Youth Bd.; mem. adv. bd. Manchester Tech. Ctr., Drug Task Force Bd., Middletown Schs; bd. dirs. Citizens Adv. Bd. Manchester Technical, 1991—, fine arts Manchester Tech. Ctr., 1993—, Middletown Fine Arts, 1993—, Dental Emergency Fund Area Children, 1994—, DEFAC Bd., 1994—. Recipient Stuart Ives Service to Youth award, 1980. Mem. LWV (pres. 1962-63), PEO (pres. 1993—), Am. Soc. Clin. Pathologists, Registry Med. Technologists, Am. Bus. Women's Assn. (pres. 1961-62), Middletown C. of C., Browns Run Country Club, Sigma Sigma Sigma. Methodist. Home: 1909 Antrim Ct Middletown OH 45042-2901

SCHAEFER, SUSAN GENE, lawyer; b. Chgo., Feb. 15; d. Oscar and Sally (Goodman) S. BA, UCLA, 1965, JD, 1968. Rsch. atty. Superior Ct., L.A., 1968-71; atty. MCA, Inc., Universal City, Calif., 1971-73; bus. affairs exec. William Morris Agy., Beverly Hills, Calif., 1975-81; ptnr., head entertainment law dept. Hufstedler, Miller, Carlson & Beardsley, L.A., 1981-84; v.p. bus. affairs Telepictures Prodns., Inc., L.A., 1984-86; prin. Law Offices of Susan G. Schaefer, L.A., 1984—. Author publs. Representing TV Writers: How to Negotiate a TV Movie Deal, 1991, Representation in the Entertainment Industry, 1992, L.A. Superior Ct. Writs and Receivers Policy and Procedural Manual, 1971; mem. adv. editorial bd. Entertainment Law Jour., 1981, 82. Named one of 50 most powerful female execs. Hollywood Reporter, 1994. Mem. Acad. TV Arts and Scis., Women in Film (bd. dirs. 1988-90), Los Angeles County Bar Assn. (chair intellectual property sect. 1982-83, trustee 1989-90), Century City Bar Assn. (pres. 1988, chair entertainment law sect. 1980-81, Spl. Achievement award 1982, Outstanding Svc. award 1989, bd. govs. 1981-91), Fin. and Adminstrv. Mgmt. Execs. (bd. dirs. 1994-95), Century City C. of C. (bd. dirs. 1988, Law Outstanding Achievement award 1990). Office: 1990 S Bundy Dr Ste 630 Los Angeles CA 90025

SCHAEFER, SUSAN TOBY, public relations executive; b. Phila., Apr. 5, 1950; d. Jack Bertram and Emma Norma (Sisken) S.; m. Robert John Ingram, Apr. 5, 1982 (div. Nov. 1988); m. Tom Vandervoort, Mar. 11, 1990 (div. 1993). BA, Temple U., 1971, MA, 1976. Cert. Conflict Mgmt., 1991; accredited Pub. Rels., 1987. Dir. bilingual English program Camden County Coll., Camden, N.J., 1976-79; editor, co-publisher South St. Star Newspaper, Phila., 1981-83; editor, writer, speechwriter Inst. for Sci. Info., Canden, 1982-83; dir. pub. rels. Provident Nat. Bank, Phila., 1983-84; pres., CEO Ingram & Picker Pub. Rels., Balacynwyd, Pa., 1984-88; sr. pres. pub. affairs Yeager, Pine & Mondale Pub. Rels., Mpls., 1988-92; prin. Schaefer Comm., Mpls., 1992—; adj. prof. English Temple U., Phila., 1974-82; prof. pub. rels. St. Joseph's U., Phila., 1987-88. Bd. dirs. Friends of the Libr. of Phila., 1984-88. Recipient Mayor's award City of Phila., 1987, Excellence award Internat. Assn. Bus. Communicators, 1989, 90, Best of Show award Minn. Pub. Rels. Soc., 1991. Mem. Pub. Rels. Soc. Am. (pres. bd. dirs. 1994—). Jewish. Office: Schafer Comm 333 Washington Ave N # 402 Minneapolis MN 55401

SCHAEFFER, BARBARA HAMILTON, retired rental leasing company executive; b. Newton, Mass., Apr. 26, 1926; d. Peter Davidson Gunn and Harriet Bennett (Thompson) Hamilton; m. John Schaeffer, Sept. 7, 1946; children—Laurie, John, Peter. Student, Skidmore Coll., 1943-46; AB in English, Bucknell U., 1948; postgrad. Montclair State U., 1950-51, Bank St. Coll. Edn., 1959-61, Yeshiva U., 1961-62; student Daytona Beach Coll., 1984. Cert. primary, secondary tchr., N.J. Dir. Pompton Plains Sch., N.J., 1959-62; adviser Episcopal Sch., Towaco, N.J., 1968-70; v.p. Deltona-DeLand Trolley, Orange City, Fla., 1980-81; pres. Monroe Heavy Equipment Rentals, Inc., Orange City, 1981—, also Magic Carpet Travel, 1985-88 cons., founder, pres. TLC Travel Club, Orange City, 1981-88; lectr. on children's art, 1959-70. Contbr. articles to profl. publs. Mem. LWV, AAUW, Internat. Platform Assn., Small Bus. Devel. Regional Ctr. (Stetson U. chpt.). Episcopalian. Avocations: restoring old homes, oil painting, piano, writing. Home: 400 Foothill Farms Rd Orange City FL 32763-5502 Address: PO Box 688 Debary FL 32713-0688

SCHAEFFER, ELAINE, environmental engineer; b. Washington; d. Maurice and Sarah (Siegel) S. BS, U. Md., 1977; MS, George Washington U., 1983. Registered profl. engr., D.C., Md., Va. From chemist to asst. mgr. chemistry Burton Parsons, Seat Pleasant, Md., 1978-80; task leader Alcon/Burton Parsons, Seat Pleasant, Md., 1980; from environ. engr. to project mgr. Benmol Corp., Alexandria, Va., 1981-83; dir., environ. svcs. County of Fairfax, Lorton, Va., 1983—; regional monitoring com. Met. Coun. Govt., Washington, 1983—. O and M Excellence award U.S. EPA, 1983. Mem. Water Environ. Fedn. (edn. com. 1990-92), Va. Water Environ. Assn. (chmn. 1989-90), The Bench Sheet (editorial adv. bd. 1989—). Office: County of Fairfax 9399 Richmond Hwy Lorton VA 22079-1825

SCHAEFFER, MARTHA, fine art gallery executive; b. Springfield, Mass., Jan. 14, 1948; d. John A. and Beverly J. (Mortland) S.; m. Paul D. Feinstein, Sept. 24, 1983; children: Laura, Samantha; 1 stepchild, Emily. BA, Herbert Lehman Coll., 1974. Co-founder, v.p. Diversified Editions, N.Y.C., 1976-79; gallery dir. Gallery 410, N.Y.C., 1976-79; pres., founder Schaeffer Editions, N.Y.C., 1979-81, Schaeffer Fine Art, N.Y.C., 1981—. Mem. Pvt. Art

Dealers Assn., Coll. Art Assn., Confederation Internat. des Negotiants en Oeuvres d'Art, 1993. Office: Schaeffer Fine Art 500 E 77th St Apt 512 New York NY 10162-0001

SCHAEFFER, SUSAN FROMBERG, author, educator; b. Bklyn., Mar. 25, 1941; d. Irving and Edith (Levine) Fromberg; BA, U. Chgo., 1961, MA with honors, 1963, PhD with honors, 1966; m. Neil J. Schaeffer, Oct. 11, 1970; children: Benjamin Adam, May Anna. Instr. English, Wright Jr. Coll., Chgo., 1964-65; asst. prof. Ill. Inst. Tech., Chgo., 1965-67; successively asst. prof., asso. prof., prof. Bklyn. Coll., 1967—; guest lectr. U. Chgo., Cornell U., U. Ariz., U. Maine, Yale U., U. Tex., U. Mass. John Simon Guggenheim fellow; recipient E.L. Wallant award, Friends of Lit. award.; Prairie Schooner's Lawrence award; O. Henry award; Poetry award Centennial Rev. Mem. PEN, Authors Guild, Poetry Soc. Am. Democrat. Jewish. Author novels: Falling, 1973; Anya, 1974; Time In Its Flight, 1978; Love, 1981; The Madness of a Seduced Woman, 1983; Mainland, 1984, The Injured Party, 1986, Buffalo Afternoon, 1989, First Nights, 1993; poetry: The Witch and the Weather Report, 1972; Alphabet For the Lost Years, 1976; Granite Lady (nominee Nat. Book award), 1974; Rhymes and Runes of the Toad, 1975; The Bible of the Beasts of the Little Field, 1980; short stories: The Queen of Egypt and Other Stories, 1980; children's novel: The Dragons of North Chittendon, 1986, The Four Hoods and Great Dog, 1988. Address: 783 E 21st St Brooklyn NY 11210

SCHAFER, ALICE TURNER, mathematics educator; b. Richmond, Va., June 18, 1915; d. John H. and Cleon (Dermott) Turner; m. Richard Donald Schafer, Sept. 8, 1942; children: John Dickerson, Richard Stone. A.B., U. Richmond, 1936, D.Sc., 1964; M.S., U. Chgo., 1940, Ph.D. (fellow), 1942. Tchr. Glen Allen (Va.) High Sch., 1936-39; instr. math. Conn. Coll., New London, 1942-44; asst. prof. Conn. Coll., 1954-57, asso. prof., 1957-61, prof., 1961-62; prof. math. Wellesley Coll., 1962-80, Helen Day Gould prof. math., 1969-80, Helen Day Gould prof. math. emerita, 1980—, affirmative action officer, 1980-82; prof. math. Marymount U., Arlington, Va., 1989—; instr. U. Mich., Ann Arbor, 1945-46; lectr. Douglass Coll., New Brunswick, N.J., 1946-48; asst. prof. Swarthmore (Pa.) Coll., 1948-51, Drexel Inst. Tech., Phila., 1951-53; mathematician Johns Hopkins Applied Physics Lab., Silver Spring, Md., 1945; lectr. Simmons Coll., Boston, 1980-88, Radcliffe Coll. Seminars, Cambridge, Mass., 1980-85. Contbr. articles on women in math. and other articles to math. jours. Recipient Disting. Alumna award Westhampton Coll., U. Richmond, 1977; NSF sci. faculty fellow Inst. for Advanced Study, Princeton, N.J., 1958-59. Fellow AAAS (math. sect. A nominating com. 1979-83, mem.-at-large 1983-86, chair-elect sect. A 1991, chair 1992, retiring chair 1993, Assn. for Women in Math. rep., 1993—), AAUP (chmn. nat. com. W 1980-83, mem. nat. coun. 1984-87), Am. Math. Soc. (chmn. postdoctoral fellowship com. 1973-76, affirmative action procedures com. 1980-82, chair com. on Human Rights of Mathematicians 1988-94), Soc. Indsl. and Applied Math., Am. Statis. Assn., Inst. Math. Stats., Nat. Coun. Tchrs. of Math. (chair com. on women 1976-81), Math Assn. Am. (adv. com. for Women and Math. program 1987-89, dir. fund raising 1989-92, lectr. 1982—, chair devel. com. 1988-92), Internat. Congress Mathematicians (mem. fund raising com. 1986), Assn. for Women in Math. (pres. 1973-75, Alice T. Schafer Prize established 1989, chair fund raising com. 1992—), leader math. del. women mathematicians to People's Rep. China 1990), Phi Beta Kappa, Sigma Xi, Sigma Delta Epsilon. Home: 2725 N Pollard St Arlington VA 22207-5038 Office: Marymount U Dept Math 2807 N Glebe Rd Arlington VA 22207-4299

SCHAFER, SHARON MARIE, anesthesiologist; b. Detroit, Mar. 23, 1948; d. Charles Anthony and Dorothy Emma (Schweitzer) Pokriefka; m. Timothy John Schafer, Nov. 12, 1977; children: Patrick Christopher, Steven Michael. BS in Biology, Wayne State U., 1971, MD, 1975. Diplomate Am. Bd. Anesthesiology. Intern, resident Sinai Hosp. Detroit, 1975-78; pvt. practice anesthesiology Troy, Mich., 1988—. Mem. AMA, Am. Soc. Anesthesiologists. Roman Catholic. Home and Office: 5741 Folkstone Troy MI 48098-3154

SCHAFER, SHIRLEY KAY, executive secretary; b. McCook, Nebr., Dec. 21, 1938; d. Henry H. and Leta (Gettman) Reinek; m. Ted L. Schafer, Dec. 20, 1959 (div. Jan. 1983). B in Music Edn., U. Nebr., 1959, M in Edn. Adminstrn., 1988. Lic. real estate salesperson, Nebr. Tchr. Dewitt (Nebr.) Pub. Schs., 1959-60, Waco (Tex.) Pub. Schs., 1960-63, Corpus Christi (Tex.) Pub. Schs., 1963-65, Lincoln (Nebr.) Pub. Schs., 1965-67, Luth. Nursery Sch., Lincoln, 1967-74; mgr. Midwest Fashions, Omaha, 1974-75; mem. senatorial staff, clk. edn. com. Nebr. Legislature, Lincoln, 1976-82; office mgr. for Supreme Ct. judge Nebr. Supreme Ct., Lincoln, 1982-93; exec. sec. State Hwy. Commn., Lincoln, 1993—; legis. liaison, coord. gov.'s task force excellence edn. Nebr. Dept. Edn. Chair edn. and art ctr. and officer Jr. League Lincoln, 1965-74, bd. dirs., chair edn. com., publicity chair 50th yr., docent Sheldon Art Gallery, rep. Lincoln Art's Coun., rep. Inter-Club Coun., rep. alcohol studies, chair creativity ctr., publ. advt. chair, chair Disney on Parade, mem. various coms.; area chair Heart Assn. Am., Lincoln, 1982; coord. collegiate leadership seminar U. Kans. Mem. Nebr. Real Estate Commn., Engring. Club, Ea. Star, Alpha Phi (nat. bd. dirs. 1969-74, mem. adv. bd. 1989-92, chpt. advisor U. Nebr. Lincoln, 1992-94, rush chair, area dir. collegiate chpts. ctrl. area U.S. and Can., internat. chair nominations, dist. gov. Nebr., Iowa, S.D., program coord., Outstanding Alumnae Nu chpt. 1986), Phi Delta Kappa, Mu Phi Epsilon. Republican. Presbyterian. Home: 1941 Devonshire Dr Lincoln NE 68506 Office: State Hwy Commn 1500 Hwy 2 Lincoln NE 68509

SCHAFF, PAULA KAY, industrial company executive; b. Cape Girardeau, Mo., Oct. 10, 1945; d. Charles Henry Sr. and Elnora Pauline (Ridge) Canine; m. Fred Jon Schaff; 1 child, Kevin Jon. Student, Washtenaw Community Coll., U. Ill., Dana U., Heidelberg (Ohio) Coll. Successively records clk. PTO div., accounts payable clk., sec., sales specialist, exec. sec., customer svc. specialist Dana Corp., Chelsea, Mich., 1967-78, supr. customer svc., 1978-79, supr. customer svc., shipping and assembly PTO div., 1979-81; distbn. mgr. Dana Corp., Athens, Ga., 1981-85, Maumee, Ohio, 1985-88; gen. mgr. warehouse ops. div. Dana Corp., 1989-91, v.p., gen. mgr. distbn. svcs. div., 1991—. Mem. NAFE, Mgmt. Forum. Republican. Methodist. Office: Dana Corp Distbn Svcs Divsn PO Box 455 Toledo OH 43697-0455

SCHAFFER, TERESITA CURRIE, federal official; b. Washington, Sept. 28, 1945; d. Francis and Teresita (Sparre) Currie; m. Howard B. Schaffer, Oct. 25, 1971; children: Michael C., Christopher S. AB, Bryn Mawr Coll., 1966; Cert., Institut d'Etudes Politiques, Paris, 1965; postgrad., Georgetown U., 1973-74. Embassy officer U.S. Embassy, Tel Aviv, 1967-69; econ. officer U.S. Embassy, Islamabad, Pakistan, 1975-77; sci. attache U.S. Embassy, New Delhi, 1977-79; polit. analyst U.S. Dept. State, Washington, 1969-71, economist, 1972-73; div. chief, dir. Office Trade U.S. Dept. State, Washington, 1980-84; dir. Office Egyptian Affairs U.S. Dept. State, Washington, 1987-89, dep. asst. sec. for Near East and South Asia, 1989-92; amb. to Sri Lanka and Maldives U.S. Embassy, Colombo, Sri Lanka, 1992—. Author: Profile of Women in Bangladesh, 1986, Survey of Development Projects and Activities for Women in Bangladesh, 1986; chmn. editorial bd. Fgn. Svc. Jour., 1972-74. Mem. Am. Fgn. Svc. Assn. Office: U S Embassy, Colombo Sri Lanka

SCHAFFNER, JOAN ELSA, law educator; b. Mineola, N.Y., Apr. 23, 1957; d. George Alvin and Harriette Catherine (Wager) S. BSME, U. So. Calif., 1979, JD, 1990; MSME, MIT, 1981. Bar: Calif. 1990, D.C. 1992. Sr. cons., supr. Energy Mgmt. Assocs., Atlanta, 1981-86; generation analyst Ga. Power Co., Atlanta, 1986-87; assoc. Irell & Manella, L.A., 1990-91; law clk. to Hon. Mariana R. Pfaelzer U.S. Dist. Ct. (ctrl. dist.) Calif., L.A., 1991-92; assoc. prof. Nat. Law Ctr., George Washington U., Washington, 1992—. Convener fed. benefits subcom. L.A. working group, gender bias task force U.S. Ct. Appeals (9th cir.), 1991-92. Recipient numerous Am. Jurisprudence awards in Criminal Procedure, Bus. Orgns., and Profl. Responsibility, 1990. Mem. Soc. Am. Law Tchrs., Am. Intellectual Property Law Assn., Gaylaw, Animal Legal Def. Fund, Mortar Bd., Order of Laurel, Order of Coif, Phi Kappa Phi, Tau Beta Pi, Pi Tau Sigma. Office: George Washington U Nat Law Ctr 2000 H St NW Washington DC 20006-4208

SCHAFFNER, LINDA CAROL, biological oceanography educator; b. Freeport, N.Y., Dec. 8, 1954; d. John Charles Schaffner and Shirley Garnet Voges Sanders; m. Stephen Marshall Bennett, Apr. 7, 1979; 1 child, William Schaffner. BA, Drew U., 1976; MA, Coll. of William and Mary, 1981, PhD, 1987. Asst. prof. Va. Inst. Marine Sci., Coll. of William and Mary, Gloucester Point, 1988—; vis scientist Swedish Environ. Protection Bd., 1988. Contbr. articles to profl. jours. Scholar Drew U., 1975-76, Houston Underwater Club, 1981, U. Wash., 1983; grantee NOAA, 1987-91, U.S. Fish and Wildlife Svc., 1991, NOAA-EPA, 1991-93, 93—, Office of Naval Rsch., 1993—. Mem. Assn. of Women in Sci., Atlantic Estuarine Rsch. Soc. (treas. 1988-90), Estuarine Rsch. Fedn., Am. Soc. Limnology and Oceanography. Office: Sch Marine Sci RR 8 Gloucester Point VA 23062

SCHAKOWSKY, JANICE, state legislator; b. Chgo., May 26, 1944; d. Irwin and Tillie (Cosnow) Danoff; m. Harvey E. Schakowsky, Feb. 17, 1965 (div. 1980); children: Ian, Mary; m. Robert B. Creamer, Dec. 6, 1980; 1 stepchild, Lauren. BS, U. Ill., 1965. Cert. elem. tchr., Ill. Tchr. Chgo. Bd. Edn., 1965-67; organizer Ill. Pub. Action Coun., Chgo., 1976-85; exec. dir. Ill. State Coun. Sr. Citizens, Chgo., 1985-90; mem. Ill. Ho. Reps., 1990—. Bd. dirs. Ill. Pub. Action, 4 C's Day Care Coun., Evanston, Ill.; steering com. mem. Cook County Dem. Women, 1986-90; del. Nat. Dem. Conv., 1988; governing coun. Am. Jewish Congress, 1990—. Named Outstanding Legislator Interfaith Coun. for Homeless, 1993, Legislator of Yr. Ill. Nurses Assn., 1992, Ill. Assn. Cmty. Mental Health Agys., 1994, Coalition of Citizens with Disabilities and Ill. Coun. Sr. Citizens, 1993, Cmty. Action Assn., 1991, Champaign County Health Care Assn., 1992, Rookie of Yr. Ill. Environ. Coun., 1991. Mem. ACLU, NOW, Nat. Coun. Jewish Women, Ill. Pro-Choice Alliance, Evanston Mental Health Assn., Evanston Hist. Soc., Evanston Friends of Libr., Rogers Park Hist. Soc. Democrat. Jewish. Home: 1101 Ridge Ave Evanston IL 60202-1231 Office: Dist Office 2100 Ridge Ave Evanston IL 60201-2796*

SCHALLER, JANE GREEN, pediatrician; b. Cleve., June 26, 1934; d. George and May Alice (Wing) Green; children: Robert Thomas, George Charles, Margaret May. A.B., Hiram (Ohio) Coll., 1956; M.D. cum laude, Harvard U., 1960. Diplomate Am. Bd. Pediatrics, Am. Bd. Med. Examiners. Resident in pediatrics Children's Hosp.-U. Wash., Seattle, 1960-63; fellow immunology and arthritis Children's Hosp.-U. Wash., 1963-65; mem. faculty U. Wash. Med. Sch., 1965-83, prof. pediatrics, 1975-83; head div. rheumatic diseases Children's Hosp., Seattle, 1968-83; prof., chmn. dept. pediatrics Tufts U. Sch. Medicine/New Eng. Med. Ctr., 1983—; pediatrician-in-chief Boston Floating Hosp., 1983—; vis. physician Med. Research Council, Taplow, Eng., 1971-72; bd. visitors Sch. of Medicine U. Pitts., 1989—. Author articles in field.; Editorial bds. profl. jours. Bd. dirs. Seattle Chamber Music Festival, 1982-85; trustee Boston Chamber Music Soc., 1985—; mem. Boston adv. coun. UNICEF. Mem. Inst. Medicine of NAS, AAAS (sci. and human rights program)), Soc. Pediatric Research, Am. Pediatric Soc., Am. Acad. Pediatrics (chmn. subcom. on children and human rights 1989—, com. on internat. child health 1990—), Am. Coll. Rheumatology, New Eng. Pediatric Soc. (pres. 1991-93), Assn. Med. Sch. Pediatric Chmn. (exec. com. 1986-89, rep. to council on govt. affairs and council of acad. socs.), Com. Health in So. Africa (exec. com. 1986—), Physicians for Human Rights (exec. com. 1986—, pres. 1986-89) Aesculapian Club (pres. 1988-89), Harvard U. Med. Sch. Alumni Council (v.p. 1977-80, pres. 1982-83), Internat. Rescue Com. (med. adv. com., women's commn. for refugee women and children, tech. adv. group for united nature study on the impact of war on children), Mass. Women's Forum, Internat. Women's Forum, Tavern Club, Saturday Club. Office: Floating Hosp for Children 750 Washington St Box 286 Boston MA 02111

SCHALLER, JOANNE FRANCES, nursing consultant; b. Columbus, Ga., July 15, 1943; d. John Frank and Ethel Beatrice (Spring) Lanzendorfer; m. Robert Thomas Schaller, Jan. 22, 1977 (div. Aug. 1987); 1 child, Amy. BS, Pacific Luth. U., 1969; M in Nursing, U. Wash., 1971. House supr. UCLA Hosp., 1971-72; outpatient supr. Harborview Hosp., Seattle, 1973-75; outpatient clinic and emergency room supr. U. Wash. Hosp., Seattle, 1975-77; coauthor, researcher with Robert Schaller MD Seattle, 1977-87; prin. Nursing Expert-Standards of Care, Seattle, 1987—; cons. Wash. State Trial Lawyers, Wash. Assn. Criminal Def. Lawyers, 1989—; founder, chief exec. officer Present Perfect, Seattle, 1991—. Contbr., editor articles to profl. jours. Bd. dirs. Pacific Arts Ctr.,1992—; vol. guardian ad litem King County Juvenile Ct., 1978—; vol. Make a Wish Found. U.S. Bank, 1984—, Multiple Sclerosis Assn., 1986—, Am. Heart Assn., 1986—, Internat. Children's Festival, 1987—, Seattle Children's Festival, 1987—, Seattle Dept. Parks and Recreation Open Space Com., 1990—, Pacific N.W. Athletic Congress, 1991—, Wash. Fed. Garden Clubs Jr. Advisor, 1992—, Fred Hutchison Cancer Rsch. Ctr., 1993; mem. parent coun. SCDS, 1986—; mem. Photo Coun. Art Mus., 1986—, Native Am. coun., 1989—; mem. N.W. coun. Seattle Mus., 1992—, mem. NAOO Coun., 1989—, Plestcheeff Inst. Decorative Arts, 1992—; mem, fundraiser Children's Hosp. Med. Ctr., 1977—, Breast Cancer Fund, 1994—, Susan G. Koaran Breast Cancer Found., 1994—; active Seattle Country Day Sch. Mem. AAUW, ANA, Wash. State Nurses Assn., U. Wash. Alumni Assn. Home and Office: 914 Randolph Pl Seattle WA 98122-5267

SCHALLER, JOYCE ANN, marketing professional; b. Ridley Park, Pa., Dec. 4, 1957; d. Joseph Adolph and Louise (Colasante) Morelli; m. James L. Schaller, June 18, 1994. BS in Mktg. cum laude, U. Pa., 1982; MBA in Pharm. Mktg., St. Joseph's U. Internat. market analyst Franklin Mint, Franklin Center, Pa., 1982-84; asst. product mgr. Hunt Mfg., Phila., 1984-85; quality assurance analyst IMS Am., Ltd./Dun and Bradstreet, Inc., Plymouth Meeting, Pa., 1986-91, nat. field mgr., 1987-90, sr. account exec., 1991-92, nat. sales mgr., 1992—. Vol. Jr. Orange Bowl, Miami, 1986, United Cerebral Palsy Assn. Annual Benefit, Phila., 1985-88. Recipient Fundraising Vol. award United Cerebral Palsy Assn., 1986; named one of Outstanding Young Women in Am., 1988. Mem. Phila. Direct Mktg. Assn., Mktg. Rsch. Assn., Am. Mktg. Assn. Republican. Office: IMS Am Ltd 660 W Germantown Pike Plymouth Meeting PA 19462

SCHANDER, MARY LEA, police official; b. Bakersfield, Calif., June 11, 1947; d. Gerald John Lea and Marian Lea Coffman; B.A. (Augustana fellow) Calif. Luth. Coll., 1969; M.A., U. Calif., Los Angeles, 1970; m. Edwin Schander, July 3, 1971. Staff aide City of Anaheim (Calif.) Police Dept., 1970-72, staff asst., 1972-78, sr. staff asst., 1978-80; with Resource Mgmt. Dept., City of Anaheim, 1980-82; asst. to dir. Pub. Safety Agy., City of Pasadena Police Dept., 1982-85, spl. asst. to police chief, 1985-88, adminstrv. comdr., 1988-92, police comdr., 1992—; freelance musician; publisher Australian Traditional Songs, 1985, Songs in the Air of Early California, 1994; lectr. Calif. Luth. Coll.; cons. City of Lodz, Poland, Internat. Assn. Chiefs of Police; assessor Nat. Commn. on Accreditation for Law Enforcement Agencies; speaker, panelist League of Calif. Cities, Pasadena Commn. on Status of Women. Producer (cable TV program) Traditional Music Showcase. Contbr. articles in field to profl. jours. Bd. dirs. Women At Work, Pasadena Pops Orch. Recipient Women at Work Medal of Excellence, 1988. Mem. Nat. Womens Political Caucus, Pasadena Arts Coun., L.A. County Peace Officers, Internat. Assn. Chiefs of Police. Home: PO Box 50151 Pasadena CA 91115 Office: Pasadena Police Dept 207 N Garfield Ave Pasadena CA 91101-1791

SCHANEY, DIANA L., accountant; b. Butler, Pa., July 31, 1947; d. Wayne Frederick and Helen Elaine (Horton) Herrit; m. C. Raymond Schaney, Feb. 8, 1969; children: Christopher Raymond, Nathan Frederick. RN, Lutheran Hosp. Sch. Nursing, 1968; BA in Acctg. magna cum laude, Edinboro U. of Pa., 1984. CPA. Oper. rm. nurse various hosps., 1968-81; staff acct. Local CPA Firm, Erie, Pa., 1984-87; ptnr. Local CPA Firm, Erie, 1988-89; sole pratitioner Diana L. Schaney, CPA, Erie, 1989-90; ptnr. Coleman Schaney & Co., Erie, 1990—. Mem. bd. dirs., treas. The Achievement Ctr., 1989—. Mem. Am. Inst. CPA's, Pa. Inst. CPA's (sec. Erie chpt.), Inst. Mgmt. Accts., Rotary Internat., Women's Roundtable of Erie. Republican. Episcopalian. Home: 307 Rice Ave Girard PA 16417 Office: Coleman Schaney & Co 1805 West 38th St Erie PA 16508

SCHANFIELD, FANNIE SCHWARTZ, community volunteer; b. Mpls., Dec. 25, 1916; d. Simon Zouberman and Mary (Schmilovitz) Schwartz; m. Melvin M. Stock, Oct. 27, 1943 (dec. Apr. 1944); 1 child, Moses Samuel Schanfield; m. Abraham Schanfield, Aug. 28, 1947; children: David Colman, Miriam Schanfield Kieffer. Student, U. Minn., 1962-75. Bd. dirs. Jewish Cmty. Ctr., Mpls., 1983—, chairperson older adult needs, 1982-88; past pres. Bnai Emet Women's League, Mpls., 1988-90; rschr., advocate Hunger Hennepin County, Mpls., 1969-75; sec. Joint Religious Legis. Coalition; v.p., bd. dirs. Cmty. Housing Svc., Mpls., 1971-85. Recipient Citation of Honor Hennepin County Commn., 1989. Mem. NOW, Lupus Found. Minn., Internat. Soc. Poets, Hadassah (prs. 1967-69, Citation 1969). Jewish. Home: 3630 Phillips Pky Minneapolis MN 55426-3776

SCHANSTRA, CARLA ROSS, technical writer; b. Berwyn, Ill., Sept. 4, 1954; d. Caroles Schanstra and Heather Millar (Thomson) Alonso. BA, Western Ill. U., 1976; postgrad., U. Ill. Circle, Chgo., 1980-81. Assoc. editor Hitchock Pub., Wheaton, Ill., 1976-80; assoc. product mgr. Advanced Systems, Inc., Elk Grove Village, Ill., 1980-81; tech. writer Profl. Computer Resources, Oak Brook, Ill., 1982; sr. tech. writer AT&T Bell Labs., Naperville, Ill., 1982—; freelance writer, 1980-85. Author: (stage plays) A Little Bit of Both, The Reversible Play, Survivors, Snakes and Apple Pie, It Should Be Obvious, Pastiche, A Model Home; contbr. articles to profl. jours. Violist DuPage Symphony, Glen Ellyn, Ill., 1984-87, 90-93, Elgin (Ill.) Symphonette, 1985-87. Mem. So. Tech. Comm. Assn. (award of excellence 1985), Dramatists Guild, Feminist Writers Western Suburbs (founder), Feminist Writers Guild Chgo. (adv. panel), Internat. Soc. Dramatists, Ill. Theatre Assn., Writers Workshop (co-founder). Office: AT&T Bell Labs IH-2C-312 2000 N Naperville Rd Naperville IL 60563-1443

SCHANZLIN, PATRICIA ROBERTS, mortgage banking company executive; b. York, Pa., Apr. 15, 1944; d. Thomas William and Mary Elizabeth (Christine) Roberts; m. Donald Nelson Schanzlin, Feb. 19, 1966; children: Todd Byron, Lauren Leigh. BS, Beaver Coll., 1966. Asst. v.p. City Fed. Savs. & Loan, Somerset, N.J., 1978-81; sr. v.p. adminstrn. City Mortgage, Somerset, 1981-82; sr. v.p. loan adminstrn. City Fed. Mortgage, Somerset, 1982-86; sr. v.p. systems and ops. Meritor Mortgage Group/Meritor Fin., Phila., 1986-88; sr. v.p. loan adminstrn. Cenlar FSB, Princeton, N.J., 1988-91; dir. mortgage svcs. Dime Savs. Bank, Uniondale, N.Y., 1991-92; exec. v.p. Meridian Mortgage Corp., Wayne, Pa., 1992—. Bd. dirs. jr. bd. Florence Crittenden Home, Trenton, N.J., 1973-76, chair, 1975-76. Mem. Mortgage Bankers of Am. (chmn. automation com. 1985-87, vice chmn. loan adminstrn. com. 1986-90, chmn. 1990-91, chmn. FHA/VA liaison com. 1988-90, gov. 1989—), Computer Power Inc. User's Group (steering com. 1985—, chairperson 1989-91). Republican. Office: Meridian Mortgage Corp 744 W Lancaster Ave Wayne PA 19087-9999

SCHAPIRO, MARY, federal agency administrator, lawyer; b. N.Y.C., June 19, 1955; d. Robert D. and Susan (Hall) S.; m. Charles A. Cadwell, Dec. 13, 1980. BA, Franklin and Marshall Coll., 1977; JD, George Washington U., 1980. Bar: D.C. 1980. Trial atty., 1980-81; counsel to chmn. Commodity Futures Trading Commn., 1981-84; gen. counsel Futures Industry Assn., 1984-88; commr. SEC, Washington, 1988-94; chmn. CFTC, Washington, 1994—. Office: CFTC Ste 800 2033 K St Nw Washington DC 20581

SCHARF-GARCIA, VERONICA, artist, registrar; b. Concepcion, Chile, June 19, 1959; came to U.S., 1979; d. Arthur and Izabella (Grabowski) Scharf; m. Luis Y. Garcia, Mar. 19, 1980; 1 child, Alexander Scharf. BFA, Colo. Coll., 1982. Mgr. La Vicuna, Inc., Colorado Springs, Colo., 1983-87; design asst. Ctr. for the Fine Arts, Miami, Fla., 1987-90; registrar and curator Mus. of Art, Ft. Lauderdale, Fla., 1991—; curator Cuzco Painting Exhbn., 1993, Ann. Art Competition, 1991-93. One-person shows include Colo. Coll., Colorado Springs, 1985; group exhbns. include Art and Cultural Ctr., Hollywood, Fla., 1990, OK South Gallery, Bal Harbor, Fla., 1989, Frances Wolfson Gallery, Miami, 1989, Park Gallery, Ft. Lauderdale, Fla., 1989, Bakehouse Complex, Miami, 1989, Broward ArtGuild, Ft. Lauderdale, 1989, Gallery Helene Grubair, Miami, 1989, Mill Gallery, Guilford, Conn., 1991, Metro-Dade Cultural Ctr., Miami, 1991, Art Collectors Inc., Miami, 1993. Home: 798 Crandon Blvd # 25 Key Biscayne FL 33149 Office: Museum of Art 1 E Las Olas Fort Lauderdale FL 33301

SCHAROLD, MARY LOUISE, psychoanalyst, educator; b. Wichita Falls, Tex., Mar. 3, 1943; d. Walter John and Louise Helen (Hartman) Baumgartner; m. William Ballew McCollum, Aug. 23, 1964 (div. 1981); m. Harry Karl Scharold, June 19, 1982; children: Margaret Louise, Walter Ballew. BA with highest distinction, U. Kans., 1964; MD, Baylor Coll. Med., 1968; postgrad. Topeka Inst. for Psychoanalysis, 1981. Diplomate Am. Bd. Psychiatry and Neurology. Intern Meml. Baptist. Hosp., Houston, 1968-69; resident in psychiatry Baylor Coll. Med., Houston, 1969-72, chief resident, 1971-72; practice of medicine specializing in psychoanalysis, Houston, 1972—; asst. prof. Baylor Coll. Med., Houston, 1973-76, asst. clin. prof., 1981-84, asso. clin. prof., 1984—; dir. Baylor Psychiat. Clinic, Houston, 1973-76; co-dir. Rice U. Psychiat. Service, Houston, 1981-82; asst. clin. prof. U. Kans. Sch. Medicine, Kansas City, 1977-81; teaching assoc. Topeka Inst. Psychoanalysis, 1980-81; instr. Houston-Galveston Psychoanalytic Inst., 1984-86, teaching analyst, 1986-90, tng. and supervising analyst, 1990—, v.p., 1994—; Adv. bd. Leavenworth Mental Health Assn., Kans., 1977-81. Watkins scholar U. Kans., 1961-64. Fellow Am. Psychiatric Assn. (chmn. Tex. peer review 1984-88); mem. Am. Psychoanalytic Assn. (cert. 1982, peer rev. com. 1985-90, prof. ins. commn. 1986-93, bd. profl. stds., 1994—, CME com., 1994—), Am. Group Psychotherapy Assn., Houston Psychiatric Soc. (v.p. 1984-85, pres. elect 1985-86, pres. 1986-87), Houston-Galveston Psychoanalytic Soc. (sec.-treas. 1984-86, pres.-elect 1986-88, pres. 1988-90), Am. Psychiat. Assn. (quality assurance com. 1986-87), Houston Group Psychotherapy Soc. (adv. bd. 1984-85), Mortar Bd., Phi Beta Kappa, Delta Phi Alpha, Alpha Omega Alpha, Hilltopper, Pi Beta Phi Alumni Assn. Republican. Lutheran. Office: 3400 Bissonnet St Ste 170 Houston TX 77005-2153

SCHARRER, BERTA VOGEL, anatomy and neuroscience educator; b. Munich, Dec. 1, 1906; d. Karl and Johanna V.; widowed. PhD in Zoology, U. Munich, 1930; MD (hon.), U. Giessen, Germany, 1976, U. Frankfurt, Germany, 1992; DSc (hon.), Northwestern U., 1977, U. N.C., 1978, Smith Coll., 1980, Harvard U., 1982, Yeshiva U., 1983, Mt. Holyoke Coll., 1984, SUNY, 1985, U. Salzburg, Austria, 1988; LLD, U. Calgary, Alta., Can., 1982. Research assoc. Research Inst. for Psychiatry, Munich, 1931-34, Neurol. Inst., Frankfurt-am-Main, 1934-37, U. Chgo. Dept. Anatomy, 1937-38, Rockefeller Inst., N.Y.C., 1938-40; instr., fellow Western Res. U. Dept. Anatomy, Cleve., 1940-46; John Guggenheim fellow U. Colo. Dept. Anatomy, Denver, 1947-48, spl. USPHS research fellow, 1948-50; asst. prof. (research) dept. anatomy U. Colo. Sch. Medicine, Denver, 1950-55; prof. anatomy Albert Einstein Coll. Medicine, 1955-77, acting chmn., 1965-67, 76-77, disting. prof. emeritus anatomy and neurosci., 1978—. Decorated Order of Merit (Free State of Bavaria); recipient Kraepelin gold medal, 1978, F.C. Koch award Endocrine Soc., 1980, Nat. Medal Sci., 1983. Mem. NAS, Am. Acad. Arts and Scis., Deutsche Acad. Naturforscher Leopoldina (Schleiden medal 1983), Am. Assn. Anatomists (pres. 1978-79, Henry Gray award 1982), Am. Soc. Zoologists (hon. mem.), Soc. Neurosci., Endocrine Soc. (F.C. Koch award 1980). Home: 1240 Neill Ave Bronx NY 10461-1736 Office: Albert Einstein Coll Med Dept Anatomy 1300 Morris Park Ave Bronx NY 10461-1975

SCHARUDA, VICTORIA, lawyer; b. Vineland, N.J., Aug. 3, 1967; d. Victor Scharuda and Elizabeth (Repin) Bennett. BA in History, Ursinus Coll., 1989; JD, Temple U., 1992. Bar: Ga. 1993. Corp. counsel Wells Fargo Armored Svc. Corp., Atlanta, 1993—. Active 1000 Lawyers for Justice, Atlanta, 1993. Recipient James D. Mandarino award Phila. Trial Lawyers Assn., 1992. Mem. NAFE. Office: Wells Fargo Armored Svc Corp 6165 Barfield Rd Ste 200 Atlanta GA 30328

SCHAUB, MARILYN MCNAMARA, religion educator; b. Chgo., Mar. 24, 1928; d. Bernard Francis and Helen Katherine (Skehan) McNamara; m. R. Thomas Schaub, Oct. 25, 1969; 1 dau., Helen Ann. B.A., Rosary Coll., 1953; Ph.D., U. Fribourg, Switzerland, 1957; diploma, Ecole Biblique, Jerusalem, 1967. Asst. prof. classics and Bibl. studies Rosary Coll., River Forest, Ill., 1957-69; prof. Bibl. studies Duquesne U., Pitts., 1969-70, 73—; participant 8 archeol. excavations, Middle East; adminstrv. dir. expedition to the Southeast Dead Sea Plains, Jordan, 1989—; hon. assoc. Am. Schs. Oriental Rsch., 1966-67, trustee, 1986-89; Danforth assoc., 1972-80. Author: Friends and Friendship for St. Augustine, 1964; translator: (with H. Richter) Agape in the New Testament, 3 vols, 1963-65. Mem. Soc. Bibl. Lit., Catholic Bibl. Assn., Am. Acad. Religion. Democrat. Home: 25 McKelvey Ave Pittsburgh PA 15218-1452 Office: Duquesne U Theology Dept Pittsburgh PA 15282

SCHAUB, MARY EMERSON, social services administrator, social worker; b. Norfolk, Va., Oct. 20, 1922; m. Charles E. Schaub, June 10, 1952; children: Mary, Margaret. B Gen. Studies cum laude, Tex. Christian U., 1976; MS in Social Work, U. Tex., Arlington, 1986. Cert. social worker, Tex.; lic. mater social worker advanced practice. Asst. coord. Johnson County Indigent Health Care, Cleburne, Tex., 1986-88, coord., 1988—; adj. prof. in social work S.W. Adventist Coll., 1992, 94; mem. Johnson County Mental Health Adv. Bd., 1988—, Johnson County Task Force Human Svcs., 1989—. Bd. dirs. Johnson County Family Crisis Ctr., 1989-93. Mem. NASW (Tex. task force on AIDS 1988-90). Office: Johnson County Indigent Health Care PO Box 709 Cleburne TX 76033

SCHAUBERGER, GINNY MARGERY, construction company executive; b. Roslyn, N.Y., Dec. 25, 1956; d. Richard Clement and Virginia Wilder (Small) Benning; m. Shelley Lee Schauberger, Aug. 20, 1988; children: Christopher Neil, David Ryan. Student, Phoenix Coll., 1990-93, Ariz. State U., 1993—. Asst. pers. dir. Hyatt Hotels, Phoenix, 1979-83; pers. dir. Heritage Hotel, Phoenix, 1983-88; v.p. Decca Constrn. Co., Phoenix, 1988—; notary public. Youth sponsor First Christian Ch., Phoenix, singles minister, 1988-90; vol. Ctrl. Ariz. Shelter Svcs., Phoenix, 1993. Mem. Valley Hospitality Pers. Dirs. (sec. 1984-86), Phi Theta Kappa. Republican. Home: 3321 W Roma Ave Phoenix AZ 85017

SCHAUBMAN, AVERI LYN, social worker; b. N.Y.C., Nov. 2, 1955; d. Gerald Eli and Toby (Cohen) S.; m. Bruce Alan Stoebner, June 18, 1989. BA, Clark U., Worcester, Mass., 1976; MSW, U. Denver, 1979. Lic. clin. social worker; cert. practitioner neuro-linguistic programming. Child care worker ARCHway, Inc., Worcester, 1976-77; social worker Cen. Denver Youth Div., 1979-80; asst. dir. Roundup Fellowship, Denver, 1980-85; clinical social worker Cherry Creek Sch. Dist., Aurora, Colo., 1985—; pvt. practice Denver, 1988—; cons. Colo. Dept. of Edn., Denver, 1982-93; pro bono mental health care Mental Health Assn. of Colo., 1988-89. Project Dir. Research-needs assessment, 1981. Bd. dirs. Chestor House, Inc., Boulder, Colo., 1985-90. Grantee Colo. Autism Project Devel. Disabilities Coun., 1981. Mem. NASW, Assn. Persons with Severe Handicaps (Colo. chpt. sec. 1984-86), Denver Assn. Retarded Citizens, Nat. Autism Soc. (Colo. chpt. bd. mem. 1979-83). Democrat. Home: 2554 Hudson St Denver CO 80207-3232

SCHAUENBERG, SUSAN KAY, educator, counselor; b. Taylor Ridge, Ill., Oct. 23, 1945; d. Albert George and Elizabeth (Stedman) Grill; m. Robert Dale Schauenberg Jr.; 1 child, Trevor Alan. BA, Marycrest Coll., 1967; MA, U. Iowa, 1968. Counselor, assoc. prof. Black Hawk Coll., Moline, Ill., 1971—; bus. cons., Rock Island, 1984—; v.p. faculty senate Black Hawk Coll., 1980-82. Planning com. United Way Orgn., Quad-Cities, Ill., 1981-84, agy. rels. com., 1981-82, allocations com., 1980-82; den mother Rock Island chpt. Boy Scouts Am., 1978-79; sponsor Christmas fundraiser for 100 children, yearly. Named one of Most Admired Women of the Quad-Cities, 1975; won L.I.V.E. Volunteerism honor for peer counselor-aide program, 1991. Mem. Assn. of Psychol. Type, Friends of Jung, Am. Fedn. Tchrs., Ill. Guidance and Personnel Assn. (Black Hawk chpt.), U. Iowa Alumni Assn., Phi Gamma Delta (mem. Parents Assn.). Home: 8428 104th Ave W Taylor Ridge IL 61284 Office: Black Hawk Coll 6600 34th Ave Moline IL 61265-5870

SCHAUER, CATHARINE GUBERMAN, public affairs specialist; b. Woodbury, N.J., Sept. 24, 1945; d. Jack and Anna Ruth (Felipe) Guberman; m. Irwin Jay Schauer, July 4, 1968; children: Cheryl Anne, Marc Cawin. AB, Miami-Dade Jr. Coll., 1965; BEd, U. Miami, 1967; postgrad. Mercer U., 1968, MPA, Troy State U., 1995. Writer, Miami (Fla.) News, 1962-63; tchr. Dade County Schs., Miami, Fla., 1967-68; coordinator pub. info. Macon Jr. Coll. (Ga.), 1968-69; writer Atlanta Jour., 1969-72; editor Ridgerunner newspaper, Woodbridge, Va., 1973-75; pub. info. specialist Dept. Interior, Washington, 1980-82; writer Dept. Army, Ft. Belvoir, Va., 1982-84, chief prodn., design and editorial, publs. div., 1984-85; head writer-editor SE region U.S. Naval Audit Service, Virginia Beach, Va., 1986; pub. affairs specialist, tech. rep. for vis. ctr. ops., NASA Langley, 1986-90, project mgr., chmn. 75th anniversary yr., 1991-92; NASA Langley Rsch. Ctr., Hampton, Va., 1987-89, acting head Office Pub. Svcs., 1989, pub. affairs officer for space NASA Langley, 1993—; columnist, writer Potomac News, Woodbridge, 1972-85. Contbr. articles to profl. jours. Historian, publicity chmn. PTO, Woodbridge, 1974; publicity chmn. Boy Scouts Am., Woodbridge, 1974-83, Girl Scouts U.S., Woodbridge, 1974-79; bd. dirs. Congregation Ner Tamid, Woodbridge, 1984-85. Recipient Outstanding Tng. Devel. Support award U.S. Army, 1983; 1st place news writing award and 1st place for advt. design Fla. Jr. Coll. Press Assn., 1964, 1st place feature writing award, 1964, 1st place news writing award Sigma Delta Chi, 1965, 70th anniversary team NASA, 1988, Long Duration Exposure Facility Team award NASA. Mem. Va. Press Women (1st Pl. Govt. Mags. 1991, 3d Pl. Govt. Brochures 1991, 1st Pl. Govt. Brochures 1993, 1st Pl. Govt. Media Campaign 1993), Women in Communications, Nat. Fedn. Press Women (1st Pl. Govt. Mags. 1991, 1st Pl. Govt. Media Campaign 1993). Democrat. Home: 120 Tide's Run Yorktown VA 23692-4333 Office: NASA Langley Rsch Ctr Mail Code 154 Hampton VA 23681-0001

SCHAUER, TONE TERJESEN, lawyer; b. Arendal, Norway, Jan. 1, 1941; came to U.S., 1958; d. Haakon and Signe (Andersen) Terjesen; children from previous marriage: Randi Vargas, Shawn Wilson, Kristina Schauer; m. John Richilano; 1 child, Jamie. BA, Colo. State U., 1969, M in French Lit., 1971; JD, U. Colo., 1977. Bar: Colo. 1977, U.S. Ct. Appeals (10th cir.) 1977. Dep. pub. defender State of Colo., Denver, 1977-83; pvt. practice Boulder, Colo., 1983-90, Denver, 1990—. Mem. ABA, Colo. Bar Assn., Denver Bar Assn. Democrat. Home: 356 Marion St Denver CO 80218-3928 Office: 150 E 10th Ave Denver CO 80203-2740

SCHAUF, VICTORIA, pediatrician, educator, researcher, consultant; b. N.Y.C., Feb. 17, 1943; d. Maurice J. and Ruth H. (Baker) Bisson; m. Michael Delaney; 2 children. BS with honors in Microbiology, U. Chgo., 1965, MD with honors, 1969. Intern pediatrics U. Chgo. Hosp., 1969-70; resident pediatrics Sinai Hosp. of Balt., 1970-71; chief resident pediatrics Children's Hosp. Nat. Med. Ctr., Washington, 1971-72; rsch. trainee NIH, Bethesda, Md., 1972; asst. prof. microbiology Rush Med. Coll., Chgo., 1972-74; prof. pediatrics, head pediatric infectious diseases U. Ill., Chgo., 1974-84; med. officer FDA, Rockville, Md., 1984-86; chmn. dept. pediatrics Nassau County Med. Ctr., East Meadow, N.Y., 1986-90; prof. pediatrics SUNY, Stony Brook, 1987—; vis. prof. Rockefeller U., 1990-92; mem. vis. faculty Chiang Mai (Thailand) U., 1978; mem. ad hoc com. study sects. NIH, Bethesda, 1981-82; bd. dirs. Pearl Stetler Rsch. Found., Chgo., 1982-84; cons. FDA, 1987-88, 93—, Can. Bur. Human Prescription Drugs, Ottawa, 1990—, biotech. investors, 1993—; course dir. pediatric infectious diseases rev. course Cornell U. Med. Coll., N.Y.C., 1994. Producer TV programs in field; contbr. articles to profl. jours., chpts. to books. Vol. physician Cook County Hosp., Chgo., 1974-84; mem. adv. com. Nat. Hansen's Disease Ctr., La., 1986, Nassau County Day Care Coun., N.Y., 1988-90; mem. adv. bd. Surg. Aid to Children of World, N.Y., 1986-90. Am. Lung Assn. grantee U. Ill., 1977; recipient contract NIH, U. Ill., 1978-81, grantee, 1979-84. Fellow Infectious Diseases Soc. Am.; mem. Pediatric Infectious Diseases Soc. (exec. bd.), Soc. Pediatric Rsch., Am. Pediatric Soc., AAAS, Am. Soc. Microbiology, Am. Acad. Pediatrics, NOW, Phi Beta Kappa, Alpha Omega Alpha.

SCHAUPP, JOAN POMPROWITZ, trucking company executive, writer; b. Green Bay, Wis., Sept. 29, 1932; d. Joseph and Helen Elizabeth (Vander-Linden) Pomprowitz; m. Robert James Schaupp, Sept. 4, 1956; children: Margaret Schaupp Siebert, Frederick, John Robert, Elizabeth Schaupp Sidles. BS cum laude, U. Wis., 1954; cert. in theology, St. Norbert Coll., 1979; MA, U. Wis., Green Bay, 1982. Rsch. asst. Calif. Inst. Tech., Pasadena, 1954-55; woman's editor Green Bay Press-Gazette, 1955-56; freelance writer Green Bay, 1957-75; sec.-treas., dir. L.C.L. Transit Co., Green Bay, 1962-70; dir. P & S Investment Co., Green Bay, 1982—, mgmt. cons., 1984-89, dir. strategic planning, 1992, vice chmn., 1994—; pres. The Manna Co., Green Bay, 1992. Author: Jesus Was a Teenager, 1972, Woman Image of Holy Spirit, 1975 (Thomas Moore Book award), Elohim: A Search for a Symbol for Human Fulfillment, 1994. Master gardener De Pere (Wis.) Beautification Com., 1991-92; lector, lay min. St. Francis Xavier Cathedral, Green Bay, 1991-92. Mem. Am. Acad. Religion, Nat. Fedn. Press Women, Nat. Press Club, Soc. Bibl. Lit., Equestrian Order of the Holy Sepulchre Jerusalem (lady, grand cross), Secular Franciscan Order (vice min. Assumption Province 1991-92). Home: PO Box 358 De Pere WI 54115-0358

SCHAUWECKER, MARGARET LIDDIE, construction company executive; b. Louisa, Ky., July 28, 1934; d. Mitchell and Mary Lou (Thompson) McKinster; m. Norman Walter Schauwecker, Aug. 30, 1953 (div. Oct. 1968); children: Johanna L., Mitchell Walter, Shawna Ann. Student, Bliss Coll., 1952-54, El Segundo Coll., 1957-59. Sec. N. Am. Aviation, Columbus, Ohio, 1952-1955, Gilfillan Electronics, Los Angeles, 1956-62; adminstrv. asst. Columbus Wood Preserving Co., 1970-78; pres. Ohio State Tie and Timber Inc., Louisa, Ky., 1978—. Named to Honorable Order Ky. Cols. Commonwealth Ky., 1984; recipient Outstanding Achievement in Sales Vol. award Ohio Dept. Econ. Devel., 1980, 81, 82; recipient Top 100 Small Bus's. in Ohio award Ohio House Reps., 1983. Mem. Am. Wood Preservers Assn., Railway Tie Assn., Bus. and Profl. Women in Constrn. Baptist. Club: Louisa Woman's. Lodges: Order Eastern Star, Rebekah. Home: 4015 Clabber Rd Columbus OH 43207-4202 Office: Ohio State Tie and Timber RR 1 Box 2360 Louisa KY 41230-9019

SCHECHTER, GERALDINE POPPA, hematologist; b. N.Y.C., Jan. 16, 1938; d. Josif and Victoria (Nosi) P.; m. Alan Neil Schechter, Feb. 6, 1965; children: Daniele Malka, Andrew M.R. AB, Vassar Coll., Poughkeepsie, N.Y., 1959; MD, Columbia U., 1963. Diplomate Am. Bd. Internal Medicine, Am. Bd. Hematology. Intern, resident Presbyn. Hosp., N.Y.C., 1963-65; resident, fellow, rsch. assoc. VA Med. Ctr., Washington, 1965-70, staff physician, 1970-74, chief hematology, 1974—; asst., assoc. prof. medicine George Washington U., Washington, 1971-81, prof. medicine, 1981—; mem. hematology com. Am. Bd. Internal Medicine, Phila., 1985-91, bd. dirs., 1990—. Mem. editorial bd. Blood, 1985-89. Contbr. articles to hematologic jours. Office: VA Med Ctr Hematology Sect 50 Irving St NW Washington DC 20422-0001

SCHECTMAN, AMY NAN, urban planner; b. Stamford, Conn., Oct. 23, 1956; d. Bernard and Marylin Helen (Gross) S.; m. Mitchell L. Rosenberg, May 27, 1984; children: Solomon Fredric Rosenberg, Noah Andrew Schectman. Bachelor's degree, Johns Hopkins U., 1978; Master of City Planning, MIT, 1982. Housing planner Cambridge (Mass.) Housing Authority, 1982-83; dir. state capital budget office Divsn. Capital Planning and Ops., Boston, 1983-87; lectr. urban planning MIT, Cambridge, 1987-92; planning dir. Boston Housing Authority, 1992—. Pres., bd. dirs. Cambridge YWCA, 1987-91; elected town meeting mem. Brookline (Mass.) Town Govt., 1992—; bd. dirs. Pierce Sch. Extended Day, Brookline, 1992—. Recipient citation outstanding performance Commonwealth Mass., 1985. Democrat. Jewish. Office: Boston Housing Authority 52 Chauncy St Boston MA 02111-2375

SCHEEDER, DONNA WILLS, library administrator; b. Buffalo, Nov. 8, 1947; d. Joseph Morris and Detta Olivia (Gorman) Wills. BS in Fgn. Svc., Georgetown U., 1969. Reference libr. Libr. of Congress, Washington, 1969-75, resource and devel. specialist, 1975-78, team leader, 1978-79, coord. congl. reference svcs., 1980—. Guest editor Spl. Librs., 1990. Mem. Adv. Neighborhood Commn., Washington, 1991-93, Civilian Complaint Rev. Bd., Washington, 1992—, vice chmn., 1994—; mem. D.C. Dem. State Com., 1985—, sec., 1988-92, vice chmn., 1992—; mem. steering com. Mayor's Pre-White House Conf. on Librs. and Info. Svcs.; mem. Dem. Nat. Com., 1992—; chmn. D.C. Women for Clinton/Gore, 1992. Mem. Spl. Librs. Assn. (mem., chmn. govt. rels. com. 1985-91, internat. rels. com. 1991-94, chmn-elect, chmn. news div. 1991—, pres.-elect, pres. Washington chpt. 1987-90, treas. 1994—), Assn. State Dem. Chairs (exec. bd. 1992—, v.p. 1994—). Roman Catholic. Home: 312 N Carolina Ave SE Washington DC 20003-2003 Office: Libr of Congress Congl Rsch Svc Washington DC 20540

SCHEER, ELAINE M., artist, educator; b. L.A., Jan. 31, 1958. Student, U. London, summer 1976; BA, Sonoma State U., 1979; MFA, San Francisco Art Inst., 1982. Lectr. U. Wis., Madison, 1988-90, asst. prof., 1990—; Sculptor's works include Peace Theater, 1986, Chess Game, 1989, Assumed Guilty, 1993; work is included in The History of American Ceramics, 1988. Sculptress works include Chess Game, 1989, Assumed Guilty, 1993; work included in Nat. Ceramics Invitational, West Chester, Pa., 1992, and Works Outside, Cin., 1990. Recipient Small Projects award Inter-Arts of Marin, San Anselmo, Calif., 1985-86; Arts-Industry residency N.J. Kohler Art Ctr., Sheboygan, Wis., 1986, Residency fellowship Mary Anderson Ctr. for Art, St. Francis, Ind., 1993, Artists fellowship Wis. Arts Bd., Madison, 1994. Mem. Internat. Sculpture Ctr., Women's Caucus for Art. Office: U Wis Art Dept 455 N Park St Rm 6241 Madison WI 53706-1483

SCHEER, TERRI LYNN, special education educator; b. St. Charles, Mo., Oct. 1, 1961; d. Michael Vincent Sr. and Christine May (Stepp) Brush. Student, U. Mo., 1984. Mental retardation profl. Community Living for Handicap, St. Charles, 1984-85; tchr. adult spl. edn. St. Louis Assn. for Retarded Citizens, 1985-86; tchr. spl. edn. Fransic Howell Sch. Dist., St. Charles, 1986-89; tchr. vocat. spl. edn. Spl. Sch. Dist., St. Louis, 1989—; mem. adv. bd. Lewis and Clark Tech. Sch., St. Charles, 1987-88; student coun. advisor West County Tech. Sch., St. Louis, 1989—, sr. class advisor, 1991—, mem. adv. bd. Vocat. Indsl. Clubs Am., 1991—. Explorer leader Boy Scouts Am., St. Louis, 1991-91. Mem. Mo. Vocat. Assn., Nat. Assn. Vocat. Edn. Spl. Needs Personnel.

SCHEETZ, SISTER MARY JOELLEN, English language educator; b. Lafayette, Ind., May 20, 1926; d. Joseph Albert and Ellen Isabelle (Fitzgerald) S. A.B., St. Francis Coll., 1956; M.A., U. Notre Dame, 1964; Ph.D., U. Mich., 1970. Tchr. English, Bishop Luers High Sch., Fort Wayne, Ind., 1965-67; acad. dean St. Francis Coll., Fort Wayne, 1967-68; pres. St. Francis Coll., Ft. Wayne, Ind., 1970-93; pres. emeritus; English lang. prof. St. Francis Coll., Ft. Wayne, Ind., 1993—. Mem. Delta Epsilon Sigma. Office: St Francis Coll 2701 Spring St Fort Wayne IN 46808

SCHEID, SUSAN ELIZABETH JEAN, mediator, lawyer; b. Chicago Heights, Ill., Jan. 31, 1949; d. Adolph Joseph and Betty Jean (Gurganus) S. BA in History, U. Chgo., 1971; JD, U. Iowa, 1974. Bar: N.Y. 1979, Iowa 1974. Internat. rep. Am. Fedn. State, County, and Mcpl. Employees, Iowa City, 1975-77; asst. gen. counsel Amalgamated Clothing and Textile Workers Union, N.Y.C., 1977-82; asst. counsel Writers Guild Am., N.Y.C., 1983-87; litigation sect. chief N.Y. State Dept. Law Charities Bur., N.Y.C., 1987-92; counsel Office of Medicaid Managed Care, N.Y.C., 1992—. Office: Medicaid Managed Care 250 Broadway Fl 14 New York NY 10007-2516

SCHEIDENHELM, CAROL ELIZABETH, academic program coordinator; b. LaSalle, Ill., July 4, 1946; d. Peter Joseph and Marjorie Lorraine (Lindbeck) Donohue; m. Lee Edgar Scheidenhelm, July 20, 1968; children: Kristen Ann, Matthew Peter. AA, Ill. Valley C.C., 1966; BS in Edn., Ill. State U., 1968; MA, U. No. Colo., 1971; student, No. Ill. U., 1980. Cert. elem. tchr., guidance counselor, alcohol and drug counselor, Ill.; nat. cert. counselor; lic. marriage and family therapist. Tchr. Ctrl. Sch., Amboy, Ill., 1968-71, Louise White Elem. Sch., Batavia, Ill., 1971-72; instr. Waunbonsee C.C., Surgar Grove, Ill., 1974-76; family therapist Luth. Social Svcs. Batavia, Ill., 1978-84, Kane-DeKalb Truancy Prevention Program, Geneva, Ill., 1984-90; guidance counselor, coord. student assistance program Glenbard Dist. # 87, Glen Ellyn, Ill., 1990—; pvt. practice marriage and family therapy, St. Charles, Ill., 1984—. Named Outstanding Young Woman Am., 1979; recipient Those Who Excel award Ill. State Bd. Edn., 1993. Mem. ACA, Am. Assn. Marriage and Family Therapy, Ill. Assn. Marriage and Family Therapy (pres. 1994—), Ill. Alcoholism and Drug Dependence Assn. Lutheran.

SCHEIN, SALLY JOY, special services and learning disabilities consultant, marriage and family counselor; b. Chgo., July 6, 1930; d. Rudolph James and Lillian (Cohen) Good; m. Michael Schein, Apr. 9, 1955; children: Jack Edward, David Lee. BA, U. Chgo., 1950, Columbia U., 1952; MS, CCNY, 1953; EdS, Seton Hall U., 1982, also doctoral coursework; EdD. Nova U., 1986. Occupational therapist Monmouth Meml. Hosp., Longbranch, N.J., 1953-54; tchr. nursery kindergarten N.Y. Dept. Welfare, N.Y.C., 1954-55; tchr. kindergarten Yonkers Pub. Sch., N.Y., 1955, Dumont Pub. Sch., N.J., 1955-56; learning disabilities teaching cons. Haworth, N.J., 1968-72, Caldwell, N.J., 1972-79, Cranford Pub. Sch., N.J., 1979-90; psychologist extern North Caldwell, Closter, N.J., 1976-77; counselor Community Mental Health Ctr., Dumont, 1981-82. Author: Welcome to Danish International Studies, 1979; (with E. Riley et al) Sparking Divergent Ability, 1985, Reducing Children's Vulnerability After Divorce, 1987. Founding mem. clin. bd. Community Mental Health Ctr., Dumont, 1958-60. Mem. Am. Assn. Marriage and Family Therapists, Nat. Assn. Sch. Psychologists, Assn. Learning Cons., Council Exceptional Children, Orton Soc. Avocations: Sculpting; art; jogging; travel. Home: 4 Harding Ave Dumont NJ 07628-1211

SCHEIN, VIRGINIA ELLEN, psychologist; b. Rahway, N.J., June 23, 1943; d. Jacob Charles and Anne S.; m. Rupert F. Chisholm. BA cum laude, Cornell U., 1965; PhD, N.Y.U., 1969. Lic. psychologist, Pa. 1 child, Alexander Nikos. Sr. research assoc. Am. Mgmt. Assn., N.Y.C., 1969-70; mgr. personnel research Life Office Mgmt. Assn., N.Y.C., 1970-72; dir. personnel research Met. Life Ins. Co. N.Y.C., 1972-75; asso. prof. Sch. Mgmt. Case Western Res. U., Cleve., 1975-76; vis. asso. prof. Sch. Orgn. and Mgmt., Yale U., New Haven, 1976-77; assoc. prof. mgmt. Wharton Sch. U. Pa., Phila., 1977-80; mgmt. cons. Virginia E. Schein, Ph.D., P.C., 1975—; assoc. prof. psychology Bernard M. Baruch Coll., City U. N.Y., 1982-85; prof. mgmt. Gettysburg Coll., Pa., 1986—, chair mgmt. dept., 1993—. Author: (with others) Power and Organization Development, 1988, Working from the Margins, 1995; mem. editorial rev. bds. Women Mgmt. Rev., Acad. Mgmt. Execs.; contbr. articles to profl. jours. Bd. dirs. Family Planning Ctr., Survivors, Inc., past pres. bd.; bd. dirs. Pvt. Industry Coun. Mem. Am. Psychol. Assn. (council reps. 1978-80, com. on women 1980-83), Met. Assn. Applied Psychology (pres. 1973-74), Acad. Mgmt., (rep. orgn. devel. div. 1979-81, mem. exec. com. women mgmt. divsn.), Internat. Assn. Applied Psychology, Am. Psychol. Soc., Psi Chi. Office: Gettysburg Coll Dept Mgmt Gettysburg PA 17325

SCHEINDLIN, SHIRA A., federal judge; b. Washington, Aug. 16, 1946; d. Boris and Miriam (Shapiro) Joffe; m. Stanley Friedman, May 22, 1982; 2 children. BA cum laude, U. Mich., 1967; MA in Far Ea. Studies, Columbia U., 1969; JD cum laude, Cornell U., 1975. Bar: N.Y. 1976. With Stroock, Stroock & Lavan, 1975-76; law clerk to Hon. Charles L. Brieant, Jr. U.S. Dist. Ct. (so. dist.) N.Y., 1976-77; asst. U.S. atty. Ea. Dist. N.Y., 1977-81; gen. counsel N.Y.C. Dept. of Investigation, 1981-82; U.S. magistrate U.S. Dist. Ct. (ea. dist.) N.Y., 1982-86; with Budd, Larner, Gross, Rosenbaum, Greenberg & Sade, Short Hills, N.J., 1986-90, ptnr., 1990; ptnr. Herzfeld & Rubin, N.Y.C., 1990-94; mem. Judicial Panel, 1992-94; judge U.S. Dist. Ct. (so. dist.) N.Y., 1994—; adj. prof. law Bklyn. Law Sch., 1983-94; mem. 2nd Cir. Conf. Planning Com., So. Dist. Adv. Com., 1991—. Bd. editors Cornell Law Rev., 1973-74. Recipient Spl. Achievement award Dept. of Justice, 1980. Mem. Fed. Bar Coun. (trustee 1986-88, 90—, v.p. 1988-90), N.Y. State Bar Assn. (chair comml. and fed. litigation sect. 1991-92), N.Y. County Lawyers Assn. (bd. dirs. 1992—, chair tort sect. 1992—), Assn. of Bar of City of N.Y. Office: US Courthouse Foley Square Rm 313 New York NY 10007*

SCHEIRER, MARY ANN, sociologist researcher; b. Akron, Ohio, July 19, 1941; d. John Marquis and Martha Lillian (White) Pittenger; m. Clark James Scheirer, July 4, 1965; children: Eric D., Laura A. BA, Coll. of Wooster, 1963; M of Pub. & Internat. Affairs, U. Pitts., 1969; MA, SUNY, Binghamton, 1973; PhD, Cornell U., 1979. Vol. U.S. Peace Corps, Philippines, 1963-66; fgn. student advisor admissions U. Pitts., 1967-70; rsch. assoc. SUNY, Binghamton, 1973-74; evaluation intern Broome Devel. Ctr., 1977-78; evaluation specialist Dept. Health, Edn. and Welfare U.S. Office of Edn., Washington, 1978-79; sr. rsch. assoc. JWK Internat., Inc., 1979-82; sr. study dir. Westat, Inc., 1982-88; spl. expert in program evaluation NIH, 1988-90; ind. cons. Annandale, Va., 1990—; invited speaker in field. Author: (book) Program Implementation: The Organizational Context, 1981; contbr. chpts. to books, articles to profl. jours. and tech. reports to profl. publs. Grantee NSF, 1981-82, 85, 88, Nat. Inst. Child Health and Human Devel., 1980, Nat. Inst. Dental Rsch., 1984-87, Nat. Bur. Stds., 1987. Mem. APHA, Am. Evaluation Assn. (bd. dirs. 1990-93), Am. Sociol. Assn., Washington Evaluators (chairperson 1993—). Home: 4616 Hillbrook Dr Annandale VA 22003-5921 Office: Evaluation & Social Rsch Cons 4616 Hillbrook Dr Annandale VA 22003-5921

SCHEITZACH, EVELYN B., manufacturing company executive; b. Seminole, Okla., June 14, 1941; d. Roy A. and Ida (Kirkpatrick) Boggs; m. James R. Mestepey (div. 1973); 1 child, Philip Todd; m. Duane R. Scheitzach; children: Michael Dean, Clay Bradley. BS in Indsl. Engring., La. State U., 1960; MBA, Ball State U., 1969; PhD, Walden U., 1983. Indsl. engr. E.I. DuPont de Nemours & Co., Inc., Orange, Tex., 1960-62, Chrysler Air Temp, Bowling Green, KY., 1967-73; ops. mgr. Popped Right, Marion, Ohio, 1978-83; cons. Dresser Ind., Marion, 1973-78, Mgmt. Co., Columbus, Ohio, 1983-84; owner S & A Enterprises, Inc., Clinton, Mich., 1984—; bd. dirs. Wyandotte Popcorn. Contbr. articles to profl. jours. Bd. dirs. Big Bros. Am., Marion, 1980-84; trustee First Presbyn. Ch., Marion, 1982-84; campaign organizer Reagan for Pres., Marion, 1983. Named Woman of Yr. Bus. and Profl. Women of Marion, 1982; Dept. Edn. grantee, 1968-69. Mem. Soc. Mfg. Engrs., Indsl. Engring. Soc. (pres. 1982-84), Am. Prodn. and Inventory Control Soc. (v.p. 1981-85). Republican. Home: 8600 Wellington Point Dr Irving TX 75063 Office: S&A Enterprises Inc PO Box 610 Guttenberg IA 52052-0610

SCHELAR, VIRGINIA MAE, chemistry educator, consultant; b. Kenosha, Wis., Nov. 26, 1924; d. William and Blanche M. (Williams) S. BS, U. Wis., 1947, MS, 1953; MEd, Harvard U., 1962; PhD, U. Wis., 1969. Instr. U. Wis., Milw., 1947-51; info. specialist Abbott Labs., North Chgo., Ill., 1953-56; instr. Wright Jr. Coll., Chgo., 1957-58; asst. prof. No. Ill. U., DeKalb, 1958-63; prof. St. Petersburg (Fla.) Jr. Coll., 1965-67; asst. prof. Chgo. State Coll., 1967-68; prof. Grossmont Coll., El Cajon, Calif., 1968-80; cons. Calif., 1981—. Author: Kekule Centennial, 1965; contbr. articles to profl. jours. Active citizens adv. coun. DeKalb Consol. Sch. Bd.; voters svc. chair League Women Voters, del. to state and nat. convs., judicial chair, election laws chair. Standard Oil fellow, NSF grantee; recipient Lewis prize U. Wis. Fellow Am. Inst. Chemists; mem. Am. Chem. Soc. (membership affairs com., chmn. western councilor's caucus, exec. com., councilor, legis. counselor, chmn. edn. com., editor state and local bulletins).

SCHELL, JACQUELYN ANN, elementary education educator; b. Binghamton, N.Y., Apr. 15, 1947; d. Robert Emory and Eleanor Bernadine (Shea) Finch; m. Michael William Schell, Aug. 30, 1969; children: Amy, Julie, Amanda, Carey, Kate. BS, Ithaca (N.Y.) Coll., 1969; MS magna cum laude, SUNY, Potsdam, 1983. Elem. tchr. pub. schs., N.Y., 1969—; tchr. Sci-Tech Ctr. of No. N.Y., Watertown, 1989—. Mem. sch. bd. Watertown City Sch. Dist., 1983—; mem. coll. coun. Oswego (N.Y.) Coll., 1990—; trustee Herrings Coll., Watertown, 1993—. Mem. AAUW, N.Y. State Sch. Bds., Jeff-Lewis Sch. Bds. Democrat. Roman Catholic. Home: 265 Paddock St Watertown NY 13601 Office: Sci-Tech of No NY 154 Stone St Watertown NY 13601

SCHELL, MERRY L., critical care and oncological nurse; b. Seminole, Tex., Sept. 16, 1946; d. Tiny Hollis and Mary Elizabeth (Yates) Odom; m. Thomas E. Schell, Jan. 17, 1965; children: Carrie Elizabeth, Thomas Wade. AS, Bakersfield Community Coll., 1977; BSBA, U. San Francisco, 1984. Cert. oncology nurse specialist. Dir. nursing Med. Pers. Pool, Bakersfield, Calif.; head nurse in oncology and hematology San Joaquin Community Hosp., Bakersfield; clin. dir. critical cre Delano (Calif.) Regional Med. Ctr. Mem. Oncology Nursing Soc.

SCHELLER, ERIN LINN, publishing company executive; b. Port Arthur, Tex., Dec. 25, 1942; d. Truman Edward Jr. and Margaret Jane (Imhoff) Linn; m. Herman Scheller, Oct. 19, 1983; 1 child, Christopher Wayne Levy. Student, Barat Coll., 1960-61; BS, U. Tex., 1964. Tchr. Cath. Sch. Dist., Houston, 1965-67; owner, pres. The Pub.'s Mark, Incline Village, Nev., 1982—; pres., chmn. bd. EduVision Inc., computer software co., Incline Village, 1994—; guest lectr. death edn. related orgns., U.S., 1982—. Author: Children Are Not Paper Dolls, 1982, I Know Just How You Feel, 1986, Dear Teacher, 1988, 150 Facts About Grieving Children, 1990, Premonitions, Visitations and Dreams, 1991. Advisor Mo. Bapt. Children's Group, St. Louis, 1980-81; chpt. leader The Compassionate Friends, Denver, 1980-81, Greeley, Colo., 1981-83; 2nd v.p. Republican Women's Club,

Incline Village, 1987-90; mem. AAUW, Incline Village, 1987-89; pres. Teester's Ladies Golf Assn., Incline Village, 1987-90; mem. Assn. for Death. Edn. and Counseling, 1985—, Grief Edn. Inst., 1981—, The Compassionate Friends, 1980—. Named Honored Author, Ill. Libr. Exposition, 1985. Republican. Lutheran. Home and Office: The Publishers Mark PO Box 6300 Incline Village NV 89450-6300

SCHELLHAAS, LINDA JEAN, toxicologist, consultant; b. South Haven, Mich., Apr. 27, 1956; d. Richard Louis and Virgene Frieda (Lietzke) Plankenhorn; m. Robert Wesley Schellhaas, May 27, 1990. BA in Biology, Albion Coll., 1978. Pathology rsch. asst. Internat. R&D Corp., Mattawan, Mich., 1978-80; toxicology rsch. coord. Borriston Labs., Inc., Temple Hills, Md., 1980-84; quality assurance coord. Tegeris Labs., Inc., Temple Hills, Md., 1984-85; good lab. practice compliance specialist, staff scientist Dynamac Corp., Rockville, Md., 1985-90; dir. quality assurance Pathology Assocs., Inc., Frederick, Md., 1992-94; pres., regulatory compliance specialist Quality Reviews, Inc., Falling Waters, W.Va., 1990—; instr. regulatory compliance tng. seminars, 1990—. Contbr. articles to profl. jours. Mem. Soc. Quality Assurance, Albion Coll. Fellows, Pi Beta Phi, Phi Beta Kappa. Home: 1204 Berkeley Dr Falling Waters WV 25419-9657 Office: Quality Reviews Inc PO Box 755 Falling Waters WV 25419-0755

SCHELLHOUS, NANCY SHICK, outplacement executive; b. Youngstown, Ohio, Feb. 15, 1940; d. Robert C. and Nell Louise (Redman) Shick; m. James H. Reed. Apr. 21, 1960 (div. May. 1972); children: Bradley, Tobin, Steven; m. Edward A. Schellhous, Oct. 4, 1974. AA, U. Cin., 1975, BS, 1979, postgrad., 1979-84. Mgr. office H. Derringer Co., Cin., 1970-72; researcher Promark Co., Cin., 1972-73; asst. to treas. Frederick Rauh & Co., Cin., 1973-75; v.p. adminstrn. Promark Co., Cin., 1975-78, pres., 1978-91; chmn. of bd., chief exec. officer Promark Co., 1991—; chmn. Outplacement Internat., Del., 1990-91, bd. dirs., 1985—. Chmn. Pvt. Industry Coun., 1989-92; vice chmn. Cin. chpt. ARC, 1989—; past chmn. adv. bd. Gt. Oaks Career Resource Ctr., 1985-89; v.p. Leadership Cin. Alumni Bd., 1989—; trustee Cin. State Tech. and C.C., 1990—, chmn. bd., 1993-94. Recipient ann. achiever award Greater Cin. C. of C., 1980-85, Career Woman of Achievement award YWCA, 1989. Mem. Internat. Assn. Personnel Women (pres. cin. 1985-86), Soc. Human Resource Mgrs. Republican. Home: 5634 Sun Valley Ln Cincinnati OH 45230-1222 Office: Promark Co 615 Elsinore Pl Ste 720 Cincinnati OH 45202

SCHELLING, JOYCE ELAINE, account executive; b. Fort Wayne, Ind., Oct. 14, 1937; d. George Martin and Lucille Alice (Schuckel) Schmeling. BA, St. Francis Coll., 1962; MA, Catholic U., 1968; PhD, NYU, 1987. Lic. tchr., Ind., N.J. Dir. drama St. Francis Coll., Ft. Wayne, 1966-70; instr. South Plainfield (N.J.) High Sch., 1970-80, NYU, N.Y.C., 1980-82; account exec. On-Line Software, Fort Lee, N.J., 1982-86, SDI, Hackensack, N.J., 1986-88, Microbank Software, Inc., N.Y.C., 1988-91, Performance Mgmt., Inc., N.Y.C., 1991—. Mem. NAFE, NOW, N.J. Network Bus. and Profl. Women, N.J. Assn. Women Bus. Owners. Democrat. Home: 2100 Linwood Ave Apt 15R Fort Lee NJ 07024-3186

SCHEMMEL, DEANNE LOUISE, city administrator; b. Rochester, Minn., Apr. 2, 1947; d. Russell Edward and Lucille Frances (Jansen) S. Student, Coll. St. Benedict, St. Joseph, Minn., 1965-67; BS in Bus. Adminstrn., Winona (Minn.) State U., 1992. Procurement clk. IBM Corp., Rochester, 1967-71; pers. asst. Rochester Pers., 1971-75; office svcs. coord. Rochester Bldg. Safety Dept., 1975-94; office mgr. City of Rochester, 1994—. Mem. exec. bd. AAU Nat. Jr. Olympics, Rochester, 1991-92; mem. exec. com. Star of the North State Summer Games, 1989-90, chair, 1993-94; mem. bldg. com. Resurrection Ch., Rochester, 1985-89. Mem. Nat. Assn. Women in Constrn. (bd. dirs. 1992-94). Democrat. Roman Catholic. Office: 2122 Campus Dr SE Rochester MN 55904-4744

SCHENEWERK, SHARON KAY, counselor; b. Jefferson City, Mo., Oct. 31, 1960; d. John T. and Arah Eloise (Wood) Martin; m. Dale Robert Schenewerk Sr., May 19, 1984; children: Dale Robert Jr., Angela Louise. BA, N.E. Mo. State U., 1983, MA, 1993. Nat. cert. counselor. Dir. careers unltd. Linn (Mo.) Tech. Coll., 1983-84; admissions counselor Wichita (Kans.) State U., 1985-87; counselor intern N.E. Mo. State U., Kirksville, 1992, asst. to dean, 1992—; supr. Kelly Svcs., Columbia, Mo., 1985, Syracuse N.Y., 1988. Mem. Big Bros./Big Sisters, Sedgwick County, Wichita, 1985-87; vol. Willard Sch. Dist., Kirksville, Mo., 1993. Named Outstanding Young Women in Am., 1983; Pershing Leadership scholar, 1979-83. Mem. ACA, Nat. Career Devel. Assn., Nat. Assn. Student Pers. Adminstrs., Assn. for Humanistic Edn. and Devel. Democrat. Baptist. Home: 2407 N Oak Ln Kirksville MO 63501-2171 Office: NE Mo State U Missouri # 120 Kirksville MO 63501

SCHENKEL, SUSAN, psychologist, educator, author; b. Wroclaw, Poland, Apr. 21, 1946; came to U.S., 1949; d. Leon and Siddi (Fiedleholz) S.; m. Alvin Helfeld, Apr. 8, 1984. BA, U. Wis., 1967; MA in Clin. Psychology, SUNY, Buffalo, 1970, PhD in Clin. Psychology, 1973. Lic. psychologist, Mass. Psychologist Fitchburg (Mass.) State Coll., 1972-75, instr. in psychology, 1973-74; staff psychologist div. of alcoholism Boston City Hosp., 1975-76; chief psychologist Cambridge (Mass.) Ct. Clinic, 1976-80; instr. in psychology dept. psychiatry Med. Sch. Harvard U., 1976-80; pvt. practice psychology Cambridge, 1976—; instr. in psychology U. Mass., Boston, 1978; speaker in field. Author: Giving Away Success, 1984, German edit., 1986, Brazilian edit., 1988, rev. edit. 1991, Chinese edit., 1991; contbr. articles to profl. jours. USPHS fellow, 1967-70; N.Y. State Regents scholar, 1968-70; SUNY Rsch. Found. grantee, 1971-72. Mem. Am. Psychol. Assn., Mass. Psychol. Assn., Am. Soc. Tng. and Devel., Assn. for Advancement of Behavior Therapy.

SCHENKEL, SUZANNE CHANCE, natural resource specialist; b. Phila., Mar. 12, 1940; d. Henry Martyn Chance II and Suzanne (Sharpless) Jameson; m. John Lackland Hardinge Schenkel, June 15, 1963; children: John Jr., Andrew Chance. BS in Edn., Tufts U., 1962. Tchr. Roland Pk. Country Sch., Balt., 1962-65; exec. dir. Mass. Citizens' Com. for Dental Health, Springfield, 1981-83; pub., editor Women's Investment Newsletter, Longmeadow, Mass., 1985-89; pub. affairs officer USDA's Soil Conservation Svc., Amherst, Mass., 1990-93; program mgr. land and water program divsn. USDA's Soil Conservation Svc., Washington, 1993—; staff Merchant Marine and Fisheries com. U.S. Ho. of Reps., Washington, 1993. Author Wetlands Protection and Management Act. Chmn. Longmeadow (Mass.) Conservation Commn., 1984-90; supr. Hampden County (Mass.) Conservation Dist., 1985-90; bd. dirs., v.p. League of Women Voters of Mass., Boston, 1974-85; exec. com. Water Supply Citizens' Adv. Com., Water Resources Authority, Mass., 1979-90. Mem. Soil and Water Conservation Soc., Nat. Assn. Conservation Dists. Episcopalian. Home: 1052 Carriage Hill Pkwy Annapolis MD 21401 Office: USDA Natural Resources Conservation Svc/Ecosystem Asst Divsn/PO Box 2890 Washington DC 20013

SCHEPIS-KORNUC, ANDREA MARTA, elementary art educator; b. Cleve., Jan. 27, 1962; d. Anthony Joseph and Irene Marta (Komarjanski) Schepis; m. Edward Joseph Kornuc, Aug. 11, 1984 (div. Oct. 1993); children: Christopher, Michael. BFA, Kent State U., 1984. Cert. tchr., Ohio. Elem. art tchr. Stow (Ohio) City Schs., 1985—; art tutor, Stow. Active Stow Sch. PTA, 1985—. Named Outstanding Educator, Stow Sch. PTA, 1994. Mem. NEA, Nat. Art Edn. Assn., Ohio Edn. Assn., Ohio Art Edn. Assn. Home: 4920-A Friar Rd Stow OH 44224 Office: Fishcreek Sch 5080 Fishcreek Rd Stow OH 44224

SCHEPPNER, KATHLEEN, metal products executive; b. Erie, Pa., Feb. 7, 1949; d. Albin C. and Dorothy (Carlson) S. Student, Denison U. V.p., sec. Carlson-Erie Corp., Erie, 1970-94, 1995—; pres. Am. Tinning & Galvanizing Co., Erie, Pa., 1984—; co-owner Cup.A.Ccino's Coffie House, Erie, 1990—. Bd. corporators St. Vincent Health Ctr.; mem. Pa. Environ. Coun., Gannon U. Ambs., Enterprise Zone Loan Rev. Commn. Mem. Am. Electroplaters and Surface Finishers Soc. (pres. Erie br. 1988-92), Am. Galvanizers Assn., Nat. Assn. Metal Finishers, Pvt. Industry Coun., Mfrs. Assn. (environ. roundtable), Erie Conf. Cmty. Devel., Aluminum Anodizers Coun. Address: 552 W 12th St Erie PA 16501-1507

SCHERDIN, MARY JANE LISKOVEC, librarian, information professional, researcher; b. LaCrosse, Wis., Sept. 29, 1940; d. Ambrose John and Martha Marie (Borgmeier) Liskovec; m. Arthur William Scherdin, Apr. 15, 1961 (div. 1976); children: James William, Laurette Therese (dec.), Amy Lynn. BS in Elem. Edn., U. Wisc., LaCrosse, 1961; MS in Libr. Sci., U. Wisc., 1972; MEd Profl. Devel. in Audiovisual Media, U. Wisc., Whitewater, 1980; PhD in Edn. Adminstrn., U. Wisc., Madison, 1989. Children's libr. LaCrosse Pub. Libr., 1961; sch. libr. LaCrosse Pub. Schs., 1961-64; media dir. Whitewater Pub. Schs., 1971-75; supr. arts media ctr. U. Wisc., Whitewater, 1975-79, head learning mater ctr., 1979-86, instr., 1976-78; asst. dean U. Wis., Milw., 1986-88; collection access coord. U. Wisc., Madison, 1988-92; libr. dir. Edgewood Coll., Madison, 1992—; researcher The Highsmith Co., Ft. Atkinson, Wis., 1983, ALA, Chgo., 1991—, Cons. Psychologists Press, Palo Alto, Calif., 1991—; cons. Myers-Briggs Type Indicator, 1992—; vis. prof. U. Wisc., Madison, 1992. Co-author: K-12 Library Curriculum, 1974; author of bio-bibliographies of Wis. authors, 1981-83; designer: instructional computer programs, 1983, 87, 89; contbr. articles to profl. jours. Pres. Jefferson (Wis.) Jaycettes, 1968-69; state and internal exec. v.p. Wis. Jaycettes, 1969-71; edn. chair Nat. Found. March of Dimes, Jefferson, 1970-74; vol. Nat. Found. Sudden Infant Death, Wis., 1975-83. Mem. AAUW (v.p. Ft. Atkinson 1974-75), Assn. Coll. and Rsch. Librs. (task force chair 1991-93), Libr. Adminstrv. and Mgmt. Assn. (ubs. and bibliography com.), Wis. Health Sci. Libr. Assn. (long range planning com. 1990-91, bd. mem. 1991-92), Wis. Libr. Assn. (chair lit. awards com. 1983, bd. dirs. 1987-88, chair edn. sect. 1993), Wis. Assn. Acad. Librs. (chair conf. planning 1985, chair publs. 1993, chair 1988), U. Wis. Sch. Libr. and Info. Studies Alumni Assn. (sec. 1993—). Home: 6111 Winnequah Rd Madison WI 53716-3459 Office: Edgewood Coll 855 Woodrow St Madison WI 53711

SCHERER, ANITA (ANITA STOCK), advertising executive; b. Cleve., Sept. 20, 1938; d. William John Stock and Gertrud Clara (Kaufmann) Bacher; m. Richard Phillip Scherer, Nov. 25, 1961; children: William Richard, Christopher Howard. Student U. Cin., 1956-57. AB Jones Bus. Coll., 1958. Account sec. Northlich, Stolley Inc., Cin., 1978-79, account asst., 1979-80, asst. account mgr., 1980-81, account mgr., 1981-84, mktg. svc. assoc., 1984-89, mgr., 1989—; lectr. local schs., univs., Cin. 1980—. Coeditor: monthly newsletter Badge, 1967-72; designer assorted notepads, 1986. Lector, Our Lady of Victory Roman Cath. Ch., Cin., 1972—; corr. sec. Delhi Police Assn. Inc., Ohio, 1967-72; pres. Delhi Hills Community Coun., Ohio, 1974-75; adv. bd. mem. Coll. Mount St. Joseph, Ohio, 1974-80; v.p. adminstr. Stagecrafters, Cin., 1983-85, publicity chmn., 1984-89; mktg. bd. mem. Contemp. Arts Ctr., 1985—, chmn. Advt./Graphic Arts div. Fine Arts Fund Campaign, 1988; trustee Arts and Humanities Resource Ctr. for Elderly, 1990—, bd. chmn., 1991-93. Winner nat. competition Am. Assn. Advt. Agys., 1980; recipient Outstanding Performance award Assn. Community Theatres, Cin., 1983, Excellence in Acting award Ohio Community Theatres Assn., 1984. Mem. Cin. Direct Mktg. Assn., Am. Mktg. Assn., Acad. Health Services Mktg. (adv. bd. dirs. 1989-91), Am. Coll. Healthcare Mktg., Cin. C. of C. (lectr. 1984-86). Avocations: travel, reading, medieval/renaissance history, community theater. Home: 5511 Palomino Dr Cincinnati OH 45238-4143 Office: Northlich Stolley LaWarre Inc 200 W 4th St Cincinnati OH 45202-2688

SCHERER, KARLA, foundation executive, venture capitalist; b. Detroit, Jan. 13, 1937; d. Robert Pauli and Margaret (Lindsey) S.; m. Peter R. Fink, Sept. 14, 1957 (div. July 1989); children: Christina Lammert, Hadley Anne Tolliver, Allison Augusta Scherer; m. Theodore Souris, Sept. 5, 1992. Student, Wellesley Coll., 1954-55; BA, U. Mich., 1957. Bd. dirs. Renaissance Club; chmn. Karla Scherer Found., Detroit, 1989—; advisor on shareholders' rights; speaker on corp. governance to various univs. and profl. assns.; condr. workshops in field; leader only successful proxy contest of maj. U.S. publicly held corp., 1988. Trustee Eton Acad., Birmingham, Mich., 1989—; mem. vis. com. Fordham U. Grad. Sch. Bus. Adminstrn.; former mem. bd. dirs. Cottage Hosp., Univ. Liggett Sch., Music Hall, Detroit League for Handicapped; former mem. adv. bd. Wellesley Coll; former mem. Rep. Dennis M. Hertel's Candidate Selection Com. for Armed Svcs. Acads.; mem. U. Mich. Ctr. for the Edn. of Women Leadership Coun. Named Outstanding Woman Leader of Yr. Oakland U., 1990, one of Metro Detroit's Dynamic Women Women's Econ. Club, 1992, Entrepreneur of Yr. Finalist, 1993. Mem. Women's Forum Mich., Econ. Club Detroit (bd. dirs. 1991—), Women's Econ. Club Detroit, Detroit Club, Detroit Athletic Club, Country Club Detroit, Grosse Pointe Club, Renaissance Club (bd. dirs. 1995—). Office: 100 Renaissance Ctr Ste 1680 Detroit MI 48243-1009

SCHERMAN, SUSAN LOUISE, nurse; b. Hoboken, N.J., Apr. 20, 1953; d. Everett Harold and Louise Annetta (Becker) S.; m. John Alfred Pendenza, Oct. 6, 1979. Student, St. Mary Hosp. Sch. Nursing, 1974, Katharine Gibbs Secretarial Sch., N.Y.C., 1976; BA, Sch. Nursing and Health Edn., Jersey City State Coll., 1978. RN, N.Y.; Lic. Real Estate Broker, N.J., 1994. Sr. Staff NYU Med. Ctr., N.Y.C., 1974-78; nurse Christ Hosp., Jersey City, 1975-78; pub. health nurse Retarded Infants Svcs., Inc., N.Y.C., 1978-80; pub. health nursing supr. Hoboken Pub. Health Nursing Service, N.J., 1980-83; nurse cons. New York County Health Services Rev. Orgn., N.Y.C., 1983-86; cons. risk mgmt. Bower & Gardner, N.Y.C., 1986-91; nurse cons. Group Health, Inc., 1992; risk mgr. Jersey City Med. Ctr., 1992; sch. nurse/health edn. tchr. T. Roosevelt Sch., N.J., 1992-95; realtor Ray Fiore Real Estate, Hoboken, N.J., 1994; nurse cons. McAllon, Friedman & Mandell, Attys., N.Y.C., 1995—. Author: Community Health Nursing Care Plans: A Guide for Home Health Care Professionals, 1984. Mem. N.Am. Nursing Diagnosis Assn., N.J. Assn. Realtors, Hudson County Bd. of Realtors, Inc., Hudson County Multiple Listing Svc., Soc. Scribes, Intravenous Nurses Soc. (N.J. chpt.), Nat. Assn. Realtors, N.J. State Bd. Realtors. Roman Catholic. Avocations: calligraphy, swimming, needlepoint, parasailing. Office: McAloon Friedman & Mandell PC 116 John St New York NY 10038

SCHERMER, JUDITH KAHN, lawyer; b. N.Y.C., Feb. 28, 1949; d. Robert and Barbara Kahn; m. Daniel Woodrough Schermer; 1 child, Sarah Nicole. BA, U. Chgo., 1971; JD, William Mitchell Coll. Law, 1987. Bar: Minn. 1987, U.S. Dist. Ct. Minn. 1987. Advt. and promotion specialist U. Chgo. Press, 1971-75; systems analyst Allstate Ins. Co., Northbrook, Ill., 1975-78, Lutheran Brotherhood, Mpls., 1980-83; polit. aide Mpls. City Coun., 1986-87; ptnr. Schermer & Schermer, Mpls., 1987—. Pres., feminist caucus Dem. Farm Labor Party, 1088—; bd. dirs. Women Candidates Devel. Coalition. Mem. Minn. Trial Lawyers Assn. (chair employment law sect.), Minn. State Bar Assn., Minn. Women Lawyers. Home: 4624 Washburn Ave S Minneapolis MN 55410-1846 Office: Schermer and Schermer Lumber Exch Bldg 10 S 5th St Ste 700 Minneapolis MN 55402

SCHETLIN, ELEANOR M., retired university official; b. N.Y.C., July 15, 1920; d. Henry Frank and Elsie (Chew) Schetlin; B.A., Hunter Coll., 1940; M.A., Tchrs. Coll., Columbia U., 1942, Ed.D., 1967. Playground dir. Dept. of Parks, N.Y.C., 1940-42; librarian Met. Hosp. Sch. Nursing, N.Y.C., 1943-44, dir. recreation, 1944-48, dir. recreation and guidance, 1948-59; coordinator student activities SUNY, Plattsburgh, 1959-63, asst. dean students, 1963-64; asst. prof., coordinator student personnel services CUNY, Hunter Coll., 1967-68; asst. dir. student personnel Columbia U., Coll. Pharm. Scis., N.Y.C., 1968-69, dir. student personnel, 1969-71; assoc. dean for students Health Scis. Center, SUNY, Stony Brook, 1971-73, asst. v.p. for student services, 1973-74, assoc. dean of students, dir. student services, 1974-85; mem. sea cliff unit 300 Nassau County Auxiliary Police. Recipient Lifetime Achievement award Nassau NOW, 1992. Mem. Nat. Assn. Women in Edn. Contbr. articles to profl. jours. Home: 20 Barberry Ln Sea Cliff NY 11579-2052

SCHEUFFELE, TRACY LYNNE, accountant; b. Battle Creek, Mich., Feb. 7, 1968; d. Kent Allan Schwartz and Marie Elaine (Decker) Dowd; m. Scott Dwight Scheuffele, Sept. 21, 1990 (div.). BA, Western Mich. U., 1990; postgrad., Ind. U. Acctg. assoc. James River Corp., Kalamazoo, Mich., 1990-91, cost acct., 1991-92; contr. James River Corp., Kendallville, Ind., 1992—. Mem. Inst. Mgmt. Accts. (sec. 1990-91, treas. 1991-92, v.p. membership 1992-93, v.p. fin. and adminstrn. 1993-94), Internat. Mgmt. Coun. Republican. Roman Catholic. Home: 1314 Village Green Dr Angola IN 46703 Office: James River Corp 301 S Progress Dr E Kendallville IN 46755

SCHEURER, ELIZABETH ANN, curator, consultant; b. Charlotte, N.C., Aug. 24, 1948; d. Clarence Ward and Helen Marjorie (Wilson) Fulcher; m. Stephen Ganim Scheurer, July 17, 1971. BA, U. Cin., 1970, MA, 1971, postgrad., 1974-78; postgrad., Ohio State U., 1981, Miami U., Oxford, Ohio, 1993. Regional preservation officer Miami Purchase Assn., Cin., 1974-78; mgr. cultural resources Ohio Historic Preservation Office, Columbus, 1978-81; prin. investigator in archeology WAPORA, Inc., Cin., 1982-85; curator Nationwide Ins. Cos., Columbus, 1982-85; archaeologist Cin. Mus. Natural History, 1985-86, curator, 1986-89; curator Contemporary Arts Ctr., Cin., 1989-92, dir. edn., 1990-91; juror Leigh Yawkey Woodson Art Mus., Wausau, Wis., 1988, Arts for the Parks, Jackson, Wyo., 1988, Ohio Designer Craftsmen, Columbus, 1991—, curator, mem. various coms. Miami U. Art Mus., Oxford, 1991, 93, guest curator, Dahl Fine Arts Ctr., Rapid City, 1992; participant New Art Forms Exhbn., Chgo., 1989; regional coord. Smithsonian's Save Outdoor Sculpture! program, 1992—. Author: (catalogues) Studio Furnituremakers, 1990; editor: (catalogue) Morphosis: Architectural Projects, 1989, The Continuous Present of Organic Architecture, 1991, Glorious Adornment, 1992. Grantee NEA, 1989, 90, Ohio Arts Coun., 1991, 92, 93, 94. Home and Office: 2754 Powell Dr Cincinnati OH 45211

SCHEWEL, ROSEL HOFFBERGER, education educator; b. Balt., Mar. 1, 1928; d. Samuel Herman and Gertrude (Miller) Hoffberger; m. Elliot Sidney Schewel, June 12, 1949; children: Stephen, Michael, Susan. AB, Hood Coll., 1949; MEd, Lynchburg Coll., 1974; EdS, 1982. Reading resource tchr. Lynchburg Pub. Schs., Va., 1967-75; adj. prof. edn. Lynchburg Coll., 1973-79; cons., seminar leader Woman's Resource Ctr., Lynchburg, 1980-92; assoc. prof. edn. Lynchburg Coll., 1980-92. Trustee, vice chair bd. trustees Lynchburg Coll., Va., 1992—; bd. dirs. Va. Found. for Humanities and Pub. Policy, 1985-90, New Vistas Sch., Lynchburg Human Rights Commn., 1992—, Lynchburg Youth Svcs., 1993—; chmn. bd. dirs. Venture Enterprising Women; trustee Va. Mus. of Fine Arts, 1985-90; appointed Commn. on Edn. for All Virginians, 1990. Recipient Disting. Svc. award NCCJ, 1973, Outstanding Woman in Edn. award YWCA, 1988, Disting. Alumni award Lynchburg Coll., 1993. Mem. Va. Family and Childrens Trust Fund Commn. Democrat. Jewish. Address: 4316 Gorman Dr Lynchburg VA 24503

SCHEXNAYDER, CHARLOTTE TILLAR, state legislator; b. Tillar, Ark., Dec. 25, 1923; d. Jewell Stephen and Bertha (Terry) Tillar; m. Melvin John Schexnayder Sr., Aug. 18, 1946; children: M. John Jr., Sarah Holden, Stephen. BA, La. State U., 1944, postgrad., 1947-48. Asst. editor La. Agrl. Extension, Baton Rouge, 1944; editor The McGehee (Ark.) Times, 1945-46, 48-53; editor, co-publisher The Dumas (Ark.) Clarion, 1954-85, publisher, 1985—; state rep. Ark. House Reps., Little Rock, 1985—; pres. Ark. Assn. Women, 1955, Nat. Newspaper Assn., Washington, 1991-92, Ark. Press. Assn., Little Rock, 1982, Nat. Fedn. Press Women, Blue Springs, Mo., 1977-78, Litte Rock chpt. Soc. Profl. Journalists, 1973; mem. pres.'s coun. Winrock Internat., 1990—. Editor: Images of the Past, 1991. 1st woman mem. Ark. Bd. Pardons and Parole, 1975-80; mem. Ark. Legis. Coun., 1985-92; v.p. Desha County Mus., 1989—; dir. Dumas Indsl. Found., 1986—; exec. com. Ark. Ctrl. Radiation Therapy Inst., 1991-92; mem. adv. bd. Ark. Profl. Women Achievement, 1992; mem. Ark. Rural Devel. Commn., 1991-93; mem. Winrock Internat. Adv. Coun., 1991—. Named Disting. Alumnus Ark. A&M Coll., 1971, Woman of Achievement Nat. Fedn. Press Women, 1970, Outstanding Arkansan C. of C., 1986; recipient Ark. Profl. Women of Distinction award No. Bank, Little Rock, 1990, Emma McKinnery award Nation's Top Cmty. Newspaper Woman, 1980, Journalist award Nat. Conf. of Christians and Jews, 1989, Lifetime Achievement award Nat. Fedn. Press Women, 1992, Outstanding Svc. award Ark. Assn. Elem. Prins.; named to La. State U. Alumni Hall of Distinction, 1994; named one Top 100 Ark. Women, Ark. Bus., 1995. Mem. Pi Beta Phi (Crest award 1992), Ark. Delta Coun. (chmn. of bd. dirs. 1989—). Democrat. Roman Catholic. Home: 322 Court Dumas AR 71639 Office: Clarion Publishing Co Inc 136 E Waterman Dumas AR 71639

SCHIAVO, A. MARY FACKLER, federal official, lawyer; b. Pioneer, Ohio, Sept. 4, 1955. AB cum laude, Harvard U., 1976; MA, Ohio State U., 1977; JD, NYU, 1980. Bar: Mo. 1980, U.S. Dist. Ct. (we. dist.) Mo. 1980, U.S. Ct. Appeals (8th cir.) 1983, U.S. Ct. Appeals (10th cir.) 1985, U.S. Supreme Ct. 1990, D.C. 1993, Md. 1994. Assoc. Watson, Ess, Marshall & Enggas, Kansas City, Mo., 1980-82; asst. U.S. atty. we. dist. Mo. U.S. Dept. Justice, Kansas City, 1982-85, fed. prosecutor organized crime and racketeering strike force, 1985-86; White House fellow, spl. asst. to U.S. Atty. Gen. U.S. Dept. Justice, Washington, 1987-88; exec. dir. Bush/Quayle '88 Campaign, State of Mo., 1988; atty. McDowell, Rice & Smith, Kansas City, 1989; asst. sec. labor-mgmt. standards U.S. Dept. Labor, Washington, 1989-90; insp. gen. U.S. Dept. Transp., Washington, 1990—; instr. U.S. Atty. Gen.'s Adv. Inst., Washington, 1986, 88, FBI Acad., Quantico, Va., 1988; guest lectr. NYU Sch. Law, 1986, 88, 91; bd. dirs. Dept. Labor Acad., 1989-90, White House Fellows Assn., 1992—, 2d v.p., 1992-93, chair ann. meeting, 1993, 1st v.p., pres.-elect, 1993-94, pres., 1994—; mem. Pres.'s Coun. on Integrity and Efficiency, 1990—, Fed. Investigators assn., Pres. Commn. on White House Fellowships, 1994—. Bd. dirs. Root-Tilden Scholarship program NYU, 1982-89. Recipient Thompson award Ohio State U. Alumni, 1988, Aviation Laurel award Aviation Week and Space Tech. mag., 1992; named one of Top Ten Coll. Women in U.S., 1975, One of Ten Outstanding Young Working Women in Am., 1987, Kansas City Career Woman of Yr., 1988; Ohio State U. fellow, 1976-77; Root-Tilden legal scholar NYU, 1977-79. Mem. ABA (ho. of dels. 1986-89, assembly del. 1986-89, litigation sect. complex crimes com.), Mo. Bar Assn. (bd. govs. 1986-89, chmn. pro bono task force 1984-86, young lawyers coun. 1983-86, Outstanding Svc. award 1986), Exec. Women in Govt., Harvard U. Alumni Assn. (bd. dirs. 1989-92), Harvard Club of Washington, Charter 100. Office: US Dept Transp Office of Insp Gen 400 7th St SW Ste 9210 Washington DC 20590

SCHIAVONE, LOUISE L., political correspondent, news analyst; b. N.Y.C., Apr. 10, 1951; d. Rocco Michael and Accursia Theresa (La Rocca) Schiavone; m. Richard Uliano, Oct. 19, 1985; 1 child, Christina Maria. BA in History, Emmanuel Coll., 1972; MS in Journalism, Columbia U., 1978. Press sec., legis. asst., speech writer Office of Congressman Paul Tsongas, Washington, 1975-77; polit. reporter anchor WGST Newsradio, Atlanta, 1978-80; senate corr., polit. reporter Associated Press Radio Network, Washington, 1980—; anchor, guest co-host Newsweek on Air, Newsweek Mag., Washington, 1980—; TV reporter AP TV Direct, 1988-91; guest commentator on polit. affairs Fox TV, C-Span TV, Cable News Network, Washington, 1992—. Mem. Congressional Radio and TV Corrs. Assn. (elected exec. com. 1993—). Roman Catholic. Office: AP Broadcast News Ctr 1825 K St NW Washington DC 20006-1202

SCHIAVONI-COLUCCI, ANNE, nursing administrator; b. Providence, Feb. 20, 1954; d. William and Doris R. (Nadeau) Schiavoni; m. Richard George Colucci, Sept. 27, 1980; children: Richard, James, Michelle. BS, Fairleigh Dickinson U., 1976; MA, NYU, 1982. Staff nurse Winthrop-U. Hosp., Mineola, N.Y.; clin. instr. Adelphi U., Garden City, N.Y.; nurse cons. Island Oxycare, West Hempstead, N.Y.; field supr. Norrell Health Care. Mem. AAUP, Sigma Theta Tau.

SCHICK, CONSTANCE JOYCE, psychology educator; b. Abilene, Tex., Apr. 11, 1939; d. Marshall F. and Velma J. (Hawes) Wilson; m. Bradford P. DeNoce, Aug. 20, 1992; 1 child, Jana Kaye Hamrick. Student, McMurray Coll., 1958; B of Bus. Adminstrn. in Acctg., Angelo State U., 1969; PhD in Exptl. Psychology, Tex. Tech. U., 1973; student, Summer Acad. Advancement Coll. Teaching, 1991. Mgr., co-owner Hamrick Photographic Studio, Graham, Tex., 1958-60; treas. Concho Camera Corp., San Angelo, Tex., 1961-63; tutor stats. and acctg. Angelo State U., San Angelo, 1968-69; part-time instr. Tex. Tech. U., Lubbock, 1971-73; from asst. to assoc. prof. psychology Bloomsburg (Pa.) U., 1973-82, prof. psychology, 1982—; pres. KC Enterprises Inc., Millville, Pa., 1991—; bd. dirs. Alternatives Counseling Svcs., Selinsgrove, Pa.; condr. workshops on team-bldg., values clarification, organization, developing positive thinking and behavior patterns; presenter in field. Contbr. articles to books and jours. Mem. People to People Internat. Citizen Amb. Program, 1988—. Grantee Profl. Devel., Bloomsburg U., 1980—. Mem. APA, Ea. Psychol. Assn., Soc. Behavioral Medicine, Rocky Mountain Psychol. Assn., Internat. Soc. for Study of Personal Relationships, Phi Kappa Phi (pres. 1977-78, treas. 1979—, founding mother 1980). Home:

RR 1 Box 209-1C Millville PA 17846 Office: Bloomsburg U Dept Psychology Bloomsburg PA 17815

SCHIEBE, BONITA ROSE, psychotherapist; b. Ashtabula, Ohio, May 10, 1940; d. William K. and Helen L. Herl; m. George K. Schiebe, Apr. 9, 1960; children: Robert S., Randall S., Russel S., Chrystal J. AA, Fullerton Coll., 1960; BS, La Verne Coll., 1982; MS, Calif. State U., Fullerton, 1985; PhD in Human Behaviour, So. Calif. Inst., 1995, D in Clin. Hypnotherapy, 1995. RN, Calif.; lic. tchr., Calif.; cert. in hypnotherapy, marriage, family and child counseling; CPR, ACLS instr. Am. Heart Assn. Staff, relief charge nurse Martin Luther Hosp., Anaheim, Calif., 1964-77, insv. dir., 1977-79, tchr., asst. dir. emergency ICU, 1979-81, nursing tchr., 1983—, adminstrv. supr., 1981-83; pschotherapist Adult Children's Ctrs., Orange, Calif., 1987—; psychotherapist, exec. dir. Crossroads Counseling, Brea, Calif., 1989—; pvt. practice Santa Ana, Calif. Contbr. nursing and counseling articles to profl. newsletters. Crisis vol., Costa Mesa, Huntington Beach, Calif., 1984-85. Mem. Calif. Assn. Marriage Family Therapists, Orange County Nursing Educators (bd. dirs., sec. 1982-83), Toastmasters Internat., Soroptomists Internat. Office: 505 N Tustin Ave # 228 Santa Ana CA 92705-3735 also: Crossroads Counseling 480 N State College Blvd Brea CA 92621-4215

SCHIEBEL, MARTHA, public relations executive; b. Sonthofen, Bavaria, Germany, Apr. 26, 1940; came to U.S., 1958; d. Josef and Thekla Ursula (Einsle) S.; m. John Norman Collins, June 11, 1961 (div. May 1980); Naomi Collins Snodgrass, Marley Collins Kercher, Arthur; m. Arthur Elliot Harrison, Jan. 5, 1994. BA in English magna cum laude, U. Mo., St. Louis, 1976; MA in Pub. Affairs Reporting, Sangamon State U., 1979. Cert. secondary English tchr. Tchr. creative writing St. Louis Pub. Schs., 1976; bur. chief Chgo. Daily Law Bulletin, Springfield, Ill., 1979-80; transp. policy analyst Jefferson County, Golden, Colo., 1990-91; policy specialist Ill. Dept. Transp., Springfield, 1980-84, sr. policy specialist, 1984-85, sect. chief fed. affairs, 1985-90, dep. dir. pub. affairs, 1991—. Mentor at-risk student Springfield Sch. Dist., 1993—; tutor, vol. tchr.'s aide University City (Mo.) Sch. Dist., 1972-73; sch. vol. Springfield S.E. H.S., 1981-84. Recipient Vol. Svc. award Springfield Pub. Schs., 1984.

SCHIER, MARY JANE, science writer; b. Houston, Mar. 10, 1939; d. James F. and Jerry Mae (Crisp) McDonald; B.S. in Journalism, Tex. Woman's U., 1961; m. John Christian Schier, Aug. 26, 1961; children—John Christian, II, Mark Edward. Reporter, San Antonio Express and News, 1962-64; med. writer Daily Oklahoman, also Oklahoma City Times, 1965-66; reporter, med. writer Houston Post, 1966-84; sci. writer, univ. editor U. Tex. M.D. Anderson Cancer Ctr., 1984—. Recipient award Tex. Headliners Club, 1969, Tex. Med. Assn., 1972-74, 76, 78, 79, 80, 82 Tex. Hosp. Assn., 1974, 82, Tex. Public Health Assn., 1976, 77, 78, others. Mem. Houston Press Club Ednl. Found. (pres 1992—). Lutheran. Home: 9742 Tappenbeck Dr Houston TX 77055-4102 Office: 1515 Holcombe Blvd Houston TX 77030-4095

SCHIEROW, LINDA-JO, environmental policy analyst; b. Milw., Aug. 17, 1947; d. Joseph August Schierow and Ruth Eleanore (Beyersdorff) Heuer. BS in Edn. with honors, U. Wis., 1969, MS in Land Resources, 1980, PhD in Land Resources, 1983. Cert. tchr., Wis. Tchr. elem. Cedarburg (Wis.) Pub. Schs., 1972-78; lectr. environ. studies U. Wis., Madison, 1984, project assoc. Water Resources Ctr., 1985; asst. prof. U. Okla., Oklahoma City, 1985-88; rsch. fellow U. Okla., Norman, 1988; rsch. assoc. MIT, Cambridge, 1989-90; ind. cons., 1990-91; policy analyst Environ. and Natural Resources Policy div. U.S. Congress Congl. Rsch. Svc., Libr. of Congress, Washington, 1991—; cons. U.S.-Can. Internat. Joint Commn., Windsor, Ont., Can., 1985; mem. editorial bd. RISK: Health, Safety & Environ., 1990—. Mem. Okla. State Groundwater Protection Strategy Com., Oklahoma City, 1985-88; bd. dirs. Ctr. for Community Tech., Madison, 1983-84. Mem. AAAS, Soc. for Risk Analysis, Sigma Xi. Democrat. Office: Congl Rsch Svc Libr of Congress Washington DC 20540-7450

SCHIESS, BETTY BONE, priest; b. Cin., Apr. 2, 1923; d. Evan Paul and Leah (Mitchell) Bone; m. William A. Schiess, Aug. 28, 1947; children: William A. (dec.), Richard Corwine, Sarah. BA, U. Cin., 1945; MA, Syracuse U., 1947; MDiv, Rochester Ctr. for Theol. Studies, 1972. Ordained priest Episcopal Ch., 1974; priest assoc. Grace Episc. Ch., Syracuse, N.Y., 1975; mem. N.Y. Task Force on Life and Law (apptd. by gov.) 1985—; chaplain Syracuse U., 1976-78, Cornell U., Ithaca, N.Y., 1978-79; rector Grace Episc. Ch., Mexico, N.Y., 1984-89; cons. Women's Issues Network Episc. Ch. in U.S., 1987—; writer, lectr., cons. religion and feminism, 1979—. Author: Take Back the Church, Indeed The Witness, 1982, Creativity and Procreativity: Some Thoughts on Eve and the Opposition and How Episcopalians Make Ethical Decisions, Plumline, 1988, Send in the Clowns, Chrysalis, Journal of the Swidenborg Foundation, 1994. Bd. dirs. People for Pub. TV in N.Y., 1978, Religious Coalition for Abortion Rights; trustee Elizabeth Cady Stanton Found., 1979; mem. policy com. Coun. Adolescent Pregnancy; mem. N.Y. State Task Force Life and the Law, 1983—. Recipient Gov.'s award Women of Merit in Religion, 1984, Ralph E. Kharas award ACLU Cen. N.Y., 1986 Goodall disting. alumna award & Hills Sch., 1988, Human Rightes award Human Rights Commn. of Syracuse and Onondaga County, N.Y., 1989; inducted into Nat. Women's Hall of Fame, 1994. Mem. NOW (Syracuse), Internat. Assn. Women Ministers (dir. 1978, pres. 1984-87), Assn. for Vol. Surg. Contraception (exec. com.), Am. Soc. Law and Medicine, Clergy Assn. Diocese of Cen. N.Y. (v.p. 1985—), Na'amat U.S. (hon. life), Mortar Bd., Theta Chi Beta. Democrat. Home and Office: 107 Bradford Ln Syracuse NY 13224-1901 Office: Grace Episcopal Ch Main St Mexico NY 13114

SCHIESSWOHL, CYNTHIA RAE SCHLEGEL, lawyer; b. Colorado Springs, July 7, 1955; d. Leslie H. and Maime (Kascak) Schlegel; m. Scott Jay Schiesswohl, Aug. 6, 1977; children: Leslie Michelle, Kristen Elizabeth. BA cum laude, So. Meth. U., 1976; JD, U. Colo., 1978; postgrad. U. Denver, 1984. Bar: Colo. 1979, U.S. Dist. Ct. (Colo.) 1979, U.S. Ct. Appeals (10th cir.) 1984, Wyo. 1986, Ind. 1988; cert. family mediator; cert. civil mediator. Rsch. clk. City Atty.'s Office, Colorado Springs, 1976; investigator Pub. Defender's Office, Colorado Springs, 1976; dep. dist. atty., 4th Jud. Dist. Colo., 1979-81; pvt. practice law, Grand Junction, Colo., 1981-82, Denver, 1983-84; assoc. Law Offices of John G. Salmon P.C., 1984-85; pvt. practice, Laramie, Wyo., 1985-88, Indpls., 1988-90; of counsel Rund & Wunsch, Indpls., 1990—; guest lectr. Pikes Peak Community Coll., 1980; adj. prof. polit. sci. and speech Butler U., Indpls., 1993—, spl. asst. to dean for pre-law, 1993—. Advisor Explorer Law Post, Boy Scouts Am., 1980-81; vol. Girl Scouts Am., 1992—; ex officio mem. ch. devel. com. Cen. Rocky Mt. region Christian Ch. (Disciples of Christ), 1986-88; mem. evangelism commn. United Meth Ch., 1987-88, fin. com. youth and music depts., 1979-81, lay del. Rocky Mountain Ann. Conf., 1986-87, academic tutor youth program, 1989—; mem. ch. and soc. com. Meridian St. United Meth. Ch., 1989-93, mem. refugee resettlement com., 1990-93; hearing officer Wyo. Dept. Edn., 1987-88; vol. Project Motivation, Dallas, 1974; chairperson Wyo. Med. Rev. Panel, 1987; lectr. Ind. Pastor's Conf., Rethinking Prisons Conf., 1990, Econ. Edn. for Clergy Conf., 1991. Named U. Scholar So. Meth. U., 1973. Mem. ABA (internat. law com.), Ind. State Bar Assn., Wyo. State Bar, Colo. Bar Assn. (ethics com. 1984-85, long range planning com. 1985-88, chairperson 1986-87), Am. Immigration Lawyers Assn. (sec. Ind. chpt. 1991-92, 93-94, chpt. vice chair 1992-93, asylum liaison 1990—, chpt. chair 1994—, bd. govs. 1994—), Indpls. Bar Assn. (internat. law sect. ethics com. 1990—), Pi Sigma Alpha, Alpha Lambda Delta, Alpha Delta Pi. Republican. Office: PO Box 88853 Indianapolis IN 46208-0853

SCHIFF, JAYNE NEMEROW, underwriter; b. N.Y.C., Aug. 8, 1945; d. Milton E. Nemerow and Shirley (Kaplan) Wachtel; m. Albert John Schiff, Mar. 7, 1971; children: Matthew Evan, Kara Anne. BS in Bus., Marymount Coll., 1981; M of Profl. Studies in Elem. and Spl. Edn., Manhattanville Coll., 1995. Corporate sec., treas. Albert J. Schiff Assocs., Inc., N.Y.C., 1970-78; field underwriter Mut. N.Y. Fin. Svcs., Greenwich, Conn., 1973—; freelance employee benefit cons. Greenwich, 1979—; regional dir. mktg., MONY Fin. Services, N.Y.C., 1978-79. Bd. dirs. N.Y. League Bus. and Profl. Women, 1976-78, Temple Sinai, Stamford, Conn., 1979-84, N.Y. Ctr. Fin. Studies; leader Webelos Cub Scouts, 1977-78; treas. Ann. Mothers Bd. Benefit Greenwich Acad., 1988, upper sch. acquisitions chmn., 1989, chmn. spl. acquisitions Greenwich Acad. Benefit, 1990-91, chmn. advt., 1992; ESL tutor Lit. Vols. Am., ESL tutor, trainer, 1993. Named Conn.'s Outstanding Young Woman, 1979. Mem. LWV, Am. Soc. Chartered Life Underwriters, N.Y. Ctr. Fin. Studies (bd. dirs.), N.Y.C. Life Underwriters Assn. (bd. dirs. 1977-78). Jewish. Office: 30 Stanwich Rd Greenwich CT 06830-4860

SCHIFF, LAURIE, lawyer; b. Newark, Apr. 24, 1960; d. Norman Nathan and Claire Jane (Schott) S.; m. Ralph Conrad Shelton II, 1992. BS in Law, We. State U., Fullerton, Calif., 1987, JD, 1988. Bar: Calif. 1989. Ptnr. Schiff Mgmt., Newport Beach, Calif., 1983-89; pvt. practice Schiff & Assocs., Irvine, Calif., 1989-91; ptnr. Schiff & Shelton, 1991—; probation monitor State Bar Ct. Calif., 1991—. Producer: (record album) Boys Just Want to Have Sex, 1984. Bd. dirs. Jewish Family Svcs. of Orange County, 1994—. Mem. ABA, Orange County Bar Assn., Am. Mensa, Am. Polocrosse Assn., Saddlebrook Polocrosse (treas. 1991), Am. Quarterhorse Assn., Internat. Cat Assn., Tonks West (v.p. 1994—). Democrat. Jewish. Office: Schiff & Shelton 3 Hutton Centre Dr Ste 400 Santa Ana CA 92707-5736

SCHIFF, MOLLY JEANETTE, artist; b. Chgo., Oct. 19, 1927; d. David Nathan and Beatrice (Aisenberg) Rice; m. Haskell Schiff, June 12, 1946; children: Darryll Nat, Lesley Nan, Brad Scott, Rae Ellyce. Student, U. Chgo., 1958-63, 68-69; BFA, Art Inst., Chgo., 1962; MFA, Art Inst., 1963, MA in Edn., 1969. Cert. art tchr. Ill. Instr. art Chgo. Bd. Edn. and Park Dist., 1962-66, Jewish Community Ctrs., Chgo., 1962-65; pvt. practice Chgo., 1962—; instr. art New Trier Extensions, Winnetka, Ill., 1965-78, Evanston (Ill.) Art Ctr., 1965, St. Tarsissus Sch., Chgo., 1968, Young Artists Studio Art Inst., Chgo., 1968-69, Ill. Visually Handicapped Inst., Chgo., 1968-73, Govs. State U., Monee, Ill., 1975-76; cons. Markal Corp., Chgo., 1968-94; cons., presenter, regional rep. Siva Corp., Chgo., 1984-87. Prin. works include Facades, 1971 (Honors award 1971), Drawn Paintings, 1976 (Honors award 1976), Acapulco Balcony, 1978 (Honors award 1980), Mexican Scenics, 1980 (Honors award 1980), Figures on Paper, 1988-89 (Honors award 1989), Low Seam, 1988 (Honors award), Later Impressions, 1989 (Honors award), Acapulco Nite View, 1989 (Honors award), Impressions, 1990 (Honors award), Mannequin Cut Outs, 1990 (Honors award), Union League, 1993 (Honors award), Jarvis Still Life, 1993 (Honors award). Pres. I.G.C. chpt. Am. Jewish Congress, Chgo., 1955. Recipient Cash award Foremost Corp., 1963, Ill. Dept. Energy and Natural Resources, 1988, Purchase award Rotarian Mag., 1978, Ill. State Mus., 1978, Nite View, 1989. Mem. Figurative Art League, Chgo. Artists Coalition, Chgo. Soc. Artists, Am. Jewish Art Assn. (program dir. 1970-74, 89-93), Dutch Folk Art Assn. (cons., juror 1979), Alumni Assn. Art Inst. Chgo., Am. Jewish Art Club, Scan Chgo. (bd. dirs. 1988-91). Home and Office: 744 Sheridan Rd Evanston IL 60202

SCHIFFMAN, SUSAN STOLTE, medical psychologist, educator; b. Chgo., Aug. 24, 1940; d. Paul R. and Mildred (Glicksman) Stolte; m. Harold Schiffman (div.); 1 child, Amy Lise; m. H. Troy Nagle, July 22, 1989. BA, Syracuse U., 1965; PhD, Duke U., 1970. Lic. psychologist, N.C. Postdoctoral fellow Duke U., Durham, N.C., 1970-72, asst. prof., 1972-77, assoc. prof., 1978-83, full prof., 1983—; cons., mem. adv. bd. Nutrasweet, Chgo., 1978—, Nestle, Vevey, Switzerland, 1990, Fragrance Rsch. Fund, N.Y.C., 1986—, and others. Author: Introduction to Multidimensional Sealing: Theory, Methods and Applications, 1981, Flavor Set-Point Weight Loss Cookbook, 1990. Nat. Inst. Aging grantee, 1972—. Mem. Assn. Chemoreception Scis., European Chemoreception Rsch. Orgn., Soc. for Neurosci. Office: Duke U Dept Psychology Durham NC 27708-0086

SCHIFLETT, MARY FLETCHER CAVENDER, health facility executive, researcher, educator; b. El Paso, Tex., Sept. 23, 1925; d. John F. and Mary M. (Humphries) Cavender; 1 son, Joseph Raymond. BA in Econs. with honors, So. Meth. U., 1946, BS in Journalism with honors, 1947; MA in English, U. Houston, 1971. Writer, historian Office Price Adminstrn., Dallas, 1946-47; asst. editor C. of C. Publs., Dallas, 1947-48; bus. writer Houston Oil, 1948-49; market analyst Cravens-Dargan, Ins., Houston, 1949-52; bus. writer Bus. Week and McGraw-Hill Pub. Co., Houston, 1952-56; freelance writer in bus. econs., banking and ins., 1956-68; spl. projects coordinator Center for Human Resources, Houston, 1969-73; dir. publs. Energy Inst., U. Houston, 1974-78; sr. research assoc. Inst. Labor and Indsl. Relations, 1973-80, adj. faculty Coll. Architecture, 1976-85, dir. Ctr. for Health Mgmt., Coll. Bus. Adminstrn., 1980-83; assoc. dir. research and planning Tex. Med. Ctr., Inc., Houston, 1984; dir. spl. projects and pub. affairs Tex. Med. Ctr., 1985-92, asst. v.p., 1993—. Bd. dirs. Third Ward Redevelopment Coun., 1993—, Houston Acad. Motion Pictures, 1986-90, Houston World Trade Assn., 1988-91. Pres., Houston Ct. Humanities, 1978-80; project dir. Houston Meets Its Authors I-IV, 1980-84; pub. program dir. Houston: Internat. City, 1980-83. Mem. Internat. Council Indsl. Editors, World Future Soc., Tex. Folklore Soc., Friends of the Library, Houston C. of C. (future studies com. 1975-84, small bus. council 1981-83), Nat. Assn. Bus. Economists, AIA (profl. affiliate), Mortar Bd., Theta Sigma Phi, Alpha Theta Phi, Delta Delta Delta. Methodist. Club: Downtown (pres. 1987-89). Lodge: Rotary. Author: (with others) Dynamics of Growth, 1977, Applied Systems and Cybernetics, 1981, The Ethnic Groups of Houston, 1984, Names and Nicknames of Places and Things, 1986. Office: Tex Med Ctr 406 Jesse H Jones Libr Bldg Houston TX 77030

SCHILBRACK, KAREN GAIL, system analyst; b. Tomahawk, Wis., Sept. 28; d. Edward Richard and Irene Angeline (Ligman) S. Student U. Calif.-Santa Barbara, 1967-69; BA in Anthropology, U. Calif.-Davis, 1971; postgrad. in Edn. and Archeology, Calif. State Poly. U., San Luis Obispo, 1971-72. Cert. tchr., computer specialist, data processing; lic. cosmetologist. Computer specialist Facilities Systems Office, Port Hueneme, Calif., 1975-78, sr. computer specialist, 1978-80, project mgr. U.S. Naval Constrn. Bn. Ctr., 1980-89, imaging systems computer specialist Comptr. Office, 1989-92; fiscal quality specialist Dept. Def. Finance and Acctg. Svc., DAO, Port Hueneme, 1992—; tng. cons. FACSO, 1981, 82; curriculum cons. Ventura Community Coll., Calif., 1981-89; instr. U.S. Navy, Port Hueneme, 1983, 91, Civil Service Commn., Port Hueneme, 1978-80. Author: AMALGAMAN Run Procedures, 1976; Cobol Programming Efficiencies, 1978, Imaging System UserManual, 1991; co-author, editor: Training Manual for Direct Data Entry System, 1983. Mem. Vols. for Camarillo State Hosp., Camarillo, 1978-88, coord. Ventura County, 1981; chmn. scholarship fund drive Ventura, Santa Barbara, Los Angeles, Counties, 1980. Named Young Career Woman of Yr., Calif. Bus. and Profl. Women, 1979. Mem. Young Ladies Inst. (pres. Santa Paula, dist. dep. Ventura/Santa Barbara Counties), Am. Biog. Inst. Research Assn. (lifetime dep. gov.). Lodge: Toastmistress. Home: 6993 Wheeler Canyon Rd Santa Paula CA 93060-9727 Office: Compt Office Code 243-A USNCBC Port Hueneme CA 93042

SCHILD, JOYCE ANNA, otolaryngologist, surgeon; b. Chgo., May 26, 1931; d. William Paul and Helen (Kammer) S.; m. John A. Hegber, Dec. 15, 1973. BS, U. Ill., Chgo., 1954, MD, 1956. Diplomate Am. Bd. Otolaryngology. Intern St. Francis Hosp., Peoria, Ill., 1956-57; residency in otolaryngology U. Ill., Chgo., 1958-61, fellow in bronchoesophagology, 1961-62, clin. instr. to assoc. prof. otolaryngology, 1958-82, interim acting head dept. otolaryngology, 1978-79, prof. otolaryngology head and neck surgery Coll. Medicine, 1982—; mem. staff U. Ill. Hosp., Chgo.; otolaryngologist, surgeon Ill. Eye and Ear Infirmary, Chgo.; from adj. to assoc. attending otolaryngologist Presbyn. St. Luke's Hosp., Chgo., 1964-76; acting head bronchoesophagology dept. Children's Meml. Hosp., Chgo., 1972-76, cons. staff, 1976—; mem. staff Michael Reese Hosp., Chgo., 1989—; courtesy staff dept. surgery sect. otolaryngology St. Joseph's Hosp., Chgo., 1961-74; numerous presentations and lectrs. in field. Mem. AMA, Am. Acad. Otolaryngol.-Head-Neck Surgery, Ill. State Med. Soc., Chgo. Med. Soc., Am. Laryngol. Assn., Soc. Univ. Otolaryngologists, Am. Laryngol., Rhinol. and Otol. Soc., Am. Soc. Pediatric Otolaryngology, Chgo. Laryngol. and Otol. Soc. (pres. elect 1983-84, pres. 1984-85, coun. mem. 1985-86), Am. Broncho-Esophagological Assn. (v.p. 1976-77, pres. elect 1978-79, pres. 1979-80, thesis com. 1981-82), Am. Coun. Otolaryngology, Soc. Ear, Nose and Throat Advances in Children, Am. Acad. Pediatrics (com. on accident and poison prevention 1982-85), Pan-Am. Assn. Oto-Rhino-Laryngology, Head and Neck Surgery. Office: Ill Eye and Ear Infirmary 1855 W Taylor St Rm 42 Chicago IL 60612-7243

SCHILLER, FRANCINE SANDRA, real estate broker; b. N.Y.C., Nov. 22, 1941; d. Frank C. and Blanche (Siegel) S.; divorced; 1 child, Lisa M. Student, Fairleigh Dickinson Coll., 1959. Salesperson Merrin Jewelry Co., N.Y.C., 1968, N.Y. Diamond Exchange, Surfside, Fla., 1976-78, Chinelly Real Estate, Hollywood, Fla., 1979-80; pres. Casino Real Estate, Inc., Hollywood, 1980—. Mem. adv. bd. Hollywood in Progress, Cen. Beach Redevel., Gold Coast Free Enterprise Coalition; mem. Jewish Fedn., mem. exec. com. Broward County Dems.; alt. del. White House; v.p. Hollywood Dem. Club, 1989-94; co-chair Dick Gephardt's Presdl. Campaign in So. Fla., 1988; del. Dem. Conv., 1988; bd. dirs. Broward Econ. Devel., So. Fla. Theatre of the Deaf; treas. Broward Forum; mem. adv. bd. Hollywood Annexation. Recipient City of Hollywood Appreciation award Mayor of Hollywood, 1985. Mem. Hollywood Area Bd. Realtors (bd. dirs. 1984, corp. sec. 1985, 2nd v.p. 1986), Fla. Assn. Realtors (bd. dirs. 1984-86), Nat. Coun. Jewish Women, Greater Hollywood C. of C. (bd. dirs. 1986, vice chmn. 1987), Kiwanis (bd. dirs. 1989-94, 95). Democrat. Office: Casino Real Estate Inc 4111 S Ocean Dr Hollywood FL 33019-3011 also: Casino Real Estate Unit 2 19011 Biscayne Blvd Aventura FL 33180

SCHILLER, MARGERY KABOT, financial planner; b. Hartford, Conn., Nov. 26, 1947; d. Ben William and Anne Lillian (Smulovitz) Kabot; m. Eugene Allan Schiller, Nov. 21, 1973; children: Jonathan Michael, Jeremy Andrew. BS, U. Conn., 1969, MA, 1975. Cert. fin planner, registered investment advisor. County agt. N.Y. State Coop. Extension, Liberty, 1969-70, Conn. Coop. Extension, Hartford, 1970-73; lectr. U. Vt., Burlington, 1975-77; extension specialist U. Conn., Storrs, 1977; cons. East Hampton, Conn., 1978-81; fin. planner, East Hampton, 1981-86, St. Paul, 1986-90, Sarasota, Fla., 1990—; fee only fin. planner Goar Endriss Walker & Wall, CPA's, Sarasota, 1990—; guest lectr. So. New Eng. Tel. Co., New Haven, 1981-86; lectr. St. Joseph Coll., New Hartford, Conn., 1981-86. Author: (with E. Carr and V. Jodoin) Consumer Education: A Green Thumb Guide, 1975: (with E. Fetterman) Let the Buyer Be Aware, 1976; Personal and Family Finance: Principles and Applications, 1981; Connecticut Guide to Curriculum Development in Comsumer Education K Through Adult, 1981; Money Management: A Packet for Teaching Adults, 1984; Guidebook for Teaching Consumer Credit, 1984; contbr. articles in to profl. jours. Recipient award Registry Fin. Planning Practitioners, 1987. Mem. Inst. Cert. Fin. Planners, Internat. Assn. Fin. Planning, Nat. Assn. Personal Fin. Advisors. Office: Goar Endriss Walker & Wall CPA's 1590 1st St Sarasota FL 34236-8502

SCHILLER, RHODA MARCIA, personnel and purchasing professional; b. N.Y.C., Apr. 21, 1945; d. Jacob and Sarah (Rosenberg) Morganstern; m. Irwin Schiller, Nov. 2, 1968 (div. May 1986); children: Geoffrey Lyle, Jared Scott. BA, Bklyn. Coll., 1966. Caseworker N.Y. Dept. Social Svcs., N.Y.C., 1967-78; chiropractic asst. Goldfarb Chiropractic Ctr., West Orange, N.J., 1985-87; dir. purchasing and pers. Daus. of Israel Geriatric Ctr., West Orange, 1987—. Editor bull. Personnely Yours, 1989—. V.p. Women's Am. ORT, West Orange, 1980s, St. Cloud PTA, West Orange, 1986; chairperson Daus. of Israel campaign United Way, 1989, Daus. of Israel-United Jewish Appeal, 1991. Democrat. Home: 8 Rutgers St West Orange NJ 07052-2512 Office: Daus Israel Geriatric Ctr 1155 Pleasant Valley Way West Orange NJ 07052-1419

SCHILLER, SARAH MILES, home designer and distributor, real estate developer; b. New Haven, Conn., June 25, 1957; d. Philip Erskine and Angela Jeanne (Ackley) M.; m. Arthur James Schiller, June 17, 1979; children: Margaret Harding, Erik Philip. BA, Carleton Coll., 1979; MBA, U. Chgo., 1982. Product mgr. Harris Trust & Savings Bank, Chgo., 1980-82; v.p. First Nat. Bank Chgo., 1982-88; mgr. product mgmt. COVIA, Rosemont, Ill., 1988-92; bus. devel. mgr. ARDIS, Lincolnshire, Ill., 1992-93; pres. Lake Shore Assocs. Ltd., Kewaunee, Wis., 1993—; mem. bd. dirs. Kewaunee C. of C., 1994—; mem. Door County C. of C., 1992—. mem. League of Women Voters, 1992—, Kewaunee Women's Club, 1994—. Mem. Brown County Home Bldrs. Assn., Door County Home Bldrs. Assn. Office: Lake Shore Assocs Ltd 231 N Main St Kewaunee WI 54216

SCHILLING, KATHERINE LEE TRACY, retired principal; b. Mitchell, S.D., May 31, 1925; d. Ernest Benjamin and Mary Alice (Courier) Tracy; BA, Dakota Wesleyan U., 1947; MA, U. S.D., 1957; postgrad. U. Wyo., U. Nebr., Kearney State Coll.; m. Clarence R. Schilling, Oct. 14, 1951; 1 child, Keigh Leigh. Tchr. elem. and secondary schs., also colls., S.D. and Nebr. Mem. staff S.D. Girls' State, 1950-51; mem. S.D. Gov.'s Com. on Library, Nebr. Gov.'s Com. on Right to Read; prin. Mitchell (S.D.) Christian Sch., until 1994; ret., 1994. Recipient Outstanding Tchr. award S.D. High Sch. Speech Tchrs., 1966. Mem. NEA, Nebr., Thurston County (pres.) edn. assns., Winnebago Tchrs. Assn., Delta Kappa Gamma. Clubs: Internat. Toastmistress (internat. dir. 1963-65, Mitchell Toastmistress of Year 1959), Order Eastern Star. Contbr. articles to profl. jours., also poetry. Home: 39 S Harmon Dr Box 578 Mitchell SD 57301

SCHIMBERG, BARBARA HODES, organizational development consultant; b. Chgo., Nov. 30, 1941; d. David and Tybe Zisook; children from previous marriage: Brian, Valery; m. A. Bruce Schimberg, Dec. 29, 1984. BS, Northwestern U., 1962. Ptnr. Just Causes, cons. not-for-profit orgns., Chgo., 1978-86; cons. in philanthropy, community involvement, and organizational devel., 1987—; Chgo. cons. Population Resource Ctr., 1978-82. Woman's bd. dirs. Mus. Contemporary Art; bd. dirs., vice chmn. Med. Rsch. Inst. Coun., Michael Reese Med. Ctr.; bd. dirs., chmn. Midwest Women's Ctr.; trustee Francis W. Parker Sch.; bd. dirs. Women's Issues Network, 1991—, pres., 1993-94; mem. honorary bd. med. rsch. inst. coun. Children's Meml. Hosp. Mem. ACLU (adv. com.). Office: 132 E Delaware Pl Ste 5002 Chicago IL 60611

SCHIMEK, DIANNA RUTH REBMAN, state legislator; b. Holdrege, Nebr., Mar. 21, 1940; d. Ralph William and Elizabeth Julia (Wilmot) Rebman; m. Herbert Henry Schimek, 1963; children: Samuel Wolfgang, Saul William. AA, Colo. Women's Coll., 1960; student, U. Nebr., Lincoln, 1960-61; BA magna cum laude, U. Nebr., Kearney, 1963. Former tchr. and realtor; mem. Nebr. Legislature, Lincoln, 1989—, chmn. govt., mil. and vets. affairs com., 1993-94, vice chair urban affairs com., 1995—. Chmn. Nebr. Dem. Com., 1980-84; past pres., sec. bd. dirs. Downtown Sr. Ctr. Found. Mem. NAACP, Nat. Conf. State Legislators Women's Network (bd. dirs.), P.E.O., Soroptomists. Democrat. Unitarian. Home: 2321 Camelot Ct Lincoln NE 68512-1457 Office: State Legislature State Capital Lincoln NE 68516

SCHINDLER, FAITH S., administrative volunteer; b. N.Y.C., Oct. 2, 1925; d. John Nevin and Kathleen Martha (Whitaker) Sayre; m. George E. Schindler, Jr., Sept. 2, 1946; children: Karen Elizabeth Schindler Baart, Heather Schindler Lovett, Sarah Schindler Nevin. AB, Vassar Coll., 1946. Asst. teen program dir. YWCA, Pitts., 1946-47, part-time program dir., 1949; part-time program dir. YWCA, Chgo., 1951-52; adminstrv. vol. YWCA, N.J. and Nat., 1954—; nat. bd. dirs. YWCA, 1976-88; pres. N.J. State Coun. YWCAs, 1974-76, 88-92, editor newsletter, 1975—, treas., 1992—. Pres. Union County Fair Housing Coun., 1988-93, Bd. Edn., New Providence, N.J., 1961-70; bd. dirs. Union County Psychiat. Clinic, Plainfield, N.J., Child Placement Rev., 1982-94; v.p. Ch. Coalition for New Providence Affordable Housing, 1993—; past pres. LWV. Democrat. Episcopalian. Home: 15 Park Edge Berkeley Heights NJ 07922

SCHINDLER, JUDITH KAY (JUDI SCHINDLER), public relations executive, marketing consultant; b. Chgo., Nov. 23, 1941; d. Gilbert G. and Rosalie (Karlin) Cone; m. Jack Joel Schindler, Nov. 1, 1964; 1 child, Adam Jason. BS in Journalism, U. Ill., 1964. Assoc. editor Irving Cloud Publs., Lincolnwood, Ill., 1963-64; asst. dir. publicity Israel Bond Campaign, Chgo., 1965-69; v.p. pub. relations Realty Co. of Am., Chgo., 1969-70; dir. pub. relations Pvt. Telecommunications, Chgo., 1970-78; pres. Schindler Communications, Chgo., 1978—; del. White House Conf. on Small Bus., Washington, 1980, 86; mem. adv. bd. Entrepreneurship Inst., Chgo., 1988-92. Bd. dirs. Friends of Chgo. Pub. Libr., 1985-88; leader luncheon coun. YWCA, Chgo., 1987, 89, 90, 92; appointee small bus. com. Ill. Devel. Bd., 1988-89. Named Nat. Women in Bus. Adv. SBA, 1986, Chgo. Woman Bus. Owner of Yr., Continental Bank and Nat. Assn. Women Bus. Owners, 1989, Ill. Finalist Entrepreneur of Yr. award, 1991, 92. Mem. Nat. Assn. Women Bus. Owners (pres. Chgo. chpt. 1980-81, nat. v.p. membership 1988-89), Ind. Bus. Assn. Ill., Ill. Coun. Growing Cos. (vice chair 1993-94), Publicity Club Chgo., Alpha Epsilon Phi. Office: Schindler Communications 500 N Clark St Chicago IL 60610-3372

SCHINE, WENDY WACHTELL, foundation administrator; b. White Plains, N.Y., May 5, 1961; d. Thomas and Esther Carole (Pickard) Wachtell; m. Jonathan Mark Schine, Sept. 2, 1990; children: Jameson Myer, Bradley Thomas. BA, Wellesley Coll., 1983; MA in Journalism, U. So. Calif., L.A., 1987. Legis. asst. U.S. House Reps., Washington, 1983-85; varied positions KCBS-TV, L.A., 1986-88; v.p. Joseph Drown Found., L.A., 1988—; bd. dirs. Arts, Inc., L.A., L.A. Urban Funders, L.A. Cities in Schs.; advisor Psychol. Trauma Ctr., L.A., 1988—, Ctr. for Talented Youth, Glendale, Calif., 1989—. Bd. dirs. L.A. Urban Funders oversight com. Pathways project Big Sisters L.A. Office: Joseph Drown Found 1999 Ave of the Stars # 1930 Los Angeles CA 90067

SCHIRMER, LINDA IRENE, accountant; b. Battle Creek, Mich., Sept. 1, 1947; d. Henry J. and Lillian H. (Muraski) Wright; m. Keith E. Schirmer, Jan. 3, 1969 (div. Apr. 1989); children: Sara, Ann. AS, Kellogg Community Coll., Battle Creek, 1969; BBA, Western Mich. U., 1980; MBA, Mich. State U., 1982. CPA, Mich. Group underwriter Fed. Home Life, Battle Creek, 1965-70; with tax dept. Plante & Moran, Battle Creek, 1982-87, tax assoc., 1987-91; sr. mgr. in tax dept. Maner, Costerisan & Ellis, P.C., Lansing, Mich., 1991—; treas. Goodwill of Battle Creek, 1984-91. Mem. AICPA, Am. Soc. Pension Actuaries (assoc.), Nat. Assn. Accts. (pres. Battle Creek chpt. 1987, nat. bd. dirs. 1988-89, v.p. Lansing Jackson chpt. 1993-95, pres. 1995—), Mich. Assn. CPAs, Calhoun County Estate Planners, Greater Lansing Estate Planners. Home: 344 Bronco Way Lansing MI 48917-2728 Office: Maner Costerisan & Ellis PC 6105 W St Joseph Hwy Lansing MI 48917-4850

SCHIRO-GEIST, CHRISANN, rehabilitation counselor; b. Chgo., Dec. 31, 1946; d. Joseph Frank and Ethel (Fortunato) Schiro; m. John J. Conway Sr., Oct. 26, 1985; children: Jennifer, Daniel; stepchildren: Patricia, Nicole, John Jr., Denise, Christine. BS, Loyola U., Chgo., 1967, MEd, 1970; PhD, Northwestern U., 1974. Registered psychologist, Ill.; cert. sex edn. cons. Tchr. sci. Northbrook (Ill.) Jr. High Sch., 1967-70; dir. career counseling and placement Mundelein Coll., Chgo., 1972-74; counselor human devel. Regional Service Agy., Skokie, Ill., 1975-87; assoc. prof. psychology, rehab. counselor Ill. Inst. Tech., Chgo., 1975-87; full prof. rehab. U. Ill., Champagne-Urbana, 1987—. Co-author: Placement Handbook for Counseling Disabled Persons, 1982; author, editor: Vocational Counseling with Special Populations, 1990. Rsch. grantee Northwestern U., 1974; Region V Short-Term Tng. grantee Rehab. Svcs. Adminstrn., 1978-79, Long-Term Tng. grantee, 1983—; Mary E. Switzer fellow NIDRR, 1989-90, VA, 1991-92, World Rehab. Fund fellow, 1993. Mem. APA, ACA, Nat. Rehab. Assn., Nat. Coun. Rehab. Edn. (named Educator of Yr. 1987), Ill. Rehab. Counseling Assn. (pres. 1979-80), Coun. on Rehab. Edn. (pres. 1982-85, editor jour. 1986-92), Ill. Rehab. Assn. (pres.-elect), Kappa Beta Gamma Alumni Assn. (nat. officer). Office: U Ill Divsn Rehab Edn 1207 S Oak St Champaign IL 61820-6901

SCHLACHTER, DEBORAH BRISTOW, special education educator, consultant; b. Ajo, Ariz., Dec. 21, 1957; d. John Edward Jr. and Anne Elizabeth (Butler) Bristow; m. James Martin Schlachter Jr., July 25, 1981; children: James Martin, Katie Elizabeth, Joshua Timothy, Jacob Leslie, Jean Nicole. BE, Stephen F. Austin, 1981; MEd, U. N. Tex., 1991. Cert. tchr., Tex. Pvt. practice spl. needs tutor Dallas/Ft. Worth, 1981-91; pvt. practice family in home child care Lancaster, Tex., 1982-89; instr., coord. Cedar Valley Coll., Lancaster, 1989—; tchr. DeSoto (Tex.) Ind. Sch. Dist., 1990-91; kindergarten tchr. Dallas Ind. Sch. Dist., 1991-92, ESL tchr. 1st grade, 1992-93; Montessori tchr. Dallas Pub. Sch., 1993—; co-leader strategic planning Lancaster Ind. Sch. Dist., 1992-93. Co-editor: Resource Handbook for Educators on American Indians, 1993-94. Vol. tutor Womens Half Way House, Nacogdoches, Tex., 1980-81; trnr. in spl. needs children PTA, Dallas/Ft. Worth, 1990—, active Dallas/Lancaster, 1984—; voting mem. Dallas Native Am. Parent Adv. Com., 1992-94. Mem. ASCD, AAUW, Nat. Assn. Edn. Young Children, Nat. Indian Edn. Assn., Nat. Mus. Am. Indian, Am. Montessori Soc., So. Assn. Children Under Six, Dallas Assn. Edn. Young Children, Native Am. Rights Funds, Am. Indian Resource and Edn. Coalition. Episcopalian. Home: 532 Laurel St Lancaster TX 75134-3220 Office: Dallas Ind Sch Dist 3807 Ross Ave Dallas TX 75204-5202

SCHLAFLY, PHYLLIS STEWART, author; b. St. Louis, Aug. 15, 1924; d. John Bruce and Odile (Dodge) Stewart; m. Fred Schlafly, Oct. 20, 1949; children: John F., Bruce S., Roger S., Phyllis Liza Forshaw, Andrew L., Anne V. BA, Washington U., St. Louis, 1944, JD, 1978; MA, Harvard U., 1945; LLD, Niagara U., 1976. Bar: Ill. 1979, D.C. 1984, Mo. 1985, U.S. Supreme Ct. 1987. Syndicated columnist Copley News Svc., 1976—; pres. Eagle Forum, 1975—; broadcaster Spectrum, CBS Radio Network, 1973-78; commentator Cable TV News Network, 1980-83, Matters of Opinion sta. WBBM-AM, Chgo., 1973-75. Author, pub.: Phyllis Schlafly Report, 1967—; author: A Choice Not an Echo, 1964, The Gravediggers, 1964, Strike From Space, 1965, Safe Not Sorry, 1967, The Betrayers, 1968, Mindszenty The Man, 1972, Kissinger on the Couch, 1975, Ambush at Vladivostok, 1976, The Power of the Positive Woman, 1977, First Reader, 1994; editor: Child Abuse in the Classroom, 1984, Pornography's Victims, 1987, Equal Pay for Unequal Work, 1984, Who Will Rock the Cradle, 1989, Stronger Families or Bigger Government, 1990, Meddlesome Mandate: Rethinking Family Leave, 1991. Del. Rep. Nat. Conv., 1956, 64, 68, 84, 88, 92, alt., 1960, 80; pres. Ill. Fedn. Rep. Women, 1960-64; 1st v.p. Nat. Fedn. Rep. Women, 1964-67; mem. Ill. Commn. on Status of Women, 1975-85; nat. chmn. Stop ERA, 1972—; mem. Ronald Reagan's Def. Policy Adv. Group, 1980; mem. Commn. on Bicentennial of U.S. Constn., 1985-91; mem. Adminstrv. Conf. U.S., 1983-86. Recipient 10 Honor awards Freedoms Found., Brotherhood award NCCJ, 1975; named Woman of Achievement in Pub. Affairs St. Louis Globe-Democrat, 1963, one of 10 most admired women in world Good Housekeeping poll, 1977-90. Mem. ABA, DAR (nat. chmn. Am. history 1965-68, nat. chmn. bicentennial com. 1967-70, nat. chmn. nat. def. 1977-80, 83-95), Ill. Bar Assn., Phi Beta Kappa, Pi Sigma Alpha. Office: Eagle Forum 7800 Bonhomme Saint Louis MO 63105

SCHLAIN, BARBARA ELLEN, lawyer; b. N.Y.C., May 28, 1948; d. William and Evelyn (Youdelman) S.; B.A., Wellesley Coll., 1969; M.A., Columbia U., 1970; J.D., Yale U., 1973. Bar: N.Y. 1974, U.S. Dist. Ct. (so. dist.) N.Y. 1974, U.S. Ct. Appeals (2d cir.) 1975, U.S. Dist. Ct. (ea. dist.) N.Y. 1977. Assoc. firm Donovan Leisure Newton & Irvine, N.Y.C., 1973-76, Graubard Moskovitz McGoldrick Dannett & Horowitz, N.Y.C., 1976-79; atty. McGraw-Hill, Inc., N.Y.C., 1979-80, asst. gen. counsel, 1980-86, v.p., assoc. gen. counsel, asst. sec., 1986—. sec. proprietary rights com. Info. Industry Assn., 1982-83. Author outlines Practicing Law Inst., 1983, 84, 85, 86, 88; contbr. numerous articles to profl. jours. Bd. dirs., v.p., sec. Dance Research Found., N.Y.C., 1983-86, chmn. 1986—. Phi Beta Kappa scholar, Durant scholar Wellesley Coll., 1967-69. Mem. Assn. Am. Pubs. (lawyers com. 1979—), Assn. Bar City N.Y. (communications law com. 1985-88), N.Y. State Bar Assn. Office: McGraw-Hill Inc 1221 Ave Of The Americas New York NY 10020-1001

SCHLAMP, KAREN LAUN, realtor; b. Milw., Nov. 28, 1941; d. Edgar Casper and Wilhelmina Louisa (Krause) Laun; m. Daryl Henry Schlamp, July 6, 1961; children: Daniel Henry, David Edgar, Dawn Elizabeth. Student, Valparaiso U., 1959-61; BS in Edn., U. Wis., Milw., 1971. Tchr. Baypoint Nursery Sch., Fox Point, Wis., 1971-75, Univ. Sch., Milw., 1975-79; salesperson Wauwatosa Realty, Glendale, Wis., 1980-82, Federated Realty, Whitefish Bay, Wis., 1982-84, Miley Real Estate, Big Pine Key, Fla., 1988-89; rental agt. The Rental Connection, Inc., Stuart, Fla., 1989—; real estate cons. Milw. Gear Co., Jensen Beach,. Fla., 1984-87. Contbr. to Bible Studies for Women, The Quar., 1993, 94. Mem. Valparaiso Guild, Greater Martin County Bd. Realtors. Lutheran. Home: 2961 SE Morningside Blvd Port St Lucie FL 34952 Office: The Rental Connection Inc 2399 SE Ocean Blvd Stuart FL 34996

SCHLATHER, MARY AGNES, librarian; b. Berea, Ohio, Jan. 12, 1961; d. Bernard Paul and H. Virginia (Bilskey) S. BA, Walsh Coll., 1983; MLS, Kent State U., 1986. Cert. elem. tchr., Ohio, Ill.; cert. media, Ohio, Ill. Tchr. St. Mary's Elem. Sch., Lorain, Ohio, 1983-84, Avon, Ohio, 1984-85; student ref. asst. Kent (Ohio) State U., 1985-86; youth svcs. libr. Granite City (Ill.) Pub. Libr. Dist., 1987-90, St. Charles (Ill.) Pub. Libr. Dist., 1990-91; youth svcs. libr., asst. dir. East Alton (Ill.) Pub. Libr. Dist., 1991-93; west br. libr. supr. Belleville (Il.) Pub. Libr., 1993—; project dir. Door to Learning family literacy grant, 1992-93; co-chair S.W. Advocates for Youth Svcs., 1993-95. Mem. So. Ill. U. at Edwardsville Community Choral Soc., 1988-90, 92—. Mem. ALA (assn. for libr. svcs. to children, pub. libr. assn., young adult libr. svcs. assn., reference and adult svcs. divsn.), Ill. Libr Assn. (youth svcs. forum, mem. I-READ com. 1990-92, mem. conf. com. 1993—, youth svcs. forum mgr.-elect 1994-95, mgr. 1995—), Metro Area Pub. Librs. Roman Catholic.

SCHLEGEL, BEVERLY FAYE, private clubs administrator; b. San Diego, May 15, 1950; d. Frederick Hugh and Fern (Bailey) Einhaus; m. Heinz Dieter Schlegel, Oct. 27, 1976; 1 child, Kailo Heinz. Student, Hollins Coll., 1990—. Cert. club mgr. Mgr. The Town Club of Salem, Va., Va., 1976-84, The Shenandoah Club, Roanoke, Va., 1984—. Contbr. articles to profl. publ. Vol. Jr. Achievement. Featured in Club Dir. mag., 1993. Mem. Nat. club Assn. (city coun. adv. bd. 1992—), Club Mgrs. Assn. Am. (cert.; 2 Blue Ribbons 1993), Nat. Restaurant Assn., Va. Restaurant Assn. Baptist. Home: RR 1 Box 55 Montvale VA 24122-9714 Office: The Shenandoah Club Inc 24 Franklin Rd SW Roanoke VA 24011

SCHLEGEL, NANCY BROWNING, small business owner; b. Camden, N.J., May 4, 1929; d. Stanley Holland and Sara N. (Finley) Browning; m. Arthur J. Schlegel, Nov. 10, 1962; children: Janice, Richard, Arthur, Joy, John, Eraka. Student, Pa. Bus. Coll., 1945, N.Mex. Pub. Sch., 1970. Bookkeeper Louis Shoe Salons, Tucson, Ariz., 1961-63; speech and hearing aide N.Mex. Pub. Schs., Moriarty, 1970-71, substitute tchr., 1971-78; field supr. Office of the Aging, Wilkes Barre, Pa., 1979-86; owner Nancy's Vinyl Repair & Restore, White Haven, Pa., 1986—. Inventor Nancy's Spaghetti Sauce. Mem. Internat. Traders, Am. Assn. Retired Persons. Republican. Episcopalian. Office: Nan Art Enterprises PO Box 242 White Haven PA 18661-0242

SCHLEGEL, PATRICIA KIM, lawyer; b. Dodge City, Kans., Dec. 10, 1959; d. Wesley Pete and Grace N. (Tuttle) S.; m. Anthony J. Bosco, May 5, 1990. BS, BMusic, Kans. State U., 1982; MBA, U. Va., 1987, JD, 1987. Assoc. Lord Day & Lord, Barrett Smith, N.Y.C., 1987-93, 93—; gen. counsel Hartstone Holdings, Inc., N.Y.C., 1993. Mem. ABA. Office: Lord Day & Lord Barrett Smith 1675 Broadway New York NY 10019-5820

SCHLEICH, DEBORAH JAN, mental health counselor; b. San Bernadino, Calif., Mar. 9, 1952; d. Joseph Walter and Sara Griffin (Dean) Coyle; m. John Francis Schleich, Apr. 12, 1982; 1 child, James John. BS, Troy State U., 1974, MS, 1976. Lic. mental health counselor, Fla.; nat. cert. clin. mental health counselor. Counselor Ctrl. Ala. Rehab. Ctr., Montgomery, 1970-74; drug counselor Youth Svcs., Montgomery, 1974-75, youth evaluator, 1975-76; vocat./ednl. coord. drug counseling program Lakeview Ctr., Pensacola, Fla., 1977-81; ombudsman coord. Navy Family Svcs., Pensacola, 1987-88; mental health counselor The Avalon Ctr., Milton, Fla., 1988-89, Charter Hosp., Pensacola, 1989-90, Rehab. Inst. West Fla., Pensacola, 1990-92, Clin. Psychology Assn., Pensacola, 1992-94; pvt. practice Pensacola, 1994—; tchr. Pensacola Jr. Coll., 1993-94. Bd. dirs. Luth. Brotherhood, Pensacola, 1990, Luth. Ministries, Pensacola, 1993; mem. adv. bd. Stephen Minister Cmty. Drug and Alcohol Commn., Pensacola, 1992—; chair mental health disaster ARC, Pensacola, 1994—. Mem. APA (assoc.), Am. Mental Health Counselors Assn. (clin. mem., pub. policy and legis. com. 1993-94, legal profl. standards com. 1993-94, chair mems. sbcs. com. 1994-95), Nat. Alliance for Mentally Ill (profl. mem.), Fla. Mental Health Assn. (clin. mem. bd. dirs. 1988—), Fla. Mental Health Counselors Assn. (bd. dirs. 1990—, Leadership award 1992-93), Fla Counseling Assn. (mem. svcs. pub. awareness chair, 1994—). Home: 3492 Mai Kai Dr Pensacola FL 32526

SCHLEICHER, NORA ELIZABETH, banker, treasurer, accountant; b. Balt., Aug. 10, 1952; d. Irvin William and Eleanor Edna S.; m. Ray Leonard Settle Jr., July 27, 1985. AA cum laude, Anne Arundel Community Coll., 1972; BS summa cum laude, U. Balt., 1975. CPA, Md. Staff auditor Md. Nat. Bank, Balt., 1975-76, sr. staff auditor, 1976-77, supr. auditing dept., 1977-78; full charge acct. Wooden & Benson, CPA's, Balt., 1978-81; asst. to treas. First Fed. Savs. & Loan Assn., Annapolis, Md., 1981, asst. treas., 1982-83, v.p., 1984; v.p., treas. First Fed. Savs. & Loan Assn. (now First Annapolis Bank), 1984—. Bd. dirs., treas. Coll. Manor Community Assn. Mem. AICPA, Md. Assn. CPA's, Fin. Mgrs. Soc., Coll. Manor Community Assn. (bd. dirs., treas.). Methodist. Office: First Annapolis Savs Bank 1832 George Ave Annapolis MD 21401-4103

SCHLEIN, MIRIAM, author; b. June 6, 1926, N.Y.C.; d. William and Sophie (Bigleisen) S.; m. Harry Weiss, 1954; children: Elizabeth Weiss, John Weiss. B.A. in Psychology, Bklyn. Coll., 1947. Author over 85 books for children, natural sci. books, concept books, story books, picture books, including: A Day at the Playground, 1951, The Four Little Foxes, 1952 (Jr. Lit. Guild selection), Shapes, 1952, Go with the Sun, 1952, Tony's Pony, 1952, Fast is Not a Ladybug, 1953 (Boys' Club Am. Jr. Book award 1953), When Will the World Be Mine?, 1953, The Sun Looks Down, 1954, How Do You Travel?, 1954, Heavy is a Hippopotamus, 1954, Elephant Herd, 1954 (Jr. Lit. Guild selection, Herald Tribune Honor Book award 1954), Oomi, the New Hunter, 1955, Little Red Nose, 1955, It's About Time, 1955, City Boy, Country Boy, 1955 (Jr. Lit. Guild selection), Puppy's House, 1955, Big Talk, 1955, Lazy Day, 1955, Henry's Ride, 1956, Something for Now, 1956, Deer in the Snow, 1956, The Big Cheese, 1957 (Jr. Lit. Guild selection), Little Rabbit, The High Jumper, 1957, Amazing Mr. Pelgew, 1957, A Bunny, A Bird, A Funny Cat, 1957, Here Comes Night, 1957, The Bumblebee's Secret, 1958, Home: The Tale of a Mouse, 1958, Herman McGregor's World, 1958, The Raggle Taggle Fellow, 1959, Little Dog Little, 1959, The Fisherman's Day, 1959, Kittens, Cubs and Babies, 1959, My Family, 1960, The Sun, the Wind, the Sea and the Rain, 1960, Laurie's New Brother, 1961, Amuny, Boy of Old Egypt, 1961, The Pile of Junk, 1962 (Jr. Lit. Guild selection), Snow Time, 1962, The Snake in the Carpool, 1963, Who?, 1963, The Big Green Thing, 1963, The Way Mothers Are, 1963, Big Lion, Little Lion, 1964, Billy, the Littlest One, 1966, The Best Place, 1968, My House, 1971, Moon-months and Sun-days, 1972, The Rabbit's World, 1973, Juju Sheep and the Python's Moonstone, 1973, What's Wrong with Being a Skunk?, 1974, Metric: The Modern Way to Measure, 1975, The Girl Who Would Rather Climb Trees, 1975, Giraffe: The Silent Giant, 1976 (Children' Book of Yr. Child Study Assn. 1976), Bobo, the Troublemaker, 1976, Antarctica: The Great White Continent, 1978, I Hate It, 1978, On the Track of the Mystery Animal, 1978, I, Tut: The Boy Who Became Pharaoh, 1979, Snake Fights, Rabbit Fights and More: A Book About Animal Fighting, 1979 (Outstanding Sci. Trade Book for Children Nat. Sci. Tchrs. Assn./Children's Book Council Joint Com. 1979), Lucky Porcupine!, 1980 (Outstanding Sci. Trade Book for Children Nat. Sci. Tchrs. Assn./Children's Book Council Joint Com. 1980), Billions of Bats, 1982 (Outstanding Sci. Trade Book for Children Nat. Sci. Tchrs. Assn./Children's Book Council Joint Com. 1982), Our Holidays, 1983, Project Panda Watch, 1984 (Children's Sci. Book award N.Y. Acad. Scis. 1985), What the Elephant Was, 1986, The Dangerous Life of the Sea Horse, 1986 (Outstanding Sci. Trade Book for Children Nat. Sci. Tchrs. Assn./Children's Book Council Joint Com. 1986), Pigeons, 1989, Big Talk, 1990, The Year of the Panda, 1990 (Outstanding Sci. Trade Book for Children Nat. Sci. Tchrs. Assn./Children's Book Council Joint Com. 1990), That's Not Goldie, 1990, Jane Goodall's Animal World: Elephants, 1990, I Sailed With Columbus, 1991, Discovering Dinosaur Babies, 1991 (Outstanding Sci. Trade Book for Children Nat. Sci. Tchrs. Assn./Children's Book Council Joint Com. 1991), Let's Go Dinosaur Tracking, 1991, Squirrel Watching, 1992, Secret Land of the Past, 1993, Just Like Me, 1993, Before the Dinosaurs, 1994, The Puzzle of the Dinosaurs-Birds: The Story of Archaeopteyx, 1995; contributor: (as Miriam Weiss) Redbook, McCall's, Ladies Home Jour., Good Housekeeping, Univ. Rev., Creative Living, Colorado Quar.; included in anthologies; transl. into Danish, Swedish, Italian, French, Dutch, Norwegian, German, Braille. Mem. Authors Guild, PEN Am. Center (children's book com.), Nat. Writers Union. Author filmstrip materials Guidance Assocs.; textbook editor Harcourt Brace Jovanovich, 1980; editor Scribner Ednl. Pubs., 1985. Home and Office: 19 E 95th St New York NY 10128-0710*

SCHLEITER, MARY KAY, sociology educator; b. Chgo., Apr. 30, 1949; d. Edward Philip and Dolores Helen (Kearney) S. BA, Loyola U., Chgo., 1971; MA, U. Chgo., 1977, PhD, 1982. Asst. prof. U. Chgo., 1982-84, Albion (Mich.) Coll., 1984-89; asst. prof. sociology U. Wis.-Parkside, Kenosha, 1989-93, assoc. prof., 1994—, dir. women's studies; cons. Madison AIDS Support Network, Madison, 1992—, Hospice Alliance, Kenosha, 1990—. Contbr. articles to profl. publs. Mem. Am. Sociol. Assn., Midwest Sociol. Soc., Sociologists for Women in Soc. (coord. mentoring program 1991—). Office: U Wis-Parkside 900 Wood Rd Kenosha WI 53141-2000

SCHLESINGER, CAROLE LYNN, elementary educator; b. Detroit, May 13, 1961; d. Robert Schlesinger and Regenia Marie (Mitchell) Comper-e. Student, Kalamazoo Coll., 1981-84; BA, U. Mich., 1986; teaching cert., Eastern Mich. U., 1992. Cert. elem. tchr., Mich. Bank teller U. Mich. Credit Union, Ann Arbor, 1987; rsch. asst. dept. postgrad. medicine U. Mich., Ann Arbor, 1987; fin. planner IDS Fin. Svcs., Ann Arbor, 1988-89; telemarketer U. Mich. Telefund, Ann Arbor, 1989-90; enumerator U.S. Bur. Census, Ann Arbor, 1990; reading and math. tutor Reading and Learning Skills Ctr., Ann Arbor, 1991-92; interpreter Living Sci. Found., Wixom, Mich., 1992—; intern planning and mgmt. info. div. Peace Corps., Washington, 1985; intern Com. for Econ. Devel., Washington, 1985. Elder 1st Presbyn. Ch., Ann Arbor, 1992-94; canvasser, vol. Pub. Interest Rsch. group in Mich., Ann Arbor, 1986-87; trainee Groundwater Edn., Eastern Mich. U., Ypsilanti, 1991, mem. dean's adv. com., 1992; mem., group leader Ann Arbor Dems., 1984-87. Mem. ASCD, Kappa Delta Pi. Home: 4406 Hillside Dr Ann Arbor MI 48105-2782

SCHLESINGER, LYNN, sociology educator; b. Plattsburgh, N.Y., Apr. 8, 1955; d. H. Leonard and Caroline Janet (Schiff) S.; m. Jonathan Nizel, Aug. 21, 1983. AB magna cum laude, Smith Coll., 1977; MA, Brandeis U., 1982, PhD, 1994. Teaching asst. Smith Coll., Northampton, Mass., 1975, Brandies U., Waltham, Mass., 1978-80, Tufts U., Medford, Mass., 1981-82; rsch. asst. dept. social gerontol. rsch. Hebrew Rehab. Ctr. for Aged, Boston, 1981-84, 85-87; rsch. asst. arthritis/fibrosis ctr. Newton (Mass.)-wellesley Hosp., 1989-90; lectr. intro sociology SUNY, Plattsburgh, N.Y., 1991—; vis. lectr. Framingham (Mass.) State Coll., 1988-89; adj. educator Trinity Coll., Burlington, Vt., 1991, U. Vt., Burlington, 1992; cons. reviewer and presenter in field. Contbr. articles to profl. jours. Office: SUNY Dept Sociology Plattsburgh NY 12901

SCHLESINGER, VIOLET M., biomedical consultant; b. Denver, June 14, 1929; d. Robert Robertson Ferguson and Virginia Lee (Murray) Corbin; m. Robert Alexander Schlesinger, June 14, 1953; children: Roberta Diane, William Alexander. BA, U. Colo., 1952; MA, Goddard Coll., 1967; mins. license, Bethesda Sch. Ministry, 1990; PhD, Columbia Pacific, 1993. Prof. Ecole Normale, Tours, France; tchr. Denver, L.A. (Calif.) City Schs.; exec. dir. Wilde Woode Children's Ctr., Palm Springs, Calif.; trustee Anderson Children's Found., Palm Springs; self employed Candle Cross Chapel, Palm Springs, Prevention Pays, Palm Springs. Author: Spiritual, Mental and Physical, 1967, A Wholistic Approach to Wellness A Needed Answer to American Healthcare Crises, 1993. Pastor Candle Cross Chapel, 1990-94. Republican. Home: 380 Pablo Dr Palm Springs CA 92262

SCHLESSINGER, KARI, physician; b. N.Y.C., May 1, 1963; d. Arthur and Susan Schlessinger. BS, SUNY, Stony Brook, 1985, MD, 1990. Intern St. Vincent's Hosp., N.Y.C., 1990-92, resident in radiology, 1992-94. Home: 250 W 19th St New York NY 10011 Office: St Vincent's Hosp 153 W 11th St New York NY 10011

SCHLEY, ARLENE DORIS, federal agency administrator; b. Aberdeen, S.D., May 17, 1937; d. Armund Theodore and Alvina Emily (erdman) S. BS, Northern State U., 1958; MBA, Rockhurst Coll., 1981. Tchr. music Sioux Falls Schs., 1958-59; edn. dir. S.D. Farmers Union, Huron, 1959-66; tng. officer, intern U.S. GSA, Kansas City, 1966-71; regional personnel officer U.S. GSA, Chgo., 1971-74; dir. personnel mgmt. staff U.S. GSA, Washington, 1974-77, regional controller, 1977-82, deputy regional adminstr., 1982-83; deputy regional adminstr. U.S. GSA, Ft. Worth, 1987-95; dir. ctrl. adminstrv. ctr. Dept. of Commerce, Kansas City, 1983-87. Combined fed. campaign chmn. Tarrant County Combined Fed. Campaign and United Way, Ft. Worth, 1989-91. Recipient Presdl. Meritorious Rank award, Washington, 1989; named Disting. Alumnus Northern State U., 1987. Mem. Am. Soc. Pub. Adminstrs. (nat. coun. 1990-93, chpt. pres. 1990-91, mem. exec. com. sect. for women 1992-95, Pub. Adminstr. of Yr. 1993), Fed. Exec. Inst. Alumni Assn., Women's Policy Forum, Federally Employed Women. Lutheran. Home: 2929 Eagles Nest Dr Bedford TX 76021-3300 Office: US GSA 819 Taylor St Fort Worth TX 76102-6114

SCHLICHTEMEIER-NUTZMAN, SUE EVELYN, training consultant; b. Omaha, May 30, 1950; d. StuarTaylor and LaVera YVaughn (Conn) S.; m. Ronald E. Sorensen, Dec. 2, 1972 (div. Aug. 1984); m. Wade Edwin Nutzman, Aug. 27, 1988. BA in Journalism, U. Nebr., 1972, MA in Tng. and Devel., 1988, postgrad., 1989—. Advt. mgr. Burton Harpsichord Co., Lincoln, 1970-71; editorial asst. Nebr. Natural Resources Commn., Lincoln, 1971-72; editor Nebr. Personnel Dept., Lincoln, 1972-73; public info. specialist Governor's Budget Office, Lincoln, 1973-74; mental health cons. Mentl Health Ctr., Lincoln, 1974-81; tng. cons., keynote speaker Lincoln, 1977—; adj. advt. instr. U. Nebr., Lincoln, 1977-81, diversity instr., 1992—, orgn. cons., 1990—, dir. math camp, 1993—. Author: Seeds of Change, 1985, Assertiveness Training, 1990, Help in the Aftermath, 1995; contbr. feature articles and reviews to newspapers and other pubs. Organist, youth music dir., trustee, historian, Nehawka (Nebr.) United Meth. Ch., 1985-93; dir. Community Youth Music Program, Nehawka, 1988-93; sec. Conestoga Found Bd., Murray, Nebr. 1988-92; treas. Conestoga Bd. Edn., Murray, 1988-92; project leader 4-H, 1993—; dir. Math Camp, U. Nebr., 1993—; mem. steering com. Conestoga, 1994—; mem. Eastern Regional Math Sci. Coalition, 1995—; many other civic and charitable roles as vol. Recipient fellowship U. Nebr., Lincoln, 1991-92. Mem. ASTD, Bus. and Profl. Women (keynote spkr. 1991-92), Nat. Music Tchrs. Assn., Lincoln Music Tchrs. Assn., Missouri Valley Adult Edn. Assn., Adult and Continuing Edn. Assn. Nebr., Internat. Platform Speakers Assn., Am. Bus. Women's Assn. (keynote speaker 1993), U. Nebr. Alumni Assn. (life). Democrat. Home and Office: Tng Cons 3412 Mount Pleasant Dr Nehawka NE 68413-2424

SCHLICHTING, NANCY MARGARET, hospital administrator; b. N.Y.C., Nov. 21, 1954. B, Duke U., 1976; M, Cornell U., 1979. Adminstrv. resident Meml. Hosp. Cancer, N.Y.C., 1978; fellow Blue Cross-Blue Shield Assn., Chgo., 1979-80; asst. dirs. ops. Akron (Ohio) City Hosp., 1980-81, assoc. dir. planning, 1981-83, exec. v.p., 1983-88; exec. v.p. Riverside Meth. Hosps., Columbus, Ohio, 1988-92, pres., COO, 1992-93; pres., CEO, 1993—. Home: 887 Neil Ave Columbus OH 43215 Office: Riverside Meth Hosps 3535 Olentangy River Rd Columbus OH 43214-3925

SCHLOESSER, PATRICIA TURK, pediatrician, consultant; b. Okmulgee, Okla., Apr. 10, 1924; d. Alonzo Benjamin and Ruth (Powe) Turk; m. Harvey Leopold Schloesser, Dec. 31, 1945; children: Lysa Lynn, Nina Ruth, Peter Ernst, Anne Carol, David Turk. Student, Okla. State U., 1941-44, BS, 1965; BA, U. Wis., 1945; MD, U. Okla., Oklahoma City, 1949. Diplomate Am. Bd. Pediatrics; lic. healing arts. Pediatric cons. Kans. Bd. Health, Topeka, 1952-58, dir. divsn. maternal and child health, 1958-71; chief of party maternal and child health USAID and U. Calif. Berkeley, Kampala, Uganda, 1971-73; med. officer Mental Retardation Svcs. Western Australia, Perth, 1973; dir. bur. maternal and child health Kans. Dept. Health & Environment, Topeka, 1974-83, med. dir. MCH programs, 1984-87, dir. divsn. health, 1987-88, dep. dir. fed. and state rels., 1988-89; pvt. practice as maternal and child health cons. Topeka, 1989—; rsch. assoc. coping project Menninger Found., Topeka, 1955-62; clin. asst. prof. dept. pediatrics med. sch. U. Kans., Kansas City, 1977-94. Author: (with others) Widening World of Childhood, 1962; author, editor: Health of Children in Day Care, 1986; contbr. chpt. to Encyc. Britannica Med. & Health Ann., 1994; contbr. articles to profl. jours. Mem. adv. com. Kans. Action Children, Topeka, 1980-94; cons. Kans. Children's Svc. League, Topeka, 1980-85. Recipient Samuel J. Crumbine award Kans. Pub. Health Assn., 1983, Kans. Action Children award, 1985. Fellow Am. Acad. Pediatrics (mem. coms. child care 1969-74); mem. APHA (chair MCH sect. 1985-86, cons. child care 1987-94, mem. action bd. 1991—, Martha May Eliot award 1992), Kans. Med. Soc. (mem. maternal health com.), Assn. Maternal & Child Health Programs (bd. dirs. 1981-87, mem. various coms.). Republican. Presbyterian. Home and Office: 1914 Warner Ct Topeka KS 66604-3267

SCHLOSSER, ANNE GRIFFIN, librarian; b. N.Y.C., Dec. 28, 1939; d. C. Russell and Gertrude (Taylor) Griffin; m. Gary J. Schlosser, Dec. 28, 1965.

BA in History, Wheaton Coll., Norton, Mass., 1962; MLS, Simmons Coll., 1964; cert. archives adminstrn. Nat. Archives and Records Service, Am. U., 1970. Head UCLA Theater Arts Library, 1964-69; dir. Louis B. Mayer Libr., Am. Film Inst., L.A., 1969-88, dir. film/TV documentation workshop, 1977-87; head Cinema-TV Libr. and Archives of the Performing Arts, U. So. Calif., L.A., 1988-91; dir. Entertainment Resources Seminar, 1990; dir. rsch. libr. Warner Bros., 1991—. Project dir.: Motion Pictures, Television, Radio: A Union Catalogue of Manuscript and Special Collections in the Western U.S., 1977. Active Hollywood Dog Obedience Club, Calif. Numerous grants for script indexing, manuscript cataloging, library automation. Mem. Soc. Am. Archivists, Soc. Calif. Archivists (pres. 1982-83), Theater Library Assn. (exec. bd. 1983-86), Women in Film Special Librs. Assn.. Democrat. Episcopalian. Avocations: running, swimming, reading, dog obedience training. Office: Warner Bros Rsch Libr 5200 Lankershim Blvd Ste 100 North Hollywood CA 91601-3100

SCHLOSSER, THEA SUSSANNE, association executive; b. Hasenfeld, Germany, June 1, 1937; d. Theodor and Anna (Poppe) Hermesmeyer; divorced; children: Ingrid, Evelyn. Ed. in home econs., Austria; attended, N.Y. Inst. Photography, Modern Sch. Photography; postgrad., Am. Coll. Nutrition. Prin. World Wide Slides, Santa Barbara; founder Chronic Fatigue Media Awareness Assn., Santa Barbara; personal adviser, advt. dir., cons. Health Consciousness Mag.; pub. rels. dir. The Kuhnan Ctr.; spkr., lectr. on chronic fatigue immune dysfunction on TV, radio, among others; bus., advt. cons.; pub. rels. dir. Mex. Soc. Traditional Medizin. Author: Dark Cloud, 1995; inventor game show Challenge Your IQ. Recipient numerous gold medals in photography; swimming champion Austria, 1950. Mem. AMA. Office: Chronic Fatigue Media Awareness Assn 14 Camino Verde Santa Barbara CA 93103

SCHLOTFELDT, ROZELLA MAY, nursing educator; b. DeWitt, Iowa, June 29, 1914; d. John W. and Clara C. (Doering) S. BS, State U. Iowa, 1935; MS, U. Chgo., 1947, PhD, 1956; DSc (hon.), Georgetown U., 1972, Adelphi U., 1979, Wayne State U., 1983, U. Ill., Chgo., 1985, Kent State U., 1987, U. Cin., 1989; LHD (hon.), Med. U. S.C., 1976. Staff nurse State U. Iowa, VA Hosp., 1935-39; instr., supr. maternity nursing (State U. Iowa), 1939-44; asst. prof. U. Colo. Sch. Nursing, 1947-48; asst., then asso. prof. Wayne State U. Coll. Nursing, 1948-55; prof., asso. dean Wayne State U. Coll. Nursing (Coll. Nursing), 1957-60; dean Frances Payne Bolton Sch. Nursing, Case Western Res. U., 1960-72, prof., 1960-82, prof., dean emeritus, 1982—; vis. prof. Rutgers U., 1984-89, 90—, U. Pa., 1985-86; spl. cons. Surgeon Gen.'s Adv. Group on Nursing, 1961-63; mem. nursing research study sect. USPHS, 1962-66; mem. Nat. League for Nursing-USPHS Com. on Nursing Edn. Facilities, 1962-64; mem. com. on health goals Cleve. Health Council, 1961-66; mem. Cleve. Health Planning and Devel. Commn., 1969-72; adv. com. div. nursing W.K. Kellog Found., 1959-67; v.p. Ohio Bd. Nursing Edn. and Nurse Registration, 1970-71, pres., 1971-72; mem. Nat. Health Services Research Tng. Com., 1970-71; mem. supply and edn. panel Health Manpower Com., 1966-67; rev. com. Nurse Tng. Act, 1967-68; bd. visitors Duke U. Med. Center, 1968-70; mem. council, exec. com. Inst. Medicine of Nat. Acad. Scis., 1971-75; mem. nat. adv. health services council Health Services and Mental Health Adminstrn., 1971-75; mem. def. adv. com. on women in services Dept. Def., 1972-75; bd. mem., treas. Nursing Home Adv. and Research Council, 1975—; mem. adv. panel Health Services Research Commn. on Human Resources, Nat. Acad. Sci., 1977-85; cons. Walter Reed Army Inst.; adv. council on nursing, U.S. VA, 1965-69, chmn., 1966-69; mem. Yale U.; Council Com. on Med. Affairs, 1981-86; mem. adv. bd. Scholarly Inquiry for Nursing Practice, 1987—. Mem. editorial bd.: Advances in Nursing Sci, Inquiry, 1982-85, Jour. Nursing Edn., 1982-91; contbr. numerous articles to profl. jours. Bd. vis. Syracuse U., 1990—. Served to 1st lt. Army Nurse Corps, 1944-46. Recipient Disting. Svc. award U. Iowa, 1973, Case Western Res. U., 1991. Fellow Am. Acad. Nursing (v.p. 1975-77), Nat. League Nursing; mem. Am. Nurses Assn. (chmn. commn. on nurse edn. 1967-70, mem. com. for studying credentialling 1976-79, adv. com. W. K. Kellogg Nat. Fellowship program 1981-85), Pi Lambda Theta, Sigma Theta Tau (nat. v.p. 1948-50, selection com., disting. lectr. program 1986-87, Founders award for creativity 1985). Home: 1111 Carver Rd Cleveland OH 44112-3635 Office: 2121 Abington Rd Cleveland OH 44106-2333

SCHLOTMAN, VIRGINIA B., academic program director; b. N.Y.C., Aug. 11, 1919; d. Roy Edwin and Mary Theresa (Malloy) Blewitt; m. William Jerome Schlotman, June 8, 1946; children: Jeffrey W., Paul M., James P., Virginia M., William J. Jr., Mary Joan, Kim Anita. BA, Coll. of New Rochelle, N.Y., 1940; postgrad., Newark St. Tchrs. Coll., UCLA, 1977; cert., Carnegie Mellon U., 1980. Cert. elem. and secondary tchr. Lectr., publicity writer Circle Line, N.Y.C., 1939-41; tchr. Acad. Mt. St. Ursula, N.Y.C., 1941-43; dir. devel. and alumnae relations Acad. of MT. St. Ursula, N.Y.C., 1985-88; interline ticketing and tariffs agt. Pa. R.R., N.Y.C., 1943-45; asst. dir. arts program Assn. Am. Colls., N.Y.C., 1945-47; elem. tchr. Holy Trinity Sch., Westfield, N.J., 1953-55; elem. and mid. sch. tchr. Our Lady of Mercy, Portchester, N.Y., 1964-75, Sts. John and Paul Sch., Larchmont, N.Y., 1975-84; drama coach Our Lady of Mercy, Portchester, 1964-75, Sts. John and Paul Sch., Larchmont, 1975-84; adult edn. tchr. Mamaroneck (N.Y.) High Sch., 1978-81; test composer Archdiocese of City of N.Y.; classroom demonstrator N.Y. State Edn. Dept. Pres. alumnae chpt. Coll. New Rochelle, 1970-85; mem. vol. coun. Castle Gallery; mem. Larchmont Hist. Soc., Ladies of Charity, Larchmont and N.Y.C.; vol. St. Vincent's Hosp., Harrison, N.Y. Recipient Ursula Laurus award Coll. of New Rochelle, 1975. Mem. Fedn. Cath. Tchrs., Retired Tchrs. Assn., Nat. Cath. Edn. Assn., Am. Assn. Retired Persons, Coll. of New Rochelle Club (pres. 1975-85). Republican. Roman Catholic. Clubs: Coveleigh (Rye, N.Y.); Larchmont Woman's. Home: 17 Revere Rd Larchmont NY 10538-1814

SCHLOTZHAUER, VIRGINIA HUGHES, parliamentarian; b. Washington, July 24, 1913; d. William and Secy Alice (Royston) Hughes; m. Elbert O. Schlotzhauer, May 16, 1936; children: Carol Schlotzhauer Hinds, Jean Schlotzhauer Sumner, Jude. AB in LS, George Washington U., 1934. Mem. libr. staff George Washington U., Washington, 1934; various clerical positions U.S. Govt., Phoenix ARC, mid. 1930s; cons. parliamentarian Washington, 1967—; cons. Nat. Parliamentarian Edn. Project for Colls. and Univs. sponsored by Am. Inst. Parliamentarians funded by William Randolph Hearst Found., 1993—; presenter seminars. Author: A Parliamentarian's Book of Limericks, 1984; (with others) Parliamentary Opinions, 1982, Parliamentary Opinions II, 1992; primary contbr./cons. column Parliamentary Jour.; contbr. articles to profl. publs. Mem. steering and bylaws coms., sec. Nominating Conv. for Endorsement of Candidates for Bd. Edn., Montgomery County, Md., 1966; election reporter ABC-LWV, Prince George's County, Md., 1970s; v.p. bylaws Planned Parenthood Am., Prince George's County, late 1960s and 70s; group leader, bd. dirs., sec., trustee Potomac Area coun. Camp Fire Girls, Md. and D.C. area, 1940s and 50s; participant nonpartisan and Dem. polit. campaigns; judge various contests Future Bus. Leaders Am., Washington, 1970s. Mem. AAUW (life, named gift Bethesda-Chevy Chase br. 1962, named gift Md. divsn. 1972), Am. Inst. Parliamentarians (cert. profl. parliamentarian AIP, mem. adv. coun. 1966—, pres. D.C. chpt. 1966-68, name changed to Virginia Schlotzhauer D.C. chpt. 1984), Nat. Assn. Parliamentarians (profl. registered parliamentarian NAP, mem. coms.), D.C. Assn. Parliamentarians (founding pres., 1st hon. pres., Achievement award 1976), Westerners. Home and Office: 9819 Indian Queen Point Rd Fort Washington MD 20744-6904

SCHLUB, TERESA RAE, minister; b. Oak Park, Ill., July 11, 1946; d. Robert Carl and Shirley Rae (Listhartke) Grupe; m. George Jonas Schlub, Aug. 29, 1981; stepchildren: Kathy Bruns, Gary, Greg, Dean. BA, Westmar Teikyo U., 1971; MDiv, Garrett Evangel. Seminary, Evanston, Ill., 1974. Ordained deacon United Meth. Ch., 1973, elder, 1978. Asst. minister First United Meth. Ch., Morris, Ill., 1974-76; minister Leaf River (Ill.) German Valley United Meth. Ch., 1976-82, East Jordan United Meth. Ch., Sterling, Ill., 1982-86, Paw Paw (Ill.) United Meth. Ch., 1986-89, Community United Meth. Ch., LaMoille, Ill., 1989—; mem. alumni coun., sec. Garrett Evangel. Theol. Seminary, Evanston, 1974-76; mem. Conf. Bd. of Evangelism, 1974-76. Bd. dirs. Green Hills coun. Girls Scouts U.S., Freeport, Ill., 1986-88, Lee County Red Cross, Dixon, Ill., 1986-89, Crossroads Counseling Ctr., Mendota, 1989-91; bd. dirs. Quad County Counseling Ctr., Princeton, 1991—, treas., 1993-94; mem. Ill. Home Extension Assn., Grundy, Ogle, Whiteside and Lee Counties, 1974-89. Home: 71 Main PO Box 270 La Moille IL 61330-0270 Office: Community United Meth Ch 73 Main La Moille IL 61330

SCHLUTTER, LOIS COCHRANE, psychologist; b. Indpls., Oct. 18, 1953; d. Roy and Mavis (Wolfe) Cochrane; m. Dennis James Schlutter, Oct. 30, 1976; 1 child, Nathan Paul. BS, U. S.D., 1974, MA, 1975, PhD, 1978. Lic. psychologist, Minn. Psychologist, asst. Neurol. Inst. and Pain Ctr., Sioux City, Iowa, 1975-77; staff Mpls. Psychotherapy Inst., St. Louis Park, Minn., 1978-80; with strategic planning Vail Place, Mpls. and Hopkins (Minn.), 1988-90; owner Schlutter & Assocs., St. Louis Park, Minn., 1994—; bd. dirs. Vail Pl.; allied health staff, cons. Meth. Hosp., St. Louis Park, 1978—, mem. hospice adv. com., 1984—, mem. child abuse consortium, 1985-89; staff psychologist Sister Kenny Inst., Mpls., 1980-81; cons. Dept. Vocat. Rehab., St. Paul, 1984-93; supr. pastoral care AAPC, St. Louis Park, 1984—; lectr. St. Mary's Hosp. and Coll., Mpls., 1984-90; psychologist, dir. Family Dynamics, St. Louis Park, 1980-94; owner Employee Assistance Programs. Co-author: (play) The Extrapolator, 1968; contbr. articles to profl. jours. Mem. task force Vinland Nat. Ctr.; chmn. adult edn., Hopkins United Meth. Ch., 1988-91. Recipient rsch. grant Lederle Pharms., 1979. Mem. APA, Minn. Psychol. Assn., Am. Assn. Pastoral Counselors (profl. affiliate), Brookside Condominium Assn., Blvd. Condominium Assn., Internat. Platform Assn., Rotary, Phi Beta Kappa, Kappa Alpha Theta, Alpha Lambda Delta, Psi Chi. Office: Schlutter & Assocs 6200 Excelsior Blvd # 202 Saint Louis Park MN 55416

SCHMEER, ARLINE CATHERINE, cancer research development chemotherapy scientist; b. Rochester, N.Y., Nov. 14, 1929; d. Edward Jacob and Madeline Margaret (Haines) S. BA, Coll. St. Mary of the Springs, Columbus, Ohio, 1951; MS in Biology, Notre Dame U., 1961; PhD in Biomedicine, U. Colo., 1969; DSc (hon.), Albertus Magnus Coll., Potsdam, 1974, SUNY, Potsdam, 1990. Chmn. sci. dept. Watterson High Sch./Diocese of Columbus, 1954-59, St. Vincent Ferrer High Sch./Archdiocese of N.Y., N.Y.C., 1959-62; chmn. dept. biology Ohio Dominican Coll., Columbus, 1963-72; chmn. dept. anti-cancer agents of marine origin Am. Cancer Rsch. Ctr., Denver, 1972-82; dir. Mercenene Cancer Rsch. Inst. Hosp. St. Raphael, New Haven, 1982-93; sr. prin. investigator Marine Biol. Lab., Woods Hole, Mass., 1962-72, corp. mem., mem. libr. com., 1964—; rsch. prof. Med. Sch., U. Würzburg, Fed. Republic Gemany, 1969-70; pres., chief exec. officer Med. Rsch. Found., 1972—; participant, contbr. Internat. Cancer Congress, 1966—. Contbr. articles to biol. publs. Grantee Am. Cancer Soc., 1965; NSF fellow, 1957-62, NIH fellow, 1966-69; recipient numerous teaching awards, Ohi Acad. Scis. and others. Fellow Royal Microscopical Soc. Eng. (life); mem. N.Y. Acad. Sci. (life), Am. Soc. Cell Biology. Roman Catholic. Office: Mercenene Cancer Rsch Inst 790 Prospect St New Haven CT 06511

SCHMELING, HELEN MARGARET, clinical social worker; b. Denver, Jan. 31, 1951; d. Herbert Henry and Lillian Anna (Meyer) Thimm; m. William Allan Schmeling, Jr., July 24, 1982 (div. Dec., 1992); children: Dustin William, Alexander Thimm. BA in Psychology, U. Colo., 1973; MSW, U. Denver, 1982. Lic. profl. social worker, Wyo. Peer counselor Met. Community Coll., Omaha, 1975-76; outreach worker South Omaha Crisis Ctr., 1976-77; child care worker Mt. St. Vincent's Youth Home, Denver, 1978-81; social work intern health scis. ctr. U. Colo., Denver, 1981-82; coord. crisis line Vol. Info. Referral Service, Rock Springs, Wyo., 1983-85; clin. social worker, coord. elderly svcs. S.W. Counseling Svc., Rock Springs, 1985-92; med. social worker Wyo. Home Health Care, Rock Springs, 1986—; pvt. practice, 1992—; facilitator Alzheimer's Family Support Group, Rock Springs, 1983-92; social work cons. Castle Rock Convalecent Ctr., Green River, Wyo., 1990, Sage View Care Ctr., 1992—; sch. counselor Desert View Sch., 1992—. Mem. NASW (regional rep. on bd. dirs. Wyo. chpt. 1991-92). Democrat. Office: Desert View Elem Sweetwater Sch Dist # 1 PO Box 1089 Rock Springs WY 82902-1089

SCHMELZ, BRENDA LEA, legal assistant; b. Washington, Mo., June 13, 1958; d. Edward G. and Wilma D. (Hektor) R.; m. Jan M. Schmelz, Oct. 7, 1978; children: Edward L., Brent T. Secretarial sci. cert. with honors, East Cen. Coll., Union, Mo., 1977. Sec., paralegal Mittendorf & Mittendorf, Union, 1976-83, Eckelkamp, Eckelkamp, Wood & Kuenzel, Washington, 1983—; mem. legal secretarial adv. bd. East Cen. Coll., 1978, chmn., 1987. Mem. Nat. Assn. Legal Assts. (cert.), Nat. Assn. Legal Secs. (cert.), Mo. Assn. Legal Secs. (v.p. 1986, 91, pres. elect 1992-94, pres. 1994—, sec. 1984-86, 89-90, dir. pub. rels. 1987-89, Legal Sec of Yr. 1987, pres. 1989-92), Union Women of Today, Phi Beta Kappa. Republican. Roman Catholic. Home: 142 Highland Dr Union MO 63084-2014 Office: Eckelkamp Eckelkamp Wood & Kuenzel Bank of Washington Bldg Main & Oak Washington MO 63084

SCHMERTZ, MILDRED FLOYD, editor, writer; b. Pitts., Mar. 29, 1925; d. Robert Watson and Mildred Patricia (Floyd) S. B.Arch., Carnegie Mellon U., 1947; M.F.A., Yale U., 1957. Archtl. designer John Schurko, Architect, Pitts., 1947-55; assoc. editor Archtl. Record, N.Y.C., 1957-65; sr. editor Archtl. Record, 1965-80, exec. editor, 1980-85, editor-in-chief, 1985-90; vis. lectr. Yale Sch. Architecture, 1979—. Editor, contbr.: New Life for Old Buildings; other books on architecture and planning. Bd. mgrs. Jr. League, City of N.Y., 1964-65; commr. N.Y. Landmarks Preservation Commn., 1988-91. Fellow AIA; mem. Archtl. League N.Y., Century Assn. (N.Y.C.). Home and Office: 310 E 46th St New York NY 10017-3002

SCHMID, LYNETTE SUE, child/adolescent psychiatrist; b. Tecumseh, Nebr., May 28, 1958; d. Mel Vern John and Janice Wilda (Bohling) S.; m. Vijendra Sundar, June 13, 1987; children: Jesse Christopher Mikaéle, Eric Lynn Kalani. BS, U. Nebr., 1979; MD, U. Nebr., Omaha, 1984; postgrad., U. Mo., 1984-89. Diplomate Am. Bd. Med. Examiners, Am. Bd. Psychiatry and Neurology. Child and adolescent psychiatrist Fulton (Mo.) State Hosp., 1990-91, Mid-Mo. Mental Health Ctr., Columbia, Mo., 1991—; clin. asst. prof. psychiatry U. Mo., Columbia, 1990—. Contbr. articles to profl. jours. Mem. Am. Psychiat. Assn., Am. Acad. Child and Adolescent Psychiatry, Ctrl. Mo. Psychiat. Assn. (sec.-treas. 1992-93, pres.- elect 1993-94, pres. 1994-95), U. Nebr. Alumni Assn., Phi Beta Kappa, Alpha Omega Alpha. Republican. Baptist.

SCHMIDT, JEAN MARIE, microbiology educator; b. Waterloo, Iowa, June 5, 1938; d. John Frederick and Opal Marie (Lowe) S. BA, U. Iowa, 1959, MS, 1961; PhD, U. Calif., Berkeley, 1965. NIH postdoctoral fellow U. Edinburgh, Scotland, 1965-66; asst. prof. Ariz. State U., Tempe, 1966-71, assoc. prof., 1971-79, prof. microbiology, 1979—, assoc. dir. for biology, 1982—, acting chair dept. microbiology, 1988-89. Author: (with others) Bergey's Manual of Systematic Bacteriology, 1989; contbr. articles to jours. NSF grantee, 1981. Fellow AAAS; mem. Am. Soc. Microbiology (div. chmn. 1979-80), Soc. Gen. Microbiology, Phi Beta Kappa, Sigma Xi. Democrat. Methodist.

SCHMIDT, JOYCE, emergency physician; b. Wadena, Minn., Nov. 26, 1955; d. Kenneth W. and Willa K. (Blacklock) S. AA, City Coll. San Francisco, San Francisco, 1977; BS summa cum laude, Tex. A&M U., 1984; postgrad., U. Tulsa, 1985; MD, U. Tex., 1990. RN. RN St. Luke's Hosp., San Francisco, 1976-77, Twin Cities Community Hosp., Templeton, Calif., 1977-79, St. Joseph Hosp., Bryan, Tex., 1979-83; intern Maricopa Med. Ctr., Phoenix, 1990-91, resident emergency medicine, 1991-94; attending physician Maricopa Med Ctr., Phoenix, 1994—; chief resident Maricopa Med Ctr., 1993-94; instr. Tex. Emergency Med. Svcs., 1983-84; mem. subcom. on edn. and tng. Brazos Valley Devel. Coun., 1982-84; asst. instr., clin. supr. Coll. Health Edn., Tex. A&M U., College Station, 1980-84. Del. San Luis Obispo County Sexual Abuse Coun., 1979. Mem. Am. Coll. Emergency Physicians (outstanding sr. med. student), Soc. Acad. Emergency Medicine (excellence in emergency medicine award), Emergency Medicine Women's Assn., Alpha Omega Alpha, Phi Kappa Phi, Am. Heart Assn. (bd. dirs.), Sierra Club. Office: Maricopa Med Ctr 2601 E Roosevelt Phoenix AZ 85001

SCHMIDT, JUNE LAUREL, minister; b. Benton Harbor, Mich., June 5, 1941; d. Laurie Hudspeth-Minton and Julia Montgomery (Rowland) Minton; m. Ronald Edward Rogers, May 28, 1967 (dec.); children: Ronald Edward, Rhonda June; m. Donald Fredrick Schmidt, Dec. 18, 1980; stepchildren: Donald, Karen, Darryl, Lori, Mark. Diplomas in ministry, Gospel Crusade Inst. Ministry, Brandenton, Fla., 1980, 81. Ordained to ministry, Gospel Crusade Ministerial Fellowship, Bradenton, Fla., 1980. Assoc. pastorial trainee Soul's Harbour Ch., Tulsa, Okla., 1980; internat. dir. City of Light Sch. of Mininstry, Houston, 1980-82; dir. missions World Bible Way Fellowship, Dallas, 1983-85; pres., chief exec. officer His Word to the Nations, Inc., Dallas, Perry (Kans.), Sacramento, and Orlando, Fla., 1983—; regional dir., Caribbean region and Venezuela Gospel Crusade Ministerial Fellowship, Brandenton, Fla., 1986—; supr. Herbalife, Internat.; bd. dirs. Gospel Crusade Ministerial Fellowship, Bradenton, Fla., 1986—, His Word to the Nations, Inc., Dallas, Perry, Sacramento and Orlando, 1983—, The Encouragers, Nashville, 1986-91; cons. various internat. ministries, 1980—, Eagles Internat., New Brunswick, Can., 1994—; supr. Herbalife Internat. Editor: The Gospel Crusader, The Shepherd's Reporter, The Harvest Communiqu'80; contbr. numerous articles to religious publs. Capt., counselor Little League Baseball, Mililani Town, Hawaii, 1970; mem. Internat. Women in Leadership; bd. dirs. various internat. ministries. Mem. Charismatic Bible Ministries, Network Christian Ministries, Gospel Crusade Ministerial Fellowship, World Bible Way Fellowship, Eagles Internat. Republican. Nondenominational Pentecostal. Home and Office: 10794 Spring Brook Ln Orlando FL 32825-8529

SCHMIDT, KAREN ANNE, travel company executive, state legislator; b. L.A., Nov. 27, 1945; d. Ernest Potter and Anne Ruth (Cieslar) Jacobi; m. Gary Manning Schmidt, Jan. 30, 1970 (div. Jan. 1984); children: Geoffrey, Gavin; m. Simeon Robert Wilson III, Mar. 20, 1993. Student, Ariz. State U., 1963-66. Stewardess TWA, Kansas City, Mo., 1966-67, Western Airlines, L.A., 1967-68; sales rep. Delta Airlines, Atlanta, 1968-70; owner Go Travel Svc., Bainbridge Island, Wash., 1971—; mem. Wash. Legislature, 1980—. Named Legislator of Yr. Hwy. Users Fedn., 1992. Mem. Bainbridge Island C. of C. (dir. 1971-81, pres. 1976), Rotary (named Woman of the Yr. 1979). Office: Go Travel Svc 155 Madrone Ln N Bainbridge Is WA 98110-1862 also: Wash Ho of Reps 314 Jlob Olympia WA 98504

SCHMIDT, MARTHA MARIE, educator, counselor; b. Cadott, Wis., Sept. 28, 1912; d. Karl Christian and Lydia Sarah (Keller) Bubeck; m. Eugene Milton Schmidt, Sept. 11, 1943; children: Eugene Karl, Fredric John. BS, U. Wis., Stout, 1934; MPhil, U. Wis., Madison, 1947, M in Psychology and Behavioral Studies, 1959. Tchr. home econs. Barron (Wis.) High Sch., 1934-37; supr. student teaching U. Wis., Stout, 1937-38; state supr. home econs. edn. Wis. State Bd. Vocat. Edn., Madison, 1938-48; instr. adult evening sch. Madison Area Tech. Coll., 1949-69; guidance counselor Madison Met. Schs., 1959-79; coord. AARP and Wis. Ret. Tchrs. Assn., Madison, 1986-90; state chmn. health/long term care action group AARP, Wis., 1990-91; coord. health advocacy svcs. AARP, 1991—; founder Future Homemakers of Am., past advisor; conducted fgn. study programs Europe, Asia, Australia, 1971-88. Bd. dirs. Madison Oakwood Retirement Ctr., 1983-89; com. mem. Wis. Legis. Study Elderly Abuse, 1985-88. Mem. AARP, Wis. Ret. Tchrs. Assn. (recording sec. 1983-89), AAUW, Nat. Honor Soc. Home Econs., Luth. Women Missionary League, Valparaiso U. Guild (state pres. 1981-85), Madison Civics Club. Lutheran. Home: 3709 Zwerg Dr Madison WI 53705-5229

SCHMIDT, NANCY ANNE JACKSON, travel consultant; b. Aurora, Ill., Nov. 20, 1936; d. Roscoe N. and Estelle B. (Rhodes) Jackson; m. Richard A. Schmidt, June 13, 1959; 1 child, Pamela Anne Schmidt Sammons. BMus, MacMurray Coll., Jacksonville, Ill., 1958. Music tchr. Wallace & Rutland Grade Schs., Ottawa, Ill., 1968-92; ret., 1992; travel cons. Royal Travel, Ottawa, 1989—; travel escort Travel With Nancy. Home: 25 Oaklane Dr Ottawa IL 61350-1134

SCHMIDT, NANCY CHARLENE LINDER, English and journalism educator; b. Canton, Ohio, May 10, 1940; d. Charles William Masters and Mona Louise (Branch) Masters Swindell; m. Walter C. Linder, Sept. 6, 1958 (div. 1974); children: Karen Linder Heard, Cynthia Linder Webb, W. Charles; m. Charles Mathew Schmidt, Aug. 19, 1978; children: John, Michael, Greta Schmidt Wacker. BS in Edn., Kent State U., 1974, BS in English, 1979, BS in Journalism, 1985. Cert. elem. tchr., English tchr., journalism tchr. Jr. high sch. reading tchr. New Philadelphia (Ohio) City Schs., 1974-77; jr. high sch. tchr. Plain Local Schs., Canton, 1977-78; high sch. tchr., advisor yearbook, newspaper Nordonia Hills City Schs., Macedonia, Ohio, 1979—. Coun. pres. Village of Boston Heights, Ohio, 1983-86; leader Girl Scouts USA, 1965-73; children's choir dir. Broadway United Meth. Ch., 1965-74, Sun. sch. supt., 1965-73; pres. New Phila. Welcome Wagon Club, 1964-66. Mem. Nat. Coun. English Tchrs., Nordonia Hills Educators Assn. (pres. 1989-91, v.p. 1991-92). Republican. Home: 630 Fairfield Rd Aurora OH 44202 Office: Nordonia High Sch 8006 S Bedford Rd Macedonia OH 44056-2094

SCHMIDT, PAMELA MARIE, lawyer; b. Waukesha, Wis., Aug. 27, 1962; d. Edward C. Jr. and Corinne T. (Klopfer) S. BA, U. Wis., 1984; JD, Harvard U., 1987. Bar: Wis. 1987, U.S. Dist. Ct. (ea. and we. dists.) Wis. 1987, U.S. Ct. Appeals (7th cir.) 1994. Assoc. Foley & Lardner, Milw., 1987-89, Frisch Dudek, Ltd., Milw., 1989-93, Whyte Hirschboeck Dudek, Milw., 1993—. Active Milw. City Bd. Ethics, 1991—. Mem. ABA, Wis. Bar Assn., Milw. Young Lawyers Assn. (law explorer), Assn. Women Lawyers, Civil Trial Counsel Wis. Democrat. Roman Catholic. Office: Whyte Hirschboeck Dudek SC 111 E Wisconsin Ave Milwaukee WI 53202-4812

SCHMIDT, PATRICIA JEAN, medical lab technician; b. Cleve., June 15, 1941. Cert. applied lab. tech., Cuyahoga C.C., Cleve., 1967. Gen. lab. tech. Meridia Euclid (Ohio) Hosp., 1967—; tutor deaf students in coll math.; meml. designer. Composer, vocal and stage presentation coach. Active voter registration Rep. Party. Recipient Acad. award Math. Assn. Am., Washington, 1959. Mem. Nat. Assn. of the Deaf, Nat. Head Injury Found., Sweet Adeline Internat. Home: PO Box 43123 Cleveland OH 44143-0123

SCHMIDT, ROSEMARY E., nursing administrator; b. St. Louis, Nov. 2, 1947; d. Vincent A. and Margaret E. (Ottinger) Knopp; m. Emil J. Schmidt III, June 19, 1971; children: Emil J. IV, Amy E., Ericka E. RN, Barnes Hosp. Sch. Nursing, 1965. Staff nurse Barnes Hosp., St. Louis, 1965-66; staff nurse-med. St. Anthony's Med. Ctr., St. Louis, 1966-67, head nurse-med., 1967-75, head nurse-gyn, 1975-77, head nurse-ob/gyn, 1977-87, supr. nursing-med./surg./PRN pool, 1987—. Mem. Mo. Coun. Nurse Mgrs. Office: St Anthony's Med Ctr 10010 Kennerly Rd Saint Louis MO 63128

SCHMIDT, RUTH ANN, retired college president; b. Mountain Lake, Minn., Sept. 16, 1930; d. Jacob A. and Anna A. (Ewert) S. B.A., Augsburg Coll., Mpls., 1952; M.A., U. Mo., 1955; Ph.D., U. Ill., 1962; LLD, Gordon Coll., 1987. Asst. prof. Spanish Mary Baldwin Coll., Staunton, Va., 1955-58; asst. prof. Spanish SUNY-Albany, 1962-67, assoc. prof., 1967-78, dean of humanities, 1971-76; prof. and provost Wheaton Coll., Norton, Mass., 1978-82; pres. Agnes Scott Coll., Decatur, Ga., 1982-94; chair Women's Coll. Coalition, 1986-88. Author: Ortega Munilla y sus novelas, 1973, Cartas entre dos amigos del teatro, 1969. Trustee Gordon Coll., Wenham, Mass., 1980-86, Lyon Coll., 1993—; bd. dirs. DeKalb C. of C., 1982-85, Atlanta Coll. Art, 1984-94; mem. exec. com. Women's Coll. Coalition, 1983-88; v.p. So. Univ. Conf., 1993. Named Disting. Alumna Augsburg Coll., 1973. Mem. Assn. Am. Colls. (dir. 1979-82, treas. 1982-83), Soc. Values in Higher Edn., Am. Coun. Edn. (commn. on women in higher edn. 1985-88), AAUW, Assn. Pvt. Colls. and Univs. Ga. (pres. 1987-89), Internat. Women's Forum, Young Women's Christian Assn. Acad. Women Achievers. Democrat. Presbyterian.

SCHMIDT, SANDRA JEAN, financial analyst; b. Limestone, Maine, Mar. 21, 1955; d. Dale Laban and Marie Audrey (Bailey) Winters; m. Lee Lloyd Schmidt, Oct. 20, 1973; children: Colby Lee, Katrina Leesa. AA summa cum laude, Anne Arundel Community Coll., 1987; BS summa cum laude, U. Balt., 1990. CPA, Md. Enlisted U.S. Army, 1973, traffic analyst, 1973-85, resigned, 1985; auditor Md. State Office of Legislative Audits, Balt., 1990-93; fin. analyst Md. Ins. Adminstrn., Balt., 1993—. Tutor Anne Arundel County Literacy Coun., Pasadena, Md., 1990—; mentor U. Balt., 1991; host family Am. Intercultural Student Exchange, 1992—. Reciepient Mary Lou Hudson award Univ. Balt., 1990. Mem. AICPA, Am. Soc. Women Accts., Md. Assn. CPAs, Soc. Fin. Examiners, U. Balt. Alumni Assn., Alpha Chi, Beta Gamma Sigma, Phi Theta Kappa. Republican. Baptist. Home: 7716 Pinyon Rd Hanover MD 21076-1585

SCHMIDT, SARA LIZABETH, financial executive, financial planner; b. Wausau, Wis., Nov. 18, 1960; d. Peter Karl and Paula (Rendenbach) S.; m. Glen William Agritelley, Apr. 10, 1993. BA in Econs., Lawrence U., 1983. CFP. Registered sales asst. Merrill Lynch Pierce Fenner & Smith, Chgo., 1983-86; fin. counselor First Nationwide Bank, Oak Brook, Ill., 1986-88; personal and bus. fin. planner IDS Fin. Svcs., Downers Grove, Ill., 1989-90; regional v.p. Kemper Fin. Svcs., Chgo., 1990—. Mem. Internat. Assn. Fin. Planners, Inst. Cert. Fin. Planners. Office: Kemper Fin Svcs Inc # 105-382 820 S Macarthur Blvd Coppell TX 75019-4216

SCHMIDT, WENDY S., marketing executive; b. Neenah, Wis., May 6, 1959; d. Allan Gilbert and Marlene Jean (Beimborn) Wohlers; m. Charles Donald Schmidt, Oct. 17, 1981; children: Michaela Marel, Mariah Marel. Grad., pvt. schs. Cert. profl. sec., fin. paraplanner. Cert. clk. AAL/Life Issue Svcs., Appleton, Wis., 1977-79, cert. verifier, 1979; corr. AAL/Premium Svcs., Appleton, 1979-81; investment analysis clk./mortgages and real estate AAL/Investment Div., Appleton, 1981-87; exec. asst. to pres. AAL Distbrs. Inc., AAL Advisors Inc., Appleton, 1987-91; mgr. corp. communications AAL Capital Mgmt. Corp., Appleton, 1991-94, mktg. mgr., 1994—. Vol. ICT (vol. orgn.) of AAL, Appleton, 1980—. Mem. Nat. Assn. Securities Dealers. Office: AAL Capital Mgmt Corp 222 W College Ave Appleton WI 54911-5827

SCHMIDT-BOVA, CAROLYN MARIE, vocational school educator, consultant; b. Jacksonville, Fla., Sept. 1, 1948; d. Leonard Stephen and Marianne Vesta (Ruscher) S.; m. Edward W. Bova. EdB, SUNY, Buffalo, 1980, MEd, 1981; cert. advanced study, SUNY, Brockport, 1988. Cert. tchr., N.Y., SDA Work Study Coord. Instr. Erie Bd. Coop. Edn. Svcs., Lancaster, N.Y., 1977-82, Orleans-Niagara Bd. Coop. Ednl. Svcs., Medina, N.Y., 1982—; adj. instr. State U. Coll., Buffalo, 1988—; cons. N.Y. Dept. Edn., Albany, 1982—, facilitator, 1982-85, regional resource person, 1985—; bd. dirs. Inst. Curriculum Advancement; mem adv. com. Sch. Dist. Reorganization Ctrl. Western Regional Study. Leader Girl Scouts U.S.A., Buffalo. Tchr. Intern award Tchrs. Ctr., Lockport, N.Y., 1989; N.Y. Disting. Occupational edn. award, 1991. Mem. ASCD, Am. Vocat. Assn., Vocat. Indsl. Clubs Am. (advisor), N.Y. State Tchrs. Vocat. Assn. (regional rep.), Buffalo State Coll. Alumni (adv. bd. dirs. vocat. tech. programs), Phi Delta Kappa, Epsilon Pi Tau, Iota Lambda Sigma. Home: 5894 Fisk Rd Lockport NY 14094 Office: Orleans-Niagara Bd Ednl Svc 4232 Shelby Basin Rd Medina NY 14103-9515

SCHMIDT-DOWLER, VALERIE WOOD, retired mental health nurse; b. Chgo., July 12, 1915; d. Walter Arthur and Ebba Amanda (Stubbs) Wood; m. Frederick Schmidt, June 15, 1940 (dec. Apr. 1978); children: Frederick W. Schmidt, Carol Lorenzen, Dianne Wiest; m. G.L. Dowler, Feb. 14, 1982. Diploma, Evanston (Ill.) Sch. Nursing, 1938. RN, Calif. Nurse on surg. ward, also mental health clinic Queens Hosp., Honolulu, 1938-41; office nurse Escondido, Calif., 1960-85. Mem. Order Eastern Star (past matron), White Shrine of Jerusalem (worthy high priestess), Daus. of the Nile, Felicita Ct. Order of the Aramanth. Republican. Methodist. Home: 1540 Birch Ave Escondido CA 92027-4602

SCHMIEDER, LINDA MARIE, therapist; b. Phoenix, Feb. 9, 1950; d. Otto and Ruby (Harkey) S. BS, Ariz. State U., 1976; MA, Antioch U., 1988, Fielding Inst., 1994; postgrad., Fielding Inst., 1995—. Cert. alcohol and drug counselor, sex offender treatment provider. Psychology asst. Maricopa County Hosp., Phoenix, 1976-77; counselor I and II Ariz. State Hosp., Phoenix, 1977-79; contract counselor Health and Social Svcs. Juneau, Alaska, 1988; therapist, program dir. Tongass Community Counseling Ctr., Juneau, 1988-90; therapist, cons. Juneau Alliance Mentally Ill, 1990-92; pvt. practice Juneau, 1990-92; therapist Boyer Marin Ledge, Woodacre, Calif., 1992-93; house mgr. Buckelew Programs, San Rafael, Calif., 1992—; inservice provider St. Ann's Nursing Home, Juneau, 1990-92; cons., group leader Shanti, Juneau, 1990-92; mem. adj. faculty U. Alaska S.E., Juneau, 1991. Bd. dirs. AWARE-Women's Svcs., Juneau, 1991. Mem. APA, Am. Counseling Assn., Marin County Psychol. Assn., Mensa. Democrat. Unitarian. Home: 414 Marin Ave Mill Valley CA 94941

SCHMITT, MARGARET SCHOMBURG, librarian; b. LaCrosse, Wis., Apr. 25, 1927; d. Frederick and Ida (Nuttleman) Schomburg; m. Elroy Henry Schmitt, Sept. 24, 1949; children: Katherine Anne, Lawrence Elroy. BA, U. Wis., 1948; MLS, Rosary Coll., River Forest, Ill., 1970. Ref. librarian, asst. libr. dir. LaGrange (Ill.) Pub. Libr., 1971-74; libr. dir. Alsip-Merrionette Park (Ill.) Pub. Libr., 1974-92; ret., 1992; mem. Ill. Authors Com., 1986-88; sec. Joint Advancement of Ill. Librs., 1987-89. Mem. ALA, Ill. Libr. Assn., South Suburban Libr. Assn. (pres. 1980-81), Phi Beta Kappa, Phi Kappa Phi, Beta Phi Mu. Lutheran. Home: 1409 53d Pl La Grange IL 60525

SCHMITT, MARILYN LOW, foundation program manager, art historian; b. Chgo., May 24, 1939; d. Abraham A. and Mae (Willett) Low. BA, Lawrence U., 1960; MA, U. Calif., Berkeley, 1962; PhD, Yale U., 1972. Instr. Dickinson Coll., Carlisle, Pa., 1964-66; acting instr. Yale Univ., New Haven, 1969-70; asst. prof. So. Conn. State U., New Haven, 1970-75; assoc. prof. U. Miami, Coral Gables, Fla., 1976-82; program officer J. Paul Getty Trust, L.A., 1983-85; program mgr. Getty Art History Info. Program, Santa Monica, Calif., 1985—; bd. dirs. Internat. Ctr. of Medieval Art, N.Y.C.; ex-officio bd. dirs. Recovery, Inc., Chgo., 1971—; 1st v.p. Abraham A. Low Inst., Chgo., 1989—. Co-author: Object, Image, Inquiry: The Art Historian at Work, 1988; co-editor: Report on Data Processing Projects in Art, 1988. Recipient Woodrow Wilson fellowship, 1960-61, AAUW fellowship, 1968-69, NEH fellowship for ind. rsch., 1981-82. Mem. Coll. Art Assn. Am., Art Librs. Soc. N.Am., Phi Beta Kappa. Home: 1440 Veteran Ave Apt 362 Los Angeles CA 90024-4832 Office: Getty Art History Info Program 401 Wilshire Blvd Ste 1100 Santa Monica CA 90401-1430

SCHMITT, MARY ELIZABETH, postal supervisor; b. Detroit, Sept. 16, 1948; d. Jerome Ferdinand and Margaret Ellen (Beauregard) S. BS, Ea. Mich. U., 1979. Waitress, hostess Mr. Steak, Westland, Mich., 1969-70; mgr. housewares K-Mart, Ypsilanti, Mich., 1971, asst. mgr., jewelry, 1972; postal clk. U.S. Postal Svc., Ann Arbor, Mich., 1972-88, postal supr., 1988—. Crisis intervention counselor Ozone House, Ann Arbor, 1978; convenor Gray Panthers of Huron Valley, Ann Arbor, 1979-80; active Greenpeace. Mem. LWV, Nat. Assn. Postal Suprs., Ann Arbor Postal Fed. Credit Union (v.p. 1987—), Sierra Club, Ancestry Club. Roman Catholic. Home: PO Box 1833 Ann Arbor MI 48106 Office: US Postal Svc 2075 W Stadium Ann Arbor MI 48106

SCHMITZ, DOLORES JEAN, educator; b. River Falls, Wis., Dec. 27, 1931; d. Otto and Helen Olive (Webster) Kreuziger; m. Karl Matthias Schmitz Jr., Aug. 18, 1956; children: Victoria Jane, Karl III. BS, U. Wis., River Falls, 1953; MS, Nat. Coll. Edn., 1982; postgrad., U. Minn., Mankato, 1969, U. Melbourne, Australia, 1989, U. Wis., Milw., 1989, Carroll Coll., 1990, Cardinal Stritch, 1990. Cert. tchr., Wis. Tchr. Manitowoc (Wis.) Pub. Schs., 1953-56, West Allis (Wis.) Pub. Schs., 1956-59, Lowell Sch., Milw., 1960-63, Victory Sch., Milw., 1964; tchr. Palmer Sch., Milw., 1966-84, 86-94, unit leader, 1984-86; ret., 1994; co-organizer Headstart Tchg. Staff Assn., Milw., 1968; insvc. organizer Headstart and Early Childhood, Milw., 1969-92; pilot tchr. for Whole Lang., Hi-Scope and Math. Their Way, 1988-93; bd. dirs. Cuurriculum Devel. Ctr. of Milw. Edn. Ctr., 1993-94. Author: (curriculum) Writing to Read, 1987, Cooperation and Young Children (ERIC award 1982), Kindergarten Curriculum, 1953. Supporter Milw. Art Mus., Milw. Pub. Mus., Milw. County Zoo, Whitefish Bay Pub. Libr., Earthwatch, Riveredge Nature Ctr.; vol. fgn. visitor program Milw. Internat. Inst., 1966-94, vol. holiday folk fair, 1976-94; vol. Earthwatch, 1989; lobbyist Milw. Pub. Sch. Bd. and State of Wis., 1986-93, 1986-93; coord. comty. Vols., 1990-94. Grantee Greater Milw. Ednl. Trust, 1989. Mem. NEA (life), ASCD, Milw. Kindergarten Assn. (rec. sec. 1986-93), Nat. Assn. for Edn. of Young Children, Tchrs. Applying Whole Lang., Wis. Early Childhood Assn., Milw. Tchrs. Ednl. Assn. (co-chmn. com. early childhood 1984-86), Assn. for Childhood Edn. Internat. (charter pres. Manitowoc chpt. 1955-56), Milw. Educating Computer Assn., Alpha Psi Omega. Roman Catholic. Home: # 9 312 8th Ave N Tierra Verde FL 33715

SCHMITZ, SHIRLEY GERTRUDE, marketing and sales executive; b. Brackenridge, Pa., Dec. 19, 1927; d. Wienand Gerard and Florence Marie (Grimm) S. BA, Ariz. State U., 1949. Tchr., guidance counselor Mesa High Sch., Ariz., 1949-51; area mgr. Field Enterprises Ednl. Corp., Phoenix, 1951-52, dist. mgr., 1952, regional mgr., 1953-55, br. mgr., Montreal, Que., Can., 1955-61, nat. supr., Chgo., 1961-63, asst. sales mgr., 1963-65, nat. sales mgr., 1965-70; v.p., gen. sales mgr. F.E. Compton Co. div. Ency. Brit., Chgo., 1970-71, exec. v.p., dir. sales, 1971-73; pres. CHB Port-A-Book Store, Inc., 1973-76; gen. mgr. Bobbs-Merrill Co., Inc., Indpls., 1976-82; v.p. sales U.S. Telephone Communications of Midwest, Inc., Chgo., 1982-83; exec. v.p. sales and market devel. Entertainment Publs., Corp., Birmingham, Mich., 1983-89, sr. v.p. mktg. and sales, Troy, Mich., 1989-92; prin. S.G. Schmitz and Assocs., Chgo., 1992—; bd. dirs. Ariz. Tech. Incubator; bd. advisors Ctr. Advancement of Small Bus., Ariz. State U. Sch. Bus; bd. dirs. Spectral, Inc., Colourtech, Inc. Recipient Twin award Nat. Bd. YWCA, 1987. Recipient Honors award Beta Gamma Sigma, 1995. Mem. USGA (assoc.), Internat. Platform Assn., Am. Mgmt. Assn., Nat. Bus. Incubation Assn., Nat. Geographic Soc., Nat. Space Soc., World Future Soc., Ariz. State U. Alumni Assn. Republican. Roman Catholic. Home: 93 Miller Rd Hawthorn Woods IL 60047-1395

SCHMOLDT, PEGGY SUE, cosmetology educator; b. International Falls, Minn., Apr. 11, 1959; d. John Herbert and Elizabeth Ann (Powers) Hauptli; m. Stephen Michael Schmoldt, Jan. 5, 1980; children: Jillian Marie, Megan Elizabeth. Student, U. Iowa, 1977-78; diploma, Capri Cosmetology Coll., 1979; student, Regis U., 1993—. Lic. cosmetologist, Colo., Fla.; cert. pvt. cosmetology tchr., vo-tech. tchr., Colo. Hair designer Fashion Ave., Dubuque, Iowa, 1979-81, A Unique Boutique, Destrehan, La., 1984-85, V.I.P. Salon, Boca Raton, Fla., 1987-89; sch. mgr., instr. LaVonne's Acad. of Beauty, Denver, 1981-83; nat. platform educator Anion Labs., Inc., Harvey, La., 1984-85; salon mgr., designer, publ. rels. specialist, educator Lord & Taylor Salons, Boynton Beach/Boca Raton, Fla., 1985-87; dir. edn. Cantwell/Creative Sch. Beauty, Pompano Beach, Fla., 1988-91; dir. cosmetology edn. Boca Raton Inst., 1991-92; freelance cosmetologist, educator Profl. Salon Svcs., Westminster, Colo., 1993—; mem., educator La. Hair Fashion Com., New Orleans, 1985; tchr. Le Team Styles Group, Ft. Lauderdale, Fla., 1986-87; mem. Colo. Edn. Com., Denver, 1993. Pres. New Orleans Cosmetology Assn., 1984; treas., membership chair Palm Beach Cosmetology Assn., 1986-88; vol. Look Good-Feel Better program Am. Cancer Soc., Palm Beach/Broward County, Fla., 1989, Denver, 1993; sec., mem. legislation/edn. com. Broward County Cosmetology Assn., 1990-92; mem. spkrs. bur. Planned Parenthood of Rocky Mountains, Denver, 1993. Mem. Denver Cosmetology Assn. (pres. 1993, 94), Colo. Cosmetology Assn. (3d v.p. 1993, 1st v.p. 1994, mem. legislation/by-laws com.). Roman Catholic.

SCHMONES, SHIRLEY See WALLACH, SHIRLEY SCHMONES

SCHNABEL, JOANN, artist, educator; b. Cleve., Oct. 26, 1957; d. Irving Dwight and Alys (Grossman) S. BFA, Alfred U., 1981; MFA, La. State U., 1986. Asst. to dir. Haystack Mountain Sch. of Craft, Deer Isle, Maine, 1986-87; artist-in-residence, studio coord. Penland (N.C.) Sch., 1987-89; vis. asst. prof. Art Tulane U., New Orleans, 1989-90; resident artist Banff (Can.) Ctr. for the Arts, 1991; vis. artist Watershed Ctr. for Ceramic Art, Edgecombe, Maine, 1992, 93, also bd. dirs.; asst. prof. Art U. No. Iowa, Cedar Falls, 1990—; vis. artist. U. Ill., Champaign, 1992, Iowa City, 1992; juror Summer Sensations ann. student exhibition, Cedar Falls, 1992. Contbr. (book) Ceramics, Mastering The Craft, 1991, Electric Kiln Ceramics, revised edit., 1994; exhibits include Northern Clay Ctr., St. Paul, 1994, Chgo. Botanic Garden, Glencoe, Ill., 1993, Drake U., Des Moines, 1993, William Traver Gallery, Seattle, Creative Arts Workshop, New Haven, Conn., Penland Overlook Asheville Mus. of Art, 1992—, Watershed Benefit Exhibition, N.Y.C., 1993, Art Show 4, Cedar Falls, 1992, Ceramics Invitational, Cedar Rapids, Iowa, 1991, Works in Clay, Wichita Falls, Tex., 1991, many others. Summer Rsch. fellow U. No. Iowa, 1993, Nanette Finger scholar, 1993, Profl. Devel. grantee Iowa Arts Coun., 1993. Mem. Coll. Art Assn., Nat. Coun. for Edn. in the Ceramic Arts, Am. Crafts Coun., La. State U. Ceramic Art Student Assn. (v.p. 1983-86). Jewish. Home: 1922 Tremont St Cedar Falls IA 50613 Office: U No Iowa Dept Art 126 Kamerick Cedar Falls IA 50614

SCHNACK, GAYLE HEMINGWAY JEPSON (MRS. HAROLD CLIFFORD SCHNACK), corporate executive; b. Mpls., Aug. 14, 1926; d. Jasper Jay and Ursula (Hemingway) Jepson; student U. Hawaii, 1946; m. Harold Clifford Schnack, Mar. 22, 1947; children: Jerrald Jay, Georgina, Roberta, Michael Clifford. Skater, Shipstad & Johnson Ice Follies, 1944-46; v.p. Harcliff Corp., Honolulu, 1964—, Schnack Indsl. Corp., Honolulu, 1969—, Nutmeg Corp., Cedar Corp.; ltd. ptnr. Koa Corp. Mem. Internat. Platform Assn., Beta Sigma Phi (chpt. pres. 1955-56, pres. city council 1956-57). Established Ursula Hemingway Jepson art award, Carlton Coll., Ernest Hemingway creative writing award, U. Hawaii. Office: PO Box 3077 Honolulu HI 96802-3077 also: 1200 Riverside Dr Reno NV 89503

SCHNACKENBERG, GJERTRUD CECELIA, poet; b. Tacoma, Aug. 27, 1953; d. Walter Charles and Doris Ione (Strom) S.; m. Robert Nozick, Oct. 5, 1987. BA summa cum laude, Mount Holyoke Coll., 1975, LittD (hon.), 1985. Author: (poetry) Portraits and Elegies, 1982, The Lamplit Answer, 1985, A Gilded Lapse of Time, 1992. Poetry fellow The Bunting Inst. of Radcliffe Coll., 1979-80, NEA, 1985-86, The Guggenheim Found., 1986-87; recipient Rome prize AAAL, 1983, Lit. Lion award N.Y. Pub. Libr., 1993. Office: care Farrar Straus & Giroux Inc 19 Union Sq West New York NY 10003*

SCHNALL, EDITH LEA (MRS. HERBERT SCHNALL), microbiologist, educator; b. N.Y.C., Apr. 11, 1922; d. Irving and Sadie (Raab) Spitzer; AB, Hunter Coll., 1942; AM, Columbia U., 1947, PhD, 1967; m. Herbert Schnall, Aug. 21, 1949; children: Neil David, Carolyn Beth. Clin. pathologist Roosevelt Hosp., N.Y.C., 1942-44; instr. Adelphi Coll., Garden City, N.Y., 1944-46; asst. med. mycologist Columbia Coll. Physicians and Surgeons, N.Y.C., 1946-47, 49-50; instr. Bklyn. Coll., 1947; mem. faculty Sarah Lawrence Coll., Bronxville, N.Y., 1947-48; lectr. Hunter Coll., N.Y.C., 1947-67; adj. assoc. prof. Lehman Coll., City U. N.Y., 1968; asst. prof. Queensborough Community Coll., City U. N.Y., 1967, assoc. prof. microbiology, 1968-75, prof., 1975—, adminstr. Med. Lab. Tech. Program, 1985—; vis. prof. Coll. Physicians and Surgeons, Columbia U., N.Y.C., 1974; advanced biology examiner U. London, 1970—. Mem. Alley Restoration Com., N.Y.C., 1971—; mem. legis. adv. com. Assembly of the State of N.Y., 1972. Mem. Community Bd. 11, Queens, N.Y., 1974—, 3d vice-chmn., 1987-92, 2nd vice chmn., 1992—; public dir. of bd. dirs. Inst. Continuing Dental Edn. Queens County, Dental Soc. N.Y. State and ADA, 1973—. Rsch. fellow NIH, 1948-49; faculty rsch. fellow, grantee-in-aid Rsch. Found. of SUNY, 1968-70; faculty rsch. grant Rsch. Found. City U. N.Y., 1971-74. Mem. Internat. Soc. Human and Animal Mycology, AAAS, Am. Soc. Microbiology (coun., N.Y.C. br. 1981—, co-chairperson ann. meeting com. 1981-82, chair program com. 1982-83, v.p. 1984-86, pres. 1986-88), Med. Mycology Soc. N.Y. (sec.-treas. 1967-68, v.p. 1968-69, 78-79, archivist 1974—, fin. advisor 1983—, pres. 1969-70, 79-80, 81-82), Bot. Soc. Am., Med. Mycology Soc. Americas, Mycology Soc. Am., N.Y. Acad. Scis., Sigma Xi, Phi Sigma. Clubs: Torrey Botanical (N.Y. State); Queensborough Community Coll. Women's (pres. 1971-73) (N.Y.C.). Editor: Newsletter of Med. Mycology Soc. N.Y., 1969-85; founder, editor Female Perspective newsletter of Queensborough Community Coll. Women's Club, 1971-73. Home: 21406 29th Ave Flushing NY 11360-2622

SCHNEEWIND, ELIZABETH HUGHES, social worker; b. Chgo., May 11, 1940; d. Everett Cherrington and Helen (MacGill) Hughes; m. Jerome Borges Schneewind, Feb. 23, 1963; children: Sarah Katherine, Rachel Miriam, Hannah Elizabeth. BA in Philosophy, U. Chgo., 1959; MA in Philosophy, Brown U., 1962; MSW, U. Md., 1985; postgrad., Yale U., 1962-63. ACSW, LCSW-C; cert. German translator. Program evaluator Coll. Human Svcs,, N.Y.C., 1976-77; rsch. asst. Fordham U. Gerontology Ctr., N.Y., 1977-80; field supr. N.Y.C. Dept. Aging Foster Grandparent Program, 1980-82; social worker Levindale Geriatric Ctr., Balt., 1985-88, Johns Hopkins Hosp., Balt., 1988; asst. dir. older adult svcs. Jewish Family Svcs., Balt., 1988—; presentor in field. Pres. Balt. Washington Soc. Psychogeriatrics, 1987-89; exec. bd. Alzheimer's Assn., Balt. chpt. 1986-92; v.p. Women in Urban Crisis, Pitts., 1972-73. Mem. NASW, Md. Soc. Clin. Social Work. Democrat. Home: 325 Woodlawn Rd Baltimore MD 21210-2308 Office: Jewish Family Svcs 5750 Park Heights Ave Baltimore MD 21215-3929

SCHNEIBEL, VICKI DARLENE, human resources administrator; b. Astoria, Oreg., Mar. 11, 1946; d. Howard Stanley and Sally (Thompson) Brandt; m. Lawrence Walter Schneibel, Mar. 18, 1967. AAS, Anchorage Community Coll., 1986; BA, Alaska Pacific U., 1991, MAT, 1994. Cert. profl. sec. Clk. typist The Oregonian, Portland, Oreg., 1964-67; statis. typist Rader Pneumatics, Inc., Portland, Oreg., 1967-71; sec., bookkeeper Larry's Custom Remodeling, Portland, Oreg., 1971-73; bookkeeper Tualatin Hills Pk. & Recreation Dist., Portland, Oreg., 1973-74; pvt. sec. Aloha (Oreg.) Community Bapt. Ch., 1974-79; exec. sec. Hyster Sales Co., Tigard, Oreg., 1979-83, 1st Nat. Bank of Anchorage, 1983-84; office mgr. Control Data Alaska, Anchorage, 1984-86; human resource liaison, corp. office mgr. Westmark Hotels, Inc., Anchorage, 1986—. Active Anchorage Women's Commn., 1995—, Alaska Worksite Wellness Alliance. Mem. ASTD, Am. Mgmt. Assn., Adminstrv. Mgmt. Soc., Soc. for Human Resource Mgmt. Lutheran. Home: 6646 Cimarron Cir Anchorage AK 99504 Office: Westmark Hotels Inc 880 H St Ste 101 Anchorage AK 99501-3450

SCHNEIDER, ADELE GOLDBERG, librarian, educator; b. N.Y.C., May 13, 1924; d. Abraham and Anna (Levy) Goldberg; B.A., Bklyn. Coll., 1945; M.L.S., Pratt Inst., 1965; M.A., L.I.U., 1971; m. Noel Schneider, Jan. 1, 1950; children: Adam Matthew, Tracy Lynn. Field interviewer Gallup Poll, N.Y.C., 1941-48; social worker N.Y.C. Dept. Social Services, 1949-52; editor Bklyn. Coll. Alumni Quarterly, 1961-65; instr. Kingsborough Community Coll. CUNY, 1965-70, asst. prof. dept. library, 1970-72, assoc. prof., 1972-88, prof., 1988-92, prof. emeritus, 1992—. Contbr. articles to profl. jours. Mem. ALA, Library Assn. City U. N.Y., N.Y. Tech. Services Librarians, Beta Phi Mu. Home: 124 Oxford St Brooklyn NY 11235-2311 Office: 2001 Oriental Blvd Brooklyn NY 11235-2336

SCHNEIDER, ADELE SANDRA, clinical geneticist; b. Johannesburg, South Africa, Mar. 21, 1949; came to U.S., 1976, naturalized, 1981; d. Michael and Annette (Sive) S.; m. Gordon Mark Cohen, July 2, 1978; children: Jeffrey, Brian, Adrienne. MB, BChir, Witwatersrand U., Johannesburg, South Africa, 1973. Intern in internal medicine Baragwanath Hosp., Johannesburg, 1974, intern in gen. surgery, 1974; sr. house officer in pediatrics Coronation Hosp., Johannesburg, 1975; sr. house officer in radiation therapy Johannesburg Gen. Hosp., 1975-76; resident in pediatrics Wilmington (Del.) Med. Ctr., 1976-78; fellow in clin. genetics and metabolic diseases Children's Hosp. of Phila., 1978-81, staff physician Cystic Fibrosis Clinic, 1987-88; staff pediatrician Children's Rehab. Hosp., Phila., 1981-82, dir. pediatrics, 1982-87, acting med. dir., 1984-85; clin. instr. dept. pediatrics Jefferson Med. Coll., Phila., 1982-84, clin. asst. prof. dept. pediatrics, 1984—; clin. geneticist Hahnemann Univ. Hosp., Phila., 1987-90, asst. clin. prof. dept. pediatrics and neoplastic diseases, 1987-90; clin. geneticist Albert Einstein Med. Ctr., Phila., 1990-92, acting dir. med. genetics, 1992-93, dir. clin. genetics program, 1993—; mem. courtesy faculty Sch. Medicine Temple U., Phila., 1987; clin. geneticist St. Christopher's Hosp. for Children, Phila., 1987; genetics cons. dept. pediatrics Bryn Mawr (Pa.) Hosp.; presenter, lectr. in field. Contbr. articles to profl. jours. Bd. dirs. Phila. Parenting Associates, 1986-93. Fellow Am. Coll. Med. Genetics; mem. Am. Soc. Human Genetics, Am. Chem. Soc. Office: Albert Einstein Med Ctr Dept Pediatrics 5501 Old York Rd Philadelphia PA 19141-3098

SCHNEIDER, CHRISTINE LYNN, customs inspector; b. Staten Island, N.Y., Feb. 3, 1960; d. Howard Thomas and Ina Elise (Beyer) S. BS, SUNY Maritime Coll., Bronx, 1984. Lic. 3d mate, U.S. Mcht. Marine; cert. U.S. customs firearms instr. Sr. inspector U.S. Customs Svc., San Diego, 1989—. Lt. USNR, 1984-87, 91—. Democrat. Lutheran. Home: 2950 Alta View Dr Apt H104 San Diego CA 92139-3365 Office: US Customs Svc 720 E San Ysidro Blvd San Ysidro CA 92173-3115

SCHNEIDER, CLARA GARBUS, dietitian, consultant; b. Paterson, N.J., Sept. 2, 1955; d. Edward George and Constance (Murray) Garbus; m. Philip John Schneider, July 22, 1978; children: Amy L., Stephen P. BS, U. Del., 1977; MS, U. Md., 1979. Registered dietitian. Nutritionist Woman, Infant & Children Feeding Program, Leesburg, Va., 1980-81, Barney Sr. Svcs., Washington, 1982-83; cons. dietitian Sharon Nursing Home, Washington, 1984-85, Nat. Acad. SCis., Washington, 1985; cons. Nat. Assn. WIC Dirs., Balt., 1990; cons. dietitian J.B. Johnson Nursing Ctr., Washington, 1990-93, Am. Inst. for Cancer Rsch., Washington, 1987—, Higher Horizons Head Start, Fairfax, Va., 1985-93, Arlington (Va.) Cmty. Action Program, 1985—; employment exch. coord. for dietitians D.C. Dietetic Assn., 1985—; cons. dietitian Hospice Vis. Nurses Assn. No. Va., 1993—. Author: Diabetic's Brand Named Food Exchange Handbook, 1991; contbr. articles to profl. jours. Active Girl Scouts U.S.A., Arlington, 1989—, Boy Scouts Am., 1992—. Mem. AAUW, Am. Dietetic Assn., Cons. Nutritionists of Chesapeake Bay Area, Arlington Nutrition Coun., Assn. of Part-Time Profls. Home and Office: 263 N Bryan St Arlington VA 22201

SCHNEIDER, DEBRA, physical therapist; b. Bklyn., July 4, 1966; d. Carl and Rena Natalie (Brown) Litt; m. Russell Wayne Schneider, May 31, 1993. BS, MA in Phys. Therapy, Touro Coll., 1989. Phys. therapist L.I. Spine/Proform Sports Medicine, St. James, N.Y., 1989-90, Louis Cress Phys. Therapy P.C., Huntington, N.Y., 1990—, Homeward Bound Phys. Therapy, Centerport, N.Y., 1990—. Active L.I. Ladies Soccer League. Mem. Am. Phys. Therapy Assn. Democrat. Jewish.

SCHNEIDER, DEBRA A., financial executive; b. Buffalo, Sept. 22, 1962; d. Albert H. Schneider and Beverly (Full) Fazio. BA in Econs., SUNY, Buffalo, 1985, BS in Acctg., 1986. CPA, N.Y. Staff acct. Ernst & Whinney, Rochester, N.Y., 1986-88; sr. acct. Price Waterhouse, Rochester, N.Y., 1988-89; fin. mgr. Rochester Mental Health Ctr., 1989-90; sr. fin. analyst Rochester Telephone Corp., 1990; controller Sunset Corp., Rochester, 1990-91; controller Wolf Mansfield Bolling Inc., Buffalo, 1991-94, pres., CFO, 1994—; ind. cons. in field. Allocations com. United Way, Rochester, 1990; treas. Community Mental Health Ctr. Systems, Rochester, 1990. Mem. AICPA, Inst. Mgmt. Accts., N.Y. State Soc. CPAs, Zontas of Amherst. Home: 640 E Youngs Rd Williamsville NY 14221 Office: Wolf Mansfield Bolling Inc 40 Fountain Plz Buffalo NY 14202-2200

SCHNEIDER, ELEONORA FREY, physician; b. Basel, Switzerland, Jan. 17, 1921; came to U.S., 1952; d. Friedrich Ernst and Clara Melanie (Heiz) Frey; m. Jurg Adolf Schneider, Aug. 22, 1946; children: Andreas George, Daphne Eleanor, Diana Veronica, Claudia Elizabeth. MD, U. Basel, 1945. Lic. MD. Pharmacologist Sandoz Pharms., Basel, 1946-47; resident in anesthesiology U. Hosp., Basel, 1950-51; resident Pediatric Dept. Del. Div., Wilmington, 1971-73; physician Wilmington Pub Schs., 1973-79, Pub. Health, Wilmington, 1975-80; staff physician student health svc. U. Del., Newark, 1979—; v.p. Pharmacon, Inc., Wilmington, 1985—. Contbr. articles to profl. jours. V.p. del. Citizens for Clean Air, 1969-71; mem. com. Gov.'s Adv. Coun. for Exceptional Children, Dover, Del.; mem. adv. panel YWCA; vol. Girl Scouts U.S.A., ARC. Mem. AAUW (study group leader 1966-67, area chmn. community problems 1967-69, edn. com. 1968-69, new mems. advisor 1969-70, bd. dirs. 1967-70), AMA, Am. Acad. Pediatrics, Med. Soc. Del., New Castle County Med. Soc. Republican.

SCHNEIDER, GRETA SARA, ergonomics consultant; b. Bklyn., May 26, 1954; d. Irving Victor and Anne Joyce (Goldberg) S. BA, MA, CUNY, 1975, MA, 1976, PhD, 1977. Writer, cons. Pitts., 1972-73; cons. Flushing, N.Y., 1973-85; sr. writer, cons. Buck Cons. Inc., N.Y.C., 1985-86; chmn., CEO Schneider Cons. Inc., N.Y.C., 1986-90; pvt. cons. Greta Schneider Cons., N.Y.C., 1991—; lectr. on personal bankruptcy The Learning Annex, 1995. Author: Exploding the Bankruptcy Mystique, 1993. Mem. Little Theatre Group, Marathon Community Ctr., Little Neck, N.Y., 1980-83. Cambridge Biographical Inst. fellow, 1993. Mem. AFTRA, Nat. Assn. Women Bus. Owners, Nat. Assn. Bus. Communicators, Internat. Platform Assn., Employee Assistance Profls. Assn., Soc. Human Resource Mgmt., U.S. C. of C., Writers Guild Am., Rotary. Home and Office: 252-37 60th Ave Little Neck NY 11362-2423

SCHNEIDER, JANE HARRIS, sculptor; b. Trenton, N.J., Jan. 2, 1932; d. Leon Harris and Dorothy (Perlman) Rosenthal; m. Alfred R. Schneider, July

25, 1953; children: Lee, Jeffry, Elizabeth. BA, Wellesley Coll. Exhibited work in numerous group and one-person shows including June Kelly Gallery, 1993, 90, 88, Nassau County Mus. Fine Art, Roslyn, N.Y., 1988, Alternative Mus., N.Y.C., 1985, Phila. Art Alliance, 1984, Atrium Gallery, St. Louis, 1993, Bill Bace Gallery, 1992, Triplex Gallery, N.Y.C., 1991, Rockland Ctr. for Arts, West Nyack, N.Y., 1990, Hudson River Mus., Yonkers, N.Y., 1989, Sculpture Ctr., N.Y.C., 1988, many others; sculpture represented in numerous pub. and pvt. collections. Office: 75 Grand St New York NY 10013

SCHNEIDER, JANET M., arts administrator, curator, painter; b. N.Y.C., June 6, 1950. d. August Arthur and Joan (Battaglia) S.; m. Michael Francis Sperendi, Sept. 21, 1985. BA summa cum laude, Queens Coll., CUNY, 1972; spl. study fine arts Boston U. Tanglewood Inst., 1971. With Queens Mus., Flushing, N.Y.C., 1973-89, curator, 1973-75, program dir., 1975-77, exec. dir., 1977-89. Collections arranged include: Sons and others, Women Artists See Men (author catalog), 1975, Urban Aesthetics (author catalog), 1976, Masters of the Brush, Chinese Painting and Calligraphy from the Sixteenth to the Nineteenth Century (author catalog), 1977, Symcho Moszkowicz: Portrait of the Artist in Postwar Europe (author catalog), 1978, Shipwrecked 1622, The Lost Treasure of Philip IV (author catalog), 1981, Michaelangelo: A Sculptor's World (author catalog), 1983, Joseph Cornell: Revisited (author catalog), 1992. Chmn. Cultural Instns. Group, N.Y.C., 1986-87; mem. N.Y.C. Commn. for Cultural Affairs, 1991-93; bd. dirs. N.Y.C. Partnership, 1987-88, Gallery Assn. N.Y. State 1979-81. Mem. Artists Choice Mus. (trustee 1979-82), Am. Assn. Mus., Phi Beta Kappa.

SCHNEIDER, JAYNE B., school librarian; b. Cin., Nov. 9, 1950; d. Neil Kendrick and Edith (Dilworth) Bangs; m. James R. Bronn, June 9, 1973 (div. 1979); m. Arthur Schneider, July 11, 1986; 1 stepdaughter, Heather. BS in Elem. Edn., Ea. Ky. U., 1973; MA in Libr. Sci., Spaulding U., 1978. Tchr., 1st & 2d grades Fort Thomas (Ky.) Pub. Schs./Ruth Moyer Elem., 1973; libr. Lassiter Middle Sch., Ky., 1973—; presenter Nat. Middle Sch. Assn., St. Louis, 1988, Denver, 1989, Assn. of Ind. Media Educators, 1992. Mem. Ky. Hist. Soc., Friends of the Libr.; co-capt. Block Watch. Named Superstar Ky. Ednl. TV; Owen Badgett grantee Louisville Community Grant, 1988. Mem. NEA, ALA, AASL, PTSA (life), Nat. Mid. Sch. Assn., Jefferson County Sch. Media Assn. (treas. 1982-83, sec. 1991-92, newsletter 1992-93, pres.-elect 1993-94, pres. 1994-95), Ky. Sch. media Assn. (bd. dirs. 1994-95). Presbyterian. Home: 2553 Kings Hwy Louisville KY 40205-2646 Office: Lassiter Mid Sch 8200 Candleworth Dr Louisville KY 40214-5599

SCHNEIDER, MARY JOE DEUTSCH, lawyer; b. Fargo, N.D., June 12, 1950; d. Joseph Charles and Geraldine Ray (Clarey) Deutsch; m. Mark Gray Schneider, June 9, 1973; children: McLain Joseph, Liberty Alexis. BS, N.D. State U., 1972; JD, Emory U., 1979. Police agt. City of Lakewood, Colo., 1972-73; dep. clk. of ct. Grand Forks (N.D.) County, 1973-74; criminal justice rschr. Midwest Rsch. Inst., Bethesda, Md., 1974-75; social svcs. caseworker Alexandria (Va.) County, 1975-76; social svcs. worker County of Dekalb, Decatur, Ga., 1976-77; staff atty. Legal Assistance of N.D., Fargo, 1980-82, mng. dir., 1982-90; exec. dir. Legal Svcs. NW Minn., Moorhead, 1990—; mem. exec. com. Legal Svcs. Coalition, St. Paul, 1990—; various coms. and task forces Minn. Bd. Aging, St. Paul, 1993—. Bd. dirs. Fargo-Moorhead Cmty. Theatre, Fargo, 1986-91, Jr. Great Books Program Hawthorne Sch., Fargo, 1993—; pres. legal asst. adv. com. Minn. State U., Moorhead, 1991—, Medicare Advocacy Project Bd., St. Paul, 1990-94. Recipient Svc. award Assn. Retarded Citizens, 1984, Exemplary Svc. plaque, 1986, Champion of Justice award, 1990, Advocacy Excellence award, 1990. Mem. LWV, Minn. State Bar Assn. (mem. legal assistance to disadvantaged com. 1992—), N.D. State Bar Assn., Women's Bar Assn., Soroptimist Internat. (bd. dirs. 1992—). Home: 1011 S 8th St Fargo ND 58103 Office: Legal Svcs NW Minn 403 Center Ave Ste 403 Moorhead MN 56561

SCHNEIDER, NILA MARIE, media consultant, communications educator; b. Knoxville, Tenn., Sept. 18, 1956; d. Erwin Henry and Jenila Marie (Adkins) S. BA, U. Iowa, 1977, MA, 1979, postgrad., 1979-84, 84-90. Cert. secondary tchr. speech and theater, Mo. Theater instr. South Harrison H.S., Bethany, Mo., 1978-79; mgr. Campus Cablevision, Iowa City, 1979-80; grad. rsch. asst. Coll. Edn. U. Iowa, Iowa City, 1980, computer lab. monitor Coll. Edn., 1981-84; instr. comm. studies Mo. Western State Coll., St. Joseph, 1984-90; media cons. St. Joseph and Harlingen, Tex., 1990—. Author: (workbook) Oral Communication, 1990; dir. (pub. svc. announcement) Music in Our Schools, 1980; segment dir.: (film) Refocus, 1976. Mem. Assn. Ednl. Comm. and Tech., Mo. Assn. Ednl. Comm. and Tech., Amateur Radio Relay League. Democrat. Lutheran. Home: # B 4205 Country Ln # B Saint Joseph MO 64506-2428 Office: Trailer 449 1203 N Expressway 77 Harlingen TX 78552-5103

SCHNEIDER, PATRICIA REED, small business owner; b. Woodbury, N.J., Sept. 16, 1952; d. Clinton Harvey and Marcella Gertrude (Crawford) Reed; m. Lewis Morris Schneider, Jr., Oct. 5, 1973; children: Zachary Charles, Wyatt Reed. Student, Cumberland Co. Coll., 1977-78. Clk. medicare The Prudential, Millville, N.J., 1970-75, computer programmer, 1975-78; methods analyst The Prudential, Millville, 1978-81; owner Video Memories, Elmer, N.J., 1982—. Vol. Spl. Olympics, 1989—, Elmer Pub. Libr., 1993; mem. Salem County HUman Rels., Bd., Salem, 1993, Elmer Sch. Bd., 1993; found. mem. Elmer Centennial Com., Elmer, 1993. Named Vol. Yr. Am. Cancer Soc., 1993. Republican. Methodist. Home: PO Box 885 Elmer NJ 08318 Office: Video Memories PO Box 478 Elmer NJ 08318

SCHNEIDER, PHYLLIS LEAH, writer, editor; b. Seattle, Apr. 19, 1947; d. Edward Lee Booth and Harriet Phyllis (Ebbinghaus) Russell; m. Clifford Donald Schneider, June 14, 1969; 1 child, Pearl Brooke. B.A., Pacific Luth. U., 1969; M.A., U. Wash., 1972. Fiction, features editor Seventeen Mag., N.Y.C., 1975-80; mng. editor Weight Watchers Mag., N.Y.C., 1980-81; editor YM mag., N.Y.C., 1981-86. Author: Parents Book of Infant Colic, 1990, Kids Who Make a Difference, 1993, Straight Talk on Women's Health: How to Get the Health Care You Deserve, 1993, Hot Health Care Careers, 1993, What Kids Like To Do, 1993. Recipient Centennial Recognition award Pacific Luth. U., 1990. Democrat. Episcopalian.

SCHNEIDER, SANDRA MCEWEN, emergency physician educator; b. Pitts., June 5, 1950; d. Fred Collier and Pearl Mae (Nycum) McEwen; m. Paul Gilbert Schneider, Aug. 26, 1972; 1 child, Kathryn Alexandra. BS in Chemistry, U. Pitts., 1971, MD, 1975. Diplomate Am. Bd. Internal Medicine, Am. Bd. Emergency Medicine. Resident internal medicine Presbyn. Univ. Hosp., Pitts., 1975-78; med. dir. family health svcs. USPHS, Nat. Health Svcs. Corps, Hazard, Ky., 1978-81; asst. prof. medicine Montefiore Hosp., U. Pitts., 1981-86, assoc. prof. medicine, dir. emergency svcs., 1986-92; assoc. prof., assoc. chief divsn. emergency medicine U. Pitts. Med. Ctr., 1992-93; prof., chair dept. emergency medicine Strong Meml. Hosp., U. Rochester, N.Y., 1993—. Contbr. chpts. in books and articles to profl. jours. Grantee Upjohn Co., 1984, Smith Kline French, 1987. Mem. World Assn. Emergency and Disaster Medicine, Soc. for Academic Emergency Medicine (bd. dirs.), Nat. Assn. EMS Physicians (exec. com.), Am. Coll. Emergency Physicians (fellow 1985), Am. Assn. Poison Control Ctrs., Am. Acad. Clin. Toxicology, Rochester Acad. Medicine. Democrat. Office: Univ Rochester 601 Elmwood Ave # 655 Rochester NY 14642-0001

SCHNEIDER, VALERIE LOIS, speech educator; b. Chgo., Feb. 12, 1941; d. Ralph Joseph and Gertrude Blanche (Gaffron) S. BA, Carroll Coll., 1963; MA, U. Wis., 1966; PhD, U. Fla., 1969; cert. advanced study Appalachian State U., 1981. Tchr. English and history Montello High Sch. (Wis.), 1963-64; dir. forensics and drama Montello High Sch., 1963-64; instr. speech U. Fla., Gainesville, 1966-68, asst. prof. speech, 1969-70; asst. prof. speech Edinboro (Pa.) State Coll., 1970-71; assoc. prof. speech East Tenn. State U., Johnson City, 1971-76, prof. speech, 1976—; instr. newspaper course Johnson City Press Chronicle, 1979, Elizabethton Star, Erwin Record, Mountain City Tomahawk, Jonesboro Herald and Tribune, 1980; mem. investor panel USA Today, 1991-92. Editor East Tenn. State U. evening and off-campus newsletter, 1984-91; assoc. editor: Homiletic, 1974-76; columnist Video Visions, Kingsport Times-News (Tenn.), 1984-86; book reviewer Pulpit Digest, 1986-90; contbr. articles on speech to profl. jours. Chmn. AAUW Mass Media Study Group Com., Johnson City, 1973-74. Recipient Creative Writing award Va. Highlands Arts Festival, 1973; award Kingsport (Tenn.) Times News, 1984, 85, Tri-Cities Met. Advt. Fedn., 1983, 84; Danforth assoc., 1977. Mem. Speech Communication Assn. (Tenn. rep. to states adv. council 1974-75), So., Tenn. (exec. bd. 1974-77, publs. bd. 1974-78, pres. 1977-78), Religious Speech Communication Assn. (Best article award 1976), Tenn. Basic Skills Council (exec. bd. 1979-80, v.p. 1980-81, pres. 1981-82), AAUW (v.p. chpt. 1974-75, pres. 1975-76, corp. rep. for East Tenn. State U. 1974-76), Am. Assn. Continuing Higher Edn., Bus. and Profl. Women's Club (chpt. exec. bd. 1972-73, v.p. 1976-77), Mensa, Delta Sigma Rho-Tau Kappa Alpha, Phi Delta Kappa, Delta Kappa Gamma, Pi Gamma Mu. Presbyterian. Home: 3201 Buckingham Rd Johnson City TN 37604-2715 Office: East Tenn State U PO Box 23098 Johnson City TN 37614-0124

SCHNEIDER, WILLYS HOPE, lawyer; b. N.Y.C., Sept. 27, 1952; d. Leon and Lillian (Friedman) S.; m. Stephen Andrew Kals, Jan. 21, 1979; children: Peter, Josefine. AB, Princeton U., 1974; JD, Columbia U., 1977. Bar: N.Y. 1978, U.S. Dist. Ct. (ea. and so. dists.) N.Y. 1978, U.S. Tax Ct. 1979. Law clk. to judge U.S. Dist. Ct. (ea. dist.), Bklyn., 1977-78; assoc. Paul, Weiss, Rifkind, Wharton & Garrison, N.Y.C., 1978-83; ptnr. Kaye, Scholer, Fierman, Hays & Handler, N.Y.C., 1983—. Contbr. articles to profl. jours. Mem. ABA, N.Y. State Bar Assn., Assn. of Bar of City of N.Y. Home: 320 West End Ave New York NY 10023-8110 Office: Kaye Scholer Fierman Hays & Handler 425 Park Ave New York NY 10022-3506

SCHNEIDER-CRIEZIS, SUSAN MARIE, architect; b. St. Louis, Aug. 1, 1953; d. William Alfred and Rosemary Elizabeth (Fischer) Schneider; m. Demetrios Anthony Criezis, Nov. 24, 1978; children: Anthony, John and Andrew. BArch, U. Notre Dame, 1976; MArch, MIT, 1978. Registered architect, Wis. Project designer Eichstaedt Architects, Roselle, Ill., 1978-80, Solomon, Cordwell, Buenz & Assocs., Chgo., 1980-82; project architect Gelick, Foran Assocs., Chgo., 1982-83; asst. prof. Sch. Architecture U. Ill., Chgo., 1980-86; exec. v.p. Criezis Architects, Inc., Evanston, Ill., 1986—. Graham Found. grantee MIT, 1977, MIT scholar, 1976-78; Prestressed Concrete Inst. rsch. grantee, 1981. Mem. AIA, Chgo. Archtl. Club, Chgo. Women in Architecture, Am. Solar Energy Soc., NAFE, Jr. League Evanston, Evanston C. of C. Roman Catholic. Office: 1007 Church St Ste 101 Evanston IL 60201-5910

SCHNEIDMAN, BARBARA SUE, psychiatrist; b. Mpls., Jan. 18, 1944; d. Norman Reuben and MIldred (Roberts) S.; m. William McAllister. BA, U. Minn., Mpls., 1966, MD, 1970; MPH, U. Wash., 1974. Diplomate Am. Bd. Psychiatry and Neurology. Resident ob-gyn. U. Wash., Seattle, 1972-74, dir. gynecology, 1974-78, resident in psychiatry, 1978-81, cons. primary care, 1981-88; pvt. practice Seattle, 1981-93; cons. Sexual Assault Ctr., Seattle, 1981-93, Cen. Area Mental Health, Seattle, 1990-92; assoc. v.p. Am. Bd. Med. Specialties, Evanston, Ill., 1993—; mem., chair Wash. State Bd. Med. Examiners, 1982-93; pres. Fedn. State Med. Bds., 1991-92. Mem. AMA, Am. Psychiat. Assn., Wash. State Med. Assn., Ill. Psychiat. Soc., King County Med. Assn. Office: ABMS 1007 Church St Ste 404 Evanston IL 60201-5913

SCHNELL, SHIRLEY LUKE, art educator; b. Mpls., Jan. 17, 1937; d. Hjalmar and Dorothy Ruth (Ledwein) Luke; m. Lloyd William Schnell, Aug. 26, 1961. BFA, Mpls. Coll. Art & Design, 1958; MFA, Yale U., 1963. Artist Northwestern Bell Telephone Co., Mpls., 1957-58, Fed. Res. Bank Mpls., 1958-60; instr. Mpls. Coll. Art & Design, 1962-65, U. Minn., Mpls., 1963-64; prof. Kansas City (Mo.) Art Inst., 1966—. One-person show Galveston (Tex.) Arts Ctr., 1977; group exhbns. include Walker Art Ctr. Biennale, Mpls., 1966, Nelson Atkins Mus. Art, Kansas City, Mo., 1966, City Art Mus. St. Louis, 1966, Krannert Art Mus., Bloomington, Ind., 1976, William Crapo Gallery, New Bedford, Mass., 1982, Mulvane Art Ctr., Topeka, Kans., 1982, Pinnacle Gallery, Rochester, N.Y., 1985, Osaka (Japan) Coll. Art, 1986, U.S.A. Invitational Easter at the White House, 1987, Leedy-Voulkos Gallery, Kansas City, Mo., 1988, Del Bello Gallery, Toronto, 1992, 94, Toward Earth Community: Ecology, Native Wisdon and Spirituality Internat. Transpersonal Assn., Internat. Art Exhbn., Killarney, Co. Kerry, Ireland, others; permanent collections include Nelson-Atkins Mus. Art, Kansas City, Mo., Smithsonian Inst., Washington, State Hist. Soc. Mo. Contbg. mem. Dem. Nat. Com., 1984—; coord., participant Kansas City (Mo.) Pub. TV Print Portfolio, 1989—; active Pub. Citizen Found., 1984—, Friends of Jung, Kansas City, 1990. MacDowell Colony fellow, 1976; 1st Mo. Arts Coun. grantee, 1977, Alliance of Ind. Colls. of Art grantee, 1982, Andrew W. Mellon grantee, 1986, 89. Home: 3917 SW Hidden Cove Cir Lees Summit MO 64082 Office: Kansas City Art Inst 4415 Warwick Blvd Kansas City MO 64111

SCHNEPF, CARRIE BIGGS, sales and marketing professional; b. Mesa, Ariz., Sept. 3, 1960; d. Robert Darrel and Carolyn Sarah (Cox) Biggs; m. Mark Edward Schnepf, Apr. 13, 1991. Student, Brigham Young U., 1979-85. Anchor Sta. KIVI-TV, Boise, Idaho, 1985-87; reporter, anchor Sta. KPHO-TV, Phoenix, 1987-89; sales and mktg. profl. Ariz. Escrowq & Title, Phoenix, 1989-91, Schnepf Tree Farms, Queen Creek, Ariz., 1991—; comml. spokesperson Robert Blaack Agy., Phoenix, 1989—; with promotions dept. Country Jam USA, Queen Creek, 1993—; pres. The Regal Group, Phoenix, 1992—. Chmn. spl. event Ariz. Spl. Olympics, Phoenix, 1991—; bd. dirs. Am. Heart Assn., Phoenix, 1993—, chmn. spl. event, 1993—; mem. fundraising com. PreHab of Ariz., Mesa, 1991—; founding mem., chmn. Project B.E.S.T., Queen Creek. Recipient chmn.'s award Ariz. Spl. Olympics, 1993. Mem. Desert Club (publicity com. 1992-93). Republican. Home and Office: 22601 E Cloud Rd Queen Creek AZ 85242-9556

SCHNETTLER, NADINE SYVONNE, employment and administration services supervisor; b. Norfolk, Va., Jan. 8, 1956; d. Herbert Frederick and Lucille Ann (Winkels) Ferrier; m. Thomas W. Schnettler, Mar. 22, 1980; 1 child, Caitlin. BS in Mgmt., Cardinal Stritch, 1993; postgrad., U. St. Thomas. Cert. profl. human resource mgmt. Human Resources Cert. Inst.; cert. mgr. suggestion systems Nat. Assn. Suggestion Systems. Design draftsperson DeZurik, Sartell, Minn., 1976-78, time study technician, 1978-80, customer order designer, 1980, corp. profit improvement adminstr., 1980-85, human resources specialist, 1985-88, supr. employment and adminstrv. svcs., 1988—. Bd. dirs. United Cerebral Palsy Ctrl. Minn. Mem. Minn. Affirmative Action Assn., St. Cloud Area Pers. Assn. (v.p., pres., past pres. 1989-91). Lutheran. Home: 26684 Theresia Ter Richmond MN 56368-8402 Office: DeZurik 250 Riverside Ave N Sartell MN 56377-1743

SCHNITGER, CONSTANCE, small business owner; b. Watertown, Wis., Nov. 18, 1943; d. Ernest and Eunice (Foss) Gruner; m. Wayne A. Schnitger, June 26, 1965; children: Michael, Kathryn. BA, Carroll Coll., Waukesha, Wis., 1965; student, Ctrl. State U., 1979-80. Instr. art YWCA, Janesville, Wis., 1965-78; free-lance cartographer and illustrator Edmond, Okla., 1979-80; instr. computer programing Oxford (Mich.) Pub. Schs., 1984-85; crew leader U.S. Census Bur., Rochester Hills, Mich., 1985; owner Artful Hand, Janesville, Wis., 1988—; writer Sta. WCLO-FM, Janesville, 1965-68; freelance artist, Janesville, 1968-78. Cartographer and artist: Memphis to Pacific Railroad, 1979, Beacon Hill, 1992, Back Bay, 1995. Bd. dirs. Young Women's Christian Assn., Janesville, 1974-78, Homeowner's Assn., Edmond, Okla., 1978-80; chair Friends of Rotary Gardens, Janesville, 1992-93, developer, 1992. Mem. AAUW (v.p. 1979-80, sec. 1992—), Profl. Picture Framers Am. (Wis. chpt.), Janesville Art League (v.p. 1976-77, 94-95), Bower City Garden Club (sec. 1992—, v.p. 1994-95).

SCHNITZER, ARLENE DIRECTOR, art dealer; b. Salem, Oreg., Jan. 10, 1929; d. Simon M. and Helen (Holtzman) Director; m. Harold J. Schnitzer, Sept. 11, 1949; 1 child, Jordan. Student, U. Wash., 1947-48; BFA (hon.) Pacific NW Coll. Art., 1988. Founder, pres. Fountain Gallery of Art, Portland, Oreg., 1951-86; sr. v.p. Harsch Investment Corp., 1951—. Apptd. to Oreg. State Bd. Higher Edn., 1987-88; former bd. dirs. Oreg. Symphony Assn., v.p. Oreg. Symphony; former bd. dirs. U.S. Dist. Ct. Hist. Soc.; bd. dirs. Boys and Girls Club, 1988—; mem. Gov.'s Expo '86 Commn., Oreg.; mem. exec. com., former bd. dirs. Artquake; former mem. adv. bd. Our New Beginnings; past bd. dirs. Artists Initiative for a Contemporary Art Collection; former trustee Reed Coll., 1982-88; mem. exec. com. bd. dirs. N.W. Bus. Com. for Arts.; trustee, mem. exec. com. Oreg. Health Scis. Univ. Found.; mem. arts acquisition and collections com. Portland Art Mus.; mem. Nat. Com. for the Performing Arts, 1995—. Recipient Aubrey Watzek award Lewis and Clark Coll., 1981, Pioneer award U. Oreg., 1985, Met. Arts Commn. award, 1985, White Rose award March of Dimes, 1987, Disting. Svc. award Western Oreg. State Coll. 1988, Oreg. Urban League Equal Opportunity award 1988, Gov's. award for Arts, 1987, Woman of Achievement award YWCA, 1987, Disting. Svc. award U. Oreg., 1991, SAFECO Art Leadership award ArtFair/Seattle, 1994; honored by Portland Art Assn., 1979. Mem. Univ. Club, Multnomah Athletic Club, Portland Golf Club. Office: Harsch Investment Corp 1121 SW Salmon St Portland OR 97205-2000

SCHNITZER, IRIS TAYMORE, financial management executive; b. Cambridge, Mass., Aug. 3, 1943; d. Joseph David and Edith (Cooper) Taymore; m. Stephen Mark Schnitzer, Sept. 10, 1966. BA in Econs., Boston U., 1967; postgrad., Mass. Sch. Law, 1992—. Lic. real estate broker, life ins. advisor, life ins. and health ins. broker; registered rep. NASD; CFP; CLU; cer. in fin. counseling, advanced pension planning. Real estate broker Woods Real Estate, Braintree, Mass., 1968; real estate broker, property mgr. Village Gate Realty, Brockton, Mass., 1969; agt. Prudential Ins., Boston, 1970-73; supr. edn. and advanced underwriting, agt. Northwestern Mutual Life, Boston, 1973-78; fin. planning cons. Iris Taymore Schnitzer Assocs., Boston, Mass., 1973-79; trainer fin. planners Gerstenblatt Co., Newton, Mass., 1978-79; founder, pres. The Fin. Forum, Inc., Boston, 1979-91, TFF, Inc. at the Chase Exchange, N.Y.C., 1980-83; pres. I&S Assocs., Boston, 1991-93; v.p. Fleet Investment Svcs., Boston, 1993—; bd. dirs., clk. Mister Tire, Inc., Abington, Mass.; arbitrator Nat. Assn. Securities Dealers, 1992—. Contbr. articles to profl. jours. Chmn. credit com., bd. dirs. Mass. Feminist Fed. Credit Union, Boston, 1975-77; bd. dirs. Ledgewood, Brookline, Mass., 1967-70, LWV, Brockton, Mass., 1968-70, NOW, Boston, 1972-73; bd. govs. Women's City Club, Boston, 1976-80; pres. Mass. div. Women's Equity Action League, 1977-79; life mem. Navy League U.S., Boston, 1985—; treas., bd. dirs. Festival of Light and Song, 1989-92; bd. dirs. Achievement Rewards for Coll. Scientists, Boston, 1991—. Named One of the Best Fin. Planners in the U.S., Money Mag., 1987, to Mutual Funds Panel, Sylvia Porter's Personal Fin. Mag., 1988, 89. Mem. Am. Assn. Individual Investors (pres. Boston chpt. 1987-89, bd. dirs. 1985—), Boston Estate Planning Coun., Boston Club. Republican. Jewish. Office: Fleet Investment Svcs MABOFO5A 75 State St Boston MA 02109-1807

SCHNITZLER, BEVERLY JEANNE, designer, art educator, writer; b. Berkeley, Calif.; children: Erich Gregory. BS, Ariz. State U., 1954; MA, Calif. State U., L.A., 1959; postgrad., Claremont Grad. Sch., 1956-59, Chouinard Art Inst., L.A., 1960-63. Spl. art tchr. and cons. Alhambra (Calif.) City Sch. Dist., 1958-60; prof. art Calif. State U., L.A., 1960—; cons. in art and creative fabric art Calif. State U., L.A., 1960—; lectr. in field; Calif. State U. del. for internat. acad. exch. guidelines to Yunnan Art Inst., Kunming, China, 1993. Author: New Dimensions in Needlework, 1978; project dir. and head designer heraldic banners Calif. State U., L.A., 1986-87; exhibiting artist in fiber art. Participant student/prof. exch. program Kunming, 1993. Calif. State U. L.A. instl. grantee, 1978, 79; AAUW Found. grantee, 1988; recipient Award for Outstanding Artistic Merit, Calif. State U. L.A. Assoc. Students, 1987; scholar conf. Spain and Portugal of the Navagators: The Age of Discovery to the Enlightenment, Georgetown U., 1990, scholar conf. participant Portugal and Spain of the Navigators: The Age of Exploration, George Washington U., 1992. Mem. Nat. Surface Design Assn., Costume and Textile Coun. of L.A. County Mus., Internat. Designers Assn., Internat. World Conf. of Educators, AAUW, Am. Craftsman's Coun., Fine Art Club of Pasadena. Office: Calif State U Art Dept 5151 State University Dr Los Angeles CA 90032

SCHOCH, CLARISSA ANTHONY, singer, educator, executive assistant; b. Redmond, Oreg., Jan. 17, 1935; d. John Henry and Eleanor (Edwards) Berning; m. Jack Williams Anthony, Jr., June 26, 1960 (dec. 1982); m. Albert E. Schoch, Mar. 22, 1986 (dec. 1993); children: Rebecca Ellen, Julia Kathleen. BA, U. Oreg., 1957, MMus, 1959. Voice instr. William Paterson Coll., Wayne, N.J., 1979-84, Fairleigh Dickinson U., Rutherford, N.J., 1983-89; pvt. practice voice and flute tchr., Upper Montclair, N.J., 1971—; exec. sec. Nat. Westminster Bancorp, 1985—; owner garden ctr. Jack and the Preacher's, Holmdel, N.J., 1972-83; profl. singer, 1959—; soprano soloist Montclair State Coll., 1981-85, William Paterson Coll., 1981-82, Temple Emanu-EL, N.Y.C., 1962-79, Union Congl. Ch., Montclair, 1973—. Chmn. youth com. Union Congl. Ch., 1983-87 (mem. membership com. 1992—, chmn. 1995—), mem. parish life, 1985-91, mem. music com., 1983-85. Winner voice and oratorio N.J. Young Artists, Nat. Fedn. Music Clubs, N.J., 1966. Mem. Nat. Assn. Tchrs. of Singing (treas. N.J. 1984-92), N.Y. Singing Tchrs. Assn. (chairperson young artists auditions 1980-86), Internat. Bach Soc. (performing fellow 1969), AAUW, Phi Beta (nat. grad. grantee 1964), Montclair Music Club (Young Artists Audition chairperson 1982—, past pres. and program chmn.), Rehearsal Club (past program chmn.). Democrat. Home: 8 Waterbury Rd Montclair NJ 07043-1714

SCHOCK, JACQUI VIRGINIA, counselor, data operations specialist; b. Atlanta, Nov. 24, 1938; d. Herman Lee and Martha Jane (Hunsecker) Turner; m. Raymond J. Torres, Oct. 20, 1990. AA in Human Svcs., Bucks County Community Coll., 1986; BA in Human Svcs., Antioch U., 1987; MS in Addictions, Chestnut Hill Coll., 1988; MA in Applied Psychology, U. Santa Monica, Calif., 1990. Counselor Bucks County Rehab. Ctr., Doylestown, Pa., 1983-88; addictions counselor Clearbrook Friendship Ctr., Phila., 1988-89; in-patient counselor Penn Found., Sellersville, Pa., 1988-89; pvt. practice Willow Grove, Pa., 1989—; outpatient therapist Westmeade Med. Ctr., 1992—; instr. self-esteem Upper Moreland Adult Eveing Sch., 1991—; founder, dir. Crossroads Counseling Svc., Willow Grove, 1990—; data entry operator SPS Techs., Jenkintown, Pa., 1963-65, data engry supr., 1965-70, data mgr., 1970-94; pvt. instr. in computer concepts, 1991—. Mem. exec. bd. Counseling Assn. Greater Phila., 1988—, pres., 1994—; exec. bd. West Phila. Fund for Human Devel., 1989-92. Mem. NAFE, APA, Am. Counseling Assn., Counseling Assn. Greater Ga. (pres. 1994-95), Pa. Counselors Assn., Data Entry Mgrs. Assn., Nat. Coun. on Self-Esteem, Fraternal Order of Police, Phi Theta Kappa Alumni Assn. Office: Crossroads Counseling Svc 1013 N York Rd Willow Grove PA 19090

SCHOCKAERT, BARBARA ANN, operations executive; b. Queens, N.Y., Dec. 13, 1938; d. Lawrence Henry and Eleanor Veronica (Tollner) Grob; children: Donna Ann, Don. Student, Ocean County Coll., Toms River, N.J., 1987, 94—. Cert. notary pub. V.p. ops. Am. Vitamin Products, Inc., Freehold, N.J., 1977-89, v.p. ops. Foods Plus div., 1990-94, sales coord., 1994—; assoc. Ocean County Realty, Toms River, N.J., 1987-90, Crossroads Realty, Toms River, 1990—. Contbg. author: Greatest Poems of the Western World, 1989 (Golden Poet award). Past pres. mayor's adv. coun., past pres. of help line Town of Jackson, N.J.; past bd. dirs. Big Bros. of Ocean County; speaker community svc. orgns. Named Woman of Yr., Jaycees, 1974; recipient Capitol award Nat. Leadership Coun., 1991. Mem. N.J. Realtors Assn. Home: 977 Fairview Dr Toms River NJ 08753-3064 Office: 500 Halls Mill Rd Freehold NJ 07728

SCHOEN, KAREN R., psychologist; b. L.A., Mar. 10, 1956; d. Max Howard and Beatrice Mildred (Hoch) S. Grad. with gt. distinction, West L.A. Coll., 1982; AB in Psychology magna cum laude, U. So. Calif., 1985, PhD in Psychology, 1990. Psychologist Curtis Psychiat. Inc., North Hollywood, Calif., 1990-93; pvt. practice L.A., 1992—; dir. clin. programs HIV/AIDS counseling Pacific Ctr., L.A., 1993—; psychologist AIDS Healthcare Found., L.A., 1994—; adj. prof. Mount St. Mary's Coll., L.A., 1994. Vol. therapist Pacific Ctr. HIV/AIDS Counseling, L.A., 1992—; vol. disaster response team ARC, L.A., 1992—. Mem. ACLU, APA, Calif. Psychol. Assn., So. Calif. Group Psychol. Assn., L.A. County Psychol. Assn. (steering com. health psychology, ethics, disaster response 1992—, treatment com. 1992—, chair conv. com. 1994, 95, bd. dirs. 1995), L.A. Group Psychotherapy Assn. Office: Ste 211 12304 Santa Monica Blvd Los Angeles CA 90025

SCHOEN, LAURA FEIO, public relations executive, consultant; b. São Paulo, Brazil, Feb. 29, 1956; came to U.S., 1981; d. Luciano and Eny Dora (Feio) S.; m. Robert R. Kaufman, Oct. 29, 1983. BA in Journalist, Faculdade da Cidade, Rio de Janeiro, 1977; MA in Internat. Rels., U. Pa., 1983. Account exec. Denison/Ted Bates, Rio de Janeiro, 1974-75; mgr. pub. rels. and spl. events Estrutural Agy., Rio de Janeiro, 1975-81; internat. coord. mgr. Burson-Marsteller, N.Y.C., 1984-88, v.p., 1988-91, sr. v.p., 1991; sr. v.p. Creamer Dickson Basford, N.Y.C., 1991—, exec. v.p., 1994. Exec. producer (documentary) Winners, 1988-89. Recipient scholarship Rotary,

1981-82. Mem. Pub. Rels. Soc. Am., Fgn. Press Assn. Office: Creamer Dickson Basford 1633 Broadway New York NY 10019

SCHOEN, LINDA ALLEN, public affairs administrator; b. Lynch, Ky., July 9, 1936; d. Wert Harvey and Mary Mabel (Ramsey) Allen; m. Stanly M. Schoen, Apr. 8, 1972 (div. 1980). BA, Northwestern U., 1958. Rsch. technician G.D. Searle & Co., Chgo., 1958-60; rsch. assoc., asst. sec. com. cutaneous health and cosmetics AMA, Chgo., 1960-75; dir. mktg. svcs. Neutrogena Corp., L.A. 1975-83, dir. mktg. svcs., 1983-87, v.p. pub. affairs, 1987-93; pres. Unltd., 1993—. Mem. IABC, Pub. Rels. Soc. Am., Soc. Cosmetic Chemists, The Fashion Group. Episcopalian. Club: Opera Assn. (Northwestern U. Alumni). Editor The Look You Like column Today's Health mag., 1962-74; The AMA Book of Skin and Hair Care, 1976, The Look You Like Book, 1989; contbr. articles to Harper's Bazaar, Vogue, Redbook, Beauty Handbook. Mem. Soc. Cosmetic Chemists, Internat. Assn. Bus. Communicators. Episcopalian. Avocations: cross country skiing, travel, opera.

SCHOEN, REGINA NEIMAN, psychotherapist; b. Bronx, N.Y., Feb. 21, 1949; d. Louis and Bertha (Hoffman) Neiman; m. Dennis Leo Schoen, Dec. 2, 1979; 1 child, Leah F. B, Hunter Coll., N.Y.C., 1969; M, Columbia U., N.Y.C., 1971; M (social work), Hunter Coll., N.Y.C., 1977. Cert. Psychoanalytic Psychotherapist, Wash. Square Inst. N.Y.C., 1983, Family Therapist, Postgrad. Ctr. for Mental Health N.Y.C., 1986. Tchr., advisor Brandeis High Sch., N.Y.C., 1972-75; family service counselor N.Y. Assn. for New Am., N.Y.C., 1978-82; psychiatric social worker Lutheran Med. Ctr., Bklyn., 1982-84; mental health practitioner Montefiore Med. Ctr., Riker's Island, N.Y., 1984-86; moderator, speaker Nat. Assn .Social Workers Alcoholism Inst. N.Y.C., 1989, 91; presenter YWCA, N.Y.C., 1987—; speaker Greater N.Y. Hosp. Assn., 1983; commentator WNYC Radio Women and Rape N.Y.C., 1982; mem. faculty Postgrad. Ctr. Mental Health, 1990—; speaker Empire Blue Cross/Blue Shield, N.Y., 1990—. Mem. Nat. Assn. Social Workers. Office: Regina Schoen CSW 488 7th Ave Apt 9A New York NY 10018-6808

SCHOENBERG, BARBARA ANNE, paralegal, public relations professional; b. Bklyn., Mar. 15, 1938; d. John Joseph and Esther (Anders) Lynch; m. Joseph Carl Schoenberg, June 13, 1970. BA in English Lit., St. Joseph's Coll., Bklyn., 1959. Cert. paralegal. Tchr. English Horace Greeley Jr. High Sch., Long Island City, N.Y., 1959-63; traffic operator Benton & Bowles, N.Y.C., 1965-66; with Grey Pub. Rels., N.Y.C., 1966; pub. rels. and prodn. asst. Hayden Pub. Co., N.Y.C., 1967-71; exec. asst. Edwin Gould Svcs. for Children, N.Y.C., 1972-83; asst. paralegal Amerace Corp., N.Y.C., 1983-85, Squadron, Ellenoff, N.Y.C., 1986, Seward & Kissel, N.Y.C., 1987; paralegal various businesses, N.Y.C., 1988-94. Author: (poetry) Dance on the Horizon, 1994. Mem. Park River Ind. Dems., N.Y.C., 1994—; mem., fund raiser West Side Peace Found., N.Y.C., 1994—. Mem. Manhattan Paralegal Assn. (pub. rels. chair 1993-94, Svc. award 1993).

SCHOENBERG, MARGARET MAIN, former English language educator; b. Winnipeg, Manitoba, Can., Apr. 2, 1923; came to U.S., 1948; d. George Knowles and Catherine Bruce (Oswald) Main; m. Emanuel Schoenberg, Oct. 23, 1953 (dec. Aug. 1977); children: Paul, Roberta. BA in English, U. Manitoba, 1946; MA, Radcliffe Coll., 1950; PhD, Harvard U., 1958; AASc, RN, Adirondack C.C., 1987; BA in Music, SUNY, Potsdam, 1992. Licentiate Royal Schs. Music, London. Lectr. English U. Manitoba, Winnipeg, 1946-48; instr. English U. Akron, Ohio, 1956-60; assoc. prof. English Kent (Ohio) State U., 1964-82, prof. emeritus, 1982—. Performer concert piano, 1965-87, dramatic readings, 1994. Departmental scholar Crane Sch. Music SUNY, 1993. Mem. Pi Kappa Lambda. Home: Rte 28 Box 372 Indian Lake NY 12842

SCHOENBERG-SWARTCHILD, COCO, sculptor; b. Paris, May 3, 1939; came to U.S., 1941; d. Heinz Ernst and Kathe (Gassman) Oppenheimer; m. Bernard Schoenberg, Aug. 11, 1963 (dec. Apr. 1979); children: Nara, Jonathan Alexander, Amanda; m. William G. Swartchild III, June 5, 1988. BS in Lit., Sci., Arts, U. Mich., 1961; MA in Art, Columbia U., 1964. Tchr. handicapped children Steven Sch., N.Y.C., 1962-63; assoc. in pottery for occupational therapy Columbia Tchrs. Coll., N.Y.C., 1963; studio potter, tchr., lectr. various cities, N.Y., 1965—; chmn. N.J. Designer Craftsman, New Brunswick, 1983-85; coord. Ctr. Crafts Fair-Old Ch., Demarest, N.J., 1983-84, ACC Craft Fair, Balt., 1985-94, West Springfield, 1985-94; juror Lincoln Ct. Craft Fair, N.Y.C., 1985, Art Rider Craft Fairs, N.Y.C., 1986, Sta. WBAI Craft Fair, N.Y.C., 1989; commd. by Gulick Group, 1988, Harrison, Star Weiner and Beitler Advt., N.Y.C., 1989; juror Am. Craft Exposition, 1992. Two-person shows include Latitude, Greenwich, Conn., Handworks Gallery, Manchester, Vt.; exhibited in group shows at Montclair (N.J.) Mus., Bergen Mus., Paramus, N.J., Morris Mus., Morristown, N.J., Noyes Mus., Oceanville, N.J., Mus. Am. Jewish History, Phila., High Mus., Atlanta, Craft and Folk Mus., L.A., Brockton (Mass.) Mus., Summit (N.J.) Art Ctr., Campbell Mus., and various other galleries, craft fairs and stores. N.J. State Coun. on the Arts grantee 1983-84; recipient Innovative Sculpture award Texaco, 1982, purchase award Noyes Mus., 1986, highest award for crafts Craft Concepts, 1986, Juror's award Summit Art Ctr., 1985, Mamoroneck Artist Guild award, 1984, Charlotte Simons Glicksman Meml. award, 1983, merit award in ceramics N.Y.C. Artist/Craftsmen of N.Y., 1987, Most Innovative Use of Medium award Toshiko Tokaezu, 1994. Home: 119 Erledon Rd Tenafly NJ 07670-2503

SCHOENE, KATHLEEN SNYDER, lawyer; b. Glen Ridge, N.J., July 24, 1953; d. John Kent and Margaret Ann (Bronder) Snyder; m. Charles Alan Schoene, Aug. 16, 1974. BA, Grinnell Coll., 1974; MS, So. Conn. State Coll., 1976; JD, Washington U., St. Louis, 1982. Bar: Mo. 1982, U.S. Dist. Ct. (we. and ea. dist. cts.) Mo. 1982, Ill. 1983. Head librarian Mo. Hist. Soc., St. Louis, 1976-79; assoc. Peper, Martin, Jensen, Maichel & Hetlage, St. Louis, 1982-88, ptnr., 1989—; bd. dirs. Legal Svcs. of Eastern Mo. Author: (with others) Missouri Corporation Law and Practice, 1985; contbr. articles to profl. jours. Trustee Grinnell (Iowa) Coll., ex officio voting mem., 1991-93. Mem. ABA, Nat. Health Lawyers Assn., Nat. Assn. Bond Lawyers, Mo. Bar Assn., Ill. Bar Assn., Bar Assn. Met. St. Louis (treas. 1991-92, sec. 1992-93, v.p. 1993-94, pres.-elect 1994-95, pres. 1995-96, chair small bus. com. 1987-88, exec. com. 1988—, chair bus. law sect. 1988-89, exec. com. young lawyers sect. 1988-90), Grinnell Coll. Alumni Assn. (bd. dirs. 1987-93, v.p. 1990-91, pres. 1991-93). Home: 7824 Cornell Ave Saint Louis MO 63130-3701 Office: Peper Martin Jensen Maichel & Hetlage 720 Olive St Fl 24 Saint Louis MO 63101-2337

SCHOENFELD, BARBARA BRAUN, lawyer; b. Phila., Apr. 17, 1953; d. Irving Leon Braun and Virginia (Parker) Sand; m. Larry Jay Schoenfeld, June 29, 1975; children: Alexander, Gordon, Max. BA cum laude, U. Pa., 1974, M in City Planning, Social Work, 1977; JD, Boston U., 1982. Bar: R.I. 1982, U.S. Dist. Ct. R.I. 1982. Assoc. planner Del. Valley Hosp. Council, Phila., 1978-79; summer assoc. Tillinghast, Collins & Graham, Providence, 1980, 81; assoc. Edwards & Angell, Providence, 1982-86, Ropes & Gray, Providence, 1986-92; dep. treas., gen. counsel State of R.I., 1993—. Chmn., bd. dirs. Com. Women's Health Concerns, Phila., 1978-79; bd. dirs. Jewish Family Svc., Providence, 1982-88, Jewish Fedn. of R.I., 1989—; assoc. treas. Jewish Community Ctr. of R.I.; Bd. of Assoc. Alumni Trustees U. Pa.; chmn. admissions com. U. Pa. Alumni Club, Providence, 1982—. Mem. ABA, R.I. Bar Assn., Ledgemont Country Club (Seekonk, Mass.). Democrat. Jewish. Office: State House Rm 102 Providence RI 02903

SCHOENING-ROESS, SUE, marketing executive; b. Freeport, Ill., Aug. 3, 1946; d. Dominic Vincent and Dorothy Margaret (Kidwell) Casciana; divorced; children: Jodi Ann Schoening Nunziata, Theresa Lynn; m. Gustav Frederick Roess III, Jan. 2, 1993. AA in Bus. and Econs., Rollins Coll., 1979. Mgr. creative svcs. Sea World, Orlando, Fla., 1976-84, dir. advt., rsch. and creative svcs., 1984-86; v.p. mktg. Cypress Gardens, Winter Haven, Fla., 1986-89, Inter Coastal Communities, Ft. Lauderdale, Fla., 1989-90, Ridgewood Properties, Atlanta, 1992-94; pres. Fla. Communities, Orlando, 1990-94, Blue Sky Mktg., Orlando, 1994—. Bd. dirs. Orlando Advt. Fedn., 1982-85, pres., 1985; mem. mktg. adv. com. 1996 Olympics, Atlanta, 1994; founding mem. Give Kids the World, Orlando, 1986; bd. dirs. Fla. Symphony Youth Orch., Orlando, 1983. Named Outstanding Businesswoman of Yr., Sales and Mktg. Execs. Assn., 1983. Mem. Fla. Manufactured Housing Assn. Home and Office: 1624 Golfside Dr Winter Park FL 32792

SCHOENRICH, EDYTH HULL, academic administrator, physician; b. Cleve., Sept. 9, 1919; d. Edwin John and Maud Mabel (Kelly) Hull; m. Carlos Schoenrich, Aug. 9, 1942; children: Lola, Olaf. AB, Duke U., 1941; MD, U. Chgo., 1947; MPH, John Hopkins U., 1971. Diplomate Am. Bd. Internal Medicine, Am. Bd. Preventive Medicine. Intern John Hopkins Hosp., Balt., 1948-49, asst. resident medicine, 1949-50, postdoctoral fellow medicine, 1950-51, chief resident, pvt. wards, 1951-52; asst. chief, acting chief dept. chronic and cmty. medicine Balt. City Hosp., Balt., 1963-66; dir. svc. to chronically ill and aging Md. State Dept. Health, Balt., 1966-74; dir. divsn. pub. health adminstrn. Sch. Pub. Health, John Hopkins U., Balt., 1974-77, assoc. dean academic affairs, 1977-86, dir. part time profl. programs and dep. dir. MPH program, 1986—, prof. dept. health policy and mgmt., 1974—, joint appointment medicine, 1978—. Contbd. articles to profl. jours. Bd. trustees Friends Life Care Cmty., 1984—; Kennedy-Krieger Inst., Balt., 1985—, Vis. Nurses Assn., 1990—. Recipient Stebbins medal John Hopkins U., 1989. Fellow Am. Col. Physicians, Am. Coll. Preventive Medicine; mem. Assn. Tchrs. Preventive Medicine, Am. Pub. Health Assn., Med. Chirurg. Soc. Md., Balt. City Med. Soc., Phi Beta Kappa, Alpha Omega Alpha, Delta Omega. Home: 1402 Boyce Ave Baltimore MD 21204-6512 Office: Johns Hopkins Hosp Sch Pub Health 615 N Wolfe St Baltimore MD 21205

SCHOETTLER, GAIL SINTON, state official; b. Los Angeles, Oct. 21, 1943; d. James and Norma (McLellan) Sinton; children: Lee, Thomas, James; m. Donald L. Stevens, June 23, 1990. BA in Econs., Stanford U., 1965; MA in History, U. Calif., Santa Barbara, 1969, PhD in History, 1975. Businesswoman Denver, 1975-83; exec. dir. Colo. Dept. of Personnel, Denver, 1983-86; treas. State of Colo., Denver, 1987-94, lt. govern., 1995—; bd. dirs. Pub. Employees Retirement Assn., Denver, Nat. Jewish Hosp., Nat. Taxpayers' Union, Mi Casa Resource Ctr., Douglas County Edn. Found.; past bd. dirs. Women's Bank, Denver, Equitable Bankshares of Colo., Equitable Bank, Littleton. Mem. Douglas County Bd. Edn., Colo., 1979-87, pres., 1983-87; trustee U. No. Colo., Greeley, 1981-87; pres. Denver Children's Mus., 1975-85. Recipient Disting. Alumna award U. Calif. at Santa Barbara, 1987. Mem. Nat. Women's Forum (bd. dirs. 1981-89, pres. 1983-85), Women Execs. in State Govt. (bd. dirs. 1981-87, chmn. 1988), Leadership Denver Assn. (bd. dirs. 1987, named Outstanding Alumna 1985), Nat. Assn. State Treas., Stanford Alumni Assn. Democrat. *

SCHOFIELD, CAROLYN WILSON, biology educator; b. Midland, Tex., July 27, 1951; d. Charles F. and Jane (Johnson) Wilson; m. John Daniel Schofield, June 30, 1973. BA with high honors in Biology, U. Tex., Austin, 1973; MS in Interdisciplinary studies, U. Tex., Tyler, 1982. Tchr. biology Meml. High Sch., Houston, 1973-81; teaching asst. U. Tex., Tyler, 1981-82; tchr. biology Robert E. Lee High Sch., Tyler, 1982—; cons. Coll. Bd. Advanced Placement Program, Austin, 1975—; test item writer, essay grader Nat. Advanced Placement Biology Exam-Ednl. Testing Svc., Princeton, N.J., 1986—. Author: Pig Tales-Dissection Guide, 1989. Facilitator City of Tyler Recycing Ctr., 1991-92. Named Outstanding Advanced Placement Biology Cons., Coll. Bd., 1988; recipient Woman in Edn. awarad City of Tyler, 1989, Tex. Excellence awarad U. Tex.-State of Tex., 1991, Excellence in Sci Tchg. award Tex. Med. Assn., 1994. Mem. AAUW, Nat. Assn. Biology Tchrs. (Outstanding Biology Tchr. of Yr. 1994), Tex. Assn. Biology Tchrs. (Tex. Biology Tchr. of Yr. 1993), Phi Beta Kappa. Home: 6902 Gleneagles Dr Tyler TX 75703-5703

SCHOFIELD, S. LYNN, librarian; b. Hamburg, Iowa, Feb. 23, 1961; d. William Walter and Dorothy Lucille (Metz) S. BA, Buena Vista Coll., 1983; MLS, Tex. Woman's U., 1985. Head audiovisual dept., pub. rels. coord. Ector County Libr., Odessa, Tex., 1985—; exec. sec. West Tex. Libr. Film Circuit, Inc., Odessa, 1985—. Developed audio book and videocassette collections. Bd. dirs. Globe of Gt. Southwest, Odessa, 1992—; mem. selection com. Permian Playhouse, Odessa, 1990-94; mem. Odessa Cultural Coun., 1988-92. Recipient Dir.'s award for vol. svc. Permian Playhouse, 1992-93. Mem. ALA, Tex. Libr. Assn., Tex. Libr. Assn. Audio Visual Round Table (sec. 1987), Order of Wetbrush (libr. 1992—). Democrat.

SCHOLEFIELD, ADELINE PEGGY, therapist; b. Bklyn., Nov. 23, 1932; d. C. Joseph and Connie (Campbell) Taylor; m. Paul Robert Scholefield, June 26, 1954; children: Debra, Robert, Scott, Colin, Colleen, Heidi, Alan, Gene, Timothy, Christina, Holly, Shawn. Cert. radiol. technician, NYU, 1953; BS, N.H. Coll., 1989; MS in Human Svc., Springfield Coll., 1991. Registered radiol. technician, N.Y. X-ray technician St. Elizabeth's Hosp., N.Y.C., 1951-53, St. Joseph' Hosp., Lowell, Mass., 1954-67; owner, operator Maplewood Farm Family Care, Peperell, Mass., 1968—, Lauranne Village, Laconia, N.H., 1979-81; issues aide Offices of Senator Edward M. Kennedy, Boston, 1984-85, health and human svc. rep., 1985-87; liaison Dept. Social Svcs., Boston, Fitchbourg, Mass., 1988—, mem. steering com. of adv. coun.; sec. Statewide Adv. Coun., 1992. Foster parent Maplewood Farm, Pepperell, 1956—; staff Dem. State Com., Boston, 1987; sec. pers. bd. Town of Pepperell, 1989-90; vol. support/group loss and bereavement therapist, Naukeag Hosp., Ashbourham, Mass., 1993—, vol. therapist, 1991—; mem. adv. com. Coun. of Aging Commn.; mem. St. Josph's Parish Coun., Pepperell; ad hoc com. VA Hosp. Named Foster Parent of Yr. State of Mass., Boston, 1985; recipient commendation for family care VA, Bedford, Mass., 1971-73, 76, 81; Goldie Rogers award Dept. Social Svcs., 1994. Mem. Mass. Assn. Profl. Foster Care, Lioness Club (charter). Roman Catholic. Home and Office: 1 Chestnut St # 183 Pepperell MA 01463-1013

SCHOLER, SUE WYANT, state legislator; b. Topeka, Oct. 20, 1936; d. Zint Elwin and Virginia Louise (Achenbach) Wyant; m. Charles Frey Scholer, Jan. 27, 1957; children: Elizabeth Scholer Truelove, Charles W., Virginia M. Scholer McCal. Student, Kans. State U., 1954-56. Draftsman The Farm Clinic, West Lafayette, Ind., 1978-79; assessor Wabash Twp., West Lafayette, 1979-84; commr. Tippecanoe County, Lafayette, Ind., 1984-90; state rep. Dist. 26 Ind. Statehouse, Indpls., 1990—; asst. minority whip, 1992-94, majority whip, 1994—; mem. Tippecanoe County Area Plan Commn., 1984-90. Bd. dirs. Crisis Ctr., Lafayette, 1984-89, Tippecanoe Arts Fedn., 1990—, United Way, Lafayette, 1990-93; mem. Lafayette Conv. and Visitors Bur., 1988-90. Recipient Salute to Women Govt. and Police award, 1986. Mem. Ind. Assn. County Commrs. (treas. 1990), Assn. Ind. Counties (legis. com. 1988-90), Greater Lafayette C. of C. (ex-officio bd. 1984-90), Sagamore Bus. and Profl. Women, LWV, P.E.O., Purdue Women's Club (past treas.), Kappa Kappa Kappa (past pres. Epsilon chpt.), Delta Delta Delta (past pres. alumnae, house corp. treas.). Republican. Presbyterian. Home: 807 Essex St West Lafayette IN 47906-1534 Office: Indiana Statehouse Rm 3A-4 Indianapolis IN 46204

SCHOLL, WENDY ZONENBLIK, personnel manager; b. Chgo., Mar. 1, 1955; d. Louis David and Barbara Lois (Stone) Zonenblik; m. Gary Lee Scholl, Aug. 24, 1975 (div. Apr. 1985); children: Stacy, Holly, Jaclyn. Student, Bradley U., 1973-74. Bur. mgr. Pinellas County Tampa (Fla.) Bay Mag., 1980-82; pub. rels., lobbyist Dissatisfied Parents Together, Vienna, Va., 1983; pres. state chpt. Dissatisfied Parents Together, St. Petersburg, Fla., 1983-86; br. mgr. Personnel Pool Am., Inc., Pinellas Park, Fla., 1985-90; mktg. mgr. employment svcs. Abilities of Fla. Inc., 1990—. Contbr. articles to Tampa Bay Mag., 1981-82; producer, writer, director video tape on vaccine injured children. Mgr., fundraiser Abilities Rehab. Ctr., Pinellas county bur. Chi-Chi Rodriegez Youth Found., 1981; with pub. rels. for Pinellas county Vietnam MIAs, 1982; with outreach program United Jewish Appeal, 1983-84 (award of merit 1983-84); media coord. Jewish Media Rels.; proposed and had imput on U.S. gov. reporting systems for adverse reaction to vaccines. Jewish. Home: 9085 109th Ave N # 408 Largo FL 34647 Office: 7907 Sailboat Key Blvd S Saint Petersburg FL 33707-6305

SCHOMMER, TRUDY MARIE, pastoral minister, religion education; b. Wayzata, Minn., May 18, 1937; d. Edward and Gertrude (Mergen) S. BA, Coll. St. Catherine, St. Paul, 1966; MA, Manhattanville Coll., 1971. Joined Order of Franciscan Sisters of Little Falls, Minn., 1955. Dir. religious edn. St. Pius X, White Bear Lake, Minn., 1971-77; campus min., theology tchr. St. Cloud (Minn.) State Univ., 1977-81; pastoral min. St. Galls, St. Elizabeth, Milw., 1981-85; dir. religious edn. St. Alexander's, Morrisonville, N.Y., 1985-90; pastoral min. of religious edn. St. Mary's, Bryantown, Md., 1990-91; diocesan dir. religious edn. Diocese of New Ulm, Minn., 1991—; exec. bd. mem. Nat. Assembly Religious Women, Chgo., 1974-78. Author: Easiest Gospel Stories Ever, 1993; book reviewer Sister's Today, 1988-91. Mem. Network, Washington, 1978—. Mem. Nat. Cath. Edn. Assn., Nat. Parish Coords. and Dirs. Democrat. Roman Catholic. Home and Office: 1725 Oxford St Apt 201 Berkeley CA 94709-1701

SCHÖNBERG, BESSIE, dance educator; b. Hanover, Germany, Dec. 27, 1906; m. Dimitry Varley (dec. 1984). Studied with Martha Hill, Martha Graham. Dancer Martha Graham Dance Co., N.Y.C., 1931; prof. dance Sarah Lawrence Coll., Bronxville, N.Y., 1941-75, head dance dept., 1941, prof. emerita, 1975—; guest tchr. Ohio State U., Wesleyan U., U. N.H., Amherst Coll., George Mason U., The Art of Movement Ctr., London, Contemporary Dance Ctr., London; presenter workshops Dance Theatre Workshop, N.Y.C., Dance Theatre Harlem, N.Y.C.; dance cons. Hunter Coll., N.Y.C., Oberlin (Ohio) Coll., Dennison U., Wesleyan U.; mem. appeals bd. N.Y. State Coun. on Arts; mem. adv. panel NEA Dance Program; chmn., bd. dirs. Dance Theatre Workshop. Appeared in Martha Graham's dances including Primitive Mysteries, Ceremonials, Project in Movement for a Divine Comedy. Mentor fellow NEA, 1994; recipient citation Assn. Am. Dance Cos., 1975, Lifetime Achievement in Dance Bessie award, 1987-88, Gov. Arts award N.Y. State, 1989, Ernie award Dance/USA, 1994; The N.Y. Dance and Performance Awards are named in her honor as The BESSIES. Office: Sarah Lawrence Coll Dept Dance 1 Meadway Bronxville NY 10708*

SCHONHOLTZ, JOAN SONDRA HIRSCH, banker, civic worker; b. N.Y.C., Sept. 8, 1933; d. Joseph G. and Mildred (Klebanoff) Hirsch; m. George J. Schonholtz, Aug. 21, 1951; children: Margot Beth, Steven Robert, Barbara Ellen. Student, Vassar Coll., 1950-52; B.A., Barnard Coll., 1954; postgrad., Am. U., 1963. Chmn. bd. dirs., founding mem. Ist Women's Bank of Md., Rockville, 1976—; chmn. FWB Bancorp., Rockville, 1982—. Pres. Ft. Benning Med. Wives, Ga., 1962-63; sec. Montgomery County Women's Med. Aux., Md., 1968; bd. dirs. Svc. Guild of Washington, 1968-77, sec., 1969-70, pres., 1975-77; bd. dirs. Pilot Sch. for Blind Multiple Handicapped Children, Washington, 1968-77; bd. dirs. Strathmore Hall Arts Ctr., N. Bethesda, Md., 1992—; spl. gifts chmn. Cancer Soc. Montgomery County, 1968, 69; mem. Washington Adv. Coun. on Deaf-Blind Children, 1972-74; chmn. Friends of Wash. Adventist Hosp., Takoma Park, Md., 1993—. Recipient Outstanding Service award Service Guild of Washington, 1969. Republican. Jewish. Clubs: Vassar, Barnard. Home: 10839 Lockland Rd Potomac MD 20854-1855

SCHOOLEY, DOLORES HARTER, entertainment administrator; b. Nora Springs, Iowa, May 2, 1905; d. Amil A. and Elizabeth (Sefert) Zemke; m. Leslie J. Harter, June 5, 1934 (dec. 1963); m. Charles Earl Schooley, Apr. 1, 1966. BE, BA, U. Colo., 1927; MA, Northwestern U., 1931. Tchr. high sch. Consol. Schs., Johnstown, Colo., 1927-28, Byers, Colo., 1928-29, Clayton, Mo., 1931-34; theatrical makeup artist, 1937-86; instr. theatrical makeup dramatic clubs, N.J. Theatre League; lectr., demonstrator theatrical makeup, dramatic and women's clubs, high schs., N.J. and N.Y. area, 1937-53; nat. officer, entertainer, dir. internat. entertainment project for mil. posts Phi Beta Nat. Profl. Fraternity for Creative & Performing Arts, 1951-61; cons. radio broadcast series Sta. WNYC, N.Y., 1962-65; dir. community rels. Wingspread Summer Theatre, Colon, Mich., 1955; co-chmn. Valley Shore Community Concerts, Conn., 1958-61, artist mgr., 1959—; founder, pres. Berkshire Hills Music and Dance Assn., Conn., 1970-78; mem. Music Mountain Corp., Falls Village, Conn., 1975-81. Trustee Sharon (Conn.) Creative Arts Found., 1970-73; hon. trustee Bar Harbor Maine Festival, 1968-80; founder, pres. Wingspread Found., Conn. 1977—; mem. adv. bd. Community Found. of Henderson County, N.C., 1990-93; trustee Brevard (N.C.) Music Ctr., 1990-93. Mem. Montclair (N.J.) Dramatic Club (chmn. and instr. makeup), Rehearsal Club (program chmn.), Montclair (N.J.) Women's Club (dir. plays, chmn. drama dept.), Sharon (Conn.) Women's Club, Sharon Rep. Women's Club (pres. 1982-85), Sharon Country Club, Hendersonville (N.C.) Country Club, Alpha Omicron Pi., Phi Beta (nat. profl. fraternity for peforming arts). Congregationalist. Address: PO Box 746 Hendersonville NC 28793-0746

SCHOOLEY, JENNIFER LYNN, broadcasting executive; b. Oakdale, Calif., Sept. 22, 1957; d. Irwin Ross and Elvira Janet (Brown) Hickman; m. Bruce G. Schooley, Apr. 21, 1991; 1 child, James Bruce. BS in Communications, Pacific Union Coll., 1981. On-air commentator Sta. KCDS, Angwin, Calif., 1983—, talk show host, 1986-88, script writer for Step Aside (formerly Mellow Majesty), 1988-92, host Step Aside, 1989—; gen. mgr. Sta. KCDS, Angwin, 1993—. Seventh-day Adventist. Office: Sta KCDS Broadcast Ctr Angwin CA 94508

SCHOONOVER, JEAN WAY, public relations consultant; b. Richfield Springs, N.Y.. AB, Cornell U., 1941. With D-A-Y Pub. Rels., Ogilvy & Mather Co., N.Y.C., 1949-91, D-A-Y Pub. Rels. Inc. and predecessor, N.Y.C., 1949—; owner, pres. Dudley-Anderson-Yutzy Pub. Rels. Inc. and predecessor, N.Y.C., 1970—; chmn. Dudley-Anderson-Yutzy Pub. Relations Inc. and predecessor, 1984-88; merger with Ogilvy & Mather, 1983; sr. v.p. Ogilvy & Mather U.S., 1984-91; vice chmn. Ogilvy Pub. Relations Group, 1986-91; ind. cons., 1992—; pres. YWCA of the City of N.Y., 1994—; mem., historian, Pub. Relations Seminar; mem. U.S. Dept. Agriculture Agribusiness Promotion Council, 1985—. Trustee Cornell U., 1975-80; mem. Def. Adv. Com. on Women in Svcs., 1987-89. Named Advt. Woman of Yr. Am. Advt. Fedn., 1972, one of Outstanding Women in Bus. & Labor, Women's Equity Action League, 1985.; recipient Matrix award, 1976, Nat. Headliner award, 1984, N.Y. Women in Communications, 1976, leadership award Internat. Orgn. Women Bus. Owners, 1980, Entrepreneurial Woman award Women Bus. Owners N.Y., 1981. Mem. Women Execs. in Pub. Rels. N.Y.C. (pres. 1979-80), Pub. Rels. Soc. Am., Pub. Rels. Soc. N.Y. (pres. 1979). Home: 25 Stuyvesant St New York NY 10003-7505

SCHOPPER, SUE FRANKS, maternal-women's health and medical-surgical nurse; b. Stigler, Okla., Mar. 25, 1938; d. Everett and Ruby (McCaslin) F.; m. Jared B. Schopper, Jan. 27, 1978; children: Robert, Jenny, Melody. Assoc. Diploma Nursing, Bacone Coll., Muskogee, Okla., 1973; BSN, Northeastern State U., Tahlequah, Okla., 1991. RN, Okla. Supr. VA Med. Ctr., Muskogee, 1973-78; charge nurse obstetrics-labor-delivery room, newborn nursery Hastings Hosp., Tahlequah, 1979; charge nurse surg. floor Tahlequah City Hosp., 1983-90; pediatric nurse Pediatric Clinic, Tahlequah, 1990—; RN cons. Green Acres Retirement Ctr., Tahlequah, 1989—. Home: 402 Wheeler St Tahlequah OK 74464-6301 Office: Pediatric Clinic 1607 S Muskogee Ave Tahlequah OK 74464

SCHOR, OLGA SEEMANN, mental health counselor, real estate broker; b. Havana, Cuba, Mar. 2, 1951; came to U.S., 1961; d. Olga del Carmen (Hernandez) S.; m. David Michael Schor, Apr. 22, 1979; 1 child, Andrew. A.A., Miami Dade Community Coll., 1971; B.A., U. Fla.-Gainesville, 1973; M.Edn., U. Miami, Fla., 1976; Psy.D., Nova U., 1981; cert. Bert Rodgers Sch. Real Estate, Miami, 1981, Gold Coast Sch. Real Estate, 1988; lic. real estate broker. Teaching asst. U. Fla., Gainesville, 1972-73; counselor U. Miami, Fla., 1974-79; assoc. psychotherapist Linda H. Jamrozy & Assocs., Miami, 1976-78, Interactive Systems, Miami, 1978-79; psychometrist Jackson Meml. Hosp., Miami, 1978-79; assoc. psychotherapist Behavioral Medicine Inst., Miami, 1979-85, Tony Ciminero & Assocs., Miami, 1985-86; lectr. U. Miami, 1976-78, Jackson Meml. Hosp. Sch. Nursing, Miami, 1976; real estate broker The Keyes Co. Realtor, Coral Gables, 1981-88, Keyes Asset Mgmt., Miami, 1988—; sec./treas. bd. dirs. BODS Inc., Miami. Recipient Assoc. of Quarter award Keyes Co. Realtors, 1986. Mem. Am. Psychol. and Guidance Assn., Keyes Comml. Roundtable, Keyes Inner Circle, Coral Gables Bd. Realtors, Gulliver Acad.'s Parents Bd., Dade County Mental Health Assn., Million Dollar Sales Club. Club: South Fla. Sailing Assn. (Miami). Avocations: sailing; diving; reading; running; theater; acting; tennis. Office: Keyes Asset Mgmt Inc 1 SE 3 Ave 11th Fl Miami FL 33131

SCHORR, LISBETH BAMBERGER, child and family policy analyst, author, educator; b. Munich, Jan. 20, 1931; d. Fred S. and Lotte (Krafft) Bamberger; m. Daniel L. Schorr, Jan. 8, 1967; children—Jonathan, Lisa. BA with highest honors, U. Calif., Berkeley, 1952; LHD (hon.), Wilkes U., 1991, U. Md., 1994. Med. care cons. U.A.W. and Community

Health Assn., Detroit, 1956-58; asst. dir. Dept. Social Security AFL-CIO, Washington, 1958-65; acting chief CAP Health Svcs., OEO, 1965-66; chief program planning Office for Health Affairs, OEO, Washington, 1967; cons. Children's Def. Fund, Washington, 1973-79; scholar-in-residence Inst. of Medicine, 1979-80; chmn. Select Panel on Promotion Child Health, 1979-80; adj. prof. maternal and child health U. N.C., Chapel Hill, 1981-85; lectr. social medicine Harvard U. Med. Sch., 1984—; dir. project on effective svcs. Harvard U., 1988—; nat. council Alan Gutmacher Inst., 1974-79, 82-85; pub. mem. Am. Bd. Pediatrics, 1978-84; vice chmn. Found. for Child Devel., 1978-84, bd. dirs. 1976-84, 86-94; mem. coun. Nat. Ctr. for Children in Poverty, 1987—; mem. children's program adv. com. Edna McConnell Clark Found., 1987—; bd. dirs. Pub. Edn. Fund Network, 1991-93; co-chair Roundtable on Effective Svcs. Aspen Inst., 1992—; mem. bd. on children and families NAS, 1993—; mem. Nat. Commn. State & Local Pub. Svc., 1992—; mem. task force on young children Carnegie Corp., 1991-94; mem. sec.'s adv. com. Head Start quality and expansion, 1993-94; mem. exec. com. Harvard Project on Schooling and Children. Author: Within Our Reach: Breaking the Cycle of Disadvantage, 1988. Recipient Dale Richmond Meml. award Am. Acad. Pediatrics, 1977, 9th Ann. Robert F. Kennedy Book award, 1989, Nelson Cruikshank award nat. Coun. Sr. Citizens, 1990, Porter prize, 1993. Mem. Inst. Medicine, NAS, Nat. Acad. on Social Ins., Phi Beta Kappa. Home: 3113 Woodley Rd NW Washington DC 20008-3449

SCHOTT, ETHEL MENDOW, wastewater district administrator; b. New Orleans, Oct. 27, 1934; d. F. Robert and Dorothy Isabel (Drawe) Mendow; m. Vincent Fabian Schott, June 28, 1956; children: James V., Carl G., Eric R., Anne F., Gary F., Vincent A., Alan L. BS in Chemistry, St. Mary's Dominican Coll., 1956. Lic. class IV wastewater plant operator, Miss. Tchr. math. and English St. Clare Sch., Waveland, Miss., 1970-72; lab. technician Waveland (Miss.) Treatment Plant, 1980-82, plant supt., 1982—; adminstr. Waveland Regional Wastewater Mgmt. Dist., 1982-93, So. Regional Wastewater Mgmt. Dist., Hancock County, Miss., 1993—. Troop leader Girl Scouts Am., Bay/Waveland, Miss., 1974-81; neighborhood chmn. Bay/Waveland Girl Scouts, 1978-82. Mem. Water Environment Fedn. (wastewater ops. divsn. 1992, program and short course com. 1991-92, nominating com. 1993-94, membership com. 1992-93), Miss. Water and Pollution Control Operator's Assn. (program and short course com. 1991-92, membership com. 1992-93, nominating com. 1993-94, dist. 6 program chmn. 1993, 94, Outstanding Water Pollution Control Operator 1992). Roman Catholic. Office: So Regional Wastewater Mgmt Dist PO Drawer 110 Waveland MS 39576

SCHOTT, MARGE, professional baseball team executive; b. 1928; d. Edward and Charlotte Unnewehr; m. Charles J. Schott, 1952 (dec. 1968). Owner Schottco, Cin.; ltd. ptnr. Cin. Reds, 1981-84, gen. ptnr., 1984-85, owner, pres., 1985—, chief exec. officer. Office: Cin Reds 100 Riverfront Stadium Cincinnati OH 45202*

SCHOWALTER, ELLEN LEFFERTS, financial planner; b. Milw., Apr. 23, 1937; d. William George and Alice (Virgin) Lefferts; m. John Erwin Schowalter, June 11, 1960; children: Jay, Bethany. BS, U. Wis., 1958, MS, 1959; MA, Yale U., 1982. Cert. fin. planner. Tchr. English West Allis (Wis.) Bd. Edn., 1959-60, New Haven (Conn.) Bd. Edn., 1960-61, Cin. Bd. Edn., 1961-63; dir. Bethesda Nursery Sch., New Haven, 1971-80; registered rep. First Investors Corp., Hamden, Conn., 1982-85; sr. rep. Jonathan Alan and Co., Inc. (name changed to Schowalter & Seymour Assocs.), White Plains, N.Y., 1985-90; cert. fin. planner Schowalter Assocs., New Haven, 1990—; seminar leader, tchr., Successful MOney MgmtSeminars, Fairfield Continuing Edn. Program, Fairfield, Conn., 1987-92; seminar leader Pace U.. Exec. Nurses,1988-92, K Mart Employees, Morrisville, Pa, North Bergen, N.J., 1994—, ,. Mem. Internat. Assn. Fin. Planners, Coll. Fin. Planning, Mortar Bd. Democrat. Lutheran. Home: 606 Ellsworth Ave New Haven CT 06511-1636 Office: Schowalter Assocs 68 Putnam Ave New Haven CT 06517-2825

SCHRADER, CAROL ANN, painter; b. Elizabethtown, Pa., Dec. 19, 1939; d. Gilbert Thomas and Margaret Mary (Thomas) Steever; m. Robert F. Schrader. BS, Pa. State U., 1961, MEd, 1963; MFA, U. N.C., 1972. Instr. art Prince George's County Pub. Schs., Beltsville, Md., 1961-71; art chair, instr. U. Alaska-S.E., Sitka, 1985-86; coord. art show C.C. Rural Edn. Ext., Sitka, 1985-86; juror S.E. Alaska Art Ann., Sitka, 1986. Contbr.: Splash III, 1994; contbr. articles to profl. jours.; paintings include Illinois Afternoon (Bristol-Myers Squibb award 1991), Margaret's July (George and Beverly Ryan award 1992). Recipient High Winds Medal and Honorarium, Am. Watercolor Soc., 1991. Mem. Nat. Watercolor Soc. (Alexander Nepote award 1989, Altfeld/Campbell award 1989), Watercolor U.S.A. Honor Soc., Midwest Watercolor Soc. (Maijaliisa Rudy award 1990), Ky. Watercolor Soc. (Ky. Artist award 1989, 90, 92), Watercolor Soc. Ala. (Emil Hess award 1993), Watercolor West, Phila. Water Color Club. Home: 113 E Harbor Dr Hendersonville TN 37075

SCHRADER, HELEN MAYE, retired municipal worker; b. Akron, Ohio, June 8, 1920; d. Simon P. and Helen Cecelia (Fennessy) Eberz; widowed; children: Alfred E., Kathleen Therese Schrader Wein. Notary pub. Inspector and clk. Fed. Govt. agys., 1940; stenographer Chem. Warfare div./USAF, Akron, 1954; clk., stenographer VA; elected clk./treas. of twp. Springfield (Ohio) Twp., 1956-92. Clk., treas. Springfield Twp., 1956-62; sec. Springfield Dem. Club, Akron, 1957—; sec., treas. Springfield Twp. Civic Club, 1980—. Mem. Summit County Assn. of Trustees and Clks. (sec. 1959-78, 83-92, Svc. plaque 1979, 92). Roman Catholic. Home: 693 Neal Rd Akron OH 44312-3709

SCHRAGE, ROSE, educational administrator; b. Montelimar, France, Apr. 15, 1942; came to U.S., 1947; d. Abraham and Celia (Silbiger) Levine; m. Samuel Schrage, Dec. 12, 1935 (dec. 1976); children: Abraham, Leon. BRE, Beth Rivkah Tchrs. Sem., Bklyn., 1968; Paralegal, Manpower Career Devel. Agy., Bklyn., 1973; MS, L.I. U., 1975; Advanced Cert. Ednl. Adminstrn., Bklyn. Coll., 1983. Cert. sch. dist. adminstr., guidance counselor, tchr., asst. prin. Sec. N.Y.C., 1964-68; police adminstrv. aide N.Y.C. Police Dept., 1974-75; coordinator state reading aid program Sch. Dist. 14, Bklyn., 1977-78, project dir. Title VII, 1978-81, asst. dir. reimbursable fed. and state programs, 1981-85, dist. bus. mgr., 1985-94, asst. prin., 1994—; chmn. N.Y.C. Bd. Edn. IMPACT Com., Bklyn., 1986—. Author (poem): Never Again, 1983; contbg. editor Chai Today; contbr. articles on current affairs and concerns to profl. jours. Del. Republican. Jud. Conf., 1968; founder, pres Concerned Parents, Bklyn., 1977; radio co-host Israeli War Heroes Fund-Radiothon, Bklyn.; family counselor local social agys., Bklyn. Recipient Cert. of Appreciation as vol. regional coord. N.Y. State Mentoring Program N.Y. Gov. Cuomo, 1991. Mem. Am. Assn. Sch. Adminstrs., Assn. Orthodox Jewish Tchrs. (v.p. exec. bd.), N.Y. State Assn. Sch. Bus. Ofcls., N.Y.C. Assn. Sch. Bus. Ofcls., Coun. Suprs. and Adminstrs.

SCHRAGER, MINDY RAE, quality assurance professional; b. Paterson, N.J., Jan. 18, 1958; d. Julius Maxwell and Miriam (Max) S.; m. Jim Flannery, 1993. BA, Dickinson Coll., 1979; MBA, Babson Coll., 1981. Cons., Nolan Norton & Co., Lexington, Mass., 1981-86; mgr. Logos Corp., Dedham, Mass., 1986-87; supr. resource ctr., customer satisfaction mgr. distribution quality mgr., dir. of quality for worldwide distribution, Motorola ISG, Mansfield, Mass., 1987-95; dir. quality Fidelity Retail Investment Svcs., Boston, 1995—. Co-author: Non Product Quality: The Cornerstone for Sucess, Continuous Improvement of the Selling Process. Mem. NAFE, Am. Soc. Quality Control (founder, chmn. 1992-94, bus. process improvement com.), Assn. for Rsch. and Enlightenment, Assn. Quality and Participation (co-founder Boston chpt. 1990, v.p. 1991-92, pres. 1992-93) Avocation: ballroom dance. Home: 43 Bradford Rd Framingham MA 01701-3381

SCHRAGER, SARA LOUISE, lighting design consultant; b. Hartford, Conn., May 9, 1952; d. Arthur and Shirley Eva (Cohen) S.; m. Bil Mikulewicz, Aug. 27, 1981; 1 child, Alexandra; 1 stepchild, Maude. AB, Conn. Coll., 1974; postgrad in Fine Arts, Parsons Sch. of Design, 1991—. Stage electrician N.Y. Shakespeare Festival, N.Y.C., 1975-76; theatrical, architectural lighting designer pvt. practice, N.Y.C., 1976-80; designer show lighting Walt Disney Imagineering, Glendale, Calif., 1980-81; assoc. Terry Chasman Lighting Design, N.Y.C., 1983; prin., owner S. Schrager Lighting Cons., N.Y.C., 1981-93, Ridgefield, Conn., 1993—; adj. instr. Fashion Inst. Tech., N.Y.C., 1988-91, in continuing edn. Parsons Sch. of Design, 1991-93. Designer of lighting; works include: Imagination Pavilion, Horizons Pavilion, Italy and Japan Pavilions at Epcot, Walt Disney Prodns., 1980-81, Whitney Mus. Am. Art at Equitable Ctr., N.Y.C., 1987, Bklyn. Hist. Soc., 1987-88, Whitney Mus. of Art, Fairfield County, Sagamore Hill Hist. Site, 1988, Am. Mus. of Moving Image, permanent exhbn., Astoria, N.Y., 1991, The Jewish Mus. N.Y. Hist. Soc., Bklyn. Children's Mus., Renovation Lighting, 1993, more. Mem. Internat. Assn. Lighting Designers (corp. mem., bd. dirs.), Illuminating Engr. Soc. N. Am. (bd. mgrs., v.p., pres. N.Y. sect.). Office: Sara Schrager Lighting Cons 133 Wilton Rd W Ridgefield CT 06877-5608

SCHRAM, MELODY JOANNE, emergency relief and development in Russia & Asia; b. Oceanside, Calif., Mar. 22, 1963; d. Albert Bruce and Norma May (Swift) S. BA in Polit. Sci. cum laude, UCLA, 1985; MA in Internat. Affairs/Soviet Studies, Columbia U., 1987. Office mgr. Cath. Relief Svcs., Washington, 1987-89; cons. pub. affairs dept. Cath. Relief Svcs., Balt., 1989; project mgr. Cath. Relief Svcs., Calcutta, India, 1990-92; dir. Cath. Relief Svcs., Vladivostok, Russia, 1992-93; country dir., Russia Cath. Relief Svcs., 1992-93; cons. Internat. Bus. and Cross-Cultural Negotiation, San Francisco, 1994; program devel. cons. Russia & Ctrl. Asia program The Asia Found., 1994—. Recipient Govs. Proclamation, Gov. of Primorskii Krai, Russian Far East, 1993. Mem. Calif. Scholarship Fedn., UCLA Alumni Assn., Gamma Phi Beta (inter-sorority rep. 1984-85, Panhellenic tuition award 1984, Gamma Phi Beta scholarship 1984). Democrat. Home: 327 Cornwall St San Francisco CA 94118

SCHRAMM, LORETTA LINGG, nursing administrator; b. Balt., Apr. 29, 1943; d. Joseph Irvin and Lillian F. (Smith) Lingg; m. Bernard H. Schramm, June 5, 1965; children: Timothy Joseph, Lori Ann. Diploma, Bon Secours Hosp. Sch. Nursing, 1964; BSN, Towson (Md.) State U., 1992. Cert. gerontology nurse. Dir. nursing, supr. Meridian Nursing Ctr. Catonsville, Balt.; staff nurse Little Sisters of Poor, Balt., Summit Nursing Home, Balt.; continuing edn. faculty Catonsville Community Coll.

SCHREIBER, CAROL MARIE HOUSER SAMS, fine artist, graphic designer, illustrator; b. Knoxville, Tenn., Sept. 28, 1952; d. Harrison Barton and Doris Marie (McFarland) Houser; m. Richard Vernon Sams, Sept. 1, 1972 (div. Nov. 1979); m. Robert William Schreiber, Nov. 3, 1990. BFA in Communication Design, U. Tenn., 1973. Graphic artist Richards Med. Co., Memphis, Tenn., 1976-84; sr. art dir. Smith & Nephew Richards, Memphis, 1984-89; prin. Square One Design, Memphis, 1989-92; prin., artist Square One Studio, Memphis, 1992—; isntr. painting Memphis State U., 1983-87; dealer Bell Gallery, Memphis, Tenn., Harbor Springs, Mich., Birmingham, Mich. Mem. Nat. Watercolor Assn., So. Watercolor Assn., Tenn. Watercolor Assn. (various offices 1982-86), Art Today. Home: 794 N Evergreen Memphis TN 38107 Office: Square One Studio 1575 Madison Ave Memphis TN 38104

SCHREIBER, EILEEN SHER, artist; b. Denver; d. Michael Herschel and Sarah Deborah (Tannenbaum) Sher; student U. Utah, 1942-45, N.Y.U. extension, 1966-68, Montclair (N.J.) State Coll., 1975-79; also pvt. art study; m. Jonas Schreiber, Mar. 27, 1945; children—Jeffrey, Barbara, Michael. Exhibited Morris Mus. Arts and Scis., Morristown, N.J., 1965-73, N.J. State Mus., 1969, Lever House, N.Y.C., 1971, Paramus (N.J.) Mus., 1973, Newark Mus., 1978, Am. Water Color Soc., Audubon Artists, N.A.D. Gallery, N.Y.C., Pallazzo Vecchio Florence (Italy), Art Expo 1987, 1988, Newark Mus., 1991-92; represented in permanent collections Tex. A&M U., Sunbelt Computers, Phoenix, Ariz., State of N.J., Morris Mus., Seton Hall U., Bloomfield (N.J.) Coll., Barclay Bank of Eng., N.J., Somerset Coll., NYU, Morris County State Coll., Broad Nat. Bank, Newark, IBM, Am. Telephone Co., RCA, Johnson & Johnson, Champion Internat. Paper Co., SONY, Mitsubishi, Celanese Co., Squibb Corp., Nabisco, Nat. Bank Phila., NYU, Data Control, Sperry Univac, Ga. Pacific Co., Public Service Co. N.J., Forms Galleries, Delray Beach, Fla., , Robin Hutchins Galleries, Maplewood, N.J., Passage West, Ft. Lauderdale, Fla., others; also pvt. collections. Recipient awards N.J. Watercolor Soc., 1969, 72, Nat. Assn. Women Artists, 1970; 1st award in watercolor Hunterdon Art Center, 1972, Best in Show award Short Hills State Show, 1976, Tri-State Purchase award Somerset Coll., 1977, Art Expo, N.Y.C. 1987, 88; numerous others. Mem. Nat. Assn. Women Artists (chmn. watercolor jury; Collage award 1983), Nat., N.J. artists equity, Printmaker Coun. Visual Artists (Boca Raton, Fla.). Home: 22 Powell Dr West Orange NJ 07052-1337 Office: 3429 Galt Ocean Dr Fort Lauderdale FL 33308

SCHREYER, NANCY KRAFT, medical science researcher; b. Chelsea, Mass., Apr. 18, 1952; d. Meyer Louis and Eileen Marguerite (McCauley) Kraft; m. Raymond Scott Schreyer, Aug. 22, 1976; children: Kraftin Ellice, Evan Kraft. BS, Simmons Coll., 1974; PhD, Hahnemann Med. Coll., 1979. Instr. Hahnemann Med. Coll., Coll. Allied Health Professions, Phila., 1977-79, sr. instr., 1979-80; asst. instr. Hahnemann Med. Coll., Phila., 1977-79, instr., 1979-80, sr. instr., 1980-81; asst. prof. Hahnemann U., Sch. Allied Health Professions, Phila., 1980-88, Hahnemann U. Sch. Medicine, Phila., 1981-88, Hahnemann U. Grad. Sch., Phila., 1983—; non-affiliated mem. animal care and use com. Bristol Myers-Squibb Co. N.J., 1988. Contbr. articles to profl. jours. Rsch. grantee Hahnemann U., 1983, Am. Heart Assn., 1986. Mem. Am. Soc. Hypertension, N.Y. Acad. Scis., Am. Soc. Primatologists, Physiol. Soc. Phila., Am. Assn. Lab. Animal Sci., Am. Physiol. Soc.

SCHRICKER, ETHEL KILLINGSWORTH, business management and public relations consultant; b. Hagerstown, Md., July 22, 1937; d. Lloyd Granville and Ethel Mull; children: Jeanne, Lori, Jerri; m. Robert Lee Schricker, June 6, 1993. BA in Mgmt., Hood Coll., 1994; postgrad. in Psychology, Hood Coll, 1994—. Specialist Frederick County Pub. Schs., Frederick, Md., 1967-95, retired specialist, 1995—. Vol. Literacy Coun., Frederick, 1976-84, Dept. Social Svcs., Frederick, 1984; bd. ruling elders Frederick Presbyn. Ch., 1989-92. Named Bus. Woman of Yr. Frederick Bus. and Profl. Women, 1992. Mem. Assn. Sch. Bus. Ofcls. (chairperson seminar devel. com. 1990-94), Frederick County Assn. Adminstrv. and Supervisory Pers., Toastmasters Internat. (area gov. 1991-92, pub. rels. 1991-93). Home: PO Box 15 Frederick MD 21705-0015

SCHROCK, BARBARA JEAN, clinical neuropsychologist; b. Odessa, Tex., July 16, 1952; d. Clarence and Lillian Bernice (Howard) S.; m. Kevin David Gerhart, Aug. 20, 1977; children: David Adam Gerhart, Kathryn Margaret Gerhart. BA, U. Redlands, 1975; MA, U. Houston, 1983, PhD, 1985. Cert. clin. neuropsychologist. Clin. co-dir. Transitional Learning Community, Galveston, Tex., 1982-84; assoc. dir. U. Houston Neuropsychology Cons., 1984-86; staff neuropsychologist Santa Clara Valley Med Ctr., San Jose, Calif., 1986-89; pvt. practice, consultation San Jose, 1989-90; pvt. practice San Diego, 1990—; head dept. rehab. psychology svcs. Sharp Rehab. Ctr., San Diego, 1991—, clin. dir. disability assessment program, 1992—; asst. clin. prof. dept. psychiatry U. Calif., San Diego, 1993—; rehab. cons. Stepping Stones, San Jose, 1988-90; neuropsychology cons. Saratoga (Calif.) Sub-Acute, 1989-90. Mem. APA, Internat. Neuropsychol. Soc., Calif. Psychol. Assn. Office: Sharp Rehab Ctr 2999 Health Center Dr San Diego CA 92123-2788

SCHROEDER, ANNE KATHERINE, glass blower, artist, educator; b. Madison, Wis., Sept. 2, 1958; d. Collin Harold and Margaret (Isabell (Roberts) S. BS, U. Wis., 1982; MFA, Mass. Coll. Art, Boston, 1987. Owner, mgr. Brick House Glass, Madison, 1989—; lectr., demonstrator Madison Art Ctr., 1992, Madison East H.S., 1992, Univ. League, 1993. Exhibited in group shows Valperine Gallery, Madison, 1992, City-County Arts, Madison, 1993, Newell Gallery, Waunakee, Wis., 1993, 94, Blue Bird Gallery, Prairie du Sac, Wis., 1994; work represented in various mags. Home: 4802 Bayfield Ter Madison WI 53705 Office: Brick House Glass 4157 Veith Ave Madison WI 53704

SCHROEDER, BETTY LOUISE, bookkeeper; b. Aldrich, Mo., Apr. 20, 1937; d. Raymond Fenton and Josie Margaret (Redman) Slagle; m. Earl Freddie Schroeder, Mar. 8, 1958 (div. 1981); children—Kathryn, David, Robert. Student pub. schs., Pleasant Hope, Mo. Head sec. Jackson Extension Ctr., Independence, Mo., 1964; typist MWM Colorpress, Aurora, Mo., 1965; income tax preparer, H&R Block, Aurora, 1969-77, preparer, owner, 1977-83, preparer, owner, West Plains, Mo., 1984—. Fund raiser Houn Dawg Band, Aurora, 1975-85. Baptist. Avocation: handcrafts. Office: H&R Block-Schroeder Bookkeeping 1406 Kentucky St West Plains MO 65775-1822

SCHROEDER, EILEEN ELIZABETH, education educator; b. Allentown, Pa., June 6, 1955; d. Randall Wisser and Betty Mae (Baker) S. BS in Edn., Kutztown State Coll., 1977; MS in Libr. and Info. Sci., Drexel U., 1982; MA in Ednl. Founds., U. N.Mex., 1987; MS, Syracuse U., 1992; PhD in Instructional Systems, Penn State, 1993. Cert. sch. libr. media specialist. Libr. Drum Point Elem. Sch., Brick Town, N.J., 1977-82; dir. Tireman Learning Materials Libr., U. N.Mex., Albuquerque, 1983-85; teaching materials reference/bibliographer SUNY, Cortland, 1985-89, 91; asst. prof. ednl. founds. U. Wis., Whitewater, 1993—. Author: Science Education, 1986. Mem. ALA, Assn. for Ednl. Comms. and Tech. (Dean and Sybil McCluskey award 1993), Am. Ednl. Rsch. Assn., Am. Assn. Sch. Librs. Office: U Wis Ednl Founds 1006 Winther Hall Whitewater WI 53190

SCHROEDER, JOYCE KATHERINE, research analyst; b. Moline, Ill., Apr. 1, 1951; d. Reinhold J. and Miriam-May Schroeder. BS in Math., U. Ill., 1973; MA in Ops. Rsch., Sangamon State U., 1978. Underwriter/programmer Springfield, Ill., 1973-76; ops. rsch. analyst Ill. Dept. Transp., Springfield, 1976-78, data analyst, 1978-80, team leader, fatal accident reporting sys., 1980-83, mgr. safety project evaluation, 1983-92, mgr. accident studies and investigation, 1992—; sys. engring. del. to China China Assn. for Sci. and Tech., 1986; mem. staff Driving While Intoxicated Adv. Coun. and Task Force, State of Ill., 1983-86, 89-92, Gov. Task Force on Occupant Protection, 1988-90; active Ill. Traffic Safety Info. Sys. Coun., 1993—. Vol. Animal Protective League, Springfield; leaderboard co-chair LPGA Rail Classic, Springfield, 1983-87. Mem. Ill. Assn. Highway Engrs., Springfield Lincoln Land Lions Club (charter pres. 1988-90, treas. 1993—), Lions Club (dist. gov. Ill. 1992-93, state membership coord. 1994—, Melvin Jones fellow 1993), Lions of Ill. Found. (amb. of goodwill 1993), Past Dist. Gov. Assn. (sec.-treas.), Phi Kappa Phi, Kappa Delta Pi. Office: Ill Dept Transp 3215 Executive Park Dr Springfield IL 62794-9245

SCHROEDER, LEILA OBIER, law educator; b. Plaquemine, La., July 11, 1925; d. William Prentiss and Daisy Lavinia (Mays) Obier; divorced; 1 child, James Michael Cutshaw; m. Martin Charles Schroeder Jr., Sept. 19, 1969. BA, Newcomb Coll., 1946; MSW, La. State U., 1953, JD, 1965. Bar: La. 1965. Exec. dir. Evangeline Area Guidance Ctr. La. Dept. Hosps., Lafayette, 1955-57; dir. social services dept. East La. State Hosp. La. Dept. Hosps., Jackson, 1957-60; cons. psychiat. social work La. Dept. Hosps., Baton Rouge, 1960-61; research assoc. La. State U., Baton Rouge, 1965-68, asst. prof., 1968-73, assoc. prof., 1973-80, prof., 1980—. Author: The Legal Environment of Social Work, 1982; contbr. articles to profl. jours. Fellow Am. Orthopsychiat. Assn.; mem. ABA, Nat. Assn. Social Workers, Acad. Cert. Social Workers, La. State Bar Assn., Baton Rouge Bar Assn. Home: 4336 Oxford Ave Baton Rouge LA 70808-4651 Office: La State U Dept Fin Baton Rouge LA 70803-6308

SCHROEDER, MARY MURPHY, federal judge; b. Boulder, Colo., Dec. 4, 1940; d. Richard and Theresa (Kahn) Murphy; m. Milton R. Schroeder, Oct. 15, 1965; children: Caroline Theresa, Katherine Emily. B.A., Swarthmore Coll., 1962; J.D., U. Chgo., 1965. Bar: Ill. 1966, D.C. 1966, Ariz. 1970. Trial atty. Dept. Justice, Washington, 1965-69; law clk. Hon. Jesse Udall, Ariz. Supreme Ct., 1970; mem. firm Lewis and Roca, Phoenix, 1971-75; judge Ariz. Ct. Appeals, Phoenix, 1975-79, U.S. Ct. Appeals (9th cir.), Phoenix, 1979—; vis. instr. Ariz. State U. Coll. Law, 1976, 77, 78. Contbr. articles to profl. jours. Mem. Am. Bar Assn., Ariz. Bar Assn., Fed. Bar Assn., Am. Law Inst., Am. Judicature Soc. Democrat. Club: Soroptimists. Office: US Ct Appeals 9th Cir 6421 Courthouse & Fed Bldg 230 N 1st Ave Phoenix AZ 85025-0230

SCHROEDER, PATRICIA SCOTT (MRS. JAMES WHITE SCHROEDER), congresswoman; b. Portland, Oreg., July 30, 1940; d. Lee Combs and Bernice (Lemoin) Scott; m. James White Schroeder, Aug. 18, 1962; children: Scott William, Jamie Christine. B.A. magna cum laude, U. Minn., 1961; J.D., Harvard U., 1964. Bar: Colo. 1964. Field atty. NLRB, Denver, 1964-66; practiced in Denver, 1966-72; hearing officer Colo. Dept. Personnel, 1971-72; mem. faculty U. Colo., 1969-72, Community Coll., Denver, 1969-70, Regis Coll., Denver, 1970-72; mem. 93d-103d Congresses from 1st Colo. dist., 1973—; co-chmn. Congl. Caucus for Women's Issues, 1976—; mem. Ho. of Reps. armed svcs. com., chair subcom. rsch. and tech., judiciary com., post office and civil svc. com. Congregationalist. Office: US Ho of Reps 2208 Rayburn House Office Bldg Washington DC 20515

SCHROEDER, RITA MOLTHEN, chiropractor; b. Savanna, Ill., Oct. 25, 1922; d. Frank J. and Ruth J. (McKenzie) Molthen; m. Richard H. Schroeder, Apr. 23, 1948 (div.); children—Richard, Andrew, Barbara, Thomas, Paul, Madeline. Student, Chem. Engring., Immaculate Heart Coll., 1940-41, UCLA, 1941, Palmer Sch. of Chiropractic, 1947-49; D. Chiropractic, Cleve. Coll. of Chiropractic, 1961. Engring.-tooling design data coordinator Douglas Aircraft Co., El Segundo, Santa Monica and Long Beach, Calif., 1941-47; pres. Schroeder Chiropractic, Inc., 1982—; dir. Pacific States Chiropractic Coll., 1978-80, pres. 1980-81. Recipient Palmer Coll. Ambassador award, 1973. Parker Chiropractic Research Found. Ambassador award, 1976, Coll. Ambassador award Life West Chiropractic Coll. Mem. Internat. Chiropractic Assn., Calif. Chiropractic Assn., Internat. Chiropractic Assn. Calif., Assn. Am. Chiropractic Coll. Presidents, Council Chiropractic Edn. (Pacific State Coll. rep.), Am. Pub. Health Assn., Royal Chiropractic Knights of the Round Table. Home: 8701 N Hwy 41 # 18 Fresno CA 93720-1010 Office: Schroeder Chiropractic Inc 2535 N Fresno St Fresno CA 93703-1831

SCHROER, MARY BERNADETTE, state representative; b. St. Marys, Ohio, Feb. 11, 1947; m. J. Michael Schroer; children: Jennifer, Amy, Rebecca. Student, Washtenaw C.C., Ea. Mich. U. Legis. asst. to State Sen. Lana Pollack Inst. Study of Mental Retardation and Related Disabilities, 1983-92; state rep. 52d dist. State of Mich., 1992—; co-vice chair pub. health com., pub. retirement com.; mem. human svcs. com., children com., ins. com., corrections com. Mem. Washtenaw County (Mich.) Dem. Party, Washtenaw County Area Auto Plant Coaltion, Ann Arbor, Pittsfield Twp. Econ. Deve. Corp. Bd.; past pres. Carpenter Sch. PTO, Ann Arbor; former bd. dirs. Ann Arbor (Mich.) Cmty. Ctr. Roman Catholic. Office: 922 Olds Plz Bldg Lansing MI 48913

SCHROM, ELIZABETH ANN, educator; b. Princeton, Minn., June 7, 1941; d. Raymond Alois and Grace Eleanor (Hayes) S. Student, U. Minn., 1960; BA, St. Scholastica Coll., Duluth, Minn., 1963; postgrad., Princeton U., 1965; MEd, Temple U., 1972; MLS, Drexel U., 1974; postgrad., NYU, 1981, Russian Temple U., 1983. Tchr. Strandquist (Minn.) High Sch., 1963-64, Hutchinson (Minn.) High Sch., 1964-65, Peace Corps, Ankara, Turkey, 1965-67, Phila. Sch. Dist., 1968-80; children's libr. Laurel (Del.) Pub. Libr., 1983. Mem. Jewish Com. on Middle East, Washington, 1988-90, 93, Nat. Coun. Returned Peace Corps. Vols., Washington, 1989-95, Nat. Taxpayers Union, Washington, 1988-92; mem. bd. policy Liberty Lobby, Washington, 1989-95; mem. Emergency Com. to Stop Immigration, Marietta, Ga., 1989-91. Populist. Roman Catholic. Home: PO Box 206 RR 2 Ortonville MN 56278-9784

SCHROTT, JANET ANN, information specialist, administrator, consultant; b. Cleve., Dec. 11, 1941; d. Louis Vincent and Amelia Jane (Lauko) Cupolo; BA, Flora Stone Mather Coll. of Case Western Res. U., 1963, MS in Social Adminstrn., 1974; MBA, Baldwin-Wallace Coll., Berea, Ohio, 1986; m. Norman Schrott, July 25, 1964. Rsch. asst. Aging Baseline Study, HEW Grant, Miami, Fla., 1964-65; caseworker Div. Social Svcs., Cuyahoga County Welfare Dept., Cleve., 1965-72, protective svcs. supr., 1974-78; dir. social svcs. Luth. Housing Corp., Cleve., 1973-74; dir. travelers aid svcs. and quality assurance Ctr. for Human Svcs., Cleve., 1978-86; tng. analyst Cleve. Electric Illuminating Co., Perry, Ohio, 1985-86, supr. support services, tng., 1986—. Bd. dirs. adv. council Adult Rehab. Svcs., Salvation Army, 1978-85. Cuyahoga County Welfare Dept. grantee, 1972-74. Mem. Assn. MBA Execs., Acad. Cert. Social Workers, Nat. Assn. Social Workers, Am. Evaluation Assn., Nat. Geographic Soc., Travelers Aid Assn. Am. (bd. dirs., Steering com. 1982-85), Theta Phi Omega. Home: 25925 Lake Rd Cleveland OH 44140-2563 Office: Perry Tng Ctr PO Box 97 Perry OH 44081-0097

SCHUBERT, HELEN C., public relations executive; b. Washington City, Wis.; d. Paul H. and Edna (Schmidt) S. BS, U. Wis., Madison. Pub. relations dir. United Cerebral Palsy, Chgo., 1961; adminstrv. dir. Nat. Design Ctr., Chgo., 1962-67; owner Schubert Pub. Relations, Chgo., 1967—; bd. dirs. Fashion Group, Chgo., 1988-92. Mem. women's bd. Am. Cancer Soc., Chgo., 1988-92, Art Resources in Teaching, Chgo., 1988-92. Recipient Communications award Am. So. Internat. Designers, Chgo., 1979, 83, 88; named to Chgo. Women's Hall of Fame, 1990. Fellow Nat. Home Fashion League; mem. Women's Ad Club of Chgo. (pres. 1981-83, Woman of Yr. award 1987), Women in Communications (pres. 1969-70), Am. Advt. Fedn. (lt. gov. 1983-85). Lutheran. Home: 1400 Lake Shore Dr Chicago IL 60610

SCHUBERT, JANET LEE, middle school educator; b. Cleve., Apr. 22, 1952; d. Melvin Gene and Lillian Ester (Adams) Jewett; m. Terry Lee Schubert, June 14, 1980; children: Jill Marie Schubert Clark, Lisa Ann. BA, Miami U., Oxford, Ohio, 1974; MA, Kent State U., 1977. Learning disabled/behaviorally disordered tchr. Berea (Ohio) City Schs., 1974-83, health specialist, 1983-90, classroom of the future tchr., 1990-93; ednl. cons. Jostens Learning, 1993-94; 6th grade team educator Ford Mid. Sch., Brook Park, Ohio, 1994—; summer sch. prin., cons. Cuyahoga County Spl. Edn., Brook Park, Ohio, 1974-79; in-svc. workshop leader. Vol. S.W. Gen. Hosp., Middleburg Heights, Ohio, 1984-89, jr. bd., 1985-87. Martha Holden Jennings Found. scholar, 1981-82, master tchr., 1982. Mem. Berea Fedn. Tchrs. (rep. 1985-91, mem. negotiating com. 1991-92), Cuyahoga County Agrl. Soc. (bd. dirs. 1985-95). Office: Ford Mid Sch 17001 Holland Rd Cleveland OH 44142

SCHUCHMANN, MARY BETH, dentist; b. Ft. Dodge, Iowa, Dec. 8, 1965; d. Harold Fredrick and Mary Anne (Feeney) S. BS in Psychology, U. Iowa, 1988, DDS, 1992. Dentist U. Iowa Coll. Dentistry Admissions Clinic, Iowa City, 1992; clin. instr., dentist U. Iowa Coll. Dentistry, Iowa City, 1992-93; pvt. practice Worthington, Ohio, 1993—; resident oral pathology Ohio State U., Columbus, 1995—. Mem. tobacco control subcom. Am. Cancer Soc., 1994. Mem. ADA, Acad. Gen. Dentistry, Am. Assn. Women Dentists, PEO, Ohio Dental Assn., Columbus Dental Soc., Worthington C. of C. Republican. Roman Catholic. Office: Drs Jerman & Schuchmann 11 W New England Ave Worthington OH 43085-2515

SCHUCK, JOYCE HABER, author; b. N.Y.C., Dec. 9, 1937; d. Frank F. and Florence (Smith) H.; m. Stephen Martin Schuck, June 15, 1958; children: William David, Thomas Allen, Ann Elizabeth. BA in Human Svcs. and Counseling, Loretto Hts. Coll., Denver, 1982. Counselor, tchr. Vision Quest, Colorado Springs, 1979-82; cons., program designer for govt. agys. Colorado Springs, 1982-85; author, 1987—; asst. to cons. Volusia County Dept. Corrections, Daytona Beach, Fla., 1982; cons. student svcs. program Pikes Peak C.C., Colorado Springs, 1982; cons., designer Juvenile Probation of El Paso County, Colorado Springs, 1982, 4th Jud. Dist./Dist. Atty.'s Office, Colorado Springs, 1984. Author: Political Wives, Veiled Lives, 1991. Cofounder Community Transitions, Colorado Springs, 1984; coord. El. Paso County Shape Up Program, 1982; v.p. Community Coun. of Pikes Peak Region, Colorado Springs, 1983, Women's Found. of Colo., Denver, 1987. Recipient Mayor's award for civic leadership City of Colorado Springs, 1983. Mem. Jr. League of Colorado Springs (sustaining), Salon de Femme (founding).

SCHUCK, MARJORIE MASSEY, publisher, editor, authors' consultant; b. Winchester, Va., Oct. 9, 1921; d. Carl Frederick and Margaret Harriet (Parmele) Massey; student U. Minn., 1941-43, New Sch., N.Y.C., 1948, N.Y. U., 1952, 54-55; m. Ernest George Metcalfe, Dec. 2, 1943 (div. Oct. 1949); m. 2d, Franz Schuck, Nov. 11, 1953 (dec. Jan. 1958). Mem. editorial bd. St. Petersburg Poetry Assn., 1967-68; co-editor, pub. poetry Venture Mag., St. Petersburg, Fla., 1968-69, editor, pub., 1969-79; co-editor, pub. Poetry Venture Quar. Essays, Vol. I, 1968-69, Vol. 2, 1970-71; pub., editor poetry anthologies, 1972—; founder, owner, pres. Valkyrie Press, Inc. (name changed to Valkyrie Pub. House 1980), 1972—; cons. designs and formats, trade publs. and ann. reports, lit. books and pamphlets, 1973—; founder Valkyrie Press Roundtable Workshop and Forum for Writers, 1975-79; established Valkyrie Press Reference Libr., 1976-80; pub., editor The Valkyrie Internat. Newsletter, 1986—; exec. dir. Inter-Cultural Forum Villanor Ctr., Tampa, Fla., 1987-94; dir. edn. The Villanor Mus. Fine and Decorative Arts, Tampa, 1994, St. Petersburg, 1994—; pres. Found. for Human Potentials, Inc., Tampa, 1988-94; representative distbr. Marg Art Publs. of India (Bombay), 1992—; mem. pres. coun. U. South Fla., 1993—; lectr. in field. Judge poetry and speech contests Gulf Beach Women's Club, 1970, Fine Arts Festival dist. 14. Am. Fedn. Women's Clubs, 1970, South and West, Inc., 1972, The Sunstone Rev., 1973, Internat. Toastmistress Clubs, 1974, 78, Beaux Arts Poetry Festival, 1983, 89, 92, 93, 94; judge poetry contest Fla. State conf. Nat. League Am. Pen Women, 1989; judge Fla. Gov.'s Screenwriters Competition, 1984—. Corr.-rec. sec. Women's Aux. Hosp. for Spl. Surgery, N.Y.C., 1947-59; active St. Petersburg Mus. Fine Arts (charter), St. Petersburg Sister City Com., St. Petersburg Arts Ctr. Assn.; mem. Orange Belt express com. 1988 Centennial Celebration for St. Petersburg; mem. Com. of 100 of Pinellas County, Inc., exec. bd., 1975-77, membership chmn., 1975-77; pub. rels. chmn. Soc. for prevention Cruelty to Animals, 1968-71, bd. dirs., 1968-71, 75-77; founder, mem. Pinellas County Arts Coun., 1976-79, chmn., 1977-78; mem. grant rev. panel for lit. Fine Arts Coun. of Fla., 1979; mem. pres.'s coun. U. South Fla., 1994—. Named One of 76 Fla. Patriots, Fla. Bicentennial Commn., 1976; a recipient 1st ann. People of Dedication award Salvation Army, Tampa, 1984; named to Poetica Hall of Fame, Tampa Bay Poetry Coun., 1994. Mem. Am. Assn. Museums, Acad. Am. Poets, Fla. Suncoast Writers' Confs. (founder, co-dir., lectr. 1973-83, adv. bd. 1984—), Com. Small Mag. Editors and Pubs., Coordinating Council Lit. Mags., Friends of Libr. of St. Petersburg, Suncoast Mgmt. Inst. (exec. bd.; chmn. Women in Mgmt. 1977-78), Pi Beta Phi. Republican. Episcopalian. Author: Speeches and Writings for Cause of Freedom, 1973. Contbr. poetry to profl. jours. Home and Office: 8245 26th Ave N Saint Petersburg FL 33710-2857

SCHUCK, TERRI MARIE, nurse, diabetes educator; b. Milw., May 27, 1960; d. Robert George and Virginia Catherine (Roberts) Huhnke; m. John E. Schuck, Aug. 17, 1991. BSN, U. Wis., Milw., 1982. RN, Wis. Pediatric nurse St. Luke's Med. Ctr., Milw., 1986-88, diabetes educator, 1988—. Mem. Am. Assn. Diabetes Educators (cert.). Roman Catholic.

SCHUELKE, CONSTANCE PATRICIA, mortgage company executive; b. Cedar Rapids, Iowa, Feb. 9, 1953; d. Enno August and Ruth Otilia (Firnhaber) S.; m. Kevin Dennis Curran, May 21, 1983 (div. Dec. 1986); 1 child, Emma Kate Schuelke-Curran. BA, U. Nebr., 1973. Asst. mgr. Jaeger Internat., Atlanta, 1973-75; pres., owner Domani of Florence (Italy), Inc., 1975-82; assoc. broker Downtown Properties, Inc., Atlanta, 1982-85; v.p. Dunwoody Mortgage, Inc., Atlanta, 1985-90; owner, exec. v.p. FSM, Inc. dba First So. Mortgage, Atlanta, 1990-91; v.p. Dunwoody Mortgage, Inc., Atlanta, 1991—. Neighborhood adv. Inman Park Civic Assn., Atlanta, 1973—, Castelberry Hill Neighborhood, Atlanta, 1988—; fund raiser Design Industry Found. for AIDS, Atlanta, 1989. Mem. Mortgage Bankers Ga., Ga. Assn. Mortgage Brokers (individual sr.), Midtown Bus. Assn., Atlanta Bd. Realtors, Ravinia Club, Pi Beta Phi, Phi Upsilon Omicron (Hon.), Nat. Honor Soc. Democrat. Home: 170 Robin Hood Rd Atlanta GA 30309 Office: Dunwoody Mortgage Ste 350 1100 Ashwood Pkwy Atlanta GA 30338

SCHUESSLER, ANNEMARIE, pianist, educator; b. Wheaton, Ill., Apr. 20, 1951; d. Joseph John and Maureen Eileen (Harrington) S. MusB, Manhattanville Coll., 1973; MusM, Northwestern U., 1980, MusD, 1987; artists diploma with honors, Hochschule für Musik, Wurzburg, Germany, 1982. Music dir. Am. Mil. Community of Kitzingen, Germany, 1976-78; tchr. Music Arts Sch., Highland Park, Ill., 1978-82, Jack Benny Fine Arts Ctr., Waukegan, Ill., 1982-88; lectr. DePaul U. Sch. Music, Chgo., 1984-88; asst. prof. La. State U. Sch. Music, Baton Rouge, 1988-89, Ithaca (N.Y.) Coll. Sch. Music, 1989-92; asst. prof., piano Ball State U. Sch. Music, Muncie, Ind., 1992—; adj. prof. Suzuki program Wheaton (Ill.) Coll., 1982-88, Triton Coll., River Grove, Ill., 1980-82; adjudicator nat. competitions; vis. asst. prof. Eastman Sch. Music, Rochester, N.Y., 1990-91; adj. instr. Northwestern U., Evanston, Ill., 1980-81; lectr. Kang Reung, South Korea, 1990; lectr., performer European Piano Tchrs. Assn., Eng., 1991; performer Maly Hall, St. Petersburg, Russia, 1993—. Contbr. articles to profl. jours. Eckstein scholar Northwestern U., 1978—. Mem. ISSTIP, EPTA, Nat. Conf. on Piano Pedagogy, Coll. Music Soc. (Sec. N.E. chpt. 1992-94), Ind. Music Tchrs. Assn. (bd. dirs.), Music Tchrs. Nat. Assn., Pi Kappa Lambda. Office: Ball State U Sch Music Muncie IN 47305

SCHUESSLER FIORENZA, ELISABETH, theology educator; b. Tschanad, Romania, Apr. 17, 1938; parents German citizens; d. Peter and Magdalena Schuessler; m. Francis Fiorenza, Dec. 17, 1967; 1 child, Chris. MDiv, U. Wuerzburg, Federal Republic of Germany, 1962; Dr of Theology, U. Muenster, Federal Republic of Germany, 1970; Lic. Theol, U. Wuerzburg, 1963. Asst. prof. theology U. Notre Dame, South Bend, Ind., 1970-75, assoc. prof., 1975-80, prof., 1980-84; instr. U. Muenster, 1966-67; Talbot prof. New Testament Episcopal Div. Sch., Cambridge, Mass., 1984-88; Krister Stendahl prof. div. in scripture and interpretation Harvard U., Cambridge, Mass., 1988—; Harry Emerson Fosdick vis. prof. Union Theol. Sem., N.Y.C., 1974-75; guest prof. U. Tuebingen, Federal Republic of Germany, 1987, Cath. Theol. faculty Luzern, Switzerland, 1990. Author: Der Vergessene Partner, 1964, Priester für Gott, 1972, The Apocalypse, 1976, Invitation to the Book of Revelation, 1981, In Memory of Her, 1983, Bread not Stone, 1984, Judgement or Justice, 1985, Revelation: Vision of a Just World, 1991, But She Said - Feminist Practices of Biblical Interpretation, 1992, Discipleship of Equals: A Critical Feminist Ekklesialogy of Liberation, 1993, Jesus: Miriam's Child and Sophia's Prophet, Critical Issues in Feminist Christology, 1994; editor: Searching the Scriptures, 2 vols, 1993, 94; founding co-editor Jour. Feminist Studies in Religion; also editor other works. Mem. Am. Acad. Religion, Soc. Bibl. Lit. (past pres.). Office: Harvard Div Sch 45 Francis Ave Cambridge MA 02138-1994

SCHUETZ, CATHERINE MARY, systems engineer; b. Breese, Ill., Oct. 6, 1965; d. Kenneth Norman and Irene Bernice (Schroer) S.; m. Steven Witaschek, Sept. 2, 1994. BS in Fin. with honors, St. Louis U., 1987, BA in Math./Computer Sci. with honors, 1987. Cert. mgmt. acct. Prodn. scheduler Anheuser-Busch, Inc., St. Louis, 1987; documentation and quality assurance specialist Citation Computer Systems, St. Louis, 1987-89; budget support Electronic Data Systems, Dallas, 1989; fin. coord. Electronic Data Systems, London, 1989-90; costing analyst Electronic Data Systems, Detroit, 1990; system engrng. tng. program Electronic Data Systems, Dallas, 1990; fin. coord. Electronic Data Systems, Russelsheim, Germany, 1991-92; bus. analyst, system engr. Electronic Data Systems, Bedminster, N.J., 1993—. Mem. Inst. Cert. Mgmt. Accts.

SCHUETZ, RHONDA LEE, assistant city clerk; b. Hiawatha, Kans., Apr. 2, 1965; d. Clifton and Ferne (Johnson) Walder; m. John M. Schuetz, July 7, 1984; children: Amy, Gabrielle. AD, Highland C.C., 1986. Asst. city clk. City of Hiawatha (Kans.), 1986—. Pres. Friends of Libr., Hiawatha, 1990. Mem. City Clks. & Mcpl. Fin. Officers Assn. Presbyterian. Office: City of Hiawatha 723 Oregon St Hiawatha KS 66434-2294

SCHUK, LINDA LEE, legal assistant; b. Scott Field, Ill., July 19, 1946; d. Frank A. Schuk and Jessie (Bumpass) Stearns; divorced; 1 child, Earl Wade. BBA, U. Tex., El Paso, 1968. Lic. life and health ins. agt., Tex. Acct., traffic mgr. Farah Mfg. Co., El Paso, 1970-71; adminstrv. asst. Horizon Corp., El Paso, 1971-76; adminstrv. asst. in charge office ops. Foster-Scwartz Devel. Corp., El Paso, 1976-78; legal sec. Howell and Fields, El Paso, 1978-80; supr. Southland Corp., San Antonio, Waco, El Paso, 1980-83; sales mgr. Southland Corp., San Antonio, 1983-84, dist. mgr., 1984-87; dist. supr. E-Z Mart Conveniance Stores, San Antonio, 1987-89; legal asst. Watkins & Brock, San Antonio, 1989—; instr. San Antonio Community Coll., 1989—. Mem. NAFE. Democrat. Baptist. Home: 5822 Burkley Springs San Antonio TX 78233 Office: Watkins & Brock 803 E Mistletoe Ave San Antonio TX 78212-9999

SCHUKER, JILL ANITA, federal official, consultant; b. N.Y.C., Feb. 5, 1946; d. Litman H. and Mildred Frances (Lehrer) S. BA, Skidmore Coll., 1966; MA, Tufts U., 1970. Legis. asst. to senate pres. Mass. Gen. Ct., Boston, 1969-70; legis. asst. Congressman Michael J. Harrington, Washington, 1970-72; exec. dir. New Eng. Congl. Caucus, Washington, 1973-77; spl. asst., dep. spokeswoman Dept. State, Washington, 1977-79; counselor press and pub. affairs U.S. Mission to UN, N.Y.C., 1979-81; press sec. Gov. Hugh L. Carey, N.Y.C. and Albany, N.Y., 1981-82; sr. counseller, sr. v.p. Hill & Knowlton Pub. Affairs Worldwide, Washington, 1984-93; asst. to sec., dir. pub. affairs Dept. Commerce, Washington, 1993—. Dep. press sec. Shriver for V.P., 1972; comm. dir. Calif. Dukakis for Pres., 1988; internat. election observer Nat. Dem. Inst. Internat. Affairs, Bulgaria, 1991; surrogate spkr. fgn. policy Clinton for Pres., 1992. Grantee European Cmty., 1976; fellow Ford Found., 1967-68. Mem. Am. Coun. Young Polit. Leaders (bd. dirs. 1990—, grantee to Soviet Union 1979), Coun. Fgn. Rels. Office: Dept Commerce Public Affairs 14th St & Constitution Ave NW Washington DC 20230

SCHULER, ALISON KAY, lawyer; b. West Point, N.Y., Oct. 1, 1948; d. Richard Hamilton and Irma (Sanken) S.; m. Lyman Gage Sandy, Mar. 30, 1974; 1 child, Theodore. AB cum laude, Radcliffe Coll., 1969; JD Harvard U., 1972. Bar: Va. 1973, D.C. 1974, N.Mex. 1975. Assoc. Hunton & Williams, Richmond, Va., 1972-75; asst. U.S. atty. U.S. Atty's. Office, Albuquerque, 1975-78; adj. prof. law U. N.Mex., 1983-85, 90; ptnr. Sutin, Thayer & Browne, Albuquerque, 1978-85, Montgomery & Andrews, P.A., Albuquerque, 1985-88; sole practice, Albuquerque, 1988—. Bd. dirs. Am. Diabetes Assn., Albuquerque, 1980-85, chmn. bd. dirs., 1984-85; bd. dirs. June Music Festival, 1980—, pres., 1983-85, 93-94; bd. dirs. Albuquerque Conservation Trust, 1986-90, N.Mex. Osteo. Found., 1993—; chairperson Albuquerque Com. Fgn. Rels., 1984-85; mem. N.Mex. Internat. Trade and Investment Coun., Inc., 1986—; mem. coun. and v.p. St. Lukes Luth. Ch., 1992, pres. 1993—. Mem. Fed. Bar Assn. (coord.), ABA, Va. Bar Assn., N.Mex. State Bar Assn. (chmn. corp., banking and bus. law 1982-83, bd. dirs. internat. and immigration law sect. 1987—, chmn. 1993-94), Harvard U. Alumni Assn. (mem. fund campaign, regional dir. 1984-86, v.p. 1986-89, chmn. clubs com. 1985-88, chmn. communications com. 1988-91), Radcliffe Coll. Alumnae Assn. Bd. Mgmt. (regional dir. 1984—, chmn. communications com. 1988-91, Harvard-Radcliffe Club (pres. 1980-84). Home: 632 Cougar Loop NE Albuquerque NM 87122-1808 Office: 5700 Harper Dr NE Ste 430 Albuquerque NM 87109-3573

SCHULER, DARETIA MARY USSELMAN, chemical engineer, management consultant; b. Breese, Ill., Nov. 8, 1953; d. Raymond Andrew and Florence Irene (Hilmes) U. B.S. in Chem. Engring., U. Ill., Champaign-Urbana, 1976; M.B.A., U. Chgo., 1982. Research chemist Amoco Chems. Corp., Naperville, Ill., 1974; research engr. Amoco Oil Co., Naperville, 1975; with domestic and internat. mktg., mgmt. dept. Standard Oil Co. (Ind.) Amoco Chems. Corp., Chgo., 1976-81; sr. mgmt. cons. Coopers & Lybrand, Inc., Houston, 1983—. Mem. fin. com. Hollywood Towers Condominium Assn., Chgo., 1979-80; staff vol. Ill. Primaries 1980 Presdl. Campaign, 1980. B.M. Compton Chem. Engring scholar, 1971; U. Ill. Assn. scholar, 1971; Ill. Benedictine Coll. Acad. Achievement scholar, 1971; Ill. State Scholarship Commn. grantee, 1971-75. Mem. Bus. and Profl. Women's Soc., Soc. Women Engrs., Am. Inst. Chem Engrs., Am. Chem. Soc., Internat. Assn. Energy Economists. Office: Coopers & Lybrand Inc 1100 Louisiana St Ste 4100 Houston TX 77002

SCHULMAN, AILEEN HADASSAH, social worker; b. Bklyn., Mar. 1, 1964; d. David Isaac Schulman. BSW, Pa. State U., 1985; MSW, Rutgers U., 1989. Lic. social worker, Pa. Med. social worker Parkview Divsn. Met. Hosp., Phila., 1985-86; oncology social worker, phys. rehab. Rolling Hill Hosp., Elkins Park, Pa., 1986-89; case mgr. Action AIDS, Phila., 1989-91, U.S. Healthcare, Blue Bell, Pa., 1991-92; dir. edn. and mktg. Option Care, State College, Pa., 1992-94; coord. social work and mental health case mgmt. Geisinger Med. Group, State College, 1994—; home health social worker Med. Social Worker Assocs., Phila., 1986, Nittany Home Health, State College, Pa., 1993-94. Support group facilitator Action AIDS, 1991-92; v.p., bd. dirs. AIDS Project, State College, 1993—, chair program svcs. com., 1994—. Mem. NASW, Acad. Cert. Social Workers. Democrat. Jewish. Home: 1719 Puddintown Rd State College PA 16801-7155

SCHULMAN, EVELINE DOLIN, psychologist, author, consultant; b. N.Y.C.; d. George and Fannie (Simon) Dolin; m. Sol Schulman, June 3, 1941; children: Mark H., Ken S. BS, CCNY, 1939, postgrad., 1940-42; postgrad., State U. Iowa, 1939-40, Am. U., 1947; MEd, U. Md., 1954, EdD, 1957, postgrad., 1979-81. Tchr. Children's Colony, N.Y.C., 1941-42; registrar-tchr. Rockwood Nursery Sch., N.Y.C., 1942-43; asst. dir. Settlement House, Juanita Kauman Nye Council House; dir./tchr. nursery sch., Washington, 1947-48; dir.-tchr. Greenway Co-op. Nursery Sch., Washington, 1947-48, Fairfax Co-op. Nursery Sch., Washington, 1948-50, Community Nursery Sch., Silver Spring, Md., 1952-54; grad. asst. U. Md., 1954-55; psychologist, cons. Prince Georges County Council of Kindergarten and Nursery Schs., 1955-57; psychologist, lectr. Am. U., Washington, 1957; instr. psychology Community Coll. Balt., 1958-62, chmn. dept., 1962-73, prof. psychology, 1964-73, dir. mental health tech. program, 1967-73; lectr. human devel. Inst. for Child Study, U. Md., 1967-68, 69-71; prof. mental health Morgan State Coll., Towson, 1971-77; dir. evaluation and tng. Md. Mental Retardation Adminstrn., Balt., 1974-76, asst. dir. adminstrn., 1976-77; dir., cons. human services Ctr. for Devel. Inter-Personal Skills, Silver Spring, 1977—; cons. Nat. Disabilities Assn., 1980. Author: Intervention in Human Services—A Guide to Skills and Knowledge, 1974, 4th edit., 1991, Focus on the Retarded Adult, 1980; contbr. articles in field to profl. jours. Mem. Clifton T. Perkins Adv. Bd., 1972-80, chmn., 1974-80; mem. Mental Health Assn. Montgomery County, 1972, Montgomery County Assn. for Retarded Citizens, 1977; chmn. Montgomery County Council of Disabled Persons Rev. Bds. of Md., 1986—, Wheaton Community Mental Health Adv. Com., 1978—; mem. Montgomery County Com. for Community Edn., about Mentally Ill, 1982-86. Fellow, U. Md., 1954-55. Mem. Am. Psychol. Assn., Ea. Psychol. Assn., Am. Assn. Mental Health Counselors Assn., Am. Counseling and Devel. Assn., Gerontol. Soc., Nat. Council on Aging, Md. Assn. Jr. Colls. (pres. 1967-69). Office: Ctr for Devel Inter-Personal Skills 1103 Caddington Ave Silver Spring MD 20901-1114

SCHULMAN, GRACE, poet, English language educator; b. N.Y.C.; d. Bernard and Marcella (Freiberger) Waldman, m. Jerome L. Schulman, Sept. 6, 1959. Student, Bard Coll., Johns Hopkins U.; BS, Am. U., 1955; MA, NYU, 1960, PhD, 1971. Prof. Baruch Coll., N.Y.C., 1971—; poetry editor The Nation, N.Y.C., 1971—; adviser Poetry Ctr., N.Y.C.; mem. Brandeis Commn., Translation Ctr. Author: (poetry) Burn Down the Icons, 1976, Hemispheres, 1984, For That Day Only, 1994, (critical study) Marianne Moore: The Poetry of Engagement; translator (postry) At the Stone of Losses, Carmi/Present Tense Award. Fellow Yaddo, 1973, 75, 77, 79, 81, 93, MacDowell Colony, 1973, 75, 77, Rockefeller Inst., 1986. Mem. PEN (past v.p.), Poetry Soc. Am., Nat. Book Critics Cir., Authors Guild. Home: 1 University Pl # 14F New York NY 10003

SCHULMAN, MELISSA A., legislative staff director; b. Detroit, Sept. 12, 1961; m. Thomas P. Mann, Aug. 12, 1990. BA in Social Sci., Mich. State U., 1983. Staff asst. to Rep. Geraldine A. Ferraro N.Y., 1984-85, legis. asst. to Rep. Thomas J. Manton, 1985-88; sr. legis. asst. to Rep. Steny H. Hoyer Md., 1988-90; assoc. dir., floor asst. Dem. Caucus, 1991-93, exec. dir., 1993—. Office: Dem Caucus 718 O'Neill House Office Bldg Washington DC 20515*

SCHULMAN, TAMMY BETH, communications executive; b. Queens, N.Y., Sept. 1, 1960; d. David Abraham and Diane Lois (Herman) Schulman; m. Kurt James Anderson, Sept. 14, 1986 (div. 1990); m. Kenneth Steven Peterson, 1990; stepchildren: Tanya, Kathleen, Amanda. Degree in comml. art, Hennepin County Vocat.-Tech., Eden Prairie, Minn., 1978; postgrad., Coll. St. Catherine, St. Paul, 1985-88, Augsburg Coll., 1991—. Corr. sec. Ross Investment Co., Edina, Minn., 1980; quality control rep. Hubbard Milling Co., Minnetonka, Minn., 1980-81; ins. insp. Underwriters Svc. Co., Hopkins, Minn., 1982-83; dir. publs., communications mgr. Lifetouch Nat. Sch. Studios, Mpls., 1984—. Author, editor: Versatile Beans, 1978, Exposure mag., 1986—. Tutor Glenwood-Lyndale Community Ctr., Mpls., 1982; women's advocate Sojourner Shelter, Minnetonka, 1984—; active Sta. KFAI-Radio, Mpls., Simon Weisenthal Ctr., Mpls., 1985-86. Mem. Women in Communications Inc., Upper Miss. Blues Soc. Democrat. Jewish. Office: Lifetouch Nat Sch Studios 7800 Picture Dr Minneapolis MN 55439-3149

SCHULTE, SISTER LORETTA, social services consultant, educator; b. Cleve., Sept. 22, 1927; d. Frank and Mary (Berendsen) S. BS in Edn., St. John Coll., Cleve., 1958, MS in Edn., 1968. Joined Congregation of St. Joseph, Roman Cath. Ch. Elem. sch. tchr. Cath. Sch. System, Akron, Lorain, Ohio, 1950-59; elem. sch. prin. Cath. Sch. System, Akron, Lorain, 1959-75; missionary Cath. Diocese of Cleve., El Salvador, 1975-78; founder, exec. dir. West Side Cath. Ctr. Shelter, Cleve., 1979-83, Transitional Housing Inc., Cleve., 1983-90; cons. Transitional Housing Inc., Cons. Svcs. Inc., 1987-90; initiator First Nat. Conf. on Transitional Housing, Cleve., 1990. Author: Inn-Between: A Manual on Transitional Housing, 1989, (with others) Vision Statement for a United States Housing Policy, 1989. Mem. Ohio Coalition for the Homeless, Columbus, 1984-87; participant Housing Activist Conf., Washington, 1989. Recipient Congl. Merit-Achievement award for Peace and Justice, U.S. Congress, Washington, 1988, Peace, Jusitce and Human Dignity award Commn. on Cath. Community Action, Cleve., 1988, Berkman-Lowry Community Achievement award Legal Aid Soc. Cleve., 1989, Peace, Justice, Merit award Cuyahoga County COmmrs., Cleve., 1988. Democrat. Home: 3430 Rocky River Dr Cleveland OH 44111-2937

SCHULTE, MARY ANN, finance executive; b. Phoenix, Feb. 6, 1953; d. Walter Barry and Norma Gladys (Caffey) S. BSBA, U. So. Calif., 1975, MBA, 1979. Mgr. acctg. Coldwell Banker, Los Angeles, 1975-78; controller Adams, Ray and Rosenberg, Inc. (now The William Morris Agy.), Century City, Calif., 1978-81; co-owner Marwal, Inc., Los Angeles, 1976-82; controller, chief fin. officer DNA Group, Inc., Pasadena, Calif., 1982-86; chief fin. officer Sukut Constrn., Inc., Santa Ana, Calif., 1986—; cons. Mikeselle DeKorff, Los Angeles, 1981-82, Hollywood (Calif.) High Sch., 1986-87; cons., bd. dirs. Inner Ear Prodns., Los Angeles, 1983-85; guest speaker Am. Soc. women Accts. Assoc. producer (documentary film) Echoes of The Ozarks, 1989; speaker in field. Staff leader drop-out prevention program Hollywood High Sch., 1986; bd. dirs., chair fin. com. STOP GAP; mem. joint budget task force City of Santa Ana, 1991-92; mem. adv. bd. Orange County Acad. Decathlon; chair vendor subcom. to master creditors com. Orange County Bankruptcy. Mem. U. So. Calif. Commerce Assocs., Alpha Chi Omega. Republican. Roman Catholic. Office: Sukut Constrn Inc 4010 W Chandler Ave Santa Ana CA 92704-5274

SCHULTHEIS, RITA VIRGINIA, artist; b. Parkersburg, W.Va., Apr. 2, 1954; m. Thomas D. Schultheis, Nov. 16, 1973; 1 child, Theresa L. Grad., Famous Artist Sch., 1973. Vet. asst., 1971-72; framing and store mgr. Marj Teague Art Gallery, Williamstown, W.Va., 1972-80. V.p. Lawrence Elem. PTL, 1992, 93, 94; bd. dirs. Humane Soc. Ohio Valley, 1989-93, chairperson Art for Animals show, 1980-93. Recipient cert. Marietta Area C. of C., 1991; recipient Nat. Nature Art award, 1980, 85, 86, 87. Mem. Marietta Area Arts and Crafts League (past sec., past v.p., past pres.), Ohio Arts and Crafts Guild. Office: RVS Art & Frames 222 Putnam St Marietta OH 45750-3014

SCHULTZ, BARBARA MARIE, insurance company executive; b. Chgo., Sept. 9, 1943; d. Edwin and Bernice (Barstis) Legner; m. Ronald J. Schultz Sr., May 1, 1965; 1 child, Ronald J. Grad. high sch., Chgo. Account rep. Met. Ins. Co., Aurora, Ill., 1981—; qualifier Met. Life Leaders Conf., 1990. Fellow Nat. Assn. Life Underwriters (edn. chmn. 1988-91, nat. quality award Robert L. Rose award 1990), Life Underwriters Tng. Coun. (chmn. 1986-88, citation 1987), South Cook County Assn. Life Underwriters (edn. chmn. 1988-91). Roman Catholic. Office: Met Ins Co 15255 94th Ave Orland Park IL 60462-3800

SCHULTZ, CARMEN HELEN, copywriter, translator; b. Caracas, Venezuela, Jan. 22, 1962; came to U.S., 1975; d. Arthur Henry and Alicia M. (Mercedes) S. BA in Fgn. Langs. cum laude, So. Meth. U., 1984; postgrad., U. Tex., Dallas, 1987—. Tech. translator Mobil Oil Exploration & Producing Svcs., Dallas, 1984-85; freelance translator/interpreter Dallas, 1985-87; abstractor/rsch. asst. Rand Corp., Santa Monica, Calif., 1987; Hispanic comm. coord. Mary Kay Cosmetics, Inc., Dallas, 1987-93; bilingual copywriter Rapp Collins Worldwide, Irving, Tex., 1993-94; translator/copy editor Ornelas & Assocs., Dallas, 1994—. Editor/translator: Belleza Total, 1992 (Internat. Mercury award); founder, editor (newsletter) Entérate, 1988 (Hispanic 100 1990, 91); contbg. writer Applause, 1992 (Award of Merit IPBC). So. Meth. U. scholar, 1980-84. Mem. Am. Translators Assn., Am.

Lit. Translators Assn., Metroplex Interpreters and Translators Assn., Dallas Hispanic C. of C., Pi Delta Phi, Sigma Delta Pi. Roman Catholic. Home: 7008 Town Bluff Dr Dallas TX 75248-5524 Office: Ornelas and Assocs 2515 McKinney Ave Ste 1400 Dallas TX 75201

SCHULTZ, CAROLE LAMB, community volunteer; b. Corning, N.Y., May 14, 1946; d. Arthur Martin and Jane Ursula (Oehler) Lamb; m. John Charles Schultz, July 13, 1968; children: David Michael, Geoffrey Brian. BS in Math. magna cum laude, St. Lawrence U., Canton, N.Y., 1968. Systems engr. IBM, Williamsport, Pa., 1968-71; invited attendee Gov.'s Cong. of Bus./Edn. Partnerships, Harrisburg, Pa., 1991. Helped establish Children's Hands-on Mus., Children's Discovery Workshop, 1979-88. Treas. Jr. League of Williamsport, Inc., 1980-82, community v.p., 1985-86, pres.-elect, 1986-87, pres., 1987-88; mem. area II coun. Assn. Jr. Leagues Internat., Inc., 1988-90, chair nominating com., 1989-90; mem. NE regional coun. United Way Am., 1993—; pers. chair Faxon-Kenmar United Meth. Ch., Williamsport, 1991-92; trustee St. Lawrence U., 1988—; chair honors com. St. Lawrence U., 1994—; mem. ednl. tech. adv. com. Williamsport Area Sch. Dist., 1994—; sec., div. chair, planning mem. Lycoming United Way, Williamsport, 1991—, vice chair Campaign 1992, chair Campaign 1993; candidate Williamsport Area Sch. Bd., 1989; panelist Leadership Lycoming, 1987, mentor, 1990—. Mem. AAUW (program v.p. 1973-75, pres. 1975-77, treas. Pa. conv. 1973, 85, Woman of Yr. 1981), Williamsport-Lycoming C. of C. (chair edn. subcom. on partnerships 1991-92), Lycoming Bus.-Edn. Coalition (exec. com., steering com., co-chair task force on skills/curriculum), Phi Beta Kappa. Methodist. Home: 300 Upland Rd Williamsport PA 17701-1852

SCHULTZ, EILEEN HEDY, graphic designer; b. Yonkers, N.Y.; d. Harry Arthur and Hedy Evelyn (Morchel) S. B.F.A., Sch. Visual Arts, 1955. Staff artist C.A. Parshall Studios, N.Y.C., 1955-57; editorial art dir. Paradise of the Pacific, Honolulu, 1957-58; graphic designer Adler Advt. Agy., N.Y.C., 1958-59; art dir. Good Housekeeping Mag., N.Y.C., 1959-82; creative dir. advt. and sales promotion Good Housekeeping Mag., 1982-86; creative dir. Hearst Promo, 1986-87; pres. Design Internat., N.Y.C., 1987—; creative dir. The Depository Trust Co., 1987—. Art dir., editor, designer, 50th Art Directors Club Annual, 1973; columnist: Art Direction, 1969—. Dir. Sch. Visual Arts, N.Y.C., 1978—; trustee Sch. Art League, 1978—; advisor Fashion Inst. Tech., 1979—; mem. adv. commn. N.Y.C. Community Colls., 1979—. Named Yonkers Ambassador of Good Will to Netherlands, 1955; recipient Outstanding Achievement Sch. Visual Arts Alumni Soc., 1976, Sch. Art League Youth award, 1976. Mem. Art Dirs. Club (pres. 1975-77), Soc. Illustrators (pres. 1991-93), Joint Ethics Com. (chmn. 1978-80), Am. Inst. Graphic Arts, Soc. Publ. Designers, Type Dirs. Club.

SCHULTZ, ELLEN B.T., legal office administrator; b. Phila., Oct. 30, 1954; d. Henry and Phyllis (Baker) Twitchell; m. Thomas A. Schultz, Oct. 17, 1981. AA, Endicott Jr. Coll., 1974; BA, U. Mass., 1977. Mgr. Rusty Scupper Restaurant, San Francisco, 1977-83; owner White Mountain Creamery, San Ramon, Calif., 1983-91; adminstrv. bookkeeper Haims, Johnson, MacGowan & McInerney, Oakland, Calif., 1983-93, office adminstr., 1993—. Mem. DAR, Assn. Legal Adminstrs., Phi Theta Kappa. Office: Haims Johnson MacGowan 490 Grand Ave Oakland CA 94610-5010

SCHULTZ, KAREN ROSE, clinical social worker, author, publisher, speaker; b. Huntington, N.Y., June 16, 1958; d. Eugene Alfred and Laura Rose (Palazzolo) Squeri; m. Richard S. Schultz, Apr. 8, 1989. BA with honors, SUNY, Binghamton, 1980; MA, U. Chgo., 1982. Lic. clin. social worker, Ill. Unit dir., adminstr. Camp Algonquin, Ill., 1981; clin. social worker United Charities Chgo., 1982-86; social worker Hartgrove Hosp., Chgo., 1986—; pvt. practice, Oak Brook, Ill., 1987—; trainer, speaker various groups, schs. and orgns., DuPage County, Ill., 1988—; group leader Optifast Program, Oak Park and Aurora, Ill., 1989-90; instr. social work Morraine Valley C.C., Palos Hills, Ill., 1989-90; isntr. eating disorders Coll. of DuPage, Glen Ellyn, Ill., 1990-92, mem. eating disorder com., 1989—. Editor, contbg. author The River Within newsletter, 1989—. Com. mem. DuPage Consortium, 1987-89. Mem. NASW (registerd, diplomate), acad. Cert. Social Workers, Nat. Speakers Assn., Profl. Speakers Ill., Toastmasters Interant., Women Entrepreneurs DuPage. Office: 900 Jorie Blvd Ste 234 Oak Brook IL 60521

SCHULTZ, MADELYN CAHN, health educator; b. Pitts., June 2, 1929; d. Abraham Cahn and Leah (Wenkert) Cahn-Katz; m. Harold Schultz, Aug. 12, 1956 (dec. Oct. 1971); 1 child, Robert Alan. BS, U. Pitts., 1950, MEd, 1956; PhD, U. Md., 1994. Cert. elem. tchr., spl. edn. tchr., Pa. Tchr. Pitts. Bd. Edn., 1950-60; spl. edn. tchr. Friendship House, Scranton, Pa., 1965-67, Lackawanna County, Scranton, 1970-71; ednl. coord. Pa. Dept. Welfare, Scranton and Harrisburg, Pa., 1971-72; devel. disabilities program specialist U.S. Dept. HHS/Adminstrv. Devel. Disabilities, Phila., 1972-78, Atlanta, 1978-81, Washington, 1981-85; desk officer U.S. Dept. HHS/Adminstrn. Children, Youth & Families, Washington, 1985-87, head start program specialist, 1987—; cons. on infant and toddler programs Head Start Bur., Washington, 1982-92. Author regulation proposals in field. Mem. AAUW, Nat. Assn. Edn. of Young Child, Soc. for Rsch. in Child Devel., Am. Cancer Soc. Office: US Dept HHS Head Start Bur 330 C St SW Washington DC 20201

SCHULTZ, PHYLLIS G., lawyer, federal government; b. Bklyn., Dec. 17, 1931; d. Louis and Ida (Finkelstein) Glass; m. Morton Schultz, Dec. 22, 1957; children: Leslie P., Eric G. BA, Bklyn. Coll., 1953, MA, 1956; JD, Md. Sch. of Law, 1976. Bar: Md. 1977, D.C. 1980. Elem. sch. tchr. N.Y.C. Pub. Schs., 1953-66; home tchr. Montgomery County (Md.) Schs., 1968-72; lawyer Judge Advocate Gen. of Navy, Washington, 1978-80, Judge Advocate Gen. of Army, Fort Meade, Md., 1980—; instr. Prince Georges County C.C., 1972-73. Founding pres. Women's Polit. Caucus of Prince Georges County, 1972. Mem. NOW. Democrat. Home: 12224 Valerie Ln Laurel MD 20708-2838

SCHULTZ, PHYLLIS MAY, financial property manager; b. Knox County, Ill., Dec. 17, 1933; d. Clarence Cleo and Mildred Ruth (Hultberg) Cooper; m. Wayne Willard Mohr, Apr. 23, 1955 (div. Sept. 1965); Jeffery Lee Mohr, Kelly Marie Mohr (dec.); m. Robert William Schultz, Sept. 14, 1968. Student, L.A. Valley Coll., 1979-82. Fire and casualty ins. lic., Calif. Keypunch operator Gale Products Outboard Marine Corp., Galesburg, Ill., 1952-55; office mgr. movie and video distbn. Rainbow Distbrs., Inc., 1965-89; fin. property mgr. and acctg. John Lamb, L.A., 1989—; co-owner Real Estate Investments, Ill., Calif., 1980-89. Mem. Lutheran Social Svcs., L.A., 1989. Republican. Home: 6309 Morella Ave North Hollywood CA 91606-3413

SCHULTZ, RUTH ANNE, home economics educator, parenting educator, consultant; b. Oneida, N.Y., Jan. 27, 1953; d. Herman Lyon and Anna Marie (Jarvis) S. BS, Cornell U., 1975; MS, Syracuse U., 1982; postgrad., Plattsburgh State U., 1986, 89, L.I. U., 1990—. Cert. tchr., N.Y.; cert. home economist. Tchr. home econs. Phelps-Clifton Springs (N.Y.) Cen. Schs., 1975-77, adult educator, 1976-77, 93; home econs. tchr. Fabius (N.Y.)-Pompey Cen. Schs., 1977-82; home econs. tchr. Chittenango (N.Y.) Cen. Schs., 1982—, adviser Future Homemakers Am. club, 1986—; parenting educator Cornell Coop. Extension, Madison County, Morrisville, N.Y., 1985—; cons. N.Y. Dept. Edn., 1988—. Primary author curriculum materials. Community rep. Madison County Head Start Policy Coun., Morrisville, 1985-88; chmn. program com. Cornell Coop. Extension, Madison County, 1990-92, Long Range Planning Com.; bd. dirs. Community Action Program of Madison County. Recipient N.Y. State Edn. Dept. Region 7 Disting. Occupational Educator ward, 1990. Mem. ASCD, N.Y. State Future Homemakers of Am. (bd. trustees, vice chair), Home Econs. Edn. Assn. (v.p. 1988-90, pres. elect 1990-91, pres. 1991-93, past pres. 1993-94), N.Y. State Home Econs. Tchrs. Assn. (pres. 1986-88, state conv. chmn. 1989-90, legislation co-chmn. 1989-90), N.Y. State Home Econs. Assn. (elem., secondary, adult chmn. 1989-93, New Achiever award, 1988, Tchr. of Yr. 1989), Am. Home Econs. Assn. (nat. leadership com. 1989-91), Cen. N.Y. Home Econs. Tchrs. Assn. (Tchr. of Yr. 1985), N.Y. State Occupational Edn. Assn. (affiliate v.p. 1986-88, state conv. chmn. 1988-89, 93, Disting. Svc. award 1990), Nat. Assn. Vocat. Home Econs. Tchrs. (spl. award of merit 1991), Am. Vocat. Assn. (region I Vocat. Tchr. of the Year 1994). Democrat. Roman Catholic. Home: RR 3 Cazenovia NY 13035-9803 Office: Chittenango Mid Sch RR 2 1732 Fyler Rd Chittenango NY 13037-9802

SCHULZ, CHRISTINE JUNE, librarian; b. Norwich, Conn., Oct. 1, 1960; d. Wallace Junior and Lillian Regina (Wojcik) Baldwin; m. Timothy Harold Schulz, Sept. 14, 1985; children: Carolyn Rebecca, Victoria Diana, Connor Timothy. BS, So. Conn. State U., 1982. Univ. libr. asst. II U. Conn. Health Ctr.-Lyman Maynard Stowe Libr., Farmington, 1983-86; asst. libr. cen. rsch. library Pfizer, Inc., Groton, Conn., 1986—; head libr. Coit Libr. Corp., Jewett City, Conn., 1990—. trustee Coit Libr. Corp., Jewett City, 1989—. Mem. Conn. Libr. Assn. Republican. Roman Catholic. Home: 24 Roosevelt Ave Preston CT 06365-8025 Office: Pfizer Inc Cen Rsch Libr Eastern Point Rd Groton CT 06340-4947

SCHULZ, KELLY LYNN, television anchor, reporter; b. Livonia, Mich., May 21, 1962; d. William Eugene and Betty Jane (Murphy) S. BA in Comm. and Vocal Music, U. Mich., 1984. Reporter Stas. WGTU-TV and WGTQ-TV, Traverse City, Mich., 1983, 84; anchor, news dir. Sta. WBKB-TV, Alpena, Mich., 1984-86; anchor Sta. WAOW-TV, Wausau, Wis., 1986-94, Sta. KCRG-TV, Cedar Rapids, Iowa, 1994—. Speaker to area schs. and svc. groups, Wausau, 1986—; telethon host St. Joseph's Hosp., Marshfield, Wis., 1990—; comm. dir. Am. Heart Assn., Wausau, 1990; mem. Wausau Mayor's Com. on Disabilities, 1990-91. Recipient media award for heart disease series Am. Heart Assn., 1990. Mem. Radio and TV News Dirs. Assn. Office: Sta KCRG-TV 2d Ave at 5th St SE Cedar Rapids IA 52401

SCHULZ, MARIANNE, accountant; b. East Orange, N.J.; d. Clifford W. Schulz; m. James A. Willits, Dec. 29, 1991; 1 child, Lukas James. BA in Bus., U. Wash., 1979. Cert. mgmt. acct. Contr. Farwest Spl. Products, Bellevue, Wash., 1974-88; acct. Lakeside Industries, Bellevue, Wash., 1988—. Mem. Inst. Mgmt. Accts. (bd. dirs. 1990-92, v.p. 1992-93).

SCHULZ, MARY ELIZABETH, lawyer; b. New Ulm, Minn., Oct. 6, 1950; d. Paul F. and Elizabeth B. (Wichtel) S. BA cum laude, Mankato State U., 1972; JD, So. Meth. U., 1976. Bar: Tex., 1976, Ky., 1992, Ohio, 1993. Atty. Kagay, Turner, Eyres & Robertson, Dallas, 1976-78; asst. regional counsel U.S. EPA, Dallas, 1978-86; atty. Gardere & Wynne, Dallas, 1986-89, Valvoline, Inc., Lexington, Ky., 1989-90; counsel Olin Corp., E. Alton, Ill., 1990-92; sr. environ. counsel B.F. Goodrich Co., Akron, Ohio, 1992—; mem. adv. bd. Bus. Forum for Environ. Health & Safety, Washington, 1994. Mem. ABA, Fed. Bar Assn. Office: B F Goodrich Co 3925 Embassy Pkwy Akron OH 44333

SCHULZE, FLORENCE ELSIE, retired educator; b. Indiana Harbor, Ind., Nov. 10, 1925; d. Frank Joseph and Anna Frances (Varshal) Lozich; divorced; 1 child, Ricki Leigh Carrington. BS, Ind. U., 1960, MS, 1961. Cert. tchr., Ind. Standard checker U.S. Steel, Gary, Ind., 1944-45, 46-47; telephone operator Keevan Sadock Interior Designer, Chgo., 1947-49; standard checker Nat. Tube Co., Gary, Ind., 1952-54; office sec. E.C. Sumereau, Huntington, N.Y., 1954-56; sec. Gary Community Schs., 1956-59, tchr., 1961-91; mem. numerous coms. including curriculum, attendance, safety, discipline Gary Community Schs., 1961-91. Vol. ACLU, Dallas, ASPCA, Dallas, Dem. Party, Dallas. Sgt. U.S. Army, 1949-52; charter mem. Nat. Mus. of Women in the Arts. Recipient Plaque for Svc., William A. Wirt High Sch. Tchrs., 1968-70. Mem. AARP, Am. Fedn. Tchrs. (mem. exec. bd., negotiating com., Viola Briley award 1985, Florence Schulze scholar 1991), Am. Legion, Ind. U. Alumni Assn. (life), Ind. Ret. Tchrs. Assn. Episcopalian.

SCHUMACHER, CYNTHIA JO, secondary education educator, retired; b. Sebring, Fla., Sept. 24, 1928; d. Floyd Melvin and Espage Love (Rogers) S. BA, Fla. State U., 1950, MA, 1951; MS, Nova U., 1978; postgrad., Fla. State U., 1968-69. Cert. elem. and secondary sch. tchr., ednl. adminstr. and supr., Ga., Fla. English tchr. Grady County Sch. System, Cairo, Ga., 1951-53; elem. tchr. Brevard County Sch. System, Melbourne, Fla., 1953-55; elem. tchr., curriculum generalist, secondary tchr. Lake County Schs., Tavares, Fla. area, 1955-85; retired, 1985; mem. Edn. Standards Commn., Fla., 1980-85, Quality Instrn. Incentives Coun., Fla., 1983-84. Author: (Poetry) Seeds from Wild Grasses, 1988, Creekstone Crossings, 1993. Pres. League of Women Voters of Lake County, 1989-91; mem. Lake Conservation Coun., The Nature Conservancy, Habitat for Humanity of Lake County. named Fla. Tchr. of Yr., Fla. Fedn. Women's Clubs, 1966, Lake County Tchr. of Yr., Lake County Sch. Systems, 1985, East Cen. Fla. Tchr. of Yr., finalist State of Fla., 1986; recipient Good Egg award Leesburg Area C. of C., 1991. Mem. Lake County Edn. Assn. (pres. 1971-72, cons. 1985—). Democrat. Roman Catholic. Office: Lake County Edn Assn PO Box 490816 Leesburg FL 34749-0816

SCHUMACHER, JESSICA ROBINS, lawyer; b. Oakland, Calif., May 22, 1955; d. John Calvin and Elizabeth (Snow) Robins; m. Robert James Schumacher, Aug. 20, 1977; children: James Edward, Charlotte Anne. BA cum laude, Vanderbilt U., 1977; JD cum laude, U. Louisville, 1986. Bar: Ky. 1986, U.S. Dist. Ct. (we. dist.) Ky. Assoc. Woodward Hobson & Fulton, Louisville, 1986-89; asst. counsel, asst. v.p. Liberty Nat. Bank and Trust Co. of Louisville, Louisville, 1989—. Editor in chief: Jour. of Family Law, Louisville, 1985-86. Recipient Edwin O. Davis award U. Louisville Sch. Law, Louisville, 1986. Mem. Ky. Bar Assn. (sec. 1992—). Office: Liberty Nat Bank Trust Co PO Box 3250 416 W Jefferson St Louisville KY 40202-3244*

SCHUMACHER, THERESA ROSE, singer, musician; b. Muskegon, Mich.; d. Boles and Marguerite (Lassard) Pietkiewicz; m. Glenn O. Schumacher, 1968 (div. 1988); children: Pamela Harrington Boller, Daniel Mark Harrington. BS in Sociology, Fairmont State Coll., 1975. Active W.Va. U. Symphony Choir, 1988—, 93 Fairmont State Coll. Choir; musician with spl. knowledge of music from 1735-1850, Nat. Park Svcs., 1989—. Mem. AAUW, W.Va. Poetry Soc., Morgantown, W.Va. Poetry Soc. Home: PO Box 162 Mannington WV 26582

SCHUMAN, PATRICIA GLASS, publishing company executive, educator; b. N.Y.C., Mar. 15, 1943; d. Milton and Shirley Rhoda (Goodman) Glass; m. Alan Bruce Schuman, Aug. 30, 1964 (div. 1973). AB, U. Cin., 1963; MS, Columbia U., 1966. Libr. trainee Bklyn. Pub. Libr., 1963-65; tchr. libr. Brandeis High Sch., N.Y.C., 1966; asst. prof. libr. N.Y. Tech. Coll., Bklyn., 1966-71; assoc. editor Sch. Libr. Jour., N.Y.C., 1970-73; sr. editor R.R. Bowker Co., N.Y.C., 1973-76; pres. Neal-Schuman Pubs., N.Y.C., 1976—; vis. prof. St. John's U., Queens, N.Y., 1977-79, Columbia U., N.Y.C., 1981-90, Pratt Inst., 1993—; cons. N.Y. State Coun. on Arts, 1987, Office Tech. Assessment, U.S. Congress, 1982, 84, Coord. Coun. Lit. Mags., N.Y.C., 1987, NEH, 1980, Temple U., 1978-80; bd. visitors Sch. Libr. and Computer Studies Pratt Inst., 1987—; juror Best of Libr. Lit., 1988; mem. adv. bd. Sch. Libr. and Info. Studies, Queens Coll., 1989-91. Author: Materials for Occupational Education, 1973, 2d edit., 1983 (Best Edn. Book award 1973), Library Users and Personnel Needs, 1980, Your Right to Know: The Call for Action, 1993; editor: Social Responsibilities and Libraries, 1976; mem. editorial bd. Urban Acad. Libr., 1987-89, Multicultural Review, 1991—; contbr. articles to profl. jours. Bd. dirs. Women's Studies Abstracts, Albany, N.Y., 1970-74; mem. Com. To Elect Major Owens to U.S. Congress, 1983, N.Y.C. Mayor's Com. for N.Y. Pub. Ctr., 1984-85. Recipient Fannie Simon award Spl. Librs. Assn., 1984, Disting. Alumni award Columbia U., 1992; U.S. Office Edn. fellow, 1969. Mem. ALA (councillor 1971-79, 84-88, exec. bd. 1984-88, 90—, treas. 1984-88, chmn. legis. com. 1989-90, 94—, v.p., pres.-elect 1990-91, pres. 1991-92, Disting. Coun. Svc. award 1979, 88, Equality award 1993), Am. Soc. Info. Sci., N.Y. Libr. Assn., Assn. for Libr. and Info. Sci. Edn., Spl. Librs. Assn. Office: Neal-Schuman Pubs Inc 100 Varick St New York NY 10013-1506

SCHUMANN, ALICE MELCHER, sheep farmer, medical technologist, educator; b. Cleve., Sept. 1, 1931; d. John Henry and Marian Louise (Clark) M.; m. Stuart McKee Struever, Aug. 21, 1956 (div. June 1983); children: Nathan Chester, Hanna Russell; m. John Otto Schumann, July 3, 1985. BS, Colby Coll., New London, N.H., 1953. Cert. tchr.; cert. med. technologist. Rschr. Lakeside Hosp., Cleve., 1953-54, Bambridge (Ohio) Schs., 1954-55, Shalersville (Ohio) Schs., 1955-56, Richtnior Sch., Overland, Mo., 1956-57; sci. tchr. Tonica (Ill.) High Sch., 1956-58, Morton Grove (Ill.) High Sch., 1958-60, Univ. Chgo. Lab Sch., 1960-65; co-founder Ctr. for Am. Archeology, dir. flotation rsch. U. Chgo. Campus, Kampsville, Ill., 1957-71, head of supplies distbn., dir. food svcs. dept.; head mailing dept. Found. for Ill. Archeology, Evanston and Kampsville, Ill., 1971-83; sheep farmer, wool processor Gravel Hill Farm, Kampsville, 1983—. Vol. Mt. Sinai Hosp., Cleve., 1948-49; tchr. Title I Dist. 40, Kampsville, 1970-71. Recipient Beverly Booth award Colby Coll., 1953, 1st prize for hand spun yarn DeKalb County Fair, Sandwich, Ill., 1987, 88. Mem. Precious Fibers Found., Natural Colored Wool Growers Assn., Farm Bur. of Calhoun County. Home and Office: Gravel Hill Farm RR 1 Box 121A Kampsville IL 62053-9720

SCHUMANN, MARY JEAN, nurse executive; b. Eau Claire, Wis., Dec. 4, 1950; d. Clarence William and Irene I. (Berger) Schlosser; m. Glen Leslie Schumann, Aug. 19, 1982 (div. 1991); children: Angela, Nicole, Britta, Kari, Tresa. BSN, U. Wis., 1973, MSN, 1975; MBA, U. Minn., 1993. RN, Mich., Wis., Md. Mem. clin. nursing faculty Ea. Mich. U., U. Wis., 1975-81; clin. adminstr. univ. health svcs. Ea. Mich. U., Ypsilanti, 1983-86; project coord., nurse mgr., ambulance care adminstr. Mich. Med. Ctr., Ann Arbor, 1986-88; dir. nursing Tomah (Wis.) Meml. Hosp., 1988-93; exec. dir. Nat. Cert. Bd. of PNP/N, Rockville, Md., 1993—; presenter in field. Contbr. articles to profl. jours. Bd. dirs. Tomah Area Pool Assn., La Crosse YMCa Swim Team; mem. nursing adv. bd. Western Wis. Tech. Coll. Community Adv. Bd. for Options in Reproductive Care. Fellow Commonwealth Fund, 1991; recipient Cert. of Merit ARC, 1986; scholar Soroptomist Club, 1972. Mem. Wis. Orgn. Nurse Execs. (legis. com. 1990-92), Am. Orgn. Nurse Execs., Nat. Assn. Nurse Assocs. and Nurse Practitioners, Toastmasters, AAUW, Sigma Theta Tau (chpt. treas. 1986-88). Home: 19300 Dubarry Dr Brookeville MD 20833-2618 Office: Nat Cert Bd PNP/N 416 Hungerford Dr Ste 222 Rockville MD 20850-4127

SCHUMANN, MARY KATHERINE, early childhood educator; b. Milw., May 7, 1947; d. Joseph P. and Regina R. (Mesenbourg) Schauble; m. Gary R. Schumann, Oct. 23, 1971; 1 child, Jessica Rae. BA in Elem. Edn., Mount Mary Coll., 1969; MS in Curriculum and Instrn., U. Wis., Milw., 1972. Cert. tchr., Wis. Classroom tchr. Milw. Pub. Schs., 1969—; univ. instr. U. Wis., Milw., 1992—; presenter workshops on math., literacy, open edn. Milw. Pub. Schs., 1985—; presenter inst. on literacy portfolio Internat. Reading Conv., Las Vegas, 1991; presenter integrated curriculum Wis. State Reading Conv., Oconomowoc, 1990; presenter manipulative math Migrant Edn. State Conv., Fond du Lac, Wis., 1989. Panel mem. on peace in community local radio program, Milw., 1994. Mem. Emergent Literacy Rsch. Group, Milw. Tchrs. Edn. Assn., Milw. Area Reading Coun., Wis. State Reading Assn., Internat. Reading Assn., Whole Lang. Umbrella. Mem. Humanist Ch. Office: Milw Pub Schs 2623 N 38th St Milwaukee WI 53010

SCHUMM, LISA ELEANOR, accountant; b. Bklyn., June 22, 1969; d. James Francis and Camilla Margaret (Arnesen) S. BS in Acctg. cum laude, St. Thomas Aquinas Coll., 1987-91; postgrad., Iona Coll., 1992—. Cert. payroll profl. Accts. receivable clk. Coachman Carting Inc., Port Jervis, N.Y., 1988; credit and collection support Nynex Mobile Communications, Orangeburg, N.Y., 1989-91, sr. acct., 1991—. Elks scholar, 1987, Regents scholar, 1987. Mem. Inst. Mgmt. Accts., Telephone Pioneers, Delta Mu Delta. Home: 104 Rose Rd West Nyack NY 10994 Office: Nynex Mobile Communications 2000 Corp Dr Orangeburg NY 10962

SCHUR, SUSAN DORFMAN, state legislator; b. Newark, Feb. 27, 1940; d. Norman and Jeanette (Handelman) Dorfman; children: Diana Elisabeth, Erica Marlene. BA, Goucher Coll., 1961. Adminstr. fed. housing, fgn. aid, anti-poverty programs, 1961-67; mem. Mass. Housing Appeals Com., 1977-86; mem., v.p. Bd. of Alderman, Newton, Mass., 1974-81; mem. Mass. Ho. of Reps., 1981-94. Mem. Newton Dem. City Com., 1970—.

SCHURTER, BETTE JO, realtor; b. Salem, Oreg., July 7, 1932; d. Walter Robert and Dixie Wayne (Gayman) Haverson; m. John J. Schurter, Oct. 2, 1954; children: John Thomas, Steven Robert, Brian Douglas. BS, Portland State U., 1980. Mgr. Ball, Ball & Brosamer, Danville, Calif., 1982-87; realtor Stan Wiley, Inc. Realtors, Wilsonville, Oreg., 1988—. Mem. Draft Bd., Aurora, Oreg., 1980—. Mem. AAUW, Clackamas County Bd. Realtors, Clackamas County Million Dollar Club, Wilsonville C. of C., Aurora Colony Hist. Soc. Home: 24979 NE Pr Dr Aurora OR 97002 Office: Stan Wiley Inc 8750 SW Citizens Dr Wilsonville OR 97070-9488

SCHUSTER, CARLOTTA LIEF, psychiatrist; b. N.Y.C., Sept. 16, 1936; d. Victor Filler and Nina Lincoln (Rayevsky) Lief; m. David Israel Schuster, Sept. 2, 1962; 1 child, Amanda. BA, Barnard Coll., 1957; MD, NYU, 1964. Cert. Am. Bd. Psychiatry and Neurology; cert. addiction psychiatry. Intern Lenox Hill Hosp., N.Y.C., 1964-65; resident St. Luke's Hosp., N.Y.C., 1965-68; fellow Inst. Sex Edn., U. Pa., Phila., 1968-69; instr. N.Y. Med. Coll., N.Y.C., 1969-72; asst. attending Met. Hosp., N.Y.C., 1969-72; assoc. attending St. Luke's-Roosevelt Hosp. Ctr., N.Y.C., 1972—; staff psychiatrist Silver Hill Found., New Canaan, Conn., 1972—; clin. assoc. instr. Columbia U., N.Y.C., 1990—; chief substance abuse svc. Silver Hill Found., New Canaan, 1976—. Author: Alcohol and Sexuality, 1988; co-author: Chapter in Advances in Alcohol and Substance Abuse, 1987; contbr. chpt. Mental Health in the Workplace, 1993. Mem. Am. Psychiat. Assn., Am. Med. Soc. on Addictions, Am. Acad. Psychiatrists in Alcohol and Addictions. Democrat. Jewish. Office: Silver Hill Found PO Box 1177 New Canaan CT 06840-1177

SCHUSTER, INGEBORG IDA, chemistry educator; b. Frankfurt, W. Ger., Oct. 30, 1937; came to U.S. 1947; d. Ludwig Karl and Mariluise (Kautetzky) S. BA, U. Pa., 1960; MS, Carnegie Inst. Tech., 1963; PhD, Carnegie Inst. Tech., 1965. Postdoctoral fellow Bryn Mawr (Pa.) Coll., 1965-67; asst. prof. chemistry Pa. State U., Abington, 1967-73; assoc. prof. chemistry Pa. State U., 1973-83, prof. chemistry, 1983—. Contbr. articles to profl. jours. Huff fellow, 1966; E. Gerry fellow, 1982. Mem. Am. Chem. Soc. Republican. Roman Catholic. Office: Pa State Univ 1600 Woodland Rd Abington PA 19001-3918

SCHUSTER-ARTIS, NANCY MARIE, medical/surgical nurse; b. Tuscola, Ill., May 14, 1961; d. Robert George and Elizabeth (Birkner) Schuster; m. David Michael Artis, Aug. 8, 1987. AA, Springfield (Ill.) Coll., 1982; diploma in nursing, St. John's Sch. Nursing, Springfield, 1982; BSN, Sangamon State U., 1984. RN, Calif., Ill. Med.-surg. staff nurse, relief charge nurse St. John's Hosp., Springfield, 1982-88; med.-surg. staff nurse, relief charge nurse Covenant Med. Ctr., Urbana, Ill., 1988-91, unit quality assurance rep., 1989-91, quality assurance dept. co-chair, 1990-91, mem. nursing coun., 1990; infection control liaison, med.-surg. nurse Sierra Hosp., Fresno, Calif., 1991-94, mem. nurse practice coun., diabetic educator, 1991—, mem. totaly quality mgmt. teams, 1993—; nutritional counselor Nutri/System, Champaign, Ill., 1988-89; lab. instr. Parkland Coll., Champaign, 1990. Nurse ARC, Ill., 1982—; advisor Springfield Area Nursing Explorer Post 727, 1985-88; mem. State Nurses Active in Politics in Ill., Springfield, 1982-87. Mem. Nat. League for Nursing (advocacy com. 1991—), Ill. Nursing Assn. (corr. sec. 9th dist. 1982-87), Profl. Nurse Forum. Home: 28700 Long Hollow Ct S Coarsegold CA 93614-9629 Office: Sierra Community Hosp 2025 E Oakota Ave Fresno CA 93726

SCHUTH, MARY MCDOUGLE, interior designer, educator; b. Kansas City, Mo., Jan. 19, 1942; d. William Darnall and Marie DeArmond (Meiser) McDougle; m. Howard Wayne Schuth, Sept. 4, 1965; 1 child, Andrew Wayne. BS in Interior Design, Communications, Northwestern U., 1964; Cert. Basic Mgmt., U. Mo., 1966. Lic. interior designer, La. Interior designer Cottington's Interiors, Glen Ellyn, Ill., 1964-65, Robnett-Putman Interiors, Columbia, Mo., 1966-67, Nu-Idea Furniture Co., New Orleans, 1973, Maison Blanche, New Orleans, 1974-75, Mary M. Schuth Interior Design, Metairie, La., 1977—; instr. interior design U. New Orleans div. Continuing Edn., 1973—; judge model homes U.S. Homes, Mandeville, La., 1978, 80; bd. dirs. Interior Design Adv. Com. Delgado Coll., New Orleans, 1981—; mem. Alpha Chi Omega Frat. housing review com., 1991—; speaker in field. Co-author: cookbook From the Privateers' Galley, 1980; design work featured in profl. jours.; contbr. to Metairie Mag., 1993-94. Recipient 3rd place Batik Design Juried Art Show Columbia (Mo.) Art League, 1969. Mem. AIA (profl. affiliate), Am. Soc. Interior Designers (profl.), La. Landmarks, Alpha Chi Omega, Alumnae Club (New Orleans).

SCHUTTE, PAMELA KAY, elementary school educator; b. Enid, Okla., June 6, 1952; d. Lawrence George Elbert and Naomi Jean (Hudson) Keener; m. David James Schutte, May 28, 1978; children: Dawn Renee, Caroleah Lynn. B in Elem. Edn., U. No. Colo., Greeley, 1977. Cert. elem. tchr., Ariz. Paraprofl. Fairmont Elem. Sch., Denver, 1974-75; instructional aide Jackson Elem. Sch., Greeley, Colo., 1975-77; 3d grade classroom tchr. Big Springs (Nebr.) Elem. Sch., 1977-79; homebound tutor, substitute Riverdale Elem. Sch., Port Byron, Ill., 1979-82; spl. edn. aide, substitute Ruth Fisher Elem. Sch., Tonopah, Ariz., 1986-87; 4th grade classroom tchr. Scott L. Libby Elem. Sch., Litchfield Park, Ariz., 1987-90, Longview (Wash.) Christian Sch.; tchr. rep. gifted task force Litchfield Park Elem. Sch. Dist., 1988-91. Vice pres. Riverdale Elem. Sch. PTA, Port Byran, Ill., 1980, Scott Libby Elem. Sch. PTA, Litchfield Park, 1988. Mem. NEA, ASCD, Ariz. Educators Assn., Litchfield Park Sch. Dist. Educators Assn. (sec. 1989). Methodist. Home: 329 E Bayshore Dr Palacios TX 77465-9241

SCHUTTE, PAULA MARION, financial planner; b. St. Paul, Oct. 29, 1941; d. Paul Maurice and Marion (McAllister) S. BA in Chemistry, Rosary Coll., River Forest, Ill., 1963; MBA, NYU, 1985; grad., Coll. for Fin. Planning, Denver, 1993. Med. research chemist Geigy Chem. Corp., Ardsley, N.Y., 1964-70; group leader, sci. systems Ciba-Geigy Corp., Ardsley, N.Y., 1970-77, mgr. sci. info., 1980-83, sr. research fellow, 1985-86, dir. end user services, 1986-87; dir. info. techs. Ciba-Geigy Corp., Ardsley, 1987-91, dir. corp. info. svcs., 1991-92; dir. med. systems pharm. div. Ciba-Geigy Corp., Summit, N.J., 1977-80; dir. sci. info. systems pharm. div. Ciba-Geigy Corp., Summit, 1985-92; counselor Svc. Corps Ret. Execs., 1993—; owner fin. planning practice; info. systems cons. St. Jude's, Thornwood, N.Y., 1985-86; adv. Pace U. Computer Sci. and Info. Systems Bd. Patentee in field. Vol. Score/SBA Svc. Corps. Ret. Execs.; ret. exec. program N.Y.C. Pub. Schs. Mem. Inst. Cert. Fin. Planners, Internat. Assn. for Fin. Planning. Office: 250 E 87th St # 26F New York NY 10128-3117

SCHUTZKY, MARILYN HORSLEY, artist; b. Soda Springs, Idaho, July 13, 1936; d. Earl James and Alta (Bollwinkel) Horsley; m. Victor Sergay Schutzky, Oct. 11, 1957; children: Allen Victor, Sandra Kristin. Student, U. Calif., Berkeley, 1954-55, U. Utah, 1955-57. Free-lance artist, 1957—. One-woman shows include Design Concepts, Alamo, Calif., 1991, Harbor Studio Gallery, Gig Harbor, 1991, Back Bay Gardens Gallery, Corte Madera, Calif., 1988, St. Paul Towers, Oakland, Calif., 1988, Marin Arts Guild, Larkspur, Calif., 1986, Two Birds, Forest Knolls, Calif., 1983, Avoir Gallery, Kirkland, Wash., 1993, 94; exhibited in groups shows at Waterworks '92, Seattle Conv. Ctr., Grand Exhbn. '92, Akron (Ohio) Soc. of Artists, Howard Mandeville Gallery, Kirkland, 1992, The Nut Tree, 1991, Kaiser Gallery, 1991, Ariz. Aqueous, Tubac, 1993, 95, Suncities Mus., Phoenix, Ariz., 1994, Western Fedn. Watercolor Socs., Phoenix, 1994, and others. Recipient 1st award Frye Art Mus., 1990, James Copley Purchase award San Diego Watercolor Soc., 1988, 2d Pl. award The Artist's Mag., 1993, Excellence award Western Fedn. Watercolor Socs., 1993. Mem. N.W. Watercolor Soc. (Past Pres.'s award 1992, Signature award 1992, Merit award 1993), Marin Soc. Artists, Ariz. Watercolor Assn. (awarded Coatimundi Soc. membership), Eastbay Watercolor Soc. (Signature award 1989), Fedn. Can. Artists, Marin County Watercolor Soc., Watercolor West. Home and Studio: 8915 N Harborview Dr # 103 Gig Harbor WA 98332-2170 also: Marilyn Schutzky Studio 7340 E Turquoise Ave Scottsdale AZ 85258-1220

SCHUUR, DIANE JOAN, vocalist; b. Tacoma, Dec. 10, 1953; d. David Schuur. Ed. high sch., Vancouver, Wash. Albums include Pilot of My Destiny, 1983, Deedles, Schuur Thing, 1986, Timeless (Grammy award for female jazz vocal 1986), Diane Schuur and the Count Basie Orchestra (Grammy award for female jazz vocal 1987), Talkin' 'Bout You, 1988, Pure Schuur, 1991 (reached #1 on Billboard contemporary jazz chart, nominated for Grammy award 1991), In Tribute, 1992, Love Songs, 1993 (Grammy nomination, Best Traditional Vocal), (with B.B. King) Heart to Heart, 1994 (entered at #1 on Billboard contemporary jazz chart); performed at the White House, Monterey Jazz Festival, Hollywood Bowl; toured Japan, Far East, South Am. and Europe.

SCHUYLER, JANE, fine arts educator; b. Flushing, N.Y., Nov. 2, 1943; d. Frank James and Helen (Oberhofer) S. BA, Queens Coll., 1965; MA, Hunter Coll., 1967; PhD, Columbia U., 1972. Asst. prof. art history Montclair State Coll., Upper Montclair, N.J., 1970; assoc. prof. C.W. Post Coll., L.I. Univ., Greenvale, N.Y., 1971-73, adj. assoc. profl, 1977-78; coord. fine arts, asst. prof. York Coll., CUNY, Jamaica, 1973-77, 78-87, assoc. prof., 1988-92, prof. 1993—. Author: Florentine Busts: Sculpted Portraiture in the Fifteenth Century, 1976; contbr. articles on occult and art to Cakes and Ale, 1978, Italian Quar., 1982, Secac Jour. on Italian Renaissance art, 1983, 85, Source, 1986-90, Studies in Iconography, 1987. Mem. Fine Arts Com. Internat. Women's Arts Festival, 1974-76; pres. United Community Dems. of Jackson Heights, 1987-89. N.Y. Columbia U. Summer Travel and Rsch. grantee, 1969; recipient PSC-CUNY Rsch. award, 1990-91. Mem. AAUP, Coll. Art Assn. Am., Women's Caucus for Art, Nat. Trust Hist. Preservation, Renaissance Soc. Am. Roman Catholic. Home: 35-37 78th St Jackson Heights NY 11372

SCHWAB, CAROL ANN, law educator; b. Washington, Mo., Mar. 2, 1953; d. Calvin George and Edith Emma (Starke) Schermann; m. Steven Joseph Schwab, May 31, 1975. BA, Southeast Mo. State U., 1975; JD, U. Mo., 1978; LLM, Washington U., St. Louis, 1985. Bar: Mo. 1979, N.C. 1986. Law clk. to presiding justice U.S. Dist. Ct. (we. dist.), Kansas City, Mo., 1979-82; assoc. Bryan, Cave, McPheeters & McRoberts, St. Louis, 1982-84, Smith, Anderson, Blount, Dorsett, Mitchell & Jernigan, Raleigh, N.C., 1985-87; assoc. prof., resource mgmt. specialist N.C. Coop. Extension Svc., N.C. State U., Raleigh, 1988—; instr. legal writing St. Louis U. Sch. Law, 1984. Contbr. articles to profl. jours. Bd. dirs., co-chair fin. com. N.C. chpt. Nat. Com. for Prevention of Child Abuse, 1988-90, pres.-elect, 1990; mem. bd. assocs. N.C. Child Advocacy Inst., 1990-93; mem. Children's Summit Steering Com., 1993. Recipient John S. Divilbiss award U. Mo., 1977. Mem. N.C. Bar Assn. (editor the Will and Way quar. publ. 1990-91, sec. estate planning and fiduciary law sect. 1991-92, mem. comm. adv. com. 1991—), Mo. Bar Assn. Republican. Roman Catholic. Office: NC State U PO Box 7605 Raleigh NC 27695

SCHWAB, EILEEN CAULFIELD, lawyer, educator; b. N.Y.C., Feb. 11, 1944; d. James Francis and Mary Alice (Fay) Caulfield; m. Terrance W. Schwab, Jan. 4, 1969; children: Matthew Caulfield, Catherine Grimley, Claire Gillespie. BA, Hunter Coll., 1965; JD, Columbia U., 1971; BA magna cum laude. Bar: N.Y. 1972, U.S. Dist. Ct. (so. and ea. dists.) N.Y. 1975, U.S. Ct. Appeals (2d cir.) 1975, U.S. Tax Ct. 1980, U.S. Ct. Appeals (10th cir.) 1993. Assoc. Poletti Friedin, N.Y.C., 1971-72, Hughes Hubbard & Reed, N.Y.C., 1972-75, Davis Polk & Wardwell, N.Y.C., 1975-81; dep. bur. chief Charities Bu., Atty. Gen. of N.Y., 1981-82; counsel Brown & Wood, N.Y.C., 1983—, ptnr., 1984; adj. prof. N.Y. Law Sch.; mediator atty. disciplinary com. first dept., N.Y. Co-chmn. gift planning adv. com. Archdiocese of N.Y.C. Fellow Am. Coll. Trust and Estate Counsel; mem. N.Y. State Bar Assn. (exec. com. trust and estate sect.), Assn. Bar City N.Y., Phi Beta Kappa. Democrat. Roman Catholic.

SCHWAB, RISE, immunologist, educator; b. N.Y.C.; d. Irving and Dorothy (Lubliner) S. BS, SUNY, Stony Brook, 1971; PhD, Cornell U., 1981. Assoc. prof. Cornell U. Med. Coll., N.Y.C., 1986—; vis. scientist Inst. Pasteur, Paris, 1993-94. Contbr. chpts. to books and articles to profl. jours. Recipient First Rsch. grant NIH, 1988-93, rsch. grant NIH, 1991-93. Mem. Am. Assn. Immunologists, Am. Soc. for Histocompatibility and Immunogenetics, Am. Fedn. for Clin. Rsch., The Harvey Soc., The Gerontol. Soc. Am. Home: 430 E 63rd St New York NY 10021-7918

SCHWAB, SUSAN CAROL, electronics company executive. BA in Polit. Economy, Williams Coll., 1976; MA in Applied Econs., Stanford U., 1977; PhD in Pub. Adminstrn., George Washington U., 1993. U.S. trade negotiator Office of Pres.'s Spl. Trade Rep., Washington, 1977-79; trade policy officer U.S. Embassy, Tokyo, 1980-81; chief economist, legis. asst. for internat. trade for Senator John C. Danforth, 1981-86, legis. dir., until 1989; asst. sec. commerce, dir. gen. U.S. and Fgn. Comml. Svc. Dept. Commerce, 1989-93; with corp. strategy office Motorola, Inc., Schaumburg, Ill., 1993—. Office: Motorola Inc Corporate Strategy Office 1303 E Algonquin Rd Schaumburg IL 60196

SCHWALLER, SHIRLEY FILES, publisher; b. Ft. Worth, Feb. 16, 1946; d. John Thomas and Janette Elizabeth (Hicks) Files; m. Leonard Edward Kowitz, Oct. 6, 1968 (div. Mar. 1979); children: Jeffrey Edward Kowitz, Kendra Denise Kowitz; m. Robert Corbett Schwaller, Sept. 17, 1983; 1 child, Mark Files Schwaller. BBA, U. Tex., 1968; BA in Comm., U. Houston, 1979. Reporter The Mirror, Houston, 1977-78; bus. editor Saudi Rsch. and Mktg., Houston, 1978-79; writer Houston Bus. Jour., 1979-81; v.p. Hart & Assocs., Houston, 1981-82; freelance writer Wall St. Jour. and Houston Bar Jour., Houston, 1982-83; editor Dallas-Ft. Worth Bus. Jour., 1983-85, Dallas Times Herald, 1985-87; co-founder, pub. SR Texas, 1987-93; prin. Horizon Comm., Dallas, 1994—. Contbr. numerous articles to profl. jours. Mem. Mayor's Task Force on Employing the Handicapped, Dallas, 1985-87; pres. Shared Housing, City of Dallas; bd. dirs. Metro Dallas YMCA Cmtys. Svc.; mem. adv. bd. Dallas Assistance League; mem. steering com. Safeguards for Srs., 1992-93. Recipient Sr. Affairs award City of Dallas. Mem. Nat. Assn. Women Bus. Owners (bd. dirs. Dallas chpt. 1994—), Nat. Assn. Bus. Editors and Writers, Dallas Press Club (finalist Best Headline Portfolio 1986, finalist Best Splty. Pub. 1986), Soc. Profl. Journalists, Dallas C. of C. (chmn. pub. rels. com. 1985—). Democrat. Office: SR Texas 6520 Southpoint Dallas TX 75248-2220

SCHWALM, RIELA LOUISE, dog trainer; b. Renton, Wash., Apr. 17, 1948; d. Gabriel Ely Smiljanich and Ardis Louise (Wiseman) Vanosse; 1 child, Dar Ling. Cert., Nat. 9-K, 1992. Cert. master dog trainer. Sec. Dept. Natural Resources, Sedro-Woolley, Wash., 1971-72; operator logging camp Huffman-Wright Logging, Stump Lake, Oreg., 1972-76; market grower Farmer's Market Douglas County, Oreg., 1981—; profl. trainer Nat. K-9, Winston, 1991—; cons. Companion Animal Clinic, Roseburg, Oreg., 1992—. Vol. Wildlife Safari, Winston, 1984—. Mem. Nat. K-9 Trainers Assn., Ollalla Hunt Club (dog master 1989—). Home: 7777 Upper Olalla Rd Winston OR 97496

SCHWAN, JUDITH ALECIA, photographic researcher; b. Middleport, N.Y., Apr. 16, 1925; d. James William and Mary Alecia (Wythers) S. BSChemE, U. Cin., 1948; MS, Cornell U., 1950. Research scientist Eastman Kodak Co., Rochester, N.Y., 1950-65, lab. head, 1965-68, asst. div. dir. emulsion research div., 1968-71, div. dir. emulsion research div., 1971-75, asst. dir. research labs., 1975-86, dir. photographic research labs., photographic products group, 1986-87, ret., 1987; bd. trustees Eastman Savs. & Loan Assn., Rochester, 1977-87. Patentee in field. Trustee St. John Fisher Coll., Rochester, 1975—; active Meml. Art Gallery, Rochester, Rochester Philharm. Orch., Rochester Mus. and Sci. Ctr., George Eastman House, Rochester; mem. task force Women in Ch. of Rochester Cath. Diocese; mem. econ. pastoral steering com. Rochester Cath. Diocese; mem. parish coun. St. Stephen's Ch., Middleport, N.Y.; mem. Diocesan Pastoral Coun., Buffalo. Recipient Disting. Alumnus award U. Cin. Coll. of Engring., 1976. Fellow Soc. Motion Picture and TV Engrs. (Herbert T. Kalmus Meml award for Outstanding Contbn. in Color Films, 1979); mem. Am. Chem. Soc., Nat. Acad. Engring. Soc. Photographic Scientists and Engrs. Clubs: Shelridge Country (Medina, N.Y.). Home: 45 Park Ave Middleport NY 14105-1354

SCHWANZ, DEBORAH ANN, psychiatric nurse; b. South Bend, Ind., Jan. 1, 1952; d. Ned Christian and Rita Jane (Witucki) S. Diploma in nursing, Meml. Hosp. Sch. Nursing, South Bend, 1973; BS in Health Arts, Coll. of St. Francis, Joliet, Ill., 1991. RN, Fla.; cert. psychiat. and mental health nurse ANCC. House float nurse Meml. Hosp., 1973; psychiat. team leader St. Anthony's Hosp., St. Petersburg, Fla., 1974-81, asst. head nurse, 1981-84, clin. mgr. psychiatry, instr. aggression control techniques, 1984-89; weekend nursing supr. Boley, Inc., St. Petersburg, 1989-92; nurse therapist various nursing homes, St. Petersburg, 1992-93, Physicians' Cmty. Hosp., St. Petersburg, 1993-94; contract psychiat. nurse St. Anthony's Home Health Care, St. Petersburg, 1986—; presenter on psychiat. nursing at seminars and workshops, St. Petersburg, Clearwater, Fla., 1984-88. Mem. NOW (past sec. Pinellas chpt.), Mental Health Assn., Tampa Bay Depressive and Manic-Depressive Assn.

SCHWARTZ, ALLYSON Y, state senator; b. N.Y.C., Oct. 3, 1948; d. Everett and Renee Perl Young; m. David Schwartz, 1970; children: Daniel, Jordan. BA, Simmons Coll., 1970; MSS, Bryn Mawr Coll., 1972. Founder, exec. dir. Elizabeth Blackwell Health Ctr. for Women, 1975-88; acting commr., 1st dep. commr. Dept. Human Svcs., 1988-90; mem. Pa. State Senate 4th dist., 1990—; minority chmn. Edn. Com., 1994—; mem. Aging and Youth Com., Pub. Health and Welfare Com., Comty. and Econ. Devel. Com. Policy. Mem. Pa. Citizen's Crime Commn. Task Force on Juvenile Justice, 1988-89, Mayor's Task Force on Juvenile Justice, 1988-89, Mayor's Pub.-Pvt. Task Force on Homelessness; bd. dirs., founding mem. Women's Way, 1976-88; chair health com. Nat. Coun. State Legislators, 1994, Ea. Regional Women's Network, 1994. Named Social Worker of Yr. Nat. Assn. Social Workers, 1990. Mem. Child Welfare League. Office: Senate State Capital Harrisburg PA 17101

SCHWARTZ, ANNA JACOBSON, economic historian; b. N.Y.C., Nov. 11, 1915; married; four children. BA, Barnard Coll., 1934; MA, Columbia U., 1935, PhD, 1964; LittD (hon.), U. Fla., 1987; ArtsD (hon.), Stonehill Coll., 1989; LLD (hon.), Iona Coll., 1992. Researcher USDA, 1936, Columbia U. Social Sci. Research Council, 1936-41; mem. sr. research staff Nat. Bur. Econ. Research Inc., N.Y.C., 1941—; instr. Bklyn. Coll., 1952, Baruch Coll., 1959-60; adj. prof. econs. grad. CCNY, 1967-69, grad. sch. CUNY, 1986—, NYU Grad. Sch. Arts and Sci., 1969-70; hon. vis. prof. City U. Bus. Sch., London, 1984—. Mem. editorial bd. Am. Econ. Rev., 1972-78, Jour. Money, Credit and Banking, 1974-75, 84—, Jour. Monetary Econs., 1975—, Jour. Fin. Svcs. Rsch., 1993—; contbr. numerous articles to profl. jours. Disting. fellow Am. Econ. Assn., 1993. Mem. Western Econ. Assn. (pres. 1987-88). Office: Nat Bur Econ Research 269 Mercer St Fl 8 New York NY 10003-6633

SCHWARTZ, BARI-LYNNE, social services specialist, social worker; b. Cambridge, Mass., Jan. 27, 1943; d. William and Pearl (Levin) Hurwitz; children: Alec, Alison. BA, U. Mass., 1964; MSW, Rutgers U., 1988. Lic. social worker, N.J.; cert. secondary edn. tchr., N.J., Mass. Coord. of monitoring Morris County Dept. Human Svcs., Morristown, N.J.; contract adminstr., intern Bergen County Dept. Human Svcs., Hackensack, N.J.; tchr. Livingston (N.J.) Bd. of Edn.; tchr. English Haddon Twp. Bd. of Edn., Westmont, N.J. Mem. NASW. Home: 181 Long Hill Rd Apt 5M Little Falls NJ 07424-2029 Office: Commission Status Women Adminstrn Bldg Ct Plz South 21 Main St Rm 115W Hackensack NJ 07601-7000*

SCHWARTZ, BRENDA KEEN, lawyer; b. Ft. Smith, Ark., Dec. 5, 1949; d. James Pritchard and Era Erline (Jones) Denniston; m. Dean Edward Keen, June 23, 1973 (dec. June 1990); 1 child, Duncan Denniston; m. Sylvan Schwartz, Jr., Apr. 26, 1992. BA, U. Houston, 1972, JD magna cum laude, 1975. Bar: Tex. 1975, U.S. Dist. Ct. (so. dist.) Tex. 1975. Assoc. Haynes & Fullenweider, P.L.C., Houston, 1975-79, v.p., ptnr., 1979-87; ptnr., officer Wallis & Keen, P.C., Houston, 1988-92; prin. Brenda Keen Schwartz P.C., Houston, 1992—. Contbr. articles to legal publs. Fellow Am. Acad. Matrimonial Lawyers (treas. Tex. chpt. 1989-91, sec. 1991-93, v.p. 1993—), Tex. Bar Found., Houston Bar Found.; mem. State Bar Tex. (family law coun. 1989-93). Roman Catholic. Office: Brenda Keen Schwartz P C 5718 Westheimer Ste 1320 Houston TX 77057

SCHWARTZ, CAROL LEVITT, former government official; b. Greenville, Miss., Jan. 20, 1944; d. Stanley and Hilda (Simmons) Levitt; m. David H. Schwartz (dec.); children: Stephanie, Hilary, Douglas. BS in Spl. and Elem. Edn., U. Tex., 1965. Mem. transiton team Office of Pres. Elect, 1980-81; con. office presdl. personnel The White House, Washington, 1981; cons. U.S. Dept. Edn., Washington, 1982; pres. sec. U.S. Ho. Reps., Washington, 1982-83; mem. at large Coun. of D.C., Washington, 1985-89; candidate for mayor, Washington, 1986, 94; vice chmn. Nat. Edn. Commn. on Time and Leaarning, 1992-94, Nat. Adv. Coun. on Disadvantaged Children, 1974-79; lectr. in field; radio commentator, 1990-91. Mem. D.C. Bd. Edn., 1974-82, v.p., 1977-80; bd. dirs. Met. Police Boys and Girls Club, 1st v.p., 1989-93, pres., 1994—, chmn. membership com., 1984-93; mem. adv. com. Am. Coun. Young Polit. Leaders, 1982-90; mem. Nat. Coun. Friends Kennedy Ctr., 1984-91; bd. dirs. Whitman-Walker Clinic, 1988—, St. John's Child Devel. Ctr., 1989-91; trustee Kennedy Ctr. Cmty. and Friends Bd., 1991—, chmn. edn. task force, 1993—; trustee Jewish Coun. on Aging, 1991-93; v.p. adv. bd. Am. Automobile Assn., 1988—. Mem. Cosmos Club. Republican. Jewish.

SCHWARTZ, CAROL VIVIAN, lawyer; b. Newark, Apr. 5, 1952; d. A. Harold and Helen (Schwartz) S.; m. Robert L. Sills, June 9, 1985. BA, Tufts U., 1974; JD, Columbia U., 1977. Law clk. to presiding justice U.S. Dist. Ct. N.Y., N.Y.C., 1978-79; assoc. DeLevoise & Plimpton, N.Y.C., 1979-81; assoc. counsel Am. Express Co., N.Y.C., now sr. counsel. Mem. ABA. Home: 140 E 83rd St 11A New York NY 10028 Office: Am Express Co World Financial Ctr New York NY 10285-4900*

SCHWARTZ, CHERIE ANNE KARO, storyteller; b. Miami, Fla., Feb. 24, 1951; d. William Howard and Dorothy (Olesh) Karo; m. Lawrence Schwartz, Aug. 12, 1979. BA in Lit., The Colo. Coll., 1973; MA in Devel. Theater, U. Colo., 1977. Tchr. English, drame, mime, creative writing, speech coach South High Sch., Pueblo, Colo., 1973-76; tchr. drama St. Mary's Acad., Denver, 1979-81; tchr. English and drama Rocky Mountain Hebrew Acad., Denver, 1981-83; full-time profl. storyteller throughout N.Am., 1982—; storyteller, docent, tchr. tng., mus. outreach Denver Mus. Natural History, 1982—; trainer, cons., performer, lectr, keynote speaker various orgns., synagogues, instns., agys., confs. throughout the country, 1982—; co-founder, chairperson Omanim b'Yachad: Artists Together, Nat. Conf. Celebrating Storytelling, Drama, Music and Dance in Jewish Edn., Denver, 1993. Storyteller: (audio casette tapes) Cherie Karo Schwartz Tells Stories of Hanukkah from Kar-Ben Books, 1986, Cherie Karo Schwartz Tells Stories of Passover From Kar-Ben Books, 1986, Miriam's Tambourine, 1988, Worldwide Jewish Stories of Wishes and Wisdom, 1988; storyteller, actor: (video tape) The Wonderful World of Recycle, 1989; author: (book) My Lucky Dreidel: Hanukkah Stories, Songs, Crafts, Recipes and Fun for Kids, 1994. Title III grantee State of Colo. Edn., Pueblo, 1975-76. Mem. Coalition for Advancement of Jewish Edn. (coord. Jewish Storytelling Conf. 1989—, coord. Nat. Jewish Storytelling Network), Nat. Assn. for Preservation and Perpetuation of Storytelling, Nat. Storytelling Assn., Rocky Mountain Storytelling Guild. Democrat. Jewish. Home: 996 S Florence St Denver CO 80231

SCHWARTZ, DORIS RUHBEL, nursing educator, consultant; b. Bklyn., May 30, 1915; d. Henry and Florence Marie (Shuttleworth) S. BS, NYU, 1953, MS, 1958. RN, N.Y. Staff nurse Meth. Hosp., Bklyn., 1942-43; pub. health nurse Vis. Nurse Assn., Bklyn., 1947-51; pub. health nurse Cornell U. Med. Coll., Cornell-N.Y. Hosp. Sch. Nursing, N.Y.C., 1951-61, tchr. pub. health nursing, geriatric nursing, 1961-80; sr. fellow U. Pa. Sch. Nursing, Phila., 1981-90. Author: Give Us to Go Blithely, 1990 (Book of Yr. award Am. Jour. Nursing 1991); sr. author: The Elderly Chronically Ill Patient: Nursing and Psychosocial Needs, 1963; co-author: Geriatrics and Geriatric Nursing, 1983 (Book of Yr. award Am. Jour. Nursing 1984); contbr. articles to profl. jours. Mem. adv. com. nursing WHO, Geneva, 1971-79; adv. com. Robert Wood Johnson Found., Teaching Nursing Home Project, Princeton, N.J., U. Pa. Wharton Sch. Study of Continuing Care Retirement Communities, 1981-83. Served to capt. N.C., U.S. Army, 1943-47, PTO. Rockefeller fellow U. Toronto, 1950-51, Mary Roberts fellow Am. Jour. Nursing, 1955, Fogarty fellow NIH, 1975-76; recipient Diamond Jubilee Nursing award N.Y. County RNs Assn., 1979. Fellow Inst. Medicine of NAS, APHA (Disting. Career award nursing sect. 1979), Am. Acad. Nursing (charter, coun. 1973-74); mem. ANA (Pearl McIver award 1979), Soroptimist (v.p. N.Y.C. club 1974-75), Sigma Theta Tau (Founders award 1979, Mentor award Alpha Upsilon chpt. 1992). Democrat. Mem. Soc. of Friends.

SCHWARTZ, ELEANOR BRANTLEY, academic administrator; b. Kite, Ga., Jan. 1, 1937; d. Jesse Melvin and Hazel (Hill) Brantley; children: John, Cynthia. Student Mercer U., Ga., 1954-55; student U. Va., 1955, Ga. Southern Coll., 1956-57, BBA, Ga. State U., 1962, MBA, 1963, DBA, 1969. Adminstrv. asst. Fin. Agy., 1954, Fed. Govt., Va., Pa., Ga., 1956-59; asst. dean admissions Ga. State U., Atlanta, 1961-66, asst. prof., 1966-70; assoc. prof. Cleve. State U., 1970-75, prof. and assoc. dean, 1975-80; dean, Harzfeld prof. U. Mo., Kansas City, 1980-87, vice chancellor acad. affairs, 1987-91, interim chancellor, 1991-92, chancellor, 1992—; disting. vis. prof. Berry Coll., Rome, Ga., N.Y. State U. Coll., Fredonia, Mons U., Belgium; cons. pvt. industry, U.S., Europe, Can.; bd. dirs. ANUHCO, Rsch. Med. Ctr., Country Club Bank, Toy and Miniature Mus., Menorah Med. Ctr. Found., NCCJ, Econ. Devel. Corp. of Kansas City, Vendo Co. Adv. Com., Midwest Grain Products, Silicon Prairie Tech. Assn. Author: Sex Barriers in Business, 1971, Contemporary Readings in Marketing, 1974; (with Muczyk and Smith) Principles of Supervision, 1984. Chmn., Mayor's Task Force in Govt. Efficiency, Kansas City, Mo., 1984; mem. community planning and research council United Way Kansas City, 1983-85; bd. dirs. Jr. Achievement, 1982-86. Recipient Disting. Faculty award Cleve. State U., 1974, Cleve., 60 Women of Achievement Girls Scouts Council Mid Continent, 1983; named Career Woman of Yr. Kansas City, Mo., 1989; recipient disting. svc. award Kansas State U., 1992. Mem. Am. Mktg. Assn., Acad. Internat. Bus., Am. Mgmt. Assn., Am. Case Research Assn., Internat. Soc. Study Behavioral Devel., Greater Kansas City C. of C. (ex. officio, bd. dirs.), Silicon Prairie Tech. Assn. (ex officio, bd. dirs.), Phi Kappa Phi, Golden Key, Alpha Iota Delta.

SCHWARTZ, ESTAR ALMA, lawyer; b. Bklyn., June 29, 1950; d. Henry Israel and Elaine Florence (Scheiner) Sutel; m. Lawrence Gerald Schwartz, June 28, 1976 (div. Dec. 1977); 1 child, Joshua (dec.). JD, N.Y.U., 1980. owner Estaris Paralegal Svc., Flushing, N.Y., 1992—. Mgr., ptnr. Scheiner, Scheiner, DeVito & Wytte, N.Y.C., 1966-81; fed. govt., social security fraud specialist DHHS, OI, OIG, SSFIS, N.Y.C., 1982-83; pensions Todtman, Epstein, et al, N.Y.C., 1983-85; office mgr., sec. Sills, Beck, Cummis, N.Y.C., 1985-86; office mgr., bookkeeper Philip, Birnbaum & Assocs., N.Y.C., 1986-87; office mgr., sec. Stanley Posses, Esq., Queens, N.Y., 1989-90. Democrat. Jewish. Home and Office: 67-20 Parsons Blvd 2A Flushing NY 11365

SCHWARTZ, FELICE N., social activist, educator; b. N.Y.C., Jan. 16, 1925; d. Albert and Rose (Kaplan) Nierenberg; m. Irving L. Schwartz, Jan. 12, 1946; children: Cornelia Ann, Tony, James Oliver. BA, Smith Coll., 1945; LHD (hon.), Pace U., 1980, Smith Coll., 1981, Marietta Coll., 1989, Chatham Coll., 1990, CUNY Grad. Ctr., 1993, Mt. Holyoke Coll., 1994. Founder, exec. dir. Nat. Scholarship Svc. and Fund for Negro Students, N.Y.C., 1945-51; v.p. prodn. Etched Products Corp., N.Y.C., 1951-54; founder, pres. Catalyst, N.Y.C., 1962-93. Author: Breaking With Tradition: Women and Work, The New Facts of Life, 1992, How To Go To Work When Your Husband Is Against It, Your Children Aren't Old Enough, There's Nothing You Can Do Anyhow, 1968; author numerous articles. Mem. adv. bd. Nat. Women's Polit. Caucus, Nat. Network of Hispanic Women; bd. visitors CUNY Grad. Ctr.; mem. adv. bd. Found. for Student Comm. Woodrow Wilson fellow, 1994—; recipient Mademoiselle medal for singular achievement in edn., 1949, Disting. Alumnae medal Smith Coll., 1976, Susan B. Anthony award NOW, 1981, Boehm Soaring Eagle award Nat. Women's Econ. Alliance, 1987, Sara Lee Corp. Front Runner award, 1987; named Human Resource Profl. of Yr. Internat. Assn. Pers. Women, 1983. Fellow Nat. Acad. Human Resources; mem. Women's Forum, Inc., Global Bus. Network (Woodrow Wilson vis. fellow). Office: 230 Park Ave S New York NY 10003

SCHWARTZ, HILDA G., retired state judge; b. N.Y.C.; d. Solomon and Anna Leah (Rubin) Ginsburg; m. Herman N. Schwartz, Feb. 21, 1930; 1 child, John Michael. BS, Washington Sq. Coll. of NYU; LLB, NYU, 1929. Bar: N.Y. 1930. Pvt. practice, 1930-46; sec., bur. head, trial commr. Bd. Estimate, N.Y.C., 1946-51; city magistrate City of N.Y., 1951-58, city treas., head dept. finance, 1958-62, dir. finance, 1962-64, judge civil ct., 1965-71; justice state supreme ct. State of N.Y., 1972-83; ret., 1983; counsel to law firm, 1984; chmn. law com. Bd. Magistrates, 1953-58; chmn. home term panel judges, 1954-56; judge adolescent ct., 1953-58. Mem. welfare adv. bd. N.Y. Jr. League, 1953-56; bd. mgrs. Greenwich House, 1946-48; v.p. Young Dem. club 1935-37; trustee Village Temple, 1956-61, chair dedication com., 1957; chair exec. bd. Coun. Org. Am. Jewish Congress, 1958; hon. chair, bd. dirs. Women's League for Histadrut, 1959; vice-chair Greenwich Village Fresh Air Fund, 1962; co-chair community breakfast State of Israel Bonds, 1956; bd. dirs. Washington Sq. Outdoor Art Exhibit, 1950-58, Washington Sq. Coll. Alumni Assn., 1967. Recipient Citation by Women for Achievement, 1951, Award of Merit Women Lawyers Assn. State of N.Y., 1957,

Scroll of Key award Key Women, 1959, Honor award Am. Jewish Congress Coun. of Orgns., 1959, Honor award Greenwich Village Community for State of Israel Bonds, 1960, Mother of Yr. award Justice Lodge Masons, 1960, First Egalitarian award Aegis Soc., Fed. Negro Civil Svc. Orgns., 1961, Honor award B'nai B'rith, 1963, Interfaith award, 1963, Alumni Achievement award NYU Washington Sq. Coll. Alumni Assn., 1968; named Woman of Achievement Fedn. Jewish Women Orgns., 1959, Patron ann. bridge, Cath. Ctr. NYU, 1960. Mem. ABA, Assn. of Bar of City of N.Y. (mem. lectr., legal aid, matrimonial law, profl. and jud. ethics coms.), N.Y. State Assn. Women Judges (hon. mem., bd. dirs., Outstanding Jud. Achievement award 1983), Supreme Ct. Justices Assn. of City of N.Y. (bd. dirs. 1976-89), Ins. Arbitrator Forums (arbitrator), N.Y. County Lawyers Assn. (profl. ethics com.), N.Y. State Bar Assn. (jud. sabbaticals com.), N.Y. Women's Bar Assn. (past pres., founder, mem. adv. bd., scroll of honor 1958, Disting. Svc. award 1977, Lifetime Contbn. to Justice award 1984), Nat. Assn. Women Judges, Assn. Supreme Ct. Justices State of N.Y. (community rels., retirement and pensions, jud. sabbaticals coms.), Hadassah (hon. mem. N.Y. chpt. 1961), United HIAS Women's Div. (life), Emerald Soc. (hon. mem. 1961), Histadrut (hon. mem. 1960), Iota Tau Tau (hon.). Office: 43 Fifth Ave New York NY 10003-4368

SCHWARTZ, ILENE, psychotherapist, educator; b. Phila., June 19, 1942; d. Israel Gerson and Susan (Soloway) Schiffman; m. Victor Schwartz, Jan. 6, 1970 (div. 1980). BS, Temple U., 1970; postgrad. U. Pa., 1981-82; MEd, Antioch U., 1990. Counselor pvt. practice, Phila., 1978—; instr. Community Coll. Phila., 1974-79; crisis counselor Women In Transition, 1988-89; cons., crisis counselor in the field. Mem. AAUW, Am. Counseling Assn., Freud Friends.

SCHWARTZ, ILSA ROSLOW, neuroscientist; b. Bklyn., Aug. 20, 1941; d. David and Lottie (Warshall) Roslow; m. Alan Gordon Schwartz, July 19, 1964; children: Leah Ellen, Seth Roslow. AB magna cum laude, Vassar Coll., 1962; MS, Yale U., 1964, PhD, 1968. Postdoctoral fellow Albert Einstein Coll. Medicine, Bronx, N.Y., 1968-69; rsch. assoc. ctr. for neural scis. Ind. U., Bloomington, 1970-73, asst. prof. anatomy and physiology, 1973-75; asst. prof. med. scis. Ind. U. Sch. Medicine, Bloomington, 1976-77; vis. rsch. anatomist UCLA Sch. Medicine, 1976-77, asst. prof. in- residence head and neck surgery, 1977-81, assoc. prof., 1981-87; assoc. prof. Yale U. Sch. Medicine, New Haven, 1987-89, prof. surgery (otolaryngology) and neurobiology, 1989—; mem. communicative disorders rev. com. Nat. Inst. Neurol. Communicative Disorders and Stroke, Bethesda, 1981-83, chair, 1983-85; sci. adv. coun. House Ear Inst., L.A., 1989, chair, 1991-94. Recipient Jacob Javits Neurosci. Investigator award Nat. Inst. Neurol. Communicative Disorders and Stroke, 1988-95; grantee NIH, 1973—; fellow Vassar Coll., 1962-63, NIH, 1962-68, 68-69. Mem. Assn. for Rsch. in Otolaryngology (coun. mem. 1986-89, pres. elect 1989-90, pres. 1990-91, past pres. 1991-92), Nat. Inst. on Deafness and Other Communication Disorders (adv. coun. 1989-93), Soc. for Neurosci. (chair Bloomington, Ind. chpt. 1975-76), Am. Assn. Anatomists, Women in Neurosci., AAAS, Friends of NIDCD, Inc. (bd. dirs.). Jewish. Office: Yale U Sch Medicine 333 Cedar St New Haven CT 06510-3289

SCHWARTZ, JUNE VIRGINIA, pediatrician, educator; b. Hempstead, N.Y., June 3, 1921; d. John Schwartz and Florence G. (Bennett) Cobb. Student, Hunter Coll., 1956; MD, N.Y. Med. Coll., 1960. Diplomate Am. Bd. Pediatrics. Intern Nassau Hosp., Mineola, N.Y., 1960-61; resident in pediatrics Meadowbrook Hosp., East Meadow, N.Y., 1961-64; pediatrician, asst. prof. N.Y. Med. Coll.-Flower Fifth Ave. Hosp., N.Y.C., 1964-85; attending pediatrician, clin. asst. prof. St. Vincent Hosp.-N.Y. Med. Coll., N.Y.C., 1985—; tchr. St. Vincent's Hosp., N.Y.C., 1985—; mentor Hunter Coll., N.Y.C., 1989—. Author: (pub. affairs pamphlets) Caring for the New Baby, 1983, When Your Child is Ill, 1983, The Very New Baby, 1983, Health Care for the Adolescent, 1987. Mem. adv. coun. Salvation Army Social Svcs. for Children, N.Y.C., 1972—. Fellow Am. Acad. Pediatrics.

SCHWARTZ, KATHERINE ANN, sales executive; b. Piscataway, N.J., June 26, 1958; d. Robert Parker and Katherine Ann (Grant) Bunker; m. Eric William Schwartz, Aug. 1, 1981 (div. Mar. 1984). BA in Music, Trenton State Coll., 1981; postgrad., Rutgers U., 1987—. Cert. tchr., N.J. Lab. technician Thema Sys., South Plainfield, N.J., 1982-87; lab. technician Engelhard Corp., Iselin, N.J., 1987-90, assoc. chemist, 1990-91, N.Am. sales specialist, 1991—. Home: 105 Overbrook Rd Piscataway NJ 08854-5527

SCHWARTZ, LILLIAN FELDMAN, artist, filmaker, art analyst, author; b. Cin., July 13, 1927; d. Jacob and Katie (Green) Feldman; m. Jack James Schwartz, Dec. 22, 1946; children: Jeffrey Hugh, Laurens Robert. RN, U. Cin., 1947; Dr. honoris causa, Kean Coll., 1988. Nurse Cin. Gen. Hosp., 1947; head supr. premature nursery St. Louis Maternity Hosp., 1947-48; cons. AT&T Bell Labs., Murray Hill, N.J., 1968—; pres. Computer Creations Corp., Watchung, N.J., 1989—; cons. Bell Communications Research, Morristown, N.J., 1984-92; artist-in-residence Sta. WNET, N.Y.C., 1972-74; cons. T.J. Watson Rsch. Lab. IBM Corp., Yorktown, N.Y., 1975, 82-84; vis. mem. computer sci. dept. U.. Md., College Park, 1974-80; adj. prof. fine arts Kean Coll., New Brunswick, N.J., 1980-82, Rutgers U., New Brunswick, N.J., 1982-83; adj. prof. dept. psychology NYU, N.Y.C., 1985-86, assoc. prof. computer sci.; guest lectr. Princeton U., Columbia U., Yale U., Rockefeller U.; mem. grad. faculty Sch. Visual Arts, N.Y.C., 1990—. Co-author: The Computer Artist's Handbook; contbr. chpts. to books, also Trans. Am. Philos. Soc., vol. 75, Part 6, 1985; one-woman shows of sculpture and paintings include Columbia U., 1967, 68, Rabin and Krueger Gallery, Newark, 1968; films shown at Met. Mus., N.Y.C., Franklin Inst., Phila., 1972, U. Toronto, 1972, am. Embassy, London, 1972, L.A. County Mus., Corcoran Gallery, Washington, 1972, Whitney Mus., N.Y.C., 1973, Grand Palais, Paris, Musee Nat. d'Art Moderne, Paris, IBM, and others. Recipient numerous art and film awards, Emmy award Mus. Modern Art, 1984, Computer Graphics World Smithsonian awards for virtual reality, art analysis, inventing computer medium for art and animation, 1993; named Outstanding Alumnus, U. Cin., 1987; grantee Nat. Endowment for Arts, 1977, 81, Corp. Pub. Broadcasting, 1979, Nat. Endowment Composers and Librettists, 1981. Fellow World Acad. of Art and Sci.; mem. NATAS, Am. Film Inst., Info. Film Prodrs. Am., Soc. Motion Picture and TV Engrs., Internat. Sculptors Assn., Centro Studi Pierfrancescani (Sansepolcro, Italy, founding mem.).

SCHWARTZ, MILDRED B., interior designer, art consultant; b. Pitts., Apr. 7, 1927; d. David and Jennie (Handelsman) Bernstein; m. Leonard Schwartz, Sept. 8, 1946; children: Debra Lynn Schwartz Bailey, Jodi Sue Schwartz Lindner. Student, U. Pitts., 1968. Pres., interior designer Millie Schwartz Assoc., Inc., Pitts., 1971-94, ret., 1994; art cons. Reynolds Gallery, Pitts., 1989-94. Home (winter): 2230 Embassy Dr West Palm Beach FL 33401 also (summer): 5526 Northumberland St Pittsburgh PA 15217

SCHWARTZ, MIRIAM CATHERINE, biology educator; b. Tarlac, Luzon, Philippines, Mar. 9, 1964; came to U.S., 1980; d. Conrado Palarca and Elena Obcena (Domingo) Estanislao; m. Jason Jay Schwartz, July 20, 1987. BS in Biology, Calif. State U., L.A., 1985; PhD, Purdue U., 1992. Rsch. assist., rsch. assoc. dept. biol. sci. Purdue U., West Lafayette, Ind., 1988-93; postdoctoral fellow sch. med. divsn. Emory U., Atlanta, 1993-94; biology lectr. Spelman Coll., Atlanta, 1994—; teaching asst., instr. Purdue U., West Lafayette, 1988-93. Contbr. articles to profl. jours. Aux. vol. Emory Univ. Hosp., Atlanta, 1993—. Mem. Phi Kappa Phi, Golden Key Nat. Honor Soc. Office: Spelman Coll Atlanta GA 30314

SCHWARTZ, NEENA BETTY, endocrinologist, educator; b. Balt., Dec. 10, 1926; d. Paul Howard and Pauline (Shulman) S. A.B., Goucher Coll., 1948, D.Sc. (hon.), 1982; M.S., Northwestern U., 1950, Ph.D., 1953. From instr. to prof. U. Ill. Coll. Medicine, Chgo., 1953-72; asst. dean for faculty U. Ill. Coll. Medicine, 1968-70; prof. physiology Northwestern U. Med. Sch., Chgo., 1973-74; Deering prof. Northwestern U., Evanston, Ill., 1974—; chmn. dept. biol. scis. Northwestern U., 1974-78. Contbr. chpts. to books, articles to profl. jours. NIH research grantee, 1955—. Fellow AAAS; mem. Am. Acad. Arts Scis., Endocrine Soc. (v.p. 1970-71, mem. coun. 1979-83, pres. 1982-83, Williams award 1985), Soc. for Study of Reprodn. (dir. 1975-77, exec. v.p. 1976-77, pres. 1977-78, Carl Hartman award 1992), Am. Physio. Soc., Soc. for Neurosci., Phi Beta Kappa. Home: 1511 Lincoln St Evanston IL 60201-2338

SCHWARTZ, RUTH WAINER, physician; b. New London, Wis.; d. Louis M. and Kathryn Ann (Schwall) W.; m. Seymour I. Schwartz, June 18, 1949; children: Richard, Kenneth, David. BS, U. Wis., 1947, MD, 1950. Diplomate Am. Bd. Ob-Gyn. Intern Genesee Hosp., Rochester, N.Y., 1950; resident Strong Meml. Hosp., Rochester, N.Y., 1951-54; pvt. practice ob-gyn. Rochester, 1954—; examiner Am. Bd. Obstetrics and Gynecology, 1976—, bd. dirs., 1981-89; dir. colposcopy, dysplasia and DES Clinic, colposcopy and laser tutor Genesee Hosp.; clin. prof. ob/gyn U. Rochester Sch. Medicine and Dentistry; pres. med. staff Genesee Hosp., 1972-74; bd. dirs. Genesee Health Svc., 1972-75, ARC, med. adv. com.; trustee Rochester Acad. Medicine, 1975-78; vis. prof. U. Kuwait Med. Sch., 1984, U. Toledo Sch. Medicine, 1985, U. N.Mex. Sch. Medicine, 1989. Contbr. numerous articles to med. jours. and chpts. to med. textbooks; cons. editor and contbr. to The Merck Manual, 15th edit., 1983, 16th edit., 1987, 17th edit., 1991. Mem. med. adv. bd. N.Y. State Task Force on Child Abuse. Named one of Best Women Doctors in Am., Harper's Bazaar mag., Nov., 1985. Mem. Am. Coll. Surgeons, Am. Coll. Obstetricians and Gynecologists (health care commn., Women in Ob/Gyn task force, patient edn. com. 1979-83, asst. sec. 1994—, task force on hysterectomy 1987-89, adv. bd. Dist. II 1982), Task Force on Aging (sec. ACOG Dist. II 1993—, sec. 1993—), Am. Soc. of Colposcopy and Colpomicroscopy, Gynecologic Laser Soc. (bd. dirs.), Am. Fertility Soc., AMA (accreditation council on continuing med. edn. 1988-93), N.Y. State Med. Assn., Monroe County Med. Soc. (maternal mortality com., pub. health com.), Am. Bd. Med. Specialties (fin. com.). Home: 18 Lake Lacoma Dr Pittsford NY 14534-3956

SCHWARTZ, SHIRLEY E., chemist; b. Detroit, Aug. 26, 1935; d. Emil Victor and Jessie Grace (Galbraith) Eckwall; m. Ronald Elmer Schwartz, Aug. 25, 1957; children: Steven Dennis, Bradley Allen, George Byron. BS, U. Mich., 1957, Detroit Inst. Tech., 1978; MS, Wayne State U., 1962, PhD, 1970. Asst. prof. Detroit Inst. Tech., 1973-78, head divsn. math. sci., 1976-78; mem. rsch. staff BASF Wyandotte (Mich.) Corp., 1978-81, head sect. functional fluids, 1981; sr. staff rsch. scientist GM, Warren, Mich., 1981—. Contbr. articles to profl. jours.; patentee in field. Recipient Gold award Engring. Soc. Detroit, 1989. Fellow Soc. Tribologists and Lubrication Engrs. (treas. Detroit sect. 1981, vice chmn. 1982, chmn. 1982-83, chmn. wear tech. com. 1987-88, bd. dirs. 1985-91, assoc. editor 1989-90, contbg. editor 1989—, Wilbur Deutsch award 1987, P.M. Ku award 1994); mem. Am. Chem. Soc., So. Invitro Biology, Soc. Automotive Engrs. (Excellence in Oral Presentation award 1986, 91, 94, Arch T. Colwell Merit award 1991, Lloyd L. Withrow Disting. Spkr. award), Mensa, Classic Guitar Soc. Mich., U.S. Power Squadrons, Detroit Navigators, Sigma Xi. Lutheran. Office: GM NAO Rsch & Devel Ctr 30500 Mound Rd Warren MI 48092-2031

SCHWARTZ, SUSAN LYNN HILL, principal; b. Portland, Ind., Aug. 15, 1951; d. Leland Alfred and Marjorie (Halberstadt) Hill; m. William Samuel Schwartz, July 6, 1974; children: Angelica Martinique, Allysia Dominica. BA, DePauw U., 1973; MA, Ball State U., 1976; postgrad., Tri-Coll. U., Fargo, N.D., 1986, Ind. U., 1993—. Cert. tchr. and aminstr., Ind., N.D. 2d and 3d grade tchr. Jay Sch. Corp., Portland, 1973-76; 1st to 3d grade tchr. Minot (N.D.) Pub. Schs., 1976-80; prin. elem. sch. Ward County Schs., Minot, 1980-82, LaPorte (Ind.) Schs., 1988-89; prin. 3d to 4th grade and spl. edn. Western Wayne Schs., Cambridge City, Ind., 1989—; mem. State Sch. Evaluation Team, Bismarck, N.D., 1980-81. Bd. dirs. Am. Cancer Soc., Muncie, Ind., 1985-88, Richmond, Ind., 1992—, Suzuki Music Assn., Muncie, 1986-87; mem./leader Work Area on Edn.-Meth., Muncie, 1985-87; philanthropic chair Delaware County Welcome Wagon, Muncie, 1982-88; treas./fin. sec. Christian Women's Club, Muncie, 1983-86; pres. N.D. State U. Sch. Adminstrs. Assn., Fargo, 1980-81; mem. Wayne County Step Ahead Edn. Com., 1991—. Named Outstanding Young Educator, Jaycees, 1980, Outstanding Young Career Woman, Bus. and Profl. Women, 1981. Mem. Phi Delta Kappa, Pi Lambda Theta, Delta Kappa Gamma, Psi Iota Xi. Methodist. Home: 12522 W Us Highway 40 # 30 Cambridge City IN 47327-9480 Office: Milton Elem Sch PO Box 308 Milton IN 47357-0308

SCHWARTZ, TERI J(EAN), clinical psychologist; b. N.Y.C., Dec. 30, 1949; d. Jerome and Shirley Ruth (Dushkind) Kraus; m. Raymond C. Schwartz; children: Rachel, Michael, Daniel. BA, Queens Coll., 1971; MS, C.W. Post Ctr., 1974; MA, New Sch. for Social Rsch., 1977, PhD, 1980. Staff psychologist to chief psychologist New Hope Guild, Howard Beach, N.Y., 1982-85, 85—; staff psychologist Queens Child Guidance Ctr., Flushing, N.Y., 1985-88; staff psychotherapist Adelphi Univ.-Postdoctoral Psychotherapy Ctr., Garden City, N.Y., 1984—; pvt. practice, clin. psychologist Briarwood and Floral Park, N.Y., 1984—; adj. clin. supr. Yeshiva U., Bronx, 1987—; clin. supr. Adelphi U., Garden City, 1991—, assoc. clin. prof., 1992—; supr. child therapy tng. program New Hope Guild, Bklyn., 1994. Mem. exec. bd. Briarwood (N.Y.) Civic Assn., 1984—; adv. bd. Queens Community Mental Health Ctr. and Area D Subcom.-Queens Hosp. Ctr., Jamaica, N.Y., 1984—. Mem. APA, N.Y. State Psychol. Assn., Adelphi Soc. for Psychoanalysis and Psychotherapy, Nassau County Psychol. Assn., Queens County Psychol. Assn. Office: 1 Holland Ave Floral Park NY 11001-1505

SCHWARTZ, VALERIE BREUER, interior designer; b. Senica, Czechoslovakia, May 13, 1912; came to U.S., 1928, naturalized, 1928; d. Jacob and Ethel (Weiss) Breuer; m. Leo Schwartz, Feb. 5, 1939; children—Catherine, Robert, William. Student State Real Gymnazium, Prague, 1925-28; Parsons N.Y. Sch. of Fine and Applied Arts, 1930-32. Cert. Am. Soc. Interior Designers. Self-employed interior designer, N.J., 1932—. Contbr. to various mags. including N.Y. Times, House & Garden, Cue Mag., Confort, Argentina; guest radio talk shows. Mem. Hadassah (life). Designed Holocaust Room, Kean Coll., N.J.

SCHWARTZMAN, GLENDA JOY, artist; b. L.A., Dec. 24, 1939; d. Morton and Thelma Lorrain (Bryer) S.; m. Leonard I. Schwartzman, June 21, 1961 (div. Sept. 1973); children: James Elliot, Eric Bennett. Student, Otis Art Inst., Calif., 1958, Chouinard Art Inst., Calif., 1959-60. One-woman shows include: Angeles Press, L.A., 1990, Boringer Gallery, Dallas, 1988, Krieger Gallery, Santa Barbara, Calif., 1987, SOMA Exhbns., Denver, 1986, De Vorsan Gallery, 1987, Inamori, Beverly Hills, Calif., 1982, Lelia Ivy Gallery, Santa Monica, Calif., 1982, others; group shows include TransAmerica Bldg., San Francisco, 1990, Wells Fargo Bank, L.A., 1990, La Jolla (Calif.) Mus., 1990, 1989, Col.-Jems Studios, others; work in pub. and pvt. collections; author: (book) Art in California, 1990. Mem. Dems., Calif., Benedict Canyon. Recipient fine art scholarship Otist Art Inst. Mem. Calif. Yacht Club, So. Calif. Women's Caucas for Art. Jewish. Office: Glenda Schwartzman Studio 807 Hampton Ave Venice CA 90291

SCHWARZ, BARBARA RUTH BALLOU, elementary school educator; b. East Orange, N.J., Aug. 8, 1930; d. Robert Ingram Ballou and Ruth Edna Sweeney; m. Eugene A. Schwarz, Jr., Dec. 24, 1954 (div. 1977); children: Ruth Ellen, Eugene A. III. BS, Trenton State Coll., 1952. Tchr. West Orange N.J. Schs., 1952-54, Franklin Sch., Ft. Wayne, Ind., 1955-56, Parliament Place Sch., North Babylon, N.Y., 1965-91; trustee welfare trust fund North Babylon Tchrs. Orgn., N.Y., 1988-91. Vol. Safe Home, L.I. Women's Coalition, Bayshore, N.Y., 1979—; sec. Victims Info. Bur., Suffolk, 1987-88, v.p., 1989-90, pres. bd. dirs., 1990-94, rep. to Women's Equal Rights Coalition, Suffolk County Human Rights Commn., 1989-94; mem. adv. bd. Suffolk County Women's Svcs., 1990—, vice-chmn., 1991-93; bd. dirs. Suffolk Abortion Rights Coun., 1992—; mem. Suffolk-Nassau Abortion Def., 1991—; mem. pub. affairs com. Planned Parenthood Suffolk County; mem. adminstrv. bd. Babylon Meth. Ch.; mem. Long Islanders for Fairness and Equality 94. Women's History Month Community Svc. honoree Town of Babylon. Mem. AAUW (mem. v.p. Islip area br. 1982-84, pres. 1984-88, legis. chmn. 1988-93, mem. com. promoting individual liberties Nassau-Suffolk dist. VI 1989-91, pro-choice coord. N.Y. state 1990-92, rep. to women on job task force 1986—, chmn. dist. VI inter-br. 1991-92, chair N.Y. state pub. policy 1992—, rep. on L.I. and N.Y. State Pro-Choice Coalitions), N.Y. State Ret. Tchrs. Assn., Western Suffolk Ret. Tchrs. Assn., Coalition Ret. Tchrs. L.I., North Babylon Tchrs. Orgn. (retirees chpt.). Republican. Home: 23 Wyandanch Ave Babylon NY 11702-1920

SCHWARZ, GRETCHEN CAROLYN, government administrator; b. Mar. 16, 1944; d. George Anthony and Grace Katherine (Mahoney) S. BS in Bus. Adminstrn. and Acctg., Kansas State U., 1966; M in Pub. Adminstrn., George Washington, 1979. Auditor, audit mgr. U.S. GAO, Washington, 1966-79; spl. asst. to the dir. bur. accounts ICC, Washington, 1979-80; spl. asst. to the insp. gen. and assoc. insp. gen. U.S. Dept. Edn., Washington, 1980—Mem. Assn. Govt. Accts. (Disting. Leadership award No. Va. chpt. 1975, pres. No. Va. chpt. 1973, nat. fin. bd. 1981-84), Inst. Internal Auditors (v.p. Wash. 1984-86, internat. membership com. 1984-88, co-chair Ea. Regional Conf., 1988, Disting. Service award 1986, mem. standards bd. 1993—), Phi Alpha Alpha. Roman Catholic. Office: US Dept Edn 400 Maryland Ave SW Washington DC 20202-0002

SCHWARZ, JOYCE ANN, marketing executive, public speaker; b. Cleve., Jan. 14, 1946; d. Frank and Ann (Stefani) Habart. BS in Journalism, Ohio U., 1968; M Profl. Writing, U. So. Calif., 1984. Assoc. editor Am. Girl, N.Y.C., 1968-70; dir. publs. U. San Francisco, 1970-77; account supr. Foote, Cone & Belding, San Francisco, 1977-79; v.p. Fawcett McDermott Cavanagh, Honolulu, 1979-82; pres. Joyce Comm., L.A., 1984—; cons. film, TV, new technology; lectr. Star Course, 1987—, career advisor, 1987—; mem. activities com. TV Acad. Co-producer: The Bonsai Tree, 1984, The Sarol Sasaki Story, 1985, On Being Woman and Mormon, 1986; assoc. producer Toulouse, 1986; dir. Blood Bond, 1985; producer: Hot Line to Bus. Show; creator Triumph of Humanism Art Exhbn. and Video, San Francisco Legion of Honor Mus., 1979; freelance writer The Christian Sci. Monitor; author: Successful Recareering, Multimedia: Gateway to the Next Millennium; contbr. articles to profl. jours. Fundraising com. U.S. Olympic Swim Meet, Honolulu, 1982; fundraising cons. Senator Inouye, 1982; fundraising chairperson Women in Film Festival; organizer World Children's Baseball Found. Nat. Endowment Arts grantee, 1976; recipient Telly Pub. Svc. award TV, 1981; named Boss of the Yr., Am. Bus. Women's Assn., 1986. Mem. PRSA (counselors acad.), Hollywood Radio and TV Assn., U. So. Calif. Cinema/TV Alumni Assn. (pres. 1989-90). Office: Joyce Comm 1714 Sanborn Ave Los Angeles CA 90027-6305

SCHWARZ CORE, PATRICIA TZUANOS, real estate company executive, local government official; b. New Orleans, Oct. 1, 1948; d. John Angelo Tzuanos and Marion Gertrude (Johnson) Rodriquez; m. Kenneth W. Zylicz Nov. 1, 1965 (div. May 1969); 1 child, Sheryl Anne; m. Erik B. Schwarz, June 1, 1970 (div. Oct. 1982); 1 child, Erika Rachael; m. Barney Leroy Core, Dec. 31, 1982. BA, U. New Orleans, 1971. Cert. real estate instr., La. Mgr., v.p. Wagner Truax Realtors, Metairie, La., 1975-77; owner, mgr. Patricia Schwarz, Inc./Realtors, Folsom, La., 1977—; dir. Miss Covington (La.) Beauty Pageant, 1988-90, Miss La. Am. Pageant, 1989—; judge for Miss America Preteen, Coed Pageants, Little Miss La., Master La. Pageants. Bd. dirs. St. Tammany Econ. and Devel. Found., 1989-90; assessor St. Tammany Parish, 1991—. Mem. Realtors Nat. Mktg. Inst. (cert. residential specialist, cert. residential broker), Nat. Assn. Realtors (life), La. Bd. Realtors (grad. realtors Inst.), La. Realtors Assn. (bd. dirs. 1989-90, bd. dirs. econ. and devel. com. 1990-92, mem. legis. com. 1990, Athena Award/GM 1991), La. Realtors Land Inst. (pres. 1992-93), Tex. and La. Realtors Land Inst. (v.p. region 1993-94), St. Tammany Bd. Realtors (bd. dirs. 1988-93, life mem. Million Dollar Club, Honor Soc. award 1988-89, 90, pres. 1992), Jefferson Bd. Realtors (life mem. Million Dollar Club). Democrat. Roman Catholic. Home: 47 Rue du Sud Madisonville LA 70447 Office: PO Box 837 Folsom LA 70437-0837

SCHWARZKOPF, GLORIA A., education educator, psychotherapist; b. Chgo., Apr. 20, 1926; m. Alfred E. Grossenbacher. BE, Chgo. State U., 1949, ME, 1956. Cert. tchr. sci. endorsement; libr. sci. endorsement; cert. hypnotherapist. Tchr. Chgo. Bd. Edn., 1949-91, inservice trainer, 1990, 91; co-therapist ATC outpatient unit Ingalls Meml. Hosp., Chgo., 1986—; recovery specialist Interaction Inst., Evergreen Park, Ill., 1993—; instr. Governors State U., 1987, 91, South Suburban Coll., Chgo., 1991, Prairie State Coll., 1993; speaker in field. Recipient Sci. Tchr. of Yr. award, 1976, Svc. Recognition award, 1985, IMSA Recognition award, 1988; grantee Chgo. Pub. Sch., 1981. Mem. NEA, Sci. Tchrs. Assn., Ill. Alcoholism Counselors Alliance, Nat. Alcoholism Coun., Am. Assn. Hypnotherapists, Am. Assn. Behavioral Therapists, Soc. of Am. for Recovery (nat. cert. recovery specialist). Home: 2216 W 91st St Chicago IL 60620

SCHWARZROCK, SHIRLEY PRATT, author, lecturer, educator; b. Mpls., Feb. 27, 1914; d. Theodore Ray and Myrtle Pearl (Westphal) Pratt; m. Loren H. Schwarzrock, Oct. 19, 1945 (dec. 1966); children: Kay Linda, Ted Kenneth, Lorraine V. BS, U. Minn., 1935, MA, 1942, PhD, 1974. Sec. to chmn. speech dept., U. Minn., Mpls., 1935, instr. in speech, 1946, team tchr. in creative arts workshops for tchrs., 1955-56, guest lectr. Dental Sch., 1967-72, asst. prof. (part-time) of practice adminstrn. Sch. Dentistry, 1972-80; tchr. speech, drama and English, Preston (Minn.) High Sch., 1935-37; tchr. speech, drama and English, Owatonna (Minn.) High Sch., 1937-39, also dir. dramatics, 1937-39; tchr. creative dramatics and English, tchr.-counselor Webster Groves (Mo.) Jr. High Sch., 1939-40; dir. dramatics and tchr.-counselor Webster Groves Sr. High Sch., 1940-43; exec. sec. bus. and profl. dept. YWCA, Mpls., 1943-45; tchr. speech and drama Covent of the Visitation, St. Paul, 1958; editor pro-tem Am. Acad. Dental Practice Adminstrn., 1966-68; guest tchr. Coll. St. Catherine, St. Paul, 1969; vol. mgr. Gift Shop, Eitel Hosp., Mpls., 1981-83, Edina Community Resource Pool, 1992—; community citizen mem. planning, evaluating, reporting com. Edina Pub. Sch. System, 1993—; tutor for reading, writing, and speaking, 1993—; cons. for dental med. programs Normandale Community Coll., Bloomington, Minn., 1968; cons. on pub. relations to dentists, 1954—; guest lectr. to various dental groups, 1966—; lectr. Internat. Congress on Arts and Communication, 1980, Am. Inst. Banking, 1981; condr. tutorials in speaking and profl. office mgmt., 1985—; owner Shirley Schwarzrock's Exec. Support Svc., 1989—; cons. to mktg. communications mgr. Ergodyne Corp., St. Paul, 1991-92; freelance editor med. support bus., 1992. Author books (series): Coping with Personal Identity, Coping with Human Relationships, Coping with Facts and Fantasies, Coping with Teenage Problems, 1984; individual book titles include: Do I Know the "Me" Others See?, My Life-What Shall I Do With It?, Living with Loneliness, Learning to Make Better Decisions, Grades, What's So Important About Them, Anyway?, Facts and Fantasies About Alcohol, Facts and Fantasies About Drugs, Facts and Fantasies About Smoking, Food as a Crutch, Facts and Fantasies About the Roles of Men and Women, You Always Communicate Something, Appreciating People-Their Likenesses and Differences, Fitting In, To Like and Be Liked, Can You Talk With Someone Else? Coping with Emotional Pain, Some Common Crutches, Parents Can Be a Problem, Coping with Cliques, Crises Youth Face Today, Effective Dental Assisting, (with L.H. Schwarzrock) 1954, 59, 67, (with J.R. Jensen) 1973, 78, 82, (with J.R. Jensen, Kay Schwarzrock, Lorraine Schwarzrock) 1990, Workbook for Effective Dental Assisting, 1960, 68, 73, (with Lorraine Schwarzrock), 1978, 82, 90, Manual for Effective Dental Assisting, 1968, 73, 78, 82, 90; (with Donovan F. Ward), Effective Medical Assisting, 1969, 76; Workbook for Effective Medical Assisting, 1969, 76, Manual for Effective Medical Assisting, 1969, 76; (with C.G. Wrenn) The Coping With Series of Books for High School Students, 1970, 73; The Coping With Manual, 1973, Contemporary Concerns, of Youth, 1980. Pres. University Elem. Sch. PTA, 1955-56. Fellow Internat. Biog. Assn.; mem. Minn. Acad. Dental Practice Adminstrn. (hon.), Minn. Historical Soc., 1992—, Minn. Geneaolgical Soc., 1992—, Zeta Phi Eta (pres. 1948-49), Eta Sigma Upsilon. Home: 7448 W Shore Dr Edina MN 55435-4022

SCHWEGMAN, MONICA JOAN, artist; b. Hamilton, OH, Apr. 19, 1958; d. David Michael and LaVerne Henrietta (Mergy) Kiley; m. Craig Alfred Schwegman, Oct. 6, 1978; children: Craig, Sarah. Student, U. Cin., 1976-78; AAS, Brookdale C.C., 1978; postgrad., Kansas City Art Inst., 1990. Mgmt. trainee coll. coop. Marshall Fields, Chgo., 1977-78; decorator, cons. Sears, Toms River, N.J., 1985-88; artist, owner studio and gallery Lampasas, Tex., 1990-94; chmn. Keystone Art Alliance, Lampasas, 1991-94; art dir. Theatre for Lampasas, 1993-94. Instr. art City of Lampasas/Sparts, 1993. Mem. Tex. Fine Artist Assn., Lampasas C. of C. (mem. tourism com. 1993). Republican. Roman Catholic.

SCHWEGMANN, MELINDA, state official; b. Austin, Tex., Oct. 25, 1946; m. John F. Schwegmann; 3 children. Student, La. State U.; grad. in Edn., U. New Orleans, 1968. Former pub. sch. tchr.; past pres. La. Soc. for Prevention of Cruelty to Animals; lt. gov. La., 1991—. Mem. bd.

Schwegmann Giant Super Markets; chmn. bd. Goodwill Industries; bd. dirs. Met. Area Com. New Orleans; sec. bd. dir.s Jr. Achievement; former mem. Jefferson Beautification Com. Office: Office of Lt Gov PO Box 44243 Baton Rouge LA 70804*

SCHWEICKERT, TINA KATHLEEN, environmental science educator; b. Ft. Wayne, Ind., May 31, 1955; d. Jack Charles McGinley and Cynthia Constance (Custard) Schmitz; m. Hudson Lee Schweickert, June 26, 1976; children: Hudson Paul, Zebulin Adam. AA in Art, Biology, Pasadena (Calif.) City Coll., 1976; BS in Environ. Sci., Willamette U., 1989. Pres. Salem (Oreg.) Community Environ. Coun., 1989-90; coord. Salem (Oreg.) Earth Day 20th Ann., 1990-91; adminstrv. analyst trainee State Oreg. Dept. Water Resources, Forestry & Land Devel., Salem, 1990-91; adminstrv. analyst environ. outreach City of Salem (Oreg.) Pub. Works Dept., 1991—; vice-chair edn. com. Oreg. Assn. Clean Water Agys., Portland, 1993—. Founding bd. dirs. Wallamet Valley Environ. Ctr., 1993—, N.W. Land Conservation Trust, 1993—; loaned exec. United Way, Salem, 1992. Recipient Collins Acad. grant Collins Found., Willamett U., 1987-89, Environ. Edn. grant EPA, N.W. Region, 1993. Mem. Am. Water Works Assn. (conservation Pacific N.W. region 1992—), Assn. Clean Water Agys. (chair edn. com. 1991—), Salem Community Environ. Coun. (governing coun.), Internat. Assn. Pub. Participation Practioners (Oreg. chpt. 1992—). Office: City Salem Pub Works Rm 325 555 Liberty St SE Salem OR 97301

SCHWEIG, MARGARET BERRIS, meeting and special events consultant; b. Detroit, Mar. 23, 1928; d. Jacob Meyer and Anne Lucille (Schiller) Berris; m. Eugene Schweig Jr., Nov. 24, 1951 (dec.); children: Eugene III, John A., Suzanne. Student, U. Mich., 1945-47. Founder, pres. St. Louis Scene, Inc., 1975-94. Mem. St. Louis Conv. and Visitors Commn., St. Louis Forum. Mem. Meeting Planners Internat., Am. Soc. Assn. Execs., Profl. Conv. Mgmt. Assn., Nat. Assn. Exposition Mgrs., Internat. Spl. Events Soc., Hotel Sales Mgmt. Assn. (bd. dirs. 1977-80), Regional Commerce and Growth Assn., The Network (pres. 1980-81).

SCHWEIGER, BARBARA GLENNON, real estate company official; b. Mobile, Ala., Dec. 21, 1916; d. James Hope and Aurelia Eulalie (Wilds) Glennon; m. Erasmus Manford Blacksher, Jr., Nov. 8, 1938 (dec. July 1960); children: James Uriah, William Glennon, Erasmus Manford III; m. John Louis Schweiger, July 7, 1969. Grad. high sch., Mobile. Sec. Irvin Jackson & Co., Mobile, 1934-36; file clk. Pan Atlantic S.S. Corp., Mobile, 1936-39; mgr. Lauren Gift Shop, Brewton, Ala., 1961-62; saleswoman Hines Realty, Brewton, 1962-71; co-owner The Carriage House, Browton, Ala., 1965-72; saleswoman Larkin Harris Real Estate, Fairhope, Ala., 1971-90, Century 21-Gulf Bay, Inc., Foley, Ala., 1990—. Past sec. Lillian (Ala.) Women's Club, Lillian Vol. Fire Aux. Home: 35936 Boykin Blvd Lillian AL 36549-4108

SCHWEINFURTH, MONIKA LIESELOTTE, banker, educator; b. Mainz, Germany, Feb. 11, 1959; came to U.S., 1964; d. Rosemary (Dooley) Sprankel. AA, Alpena Coll., 1985, AS magna cum laude, 1987; BA in Math., U. Tex., 1990, postgrad studies, 1991—. Adminstr. Longhorn Coun. Boy Scouts Am., Fort Worth, 1992; internal auditor Citizens Nat. Bank, Weatherford, Tex., 1992—; dir. Discovery Station, Weatherford, Tex., 1993—. Mem. NAFE, Sci. Tchrs. Assn. Tex., Inst. Mgmt. Accts.

SCHWEITZER, JOYCE ANN, physical therapist, educator; b. Balt., Oct. 20, 1958; d. Ted Howard and Freda Joan (Herman) S. BA, U. Md., 1980; BS, U. Md., Balt., 1985; postgrad., Towson State U., 1981-83. Lic. phys. therapist. Nursing aide Md. Inst. Emergency Svcs. Systems, Divsn. Shock & Trauma, Balt., 1983, staff phys. therapist, 1985-88, sr. phys. therapist, 1988-91, grant coord., 1990-91; part time staff phys. therapist Bay Area Health Care, Balt., 1988-89; clin. instr. U. Md. Sch. of Medicine, Dept. Phys. Therapy, Balt., 1988—; part time staff phys. therapist Montebello Rehab. Hosp., Balt., 1989-90, assoc. dir. dept. phys. therapy, 1991—; co-rschr. various projects Md. Inst. Emergency Svcs. Systems, Balt., 1990-91, Montebello Rehab. Hosp., Balt., 1991—. Contbr. articles to profl. jours. vol. CPR instr. Am. Heart Assn., College Park, Md., 1979-91. Mem. Am. Phys. Therapy Assn., Am. Trauma Soc. Office: Montebello Rehab Hosp Dept Phys Therapy 2201 Argonne Dr Baltimore MD 21218

SCHWENDINGER, JULIA ROSALIND SIEGEL, sociology researcher; b. Rockaway Beach, N.Y., Sept. 3, 1926; d. Jacob and Lena (Pliskin) Siegel; m. Herman Schwendinger, Nov. 26, 1946; children: Jane Leni, Joseph Tom. BA, Queens Coll., 1947; MSW, Columbia U., 1950; D Criminology, U. Calif., Berkeley, 1975. Cert. tchr., Calif. Project dir. Adolescent Cmty. Survey U. Calif., Berkeley, 1963-67; dir. Women's Resource Ctr., San Francisco Sheriff's Office, 1975-76; dep. parole commr. San Francisco Bd. Parole, 1976; asst. prof. U. Nev., Las Vegas, 1976-77; vis. scholar Humboldt U., Berlin, summer 1979; adj. prof., lectr. SUNY, New Paltz, 1978-88; rsch. assoc. Inst. for Study of Social Change, Berkeley, 1986—; vis. prof. Vassar Coll., Poughkeepsie, N.Y., spring 1980, 82; vis. scholar Moscow State U., fall 1988; cons. criminologist, Berkeley, 1988; cons. Women's Crisis Ctr., SUNY, New Paltz, 1983-86, Nat. Inst. for Juvenile Justice and Delinquency Prevention, Washington, 1981-84; criminal justice planning cons. San Francisco Sheriff's Dept., 1974. Co-author: The Sociologists of the Chair, 1974, Rape and Inequality, 1983, Delinquency and Adolescent Subcultures, 1985. Recipient Outstanding Scholarship award Soc. Study of Social Problems, 1986, Career award Women's divsn. Am. Soc. Criminology, 1994. Mem. Am. Sociol. Assn. (Disting. Scholar award 1987), Western Soc. Criminology (Paul Tappan award for Most Original and Seminal Contbn. to Criminology, 1984).

SCHWIER, PRISCILLA LAMB GUYTON, television broadcasting company executive; b. Toledo, Ohio, May 8, 1939; d. Edward Oliver and Prudence (Hutchinson) L.; m. Robert T. Guyton, June 21, 1963 (dec. Sept. 1976); children—Melissa, Margaret, Robert; m. Frederick W. Schwier, May 11, 1984. B.A., Smith Coll., 1961; M.A., U. Toledo, 1972. Pres. Gt. Lakes Communications, Inc., 1982—; vice chmn. Seilon, Inc., Toledo, 1981-83, also dir. Contbr. articles to profl. jours. Trustee Wilberforce U., Ohio, 1983—, Planned Parenthood, Toledo, 1979-83, Maumee Valley Country Day Sch., Toledo; bd. dirs. N.W. Ohio Hospice, 1991—. Episcopal Ch., Maumee, Ohio, 1983—; bd. trustees Toledo Hosp., Maumee Country Day Sch., 1986-92; pres. Edward Lamb Found., 1987—. Democrat. Episcopalian. Home: 345 E Front St Perrysburg OH 43551-2131 Office: 129 W Wayne St Ste 100 Maumee OH 43537-2150

SCHWIND, JANET KAY, writer; b. South Bend, Ind., Oct. 1, 1962; d. Robert Dale and Catherine (Carlino) S. BA in Journalism, English, Ind. U., 1984. Copy editor South Bend Tribune, 1984-85; jr. copywriter, copy editor Juhl Advt., Elkhart, Ind., 1985-86; freelance writer South Bend, 1986, 92-93; copywriter, producer Nitz, Rosheck, McLaughlin & Bowers, South Bend, 1986-87, Juhl Mktg. Communications, Mishawaka, Ind., 1987-91; copywriter Communico, Indpls., 1993—. Vol. spl. events United Way St. Joseph County, South Bend, 1992-93. Recipient 1st Pl. award (copr. video) Bus. Profls. Advt. Assn., Cin., 1992, 1st Pl. Tower Arlend Video award, Chgo., 1992. Office: Communico 5804 Churchman By-Pass Indianapolis IN 46203

SCHWINN-JORDAN, BARBARA (BARBARA SCHWINN), painter; b. Glen Ridge, N.J.; d. Carl Wilhelm Ludwig and Helen Louise (Jordan) Schwinn; m. Frank Bertram Jordan, Jr.; children: Janine Jordan, Frank Bertram III. Grad. N.Y. Sch. Fine and Applied Art (Parsons), N.Y. and Paris; student Grand Cen. Art Sch., Art Students League, Grand Chaumiere, Academie Julien-Paris, Columbia U., NAD. Illustrator mags. including Vogue, 1930's, Ladies Home Jour., Saturday Evening Post, Colliers, Good Housekeeping, Cosmopolitan, McCall's, American, Town and Country, 1940's-60's. Women's Jour., Eng., Hors Zu, Fed. Republic Germany, Marie Claire, France, other fgn. publs., 1950's-60's. Portrait painter, including Queen Sirikit, Princess Margaret, Princess Grace; freelance painter, 1970—; one-man shows include Soc. of Illustrators, 1940, 50, Barry Stephens Gallery, 1950, Bodley Gallery, N.Y.C., 1971, 80, Community Coll., West Mifflin, Pa., 1973, Duquesne U., 1973, Mus. Am. Illustration, N.Y.C., 1991, Illustration House, N.Y.C., 1991, Giraffics Gallery, East Hampton, N.Y., 1991,92, 93, 94, 95 (also rep.); exhibited in group shows including NAD, 1955, Royal Acad., London, Guild Hall, N.Y., 1981, Summit N.J. Art Ctr., 1981, Meredith Long Gallery, Houston, 1983, Mus. Soc. Illustrators, N.Y., 1985, The Marcus Gallery, Sante Fe, 1985, 86, The Gerald Peters Gallery, Santa Fe, 1985, 86, Brandywine Mus., Pa., 1986, New Britain (Conn.) Mus. Am. Art, 1986, Armory Show, N.Y.C., 1992, 93, 94, The Women's Ctr., Chapel Hill, N.C., 1993, 94, Greenville County Mus. Art, S.C., 1995, The Soc. of the Four Art, Palm Beach, Fla., 1995, The Hyde Collection, Glens Falls, N.Y., 1995, Ga. Mus. Art, 1995, Heckscher Mus., L.I., N.Y., 1995; works represented Holbrook Collection, Ga. Mus. Art, Eureka Coll., Ill., New Britain Mus. Am. Art, Mus. of Soc. of Illustrators, N.Y.C., Brandywine Mus., Pa., Sanford Low Meml. Collection, Del. Art Mus., Wilmington, Mus. Am. Illustration, N.Y.C., Glenbow Mus., Calgary, Alberta, Can.; represented in traveling show Del. Art Mus. 1994, 95; various pvt. and gallery collections; work featured in America's Great Women Illustrators 1850-1950, 1985; lectr., instr. illustration Parsons Sch., 1952-54; founder adv. coun. Art Instrn. Sch., 1956-70. Chmn. art com. UNICEF greeting cards, 1950-61 mem. com. Spence Chapin Sch., Philharm. Soc., 1950's-60's. Winner prizes Art Dirs. Club, 1950, Guild Hall, 1969. Assoc. mem. Guggenheim Mus. Mem. Cosmopolitan Club N.Y. Author: Technique of Barbara Schwinn, 1956; World of Fashion Art, 1968. Home and Studio: 579 Fearrington Post Fearrington V NC 27312-8570

SCHWOERER, LOIS GREEN, history educator; b. Roanoke, Va.; d. Edward Shelley and Emma Lois (Hester) Green; m. Frank Schwoerer, June 25, 1949; 1 child, John Arnold. B.A. summa cum laude, Smith Coll., 1949; M.A., Bryn Mawr Coll., 1952, Ph.D., 1956. Tchr. social studies Shipley Sch., Bryn Mawr, Pa., 1949-51; instr. dept. history Bryn Mawr Coll., 1954-55; lectr. dept. history U. Pitts., 1962-63; assoc. professorial lectr. George Washington U., Washington, 1964-65, asst. prof. history, 1965-68, assoc. prof., 1968-76, prof., 1976—, chmn. dept., 1979-81, Elmer Louis Kayser chair, 1992—. Author: No Standing Armies! The Anti Standing Army Ideology in Seventeenth-Century England, 1975 (Berkshire Conf. Women Historians prize 1975); The Declaration of Rights 1689, 1981; Lady Rachel Russell (1637-1723), 1988; editor: The Revolution of 1688-89: Changing Perspectives, 1992; co-editor: The Varieties of British Political Thought, 1994. Contbr. articles to profl. jours. Chmn. Allegheny County council LWV, 1962-63, mem. state bd., 1961, pres. Mt. Lebanon, Pa. chpt., 1957-61; sr. fellow Nat. Endowment for Humanities, 1975, Folger Shakespeare Libr., 1978. Recipient Albert Love Prize, 1985, Carolinas Symposium Prize, 1987; grantee Am. Philosophical Soc., 1971-72, Nat. Endowment for Humanities. Fellow Royal Hist. Soc.; mem. N.Am. Conf. Brit. Studies (pres. 1987-89), Ctr. for Study of Brit. Polit. Thought, Am. Hist. Assn., Renaissance Soc. Am., Cosmos Club, Phi Beta Kappa. Office: George Washington U Dept History Washington DC 20052

SCIACCA, KATHLEEN, psychologist; b. N.Y.C., Jan. 19, 1943; d. Rosario and Angela (Pucciarelli) S.; children: Kenneth Mortellaro, Cheryl Ann Mortellaro. BS in Psychology, SUNY, Empire State, 1976; MA in Psychology, New Sch. for Social Rsch., 1980, postgrad., 1980. Pvt. practice, 1976—; primary therapist, vocat. coord., program developer Bronx-Lebanon Hosp., South Bronx, N.Y., 1977-84; mental health program specialist N.Y. State Office of Mental Health, N.Y. statewide, 1984-92; founding exec. dir. Sciacca Comprehensive Svc. Devel. Mental Illness, Drug Addiction and Alcoholism, N.Y.C., 1990—, nat. lectr., program devel. for dual and multiple disorders; fellow New England, Providence, R.I., 1992-93; cons. program devel. Am. Assn. for Partial Hospitalization, Washington, 1987-91, Columbia U., N.Y.C., 1991, Southcentral Counseling Ctr., Anchorage, Alaska, 1991—, Alaska Dept. Mental Health, 1992—, Jackson-Hillsdale Mental Health, Mich., 1993—, Southeastern Conn. Community Mental Health, 1993—, Advocates, Framingham, Mass., 1993—, numerous mental depts. and substance abuse depts. accross the country; nat. and internat. presenter and cons. in field. Author/developer: (manual-book) Mental Illness, Drug Addiction and Alcoholism (MIDAA) Service Manual, 1990; prodr. (edn. and tng. video) Integrated Treatment for MIDAA across Alaska; contbr. articles to profl. jours., chpts. to books. Mem. APA (assoc.), N.Y. State Psychol. Assn. (assoc., com. on Alcoholism, Drug Abuse and other Addictions), Nat. Assn. Masters in Psychology, Soc. Psychologists in Addictive Behaviors. Home and Office: 299 Riverside Dr Apt 3E New York NY 10025-5289

SCIANNAMEO, MARIA LUIGIA, secondary education educator; b. Gravina, Italy, Mar. 8, 1952; d. Nicola and Rosalia (Grassi) S. AA in Liberal Arts, Quinsigamond C.C., Worcester, Mass., 1972; BS in Secondary Edn., Worcester State Coll., 1974; diploma in acctg., New England Sch. Acctg., Worcester, Mass., 1981; MBA in Bus. Adminstrn., Anna Maria Coll., Paxton, Mass., 1985. Cert. secondary education, math., English, Mass. Tchr., math., computers Worcester Pub. Schs., Mass., 1974-82, 86—; staff acct. Elkay Products, Inc., Shrewsbury, Mass., 1980, 86; part-time instr. in acctg, New England Sch. Acctg., 1980-81, 93-94, Ctrl. New England Coll., 1984-89; Dudley Hall Car. Inst., 1990-91; mem. curriculum devel. com. Math. and Sci. K-12, Worcester, 1994—. Coord., organizer religious edn. for adult converts Our Lady of Mt. Carmel, St. Ann Parish, Worcester, 1970—. Fulbright Tchr. grant U.S. Info. Agy. Tchr. Exchange, Washington, 1994. Mem. Nat. Tchrs. Assn., Mass. Tchrs. Assn., Edn. Assn. Worcester. Roman Catholic. Home: 35 General Ave Shrewsbury MA 01545

SCOBELL, ELIZABETH HIGHT, librarian; b. Bluefield, W.Va.; d. Joel E. and Louise Ellen (Allen) Hight; m. Emmett W. Denerson, June 5, 1955 (div. Feb., 1962); 1 child, Emmett W.; m. Scott E. Scobell, Aug., 1969. BA, Bennett Coll., 1952; MS in Libr. Sci., Atlanta U., 1955. Cert. tchr., Ga. Tchr., libr. Morristown (Tenn.) Coll., 1953-54; asst. libr. Ft. Valley (Ga.) State Coll., 1954-57; libr. Peter G. Appling High Sch., Macon, Ga., 1958-62; asst. libr. W.Va. State Coll., Inst., Institute, 1962-71, 1971-74; dir. devel. W.Va. State Coll., Institute, 1971-74, reference libr., 1974-88, dir. libr., 1988—. Rsch. asst. (book) From the Grove to the Stars, 1991. Active Equal Opportunity Affirmative Action Coun., W.Va. Bd. Regents, Charleston, W.Va., 1988-91, adv. bd. W.Va. Hist. Records. Grantee Coll. Libr. Tech. and Cooperation, Grant Program U.S. Office of Edn., 1990, NEH, 1994. Mem. W.Va. Libr. Assn., Am. Libr. Assn., Soc. Am. Archivist. Methodist. Home: 2135 Pennsylvania Ave Saint Albans WV 25177-3557 Office: WVa State Coll Drain-Jordan Libr Institute WV 25112-1002

SCOBEY, JOAN MOISSEIFF, writer, editor; b. N.Y.C.; d. Siegfried and Frieda (Loewe) Moisseiff; children: David, Richard. BA, Smith Coll. Author: Stained Glass, 1979, Short Rations, 1980, I'm A Stranger Here Myself, 1984, Fannie Farmer Junior Cookbook, 1993, numerous others; editor: Cooking with Michael Field, 1978; contbr. numerous articles to mags. Mem. PEN, Authors Guild, Am. Soc. Authors and Journalists, Soc. Am. Travel Writers.

SCOBEY, SALLY ESTELLE, speaker; b. Grand Rapids, Mich., June 19, 1954; d. Clinton H. and Betty Jane (Davies) S.; m. Philip H. Biggs, Sept. 15, 1984; 1 child, Christopher James. BS in Radio and TV cum laude, Butler U., 1976. Documentary writer, prodr. Am. Cable, Traverse City, Mich., 1976; reporter WXEX-TV, Richmond, Va., 1976-78; reporter, anchor, prodr. WOOD-TV, Grand Rapids, 1978-84; freelance writer Sally Scobey and Assocs., Grand Rapids, 1984-89; prin. Total Comm. Svcs., Milw., 1987-89; owner Communication Works, West Dundee, Ill., 1989—; speaker, trainer Dun & Bradstreet, N.Y.C., 1987-89, Career Track, Boulder, Colo., 1988—; freelance writer USA Today, Washington, 1986, Chgo. (Ill.) Trib., 1990—. Author: (workbook) Power Writing, 1987; (audio tape albums) Profitable Publicity, 1992, Focused Listening Skills, 1995. Media trainer Kent County Commrs., Grand Rapids, 1986. Recipient Journalism Excellence award Indpls. Press Club, 1976. Mem. Profl. Speakers Ill. (speaking profl. designation), Nat. Speakers Assn. Office: Communication Works PO Box 1023 West Dundee IL 60118-7023

SCOLLARD, DIANE LOUISE, educator; b. Seattle, Mar. 12, 1945; d. James Martin and Viola Gladys (Williams) S. BA in Edn., Wash. State U., 1967; 5th yr. cert. in edn., U. Wash., 1970; cert. edn., Oakland U., 1977. Tchr. Battle Ground (Wash.) Sch. Dist., 1967-70, Lapeer (Mich.) Community Schs., 1970—. Mem. AAUW, NEA, NAFE, Am. Bus. Women's Assn., Mich. Edn. Assn., Lapeer Edn. Assn. (bldg. rep. 1985, 89), Beta Sigma Phi. Democrat. Episcopalian. Office: Elba Elem Sch 300 N Elba Rd Lapeer MI 48446-8052

SCOTCHLAS, JOANNE MARIE, nurse; b. Carbondale, Pa., Nov. 25, 1958; d. Joseph Charles and Leona Eleanor Alice (Perkowski) S. Diploma in nursing, Allentown (Pa.) Hosp. Sch. of Nursing, 1979; BS, St. Joseph Coll., 1990. RN, Pa.; cert. case mgr. Staff nurse Lehigh Valley Hosp., Allentown, Pa., 1979-81, 82-84, home health nurse, 1984-90; dir. profl. svcs. Kimberly Quality Care, Allentown, 1990-91; charge nurse medication treatment Fellowship Manor, Whitehall, Pa., 1991-92; pvt. duty pediatric nurse SNI, Flourtown, Pa., 1991; case mgr. Aetna Ins. Co., Allentown, 1991-92; charge nurse head trauma unit Good Shepard Rehab. Hosp., Allentown, 1992-93; nurse case mgr. CNA Ins. Co., Reading, Pa., 1993-94; nursing supr. VNA Easton, Easton, Pa., 1994—; vis. nurse Visiting Nurses Assn., Allentown, 1981, Easton, 1993—. Sec. Pulaski Found., Bethlehem, Pa., 1980. Mem. Nat. Assn. Rehab. Nurses, Cath. Nurses Assn. (bd. dirs. 1992-94), Home Healthcare Nurse Assn., Mack Ski Club. Home: 437 E Belvidere St Nazareth PA 18064

SCOTT, ADRIENNE, social worker, psychotherapist; b. N.Y.C., Apr. 17, 1937; d. William and Anne Scott; m. Ross F. Grumet, Nov. 10, 1957 (div. Aug. 1969). BA, Finch Coll., 1957; postgrad., NYU, 1958-62, MA in English, 1958; MSW, Adelphi U., 1988. Mem. English faculty Fordham U., N.Y.C., 1966-68; editor Blueboy Mag., Miami, Fla., 1974; freelance writer N.Y.C., 1958-66; mem. English faculty NYU, 1958-65; pres. Googolplex Video, N.Y.C., 1981-86; social worker Mt. Sinai Hosp., N.Y.C., 1988-93, Cabrini Hosp., N.Y.C., 1993—; presenter Nat. Methadone Conf., 1992. Author: Film as Film, 1970; contbr. articles to profl. jours. Mem. NASW (cert.), AAUW, Assn. for Psychoanalytic Self Psychology. Home: 165 E 66th St New York NY 10021 Office: 7 Patchin Pl New York NY 10011

SCOTT, ALICE H., librarian; b. Jefferson, Ga.; d. Frank D. and Annie D. (Colbert) Holly; m. Alphonso Scott, Mar. 1, 1959; children—Christopher, Alison. A.B., Spelman Coll., Atlanta, 1957; M.L.S., Atlanta U., 1958; Ph.D., U. Chgo., 1983. Librarian Bklyn. Pub. Library, 1958-59; br. librarian Chgo. Pub. Library, 1959-72, dir. Woodson Regional Library, 1974-77, dir. community relations, 1977-82, dep. commr., 1982-87, asst. commr., 1987—. Doctoral fellow, 1973. Mem. ALA (councilor 1982-85), Ill. Library Assn., Chgo. Spelman Club, DuSable Mus., Chgo. Urban League. Democrat. Baptist. Office: Chgo Pub Library 400 S State St Chicago IL 60605-1203

SCOTT, AMY ANNETTE HOLLOWAY, nursing educator; b. St. Albans, W.Va., Apr. 10, 1916; d. Oliver and Mary (Lee) Holloway; m. William M. Jefferson, June 22, 1932, (div. Oct. 1933); 1 child, William M. Jefferson, m. Vann Hyland Scott, Mar. 15, 1952, (dec. Dec. 1972). BS in Nursing Edn., Cath. U., Washington, 1948; cert. in psychiat. nursing, U. Paris, Paris, 1959. Indsl. nurse Curtiss Wright Air Plane Co., Lambert Field, St. Louis, 1941-44; faculty St. Thomas U., Manila, Philippines Island, 1948-50; pub. health nurse St. Louis Health Dept., 1951-56; capt. USAF Nursing Corps, Paris, 1956-60; resigned as maj. USAF (Nurse Corps), 1960, 1960; faculty St. Louis State Hosp., 1960-67; dept. head St. Vincents Hosp., St. Louis, 1967-68; faculty RN, creator psychiat. program Sch. of Nursing Jewish Hosp., 1968-72; adminstrv. nurse St. Louis State Hosp., 1972-84; initiated first psychiatric program sch. nursing, Jewish Hosp. Author: (short story) Two Letters, 1962, (novel) Storms, 1987, Life's Journey, 1993. Past bd. dirs. county bd. Mo. U., 1984-88; hon. citizen Colonial Williamsburg, Va.; mem. Rep. Presdl. Task Force; mem. Women in the Arts '94. Recipient Key to Colonial Williamsburg, Va., Medal of Merit, Rep. Presdl. Task Force, 1992; named to Rep. Presdl. Task Force Honor Roll, 1993. Mem. AAUW, NAFE, Internat. Fedn. Univ. Women, Internat. Soc. Quality Assurance in Health Care, Am. Biog. Inst. (life, governing bd.), Cambridge Centre Eng., Internat. Platform Assn. Roman Catholic.

SCOTT, ANNA MARIE PORTER WALL, sociology educator; b. South Fulton, Tenn.; d. Thomas Madison and Jevvie Roggie (Patton) P.; m. John T. Scott Sr. (dec.); 1 child, Harvey G. BA, U. Ill., MEd, MSW. Cert. tchr. and social worker, Ill. Caseworker Dept. Pub. Aid, Champaign, Ill.; psychiat. social worker Vets. Hosp., Danville, Ill.; prof. sociology Parkland Coll., Champaign, Ill. Mem. Dem. Cen. Com., 1974-78; head Dem. 21st Congl. Dist., 1974-78; del. Nominating Conv./Mini Conv., 1975, 76; vol. Nominating Com., 1988; mem. AME Ch., Hadassah; mem. Vet. of Armed Svcs. Named Outstanding Black Alumni, U. Ill., Urbana, 1977. Mem. LWV, NAACP, Nat. Coun. Negro Women (past pres.), Am. Legion, AMVETS, Champaign-Urbana Symphony Guild, Order Ea. Star (grand organist Eureka Grand chpt.). Home: 309 W Michigan Ave Urbana IL 61801-4945 Office: Parkland Coll 2400 W Bradley Ave Champaign IL 61821-1806

SCOTT, ANNE BYRD FIROR, history educator; b. Montezuma, Ga., Apr. 24, 1921; d. John William and Mary Valentine (Moss) Firor; m. Andrew Mackay Scott, June 2, 1947; children: Rebecca, David MacKay, Donald MacKay. AB, U. Ga., 1941; MA, Northwestern U., 1944; PhD, Radcliffe Coll., 1958; LHD (hon.), Lindenwood Coll., 1968, Queens Coll., 1985, Northwestern U., 1989, Radcliffe Coll., 1990, U. of the South, 1990, Cornell Coll., 1991. Congressional rep., editor LWV of U.S., 1944-53; lectr. history Haverford Coll., 1957-58, U. N.C., Chapel Hill, 1959-60; asst. prof. history Duke U., Durham, N.C., 1961-67; assoc. prof. Duke U., 1968-70, prof., 1971-80, W.K. Boyd prof., 1980-91, W.K. Boyd prof. emerita, 1992—, chmn. dept., 1981-85; Gastprofessor Universität, Bonn, Germany, 1992-93; vis. prof. Johns Hopkins U., 1972-73, Stanford U., 1974, Harvard U., 1984, Cornell U., 1993, Williams Bernhard Coll., 1994; vice chmn. Nat. Humanities Ctr., 1991—; mem. adv. com. Schlesinger Libr.; Fulbright lectr, 1984, 92-93. Author: The Southern Lady, 1970, (with Andrew MacKay Scott) One Half the People, 1974, Making the Invisible Woman Visible, 1984, Natural Allies, 1991; editor: Jane Addams, Democracy and Social Ethics, 1964, The American Woman, 1970, Women in American Life, 1970, Women and Men in American Life, 1976, Unheard Voices, 1993; mem. editorial bd. Revs. in Am. History, 1976-81, Am. Quar., 1974-78, Jour. So. History, 1978-84; contbr. articles to profl. jours. Chmn. Gov.'s Commn. on Status of Women, 1963-64; mem. Citizens Adv. Council on Status of Women U.S., 1964-68. AAUW fellow, 1956-57; grantee NEH, 1967-68, 76-77, Nat. Humanities Ctr., 1980-81; fellow Ctr. Advanced Study in Behavioral Sci., 1986-87; Fulbright scholar, 1984, 92-93. Mem. Am. Antiquarian Soc., Orgn. Am. Historians (exec. bd. 1973-76, pres. 1983), So. Hist. Assn. (exec. bd. 1976-79, pres. 1989), Soc. Am. Historians, Phi Beta Kappa. Democrat. Office: Duke U Dept History Durham NC 27708

SCOTT, BERNICE PARKER, nurse; b. Jasper, Fla., Jan. 31, 1939; d. Samuel James and Louise (Roberson) Parker; divorced; children: Erroll Dewayne Scott, Darryl Andre Scott. Diploma, Brewster Dural Sch. Nursing, Fla., 1959; BSN, U. Fla., 1976; MEd, U. Ctrl. Fla., 1986. Staff nurse Christian Hosp., Miami, Fla., 1959-61; staff nurse to head nurse Jackson Meml. Hosp., Miami, Fla., 1961-68; head nurse Orlando (Fla.) Regional Med. Ctr., 1968-80; staff nurse outpatient clinic Dept. Vet. Affairs, Orlando, Fla., 1980—. Sec. Orlando Women Civic Club, Fla., 1975-86, pres. 1986—. Mem. Nat. Black Nurses Assn. (scholarship chairperson local chpt.), Ctrl. Fla. Black Nurses Assn. (sec. 1985, 87). Democrat. Baptist. Home: 439 Ventura Ave Orlando FL 32805

SCOTT, BETTINA VARNELL MONROE, federal agency administrator; b. Balt., Jan. 4, 1941; d. Robert Henry and Lillie Daisey (Conyers) Monroe; m. Joseph Clayton Scott, Jr., May 20, 1967 (div. May 1992); children: Joseph, III, Jason-Robert. AA, C.C. Balt., 1961; BS, Towson State U., 1963; MA in History, Morgan State U., 1967; PhD, U. Md., 1979. Tchr. Balt. City Pub. Schs., 1963-72, 75-78; mgmt. cons. ABT Assocs., Washington, 1972-75; cons. Dynamac/Informatics Corp., Rockville, Md., 1978-83, Univ. Rsch. Corp., Chevy Chase, Md., 1983-87; br. chief Alcohol, Drug Abuse and Mental Health Svcs. Adminstrn./Substance Abuse and Mental Health Svcs. Adminstrn., Rockville, 1987-92; acting assoc. adminstr. Substance Abuse and Mental Health Svcs. Adminstrn., Rockville, 1992—. Author: (children's book) Buzzy's Rebound, 1986, (booklet) Ten Steps to Help Your Child, 1988; contbr. articles to profl. jours. Bd. trustees Concord Bapt. Ch., Balt., 1989—; bd. mgrs. Nat. Edn. Found., Washington, 1990—; trustee Myrtle Tyler Faithful Fund, Balt., 1994. Recipient Sec.'s Commendation award U.S. Dept. Health and Human Svcs., 1989, Dir.'s award Ctr. Substance Abuse Prevention, 1990. Fellow Phi Delta Kappa; mem. APHA (com. chair 1991-94, Svc. award 1994), Fed. Exec. Inst. Alumni Assn., PAMS Social Club (pres. 1967, treas. 1969), Zeta Phi Beta (treas. 1983-87, Svc. award 1987, 90, Cmty. Forum award 1990). Office: Sub Abuse & Mental Health Svcs Adminstrn 5600 Fishers Ln Rockville MD 20857

SCOTT, BONNIE CELESTE, geriatrics nurse; b. Tampa, Fla., June 28, 1948; d. James Louis and Elizabeth Dendy (Snyder) Billups; m. George Vincent Scott, June 29, 1970; children: Laura Elizabeth, Michael Sean, Sara

Joy. BA in Psychology summa cum laude, U. North Fla., 1990. RN, Fla. Staff nurse Richmond (Va.) Meml. Hosp., 1971-72, Upjohn Homemakers, Seattle and Norfolk, Va., 1972-73; charge nurse Crest House, Seattle, 1974-75; sch. nurse Dept. Def. Sch., Pusan, Korea, 1980-81; campus nurse U. North Fla., Jacksonville, 1982; nursing supr. Orange Park (Fla.) Care Ctr., 1986-87, staff developer, 1987-88, asst. dir. nursing, 1989-90; dir. nursing Arbors at Orange Park, 1990-92, staff devel. dir., 1992; care plan coord. and patient educator Heartland Health Care Ctr., Orange Park, Fla., 1993—. Contbg. author CME Resource. Mem. Nat. Gerontol. Nursing Assn., Phi Kappa Phi. Republican. Baptist. Home: 626 Tara Farm Dr Doctors Inlet FL 32068 Office: Heartland Health Care Ctr 570 Wells Rd Orange Park FL 32073

SCOTT, CAROL LEE, child care educator; b. Monte Vista, Colo., Jan. 10, 1944; d. Robert A. and Thelma G. (Allen) Jay; m. Bates E. Shaw, June 4, 1966 (dec. Feb. 1976); children: Crystal A., Sharon L.; m. James W. Scott, July 23, 1977. BA in Home Econs., Friends U., 1965; MS, Okla. State U., 1973. Cert. home economist; lic. profl. counselor. Receptionist Cen. Assembly of God Ch., Wichita, Kans., summer 1965; office worker Henry's Inc., Wichita, 1965-66; tchr. home econs. Wichita High Sch. South, 1966, Cir. High Sch., Towanda, Kans., 1966-68, Fairfax (Okla.) High Sch., 1968-74; tchr. vocat. home econs. Derby (Kans.) High Sch., 1974-75; child devel. specialist Bi-State Mental Health Found., Ponca City, Okla., 1975-87; instr. child care Pioneer Tech. Ctr., Ponca City, 1987—, dir., 1987-89, 93—; cons. Phil Fitzgerald Assocs. Archs., Ponca City, 1980, Head Start Okla., 1981-86; trainer, paraprofl. Child Care Careers, 1980—. Contbg. author Child Abuse Prevention Mini Curriculum. Mem. sch. bd. Ponca City Schs., 1982-85, title IV-A parent com., 1985-89; area chmn. Heart Fund, 1985; chmn. edn. com. Dist. XVII Child Abuse Prevention Task Force, Okla., 1985—, treas., 1989—; mem. cultural affairs com. Ponca City Adv. Bd., 1986-89; co-chair Week of the Young Child Com. for Kay County, 1991—. Mem. NEA, Am. Vocat. Assn., Am. Assn. Family and Consumer Scis., Okla. Assn. Family and Consumer Scis., Okla. Vocat. Assn., Okla. Assn. Vocat. Home Econs. Tchrs., Okla. Edn. Assn., Okla. Asn. for the Edn. Young Children, Okla. Early Childhood Assn., So. Early Childhood Assn., No. Okla. Early Childhood Assn. (chair 1992-93, past chair 1993-94), Nat. Assn. Vocat. Home Econs. Tchrs., Nat. Assn. for the Edn. Young Children (validator for early childhood programs seeking accreditation by divsn. Nat. Acad. Early Childhood Programs 1992—), Friends of Day Care, LWV. Republican. Methodist. Home: 414 Virginia Ave Ponca City OK 74601-3436

SCOTT, CATHERINE DOROTHY, librarian, information consultant; b. Washington, June 21, 1927; d. Leroy Stearns Scott and Agnes Frances (Meade) Scott Schellenberg. AB in English, Cath. U. Am., 1950, MS in Library Sci., 1955. Asst. Librarian Export-Import Bank U.S.A., Washington, 1951-55; asst. librarian Nat. Assn. Home Builders, 1955-62, reference librarian, 1956-62; founder, chief tech. librarian, Bellcomm, Inc., subs. AT&T, Washington, 1962-72; chief librarian Nat. Air and Space Mus., Smithsonian Instn., Washington, 1972-82, chief librarian Mus. Reference Ctr., 1982-88, sr. reference librarian, 1989—; bd. visitors Cath. U. Am. Library Sci. Sch. and Libraries, 1984-93; apptd. by Pres., mem. Nat. Commn. Libraries and Info. Sci., 1971-76. Editor International Handbook of Aerospace Awards and Trophies, 1980, 81; guest editor Aeronautics and Space Flight Collections, 1985, in Spl. Collections, 1984. Vice-chmn. D.C. Rep. Com., 1960-68; mem. platform com. Rep. Nat. Com., 1964, sec., 1968; del. Rep. Nat. Conv., San Francisco, 1964, Miami, Fla., 1968. Recipient Sec.'s Disting. Service award Smithsonian Instn., 1976, Alumni Achievement award Cath. U. Am., 1977, Disting. Fed. Svc. Nat. Comm. Libr. and Info. Sci. medal, 1985. Mem. Spl. Librs. Assn. (pres. Washington chpt. 1973-74, cons. 1976-89, chmn. cons. com. 1994—, chmn. aerospace div. 1980-81, aerospace divsn. 30th anniversary com. 1995, Disting. Svc. award 1982, nat. dir. 1986-89, bd. dirs. 1986-89, 91-94, Washington chpt. awards com. 1990-91, assn. pres.-elect 1991-92, pres. 1992-93, immediate past pres. 1993-94, chair assn. awards and honors 1994-95), Am. Soc. Assn. Execs. (internat. roundtable), Am. Soc. Info. Scis. (com. chmn.), Internat. Fedn. Library Assns. (del. 1976, 83, 85, 88, 89), Friends of Cath. U. Libraries (founder, pres. 1984-88, exec. coun. 1984—), Nat. Fedn. Rep. Women, Rep. Women's Fed. Forum, League Rep. Women D.C. (dir. mem. 1995—), Capital Yacht Club (Washington). Roman Catholic. Office: Smithsonian Instn Cen Ref and Loan SI Librs NHB 27 Washington DC 20560

SCOTT, DEBORAH EMONT, curator; b. Passaic, N.J.; d. Harold and Rhoda (Baumgarten) Emont; m. George Andrew Scott, June 4, 1983; children: Meredith Suzanne, Diana Faith. BA, Rutgers U., 1973; MA, Oberlin Coll., 1979. Asst. curator Allen Meml. Art Mus., Oberlin, Ohio, 1977-79; curator collections Memphis Brooks Mus. Art, 1979-83; curator The Nelson-Atkins Mus. Art, Kansas City, 1983—; project dir. Henry Moore Sculpture Garden, 1986—. Author: (catalogue) Alan Shields, 1983, (essay) Jonathan Borofsky, 1988, (essay) Judith Shea, 1989, (interview) John Ahearn, 1990, (essay) Gerhard Richter, 1990, (essay) Kathy Muehlemann, 1991, (essay) Nate Fors, 1991, (essay) Julian Schnabel, 1991, (essay) Louise Bourgeois, 1994. Office: Nelson-Atkins Mus Art 4525 Oak St Kansas City MO 64111-1818

SCOTT, ELIZABETH, social service administrator; b. Aberdeen, Md., Sept. 28, 1954; d. Thomas and Mary Alberta (Adams) S.; 1 child, Cha Rae L'Nise. Student, Md. Inst. Coll. Art, Balt., 1972-75, U. Balt., 1977-79. Employment counselor City of Balt., 1976-78; supr. U.S. Postal Svc., Balt., 1978-83; work study counselor Westside Skill Ctr., Balt., 1984-85; gen. mgr. 32d St. Pla., Balt., 1985-87; office mgr. Md. Citizen Action Coalition, Balt., 1988-89; exec. dir. Coalition of Peninsula Orgns., Balt., 1989-93, Heart, Body and Soul, Inc., Balt., 1993; legis. coord. Planned Parenthood of Md., Balt., 1993-94; exec. dir. Balt. Housing Roundtable, 1994—; faculty assoc. Johns Hopkins U., Balt., 1993—; cons. Johns Hopkins U. Sch. of Pub. Health, Balt., 1993—; exec. com. Inner City Community Devel. Corp., 1990-92. Bd. dirs. Light St. Housing Corp., Balt., Balt. Cable Access Corp.; media rep. Save Our Cities March on Washington, 1991-92; mem. jazz comm. Md. Mus. of African Art, Columbia, 1994—; mem. Walters Art Gallery, Balt., Md.; charter mem. Libr. of Congress, Washington; mem. gubernatorial transition team subcom. neighborhood revitalization and cmty. devel. Md. Forward, 1994. Recipient Contbn. award Balt. Commonwealth, 1992, Balt. City Pub. Schs., 1990, Community Svc. award State of md., 1990, 91, 92, Svc. award United Way of Cen. Md., 1991, Svc. award U.S. Postal Svc., 1983. Mem. Balt. Recycling Coalition, Md. Citizen Action Coalition (bd. dirs.), S. Balt. Youth Ctr. (bd. dirs., pres. 1992—), Jobs With Peace (bd. dirs. 1989-91), Md. Low Income Housing Info. Svc. (bd. dirs. 1989-91). Office: Balt Housing Round Table 1714 St Paul St Baltimore MD 21202

SCOTT, ELOISE HALE, state legislator; b. Benton County, Miss., Jan. 24, 1932; m. Lex B. Scott; children: Kenny, Kimble. BS, Miss. U. for Women; MA, U. Miss. Mem. Miss. Ho. of Reps.; vice chmn. edn. com., mem. appropriations, banks and banking, and ethics coms. Active Lee County Ext. Svc. Mem. LWV, Dem. Women. Methodist. Democrat. Home: Rte 3 Box 102 Tupelo MS 38801 Office: Miss State Senate State Capitol Jackson MS 39201*

SCOTT, EMILY WALKER, nurse, infection control and employee health director; b. Stevensville, Va., Oct. 1, 1936; d. Lewis Edward and Ruth Garnett (Fleet) Walker; m. George Henderson Stowe, Jr., Aug. 6, 1954 (div. 1957); 1 child, Elizabeth Darlene Stowe; m. Conrad Benton Scott, Aug. 8, 1960; children: Randolph Edward, Patricia Lee, Ruth Michelle. LPN, Med. Coll. Va., 1959; ADN, Rockingham C.C., 1979. RN, cert. nurse adminstr., N.C. Labor and delivery nurse Med. Coll. of Va., Richmond, 1959-62; med. surg. nurse Morehead Meml. Hosp., Eden, N.C., 1965-75, med. surg., labor and delivery nurse, 1975-80, dir. inservice edn., employee health, 1980-89, dir. infection control, employee health, 1989—; bd. dirs. Rockingham County HIV/AIDS Coalition, Wentworth, N.C., 1992-94, pres. 1995-96; cons. occupl. health classes McMichael, Morehead, Rockingham County schs. and Rockingham C.C., 1986-94. Choir mem. Spray Bapt. Ch., 1982-94, Sunday sch. tchr., 1985-94, bd. trustees, 1987-88; activities com. Morehead Meml. Hosp., Eden., 1988-94. Mem. Assn. Practitioners in Infection Control & Epidemiology. Office: Morehead Meml Hosp 117 E Kings Hwy Eden NC 27288-5299

SCOTT, GLORIA, publishing marketing consultant; b. N.Y.C., May 22, 1927; d. Matthew and Ethel Lindenberg; m. Sidney Steinberg, Mar. 2, 1947 (dec. 1969); children: Marcy Lea Chessler, Cindy Ann Sachs; m. John Lenard Scott, Dec. 1, 1974 (div. May 1991). BBA, CCNY, 1947; MEd, Temple U., 1963. Adminstr. Rahmani Trading Corp., N.Y.C., 1947-50; acct. Pola Stout Corp., Phila., 1950-54; adminstr. Bristol Twp. Police Dept., Pa., 1954-58; acct. Odora Corp., N.Y.C., 1958-59, Middletown Twp., Neshaminy, Pa., 1959-60; tchr., chmn. social studies dept. Pennsbury Schs., Falls Twp., Pa., 1960-70; mktg. dir., dir. profit ctr. Bantam Books, N.Y.C., 1970-77; exec. officer Infocom Broadcast Svc., Hawley, Pa., 1977-89; ind. mktg. cons. Bantam, Doubleday, Dell Publishing Group, Random House, Assn. Am. Pubs., N.Y.C., 1989—; ptnr. Scott/Satz Group, Walnut Creek, Calif., 1991—, LetterLink, Walnut Creek, Calif., 1992—; mem. negotiating team Pa. Tchrs. Assn., 1963-67. Contbr. articles to profl. jours. Active Pa. Bd. Edn. Mem. AAUW, LWV, Nat. Women's Polit. Caucus, Great Books Club (sec. 1986—), Walnut Creek C. of C., Rotary Internat. Avocations: running, aerobics, reading. Home and Office: 539 Monarch Ridge Dr Walnut Creek CA 94596-2955

SCOTT, IRENE FEAGIN, federal judge; b. Union Springs, Ala., Oct. 6, 1912; d. Arthur H. and Irene (Peach) Feagin; m. Thomas Jefferson Scott, Dec. 27, 1939 (dec.); children: Thomas Jefferson, Irene Scott Carroll. A.B., U. Ala., 1932, LL.B., 1936, LL.D., 1978; LL.M., Catholic U. Am., 1939. Bar: Ala. 1936. Law libr. U. Ala. Law Sch., 1932-34; atty. Office Chief Counsel IRS, 1937-50, mem. excess profits tax coun., 1950-52, spl. asst. to head appeals div., 1952-59, staff asst. to chief counsel, 1959-60; judge U.S. Tax Ct., 1960-82, sr. judge serving on recall, 1982—. Contbr. articles to Women Lawyers Jour. Bd. dirs. Mt. Olivet Found., Arlington. Mem. ABA (taxation sect.), Ala. Bar Assn., Fed. Bar Assn., D.C. Bar Assn. (hon.), Nat. Assn. Women Lawyers, Nat. Assn. Women Judges, Kappa Delta, Kappa Beta Pi. Office: US Tax Ct 400 2nd St NW Washington DC 20217

SCOTT, JUDITH MYERS, elementary education educator; b. Loredo, Mo., Dec. 29, 1940; d. Wilbur Charles and Dora Emma (Frazier) Myers; m. David Ronald Scott, Dec. 18, 1965; children: Russell Myers, Geoffrey Douglas. BA in Edn., Ariz. State U., 1962, MA in edn., 1970. Cert. tchr., Ariz. Tchr. 2d grade Scottsdale (Ariz.) Elem. Dist., 1962-64; tchr. 1st grade Cahuilla Sch., Palm Springs, Calif., 1965, Palm Crest Sch., La Canada, Calif., 1968-69; tchr. Ak Chin Community Sch., Maricopa, Ariz., 1969-70; grad. asst. Ariz. State U., Tempe, 1970-71; pvt. tutor Tempe, 1970-77; tchr. Dayspring Presch., Tempe, 1978-83; tchr. 3d grade Waggoner Elem. Sch., Kyrene, Ariz., 1984-86; reading specialsit Tempe Elem. Sch. Dist., 1986-90, tchr., trainer collaboratve literacy intervention program, 1990—; exec. dir. Beauty for All Seasons, Tempe, 1982-86. Coord. New Zealand Tchr. Exch., Tempe Sister Cities, 1992—. Mem. NEA, ASCD, Ariz. Sch. Adminstrs., Ariz. Edn. Assn., Tempe Edn. Assn., Internat. Reading Assn. Methodist. Home: 1940 E Calle De Caballos Tempe AZ 85284-2507 Office: Tempe Elem Sch Dist 3205 N Rural Rd Tempe AZ 85282

SCOTT, KATHEY ELAINE, real estate company executive; b. Denison, Tex., Aug. 31, 1945; d. Robert Lee and Lois Evelyn (Nelson) Johnson; m. Burt Clifford Scott, Feb. 12, 1965; children: Lea Evelyn, Burt Christopher. Grad. high sch., Denison, 1963. Clk., typist City of Sherman, Tex., 1980, gen. sec., 1980-81, adminstrv. sec., 1981-82, pers. technician, 1982-83, activities coord., 1983-87; exec. dir. The Renaissance, Sherman, 1987-94; adminstr., br. mgr. Home Health, 1994—. Adv. bd. Ret. Sr. Vol. Program, Grayson, Tex., 1986-90, Texoma Area Agy. Aging, Grayson, 1988-90; reporter S.W. Soc. on Aging, 1986-88; active program bldg. com. County Extension, Grayson, 1984-88; facilitator local White House Conf. on Aging, Grayson, 1989; club adminstr. Grayson County 4-H Club, Sherman, 1976-86; speaker Nat. Assn. Sr. Living Industries. Mem. Tex. Assn. Retirement Communities, Rotary (community svc. com. 1990, dir. vocat. svc. 1992—). Republican. Baptist. Office: The Renaissance 3701 Loy Lake Rd Sherman TX 75090-2500

SCOTT, LINDA ANN, assistant principal, elementary education educator; b. St. Louis, Jan. 21, 1955; d. Jay R. and Bernadette (Hogan) S. BS, Youngstown State U., Ohio, 1979; MS, Gov.'s State U., Park Forest, Ill., 1991. Tchr. Bishop Blanchette, Joliet, Ill., 1981-85, St. Joseph's, Joliet, Ill., 1985-86, Hufford Jr. High Sch., Joliet, Ill., 1986-93; asst. prin. Washington Jr. H.S., Joliet, 1992—; ednl. coord. Warren-Sharpe Community Ctr., Joliet, 1990—. Mem. life PTA, 1990—. No. Ill. U. grantee, 1990, Argonne Nat. Lab. grantee, 1990, U. Ill. grantee, 1991. Mem. Ill. Coun. Tchrs. of Math. Home: 7324 Heritage Ct Frankfort IL 60423-9587 Office: Washington Jr HS 402 Richards St Joliet IL 60433

SCOTT, LINDA KAY See GRANT, LINDA KAY

SCOTT, MARGARET SIMON, mortgage broker; b. Boston, May 12, 1934; d. Frank A. and Margaret Alice (Gotham) Simon; m. Walter Neil Scott, Nov. 21, 1959; 1 child, Walter David Kimbley. BA in Physics, Wellesley Coll., 1956; MA in Polit. Sci., Boston U., 1965; MS in Human Resources Mgmt., U. Utah, 1974. Registered mortgage broker, N.Y. Rsch. asst. Bell Tel. Labs., Whippany, N.J., 1956-58; rsch. asst. med. sch. U. Louisville, 1959-60, Harvard U., Boston, 1960-64; instr. polit. sci. Trinity U., San Antonio, 1966-67; cons. info. systems U.S. Dept. Labor, Washington, 1968; dir. manpower planning N.Y.C. Human Resources Adminstrn., 1968-71; asst. v.p. First Nat. City Bank, N.Y.C., 1972-77; v.p. Citibank, N.A., N.Y.C., 1978-86, AMEV Asset Mgmt., Inc., N.Y.C., 1986-88; pres. Mortgage Adv. Svcs., Inc., N.Y.C., 1988—. Vol. Jr. League, Louisville, N.Y.C., 1957—; bd. mgr. N.Y. Jr. League, N.Y.C., 19720-74; sec. 1095 Park Ave Corp., N.Y.C., 1976-86; bd. dirs. N.Y.C. YWCA, 1980-85; trustee The First Presbyn. Ch. in the City of N.Y. Mem. Nat. Assn. Mortgage Brokers (cert. mortgage cons.), N.Y. Assn. Mortgage Brokers, Met. N.Y. Mortgage Brokers Assn. (founding pres. 1990-91), Am. Assn. Residential Mortgage Regulators, Nat. Assn. Women Bus. Owners, Assn. Real Estate Women, Fin. Women's Assn., Women's Econ. Roundtable, Spinsters' Cotillion Club, Wellesley Club. Democrat. Home: 441 W 24th St New York NY 10011-1253

SCOTT, MARIANNE FLORENCE, librarian, educator; b. Toronto, Dec. 4, 1928; d. Merle Redvers and Florence Ethel (Hutton) S. BA, McGill U., Montreal, Que., Can., 1949, BLS, 1952; LLD (hon.), York U., 1985, Dalhousie U., 1989; DLitt (hon.), Laurentian U., 1990. Asst. librarian Bank of Montreal, 1952-55; law librarian McGill U., 1955-73, law area librarian, 1973-75, dir. libraries, 1975-84, lectr. legal bibliography faculty of law, 1964-75; nat. librarian Nat. Library of Can., Ottawa, Ont., 1984—; officer Order of Can., 1995. Co-founder, editor: Index to Can. Legal Periodical Lit, 1963—; contbr. articles to profl. jours. Decorated Officer of the Order of Can. Mem. Internat. Assn. Law Libraries (dir. 1974-77), Am. Assn. Law Libraries, Can. Assn. Law Libraries (pres. 1963-69, exec. bd. 1973-75, honored mem. 1980—), Can. Library Assn. (council and dir. 1980-82, 1st v.p. 1980-81, pres. 1981-82), Corp. Profl. Librarians of Que. (v.p. 1975-76), Can. Assn. Research Libraries (pres. 1978-79, past pres. 1979-80, exec. com. 1980-81, sec.-treas. 1983-84), Ctr. for Research Libraries (dir. 1980-83), Internat. Fedn. Library Assns. (honor com. for 1982 conf. 1979-82), Conf. of Dirs. of Nat. Libraries (chmn. 1988-92). Home: 119 Dorothea Dr, Ottawa, ON Canada K1V 7C6 Office: Nat Libr Can, 395 Wellington St, Ottawa, ON Canada K1A 0N4

SCOTT, MARY DAVIES, federal judge; b. 1944. BA, Trinity U., San Antonio, 1968; JD, U. Ark., Little Rock, 1978. Admitted to bar, 1979. Bankruptcy judge U.S. Dist. Ct. Ark., Little Rock, 1987—. Office: US Dist Ct 600 W Capitol St PO Box 3201 Little Rock AR 72201*

SCOTT, MARY JANE GOMEZ, human resources executive; b. Hartford, Conn., Aug. 12, 1944; d. Juan and Marion Priscilla (Jewett) Gomez; m. Jeffery Anderson Scott, Jan. 27, 1967. BS in Edn., U. Conn., 1966. Tchr. elem. schs. Stamford (Conn.) Bd. Edn., 1966-69; coll. relations asst. Olin Corp., Stamford, 1969-73, compensation analyst, 1973-77, mgr. salary programs, 1977-78, mgr. internal placement, 1978-80; mgr. salaried personnel Olin Corp., New Haven, 1980-82; mgr. staffing GTE Communication Systems Corp., Stamford, 1982-84; dir. personnel TransKrit Corp., Roanoke, Va., 1984-89, v.p. human resources, 1989—. Mem. Am. Compensation Assn., Soc. for Human Resource Mgmt. Home: 285 N Salem Rd Ridgefield CT 06877-3125 Office: TransKrit Corp P O Box 40020 Roanoke VA 24022-0020

SCOTT, MARY LOUISE, educator, writer; b. Ft. Worth, Tex., Oct. 15, 1932; d. Edward Hughes and Gertrude Elizabeth (Wiltshire) S. AB, U. San Diego, 1955; MA, San Diego State U., 1961; JD, U. San Diego, 1970. Bar: Calif. Tchr. San Diego Unified Sch. Dist., 1955-89; rsch. assoc. San Diego Aerospace Mus., 1989-94, edn. specialist, 1994—; curriculum writer San Diego City Schs., 1972, 73, 80-89. Author: San Diego: Air Capital of the West, 1991; co-author: Young Adults in the Marketplace (2 vols.), 1979; contbr. articles to profl. jours. Recipient Citation of Honor Diocese of San Diego, 1955, cert. of appreciation San Diego State U., 1985, recognition Calif. State Assembly, 1991; ednl. mentor Old Globe Theatre, San Diego, 1987, 88, 89. Mem. Am. Aviation Hist. Soc., U.S. Naval Inst., Navy League U.S., Zool. Soc. San Diego, San Diego Natural History Soc. Republican. Roman Catholic. Home: 4702 Norma Drive San Diego CA 92115 Office: San Diego Aerospace Museum Balboa Park 2001 Pan American Plz San Diego CA 92101

SCOTT, MILDRED HOPE, nurse; b. Miami, Fla., July 5, 1926; d. Enos R. and Ruth (Sommers) Eby; m. Thomas Wayne Scott, Dec. 19, 1958; children: Linda Joy Scott Day, Daniel Dean. ThB in Bible Theology, Internat. Bible Inst. and Sem., Plymouth, Fla., 1982. Lic. practical nurse, Fla. Lic. practical nurse various hosps. and nursing homes, Fla. and Mo., 1969-86; sch. nurse Orange County Sch. Bd., Orlando, Fla., 1974-78; pvt. duty nurse Upjohn Healthcare Services, Kansas City, Mo., 1985-89; allergy nurse Agarwal Allergy Clinic, Raytown, Mo., 1987-89, 92—; sec. to Dr. Lottie McWherter Mission, Kans., 1989-92; staff writer Majestic Records-Countrywine Pub., Linden, Tex., 1987—. Served as cpl. USMC, 1957-59. Mem. ASCAP, Assn. Internat. Gospel Assemblies Inc. (ordained minister). Democrat. Home: PO Box 143 43 Aspen St Belton MO 64012-2091

SCOTT, MIMI KOBLENZ, actress, psychotherapist; b. Albany, N.Y., Dec. 15, 1940; d. Edmund Akiba and Tillie (Paul) Koblenz; m. Barry Stuart Scott, Aug. 13, 1961 (dec. Nov. 1991); children: Karen Scott Zantay, Jeffrey B. BA in Speech, English Edn., Russell Sage Coll., 1962; MA in Speech Edn., SUNY, Albany, 1968; M in Social Welfare, SUNY, 1985; PhD in Psychology, Pacific Western U., Encino, Calif., 1985. Cert. tchr., social worker. Tchr. English, speech Albany Pub. Schs., 1961-63; hostess, producer talkshow Sta. WAST-TV 13, Albany, 1973-75; freelance actress N.Y.C., 1975-77; producer, actress Four Seasons Dinner Theater, Albany, 1978-82; instr. of theatre Albany Jr. Coll., 1981-83; pvt. practice psychotherapy Albany, N.Y., 1985-92; exec. producer City of Albany Park Playhouse, 1989-92; actor self-employed N.Y.C., 1992—; press rep. Jeffrey Richards Assocs., N.Y.C., 1994—; guest psychotherapist Sally Jessy Raphael Show, 1992, 93, Jane Whitney Show, 1994. Scriptwriter, dir., actress TV movie, 1984. Event organizer AmFar, 1985; co-chmn. March of Dimes Telethon, 1985-86; fundraiser Leukemia Found., 1987, Aids Benefit, N. Miami Beach, Fla., 1988; elected to SUNY Albany U. Found., 1990. Recipient FDR Nat. Achievement award March of Dimes, 1985, Recognition Cert. Capital Dist. Psychiat. Ctr., 1983, 84, 85; named Woman of Yr. YWCA, 1986, Commr. Albany Tricentennial Celebration, 1986; Mimi Scott Day proclaimed by Mayor of Albany, 1989. Mem. AEA, SAG, AFTRA, NASW. Jewish. Home and Office: 155 W 70th St Apt 8G New York NY 10023-4422

SCOTT, OMERIA MCDONALD, state legislator; m. Charles Scott. Mem. Miss. Ho. of Reps. Mem. Nat. Coun. Negro Women, Federated Women Am., Assn. Excellence in Edn., Eastern Star. Democrat. Baptist. Address: 615 E 19th St Laurel MS 39440 Office: Miss Ho of Reps State Capitol Jackson MS 39205*

SCOTT, PAMELA MOYERS, physician assistant; b. Clarksburg, W.Va., Jan. 5, 1961; d. James Edward and Norma Lee (Holbert) Moyers; m. Troy Allen Scott, July 19, 1986. BS summa cum laude, Alderson-Broaddus Coll., 1983. Cert. physician asst. Physician asst. Weston (W.Va.) State Hosp., 1983-84, Rainelle (W.Va.) Med. Ctr., 1984—; part-time faculty physician asst. program Coll. W.Va., 1994—; keynote speaker Alderson-Broadous Coll. Ann. Physician Assn. Banquet, 1992; presenter W.Va. Task Force on Adolescent Pregnancy and Parenting State Meeting, Charleston, 1992, W.Va. Primary Care Assn. Ann. Conf., Beckley, W.Va., 1994, W.Va. State Rural Health Conf., Morgantown, 1992, Chinese Med. Soc., Bejing, 1992; guest Lifetime TV med. program Physician Jour. Update, 1993; adv. coun. W.Va. Rural Health Networking, 1994—. Contbr. articles to profl. jours. Mem. W.Va. State Task Force on Adolscent Pregnancy and PArenting, 1992-94. Named Young Career Woman of Yr. Rainelle chpt. and Dist. V of W.Va., Citation of Honor at State Level of Competition, Bus. and Profl. Woman Clubs, 1986, Outstanding Physician Asst. of Yr. Am. Acad. Physician Assts., 1991; nominated for Rural Physician Asst. of Yr., 1992. Fellow Am. Acad. Physician Assts. (del. to People's Rep. China 1992, W. Va. chief del. Ho. of Dels. Nat. Conv. 1992, 94-95, W.Va. Del. 1993, mem. rural health caucus 1991—, pub. edn. com., 1992—, presenter ann. CME conf., San Antonio 1994), W.Va. Assn. Physician Assts. (chair membership com. 1989-91, nominations and elections com. 1990-91, pres. 1991-94, immediate past pres. 1994-95, presenter Continued Med. Edn. Conf. 1993), Coll. W.Va. Physician Asst. Adv. Coun., 1993—. Republican. Baptist. Home: PO Box 43 Williamsburg WV 24991-0043 Office: Rainelle Med Ctr 645 Kanawha Ave Rainelle WV 25962-1095

SCOTT, REBECCA ANDREWS, biology educator; b. Sunny Hill, La., June 4, 1939; d. Hayward and Dorothy (Nicholson) Andrews; m. Earl P. Scott, June 8, 1957; children: Stephanie Scott Dilworth, Cheryl L. BS, So. U., 1962; MS, Eastern Mich. U., 1969. Biology tchr., Detroit, 1966-68; sci. tchr. Ann Arbor (Mich.) Pub. Schs., 1968-69; biology tchr. North High Sch., Mpls., 1972—, coord. math., sci. tech. magnet, 1986—, advisor Jets Sci. Club. Mem. LVW (pres. 1981-83, 87-89, treas. 1989—), Nat. Sci. Tchrs. Assn., Minn. Sci. Tchrs. Assn., Minn. Acad. Sci., Nat. Assn. Biology Tchrs., Iota Phi Lambda. Democrat. Presbyterian. Home: 3112 Wendhurst Ave Minneapolis MN 55418-1726 Office: 1500 James Ave N Minneapolis MN 55411

SCOTT, SHARON, training consultant, counselor; b. Sherman, Tex., Oct. 19; m. John W. Przywara, Jan. 5, 1980. BA in Sociology, U. Tex., Arlington, 1970; MA in Human Rels., Am. Internat. Coll., Springfield, Mass., 1977. Lic. marriage and family therapist, Tex.; lic. profl. counselor, Tex. Case worker Dallas County Dept. of Human Svcs., Dallas, 1970-74; dir. 1st offender program Dallas Polic Dept., 1974-80; internat. trainer, speaker Sharon Scott and Assocs., Garland, Tex., 1980—. Author: Peer Pressure Reversal, 1985, How To Say No and Keep Your Friends, 1986, Positive Peer Groups, 1987, When To Say Yes! And Make More Friends, 1988, Too Smart for Trouble, 1990, Not Better...Not Worse...Just Different, 1992, Too Cool For Drugs, 1993. Recipient Tex. Gubernatorial Cert. of Appreciation, 1982, Heart of Am. award, St. Louis, 1987, Profl. Writing award Tex. Counseling Assn., 1987. Mem. ACA, Tex. Counseling Assn., Internat. Assn. Marriage and Family Therapists. Office: Sharon Scott and Assocs 2709 Woods Ln Garland TX 75044

SCOTT, SHERYL ANN, mental health educator; b. Elkhart, Ind., Aug. 10, 1950; d. George and Kathryn Louise (Glass) S. BS, Ind. State U., 1972; MEd, Ga. State U., 1976. Speech therapist Drs. Meml. Hosp., Spalding County Schs., Elkhart Rehab. Ctr., Atlanta, Griffin, Ga., 1972-76; assoc. trainer Dr. Richard Smith Ga. State U., Atlanta, 1976-77; edn./tng. specialist Neuse Mental Health Ctr., New Bern, N.C., 1977-83; pres. Performance Tng. Systems, New Bern, 1983-84; instr. Craven Community Coll., Pamlico Tech. Coll., New Bern, Bayboro, N.C., 1978-84, Carteret Tech. Coll., Morehead City, N.C., 1978-84; computer mktg. rep. Radio Shack divsn. of Tandy Corp., New Bern, 1984-85; dir. mental health edn. Coastal Area Health Edn. Ctr., Wilmington, N.C., 1986—; clin. instr. dept. psychiatry sch. medicine U. N.C., Chapel Hill, 1986—; presenter in field. Mem. ASTD, Atlanta Area Counseling Ctr. (bd. dirs., founder 1976), Parents Supporting Parents (bd. dirs. 1987-88), Family Support Network Southeastern N.C. Inc. (bd. dirs. 1991, pres., chmn. bd. 1992-94), Nat. Assn. for Rural Mental Health (bd. dirs. 1993, sec. 1993). Home: 221 Inlet Dr Wilmington NC 28405-6825 Office: Coastal AHEC PO Box 9025 Wilmington NC 28402-9025

SCOTT, SUSAN, lawyer; b. Orange, N.J., July 25, 1943; d. Bailey Bartlett and Regina Margaret (Butler) S.; m. Robert John Gillispie, Aug. 20. 1966 (div. 1979); children: Robert John Jr., Megan Anne. BA in Math, Catholic U. Am., 1965; JD, Rutgers U., 1975. Bar: N.J. 1975, U.S. Dist. Ct. N.J.

1975, U.S. Ct. Appeals (3d cir.) 1988, U.S. Supreme Ct. 1993. Applied math. CIA, Washington, 1965-68; assoc. Pitney, Hardin, Kipp & Szuch, Morristown, N.J., 1975-76; assoc. Riker, Danzig, Scherer, Hyland & Perretti, Morristown, 1979-85, ptnr., 1986—; corp. counsel Allied-Signal, Inc., Morristown, 1977-78; mem. Child Placement Rev. Bd., Morristown,1992—; commr. Morris County Bd. Condemnation, Morristown, 1989—. Mem. ABA, N.J. State Bar Assn., Morris County Bar Assn. Democrat. Roman Catholic. Home: 20 Vinton Rd Madison NJ 07940-2506 Office: Riker Danzig Scherer Hyland & Perretti Headquarters Plz 1 Speedwell Ave Morristown NJ 07960-6838

SCOTT, SUSAN ANNETTE, museum curator, writer; b. Lompoc, Calif., Mar. 27, 1955; d. William Mollyneaux and Irene Annette (Olson) S. BA, U. Okla., 1977; MA in Art History, U. Va., 1980; postgrad., Ctrl. State U., Edmond, Okla., 1986-88. Asst. curator Mus. of Art U. Okla., Norman, 1982-83; curator of exhbns. Okla. Art Ctr., Oklahoma City, 1984-88; curator of collections Orlando (Fla.) Mus. of Art, 1988-90, cons. curator of contemporary art, 1990—; critic, exhbn. reviewer Art News, N.Y.C., 1992-94; exhbn. reviewer Artpapers, Atlanta, 1992-94; guest curator Va. Beach Ctr. for the Arts, 1991. Author: (exhbn. catalogue) Motion as Metaphor: The Automobile in Art, 1990; author, editor: Alex Katz: Paintings, Drawings, and Cut Outs, 1990, Washington Color Painters: The First Generation, 1991, Jennifer Bartlett: A Print Retrospective, 1993, (plays) Untitled, 1990, The Source, 1994. Named one of Outstanding Young Women in Am., 1978; grantee Ind. Rsch. on the Washington Gallery of Modern Art, Nat. Endowment Arts, 1988-90. Mem. Coll. Art Assn. Home: 498 Hudson St # 3 New York NY 10014-2818

SCOTT, SUZANNE, writer; b. Athens, Ga., Mar. 1, 1940; d. Jane Scott (Terrell) Overby; divorced; children: Elizabeth Atwell, William F. Atwell Jr., Stephanie Atwell Zehr, David Allan Atwell; life ptnr. Lynne Mary Constantine. BA in English, Eastern Mennonite Coll., 1979; MA in English Lit., James Madison U., 1986. Continuity writer WSVA TV-AM-FM, Harrisonburg, Va., 1966-68, 71-72, WBTX-FM, Broadway, Va., 1972; instr. English as 2d lang. Eastern Mennonite Coll., Harrisonburg, 1977-78, instr. English, 1979; teaching asst. English James Madison U., Harrisonburg, 1979-81; writer Psychiatric Insts. Am., Washington, 1981-84; founding ptnr. Community Scribes, Arlington, Va., 1984—. Co-author: Migraine: The Complete Guide, 1994; contbr. articles to profl. jours. Mem. Nat. Gay & Lesbian Task Force, Washington, 1992—. Meth. Ch. Coll. scholar, 1958; Teaching fellow James Madison U., 1979, 80. Mem. NAFE, Arlington C. of C., Arlington Arts Ctr. Democrat. Methodist. Office: Community Scribes Penthouse Ste 1001 N Highland St Arlington VA 22201

SCOTT, VANESSA KATHLEEN, writer; b. Flushing, N.Y., Aug. 28, 1963; d. John Crennan and Sonia (Rossi) Scott. BA, Hunter Coll., 1990; MA, N.Y.U., 1993. Author: Pneuma, 1989, The Returning Woman, 1989, Olive Tree Review, 1990, Icarus, 1993. Recipient Honorary Mention Creative Writing Silver Quill Writing Contests, 1993. Home: 94-32 133rd Ave Ozone Park NY 11417

SCOTT, VICKI SUE, school system administrator; b. Pine Bluff, Ark., Feb. 16, 1946; d. John Wesley and Ruby Gray (Whitehead) and Hannah (Lewis) S. BA, Hendrix Coll., 1968; MS in Edn., U. Cen. Ark., 1978, postgrad., 1979-84; postgrad., U. Ark., 1983-85, Ark. State U., 1993-94. Cert. adminstrn., secondary sch. prin., middle sch., secondary health and phys. edn. Tchr., coach Brinkley (Ark.) Pub. Schs., 1968-76, Lonoke (Ark.) Jr. and Sr. High Schs., 1976-77; tchr., coach S.E. Jr. High Sch., Pine Bluff, 1978-92, asst. prin., 1992—, dir. summer sch., 1991, 92; AIDS educator Arkansas River Edn. Svc. Coop., Pine Bluff, 1989-92. Active Leadership Pine Bluff, 1993-94. Scholar Assn. Women Ednl. Suprs., 1985; named Outstanding Young Women of Am., 1974. Mem. ASCD, DAR, Ark. Assn. Ednl. Adminstrs., Nat. Assn. Secondary Prins., Order Ea. Star, Delta Kappa Gamma (scholar 1984), Phi Delta Kappa. Baptist. Home: 3215 S Cherry St Pine Bluff AR 71603-5983 Office: SE Jr High Sch 2001 S Ohio St Pine Bluff AR 71601-6901

SCOTT, WILLODENE ALEXANDER, retired library administrator; b. Ethridge, Tenn., Sept. 4, 1922; d. Jesse Cary and Maud (Goff) Alexander; m. Ray Donald Scott, Nov. 27. 1959; 1 child, Pamela Dean. B.A., George Peabody Coll. for Tchrs., 1946, BS in Lib. Sci., 1947, MA, 1949, EdS, 1972, PhD, 1986. Libr. Sylvan Park Elem. Sch., Nashville, 1947-51, Waverly Belmont Jr. High Sch., Nashville, 1951-54, Howard High Sch., Nashville, 1954-62, Peabody Demonstration Sch., Nashville, 1962-63; libr. McCann Elem. Sch., Nashville, 1963-66; supr. instructional materials, libr. div. Metro Nashville-Davidson County Schs., Nashville, 1966-73, dir. instructional materials and libr. svcs., 1973-87; dir. librs. Watkins Inst., Nashville, 1987-88, ret.; lectr. Peabody Coll. Libr. Sch., Nashville, 1950-66, 71, 72, 76, U. Tenn., Nashville Ctr., 1970; Tenn. rep. White House Conf., 1970. Pub. Experiencing Literature With Children, Elementary English, 1967, Instructional Materials Center, Tennessee Librarian, 1969. Chmn. nat. alumni fund-raising George Peabody Coll. for Tchrs., 1975-76, nat. alumni pres., 1977-78, trustee, 1976-78; bd. dirs. Friends of Music, 1977-79; mem. vis. com. bd. trustees Vanderbilt U., 1979-85. Recipient Disting. Alumni award Peabody Libr. Sch., 1987, Tenn. Libr. Assn. honor award, 1986. Mem. ALA, AAUW, NEA (life), DAR (organizing treas. Buffalo River chpt. 1967-69), Southeastern Libr. Assn. (scholarship com. 1968-70), Tenn. Libr. Assn. (membership chmn. 1955, 64, treas. 1977-78, honor award 1986), Tenn. Edn. Assn. (libr. sect. pres. 1954), Met. Nashville Ret. Tchrs. Assn., Woman's Nat. Book Assn. (charter mem.), Delta Kappa Gamma (v.p. 1984-86), Embroidery Guild of Am. (vol. libr. Cheekwood chpt.), Nashville Libr. Club (pres. 1952-53). Baptist. Home: 525 Clematis Dr Nashville TN 37205-3163

SCOTT-FINAN, NANCY ISABELLA, government administrator; b. Canton, Ohio, June 13, 1949; d. Milton Kenneth and Gertrude (Baker) Scott; m. Robert James Finan II, Aug. 23, 1986. Student, Malone Coll., 1970-73; BA magna cum laude, U. Akron, 1976, postgrad., 1976; postgrad., Kent State U., 1977; MA in Internat. Transactions, George Mason U., 1995. Legal sec. Krugliak, Wilkins, Griffiths & Dougherty, Canton, 1969, Amerman, Burt & Jones, Canton, 1970-77; legal sec., paralegal Black, McCuskey, Souers & Arbaugh, Canton, Ohio, 1977-81; adminstrv. staff mem. com. on judiciary U.S. Senate, Washington, 1981-86; adminstrv. asst. to counsel to Pres., The White House, Washington, 1986-89; adminstrv. asst. to former counsel to pres. O'Melveny & Myers, Washington, 1989; asst. dir. congl. rels. Office Legis. Affairs U.S. Dept. Justice, Washington, 1989-91; spl. asst. to asst. atty. gen. U.S. Dept. of Justice, Washington, 1991—; substitute tchr. North Canton City Sch. System, 1979-80; residential tutor Canton City Sch. System, 1980-81, Fairfax (Va.) County Sch. System, 1983;instr. dance and exercise Siffrin Home for Developmentally Disabled, Canton, 1980. East coast regional v.p. for spl. projects Childhelp U.S.A., Washington, 1988-90; mem. Rep. Women of Capitol Hill, Washington, 1984—; bd. mem. Have a Heart Homes for Abused Children, Washington, 1990-91. Mem. AAUW, Women of Washington. Presbyterian. Office: US Dept Justice 10th and Constitution Washington DC 20530

SCOTTO, RENATA, soprano; b. Savona, Italy, Feb. 24, 1935; m. Lorenzo Anselmi. Studied under, Ghirardini, Merlino and Mercedes Llopart, Accademia Musicale Savonese, Conservatory Giuseppe Verdi, Milan. Debut in La Traviata, Teatro Nuevo, Milan, 1954; then joined La Scala Opera Co.; appeared with Met. Opera, N.Y.C., 1965, Convent Garden, Hamburg (Fed. Republic of Germany) State Opera, Vienna (Austria) State Opera, Nat. Theatre Munich, San Francisco Opera, Chgo. Lyric Opera, 1988; roles include: Ballo in Maschera, La Sonnambula, I Puritani, L'Elisir d'amore, Lucia di Lammermoor, La Boheme, Turandot, Otello (Verdi), Trovatore, Le Prophete, Madama Butterfly, Adriana Lecouvreur, Norma, Tosca, Manon Lescaut, Rosenkavalier (Marschallin), La Voix Humaine, Pirata; dir. Madama Butterfly, N.Y. Met. Opera, 1986; recordings include Christmas at St. Patrick's Cathedral, French Arias with Charles Rosekrans, Live in Paris with Ivan Davis, Great Operatic Scenes with Jose Carreras. Office: care Robert Lombardo Assocs 61 W 62d St Ste 6F New York NY 10023 also: care Il Teatro la Scala, via Filodrammatici 2, Milan Italy*

SCOTT-WILSON, SUSAN RICE, educator; b. Brownsville, Tenn., Aug. 11, 1942; d. Moreau Estes and E. Estelle (Walker) Rice; m. Charles E. Scott, Feb. 28, 1969 (div. July 1985); children: Tamera W., David W.; m. Lloyd Curlin Wilson, Apr. 7, 1994. BS, U. Tenn., Martin, 1964; EdM, Memphis State U., 1979, EdD, 1989. Cert. master tchr., Tenn. Elem. tchr. Lauderdale County Bd. Edn., Ripley, Tenn., 1964-65; exchange tchr. USIA, Washington, Netherlands, 1986-87; chmn. English dept. Am. Sch. of The Hague, Netherlands, 1987-88; secondary tchr. Haywood County Bd. Edn., Brownsville, Tenn., 1974-86, tchr. vocat. English, 1989-90, dir. adult basic edn., 1990—; mem. curriculum task force Tenn. Dept. Edn., Nashville, 1985-86, mem. collaborative task force, 1989-92. Local elector Tenn. President's Trust, Knoxville, 1989—; mem. Sister Cities Commn., Brownsville, 1990; com. mem. Ptnrs. in Edn., Brownsville, 1992-93; active West Star Leadership, 1993, Tenn. Reporting and Improvement Mgmt. Sys., 1994-95; mem. steering com. Fayette-Haywood County Enterprise Com., 1994—. Named Outstanding Tchr. by students U. Chgo., 1989. Mem. NEA, Nat. Coun. Tchrs. English (regional composition judge 1984-86), Am. Assn. Adult and Continuing Edn., Tenn. Edn. Assn., Tenn. Assn. Adult and Continuing Edn., Tenn. Tchrs. Study Coun. (state steering com. 1984-86), Sigma Tau Delta, Phi Delta Kappa, Kappa Delta Pi. Methodist. Home: 321 N Washington St Brownsville TN 38012-2063 Office: Haywood County Bd Edn 900 E Main St Brownsville TN 38012-2647

SCOVEL, MARY ALICE, music therapy educator; b. Grand Rapids, Mich., Jan. 28, 1936; d. Carl Edward and Alice Bertha (Bieri) Sennema; m. Ward Norman Scovel, July 7, 1956; children: Marcia, Katherine. MusB, Western Mich. U., 1969; MusM, Mich. State U., 1975. Registered music therapist; bd. cert. Asst. prof. music Grand Valley State U., Allendale, Mich., 1969-75; instr. U. Dayton (Ohio), 1975-78, Muskegon (Mich.) Community Coll., 1978-80; intern dir. Battle Creek (Mich.) Adventist Hosp., 1980-84; prof. music therapy Western Mich. U., Kalamazoo, 1984—; cons. Pre-sch. Physically Handicapped, Wyoming, Mich., 1974, Doris Klausen Devel. Ctr., Battle Creek, 1985-86; chmn. Multi-clinic, Kalamazoo, 1988-89. Author: Music Therapy in Treatment of Adults, 1990; co-editor Music Therapy Perspectives; contbr. articles to profl. jours. Lay del. United MEth. Ch., Albion, Mich., 1991. Mem. Nat. Assn. Music Therapy (del.), Nat. Assn. Mental Illness, AAUW, Great Lakes Region Music Therapy, Mich. Music Therapists, Pi Delta Alpha, Pi Kappa Lambda. Office: Western Mich U Sch Music Kalamazoo MI 49008

SCRANTON, LYNDA KAY, secondary physical education educator; b. Quincy, Ill., Aug. 6, 1947; d. Charles Leslie and Dorothy Blanche (Schnellbecher) S. BS in Phys. Edn., U. Ill., 1970; MA in Guidance, Roosevelt U., 1981. Cert. tchr., Ill. Phys. edn. tchr., coach Barrington (Ill.) High Sch., 1970—; orchesis sponsor Barrington (Ill.) High Sch., 1971-78, girls tennis coach, 1973-88; mem. adv. bd. Ill. High Sch. Assn. Tennis, Bloomington. Mem. NEA, Ill. Edn. Assn., Am. Assn. Health, Phys. Edn., Recreation and Dance, Ill. Assn. Health, Phys. Edn., Recreation and Dance. Home: 670 South Rd Palatine IL 60074 Office: Barrington High Sch 616 W Main Barrington IL 60010

SCRANTON, RITA SUSAN, counselor, enterpreneur; b. Oklahoma City, Okla., Apr. 1, 1957; d. William Lansing and Dorothy Mary (Welsh) S. BBA, U. Okla., 1979, MEd, 1993. Owner, mgr. Gemini Industries, Oklahoma City, 1976-92, ARES Mil. Surplus, Oklahoma City, 1979-92, Scranberry Collectibles, Oklahoma City, 1992—; ptnr. Scranton Assocs., Oklahoma City, 1986—. Umpire City of Norman, Oka., 1991—; vol., student intern Griffin Meml. Hosp., Norman, 1992—, Kids Kore Children's Hosp.; actor, co-dir. Okla. Sign Theatre, Unltd., Moore, 1991—; entertainer Signs of Music, Oklahoma City, 1992—; mem. Okla. Com. on HIV/AIDS and Deafness, 1992—, "Just Say Ho" Clown Orgn. Mem. Am. Counseling Assn., Nat. Assn. of the Deaf, Oklahoma City Assn. of the Deaf, Ctrl. Okla. Assn. for the Deaf and Hearing Impaired, Am. deafness and Rehab. Assn. Methodist. Home: 1306 Regent St Norman OK 73069-7538

SCRIBNER, JEAN ELIZABETH, retired vocational counselor, English educator; b. Leroy, Mich., Dec. 18, 1922; d. Cassius Mayne and Bessie Belle (Bowen) Kenney; m. Delbert Paul Scribner, Oct. 8, 1943. BS in Edn., Goshen Coll., 1961; M in Eng., Montclair State Coll., 1969. Cert. Eng. tchr., vocat. counselor. Tchr. Penn-Harris-Madison Schs., Mishawaka, Ind., 1961-66, W. Orange-Maplewood Schs., West Orange, N.J., 1967-69, Graham High Sch., St. Paris, Ohio, 1969-71; vocat. counselor Chgo., Aurora, Ill., 1972-88. Vol. probation officer Elkhart County (Ind.) Cts., 1989—, tax preparer numerous Elkhart County locations, 1989—, Elkhart Coun. on Aging (recipient vol. month award, Feb., 1992); ins. preparer YMCA County Coun. on Aging, Elkhart, 1990—. Mem. LWV (editor, mem. bd. dirs. Elkhart chpt. 1990—), AAUW (treas. Elkhart chpt. 1990—), AFSCME, Women for Meaningful Summits, Learning Soc. of Elkhart.

SCRIMENTI, BELINDA JAYNE, lawyer; b. Dayton, Ohio, Jan. 30, 1956. BS in Journalism, Ohio U., 1978; JD, Ohio State U., 1981. Bar: Ohio 1981, U.S. Dist. Ct. (no. dist.) Ohio 1981, U.S. Dist. Ct. (ea. dist.) Mich. 1983, U.S. Ct. Appeals (3d and 6th cirs.) 1984, U.S. Dist. Ct. Md. 1988, D.C. 1989, U.S. Dist. Ct. D.C. 1989. Assoc. Baker & Hostetler, Cleve., 1981-88; assoc. Baker & Hostetler, Washington, 1988-90, ptnr., 1991—. Contbr. articles to profl. jours. Sec. Chagrin Condominiums Homeowners' Assn., Chagrin Falls, Ohio, 1985-87. Mem. ABA (sect. on litigation, patent, trademarks and copyritghts, entertainment and sports law), D.C. Bar Assn. (sects. on copyright, trademarks, patent and entertainment and sport law), Internat. Trademark Assn. (firm rep., coms. 1990—), Internat. Anti-Counterfeiting Coaliton (firm rep.), Womens Bar Assn. D.C. Office: Baker & Hostetler 1050 Connecticut Ave NW Ste 1100 Washington DC 20036

SCROGGS, DEBBIE LEE, communications professional; b. Norton, Va., Sept. 27, 1953; d. Jennings Eugene and Edith Marie (Harris) S.; m. John L. Price, Apr. 1, 1984. AAS in Acctg., C.C. of Denver, 1981; BSBA magna cum laude, Regis Coll., 1987; MSS in Applied Comms., U. Denver, 1992. Bookkeeper Am./Trayer, Inc., Bristol, Va., 1972-74; assessment transcriber Dept. of Interior, Bristol, 1974-78; supr. computer asst. Dept. of Labor, Mine Safety and Health Adminstrn., Lakewood, Colo., 1978-82; lead tech. writer OAO Corp., Lakewood, 1982-83; tech. writer, editor Tele-Communications, Inc., Denver, 1984-85, Integrated Svcs., Inc., Aurora, Colo., 1985-87; sr. documentation specialist AT&T Customer Edn. Tng., Denver, 1988-89; sr. project mgr. AT&T Customer Edn. and Tng., Denver, 1989-94; tng. facilitator AT&T Customer Edn. Tng., Denver, 1993-94; transmission dept. mgr. AT&T Customer Edn. & Tng., Denver, 1994—. Contbr. articles to profl. jours., publs. Vol. Art Reach of Denver, 1988—, Channel 6 TV, Denver, 1989—. Mem. NAFE, Nat. Soc. Performance and Instrn., Assn. Computing Machinery, Soc. Tech. Comm. (Achievement award for user manual 1986, Achievement award for mktg. brochure 1986, Merit award for user manual 1988, moderator nat. conf. 1991, co-presenter nat. conf. 1991, 93, presenter nat. conf. 1995, networking lunch coord./nat. conf. 1992-95). Office: AT&T 67 Whippany Rd Rm 14E-202 Whippany NJ 07981

SCRUPE, MARA A. (MARY SCRUPE), visual artist, sculptor; b. Mpls., Feb. 19, 1955; d. Carolyn A. (Hanson) Sankey; m. Daniel J. Holm, July 19, 1986. BA, Macalester Coll., 1977; MFA, Bard Coll., 1995. Founder, dir. WAVE Gallery, St. Paul, 1984; instr. The Hand Workshop, Richmond, Va., 1988-90; exec. dir. Greater Reston (Va.) Arts Ctr., 1990-91, Second St. Gallery, Charlottesville, Va., 1991-92; visual artist, curator, educator, 1992—; artist-in-residence Mpls. Pub. Schs., 1982-84, Minn. State Arts Bd., 1983-87, 89, Sculpture Space, Utica, N.Y., 1986, Del. Ctr. for Contemporary Arts, Wilmington, 1994; guest lectr. Coll. of Associated Arts, St. Paul, 1983, Macalester Coll., St. Paul, 1983, Colgate U., Hamilton, N.Y., 1986, Munson-Williams-Proctor Art Inst. Sch., Utica, 1986, Vanderbilt U., Nashville, 1988, U. Tenn., Knoxville, 1989, Appalachian State U., Boone, N.C., 1990, Radford (Va.) U., 1991, Sawhill Gallery, James Madison U., Harrisongburg, Va., 1992, Fayerweather Gallery, U. Va., Charlottesville, 1992, others; vis. artist The Miami U., Oxford, Ohio, 1993, Western Mich. U., Kalamazoo, 1993, Walters State C. C., Morristown Tenn., 1993, Va. Commonwealth U., Richmond, 1995; adj. prof. sculpture Longwood Coll, Farmville, Va., 1995. One-woman shows include Arts Ctr. Minn., Mpls., 1982, Coll. Associated Arts, St. Paul, 1983, WAVE Gallery, St. Paul, 1984, PLUG-IN, Inc., Winnipeg, Can., 1985, Adirondack State Park, Old Forge, N.Y., 1988, Foundry Gallery, Washington, 1990, U. Calif., Riverside, 1991, Peninsula Fine Arts Ctr., Newport News, Va., 1993, Del. Ctr. Contemporary Arts, Wilmington, 1994, Virginia Beach (Va.) Ctr. Arts, 1995; exhibited in group shows at W.A.R.M. Gallery, Mpls., 1982, Fed. Res. Bank Exhbn. Program, Mpls., 1985, C.G. Rein Gallery, Mpls., 1985, Martin Gallery, Washington, 1986, Anderson & Anderson Gallery, Mpls., 1986, Macalester Coll. Alumni Invitational, St. Paul, 1987, Second St. Gallery, Charlottesville, Va., 1988, Sarratt Gallery, Vanderbilt U., Nashville, 1988, Chrysler Museum, Norfolk, 1988, Washington Sq. Exhbn. Program, Washington, 1988, 90, Peninsula Fine Arts Ctr., Newport News, Va., 1990, Nat. Ornamental Metals Mus., Memphis, 1991, Sawhill Gallery, James Madison U., Harrisonburg, Va., 1992, U., Tenn., Knoxville, 1992-94, Fayerweather Gallery, U. Va., Charlottesville, 1992, Walters State C. C., Morristown, 1993, Western Mich. State U., Kalamazoo, 1993, Thomas J. Walsh Art Gallery, Fairfield Conn., 1993, Laguna Gloria Art Mus., 1993, Frederic Layton Art Gallery, Milw., 1993, The Ellipse Art Ctr., Arlington Va., 1994, Miami-Dade C.C., Fla., 1994, N.Y. (N.Y.C.) Open Ctr., 1994, Nexus Found. for Today's Art, Phila., 1994, Pyramid Atlantic Art Ctr., Washington, 1995, Peconic Gallery of Suffolk C.C., Albany, N.Y., 1995, Sage Jr. Coll., Rathbone Gallery, Albany, 1995; represented in permanent collections including Western Mich. U., Va. Commonwealth U., Med. Coll. Va. Mem. fundraising com. AIDS Support Group Charlottesville, 1992—; active Nat. Mus. Women in the Arts, Washington. Recipient Artist-in-Residence award Villa Montalvo Ctr. for Arts, 1987, Artist-in-Residence award Tyrone Guthrie Ctr.-Ireland, 1991, Nat. Site-Specific Sculpture Competitiion award U. Calif.-Riverside, 1991, Mildred Victor prize Nat. Sculpture Soc. Centennial Exhbn., 1993, Nat. Outdoor Sculpture Competition award Miami U., 1993, Installation Exhbn. award Sch. 33 Art Ctr., 1994; workshop grantee Film in the Cities Performance Program, 1984; grantee COMPAS Comm. Arts Fund, St. Paul, 1984, Minn. State Arts B., 1985, 86, The Ruth Chenven Found., Inc., 1986, Artists Space, N.Y.C., 1988, 89; Artist-In-Residence grantee Mid-Atlantic Arts Found, 1989, Visual Arts Residency grantee Mid Atlantic Arts Found., 1994; fellow Djerassi Found., 1990, 91, ACTS Inst., 1991; Artist-In-Residence fellow MacDowell Colony, 1993. Mem. Internat. Sculpture Ctr., Washington Sculptors Group, Washington Project for Arts, Second St. Gallery, 1708 E. Main Artists Collectivie, Tri-State Sculors Guild. Home: 3601 Connecticut Ave Apt 517 Washington DC 20008

SCUDIERI, LOUISE M., nurse anesthetist; b. Lewiston, N.Y., July 9, 1964; d. Louis F. and Nancy J. (Sanfilippo) S. BS, SUNY, Brockport, 1987; MS, SUNY, Buffalo, 1994. RN U. Rochester, Strong Meml. Hosp., N.Y., 1987-88; RN-SICU Buffalo Gen. Hosp., 1988-91; cert. RN anesthetist Erie County Med. Ctr., Buffalo, 1991-94, Meth. Med. Ctr., Dallas, 1994—. Supporter YMCA, Niagara Falls, N.Y., 1992-94. Mem. ANA, Am. Assn. Nurse Anesthetists, Soc. Critcal Care Medicine, N.Y. State Assn. Nurse Anesthetists (sec. Niagara edn. dist. 1993-94).

SCULL, PATRICIA DANA, artist; b. Bethesda, Md., Mar. 7, 1953; d. Donald Marshall and Ann Marie (White) Clifford; m. Charles Joseph Scull, Nov. 27, 1976; children: Brooks Patrick, Christopher Mathew. BFA in Painting and Printmaking, Carnegie Mellon U., 1975; grad., Tex. Acad. Art, 1978; postgrad., Corcoran Sch. Art, 1976-78, U. N.C., 1991-93. Graphic artist Studio Graphics, Toronto, Can., 1979-80; freelance graphic artist Southam Bus. Pub., Toronto, 1979-81; profl. artists Artspace, Raleigh, 1993—. Exhibited in group shows Corcoran Gallery, 1990, Art Space, Raleigh, N.C., 1991-93, U. N.C. Hanes Glass Gallery, Chapel Hill, 1992, Durham (N.C.) Art Guild, 1992-93, Little Cafe, Raleigh, Sertoma Arts Ctr., Raleigh, 1993, Wake Visual Arts Assn., Raleigh, 1992, Raleigh Fine Arts Soc. Artists Exhbn., 1994; represented in permanent collections 1st City Bank, Houston, Nylos Can. Inc., Alta, Can., Long & Foster Realtors, Va., Burroughs Wellcome and Glaxco, Inc., Research Triangle Park, N.C. Docent N.C. Mus. Art, Raleigh, 1993. Mem. ArtSpace (Merit award York Properties 1991, Purchase award Burroughs Wellcome 1992), Wake Visual Artists Assn., Durham Art Guild. Office: ArtSpace 201 E Davie St Raleigh NC 27601-1869

SCULLION, ANNETTE MURPHY, lawyer, educator; b. Chgo., Apr. 6, 1926; d. Edmund Patrick and Anna (Nugent) Murphy; 1 son, Kevin. B.Ed., Chgo. Tchrs. Coll., 1960; J.D., DePaul U., 1964, M.Ed., 1966; M.Ed., Loyola U., Chgo., 1970; Ed.D., No. Ill. U., 1974. Bar: Ill. 1964, U.S. Dist. Ct. (no. dist.) Ill. 1965, U.S. Ct. Appeals (D.C. cir.) 1978. Lectr. Chgo. Community Coll., 1964-68; pvt. practice law, Chgo., 1964—; asst. prof. bus. edn. Chgo. State U., 1966-69, assoc. prof., 1970-73, prof., 1974—. Club founder, adviser Bus. Edn. Students Assn., Chgo. State U., 1976—; sch. law workshop coordinator Ill. Div. Vocat. and Tech. Edn., 1981. Mem. Nat. Bus. Edn. Assn., Women's Bar Assn. Ill., ABA, Am. Tchr. Edn., Beta Gamma Sigma Home: 386 Muskegon Ave Calumet City IL 60409-2347 Office: Chgo State U 95 And King Dr # 203 Chicago IL 60601

SCULLION, TSUGIKO YAMAGAMI, non-profit organization executive; b. China, June 30, 1946; d. Hajime and Akemi (Murazumi) Yamagami; m. William James Scullion, Nov. 26, 1971; 1 child, James. BA, Baldwin-Wallace Coll., 1970; MA, Sch. Internat. Tng., 1971. Area cons. Conn. AFS Internat./Intercultural Programs, N.Y.C., 1972-73, regional mgr. for Asia and Pacific, 1973-78, dir. internat. ops., 1978-81, v.p. Europe, Africa, Middle East, 1981-83, v.p. program svcs., 1083-85, exec. v.p., 1985-87; exec. v.p. U.S. Com. UNICEF, N.Y.C., 1988—. Bd. dirs. Oberlin Shansi Meml. Assn. Home: 7 Chasmar Rd Old Greenwich CT 06870

SEABOLT, PATRICIA ANN, perioperative nurse; b. Richwood, W.Va., Mar. 11, 1955; d. Jack E. and Mildred Ruth (Cowger) S. BSN, Alderson-Broaddus Coll., 1977; MEd, W.Va. U., 1979; M in Nursing Adminstrn., U. S.C., 1987. Staff nurse med. unit W.Va. U. Hosp., Morgantown, 1977-78, staff nurse surgery, 1983-84, asst. nurse mgr., 1984-85; staff nurse ICU/CCU St. Francis Hosp., Charleston, W.Va., 1979-80, asst. dir., dir. staff devel., 1980-83; staff nurse surgery Richland Meml. Hosp., Columbia, S.C., 1985-87; grad. rsch. asst. U. S.C., Columbia, 1986-87; nurse mgr. surgery Charleston Area Med. Ctr., 1987-88; dir. nursing and surg. svcs. Spartanburg (S.C.) Regional Med. Ctr., 1988-90; dir. surg. svcs. St. Joseph Hosp., Lexington, Ky., 1990-93; operational dir. oper. rm. svcs. U. Ky. Med. Ctr., Lexington, 1993—. Mem. Assn. Oper. Room Nurses, Ambulatory Care Forum, Sigma Theta Tau. Republican. Baptist. Office: U Ky Chandler Med Ctr Oper Rm Svcs 800 Rose St Lexington KY 40514

SEABROOK, DEBORAH JEAN, psychotherapist; b. Charleston, S.C., Jan. 25, 1949; d. Richard Eugene and Ellen Rae (Scott) S.; m. Robert Joseph Meyer, Aug. 4, 1965 (div. 1971); 1 child: Lisa Ann Meyer Potts; m. Thomas Ballard Lesemann, Jr., Nov. 27, 1986. BA, U. S.C., 1971; MEd, The Citadel, Charleston, 1974. Lic. profl. counselor; cert. elem. tchr. 1-8, spl. edn., principal high sch. Tchr. emotionally handicapped Ablemarle Elem., Charleston, 1973-75; intern child and adolescent unit Charleston Area Mental Health Ctr., 1977; head tchr. emotionally handicapped Charleston County Schs. Substance Abuse, 1978-79; counselor Charleston Higher Edn. Consortium, 1979-84; aftercare coord., work/industry coord., alumni coord. Fenwick Hall Hosp., Charleston, 1984-85, work industry coord., staff devel. coord., 1985-87; grant coord. Coll. Charleston, 1987-88; psychotherapist Lowcountry Psychotherapy Assocs., Charleston, 1988—; adj. faculty Coll. Charleston, 1989—. Com. mem. Mayor's Task Force for the Homeless, Charleston, 1990—; bd. dirs. Charleston County Substance Abuse Commn., 1988-90, Charleston County Schs. Drug & Alcohol Adv. Bd., 1988—. Recipient cert. of merit Senate of State of S.C., 1993. Mem. Am. Assn. Guidance Counseling, Internat. Soc. Study of Dissociative Disorders. Office: Lowcountry Psychotherapy Assocs 21 Gamecock Ave Charleston SC 29407

SEAGER, KATHLEEN MULEADY, psychotherapist; b. L.A., Apr. 4, 1950; d. Thomas William and Eileen (Shelley) Muleady; m. Robert Donald Seager, Sept. 9, 1972; children: Danielle Marie, Michael Donald. BA in Cultural Anthropology, U. Calif., Santa Barbera, 1972, BA in History, 1974; postgrad., U. Calif., Berkeley, 1976; MA in Counseling, U. No. Iowa, 1985. Diplomate Am. Bd. Med. Psychotherapy. Counselor CUH, Waterloo, Iowa, 1987-92; coord. grief support svcs. Cedar Valley Hospice, Waterloo, 1992—. Author: (tng. manual) Psycho-Social Issues of AIDS, 1987. Bd. dirs. Stage Inc., Cedar Falls, Univ. No. Iowa, 1992-95, pres. bd., 1993; mem. Symphony Guild Waterloo-Cedar Falls Symphony, 1986—. Recipient scholarship Kennedy Found., 1987. Mem. ACA, Am. Mental Health Counseling Assn. Democrat. Episcopalian. Office: Cedar Valley Hospice Ste 401 2101 Kimball Ave Waterloo IA 50702

SEAGRAVE, JANET LEE, economic developer; b. Okinawa, Japan, Dec. 31, 1951; (parents Am. citizens); d. Rodman Gamble and Patricia Jane (McDonald) S. Student, Maple Woods Coll., 1974-78, Del Mar Coll., 1978-79. Cert. econ. developer. Exec. sec. Am. Indsl. Devel. Coun., Kansas City,

Mo., 1973-78; dir. western sales Indsl. Properties Report, Corpus Christi, Tex., 1978-79; indsl. devel. location cons. Amarillo (Tex.) Bd. Devel., 1979-81; dir. econ. devel. divsn. Roswell (N.Mex.) C. of C., 1981-86; exec. dir. Sheridan (Wyo.) City Econ. Devel. Coun., 1986-90, High Plains Devel. Authority, Great Falls, Mont., 1990-94, Indsl. Devel. Corp. of Lea County, Hobbs, N.Mex., 1994—; mem. faculty Ariz. Basic Econ. Devel. course, U. Ariz., Tucson, 1983-93. Bd. regents Am. Indsl. Devel. Coun., 1981-83, bd. dirs., 1984-88; chmn., bd. dirs., mediator, treas. Great Falls Area Labor/Mgmt. Com., 1991—; mem. Pres.'s coun. Coll. of Great Falls, 1991—. Ninetieth woman in N.Am. to obtain Cert. Econ. Developer designation, 1982. Mem. Mont. Profl. Econ. Devel. Assn. (bd. dirs. 1993-94), Am. Devel. Coun. (bd. dirs. 1982-86, bd. regents 1982-84), N.Mex. Indsl. Devel. Execs. (bd. dirs. 1994—), N.Mex. Commerce and Industry Assn., Hobbs Rotary, Order of Eastern Star. Republican. Baptist. Home: PO Box 294 Hobbs NM 88241 Office: 2702 B Grimes St Hobbs NM 88240

SEAGREN, ALICE, state legislator; b. 1947; m. Fred Seagren; 2 children. BS, SE Mo. State U. Mem. Minn. Ho. of Reps., 1993—. Active Bloomington (Minn.) Sch. Bd., 1989-92. Mem. Bloomington C. of C. (bd. dirs. 1990-92), Phi Gamma Nu, Alpha Chi Omega. Republican. Home: 9730 Palmer Cir Bloomington MN 55437 Office: Minn Ho of Reps State Capitol Saint Paul MN 55155*

SEAMAN, EMMA LUCY, artist, poet; b. West Freedom, Pa., Dec. 5, 1932; d. Roger Leslie and Lillian Emeline (Phillips) Eddinger; m. Roger John Seaman, Sept. 14, 1958; 1 child, Roger Kent. Grad. H.S., Seneca, Pa. Sec. to supt. Cranberry H.S., Seneca, 1951-56; flight attendant, hostess Trans World Airlines, Newark, 1956-57; copy writer Radio St. WFRA, Franklin, Pa., 1957-58. Works have been exhibited at Art League of Marco Island, Fla., 1985-93, Sussex County Arts and Heritage Coun. Fine Arts Exhbns., Newton, 1990-94, N.J. Herald Art Show, Newton, 1990, Annual Sparta (N.J.) Day Event, 1990, St. Mary's Art Festival, Sparta, 1991-94, Hilltop Art Exhibit, Sparta, 1991-94, Edison Festival of Light, Ft. Myers, Fla., 1992; one women show: Sparta Libr., N.J., 1994; contbr. numerous poems to publs. Sunday sch. tchr., Sparta, 1965-74; organizer, operator Paper Drives, Sparta, 1965-74. Recipient First Pl. Beginners Oils award Creative Canvas Art Assn., Newton, 1982, Purchase award St. Mary's Art Festival, Sparta, N.J., 1991, honorable mention, 1993. Mem. ASPCA, AARP, People for the Ethical Treatment Animals, Art League Marco Island, Sussex County Arts and Heritage Coun., Sussex County Arts Assn., Studio A Art Assn., Edison Festival of Light, Nat. Humane Edn. Soc., Human Soc. U.S., Doris Day Animal League, Animal Legal Def. Fund, Women's Mus. Art, Smithsonial Assn., Antique Airplane Assn., Newton (N.J.) Meml. Hosp. Aux., Sparta (N.J.) Woman's Club, Lake Mohawk Country Club. Home: 54 Alpine Trail Sparta NJ 07871

SEAPKER, JANET KAY, museum director; b. Pitts., Nov. 2, 1947; d. Charles Henry and Kathryn Elizabeth (Dany) S.; m. Edward F. Turberg, May 24, 1975. BA, U. Pitts., 1969; MA, SUNY, Cooperstown, 1975. Park ranger Nat. Park Svc., summers 1967-69; archtl. historian N.C. Archives and History, Raleigh, 1971-76, hist. preservation adminstr., 1976-77, grant-in-aid adminstr., 1977-78; dir. Cape Fear Mus. (formerly New Hanover County Mus.), Wilmington, N.C., 1978—; bd. dirs. Bellamy Mansion Found., Wilmington, 1986-89, 91—, Lower Cape Fear Hist. Soc., Wilmington, 1985-88; N.C. rep. S.E. Mus. Conf., 1986-90; field reviewer Inst. Mus. Svcs., 1982—. Contbr. articles to profl. jours. Bd. dirs. Downtown Area Revitalization Effort, Wilmington, 1979-81, Hist. Wilmington Found., 1979-84, pres., 1980-81; mem. Community Appearance Commn., Wilmington, 1984-88, 250 Ann. Commn., Wilmington, 1986-90. Grad. program fellow SUNY, Cooperstown, 1969-70; recipient Profl. Svc. award N.C. Mus. Coun., 1982, Woman of Achievement award YWCA, 1994. Mem. Am. Assn. Mus. (accreditation vis. com. 1983—, reviewer mus. assessment program 1982—), Nat. Trust Hist. Preservation, Southeastern Mus. Conf. (N.C. state rep. 1986-90), N.C. Mus. Coun. (sec.-treas. 1978-84, pres. 1984-86), Hist. Preservation Found N.C. (sec. 1976-78). Democrat. Presbyterian. Home: 307 N 15th St Wilmington NC 28401-3813 Office: Cape Fear Mus 814 Market St Wilmington NC 28401

SEARIGHT, CAROL CHIPMAN, mortgage banker; b. Ashland, Ohio, July 21, 1942; d. Kenneth Gordon Chipman and Ruth Collins Canzonari; m. Nicholas Reis Snyder, Sept. 15, 1962 (div. 1971); children: Nicholas Scott Snyder, Kenneth Matthew Snyder; m. Scott Charles Searight, July 11, 1993. AS in Fine Arts, Penn Hall, Chambersburg, Pa., 1962. Lic. real estate broker, Calif. V.p. Anaheim (Calif.) Savs., 1976-84; sr. v.p. Meritor Mortgage Corp., Phila., 1984-89, M-West Mortgage Corp., Orange, Calif., 1989-93; exec. v.p. MCS Fin., Dallas, 1993—. Bd. dirs. Santa Ana Community Housing Authority, 1985. Gold medalist in Art, 1962. Mem. Western Assn. Affiliated Agys., Calif. Mortgage Bankers Assn. (ins. com. 1991-93), Am. Assn. Residential Mortgage Regulators, Am. Soc. Quality Control. Home: 2 Monticello Irvine CA 92720 Office: MCS Financial 5485 Belt Line Rd Ste 225 Dallas TX 75240-7656

SEARIGHT, MARY DELL (MRS. PAUL JAMES SEARIGHT), nursing educator; b. Cordell, Okla., Jan. 4, 1918; d. John Quitman and Grace Jewel (Giles) Williams; diploma St. Francis Hosp. Sch. Nursing, 1940; B.S. with honors, U. Calif. at Berkeley, 1960; M.S., U. Calif. at San Francisco, 1961; Ed.D., U. San Francisco, 1980; m. Paul James Searight, June 12, 1953; children—Gregory Newton, Sara Ann. Clin. nursing in various hosps., clinics, industries, drs. offices, 1940-59; instr. nursing Merritt Coll., Oakland, Calif., 1961-66; lectr. U. Calif. at San Francisco Sch. Nursing, 1966-68; nursing cons. regional med. programs, lectr. U. Minn., Mpls., 1968-71; chmn. dept. Sonoma State U., 1971-77, prof. nursing, 1971-87, prof. emeritus, 1987—; mem. acad. senate, 1972-75, cons. nursing edn., 1972-77; project dir. Nat. 2d Step Project, 1978-81; cons. Bur. Health Resources Devel., San Francisco, 1973-75; mem. chancellor's liaison com. nursing edn. Calif. State U. and Colls. Office of Chancellor, Los Angeles, 1973-76; chmn. Sonoma County Health Facilities Planning Com., Santa Rosa, Calif., 1970-72; mem. planning com. Sonoma Health Services/Edn. Activities, Santa Rosa, 1972; mem. exec. com., bd. dirs. Sonoma County Comprehensive Health Planning Com., 1970-72. Mem. Nat. League Nursing, Am. Assn. Colls. Nursing, Am., Calif. (Lulu Hassenplug award 1975) Nurses Assns., Santa Rosa Symphony League, Sigma Theta Tau. Author: Your Career in Nursing, 1970, 2d edit., 1977; editor, contbg. author: The Second Step, Baccalaureate Education for Registered Nurses (Book of Year, Am. Jour. Nursing), 1976; contbr. articles to profl. jours. Address: 301 White Oak Dr # 165 Santa Rosa CA 95409

SEARIGHT, PATRICIA ADELAIDE, retired radio and television executive; b. Rochester, N.Y.; d. William Hammond and Irma (Winters) S. BA, Ohio State U. Program dir. Radio Sta. WTOP, Washington, 1952-63, gen. mgr. info., 1964; radio and TV cons., 1964-84; ret., 1984; producer, dir. many radio and TV programs; spl. fgn. news corr. French Govt., 1956; v.p. Micro Beads, Inc., 1955-59; sec., dir. Dennis-Inches, Corp., 1955-59; exec. dir. Am. Women in Radio and TV, 1969-74; fgn. service officer U.S. Dept. State, ret., AEC, ret. Mem. pres.'s coun. Toledo Mus. Art. Recipient Kappa Kappa Gamma Alumna achievement award. Mem. Am. Women in Radio and TV (program chmn.; corrs. sec.; dir. Washington chpt.; pres. 1958-60, nat. membership chmn. 1962-63, nat. chmn. Industry Info. Digest 1963-64, Mid-Eastern v.p. 1964-66), Soc. Am. Travel Writers (treas. 1957-58, v.p. 1958-59), Nat. Acad. TV Arts and Scis., Women's Advt. Club (Washington, pres. 1959-60), Nat. Press Club, Soroptimist, Kappa Kappa Gamma. Episcopalian. Home: 9498 E Via Montoya Dr Scottsdale AZ 85255-5074

SEARING, MARJORY ELLEN, government official, economist; b. N.Y.C., Mar. 29, 1945; d. William Edgar Searing and Jean Frances (Smith) Searing Fusaro; m. Warren Eugene Lane, Mar. 3, 1977; children—Gary Francis, Jennifer Rebecca, Stephanie Anne. B.A. in Econs., SUNY-Binghamton, 1966; M.A. in Econs., Georgetown U., 1969, Ph.D. in Econs., 1972. Economist Bur. Econs. Analysis U.S. Dept. Commerce, Washington, 1967-73, internat. economist Bur. East-West Trade, 1973-74, dir. Office Internat. Sector Policy, 1980-84, dir. Office Industry Assessment, 1984-86, acting dep. asst. sec. for sci. and electronics, 1984-85, dir. Office Multilateral Affairs, 1986-90; dep. asst. sec. for Japan U.S. Dept. Commerce, 1991—; sr. internat. economist Office Trade Policy U.S. Dept. Treasury, Washington, 1974-76, dir. Office East-West Econ. Policy, 1976-79. Contbr. numerous articles to profl. publs. N.Y. State Regents scholar, 1962-65; Georgetown U. fellow, 1966-71. Office: US Dept Commerce Rm 2318 14th & Constitution Ave NW Washington DC 20230-0002

SEARLE, ELEANOR MILLARD, history educator; b. Chgo., Oct. 29, 1926; married. BA, Harvard U., 1948; Licentiate Medieval Studies, Pontifical Inst. Medieval History, 1961, D Medieval Studies, 1972. Lectr. history Calif. Inst. Tech., Pasadena, 1962-63, prof. history, 1979-87, Edie and Lou Wasserman prof. history, 1987—; rsch. fellow Rsch. Sch. Social Sci., Australian Nat. U., 1963-65, fellow, 1965-68; assoc. prof. UCLA, 1969-72, prof., 1972-79; vis. fellow Cambridge U., 1976, 81; sr. rsch. fellow Hungtington Libr., 1986—; cons. Huntington Libr., 1980-82. Author: Lordship and Community: Battle Abbey and Its Banlieu, 1066-1538, 1974; editor: The Chronicle of Battle Abbey, 1980; co-editor: Accounts of the Cellarers of Battle Abbey, 1967, Predatory Kinship and the Creation of Norman Power, 840-1066, 1988; contbr. articles to profl. jours. Fellow Royal Hist. Soc., Royal Soc. Antiquaries of London; mem. Am. Hist. Soc., Medieval Acad. Am. (pres. 1985-86), Econ. History Soc., Am. Soc. Legal History, Haskins Soc. (bd. dirs. 1982—, pres. 1990—). Office: Calif Inst Tech Dept History Pasadena CA 91125

SEARLE, EVE KAPRAL, small business owner; b. Brno, Czechoslovakia, Oct. 24, 1934; came to U.S., 1973; d. Ales Maria and Zdena Maria (Sramek) Kapral; m. Gerald Searle, May 7, 1983. Sales mgr. Willmore & Randell, Melbourne, Australia, 1961-63, Devel. Underwriting, Ltd., Melbourne, Australia, 1963-65; chief flight instr. Groupair Ltd., Casey Airfield Berwick, Victoria, Australia, 1968-70; rancher, 1970-85; mgr., CEO Grapevine Canyon Ranch Inc., Pearce, Ariz., 1986—, sec.-treas., 1990—; sec.-treas. Grapevine Canyon Land Corp., Pearce, 1990—. Office: Grapevine Canyon Ranch Inc PO Box 302 Pearce AZ 85625

SEARLES, ANNA MAE HOWARD, educator, civic worker; b. Osage Nation Indian Terr., Okla., Nov. 22, 1906; d. Frank David and Clara (Bowman) Howard; A.A., Odessa (Tex.) Coll., 1961; B.A., U. Ark., 1964; M.Ed., 1970; postgrad. (Herman L. Donovan fellow), U. Ky., 1972—; m. Isaac Adams Searles, May 26, 1933; 1 dau., Mary Ann Rogers (Mrs. Herman Lloyd Hoppe). Compiler news, broadcaster sta. KJBC, 1950-60; corr. Tulsa Daily World, 1961-64; tchr. Rogers (Ark.) High Sch., 1964-72; tchr. adult class rapid reading, 1965, 80; tchr. adult edn. Learning Center Benton County (Ark.), Bentonville, 1973-77, supr. adult edn., 1977-79; tchr. North Ark. Community Coll., Rogers, 1979-90, CETA, Bentonville, 1979-82; tchr. Joint Tng. Partnership Act, 1984-85; coordinator adult edn. Rogers C. of C. and Rogers Sch. System, 1984—. Sec. Tulsa Safety Council, 1935-37; leader, bd. dirs. Girl Scouts U.S.A., Kilgore, Tex., 1941-44, leader, Midland, Tex., 1944-52, counselor, 1950-61; exec. sec. Midland Community Chest, 1955-60; gray lady Midland A.R.C., 1958-59; organizer Midland YMCA, Salvation Army; dir. women's div. Savings Bond Program, Midland; mem. citizens com. Rogers Hough Meml. Library, women's aux. Rogers Meml. Hosp.; vol. tutor Laubach literacy orgn., 1973—; sec. Beaver Lake Literacy Council, Rogers, 1973-83, Little Flock Planning Commn., 1975-77, Benton County Hist. Soc., 1981—; pub. relations chmn. South Central region Nat. Affiliation for Literacy Advance, 1977-79; bd. dirs. Globe Theatre, Odessa, Tex., Midland Community Theatre, Tri-County Foster Home, Guadalupe, Midland youth centers, DeZavala Day Nursery, PTA, Adult Devel. Center, Rogers CETA, 1979-81; vol. recorder Ark. Hist. Preservation Program, 1984—; docent Rogers Hist. Mus., 1988—. Recipient Nice People award Rogers C. of C., 1987, Thanks badge Midland Girl Scout Assn., 1948, Appreciation Plaque award Ark. Natural Heritage Commn., 1988; Cert. of recognition, Rogers Pub. Schs., 1986, Cert. of Recognition, Beaver Lake Literacy Coun., 1993; Instr. of Yr. award North Ark. Community Coll. West Campus, Conservation award Woodmen of the World Life Ins. Soc., 1991, Vol. of Yr. award Rogers Hist. Mus., 1993. Mem. NEA (del. conv. 1965), Ark. Assn. Public Continuing and Adult Edn. (pres. 1979-80), South Central Assn. for Lifelong Learning (sec. 1980-84), PTA (life), Future Homemakers Am. (life; sec. 1980—), Delta Kappa Gamma (Disting. Achievement award Beta Pi chpt. 1992). Episcopalian. Clubs: Altrusa (pres. 1979—), Apple Spur Community (Rogers). Home: 2808 N Dixieland PO Box 03319400 Rogers AR 72756

SEARLES, LYNN MARIE, nurse; b. Cherryvale, Kans., Oct. 29, 1949; d. Darrell Eugene and Beva Caroline (Waller) Stringer; m. Martin Dale Searles, Aug. 23, 1970; children: Jeremy Dale, Michelle Le Anne. Assoc. in Fine Arts, Labette Community Jr. Coll., Parsons, Kans., 1969; ADN, Labette Community Jr. Coll., 1970. RN, Kans., Calif. Evening med.-surg. charge nurse Coffeyville (Kans.) Meml. Hosp., 1970-72, med.-surg. head nurse, 1972-73, relief evening house supr. and emergency rm. nurse, 1974, head nurse recovery rm., 1974-81; head nurse recovery rm., ambulatory care unit Coffeyville Meml. Med. Ctr., 1981-83, head nurse recovery rm., ambulatory care unit and surgery, 1983-84; dir. family planning, rural home health aide and multi phasic screening clinics, AIDS edn. and counseling Jefferson County Health Dept., Oskaloosa, Kansas, 1984-87; nurse III, health facility surveyor Lawrence dist. Kans. Dept. Health and Environ., Lawrence, Kans., 1988—. Mem. Internat. Platform Assn., Kans. Pub. Health Assn., Am. Soc. Post Anesthesia Nurses (charter mem.). Republican. Nazarene Ch. Office: Kans Dept Health and Environment 808 W 24th St Lawrence KS 66046-4417

SEARLS, EILEEN HAUGHEY, lawyer, librarian, educator; b. Madison, Wis., Apr. 27, 1925; d. Edward M. and Anna Mary (Haughey) S.; BA, U. Wis., 1948, JD, 1950, MS in Libr. Sci., 1951. Bar: Wis. 1950. Cataloger Yale U., 1951-52; instr. law St. Louis U., 1952-53, asst. prof., 1953-56, asso. prof., 1956-64, prof., 1964—, law librarian, 1952—. Mem. Am. Lib. Assn., Wis. Bar Assn., Bar Assn. Met. St. Louis, Am. Assn. Law Librs., Mid-Am. Assn. Law Librs., Southwestern Assn. Law Librs., Altrusa Club. Office: 3700 Lindell Blvd Saint Louis MO 63108-3478

SEARS, ANNE MORGAN, college administrator; b. Norristown, Pa., Sept. 14, 1947; d. Lewis Hinkel and Gladys Elizabeth (Tregea) Dyer; m. Thomas Ananda Dorlon; 1 child, Michelle Tregea Dorlon; m. John Thomas Sears, Aug. 21, 1982. BA, Trenton (N.J.) State Coll., 1979. Dir. pub. rels. Cybis, Trenton, 1979-86; dir. external affairs Westminster Choir Coll. of Rider U., Princeton, N.J., 1986—; cons. Am. Boychoir Sch., Princeton, 1987-90. Editor newsletter Westminster Notes, 1986—. Bd. dirs. Delaware Valley Philharm., 1991-93. Recipient Tribute to Women of Industry award YWCA of Trenton, 1985. Mem. N.J. Comms., Mktg. and Advt. Assn. (bd. dirs., pres. 1990-91), Nuvisions for Disabled Adults (bd. dirs., v.p. 1991—). Office: Westminster Choir Coll Rider U 101 Walnut Ln Princeton NJ 08540-3899

SEARS, DONNA MAE, technical writer and illustrator; b. St. Paul, Oct. 23, 1951; d. Raymond and Shirley Marie (Dupre) Waldoch; m. Mark D. Sears, Sept. 4, 1993. BA in Art and Edn., Cardinal Stritch Coll., Milw., 1969-73; postgrad., Rock Valley Coll., Rockford, Ill., 1985, 87, 89-90, So. Ill. U., 1983; cert. of tng., Computervision Tech. Ctr., Itasca, Ill., 1986, 88. Electronic assembler Warner Electric Co., Marengo, Ill., 1973-75, machine hand, 1976-78, quality assurance lead insp., 1978-80, draftswoman, 1980-86, CAD-sr. draftswoman, 1986-87; tchr. art Stephen Mack Sch. Dist., Rockford, 1975, Harrison Sch. Dist., Wonder Lake, Ill., 1975-76; CAD specialist Greenlee Textron Inc., Rockford, 1988-89, resigned, 1989; asst. buyer Ingersoll Milling, Rockford, 1989-90; asst. office mgr. and sign maker Shake-A-Leg Signs, Rockford, 1990-92; tech. writer and illustrator Mathews Co., Crystal Lake, Ill., 1992; tech. writer and CAD support Clinton Electronics, Loves Park, Ill., 1993—. Author: (with others) Treasured Poems of America, 1990, Poetic Voices of America, spring 1992, Anthonology of American Poetry, fall 1991 (awards of Poetic Excellence 1992), Distinguished Poets of America, spring 1993, The Sound of Poetry, spring 1993. Vol. Boone County Conservation Dist.; mem. choir St. James Ch., Belvidere, Ill., 1985-93; assoc. mem. Spl. Olympics. Recipient Leadership award YWCA, Rockford, 1988. Mem. Internat. Soc. Poets, Exptl. Aircraft Assn., Nat. Right to Life Assn. Roman Catholic.

SEARS, SANDRA LEE, computer consultant; b. Rochester, N.Y., Apr. 25, 1952. AB with distinction, Cornell U., 1974; MA, U. Conn., 1976, postgrad., 1976-81. Cert. in data processing, 1983. Tng. cons. Ins. Crime Prevention Inst., Westport, Conn., 1977-78; systems analyst Data Directions, Bloomfield, Conn., 1978-79; prin. S. S. Prindle Consulting, Manchester, Conn., 1979-81; dir. info. svcs. Conn. Attys. Title Ins., Rocky Hill, Conn., 1981-85; mgr., systems, programming Community Health Care Plan, Inc., Wallingford, Conn., 1985-87; assoc. dir. Mass. Mutual Life Ins., Springfield, Mass., 1987-91; cons. mgr. Coopers & Lybrand Cons., East Hartford, Conn., 1991—; adj. faculty U. New Haven, West Haven, Conn., 1976-77, Eastern Conn. State U., Willimantic, 1986—, Manchester Community Coll., 1989—; participant Tex. Instruments' Case Satellite Seminar, 1989. Mentor Career Beginnings, Hartford, 1991—. Presdl. scholar Nat. Merit Program, 1970, William Stout scholar Cornell U., 1973, AAUW fellow U. Conn., 1981. Mem. Cornell Club of Greater Hartford (mem. admissons vol. programs alumni adv. com., exec. bd., book award chair 1987—), Cornell Alumni Admissions Amb. Network (chair 1983-86), Mortar Board, Phi Kappa Phi, Pi Mu Epsilon. Office: Coopers & Lybrand LLP 333 E River Dr East Hartford CT 06108

SEARS-COLLINS, LEAH J., state supreme court justice; b. Heidelberg, Germany, June 13, 1955; d. Thomas E and Onnye J. Sears; m. Love Sears-Collins III; children: Addison, Brennan. BS, Cornell Univ., 1976; JD, Emory Univ., 1980; postgrad., Nat. Judicial Coll., U. Va.; LLD (hon.), Morehouse Coll., 1993. Assoc. Alston & Bird, Atlanta; judge Superior Ct of GA, Atlanta, GA, 1988-1992; assoc. justice Ga. Supreme Ct., Atlanta, GA, 1992—. Contbr. articles to profl. jours. Adv. bd. United Way Drug Abuse Action Ctr., Outdoor Activity Nature Ctr.; bd. dirs. Sadie G. Mays Nursing Home, Ga. chpt. NCCJ; active Cornell U. Women's Coun., Children's Def. Fund's Black Community Crusade for Children, steering com. Ga. Women's History Month; founder Battered Women's Project, Columbus, Ga. Recipient Community Svc. award Atlanta chpt. NAACP, Disting. Leadership award for Outstanding Svc. in the Judiciary, 1988, Drum Major for Justice award SCLC Women, 1992, Excellence in Pub. Svc. award Ga. Coalition of Black Women, 1992; named Black Woman of Achievement, Southern Bell 1990, Outstanding Young Alumna, Ga. Speaker of Yr., Emory U., One of 100 Most Influential Georgians, Ga. Trend Mag., Atlantan on the Move, 100 Black Men of Am., One of 10 Outstanding Women of Achievement, YMCA of Greater Atlanta. Mem. ABA (chair bd. elections, Margaret Brent Women Judge Achievement award), Nat. Bar Assn., Nat. Assn. Women Judges, State Bar Ga., Atlanta Bar Assn. (past chair jud. sect., minority clerkship program), Ga. Assn. Black Women Attys. (founding pres.), Women's Forum Ga., Gate City Bar Assn., Links, Inc. (Atlanta chpt.), Fourth Tuesday Group, Jack and Jill of Am. (Atlanta chpt.), Alpha Kappa Alpha. Baptist. Office: Supreme Ct Ga 514 State Judicial Bldg Atlanta GA 30334*

SEASHORE, MARGRETTA, physician; b. Red Bank, N.J., June 20, 1939; d. Robert Clark and Lillie Ann (Heaviland) R.; m. John Seashore, Dec. 26, 1964; children: Robert H., Carl J., Carolyn L. BA, Swarthmore Coll., 1961; MD, Yale U., 1965. Diplomate Am. Bd. Pediatrics, Am. Bd. Med. Genetics, Nat. Bd. Med. Examiners. Intern in pediatrics Yale U. Sch. Medicine, Haven, Conn., 1965-66, asst. resident in pediatrics, 1966-68; postdoctoral fellow in genetics and metabolism, depts. of pediatrics and medicine Yale U. Sch. Medicine, 1968-70; clin. asst. prof. pediatrics U. Fla. Coll. Medicine, Gainesville, 1970-71; attending physician Hope Haven Children's Hosp., Jacksonville, Fla., 1970-73; asst. prof. pediatrics Duval Med. Ctr., Jacksonville, Fla., 1970-71; attending physician Duvall Med. Ctr. U. Hosp. Jacksonville, 1970-73; asst. prof. pediatrics U. Fla. Coll. Medicine, 1971-73; attending physician Shands Teaching Hosp., Gainesville, Fla., 1971-73; asst. clin. prof. human genetics and pediatrics Yale U. Sch. Medicine, 1974-78; attending physician Yale-New Haven Hosp., 1974—; cons. physician Bridgeport (Conn.) Hosp., 1974—; attending physician Danbury (Conn.) Hosp., 1977—; dir. Genetic Consultation Svc. Yale-New Haven Hosp., 1977-86; from asst. prof. to assoc. prof. human genetics and pediatrics Yale U. Sch. Medicine, 1978-90; cons. physician Lawrence and Meml. Hosp., New London, Conn., 1979—, Norwalk (Conn.) Hosp., 1981—; dir. Genetic Consultation Svc. Yale-New Haven Hosp., 1989—; prof. genetics and pediatrics Yale U. Sch. Medicine, 1990—. Contbr. chpts. to books. Fellow Am. Acad. Pediatrics (chair com. on genetics, 1990-94, mem. screening com. Conn. chpt. 1977—, mem. genetics com. 1989—), Am. Coll. Med. Genetics (founder, mem. screening sub-com. 1993—); mem. AMA, AAAS, Am. Soc. Human Genetics (mem. genetic svcs. com. 1986-91), Soc. Inherited Metabolic Disorders (mem. bd. dirs. 1989—, sec. 1991—), Soc. for the Study of Inborn Errors of Metabolism, New England Genetics Group (co-dir. 1992—, chmn. outreach com. 1979-89, chmn. screening com. 1989-93, mem. steering com. 1979—). Office: Yale U Sch Med Dept Genetics 333 Cedar St New Haven CT 06510-3206

SEASTRAND, ANDREA, congresswoman; b. Chgo., Aug. 5, 1941; m. Earl Seastrand (dec.); children: Kurt, Heidi. BA in Edn., DePaul U., 1963. Prof. religion U. Santa Barbara; mem. Calif. Assembly, 1990-94, U.S. Ho. of Reps., 1995—; asst. Rep. leader; mem. Rep. caucus; mem. edn. com., agr. com., consumer protection com., new tech. com., govtl. efficiency com., and ways and means com.; mem. rural caucus and select com. on marine resources. Mem. Calif. Fedn. Rep. Women (past pres.). Office: US Ho of Reps 113 Cannon HOB Washington DC 20515-0522*

SEATON, KATHLEEN CASEY, newspaper publisher; b. Stockton, Calif., Sept. 25, 1949; d. Finis Edward Bumgarner and Evelyn Lucille (Rule) Dockter. BS in Biol. Scis., Calif. State U. Stanislaus, Turlock, 1977. Lic. gen. bldg. contractor. Founder, co-owner, mgr. The Wood Works, Modesto, Calif., 1978-83, Havasu Hills Herb Farm, Coulterville, Calif., 1982-90; founder, co-editor, pub. Yosemite Hwy. Herald, Coulterville, 1988—. Mem. Blue Ribbon Com. Studying Ambulance County Wide Svc., Mariposa, Calif., 1988; vol. AARP-Tax Assistance for the Elderly, Coulterville, 1991-92. Recipient Grand Cross of Color, Internat. Order of Rainbow for Girls, Fresno, 1968, NSF Rsch. grant NSF, Eagle Lake, Calif., 1977. Mem. AAUW, NOW, Nat. Mus. Women in the Arts, Sierra Club, Northside Ambulance Assn. (dir. 1986-88), Gold Country Singers (treas. 1990—). Office: Yosemite Hwy Herald 3717 Stoney Oak Rd Coulterville CA 95311

SEATS, PEGGY CHISOLM, marketing executive; b. Lisman, Ala., Oct. 12, 1951; d. William H. and Bernice (Berry) Chisolm; m. Melvin Seats (div.). BA in Communications cum laude, Lewis U., 1974. Account exec. Globe Broadcasting, Chgo., 1976-78, Merrill Lynch, Chgo., 1978-79, Transp. Displays, Inc., Chgo., 1979-81; nat. accounts mgr. Soft Sheen Products Co., Chgo., 1981-83; mktg. cons. Reverie, Inc., Chgo., 1983-85; pres., mktg. cons. Reverie, Inc., Atlanta, 1987—; pub. rels., mktg. mgr. Proctor & Gardner Advt., Chgo., 1985-86; dir. pub. rels., mktg. Morris Brown Coll., Atlanta, 1986-87; mgr. mktg. Howard U. Press, Washington, 1989-90; cons. White House Initiative on Historically Black Colls., Univs., 1990—; founder Black Pub. Rels. Soc., Atlanta, 1987. Contbr. numerous articles to newspapers and mags. Bd. dirs Lewis U. Alumni, Ill., 1979; state advisor U.S. Congl. Adv. Bd., Ill. 1982. Recipient Kizzie award Black Women Hall of Fame, Chgo., 1981, Svc. award Nat. Assn. Women in Media, Chgo., 1982; inductee Outstanding Women of Am., 1975, 87. Mem. Internat. Platform Assn., Internat. Assn. Bus. Commmunicators, Pub. Rels. Soc. Am., Black Pub. Rels. Soc. (Atlanta Chpt. pres. emeritus), Nat. Assn. Market Developers. Democrat. Baptist. Home: 2020 Pennsylvania Ave NW Washington DC 20006-1846

SEAVY, MARY ETHEL INGLE, art educator; b. Alpena, S.D., Mar. 23, 1910; d. James Albert and Mollie (Ceny) Ingle; m. Donald Lee Seavy, Mar. 19, 1940; 1 child, Judith Ann. BS, No. State Tchrs. Coll., Aberdeen, S.D., 1934; MA in Art, U. Iowa, 1937, postgrad., 1949-53; postgrad., Columbia U., 1940. Cert. permanent profl. tchr., Iowa. Art coord. pub. schs., Decorah, Iowa, 1937-38, Waterloo, Iowa, 1938-40, Whiting, Ind., 1940-41; instr. art Luther Coll., Decorah, 1942-43, U. Iowa, Iowa City, 1945-47; tchr. Solon (Iowa) Elem. Sch., 1949-53; art coord. Mil. Sch., Aschaffenburg, Fed. Republic Germany, 1962-64; tchr. Iowa City Pub. Schs., 1965-75; artist, tchr. Stauffenburg Studio, Marengo, Iowa, 1987-90. One-woman show Hawkeye State Bank, Coralville, Iowa, 1987; exhibited in group shows State Fair, Des Moines, 1989, Cmty. Theatre, 1990, Heart Ctr. for Arts, Cedar Falls, 1992, Fern Hill Gallery, 1992, Dubuque (Iowa) Art Show, 1993, Iowa City Art Ctr., 1994, Hawkeye State Bank, 1994, art show, Iowa City, 1994, Cedar Rapids Art Show, 1994. Recipient award for short story State Federated Women's Club, 1987, 90, award for essay, 1987, 90; 1st place print, 2d place oil State Regional Art Show, Dubuque, 1994, 2d place award, Cedar Rapids, 1994; Mil. Edn. Achievement award, 1994; named to Internat. Profl. and Bus. Women's Hall of Fame, 1994. Mem. AAUW, DAR (past regent Iowa City), Iowa Watercolor Soc., Iowa City Women's Club, Order Ea. Star, Order White Shrine of Jerusalem (past worth high priestess), Order of Amaranth, Delta Kappa Gamma, Zeta Tau Alpha (v.p. Alpha Omicron chpt. 1970-71). Christian Scientist. Home and Studio: 534 Clark St Iowa City IA 52240

SEBASTIAN, NANCY SMITH TOMSON, guidance counselor, consultant; b. Hammond, Ind., Jan. 4, 1947; d. Robert Ellsworth Smith and Norma J. (Gattoli) Blackman; m. Douglas Sebastian, Dec. 17, 1994; children: Tami Lee Tomson, Troy Dustin Tomson. BA in English with distinction, Purdue U., 1969; MA in English, Ball State U., 1973; MA in Counseling, Ind. U., Ft. Wayne, 1986. Program dir. Miami County Mus., Peru, Ind., 1985-87; guidance counselor Maconaquah Sch. Corp., Bunker Hill, Ind., 1987—; mem. adj. faculty Ball State U., Muncie, Ind., 1987, Ind. U., Kokomo, 1989; cons. Lilly Endowment, Indpls., 1989—, Ind. Youth Inst.; trainer Trustee Leadership Devel., Indpls., 1988—, Community-Youth Partnerships, Ft. Wayne, 1991—; workshop presenter on youth and parenting to local and state orgns.; cons. on youth programming. Author: Leadership Partners, 1993. Mem. Ind. Parent Project. Named Sagamore of Wabash, State of Ind., 1989; Lilly leadership edn. fellow Lilly Endowment, 1987. Mem. ACA, Am. Sch. Counselor Assn., Ind. Sch. Counselor Assn., Ind. Counseling Assn. Office: Maconaquah Mid Sch RR 1 Bunker Hill IN 46914

SEBELA, VICKI D., association executive; b. Des Plaines, Ill., Mar. 7, 1964; d. James Edward and Mary Nell (Davis) S.; m. Julius Michael Colangelo, Oct. 8, 1988. AA, AS, Harper Coll., 1984; BS, Roosevelt U., 1986; student, Inst. Orgnl. Mgmt., Boulder, Colo., 1991-93. Adminstrv. asst. McDonald's Corp., Rolling Meadows, Ill., 1979-83; info. specialist William Rainey Harper Coll., Palatine, Ill., 1983-84; teller Arlington Fed. Savs. and Loan, Arlington Heights, Ill., 1984-85; asst. to the pres. Ill. Women's Agenda, Chgo., 1984-85; student outreach coord. William Rainey Harper Coll., Palatine, 1985-86; adminstrv. asst. women's affairs Office of the Gov., Chgo., 1986-88; exec. adminstr. Social Engring. Assocs., Inc., Chgo., 1988-89; exec. dir. Greater Wheaton (Ill.) C. of C., 1989-94; internat. conf. dir. Environ. Planning Group, Barrington, Ill., 1994—; founder Wheaton Womens Bus. Coun. Columnist, Daily Herald, 1992—; contbr. articles to Ency. Brit. Cert. paraprofl. Talk Line/Kids Line Crisis Hot Line, Elk Grove Village, Ill., 1983; plan commr. City of Wheaton, 1994—; mem. Wheaton History Ctr. Harper Coll. scholar, 1982, Roosevelt U. scholar, 1984. Mem. APA, Chgo. Women in Govt. Rels. (membership chair, bd. dirs. 1988-89), Women's Opportunity Internat., Greater Wheaton C. of C. (hon., life), South Wheaton Bus. Assn., Phi Theta Kappa. Republican. Office: Environmental Planning Group Inc 205 Park Ave Barrington IL 60010-4332

SEBELIUS, KATHLEEN GILLIGAN, state legislator; b. Cin., May 15, 1948; d. John J. and Mary K. (Dixon) Gilligan; m. Keith Gary Sebelius, 1974; children: Edward Keith, John McCall. BA, Trinity Coll., 1970; MA, U. Kans., 1977. Dir. planning Ctr. for Cmty. Justice, Washington, 1971-74; spl. asst. Kans. Dept. Corrections, Topeka, 1975-78; mem. Kans. Ho. of Reps., 1987—. Founder Women's Polit. Caucus; mem. cmty. adv. com. Youth Ctr. Topeka, Kans. Children's Coalition; precinct committeewoman, 1980-86; mayor-elect, Potwin, 1985-87. Mem. Common Cause (state bd., nat. gov. bd. 1975—), Phi Sigma Alpha. Democrat. Roman Catholic. Home: 224 SW Greenwood Ave Topeka KS 66606-1228*

SEBRING, MARJORIE MARIE ALLISON, home furnishings company executive; Burnsville, N.C., Oct. 8, 1926; d. James William and Mary Will (Ramsey) Allison Shockey; student Mars Hill Coll., 1943, Home Decorators Sch. Design, N.Y.C., 1948, Wayne State U., 1953; cert. home furnishings rep. U. Va., 1982; 1 child, Patricia Louise Banner Krohn. Dir. decorating div. Robinson Furniture, Detroit, 1949-57; head buyer Tyner Hi-Way House, Ypsilanti, Mich., 1957-63; head buyer Town and Country, Dearborn, Mich., 1963-66; instr. Nat. Carpet Inst., 1963-71; owner Adams House, Inc., Plymouth, Mich., 1966-72; exec. v.p. mktg. and sales, regional sales and mktg. mgr. Triangle Industries, L.A., 1972-89; co-owner Markham-Sebring, Inc., St. Petersburg, Fla., 1983-89; dir. contract div. Kane Furniture, 1984-85; co-owner Accessories, Etc., 1985-89; chmn. bd. Heritage Lakes, U.S. Home. Vol. coord. Pasco County Clerk Ct., Suncoast Theatre; mem adv. bd. Webster Coll; charter mem. Presdl. Task Force; pres. Presbyn. Ch. Seven Springs; bd. dirs. Fla. Health and Human Svc.; chmn. bd. dirs. Two Westminster Condominium Assn., Inc. Recipient nat. sales awards, recognition for work with youth and aged; named to Fla. Finest list by Fla. Gov., 1994. Mem. Internat. Home Furnishings Assn., Fla. Home Furnishings Rep. Assn. (officer), Am. Security Coun. (coun.), Williamsburg Found., USCG Aux., Nat. Audubon Soc., Internat. Platform Assn. Republican. Contbr. creative display to Better Homes and Gardens, 1957-64. Home: 4902 Cathedral Ct New Port Richey FL 34655-1486

SEBRING, PATRICIA LOUISE, technical writer and editor; b. N.Y., Oct. 3, 1956; d. Ray McCarty and Louise Arlene (Bender) S. BA, Wilkes Coll., 1978; MS, East Stroudsburg State U., 1981. Environ. compliance coord. Bechtel Power Corp., Berwick, Pa., 1981-84; safety engr. Dynamac Corp., Rockville, Md., 1984; exec. dir. Susquehanna-Wyoming Counties Solid Waste Authority, Tunkhannock, Pa., 1985-88; bus. devel. rep. Bechtel Civil, Inc., Vienna, Va., 1988-89; supr. pubs. Bechtel Power Corp., Gaithersburg, Md., 1989-94; bus. devel. rep. Bechtel Power Corp., 1994—. Adult ministries coord. Grace United Meth. Ch., Gaithersburg, 1994—. Mem. Nat. Mgmt. Assn. (chmn. bd. dirs. 1993—). Methodist. Office: Bechtel Power Corp 9801 Washingtonian Blvd Gaithersburg MD 20878

SECCARECCIA, LUCILLE DINA, game manufacturing company executive; b. Hartford, Conn., June 27, 1958; d. Dino and Lucille (Gallicchio) S. BFA, U. Hartford. Lic. master type-setter Printing Industry Am. Paste-up artist, typesetter Gamer Publications, West Hartford, Conn., 1980; typesetter, supr. system Allied Printing Svc., Manchester, Conn., 1980-88; v.p. Lombard Mktg., Bloomfield, Conn., 1988-93; COO Gamewright, Inc., Chestnut Hill, Mass., 1993—. vol. career counselor U. Hartford, 1991—. Office: Gamewright, Inc PO Box 370219 West Hartford CT 06137-0219

SEDACCA, ROSALIND PEARL, marketing professional, copywriter, consultant; b. Bklyn., Mar. 7, 1947; d. Sidney J. and Dorothy Lipson; m. divorced; 1 child, Cassidy Daniel. BFA, Pratt Inst., 1967; postgrad., NYU, 1967-68. Creative dir. circulation promotion dept. The Condé Nast Pub., N.Y.C., 1967-70; direct response copywriter Altman, Vos & Reichberg, N.Y.C., 1970-72; advt., freelance copywriter The Parker Group, Nashville, 1973-78; pres. Creative Copywriting Services, St. Louis, 1978-80; copy dir. MBI Advt., Palm Beach Gardens, Fla., 1981-84; pres. Rosalind Sedacca & Assocs., Advt., Mktg., Pub. Rels., Lake Worth, Fla., 1984—; cons. small bus. devel. ctr. Fla. Atlantic U., 1986—. speaker in field. Recipient numerous awards Advt. Fedn. Am. Mem. Fla. Freelance Writer Assn., Am. Mktg. Assn. (program dir. Palm Beach County chpt. 1989-91), Fla. Spkrs. Assn. (comm. workshop), Nat. Spkrs. Assn. Office: Rosalind Sedacca & Assocs 2003 20th Ln Lake Worth FL 33463-4259

SEDDON, JOHANNA MARGARET, ophthalmologist, epidemiologist; b. Pitts.; m. Ralph Hingson, 1974. BS, U. Pitts., 1970, MD, 1974; MS in Epidemiology, Harvard U., 1976. Diplomate Am. Bd. Ophthalmology. Intern Framingham (Mass.) Union Hosp., 1974-75; resident Tufts New Eng. Med. Ctr., Boston, 1976-80; fellow ophthalmic pathology Mass. Eye and Ear Infirmary, Boston, 1980-81, clin. fellow vitreoretinal Retina Svc., 1981-82; instr. clin. ophthalmology Harvard Med. Sch., Boston, 1982-84, asst. prof., asst. surgeon ophthalmolgy, 1984, assoc. prof., 1989—; assoc. surgeon, dir. ultrasound svc. Mass. Eye and Ear Infirmary, Boston, 1989—, orgn. epidemiology rsch. unit, 1984-85, dir. epidemiology unit, 1985—, surgeon in ophthalmology, 1992—; assoc. prof. faculty dept. epidemiology Harvard Sch. Pub. Health, Boston, 1992—; mem. com. vision Commn Behavioral and Social Scis. and Edn., NRC, Washington, 1984; mem. div. rsch. grants NIH, 1987-89, 94—. Author books and articles in field; mem. editl. staff ophthalmic jours. Recipient awards NIH Nat. Svc. Rsch., 1975, 80-81; grantee and prin. investigator Nat. Eye Inst., 1984-95, Nat. Cancer Inst., 1986; med. sch. scholar, 1970-74, Henry H. Clark Med. Edn. Found., 1973. Mem. AMA, APHA, Am. Acad. Ophthalmology (Honor award 1990), Am. Med. Women's Assn., Assn. Rsch. in Vision and Ophthalmology (elected, chair epidemiology sect. 1990, trustee clin. vision epidemiology sect. 1992—), Soc. Epidemiologic Rsch., New Eng. Ophthal. Soc., Am. Coll. Epidemiology, Retina Soc., Macula Soc. Home: 4 Louisburg Sq Boston MA 02108-1203

SEDLACEK, EVELYN ANN, library developer; b. Mpls., Sept. 18, 1919; d. Guy Galen and Eleanor Rose (Stein) Harper; m. James Arthur Sedlacek, June 6, 1945; children: Judith, Joan, Karen. BS, U. Nebr., Omaha, 1973, MS, 1981. Rsch. libr. Joslyn Art Mus., Omaha, 1974-75; law libr. Smith, Peterson Law Firm, Council Bluffs, Iowa, 1977-84; libr. developer Papio Natural Resources Devel., Omaha, 1977-81; pres. BHS and Assocs., Omaha, 1982—. Bd. dirs. Etc. Camp Fire Girls, Omaha, 1955-76; mem. Omaha Opera, 1959—; mem. coms. Omaha Symphony Guild, 1946-49; sewing com. Omaha Home for Girls, 1958-66; sorting com. Friends of the Omaha Pub. Libr. (Vol. of Yr. award 1994); vol. arhival/photogrpahy dept. Western Heritage Mus. Omaha History Mus., Joslyn Art Mus. Mem. AAUW, Omaha History Mus., Nebr. Libr. Assn., Mountain Plains Libr. Assn., Civil War Round Table of Omaha, Daus. of Union Vets. of Civil War 1861-1865, Phi Alpha Theta, Kappa Delta Pi, Phi Delta Gamma. Home: 8628 Broadmoor Dr Omaha NE 68114-4243

SEDLAK, VALERIE FRANCES, English language educator, university administrator; b. Balt., Mar. 11, 1934; d. Julian Joseph and Eleanor Eva (Pilot) Sedlak; 1 child, Barry. AB in English, Coll. Notre Dame, Balt., 1955; MA, U. Hawaii, 1962; PhD, U. Pa., 1992. Grad. teaching fellow East-West Cultural Ctr. U. Hawaii, 1959-60; adminstrv. asst. Korean Consul Gen., 1959-60; tchr. Boyertown (Pa.) Sr. High Sch., 1961-63; assoc. prof. English U. Balt., 1963-69; assoc. prof. Morgan State U., Balt., 1970—, sec. to faculty, 1981-83, faculty research scholar, 1982-83, 92-93, communications officer, 1989-90, dir. writing for TV program, 1990—, asst. dean coll. arts and scis., 1995—; cons. scholar Md. Humanities Coun., 1992—. Author poetry and lit. criticism; asst. editor Mid. Atlantic Writer's Assn. Rev., 1989—; assoc. editor Md. English Jour., 1994—, Morgan Jour. of Undergrad. Rsch., 1995—. Coord. Young Reps., Berks County, Pa., 1962-63; chmn. Md. Young Reps., 1964; election judge Baltimore County, Md., 1964-66; regional capt. Am. Cancer Soc., 1978-79; mem. adv. bd. Md. Our Md. Anniversary, 1984, The Living Constitution: Bicentennial of the Fed. Constitution, 1987. Fellow Morgan-Penn Faculty, 1977-79, Nat. Endowment Humanities, 1984; named Outstanding Teaching Prof., U. Balt. Coll. Liberal Arts, 1965, Outstanding Teaching Prof. English, Morgan State U., 1987. Mem. MLA, South Atlantic MLA, Coll. Lang. Assn., Coll. English Assn. (v.p. Mid-Atlantic Group 1987-90, pres. 1990-92, exec. bd. 1992—), Women's Caucus for Modern Langs., Md. Coun. Tchrs. English, Md. Poetry and Lit. Soc., Md. Assn. Depts. English (bd. dirs. 1992—), Mid. Atlantic Writers' Assn. (founding 1981, asst. editor Mid Atlantic Writers' Assn. Review 1989—), Delta Sigma Epsilon (v.p. 1992-94, pres. 1994—). Roman Catholic. Home: 102 Gorsuch Rd Lutherville Timonium MD 21093-4318 Office: Morgan State U Dept English Baltimore MD 21239

SEDLOCK, JOY, psychiatric social worker; b. Memphis, Jan. 23, 1958; d. George Rudolph Sedlock and Mary Robson; m. Thomas Robert Jones, Aug. 8, 1983. AA, Ventura (Calif.) Jr. Coll., 1978; BS in Psychology, Calif. Luth. U., 1980; MS in Counseling and Psychology, U. LaVerne, 1983; MSW, Calif. State U., Sacramento, 1986. Research asst. Camarillo (Calif.) State Hosp., 1981, tchr.'s aide, 1982; sub. tchr. asst. Vertura County Sch. Dist., 1981; teaching asst. Ventura Jr. Coll., 1980-82, tchr. adult edn., 1980-84; psychiatric social worker Yolo County Day Treatment Ctr., Broderick, Calif., 1986, Napa (Calif.) State Hosp., 1986—. Bd. dirs. Napa County Humane Soc. Mem. NOW. Home: PO Box 1095 Yountville CA 94599-1095 Office: Napa State Hosp Napa/Vallejo Hgwy Napa CA 49558

SEDRAN, CINDY LISA, orthopedic sales executive, radiologic technologist; b. Greenville, S.C., Dec. 12, 1953. BA, Oglethorpe U., Atlanta, 1975; AMS in Radiologic Technology, Emory U., Atlanta, 1980; cert. in Basic Lab. Techniques, Dekalb Coll., Atlanta, 1981. Registered Radiologic Tech., Ga. Personnel, sales Davison's Dept. Store, Atlanta, 1972-76; x-ray technologist, med. asst. Dr. Louis Levy and Dr. Terry Golden, Atlanta, 1977; radiologic technologist, emergency on call Grady Hosp., Atlanta, 1978-82; radiologic technologist, med. asst. Dr. Quentin Pirkle, Dr. Harold Sours and Dr. Roy Wiggins, Atlanta, 1980-81, Dunwoody Family Practice, Dunwoody, Ga., 1981, White-Hancock Orthopedics, P.C., Atlanta, 1981-84; sales rep. DePuy Orthopedics, Atlanta, 1985—; emergency on call radiologic technologist Met. Hosp. and Physicians in the area, Atlanta, 1982-92. Vol. to build playground Sterling Community, 1992, 93; Vol., team leader Hands on Atlanta, 1994; vol. Atlanta Food Bank, Cabbagetown Shoe Fitting, Red Cross Disaster Action Team, Flying Doctors of Am. to Dominican Republic, Am. Cancer Soc., High Mus. Art. Merit scholar Oglethorpe U., Emory U. Mem. Am. Registry Radiologic Technologists, Am. Soc., Atlanta Soc., Ga. Soc., Nat. Assn. Female Execs., Atlanta Women in Bus., Women's Am. ORT. Home: 4952 Mill Brook Dr Atlanta GA 30338-4908

SEE, KAREN MASON, federal judge; b. Springfield, Mo., Jan. 31, 1952; d. Robert Wayne and Mildred Lucille (Stockstill) Mason; m. Andrew B. See, Nov. 24, 1979. BS in Edn. cum laude, SW Mo. State U., 1973; JD, U. Mo., 1978. Bar: Mo. 1978. Tchr. Springfield (Mo.) Dist., 1973-75; law clk. Judge William E. Turnage, Mo. Ct. of Appeals, Kansas City, 1978-79; assoc. atty. Slagle & Bernard, Kansas City, 1979-84, ptnr., 1984-86; judge U.S. Bankruptcy Ct., Kansas City, 1986—; adj. prof. U. Mo. Law Sch., Kansas City. Active Mo. Bicentennial Commn., Jefferson City, 1987—, Kansas City Bicentennial Commn., 1987—; mem. adv. bd. Greater Mo. Focus on Leadership; bd. dirs. Mo. Found. for Women's Resources, Inc.; bd. dirs. Mid-Continent Coun. Girl Scouts U.S.A. Named an Outstanding Young Alumnus S.W. Mo. State U., 1988. Mem. ABA, Mo. Bar Assn. (vice chmn. comml. law com., bd. editors Mo. Bar Jour.), Kansas City Met. Bar Assn., Kansas City Lawyers Assn., Nat. Conf. of Bankruptcy Judges, Am. Judicature Soc., Order of Coif. Office: US Bankruptcy Ct 811 Grand Ave Rm 905 Kansas City MO 64106-1909

SEE, SAW-TEEN, structural engineer; b. Georgetown, Penang, Malaysia, Mar. 23, 1954; came to U.S., 1974; d. Hock-Eng and Ewe-See (Lim) S.; m. Leslie Earl Robertson, Aug. 11, 1982; 1 child, Karla Mei. BSc in Civil Engring., Cornell U., 1977, M in Civil Engring., 1978. Registered profl. engr., N.Y., Calif., Conn., Fla., Md., N.J., Ohio, Pa., Wash. Design engr. Leslie E. Robertson Assocs., N.Y.C., 1978-81, assoc., 1981-85, ptnr., 1986—, mng. ptnr., 1990—. Contbr. articles to profl. jours. Named to Those Who Made Marks in the Constrn. Industry in 1988, Engring. News Record, N.Y.C., 1989. Mem. ASCE, Archtl. League, Coun. on Tall Bldgs. and Urban Habitat (past chairperson com. on gravity loads and temperature effects 1982-85), Architects, Designers, Planners for Social Responsiblity, N.Y. Assn. Cons. Engrs. (dir. 1989-93, structural codes com. 1991—). Home: 45 E 89 Apt 25C New York NY 10128 Office: Leslie E Robertson Assocs 211 E 46 St New York NY 10017

SEEBACH, LYDIA MARIE, internist; b. Red Wing, Minn., Nov. 9, 1920; d. John Henry and Marie (Gleusen) S.; m. Keith Edward Wentz, Oct. 16, 1959; children: Brooke Marie, Scott Seebach. BS, U. Minn., 1942, BM, 1943, MD, 1944, MS in Medicine, 1951. Diplomate Am. Bd. Internal Medicine. Intern Kings County Hosp., Bklyn., 1944; fellow Mayo Found., Rochester, Minn., 1945-52; pvt. practice Oakland, Calif., 1952-60, San Francisco, 1961—; asst. clin. prof. U. Calif., San Francisco, 1981—. Contbr. articles to med. jours. Fellow ACP; mem. AMA, Am. Med. Womens Assn. (pres. Calif. chpt. 1968-70), Pan Am. Med. Womens Assn. (treas.), Calif. Med. Assn., San Francisco Med. Assn., Mayo Alumni (bd. dirs. 1983-89), Iota Sigma Pi. Republican. Lutheran. Office: 490 Post St # 939 San Francisco CA 94102-1410

SEEBERT, KATHLEEN ANNE, international marketing director; b. Chgo.; d. Harold Earl and Marie Anne (Lowery) S. BS, U. Dayton, 1971, MA, U. Notre Dame, 1976; MM, Northwestern U., 1983. Registered commodity rep. Publs. editor ContiCommodity Services, Inc., Chgo., 1977-79, supr. mktg., 1979-82; dir. mktg. MidAm. Commodity Exchange, 1982-85; internat. trade cons. to Govt. of Ont., Can., 1985-90; dir. mktg. and program devel. Internat. Orientation Resources. 1990-94; with Am. Internat. Group, 1995—. guest lectr. U. Dayton, U. Notre Dame, Northwestern U., Kellogg Alumni Chgo., French-Am. C. of C., Internat. Employee Relocation Coun., Soc. Intercultural Educators, Trainers and Researchers, Am. Soc. Tng. and Devel., Ill. CPA Soc., SBA, KPMG Peat Marwick, Price Waterhouse, Nat. Fgn. Trade Coun., William M. Mercer, Inc., Minn. Employee Relocation Coun., MRA, CRC, Chgo. Relocation Coun., Ky. Relocation Coun., Mpls. Employee Relocation Coun., Chgo.-Midwest Credit Mgmt. Assn. Mem. Futures Industry Assn. Am. (treas.), Greater Cin. C. of C., Notre Dame Club Chgo., Kellogg Mgmt. Club Chgo. Republican. Roman Catholic. Office: 707 Skokie Blvd Ste 350 Northbrook IL 60062-2838

SEEGER, LEINAALA ROBINSON, law librarian, educator; b. Wailuku, Hawaii, July 2, 1944; d. John Adam and Anna Hiilani (Leong) Robinson; 1 child, Maile Lea. BA, U. Wash., 1966; JD, U. Puget Sound, 1977; M in Law Librarianship, U. Wash., 1979. Bar: Wash. 1977. Reference librarian U. Puget Sound Sch. Law., Tacoma, 1977-79, assoc. law librarian, 1981-86; asst. librarian McGeorge Sch. Law, U. of Pacific, Sacramento, 1979-81; assoc. librarian pub. svc. Harvard Law Sch., Cambridge, Mass., 1986-89; dir. law library, assoc. prof. law U. Idaho Coll. Law, Moscow, 1989—; bd. dirs. Inlan, Spokane, Wash., 1989—. Mem. Palouse Asian-Ams. Assn., Moscow, 1989—. Mem. Wash. STate Bar Assn., Am. Assn. Law Librs. (chmn. minority com. 1990-91, v.p., pres.-elect Western Pacific chpt. 1985-86, 90-91, pres. 1991-92, vice chmn. edn. com. 1991-92, chmn. 1992-93), Idaho Coun. Acad. Librs. Office: U Idaho Coll Laws Moscow ID 83844-2324

SEEGER, MELINDA WAYNE, realtor; b. Albert Lea, Minn., Dec. 31, 1940; d. Oscar Earnest and Evelyn Josephine (Pihl) Wayne; BS, U. Minn., 1963; m. Robert Charles Seeger, Mar. 16, 1964; 1 child, Jeffrey Wayne. Chief occupational therapy Rehab. Inst. Oreg., Portland, 1964-66; supr. phys. disabilities and gen. medicine and surgery occupational therapy Mpls. VA Hosp., 1966-68; supr. phys. disabilities occupational therapy Nat. Naval Med. Ctr., Bethesda, Md., 1968-71; assoc. chief rehab. svcs., dir. occupational therapy UCLA Med. Center, 1974-85, cons., prin. investigator rheumatology div. dept. medicine, 1985-86; realtor Merrill Lynch Realty, Los Angeles, 1987—. Mem. utilization rev. com. Vis. Nurse Assn. Los Angeles, 1975-85, mem. profl. adv. com., 1979-80; mem. exec. com. Allied Health Professions sect. Arthritis Found., 1980-85, chmn. edn. com., 1982-85, mem. profl. edn. com.; bd. dirs. Calif. Occupational Therapy Found., 1984-85, Westwood-Holmby Hills Homeowners Assn., Los Angeles. Recipient Spl. Achievement award Nat. Naval Med. Ctr., 1971, Outstanding Performance award, 1971; Spl. Performance award UCLA, 1980, 84; Addie Thomas Service award for outstanding service to rheumatology community Arthritis Found., 1986, Cert. of Appreciation award, 1989; mem. Million Dollar Club. Mem. Am. Occupational Therapy Assn., Occupational Therapy Assn. Calif., Allied Health Professions Assn. (chmn. edn. com. 1982—), Los Angeles Bd. Realtors, San Fernando Valley Bd. Realtors, West Los Angeles C. of C., Blue Diamond Club. Author, editor articles in field. Office: 1401 Westwood Blvd Los Angeles CA 90024-4948

SEEGER, SONDRA JOAN, artist; b. L.A., May 27, 1942; d. Reinhold Josheph and Bertha Catherine (Monese) S.; m. Richard John Pahl, Aug. 18, 1961 (div. 1974); children: Catherine Marie, Douglas Richard, Angela Gay, Susan Joan; m. David Ernest Matteson, Apr. 25, 1990. Student, Marylhurst Coll., 1960. Pvt. practice musician various locations, 1973-81; security guard MGM Hotel, Las Vegas, 1981-82; real estate salesperson Century 21, Kent, Wash., 1983-85; mgr. Viera Land & Cattle, Inc., La Grande, Oreg., 1984-92; freelance artist, Casper, Wyo., 1991—; ptnr. Old West Saddle Shop, Casper, 1989-93, Casper, Wyo., 1993—; com. mem. Oreg. State Forest Practices Com., N.E. Region, 1990-91. Named Union Co. Tree Farmer of Yr., Am. Tree Farm System, 1987. Mem. NRA, Mont. Miniature Art Soc., Small Woodlands Assn., Knickerbocker Artists (assoc.), United Pastelists of Am., The Art League of Alexandria, Va., Miniature Art Soc. Fla., Oil Painters Am., Casper Artists Guild, Wyo. Fly Casters, Oreg. Forest Resources Inst. Republican. Home and Office: Old West Saddle Shop PO Box 4300 Casper WY 82604

SEELER, RUTH ANDREA, pediatrician, educator; b. N.Y.C., June 13, 1936; d. Thomas and Olivia (Patten) S. BA, U. Vt., 1959, MD, 1962. Diplomate Am. Bd. Pediatrics, Am. Bd. Pediatric Hematology/Oncology. Intern Bronx (N.Y.) Mcpl. Hosp., 1962-65; pediats. hematology/oncology fellow U. Ill., 1965-67; dir. pediatric hematology/oncology Cook County Hosp., 1967-84; prof. pediatrics, dir. pediatric edn. coll. medicine U. Ill., Chgo., 1984—; course coord. pediatrics Nat. Coll. Advanced Med. Edn., Chgo., 1987—; mem. subboard Pediatric Hematology/Oncology, Chapel Hill, 1990—. Mem. editorial bd. Am. Jour. Pediatric Hematology/Oncology, 1985—. Jr. and sr. warden, treas. Ch. Our Saviour, Chgo., 1970-92; founder camp for hemophiliacs Hemophilia Found., Ill., 1973—; pres. Hemophilia Found. Ill., 1981-85. Mem. Gamma Phi Beta Found. (trustee 1994—), Phi Beta Kappa. Office: Michael Reese Pediatrics 2929 S Ellis Chicago IL 60616

SEELMAN, KATHERINE DOLORES, institute administrator; b. Boston, May 26, 1938; d. Frederick George and Loretta (Tetu) S. BA, Hunter Coll., 1964; MA, NYU, 1970, PhD, 1982. Tchr. N.Y.C. Schs., 1966-73; instr., rschr. N.Y. Inst. Tech., NSF, N.Y.C., 1973-75; project mgr. Nat. Coun. Chs., N.Y.C., 1976-82; cons. Am. Assn. Retired Persons, Washington, 1982-83; rsch. scholar Gallaudet U., Washington, 1984-86; dir. pub. edn. Mass. Commn. for Deaf and Hard of Hearing, Boston, 1986-89; rsch. specialist Nat. Coun. on Disability, Washington, 1989-93; dir. program devel. Adminstrn. on Devel. Disability, Washington, 1993-94; dir. Nat. Inst. on Disability and Rehab. Rsch., Washington, 1994—. Switzer scholar Nat. Rehab. Assn., 1991, Disting. Switzer fellow Dept. Edn. Nat. Inst. Disability and Rehab. Rsch., 1985-86; recipient Scholarships NYU, 1973, Am. Law Inst./ABA, 1977, Fellowships NSF, 1974, Resources for the Future, 1976; named to Hall of Fame Alumni Assn. Hunter Coll., 1995. Mem. RESNA, AAAS, Assn. for Advancement of Sci., Soc. for Disability Studies, Nat. Assn. for the Deaf, Self-Help for Hard of Hearing. Home: PO Box 1056 404 Grove Ave Washington Grove MD 20880 Office: Nat Inst Disability and Rehab Rsch 600 Maryland Ave SW Washington DC 20202-2572

SEEMAN, LINDA KAMSKY, counselor; b. Richmond, Va., Apr. 19, 1950; d. David and Margaret (Rosenberg) Kamsky; m. Irvin Jay Seeman, July 25, 1971; children: Benjamin Gary, Paul Lawrence. BSEd, U. Ga., 1971; MS, U. Tex., 1977; PhD, Va. Commonwealth U., 1987. Lic. profl. counselor, cert. rehab. counselor, cert. clin. mental health counselor. Spanish and English tchr. Glenn Hills High Sch., Augusta, Ga., 1971-74; vocat. rehab. program dir. El Centro Coll. Texas. Rehab. Commn., Dallas, 1978-80; mental health counselor Richmond Rehab. Svcs., 1981-84; pvt. practice Richmond, 1984—; bd. dirs. Dallas Epilepsy Assn., 1978-80, Va. Rehab. Counselors Assn., 1980-92, Women's Resource Ctr. and U. Richmond, 1986-92; bd. dirs. Jewish Family Svcs., 1987—, chmn. adoption com., 1993—, sec., 1994—. Developer, chair ann. leadership symposium Women's Resource Ctr., U. richmond, 1986, 88, com. mem. Va. Women's Conf., 1990—; active Policy Bd. for Societ Resettlement, 1990-93; chair Vol. Recognition for Soviet Resettlement, 1991. Mem. AACD, Va. Counselors Assn., Va. Mental Health Counselors Assn., Phi Kappa Phi, Phi Delta Kappa. Jewish. Home: 2400 Loreines Landing Ln Richmond VA 23233-1700 Office: 5700 W Grace St Ste 100 Richmond VA 23226-1832

SEFEL-MARTEL, MICHAILINA, marketing and corporate consultant, investment banker; d. Basil and Stephania Sefel. Student, U. Pa., NYU; grad. summa cum laude, McGrathis Inst. Fin. Dir. fin. planning and corp. mktg. Camera Corp. Am.; exec. v.p., co-owner Micha-Lind Enterprises, N.Y.C., Corp. Forum, Inc., N.Y.C.; fin. cons. Eltro-Marine Corp., N.Y.C.; dir. fin. planning Capsule Tng. Systems, Inc., N.Y.C.; exec. v.p., dir. fin. planning Challenger Marine Corp., N.Y.C.; pres., owner M. Martel Capital Corp. Hostess tv show and numerous radio talk shows; performer in comls. and films. Sponsor, fund-raiser Assn. Help for Retarded Children, United Cerebral Palsy, East Side Settlement House; active Heart Fund Assn., Am. Cancer Soc., Spl. Olympics., Fedn. of Handicapped, March of Dimes; mem. benefit com. Nat. Chpt. Met. Hemophilia Found.; patron Am. Mus. and Dramatic Acad., Met. Mus. Art, ASTA Magna Found.; mem. hon. com. Franklin D. Roosevelt Four Freedoms Awards. Recipient Goodwill Amb. award State of Ark., Peace medal Office of U.S. Amb. to UN, 4 Woman of the Yr. awards Marine Industry; named to Ceasar's Marine Acad. Hall of Fame, 1993. Mem. SAG, AFTRA, NATAS, Actors' Fund Am. (life), Am. Women in Radio and TV, Am. Powerboat Assn., Am. Inst. Corp. Contrs., Nat. Assn. Securities Broker Dealers (principle lic.), Internat. Platform Assn. Address: 7 Sefel Ave Creamridge NJ 08514-9446

SEFTON, AMELIA KATHLEEN, librarian, performing artist; b. Hammond, Ind., Apr. 1, 1950; d. George William and Elizabeth Margaret (Huie) S.; m. Freff, May 1976 (div. May 1986); m. James Peter Killus Jr., Aug. 29,

1991. Student, U. Galway, Ireland, 1970; BA, Aquinas Coll., 1971; MLS, U. Mich., 1972. Libr. Deershead State Hosp., Salisbury, Md., 1972-73; part-time asst. libr. Mt. Vernon Jr. Coll., 1973-74; music libr., prop mistress Dupont Cir. Consortium, Washington, 1973-75; asst. libr. Gt. Oak Ctr., Silver Spring, Md., 1974-75; intern libr. Ft. Belvoir (Va.) Post Libr., 1975-76; libr. U.S. Army, Ft. Rucker, Ala., 1976-78; dir. libr. activities Hdqrs. N.Y. Area Command and Ft. Hamilton, 1978-91, mgr. fed. women's program, 1984-87, dir. community recreation div., 1987, dir. libr. activities, 1978-91. Author, performer Madame Ovary Presents Egg Folk, 1982-91, Madame Ovary's Cat-Egglog of Egg-Zotic Delights, 1990-91; author summer reading program Castles in the Air: A Reading Renaissance, 1989. Performer N.Y. Renaissance Festival, Sterling Forest, 1982-91, Cloisters Medieval Faire, N.Y.C., 1985-90, Pa. Renaissance Faire, Mt. Hope Winery, 1991. Mem. Kings County Shakespeare Co. (assoc.), Witchworks (head mistress 1988—). Home: 2305 Helena Ct Pinole CA 94564-1814

SEGAL, CHARLOTTE BEVERLY EDISON, artist, educator; b. South Norwalk, Conn., Dec. 3, 1931; d. Benjamin Harold and Marsha Vera (Racher) Edison; m. Donald Segal, Aug. 30, 1952; children: Jeffery, Barbara. BA, Barat Coll., Lake Forest, Ill., 1976; student, Sch. Art Inst. Chgo., 1981-82. Teaching asst. edn. dept. Barat Coll., 1975-76, asst. to dir. Continuing Edn. Office, 1976; adminstr. children's art camp Suburban Fine Arts Ctr., Highland Park, Ill., 1978-79, dir. faculty and curriculum, 1981; instr. to adults Northbrook (Ill.) Park Dist., 1981-84, instr. adults and children's summer art camp, 1984; instr. for srs. Bernard Horwich Ctr., 1984; instr. Brandeis Women's Studies, 1986; pvt. tchr. painting, 1985-87; instr. art and color fundamentals Internat. Acad. Design, Chgo., 1987—. One-woman shows include Freeport (Ill.) Art Mus., 1981, U. Ill., Chgo., 1982, ARC Gallery, Chgo., 1987, Steiner Gallery, Chgo., 1987, Carol Jones Gallery, Chgo., 1993, also retrospective, 1994; 2-woman shows include Ditmar Gallery, Northwestern U., Evanston, Ill., 1982; exhibited in numerous group shows, 1977—, including Art Inst. Chgo., 1979, 86, Carol Jones Gallery, 1992, Bower Mus., Orange County, Calif., 1993-95; represented in corp. and pvt. collections; represented by Carol Jones Gallery. Recipient hon. mention Beverly Arts Ctr., Galesburg, Ill., 1979; design selected for Easter Seals Found., 1993. Mem. Chgo. Soc. Artists. Home: 3150 N Lake Shore Dr Chicago IL 60657-4829 Studio: 1525 W Homer St Chicago IL 60622-1221

SEGAL, GERALDINE ROSENBAUM, sociologist; b. Phila., Aug. 26, 1908; d. Harry and Mena (Hamburg) Rosenbaum; m. Bernard Gerard Segal, Oct. 22, 1933; children: Loretta Joan Cohen, Richard Murry. BS in Edn., U. Pa., 1930, MA in Human Rels., 1963, PhD in Sociology, 1978; MS in Libr. Sci., Drexel U., 1968; Dr. Letters (Hon.), Franklin & Marshall Coll., 1990. Social worker County Relief Bd., Phila., 1931-35; sociologist, Phila., 1935—; cons. and lectr. in field. Author: In Any Fight Some Fall, 1975; Blacks in the Law, 1983. Bd. dirs. NCCJ, 1937-47, 82—, sec., 1983-91; bd. overseers U. Pa. Sch. Social Work, 1983—; bd. dirs., Juvenile Law Ctr., 1984—; chair Phila. Tutorial Project, 1966-68; 1st v.p. U. Pa. Alumnae Assn., 1967-70. Co-recipient Nat. Neighbors Disting. Leadership in Civil Rights award, 1988; recipient Drum Major award for Human Rights, Phila. Martin Luther King, Jr. Assn. for Nonviolence, 1990, Brotherhood Sisterhood award NCCJ, 1994. Democrat. Jewish. Home: Apt 19-C-44 2401 Pennsylvania Ave Philadelphia PA 19130-3003

SEGAL, JOAN SMYTH, library association executive, consultant, organization adminstrator; b. Bklyn., Sept. 14, 1930; d. John Patrick and Anna Catherine (Green) Smyth; m. William Segal, June 25, 1955; children: Harold M., Nora A. BA, Douglass Coll., Rutgers U., 1951; MS in LS, Columbia U., 1955; PhD, U. Colo., 1978. Cert. assn. exec., 1988. Librarian, Math Inst., NYU, 1955-58, Western Interstate Commn. for Higher Edn., Boulder, Colo., 1970-76; library cons., Boulder, 1976-78; resource sharing program mgr. Bibliog. Ctr. for Research, Denver, 1978-80, exec. dir., 1980-84; exec. dir. Assn. for Coll. and Research Libraries, ALA, Chgo., 1984-90; assoc. exec. dir. programs ALA, 1990-93; owner Vintage Ventures, 1993—; trainer library automation, group devel., resource sharing; cons. in field. Contbr. articles to profl. publs. Named Colo. Librarian of Yr., Colo. Library Assn., 1984; named to Douglass Soc. Mem. ALA, Spl. Libraries Assn. (chmn. edn. div. 1981-82, pres. Rocky Mountain chpt. 1981-82, 1994—, bd. dirs. 1983-86), OCLC Network Dirs. (chmn. 1983), Mountain Plains Library Assn., Am. Soc. Assn. Execs. Colo. Soc. Assn. Execs.

SEGAL, LYNNE NICOLAU, law librarian; b. Camden, N.J., Mar. 27, 1957; d. Nick George Nicolau and Nancy Rae Rhys; m. Donald Frank Segal, Nov. 13, 1977. BA, U. N.Mex., 1986; JD, Harvard U., 1989. Law clk. to chief judge U.S. Ct. Appeals (10th cir.), Oklahoma City, 1989-90; assoc. Meyer, Hendricks, Victor, Osborn and Maledon, Phoenix, 1990-93; law librarian DNA People's Legal Svcs., Inc., Window Rock, Ariz., 1993—. Mem. ABA, Ariz. Bar Assn. (membership assistance com. 1991—), Maricopa County Bar Assn., Ariz. Women Lawyers Assn., Phi Kappa Phi, Golden Key Soc.

SEGAL, NANCY LEE, psychology educator, twin researcher; b. Boston, Mar. 2, 1951; d. Alfred Maurice and Esther (Rubenstein) S. BA in Psychology and English, Boston U., 1973; MA in Social Sci., U. Chgo., 1974, PhD in Human Devel., 1982. Asst. dir., rsch. assoc. Minn. Ctr. for Twin and Adoption Rsch., Mpls., 1985-91; prof. dept. psychology Calif. State U., Fullerton, 1991—; cons. on twin loss, Mpls., 1984, 87. Contbg. editor Twins Mag., 1984—, mem. editorial bd., 1985—; contbr. articles to profl. jours. Recipient Disting. Alumni award Boston U., 1990. Fellow Am. Psychol. Soc., APA (divsn. 7); mem. Twins Found., Internat. Soc. for Twin Studies, Internat. Soc. for Human Ethology (membership chair), N.Y. Road Runners Club, Sigma Delta Epsilon (rsch. award 1989), Sigma Xi. Office: Calif State U Dept Psychology 800 N State College Blvd Fullerton CA 92634-9999

SEGAL, SYLVIA OZNER, songwriter, publisher, producer, inventor; b. Bronx, N.Y.; m. Melvin Casey Segal; children: Michael Ozner, Laurence Ozner. Grad. high sch., Bronx. Pres., founder Glamortop Fashions Miami dba Ostel Enterprises, Inc., Fla., 1952-79; pres. SOS Worldwide Prodns., Inc., 1985; CEO, pres. children's divsn. Ednl. Songs. Internat., Inc., 1994—; founder Indie Label. Music writer, pub., prodr. records including My Love Song (recorded by Vic Damone 1952, a.k.a. You Belong To Me), Olympic Fever (song of U.S. Olympic Team 1988), Winning Fever, We Must Unite World, USA's For Me, others; creator The Safe Song Program, audio, video, booklet package, all langs. Recipient various awards Billboard Mag. Patentee for 12 Fashion Glamortop scarf. Mem. ASCAP, Songwriters Guild, Assn. Fla. Poets, Inc. Office: 20416 NE 10th Court Rd Miami FL 33179-2524

SEGEL, KAREN LYNN JOSEPH, tax professional, lawyer; b. Youngstown, Ohio, Jan. 15, 1947; d. Samuel Dennis and Helen Anita Joseph; m. Alvin Gerald Segel, June 9, 1968 (div. Sept. 1976); 1 child, Adam James. BA in Soviet and East European Studies, Boston U., 1968; JD, Southwestern U., 1975. Cert. tax profl. Adminstrv. asst. Olds Brunel & Co., N.Y.C., 1968-69, U.S. Banknote Corp., N.Y.C., 1969-70; tax acct. S.N. Chilkov & Co. CPA's, Beverly Hills, Calif., 1971-74; intern Calif. Corps. Commr., 1975; tax. sr. Oppenheim Appel & Dixon CPA's, L.A., 1978, Fox, Westheimer & Co. CPA's, L.A., 1978, Zebrak, Levine & Mepos CPA's, L.A., 1979; ind. cons. acctg., taxation specialist Beverly Hills, 1980—; bd. dirs. World Wide Motion Pictures Corp., L.A. Editorial adv. bd. Am. Biog. Inst. High sch. amb. to Europe People-to-People Orgn., 1963. Named 1991, 93 Woman of Yr., Am. Biog. Inst. Mem. Nat. Soc. Tax Profls., Nat. Trust for Hist. Preservation, Am. Mus. Natural History, Winterthur Guild, Women's Inner Circle of Achievement.

SEGGERMAN, ANNE CRELLIN, foundation executive; b. Los Angeles, May 13, 1931; d. Curtin Vergil and Yvonne (LaGrave) Crelin; m. Harry G.A. Seggerman, Apr. 14, 1951; children: Patricia, Henry, Marianne, Yvonne, Suzanne, John. Studies with Albert Levesque, Paris, 1948-50; Student, Sch. Decorative Arts, Paris, 1950, Sch. of the Louvre, Paris, 1950, Albert Magnus Coll., 1951; D.H.L. (hon.), Sacred Heart U., 1980. French tchr. Beverly Hills, Calif., 1958-60; translator World Affairs Council, Los Angeles, 1958-60; staff mem. West Side Sch. Gifted Children, Beverly Hills, 1958-60; pres. Huxley Inst. for Bio-Social Research, Fairfield, Conn., 1972—, 4th World Found. Interfaith Media Action, Fairfield, 1977—, Steiner Prodns., Fairfield, 1981—; founder The Com. for Guadalupe Research, Fairfield, 1982—; bd. dirs. Anuk, Inc. Fundraiser Rep. Party; co-founder Christian/Jewish ctr. understanding Sacred Heart U., Fairfield, Conn.; active Pres. Reagan's Health Task Force Resources Com. on Health Adv. Councils of U.S. Dept. Health and Human Services; mem. Pres.'s Com. Mental Retardation, 1981-86, Com. Housing Handicapped Families, 1989; bd. dirs. Easter Seal Rehab. Ctr., Fairfield, Internat. Coll. Applied Nutrition, World Health Med. Group, Cath. League for Religion and Civil Rights. Recipient Am. Assn. Sovereign Mil. Order of Malta, 1991, Lady of Equestrian Order of Holy Sepulchre of Jerusalem, 1991. Mem. Nat. Health Fedn., Nat. Coun. Disability, The Inst. for Study of Human Knowledge, Am. Holistic Med. Inst., Internat. Acad. Preventive Medicine, Calif. Orthomolecular Soc., Am. Psychical Reasearch, Fairfield County Organic Gardeners.

SEGGERMAN, MARY BETH, elementary school counselor; b. Osceola, Iowa, Apr. 5, 1939; d. Ray Alfred and Grace Elizabeth (King) Allen; m. Lowell D. Seggerman, Mar. 8, 1959; children: David, Leslie Ann, Karl. BA, Westmar Coll., 1977; MA, U. S.D., 1988. Cert. tchr. music K-12, secondary English, guidance counselor elem. and secondary. Estate planner Penn Corp. Fin., Sioux City, Iowa, 1978-81; K-12 vocal music instr. Hinton (Iowa) Community Sch., 1979-89; elem. guidance counselor Marcus-Meriden-Cleghorn Schs., Meriden, Iowa, 1989—; music instr. Kingsley (Iowa) Pierson Cmty. Sch., 1977-79. Chmn. bd. dirs., mother adv. Rainbow Girls; coun. chmn., leader Cub Scouts, Campfire Girls; organizer ch. jr. choir, jr. high fellowship group. Mem. Am. Counseling Assn., Am. Sch. Counseling Assn., Order of the Eastern Star (worthy matron 1968-69, grand organist 1973), DAR (recording sec.). Home: 44232 330th St Kingsley IA 51028

SEGIL, LARRAINE DIANE, former materials company executive; b. Johannesburg, South Africa, July 15, 1948; came to U.S., 1974; d. Jack and Norma Estelle (Cohen) Wolfowitz; m. Clive Melwyn Segil, Mar. 9, 1969; 1 child, James Harris. BA, U. Witwatersrand, South Africa, 1967, BA with honours, 1969; JD, Southwestern U., L.A., 1979; MBA, Pepperdine U., 1985. Bar: Calif. 1979, U.S. Supreme Ct. 1982. Cons. in internat. transactions, L.A., 1976-79; atty. Long & Levit, L.A., 1979-81; chmn., pres. Marina Credit Corp., L.A., 1981-85; pres., chief exec. officer Electronic Space Products Internat., L.A., 1985-87; mng. ptnr. The Lared Group, L.A., 1987—. Bd. govs. Cedars Sinai Med. Ctr., L.A., 1984—; bd. dirs. So. Calif. Tech. Execs. Network, 1984-86. Mem. ABA (chmn. internat. law com. young lawyers div. 1980-84), Internat. Assn. Young Lawyers (exec. coun. 1979-81, coun. internat. law and practice 1983-84), World Tech. Execs. Network (chmn.), Regency Club (house com. 1986). Avocations: piano, horseriding. Office: The Lared Group 1901 Ave of The Stars Ste 280 Los Angeles CA 90067

SEGRÈ, NINA, lawyer; b. New Haven, Apr. 4, 1940; d. Victor M. and Naomi (Berlin) Gordon; m. Gino Segrè, Dec. 31, 1962 (div. 1983); children: Katia, Julie, Michele; m. Frank F. Furstenberg, Jr., Feb. 2, 1985; stepchildren: Sarah Furstenberg, Ben Furstenberg. BA, Radcliffe Coll., 1961; MAT, Harvard U., 1963; JD, U. Pa., 1974. Bar: Pa. 1974, U.S. Dist. Ct. (ea. dist.) Pa. 1974. Law clk. U.S. Ct. Appeals (3d cir.), Phila., 1974-75; assoc. Dechert Price & Rhoads, Phila., 1976-83, ptnr., 1983-93; ptnr. Segrè & Senser, P.C., Phila., 1993—; adj. prof. Temple U., Sch. Law, 1991; course preparer, panelist Phila. (Pa.) Bar Edn. Ctr., 1994—. Trustee Radcliffe Coll., Cambridge, Mass., 1991—, chair fund com., chair program com.; mem. fin. com. Lynn Yeakel for U.S. Senate, Phila., 1992, Lynn Yeakel for Gov. Pa., 1994. Mem. Phila. Bar Assn. (mem. real property sec., mem. exec. bd.), The Harvard-Radcliffe Club (v.p., mem. exec. bd.), College Works (founder, bd. dirs.). Home: 2316 Delancey Pl Philadelphia PA 19103-6407 Office: Segrè & Senser PC Ste 414 2 Penn Center Plz Philadelphia PA 19102-1704

SEHRING, HOPE HUTCHISON, library science educator; b. Akron, Ohio; d. Wesley Harold and Jane (Brown) H.; m. Frederick Albert Sehring, July 15, 1978. BS, Slippery Rock U., 1968; MEd, U. Pitts., 1973, MLS, 1984. Cert. instructional media specialist. Reference libr.-intern Carnegie Mellon U., Pitts., 1981; libr. media specialist Gateway Sch. Dist., Monroeville, Pa., 1968—. Contbr. articles to profl. jours. Active Pa. Citizens for Better Libraries. Recipient Henry Clay Frick Found. U. of London scholarship, 1969, 73, Gift of Time tribute Am. Family Inst., 1992; U. Pitts. Evaluation Inst. grantee, 1976. Mem. NEA, ALA, Pa. Sch. Librs. Assn. (treas. 1982-84), Pa. State Edn. Assn., Gateway Edn. Assn., Alpha Xi Delta. Home: PO Box 74 Delmont PA 15626-0074 Office: Gateway Sch Dist Mosside Blvd Monroeville PA 15146

SEIBERT, MARY LEE, college official; b. Evansville, Ind., Jan. 30, 1942; d. Ernest Hensley and Lillian (Schmadel) S.;. BS, Ind. U., 1963, MS, 1973, EdD, 1979. Cert. med. technologist, med. asst. Lab. supr. Wishard Meml. Hosp., Indpls., 1964-67; chmn. life scis. div. Ind. Vocat. Tech. Coll., Indpls., 1967-73; assoc. prof., program dir. Ind. U. Sch. Medicine, Indpls., 1973-79; assoc. project coordinator Am. Assn. State Colls. and Univs., Washington, 1979-81; dean coll. allied health professions Temple U., Phila., 1981-90; assoc. provost, dean grad. studies Ithaca (N.Y.) Coll., 1990—; vis. prof. U. Tex. Med. Br., Galveston, 1985. Assoc. editor Jour. Med. Tech., 1985-86. Fellow Am. Soc. Allied Health Profls. (hon., chmn. forum on allied health data, rsch. com. 1983-89, bd. dirs. 1990-92, Outstanding Mem. award 1986); mem. Am. Soc. Med. Technologists (profl. affairs com. 1986-89), Am. Assn. Med. Assts. (hon.), Nat. Coun. on Health Professions Edn., Nat. Acad. Scis. (bd. health care svcs. inst. of medicine 1993—), Phi Delta Kappa, Pi Lambda Theta. Republican. Home: 16 Bean Hill Ln Ithaca NY 14850-9750

SEIDEL, DIANNE MARIE, finance executive; b. Reading, Pa., Feb. 1, 1959; d. Frederick Jacob and Claire Marie (Paskey) S. ASBA, Pa. State U., 1986; BA, Alvernia Coll., Reading, Pa., 1988. Office asst. Berks-Lehigh Valley Farm Credit Service, Fogelsville, Pa., 1977-80, sr. office asst., 1980, office supr., 1980-83, office mgr., 1983-86; chief fin. officer, 1986-88; exec. v.p. Keystone Farm Credit ACA, Lancaster, 1989-92, sr. v.p. fin. svcs., CFO, 1992—. Mem. Pa. State U. Alumni Assn. Home: 218 Candalwood Ln Exton PA 19341

SEIDEL, JOAN BROUDE, stockbroker, investment advisor; b. Chgo., Aug. 16, 1933; d. Ned and Betty (Treiger) Broude; m. Arnold Seidel, Aug. 18, 1957; children: David, Craig. BA, UCLA, 1954; postgrad., N.Y. Inst. Fin. Registered prin., investment advisor Morton Seidel & Co. Inc., L.A., 1970-74, v.p., 1974-93; pres., 1993—; also bd. dirs. Morton Seidel & Co. Inc., L.A.; instr. UCLA Extension, 1979-84. Treas. City of Beverly Hills, Calif., 1990—, chmn. rent adjustment bd., 1989-90, mem., 1983-89; mem. investment com. YWCA, L.A., 1987—, chmn. bd. dirs., 1989—, treas. Greater L.A., 1992—; bd. dirs. Discovery Fund for Eye Rsch., L.A., 1987—. Named Citizen of Yr. Beverly Hills C. of C., 1993. Fellow Assn. for Investment Mgmt. and Rsch.; mem. Nat. Assn. Security Dealers (dist. bus. conduct com. 25 1993—), L.A. Soc. Fin. Analysts, Orgn. Women Execs., Women in Bus., City Club, Bond Club, Phi Sigma Alpha. Home: 809 N Bedford Dr Beverly Hills CA 90210-3023 Office: Morton Seidel & Co Inc 350 S Figueroa St Bldg 499 Los Angeles CA 90071-1203

SEIDEL, KATHLEEN JO, nurse; b. Bismarck, N.D., Mar. 9, 1956; d. Ervin and Phyllis Mae (Marquart) Roemich; m. Kevin Niles Seidel, July 28, 1984; children: Jennifer, James, Joslin. BSN, U. N.D., 1978. RN, N.D. Med. nurse St. Alexius Med. Ctr., Bismarck, 1979-80, telemetry nurse, 1980-89, asst. dir. telemetry, 1989-94, dir. emergency trauma ctr., 1994—. Mem. PAC Saxvik Grade Sch., Bismarck, 1991-94; sec. 1993-94; asst. leader Rising Sun Sakawea Girl Scouts, Bismarck, 1993-94; leader Girl Scouts, 1994-95. Mem. ANA, N.D. Nurses Assn. (nominating com. chair 1993-94, v.p. dist. #6 1993-94, pres.-elect dist. #6 1994-95, Search for Excellence award 1994), Nat. Mgmt. Assn. (mem. pub. com. Dakota West chpt. 1993-94). Roman Catholic. Office: St Alexius Med Ctr 900 E Broadway Bismarck ND 58502

SEIDELMAN, SUSAN, film director; b. Pa., Dec. 11, 1952. Student, Drexel U., NYU. Dir. films Smithereens, 1982, Desperately Seeking Susan, 1985, Cookie, 1989, She-Devil, 1990; dir., co-exec. producer Making Mr. Right, 1987; dir. debut with short film and You Act Like One, Too (Student film award Acad. Motion Picture Arts and Scis.). Office: care Michael Shedler 225 W 34th St Ste 1012 New York NY 10122-0049 also: William Morris Agy 151 El Camino Los Angeles CA 90048*

SEIDEN, MARLA, public relations executive; b. N.Y.C., Mar. 25, 1951. BA in Speech/English, SUNY, Albany, 1972; MA in Comm., Queens Coll., 1976. Pres. Seiden Comm., 1980—. Mem. Healthcare Pub. Rels. and Mktg. Soc. Greater N.Y. Office: Seiden Comm PO Box 358 New Hyde Park NY 11040*

SEIDL, JANE PATRICIA, lawyer; b. Stamford, Conn., June 9, 1958; d. Francis Xavier and Frances (Nizolek) S. BA magna cum laude, Boston Coll., 1980; JD, U. Conn., 1985. Bar: Conn. 1985, U.S. Dist. Ct. Conn. 1985. Fin. editor Fin. Acctg. Standards Bd., Stamford, 1980-82; assoc. Schatz & Schatz, Ribicoff & Kotkin, Hartford, Conn., 1985-92; sr. counsel Northeast Utilities, Hartford, Conn., 1992—. Mem. ABA, Conn. Bar Assn., Hartford County Bar Assn., Hartford Assn. Women Attys. (pres. dir 1992—). Office: Northeast Utlities PO Box 270 Hartford CT 06141-0270

SEIDLE, JEAN H., accountant, operational consultant; b. Balt., Aug. 2, 1956; d. Robert Haynes and Agnes May (Smith) Henning; m. Michael John Seidle, Apr. 26, 1980; children: Vincent Robert, Christopher Michael, Alaina Marie. BBA, Temple U., 1986. CPA, Pa. With restaurant mgmt. Stouffer's, 1975-83; CPA, auditor, cons. Arthur Andersen & Co., Phila., 1986-91; CPA, ops. mgr., regional mgr. no. Europe Am. Internat. Group (Am. Life Ins. Co.), Wilmington, Del., 1991—; cons., acct. Chamberlain's, Boothwyn, Pa., 1993—. Mem. AICPA, Ins. Acctg. & Sys. Assn. (chairperson 1991—). Republican. Roman Catholic. Home: 2610 Epping Rd Wilmington DE 19810

SEIDLING, SUSAN MARY, state official; b. Duquesne, Pa., July 24, 1929; d. John and Maria (Sokolovsky) Boronkay; m. Jack Cleon Seidling, Sept. 18, 1949 (dec. 1979); children: Cheryl Susan, Janet Marie, David John; m. Ronald John Eisenberg, Sept. 26, 1992. Student, LaSalle Inst., Pitts., 1949, N.Y. Inst. Fin., 1964. Lic. ins. agt.; stock broker. Paralegal A.J. Rosenbleet, Esq., McKeesport, Pa., 1949-51, Stokes & Lurie, Clairton, Pa., 1952-56; asst. mgr. Bernstein & Co., McKeesport, 1963-64; stockbroker Chaplin-McGuiness Co., Pitts., 1965-66; account exec. Bache & Co., Pitts., 1966-75; employment rep. Pa. Office Employment Security, McKeesport, 1975-91; ret., 1991. Author/editor newsletter Sr. Ams. Newsletter, 1981—. Founder, dir., past pres. Sr. Ams., Inc., North Versailles, Pa., 1981-91; pres. St. Stephens Ladies Guild, 1983; troop cons., leader Girl Scouts. Recipient Senatorial Citation Pa. Senate, 1988, Lt. Gov.'s Proclamation State of Pa., 1988, People Who Care award Sec. of Labor, 1990. Mem. Am. Legion (founder, travel chmn. post 701 srs. 1982—, v.p. 1982-83, 93-94), Rotary (v.p. 1993-94), Lost Chord Club (entertainment chmn. 1994-95). Home: 1000 Taylor St North Versailles PA 15137-2130

SEIDMAN, AUDREY NADINE, public relations executive; b. N.Y.C., Sept. 20, 1953; d. Elliot Solomon and Hazel Selma (Lipsky) S.; ptnr. Sarah E. Bratspis; children: Stephen, Jeffrey, David. BA, SUNY, Albany, 1975; MA, Syracuse U., 1976. Pub. info. specialist Jewish Assn. for Svcs. for the Aged, N.Y.C., 1976-80; pub. rels. assoc. Jewish Bd. Family and Children's Svcs., N.Y.C., 1980-84; dir. pub. affairs and cmty. programs Ctr. for Women in Govt., Albany, 1984-93; dept. dir. comm. N.Y. State Office of Pks., Recreation and Hist. Preservation, Albany, 1993-95; pres. Cmty. Pub. Rels. Assn. Agys., N.Y.C., 1982-84. Bd. mem., officer Sr. Action in a Gay Environment, N.Y.C., 1979-83, Holding Our Own: A Fund for Women, Albany, 1988-94. Democrat. Jewish. Home: 186 S Main Ave Albany NY 12208

SEIDMAN, ELLEN SHAPIRO, lawyer, government official; b. N.Y.C., Mar. 12, 1948; d. Benjamin Harry Shapiro and Edna (Eysen) Stern; m. Walter Becker Slocombe, June 14, 1981; 1 child, Benjamin William. AB, Radcliffe Coll., 1969; JD, Georgetown U., 1974; MBA, George Washington U., 1988. Bar: D.C., 1975. Law clk. U.S. Ct. of Claims, Washington, 1974-75; assoc. Caplin & Drysdale, Washington, 1975-78; atty., advisor U.S. Dept. of Transportation, Washington, 1978-79, dep. asst. gen. counsel, 1979-81; assoc. gen. counsel Chrysler Corp Loan Guaranty Bd., Washington, 1981-84; atty., advisor U.S. Dept. of Treasury, Washington, 1981-86, spl. asst. to the Under Sec. Fin., 1986-87; dir. strategic planning Fed. Nat. Mortgage Assn., Washington, 1987-88, v.p., asst. to chmn., 1988-91, sr. v.p. regulation rsch. and econs., 1991-93; spl. asst. to the pres. for econ. policy The White House, Washington, 1993—. Mem. Women in Housing and Fin. Office: Nat Econ Coun The White House Washington DC 20500

SEIFER, JUDITH HUFFMAN, sex therapist, educator; b. Springfield, Ill., Jan. 18, 1945; d. Clark Lewis and Catherine Mary (Fisher) Huffman; married; children: Christopher, Patrick, Andrea. RN, St. John's Hosp./Quincy Coll., 1965; MHS, Inst. Advanced Study Human Sexuality, 1981, PhD, 1986. RN, Ohio; Diplomate Am. Bd. Sexology. Charge nurse Grandview Hosp., Dayton, Ohio, 1967-70; v.p. Sego, Inc., Dayton, 1970-84, pres., 1984—; marital and sex therapist Grandview Ob-Gyn., Inc., Dayton, 1975-87; asst. clin. prof. psychiatry and ob-gyn Wright State U. Sch. Medicine, Dayton, 1985-93; edn. cons., screenwriter The Learning Corp., Ft. Lauderdale, Fla., 1990—; adj. prof. psychology U. Dayton, 1985-90; profl. speaker The Upjohn Co., Kalamazoo, 1986—, CIBA-GEIGY Co., 1987-90; chmn. tech. adv. com. Mercari Comm., Inc., Englewood, Colo., 1988-89; cons. dept. psychology VA Hosp., Dayton, 1990-93. Author, screenwriter film script: Mercari Communications, 1988; guest editor: The D.O., 1985, contbr. articles to profl. jours. Pres. Dayton Osteopathic Aux., 1974-75, Aux. Ohio Osteopathic Assn., Columbus, 1981-82, Sister City Assn., Oakwood, Ohio, 1985-86; bd. dirs. Grace House Sexual Abuse Resource Ctr., Dayton, 1987-89, Planned Parenthood Miami Valley, Ohio, 1985-86, Social Health Assn., Dayton, 1976-87. Grantee Dayton Found., 1980-82; fellow Masters and Johnson Inst., 1984. Fellow Internat. Coun. Sex Educators, Am. Acad. Clin. Sexologists; mem. Am. Assn. Sex Educators, Counselors and Therapists (cert., rec. sec. 1986-91, pres. 1994—), Am. Coll. Sexologists. Roman Catholic. Office: Sego Corp 2 Deerfield Rd PO Box 426 Lewisburg WV 24901-0426

SEIFERT, CAROL JOY, goverment administrator; b. Paducah, Tex., July 21, 1953; d. Charles Gene Bragg and Anita Joy (Bates) Hurta; m. Stephen Charles Seifert. BA in Psychology, U. Tex., 1974. Contract specialist NASA, Houston, 1974-77; collections supr. U.S. Dept Edn., Dallas, 1977-80, lender examiner, 1980-84; chief, fin. mgmt. sect. U.S. Dept Edn., Washington, 1984-86, chief, guaranteed student loan policy br., 1986-87, chief, guaranteed student loan ops. br., 1987-92; dir. div. Guaranteed Student Loan Systems U.S. Dept. Edn., Washington, 1992—. Baptist.

SEIFERT, CAROLINE HAMILTON, community health nurse, school nurse; b. Warren, Ohio, May 28, 1937; d. Oliver L. and Martha (Moran) Hamilton; m. Dale E. Seifert, Sept. 5, 1959; children: Brian Dale, Joan Kimberly. Diploma, Youngstown (Ohio) Hosp. Assn., 1959; BSN, U. Cin., 1964, MEd, 1979. Cert. sch. nurse, health educator, spl. edn. educator. Caseworker Children's Svcs. div. Dept. Health and Human Svcs., Batavia, Ohio, 1966-68; dir. Happy Days Nursery Sch. Bethel (Ohio) United Meth. Ch., 1970-73; social worker Clermont County Bd. Mental Retardation/Devel. Disabilities, Batavia, 1973—; sch. nurse, health educator Thomas A. Wildey Sch., Owensville, Ohio, 1973—; instr. Sch. Health Svcs. U. Cin., 1976, preceptor nursing students, 1992—. Mem. Hamilton/Clermont Sch. Nurses Orgn. (v.p.), S.W. Ohio Sch. Nurses Assn. (program chmn.), Profl. Assn. for Retardation (v.p. nursing div., Nurse of Yr.). Home: 2631 Oldforge Ln Cincinnati OH 45244-2831 Office: Thomas A Wildey Sch PO Box 8 Owensville OH 45160-0008

SEIGLER, RUTH QUEEN, state agency administrator, consultant, nurse; b. Conway, S.C., July 31, 1942; d. Charles Isaac and Berneta Mae (Weaks) Queen; m. Rallie Marshall Seigler, Sept. 1, 1963; children: Rallie Marshall Jr., Scot Monroe. ADN, Lander Coll., 1962; BSN, U. S.C., 1964, MSN, 1980. Pub. health nurse Richland County Health Dept., Columbia, S.C., 1964-66; dir. nurses Columbia Area Mental Health Ctr., 1966-69; program nurse specialist Midlands Health Dist., 1969-72; discharge planner Richland Meml. Hosp., 1972-73, clin. dir., 1973-75; exec. dir. S.C. State Bd. Nursing, 1976-83; v.p. nursing dept. Self Meml. Hosp., Greenwood, S.C., 1983-86; exec. dir. S.C. Commn. on Aging, Columbia, 1986—; bd. dirs. Queen Gas Co., Barnwell, S.C.; nurse cons. Creative Nursing Mgmt., Mpls., 1984—. Advisor: The Role of County Mental Health Nurse, 1971. Recipient Disting. Alumni award Lander Coll., 1978, career Woman recognition award Columbia YWCA, 1980, William S. Hall award S.C. Assn. Residential Care Homes, 1988, U. S.C. Coll. Nursing Disting. Alumni award, 1993; named one of Ten Women of Achievement, S.C., March of Dimes, 1987. Mem. Am.

Nurses Assn., S.C. Nurses Assn. (sec. 1965-68, bd. dirs. 1986-88, Excellence award 1984, Recognition award 1984), S.C. Hosp. Assn., S.C. Gerontol. Soc., Am. Pub. Health Assn., Columbia Luncheon Club, S.C. Fedn. Older Ams., Evening Mission Action Group, Bd. Nursing Home Examiners, Pilot Club, Inc. (pres. 1988-89), Rotary Internat., Sigma Theta Tau. Presbyterian. Home: 2220 Bermuda Hills Rd Columbia SC 29223-6710 Office: SC Govs Divsn Aging 202 Arbor Lake Dr Ste 301 Columbia SC 29223-4554

SEILER, CHARLOTTE WOODY, retired English language educator; b. Thorntown, Ind., Jan. 20, 1915; d. Clark and Lois Merle (Long) Woody; m. Wallace Urban Seiler, Oct. 10, 1942; children: Patricia Anne Seiler Bootzin, Janet Alice Seiler Sawyer. AA, Ind. State U., 1933; AB, U. Mich., 1941; MA, Cen. Mich. U., 1968. Tchr. elem. schs., Whitestown, Ind., 1933-34, Thorntown, Ind., 1934-37, Kokomo, Ind., 1937-40, Ann Arbor, Mich., 1941-44, Willow Run, Mich., 1944-46; instr. English div. Delta Coll., University Center, Mich., 1964-69, asst. prof., 1969-77, ret., 1977; organizer, dir. Delta Coll. Puppeteers, 1972-77. Mem. Friends of Grace A. Dow Meml. Library, 1974—, treas. 1974-75, 77-79, corr. sec., 1975-77; mem. Midland Art Assn.; adv. bd. Salvation Army, 1980-91, sec., 1984-87; leader Sr. Ctr. Humanities program Midland Sr. Ctr., 1977—. Mem. AAUW (fellowship honoree 1979), Mich. Libr. Assn., Midland Symphony League, Tuesday Rev. Club (pres. 1979-80), Seed and Sod Garden Club (v.p. 1986-87, pres. 1987-88), Pi Lambda Theta, Chi Omega. Presbyterian. Home: 5002 Sturgeon Creek Pky Midland MI 48640-2229

SEILER, MARILYN, advertising professional; b. Bklyn.; d. Joseph A. and Felicia (Perrone) Sileo. BA in Psychology, UCLA, 1970; MA in Psychology, Columbia U., 1973, MPhil. in Psychology, 1976, PhD in Psychology, 1978. Project dir. Bus. Sci. Internat., N.Y.C., 1979-80; assoc. research supr. Doyle Dane Bernbach, Inc., N.Y.C., 1979-80; research supr. Doyle Dance Bernbach, Inc., N.Y.C., 1981-82; research acct. exec. Young & Rubicam, N.Y.C., 1982-83, research acct. supr., 1983-86, assoc. rsch. dir., 1986-88; v.p., dir. consumer behavior dept. J. Walter Thompson, N.Y.C., 1988-94; v.p., dir. account planning Cline, Davis & Mann, N.Y.C., 1994—. Contbr. articles to profl. jours. Mabel Wilson Richards scholar UCLA, 1967-70, UCLA scholar, 1969-70; NIMH fellow, 1971-75. Mem. Am. Mktg. Assn., Am. Psychol. Assn., Ea. Psychol. Assn. Home: 225 E 57th St New York NY 10022-2862 Office: Cline Davis & Mann 450 Lexington Ave New York NY 10017-3911

SEITNER, RITA A., management consultant, researcher; b. Milw., July 11, 1940; d. Robert and Esther (Steren) Seitner; m. Alfred F. Huete, Nov. 3, 1973 (div.). BA, Beaver Coll., 1962; MS, U. Wis., Milw., 1977. Mktg. asst. Advanced Learning, Milw., 1972-75; adminstv. asst. J. Walter Thompson, N.Y.C., 1962-67; assoc. planner David M. Walker, Phila., 1967-68; urban analyst HUD, Phila., 1968-70; market analyst Gen. Electric, Milw., 1977-82; mgr. research Hoffman, York & Compton, Milw., 1982-84, pres. RS Research Cons., Inc., Milw., 1984—. Fellow Am. Mktg. Assn., Am. Mgmt. Assn., Direct Mktg. Club. Jewish.

SEITZ, SHARON ELIZABETH, elementary school educator; b. Newton, N.C., Dec. 12, 1950; d. Glenn Lloyd and Lorene Elizabeth (Sigmon) S. BS magna cum laude, Appalachian State U., 1973, MA, 1974. Cert. tchr., N.C. Intern tchr. corps. project Mable Sch., Zionville, N.C., 1972-74; tchr. Asheboro (N.C.) City Schs., 1974—; mem. Sch. Leadership Team, 1991-93; cons. Comm. Skills Com. New Curriculum, Asheboro, 1992-93; sch. rep. Supt.'s Adv. Coun., Asheboro, 1992-93. Vol. ARS, Asheboro, 1988-90; mem. Luth. Ch. coun., 1988-90, witness com. chairperson, 1994—. Mem. N.C. Assn. Educators (treas., chair com. 1983-84), N.C. Coun. Tchrs. Maths., N.C. Zool. Soc., Internat. Assn. Childhood Edn. (treas. 1985-86), Community Concert Assn., Randolph Arts Guild. Office: Donna Lee Loflin Sch 405 S Park St Asheboro NC 27203

SEITZ, VICTORIA MARIE, judge; b. Tacoma, Wash., Mar. 28, 1951; d. Victor Clement and Mary G. (Drange) Sunich; m. Jerome Boniface Seitz, Dec. 29, 1971; 3 children. B in Pub. Adminstrn., Seattle U., 1973; JD, U. Puget Sound, 1976. Bar: Wash. 1974, U.S. Dist. Ct. (we. dist.) Wash. 1976, U.S. Ct. Appeals (9th cir.) 1988. Pub. defender Assoc. Coun. for the Accused, Seattle, 1976-80; city pros. Seattle City Atty.'s Office, 1980-83, civil trial atty., 1985-91; dep. pros. atty. King County Pros. Office, Seattle, 1983-85, dist. ct. judge, 1991—. Mem. steering com. Mothers Against Violence in Am., Seattle, 1994; mem. Mt. Rainier H.S. PTA, Des Moines, Wash., 1992—. Mem. King County Dist. Ct. Judges Assn. (exec. com. 1994—), Wash. State Dist. Ct. Judges (legis. com. 1991—), King County Bar Assn. (diversity task force 1994), Kiwanis. Roman Catholic. Office: King County Dist Ct 601 SW 149th St Burien WA 98166

SEKHON, KATHLEEN, state legislator; b. 1948; m. David Sekhon; 3 children. BS, U. Minn. Mem. Minn. Ho. of Reps., St. Paul, 1992—, mem. environ. and natural resources com., labor and mgmt. rels. com.; tchr. Home: 6619 189th Ln NW Anoka MN 55303-9519 Office: Minn Ho of Reps 593 State Office Bldg Saint Paul MN 55155*

SEKOWSKI, CYNTHIA JEAN, corporate executive, contact lens specialist; b. Chgo., Feb. 14, 1953; d. John L. and Celia L. (Matusiak) S. PhD in Health Svcs. Adminstrn., Columbia Pacific U., 1984, PhD in Health Scis., 1984. Chief contact lens dept. Lieberman & Kraff, Chgo., 1974-87; pres., chief exec. officer Seko Eye Care, Inc., Chgo., 1988—; researcher, technologist U. Ill., Chgo., 1976-78. Mem. Chgo. Zool. Soc., 1984—, Little City Inner Circle, 1991—; sponsor Save the Children Orgn., 1983—; asst. to campaign mgr. Rep. State Senatorial candidate, Chgo., 1972. Fellow Contact Lens Soc. Am.; mem. Ill. Soc. Opticianry, Opticians Assn. Am., Better Vision Inst., Nat. Contact Lens Examiners, Nat. Geog. Soc., Columbia Pacific U. Alumnae Assn., Nat. Wildlife Fedn. Roman Catholic. Office: Seko Eye Care Inc 4200 N Central Ave Ste 107 Chicago IL 60634-1810

SELBER, ARLENE BORK, environmental services company executive; b. Jacksonville, Fla., June 24, 1942; d. Morris and Ethyl (Sigal) Bork; m. H. Joel Selber, Nov. 22, 1964 (div. 1982); children: Blair C., Robin A. BS, Tufts U., 1964; MBA, Jacksonville U., 1983. Internat. mktg. dir. Clow Corp., Jacksonville, 1984-85; dir. mktg. Haztech Inc., Atlanta, 1985-87; asst. v.p. Nuclear Assurance Corp., Atlanta, 1987-88; dir. bus. devel. Ecotek, Inc., Atlanta, 1988-90; v.p. bus. devel. Parsons Engrng. Sci., Inc., Charlotte, N.C., 1990—. Advisor, Adv. Com. for Internat. Trade, Sen. Paula Hawkins, Washington, 1984; mem. trade adv. coun. U.S. Dept. Commerce Environ. Techs. Mem. ASME (mixed waste com., vice chmn.), Am. Nuclear Soc., Hazardous Materials Control Resources Inst. (bd. dirs.), Women's Execs., Internat. Soc. for Decontamination and Decommissioning Profls., Laubach Tutor, Charlotte C. of C. (Far East task force 1983-84), High Mus., Jacksonville Track Club (bd. dirs. 1977-83), Women's Execs. Golf League. Office: Parsons Engring Sci Inc 4701 Hedgemore Dr Charlotte NC 28209-3281

SELBER, SARANNE SPEER, social services professional; b. Houston, May 24, 1957; d. Marvin J. and Beverly (Kaplan) Speer; m. Mandel Selber, Nov. 21, 1982; children: Peter, Jennifer. BA, Tulane U.; MA in Lang. Pathology, U. Houston. Co-owner Selko and Assocs., Midland and Houston, 1986—; devel. dir. Planned Parenthood, Oklahoma City, 1992-94; exec. dir. AIDS Found., Houston, 1994—. Participant Leadership Oklahoma City, 1993-94; bd. dirs. Jewish Fedn. of Oklahoma City, 1993-94, Temple B'nai Israel, Oklahoma City, 1993-94; mem. Young Leadership Cabinet of UJA, 1992-94. Named to Outstanding Young Women in Am., 1983. Mem. Jr. League of Midland (bd. dirs. 1988-89), Jr. League of Oklahoma City, AIPAC, Hockaday Sch. Alumni (bd. dirs. 1992-94). Jewish. Home: 5323 Yarwell Dr Houston TX 77096-5118

SELBERG, JANICE KAY, law librarian, educator; b. Pontiac, Mich., Dec. 6, 1953; d. Alfred Nels and Regina Lee (Gibbs) S.; m. Anthony Augustus Muraski, Nov. 25, 1978; 1 child, Emily Jo Muraski. AB, Mich. State U., 1976; MLS, U. Mich., 1977; JD, Detroit Coll. Law, 1985. Bar: Mich. 1985. Account rep. Mead Data Cen., Detroit, 1982-85; info. specialist GM, Detroit, 1985-87; pub. svcs. law libr. Wayne State U., Detroit, 1987—, instr. libr. sci. program, 1990—. Editor: Directory of Michigan Law Libraries, 1989; contbr. articles to profl. jours. Recipient Graylyn Conf. grant Mead Data Cen., Winston-Salem, N.C., 1989. Mem. Women Lawyers Assn. of Mich., Mich. Assn. Law Librs. (pres. 1991-92), Mich. State Bar Assn. (asst. editor internat. law sect. 1990—). Democrat. Lutheran. Home: 1603 Westminster Pl Ann Arbor MI 48104-4358 Office: Wayne State U Law Libr 468 E Ferry St Detroit MI 48202-3814

SELBY, CECILY CANNAN, dean, educator, scientist; b. London, Feb. 4, 1927; d. Keith and Catherine Anne Cannan; m. Henry M. Selby, Aug. 11, 1951 (div. 1979); children: Norman, William, Russell; m. James Stacy Coles, Feb. 21, 1981. A.B. cum laude, Radcliffe Coll., 1946; Ph.D. in Phys. Biology, MIT, 1950. Teaching asst. in biology MIT, 1948-49; adminstrv. head virus study sect. Sloan-Kettering Inst., N.Y.C., 1949-50; asst. mem. inst. Sloan-Kettering Inst., 1950-55; research assoc. Sloan-Kettering div. Cornell U. Med. Coll., N.Y.C., 1953-55; instr. microscopic anatomy Cornell U. Med. Coll., 1955-57; tchr. sci. Lenox Sch., N.Y.C., 1957-58; headmistress Lenox Sch., 1959-72; nat. exec. dir. Girl Scouts U.S.A., N.Y.C., 1972-75; adv. com. Simmons Coll. Grad. Mgmt. Program, 1977-78; mem. Com. Corp. Support of Pvt. Univs., 1977-83; spl. asst. acad. planning N.C. Sch. Sci. and Math., 1979-80, dean acad. affairs, 1980-81, chmn. bd. advisors, 1981-84; cons. U.S. Dept. Commerce, 1976-77; dir. Avon Products Inc., RCA, NBC, Loehmanns Inc., Nat. Edn. Corp. pres. Am. Energy Ind., 1976; co-chmn. commn. precoll. math. and sci. Nat. Sci. Bd., 1982-83; adj. prof. NYU, 1984-86, prof. sci. edn., 1986—; mem. policy steering com. Gov. Cuomo's Conf. on Sci. and Engrng., 1989-90. Contbr. articles to profl. jours., chpt. to book. Founder, chmn. N.Y. Ind. Schs. Opportunity Project, 1968-72; mem. invitational workshops Aspen Inst., 1973, 75, 77, 79; trustee MIT, Bklyn. Law Sch., Radcliffe Coll., Woods Hole Oceanographic Instn., Women's Forum N.Y., Skin Disease Found., N.Y. Hall of Sci., 1982—, vice chmn., 1989—; trustee Girls Inc., 1992—, Nat. Coun. Women in Medicine, 1990—; mem. Yale U. Peabody Mus. Adv. Coun., 1981-89. Recipient Woman Scientist of Yr. award N.Y. chpt. Am. Women in Sci., 1992. Mem. Headmistresses of East (hon., pres. 1970-72), Sigma Xi, Phi Delta Kappa. Clubs: Cosmopolitan (N.Y.C.). Home and Office: 45 Sutton Pl S New York NY 10022-2444 also: 100 Ransom Rd Falmouth MA 02540

SELBY, NAOMI ARDEAN, women's health nurse, medical/surgical nurse; b. Duncan, Okla., Jan. 17, 1946; d. Orbie J.N. Sr. and Dorothy Naomi (Foster) S. BSN, Tex. Woman's U., 1969. Staff nurse, head nurse labor and delivery Meth. Med. Ctr., Dallas; cons., staff nurse ob-gyn. Southeastern Meth. Hosp., Dallas, staff nurse, operating room; head nurse ob-gyn. Yukon Delta Regional Hosp./USPHS/Indian Health Svc., Bethel, Alaska; nurse mgr. cen. supply rm./oper. rm. Yukon Kuskokwim Delta Regional Hosp./ USPHS Indian Health Svc. Mem. NAACOG, Assn. Operating Room Nurses. Home: PO Box 287 Unit 3114 Bethel AK 99559-0287

SELDES, MARIAN, actress; b. N.Y.C.; d. Gilbert and Alice (Hall) S.; m. Julian Claman, Nov. 3, 1953 (div.); 1 child, Katharine; m. Garson Kanin, June 19, 1990. Grad., Neighborhood Playhouse, N.Y.C., 1947; D.H.L., Emerson Coll., 1979. Mem. faculty drama and dance div. Juilliard Sch. Lincoln Center, N.Y.C., 1969-91. Appeared with Cambridge (Mass.) Summer Theatre, 1945, Boston Summer Theatre, 1946, St. Michael's Playhouse, Winooski, Vt., 1947-48, Bermudiana Theatre, Hamilton, Bermuda, 1951, Elitch Gardens Theatre, Denver, 1953; Broadway appearances include Medea, 1947, Crime and Punishment, 1948, That Lady, 1949, Tower Beyond Tragedy, 1950, The High Ground, 1951, Come of Age, 1952, Ondine, 1954, The Chalk Garden, 1955, The Wall, 1960, A Gift of Time, 1962, The Milk Train Doesn't Stop Here Any More, 1964, Tiny Alice, 1965, A Delicate Balance, 1967 (Tony award for best supporting actress), Before You Go, 1968, Father's Day, 1971 (Drama Desk award), Mendicants of Evening (Martha Graham Co.), 1973, Equus, 1974-77, The Merchant, 1977, Deathtrap, 1978; off-Broadway appearances include Diff'rent, 1961, The Ginger Man, 1963 (Obie award), All Women Are One, 1964, Juana LaLoca, 1965, Three Sisters, 1969, Am. Shakespeare Festival, Stratford, Conn., Mercy Street at Am. Place Theater, N.Y.C., 1969, Isadora Duncan, 1976 (Obie award), Painting Churches, 1983, 84 (Outer Critics Circle award 1984), Other People, Berkshire Theatre Festival, 1969, The Celebration, Hedgerow Theater, Pa., 1971, Richard III, N.Y. Shakespeare Festival, 1983, Remember Me, Lakewood Theatre, Skowhegan, Maine, Gertrude Stein and a Companion, White Barn Theatre, Westport, Conn., 1985, Lucile Lortel Theatre, N.Y.C., 1986, Richard II, N.Y. Shakespeare Festival, 1987, The Milk Train Doesn't Stop Here Anymore, WPA Theatre, N.Y.C., 1987, Happy Ending, Bristol (Pa.) Riverside Theatre, 1988, Annie 2 John F. Kennedy Ctr., Washington, 1989-90, Goodspeed Opera House, Chester, Conn., 1990, A Bright Room Called Day, N.Y. Shakespeare Festival, 1991, Three Tall Women, River Arts, Woodstock, N.Y., 1992, Another Time, Am. Jewish Theatre, 1993, Breaking the Code, Berkshire Theatre Festival, 1993, Three Tall Women, Vineyard Theatre, N.Y.C., 1994, Promenade Theatre, 1994; engaged in nat. tour Medea, 1947; U.S. entry Berlin Festival, 1951; motion picture appearances include The Greatest Story Ever Told, Gertrude Stein and a Companion, 1988, In a Pig's Eye, 1988, The Gun in Betty Lou's Handbag, 1992; (ABC series) Good and Evil, 1991, Murphy Brown, 1992; also appeared on CBS Radio Mystery Theater, 1976-81, as well as numerous dramatic shows; author: The Bright Lights, 1978, Time Together, 1981. Bd. dirs. Neighborhood Playhouse, The Acting Co., nat. repertory theatre. Mem. Players Club, Century Assn.

SELDIN, MABEL ALICE, education educator; b. Osceola, Iowa, May 7, 1909; d. Charles William and Rose (Ehret) Hinsey; m. Morris P. Seldin, July 6, 1941 (dec. July 1967). BA, No. Colo. U., 1933; MA, U. Denver, 1958. Tchr. Colo. Pub. Schs., Larimer, 1928-31, Logan, 1932-35; tchr. Denver Pub. Schs., 1935-65, ret., 1965. Mem. Kappa Delta Pi. Democrat.

SELECMAN, BARBARA ANN, private investor; b. St. Louis, Sept. 26, 1942; d. August and Mary Barbara (Whitman) Midden; m. Ronald F. Calvert, Sept. 28, 1959 (div. 1980); 1 child, Bradley S. Calvert; m. Charles Edward Selecman, Apr. 18, 1985. Student, Maryville Coll., 1974-75, Rollins Coll., 1976-77, St. Edwards U., 1988-89. Home: 26 Island Estates Pkwy Palm Coast FL 32137

SELES, MONICA, tennis player; b. Novi Sad, Yugoslavia, Dec. 2, 1973; came to U.S., 1986; d. Karol and Esther Seles. Winner Italian Open, 1990, German Open, 1990, French Open, 1990, 91, 92, Va. Slims, 1990, 91, 92, U.S. Open, 1991, 92, Australian Open, 1991, 92, 93; named Yugoslavia's sportswoman of yr., 1985. Office: care Internat Mgmt Group 1 Erieview Plz Cleveland OH 44114-1715*

SELESKI, DOROTHY MARIE, health care administrator; b. Washington, Mar. 22, 1962; d. John and Dorothy Pauline (Papson) S. BA, U. Md., 1984; MBA, UCLA, 1987, MPH, 1987. Mgmt. intern FHP, Long Beach, Calif., 1985; mgmt. engr. intern UCLA Med. Ctr., 1985-87; spl. asst. to COO U. Chgo. Hosps., 1987-89; sr. contract adminstr. PacifiCare, Cypress, Calif., 1989-91; contracts mgr. VertiHealth, Burbank, Calif., 1991-94, adminstrv. dir., 1994—; speaker at seminars. Columnist Jour. Med. Practice Mgmt., 1988—. Mem. UCLA Sch. Pub. Health Alumni Assn., Phi Beta Kappa, Delta Omega. Democrat. Catholic. Office: VertiHealth 4000 W Alameda Blvd Burbank CA 91505

SELIG, MARTHA KEISER, social work consultant; b. N.Y.C., Dec. 25, 1912; d. Jacob H. and Sadie (Hammer) Keiser; B.A., Hunter Coll., N.Y.C., 1932; M.S., CCNY, 1933; postgrad. Columbia U., 1933-38; diploma N.Y. Sch. Social Work, 1939; m. Kalman Selig, Mar. 23, 1935; children—Judith Selig Rubenstein, Elaine Selig Gould. Clin. psychologist Edn. Clinic, CCNY, 1932-44; exec. dir. Jewish Community Services L.I., 1944-46; exec. dir. community services Fedn. Jewish Philanthropies N.Y., 1946-74; vis. prof. Adelphia U., Garden City, N.Y., also Jewish Theol. Sem., N.Y.C., 1974—; guest lectr. Columbia U., Wurzweiler Sch. Social Work, Hunter Coll. Sch. Social Work, 1974-79; cons. health and welfare agys. and founds., 1974—, exec. dir. S.H. and Helen R. Scheuer Family Found., 1979-87; exec. bd. Am. Jewish Com.; bd. dirs. Council Vol. Child Care Agys. N.Y.C., Henry Kaufman Campgrounds, Hebrew Arts Sch., Nat. Found. for Jewish Culture; mem. Mayor's Commn. on Child Care, N.Y. State Adv. Commn. on Welfare, N.Y. State Gov.'s Commn. on Alcohol and Drug Abuse N.Y.C. Commn. on Mental Health. Recipient Naomi Lehman Meml. award, 1960, Samuel W. and Rose Hurowitz award Fedn. Jewish Philanthropies N.Y., 1975; named to Hunter Coll. Hall of Fame, 1976; hon. mem. psychol. assn., also ednl. assn. CCNY. Mem. Nat. Assn. Social Workers, Acad. Cert. Social Workers, Nat. Conf. Jewish Communal Service (past pres.). Author papers in field. Home: 22 E 88th St New York NY 10128-0502 Office: 120 W 57th St New York NY 10019

SELIG, PHYLLIS SIMS, architect; b. Topeka, Nov. 16, 1931; d. Willis Nolan and Victoria Clarinda (Oakley) Sims; m. James Richard Selig, Mar. 31, 1957; children: Lin Ann, Susan Nan, Sarah Jo. BS in Architecture, U. Kans., 1956. Realtor Assoc. Realty, Lawrence, Kans., 1965-70; v.p. finance and housing Alpha Phi Internat. Fraternity, Inc., Evanston, Ill., 1968-74, chief exec. officer, internat. pres., 1974-78, trustee, 1978-80; sr. engr. tech. Nebr. Pub. Power, Columbus, 1980-86, staff architect, 1986-89, archtl. supr., 1989—. Republican. Lutheran. Office: Nebr Pub Power 1414 15th St Columbus NE 68601-5226

SELK, ELEANOR HUTTON, artist; b. Duboise, Nebr., Oct. 21, 1918; d. Anderson Henry and Florence (Young) Hutton; R.N., St. Elizabeth Hosp., Lincoln, Nebr., 1938; m. Harold Frederick Selk, Aug. 3, 1940; children: Honey Lou, Katherine Florence. Nurse, Lincoln, 1938-40, Denver, 1940-50; with Colo. Bd. Realtors, 1956-66; owner, mgr. The Pen Point, graphic art studio, Colorado Springs, 1974-94; instr. history and oil painting, 1994—; one-woman shows: Colo. Coll., 1970, 72, Nazarene Bible Coll., 1973, 1st Meth. Ch., 1971 (all Colorado Springs); exhibited in group shows: U. So. Colo., 1969, 70, 71, 72, Colorado Springs Art Guild, 1969-72, Pike's Peak Artists Assn., 1969-73, Mozart Art Festival, Pueblo, Colo., 1969-74, numerous others; represented in permanent collection U.S. Postal Service, Pen-Arts Bldg., Washington, Medic Alert Found. Internat. Hdqrs., Turlock, Calif. Rec. sec. Colo. chpt. Medic Alert Found. Internat., 1980-90, chairperson El Paso County and Colorado Springs chpt., 1980-90, Colo. bd. dirs., 1980-89, rec. sec., 1980-89. Recipient 3d pl. award Nat. Tb and Respiratory Disease and Christmas Seal Art Competition, 1969, finalist award Benedictine Art competition Hanover Trust Bank, N.Y.C., 1970, numerous awards and certs. for pub. service and art, award Music of the Baroque, 1991, Editors Choice award Nat. Libr. Poetry, 1993. Mem. Nat. League Am. Pen Women (rec. sec. 1972-74, travelling art slide collection 1974—, designer jewelry, awards for book cover art, numerous Gold Bangle awards). Contbr. med. articles, short stories, poetry to newspapers. Home and Studio: 518 Warren Ave Colorado Springs CO 80906-2343

SELKE-KERN, BARBARA ELLEN, university official, writer; b. Houston, Dec. 14, 1950; d. Oscar Otto Jr. and Edith Hicks (Hardey) Selke; m. Homer Dale Kern, May 31, 1985. BS, U. Colo., 1973; MA, U. Tex., 1981, PhD, 1986. Cert. elem. and secondary tchr., Tex. Co-owner Colo. Sound, Denver, 1972-76; tchr. Jefferson County Schs., Lakewood, Colo., 1974-76; dir. Harvest Time Day Care Ctr., Austin, 1976-77; mgr. TourService, Inc., Austin, 1977-82; curriculum specialist U. Tex., Austin, 1982-87, ednl. resources coord., 1987-88, ednl. resources dir., 1988-92; coord. adult vocat. programs Austin (Tex.) C.C., 1992-94, coord. grant devel., 1994—. Author (books): Retail Travel Marketing, 1983, Communication Skills, 1984, Orientation to Cosmetology Instructor Training, 1984, Resumes and Interviews, 1984, Competency in Teaching, 1985, Guidelines for the Texas Cosmetology Commission Instructor Licensing Examination, 1985, Effective Communication, 1986, Effective Teaching, 1986, Balancing the Curriculum for Marketing Education, 1987, Bulletin Board Designs for Marketing Education, 1987, Marketing Education I, 1988, Flashcards for Marketing Education, 1988, Glossary for Marketing Education, 1988, Validated Task Lists for Apparel And Accessories Marketing, 1991; co-author: Higher Level Thinking in Marketing Education, 1990; author (computer software): Emergency Aid, 1986, 2nd edit., 1989, Measuring Employee Productivity, 1986, Retail Pricing in Action, 1987, Marketing Fibers and Fabrics, 1989, Physical Distribution, 1991; editor: Training Plans for Marketing Education, 1987, Correspondence, 1988, Instructional Planning, 1988; contbr. articles to profl. jours. Recipient scholarship Am. Bus. Women's Ass., 1985. Mem. Am. Assn. Adult and Continuing Edn., Nat. Coun. Resource Devel., Tex. Jr. Coll. Tchrs. Assn., Phi Delta Kappa, Kappa Delta Phi, Phi Kappa Phi. Home: 6518B Hart Ln Austin TX 78731-3139 Office: Austin CC 5930 Middle Fiskville Rd Austin TX 78752-7218

SELL, JOAN ISOBEL, mobile home company owner; b. Johnson City, Tenn., May 5, 1936; d. Earl Walter and Jeanne Mason (Lyle) S.; m. Dale L. Moss, Jan. 15, 1956 (div. Nov. 1977); children: Carol Anne, John D. BS, East Tenn. State U., Johnson City, 1961. Cert. tchr., Tenn., Ga. Tchr. Asbury Sch., Johnson City, 1961-62, Richard Arnold High Sch., Savannah, Ga., 1964-66, Windsor Forest High Sch., Savannah, 1966-67, Boones Creek High Sch., Jonesborough, Tenn., 1967-77; co-owner Moss-Sell Mobile Homes, Johnson City, 1978-88; co-owner Biddix Budget Homes, Inc. (formerly Budget Mobile Homes), Johnson City, 1978-87, v.p., sec., 1987—; pres., treas. Budget Homes, Inc. (formerly Biddix Budget Homes), Johnson City, 1988-92; owner McKinley Park, Johnson City. Mem. Tenn. Manufactured Housing Assn. (state bd. dirs. 1993—), N.E. Tenn. Manufactured Housing Assn. (pres.), DAR, UDC, Order Ea. Star. Mem. Brethren Ch. Home: 3 Caitlin Ct Johnson City TN 37604-1147 Office: McKinley Park PO Box 5189 Johnson City TN 37603-5189

SELLERS, BARBARA JACKSON, federal judge; b. Richmond, Va., Oct. 3, 1940; m. Richard F. Sellers; children: Elizabeth M., Anne W., Catherine A. Attended, Baldwin-Wallace Coll., 1958-60; BA cum laude, Ohio State U., 1962; JD magna cum laude, Capital U. Law Sch., Columbus, Ohio, 1979. Bar: Ohio 1979, U.S. Dist. Ct. (so. dist.) Ohio 1981, U.S. Ct. Appeals (6th cir.), 1986. Jud. law clk. Hon. Robert J. Sidman, U.S. Bankruptcy Judge, Columbus, Ohio, 1979-81; assoc. Lasky & Semons, Columbus, 1981-82; jud. law clk. to Hon. Thomas M. Herbert, U.S. Bankruptcy Ct., Columbus, 1982-84; assoc. Baker & Hostetler, Columbus, 1984-86; U.S. bankruptcy judge So. Dist. Ohio, Columbus, 1986—; lectr. on bankruptcy univs., insts., assns. Recipient Am. Jurisprudence prize contracts and criminal law, 1975-76, evidence and property, 1976-77, Corpus Juris Secundum awards, 1975-76, 76-77. Mem. ABA (corp., litigation sect. 1986—, banking and bus. law sect. 1981—, jud. adminstrv. sect. 1983-84), Columbus Bar Assn., Comml. Law League of Am., Am. Bankruptcy Inst., Nat. Conf. Bankruptcy Judges, Order of Curia, Phi Beta Kappa. Office: US Bankruptcy Ct 124 US Courthouse 85 Marconi Blvd Columbus OH 43215-2823

SELLERS, BEVERLY BURCH, university administrator; b. Geneva, Ala., July 23, 1962; d. Robert and Eris Lucille (Reeves) B.; m. James T. Sellers, Sept. 22, 1984. AA, Enterprise (Ala.) Jr. Coll., 1982; BA, Troy State U., 1984; MA, La. State U., 1989. Nat. cert. counselor. Career counselor Southeastern La. U. Comprehensive Counseling Ctr., Hammond, 1989-94; asst. dir. career devel. svcs. Southeastern La. U., 1994—; conduct career decision making, resume writing, job search and interviewing, and Myers-Briggs Type Indicator workshops and presentations for campus and cmty. orgns. Home: Hwy 38 E Kentwood LA 70444 Office: Southeastern La U PO Box 492 Hammond LA 70402

SELLERS, PATRICIA ANN, surgical nurse; b. Salamanca, N.Y., May 22, 1946; d. Elmer Ellsworth Long and Elizabeth June (Anderson) Eckman; m. William Russell Sellers, Apr. 21, 1967; children: Donna Sue, Joanne Marie. Diploma, Oil City Sch. Nursing, 1967; stroke nurse, West Pa. Reg. Med. Program, 1971. RN, Pa. Staff nurse Oil City Hosp., Oil City, Pa., 1967-68, Butler County Meml. Hosp., Butler, Pa., 1968-70; asst. head nurse Grove City Hosp., Grove City, Pa., 1970-81; clin. coord. United Community Hosp., Grove City, 1981-82, asst. head nurse in surg. unit, 1982-90, nurse mgr. in surg. unit, 1990-93; staff nurse in home health svc. United Community Hosp., 1993—; chmn. audit com. United Community Hosp., 1975-80, chmn. patient edn. com., 1980-81. Mem. Order of Ea. Star. Democrat. Presbyterian. Home: 3325 Oneida Valley Rd Emlenton PA 16373-2111 Office: United Community Hosp 631 N Broad Street Ext Grove City PA 16127-9793

SELLET, REBECCA CAROL, tour manager, tour leader; b. Mt. Kisko, N.Y., Oct. 3, 1960; d. Lawrence Randall and Carol Audrey (Rossiter) S. AA, Am. U. Paris, 1980. Office mgr. Wilton (Conn.) Ctr. Travel, 1981-89; ops. mgr. Passages Unltd., Boston, 1989-90; office mgr. Caboose Travel Svc., Gloucester, Mass., 1990-92; tour mgr. Travel Dynamics, N.Y.C , 1992—; instr. Conn. Acad. Travel, Norwalk, 1988. Vol. project up-lift Action, Inc., Gloucester, 1992.

SELL-LAUBACH, CHERYL DAWN, state official; b. Allentown, Pa., Feb. 18, 1953; d. Dale F. and Paula A. (Zeart) Sell; m. Gregory J. Laubach, May

31, 1986; 1 child, Whitney S. BA, Mansfield U., 1974; BS, Cedar Crest Coll., Allentown, Pa., 1989. With Commonwealth of Pa., Allentown, 1975-76, 86, unemployment compensation tax agt, 1992—; with Commonwealth of Pa., Reading, Pa., 1980-83; planner, researcher City of Allentown, 1976-79; staff acct. Concannon, Gallagher, Miller, Allentown, 1989-91. Recipient Acctg. award Nat. Assn. Accts., Lehigh Valley, 1989. Mem. Inst. Mgmt. Accts. (dir. pub. rels. 1989-92), Lehigh Valley ZTA Alumnae (sec.-treas. 1993-94). Mem. Ch. of Christ. Office: Bur Employer Tax FAS 160 W Hamilton St Ste 300 Allentown PA 18101-1939

SELMAN, MINNIE CORENE PHELPS, educator; b. Freedom, Okla., Mar. 25, 1947; d. Maxwell Jack and Mary Elizabeth (Mountain) Phelps; m. Thomas O. Selman, Aug. 8, 1966; children: T. Justin, Jeffrey L. BS in Elem. Edn., Northwestern Okla. State U., 1969. Cert. elem. tchr., early childhood edn. tchr., Okla.; cert. early experiences in sci., Okla. Tchr. Woodward (Okla.) Pub. Sch., 1969-72; pre-sch. tchr. Free Spirit Pre-sch., Woodward, 1974-75; tchr. Montessori Discovery World Pre-sch., Woodward, 1975-78; tchr. kindergarten Woodward Pub. Sch., Woodward, 1978—; host Leaderhip Okla. in the Classroom, 1991; tng. tchr. Okla. State U., Stillwater, 1987, 90. Benefit vol. Western Plains Shelter Orgn., Woodward, 1990, 91; life mem. Plains Indians and Pioneers Hist. Found., Woodward. Woodward Pub. Schs. Ednl. Found. grantee, 1990, 91, 92. Mem. NEA, Okla. Edn. Assn., Woodward Edn. Assn. (pub. rels. com. 1990—). Democrat. Home: 318 Spruce Park Dr Woodward OK 73801-5945

SELTZER, VICKI LYNN, obstetrician-gynecologist; b. N.Y.C., June 2, 1949; d. Herbert Melvin and Marian Elaine (Willinger) S.; m. Richard Stephen Brach, Sept. 2, 1973; children: Jessica Lillian, Eric Robert. BS, Rensselaer Poly. Inst., 1969; MD, NYU, 1973. Diplomate Am. Bd. Ob-Gyn. Intern Bellevue Hosp., N.Y.C., 1973-74, resident in ob-gyn, 1974-77; fellow gynecol. cancer Am. Cancer Soc., N.Y.C., 1977-78, Meml. Sloan Kettering Cancer Ctr., N.Y.C., 1978-79; assoc. dir. gynecol. cancer Albert Einstein Coll. Medicine, N.Y.C., 1979-83; assoc. prof. ob-gyn., SUNY, Stony Brook, N.Y.C., 1983-89; prof. ob-gyn. Albert Einstein Coll. Medicine, 1989—; chmn. ob-gyn. L.I. Jewish Med. Ctr., 1993—; dir. ob-gyn., Queens Hosp. Ctr., Jamaica, N.Y., 1983—, pres. med. bd., 1986-89. Author: Every Woman's Guide to Breast Cancer, 1987; editor-in-chief: Primary Care Update for the Ob-Gyn, 1993—; editor: Women's Primary Health Care, 1995; mem. editorial bd. Women's Life mag., 1980-82, Jour. of the Jacobs Inst. Women's Health, 1990—; contbr. over 75 articles to profl. jours.; host Weekly Ob-Gyn. TV Program, Lifetime Med. TV. Chmn. health com. Nat. Coun. Women, N.Y.C., 1979—; mem. Mayor Beame's Task Force on Rape, N.Y.C., 1974-76; bd. govs. Regional Coun. Women in Medicine, 1985—; chmn. Coun. on Resident Edn. in Ob-Gyn., 1987—. Galloway Fund fellow 1975; recipient citation Am. Med. Women's Assn., 1973, Nat. Safety Coun., 1978, Achiever award Nat. coun. Women, 1985, Achiever award L.I. Ctr. Bus. and Profl. Women, 1987. Fellow N.Y. Obstet. Soc., Am. Coll. Ob-Gyn (v.p. 1993—, gynecol. practice com. 1981, examener Am. Bd. Obstetrics and Gynecology 1988—); mem. Women's Med. Assn. (v.p. N.Y. 1974-79, editorial bd. jour. 1985—, resident review com. for obstetrics and gynecology 1993—), Am. Med. Women's Assn. (com. chmn. 1975-77, 78-79, editorial bd. jour. 1986—), N.Y. Cancer Soc., NYU Sch. Med. Alumni Assn. (bd. govs. 1979—, v.p. 1987—, pres. 1992—), Alpha Omega Alpha. Office: LI Jewish Med Ctr New Hyde Park NY 11040

SELTZER, VIVIAN CENTER, psychology educator; b. Mpls., May 27, 1931; d. Aaron M. and Hannah (Chazanow) Center; m. William Seltzer; children: Jonathan, Francesca S. Rothseid, Aeryn S. Fenton. BA summa cum laude, U. Minn., 1951; MSW, U. Pa., 1953; PhD, Bryn Mawr Coll., 1976. Lic. psychologist; cert. sch. psychologist; lic. social worker, Pa.; cert. marriage and family therapist. Family counselor Phila. and Miami, Fla., 1953-60; pvt. practice psychology cons. Phila., 1965—; prof. human devel. and behavior U. Pa., Phila., 1976—; exch. prof. U. Edinburgh, 1979-80; vis. prof. Hebrew U. Jerusalem, 1984-85; chair internat. com. U. Pa., various other coms. Author: Adolescent Social Development: Dynamic Functional Interaction, 1982, The Psychosocial Worlds of the Adolescent, 1989; contbr. articles to profl. jours. Mem. bd. overseers Gratz Coll., Phila., 1965—, v.p., 1989—, chair acad. affairs com., 1980—. Mem. APA, Pa. Psychol. Assn., Phila. Soc. Clin. Psychologists (bd. dirs. 1975-86, program chair 1980-86), Phi Beta Kappa. Office: U Pa 3701 Locust Walk Philadelphia PA 19104-6214

SELVY, BARBARA, dance instructor; b. Little Rock, Jan. 20, 1938; d. James Oliver and Irene Balmat Banks; m. Franklin Delano Selvy, Apr. 15, 1959; children: Lisa Selvy Yeargin, Valerie Selvy Miros, Lauren, Franklin Michael. Student, U. Ctrl. Ark., 1955-57. Founder, dir. Carolina Ballet Theater, Greenville, S.C., 1973—; Advisory bd. dirs. Met. Arts Council and S.C. Governors Sch. Appeared in numerous TV commls., on Goodson-Toddman game show Play Your Hunch, 1958-59; toured Far East with TV show Hit Parade, 1958; named Miss Ark., 1956, Mrs. S.C., 1981; dir. and staged Mrs. Va., Mrs. N.C., Mrs. S.C. pageants; choreographed Little Theater prodns., Furman U. Opera. Mem. So. Assn. Dance Masters (ballet adviser, regional dir.), Dance Educators Am., Dance Masters of Am., Profl. Dance Tchrs. Home: 206 Honey Horn Dr Simpsonville SC 29681-5814 Office: Carolina Ballet Theatre 872 Woodruff Rd Greenville SC 29607-3538

SEMBER, JUNE ELIZABETH, retired elementary education educator; b. Apr. 3, 1932; d. Charles Benjamin and Cora Emma (Miller) Shoemaker; m. Eugene Sember, Oct. 18, 1975. BS with honors, Ea. Mennonite, 1957; post-grad., Columbia U., 1958, U. W.Va., 1960. Tchr. grades 1-6 Cross Roads Pvt. Sch., Salisbury, Pa., 1953-55; tchr. grade 5 Connellsville (Pa.) Area Schs., 1957-58, tchr. grade 2, 1958-66, tchr. grade 1, 1967-92, classroom vol., 1992—; supervising tchr. California (Pa.) U., 1970-90. Mem. Delta Kappa Gamma (pres. 1978-80). Presbyterian. Home: 1125 Pittsburgh St Scottdale PA 15683-1630 Office: Connellsville Area Schs 7th Ave Connellsville PA 15425

SEMMLER, CARYL J., occupational therapist; b. Portland, Oreg., Sept. 15, 1949; d. Hardie Justus Sickles and Elna Gertrude (Kohlstedt) Linville; m. Maynard Jonathan Semmler, Aug. 22, 1970; children: Emma, Desireé, Kristoffer, Damon, Shane, Micah. BS, U. Kans., 1972; MS, Boston U., 1975; PhD, U. Tex., Dallas, 1984. Lic. occupational therapist, Tex. Occupational therapist St. Frances Hosp., Tulsa, 1972-74; instr. occupational therapy Tex. Women's U., Dallas, 1975-76; asst. prof. pediatrics U. Tex. Southwestern Med. Sch., Dallas, 1976-90; pvt. practice Dallas, 1990—; cons. phys. mgmt. adv. com. Tex. Dept. Mental Health/Mental Retardation, Austin, 1989-94; adj. prof. occupl. therapy Tex. Women's U., 1991-94; ind. contractor Comprehensive Home Health Svcs., AccuCare, Leisure Lodge Nursing Home; vol. occupl. therapist Children;s Rehab. Clinic, Ryazan, Russia, 1994. Author: Handle with Care, 1990, Early O.T. Intervention, 1991; author, editor: A Guide to Care and Management of Very Low Birth Weight Infants, 1989; contbr. numerous articles to profl. jours. Flutist Mesquite (Tex.) Symphony Orch., 1986—, North Dallas Symphony, 1993—; v.p. Mesquite Symphony Orch. Assn., 1989-91; bd. dirs. Mesquite Arts Coun., 1991-93. Grantee Maternal Child Health divsn. Boston U., 1974-75, North Ctrl. Tex. March of Dimes, 1983-85, NIH, 1986, Ronald McDonald Charities, 1989. Mem. Am. Occupl. Therapy Assn. (pediatric splty. cert. exam. com. 1990—), World Fedn. Occupl. Therapists. Office: Ste 205 12820 Hillcrest Rd Dallas TX 75230

SEMORE, MARY MARGIE, abstractor; b. Cowlington, Okla., Feb. 11, 1920; d. William Leonard and Bessie Mae (Bellah) Barnett; m. Jack Sanford Semore, Mar. 3, 1940 (dec. Jan. 1985). Grad. high sch., Wagoner, Okla., 1938. Legal sec. W.O. Rittenhouse, Wagoner, Okla., 1938-40; abstractor Wagoner County Abstract Co., 1941—. Mem. Title Industry Polit. Action Com., Washington, 1986, Am. Legion Women's Aux., Wagoner Hist. Soc. Mem. Okla. Land Title Assn., Am. Land Title Assn., Wagoner C. of C., DAR, Daus. Am. Colonists. Democrat. Methodist. Home: 902 S White Ave Wagoner OK 74467-7239 Office: Wagoner County Abstract Co 219 E Cherokee PO Box 188 Wagoner OK 74477

SEMPLE, HELEN ARLENE, accountant, educator; b. Lake Milton, Ohio, May 21, 1940; d. Donald L. and Janette V. (Ripley) Donaldson; m. Scott D. Semple. BS in Home Econs. Edn., Ohio U., 1962; MS, Calif. State U., Northridge, 1983; AA, Moorpark Coll., 1983; postgrad., Caif. Luth. U., 1984-85. Cert. lifetime teaching credential. Tchr. high sch. Wayne Twp. Schs., Dayton, Ohio, 1964-67; salesperson Simi Valley, Calif.; cons. Canyon Rsch. Group, Westlake Village, Calif.; acct. Giga Bit Logic, Inc., Thousand Oaks, Calif., 1983-88, Rockwell Internat., Canoga Park, Calif., 1988-89, GTE-CA, Thousand Oaks, 1989—; instr. Moorpark (Calif.) Coll., 1989-90, Learning Tree U., Thousand Oaks, 1991-93. Dir. Simi Valley Ednl. Found., 1993; elected ofcl. Ventura County (Calif.) Rep. Ctrl. Com., 1993; officer Las Manitas Aux., 1972-92, Dr.'s Hosp. Aux., 1971-73. Mem. AAUW (officer 1969-93), Children's Home Soc. (mem. steering com. 1991-92). Home: 410 Capri Dr Simi Valley CA 93065

SENDER, LORI JO, chiropractor; b. L.A., May 30, 1963; d. Arthur Irwin and Lillian (Sender) S. AA, Santa Barbara City Coll., 1983; diploma, Pasadena Coll. of Chiropractic, 1984; BS, L.A. Coll. of Chiropractic, 1986; DC, Life Chiropractic Coll., 1987. Diplomate Nat. Bd. Chiropractic Examiners. Asst. athletic trainer Santa Barbara City Coll., Calif., 1981-83; chiropractic assoc. Chiropractic Assocs., Walnut Creek, Calif., 1987-89; faculty instr. Life Chiropractic Coll.-West, San Lorenzo, Calif., 1987-89; owner, dir. Sender Chiropractic, Goleta, Calif., 1989-94; industry cons. local bus., Santa Barbara, Goleta, 1989-94; lectr. in field. active Jr. League of Santa Barbara, 1992—; mem. Gov's. Coun. on Physical Fitness & Sports, Ventura, 1994—; mem. bd. dirs. Life Chiro-Coll.-West Alumni, 1994—. Recipient Internat. Gymnastics Competitor USGF, 1972-78. Mem. Internat. Chiropractic Assn., Goleta U.S. C. of C., South Coast Bus. Network. Office: Sender Chiropractic Clinic 25 Carlo Dr Santa Barbara CA 93117

SENDRA-ANAGNOST, TERESA AMOR, nurse, writer; b. Mt. Pleasant, N.Y., Nov. 20, 1936; d. Fernando Miralles Sendra and Hazel Ellene (Rice) Estruch; div. Oct. 1985; children: James Christopher, Karen Ellen, Andrew John. AA cum laude, Los Angeles Valley Coll., 1971; BS, Calif. State U., Northridge, 1979. Registered nurse practitioner, Calif. Nurse So. Calif. Permanente Med. Group, Panorama City, 1971-75, nurse practitioner adult medicine, 1975—; mgr. high risk hypelipidemia patients, 1989—. Active Am. Cancer Soc. Project Outreach, L.A., 1986-87. Mem. United Nurses Assn. Calif., ANA (nat. cert.), Calif. Coalition of Nurse Practitioners, Am. Acad. Nurse Practitioners. Home: 5630 Ranchito Ave Van Nuys CA 91401-4710 Office: So Calif Permanente Med Group 13652 Cantara St Panorama City CA 91402-5423

SENECHAL, ALICE R., judge, lawyer; b. Rugby, N.D., June 25, 1955; d. Marvin William and Dora Emma (Erdman) S. BS, N.D. State U., 1977; JD, U. Minn., 1984. Bar: Minn. 1984, U.S. Dist. Ct. Minn. 1984, N.D. 1986, U.S. Ct. Appeals (8th cir.) 1987. Law clk. U.S. Dist. Judge Bruce M. Van Sickle, Bismarck, N.D., 1984-86; assoc. Robert Vogel Law Office, Grand Forks, N.D., 1986—; U.S. magistrate judge, 1990—. Office: Robert Vogel Law Office 106 N 3rd St Ste M102 Grand Forks ND 58203-3798

SENEKER, KAY ANN, critical care, home health nurse; b. Omer, Mich., Mar. 4, 1948; d. Herbert Arthur and Alvina Eleanor Elizabeth (Silk) Deckett; m. James Lee Seneker, Nov. 23, 1986; 1 child, Michelle Denise Coates. Diploma, St. Mary's Sch. Nursing, Knoxville, Tenn., 1970; student, U. Mich., 1966-68; BS in Edn., U. Tenn., Knoxville, 1975. Cert. CPR instr. Instr. LPNs Sevier County, Sevierville, Tenn.; nursing svc. mgr. East Tenn. Bapt. Hosp., Knoxville; staff nurse in acute care and emergency room Blount Meml. Hosp., Maryville, Tenn.; dir. health care svcs. Priority Healthcare, Knoxville. Mem. Tenn. Nurses Assn., Tenn. Assn. Home Care (medicare part A com.), Region II Coun. Home Health Agencies. Home: 2311 Old Chilhowee Rd Seymour TN 37865-3722

SENG, ANN FRANCES, civic organization executive; b. Chgo., Jan. 5, 1936; d. William John and Helen Christine (Steger) S. BA, Alverno Coll., Milw., 1957; MA, Loyola U., Chgo., 1970. Tchr. Alvernia High Sch., Chgo., 1958-65; exec. dir. Community House Cath. Charities, Chgo., 1965-67; adminstr. Sch. Sisters St. Francis, Chgo., 1967-69; dir. uptown advocacy program Chgo. Cath. Interracial Coun., 1970-71; community devel. dir. Uptown Ctr. Hull House, Chgo., 1971-81; dir. rsch. and pub. policy Hull House Assn., Chgo., 1981-88; pres., chief exec. officer Chgo. Coun. Urban Affairs, 1988—; bd. dirs. Jane Addams Conf., Chgo., 1987—, Chgo. Capital Fund, 1988—, Women Employed Inst., Chgo., 1988-91. Mem. Pvt. Industry Coun., Chgo., 1988—; vice-chair Chgo. Com. Urban Opportunity, 1988-92. Mem. LWV, NOW, Ill. Women's Agenda (chair 1983-84),. Office: Chgo Coun Urban Affairs 6 N Michigan Ave Ste 1308 Chicago IL 60602-4808

SENICH, JENNY LOU, accountant; b. Oklahoma City, May 20, 1948; d. Howard B. and Mary Lucille (Shoop) Kirby; m. Robert J. Senich III (div. 1975); children: Stephanie, Jennifer. AS, Grayson Jr. Coll., Denison, Tex., 1968; BS in Acctg., Southeastern Okla. State U., 1984. Bookkeeper, teller State Nat. Bank, Denison, Tex., 1969-79; with finance J-M Mfg., Denison, 1979-87; asst. controller Plano (Tex.) Savs. and Loan, 1987-88; gen. acct. Kwikset Corp., Denison, 1989—. Active United Way Com., 1993—. Mem. Inst. Mgmt. Accts. Office: Kwikset Corp 2600 N Highway 75A Denison TX 75020-9042

SENIOR, SHEILA MATHILDA, nurse; b. Phila., May 28, 1947; d. Robert F. and Georgiana Marie (Stewart) Riskie; children by previous marriage: Harry Brooks, Georgianna Brooks; m. Matthew J. Senior (div. 1979); 1 child, Melissa. AAS, Delaware County Community Coll., Media, Pa., 1979. Staff med.-surg. nurse Hahnemann U. Hosp., Phila., 1979, cardiology staff nurse, 1979-82, nurse educator, cardiology, 1982-83, rsch. nurse clinician, clin. cardiac electrophysiology, 1983—, head rsch. nurse sudden death prevention program and clin. cardiac electrophysiology, 1985-86; clin. rsch. assoc. DuPont Pharm., 1986-88; cardiovascular rsch. coord. Beecham Labs., 1988-93; clin. rsch. mgr. microbiology-virology Abbott Labs., 1989-93, medical liason infectious diseases Abbott Labs, 1993—; staff nurse Lake Forest Hosp., Chgo., 1992-93; staff nurse cardiology Princeton Med. Ctr., 1993—; numerous presentations in field; coord. First Nursing Presentation of the Yugoslav-U.S. Med. Assn., 1982; acting chmn. Third European Symposium on Cardiac Pacing, Torremolinos, Malaga, Spain, 1985. Author: (with P. Wilson) Understanding your Heart: Facts, Testing, Treatment, 1985; also articles; reviewer jours. Vol. instr. for prison inmate reform Thresholds, 1977; mem. St. Francis Players. Recipient Mayor's Svc. award, Phila., 1980, Humanitarian award Optimists Internat., 1980, Citizen of Yr. award Am. Legion, 1980. Mem. ACA. Avocations: skiing; target shooting; dancing. Home: 515 Brickhouse Rd Princeton NJ 08540 Office: Abbott Labs 1 Abbott Park Rd North Chicago IL 60064-3500

SENSABAUGH, MARY ELIZABETH, financial consultant; b. Eastland, Tex., Aug. 15, 1939; d. Johnnie and L.G. (Tucker) Roberts; m. Dwight Lee Sensabaugh, Dec. 22, 1956; children: Robert Lee, Mark Jay. Student, Odessa Jr. Coll., 1959-63, U. North Tex., 1963-67. Sr. acct. Braniff Internat. Airlines, Dallas, 1967-68; acct. Computer Bus. Services, Dallas, 1968-72; sec.-treas. Robert D. Carpenter, Inc., Dallas, 1972-76; controller Broadway Warehouses, Dallas, 1976-78; asst. controller S.W. Offset, Dallas, 1978-79; sec.-treas., cons. Carpenter, Carruth & Hover, Inc., Dallas, 1979-92; sec.-treas. Roberts, Taylor and Sensabaugh, Inc., Hurst, Tex., 1992—. Mem. Nat. Assn. Women in Constrn. (bd. dirs. Dallas chpt. 1983-84), Internat. Platform Assn., Beta Sigma (pres. Irving, Tex. chpt. 1973-74), NAFE. Home: 702 Hughes Dr Irving TX 75062-5601 Office: 204 W Bedford Euless Rd Ste E Hurst TX 76053-4042

SENSENICH, ILA JEANNE, lawyer, magistrate judge; b. Pitts., Mar. 6, 1939; d. Louis E. and Evelyn Margaret (Harbourt) S. BA, Westminster Coll., 1961; JD, Dickinson Sch. Law, 1964, JD (hon.), 1994. Bar: Pa. 1964. Assoc. Stewart, Belden, Sensenich and Herrington, Greensburg, Pa., 1964-70; asst. pub. defender Westmoreland (Pa.) County, 1970-71; U.S. magistrate judge for We. Dist. Pa., Pitts., 1971—; adj. prof. law Duquesne U., 1982-87. Trustee emeritus Dickinson Sch. Law. Mem. ABA, Fed. Magistrate Judges Assn. (sec. 1979-81, sec. 1988-89, treas. 1989-90, 2d v.p. 1990-91, pres.-elect 1992-93, pres. 1993-94), Pa. Bar Assn., Allegheny County Bar Assn. (fed. ct. sect.), Nat. Assn. Women Judges, Westmoreland County Bar Assn., Allegheny Bar Assn. (civil litigation sect., com. women in law), Am. Judicature Soc., 3d Cir. Jud. Coun. Democrat. Presbyterian. Avocations: skiing, sailing, bicycling, classical music, cooking. Author: Compendium of the Law of Prisoner's Rights, 1979; contbr. articles to profl. jours. Office: 518B Us PO And Courthouse Pittsburgh PA 15219

SENTENNE, JUSTINE, corporate ombudsman; b. Montreal, Que., Can.; d. Paul Emile and Irene Genevieve (Laliberte) S. MBA, U. Que., Montreal, 1993, postgrad. McGill U., Ecole Nat. d'Adminstrn. Publique, 1989-91. Fin. analyst, assoc. mgr. portfolio Bush Assocs., Montreal, 1970-82; city councillor, mem. exec. com. City of Montreal and Montreal Urban Com., 1978-82; adminstrv. asst. Montreal Conv. Ctr., 1983; dir. sponsorship Cen. Com. for Montreal Papal Visit, 1984; dir. pub. rels. Coopers & Lybrand, Montreal, 1985-87; exec. dir. Que. Heart Found., 1987-89; corp. ombudsman Hydro-Que., Montreal, 1991—; tchr. DSA program Concordia U.; v.p., bd. dirs. Armand Frappier Found., Can., Chateau Dufresne Mus. Decorative Arts, Montreal, 1985-90; chmn. bd. Wilfrid Pelletier Found., Montreal, 1986-91; bd. dirs. St. Joseph's Oratory, 1979-92, Caisse Populaire Desjardins Notre Dame de Grace, Montreal, 1980—; mem. jury John Labatt Ltd., London, Ont., 1982-86. Notre Dame de Grace v.p. riding assoc. Liberal Party of Can., chairperson Women's Commn.; mem. bd. govs. Youth and Music Can., Montreal, 1981-86; chmn. bd. The Women's Ctr., Montreal, 1986-88, Vol. Bur. Montreal, 1986-87; bd. dirs. Palais des Congres de Montreal, 1981-89, Port of Montreal, 1983-84, Can. Ctr. for Ecumenism, Montreal, 1968-85, Villa Notre-Dame de Grace, Montreal, 1979-87, Montreal Diet Dispensary, 1989—, Pathways to Faith, 1990—; bd. mgmt. Saidye Bronfman Ctr. for Arts, 1994—. Named Career Woman of Yr., Sullivan Bus. Coll., 1979; recipient Silver medal Ville de Paris, 1981, Women's Kansas City Assn. for Internat. Rels. and Trade medal, 1982. Fellow Fin. Analysts Fedn. N.Y., Inst. Fin. Analysts, Montreal Soc. Investment Analysts; mem. Cercle Fin. et Placement, Corporation Professionelle des adminstrs. agrées, Assn. Profl. Adminstrs., The Ombudsman Assn. Roman Catholic.

SENTER, MERILYN P(ATRICIA), state legislator, retired freelance reporter; b. Haverhill, Mass., Mar. 17, 1935; d. Paul Barton and Mary Etta (Herrin) Staples; m. Donald Neil Senter, Apr. 23, 1960; children: Karen Anne Hussey, Brian Neil. Grad., McIntosh Bus. Coll., 1955. Sec. F.S. Hamlin Ins. Agy., Haverhill, Mass., 1955-60; free lance reporter Plaistow-Hampstead News, Rockingham county newspapers, Exeter and Stratham, N.H., 1970-89; state legislator N.H. Gen. Ct., Rockingham Dist. 9, 1989-90. Sec. Hwy. Safety Com., Plaistow, N.H., 1976—; state rep. N.H. Gen. Ct., Rockingham Dist. 16, 1993—, Rep. com. leader, state rep. Dist. 9, 1991-92, floor leader; sec., bd. dirs. Region 10 Commn. Support Svcs. Inc., Atkinson, N.H., 1982-88; chmn. Plaistow Area Transit Adv. Com., 1990-93; active Devel. Disabilities Coun., 1993—. Named Woman of Yr., N.H. Bus. and Profl. Women, 1983, Nat. Grange Citizen of Yr., 1992. Republican. Home and Office: 11 Maple Ave Plaistow NH 03865-2221

SENTURIA, YVONNE DREYFUS, pediatrician, epidemiologist; b. Houston, Jan. 16, 1951. BA in Biology and Sociology, Rice U., 1973; MD, U. Tex., San Antonio, 1977; MSc in Epidemiology, London Sch. Hygiene and Tropical Medicine, 1985. Diplomate Am. Bd. Pedias. Pediat. resident Shands Tchg. Hosp., Gainesville, Fla., 1977-79, Tex. Children's Hosp., Houston, 1979-80; instr., asst. prof. Coll. Medicine, Baylor U., Houston, 1980-82; sr. clin. med. officer Hammersmith and Fulham Health Authority, London, 1982-83; cons. pediatrician Kingston (Eng.) Hosp., 1983, Northwick Park Hosp., London, 1983; rsch. pediatrician Charing Cross Hosp. Med. Sch., London, 1984-85; clin. lectr. Inst. Child Health, London, 1985-88; attending pediatrician and epidemiologist Children's Meml. Hosp., Chgo., 1989—. Fellow Am. Acad. Pediats.; mem. Ambulatory Pediat. Assn., Midwest Soc. Pediat. Rsch. Office: Children's Meml Hosp PO Box 103 2300 Childrens Plz Chicago IL 60614

SEPAHPUR, HAYEDEH C(HRISTINE), investment executive; b. Lincoln, Nebr., Dec. 8, 1958; d. Bahman and Marylin Lou (Duffy) S.; m. Bahman Robert Kosrovani, May 2, 1992. BS, Lehigh U., 1983. V.p. Drexel Burnham Lambert Inc., N.Y.C., 1982-90, Donaldson, Lufkin & Jenrette, New York City, 1990-92, Lehman Bros., Inc., N.Y.C., 1992—. Sponsor Jr. Statesmen of Am. Found., Washington, 1976—; charter mem. Nat. Mus. Women in the Arts, Washington, 1985—; bd. dirs. Coll. Express Project, Bronx, N.Y., 1987—; mem. Inst. Asian Studies, St. Thomas Episc. Ch. Mem. Nat. Trust Hist. Preservation, The Asia Soc., Women's Campaign Fund, N.Y. Hist. Soc., Mcpl. Art Soc., French Inst., English Speaking Union, WISH List, U.S. Fencing Assn., Fin. Women's Assn. (N.Y. chpt.), Persian Heritage Found., Mensa, Gamma Phi Beta. Club: Downtown Athletic (N.Y.C.). Home: 220 E 67th St Apt 12-D New York NY 10021-6263 Office: Lehman Bros Inc 3 World Fin Ctr 200 Vesey St 6th fl New York NY 10285-0600

SEPARK, ELAINE FRICKS, office manager; b. Chamblee, Ga., Dec. 19, 1949; d. William Dean Jr. and Betty Ann (Creel) Fricks; m. Willis Allen Separk, Jan. 24, 1970 (div. 1985); 1 child, Gregory Allen. Student, U. Tenn., 1967-70; BA, Ga. State U., 1971. Social studies tchr. Cherokee H.S., Canton, Ga., 1971-72; office mgr. Gaston de Lemos, MD, Marietta, Ga., 1973-74, Arthur Melich, MD, and Sig Rosenbloom, MD, Austell, Ga., 1976-77, Mt. Bethel United Meth. Ch., Marietta, 1983-94, Profl. Practice Cons., Ltd., Roswell, Ga., 1994—; bookkeeper W. Allen Separk, Atty., Smyrna, Ga., 1977-79; alphatype operator AdverGraphics, Inc., Smyrna, 1979-83. mem. fin. com., treas. Wesley Chapel United Meth. Ch., 1975-80; co-sec. Kennestone Hosp. Guild, Marietta, 1978, co-2nd v.p., 1979, co-1st v.p., 1980, co-pres., 1981-83; with Nat. Inst. in Ch. and Fin. Adminstrn., 1992; mem. adminstrv. bd., mem. coun. mins. Mt. Bethel United Meth. Ch., 1992—; life mem. Kennestone Hosp. Vols., 1978—, Kennestone Guild Found., 1978—. Mem. Am. Bus. Womens Assn. (program chmn.). Democrat. Home: 2733 Old Mill Trl Marietta GA 30062 Office: Profl Practice Cons Ltd 11285 Elkins Rd F4 Roswell GA 30076

SEPKO, KAREN LUCIA, chemical engineer, consultant; b. Moses Lake, Wash., Apr. 9, 1962. BS in Chem. Engring., U. Ariz., 1987. Project engr. Manville Sales Corp., Corona, Calif., 1987-90; plant engr. NCR Corp., Brea, Calif., 1990-91; compliance/permit specialist Envirosafe Svcs. Ohio, Oregon, Ohio, 1993-94; process engr. Martin Marietta Magnesia Specialties, Woodville, Ohio, 1994—; environ. cons., Fontana, Calif., 1991. Author: (book) Paint Tng. Manual, 1985. Home: 6801 Cloister Ct Toledo OH 43617 Office: 755 Lime Rd Woodville OH 43469

SEPPALA, KATHERINE SEAMAN (MRS. LESLIE W. SEPPALA), retail executive, clubwoman; b. Detroit, Aug. 22, 1919; d. Willard D. and Elizabeth (Miller) Seaman; B.A., Wayne State U., 1941; m. Leslie W. Seppala, Aug. 15, 1941; children: Sandra Kay, William Leslie. Mgr. women's bldg. and student activities adviser Wayne State U., 1941-43; pres. Harper Sports Shops, Inc., 1947-85, chmn. bd., treas., sec., v.p. 1985—; ptnr. Seppala Bldg. Co., 1971—. Mich. service chmn. women grads. Wayne State U., 1962—, 1st v.p., fund bd., Girl and Cub Scouts; mem. Citizen's adv. com. on sch. needs Detroit Bd. Edn., 1957—, mem. high sch. study com., 1966—; chmn., mem. loan fund bd. Denby High Sch. Parents Scholarship; bd. dirs., v.p. Wayne State U. Fund; precinct del. Rep. Party, 14th dist., 1956—, del. convs.; mem. com. Myasthenia Gravis Support Assn. Recipient Ann. Women's Service award Wayne State U., 1963. Recipient Disting. Alumni award Wayne State U., 1971. Mem. Intercollegiate Assn. Women Students (regional rep. 1941-45), Women Wayne State U. Alumni (past pres.), Wayne State U. Alumni Assn. (dir., past v.p.), AAUW (dir. past officer), Council Women as Public Policy Makers (editor High lights) Denby Community Ednl. Orgn. (sec.), Met. Detroit Program Planning Inst. (pres.), Internat. Platform Assn., Detroit Met. Book and Author Soc. (treas.), Mortar Bd. (past pres.), Karyatides (past pres.), Anthony Wayne Soc., Alpha Chi Alpha, Alpha Kappa Delta, Delta Gamma Chi, Kappa Delta (chmn. chpt. alumnae adv. bd.). Baptist. Clubs: Zonta (v.p., dir.); Les Cheneaux. Home: 22771 Worthington Ct Saint Clair Shores MI 48081-2603 Office: Harper Sport Shop Inc 23208 Greater Mack Saint Clair Shores MI 48080-1914

SEPRODI, JUDITH CATHERINE, accounting administrator; b. Terre Haute, Ind., June 16, 1955; d. Ferris Lee and Mary Ann (Tully) Roberson; m. Donald Matthew Seprodi, Aug. 1, 1972 (div. Oct. 1994); children: Antoinette, Autumn, Jacob, Brooklyn. AA, Ivy Tech., 1990; grad., Dale Carnegie Course. Lic. property/casualty ins. agt.; notary public. Sec. Equifax, Oklahoma City, 1975-76; ins. clk. Northside Family Medicine, Del City, Okla., 1976; office mgr. Dick Clark Ins., Terre Haute, 1981, Simrell's, Terre Haute, 1981-85; ADC acctg. clk./typist V Vigo County Welfare, Terre Haute, 1985-86, head ADC acctg. clk./typist IV, 1986-87; purchasing agt. Bruce Fox, Inc., New Albany, Ind., 1987-88; acctg. mgr. Terre Haute Coke and Carbon, 1988—, acting sec. bd. dirs., 1989; ptnr., owner Thistlehare; bookkeeper Seprodi Constrn., Terre Haute, 1989—; grad. asst. Dale Carnegie

Inst. Author employee manuals. Coach, Terre Haute Youth Soccer Assn., 1979-82, bd. dirs., 1979-82; player North Tex. Women's Soccer Assn., Plano, 1977-78. Mem. NAFE, AIPB, Am. Notary Assn., Profl. Bookkeepers Assn., Vigo County Taxpayers Assn. Democrat. Roman Catholic. Home: PO Box 3527 Terre Haute IN 47803-0527

SERAFINE, MARY LOUISE, psychologist, educator, lawyer; b. Rochester, N.Y., July 2, 1948. B.A. with honors in music, Rutgers U., 1970; Ph.D., U. Fla., 1975; JD, Yale U., 1991. Bar: Calif., D.C.; U.S. Tax Ct. Teaching and research fellow U. Fla., Gainesville, 1970-76; vis. asst. prof. U. Tex.-San Antonio, 1976-77; asst. prof. U. Tex.-Austin, 1977-79; postdoctoral fellow dept psychology Yale U., New Haven, 1979-83, lectr., 1981-83; asst. prof. dept. psychology Vassar Coll. Poughkeepsie, N.Y., 1983-88; with O'Melveny & Myers, L.A., 1988—. Author: Music as Cognition: The Development of Thought in Sound, 1988. Contbr. articles to profl. jours. Editorial reviewer Child Devel., Devel. Psychology, Am. Scientist, Jour. Experimental Child Psychology, Jour. Applied Developmental Psychology, Yale Law Jour. Grantee State of Fla., 1974-75, U. Tex.-Austin, 1977, Spencer Found., 1979-85. Office: O'Melveny & Myers 1999 Avenue Of The Stars Los Angeles CA 90067-6022

SERBUS, PEARL SARAH DIECK, former free-lance writer, former editor; b. Riverdale, Ill.; d. Emil Edwin and Pearl (Kaiser) Dieck; m. Gerald Serbus, Jan. 26, 1946 (dec. Aug. 1969); children—Allan Lester, Bruce Alan, Curt Lyle. Mem. home econs. staff, writer Chgo. Herald Examiner, 1934-39; operator test kitchen Household Sci. Inst., Mdse. Mart, Chgo., 1940-45; free-lance writer grocery chains, Chgo., 1945-49; Riv.-Dolton corr. Calumet Index, Chgo., 1953-58, editorial asst., 1958-60, asst. editor, 1960-68, editor, 1968-72; with Suburban Index, Chgo., 1959-72, editor, 1960-72; mng. editor Index Publs., 1972-74; free lance writer, 1974-94, ret., 1994. Public relations vol. New Hope Sch., 1959-67; bd. dirs. United Fund of Riverdale, Roseland Mental Health Assn., Thornton chpt. Am. Field Service. Recipient Disting. Service Meml. scroll PTA, 1959, Sch. Bell award Ill. Edn. Assn., 1965, Outstanding Citizen award Chgo. South C. of C., 1972. Named Outstanding Civic Leader Am.; recipient Vol. citation Ctrl. Ark. Radiation Therapy Inst., 1994. Mem. Ill. Woman's Press Assn. (past pres. Woman of Distinction 1968, recipient 46 state awards, 3 nat. awards), Ark. Press Women (Communicator of Achievement award 1991, honored 50 Yr. member 1994), Nat. Fedn. Press Women (past pres. parley past presidents 1981, past dir. protocol, Honors 50 Yrs. Membership 1994), Riverdale (v.p. 1966-68), Chgo. South (v.p., dir.) chambers commerce. Home: 1421 N University Ave Apt 215N Little Rock AR 72207-5253

SERIO VARGUS, SUSAN, television anchor, reporter; b. Balt., Aug. 16, 1958; d. Joseph Anthony and Nancy Ann (O'Donnell) S.; m. William D. Vargus, Dec. 31, 1994. BA, Towson State U., 1980. Mid-day radio host Sta. WBAL-AM, Balt., 1981-82; morning disc jockey Sta. WNAV-AM, Annapolis, Md., 1982-84; morning show co-host Sta WQSR-FM, Balt., 1984-86, Sta. WSTW-FM, Wilmington, Del., 1986-89, Sta. WKSZ-FM, Phila., 1992-93; nightly music show host Sta WMGK-FM, Phila., 1989-92; weather anchor, feature reporter Sta. WHYY-TV, Phila., 1988-94; morning show anchor, weather forcaster, feature reporter Sta. WIVB-TV, Buffalo, 1994—. Fund raiser Leukemia Soc., Phila., 1989-94; walk chair Juvenile Diabetes Found., Wilmington, Del., 1992, AIDS Walk, Wilmington, 1993. Recipient Mid-Atlantic Emmy award NATAS, 1994. Mem. AFTRA, NATAS. Office: Sta WIVB-TV 2077 Elmwood Ave Buffalo NY 14207

SERONDE, ADELE HERTER, artist; b. Manchester, Mass., June 17, 1925; d. Christian A. and Mary Caroline (Pratt) Herter; m. Joseph Seronde, Aug. 26, 1945; children: Antoine, Jacques, Pierre, Dorée, Jeanne. Student, Bennington Coll., 1943-45. One-woman show DeCordova Mus., Lincoln, Mass., 1956, Nova Gallery, Boston, 1958, Galleria Vigna Nuova and Galleria Santa Croce, Florence, Italy, 1964, 66, Herbert Benevy Gallery, N.Y.C., 1976; 2-person show Art Directions Gallery, N.Y.C., 1966, S.W. Symphony Gallery, Sedona, 1985; exhibited in group shows Sedona (Ariz.) Arts Ctr., 1988, 92; one-woman show and group shows Wingspread Gallery, Gallery 68, Belfast, Maine, 1969, 73, 76, 80, 83, 88, 90, 93; also others; represented in permanent collections Phillips Mus., Washington, also numerous pub. and pvt. instns. Co-coord. visual arts Summerthing, neighborhood arts program, Boston, 1968-71; pres. Christian Herter Ctr.; mem. Sedona Cultural Arts Commn., 1989-90; sec., v.p., bd. dirs. Internat. Friends of Transformative Art, Phoenix, 1989-95; organizer show Sedona Art Mus., 1993. Home and Studio: 345 Longwood Dr Sedona AZ 86351-7208

SEROTA, SUSAN PERLSTADT, lawyer; b. Chgo., Sept. 10, 1945; d. Sidney Morris and Mildred (Penn) Perlstadt; m. James Ian Serota, May 7, 1972; children: Daniel Louis, Jonathan Mark. AB, U. Mich., 1967; JD, NYU, 1971. Bar: Ill. 1971, D.C. 1972, N.Y. 1981, U.S. Dist. Ct. (no. dist.) Ill. 1971, U.S. Dist. Ct. (so. dist.) N.Y. 1981, U.S. Dist. Ct. (ea. dist.) N.Y. 1985, U.S. Ct. Claims 1972, U.S. Tax Ct. 1972, U.S. Ct. Appeals (D.C. cir.) 1972. Assoc. Gottlieb & Schwartz, Chgo., 1971-72, Silverstein & Mullens, Washington, 1972-75, Cahill Gordon & Reindel, N.Y.C., 1975-82; assoc. Winthrop, Stimson, Putnam & Roberts, N.Y.C., 1982, ptnr., 1983—; adj. prof. Sch. Law, Georgetown U., Washington, 1974-75; mem. faculty Practicing Law Inst., N.Y.C., 1983—. Assoc. editor Exec. Compensation Jour., 1973-75; dep. editor Tax Mgmt., Estate and Gift Taxation and Exec. Compensation, 1972-75; mem. editorial adv. bd. Benefits Law Jour., 1988—, Tax Mgmt. Compensation Jour., 1993—; mem. bd. editors ERISA and Benefits Law Jour., 1992—; contbr. articles to profl. jours. Mem. ABA (chmn. joint com. employee benefits 1988-89, chair com. employee benefits taxation sect. 1991-92, coun. mem. taxation sect. 1994—), Internat. Pension and Employee Benefits Lawyers Assn. (co-chair 1993—), N.Y. State Bar Assn. (exec. com. tax sect. 1988-92), Am. Bar Retirement Funds (dir. 1994—). Democrat. Office: Winthrop Stimson Putnam & Roberts One Battery Park Pla New York NY 10004-1490

SERPE-SCHROEDER, PATRICIA L., elementary education educator; b. La Porte, Ind., Feb. 1, 1949; d. Fred J. and Priscilla (Nowak) Serpe; children: Matthew Aaron, Scott Allan. BA, Purdue U., 1971, MS in Edn., 1976. Cert. tchr., administr., Ind. Tchr., grades 1-2 Westville (Ind.) Sch.; tchr., grade 2 Lincoln Sch., Highland, Ind.; tchr. grades 1, 2, 4 Iddings Sch., Merrillville, Ind., 1985-92; prin. Hudson Lake Elem. Sch., New Carlisle, Ind., 1992-94; chpt. I coord. New Prairie Sch. Corp., New Carlisle, 1994—; mem. drug-free, sci. textbook, elem. computer coms. New Prairie United Sch. Corp.; presenter in field. Recipient Ind. State grant. Mem. NEA, ASCD, Ind. Tchrs. Assn., Merrillville Tchrs. Assn. (sec., membership chmn., mem. computer and tech. coms. for sch. corp., bldg. adv. com.), Nat. Assn. Sch. Prins., Ind. Assn. Sch. Prins., Ind. Prins. Leadership Acad., Kappa Delta Pi, Delta Kappa Gamma, Pi Delta Phi. Home: PO Box 1076 New Carlisle IN 46552 Office: New Prairie United Sch Corp 5329 N Cougar Rd New Carlisle IN 46552

SERRETTE, CATHY HOLLENBERG, lawyer; b. Scranton, Pa., Apr. 28, 1954; d. Herbert Saul and Lee (Weisberger) Hollenberg; m. Dennis Louis Serrette, July 27, 1985; children: Kyle Malcolm, Desmond Harold, Malcolm Mandela. BS summa cum laude, U. Pitts., 1975; JD, George Washington U., 1980; LLM in Internat. Legal Studies, Am. U., 1991. Bar: N.Y. 1980, D.C. 1986, Md. 1986, U.S. Dist. Ct. D.C. 1987. Assoc. Advs. for Children, N.Y.C., 1980-81; ptnr. Kresky, Sinawski & Hollenberg, N.Y.C., 1981-84; legis. dir. Congressman Savage, Washington, 1985-86; pvt. practice Oxon Hill, Md., 1987—. Writer ABA Commn. on the Disabled, 1978-79. Co-chairperson edn. com. NAACP, Prince Georges County, Md., 1987-88; chairperson parent's adv. com. Apple Grove Elem. Sch., 1987-88; co-coord. 26th legis. dist. Prince Georges County Rainbow Coalition, 1988; bd. dirs. Prince Georges County chpt. ACLU, 1994—. Mem. Nat. Lawyers Guild (D.C. chpt. chair So. Africa com. exec. bd., pres. South African Women's Day com. 1988—), D.C. Bar Assn., Md. Bar Assn., Prince Georges County Bar Assn., Md. Women's Bar Assn., Phi Beta Kappa. Jewish. Home: 1809 Clayton Dr Oxon Hill MD 20745-3724 Office: Hollenberg Serrette & McDermott 6192 Oxon Hill Rd Ste 511 Oxon Hill MD 20745-3114

SERSHEN, CHERYL LYNN, financial analyst; b. Scranton, Pa., Nov. 7, 1963; d. Francis Christopher Sershen and Carol Frounfelker/Caughill. BA in Econs. cum laude, U. Pa., 1994; postgrad., Columbia U., 1993—; student, Julliard Sch. Music. Fin. mgr. Time Inc., N.Y.C., 1986-88, bus. analyst, 1990-91, asst. bus. mgr., 1991-93; statis. analyst AIG, N.Y.C., 1988-90; risk analyst Time Warner Inc., N.Y.C., 1993-95; bus. mgr. Columbia U. Health Svcs., N.Y.C., 1995—. Treas., founder Manhattan Internat. Cultural Studies, N.Y.C., 1988-92; campaign organizer Fletcher for City Coun., N.Y.C., 1989; tutor Time Warner Inc., 1990, Consortium For Worker Edn., N.Y.C., 1994-95; family rep. Beth Israel Med. Ctr., N.Y.C., 1994—. Mem. Andover Abbott Assn. Democrat. Home: 720 Ft Washington Ave # 2N New York NY 10040 Office: Columbia U John Jay Hall New York NY 10027

SERSTOCK, DORIS SHAY, retired microbiologist, educator, civic worker; b. Mitchell, S.D., June 13, 1926; d. Elmer Howard and Hattie (Christopher) Shay; B.A., Augustana Coll., 1947; postgrad. U. Minn., 1966-67, Duke U., summer 1969, Communicable Disease Center, Atlanta, 1972; m. Ellsworth I. Serstock, Aug. 30, 1952; children—Barbara Anne, Robert Ellsworth, Mark Douglas. Bacteriologist, Civil Service, S.D., Colo., Mo., 1947-52; research bacteriologist U. Minn., 1952-53; clin. bacteriologist Dr. Lufkin's Lab., 1954-55; chief technologist St. Paul Blood Bank of ARC, 1959-65; microbiologist in charge mycology lab. VA Hosp., Mpls., 1968-93; instr. Coll. Med. Scis., U. Minn., 1970-79, asst. prof. Coll. Lab. Medicine and Pathology, 1979-93. Mem. Richfield Planning Commn., 1965-71, sec., 1968-71. Contbr. articles to profl. jours. Extended ministries commn. Wood Lake Luth. Ch., Richfield, Minn., 1993-94; rep. religious coun. Mall Am., Bloomington, Minn., 1993-94. Fellow Augusta Coll.; named to Exec. and Profl. Hall of Fame; recipient Alumni Achievement award Augustana Coll., 1977; Superior Performance award VA Hosp., 1978, 82, Cert. of Recognition, 1988; Golden Spore awards Mycology Observer, 1985, 87. Mem. Minn. Planning Assn. Republican. Clubs: Richfield Women's Garden (pres. 1959), Wild Flower Garden (chmn. 1961). Home: 7201 Portland Ave Minneapolis MN 55423-3218

SERYLO, JANET MARIE, critical care nurse; b. Bayonne, N.J., Nov. 25, 1954; d. Bernard Michael and Eleanor Emily (Molcan) Baron; m. Joseph Peter Serylo, Apr. 6, 1986. AAS, Pace U., 1974; BSN, Felician Coll., Lodi, N.J., 1980. BLS, CCRN. Staff nurse med.-surg. Jersey City (N.J.) Med. Ctr., 1974-76, charge nurse, 1976-80, staff nurse SICU, 1980-85, head nurse, 1985-87, head nurse mgr. MICU, 1987—. Mem. AACN, No. N.J. Chpt. AACN. Roman Catholic. Office: Jersey City Med Ctr 50 Baldwin Ave Jersey City NJ 07304-3154

SESSA, JANE THOMAS, library director; b. Miami, Fla., Nov. 9, 1951; d. Frank Bowman and Anne Marshall (Johnston) S.; m. Steven Allen Hawkins, June 1, 1974; 1 child, Margaret Anne Sessa Hawkins. AB in Anthropology, U. Miami, 1973; MLS, Cath. U., 1976; MBA, Am. U., 1986. Libr. dir. Congressional Budget Office, Washington, 1978-92, Securities & Exch. Com., Washington, 1992—; chair Microcomp Users Int. Group, Chgo., 1991-92; dir. Fed. Librs. Round Table, Washington, 1993—. Mem. ALA, Fed. Libr. and Info. Ctr. Com., Libr. and Info. Tech. Assn. (membership com. 1992—). Office: Securities & Exch Commn 450 5th St NW Washington DC 20549

SESSIONS, JUDITH ANN, librarian, university library dean; b. Lubbock, Tex., Dec. 16, 1947; d. Earl Alva and Anna (Mayer) S. BA cum laude, Cen. Fla. U., 1970; MLS, Fla. State U., 1971; postgrad., Am. U., 1980, George Washington U., 1983. Head libr. U. S.C., Salkehatchie, 1974-77; dir. Libr. and Learing Resources Ctr. Mt. Vernon Coll., Washington, 1977-82; planning and systems libr. George Washington U., Washington, 1981-82, asst. univ. libr. for adminstrn. svcs., acting head tech. svcs., 1982-84; univ. libr. Calif. State U., Chico, 1984-88; univ. libr., dean of libr. Miami U., Oxford, Ohio, 1988—; cons. Space Planning, S.C., 1976, DataPhase Implementation, Bowling Green U., 1982, TV News Study Ctr., George Washington U., 1981; asst. prof. Dept. Child Devel., Mt. Vernon Coll., 1978-81; mem., lectr. U.S.-China Libr. Exch. Del., 1986, 91; lectr., presenter in field. Contbr. articles, book revs. to profl. jours. Trustee Christ Hosp., Cin., 1990-94, Hamilton YMCA, Deaconess Gamble Rsch. Ctr., Cin., 1990-94. Recipient award for outstanding contbn. D.C. Libr. Assn., 1979; rsch. grantee Mt. Vernon Coll., 1980; recipient Fulbright-Hayes Summer Travel fellowship to Czechoslovakia, 1991. Mem. ALA (Olofson award 1978, councillor-at-large policy making group 1981-94, coun. com. on coms. 1983-84, intellectual freedom com. 1984-88, directions and program rev. com. 1989-91, fin. and audit subcom. 1989-90, mem. exec. bd. 1989-94), Assn. Coll. and Rsch. Librs. (editorial bd. Coll. and Rsch. Librs. jour. 1979-84, nominatins and appointments com. 1983-85, faculty status com. 1984-86), Libr. and Info. Tech. Assn. (chair legis. and regulation com. 1980-81), Libr. Adminstrn. and Mgmt. Assn. (bd. dirs. libr. orgn. and mgmt. sect. 1985-87), Calif. Inst. Librs. (v.p., pres. elect 1987-88), Mid-Atlantic Regional Libr. Fedn. (mem. exec. bd. 1982-84), Jr. Mems. Round Table (pres. 1981-82), Intellectual Freedom Round Table (sec. 1984-85), Freedom to Read Found. (trustee 1984-88, v.p. 1985-86, treas. 1986-87, pres. 1987-88), Rotary, Beta Phi Mu. Home: 45 Waters Way Hamilton OH 45013-6324 Office: Miami U Edgar W King Oxford OH 45056

SESSOMS, TONI LYNN, lawyer; b. Chapel Hill, N.C., Mar. 1, 1957; d. Richard Darrow and Nancy Jean (Howe) S. BSN, U. N.C., Greensboro, 1979; MDiv, Nyack Coll., 1986; JD, Wake Forest U., 1993. Bar: Mich. 1993; RN, Mich. Staff nurse VA Hosp., Durham, N.C., 1979-80; staff nurse pediatrics, PICU Wake County Med. Ctr., Raleigh, N.C., 1981-83; staff nurse neurol. ICU Wake County Med. Ctr., Raleigh, 1986-93; staff nurse pediatrics Nyack (N.Y.) Hosp., 1983-86; assoc. Wisti & Jaaskelainen, Houghton, Mich., 1993—. Mem. ABA, Copper Country Bar Assn., Nat. Assn. Women Lawyers (Outstanding Woman Law Grad. 1993). Office: Wisti & Jaaskelainen 101 Quincy St Hancock MI 49930

SETSER, CAROLE SUE, food science educator; b. Warrenton, Mo., Aug. 26, 1940; d. Wesley August and Mary Elizabeth (Meine) Schulze; m. Donald Wayne Setser, June 2, 1969; children: Bradley Wayne, Kirk Wesley, Brett Donald. BS, U. Mo., 1962; MS, Cornell U., 1964; PhD, Kans. State U., 1971. Grad. asst. Cornell U., Ithaca, N.Y., 1962-64; instr. Kans. State U., Manhattan, 1964-72, asst. prof., 1974-81, assoc. prof., 1981-86, prof., 1986—. Recipient Rsch. Excellence award Coll. of Human Ecology, Manhattan, 1990. Mem. Am. Assn.Cereal Chemists (assoc. editor 1989-93), Inst. Food Techs. (chmn. sensory evaluation divsn. edn. com. 1989-92, continuing edn. com. 1992—, other offices), Kappa Omicron Nu (Excellence for Rsch. award 1987), Sigma Xi, Phi Upsilon Omicron, Gamma Sigma Delta, Phi Tau Sigma. Office: Kansas State U Justin Hall Dept Foods Nutrition Manhattan KS 66506

SETTERGREN, TAMARA KAY, technical writer, electronics educator; b. Yakima, Wash., June 24, 1962; d. Bliss Nathanial Eugene and Joyce Marie (Austin) S. ATA in Electronics, Edmonds C.C., Lynnwood, Wash., 1982; BS in Tech. Comm., U. Wash., 1994. Computer svc. technician Computerland, Lynnwood, 1982-94; instr. electronics Edmonds C.C., 1984-94; engring. writer John Fluke Mfg. Co., Inc., Everett, Wash., 1994—. Recipient Cert. of Achievement in tech. comm. Soc. for Women in Engring., 1994. Home: 906 11th St Mukilteo WA 98275-2209

SETTLE, MARY LEE, author; b. Charleston, W.Va., July 29, 1918; d. Joseph Edward and Rachel (Tompkins) S.; m. Rodney Weathersbee, 1939 (div. 1946); 1 child, Christopher Weathersbee; m. Douglas Newton, 1946 (div. 1956); m. William Littleton Tazewell, Sept. 2, 1978. Student, Sweet Briar Coll., 1936-38. Editor Harper's Bazaar, 1945; Eng. corres. Flair, 1950-51; assoc. prof. Bard Coll., Annandale-on-Hudson, N.Y., 1956-76; vis. lectr. U. Va., 1978, U. Iowa. Author: The Love Eaters, 1954, The Kiss of Kin, 1955, O Beulah Land, 1956, Know Nothing, 1960, Fight Night on a Sweet Saturday, 1964, (play) Juana La Loca, 1965, All the Brave Promises, 1966, The Story of Flight, 1967, The Clam Shell, 1971, The Scopes Trial: The State of Tennessee vs. John Thomas Scopes, 1972, Prisons, 1973, Blood Tie, 1977 (Nat. Book award 1978), The Scapegoat, 1981, The Killing Ground, 1982 (Janet Heidinger Kafka Prize in fiction 1983), Water World, 1984, Celebration, 1986, Maugham, 1987, The Search for Beulah Land, 1988, Charley Bland, 1989, Turkish Reflections, 1991, Choices, 1995; (with Raymond W. Settle) War Drums and Wagon Wheels: The Story of Russell, Majors, and Waddell, 1966, Saddles and Spurs: The Pony Express Saga, 1972. Served with Womens Aux., RAF, 1942-43. Recipient Merrill Found. award, 1975; John Simon Guggenheim fellow, 1958, 60. Democrat. Office: care Farrar Straus & Giroux 19 Union Sq W New York NY 10003-3304*

SEVALSTAD, SUZANNE ADA, accounting educator; b. Butte, Mont., Mar. 26, 1948; d. John Cornelius and Ivy Jeanette (Cloke) Pilling; m. Nels Sevalstad, Jr., Mar. 11, 1975. BS in Bus. with high distinction, Mont. State U., 1970, MS in Bus., 1972. CPA, Mont. Internal auditor Anaconda Co., Butte, 1970-71; mgr. Wise River (Mont.) Club, 1976-79; instr. acctg. Bozeman (Mont.) Vocat./Tech. Ctr., 1970-72, Ea. Mont. Coll., Billings, 1972-73, Mont. State U., Bozeman, 1973-76, U. Nev., Las Vegas, 1979—. Recipient Women of Month award Freshman Class Women, 1976, Disting. Tchr. Coll. Bus. U. Nev., 1983, 86, 89, 93, Prof. of Yr. award Student Acctg. Assn. U. Nev., 1984, 87, 88, 90, 91, Outstanding Acctg. Prof. award Acctg. Students of U. Nev., 1987, 88, 89, Spanos Disting. Teaching award, 1989. Mem. AICPA, Am. Acctg. Assn., Nat. Inst. Mgmt. Acctg. (campus coord. 1988—), Inst. Mgmt. Accts., Assn. for Female Execs., Golden Key Soc. (hon.). Office: U Nev Dept Acctg 4505 Maryland Pkwy Las Vegas NV 89154-6003

SEVERIN, CHARLOTTE WOOD, nurse, health consultant, artist; b. Evanston, Ill., Oct. 25, 1936; d. Emerson and Lydia (Weber) Wood; m. Gerald Lang Severin, June 14, 1958; children: John Gerald, Kimberly Sue, Juliana Leigh. BS with honors, Stanford U., 1959. RN, Calif.; lic. pub. health nurse; lifetime school health credential. Staff nurse Stanford U. Hosp., San Francisco, 1959; vis. pub. health nurse Mpls., 1959-60; clinic coordinating nurse Stanford U. Hosp. Neurology Clinic, Palo Alto, Calif., 1965-66; sch. health cons. Livermore (Calif.) Sch. Dist., 1967-69, Pleasanton (Calif.) Unified Sch. Dist., 1969-94; artist in residence, watercolor instr. Pleasanton and Livermore Sch. Dists., 1969—; art tchr. City of Pleasanton Pks. and Community Svcs., 1992—. One-woman shows include Concannon Vineyard; represented in pvt. and corp. collections in U.S., Japan, Guatemala, France, Germany, Mexico as well as fgn. Consulates and Embassies in San Francisco. Chairperson Bicentennial Festivals Com., Pleasanton, 1976; founder Pleasanton Cultural Arts Coun., pres., bd. dirs., 1973-94; vol. instr. Am. Cancer Soc., 1976—; chairperson renovation Amador Theater, 1981-89; founding chairperson board Pub. Access TV Channel, 1983—; founder Arts in the Schs. Program, Tri-Valley, Calif., 1984-94. Recipient Gen.'s commendation 3d inf. divsn. arty. 7th Army Germany, 1962, commendation City of Pleasanton, 1976, 89, Edn. award Bay Area Sch. Adminstrs. and Phi Delta Kappa, 1983, 86, award Am. Cancer Soc., 1983, 85; named Woman of Yr., City of Pleasanton, 1976, Woman of Distinction, Pleasanton Soroptimists, 1986. Mem. AAUW (pres. 1972-74, state officer 1973-74, Fellowship award 1974, 89), East Bay Watercolor Soc. (Signature award 1992), Pleasanton Art League (charter), Stanford U. Nurse Alumnae Assn. Presbyterian.

SEVERINO, ELIZABETH FORREST, consulting company executive; b. Bryn Mawr, Pa., Dec. 29, 1945; d. John Joseph and Elizabeth (Patton) Girard-diCarlo; m. Joseph Domenic Severino, Oct. 20, 1973 (div. Oct. 1983); 1 child, Nicole Marie. AB, Vassar Coll., 1967; MS in Computer Sci., Syracuse U., 1969. Systems programmer IBM Corp., Poughkeepsie, N.Y., 1967-71; competitive analyst IBM Corp., Phila., 1977-79; systems analyst Fidelity Bank, Phila., 1971-72; mng. editor Auerbach Pubs., Phila., 1972-77; v.p. editorial and technology McGraw-Hill Pubs., Delran, N.J., 1979-81; v.p. Symcro Systems, Pennsauken, N.J., 1981-82; pres. The PC Group, Inc., Cherry Hill, N.J., 1982—, also bd. dirs.; bd. dirs. CompCar Leasing, Cherry Hill, Life Mgmt. Systems, Inc., Cherry Hill, Soc. for Grateful Living, Cherry Hill. Author: Do-It-Yourself Vibrant Mind/Body/Spirit Health, 1995; contbr. over 125 articles to profl. jours.; choreographer Faust, Der Vampry, Sound of Music. Mem. Assn. of Personal Computers Cons. (bd. dirs. Phila. chpt., pres. 1987-90), NAFE, Phila. Area Computer Soc. Republican. Episcopalian. Office: The PC Group Inc 715 Kings Croft Cherry Hill NJ 08034-1108

SEVERINO, ELIZABETH MARY, health care company executive; b. Camden, N.J., July 27, 1944; d. Anthony J. and Violet J. (Baker) DiIelsi; m. Lucio R. Severino, Sept. 14, 1968 (div. 1975); 1 child, Antonio R. BS in Biology, U. Pa., 1967; MSW in Planning, Adminstrn., Rutgers U., 1978; postgrad., Temple U., 1968. Activity therapist Camden County Psychiat. Hosp., Camden, 1962-67; instr. biology Temple U., Phila., 1968-69; tchr. sci. Forrest Sherman John F. Kennedy High Sch., Naples, Italy, 1971-73; dir. therapy services Camden County Health Services Ctr., 1973-78; dir. profl. services AID Health Care Ctrs., Wayne, Pa., 1979-81, Western Div. Beverly Enterprises, Fresno, Calif., 1981-82; v.p. ops. Health Group Care Ctrs. Inc., Chadds Ford, Pa., 1982-85; v.p., gen. mgr. Eastern Div. Health Care Retirement Corp., Chadds Ford, 1985; pres. Concord Healthcare Corp., Wilmington, Del., 1985-91; sr. v.p. Genesis Health Ventures, Kennett Square, Pa., 1991—; mem. editorial bd. D.O.N. Mag.; bd. dirs. Concord Healthcare Corp., Camden County Health Services System. Vol. tutorial program for Hispanic and Black children. Mem. Nat. Assn. Social Workers (cert.), Gerontol Soc. Roman Catholic. Home: PO Box 332 Gwynedd PA 19436-0332 Office: Genesis Mgmt Resources 144 W State St Kennett Square PA 19348

SEVERINO, SUSAN DANETTE, legislative staff member; b. Topeka, Kans., Apr. 10, 1965; d. Frank Stephan and Margaret Marylin (Hagie) S. BS in Polit. Sci., Drake U., 1988. Field dir. Congressman Jim Leach, Iowa Campaign, Davenport, 1988; rsch. analyst Iowa Ho. of Reps., Des Moines, 1989-93, chief of staff House Majority, Brent Siegrist, 1993—. Youth dir. Branstad for Gov., Des Moines, 1982; youth dir. Grassley for Senate, Des Moines, 1986; pres. Coll. Reps., Simpson Coll., 1984, 85; exec. bd. Polk County Reps., 1990-92. Mem. PEO, Pi Beta Phi. Roman Catholic. Home: 1411 47th St Des Moines IA 50311-2432 Office: Iowa Ho of Reps State Capital Bldg Des Moines IA 50319

SEVERNS, PENNY L., state legislator; b. Decatur, Ill., Jan. 21, 1952. BS in Polit. Sci. and Internat. Relations, So. Ill. U., 1974. Spl. asst. to adminstr. AID, Washington, 1977-79; city councilwoman Decatur, from 1983; mem. 51st dist. Ill. State Senate, 1987—, chief budget negotiator for Senate Dems., 1993—, minority spokesperson appropriations com., 1994—. Office: Ill State Senate State Capitol Springfield IL 62706*

SEVERY, ISABEL TERESA, counselor; m. Raymond O. Severy; children: Michael Thomas, Ian Patrick. BS, U. Maine, 1967; MA, Ctrl. Mich. U., 1992. Lic. profl. counselor; cert. tchr. Tex., Wash., Mich. Counselor Perry Pub. Schs., 1992—. Named one of Outstanding Young Women Am., 1982, 83. Mem. ACA, Am. Sch. Counselors Assn., Mich. Counseling Assn., Mich. Sch. Counselors Assn., Mich. Mental Health Counselors Assn., Order of Omega, Delta Zeta. Home: 3953 White Pine Dr DeWitt MI 48820 Office: Perry Pub Schs 7380 Beard Rd Shaftsburg MI 48882

SEWARD, ANN MARIE, lawyer; b. Norfolk, Conn., Nov. 20, 1955; d. Sebastiano Raymond Giansiracusa and Dolores Bonn; m. Mark A. Seward. Student, U. Exeter, Eng., 1978; BA, U. Ariz., 1977, JD, 1980. Asst. staff judge adv. USAF, Travis AFB, Calif., 1981-83; asst. staff judge adv. USAF, Howard AFB, Panama, 1983-84, area def. counsel, 1984-85; adminstrv. law judge Ariz. Dept. Econ. Sec., Tucson, 1985-88; atty. Edwards & Kolesar, Chtd., Las Vegas, Nev., 1988-93; atty., founder Seward & Assocs., P.C., Las Vegas, 1993—; adj. prof. Panama br. U. Miami, Panama City, 1983, 84, U. Nev., Las Vegas, 1989; lectr. Bus. Entity Seminars, Las Vegas, 1992, 94, Nat. Bus. Inst., Las Vegas, 1991; arbitrator Nev. Arbitration Assn., NASD, U.S. Arbitration and Mediation, Am. Arbitration Assn., Las Vegas, 1988—. Contbr. articles to law jours. Mem. Nat. Assn. Women Bus. Owners, Associated Gen. Contractors, Nev. Bar Assn., Ariz. Bar Assn., Mo. Bar Assn., Mensa, Phi Beta Kappa. Office: Seward & Assocs Ste D-31 601 S Rancho Dr Las Vegas NV 89106

SEWARD, TROILEN GAINEY, psychologist; b. Petersburg, Va., Nov. 26, 1941; d. Troy L. and Mary (Nester) Gainey; m. William E. Seward III, June 29, 1963; children: Susan Blair, William E. IV. BA, Coll. William and Mary, 1963, MEd, 1980, EdS, 1980; MEd, Va. Commonwealth U., 1977. Elem. tchr. Petersburg, 1963-67; secondary tchr. Surry (Va.) Acad., 1967-76, guidance counselor, 1976-77; headmistress Tidewater Acad., Wakefield, Va., 1977-79; psychologist Peninsula Child Devel. Clinic, Newport News, Va., 1980-82; sch. psychologist Dinwiddie (Va.) Pub. Sch., 1982-89, dir. pupil pers. svcs., spl. edn., 1990-93, dir. student svcs., 1993—; mem. human rights com. Southside Tng. Ctr., Petersburg, 1986—. Trustee Ritchie Meml. ch., Claremont, Va., 1971—; mem. Town Coun., Claremont, 1984-90, mem. fin. com., 1984-90. Mem. Nat. Assn. Sch. Psychologists (del. 1992-94), Va.

Assn. Sch. Psychologists (chair cert. and licensure com. 1985-87, legis. chair 1987—, pres. 1989-91), Delta Kappa Gamma, Phi Kappa Phi. Episcopalian. Home: PO Box 266 Claremont VA 23899-0266

SEWELL, BETTY DAVENPORT, special education educator; b. Birmingham, Ala., Feb. 15, 1953; d. William Harry and Edna Earl (Staggs) Davenport; children: David, Daniel. Dental technician, Carrer Acad., Atlanta, 1973; BS in Spl. Edn. with honors, Auburn U., Montgomery, 1992, M in Mild Learning Handicapped, 1994. Cert. spl. edn. tchr., Ala. Dental technician Clanton (Ala.) Dental Lab., 1973-86; tchr. asst. Clanton Elem. Sch., 1988—, tchr. spl. edn., 1992—; tchr. emotionally conflicted Children's Harbor (Ala.) Sch.; edn. coord. Cmty. Intensive Treatment for Youth, Clanton, Ala., 1995—. Sec. Thorsby (Ala.) Band Boosters, 1989-91; parade organizer Thorsby Swedish Heritage Com., 1992-93. Mem. NEA, Ala. Edn. Assn., Coun. for Exceptional Children, Kappa Delta Phi, Phi Kappa Phi. Baptist. Home: 804 Ware Ave Clanton AL 35045

SEWELL, BEVERLY JEAN, financial executive; b. Oklahoma City, July 10, 1942; d. Benjamin B. Bainbridge and Faith Marie (Mosier) Allision; m. Ralph Byron Sewell, Jan. 23, 1962; children: M. Timothy, Pamela J. Student, U. Okla., 1960-61, Jackson Community Coll., 1973-77; BA in Bus., Mesa Coll., 1982; cert., Coll. Fin. Planning, 1984, MS in Fin. Planning, 1994. Sole practice fin. planning Grand Junction, Colo., 1985-87; fin. planner, broker Interpacific Investors Services, Grand Junction, 1987-88; investment broker A.G. Edwards & Sons, Inc., Grand Junction, 1988-92, v.p., 1992—; MS in Fin. Planning, 1994. Mem. ctrl. com. Grand Junction Rep. Orgn., 1988; mem. Grand Junction Planning Commn., 1987-89; bd. dirs. Grand Junction Symphony, 1991-94, Downtown Devel. Authority, St. Mary's Hosp. Mem. Inst. Cert. Fin. Planners, Internat. Assn. Fin. Planning. Home: 717 Wedge Dr Grand Junction CO 81506-1866 Office: A G Edwards & Sons Inc 501 Main St Grand Junction CO 81501-2607

SEWELL, PHYLLIS SHAPIRO, retail chain executive; b. Cin., Dec. 26, 1930; d. Louis and Mollye (Mark) Shapiro; m. Martin Sewell, Apr. 5, 1959; 1 child, Charles Steven. B.S. in Econs. with honors, Wellesley Coll., 1952. With Federated Dept. Stores, Inc., Cin., 1952-88, research dir. store ops., 1961-65, sr. research dir., 1965-70, operating v.p., research, 1970-75, corp. v.p., 1975-79, sr. v.p., research and planning, 1979-88; bd. dirs. Lee Enterprises Inc., Davenport, Iowa, Pitney Bowes Inc., U.S. Shoe Corp., SYSCO Corp. Bd. dirs. Nat. Cystic Fibrosis Found., Cin., 1963—; chmn. divsn. United Appeals, Cin., 1982; mem. bus. adv. coun. Sch. Bus. Adminstrn., Miami U., Oxford, Ohio, 1982-84; trustee Cin. Community Chest, 1984-94, Jewish Fedn., 1990-92, Jewish Hosp., 1990—. Named One of 100 Top Corp. Women Bus. Week mag., 1976; named Career Woman of Achievement YWCA, 1983; recipient Alumnae Achievement award Wellesley Coll., 1979, Disting. Cin. Bus. and Profl. Woman award, 1981; named to Ohio Women's Hall of Fame, 1982.

SEWER, DORIS E., critical care nurse, educator; b. Charlotte, St. Thomas, V.I., Oct. 23, 1934; d. Richard and Rachel (Callwood) Donovan; m. Edmundo Valerius Sewer, Mar. 19, 1959; children: Milagros Holden, Melinda Muganzo Mignel Sewer, Maria Vantine. Diploma, Bella Vista Sch. Nursing, Mayaguez, P.R., 1969; BSN, Andrews U., 1975; MA in Edn., Counseling, Calif. State U., San Bernardino, 1979; cert. in clin. pastoral edn., Loma Linda U., 1989. Staff nurse ICU Lincoln (Nebr.) Gen. Hosp., 1969-72; charge nurse ICU Loma Linda (Calif.) Community Hosp., 1974-75; staff nurse ICU Loma Linda U. Med. Ctr., 1975-77; dir. nursing Mountain View Child Care Ctr., Loma Linda, 1977-79; asst. prof. nursing Chaffey Coll., Ont., Calif., 1979-82; nursing instr., missionary nurse Antillian Coll., Mayaguez, P.R., 1982—; counselor, lectr. Suicide and Crisis Intervention, San Bernardino, Calif., 1977-80; part-time clin. instr. psychiat. nursing Riverside (Calif.) City Coll., 1976-78; instr. ICU course Bella Vista Hosp., Mayaguez, 1984, 86, 88, 89; participating instr. Intensive Care Course Antillian Coll., Mayaguez, 1989; mem. San Bernardino Adv. Com. Drug Abuse, 1979-82; vis. prof. nursing U. V.I., St. Thomas, 1991. Mem. Nat. League Nursing.

SEXSON, SANDRA GRIFFIN BISHOP, child psychiatrist, educator; b. Baldwyn, Miss., Sept. 16, 1945; d. Horace Omer Bishop and Correne Griffin; m. William R. Sexson, June 24, 1972; children: Kristen, Ryan. BS in Phys. Scis., Miss. State Coll. for Women, 1967; MD, U. Miss., 1971. Intern in pediat. U. Miss. Sch. Medicine, Jackson, 1971-72; resident in gen. psychiatry U. Tex. Health Sci. Ctr., San Antonio, 1972-74; fellow in child devel. Child Devel. Clinic U. Hosp.-U. Miss., Jackson, 1974-75; fellow in child psychiatry, asst. in psychiatry Wash. U. Sch. Medicine, St. Louis, 1976-78; asst. prof. in pediats. psychiatry Wright State U., Dayton, Ohio, 1978-83, assoc. prof. psychiatry, 1983-84; asst. prof. child psychiatry Sch. Medicine, Emory U., Atlanta, 1984-93, assoc. prof. child psychiatry, 1993—, chief child psychiatry, 1994. Recipient Spl. Achievement award YWCA Salute to Career Women, 1984, Outstanding Mentor award Am. Acad. Child and Adolescent Psychiatry, 1990; named Ohio Outstanding Young Woman of Am., 1981. Mem. Am. Assn. Dirs. Psychiatry, Am. Acad. Child Psychiatry, Soc. Rsch. in Child Devel. (assoc. chair), Assn. Acad. Psychiatry, Ga. Coun. Child and Adolescent Psychiatry (pres.). Office: Emory U Sch Medicine 2215 Ridgewood Dr NE Atlanta GA 30322

SEXTER, DEBORAH RAE, lawyer; b. Bklyn., May 28, 1939; d. Benjamin and Minnie (Popkewitz) Rochkin; m. Jay Sexter, Apr. 14, 1957; children: David, Michael. BBA, CCNY, 1961; AAS, Bergen C.C., 1975; MS, Fordham U., 1978, JD, 1987; profl. diploma, United Hosps. Sch. Nurse Anesthesia, 1980. Bar: N.J. 1987, U.S. Dist. Ct. N.J. 1987, N.Y. 1988; RN, N.J., N.Y.; cert. RN anesthetist, Am. Assn. Nurse Anesthetists; cert. fraud examiner, Assn. Cert. Fraud Examiners. Community organizer N.Y.C., 1965-70; staff nurse community hosps., Bergen County, N.J., 1975-78; staff anesthetist Columbia-Presbyn. Med. Ctr., N.Y.C., 1980-83, Manhattan Eye, Ear, Throat Hosp., N.Y.C., 1983-84; chief nurse anesthetist Anesthesia Assocs., Nyack, N.Y., 1984-87; pvt. practice law Grand View-on-Hudson, N.Y., 1987-90; sr. asst. gen. counsel, inspector gen. Met. Transp. Authority, N.Y.C., 1990-94; pvt. practice Irvington, N.Y., 1994—. Village justice Village of Grand View-on-Hudson, 1986-92; vice chmn. ethics com. Village of Irvington, N.Y., 1992—; mem. ethics com. Cmty. Hosp., Dobbs Ferry, N.Y., 1995—. Mem. Nat. Assn. Scholars, Fedn. Am. Immigration Reform, N.Y. State Magistrates Assn. Home: 2 Hudson Rd E Irvington NY 10533 Office: 2 Hudson Rd E Irvington NY 10533

SEXTON, AMY MANERBINO, computer analyst; b. Denver, Sept. 21, 1957; d. George Anthony and Victoria Violet (Marolt) Manerbino; m. Lindel Scott Sexton, May 29, 1982; 1 child, Monica Marie. Student, Colo. Sch. Mines, 1975-79; BS, Ft. Lewis Coll., 1980; M in Computer Info. Systems, U. Denver, 1989. Phys. sci. aid U.S. Geol. Survey, Golden, Colo., 1977-79; geologist Am. Stratigraphic Co., Denver, 1981-89; cons. geologist Denver, 1989-90; programmer Covia Partnership, Denver, 1990-91, computer analyst, trainee mentor, 1991-92; computer tech. analyst Covia Partnership, 1992-93; sr. programmer, analyst United Airlines, Denver, 1993—. Republican. Roman Catholic. Office: United Airlines 5347 S Valentia Way Englewood CO 80111

SEXTON, CAROL BURKE, financial institution executive; b. Chgo., Apr. 20, 1939; d. William Patrick and Katharine Marie (Nolan) Burke; m. Thomas W. Sexton Jr., June 30, 1962 (div. June 1976); children: Thomas W., J. Patrick, M. Elizabeth. BA, Barat Coll., 1961; cert. legal, Mallinckrodt Coll., 1974. Tchr. Roosevelt High Sch., Chgo., 1961-63, St. Joseph's Sch., Wilmette, Ill., 1975-80; dir. Jane Byrne Polit. Com., Chgo., 1980-81; mgr. Chgo. Merc. Exch., 1981-84, sr. dir. govt. and civic affairs, 1984-87, v.p. pub. affairs, 1987-94, sr. v.p. corp. rels., 1994—; mem. internat. trade an investment subcom. Chgo. Econ. Devel. Commn., 1989, 90. Bd. dirs. Chgo. Sister Cities, 1992—; chmn. Chgo.-Toronto Sister Cities Com., 1992—; bd. dirs. Ill. Ambs., 1991—, pres., 1994; bd. dirs., sec. Internat. Press Ctr., 1992—, chmn. bd., 1994. Mem. Exec.'s Club of Chgo. (bd. dirs.), Chgo. Conv. and Tourism Bur. (sec. 1989—, exec. com. 1987—, chmn. elect 1990, chmn. 1991-92), Chgo.-Toronto Sister Cities Internat. (chmn.). Roman Catholic. Office: Chgo Merc Exch 30 S Wacker Dr Chicago IL 60606-7402

SEXTON, DEBORAH ANNE, psychotherapist, social worker; b. Bklyn., Nov. 12, 1947; d. Joseph Edward and Evelyn Dorothy (Feibel) Gunn; m. Michael A. Sexton, Oct. 21, 1972; children: Timothy Michael, William Michael, Brendan Liam. AA, Nassau Community Coll., Garden City, N.Y., 1973; BS, St. Joseph's Coll., Patchogue, N.Y., 1985; MSW, SUNY, Stony Brook, 1988; cert. alcoholism-substance abuse counseling, Molloy Coll., 1990; studeint, Inst. Modern Psychoanalysis, N.Y.C., 1987—. Qaulified clin. social worker, N.Y.; acad. cert. scial worker. Social worker Kings Park (N.Y.) Psychiat. Ctr., N.Y. State Office Mental Health, 1988-89, 90-91; social worker Creedmoor Psychiat. Ctr., N.Y. State Office Mental Health, Queens, 1989-90; therapist L.I. Ctr., Inc., Huntington, N.Y., 1989-90; psychotherapist Commack (N.Y.) Consultation Ctr., 1989—; social worker Prilgrim Psyciat. Ctr., N.Y., 1991-93. Mem. NASW, Acad. Cert. Social Workers, N.Y. State Soc. Clin. Social Work Psychotherapists. Home: 350 Park Ln Massapequa Park NY 11762-1426 Office: Commack Cons Ctr 283 Commack Rd Ste 215 Commack NY 11725-3400

SEXTON, VIRGINIA STAUDT, retired psychology educator; b. N.Y.C., Aug. 30, 1916; d. Philip Henry and Kathryn Philippa (Burkard) Staudt. B.A., Hunter Coll., 1936; M.A., Fordham U., 1941, Ph.D., 1946; L.H.D., Cedar Crest Coll., 1980. Elem. tchr. St. Peter and St. Paul's Sch., Bronx, N.Y., 1936-39; clk. N.Y.C. Dept. Welfare, 1939-44; lectr., asst. prof., assoc. prof. psychology Notre Dame Coll. of S.I., 1944-52; instr. Hunter Coll. of CUNY, 1953-56, asst. prof., 1957-60, assoc. prof., 1961-66, prof., 1967-68; prof. psychology Herbert H. Lehman Coll., 1968-79, prof. emeritus, 1979—; disting. prof. St. John's U., Jamaica, N.Y., 1979-92; mem. profl. conduct rev. bd. N.Y. State Bd. for Psychology, 1971-78; mem. adv. bd. Archives of History Am. Psychology, 1966—. Author: (with H. Misiak) Catholics in Psychology; A Historical Survey, 1954, History of Psychology: An Overview, 1966, Historical Perspectives in Psychology: Readings, 1971, Phenomenological, Existential and Humanistic Psychologies: A Historical Survey, 1973, Psychology Around the World, 1976. Editor: (with J. Dauben) History and Philosophy of Science: Selected Papers, 1983, (with R. Evens, T. Cadwallader) 100 Years: The American Psychology Assn., 1992, (with J. Hogan) International Psychology: Views From Around The World, 1992; mem. editorial bd. Jour. Phenomenological Psychology, 1977—, Jour. Mind and Behavior, 1979—, Interamerican Jour. Psychology, 1982—, The Humanistic Psychologist, 1984—, Professional Psychology: Research and Practice, 1984-89, Clinician's Research Digest, 1984-92. Contbr. articles to profl. jours. Fellow Am. Psychol. Assn., AAAS, N.Y. Acad. Scis.; mem. Am. Hist. Assn., AAUP, AAUW, Am. Assn. for Advancement Humanities, Internat. Assn. Applied Psychology, Internat. Council Psychologists (pres. 1981-82), Interam. Soc. Psychology, Internat. Soc. History of Behavioral and Soc. Scis., Eastern Psychol. Assn., N.Y. Soc. Clin. Psychologists, N.Y. Psychol. Assn., N.Y. Assn. Applied Psychologists, Assn. for Women in Psychology, N.Y. Acad. Scis., Psychologists Social Responsibility, Phi Beta Kappa, Psi Chi (v.p. eastern region 1982-86; pres. 1986-87). Roman Catholic. Avocation: stamp collecting. Home: 188 Ascan Ave Flushing NY 11375-5947

SEYBERT, JOANNA, judge; b. Bklyn., Sept. 18, 1946; married; 1 child. BA, U. Cin., 1967; JD, St. John's U., 1971. Bar: N.Y. 1972, U.S. Dist. Ct. (ea. and so. dists.) N.Y. 1973, U.S. Ct. Appeals (2d cir.) 1973. Trial staff atty. Legal Aid Soc., N.Y.C., 1971-73; sr. staff atty. Legal Aid Soc., Mineola, N.Y., 1976-80; sr. trial atty. Fed. Defender Svc., Bklyn., 1973-75; bur. chief Nassau County Atty's Office, Mineola, 1980-87; judge Nassau County Dist. Ct., Hempstead, N.Y., 1987-92, Nassau County Ct., Mineola, 1992-94, U.S. Dist. Ct. (ea. dist.) N.Y., Bklyn., 1994—. Active environ. bd. Town of Oyster Bay; mem. Rep. com. Nassau County, 1979-87. Recipient Norman F. Lent award Criminal Cts. Bar Assn., 1991. Mem. ABA, N.Y. State Bar Assn., Nassau County Women's Bar Assn., Theodore Roosevelt Inns of Ct., Fed. Judges Assn., Nassau Lawyer's Assn. (past pres.). Office: 225 Cadman Plz E Brooklyn NY 11201

SEYFFARTH, LINDA JEAN WILCOX, corporate executive, controller; b. Montour Falls, N.Y., May 10, 1948; d. Maurice Roscoe and Theodora (Van Tassell) Wilcox; m. P. Tomlin Agnew, June 29, 1991; 1 child by previous marriage, Kristin. BA magna cum laude, Syracuse (N.Y.) U., 1970; MBA with honors, NYU, 1977. Programmer Prudential Ins. Co., Newark, 1970-73; with Hoffmann-La Roche Inc., Nutley, N.J., 1973—, corp. controller, 1985-88, v.p., controller, 1989—. Bd. dirs., treas. St. Barnabas Burn Found., West Orange, N.J., Glen Ridge (N.J.) Ednl. Found., Ind.Coll. Fund, Summit, N.J. Mem. Nat. Assn. Accts., Fin. Execs. Inst., Leadership N.J., Phi Beta Kappa, Beta Gamma Sigma. Office: Hoffmann-LaRoche Inc 340 Kingsland St Nutley NJ 07110-1150

SEYKORA, MARGARET S., psychotherapist; b. N.Y.C., June 18, 1947; d. Stanley Sneider and Janet Pick (Sneider) Smith; m. Sern A. Seykora, Jan. 19, 1968 (div. 1984); m. H. Lester Mower, Jr., Nov. 19, 1993. BS in Journalism, U. Fla., 1970; MA in Edn. and Human Devel. Counseling, Rollins Coll., 1991. Lic. mental health counselor, Fla.; lic. mortgage broker, Fla., lic. real estate broker, Fla. Advt. profl. Gainesville (Fla.) Sun, 1968-75, TV mag. editor, 1968-75, Sunday/lesiure/book editor, 1970; stoneware potter, owner Old Town (Fla.) Pottery, 1975-82; real estate salesperson Jack McCormick Realty, Chiefland, Fla., 1982-85, Coldwell Banker, Orlando, Fla., 1985-90; real estate broker The Hood Group, Inc., Orlando, 1990-92; psychotherapist, facilitator, pres. Personal Dynamics Inst., Altamonte Springs, Fla., 1989—; career instr. The Knowledge Shop, Winter Park, Fla., 1992—; outpatient mental health therapist Lakeside Alternatives, Winter Park, Fla., 1992—; adj. instr. Seminole C.C., Sanford, Fla., 1992—, Valencia C.C., Winter Park, 1992—. Author/facilitator workshops in field. Mem. Nat. Bd. Counselors, Am. Counseling Assn., Assn. for Specialists in Group Work, Nat. Bd. Realtors. Mem. Ch. of Religious Sci. Office: Personal Dynamics Inst 421 Montgomery Rd # 105 Altamonte Springs FL 32717

SEYMOUR, BARBARA MAYNARD, artist, landscape designer; b. Ft. Worth, Dec. 19, 1940; d. Richard Maynard and Barbara (Muggleton) S.; m. William J. Morehouse, June 12, 1963 (div. 1979). BA with honors, Swarthmore Coll., 1963; M of Landscape Architecture, U. Pa., 1982. Landscape designer Wallace Roberts & Todd, Phila., 1982-83; owner Barbara Seymour Landscapes, Moylan, Pa., 1987—; lectr. Calif. Poly State U., San Luis Obispo, 1984-85, Temple U., Ambler, Pa., 1987-88. Author, illustrator: Portrait of a Place: San Luis Obispo, 1986; illustrator Phila. Inquirer, 1989-94; illustrator: The Exhuberant Garden, 1992, Susquehanna: River of Dreams, 1993; watercolors exhibited in solo show Swarthmore Coll. List Gallery, 1993. NEA grantee, Washington, 1985-86. Mem. Media Hist. Preservation. Democrat.

SEYMOUR, JANE, actress; b. Hillingdon, Middlesex, Eng., Feb. 15, 1951; came to U.S., 1976; d. John Benjamin and Mieke Frankenberg; m. David Flynn, July 18, 1981 (div. 1991); 2 children; m. James Keach, May 15, 1993. Student, Arts Ednl. Sch., London. Appeared in films Oh What A Lovely War, 1968, The Only Way, 1968, Young Winston, 1969, Live and Let Die, 1971, Sinbad and the Eye of the Tiger, 1973, Somewhere in Time, 1979, Oh Heavenly Dog, 1979, Lassiter, 1984, Head Office, Scarlet Pimpernel, Haunting Passion, Dark Mirror, Obsessed with a Married Woman, Killer on Board, The Tunnel, 1988, The French Revolution; TV films include Frankenstein, The True Story, 1972, Captains and The Kings, 1976 (Emmy nomination), 7th Avenue, 1976, The Awakening Land, 1977, The Four Feathers, 1977, Battlestar Galactica, Dallas Cowboy Cheerleaders, 1979, Our Mutual Friend, PBS, Eng., 1975, Jamaica Inn, 1982, Sun Also Rises, 1984, Crossings, 1986, Keys to Freedom, Angel of Death, 1990, Praying Mantis, 1993; A Passion for Justice: The Hazel Brannon Smith Story, 1994; Broadway appearances include Amadeus, 1980-81, I Remember You, 1992, Matters of the Heart, 1991, Sunstroke, 1992, Praying Mantis, 1993, Heidi, 1993; TV mini-series include East of Eden, 1980, The Richest Man in the World, 1988 (Emmy award), The Woman He Loved, 1988, Jack the Ripper, 1988, War and Remembrance, 1988, 89; host PBS documentary, Japan, 1988; TV series: Dr. Quinn: Medicine Woman, 1993— (Emmy nomination, Lead Actress - Drama, 1994); author: Jane Seymour's Guide to Romantic Living, 1986. Named Hon. Citizen of Ill., Gov. Thompson, 1977. Mem. Screen Actors Guild, AFTRA, Actors Equity, Brit. Equity. Office: Metropolitan Talent Agency 4526 Wilshire Blvd Los Angeles CA 90010*

SEYMOUR, JANET MARTHA, psychologist; b. Mineola, N.Y., June 13, 1957; d. John Andrews and Eileen (Brudie) S.; children: Heidi Lynn Adams, Hartley Ann Adams. BA in Psychology and Music, Wheaton Coll., 1979; MA in Clin. Psychology, Rosemead Sch. Psychology, La Mirada, Calif., 1981, PsyD in Clin. Psychology, 1988. Lic. psychologist, Calif. Psychology intern Colmery Oneil VA Med. Ctr., Topeka, 1985-86; psychotherapist Concord (N.H.) Psychol. Assocs., 1987-88; psychologist Jolliffe & Assocs., Long Beach, Calif., 1989—. Sunday sch. tchr. 1st Evang. Free Ch. Fullerton, Calif., 1990-91, orch. flutist, 1980—; coach Pony Baseball, Whittier, Calif., 1989; mem. Flutes Fantastiques Trio, 1993—; instr. flute tones course Whittier Cmty. Ctr., 1994—. Mem. APA, Calif. Assn. Marriage and Family Therapy. Republican. Office: Jolliffe & Assocs 3740 Atlantic Ave Ste 200 Long Beach CA 90807-3440

SEYMOUR, MARY FRANCES, lawyer; b. Durand, Wis., Oct. 20, 1948; d. Marshall Willard and Alice Roberta (Smith) Thompson; m. Marshall Warren Seymour, June 6, 1970; 1 foster child, Nghia Pham. BS, U. Wis., LaCrosse, 1970; JD, William Mitchell Coll., 1979. Bar: Minn. 1979, U.S. Dist. Ct. Minn. 1979, U.S. Ct. Appeals (8th cir.) 1979, U.S. Supreme Ct. 1986. With Cochrane and Bresnahan, P.A., St. Paul, 1979-94, Loper & Seymour, P.A., 1994—. Mem. Assn. Trial Lawyers Am., Minn. Bar Assn., Ramsey County Bar Assn., Minn. Trial Lawyers Assn., Assn. of Cert. Fraud Examiners. Office: Loper & Seymour PA 24 E 4th St Saint Paul MN 55101-1099

SEYMOUR, STEPHANIE KULP, federal judge; b. Battle Creek, Mich., Oct. 16, 1940; d. Francis Bruce and Frances Cecelia (Bria) Kulp; m. R. Thomas Seymour, June 10, 1972; children: Bart, Bria, Sara, Anna. BA magna cum laude, Smith Coll., 1962; JD, Harvard U., 1965. Bar: Okla. 1965. Practice Boston, 1965-66, Tulsa, 1966-67, Houston, 1968-69; assoc. Doerner, Stuart, Saunders, Daniel & Anderson, Tulsa, 1971-75, ptnr., 1975-79; judge U.S. Ct. Appeals (10th cir.) Okla., Tulsa, 1979—, now chief justice; assoc. bar examiner Okla. Bar Assn., 1973-79; trustee Tulsa County Law Library, 1977-78; mem. U.S. Jud. Conf. Com. Defender Svcs., 1985-91, chmn., 1987-91. Mem. various task forces Tulsa Human Rights Commn., 1972-76, legal adv. panel Tulsa Task Force Battered Women, 1971-77. Mem. Am. Bar Assn., Okla. Bar Assn., Tulsa County Bar Assn., Phi Beta Kappa. Office: US Courthouse 333 West 4th St Rm 4-562 Tulsa OK 74103*

SEYMOUR, SUSAN CHRISTINE, academic administrator, anthropology educator; b. San Francisco, Aug. 1, 1940; d. Kent Osborn and Helen Rosalie (Close) S.; m. Laurence Drell Graham, June 16, 1973; 1 child, Elliot Close. BA, Stanford U., 1962; PhD, Harvard U., 1971. Instr. Whittier (Calif.) Coll., 1970-71, asst. prof., 1971-73; asst. prof. U. So. Calif., L.A., 1973-74; asst. prof. Pitzer Coll., Claremont, Calif., 1974-76, assoc. prof., 1976-81, prof. anthropology, 1981—; coord. women's studies Claremont Coll., 1983-85; v.p. for acad. affairs, dean faculty Pitzer Coll., Claremont, Calif., 1994—; rsch. cons. Asian Women's Inst., Lahore, Pakistan and Madras, India, 1981-86; lectr. in field. Author, editor: The Transformation of a Sacred Town, 1980, Women, Education and Family Structure in India, 1994; contbr. articles to profl. jours. and chpts. to books. Grantee, Radcliffe Coll., 1962-63, 70, Haynes Found., 1972-81; NIMH rsch. tng. fellow, 1963-67, Fulbright fellow, 1989. Fellow Soc. for Applied Anthropology, Am. Anthropol. Assn.; mem. Soc. for Psychol. Anthropology (sec.-treas. 1991-94, bd. dirs. 1995—), Southwestern Anthropol. Assn. (bd. dirs. 1987-89), LWV. Democrat. Office: Pitzer Coll 1050 N Mills Ave Claremont CA 91711-6101

SEYMOUR-HARRIS, BARBARA LAVERNE, lawyer; b. Columbia, S.C., July 9, 1953; d. Leroy Semon and Barbara Lucile (Youngblood) Seymour; m. Canaan L. Harris. BS, S.C. State Coll., 1975; JD, Georgetown U., 1979; MBA, Harvard U., 1985. Bar: S.C. 1979, Tex. 1984, U.S. Dist. Ct. (ea. dist.) Tex. 1983, U.S. Dist. Ct. (so. dist.) Tex. 1985, U.S. Tax Ct. 1986, U.S. Claims Ct. 1991. Tax atty. Texaco Inc., White Plains, N.Y., 1979-80, Houston, 1980—; loaned exec. for task force to audit Tex. Employment Commn. by Gov. of Tex., 1987-88. Troop leader Girl Scouts U.S., White Plains, 1979-80, asst. troop leader, Houston, 1981-82; bd. dirs Sickle Cell Disease Rsch. Found. Tex., Houston, 1986-92, treas., 1986-88, pres., 1988-90; allocation panel vol. United Way of the Tex. Gulf Coast; mem. Black Exec. Exch. program Nat. Urban League, 1980—; mem. bus. adv. coun. S.C. State Coll. Sch. Bus., 1990—; trustee Houston Grand Opera. Named One of 50 Outstanding Young Leaders of the Future, Ebony Mag., 1983, Disting. Bus. Alumnus award S.C. State Coll., 1991; selected for Leadership Houston, Leadership Am., 1990; finalist Five Outstanding Young Houstonians award Jaycees, 1988, one of 10 Foremost Fashionables in Houston, Alpha Kappa Alpha, 1994. Mem. ABA, Houston Black Women Lawyers Assn. (sec. 1981-82, treas. 1982-83), Houston Bus. Forum (bd. dirs. 1983, 87-90, treas. 1988-89, sec. 1989-90), Nat. Bar Assn. (com. chmn. 1982-83), S.C. Bar Assn., Tex. Bar Assn., Harvard U. Bus. Sch. Black Alumni Assn. (historian 1985-86), Black Law Alumni Coun. of Georgetown U. Law Ctr., W.J. Durham Soc., The Links, Inc. (parliamentarian of Houston chpt., chair 1995 Cotillion). Democrat. Roman Catholic. Office: Texaco Inc 1111 Bagby St Houston TX 77002-2543

SFURM, JULIA KAY, workers compensation administrator; b. Joliet, Ill., Jan. 29, 1961; d. John Louis and Flora Darlene (Mason) S. BA in Bus., North Ctrl. Coll., 1992; postgrad., DePaul U., 1993—. Claims examiner Royal Ins., Aurora, Ill., 1986-88; sr. claims examiner Sedgwick James, Chgo., 1988-89, supr., 1989-91, assst. v.p., 1991—. Vol. Red Cross, Chgo., 1993. Mem. NAFE, Women in Workers Compensation, Workers' Compensation Claims Assn. Methodist. Office: Sedgwick James 230 W Monroe St Chicago IL 60606-4703

SGARLAT, MARY ANNE E. A., marketing professional; b. Boston, Apr. 5, 1958; d. Francis Abbott and Elizabeth Maria (Paragallo) S. Diploma, Milton Acad., 1974; student, Roedean Sch., Brighton, Eng., 1975; BA, Bennington Coll., 1979. Adminstr. Harvard U., Cambridge, Mass., 1979-86; pub. rels. dir. Graham Gund Architects, Cambridge, 1986-89; mktg. and comms. mgr. Elkus/Manfredi Architects, Boston, 1989-90; comms. mgr. Turan Corp., Boston, 1990-92; mktg. mgr. The Design Partnership of Cambridge, 1992—. Mem. Bennington Coll. Alumni Assn. (regional dir. 1993—, exec. com. 1986-93). Home: 1214 Brook Rd Milton MA 02186-4136

SHABAZZ, AIYSHA MUSLIMAH, social work administrator; b. Columbia, S.C., Aug. 9, 1942; d. Jerry James Gadson and Edna Louise (Bellinger) Gadson Smalls; m. Abdullah Muslim Shabazz; children: Ain, Wali. BA, Fed. City Coll., Washington, 1973; MSW with honors, U. S.C., 1994. Cert. child protective svcs. investigator, S.C., adoption investigator, S.C.; lic. social worker and ACBSW; cert. AIDS instr. ARC; lic. notary pub., S.C. Social work asst. Family Service Ctr., Washington, 1966-68; admission counselor Washington Tech. Inst., Washington, 1968-70; program dir. Park Motor Community Ctr., Washington, 1970-75; adminstrv. asst. Neighborhood Planning Council, Washington, 1974-75; substitue tchr. D.C. Pub. Sch. System, Washington, 1974-75; substitute tchr. Dist. I Pub. Schs., Columbia, 1977; home sch. program dir. Community Care, Inc., Columbia, 1977-81; monitor summer program U. S.C., Columbia, 1982; program dir. Dept. Social Services, Columbia, 1984—, case auditor, 1987-88, social worker supr., 1988—; writer Acad. of Bacholu-Social Workers Exam, 1991; speaker in field. Bd. dirs. Frederick Douglas Inst., Washington, 1968-69; pres. Park Motor Resident Coun., Washington, 1972-75; expert witness Family Ct.; bd. dirs. Coun. on Child Abuse and Neglect; adv. com., v.p. Benedict Coll. Sch. Social Work, S.C. Protection and Advocacy Handicapped Children; vol. AIDS instr. ARC, 1994. Mem. NASW (bd. dirs. 1993—), S.C. Child Abuse Neglect Task Force, AIDS Task Force (chmn. 1987-89). Democrat. Office: Dept Social Services 3220 Two Notch Rd Columbia SC 29204-2826

SHACKLETON, MARY JANE, small business owner; b. Colorado Springs, Colo., Oct. 20, 1934; d. James Emrie and Thelma Isabella (Vittetoe) Mc Carty; m. William H. Shackleton, Apr. 25, 1953; children: Denise, Dennis, Danette, Donna, Donald. Grad. high sch., Montebello, Calif. Owner Chi Town/Radio Shack, Oscoda, Mich., 1978—, East Tawas, Mich., 1983—. Bd. dirs. Oscoda Downtown Devel. Authority. Mem. Toastmasters CTM (sec. Lake Huron chpt. 1988-89, sec.-treas. 1991-92), Oscoda C. of C. (bd. dirs. 1985-90), Oscoda Merchants Assn. (sec.-treas.), Quota Club Iosco (bd. dirs. 1990-91). Republican. Roman Catholic. Home: 3852 N Huron Rd Oscoda MI 48750-9480

SHADE, LYN CASSANDRA, medical rehabilitation services professional; b. Tuskegee, Ala., May 30, 1952; d. George and Bertha (Thorpe) S.; m. Euris Carmichael, Feb. 14, 1983 (div. Sept. 1987); 1 child, Omari. BA, Rutgers U., 1974; MA, Atlanta U., 1977. Counselor, instr. Miss. State U., Starksville, 1977-80; med. rehab. couns. Internat. Rehab., Norcross, Ga., 1984-89; rehab. case mgr. Taylor-Mehl Assocs., Tucker, Ga., 1990—; fin. svcs. mgr.

Primerica Fin. Svcs., Kithonia, Ga., 1991—. Mem. ACA, Am. Rehab. Assn. Home: 5607 Boggs Dr Stone Mountain GA 30087

SHADEROWFSKY, EVA MARIA, photographer, writer; b. Prague, Czechoslovakia, May 20, 1938; came to U.S., 1940; d. Felix Resek and Gertrude (Telatko) Frank; children: Tom, Paul. Student, Oberlin Coll., 1955-56; BA, Barnard Coll., 1960. moderator America Online: Women's Issues Conf., The Women's Room: Women's Wire, Chat in Real Time. Exhibited in one-person shows at The Left Bank Gallery, Wellfleet, Mass., 1974, Art Ctr. No. N.J., Tenafly, 1975 Soho Photo, N.Y., 1974, 80, Esta Robinson Gallery, 1982, Fairleigh Dickinson U., 1983, Donnell Libr., N.Y.C., 1985, Piermont (N.Y.) Libr., 1987, The Turning Point, Piermont, N.Y., 1988, Hopper House, Nyack, N.Y., 1989, Puchong Gallery, N.Y., 1991; group shows include Soho Photo Gallery, N.Y., 1974, Fashion Inst. Tech., N.Y.C., 1975, Portland (Maine) Mus. Art, 1977, Maine Photog. Workshop, Rockport, 1978, Marcuse Pfeifer, N.Y., 1977, 78, Chrysler Mus., Norfol,, Va., 1978, Exposure Gallery Wellfleet, 1978, 79, The Art Ctr. No. N.J., Tenafly, 1980, Neuberger Mus., Purchase, N.Y., 1982, Hudson River Mus., 1982, Foto, N.Y., 1982, Barnard Coll., N.Y.C., 1983, Rockland Ctr. for Arts, 1978, 89, Print Club, Phila., 1988; represented in collections at Bklyn. Mus., Portland (Maine) Mus. Art, Met. Mus. Art, N.Y.C.; author and photographer (book) Suburban Portraits, 1977; photographer Women in Transition, 1975, (book) Earth Tones, 1993; poetry critic/essayist Contact II, 1980—; contbr. story to anthology, 1980-93, Touching Fire, 1989, Sexual Harassment: Women Speakout, 1992, Lovers, 1992, The Time of Our Lives, 1993; contbr. photography to Camera 35 mag., Shots mag., Shutterbug. Recipient Photography award Rockland Ctr. for Arts, 1978, Gt. Am. Photo Contest, 1981, Demarais Press, 1982, Harrison Art Coun., SUNY-Purchase, 1982, The Cape Codder, 1976, 79-82. Home and Office: 265 Maple Rd Valley Cottage NY 10989

SHAEFFER, THELMA JEAN, primary school educator; b. Ft. Collins, Colo., Feb. 1, 1949; d. Harold H. and Gladys June (Ruff) Pfeif; m. Charles F. Shaeffer, June 12, 1971; 1 child, Shannon Emily. BA, U. No. Colo., 1970, MA, 1972. Cert. profl. tchr., type B, Colo. Primary tchr. Adams County Dist #12 Five Star Schs., Northglenn, Colo., 1970-84; chpt. I (lang. arts) tchr. Adams County Dist #12 Five Star Schs., Northglenn, 1984-92, chpt. I, read succed tchr., 1992—; mem. policy coun. Adams County Dist. # 12 Five Star Schs., Northglenn, 1975-79, dist. sch. improvement team, 1987-89; presenter Nat. Coun. Tchrs. of English, 1990; alumni adv. career connections U. No. Colo. Vol. 1992 election, Denver, alumni advisor for Career Connections U. No. Colo., 1993—. Mem. Colo. Tchrs. Assn. (del. 1992), Dist. Tchrs. Edn. Assn. (exec. bd. mem. 1991-93), Internat. Reading Assn. (pres. Colo. coun. 1988), Internat. Order of Job's Daughters (coun. mem.), Order of Eastern Star, Delta Omicron. Episcopalian. Home: 6502 Perry St Arvada CO 80003-6400 Office: Hulstrom Elem Sch 10604 Grant Dr Northglenn CO 80233-4117

SHAER, PATRICIA ANN BLACHA, radio producer, writer; b. Hartford, Conn., Sept. 12, 1941; d. Antoni and Mary (Tricka) Blacha; m. Robert Noel Shaer, Aug. 10, 1963; children: Kathryn Ann, Deborah Marie. BA, Albertus Magnus Coll., 1963; postgrad., Syracuse U., 1972, Middletown (Ohio) Fine Arts Ctr., 1974-79, Rice U., 1986. Asst. underwriter Travelers Ins. Co., Hartford, 1963-64; tchr. various schs., Conn. and Ohio, 1963-75; reporter, photographer Monroe (Ohio) Jour., 1976-77; arts reporter WGUC-FM, Cin., 1982-83; news dir. WPFB-AM/FM, Middletown, 1983-85; news anchor, reporter WRMZ-FM/WMNI-AM, Columbus, Ohio, 1985; arts reporter KUHF-FM, Houston, 1987-90; freelance reporter, writer Houston, 1990—; owner Rubber Tree Prodns., Kingwood, Tex., 1990—; cons. La. State U. Communications Dept., Baton Rouge, 1989; active S.W. Ohio Speakers Bur.; pub. rels. coord. Very Spl. Arts, Houston, 1990-91. Pres. Lemon-Monroe High Sch. Booster Assn., 1979-83; dir. art show Apple Butter Festival, Monroe, 1979-80; dir., newsletter editor Sand Creek Community Assn., 1987—. Mem. AAUW (Lake Houston br. program v.p. 1991-92, pres. 1992-93, Tex. state bd. dirs., dir. internat. affairs 1992-94), Internat. Assn. Bus. Communicators, Women in Communications (Houston chpt. v.p. membership 1990-91, co-chmn. MATRIX competition 1990, sec. 1989), Soc. Profl. Journalists, Beta Sigma Phi. Home: 2723 Cedarville Dr Kingwood TX 77345-1452

SHAEUMIN, MINAYA, customer service representative; b. San Francisco, July 11, 1928; d. John Jesse and Helen Elizabeth (Forsyth) McNeil; m. Maurice Loren Turner, July 28, 1949 (div. Nov. 1955); 1 child, Colleen Ann; m. Rayee Shaeumin, Feb. 13, 1973. Student, Santa Rosa (Calif.) Jr. Coll., 1958-60; AA, Tanana Valley C.C., Fairbanks, Ark., 1987; BS in Anthropology, Oreg. State U., 1992. Lic. life ins. agt., health and accident agt. Intern tchr. 2d grade Primrose Elem. Sch., Santa Rosa, 1961-62; floor clk. surg. wing Santa Rosa Meml. Hosp., 1962; lab. technician Optical Coating Labs., Santa Rosa, 1962-63; live-in practical nurse, housekeeper, sch. tchr. Healsburg, Calif., 1963-65; saleslady, mgr. cosmetic dept. Empire Drug Store, Santa Rosa, 1965-67; community ctr. aide, coord. Community Ctr., Ukiah, Calif., 1968-69; picture framer New Horizons Art Gallery, Fairbanks, Alaska, 1985; seed analyst Oreg. State U. Seed Lab., Corvallis, 1988; owner, operator Best Publs., 1991-92; agt., rep. Bus. Network Comms. Inventor matchbook holder-dispensor; inventor-designer free standing mag. rack; writer songs. Active mem. Pro-Choice Orgn., 1991—; mem. The Planetary Soc., 1989-91, Nat. Space Soc., 1990-91; mem. gold club North Shore Animal League, N.Y., 1985—. Recipient Benefactor award North Shore Animal League, 1991, Cert. of Appreciation, Nat. Cm. to Preserve Social Security and Medicare, 1991. Mem. Amnesty Internat. USA, Ams. to Limit Congl. Terms, Am. Policy Inst. "We the People", World Future Soc., LWV, Srs. Coalition, So. Poverty law Ctr., Nat. Com. to Preserve Social Security and Medicare. Home: 205 NW 11th St Apt 2 Corvallis OR 97330

SHAFER, KATHLEEN MARY, medical marketing executive; b. Chgo., Dec. 29, 1948; d. James Albert and Irene Jeanne (Yurcega) S.; m. Kenneth Alan Petras, Sept. 24, 1983 (div. Jan. 1990). BS in Speech Edn., Northwestern U., 1970. Lic. nursing home adminstr., Ill. Benefits counselor Hosp. Svc. Corp., Chgo., 1970-73; pers. rep. V. Mueller divsn. Baxter Healthcare Corp. (formerly divsn. Am. Hosp. Supply Corp.), Niles, Ill., 1973-74; inventory coord. Niles, Ill., 1974-77, from assoc. product mgr. to market mgr. gen. products, 1977-87; mktg. mgr. Bioproducts for Medicine, Inc. and Bioproducts, DVM, Inc., Tempe, Ariz., 1987-90; dir. sales and mktg. V-Tech, Inc., Tempe, 1990-91; western divsn. mgr. sales and mktg. Alko Equipment, Inc., Gilbert, Ariz., 1992-93; sr. mktg. mgr. Paragon Vision Scis., Phoenix, 1994—. Mem. Med. Mktg. Assn. Republican. Roman Catholic. Home: 1002 S Lagoon Dr Gilbert AZ 85234 Office: 1100 E Bell Rd Phoenix AZ 85022

SHAFER, SUSAN WRIGHT, educator; b. Ft. Wayne, Dec. 6, 1941; d. George Wesley and Bernece (Spray) Wright; 1 child, Michael R. BS, St. Francis Coll., Ft. Wayne, 1967, MS in Edn., 1969. Tchr. Ft. Wayne Community Schs., 1967-69, Amphitheatre Pub. Schs., Tucson, 1970—; odyssey of the mind coord. Prince Elem. Sch., Tucson, 1989-91, future problem solving, 1991-94. Tchr. Green Valley (Ariz.) Cmty. Ch., Vacation Bible Sch., 1987-89, dir. vacation bible sch., 1989-93. Mem. AAUW, NEA (life), Delta Kappa Gamma (pres. Alpha Rho chpt.), Alpha Delta Kappa (historian Epsilon chpt. 1990—), Phi Delta Kappa (life, Tucson chpt.). Republican. Methodist. Home: 603 W Placita Nueva Green Valley AZ 85614-2827 Office: Prince Elem Sch 125 E Prince Rd Tucson AZ 85705-2626

SHAFF, BEVERLY GERARD, educational administrator; b. Oak Park, Ill., Aug. 16, 1925; d. Carl Tanner and Mary Frances (Gerard) Wilson; m. Maurice A. Shaff, Jr., Dec. 20, 1951 (dec. June 1967); children: Carol Maureen, David Gerrard, Mark Albert. MA, U. Ill., 1951; postgrad., Colo. Coll., 1966, 73, Lewis and Clark Coll., 1982, Portland State U., 1975-82. Tchr. Haley Sch., Berwyn, Ill., 1948-51; assoc. prof. English, Huntingdon Coll., Montgomery, Ala., 1961-62; tchr. English, William Palmer High Sch., Colorado Springs, Colo., 1964-67, 72-76, dir., 1967-72; tchr. English, Burns (Oreg.) High Sch., 1976-78; tchr. English as 2d lang. Multnomah County Ednl. Svc. Dist., Portland, Oreg., 1979-85; coord. gen. studies Portland Jewish Acad., 1984-90; with Indian Edn. Prog./Student Tng. Edn. Prog. (STEP) Portland Pub. Schs., 1990-92; tchr. St. Thomas More Sch., Portland, 1992—. Del. Colorado Springs Dem. Com., 1968, 72; active Rainbow Coalition, Portland. Mem. Nat. Assn. Admnstrs., Nat. Assn. Schs. and Colls., Nat. Coun. Tchrs. Math., Nat. Coun. Tchrs. English. Home: 1 Jefferson Pky Apt 125 Lake Oswego OR 97035-8810

SHAFFER, ANITA MOHRLAND, counselor; b. Racine, Wis., Apr. 5, 1939; d. Milton Arthur and Gudrun Amanda (Sundvoll) Stoffel. BS magna cum laude, U. Wis.-Madison, 1961; MEd, U. Wash., 1966; postgrad. Ariz. State U., 1971-76. Cert. in elem. edn., social sci. secondary edn., spl edn., Tex., Ariz.; lic. profl. counselor, Tex.; diplomate Internat. Acad. Behavioral Medicine, Counseling and Psychotherapy. Tchr. Racine Unified Dist. 1, 1961-63, Edmonds Sch. Dist. 15, Alderwood Manor, Wash., 1963-70; tchr. Ariz. Dept. Corrections, Phoenix, 1971-77; tchr. spl. edn. Pasadena Ind. Sch. Dist. (Tex.); 1977-78, spl. edn. counselor, 1978-90, elem. counselor, 1990—. Mem. Am. Counseling Assn., Am. Sch. Counselor Assn., Tex. Counseling Assn., Internat. Platform Assn., NAFE, Mus. Fine Arts Houston (patron), Beta Sigma Phi, Pi Lambda Theta. Home: 260 El Dorado Blvd H 801 Webster TX 77598 Office: Pasadena Ind Sch Dist 1515 Cherrybrook Ln Pasadena TX 77502-4099

SHAFFER, FERN JOAN, artist; b. Chgo., Mar. 29, 1944; d. Albert L. Goldsand and Ruth Arkin; m. Michael Jay Shaffer, Mar. 21, 1965 (div. 1994); children: Jeffrey, Stacy, Samuel. Student, U. Ill., 1962-64, 64-65, BFA, 1981, postgrad., 1983-89; MA in Interdisciplinary Arts Edn., Columbia Coll., 1991. Instr. Art Resources in Teaching, Chgo., 1985-87; curator Morton Coll. Gallery, Cicero, Ill., 1987-88; program dir. Humanitas Instn., Chgo., 1989-91, Selfhelp Home for the Aged, Chgo., 1992—; pres. Artemisia Gallery, Chgo., 1982-92; guest lectr. Sch. of Art Inst., Chgo., 1986, 89, 90, 91, 93, 94, Va. Tech. Sch., Blacksberg, 1989, Harper Coll., Palatine, Ill., 1991, Columbia Coll., Chgo., 1991, 93, 94; keynote speaker No. Ill. U., Dekalb, 1986, Wichita (Kans.) Art Assn., 1989; panelist Sch. of Art Inst. of Chgo., 1987, Midwest Socialists for Women in Soc., Chgo., 1987, U. Wis., Whitewater, 1988, Women's Caucus for Art, Nat. Conf., Washington, 1991, chmn. nat. conf., 1992. One woman shows include Artemisia Gallery, Chgo., 1981, 83, 85, 86, 88, 91, Common Boundary Conf., Washington, 1989; exhibited in group shows Evanston (Ill.) Art Ctr., 1976, 77, 87, Chgo. Abstract Artist's Invitational, Bensonville, Ill., 1980, Hallwalls, Buffalo, 1985, Ea. Ill. U., Charleston, 1987, Monmouth (Ill.) Coll., 1987, Artemisia Gallery, Chgo., 1988, 89, 90, 93, Ceres Gallery, N.Y., 1992, others. Fellow Columbia Coll., 1990; Katherine J. Horwich scholar, 1990, Weisman Meml. scholar, 1990; grantee Internat. Friends of Transformative Art, 1992. Democrat. Jewish. Office: Fern Shaffer Studio 1524 S Peoria Chicago IL 60608

SHAFFER, GAIL S., state government official; b. Kingston, N.Y., Aug. 1, 1948; d. Robert E. and Marion (Gallagher) S. BA summa cum laude, Elmira Coll., 1970; student, U. Paris, 1968-69. Editor Sam Har Press, 1972-76; legal asst. Rahmas Law Firm, 1973-76; spl. asst. to commr. N.Y. State Environ. Conservation, 1977-79; exec. dir. N.Y. State Rural Affairs Council, 1979-80; mem. N.Y. State Assembly, 1981-83; sec. state State of N.Y., Albany, 1983—. Mem. N.Y. State Dem. Com., 1976—; chair Yonkers Emergency Fin. Control Bd., 1985—. Mem. Women Execs. in State Govt., N.Y. State Assn. Women Officeholders (pres.). Presbyterian. Office: Sec of State NY 162 Washington Ave Albany NY 12210-2304

SHAFFER, JILL, clinical psychologist; b. Columbus, Ohio, May 18, 1958; d. Melvin Warren and Emily (White) S.; m. Robert K. Yost, Jan. 9, 1991; 1 child, Melanie Jill. BS in Psychology with honors, Wright State U., 1984, PsyD, 1988. Lic. psychologist, Ohio. Psychology talk show producer/participant Sta. WHIO-AM, Dayton, Ohio, 1981-83; psychology asst. and organizer Terrap S.W. Ohio, Dayton, 1981-83; psychology trainee Oakwood Forensic Ctr., Lima, Ohio, 1984-85, Wright State U., Dayton, 1984-87; predoctoral resident South Community Mental Health Ctr., Dayton, 1987-88; postdoctoral trainee Fulero and Assoc., Dayton, 1988-89; pvt. practice Dayton, 1989—; supervising psychologist GERI-Tech of Dayton, 1990-92; cons. psychologist disability evaluations for worker's compensation and social security disability, 1989-94; state examiner Indsl. Commn. of Ohio, 1989—; owner, mgr. rental properties, 1988—. Author: (article) Strategic Intervention with Transvestism, 1989. Recipient scholarship Sch. of Profl. Psychology, 1985. Mem. APA, NOW, Ohio Psychol. Assn., Dayton Area Psychol. Assn. Office: 2705 Far Hills Ave Ste 4 Dayton OH 45419-1606

SHAFFER, JULIET POPPER, statistics educator; b. N.Y.C., May 23, 1932; d. Abraham Louis and Harriet Estelle (Marcus) P.; m. Harry George Shaffer, Aug. 11, 1960 (div. May 1975); children: Ronald Eric, Leonard Joseph, Tanya Elaine; m. Erich Leo Lehmann, Feb. 24, 1977. BA in Psychology, Swarthmore Coll., 1953; PhD in Psychology, Stanford U., 1957. NSF postdoctoral rsch. fellow Ind. U., 1957-58; asst. prof. U. Kans., Lawrence, 1958-65, assoc. prof., 1965-74, prof., 1974-77; lectr. stats. U. Calif., Berkeley, 1977-81, sr. lectr., 1981—; vis. scholar U. Calif., Berkeley, 1973-74, vis. prof. stats., 1976-77, initiator, faculty supr. statis. cons. svc., 1977; vis. lectr. psychology U. Munich, winter 1964-65; vis. prof. math. U. Calif., Davis, 1975-76; chairperson bd. to devel. affirmative action plan U. Kans., 1972; mem. vis. panel on rsch. Ednl. Testing Svc., 1987-89; apptd. design and analysis com. Nat. Assessment Ednl. Progress, 1991—; apptd. dept. stats. vis. com. Harvard U., 1993—; cons. in field. Stats. editor Computer Studies in Humanities and Verbal Behavior, 1970-74; assoc. editor Jour. Ednl. Stats., 1980-85, 90—, editor, 1986-89; assoc. editor Psychometrika, 1983-85; contbr. articles to profl. jours. NSF-Am. Statis. Assn. fellow Nat. Ctr. for Edn. Stats., 1993. Fellow AAAS (mem. electorate nominating com. stats. sect. 1992—), Am. Statis. Assn. (rep. social stats. sect. at winter conf. 1989, bd. dirs. 1984-86, apptd. coom. on women in stats. 1991-93, 94—, apptd. com. on fellows 1991—, chair 1995), Am. Psychol. Soc.; mem. Psychometric Soc. (mem. bd. trustees 1982-84, 92—, mem. editl. coun. 1993—, chair 1994—), Caucus for Women in Stats. (rep.-at-large 1988-90, pres. 1994), Inst. Math. Stats. (apptd. nominations com. 1991-92). Office: Univ Calif Dept Stats Berkeley CA 94720

SHAFFER, KAREN ELIZABETH, urban planning assistant director; b. Pensicola, Fla., July 18, 1964; d. Carl Kristian and Linda Rae (McNew) Hansen; m. John E. Shaffer, Oct. 9, 1993. BA in Urban Affairs, Va. Poly. Inst. and State U., 1986. Asst. planner County of James City, Williamsburg, Va., 1987; planner City of Chesapeake, Va., 1987-91, planner II, 1991-92, asst. planning dir., 1992—. Mem. Am. Planning Assn. Office: City of Chesapeake Planning Dept PO Box 15225 Chesapeake VA 23328

SHAFFER, MARGARET MINOR, library director; b. New Orleans, Sept. 20, 1940; d. Milhado Lee and Margaret Minor (Krumbhaar) S. BS, Nicholls State U., Thibodaux, La., 1962; MLS, La. State U., 1965. Asst. dir. Terrebonne Parish Pub. Libr., Houma, La., 1965-72, dir., 1973—. Named Woman of Yr., Houma Bus. and Profl. Women's Club, 1981. Mem. ALA, La. Libr. Assn. (chmn. pub. libr. com. 1986-87), Southeastern Libr. Assn. Democrat. Episcopalian. Home: 1726 Hwy 311 Schriever LA 70395 Office: Terrebonne Parish Pub Libr 424 Roussel St Houma LA 70360-4552

SHAFFER, ROBERTA IVY, law librarian; b. Oceanside, N.Y., Nov. 27, 1953; d. Joseph Ceicel and Gladys (Dellerson) Shaffer. AB in Econs., Vassar Coll., 1973; M of Librarianship, Emory U., 1975; JD, Tulane U., 1980; cert. in arts mgmt., Am. U., 1987. Bar: Tex. 1982, U.S. Dist. Ct. (so. dist.) Tex., U.S. Ct. Appeals (5th cir.), U.S. Supreme Ct. Dir. legal communications U. Houston Law Ctr., 1980-84, assoc. dir. law and tech., 1982-84; spl. asst. to law libr. Libr. of Congress, Washington, 1984-87; Fulbright sr. researcher Tel Aviv Faculty Law, 1987-88; pvt. practice cons. Washington, 1988-89; dir. devel. Washington Project for the Arts, 1989; acting libr. dir. George Washington U. Law Ctr., Washington, 1990; asst. dean U. Washington, Seattle, 1990-91; dir. libr. svcs. Covington & Burling, Washington, 1991—; cons. Coca-Cola Co., Atlanta, 1975-76, Research Info. Service, Houston, 1982-84; edn. rep. Westlaw, St. Paul, 1982-83. Bd. dirs. Friends of Torpedo Factory Arts Ctr. Mem. ABA, Am. Assn. Law Librs., Internat. Assn. Law Librs. (sec. 1992—). Home: 4909 Crescent St Bethesda MD 20816 Office: Covington & Burling 1201 Pennsylvania Ave NW Washington DC 20004-2401

SHAFNER, JANET, artist, museum official; b. N.Y.C., Aug. 30, 1931; d. Herman and Sonia (Glantz) Schreier; m. Sholom Shafner, June 8, 1952; children: Samuel, David, Jonathan, Hyim. BA, Barnard Coll., 1953; MA, Conn. Coll., 1975. Lectr. U. Conn., Groton, 1970, Mohegan C.C., Norwich, Conn., 1971-77; vis. asst. prof. Conn. Coll., New London, 1972-79; dir., coord. adult student art program Lyman Allyn Art Mus., New London, 1968—, curator, 1988, 89. One-woman shows include Lyman Allyn Art Mus., 1981, retrospective, 1989, Housatonic Mus. Art, Bridgeport, Conn., 1981, Hoxie Gallery, Westerly, R.I., 1994; exhibited in numerous groups, including Slater Mus., Norwich, Conn., 1981, 90, 93, 94, Lyman Allyn Art Mus., 1984, 88, 89, 91, 94, Silvermine Guild, New Canaan, Conn., 1986, Yeshiva U. Mus., N.Y.C. (also travelling to 5 cities in U.S. and Can., 1994-96), 1993-94, U.S. and Can. 1994—; represented in permanent collections Slater Mus., Mus. Fine Arts, Springfield, Mass., Housatonic Mus. Art, Lyman Allyn Mus. Fine Art, also others. Yaddo fellow, Saratoga Springs, N.Y., 1977; grantee Falk Found. for Creative Excellence, 1986, Meml. Found. for Jewish Culture, 1990. Mem. Conn. Acad. Fine Arts. Home: 40 Glenwood Pl New London CT 06320-2907 Office: Lyman Allyn Art Mus 625 Williams St New London CT 06320-4199

SHAHEEN, C. JEANNE, state legislator; b. St. Charles, Mo., Jan. 28, 1947; m. William H. Shaheen; 3 children. BA, Shippensburg U., 1969; MSS, U. Miss., 1973. Mem. N.H. Senate. Democrat. Protestant. Office: NH State Senate State Capital Concord NH 03301*

SHAHEEN, LISA, public relations consultant; b. Methuen, Mass., Nov. 4, 1963; d. Mansour James and Carmelina Bernadette (Pennisi) S. BS, Providence Coll., 1985. Sales rep. NCR, Hartford, Conn., 1985-86; v.p. Add-On-Data, Boston, 1986-88; pub. rels. cons. Brucado Comms., Boston, 1988—; dir. pub. rels. BDO Seidman, Boston, 1988-89; R&D assoc. Am. Bankers Ins., Miami, Fla., 1989-91; account exec. J. Berg Creative Group, Miami, 1991; account mgr. Kreps & Adams, Miami, 1991-94; supr. Rubin Barney & Birger, Miami, 1994—. Bd. dirs. Bus. Vols. for the Arts, Miami, 1993-94, New Directions of Am. Cancer Soc., Miami, 1993-94. Mem. Am. Mktg. Assn. (bd. dirs., v.p. comm. 1992-93), Greater Miami C. of C. (mem. mktg. com., co-chair com. recognition com. 1993-94).

SHAHZADE, ANN MARY, retired speech and language pathologist; b. Arlington, Mass., Jan. 25, 1928; d. Nazar Michael and Mary (Israelian) Skenian; m. Herbert Sarkis Shahzade, Aug. 28, 1955 (div.); children: Joyce, John, David, Edward. AB, Emerson Coll., 1949, MA, 1950; postgrad., Boston U., 1952-72. Speech pathologist Lynn (Mass.) Pub. Schs., 1949-56, Somerville (Mass.) Sch. Dept., 1957-58, Cambridge (Mass.) Sch. Dept., 1969-74; co-founder speech clinic Children's Hosp., Boston, 1952-57; asst. dir. Inst. for Speech Correction, Boston, 1949-59; dir. speech and lang. dept. Cambridge Pub. Schs., 1974-89, ret., 1989; instr. pub. speaking John Roberts Powers Sch., Boston, 1950-55; speech pathology cons. to pediatricians, Arlington, 1949-60; pvt. practice, Boston, 1957-69. Author: Oral Language Development, 1982, also kindergarten screening test. Mem. NEA, Mass. Tchrs. Assn., Cambridge Tchrs. Assn. (Disting. Svc. award 1989). Democrat. Mem. Armenian Apostolic Ch. Home: 60 Clear Pond Rd Falmouth MA 02540-2335

SHAINESS, NATALIE, psychiatrist, educator; b. N.Y.C., Dec. 2, 1915; d. Jack and Clara (Levy-Hart) S.; div.; children: David Spiegel, Ann Spiegel. BA in Chemistry, NYU, 1936; MD, Va. Commonwealth U., 1939. Diplomate in psychiatry; cert. in psychoanalysis. Pvt. practice N.Y.C., 1955—; faculty William Alanson White Inst. Psychiatry, Psychoanalysis, N.Y.C., 1961-81; asst. clin. prof. psychiatry N.Y. Sch. Psychiatry, N.Y.C., 1964-67; faculty med. edn. div. N.Y. Acad. Medicine, 1966-67; lectr. psychiatry Columbia U. Coll. Physicians and Surgeons, N.Y.C., 1966-80; faculty, supervising analyst L.I. Inst. Psychoanalysis, N.Y., 1980—; invited participant 1st and 2nd Internat. Conf. on Abortion, 1967, 68; research project on menstruation. Editorial bd. Jour. of the Am. Women's Med. Assn., 1985—; author: Sweet Suffering: Woman as Victim, 1984; contbr. over 100 articles to profl. jours. and over 90 profl. book revs. Mem. Physicians for Social Responsibility, Nuclear Freeze, several other anti-nuclear orgns. Fellow Am. Acad. Psychoanalysis (former trustee, organizer several panels), Am. Psychiat. Assn. (life mem.; organizer several panels), N.Y. Acad. Medicine (hon.), Soc. Med. Psychoanalysts (honored for keen erudition, lively imagination and professionalism 1993, councillor); mem. Assn. for Advancement of Psychotherapy, Women's Med. Assn. N.Y.C. (fin. assistance com., 1st Pres.'s award 1990). Home and Office: 140 E 83rd St New York NY 10028-1924

SHALACK, JOAN HELEN, psychiatrist; b. Jersery City, Mar. 6, 1932; d. Edward William and Adele Helen (Karski) S.; m. Jerome Abraham Sheill. Student, Farleigh Dickinson U., 1950-51; BA cum laude, NYU, 1954; MD, Women's Med. Coll. Pa., 1958. Intern Akron (Ohio) Gen. Hosp., 1958-59; resident in psychiatry Camarillo (Calif.) State Hosp., 1959-62; resident in phsychiatry UCLA Neuropsychiat. Inst., 1962, U. So. Calif., L.A., 1963; pvt. practice Beverly Hills, Calif., 1963-83, Century City L.A., Calif., 1983-86, Pasadena, Calif., 1986—; pres., chair bd. dirs. Totizo Inc., Beverly Hills, 1969-71; mem. staff Westwood Hosp., 1970-75. Mem. AMA, Calif. Med. Assn., L.A. County Med. Assn., Physicians for Social Responsibility, Phi Beta Kappa, Mu Chi Sigma. Home and Office: 1405 Afton St Pasadena CA 91103-2703

SHALALA, DONNA EDNA, federal official, political scientist, educator, university chancellor; b. Cleve., Feb. 14, 1941; d. James Abraham and Edna (Smith) S. AB, Western Coll., 1962; MSSC, Syracuse U., 1968, PhD, 1970; 16 hon degrees, 1981-91. Vol. Peace Corps, Iran, 1962-64; asst. to dir. met. studies program Syracuse U., 1965-69; instr. asst. to dean Syracuse U. (Maxwell Grad. Sch.), 1969-70; asst. prof. polit. sci. CUNY, 1970-72; assoc. prof. politics and edn. Tchrs. Coll. Columbia U., 1972-79; asst. sec. for policy devel. and research HUD, Washington, 1977-80; prof. polit. sci., pres. Hunter Coll., CUNY, 1980-88; prof. polit. sci., chancellor U. Wis., Madison, 1988-93; Sec. Dept. of Health and Human Services, Washington, 1993—. Author: Neighborhood Governance, 1971, The City and the Constitution, 1972, The Property Tax and the Voters, 1973, The Decentralization Approach, 1974. Bd. govs. Am. Stock Exch., 1981-87; trustee TIAA, 1985-89, Com. Econ. Devel., 1981-93; bd. dirs. Inst. Internat. Econs., 1981-93, Children's Def. Fund, 1980-93, Am. Ditchley Found., 1981-93, Spencer Found., 1988-93, M&I Bank of Madison, 1991-93, NCAA Found., 1991; mem. Trilateral Commn., 1988-93, Knight Commn. on Intercollegiate Sports, 1990-93; trustee Brookings Inst., 1989-93. Ohio Newspaper Women's scholar, 1958, Western Coll. Trustee scholar, 1958-62; Carnegie fellow, 1966-68; Nat. Acad. Edn. Spencer fellow, 1972-73; Guggenheim fellow, 1975-76; recipient Disting. Svc. medal Columbia U. Tchrs. Coll., 1989. Mem. Am. Polit. Sci. Assn., Am. Soc. Pub. Adminstrn., Nat. Acad. Pub. Adminstrn., Coun. Fgn. Rels., Nat. Acad. Edn. Office: Dept Health and Human Svcs Office of Sec 200 Independence Ave SW Rm 615F Washington DC 20201-0004

SHALHOUP, JUDY LYNN, marketing communications executive; b. Charleston, W.Va., Oct. 25, 1940; s. George Ferris and Mary Margaret (Moses) S.; BA, Morris Harvey Coll., Charleston, 1967; MS, W.Va. U., 1970. With Union Carbide Corp., 1960-92, publicity mgr. plastics, N.Y.C., 1971-73, coatings materials div. advt. mgr., 1973-82, mgr. mktg. comm. splty. chems. div., 1982-85; mgr. mktg. comm., solvents and coatings materials div., 1982-92; pres. GMJC Assocs., 1992—. v.p., gen. mgr. Fruit Bowl, Charleston, 1975-78. Recipient Best Teller award Bus. Profl. Advt. Assn., 1978-84, 86-87, Pro-Com. award, 1991, Excellence in Bus.-to-Bus. Advt. award, 1989, Objectives and Results Advt. award Am. Bus. Press, 1978, Clio Advt. Recognition award, 1978-86, Clio award, 1984, Andy award, 1983, 84, Nutmegger award, 1985 . Mem. Telefood Assn., Internat. Platform Assn., Assn. Nat. Advt., Inc., SSPC, AAAS, Nat. Paint and Coatings Assn. (comm. com.), Fedn. Socs. Coatings Tech., Bus. Profl. Advt. Assn. (Star awards for excellence 1989-90, Procom award 1990).

SHALLCROSS, DORIS JANE, creative behavioral educator; b. Cranford, N.J., Feb. 28, 1933; d. John William and Ethel Belle (Ruth) S. BA, Montclair State Coll., 1955; MA, Wesleyan U., Middletown, Conn., 1962; EdD, U. Mass., 1973. Tchr. Hunterdon Cen. High Sch., Flemington, N.J., 1955-61, Roosevelt Jr. High Sch., Cleveland Heights, Ohio, 1961-65, Cleveland Heights H.S., 1965-67; adminstr. Cleveland Heights Pub. Schs., 1967-69; dir. humanistic edn. Montague (Mass.) Pub. Schs., 1972-75; program devel. specialist Tchr. Corps., SUNY, Oneonta, N.Y., 1976-78; asst. prof. edn. divsn. home econs. U. Mass., Amherst, 1978-82, prof., dir. grad. studies in creativity, 1982—; pres. bd. trustees Creative Edn. Found., Buffalo, 1989-94; co-dir. Global Odyssey, 1992—; bd. dirs. Ctr. for Critical and Creative Thinking, Hartford, Conn., 1989-92. Author: Teaching Creative Behavior, 1981; co-author: The Growing Person, 1985, Leadership: Making Things

Happen, 1987, Intuition: An Inner Way of Knowing, 1989; cons. editor Jour. Creative Behavior, 1967—; contbr. articles to profl. jours. Mem. Planning Bd., Town of Williamsburg, 1981-89. Recipient Disting. Leader award, Creative Edn. Found., 1986; grantee, NSF, 1987-89, U. Mass., 1987-89. Mem. NEA, Mass. Soc. of Profs., Assn. for Transpersonal Psychology, Inst. for Noetic Scis., World Coun. for Gifted Chidlren, Am. Creativity Assn. (bd. dirs. 1990-93). Home: 26 S Main St Haydenville MA 01039-9735 Office: U Mass 361 Hills S Amherst MA 01003

SHAMASH, ANN R., craftsperson; b. Bklyn., Aug. 23, 1945; d. William and Rose (Albert) Shulman; m. Maurice Baruch Shamash, Jan. 29, 1967; children: Elizabeth M., Brian B. BA in Fine Arts, Hofstra U., 1967; M Art Edn., Towson (Md.) State U., 1973. Cert. tchr., Md. Tchr. art Ann Arundel County (Md.) Schs., 1967-70, Baltimore County (Md.) Schs., 1970-71, 90; tchr. Jewish Cmty. Ctr., Balt., 1972-78; instr. art Catonsville C.C., Balt., 1983-90; owner, mgr. Ann Shamash, Creative Clay Concepts, Owings Mills, Md., 1971—. Prodr. video The Edge in the Artists and Craftsman's Market Place: Tibbles, Tips, and Tricks, 1994. Pres. Orgn. for Rehab. through Tng., Balt., 1972-78; mem. Child Study, Balt., 1972-78. Mem. Toastmasters. Jewish. Home and Office: 24 Pinewood Farm Ct Owings Mills MD 21117

SHANAFELT, NANCY SUE, organizational development specialist, career counselor; b. Northampton, Mass., Nov. 21, 1947; m. John D. Shanafelt; children: Amy, Nicholas. BS, U. Mass., 1969; MA in Human Resources/Orgnl. Devel., U. San Francisco, 1991. Tchr. Southwick (Mass.) Pub. Schs., 1969-70; acctg. asst. Maricopa County Schs., Phoenix, Ariz., 1973-74; tax auditor to br. chief IRS, San Jose, 1974-89; enrolled agt., 1984-85; OD specialist IRS, Phoenix, 1991-93; creator IRS Women's Network, San Francisco, 1981—. Leader Girl Scouts U.S., Santa Clara, 1980-81, cons., 1981-82, svc. mgr., 1982-84, trainer, 1982-84; leader Boy Scouts Am., 1992; facilitator Unwed Parents Anonymous, 1992—; master catechist Diocese of San Jose, 1992—. Recipient Disting. Performance award IRS, 1993. Mem. AAUW, NAFE, ASTD, Federally Employed Women, Commonwealth Club Am., Italian Cath. Fedn. (sec. 1991—), Bay Area Orgnl. Devel. Network, Medugorje PGL. Office: IRS 55 S Market St Ste 812 San Jose CA 95113-2326

SHANAHAN, EILEEN F., internal auditor; b. Darby, Pa., May 11, 1965; d. William F. and Sandra L. (Sloan) S. BS in Acctg./Econs., West Chester (Pa.) U., 1987; postgrad., U. Pa. CPA, Pa. Staff acct. Wyeth-Ayerst Internat. Inc., Radnor, Pa., 1988; semi-sr. auditor Fishbein & Co., P.C., Elkins Park, Pa., 1989-92; internal auditor The Devereux Found., Devon, Pa., 1992-94; sr. auditor U. Pa. Health System, Phila., 1995—. Mem. AICPA, ASTD (svcs. com. Phila. chpt.), Phila. Region Orgns. Devel. Network (fin. head), Inst. Internal Auditors, Pa. Inst. CPAs.

SHANAHAN, EILEEN FRANCES, secondary education educator; b. Bethlehem, Pa., Sept. 10, 1949; d. Edward Vincent and Geraldine Mary (Gilligan) S. BA, Moravian Coll., 1971. Cert. secondary tchr. in Spanish, English, N.J. Tchr. Kingsway Regional High Sch. Dist., Swedesboro, N.J., 1971—. Mem. NEA, N.J. Edn. Assn., Gloucester County Edn. Assn., Fgn. Lang. Educators N.J., Kingsway Edn. Assn. (sec. membership), Hellertown Hist. Soc. Democrat. Roman Catholic.

SHANAHAN, ELIZABETH ANNE, art educator; b. High Point, N.C., Apr. 5, 1950; d. Joe Thomas and Nancy Elizabeth (Moran) Gibson; m. Robert James Shanahan, Aug. 31, 1969 (div. Mar. 1987); children: Kimberly Marie Shanahan Stanley, Brigette Susanne. Student, Forsyth Tech. Coll., 1974-83, Tri-County Tech. Coll., 1989, Inst. of Children's Lit., 1989. Owner cleaning bus. Winston-Salem, N.C., 1985-86, 87; instr. Anderson (S.C.) Arts Coun., 1987—, Tri-County Tech. Coll., Pendleton, S.C., 1987—. Artist Wild Geese, 1985 (Best in Show). Active Libr. of Congress, 1994. Mem. Anderson Art Assn. (con. 1987—), Met. Arts Coun. (Upstate Visual Arts divsn.), Triad Art Assn. (pres. Kernersville, N.C. chpt. 1984-85), Nat. Mus. Women in Arts (charter), Libr. of Congress (charter). Home: 7 Woodbridge Ct Anderson SC 29621-2260 Office: Tri County Tech Coll PO Box 587 Pendleton SC 29670-0587

SHANAHAN, TERESA ANN, therapist; b. Scotia, Calif., Nov. 23, 1955; d. Laurence and Katherine (Nansel) S. BA, San Diego State U., 1981, MS in Counseling, 1983; postgrad., U. Humanistic Studies, 1989—. Cert. fitness instr., health mgmt. Therapeutic recreation specialist Grossmont Hosp., La Mesa, Calif., 1980-85, Sharp Cabrillo Hosp., San Diego, 1984-89; owner, founder, operator Lifeline Healthcare, San Diego, 1986-; cons. to skilled nursing therapy and case mgmt. to geriatric population facilities, San Diego, 1982—; fitness instr. San Diego Community Coll., 1984-86; lectr., educator in field. Columnist Calendar Mag., 1986-89. Chmn. San Diego Stroke Club Facilitators, Am. Heart Assn., 1987-89; mem. spl. events com.; parade announcer La Jolla (Calif.) Town Coun., 1987—. Mem. Am. Therapeutic Recreation Assn., Toastmasters (pres. La Jolla chpt. 1985—, Best Serious Speaker award 1987). Home: 4914 Lamont St San Diego CA 92109-1403

SHANAS, ETHEL, sociology educator; b. Chgo., Sept. 6, 1914; d. Alex and Rebecca (Rich) S.; m. Lester J. Perlman, May 17, 1940; 1 child, Michael Stephen. AB, U. Chgo., 1935, AM, 1937, PhD, 1949; LHD (hon.), Hunter Coll., N.Y.C., 1985. Instr. human devel. U. Chgo., 1947-52, rsch. assoc. prof., 1961-65; sr. rsch. analyst City of Chgo., 1952-53; sr. study dir. Nat. Opinion Rsch. Ctr., Chgo., 1956-61; prof. sociology U. Ill., Chgo., 1965-82, prof. emerita, 1982—; vice chmn. expert com. on aging UN, 1974; mem. com. on aging NRC, Washington, 1978-82, panel on statistics for an aging population, 1984-86; mem. U.S. Com. on Vital and Health Stats., Washington, 1976-79. Author: The Health of Older People, 1962; (with others) Old People in Three Industrial Societies, 1968; editor: (with others) Handbook of Aging and the Social Sciences, 1976, 2d edit., 1985. Bd. govs. Chgo. Heart Assn., 1972-80; mem. adv. council on aging City of Chgo., 1972-78. Keston lectr. U. So. Calif., 1975; recipient Burgess award Nat. Council on Family Relations, 1978; Disting. Chgo. Gerontologist award Assn. for Gerontology in Higher Edn., 1988. Fellow Gerontol. Soc. Am. (pres. 1974-75, Kleemeier award 1977, Brookdale award 1981), Am. Sociol. Assn. (chmn. sect. on aging 1985-86 Disting. Scholar award, 1987); mem. Midwest Sociol. Soc. (pres. 1980-81), Inst. Medicine of Nat. Acad. Scis. (sr. mem.). Home: 222 Main St Evanston IL 60202-2488 Office: U Ill Chgo Dept Sociology M/C 312 4112 Behavioral Sci Bldg Chicago IL 60607-7140

SHANE, BEVERLY JEAN, planning director; b. Kewanee, Ill., Jan. 12, 1956; d. Francis Edmund and Ardis Louise (Meeker) S.; m. John Joseph Maschi, June 30, 1979 (div. Apr. 1987). B of Landscape Architecture, U. Ill., 1978; MPA, Calif. State U., 1993. Landscape designer, crew foreman Smith Landscaping, 1977; landscape architect JMD Landscape Architects, 1978-79; draftsman Andrew Marshall Engring., 1979; landscape architect U.S. Forest Svc., 1980; sr. planner County of Tuolumne, 1980-87, asst. planning dir., 1988-93, planning dir., 1993—. Mem. Tuolumne County Friends of the Libr., Leadership Tuolumne County. Mem. AICP, Am. Planning Assn., Am. Soc. Landscape Architects, Tuolumne County Humane Soc. Home: 14209 Stanton Circle Sonora CA 95370 Office: Tuolumne County Planning Dept 2 South Green St Sonora CA 95310

SHANE, RITA, opera singer; b. N.Y.C.; d. Julius J. and Rebekah (Milner) S.; m. Daniel F. Tritter, June 22, 1958; 1 child, Michael Shane. BA, Barnard Coll., 1958; postgrad., Santa Fe Opera Apprentice Program, 1962-63, Hunter Opera Assn., 1962-64; pvt. study with, Beverly Peck Johnson, Elizabeth Schwartzkopf. Prof. voice Manhattan Sch. of Music, 1993—; prof. voice Eastman Sch. Music Rochester U., 1989—; pvt. teachng, N.Y.C., 1978—. Performer with numerous opera cos., including profl. debut, Chattanooga Opera, 1964, Met. Opera, San Francisco Opera, N.Y.C. Opera, Chgo. Lyric Opera, San Diego Opera, Santa Fe Opera, Teatro alla Scala, Milan, Italy, Bavarian State Opera, Netherlands Nat. Opera, Geneva Opera, Vienna State Opera, Phila., New Orleans, Balt. Opera, Opera du Rhin, Strasbourg, Scottish Opera, Teatro Reggio, Turin, Opera Metropolitana, Caracas, Portland Opera, Minn. Opera, also others; world premiere Miss Havisham's Fire, Argento; Am. premieres include Reimann-Lear, Schat-Houdini, Henze-Elegy for Young Lovers; participant festivals, including Mozart Festival, Lincoln Center, N.Y.C., Munich Festival, Aspen Festival, Handel Soc., Vienna Festival, Salzburg Festival, Munich Festival, Perugia Festival, Festival Canada, Glyndebourne Festival, performed with orchs. including Santa Cecilia, Rome, Austrian Radio, London Philharmn., Louisville, Cin., Cleve., Phila., RAI, Naples, Denver, Milw., Israel Philharm.; rec. artist, RCA, Columbia, Louisville, Turnabout labels, also radio and TV. Recipient Martha Baird Rockefeller award, William Matheus Sullivan award. Mem. Am. Guild Mus. Artists, Screen Actors Guild. Office: care Daniel F Tritter 545 5th Ave New York NY 10017-3609

SHANE, SANDRA KULI, postal service administrator; b. Akron, Ohio, Dec. 12, 1939; d. Amiel M. and Margaret E. (Brady) Kuli; m. Fred Shane, May 30, 1962 (div. 1972); 1 child, Mark Richard; m. Byrl William Campbell, Apr. 26, 1981 (dec. 1984). BA, U. Akron, 1987, postgrad., 1988-90. Scheduler motor vehicle bur. Akron Police Dept., 1959-62; flight and ops. control staff Escort Air, Inc., Akron and Cleve., 1972-78; asst. traffic mgr. Keen Transport, Inc., Hudson, Ohio, 1978-83; mem. ops. and mktg. staff Shawnee Airways and Essco, Akron, 1983-86; in distbn. U.S. Postal Svc., Akron, 1986—; rec. sec. Affirmative Action Coun., Akron, 1988-90. Asst. art tchr. Akron Art Mus., 1979; counselor Support, Inc., Akron, 1983-84; com. chmn. Explorer post Boy Scouts Am., Akron, 1984-85. Mem. Bus. and Profl. Women's Assn. (pres.), Delta Nu Alpha. Democrat. Roman Catholic. Home: 455 E Bath Rd Cuyahoga Falls OH 44223-2511

SHANGE, NTOZAKE (PAULETTE WILLIAMS), playwright, poet; b. Trenton, N.J., Oct. 18, 1948; d. Paul T. and Eloise Williams; m. David Murray, July 4, 1977 (div.); 1 child: Savannah. BA in Am. Studies cum laude, Barnard Coll., 1970; MA in Am. Studies, U. So. Calif., 1973. mem. faculty Sonoma State U., 1973-75, Mills Coll., 1975, CCNY, 1975, Douglass Coll., 1978; lectr. in field. Author: (plays) for colored girls who have considered suicide/when the rainbow is enuf, 1975 (Obie award for best play 1977, Outer Critics Circle award for best play 1977, Audelco award 1977, Tony award nomination for best play 1977, Grammy award nomination for best spoken word rec. 1977), Melissa and Smith, 1976, A Photograph: A Study of Cruelty, 1977, (with Thulani Nkabinde and Jessica Hagedorn) Where the Mississippi Meets the Amazon, 1977, Boogie Woogie Landscapes, 1978, From Okra to Greens, 1978, Spell #7: A Geechee Quick Magic Trance Manual, 1979, Black and White Two Dimensional Planes, 1979, Mouths, 1981, A Photograph: Lovers in Motion, 1981, Three For a Full Moon, 1982, Bocas, 1982, Three Views of Mt. Fuji, 1987; (adaptations) Mother Courage and Her Children (Brecht), 1980 (Obie award for best play 1981), Educating Rita, 1982; (operetta) Carrie, 1981; (novels) Sassafrass, 1976, Sassafrass, Cypress and Indigo, 1982, Betsey Brown, 1985, Liliana: Resurrection of the Daughter, 1994; (poems) Natural Disasters and Other Festive Occasions, 1977, Nappy Edges, 1978, Three Pieces, 1981 (L.A. Book prize for poetry 1981), A Daughter's Geography, 1983, From Okra to Greens, 1984, The Love Space Demands, 1991, I Live in Music, 1994; (non-fiction) See No Evil: Prefaces, Essays and Accounts 1976-1983, 1984, Ridin' the Moon in Texas: Word Paintings, 1987; contbr. poetry, essays and short stories to numerous mags. and anthologies, including Third World Women, Chgo. Rev., Am. Rag, Sojourner, Womansports; actress: For Colored Girls Who Have Considered Suicide/When the Rainbow is Enuf, 1976, Where the Mississippi Meets the Amazon, 1977; dir.: The Mighty Gents, 1979, A Photograph: A Study in Cruelty, 1979, The Issue, 1979, The Spirit of Sojourner Truth, 1979; writer: An Evening with Diana Ross: The Big Event, 1977 (Emmy award nomination 1977); performing mem.: Sounds in Motion Dance Co.; performed in various jazz/poetry collaborations; dancer with Third World Collective, Raymond Sawyer's Afro-American Dance Co., Sound in Motion, West Coast Dance Works; founder, dancer For Colored Girls Who Have Considered Suicide. Recipient Frank Silvera Writer's Workshop award, 1978, Excellence medal Columbia U., 1981, Taos World Poetry Heavyweight Champion, 1992, 93, 94; NDEA fellow, 1973, Guggenheim fellow, 1981. Mem. Actors Equity, Nat. Acad. TV Arts and Scis., Acad. Am. Poets, Dramatist's Guild, PEN Am Center, Poets and Writer's, Inc., N.Y. Feminist Art Guild. Office: care St Martins Press 175 Fifth Ave New York NY 10010*

SHANK, CLARE BROWN WILLIAMS, political leader; b. Syracuse, N.Y., Sept. 19, 1909; d. Curtiss Crofoot and Clara Irene (Shoudy) Brown; m. Frank E. Williams, Feb. 18, 1940 (dec. Feb. 1957); m. Seth Carl Shank, Dec. 28, 1963 (dec. Jan. 1977). B in Oral English, Syracuse U., 1931. Tchr., 1931-33, merchandising exec., 1933-42; Pinellas County mem. Rep. State Com., 1954-58; life mem. Pinellas County Rep. Exec. Com.; exec. com. Fla. Rep. Com., 1954-64; Fla. committeewoman Rep. Nat. Com., 1956-64, mem. exec. com., 1956-64, asst. chmn. and dir. women's activities, 1956-58; alt., mem. exec. arrangements com., major speaker Rep. Nat. Conv., Chgo., 1960; alt., program and arrangement coms. Rep. Nat. Conv., 1964. Pres. St. Petersburg Women's Rep. Club, 1955-57; Mem. Def. Adv. Com. on Women in Services, 1959-65; trustee St. Petersburg Housing Authority, 1976-81. Recipient George Arents medal Syracuse U., 1959; citation for patriotic civilian service 5th U.S. Army and Dept. Def.; 1st woman to preside over any part of nat. polit. conv., Rep. Nat. Conv., Chgo., 1960. Mem. AAUW, DAR, Gen. Fedn. Women's Clubs, Colonial Dames 17th Century, Fla. Fedn. Women's Clubs (dist. pres. 1976-78), Women's Club (St. Petersburg, pres. 1974-76, Yacht Club, Lakewood Country Club (St. Petersburg). Methodist. Home: 939 Beach Dr NE Apt 409 Saint Petersburg FL 33701-2009

SHANK, SUZANNE ADAMS, lawyer; b. Kansas City, Mo., Nov. 13, 1946; d. Howard Howe and Bettie Ann (Winkler) Hettick; m. Martin Smoler, May 18, 1991. BJ, U. Mo., 1972; MPA in Health Adminstrn., U. Mo.-Kansas City, 1982, JD, 1982. Bar: Mo. 1982, U.S. Dist. Ct. (we. dist.) Mo. 1982. Journalist, U. Kans. Med. Ctr., Kansas City, 1972-73; asst. editor Am. Family Physician, Kansas City, Mo., 1973-75; exec. dir. Lambert Med. Clinic, Kansas City, Mo., 1975-80; assoc. firm Shughart, Thomson & Kilroy, Kansas City, 1982-85; second v.p. GE/Employers Reins Corp., Overland Park, Kans., 1985—. Mem. Friends of Zoo, Kansas City., Mo., 1981—, Menorah Med. Ctr. Aux., Kansas City., 1982—, Harvesters, Kansas City, Mo., 1989—. Mem. ABA, Am. Soc. Hosp. Attys., Mo. Soc. Hosp. Attys., Mo. Bar Assn., Kansas City Bar Assn. (chmn. hosp. law com.), Am. Soc. Hosp. Risk Mgrs. (mem. risk financing com.), Nat. Health Lawyers Assn., Kappa Tau Alpha. Office: Employers Reins Corp PO Box 2991 Shawnee Mission KS 66201-1391

SHANKS, ANN ZANE, filmmaker, photographer, writer; b. N.Y.C.; d. Louis and Sadye (Rosenthal) Kushner; m. Ira Zane (dec.); children—Jennifer, Anthony; m. Robert Horton Shanks, Sept. 25, 1959; 1 child, John. Student, Carnegie-Mellon U., Columbia U., 1949. tchr., moderator spl. symposiums Mus. Modern Art, N.Y.C.; tchr. New Sch. for Social Research. Photographer, writer for numerous mags. and newspapers; producer, dir.: (movie shorts) Central Park, 1969 (U.S. entry Edinburgh Film Festival, Cine Golden Eagle award, Cambodia Film Festival award), Denmark... A Loving Embrace (Cine Golden Eagle award 1973), Tivoli, 1972-79 (San Francisco Film Festival award, Am. Film Festival award), (TV series) American Life Style (Silver award, 5 Gold medal awards Internat. TV and Film Festival N.Y., 2 Cine Golden Eagle awards), He's Fired, She's Hired; producer CBS TV Drop-Out Mother; producer, dir., writer (TV short) Mousie Baby; dir. (TV movie) Friendships, Secrets and Lies, NBC; producer: (TV movie) Drop-out Father, CBS, (video spl.) The Avant-Garde in Russia 1910-1930, Arts and Entertainment channel, ABC Morning Show, Good Afternoon Detroit; producer, dir. (TV spl.) A Day in the Country, PBS, (Emmy award nomination); producer, dir. play S.J. Perelman in Person; producer Broadway play, Lillian; exhibited photographs Mus. Modern Art, Mus. City N.Y., Met. Mus. Art, Jewish Mus.; author: (photographs and text) The Name's the Game, New Jewish Ency; author, photographer, writer Old Is What You Get, Busted Lives...Dialogues with Kids in Jail, 1983; writer, photographer Garbage and Stuff. Recipient awards from internat. competitions. Mem. Am. Soc. Mag. Photographers (bd. govs.), Overseas Press Club Am., Women in Film (v.p.), Dirs. Guild Am.

SHANKS, ARDIS MAUREEN, artist; b. Tahlequah, Okla., May 28, 1932; d. John Oscar and Berniece (Scott) S.; m. David L. Settle, Feb. 9, 1952 (div. 1969); children: Linda Speck, Scott Settle, Philip Settle, Sara Beth Settle. Student, Moore Coll., Phila., U. Mich., Malden Bridge Sch. Art; pvt. study with J. Nelson Shanks. VIP press photographer JCNS News Svc., 1970-80; artist pvt. classes, Houston, 1968-78, Layety Lodge HEB Found., Hill County, Tex., 1982—. Doll maker under contract with House of Hatten; exhibited in group show at Internat. Doll Expo, Dallas, 1994, 95, Idex, Washington, 1994; various portrait commns. Home: 123 Shalako Kerrville TX 78028

SHANKS, JUDITH WEIL, editor; b. Montgomery, Ala., Nov. 2, 1941; d. Roman Lee and Charlotte (Alexander) Weil; m. Hershel Shanks, Feb. 20, 1966; children: Elizabeth Jeannette, Julia Emily. BA in Econs., Wellesley Coll., 1963; MBA, Trinity Coll., 1980. Econs. asst. Export-Import Bank, Washington, 1963-68; cons. econs. and social sci., 1968-76; researcher Time-Life Books, Alexandria, Va., 1976-80, prin. researcher, 1980-83, illustrations editor, 1983, adminstrv. editor, 1984—. Vol. dinner program for homeless women; bd. dirs. Anne Frank House, for formerly homeless women. Mem. Garden Writers Am., Internat. Alliance, Washington Alliance Bus. Women, Leadership Greater Washington, Washington Wellesley Club (career caucus). Democrat. Jewish. Home: 5208 38th St NW Washington DC 20015-1812

SHANKS, KATHRYN MARY, health care administrator; b. Glens Falls, N.Y., Aug. 4, 1950; d. John Anthony and Lenita (Combs) S. BS summa cum laude, Spring Hill Coll., 1972; MPA, Auburn U., 1976. Program evaluator Mobile Mental Health, Ala., 1972-73; dir. spl. projects Ala. Dept. Mental Health, Montgomery, 1973-76; dir. adminstrn. S.W. Ala. Mental Health/Mental Retardation, Andulusia, Ala., 1976-78; adminstr. Mobile County Health Dept., 1978-82; exec. dir. Coastal Family Health Ctr., Biloxi, Miss., 1982—; ptnr. Shanks & Allen, Mobile, 1979—; cons. S.W. Health Agy., Tylertown, Miss., 1984-86; preceptor Sch. Nursing, U. So. Miss., Hattiesburg, 1983, 84; advisor Headstart Program, Gulfport, Miss., 1984—, LPN Program, Gulf Coast C.C., 1984—; lectr. Auburn U., Montgomery, 1977-78. Bd. dirs. Mobile Cmty. Action Agy., 1979-81, Moore Cmty. House; mem. S.W. Ala. Regional Goals Forum, Mobile, 1971-72, Cardiac Rehab. Study Com., Biloxi, Miss., 1983-84, Mothers and Babies Coalition, Jackson, Miss., 1983—, Gulf Coast Coalition Human Services, Biloxi, Miss., 1983—; exec. dir. Year for Miss., 1993-94. Spring Hill Coll. Pres.'s scholar, 1972. Mem. Miss. Primary Health Care Assn. (pres.), Med. Group Mgmt. Assn., Biloxi C. of C., ACLU, Soc. for Advancement of Ambulatory Care, Spring Hills Alumni Assn. Avocations: tennis, home restoration, golf. Office: Coastal Family Health Ctr PO Box 475 1046 Division St Biloxi MS 39533

SHANNON, IRIS REED, nursing educator; b. Chgo.; d. Ira Paul and Iola Sophia (Williams) S.; m. Robert Alwood Shannon, Aug. 21, 1953. BS in Nursing, Fisk U.-Meharry Med. Coll., 1948; MA, U. Chgo., 1954; PhD, U. Ill., Chgo., 1987; D in Pub. Svc. (hon.), Elmhurst Coll., 1993. Staff nurse Chgo. Bd. Health, 1948-50; instr. pub. health nursing Meharry Med. Coll., Nashville, 1951-56; tchr.-nurse, health coordinator child devel. Head Start, Chgo. Bd. Edn., 1957-66; dir. community nursing Mile Sq. Neighborhood Health Center, Presbyn.-St. Luke's Hosp., Chgo., 1966-69; co-dir. nurse assoc. programs Rush Presbyn.-St. Luke's Hosp., 1971-76; chairperson community nursing Rush U., Chgo., 1972-77; acting chairperson Rush U., 1988-90; asst. prof. pub. health nursing U. Ill., 1971-74; assoc. prof. community nursing Rush U., 1974—; adj. faculty Sch. Public Health, U. N.C., 1977-85; mem. profl. adv. bd. Vis. Nurse Assn. Chgo., 1973-75; cons. Video Nursing, Inc.; mem. profl. adv. com. Mile Sq. Home Health Unit, Chgo., 1975-77; mem. Nat. Adv. Council on Nurse Tng., HEW, 1978-81; Mem. Nat. Task Force on Credentialing in Nursing, 1979-82; mem. Chgo. regional com. Ill. White House Conf. on Children, 1979-80. Recipient award of merit Ill. Public Health Assn., 1979, Outstanding Achievement award YWCA of Met. Chgo., 1988, Disting. Svc. award Chgo. chpt. Meharry Alumni, 1989, Lowenberg Chair of Excellence in nursing Memphis State U., 1993; Rockefeller fellow, 1953-54. Fellow Am. Pub. Health Assn. (chmn. pub. health nursing sect. 1977-79, governing coun. 1980-82, exec. bd. 1985-87, pres. 1988-89), Royal Soc. Health (hon. 1989), Am. Acad. Nursing; mem. Am. Nurses Assn., Inst. Medicine of Nat. Acad. Scis., Delta Sigma Theta, Sigma Theta Tau.

SHANNON, SHERRI GALE, business consultant; b. Charleston, W.Va., Feb. 3, 1957; d. Clyde Roy and Ida May (Cyrus) Bird; m. Robert William Shannon, June 2, 1984; 1 child, Michael Robert. BA in Acctg. and Fin. summa cum laude, W.Va. State Coll., 1978. CPA, W.Va. Chmn. supr. com., acct. Charleston (W.Va.) Area Med. Ctr., 1979-84, ops. auditor, 1983-88, auditor, 1988, dir. internal audit, 1988-90; pvt. practice acct., 1990-92; pvt. practice bus. cons. Winfield, W.Va., 1992—. Mem. Am. Inst. CPA's, W.Va. Soc. CPA's, Inst. Internal Auditors (W.Va. chpt., mem. Directory 1984-85), Health Care Internal Audit Group, Hosp. Fin. Mgmt. Assn., Alpha Kappa Mu. Democrat. Baptist.

SHANNON, SUSAN CHRISTINE, association executive; b. Detroit, Dec. 20, 1949; d. Harold Raymond and Gloria Mae Shannon; children: Eric Anton III, Darin Shannon, Carrie Marie. BS, Eastern Mich. U., 1980; MBA, Western Mich. U., 1987. Admin. asst. City of Grand Rapids, Mich., 1981-84; mgmt. analyst city of Grand Rapids, Mich., 1984-88; exec. dir. YWCA of Grand Rapids, 1988—. Treas. Fountain St. Ch., v.p. Downtown Mgmt. Bd.; mem. Met. Hosp. Found., Western Mich. Found., Cable TV Adv. Forum. Office: YWCA of Grand Rapids 25 Sheldon Blvd SE Grand Rapids MI 49503-4209

SHANTZ, CAROLYN UHLINGER, psychology educator; b. Kalamazoo, Mich., May 19, 1935; d. James Roland and Gladys Irene (Jerrett) Uhlinger; m. David Ward Shantz, Aug. 17, 1963; children: Catherine Ann, Cynthia Anne. BA, DePauw U., 1957; MA, Purdue U., 1959, PhD, 1966. Rsch. assoc. Merrill-Palmer Inst., Detroit, 1965-71; prof. Wayne State U., Detroit, 1971—; com. mem. grant rev. panel NIMH, NIH, Washington, 1979-81, 84-86; reviewer grant proposals NSF, Washington, 1978—; cons. Random House, Knopf, Guilford, others. Editor Merrill-Palmer Quar., 1981—; contbr. articles to profl. jours. Rsch. grantee NSF, NICHHD, OEO, Edn., Spencer Found., 1966-89. Fellow Am. Psychol. Assn. (pres. div. on devel. psychology 1983-84), Am. Psychol. Soc.; mem. Soc. for Rsch. in Child Devel., Sigma Xi, Phi Beta Kappa. Office: Wayne State U Dept Psychology Detroit MI 48202

SHAPIRO, BETH JANET, librarian; b. Newton, Mass., July 18, 1946; d. Harold H. and Marilyn Ann (Katz) S.; m. Russell Carl Barnes, May 15, 1987; children: Gabrielle Alexandra Barnes. BS in Sociology, Mich. State U., 1968, MA in Sociology, 1971; MLS, Western Mich. U., 1974; PhD in Sociology, Mich. State U., 1981. Urban affairs bibliographer Mich. State U. Librs., East Lansing, 1972-76, urban policy and planning librarian, 1976-79, social sci. coord., 1979-81, asst. dir., 1981-85, assoc. dir., 1985-87, deputy dir., 1987-90; univ. libr. Rice U., Houston, 1991—; mem. rsch. librs. adv. com. Online Coll. Libr. Ctr., Inc., 1992—; bd. dirs. Ctr. for Rsch. Librs., 1994—. Editor: Selection of Library Materials in the Humanities, Social Sciences. and Sciences., 1985, Selection of Library Materials in Applied and Interdisciplinary Fields, 1987. Mem. Ingham County Equal Opportunity Com., Mason, Mich., 1974-75, Lansing Com. on Affirmative Action, 1976-78, Capital City Revitalization Task Force, Lansing, 1986; mem. Mich. Consumers Coun., Lansing, 1982-88, chmn., 1987-88; bd. dirs. Interracial Family Alliance of Houston, 1993—. Grantee Coun. on Libr. Resources, 1978, 83, 93. Mem. ALA (councilor 1991-95), N.Am. Soc. for Sociology Sport. Office: Rice University Fondren Library MS44 6100 Main St Houston TX 77005

SHAPIRO, FLORENCE, state legislator, advertising, public relations executive; b. N.Y.C., May 2, 1948; d. Martin Nmi and Ann (Spiesman) D.; m. Howard Nmi Shapiro, Dec. 28, 1969; children: Lisa, Todd, Staci. BS, U. Tex., 1970. Tchr. Richardson High Sch., Tex., 1970-72; advt., pub. rels. Shapiro, Small and Assocs., Plano, Tex., 1982—; formerly mayor and mem. city coun. City of Plano, Tex.; now mem. Tex. Senate, 1992—. Bd. dirs. Plano C. of C., Presbyterian and Children's Healthcare Ctr., Plano Econ. Devel. Bd., U. Tex. at Dallas Adv. Coun., The North Tex. Commn., The Dallas Regional Mobility Coalition, Nat. Bd. of the Susan B. Komen Breast Cancer Found. Recipient Plano Vol. of the Yr. award, 1983, Plano Citizen of the Yr. award 1985, Athena award Plano C. of C. for Businesswoman of the Yr., 1990. Mem. Alpha Epsilon Phi (v.p., soc. chmn. 1968-69), Plano Rotary Club (Paul Harris fellow award 1990). Republican. Jewish. Home: 2005 Crown Knoll Plano TX 75093 Office: Senate House State Capitol Austin TX 78769*

SHAPIRO, JOAN ISABELLE, laboratory administrator, nurse; b. Fulton, Ill., Aug. 26, 1943; d. Macy James and Frieda Lockhart; m. Ivan Lee Shapiro, Dec. 28, 1968; children: Audrey, Michael. RN, Peoria Methodist

Sch. Nursing, Ill., 1964. Nurse, Grant Hosp., Columbus, Ohio, 1975-76; nurse Cardiac Thoracic and Vascular Surgeons Ltd., Geneva, Ill., 1977—, mgr. non-invasive lab., 1979—; owner, operator Shapiro's Mastiff's 1976-82; sec.-treas. Sounds Svcs., 1976—, Mainstream Sounds Inc., 1980-84; co-founder Cardio-Phone Inc., 1982—, Edgewater Vascular Inst., 1987-89, Associated Profls., 1989-92; v.p., bd. dir. Computer Specialists Inc., 1986-89; founder, pres. Vein Ctr., Edema Ctr. Ltd. Mem. Soc. Non-invasive Technologists, Soc. Peripheral Vascular Nursing (community awareness com. 1984—), Oncology Nursing Soc., Internat. Soc. Lymphology, Kane County Med. Soc. Aux. (pres. 1983-84, adviser, 1984-85). Lutheran. Office: Cardiac Thoracic and Vascular Surgeons Ltd PO Box 564 Geneva IL 60134-0564

SHAPIRO, JUDITH R., anthropology educator, university official; b. N.Y.C., Jan. 24, 1942. Student Ecole des Haute Etudes Institut d'Etudes Politiques, Paris, 1961-62; BA, Brandeis U., 1963; PhD, Columbia U., 1972. Asst. prof. U. Chgo., 1970-75; postdoctoral fellow U. Calif.-Berkeley, 1974-75; Rosalyn R. Schwartz lectr., asst. prof. anthropology Bryn Mawr Coll., Pa., 1975-78, assoc. prof., 1978-85, prof., 1985—, chmn. dept., 1982-85, acting dean undergrad coll., 1985-86, provost, 1986-94; pres. Barnard Coll., N.Y., 1994—; contbr. articles to profl. jours., chpts. to books. Fellow Woodrow Wilson Found., 1963-64, Columbia U., 1964-65, NEH Younger Humanist, 1974-75, Am. Coun. Learned Socs., 1981-82, Ctr. for Advanced Study in the Behavioral Scis., 1989; grantee NSF summer field tng., 1965, Ford Found. 1966, NIMH, 1974-75, Social Sci. Rsch. Coun., 1974-75. Mem. Phila. Anthrop. Soc. (pres. 1983), Am. Ethnol. Soc. (nominations com. 1983-84, pres. elect 1984-85, pres. 1985-86), Am. Anthrop. Assn. (ethics com. 1976-79, bd. dirs. 1984-86, exec. com. 1985-86), Social Sci. Rsch. Coun. (com. social sci personnel 1977-80), Women's Forum, Phi Beta Kappa, Sigma Xi. Office: Barnard Coll Office of the Pres 3009 Broadway New York NY 10027-6598

SHAPIRO, LINDA, clinical psychologist; b. Phila., Sept. 29, 1959; d. Walter E. and Marilyn Simon; m. Neil R. Shapiro, May 27, 1984; children: Ariel P., Joel A. BA, Cornell U., 1981; PhD, SUNY, Albany, 1986. Lic. psychologist. Staff psychologist Montgomery County Mental Health Clinic, Amsterdam, N.Y., 1986-89; cons. St. Catherine's Ctr. for Children, Albany, 1989-92; pvt. practice psychology N.E. Psychol. Assocs., Albany, 1991—. Mem. APA, Psychol. Assn. Northeastern N.Y. Office: NE Psychol Assocs 435 New Karner Rd Albany NY 12205

SHAPIRO, LINDA TAYLOR, academic administrator; b. Boston, Feb. 13, 1947; d. Myer and Beatrice (Wolbarst) S.; m. James S. Eiseman, Sept. 2, 1968 (div. 1982); 1 child, Kara A. Eiseman; m. Robert L. Taylor, Oct. 28, 1988. AB, Boston U., 1968, MEd, 1971; EdD, U. Louisville, 1991. Team leader Jewel Manor Day Treatment Ctr., Louisville, 1972-74; counselor Jefferson C.C., Louisville, 1976-78; counselor U. Louisville, 1978-79, dir. career planning, 1980-86, exec. asst. to provost, 1986-90, asst. univ. provost, 1990-94; project dir. Displaced Homemaker Project, Louisville, 1979-80; assoc. univ. provost, 1994—; cons. Right Assocs., Louisville, 1980-85, others; instr., adj. asst. prof. U. Louisville, 1980—. Pres. Bus. and Profl. Women U. Louisville, 1986; bd. dirs. B'nai B'rith Hillel, U. Louisville; participant, Leadership Louisville, 1994-95. Mem. ACA, ACLU (membership com.), Am. Coll. Pers. Assn., Nat. Career Devel. Assn., Phi Kappa Phi. Office: U Louisville 209 Grawemeyer Hall Louisville KY 40292

SHAPIRO, LUCILLE, molecular biology educator; b. N.Y.C., July 16, 1940; d. Philip and Yetta (Stein) Cohen; m. Roy Shapiro, Jan. 23, 1960 (div. 1977); 1 child, Peter; m. Harley H. McAdams, July 28, 1978; stepchildren: Paul, Heather. BA, Bklyn. Coll., 1961; PhD, Albert Einstein Coll. Medicine, 1966. Asst. prof. Albert Einstein Coll. Medicine, N.Y.C., 1967-72, assoc. prof., 1972-77, Kramer prof., chmn. dept. molecular biology, 1977-86, dir. biol. scis. div., 1981-86; Eugene Higgins prof., chmn. dept. microbiology, Coll. Physicians and Surgeons Columbia U., N.Y.C., 1986-89; Joseph D. Grant prof., chmn. dept. devel. biology Sch. Medicine, Stanford U., 1989—; mem. bd. sci. counselors NIH, Washington, 1980-84, DeWitt Stetten disting. lectr., 1989; mem. bd. sci. advisors G.D. Searle Co., Skokie, Ill., 1984-86; mem. sci. adv. bd. Mass. Gen. Hosp., 1990-93, SmithKline Beecham, 1993—; trustee Scientists Inst. for Pub. Info., 1990-94; lectr. Harvey Soc., 1993; commencement speaker U. Calif., Berkeley, 1994; co-chmn. adv. bd. biology directorate, NSF, 1988-89; mem. sci. bd. Helen Hay Whitney Found., N.Y., 1986—; mem. sci. bd. Whitehead Inst., MIT, 1988-93. Editor: Microbiol. Devel., 1984; mem. editorial bd. Jour. Bacteriology, 1978-86, Trends in Genetics, 1987—, Genes and Development, 1987-91, Cell Regulation, 1990-92, Molecular Biology of the Cell, 1992—, Molecular Microbiology, 1991—, Current Opinion on Genetics and Devel., 1991—; contbr. articles to profl. jours. Mem. vis. com., bd. overseers Harvard U., Cambridge, Mass., 1987-90; mem. sci. rev. bd. Howard Hughes Med. Inst., 1990-94; mem. presidio coun. City of San Francisco, 1991-94; mem. president's coun. U. Calif., 1993—; bd. dirs. Silicon Graphics, Inc., 1993—. Recipient Hirschl Career Scientist award, 1976, Spirit of Achievement award, 1978, Excellence in Sci. award Fedn. Am. Socs. Exptl. Biology, 1994; Jane Coffin Child fellow, 1966. Fellow AAAS, Am. Acad. Arts and Scis., Am. Acad. Microbiology; mem. NAS, Inst. Medicine of NAS, Am. Soc. Biochemistry and Molecular Biology (nominating com. 1982, 87, coun. 1990—), Am. Heart Assn. (sci. adv. bd. 1984-87). Office: Stanford U Sch Medicine Beckman Ctr Dept Devel Biology Stanford CA 94305

SHAPIRO, MARCIA HASKEL, speech and language pathologist; b. N.Y.C., Nov. 6, 1949; d. Ben and Edna Haskel; m. Louis Shapiro, Aug. 1, 1981. BA, Hunter Coll., 1982; MA, NYU, 1983; MA in Speech Pathology, U. Cen. Fla., 1991. Cert. deaf educator, Fla. Tchr. deaf Pub. Sch. 47, N.Y.C., 1983-84; speech pathologist St. Francis Sch. for the Deaf, Bklyn., 1984-86, Seminole County Schs., 1986-87, Lake County Schs., 1987-89, Orange County Schs., Orlando, Fla., 1989-91, West Volusia Meml. Hosp., Deland, Fla., 1991-93, Orlando Regional Med. Ctr., 1993, Sand Lake Hosp., 1993—; staff head swallowing dept. Leesburg Regional Med. Ctr., 1994—; dir. speech pathology Fla. Hosp., Waterman, 1994—. Mem. ASHA, AFTRA, EQITY, Annals of Deaf, CAID, Alexander Graham Bell Assn. for Deaf.

SHAPIRO, MARIAN KAPLUN, psychologist; b. N.Y., July 13, 1939; d. David and Bertha Rebecca (Pearlman) Kaplun; m. Irwin Ira Shapiro, Dec. 20, 1959; children: Steven, Nancy. BA, Queens Coll., 1959; MA in Teaching, Harvard U., 1961, EdD, 1978. Cert. psychologist. Tchr. North Quincy High Sch., Quincy, Mass., 1962-64; instr. Carnegie Inst., Boston, 1968-74; staff psychologist South Shore Counselling Assn., Hanover, Mass., 1978-80; pvt. practice psychologist Lexington, Mass., 1980—; adj. instr. Mass. Sch. Profl. Psychology, Dedham, 1985—. Author: 2nd Childhood: Hypnoplay Therapy with Age--Regressed Adults, 1989; contbr. articles on teaching reading, hypnotherapy, multiple personality and other clin. issues to profl. jours. Fellow Am. Orthopsychiat. Assn.; mem. APA, Mass. Psychol. Assn., N.E. Soc. Group Psychotherapy, Am. Soc. Group Psychotherapy (clin.), Am. Soc. Clin. Hypnosis (cert. cons.), New Eng. Soc. for the Study of Multiple Personality Disorders, Internat. Soc. for the Study of Multiple Personality Disorders, New Eng. Soc. Clin. Hypnosis, Sigma Alpha, Pi Lambda Theta. Jewish. Home and Office: 17 Lantern Ln Lexington MA 02173-6029

SHAPIRO, MARJORIE MACKAY, musicologist, educator; b. Jamaica, N.Y., Nov. 3, 1929; d. Hugh Alexander and Violet (Kemble) Mackay; m. Jerome Gerson Shapiro, Dec. 31, 1959; children: Jeffrey Kemble, Jill Dara, Eric Paul. BS, SUNY, Oswego, 1950; MA, Columbia U., 1954; MusM, Manhattan Sch. Music, 1982; postgrad., CUNY, 1989—. Lic. tchr., N.Y. Tchr. various pub. schs., New Canaan, Conn., 1950-54; tchr. high sch. music and English various pub. schs., Great Neck, N.Y., 1954-56; tchr. Le Coll. de Jeunes Filles, St. Gauthier, France, 1956-57; singer various light opera houses and chs., Paris, 1957-59; singer, prin. Village Light Opera Group, N.Y.C., 1959-64; singer Ch. of the Resurrection, N.Y.C., 1959-74; founder, prin. singer The Hopewell Consort, N.Y.C., 1970-76; founder ednl. co. Ventures in Music, N.Y.C., 1984-90; mem. Am. Recorder Soc., N.Y.C., 1979-85; staff lectr. on music Manhattan Sch. of Music, N.Y.C., 1984-86, Berkshire Choral Inst., Sheffield, Mass., 1984-86, Aristocrat Tours, Inc., 1984-87, AAUW, 1986-89, The New Sch., N.Y.C., 1986-91, The N.Y. Philharmonic, N.Y.C., 1987-91. Performer (record album) The Art of Heinrich Schutz Vol. I and II, 1965; contbr. articles to profl. publs. Organizer Head Start program James Weldon Johnson Settlement House, N.Y.C., 1970-74; rschr., active mem. Citizens' Com. for Children, N.Y.C., 1972—. Frick Mus. fellow, 1990—. Mem. AAUW, Am. Composers Orch. (adv. coun. 1982—), Am. Music Ctr., Music Libr. Assn., Sonneck Soc. (area rep. 1983—, bd. trustees), English Speaking Union, Cosmopolitan Club (music com. 1986-89, 92). Episcopalian. Home: 200 E 66 St #A-701 New York NY 10021

SHAPIRO, MARY J., writer, researcher, speech writer; b. Buffalo, Oct. 30, 1945; d. Peter J. and Margaret (McMahon) Crotty; m. Barry H. Shapiro, Apr. 22, 1972; children: Michael, Eben. BA, Manhattanville Coll., 1967; MFA, NYU, 1970. Editor Francis Thompson, Inc., N.Y.C., 1973-76; exhbn. coord., writer, researcher Chermayeff & Geismar, Inc., N.Y.C., 1987-92; writer, researcher Edwin Schlossberg Inc., N.Y.C., 1991-92, Ralph Appelbaum Assocs. Inc., N.Y.C., 1994—; exhbn. coord. Mus. Jewish Heritage, N.Y.C., 1987-88, Carnegie Hall Mus., N.Y.C., 1990; writer Ellis Island Immigration Mus., N.Y.C., 1988-90, Johnston (Pa.) Flood Mus., 1989, Chickamauga (Ga.) Battlefield Visitor Ctr., 1991, Oklahoma City Zoo Great Apes Habitat, 1992, Sony Wonder Tech. Mus., N.Y.C., 1993; writer, rschr. Women's Rights Nat. Hist. Park, Seneca Falls, N.Y., 1988-91. Author: Picture History of the Brooklyn Bridge, 1983, How They Built The Statue of Liberty, 1985, Gateway to Liberty, 1986, Ellis Island: An Illustrated History of the Immigrant Experience, 1991. Recipient Outstanding Science Trade Book citation Children's Book Coun., 1985, Garden State Children's Book award N.J.. Libr. Assn., 1986. Home: Apt 4B 370 1st Ave New York NY 10010

SHAPIRO, MYRA STEIN, poet; b. Bronx, N.Y., May 21, 1932; d. David M. and Ida Betty (Leader) Stein; m. Harold M. Shapiro, Feb. 15, 1953; children: Karen S., Judith M. BA, U. Tenn., 1968; MA in English, Middlebury Coll., 1973; MFA, Vt. Coll., 1993. reader, Internat. Women's Day, Jefferson Market Libr., N.Y.C., 1989; reading performance Midday Muse Series, Folger Shakespeare Libr., Washington, 1983, NEA Hunter Mus., Chattanooga, 1985, Bower's Mus., Santa Ana, Calif., 1986, 88. Author: (poetry) The Ohio Review, 1989, Education for Peace, 1988, Kalliope, 1988, Ploughshares, 1990-91, The Harvard Review, 1994. Recipient Dylan Thomas Poetry award, The New Sch., N.Y.C., 1981, The MacDowell Colony Fellowship, The MacDowell Colony, Peterborough, N.H., 1985, 87. Mem. Poetry Soc. Am., Poets House (bd. dirs.). Office: 111 4th Ave Apt 12I New York NY 10003-5240

SHAPIRO, NELLA IRENE, surgeon; b. N.Y.C., Nov. 13, 1947; d. Eugene and Ethel (Pearl) S.; m. Jack Schwartz, Oct. 16, 1977; children: Max, Molly. BA, Barnard Coll., 1968; MD, Albert Einstein Coll., 1972. Resident in gen. surgery Montefiore Hosp., N.Y.C., 1972-76; mem. staff North Cen. Hosp., Bronx, N.Y., 1976-77, Bronx Mcpl. Hosp., Bronx, 1977-87; chief gen. surgery Bronx Mcpl. Hosp. Ctr., 1983-87; mem. staff in gen. surgery Albert Einstein Coll. Hosp., Bronx, 1977-93, chief gen. surgery, 1991-93; pvt. practice Lear Surg. Assocs., 1993—; asst. prof. surgery Albert Einstein Coll., Bronx, 1980—; assoc. dir. gen. surgery Weller Hosp., Bronx, 1991—; co-founder Whaecom Breast Ctr., Bronx, 1991—. Fellow Am. Coll. Surgeons. Office: Lear Surg Assocs Ste 304 1695 Eastchester Rd Bronx NY 10461

SHAPIRO, NORMA SONDRA LEVY, federal judge; b. Phila., July 27, 1928; d. Bert and Jane (Kotkin) Levy; m. Bernard Shapiro, Aug. 21, 1949; children: Finley, Neil, Aaron. BA in Polit. Theory with honors, U. Mich., 1948; JD magna cum laude, U. Pa., 1951. Bar: Pa. 1952, U.S. Supreme Ct. 1978. Law clk. to presiding justice Pa. Supreme Ct., 1951-52; instr. U. Pa. Law Sch., 1951-52, 55-56; assoc. Dechert Price & Rhoads, Phila., 1956-58, 67-73; ptnr. Dechert Price & Rhoads, 1973-78; judge U.S. Dist. Ct. (ea. dist.) Pa., 1978—; assoc. trustee U. Pa. Law Sch., 1978-93; former trustee Women's Law Project, Albert Einstein Med. Ctr.; v.p. Jewish Pub. Soc.; trustee Fedn. Jewish Agys., 1980-83; mem. lawyers adv. panel Pa. Gov.'s Commn. on Status of Women, 1974; legal adv. regional Coun. Child Psychiatry, bd. dirs. Women Judges' Fund for Justice. Guest editor: Shingle, 1972. Mem. Lower Merion County (Pa.) Bd. Sch. Dirs., 1968-77, pres., 1977, v.p., 1976; v.p. Jewish Community Relations Council of Greater Phila., 1975-77; chmn. legal affairs com., 1978; pres. Belmont Hills Home and Sch. Assn., Lower Merion Twp.; legis. chmn. Lower Merion Sch. Dist. Intersch. Council; mem. Task Force on Mental Health of Children and Youth of Pa.; treas., chmn. edn. com. Human Relations Council, Lower Merion; v.p., parliamentarian Nes Ami Penn Valley Congregation, Lower Merion Twp. Named Woman of Yr., Oxford Circle Jewish Community Center, 1979, Woman of Distinction, Golden Slipper Club, 1979; Gowen fellow, 1954-55; recipient Hannah G. Solomon award Nat. Coun. Jewish Women, 1992. Mem. Am. Law Inst., Am. Bar Found., ABA (ho. dels. 1990—, coun./chmn. conf. fed. judges 1986-87, vice-chmn. com. law and mental health sect. family law), Pa. Bar Assn. (ho. of dels. 1979-81), Phila. Bar Assn. (chmn. com. women's rights 1972, 74-75, chmn. bd. govs. 1977-78, chmn. pub. rels. com. 1978), Fed. Bar Assn. (Bill of Rights award 1991), Nat. Assn. Women Lawyers, Phila. Trial Lawyers Assn., Am. Judicature Soc., Phila., Nat. Assn. Women Judges, Fellowship Commn., Order of Coif (chpt. pres. 1973-75), Tau Epsilon Rho, Jurisprudence. Office: US Dist Courthouse Independence Mall West 601 Market St Rm 10614 Philadelphia PA 19106-1723*

SHAPIRO, PAULA, former maternal and women's health nurse; b. Pitts., Nov. 16, 1927; d. Ben and Esther (Halpert) Cohn; m. Bernard Shapiro, July 17, 1982; children: Eugene Hershorin, Gary Hershorin, Marc Hershorin, Jay Hershorin, Ellen Fenerty, Kenneth, Fred, Stacy Pierce. RN, Menorah Hosp. Sch. Nursing, 1948; BS, Phila. Coll. Textile & Sci., 1987. RN, Pa. Nursing care coord. Thomas Jefferson U. Hosp., Phila.; asst. supr. operating rm. Wakefield (R.I.) Gen. Hosp.; staff RN operating rm. Jefferson Hosp., Phila.; ret., 1993. Contbr. articles to profl. jours. Vol. TJUH. Home: 1500 Locust St Apt 2216 Philadelphia PA 19102-4317

SHAPIRO, ROBYN SUE, lawyer, educator; b. Mpls., July 19, 1952; d. Walter David and Judith Rae (Sweet) S.; m. Charles Howard Barr, June 27, 1976; children: Tania Shapiro-Barr, Jeremy Shapiro-Barr, Michael Shapiro-Barr. BA summa cum laude, U. Mich., 1974; JD, Harvard U., 1977. Bar: D.C. 1977, Wis. 1979. Assoc. Foley & Lardner, Washington, 1977-79; ptnr. Barr & Shapiro, Menomonee Falls, Wis., 1980-87; assoc. Quarles & Brady, Milw., 1987-92; ptnr. Michael Best & Friedrich, Milw., 1992—; adj. asst. prof. law Marquette U., Milw., 1979-83; assoc. dir. bioethics ctr. Med. Coll. Wis., Milw., 1982-85, dir., 1985—; asst. prof. bioethics Med. Coll. Wis., 1984-89, assoc. prof. bioethics, 1989—; dir. Wis. Ethics Com. Network, 1987—; bd. mem. Wis. Health Decisions, 1990-93. Editorial bd. mem: Cambridge Quarterly, 1991—, HEC Forum, 1988-91; contbr. articles to profl. jours. Mem. ethics com. St. Luke's Hosp., Milw., 1983—, Elmbrook Meml. Hosp., Milw., 1983-86, Community Meml. Hosp., Menomonee Falls, 1984—, Sinai Samaritan Hosp., Milw., 1986—, Milw. County Med. Complex, 1985—, Froedtert Meml. Luth. Hosp., 1985—; mem. subcom. organ transplantation Wis. Health Policy Coun., Madison, Wis., 1984, bioethics com., 1986—; mem. com. study on bioethics Wis. Legis. Coun., Madison, 1984-85; bd. dirs. Jewish Home and Care Ctr., 1994—, chair ethics com., 1994—; chair Bayside Ethics Bd., 1994—. James B. Angell scholar, 1971-72. Mem. ABA (forum com. health law, individual rights and responsibilities sec., health rights com. chair 1994—, mem. coordinating com. on bioethics and the law), Nat. Health Lawyers Assn.. Am. Soc. Law & Medicine, Am. Hosp. Assn. (bioethics tech. panel 1991-94, spl. com. HIV & practitioners 1991-93) Wis. Bar Assn. (coun. Wis. health law sect. 1984-87, chair health law sect. 1988-89, individual rights sect. coun. 1987-90), Assn. Women Lawyers, ACLU, Wis. Found. (Atty. of Yr. 1988), Milw. Acad. Medicine (coun. 1992—, chair bioethics com. 1992—), Milw. AIDS Coalition (steering com. 1988-91), Internat. Bioethics Assn. (chair task force on ethics coms.), Phi Beta Kappa, others. Home: 9474 N Broadmoor Rd Milwaukee WI 53217-1309 Office: Med Coll Wis Bioethics Ctr 8701 W Watertown Plank Rd Milwaukee WI 53226-3548

SHAPIRO, SANDRA, lawyer; b. Providence, Oct. 17, 1944; d. Emil and Sarah (Cohen) S. AB magna cum laude, Bryn Mawr Coll., Pa., 1966; LLB magna cum laude, U. Pa., 1969. Bar: Mass. 1970, U.S. Dist. Ct. Mass. 1971, U.S. Ct. Appeals (1st cir.) 1972, U.S. Supreme Ct. 1980. Law clk. U.S. Ct. Appeals (1st cir.), Boston, 1969-70; assoc. Foley, Hoag & Eliot, Boston, 1970-75, ptnr., 1976—; bd. dirs. Mass. Govt. Land Bank; mem. Bd. Bar Overseers Mass. Supreme Judicial Ct., 1988-92, Gender Bias Study Com., 1986-89. Contbr. articles to profl. jours. Bd. dirs. Patriots' Trail coun. Girl Scouts U.S., 1994—; mem bd. overseers Boston Lyric Opera, 1993—. Woodrow Wilson fellow, 1966. Mem. ABA (ethics, professionalism and pub. edn. com. 1994—), Women's Bar Assn. of Mass. (prs. 1985-86), New Eng. Women in Real Estate, Nat. Women's Law Ctr. Network, Mass. Bar Assn. (chmn. real property sect. coun., com. on profl. ethics), Boston Bar Assn. (mem. coun.), U. Pa. Law Sch. Alumni Assn. (bd. mgrs. 1990—), Order of Coif, Boston Club. Office: Foley Hoag & Eliot 1 Post Office Sq Boston MA 02109-2170

SHAPO, HELENE S., law educator; b. N.Y.C., June 5, 1938; d. Benjamin Martin and Gertrude (Kahaner) Seidner; m. Marshall S. Shapo, June 21, 1959; children: Benjamin Mitchell, Nathaniel Saul. BA, Smith Coll., 1959; MA in Teaching, Harvard U., 1960; JD, U. Va., 1976. Bar: Va. 1976, U.S. Dist. Ct. (we. dist.) Va. 1977, Ill. 1993. Tchr. Dade County, Miami, Fla., 1960-64; assoc. Robert Musselman & Assocs., Charlottesville, Va., 1976-77; law clk. to presiding justice U.S. Dist. Ct. Va., Charlottesville, 1977-78; asst. prof. law Northwestern U., Chgo., 1978-81, assoc. prof. law, 1981-83, prof. law, 1983—; instr. Sweet Briar Coll., Va., 1976-77, U. Va., Charlottesville, 1976-78; mem. com. law sch. admissions council/testing and devel., 1983—; cons. in field. Mem. ABA, Va. Bar Assn., Assn. of Am. Law Schs. (sect. chairperson 1985—), Women's Bar Assn. Chgo. Office: Northwestern U Sch Law 357 E Chicago Ave Chicago IL 60611-3008

SHARBEL, JEAN M., editor; b. Lansford, Pa.; d. Joseph and Star (Nemr) Sharbel. BA in Journalism, Hunter Coll., N.Y.C. Editorial dir., v.p. Dauntless Books, N.Y.C., 1962-75; editor romance mags., True Confessions Mag., Macfadden Holdings, Inc., N.Y.C., 1976-92; freelance editor romance books, 1989—. Home: 165 E 66th St New York NY 10021-6132

SHARBONEAU, LORNA ROSINA, artist, educator, writer; b. Spokane, Wash., Apr. 5, 1935; d. Stephen Charles Martin and Midgie Montana (Hartzel) Barton; m. Thomas Edward Sharboneau, Jan. 22, 1970; children: Curtis, Carmen, Chet, Cra, Joseph. Student, Delta Coll., 1983—; studies with Steve Lesnick, Las Vegas, Nev.; studies with Bette Myers/Zimmerman, Phoenix and Bonners Ferry, Idaho. Prin. Sharboneau's Art Gallery, Spokane, 1977-80; tchr. art Michell's Art Gallery, Spokane, 1978-79; art therapist Vellencino Sch. Dist., Calif., 1981-83; ind. artist Lind, Wash., 1948—; dir., producer, stage designer Ch. of Jesus Christ of LDS, San Jose, Sonora, Modesto, Calif., 1978 (1st. place road show San Jose); dir. Sharboneau's Art Show, Spokane, 1979, Hands On-Yr. of the Child; platform spkr., poet, fundraiser, libr., 1984-87; asst., apprentice to Prof. Rowland Cheney, Delta Coll. Arts, Stockton, Calif., 1985, 86, 87; demonstrated drip oil technique, Bonners Ferry, Idaho, Spokane, Wash., Stockton, Calif., Delta Coll. Author, illustrator: Through the Eyes of the Turtle Tree, The One-Armed Christmas Tree, The Price of Freedom, William Will, Bill Can, Song of the Turtle Tree, Chet's Ottle-Bottle: The Unbreakable Bottle, One Drop of Water and a Grain of Sand; poet; prolific artist completed over 3000 paintings and drawings, displayed works in galleries through western states; featured in Magnolia News, Seattle, Delta Coll. Impact, Stockton, Calif., Stockton Record, Union Democrat, Sonora, Calif., Lincoln Center Chronicle, Stockton, Calif., Spokesman Rev., Spokane, Wash., Modesto (Calif) Bee, Angels Camp, Calif., Union Democrat, Sonora, Calif., New-Letter, Ch. of Jesus Christ of L.D.S 1st ward, Sonora; artist mixed media, oil, drip oil works, sculptures, pastel, watercolor; illustrations pen and ink, acrylic; sculpter bronze, lost wax method, ceramic art, soap stone, egg-tempra, original techniques. Dir., programmer, fundraiser Shelter Their Sorrows, Sonora, Calif., 1989-92, vol. Community Action Agency and Homeless Shelter. Recipient Golden Rule award J.C. Penny, 1991, Recognition award Pres. George Bush, cert. Spl. Congl. Recognition Congressman Richard H. Lehman, 3rd Pl. Best Show East Valley Artists/Pala Show, 1973, 74, 75, 3d Pl. Artist of Yr., 1974, Valley Fair, Santa Clara, Calif., 1974, 1st and 2d Pl. Spokane County Fair, 1978, 3 honorable mentions, 4 premiums, 1979, 3 1st Pl., 3 2d Pl., 2 3d Pl., honorable mention Calaveras County Fair/Angels Camp, Calif., 1983, 1st and 3d Pl. Unitarian Art Festival, Stockton, Calif., 1984, 2nd Pl., 1985, 3d Pl., 1986, 1st Pl. Lodi Art Ann., 1985, 3d Pl., 1986, 1st Pl., 1987, 1st Pl., 1988, honorable mention SJCAC Junque Art Show, Stockton, 1985, 1st Pl. Central Calif. Art League, Modesto, 1986, 88; 3d Pl. Camilla Art Show, San Jose, Calif., 1974; 1st, 2d, and 3d Pl., Spokane County Fair, 1978; 4 honorable mentions, Mother Lode Art Show, 1991, 2 hon. mentions, Sonora, Calif., 1993; homeless shelter kitchen named in her honor, Sonora. Mem. Cen. Sierra Arts Coun., Mother Lode Artists Assn., Internat. Platform Assn. (Judges Choice conv. arts competition 1993), The Planetary Soc.-Carl Sagan (pres.). Mem. Ch. of Jesus Christ of LDS. Home and Studio: 400 Mono Way Sonora CA 95370-5235 Office: Internat Platform Assn PO Box 250 Winnetka IL 60093-0250

SHARKEY, KATHLEEN, accountant; b. Phila., Jan. 25, 1951; d. Joseph Philip and Florence Veronica (Noykoff) Sharkey; m. Joel David Delpha, Sept. 24, 1977; children: Daniel Joseph, Madeleine Day. BA, John Carroll U., 1973. Tchr. St. Michael's Sch., St. Louis, 1976-79; acct. Citicorp Acceptance, St. Louis, 1986-89; fin. dir., adminstr. Women's Self Help Ctr., St. Louis, 1989—. Bd. dirs. Mo. Religious Coalition for Reproductive Choice, St. Louis, 1992—; co-chair St. Louis Caths. for a Free Choice, 1992—; treas. Shaw Neighborhood Improvement Assn., 1994—. Democrat. Roman Catholic. Home: 4047 Magnolia Pl Saint Louis MO 63110 Office: Women's Self Help Ctr Inc 2838 Olive St Saint Louis MO 63103

SHARMA, SANTOSH DEVRAJ, obstetrician and gynecologist, educator; b. Kenya, Feb. 24, 1934; came to U.S., Jan. 1972; d. Devraj Chananram and Lakshmi (Devi) S. BS, MB, B.J. Medical Sch., Pune, India, 1960. House surgeon Sasson Hosp., Poona, India, 1960-61; resident in ob-gyn. various hospitals, England, 1961-67; house officer Maelor Gen. Hosp., Wrexham, U.K., 1961-62; asst. prof. ob-gyn. Howard U. Med. Sch., Washington, 1972-74; assoc. prof. John A. Burns Sch. Med., Honolulu, 1974-78, prof., 1978 --. Fellow Royal Coll. Ob-Gyn., Am. Coll. Ob-Gyn. Office: 1319 Punahou St Rm 824 Honolulu HI 96826-1032

SHARON, MARGARET MILAM (PEGGY SHARON), interior architect; b. Versailles, Ky., Sept. 25, 1954; d. Leslie Murphy and Jean (Clifton) S.; 1 child, Kristina Alyse. BS, Eastern Ky. U., 1976; MA, U. Ky., 1981, EdD, 1992. Archt. designer Commonwealth of Ky., Frankfort, 1972-76; archt. design, preservationalist City of Louisville, 1977-78; owner, designer, contractor Milam Interiors, Ltd., Louisville, 1978-80; instr. edn. U. Louisville Interior Design Program, 1981-82; ednl. instr. Georgetown Coll. (Ky.) Design & Art, 1982-83; asst. prof., coord. interior design program Eastern Ky. U., Richmond, 1983-88; archtl. designer Meyer Wright & Assocs., Frankfort, 1988-89; dir. interior architecture Sherman, Carter, Barnhart Architects, Lexington, Ky., 1990-92; owner, designer, ergonomic & ednl. cons. Interior Spaces, Midway, Ky., 1992—; exec. asst., commr.'s office fin. cabinet Commonwealth of Ky. Dept. Facilities Mgmt., Frankfort, 1993—; dir. Main St. program City of Georgetown, 1987. Mem. Am. Soc. Interior Designers (profl.), Inst. Bus. Designers (Lackawanna Leather recipient 1986), Internat. Interior Design Assn. (profl.). Baptist. Home: 109 N Winter St PO Box 707 Midway KY 40347 Office: Commonwealth of Ky Dept Facilities Mgmt 403 Wapping St Frankfort KY 40601

SHARP, ANNE CATHERINE, artist, educator; b. Red Bank, N.J., Nov. 1, 1943; d. Elmer Eugene and Ethel Violet (Hunter) S. BFA, Pratt Inst., 1965; MFA (teaching fellow 1972), Bklyn. Coll., 1973. tchr. art Sch. Visual Arts, 1978-89, NYU, 1978, SUNY, Purchase, 1983, Pratt Manhattan Ctr., N.Y.C., 1982-84, Parsons Sch. Design, N.Y.C., 1984-90, Visual Arts Ctr. of Alaska, Anchorage, 1991, Anchorage Mus. Hist. and Art, 1991, 93, 94, U. Alaska, Anchorage, 1994, 95. One-person shows Pace Editions, N.Y.C., Ten/Downtown, N.Y.C., Katonah (N.Y.) Gallery, 1974, Contemporary Gallery, Dallas, 1975, Art in a Public Space, N.Y.C., 1979, Eatontown Hist. Mus., N.J., 1980, N.Y. Pub. Library Epiphany Br., 1988, Books and Co., N.Y., 1989, The Kendall Gallery, N.Y.C., 1990, Alaska Pacific U., Carr-Gottstein Gallery, Anchorage, 1993, Internat. Gallery Contemporary Art, Anchorage, 1993, Art Think Tank Gallery, N.Y.C., 1994, U.S. Geol. Survey, Reston, Va., 1994, Stonington Gallery, Anchorage, 1994; group shows include Arnot Art Mus., Elmira, N.Y., 1975, Bronx Mus., 1975, Mus. Modern Art, N.Y.C., 1975-76, Nat. Arts Club, N.Y.C., 1979, Calif. Mus. Photography, Riverside, 1983-92, Jack Tilton Gallery, N.Y.C., 1983, Lincoln Ctr., N.Y.C., 1983, Cabo Frio Print Biennale, Brazil, 1983, Pratt Graphic Ctr., N.Y.C., 1984, State Mus. N.Y., Albany, 1984, Kenkeleba Gallery, N.Y.C., 1985, Hempstead Harbor Art Assn., Glen Cove, N.Y., 1985, Mus. Modern Art, Weddel, Fed. Republic of Germany, 1985, Kenkeleba Gallery, N.Y.C., 1985, Paper Art Exhbn. Internat. Mus. Contemporary Art, Bahia, Brazil, 1986,

Mus. Salon-de-Provence, France, 1987, Mus. Contemporary Art, Sao Paulo, Brazil, 1985-86, Salon de Provence, France, 1987, Adirondack Lakes Ctr. for Arts, Blue Mountain Lake, N.Y., 1987, Kendall Gallery, N.Y.C., 1988, Exhibition Ctr. Parsons Sch. Design, N.Y.C., 1989, F.M.K. Gallery, Budapest, Hungary, 1989, Galerie des Kulturbundes Schwarzenberg, German Dem. Republic, Q Sen Do Gallery, Kobe, Japan, 1989, Anchorage (Alaska) Mus. History and Art, 1990-91, U. Alaska, Anchorage, 1990, 91, Coos Art Mus., Coos Bay, Oreg., 1990, Spaceship Earth, Mus. Internat. de Neu Art, Vancouver, Can., 1990, Councourse Gallery, Emily Carr Coll. Art and Design, 1990, Nat. Mus. Women in the Arts, Washington, 1991, Visual Arts Ctr. Alaska, 1991, 92, Nomad Mus., Lisbon, Portugal, 1991, Mus. Ostdeutsche Gallery, Regensberg, Germany, 1991, Mcpl. Mus. Cesley Krumlov (So. Bohemia) CSFK, Czechoslovakia, 1991, Böltmiche Dörter Exhbn. Hochstrass 8, Munich, 1992, BBC-TV, Great Britain, U.K., Sta. WXXI-TV, Rochester, N.Y., 1992-93, Site 250 Gallery Contemporary Art., Fairbanks, Alaska, 1993, The Rochester (N.Y.) Mus. and Sci. Ctr., 1990-94, Anchorage Mus. History and Art, 1994, Space Arc: The Archives of Mankind, Time Capsule in Earth Orbit, Hughes Comm., Divec TV Satellite Launch, 1994—, Stonington Gallery, Anchorage, 1994; represented in permanent collections Smithsonian Instn., Nat. Air and Space Mus., Washington, Albright Knox Gallery, Buffalo, St. Vincent's Hosp, N.Y.C., N.Y. Pub. Libr., N.Y.C., U.S. Geol. Survey, Reston, Va., White House (Reagan, Bush adminstrns.), Site 250 Gallery Contemporary Art, Fairbanks, others; Moon Shot series to commemorate moon landing, 1970-76, Cloud Structures of the Universe Painting series, 1980-86, Am. Landscape series, 1987-89, Thoughtlines, fall 1986, Swimming in the Mainstream with Her, U. Va., Charlottesville; author: Artist's Book - Travel Dreams U.S.A., 1989, Artworld-Welt Der Kunst, Synchronicity, 1989—, Art Think Tank: Projects in Art and Ecology, 1990—, The Alaska Series, 1990—, Potraits in the Wilderness, 1990—. Mem. IDITOROD trail com., Alaska Photographic Ctr. Artist-in-residence grantee Va. Center for Creative Arts, 1974, Artpark, Lewiston, N.Y., 1980, Vt. Studio Colony, 1989; recipient Pippin award Our Town, N.Y.C., 1984. Mem. Nat. Space Soc., Nat. Mus. Women in Arts, Alaska Natural History Assn., Alaska Photography Ctr., Pratt Inst. Alumni Assn., Mus. Modern Art, Internat. Assn. for Astron. Artists, The Planetary Soc., Internat. Assn. Near-Death Studies, Art and Sci. Collaborations, The Internat. Gallery of Contemporary Art. Address: PO Box 100480 Anchorage AK 99510-0480

SHARP, JANE SHRIVER, artist; b. Dechard, Tenn., Oct. 14, 1931; d. Paul and Jane (Brown) Shriver; m. Benjamin Thomas Sharp, Sept. 26, 1953; children: Jane Ashton Sharp-Hersey, Anne Dudley, Julia Shriver. Student, Art Acad., Cin., 1948, Wesleyan Women's Coll., Macon, Ga., 1949-52, U. Chattanooga, 1953, Ecole Beaux Arts, Geneva, 1968-70. Transp. line designer TVA, Chattnooga, 1952-55; founder Artist's Studio Gallery, Palos Verdes Art Ctr., Palos Verdes Estates, Calif., 1987, bd. dirs., 1985-88; coord. art displays Hall of Adminstrn., L.A., 1987—. One-woman show includes Security Pacific Bank, Palos Verdes Estates, 1988; juried shows include Palos Verdes Art Ctr., 1988, 89; group exhbns. include The Artist's Studio Gallery, Rancho Palos Verdes, 1991; permanent collections include Wesleyan Coll., Macon, Ga., City Hall Palos Verdes Estates; pvt. collections in Geneva, Switzerland and Wilmington, Del.; executed mural Children at Play, Nemours Inst., 1961. Artistic cons. Peninsula Beautification Com., Palos Verdes Estates, Calif., 1987—. Recipient Profl. Artist award Los Angeles County Suprs., 1989; tchr.'s scholar Art Acad., 1948. Mem. Los Angeles County Mus. Art, Mus. Contemporary Art (charter), Armand Hammer Mus. (charter), Beverly Hills Art League, 242 Art Gallery Palos Verdes, Jr. League L.A. (sustaining), Pacific Arts Group (pres. 1976-78), Peninsula Six Artists Groups (pres. 1985-88). Republican. Episcopalian. Home and Studio: 2405 Via La Selva Palos Verdes Estates CA 90274-1017

SHARP, JOANN M., county official; b. Lynn, Mass., Sept. 30, 1942; d. Joseph M. and Theresa S. (Angelone) Foti; m. John S. Sharp, May 8, 1970; children: Jocelyn, Jacqueline, Joanna, Julianne. Selectman Northborough, Mass., 1986-92, chmn. bd. selectmen, 1990-91; commr. Worcester (Mass.) County, 1992—. Chmn. Northborough to Feed the Hungry, 1987-91, Rep. town com., 1991-92. Mem. Jr. Women's Club (hon.). Roman Catholic. Home: Box 132 51 Cherry St Northborough MA 01532 Office: Worcester County Commrs Courthouse 2 Main St Worcester MA 01608

SHARP, PAMELA ANN, quality assurance engineer; b. Pullman, Wash., Dec. 20, 1950; d. Robert Melvin and Vivian Lois (Steele) Olson; m. David William Sharp, June 16, 1973; children: Jaime David, Erik Scott. Student, Big Bend C.C., Moses Lake, Wash., 1969-70; BS in Zoology, Wash. State U., 1973; postgrad., Portland State U., 1976. Lab. technician The Carter Mining Co., Gillette, Wyo., 1977-79, lab. supr., 1979-80, quality control supr., 1980-81, engring. analyst, 1982-88; engr. quality control The Carter Mining Co., Gillette, 1988-89; owner Sharp Consulting, Gillette, 1989—, Landscape Design, 1993—; leader auditor tng. ISO 9000; obedience dog tng. instr., 1990—. Supt. Campbell County Fair, Gillette, 1985-87. Mem. AIME, ASTM (proximate analysis chmn. 1985—, chmn. on-line analysis com.), Am. Water Ski Assn. (regular judge 1974-91, eastern regional water ski trick record 1975, 3d nat. trick title 1962, state champion in tricks Wash., Idaho, Mont. 1961-73, 2d 1987 Western region women's III tricks). Republican. Presbyterian. Office: Sharp Consulting 2406 Hillcrest Gillette WY 82718

SHARP, SHARON LEE, gerontology nurse; b. Beatrice, Nebr., Jan. 14, 1939; d. Clarence Alfred and Edna Clara (Grosshuesch) Wolters; m. Philip Butler, June 27, 1959 (div. 1964); m. Ted C. Sharp, Sept. 21, 1966 (div. 1988); children: Sheryl Butler, Philip Butler. Diploma, Lincoln Gen. Hosp., 1959. RN Nebr. Charge nurse Mary Lanning Meml. Hosp., Hastings, Nebr., 1960-61; asst. head nurse Ingleside State Hosp., Hastings, Nebr., 1961-62; charge nurse Rio Hondo Meml. Hosp., Downey, Calif., 1969-71, Santa Barbara (Calif.) Cottage Hosp., 1974-78; supr. Marlora Manor Convalescent Hsop., Long Beach, Calif., 1979-80; supr. Marlinda Nursing Home, Lynwood, Calif., 1982-84, dir. nursing, 1984-89; dir. nursing Ramona Care Ctr., El Monte, Calif., 1989-90, Oakview Convalescent Hosp., Tujunga, Calif., 1990-91, North Valley Nursing Ctr., Tujunga, Calif., 1992—; asst. dir. nursing Skyline Health Care Ctr. (Gran Care), L.A., 1993-94; MDS coord. Country Villa Rehab. Ctr., L.A., 1994—; mem. adv. bd. Regional Occupational Program, Downey, 1985-86. Home: 2875 E Delmar Blvd Pasadena CA 91107

SHARPE, KATHRYN MOYE, psychologist; b. Barnesville, Ga., Nov. 27, 1922; d. Herbert Johnston and Henri Lucile (Winter) Moye; m. William Herschel Sharpe, Mar. 2, 1946; children: William Herschel Jr., Mark Stephens. AB, Piedmont Coll., Demorest, Ga., 1942; MA, U. N.C., 1947; PhD, U. S.C., 1975. Tchr., guidance counselor Charleston (S.C.) Pub. Schs., 1947-66; prof. sociology, chmn. dept. Bapt. Coll. at Charleston, 1966-88, prof. emeritus, 1988—; pvt. practice psychology, Charleston, 1975—. Kathryn Moye Sharpe scholarship given in her honor Bapt. Coll. at Charleston, 1988. Fellow Am. Assn. for Marriage and Family Therapy (approved supr., pres. S.C. div. 1975-77). Congregationalist. Home and Office: 6 Cavalier Ave Charleston SC 29407-7702

SHARPE, MARGARET HUGHES, real estate appraiser; b. Miami, July 1, 1948; d. Arthur Neal and Dorothy Agnes (Sullivan) Hughes; m, Thomas W. Adair, Aug. 12, 1969 (div. Aug. 1974); 1 child, Heather Neale Adair; m. Thomas R. Sharpe, Aug. 20, 1983. BA in Banking and Fin., U. Miss., 1983, postgrad in Bus. Adminstrn., 1993—. Lic. real estate appraiser, Miss. Mgr. money desk Bank Miss., Jackson, 1977-80; adminstrv. asst. Rsch. Inst. Pharm. Scis., University, Miss., 1980-83; appraiser, mgr. property, owner Magnolia Mgmt. Co., Oxford, Miss., 1985—; interim dir. Small Bus. Devel. Ctr., Oxford, 1989; chmn. multiple listing com. No. Ctrl. Miss. Bd. Realtors, Oxford, 1993-94. Pres. Oxford Downtown Coun., 1988; sec. Oxford Tourism coun., 1992-93. Mem. DAR, No. Ctrl. Miss. Home Builders Assn., Oxford C. of C., Lift, Inc., Golden Key, Phi Kappa Phi, Omicron Delta Epsilon. Democrat. Episcopalian. Home and Office: 1534 Jefferson Ave Oxford MS 38655

SHARPE, REGINA PAULA, accountant; b. Dayton, Ohio, Apr. 4, 1962; d. Carl and Alberta G. (Wells) S.; m. David W. Neiswender; 1 child, Carley. BS in Acctg., Wright State U., 1990. CPA, Ohio. Office mgr. Towne & Country Constrn., Inc., Kettering, Ohio, 1984; acctg. clk. Montgomery County Combined Health Dist., Dayton, 1984-87; acct. Montgomery County Community Human Svcs., Dayton, 1987-93; office mgr. Quality Aluminum Svcs., Dayton, 1991—; fiscal officer Montgomery Developmental Ctr., Huber Heights, Ohio, 1993—; prin. Sharp Tax Svcs., 1993—. Asst. treas. United Negro Coll. Fund, 1988-92. Mem. AICPA, Ohio Soc. CPAs, Profl. Tax Preparers Ohio. Home: 5215 Millcreek Rd Kettering OH 45440

SHARPE, ROCHELLE PHYLLIS, journalist; b. Gary, Ind., Apr. 27, 1956; d. Norman Nathaniel and Shirley (Kaplan) S. BA, Yale U., 1978. Reporter Concord (N.H.) Monitor, 1979-81; statehouse rep. Wilmington News Jour., Dover, Del., 1981-85; statehouse corr. Gannett News Svc., Albany, N.Y., 1985; nat. reporter Gannett News Svc., Washington, 1986-93; staff reporter social issues The Wall St. Jour., Washington, 1993—. Contbr. articles to profl. jours. Recipient Pulitzer prize for series in child abuse, Columbia U., 1991. Home: 2500 Q St NW #315 Washington DC 20007 Office: Wall St Jour Washington Bur 1025 Connecticut Ave NW Ste 800 Washington DC 20036

SHARPE, SAXON ELISABETH, paleoecologist; b. St. Louis, Feb. 8, 1954; d. Russell Thornley and Betty (Ward) S. BA in Environ. Planning, The Colo. Coll., 1976; MS in Quaternary Studies, No. Ariz. U., 1991. Paleoecologist Desert Rsch. Inst., Reno, 1992—. Author: (procs.) First Biennial Conf. on Rsch. in Colo. Plateau Nat. Pks., 1993, Fifth Ann. Internat. High-Level Radioactive Waste Mgmt. Conf. and Exposition, 1994. Planning commr. Castle Valley Town, Utah, 1985-88, coun. mem., 1986-88. Mem. AAUW, Am. Quaternary Assn., Ariz.-Nev. Acad. Scis., Assn. for Women in Sci., Geol. Soc. Am., Western Soc. Malacologists. Office: Desert Rsch Inst Quaternary Scis Ctr 7010 Dandini Blvd Reno NV 89512

SHARRAR, VICTORIA ANNE, publishing company executive; b. San Jose, Calif., June 2, 1958; d. Hans Christian Gunnar and Dolores Valerie (Barton) Sorensen; m. Kenneth Andrew Sharrar, Aug. 6, 1983. BS, U. So. Calif., 1981. Office adminstv. mgr. nat. radio div. CBS, Inc., Los Angeles, 1982-84; account exec. Orange (Calif.) Broadcasting Corp., 1984-85; account exec. Dun and Bradstreet/Donnelley Info. Pub., Garden Grove, Calif., 1985, sales tng mgr., 1985-86, sales tng. mgr., 1986-89, area sales mgr., 1989-91, gen. tng. mgr., 1991-92; gen. sales mgr. Reuben H. Donnelley, Orange, Calif., 1992-94, asst. v.p., 1994—. Mem. NAFE, Broadcast Music Inc. (writer), Long Beach C. of C. Republican. Office: Reuben H Donnelley 681 S Parker St Orange CA 92668

SHARROW, MARILYN JANE, library administrator; bd. Oakland, Calif.; d. Charles L. and H. Evelyn S.; m. Lawrence J. Davis. BS in Design, U. Mich., 1967, MALS, 1969. Librarian Detroit Pub. Libr., 1968-70; head fine arts dept. Syracuse (N.Y.) U. Librs., 1970-73; dir. libr. Roseville (Mich.) Pub. Libr., 1973-75; asst. dir. librs. U. Wash., 1975-77, assoc. dir. librs., 1978-79; dir. libraries U. Man., Winnipeg, Can., 1979-82; chief libr. U. Toronto, Can., 1982-85; univ. libr. U. Calif., Davis, 1985—. Recipient Woman of Yr. in Mgmt. award Winnipeg YWCA, 1982; named Woman of Distinction, U. Calif. Faculty Women's Rsch. Group, 1985. Mem. ALA, Assn. Rsch. Librs. (bd. dirs., v.p., pres-elect 1989-90, pres. 1990-91, chair sci. tech. work group 1994—, rsch. collections com. 1993—), Online Computer Libr. Ctr.-Rsch. Librs. Adv. Com. (vice chmn. 1992-93, chair 1993-94). Office: U Calif Shields Lib Davis CA 95616

SHASKY, LISA MARIE, insurance training specialist; b. Mpls., July 11, 1961; d. John Vincent and Joan Laurel (Hawkinson) S. BA in Zoology, Miami U., 1984; MS in Sports Medicine, Ill. State U., 1985. Athletic trainer Ill. State U., Normal, 1984-85; staff counselor Northside Ch. of Christ, Normal, 1985-87; health ins. underwriter State Farm Ins. Cos., Bloomington, Ill., 1987-90, health ins. supr., 1990-91, tng. specialist, 1991—; owner Laurel Publs., Normal, 1992—. Author: (pamphlet) Money Tips, 1993; contbr. articles to bus. mags. Mem. NAFE, Health Ins. Assn. Am. (assoc.), Womens Sports Found.

SHASTRI, KAREN ANDREA, finance educator; b. Balt.; d. Charles M. and Leona B. (Smidt) Connor; m. Kuldeep Shastri; 1 child, Joseph Kiran. BSBA magna cum laude, U. Balt., 1977; MBA, U. Pitts., 1982, PhD, 1990. CPA, Pa., Md. Sr. acct. Grant Thornton, Balt., 1978-81; instr. Robert Morris Coll., Pitts., 1982-85; lectr. Katz Grad. Sch. Bus. U. Pitts., 1981-90; instr. Sch. Bus. and Adminstrn. Duquesne U., Pitts., 1985-88; asst. prof. Coll. Bus. & Econs. W.Va. U., Morgantown, 1988-90; asst. prof. H. John Heinz III Sch. Pub. Policy & Mgmt. Carnegie Mellon U., Pitts., 1990—; instr. managerial acctg. grad. students Czechoslavak Mgmt. Ctr., 1992; cons. Feldstein, Grinberg, Stein & McKee, 1993, Meyer, Darragh, Buckler, Bebenek & Eck, 1989, 91, Rockwell Internat., summer 1986, 88, 89; speaker in field. Tutor, trainer Literacy Campaign, McKees Rock, Pa., 1988-91; bd. dirs. Renewal, Inc., Pitts., mem. fin. com. Senate rsch. grantee, 1990, US AID Case Study grantee, 1992, grad. fellow U. Pitts., 1981-82, Beta Alpha scholar U. Balt., 1977. Mem. Am. Acctg. Assn., AICPA, Ea. Fin. Assn., Fin. Mgmt. Assn., Inst. Mgmt. Accts., Pa. Inst. CPAs, Western Fin. Assn. Office: Carnegie Mellon U H John Heinz III Sch Pub Policy Mgmt Hamburg Hall Pittsburgh PA 15213

SHATTO, GLORIA MCDERMITH, college administrator, economist; b. Houston, Oct. 11, 1931; d. Ken E. and Gertrude (Osborne) McDermith; m. Robert J. Shatto, Mar. 19, 1953; children: David Paul, Donald Patrick. BA with honors in Econs., Rice U., 1954, PhD (fellow), 1966. Mkt. rsch. Humble Oil & Refining Co., Houston, 1954-55; tchr. pub. sch. C.Z., 1955-56; tchr. Houston Ind. Sch. Dist., 1956-60; asst. prof. econs. U. Houston, 1965-69, assoc. prof., 1969-72; prof. econs., assoc. dean Coll. Indsl. Mgmt., Ga. Inst. Tech., Atlanta, 1973-77; George R. Brown prof. bus. Trinity U., San Antonio, 1977-79; pres. Berry Coll., Mt. Berry, Ga., 1980—; small bus. adv. com. U.S. Treasury, 1977-81; trustee Joint Coun. Econ. Edn., 1985-88; dir. Ga. Power Co., Kmart Corp., So. Co., Becton Dickinson and Co., Tex. Instruments, Inc. Contbr. articles to profl. jours.; Editor: Employment of the Middle-Aged, 1972; mem. editorial bd.: Ednl. Record, 1980-82. Mem. Tex. Gov.'s Commn. on Status of Women, 1970-72, Gov.'s Commn. on Economy and Efficiency in State Govt., 1991, State Ethics Com., 1995—; trustee Ga. Tech. Rsch. Inst., 1975-77, Berry Coll., Ga., 1975-79, Ga. Forestry Commn., 1987-95; mem. Ga. Gov.'s Commn. on Status of Women, 1975; mem. commn. on women in higher edn. Am. Council on Edn., 1980-82, chmn., 1982; mem. Ga. Study Com. on Public Higher Edn. Fin., 1981-82; v.p. Ga. Found Ind. Colls., 1981, pres., 1982, 94; mem. adv. bd. to Sch. Bus. Adminstrn., Temple U., Phila., 1981-83; mem. Study Com. on Ednl. Processes, So. Assn. Colls. and Schs., 1981-82, Ga. United Meth. Commn. on Higher Edn. and Campus Ministry, 1981-82; trustee Redmond Park Hosp., Rome, Ga., 1981-87, 1st United Meth. Ch., 1986-89. Recipient Disting. Alumni award Rice U., 1987; OAS fellow, summer 1968. Mem. Royal Econ. Assn., Am. Econ. Assn., So. Econ. Assn., Southwestern Econ. Assn. (pres. 1976-77), Am. Fin. Assn. (nominating com. 1976), Southwestern Social Scis. Assn., Fin. Execs. Inst. (chmn. Atlanta edn. com. 1976-77, mem. com. on profl. devel. 1981), AAUW (area rep. 1967-68, Tex. chmn. legis. program 1970-71, mem. internat. fellowships-awards com. 1970-76, chmn. 1974-76), Ga. Newcomen Soc. (chmn. 1991—), Newcomen Soc. U.S. (trustee), Phi Beta Kappa, Phi Kappa Phi, Omicron Delta Epsilon. Office: Berry Coll Office of the President 39 Mt Berry Sta Mount Berry GA 30149-0039

SHATTUCK, CATHIE ANN, lawyer, former government official; b. Salt Lake City, July 18, 1945; d. Robert Ashley S. and Lillian Culp (Shattuck). B.A., U. Nebr., 1967, J.D., 1970. Bar: Nebr. 1970, U.S. Dist. Ct. Nebr. 1970, Colo. 1971, U.S. Dist. Ct. Colo. 1971, U.S. Supreme Ct. 1974, U.S. Ct. Appeals (10th cir.) 1977, U.S. Dist. Ct. D.C. 1984, U.S. Ct. Appeals (D.C. cir.) 1984. V.p., gen. mgr. Shattuck Farms, Hastings, Nebr., 1967-70; asst. project dir. atty. Colo. Civil Rights Commn., Denver, 1970-72; trial atty. Equal Employment Opportunity Commn., Denver, 1973-77; vice chmn. Equal Employment Opportunity Commn., Washington, 1982-84; pvt. practice law Denver, 1977-81; mem. Fgn. Svc. Bd., Washington, 1982-84, Presdl. Personnel Task Force, Washington, 1982-84; ptnr. Epstein, Becker & Green, L.A. and Washington, 1984—; lectr. Colo. Continuing Legal Edn. Author: Employer's Guide to Controlling Sexual Harrassment, 1992; mem. editorial bd. The Practical Litigator, 1988—. Bd. dirs. KGNU Pub. Radio, Boulder, Colo., 1979, Denver Exchange, 1980-81, YWCA Met. Denver, 1979-81. Recipient Nebr. Young Career Woman Bus. and Profl. Women, 1967; recipient Outstanding Nebraskan Daily Nebraskan, Lincoln, 1967. Mem. ABA (mgmt. chair labor and employment law sect. com. on immigration law 1988-90, mgmt. chair com. on legis. devels. 1990-93), Nebr. Bar Assn., Colo. Bar Assn., Colo. Women's Bar Assn., D.C. Bar Assn., Nat. Women's Coalition, Delta Sigma Rho, Tau Kappa Alpha, Pi Sigma Alpha, Alpha Xi Delta, Denver Club.

SHAUGHNESSY, AMY ELISABETH, retired association administrator; b. N.Y.C., Dec. 6, 1942; d. John Arthur and Alice (Miller) S.; m. David T. Humes, June, 14, 1984; 1 stepchild, Amy Elizabeth Humes. BS in Linguistics, Georgetown U., 1964, MS in Linguistics, 1970. Editorial assoc. Ctr. Applied Linguistics, Washington, 1964-70; asst. mng. editor Am. Jour. Psychiatry, Am. Psychiat. Assn., Washington, 1970-74; mng. editor, bus. mgr. Ctr. Personalized Instrn. Georgetown U., Washington, 1974-76; sr. editor Transp. Research Bd. Nat. Acad. Scis., Washington, 1976-81; free-lance editor, writer Washington, 1982-83; dir. publs. Am. Ednl. Research Assn., Washington, 1983-88; mng. editor Am. Soc. for Parenteral and Enteral Nutrition, 1990-91; free-lance editor, writer Washington, 1991—; judge typographic excellence competition Nat. Composition Assn., Washington, 1972-75. Vol. income tax assistance, 1989—. Mem. AAUW, Mensa (officer Washington chpt. 1978-79, pres. Washington chpt. 1979-81, nat. gov. com. 1981-93, 1st vice chmn. 1983-85, chief exec. officer nat. chpt. 1985-89, internat. bd. dirs. 1985—). Home: 369 0 St SW Washington DC 20024

SHAUGHNESSY, MARIE KANEKO, artist, business executive; b. Detroit, Sept. 14, 1924; d. Eishiro and Kiyo (Yoshida) Kaneko; m. John Thomas Shaughnessy, Sept. 23, 1959. Assocs. in Liberal Arts, Keisen Women's Coll., Tokyo, 1944. Ops. mgr. Webco Alaska, Inc., Anchorage, 1970-88; ptnr. Webco Partnership, Anchorage, 1983—, also bd. dirs. Paintings include Lilacs, 1984, Blooms, 1985, The Fence, 1986 (Purchase award 1986). Bd. dirs. Alaska Artists Guild, 1971-87; commr. Mcpl. Anchorage Fine Arts Commn., 1983-87; organizing com. Japanese Soc. Alaska, 1987. Recipient arts affiliates award Anchorage C.C., 1975, 78, 84, Univ. Artists award Alaska Pacific U., 1986, Am. Juror's Choice award Sumi-E Soc. Am., 1994, Ikebana Internat. award, 1994. Mem. Potomac Valley Watercolorists (bd. dirs., awards 1989, 91), Va. Watercolor Soc. (pres.), Sumi-E Soc. Am. (past pres., bd. dirs., Nat. Capital Area Chpt. award 1990, 91, 92, 94, Purchase award 1993), Vienna Art Soc. (bd. dirs.), Alaska Watercolor Soc. (charter and life mem., Grumbacher Silver medal 1989), McLean Arts Club (1st Pl. award 1991), Nat. League Am. Penwomen (Grumbacher Gold medal award Excellence 1993), Potomac Valley Watercolorists (bd. dirs. 1995). Republican. Episcopalian.

SHAUGHNESSY, RITA HOLMES, association executive; b. Chgo., Sept. 10, 1947; d. Harry Brennon and Mildred Delores (Zuanic) Holmes; m. Dennis Shaughnessy, Mar. 10, 1984. AB, St. Louis U., 1969; MEd, U. Mo., St. Louis, 1976. Cert. tchr. spl. edn. K-12, sch. psychol. examiner, elem. prin., Mo. Tchr. Spl. Sch. Dist., St. Louis, 1969-76; learning specialist Operation S.A.I.L., Jennings, Mo., 1976-78, dir., 1978-79; coord. student svcs. Miriam Sch., Webster Groves, Mo., 1979-84, dir., 1984-86; exec. dir. YWCA of Darien-Norwalk, Darien, Conn., 1987—. Mem. NAFE, Nat. Assn. YWCA Execs. Office: YWCA of Darien-Norwalk 49 Old Kings Highway N Darien CT 06820-4687

SHAVIN, KARNE LEE, academic administrator; b. Chattanooga, Dec. 7, 1949; d. Seamour and Gertrude (Horowitz) S.; m. Thomas Jefferson Crabtree, Oct. 6, 1974; children: Lauren, Seth, Zachary. BA in Liberal Arts, St. Johns Coll., 1972; MEd, Johns Hopkisn U., 1978. Cert. tchr., Md. Tchr. Balt. City Pub. schs., 1978-80; head tchr. Dundalk (Md.) C.C., 1980-82; instr. C.C. Balt., 1985; assoc. Disegno, Inc., Balt., 1986-92; rsch. asst. U. Md., Balt., 1992; child devel. specialist Balt. County Dept. Social Svcs., Towson, Md., 1992-94; ednl. cons. Head Start, Balt., 1994; dir. edn. St. Vincent's Children's Learning Ctr., Timonium, Md., 1994—. Mem. Parent Action Pub. Policy, Balt., 1993—; co-leader great books Montessori Soc. Ctrl. Md., Balt., 1987-89, bd. dirs., 1988-89; edn. com. Bolton St. Synagogue, Balt., 1992-93. U.S. Govt. grantee, 1993-95. Mem. Nat. Assn. Edn. Young Children, Parent Action. Home: 404 Dunkirk Rd Baltimore MD 21212-1815

SHAW, ANNETTE MARIE, realtor; b. Panama City, Fla., July 24; d. Winfred A. and Eunice M. (Merchant) Ramsey; children: Lani, Peter. Cert. in real estate, Career Coll., 1978. Realtor C-21, Bedford, Tex., Coldwell Banker, Hurst, Tex., Network 100, San Antonio, 1993—. Scrap book chmn. Womens Coun. Realtors, San Antonio. Home: 14019 Sunny Gln San Antonio TX 78217-1553 Office: Network 100 15600 San Pedro Ave Ste 400 San Antonio TX 78232-3788

SHAW, BARBARA SUSAN, community nurse; b. Queens, N.Y., July 3, 1956; d. David and Marcia Harriet (Mattis) S. BA cum laude, Mt. Holyoke Coll., 1978; MA, U. Chgo., 1980; MSN, Yale U., 1988. Rsch. dir. Midwest Women's Ctr., Chgo., 1980-81; pub. affairs assoc., pub. rels. dir. Planned Parenthood, Chgo., 1981-85; family nurse practitioner Joseph Smith Health Ctr., Boston, 1988-91, Brigham Women's Hosp., Boston, 1991-94; clinic coord. Esperanza Family Ctr., Chgo., 1994—; cons. Boston U. Midwifery Program, 1993; adj. clin. instr. Simmons Coll., Boston, 1992—. Mem. ANA, Mass. Nurse Practitioner Assn., Tex. Nurse Practitioner Assn.

SHAW, CAROLE, editor, publisher; b. Bklyn., Jan. 22, 1936; d. Sam and Betty (Neckin) Bergenthal; m. Ray Shaw, Dec. 27, 1957; children: Lori Eve Cohen, Victoria Shaw Locknar. BA, Hunter Coll., 1962. Singer Capitol Records, Hilton Records, Rama Records, Verve Records, 1952-65; TV appearances Ed Sullivan, Steve Allen, Jack Paar, George Gobel Show, 1957; owner The People's Choice, L.A., 1975-79; founder, editor-in-chief Big Beautiful Woman mag., Beverly Hills, Calif., 1979—; creator Carole Shaw and BBW label clothing line for large-size women. Author: Come Out, Come Out Wherever You Are, 1982. Office: BBW Mag PO Box K-298 Tarzana CA 91356

SHAW, CHARLOTTE DENISE, accountant; b. Birmingham, Ala., June 21, 1961; d. Fred Franklin and Edith (Williams) Self; m. Robert Neal Shaw, Sept. 7, 1984. BS in Commerce summa cum laude, U. Ala., 1983. CPA; cert. mgmt. acct., cert. internal auditor. Audit mgr. Coopers & Lybrand, Dallas, 1983-91; mgr. fin. reporting Aegon, U.S.A., Dallas, 1991-93; dir. accounting NCH Corp., Irving, Tex., 1993—. Mem. AICPA, Inst. Mgmt. Accts., Tex. Soc. CPA, Beta Gamma Sigma, Beta Alpha Psi. Republican. Baptist. Home: 917 McCoy Dr Irving TX 75062 Office: NCH Corp 2727 Chemsearch Blvd Irving TX 75062

SHAW, DORIS BEAUMAR, film and video producer, executive recruiter; b. Pitts., July 13, 1934; d. Emerson C. and Doris Llorene (Rees) Beaumar; m. Robert Newton Shaw, July 6, 1957. BA summa cum laude, Lindenwood Coll., St. Charles, Mo., 1955. Writer, asst. to pres. Baker Prodns., Benton Harbor, Mich., 1955; asst. prodn. mgr. Condor Films, Inc., St. Louis, 1955-57; chief editor, asst. to v.p. Frederick F. Watson Inc., N.Y.C., 1957-58; v.p. Gen. Pictures Corp., Cleve., 1958-71; dir., editor, unit mgr. Cinecraft Inc., Cleve., 1971-72; mgr. audio-visual dept. Am. Greetings Corp., Cleve., 1972-73; proprietor Script to Screen Svcs., Chagrin Falls, Ohio, 1973-76; pres. D & B Shaw, Inc., Chardon, Ohio, 1976-87, Hudson, Ohio, 1987—; pres. Execusearch, Inc., Hudson, 1987—, Infosearch Svcs., Hudson, 1994—; film festival judge, tchr. Martha Holden Jennings Found./Hawken Sch., Gates Mills, Ohio, 1970-85; advisor teenage film contests, seminars Cleve. Bd. Edn., 1970-88; contest judge/film and video WVIZ-TV, Channel 25, Parma, Ohio, 1971—; guest lectr. Lindenwood Coll., 1973-80; adj. prof. U. Akron, 1990—. Writer, dir., editor, prodr. film, video, multi-image, multi-media, audio/visual prodn., radio, TV, commls. and programs; contbr. articles to profl. jours. Bd. trustees Ohio Boys Town, Cleve., 1957-68; mem. alumnae coun. Lindenwood Coll., 1973-77; publicity chmn. Geauga County Preservation Soc., 1984-91; active various charitable orgns. Named Outstanding Young Woman of Am., Fedn. of Women's Clubs, 1965, Alumna of Yr. Merit award Lindenwood Coll., 1971; recipient numerous awards and grants for film, video projects including Gold Camera Best Documentary award, 1979. Mem. Soc. Motion Picture and TV Engrs., Info. Film Prodrs. Am., Assn. for Multi Image (charter), Detroit Prodrs. Assn., Internat. TV and Video Assn. (charter), Internat. Comm. Industries Assn., Alpha Epsilon Rho. Republican. Office: D & B Shaw Inc 118 W Streetsboro Rd Hudson OH 44236

SHAW, ELIZABETH ORR, lawyer; b. Monona, Iowa, Oct. 2, 1923; d. Harold Topliff and Hazel (Kean) Orr; m. Donald Hardy Shaw, Aug. 16,

1946; children: Elizabeth Ann, Andrew Hardy, Anthony Orr. AB, Drake U., 1945; postgrad. U. Minn., 1945-46; JD, U. Iowa, 1948. Bar: Ill. 1949, Iowa 1956, U.S. Dist. Ct. (so. dist.) Iowa 1977. Assoc. Lord Bissell & Brook, Chgo, 1949-52; pvt. practice law, Arlington Heights, Ill., 1952-56; ptnr. Wood & Shaw, Davenport, Iowa, 1968-72; mem. Iowa Ho. of Reps., Des Moines, 1967-72; mem. Iowa Senate, Des Moines, 1972-77; county atty. Scott County, Davenport, 1977-78; corp. atty. Deere & Co., Moline, Ill., 1979-89; pvt. practice, Davenport, 1990—. Mem. ABA, Scott County Bar Assn. (com. chmn. 1970-72), Iowa State Bar Assn. (com. chmn. 1970-76), Order of Coif, Phi Beta Kappa, Kappa Kappa Gamma, PEO. Republican. Mem. United Ch. Christ. Home and Office: 29 Hillcrest Ave Davenport IA 52803-3726

SHAW, GINA LOUISE, wallpaper designer; b. Ephrata, Pa., Sept. 26, 1960; d. Brenda L. (Enck) Roach; m. Jonathan Wayne Shaw, Sept. 28, 1985; 1 child, Cameron. BFA, Moore Coll. of Art, 1982. V.p. design Eisenhart Wallcoverings Co., Hanover, Pa., 1982—. Named 1 of 12 Achievers of Yr., Wallcoverings Windows & Interior Fashion mag., 1994. Mem. Color Mktg. Group. Home: 2 Timber Ln Hanover PA 17331-9381 Office: Eisenhart Wallcoverings Co PO Box 464 Hanover PA 17331-0464

SHAW, GLORIA DORIS, art educator; b. Huntington, W.Va., Nov. 10, 1928; d. Charles Bert and Theodosia Doris (Shimer) Haley; m. Arthur Shaw, July 13, 1954 (dec. Aug. 1985); children: Deirdra E. Franz, Stewart N. Student, SUNY, 1969-70, Art Students League, N.Y.C., 1969-70, 74; BA, SUNY, N.Y.C., 1980; postgrad., U. Tenn., 1982, Nat Kaz, Pietrasanta, Italy, 1992. Sculptor replicator Am. Mus. Natural History, N.Y.C., 1976-77; adj. prof. sculpture Fla. Keys C.C., Key West, 1983—; prof. TV art history Fla. Keys Community Coll., 1989-91. Sculptor (portrait) Jimmy Carter, Carter Meml. Libr., 1976, Tennessee Williams, Tennessee Williams Fine Arts Ctr., 1982, UNICEF, 1978-79, (series) Fla. Panther and Audubon Wall Relief, 1985, (bust) AIDS Meml., 1990; one woman shows includes Bank Street Coll., 1979, Hollywood Mus. of Art, 1985, Islander Gallery, 1983, Martello Mus., 1984, Greenpeace, 1987; exhibited in group shows at Montoya, West Palm Beach, Fla., 1989, N.Y.C. Bd. of Edn. Tour of Schs., 1979, Earthworks East, N.Y., 1987, Man and Sci., 1978, Cuban Club, Key West, Fla., 1991, Leda Bruce Gallery, Big Pine, 1992, Kaz, Pietrasanta, Italy, 1992, Fla. Keys C.C. Gallery, 1993, Tennessee Williams Fine Arts Ctr., Key West, 1993, Internat. Woman's Show, Fla. Keys, 1994, Joy Gallery, 1994. Host, moderator Channel 5 TV, Fla. Keys, 1982—, Humanities Channel 19 TV, 1995—; designer Windows at Greenpeace Bldg., Key West, 1985-88. Recipient Children and Other Endangered Species award Thomas Cultural Ctr., 1980, Purchase award Cuban C. of C., 1982, Sierra Club, 1983, Blue Ribbon, Martello Towers Art and Hist. Soc., 1985, Red Ribbon, South Fla. Sculptors, 1986, Endangered Species award Greenpeace, 1986. Mem. Nat. Sculpture Soc. of N.Y.C., Internat. Sculpture Ctr., Art Students League of N.Y.C. (life), Art and Hist. Soc. Democrat. Office: Fla Keys CC Stock Island Key West FL 33040

SHAW, GRACE GOODFRIEND (MRS. HERBERT FRANKLIN SHAW), publisher, editor; b. N.Y.C.; d. Henry Bernheim and Jane Elizabeth (Stone) Goodfriend; m. Herbert Franklin Shaw (dec. 1992); 1 son, Brandon Hibbs. Student, Bennington Coll.; BA magna cum laude, Fordham U., 1976, MS, 1991. Reporter Port Chester (N.Y.) Daily Item; editorial coordinator World Scope Ency., N.Y.C.; assoc. editor Clarence L. Barnhart, Inc., Bronxville, N.Y.; freelance-writer for reference books; editing supr. World Pub. Co., mng. editor, sr. editor; mng. editor Peter H. Wyden Co., N.Y.C., 1969-70; assoc. editor Dial Press, N.Y.C., 1971-72; sr. editor Dial Press, 1972, David McKay Co., N.Y.C., 1972-75, Grosset & Dunlap, 1975-79; chief editor Today Press (Grosset), 1977-79; sr. editor, coll. dept. Bobbs-Merrill, N.Y.C., mng. editor, exec. editor trade div., 1979-80; pub. Bobbs-Merrill, 1980-84; mng. editor Rawson Assocs. div. Macmillan Pub., 1985-91; pres. Grace Shaw Assocs., Scarsdale, N.Y., 1991—. Home and Office: 85 Lee Rd Scarsdale NY 10583-5212

SHAW, HELEN LESTER ANDERSON, nutrition educator; b. Lexington, Ky., Oct. 18, 1936; d. Walter Southall and Elizabeth (Guyn) Anderson; m. Charles Van Shaw, Mar. 14, 1988. BS, U. Ky., 1958; MS, U. Wis., 1965, PhD, 1969. Registered dietitian. Dietitian Roanoke (Va.) Meml. Hosp., 1959-60, Santa Barbara (Calif.) Cottage Hosp., 1960-61; dietitian, unit mgr. U. Calif., Santa Barbara, 1961-63; rsch. asst., NIH fellow U. Wis., Madison, 1963-68; from asst. prof. to prof. U. Mo., Columbia, 1969-88, assoc. dean, prof., 1977-84; prof., chair dept. food and nutrition U. N.C., Greensboro, 1989-94, dean Sch. Human Environ. Scis., 1994—; cluster leader Food for 21st Century rsch. program U. Mo., 1985-88. Contbr. articles to rsch. publs. Elder 1st Presbyn. Ch., Columbia, 1975-89, Greensboro, 1992-94. Recipient Teaching award Home Econ. Alumni Assn., 1981, Gamma Sigma Delta, 1984; rsch. grantee Nutrition Found., 1971-73, NIH, 1972-75, NSF, 1980-83. Mem. Am. Inst. Nutrition, Am. Bd. Nutrition, Am. Soc. for Clin. Nutrition, Am. Dietetic Assn., Am. Home Econs. Assn., Soc. for Nutrition Edn., Sigma Xi, Phi Upsilon Omicron, Omicron Nu. Democrat.

SHAW, HELEN LOUISE HAITH, educational administrator; b. Glen Raven, N.C., Oct. 6, 1931; d. Samuel and Robie (Summers) Haith; m. Benjamin Franklin Shaw, Apr. 9, 1954 (div. Dec. 1991); children: Ronald Elliott, Roland Eric. BS cum laude, N.C. Agrl. and Tech. State U., Greensboro, 1953; postgrad., D.C. Tchrs. Coll., 1962-64, Monterey Peninsula Coll., 1966, 86. 91, LaVerne Coll., 1975-77, Gavilan Coll., 1985-87. Cert. child devel. tchr., Calif. Elem. tchr. Lynchburg (Va.) City Schs., 1953-54, D.C. Pub. Schs., Washington, 1960-65; receptionist, dental asst. Dr. Benjamin Franklin Shaw, Seaside, Calif., 1970-85; from office pers. to adminstrv. asst. Infant Care Ctr., Inc., Seaside, 1984-92. Vol. Reach to Recovery; past stewardess, steward, sec. ch. conf., sec. ofcl. bd., sec. quar. conf., past pres. Women's Missionary Soc., now v.p.; ch. treas., mem. choir, sec.; mem. Lay Coun., adminstrv. asst. to pastor Hays Christian Meth. Episcopal Ch. Named Woman of Yr., Hays Christian Meth. Episcopal Ch., 1982, 91, 1st pl. award state rally, 1991, 92, 93, 2d pl. award 1994, stewardess award, 1992; honoree for outstanding cmty. svc. Sun St. Ctrs., Inc.-Sea Rina Cmty. Recovery Ctr., 1994. Mem. NAACP (Golden Heritage), Am. Assn. Ret. Persons, Am. Legion Aux. (pres. 1993—), Seaside Bus. and Profl. Women, Nat. Coun. Negro Women, Citizen's League for Progress (life), Order Ea. Star (past matron Golden State Grand chpt., honoree for contbns. to cmty. 1994), Heroines of Jericho (most ancient matron and grand dep.), Alpha Kappa Alpha (past basileus and currently corres. sec. Kappa Gamma Omega chpt.), Sigma Rho Sigma. Democrat. Address: PO Box 331 Seaside CA 93955-0331

SHAW, LAQUETTA AVEITTE, computer specialist; b. Dallas, June 20, 1964; d. Lawrence James and Lillian Marie (Jefferies) S. BBA, East Tex. State U., 1985, MEd, 1992. Cert. tchr., adminstr., Tex. With Dallas County, Dallas, 1986-87, City of Dallas, 1987-88; tchr. Allstate Bus. Coll., Dallas, 1988-90, Phillips Sch. Bus. and Tech., Dallas, 1990, Nat. Edn. Ctr., Dallas, 1991; tchr., computer specialist Dallas Ind. Sch. Dist., 1988—; personal computer cons., Dallas, 1985—. Program cons., troop leader Tejas coun. Girl Scouts U.S.A., 1991—. Recipient Pub. Svc. award Tejas coun. Girl Scouts U.S.A., 1992. Mem. ASCD, Assn. for System Mgrs., Delta Sigma Theta (Pub. Svc. award 1990). Office: Sequoyah Learning Ctr 3635 Greenleaf St Dallas TX 75212-1520

SHAW, LAURIE JO, grant project director; b. Morris, Minn., Feb. 23, 1956; d. Edgar Allen and Dorothy Ruth (Harms) S.; m. Grant William Carlson, July 23, 1983 (div. Feb. 1986). Tchr. aide degree, Hutchinson Area Vocat. Tech., Minn., 1975; audio visual prodn., Hutchinson (Minn.) AVTI, 1976; BA in Psychology, S.W. State U., 1982; MA in Counseling, N.Mex. State U., 1987. Libr. tech. S.W. State U., Marshall, Minn., 1976-84; student svcs. coord. Mohave C.C., Bullhead City, Ariz., 1987-91; counselor, instr. Prestonsburg C.C., Pikeville, Ky., 1992-93; project dir. So. W.Va. C.C., Williamson, 1993—. Mem. AAUW (v.p. 1990-92), Nat. Assn. Student Pers. Adminstrs., Ky. Assn. Student Fin. Aid Adminstrs., Bus. and Profl. Women (pres. 1990-91, Young Career Woman award 1989), W.Va. Assn. Edn. Opportunity Program Pers., Mid.-East Assn. Edn. Opportunity Program Pers. Democrat. Methodist. Office: So WV Community Coll Armory Dr Williamson WV 25661

SHAW, LILLIE MARIE KING, vocalist; b. Indpls., Nov. 27, 1915; d. Earl William and Bertha Louise (Groth) King; m. Philip Harlow Shaw, June 26, 1940. Student, Jordan Conservatory Music, Indpls., 1940-43; BA, Ariz. State U., 1959; MA, Denver U., 1962; pvt. vocal study, 1944-70. Educator, libr. Glendale (Ariz.) Schs., 1959-67; lectr. libr. sci. Ariz. State U., Tempe, 1962-68. Concertizing, oratorio, symphonic soloist, light opera, 1965-82; soloist First Ch. of Christ Scientist, Sun City West, Ariz., 1980—. Monthly lectr. Christian Women's Fellowship, Phoenix, 1989—; World Conf. del. Soc. of Friends, 1967. Mem. Nat. Soc. Arts and Letters (sec. 1990-94, nat. del. 1992), Am. Philatelic Assn. (life), Am. Topical Assn., Phoenix Philatelic Soc., Auditions Guild Ariz. (sec. 1989-93), Phoenix Opera League, Phoenix Symphony Guild (bd. mem. youth activities 1986—), Sigma Alpha Iota Alumnae (Phoenix chpt., life, treas. 1988—, Sword of Honor 1972, Rose of Honor 1982). Republican. Home: 6802 N 37th Ave Phoenix AZ 85019-1103

SHAW, MARILYN MARGARET, artist, photographer; b. San Diego, Dec. 19, 1933; d. George Louis and Helen Frances (Wright) Mitchell; m. Robert Dale Shaw, Feb. 19, 1952; children: Austin Allen, Kenneth Duane, Frank Lloyd. BA in Fine Arts and Photography, Juniata Coll., 1989. Photographer The Daily News, Huntingdon, Pa., 1988-92; owner, tchr. Marilyn Shaw Studios, Marklesburg, Pa., 1989—; photographer The Jamesyouth, St. James. Luth. Ch., Huntingdon, 1987-92; photojournalist Easter Seals Telethon, 1991-92; art dir. Allegheny Riding Camp-The GrierSch., Tyrone, Pa., 1992. One-woman shows include Shoemaker Gallery, Huntingdon, 1989; group shows include Standing Stone Art League, Huntingdon, 1978-92, Washington St. Art Gallery, Huntingdon, 1991, 94; author, illustrator The Prize, 1989. Vol. The Huntingdon House, 1992—, The Presbyn. Ch., Huntingdon, 1992-94. Recipient numerous ribbons Huntingdon County Fair, 1978, 90, 91, Sinking Valley Farm Show, 1992, 94, Huntingdon County Arts Coun., 1989, 90, 91, Merit cert. Photographers Forum, 1989, Vila Gardner Metzger art award, 1989, others. Mem. Standing Stone Art League, Huntingdon County Arts Coun., Women's League Juniata Coll., , Nat. Mus. of Women in the Arts (charter mem.). Home: PO Box 7 28 N Bedford Rd James Creek PA 16657-0007 Office: The Marilyn Shaw Studios PO Box 7 28 N Bedford Rd James Creek PA 16657-0007

SHAW, MARY TODD, art educator; b. Gadsden, Ala., Feb. 9, 1921; d. Oscar E. and Jennie (Harris) T.; m. Edward H. Shaw; children: Barbara Shaw Brinson, George N. BCA, Atlanta Coll. Art, 1942; BFA, U. N.C., 1974; postgrad., Ga. Inst. Tech., U. N.C., Greensboro. Draftsman So. Bell, Atlanta, 1941-42, U.S. Warfare, Atlanta, 1942-43; comml. artist Maurice Coleman & Assocs., Atlanta; instr. art Mint Mus., Charlotte, N.C., 1966-76, Spirit Square, Charlotte, 1976-93; One person shows at Mint Mus., Charlotte, N.C., 1967, Herman Art Gallery, Statesville, N.C., 1972, Queens Coll., Charlotte, 1973, Harold Decker Gallery, Norfolk, Va., 1973, The Arts Works, Statesville, N.C., 1978, Spirit Sq., Charlotte, 1977, 81, Lancaster (S.C.) Gallery, 1983, Queen's Coll. Paul Klapper Art Libr., Flushing, N.Y., 1985, Secca, Winston Salem, N.C., 1982, Milliken Gallery, Spartanburg, S.C., 1986, Upstairs Gallery, Tryon, N.C., 1988, Asheville (N.C.) Mus. Art, 1990, The Waterworks, Salisbury, N.C., 1991, Mus. York County, 1994, others. Group exhbns. include Nat. Acad., N.Y.C., Atlanta Art Inst., Winston-Salem Gallery of Fine Arts, Richmond Mus., Collectors' Gallery, Washington, Riverside Mus., N.Y.C., Museo de Bella Artes, Buenos Aires, Winston-Salem, Art and Sci. Mus., Statesville, Columbia (S.C.) Mus. Art, Columbus (Ga.) Mus. Art, Birmingham (Ala.) Mus. Art, Dulin Gallery of Art, Knoxville, Mint Mus. Art, Charlotte, Atlier-Galerie, Dijon, France, Pallazzo Ducale, Venezia, Italy, Mark Milliken Gallery, others. Recipient Henri Bendel award Nat. Acad., N.Y., 1961, 1st prize Drake House Pub. Co., Charlotte, 1971, Purchase award U. N.C., 1973, Charlotte Open Exhbn., 1980, Best in Show award Spring Fest, Charlotte, 1986, numerous others; fellow Yaddo, 1980, 81, Va. Ctr. for Arts, Sweet Briar, 1984, 86, 93, Tyrone Guthrie Found., 1986, Banff Ctr. for Arts, Can., 1987, Atlantic Ctr. for Arts, 1983, others. Mem. Tri-State Sculptors Assn., So. Graphics Assn. Home: 6611 Burlwood Rd Charlotte NC 28211-5607

SHAW, NANCY RIVARD, museum curator, art historian, educator; b. Saginaw, Mich.; d. Joseph H. and Jean M. (O'Boyle) Marcotte; m. Danny W. Shaw, Feb. 29, 1980; 1 stepchild, Christina Marie. BA magna cum laude, Oakland U., 1969; MA, Wayne State U., 1973. Asst. curator Am. art Detroit Inst. Arts, 1972-75, curator, 1975—; adj. prof. art and art history Wayne State U., Detroit, 1991—. Contbg. author: American Art in the Detroit Institute of Arts, 1991; contbr. articles to exhbn. catalogues and profl. jours. Mem. Wayne State U. Alumni Assn. Roman Catholic. Office: Detroit Inst Arts 5200 Woodward Ave Detroit MI 48202-4094

SHAW, PATRICIA MARIE, home care nurse; b. McLeansboro, Ill., Oct. 4, 1950; d. Henry Paul and Rita Marie (Rapp) Kiefer; m. Charles H. White, Aug. 26, 1970 (div. Sept. 1979); children: Christopher, Gregory; m. Larry N. Shaw, Nov. 27, 1981; children: Mark, Angie, Sarah. Student, Rend Lake Coll., 1969-71; ADN, Frontier Community Coll., Fairfield, Ill., 1980; student, McKendree Coll., 1993—. From CNA to lic. practical nurse to RN Good Samaritan Hosp., Mt. Vernon, Ill., 1972-80; RN Hamilton Meml. Hosp., McLeansboro, Ill., 1980-81, Crossroads Hosp., Mt. Vernon, 1981-84, Jeffersonian Nursing Home, Mt. Vernon, 1985-88, Olson Kimberly Quality Care, Marion, Belleville, Ill., 1988-94, Staff Builders, Edwardsville, Ill., 1989—, Ptnrs. Home Health, Marion, Ill., 1989—; nurse Home House Calls, Fairview Heights, Ill., 1993—. Former head birthday com., charge Sunday sch. class activity, choir mem. First Freewill Bapt. Ch. Mem. Ladies Aux. (former sec.-treas.). Baptist. Home: Box 185 Ina IL 62846

SHAW, PEGGY NAHAS, clergywoman; b. Merced, Calif., Feb. 3, 1958; d. Edward Nahas and Edith Candler (Stebbins) Paxman; m. Albert A. Polhamas, Sept. 18, 1977 (div. 1979); m. Michael Steven Shaw, May 25, 1980; children: Danica, Brandy Rae, Adria. Grad. high sch., Davis, Calif. Dianetics counselor Ch. Scientology Mission of Davis (Calif.), 1975-76, dir. processing, 1976-77, registrar, 1977-78, dissemination dir., 1978-82; dir. pub. svcs. Ch. Scientology Mission of Sacramento Valley, Davis, 1982-83, orgnl. exec., 1983-84, HCO exec., 1984-85; exec. dir. Ch. Scientology Missions Sacramento Valley-River Park-Chico, Vacaville, Calif., 1985—; also pres. bd. dirs. Ch. Scientology Missions Sacramento Valley-River Park-Chico, Vacaville, 1985—. Mem. Internat. Assn. Scientology (honor roll 1987). Home: 4132 Mindt Ct Carmichael CA 95608-2400 Office: Ch of Scientology 1485 River Park Dr Sacramento CA 95815-4501

SHAW, ROSLYN LEE, elementary education educator; b. Bklyn., Oct. 1, 1942; d. Benjamin Biltmore and Bessie (Banilower) Deretchin; m. Stephen Allan Shaw, Feb. 1, 1964; children: Laurence, Victoria, Michael. BA, Bklyn. Coll., 1964; MS, SUNY, New Paltz, 1977, cert. advanced study, 1987; cert. gifted edn., Coll. New Rochelle, 1986. Cert. sch. adminstr., supr., sch. dist. adminstr., reading tchr., tchr. N-6. Tchr. Hillel Hebrew Acad., Beverly Hills, Calif., 1965-66, P.S. 177, 77, Bklyn., 1964-65, 66-67; tchr. Middletown (N.Y.) Sch. Dist., 1974-77, reading specialist, 1977—, compensatory edn. reading tchr., 1977-86, tchr. gifted children, 1984-87, asst. project coord. pre-K, 1988-89, instrnl. leader, 1989-93. Pres. Middletown H.S. Parents' Club, 1983-86; bd. dirs. Mental Health Assn., Goshen, N.Y., 1980-81; mem. Middletown Interfaith Coun., 1983-85. Mem. ASCD, Amy Bull Crist Reading Coun. (pres. 1989-91, 93—), N.Y. State Reading Assn. (Coun. Svc. award 1990, regional dir. 1991-93, bd. dirs. 1991—, chair reading tchrs. spl. interest group 1993—), Internat. Reading Assn., Univ. Women's Club, Delta Kappa Gamma. Home: 133 Highland Ave Middletown NY 10940-4712 Office: Liberty St Sch 6 Liberty St Middletown NY 10940

SHAW, RUTH JEAN, librarian, library consultant; b. Glasgow, Mont., Jan. 12, 1943; d. Jerold B. and Ruth (Shanahan) Van Faasen; m. Robert D. Shaw, Aug. 28, 1964; 1 child, Douglas Bryan. BS, East Tex. State U., 1966; MLS, U. Okla., 1967. Cataloger East Tex. State U., Commerce, 1965-66; acquisitions asst. U. Okla., Norman, 1966-67; libr. dir. Coll. of Great Falls, Mont., 1967-70; spl. projects libr. Wash. State U., Pullman, 1970-78; mgr., libr. resources Anchorage Sch. Dist., 1979—; pvt. piano tchr., organist, Anchorage. Editor: Sourdough/Alaska Libr. Assn. Quarterly, 1990-91, Acticulation/Alaska Press Women, 1991-92; contbr. articles to profl. jours. Chmn. Access Task Force, Anchorage Link, 1989-90; mem. Lifelong Learning Task Force, WISE Project, Anchorage, 1991. Mem. ALA, Am. Assn. Sch. Librs. (publs. com. 1992—), Am. Organists Guild, Alaska Libr. Assn., Pacific N.W. Libr. Assn. Home: 5430 E 32nd Ave Anchorage AK 99508-4719 Office: Anchorage Sch Dist 1800 Hillcrest Dr Anchorage AK 99517-1347

SHAW, SALLYE BROWN, women's health nurse; b. Charlotte, N.C., Oct. 14, 1941; d. Robert Cotten III and Nannie Lee (Phillips) Brown; m. Phillip A. Shaw, III, July 19, 1986. BS, Queens Coll., Charlotte, 1964; M in Nursing, Emory U., Atlanta, 1967. Instr. nursing edn. Western Carolina Ctr., Morganton, N.C., 1964; staff nurse York Gen. Hosp., Rock Hill, S.C., 1965-66; assoc. prof. Fla. State U., Tallahassee, 1967-81; exec. dir. NAACOG, Washington, 1981-92; assoc. dir. collaborative practice ACOG, 1993—; cons. Edn. in Childbirth Assn., Tallahassee, 1972-74, Gadsden County Hosp., Ft. Walton, Fla., 1974-75, Fla. State U. Sch. of Nursing and Community Agys., Tallahassee, 1974-75, task force Common Course Numbering, State of Fla., 1975-77; adv. panel Maternal-Child Core Competencies, 1986-88; adv. bd. ParentSource, Waltham, Mass., 1993-94, Vida Health Comm., 1989-91, Williams and Wilkins Pub., 1987-89; speaker in field. Contbr. articles to profl. jours. Vol. Telephone Pollsters, Alexandria, Va., 1990-93; pres. Presbyn. Women Westminster Ch., Alexandria, 1992-94. Mem. ANA, NAACOG (pres. 1977), Nat. League Nursing (bd. dirs. D.C. League 1986-87), Sigma Theta Tau (bd. dirs. Pi chpt. 1977-79), Am. Soc. Assn. Execs. Home: 3212 Old Dominion Blvd Alexandria VA 22305-1316 Office: ACOG 409 12th St SW Washington DC 20024-2188

SHAW, SUSAN MARY, sales executive; b. Milw., Aug. 17, 1963; d. Leonard F. and Shirley Mae (Hendricks) S. BBA in Mktg., U. Wis., Milw., 1985. Sales rep. Johnson Bros. Beverages, Milw., 1985-90, Ethicon, Inc., Chgo., 1990-92, McGaw Inc., Chgo., 1992-94, Cryolife, Inc., Milw., 1994—.

SHAW, VALEEN JONES, special education educator, elementary school educator; b. Coalville, Utah, June 19, 1930; d. G. Allen and Mabel Leon (Clark) Jones; m. Melvin Francis Shaw, June 21, 1948; children: C. Allene Shaw Fuhriman, Denise Ellen Shaw Call, Sharon Marie Shaw Williams. BS, Weber State U., Ogden, Utah, 1966; postgrad., U. Utah, Utah State U., Brigham Young U. Cert. tchr. elem. edn., early childhood edn., spl. edn. Tchr. 3rd grade Morgan (Utah) Sch. Dist., 1965-66; tchr. 6th grades N. Summit Sch. Dist., Coalville, Utah, 1966-67, tchr. 2d grades, 1967-82, tchr. resource, spl. edn., 1982-92, teaching specialist elem. summer sch. prog., 1967-92; elementary resource and spl. edn. tchr. North Summit Sch. Dist., Coalville, 1982-92; mentor N. Summit Elementary Sch., 1988-89. Tchr./trainer Coalville Ch. of Jesus Christ of Latter-day Saints. &D. Mem. NEA, ASCD Inst., Utah Edn. Assn., Morgan Edn. Assn., North Summit Edn. Asssn, Utah Fedn. Coun. for Exceptional Children.

SHAW, VIRGINIA RUTH, clinical psychologist; b. Salina, Kans., Dec. 10, 1952; d. Lawrence Eugene and Gladys (Wilbur) S.; m. Joseph Eugene Scuro Jr., July 14, 1990. BA magna cum laude, Kans. Wesleyan U., 1973; MA, Wichita State U., 1975; PhD, U. Southern Miss., 1984. Diplomate Am. Bd. Med. Psychotherapists (fellow). Rsch. fellow Wichita (Kans.) State U., 1973-75; rsch. fellow, teaching fellow U. So. Miss., 1978-79, 80-81; staff psychologist Big Spring (Tex.) State Hosp., 1976-78; predoctoral clin. psychology intern U. Okla. Health Scis. Ctr., Oklahoma City, 1981-82; postdoctoral fellow in neuropsychology Neuropsychiat. Inst., UCLA, 1982-83; rsch. psychologist, neuropsychologist L.A. VA Med. Ctr. Wadsworth Div., 1983-84; clin. neuropsychologist Patton (Calif.) State Hosp., 1984-85; clin. neuropsychologist Brentwood div. LA VA Med. Ctr., 1985; clinical, neuropsychologist Timberlawn Psychiatric Hosp., Dallas, 1985-87, Dallas Rehab. Inst., 1987-93; cons. clin. neuropsychology Dallas area hosps., Willowbrook Hosp., Waxahachie, Tex., Cedars Hosp., Waxahachie, 1988—; presenter profl. meetings, 1975—. Contbr. articles to profl. jours. Mem. Dallas Mayor's Com. for Employment of the Disabled (cert. appreciation), 1987, 500 Inc., Dallas, 1988—. Remiatte Meml. scholar Kans. Wesleyan U., 1970-73; recipient Nat. Disting. Svc. Registry award in rehab., 1989, Early Career Contbns. to Clin.Neuropsychology award candidate, Nat. Acad. Neuropsychologists, 1993, 94. Mem. APA, Internat. Neuropsychol. Soc., Nat. Head Injury Found., Tex. Head Injury Found., Dallas Head Injury Found. (Vol. award, cert. appreciation 1991), Am. Congress Rehab. Medicine, Nat. Rehab. Assn., Nat. Acad. Neuropsychologists (membership com. 1991-94, rsch. consortium 1991—). Office: PO Box 543202 Dallas TX 75354-3202

SHAW-COHEN, LORI EVE, magazine editor; b. Manhattan, N.Y., Apr. 22, 1959; d. Ray and Carole (Bergenthal) Shaw; m. Robert Mark Cohen, Sept. 20, 1981; children: Joshua Samuel, Drew Taylor, Logan Shaw. BA in Journalism, U. So. Calif., 1981. Editorial asst., writer BBW: Big Beautiful Woman Mag., Los Angeles, 1979-80; editorial asst., writer Intro Mag., Los Angeles, 1980-81; mng. editor 'Teen Mag., Los Angeles, 1981-86; writer, interviewer Stan Rosenfeld & Assocs. Pub. Relations, Los Angeles, 1980-81; cons. BBW: Big Beautiful Woman Mag., Los Angeles, 1981—, Media Research Group, Los Angeles, 1984; condr. seminars Women in Communication, Los Angeles, 1983, Pacific N.W. Writers Conf., Seattle, 1984. Patentee children's toy, 1971; lyricist for songs, 1977—; contbr. articles and poems to profl. jours. and mags. Office: BBW: Big Beautiful Woman Mag 19528 Ventura Blvd # 298 Tarzana CA 91356-2917

SHAW-GALLANT, CATHARINE, marriage and family therapist, freelance writer; b. Washington, Feb. 13, 1944; d. Earl Wilbur and Catharine Estelle (Bishop) Shaw; children: Shannon, Jason. BFA, Md. Inst. Art, Balt., 1975; MEd, Lynchburg (Va.) Coll., 1980, Johns Hopkins U., 1984. Cert. art, English and counseling tchr. Head art dept. Chatham (Va.) Hall, 1982-84, counselor, 1982-84; counselor Bedford Schs., Forest, Va., 1983-84; specialist fine arts and antiques, reporter Mayhill Publs., Knightsville, Ind., 1985-91; pvt. practice therapy, free-lance writer, counselor Lynch Station, Va., 1986—. Mem. ACA, DAR, Jamestown Soc., Va. Poetry Soc. Address: Mount Hermon Farm Lynch Station VA 24571

SHAY, E. KATHARYN, engineering manager; b. Louisville, July 8, 1942; d. Harry Lewis and Elizabeth Ann (Clubb) S. BA in Math. and Phys. Edn., Transylvania U., Lexington, Ky., 1964. Cert. tchr.; cert. real estate sales assoc. Tchr. 8th and 9th grade math. Baltimore County (Md.) Schs., 1964-65; cost acct. Md. Cup Corp., Owings Mills, 1966-68; sr. lead engr. Westinghouse Electric Corp., Balt., 1968-80, health care cons., 1970-74, quality and reliability assurance mgr., 1980-85; lead staff engr., spl. info. program IBM, Sunnyvale, Calif., 1985-88; engring. mgr. Computer Scis. Corp., Greenbelt, Md., 1989-94; dir. product assurance office IM/DE State Dept., Washington, 1995—; math. tutor, Columbia, Md., 1964-70; owner, pres., bd. dirs. Balt. Adhesives Corp., Owings Mills, 1988—, Lewis Marr Corp., Owings Mills, 1988—. Author: (manuals) Maternal and Infant Care Clinic, 1975, WEC SQE Procedures, 1980, revised, 1983, IBM Site CM Data Base Procedures, 1986, rev., 1988. Vol. Little Sister Program, Catonsville, Md., 1974-78; spkr. St. Timothy's Sch., Stevenson, Md., 1991. Recipient awards Goddard Space Flight Ctr., Greenbelt, 1993, Seas TQM award, 1992. Mem. Nat. Mgmt. Assn., Air Force Comms. and Electronics Assn., Soc. Women Engrs. (local fund raising chair 1983). Democrat. Methodist. Home: 10170 Pasture Gate Ln Columbia MD 21044-1708 Office: State Dept Annex 1250 23d St NW Washington DC 20037

SHEA, ANNE JOAN, fashion editor; b. Beacon, N.Y., Dec. 29, 1907; d. Patrick Henry and Mary Loretta (Walsh) S. AB in Liberal Arts, Syracuse (N.Y.) U., 1929. Fashion editor The Bride's Mag., N.Y.C., 1952-63; dir. fashion promotion Angelo Bridals, N.Y.C., 1964-65; asst. to N.Y. mgr. Nat. Home Fashions League, 1965; freelance sec. to mgr. Union League Club of N.Y., 1963, 65; fashion cons. to pub. rels. dir. French Lace Inst., Paris, 1965-67; freelance fashion cons., stylist, 1966-70. Bd. dirs. Dag Hammerskjold Fund; mem. mobile blood bank unit ARC; vol. Svcs. for Children, Bide-A-Wee Home, Fairchild Tropical Gardens, Miami Heart Inst. Aux., Am. Mus. Natural History. Mem. Women in Communications, Fashion Group (bd. dirs. Fashion Critics award), Syracuse U. Alumni Assn., AAUW, Am. Assn. Ret. Persons, English Speaking Union, Internat. Platform Assn., Lucy Stone League, Smithsonian Assocs., Theta Phi Alpha. Home: 948 Bay Dr Miami FL 33141-5647

SHEA, B(ARBARA) CHRISTINE, communications educator, consultant; b. Washington, Nov. 28, 1961; d. Edward Vincent and Micheline Marie (Simplicio) S. BA summa cum laude, Towson State U., 1983; MA, Ohio U., 1985; postgrad., U. Calif., Santa Barbara, 1992—. Teaching assoc. Ohio U., Athens, 1983-84; instr. Clarion U. Pa., 1985; lectr. Calif. Poly. State U., San Luis Obispo, 1985—; cons. for corp. non-profit and ednl. orgns., 1984—, presenter in field. Assoc. editor Cross-Exam. Debate Yearbook, 1986-92; contbr. articles to scholarly jours., chpts. to books and procs. Regents fellow U. Calif., 1994-95. Mem. AAUP, Internat. Comm. Assn., Internat. Soc. for Study Argummentation, Orgn. for Study Comm., Lang. and Gender, Speech Comm. Assn., Western States Comm. Assn., Acad. Mgmt., Nat. Coun. for Rsch. on Women, Phi Kappa Phi. Office: Calif Poly State U Speech Comm Dept San Luis Obispo CA 93407

SHEA, CHRISTINA ELIZABETH, office manager; b. Littleton, N.H., July 29, 1949; d. Frank George and Patricia (Weisner) Childs; children: Stephen Allen, Leanne. Student, Keene State Coll., 1968. Licensed real estate agt., N.H., Mass. Tax examiner, collections rep., auditor IRS, Andover, Manchester, Mass., N.H, 1970-84; credit and collections mgr. Dean's Carpets, Manchester, 1984-90; office mgr., credit mgr. Tom Rich's Flooring, Lowell, Mass., 1990—; salesperson, office mgr. Boutwell Real Estate, Pelham, N.H., 1991-92; owner, operator Creative Treasure Crafts, Pelham, 1983-88. Leader Girl Scouts U.S.A., Pelham, 1978-82; chairperson fundraisers Dracut (Mass.) Youth Hockey and Skating, 1975-78; active pub. schs., Pelham, 1976-80, Am. Cancer Soc., 1991. Mem. Greater Salem Area Realtors. Home: 13 Hillcrest Ln Pelham NH 03076-3519 Office: Tom Richs Flooring 133 Congress St Lowell MA 01852-4010

SHEA, NANCY ELAINE, computer consultant; b. Waltham, Mass., May 21, 1953; d. Jeremiah G. and Marilyn E. (Leach) S. AS in Bus. and Acctg., Manchester Tech. Sch., 1980, AS in Computer Sci., 1982; postgrad., Ctrl. Conn. State U., 1983-85. Acctg. supr. Rourke-Eno Paper Co., Hartford, Conn., 1974-82; assoc. programmer Aetna Life & Casualty, Hartford, 1982-83; programmer Conn. Bank & Trust, Hartford, 1984-86; programmer/analyst Barnett Techs., Jacksonville, Fla., 1986-89, Telecredit, Inc., Tampa, Fla., 1990-92; sr. programmer/analyst Total System Svcs., Columbus, Ga., 1992-93; pres., owner Premier Computer Cons., Inc., Raleigh, N.C., 1993—. Vol. United Way of Atlanta, Tampa Bay Harvest food delivery program, 1991, Upbeat, Jacksonville, 1990, Conn. Pub. TV, Hartford, 1985. Aetna scholar, 1981. Mem. Data Processing Mgmt. Assn., Ind. Computer Cons. Assn., Alpha Beta Gamma. Home: 5635 Hamstead Crossing Dr Raleigh NC 27612

SHEAHAN, MAUREEN ALMA, labor management project administrator; b. Detroit, Sept. 21, 1954; d. James Bernard and Mary Helen (Shandilis) S. BA in English, Wayne State U., 1976. Tchr. Immaculata High Sch., Detroit, 1977; sec. Children's Hosp., Detroit, 1978-79; office mgr. Samalona Clinic, Birmingham, Mich., 1979; coord. Cass Corridor Food Coop, Detroit, 1979-80; gen. mgr. Sun Press, Detroit, 1980-85; life edn. advisor UAW-Ford U. Mich., Dearborn, 1985-89; asst. dir. ACLU of Mich., Detroit, 1989-90; exec. dir. Labor Mgmt. Coun. for Econ. Renewal, Taylor, Mich., 1990—; bd. dirs. SE Mich. Coalition on Occupational Safety and Health, Detroit. Coord. Detroit Internat. Women's Day Celebration, Detroit, 1987—; mem., vol. Orgn. in Solidarity in Cen. Am., Detroit, 1981—; co-coord. Mich. Fenastras Support Group, Taylor, 1990—, UAW Region IA Internat. Labor Solidarity Network. Mem. NOW (Feminist of Yr. 1993), ACLU, NAACP, Nat. Writers Union-UAW Local 1981, Am. Mus. Natural History, Coalition of Labor Union Women. Office: Labor Mgmt Coun 9650 Telegraph Rd Taylor MI 48180-3333

SHEAHAN, MELODY ANN, transportation executive; b. Cin., Aug. 5, 1959; d. Earl Sterling and Willie Catherine (Stonestreet) McCoy. AA in Mech. Engring. Tech., U. Cin., 1979; student, Marshall U., 1980-86, U. North Fla., 1987-89, Fla. C.C., 1988-91. Engring. tech. Chessie System R.R., Huntington, W.Va., 1979-81, asst. supr. motor vehicles, 1981-86; staff asst. CSX Transp., Jacksonville, Fla., 1986, engr. system material, 1986-91, mgr. work equipment, budget and planning, 1991-94; mgr. work equipment stds., specifications and tng., 1994—. Named one of Outstanding Young Women of Am., 1985, Woman of Yr. Am. Coun. R.R. Women, 1992. Mem. Am. Coun. R.R. Women (sec. 1984-86, 1st v.p. 1986-88, pres. 1988-90), Am. R.R. Engring. Assn., U. Cin. Alumni Assn., Marshall U. Alumni Assn., Order of Eastern Star. Home: 8986 Kings Charter Dr Mechanicsville VA 23111 Office: CSX Transp 1 CSX Rd Richmond VA 23230

SHEAR, IONE MYLONAS, archaeologist; b. St. Louis, Feb. 19, 1936; d. George Emmanuel and Lella (Papazoglou) Mylonas; B.A., Wellesley Coll., 1958; M.A., Bryn Mawr Coll., 1960, Ph.D., 1968; m. Theodore Leslie Shear, June 24, 1959; children—Julia Louise, Alexandra. Research asst. Inst. for Advanced Study, Princeton, N.J., 1963-65; mem. Agora Excavation, Athens, 1967, 72-94; lectr. art and archaeology Princeton U., 1983-84; lectr. Am. Sch. Classical Studies, Athens, summers 1989—; also excavator various other sites in Greece and Italy. Mem. Archaeol. Inst. Am., Greek Archaeol. Soc. (hon.). Author: The Panagia Houses at Mycenae, 1987; contbr. articles to profl. jours. Address: 87 Library Pl Princeton NJ 08540-3015

SHEAR, NATALIE PICKUS, public relations executive; b. N.Y.C., Oct. 18, 1940; d. Sam and Mildred (Shulman) Pickus; m. Daniel H. Shear, Dec. 14, 1968 (dec. Apr. 1989); children: Adam Brian, Tamara Beth. BA in Journalism, Fairleigh Dickinson U., 1962. Editorial asst. Show Bus. Newspaper, N.Y.C., 1962-64, The Jewish News, Newark, 1964-66; dir. Manhattan women's div., program asst. Am. Jewish Congress, N.Y.C., 1966-68; mng. editor The Jewish Week, Washington, 1968-71; dir. pub. rels. United Jewish Appeal, Washington, 1973-74; pub. affairs dir. Leadership Conf. on Civil Rights, Washington, 1977-83; pres. Natalie P. Shear Assocs., Inc., Washington, 1983—. Editor (newspaper) Books Alive, 1973-74; editor, pub. (newsletter) Trends, Inc., 1989—. Vol. Nat. Jewish Dem. Coun., Washington, 1992—, D.C. Jewish Cmty. Ctr.; chairperson women's task force Am. Jewish Congress, Washington, 1984-86, mem. nat. women's task force, 1989—; v.p. Nat. Child Rsch. Ctr., Washington, 1974-76; pres. Ohr Kodesh Sisterhood, Chevy Chase, Md., 1980-82. Mem. Am. Jewish Pub. Rels. Soc., Jewish Cmty. Ctr. Home: 4701 Willard Ave Chevy Chase MD 20815 Office: 1629 K St NW # 802 Washington DC 20006-1602

SHEARER, CYNTHIA HODGE, lawyer; b. Midland, Mich., Sept. 18, 1950; d. John Austin Jr. and Mary Jean (Bale) Hodge; m. Richard L. Shearer, Aug. 26, 1978; children: Whitney Marie, James Michael. BA, Western Mich. U., 1972; JD, U. Denver, 1980. Bar: Colo. 1981, U.S. Dist. Ct. Colo. 1981. Assoc. Hall & Evans, Denver, 1980-83, Constantine, Anderson & Tobey, Denver, 1983-85; atty. Colo. Nat. Bank, Denver, 1985—. Mem. ABA, Colo. Bar Assn., Denver Bar Assn. Office: Colorado Nat Bank PO Box 5168 TA Denver CO 80217

SHEARER, VELMA MILLER, clergywoman; b. Hines, Minn., Jan. 2, 1921; d. Floyd and Mary (Ross) M.; m. Byron C. Shearer, Nov. 3, 1946; 1 child, Mary Jane. RN, Rockford (Ill.) Meml. Hosp., 1944; BFA, U. Dayton, Ohio, 1968; MDiv, United Theol. Sem., Dayton, 1984, DMin, 1987. Ordained to ministry Ch. of the Brethren, 1987. Staff nurse, supr. Castaner (P.R.) Gen. Hosp., 1945-47; staff nurse, oper. rm. supr. Dettmer Hosp., Troy, Ohio, 1954-58; nursing instr. Miami Valley Hosp., Dayton, 1970-72; clergy So. Ohio dist. Ch. of the Brethren, 1983—, Neighbors in Need, 1990—; field edn. supervisor Bethany Theol. Sem., Richmond, Ind., 1994—. Author: Nuc Radiation and Cancer, 1981; artist numerous paintings and drawings. Mem. nuclear study com. Ch. of the Brethren, So. Ohio, 1978-92; bd. dirs. Ohio Environ. Coun. Recipient Ann. Peace award Wright State U.; Ohio Humanities Coun. grantee, 1989-90. Mem. Internat. Assn. Women Ministers, Ohio Environ. Coun. (bd. dirs. 1994—). Home and Office: 124 Chestnut St Apt 210 Englewood OH 45322-1410

SHEARIN, BETTY SPURLOCK, volunteer services administrator; b. Salem, Va., Nov. 7, 1931; d. Thomas Shirley and Willie Ann (Borden) Spurlock; m. Alexander Moore Shearin Jr. (dec.), June 1 1957; 1 child, Victoria Louise. BS, Va. State U., 1954. Mem. staff Benedict Coll., Columbia, S.C., 1957-94; acting pres. Benedict Coll., 1984-85, v.p. adminstrn., 1986-87, coord. archives, telecommunications, 1987-88, spl. asst. to v.p. bus. affairs, 1988-90; cons., 1990-94; vol. coord. Richland County Pub. Libr., Columbia, 1991—. Bd. dirs. Benedict Coll. Fed. Credit Union, 1974-79, 84-91; asst. sec. bd. trustees Benedict Coll., 1976-85, sec., 1985-86; sec. Colonial Park Community Home Assn., Columbia, 1988—; vol. Friends Richland County Pub. Libr., 1991—, Harvest Hope Food Bank, S.C. State Mus. Mem. NAFE, Assn. Records Mgrs. and Adminstrs. (sec. bd. dirs. 1983-85), Assn. Vol. Adminstrs. S.C. Assn. Vol. Adminstrs. (Historian), S.C. Libr. Assn., Alpha Kappa Alpha. Democrat. Episcopalian. Home: 4116 Grand St Columbia SC 29203-6656

SHEARING, MIRIAM, judge; b. Waverly, N.Y., Feb. 24, 1935. BA, Cornell U., 1956; JD, Boston Coll., 1964. Bar: Calif. 1965, Nev. 1969. Justice of peace Las Vegas Justice Ct., 1977-81; judge Nev. Dist. Ct., 1983-92, chief judge, 1986; justice Nevada Supreme Ct., Carson City, 1993—; alt. referee Juvenile Ct., Clark County, 1975-76. Mem. ABA, Am. Judicature Soc., Nev. Judges Assn. (sec. 1978), Nev. Dist. Ct. Judges Assn. (sec. 1984-85, pres. 1986-87), State Bar Nev., State Bar Calif., Clark County Bar Assn. Democrat.

SHEARWATER, DEBRA LOVE, naturalist, tour guide; b. Upland, Pa., Sept. 13, 1951; d. C. Richard Millichap and Dolores E. (Johnson) Trovatore. AA, Monterey Peninsula Coll., 1980; AS, Cabrillo Coll., 1982; postgrad., U. Calif., Santa Cruz, 1981. Registered dental hygienist. rsch. assoc. Earthwatch, Monterey, Calif., 1987. Co-writer, co-videographer (video) Through the Seasons. Founder, leader W.I.N.G.S./Suicide Prevention Svc., Santa Cruz, 1991. Mem. Am. Birding Assn., Am. Cetacean Soc. (founder biennal conf. 1982), Assn. of Dental Hygienists of Am. Office: Shearwater Journeys PO Box 1445 Soquel CA 95073

SHEA-STONUM, MARILYN, judge; b. Anaconda, Mont., June 6, 1947. AB, U. Calif., Santa Cruz, 1969; JD, Case Western Res. U., 1975. Bar: Ohio 1975, Calif. 1976. Law clk. to Hon. Battisti U.S. Dist. Ct. (no. dist.), Ohio, 1975-76; ptnr. Jones, Day, Reavis & Pogue, Cleve.; judge ea. divsn. U.S. Bankruptcy Ct. (no. dist.) Ohio, Akron, 1984-94, bankruptcy judge, 1994—. Office: US Bankruptcy Ct No Dist Ohio Ea Divsn 2 S Main St Ste 240 Akron OH 44308

SHEBAN, LYNNE ROSENZWEIG, psychologist; b. Hicksville, N.Y., Jan. 7, 1958; d. Louis and Gloria Rosenzweig; m. Christopher Sheban. BA, U. Rochester, 1979; MA, U. Ill., Chgo., 1982, PhD, 1984. Lic. clin. psychologist. Staff psychologist Inst. for Juvenile Rsch., Chgo., 1985-91; pvt. practice clin. psychologist Chgo. and Skokie, Ill., 1986—; clin. instr. U. Ill., Chgo., 1986—; cons. psychologist valve behavioral health, 1994—. Mem. APA, Phi Beta Kappa, Sigma Xi, Phi Kappa Phi. Office: 343 S Dearborn Chicago IL 60604 also: 4711 Golf Rd Skokie IL 60076

SHEBESTA, LYNN MARIE, school administrator; b. Manitowoc, Wis., Dec. 16, 1955; d. Joseph J. Shebesta and Shirley Ann (Pietras) Kent. BS, U. Wis., La Crosse, 1978; MS, Mankato State U., 1986; postgrad. study Admissions, Harvard Grad. Sch. Edn., 1992. Admissions counselor Silver Lake Coll., Manitowoc, Wis., 1980-83; asst. dir. admissions Mankato (Minn.) State U., 1983-88; dir. admissions Lakeland Coll., Sheboygan, Wis., 1988-90; dean of admissions and fin. aid Wayland Acad., Beaver Dam, Wis., 1990—; cons. to admissions Northwestern Military/Naval Acad., Lake Geneva, Wis., 1992; presenter Nat. Assn. Luth. Coll. Admission Officers, Concordia U. Wis., Mequon, Wis., 1993. Editor, designer, publisher (endl. insts. brochures, viewbooks), 1986-93. Bd. dirs., founder Civitan, Mankato, 1986-88; bd. dirs. Big Brothers/Big Sisters, Manitowoc, Wis., 1989. Mem. Wis. Assn. Secondary Sch. and Coll. Admissions Counselors, Secondary Sch. Admission Test Bd., Midwest Boarding Schs. (bd. dirs.), Nat. Assn. Student Affairs Profls. Home: 240 Cherokee Rd Beaver Dam WI 53916-1057 Office: Wayland Acad 101 N University Ave Beaver Dam WI 53916-2253

SHEDLOCK, KATHLEEN JOAN PETROUSKIE, community health/research nurse; b. Victorville, Calif., Jan. 22, 1952; d. Frank A. and Joan O. (Bird) Petrouskie; m. Ronald Francis Shedlock, Dec. 1, 1973; children: Pamela, Alison. Diploma, York Hosp. Sch. Nursing, 1973; BS in Nursing, SUNY, Utica, 1978; MS in Community Health Nursing, Syracuse U., 1991; MPA in Health Care, Maxwell Sch., 1991. Cert. adult practitioner ANCC; cert. community health nurse. Staff nurse, charge nurse emergency rm. Doctors' Hosp., Freeport, N.Y., 1973; staff nurse ICU SUNY Health Sci. Ctr., Syracuse, 1974-76; primary care nurse with pvt. practice ob.-gyn. physician Liverpool, N.Y., 1977-79; staff nurse post anesthesia care unit, diabetes educator Community Gen. Hosp., Syracuse, 1978-87; trainer, supr. home health aides Upjohn Health Care Svcs., Liverpool, 1986; staff nurse, health educator Syracuse U. Health Svcs., 1986-88; mem. faculty Crouse Irving Meml. Hosp. Sch. Nursing, Syracuse, 1987-93; rsch. coord. Hematology-Oncology Assocs. of Cen. N.Y., Syracuse, 1993—; Syracuse coord. Breast Cancer Prevention Trial; cons., planner Oneida (N.Y.) Nation Healthcare Program, 1990; reviewer Mosby Year Book Med. Pub., St. Louis, 1991; presenter at profl. confs., workshops; cons. Ctrl. N.Y. Coun. Occupational Safety and Health, Syracuse, 1987-90; childbirth educator Childbirth Edn. Assn. Greater Syracuse, 1976-81, consumer rep., 1977; bd. dirs. Onondaga County chpt. Am. Cancer Soc. Mem. ANA, Oncology Nursing Soc., Transcultural Nursing Soc., N.Y. State Nurses Assn. (chair coun. on ethical practice 1990-94, dist. treas. 1990-94, Excellence in Nursing award 1991), Syracuse U. Nursing Alumni Assn., York Hosp. Sch. Nursing Alumni Assn., Sigma Theta Tau. Home: 8544 E Seneca Turnpike Manlius NY 13104 Office: Hematology-Oncology Assocs Ctrl NY 1000 E Genesee St Ste 400 Syracuse NY 13210

SHEDRICK, MARY BERNICE, state legislator; b. Chickasha, Okla., Aug. 9, 1940; m. R. Mike Shedrick; children: Crystal Shedrick Hayes, Michael Scott (dec.), Steven Link. BS, Okla. State U., 1969, MS, 1972; JD, Okla. City U. Law Sch., 1983. Educator, 1969-80, atty., mem. Okla. State Senate. Mem. Stillwater Okla. C. of C., Stillwater Arts and Humanities Council, Okla. State U. Alumni Found., Delta Kappa Gamma, Kappa Kappa Iota. Democrat. Baptist. Office: PO Box 843 Stillwater OK 74076-0843

SHEEHAN, ANNE MORISON, newspaper editor, journalist; b. Brookline, Mass., Sept. 12, 1950; d. William Keniston and Mary Carolyn (Porter) Morison; m. Robert Frederick Coe, 1971; 1 child, Carolyn Porter Coe; m. Kevin John Sheehan, June 7, 1986; children: Elizabeth Pendleton, Kate DeCorse. Grad. high sch., Concord, N.H., 1968. Sec. to pres. Yale U., New Haven, Conn., 1975-77; bus. mgr. Yale U.-UPI, New Haven, Conn., 1980-84; journalist Register-Star newspaper, Hudson, N.Y., 1985-86; exec. editor The Chatham (N.Y.) Courier, 1986—. Vol. Berkshire Farm Ctr. for Youth, Canaan, N.Y., 1988-93; founder Chatham Theater Co., 1984, Children's Theater of Cheshire, Conn., 1973. Mem. Rotary. Home: PO Box 66 43 Spring St Chatham NY 12037

SHEEHAN, DEBORAH ANN, radio station and theater executive; b. Paterson, N.J., Mar. 29, 1953; d. John J. and Ruth (Badertschier) S.; m. Emidio S. Quattrocchi, Mar. 15, 1985; 1 child, Deirdre Emily Sheehan. B.A., William Paterson Coll., 1975. With radio Sta. WWDJ, Hackensack, N.J., 1980-83, Shadow Traffic, N.Y.C., 1981-83; dir. news, community affairs WPAT-AM/FM, N.Y.C., 1979—. Actress-tchr. Paterson Arts Ctr., 1975-79; host radio show Bus. Jour. N.J., 1984; host, producer radio show Debbie Sheehan mag., 1983; host FDU Focus, Cable Network N.J.; writer plays. Exec. dir., actress Learning Theater Co., Paterson, 1975—; sec. bd. dirs. YMCA Passaic Valley, Paterson, 1983-89; mem. N.J. Legal Bd., Montclair, N.J., 1984-86; mem. Paterson Edn. Found., 1984-89; bd. dirs. United Way Passaic Valley, Conn., 1985, chair allocations com., 1985-92. Recipient Edward R. Murrow Gold medal B'nai B'rith, 1983, finalist 1984-85; Gold medal Internat. Radio Festival, 1983; Best Reporter award Sigma Delta Chi, 1985-87, Personality Profile award local chpt., 1987, Best Pub. Service award, 1987; Best Feature award AP, 1985, 87; Angel Excellence award, Los Angeles, 1985, 87; Internat. Press Assn. fellow, Japan, 1985, New Zealand, 1988. Club: Zonta. Avocations: weaving; travel; acting. Office: WPAT-AM-FM 1396 Broad St Clifton NJ 07013-4222

SHEEHAN, PATRICIA LYNNE, therapist, writer; b. Montclair, N.J., Nov. 11, 1945; d. William Palmer and Florence Louise (Muller) S.; m. Bud Burns, Dec. 23, 1976 (div. Oct. 1978). BA, Fla. Atlantic U., 1967, MEd, 1975. Elem. tchr. Fla. Pub. Schs., West Hollywood, 1967-69, N.C. Pub. Schs., Chapel Hill, 1969-70; ESL tchr. N.Am. Inst., Barcelona, Spain, 1971-73, Panama Cultural Inst., Panama City, 1974-75; counselor Opportunities Industrialization Orgn., Albuquerque, 1975-77; kindergarten tchr. Albuquerque Pub. Schs., 1977-87; pvt. practice Albuquerque, 1987—. Author: (children's books) Kylie's Song, 1988 (Coors' Family Literacy award 1989), Albuquerque Then and Now, 1990, Gwendolyn's Gifts, 1990, Kylie's Concert, 1993, Shadow and the Ready Time, 1994; editor Families in Recovery mag., 1989-91. Mem. Am. Counseling Assn., Am. Assn. for Group Therapists, S.W. Writers Assn., Albuquerque Assn. for Edn. of Young Children (pres. 1978), Soc. for Childrens Book Writers and Illustrators, Population-Environment Network. Home and Office: PO Box 3848 Albuquerque NM 87190

SHEEHAN, SUSAN, writer; b. Vienna, Austria, Aug. 24, 1937; came to U.S., 1941, naturalized, 1946; d. Charles and Kitty C. (Herrmann) Sachsel; m. Neil Sheehan, Mar. 30, 1965; children—Maria Gregory, Catherine Fair. BA (Durant scholar), Wellesley Coll., 1958; DHL (hon.), U. Lowell, 1991. Editorial researcher Esquire-Coronet, N.Y.C., 1959-60; free-lance writer N.Y.C., 1960-61; staff writer New Yorker mag., N.Y.C., 1961—. Author: Ten Vietnamese, 1967, A Welfare Mother, 1976, A Prison and a Prisoner, 1978, Is There No Place on Earth for Me?, 1982, Kate Quinton's Days, 1984, A Missing Plane, 1986, Life For Me Ain't Been No Crystal Stair, 1993; contbr. articles to various mags., including N.Y. Times Sunday Mag., Washington Post Sunday Mag., Harper's, Atlantic, New Republic, McCall's, Holiday, Boston Globe Sunday Mag., Life. Judge Robert F. Kennedy Journalism awards, 1980, 84; mem. lit. panel D.C. Commn. on Arts and Humanities, 1979-84; mem. pub. info. and edn. com. Nat. Mental Health Assn., 1982-83; mem. adv. com. on employment and crime Vera Inst. Justice, 1978-86; chair Pulitzer Prize nominating jury in gen. non-fiction for 1988, 1994, mem., 1991. Recipient Sidney Hillman Found. award, 1976, Gavel award ABA, 1978, Individual Reporting award Nat. Mental Health Assn., 1981, Pulitzer prize for gen. non-fiction, 1983, feature writing award N.Y. Press Club, 1984, Alumnae Assn. Achievement award Wellesley Coll., 1984, Carroll Kowal Journalism award NASW, 1993; fellow Guggenheim Found., 1975-76, Woodrow Wilson Ctr. for Internat. Scholars, 1981. Mem. Soc. Am. Historians, Phi Beta Kappa, Authors Guild. Home: 4505 Klingle St NW Washington DC 20016-3580 Office: New Yorker Mag 20 W 43rd St New York NY 10036-7400

SHEEHY, GAIL HENION, author; b. Mamaroneck, N.Y., Nov. 27, 1937; d. Harold Merritt and Lillian Rainey (Paquin) Henion; m. Albert F. Sheehy, Aug. 20, 1960 (div. 1967); 1 dau., Maura; 1 adopted dau., Mohm; m. Clay Felker, Dec. 16, 1984. B.S., U. Vt., 1958; fellow, Journalism Sch., Columbia U., 1970. Traveling home economist J.C. Penney & Co., 1958-60; fashion editor Rochester Democrat & Chronicle, 1961-63; feature writer N.Y. Herald Tribune, N.Y.C., 1963-66; contbg. editor New York mag., 1968-77. Sometime contbr. to: N.Y. Times Mag., Parade, New Republic, Washington Post; polit. contbg. editor Vanity Fair mag., 1988—; author: books include (novel) Lovesounds, 1970; Panthermania: The Clash of Black Against Black in One American City, 1971, Speed Is of the Essence, 1971, Hustling: Prostitution in Our Wide-Open Society, 1973, Passages: Predictable Crises of Adult Life, 1976, Pathfinders, 1981, Spirit of Survival, 1986, Character: America's Search for Leadership, 1988, Gorbachev: The Man Who Changed the World, 1990, (play) Maggie and Misha, 1991, The Silent Passage: Menopause, 1992. Adv. bd. Women's Health Initiative, NIH; bd. dirs. Girls, Inc., Poets and Writers; eminent citizen's com. UN Internat. Conf. on Population and Devel., 1994. Recipient 4 Front Page awards Newswomen's Club N.Y., Nat. Mag. award Columbia U., 1973, Penney-Mo. Journalism award U. Mo., 1975, Anisfield-Wolf Book award, 1986, Best Mag. Writer award Washington Journalism Rev., 1991, N.Y. Pub. Libr. Literary Lion, 1992; Columbia U. fellow, 1970; Alicia Patterson Found. grantee, 1974. Mem. PEN, NOW, Authors Guild.

SHEEHY, PATRICIA ANN, environmental services manager; b. Rockaway Park, N.Y., July 6, 1960; d. James Patrick and Margaret Patricia (Maloney) Boyle; m. Neil Edward Sheehy, May 24, 1991; children: Patrick Joseph and Megan Eileen (twins). BS in Biology and Biochemistry, SUNY, Stony Brook, 1983; MS in Environ. Studies, L.I. U., 1985. Sec. Met. N.Y. Assn. Environ. Profls., Greenvale, 1984-85; intern Suffolk County Dept. Health Svcs., Hauppauge, N.Y., 1984-85; regulatory specialist Prentiss Drug & Chem. Co., Inc., Floral Park, N.Y., 1986-89; mgr. regulatory affairs Roussel Bio Corp., Lincoln Park, N.J., 1989-90; mgr. internat. regulatory affairs Merck & Co., Inc., Three Bridges, N.J., 1990-93, mgr. regulatory coord. and planning, 1993—; spokesperson endangered species task force Prentiss Drug & Chem. Co., Inc., Washington, 1986-89. Freelance designer. Mem. Nat. Agrl. Chems. Assn., Met. N.Y. Assn. Environ. Profls. (sec.), Chem. Spltys. and Mfr.'s Assn. (steering com. Washington chpt. 1989-90), Chem. Producers and Distbrs. Assn. (minor use com. Washington chpt. 1988), Codex Com. of Pesticide Residues. Office: Merck & Co Inc PO Box 450 Hillsborough Rd Three Bridges NJ 08887-0450

SHEEHY, VERONICA GARVEY, nursing administrator; b. Waterbury, Conn., Oct. 18, 1937; d. William Nelson and Mae Theresa (Caffrey) Garvey; children: Mark D., Shawn Colleen, Erin A. Diploma in nursing, Waterbury Hosp., 1952; BSN, So. Conn. State U., 1971, MS in Health Edn., 1974. RN, Conn., Fla. Staff nurse Waterbury Hosp., 1952-53; pvt. duty nurse Waterbury Hosp. Registry, 1953-73; nursing supr. Waterbury Hosp. Health Ctr., 1973-78; nursing supr. psychiatry Waterbury Hosp., 1981-90, admissions coord., 1990-93, asst. pediatric nursing, 1993—; asst. prof. nursing Quinnipiac Coll., Hamden, Conn., 1977—; asst. dir. nursing Mt. Sinai Hosp., Hartford, Conn., 1978-80; clin. dir. nursing Danbury (Conn.) Hosp., 1980-82; asst. prof. nursing So. Conn. State U., New Haven, 1987-90. V.p., sec. Bunker Hill Athletic Club, Waterbury, 1965-75, coord. cheerleading competitions, 1970-75; treas. Bunker Hill Community Club, Waterbury, 1969-74; coord. Brownies Girl Scouts Am., New Haven, 1973-79. Fellow ANA (cert. nursing adminstr.), Waterbury Hosp. Alumnae Assn., Conn. State Nurses Assn. Roman Catholic. Home: 3-12 Lake Hills Vlg Wolcott CT 06716 Office: Waterbury Hosp Psychiatric Resource 88 Grandview Ave Waterbury CT 06708-2509

SHEERAN-EMORY, KATHLEEN MARY, executive consultant; b. Wilmington, Del., Feb. 27, 1948; d. Stanley Robert and Eileen Ann (Walsh) Sheeran. BA, St. Mary's Coll., Notre Dame, Ind., 1970. Asst. editor Conde Nast Publs., N.Y.C., 1970-76; account exec. Working Woman mag., N.Y.C., 1976-77; account exec. Foote Cone & Belding Communications, Inc., N.Y.C., 1977-78; v.p. John P. Holmes & Co., Inc., N.Y.C., 1978-83, Korn Ferry Internat., N.Y.C., 1983-84, Sheeran-Emory Assocs., N.Y.C., 1984—; mem. faculty YWCA, 53d St. chpt., N.Y.C., 1980—. Mem. nominating com. Girl Scouts Greater N.Y. Fellow Internat. Biog. Assn.; mem. MIT Enterprise Forum, Nat. Assn. for Female Execs., Women's Nat. Rep. Club, Am. Soc. Profl. and Exec. Women. Roman Catholic. Home and Office: Sheeran-Emory Assocs 244 Nassau St Apt 7 Princeton NJ 08542

SHEERIN, MAGGIE, small business owner, artist; b. Vernon, Tex., Sept. 22, 1940; d. Leslie L. and Sue Maxcy (Watters) Speir; m. James O. Davis, Sept. 14, 1957 (div.); m. Robert M. Sheerin, Jan. 3, 1967; children: James Maxcy, Cynthia Kathleen, John Malcolm. Owner Mag Ties, San Antonio, 1989—; bd. dirs. Tex. Bank North, San Antonio, 1982-85; founder, chmn. Winston Sch. of San Antonio, 1985—. Founding com. St. Mary's Hall Summer Arts, San Antonio, 1979-81; advisor Hugh O'Brien Youth Found., San Antonio, 1981; bd. dirs. Joffrey Workshop Com., 1982-83, Cancer Ctr. Coun., 1982-83, S.W. Found. Forum, 1971-76, Project ABC & ABC Alliance, 1983-84; bd. dirs., crusade chmn. Am. Cancer Soc., 1978-83; bd. dirs. Gallery of the McNay, 1992-94. Recipient Sword of Hope, Am. Cancer Soc., 1981, Golden Rule, J.C. Penney Co., 1985, Outstanding Svc. award Winston Sch., 1989, ABC Alliance, 1986, Profiles in Leadership, San Antonio, 1991. Mem. San Antonio Mus. Assn., San Antonio Art League, McNay Mus., N.Y. Drama League, Assn. of Children with Learning Disabilities, Am. Rsch. Ctr. in Egypt, Egypt Exploration Soc. (London), Harry's Bar London, Annabels London, Doubles N.Y., The Argyle. Republican. Home and Office: Mag Ties 17 Auburn Pl San Antonio TX 78209-4739

SHEETS, DIANA ELAINE, sales and marketing professional; b. Westerly, R.I., Apr. 11, 1954; d. Herman E. and Norma (Sams) S.; m. Stephen E. Levinson, June, 1976. BA, U. Colo., 1976; MA, Columbia U., 1980, MPhil, 1982, PhD, 1985. Paralegal Middlesex County Legal Svcs., New Brunswick, N.J., 1976-77; asst. to dean, dir. women's ctr. Princeton (N.J.) U., 1977-78; lectr. and rsch. asst. Columbia U., N.Y.C., 1981-82; sales rep. Savin Corp., N.Y.C., 1986, Ameritech, Pontiac, Mich., 1987-89; sales mgr. N.Y., N.J., Conn. Ameritech, Pontiac, 1989-93; sales mgr. mid-Atlantic region Ameritech, Troy, Mich., 1993; account exec. Navco Security Sys., Anaheim, Calif., 1994—. Recipient Pre-Dissertation fellowship Coun. of European Studies, Columbia U., N.Y.C., 1982. Mem. NAFE. Home: 320 N Chestnut St

Westfield NJ 07090-2413 Office: Navco Security Sys Ste A 1300 Kellogg Dr Anaheim CA 92807

SHEETS, MARTHA LOUISE, civic activist; b. Toledo, Mar. 25, 1923; d. Ira Elmo and Nellie Gertrude Merrill; m. Ted Charles Sheets, Dec. 21, 1946; children: Thomas Merrill, Susan Ruth, Laura Louise, Charles Ira. B in Edn., U. Toledo, 1945. speaker in field. Charter mem., trustee, sec.-treas., v.p., pres. Citizens for Metroparks, Inc.; commr. Met. Park Dist. Bd., 1976; mem. Gov.'s Commn. Restoration of State Capitol Bldg., Nashville, 1986; historian designer show houses Chattanooga Symphony and Opera Guild, 1981-93; appointee City Commn. to Greenway Adv. Bd., 1989, re-appointed, 1992-93; active numerous civic orgns. including garden clubs and ch. groups; active Save Outdoor Sculpture project Tenn. State Mus. and Smithsonian Inst., 1992-93. Mem. AAUW (chmn. 75th birthday luncheon 1982, grantee Ednl. Found prog.), ASME (chmn., pres. Northwest Ohio sect. women's aux.), Jr. Coterie Club (founding pres.), Zonta Internat. Svc. Club, Little Theatre Assocs. (past pres.), Murray Hills Garden Club (pres. 1991-92, 92-93), Tenn. Fedn. Garden Clubs (dist. hist. preservation chmn. 1981-85, state hist. preservation chmn. 1987-89, dist. III hist. preservation chmn. 1992-94), Chattanooga Coun. Garden Clubs (awards chmn., hist. preservation chmn. 1992-94).

SHEFFIELD, BENITA CARROLL, bank officer; b. Lexington, Mo., June 5, 1950; d. Bruce Byron and Willie Otella (Lorren) Carroll; m. James Wilbur Sheffield, Jr., May 8, 1982. Student, Jacksonville (Fla.) U., 1968-69; AA, Fla. Jr. Coll., 1980; BBA cum laude, U. North Fla., 1987; MBA summa cum laude, U. of North Fla., 1991. Cert. fraud examiner. Authorization and control clk. First Union Nat. Bank Fla., Jacksonville, 1970-74, supr. ops. and control, 1974-78; bankcard acctg. mgr. First Union Nat. Bank of Fla., Jacksonville, 1978-80; loss prevention officer First Union Nat. Bank Fla., Jacksonville, 1980-87, asst. v.p., 1987—. Presdl. scholar Jacksonville U., 1968-69. Mem. Bank Security Assn. of N.E. Fla. (pres. Jacksonville chpt. 1986-87), Phi Kappa Phi, Beta Gamma Sigma, Golden Key Nat. Honor Soc. Home: 2331 Herschel St Jacksonville FL 32204-4313 Office: 1st Union Nat Bank Fla 214 N Hogan St Jacksonville FL 32202

SHEI, JULIANA CHIANG, research and development manager; b. Tokyo, Aug. 27, 1948; d. Wellington J. and Yoshiko (Araki) Chiang; m. Shen-Ann Shei; children: Irene, Ryan. BS, Nat. Cheng Kung U., Taiwan, 1971; MS, Southeastern Mass. U., 1975; MBA, Rensselaer Poly. Inst., 1987. Tech. interpreter Shionogi Pharm. Co., Taiwan, 1971-73; gen. mgr. Enterpreneurial Pub. Co., Los Alamitos, Calif., 1975-77; asst. chemist Ames lab. Iowa State U., 1977-81; rsch. scientist Tech. Ctr. U.S. Steel Corp., Monroeville, Pa., 1982-85; group coord. Sterling Drug Inc., Rensselaer, N.Y., 1986-91; mgr. tech. coun. resources GE Corp. R & D, Schenectady, N.Y., 1991—. Contbr. to tech. publs. Mem. NAFE, Assn. Women in Sci., Am. Chem. Soc. (sec.-treas. Pitts sect. 1983-84), Am. Mgmt. Assn., Profl. Women's Network (pres. Capital dist. N.Y. 1986—).

SHEI, VICKIE IRENE, accountant; b. Highland, Ill., Nov. 15, 1949; d. Gerard Conrad and Alice Irene (Lee) Mueller; m. Edwin Arthur Shei, July 5, 1969. BS in Math., Loyola U., Chgo., 1971. Officer mgr., acct. Clawson Mfg. Co., Missoula, Mont., 1976-79, Roemer's Tire Ctr. Inc., Missoula, Mont., 1979-83, Agy. Tile Co., Spring Valley, N.Y., 1983-84; sr. acct. Ford Products Corp., Valley Cottage, N.Y., 1984-88; acct. Christiania K. Nietz, C.P.A., Bowling Green, Ohio, 1989-94. Republican.

SHEININ, ROSE, biochemist, educator; b. Toronto, Ont., Can., May 18, 1930; d. Harry and Anne (Szyber) Shuber; BA, U. Toronto, 1951, MA (scholar), 1953, PhD in Biochemistry, 1956, L.H.D., 1985; DHL (hon.), Mt. St. Vincent U., 1985; DSc (hon.) Acadia U., 1987, DSc (hon.) U. Guelph, 1991; m. Joseph Sheinin, July 15, 1951; children—David Matthew Khazanov, Lisa Basya Judith, Rachel Sarah Rebecca. Demonstrator in biochemistry U. Toronto (Ont., Can.), 1951-53, asst. prof. microbiology, 1964-75, asst. prof. med. biophysics, 1967-75, prof. microbiology, 1975-90, prof. med. biophysics, 1978-90, assoc. prof. med. biophysics, 1975-78, chmn. microbiology and parasitology, 1975-82, vice dean Sch. Grad. Studies, 1984-89; vice-rector acad., Concordia U., Montreal, Que., Can., 1989-94, prof. dept. biology, 1989—; mem. Health Scis. Com.; vis. rsch. assoc. chem. microbiology, Cambridge U., 1956-57, Nat. Inst. Med. Rsch., London, 1957-58; rsch. assoc. fellow div. biol. research Ont. Cancer Inst., 1958-67; sci. officer cancer grants panel Med. Research Council Can.; mem. Can. Sci. Del. to People's Republic of China, 1973; mem. adv. com. Provincial Lottery Health Research Awards; mem. adv. com. on biotech. NRC Can., 1984-87; mem. Sci. Council Can., 1984-87; adv. com. on sci. and tech. CBC, 1980-85; mem. bd. dirs. Can. Bacterial Disease Network, 1989-94; vis. prof. biochemistry U. Alta., 1971. Nat. Cancer Inst. Can. fellow, 1953-56, 58-61; Brit. Empire Cancer Campaign fellow, 1956-58; Recipient Queen's Silver Jubilee medal, 1978, Woman of Distinction award Health and Edn., YWCA, 1988; Josiah Macy Jr. Faculty scholar, 1981-82; fellow Ligue Contre le Cancer, France, 1981-82, Massey Coll. U. Toronto, 1981—, resident sr. fellow, 1994—; hon. fellow Ryerson Polytech. U., 1993. Fellow Am. Acad. Microbiology, Royal Soc. Can. (chair women in scholarship com. 1990-93); mem. Can. Biochem. Soc. (pres. 1974-75), Can. Soc. Cell Biology (pres. 1975-76), Am. Soc. Virology, Am. Soc. Microbiologists, Canadian Assn. Women in Sci., Internat. Assn. Women Bioscientists, Sigma Xi Rsch. Soc., Scitech, Soc. Complex Carbohydrates, Toronto Biochem. and Biophys. Soc. (pres. 1960-70, council 1970-74). Assoc. editor Can. Jour. Biochemistry, 1968-71, Virology, 1969-72, Intervirology, 1974-85; editorial bd. Microbiol. Revs., 1977-80; author, co-author various publs. Office: U Toronto Massey Coll, 4 Devonshire Pl, Toronto, ON Canada M55 2E1

SHEIRR, OLGA, artist; b. N.Y.C., June 7, 1931; d. Edward E. and Lillian (Tobias) S.; m. Maurice Krolik, Jan. 28, 1973. Student, Arts Students League, 1948-50; BA, Bklyn. Coll., 1953; postgrad., N.Y. Inst. Fine Arts, 1954, NYU, 1964, Pratt Graphic Ctr., 1965-72. guest lectr. and tchr. Fla. Gulf Coast Art Ctr. seminar and art workshop, Belleair, 1987, The Ednl. Alliance, N.Y.C., 1989, Rutgers U., New Brunswick, N.J., 1990, The Barkley Art Ctr., Custer, S.D., 1990, The Art Student's League, N.Y. Artists Equity Symposium Homage to Kaldis, 1993, N.Y. Artists Equity Sacred Places, 1995. One-woman exhbns. include: Internat. Art Exchange, N.Y.C., 1962-63, Noho Gallery, N.Y.C., 1975-76, 78-80, 82-83, 87, 89, 92, New Sch. Social Research, N.Y.C., 1984, Barbizon Gallery, Greenwich, Conn., 1984, Fairleigh Dickinson U., 1985, 90-91, The Kendall Gallery, 1986, Passaic County C.C., Paterson, N.J., 1990, Ashawagh Hall, East Hampton, N.Y., 1993; group exhbns. include A.A.A. Gallery, N.Y.C., 1965, 71, Silvermine Guild Artists, New Canaan, Conn., 1966, 76, 93, Springville (Utah) Mus. Art, 1981, 83, Riyadh, Saudi Arabia, 1982, KenKeleba Gallery, 1985, Fed. Pla., 1986, Lever House, 1986, 88-94, Nat. Arts Club, 1988, Nabisco Brands 1989, Guild Hall, 1989-95, Nat. Acad. Design, 1990, Heckscher Mus., Huntington, N.Y., 1990, 94, Compagnie Moderne et Contemporaine, Paris, 1991, Ctr. Culturo Recoleta, Buenos Aires, 1992, Newark Mus., 1992, Patterson Mus., 1993, San Giorgio Island, Venice, Italy, 1994, Schering-Plough, Madison, N.J., 1995, Krasdale Gallery, White Plains, N.Y., 1995; represented in permanent collections: Mus. City of N.Y., St. Vincent's Hosp., N.Y.C., Greenville County (S.C.) Mus., NYU Hosp., others; reviewer Artists View Art, 1976-80. Founding mem., bd. dirs., treas., publicity chair Noho Gallery, 1975-93, chair invitational exhbns. for Noho for the Arts; bd. dirs., v.p., sec., reviewer for Artists View Art, Assn. of Artist Run Galleries, 1976-92. Mem. N.Y. Artists Equity (bd. dirs. 1985-91, sec. 1988-91), Women in Arts, N.Y. Soc. Women Artists (rec. sec., asst. v.p., bd. dirs. 1984—, now treas.). Home: 360 1st St 11 G New York NY 10010

SHEKLETON, MAUREEN E., respiratory nurse, educator; b. Cleve., Oct. 26, 1947; d. Raymond S. and Marjorie Anne (Hogue) Gurnick; m. Gerald T. Shekleton, Dec. 27, 1968; 1 child, Thomas. BSN, Coll. Mt. St. Joseph, 1969; MSN, Case Western Res. U., 1973; DNSc, Rush U., 1982. RN, Ill. Dir. nursing grad. program Coll. Nursing Rush U., Chgo., 1984-85; asst. chair dept. oper. rm., surg. nursing Rush Presbyn. St. Luke's Med. Ctr., Chgo., 1983-85, practitioner, tchr., 1981-83, 85-86; asst. prof. nursing U. Ill., Chgo., 1989-92; adj. clin. faculty Rush U. & U. Ill., Chgo., 1992—; satellite site coord. DuPage Cmty. Clinic, Wheaton, Ill., 1992—. Author: (with M. Groer) Basic Pathophysiology: A Holistic Approach, 1989; (with K. Litwack) Critical Care Nursing of the Surgical Patient, 1991. Named Med. Surg. Nurse of Yr. ANA, 1989, Golden Apple award for excellence in teaching, 1991, Disting. Alumna Rush U., 1992, Jesse Scott award ANA, 1994; postdoctoral fellow Nat. Rsch. Svc., 1987-88. Mem. Ill. Nurses Assn. (pres. 1989-91), Respiratory Nursing Soc. (pres. 1992-94), Sigma Theta Tau (ANF Internat. scholar 1987). Home: 805 Edgewood Dr Glen Ellyn IL 60137-4214

SHELDON, BETTY CAROL, marketing manager, editor; b. Chgo., May 6, 1946; d. Richard A. And Beatrice G. (Gutensky) S. BA, U. Rochester, N.Y., 1970; MBA, DePaul U., 1983. Editorial asst. AMA, Chgo., 1970-71; mng. editor Joint Commn. on Accreditation of Hosps., Chgo., 1971-76; comm. coord. Arthur Andersen & Co., Chgo., 1977-80, planning coord., 1980-82, planning mgr., 1982-88; adminstrv. mgr. Andersen Consulting, Chgo., 1988-91, mktg. mgr., 1991—. Mng. editor: (manuals) Accreditation Manual for Hospitals, 1972, 75, Accreditation Manual for Long Term Care Facilities, 1973, Accreditation Manual for Psychiatric Facilities, 1973; editor Continuing Med. Edn. Newsletter, 1970-71, Perspectives on Accreditation, 1971-76, Strategic Svcs. Insights, 1988—. Supporting mem. The Orchestral Assn., 1983—, Lyric Opera of Chgo., 1983—. Mem. ABA (assoc.), The Planning Forum (sec. Chgo. chpt. 1984-86), Women in Comm., Internat. Assn. Bus. Communicators. Republican. Office: Andersen Cons 69 W Washington St Chicago IL 60602

SHELDON, BROOKE EARLE, librarian, educator; b. Lawrence, Mass., Aug. 29, 1931; d. Leonard Hadley and Elsie Ann (Southerl) Earle; m. George Duffield Sheldon, Mar. 28, 1955 (dec.); children: L. Scott, G. Stephen. B.A., Acadia U., 1952, D.C.L. (hon.), 1985; M.L.S., Simmons Coll., 1954; Ph.D., U. Pitts., 1977. Base librarian Ent AFB, Colorado Springs, Colo., 1955-57, U.S. Army, Germany, 1956-57; br. librarian Albuquerque Public Library, 1959-61; coordinator adult services Santa Fe Public Library, 1965-67; head library devel. N.Mex. State Library, Santa Fe, 1967-72; asst. dir. leadership tng. inst. U.S. Office Edn., Washington, 1971-73; head tech. svcs. and tng. Alaska State Library, Juneau, 1973-75; dean Sch. Library Info. Studies Tex. Woman's U., Denton, 1977-90; acting provost Library Info. Studies, Tex. Woman's U., Denton, 1979-80; dean Grad. Sch. Libr. Info. Sci. U. Tex., Austin, 1991—. Author: Leaders in Libraries: Styles and Strategies for Success, 1991; contbr. articles to profl. jours. Bd. dirs. Am. Libr. in Paris, 1992—. Recipient Alumni Achievement award Simmons Coll., 1983; Disting. Alumni award Sch. Library Info. Sci., U. Pitts., 1986. Mem. ALA (pres. 1983-84), Tex. Libr. Assn., Rotary Internat., Beta Phi Mu. Democrat. Episcopalian.

SHELDON, CYNTHIA COLLINS, artist; b. Liberty, Tex., Sept. 6, 1956; d. George Bert and Shirley Ann (Blanchard) Collins; m. Scot Edward Sheldon, June 6, 1975; 1 child, Collin Blume. BS, Lamar U., 1982. Sec. Rondell Homes, Anaheim, Calif., 1976-78; surg. & office asst. Beaumont (Tex.) Eye Assocs., 1982-83; tech. asst. II Tex. A&M U. Agrl. Rsch. & Extension Ctr., Beaumont, 1984-85; artist, designer Blumers, Beaumont, 1988—. Home and Office: 4655 Littlefield Beaumont TX 77706

SHELDON, ELEANOR HARRIET BERNERT, sociologist; b. Hartford, Conn., Mar. 19, 1920; d. M.G. and Fannie (Myers) Bernert; m. James Sheldon, Mar. 19, 1950 (div. 1960); children: James, John Anthony. A.A., Colby Jr. Coll., 1940; A.B., U. N.C., 1942; Ph.D., U. Chgo., 1949. Asst. demographer Office Population Rsch., Washington, 1942-43; social scientist USDA, Washington, 1943-45; assoc. dir. Chgo. Community Inventory, U. Chgo., 1947-50; social scientist Social Sci. Rsch. Coun., N.Y.C., 1950-51, rsch. grantee, 1953-55, pres., 1972-79; rsch. assoc. Bur. Applied Social Rsch. Columbia U., 1950-51, lectr. sociology, 1951-52, vis. prof., 1969-71; social scientist UN, N.Y.C., 1951-52; rsch. assoc., lectr. sociology UCLA, 1955-61; assoc. rsch. sociologist, lectr. Sch. Nursing U. Calif., 1957-61; sociologist, exec. assoc. Russell Sage Found., N.Y.C., 1961-72; vis. prof. U. Calif., Santa Barbara, 1971; dir. Equitable Life Assurance Soc., Mobil Corp., H.J. Heinz Co. Author: (with L. Wirth) Chicago Community Fact Book, 1949, America's Children, 1958, (with R.A. Glazier) Pupils and Schools in N.Y.C, 1965; editor: (with W.E. Moore) Indicators of Social Change, Concepts and Measurements, 1968, Family Economic Behavior, 1973; contbr. (with W.E. Moore) articles to profl. jours. Bd. dirs. Colby-Sawyer Coll., 1979-85, UN Rsch. Inst. for Social Devel., 1973-79; trustee Rockefeller Found., 1978-85, Nat. Opinion Rsch. Ctr., 1980-87, Inst. East-West Security Studies, 1984-88. William Rainey Harper fellow U. Chgo., 1945-47. Fellow Am. Acad. Arts and Scis., Am. Sociol. Assn., Am. Statis. Assn.; mem. AAAS, U. Chgo. Alumni Assn. (Profl. Achievement award), Sociol. Rsch. Assn. (pres. 1971-72), Coun. on Fgn. Rels., Am. Assn. Pub. Opinion Rsch., Ea. Sociol. Soc., Internat. Sociol. Assn., Internat. Union Sci. Study of Population, Population Assn. Am. (2d v.p. 1970-71), Inst. of Medicine (chmn. program com. 1976-77), Cosmopolitan Club. Home and Office: 630 Park Ave New York NY 10021-6544

SHELDON, INGRID KRISTINA, mayor; b. Ann Arbor, Mich., Jan. 30, 1945; d. Henry Ragnvald and Virginia Schmidt (Clark) Blom; m. Clifford George Sheldon, June 18, 1966; children: Amy Elizabeth, William David. BS, Eastern Mich. U., 1966; MA, U. Mich., 1970. Cert. tchr., Mich. Tchr. Livonia (Mich.) Pub. Schs., 1966-67, Ann Arbor Pub. Schs., 1967-68; bookkeeper Huron Valley Tennis Club, Ann Arbor, 1978—; acct. F.A. Black Co., Ann Arbor, 1984-88; coun. mem. Ward II City of Ann Arbor, 1988-92, mayor, 1993—; chair Housing Bd. Appeals, Ann Arbor, 1988-91; del. S.E. Mich. Coun. of Govts., 1989. Mem. Ann Arbor Planning Commn., 1988-89, Parks Adv. Commn. 1987—, Ann Arbor Hist. Found., 1985—, Huron Valley Child Guidance Clinic, Ann Arbor, 1984—, excellence com. Ann Arbor Pub. Schs. reorgn., 1985; treas. SOS Community Crisis Ctr., Ypsilanti, Mich., 1987—; precinct ward city vice-chair Ann Arbor Rep. City Com., 1978—. Recipient Community Svc. award Ann Arbor Jaycees, 1980; AAUW fellowship, 1982. Mem. Mich. Mcpl. League (del. 1989—), Ann Arbor Women's City Club (chair endowment com. 1989-90, fin. com. 1987-90, treas.), Rotary (dir.-elect Ann Arbor chpt.), Kappa Delta Pi, Alpha Omnicron Pi. Republican. Methodist. Home: 1416 Folkstone Ct Ann Arbor MI 48105-2848

SHELDON, NANCY WAY, environmental management consultant, real estate developer; b. Bryn Mawr, Pa., Nov. 10, 1944; d. John Harold and Elizabeth Semple (Hoff) W.; m. Robert Charles Sheldon, June 15, 1968. BA, Wellesley Coll., 1966; MA, Columbia U., 1968, M in Philosophy, 1972. Cert. hazardous materials mgr., environ. auditor, Calif.; registered environ. profl., environ. assessor, Calif. Mgmt. cons. ABT Assocs., Cambridge, Mass., 1969-70; mgmt. cons. Harbridge House, Inc., 1970-79, L.A., 1977-79, v.p., 1977-79; mgmt. cons., pres. Resource Assessment, Inc., 1979—; ptnr., real estate developer Resource Devel. Assocs., 1980—. Author: Social and Economic Benefits of Public Transit, 1973. Contbr. articles to profl. jours. Columbia U. fellow, 1966-68; recipient Nat. Achievement award Nat. Assn. Women Geographers, 1966. Mem. DAR, Nat. Environ. Health Assn., Air and Waste Mgmt. Assn., Nat. Ground Water Assn., Water Pollution Control Fedn., Water Environment Fedn., Fla. Pollution Control Assn., Grad. Faculties Alumni Assn. Columbia U. Office: Resource Assessment Inc 1192 Kittiwake Cir Sanibel FL 33957-3606

SHELLEY, CAROLE AUGUSTA, actress; b. London, Aug. 16, 1939; came to U.S., 1964; d. Curtis and Deborah (Bloomstein) S.; m. Albert G. Woods, July 26, 1967 (dec.). Student, Arts Ednl. Sch., 1943-56, Prepatory Acad. Royal Acad. Dramatic Art, 1956-57; studies with Iris Warren. Studied with Iris Warren and Eileen Thorndike; Trustee Am. Shakespeare Theatre., 1974-82. Appeared in revues, films, West End comedies, including Mary Mary at the Globe Theatre; appeared as Gwendolyn Pigeon in stage, film and TV versions of The Odd Couple, Absurd Person Singular; The Norman Conquests (Los Angeles Drama Critics Circle award 1975); appeared as Rosalind in As You Like It, as Regan in King Lear, as Neville in She Stoops to Conquer, Stratford, Ont., Can., 1972, as Mrs. Margery Pinchwife in The Country Wife, Am. Shakespeare Festival, Stratford, Conn., 1973, as Nora in A Doll's House, Goodman Theatre, Chgo., as Ann in Man and Superman, as Lena in Misalliance, Zita in Grand Hunt; appeared at Shaw Festival, 1977, 80, Stepping Out, 1986 (Tony nomination 1986), Broadway Bound, 1987-88; appeared in: The Play's the Thing, Bklyn. Acad. Music, 1978; played Eleanore in stage prodn. Lion in Winter, 1987; other stage appearances include Nat. Co. of The Royal Family (L.A. Drama Citics Circle award 1977), The Elephant Man (Outer Critics Circle award 1978-79 season, Tony award for best actress 1978-79 season), What the Butler Saw, 1989; appeared inaugural season, Robin Phillips Grand Theatre Co., London, Ont., Can., 1983-84, Broadway and Nat. Co. of Noises Off, 1985, Waltz of the Toreadors, 1986, Oh Coward, 1986-87 ; appeared as Kate in Broadway Bound by Neil Simon The Nat. Co. and L.A. Premiere, 1987-88; played Lettice in Lettice and Lovage Globe Theatre, London, 1989-90, Frosine in The Miser, 1990, Cabaret Verboten, 1991, The Destiny of Me, 1992-93, Later Life, 1993 (Outer Critics nominee), Richard II, 1994, London Suite, 1994, N.Y. Shakespeare Festival; films include: The Boston Strangler, The Odd Couple, The Super, 1990, Devlin, 1991, Quiz Show, 1993, The Road to Wellville, 1993; created: voice characters in Walt Disney films Robin Hood, The Aristocats. Recipient Obie Award for Twelve Dreams N.Y. Shakespeare Festival, 1982. Jewish. Office: care Duva-Flack Assocs Inc 200 W 57th St New York NY 10019-3211

SHELLHORN, RUTH PATRICIA, landscape architect; b. L.A., Sept. 21, 1909; d. Arthur Lemon and Lodema (Gould) S.; m. Harry Alexander Kueser, Nov. 21, 1940. Student dept. landscape architecture, Oreg. State Coll., 1927-30; grad. landscape architecture program, Cornell U. Coll. Architecture, 1933. Pvt. practice landscape architecture, various cities Calif., 1933—; exec. cons. landscape architect Bullocks Stores, Calif., 1945-78, Fashion Sqs. Shopping Ctrs., Calif., 1958-78, Marlborough Sch., L.A., 1968—, El Camino Coll., Torrance, Calif., 1970-78, Harvard Sch., North Hollywood, Calif., 1974-90; cons. landscape architect, site planner Disneyland, Anaheim, Calif., 1955, U. Calif., Riverside Campus, 1956-64, numerous others, also numerous gardens and estates; landscape architect Torrance (Calif.) City Goals Com., 1969-70; cons. landscape architect City of Rolling Hills (Calif.) Community Assn., 1973-93. Contbr. articles to garden and profl. publs.; subject of Oct. 1967 issue Landscape Design & Constrn. mag. Named Woman of Year, Los Angeles Times, 1955, Woman of Year, South Pasadena-San Marino (Calif.) Bus. Profl. Women, 1955; recipient Charles Goodwin Sands medal, 1930-33, Landscape Architecture award of merit Calif. State Garden Clubs, 1984, 86, Horticulturist of the Yr. award So. Calif. Hort. Inst., numerous nat., state, local awards for excellence. Fellow Am. Soc. Landscape Architects (past pres. So. Calif. chpt.), Phi Kappa Phi, Kappa Kappa Gamma (Alumni Achievement award 1960). Home and Office: 362 Camino De Las Colinas Redondo Beach CA 90277-6435

SHELLY, CHRISTINE DEBORAH, foreign service officer; b. Pontiac, Mich., May 1, 1951; d. Chester Price and Margaret Alice (Neafie) S.; m. Jose Manuel San-Bento Menezes, July 19, 1987; 1 stepchild, Ana Ferreira San-Bento Menezes. BA cum laude, Vanderbilt U., 1973; MA, Tufts U., 1974, MA in Diplomacy, 1975. Fgn. affairs analyst Intelligence and Rsch. Bur. Dept. State, Washington, 1975-77, desk officer Near Eastern Affairs, 1977-79; fin. attache Am. Embassy Dept. State, Cairo, 1979-81; asst. v.p. BankAmerica Internat., N.Y.C., 1981-82; spl. asst. Near Eastern Affairs Dept. State, Washington, 1982-83; econ., polit. officer Am. Embassy Dept. State, Lisbon, Portugal, 1983-87; dep. econ. advisor U.S. Mission to NATO, Brussels, 1987-90, dep. cabinet dir. Sec. Gen., 1990-93; dep. spokesman, dep. asst. sec. pub. affairs Dept. State, Washington, 1993—. Office: Bur Pub Affairs Dept State 2201 C St NW Rm 6800 Washington DC 20520

SHELSTA, JOAN STAPLETON, hotel executive; b. Cheyenne, Wyo., July 29, 1935; d. Roy Joseph and Laretta (Milan) Stapleton; m. Harold D. Engstrom, June 3, 1957 (div. 1979); children: Lisa, James, Christina, Hardy, Kevin, Lael; m. Rodney Leigh Shelsta, Feb. 6, 1983. BA, Lone Mountain Coll., 1956. Tchr. secondary sch. Casper, Wyo., 1956-68; stockbroker N.A.S.D., Casper, 1968-73; hotel salesperson Vail (Colo.) Resort Hotels, 1973-80; gen. mgr. Fall Ridge Hotel, Vail, 1980-90; gen. mgr., dir. sales and mktg. John Muir Inn, Napa, Calif., 1990—. Mem. Jr. League, Casper, 1959-65. Mem. Vail, Colo. Resort Assn. (bd. dirs. 1981-90). Office: John Muir Inn 1998 Trower Ave Napa CA 94558-2209

SHELTON, BESSIE ELIZABETH, school system administrator; b. Lynchburg, Va.; d. Robert and Bessie Ann (Plenty) Shelton; B.A. (scholar), W.Va. State Coll., 1958; student Northwestern U., 1953-55, Ind. U., 1956; M.S., SUNY, 1960; diploma Profl. Career Devel. Inst., 1993. Young adult libr. Bklyn. Pub. Libr., 1960-62; asst. head cen. ref. div. Queens Borough Pub. Libr., Jamaica, N.Y., 1962-65; instructional media specialist Lynchburg (Va.) Bd. Edn., 1966-74; ednl. research specialist, 1974-77; ednl. media assoc. Allegany County Bd. Edn., Cumberland, Md., 1977—. Guest singer Sta. WLVA, 1966—, WLVA-TV Christmas concerts, 1966—;cons. music and market rsch. Mem. YWCA, Lynchburg, 1966—, Fine Arts Ctr., Lynchburg, 1966—; ednl. adv. bd., nat. research bd. Am. Biog. Inst.; mem. U.S. Congl. Adv. Bd., USN Nat. Adv. Coun.; amb. goodwill Lynchburg, Va., 1986. Named to Nat. Women's Hall of Fame. Mem. AAUW, NEA, NAFE, Md. Tchrs. Assn., Allegany County Tchrs. Assn., Va. Edn. Assn., State Dept. Sch. Librarians, Internat. Entertainers Guild, Music City Songwriters Assn., Vocal Artists Am., Internat. Clover Poetry Assn., Internat. Platform Assn., Nat. Assn. Women Deans, Adminstrs. and Counselors, Intercontinental Biog. Assn., World Mail Dealers Assn., N.Am. Mailers Exch., Am. Assn. Creative Artists, Am. Biog. Inst. Research Assn., Tri-State Community Concert Assn. Pi Delta Phi, Sigma Delta Pi. Contbr. poems to various publs. Democrat. Baptist. Clubs: National Travel, Gulf Travel. Home: PO Box 187 Cumberland MD 21502-0187

SHELTON, BILLIE ANN HOFFMAN GOLLNER, elementary education counselor; b. Grant, Nebr., May 10, 1944; d. Darryl and Alma Marie (Friesen) Hoffman; m. Martin Patrick Shelton, Aug. 13, 1994; children: Brent, Donya. BA in Edn., U. Nebr., Kearney, 1978, MS in Counseling, 1988. Tchr. spl. edn. Ednl. Svc. Unit # 9, Hastings, Nebr., 1978-89; secondary edn. counselor Sch. Dist. OR 1, Palmyra, Nebr., 1989-93; elem. edn. counselor Council Bluffs (Iowa) Pub. Schs., 1993—; tchr. parenting class Council Bluffs-Palmyra Sch. Dist., Carter Lake, Iowa and Palmyra, 1990-93; facilitator Art Expression Workshop, 1990-94; Nebr. state coord. Counseling for High Skills, Manhattan, Kans., 1992—. Bd. dirs. Carter Lake Cmty. Resource Ctr., 1994—. Mem. ACA, Am. Sch. Counselor Assn., Iowa Edn. Assn., Nebr. Counseling Assn. (bd. dirs. Profl. Recognition Award chair 1993—), Nebr. Sch. Counselor Assn. (pres. 1992-93, editor newsletter 1992-93, career-life chair 1993-94). Democrat. Home: 409 S 38th Ave Omaha NE 68131-3808

SHELTON, DEBORAH KAY, elementary education educator; b. Lynchburg, Va., July 10, 1952; d. Edward O. and Gloria (Keesee) S. BS, Nova U., 1979, MS, 1983, postgrad., 1992—. Cert. elem. tchr., elem. prin., supr. Legal sec. Bunnell & Assocs., Ft. Lauderdale, Fla., 1978-79; tchr. Davie Elem. Sch., Ft. Lauderdale, 1979-87, Altavista (Va.) Elem. Sch., 1987—; mem. Supt.'s Adv. Com., 1989—. Mem. ASCD, Am. Ednl. Rsch. Assn., Va. Edn. Assn. (state com., lobbyist), Campbell County Edn. Assn. (pres. 1988-91, faculty rep. 1992—), Phi Delta Kappa (v.p. membership). Home: 315 Kitty Hawk Sq Lynchburg VA 24502 Office: Altavista Elem Sch School Rd Altavista VA 24517

SHELTON, DOROTHY DIEHL REES, lawyer; b. Manila, Sept. 16, 1935; came to U.S., 1945; d. William Walter John and Hedwig (Glienecke) Diehl; m. Charles W. Rees, Jr., June 15, 1957 (div. 1971); children: Jane Rees Stebbins, John B., Anne Rees Slack, Esq., David C., Esq.; m. Thomas C. Shelton, Mar. 4, 1977 (dec.). BA in Music, Stanford Univ., 1957; JD, Western State Univ. Coll. Law, 1976. Bar: Calif. 1977, U.S. Dist. Ct. (so. dist.) Calif. 1977. Pvt. practice, San Diego, 1977—. Mem. ABA, Calif. State Bar, Am. Trial Lawyers Assn., Calif. Trial Lawyers Assn., Calif. Attys. for Criminal Justice, San Diego County Bar Assn., San Diego Trial Lawyers Assn., Stanford U. Alumni Assn., Jr. League San Diego, Gt. Pyrenees Club Am., Dachshund Club Am., Nu Beta Epsilon. Roman Catholic. Office: 110 W C St Ste 918 San Diego CA 92101-3959

SHELTON, MARILYN J., counselor; b. Clinton, Miss., Dec. 28, 1955; d. Walter Shelton Sr. and Ruby (Gorman) Martin. AA, Coahoma Jr. Coll., 1974; BA, Alcorn State U., 1976, MEd, 1980. Counselor, outreach worker Talent Search project Mary Holmes Coll., West Point, Miss., 1980-82; guidance counselor in residential living Batesville (Miss.) Job Corps. Ctr., 1982-85; counselor, assoc. program mgr. ROTC enhanced skills tng. Alcorn State U., Lorman, Miss., 1985-87; counselor Gen. Coll. for Excellence Alcorn State U., Lorman, 1987—. Mem. AACD, Miss. Counseling Assn., Miss. Assn. Multicultural Counseling and Devel., Assn. for Multicultural Counseling and Devel., Alcorn State U. Nat. Alumni Assn. Baptist. Home: PO Box 664 Lorman MS 39096-9998 Office: Alcorn State U Lorman MS 39096

SHELTON, MURIEL MOORE, religious education administrator; b. Freeport, N.Y., May 29, 1921; d. Samuel Talbott and Agnes Jerolean (Trigg) Payne; m. Ernest William Moore, May 29, 1944 (dec. Apr. 2, 1978); children: Diana Moore Williams, David E. Moore, Cathi Moore Mount, Douglas L. Moore; m. Malcolm Wendell Shelton, Aug. 9, 1987. AB, Eastern Nazarene Coll., 1942; MusM, U. Tex., 1966. Cert. educator gen. and choral music, English, Tex., Tenn., Ark., Kans. Music dir. Coll. Ave. United Meth. Ch., Manhattan, Kans., 1969-71, Cen. United Meth. Ch., Lawrence, Kans., 1971-75, First United Meth. Ch., Horton, Kans., 1975-78; dir. Christian edn. St. Mark's United Meth. Ch., Bethany, Okla., 1980—; chmn. bd. dirs. Northwest Food Pantry, Oklahoma City, 1987-88; rep. St. mark's United Meth. Ch. Labor Link Ctr., 1989—; lectr. in field. Contbr. articles to quar. mags.; author: Song of Joy, 1985, Promises of Good, 1989, Healing in His Wings, 1992. Mem. Christian Educators' Fellowship. Home: 6404 NW 35th St Bethany OK 73008-4136 Office: St Mark's United Meth Ch 8140 NW 36th St Bethany OK 73008-3500

SHELTON, SLOANE, actress; b. Hahira, Ga., Mar. 14, 1934; d. Clarence Duffie and Ruth Evangeline (Davis) S. Student, Berea Coll., 1955; honors diploma, Royal Acad. Dramatic Art, London, 1959. Mem. O'Neill Found., Waterford, Conn., 1981-83, 85, 89, 91, 94; mem. theater panel N.Y. State Coun. on the Arts, 1979-81. Producer: (with Kevin Brownlow and Norma Millay Ellis) (documentary film) Millay at Steepletop, 1976; appearances in Broadway plays include: I Never Sang for My Father, Sticks & Bones, The Runner Stumbles, The Shadow Box, Orpheus Descending, Passione, Open Admissions; films include: All That Jazz, All the President's Men, Tiger Warsaw, Running on Empty, Jacknife, Lean on Me. Pres. Bevilla Kew Found., Millay Colony for the Arts. Mem. Actors Equity Assn., Screen Actors Guild, Actors Fund Am., AFTRA. Democrat.

SHELTON, STEPHANI, broadcast journalist, consultant; b. Boston; d. Phil and Babette (Belloff) Saltman; m. Frank Herold. BS, Boston U. Reporter, news broadcaster Sta. WPAT, Paterson, N.J., 1972-73; corr. CBS News, N.Y.C., 1973-84; news corr. WOR-TV, N.Y.C., 1984-88; corr., anchor Fin. News Network, N.Y.C., 1989-91; ind. broadcast journalist, producer, cons., 1991—; freelance reporter Sta. WPIX-TV, 1991—, Sta. WNBC-TV, 1993; freelance radio documentary writer Westinghouse Group W Broadcasting, N.Y.C., 1970-73. Recipient Peabody award, 1972, N.J. Best Spot News award AP, 1987, 88, N.J. Working Press award, 1992, 93, 94. Mem. Radio and TV Working Press Assn. (v.p. 1985—), Soc. Profl. Journalists.

SHELTON, THERESE NOEL SULLIVAN, mathematics and computer science educator; b. Wichita Falls, Tex., Nov. 23, 1959; d. Daniel Henry and Dorothea Margaret (Callanan) Sullivan; m. Drew Curtis Shelton, May 26, 1984; 1 child, Jennifer Michele. BS, Tex. A&M U., 1982; MS, Clemson (S.C.) U., 1984, PhD, 1987. Assoc. prof. math. and computer sci. Southwestern U., Georgetown, Tex., 1987—. Contbr. articles to profl. jours. Mem. AAUW, Math. Assn. Am., Am. Math. Soc., Soc. for Indsl. and Applied Math., Assn. Women in Math., Assn. Women in Sci. Roman Catholic. Office: Southwestern U Georgetown TX 78626

SHEMA, VIRGINIA KING, lawyer; b. Terre Haute, Ind., Aug. 20, 1957; d. Thomas Frederick and Mary Kathryn (Milner) King; m. Christopher P. Shema, Sept. 17, 1988. BS in Environ. Health Scis., Ind. State U., 1979, BS in English, 1984; JD, Ind. U., Indpls., 1987. Bar: Ind. 1987, U.S. Dist. Ct. (no. and so. dists.) Ind. 1987, Va. 1988, U.S. Dist. Ct. (ea. dist.) Va. 1988, U.S. Ct. Appeals (4th cir.) 1989. Assoc. Breit, Rutter & Montagna, Norfolk, Va., 1987, Breit, Drescher & Breit, Norfolk, 1987-92, Shema & Shema P.C., Norfolk, 1992—. Mem. ABA, Ind. Bar Assn., Va. Bar Assn., Norfolk-Portsmouth (Va.) Bar Assn., Assn. Trial Lawyers Am., Va. Trial Lawyers Assn. Democrat. Roman Catholic. Home: 128 Old Dr Chesapeake VA 23320-5228 Office: Shema & Shema PC 860 Greenbriar Cir Ste 506 Chesapeake VA 23320

SHEMCHUK, PAULA J., training and education coordinator; b. Meriden, Conn., Aug. 8, 1962; d. Paul and Rose Virginia (Piccolo) S. AS, Bay State Jr. Coll., 1980-82. Sales assoc. D & L Stores Corp., Meriden, 1982-83; clerk, typist Corometrics Med. Systems, Wallingford, Conn., 1983-84; plasticware packer UniSet, Inc., Wallingford, 1984-86; human resources sec. Gaylord Hosp., Wallingford, 1986-88, mktg. devel. sec., 1988; internat. sales sec. Novametrix Med., Wallingford, 1988-89, corp. travel sec., 1989; adminstrv. asst. Housing Authority Ins., Cheshire, Conn., 1990-92, tng. asst., 1992-93, tng. & edn. coord., 1994—. Article coord. (newsletter) Risk News, 1992-93. Vol. St. Vincent De Paul Shelter for Homeless, Meriden, 1989—. Mem. Profl. Conv. Mgmt. Assn. Home: 42 Antonio Ave Meriden CT 06451 Office: Housing Authority Ins 189 Commerce Ct PO Box 189 Cheshire CT 06410

SHEMET, KAREN ANASTASIA, anthropologist, archaeologist; b. Queens, N.Y., Jan. 11, 1961; d. Arthur Anthony and Lillian Emma (Mahler) S. BA with honors, Alfred U., 1983; MA, Am. U., 1987. Archaeologist The Pub. Archaeology Lab., Inc., Pawtucket, R.I., 1987-88, R.I. Coll. Pub. Archaeology Program, Providence, 1988-89; vol. U.S. Peace Corps Agriculture Ext., Ifugao, Philippines, 1989-90; archaeologist SUNY, Stony Brook, 1991-92; anthropology instr. Dowling Coll., Oakdale, N.Y., 1992; archaeologist Alaska Native Claims Settlement Office Dept. of Interior, Bur. Indian Affairs, Anchorage, 1992-94; coord. Bur. Indian Affairs, Alaska Archaeology Week with U.S. Park Svc., Anchorage, 1992-94. Mem. Alaska Tibet Com., Homer, 1993-94; participant Run for Human Rights, Amnesty Internat., Anchorage, 1994; vols. Alaska Aviation heritage Mus., Oscar Anderson House Mus., Salvation Army, Anchorage. Mem. Alaska Anthropol. Assn., Aircraft Owners and Pilots Assn. Home: 215 W 13th Ave Anchorage AK 99501

SHEMORRY, CORINNE JOYNES, marketing executive; b. Rolla, N.D., Jan. 24, 1920; d. William H. and Edna Ruth (Conn) Joynes; children: Gay, Jan. Publisher, Williston (N.D.) Plains Reporter, 1953-78; mktg. dir. Western Credit Union, 1979-91; journalist, lectr., cons., author, reporter. Recipient numerous awards in journalism on state and nat. level, including Outstanding Woman in Journalism in N.D., 1987, 1st Place Golden Mirror award Credit Union Nat. Assn., Rough Rider Gov.'s Individual Community Pride Leadership award N.D. Gov. George A. Sinner, 1988. Chmn. Rough Rider Internat. Art Show & Auction, 1985—. Mem. N.D. Press Assn., N.D. Press Women (past pres.), Nat. Press Women, Williston C. of C., NAFE, Fin. Mktg. Assn. (charter). Club: Bus. and Profl. Women's (past pres.). Home: 210 E 14th St PO Box 1030 Williston ND 58801

SHEN, GRACE CHI-MEI, technical writer; b. St. Louis, Nov. 23, 1950; d. Kwan-ting and Nai-hsuan (Chang) S. AB magna cum laude, Georgian Court Coll., Lakewood, N.J., 1977. Sr. tech. assoc. Bell Labs., Holmdel, N.J., 1977-79; mem. adminstrv. group Bell Labs., Murray Hill, N.J., 1979-80; sr. tech. assoc. Bell Labs., South Plainfield, N.J., 1980-82; systems analyst Sea-Land Corp., Elizabeth, N.J., 1982-85; systems cons. CIGNA Systems, Phila., 1985-88, bus. sys. specialist, 1988-91; FOCUS release analyst Info. Builders, Inc., N.Y.C., 1991-93; quality assurance analyst, 1993-95, EDA/SQL tech. writer, 1995—. Mem. Nat. Women's Polit. Caucus. Mem. NOW, Assn. for Women in Computing (convener N.J. 1980), AAUW, Lower Camden County Bus. and Profl. Women (2d v.p. 1988-89, 1st v.p. 1989-90, corr. sec. 1990-91), Hightstown/East Windsor Bus. and Profl. Women. Home: 63-21 Ravens Crest Dr Plainsboro NJ 08536-2429 Office: Information Builders Inc 1250 Broadway New York NY 10001-3701

SHENTON, MARTHA ELIZABETH, research psychologist; b. Concord, N.H., Nov. 11, 1952; d. Enoch and Loretta Marie (Halle) S., m. George Santiccioli; 1 child, Jessica. AB, Wellesley Coll., 1973; MS, Tufts U., Medford, Mass., 1976; MA, Harvard U., 1981, PhD, 1984. Research fellow Mclean Hosp. Mailman Research Ctr., Belmont, Mass., 1979-84; lecturer Brandis U., Walton, Mass., 1984-85; post doctoral research fellow Harvard Med. Sch., Mass. Mental Health Ctr., Boston, 1984-86; rsch. assoc. Harvard Med. Sch., VA Med. Ctr., Boston, 1986-88, instr. dept. psychiatry, 1988—; asst. prof. psychology, dept. psychiatry Med. Sch. Harvard U., now assoc. prof psychology. Contbr. articles to profl. jours. Mem. Am. Psychol. Assn., Mass. Psychol. Assn., Phi Beta Kappa. Office: VA Med Ctr Dept Psychiatry 116A 940 Belmont St Cambridge MA 02140-1704

SHEPARD, ELAINE ELIZABETH, writer, lecturer; b. Olney, Ill.; d. Thomas J. and Bernice E. (Shadle) S.; m. Terry D. Hunt, Apr. 16, 1938; m. George F. Hartman, Oct. 1, 1943 (div. June 1958). Covered nat. polit. convs. for Stas. WTTG-TV and WINS, Chgo., 1952, 1956; polit. reporter for NANA and WINS, Chgo. and Los Angeles, 1960; reporter Congo rebellion for N.Am. Newspaper Alliance and N.Y. Mirror, 1960-61; corr. covering Pres. Eisenhower's Middle East, Far East and S. Am. tour, 1959-60; Vietnam corr. MBS, 1965-66; granted interviews with Khrushchev, Castro, Tito, Chou En-lai, Nasser, Shah of Iran, King Hussein, King Faisel, Duvalier, Lumumba, Chiang-Kai-Shek, Nehru, Menzies, John F. Kennedy, Richard M. Nixon, others; mem. White House Press Corps accompanying Pres. Nixon to, Austria, Iran, Poland, Moscow, 1972. Film and theater actress, Hollywood, N.Y.C., Europe, 1939-50, cover girl, John Robert Powers, 1939-43, under contract to, RKO and Metro-Goldwyn-Mayer, 1940-45, guest commentator for, Voice of Am.; contbr.: feature articles to various mags., including N.Y. News Sunday Mag, 1953—; columnist, contbg. editor: feature articles to various mags., including Nat. Cath. Press, 1969-74; author: Forgive Us Our Press Passes, 1962, The Doom Pussy, 1967, The Doom Pussy II, 1991. Recipient 2 citations for participating in armed helicopter assaults with 145th Aviation Bn. Vietnam. Mem. Screen Actors Guild, AFTRA, Actors Equity. Club: Overseas Press (N.Y.C.). Home: 12 E 62nd St New York NY 10021-7218

SHEPARD, JANIE RAY (J. R. SHEPARD), software development executive; b. Montebello, Calif., Feb. 23, 1954; d. George Allen and Ada Janette (Barrow) Ray; 1 child, April Lynn. Grad. high sch., Albany, Ga., 1972. Adminstrv. asst. to pres. FRC Office Products, Jacksonville, Fla., 1979-82; adminstrv. asst. to v.p. comml. lending Stockton Savs., Dallas, 1983-84; exec. sec. to v.p. ops. Metromedia Long Distance, Ft. Lauderdale, Fla., 1985-87; owner, pres. RaceCom, Inc., Ormond Beach, Fla., 1986—, April Lynn Advt., Ormond Beach, 1986—. Developer computer text file editing system and computer artificial intelligence; developer optical character recognition neural network software. Active Jacksonville and Dallas areas Girl Scouts U.S., 1980-96; vol. co-chair, 1992-94, adv. coord. 1995, Jazz Matazz, City of Ormond Beach. Mem. Ormond Beach C. of C. Democrat. Methodist. Home: 10 Cypress View Trl Ormond Beach FL 32174-8295 Office: RaceCom Inc 555 W Granada Blvd Ste 10E Ormond Beach FL 32174-9403

SHEPARD, JEANNIE, elementary school educator; b. Lee County, S.C., Mar. 24, 1950; d. Leroy and Helen (Myers) Butler; m. Sept. 27, 1980; 1 child, LaVaughn Emil Blanding. BA in Edn., St. Peter's Coll., 1979. Cert. elem. tchr., early childhood, English, home health care. Tchr. kindergarten, tchr. pre-kindergarten Sch. #5, Linden, N.J., 1979-81; tchr. basic skills Sch. #2, Linden, N.J., 1981-82; tchr. grade 4 Sch. #4 Annex, Linden, N.J., 1982-83; tchr. grade 4, grade 2 Public Sch. #8, Jersey City, 1983-84; tchr. pre-sch. JFK Day care Ctr. Rahway (N.J.) Community Action Orgn. Inc., 1986-87; tchr. grade 7 18th Ave. Sch., Newark, 1987-89; tchr. grade 5 South 17th St. Sch., Newark, 1989-90, tchr. grade 6, 1989—; coord. JFK Day Care Ctr., Rahway, N.J., 1987—. Treas. PTA South 17th St. Sch., 1992—, ch. community rels. com. First Bapt. Ch. of Linden, 1992—. Mem. N.J. Edn. Assn., Newark Tchrs. Edn. Assn., Operation PUSH. Home: 307 Carnegie St Linden NJ 07036-2213

SHEPARD, KATHRYN IRENE, public relations executive; b. Tooele, Utah, Jan. 6, 1956; d. James Lewis and Glenda Verleen (Slaughter) Clark; m. Mark L. Shepard, June 5, 1976. BA in History, Boise State U., 1980. On-air writer Sta. KTTV, Channel 11, L.A., 1982-85; publicity dir. Hollywood (Calif.) C. of C., 1985-87; pres. Kathy Shepard Pub. Rels., Burbank and Portland, 1987-93; dir. public relations Las Vegas Hilton; instr. pub. rels. ext. program UCLA, 1991-92. Contbr. articles to profl. publs. Mem. Publicity Club L.A. (pres. 1991-92, bd. dirs. 1987-91). Office: Las Vegas Hilton PR Dept 3000 Paradise Rd Las Vegas NV 89109

SHEPARD, MARGO ANN, financial consultant; b. Starke, Fla., Dec. 6, 1957; d. Michael Joseph and Carroll May (Emerson) Warhola; m. Michael Eugene Shepard, Sept. 4,1982; children: Andrew Eugene, Ann Emerson, Emily Catherine. BSBA, U. N.C., 1978; MBA, U. Kans., 1981. Cert. fin. planner. Product planner Hallmark Cards, Kansas City, Mo., 1979-81; grad. tchg. asst. Sch. Bus. U. Kans., Lawrence, 1981; account exec. Kidder, Peabody Co., Kansas City, 1981-83; v.p., fin. cons. Smith Barney, Kansas City, 1983—. Bd. dirs. Mid-Continent coun. Girl Scouts U.S., 1987-90, Greater Mo. Focus on Leadership, 1990; bd. dirs., treas. Mo. Found. for Women's Resources. Named One of Am.'s Best Stockbrokers Money Mag., 1987. Mem. Am. Inst. Cert. Fin. Planners, Greater Kansas City C. of C., Kansas City Club, Zonta (pres. found. devel. com. Kansas City chpt. 1983-84), Phi Beta Kappa, Beta Gamma Sigma. Republican. Roman Catholic. Home: 3706 Locust St Kansas City MO 64109-2626 Office: Smith Barney 401 Ward Pky Ste C Kansas City MO 64112-2102

SHEPARD, MARGUERITE AUWERTER (MIDGE SHEPARD), computer systems specialist; b. Cleve., June 25, 1946; d. Jay Pearce and Ida (Armstrong) Auwerter; m. William Brown Shepard Jr., June 14, 1969; children: Trip, Jay, Susan. BA, Conn. Coll., 1968; MBA, U. Conn., 1993. Sys. programmer AT&T, White Plains, N.Y., 1968-73; programmer Turnkey Sys., Inc., Norwalk, Conn., 1973-77; mktg. cons. Gen. Electric, Tokyo, 1977-80; sr. cons., dir. Real Decisions Corp., Darien, Conn., 1980-93; project leader Mercedes-Benz Credit Corp., Norwalk, 1993—. Mem. Country Club of Darien, Phi Kappa Phi, Beta Gamma Sigma. Home: 9 Beach Dr Darien CT 06820 Office: Mercedes-Benz Credit Corp 201 Merritt 7 Ste 700 Norwalk CT 06856

SHEPARD, MARIDEAN MANSFIELD (MARI SHEPARD), data processing executive, advocate for rights for the disabled; b. Enid, Okla., Jan. 20, 1952; d. Howard Ernest and Nadine (Miller) Mansfield; m. Kent Lee Shepard, June 25, 1977. Student, Ventura Coll., 1969-72, Mission Coll., 1979-81, 93, Learning Tree U., 1990-92. Spl. edn. aide, Braille transcriber, Spanish interpreter Hueneme Sch. Dist., Port Hueneme, Calif., 1970-76; entertainer, musician, 1972-87; spl. edn. tchr. Found. for Jr. Blind, L.A., 1977-78; music tchr. Pinecrest Sch., Northridge, Calif., 1978-79; libr./textbook clk. Burbank (Calif.) Sch. Dist., 1980-81; receptionist, sec. Van Nuys (Calif.) Coll. Bus., 1981-84; bookkeeper, computer operator, sec. Pacific Coast Tech. Inst., Van Nuys, 1984-85; sec. tng. dept., computer operator, transcriber Braille, interpreter sign lang. Internat. Guiding Eyes, Sylmar, Calif., 1985-86; computer operator, bookkeeper Engelhard Corp., Sylmar, 1989—; founder, disABILITIES Info. Svcs., at Quantum, 1986, at Am. OnLine, 1990, at GEnie, 1989—; producer, host disABILITIES Roundtable and Equal Access Cafe BBS, 1990—; speaker World Inst. on Disabilities, Oakland, Calif., 1990, Abilities Expo, Anaheim, 1992, Calif. State U. Northridge Conf. Tech. and Disabilities, 1993; session chair Accessing Tech. Through Online Svcs., ADA Conf., Washington, 1993. Co-author: (computer database program) Johns Hopkins Technology Search Regional Finals, 1991. Vol. voter registration LWV, Ventura County, Calif., 1978; vol. tchr. Pleasant Valley Convalescent Hosp., Port Hueneme, 1971; vol. transcriber Ventura County Braille Transcribers Assn., 1963-76; volunteer relay/interpreter Greater L.A. Coun. on Deafness, Van Nuys, 1980-82; vol. writer, decorator Ventura County USO, Oxnard, 1969-71; Sunday sch. tchr. 1st Presbyn. Ch., Oxnard, 1973-74. Scholar Ventura County Bus. and Profl. Women, 1973; recipient 1st place mixed media Ventura County Fair, 1970. Office: disABILITIES Info Svc 9840 Stanwin Ave Arleta CA 91331-5303

SHEPARD, MIKKI MAUREEN ALLISON, personal care company executive; b. Queens, N.Y., May 12, 1951; d. George William and June Rita (Ferrary) S.; m. Tom C. Blankenheim, July 2, 1983; 1 child, Jeffrey Thomas. BA, U. Colo., 1982. Cert. real estate brokerage mgr. Employment counselor Centennial Personnel, Colorado Springs, Colo., 1977-78; ins. auditor Associated Ins. Utah, Colorado Springs, 1978-79; broker, co-owner TCB Realty and Investment Co., Inc., Colorado Springs, 1979-90; exec. NuSkin, Castles of Am., Inc., Colorado Springs, Colo., 1989—; speaker Nat. Assn. Realtors, Chgo., 1985—. Contbr. articles to Real Estate Today, Colo. Realtor News Communiqué, Gazette Telegraph. Pres. Christmas Unlimited, Colorado Springs, 1988, 89; campaign worker El Paso County Reps., Colorado Springs, 1977-78; mem. Realtors Polit. Action Com., Chgo., 1979—; mem. Profl. Women's Rep. Club, Colorado Springs, 1987. Served with USAF, 1970-74. Mem. Colo. Assn. Realtors (dir. 1988—), Colorado Springs Bd. Realtors (bd. dirs. 1981, 84, treas. 1985-86, sec. 1987-88, pres. 1989-90), Realtors Nat. Mktg. Inst., Women's Coun. Realtors (Colo. chpt. pres. 1989—, gov. 1990, Pikes Peak chpt. treas. 1984-85, pres. 1986-87, Woman of Yr. Pikes Peak chpt. 1986, Woman of the Yr. Colo. State chpt. 1990), Nat. Women's Coun. Realtors (leadership tng. grad. 1987, edn. chmn. 1987-88). Methodist. Office: Castles of Am Inc PO Box 241 Manitou Springs CO 80829-0241

SHEPHARD, DOREEN LOY, community health nurse, educator; b. York, Nebr., Apr. 16, 1936; d. Daniel R. Friesen and Marie Mildred (Janzen) Friesen Siebert; m. Raymond C. Shephard, Aug. 24, 1985. Diploma in nursing, Lincoln Gen. Hosp. Sch., 1957; student, U. Nebr., 1954-57, Portland State Coll., 1961-63; BSN, U. Oreg., 1963; postgrad., Tex. Christian U., 1964-65, U. Tex., 1965-66; MPH, U. Hawaii, 1975; PhD, Tex. Woman's U., 1987. RN, Nebr., Tex. Staff nurse Lincoln (Nebr.) Gen. Hosp., 1957-59, VA Hosp., Fargo, N.D., 1959-61; clinic nurse Kaiser Permanente Clinic, Portland, Oreg., 1962-63; staff nurse VA Hosp., Portland, 1963-64; night float nurse All Saints Hosp., Ft. Worth, 1965; missionary nurse United Christian Missionary Soc., Indpls., 1966-73; operating room instr. CMC Hosp., Ludhiana, Punjab, India, 1966-67; instr. MIBE Sch. for Grad. Nurses, 1968, Sch. of Nursing Mission Hosp., Tilda, India, 1969-72; community health nurse Holy Family Hosp., Community Health Project, New Delhi, 1971-72; staff nurse St. Elizabeth's Health Care Ctr., 1973; pub. health nurse II Lincoln Lancaster Health Dept., 1973-74; instr. U. Hawaii Coll. Nursing, Honolulu, 1975-77; tester, reader U. Hawaii Rsch. Corp., Honolulu, 1980; vis. nurse Tabitha Home Health Care, Lincoln, 1980; night staff nurse York (Nebr.) Gen. Hosp., 1980-81; instr. nursing Kearney (Nebr.) State Coll., 1981-84; supr. North Cen. Tex. Home Health Agy., Ft. Worth, 1986-87; asst. prof. nursing West Tex. State U., Canyon, 1987-88; assoc. prof. nursing U. Guam, Mangilao, 1988; asst. prof. nursing Stephen F. Austin State U., Nacogdoches, Tex., 1989-93; asst. prof. U. Tex. Pan Am., Edinburg, 1994—; attendee numerous nursing confs., seminars and workshops. Contbr. articles to profl. jours. Mem. Nat. League for Nursing, N.Am. Nursing Diagnosis Assn. Home: 118 Gastel Cir Apt 2 Edinburg TX 78539 Office: U Ten Pan Am Dept Nursing 1201 W University Dr Edinburg TX 78539

SHEPHERD, CYBILL, actress, singer; b. Memphis, Feb. 18, 1950; d. William Jennings and Patty Shobe (Micci) S.; m. David Ford, Nov. 19, 1978 (div.); 1 child, Clementine; m. Bruce Oppenheim, March 1, 1987; children: Molly Ariel and Cyrus Zachariah (twins). Student, Hunter Coll., 1969, Coll. of New Rochelle, 1970, Washington Sq. Coll., NYU, 1971, U. So. Calif., 1972, NYU, 1973. Appeared in motion pictures Last Picture Show, 1971, The Heartbreak Kid, 1973, Daisy Miller, 1974, At Long Last Love, 1975, Taxi Driver, 1976, Special Delivery, 1976, Silver Bears, 1977, The Lady Vanishes, 1978, Earthright, 1980, The Return, 1986, Chances Are, 1988, Texasville, 1990, Alice, 1990, Once Upon a Crime, 1992, Married to It, 1993; star TV series The Yellow Rose, 1983-84, Moonlighting, 1985-89, Cybill, 1994—; TV films include A Guide for the Married Woman, 1978, Secrets of a Married Man, 1984, Seduced, 1985, The Long Hot Summer, 1985, Which Way Home, 1991, Memphis, 1992 (also co-writer, co-exec. prodr.), Stormy Weathers, 1992, Telling Secrets, 1993, There Was a Little Boy, 1993; record albums include Cybill Does It To Cole Porter, 1974, Cybill and Stan Getz, 1977, Vanilla with Phineas Newborn, Jr, 1978; appeared in stage plays A Shot in the Dark, 1977, Picnic, 1980, Vanities, 1981. Office: Rogers and Cowan 10000 Santa Monica Blvd Los Angeles CA 90067*

SHEPHERD, ELIZABETH POOLE, health science facility administrator; b. Bulape, Kasai, Zaire, Mar. 16, 1937; (parents Am. citizens); d. Mark Keller and Sara Amelia (Day) Poole; m. Donald Ray Shepherd, June 6, 1958; children: Lisa, Stephanie, Leslie, Don Poole. BA magna cum laude, Austin Coll., 1958. Cert. secondary and elem. tchr., Tex. Tchr. Thomas Jefferson High Sch., Dallas, 1958, Edward H. Cary Jr. High Sch., Dallas, 1959-60; bus. mgr. Donald R. Shepherd, M.D., P.A., Conroe, Tex., 1972—; bus. mgr., co-owner Profl. Labs, Inc., Houston, 1975-82. Brownie leader Girl Scouts Am., 1967-69; dist. chmn. San Jacinto council Boy Scouts Am., Conroe, 1977; pres. Women of Ch. First Presbyn. Ch., Conroe, 1973-74, Montgomery County Med. Soc., Conroe, 1974-75; bd. dirs. ARC, Conroe, 1970-80; bd. dirs., officer Med. Ctr. Hosp. Vols., Conroe, 1978-81. Mem. AAUW, Alpha Chi, Alpha Delta. Republican. Presbyn. Home: 704 Longmire Rd Conroe TX 77304

SHEPHERD, ELSBETH WEICHSEL, manufacturing consultant; b. Youngstown, Ohio, Dec. 5, 1952; d. Richard Henry and Lesley Frances (Lynn) Weichsel; BS in Math., Carnegie-Mellon U., 1974; MBA, U. Cin., 1979; m. Gordon Ray Shepherd, Aug. 28, 1976. Asst. indsl. engr. Armco, Inc., Middletown, Ohio, 1974-76, asso. indsl. engr., 1976-78, indsl. engr., 1978-82, sr. ops. engr., 1982-86, supr. process planning, 1986-88; project mgr. Integrated Mfg., 1988-91, supt. primary ops. scheduling, 1991-92; sr. assoc. Coopers & Lybrand, Cin., 1992-93, mng. assoc., 1993-94; sr. cons. CSC Consulting, 1995—. Mem. news mag. staff Jr. League Cin., 1980-81; vol. Miami Purchase Assn. Am. Iron and Steel Inst. fellow, 1978-81. Mem. Soc. Women Engrs. (pres. sect. 1981-82, provisional regional dir. 1983-84), Assn. Computing Machinery, Am. Inst. Indsl. Engrs. (v.p. services, pres. 1985-86), Tech. Socs. Council of Cin. (pres. 1986-87, 1st v.p. 1985-86, 2d v.p. 1984-85, treas. 1983-84), Engrs. and Scientists of Cin. (sec. 1986-87, pres. elect 1987-88, pres. 1988-89, treas. 1990—). Home: 7382-4 Ridgepoint Dr Cincinnati OH 45230-4398 Office: 1500 Atrium One 201 E 4th St Cincinnati OH 45202

SHEPHERD, EMILIE KAY, investment advisor, financial planner; b. Freeport, Ill.; d. Robert Marston and Vivian Elizabeth (Youngblood) Hopkins; m. Jon Martin Shepherd, Feb. 17, 1962 (dec. May 1991); children: Jon, Stephen, Amy. BS with honors, U. Wis., 1956; postgrad., UCLA, 1958, U. Mich., 1959. CLU, chartered fin. cons. Speech therapist Troy (Mich.) Sch. Dist., 1956-59; med. rsch. asst. Kresge Eye Inst., Detroit, 1959-61; ins. sales asst. Jeb Bruce Robertson Assocs., Glenview, Ill., 1983-84; ins. cons. fin. inst. John J. Smith & Assocs., Wilmette, Ill., 1984-85; v.p. Horizon Fin. Svcs., Wilmette, 1985-91; pres. Shepherd & Vitek, Wilmette, 1991; investment advisor, fin. planner Bank One, Wilmette, 1992-94. Mem. svc. bd. Hospice of North Shore, Evanston, Ill., 1990-91. Mem. Inst. for Cert. Fin. Planners (assoc.). Address: 1020 Ashland Ave Wilmette IL 60091

SHEPHERD, JUNE ELLEN, psychologist; b. Dallas, Nov. 5, 1950; d. Max A. Shepherd and Mary E. Shepherd Graves; m. Stephen Porter (div.). BS in Edn., Tex. Woman's U., 1973, MEd, 1977, MA in Psychology, 1985, PhD in Psychology, 1989. Lic. psychologist, Tex., lic. marriage and family therapist, Tex. Tchr. spl. edn. pub. schs. Dallas and Plano, Tex., 1973-79; developmental lab. asst. dir. Richland Coll., Dallas, 1979; instr. Richland Coll., Tex. Woman's U., 1979-87; cons. sch. psychologist Irving (Tex.) Schs., 1987-88; psychology intern U. Nebr. Med. Sch., Omaha, 1988-89; psychologist Boys Town Nat. Rsch. Hosp., Omaha, 1989-91; postdoctoral fellow Johns Hopkins Hosp., Balt., 1991-92; pvt. practice Austin, Tex., 1993—. Mem. APA (clin. mem.), Am. Assn. Marriage and Family Therapists, Tex. Psychol. Assn., Capital Area Psychol. Assn. Office: Ste 280 8200 N Mopac Austin TX 78759

SHER, LINDA ROSENBERG, lawyer; b. Chgo., May 16, 1938; d. Sidney and Rebecca Rosenberg; B.A., U. Chgo., 1959; LL.B., Yale U., 1962; m. Stanley O. Sher, Aug. 11, 1963; children—Jeremy Jay, Hellyn Sue. Admitted to D.C. bar, 1962; counsel constl. rights subcom. Senate Judiciary Com., 1962-64; atty. NLRB, 1964-77, asst. gen. counsel supreme ct. br., 1977-93, acting assoc. gen. counsel, 1994—. Office: NLRB 1099 14th St NW Washington DC 20570-0001

SHER, PATRICIA RUTH, state legislator; b. Washington, June 19, 1931; d. Harry Eugene Hesse and Beatrice Ruth (Whitcomb) Cooper; m. William Sher, Feb. 13, 1955; children: Mark Stephen, Hunter Neal, Valerie Lynn, Tod David. Student, Montgomery Coll.; BS in Human Ecology and Applied Design, U. Md., 1983. Mem. House of Dels., Annapolis, Md., 1979-90, dep. majority whip, 1987-89, dep. majority leader, 1989-90, vice-chair task force to study deaths resulting from bldg. fires, 1985-88, mem. interdept. com. mandated health ins. benefits, spl. com. drug and alcohol abuse, chair nat. legis. task force fire gas toxicity, 1983-85; mem. Md. State Senate, 1991—; mem. finance com., state employees' health ins. adv. coun., spl. joint com. legis. data sys., 1991—. Founder Friends of RAP-Regional Addiction Prevention, 1971; mem. Com. to Repeal Blue Laws, 1976; mem. adv. coun. Drug Abuse, 1972-78; Dem. precinct chair, 1966-78. Recipient Ann London

Scott Meml. award, Md. NOW, 1989, Pres. Recognition award Md. Soc./ AIA, 1991, Md. Senate Legis. Law Enforcement Friend of Yr. award Fraternal Order of Police, 1991, Child Advocacy award Md. chpt. Am. Acad. Pediat., 1992, Betty Tyler Pub. Affairs award Planned Parenthood Md., 1992. Democrat. Office: 2905 Barker St Silver Spring MD 20910-1004 also: Presdl Wing P W James Senate Office Bldg 110 College Ave Annapolis MD 21401-1676*

SHERBELL, RHODA, artist, sculptor; b. Bklyn.; d. Alexander and Syd (Steinberg) S.; m. Mervin Honig, Apr. 28, 1956; 1 child, Susan. Student, Art Students League, 1950-53, Bklyn. Mus. Art Sch., 1959-61; also; pvt. study art, Italy, France, Eng., 1956. cons., coun. mem. Emily Lowe Gallery, Hofstra U., Hempstead, N.Y., 1978, pres., 1989-81, instr., 1991—, life mem. bd. friends, pres. bd. trustees; tchr. instr. Mus. Modern Art, N.Y.C., 1959, NAD Art Sch., N.Y.C., 1985—, Art Students League, N.Y.C., 1980—. Exhibited one-woman shows Country Art Gallery, Locust Valley, N.Y., Bklyn. Mus. Art Sch., 1961, Adelphi Coll., A.C.A. Galleries, N.Y.C., 1967, Capricorn Galleries, Rehn Gallery, Washington, 1968, Huntington Hartford Mus., N.Y.C., 1969, Morris (N.J.) Mus. Arts and Scis., 1980, Bergen Mus. Arts and Scis., N.J., 1984, William Benton Mus., Conn., 1985, Palace Theatre of the Arts, Stamford, Conn., Bronx Mus. Arts, 1986, Hofstra Mus. Art, L.I., N.Y., 1989, 90, County Art Gallery, N.Y.C., 1990; one-woman retrospective at N.Y. Cultural Ctr., 1970, Nat. Arts Collection, Washington, 1970, Montclair Mus. of Art, 1976, Nat. Art Mus. of Sport, 1977, Jewish Mus. of N.Y.C., 1980, Black History Mus., 1981, Queens Mus., 1981, 82, Nat. Portrait Gallery, Washington, 1981, 82, Bronx Mus., N.Y., Bklyn. Mus., Mus. Modern Art, N.Y.C., Country Art Gallery, 1990, Port Washington Library, Nat. Mus. Am. Art, The Smithsonian Instn., 1982, Nat. Acad. Design, N.Y.C., 1984, 89, Castle Gallery Mus., N.Y.C., 1987, Emily Lowe Mus., N.Y.C., 1987, Heckshire Mus., N.Y.C., 1989, Islip Art Mus., N.Y.C., 1989, Gallery Emanuel, N.Y.C., 1993, Sundance Gallery, Bridgehampton, N.Y.; exhibited group shows Heckscher Mus., 1989, Islip Mus., 1989, Nassau Dept. Recreation and Parks, 1989, Downtown Gallery, N.Y.C., Maynard Walker Gallery, N.Y.C., F.A.R. Gallery, N.Y.C., Provincetown Art Assn., Detroit Inst. Art, Pa. Acad. Fine Arts, Bklyn. and L.I. Artists Show, Old Westbury Gardens Small Sculpture Show, Audubon Artists, NAD, Allied Artists, Heckscher Mus., Nat. Art Mus. Sports, Mus. Arts and Scis., L.A., Am. Mus. Natural History, Post of History Mus., 1987, 88, Caslte Gallery Mus., N.Y.C., 1987, Emiloy Lowe Gallery Mus., N.Y., 1987, Bronx Mus. Arts, 1987, Chgo. Hist. Soc., Mus. of Modern Art, N.Y.C., 1988, Sands Point Mus., L.I., NAD, Hofstra Mus., 1990, Nat. Mus. Sports Art, 1991, Indpls. Art Mus., Phoenix Mus. Art, Corcoran Mus. Art, Washington, IBM, N.Y.C., Fire House Gallery Mus. Nassau Community Coll., L.I., 1992, Nat. Arts Club Ann. Exhbn., 1992, Sports in Art From Am. Mus. at IBM, N.Y.C., 1992, Nat. Sculpture Soc. and The Regina A Quick Ctr. for The Arts Fairfield U.Centennial Anniversary Exbn., 1993, Mus. Modern Art, N.Y.C., Nat. Sculpture Soc. 100 Anniversary Exhbn., 1993, Italy, 1994, Provincetown Assn. and Art Mus., 1993, Kyoto (Japan) Mus. Sculpture Guild, 1993, Nat. Sculpture Soc. Exhbn. in Italy, Lucca, 1994, Sculptures Guild, N.Y.C., 1994-95; represented permanent collections, Stony Brook Hall of Fame, William Benton Mus. Art, Colby Coll. Mus., Oklahoma City Mus., Montclair (N.J.) Mus., Schonberg Library Black Studies, N.Y.C., Albany State Mus., Hofstra U., Bklyn. Mus., Colby Coll. Mus., Nat. Arts Collection, Nat. Portrait Gallery, Smithsonian Instn., Baseball Hall of Fame Cooperstown, N.Y., Nassau Community Coll., Hofstra U. Emily Lowe Gallery, Art Students League, Jewish Mus., Queens Mus., Black History Mus., Nassau County Mus., Stamford Mus. Art and Nature Ctr., Jericho Pub. Library, N.Y., African-Am. Mus., Hempstead, N.Y., 1988, Stamford (Conn.) Mus. Art and Scis., Silvermine Artists North East exhibition, 1989, Nassau Community Coll. Fire House Gallery Exbn., 1992, Nat. Portrait Gallery Smithsonian Instn.; also pvt. collections, TV shows, ABC, 1968, 81; ednl. TV spl. Rhoda Sherbell-Woman in Bronze, 1977; important works include Seated Ballerina, portraits of Aaron Copland (Bruce Stevenson Meml. Best Portrait award Nat. Arts Club 1989), Eleanor Roosevelt, Variations on aeme (36 works of collaged sculpture), 1982-86; appeared several TV shows; guest various radio programs; contbr. articles to newspapers, popular mags. and art jours. Council mem. Nassau County Mus., 1978, trustee, 1st v.p. council; asso. trustee Nat. Art Mus. of Sports, Inc., 1975—; cons., community liaison WNET Channel 13, cultural coordinator, 1975-83; host radio show Not for Artists Only, 1978-79; trustee Women's Boxing Fedn., 1978; mem. The Art Comm of The City of New York, 1993. Recipient Gold medal Allied Artists of Am., 1989, Alfred G. B. Steel Meml. award Pa. Acad. Fine Arts, 1963-64; Helen F. Barnett prize NAD, 1965, Jersey City Mus. prize for sculpture, 1961, 1st prize sculpture Locust Valley Art Show, 1966, 67, Ann. Sculpture prize Jersey City Mus., Bank for Savs. 1st prize in sculpture, 1950, Ford Found. purchase award, 1964, 2 top sculpture awards Mainstreams 77, Cert. of Merit Salmagundi Club, 1978, prize for sculpture, 1980, 81, award for sculpture Knickerbocker Artists, 1980, 81, top prize for sculpture Hudson Valley Art Assn., 1981, Sawyer award NAD, 1985, Gold medal of honor Audubon Artists, 1985, 39th Ann. Silvermine Exhbn. award, Gold medal Allied Artists Am., 1990, Pres' award Nat arts Club N.Y.C.; MacDowell Colony fellow, 1976 Am. Acad. Arts and Letters and Nat. Arts and Letters grantee, 1960, Louis Comfort Tiffany Found. grantee, 1962, Ford Found. grantee, 1964, 67, also award; named one of top 5 finalist World Wide Competition to do Monument of Queen Catherine of England, 1991. Fellow Nat. Sculpture Soc.; mem. Sculpture Guild (dir.), Nat. Assn. Women Artists (Jeffery Childs Willis Meml. prize 1978), Allied Artists Soc. (dir., Gold medal 1990), Audubon Artists (Greta Kempton Walker prize 1965, Chaim Gross award, award for disting. contbr. to orgn. 1979, 80, Louis Weskeem award, dir.), Woman's Caucus for Art, Coll. Art Assn., Am. Inst. Conservation Historic and Artistic Works, N.Y. Soc. Women Artists, Artists Equity Assn. N.Y., Nat. Sculpture Soc. (E.N. Richard Meml. prize 1989), Internat. Platform Assn., Profl. Artists Guild L.I., Painters and Sculptors Soc. N.J. (Bertrum R. Hulmes Meml. award), Am. Watercolor Soc. (award for disting. contbn. to orgn.), Catharine Lorillard Wolfe Club (hon. mention 1968), Nat. Arts Club (N.Y.C., Stevenson Meml. award 1989, Pres. award 1992), NAD Design (Leila Gordon Sawyer prize 1989; The Dessle Green Prize 1993). Home: 64 Jane Ct Westbury NY 11590-1410

SHERBINSKI, LINDA ANNE, nurse anesthetist, nursing educator; b. Rochester, N.Y., Jan. 17, 1956; d. Edward Marion and Helen Marie (Kindzera) S. Student, Genesee Hosp. Sch. Nursing, Rochester, N.Y., 1977; BSN, Alfred U., 1978; grad. in anesthesia, Univ. Health Ctr. Pitts., 1987; MSN, Duquesne U., 1991. RN, Pa. Leader day team CCU The Genesee Hosp., 1978-84, staff nurse operating rm., 1984-85; staff nurse ICU Forbes Met. Hosp., Pitts., 1985-87; staff anesthetist Presbyn. Univ. Hosp., Pitts., 1987-92, preceptor anesthetist, 1991-92; instr. Univ. Health Ctr. Pitts. Sch. Anesthesia, 1987-90, U. Pitts. Grad. Anesthesia Program, 1990-92; staff anesthetist Meml. Med. Ctr., Springfield, Ill., 1992—; item writer Acad. Item Writers AANA, Chgo., 1991—. Contbr. articles to profl. jours., chpt. to book. Med. vol. Pitts. Marathon, 1990, 91. Mem. Am. Assn. Nurse Anesthetists (cert. nurse anesthetist, program dir. internship grant 1990), Nat. League Nursing, Sigma Theta Tau (sec. Delta Sigma chpt. 1978-80, Rsch. scholar Epsilon Phi chpt. 1991). Roman Catholic. Home: 1955 Stonehenge Rd Springfield IL 62702-2052 Office: U Pitts Sch Nursing Victoria St Pittsburgh PA 15261

SHERBY, KATHLEEN REILLY, lawyer; b. St. Louis, Apr. 5, 1947; d. John Victor and Florian Sylvia (Frederick) Reilly; m. James Wilson Sherby, May 17, 1975; children: Michael R.R., William J.R., David J.R. AB magna cum laude, St. Louis U., 1969, JD magna cum laude, 1976. Bar: Mo. 1976. Assoc. Bryan Cave, St. Louis, 1976-85, ptnr., 1985—. Contbr. articles to profl. jours. Bd. dirs. Jr. League, St. Louis, 1989-90, St. Louis Forum, 1992—. Fellow Am. Coll. Trust and Estate Coun., Estate Planning Council of St. Louis (pres. 1986-87), Bar Assn. Met. St. Louis (chmn. probate sect. 1986-87), Mo. bar Assn. (probate coun. 1985-87, 89—, chmn. probate law revision subcom. 1988—). Episcopalian. Home: 47 Crestwood Dr Saint Louis MO 63105-3032 Office: Bryan Cave 1 Metropolitan Sq Ste 3600 Saint Louis MO 63102-2750

SHERFEY, GERALDINE RICHARDS, educational administrator; b. Pontiac, Mich., Dec. 11, 1929; d. William and Ethel (Spurr) Richards; m. William E. Sherfey, Aug. 4, 1950 (div.); children: Emily J., Laura A., Susan E., William E. B.S., Ind. State U., 1963, M.S., 1965; Ed.S., U. Ga., 1973, Ed.D., 1978. Biology and gen. sci. instr. Hammond (Ind.) Tech.-Vocat. High Sch., 1963-65; advanced biology instr. Griffith (Ind.) Sr. High Sch., 1965-70, dept. chmn. grades K-12, acting sci. cons., 1968-70; mgr. sch. programs (asst. supt. for curriculum and instrn.) Greenville (S.C.) Pub. Schs., 1972-73; instr. edn. Purdue U., Calumet Campus, Hammond, Ind., 1973-75; guest lectr. Purdue U. Calumet Campus and Ind. U. N.W., Gary, 1975-78; sci. instr. grades 7 and 8, Spohn Middle Sch., Hammond, 1975-78, prin. A.L. Spohn Elem./Middle Sch., 1978-80, adminstrv. asst. for curriculum and instruction Hammond Schs., 1980-82, coord. vocat. program devel. and extended programs 1982-85, dir. curriculum/ops. area career ctr., 1985—; dir. curriculum and plan mgmt., 1985-87; pres. Sherfey-Chirinos Corp., 1986—; biology instr. Gavit MS/HS, 1987-89; coord./mentor Program Reaching Indiviual Middle Sch. Student. Co-editor Ind. State newsletter for adult and continuing edn., 1985; contbr. articles to profl. jours. Ind. State U. teaching fellow, 1964-65; U. Ga. grad. asst., 1970-72. Mem. World Coun. for Curriculum and Instruction, Assn. for Supervision and Curriculum Devel., Nat. Sci. Tchrs. Assn., Nat. Middle Schs. Assn., Ind. Middle Schs. Assn., Ind. Assn. Adult and Continuing Edn. (recipient Outstanding Contbn. award 1986. Democrat. Roman Catholic. Home: 540 W 56th Ave Gary IN 46410-2029 Office: 5727 Sohl Ave Hammond IN 46320-2356

SHERIDAN, DEBRA JEAN, video producer and director, videographer; b. Meridian, Miss., Nov. 4, 1962; d. Joseph Dale Sheridan and Della Mae (Holmes) Davis; m. Philip C. Brinkman, July 15, 1986; 1 child, Stephen Forrest Brinkman. BS, U. Fla., 1984. Asst. prodr., designer Multivision Prodns., Miami, Fla., 1985-86; broadcast coord. Fla. Internat. U., Miami, 1985—. Mem. Assn. Ednl. Comm. Tech., Internat. TV Assn. (editor, sec. pres. 1986—, Appreciation award 1989). Office: Fla Internat Univ University Park AT136 Miami FL 33199

SHERIFF, LINDA LEPPER, real estate property manager; b. Cin., May 31, 1954; d. Milton Webster and Marie Hinz (Becker) Lepper; m. Richard William Briggs, June 30, 1981 (div. Mar. 1983); m. Warren Calvin Sheriff, July 10, 1987 (div. 1990). BA in History, Stephens Coll., 1977. Cert. apartment mgr. Property supr. Chelsea Moore Corp., Cin., 1980-85; regional property mgr. The Mayerson Co., Cin., 1987-94; property mgr. Molique Mgmt. Corp., Ft. Wright, Ky., 1994—. Mem. Young Reps., Columbia, Mo., 1975-76; bd. dirs. Apt. Assn. No. Ky., 1991—. Mem. No. Ky. Apt. Assn. (v.p. 1989, gov. 1989—, bd. dirs. 1991), Greater Cin. Apt. Assn. (bd. dirs. 1989—, Cert. Apt. Mgr. of Yr. award 1989), Apt. Assn. No. Ky. (bd. dirs. 1991). Presbyterian. Home: 6810 Vantage Ct Florence KY 41042 Office: Molique Mgmt Corp 1530 Amsterdam Rd Fort Wright KY 41001

SHERLOCK, PHYLLIS KRAFFT, psychologist; b. Chgo., Dec. 22, 1936; d. Lee M. and Beatrice Elliott (Hasenstab) Krafft; m. Hugh Paul Sherlock, June 4, 1960 (dec. Oct. 1991); children: William, John, James. BA in Philosophy and Religious Studies, U. N.C., 1958; postgrad., Boston U., 1959-60; PhD in Clin. Psychology, Pacific Grad. Sch. Psychology, 1980. Lic. psychologist, marriage, family and child counselor. Social work trainee ARC, Chgo., 1959-60; child welfare worker Santa Clara County Social Svcs., San Jose, Calif., 1961-62; counselor Diabesis, San Francisco, 1973-75; counselor chaplaincy svc. Stanford (Calif.) U. Med. Ctr., 1977-79; intern North County Community Mental Health Clinic, Palo Alto, Calif., 1977-78; postdoctoral intern counseling and psychol. svcs. Cowell Health Svcs., Stanford U., 1980-81; clin. faculty Pacific Grad. Sch. Psychology, 1989—; pvt. practice, 1979—; core founding mem. Pacific Grad. Sch. Psychology, Palo Alto, 1975-76; group facilitator Grad. Sch. Bus., Stanford U., 1980-82; supr. psychol. assts., 1988-91; adj. clin. faculty Sch. Edn., U. San Francisco, 1990—. Vol. Agnew State Hosp., 1971. Mem. APA, Calif. Psychol. Assn., Assn. Psychol. Type, Santa Clara County Assn. Focusing Inst. Democrat. Office: 1275 Dana Ave Palo Alto CA 94301

SHERMAN, ARLENE, television producer; b. Washington, Sept. 12, 1947; d. Burton H. and Ann M. (Butt) S. BFA, NYU, 1970. Free lance film editor U.S., France, Eng., 1970-78; prodn. coordinator Children's TV Workshop, N.Y.C., 1978-81, assoc. producer, 1981-85, producer, 1985—; exec. producer PBS primetime spl. Sesame St. Jam, 1994; assoc. dir. TV programs, 1985—. Producer TV series Sesame St., 1988 (Emmy award); dir. film The Machine, 1970 (Cannes Film Festival award 1970). Recipient Emmy for Producing Sesame St., 1990, 91, 92, 94; nominee Emmy for Sesame St. Jam. Mem. Am. Film Inst., Nat. Acad. TV Arts and Scis., Dirs. Guild Am. Office: Children's TV Workshop 1 Lincoln Plz New York NY 10023-7170

SHERMAN, BEATRICE ETTINGER, business executive; b. N.Y.C., May 29, 1919; d. Max and Stella (Schrager) Ettinger; m. Herbert Jacob Howard, Feb. 15, 1942 (dec. 1971); children: Robert David Howard, Carolyn Howard Smith; m. Ernest John Sherman, Dec. 29, 1974. Student, Gulf Park Jr. Coll., Gulfport, Miss., 1934-35, Shimer Jr. Coll., Mt. Carroll, Ill., 1936-38; BA, U. Miami, Fla., 1940; postgrad. Harvard U., 1940, Paris-Am. Acad., Paris, 1972, Alliance Française, Paris, 1973. Corp. sec., dir. Save Electric Corp., Toledo, 1940-67, Verd-A-Ray Corp., Toledo, 1944-67, Penetray Corp., Toledo, 1962-67; ptnr. Stella Assocs., Newark, 1960-80, BHS Ptrns., Miami, 1983—; pres. Besman Inc., Coral Gables, Fla., 1975—, All Am. Mobile Tel. Co., Coral Gables, 1986—, Besman Hospitality, Coral Gables, 1993—, Archer House, Gainesville, Fla., 1994. Vol. worker Jewish Welfare Fedn., Toledo, 1942-69; nat. speaker United Jewish Appeal; mem. womens div. Greater Miami Jewish Fedn., 1969—, trustee, 1986; active Miami advertiser adv. bd. Bell South Advt. and Pub. Co. Recipient Lion of Judah award Greater Miami Jewish Fedn., 1986. Mem. Assn. Telemessaging Svcs. Internat., Pioneers of Miami Beach, Biltmore Club (Coral Gables, Fla.). Home: 5108 SW 72d Ave Miami FL 33155 Office: Besman Inc 2355 Salzedo St Ste 308 Coral Gables FL 33134

SHERMAN, DAWN DENISE, mental health services professional; b. West Point, N.Y., May 16, 1964; d. Robert James and Diane Elaine (Haylock) S.; m. Carl Frederick Schultz, Nov. 13, 1982 (div. 1992); 1 child, DeAndra Elaine Schultz. Resident counselor Assn. for Help of Retarded Children, Middletown, N.Y., 1984-85; therapy aide Middletown Psychiatric Ctr., Middletown, N.Y., 1986-92; residential counselor Occupations, Inc., Middletown, N.Y., 1992-94, sr. counselor, 1994, site supr., 1994—. Democrat. Methodist. Office: Occupations Inc Brola Rd RD 5 Box 371 Middletown NY 10940

SHERMAN, ELAINE C., gourmet foods company executive, educator; b. Chgo., Aug. 1, 1938; d. Arthur E. and Sylvia (Miller) Friedman; m. Arthur J. Spiegel, Jan. 1989; children: Steven J., David P., Jaime A. Student, Northwestern U., 1956-58; diploma in cake decorating, Wilton Sch. Profl. Cake Decorating, 1973; diploma, Dumas Pere, L'école de la Cuisine Française. Tchr. cooking and adult edn. Maine, Oakton, Niles Adult and Continuing Edn. Program, Park Ridge, Ill., 1972-82; corp. officer The Complete Cook, Glenview, Ill., 1976-82, Madame Chocolate, Glenview, 1983-87; food columnist Chgo. Sun Times, 1985-87; dir. mktg. Sue Ling Gin, Chgo., 1987-88; co-owner Critical Eye, Chgo., 1988—; v.p., dir. merchandising, gen. mgr. Foodstuffs, Inc., Evanston, Ill., 1990-91, food cons. mgmt. and mktg., 1991—. Author: Madame Chocolate's Book of Divine Indulgences, 1984 (nominated Tastemaker award 1984). Bd. dirs. Chgo. Fund on Aging and Disability, 1989—; co-chmn. Meals on Wheels, 1989-90, 91. Mem. Les Dames D'Escoffier (founding pres.), Women's Foodservice Network (pres.), Confrerie de la Chaine Des Rotisseurs (vice conselliere gastronomique), Am. Inst. Wine and Food (bd. dirs.). Home and Office: 1728 Wildberry Dr # D Glenview IL 60025-1748

SHERMAN, JUDITH ZEHMAN, child advocate; b. Cleve., Sept. 9, 1931; d. Sidney and Irene (Ratner) Zehman; m. Harlan Edwin Sherman, Aug. 31, 1952; children: Charles Evan, Charna Eve, Scott Allen. BA in Econs., Case Western Res. U., 1953, MS in Edn., 1968. Spl. edn. tchr. Beachwood (Ohio) Bd. Edn., 1967-68; founder, dir. Suburban East Sch. for the Retarded, Cleve., 1969-75; planning assoc. Fedn. of Cmty. Planning, Cleve., 1977-84. Commr. Ohio Commn. for Children, Columbus, 1978-81; chmn. Ohio White House Conf. on Children, Columbus, 1980-81; bd. dirs. Cuyahoga County Bd. of Mental Retardation, Cleve., 1975-78; pres., founder Parent Vol. Assn.-Women's Aux., Cleve., 1970-73; mem. vis. com. Sch. Applied Social Scis., Case Western Res. U., Cleve., 1978-80; pres. Bellefaire/Jewish Children's Bur., Cleve., 1981-85; chmn. capital campaign, 1986-91; bd. dirs. Jewish Cmty. Fedn., 1980—, Fairmount Temple, v.p., 1978—. Mem. Child Welfare League of Am. (trustee 1986—, v.p. 1992—, Child Advocate of Yr. 1985). Home: 26720 Hendon Rd Beachwood OH 44122

SHERMAN, MARY ANGUS, public library administrator; b. Lawton, Okla., Jan. 3, 1937; d. Donald Adelbert and Mabel (Felkner) Angus; m. Donald Neil Sherman, Feb. 8, 1958; children: Elizabeth Sherman Cunningham, Donald Neil II. BS in Home Econs., U. Okla., 1958, MLS, 1969. Br. head Pioneer Libr. System, Purcell, Okla., 1966-76; regional libr. Pioneer Libr. System, Norman, Okla., 1976-78, asst. dir., 1978-80, dir., 1987—. Named one of Distinguished Alumni Sch. Home Econs., U. Okla., 1980. Mem. ALA (councilor 1988—, planning and budget assembly 1990-91, internat. rels. com. 1992—), AAUW (pres. Okla. chpt. 1975-77, nat. bd. dirs. 1983-87, S.W. cen. region dir. 1983-85, v.p. nat. membership 1985-87, Woman of the Yr. Purcell chpt. 1982), Okla. Library Assn. (pres. 1982-83, interlibrary cooperation com. 1993—, chair 1994-95, Disting. Service award 1986), Norman C. of C. (bd. dirs. 1988—, pres. 1994-95), Altrusa Internat., Rotary (program chair 1991-92, bd. dirs. 1993—, pres. 1995—, Paul Harris fellow), Norman Assistance League Club (community assoc.), Norman, Okla. Sisters City Com., 1994—, Delta Gamma Mothers (pres. 1978-79), Kappa Alpha Theta (pres. Alpha Omicron House Corp. 1984-87, nat. dir. house corps. 1987-88), Beta Phi Mu, Phi Beta Kappa. Democrat. Methodist. Office: Pioneer Libr System 225 N Webster Ave Norman OK 73069-7133

SHERMAN, MONA DIANE, school system administrator; b. N.Y.C., Aug. 28, 1941; d. Hyman and Lillian (Baker) Ginsberg; m. Richard H. Sherman, May 9, 1964; children: Holly Baker, Andrew Hunter. BS, Hunter Coll., CUNY, 1962; MS, CUNY, 1965. Cert. elem. tchr., K-12 reading endorsement specialist, ESL tchr., elem. adminstrn. and supervision, instrnl. supervision, spl. edn. learning disabilities and neurologically impaired edn., Ind. Elem. tchr. N.Y.C. Pub. Schs., 1962-77; team leader Tchr. Corps Potsdam (N.Y.) State Coll., SUNY, 1977-79; dir. Tchr. Ctr., Sch. City of Hammond, Ind., 1979-87; lab. coord. PALS, Gary (Ind.) Sch. Corp., 1987-93, mentor, 1988—, facilitator of staff devel., 1993—; instr. Tex. Instrument Computer Co., Lubbock, 1983-84, Performance Learning System, Emerson, N.J., 1984—; cons. in classroom discipline and computer instrn. Gary Staff Devel. Ctr., 1987—; mentor Urban Tchr. Edn. program Ind. U. N.W., Gary, 1991—; chair sch. improvement team, tchr. of yr. com., 1993-94; mem. Gary Tech. Com., Gary Distance Learning Com. Mem. Lake Area United Way Lit. Coalition NW Ind., 1990, Gary Reading Textbook Adoption Com.; sec. Martin Luther King Jr. Acad. PTSA, mem. sch. improvement team. Recipient Recognition NW Ind. Forum, 1988, Tchr. of Yr. award Merrillville (Ind.) Lions Club, 1988, Outstanding Tchr. of Yr. award Inland Ryerson, East Chicago, Ind., 1989. Mem. Ind. Reading Assn., Gary Reading Assn., Phi Delta Kappa, Delta Kappa Gamma. Home: 1112 Fran Lin Pky Munster IN 46321-3607

SHERMAN, RUTH TENZER, artist, fixtures company executive; b. Chgo., Sept. 11, 1920; d. Philip and Jennie (Greitzer) Tenzer; m. Samuel Sherman, May 18, 1946 (dec. Nov. 1974); children: Patricia (dec.), Randy Mitchell. Art student, Pratt Inst., 1938-42, Art Students League, N.Y.C., 1942-45; studies with Raphael Soyer, N.Y.C., 1943, studies with Harold Baumbach, 1947-49; studies with Ruth Connery, Mamaroneck, N.Y., 1955; studies with Rudolph Baranik, White Plains, N.Y., 1961-63, studies with George Koras, 1966. Cert. artist Dept. Cultural Affairs. Pres. Pioneer Fixture Corp., Paterson, N.J., 1975-86. Exhbns. include Mamaroneck Artists Guild, 1963, Jr. League Artists of North Westchester, 1964, Westchester C.C., Valhalla, N.Y., 1964, The New Rochelle (N.Y.) Art Assn., 1964, Silvermine Guild Artists, New Canaan, Conn., 1964-88, Westchester Art Soc., White Plains, 1964-72, Hudson River Mus., Yonkers, N.Y., 1965, First Westchester Nat. Bank, New Rochelle, 1967, Conn. Acad. Fine Arts, Hartford, 1967, Stern Bros., N.Y.C., 1967, Nat. Jewish Hosp. Denver, Woodmere, N.Y., 1968, Quaker Ridge Sch., Scarsdale, N.Y., 1970, Gallery Shop, Westport, Conn., 1976, Mari Gallery, Woodstock, N.Y., 1978, The Village Gallery, Ardsley, N.Y., 1979, Todd Gallery, Kiamesha Lake, N.Y., 1980, Norwalk Mchts. Bank, New Canaan, 1980, Mchts. Bank, Norwalk, 1980, Emery Air Freight Hdqs., Conn., 1981, Mari Hube Gallery, N.Y., 1990, Helio Gallery, N.Y.C., 1991, Maska Gallery, Seattle, 1991, Rockefeller Town House, N.Y.C., 1992, Denise Bibro Fine Art Gallery, Soho, N.Y., 1993, Musée D'Art Moderne, Tonniens, France, 1993, Salon du Vieux Colombier, Paris, 1993, Md. Fedn. Art, Cardinal Gallery Md. Hall, Annapolis, 1993, Mus. Modern Art, Coral Gables, Fla., 1994, Wirtz Gallery, South Miami, Fla., 1994. Recipient Merit award Westchester Art Soc., 1964, Cert. of Honor, Museé d'Art Moderne, 1994, Gold Record of Achievement ABI, 1994, Disting. visitor award Mayor of Miami, Fla., 1994. Home: 58 Village Dr Stroudsburg PA 18360-1566

SHERMAN, SIGNE LIDFELDT, former research chemist, securities analyst; b. Rochester, N.Y., Nov. 11, 1913; d. Carl Leonard Broström and Herta Elvira Maria (Thern) Lidfeldt; m. Joseph V. Sherman, Nov. 18, 1944 (dec. Oct. 1984). BA, U. Rochester, 1935, MS, 1937. Chief chemist Lab. Indsl. Medicine and Toxicology Eastman Kodak Co., Rochester, 1937-43; chief rsch. chemist Chesebrough-Pond's Inc., Clinton, Conn., 1943-44; ptnr. Joseph V. Sherman Cons., N.Y.C., 1944-84; investment strategist Signe L. Sherman Cons., Troy, Mont., 1984—. Author: The New Fibers, 1946. Fellow Am. Inst. Chemists; mem. AAAS, AAUW (life), Am. Chem. Soc., Am. Econ. Assn., Am. Assn. Ind. Investors (life), Fedn. Am. Scientists (life), Union Concerned Scientists (life), Western Econ. Assn. Internat., Earthquake Engring. Rsch. Inst., Nat. Ctr. for Earthquake Engring. Rsch., N.Y. Acad. Scis. (life), Internat. Platform Assn., Cabinet View Country Club. Office: Signe L Sherman Cons Angel Island 648 Halo Dr Troy MT 59935-9415

SHERMAN, SUSAN ROTH, social welfare educator; b. N.Y.C., Oct. 5, 1939; d. Lester and Louise (Klein) Roth; m. Malcolm J. Sherman, Sept. 8, 1963; children: Barbara, Michael. AB, U. Chgo., 1960; PhD, U. Calif., Berkeley, 1964. Asst. prof. Sch. Pub. Health UCLA, 1965-68; assoc. and sr. rsch. scientist N.Y. State Dept. Mental Hygiene, Albany, 1969-75; from lectr. to prof. Sch. Social Welfare U. Albany, 1974; mem. rsch. rev. com. N.Y. State Health Planning Commn., Albany, 1982-87; mem. adv. bd. Health Systems Agy., Albany, 1979-82; cons. N.Y. State Office for Aging, Albany, 1973-74, 79-80, 87; vis. scholar Columbia U., 1986. Co-author: Foster Families for Adults, 1988, Environment for Aging, 1988; contbr. articles to profl. jours. Bd. dirs. Sr. Svc. Ctr., Albany, 1980-86, B'nai B'rith Parkview Sr. Apts., Albany, 1988-95; mem., bd. dirs., com. aging United Jewish Fedn., Albany, 1992. Grantee SUNY, N.Y. State Health Rsch. Coun., NIMH, AOA, 1975-88. Fellow Gerontol. Soc. Am. (mem.-at-large of sect. exec. com. 1980-82); mem. Assn. for Gerontology in Higher Edn. (pres. 1989-90, treas. 1981-83, chair nominations com., long-range planning com., pers. com., program evaluation com. 1979-91), State Soc. on Aging (pres. 1979-80, Beattie award 1990). Office: U Albany Sch Social Welfare 135 Western Ave # 211 Albany NY 12203-1011

SHERN, STEPHANIE MARIE, accountant; b. Taylor, Pa., Jan. 7, 1948; d. Joseph and Stephanie (Malodovitch) Andrews; m. George Emil Shern, Sept. 25, 1971. AA, Keystone Jr. Coll., 1967; BS, Pa. State U., 1969. CPA, N.Y. Staff accountant to ptnr., nat. dir. consumer products industry svcs. Ernst & Young , N.Y.C., 1969—; dir. Met. Retail Fin. Execs., N.Y.C. Contbr. articles to profl. jours. Named Keystonian of Yr., Keystone Jr. Coll., 1984. Mem. N.Y. State Soc. CPAs (bd. dirs. 1985—), Am. Inst. CPAs, Women's Econ. Round Table, Beta Alpha Psi (mem. adv. forum 1984—). Republican. Ukrainian Orthodox. Club: Panther Valley Golf (Allamuchy, N.J.). Home: 113 Prospect St Little Falls NJ 07424-1541 Office: Ernst & Young 787 7th Ave New York NY 10019-6018

SHERR, LYNN BETH, TV news correspondent; b. Phila., Mar. 4, 1942; d. Louis and Shirley (Rosenfeld) S.; m. Lawrence B. Hilford, Jan. 11, 1980. B.A., Wellesley Coll., 1963. Writer, editor Conde Nast Publications, N.Y.C., 1963-65; writer, reporter AP, N.Y.C., 1965-72; corre. Sta. WCBS-TV News, N.Y.C., 1972-74; anchor, corre. Pub. Broadcasting System, N.Y.C., 1975-77; nat. corre. ABC News, N.Y.C., 1977—. Author: (with Jurate Kazickas) The Liberated Woman's Appointment Calendar, 1971-82, The American Woman's Gazetteer, 1976, Susan B. Anthony Slept Here, 1994, Failure is Impossible: Susan B. Anthony in Her Own Words, 1995. Recipient Ohio State award Ohio State U., 1976; recipient spl. commendation Am. Women in Radio & TV, 1979, Emmy for Post Election Spl., 1980, numerous others. Office: 20/20 147 Columbus Ave Fl 10 New York NY 10023-5900

SHERR, VIRGINIA TRUITT, psychiatrist; b. Washington, Mar. 19, 1931; d. Reginald Van Trump and Mary Harrington Truitt; m. Paul C. Sherr, Apr.

28, 1957; children: Donald, Paul B., Suzanne, Gregory. BS, U. Md., 1952; MD, U. Md., Balt., 1956. Diplomate Am. Bd. Psychiatry and Neurology. Intern Allentown Gen. Hosp.; adminstrv. officer Norristown (Pa.) State Hosp.; pvt. practice, 1976—; mem. Montgomery County Task Force Aged; speaker in field. Contbr. articles to profl. jours. Mem. med. bd. George Sch.; bd. dirs. Sr. Adult Activity Ctr. Montgomery County. Recipient Ann. Clin. Rsch. award Montgomery County Med. Soc., 1975. Fellow APA (life); mem. Physicians Social Responsibility, Internat. Physicians Prevention Nuclear War. Office: 47 Crescent Dr Holland PA 18966

SHERREN, ANNE TERRY, chemistry educator; b. Atlanta, July 1, 1936; d. Edward Allison and Annie Ayres (Lewis) Terry; m. William Samuel Sherren, Aug. 13, 1966. BA, Agnes Scott Coll., 1957; PhD, U. Fla.-Gainesville, 1961. Grad. teaching asst. U. Fla., Gainesville, 1957-61; instr. Tex. Woman's U., Denton, 1961-63, asst. prof., 1963-66; rsch. participant Argonne Nat. Lab., 1973-80, 93, 94; assoc. prof. chemistry N. Cen. Coll., Naperville, Ill., 1966-76, prof., 1976—. Clk. of session Knox Presbyn. Ch., 1976-94, ruling elder, 1971—. Mem. AAAS, AAUP, Am. Chem. Soc., Am. Inst. Chemists, Ill. Acad. Sci., Sigma Xi, Delta Kappa Gamma, Iota Sigma Pi (nat. pres. 1978-81, nat. dir. 1972-78, nat. historian 1989—). Presbyterian. Contbr. articles in field to profl. jours. Office: North Ctrl Coll Dept Chemistry Naperville IL 60566

SHERROD, SUSAN, banker; b. N.Y.C., Apr. 29, 1941; d. Nomer and Emelia (Freberg) Gray; m. John Hudson Sherrod, June 17, 1961 (div. 1977); children: Amy Elizabeth, William Gray. BS in Chemistry, U. Pa., 1963; MBA, U. Pitts., 1977, postgrad., 1980—. Comml. lending officer Equibank, Pitts., 1977-82, PNC Bank, N.A., 1982-86; v.p., mgr. cash mgmt. mktg. Pitts. Nat. Bank, 1986-89; mgr. credit quality adminstrn., 1989—. Bd. dirs. Pitts. Dance Coun., 1982—, Housing Opportunities, Inc., Pitts., 1982—, Katz Sch. Bus., U. Pitts., 1985—, Pitts. YWCA, 1986-89; trustee Sewickley Acad., Pitts., 1971-80. Republican. Episcopalian. Home: 25 Briar Cliff Rd Pittsburgh PA 15202-1305 Office: Pitts Nat Bank PNC Bank NA Pittsburgh PA 15265

SHERWIN, JULIE KAY, systems analyst; b. Tigerton, Wis., Nov. 28, 1958; d. Gerald Vilas and Kay Valeska (Peterson) Krueger; m. David Forrest Sherwin, May 7, 1983 (div. Apr. 1992); children: Kimberly Kay, Kristine Marie, Katelynn Ann. BS in Computer Sci., U. Wis., 1982. Cons. Advanced Info. Mgmt., Menasha, Wis., 1982-83; programmer Winnebago County, Oshkosh, Wis., 1983-85; application systems specialist Aid Assn. Luths., Appleton, Wis., 1985-90, application systems analyst, 1990—; devel. analyst Am. Family Ins., Madison, Wis., 1990. Active PTA, Appleton, 1992—; tchr. Sunday Sch. Faith Luth. Ch., Appleton, 1993—. Home: 418 Weiland Ave Appleton WI 54911

SHERWOOD, LILLIAN ANNA, librarian, retired; b. South Bend, Ind., Dec. 22, 1928; d. Julius Andrew and Mary (Kerekes) Takacs; m. Neil Walter Sherwood, May 31, 1953; children: Susan Kay Huff, Nancy Ellen Coney, James Walter. AB in Home Econs., Ind. U., 1951, postgrad., 1978-83. Cert. libr. IV, Ind., 1984. Lab. tech. Lobund Inst., Notre Dame (Ind.) U., 1951-53; substitute tchr. Plymouth (Ind.) Community Schs., 1969-73; bookkeeper, processing clk. Plymouth (Ind.) Pub. Libr., 1973-76, audio-visual coord., 1976-79, reference and genealogical libr., 1980-93; retired, 1994; project dir. Ind. Heritage rsch. grant, Ind. Humanities Coun. and Ind. Hist. Soc., 1992-93; orgn. and verification com. Geneal. Socs., Pioneer Soc., Marshall County, Ind., Plymouth, 1988—. Mem. bd. dirs. Child Day Care Ctr. of Plymouth, 1971-75, pres., 1974. Mem. AAUW (v.p. 1966-68, pres. 1971-73, 85-87, 91-93), Marshall County Geneal. Soc. (v.p. 1986-87), Omicron Nu. Methodist. Home: 808 Thayer St Plymouth IN 46563-2859

SHERWOOD, PATRICIA WARING, artist, educator; b. Columbia, S.C., Dec. 19, 1933; d. Clark du Val and Florence (Yarbrough) Waring; divorced; children: Cheryl Sherwood Kraft, Jana Sherwood Kern, Marikay Sherwood Taitt. BFA magna cum laude, Calif. State U., Hayward, 1970; MFA, Mills Coll., Oakland, Calif., 1974; postgrad., San Jose State U., 1980-86. Cert. tchr., Calif. Tchr. De Anza Jr. Coll., Cupertino, Calif., 1970-78, Foothill Jr. Coll., Los Altos, Calif., 1972-78, West Valley Jr. Coll., Saratoga, Calif., 1978—; artist-in-residence Centrum Frans Masereel, Kasterlee, Belgium, 1989. One-woman shows include Triton Mus., Santa Clara, Calif., 1968, RayChem Corp., Sunnyville, Calif., 1969, Palo Alto (Calif.) Cultural Ctr., 1977, Los Gatos (Calif.) Mus., 1992, Stanford U. faculty club, Palo Alto, 1993; exhibited in group shows at Tressider Union Stanford U., 1969, Oakland (Calif.) Mus. Kaiser Ctr., 1969, Sonoma (Calif.) State Coll., 1969, Bank Am., San Francisco, 1969, San Francisco Art Festival, 1969, 70, U. Santa Clara, 1967, Charles and Emma Frye Mus., Seattle, 1968, Eufrat Gallery DeAnza Coll., Cupertino, 1975, San Jose (Calif.) Mus. Art, 1976, Lytton Ctr., Palo Alto, 1968 (1st award), Zellerbach Ctr., San Francisco, 1970, Works Gallery, San Jose, 1994; represented in permanent collections Mills Coll., Bank Am., San Francisco. Art judge studnet show Stanford U., Palo Alto, 1977; mem. d.p. Fong Gallery, San Jose, Calif., 1994. Nat. Endowment for Arts/We. States Art Fedn. fellow, 1994. Mem. Calif. Print Soc., Womens Caucus for Arts. Home: 1500 Arriba Ct Los Altos CA 94024 Office: West Valley Jr Coll 14000 Fruitvale Ave Saratoga CA 95070-5698

SHEY, JANE ELIZABETH, trade specialist; b. Algona, Iowa, Dec. 2, 1956; d. Daniel Jeremiah and Jean Lois (Balgeman) S. BA, Briar Cliff Coll., 1979. Caseworker Congressman Berkley Bedell, Sioux City, 1979-81; pastoral minister St. Cecelia's Ch., Algona, 1981-84; chaplain Washington Hosp. Ctr., 1984-86; congl. candidate 6th Congl. Dist. of Iowa, Algona, 1986; legis. asst. congressman Berkley Bedell, Washington, 1986; legis. asst. congressman Tim Penny, Washington, 1986-88, 92, staff dir. subcom. fgn. agriculture and hunger, 1993-94; dir. govt. affairs Corn Refiners Assn., Washington, 1988-92; agriculture policy and trade specialist Hessian, McKasy and Soderberg, Washington, 1994—. Mem. Women in Govt. Rels. (co-chair agrl. task force Washington chpt. 1988-89, 90-91), Women in Internat. Trade. Democrat. Roman Catholic. Office: Hessian McKay and Soderberg 403 1st St SE Washington DC 20003

SHIAW, EMMA, corporate executive; b. Taiwan, Republic of China, July 27, 1954; came to U.S., 1976; BA, Chinese Culture Coll., 1976; MA, SUNY, Binghamton, 1980. Realtor assoc. Lewis and Silverman Realtors, Bethesda, Md., 1979-81, Merrill Lynch Realtors, Bethesda, Md., 1981-82, Long and Foster Realtors, Potomac, Md., 1983-85; exec. v.p. DIGICON Corp., Bethesda, 1985—. Mem. NAt. Assn. Minority Bus., U.S. Pan Asian Am. C. of C., Nat Contract Mgmt. Assn., Armed Forces Communication and Electronics Assocs. Office: DIGICON Corp 6903 Rockledge Dr Ste 600 Bethesda MD 20817-1129

SHIBLEY, GAIL ROSE, state legislator; b. North Bend, Oreg., Apr. 7, 1958; d. Lyle Donald and Rosemarie Elizabeth (Duban) S.; life ptnr. Kelly Sue Rogers. BA, U. Oreg., 1980. Congrl. aide U.S. rep. Jim Weaver U.S. Ho. Reps., Washington and Eugene, Wash., 1980-86; acct. exec. Ryan, Hutchins, Southwick, Portland, 1987-90; program mgr. City of Portland, Oreg., 1990—; mem. Oreg. Ho. Reps., Portland, 1991—; mem. Multi County Community Action Com., Portland, 1992—, Gov.'s Coun. DUII, Portland, 1992—, Breast and Cervical Cancer Coalition, Portland, 1992—. Dem. precinct leader, Multnomah County, Oreg., 1991—; fundraiser, mem. Right ot Privacy, Oreg., 1985—; mem. Gay and Lesbian Victory Fund, 1992—; trustee No On 13 Com., Oreg., 1994—; bd. dirs. Neighborhood Partnership Fund, Portland, 1994. Recipient Legis. Excellence award Multnomah County Community Action Agy., 1991, Nan Wood Honeyman award Oreg. Women's Polit. Caucus, 1991, Torch award Human Rights Campaign Fund, 1992; named to Legis. Honor Roll Oreg. Environ. Coun., 1991. Fellow Am. Leadership Forum, 1994-95, Oreg. Women's Polit. Caucus, Oreg. Hist. Soc., City Club Portland. Democrat. Home: PO Box 6805 Portland OR 97228 Office: Oreg Ho of Reps H-395 State Capitol Salem OR 97310

SHIELDS, BROOKE CHRISTA CAMILLE, actress, model; b. N.Y.C., May 31, 1965; d. Francis A. and Teri (Schmon) S. BA, Princeton U., 1987. Model for Ivory Soap commls. starting in 1966, later for Calvin Klein jeans and Colgate toothpaste commls.; actress: (films) Alice, Sweet Alice, 1975, Pretty Baby, 1977, King of the Gypsies, 1978, Wanda Nevada, 1978, Just You and Me Kid, 1978, Blue Lagoon, 1979, Endless Love, 1980, Sahara, 1983, Backstreet Strays, 1989, Brenda Starr, 1992, Seventh Floor, 1993, Running Wild, 1993, Freaked, 1993; (TV movies) The Prince of Central Park, 1977, After the Fall, Wet Gold, I Can Make You Love Me: The Stalking of Laura Black, 1993, (TV shows) The Tonight Show, Bob Hope spls., The Diamond Trap, 1988; appeared on Broadway in Grease, 1994-95. Office: Christa Inc PO Box 6 Dumont NJ 07628 also: Christa Inc Ste 630 2300 West Sahara Box 18 Las Vegas NV 89102*

SHIELDS, CYNTHIA ROSE, college administrator; b. Monterey, Calif., June 1, 1954; d. William Lawrence and Rose Virdell (Turner) Jackson; m. Franklin Shields, Sept. 19, 1981; 1 child, Brett. AA, San Francisco City Coll., 1980; BS, U. San Francisco, 1986; MPA, Golden Gate U., 1988; MS, Nat. U., 1994; doctoral student, Calif. State U., Fresno, 1994—. Cert. community coll. instr., supr., Calif. Acct. exec. KFSN-TV, Fresno, Calif., 1982-85; instr. Merced County (Calif.) Schs., 1985-89; gen. mgr., owner Ad Line Advt., Merced, 1986—; instr. Merced Coll., 1989-90; youth outreach specialist N000, 1990-91, re-entry coord., 1991—; sr. assoc. Sch. Leadership Ctr., Calif. Sch. Leadership Acad., 1989-92. Author curriculum materials. Bd. dirs. Merced Comty. Med. Ctr. Found., 1991, MUHSD Found., 1992—, Merced City Sch. Dist. Citizens Adv. Bd., 1985-87; chmn. Merced Conv. and Visitors Bur., 1991; coord. Merced County Comty. Housing Resource Bd., 1988-90. Mem. AAUW, Merced City C. of C. (bd. dirs. 1991-93, v.p. fin. and ops. 1993-94), Phi Delta Kappa. Democrat. Office: Ad Line Advt PO Box 3346 Merced CA 95344-1346

SHIELDS, LAURA AULL, public relations counselor; b. Taylorville, Ill., Oct. 24; d. Frank and Gladys (Montgomery) Aull; m. Roger V. Shields, Nov. 20, 1940 (div.); children: Deborah, Beth, Roger, Clark, Constance. Owner Shields Communications, Santa Monica, Calif., 1974—; speaker in field. Mem. Santa Monica Bay Area C. of C. Office: 2627 26th St # D Santa Monica CA 90405-2821

SHIELDS, MARGARET AGNES, association executive; b. Bloomsburg, Pa., Apr. 21, 1946; s. Robert James Alexander and Isabel Corley (Davey) S.; m. William F. Dengler Jr., Apr. 21, 1975 (div. May 1982). BS in Music Edn., Susquehanna U., 1967. Tchr. music Boyertown (Pa.) Area Schs., 1967-68; tchr. jr. high sch. music Abington (Pa.) Schs., 1969; tchr. instrumental music Ft. Washington Sch. Dist., Upper Dublin, Pa., 1969-70, Warwick Sch. Dist., Lititz, Pa., 1970-73, Pittsford (N.Y.) Cen. Schs., 1973-76; v.p., bus. mgr. Dengler Studios Inc., Rochester, N.Y., 1976-81; owner MAS Enterprises, Syracuse, 1981—; exec. adminstr. N.Y. State Assn. Profl. Land Surveyors, Syracuse, 1982—. Mem. Nat. Soc. Profl. Surveyors (chmn., editor 1987—), Sigma Alpha Iota. Home and Office: 204 Westwood Ave Syracuse NY 13211

SHIELDS, MARLENE SUE, elementary school educator; b. Denver, Apr. 7, 1939; d. Morris and Rose (Sniderman) Goldberg; m. Charles H. Cohen, Dec. 22, 1957 (dec.); children: Lee, Richard, Monica; m. Harlan Shields. BA magna cum laude, Met. State Coll., 1980; MA, U. No. Colo., 1986. Preschool tchr. Temple Emanuel, Denver, 1970-75; tchr. Kindergarten Temple Sinai, Denver, 1975-80; tchr. pre-Kindergarten St. Mary's Acad., Englewood, Colo., 1980-83; tchr. Beach Court Elem., Denver, 1983-86, Valverde Sch., Denver, 1984-85; tchr. third grade Brown Elem., Denver, 1985-86; tchr. learning disabilities Cowell Elem. Sch., Denver, 1986-87, Sabin Elem. Sch., Denver, 1987-88; tchr. second grade Sabin Elem., Denver, 1988—; mem. curriculum com. Denver Pub. Sch., 1989—, pers. subcom., 1991—. Mem. Colo. Copun. Internat. Reading Assn., Nat. Assn. for Young Children, Nat. Tchrs. Colo. Math., Internat. Reading Assn., Carousel of Intervention, Delta kappa Gamma (impact com.), PRIDE (lang. curriculum com., math curriculum com., impact com., CDM rep. 1993-94). Home: 5800 Big Canon Dr Englewood CO 80111-3516

SHIENTAG, FLORENCE PERLOW, lawyer; b. N.Y.C.; d. David and Ester (Germane) Perlow; m. Bernard L. Shientag, June 8, 1938. BS, NYU, 1940, LLB, JD. Bar: Fla. 1976, N.Y. Law aide Thomas E. Dewey, 1937; law sec. Mayor La Guardia, 1939-42; justice Domestic Relations Ct., 1941-42; mem. Tchrs. Retirement Bd., N.Y.C., 1942-46; asst. U.S. atty. So. dist. N.Y., 1943-53; cir. ct. mediator Fla. Supreme Ct., 1992; pvt. practice N.Y.C., 1994—, Palm Beach, Fla., 1994—; lectr. on internat. divorce; mem. Nat. Commn. on Wiretapping and Electronic Surveillance, 1973—, Task Force on Women in Cts., 1985-86; circuit ct. mediator Fla. Supreme Ct., 1992. Contbr. articles to profl. jours. Candidate N.Y. State senate, 1954; bd. dirs. UN Devel. Corp., 1972-95; bd. dirs., assoc. treas. YM and YWHA.; hon. commr. commerce, N.Y.C. Mem. ABA, Fed. Bar Assn. (exec. com.), Internat. Bar Assn., N.Y. Women's Bar Assn. (pres., Life Time Achievement award 1994), N.Y. State Bar Assn., N.Y.C. Bar Assn. (chmn. law and art sect.), N.Y. County Lawyers Assn. (dir.), Nat. Assn. Women LAwyers (sec.). Home: 737 Park Ave New York NY 10021-4256

SHIER, GLORIA BULAN, mathematics educator; b. Philippines, Apr. 20, 1935; came to U.S., 1966.; d. Melecio Cauilan and Florentina (Cumagun) Bulan; m. Wayne Thomas Shier, May 31, 1969; children: John Thomas, Marie Teresita, Anna Christina. BS, U. Santo Tomas, Manila, Philippines, 1956; MA, U. Ill., 1968; PhD, U. Minn., 1986. Tchr. Cagayan (Philippines) Valley Coll., 1956-58, St. Paul Coll., Manila, 1959-62, Manila Div. City Schs., 1958-64; asst. prof. U. of East, Manila, 1961-66; rsch. asst. U. Ill., Urbana, 1968-69; instr. Miramar Community Coll., San Diego, 1974-75, Mesa Community Coll., San Diego, 1975-80, Lakewood Community Coll., St. Paul, 1984, U. Minn., Mpls., 1986-87, North Hennepin Community Coll., Brooklyn Park, Minn., 1987—; cons. PWS Kent Pub. Co., Boston, 1989—. Chairperson Filipino Am. Edn. Assn., San Diego, 1978-79. Fulbright scholar U.S. State Dept., U. Ill., 1966-70; fellow Nat. Sci. Found., Oberlin Coll., 1967; recipient Excellence in Teaching award UN Ednl. Scientific Cultural Organ., U. Philippines, 1960-62, Cert. Commendation award The Gov. of Minn., 1990, Outstanding Filipino in the Midwest Edn. Cat. award 1992, Cavite Assn. Mem. Am. Math. Soc., Math. Assn. Am., Phi Kappa Phi, Sigma Xi Rsch. Honor Soc., Nat. Coun. Tchrs. Math., Am. Math. Assn. for Two Yr. Colleges, Internat. Group for Psychology of Math. Edn., Minn. Coun. of Tchrs. Math., Minn. Math. Assn. of Two Yr. Colleges, Filminnesotan Assn (bd.dirs. 1991—), Am. Statistical Assn. Roman Catholic. Home: 1715 Heritage Ln New Brighton MN 55112

SHIFFMAN, LESLIE BROWN, management executive; b. Fresno, Calif., Dec. 9, 1936; d. Albert Brown and Marion Jean (Riese) Brown-Propp; married, Jan. 20, 1957 (div. 1972); m. Sydney Shiffman, July 4, 1994; children: Susan, Steven, David, Thomas. BS, U. So. Calif., 1958. Office mgr. pvt. practice physician, Long Beach, Calif., 1971-73; cost acct. Panavision, Inc., Tarzana, Calif., 1974-76; exec. sec. Hartman Galleries, Beverly Hills, Calif., 1976-78; adminstrv. asst. Galanos Originals, L.A., 1978—. Named L.A. Alumnae Panhellenic Assn. Women of Yr., 1977. Mem. Alpha Epsilon Phi (nat. pres. 1985-89, trustee, sec. found. 1990-91, pres. found. 1991—, Woman of Distinction award 1993). Republican. Jewish. Home: 1745 S Bentley Ave # 1 Los Angeles CA 90025-4323 Office: Galanos Originals 2254 S Sepulveda Blvd Los Angeles CA 90064-1812

SHIFMAN, SANDRA LYNNETTE, English language educator; b. Calgary, Alberta, Can., Sept. 29, 1947; d. Gedaliaha and Bertha (Chester) Held; m. Samuel Shifman, Aug. 9, 1970 (div. Dec. 1990); children Ruth Miri, Mark Issac. BA, UCLA, 1969, MA, 1971. Cert. secondary tchr., Calif. English tchr. Conejo Unified Sch. Dist., Thousand Oaks, Calif., 1972—; journalist Internat. Press, Israel, 1976-80; real estate agent Century 21, Thousand Oaks, Calif. 1983-93. Journalist, Columnist Scripps Howard Publisher, Thousand Oaks, Calif., 1983-93; writer articles to newspapers L.A. Times, News Chronicle, Star, Jerusalem Post, 1970—. Tchr. rep. PTA, 1994; advocate Thousand Oaks Civic Art Ctr., Calif., 1994—. Recipient Outstanding Journalism Tchr. award Assn. Jouralism Educators, 1975. Mem. Calif. Tchrs. Assn., Grassroots for Crime Prevention (founder). Home: 3235 Sunburst Pl Thousand Oaks CA 91360 Office: Conejo Unified Sch Dist 1400 E Janss Rd Thousand Oaks CA 91360

SHIH, J. CHUNG-WEN, Chinese language educator; b. Nanking, China; came to U.S., 1948, naturalized, 1960; d. Cho-kiang and Chia-pu (Fang) S. B.A., St. John's U., Shanghai, 1945; M.A., Duke U., 1949, Ph.D., 1955. Asst. prof. English Kings Coll. N.Y., 1955-56; asst. prof. U. Bridgeport, Conn., 1956-60; postdoctoral fellow East Asian Studies Harvard, 1960-61; asst. prof. Chinese Stanford, 1961-64; asso. prof. Chinese Pomona Coll., 1965-66; asso. prof. George Washington U., Washington, 1966-71, prof., chmn. dept. East Asian langs. and lit., 1971-93, prof. emeritus, 1993—, chmn. dept. East Asian langs. and lit., 1971-93, rsch. prof., 1994—. Author: Injustice to Tou O, 1972, the Golden Age of Chinese Drama: Yuan Tsa-chu, 1976, Return from Silence: China's Writers of the May Fourth Tradition, 1983. Bd. dirs. Sino-Am. Cultural Soc., Washington, 1971-80. AAUW fellow, 1964-65; Social Sci. Rsch. Coun. fellow, 1976-77; grantee NEH, 1979-80, 89-91, Annenberg/CPB Project, 1989-92; sr. scholars exchange program NAS, China, spring 1980. Mem. Assn. Asian Studies, Am. Council Fgn. Lang. Tchrs., Chinese Lang. Tchrs. Assn. (chmn. exec. bd. 1976-78). Home: 2500 Virginia Ave NW Washington DC 20037-1901 Office: George Washington U Dept East Asian Langs E Washington DC 20052

SHIH, MARIE, metaphysical healer; b. Florence, Ariz., Jan. 24, 1959; d. John Cecil and Josephine Marie (Carter) Lewis; m. Ravi Sundervardan Candadai, Aug. 13, 1982 (div. Aug. 1984); m. Tony Hu-Tung Shih, July 11, 1987 (div. Sept. 1991); m. Jack Hunter Caldwell, Jan. 2, 1995; 1 child, John Lewis Caldwell; step-children: Trevor Hunter, Levi Robert. BA, U. Ariz., 1982, postgrad., 1982-84. Musician, writer, illustrator, Tucson and Seattle, 1978—; front desk clk. Ghost Ranch Lodge, Tucson, 1982-83; adminstrv. sec. Starnet Corp., Seattle, 1985-86; vol. U.S. Peace Corps, Mbalmayo, Cameroun, Africa, 1986; practitioner Christian Science Ch., 1994—; ind. team mgr. Noevir Natural Herbal Cosmetics, Seattle, 1987-92, author, editor mo. newsletter, 1989-92, attended nat. convs., 1989-92; lectr. So. Seattle Cmty. Coll., 1990-92. Author press releases, bus. forms local orgns., Tucson, Seattle, 1978-93; editor letters, speeches local orgns., Seattle; author, editor, designer mo. newsletter Fairmount News and Views, 1993-94; contbr. articles to jours. Bd. dirs., com. chmn. S.W. Seattle Liberacy Coalition, 1989-90; active ArtsWet, United Way, West Seattle Totem Theatre, 1990-94; bus. sponsor West Seattle Hi-Yu, 1991; active 6th Ch. of Christ, Scientist, Seatle, 1987—, 1st reader, 1991-94; active 1st Ch. of Christ, Scientist, Boston, 1990—; mem. steering com. Constellation Park and Marine Res. at Ritchey Viewpoint, 1993-94; founding mem. Fairmount Ravine Preservation Group, 1993-94. Mem. NAFE, West Seattle C. of C. (area dir. 1990-91, com. mem. 1990-93, com. chair 1992-93), Neighborhood Promotion Com. Republican. Address: 582-C Winston Creek Rd Mossyrock WA 98564

SHIH-CARDUCCI, JOAN CHIA-MO, cooking educator, biochemist, medical technologist; b. Rukuan, Chunghua, Republic of China, Dec. 21, 1933; came to U.S., 1955; d. Luke Chiang-hsi and Lien-chin (Chang) Shih; m. Kenneth M. Carducci, Sept. 30, 1960 (dec. July 1988); children: Suzanne R., Elizabeth M. BS in Chemistry, St. Mary Coll., Xavier, Kans., 1959; intern in med. tech., St. Mary's Hosp., Rochester, N.Y., 1960. Med. researcher Strong Meml. Hosp. (U. Rochester), 1960-61; pharm. chemist quality control Strasenburgh Labs., Rochester, 1961-62; cooking tchr. adult edn. Montgomery County Pub. Schs., Rockville, Md., 1973-79; cooking tchr. The Chinese Cookery Inc., Rockville, 1975-86; cooking tchr. The Chinese Cookery Inc., Silver Spring, Md., 1986—, pres., bd. dirs., 1975—; chemist NIH, Bethesda, 1987-94; analytical chemist NIH/WRAIR, Rockville, Md., 1994—. Author: The Chinese Cookery, 1981, Hunan Cuisine, 1984. Mem. Internat. Assn. Cooking Profls. Republican. Roman Catholic. Home and Office: The Chinese Cookery Inc 14209 Sturtevant Rd Silver Spring MD 20905-4448

SHILDNECK, BARBARA JEAN, accounting magazine editor; b. Waynesboro, Pa., Apr. 1, 1937; d. Barry Price and Helen Matilda (Armstrong) S. BA in English Lit., Wilson Coll., Chambersburg, Pa., 1959. With AICPA, N.Y.C., 1959—, jr. prodn. asst., 1959-62, sr. prodn. asst., 1962-66, editor The CPA, 1969-73, asst. editor to manuscript editor Jour. of Accountancy, 1966-79, from mng. editor to exec. editor, 1979—; editor Centennial issue AICPA, May, 1987; panelist edn. program video tapes in Can. and U.S.; lectr. in field. Contbr. articles to profl. jours. Recipient Gold Circle award Am. Soc. Assn. Execs., 1986, Bronze Ozzie for spl. issue Mag. Design and Prodn., May 1987, Soc. Nat. Assn. Publs. award, 1987, award of distinction Soc. Tech. Communication, 1987. Mem. NAFE, Am. Soc. Bus. Press Editors, Am. Acctg. Assn., Ocean Grove (N.J.) Civic League. Democrat. Office: Harborside Fin Ctr 201 Plaza Three Jersey City NJ 07311

SHILLINGS, GAIL, school counselor; b. Kingsville, Tex., Oct. 1, 1946; d. Nolan Woodroe and Anne (Kennedy) Petty; m. Kenneth Joe Shillings, July 13, 1968 (div. Mar. 1988); children: Jon Brandon, Justin. B Teaching, Sam Houston State U., 1971; M in Guidance and Counseling, Tex. A&M U., Corpus Christi, 1993. Lic. counselor. Tchr 3d grade Bloomington (Tex.) Elem. Sch., 1971-72, Odem (Tex.) Elem. Sch., 1972-73; tchr. 4th grade Tivoli (Tex.) Elem. Sch., 1973-81; tchr. 6th, 7th and 8th grade Travis Mid. Sch., Port Lavaca, Tex., 1981-92; counselor pre-K to 12th grade Ganado (Tex.) Ind. Sch. Dist., 1992—; mem. Tchr. Adv. Com., Port Lavaca, 1983-86. Election judge Rep. Primary of Calhoun County, Port Lavaca, 1984; com. chmn. Port Lavaca Bicenntenial Celebrtion Orgn., Port Lavaca, 1990. Mem. Tex. Counseling Assn., Tex. Sch. Counselors Assn., Tex. State Tchrs. Assn. (treas. 1983-84), LaBahia Counseling Assn. Methodist. Office: Ganado Ind Sch Dist 501 W Devers Ganado TX 77962

SHILLINGSBURG, MIRIAM JONES, educator; b. Balt., Oct. 5, 1943; d. W. Elvin and Miriam (Reeves) Jones; BA, Mars Hill Coll., 1964; MA, U. S.C., 1966, PhD, 1969; m. Peter L. Shillingsburg, Nov. 21, 1967; children: Robert, George, John, Alice, Anne Carol. Asst. prof. Limestone Coll., Gaffney, S.C., 1969; asst. prof. Mississippi State (Miss.) U., 1970-75, assoc. prof., 1975-80, prof. English, 1980—, asst. to provost, 1987-88, assoc. v.p. for acad. affairs, 1988—, dir. summer sch., 1991—; vis. fellow Australian Def. Force Acad., 1989; Fulbright lectr. U. New South Wales, Duntroon, Australia, 1984-85. Nat. Endowment Humanities fellow in residence, Columbia U., 1976-77. Mem. Soc. Study So. Lit., Nat. Acad. Advising Assn., South Atlantic Modern Lang. Assn., Australia-New Zealand Am. Studies Assn., Phi Kappa Phi. Author: Mark Twain in Australasia, 1988; editor: Conquest of Granada, 1988; mem. editorial bd. Works of W.M. Thackeray; assoc. editor Miss. Quarterly; contbr. articles to profl. jours. and mags.

SHIMANDLE, SHARON ANNE, critical care nurse; b. Cleve., Mar. 12, 1959; d. Harry William and Dorothy May (McGivney) Dowdell; m. James Edward Shimandle Jr., Dec. 22, 1979; children: Jason Michael, Jillian Lyn. ADN, Cuyahoga C.C., Parma, Ohio, 1980; MSN, Case Western Reserve U., 1990. RN, Ohio; cert. ACLS, BLS instr. Staff nurse SICU St. Vincent Charity Hosp., Cleve., 1980; staff nurse ICU Kaiser Hosp., Parma, 1981-82, staff nurse oper. rm., 1982-85; staff nurse post anesthesia care unit/ambulatory surgery unit Deaconess Hosp., Cleve., 1985-86, asst. dir. post anesthesia care unit/ambulatory surgery unit, 1986-87, critical care educator, 1987-90; critical care instr. Mt. Sinai Med. Ctr., Cleve., 1990-92; clin. nurse CCU Lorain (Ohio) Cmty. Hosp., 1992-94; critical care instr. Lorain (Ohio) Cmty. St. Joseph's Regional Health Ctr., 1994—. Mem. AACN, Nursing Staff Devel. Orgn. Home: 290 B2 Yorktown Pl Vermilion OH 44089 Office: Loran Community St Josephs Regional Health Ctr 3700 Kolbe Rd Lorain OH 44053

SHIMELMAN, SUSAN FROMM, state administrator; b. N.Y.C., May 5, 1942; m. Myer M. Shimelman, Aug. 14, 1965; children: Wendy, Amy. BA, McGill U., Montreal, 1964; MS, Columbia U., 1970. Fellow Harvard U., Cambridge, Mass., 1964-65; Can. coun. fellow McGill U., Montreal, 1965-68; asst. dir. Yale-New Haven Hosp., 1970-80; exec. dir. New Haven Jewish Fedn., 1980-90; undersec. Office Policy and Mgmt., State of Conn., Hartford, 1991-94, sec., 1994—; chair Prison and Jail Overcrowding Commn., Hartford, 1990—, Health Care State Conn., Hartford, 1992—, Exec. Com. Info. and Tech., Hartford, 1994; vice chair Cmty. Econ. Devel. Found., Hartford, 1994. Bd. dirs. Fedn. United Way, New Haven, 1970-94; alt. N.E. Regional Compact, N.J. and Conn., 1991-94; active A Conn. Party, Hartford, 1990-94. Recipient Pres. award New Haven Jewish Fedn., 1990; named Powerful Woman of Vision, YWCA, 1988. Democrat. Home: 11 Forest Trl Woodbridge CT 06525 Office: State of Conn Office Policy and Mgmt 80 Washington St Hartford CT 06106

SHIMMIN, MARGARET ANN, women's health nurse; b. Forbes, N.D., Oct. 26, 1941; d. George Robert and Reba Aleda (Strain) S. Diploma in Nursing, St. Luke's Hosp. Sch. Nursing, Fargo, N.D., 1962; BSW, U. West Fla., 1978; cert. ob-gyn nurse practitioner, U. Ala., Birmingham, 1983, MPH, 1986. Lic. nurse, Fla., N.D., Ala. Head nurse, emergency room St. Luke's Hosps., Fargo, 1962-67; charge nurse, labor and delivery, perinatal nurse educator Sacred Heart Hosp., Pensacola, Fla., 1970-82; ARNP Escambia County Pub. Health Unit, Pensacola, 1983-89; cmty. health nursing cons. Dist. 1 Health and Rehab. Svcs., Pensacola, 1989—. Capt. nurse corps U.S. Army, 1967-70, Japan. Mem. NAACOG (cert. maternal-gynecol.-neonatal nursing 1978, ob-gyn nurse practitioner 1983), Fla. Nurses' Assn., ANA, N.W. Fla. ARNP (past sec./treas.), Fla. Perinatal Assn., Nat. Perinatal Assn., Healthy Mothers/Healthy Babies Coalition, Fla. Pub. Health Assn., U. West Fla. Alumni Assn., U. Ala. at Birmingham Sch. of Public Health Alumni Assn., Phi Alpha. Republican. Presbyterian. Home: 8570 Olympia Rd Pensacola FL 32514 Office: Dist 1 HRS 160 Governmental Ctr Pensacola FL 32501

SHIMP, KAREN ANN, accountant, municipal financial executive; b. Atlantic, Iowa, July 17, 1959; d. Emerson Arnold and Verna Louise (Schmeling) Fett; m. Philip Kenneth Shimp, Jan. 30, 1988 (div.); 1 child, Keith Emerson. BSBA, Drake U., 1981. Acct. Midwest Mut. Ins. Co., West Des Moines, Iowa, 1981-84; staff acct. Deborah J. Kent, CPA, Palm Desert, Calif., 1985; fin. analyst Massey Sand & Rock Co., Indio, Calif., 1986-88; supr. interline Greyhound Lines, Inc., West Des Moines, 1989-93; fin. dir. City of Pella, Iowa, 1993—; coord. Drake U. Bus. Aid Soc., 1980; mem. Inland Soc. Tax Consultants, 1987-91. Treas. Luth. Women's Missionary League, Indio, 1986-88, sec., 1988-89; v.p. Aid Assn. for Lutherans, Indio, 1988-89. State of Iowa scholar, 1977. Mem. NAFE, Inst. Mgmt. Accts. (bd. dirs.), Kiwanis Internat. Democrat. Home: 610 W 1st St Pella IA 50219 Office: City of Pella 717 Main St Pella IA 50219

SHINEVAR, KAREN KAY, lawyer; b. Marshall, Mich., Mar. 16, 1956; d. Wayne Alden and Elizabeth Marilyn (Albrecht) Coats; m. Peter O'Neil Shinevar, Aug. 25, 1979; children: Thomas Scott, William Joseph. BA in History and Econs., Albion Coll., 1978; JD, U. Mich., 1981. Bar: D.C. 1981, Md. 1982, N.Y. 1994. Assoc. Seifman, Semo & Slevin, Washington, 1981-82; atty. MCI Airsignal, Inc., Washington, 1983-86; v.p. McCaw Cellular Comm., Washington, 1986-91; v.p., gen. counsel Cellular Telephone Co., Paramus, N.J., 1992—. Mem. Md. Bar Assn., D.C. Bar Assn., N.Y. Women in Utilities, N.J. Corp. Counsel Assn., Phi Beta Kappa. Office: Cellular Telephone Co 15 E Midland Ave Paramus NJ 07652

SHINN, DOROTHY GRAY, art critic; b. Charlotte, N.C., Oct. 26, 1943; d. David Graham and Dorothy Elizabeth (Tillotson) Gray; m. William Herman Pell, May 25, 1962 (div. 1966); m. Ronald Wyane Shinn, Dec. 28, 1974; 1 child, Nancy Cannon. BA in Journalism, U. N.C., 1970; MFA in Painting, Kent State U., 1986, MA in Art History, 1994. Fund raiser, pub. rels. Am. U. in Cairo, N.Y.C., 1966-68; reporter, editor LaFollette (Tenn.) Press, 1970-72; reporter Palm Beach (Fla.) Daily News, 1972-74; copy editor Akron (Ohio) Beacon Jour., 1977-78, art critic, 1978—. Author catalog essays; curator art shows. Mem. League Women Voters (publicity chair 1992-94, bd. dirs., edn. com. 1993-95). Home and Office: 905 Genesee Rd Akron OH 44303

SHINOLT, EILEEN THELMA, artist; b. Washington, May 18, 1919; d. Edward Lee and Blanche Addie (Marsh) Bennett; m. John Francis Shinolt, June 14, 1956 (dec. Aug. 1969). Student, Hans Hoffman Sch Art, 1949, Pa. Acad. Arts, 1950, Corcoran Sch. Art, 1945-51, Am. U., 1973-77. Sect. chief Dept. Army, Washington, 1940-73, retired, 1973. One-woman shows include various locations, 1982, 83, 85, 90, 94; group shows include Perlmutter & Co., 1981, Fitch Fox and Brown, 1986, Foundry Gallery, 1987, Ann. Add Arts, 1986; represented in permanent collections Women's Nat. Mus., Washington, Cameo Gallery, Columbia, S.C., others. Mem. Woman's Nat. Dem. Club, Washington, 1980—. Mem. Am. Art League (editor newsletter 1985-86, 1st pl. 1987, 2d pl. 1986), Arts Club Washington (exhbn. com. 1985—, admissions com. 1987-88), Miniature Painters, Sculptors & Gravers Soc. (historian 1989—, editor newsletter 1986-89). Roman Catholic. Home: 4119 Davis Pl NW Apt 203 Washington DC 20007-1254

SHIPLEY, LUCIA HELENE, retired chemical company executive; b. Boston, Oct. 26, 1920; d. Harry Jacob and Helen Merrill (Dillingham) Farrington; m. Charles Raymond Shipley, Oct. 11, 1941; children: Helen Merrill, Richard Charles. Student, Smith Coll., 1938-41. Chief exec. officer, treas. Shipley Co. Inc., Newton, Mass., 1957-92, also bd. dirs. Patentee for immersion tin, electroless copper. Recipient Winthrop Sears award Chem. Industry Assn., 1985, Semi award Semicon West, 1990. Mem. Garden Club (pres. 1954-56). Republican. Congregationalist.

SHIPLEY, SHELIA, record company executive; b. Scottsville, Ky., Oct. 2, 1952; d. Robert Shelby Davis and Pauline (Powell) Willoughby; divorced; 1 child, Michael. Student U. Tenn., 1975-77, Nashville Tech. Inst., 1978-79. Adminstrv. asst. Monument Records, Nashville, 1976-79; promotion/sales coord. RCA Records, Nashville, 1979-83; dir. career devel. Hallmark Direction Co., Nashville, 1983-84; sr. v.p. nat. promotion MCA Records, Nashville, 1984-94; sr. v.p., gen. mgr. Decca Records, 1994—. Author poetry. Mem. NARAS, Country Music Assn., Acad. Country Music, Country Radio Bd. Dirs., Nat. Assn. Talent Buyers, Source, Leadership Music. Republican. Baptist. Office: Decca Records 60 Music Sq E Nashville TN 37203-4325

SHIPMAN, SUSAN, marine fisheries administrator, association executive; b. Dyersburg, Tenn., Feb. 4, 1954; d. William Len and Virginia (Dickinson) S.; m. Mark Alan Jicha, Jan. 24, 1952. BS in Zoology, U. Ga., 1976. Rsch. asst. U. N.C., Chapel Hill, 1976-78; rsch. assoc. Ga. Dept. Natural Resources, Brunswick, 1979-80, marine biologist, 1980-81, comml. fisheries program leader, 1981-83, chief marine fisheries sect., 1983—. Mem. adv. bd. Leadership Glynn, Brunswick, 1988-92, Glynn Clean and Beautiful, 1989-93; bd. dirs. Brunswick YWCA, 1991—, pres., 1994. Recipient Outstanding Svc. State Govt. award Gov. of Ga., 1983; named Bd. Mem. of Yr., Brunswick YWCA, 1991. Mem. Am. Fisheries Soc. (sec., treas. 1987-89, pres.-elect 1989-90, pres. 1990-91, So. Div. Outstanding Achievement award 1993, Disting. Svc. award 1993), Atlantic States Marine Fisheries Commn. (mem. mgmt. and sci. com. 1983-93, commr. 1994), South Atlantic Fishery Mgmt. Coun. (vice-chmn. 1990-91, chmn. 1991-92), Leadership Ga. Alumni Assn., Leadership Glynn Alumni Assn., Pilot Club Brunswick. Episcopalian. Home: 920 Rose Cottage Rd Saint Simons Island GA 31522

SHIPPEY, LYN, reading center director; b. Childress, Tex., Mar. 6, 1927; d. Robert Coke and Alta Edna (Timmons) Elliott; m. James George Shippey, Mar. 29, 1947; children: James Robert, Deborah Shippey Meyer, Marilyn Shippey Buron. BS, U. Corpus Christi, 1963; MA in Edn., San Diego State U., 1977; EdD, U. San Diego, 1993. Cert. tchr., reading specialist, tchr. of learning handicapped, Calif. Substitute tchr. Dept. Edn., Guam, 1958-61; tchr. counselor Robstown Ind. Sch. Dist., Tex., 1964-65; elem. tchr. Cupertino Union Sch. Dist., Calif., 1965-68, tchr., secondary, 1968-71; dir. PIRK Reading Center, Poway, Calif., 1973—; cons., workshop presenter PIRK Reading Programs, Calif., Tex., 1974—. Author: Perceptual Integration Reading Kits, 1971, PIRK Reading Program, 1977, rev. 1987. Mem. ASCD, Coun. for Exceptional Children, Alcala Soc. U. San Diego (scholar), Orton Dyslexia Soc. Office: PIRK Reading Center 16957 Cloudcroft Dr Poway CA 92064-1306

SHIPPEY, SANDRA LEE, lawyer; b. Casper, Wyo., June 24, 1957; d. Virgil Carr and Doris Louise (Conklin) McC.; m. Ojars Herberts Ozols, Sept. 2, 1978 (div.); children: Michael Ojars, Sara Ann, Brian Christopher; m. James Robert Shippey, Jan. 13, 1991. BA with distinction, U. Colo., 1978; JD magna cum laude, Boston U., 1982. Bar: Colo. 1982, U.S. Dist. Ct. Colo. 1985. Assoc. Cohen, Brame & Smith, Denver, 1983-84, Parcel, Meyer, Schwartz, Ruttum & Mauro, Denver, 1984-85, Mayer, Brown & Platt, Denver, 1985-87; counsel western ops. GE Capital Corp., San Diego, 1987-94; assoc. Page, Polin, Busch & Boatwright, San Diego, 1994—. Active Pop Warner football and cheerleading. Mem. Phi Beta Kappa, Phi Delta Phi. Republican. Mem. Ch. of Christ. Home: 11878 Glenhope Rd San Diego CA 92128-5002 Office: Page Polin Busch & Boatwright 350 W Ash St #900 San Diego CA 92101

SHIREMAN, JOAN FOSTER, social work educator; b. Cleve., Oct. 28, 1933; d. Louis Omar and Genevieve (Duguid) Foster; m. Charles Howard Shireman, Mar. 18, 1967; 1 child, David Louis. BA, Radcliffe Coll., 1956; MA, U. Chgo., 1959, PhD, 1968. Caseworker N.H. Children's Aid Soc., Manchester, 1959-61; dir. research Chgo. Child Care Soc., 1968-72; assoc. prof. U. Ill., Chgo., 1972-85; prof. Portland (Oreg.) State U., 1985—, dir. PhD program, 1992—; interim exec. dir. Partnership for Rsch., Tng. and Grad. Edn. in Child Welfare, 1994; research cons. child welfare orgns., Ill., 1968-85, Oreg. 1985—; lectr. U. Chgo., 1968-72. Co-author: Care and Commitment: Foster Parent Adoption Decisions, 1985; mem. editorial bd. Jour. Sch. Social Work, 1978-81, Social Work Rsch. and Abstracts, 1990-93, Children and Youth Svcs. Rev., Jour. of Social Work Edn., 1990—; contbr. chpts. to books and articles to profl. jours. Bd. dirs. Oreg. chpt. Nat. Assn. for Prevention of Child Abuse, 1985-87, Friendly House, Portland, 1992—; mem. adv. com. Children's Svcs. div. State of Oreg., 1985—. Grantee HEW, 1980-82, Chgo. Community Trust, 1982-86, Oreg. Children's Trust Fund, 1991—. Mem. Nat. Assn. Social Workers, AAUP, Citizens for Children, Acad. Cert. Social Workers, Council on Social Work Edn., Phi Beta Kappa. Home: 2535 SW Sherwood Dr Portland OR 97201-1679 Office: Portland State U Grad Sch Social Work PO Box 751 Portland OR 97207-0751

SHIREY, MARGARET (PEGGY SHIREY), elementary school educator; b. Sussex, N.J., Nov. 24, 1950; d. Steve and Grace (McGlew) Piniaha; children: Todd, Jessica. BS, Marymount Coll., Salina, Kans., 1972; M Elem. Edn., Ctrl. State U., 1985. Cert. elem. tchr., Okla. Tchr. Putnam City Sch. Dist., Oklahoma City, 1980—. Active Putnam City Reading Coun.; bargaining mem. Putnam City, 1993-95. Named One of Okla.'s Best Tchrs. Channel 5 Alive, Oklahoma City, 1991. Mem. NEA, ASCD, Okla. Edn. Assn., Putnam City Assn. Classroom Tchrs. (bldg. rep. 1983-86, legis. chairperson 1989-92). Democrat. Home: 3720 Eagle Ln Bethany OK 73008 Office: Putnam City Sch Dist 5401 NW 40th Oklahoma City OK 73122

SHIREY, MINDYANNE BERMAN, psychologist; b. N.Y.C., Feb. 26, 1958; d. Irwin and Adele (Yanuck) Berman; m. Paul Martin Shirey, July 6, 1991; 1 child, Rebecca Olivia. BA, Hofstra U., 1980; MA, U. Pitts., 1985, PhD, 1991. Cert. sch. psychologist. Therapist Citizens Addiction Rehab. and Edn., Washington, 1985-87, Greenbriar, Washington, 1987-88, St. Francis Hosp., Pitts., 1988-89; psychologist Moniteau Sch. Dist., West Sunbury, Pa., 1989—. Vice-chair Butler County (Pa.) Mental Health and Mental Retardation Bd., 1991—. Mem. NASP, Assn. Sch. Psychologists Pa., Western Pa. Sch. Psychologists Assn. Office: Moniteau Sch Dist 1810 W Sunbury Rd West Sunbury PA 16061

SHIRK, ANNADORA VESPER, English educator; b. Altoona, Pa., Aug. 9, 1918; d. Harry M. and Jessie (Birchfield) Spengler; m. Albert R. Vesper (dec.); m. Eugene L. Shirk, 1949; children: Albert, Thea. PhD in Rhetoric, Temple U., 1977. Instr. English, Albright Coll., Reading, Pa., 1946, asst. prof., 1949-66, assoc. prof., 1966-76, prof., 1976—, chmn. dept., 1978-82, faculty chmn., 1980-82; speaker, 1955—. Mem. Reading Sch. Bd., 1955-61. Named Coll. Prof. of Yr., Reading C. of C., 1980; Lindback fellow, 1978; recipient Beacon award (Outstanding Woman of Yr.), Berks Women's Network, 1991, Albright Alumni Citation for Disting. Svc., 1992, Thiel Coll. Disting. Alumni award, 1989. Mem. AAUW (pres. Reading, 1976-78). Republican. Methodist. Home: 1503 N 12th St Reading PA 19604 Office: Albright Coll Dept English 13th St Reading PA 19604

SHIRK, EVELYN URBAN, retired philosophy educator; b. Flushing, N.Y., Sept. 12, 1918; d. Amos Urban and Mary Jane (Welchans) S.; m. Justus Buchler, Feb. 20, 1943; 1 child, Katherine Urban. B.A., Wilson Coll., 1940; M.A., Columbia U., 1942, Ph.D., 1949. Instr. Bklyn Coll., 1942-48; asst. prof. Hofstra Coll., Hempstead, N.Y., 1949-53, assoc. prof., 1953-63; prof. Hofstra U. (formerly Hofstra Coll.), 1963—, dept. chmn., 1980-89, ret. Hofstra U. Contbg. editor: Readings in Philosophy, 1946; Adventurous Idealism: The Philosophy of Alfred Lloyd, 1952; The Ethical Dimension, 1965; In Pursuit of Awareness, 1967, After the Stroke: Coping With America's Third Leading Cause of Death, 1991. Mem. Am. Philos. Assn., Soc. Advancement Am. Philosophy (program chmn. 1976, exec. com 1977-79), L.I. Philos. Soc. (exec. com.), AAUP, Phi Beta Kappa. Home: 3 Homestead Ave Garden City NY 11530-1002

SHIRLEY, NORMA, librarian, bibliographer; b. Chatham, N.Y., Mar. 22, 1935; d. George and Bertha (Shattuck) Shirley. B.A., Russell Sage Coll., 1962; M.L.S., SUNY-Albany, 1963, M.S. in Ednl. Adminstrn., 1980. Asst. reference librarian Jr. Coll. Albany, 1963-65; librarian Hudson Area Library (N.Y.), 1966-67; reference librarian Russell Sage Coll., Troy, N.Y., 1967-69; librarian Poughkeepsie High Sch. (N.Y.), 1970-71; library media specialist Spl. Edn. Ctr., Dutchess County BOCES, Poughkeepsie, 1971-92. Co-author: Checklist of Serials in Psychology and Allied Fields, 1969; Serials in Psychology and Allied Fields, 1976. Bd. dirs. Friends of Locust Grove, Deyo Family Assn., Huguenot Hist. Soc. Mem. Dutchess County Library Assn. (past pres.), Sch. Library Media Specialists Southeastern N.Y. (past pres.), ALA, N.Y. Library Assn., Dutchess County Mental Health Assn. Home: PO Box 2401 Poughkeepsie NY 12603-0881

SHIRLEY, VIRGINIA COLLIER, artist; b. Montgomery, Ala., Sept. 11, 1956; d. Olaf Edward and Mary Virginia (Caldwell) Collier; m. Philip A. Shirley, June 30, 1982. BA, U. Ala., 1980; postgrad., Miss. Coll. Prog. assoc. Ala. Humanities Found., Birmingham, 1980-84; exhibit designer U. Ala. Law Ctr., Tuscaloosa, 1984; writers conf. coord. Birmingham-So. Coll., 1984-85; account exec. Shirwood Advt., Montevallo, Ala., 1984-86; asst. curator Sloss Furnaces Mus., Birmingham, 1986-89; cons., researcher Arts Alliance of Jackson & Hinds County, Jackson, Miss., 1989; dir. community arts prog. Miss. Arts Commn., Jackson, 1989-91; exec. dir. Arts Alliance of Jackson and Hinds County, 1991-93; ceramics artist Jackson, Miss., 1993—; bd. dirs. New Stage Theatre; advisor/cons. Birmingham Mus. Art, 1983-84, Birmingham Hist. Soc., 1986-89, Birmingham Bot. Soc., 1986-89. Author, editor, photographer: Jackson Arts Directory, 1989; author, editor children's book: Sloss Furnaces Coloring Book, 1989; author, editor: Sloss Furnaces Teacher's Guide, 1988, Sloss Furnaces Docent Manual, 1988. Mem. task force Mayor's Commn. on Women, 1984-85; adv. mem. Greater Birmingham Dirs. of Vol. Svcs., 1986-89; Miss. del. Nat. Assy. of Local Arts Agencies, Washington, nat. conv., 1990. Recipient Cert. of Outstanding Svc., Mayor's Office of Birmingham, 1985, Cottonlandia Mus. Sunburst Purchase award, 1989, Cottonlandia Mus. Trustmark Purchase award, 1993; NEH scholar, 1981. Mem. AAUW (v.p. 1985-86), Miss. Mus. Art, Miss. Mus. Assn., Arts Alliance of Jackson and Hinds County, Bus. and Profl. Women. Home: 4424 Northover Dr Jackson MS 39211-6120 Studio: 4424 Northover Dr Jackson MS 39211

SHIRLEY, VIRGINIA LEE, advertising executive; b. Kankakee, Ill., Mar. 24, 1936; d. Glenn Lee and Virginia Helen (Ritter) S. Student, Northwestern U., 1960-61. With prodn. control dept. Armour Pharm., Kankakee, 1954-58; exec. sec. Adolph Richman, Chgo., 1958-61; mgr. media dept. Don Kemper Co., Chgo., 1961-63, 65-69; exec. sec. Playboy mag., Chgo., 1964-65; exec. v.p. SMY Media Inc., Chgo., 1969—. Mem. Pla. Club. Home: 800 S Wells St Chicago IL 60607-4529 Office: SMY Media Inc 333 N Michigan Ave Chicago IL 60601-3901

SHIRTCLIFF, CHRISTINE FAY, healthcare facility executive; b. Greenfield, Mass.; d. Francis E. and Doris E. (Olsen) S.; 1 child, Danielle Elizabeth. BS in Pub. Health, U. Mass., 1973, MBA, 1987; MEd, Antioch U., 1978. Lic. nursing home adminstr., social worker. Health program rep. Fulton County Health Dept., Atlanta, 1973-74; home health aide supv. County Health Care, Greenfield, Mass., 1974-77; adminstrv. asst. Mary Lane Hosp., Ware, Mass., 1977-79, asst. exec. dir., 1979-85, exec. v.p., 1985—; founder, mem. steering com. We. Mass. Healthcare Mgrs. Group, 1983-86; active Mass. Rural Devel. Social Svcs. Subcom., 1986, Mass. Coun. Homemaker/Home Health Aide Svcs., 1976-85, bd. dirs., 1976-77, We. Mass. Health Planning Coun., 1974-78. Trustee Congl. Ch. in Belchertown, Mass., 1993—; mem. Belchertown Collaboration for Excellence in Edn., 1993; mem. blue ribbon com. on excellence in edn. Pioneer Valley Planning Commn. Fellow Am. Coll. Healthcare Execs.; mem. New England Women Healthcare Execs. Office: Mary Lane Hosp 85 South St Ware MA 01082-1697

SHIVELY, JOYCE MARIE, critical care nurse; b. Portland, Oreg., Nov. 22, 1958; d. Thomas Merritt and Shirley Ann (White) Rodda; m. Michael Thomas Shively, June 25, 1983. BSN, U. Portland, 1981; M Nursing, U. Wash., 1991. RN, Oreg., CCRN. Staff nurse Woodland Park Hosp., Portland, 1981-82; commd. 2d lt. USAF, 1981, advanced through grades to maj., 1992; staff nurse female medicine David Grant Med. Ctr., Travis AFB, Calif., 1982-83, staff nurse CCU, 1983-86; flight nurse 57th Aeromed. Evacuation Squadron, Scott AFB, Ill., 1986-89, flight clin. coord., 1987-89; charge nurse ICU Keesler Med. Ctr., Keesler AFB, Miss., 1991—. Mem. AACN (cert.), Air Force Assn., Arbor Day Soc., Nat. Wildlife Assn., Sigma Theta Tau. Home: 3503 Tyler Dr Ocean Springs MS 39564 Office: 81st Med Group 301 Fisher St Ste 201 Kessler AFB MS 39534

SHIVELY, JUDITH CAROLYN (JUDY SHIVELY), office assistant, billing clerk; b. Wilkinsburg, Pa., Jan. 30, 1962; d. John Allen and Edith (Crowell) S. BA in English, U. Nev., Las Vegas, 1984. Circulation aide Charleston Heights Libr., Las Vegas, 1979-86; asst. food editor Las Vegas Sun Newspaper, 1985-88, asst. horse racing editor, 1985-90, features writer, page editor, 1988-89, editor youth activities sect., 1989-90; racebook ticket writer, cashier Palace Sta. Hotel Racebook, Las Vegas, 1989-92; billing clk., gen. office asst. Loomis Armored, Inc., Las Vegas, 1992—; horse racing historian, researcher, Las Vegas, 1985—; vol. rsch. asst. Dictionary of Gambling and Gaming, 1982-84; part-time clk. Hometown News, Las Vegas, 1994—. Staff writer horse race handicaps, columns, articles, feature stories Las Vegas Sun Newspaper, 1985-90; freelance writer for monthly horse racing publ. Inside Track, 1992—. Mem. Phi Beta Kappa. Republican. Home: PO Box 26426 Las Vegas NV 89126-0426

SHIVERS, JANE, corporate executive, director; b. Georgetown, Tex., June 29, 1943; d. Marvin Bishop and Jewell (Petrey) Edwards; m. Harold E. Shivers; children: Clay Houston, Will Davis; m. Don Evans Hutcheson. BA, U. Md., 1965. Reseacher Amex Broadcasting Co., San Francisco, 1965-67; pub. info. officer Semester at Sea, Orange, Calif., 1967-69; dir. pub. rels. Atlanta Arts Alliance, 1974-78, RSVT, Atlanta, 1978-82; pres. Shivers Communications, Atlanta, 1982-84; exec. v.p., dir. Ketchum Pub. Rels., Atlanta, 1985—; pres. Midtown Bus. Assocs., Atlanta, 1987-91; bd. dirs. Crown Cryts, Inc. Trustee Alliance Theatre Co., Atlanta, 1980-93, Care, Internat., Atlanta, 1988-89; bd. dirs. Piedmont Park Conservancy, Emory Sch. Pub. Health. Recipient Mgmt. Woman Achievement award Women in Communication, Atlanta, 1984. Mem. Pub. Rels. Soc. Am. (bd. dirs.), Cen. Atlanta Progress Club, Commerce Club, Peachtree Club, Crown Crafts, Inc. (bd. dirs.). Episcopalian. Home: 238 15th St NE Atlanta GA 30309-3594 Office: Ketchum Pub Rels 999 Peachtree St NE Atlanta GA 30309-3964

SHKURKIN, EKATERINA VLADIMIROVNA (KATIA SHKURKIN), social worker; b. Berkeley, Calif., Nov. 20, 1955; d. Vladimir Vladimirovich and Olga Ivanovna (Lisenko) S. Student, U. San Francisco, 1972-73; BA, U. Calif., Berkeley, 1974-77; MSW, Columbia U., 1977-79; postgrad., Union Grad. Sch., 1986. Cert. police instr. domestic violence, Alaska. Social worker Tolstoy Found., N.Y.C., 1978-79, adminstr., 1979-80; program supr. Rehab. Mental Health Ctr., San Jose, Calif., 1980-81; dir. svc. counselor Kodiak (Alaska) Crisis Ctr., 1981-82; domestic violence counselor Abused Women's Aid in Crisis, Anchorage, 1982-85; pvt. practice social work specializing in feminist therapy Susitna Therapy Ctr., Anchorage, 1985—; pvt. practice, 1985-89; field instr. Abused Women's Aid in Crisis, Anchorage, 1983-88, Divsn. Family and Youth Svcs., State of Alaska, 1989-91, South Cen. Found.-Dena A. Coy Prematernal Alcohol Treatment Ctr., 1991-92; expert witness Anchorage Mcpl. Cts., 1982—; interim faculty mem. U. Alaska, Anchorage, summer 1985, fall 1988—, LaVerne U., Anchorage, 1986—; family therapist Anchorage Ctr. for Families, 1994—. Coordinator Orthodox Christian Fellowship, San Francisco, 1972-76; pub. speaker Abused Women's Aid in Crisis, Anchorage, 1982—; active nat. and local election campaigns, 1968—. Mem. NASW (cert.). Democrat. Russian Orthodox. Home and Office: 3605 Arctic Blvd # 768 Anchorage AK 99503-5789

SHOBE, JANICE W., business educator; b. McCook, Nebr., Oct. 23, 1950; d. Carl William and Nila Fay (Post) Wesch; m. Kenneth M. Shobe, Aug. 23, 1969; children: Mark, Emily. BS in Edn., Kans. State U., 1971; MBA, U. S.D., 1982. Sr. trainer Mut. of Omaha, 1988-91; instr. bus. mgmt. Met. C.C., Omaha, 1991—; adj. instr. Bellevue Coll., Coll. of St. Mary, Omaha, 1987-88, Merced (Calif.) C.C., 1985-86, Black Hills (S.D.) State Coll., 1982-83. Mem. ASTD. Democrat. Methodist. Home: 1002 Rogers Dr Papillion NE 68128-6112 Office: Met CC PO Box 3777 Omaha NE 68103-0777

SHOBE-WESTBROOK, KAREN LYNN, special education educator; b. Gainesville, Tex., Oct. 13, 1938; d. Paul Joseph and Linnie P. (Billingsley) Shobe; children: Tammy Rivera, Terrence Proffer, Sheree Shobe Hazlewood, Paula Brant, Dava Westbrook. BS, U. North Tex., 1959; cert., Tex. Women's U., 1976; postgrad., Tex. A&M, 1982. Cert. elem. edn. tchr., lang./learning disabilities tchr., mentally retarded and emotionally disturbed tchr. Tchr. Ft. Worth Christian Acad., 1958, Colleyville-Grapevine (Tex.) Schs., 1963, Malta (Europe) Internat. Sch., 1977-79; resource tchr. Tex. A&M Consolidated Sch., College Station, 1980-82, 85-89; cons. Jakarta (Indonesia) Internat. Sch., 1982-83; emotionally disturbed educator Midland (Tex.) Ind. Sch. Dist., 1989-91; resource tchr. Aransas County Ind. Sch. Dist., Rockport, Tex., 1991—. Mem. Tex. State Tchrs. Assn. (sec. 1993-94, membership com. 1991-92), Eastern Star (color station 1988-89, line officer, Svc. award 1989), Bus. and Profl. Women (Svc. award 1993), Am. Women's Club Malta (sec. 1977-78, Silver Tray Svc. award 1978). Home: 146 West Lake # 106 Rockport TX 78382

SHOCKLEY, CAROL FRANCES, psychologist, psychotherapist; b. Atlanta, Nov. 24, 1948; d. Robert Thomas and Frances Lavada (Scrivner) S. BA, Ga. State U., 1974, MEd, 1976; PhD, U. Ga., 1990. Cert. in gerontology. Counselor Rape Crisis Ctr., Atlanta, 1979-80; emergency mental health clinician Gwinnett Med. Ctr., Lawrenceville, Ga., 1980-86; psychotherapist Fla. Mental Health Inst., Tampa, 1987-89, Tampa Bay Acad., Riverview, Fla., 1990-91; sr. psychologist State of Fla. Dept. of Corrections, Bushnell, 1991-92; ind. practice psychology St. Marys, Brunswick, Ga., 1992—; mem. Adv. Bd. for Mental Health/Mental Retardation, 1992-94. Author: (with others) Relapse Prevention with Sex Offenders, 1989. Vol. Ga. Mental Health Inst., Atlanta, 1972; leader Alzheimer's Disease Support Group, Athens, Ga., 1984; vol. therapist Reminiscence Group for Elderly, Athens, 1984-85. Recipient Meritorious Svc. award Beta Gamma Sigma, 1975. Mem. Am. Counseling Assn., Am. Psychol. Assn., Ga. Psychol. Assn., Sigma Phi Omega, Psi Chi. Office: 14 Saint Andrews Court Brunswick GA 31520

SHOCKLEY, LEILA MAHSHI, insurance broker executive; b. Flint, Mich., Nov. 5, 1958; d. Amin and Janet (Deek) Mahshi; m. Everett Wayne Shockley, May 27, 1989. CPCU. Exec. sec. Al-Ghanim, Kuwait, Kuwait, 1977-78; paralegal sec. Brobeck, Phelger & Harrison, San Francisco, 1978; adminstrv. sec. Corroon & Black, San Francisco, 1979-81, account asst., 1981-84, mgr. small comml. and personal lines, 1984-89; acct. exec., asst. v.p. Willis Corroon, San Francisco, 1989-92, acct. exec., v.p. oper., property and casualty divsn., 1992-94, sr. v.p., 1994—. Mem. San Francisco Ins. Womens Assn. (pres. 1985-86), Women Constrn. Owners and Execs. U.S.A. (bd. dirs. 1990-93), CPCU Soc. (chmn. Ins. Industry Day Golden Gate chpt. 1992, co-chmn. 1993).

SHOCKLEY, SARAH ANNE, publishing company executive; b. Greenwich, Conn., Oct. 30, 1954; d. Robert Bartlett and Cora Merritt (Keith) S. BA in German, U. Vt., 1976; MBA in Internat. Mktg., Monterey Inst. Internat. Studies, 1982. Mgr. Caribbean, Ams. and Far East Computerland Corp., Hayward, Calif., 1984-85, mgr. internat. product mktg., 1985-86; contracts and grants adminstr. Lawrence Berkeley (Calif.) Lab., 1990-92; co-owner Dancing Video, El Cerrito, Calif., 1994—; owner Any Road Press, El Cerrito, 1994—. Author: Traveling Incognito, 1994; dir. video documentary Dancing From the Inside Out, 1994. Recipient Chris award Colombus Internat. Film and Video Festival, 1994, Golden plaque Intercom Chgo. Internal Film Festival, 1994. Office: 1138C Hearst Ave Berkeley CA 94702 Office: Any Road Press 190 El Cerrito Plz Ste 204 El Cerrito CA 94530

SHOCKLEY, VALERIE DAWN, software developer; b. Denver, Feb. 11, 1966; d. Ted D. and Virginia R. (Senty) S. BS in Computer Sci., U. Denver, 1988. Tech. analyst Galileo Internat., Englewood, Colo., 1988—. Mem. Rocky Mountain Rd. Runners, Colo. Mountain Club, Alpha Chi Omega, Phi Beta Kappa. Mem. Cherry Hills Community Ch. Office: Galileo Internat 5350 S Valentia Way Englewood CO 80111-3102

SHOE, MARGARET ELLEN, accountant; b. Phila., Feb. 10, 1944; d. Francis James and Margaret Edna (Hathaway) Wiedenmann; m. Richard Alan Shoe, Feb. 14, 1964 (div. Aug. 1975). Associates, Burlington County Coll., 1978; BS, Trenton State Coll., 1982. Lic. pub. acct.; lic. real estate salesperson. Acct., office mgr. Philmar Constrn. Co., Somerdale, N.J., 1967-72; acct. Microcircuit Engring., Medford, N.J., 1972-73, R.L. Fitzwater and Son, Inc., Merchantville, N.J., 1973-75; asst. contr. Bancroft Sch. and Instrn., Haddonfield, N.J., 1976-79; corp. contr. Paparone Constrn. Co. Inc., Mt. Laurel, N.J., 1979; asst. contr. Reutter Engring. Inc., Camden, N.J., 1979-80; corp. contr. CSI Electronics, Inc., Cinnaminson, N.J., 1980, Wagner Holm and Inglis, Inc., Mt. Holly, N.J., 1980-81; pub. acct. Shoe Acctg. and Consulting Svc., Mt. Laurel, N.J., 1981—; acctg. clk. Robert C. Perina, CPA, Camden, 1968-69; bookkeeper, acctg. clk. Lantern Lane Interiors, Cherry Hill, N.J., 1967; bookkeeper, cost acctg. clk. Drew Constrn. Co., Inc., Cherry Hill, 1964-66; bookkeeper, time study clk. Mailing Svcs., Inc., Pennsauken, N.J., 1963-64. Recipient Woman of Achievement award Burlington County Freeholders, 1990. Mem. N.J. Assn. Pub. Accts. (pres. 1992-93, bd. dirs. 1988—, Camden pres., v.p. 1988-91), N.J. Assn. Women Bus. Owners (bd. dirs. 1981—, del. White House conf. on small bus. 1984), Burlington County Bd. Realtors, Inst. Managerial Accts. (assoc.). Lutheran. Home and Office: Shoe Acctg and Consulting 623 Union Mill Rd Mount Laurel NJ 08054

SHOEMAKER, CHRISTINE A., civil and environmental engineering educator; b. Berkeley, Calif., July 2, 1944; children: Erica, Greg. BS in Math., U. Calif., 1966; student, U. Goettingen, W. Germany, 1964-65; MS in Math., U. So. Calif., 1969, PhD in Math., 1971. Asst. prof., Sch. of Civil and Environ. Engring. Cornell U., Ithaca, N.Y., 1972-79, assoc. prof., Sch. of Civil and Environ. Engring., 1979-85, assoc. dir., Sch. of Civil and Environ. Engring., 1983-85, chair, dept. environ. engring., 1985-88, prof., Sch. of Civil and Environ. Engring., 1985—; co-chmn. Internat. Groundwater Contamination Project for Sci. Com. on Problems of Environ. (SCOPE), 1987—; vis. fellow Dambridge (Eng.) U., 1988, life fellow Clare Hall, 1990—; mem. panel on groundwater contamination NAS, 1984-86, study on pest ctrl., 1973-75; mem. UN panel on pest mgmt. FOA, 1981-84; cons. World Bank, Internat. Irrigation Mgmt. Inst.; prin. investigator on rsch. grants from NSF, EPA, U.S. Geol. Survey, USDA, Ford Found., IBM. Contbr. to profl. jours. Recipient Disting. Educator award Soc. Women Engrs., 1991. Mem. IEEE, ASCE, Am. Assn. Environ. Engring. Profs., Operations Rsch. Soc. Am., Am. Geophysical Union, Soc. Indsl. and Applied Math., Entomology Soc. Am. Office: Cornell U Sch Civil and Environ Engring Hollister Hall Ithaca NY 14853

SHOEMAKER, CLARA BRINK, retired chemistry educator; b. Rolde, Drenthe, The Netherlands, June 20, 1921; came to U.S., 1953; d. Hendrik Gerard and Hendrikje (Smilde) Brink; m. David Powell Shoemaker, Aug. 5, 1955; 1 child, Robert Brink. PhD, Leiden U., The Netherlands, 1950. Instr. in inorganic chemistry Leiden U., 1946-50, 51-53; postdoctoral fellow Oxford (Eng.) U., 1950-51; rsch. assoc. dept. chemistry MIT, Cambridge, 1953-55, 58-70; rsch. assoc. biochemistry Harvard Med. Sch., Boston, 1955-56; project supr. Boston U., 1963-64; rsch. assoc. dept. chemistry Oreg. State U, Corvallis, 1970-75, rsch. assoc. prof. dept. chemistry, 1975-82, sr. rsch. prof. dept. chemistry, 1982-84, prof. emerita, 1984—. Sect. editor: Structure Reports of International Union of Crystallography, 1967, 68, 69; co-author chpts. in books; author numerous sci. papers. Bd. dirs. LWV, Corvallis, 1980-82, bd. dirs., sec., Oreg., 1985-87. Fellow Internat. Fedn. Univ. Women, Oxford U., 1950-51. Mem. Metall. Soc. (com. on alloy phases 1969-79), Internat. Union of Crystallography (commn. on structure reports 1970-90), Am. Crystallographic Assn. (crystallographic data com. 1975-78, Fankuchen award com. 1976), Sigma Xi, Iota Sigma Pi (faculty adv. Oreg. State U. chpt. 1975-84), Phi Lambda Upsilon. Office: Oreg State U Dept Chemistry Corvallis OR 97331

SHOEMAKER, ELEANOR BOGGS, television production company executive; b. Gulfport, Miss., Jan. 20, 1935; d. William Robertson and Bessie Eleanor (Ware) Boggs; m. D. Shoemaker, April 9, 1955 (div. 1987); children: Daniel W., William Boggs. Student in protocol, Southeastern U., 1952-53; student, George Washington U., Washington, 1953-56; BA in Communications and Polit. Sci. with honrs, Goucher Coll., 1981; postgrad., Villanova U. Feature writer Washington Times Herald, 1951-54; dir. Patricia Stevens Modeling Agy., Washington, 1955-56; free-lance model Julius Garfinkel, Woodward & Lothrop, Washington, 1951-56; research analyst Balt. County Council, Towson, Md., 1980-81; feature news reporter Sta. WGCB-TV, Red Lion, Pa., 1980—; pub. speaker, protocol The Reliable Corp., Columbia, Md., 1982-86; media cons. The Enterprise Found., Columbia, Md., 1985-86; faculty, TV prodn. and communication St. Francis Prep Sch., Spring Grove, Pa., 1985-88; owner Windswept Prodns. Co., Felton, Pa., 1984—; mktg. svcs. coord. Yorktowne, Inc., Red Lion, Pa., 1993—; mem. conservation bd. Pa. Parks and Recreation Soc., 1984—; prodr. The Pa. County TV Prodn., 1981; prodr., host Westar 4 Channel 9 half hour weekly news program Keystone Report. Prodr. The Pa. County TV Prodn., 1981, The Pa. County TV Prodn., 1981, documentary Human Rights: A Special Report, Sta. WGCB-TV, 1989; prodr., host Westar 4 Channel 9 half hour weekly news program Keystone Report, 1990. Bd. dirs. York (Pa.) County Parks and Recreation, 1972-87, YWCA, York, 1957-82, Hist. York, 1990—; mem. exec. com. York County Reps., 1972-82; accreditation adv. com. York Coll. of Pa.; instr. YWCA Women in Politics; founder, mem. Child Abuse Task Force, York, 1983—; mem. select com. Pa. Agrl. Zoning, 1988; mem. steering com. York Forum, 1989—; co-chmn. Cross Mill Restoration, 1987—; mem. Displaced Homemaker's Bd., 1989—, pres., 1993—; bd. dirs. Hist. York, 1990—; founder, host Old Rose Tree Pony Club, 1967—; chair Spring Valley County Pk. Task Force, 1972; master of fox hounds Mrs. Shoemaker's Hounds, 1969—; master of beagles Mrs. Shoemaker's Weybright Beagles, 1988—. Recipient pro bono child legal representation grant Pa. Bar Assn., 1983, Pa. Tree Farmer of Yr. award, 1987, Outstanding Achievement in Broadcasting award Am. Women in Radio and TV, 1992, Lay Person of Yr. award Pa. Recreation and Parks Assn. and Gov. Thornburg, 1982, Jefferson award, 1992, Matrix award Ctrl. Pa. Women in Comm., 1993, First pl. corp. video prodn. Ctrl. Pa. Women in Comm., 1993; selected journalist for Novosti Press USSR-U.S. Press Exch. program, 1989. Mem. Am. Polled Hereford Assn., York Area C. of C., York County C. of C. (publicity com. 1985—, agri. bus. com.), Masters of Foxhounds Assn. Episcopalian. Home and Office: PO Box 167 Felton PA 17322-0167

SHOEN, JUDITH ANNE, marketing company executive; b. Rockford, Ill., Dec. 25, 1940; d. Abe J. and Bertha Deborah (Polinsky) S. B.S., U. Wis., 1962. Editorial asst. Mademoiselle Mag., N.Y.C., 1962-63; food editor Restaurants & Instns. mag., Chgo., 1963-64, merchandising editor, 1964-66, sr. editor, 1971-74; Eastern editor, internat. editor Svc. World Internat. mag., N.Y.C., 1966-71, editor-in-chief, N.Y.C., 1967-71, Chgo., 1971-74; dir. pub. rels. Dispenser Juice Distbrs./Consol. Foods, San Francisco, 1974-75; pres. Judith Shoen Assocs., San Francisco, 1975-78; v.p. Foote, Cone & Belding, San Francisco, 1978-81, also dir. FCB Foodservice; dir. mktg. Telstar Corp., San Francisco, 1981-82; pres. Foodsvc. Promotions, Inc., Mill Valley, Calif., 1982-85, Washington, 1985-89, Scottsdale, Ariz., 1989—; pres., chief exec. officer Foodsvc. Focus Inc., Scottsdale, 1989—; pres., founder Summit Leadership Confs., Inc. (divsn. of Foodsvc. Focus), 1992—. Mem. Internat. Foodsvc. Mfrs. Assn., Internat. Foodsvc. Editors Coun., Mktg. Execs. Group Nat. Restaurant Assn., Les Dames d'Escoffier, Alpha Epsilon Phi, Theta Sigma Phi. Office: 10279 N 79th St Scottsdale AZ 85258-1241

SHOENBERGER, BARBARA FRANCES, artist, educator; b. Cin., Jan. 16, 1938; m. Charles Edward Shoenberger, Jan. 3, 1959 (div.); 1 child, Susan. BS in Design, U. Cin., 1961, postgrad., 1961-83, 86-88; postgrad., Art Acad. Cin., 1974. Art instr. Operation Head Start, Cin., 1964-66; grad. teaching asst. U. Cin., 1977-79; substitute tchr. Cin. Pub. Schs., 1979-80; instr. in art history and fine art Thomas More Coll., Ft. Thomas, Ky., 1980-81, 83-84; art instr. Arts Consortium of Cin., 1983-86; painting instr. Cin. Women's Club, 1987, 88; tutor U. Cin., 1979-81, part-time instr. in fine arts, 1983—, lectr. in fine art, evening coll., 1980-81; cons. Ohio Arts Coun., Columbus, 1980; mem. com. Cin. Zoo Arts; tour guide Cin. Art Mus. One-woman shows include U. Cin. Coll. Medicine, 1985, 92, numerous others; exhibited in group shows at Conf. Cin. Women, 1986, 87, 88, 89, Nantucket, Mass. juried group show, 1987, U. Cin. Coll. Medicine, 1994; contbr. photographs to MacDowell Colony Newsletter, drawing to Cin. Mag. Recipient Cert. of Merit, Pres. Lyndon B. Johnson, 1966, 1st award for art Conf. Cin. Women, 1987; grantee U. Cin., 1980; MacDowell Colony fellow, 1986. Home: 274 Senator Pl Apt 15 Cincinnati OH 45220-1721

SHOENIGHT, PAULINE ALOISE SOUERS (ALOISE TRACY), author; b. Bridgeport, Ill., Nov. 20, 1914; d. William Fitch and Carrie (Milhouse) Souers; m. James Richard Tracy, Sept. 18, 1946 (dec. Aug. 1972); m. 2nd, Hurley F. Shoenight, June 25, 1976. BEd, Eastern Ill. U., 1937 . Mem. hon. bd. advs. Am. Biog. Inst; active Nat. Arbor Day Found. Mem. Nat. Ret. Tchrs. Assn., Eastern Ill. Alumni Assn. (life), PEO Sisterhood, Am. Bible Soc., Am. Poets Fellowship Soc. (hon. life mem.), Pleasure Island Sr. Citizens Club (charter), Ill. Poetry Soc. (charter), Ala. State Poetry Soc., Acad. Am. Poets, Baldwin Heritage Mus. Assn. (charter life), Friends of U. Mo. Libraries (life), Friends of Foley Library, 1000 Club. Republican. Baptist. Club: Bible-A-Month. Author: His Handiwork, 1954, Memory is a Poet, 1964, The Silken Web, 1965, A Merry Heart, 1966, In Two or Three Tomorrows, 1968, All Flesh Is Grass, 1971, Beyond The Edge, 1973. Address: 7425 Riverwood Dr W Foley AL 36535-4075

SHOHEN, SAUNDRA ANNE, health care communications and public relations executive; b. Washington, Aug. 22, 1934; d. Aaron Kohn and Malvina (Kleiman) Kohn Blinder; children: Susan, Brian. BS, Columbia Pacific U., 1979, MS in Health Svcs. Adminstrn., 1981. Adminstr. social work dept. Roosevelt Hosp., N.Y.C., 1978-79; adminstr. emergency dept. St. Luke's-Roosevelt Hosp. Ctr., N.Y.C., 1979-83, assoc. dir. pub. rels., 1983-87; pres. Saundra Shohen Assocs., Ltd., N.Y.C., 1987—; bd. dirs. Tureck Bach Inst., N.Y.C., 1985—; panelist ann. Emmy awards NATAS, N.Y.C., 1983, 84; tchr. healthcare mktg. Baruch Coll., N.Y.C., 1994. Author: EMERGENCY!, 1989, (health scripts for radio) Voice of America, 1983 (Presdl. Recognition award 1984), (with others) AIDS: A Health Care Management Response, 1987. Mem. NATAS, Internat. Hosp. Fedn., Am. Soc. Hosp. Mktg. and Pub. Rels., Vols. in Tech. Assistance. Democrat. Jewish. Home: 240 Central Park S New York NY 10019-1413 Office: 488 Madison Ave New York NY 10022-5702

SHOJI, JUNE MIDORI, import and export trading executive; b. Long Beach, Calif., June 21, 1957; d. Sam Masatsugu and Tomiyo (Kinoshita) S. BA in Psychology and Econs., UCLA, 1975-79; cert. Japanese, Waseda U., Tokyo, 1980-82; Grad. Gemologist, Gemol. Inst., Santa Monica, Calif., 1984. Mktg. rep. IBM Corp., L.A., 1982-84, Xerox Corp., El Monte, Calif., 1984-86; adminstrv. drilling analyst Arco Internat. Oil & Gas, L.A., 1986-89; buyer OEM components & machinery Honda Trading Am., Torrance, Calif., 1989-94, asst. mgr. OEM components machinery and non-ferrous metals, 1994—. Home: 1865 W 166th St Gardena CA 90247-4664

SHOLAR, ELIZABETH ANN, newspaper executive; b. Middletown, Ohio, Nov. 22, 1960; d. James Rodman and Ellen Elizabeth S. BA, U. Ill., 1985; postgrad. in Info. Systems, Allentown Coll., 1993—, Am. Press Inst., 1995. Art dept. coord. Crouse Printing Co., Champaign, Ill., 1982-83; paste-up artist Omegatype Typography, Champaign, 1983-85; prodn. systems ops. supr. Chgo. Tribune, 1985-87; mgr. pre-press The Morning Call, Allentown, Pa., 1987—. Vol. Big Bros./Big Sisters, Allentown, 1990-91; mem. Hawk Mt. Sanctuary, Kempton, Pa., 1990—, Allentown Art Mus., 1994—; participant in Leadership Lehigh Valley, 1994-95. Mem. Sigma Kappa Lehigh Valley Alumnae (Triangle corr. 1989-94, coll. province officer Indpls. 1991-93). Republican. Roman Catholic. Office: The Morning Call 101 N 6th St Allentown PA 18101-1403

SHOMO, CAROLE, association executive; b. Syracuse, N.Y., Dec. 3, 1946; d. Matthew B. and Mary (Degnan) Cooke; m. Douglas A. Shomo, Dec. 19, 1970; 1 child, Matthew John. BS in Health and Human Svcs. magna cum laude, Roger Williams Coll., 1977; MSW in Adminstrn., U. Conn., 1986. Asst. dir. crisis nursery Family Svc. Agy. Greater Waterbury, Inc., 1977-78; coord. child protection team Manchester Community Svc. Coun., 1978-81; dir. Time Out for Parents, 1981-86; dir. YWCA Hartford (Conn.) Region, 1986-87, dir. ops., 1988-91; assoc. exec. dir. United Way, Conn., 1987-88; exec. dir. YWCA, Manchester, N.H., 1991—; faculty advisor U. N.H., 1994—. Recipient Child Adv. award Manchester Community Svc. Coun., 1984, Nat. Program award Am. Assn. Protecting Children, 1986. Office: YWCA of Manchester 72 Concord St Manchester NH 03101-1823

SHONO, FUJIKO, architect; b. Japan, Sept. 22, 1953; came to U.S., 1976; d. Kaneshi and Harue (Otsuka) S.; m. Richard D. Browning, Aug. 24, 1982. Med. sci., Kyushu U., Fukuoka, Japan, 1975; BArch, Fla. A&M U., 1981; MArch, U. Oreg., 1987. Lic. med. technologist, Japan; registered architect, Oreg. Intern architect Robertson/Sherwood Architects, Eugene, Oreg., 1987-90; architect MCM Architects, Portland, Oreg., 1991-93; ptnr. Browning & Shono Architects, Portland, 1993—.

SHOOK, ANN JONES, lawyer; b. Canton, Ohio, Apr. 18, 1925; d. William M. and Lura (Pontius) Jones; m. Gene E. Shook Sr., Nov. 30, 1956; children: Scott, William, Gene Edwin Jr. AB, Wittenberg U., 1947; LLB, William McKinley Law Sch., 1955. Bar: Ohio 1956, U.S. Dist. Ct. (no. dist.) Ohio 1961, U.S. Ct. Appeals (6th cir.) 1981. Cost acct. Hoover Co., North Canton, Ohio, 1947-51; asst. sec. Stark County Prosecutor's Office, Canton, Ohio, 1951-53; ins. adjuster Traveler's Ins. Co., Canton, 1953-56; ptnr. Shook & Shook Law Firm, Toledo, 1958-62, North Olmsted, Ohio, 1962—. Mem. at large coun. Olmsted Community Ch., Olmsted Falls, Ohio, 1987-90; chmn. ways and means com. North Olmsted PTA, 1968; area chmn. United Way Appeal, North Olmsted, 1963; v.p. LWV, Toledo, 1960-62. Mem. Cleve. Bar Assn.

SHOPE, CLAUDIA, property specialist; b. Montreal, Que., Can., June 16, 1954; came to U.S., 1955; d. Richard Allan and Patricia Ray (Palmer) S. Student, Rider Coll., 1972-73; BA cum laude, Boston U., 1976; paralegal cert., Bentley Coll., 1977; postgrad., Oxford (Eng.) U., 1980; JD, Santa Clara Law Sch., 1982. Substitute tchr. City of Boston, 1976; weekend mgr. Bostonian Soc. Old State House Mus., Boston, 1976-79; graphic computer builder Adage, Boston, 1977; spl. svc. worker Mass. Parole Bd., Boston, 1978-79; law clk. Atwood & Hurst, Sharon Hermosilo, Mattews & Marzula, San Jose, Calif., 1981, Comty. Legal Svcs., San Jose, 1981-82; housing counselor mortgage default San Jose Housing Svc. Ctr., 1982-84; sr. property specialist Santa Clara (Calif.) County, 1984—; program developer N.J. State Home for Girls, Trenton, 1973; mem. Santa Clara Pub. Interest Law Found., 1980-82; negotiator local 715 Social Svcs., San Jose, 1985-87, asst. chief steward, 1989—, union steward, 1984—. Editor, dir.: (periodical) Parole Scroll, 1978-79; filmmaker: (ednl. film) How to Handle Your Own Landlord Tenant Or Small Claims Case, 1982. Bd. dirs. Dawn Dem. Activist Women Now, San Jose, 1993—; active Dem. Ctrl. Com., San Jose, 1994-95; bd. dirs. Pro-Choice Coalition, San Jose; mem. South Bay AFL-CIO Labor Coun., 1994—. Mem. NOW, Nat. Lawyers Guild, Sierra Club. Unitarian. Home: 1206 Plum St San Jose CA 95110-3414 Office: County Santa Clara Recovery & Legal Svcs 300 S 2d St San Jose CA 95113

SHORE, CAROLE JEAN, nutritionist; b. Dayton, Ohio, Dec. 7, 1948; d. Erroll Victor and Mabell B. (Pallanch) Black; m. Michael J. Shore, June 5, 1976; 1 child, Victoria Jean. BS, Ohio State U., 1971, MS, 1975. Intern Harvard U. Med. Ctr., Boston, 1971-72; pub. health nutritionist Polk County (Fla.) Health Dept., Winter Haven, 1972-73; asst. prof., program dir. Hood Coll., Frederick, Md., 1975-76; nutrition analyst USDA Consumer and Food Econs. Inst., Hyattsville, Md., 1976-79, USDA Human Nutrition Info. Service, Hyattsville, 1979-82; tech. info. specialist USDA Nat. Agrl. Library, Beltsville, Md., 1982-90; coord. Nat. Food Irradiation Info. Ctr.; chief of quality mgmt. for clin. nutrition-computer programs Dept. Vets. Affairs, Washington, 1990—. Author: (with others) Promoting Nutrition Through Education, 1985, Practice Guidelines for VA Dietetic Services, 1994, 95, Nutrition Status Classification Scheme, 1995; contbr. articles to profl. jours. Mem. ASTD, Am. Dietetic Assn. (Recognized Young Dietitian 1979, treas. Comty. Nutrition Rsch. Group 1981-83, chair 1984-85), Clin. Nutrition Mgmt., D.C. Met. Area Dietetic Assn. (chair coun. on practice 1980-82, 87-88, treas. 1982-84, pres. elect 1988-89, pres. 1989-90, chair state adv. com. Am. Dietetic Assn. conv. 1991), Soc. for Nutrition Edn., Inst. Food Technologists, Omicron Nu, Phi Upsilon Omicron. Republican. Roman Catholic. Home: 6356 Crosswoods Dr Falls Church VA 22044-1210 Office: Dept Vets Affairs Washington DC 20420

SHORE, CARON DEAN, commercial real estate executive; b. Tillamook, Oreg., Oct. 24, 1949; d. Wayne Dickerson and Louise Margaret (Burge) Dean; 1 child, Jacqueline Lisa. BS, U. Oreg., 1971; MA, Washington U., 1973. Rsch. analyst Ind. Colls. and Univs. of Mo., St. Louis, 1972-74; purchasing agt. Paragon Group, Inc., St. Louis, 1974-75, property mgr., 1975-77, mgr. of residential adminstrn., 1977-81, mgr. of corp. adminstrn., 1982-84; asst. v.p. corp. adminstrn. and human resources Paragon Group, Inc., 1984-91; v.p. adminstrn. and human resources Paragon Group Inc., St. Louis, 1991-94, Paragon Group Property Svcs., Inc., St. Louis, 1994—; v.p. Paragon Group Property Svcs., Inc., Dallas, 1995—; v.p. Tex. PGI, Inc., St. Louis, 1994—, Dallas, 1995—. Contbr. articles to profl. jours. Course dir. Paragon Run for Juvenile Diabetes, St. Louis, 1985, Paragon Run for Spl. Olympics, St. Louis, 1986, Paragon Run to benefit U.S. Olympics, St. Louis, 1987-88, Old Newsboys; Day for United Way, 1987-94; vol. Berean House, 1991-93, U.S. Olympic Festival, 1994. Mem. Am. Assn. Indsl. Mgmt., Comml. Real Estate Women (bd. dirs. 1993-95), Soc. for Human Resource Mgmt., Assn. Legal Adminstrs., Order Ea. Star. Republican. Home: 5750 East University Apt 524 Dallas TX 75206 Office: Paragon Group Property Svcs Inc 7557 Rambler Rd Ste 1300 Dallas TX 75206

SHORE, MELISSA CLAIRE, accountant; b. St. Louis, Jan. 5, 1966; d. Richard Eugene and Victoria Pearl (Whiteside) S. BS in Acctg., U. Ky., 1988; MBA in Fin., U. Mo., 1990. Tax analyst IBM, Southbury, Conn., 1990-92; cost staff acct. Universal Fasteners, Inc., Lawrenceburg, Ky., 1992—. Lector Christ Ch. Cathedral Episcopal, contbr. newsletter; usher Actors Theatre, Louisville; mem. Wieker Groark Election Com., Waterbury, Conn., 1990-91. Mem. Inst. Mgmt. Accts., Lexington Jaycees (bd. dirs. 1993—, artistic dir. Haunted House project 1994), Delta Zeta Soc. (Alpha Theta chpt., adv. new mem. educator). Democrat. Home: 1585 Alexandria Dr Apt 2 Lexington KY 40504 Office: Universal Fasteners Factory Ave Lawrenceburg KY 40342

SHORENSTEIN, ROSALIND GREENBERG, physician; b. N.Y.C., Jan. 14, 1947; d. Albert Samuel and Natalie Miriam (Sherman) Greenberg; m. Michael Lewis Shorenstein, June 18, 1967; children: Anna Irene, Claire Beth. BA in Chemistry, Wellesley Coll., 1968; MA in Biochemistry and Molecular Biology, Harvard U., 1970, PhD in Biochemistry and Molecular Biology, 1973; MD, Stanford U., 1976. Diplomate Am. Bd. Internal Medicine. Resident in internal medicine UCLA Med. Ctr., 1976-79; pvt. practice internal medicine Santa Cruz, Calif., 1979—; mem. dept. internal medicine Dominican Hosp., Santa Cruz, 1979—; co-dir. med. svcs. Health Enhancement & Lifestyle Planning Systems, Santa Cruz, 1983—. Contbr. articles to profl. journals. Dir. Santa Cruz Chamber Players, 1993-94, pres., bd. dirs., 1994—. Recipient Charlie Parkhurst award Santa Cruz Women's Commn., 1989; NSF fellow, 1968-72, Sarah Perry Wood Med. fellow Wellesley Coll., 1972-76. Mem. Am. Soc. Internal Medicine (del. 1994), Calif. Soc. Internal Medicine (trustee 1994—), Am. Med. Women's Assn. (Outstanding Svc. award 1987, br. #59 pres. 1986—), Calif. Med. Assn. (com. on women 1987-93), Santa Cruz County Med. Soc. (mem. bd. govs. 1993—), Phi Beta Kappa, Sigma Xi. Jewish. Office: 700 Frederick St Ste 103 Santa Cruz CA 95062-2239

SHORES, JANIE LEDLOW, state supreme court justice; b. Georgiana, Ala., Apr. 30, 1932; d. John Wesley and Willie (Scott) Ledlow; m. James L. Shores, Jr., May 12, 1962; 1 child, Laura Scott. J.D., U. Ala., Tuscaloosa, 1959; LLM, U. Va., 1992. Bar: Ala. 1959. Pvt. practice Selma, 1959; mem. legal dept. Liberty Nat. Life Ins. Co., Birmingham, Ala., 1962-66; asso. prof. law Cumberland Sch. Law, Samford U., Birmingham, 1)66-74; asso. justice Supreme Ct. Ala., 1975—; legal adviser Ala. Constn. Revision Commn., 1973; mem. Nat. Adv. Council State Ct. Planning, 1976—. Contbr. articles to legal jours. Mem. Am. Bar Assn., Am. Judicature Soc., Farrah Order Jurisprudence. Democrat. Episcopalian. Office: Ala Supreme Ct 300 Dexter Ave Montgomery AL 36104-3742

SHORR, MIRIAM KRONFELDT, artist; b. N.Y.C.; m. Eli Yale Shorr, 1931. Student, Hunter Coll., 1921-25. Exhibited in ann. shows Audubon Artists, City Ctr. Gallery, N.Y.C., Nat. Soc. Painters in Casein; Knickerbocker, Whitney, Bklyn. and Norfolk Mus., Five Arts Soc., Sarasota, 1991-92; one man shows Brandeis U., Bklyn. Coll., U. Maine, Rutgers U., LaSalle Coll., Hillside U., Gettysburg Coll., U. Tampa, Miami, R.I., Albany, Ga. and Colby U. One-man shows throughout U.S.; one-man showing of tapestries Cen. Libr., St. Petersburg, Fla., 1982, Plymouth Harbor Gallery, Sarasota, 1990; one-man show paintings Ctr. Libr., Bradenton, Fla., 1988; numerous group shows. Recipient 1st prize for drawing Nat. Assn. Women Artists, 1962, Lena Newcastle award, 1961, 65, Aileen O. Webb prize, 1974, 1st prize Fibres and Fabrics, Longboat Key Art Assn., 1979, 1st prize enamels Venice (Fla.) Art Assn., 1982, 2d prize for painting Sarasota Art Assn., 1983, 1st prize Venice Art League, 1985, Ann. Parade of Prize Winners, 1982-88, Longboat Key Art Assn., 1982-88. Mem. Artists Equity Assn. (bd. dir. 1958-64), Nat. Assn. Women Artists (bd. dir. 1970-72), Sarasota Art Assn. (chmn. exhbns. 1976-78, editor The Bull. 1979-81), Art League Manatee County, Fla. Artists Group, Longboat Key Art Assn., Venice Art League. Home: 3435 Fox Run Rd Apt 102 Sarasota FL 34231

SHORT, ELIZABETH M., physician, educator, federal agency administrator; b. Boston, June 2, 1942; d. James Edward and Arlene Elizabeth (Mitchell) Meehan; m. Herbert M. Short, Sept. 2, 1963 (div. 1969); 1 child, Timothy Owen; m. Michael Allen Friedman, June 21, 1976; children: Lia Gabrielle, Hannah Ariel, Eleanor Elana. BA Philosophy magna cum laude, Mt. Holyoke Coll., 1963; MD cum laude, Yale U., 1968. Diplomate Am. Bd. Internal Medicine, Am. Bd. Med. Genetics. Intern, jr. resident internal medicine Yale New Haven Hosp., 1968-70; postdoctoral fellow in human genetics Yale Med. Sch., 1970-72; postdoctoral fellow in renal metabolism U. Calif., San Francisco, 1972-73; sr. resident in internal medicine Stanford (Calif.) Med. Sch., 1973-74, chief resident in internal medicine, 1974-75; staff physician Palo Alto Veterans Med. Ctr., Stanford, Calif., 1975-80; asst. prof. of medicine Stanford Med. Sch., 1975-83, asst. dean Student Affairs, 1978-80, assoc. dean Students Affairs/Medical Education, 1980-83; dir. biomed. rsch. and faculty devel. Assn. Am. Med. Colls., Washington, 1983-87, dep. dir. dept. acad. affairs, 1983-87, dep. dir. biomedical rsch., 1987-88; dep. assoc. chief med. dir. for acad. affairs VA, Washington, 1988-92, assoc. chief medical dir. for acad. affairs, 1992—; vis. prof. Human Biology, Stanford U., 1983-86; resource allocation com. Veteran's Health Adminstrn., 1989-91; budget planning and policy review coun. 1991—; planning review com. Veterans Health Adminstrn., 1991—; chair resident work limit task force 1991—; managed care task force, 1993-94; co-chair com. status women Am. Fedn. Clin. Rsch., 1975-77; mem. numerous adminstrv. coms., Yale Med. Sch., Stanford U.; accreditation coun. grad. med. edn., 1988—; mem. public policy com. Am. Soc. Human Genetics, 1984—, chair, 1986-94; mem. White House Task Force on Health Care Reform, 1993-94. assoc. editor Clin. Rsch. Jour., 1976-79, editor elect, 1979-80, editor 1980-84; contbr. articles to profl. jours. Mem. nat. child health adv. coun. NIH, 1991—; mem. com. edn. and tng. Office Sci. and Tech. Policy, 1991—. Recipient Maclean Zoology award Mt. Holyoke Coll.; Munger scholar, Markle scholar, Sara Williston scholar Mt. Holyoke Coll., 1959-63, Yale Men in Medicine scholar, 1964-68; Bardwell Meml. Med. fellow, 1963. Mem. AAAS, Am. Soc. Human Genetics, Am. Fedn. Clin. Rsch. (bd. dirs. 1973-83, editor 1978-83, nat. coun., exec. com., pub. policy com. 1977-87), Am. Assn. Women in Scis., Western Soc. Clin. Investigation, Calif. Acad. Medicine, Phi Beta Kappa, Alpha Omega Alpha. Home: 6807 Bradley Blvd Bethesda MD 20817-3004 Office: Dept Veterans Affairs Vets Health Adminstrn Acad Affairs 810 Vermont Ave VHA 14 Washington DC 20420

SHORT, JILL MARIE, critical care nurse; b. Manitowoc, Wis., June 9, 1964; d. William Arnold and Janice Marie (Kuehl) S. BSN, U. Wis., Milw., 1987; postgrad., U. Md., Balt. CCRN. Staff RN Good Samaritan Hosp., Milw., 1987-88, Holy Cross Hosp., Silver Spring, Md., 1989—; informatics specialist ISSC-IBM, 1995—. Mem. Capital Area Roundtable in Nursing Informatics, Sigma Theta Tau. Democrat. Home: 8270 Ahearn Dr Millersville MD 21108

SHORT, MARION PRISCILLA, neurologist; b. Milford, Del., June 12, 1951; d. Raymond Calistus and Barbara Anne (Ferguson) S.; m. Michael Peter Klein. BA, Bryn Mawr Coll., 1973; diploma, U. Edinburgh (Scotland), 1975; MD, Med. Coll. Pa., 1978. Diplomate Am. Bd. Psychiatry and Neurology, Am. Bd. Internal Medicine. Intern in internal medicine

Hahnemann Med. Coll. Hosp., Phila., 1978-79; med. resident in internal medicine St. Lukes-Roosevelt Hosp., N.Y.C., 1979-81; neurology resident U. Pitts. Health Ctr., 1981-84; fellow in med. genetics Mt. Sinai Med. Ctr., N.Y.C., 1984-86; fellow in neurology Mass. Gen. Hosp., Boston, 1986-90, asst. neurologist, 1990—; asst. prof. dept. neurology Harvard Med. Sch., 1990—; cons. Spaulding Rehab. Hosp., Boston. Recipient Clin. Investigator Devel. award NIH, 1988-93. Mem. Am. Acad. Neurology, Am. Soc. for Human Genetics. Office: Mass Gen Hosp Dept Neuropathology Warren 329 Mgh Fruit St Boston MA 02114

SHORT, NANCY KATHRYN, accountant; b. Pine Twp., Mo., June 13, 1945; d. Elmer Bruce and Elsie Nadine (Dodgen) Huffstutter; m. Donald Gene Short, Oct. 31, 1964 (div. June 22, 1992); children: Donald Bruce, Steven Craig, Jacquelyn Denise. BSBA, Mo. So. State Coll., 1994. Bookkeeper Don's Oil Co., Liberal, Mo., 1976-91; acct. Ken Reynolds Pharmacy, Joplin, Mo., 1992—; coord. VITA-Mo. So. State Coll., Joplin, 1994—, tax preparer, 1993—. Recipient IMA scholarship Joplin Tri County Chpt., 1992, 93, scholarship to Oxford U., Mo. So. State Coll., 1993; named to summer program Oxford, Fla. State U., 1993. Mem. Inst. Mgmt. Accts., Mo. So. State Coll. Acctg. Club. Home: 969 NW 40th Rd Liberal MO 64762

SHORTAL, HELEN MARY, editor; b. Hartford, Conn., July 10, 1961; d. James Patrick and Helen Mary (Daly) S. BA in Film Studies, Yale U., 1986. Asst. producer Holiday Parade Series Md. Pub. TV, Owings Mills, 1986-87, fl. dir. A.M. Weather, 1987-88; editorial asst. In Motion, Annapolis, 1988-89, staff reporter, assoc. editor, 1989-90, tech. editor, 1990—; ptnr. Patrick/Daly Pub. Rels., 1991—; co-founder Impossible Indsl. Action Theater Co., Balt., 1987-88; writer, critic Md. Art Place Vis. Critics Residency Program, Balt., 1988. Contbr. articles, revs. to nat. and regional publs. Office: In Motion Mag 1201 Seven Locks Rd # 300 Potomac MD 20854-2931

SHORTER, BARBARA LUCILE, high school principal; b. St. Petersburg, Fla., May 29, 1936; d. Frank and Jannie (Willis) Cubby; m. Charles D. Shorter, Dec. 22, 1958 (div. July 1980); children: Gary T., Reginald C., Lynda C., Monica G. BS in Bus. Edn., Fla. A & M U., 1957, MS in Guidance, 1971; postgrad., U. South Fla., 1981. Cert. prin., Fla. Exec. sec. Fla. A & M U., Tallahassee, 1957-58, 59-61; tchr. Lincoln High Sch.-Manatee County, Palmetto, Fla., 1958-59; computer clk. Honeywell, Inc., St. Petersburg, 1961-65; vocat. counselor Fla. State Rehab./Health, St. Petersburg, 1965-67; tchr., counselor, dean, asst. prin. N.E. High Sch.-Pinellas County, St. Petersburg, 1968-85; asst. prin. Boca Ciega High Sch.-Pinellas County, St. Petersburg, 1985—. Mem. Dem. Women's Club of Pinellas County, St. Petersburg, 1980-88. Mem. Fla. Assn. Secondary Adminstrs., Pinellas Adminstr. Assn., Nat. Assn. of Secondary Prins., Pinellas County Asst. Prins. (sec., pres. 1982-91), Fla. A&M Alumni Assn. (sec. 1990—), Phi Delta Kappa, Delta Sigma Theta, Delta Kappa Gamma. Baptist. Office: Gibbs Sr High Sch 850 34th St S Saint Petersburg FL 33711-2208

SHORTINO, JOHNNA MARIE, physiologist; b. Rochester, N.Y., Sept. 22, 1963; d. John Joseph and Salvatrice Jane (Infantino) Shortino. Student, Stony Brook U., 1984; BS cum laude, Brockport State U., 1985; postgrad., Touro Law Sch., 1988-90; MA in Exercise Physiology, Adelphi U., 1992. Cert. health fitness instr, Am. Coll. Sports Medicine. Program mgr. Devel. Disabilities Inst., East Hills, N.Y., 1985-90; fitness instr. Cedarhurst (N.Y.) Atrium Club, 1990-92; personal trainer Body Works, East Meadow, N.Y., 1991-93; prin. The Fitness Solution, North Bellmore, N.Y., 1991—. Environ. activist Greenpeace, World Wildlife Fund, Conservation Soc., ASPCA. Mem. Am. Coll. Sports Medicine, Greater N.Y. Am. Coll. Sports Medicine, Nat. Strength and Conditioning Assn. Home: 1986 Hancock Ave North Bellmore NY 11710

SHORT-MAYFIELD, PATRICIA AHLENE, business owner; b. Fort Benning, Ga., Oct. 12, 1955; d. William Pressley and Ilse Marie (Hofmann) Short; m. Thomas Hicks Fort, June 2, 1973 (div. Jan. 1981); m. Michael Patrick Mayfield, Aug. 11, 1984; 1 child, William Zachary. Grad. high sch., Butler, Ga., 1973. Notary pub., Ga. Staff mem. Fairyland Day Care, Canton, Ga., 1973-74, Small World Child Care, Thomaston, Ga., 1974-77; nurses aide Kenneston Hosp., Marietta, Ga., 1978-80; staff worker Mental Health Ctr., Smyrna, Ga., 1980-81; dir. Kiddie Kollege, Marietta, 1981-85; bus. owner, mgr. Spiffy Clean by Mayfield, Marietta, 1985—, Petsmart, Kennesaw, Ga., 1994—. Choir staff Eastside Bapt. Ch., Marietta, 1988-89; vol. East Valley Elem. Sch., 1989—, chorus vol., 1994—; active Nat. Congress Parents and Tchrs., Cobb County Humane Soc., 1991—. Mem. NAFE, Cobb County C. of C., Atlanta High Mus. Art. Republican. Baptist. Home: 2791 Georgian Ter Marietta GA 30068-3625 Office: Spiffy Clean By Mayfield PO Box 72461 Marietta GA 30007-2461

SHOSS, CYNTHIA RENÉE, lawyer; b. Cape Girardeau, Mo., Nov. 29, 1950; d. Milton and Carroll Jane (Duncan) S.; m. David Goodwin Watson, Apr. 13, 1986; 1 child, Lucy J. Watson. BA cum laude, Newcomb Coll., 1971; JD, Tulane U., 1974; LLM in Taxation, NYU, 1980. Bar: La. 1974, Mo. 1977, Ill. 1978, N.Y. 1990. Law clk. to assoc. and chief justices La. Supreme Ct., New Orleans, 1974-76; assoc. Stone, Pigman et al, New Orleans, 1976-77, Lewis & Rice, St. Louis, 1977-79, Curtis, Mallet-Prevost, et al, N.Y.C., 1980-82; ptnr. LeBoeuf, Lamb, Greene & MacRae, N.Y.C., 1982—; mng. ptnr. London office LeBoeuf, Lamb, Leiby & MacRae, N.Y.C., 1987-89; assoc. editor Tulane Law Rev., 1972-74; frequent speaker before profl. orgns. and assns. Contbr. articles to profl. jours. Mem. ABA, Internat. Tax Planning Assn., Am. Mgmt. Assn. (ins. and risk mgmt. coun.), Corp. Bar Westchester and Fairfield (pro bono steering com.), Tax Rev., Lawyers Alliance N.Y. (bd. dirs.). Office: LeBoeuf Lamb Greene & MacRae 125 W 55th St New York NY 10019-5369

SHOTWELL, JANICE BOLTE, law librarian; b. Bklyn., Nov. 8, 1948; d. Henry Frederick and Anna Marie (Knickerbocker) B.; m. Richard Thomas Shotwell, May 23, 1975; 1 child, Andrew Henry. BA, Wilson Coll., Chambersburg, Pa., 1970; MS in Libr. Sci., U. N.C., 1972; paralegal cert., Roosevelt U., Chgo., 1984. Cataloger Towson State Coll., Balt., 1973-76; asst. libr. Florence (S.C.)-Darlington Tech. Coll., 1977; cataloger South Portland (Maine) Pub. Libr., 1977-78, br. libr., 1978-80; children's libr. Schlow Meml. Libr., State College, Pa., 1980-83; adult svcs. libr. C. Berger & Co., Wheaton, Ill., 1985-88; reference libr. Coll. of DuPage, Glen Ellyn, Ill., 1987-88; law libr. Berkshire Law Libr., Mass. Trial Ct., Pittsfield, Mass., 1989—. Editor: Living With the Law, 1992, supplement, 1994; co-author: How to Grow a Law Collection, 1994. Mem. Am. Assn. Law Librs. (sec.-treas. legal info. svcs. to pub. sect. 1993-94, stds. com. state, ct. and county sect. 1993-94, co-recipient publs. award 1993). Democrat. Lutheran. Office: Berkshire Law Libr 76 East St Pittsfield MA 01201

SHOUB, JENNIFER ANNE, association executive; b. Flint, Mich., Feb. 8, 1960; d. Donald Arthur and Alice Arlene (Laughlin) Shoub. BS, Bowling Green State U., 1982. Social worker Butler County Bd. Mental Retardation and Devel. Disabilities, Fairfield, Ohio, 1983-85; exec. dir. N.W. Ohio Crisis Line, Inc., Defiance, 1985-91, YWCA, Kalamazoo, Mich., 1991—. Bd. dirs. N.W. Ohio Family Planning, Defiance, 1986-88, 5 County Alcohol/Drug Program, Defiance, 1988, City of Defiance Human Rels. Commn., 1988-91; founding mem. Nat. Mus. Women in Arts, Nat. Holocaust Meml. Mem. NOW, ACLU (mem. S.W. Mich. br. 1994—), Nat. Abortion Rights Action League, Nat. Women's Health Network, Kalamazoo Women's Edn. Coalition, Kiwanis. Office: YWCA of Kalamazoo 353 E Michigan Ave Kalamazoo MI 49007-3832

SHOUSHA, ANNETTE GENTRY, critical care nurse; b. Nashville, May 25, 1936; d. Thurman and Laura (Pugh) Gentry; m. Alfred Shousha, May 29, 1959; children: Mark André, Anne, Mary, Melanie. Diploma, St. Thomas Hosp., Nashville, 1957; student, Belmont Coll., Nashville, 1958, No. State U., Aberdeen, S.D., 1973; BSN, S.D. State U., 1985. Cert. coronary care. Instr. med. nursing Nashville Gen. Hosp., 1958-59, ob-gyn. nurse, 1959-60; insvc. educator Tri County Hosp., Ft. Oglethorpe, Ga., 1960-61; clin. mgr., office nurse Britton, S.D., 1962-90; med. nursing Nashville VA Hosp., 1990-92, gastrointestinal nurse, 1992-94, critical care nurse ICU, 1994—. Contbr. essays to S.D. Jour. Medicine. Del., S.D. Dem. Conv. Recipient Gov.'s Recognition award for outstanding vol. svc. Mem. ANA, AMA Aux. (state pres.), Nat. Hospice Assn., Nurses Orgn. VA, Donelson/Hermitage C. of C. Home: 2809 Lealto Ct Nashville TN 37214-1813

SHOWALTER, ELAINE, humanities educator; b. Cambridge, Mass., Jan. 21, 1941; married; 2 children. BA, Bryn Mawr Coll., 1962; MA, Brandeis U., 1964; PhD in English, U. Calif., Davis, 1970. Teaching asst. English U. Calif., 1964-66, from instr. to assoc. prof., 1967-78; prof. English Rutgers U., from 1978; prof. English, Avalon Found. prof. humanities, Princeton (N.J.) U., 1984—; Avalon Found. prof. humanities Princeton (N.J.) U., 1987—; vis. prof. English and women's studies U. Del., 1976-77; vis. prof. Sch. Criticism and Theory, Dartmouth Coll., 1986; prof. Salzburg (Austria) Seminars, 1988; Clarendon lectr. Oxford (Eng.) U., 1989; vis. scholar Phi Beta Kappa, 1993-94; numerous radio and TV appearances. Author: A Literature of Their Own, 1977, The Female Malady, 1985, Sexual Anarchy, 1990, Sister's Choice, 1991; co-author: Hysteria Beyond Freud, 1993; editor: These Modern Women, 1978, The New Feminist Criticism, 1985, Alternative Alcott, 1987, Speaking of Gender, 1989, Modern American Women Writers, 1991, Daughters of Decadence, 1993; also articles and revs. Recipient Howard Behrman humanities award Princeton U., 1989; faculty rsch. coun. fellow Ruthers U., 1972-73, Guggenheim fellow, 1977-78, Rockefeller humanities fellow, 1981-82, fellow NEH, 1988-89. Mem. MLA. Office: Princeton U Dept of English Princeton NJ 08544

SHOWALTER-KEEFE, JEAN, data processing executive; b. Louisville, Mar. 11, 1938; d. William Joseph and Phyllis Rose (Reis) Showalter; m. James Washburn Keefe, Dec. 6, 1980. BA, Spalding U., 1963, MS in Edn. Adminstrn., 1969. Cert. tchr., Ky. Tchr., asst. prin. Louisville Cath. Schs., 1958-71; cons. and various editorial positions Harcourt Brace Jovanovich Co., Chgo. and N.Y.C., 1972-82; dir. editorial Ednl. Challenges, Alexandria, Va., 1982-83; mgr. project to cons. Xerox Corp., Leesburg, Va., 1983-88, mgr. systems edn., 1988-89; curriculum devel. mgr. corp. edn. and tng. Xerox Corp. Hdqrs., Stamford, Conn., 1989-94; mgmt. and sys. cons. Reston, Va., 1995—; mem. adv. bd. Have a Heart Homes for Abused Children, 1991-93; instr. Sales Exec. Club N.Y., 1974-79; cons., Houston, 1980-83. Moderator Jr. Achievement, Louisville, 1968-70; cons. Future Bus. Leaders Am., Dade County, Fla. 1983. Named Outstanding Young Educator Louisville Jaycees, 1968. Mem. Nat. Assn. Female Execs., Am. Soc. Tng. and Devel., Am. Mgmt. Assn. Home: 1419 Belcastle Ct Reston VA 22094-1245 Office: 1419 Belcastle Ct Reston VA 22094-1245

SHOWS, WINNIE M., public relations company executive, professional speaker; b. L.A., Apr. 2, 1947; d. William Marion Arvin and Joan Catherine (Sperry) Wilson; m. George Albert Shows, Mar. 18, 1967 (div. May 1980); 1 child, Sallie; m. Michael P. Florio, Jan. 1, 1990. BA in English, UCLA, 1969; MEd, Calif. State U., Long Beach, 1976. Tchr. St. Joseph High Sch., Lakewood, Calif., 1969-71; tchr. high sch. Irvine (Calif) Unified Sch. Dist., 1972-79; freelance writer, 1979-80; mgr. pub. rels. Forth, Inc., Hermosa Beach, Calif., 1980-81; account mgr., account supr., dir. mktg. Franson & Assoc., San Jose, Calif., 1981-84; v.p., pres. Smith & Shows, Menlo Park, Calif., 1984—. Author (newsletter) Smith & Shows Letter, 1989-94. Vol. Unity Palo Alto (Calif.) Cmty. Ch., 1989-94, Newcomers, Menlo Park, 1990-93, Kara, Palo Alto, 1991-94, Menlo Park Sch. Dist., 1993—. Named Woman of Vision, Career Action Ctr., 1994. Mem. Nat. Spkrs. Assn., Bus. Mktg. Assn. (program dir. 1985-87). Office: Smith & Shows 535 Middlefield Rd Ste 200 Menlo Park CA 94025

SHRAUNER, BARBARA WAYNE ABRAHAM, electrical engineering educator; b. Morristown, N.J., June 21, 1934; d. Leonard Gladstone and Ruth Elizabeth (Thrasher) Abraham; m. James Ely Shrauner, 1965; children: Elizabeth Ann, Jay Arthur. BA cum laude, U. Colo., 1956; AM, Harvard U., 1957, PhD, 1962. Postdoctoral researcher U. Libre de Bruxelles, Brussels, 1962-64; postdoctoral researcher NASA-Ames Rsch. Ctr., Moffett Field, Calif., 1964-65; asst. prof. Washington U., St. Louis, 1966-69, assoc. prof., 1969-77, prof., 1977—; sabbatical Los Alamos (N.Mex.) Sci. Lab., 1975-76, Lawrence Berkeley Lab., Berkeley, Calif., 1985-86; cons. Los Alamos Nat. Lab., 1979, 84, NASA, Washington, 1980, Naval Surface Weapons Lab., Silver Spring, Md., 1984. Contbr. articles on transport in semiconductors, hidden symmetries of differential equations, plasma physics to profl. jours. Mem. IEEE, AAUP (local sec.-treas. 1980-82), Am. Phys. Soc. (div. plasma physics, exec. com. 1980-82), Am. Geophys. Union, Univ. Fusion Assn., Phi Beta Kappa, Eta Kappa Nu, Sigma Xi, Sigma Pi Sigma. Home: 7452 Stratford Ave Saint Louis MO 63130-4044 Office: Washington U Dept Elec Engring 1 Brookings Dr Saint Louis MO 63130-4862

SHREEVE, JEAN'NE MARIE, chemist, educator; b. Deer Lodge, Mont., July 2, 1933; d. Charles William and Maryfrances (Briggeman) S. BA, U. Mont., 1953, DSc (hon.), 1982; MS, U. Minn., 1956; PhD, U. Wash., 1961; NSF postdoctoral fellow, U. Cambridge, Eng., 1967-68. Asst. prof. chemistry U. Idaho, Moscow, 1961-65; assoc. prof. U. Idaho, 1965-67, prof., 1967-73, acting chmn. dept. chemistry, 1969-70, 1973, head dept., and prof., 1973-87, vice provost rsch. and grad. studies, prof. chemistry, 1987—; Lucy W. Pickett lectr. Mt. Holyoke Coll., 1976, George H. Cady lectr. U. Wash., 1993; mem. Nat. Com. Standards in Higher Edn., 1965-67, 69-73. Mem. editl. bd. Jour. Fluorine Chemistry, 1970—, Jour. Heteroatom Chemistry, 1988—, Accounts Chem. Rsch., 1973-75, Inorganic Synthesis, 1976—; contbr. articles to sci. jours. Mem. bd. govs. Argonne (Ill.) Nat. Lab., 1992—. Recipient Disting. Alumni award U. Mont., 1970; named Hon. Alumnus, U. Idaho, 1972; recipient Outstanding Achievement award U. Minn., 1975, Sr. U.S. Scientist award Alexander Von Humboldt Found., 1978, Excellence in Teaching award Chem. Mfrs. Assn., 1980; U.S. hon. Ramsay fellow, 1967-68, Alfred P. Sloan fellow, 1970-72. Mem. AAAS (bd. dirs. 1991—), AAUW (officer Moscow chpt. 1962-69), Am. Chem. Soc. (bd. dirs. 1985-93, chmn. fluorine divsn. 1979-81, Petroleum Rsch. Fund adv. bd. 1975-77, women chemists com. 1972-77, Fluorine award 1978, Garvan medal 1972, Harry and Carol Mosher award Santa Clara Valley sect. 1992), Phi Beta Kappa. Office: U Idaho Rsch Office 111 Morrill Hall Moscow ID 83843

SHREVE, ALLISON ANNE, air traffic control specialist; b. Sturgeon Bay, Wis., Aug. 29, 1961; d. Kendil McLaren and Barbara Gail (Kellner) S. Student, U. Wis., Oshkosh, 1979-82, 1995, Madison Area Tch. Coll., 1993. Cert. control tower operator; nat. registered/state lic. emergency med. technician. Air traffic asst. FAA, Green Bay, Wis., 1985-87, air traffic control specialist, 1987—. Active Earth Share Fund, Humane Assn., ASPCA. Mem. Profl. Women Contrs. (dist. rep. 1991-94), Wis. Emergency Med. Technicians Assn. Home: 411 S Francis St Brillion WI 54110-1338 Office: Green Bay Air Traffic Control Tower 2077 Airport Dr Green Bay WI 54313-5596

SHREVE, CHRISTINE TRUESDELL, artist; b. Hastings, Mich., July 13, 1956; d. Charles Henry and Patricia Anne (O'Connor) Truesdell; m. Bradley Jay Shreve, July 29, 1978; 1 child, Alexander. BFA, Mich. State U., 1978. juror Art Show at the Dog Show, Wichita, Kans., 1994. Exhibited in group shows at Festival of the Arts, Grand Rapids, Mich., 1981, Art Show at The Dog Show, Wichita, 1988-93 (1st place drawing award 1992, best in show 1993), The Dog Mus., St. Louis, 1992, 94; represented in permanent collection The Dog Mus. Vol. We. Mich. Environ. Action Coun., Grand Rapids, 1988-90; Bursley Elem. Sch. Pub. Ctr. coord. Jenison Pub. Schs., Georgetown Twp., Mich., 1990-92; art docent Grand Rapids Art Mus., 1991; fundraising co-chair Hager Park Age of Discovery Playground, Georgetown, 1992. Mem. Nat. Button Soc. Home: 6508 Orchid Dr Jenison MI 49428-9333

SHREVE, PEG, retired elementary school educator; b. Spencer, Va., July 23, 1927; d. Hubert Smith and Pearl (Looney) Adams; m. Don Franklin Shreve, June 17, 1950 (dec. Sept. 1970); children: Donna, Jennifer, John, Don. BA, Glenville State U., 1948. Cert. elem. tchr., Va., Wyo. Reading tchr. Wood County Bd., Parkersburg, W.Va., 1948-50; elem. tchr. Mt. Solon, Va., 1950-52, Bridgewater, Va., 1952-53, Cody, Wyo., 1970-86. Mem. coun. Girl Scouts U.S., White Pulpher Springs, W.Va., 1962-65; chair com. travel, recreation and wildlife Wyo. Ho. of Reps., 1983-91, majority ship, 1992-94, speaker pro tempore, 1995—; co-chair Legis. Exec. Conf., Wuo., 1987; mem. Nat. Com. State Legislatures, 1982—, Nat. Women Legislators, 19876, Rep. Women, 1975—. Mem. AAUW (exec. bd.), Beta Sigma Phi (Lady of Yr. award 1986). Presbyterian. Lodge: Soroptimist (Women Helping Women award 1985). Home: PO Box 2257 Cody WY 82414-2257

SHREVE, SUSAN RICHARDS, author, English literature educator; b. Toledo, May 2, 1939; d. Robert Kenneth and Helen (Greene) Richards; children—Porter, Elizabeth, Caleb, Kate. U. Pa., 1961; MA, U. Va., 1969. Prof. English lit. George Mason U., Fairfax, Va., 1976—; vis. prof. Columbia U., N.Y.C., 1982—, Princeton U., 1991, 92, 93. Author: (novels) A Fortunate Madness, 1974, A Woman Like That, 1977, Children of Power, 1979, Miracle Play, 1981, Dreaming of Heroes, 1984, Queen of Hearts, 1986, A Country of Strangers, 1989, Daughters of the New World, 1992, The Train Home, 1993, Skin Deep: Women & Race, 1994; (children's books) The Nightmares of Geranium Street, 1977, Family Secrets, 1979, Loveletters, 1979, The Masquerade, 1980, The Bad Dreams of a Good Girl, 1981, The Revolution of Mary Leary, 1982, The Flunking of Joshua T. Bates, 1984, How I Saved the World on Purpose, 1985, Lucy Forever and Miss Rosetree, Shrinks, Inc., 1985, Joshua T. Bates In Charge, 1992, The Gift of the Girl Who Couldn't Hear, 1991, Wait for Me, 1992, Amy Dunn Quits School, 1993, Lucy Forever & the Stolen Baby, 1994. Recipient Jenny Moore award George Washington U., 1978; John Simon Guggenheim award in fiction, 1980; Nat. Endowment Arts fiction award, 1982. Mem. PEN/Faulkner Found. (pres.), Phi Beta Kappa.

SHRIER, DIANE KESLER, psychiatrist; b. N.Y.C., Mar. 23, 1941; d. Benjamin Arthur and Mollie (Wortman) Kesler; BS magna cum laude in Chemistry and Biology (Regents scholar 1957-61), Queen's Coll., CUNY, 1961; student Washington U. Sch. Medicine, St. Louis, 1960-61; M.D., Yale U., 1964; m. Adam Louis Shrier, June 10, 1961; children: Jonathan Laurence, Lydia Anne, Catherine Jane, David Leopold. Pediatric intern Bellevue Hosp., N.Y.C., 1964-65; psychiat. resident Albert Einstein Coll. Medicine-Bronx (N.Y.) Mcpl. Municipal Hosp. Center, 1966-68, child psychiatry fellow, 1968-70; staff cons. Family Service and Child Guidance Center of the Oranges, Maplewood, Milburn-Orange, N.J., 1970-73, cons., 1973-79; pvt. practice, Montclair, N.J., 1970-92; cons. Community Day Nursery, E. Orange, 1970-79, Montclair State Coll., 1976-78; psychiat. cons. Bloomfield (N.J.) public schs., 1974-75; clin. instr. Albert Einstein Coll. Medicine, 1970-73; clin. asst. prof. psychiatry U. Medicine and Dentistry N.J., 1978-82, clin. assoc. prof., 1982-89, prof. clin. psychiatry, 1989-92; vice chmn., dir. clin. psychiat. svcs. Dept. Psychiatry Children's Nat. Med. Ctr., 1992-94, attending staff, 1994—; prof. psychiatry and pediatrics George Washington U. Med. Ctr., 1992—, clin. prof. psychairty and pediatrics, 1994—. cons. Walter Reed Med. Ctr., 1994—. Trustee, Montessori Learning Center, Montclair, 1973-75. Diplomate Am. Bd. Psychiatry and Neurology. Fellow Am. Psychiat. Assn., Am. Orthopsychiat. Assn., Acad. Child Psychiatry; mem. Tri-County Psychiat. Assn. (exec. com., rec. sec. 1977-78, 2d v.p. 1978-79, 1st v.p. 1979-80, pres. 1977-81), N.J. Psychiat. Assn. (councillor 1981-84), Am. Acad. Child and Adolescent Psychiatry (councillar at large), Phi Beta Kappa. Contbr. articles to med. jours. Home: Apt E 4000 Cathedral Ave NW Washington DC 20016-5249 Office: 1616 18th St NW Ste 104 Washington DC 20009

SHRIVER, EUNICE MARY KENNEDY (MRS. ROBERT SARGENT SHRIVER, JR.), civic worker; b. Brookline, Mass.; m. Robert Sargent Shriver, Jr., May 23, 1953; children: Robert Sargent III, Maria Owings, Timothy Perry, Mark Kennedy, Anthony Paul Kennedy. BS in Sociology, Stanford U., 1943; student, Manhattanville Coll. of Sacred Heart, LHD, 1963; LittD, U. Santa Clara, 1962; LHD, D'Youville Coll., 1962; LLD, Regis Coll., 1963; LHD, Newton Coll., 1973, Brescia Coll., 1974, Holy Cross Coll., 1979, Princeton U., 1979, Boston Coll., 1990; also hon. degrees, U. Vt., Albertus Magnus Coll., St. Mary's Coll. With spl. war problems div. State Dept. Washington, 1943-45; sec. Nat. Conf. on Prevention and Control juvenile Delinquency, Dept. of Justice, Washington, 1947-48; social worker Fed. Penitentiary for Women, Alderson, W.Va., 1950; exec. v.p. Joseph P. Kennedy, Jr. Found., 1956—; founder (1968) Spl. Olympics Internat.; social worker House of Good Shepherd, Chgo., also Juvenile Ct., Chgo., 1951-54; regional chmn. women's div. Community Fund-Red Cross Joint Appeal, Chgo., 1958; mem. Chgo. Commn. on Youth Welfare, 1959-62; cons. to Pres. John F. Kennedy's Panel on Mental Retardation, 1961; founder Community & Caring, Inc., 1986. Editor: "A Community of Caring", 1982, 85, "Growing Up Caring, 1990. co-chmn. women's com. Democratic Nat. Conv., Chgo., 1956. Decorated Legion of Honor; recipient Lasker award, Humanitarian award A.A.M.D., 1973, Nat. Vol. Service award, 1973, Phila. Civic Ballet award, 1973, Prix de la Couronne Française, 1974, Presdl. Medal of Freedom, 1984, others. Office: care Joseph P Kennedy Jr 1350 New York Ave NW Ste 500 Washington DC 20005-4709

SHRIVER, MARIA OWINGS, news correspondent; b. Chgo., Nov. 6, 1955; d. Robert Sargent and Eunice Mary (Kennedy) S.; m. Arnold Schwarzenegger, Apr. 26, 1986; children: Katherine Eunice, Christina Aurelia, Patrick. BA, Georgetown U. Coll. Am. Studies, Washington, 1977. News producer Sta. KYW-TV, 1977-78; producer Sta. WJZ-TV, 1978-80; nat. reporter PM Mag., 1981-83; news reporter CBS News, Los Angeles, 1983-85; news correspondent, co-anchor CBS Morning News, N.Y.C., 1985-86; co-host Sunday Today, NBC, 1987-90; anchor Main Street, NBC, 1987; co-anchor Yesterday, Today, and Tomorrow, NBC, 1989; anchor NBC Nightly News Weekend Edition, 1989-90, Cutting Edge with Maria Shriver, NBC, 1990, First Person with Maria Shriver, NBC, 1991—; co-anchor summer olympics, Seoul, Korea, 1988; substitute anchor NBC News at Sunrise, Today, NBC Nightly News with Tom Brokaw. Recipient Christopher award for "Fatal Addictions", 1990, Exceptional Merit Media award Nat. Women's Political Caucus. Democrat. Roman Catholic. Office: NBC News First Person with Maria Shriver 30 Rockefeller Plz New York NY 10112*

SHRIVER, PAMELA HOWARD, professional tennis player; b. Balt., July 4, 1962. Profl. tennis player, 1979—; winner 21 career singles, 92 career doubles titles, 7 Australian Opens (with Martina Navratilova), 4 French Opens (with Navratilova), 5 Wimbledons (with Navratilova), 6 U.S. Opens, French Open mixed doubles (with Emilio Sanchez); mem. U.S. Fedn. Cup Team, 1986-87, 89, 92, U.S. Wightman Cup Team, 1978-81, 83, 85, 87. V.P. Internat. Tennis Hall of Fame; pres. of Women's Tennis Association, 1991, 92, 93. Recipient Gold medal 1988 Olympic Games in doubles (with Zina Garrison). Mem. Women's Tennis Assn. address: c/o PHS Ltd 2324 W Joppa Rd Ste 650 Lutherville Timonium MD 21093-4622

SHROPSHIRE, HELEN MAE, historian; b. Prosser, Nebr., May 7, 1909; d. William Pearl and Dicy Belle (Myer) Stafford. Grad., Rogers Bus. Coll., Everett, Wash., 1928. Co-owner Camera Exchange, Pacific Grove, Calif., 1947-62; co-owner, photographer, writer Shropshire Film Prodns., Pacific Grove, 1950-76; pilot, co-owner Monarch Aviation, Monterey, Calif., 1962-63; co-founder, mgr. Calif. Heritage Guides, Monterey, Calif., 1971—. Mem. Ninety Nines Inc. (life). Republican. Home: 1623 Josselyn Canyon Rd Monterey CA 93940-5273 Office: Calif Heritage Guides 10 Custom House Plz Monterey CA 93940-2430

SHROUT, LOIS GLENN, administrator; b. Beaumont, Tex., Apr. 5, 1941; d. Dennie D. and Lucile L. (White) G.; m. Loyd A. Shrout, Feb. 19, 1983; 1 stepchild, John Andrew. BA, Lamar U., 1963; MA, Tex. Tech. U., 1966, PhD, 1972. Tchr. Tex. Pub. Schs., 1962-65; teaching asst., instr. Tex. Tech. U., 1965-70; asst. prof. U. So. Miss., 1970-72; editor, pub. Nefertiti Head Press, 1973-74; mng. editor U. Tex., Bur. Bus. Rsch., Austin, 1975-77, publs. mgr., 1977-86, editor Tex. Bus. Rev., 1985—, assoc. dir., 1986-88, dir. pubs., ops. and assoc. dir., 1988—; v.p. Tex. Econ. Forum, Austin, 1989-91; judge nat. pub. awards Assn. Univ. Bus. and Econ. Rsch., 1987-88, 89-91, mem. publs. com., 1992—; acad. advisor Pflugerville Ind. Sch. Dist., 1993-94. Author: Charles W.S. Williams, 1975; contbr. articles to profl. jours. Mem. tech. com. Pflugerville Ind. Sch. Dist., 1993-94. Democrat. Home: 16216 Malden Dr Pflugerville TX 78660-2446 Office: U Tex Bureau Bus Rsch Austin TX 78712

SHRUM, ALICIA ANN, elementary school educator, librarian; b. Miami, Okla., Sept. 8, 1946; d. Harold Richard Moye and Novella (Fields) Steen; m. Jimmie Ray Shrum, May 15, 1971. BS in Elem. Edn., Northeastern State U., Tahlequah, Okla., 1969, MS in Elem. Edn., 1978; student pubs. course, Inst. Children's Lit., 1990-91. Cert. elem. tchr., libr. media specialist, Okla. Tchr. 1st grade Justus Sch., Claremore, Okla., 1969-74, tchr. 3rd grade, 1974-81, tchr. remedial math., libr., 1981-83, libr./enrichment educator, 1983—; co-chairperson centennial com., Justus Sch., 1989; coach 6th/7th grades and 7th/8th grades teams Acad. Bowl, 1993-94. Justus Sch. rep. United Way, 1989-93. Mem. NEA, Okla. Edn. Assn. (grantee to establish new libr. 1984-87), Justus Edn. Assn. (sec./treas. 1988-90, pres. 1990-91). Democrat. Office: Justus Libr 3 Mile E Hwy # 20 Claremore OK 74018

SHUART, THERESA AILEEN, counselor; b. Arlington, Va., July 30, 1962; d. Francis James Jr. and Mary Alice (Lyman) O'Neill; m. Glen Dimitri Shuart, May 28, 1988; children: Nicholas Dimitri, Elana Kathleen. BS, James Madison U., 1984; MEd, U. Va., 1986. Nat. cert. counselor; lic. profl. counselor, Va. Substance abuse counselor Northwestern Community Svcs., Winchester, Va., 1986-90, supr. residential crisis home, 1990; supr. home based family therapy program Prince William Community Svcs., Manassas, Va., 1990-92; regional mgr. Employee Asst. Svc., Inc., McLean, Va., 1992—; counselor, pres. Brief Counseling Ctr., Warrenton & Winchester, Va., 1992—; speaker in field. Bd. dirs. Community and Law Enforcement Against Narcotics, Winchester, 1988-90. Mem. Am. Counseling Assn., Va. Counselors Assn., Internat. Assn. Marriage and Family Counselors, Employee Assistance Programs Am., Fauquier Bus. and Profl. Women's Assn. Presbyterian. Home: 7519 Albrecht Ln Warrenton VA 22186 Office: Brief Counseling Ctr 12 E Clifford St Winchester VA 22601

SHUBART, DOROTHY LOUISE TEPFER, artist, educator; b. Ft. Collins, Colo., Mar. 1, 1923; d. Adam Christian and Rose Virginia (Ayers) Tepfer; m. Robert Franz Shubart, Apr. 22, 1950; children: Richard, Lorenne. Grad., Cleve. Inst. Art, 1944-46; AA, Colo. Women's Coll., 1944; grad., Cleve. Inst. Art, 1946; student, Western Res. U., 1947-48; BA, St. Thomas Aquinas Coll., 1974; MA, Coll. New Rochelle, 1978; grad., Cleve. Inst. Art. Art tchr. Denver Mus., 1942-44, Cleve. Recreation Dept., 1944-50; ind. artist, portrait painter Colo., Cleve., N.Y., and N.Mex., 1944—; adult edn. art tchr. Nanuet (N.Y.) Pub. Schs., 1950-65, Pearl River (N.Y.) Adult Edn., 1950-51; rec. sec. Van Horten Fields Assn., West Nyack, N.Y., 1969-74. Exhbns. include Hopper House, Rockland Ctr. for Arts, CWC, Cleve. Inst. Art, Coll. New Rochelle. Leader 4-H Club, Nanuet, 1960-80, Girl Scouts, Nanuet, 1961-68; mem. scholarship and gen. com. PTA, Nanuet, 1964-68; recording sec. Van Houten Fields Assn., West Nyack, N.Y., 1969-74; com. mem. Eldorado (Santa Fe) Cmty. Involvement Assn.-Arterial Rd. Planning Com., 1992-94; capt. Neighborhood Watch, local organizer Eldorado chpt. Gund scholar Cleve. Inst. Art, 1946. Mem. AAUW, NOW, Wilderness Club, El Dorado ARPC Com., Delta Tau Kappa, Phi Delta Kappa. Democrat. Home: 8 Hidalgo Ct Santa Fe NM 87505-8898

SHUCART, EVELYN ANN, sales and marketing professional; b. Covington, Ky., May 29, 1942; d. Frederick Holroyd and Evelyn Ann (Thomson) Eastabrooks; m. Rexford Lee Hill III, Sept. 12, 1964 (div. 1983); children: Eric Douglas, Rexford Alan, Gerald Alexander, Andrew David; m. James Wood Shucart, Sept. 21, 1991. BS in Design, U. Cin., 1965. Freelance artist St. Louis, 1960—; office mgr. United Ch. of Christ, St. Louis, 1983-84; program coord. Acme Premium Supply, St. Louis, 1984-86, mgr., 1986-93; v.p. I.B.A. Inc., St. Louis, 1993—. Illustrator: Life Through Time, 1975. Coord./advisor Guardian Angels N.Y., St. Louis, 1981-82; advisor Pres.'s Commn. on Continuing Edn., Eden Sem., St. Louis, 1982-83; advisor Ecumenical Task Force on Hunger, 1982; cons. Women's Task Force on Employment, 1975-76; cons. Nat. Bd. Homeland Ministries, United Ch. of Christ, 1982, mem. St. Louis Assn. United Ch. of Christ, pres., 1981-82. Best of Show award Siegfried Reinhardt County Artists, 1976. Mem. NAFE, LWV, Direct Mktg. Assn., Am. Mgmt. Assn., Amnesty Internat., Sierra Club. Home and Office: 2039 Brookcreek Ln Saint Louis MO 63122-2254

SHUHLER, PHYLLIS MARIE, physician; b. Sellersville, Pa., Sept. 25, 1947; d. Raymond Harold and Catherine Cecilia (Virus) S.; m. John Howard Schwarz, Sept. 17, 1983; 1 child, Luke Alexander. BS in Chemistry, Chestnut Hill Coll., 1971; MD, Mich. State U., 1976; diploma of Tropical Medicine and Hygiene, U. London, 1980. Diplomate Am. Bd. Family Medicine. With Soc. Cath. Med. Missionaries, Phila., 1966-82; ward clk., nursing asst. Holy Family Hosp., Atlanta, 1971-72; resident in family practice Somerset Family Med. Residency Program, Somerville, N.J., 1972-76; physician East Coast Migrant Health Project, Newton Grove, N.C., 1980; physician, missionary SCMM, Diocese of Sunyani, Berekum, Ghana, West Africa, 1980-81; emergency rm. physician Northeast Emergency Med. Assn., Quakertown, Pa., 1981-82; founder, physician Family Health Care Ctr., Inc., Pennsburg, Pa., 1982-90; physician Lifequest Med. Group, Pennsburg, 1990-93; pvt. practice Pennsburg, 1993—. Fellow Royal Soc. Tropical Medicine and Hygiene; mem. Am. Acad. Family Practice, Am. Bd. Family Practice, Am. Med. Women Assn. Pa. Acad. Family Practice, Lehigh Valley Women Med. Assn. Roman Catholic. Office: 101 W 7th St Ste 2C Pennsburg PA 18073

SHULER, SALLY ANN SMITH, telecommunications, computer services and software company executive; b. Mt. Olive, N.C., June 11, 1934; d. Leon Joseph and Ludia Irene (Montague) Simmons; m. Henry Ralph Smith Jr., Mar. 1, 1957 (div. Jan. 1976); children: Molly Montague, Barbara Ellen, Sara Ann, Mary Kathryn; m. Harold Robert Shuler, Aug. 2, 1987. BA in Math., Duke U., 1956; spl. studies, U. Liège, Belgium, 1956-57; postgrad. in bus. econs., Claremont Grad Sch., 1970-72. Mgr. fed. systems GE Info. Svcs. Co., Washington, 1976-78; mgr. mktg. support GE Info. Svcs. Co., Rockville, Md., 1978-81; dir. bus. devel. info. tech. group Electronic Data Systems, Bethesda, Md., 1981-82; v.p. mktg. optimum systems div. Electronic Data Systems, Rockville, 1982-83; v.p. planning and communications Electronic Data Systems, Dallas, 1983-84; exec. dir. comml. devel. U.S. West Inc., Englewood, Colo., 1984-90; v.p. mktg. devel. Cin. Bell Info. Systems Inc., 1990-92; mgmt. cons. in mergers and acquisitions Denver, 1992-93; v.p. major accounts U.S. Computer Svcs., Englewood, 1993—. Recipient GE Centennial award, Rockville, 1978. Mem. Women in Telecommunications, Rotary (fellow Internat. Found.), Phi Beta Kappa, Tau Psi Omega, Pi Mu Epsilon. Democrat. Presbyterian. Office: US Computer Svcs 5575 DTC Pky Ste 326 Englewood CO 80111-3008

SHULGASSER, BARBARA, writer; b. Manhasset, N.Y., Apr. 10, 1954; d. Lew and Luba (Golante) S. Student, Sarah Lawrence Coll., 1973-74; BA magna cum laude, CUNY, 1977; MS, Columbia U., 1978. Feature writer Waterbury (Conn.) Rep., 1978-81; reporter, feature writer Chgo. Sun Times, 1981-84; film critic San Francisco Examiner, 1984—; freelance book critic N.Y. Times Book Rev., N.Y.C., 1983—; guest interviewer City Arts and Lectures of San Francisco, 1990—. Co-author: (screenplay, with Robert Altman) Ready to Wear, 1994; freelance video columnist N.Y. Times Sunday Arts & Leisure, 1989, features for Vanity Fair and Mirabella mags. Office: San Francisco Examiner 110 5th St San Francisco CA 94103-2918

SHULL, JANICE KAY, law librarian; b. Elkhart, Ind., Oct. 28, 1945; d. Robert R. and Lois C. (Ebey) Thompson; m. Steven A. Shull, May 29, 1966; children: Theodore, Amanda. BA, Ball State U., 1968; MLS, U. Ill., 1969. Cataloguer Millikin U. Library, Columbus, Ohio, 1970-74; circulation librarian New Orleans Pub. Library, 1974-77, U. New Orleans, 1978-82; catalog and reference librarian Law Library of La., New Orleans, 1984—. Mem. New Orleans Assn. Law Librarians (v.p., pres. 1988-90), Am. Assn. Law Libraries (southeastern chpt.). Home: 5840 Kensington Blvd New Orleans LA 70127-2809 Office: Law Library of La 301 Loyola Ave New Orleans LA 70112-1800

SHULMAN, ANITA, nurse midwife; b. Waterloo, Iowa, Mar. 14, 1957; d. Herbert and Deana Shulman. RN, Hasharon Sch. Nursing, Petah Tikva, Israel, 1979; Israel cert. midwife, Hebrew U. Jerusalem, 1981; cert. nurse midwife, Frontier Sch. Midwifery, Hyden, Ky., 1989. Staff nurse, midwife Hadassah Med. Orgn., Jerusalem, 1980-86; pvt. midwifery practice assoc. Cynthia K. Monshower & J. Emerling CNM, Balt., Balt., 1989-90; midwife Planned Parenthood, Balt., 1989-90; staff midwife Johns Hopkins Med. Svcs. Corp., Balt., 1990-93; midwife privileges Johns Hopkins Hosp., Balt., 1991—. Mem. Am. Coll. Nurse Midwives, HMO Hadassah Med. Orgn. (life). Democrat. Jewish. Home: 2213 WicOmico Rd Baltimore MD 21221

SHULMAN, ELLEN L., speech pathologist; b. Rochester, N.Y., Nov. 21, 1957; d. Sherwood L. and Esther (Ouriel) S. BS, SUNY, Buffalo, 1979, MS, 1980; cert. advanced studies in ednl. adminstrn., SUNY, Brockport, 1987, cert. sch. dist. adminstr., 1991. Lic. speech pathologist; cert. tchr. speech and hearing handicapped. Speech-lang. pathologist Rochester (N.Y.) City Sch. Dist., 1980—, bilingual speech pathologist in Spanish and English, 1987—; pvt. practice Rochester, 1988—. Creator ednl. game Incredible City. Mem. Am. Speech-Lang. Hearing Assn., Nat. Assn. Bilingual Edn., State Assn. Bilingual Edn., N.Y. State Speech-Lang. Hearing Assn., Genesee Valley Speech-Lang. Hearing Assn. Home: 70 Kansas St Rochester NY 14609 Office: City Sch Dist 131 W Broad St Rochester NY 14614

SHULTZ, LEILA MCREYNOLDS, botanist, educator; b. Bartlesville, Okla., Apr. 20, 1946; 1 child, Kirsten. BS, U. Tulsa, 1969; MA, U. Colo., 1975; PhD, Claremont Grad. Sch., 1983. Curator Intermountain Herbarium Utah State U., 1973-92; rschr. Harvard U., Cambridge, Mass., 1994—. Co-author: Atlas of the Vascular Plants of Utah, 1988; taxon editor: Flora of North America (12 vols.), 1987. Mem. Am. Bot. Soc. (systematics rep. 1988-90), Am. Soc. Plant Taxonomists (coun. 1990-92). Office: Harvard U Herbaria 22 Divinity Ave Cambridge MA 02138

SHULTZ, MARTHA JANE See DIETRICH, MARTHA JANE

SHULTZ, MARY ELIZABETH, medical technologist, consultant; b. Colorado Springs, Colo., Nov. 17, 1922; d. Lyle Thornton and Mary Elizabeth (Simms) Lowe; m. Norman E. Shultz, Feb. 16, 1946 (div. July 1969); children: Mary Ellen, Joan, Elizabeth Anne. BS in Med. Tech., Colo. U., 1944; MA in Health Edn., Ctrl. Mich. U., 1978. Med. technologist Dee Hosp. (now named McKay-Dee Hosp.), Ogden, Utah, 1944-46, Drs. Aschmann and Lee, Kansas City, Mo., 1946-47, Meml. Hosp., Colorado Springs, 1965-66, Penrose Hosp., Colorado Springs, 1966-70; researcher I, II Colo. State U., Ft. Collins, 1970-89; med. technologist Met West Labs., Greeley, Colo., 1989-91, Ft. Collins Youth Clinic, 1991—; cons. Poudre Valley Creamery, Ft. Collins, 1991—. Active GSA, various locations, 1954-81, PTA, Colorado Springs, 1954-70, Dem. Party, Ft. Collins, 1985—. Mem. AAUW (pres. 1972, 89-91, 93—), NOW, Am. Soc. for Clin. Pathologists (assoc., cert. med. technologist), Colo. Assn. for Continuing Med. Lab. Edn., Nat. Abortion Rights Action League, Rocky Mountain Planned Parenthood. Congregational. Office: Ft Collins Youth Clinic 1200 E Elizabeth Fort Collins CO 80524

SHULTZ, RETHA MILLS, retired missionary; b. Anderson, Ind., Apr. 22, 1914; d. Raymond White and Mary Beulah (Yoder) Mills; m. Clair Wilson Shultz, Dec. 25, 1935; children: Carol Ann Shultz Lehner, David Clair. BA, Anderson U., 1937. Missionary, bookkeeper Ch. of God Mission, Trinidad, W.I., 1945-58, Jamaica, W.I., 1958-62, Kenya, East Africa, 1962-70, 85-86; co-founder, tchr. music, bookkeeping W.I. Bible Inst., Trinidad, 1950-58; mem. missionary bd. Ch. of God, Anderson, Ind., 1980-90; missionary speaker, various churches in U.S., W.I., East Africa. Republican.

SHUMATE, GLORIA JONES, retired educational administrator; b. Meridian, Miss., Jan. 8, 1927; d. Thomas Marvin and Flora E. (Suggs) Jones; m. Jack B. Shumate, Nov. 19, 1946; children: Jack B. Jr., Thomas Edward. BS, Miss. State U., 1960; MA, U. South Fla., 1969, postgrad. in vocat. edn., 1970-72. Cert. guidance counselor, psychology and social studies specialist, Fla. High sch. tchr. Lauderdale County Schs., Meridian, 1952-56; tchr. vocat. edn. Manpower Devel. and Tng., St. Petersburg, Fla., 1964-69; counselor City Ctr. for Learning St. Petersburg Vocat.-Tech. Inst., 1969-70, registrar, 1970-72, asst. dir., 1972-80, exec. dir., 1980-85; dir. vocat.-tech., adult edn. ops. Pinellas County Schs., Largo, Fla., 1985-89; chmn. Fla. Equity Council, 1980-81; mem. Fla. Adv. Council on Vocat. Edn., 1980-85, Fla. Job Tng. Coordinating Council, 1983-84. Named Outstanding Educator Pinellas Suncoast C. of C., 1980. Mem. Nat. Council Local Adminstrs., Am. Vocat. Assn., Fla. Vocat. Assn., So. Assn. Colls. and Schs. (standards com. 1975-81), Phi Delta Kappa, Kappa Delta Pi. Democrat. Baptist. Home: 900 63d St S Saint Petersburg FL 33707

SHUMICK, DIANA LYNN, computer executive; b. Canton, Ohio, Feb. 10, 1951; d. Frank A. and Mary J. (Mari) S.; 1 child, Tina Elyse. Student, Walsh Coll., 1969-70, Ohio U., 1970-71, Kent State U., 1971-77. Data entry clk. Ohio Power Co., Canton, 1969-70; clk. City of Canton Police Dept., 1971-73; system engr. IBM, Canton, 1973-81; adv. market support rep. IBM, Dallas, 1981-89; system engr. mgr. IBM, Madison, Wis., 1989-93; mktg. customer satisfaction mgr. IBM, Research Triangle Park, N.C., 1993; HelpCenter mgr. oper. sys. IBM Personal Computer Co., Research Triangle Park, 1993—. Author: Technical Coordinator Guidelines, 1984. Pres., bd. dirs. Big Bros. and Sisters of Denton (Tex.) County, 1989, v.p.,, 1988, sec., 1987; mem. St. Philip Parish Coun., Lewisville, Tex., 1988-89, Western Stark County Red Cross, Canton, 1980; v.p. Parents Without Ptnrs., Madison, 1991; founding bd. mem. Single Parents Network, 1991; vol. ARC, 1985—; mem. bd. dirs. Rape Crisis Ctr. Dane County, sec., 1990-91; vol. Paint-A-Thon, Dane County, 1990, Badger State Games Challenge, 1992, Cystic Fibrosis Found. Great Strides, 1992, 93, 94.

SHURE, MYRNA BETH, psychologist, educator; b. Chgo., Sept. 11, 1937; d. Sidney Natkin and Frances (Laufman) S.; student U. Colo., 1955; BS, U. Ill., 1959; MS, Cornell U., 1961, PhD, 1966. Asst. prof. U. R.I., head tchr. Nursery Sch., Kingston, 1961-62; asst. prof. Temple U., Phila., 1966-67, assoc. prof., 1967-68; instr. Hahneman Med. Coll., Phila., 1968-69, sr. instr. psychology, 1969-70, asst. prof., 1970-73, assoc. prof., 1973-80, prof., 1980—. NIMH research grantee, 1971-75, 77-79, 82-85, 87, 88-93. Recipient Lela Rowland Prevention award Nat. Mental Health Assn., 1982; . lic. psychologist, Pa. Fellow Am. Psychol. Assn. (Disting. Contbn. award div. community psychology 1984), Am. Psychol. Assn. (divsn. clin. psychology, child sect. 1994, Task Force on Prevention award 1987, Task Force on Model Programs award 1994); mem. Eastern Psychol. Assn., Soc. Research in Child Devel., Phila. Soc. Clin. Psychologists. Author: (with George Spivack) Social Adjustment of Young Children, 1974; (with George Spivack and Jerome Platt) The Problem Solving Approach to Adjustment, 1976; (with George Spivack) Problem Solving Techniques in Childrearing, 1978, (child curricula manual) I Can Problem Solve, 1992, (trade book) Raising a Thinking Child, 1994; mem. editl. bd. Jour. Applied Developmental Psychology; spl. cons. to The Puzzle Place PBS Children's TV Show.

SHUSTER, DIANNA, opera company executive. Artistic dir. San Jose Civic Light Opera, San Jose, Calif. Office: San Jose Ctr for Performing Arts 1717 Technology Dr San Jose CA 95113*

SHUTLER, MARY ELIZABETH, academic administrator; b. Oakland, Calif., Nov. 14, 1929; d. Hal Wilfred and Elizabeth Frances (Gimbel) Hall; m. Richard Shutler Jr., Sept. 8, 1951 (div. 1975); children: Kathryn Allice, John Hall, Richard Burnett. BA, U. Calif., Berkeley, 1951; MA, U. Ariz., 1958, PhD, 1967. Asst., assoc., full prof. anthropology, chmn. dept. San Diego State U., 1967-75; prof. anthropology, dept. chmn. Wash. State U., Pullman, 1975-80; dean Coll. Arts and Scis., prof. anthropology U. Alaska, Fairbanks, 1980-84; vice chancellor, dean of faculty, prof. anthropology U. Wis. Parkside, Kenosha, 1984-88; provost, v.p. for acad. affairs, prof. anthropology Calif. State U., L.A., 1988-94; provost West Coast U., L.A., 1994—; mem. core staff Lahav Rsch. Project, Miss. State U., 1975—. Co-author: Ocean Prehistory, 1975, Deer Creek Cave, 1964, Archaeological Survey of Southern Nevada, 1963, Stuart Rockshelter, 1962; contbr. articles to jours. in field. Mem. coun. Gamble House. Fellow Am. Anthropol. Assn.; mem. Soc. for Am. Archaeology, Am. Schs. for Oriental Rsch., Am. Coun. Edn., Am. Assn. for Higher Edn., Am. Assn. State Colls. and Univs., Delta Zeta. Republican. Roman Catholic. Office: West Coast U 440 Shatto Pl Los Angeles CA 90020

SHUTTLEWORTH, REBECCA SCOTT, English language educator; b. Eupora, Miss., Aug. 18, 1919; d. Thaddeus William and Frances Lucinda (Willingham) Scott; m. Wallace Shuttleworth, June 12, 1943 (dec. Aug. 1961); children: Sally, Rebecca. BA, Miss. U. for Women, 1941, MEd, 1962. Tchr. Okolona (Miss.) High Sch., 1941-42, Indianola (Miss.) High Sch., 1942-43, 45-70; tchr. Miss. Delta Community Coll., Moorhead, 1970-89, chmn. lang. arts, 1978-89, tchr. extended learning, 1989—; asst. organizer Miss. Community Coll. Creative Writing Assn., 1978. Past pres. Twentieth Century Club, Indianola, 1947-94. Mem. AAUW (Woman of Achievement 1992, Scholarship award 1989), DAR (Am. history chmn. 1990-92, vice-regent 1994—). Republican. Methodist. Home and Office: 401 Lee St Indianola MS 38751-2739

SHWAYDER, ELIZABETH YANISH, sculptor; b. St. Louis; d. Sam and Fannie May (Weil) Yaffe; m. Nathan Yanish, July 5, 1944 (dec.); children: Ronald, Marilyn Ginsburg, Mindy; m. M.C. Shawayder, 1988. Student, Washington U., 1941, Denver U., 1960; pvt. studies. One-woman shows include Woodstock Gallery, London, 1973, Internat. House, Denver, 1963, Colo. Women's Coll., Denver, 1975, Contemporaries Gallery, Santa Fe, 1963, So. Colo. State Coll. Pueblo, 1967, others; exhibited in group shows: Salt Lake City Mus., 1964, 71, Denver Art Mus., 1961-75, Oklahoma City Mus., 1969, Joslyn Mus., Omaha, 1964-68, Lucca (Italy) Invitational, 1971, others; represented in permanent collections include Colo. State Bank, Bmh Synagogue. Denver, Colo. Women's Coll., Har Ha Shem Congregation, Boulder, Colo., Faith Bible Chapel, Denver, others. Chmn. visual arts Colo. Centennial-Bicentennial, 1974-75; pres. Denver Council Arts and Humanities, 1973-75; mem. Mayor's Com. on Child Abuse, 1974-75; co-chmn. visual arts spree Denver Pub. Schs., 1975; trustee Denver Center for the Performing Arts, 1973-75; chmn. Concerned Citizens for Arts, 1976; pres. Beth Israel Hosp. Aux., 1985-87; organizer Coat Drive for the Needy, Denver and N.Y.C., 1982-87, Common Cents penny dirve for homeless, 1991-93; bd. dirs. Mizel Mus., Srs., Inc.; active Mayor's Com. on Cultural Affairs, Nat. Mus., Women in the Arts Mus., Freedom Found. at Valley Force, Hospice of Metro Denver. Humanities scholar Auraria Librs.-U. Colo.; recipient McCormick award Ball State U., Muncie, Ind., 1964, Purchase award Color Women's Coll., Denver, 1963, Tyler (Tex.) Mus., 1963, 1st prize in sculpture 1st Nat. Space Art Show, 1971, Humanitarian award Milehi Denver Sertoma, 1994, The Gleitsman Found., 1994, Svc. to Mankind awards Freedom Found. at Valley Forge, Mile Hi Sertoma Club, Minoruyasui Found., Gleitsman Found. Mem. Artists Equity Assn., Rocky Mountain Liturgical Arts, Allied Sculptors Colo., Allied Arts Inc. Hist. Denver, Symphony Guild, Parks People, Beth Israel Aux. Home: 131 Fairfax St Denver CO 80220-6331

SIBLEY, CELESTINE (MRS. JOHH C. STRONG), columnist, reporter; b. Holly, Fla., May 23, 1917; d. W.R. and Evelyn (Barber) S.; m. James W. Little (dec. 1953); children: James W., Susan Little Bazemore, Mary Little Vance; m. John C. Strong (dec. 1988). Attended, U. Fla., Spring Hill Coll.; LHD (hon.), Spring Hill Coll. Columnist, reporter Atlanta Constitution, 1941—; twice juror Pulitzer Pirze newspaper awards. Author: The Malignant Heart, 1957, Peachtree Street, U.S.A.: An Affectionate Portrait of Atlanta, 1963, (stories) Christmas in Georgia, 1964, A Place Called Sweet Apple, 1967, Dear Store: An Affectionate Portrait of Rich's, 1967, Especially at Christmas, 1969, Mothers are Always Special, 1970, The Sweet Apple Gardening Book, 1972, Day by Day with Celestine Sibley, 1975, Small Blessings, 1977, Ah, Sweet Mystery: A Kate Mulcay Novel of Suspense, 1991, Straight As an Arrow: A Kate Mulcay Mystery, 1992, Dire Happenings at Scratch Ankle, 1993, others. Bd. vis. Grady Hosp.; mem. adv. bd. Neighborhood Justice Ctr.; mem. literary panel Ga. Coun. Arts; head fund appeal Atlanta Area Svcs. for Blind. Recipient Literary Achievement award Ga. Writers Assn., 1964, 2 Recognition awards Dixie Coun. Authors and Journalists, 2 AP awards, Radio and TV Big Story award Pall Mall, 2 awards Ga. Conf. Social Work, Nat. Christopher award, Wesley Woods award, Ralph McGill award Lifetime Achievement in Journalism by Soc. Profl. Journalists, numerous others; named Woman of Yr. in Arts, Atlanta, 1956. Democrat. Presbyterian. Office: Atlanta Constitution Metro Desk 72 Marietta St NW Atlanta GA 30303-2804

SIBOLSKI, ELIZABETH HAWLEY, university administrator; b. Gt. Barrington, Mass., Aug. 18, 1950; d. William Snyder and Frances Harrington (Smith) Gallup; m. John Alfred Sibolski Jr. Aug. 15, 1970. BA, The Am. U., 1973, MPA, 1975, PhD, 1984. Acting dir. acad. adminstrn. The Am. U., Washington, 1974, planning analyst, 1974-79, asst. dir. budget and planning, 1980-83, dir. instl. rsch., 1984-85, dir. planning and instl. rsch., 1985—; trustee Mortar Bd. Nat. Found., 1989—. Recipient Comencement award Am. U. Women's Club, 1973. Mem. ASPA, Assn. Instl. Rsch., Soc. Coll. and Univ. Planning (regional coun. mem. 1990—), Am. Assn. for Higher Edn., Mortar Bd. (sect. coord. 1975-82), Pi Alpha Alpha, Phi Kappa Phi (chpt. officer 1986-92), Pi Sigma Alpha, Omicron Delta Kappa. Home: 565 Wayward Dr Annapolis MD 21401-6747 Office: The Am Univ Office of Planning 4400 Massachusetts Ave NW Washington DC 20016-8001

SICHEL, BEATRICE BONNE, librarian; b. Nuremburg, Fed. Republic Germany, May 26, 1934; came to U.S., 1939; d. Martin and Meta (Hoenlein) Bonne; m. Werner Sichel, Feb. 22, 1959; children: Lawrence, Linda. BS, CCNY, 1955; MA, Brandeis U., 1957; MLS, Western Mich. U., 1972. Rsch. chemist Lederle Labs., Pearl River, N.Y., 1957-59; lab. chemist Baxter Labs., Morton Grove, Ill., 1959-60; libr. Kalsec, Kalamazoo, Mich., 1973, Western Mich. U., Kalamazoo, 1974—. Author: Economics Journals and Serials, 1986. Named for Outstanding Reference Book of 1986, Choice Mag., 1987. Mem. Spl. Libraries Assn., Phi Beta Kappa, Beta Phi Mu, Phi Kappa Phi. Office: Western Mich U Waldo Libr Dept Circulation Kalamazoo MI 49008

SIDDAYAO, CORAZÓN MORALES, economist, educator; b. Manila, July 26, 1932; came to U.S., 1968; d. Crispulo S. and Catalina T. (Morales) S. Cert. in elem. teaching, Philippine Normal Coll., 1951; BBA, U. East, Manila, 1962; MA in Econs., George Washington U., 1971, MPhil, PhD, 1975; postgrad., Inst. de Français, 1989. Tchr. pub. schs. Manila, 1951-53; asst. pensions officer IMF, Washington, 1968-71; cons. economist Washington, 1971-75; rsch. assoc. Policy Studies in Sci. and Tech. George Washington U., Washington, 1971-72, teaching fellow dept. econs., 1972-75; natural gas specialist U.S. Fed. Energy Adminstrn., Washington, 1974-75; sr. rsch. economist, assoc. prof. Inst. S.E.A. Studies, Singapore, 1975-78; sr. rsch. fellow energy/economist East-West Ctr., 1978-81, acad. staff coord. energy and industrialization, 1981-86; vis. fellow London Sch. Econ., 1984-85; sr. energy economist in charge energy program Econ. Devel. Inst., World Bank, Washington, 1986-94, ret., 1994; affiliate prof. econs. U. Hawaii, 1979—; vis. prof. econs. U. Philippines, intermittently 1989—; vis. prof. U. Montpellier, France, 1992; cons. internat. orgns. and govts. Author: Increasing the Supply of Medical Personnel, 1973, The Offshore Petroleum Resources of Southeast Asia: Some Potential Conflicts and Related Economic Factors, 1978, Round Table Discussion on Asian and Multinational Corporations, 1978, The Supply of Petroleum Reserves in Southeast Asia: Economic Implications of Evolving Property Rights Arrangements, 1980, Critical Energy Issues in Asia and the Pacific: the Next Twenty Years, 1982, Criteria for Energy Pricing Policy, 1985, Energy Demand and Economic Growth, 1986; editor: Energy Policy and Planning series, 1990-92, Energy Investments and the Environment, 1993; co-editor: Investissements Energetiques et Environnement, 1993; co-editor (series) Energy Project Analysis for CIS Countries (Russian), 1993, Materiel Pedagogique sur la Politique d'Efficacité de l'Energie et d'Efficacité de l'Energie et l'Environnement, Energy Efficiency Policy and Environment, 1994; contbr. chpts. to books, articles to profl. jours. Grantee in field. Mem. Am. Econ. Assn., Internat. Assn. Energy Economists, Alliance Francaise, Omicron Delta Epsilon. Roman Catholic.

SIDEMAN, EVA STERN, marketing executive; b. Bucharest, Romania; d. Ernest and Rose Stern; m. Daniel Sideman, Oct. 27, 1974; children: Dawn Stern, Stephanie Ann. BA cum laude, U. Minn., 1968; MA, Ind. U., 1970, PhD, 1973; M. Mgmt., Northwestern U., 1982. Instr. English dept. U. Cin., 1970-71; instr. Ind. U., 1972-73; sr. rsch. analyst Amoco Corp., Chgo., 1973-77; communications and rsch. cons. Chgo., 1977-87; tech. writer Walgreen Co., Deerfield, Ill., 1987-90; tng. devel. specialist Covia Corp., Rosemont, Ill., 1990-93; tng. cons., 1994—; lectr. Northwestern U., 1975-79. Trustee Northbrook (Ill.) Pub. Libr., 1986-91. Mem. ASTD, Nat. Soc. for Performance & Instrn., Soc. for Tech. Communications.

SIDNEY, CORINNE ENTRATTER, journalist, actress; b. L.A., Apr. 13, 1937; d. Carl Smith and Alice (Polk) Kegley; m. Jack Entratter (dec. 1971); m. Robert Heffron, 1973 (div. 1980); 1 child, Benjamin Jack; m. George Sidney, Oct. 12, 1991. Student, U. Calif., Berkeley; Grad., U. Judaism, L.A., 1971; postgrad., UCLA, 1983. Feature editor Univ. Man fashion mag., 1972-86; columnist Beverly Hills, 1986-89; writer syndicated entertainment column Real to Real Capital News Svc., 1988-91; stringer USA Today, People weekly, Beverly Hills (Calif.) Post, 1990-91; pub. rels. cons., 1972-86. Film appearances include Murderers' Row, North to Alaska, Speed Limit 65, That Funny Feeling, The Big Mouth, The Journey, (with Peter Sellers) The Party, Road House, (George Sidney's film) The Swinger, Who's Minding the Mint?; TV appearances include Steve Allen, Caine's 100, Cannon, Bob Hope, Hazel, Home Show, Ironside, Monkees, Ozzie and Harriet, Bachelor Father, Tennessee Ernie Ford, General Hospital, FBI, Larry King, Bob Newhart, Shower of Stars, Johnny Carson Players, This is Alice; stage appearances include Born Yesterday, Seven Year Itch, Ninety Day Mistress, Tender Trap,

Who Was That Lady I Saw You With?, Getting It; toured with Las Vegas lounge act The New Yorkers, also toured 1990-TV cir. with playmates of each decade; hostess TV talk show Westcoasting... with Corinne, 1991; co-host Real to Reel. Active civic orgns.; candidate Beverly Hills City Coun., 1980; mem. El Rodeo Sch. PTA, El Rodeo YMCA. 1st runner-up Miss U.S.A. Contest; named Playboy Ctr. Fold of 50's Decade, 1958; named Pin-up Girl of Atomic Nuclear Submarine Nautilus, 1958, one of 7 Top Playmates Fox-TV Am. Chronicles., 1990. Mem. AFTRA (women's com.), SAG, LWV, Women in Film, Am. Film Inst., C. of C. and Civic Assn., Hollywood Women's Press Club, Bus. and Profl. Women (conv. del., Olympic com., program chmn., founder West Side chpt. 1985), Hadassah (v.p., membership chmn., co-chmn. dinner-dance honoring Barbara Sinatra, founder & pres. Haifa chpt.), Israel Tennis Ctrs., UCLA Theatre Arts Alumni Assn.

SIDON, CLAUDIA MARIE, psychiatric-mental health nursing educator; b. Bellaire, Ohio, Feb. 6, 1946; d. Paul and Nell (Bernas) DePaulis; m. Michael Sidon; children: Michael II, Babe. Diploma, Wheeling (W.Va.) Hosp. Sch., 1966; BS in Nursing summa cum laude, Ohio U., Athens, 1979; MS in Nursing, W.Va. U., Morgantown, 1982. Cert. social worker. Various staff positions Bellaire City Hosp., 1966-67, 72-77; adj. nursing faculty W.Va. No. Community Coll., Wheeling, 1977-82; nurse clinician, psychotherapist Valley Psychol. and Psychiat. Svcs., Moundsville, W.Va., 1984; psychotherapist, nurse clinician, case mgr. No. Panhandle Behavioral Health Ctr., Wheeling, 1984-88; assoc. prof. ADN program Belmont Tech. Coll., St. Clairsville, Ohio, 1988—; presenter in field. Mem. Tri-State Psychiat. Nursing Assn. (pres., v.p., program chmn.), Am. Orthopsychiat. Assn., Nat. League for Nursing (presenter), Phi Kappa Phi, Sigma Theta Tau. Home: 52295 Sidon Rd Dillonvale OH 43917-9538 Office: Belmont Tech Coll 120 Fox Shannon Pl Saint Clairsville OH 43950-8751

SIDRAN, MIRIAM, retired physics educator, researcher; b. Washington, May 25, 1920; d. Morris Samson and Theresa Rena (Gottlieb) S. BA, Bklyn. Coll., 1942; MA, Columbia U., N.Y.C., 1949; PhD, NYU, 1956. Rsch. assoc. dept. physics NYU, N.Y.C., 1950-55, postdoctoral fellow, 1955-57; asst. prof. Staten Island Community Coll., Richmond, N.Y., 1957-59; rsch. scientist Grumman Aerospace Corp., Bethpage, N.Y., 1959-67; prof. N.Y. Inst. Tech., N.Y.C., 1967-72; NSF rsch. fellow Nat. Marine Fisheries Svc., Miami, Fla., 1971-72; assoc. prof. then prof. physics Baruch Coll., N.Y.C., 1972-89, chmn. dept. natural scis., 1983-89, prof. emerita, 1990—; v.p. Baruch chpt. Profl. Staff Congress, 1983-89. Contbr. numerous articles to profl. and govtl. publs., chpts. to books. N.Y. State Regents scholar, 1937-41; NSF summer fellow, Miami, 1970. Mem. N.Y. Acad. Scis., Am. Assn. Physics Tchrs. Home: 210 W 19th St Apt 5G New York NY 10011-4009

SIDUN, NANCY MARIE, clinical psychologist, art therapist; b. Newark, July 9, 1955; d. Albert and Mae (Clement) S. BA, Colo. Womens Coll., 1976; MS, Emporia State U., 1978; PsyD, Ill. Sch. Profl. Psychology, 1986. Art therapy intern The Menninger Found., Topeka, 1978-79; art psychotherapist Childrens Med. Ctr., Tulsa, 1979-82; clin. psychologist, pvt. practice Chgo., 1983—; chief psychologist, adminstr. Ill. State Psych. Inst., Chgo., 1987-91; dir. practicum tng., mem. core faculty Chgo. Sch. Profl. Psychology, 1991—; adj. asst. prof. U. Ill., Chgo., 1982-84, 91-93; part-time asst. prof. Sch. Art Inst. Chgo., 1984—; clin. dir. Young Expressions, Chgo., 1985-87; psychologist Henry Horner Childrens Ctr., Chgo., 1986-87; cons. Weight Mgmt. Svcs., Chgo., 1988-89, Touchstone Group, Chgo., 1987, Creative Devel. Ctr., Chgo., 1985-88. Contbr. articles to profl. jours. Mem. APA, Am. Art Therapy Assn., Ill. Psychol. Assn., Ill. Art Therapy Assn., Nat. Coalition Art Therapies Assn. Office: 3170 N Sheridan Rd Apt 210 Chicago IL 60657-4825

SIEBERT, DIANE DOLORES, author, poet; b. Chgo., Mar. 18, 1948; m. Robert William Siebert, Sept. 21, 1969. RN. Author: Truck Song, 1984 (Notable Children's Book award ALA, 1984, Sch. Libr. Jour. one of Best Books 1984, Outstanding Children's Book award N.Y. Times Book Rev. 1984, Reading Rainbow Selection book 1991), Mojave, 1988 (Children's Editor's Choice 1988, Internat. Reading Assn. Tchrs.' Choice award 1989, others), Heartland, 1989 (award Nat. Coun. for Social Studies/Children's Book Coun. 1989, on John Burroughs List Nature Book for Young Readers 1989, award Ohio Farm Bur. Women 1991), Train Song, 1990 (Notable Children's Book award ALA, 1990, Redbook Mag. one of Top Ten Picture Books 1990, one of Best Books award Sch. Libr. Jour. 1990, others), Sierra, 1991 (Outstanding Sci. Trade Book for Children award Nat. Sci. Tchrs.' Assn. 1991, Notable Children's Trade Book in Field Social Studies award Nat. Coun. Social Studies 1991, Beatty award Calif. Libr. Assn. 1992), Plane Song, 1993 (Outstanding Sci. Trade Book for Children 1994, Platinum award Oppenheim Toy Portfolio). Home: PO Box 758 Terrebonne OR 97760-0758

SIEBERT, MURIEL, business executive, former state banking official; b. Cleve.; d. Irwin J. and Margaret Eunice (Roseman) Siebert; student Western Res. U., 1949-52; DCS (hon.), St. John's U., St. Bonaventure U., Molloy Coll., Adelphi U., St. Francis Coll., Mercy Coll., Coll. New Rochelle, St. Lawrence U., Manhattan Coll. Security analyst Bache & Co., 1954-57; analyst Utilities & Industries Mgmt. Corp., 1958, Shields & Co., 1959-60; partner Stearns & Co., 1961, Finkle & Co., 1962-65, Brimberg & Co., N.Y.C., 1965-67; individual mem. (first woman mem.) N.Y. Stock Exchange, 1967; chmn., pres. Muriel Siebert & Co., Inc., 1969-77; trustee Manhattan Savs. Bank, 1975-77; supt. banks, dept. banking State of N.Y., 1977-82; dir. Urban Devel. Corp., N.Y.C., 1977-82, Job Devel. Authority, N.Y.C., 1977-82, State of N.Y. Mortgage Agy., 1977-82; chmn., pres. Muriel Siebert & Co., Inc., 1983—; assoc. in mgmt. Simmons Coll.; mem. adv. com. Fin. Acctg. Standards Bd., 1981-84; guest lectr. numerous colls. Former mem. women's adv. com. Econ. Devel. Adminstrn., N.Y.C.; former trustee Manhattan Coll.; v.p., former mem. exec. com. Greater N.Y. Area council Boy Scouts Am.; mem. N.Y. State Econ. Devel. Bd., N.Y. Coun. Economy; bd. overseers NYU Sch. Bus., 1984-88; former bd. dirs. United Way of N.Y.C.; trustee Citizens Budget Commn., L.I. U.; mem. bus. com. Met. Mus., bus. com. of N.Y. State Bus. Coun.; active Women's Campaign Fund; bd. dirs. N.Y. Women's Agenda. Recipient Spirit of Achievement award Albert Einstein Coll. Medicine, 1977; Women's Equity Action League award, 1978; Outstanding Contbns. to Equal Opportunity for Women award Bus. Council of UN Decade for Women, 1979; Silver Beaver award Boy Scouts Am., 1981; Elizabeth Cutter Morrow award YWCA, 1983; Emily Roebling award Nat. Women's Hall of Fame, 1984; Entrepreneural Excellence award White House Conf. on Small Bus., 1986; NOW Legal Def. and Edn. Fund award, 1981, Brotherhood award Nat. Conf. of Christians and Jews, 1989, Women on the Move award Anti-Defamation League, 1990., award Borough of Manhattan, 1991, Benjamin Botwinick prize Columbia Bus. Sch.'s, 1992, Women in Bus. Making History award Women's Bus. Coun. N.Y. C. of C., 1993, Disting. Woman of the Yr. award Greater N.Y. Boy Scouts of Am., 1993, Woman of the Yr. award Fin. Women's Assn. N.Y., 1994, Medal of Honor award Ellis Island, 1994, Bus. Philanthropist of the Yr. award So. Calif. Conf. for Women Bus. Owner's,, 1990, Corning Excellence award N.Y.S. Bus. Coun., 1993, Star award N.Y. Women's Agenda, Established Siebert Entrepreneurial Philanthropic Plan, N.Y. Urban Coalition's Achievement award, 1994, Women of Distinction award Crohn's and Colitis Found., Entrepreneurial Leadership award Nat. Found. Teaching Entrepreneurship, 1994; inductee Nat. Woman's Hall of Fame, 1994, Internat. Women's Forum Hall of Fame, 1994. Mem. Women's Forum (founding mem., pres.), Com. 200, Fin. Women's Assn. (Community Svc. award 1993), River Club, Doubles Club, Westchester Country Club, West Palm Beach Polo and Country Club, Nat. Assn. Women Bus. Owners (Veuve Clicquot Bus. Women of Yr. award 1992, Lifetime Achievement award 1993), Econ. Club. Home: 435 E 52nd St New York NY 10022-6445 Office: Muriel Siebert & Co Inc 885 3rd Ave New York NY 10022-4834

SIEBERT, STEPHANIE RAY, video production company executive; b. Phoenix, Sept. 17, 1949; d. Richard and Jacquelyn (Schmunk) S. AA, Yavapai Community Coll., 1967; BS, U. Minn., 1970. Acctg. mgr. Ski Mart of Newport Beach, Calif.; contr. Brown Jay Prodns., L.A.; gen. mgr. Video Tape Libr., Ltd., L.A.; pres. Film & Video Stock Shots Inc., L.A.; pres., chmn. Unfettered Mind, non-profit Calif. corp. Bd. dirs., officer Buddhist orgn. Mem. NAFE, NOW (past pres. Laguna Beach), Women's Bus. Enterprises, Assn. Women Entrepreneurial Developers, Am. Film Inst., Am. Mgmt. Assn., Am. Assn. Female Execs., Nat. Assn. Women Bus. Owners, Women in Film, Hollywood C. of C., Bus. and Profl. Women's Assn., Women in Show Bus. Office: Film & Video Stock Shots 10442 Burbank Blvd North Hollywood CA 91601-2177

SIEBRANDS, WENDY LUCILLE, education educator; b. Camrose, Alberta, Can., Mar. 16, 1951; came to U.S., 1983; d. John Arthur Storwick and Marion Irene (Persinger) Belle; m. Calvin Grant Olmstead, May 12, 1973 (div. Oct. 1, 1985); children: Clarie, Alana, Graham; m. Larry Dean Siebrands, Dec. 21, 1990. BEd, U. Alberta,, Can., 1973; MA in English, Wichita State U., 1990; PhD in Adult and Continuing Edn., Kans. State U., 1994. Tchr. Walter Murray Collegiate, Saskatoon, Sask., Can., 1973-76, Sir John A. MacDonald Middle Sch.,, Calgary, Alberta, Can., 1976-78; dir. East Edn Presch., Galveston, Tex., 1980-83; substitute tchr. Trinity H.S., Hutcinson, Kans., 1984-89; grad. teaching asst. Wichita State U., 1987-89; instr. Kans. Newman Coll., Wichita, 1990-93, dir. grad. studies, 1993—; scholar Kans. Com. for the Humanities, Book Talk Series. Home: 1075 Patricia St Wichita KS 67208-2640 Office: Kans Newman Coll 3100 Mccormick St Wichita KS 67213-2008

SIEBURTH, JANICE FAE, librarian, educator; b. Ellensburg, Wash., Jan. 26, 1927; d. Monta Earl and Emma Frances (Huston) Boston; married; children: Heather L., Scott, Peggy J., Leslie E., Huston Clark. BS, Wash. State U., 1949, MS, 1951; MLS, U. R.I., 1972. Instr., reference bibliographer phys. and engrng. scis. U. R.I. Libr., Kingston, 1974-76, asst. prof., ref. libr., 1977-81, assoc. prof., 1982-88, head reference unit, 1985-87; head Pell Marine Sci. Libr. U. R.I. Libr., Narragansett, 1987—, prof., 1988—; mem. adv. com. Nat. Sea Grant Depository, Narragansett, 1984—, URI Marine Programs staff, 1994—; mem. Friends Oceanography Exec. Bd., 1995—. Author: Online Search Services, 1988; (with others) Basic Business Library, 1989; (bibliography) Bay Bib: Narragansett Bay, 1991. Recipient Disting. Alumna award Grad. Sch. Libr. and Info. Studies U. R.I., 1989; grantee Narragansett Bay Project, 1989. Mem. ALA, Internat. Assn. Aquatic and Marine Sci. Librs. and Info. Ctrs., Assn. Coll. and Rsch. Librs., New Eng. Libr. Assn. (pres. 1983-84), R.I. Libr. Assn. (NELA councilor 1978-80). Home: 408 Barbers Pond Rd West Kingston RI 02892-1615 Office: U RI Pell Marine Sci Libr Narragansett RI 02882-1197

SIEFERT, DIANE LYNN, accountant, marketing professional; b. S.I., N.Y., Nov. 8, 1948; d. George Vincent and Dorothy (Bauer) Stergious; m. Edward George Siefert, Nov. 9, 1968; children: Jennifer Lynn, Edward Charles. BS in Acctg. and Sociology, La. State U., 1983. Credit analyst Hallgarten and Co., N.Y.C., 1967-69; acctg. supt. comml. air conditioning div. Singer Co., Carteret, N.J., 1969-74; owner, pres. D.L. Siefert Acctg., Carteret, N.J., 1971-80, Baton Rouge, 1980-90; Daphne, Ala., 1990—; acctg. mgr. Kean Miller Hawthorne D'Armond, McCowan & Jarman, Baton Rouge, 1983-85; v.p. fin. KJM Inc. doing bus. as Baton Rouge Mag., 1985-88; owner, pres. DLS Mktg. Co., Baton Rouge, 1987-89; contr. Resort Mgmt. and Mktg., Gulf Shores, Ala., 1990-93; realtor Prudential/Nichols Real Estate, Daphne, Ala., 1994—; agt. Aflac Ins., Mobile, 1994—; prin. D.L. Siefert Acctg., Baton Rouge, 1980-90, Mobile, Ala., 1990—; substitute tchr. East Baton Rouge Parish Sch. Bd., 1988-90. Mem. NAFE, Nat. Assn. Accts., Am. Soc. Women Accts., Women's Info. and Networking Groups (co-founder, pres. 1987—), Am. Bus. Women's Assn. (past treas., v.p., pres., del. nat. conv. 1985-86, 87-88, 93-94, pres. Ala. Gulf Beach chpt. 1993-94, Woman of Yr. award Baton Rouge 1983, Ala. Gulf Beach chpt. 1993), La Luna Servante, La. State U. Alumni Found., Camelot Garden Club (pres. Baton Rouge 1983). Home: 217 Maplewood Loop Daphne AL 36526-8155 Office: PO Box 1454 Daphne AL 36526-1454

SIEFERT-KAZANJIAN, DONNA, corporate librarian; b. N.Y.C.; d. Merrill Emil and Esther (Levins) S.; m. George John Kazanjian, June 15, 1974; 1 child, Merrill George. BA, NYU, 1969; MSLS, Columbia U., 1973; MBA, Fordham U., 1977. Asst. librarian Dun & Bradstreet, N.Y.C., 1969-73; research assoc. William E. Hill & Co., N.Y.C., 1973-76; sr. info. analyst Info. for Bus., N.Y.C., 1976-77; librarian Handy Assocs., N.Y.C., 1979-90; mgr. Infoserve Fuchs Cuthrell & Co., Inc., N.Y.C., 1991-94; libr. Heidrick & Struggles, Inc., N.Y.C., 1994—. Mem. Spl. Librs. Assn., Rsch. Roundtable, Am. Mensa Ltd. Roman Catholic. Office: Heidrick & Struggles Inc 245 Park Ave New York NY 10167

SIEGAL, RITA GORAN, engineering company executive; b. Chgo., July 16, 1934; d. Leonard and Anabelle (Soloway) Goran; m. Burton L. Siegal, Apr. 11, 1954; children: Norman, Laurence Scott. Student, U. Ill., 1951-53; BA, DePaul U., 1956. Cert. elem. tchr., Ill. Tchr. Chgo. Public Schs., 1956-58; founder, chief exec. officer Budd Engring. Corp., Skokie, Ill., 1959—; founder, pres. Easy Living Products Co., Skokie, 1960—; pvt. practice in interior design, Chgo., 1968-73; dist. sales mgr. Super Girls, Skokie, 1976; lectr. Northwestern U., 1983; guest speaker nat. radio and TV, 1979—. Contbr. to profl. jours. Mem. adv. bd. Skokie High Schs., 1975-79; advisor Cub Scouts Skokie coun. Boy Scouts Am., 1975; bus. mgr. Nutrition for Optimal Health Assn., Winnetka, Ill., 1980-82, pres., 1982-84, v.p. med./profl., 1985-93; leader Great Books Found., 1972; founder Profit Plus Investment, 1970; bd. dirs. Noha, Internat. Recipient Cub Scout awards Boy Scouts Am., 1971-72, Nat. Charlotte Danstrom award Nat. Women of Achievement, 1988, Corp. Achievement award, 1988. Mem. North Shore Women in Mgmt. (pres. 1987-88), Presidents Assn. Ill. (bd. dirs. 1990-94, membership chairperson 1991-93), No. Ill. Indsl. Assn., Ill. Mfrs. Assn., Inventors Coun. Office: Budd Engring Corp 8707 Skokie Blvd Skokie IL 60077-2269

SIEGEL, BARBARA Z(ENZ), biology research scientist, educator; b. Detroit, July 22, 1931; d. Joseph and Barbara (Justh) Zenz; m. Sanford Marvin Siegel, June 24, 1950 (dec. 1990); children: Stephanie Siegel Morgan, Andrea, Peter Mark, David Nathaniel. AB in Philosophy, U. Chgo., 1960; MA in Zoology, Columbia U., 1963; PhD in Biology, Yale U., 1966. Postdoctoral fellow Yale U., New Haven, 1966-67; dir. biology program U. Hawaii, Honolulu, 1967-72, sr. researcher Pacific Biomed. Research Ctr., 1975-87, interim dir. research adminstrn., dean grad. sch., 1979-82, dir. pesticide hazard assessment project, 1983-87, prof. microbiology and botany grad. dept. pub. health, 1986-89, assoc. dean sch. pub. health, 1989—, dean Sch. Pub. Health, 1992—; prof. pub. health sci. and environ./occupational health Pacific Biomed. Rsch. Ctr., 1989—; had environ./occupational health Pacific Biomed. Research Ctr., 1989—; co-chmn. radiation sub-com. Com. Space Research Hdqrs., Paris, 1975-82; vis. prof. Heidelberg (Fed. Republic of Germany), 1973, Weizmann Inst., Rehovot, Israel, 1986, vis. prof. Geology, Botany, U. Brit. Columbia, 1982; vis. scholar People's Republic of China, 1985; vis. colleague Nat. Research Council of Italy, Pisa, 1987—; sr. lectr. Fulbrights-Hays, Finland, 1988. Editor: Hawaii Energy Resource Overviews: Geothermal Development, 1980; contbr. numerous articles to profl. jours. Chmn. Gov.'s Panel on Pesticides, Honolulu, 1985; mem. Commn. on Pesticides, Honolyly, 1986-88; mem. Peace Inst., Honolulu, 1985—; chmn. Masumnaga Inst. for Peace, 1992; mem. univ. commn. on status of women Hawaii Assn. Women in Sci. and Faculty Women's Caucus, 1986; co-investigator U.S./Israel Bionat., 1988—. Fulbright-Hays scholar, Yugoslavia, 1972; Fulbright rsch. fellow USIS, Yugoslavia and Fed. Republic of Germany, 1972-73; scholar to Finland, 1988-89. Mem. Am. Chem. Soc., Internat. Chem. Ecology Assn., Hawaii Acad. Scis. (chair 1993—), Sigma Xi (Cloptin award for Disting. Community Svc., Disting. Nat. lectr. 1994-95). Home: 3119 Beaumont Woods Pl Honolulu HI 96822-1421 Office: U Hawaii Sch Pub Health Biomed 208 Honolulu HI 96822

SIEGEL, BETTY LENTZ, college president; b. Cumberland, Ky., Jan. 24, 1931; d. Carl N. and Vera (Hogg) Lentz; m. Joel H. Siegel, June 6; children: David Jonathan, Michael Jeremy. B.A., Wake Forest Coll., 1952; M.Ed., U. N.C., 1953; Ph.D., Fla. State U., 1961; postgrad., Ind. U., 1964-66; hon. doctorate, Miami U., 1985, Cumberland Coll., 1985, Ea. Ky. U., 1992. Asst. prof. Lenoir Rhyne Coll., Hickory, N.C., 1956-59; assoc. prof., 1961-64; asst. prof. U. Fla., Gainesville, 1967-70; assoc. prof. U. Fla., 1970-72, prof., 1973-76, dean acad. affairs for continuing edn., 1972-76; dean Sch. Edn. and Psychology Western Carolina U., Cullowhee, N.C., 1976-81; pres. Kennesaw State Coll., Marietta, Ga., 1981—; bd. dirs. Atlanta Gas Light Co., Equifax Inc., Nat. Services Industries, Acordia Benefits of the South Inc.; cons. numerous sch. systems. Author: Problem Situations in Teaching, 1971; contbr. articles to profl. jours. Bd. dirs. Boy Scouts Am., Ga. Acad. Children and Youth Profls., Ga. Coun. Econ. Edn., United Way, Northside Hosp. Found., Nat. Ctr. for Excellence in Edn. Recipient Outstanding Tchr. award U. Fla., 1969; Mortar Bd. Woman of Yr. award U. Fla., 1973, Mortar Bd. Educator of Yr., Ga. State U., 1983, CASE award, 1986, Alumna of Yr. award Wake Forest U., 1987, "Grad Made Good" award Fla. State U. Alumni Assn, Omicron Delta Kappa, 1991, Spirit of Life award City of Hope, 1992, Woman of Achievement award Cobb Chamber YWCA, 1992; named One of 100 Most Influential People in State of Ga., Ga. Trend Mag., Outstanding Alumni, Fla. State U. Coll. Edn. Alumni Assn., 1992. Mem. ASCD, Am. Psychol. Assn., Am. Assn. State Colls. and Univs. (bd. dirs., chmn. 1990), Am. Coun. Edn. (bd. dirs., bd. advisors), Am. Inst. Mng. Diversity (bd. dirs.), Soc. Internat. Bus. Fellows, Internat. Alliance for Invitational Edn. (cofounder, co-dir.), Bus./Higher Edn. Forum, Assn. Tchr. Educators' Commn. on Leadership in Interprofl. Edn. (task force on tchr. edn.), Cobb C. of C., Atlanta C. of C., Phi Alpha Theta, Pi Kappa Delta, Alpha Psi Omega, Kappa Delta Pi, Pi Lambda Theta, Phi Delta Kappa, Delta Kappa Gamma, Kiwanis (Atlanta chpt.). Baptist. Office: Kennesaw State Coll Office of the President PO Box 444 Marietta GA 30061-0444

SIEGEL, CAROLE ETHEL, mathematician; b. N.Y., Sept. 29, 1936; d. David and Helen (Mayer) Schore; m. Bertram Siegel, Aug. 18, 1957; children: Sharon, David. BA in Math., NYU, 1957, MS in Math., 1959, PhD in Math., 1963. With computer dept. Atomic Energy Commn., 1957-59; rsch. asst. Courant Inst. of Math. Sci., 1959-63; rsch. scientist dept. of engrng. NYU, N.Y.C., 1963-64; rsch. math. Info. Scis. Div. Rockland Rsch. Inst., Orangeburg, N.Y., 1965-74; head Epidemiology and Health Svcs. Rsch. Lab Stat. Scis., Epidemiology Divsn./Nathan S. Kline Inst. Rsch., Orangeburg, N.Y., 1974—; rsch. prof. dept. psychiatry NYU, 1987—; dep. dir. WHO Collaborating Ctr., Nathan S. Kline Inst., 1987—; grant reviewer NIHM, 1988—. Editor: (with S. Fischer) Psychiatric Records in Mental Health Care, 1981; contbr. articles to profl. jours. Recipient grants NIMH, 1993—, 88-91, Nat. Ctr. for Health Svcs. Rsch., 1979-82, Nat. Inst. Alcohol Abuse, 1978-82. Mem. Assn. for Health Svcs. Rsch., Am. Soc. Clin. Pharmacology and Therapeutics, Assn. Women in Math., Am. Statis. Assn. Office: Nathan S Kline Inst Orangeburg NY 10962

SIEGEL, LUCY BOSWELL, public relations executive; b. N.Y.C., July 5, 1950; d. Werner Leiser and Carol (Fleischer) Boswell; m. Henry Winter Siegel, Nov. 11, 1979 (div.); children: David Alan Siegel, Joshua Adam Siegel. BA, Conn. Coll., 1972. Assoc. editor Conn. Western, Litchfield, Conn., 1972-73; assoc. editor, editor United Bus. Publ., N.Y.C., 1974-78; mgr. external communications Equitable Life Assurance Soc., N.Y.C., 1978-86; mgr. internat. affairs Cosmo Pub. Relations Corp., Tokyo, Japan, 1986-87; dir. internat. affairs Cosmo Pub. Relations Corp., Tokyo, 1987-88; mng. dir. Cosmo Pub. Rels. Corp., N.Y.C., 1988-90; pres. Siegel Assocs. Internat., N.Y.C., 1991—; bd. dirs. Cosmo Pub. Rels. Corp., Tokyo, N.Y.C., 1987-91. Contbr. articles to jours. and mags. Bd. dirs., Am. Jewish Com. (N.Y.C. chpt.) 1993-94. Mem. Pub. Rels. Soc. Am., Women Execs. in Pub. Rels., Japan Soc., NY, Am. C. of C. in Japan. Democrat. Jewish. Home: 41 W 96th St Apt 12B New York NY 10025-6519 Office: Siegel Assocs Internat Ltd 38 E 29th St 7th Fl New York NY 10016-7986

SIEGEL, MARGOT, journalist, real estate executive; b. St. Paul, Apr. 2, 1923; d. William and Jeanne (Braunschweig) Auerbacher; m. Charles Raddock (dec.); m. Harold Siegel (dec.); children: William Joseph, Sandra Marguerite. BA in Journalism, U. Minn., 1944. Feature writer ARC News, St. Louis, 1944-45; fgn. corr., editor/reporter Women's Wear Daily Fairchild Publs., N.Y.C., 1946-60; pub. rels. dir. Walker Art Ctr., Mpls., 1962-66; freelance writer Mpls., 1966-89; ptnr. Siegel-Hogan Enterprises, Mpls., 1970-89; columnist Skyway News, Mpls., 1989—; owner Siegel Properties, Mpls., 1989—. Author: Look Forward to a Career: Fashion, 1970. Founder, past pres. Friends of Goldstein Gallery, St. Paul, 1974; past pres. Mpls.-St. Paul Fashion Group; founder Palm Springs (Calif.) Fashion Group, 1987. Named one of 1940's Alumni of Notable Achievement, Coll. Lit. and Theatre, U. Minn., 1994. Mem. Pres.'s Club U. Minn. Home: 25 Park Ln Minneapolis MN 55416 Office: Siegel Properties 83 S 10th St Minneapolis MN 55403

SIEGEL, SYLVIA, law librarian; b. Siberia, Russia, Mar. 8, 1946; came to U.S., 1950; d. Harry and Greta (Gersten) S. AA of Law Libr., Columbia U., 1968. Law libr. Weil Gotshal Manges, N.Y.C., 1963—. Mem. Am. Libr. Assn., N.Y. Libr. Assn., Law Libr. Assn. Greater N.Y. (chair pro bono com.), Spl. Librs. Assn. Jewish. Home: 238 6th Ave Brooklyn NY 11215-2149 Office: Weil Gotshal & Manges 767 5th Ave New York NY 10153-0001

SIEGELMAN, ALLISON STACEY, financial planner; b. Newark, N.J., Sept. 30, 1962; d. Monroe Aaron and Mona Royce (Bengelsdorf) G.; m. Bryan Marshall Siegelman, Oct. 19, 1986; 1 child, Ariel Rachel. BSBA, Muhlenberg Coll., 1984. Cert. fin. planner, Pa. Fin. cons. EF Hutton, Inc., Short Hills, N.J., 1985-88, Smith Barney Shearson, York, Pa., 1988—; lectr. in field. Contbr. articles to profl. jours., newspapers, mags. Publicity chair York County Dental Aux., 1991—; membership bd. York Jewish Community Ctr., 1991—; donor chair Temple Bethel Sisterhood. Mem. Internat. Assn. Fin. Planners, Cen. Pa. Assn. Fin. Planners, Women's Network York, York Jewish Cmty. Investment Club (pres. 1991-92). Office: Smith Barney Shearson 135 N George St York PA 17401-1132

SIEGERT, BARBARA (MARIE), health care administrator; b. Boston, May 22, 1935; d. Salvatore Mario and Mary Kathleen (Wagner) Tartaglia; m. Herbert C. Siegert (dec. Apr. 1974); children: Carolyn Marie, Herbert Christian Jr. Diploma, Newton-Wellesley (Mass.) Hosp. Sch. Nursing, 1956; MEd, Antioch U., 1980. Diplomate Am. Bd. Med. Psychotherapists. Supr. nursing Hogan Regional Ctr., Hathorne, Mass., 1974-78; community mental health nursing advisor Cape Ann area office Dept. Mental Health, Beverly, Mass., 1978-79; dir. case mgmt. Dept. Mental Health, Beverly, 1979-87, dir. case mgmt. north shore area office, 1988-91; dir. case mgmt. Dept. Mental Health-north shore area-Lynn (Mass.) site, Lynn, Mass., 1991-92; mem. interdisciplinary faculty, profl. cons. com., lecture staff clin. pastoral counseling program Danvers State Hosp./Hogan/Berry Regional Ctrs., Hathorne, Mass., 1982-86; nursing edn. adv. com. North Shore Community Coll., Beverly, 1983-91; tng. staff Balter Inst., Ipswich, Mass., 1987-88. Mem. Internat. Cultural Diploma Honor, 1989—. Recipient Spl. Recognition award Lexington (Mass.) Pub. Schs., 1973, Peter Torci award Lexington Friends of Children in Spl. Edn., 1974; named Internat. Biog. Roll. of Honor, 1989—. Fellow Am. Biog. Inst. (life, Woman of Yr. 1990); mem. World Inst. Achievement. Home: 63 Willow Rd # B Boxford MA 01921-1218

SIEGLER, AVA LEE, psychologist; b. Lakewood, N.J., Dec. 17, 1939; d. Philip Jerome and Charlotte Francis (Gunsberg) Heyman; m. Robert Siegler, July 5, 1959; children: Dan Adam, Jess Gabriel. BA, Bennington Coll., 1959; MA, Columbia U., 1960; PhD, NYU, 1972. Lic. psychologist, N.Y., 1973. Liaison supr. Bellevue Hosp. Pediatric Project, 1971-75; dir. N.Y.C. Day Care, Prescott Early Intervention Project, 1972-87; assoc. clin. prof. NYU, 1976-88; dir. suicide prevention team Stuyvesant High Sch./LaGuardia High Sch., 1982-84; sr. supr. Postgrad. Ctr. Mental Health, 1985-90, dir. child adolescent and family clinic, 1981-88, dean tng., v.p. profl. acad. affairs, 1988-90; clin. psychologist, 1973—; dir. Inst. Child Adolescent and Family Studies, 1991—; cons. Childrens Aid Soc., 1971-73; cons. family project Bethlehem Day Care Ctr., 1971-75, Spence-Chapin Agy., 1973-76; lectr. NYU Med. Sch., 1983-88; forensic cons. N.Y. State Supreme Ct., 1987—; speaker in field. Author: What Should I Tell the Kids A Parent's Guide to Real Problems in the Real World, 1993; contbr. editor, columnist Child mag.; contbr. articles to profl. jours. Mem. APA, N.Y. State Psychol. Assn., NYU Postdoctoral Soc., N.Y. Freudian Soc., Internat. Psychoanalytic Assn. Office: 15 Charles St Ste 7E New York NY 10014

SIEGMAN, MARION JOYCE, physiology educator; b. Bklyn., Sept. 7, 1933; d. C. Joseph and Helen (Wasserman) S. BA, Tulane U., 1954; PhD, SUNY, Bklyn., 1966. Instr. physiology Med. Coll. Thomas Jefferson U., Phila., 1967-68, asst. prof., 1968-71, assoc. prof., 1971-77, prof., 1977—; mem. physiology study sect. NIH. Editor: Regulation and Contraction of Smooth Muscle, 1987. Recipient award for excellence in rsch. and teaching Burlington No. Found., 1986, award for excellence in teaching Lindback Found., 1987, Outstanding Alumna award, Newcomb Coll./Tulane U., 1990; grantee NIH, 1967—. Mem. Am. Physiol. Soc., Biophys. Soc., Soc. Gen. Physiologists, Physiol. Soc. Phila. (pres. 1972-73). Office: Jefferson Med Coll 1020 Locust St Philadelphia PA 19107-6799

SIEGMUND, MELINDA GAYLE, marketing executive; b. Ft. Worth, Apr. 14, 1962; d. Grant and Betty Jean (Beil) Johnson; m. Martin Scott Siegmund, Nov. 9, 1985; 1 child, Rachel Elizabeth. BA in Advt. and Pub. Rels., Tex. Tech U., 1983; MA in Communications, U. Fla., 1984. Account exec. Phillip Poole and Assocs., Ft. Worth, 1984-85; account supr. Graphic Concepts, Ft. Worth, 1985-86; from mktg. mgr. physician svcs. to mktg. analyst satellite network Vol. Hosps. of Am., Irving, Tex., 1986-89; asst. mktg. dir. Bedford Meadows Hosp., Bedford, Tex., 1989-90; pvt. practice mktg. svcs. Bedford, Tex., 1991—; cons. Vol. Hosps. of Am., Irving, Tex., 1988—. Exec. dir. Miss Hurst-Euless-Bedford Scholarship Found., 1987—; vice chmn. Cen. Bus. Dist. Planning Com., Bedford, 1990—; active Hurst-Euless-Bedford Econ. Devel. Com., 1988—. Mem. Profl. Models Am. (charter adv., historian 1990-91), Hurst-Euless-Bedford C. of C., State Assn. Local Miss Tex. Scholarship Pageants (pres. 1992—). Baptist. Office: Siegmund Mktg Svcs 3816 Hillwood Way Bedford TX 76021-2529

SIEKMAN, GRACE ANNE, nursing administrator; b. Nebr., Aug. 1, 1952; d. Frank E. and Lucille C. (Wegehoeft) Cherry; m. Dana M. Siekman, Jan. 7, 1972; children: Meredith, Michelle, Marlayna. LPN, S.E. Community Coll., 1974; ADN, SUNY, 1986; BSN, U. Phoenix, 1994. RN, Colo.; cert. ACLS instr., BLS instr., EMT instr.; cert. neonatal resuscitation instr., ABLS trauma care nurse, EMT-intermediate. Staff nurse Teamsters Hosp., Anchorage, 1975-77, Westside Manor, Lexington, Nebr., 1978-80; neonatal nurse Good Samaritan Hosp., Kearney, Nebr., 1980-81; staff nurse, Lamaze instr. Jennie Melham Meml. Med. Ctr., Broken Bow, Nebr., 1981-85, Med. Ctr., Holyoke, Colo., 1985-87; charge nurse, Lamaze instr. Chase County Hosp., Imperial, Nebr., 1987-88; charge nurse med./surg. Kit Carson County Hosp., Burlington, Colo., 1988-93, home health coord., 1993, obstetrics supr., 1993—; paraprofl. Stratton Schs., 1989-92; EMT instr. Morgan Community Coll., Ft. Morgan, 1989—. Vol. EMT-I Stratton Ambulance Svc., 1988—; pianist, organist Stratton Meth. Ch., 1988—. Named Outstanding Nurse of Yr., Kit Carson County, 1991, 92; recipient Northeastern Plains Nurse award, 1993. Mem. AWHONN, Emergency Med. Assn. Colo. (EMT Intermediate of Yr. 1991), Order Eastern Star. Home: PO Box 284 Stratton CO 80836

SIELOFF, ANDREA KATHLEEN, social worker; b. Detroit, Nov. 30, 1951; d. Francis Anthony and Eleanora Mary (Skotzke) S. BS, Detroit Mercy, 1976. Cert. social worker, Mich.; cert. geriatric resources specialist; joined Sisters of Mercy, 1970. Dir. religious edn. Immaculate Heart Parish, Detroit, 1976-78; houseparent Frontier Apostalate, Prince George, B.C., Can., 1978-80; co-dir., help office Sisters of Mercy, Benton Harbor, Mich., 1980-82; dir. White Gates Retreat Ctr. Sisters of Mercy, Battle Creek, Mich., 1982-89; support svc. tech. Mercy Hosp., Owensboro, Ky., 1989-91; case mgr. for elderly Green River Area Devel. Dist., Owensboro, 1991—. Bd. trustees Mercy Hosp., Battle Creek, 1986-89, ARC, Benton Harbor, Mich., 1980-82. Roman Catholic. Office: Green River Area Devel Dist 3860 US Hwy 60 W Owensboro KY 48301

SIEMER, DEANNE CLEMENCE, lawyer; b. Buffalo, Dec. 25, 1940; d. Edward D. and Dorothy J. (Helsdon) S.; m. Howard P. Willens; 1 child, Jason L. BA, George Washington U., 1962; LLB, Harvard U., 1968. Bar: N.Y. 1968, D.C. 1969, Md. 1972, Trust Ter. 1976. Economist Office of Mgmt. and Budget, Washington, 1964-67; assoc., then ptnr. Wilmer, Cutler & Pickering, Washington, 1968-90; ptnr. Pillsbury, Madison & Sutro, Washington, 1990—; gen. counsel U.S. Dept. of Def., Washington, 1977-79; spl. asst. to sec. U.S. Dept. of Energy, Washington, 1979-80. Author: Tangible Evidence, 1984, 2d edit., 1989, Understanding Modern Ethical Standards, 1985, Manual on Litigation Support Databases, 1986, supplement, 1992. Mem. Lawyers Com. for Civil Rights, Washington, 1973—; mediator D.C. Superior Ct., Washington, 1986—, U.S. Ct. Appeals, Washington, 1988—; chair Nat. Inst. Trial Advocacy, Am. Law Inst. Recipient Citation Air Force Assn., 1977, Dist. Pub. Service medal Sec. of Def., 1979, Commendation Pres. of U.S. 1981. Mem. ABA, ATLA, D.C. Bar Assn., No. Marianas Bar Assn., Womens Bar Assn. Episcopalian. Office: Pillsbury Madison & Sutro 1667 K St NW Washington DC 20006-1605

SIEMON, JOYCE MARILYN, lawyer, writer; b. Bridgeport, Conn., Dec. 4, 1944; d. George Lewis and Rita (Siegel) Nissenson; 1 child, Alyssa Karen. BA in English, Carnegie Inst. Tech., 1966; JD with high honors, Fla. State U., 1980. Bar: Fla. Tech. writer Computer Sci. Research Ctr. Carnegie Inst. Tech., Pitts., 1966-67; tchr. Leesville (La.) Jr. High Sch., 1967-68, Leesville State Sch., 1968; mag. editor VanTrump, Zeigler and Shane, Pitts., 1969; news editor Pitts. Press, 1970; staff writer Dade County Pub. Safety Dept., Miami, 1971-75; reporter North Dade Jour., Miami, 1977; freelance writer, 1977—; instr. legal writing and research Coll. Law Fla. State U., Tallahassee, 1979-80; intern. Fla. Supreme Ct., 1980; law clk. Office Gen. Counsel, Fla. Dept. Gen. Services, Tallahassee, 1980; assoc. Young, Stern & Tannenbaum, P.A., North Miami Beach, Fla., 1981, Greenberg, Traurig, Askew, Hoffman, Lipoff, Quentel & Wolff, P.A., Miami, Fla., 1981-82, Hornsby & Whisenand, Miami, 1982-85; pvt. practice, North Miami Beach, 1985-92, Boca Raton, 1992—. Editor: Lawrenceville: A Short History, 1969; author weekly humor column Siemon Says, North Dade Jour., 1977; author employee manual, advt. brochures, newspaper articles and ads, book revs.; author, editor, contbr. articles to legal and non-legal publs. Dade County coord. Network, 1983. Mem. ABA, Fla. Bar (various coms.), Am. Judicature Soc., Dade County Bar Assn., Am. Jewish Congress (v.p. S.E. region), Internat. Platform Assn., Order of Coif, Phi Alpha Delta, Kiwanis Internat. (bd. dirs.). Office: 1200 N Federal Hwy Ste 200 Boca Raton FL 33432-2845

SIEWERT, ROBIN NOELLE, chemical engineer; b. Heidelberg, Fed. Republic Germany, Dec. 14, 1956; (parents Am. citizens); d. Orville Ray and Norma Idella (Sprink) S. BSChemE, U. Tex., 1979; MA in Christian Edn., So. Bapt. Theol. Sem., 1993. Registered profl. engr. Start-up engr. Cen. Power and Light Co., Fannin, Tex., 1979-81; chem. engr. Cen. Power and Light Co., Corpus Christi, Tex., 1981-85, performance analysis engr., 1985-87, performance analysis supr., 1987-91; budget analyst Louisville Gas & Electric, 1992-93, chem. engr., 1994—. Republican. Baptist. Home: 8307 Delido Rd Louisville KY 40219

SIFF, MARLENE IDA, artist; b. N.Y.C., Sept. 20, 1936; d. Irving Louis and Dorothy Gertrude (Lahn) Marmer; m. Elliott Justin Siff, July 11, 1959; children: Bradford Evan, Brian Douglas. BA, Hunter Coll., 1957. Cert. elem. tchr., N.Y., N.J. Tchr. Stewart Manor (N.Y.) Sch. System, 1957-59, Teaneck (N.J.) Sch. System, 1959-60; free-lance interior designer Westport, Conn., 1966-70; designer indsl. plant Varo Inertial Products, Trumbull, Conn., 1970; corp. sec., treas. Belmar Corp., Westport, 1972—, also bd. dirs.; chmn. bd. Marlene Designs Inc., Westport, 1973-77; owner Marlene Siff Design Studio, Westport, 1978—; designer Signature Collections, J.P. Stevens & Co., Inc., 1974-78, J.C. Penney Co., N.Y.C., 1978, C.R. Gibson Co., Norwalk, Conn., 1980; aesthetic cons. ALCIDE Corp., Norwalk, 1980-88. One-woman shows include David Segal Gallery, N.Y.C., 1987, Conn. Pub. TV Gallery 24, Hartford, 1987, Paul Mellon Art Ctr. at Choate Rosemary Hall, Wallingford Conn., 1989, Conn. Nat. Bank Hdqrs., Norwalk, 1990. The Michael Stone Collection, Washington, 1992, Bergdorf Goodman, N.Y.C., 1993, Joel Kessler Fine Art, Miami Beach, Fla., 1994. Decorator ann. charity ball Easter Seal Home Svc., 1976; bd. dirs. United Jewish Appeal, Westport, 1982-86; mem. com. Levitt Pavillion Performing Arts, Westport, 1982-89. Recipient award Lower Conn. Mfrs. Assn., 1970. Mem. Kappa Pi. Home: 15 Broadview Rd Westport CT 06880-2303

SIFF, PATSY HARRIS, elementary educator; b. Charleston, W.Va., Mar. 8, 1938; d. Joseph Harris and Ruth Lillian (Mendelson) Harris; m. Alan Lewis Siff, June 17, 1962; children: Jonathan Edward, Andrew Michael. Degree, Northwestern U., 1959; postgrad., U. Cin., 1955-63, U. Akron, 1978-83, Cleve. State U., 1983, Ashland U., 1994. Cert. elem. tchr., spl. edn. tchr., social studies and computer tchr., Ohio. 8th grade lang. arts and social studies tchr. Norwood (Ohio) Bd. Edn., 1959-60; 8th grade tchr. Laguna Salada Bd. Edn., Pacifica, Calif., 1960-61; 5th grade tchr. Wyoming (Ohio) Bd. Edn., 1962-65, Lincolnwood (Ill.) Bd. Edn., 1965-68; learning disability tutor Akron (Ohio) Bd. Edn., 1974-78; tchr. learning disability class Highland Local Schs., Medina, Ohio, 1978-88, 4th grade tchr., 1988—. Mem. Jewish Family Svc. Bd.; vol. Nat. Office Robert Kennedy Presdl. Campaign, Washington, 1968. Martha Holden Jennings Found. grantee for computer edn./spl. edn., 1983. Mem. NEA (sec. Highland chpt. 1993-94, treas. Lincolnwood chpt. 1967-68), Jewish Cmty. Fedn. (v.p. edn. women's divsn.), Women's History Project (rep.), Mensa. Office: Sharon Ctr Elem Sch 6335 Ridge PO Box 179 Sharon Center OH 44274-0179

SIFTON, ELISABETH, book publisher; b. N.Y.C., Jan. 13, 1939; d. Reinhold and Ursula (Keppel-Compton) Niebuhr; m. Charles P. Sifton, 1962 (div. 1984); children: Peter Samuel, Charles Tobias, John Paul Gustav. B.A. magna cum laude, Radcliffe Coll., Cambridge, Mass., 1960; postgrad., U. Paris, 1960-61. Asst. to dep. asst. sec. of state U.S. Dept. of State, Washington, 1961-62; editorial asst., assoc. editor, editor, sr. editor Frederick A. Praeger Pubs., N.Y.C., 1962-68; editor, sr. editor, editor-in-chief The Viking Press, N.Y.C., 1969-83; v.p., pub. Elisabeth Sifton Books, Viking Penguin, N.Y.C., 1984-87; exec. v.p. Alfred A. Knopf, Inc., N.Y.C., 1987-92; sr. v.p. Farrar, Straus & Giroux, 1993—; pub. Hill & Wang, 1993—. Fulbright fellow, 1960-61. Democrat. Episcopalian. Home: 15 Claremont Ave New York NY 10027 Office: Farrar Straus & Giroux 19 Union Sq W New York NY 10003-3304

SIGALA, STEPHANIE CHILDS, art librarian; b. Berkeley, Calif., Nov. 1, 1947; d. Henry Everett and Mary Elizabeth (Baeck) Childs; m. Donald R. Allen, Aug. 19, 1980. BA in Art History, UCLA, 1968, MA, 1970; MSLS, U. Ill., 1984. Instr. art dept. U. Wis., Whitewater, 1971-73; slide curator art history dept. U. Wis., Milw., 1973-74; asst. prof. dept. art Ill. State U., Normal, 1978-83; head libr. architecture and fine arts libr. Auburn (Ala.) U., 1984-85; head libr. Richardson Meml. Libr. St. Louis Art Mus., 1985—; adj. prof. sch. libr. and info. sci. U. Mo., Columbia, 1988, 90, 92, 94; lectr. in art evening coll. U. Mo., St. Louis, 1990; instr. continuing edn. program Auburn U., 1985; student asst. classics libr. U. Ill., Urbana-Champaign, 1983-84, 76-78, grad. teaching asst., 1975-78; slide cataloger UCLA Visual Resources Ctr., 1970-71; student asst. UCLA Art Libr. and Belt Libr. of Vinciana, 1967-70; mem. edn. com. St. Louis Regional Libr. Network, 1986-88; speaker in field. Contbg. writer: A History of American Mass Market Magazines, 1990; editor, chief writer: The Museum Building: Inside and Out, Then and Now, 1990, Art of the Ancient World, 1989; editor: Art Documentation, 1985-88; contbr. articles and revs. to profl. jours. Mem. auction steering com. Mo. NARAL, St. Louis, 1993. Grantee Samuel H. Kress Found., 1969, NDEA Title II, 1970. Mem. ALA, Visual Resources Assn., Art Librs. Soc. N.Am. (collection devel. com. 1993—, art documentation adv. com. 1989-92), Art Librs. Soc. N.Am. (vice chair cen. plains chpt. 1987-88, chair 1988-89), Spl. Librs. Assn. (program com. chair St. Louis Metro chpt. 1993—, dir.-at-large 1989-90), Archaeol. Inst. Am. (bd. local chpt. 1975-76), Mid-West Art History Assn., Art History Assn. Champaign-Urbana (pres. 1977-78), AAUP (chpt. treas. 1979-80), Beta Phi Mu, Phi Kappa Phi. Office: Saint Louis Art Mus 1 Fine Arts Dr Saint Louis MO 63110-1380

SIGHOLTZ, SARA O'MEARA, non-profit organization executive; b. Knoxville, Tenn.; m. Robert Sigholtz; children: John; stepchildren: Taryn, Whitney. Attended, Briarcliff Jr. Coll.; BA, The Sorbonne, Paris. Co-founder, chmn. bd., CEO CHILDHELP USA/Internat. (formerly Children's Village USA), Woodland Hills, Calif., 1974—. Bd. dirs. Internat. Soc. Prevention Child Abuse and Neglect, Children to Children, Inc.; hon. com. mem. Learning Disabilities Found., Inc.; mem. Mayor's adv. bd., Defense for Children Internat., Nat. Soc. Prevention Cruelty to Children, World Affairs Coun.; adv. bd. mem. Ednl. Film Co.; bd. dirs. Internat. Alliance on Child Abuse and Neglect; sustaining mem. Spastic Children's League, past pres.; mem., past recording sec. Assistance League So. Calif. Recipient Cross of Merit, Knightly Order of St. Brigitte, 1967, Victor M. Carter Diamond award Japan-Am. Soc., 1970, Dame Cross of Merit of Order of St. John of Denmark, 1980, Official Seal of 34th Gov. Calif., 1981, Woman of Achievement award Career Guild, 1982, Women Making History award Nat. Fedn. Bus. Profl. Women's Clubs, 1983, Disting. Am. award for svc., 1984, Humanitarian award Nat. Frat. Eagles, 1984, Nat. Recognition award outstanding leadership Am. Heritage Found., 1986, Notable Am. award svc. to Calif., 1986, Dove of Peace award Pacific Southwest and Ctrl. Pacific Regions B'nai B'rith, 1987, Paul Harris fellow award Rotary Found., 1989, Love and Help the Children award, 1990, Presdl. award, 1990, Hubert Humphrey award Touchdown Club Washington, 1994, numerous others. Mem. SAG, AFTRA, Victory Awards (exec. com.), Am. Biographical Inst. (nat. bd. advisors), Alpha Delta Kappa (hon.). Office: Childhelp USA 6463 Independence Ave Woodland Hls CA 91370-0002

SIGLAIN, HELEN See DE LUCA, ANDREA

SIGMAN, SANDRA PERRY, human resources specialist; b. Burbank, Calif., Aug. 14, 1954; d. Jack Wayne and Donna Jane (Brandt) Perry; m. David Douglas Sigman, June 27, 1987; 1 child, Ryan Anderson. BA in Polit. Sci. and Psychology, Central Coll., 1976; MA in Labor and Indsl. Rels., U. Ill., 1978. Adminstrv. trainee Chrysler Corp., Highland Park, Mich., 1978-80; human resources analyst, coord. Exxon Chem., Baton Rouge, La., 1980-85, Houston, 1985-92; human resources analyst, coord. Exxon Co., Houston, 1992—. Mem. Houston Bus. Forum.

SIGMUND, DIANE WEISS, judge; b. N.Y.C., Mar. 1, 1943. BS, Pa. State U., 1963; JD magna cum laude, Temple U., 1977. Bar: Pa. 1977. Lawyer Blank, Rome, Cominsky & McCauley, Phila.; judge U.S. Bankruptcy Ct. (Pa. ea. dist.), 3rd circuit, Phila., 1993—; course planner Pa. Bar Inst., 1991; treas. Ea. Dist. Pa. Bankruptcy Conf., 1992. Office: US Courthouse 601 Market St Rm 3902 Philadelphia PA 19106*

SIKES, CYNTHIA LEE, actress, singer; b. Coffeyville, Kans., Jan. 2, 1954; d. Neil and Pat (Scott) S.; m. Alan Bud Yorkin, June 24, 1989. Student, Am. Conservatory Theater, San Francisco, 1977-79. Appeared in TV series St. Elsewhere, 1981-83, L.A. Law, 1989; TV movies include His Mistress, s1990; films include Man Who Loved Women, That's Life, Arthur On The Rocks, Love Hurts, 1988; also Broadway show Into The Woods, 1988-89. Active Hollywood Women's Polit. Com. Recipient Gov.'s Medal of Merit, Kans., 1986. Mem. Environ. Media Assn. (bd. dirs.). Democrat.

SIKES, MARY ALICIA, airline pilot; b. Richmond, Va., Nov. 29, 1961; d. Olen Herman and Mary Montague (Hudson) S. BS in Computer Sci. cum laude, U. S.C., 1983. Flight instr. Eagle Aviation, West Columbia, S.C., 1983-84, Midlands Aviation, Columbia, S.C., 1984-85; asst. chief pilot Napier Air Svc., Dothan, Ala., 1985; pilot, capt. Air New Orleans, Birmingham, Ala., 1985-88; pilot, 1st officer Trans World Airlines, Kansas City, Mo., 1988—. Mem. Airline Pilots Assn., Internat. Soc. Women Airline Pilots, Phi Beta Kappa.

SIKES, RUTH COX, financial company official; b. Macon, Ga., Sept. 29, 1952; d. Z. Sweeney and Louise (Cox) S.; m. Eugene W. Dabbs, IV, Apr. 1978 (div. 1981); m. Dennis L. Crow, July 1994. BA, Emory U., 1974; MSW, Tulane U., 1975. CLU; chartered fin. cons. Social worker Brawner Psychiat. Inst., Atlanta, 1976-77, Griffin (Ga.) Hosp., 1977-78, Personnel Growth Ctr., Griffin, 1978-79; agt., rep. Equitable Fin. Cos., Griffin, 1979-92, master agt., dist. asst., 1979-92; S.E. regional dir. ins. sales Waddell & Reed Inc., Atlanta, 1992-93; divsn. mgr. Waddell & Reed Inc., Marietta, Ga., 1993-94; dist. mgr. Waddell & Reed Inc., Atlanta, 1994—. Mem. Am. Soc. CLU and ChFC (Atlanta chpt.), Nat. Assn. Life Underwriters (nat. quality award 1984), Ga. Assn. Life Underwriters, Atlanta Assn. Life Underwriters, Women's Life Underwriters Confedn. (Atlanta chpt., pres.-elect). Republican. Office: Waddell & Reed Inc 1785 The Exchange NW Ste 300 Atlanta GA 30339

SIKES, SANDRA ANN, controller; b. Bowling Green, Ky., Oct. 31, 1960; d. John William and Edna Alma (Smith) S. BS, Western Ky. U., 1982, MBA, 1987. CPA, Tenn.; cert. mgmt. acct. Staff acct. Rexplore Drilling Co., Lexington, Ky., 1981-85, Marcoin Bus. Svcs., Bowling Green, 1985-87; staff acct. Ingersoll-Rand, White House, Tenn., 1987-89, supr. assembly ops., 1989-91, supr. acctg. ops., 1991-94, supr. fin. support, 1994-95; contr. Byron's Inc., Gallatin, Tenn., 1995—; cons. Sikes Tire, Inc., Bowling Green, 1983—; fin. ptnr. Investment Opportunities Unltd., White House, 1994—. Mem. fin. com. Long Hollow Bapt. Ch., Hendersonville, Tenn., 1994. Mem. Inst. Mgmt. Accts., Tenn. Soc. CPAs. Republican. Home: 499 Marlin Rd White House TN 37188 Office: Byron's Inc PO Box 1747 Gallatin TN 37066

SIKORA, SUZANNE MARIE, dentist; b. Kenosha, Wis., Dec. 4, 1952; d. Leo F. and Ida A. (Dupuis) S. BS, U. Wis., Parkside, 1975; DDS, Marquette U., 1981. Assoc. Paul G. Hagemann, DDS, Racine, Wis., 1981-84; pvt. practice dentistry Racine, 1984—; cons. Westview Health Care Ctr., Racine, 1981-89, Lincoln Luth. Home, Racine, 1981—, Becker-Shoop Ctr., Racine, 1981—, Lincoln Village Convalescent Ctr., Racine, 1986—, Racine Community Care Ctr., 1989—. Mem. ad hoc study com. County Health Dept., Racine, 1982-83. Mem. ADA, Wis. Dental Assn. (coun. on access prevention and wellness com. 1984-86, impaired provider program intervenor 1990—, del. 1993—). Office: 1900 Lathrop Ave Racine WI 53405-3707

SILAGI, BARBARA WEIBLER, corporate administrator; b. Chgo., June 26, 1930; d. Carleton Thomas and Catherine Josephine (Wolph) Weibler; m. Joseph Edward Sturgulewski (Sturgus), Feb. 12, 1953 (div. Aug. 1954); 1 child, Mariann Catherine; m. John Louis Silagi, Jr., July 2, 1960 (div. July 1968). BM in Edn., Northwestern U., 1958; MS in Edn., No. Ill. U., 1965. Cert. K-14 supervisory teaching, spl. edn. tchr., airline transport pilot, FAA dispatcher. Elem. sch. tchr. St. Mary's Sch., Chgo., 1947-49, Kingman, Ariz., 1949-52; legal sec. Judge Edward J. Mahoney, Quincy, Ill., 1954-55; elem. sch. tchr. C.M. Bardwell Sch., Aurora, Ill., 1955-76; flight instr. flight schs. Chgo., Aurora and Frankfort, Ill., Clinton, Iowa, 1960-77; aircraft dispatcher Transcontinental Airlines, Zantop Internat. Airlines, Ypsilanti, Mich., 1977-81; airline pilot Mannion Air Charter, Ypsilanti, 1977-80; head night auditor Howard Johnson, Quality Inn, Travelodge, BestWestern, others, Ocala, Fla., Silver Springs, Fla., 1983-87; sec.-treas. Diamond Design Svcs., Inc., Ocklawaha, Fla., 1985—; pub. Forest Shopper, Springs Shopper, Belle Shopper. Author: Dispatch Training, 1989; editor tng. manuals, 1977-85. Violist Chgo. Suburban Symphony, Naperville, Ill., 1956-60; contralto Palestrina A cappella Choir, Aurora, Ill., 1956-60; life mem. Ill. PTA, Aurora, 1974—; apptd. mem. adv. bd. Dunnellon Airport and Indsl. Park, 1992. Recipient 1st place Suburban Aviation Assn., Chgo., 1975, 5th place Illi-Nines Air Derby, Chgo., Moline, Ill., 1973, 2d place Leg prize Powder Puff Derby, McLean to Lincoln, Nebr., 1971; Eckstein scholar Northwestern U., 1952. Mem. AAUW (life), NEA (life), Ill. Edn. Assn., Ninety-Nines Internat. (life), Illi-Nines Air Derby (handicap chmn. 1972-76, air marking chmn. 99's Chgo. chpt. 1972-76, corr. sec. Chgo. chpt. 1976-77, 1st pl. achievement awards 1972-78), Aircraft Owners and Pilots Assn., Ocala Orchid Soc. (sec.), Suburban Aviation Assn., East Marion C. of C., Fla. Aero Club (v.p., sec.-treas. Ocala chpt. 1989-91), Fla. Native Plant Soc., Lake Weir Garden Club, Pi Lambda Theta (charter, life, rsch. chmn. Beta Delta chpt. DeKalb, Ill. 1962-63). Roman Catholic. Home: RR 2 Box 1837 A Ocklawaha FL 32179-8757 Office: Diamond Design Svcs Inc PO Box 186 Ocklawaha FL 32179-0186

SILAK, CATHY R., judge; b. Astoria, N.Y., May 25, 1950. BA, NYU, 1971; M in City Planning, Harvard U., 1973; JD, U. Calif., 1976. Bar: Calif. 1977, U.S. Dist. Ct. (no. dist.) Calif. 1977, D.C. 1979, U.S. Ct. Appeals (D.C. cir.) 1979, U.S. Dist. Ct. (so. dist.) N.Y. 1980, Idaho 1983, U.S. Dist. Ct. Idaho 1983, U.S. Ct. Appeals (2nd cir.) 1983, U.S. Ct. Appeals (9th cir.) 1985. Law clk. to Hon. William W. Schwarzer U.S. Dist. Ct. (no dist.), Calif., 1976-77; pvt. practice San Francisco, 1977-79, Washington, 1979-80; asst. U.S. atty. So. Dist. of N.Y., 1980-83; spl. asst. U.S. atty. Dist. of Idaho, 1983-84; pvt. practice Boise, Idaho, 1984-90; judge Idaho Ct. Appeals, 1990-93; justice Idaho Supreme Ct., Boise, 1993—; assoc. gen. counsel Morrison Knudsen Corp., 1989-90; mem. fairness com. Idaho Supreme Ct. and Gov.'s Task Force on Alternative Dispute Resolution; instr. and lectr. in field. Assoc. note and comment editor Calif. Law Rev., 1975-76. Land use planner Mass. Dept. Natural Resources, 1973; bd. dirs. United Way Ada County, Jr. League of Boise; founder Idaho Coalition for Adult Literacy; active adv. coun. Idaho Family and Workplace Consortium. Recipient Joyce Stein award Boise YWCA, 1992. Fellow Idaho Law Found (ann., lectr.); mem. ABA (nat. conf. state trial judges jud. adminstrn. divsn.), Nat. Assn. Women Judges, Idaho State Bar (corp./securities sect., instr.). Office: 451 W State St Boise ID 83702-6006*

SILBER, JUDY G., dermatologist; b. Newark, July 26, 1953. MD, SUNY, Bklyn., 1978. Intern Brookdale Med. Ctr., Bklyn., 1978-79; resident in dermatology Kings County Hosp., Bklyn., 1979-82; pvt. practice dermatology; affiliated with Meadowlands Med. Ctr., Secaucus, N.J. Fellow Am. Acad. Dermatology; mem. AMA, N.J. Med. Soc. Office: 992 Clifton Ave Clifton NJ 07013

SILBERBERG, INGA, dermatologist; b. Kassel, Germany, Sept. 16, 1934; came to U.S., 1938; d. Willi and Erna (Rosenbaum) S.; m. Herbert M. Sinakin, Feb. 16, 1969; 1 child, William Elias. BA, Hunter Coll., 1955; MD, SUNY, 1959; MS in Dermatology, NYU, 1965. Diplomate Am. Bd. Dermatologists, 1964. Instr., clin. dermatology NYU Med. Ctr., N.Y.C., 1963-65, clin. asst. prof., 1965-66, asst. prof. dermatology, 1966-71, clin. assoc. prof. dermatology, 1971-76; cons., dermatology Newcomb Hosp., Vineland, N.J., 1975—. Jonas Salk scholar, City of N.Y., 1955-59, Henry Silver award, Dermatologic Soc. Greater N.Y., 1962, 65, Dermatology Found. Discovery award, 1993. Fellow Am. Acad. Dermatology; mem. AMA. Jewish.

SILBERMAN, ROSALIE GAULL, federal official; b. Jackson, Miss., Mar. 31, 1937; d. Samuel and Alice (Berkowitz) Gaull; m. Laurence H. Silberman, Apr. 28, 1957; children: Katherine, Anne, Robert. BA, Smith Coll., 1958. Tchr., 1967-72; with Natl. Adv. Coun. on Edn. of Disadvantaged Children, 1973-75; bd. dirs. Widening Horizons, 1973-75; dir. comm., press sec. Sen. Robert Packwood, 1977-79; exec. dir., sec., treas. New Coalition for Econ. and Social Change, 1981-83; dir. pub. rels. San Francisco Conservatory of Music, 1982-83; spl. asst. Commr. Mimi Weyforth Dawson FCC, 1983-84; with EEOC, 1984-86, vice chmn., 1986—, now commr. Office: EEOC Office of Commr 1801 L St NW Washington DC 20507-0002*

SILBERT, LINDA BRESS, educational counselor, therapist; b. New Rochelle, N.Y., Sept. 14, 1944; d. Abram H. and Ann (Dreizen) Bress; m. Alvin Jay Silbert, Aug. 14, 1966; children: Brian R., Cheryl J. BS, SUNY, New Paltz, 1966; MS, We. Conn. State U., Danbury, 1989; PhD in Ednl. Adminstrn., Walden U., Mpls., 1993. Cert. in sch. counseling and elem. edn., N.Y. Children's writer Phone Programs, N.Y.C., 1984-86; owner, pub. Silbert & Bress, Inc., Mahopac, N.Y., 1976—, children's author, 1976—; owner, dir. Silbert Tutoring and Guidance Svc., Mahopac, 1968—; part-time prin. Temple Beth Shalom Hebrew Sch., Mahopac, 1985—; leader parent workshops Silbert Tutoring and Guidance, 1985—, leader gifted program, 1989; cons. Mahopac Ctrl. Sch. Dist., 1983-84; cons., developer Author in Your Sch. program, 1983-87. Author: Creative Thinking Workbooks, 1976, Understanding People Storybooks, 1978, (lifeskills programs) Strong Kids Program, 1991, Strong Kids Early Childhood Programs, 1993, Passport to Emotionally and Socially Strong Kids - Teacher's Handbook, 1995. Membership chair Temple Beth Shalom, Mahopac, 1980-85. Recipient Gabriel Schonfeld award for educator excellence Bd. of Jewish Edn. of Greater N.Y., 1991. Mem. Am. Counseling Assn., Orton Dyslexia Soc., Am. Mental Health Counselors Assn., United Jewish Fedn. (award 1983). Office: Silbert & Bress Inc PO Box 68 Mahopac NY 10541-0068

SILEO, HELENA ESTES, library director; b. L.A., Aug. 18, 1948; d. Rice Smith and Eleanor (Rosenfeldt) Estes; m. Stephen Richard Haeseler, May 22, 1971 (dec. 1979); m. Patrick William Sileo, June 9, 1985; 1 child, Polly Gee. BA, U. R.I., 1970; MLS, L.I. U., 1973; postgrad., CUNY, 1981—. Reference libr. Elmont (N.Y.) Pub. Libr., 1971-75, children's libr., 1976-78; reference libr. Westport (Conn.) Pub. Libr., 1979-81, N.Y.C. Tech. Coll./CUNY, Bklyn., 1981-89; head Voorhees br. N.Y.C. Tech. Coll., 1983-87; head libr. Ellis Sch., Pitts., 1990—; mem. Buhl Adv. Coun.: Continuing Edn. for Sch. Libr. Media Specialists in Western Pa., Sch. Libr. and Info. Sci. U. Pitts., 1992—. Mem. ALA, Libr. Assn. City N.Y. (sec. 1987-88), Pa. Sch. Libr. Assn. Democrat. Episcopalian. Office: Ellis Sch 6425 5th Ave Pittsburgh PA 15206-4499

SILER, JOYCE REYNOLDS, advertising and promotional specialists executive; b. Sacramento, Calif., Oct. 23, 1949; d. Marion H. Reynolds and Rosa R. (Leslie) Scarborough; m. Carl E. Siler (div. june 1979); 1 child, Tammi L. BBA, N.C. Cen. U., 1984. Project coord. Employment and Tng. Adminstrn., Graham, N.C., 1976-80; adminstrv. asst. to dir. fin. aid. N.C. Cen. U., Durham, 1980-82; mktg. and tng. rep. Systems Rsch. and Devel. Corp., Research Triangle Park, N.C., 1984-86; pres. Office Plus, Durham,

1987-89, Joyce's Specialties, Durham, N.C., 1988—. Pres. Riverwalk Homeowners Assn., Durham, 1986-88; mem. adv. bd. Triangle March of Dimes, Durham, 1987—; mem. Coal. Battered Women, Durham, 1984—, co-facilator, 1988. Mem. NAFE, Durham C. of C., N.C. Cen. U. Alumni Assn. (chairperson fundraising com. 1986—), Delta Sigma Theta, Alpha Kappa Mu. Home: 16 Riverwalk Ter Durham NC 27704-1181

SILLS, BEVERLY (MRS. PETER B. GREENOUGH), opera company director, coloratura soprano; b. Bklyn., May 25, 1929; d. Morris and Sonia (Bahn) Silverman; m. Peter B. Greenough, 1956; children: Meredith, Peter B.; stepchildren: Lindley, Nancy, Diana. Grad. pub. schs.; student voice, Estelle Leibling; student piano, Paolo Gallico; student stagecraft, Desire Defrere; hon. doctorates, Harvard U., NYU, New Eng. Conservatory, Temple U. Gen. dir. N.Y.C. Opera, 1979-1989; pres. N.Y.C. Opera Bd., 1989-90; mng. dir. Met. Opera, N.Y.C., 1991-94; chairwoman Lincoln Ctr., N.Y.C., 1994—; Bd. dirs. Am. Express, Macy's, Time/Warner Comm., Met. Opera; cons. Nat. Coun. on Arts. Radio debut as Bubbles Silverman on Uncle Bob'sRainbow House, 1932; appeared on Major Bowes Capitol Family Hour, 1934-41, on Our Gal Sunday; toured with Shubert Tours, Charles Wagner Opera Co., 1950, 51; operatic debut Phila. Civic Opera, 1947; debut, N.Y.C. Opera Co. as Rosalinda in Die Fledermaus, 1955; debut San Francisco Opera, 1953; debut La Scala, Milan as Pamira in Siege of Corinth, 1969, Royal Opera, Covent Garden in Lucia di Lammermoor, London, 1971, Met. Opera, N.Y.C., 1975, Vienna State Opera, 1967, Teatro Fenice in La Traviata, Venice; appeared Teatro Colon, Buenos Aires; recital debut Paris, 1971, London Symphony Orch., 1971; appeared throughout U.S., Europe, S. Am. including Boston Symphony, Tanglewood Festival, 1968, 69, Robin Hood Dell, Phila., 1969; title roles in: Don Pasquale, Norma, Ballad of Baby Doe, Thais, Traviata, Anna Bolena, Maria Stuarda, Lucia de Lammermoor, Barber of Seville, Manon, Louise, Tales of Hoffmann, Daughter of the Regiment, The Magic Flute, Elizabeth in Roberto Devereaux, I Puritana, Julius Caesar, Suor Angelica, Il Tabarro, G. Schicchi, Faust, La Loca, Merry Widow, Turk in Italy, Rigoletto, I Capuleti e I Montecchi, Lucrezia Borgia, Ariodante, Le Coq D'Or, others; recordings include The Art of Beverly Sills, Welcome to Vienna, Great Scores (with Placido Domingo); ret. from opera and concert stage, 1980; numerous TV spls; author: Bubbles-A Self-Portrait, 1976, autobiography Beverly, 1987. Chmn. bd. March of Dimes, nat. chmn. Mothers' March on Birth Defects; chmn. Lincoln Ctr. Recipient Handel medallion, 1973, Pearl S. Buck Women's award, 1979, Emmy award for Profiles in Music, 1976, Emmy award for Lifestyles with Beverly Sills, 1978, Medal of Freedom, 1980, Kennedy Ctr. honors. Office: care Edgar Vincent 157 W 57th St New York NY 10019-2210*

SILLS, NANCY MINTZ, lawyer; b. N.Y.C., Nov. 3, 1941; d. Samuel and Selma (Kahn) Mintz; m. Stephen J. Sills, Apr. 17, 1966; children: Eric Howard, Ronnie Lynne. BA, U. Wis., 1962; JD cum laude, Albany Law Sch., 1976. Bar: N.Y. 1977, U.S. Dist. Ct. (no. dist.) N.Y. 1977, U.S. Tax Ct. 1984. Asst. editor fin. news Newsweek mag., N.Y.C., 1962-65; staff writer, reporter Forbes mag., N.Y.C., 1965; research assoc. pub. relations Eastern Airlines, N.Y.C., 1965-67; asst. editor Harper & Row, N.Y.C., 1968-69; freelance writer, editor N.Y.C. and Albany, N.Y., 1967-70; confidential law sec. N.Y. State Supreme Ct., Albany, 1976-79; assoc. Whiteman, Osterman & Hanna, Albany, 1979-81, Martin, Noonan, Hislop, Troue & Shudt, Albany, 1981-83; ptnr. Martin, Shudt, Wallace & Sills, Albany, 1984; of counsel Krolick and DeGraff, Albany, 1984-89; ptnr. Hodgson, Russ, Andrews, Woods & Goodyear, Albany, 1990-91; pvt. practice Albany, 1991—; of counsel Lemery & Reid, Albany and Glens Falls, N.Y., 1993-94; asst. counsel N.Y. State Senate, 1983-88; cons. The Ayco Corp., 1975; bd. dirs. Albany Law Sch. Estate Planning Inst., 1980-86. Editor: Reforming American Education, 1969, Up From Poverty, 1968; researcher The Negro Revolution in America, 1963; contbr. articles to mags. Bd. dirs. Jewish Philanthropies Endowment, 1983-86, United Jewish Fedn. N.E. N.Y. Endowment Fund, 1992—; bd. dirs. Daus. of Sarah Found., 1994—, Albany Jewish Cmty. Ctr., 1984-87; mem. Guilderland (N.Y.) Conservation Adv. Coun., 1993—; mem. planned giving tech. adv. com. Albany Law Sch., 1991—, chmn., 1992—; mem. regional cabinet State of Israel Bonds Devel. Corp. for Israel, 1991-92. Mem. ABA, N.Y. State Bar Assn., Albany County Bar Assn., Warren County Bar Assn., Estate Planning Coun. Ea. N.Y., Womens Aux. Albany County Med. Soc., Capital Dist. Trial Lawyers Assn., Capital Dist. Women's Bar Assn., Phi Beta Kappa, Sigma Epsilon Sigma. Republican. Home: 16 Hiawatha Dr Guilderland NY 12084-9526 Office: 126 Stare St Albany NY 12207-1606

SILVA, ENEIDA MARIA, psychologist; b. Vagos, Portugal, Jan. 22, 1961; came to U.S., 1971; d. Jacinto and Alice Pimentel (Calisto) Rocha da Silva. BA, Rutgers Coll., 1983; MA, U. Conn., 1988, PhD, 1990. Lic. psychologist. Phychotherapist United Svcs., Willimantic, Conn., 1990-91; rsch. assoc. Casey Family Svcs., Hartford, Conn., 1991-92; psychologist Charter Oak Terrace Health Ctr., Hartford, 1993—; psychologist in pvt. practice West Hartford, Conn., 1991—; clin. supr. U. Conn., Storrs, 1993—. Author rsch. study on women's issues, 1990. Mem. APA, Conn. Psychol. Assn., Phi Beta Kappa, Phi Sigma Iota. Democrat. Office: West Hartford Psychol Svcs 10 N Main St Ste 305 West Hartford CT 06107-1901

SILVA, NANCY WILSON, psychotherapist; b. Wellesley, Mass., Feb. 27, 1947; d. William Smith and Phyllis Marie (Donahue) Wilson; m. Leonard Charles Silva, May 15, 1975; 1 child, Jennifer Lee. Student, Hartwick Coll., 1965-67; AA, St. Petersburg Jr. Coll., 1969; BA, U. South Fla., 1981, MA, 1992. Lic. mental health counselor, Fla. Owner, instr. No-Fail Swim Sch., Largo, Fla., 1979-89; social svcs. coord. Pinellas Assn. for Retarded Citizens, St. Petersburg, Fla., 1981-82; tchr. Largo (Fla.) High Sch., 1982-89; counselor, grad. asst. Fla. Mental Health Inst., Tampa, 1989-90; therapist The Harbor Behavioral Inst., Dade City, Fla., 1991-92, supr., therapist, 1992-93; supr. outpatient svcs., therapist Profl. Therapy Ctrs., Spring Hill, Fla., 1993-94; psychotherapist pvt. practice, cons., Spring Hill, 1993—. Contbr. articles to newspapers. Canvaser Local Dem. Party, Clearwater, Fla., 1988. Recipient Grad. assistantship U. South Fla., 1989-90. Mem. Am. Mental Health Counselors, Fla. Alcohol and Drug Assn., Phi Kappa Phi Nat. Honor Soc. Democrat. Home: 27120 La Paloma Ln Brooksville FL 34602-7106 Office: 1230 Mariner Blvd Spring Hill FL 34609

SILVA, OMEGA LOGAN, physician; b. Washington, Dec. 14, 1936; d. Louis Jasper and Ruth (Dickerson) Logan; m. C. Francis A. Silva, Oct. 25, 1958 (div. 1981); 1 child, Frances Cecile; m. Harold Bryant Webb, Nov. 28, 1982. Grad., Howard U., Washington, 1958, MD, 1967. Bio-chemist NIH, Bethesda, Md., 1958-63; asst. chief endocrinology Vets. Affairs Med. Ctr., Washington, 1967—; assoc. prof. George Washington U., Washington, 1975-91, prof. 1991—; prof. Howard U., Washington, 1977—. Author: (with others) Endocrinology, 1990; contbr. articles to profl. jours. Charter mem. Nat. Mus. of Women in the Arts, Washington, 1986; health cons. River Pk. Mutual Homes, Inc., Washington, 1987; vol. Career Day Chillum Elem. Sch., Career Week, George Washington U., Washington, 1988; trustee Howard U., 1991—. Fellow ACP (Best Sci. Presentation award 1974); mem. Am. Chem. Soc., Am. Med. Women's Assn. (br. I v.p. 1986-87, pres. 1987-88, anti-smoking task force 1989—, chair govtl. affairs nominations com. 1992), Howard U. Med. Alumni (pres. 1983-88), Alpha Omega Alpha. Office: Veterans Affairs Med Ctr 50 Irving St NW Washington DC 20422-0002

SILVER, BELLA WOLFSON, day care center executive; b. N.Y.C., Mar. 10, 1937; d. David Michael and Edith (Bienenstock) Wolfson; m. Kenneth A. Silver, Oct. 19, 1958; children: James, Daniel. BS, Adelphi U., 1958; postgrad. Bank St. Coll., 1958-59, Nova U. Cert. tchr., N.Y., Ill., Wis. Kindergarten tchr., N.Y.C., 1958, Madison (Wis.) Pub. Schs., 1959-61, White Fish Bay (Wis.) Public Schs., 1961-65; nursery sch. tchr., Deerfield, Ill., 1975-77; substitute tchr. Deerfield Pub. Schs., 1975-77; founder., dir., pres. Deerfield Day Care Ctr., 1978-94; founder Bella W. Silver and Assocs., 1990—, child care cons. for the nineties; pres., founder B & K E.C.E Enterprises 1993—; corp. cons. Day Care/Child Care Svcs., 1983—; pub. speaker on child care to North Shore High Schs., 1984; speaker, presenter Hawaiian Assn. for Edn. Young Children, 1992, 93, Chgo. Assn. for Edn. Young Children, 1993—, Mid West Assn. for Edn. Young Children, 1994; chmn. publicity, fundraiser, promoter 1st Ann. Craft Show, Deerfield Day Care Ctr., 1978—. Author series of books on child care, 1993—. Mem. Deerfield Caucus; active Cub Scouts, Deerfield, Outstanding Service award 1973-77; mem. exec. bd. Jewish United Fund; sec. Parents-Tchrs. Orgn. Recipient award Bahais of Deerfield, 1981; mem. "Com. of 200" Child Care Info. Exchange Mag., 1985—. Mem. NAFE, AAUW, Assn. Childhood Edn. Internat., Nat. Assn. Edn. Young Children, Chgo. Assn. Edn. Young Children (early childhood conf. presenter 1993, 94), Assn. Child Care Con. Internat., Nat. Assn. Child Care Profl., Assn. Supervision and Curriculum Devel.,, Wis. Early Childhood Assn., Dirs. Network of Childcare Info. Exch., Deerfield C. of C., Phi Sigma Sigma (Pyramid award 1965). Jewish. Home: 309 Willow Rd Deerfield IL 60015-4839

SILVER, HELENE MARCIA, health educator, speaker, author; b. Oakland, Calif., Apr. 2, 1947; d. Sam and Shirley Betty (Kerns) S. BA, UCLA, 1968; postgrad., San Francisco State Coll., 1970-72, Holistic Life U., 1978-79, Antioch U., 1979-80. Tchr. pub. schs. Oakland, 1968-76; nutritional counselor Mill Valley, Calif., 1976—; creator Women's Health Intensive, Mill Valley, 1977-79; project dir. nutrition edn. project Calif. Dept. Edn., San Rafael, Calif., 1979-80; founder, dir. Inner Beauty Inst., Sausalito, Calif., 1980—; health edn. cons., 1976—; founder Inner Beauty Mountain Retreat, 1987—; mem. Health Task Force in Marin County, 1978-80. Author: Inner Beauty/Outer Beauty, The Body Smart System, 1990; creator Body Smart System Nutritional Kit. Mem. AAUW, Soc. Nutrition Edn., Nat. Health Fedn. Office: 3A Gate 3 Rd # 5 Sausalito CA 94965-1768

SILVER, JEAN, state legislator, accountant; b. Spokane, Wash., July 25, 1926; d. Harlow Eugene and Helen Grace (Merten) Merrill; m. Charles Wesley Silver; children: Douglas W., Mitchell C., Kipp E. BBA, Eastern Wash. U., 1975, postgrad., 1980-87. CPA, Wash. Prin. Jean Silver Acctg. Svc., Spokane, 1950—; acct. Coopers & Lybrand, Spokane, 1976-80; state legislator State of Wash., Olympia, 1983—; cons. econ. devel. financing City and County of Spokane, 1980-86; bd. dirs. Wash. Water Power Co.; chmn. govt. ops. and pension com. Nat. Conf. State Legislators, 1989—. Bd. dirs. Greater Spokane Bus. Devel. Assn., 1984—, Holy Names-Ft. George Wright, Spokane, 1984—; trustee Holy Family Hosp., Spokane, 1986-87, Jr. League, 1987—; mem. adv. bd. Spokane Incubator Assn., 1987-89. Named Legislator of Yr., Assn. Builders and Contractors, 1985, Outstanding Govt. Woman of Yr., YWCA, 1988, Hosp. and Health Care award 1989. Mem. Wash. CPAs Soc. Republican. Office: Wash State Legislature HOB # 413 State Capitol Olympia WA 98504

SILVER, JOAN MICKLIN, film director, screenwriter; b. Omaha, May 24, 1935; d. Maurice David and Doris (Shoshone) Micklin; m. Raphael D. Silver, June 28, 1956; children: Dina, Marisa, Claudia. BA, Sarah Lawrence Coll., 1956. Writer, dir. (movies) Hester Street, 1975 (Writers Guild best screenplay nomination), Chilly Scenes of Winter, 1981, (TV film PBS) Bernice Bobs Her Hair starring Shelly Du Vall, 1975; dir. (TV films HBO) Finnegan, Begin Again with Robert Preston and Mary Tyler Moore, Parole Board, A Private Matter with Sissy Spacek and Aidan Quinn (films) Between the Lines, 1976, Crossing Delancey with Amy Irving, 1988, Loverboy, 1989, Stepkids, 1991; dir. stage plays and musicals including Album, Maybe I'm Doing It Wrong, Off-Broadway prodn. A...My Name is Alice; prod. On The Yard. Office: Silverfilm Prodns Inc 477 Madison Ave New York NY 10022-5802*

SILVER, JOY ELLEN, pediatrician; b. Chgo., July 4, 1954; d. Sam and Audrey Pearl (Joseph) S.; m. Bruce Jay Goldberg, Nov. 19, 1983; children: Peter, Leslie. BS, U. Ill., 1976; MD, Loyola U., Maywood, Ill., 1981. Intern Milw. Children's Hosp., 1981-82, resident in pediat., 1982-84; assoc. prof. Foster McGaw Hosp., Maywood, 1984-90; pvt. practice Rockville, Md., 1990-91; pediatrician Am. Family Doctor, Chgo., 1991-93, North Suburban Clinic, Hoffman Estates, Ill., 1993—. Fellow Am. Acad. Pediatrics; mem. AMA, Am. Med. Women's Assn., Am. Diabetic Assn. Office: North Suburban Clinic 1786 Moon Lake Blvd Hoffman Estates IL 60194

SILVER, LINDA, guidance director, educational consultant; b. N.Y.C., Jan. 11, 1954; d. Victor Paul and Mina (Levin) Berk; children: Brooke, Joshua. BA in Spanish and Secondary Edn., Hofstra U., 1976; MS in Guidance and Counseling, Nova U., 1979. Cert. guidance counselor grades K-12, Spanish tchr. grades 7-12. Spanish tchr. Ponus Ridge Middle Sch., Norwalk, Conn., 1976-77, West Hollywood (Fla.) Pvt. Sch., 1977-79; guidance counselor Collins Elem., Dania, Fla., 1979-89; adult edn. tchr. GED-Off Campus, Ft. Lauderdale, Fla., 1989-90; guidance dir. Bethune Elem., Hollywood, 1989—; family counselor Family Counseling Ctr., Hollywood, 1990-94; ednl. cons. Maimonides Community Sch., Hollywood, 1992—; workshop leader and presenter in field. Named Broward County Elem. Counselor of Yr., Broward Counseling Assn., Ft. Lauderdale, 1990, Fla. Elem. Counselor of Yr., Fla. Sch. Counselors Assn., Orlando, 1992. Mem. ACA, Am. Sch. Counselor Assn., Fla. Sch. Counselors Assn., Broward County Counselors Assn., Fla. Counseling Assn., Exec. Bd. Elem. Counselors (co-chairperson 1992—), Exec. Bd. Maimonides Community Sch. (bd. mem. 1992—), Maimonides Community (chairperson edn. com. 1992—), Hofstra U. South Fla. Alumni Assn. (pres. 1985), Delta Kappa Gamma, Phi Delta Kappa, Sigma Delta Phi. Home: 2010 N 47th Ave Hollywood FL 33021-4128 Office: Bethune Elem 2400 Meade St Hollywood FL 33020-1246

SILVER, MARY WILCOX, oceanography educator; b. San Francisco, July 13, 1941; d. Philip E. and Mary C. (Kartes) Wilcox; m. Eli A. Silver (div. 1984); children: Monica, Joel. BA in Zoology, U. Calif., Berkeley, 1963; PhD in Oceanography, U. Calif., La Jolla, 1971. Asst. prof. biology San Francisco State U., 1971-72; prof. marine sci. U. Calif., Santa Cruz, 1972—, chmn. dept., 1983-89, 92—. Contbr. numerous articles on biol. oceanography to profl. jours. Grantee NSF, 1979—; recipient Bigelow medal, 1992. Mem. AAAS, Am. Soc. Limnology and Oceanography, Am. Phycological Soc. Office: U Calif Dept Marine Sci Santa Cruz CA 95064

SILVER, STARR ESTELLE, social science educator; b. Bklyn., Feb. 16, 1954; d. Leon Isadore and Pauline (Mayo) S.; m. Roy V. Boyes, June 30, 1984 (div. Nov. 1992); 1 child, Bryan Silver-Boyes. BA, U. Fla., 1976, MA, 1980, PhD, 1983; postgrad., U. Calif., San Francisco, 1984. Rsch. assoc. Sociometrics Corp., Palo Alto, Calif., 1984-85; asst. prof. Coll. Pub. Health, U. South Fla., Tampa, 1985-86; dir. rsch. in child mental health Rsch. and Tng. Ctr. for Children's Mental Health, Tampa, 1986-90; co-dir. rsch. U. South Fla., Tampa, 1990-92, rsch. assoc. prof. dept. child and family studies, 1992—; ind. rsch. cons., Tampa, 1992—. Contbr. articles to profl. jours. Faculty scholar Fla. Atlantic U., 1973; postdoctoral fellow U. Calif., 1984. Mem. APA (program chmn. population and environ. psychology 1987), APHA, Population Assn. Am., Phi Kappa Phi. Democrat. Jewish. Office: U South Fla FMHI 13301 Bruce B Downs Blvd Tampa FL 33612-3899

SILVERMAN, AYN, director of product development; b. N.Y.C., Jan. 24, 1946; d. Sidney and Miriam (Lazarus) S. A of Mktg., Westchester C.C., 1965. Market rep. Frederick Atkins, N.Y.C., 1965-84; product mgr. Associated Merchandising Corp., N.Y.C., 1984-86, La Tique, N.Y.C., 1987-88; dir. product devel. York Luggage Co., Lambertville, N.J., 1988—; cons. Luggage and Leather Goods Mfrs. of Am., N.Y.C., 1988. Recipient Alumni Assn. Achievement award Westchester C.C. Alumni Assn., 1965. Home: 279 E 44th St New York NY 10017

SILVERMAN, DEBORAH R., medical center administrator; b. Bklyn., Oct. 13, 1950; d. Norman and Beatrice (Cohen) S. BA, SUNY, Binghamton, 1972; MD, SUNY, Syracuse, 1977. Diplomate Am. Bd. Family Practice. Resident in family practice U. Tenn., Jackson, 1981; fellow adolescent medicine Children's Hosp. Med. Ctr., Cin., 1982; assoc. med. dir. Urgent Care Ctr., Cin., 1982-83; pvt. practice adolescent medicine and family practice Cin., 1984-94; med. dir. Campus Health Ctr. U. Cin., 1994—; cons. adolescent gynecology Emerson North Psychiatric Hosp., Cin., 1985—; asst. prof. family medicine U. Cin., 1990—; educator sexuality Med. Sch. U. Cin., Jackson and Cin., 1980—. Co-author, editor: (booklet) Highways to Health, 1994; contbr. articles to profl. jour. Recipient Outstanding Cmty. Svc. award Student AMA-CIBA, 1973. Fellow Am. Acad. Family Physicians; mem. Am. Med. Women's Assn., Ohio Acad. Family Physicians (chmn., founder adolescent medicine com. 1987-92, instr. clin. hypnosis 1980—), Cin. Hypnosis Soc., Soc. Adolescent Medicne. Jewish. Office: U Cin Campus Health Ctr 2920 Scioto St ML 0010 Cincinnati OH 45221

SILVERMAN, ELLEN, speech and language pathologist; b. Milw., Oct. 12, 1942; d. Roy and Bettie (Schlaeger) Loebel; m. Feb. 5, 1967 (div.); 1 child, Catherine Bette. BS, U. Wis., Milw., 1964; MA, U. Iowa, 1967, PhD, 1970. Rsch. assoc. U. Ill., Urbana, 1969-71; asst. prof. speech pathology Marquette U., Milw., 1973-79; assoc. prof. speech pathology Marquette U., 1979—; pvt. practice speech and lang. pathology, Milw., 1985—. Contbr. articles to profl. jours., chpts. to books. Marquette U. grantee, 1982. Fellow Am. Speech, Hearing, Lang. Assn.; mem. Wis. Speech, Hearing, Lang. Assn., Sigma Xi.

SILVERMAN, MARCIA, public relations executive; b. Lexington, Ky., Dec. 4, 1943. AB, U. Pa., 1965, MA, 1966. With J. Walter Thompson, 1979-81; sr. v.p., v.p. and account exec. Adams & Rinehart; COO/vice chmn. Powell Adams & Rinehart, 1989-92; pres. Ogilvy Adams & Rinehart, 1992—. Office: Ogilvy Adams & Rinehart 1901 L St NW #300 Washington DC 20036*

SILVERMAN, VALERIE, public relations executive; b. N.Y.C., July 18, 1962; d. Rogers and Anne (Kaufman) S. BA with honors, Vassar Coll., 1984; postgrad., New Sch. for Social Rsch., 1986, NYU, 1988. Reporter, editor Miscellany News, Poughkeepsie, N.Y., 1980-84; talk show host, producer Sta. WVKR-FM, Poughkeepsie, 1982-84; pub. relations intern ABC-TV, N.Y.C., 1982; pub. relations asst. Burson-Marsteller, N.Y.C., 1983; account exec. Jack Hilton Inc., N.Y.C., 1984-86; media exec. Howard J. Rubenstein Assocs., N.Y.C., 1986-87, sr. media exec., 1987-88, v.p. media, 1988—; lectr. NYU, 1988—; mem. bd. dirs. Vassar Coll., 1994—. Columnist: Vassar Quarterly, 1984-90. Mem. Internat. Radio and TV Soc., Pub. Relations Soc. Am., NATAS, Women in Communications. Office: Howard J Rubenstein Assocs 1345 Ave Of The Americas New York NY 10105-0099

SILVERS, EILEEN S., lawyer; b. N.Y.C., Sept. 21, 1948; d. Sidney and Ethel Lynne (Starobin) Swertloff; children: Steven Jay, Sharron Roth. B.A. magna cum laude, SUNY-Buffalo, 1970; J.D., Columbia U., 1975. Bar: N.Y. 1977, U.S. Tax Ct. 1981, U.S. Ct. Claims 1983, D.C., 1984. Assoc., Paul, Weiss, Rifkind, Wharton & Garrison, N.Y.C., 1975-83, ptnr., 1983-94; v.p. taxes Bristol-Myers Squibb Co., N.Y.C., 1994—. Mem. ABA (tax sect. mem. of coms. on Fgn. Activities of U.S. Taxpayers and U.S. Activities of Foreigners and Tax Treaties 1986—), N.Y. State Bar Assn. (chmn. personal income com. tax sect. 1983-85 , exec. com. 1982-85, 1990-91), D.C. Bar Assn. Home: 20 Mountain Peak Rd Chappaqua NY 10514-2110 Office: Bristol-Myers Squibb Co 345 Park Ave New York NY 10154-0037

SILVERS, SALLY, choreographer, performing company executive; b. Greeneville, Tenn., June 19, 1952; d. Herbert Ralston and Sara Elizabeth (Buchanan) S.; life ptnr. Bruce Erroll Andrews. BA in Dance and Polit. Sci., Antioch Coll., 1975. Artistic dir. Sally Silvers & Dancers, N.Y.C., 1980—; mem. faculty Leicester Poly., 1986, 87, 89, summer choreography project Bennington Coll., 1988-92, Chisenhale Dance Space, London, 1989, 91, Am. Dance Festival, Durham, N.C., 1990, 92; guest tchr. European Dance Devel. Ctr., Arnhem, The Netherlands, 1992—. Choreographer: Politics of the Body Microscope of Conduct, 1980, Social Movement, 1981, Connective Tissue, 1981, Less Time You Know Praxis, 1981, Don't No Do And This, 1981, Lack of Entrepreneurial Thrift, 1982, Celluloid Sally and Mr. E, 1982, Mutate, 1982, Being Red Enough, 1982, Disgusting, 1982, Bedtime at the Reformatory, 1982, Eat the Rich, 1982, They Can't Get It in the Shopping Cart, 1982, Blazing Forces, 1982, And Find Out Why, 1983, Tips for Totalizers, 1983, Choose Your Weapons, 1984, And Find Out Why, 1984, Extend the Wish for Entire, 1985, No Better Way, 1985, Every All Which is Not Us, 1986, Swaps Ego Say So, 1986, Be Careful Now, You Know Sugar Melts in Water, 1987, Fact Confected, 1987, Both, Both, 1987, Tizzy Boost, 1988, Moebius, 1988, Whatever Ever, 1989, Get Tough, Sports and Divertissement, 1989, Flap, 1989, Swan's Crayon, 1989, Fanfare Tripwire, 1990, Harry Meets Sally, 1990, Along the Skid Mark of Recorded History, 1990, Matinee Double-You, 1991, Grand Guignol, 1991, Dash Dash Slang Plural Plus, 1992, The Bubble Cut, 1992, Vigilant Corsage, 1992, Oops Fact, 1992, Small Room, 1993, Exwhyzee, 1993, Elegy, 1993, Now That It Is Now, 1994, Give Em Enough Rope, 1994, Swoon Noir, 1994, others; filmmaker: Little Lieutenant, 1993 (Silver award N.Y. Dance on Camera Festival; co-author: Resurgant New Writings By Women, 1992; contbr. articles to profl. jours. Grantee Nat. Endowment Arts, 1987, 89, 90, 91, Jerome Found., 1993, Meet the Composer fellow Nat. Endowment Arts, 1988-91; Guggenheim Found. fellow, 1988. Mem. Segue Found. (bd. dirs. Segue Performance Space 1992—). Home: 303 E 8th St # 4F New York NY 10009

SILVERSTEIN, BARBARA ANN, conductor, artistic director; b. Phila., July 24, 1947; d. Charles and Selma (Brenner) S.; m. Bernard J. Taylor II, Aug. 19, 1978. Student Bennington Coll., 1965-67; B.Mus., Phila. Coll. Performing Arts, 1970. Assoc. music dir. Suburban Opera Co., Chester, Pa., 1967-75; asst. condr. Toledo Opera Assn., 1975-76; asst. condr., coach Curtis Inst. Music, Phila., 1973-77; asst. condr. Phila. Lyric Opera, 1971-74, Des Moines Opera Festival, Indianola, Iowa, 1974-78; music dir., condr. Savoy Co., Phila., 1977-80, Miss. Opera, Jackson, 1979-82; artistic dir., condr. Pa. Opera Theater, Phila., 1976-93; guest condr. Anchorage Opera, 1982, Opera Del., Wilmington, 1981, 83, Utah Festival Opera Co., 1993—, Lyric Opera of Kansas City, 1994—. Mem. Am. Fedn. Musicians, Music Fund Soc., Pa. Council on the Arts (adv. panel 1987-90) OPERA Am. (bd. dirs. 1987-93, exec. com. 1988-93), Alumni award U. of Arts 1989, Wash., H.S., 1991 (Phila.), Cultural Alliance bd. dirs., 1991-93. Jewish. Avocations: scuba diving; reading.

SILVEY, ANITA LYNNE, editor; b. Bridgeport, Conn., Sept. 3, 1947; d. John Oscar and Juanita Lucille (McKitrick) S.; m. Bill Clark, 1988. BS in Edn., Ind. U., 1965-69; MA in Comm. Arts, U. Wis., 1970. Editorial asst. children's book dept. Little Brown and Co., Boston, 1970-71; asst. editor Horn Book Mag., Boston, 1971-75; mng. editor, founder New Boston Rev., 1975-76; mktg. mgr. children's books, libr. svcs. mgr. trade divsn. Houghton Mifflin, Boston, 1976-84; editor-in-chief Horn Book Mag., Boston, 1985—; Editor: Children's Books and Their Creators, 1995; contbr. articles to profl. jours. Editor: A Companion to Children's Books and Their Creators, 1995; contbr. articles to profl. jours. Named one of 70 Women Who Have Made a Difference, Women's Nat. Book Assn., 1987. Mem. ALA (chmn. children's librs., Laura Ingalls Wilder award 1987-89), Internat. Reading Assn. (mem. IRA Book award com. 1985-87), Assn. Am. Pubs. (libr. com.), New England Round Table (chmn. 1978-79). Office: Horn Book Mag 11 Beacon St Boston MA 02108-3001

SILVIS, CAROL A., business educator; b. Natrona Heights, Pa., Nov. 10, 1949; d. Edward M. Baer and Rosella M. (Schweitzer) Miller; m. Timothy N. Silvis, Sept. 29, 1973 (div.); children: Ryan S., Nicole R. AS, Duff's Bus. Inst., 1969; BS, U. Pitts., 1974; MS, Pa. State U., 1993. Cert. tchr., Pa. Sec. Aluminum Co. Am., Pitts., 1969-74; bus. instr. Boyd Career Sch., Pitts., 1974-75, Secondary Highlands Sch. Dist., Natrona Heights, Pa., 1975-80, New Kensington (Pa.) Comml. Sch., 1983—; part-time instr. C.C. of Allegheny County, Pitts., 1974-91, Pa. State U., Parks Twp., Pa., 1993-94; part-time cons., spkr. in field. Author: (textbook and instr. manual) General Office Procedures, 1990, 2d edit., 1995. Organizer Family Life Team OLOJ Ch., Holiday Park, Pa., 1990—, also spkr. Named Key Person of Yr., New Kensington C. of C., 1989. Mem. Pa. Bus. Edn. Assn., Tri-State Bus. Edn. Assn., Allegheny-Kiski Pers. Assn. Roman Catholic. Office: New Kensington Comml Sch 945 Greensburg Rd New Kensington PA 15068

SIMECKA, BETTY JEAN, convention and visitors bureau executive; b. Topeka, Apr. 15, 1935; d. William Bryan and Regina Marie (Rezac) S.; m. Alex Pappas, Jan. 15, 1956 (div. Apr. 1983); 1 child, Alex William. Student, Butler County Community Coll., 1983-85. Freelance writer and photographer L.A., also St. Marys, Kans., 1969-77; co-owner Creative Enterprises, El Dorado, Kans., 1977-83; coord. excursions into history Butler County Community Coll., El Dorado, 1983-84; dir. Hutchinson (Kans.) Conv. & Visitors Bur., 1984-85; dir. mktg. div. Exec. Mgmt., Inc., Wichita, 1985-87; exec. dir. Topeka Conv. and Visitors Bur., 1987-91, pres., chief exec. officer, 1991—; dir. promotion El Dorado Thunderboat Races, 1977-78. Contbr. articles to jours. and mags.; columnist St. Marys Star, 1973-79. Pres. El Dorado Art Assn., 1984; chmn. Santa Fe Trail Bike Assn., Kans., 1988-90; co-dir. St. Marys Summer Track Festival, 1973-81; chmn. spl.

events Mulvane Art Mus., 1990, sec., 1991-92, membership chmn., 1993-94; bd. dirs. Topeka Civic Theater, 1991, co-chmn. spl. events, 1992; Kans. chmn. Russian Festival Com., 1992-93; vice chmn. Kans. Film Commn., 1993-84, chmn., 1994; bd. dirs. Kans. Expoctr. Adv. Bd. Recipient Gov.'s Tourism award, 1993. Mem. Nat. Tour Assn., Sales and Mktg. Execs. (bd. dirs. 1991-92), Internat. Assn. Conv. and Visitors Burs. (co-chmn. rural tourism com. 1994—), Am. Soc. Assn. Execs., Travel Industry Assn. Kans. (membership chmn. 1988-89, sec. 1990, pres. 1991-92, Outstanding Merit award 1994), St. Marys C. of C. (pres. 1975), I-70 (v.p. 1989, pres. 1990), Optimists (social sec. Topeka chpt. 1988-89). Republican. Methodist.

SIMKINS, LISA KAREN, environmental engineer; b. Morristown, N.J., Mar. 30, 1955; d. Quinton William and Suzanne Simkins; m. Michael John Barnes, June 30, 1984. BSCE, U. Vt., 1977; MS in Environ. Health Sci., Harvard U., 1981; MBA, St. Mary's Coll., Moraga, Calif., 1986. Registered profl. engr., Maine, Calif.; cert. Am. Bd. Ind. Hygiene. Head engring. controls Mare Island Naval Shipyard, Vallejo, Calif., 1981-85; indsl. hygiene engr. New United Motor Mfg., Inc., Fremont, Calif., 1985-86; mgr. indsl. hygiene svcs. Clayton Environ. Cons., Inc., Pleasanton, Calif., 1986-90, dir. Western ops., 1990-93, nat. dir. environ. mgmt. svcs., 1993—; environ. engr. Metcalf Eddy, Boston, 1977-80. Contbr. 2 chpts. to: Patty's Industrial Hygiene and Toxicology, 1991. Mem. Am. Indsl. Hygiene Assn., Am. Conf. Govtl. Indsl. Hygienists. Office: Clayton Environ Cons Inc PO Box 9019 Pleasanton CA 94566

SIMMONS, ADELE SMITH, foundation president, former educator; b. Lake Forest, Ill., June 21, 1941; d. Hermon Dunlap and Ellen T. (Thorne) Smith; m. John L. Simmons; children—Ian, Erica, Kevin. BA in Social Studies with honors, Radcliffe Coll., 1963; PhD, Oxford U., Eng., 1969; LHD (hon.), Lake Forest Coll., 1976, Amherst Coll., 1977, Franklin Pierce Coll., 1978, U. Mass., 1978, Alverno Coll., 1982, Marlboro Coll., 1987, Smith Coll., 1988, Mt. Holyoke Coll., 1989, Am. U., 1992, Tufts U., 1994. Asst. prof. Tufts U., Boston, 1969-72; dean Jackson Coll., Medford, Mass., 1970-72; asst. prof. history, dean student affairs Princeton U., N.J., 1972-77; pres. Hampshire Coll., Amherst, Mass., 1977-89, John D. and Catherine T. MacArthur Found., Chgo., 1989—; bd. dirs. Marsh & McLennan, N.Y.C., 1st Chgo. Corp., Synergos; cons. Ford. Found., Stockholm Internat. Peace Rsch. Inst., Radcliffe Coll.; former corr. in Mauritius and Tunisia for N.Y. Times, The Economist; high level adv. bd. UN, 1993—. Co-author: (with Freeman, Dunkle, Blau) Exploitation from 9 to 5: Twentieth Century Fund Task Force Report on Working Women, 1975; author: Modern Mauritius, 1982; contbr. articles on edn. and pub. policy in The N.Y. Times, Christian Sci. Monitor, The Bulletin of Atomic Scientist, Harper's, The Atlantic Monthly and others. Commr. Pres.'s Commn. on World Hunger, Washington, 1978-80, Pres.'s Commn. on Environ. Quality, 1991-92; mem. Commn. Global Governance; trustee Carnegie Found. for Advancement Teaching, 1978-86; trustee Union Concerned Scientists, 1983—; chair Mayor Richard Daily's Youth Devel. Task Force, 1993—. Fellow Am. Acad. Arts and Scis.; mem. Phi Beta Kappa. Office: MacArthur Found 140 S Dearborn St Ste 1100 Chicago IL 60603-5206

SIMMONS, ANNE L., federal official; b. Spencer, Iowa, Jan. 4, 1964; d. Donald Lewis and Lois Amber (Blass) S. B in Spl. Studies, Cornell Coll., 1986. Intern for Congressman Berkley Bedell Washington, 1986; field staff Iowans for Clayton Hodgson, Sioux City, Iowa, 1986; exec. sec. Atomic Indsl. Forum, Bethesda, Md., 1986-87; staff asst. House Armed Svcs. Com., Washington, 1987; legis. asst. to Congressman Tim Johnson Washington, 1988-93; staff dir. gen. farms commodities subcom. House Agriculture Com., Washington, 1993, staff dir. environ., credit and rural devel. subcom., 1994, minority cons. rsch. conservation rsch. and forestry subcom., 1995—. Music scholar Cornell Coll., 1982-86. Mem. Delta Phi Alpha. Democrat. Office: House Agriculture Com 1301 Longworth House Office Bldg Washington DC 20515

SIMMONS, BETTY JO, materiel manager; b. Caddo, Okla., Dec. 13, 1936; d. Robert Lee and Beatrice (Alexander) S.; m. Donald Sherrill Stauffer, Jan. 3, 1959 (div. 1963); m. Daniel Oliver Amos, Oct. 20, 1972 (div. 1975). BA, City Coll.; student, U. Calif. Drafting clk. PacBell, 1956-59, jr. civil engr. draftsperson, 1959-61, sr. civil engr. draftsperson, 1961-62, civil engr. draftsperson, 1962-82, EEO counselor, 1973-77, supr., civil engr. draftsperson, 1982-83, liaison cons. civil rights, 1983-87; project adminstr. pre-apprenticeship tng. program Caltrans, Compton, Calif., 1987-89; coord. govtl. affairs Caltran, L.A., 1989, chief facilities ops., 1989-93, dist. claims officer, 1993-94, dist. materiel mgr., 1994—; facilitator Govs. Commn. on the Status of Women, Fresno, Calif., 1980. Producer: Building a Future, 1988 (bronze Cindy award Assn. Visual Communicators). Bd. dirs. Morgan Canyon Inst. of Higher Learning, Fresno, 1978-82; fund raiser Hunger Project, L.A., Fresno, 1980—, Youth at Risk, L.A., 1986—. Recipient Excellence in Transp. Facilities award, 1993. Office: Caltrans 120 S Spring St Los Angeles CA 90012-3606

SIMMONS, CAROLINE THOMPSON, civic worker; b. Denver, Aug. 22, 1910; d. Huston and Caroline Margaret (Cordes) Thompson; m. John Farr Simmons, Nov. 11, 1936; children: John Farr (dec.), Huston T., Malcolm M. (dec.). AB, Bryn Mawr Coll., 1931; MA (hon.), Amherst Coll. Chmn. women's com. Corcoran Gallery Art, 1965-66; vice chmn. women's com. Smithsonian Assos., 1969-71; pres. Decatur House Council, 1963-71; mem. bd. Nat. Theatre, 1979-80; trustee Washington Opera, 1955-65; bd. dirs. Fgn. Student Svc. Coun., 1956-79; mem. Washington Home Bd., 1955-60; bd. dirs. Smithsonian Friends of Music, 1977-79; commr. Nat. Mus. Am. Art, 1979-89; mem. Folger com. Folger Shakespeare Libr., 1979-86, trustee emeritus, 1986—; mem. Washington bd. Am. Mus. in Britain, 1970—; bd. dirs. Found. Preservation of Historic Georgetown, 1975-89; trustee Marpat Found., 1987—, Amherst Coll., 1979-81, Dacor-Bacon House Found., Phillips Collection, 1990—, Georgetown Presbyn. Ch., 1989-91; v.p. internat. coun. Mus. Modern Art, N.Y.C., 1964-90; bd. dirs. Alliance Francaise. Recipient award for eminent svc. Folger Shakespeare Libr., 1986. Mem. Soc. Women Geographers, Sulgrave Club, Chevy Chase Club. Address: 1508 Dumbarton Rock Ct NW Washington DC 20007-3048

SIMMONS, CYNTHIA FRANCENE, Slavic languages and literature educator; b. Pitts., Oct. 1, 1949; d. Raymond Arthur and Ligia Adele (DeSimone) S.; m. Timothy Kevin Stanton, Aug. 20, 1978; children: Liam, Emma. Student, U. Zagreb, Yugoslavia, 1970-71; AB, Ind. U., 1972; AM in Russian Lang. and Lit., Brown U., 1972, PhD in Slavic Langs., 1979. Lectr. dept. German and Russian U. N.H., 1973-74; asst. to dir. summer program U. Kansas, Zagreb, 1976; from asst. prof. to assoc. prof. dept. Slavic langs./lits. U. Wis., Madison, 1980-90; vis. assoc. prof. MIT, Cambridge, Mass., 1990-94; assoc. prof. Boston Coll., 1994—. Author: Their Fathers' Voice: Vassily Aksyonov, Venedikt Erofeev, Eduard Limonov, and Sasha Sokolov, 1993; editor: (with Andrew Mackie and Tatyana McAuley) For Henry Kucera: Studies in Slavic Philology and Computational Linguistics, 1992; contbr. articles and revs. to profl. publs. Chair/mem. various com. 1st Parish in Duxbury, 1989—. U. Wis. Grad. Sch. rsch. grantee, 1982, 84, 85, 87; Internat. Rsch. & Exchs. Bd. grantee for short-term travel and rsch. in Russia, 1993; fellow Harvard Russian Rsch. Ctr., 1988-90, 91-94. Mem. MLA, Am. Assn. Advancement of Slavic Studies, Am. Assn. Tchrs. Slavic and East European Langs., Phi Beta Kappa. Unitarian-Universalist. Home: PO Box 2437 Duxbury MA 02331-2437 Office: Boston College Slavic & Eastern Languages Chestnut Hill MA 02167-3806

SIMMONS, DEIDRE WARNER, performing company executive; b. Easton, Pa., May 11, 1955; d. Francis Joseph and Irene Carol (Burd) Mooney; m. Robert D. Jacobson, June 27, 1981 (div. Mar. 1989); m. William Richard Simmons, Aug. 18, 1990; children: Caitlin Dawn, Abigail Patricia, Samantha Irene. BA in Music, Montclair State Coll., 1978. Music tchr. Warren Hills Regional Sch., Washington, N.J., 1978-80; devel. dir. N.J. Shakespeare Festival, Madison, 1981-83; dir. contbns. Parent Found., Lancaster, Pa., 1983-86; exec. dir. Fulton Opera House, Lancaster, 1986—, capital campaign counsel, 1990—. Vice chmn. bd. dirs. Ind. Eye, Lancaster, 1986-89; mem. adv. com. Lancaster Cultural Coun., 1988—. Mem. Theatre Communications Group, League Hist. Theatres. Office: Fulton Opera House 12 N Prince St PO Box 1865 Lancaster PA 17603

SIMMONS, DIANE EILEEN, corporate executive; b. New Smyrna Beach, Fla., Jan. 28, 1950; d. George Andrew and Carolyn Margaret (Cross) Naser; A.A., Daytona Beach Community Coll., 1971; student U. N.C., 1978, U. South Fla., 1980; m. Paul L. Simmons, June 2, 1973; children—Thomas David (dec.), Paula Kay. Pres., Fla. Trade Publ., Daytona Beach, Fla., 1971-74; project engr. Pollak & Skan Inc., Rosemont, Ill., 1977-78; mgr. S.E. region, 1978-79; exec. dir. Internat. Soc. Pharm. Engrs., Tampa, Fla., 1979-81; exec. dir. Seminars, Inc., Tampa, Fla., 1978-84; exec. sec., treas. ROST Inc., 1977-91, Carpet Sculpture Gallery of Fla, 1991—; pres. Regulatory Info. Systems, Inc., 1983-84; sec.-treas. Tam-Rock Devel., Inc.; exec. dir. Internat. Ctr. for Tech. Transfer, Inc. (ICT-2), Tampa, 1985—; bd. dirs. Veridien Corp., 1989—. Recipient Woman of Achievement award Nat. Bus. and Profl. Womans Assn., 1992. Mem. ASME, Nat. Assn. Female Execs. Republican. So. Baptist. Pub., FACT mag., 1971-74; editor Pharm. Engring. Jour., 1979-81, Bio Process Engring., 1984-85. Office: Carpet Sculpture Gallery Fla. 3550 Morris St N Saint Petersburg FL 33713-1629

SIMMONS, DONNA MARIE, neurobiology researcher, histotechnologist; b. Hartford, Conn., Oct. 13, 1943; d. John Henry and Ellen Louise (Meehl) Strayer; m. Corvin Gale Simmons, Sept. 17, 1964. Student, U. Wash., Western Wash. State U.; postgrad. U. Southern Calif., 1994—. Histologic technician, instr. Tacoma Gen. Hosp. Sch. Med. Tech., Tacoma, Wash., 1963; lab. technician Med. Sch. U. Wash., 1964; histologic technician Northgate Med. Lab., Seattle, 1964-67; rsch. technologist in neuroanatomy Regional Primate Rsch. Ctr., U. Wash., 1967-82; rsch. asst. Devel. Neurobiology Lab. Salk Inst., La Jolla, Calif., 1982-85; sr. technician, lab. mgr. Neural Systems Lab. Howard Hughes Med. Inst. at Salk Inst., 1985-90; rsch. assoc. dept. of biol. scis.-neurobiology, U. So. Calif., L.A., 1990—; cons., lectr. in field.; judge Greater San Diego Sci. and Engring. Fair, 1987-89, Calif. Sci. Fair, 1992; leader sci. del. to People's Rep. of China, 1986; chair China Scientist Exchange Fund, 1986-87; mem. Swiss Histology Meeting Exch., 1990. Author tech. articles, revs. in field; mem. editorial bd. Jour. histotech. Recipient Diamond Cover award Jour. of Histotech., 1990; various svc. awards; best non-clin. pub. in field, 1985. Mem. AAAS, Am. Soc. Clin. Pathologists (affiliate), Wash. State Histology Soc. (past pres., histology liaison Am. Soc. Med. Tech.), Nat. Soc. Histotech. (charter mem., regional dir. 1980-82, jud. chair 1983-86), Calif. Soc. Histotech. (San Diego dir. protem 1985-86), Assn. Women in Sci. (San Diego charter mem., bd. dir. 1985-90), Soc. for Neurosci., Swiss Soc. for Histotech., Women in Neurosci., N.Y. Acad. Sci., NOW, Am. Alpine Club, J.B. Johnston Club. Office: U So Calif Hedco Neurosci Bldg MC 2520 Los Angeles CA 90089

SIMMONS, ELIZABETH H., physics educator; b. Buffalo, N.Y., Oct. 22, 1963; d. Peter and Ruth J. S.; m. R. Sekhar Chivukula, June 16, 1990; 1 child, Ari S. Chivukula. AB, Harvard U., 1985, MA, 1987, PhD, 1990; MPhil, U. Cambridge, 1986. Rsch. assoc. Harvard U., Cambridge, Mass., 1990-93; asst. prof. physics Boston U., 1993—; mem. sci. adv. bd. Aspen Ctr. for Physics, 1994—; mem. collaboration coun. GEM Collaboration at Superconducting Super Collider Lab., Dallas, 1991-93. Contbr. articles to profl. jours. Grad. fellow NSF, Harvard U., 1985-89, SSC Nat. Rsch. fellow Tex. Nat. Rsch. Lab., 1990-91; grad. rsch. program for women AT&T Bell Labs, 1985-90; Churchill scholar Winston Churchill Found., U. Cambridge, 1985-86. Mem. AAUW (Curie fellow 1993-94), Am. Phys. Soc., Assn. Women in Sci. Office: Boston U Physics Dept 590 Commonwealth Ave Boston MA 02215-2507

SIMMONS, JEAN, actress; b. London, Jan. 31, 1929; d. Charles and Winifred Ada (Loveil) S.; m. Stewart Granger, Dec. 20, 1950 (div. June 1960); 1 dau., Tracy; m. Richard Brooks, Nov. 1, 1960; 1 dau., Kate. Ed., Orange Hill Sch., Burnt Oak, London. Motion picture actress, appearing in English and Am. films including Great Expectations, 1946, Black Narcissus, 1947, Hamlet, 1948 (Acad. award nomination), Adam and Evelyn, 1949, The Actress, 1953, Young Bess, 1953, Guys and Dolls, 1956, The Big Country, 1958, Home Before Dark, 1958, Spartacus, 1960, Elmer Gantry, 1960, The Grass Is Greener, 1960, All the Way Home, 1963, Rough Night in Jericho, 1967, Divorce American Style, 1967, The Happy Ending, 1969 (Acad. award nomination), The Dawning, 1989; also theatre appearance A Little Night Music, Phila. and on tour, 1974; appeared in: TV mini-series The Dain Curse, 1978, A Small Killing, 1981, Valley of the Dolls, 1981, The Thornbirds, 1983 (Emmy award), North and South, 1985, North and South Book II, 1986; TV film: December Flower, 1987, The Legend of Lost Loves, 1988, Great Expectations, 1989; guest TV series Murder She Wrote, 1989, In the Heat of the Night, 1993; TV series Dark Shadows, 1991. Office: care Geoffrey Barr 9400 Readcrest Dr Beverly Hills CA 90210-2552 also: Susan Smith & Assocs 121 N San Vicente Blvd Beverly Hills CA 90211-2303*

SIMMONS, JEAN ELIZABETH MARGARET (MRS. GLEN R. SIMMONS), chemistry educator; b. Cleve., Jan. 20, 1914; d. Frank Charles and Sarah Anne (Johnston) Saurwein; m. Glen R. Simmons, Nov. 14, 1935; children: Sally Anne, (Frank) Charles, James Fraser. B.A., Western Reserve U., 1933; Ph.D. (Stieglitz fellow 1935-37), U. Chgo., 1938. Faculty Barat Coll., Lake Forest, Ill., 1938-58; prof., chmn. dept. chemistry Barat Coll., 1948-58; faculty Upsala Coll., East Orange, N.J., 1959—; prof. Upsala Coll., 1963-84, prof. emeritus, 1984—, chmn. dept. chemistry, 1965-71, 74, 76-81, chmn. sci. curriculum study, Luth. Ch. Am. grantee, 1965-68, chmn. div. natural scis. and maths., 1965-69, asst. to pres., 1968-73, 78-86; Coordinator basic scis. Evang. Hosp. Sch. Nursing, Chgo., 1943-46; lectr. sci. topics; participant various White House Confs. Contbr. articles to publs. in field. Troop leader Girl Scouts U.S.A., Wheaton, Ill., 1952-58, neighborhood chmn., 1956-57, dist. chmn., DuPage County, 1958; chmn. U. Chgo. Alumni Fund Dr., Wheaton, 1957, 58, Princeton, N.J., 1964, 65; mem. nursing adv. com. East Orange (N.J.) Gen. Hosp., 1963-73; pres. Virginia Gildersleeve Internat. Fund, 1975-81, bd. dirs., 1969-83, chmn. nominating com., 1985-87, oral history com., 1981. Recipient Lindback Found. award for disting. teaching, 1964; vis. fellow Princeton U., 1977. Fellow Am. Inst. Chemists, AAAS (council 1969-71); mem. Am. Chem. Soc., AAUW (br. treas. 1960-62, chmn. sci. topic 1963-65, state v.p. program 1964, nat. sci. topic implementation chmn. 1965, 66, state dir. 1967-68, 71-72, state pres. 1968-70, 50 Yr. Cert. 1989), Fedn. Orgns. Profl. Women (nat. pres. 1974-75), Internat. Fedn. Univ. Women (alt. del. for U.S. at conf. 1968, 77, 83, del. conf. 1974, ofcl. observer UN Conf. Vienna 1979, Nairobi 1981, convenor membership com. 1980-84, adv. bd. 1980—, oral history com. 1990), AAUP (charter, past chpt. pres.), Phi Beta Kappa (pres. North Jersey alumni assn. 1973-74), Sigma Xi, Sigma Delta Epsilon (nat. pres. 1970-71, dir. 1972-78, edn. liaison 1978-87, chmn. nom. 1986-87, hon., award sci. edn. 1989). Episcopalian. Home: 40 Balsam Ln Princeton NJ 08540-5327 Office: Upsala Coll East Orange NJ 07019

SIMMONS, LORNA WOMACK, elementary school educator; b. Enid, Okla., Dec. 25, 1954; d. Doyle Alex and Ruth Phyllis (Wiens) Nunneley; m. Daniel Bruce Womack, June 7, 1975 (widowed Jan. 1981); children: Zachary Womack, Travis Womack, Shawn Simmons, Shayla Simmons; m. H. Lynn Simmons, Feb. 14, 1982. BS cum laude, U. Tex., 1977. Spl. edn. tchr. Sand Springs (Okla.) I.S.D., 1977-78; pvt. therapist Alphabetic Phonics, Big Spring, Tex., 1981-87; dyslexia cons. Big Spring (Tex.) I.S.D., 1987-88; chpt. I tchr. Forsan I.S.D., Big Spring, Tex., 1988-91; cons. Classroom Phonics, Big Spring, Tex., 1991—. Author: Classroom Phonics, 1989, Classroom Phonics II, 1991, Classroom Phonics Spelling, 1991, Classroom Phonics Kid Cards, 1994, Classroom Phonics Comprehension Tests, 1994. Mem. Assn. Tex. Profl. Educators. Republican. Mem. Ch. of God. Home: 3200 Wasson Dr Big Spring TX 79720

SIMMONS, LYNDA MERRILL MILLS, educational administrator; b. Salt Lake City, Aug. 31, 1940; d. Alanson Soper and Madeline Helene (Merrill) Mills; m. Mark Carl Simmons, Nov. 17, 1962; children: Lisa Lynn Simmons Morley, William Mark, Jennifer Louise, Robert Thomas. BS, U. Utah, 1961, MS, 1983. Cert. sch. adminstr., Utah. Tchr. Wasatch Jr. High Sch./Granite Dist., Salt Lake City, 1961-64, Altamont (Utah) High Sch./Duchesne Dist., 1964-66; tchr. spl. edn. Park City (Utah) High Sch., 1971-73; resource tchr. Eisenhower Jr. High Sch., Salt Lake City, 1979-88; tchr. specialist Granite Sch. Dist., Salt Lake City, 1985-90; asst. prin. Bennion Jr. High Sch., Salt Lake City, 1990-93; prin. Hartvigsen Sch./Jones Ctr., Salt Lake City, 1993—; adj. prof. spl. edn. U. Utah, Salt Lake City, 1985—; mentor tchr. Utah Mentor Tchr. Acad., Salt Lake City, 1987—, Utah Prin. Acad., 1994—; co-chair Utah Spl. Educators for Compuer Tech., Salt Lake City, 1988-90; mem. adv. com. on handicapped Utah State Office Edn., 1990-93; presenter at confs. Author: Setting Up Effective Secondary Resource Program, 1985; contbr. articles to profl. publs. Dist. chmn. Heart Fund, Cancer Dr., Summit Park, Utah, 1970-82; cub pack leader Park City area Boy Scouts Am., 1976-80; bd. dirs. Jr. League Salt Lake City, 1977-80; cookie chmn. Park City area Girl Scouts U.S., 1981; dist. chmn. March of Dimes, 1982—. Recipient Amb. award Salt Lake Conv. and Vis. Bur., 1993. Mem. Nat. Assn. Secondary Sch. Prins., Park City Young Women's Mut. (pres. 1989-93, family history cons. 1993—), Women's Athenaeum (v.p. 1990-93, pres. 1994—), Coun. for Exceptional Children (pres. Salt Lake chpt. 1989-90, pres. Utah Fedn. 1991-93), Granite Assn. Sch. Adminstrs. (sec.-treas. 1992-94). Mem. LDS Ch. Office: Hartrigsen Sch 350 E 3605 S Salt Lake City UT 84115

SIMMONS, MARCIA ANN, reporter; b. Topeka, Kans., Oct. 29, 1954; d. William Eugene Simmons and Ruth Mae (Engle) Shaw; m. George Z. Guzowski, Mar. 20, 1982 (dec. Nov. 1987); children: Kevin King, Stefan Guzowski, William Lindstedt. BA, U. N.Mex., 1977. Anchor, reporter KUNM Radio, Albuquerque, 1975-76; anchor reporter KNWZ Radio, Albuquerque, 1976-77, KOAT-TV, Albuquerque, 1981-88, KOA, Denver, 1991—; reporter, editor Old Town Times, Albuquerque, 1976; assignments editor, anchor KGGM-TV, Albuquerque, 1977-81; reporter KOB-TV, Albuquerque, 1990; media advisor N.Mex. Games, Albuquerque, 1988. Writer, reporter Nativity Newspaper, Broomfield, Colo., 1994. Bd. dirs. Gov.'s Task Force on Developmentally Disabled, Santa Fe, N.Mex., 1988-89, N.Mex. Animal Humane Assn., Albuquerque, 1986; media advisor Bob Schwartz for Dist. Atty. Campaign, Albuquerque, 1988. Recipient Nat. Gavel award ABA, 1982, Reporting award AP, 1985. Mem. Am. Women in Radio and TV. Democrat. Roman Catholic. Home: 1162 Clubhouse Dr Broomfield CO 80020

SIMMONS, MARGUERITE SAFFOLD, pharmaceutical sales professional; b. Montgomery, Ala., Oct. 21, 1954; d. Arthur Edward and Gwendolyn Jane (Saffold) S. BS in Communications, U. Tenn., 1976. Press sec. Met. Mayor's Office, Nashville, 1976-77; advt. copywriter United Meth. Pub. House, Nashville, 1977-78; sales rep. No Nonsense Pantyhose, Houston, 1978-81, Breon Labs., Houston, 1981-82; profl. sales rep. Janssen Pharmaceutica, Inc., Houston, 1982-88, sr. sales rep., 1988—. Vol. Dem. Nat. Conv., Atlanta, 1988. Named to Outstanding Young Women in Am., 1981, 87. Mem. NAFE, U. Tenn. Alumni Assn. (bd. dirs. Atlanta chpt. 1989-90), U. Tenn. Black Alumni Assn. (bd. dirs. Atlanta chpt. 1989—, pres.- elect bd. dirs. 1995), Ga. Trust Hist. Soc., Ala. Geneal. Soc., Ga. Geneal. Soc., Nat. Trust Hist. Preservation, Delta Sigma Theta. Baptist. Office: PO Box 16934 Atlanta GA 30321-0934

SIMMONS, MIRIAM QUINN, state legislator; b. Jackson, Miss., Mar. 28, 1928; d. Charles Buford and Viola (Hamill) Quinn; m. Willie Wronal Simmons, July 10, 1952; children: Dick, Sue, Wronal. BS, Miss. U. for Women, 1949. Tchr. Columbia (Miss.) City Schs., 1949-51, 53-54, literacy coord., 1986-87; home demonstration agt. Coop. Extension Svc., Bay Springs, Miss., 1951-52; tchr. Marion County Schs., Columbia, 1952-53, 54-55, Columbia Tng. Sch., 1961-63, Columbia Acad., 1970-73; rep. Miss. Ho. of Reps., Jackson, 1988—; adv. bd. Magnolia Fed. Bank for Savs; trustee State Inst. Higher Learning, Jackson, 1972-84; dir. Miss. Authority for Ednl. TV, Jackson, 1976-88. Named Marion County Outstanding Citizen Columbia Jr. Aux., 1981. Mem. Miss. Fedn. Women's Clubs, Bus. and Profl. Women's Club, Hilltop Garden Club, Delta Kappa Gamma. Democrat. Methodist. Home: 45 Old Highway 98 E Columbia MS 39429-8172

SIMMONS, RUTH DORIS, women's health nurse, educator; b. Bklyn., July 30, 1942; d. Stanley George and Doris Louise (Beckert) S. LPN, Glen Cove (N.Y.) Community, 1964; AD, SUNY, Farmingdale, 1976; BSPA, St. Joseph's Coll., 1994. Nurse labor/delivery unit Syosset (N.Y.) Hosp., 1964-66; staff nurse ob./gyn. and pediatrics unit Glen Cove Community Hosp., 1966-76; staff nurse ob./gyn. Mercy Hosp., Scranton, Pa., 1976—. Home: RR 2 Box 2770 Factoryville PA 18419-9658

SIMMONS, RUTH J., academic administrator; b. Grapeland, Tex., 1945; 2 children. Student, Universidad Internacional, Saltillo, Mex., 1965, Wellesley Coll., 1965-66; BA, Dillard U., 1967; postgrad., George Washington U., 1967-68; AM, Harvard U., 1970, PhD in Romance Langs., 1973. Interpreter lang. svcs. divsn. U.S. Dept. State, Washington, 1968-69; instr. French George Washington U., 1968-69; admissions officer Radcliffe Coll., 1970-72; asst. prof. French U. New Orleans, 1973-75, asst. dean coll. liberal arts, asst. prof., 1975-76; adminstrv. coord. NEH liberal studies project Calif. State U., Northridge, 1977-78, acting dir. internat. programs, vis. assoc. prof. Pan-African studies, 1978-79; asst. dean grad. sch. U. So. Calif., 1979-82, assoc. dean grad. sch., 1982-83; dir. studied Butler Coll. Princeton (N.J.) U., 1983-85, acting. die. Afro-Am. studies, 1985-87, asst. dean faculty, 1986-87, assoc. dean faculty, 1987-90, vice provost, 1992-95; provost Speilman Coll., 1990-91; pres. Smith Coll., Northhampton, Mass., 1995—; peer reviewer higher edn. divsn. NEH, 1980-83, bd. cons., 1981; mem. grad. adv. bd. Calif. Student Aid Commn., 1981-83; chair com. to visit dept. African-Am. studies Harvard U., 1991—; mem. strategic planning task force N.J. Dept. Higher Edn., 1992-93; mem. nat. adv. commn. EQUITY 2000, Coll. Bd., 1992—; mem. adv. bd. ctrl. N.J. com. NAACP Legal Def. Fund, 1992—; mem. Mid. States Assn. Accreditation Team, Johns Hopkins U., 1993; chair rev. panel for model instns. planning grants NSF, 1993. Mem. editorial bd. World Edn. series Am. Assc. Collegiate Registrars and Admissions Officers, 1984-86; contbr. articles to profl. jours.; presenter, speaker and panielist in field. Mem. adv. bd. N.J. Master Faculty program Woodrow Wilson Nat. Fellowship Found.,m 1987-90, bd. trustees, 1991—. KYOK scholar, 1963; Worthing Found. scholar, 1963-67; Danforth fellow, 1967-73; Fulbright scholar U. Lyon, 1967-68; Sr. Fulbright fellow, 1981; Rsch. grantee AACRAO, 1987-88; recipient Disting. Svc. award Assn. Black Princeton Alumni, 1989, Dillard U., 1992, Pres.'s Recognition award Bloomfield Coll., 1993, TWIN award Princeton Area YWCA, 1993. Office: Smith College Office of the President Northampton MA 01063*

SIMMONS, SUZAN BERYL, psychologist; b. Helena, Mont., Nov. 26, 1951; d. Paul H. and R. Ellen (Berry) Cresap. BA in Elem. Edn., Jamestown Coll., 1976; MS in Student Pers. and Guidance, Okla. State U., 1980, PhD in Counseling Psychology, 1983. Cert. health svc. provider in psychology, psychologist, Iowa. Counselor II student counseling svc. Iowa State U., Ames, 1983-86; psychologist Ctrl. Iowa Psychiat. Svcs., Des Moines, 1987-90, Iowa Physicians Clinic, Des Moines, 1991—; psychologist/clin. dir. Spectrum, Iowa Meth. Med. Ctr., Des Moines, 1990. Mem. multicultural nonsexist adv. com. Ankeny (Iowa) Community Schs., 1992-94. Mem. APA, Iowa Psychol. Assn., Alliance Mentally Ill. Methodist. Office: Iowa Physicians Clinic Med Found 1221 Pleasant St Ste 200 Des Moines IA 50309-1425

SIMMONS, SYLVIA JEANNE QUARLES (MRS. HERBERT G. SIMMONS, JR.), university administrator, educator; b. Boston, May 8, 1935; d. Lorenzo Christopher and Margaret Mary (Thomas) Quarles; B.A., Manhattanville Coll., 1957; M.Ed., Boston Coll., 1962, PhD, 1991; m. Herbert G. Simmons, Jr., Oct. 26, 1957; children: Stephen, Alison, Lisa. Montessori tchr. Charles River Park Nursery Sch., Boston, 1965-66; registrar Boston Coll. Sch. Mgmt., Chestnut Hill, Mass., 1966-70; dir. fin. aid Radcliffe Coll., Cambridge, Mass., 1970-75, assoc. dean admissions and fin. aid, 1972-75, assoc. dean admissions, fin. aid and women's edn., 1975; assoc. dean admissions and fin. aid Harvard and Radcliffe, from 1975; assoc. v.p. for acad. affairs, central adminstrn. U. Mass., Boston, 1976-79, spl. asst. to chancellor, 1979; v.p. field services Am. Student Assistance, 1982-84, sr. v.p., 1984-93, exec. v.p. 1993—; mem. faculty Harvard U., 1970-77; cons. Mass. Bd. Higher Edn., 1973-77. Bd. dirs. Rivers Country Day Sch., Weston, Mass., Simon's Rock Coll., Great Barrington, Mass., Wayland (Mass.) Fair Housing, Cambridge Mental Health Assn., Family Service Greater Boston, Concerts in Black and White, Mass. Higher Edn. Assistance Corp.; chmn. bd. dirs. North Shore Community Coll., 1986-88, mem. bd. dirs., 1985—; trustee and alumnae bd. dirs. Manhattanville Coll., 1986—. Mem. adv. com. Upward Bound, Chestnut Hill Boston Coll., 1972-74; Camp Chimney Corners, Becket, Mass., 1971-77; bd. dirs. Am. Cancer Soc., Mass., 1987-89, Boston Coll., 1990—, Merrimack Coll., 1992—, Mass. Found. for the Humanities, 1990-92, Mass. Bay United Way, 1990-94; overseer Mt. Ida Coll., 1990—. Named One of Ten Outstanding Young Leaders, Boston Jr. C. of C., 1971; recipient Bicentennial medal Boston Coll., 1976; Achievement award Greater Boston YMCA, 1977, Human Rights award Mass. Tchrs. Assn., 1988, Pres'. award Mass Ednl. Opportunity Assn., 1988. Mem.

Women in Politics, Nat. (exec. council 1973-75), Eastern (1st v.p. 1973) assns. financial aid officers, Coll. Scholarship Service Council, Links, (pres. local chpt. 1967-69), Nat. Inst. Fin. Aid Adminstrs. (dir. 1975-77), Jack and Jill Am. (pres. Newton chpt. 1972-74, Delta Sigma Theta, Delta Kappa Gamma (pres. 1988-90). Club: Manhattanville (pres. Boston 1966-68). Home: 3 Dean Rd Wayland MA 01778-5007 Office: 330 Stuart St Boston MA 02116-5229

SIMMONS, TRACY DIANE, systems analyst, writer; b. Albuquerque, Feb. 13, 1959; d. John Fletcher and Welda Jeanette (Haynes) Abernathy; m. Philip Eugene Simmons, Jan. 14, 1984; children: Kristin Amanda, Timothy Scott. BA, U. N.Mex., 1982, student, 1987—. Tech. writer JAYCOR, Albuquerque, 1988—, computer systems test analyst, 1993—. Author various manuals and courses, 1990-94. Asst. Brownie leader Girl Scouts U.S., Albuquerque, 1994. With U.S. Army, 1983-86. Decorated Achievement medal. Home: 5 Cedar Pl Los Lunas NM 87031

SIMMS, AMY LANG, journalist, editor; b. Bryn Mawr, Pa., Sept. 21, 1964; d. Eben Caldwell and Anna Mary (Fussell) L.; m. Donald Gardner Simms, July 15, 1989; children: Harrison Lang, Maud Whittington. BA in French and Sociology, Bucknell U., 1986; postgrad., Sch. Museum of Fine Arts, 1988, Cambridge Ctr. Adult Edn., 1988, Bryn Mawr Coll., 1988, Vassar Coll., 1993. Copywriter, media and prodn. asst. DBM Assocs., Cambridge, Mass., 1986-88; teaching asst. sociology dept. Bucknell U., Lewisburg, Pa., 1989; staff reporter Lewisburg Daily Jour., 1989-92, asst. editor, 1991; asst. editor Milton (Pa.) Standard, 1991; co-founder, co-editor Lewisburg Holiday Herald, 1990; co-founder Environ. Advisor Newsletter, Lewisburg, 1990-91. Contbr. articles to profl. jours. Media corr. Elem. Related Arts Com., Lewisburg, 1989; mem. Orgns. United for the Environment, Allenwood, Pa., 1990—; adv. bd. Union County Children and Youth Svcs., Lewisburg, 1991-92; trustee Sarah Hull Hallock Meml. Libr., Milton, N.Y., 1993—. Recipient Hon. Speakers award Lewisburg Lions Club, 1990. Mem. AAUW. Republican. Roman Catholic. Home and Office: 583 Lattintown Rd Apt 3 Marlboro NY 12542-5105

SIMMS, MARIA ESTER, health services administrator; b. Bahia Blanca, Argentina; came to U.S., 1963; d. Jose and Esther (Guays) Barberio Esandi; m. Michael Simms, July 15, 1973 (Aug. 1993); children: Michelle Bonnie Lee Carla, Michael London Valentine, Matthew Brandon. Degree medicine, Facultad del Centenario, Rosario, Argentina, 1962; Physician Asst. Cert. (hon.), U. So. Calif., 1977. Medical diplomate. Pres. Midtown Svcs. Inc., L.A., 1973—. Chmn. bd. dirs. Am.'s Film Inst., Washington. Fellow Am. Acad. Physicians' Assts.; mem. Bus. for Law Enforcement (northeast divsn.), Physicians for Social Responsibility, Mercy Crusade Inc., Internat. Found. for Survival Rsch., Noetic Scis. Soc., Inst. Noetic Scis., So. Calif. Alliance for Survival, Supreme Emblem Club of U.S., Order Eastern Star, Flying Samaritans, Shriners.

SIMMS, MARIA KAY, publishing and computer services executive; b. Princeton, Ill., Nov. 18, 1940; d. Frank B. and Anna (Haurberg) S.; m. Neil F. Michelsen, Oct. 2, 1987 (dec. 1990); children: Shannon Sullivan Stillings, Molly A. Sullivan, Elizabeth Maria Jossick. BFA, Ill. Wesleyan U., 1962. Cert. cons. profl. astrologer; ordained min. L.A. Cmty. Ch. of Religious Sci. Art tchr. elem. and jr. high pub. schs., Dundee, Northbrook, Ill., 1962-65; high sch. art tchr. Danbury, Conn., 1975-76; self employed gallery painter various cities, 1962-77, free-lance comml. illustrator, 1972-74, 86-87; shop, gallery, café owner Conn., 1976-79; art dir. ACS Pubs., Inc., San Diego, Calif., 1987-90; pres. Astro Comm Svcs., Inc. (formerly ACS Pubs.), San Diego, 1990—; conf. lectr. United Astrology Congress, Washington, 1992, Am. Fedn. Astrologers Internat. Conv., Chgo., 1992. Author: Twelve Wings of the Eagle, 1988, Dial Detective, 1989; co-author: Search for the Christmas Star, 1989, Circle of the Cosmic Muse, 1994, Your Magical Child, 1994; contbr. numerous articles to mags. High priestess Cir. of the Cosmic Muse; chairperson pub. outreach focus group Wiccan Ind. Network. Recipient numerous art awards. Mem. Nat. Assn. Women Bus. Owners, Nat. Coun. Geocosmic Rsch. Inc. (dir., pubs. dir. 1981-92, editor jour. 1984-92), Am. Fedn. Astrologers, Internat. Soc. Astrol. Rsch., New Age Pubs. Assn. Office: Astro Comm Svcs Inc 5521 Ruffin Rd San Diego CA 92123

SIMON, CARLY, singer, composer, author; b. N.Y.C., June 25, 1945; d. Richard S.; m. James Taylor, 1972 (div. 1983); children: Sarah Maria, Benjamin Simon; m. James Hart, Dec. 23, 1987. Studied with Pete Seeger. Singer, composer, rec. artist, 1971—. Appeared in film No Nukes, 1980; albums include Carly Simon, 1971, Anticipation, 1972, No Secrets, 1973, Hotcakes, 1974, Playing Possum, 1975, The Best of Carly Simon, 1975, Another Passenger, 1976, Boys in the Trees, 1978, Spy, 1979, Come Upstairs, 1980, Torch, 1981, Hello Big Man, 1983, Spoiled Girl, 1985, Coming Around Again, 1987, Greatest Hits Live, 1988, My Romance, 1990, Have You Seen Me Lately?, 1990, Carly Simon, This Is My Life, 1992, Letters Never Sent, 1994; single records: Nobody Does It Better, 1977, Let the River Run, 1988 (Academy award best original song, 1989), (with Frank Sinatra) In the Wee Small Hours of the Morning, 1993; recipient Grammy award as best new artist 1971; TV appearance: Carly in Concert: My Romance, 1990; author: Amy the Dancing Bear, 1988, The Boy of the Bells, 1990, The Fisherman's Song, 1991, The Nightime Chauffeur, 1993; created opera Romulus Hunt, 1993.

SIMON, CATHY JENSEN, architect; b. Los Angeles, Sept. 30, 1943; d. Bernard Everett and Bitten Hanne (Smith) S.; m. Michael Palmer, Nov. 23, 1972; 1 child, Sarah Marina. B.A. Wellesley Coll., 1965; M. Arch., Harvard U., 1969. Registered architect, Calif. 1974, N.Y. 1988, Mass. 1988. Architect Cambridge 7 Assocs., Mass., 1968-69, Building Systems Devel., San Francisco, 1970-72, Mackinlay Winnacker McNeil, Oakland, Calif., 1973-74; prin. Marquis Assocs., San Francisco, 1974-85; prin. Simon Martin-Vegue Winkelstein Moris, 1985—; sr. lectr. architecture U. Calif., Berkeley, 1982-85, vis. lectr., 1973-82; teaching coordinator Women's Sch. Planning and Arch., Santa Cruz, Calif., 1976; speaker ALA Nat. Conv., 1992, Les Grandes Bibliotheques de L'Avenin, Paris, 1991. Prin. works include Yerba Buena Gardens Retail and Entertainment Complex, San Francisco, Mus. N.Mex. Master Plan, Santa Fe, San Francisco Ballet Pavilion, Lick Wilmerding High Sch. Master Plan, San Francisco, Bothell Br. Campus, Bothell, Wash., San Francisco New Main Libr., Oceanside Water Pollution Control Project, San Francisco, Newport Beach (Calif.) Ctrl. Libr., Coll. 8 U. Calif., Santa Cruz, Olin Humanities Bldg. Bard Coll., N.Y., San Francisco Day Sch., Fremont (Calif.) Main Libr., Peter J. Shields Libr. U. Calif., Davis, Elena Baskin Visual Art Studios U. Calif., Santa Cruz, Primate Discovery Ctr., San Francisco Zoo, Braun Music Ctr., Stanford U. The Premier, La Jolla Colony, La Jolla, Calif. Mem. exec. com. San Francisco Mus. Modern Art; active Leadership Commn. Design Industry; mem. tech. assistance com., San Francisco Redevel. Agy., San Francisco, 1982—; mem. adv. panel Calif. Bd. Archtl. Examiners; bd. dirs. Golden Gate Nat. Park Assn. Recipient Calif. Preservation award Chambord Apartments, 1984, Adaptive Re-use award Engr. Offices, Am. Soc. Interior Designer, 1982, Commodore Sloat Sch. Honor award Nat. Sch. Bds. Assocs., 1980, Marcus Foster Mid. Sch. Honor award East Bay AIA, 1980; NEA grantee 1983. Mem. Orgn. Women Architects (founding 1972), San Francisco chpt. AIA, AIA (jury mem. nat. honor awards 1980, Los Angeles chpt. awards jury 1984). Home: 265 Jersey St San Francisco CA 94114-3822 Office: Simon Martin-Vegue Winkelstein Moris 501 2nd St San Francisco CA 94107-1431

SIMON, DEBRA WAGNER, accountant; b. Phila., July 24, 1959; d. Joseph and Annette (Schmerling) Wagner; m. Paul Stephen Simon, Sept. 5, 1982; 1 child, Jessica M. BSBA, Drexel U., 1982. CPA, Pa. Jr. acct. Mann Judd Landau, Phila., 1983-84, staff acct., 1984, sr. acct., 1985-88, BDO Seidman, Phila., 1989—. Mem. Surrey Pl. Civic Assn., Cherry Hill, N.J., 1985-91. Mem. AICPA, Pa. Inst. CPA's, Am. Women's Soc. CPA's, Am. Soc. Women Accts., Beta Alpha Psi. Avocations: tennis, computers. Office: BDO Seidman 1601 Market St Philadelphia PA 19103-2339

SIMON, DORIS MARIE TYLER, nurse; b. Akron, Ohio, Jan. 24, 1932; d. Gabriel James and Nannie Eliza (Harris) Tyler; m. Matthew Hamilton Simon, Apr. 20, 1952; children: Matthew Derek, Denise Nanette, Gayle Machele, Doris Elizabeth. ADN, El Paso (Tex.) Coll. Media, 1969, El Paso Community Coll., 1976; BSPA in Health Care Adminstrn., St. Joseph's Coll., North Windham, Maine, 1991. Med. asst. Dr. Melvin Farris, Akron, 1962-63, Dr. Samuel Watt, Akron, 1967-68, Drs. May, Fox and Buchwald, El Paso, 1972-76; head nurse, home dialysis and transplant coord. Hotel Dieu Med. Ctr., El Paso, 1977-87; nurse mgr., transplant coord. Providence Meml. Hosp., El Paso, 1987-94, nurse clinician neurology, 1994—; med. asst. instr. Bryman Sch. Med. Assts., El Paso, 1970-72. Youth choir dir. Ft. Sill, Okla., 1964-67; choir dir. Ft. Sill area and Ft. Bliss, Tex., 1964-74; instr. in piano and music theory, Ft. Sill, 1964-67; leader Ft. Sill coun. Girl Scouts U.S., 1965-67; instr. Sch. for Handicapped, Lawton, Okla., 1965-67; nephrology nurse del. to People's Republic China Citizen Amb. Program, People to People Internat., 1988, to Russia and the Baltics Citizen Amb. Group Project Asst. Healthcare, 1992. Recipient Molly Pitcher award U.S. Army, 1963-67, Martin Luther King Jr. Share a Dream Svc. award, 1993, Delta Sigma Theta Outstanding Profl. of 1993 award; named One of 12 Outstanding Personalities of El Paso El Paso Times, 1993. Mem. ANA, Am. Med. Assts. Assn., Am. Nephrology Nurses Assn., Les Charmantes (Akron) (pres./sec. 1950-52), Links Inc. (pres. El Paso chpt. 1992—), Interclub Coun. (pres. 1992—), Donor Awareness Coalition 1992—. Baptist. Home: 8909 Parkland Dr El Paso TX 79925-4012 Office: Providence Meml Hosp 2001 N Oregon St El Paso TX 79902-3320

SIMON, JACQUELINE ALBERT, political scientist, journalist; b. N.Y.C.; d. Louis and Rose (Axelroad) Albert; m. Pierre Simon; children: Lisette, Orville. BA cum laude, NYU, MA, 1972, PhD, 1977. Adj. asst. prof. Southampton Coll., 1977-79; mng. editor Point of Contact, N.Y.C., 1975-76; assoc. editor, U.S. bur. chief Politique Internationale, Paris, 1979—; sr. rsch. assoc. Inst. French Studies, NYU, 1980—, asst. prof. govt., 1982-83; assoc. Inst. on the Media for War and Peace; frequent appearances French TV and radio. Contbg. editor Harper's, 1984-92; contbr. numerous articles to French mags., revs., books on internat. affairs. Bd. dirs. Fresh Air Fund, 1984—. Mem. Ams. for Dem. Action, Overseas Press Club (bd. govs.), Phi Beta Kappa. Home: 988 Fifth Ave New York NY 10021-0143

SIMON, JANICE MYLES, federal agency administrator; b. Detroit, Mar. 14, 1956; d. William Lester and Mildred (Harris) Myles; m. Arthur James Simon, Mar. 27, 1978 (div. June, 1989); children: Janiqua Loraine, Arthur James Jr. Student, Wayne County C.C., Detroit, 1974-76, So. U., 1988-89, Wayne State U., 1989—. Med. asst. Family Med. Ctr., Detroit, 1975-76; med. adminstr. Carswell AFB, Ft. Worth, 1976-80; sec. Dept. Vets. Affairs, Shreveport, La., 1988-89; adminstrv. clk. FDA, Detroit, 1989—. Mem. Brazeal Dennard Community Chorus, 1991, Brazeal Dennard Chorale, 1992. Recipient 2d place female vocalist, vocal group categories Mather AFB Talent Show, Sacramento, 1978, 1st place female vocalist Carswell AFB Talent Show, 1979, 1st place female vocalist, duo group categories, 1980. Mem. New Dimension Choral Soc. (tel. com. 1989—, recipient Delta Pearl award 1989), Zeta Phi Beta (vis. scholarship award 1989). Democrat. Baptist. Home: 5168 Cooper St Detroit MI 48213-3086 Office: US FDA 1560 E Jefferson Ave Detroit MI 48207-3154

SIMON, JEANNE HURLEY, federal commissioner; m. Paul Simon; 2 children. BA, Barat Coll.; JD, Northwestern U. Legis. analyst Nat. Adv. Coun. Women's Ednl. Programs; govtl. rels. rep. Ill. Atty. Gen. Neil Hartigan; mem. Ill. Gen. Assembly; chair Nat. Commn. Librs. and Info. Sci., Washington, 1993—; cons. women's initiative Am. Assn. Ret. Persons, Nat. Security Archive, Emeritus Found.; mem. adv. com. White Ho. Conf. Libr. and Info. Svcs., 1979. Mem. ALA, AAUW, LWV, Il. Bar Assn., Women's Bar Assn. Ill., D.C. Bar Assn., Women's Nat. Dem. Club. Office: Nat Comm on Libraries 1110 Vermont Ave NW Ste 820 Washington DC 20005-3522*

SIMON, JEWEL WOODARD, artist; b. Houston, July 28, 1911; d. Chester Arthur and Rachel (Williams) Woodard; m. Edward Lloyd Simon, Feb. 19, 1939 (dec. Sept. 1984); children: Edward Lloyd Jr., Margaret Jewel Simon Summerour. AB summa cum laude, Atlanta U., 1931; BFA, Atlanta Coll. of Art, 1967. Head math. dept. Jack Yates High Sch., Houston, 1931-39; lectr. in field. One-woman shows at Clark Coll., 1973, Carver Mus., 1974, Huntsville Mus., 1979, Internat. Soc. Artists, 1979, Ariel Gallery, Soho, N.Y., 1990, 91; exhibited in group shows at Ringling Mus., Sarasota, Fla., Atlanta U. Gallery, Du Sable Mus., Chgo., Carver Mus., Tuskegee; sculpture "The Tusi Princess" exhibited in Art U.S.A. 58, N.Y., "Paula-Paulina" exhibited in Internat. Artists Show, N.Y.; numerous others; author: (poems) Flight-Preoccupation with Death, Life and Life Eternal, 1990. Chair, vice-chair, emeritus deaconess bd. First Congl. Ch., Atlanta, chmn. social club, 1948; v.p. bd. dirs. Nat. Girls Clubs; pres. E. R. Carter Elem. Sch. PTA, Atlanta, 1946, Jack & Jill Nat. Projects, Atlanta. Recipient Arts Svc. award Phoenix Arts and Theater Co., 1978, Bronze Jubilee award, 1981, James Weldon Johnson award in art, 1977, Golden Poets award, 1985-92, Golden Poet award, 1990, 91, Golden Seal award Nat. Assn. Chiefs of Police, 1994, Editors Choice award, Nat. Libr. Poetry, 1994. Mem. Alpha Kappa Alpha (Golden Girl award, Gold Dove Heritage award 1979). Home: 67 Ashby St SW Atlanta GA 30314-3737

SIMON, JUDITH CAROL, nursing administrator; b. Detroit. BSN, U. Mich., 1974. Cert. ins. rehab. specialist; cert. case mgr. Head nurse Glacier Hills, Ann Arbor, 1974-80; clinic nursing supr. Henry Ford Hosp.- Fairlane, Dearborn, Mich., 1980-83; med. svcs. cons./account rep. Crawford & Co., Southfield, Mich., 1984-88; mgr. Med. Mgmt. & Re-Employment, Inc., Southfield, Mich., 1988-90; corp. med. mgmt. specialist Crum & Forster, Parsippany, N.J., 1990-93; corp. sr. med. mgmt. specialist The Zenith, Woodland Hills, Calif., 1993—. Mem. AAOHN, Assn. Rehab. Nurses, Ins. Rehab. Study Group. Office: The Zenith 21255 Califa St Woodland Hills CA 91367

SIMON, KATHRYN IRENE, small business owner, management consultant; b. Oakland, Calif., Apr. 22, 1953; d. Charles Edward and Ruth (Fite) Kerwin; m. James Ernest Simon, Apr. 11, 1981; 1 child, Brooke Ainsley. BA, U. Calif., Santa Barbara, 1974; MA, U. Nev., 1983. Acad. dean Sierra Nev. Coll., Incline Village, 1977-80; adminstrv. analyst County of Washoe, Reno, Nev., 1980-81, asst. to county mgr., 1981-83; budget dir. Washoe Med. Ctr., Reno, 1983-85, dir. mgmt. devel., 1985-87; corp. dir. mktg. and planning Washoe Health System, Reno, 1987-89, assoc. exec. dir. Art of Living Inst., 1989-90; pres. Simon & Assocs., Reno, Nev., 1990—; instr. U. Nev., 1983, Truckee Meadows Community Coll. Mem. community allocations com. United Way, Reno, 1989-90; bd. dirs. Children's Cabinet Rsch. Inst., Reno, 1990—. Named Woman Ambassador, March of Dimes, 1991—. Mem. Truckee Alliance for Mus. Arts (bd. dirs., v.p. 1988-90), Soroptimist (pres. Reno chpt. 1990-91), Nev. Self-Employment Trust (chmn. bd. 1991—). Democrat. Methodist. Office: 955 S Virginia St Ste 204 Reno NV 89502-2476

SIMON, LINDA JANE WOLK, museum curator; b. Detroit, May 18, 1958; d. William Abraham and Roberta Lee (Snyder) Wolk; m. Joseph Walter Simon; 1 child, Caroline Elizabeth. BA, U. Mich., 1980, MA, 1981, PhD, 1987. Curator Met. Mus. Art, N.Y.C., 1988—. Revs. editor Master Drawings, N.Y.C., 1991—; author: (exhbn. catalogue) Sixteenth Century Italian Drawings in N.Y. Collections, 1994, Italian Old Master Drawings, Horvitz Collection, 1991; contbr. articles on 16th Century Italian Art. Fulbright grantee, Rome, 1981-83; Mary Davis fellow Samule Kress Found. Nat. Gallery Art, Washington, 1983-85.

SIMON, MARILYN WEINTRAUB, art educator, sculptor; b. Chgo., Aug. 25, 1927; d. William and Caroline Mabel (Bergman) Weintraub; m. Walter E. Simon, Mar. 19, 1950 (div. Sept. 1990); children: Nina Fay Simon-Rosenthal, Jacob Aaron, Maurine Joy Simon Rubinstein, Linda Gay Simon Shapiro. PhB, U. Chgo., 1947; MEd, Temple U., 1969. Cert. tchr., Pa. Bd. sec. Delaware Valley Smelting Corp., Bristol, Pa., 1957-89; art tchr. Calumet Sch. Dist., Ill., 1951-53; art tchr., chmn. elem. art program Cheltenham (Pa.) Sch. Dist., 1969—; real estate agt., Tullytown, Pa.; speaker in field; devel. dir., exec. bd. Art Forms, Manayunk, Pa. One woman show Hahn Gallery, Phila., 1985; permanent exhibits Elkins Park (Pa.) Libr., Univ. Hosp., Cleve.; also represented in med. offices, private collections; author publs. on using art reproductions in edn. Chmn. Phila. chpt. U. Chgo. Alumni Fund Assn., 1978-84. Recipient numerous art awards including 1st prize Doylestown Art League, 1986-87, Best Sculpture award Mummers's Mus. Phila., 1987, Juror's award Cheltenham Art Ctr., 1987-88, 3d prize Abington Art Ctr., 1988, 1st prize for sculpture Art Assn. of Harrisburg, 1989. Mem. Nat. Art Edn. Assn., Pa. Art Educators Assn. (regional rep. 1988-89, Outstanding Art Educator of Yr. award 1987), Oil Pastel Assn. N.Y.C. (invited mem.). Democrat. Jewish. Office: PO Box 29722 Philadelphia PA 19117-0922

SIMON, MICHELE JOHANNA, computer systems specialist; b. Reading, Pa., Nov. 28, 1957; d. Joseph Aloysius and Mildred Adella (White) S. BS, BA, Albright Coll., 1983. Adminstr. Dept. Def., Washington, 1979-81, Dept. Labor, Washington, 1981-83; programmer Berkshire Health Systems, Reading, 1983-85; computer systems analyst Reading Hosp. and Med. Ctr., 1985—; toy inventor, owner Designs by Natural Selection, 1992—; owner, mgr. Intervilla Apts., West Lawn, Pa., 1979—. Co-author (with Richard Murphy, screenplays) Fat Chance, 1987, Base Instinct, 1991. Vol. Meals on Wheels, Reading, 1992. Nat. Merit scholarship finalist, 1974. Mem. Supporters of Emo Philips (pres. 1986—). Democrat.

SIMON, NORMA PLAVNICK, psychologist; b. Washington, Sept. 20, 1930; d. Mark and Mary Plavnick; m. Robert G. Simon, Dec. 18, 1949; children: Mark Allan, Susan. BA, NYU, 1952, cert. in psychoanalysis, 1977; MA, Columbia U., 1953, EdD, 1968. Diplomate Am. Bd. Profl. Psychology, 1988. Psychologist Queens Coll. Counseling Ctr., Flushing, N.Y., 1968-70, asst. dir., 1970-76, dir., 1976; gen. practice psychology N.Y.C., 1976—; faculty, supr. New Hope Guild, Bklyn., 1976—, dir. child and adolescent tng. prog., 1988—; adj. prof. clin. psychology Columbia U., N.Y.C., 1986—; supr. NYU Postdoctoral Prog. in Psychoanalysis, 1988—. Author: (with Robert G. Simon): Choosing a College Major: Social Science, 1981; mem. editorial bd. The Counseling Psychologist jour., 1986-89. Vice chairperson N.Y. State Bd. for Psychology State Edn. Dept., Albany, 1978-82, chairperson 1982-88; bd. dirs. Pelham (N.Y.) Guidance Coun., 1980-83; pres.-elect Am. Assn. State Psychology Bd., 1990, pres. 1991. Recipient Karl Heiser award, 1993. Fellow APA (mem. bd. profl. affairs 1987-89, policy and planning bd. 1991-93, mem. ethics com. 1995—, John Black award 1994), ACAD, Nat. Acads. of Practice. Office: 500A E 87th St # 5A New York NY 10128-7626

SIMON, SANDRA RUTH BLACKWELL, home and community health, correctional, pediatrics and medical-surgical nurse; b. Jacksonville, Fla., Sept. 8, 1936; d. William Harold Blackwell and Ruth (Norris) Blackwell; m. Verne Allen Simon, Dec. 27, 1958; children: Victor, Katelan, Stephen, Jacqueline. BS, Fla. State U., 1959; AAS in Nursing, Morehead (Ky.) State U., 1976. RN, Fla.; cert. BLS, IV therapy. Social worker Am. Assn. Retarded Persons, Rochester, N.Y.; dir. partial hosp., individual therapist, med. nurse Cave Run Comprehensive Care Ctr., Morehead; nurse Westinghouse Health Systems, Pusan, Republic of Korea; nursing supr. Hispanic Clinic, Toledo; sr. community health nurse Duval Regional Detention Ctr., Jacksonville, Fla.; nurse case mgr. Kimberly/Quality Care Home Health Agy.; ind. contract nurse, home and cmty. health nurse. Mem. ANA, Fla. Nurses Assn. Home and Office: 208 35th Ave S Jacksonville FL 32250-6053

SIMONDS, MARIE CELESTE, architect; b. Miami, Fla., Mar. 30, 1947; d. Hinton Joseph and Frances Olivia (Burnett) Baker; m. Albert Rhett Simonds, Jr., Oct. 9, 1974; children: Caroline Lamar, Frances Rhett. BA, U. Pa., 1968; BArch, U. Md., 1973. Registered architect, Va. Architect Harry Weese & Assocs., Washington, 1973-75; pvt. practice Alexandria, Va., 1976—. Com. chmn. Jr. Friends Alexandria YWCA, 1974-78; mem. Jr. League Washington, 1978—. NSF grantee, 1972; recipient Design award No. Va. Chpt. AIA, 1990. Mem. AIA (scholar 1971, Design award No. Va. 1990), Va. Soc. AIA, West River Sailing Club (Galesville, Md.), Sierra Club. Episcopalian. Home and Office: 624 S Lee St Alexandria VA 22314-3820

SIMONE, ANGELA PAOLINO, elementary education educator; b. New Haven, Jan. 27, 1953; d. John L. and Mary (Solli) Paolino; 1 child, Dennis. BS, So. Conn. U., 1974, MS in Reading, 1976; AS, S. Cen. Community Coll., New Haven, 1972. Substitute tchr. City of West Haven, Conn., 1976-77, elem. tchr. St. Brenden's Sch., New Haven, 1985; elem. tchr. St. Lawrence Sch., West Haven, 1985—, co-coord. Writing to Read Program, 1994—, primary sci. coord.; facilitator Rainbow Program for All God's Children. Mem. We Are the World Com. of West Haven Pub. Schs. Mem. AAUW, ASCD, Nat. Cath. Edn. Assn. Office: St Lawrence Sch 231 Main St West Haven CT 06516-4597

SIMONE, GAIL ELISABETH, research analyst; b. Boston, Dec. 3, 1944; d. Hugh Nelson and Louise Amelia (Shedrick) Saunders; m. Edburne R. Hare, Sept. 7, 1968 (div. 1974); m. Joseph R. Simone, June 27, 1987. BA, The King's Coll., 1966; postgrad., Harvard U., 1976-77, N.H. Coll., 1991—. Placement dir. Boston Bar Assn., 1966-67; pub. relations Emerson Coll., Boston, 1967-69; asst. to v.p. Vance, Sanders, Inc., Boston, 1969-70; office mgr. Trans. Displays, Inc., Boston, 1970-71; seminar coordinator Assn. Trial Lawyers Am., Cambridge, Mass., 1971-74; writer, researcher Ednl. Expeditions Internat., Belmont, Mass., 1975-76; analyst United Brands Co., N.Y.C., 1976-80; analyst Mil. Sealift Commd., USN, Washington, 1980-84, legis. affairs officer, 1984-88; rsch. analyst Bath (Maine) Iron Works Corp., 1988—; free-lance writer, editor, Boston, 1970-73. Active Childreach, Warwick, R.I., 1986—; mem. Amnesty Internat., N.Y.C., 1987—, various other orgns. Mem. AAUW, NAFE. Office: Bath Iron Works 700 Washington St Bath ME 04530

SIMONE, JACQUELINE ANN, conventions/meeting planning manager; b. Chgo., Feb. 8, 1957; d. Daniel Anthony and Marion Francis (Granato) S. BA in Elem. Edn., St. Mary's Coll., Notre Dame, Ind., 1979. Acctg. clk. Motorola Inc.-Comm. Sector, Schaumburg, Ill., 1973-74, 78-79, credit analyst, 1979-81; claims mgr. Motorola Inc.-Automotive and Indsl. Electronics Group, Schaumburg, Ill., 1981-82, sr. credit analyst, 1982-86; product promotions coord. Motorola Inc.-Cellular Subscriber Group, Schaumburg, Ill., 1986-88; promotional materials mgr. Motorola Inc.-Cellular Subscriber Group, Arlington Heights, Ill., 1988-90, bus. and convs. mgr., 1990-92; bus. and convs./meeting planning mgr. Motorola Inc.-Cellular Subscriber Group, Libertyville, Ill., 1992—; mem. day care com. Motorola Inc., Libertyville, Ill., 1993—; mem. exhibitor com. Cellular Telecomm. Industry Assn., Washington, 1987—; Motorola Western Open golf tournament coord. Motorola Inc., Libertyville, 1994. Recipient Cert. of Merit, Bus./Profl. Advt. Assn., 1988, Award of Excellence award Consolidated Papers Inc., 1988. Home: 1621 Pheasant Trail Dr Arlington Heights IL 60004 Office: Motorola Inc Cellular Subscriber Group 600 N US Hwy 45 # AN450 Libertyville IL 60048

SIMONES, PAMELA SUE, librarian, playwright; b. Chillicothe, Ohio, Jan. 17, 1951. BA, Vassar Coll., 1973; MLS, Kent State U., 1977. Ref. libr. Kent Free Libr., 1977-80, asst. dir., 1989—; libr. II Akron Summit County Pub. Libr., 1980-86. Contbr. Torch to the Heart, 1994; author: (plays) Sins of the Mothers, Hysterical Women, Living My Life, Everywoman, Frost from Fire. Co-founder Low Budget Theatre, 1993. Mem. Dramatists Guild, Lesbian and Gay Alumnae of Vassar Coll. (pres. 1992-94, v.p. 1994—). Home: 671 Copley Rd Akron OH 44320-2351

SIMONETTI, MICHELLE KRISTA, tax accountant; b. Weehawken, N.J., Sept. 28, 1963; d. Joseph Anthony and Denise (Collelo) S. BSBA in Acctg., Ramapo Coll. N.J., 1984; MS in Taxation, Fairleigh Dickinson U., 1988. CPA, Md. Revenue auditor Ill. Dept. Revenue, Paramus, N.J., 1984-88; sr. tax acct. Sequa Corp., Hackensack, N.J., 1988-94; sr. tax specialist Automatic Switch Co., Florham Park, N.J., 1994—; pvt. practice, Glen Rock, N.J., 1984—. Mem. Md. Assn. CPAs. Office: Automatic Switch Co 50-60 Hanover Rd Florham Park NJ 07932

SIMONICH, SUSAN MCCAMMON, psychotherapist; b. Greensburg, Ind., Oct. 29, 1960; d. Leon Sheridan and Martha May (Foster) McCammon; m. Patrick Farrell Simonich, Sept. 1, 1990. AA, Findlay Coll., 1980; BA, Ohio No. U., 1982; MA, Morehead State U., 1985. Psychotherapist Area Mental Health Ctr., Dodge City, Kans., 1985-87, Wilson Ctr., Faribault, Minn., 1987-90; psychotherapist, supr. Zumbro Valley, MHC, Red Wing, Minn., 1990—; cons. Wilson Ctr., Red Wing, 1991—; supr. Goodhue Co. Ed. Dist., Cannon Falls, Minn., 1993—. Mem. APA. Republican. United Methodist. Office: Zumbro Valley MHC 419 Bush St Red Wing MN 55066

SIMONS, BARBARA M., lawyer; b. N.Y.C., Feb. 7, 1929; d. Samuel A. and Minnie (Mankes) Malitz; m. Morton L. Simons, Sept. 2, 1951; 1 child,

Claudia. BA, U. Mich., 1950, JD, 1952. Bar: N.Y. 1953, U.S. Supreme Ct. 1963, U.S. Ct. Appeals (D.C. cir.) 1971, (5th cir.) 1992, (1st cir.) 1994. Ptnr. Simons & Simons, Washington, 1962—. Mem. Forest Hills Citizens Assn., Washington, Clean Air Project; past pres. D.C. chpt. U. Mich. Alumnae, Washington. Alumnae scholar U. Mich., 1946-50. Mem. Washington Coun. Lawyers, Women's Legal Def. Fund, Phi Beta Kappa, Phi Kappa Phi, Alpha Lambda Delta. Office: Simons & Simons 5025 Linnean Ave NW Washington DC 20008-2042

SIMONS, DONA, artist; b. Bryn Athyn, Pa., Aug. 10, 1953; d. Keneth Alden and Reta Isabel (Evens) S.; m. John Louis Vigo, May 17, 1986. Student, Phila. Coll. Art, 1974, Moore Coll. Art, 1976, Pa. Acad. Fine Arts, 1977-79. Represented by The Rittenhouse Galleries, Phila., Sylvia Schmidt Gallery, New Orleans. One-woman shows include Frank Tanzer Gallery, Boston, 1975, The Curaçao Mus., Netherlands Antilles, 1991, The Curaçao Seaquarium, Netherlands Antilles, 1991, Sylvia Schmidt Gallery, New Orleans, 1992; exhibited in group shows at Berg Gallery, Jenkintown, Pa., 1973, United Artisans Gallery, Chalfont, Pa., 1974, 75, Arthur Roger Gallery, New Orleans, La., 1980, Arts Coun. New Orleans C. of C., 1980, Acad. Gallery, New Orleans Acad. Fine Arts, La., 1982, Am. Italian Renaissance Found., New Orleans, 1985, Found. Prince Pierre de Monaco, Monaco, 1985, The Rittenhouse Galleries, Phila., 1993, 94; commn. portrait of Manuel Piar, Curaçao, Netherlands Antilles, 1990. Office: Sylvia Schmidt Gallery 400-A Julia St New Orleans LA 70130

SIMONS, ELIZABETH R(EIMAN), biochemist, educator; b. Vienna, Austria, Sept. 1, 1929; came to U.S., 1941, naturalized, 1948; d. William and Erna Engle (Weisselberg) Reiman; B.Ch.E., Cooper Union, N.Y.C., 1950; M.S., Yale U., 1951, Ph.D., 1954; m. Harold Lee Simons, Aug. 12, 1951; children—Leslie Ann Mulert, Robert David. Research chemist Tech. Operations, Arlington, Mass., 1953-54; instr. chemistry Wellesley (Mass.) Coll., 1954-57; rsch. asst. Children's Hosp. Med. Center and Cancer Rsch. Found., Boston, 1957-59, rsch. assoc. pathology, 1959-62; research assoc. Harvard Med. Sch., 1962-66, lectr. biol. chemistry, 1966-72; tutor biochemical scis. Harvard Coll., 1971—; assoc. prof. biochemistry Boston U., 1972-78, prof., 1978—. Contbr. articles to profl. jours. Grantee in field. Mem. AAAS, Am. Chem. Soc., Am. Heart Assn., Am. Soc. Biol. Chemists, Am. Soc. Cell Biology, Am. Soc. Hematology, Am. Fedn. Clin. Rsch., Assn. Women in Sci., Biophys. Soc., Internat. Soc. Thrombosis and Hemostasis, N.Y. Acad. Sci., Sigma Xi. Office: Boston U Sch Medicine 80 E Concord St Roxbury MA 02118-2394

SIMONS, LYNN OSBORN, state education official; b. Havre, Mont., June 1, 1934; d. Robert Blair and Dorothy (Briggs) Osborn; BA, U. Colo., 1956; postgrad. U. Wyo., 1958-60; m. John Powell Simons, Jan. 19, 1957; children: Clayton Osborn, William Blair. Tchr., Midvale (Utah) Jr. High Sch., 1956-57, Sweetwater County Sch. Dist. 1, Rock Springs, Wyo., 1957-58, U. Wyo., Laramie, 1959-61, Natrona County Sch. Dist. 1, Casper, Wyo., 1963-64; credit mgr. Gallery 323, Casper, 1972-77; Wyo. state supt. public instrn., Cheyenne, 1979-91; sec.'s regional rep. region VIII U.S. Dept. Edn., Denver, 1993—; mem. State Bds. Charities and Reform, Land Commrs., Farm Loan, 1979-91; mem. State Commns. Capitol Bldg., Liquor, 1979-91; Ex-officio mem. bd. trustees U. Wyo., 1979-91; ex-officio mem. Wyo. Community Coll. Commn., 1979-91; mem. steering com. Edn. Commn. of the States, 1988-90; mem. State Bd. Edn., 1971-77, chmn., 1976-77; advisor Nat. Trust for Hist. Preservation, 1980-86. Mem. LWV (pres. 1970-71). Democrat. Episcopalian. Office: US Dept Edn Ste 310 1244 Speer Blvd Denver CO 80204-3582

SIMONS, MARLENE J., state legislator, rancher; b. Deadwood, S.D., July 1, 1935; d. Royal B. Mills and Elsie M. Snook; m. Frank Simons, Sept. 24, 1951; children: Greg, Linda, Sully. Grad. high sch., Sundance, Wyo. Pres. Outdoors Unltd., Kaysville, Utah; mem. Wyo. Ho. of Reps., 1979-94, appropriation com., 1994—; mem. rules com., chmn. agrl. com., mem. appropriations com., mem. western legis. state conf. com., mem. water policy com.; vice chmn. Pub. Lands Adv. Coun., 1986—; stockgrower Farm Bur., Wyo., 1969—; rancher, outfitter. Pres. Wyo. Multiple Use Coalition, Ranch A Restoration Found.; sec. Black Hills Multi-Use Coalition; mem. Madison water steering com. Black Hills Hydrology Study; leader 4-H. Republican. Home: Windy Acres Ranch 5480 Hwy 14 Beulah WY 82712 Office: Outdoors Unltd PO Box 373 Kaysville UT 84037-0373

SIMONS, R. KAYE, health care administrator; b. Marquette, Mich.; d. William and Dorothy (Maynard) S.; 1 child, Eric Thomas. BSN, Mich. State U., 1961; M in Health Care Adminstrn., Johns Hopkins U., Balt., 1981. Health sys. cons. Pub. Sector Cons., Lansing, Mich.; exec. dir. E. Cen. Mich. Health Sys. Agy., Saginaw, Mich.; dir. Dept. Health Systems Planning, Rockville, Md.; independent health cons. Bridgeport, Mich.; regional dir. for expanded svcs. ABC Home Health; dir. Health Ptnrs., Inc. Patentee in field. Mem. Am. Assn. Critical Care Nurses, Am. Assn. Nurse Execs.

SIMONSON, DONNA JEANNE, accountant; b. Malden, Mass., Sept. 6, 1947; d. George Francis and Dorothy Josephine (Bridges) Yost; m. Scott N. Simonson, June 30, 1967 (div. Feb. 1989); children: Stephanie Louise Burke, Kelly Lynn. AA Bus. Adminstrn., Corning Community Coll., 1979; BS in Mgmt., Keuka Coll., 1981. Bus. office supr. Steuben Allegany B.O.C.E.S., Bath, N.Y., 1969-75; staff acct. David L. Snyderwine & Co. CPA's, Bath, 1979-82; fin. dir. Steuben Assoc. for Retarded Children, Inc., Bath, 1982—; owner Donna J. Simonson, Taxes, & Acctg., Bath, 1982—. Pres. Pulteney Vol. Firemen's Auxiliary, 1973. Mem. Am. Assn. Univ. Women, Bath Area Humane Soc., Pulteney Free Library Assn., Fiscal Mgrs. Assn. Democrat. Presbyterian. Home: 1 Ellis Ave Bath NY 14810-1107 Office: Steuben ARC 6838 Industrial Park Rd Bath NY 14810

SIMONSON, SUSAN KAY, hospital administrator; b. La Porte, Ind., Dec. 5, 1946; d. George Randolph and Myrtle Lucille (Opfel) Menkes; m. Richard Bruce Simonson, Aug. 25, 1973. BA with honors, Ind. U., 1969; MA, Washington U., St. Louis, 1972. Perinatal social worker Yakima Valley Meml. Hosp., Yakima, Wash., 1979-81, dir. patient support and hospice program, 1981—, dir. social svc., 1982—; instr. Spanish, ethnic studies, sociology Yakima Valley Coll., Yakima, Wash., 1981—; pres. Yakima Child Abuse Council, 1983-85; developer nat. patient support program, 1981. Contbr. articles to profl. jours. Mem. Jr. League, Yakima; mem. adv. council Robert Wood Johnson Found. Rural Infant Health Care Project, Yakima, 1980, Pregnancy Loss and Compassionate Friends Support Groups, Yakima, 1982—, Teen Outreach Program, Yakima, 1984—. Recipient NSF award, 1967, discharge planning program of yr. regional award Nat. Glasrock Home Health Care Discharge Planning Program, 1987; research grantee Ind. U., 1968, Fulbright grantee U.S. Dept. State, 1969-70; Nat. Def. Edn. Act fellowship, 1970-73. Mem. AAUW, Soc. Med. Anthropology, Soc. Hosp. Social Work Dirs. of Am. Hosp. Assn. (regional award 1989), Nat. Assn. Social Workers, Phi Beta Kappa. Office: Yakima Valley Meml Hosp 2811 Tieton Dr Yakima WA 98902-3799

SIMONTACCHI, CAROL NADINE, retail store executive; b. Bellingham, Wash., July 6, 1947; d. Ralph Eugene and Sylvia Arleta (Tyler) Walmer; m. Bob Simontacchi, Oct. 3, 1981; children: Caryl Anne, Bobbie Anne, Melissa Anne, Laurie Anne. BS in Health and Human Svcs., Columbia Pacific U., 1995, postgrad., 1995—. Cert. nutritionist, Wash. CEO The Health Haus, Inc., Vancouver, Wash., 1985—; host radio program Back to the Beginning, Vancouver, 1990—. Author: Your Fat is Not Your Fault, 1994. Mem. Soc. of Cert. Nutritionists (pres. bd. 1992-93), Nat. Nutritional Foods Assn. (N.W. region legis. chair 1991—). Republican. Christian Ch. Office: The Health Haus Inc Ste 250 101 E 8th St Vancouver WA 98660

SIMPSON, ALLYSON BILICH, lawyer; b. Pasadena, Calif., Feb. 5, 1951; d. John Joseph and Barbaran Rita (Bessolo) Bilich; m. Roland Gilbert Simpson, Aug. 11, 1979; children: Megan Elise, Erin Marie, Brian Patrick. BS, U. So. Calif., L.A., 1973, JD, 1976. Bar: Calif. 1976. Staff atty. Gen. Telephone Co., Thousand Oaks, Calif., 1978-79; group staff atty., dir. legis. compliance Pacific Mut. Life Ins. Co., Newport Beach, Calif., 1980-86; corp. counsel and sec. Amicare Ins. Co., Beverly Hills, Calif., 1986; assoc. Leboeuf, Lamb, Leiby & MacRae, L.A., 1986-87; from assoc. to ptnr. Musick, Peeler & Garrett, L.A., 1988-94; ptnr. Sonnenschein Nath & Rosenthal, L.A., 1994—; vis. pro. bus. law U. So. Calif., L.A., 1981. Trustee St. Anne's Maternity Home Found., L.A., 1991—; bd. dirs. St. Anne's Maternity Home, L.A., 1993—. Mem. Western Pension & Benefits Conf., Conf. of Ins. Counsel. Republican. Roman Catholic. Office: Sonnenschein Nath & Rosenthal Ste 1500 601 S Figueroa St Los Angeles CA 90017*

SIMPSON, ANDREA LYNN, energy communication executive; b. Altadena, Calif., Feb. 10, 1948; d. Kenneth James and Barbara Faries Simpson; m. John R. Myrdal, Dec. 13, 1986; 1 child, Christopher Ryan Myrdal. BA, U. So. Calif., 1969, MS, 1983; postgrad. U. Colo., Boulder Sch. Bank Mktg., 1977. Asst. cashier United Calif. Bank, L.A., 1969-73; asst. v.p. mktg. 1st Hawaiian Bank, Honolulu, 1973-78; v.p. corp. comm. BHP Hawaii, Inc. (formerly Pacific Resources, Inc.), Honolulu, 1978—. Bd. dirs. Arts Coun. Hawaii, 1977-81, Hawaii Heart Assn., 1978-83, Coun. Pacific Girl Scouts U.S., 1982-85, Child and Family Svcs., 1984-86, Honolulu Symphony Soc., 1985-91, Kapiolani Women's and Children's Hosp., 1988—, Sta. KHPR Hawaii Pub. Radio, 1988-92, Kapiolani Found., 1990-95, Hanahauoli Sch., 1991—; bd. dirs., 2nd. v.p. Girl Scout Coun. Hawaii, 1994—; trustee Hawaii Loa Coll., 1984-86, Hawaii Sch. For Girls at LaPietra, 1989-91; commr. Hawaii State Commn. on Status of Women, 1985-87, State Sesquecentennial of Pub. Schs. Commn., 1990-91; bd. dirs. Hawaii Strategic Devel. Corp., 1991—, Hawaii Children's Mus., 1994—, Pacific Asian Affairs Coun., 1994—; adv. dir. Hawaii Kids at Work, 1991—, Hawaii Mothers Against Drunk Driving, 1992—. Named Panhellenic Woman of Yr. Hawaii, 1979, Outstanding Woman in Bus. Hawaii YWCA, 1980, Outstanding Young Woman of Hawaii Girl Scouts Coun. of the Pacific, 1985, 86, Hawaii Legis., 1980. Mem. Am. Mktg. Assn., Pub. Rels. Soc. Am. (bd. dirs. Honolulu chpt. 1984-86, Silver Anvil award 1984, Pub. Rels. Profl. Yr. 1991), Pub. Utilities Communicators Assn. (Communicator of Yr. 1984), Honolulu Advt. Fedn. (Advt. Woman of Yr. 1984), U. So. Calif. Alumni Assn. (bd. dirs. Hawaii 1981-83), Outrigger Canoe Club, Pacific Club, Kaneohe Yacht Club, Rotary (pub. rels. chmn. 1988—, Honolulu chpt.), Alpha Phi (past pres., dir. Hawaii), Hawaii Jaycees (Outstanding Young Person of Hawaii 1978). Office: BHP Hawaii Inc 733 Bishop St Ste 2700 Honolulu HI 96813-4025

SIMPSON, BEVERLY J., advertising executive; b. Wash., Nov. 2, 1951; d. William Denny and Mary Jane (Gilmore) S. BA magna cum laude, Ind. U. Pa., 1973. Adminstrn. Mesta Machine Co., Pitts., 1973-81; supr., advt. mgr. Jones & Laughlin LTV Steel, Pitts., 1981-84; advt. mgr. LTV Steel, Cleve., 1984—; chmn. Pipe Mktg. Communications, Wash. 1982-83; communications panel AAC-AISI, Det. 1987—. Mem. Bus. & Profl. Advt. Assn., AISI. Office: LTV Steel 25 Prospect Ave NW Rm 902L Cleveland OH 44115-1018

SIMPSON, BEVERLY TAYLOR, academic dean; b. Hannibal, Mo., Jan. 29, 1937; d. William Arlie and Mary Jane (Harding) Taylor; m. William Tilden Simpson, Aug. 18, 1956; children: William Dean, Cheryl Lynn, Catherine Sue. A in Edn., Hannibal-LaGrange Coll., 1956; BEd, U. Miami, 1972; MEd, U. Mo., 1983, EdD, 1988. Cert. elem. tchr., Mo. Tchr. 1st grade Dade County Pub. Schs., Miami, Fla., 1971-72; pre-sch. tchr. Wayside Bapt. Pre-Sch., Miami, 1972-73; kindergarten tchr. Perrine Bapt. Acad., Miami, 1973-75, dir., prin., 1975-82; fin. aid dir. Hannibal-LaGrange Coll., Hannibal, 1982-83, assoc. prof., 1983-88, div. chair, 1985-88, assoc. acad. dean., 1989-91, acad. dean, 1991—. Author tng. materials. Mem. ASCD, Am. Assn. Higher Edn., Am. Assn. Collegiate Registrars and Admissions Officers, Delta Kappa Gamma (v.p. 1985-89). Baptist. Home: 2 Mockingbird Ln Hannibal MO 63401-2310 Office: Hannibal-LaGrange Coll 2800 Palmyra Rd Hannibal MO 63401-1999

SIMPSON, CAROL LOUISE, investment company executive; b. Phila., Jan. 30, 1937; d. William Huffington and Hilda Agnes (Johnston) S. Student, Community Coll., 1985, 86, 87, U. Minn., 1986, 87, 88. Cert. Nat. Assn. Securities Dealers, Inc., Washington; registered options, mcpl. securities, gen. securities, fin. and ops. prin.; lic. life, accident, health ins. Exec. asst. Germantown Fed. Savs., Phila., 1954-67; asst. sec. Am. Med. Investment Co., Inc. (formerly Cannon and Co., Inc.), Blue Bell, Pa., 1967-91; also bd. dirs. Cannon & Co., Inc., 1986; v.p., sec. AMA Investment Advisers, Inc. (formerly Pro Svcs., Inc.), Blue Bell, Pa., 1967-91; also bd. dirs. AMA Investment Advisers, Inc. (formerly PRO Svcs., Inc.), Blue Bell, Pa., 1984-86; fin. svcs. compliance cons., 1991; exec. v.p., sec. Rutherford Fin. Corp., Phila., 1991—, Rutherford, Brown & Catherwood Inc., Phila., 1991—, Walnut Asset Mgmt. Inc., Phila., 1991—. Mem. World Affairs Coun., Investment Co. Inst. (fed. legis. com. 1984-91, investment advisers com. 1988—, compliance com. 1990—), Internat. Assn. Fin. Planners, Investment Women's Club, Nat. Notary Assn., Pa. Assn. Notaries, Nat. Soc. Compliance Profls. (assoc.), Whitemarsh Valley Country Club. Republican. Home: 7701 Lawnton St Philadelphia PA 19128-3105 Office: Rutherford Fin Corp Ste 500 1617 John F Kennedy Blvd Philadelphia PA 19103-1805

SIMPSON, CAROL MANN, librarian, consultant, editor; b. Aberdeen, Md., Nov. 28, 1949; d. Joey Mathew and Grace Winifred (Fielman) Pirrung; m. Robert Smith Mann, Jan. 4, 1969 (div. May 1986); children: Stephen, David, Sarah; m. Douglas Michael Simpson, Jan. 18, 1992; stepchildren, Brian, Kevin. BS in Edn., Southwestern U., 1971; MA, U. Tex., 1975, MLS, 1977; EdD, East Tex. State U., 1987. Cert. art and French tchr., libr., learning resources specialist, supr., Tex. Tchr. Round Rock (Tex.) Ind. Sch. Dist., 1970-74; teaching asst. U. Tex., Austin, 1974; libr. Mesquite (Tex.) Ind. Sch. Dist., 1977-90, coord. libr. and media svcs., 1990-92, facilitator libr. tech., 1992—; adj. prof. Tex. Women's U., 1992—; cons. Orex Petroleum, Dallas, 1988, Mesquite Pub. Libr., 1989-90, HBW Assocs., Dallas, 1988—; reviewer Booklist, 1984—, Sch. Libr. Jour., 1984—, Video Rating Guide for Librs., 1989-92. Editor: Technology Connection, 1995—, Copyright for School Libraries, 1994, Internet for School Libraries, 1995; contbr. articles to profl. jours. Mem. ALA, AECT, Tex. Libr. Assn., Am. Assn. Sch. Librs., Tex. Assn. Sch. Librs. Methodist. Home: 1086 Holly Ln Lewisville TX 75067-5710 Office: Mesquite Ind Sch Dist 800 E Kearney Mesquite TX 75149

SIMPSON, CAROLE, broadcast journalist; b. Chgo., Dec. 7, 1940; d. Lytle Ray and Doretha Viola (Wilbon) S.; m. James Edward Marshall, Sept. 3, 1966; children: Mallika Joy, Adam. BA in Journalism, U. Mich., 1962; postgrad., U. Iowa, 1964-65. News reporter WCFL Radio, Chgo., 1965-68; reporter/anchorwoman WBBM Radio, Chgo., 1968-70; TV news reporter WMAQ-TV, Chgo., 1970-74; NBC news network corr. Midwest Bur., transferred to Washington, from 1974; anchorwoman World News Saturday, Washington, 1988-93, World News Sunday, Washington, 1993—; instr. journalism Tuskegee Inst., Ala., 1962-64; faculty Medill Sch. Journalism, Northwestern U., 1972-74; moderator 1992 Town Mtg. Presdl. Debate. Recipient med. journalism award AMA, Emmy award, Dupont award, Milestone in Broadcasting award Nat. Commn. on Working Women, Disting. Journalist award U. Mo., Star award Am. Women in Radio and TV, Journalist of Yr. award Nat. Assn. Black Journalists, 1992; named Outstanding Woman in Comm., YWCA Met. Chgo., 1974; named to U. Iowa Comm. Hall of Fame; established several coll. scholarships for women and minorities in broadcast journalism. Mem. Internat. Women's Media Found. (bd. of RFK Journalism awards), NAS (mem. of bd. of children and families), Radio TV News Dirs. Found. (trustee), Radio-TV Corrs. Assn. Washington. Office: ABC News Washington Bureau 1717 De Sales St NW Washington DC 20036*

SIMPSON, DIANE JEANNETTE, social worker; b. Denver, Sept. 20, 1952; d. Arthur Henry and Irma Virginia (Jordan) S.; 1 child, Shantè N. BS, Nebr. Wesleyan U., 1974; MSW, U. Denver, 1977. Asst. Mile Hi coun. Girl Scouts U.S.A., Denver, 1971-77; social worker asst. Denver Pub. Schs., 1974-75, social worker, 1977—; field instr. Grad. Sch. of Soc. Work, U. Denver, 1984—. Tour leader Kenyan Safari to Kenya, East Africa, 1988. V.p. United Meth. Women, Christ United Meth. Ch., Denver, 1989-91; chmn. Christian action com., 1985-88; active Girl Scouts U.S.A., 1959—; mem. collaborative decision making com. Denver Pub. Schs., 1993—. Mem. NEA, NASW, Colo. Edn. Assn., Denver Classroom Tchrs. Assn., Nat. Assn. Black Social Workers. Democrat. Home: 6865 E Arizona Ave # D Denver CO 80224-1829 Office: Denver Pub Schs 900 Grant St Denver CO 80203-2907

SIMPSON, ELIZABETH ANN, pharmacist, educator; b. Steubenville, Ohio, Nov. 11, 1941; d. Robert Thompson and Elizabeth Ann (Rogers) Lucas; m. James Lewis Simpson, Nov. 8, 1963; children: James L., Mary Elizabeth. BS in Pharmacy, W.Va. U., 1963; postgrad., U. Tex., 1986. Staff pharmacist, Mich., Pa., N.J.; staff pharmacist Mass., W.Va., 1964-80; staff pharmacist St. John Hosp. and Med. Ctr., Detroit, 1980-83, dir. pharmacy svcs. St. John Outpatient Corp., 1983-93; asst. dir. div. pharmacy svcs. St. John Health System, 1993—; adj. clin. instr. dept. pharmacy practice Coll. Pharmacy and Allied Health Professions, Wayne State U., Detroit, 1982—; presenter in field, 1986—; mem. pharmacy and therapeutics com. Georgian East Nursing Home, 1987-89. Contbr. articles to profl. jours. Pres. bd. dirs. Meml. Co-Op Nursery Sch., 1973-75; mem. various PTO coms. and bds. Grosse Pointe (Mich.) Sch. System, 1975-89; chmn. pub. affairs com. Jr. League Detroit, 1975-76, mem. exec. com., 1978-80; chmn. pub. affairs com. Jr. Leagues Mich., 1976-78; mem. adv. bd. Chesterfield Twp. Police, 1992-93; mem. zoning bd. appeals Chesterfield Twp., 1993—. Recipient Vol. of Yr. award Jr. League Detroit, 1976, Torch Drive Communication award United Found., 1985. Fellow Am. Coll. Cons. Pharmacists, Acad. Pharmacy Practice and Mgmt. (policy com. 1987, chmn. instnl. practice sect. 1990—, mem. edn. com. 1988-89); mem. Am. Soc. Hosp. Pharmacists, Am. Pharm. Assn. (ho. of dels. 1987—, William S. Apple program fellow 1986), Mich. Pharmacists Assn. (physician dispensing adv. com. 1988-91, chmn. profl. and pub. affairs com. 1987-90, chmn. pharm. care task force), Mich. Soc. Hosp. Pharmacists (profl. and legal affairs com. 1987-90), Southeastern Mich. Soc. Hosp. Pharmacists, Lambda Kappa Sigma. Republican. Presbyterian. Home: 46978 Jans Dr Chesterfield MI 48047 Office: St John Hosp and Med Ctr 22101 Moross Rd Grosse Pointe MI 48236-2144

SIMPSON, JOAN YÉ VONNE, accountant, educator, business owner; b. Fairfield, Ill., Dec. 7, 1952; d. Harold M. and Pauline (Trailor) Reeder; children from previous marriage: Tammy Ann, James Edward; m. Roy E. Simpson, Dec. 28, 1990. AS, Vol. State Community Coll., 1984; postgrad., Am. Inst. Bankers, 1987; Austin Peay STate U. Owner Springfield Bookkeeping Svcs., 1978-82; jr. audit staff mem. Duane M. Brown, Springfield, Tenn., 1985-86; ops. supt. Joint Indsl. Techs., Portland, Tenn., 1986-88; tchr. Nashville State Tech. Inst., 1982-93; owner J.B.S. Bookkeeping and Mgmt., 1989—; pres. The Driver Leasing Co., Inc., 1992—, Carousel Creations Co., Inc., 1990—; speaker Women's Bus. Ownership Conf., Home and Minister's Inst. Copyrights rsch.: bus. devel. home based and home bound. Active Girl Scouts U.S. Gamma Beta Phi. Home: 2735 Browning Branch Rd Bethpage TN 37022-4523

SIMPSON, JOANNE MALKUS, meteorologist; b. Boston, Mar. 23, 1923; d. Russell and Virginia (Vaughan) Gerould; m. Robert H. Simpson, Jan. 6, 1965; children by previous marriage: David Starr Malkus, Steven Willem Malkus, Karen Elizabeth Malkus. B.S., U. Chgo., 1943, M.S., 1945, Ph.D., 1949; D.Sc. (hon.), SUNY, Albany, 1991. Instr. physics and meteorology Ill. Inst. Tech., 1946-49, asst. prof., 1949-51; meteorologist Woods Hole Oceanographic Instn., 1951-61; prof. meteorology UCLA, 1961-65; dir. exptl. meteorology lab. NOAA, Dept. Commerce, Washington, 1965-74; prof. environ. scis. U. Va., Charlottesville, 1974-76; W.W. Corcoran prof. environ. scis. U. Va., 1976-81; head Severe Storms br. Goddard Lab. Atmospheres, NASA, Greenbelt, Md., 1981-88, chief scientist for meteorology, 1988—; Goddard sr. fellow, earth scis. dir. Goddard Space Flight Ctr., NASA, 1988-93; project scientist tropical rainfall measuring mission, 1986—; mem. Bd. on Atmospheric Scis. and Climate, NRC/NAS, 1990-93, Bd. on Geophys. and Environ. Data, 1993—. Author: (with Herbert Riehl) Cloud Structure and Distributions Over the Tropical Pacific Ocean; assoc. editor: Revs. Geophysics and Space Physics, 1964-72, 75-77; contbr. articles to profl. jours. Mem. Fla. Gov.'s Environ. Coordinating Coun., 1971-74. Recipient Disting. Authorship award NOAA, 1969, Silver medal Dept. Commerce, 1967, Gold medal, 1972, Vincent J. Schaefer award Weather Modification Assn., 1979, Cmty. Headliner award Women in Comm., 1973, Profl. Achievement award U. Chgo. Alumni Assn., 1975, 92, Lifetime Achievement award Women in Sci. Engrng., 1990, Exceptional Sci. Achievement award NASA, 1982, William Nordberg award NASA, 1994; named Woman of Yr. L.A. Times, 1963; Guggenheim fellow, 1954-55, Goddard Sr. fellow, 1988—. Fellow Am. Meteorol. Soc. (Meisinger award 1962, Rossby Rsch. medal 1983, coun. 1975-77, 79-81, exec. com. 1977, 79-81, commr. sci. and tech. activities 1982-88, pres.-elect 1988, pres. 1989, Charles Franklin Brooks award 1992, publs. commr. 1992—, hon. mem.), Am. Peophys. Union; mem. NAE, Oceanography Soc., Cosmos Club, Phi Beta Kappa, Sigma Xi. Home: 540 N St SW Washington DC 20024-4557 Office: NASA Goddard Space Flight Ctr Earth Scis Dir Greenbelt MD 20771

SIMPSON, JOCELYN YVETTE, pediatric medical/surgical and hematology/oncology nurse; b. L.A., Oct. 29, 1966; d. James Earl and Elena Jane (Rowland) S. BA in Biol. Scis., U. Calif., Santa Barbara, 1988; ADN, Santa Barbara City Coll., 1991; BS in Health Svcs. Mgmt., U. La Verne, 1995. RN, Calif.; cert. PALS. Lab. asst. U. Calif. Santa Barbara Student Health Svcs., 1985, asst. Eye Clinic, 1987-88; med. asst. Santa Barbara Med. Found. Clinic, 1988-89, Children's Med. Clinic Santa Barbara, 1989-91; staff nurse Children's Hosp. L.A., 1991—. Scholar Ventura County Black Nurses Assn. Mem. NAFE, Nat. Coun. Negro Women Inc., U. Calif.-Santa Barbara Alumni Assn., U. Calif.-Santa Barbara Black Alumni Club.

SIMPSON, JULIETTE RICH, elementary educator; b. Bainbridge, Ga., Jan. 9, 1944; d. Robert Lloyd Jr. and Juliette (Lane) Rich; m. Ralph Felward Simpson, Aug. 13, 1966; children: Juliette, Elena. AB in Elem. Edn., Wesleyan Coll., 1966. 2d grade tchr. Bibb County Sch. System, Macon, Ga., 1966-69; title I tchr. Tift County Sch. System, Tifton, Ga., 1974-77, 3d grade tchr., 1977—; mem. sci. curriculum writing com. Tift County Bd. Edn., Tifton, 1989-90, mem. lang. arts curriculum writing com., 1990-91, mem. social studies curriculum writing com., 1991-92. Alt. del. Nat. Rep. Conv., Houston, 1992; del. Ga. Rep. Conv., Atlanta, 1992; mem. State Rep. Com., 1994—; co-pres. Tifton Cir Bar Assn., 1990-91; active Annie Belle Clark Sch. PTO; v.p. Tifton Choral Soc., 1994—. Mem. Profl. Assn. Ga. Educators, Internat. Reading Assn., Tift County Found. for Ednl. Excellence (Outstanding Tchr. award), Ga. Coun. for Social Scis., Dogwood Garden Club (alt. del.). Republican. Presbyterian. Home: 1020 N College Ave Tifton GA 31794-3942 Office: Annie Belle Clark Sch 506 W 12th St Tifton GA 31794-3999

SIMPSON, LAVADA CRAIN, nurse; b. Hollis, Ark., Mar. 5, 1938; d. Raymond Leslie and Lucy Viola (Davis) Crain; m. Cecil Edward Simpson, Dec. 20, 1958; children: Gregory Kent, Randall Scott, Lavada Suzanne. Diploma, Bapt. Meml. Hosp., 1958. RN, Ark. Staff nurse Desha County Hosp., Dumas, Ark., 1958-66, dir. nursing, 1959; staff nurse McGehee (Ark.) Desha County Hosp., 1967; sch. nurse Delta Sch. Dist., Rohwer, Ark., 1969-77, 86—; home health nurse McGehee Hosp. Home Health, 1986—; sch. nurse Tillar (Ark.) Sch. Dist., 1987-89; mem. Desha County Pub. Health Adv. Bd., 1973-78. Bd. dirs. Am. Cancer Soc., Desha County, 1980—. Mem. Delta Warrior Booster Club (v.p. 1969-92). Democrat. Baptist. Home: PO Box 502 Rohwer AR 71666 Office: McGehee Hosp Home Health PO Box 351 McGehee AR 71654

SIMPSON, MADELINE LOUISA, psychologist; b. Norfolk, Va., June 22, 1923; d. David Edward and Zenobia Eleanor (Ross) S. BA, Fisk U., 1944; MS, Boston U., 1951; MA, The New Sch., 1967; PhD, U. Md., 1981; MPA, Va. Commonwealth U., 1985. Cert. psychologist, N.Y. Practitioner Norfolk County Dept. Pub. Welfre N.Y.C. Dept. Hosps. and the Hosp. for Joint Diseases, N.Y.C. and Norfolk County, Va., 1946-56; founder, dir. Centre d'Etudes Sociales, Port-au-Prince, Haiti, 1959-61; social work practitioner and supr. Child Welfare Agy., N.Y.C., 1961-68; asst. prof. pscyhol. Del. State Coll., Dover, 1969-71; assoc. prof. psychol. Cheyney (Pa.) State Coll., 1972-75, 78; asst. prof. psychol. Longwood Coll., Farmville, Va., 1979-85; assoc prof. St. Paul's Coll., Lawrenceville, Va., 1985-90. Mem. local human rights com. Va. Dept. Mental Health, Mental Retardation and Substance Abuse Svcs., Piedmont Geriatric Hosp., Burkeville, Va., 1983-89, recipient Cert. of Recognition, 1988. Recipient Gold Circle. Mem. Am. Psychol. Assn., Delta Sigma Theta.

SIMPSON, MARY ANN JORDAN, nursing educator; b. Charlotte, N.C., Nov. 10, 1938; d. Ralph Biggers and Sarah Helen (Abee) Jordan; m. Melvyn C. Simpson, Apr. 19, 1964; children: Bryan Todd, Pamela Ann. Diploma, Charlotte Meml. Hosp. Sch. Nursing, 1960; student, Advanced Studies Inst. for Diabetes Edn., 1989; BS in Profl. Arts, St. Joseph's Coll., Windham, Maine, 1990. Cert. diabetes educator, BCLS instr. Am. Heart Assn. Clin. instr. Sch. Nursing Rex Hosp., Raleigh, N.C., 1964-66, in-svc. edn. dept. instr., 1966-70; clin. instr.LPN program Forsyth Tech. Inst., Winston-Salem, N.C., 1971-76; instr. edn. svc. dept. Rex Hosp., Raleigh, N.C., 1976-87, diabetes educator, 1987—. Mem. adv. bd. Diabetes Prevention Project Wake

County, 1991-94; bd. dirs. Triangle chpt. Am. Diabetes Assn., 1984-87, N.C. affiliate bd. dirs., 1985-88, 90-94, chair patient edn. com., 1986-91, pres., 1992-93. Recipient Outstanding Diabetes Educator award, 1991, the Great 100-RN Excellence in N.C., 1991. Mem. Am. Assn. Diabetes Educators, Am. Diabetes Assn. (N.C. Affiliate Vol. of Yr. 1994), Rsch. Triangle Assn. Diabetes Educators. Methodist. Home: 6601 Brookhollow Dr Raleigh NC 27615-6610 Office: Rex Hosp 4420 Lake Boone Trl Raleigh NC 27607-6599

SIMPSON, MARY MICHAEL, priest, psychotherapist; b. Evansville, Ind., Dec. 1; d. Link Wilson and Mary Garrett (Price) S. B.A., B.S., Tex. Women's U., 1946; grad. N.Y. Tng. Sch. for Deaconesses, 1949; grad., Westchester Inst. Tng. in Psychoanalysis and Psychotherapy, 1976; S.T.M., Gen. Theol. Sem., 1982. Missionary Holy Cross Mission, Bolahun, Liberia, 1950-52; mem. Order of St. Helena, 1952—; acad. head Margaret Hall Sch., Versailles, Ky., 1958-61; sister in charge Convent of St. Helena, Bolahan, 1962-67, novice dir., 1968-74; pastoral counselor on staff Cathedral St. John the Divine, N.Y.C., 1974-87, canon residentiary, canon counselor, 1977-87, hon. canon, 1988—; ordained priest Episcopal Ch., 1977; cons. psychotherapist Union Theol. Sem., 1980-83; dir. Cathedral Counseling Service, 1975-87; priest-in-charge St. John's Ch. Wilmot, New Rochelle, N.Y., 1987-88; pvt. practice psycholanalyst, 1974—; Bd. dirs. Westchester Inst. Tng. in Psychoanalysis and Psychotherapy, 1982-84; trustee Council on Internat. and Pub. Affairs, 1983-87; interim pastor St. Michael's Ch., Manhattan, 1992-94; cons. Diocese of N.Y., 1992—. Mem. Nat. Assn. Advancement of Psychoanalysis, N.Y. State Assn. Practicing Psychotherapists, N.Y. Soc. Clin. Psychologists. Author: The Ordination of Women in the American Episcopal Church: the Present Situation, 1981; contbg. author: Yes to Women Priests, 1978. Home and Office: 151 E 31st St Apt 8H New York NY 10016-9502

SIMPSON, SUSAN ANITA, primary school educator; b. Danville, Ill., Feb. 14, 1950; d. William Charlton and Anita Jane (Barrows) S. AA, Danville Jr. Coll., 1971; BSE, Ark. State U., 1974, MSE, 1974. Cert. tchr., Ark., Mo. Kindergarten tchr. Clay County Ctrl. Elem. Sch., Rector, Ark., 1974—. Mem. NEA, Kappa Delta Pi. Democrat. Home: 6510 Kimberly Blvd North Lauderdale FL 33068

SIMPSON, VI, state senator; b. Los Angeles, Mar. 18, 1946; d. Lloyd M. and Helen (Chacon) Sentman; m. William D. McCarty; children—Jason, Kristina. attended Ind. U. Sch. of Law, Indpls. Asst. to chmn. Com. on Status of Women, Calif., 1974-75; dir. pub. affairs Calif. Parks and Recreation Soc., Sacramento, 1975-77; county auditor Monroe County, Ind., 1980-84; mem. Ind. Senate, 1984—; exec. dir. Heritage Edn. Found., Indpls., 1989—. Editor: Equal Rights Monitor mag., 1974-76. Syndicated newspaper columnist Know Your Rights, 1975-76. Named Freshman Democrat Senator of Yr., Ind. broadcasters Assn., 1985, Legis. of Yr., Ind. State Employees Assn., 1985, various Legis. awards Sierra Club, Ind. Wildlife Fedn., Isaac Walton League, Ind. Parks and Recreation Assn. Mem. NAACP, AAUW. Methodist. Avocations: gardening, cooking. Office: Heritage Edn Found 7821 W Morris St Indianapolis IN 46231

SIMPSON, ZELMA ALENE, librarian; b. Bristow, Okla., Nov. 2, 1923; d. Robert E. and Zelma (Wolfe) Tidrow; m. Eugene Lester Simpson, Dec. 26, 1945 (dec. 1967); 1 son, Lantz Eugene. B.S. in Edn., Central State U., Edmond, Okla., 1948, postgrad., 1961—. Sch. tchr. Oklahoma County, Okla., 1948-65; library dir. Okla. Hist. Soc., Oklahoma City, 1965-79; tchr. Oscar Rose Junior Coll., Midwest City, Okla., 1972-73; librarian Lawton (Okla.) Pub. Library, 1982-89, ret., 1989; family history cons., researcher, 1989—; lectr. history and geneaology. Chmn. Hist. and Geneal. Fair Oklahoma City, 1976; sec.-treas. Broncho Basketball Booster Club, Central State U., 1967-78. Recipient Certificate of Recognition D.A.R., 1975, Award of Honor Oklahoma City Bicentennial Commn., 1975; named Distinguished Former Student Central State U., 1977. Mem. Okla. Geneal. Soc. (life, past acquisition's chmn., past 1st v.p., pres. 1972-73), DAR (lineage rsch. chmn. Samuel King chpt. 1977—, regent 1978-80, geneal. chmn. 1978-85, registrar Lawton chpt. 1986-88, co-chmn. family history fair in Lawton mall 1988), Okla. Hist. Soc., Central State U. Alumni Assn. (life), S.W. Okla. Geneal. Soc. (libr. rep. 1982-88), Edmond Geneal. Soc. (charter 1991—). Address: 33 E 9th St Edmond OK 73034-3912

SIMPSON MARTIN, TINA DEE, psychology educator; b. Elgin, Ill., Mar. 4, 1966; d. Roy Edward and Vicki Sue (Overfelt) Simpson; m. Lance Michael Martin, Aug. 12, 1989; 1 child, Jase Barter. AA, Southeastern Ill. Coll., Harrisburg, 1986; BA, So. Ill. U., Carbondale, 1988, MS, 1992. Nat. cert. counselor., qualified treatment supr., qualified treatment provider. Vol. Network Crisis Intervention, Carbondale, 1987-88, Choate Mental Health, Anna, Ill., 1987-88; youth svc. counselor Egyptian Health Dept., Eldorado, Ill., 1988-89; substance abuse counselor Substance Abuse Svcs., Marion, Ill., 1989-92, coord. treatment program, 1992-94; part time psychology instr. Southeastern Ill. Coll., Harrisburg, 1994—; chairperson Parents Assn. Com., Carbondale, 1991-92; vice chairperson Students Orgn. Com., Carbondale, 1991-92; sec. Student Govt., Harrisburg, 1985-86. Designer group counseling Adolescent Grief Group, 1992. Mem. ACA, Assn. for Specialists in Group Work. Home: 235 New Hope Church Rd Galatia IL 62935

SIMS, CAROLYN DENISE, lawyer; b. Snowhill, N.C., Sept. 29, 1960; d. James Henry and Elnora (Jackson) Sims. BA, U. N.C., 1981; JD, N.C. Cen. U., 1984; LLM in Labor Law, Georgetown U., 1988. Bar: D.C. 1985, U.S. Dist. Ct. D.C. 1985, U.S. Dist. Ct. Nebr. 1985, U.S. Dist. Ct. Hawaii 1985, U.S. Tax Ct. 1985, U.S. Claims Ct. 1985, U.S. Mil. Appeals 1985, U.S. Army Ct. Mil. Rev. 1985, U.S. Ct. Appeals (D.C., 3d, 4th, 5th, 6th, 7th, 8th, 9th, 10th, 11th, fed. and D.C. cirs.) 1985, Va. 1986. Legal rsch. asst., law libr. asst. N.C. Cen. U., Durham, 1982-84; civil litigation intern City of Greensboro, N.C., 1983; criminal pros. litigation intern City of Durham, 1984; gen. atty. Office of the Solicitor U.S. Dept. Labor, Washington, 1984-88; asst. corp. counsel Office Corp. Counsel, Washington, 1988—. Contbr. articles to profl. jours. Mem. ABA, Nat. Bar Assn., Fed. Bar Assn., Bar Assn. of D.C., Nat. Assn. Black Women Attys., Delta Sigma Theta. Democrat. A.M.E. Home: 2801 Quebec St NW Apt 110 Washington DC 20008-1241

SIMS, KAY ELLEN, critical care nurse; b. Tacoma Park, Md., Oct. 31, 1949; d. Paul Frederick and Shirley Eileen Smith; divorced; 1 child, Steffanie Gayle. Diploma, Johns Hopkins Sch. Nursing, 1970; BSN, Union U., 1991; MSN, U. Tenn., 1993. RN, Tenn., Md.; cert. critical care; cert. continuing educator and staff devel. Staff nurse Washington Adventist Hosp., Takcoma Park; instr. Bapt. Hosp. Sch. Nursing, Memphis; staff and head nurse Bapt. Meml. Hosp., Memphis, staff devel. instr. cardiovascular intensive care unit and telemetry, 1980-94; edn. specialist, 1994—. Mem. AACN (regional advisor, chpt. pres., newsletter editor, seminar spkr.), Soc. Critical Care Medicine, Sigma Theta Tau, Alpha Chi. Methodist. Office: Bapt Meml Hosp 899 Madison Ave Memphis TN 38146

SIMS, KONSTANZE OLEVIA, social worker; b. Dallas, Dec. 20, 1944; d. Kenneth Winn and Odie Lee (Wells) S. Student, U. Dallas, 1963-64; BA, U. Tex., Arlington, 1968; MEd, U. North Tex., 1972. Sec. Stillman Coll. Regional Campaign Fund, Dallas, 1969; employment interviewer Zale Corp., Dallas, 1969-71; sch. counselor Bishop Dunne High Sch, Dallas, 1973-78; dir. guidance Notre Dame High Sch., Wichita Falls, Tex., 1978-81; taxpayer svc. rep. IRS, Dallas, 1981-83, acct. analyst, 1983-88; freelance Dallas, 1989-90; social worker Tex. Dept. Human Svcs., Dallas, 1991—. Reader, North Tex. Taping & Radio for the Blind, Dallas, 1991—; mem. choir St. Peter the Apostle Cath. Ch.; mem. Whale Adoption Project. Mem. AAUW, Am. Counseling Assn., Nat. Specialty Merchandising Assn., Am. Multicultural Counseling Assn., Am. Bible Tchrs. Assn., Tex. Counseling Assn., Tex. Multicultural Counseling Assn., Assn. Rsch. and Enlightenment, Inc., Assn. for Spiritual, Ethical, and Religious Values in Counseling, U. Tex Arlington Alumni Assn., U. North Tex. Alumni Assn. Office: Tex Dept Human Svcs 4533 Ross Ave Dallas TX 75204

SIMS, LINDA GERALDINE, therapist, educator; b. L.A., Dec. 22, 1946; d. Douglas A. and Geraldine E. (Rainwater) Westmoreland; m. David A. Myers, July 30, 1966 (div. Jan. 1973); 1 child, Kenneth David; m. LeBron Sims, Sept. 4, 1976; 1 child, Jennifer Louise. BA in Psychology, San Diego State U., 1977; MEd in Pastoral Counseling, U. Puget Sound, 1987. Clin. intern Christian Counseling Svc., Tacoma, Wash., 1985-87, resident, 1987-88; clin. staff counselor N.W. Pastoral Counseling (formerly Christian Counseling Svc.), Tacoma, Wash., 1988—, dir. adminstrn., 1990—; workshop presenter N.W. Pastoral Counseling, Tacoma, Wash., 1988—; workshop presenter Assoc. Ministries, Tacoma, 1989—. Mem. Am. Counseling Assn., Internat. Assn. Marriage and Family Counselors, Assn. for Spiritual, Ethical and Religious Values in Counseling, Wash. Counseling Assn., Wash. Mental Health Counselors Assn. Democrat. Presbyterian. Office: NW Pastoral Counseling 3549 Bridgeport Way W Tacoma WA 98466

SIMS, MARTHA J., library director; b. Portsmouth, Va., Oct. 29, 1946; m. Hunter Sims; children: Hunter, Clara. BA in English, Mary Baldwin Coll.; MS in Libr. Sci., U. N.C.; MA in Pub. Adminstrn., Old Dominion U. Reference asst. U. N.C., Chapel Hill, 1968-69; libr. art and music dept. Richmond Pub. Libr., 1969-71; br. libr. Virginia Beach Pub. Libr., 1971-74, asst. dir., 1974-76, dir., 1976—; mem. adv. bd. New Va. Review, 1976-80. Contbr. articles to profl. jours. Bd. dirs. Va. Beach Arts Ctr., 1971-82, treas., 1974-75; mem. Va. Beach Bicentennial Commn., 1975-76, Jr. League Norfolk, Virginia Beach, 1976-82; sec. Tidewater Area Libr. Dir.'s Coun., 1984-85; bd. dirs. Boys Club Norfolk/Virginia Beach, 1986-90, Literacy Action South Hampton Roads, 1988—, Va. Ctr. for the Book, 1987—, Va. Literacy Found., 1989—; mem. steering com. Virginia Beach Roundtable, 1988-92; census chairperson Mayor's Complete Count Com. 1990, 1989-90; lead agt. region 12 literacy coord. com. State Office Adult Literacy, 1989-92; trustee, sec. Va. Beach Pub. Libr. Endowment Found., 1982—; mem. adv. bd. Tidewater Literacy Coun., 1984—; tchr. Sunday sch. 1st Presbyn. Ch., 1988—; mem. steering com. Adult Literacy Lab, Adult Lng. Ctr. Va. Beach Pub. Schs., 1989—; keel divsn. leader United Way, 1991-92; bd. trustees Norfolk Acad., 1991—; keel club chairperson United Way, Virginia Beach, 1992-93; vice chmn. United Way, Virginia Beach, 1995. Mem. ALA, Am. Soc. Pub. Adminstrs., Southeastern Libr. Assn., Va. Libr. Assn. (sec. 1976-78, legis. com. 1979-85, local arrangements 1982 conv. 1981-82, chmn. pub. libr. sect. 1982-84, state libr. bd. liaison com. 1984-88). Home: 1160 Cedar Point Dr Virginia Beach VA 23451 Office: Municipal Ctr Virginia Beach VA 23456

SIMS, NATALIE KAYE BLIZZARD, nurse supervisor; b. Miami, Sept. 19, 1958; d. Donald Wayne and Sammie Lea (Barrett) Blizzard; m. David Glenn Sims, May 26, 1979; 1 child, David Scott. Student, Cameron U., 1976-79; lic. vocat. nurse, Grayson Coll., 1981, AAS in Criminal Justice cum laude, 1994. Cert. BLS, med. care analyst. Nurse ICU WNJ Hosp., Sherman, Tex., 1982-86, utilization rev. nurse, 1986-90; grad. cum laude Grayson County Sheriff's Office, Sherman, Tex., 1994; HIV counselor Grayson County Sheriff's Office, Sherman, 1990—, med. proctor, 1990—; med. instr. Jail Sch. Grayson County, 1990—. Guest spkr. Mental Health/Mental Retardation, Sherman, 1991; vol. nurse Juvenile Alternatives, Sherman, 1990, 91; team mother Little League, Sherman, 1991, 92; mem. Sherman Citizen's Task Force. Recipient Commendation, Grayson County Sheriff's Dept., 1991, 94, WNJ Hosp., 1989. Mem. Phi Theta Kappa Honor Soc. Democrat. Office: Grayson County Sheriff 200 S Crockett Sherman TX 75090

SIMS, TERRE LYNN, insurance company executive; b. Madison, Wis., Dec. 26, 1951; d. Roy Charles and Ruth Marie (McCloskey) Pierstorff; m. Gary Peter Laufenberg, Feb. 15, 1969 (div.); children: Amie, Monte, Tawna; m. Perry Allen Sims, May 3, 1994. Sales agt. Bankers Life and Casualty, Madison, 1977-80, asst. mgr., 1981-84; br. mgr. Bankers Life and Casualty, Peoria, 1984-91; co-owner Complete Ins. Svcs., Inc., Madison, Wis., 1991—; owner, operator Ohio Tavern, Madison, 1993—. Office: Complete Ins Svcs Inc 6400 Gisholt Dr Madison WI 53713-4800

SIMSON, JO ANNE, anatomy and cell biology educator; b. Chgo., Nov. 19, 1936; d. Kenneth Brown and Helen Marjorie (Pascoe) Valentine; m. Arnold Simson, June 1961 (div.); 1 child, Maria; m. Michael Smith, Nov. 10, 1971 (div.); children: Elizabeth Smith, Briana Smith. BA, Kalamazoo Coll., 1959; MS, U. Mich., 1961; PhD, SUNY, Syracuse, 1969. Postdoctoral fellow Temple U. Health Sci. Ctr., Phila., 1968-70; asst. prof. Med. U. S.C., Charleston, 1970-76, assoc. prof., 1976-83, prof. anatomy and cell biology, 1983—; featured in Smithsonian exhibit, Sci. in Am. Life, 1994—. Author short stories and poems; contbr. articles to profl. jours. Active adult edn. Unitarian Ch., Charleston, 1973-75, social action, 1990-92. Grantee NSF, 1959-60; grantee NIH, 1966-67, 72-87, 91—, postdoctoral fellow, 1968-70. Mem. Am. Assn. Anatomists, Am. Soc. Cell Biology, Histochem. Soc. (sec. 1979-82, exec. coun. 1985-89), Fogarty Internat. Fellowship Bioctr. (Basel, Switzerland 1987-88), Amnesty Internat. (newsletter editor Group 168 1982-86), Phi Beta Kappa. Home: 1760 Pittsford Cir Charleston SC 29412-4110 Office: Med U SC Anatomy 171 Ashley Ave Charleston SC 29425-0001

SIMUNICH, MARY ELIZABETH HEDRICK (MRS. WILLIAM A. SIMUNICH), public relations executive; b. Chgo.; d. Tubman Keene and Mary (McCamish) Hedrick; m. William A. Simunich, Dec. 6, 1941. Student Phoenix Coll., 1967-69, Met. Bus. Coll., 1938-40. Exec. sec. sales mgr. Sta. KPHO radio, 1950-53; exec. sec. mgr. Sta. KPHO-TV, 1953-54; account exec. Tom Rippey & Assos., 1955-56; pub. rels. dir. Phoenix Symphony, 1956-62; co-founder, v.p. Paul J. Hughes Pub. Rels., Inc., 1960-65; owner Mary Simunich Pub. Rels., Phoenix, 1966-77; pub. rels. dir. Walter O. Boswell Meml. Hosp., Sun City, Ariz., 1969-85; pub. rels. cons., 1985—; pres. Darci PR, Phoenix, 1994—, Citynet, Inc., 1994—; instr. pub. rels. Phoenix Coll. Evening Sch., 1973-78. Bd. dirs. Anytown, Ariz., 1969-72; founder, sec. Friends Am. Geriatrics, 1977-86. Named Phoenix Advt. Woman of Year, Phoenix Jr. Advt. Club, 1962; recipient award Blue Cross, 1963; 1st Pl. award Ariz. Press Women, 1966. Mem. NAFE, Women in Comm., Internat. Assn. Bus. Communicators (pres. Ariz. chpt. 1970-71, dir.), Pub. Rels. Soc. Am. (sec., dir. 1976-78), Am. Soc. Hosp. Pub. Rels. (dir. Ariz. chpt. 1976-78), Nat., Ariz. Press Women. Home: 4133 N 34th Pl Phoenix AZ 85018-4771 Office: Darci Group 2425 E Camelback Ste 450 Phoenix AZ 85016

SINCLAIR, DAISY, advertising executive, casting director; b. Penth Amboy, N.J., Mar. 22, 1941; d. James Patrick and Margaret Mary (McAniff) Nieland; m. James Pratt Sinclair, May 25, 1978; children: Duncan, Gibbons. BA, Caldwell Coll., 1962. Jr. copywriter Young & Rubican, N.Y.C., 1962-64; various positions in casting dept. Ogilvy & Mather, N.Y.C., 1964-90, sr. v.p., dir. casting, 1990—. Mem. Am. Assn. Advt. (talent agt. com. 1972—), Drama League N.Y. (3d v.p. 1982—), The Knickerbocker Greys (v.p.), Edgartown Yacht Club, Chapaquoit Yacht Club, The Tuxedo Club. Republican. Episcopalian. Home: 4 E 95th St New York NY 10128-0705 Office: Ogilvy & Mather Advt Worldwide Plz 309 W 49th St New York NY 10019-7316

SINCLAIR, HEIDI, public relations executive; b. Denver, Jan. 24, 1958. BA in English Lit./Creative Writing, Stanford U., 1980. Editor, writer Women's Sports Mag., 1980-81; account exec., writer Regis McKenna Pub. Rels., 1981-82; dir. comm. Sofalink Corp., 1982; pres. New Venture Comm., 1982-84; exec. v.p., dir. Ketchum Pub. Rels., 1984-88; sr. v.p. advanced tech. divsn. Hill and Knowlton, 1988; v.p. corp. comm. Lotus Devel. Corp., 1988-92; v.p. corp. comm. Borland Internat., Inc., 1992-93, v.p. corp. strategy, 1993—. Recipient Pub. Rels. Gold Key award, 1989. Mem. Pub. Rels. Seminar, Conf. Bd. Coun., Software Pub.'s Assn. (bd. dirs.), Software Industry Coalition. Office: Borland Internat Inc 100 Borland Way Scotts Valley CA 95067*

SINCLAIR, SARA VORIS, health facility administrator, nurse; b. Kansas City, Mo., Apr. 13, 1942; d. Franklin Defenbaugh and Inez Estelle (Figenbaum) Voris; m. James W. Sinclair, June 13, 1964; children: Thomas James, Elizabeth Kathleen, Joan Sara. BSN, UCLA, 1965. RN, Utah; lic. health care facility adminstr.; cert. health care adminstr. Staff nurse UCLA Med. Ctr. Hosp., 1964-65; charge nurse Boulder (Colo.) Meml. Hosp., 1966, Boulder (Colo.) Manor Nursing Home, 1974-75, Four Seasons Nursing Home, Joliet, Ill., 1975-76; dir. nursing Home Health Agy of Olympia Fields, Joliet, Ill., 1977-79; dir. nursing Sunshine Terr. Found., Inc., Logan, Utah, 1980, asst. adminstr., 1980-81, adminstr., 1981-93; dir. divsn. health systems improvement Utah Dept. Health, Salt Lake City, 1993—; mem. long term care profl. and tech. adv. com. Joint Commn. on Accreditation Healthcare Orgns., Chgo., 1987-91, chmn., 1990-91; adj. lectr. Utah State U., 1991-93; mem. adj. clin. faculty Weber State U., Ogden, Utah; moderator radio program Healthwise Sta. KUSU-RM, 1985-93; spkr. Nat. Coun. Aging, 1993, Alzheimer's Disease Assn. Ann. Conf., 1993; presenter in field. Contbg. author: Associate Degree Nursing and The Nursing Home, 1988. Mem. dean's adv. coun. Coll. Bus. Utah State U., Logan, 1989-91, mem. presdl. search com., 1991-92; chmn., co-founder Cache Community Health Coun., Logan, 1985; chmn. bd. Hospice of Cache Valley, Logan, 1986; mem. Utah State Adv. Coun. on Aging, 1986—; apptd. chmn. Utah Health Facilities Com., 1989—; mem. Utah Adv. Coun. on Aging, 1987—; chmn. Bear River Dist. Adv. Coun. on Aging, 1989-91; chmn. health and human svcs. subcom. Cache 2010, 1992-93. Recipient Disting. Svc. award Utah State U., 1989. Fellow Am. Coll. Health Care Adminstrs. (presenter 1992-93, 95, v.p. Utah chpt. 1992-94, convocation and edn. coms. 1992-94, region IX vice gov. 1994—); mem. Am. Healthcare Assn. (non-proprietary v.p. 1986-87, region v.p. 1987-89, presenter workshop convs. 1990-93, exec. com. 1993—), Am. Coll. Health Care Administrators (vice gov. region 9 1994—), Utah Health Care Assn. (pres. 1983-85, treas. 1991-93, Disting. Svc. award 1991), Utah Gerontol. Soc. (bd. dirs. 1992-93, chmn. nominating com. 1993-94), Cache C. of C. (pres. 1991), Logan Bus. and Profl. Women's Club (pres. 1989, Woman of Achievement award 1982, Woman of Yr. 1982), Rotary (Logan chpt., chair community svc. com. 1989-90). Office: Utah Dept Health Divsn Health Systems Improvement 288 N 1460 W Salt Lake City UT 84114-2857

SINDEROFF, RITA JOYCE, property management company executive, real estate broker, mortgage broker; b. Bklyn., June 22, 1932; d. Joseph George and Mary (Cohen) Rothkopf; m. Arthur B. Schneider, Oct. 18, 1953 (div. Sept. 1973); children: Linda Ellen, Debra Carol. Degree in comml. art Pratt Inst., 1953; BA in Acctg., Bklyn. Coll., 1954. Contr. Central Funding Co., Bklyn., 1973-80; owner, contr. Riteway Mgmt. Inc., Coral Springs, Fla., 1980-86; realtor Riteway Internat. Realty Corp., Coral Springs, 1985-86, ERA Regal Internat. Realty Inc.; realtor, mortgage broker Regal Fin. Svcs. and LCAM Regal Assn. Svcs., Coral Springs, Fla., 1986—; cons. in field. Active Cancer Soc., Bklyn., 1954-73, March of Dimes, Bklyn., 1960-70. Recipient 1st art award City of N.Y., 1950. Mem. Nat. Bd. Realtors, North Broward Bd. Realtors, Fla. Assn. Mortgage Brokers, Nat. Real Estate Assn., Fla. Assn. Community Mgrs. (lic.), Community Assn. Inst. Democrat. Jewish. Avocations: reading, dancing, swimming. Office: Regal Fin Svcs 1515 University Dr Coral Springs FL 33071

SING, LILLIAN KWOK, municipal judge; b. Shanghai, China, Nov. 13, 1942. BS, Occidental Coll., 1964; MSW, Columbia U., 1966; JD, U. Calif. San Francisco, 1975. Assoc. dir. Chinese New Comer Svc. Ctr., San Francisco, 1969-71; lawyer Simmons & Ungar, San Francisco, 1975-77; lawyer solo practitioner San Francisco, 1977-81; presiding judge San Francisco Mcpl. Ct., 1988-89, judge, 1981—. Founding mem. Chinese for Affirmative Action, San Francisco, 1971; vice chair San Francisco Civil Svc. Commn., 1978; bd. dirs. Gay Asian Pacific Alliance, Cmty. HIV Project, San Francisco, 1993—. Named First Asian Woman Judge in No. Calif., Asian Am. Bar Assn., 1985; recipient Trial Judge of Yr. award, Trial Lawyers Assn., 1989, Presiding Judge award Lawerys' Club of San Francisco, 1989, Outstanding Jurist award San Francisco Women Lawyers Alliance, 1993. Office: San Francisco Mcpl Ct 400 Van Ness Ave San Francisco CA 94102

SINGER, ANITA LOUISE HOVANEC, educator; b. Swoyersville, Pa., Nov. 8, 1942; d. Louis G. and Anita T. (Santarelli) Hovanec; m. Russell John, June 8, 1963; children: Sandra Maria, Louis John, Russell Jonathan. BS in Elem. Edn., Wilkes Coll., 1964; BS in Acctg., King's Coll., 1986; MBA in Acctg./Fin., Wilkes U., 1992. Cert. libr.; CPA. Elem. tchr. Manville (N.J.) Pub. Sch., 1964, Wyo. Valley West Schs., Kingston, Pa., 1966-73, Diocese of Scranton, Swoyesville, Pa., 1983; pub. acct. Mangan and Schuler, CPA's, Wilkes-Barre, Pa., 1985-88; bus. sch. tchr. McCann Sch. of Bus., Wyoming, Pa., 1986-90; asst. prof. acctg. King's Coll., Wilkes-Barre, 1990—; moderator King's Coll. Acctg. Assn., Wilkes Barre, 1994. Mem. Confredemity of Christian Mothers, Swoyesville, 1979—. Mem. Pa. Inst. CPAs, Inst. Mgmt. Accts., Pa. State Edn. Assn., Delta Epsilon Sigma, Alpha Sigma Lambda. Roman Catholic. Home: 203 Owen St Swoyersville PA 18704

SINGER, BETH YVONNE, educator; b. Hempstead, N.Y., July 7, 1965; d. Donald Howard and Marsha (Kreizelman) S. BA, U. Del., 1987; MS, Hofstra U., 1991. Adminstr. Bruce H. Sobel, CPA, N.Y.C., 1987-90; tchr. Riverhead (N.Y.) Cen. Sch. Dist., 1991—; group leader, tchr. Crestwood County Day Sch., Melville, N.Y., 1991—. Mem. Nassau Reading Coun., Nassau County, N.Y., 1991—; co-founder The Kadimah Found., N.Y.C., 1989—; bd. dirs. Camp Louemma, Sussex, N.J., 1991—; com. mem. U.J.A., N.Y.C., 1992—. Mem. Sierra Club, Camp Louemma Alumni Assn. (v.p. 1991—), Kappa Delta Pi, Alpha Sigma Alpha Alumni. Republican.

SINGER, CECILE D., state legislator. BA, Queens Coll. Past rep. Spl. Svcs. for Children, N.Y.C.; past exec. dir. N.Y. State Assembly Social Svcs. and Judiciary Coms., Joint Legis. Com. on Corps., Authorities and Commns.; past pub. rep. Yonkers (N.Y.) Emergency Control Bd.; past coord. Westchester County Assembly Dels.; past chief of staff for dep. minority leader; mem. N.Y. State Assembly, Albany, 1988—, leadership sec. Rep. Conf., mem. assembly children & families com., mem. various other coms.; past rep. Temp. Commn. To Revise Social Svcs. Law; mem. Presdl. Commn. on Privacy Conf., N.Y. State Senate Transp. Conf.; mem. task force on substance abuse Am. Legis. Exch. Coun., task force on econ. devel., on crime victim's rights, on hosp. crisis, on women's issues, com. on mass. transit.; sec. Rep. Conf. Nat. Adv. Panel Child Care Action Campaign. Mem. adv. bd. Legal Awareness for Women, Big Bros. and Big Sisters; mem. task force on certiorari Westchester County Sch. Bds. Assn.; sch. and community chmn. Yonkers PTA; bd. dirs. Yonkers Gen. Hosp., Yonkers chpt. United Jewish Appeal. Recipient Jenkins Meml. award, Nat. PTA award. Mem. Mental Health Assn. (bd. dirs., mem. nominating and pub. affairs coms. Westchester County chpt.), Rotary. Home: 117 Cliffside Dr Yonkers NY 10710-3144 Office: NY State Assembly Lob Rm 720 Albany NY 12248

SINGER, DIANA ROSE, jewelry industry executive; b. N.Y.C., Aug. 25, 1953; d. Leonard Rothblum and Tina Singer; m. Robert Kushner, Apr. 12, 1981. B in French magna cum laude, NYU, 1975, B in Polit. Sci. magna cum laude, 1975; cert., Gemological Inst. Am., 1982. Salesperson, mgr.-in-tng. Halston dept. Bloomingdales, N.Y.C., 1969-71; asst. mgr. Women's Haberdasher's, N.Y.C., 1973; mgr., buyer Antoinette's Heirloom Jewelry, San Francisco, 1975-80; salesperson, buyer, dir. estate jewelry promotions, advt. M & L Singer, Inc., N.Y.C., 1980-89; pres., chief exec. officer D & E Singer, Inc., N.Y.C., 1989—; asst. sec. M & L Singer, Inc., N.Y.C., 1984—; sec.-treas. Antoinette's Heirloom Jewelry of Washington, 1986—; treas. Matthews Jewelry, N.Y.C., 1985—; pastry chef restaurant, N.Y.C., 1981-82; instr., lectr. appraisal studies program jewlry conf., NYU, 1989. Contbr. articles, recipes to various mags. Vol. Project Dorot, N.Y.C., 1988, Friday Breakfast for Homeless Program Cen. Synagogue, 1987-88. Recipient silver medal Maccabian Games, 1974. Mem. Women's Jewelry Assn. (bd. dirs. 1987—, dir. ann. awards dinner 1983-86, Excellency in Retailing award 1987), Circolo Italiano (v.p. 1975). Democrat. Jewish. Office: D & E Singer Inc 580 5th Ave New York NY 10036-4701

SINGER, DONNA LEA, writer, editor, educator; b. Wilmington, Del., Oct. 6, 1944; d. Marshall Richard and Sara Emma (Eppihimer) S. BA in English cum laude, Gettysburg Coll., 1966; postgrad., Montclair State Coll., 1972-73, U. Birmingham, Eng., 1977; M of Letters, Drew U., 1985. Asst. to dir. student activities Fairleigh Dickinson U., Madison, N.J., 1966-68; tchr., drama coach Morris Hills High Sch., Rockaway, N.J., 1968-84; free-lance editor Basic Books, Inc., N.Y.C., 1983-86; adj. instr. Fairleigh Dickinson U., Madison, 1986-87; free-lance writer, editor Visual Edn. Corp., Princeton, N.J., 1988—, Fact's on File, Bantam, Random House, Fodor's Travel Books, N.Y.C., 1990—, John Wiley & Sons, N.Y.C., 1990—; co-founder, co-dir. Traveling Hist. Troupe, Rockaway, 1976-78; tour leader Am. Leadership Study Groups, 1976, 78, 82; theatre studies participant Royal Shakespeare Co., Stratford, Eng., 1978, 79, 81; docent, lectr. acting co. Hist. Spanish Point, Osprey, Fla., 1989—. Contbg. author: (poetry) Chasing Rainbows, 1987, An American Heritage, 1994, (biographies) Past and Promise: Lives of New Jersey Women, 1990, American Cultural Leaders, 1993. Big sister Big Bros./Big Sisters, Sarasota, Fla., 1990—. Mem. Internat. Women's Writing Guild, Gulf Coast Writers Forum, Met. Mus. Art, Royal Shakespeare Company Assocs.

SINGER, ELEANOR, sociologist, editor; b. Vienna, Austria, Mar. 4, 1930; came to U.S., 1938; d. Alfons and Anna (Troedl) Schwarzbart; m. Alan

Gerard Singer, Sept. 8, 1949; children: Emily Ann, Lawrence Alexander. BA, Queens Coll., 1951; PhD, Columbia U., 1966. Asst. editor Am. Scholar, Williamsburg, Va., 1951-52; editor Tchrs. Coll. Press, N.Y.C., 1952-56, Dryden-Holt, N.Y.C., 1956-57; rsch. assoc., sr. rsch. assoc., sr. rsch. scholar Columbia U., N.Y.C., 1966-94; rsch. scientist Inst. for Social Rsch. U. Mich., Ann Arbor, 1994—; editor Pub. Opinion Quar., N.Y.C., 1975-86. Author: (with Carol Weiss) The Reporting of Social Science in the Mass Media, 1988, (with Phyllis Endreny) Reporting On Risk, 1993; editor: (with Herbert H. Hyman) Readings in Reference Group Theory and Research, 1968, (with Stanley Presser) Survey Research Methods: A Reader, 1989; contbr. articles to profl. jours. Mem. Am. Assn. Pub. Opinion Research (pres. N.Y.C. chpt. 1983-84, pres. 1987-88), Am. Sociol. Assn., Am. Statis. Assn. Office: U Mich Inst Social Rsch Box 1248 Survey Rsch Ctr Ann Arbor MI 48106

SINGER, EMEL, staffing industry executive; b. Gaziantep, Turkey, Apr. 7, 1944; came to U.S., 1960; d. Mehmet Resit and Nesrin (Kescioglu) Tuzun; m. James Michael Singer, Apr. 28, 1968 (dec. 1987); children: Justin Michael, Jodi Michelle. BBA, Bradley U., 1968. Adminstrv. asst. U. Ky. Med. Ctr., Lexington, 1968; exec. sec. Hoffman Products/Cortron Industries, Chgo., 1968-70; co-founder, adminstr. Banner Personnel Svc., Inc., Chgo., 1970-87, chmn., CEO, 1988—; guest speaker Chgo. Entrepreneurship Program, U. Ill., Chgo., 1993, 94, 95. Parents bd. Bradley U., Peoria, Ill., 1989-90, assoc. trustee, 1992—, alumni master, 1993, Bradley coun., 1993—. Listed in Crains Chgo. Bus. as a Top Woman-Owned Firm, 1989, 90, 91; finalist Entrpreneur of the Year award Ernst & Young, Inc. magazine, Merrill Lynch, 1993, 94; name0 to Entrepreneurship Hall of Fame, 1993. Mem. Nat. Assn. Pers. Svcs., Nat. Assn. Temp. Svcs., Ill. Assn. Pers. Svcs., Ill. Assn. Temporary Svcs. Home: 165 Maple Hill Rd Glencoe IL 60022-1252 Office: Banner Personnel Svc Inc Banner Temporary Svc Inc 122 S Michigan Ave Chicago IL 60603

SINGER, HEDY KAREN, psychologist; b. Phila., Apr. 15, 1954; d. Aaron Norman and Lillian Sarah (Goldman) S. BS, Temple U., 1975; BHL, Gratz Coll., 1975; PhD, Temple U., 1988; MA, Villanova U., 1977. Lic. psychologist, Pa. Tchr. Sch. Dist. Phila., 1975-77; counselor Montgomery County Intermediate U., Bluebell, Pa., 1978-80; intake supv., counselor Jewish Employment and Vocat. Svc., Phila., 1979-84; grad. asst. counseling ctr. Temple U., Phila., 1984-85; psychology intern Friends Hosp., Phila., 1985-86; staff psychologist Hall-Mercer Community Mental Health-Mental Retardation Pa. Hosp., Phila., 1986-87, Abington (Pa.) Psychol. Assocs., 1987-88; sr. instr., staff psychologist div. adolescent psychiatry, cons. adolescent suicide prevention Hahnemann U., Phila., 1988-89; asst. prof. psychiatry Med. Coll. Pa., Phila., 1989-91; coord. psychology Chestnut Hill Rehab., 1989-91; pvt. practice Jenkintown, Pa., 1991—; asst. prof. psychiatry, chief psychologist dept. phys. medicine and rehab. Temple U. Sch. Medicine, Phila., 1992—. Mem. Am. Jewish Congress, 1988—, Jewish Community Rels. Coun., 1990—, Urban Coalition, Interfaith Coun., 1990—. Presdl. scholar, 1974; Temple U. fellow, 1984; Rsch. grantee Phila. Geriatric Ctr., 1990. Fellow Pa. Psychol. Assn.; mem. APA, Nat. Register Health Providers in Psychology, Phila. Soc. Clin. Psychologists, Delaware Valley Group Psychotherapy Soc. (dir. tng.), Soc. Personality Assessment (Walter Klopfer Disting. Contbn. award), Am. Group Psychotherapy Assn., Kappa Delta Pi. Office: Temple Univ Sch Medicine Dept Psychiatry Broad & Tioga Sts Philadelphia PA 19140

SINGER, JEANNE (JEANNE WALSH), composer, concert pianist; b. N.Y.C., Aug. 4, 1924; d. Harold Vandervoort and Helen (Loucks) Walsh; m. Richard G. Singer, Feb. 24, 1945 (dec.); 1 son, Richard V. BA magna cum laude, Barnard Coll., 1944; artist diploma Nat. Guild Piano Tchrs., 1954; student in piano Nadia Reisenberg, 1945-60, composition, Douglas Moore, 1942-44, PhD (hon.) in Music World U., 1984. Composer, concert pianist solo chamber ensembles N.Y., 1947—; tchr. piano Manhasset, N.Y., 1960—; found, dir. Musinger Players Chamber Ensemble, 1986—, over 100 concerts performed by this ensemble; lectr. in field. Recipient spl. award merit Nat. Fedn. Music Clubs, 1st prize in nat. competition Composers Guild, 1979, Grand prize Composers Guild, 1982, 1st prize Composers and Songwriters Internat., 1985, also various nat. awards; honored at all-Singer concert, Bogotá, Colombia, 1980; N.Y. Council Arts grantee. Fellow Internat. Biog. Assn.; mem. ASCAP (awards 1978—), Am. Music Center, Internat. League Women Composers, Nat. League Am. Pen Women (nat. music chmn.), Composers, Authors and Artists Am. (v.p. N.Y.C., music mag. editor 1972-80, nat. award 1981), Am. Women Composers, L.I. Composers Alliance, Pen and Brush, Barnard Coll. Club, Bohemians, Phi Beta Kappa. Composed numerous instrumental, vocal works including: Summons (baritone), 1975, A Cycle of Love (4 songs with piano), 1976, Suite in Harpsichord Style, 1976, From The Green Mountains (trio), 1977, (choral work) Composers' Prayer, Nocturne for Clarinet, 1980, Suite for Horn and Harp, 1980, From Petrarch (voice, horn, piano), 1981, Quartet for Flute, Oboe, Violin, Cello, 1982, Trio for Viola, Oboe, Piano, 1984, Come Greet the Spring (choral), 1981, An American Vision (song cycle), 1985, Wry Rimes (voice and Bassoon), 1986, The Lost Garden (voice, piano, cello), 1988, To Be Brave Is All (orch. and voice), 1993; 23 art songs recorded on CD To Stir a Dream, 1991; performed Lincoln Center, radio, TV. Home and Office: 64 Stuart Pl Manhasset NY 11030-2620

SINGER, JOY DANIELS, writer, consultant; b. N.Y.C., Feb. 22, 1928; d. Maurice Blumberg and Anna S. (Kleegman) Daniels. B.A., Cornell U., 1948; postgrad., Sorbonne, 1949; m. Jack Singer, July 30, 1955; children: Meriamne B., Daniel C., Richard K. Advt. copywriter Franklin Spier, George Knoerr & Assocs., Parents Mag., Diener & Dorskind, March Advt., N.Y.C., 1950-68; chief exec. officer J.D. Singer, N.Y.C., 1968—. Scriptwriter Can. TV show, Magistrate's Court, 1968-69; syndicated columnist with Marlies Wolf, Women at Work, Feature Assocs., San Rafael, Calif., 1979—. Author: My Mother, the Doctor, 1970. Dem. county committeewoman, 1960-61. Mem. Direct Mktg. Creative Guild (v.p., corp. sec.), Friends Com., Gen. Soc. Libr. (chmn.), NATAS. Home and Office: 1725 York Ave Apt 19E New York NY 10128-7811

SINGER, KAREN CHOY, systems analyst; b. San Francisco, Jan. 22, 1960; d. Jack and Mary Rita Choy; m. John Robert Singer, Sept. 18, 1993. BS, San Francisco State U., 1983. Analyst The Tomorrow Group, San Francisco, 1982-83; tech. support Mission Computer Corp., Mountain View, Calif., 1983-84; field tng. specialist Analytica Corp., Fremont, Calif., 1984-85; edn. specialist Henco Software, Inc., San Mateo, Calif., 1985-87; tech. cons. BBN Software Prod., Mountain View, 1987-89; systems cons. Filenet Corp., San Francisco, 1989—. Black belt instr., 1977-79 (numerous championship titles).

SINGER, LINDA ASCHER, school library information systems specialist; b. Chgo., Apr. 16, 1937; d. Louis Irving and Elaine M. (Metz) Ascher; m. Jerome Everett Singer, Dec. 28, 1957; children: Judith Moira, Matthew Anders, Daniel Liam. BS, U. Minn., 1958; cert. in Sch. Libr. Media, George Mason U., 1979. Group social worker Wells Meml., Mpls., 1959-61; reference libr. Pa. State U., State Coll., 1961-63; jr. mus. dir. Ctrl. Pa. Jr. Mus., State Coll., 1963-65, Princeton (N.J.) Jr. Mus., 1965-66; libr. searcher SUNY, Stony Brook, 1966-68, serials cataloger, 1968-69; sch. libr. Fairfax (Va.) County Pub. Schs., 1979-90, info. systems specialist, 1990—; speaker in field, 1990—. Columnist, writer CD-ROM Profl. Mag., 1991—, Multimedia Schs., 1994—. Sec. Va. State Bd. Social Svcs., 1992-94; mem. human svcs. coun. Fairfax County Bd., 1988-92, chair libr. bd. trustees, 1985-92. Recipient Dedicated Svc. award Fairfax County Bd. of Suprs., 1992, Dedicated Svc. award Fairfax County Libr. Bd. Trustees, 1992, Dedicated Svc. award Fairfax County Dept. Community Action, 1992; named Reston Citizen of Yr., Reston Community Assn., 1987. Mem. ALA, AASL, Childrens Def. Fund, Med. Care for Children Bd. Democrat. Jewish. Home: 2072 Bingham Ct Reston VA 22091-1304 Office: Fairfax County Pub Schs 4414 Holborn Ave Annandale VA 22003-4551

SINGER, MAXINE FRANK, biochemist; b. N.Y.C., Feb. 15, 1931; d. Hyman S. and Henrietta (Perlowitz) Frank; m. Daniel Morris Singer, June 15, 1952; children: Amy Elizabeth, Ellen Ruth, David Byrd, Stephanie Frank. AB, Swarthmore Coll., 1952, DSc (hon.), 1978; PhD, Yale U., 1957; DSc (hon.), Wesleyan U., 1977, Swarthmore Coll., 1978, U.Md.-Baltimore County, 1985, Cedar Crest Coll., 1986, CUNY, 1988, Brandeis U., 1988, Radcliffe Coll., 1990, Williams Coll., 1990, Franklin and Marshall Coll., 1991, George Washington U., 1991, NYU, 1992, Lehigh U., 1992, Dartmouth Coll., 1993, Yale U., 1994, Harvard U., 1994. USPHS postdoctoral fellow NIH, Bethesda, Md., 1956-58; rsch. chemist biochemistry NIH, 1958-74; head sect. on nucleic acid enzymology Nat. Cancer Inst., 1974-79; chief Lab. of Biochemistry, Nat. Cancer Inst., 1979-87, rsch. chemist, 1987-88; pres. Carnegie Inst. Washington, 1988—; Regents vis. lectr. U. Calif., Berkeley, 1981; bd. dirs. Johnson & Johnson; mem. sci. coun. Internat. Inst. Genetics and Biophysics, Naples, Italy, 1982-86; Chulabhorn Rsch. Inst. (adv. bd. 1990—). Mem. editorial bd. Jour. Biol. Chemistry, 1968-74, Sci. mag., 1972-82; chmn. editorial bd. Procs. of NAS, 1985-88; author (with Paul Berg) 2 books on molecular biology; contbr. articles to scholarly jours. Trustee Wesleyan U., Middletown, Conn., 1972-75, Yale Corp., New Haven, 1975-90; bd. govs. Weizmann Inst. Sci., Rehovot, Israel, 1978—; bd. dirs. Whitehead Inst., 1985-94; chmn. Smithsonian Coun., 1992-93. Recipient award for achievement in biol. scis. Washington Acad. Scis., 1969, award for research in biol. scis. Yale Sci. and Engring. Assn., 1974, Superior Service Honor award HEW, 1975, Dirs. award NIH, 1977, Disting. Service medal HHS, 1983, Presdl. Disting. Exec. Rank award, 1987, U.S. Disting. Exec. Rank award, 1987, Mory's Cup Bd. Govs. Mory's Assn., 1991, Wilbur Lucius Cross Medal of Honor Yale Grad. Sch. Assn., 1991, Nat. Medal Sci. NSF, 1992. Fellow Am. Acad. Arts and Scis.; mem. NAS (coun. 1982-85, com. Sci., Engring and Pub. Policy 1989-91), AAAS (Sci. Freedom and Responsibility award 1982), Am. Soc. Biol. Chemists, Am. Soc. Microbiologists, Am. Chem. Soc., Am. Philos. Soc., Inst. Medicine of NAS, Pontifical Acad. of Scis, Human Genome Org, N.Y. Acad. Scis. Home: 5410 39th St NW Washington DC 20015-2902 Office: Carnegie Inst Washington 1530 P St NW Washington DC 20005-1933

SINGER, NIKI, publishing executive, public relations executive; b. Rochester, N.Y., Sept. 10, 1937; d. Goodman A. and Evelyn (Simon) Sarachan; BA cum laude, U. Mich., 1959; m. Michael J. Sheets, 1973; children: Romaine Kitty, Nicholas Simon Feramorz. Mgr. advt. sales promotion Fairchild Publs., N.Y.C., 1959-67; account exec., account supr. Vernon Pope Co., N.Y.C., 1967-69, v.p., 1969-71; pres. Niki Singer, Inc., N.Y.C., 1971-93; sr. v.p. M. Shanken Comm., 1994—. Mem. Am. Inst. Wine and Food (bd. dirs.), Les Dames d'Escoffier. Home: 1035 5th Ave New York NY 10028-0135 Office: M Shanken Comm 387 Park Ave S New York NY 10016

SINGER, PAULETTE FRANCES, artist; b. Newark, Oct. 24, 1941; d. Louis Harold and Gertrude Sarah (Ziger) Lasher; m. Michael H. Singer, Mar. 22, 1964; 1 child, Joshua David. BFA, Boston U., 1963; postgrad., Monmouth Coll., 1971-73; MA, L.I. U., 1977. Instr. drawing Great Neck (N.Y.) Union Free Schs., 1979-85; asst. Ruth Leaf Studios, Douglaston, N.Y., 1986-90; instr. art Rockville Centre (N.Y.) Sr. Svcs., 1984-89, 92-93; instr. printmaking Great Neck Union Free Schs., 1985—; instr. workshop Queens Art Alliance, Forest Hills, N.Y., 1989, 90, L.I. Art Tchrs. Assn., Garden City, N.Y., 1991; coord. faculty exhbn. Great Neck Union Free Schs., 1991; curator, organizer One Over One/Monotypes, Great Neck House, 1994; speaker in field. Exhbns. include Snug Harbor Cultural Ctr., 1994, Silvermine, New Canaan, Conn., 1994, Firehouse Galleries, Garden City, 1994, Islip (N.Y.) Art Mus., 1993, Walsh Gallery, Fairfield, Conn., 1993. Art chair Great Neck Breast Cancer Coalition, 1993—. Recipient Chase Manhattan Bank Community award in Art, 1988, Fine Arts Mus. L.I. award 1990, Network Exhbn. Nassau Mus. Art award Honor, 1992, Southwest Tex. State U. Purchase award, 1993. Mem. Nat. Drawing Assn. (exhbns. exec. bd. 1991—), Artist Network Great Neck. Home: 44 Colgate Rd Great Neck NY 11023

SINGER, SARAH BETH, poet; b. N.Y.C., July 4, 1915; d. Samuel and Rose (Dunetz) White; m. Leon Eugene Singer, Nov. 23, 1938; children: Jack, Rachel. B.A., NYU, 1934; postgrad., New Sch. Social Research, 1961-63. Tchr. creative writing Hillside Hosp., Queens, N.Y., 1964-75, Samuel Field YMHA, Queens, 1980-82. Author: Magic Casements, 1957, After the Beginning, 1975, Of Love and Shoes, 1987, The Gathering, 1992; contbr. poetry to anthologies, poetry mags. and quars. including American Women Poets, 1976, Yearbook of American Poetry, 1981, The Best of 1980, 1981, Filtered Images, 1992, The Croton Rev., The Lyric, Bitterroot, Judaism, Encore, The Jewish Frontier, Yankee, Hartford Courant, Poet Lore, N.Y. Times, Christian Sci. Monitor, Voices Internat., The Round Table, Orphic Lute, Brussels Sprout, Poetry and Medicine Column Jour. AMA, The Shakespeare Newsletter Midstream; cons. editor Poet Lore, 1975-81. Recipient Stephen Vincent Benet award Poet Lore, 1968, 71, Dellbrook award Shenandoah Valley Acad. Lit. and Dellbrook-Shenandoah Coll. Writers' Conf., 1978, 79, C.W. Post poetry award, 1979, 80, award for best poem Lyric quar., 1981, biennial award for achievement in poetry Seattle Br. Nat. League of Am. Penwomen, 1988, award for traditional poetry Wash. Poets Assn., Cert. of Merit Muse Mag., 1990, Editor's Choice award for haiku Brussels Sprout, 1992, poem chosen for Metro Bus. Poetry Project Seattle, 1992, poem Upon My Demise translated into Russian, recorded; recipient 1st prize Marj McAlister award Voices Internat., 1993, Honorable Mention, Lily Peter Meml. award, 1993. Mem. PEN, Nat. League Am. Penwomen (poetry chmn. L.I. br. 1957-87, publicity chmn. 1990, sec. Seattle br. 1990, pres. 1992—, v.p. 1994—, publicity chmn. for State of Wash. 1992—, Marion Doyle Meml. award 1976, 1st prize nat. poetry contest 1976, Drama award 1977, Poetry award 1977, 1st prize for modern rhymed poetry 1978, Lectr. award 1980, Sonnet award Alexandria br. 1980, 81, Catherine Cushman Leach award 1982; poetry award Phoenix br. 1983, Pasadena br. 1984, Alexandria br. 1985, 1st prize award Portland br. 1990, structured verse award Spokane br. 1992, Della Crowder Miller Meml. Petrarchan Sonnet award 1994, 2d prize Catherine Cushman Leach Poetry award 1994, Honorable Mention Anita Marie Boggs Meml. award 1994, Owl award Seattle br. 1994), Poetry Soc. Am. (v.p. 1974-78, exec. dir. L.I. 1979-83, James Joyce award 1972, Consuelo Ford award 1973, Gustav Davidson award 1974, 1st prize award 1975, Celia Wagner award 1976), Poets and Writers, Annual award for Achievement in Poetry Seattle Branch Nat. League Am. Penwomen, 1994. Address: 2360 43rd Ave E Apt 415 Seattle WA 98112-2703

SINGER, SHELLEY, author; b. Mpls., Feb. 6, 1939; d. Ralph Singer and Dorothy Rose (Lewis) Singer Fenick; 1 child, Sonya Drew Singer-Solomon. BA, U. Minn., 1961. Book critic KPFA Radio, Berkeley, Calif., 1989—; instr. of mystery writing U. Calif. Extension, Berkeley, 1993—; Coll. of Marin, Calif., 1994—; writing cons., Fairfax, Calif., 1990—. Author: The Demeter Flower, 1980, Samson's Deal, 1983, Free Draw, 1984, Full House, 1986, Spit in the Ocean, 1987, Suicide King, 1988, Following Jane, 1993, Picture of David, 1993, Searching for Sara, 1994. Mem. Mystery Writers Am., Sisters in Crime, Am. Crime Writers' League, Nat. Writers' Union. Home and Office: 7 Upper Ridgeway Fairfax CA 94930

SINGER, SUSANNA ESMAN, artists agent; b. N.Y.C., Oct. 5, 1952; d. Aaron Hirsch and Rosa Hannah (Mencher) E.; m. Peter Entin Singer, Sept. 15, 1974; 1 child, Max Esman. BA, U. Pitts., 1974. Sec. John Weber Gallery, N.Y.C., 1975-77, dir., 1977-80; pres. Susanna Singer Inc., N.Y.C., 1980—; bd. dirs. Watanabe Studio, Bklyn. Co-editor: Robert Mangold Paintings, 1968-82; editor: Sol Lewitt Wall Drawings, 1968-84, 84, Sol Lewitt Wall Drawings, 1984-92, 92, Sol Lewitt Drawings, 1958-92; curator, editor (exhibition and catalogue) Drawings for Outdoor Sculpture, 1977. Mem. Arttable Inc., Fieldson Sch. Alumni Bd. (v.p. 1990-93). Home and Office: 50 Riverside Dr New York NY 10024

SINGER, SUZANNE FRIED, editor; b. N.Y.C., July 9, 1935; d. Maurice Aaron and Augusta G. (Ginsberg) Fried; m. Max Singer, Feb. 12, 1959; children: Saul, Alexander, Daniel, Benjamin. BA with honors, Swarthmore Coll., 1956; MA, Columbia U., 1958. Program asst. NSF, Washington, 1958-60; assoc. editor Bibl. Archaeology Rev., Washington, 1979-84, mng. editor, 1984—; mng. editor Bibl. Rev., Washington, 1985-94, exec. editor, 1994—; mng. editor Moment, Washington, 1990—. Mem. Am. Schs. Oriental Rsch., Soc. Bibl. Lit. Jewish. Office: Bibl Archaeology Soc 4710 41st St NW Washington DC 20016

SINGH, CAROLYN DIANA SCHMITZ, artist, educator; b. St. Paul, May 11, 1947; d. Gordon Rudolph Schmitz and Shirley Kay (Lawrence) Woolf; m. Vijay Pal Singh, Dec. 22, 1972; children: Vincent Ajay Pal, Gordon Ranjeet Rampal. BA, BFA, U. Minn., 1972. Artist U.S. and Mex., 1972—; tchr. Alice P. Smyth Ctr., Newark, Del., 1974-76, Carolyn Singh Studio, El Paso, 1976—, El Paso Mus. Art, 1983—, Western Hills Elem. Sch. After Sch. Enrichment, El Paso, 1990, Ft. Hancock Ind. Sch. Dist. Enrichment, Ft. Hancock and El Paso, 1994, Divsn. Profl. and Continuing Edn., U. Tex., El Paso, 1994—; coord. Seven Points of View, Americana Mus., El Paso, 1993, West Tex. Artists in Berlin, Germany, 1994—. Exhibited in solo shows at Dallas Ford Gallery, 1993, Corbett Ctr. Gallery, 1984; group shows include Americana Mus., 1993, Univ. Art Gallery, N.Mex. State U., 1994; works included in Artists on Art series, 1993, Seven Points of View, 1993. Mem. co. Sta. KCOS Pub. TV Arts Auction Com., El Paso, 1982; report writer artists com. El. Paso Com. for Arts, El Paso, 1985-86. Mem. S.W. Watercolor Soc., Tex. Watercolor Soc. (signature mem., Nat. Bank of Commerce prize 1984), N.Mex. Watercolor Soc. (signature mem., 1st pl. award 1989), Rio Bravo Watercolorists (pres. 1987-88, 93-94, 1st v.p. 1991-92, 1st pl. award 1984, 2d pl. award 1994). Studio: Carolyn Singh Studio 716 La Mancha Ct El Paso TX 79922

SINGH, HARJEET KAUR, artist; b. Nanital, India, May 15, 1935; came to U.S., 1967; d. Balwant and Dharam (Kaur) Singh; m. Avtar Singh, Apr. 13, 1956; children: Gobind Sharan Singh, Harsharan Kaur Singh. Grad., Bangla Sahib, Delhi, India, 1952. Instr. gourmet cooking. Exhibited in Beaufort County Arts Coun. Fine Arts Show, Washington, N.C., 1994. Organizer, condr. discussion seminars East West Fellowship, Starkville, Miss., 1968-70; performer India music concerts U. Ala., Tuscaloosa, 1968-70; in-charge sect. Asian Studies Program, Greenville, N.C., 1973—; vol. Easter Seals, 1988, 90, Heart Fund, 1992. Mem. Univ. Women's Club (pres. knitting sect. 1982-87), Greenville Woman's Club. Sikh. Home and Studio: PO Box 2801 Greenville NC 27836

SINGLEHURST, DONA GEISENHEYNER, horse farm owner; b. Tacoma, June 19, 1928; d. Herbert Russell and Rose Evelyn (Rubish) Geisenheyner; m. Thomas G. Singlehurst, May 16, 1959 (dec.); 1 child, Suzanna Singlehurst. BA in Psychology, Whitman Coll., 1950. With pub. rels. and advt. staff Lane Wells, L.A., 1950-52; staff mem. in charge new bus. Bishop Trust Co., Honolulu, 1953-58; mgr. Town & Country Stables, Honolulu, 1958-62; co-owner, v.p. pub. rels. Carol & Mary, Ltd., Honolulu, 1964-84; owner Stanhope Farms, Waialua, Hawaii, 1969—; internat. dressage judge, sport horse breeding judge Am. Horse Shows Assn.; sr. judge Can. Dressage Fedn. Chmn. ways and means com. The Outdoor Cir., Hawaii, 1958-64, life mem.; pres. emeritus Morris Animal Found., Englewood, Colo., 1988—, pres., 1984-88; bd. dirs., pres. Delta Soc., 1994—; mem. Jr. League of Honolulu. Recipient Best Friends award Honolulu Vt. Soc., 1986, Spl. Recognition award Am. Animal Hosp. Assn., 1988, Recognition award Am. Vet. Med. Assn., 1992. Mem. NAFE, Hawaii Horse Show Assn. (Harry Hutaff award 1985, past pres., bd. dirs.), Hawaii Combined Tng. Assn. (past pres. bd. dirs.), Calif. Dressage Soc., U.S. Dressage Fedn., U.S. Equestrian Team (area chmn. 1981-85), Hawaiian Human Soc. (life), U.S. Pony Clubs (dist. commr. 1970-75, nat. examiner 1970-75), Pacific Club, Outrigger Canoe Club. Republican. Episcopalian. Home and Office: Stanhope Farms Waialua HI 96791

SINGLETON, DEBRA LYNN, accountant; b. Oscado, Mich., May 19, 1963; d. Richard Raymond and Judith Ann (Julius) Steele; m. George William Singleton, July 11, 1992. BSBA, U. N.C., 1985; postgrad., Francis Marion U., 1992-95. CPA, S.C. Gen. acct. Sonoco Products Co., Hartsville, S.C., 1985-87, jr. internal auditor, 1987-88, ops. acct. II, 1988-90, ops. acct. III, 1990—. Mem. bldg. fund St. Mary's Cath. Ch., Hartsville, 1990—, pres. fin. com., 1992-94. Mem. AICPA, Nat. Assn. Accts. (pres. 1990-91), Inst. Mgmt. Accts. (treas., v.p. adminstrn., various other positions). Office: Sonoco Products Co N 2d St W23 Hartsville SC 29550

SINGLETON, SARA, banker; b. Reading, Pa., Feb. 19, 1940; d. Walter S. and Sarah (Hain) Shearer; m. John H. Singleton, Nov. 9, 1957; children: Joanne Reagan, Suzanne Oliver. Student, Ursinus Coll., 1979-86. Teller, customer svc. rep. S.E. Nat. Bank, Phoenixville, Pa., 1972-81; mgmt. trainee Red Hill (Pa.) Savs. and Loan Assn., 1981, asst. mgr. ops., 1982-84; mgr. deposit acctg. Sovereign Bank, FSB, Wyomissing, Pa., 1984, asst. v.p. deposit svcs., 1984-86, v.p. deposit svcs., 1987—; mem. check product adv. group Phila. Res. Bank, 1988—. Pres. Mont Clare (Pa.) Home and Sch. Assn., 1973-75; officer, bd. dirs. Holy Ghost Ch., Phoenixville, 1974-84; cons. Greater Valley Coun. Girls Scouts U.S., Reading, 1988—. Mem. Nat. Assn. Banking Women (treas. Reading 1988), Berks County C. of C. (amb. com. 1986-88, edn. com. 1988—), Fin. Women Internat. (co-chair Berks County job fair 1990). Home: 310 Woodlyn Dr Collegeville PA 19426-2722 Office: Soverign Bank FSB 1130 Berkshire Blvd Reading PA 19610-1200

SINGREEN, SHIRLEY ANN BASILE (MRS. HARRY VOSS SINGREEN), lawyer; b. New Orleans, Apr. 10, 1941; d. Dominick Joseph and Rose Aile (O'Reilly) Basile; m. Harry Voss Singreen, May 12, 1979; children: Michael Harry, Elizabeth Alexandra. AB, Loyola U., New Orleans, 1962, JD, 1964. Bar: La. 1964. Law clk. Civil Dist. Ct., 1964-65; assoc. Doyle, Smith & Doyle, New Orleans, 1965-66; staff counsel U.S. Ct. Appeals (5th cir.), New Orleans, 1966-68; assoc. Plaintiff's Personal Injury Firm, New Orleans, 1968-71; spl. rsch. cons. Henican, James & Cleveland, New Orleans, 1972-73; sr. law clk. 24th Jud. Dist. Ct., Jefferson Parish, La., 1973-76; appellate counsel, legal cons., trial analyst, New Orleans. Mem. La. State Bar Assn., New Orleans Notaries Assn., Phi Alpha Delta. Republican. Roman Catholic. Office: 260 Audubon Blvd New Orleans LA 70125-4125

SINK, CATHY ROBERTS, psychologist; b. L.A., Dec. 25, 1952; d. Walter Lusk and Charlotte (Rasmussen) Roberts; m. Jeffrey Carter Sink, June 22, 1974; 1 child, Ian Matthew. BA in Psychology, UCLA, 1974; PhD in Clin. Psychology, Fuller Grad Sch., 1979. Lic. psychologist Alaska. Intern Camarillo (Calif.) State Hosp., 1978-79; staff counselor, asst. prof. psychology U. Alaska, Fairbanks, 1990-94. Postdoctoral fellow Pasadena (Calif.) Community Counseling Clinic, 1979-80. Mem. Am. Psychol. Assn., Internat. Psychol. Assn. Home: 3220 Oakshire Ln Chino Hills CA 91709

SINKFORD, JEANNE CRAIG, dentist, educator; b. Washington, Jan. 30, 1933; d. Richard E. and Geneva (Jefferson) Craig; m. Stanley M. Sinkford, Dec. 8, 1951; children: Dianne Sylvia, Janet Lynn, Stanley M. III. BS, Howard U., 1953, MS, 1962, DDS, 1958, PhD, 1963; DSc (hon.), Georgetown U., 1978; DSc (Hon.), U. Med. and Dentistry of N.J., 1992. Instr. prosthodontics Sch. Dentistry Howard U., Washington, 1958-60, mem. faculty dentistry, 1964—, rsch. coord., co-chmn. dept. restorative dentistry, assoc. dean, 1968-75, dean, 1975-91, prof. Prosthodontics Grad. Sch., 1977-91; dean emeritus, prof. Sch. Dentistry Howard U.; spl. asst. Am. Assn. Dental Schs., 1991-93, dir. office women and minority affairs, 1993—; instr. rsch. and crown and bridge Northwestern U. Sch. Dentistry, 1963-64; cons. prosthodontics and rsch. VA Hosp., Washington, 1965—; resident Children's Hosp. Nat. Med. Ctr., 1974-75; cons. St. Elizabeth's Hosp.; mem. attending staff Freedman's Hosp., Washington, 1964—; adv. bd. D.C. Gen. Hosp., 1975—; mem. Nat. Adv. Dental Rsch. Coun., Nat. Bd. Dental Examiners; mem. ad hoc adv. panel Tuskegee Syphilis Study for HEW; sponsor D.C. Pub. Health Apprentice Program; mem. adv. coun. to dir. NIH; adv. com. NIH/NIDR/NIA Aging Rsch. Coun.; mem. dental devices classification panel FDA; mem. select panel for promotion child health, 1979-80; mem. spl. med. adv. group VA; bd. overseers U. Pa. Dental Sch., Boston U. Dental Sch.; bd. advs. U. Pitts. Dental Sch.; mem. anat. rev. bd. for D.C. NRC Gov. Bd.; cons. Food and Drug Adminstrn.; Nat. Adv. Rsch. Coun., 1993—; active Nat. Rsch. Coun. Governing Bd. Mem. editorial rev. bd. Jour. Am. Coll. Dentists, 1988—. Adv. bd. United Negro Coll. Fund, Robert Wood Johnson Health Policy Fellowships; mem. Mayor's Block Grant Adv. Com., 1982; mem. parents' coun. Sidwell Friends, 1983; mem. adv. bd. D.C., mem. Women's Health Task Force, NIH; bd. dirs. Girl Scouts U.S.A., 1993—. Louise C. Ball fellow grad. tng., 1960-63. Fellow Am. Coll. Dentists (sec.-treas. Wash. met. sect.), Internat. Coll. Dentists (award of merit); mem. ADA (chmn. appeal bd. coun. on dental edn. 1975-82), Am. Soc. for Geriatric Dentistry (bd. dirs.), Internat. Assn. Dental Research, Dist. Dental Soc., Am. Inst. Oral Biology, North Portal Civic League, Inst. Grad. Dentists (trustee), So. Conf. Dental Deans (chmn.), Wash. Coun. Adminstrv. Women, Assn. Am. Women Dentists, Am. Pedodontic Soc., Am. Prosthodontic Soc., Fed. Prosthodontic Orgn., Nat. Dental Assn., Inst. Medicine (coun.), Am. Soc. Dentistry for Children, N.Y. Acad. Scis., Smithsonian Assocs., Dean's Coun., Proctor and Gamble, Golden Key Honor Soc., Links Inc., Sigma Xi (pres.), Phi Beta Kappa, Omicron Kappa Upsilon, Psi Chi, Beta Kappa Chi. Address: 1765 Verbena St NW Washington DC 20012-1048

SINKIN, FAY MARIE, environmentalist; b. N.Y.C., Mar. 24, 1918; d. Joseph E. and Amelia (Kronish) Bloom; m. William R. Sinkin, May 31, 1942; children: Richard, Lanny. BA, Syracuse U., 1938. Pres. LWV, San Antonio, 1947-51; pres., organizer Vis. Nurse Assn., San Antonio, 1952-54; pres. Brandeis U. Women's Com., San Antonio, 1954-56; recruiter, cons. U.S. State Dept. (A.I.D.), Washington, 1963-67; pres. Aquifer Protection Assn., San Antonio, 1974-80, Portrait of Am. Women, San Antonio, 1976-82; chair Bexar County/Edwards Underground Water Dist., San Antonio, 1983-89; chairwoman Edwards Aquifer Preservation Trust, San Antonio, 1990. Editor (pamphlet) Is Applewhite Necessary?, 1978. Named Woman of Yr. Express New Publ., 1964, Sunday Woman San Antonio Light, 1965, Mother of Yr. Avance, 1988; recipient WICI award Women in Comm., 1989, Spirit of Giving award J.C. Penney, 1993; elected to Women's Hall of Fame, San Antonio, 1985. Mem. San Antonio 100, Tex. Internat. Woman's Forum. Democrat. Jewish. Home: 125 Saint Dennis Ave San Antonio TX 78209-5253

SINKIS, DEBORAH MARY, principal; b. Worcester, Mass., May 13, 1949; d. Peter Paul and Joanne Mary (Dumphy) Shemeth; m. Ben J. Sinkis, June 8, 1969; 1 child, Russell John. BS in Elem. Edn., Worcester State Coll., 1970, MEd, 1977, cert. in curriculum, 1981; cert. in interactive tech., Harvard U., 1989; EdD in Ednl. Adminstrn., U. Mass., 1993. Tchr. Worcester Pub. Schs., 1971-83, computer assisted instr., 1983-86, tchr. trainer for computers, 1986, citywide computer coord., 1986-89; prin. Millbury St. Sch., Worcester, 1989-90, F.J. McGrath Sch., Worcester, 1990—; cons. in computer edn. Author curriculum materials. Mem. computer coop. regional adv. coun. Mass. Commn. for Deaf and Hard of Hearing, 1989-90. Named Woman of Distinction Montachusett Girl Scout Coun., 1994. Mem. ASCD, NEA, Mass. Tchrs. Assn., Internat. Soc. Tech. in Edn., Internat. Cath. Deaf Assn., Harvard/Radcliffe Club, Quota Internat. (Deaf Woman of Yr. award 1991), Phi Delta Kappa (Adminstr. of Yr. 1994). Office: Worcester Pub Schs 20 Irving St Worcester MA 01609-2493

SIPKA, JULIE K., architect; b. Akron, Ohio, July 29, 1964; d. Aldo Joseph Tersigni and Joanne Ruth (Circullo) Kelley; m. Gerald B. Sipka, June 16, 1989. BS in Architecture, Kent State Univ., 1982-87. Registered architect, Ohio. Archtl. intern K. Anthony Hayek Assocs., Youngstown, Ohio, 1987-88, Chemstress Consulting Co., Akron, 1988-89, Peterson/Raeder Architects, Akron, 1989, Illes Architects, Medina, Ohio, 1989-91; architect Illes Architects, Medina, 1994—; archtl. intern David Pelligra & Architects, Cuyahoga Falls, Ohio, 1991-94; notary public. Chair Bd. Zoning Appeals, Fairlawn, Ohio, 1992—. Mem. Medina Sunrise Rotary Club. Office: Kerry Illes Architects 5000 Gateway Dr Medina OH 44256-8638

SIPPEL, FRANCES MARIE, microbiologist, business owner; b. Phila., Apr. 17, 1930; d. Jacob Harry Jr. and Catharine Seachrist (Hershey) Pickle; m. Roy Joseph Sippel, Feb. 8, 1958 (div. June 1979). BA in Biology and Chemistry with honors, Hood Coll., 1952; MS in Microbiology, U. Pitts., 1956. Rsch. asst. to Dr. Jonas Salk U. Pitts., 1955; rsch. asst. to Dr. T.S. Danowski Children's Hosp., Pitts., 1956; bacteriologist Shadyside Hosp., Pitts., 1956-57; rsch. asst. to Dr. Leonard Hayflick Wistar Inst., Phila., 1958-59; asst. editor Biol. Abstracts, Phila., 1959-60; lit. chemist E.I. du Pont de Nemours & Co., Wilmington, Del., 1960-66; sec.-treas. Can-Am Sales Corp., West Chester, Pa., 1972-73; sales rep. Quick Courier Svc., Phila., 1977-82; owner Color Profile, West Chester, 1982—. Bd. dirs. Chester County (Pa.) Emergency Med. Svcs., 1980—; chair Chester County coun. LWV, 1993—; co-chair Holiday House Tour, 1989-93; vol. YWCA. Mem. AAUW (Outstanding Woman from West Chester br. 1991), Am. Soc. Microbiologists, Phila. Hood Coll. Club (past pres.), Chester County Hist. Soc. (antiques show com.), Wilmington Country Club. Republican. Unitarian Universalist. Home and Office: 975 Penn Dr S West Chester PA 19380-4339

SIPPEL, SANDRA LYNNE, industrial food broker; b. Charlotte, N.C., Sept. 16, 1947; d. Richard Oliver McCorkle and Norma Terry (Hardie) Howard; m. Nickie B. Penrod, Oct. 15, 1967 (div. June 1975); children: Debrah L., Richard P.; m. John H. Murray, July 4, 1981 (div. Sept. 1982); m. David Lee Sippel, Apr. 17, 1993. Student, U. S.C., 1966, Meramec Community Coll., St. Louis, 1971. Office clk. G.S. Suppiger Co., St. Louis, 1967-69, Comml. Printing Co., St. Louis, 1969-70; office mgr. St. Louis Food Sales, Inc., 1970-84, v.p., 1981-84; pres. Midwest Indsl. Food Sales, Inc., 1984-85, Indsl. Food Ingredients, Inc., Arnold, Mo., 1985—. Author: Great Poets of Today, 1987 (Golden Poet award 1987), World Poetry Anthology, 1987. Pres., bd. dirs. Jefferson County no. unit Am. Cancer Soc., 1989-92; vol. counselor women's shelter A Safe Place; sec. bd. dirs. Rocky Ridge Ranch Property Owner's Assn. Trustees, 1993-94; tutor Project Literacy, 1988-90. Recipient Cert. Recognition Mo. Ho. Reps., 1992. Mem. Arnold C. of C. (v.p. bd. dirs. 1993, office dir. 1985—, co-editor newsletter 1990-91, editor 1991-93, chmn. Easter program, v.p. bd. dirs. Arnold Days Parade com., v.p. 1993). Office: PO Box 467 Arnold MO 63010

SIPPEL, SUSAN ANN, public relations executive, speaker; b. Milw., Apr. 6, 1951; d. Richard Frederick and Virginia Catherine (Lange) Kuether; m. Leonard Claude Sippel, Jan. 14, 1978 (div. Mar. 1980); children: Benjamin, Elizabeth. BS, U. Wis., 1973. Field dir. Woodland Girl Scout Coun., Wisconsin Rapids, 1973-75; assoc. dir. U. Wis. Alumni Assn., Stevens Point, 1975-76; field/residential camp dir. Girl Scout Coun. Pacific, Honolulu, 1977-79; with Discovery Toys, Detroit and Virginia Beach, Va., 1981-89; dir. comm. CAP Svcs., Stevens Point, 1990—. Yearround com. chair United Way, Stevens Point, 1993-94; chair pub. rels. comm. WISCAP, Madison, 1994; commr. Stevens Point Housing Authority, 1994. Mem. Ctrl. Wis. Network (pres., v.p., social com. chair, pub. rels. com. 1990-94, sec.). Office: CAP Svcs Inc 5499 Hwy 10 E Stevens Point WI 54481

SIRIANNI, BRIDGET ANN, radiologic technologist; b. Sunbury, Pa., Aug. 25, 1962; d. Joseph Jerome and June Marie (Daddario) Costello; m. David Scott Sirianni, Apr. 15, 1994. Grad. in radiol. tech., Sch. Radiology, Mercy Med. Ctr., 1993. Registered radiol. technologist. Radiol. technologist Sunbury (Pa.) Cmty. Hosp., 1993—. Mem. Am. Soc. Radiol. Technologists, Pa. Soc. Radiol. Technologists. Roman Catholic. Home: 822 Lincoln St Milton PA 17847

SIRO, CAROL MARIE, language arts educator; b. Flushing, N.Y., Apr. 11, 1947; d. William Joseph and Carolina A. (Brouwers) Taubert; m. Francis A. Siro, Aug. 2, 1969; children: Matthew, Christel, Laura, Stephanie. BA in Elem. and Spl. Edn., St. Joseph Coll., 1969; M of Edn., cert. reading specialist, East Stroudsburg U., 1988. Tchr. 3d grade Rockaway (N.J.) Borough Pub. Schs., 1969-70; tchr. 3d and 6th grade St. John's Sch., Waterloo, Belgium, 1970-72; tchr. spl. edn. 9-12 grade Oscoda (Mich.) Pub. Schs., 1979-80; tchr. spl. edn. 7th and 8th grade Sussex (N.J.)-Wantage Schs., 1980-85, tchr. 6th grade, 1985-93, tchr. lang. arts 7th and 8th grade, 1993—. Mem. NEA, Internat. Reading Assn., N.J. Edn. Assn., N.W. N.J. Reading Coun. Roman Catholic. Office: Sussex Middle Sch Loomis Ave Sussex NJ 07461

SIROIS, PATRICIA A., psychologist; b. Miami, Fla., Aug. 12, 1951; d. Patrick S. and Dorothy (Laliberte) S. BA, Loyola U., New Orleans, 1973; MS, U. New Orleans, 1986, PhD, 1991. Clin. asst. dept. psychology Children's Hosp., New Orleans, 1988-91; tech. rsch. specialist dept. medicine Tulane U. Med. Ctr., New Orleans, 1991-92, rsch. instr., 1992—; adj. instr. dept. pediatrics Tulane U. Med. Ctr., 1993—; adj. prof. The Union Inst., Cin., 1992—; cons. Tulane U. Med. Ctr., 1988-91. Mem. NO-AIDS Task Force, New Orleans, 1986—; mem. Faubourg Marigny Improvement Assn., New Orleans, 1990—, Vieux Carre Property Owners, Residents and Assocs., New Orleans, 1990—. Mem. Am. Psychol. Assn., Am. Psychol. Soc., So. Soc. Philosophy and Psychology, Am. Assn. Applied and Preventive Psychology, Soc. for Rsch. in Child Devel., Sigma Xi. Office: Tulane U Med Ctr 1430 Tulane Ave (SL-78) New Orleans LA 70112

SIROWER, BONNIE FOX, fundraising executive; b. Bklyn., Jan. 9, 1949; d. Stanley S. and Harriet (Fischer) Fox; m. Martin Alan Sirower, Sept. 20, 1970; children: Kenneth, Daniel. AB, Barnard Coll., 1970; MA, Columbia U., 1971. Tchr. United Cerebral Palsy, N.Y.C., 1970-73, Bergen County Bd. Spl. Svcs., Paramus, N.J., 1973-76; spl. events coord. Am. Heart Assn., Glen Ridge, N.J., 1979-81; dir. devel. Goodwill Industries, Astoria, N.Y., 1981-83; pres. Access Unltd., 1984-85; dir. devel. Cheshire Home, Inc., 1986-89, Barnert Hosp., Paterson, N.J., 1989—. Commr. Paterson (N.J.) Coun. for Disabled, 1994; trustee YMCA of Paterson, 1991—. Mem. N.J. Soc. Fund Raising Execs. (bd. dirs. 1989, chmn. mentoring com., chmn. N.J. Conf. on Philanthropy 1994), Assn. Fund Raisers for Disabled (pres. 1981-83), N.J. Puzzlers' League (pres.), Barnard Coll. Class of '70 (pres. 1990—), Rotary Internat. (v.p. Paterson), Bergen Women of Accomplishment, Phi Beta Kappa. Jewish. Home: 69 Godfrey Ter Glen Rock NJ 07452-3510

SISCHY, INGRID BARBARA, magazine editor, art critic; b. Johannesburg, Republic of South Africa, Mar. 2, 1952; came to U.S., 1967; d. Benjamin and Claire S. BS, Sarah Lawrence Coll., 1973; PhD (hon.), Moore Coll. Art, 1987. Assoc. editor Print Collector's Newsletter, N.Y.C., 1974-77; dir. Printed Matter, N.Y.C., 1977-78; curatorial intern Mus. Modern Art, N.Y.C., 1978-79; editor ArtForum Mag., N.Y.C., 1979-88; editor-in-chief Interview, N.Y.C., 1989—. Office: Interview Magazine 575 Broadway 5th Fl New York NY 10012-3230*

SISEMORE, CLAUDIA, producer-director educational films and videos; b. Salt Lake City, Sept. 16, 1937; d. Darrell Daniel and Alice Larril (Barton) S. BS in English, Brigham Young U., 1959; MFA in Filmmaking, U. Utah, 1976. Cert. secondary tchr., Utah. Tchr. English, drama and writing Salt Lake Sch. Dist., Salt Lake City, 1959-66; tchr. English Davis Sch. Dist., Bountiful, Utah, 1966-68; ind. filmmaker Salt Lake City, 1972—; filmmaker-in-residence Wyo. Coun. for Arts and Nat. Endowment for Arts, Dubois, Wyo., 1977-78; prodr., dir. ednl. films Utah Office Edn., Salt Lake City, 1979-93, Canyon Video, 1993—. Prodr., dir. Beginning of Winning, 1984 (film festival award 1984), Dancing through the Magic Eye, 1986, Se Hable Espanol, 1986-87; writer, dir., editor (film) Building on a Legacy, 1988, (videos) Energy Conservation, 1990, Alternative Energy Sources, 1990, Restructuring Learning, 1991, Kidsercise, 1991, Traditional Energy Sources, 1992, A State Government Team, 1992, Problem Solving Using Math Manipulatives, 1993, Canyon Video, 1993—; videos Western Mountains and Basins, 1994, Bikes, Boards and Blades, 1994; exhibited (abstract paintings) in group show Phillips Gallery; represented in numerous pvt. and pub. collections. Juror Park City (Utah) Arts Festival, 1982, Utah Arts Festival, Salt Lake City, 1982, Am. Film Festival, 1985-86, Best of West Film Festival, 1985-86; bd. dirs. Utah Media Ctr., Salt Lake City, 1981-87; mem. multidisciplinary program Utah Arts Coun., Salt Lake City, 1983-87. Recipient award Utah Media Ctr., 1984, 85; Nat. Endowment for Arts grantee, 1978, Utah Arts Coun. grantee, 1980. Mormon.

SISKIN, CARYL F., women's health primary care nurse practitioner; b. Louisville, June 2, 1939; d. Ralph E. and Esther Marian (Binder) Flumbaum; m. Michael Baggish, 1960 (div. 1983); children: Jeffrey Steven Baggish, Mindy Ann Baggish, Cindy Beth Baggish, Stuart Harrison Baggish; m. Robert S. Siskin, 1985. Diploma, St. Anthony Hosp. Sch. Nursing, 1960; student, Nazareth Coll., Johns Hopkins U.; BSN summa cum laude, U. Hartford, 1980. Cert. NCC, oby-gyn NP. Head nurse Womens Clinic Johns Hopkins Hosp., Balt.; clin. instr., ob-gyn. dept. Mt. Sinai Hosp., Hartford, Conn.; mem. inernat. health care team S.E. Asia U.S. AID, 1973-74; ob-gyn. N.P. collaborative practice George Bacall, M.D., Hartford, 1974-90; pvt. practice Bloomfield, Conn., 1990-94. Vol. local soup kitchen. Mem. ANA, Nurses Assn. of Am. Coll. Ob-Gyn., Am. Acad. Nurse Practitioners, Assn. Reproductive Health Profls., Am. Fertility Soc., Jewish Arts Found., Temple Israel Sisterhood, Sigma Theta Tau (1st pres. Iota Upsilon chpt.). Home: 20 Kensington Park Bloomfield CT 06002-2146

SISKO, MARIE FERRARIS, fund raising executive; b. N.Y.C.; d. Joseph and Jean (Boaro) F. B.A., Queens Coll., 1975; postgrad. Adelphi U., 1976; divorced; children—Warren Joseph, Robert Edward. Pers. dir. Daypac Inc., 1969-70; sales asst. Ponder & Best, 1971-73; sales adminstr. Ampacet Corp., 1973-75; mktg. rep. Better Bus. Bur., 1975-77; ast. dir. Leukemia Soc. Am., 1978-82; campaign dir. Ketchum, Inc., 1982-85; dir. maj. gifts Seton Hall U., 1985-88; program dir. Brakeley, John Price Jones, 1988-93; v.p. Sisko Enterprises N.Y. World's Fair, 1963-65. Mem. Nat. Soc. Fund Raising Execs. (CFRE), Queens Coll. Alumni Assn. (pres. Ace chpt. 1977-79). Lutheran. Home: 32 Center Dr Flushing NY 11357-1005

SISLEY, BECKY LYNN, physical education educator; b. Seattle, May 10, 1939; d. Leslie James and Blanche (Howe) S.; m. Jerry Newcomb, 1994. BA, U. Wash., 1961; MSPE, U. N.C., 1964, EdD, 1973. Tchr. Lake Washington High Sch., Kirkland, Wash., 1961-62; instr. U. Wis., Madison, 1963-65, U. Oreg., Eugene, 1965-68; prof. phys. edn. U. Oreg., 1968—, women's athletic dir., 1973-79, head undergrad. studies in phys. edn., 1985-92. Co-author: Softball for Girls, 1971; contbr. articles to profl. jours. Admitted to Hall of Fame, N.W. Women's Sports Found., Seattle, 1981, Honor Awad, N.W. Dist. Assn. for Health, Phys. Edn., Recreation and Dance, 1988. Mem. AAHPERD, Oreg. Alliance Health, Phys. Edn., Recreation and Dance (hon. life mem.), Western Soc. for Phys. Edn. of Coll. Women (exec. bd. 1982-85), Oreg. High Sch. Coaches Assn., Nat. Softball Coaches Acad., N.W. Coll. Women's Sports Assn. (pres. 1977-78), Oreg. Women's Sports Leadership Network (dir. 1987—), Phi Epsilon Kappa, others. Office: University of Oregon Phys Activity & Recreation Svcs Eugene OR 97403

SISLEY, EMILY LUCRETIA, psychologist, medical writer; b. North Charleroi, Pa., May 7, 1930; d. Frederick William and Harriet Watkins (Litman) S. PhD in Clin. Psychology, L.I. U., 1972. Diplomate Am. Bd. Med. Psychotherapists. Mng. editor Med. Jours., Harper & Row, N.Y.C., 1960-67; freelance med. writer-editor N.Y.C., 1967—; supervising psychologist, dept. psychiatry Roosevelt Hosp., N.Y.C., 1972-77; clin. instr. Columbia Univ. Coll. Physicians and Surgeons, N.Y.C., 1975-77; chief psychologist Gramercy Park Inst., N.Y.C., 1978-84; staff therapist MedcoBehavioral Care Sys., N.Y.C., 1984—; cons. Internat. Jour. Group Tensions, N.Y.C., 1968-72. Illustrator: You and Your Brain, 1963, Thomas Alva Edison award, 1963; co-author: The Vitamin C Connection, 1983; contbr. articles to profl. jours. Fellow Am. Bd. Med. Psychotherapists; mem. APA, N.Y. Acad. Scis. Democrat. Episcopalian.

SISLEY, NINA MAE, physician, public health officer; b. Jacksonville, Fla., Aug. 19, 1924; d. Leonard Percy and Verna (Martin) S.; m. George W. Fischer, May 16, 1962 (dec. 1990). BA, Tex. State Coll. for Women, 1944; MD, U. Tex., Galveston, 1950; MPH, U. Mich., 1963. Intern City of Detroit Receiving Hosp., 1950-51; resident in gen. practice St. Mary's Infirmary, Galveston, Tex., 1951-52; sch. physician Galveston Ind. Sch. Dist., 1953-56; dir. med. svcs. San Antonio Health Dept., 1960-63, acting dir., 1963-64; resident in pub. health Tex. Dept. Pub. Health, San Antonio, 1963-65; dir. community health svcs. Corpus Christi-Nueces County (Tex.) Health Dept., 1964-67; dir. Corpus Christi-Nueces County (Tex.) Dept. Pub. Health, 1987—; dir. Tb control region 5 Tex. Dept. Health, Corpus Christi, 1967-73; dir. pub. health region 11 Tex. Dept. Health, Rosenberg, 1978-87; chief chronic illness control City of Houston Health Dept., 1973-78; lectr. Incarnate Ward Coll., San Antonio, 1963-64; adj. prof. U. Tex. Sch. Pub. Health, Houston, 1980—; guest lectr. Corpus Christi State U., 1987—; pvt. practice, Galveston, Stockdale, Hereford, Borger, Tex., 1952-59. Bd. dirs. Coastal Bend chpt. ARC, Corpus Christi, 1990-94, United Way-Coastal Bend, Coastal Bend Coalition on AIDS, 1988—, Coastal Bend chpt. Am. Diabetes Assn., 1990—. Fellow Am. Coll. Preventive Medicine; mem. AMA, Tex. Med. Assn. Nueces County Med. Soc., Am. Assn. Pub. Health Physicians, Tex. Assn. Pub. Health Physicians, Am. Pub. Health Assn., Tex. Pub. Health Assn. Episcopalian. Home: 62 Rock Creek Dr Corpus Christi TX 78412 Office: Corpus Christi-Nueces County Dept Health 1702 Horne Rd Corpus Christi TX 78416-1902

SITARZ, ANNELIESE LOTTE, pediatrics educator, physician; b. Medellin, Colombia, Aug. 31, 1928; came to U.S., 1935; d. Hans and Elisabeth (Noll) S. BA cum laude, Bryn Mawr (Pa.) Coll., 1950; MD, Columbia U., 1954. Diplomate Nat. Bd. Med. Examiners, Am. Bd. Pediatrics, Am. Bd. Pediatric Hematology and Oncology. With Columbia U., N.Y.C., 1957—, assoc. prof. clin. pediatrics, 1974-83, prof. clin. pediatrics, 1983—; cons. pediatrics, hematology and oncology Harlem Hosp., N.Y.C., 1967-72, Overlook Hosp., Summit, N.J., 1975—. Contbr. numerous articles to profl. jours. Pres. Mt. Prospect Assn., Summit, 1987—. Fellow Am. Acad. Pediatrics; mem. Am. Assn. Cancer Rsch., Am. Soc. Clin. Oncology, Am. Soc. Hematology, Internat. Soc. Hematology, Harvey Soc. Republican. Episcopalian. Office: Babies and Children's Hosp 3959 Broadway New York NY 10032-1537

SITARZ, PAULA GAJ, writer; b. New Bedford, Mass., May 25, 1955; d. Stanley Mitchell and Pauline (Rocha) Gaj; m. Michael James Sitarz, Aug. 26, 1978; children: Andrew Michael, Kate Elizabeth. BA, Smith Coll., 1977; MLS, Simmons Coll., 1978. Children's libr. Thomas Crane Pub. Libr., Quincy, Mass., 1978-84; dir. Reader's Theatre Workshop Thomas Crane Pub. Library, Quincy Mass., 1985. Author: (book) Picture Book Story Hours: From Birthdays to Bears, 1986, More Picture Book Story Hours, 1989, The Curtain Rises: A History of Theater From Its Origins in Greece and Rome Through the English Restoration, 1991, The Curtain Rises Volume II: A History of European Theater from the Eighteenth Century to the Present, 1993; contbr. monthly column Bristol County Baby Jour., 1992—, South Shore Baby Jour., 1992—, First Tchr., 1993—. Mem. New Eng. Libr. Assn., Libr. Sci. Honor Soc., Smith Club of Southeastern Mass. (v.p. 1987-89, pres. 1989-91), Beta Phi Mu. Roman Catholic. Home and Office: 25 Stratford Dr North Dartmouth MA 02747-3843

SIVE, REBECCA ANNE, public affairs company executive; b. N.Y.C., Jan. 29, 1950; d. David and Mary (Robinson) S.; m. Clark Steven Tomashefsky, June 18, 1972. BA, Carleton Coll., 1972; MA in Am. History, U. Ill., Chgo., 1975. Asst. to chmn. of pres.' task force on vocations Carleton Coll., Northfield, Minn., 1972; asst. to acquisitions librarian Am. Hosp. Assn., Chgo., 1973; rsch. asst. Jane Addams Hull House, Chgo., 1974; instr. Loop Coll., Chgo., 1975, Columbia Coll., Chgo., 1975-76; cons. Am. Jewish Com., Chgo., 1975, Ctr. for Urban Affairs, Northwestern U., Evanston, Ill., 1977, Ill. Consultation on Ethnicity in Edn., 1976, MLA, 1977; dir. Ill. Women's History Project, 1975-76; founder, exec. dir. Midwest Women's Ctr., Chgo., 1977-81; exec. dir. Playboy Found., 1981-84; v.p. pub. affairs/pub. rels. Playboy Video Corp., 1985; v.p. pub. affairs Playboy Enterprises, Inc., Chgo., 1985-86; pres. The Sive Group, Inc., Chgo., 1986—; guest speaker various ednl. orgns., 1972—; instr. Roosevelt U., Chgo., 1977-78; dir. spl. projects Inst. on Pluralism and Group Identity, Am. Jewish Com., Chgo., 1975-77; cons. Nat. Women's Polit. Caucus, 1978-80; bd. dirs. NOVA Health Systems, Woodlawn Community Devel. Corp.; trainer Midwest Acad.; mem. adv. bd. urban studies program Associated Colls. Midwest; proposal reviewer NEH. Contbr. articles to profl. jours. Commr. Chgo. Park Dist., 1986-88; mem. steering com. Ill. Commn. on Human Rels., 1976; mem. structure com. Nat. Women's Agenda Coalition, 1976-77; del.-at-large Nat. Women's conf., 1977; mem. Ill. Gov.'s Com. on Displaced Homemakers, 1979-81, Ill. Human Rights Com., 1980-87, Ill. coordinating com., Internat Womens Yr.; coord. Ill. Bicentennial Photog. Exhbn., 1977; mem. Ill. Employment and Tng. Coun.; mem. employment com. Ill. Com. on Status of Women; bd. dirs. Nat. Abortion Rights Action League and NARAL Found., Ill. div. ACLU, Midwest Women's Ctr. Recipient award for outstanding community leadership YWCA Met. Chgo., 1979, award for outstanding community leadership Chgo. Jaycees, 1988. Home: 3529 N Marshfield Ave Chicago IL 60657-1224 Office: The Sive Group 359 W Chicago Ave Ste 201 Chicago IL 60610-3025

SIZEMORE, CAROLYN LEE, nuclear medicine technologist; b. Indpls., July 22, 1945; d. Alonzo Chester and Elsie Louise Marie (Osterman) Armstrong; m. Jessie S. Sizemore Sr., June 9, 1966; 1 child, Jessie S. Jr. AA in Nuclear Medicine, Prince George's Community Coll, Largo, Md., 1981; BA in Bus. Adminstrn., Trinity Coll., 1988. Registered technologist (nuclear medicine); cert. nuclear medicine technologist, Md.; lic. nuclear med. technologist. Nuclear med. technologist Washington Hosp. Ctr., 1981-88; chief technologist, mem. com. Capitol Hill Hosp., Washington, 1988-91; chief technologist, asst. radiation safety officer Nat. Hosp. Orthopaedics and Rehab., Arlington, Va., 1991—; mem. Am. Registry of Radiologic Technologists Nuclear Medicine Exam. Com., 1990-93. Contbr. articles to profl. jours. Mem. com. Medlantic Rsch. Found., Washington, 1989-93; sec. Crestview Area Citizens Assn., 1994—. Mem. Va. Soc. Radiol. Technologists, Potomac Dist. Soc. Radiol. Technologists, Md. Soc. Radiol. Technologists, Md. Soc. Nuclear Medicine Technologists, Soc. Nuclear Medicine (chmn. mem. 1983-85, sec. 1985-87, 88-89, co-editor Isotopics 1991, editor Isotopics 1992—), Nuclear Medicine Adv. Bd. Am. Legion Aux. (exec. com. 1975-76), Internat. Platform Assn., Crestview Area Citizens Assn. (sec. 1994—). Republican. Lutheran. Home: 6700 Danford Dr Clinton MD 20735-4019

SJÖLANDER, LINDA ARLENE, marketing executive; b. Portland, Oreg., Aug. 7, 1943; d. Nathaniel David and Ardis Margaret (Gisselberg) S.; m. James Earl Pennington, Aug. 7, 1965 (div. Sept. 1974); m. John Derek Lyons, Feb. 14, 1986. BA in English, U. Oreg., 1965; MEd in English, Boston U., 1970. Tchr., David Douglas Schs., Beaverton, Oreg., 1965-69; clin. supr., Portland State U., 1965-69; tchr., Winchester Schs., Mass., 1970-73; co-dir., counselor John F. Kennedy Sch., Queretaro, Mex., 1973-74; asst. v.p. pub. rels. Newspaper Advt. Bur., N.Y.C., 1975-76; self-employed, Boston, 1977; editor, writer Intermetrics, Inc., Cambridge, Mass., 1978-85; cons., propr., by Sjolander, Belmont, Mass., 1983-85, Sjolander Lyons Comm., Concord, Mass., 1986-88, mktg. cons. Parks and Recreation Dept. Town of Mashpee, Mass., 1988—; guest lectr. U. Lowell, Mass., 1985, Northeastern U., Mass., 1987; mem. Decordova Art Mus., Lincoln, Mass. One-person show Lincolm (Mass.) Libr., Concord Cooperative Bank; group shows include de Havilland Fine Art Gallery, Boston, Arts & More, Jamaica Plain, Mass., Concord (Mass.) Art Assn. ; paintings in permanent collections; contbr. articles to profl. jours. Mem. Belmont Citizens Com., Mass., 1983-85; chmn. adv. com. Town of Mashpee. Recipient Outstanding Performance award NASA, 1983. Mem. Am. Mktg. Assn., Concord Art Assn. (artist), Alpha Omicron Pi. Republican. Episcopalian. Avocations: art, music, dance, literature. Home and Office: 82 Sandy Pond Rd Concord MA 01742-3718

SKAAR, SARAH HENSON, editor; b. Bryan, Tex., June 19, 1958; d. James Bond Henson and Evie Leone (Callihan) Miller; m. Kent Skaar, Apr. 7, 1990. BS, Wash. State U., 1983, M in Adult and Continuing Edn., 1986. Asst. prof. U. Idaho Coop. Extension System, 1984-91; editor Intermountain Horse and Rider, Idaho Falls, 1994—. Author: Risk Management: Strategies for Managing Volunteer Programs, 1988. Recipient Pub. Info. award Nat. Assn. County Agrl. Agts., 1989.

SKAER, LAURA ELIZABETH, lawyer; b. Kermit, Tex., Feb. 28, 1948; d. Arthkur Tine and Edathy Lorine (Bixier) S.; children: Brittney, Mackenzie. BS in Bus. Adminstrn., U. Mo., 1970, JD cum laude, 1974. Bar: Mo., Colo. Assoc. Blackwell, Sanders, Matheny, Weary & Lombardi, Kansas City, Mo., 1974-79; gen. coun. and COO Skaer Enterprises, Inc., Denver, 1979-93; gen. counsel, bus. cons. Pease Oil & Gas, Co., Denver, 1993—; bd. dir. Eagle Bank, Broomfield, Colo., 1985—; chair minerals, energy and geology policy adv. bd. Colo. Dept. Nat. Resources, Denver, 1992—. Recipient Disting. Svc. award Colo. Oil and Gas Assn., 1990, Faculty Alumni award U. Mo., 1991. Mem. Indep. Petroleum Assn. Mt. States (pres. 1991-92), Colo. Bar Assn., Colo. Women's Bar Assn., Colo. Oil and Gas Assn., Ind. Petroleum Assn. Am. (regional v.p. 1989-91), Denver Petroleum Club (bd. dir.). Office: Pease Oil & Gas Co 633 17th St #1500 Denver CO 80202

SKAGGS, ARLINE DOTSON, elementary school educator; b. Houston, Sept. 10, 1935; d. Gordon Alonzo and Fannie Mae (O'Kelley) Dotson; m. May 24, 1958 (div. Dec. 1969); children: Fred Mack, Ray Gordon. BS, U. Houston, 1957. Recreation leader VA Hosp., Houston, 1957-59; 4th and 5th grade tchr. Houston Ind. Sch. Dist., 1967-91; ret., 1991—; sponsor Number Sense, 1975-87, Sci. Fair, 1984-85. Auditor PTA, 1985, 87, 88; treas. Mt. Olive Luth. Sch. PTO, 1967-68; pres. Gulfgate Lioness Club, 1966-67; mem. Delphian Soc., 1965, Ch. of Houston Bread Distbn. program, 1990-91; treas. Houston Night Chpt. Women's Aglow, 1982; tchr. Children's Ch., 1972, 83, 84; prayer ptnr. Trinity Broadcasting Network, 1989-90, Christian Broadcasting Network, 1982-83; Braves scorekeeper Brays Bayou Little League, 1969-71; mem. United Way Funding Com., Salvation Army, Star of Hope & United Svcs. Orgn., 1974-76. Winning sponsor Citywide Math. Competition, Houston Ind. Sch. Dist., 1982, N.E. Area Math. Competition, 1976, 78, 79, 81, 82, 83, Lockhart Math. Contest, 1987. Mem. NEA (del. 1974), Houston Tchrs. Assn. (sch. rep. 1968-77, exec. bd. 1972-74, dir. N.E. area 1972-74, by-laws chmn. 1976), Tex. State Tchrs. Assn. (life, del. convs. 1968-75). Home: 4437 Vivian St Bellaire TX 77401-5630

SKAGGS, KAREN GAYLE, elementary school educator; b. Campbellsville, Ky., Sept. 29, 1956; d. E. Edward and Mary Virginia (Kearney) Davis; m.

Stephen Douglas Skaggs, July 30, 1976. BA in English, French and Journalism, Campbellsville Coll., 1977, elem. edn. endorsement 1-8, 1989; MA in Secondary Edn. and Psychology, Western Ky. U., 1980, reading specialist degree, 1986, rank 1 in edn., 1990. Cert. secondary tchr., Ky. Tchr. English, French, journalism Taylor County Bd. Edn., Campbellsville, 1978-81; adult edn. tchr. Taylor County Bd. Edn., 1981-89; elem. tchr. Campbellsville Bd. Edn., 1989—. Mem. Campbellsville Site Based Coun., 1993—. Recipient Outstanding Tchr. award State Dept. of Edn. Mem. NEA, Internat. Reading Assn., Ky. Edn. Assn., Campbellsville Edn. Assn. (v.p.), Taylor County Lit. Coun. (pres.), Taylor County Bus. and Profl. Women's Club (chmn. young careerist com. 1987-88, Outstanding Young Career Woman award 1987, Tchr. of Yr. award 1993, Excellence in Tchg. award 1994). Democrat. Baptist. Home: 901 S Columbia Ave Campbellsville KY 42718-2410

SKALE, LINDA DIANNE, elementary educator; b. Lansing, Mich., May 24, 1947; d. Louis and Dolores Louise (Clum) Pascotto; m. Arthur Skale, Sept. 9, 1967; children: Michelle, John, David, Jennifer. BA, Mich. State U., 1969, MA, 1971. Tchr. 3rd grade Ionia (Mich.) pub. schs.; reading cons. Benton Harbor (Mich.) schs.; elem. tchr. 3rd-5th grades, curriculum chair lang. arts portfolio assessment Berrien Springs (Mich.) Sch., reading tchr., coord.; interim prin. Sylvest Elem., 1994-95. Named 1989 Outstanding Employee of the Yr., Berrien Springs Schs., 1988. Mem. ASCD, Internat. Reading Assn., Mich. Reading Assn. (lectr.), Tri-County Reading Assn. Home: 4384 Laurel Dr Saint Joseph MI 49085-9311

SKALKA, ANNA MARIE, molecular biologist, virologist; b. N.Y.C., July 2, 1938. AB, Adelphi U., 1959; PhD in Microbiology, NYU, 1964. Am. Cancer Soc. fellow molecular biology genetics rsch. unit Carnegie Inst., 1964-66, fellow, 1966-69; asst. mem. dept. cell biology lab. molecular and biochemical genetics Roche Inst. Molecular Biology, 1969-71, assoc. mem., 1971-76, mem., 1976-80, head, 1980—; now dir. Inst. Cancer Rsch., Phila.; vis. prof. dept. molecular biology Albert Einstein Coll. Medicine, 1973—, Rockefeller U., 1975. Mem. AAAS, Am. Soc. Microbiology, Am. Soc. Biol. Chem., Assn. Women Sci., Sigma Xi. Office: Inst for Cancer Rsch Fox Chase Cancer Ctr 7701 Burholme Ave Philadelphia PA 19111-2497*

SKEANS, CAROLOU, business educator; b. Dayton, Ohio, Nov. 26, 1932; d. Ledford and Sue Ann (Brown) Smith; children: Max Howard, Mark Timothy. BA, Georgetown Coll., 1964; MEd, U. Cin., 1969, EdD, 1980. Cert. tchr. bus. and music; cert. supr. bus. office edn. Tchr. Johnsonville New Lebanon (Ohio) High Sch., 1964-65; coord. bus. Trotwood (Ohio)-Madison High Sch., 1965-75; assoc. prof. Miami U., Middletown, Ohio, 1975—; tchr. internat. bus. Miami U. European campus, Luxembourg, 1992-93; vis. scholar European Ctr. Miami U., 1992; cons. Nat. Adv. Coun., Columbus, Ohio, 1967, Armco Steel Corp., Middletown, 1977-78, Fifth Third Bank, Cin., 1979-80; U.S. del. to Helsinki, Finland for Internat. Bus. Edn. Soc., 1985. Co-author: Advanced Information Processing, 1980; editor (book) Office Procedures, 1984. Choir dir. Triumphant Luth. Ch., Trotwood, 1964-66, Ft. McKinley Meth. Ch., Dayton, 1967-75. Scholar Georgetown Coll., 1961, U. Cin., 1977. Mem. Adminstrv. Mgmt. Soc. (coll. advisor), Internat. Soc. Bus. Educators' Congress (U.S. del. to Finland 1984), Beta Gamma Sigma, Delta Omicron (scholarship coord. 1981-83), Delta Pi Epsilon. Republican. Baptist. Office: Miami U 4200 E University Blvd Middletown OH 45042-3458

SKELTON, DOROTHY GENEVA SIMMONS (MRS. JOHN WILLIAM SKELTON), art educator; b. Woodland, Calif.; d. Jack Elijah and Helen Anna (Siebe) Simmons; BA., U. Calif., 1940, MA, 1943; m. John William Skelton, July 16, 1941. Sr. rsch. analyst War Dept., Gen. Staff, M.I. Div. G-2, Pentagon, Washington, 1944-45; vol. rschr. monuments, fine arts and archives sect. Restitution Br., Office Mil. Govt. for Hesse, Wiesbaden, German, 1947-48; vol. art tchr. German children in Bad Nauheim, Germany, 1947-48; art educator, lectr. Dayton (Ohio) Art Inst., 1955; art educator Lincoln Sch., Dayton, 1956-60; instr. art and art edn. U. Va. Sch. Continuing Edn., Charlottesville, 1962-75; rschr. genealogy, exhibited in group shows, Calif., Colo., Ohio, Washington and Va.; represented in permanent collections Madison Hall, Charlottesville, Madison (Va.) Center. Mem. Nat. League Am. Pen Women, AAUW, Am. Assn. Museums, Coll. Art Assn. Am., Inst. for Study of Art in Edn., Dayton Soc. Painters and Sculptors, Nat. Soc. Arts and Letters (life), Va. Mus. Fine Arts, Cal. Alumni Assn., Air Force Officers Wives Club. Republican. Methodist. Clubs: Army Navy Country, Lake of the Woods (Va.) Golf and Country. Chief collaborator: John Skelton of Georgia, 1969; author: The Squire Simmons Family, 1746-1986, 1986. Address: Lotos Lakes Brightwood VA 22715

SKIBINSKI, OLGA, artist, art conservator; b. Bucharest, Romania, Sept. 15, 1939; came to U.S., 1986; d. Alois Skibinski and Marina Barbulescu; divorced; 1 child, Stefan. BA, Fine Arts Coll., 1963; diploma in art conservation, Nat. Mus. Art, 1967. Sr. art conservator Nat. Mus. Art, Bucharest, 1964-86; freelance artist and art conservator N.Y.C., 1986—; lectr. on art conservation. One woman shows at Orizont Gallery, Bucharest, Romania, 1978, Mus. Fine Arts, Craiova, Romania, 1981, Simeza Gallery, Bucharest, 1984, Romanian Cultural Ctr., N.Y.C., 1993; contbr. articles to art mags. Mem. Internat. Inst. for Conservation London, Am. Inst. for Conservation, West Side Art Coalition, Ward-Nasse Gallery. Republican. Home: Apt 4A 78-12 35th Ave Jackson Heights NY 11372

SKIER, PAULA S., automotive marketing executive; b. Hackensack, N.J., Oct. 11, 1964; d. J. Norman and Carole E. (Rabins) Schwarz; m. Chad N. Skier, Jan. 8, 1994. MusB summa cum laude, Syracuse U., 1986; diploma in direct mktg., NYU, 1989. Pub. rels. coord. WEA Internat., Inc., N.Y.C., 1986-87; acct. exec. Wells, Rich, Greene, N.Y.C., 1987-89; mng. dir. European imports R.L. Polk & Co., Montvale, N.J., 1989—. Mem. NAFE, Direct Mktg. Assn., Direct Mktg. Club N.Y. Office: RL Polk & Co 221 E Grand Ave Montvale NJ 07645

SKIGEN, PATRICIA SUE, lawyer; b. Springfield, Mass., June 16, 1942; d. David P. and Gertrude H. (Hirschhaut) S.; m. Irwin J. Sugarman, May 1973 (separated May 1992); 1 child, Alexander David. BA with distinction, Cornell U., 1964; LLB, Yale U., 1968. Bar: N.Y. 1968, U.S. Dist. Ct. (so. dist.) N.Y. 1969. Law clk. Anderson, Mori & Rabinowitz, Tokyo, 1966-67; assoc. Rosenman Colin Kaye Petschek Freund & Emil, N.Y.C., 1968-70; assoc. Willkie Farr & Gallagher, N.Y.C., 1970-75, ptnr., 1977—; dep. supt., gen. counsel N.Y. State Banking Dept., N.Y.C., 1975-77, 1st dep. supt. banks, 1977; adj. prof. Benjamin Cardozo Law Sch. Yeshiva U., 1979. Contbr. articles to profl. jours. Cornell U. Dean's scholar, 1960-64, Regent's scholar, 1960-64, Yale Law Sch. scholar, 1964-68. Mem. ABA (corp. banking and bus. law sect.), Assn. of Bar of City of N.Y. (chmn. com. banking 1991-94, mem. long range planning com. 1994—), Phi Beta Kappa, Phi Kappa Phi. Office: Willkie Farr & Gallagher One Citicorp Ctr 153 E 53rd St New York NY 10022-4669

SKILBECK, CAROL LYNN MARIE, elementary educator and small business owner; b. Seymour, Ind., May 1, 1953; d. Harry Charles and Barbara Josephine (Knue) S.; div.; 1 child, Michael Charles. BS in Elem. Edn., U. Cin., 1977; postgrad. in Psychology, Wright State U., 1985-86; postgrad., Northern Ky. U. Cert. tchr., Ohio. Sec. Procter & Gamble, Cin., 1971-76; classified typist The Cin. Enquirer, Cin., 1976; tchr. St. Aloysius Sch., Cin., 1977-79, St. William Sch., Cin., 1979-82; legal sec. County Dept. Human Svcs., Cin., 1982-86; tchr. St. Jude Sch., Cin., 1986-91; educator, owner CLS Tutoring Svcs., Cin., 1991—; tchr. St. Martin Gifted Program, Cin., 1992-93, Oak Hills Schs. Community Edn., Cin., 1990—, Super Saturday Gifted Program, Cin., 1990—; adult leader antidrug program Just Say No, Cin., 1989-92. Author: Study Skills Workshop, 1993; writer, dir. Christmas play, 1993. Vol. interior designer for homeless shelter St. Joseph's Carpenter Shop, Cin., 1990; mem. LaSalle PTA, 1993—; vol. Habitat for Humanity. Mem. Nat. Tchrs. Assn. Democrat. Roman Catholic. Home and Office: 3801 Dina Ter Cheviot OH 45211

SKILLIN, THERESE JENO, elementary school educator; b. San Jose, Calif., Feb. 16, 1956; d. Joseph John and Eloise Martha (Holden) Jeno; m. Robert Hance Skillin, Sept. 28, 1985;; children: Paul Holden, Julia Rose, Anna Katherine. BA, San Francisco State U., 1978, MA, 1983. Cert. Calif. multiple subject life tchr. Tchr. Lost Hills (Calif.) Union Sch., 1979-81, Panama Unified Sch. Dist., Bakersfield, Calif., 1981-85, Santa Paula (Calif.) Sch. Dist., 1985-90; adult literacy tutor Family Literacy Aid to Reading Program, Bakersfield, 1986, 87; cons. Ventura (Calif.) County Farm Bus., 1987-88, Ventura County Supt. County Schs.; sci. specialist, chair Ventura County Environ. and Energy Edn. Coun., 1990; originator, presenter Farm Day, Kern and Ventura Counties; presenter Ventura County Creative Arts Seminar, 1990, Calif. Kindergarten Conf., San Francisco, 1995; tchr. agrl. seminar, Ker County, 1992-94. Author children's books. Mem. AAUW (mem. Camarillo Creative Arts Workshop 1988), Ventura County Reading Assn., Northern Calif. Kindergarten Assn., So. Calif. Assn. Sci. Specialists, Wasco Jr. Woman's Club (sec. 1982-83, v.p. 1983-84, dir. Annual Fun Run, named Woman of Yr. 1982), Santa Barbara Cactus and Succulent Soc. (cons.), Petroleum Wives Assn. (com. chairperson 1993-94). Democrat. Roman Catholic. Home and Office: 2901 22nd St Bakersfield CA 93301-3237

SKILLINGSTAD, CONSTANCE YVONNE, social services administrator, educator; b. Portland, Oreg., Nov. 18, 1944; d. Irving Elmer and Beulah Ruby (Aleckson) Erickson; m. David W. Skillingstad, Jan. 12, 1968 (div. Mar. 1981); children: Michael, Brian. BA in Sociology, U. Minn., 1966; MBA, U. St. Thomas, St. Paul, 1982. Cert. vol. adminstr.; lic. social worker. Social worker Rock County Welfare Dept., Luverne, Minn., 1966-68; social worker Hennepin County Social Svcs., Mpls., 1968-70, vol. coord., 1970-78; vol. coord. St. Joseph's Home for Children, Mpls., 1978-89, mgr. community resources, 1989-94; exec. dir. Mpls. Crisis Nursery, 1994—; mem. community faculty Met. State U., St. Paul and Mpls., 1982—; faculty U. St. Thomas Ctr. for Non Profit Mgmt., 1990—; trainer, mem. adv. commn. Mpls. Vol. Ctr., 1978-90, cons., 1980—, chmn. Contbr. articles to Jour. Vol. Adminstrn. Mem. adv. bd. Mothers Against Drunk Driving, Minn., 1986-88; vice chmn., chmn. adminstrv. coun., lay leader Hobart United Meth. Ch.; lay rep. to Minn. Ann. Conf. of Meth. Chs., 1989-92; active Park Ave United Meth. Ch., 1992—. Named one of Oustanding Young Women Am., 1974, Woman od Distinction Mpls. St. Paul Mag./KARE-TV, 1995. Mem. Minn. Assn. Vol. Dirs. (pres. 1975, sec., ethics chmn. 1987—), Assn. for Vol. Adminstrn. (v.p. regional affairs 1985-87, mem. assessment panel 1986—, coord. nat. tng. team, cert. process for vol. adminstrs. 1988-92, profl. devel. chair 1990-92), Minn. Social Svcs. Assn. (pres. 1981, Disting. Svc. award 1987). Mem. Dem.-Farmer-Labor Party. Methodist. Office: Mpls Crisis Nursery 4255 3d Ave S Minneapolis MN 55409

SKILLMAN, BECKY SUE, state legislator; b. Bedford, Ind., Sept. 26, 1950; d. Jack Delmar and Catherine Louise (Flinn) Foddrill; m. Stephen E. Skillman, 1969. Dep. recorder Lawrence County, 1971-76, county recorder, 1977-84; clerk Lawrence County crct. ct., 1985—; mem. Ind. State Senate, 1992—. Co-dir. Lawrence County Young Reps., 1973-78; co-chmn. State Young Reps. Conv., 1975, 77; vice chmn. Lawrence County Rep. Ctrl. Com. Office: RR 16 Box 76 Bedford IN 47421-9589

SKILLMAN, JOANNE GARCIA, assistant principal; b. Las Cruces, N.Mex., Dec. 5, 1949; d. Benjamin Maldonado and Viola Jane (Camuñez) Garcia; m. Richard Charles Skillman, Nov. 28, 1968; children: Amy Kathleen, Alison Michelle. BS in Edn., N.Mex. State U., 1971; MA in Edn., Pembroke State U., 1989. Cert. elem. tchr., supr., prin. N.C., S.C. Tchr. 8th and 9th grades Spanish Las Cruces Pub. Schs., 1971; tchr. kindergarten Redstone Arsenal (Ala.) Children's Ctr., 1976-78; tchr. 5th grade Holy Spirit Sch., Huntsville, Ala., 1978-81, Dept. Def. Dependent Schs., Zweibrücken, Germany, 1981-84; tchr. 1st grade, K-2 Spanish, 5th grade Cumberland County Schs., Fayetteville, N.C., 1985-92; tchr. 5th grade Aiken (S.C.) County Schs., 1992-93, asst. prin., 1993—; presenter Results of So. Assn. Colls. and Schs. Self Study, Pirmasens, Germany, 1983, Fgn. Lang. Assn. N.C. Conf., Raleigh, 1991. Pres. Friends of the Orch., Cumberland County, 1991; neighborhood rep. Am. Heart Assn., Fayetteville, 1990-91, Am. Cancer Soc., Aiken, 1994. Jr. Women's League grantee, 1991. Mem. AAUW, ASCD, NEA, S.C. Edn. Assn., Internat. Reading Assn., S.C. Assn. Sch. Adminstrs., Phi Delta Kappa. Democrat. Roman Catholic. Home: 2232 Beaver Creek Ln Aiken SC 29803-9446

SKINNER, ANITA MARIER, talk show host, law enforcement official; b. Portland, Maine, Feb. 23, 1933; d. Rene Ernest and Eva (Boivin) Marier; m. Andrew Y. Skinner III, Jan. 17, 1953 (div. Aug. 1986); children: Drew, Dean Brien, Jamie. Student, Georgetown U., 1955-57. Cert. TV producer, camera operator. Exec. sec. Dept. Navy, Washington, 1951-57; dep. sheriff Tampa (Fla.) Sheriff's Office, 1985—; talk show host Jones Intercable, Inc., Tampa, 1985—, producer Personality Profiles, 1988—; pres. Anita Skinner Prodns., 1989—; freelance videographer, Tampa, 1990—; treas. Micah Prodns., 1987-91. Prodr. (videos) Medjugorje, Yugoslavia, 1988, Maine-Lobsters, 1989, (TV spl.) The Lamb That Was Slain, 1989 (Golden Cassette award, finalist for Home Town USA, 1990); prodr., camera operator (TV spls.) Person of Vision, 1989, Stamping Out Aids, 1989, America This Is What We Declare, 1989, Sing Noel, 1989, Russian Orthodox Divine Liturgy, 1990, Standing Room Only, 1990, Cheval Polo Tournament for LUPUS, 1990 (Golden Cassette award, 1990), Universal Studios Orland Grand Opening, 1990, Shake Rattle and Roll, 1990 (Golden Cassette award, 1990), Producers Three, The Entertainment Revue, (videos) Welcome Home Gen. H.N. Schwarzkopf & Troops, 1991, Queen Elizabeth's Arrival on the Britania, 1991, USA and USSR Athletes Exhbn., 1991; prodr., talk show host Personality Profile, 1992 (Golden Cassette award 1993). Mem. Fla. Motion Picture and TV Assn., Pub. Access (sec. 1987-90, membership treas. 1992). Democrat. Roman Catholic. Home: 815 Country Club Dr Tampa FL 33612-5629 Office: Jones Intercable Inc 1001 N B St Tampa FL 33606

SKINNER, CORNELIA BENNETT, librarian; b. El Paso, Aug. 26, 1928; d. John Thomas and Lucille (Pierson) Bennett; m. John Shaw Skinner, Aug. 20, 1946 (dec. Jan. 1978); children: John Shaw, Mary Jacobina, Walter William, Nelson Pierson. BS, Sul Ross State U., 1966, MA, 1971. Reading tchr. Centennial Sch., Alpine, Tex., 1966-69; tchr. classroom 5th grade Alpine Elem., 1969-71; tchr. English grades 6, 7, 8 Alpine Jr. High, 1971-81; tchr. classroom grades 1, 2 Our Lady of Peace Sch., Alpine, 1982-83; libr. elem. schs. Pecos (Tex.) Ind. Schs., 1983-88; libr. supr. 1st-12th grades Franco Jr. High, Presidio, Tex., 1988—; libr. sci. tchr. Presidio Elem., 1988—; libr. media ctr. Presidio High Sch., 1988—; libr. bookmobile Candelaria Elem., Presidio, 1988—; beekeeper, Marathon, Tex., 1953-63; camp asst. AFTOSA Eradication Patrol, Hot Springs, Tex., support personnel Bur. Animal Industry Big Bend Nat. Park, Tex., 1948-51; corr. area newspapers, 1950-54; libr. media specialist Rotan (Tex.) Ind. Sch. Dist., 1993-95. Cub scout leader Boy Scouts Am., Alpine, 1961-63; girl scout leader Girl Scouts U.S., Alpine, 1959-60; mem. adv. bd. Redford (Tex.) Devel. Assn. Dairy Goat Coop., 1992-93. Mem. Tex. State Tchrs.' Assn. (v.p. and prees. Alpine dist. 1972-91), Nat. Trust for Hist. Preservation, Native Plant Soc. Tex., Chihuahuan Desert Rsch. Inst., Presidio Valley Woman's Club Federated Internat. (v.p. (1988-92, pres. 1992-94), Am. Legion Aux. (v.p. 1960, pres. Alpine unit 79 1961). Democrat. Roman Catholic. Home: PO Box 1527 Alpine TX 79831-1527

SKINNER, HELEN CATHERINE WILD, biomineralogist; b. Bklyn., Jan. 25, 1931; d. Edward Herman and Minnie (Bertsch) Wild; m. Brian John Skinner, Oct. 9, 1954; children: Adrienne W.S. Scott, Stephanie Skinner, Thalassa Skinner. BA, Mt. Holyoke Coll., 1952; MA, Radcliffe/Harvard, 1954; PhD, Adelaide (Australia) U., 1959. Mineralogist sect. molecular structure Nat. Inst. Arthritis and Metabolic Diseases, NIH, 1961-65; mem. sect. crystal chemistry Lab. Histology and Pathology Nat. Inst. Dental Rsch., NIH, 1965-66; lectr. dept. geology and geophysics Yale U., 1967-69, rsch. assoc. dept. surgery, 1967-72, sr. rsch. assoc. dept. surgery, 1972-75; Alexander Agassiz vis. lectr. dept. biology Harvard U., 1976-77; lectr. dept. biology Yale U., 1977-83; assoc. prof. biochemistry in surgery Yale U., New Haven, 1978-84, lectr. dept. orthopaedic surgery, 1977—, rsch. assoc. in geology and geophysics, 1985—; pres. Conn. Acad. Arts and Scis., 1986-94; mineralogist AEC, summer 1953; master Jonathan Edwards Coll., Yale U., 1977-82; vis. prof. sect. ecology and systematics dept. biology Cornell U., 1980-83; dental adv. com. Yale-New Haven Hosp., 1973-80; mem. faculty adv. com. Yale-New Haven Tchrs. Inst., 1983—; chmn. site visit team Nat. Inst. Dental Rsch., 1974-75. Author: (with others) Asbestos and other Fibrous Materials: Mineralogy, Crystal Chemistry and Health Effects, 1988; co-editor: Biomineralization Process of Iron and Manganese: Modern and Ancient Environments, 1992; tech. abstractor Geol. Soc. Am., 1961-65; sect. editor Am. Mineralogist, 1978-82; contbr. over 40 articles to profl. jours. Mem. bd. edn. com. Conn. Fund for Environ., 1983-89, mem. sci. adv. com., 1989-92; founder, pres. Investor's Strategy Inst., New Haven, 1983-85; trustee Miss Porter's Sch., Farmington, Conn., mem. edn. com., 1986-88, mem. salaries and benefits com., 1988-91; treas. YWCA, New Haven, 1983-84. Fellow AAAS, Geol. Soc. Am., Mineral. Soc. Am. (fin. counsel 1981-86); mem. Am. Soc. Bone and Mineral Rsch., Am. Assn. Crystal Growth, Am. Assn. Dental Rsch., Internat. Assn. Dental Rsch., Mineral Soc. Can. Home: PO Box 894 Woodbury CT 06798-0894 Office: Yale U Dept Geology Geophysics P O Box 208109 New Haven CT 06520-8109

SKINNER, LINDA WALKUP, librarian; b. Timmonsville, S.C., Oct. 3, 1947; d. William Carothers and Dorothy Alice (Anderson) Walkup m. Thomas Fry Skinner, June 26, 1971; children: John Alexander, Samuel Lonnie, Emily Norvell. BA, Winthrop Coll., Rock Hill, S.C., 1969; MLS, U. S.C., 1991. Librarian Jonesboro (Ga.) Sr. High Sch., 1969-71; libr. tech. asst. Louis Round Wilson Libr., U. N.C., Chapel Hill, 1971-72; bookmobile librarian New Hanover County Pub. Libr., Wilmington, N.C., 1972-73; libr. tech. asst. U. S.C., Aiken, 1976-77; librarian Charlotte Mecklenburg Sch., Charlotte, N.C., 1982-83, Duke Power Co., Charlotte, 1984—. Docent Hezekiah Alexander Homesite, Charlotte, 1980-90. Mem. Metrolina Libr. Assn., Spl. Libraries Assn., Southeastern Libr. Assn. Presbyterian. Office: Duke Power Co 401 S College St Charlotte NC 28202-1908

SKINNER, NANCY JO, recreation executive; b. Ogallala, Nebr., Nov. 5, 1956; d. Dale Warren Skinner and Beverly Jane (Fister) Berry. AA, Platte Community Coll., 1977; BS, U. Ariz., 1981; MBA, U. Phoenix, 1990; diploma, Nat. Exec. Devel. Sch., 1992. Cert. leisure profl. Sports specialist YWCA, Tucson, 1981, asst. dir. summer day camp, 1981, dir. health, phys. edn. and recreation, 1981-82; sr. recreation specialist Pima County Parks and Recreation Dept., Tucson, 1983, recreation program coord., 1983-90; recreation coord. III Phoenix Parks, Recreation and Libr. Dept., 1990-94, recreation supr., 1994—; labor mgmt. quality of work life rep. Pima County Govt., 1987; dist. coord. Atlantic Richfield Co. Jesse Owens Games, Tucson, 1986-89; adv. Pima County Health Dept. Better Health Through Self Awareness, 1982-83. Dir. tournament Sportsman Fund-Send a Kid to Camp, Tucson, 1984, 85, 86; mem. labor mgmt. quality of working life com. Pima County Govt., 1987; dist. coord. Nat. Health Screening Coun., Tucson, 1982-85; event coord. Tucson Women's Commn. Saguaro Classic, 1984; com. mem. United Way, Tucson, 1982-83; panelist Quality Conf. City of Phoenix, 1992. Musco/APRf Grad. scholar; recipient City of Phoenix Excellence award, 1994. Mem. Nat. Recreation and Parks Assn., Ariz. Parks and Recreation Assn. (cert., treas. dist. IV 1987, pres. 1988, 89, state treas. 1990, pub. rels. chair 1993, Tenderfoot award 1984, co-chair state conf. ednl. program com. 1995), Delta Psi Kappa. Democrat. Methodist. Office: Phoenix Pks Recreation & Libr Dept 3901 W Glendale Phoenix AZ 85051

SKINNER, PAMELA WELCH, systems analyst; b. Washington, May 5, 1965; d. James Stallings Jr. and Noreen O'hara Welch; m. Bruce Henry Skinner, Dec. 22, 1991. BA in Polit. Sci., Grinnell Coll., 1986; MS in Info. Systems Engrng., George Mason U., 1992. Adminstrv. asst. Ketron, Inc., Rosslyn, Va., summers 1979-83; statis. clk. IRS, Washington, summers 1984-86; jr. systems analyst Shorts Bros. USA, Inc., Crystal City, Va., 1986-88; sr. cons. Booz, Allen & Hamilton, Inc., Bethesda, Md., 1988-93; bus. analyst Nat. Assn. of Securities Dealers, Rockville, Md., 1993—; chair staff com. NASD, Rockville, 1993-94; mem. several orgn. devel. coms. NASD, 1993—; cons. in field. Contbr. articles to profl. jours. Bd. dirs. Potomac River Jazz Soc., Washington, 1990-93; fundraiser Leukemia Soc., Arlington, Va., 1989-92. Named to Outstanding Young Women of Am., 1988. Mem. IEEE, Assn. Computing Machinery, Armed Forces Computing and Electronics Engrng. Democrat. Methodist. Home: 12004 Lofting Ct Bowie MD 20720-4462 Office: Nat Assn Securities Dealers 9513 Key West Ave Rockville MD 20850-3351

SKINNER, PATRICIA MORAG, state legislator; b. Glasgow, Scotland, Dec. 3, 1932; d. John Stuart and Frances Charlotte (Swann) Robertson; m. Robert A. Skinner, Dec. 28, 1957; children: Robin Ann, Pamela. BA, NYU, 1953. Mdse. trainee Lord & Taylor, N.Y.C., 1955-59; adminstrv. asst. Atlantic Products, N.Y.C., 1954-59; newspaper corr. Salem Observer, N.H., 1964-84; mem. N.H. Ho. of Reps., 1973-94, chmn. labor, human resources and rehab. com., 1975-86, House Edn. Com., 1987, chmn., 1989-94, exec. com. Nat. Conf. State Legislatures, 1987-90; chmn. N.H. Adv. Council Unemployment Compensation. Bd. dirs. chmn. Castle Jr. Coll., 1975, chmn. bd., 1988—; v.p. bd. Swift Water council Girl Scouts U.S., v.p. 1987-92; mem. chmn. coun. N.H. Voc-Tech. Coll., Nashua, 1978-83; trustee Nesmith Library, Windham, N.H., 1982—, chmn. bd. trustees, 1994. Mem. N.H. Fedn. Women's Clubs (parliamentarian, legis chmn. 1984—), N.H. Fedn. Republican Women's Clubs (pres. 1979-82). Christian Scientist. Club: Windham Woman's (pres. 1981-83). Lodge: Order Eastern Star.

SKINNER, PEGGY JUNE, psychology educator, development consultant; b. Portales, N.Mex., Nov. 29, 1950; d. Arthur F. and Betty C. (Rogers) Rowland; m. Don Stroud, May 27, 1984 (dec. Oct. 2, 1991); children: Shannon, Derek; m. William Fietz, Apr. 17, 1993. BS, Ea. N.Mex. U., 1973, MA, 1974; PhD, Tex. Tech U., 1983. Lic. profl. counselor; registered sex offender therapist. Prof., counselor Ea. N.Mex. U., Portales, 1973-78; prof. psychology South Plains Coll., Levelland, Tex., 1978—; cons. Levelland Devel. Ctr., 1983—; cons., developmentalist Dept. Human Resources, Levelland, 1987—; therapist West Tex. Children's Assessment Ctr., Terry County Juvenile Probation, Hockley County Adult Probation; textbook supplement author McGraw-Hill, Harper Collins. Bd. dirs. Women's Protective Svcs., Lubbock, Tex., 1984—; vol. Family Outreach, Levelland, 1988—. Named Outstanding Tchr., Phi Theta Kappa, 1986, 87, 89. Mem. APA, Soc. for Rsch. in Child and Human Devel., Tex. Conf. on Family Rels., South Plains Perinatal Assn. (bd. dirs., pres. 1978—). Democrat. Home: 2042 Longhorn Dr Levelland TX 79336-6702 Office: South Plains Coll Levelland TX 79336

SKJERVOLD, GERALDINE REID See REID, GERALDINE WOLD

SKLADAL, ELIZABETH LEE, elementary school educator; b. N.Y.C., May 23, 1937; d. Angier Joseph and Julia May (Roberts) Gallo; m. George Wayne Skladal, Dec. 26, 1956; children: George Wayne Jr., Joseph Lee. BA, Sweet Briar Coll., 1958; EdM, U. Alaska, 1976. Choir dir. Main Chapel, Camp Zama, Japan, 1958-59, Ft. Lee, Va., 1963-65; choir dir. Main Chapel and Snowhawk, Ft. Richardson, Alaska, 1968-70; tchr. Anchorage (Alaska) Sch. Dist., 1970—. Active Citizens' Adv. Com. for Gifted and Talented, Anchorage, 1981-83, music com. Anchorage Sch. Dist., 1983-86; soloist Anchorage Opera Chorus, 1969—, Community Chorus, Anchorage, 1968-80; mem. choir First Presbyn. Ch., Anchorage, 1971—, deacon, 1988—; participant 1st cultural exch. from Anchorage to Magadan, Russia with Alaska Chamber Singers, 1992. Named Am. Coll. Theater Festival winner Amoco Oil Co., 1974. Mem. AAUW, Anchorage Concert Assn. Patron Soc. (assocs. coun. of dirs.), Alaska Chamber Singers, Am. Guild Organists (former dean, former treas.). Republican. Presbyterian. Home: 1841 S Salem Dr Anchorage AK 99508-5156

SKLAR, DORIS ROSLYN, conference planning executive; b. N.Y.C., Feb. 15, 1936; d. Philip and Anna (Donn) S. BA, Hunter Coll., 1957. Sec. GE Co., N.Y.C., 1957-69; exec. sec. Behavioral Sci. Applications, Inc., N.Y.C., 1969-72; conf. planning specialist GE Co., N.Y.C., 1972-76, conf. planning cons., 1976-82, mgr. conf. planning, 1982—; adj. asst. prof. mgmt. inst. Sch. Continuing Edn., NYU, 1988-91. Contbr. articles to profl. publs. Recipient Pacesetter award Hospitality Sales and Mktg. Assn. Internat., 1994. Mem. Meeting Profls. Internat. (Internat. Planner of Yr. award 1988, bd. dirs.), Acad. Women Achievers, Internat. Assn. Conf. Ctrs. (pres.'s coun. 1992—).

SKLAR, ETHEL (DUSTY SKLAR), writer; b. Sokol, Poland, Mar. 11, 1928; came to U.S., 1930; d. Max and Lena (Charap) K.; m. David Sklar, Nov. 27, 1949 (div. June 1988); children: Steven, Leeza, Joseph. Grad. high sch., 1945. Author: Gods and Beasts, 1977, The Nazis and the Occult, 1990. Mem. Am. Soc. Journalists and Authors, Investigative Reporters and Editors. Home: 1043 Wilson Ave Teaneck NJ 07666-1810

SKLAR, HOLLY L, nonfiction writer; b. N.Y., May 6, 1955. BA, Oberlin Coll., 1977; MA in Polit. Sci., Columbia U., 1980. Researcher UN Ctr. Transnat. Corps., N.Y., 1978; writer, rschr. N. Am. Congress Latin Am., N.Y., 1981-82; exec. dir. Inst. New Communications, N.Y., 1982-84; writer, lectr. N.Y., Boston; review panelist Nat. Endowment Humanities, Washington, 1989; del. Soviet-Am. Women's Summit, N.Y., Washington, 1990. Author, co-author books including Trilateralism, 1980, Poverty in the American Dream: Women and Children First, 1983, Washington's War on Nicaragua, 1988, Streets of Hope: The Fall and Rise of an Urban Neighborhood, 1994, Chaos or Community? Seeking Solutions, Not Scapegoats for Bad Economics, 1995. Mem. adv. bd. Nationwide Women's Program, Am. Friends Svc. Com., The Progressive Media Project, Polit. Rsch. Assocs.; mem. steering com. Caribbean Basin Info. Project, 1982-85. Recipient Outstanding Book award Gustavus Myers Ctr. for Study Human Rights in U.S., 1988, Assocs. award Polit. Rsch. Assocs., Cambridge, 1991-95; fellow Columbia U. Grad. Sch. Arts and Scis., 1978-80. Mem. Nat. Writers Union, Acad. Polit. Sci., Latin Am. Studies Assn. Office: 97 Sheridan St Boston MA 02130-1857

SKLAR, KATHRYN KISH, historian, educator; b. Columbus, Ohio, Dec. 26, 1939; d. William Edward and Elizabeth Sue (Rhodes) Kish; m. Robert A. Sklar, 1958 (div. 1978); children: Leonard Scott, Susan Rebecca Sklar Friedman; m. Thomas L. Dublin, Apr. 30, 1988. B.A. magna cum laude, Radcliffe Coll., 1965; Ph.D., U. Mich., 1969. Asst. prof., lectr. U. Mich., Ann Arbor, 1969-74; assoc. prof. history UCLA, 1974-81, prof., 1981-88, chmn. com. to administer program in women's studies Coll. Letters and Sci., 1974-81; Disting. Prof. history SUNY, Binghamton, 1988—; Pulitzer juror in history, 1976; fellow Newberry Libr. Family and Community History Seminar, 1973; NEH cons. in women's studies U. Utah, 1977-79, Santa Clara U., 1978-80, Roosevelt U., 1980-82; hist. cons. AAUW; active Calif. Coun. for Humanities, 1981-85, N.Y. Coun. for Humanities, 1992—. Author: Catharine Beecher: A Study in American Domesticity, 1973 (Berkshire prize 1974); editor: Catharine Beecher: A Treatise on Domestic Economy, 1977, Harriet Beecher Stowe: Uncle Tom's Cabin, or Life Among the Lowly: The Minister's Wooing, Oldtown Folks, 1981, Notes of Sixty Years: The Autobiography of Florence Kelley, 1849-1926, 1984, (with Thomas Dublin) Women and Power in American History: A Reader (2 vols.), 1991; co-editor: The Social Survey Movement in Historical Perspective, 1992; mem. editorial bd. Jour. Women's History, 1987—, Women's History Rev., 1990—, Jour. Am. History, 1978-81; contbr. chpts. books. Fellow Woodrow Wilson Found., 1965-67, Danforth Found., 1967-69, Radcliffe Inst., 1973-74, Nat. Humanities Inst., 1975-76, Rockefeller Found. Humanities, 1981-82, Woodrow Wilson Internat. Ctr. for Scholars, 1982, 1992-93, Guggenheim Found., 1984, Ctr. Advanced Study Behavioral and Social Scis., Stanford U., 1987-88, AAUW, 1990-91; Daniels fellow Am. Antiquarian Soc., 1976, NEH fellow Newberry Library, 1982-83; Ford Found. faculty rsch. grantee, 1973-74; grantee NEH, 1976-78, UCLA Coun. for Internat. and Comparative Studies, 1983. Mem. Am. Hist. Assn. (chmn. com. on women historians 1980-83, v.p. Pacific Coast br. 1986-87, pres. 1987-88), Orgn. Am. Historians (exec. bd. 1983-86, Merle Curti award com. 1978-79, lectr. 1982—), Am. Studies Assn. (coun. mem.-at-large 1978-80), Berkshire Conf. Women Historians, Am. Antiquarian Soc., Phi Beta Kappa. Office: SUNY Dept History Binghamton NY 13902

SKLARIN, ANN H., artist; b. N.Y.C., May 21, 1933; d. Sidney and Revera (Myers) Hirsch; m. Burton S. Sklarin, June 29, 1960; children: Laurie Sklarin Ember, Richard, Peter. BA in Art History, Wellesley Coll., 1955; MA in Secondary Art Edn., Columbia U., 1956. Art tchr. jr. high sch. N.Y.C. Sch. System, 1956-61, chmn. art. dept. jr. high sch., 1957-61. One-woman shows include Long Beach (N.Y.) Libr., 1973, Silvermine Guild Ctr. Arts, New Canaan, Conn., 1986, Long Beach Mus. Art, 1986, Discovery Art Gallery, Glen Cove, N.Y., 1987—; exhibited in juried shows at Nassau C.C., Garden City, N.Y., 1970, Nassau County (N.Y.) John F. Kennedy Ctr. Performing Arts, 1970 (1st Pl. award 1970), Long Beach Art Assn., 1970 (1st Pl. award 1970), Gregory Mus., 1973-74, L.I. Arts 76, Hempstead, N.Y., 1976, 5 Towns Music and Art Found., Woodmere, N.Y., 1980 (1st Pl. award 1981, Honorable Mention award 1981), 83 (3d Pl. award 1983), 85, Long Beach Art Assn. and Long Beach Mus. Art, 1982 (1st Pl. award 1982), 84, 85 (3d Pl. award 1985), Silvermine Guild Arts, 1984 (Richardson-Vicks Inc. award 1985), 87 (Pepperidge Farm Inc. award 1987), Long Beach Mus. Art, 1985 (Best in Show-Grumbacher award 1985), Heckscher Mus., Huntington, N.Y., 1985, 87, Fine Arts Mus. L.I., Hempstead, 1985, 91, Long Beach Art League and Long Beach Mus. Art, 1986 (2d Pl. award 1986), Wunsch Arts Ctr., Glen Cove, 1986, 87, Smithtown Twp. Arts Coun., St. James, 1989 (Honorable Mention award 1989); exhibited in group shows at Hewlett-Woodmere Libr., 1969, B.J. Spoke Gallery, Port Washington, N.Y., 1985, Shirley Scott Gallery, Southampton, N.Y., 1986, Smithtown Twp. Arts Coun., St. James, N.Y., 1988, 90, N.Y. Inst. Tech., Old Westbury, N.Y., 1989, Dowling Coll., Oakdale, N.Y., 1990, Discovery Art Gallery, 1992, 93, 94, Silvermine Guild Arts Ctr., 1992, Sound Shore Gallery, Stamford, Conn., 1993, Krasdale Foods Gallery, N.Y.C., 1993. Mem. exec. bd. 5 Towns Music & Art Found., 1960—, pres., 1971-74. Mem. Silvermine Guild Artists, Discovery Gallery (artist mem.). Studio: 501 Broadway Lawrence NY 11559

SKLAROV, DIANE MARIE, nursing administrator, emergency care nurse; b. Chgo., July 18, 1957; d. Edward and Anna Maria (Linehan) S. BSN, Duke U., 1978; MS in Nursing, U. Tex., Houston, 1984. RN, N.C., Tex., Fla.; cert. ACLS provider, trauma nurse core curriculum instr. Staff nurse emergency dept., asst. head nurse Charlotte (N.C.) Meml. Hosp. and Med. Ctr.; staff nurse emergency dept. Hermann Hosp., Houston; mgr. patient care emergency dept. North Miami (Fla.) Med. Ctr.-Parkway Med. Ctr.; adminstrv. ladm, dir. emergency/endoscopy svcs. Miami Heart Inst., Miami Beach, Fla.; adv. com. EMS MDCC. Contbg. author: Trauma Nursing: The Art and Science, 1993. Bd. dirs. Chaminade-Madonna Coll. Prep. Named to Alumni Hall of Fame, Chaminade-Madonna, 1994. Mem. Emergency Nurses Assn. (cert., bd. dirs. Dade-Broward chpt.), Sigma Theta Tau, Kappa Alpha Theta. Home: 34103 Ives Dairy Rd Miami FL 33179

SKODRAS, VICKI HERRING, banker; b. South Bend, Ind., June 4, 1958; d. David Lee and Ruth Irene (Ross) Herring; m. Dan Peter Skodras, June 24, 1989; 1 child, Jonathan David. BS, Ball State U., 1981. Asst. br. mgr. ITT Fin. Svcs., Cin., 1982-83; br. mgr. Transam. Fin. Svcs., Atlanta, 1983-85; loan officer lst Source Bank, South Bend, 1985-86, br. mgr., asst. v.p., 1986-88, br. mgr., bus. devel. mgr., 1988-90, asst. v.p., br. mgr. main office, 1990-92; asst. v.p., br. mgr. Roseland br. 1st Source Bank, 1992. Vol. United Way, 1985-87, 90, Jr. League, 1991—; parent aide Child Abuse and Neglect Coun., 1987—; casa program Youth Svc. Bur., 1992—. Named Boss of Yr., Am. Bus. Woman's Assn., Potawotomi chpt., 1990-91. Mem. Jr. League South Bend. Home: 17570 Irongate Ct Granger IN 46530

SKOLAN-LOGUE, AMANDA NICOLE, lawyer, consultant; b. Los Angeles, Feb. 19, 1954; d. Carl Charles and Estelle (Lubin) Skolan; m. James Edward Logue, Dec. 10, 1983. BS, U. Calif., Los Angeles, 1973; MBA, U. So. Calif., 1976; JD, Southwestern U., Los Angeles, 1982. Bar: Calif. 1982, U.S. Dist. Ct. (cen., no. and ea. dists.) Calif. 1982, N.Y. 1986. Sr. internal cons. Getty Oil Co., Los Angeles, 1976-80; atty. litigation ACLU of So. Calif., Los Angeles, 1982-83; corp. atty. Am. Can Co., Greenwich, Conn., 1983-86; assoc. Shereff, Friedman, Hoffman & Goodman, N.Y.C., 1986-88; region counsel Gen. Electric Capital Corp., Danbury, Conn., 1988—. Mem. ABA, N.Y. State Bar Assn. Republican. Home: 33 Musket Ridge Rd New Fairfield CT 06812-5101 Office: Gen Electric Capital Corp 44 Old Ridgebury Rd Danbury CT 06810-5107

SKOLER, CELIA REBECCA, art gallery director; b. Sioux City, Iowa, Apr. 7, 1931; d. Jacob and Flora (Gorchow) Stern; m. Louis Skoler, Aug. 24, 1952; children: Elisa Anne, Harry Jay. BFA in Art and Music magna cum laude, Syracuse U., 1976. Fin. planner Architects' Partnership, Syracuse, N.Y., 1969-71; bus. mgr. Skoler & Lee Architects P.C., Syracuse, 1971-89; owner, dir. New Acquisitions Gallery, Syracuse, 1981—; ptnr. Gallery Metro, Syracuse, 1991-93, mng. ptnr., 1992-93; contbg. writer Syracuse Herald and Syracuse Newtimes, Syracuse, 1989-91; art cons. IBM, Syracuse, Rochester, Albany, 1983-86, Costello, Cooney & Fearon, Syracuse, 1981-83, Menter, Rudin & Trivelpiece, Syracuse, 1987-88, Blue Cross/Blue Shield Ctrl. N.Y., Syracuse, 1990, Syracuse Newspapers, 1992-94; with cmty. internship program Syracuse U., 1981-87, directed mayoral portrait City of Syracuse,1983, Gelling Meml. Portrait U. Coll., 1984, Levine Meml. Commn. Temple. Concord, 1984; TV producer Syracuse U. Friends of Art, 1979-80; curated 45 exhibits, 1981-90; panelist for art critique Everson Mus. Art, Syracuse, 1989; lectr. on gallery mgmt. Syracuse U. Sch. Art., 1989; juror Fine Art N.Y. State Fair, 1989. One-man shows include Camillus Plaza, 1972, The Associated Artists Gallery, Syracuse, 1973, Library of Fayetteville, N.Y., 1974; exhibited in group show at N.Y. State Fair (1st prize 1974), U. Coll, 1967, 69, 71, Rochester Meml. Gallery, 1969, 70, 71, 72, 74, The Associated Artists, 1971, 72, Cen. N.Y. Art Open, 1970, 71, (Purchase prize 1970, 71), Munson Williams Protor Inst, Utica, N.Y., 1971, 72, Cayuga Mus., Auburn, N.Y., 1972, Oneida (N.Y.) Art Festival, 1969, (1st prize), Jewish Community Ctr., Syracuse, 1968 (1st prize 1969), St. David's Invitational, Dewitt, N.Y., 1970, 71, 72, 73, 74, 75, Cooperstown Art Inst., Nat. Show, 1973, 74, Arena Nat. Show, Binghamton, N.Y., 1975 (Purchase prize 1975). Peer counselor Univ. Coll., Syracuse, 1980-85; Telauc auctioneer Sta. WCNY-TV, Liverpool, N.Y., 1982; mem. steering and implementation com. Gelling Meml. Lounge U. Coll., 1984-85; exec. bd. Syracuse U. Friends of Art, 1977-80; fine art juror N.Y. State Fair, Syracuse, 1982, Downtown Com., Syracuse, 1982, Oswego (N.Y.) Art Guild, 1984. Recipient Purchase prize Marine Midland Bank, 1974, Crouse-Irving Hosp., 1974. Mem. Everson Mus. Art (corp.) mem. Phi Kappa Phi, Alpha Sigma Lambda (pres. 1980-81). Home: 213 Scottholm Ter Syracuse NY 13224-1737 Office: New Acquisitions Gallery Ste 1004 120 E Washington St Syracuse NY 13202-4000

SKOLFIELD, MELISSA T., government official; b. New Orleans, June 25, 1958; m. Frank W. Curtis. BA in Econ. and Behavioral Sci., Rice U., 1980; MA in Pub. Affairs, George Washington U., 1986. Account exec. McDaniel & Tate Pub. Rels., Houston, 1981-84; press sec. Rep. Michael Andrews of Tex., 1985-87; press. sec. Senator Dale Bumpers of Ark., 1987-93; dep. asst. sec. for pub. affairs for policy and strategy Dept. Health and Human Svcs., Washington, 1993—. Press asst. Dem. Nat. Com., Dem. Nat. Conv., 1988, Clinton Pres. Campaign, Dem. Nat. Com., 1992. Mem. Senate Press Secs. Assn. (pres.), Assn. Dem. Press Assts., Pub. Rels. Soc. Am. Office: Dept Health & Human Svcs 200 Indendence Ave SW Washington DC 20201

SKOLNICK, JUDITH A. COLTON, artist; b. Washington, Jan. 31, 1947. BA with honors, U. Md., 1972. represented by Agora Gallery, N.Y.C., Artists Space, N.Y.C., Md. Arts Place, Balt., Paranteze, Chgo., Sodarco, Montreal, Que., Can., Very Spl. Arts, Washington, Washington Project for Arts; resident Contemporary Artists Ctr., North Adams, Mass., 1993, Vt. Studio Ctr., Johnson, 1993; speaker, presenter workshops in field; work included in Women's Issues course Marymount Manhattan Coll., N.Y.C., July 1994. One woman shows include Capitol Hill Art League, Washington, 1994; exhibited in numerous group shows, including Montpelier Arts Ctr., Laurel, Md., 1994, U. Md., Balt., 1994, U. Del., 1994, Jacob Javitz Ctr., N.Y.C., 1994, Monteral Internat. Visual Arts Competition, Sodarco, 1994, Owen Patrick Gallery, Phila., 1994, Mary Anne Reilly Gallery, Washington, 1994, Women's Caucus for Arts, Rockville, Md., 1994, Office Rep. Eleanor Holmes Norton, Harrisburg, Pa., 1994, Franklin Ct. Lobby Gallery, 1994, Univ. North Galleria, 1994, Santa Barbara (Calif.) Mus., Nat. Mus. Women in Arts, Washington, 1995, numerous others; represented in corp. and pvt. permanent collections. Mem. Am. Artists Registry, Capitol Hill Arts League, Corcoran Sch. Art Alumni Assn., Nat. Mus. Women in the Arts, Nat. Trust for Hist. Preservation, Pandora (curator spring performance art season 1994), New D.C. Collage Soc. (v.p. 1993-94), Washington Project for Arts, Women's Caucus for Arts, Nat. Assn. Women Artists Inc. (juried mem.), Unity in Diversity (founder 1993). Address: 1601 Argonne Pl NW # 233 Washington DC 20009

SKOLNICK, MARILYN, civic worker; b. N.Y.C., Jan. 17, 1925; d. Max and Annie Ruth (Stern) Kassel; m. Herbert Skolnick, Aug. 2, 1948; 1 child, Tamara. BA, Bklyn. Coll., 1946; MA, U. Okla., 1948; postgrad., State U. Iowa, 1948-52. Host, producer cable TV program Focus on Issues, 1983—. Chair citizen participation com. Transp. Rsch. Bd., Nat. Acad. Sci., 1987-94, sec. local transp. fin. com., 1985-87, mem. air quality in transp. com., 1987—; bd. dirs. Port Authority of Allegheny County, 1983—; chair Monroeville Planning Commn., 1983-85; bd. dirs. Pa. Planning Assn., 1983-85; mem. Allegheny County Hazardous Waster Task Force, 1983-85; mem. air pollution control adv. com. Allegheny County Health Dept., 1985—; mem. Allegheny County Local Emergency Planning Com., 1987—; bd. dirs. Group Against Smog and Pollution; mem. Pa. Transp. Adv. Com., 1983—. Mem. LWV (bd. dirs. 197-86), N.Y. Acad. Sci., Pa. Acad. Sci., Sierra Club (bd. dirs. Pa. chpt. 1986—, chair Allegheny Group 1988-91), Sigma Xi. Home: 109 S Ridge Dr Monroeville PA 15146

SKORUPSKI, DIANE CHRISTINE, school library media specialist; b. Southbridge, Mass., Mar. 24, 1948; d. Axel Hector and Naomia Maxine (Willis) Johnson; m. Alfred Robert Skorupski, Oct. 9, 1971; children: Kurt (dec.), Gregory R., Kayle J. BS in Edn., North Adams State Coll., 1970; MLS, U. Ariz., 1988. Tchr., Libr., Ariz. Tchr. Town of Dudley, Mass., 1970-71, Sowest Supervisory Sch. Union, Bennington, Vt., 1971-73; sch. libr. media specialist Sunnyside Sch. Dist. # 12, Tucson, 1987—; bd. mem. Sch. Libr. Media Divsn., 1988-91, pres.-elect, 1992-93, pres. 1993-94. Contbr.: Information Literacy: Educating Children for the 21st Century, 1994. Brownie/Jr. Scout Leader Sahuaro Girl Scout Coun., Tucson, 1985-92. Grantee Tech. for Tchg. US West, Am. Assn. Sch. Adminstrs., Autodesk, AT&T, 1991-93. Mem. ALA, NEA, Am. Assn. Sch. Librs., Ariz. State Libr. Assn., Ariz. Reading Assn., Tucson Area Reading Coun. Home: 7810 N Rasmussen Ave Tucson AZ 85741-1448 Office: Liberty Elem School 5495 S Liberty Ave Tucson AZ 85706

SKRATEK, SYLVIA PAULETTE, mediator, arbitrator, dispute systems designer; b. Detroit, Dec. 23, 1950; d. William Joseph and Helen (Meskauskas) S.; m. John Wayne Gullion, Dec. 21,1984. BS, Wayne State U., 1971; MLS, Western Mich. U., 1976; PhD, U. Mich., 1985. Media specialist Jackson (Mich.) Pub. Schs., 1971-79; contract specialist Jackson County Edn. Assn., 1976-79; field rep. Mich. Edn. Assn., E.Lansing, 1979-81; contract adminstr. Wash. Edn. Assn., Federal Way, 1981-85, regional coord., 1985-88, program adminstr., from 1988; dir. mediation svcs. Conflict Mgmt. Inst., Lake Oswego, Ore., 1986-87; exec. dir. N.W. Ctr. for Conciliation, 1987-88; served in Wash. State Senate, 1990-94; tng. cons. City of Seattle 1986—; trustee Group Health Coop. of Puget Sound, Wash., 1984-87; sole proprietor Skratek & Assocs., 1980—; pres. Resolutions Intenat., 1990—. Contbr. articles to legal jours. Mem. Soc. for Profls. in Dispute Resolution, Indsl. Rels. Rsch. Assn.

SKURDENIS, JULIANN VERONICA, librarian, educator, writer, editor; b. Bklyn., July 13, 1942; d. Julius J. and Anna M. (Zilys) S.; A.B. with honors, Coll. New Rochelle, 1964; M.S., Columbia U., 1966; M.A., Hunter Coll., 1974; m. Lawrence J. Smircich, Aug. 21, 1965 (div. July 1978); m. 2d, Paul J. Lalli, Oct. 1, 1978; 1 adopted dau., Kathryn Leila Skurdenis-Lalli. Young adult librarian Bklyn. Pub. Library, 1964-66; periodicals librarian, instr. Kingsborough Community Coll., Bklyn., 1966-67; acquisitions librarian Pratt Inst., Bklyn., 1967-68; acquisitions librarian, asst. prof. Bronx (N.Y.) Community Coll., 1968-75, head tech. services, assoc. prof., 1975—, acting dir. Libr. Resource Learning Ctr., 1994—. N.Y. State fellow, 1960-66, Columbia U. fellow, 1964-66, Pratt Inst. fellow, 1965. Mem. AAUP, NOW, Library Assn. CUNY (chairwoman numerous coms.), Archaeol. Inst. Am., CUNY Women's Coalition. Author: Walk Straight Through the Square, 1976, More Walk Straight Through the Square, 1977; contbg. editor Internat. Travel News, 1989—; travel editor Archaeology mag., 1986-89; contbr. over 200 travel, hist., and archaeol. pieces. Avocations: archaeology, travel, travel writing. Office: CUNY Bronx CC University Ave Bronx NY 10453-6994

SKURKA, KATHLEEN, sculptor, educator; b. Pitts., Pa., Jan. 23, 1947; d. Cornelius Albert and Ruby Nell (Spencer) S. BFA, U. Ala., Tuscaloosa, 1969, MA, 1970, MFA, 1971. Asst. prof. art Ala. State U., Montgomery, 1971—; pottery instr. Montgomery Sch. Fine Arts, 1989-90, Armory Learning Arts Ctr., Montgomery, 1990—. Exhibited sculpture in one-person exhbn. Other-Worldly Creatures and Forms, 1988, Sculpture in Black and White, 1989, Odd Icons, 1992, Ala. City Invitational, 1992, 93, El Dorado Gallery, Colorado Springs, Colo., 1992, Gallery La Luz, N.Mex., 1992, South Bend (Ind.) Regional Mus. Art, 1992, Catskill Arts Soc., Hurleyville, N.Y., 1992, Jacksonville (Ala.) State U., 1994. Recipient 1st pl. award and Best Media ward Roswell Fine Arts LEague, N.MEx. Miniatrue Art Soc., 1992, Ala. Originality award, 1993, 3d pl. award Women Artists Exhbn., Ala., 1993. Mem. Internat. Sculpture Ctr., Ala. Craftsman Assn., Artifice Rex, Women's Caucus Art. Roman Catholic. Home: PO Box 6085 Montgomery AL 36106-0085

SKUZA, KATHRYN ANN, pediatric endocrinologist, educator; b. Newark, July 17, 1957; d. Voytek Stanislaw and Marta Irena (Nakoneczna) Kasznica; m. Christopher Skuza; 1 child, Anne Christine. MD, Warsaw Med. Sch., 1982. Diplomate Am. Bd. Pediatrics, Am. Bd. Pediat. Endocrinology. Pediatric resident U. Medicine and Dentistry N.J. and Children's Hosp. of N.J., Newark, 1982-85, fellow pediatric endocrinology, 1985-88, asst. prof. pediatrics, 1992—; clin. asst. pediatrics U. Medicine and Dentistry N.J., N.J. Med. Sch., Newark, 1990-92; cons. pediatric endocrinologist Newark (N.J.) Beth Israel Med. Ctr., 1992—, Joslin Diabetes Clinic, West Orange, N.J., 1992—, St. Barnabas Med. Ctr., Livingston, N.J., 1993—. Contbr. articles to profl. jours. Office: Childrens Hosp of NJ 15 S 9th St Newark NJ 07107

SKY, ALISON, artist, designer; b. N.Y.C.. BFA, Adelphi U., 1967; student, Art Students League, 1967-69, Columbia U. Co-founder, v.p. Sculpture in the Environ./SITE, N.Y.C., 1969-91; co-founder, prin. SITE Projects, N.Y.C., 1970-91; art educator Parsons Sch. Design, N.Y.C., 1994, Cooper Union, N.Y.C., 1995; vis. artist Purchase Coll., SUNY, 1994-95; artist in residence Urban Glass, 1994-95; lectr. in field. Exhbns. include The Venice Biennale, 1975, The Pompidou Ctr. and Louvre, Paris, 1975, The Mus. Modern Art, N.Y.C., 1979, 84, Ronald Feldman Fine Arts, N.Y.C., 1980, 83, The Wadsworth Atheneum, Hartford, Conn., 1980, The Va. Mus. Fine Arts, Richmond, Va., 1980, Neuer Berliner Kunstverein, 1982, Castello Sforzesco, Sala Viscontea, 1983, Victoria and Albert Mus., London, 1984, Nat. Mus. Modern Art, Toyko, 1985-86, The Triennale di Milano, Italy, 1985, Whitney Mus. Am. Art, N.Y.C., 1985-86, Grey Art Gallery, N.Y.C., 1987-88, Documenta 8, Kassel, Germany, 1987; permanent collections include: Williwear Ltd., N.Y.C. and London, 1982-89, The Mus. Borough of Bklyn., N.Y., 1985, Laurie Mallet House Memories, N.Y.C., 1986, Hwy. 86, Vancouver, Can., 1986, Pershing Sq., L.A., 1986, MTV Sets, N.Y.C., 1988, SWATCH, N.Y.C. and Zunich, Switzerland, 1988-90, Rockplex, Music Complex, Universal City, Calif., 1989, Peace Garden, Washington, 1989, NASA Exhibit, Sevilla, Spain, 1990, N.Y.C. Pub. Libr., 1990, Franz Mayer, Munich, Germany, 1991, Smithsonian Instn., Washington, Mus. Modern Art, N.Y.C., Avery Libr. Columbia U., N.Y.C., Formica Corp., N.J.; projects include BEST Products, 1979-84, SITE Studio, 1984; author: (series of books) Onsite, 1971-76, Unbuilt America, 1976; pub. numerous books on art, 1971-76. Artery Arts finalist, Boston, 1994-95, RTA Arts-in-Transit finalist, Cleve., 1994, Pub. Art Commn. finalist, Cleve., 1994; Design fellow NEA, 1984, 90, Pollock-Krasner Found. fellow, 1991, Fulbright Indo-Am. fellow, 1992. Fellow Am. Acad. Rome. Studio: 60 Greene St New York NY 10012-4301

SKYLAR, ALAYNE, television producer; b. N.Y.C., July 12, 1957; d. Ralph and Verra (Finkenberg) Katz. BA, Hunter Coll., 1979. Talent agent Funny Face, N.Y.C., 1984-85; owner, pres. Skylar Talent, N.Y.C., 1985-91; freelance TV prodr. various mag. and talk shows, N.Y.C., 1991—; speaker in field. Talent coord. breast cancer benefit Susan G. Komen Found., humanitarian awards benefit for AIDS awareness N.Y. Bd. Edn.; vol. pediatrics St. Vincents Hosp., N.Y.C., 1991; active People Ethical Treatment Animals, battered women's charities. Regents scholar, 1975.

SLABY, LILLIAN FRANCES, home finance counselor, real estate professional; b. Cleve., June 9, 1931; d. Bismarck Von Otto and Marie Theresa (Emeaux) Newman; m. Jack Glenn Slaby, Sept. 22, 1951; children: Lonna, Jan, Jeffrey, James, Jack. Student, Dyke Coll., 1949-50. Lic. realtor, Ohio. Home fin. counselor, real estate assoc. HGM Hilltop, Rocky River, Ohio, 1978-88, Realty One, Westlake, Ohio, 1988-91; with Riveredge Realty, Rocky River, Ohio, 1993—. Mem. Internat. Graphoanalysis Soc. (cert.), World Assn. of Document Examiners. Roman Catholic. Home: 5106 NW 16th Pl Gainesville FL 32605-3302 Office: Riveredge Realty Detroit Rd Rocky River OH 44116

SLACK, FRANCES SPIVEY, maternal/women's health and medical/surgical nurse; b. Ouachita Parish, La., Mar. 2, 1947; d. Jack Shelton and Ethel Mae (Thompson) Spivey; m. Roosevelt Slack, Jr., Feb. 4, 1966; children: Rodney J., Shannon N. Student, Gramblin U., 1965-66; BA, NE La. U., 1980, BSN, 1985. RN, La. Staff nurse No. La. Dialysis Ctr., Monroe, St. Francis Med. Ctr., Monroe; charge nurse labor and delivery room Glenwood Med. Ctr., West Monroe, La.; charge nurse med.-surg. unit E.A. Conway Hosp., Monroe; dir. nursing svc. Ridgecrest Nursing Home, West Monroe, La.

SLADE, LINDA E. MOREHEAD, postmaster; b. Reidsville, N.C., June 4, 1949; d. Daniel and Clorean (Lawson) Morehead; m. Lawrence E. Slade, Oct. 25, 1972 (div.); 1 child, Lachelle E. BA, Bennett Coll., Greensboro, N.C., 1971. Sec.-treas. Guilford County Bd. Edn., Greensboro, 1973-77; bookkeeper Carolina Gasket & Rubber, Greensboro, 1973-77; acctg. clk. Loman-Garrett Air Conditioning, Greensboro, 1977-78; jr. acct. Sperry & Hutchinson, High Point, N.C., 1978-79; automated mark-up clk. U.S. Postal Svc., Greensboro, 1978-81, 81-82, sec.-typist fin., 1982-84, acctg. svcs. specialist, 1984-87; postmaster U.S. Postal Svc., McLeansville, N.C., 1987—; rural carrier facilitator, U.S Postal Svc., Greensboro, 1987-93. Fundraiser United Way, 1993; trustee Chapel Hill United Methodist Ch., Reidsville, 1990-93, adm. bd., sec. fin. program.; vol. L. Richardson Hosp., Greensboro. Mem. Nat. Assn. Postmasters U.S. Democrat. Home: 221 Slade Dr Reidsville NC 27320-1653

SLADZINSKI, MARIANNE, corporate executive, consultant; b. Wilkes-Barre, Pa., Nov. 23, 1942; d. Peter Anthony and Anna (Turinski) S. BS in Elem. Edn. and English, Misericordia Coll., 1963; MEd in Ednl. Psychology, Rutgers U., 1967; postgrad. Temple U., 1977, U. Mich., 1984, George Washington U., 1985; MA in Applied Psychology, U. Santa Monica, 1988. Tchr. Hillsborough Twp., N.J., 1963-67; counselor, coordinator RCA Service Co., Drums, Pa., 1967-68, mgr. various depts., 1968-75, adminstr. orgn. devel. and tng., Cherry Hill, N.J., 1975-77, dir. orgn. and devel., 1977-80, dir. orgn. devel. and employment, 1980-84, corp. dir. quality edn. and communication, 1984-87; pres. Sladzinski Assocs., Cherry Hill, N.J., 1987—; external cons. Monet Jewelry, N.Y.C., Barra Internat., RMR Assocs., RCA, Thompson S.A., Gen. Electric, U. Pa., AT&T, N. Y. Life, other cos., also internat. cons. Korea, Taiwan, The Netherlands, Spain, England, Brazil, Japan, Singapore. Rep. of Voorhees Twp. to County Democratic Com., Camden County, N.J., 1981—. Recipient Acad. Women Achievers award YWCA of N.Y.C., 1982; Pres.'s Seal, RCA Service Co., 1983-84. Mem. Orgn. and Devel. Network, Orgn. Transformation Network, Phila. Women's Network, Am. Soc. Tng. and Devel., Am. Soc. Quality Control, Assn. Internal Mgmt. Cons. Club: Fall Line Ski (Cherry Hill) (pres. 1982-83, bd. dirs. 1980-83). Office: PO Box 3850 Cherry Hill NJ 08034-0595

SLATEN, PAMELA GAIL, artist; b. Winter Haven, Fla., May 9, 1964; d. L. Lee and Priscilla Jane (Phillips) Collins. Grad., Flint Tech. Inst., 1990. Artist The Pub., Senoia, Talbot, Ga., 1982-89, Thomaston, Ga., 1988-93; artist Bostwick Tigers, Thomaston, Ga., 1992-93; artist Thomaston Upson Arts Coun., 1993, Upson County Commrs., 1993. Paintings exhibited in group shows including Cherry Blossom Festival, Macon, Ga., 1994; paintings represented in permanent collections including Epilepsy Found., Charles Kass Co. Dress Shop, Ga. State Capitol, Roosevelt Warm Springs Rehab. Vol. Epilepsy Found. Am., arts & crafts dept. Wal-Mart, 1994, St. Jude's Hosp., 1993, 94, Upson County Child Abuse Program, 1994. Recipient Cert. of Appreciation Pilot Club Metro Atlanta, 1993, Ga. State Capitol, 1994, Roosevelt Warm Springs Rehab. Ctr., 1995. Mem. Epilepsy Found. of Am., The Nat. Mus. of Women in the Arts, Thomaston-Upson Arts Coun. Home: 368 Sheila Cir Thomaston GA 30286-9593

SLATER, DORIS ERNESTINE WILKE, business executive; b. Oakes, N.D.; d. Arthur Waldemar and Anna Mary (Dill) Wilke; m. Lawrence Bert Slater, June 4, 1930 (dec. 1960). Grad. high sch. Sec. to circulation mgr. Mpls. Daily Star, 1928-30; promotion activities Lions Internat. in U.S., Can., Cuba, 1930-48; exec. sec. parade and spl. events com. Inaugural Com., 1948-49; exec. sec. Nat. Capital Sesquicentennial Commn., 1949-50, Capitol Hill Assos., Inc., 1951, Pres.'s Cup Regatta, 1951; adminstrv. asst. Nat. Assn. Food Chains, 1951-60; v.p., sec.-treas. John A. Logan Assos., Inc., Washington, 1960—; v.p., sec.-treas. Logan, Seaman, Slater, Inc., 1962—; mng. dir. Western Hemisphere, Internat. Assn. Chain Stores, 1964—. With pub.

relations div. Boston Met. chpt. ARC, 1941-42; mem. Nat. Cherry Blossom Festival Com., 1949—; mem. Inaugural Ball Com., 1953, 57, 65. Methodist. Lion. Home and Office: 2500 Wisconsin Ave NW Washington DC 20007-4505

SLATER, HELEN RACHEL, actress; b. N.Y.C., Dec. 15, 1963; d. Gerald and Alice Joan (Chrin) S. Stage appearances include Responsible Parties, 1985, Almost Romance, 1987; films: Supergirl, 1984, The Legend of Billie Jean, 1985, Ruthless People, 1986, The Secret of My Success, 1987, Sticky Fingers, 1988, Happy Together, 1989, City Slickers, 1991, Lassie, 1994; TV appearances include (series) Capital News, 1990, (movies) Chantilly Lace, 1993, 12:01, 1993. Office: Gersch Agy 232 N Canon Dr Beverly Hills CA 90210-5302*

SLATER, JILL SHERRY, lawyer; b. N.Y.C., Apr. 8, 1943. BA with distinction and honors, Cornell U., 1964; JD cum laude, Harvard U., 1968. Bar: Mass. 1968, Calif. 1971, U.S. Dist. Ct. (cen. dist.) Calif. 1971, U.S. Ct. Appeals (9th cir.) 1974, U.S. Dist. Ct. (so. dist.) Calif. 1977, U.S. Dist. Ct. (ea. dist.) Calif. 1984, U.S. Dist. Ct. (no. dist) Calif. 1985, U.S. Ct. Appeals (Fed. cir.) 1982, U.S. Supreme Ct. 1986, N.Y. 1988. Atty. Boston Redevel. Authority, 1968-70; from assoc. to ptnr. Latham & Watkins, L.A., 1970—. Woodrow Wilson fellow, 1964. Mem. ABA, L.A. County Bar Assn. (exec. com. litigation sect., fed. cts. com.), Am. Intellectual Property Law Assn., Assn. Bus. Trial Lawyers, Phi Beta Kappa. Office: Latham & Watkins 633 W 5th St Ste 4000 Los Angeles CA 90071-2007

SLATER, KRISTIE, construction company executive; b. Rock Springs, Wyo., Nov. 14, 1957; d. Fredrick Earl and Shirley Joan (McWilliams) Alexander; m. C. James Slater, May 11, 1992. A in Bus. Adminstrn., Salt Lake City Coll., 1978. EMT, Wyo. Cost engr., material coord. Project Constrn. Corp., LaBarge, Wyo., 1985; cost engr., scheduler Flour Daniel Constrn. Co., Salt Lake City, 1985-86, Bibby Edible Oils, Liverpool, Eng., 1986-87; cost engr., safety technician Sunvic, Inc./I.S.T.S., Inc., Augusta, Ga., 1987-88; cost engr. Brown & Root, Inc., Ashdown, Ark., 1988-89, Wickliffe, Ky., 1989; sr. cost engr. Brown & Root, Inc., Pasadena, Tex., 1989-90, LaPorte, Tex., 1990-91; project controls mgr. Yeargin Inc., Thousand Oaks, Calif., 1991-92; corp. controls mgr. Suitt Constrn. Co., Greenville, S.C., 1993—. Pres. 4-H State Coun., Laramie, Wyo., 1976; mem. com. Houston Livestock Show and Rodeo. Baptist. Office: Suitt Constrn Co 1400 Cleveland St Greenville SC 29604

SLATER, MARILEE HEBERT, theatre administrator, producer, director, consultant; b. Laredo, Tex., Feb. 25, 1949; d. Minos Joseph and Eulalie (Fisher) Hebert; m. Stewart E. Slater, Dec. 3, 1972 (div. July 1978). BA, Baylor U., 1970, MA, 1972. Cert. secondary sch. tchr., Tex. Actress, dir., assoc. producer Everyman Players, Ky. and La., 1972-80; community rels. dir. Actors Theatre of Louisville, 1973-74, dir. children's theatre, lunchtime & cabaret theatre, 1974-76, dir., apprentice intern program, 1974-77, new play festivals coord., 1979-81, mgr. internat. touring, 1980—, assoc. dir., 1981—; guest dir. Louisville Children's Theatre, 1978; grants panelist Ky. Arts Coun., La. Arts Coun.; conf. lectr. Ky. Arts Coun., Va. Arts Commn., Southeastern Theatre Conf., S.W. Theatre Conf., So. Arts Fedn. Author: (play) Hey Diddle Diddle!, 1976. Pres. Ky. Citizens for Arts, 1985-86, 90-92; co-chmn. subcom. on arts Edn. Workforce, 1990-93; mem. program com. Leadership Louisville, 1989-94, bd. dirs., 1992—; vice chmn. Focus Louisville, 1994—; vice chair Louisville Downtown Mgmt. Dist., 1995—; mem. Downtown Devel. Implementation Com., Louisville, 1991-93; pres. Park IV Condo Assn., 1989-91, sec. Main St. Assn., 1992—; staging dir., cons. Walnut St. Bapt. Ch., 1980—. Recipient Outstanding Alumna award Baylor U., Waco, Tex., 1986. Democrat. Baptist. Office: Actors Theatre Louisville 316 W Main St Louisville KY 40202-2916

SLATER, SHELLEY, engineering specialist, network analyst; b. Ogden, Utah, June 26, 1959; d. Lynn Russell and Darlene (Allen) Slater; m. Dale Thomas Hansen, Jan. 26, 1977 (div. Feb. 1979); 1 child, Thomas Arthur; m. Eugene Allan DuVall, Mar. 8, 1981 (div. Dec. 1985); 1 child, Gregory Allan; m. Steven Blake Allender, June 9, 1990 (div. May 1993). BBA cum laude, Regis U., 1992, postgrad., 1992—. Installation, repair technician MT Bell, Clearfield, Utah, 1977-81; ctrl. office technician MT Bell, Salt Lake City, 1981-83, engring. specialist, 1983-86; engring. specialist U.S. West Comm., Englewood, Colo., 1986-93; network analyst Time Warner Comm., Englewood, Colo., 1993—; bus. cons. Jr. Achievement, Denver, 1988-89. Day capt. AZTEC Denver Mus. of Natural History, 1992; loaned exec. Mile High United Way, 1993. Democrat. Home: 9618 Cordova Dr Highlands Ranch CO 80126 Office: Time Warner Comm 160 Inverness Dr W Englewood CO 80112

SLATKIN, NORA, government official; b. Glen Cove, N.Y., May 5, 1955; d. Carl L. and Muriel (Breen) S.; m. Deral Willis, July 4, 1982; stepchildren: Nick, Lisa, Kelly. BA in Internat. Rels., Lehigh U., 1977; MS in Fgn. Svc., Georgetown U., 1979. Def. analyst Congl. Budget Office, Washington, 1977-84; mem. profl. staff House Armed Svcs. Com., Washington, 1984-93; asst. Sec. of Navy for rsch., devel., acquisition Washington, 1994—; spl. asst. to under sec. of def. for acquisition Office Sec. Def., Washington, 1993. Grad. fellow Nat. Security Coun. Dept. State CIA. Mem. Phi Beta Kappa. Home: 36 Chesapeake Landing Annapolis MD 21403 Office: Asst Sec Navy Rsch Devel Acquisition 1000 Navy Pentagon Washington DC 20350

SLATON, GWENDOLYN CHILDS, librarian; b. Phila., June 19, 1945; d. George Alexander and LaFronia (Dunbar) Childs; m. Harrison Allen Slaton, Sept. 17, 1966; children: Kimberly Dawn, Leigh Alison. BA in History, Pa. State U., 1970; MA in Edn., Seton Hall U., 1976; MLS, Rutgers U., 1981. Lic. profl. librarian, N.J. Tchr. Project A.C.T.I.O.N., New Brunswick, N.J., 1969-70; prodn. coord. Essex County Coll., Newark, 1972-75, non-print media spl., 1975-81, dir. libr., 1981—. Sec. Maplewood Cultural Commn., 1983-89; mem. adv. bd. Family Svc. Child Guidance Ctr. of the Oranges, Maplewood and Millburn, 1976-82. Mem. ALA, N.J. Libr. Assn. (sec. Coll. and Univ. sect. 1993—), Essex Hudson Regional Libr. Coop. (sec. exec. bd. 1988-89), Assn. Two Yr. Coll. Libr. Dirs. (pres. 1984), Delta Sigma Theta. Office: Essex County Coll 303 University Ave Newark NJ 07102-1798

SLATTEN, LISE ANNE DUMOND, communications executive, association executive; b. New Iberia, La., Dec. 12, 1960; d. Lindsey Luke and Carol Ann (Roberts) Dumond; m. James E. Slatten III, Mar. 15, 1986. BS, St. Mary's Dominican Coll., 1982; cert. in politics, Loyola U., New Orleans, 1985; cert. in agy. mgmt., U. Southwestern La., 1993; postgrad., Tulane U., 1995. Asst. pub. rels. dir. Audubon Park and Zool. Gardens, New Orleans, 1982-83; state youth campaign dir. People for Gov. Dave Treen, Baton Rouge, 1983-84; caseworker New Orleans City Coun., 1984-85; leasing rep. Maurin-Ogden, Inc., New Orleans, 1985-87; membership dir. Lafayette (La.) Conv. and Visitors Com., 1987-91; membership dir. Acadian Home Builders Assn., Lafayette, 1991-93, comms. dir., 1993—. Mem. steering com. Dirs. Vols. in Agys. of Acadiana, 1993—; mem. exec. com. Lafayette Parish Rep. Ctrl. Com., 1988-92; bd. dirs. Jr. League of Lafayette, 1990-94; bd. dirs. Festival Internat. de Louisiane, Lafayette, 1991-94. Paul Harris fellow, Rotary Club of Lafayette, 1994. Mem. La. Soc. Assn. Execs., Am. Soc. Assn. Execs. Republican. Roman Catholic. Office: Acadian Home Builders Assn 135 N Domingue Ave Lafayette LA 70506

SLAUGHTER, KATHERINE EWING, lawyer; b. Richmond, Va., Dec. 1, 1939; d. John Mercer and Margaret Anna (Miller) S.; m. Ian Edler McNett, Nov. 10, 1962 (Dec. 1984); children: Ian E. McNett Jr., Margaret Alma McNett. BA, U. N.C., 1961; JD, U. Va., 1986. Bar: Va. 1986. News reporter Harrisburg Pa. Patriot News, 1961-62; editorial asst. Am. Scholar, Washington, 1962, 69; freelance writer, 1971-75; job counselor men dir. OIC Outreach, Madison, Va., 1975-78; dir. Sevenoaks Ctr., Madison, 1978-84; staff atty. So. Environ. Law Ctr., Charlottesville, Va., 1986—. Mem. City Coun. of Charlottesville, 1990—, vice mayor, 1992-94; chair Thomas Jefferson Planning Dist. Commn.; bd. dirs. Charlottesville-Albermarle Recycle Together; bd. dirs. Piedmont Va. C.C.; mem. Downtown Bus. Revitalization Task Force; past chair North Downtown Residents Assn.; state ctrl. com. 7th Dist. Dem. Com.; mem. St. Paul's Episcopal Ch. Mem. Charlottesville Area Women's Bar Assn., Charlottesville-Albermarle Bar Assn., Phi Beta Kappa, Omicron Delta Kappa. Episcopalian. Home: 1501 Short 18th St Charlottesville VA 22902 Office: So Environ Law Ctr 201 W Main St #14 Charlottesville VA 22902

SLAUGHTER, LOUISE MCINTOSH, congresswoman; b. Harlan County, Ky., Aug. 14, 1929; d. Oscar Lewis and Grace (Byers) McIntosh; m. Robert Slaughter, 1956; children: Megan Rae, Amy Louise, Emily Robin. BS, U. Ky., 1951, MS, 1953. Bacteriologist Ky. Dept. Health, Louisville, 1951-52, U. Ky., 1952-53; market researcher Procter & Gamble, Cin., 1953-56; mem. staff Office of the Lt. Gov. N.Y., Albany, 1978-82; state rep. N.Y. Gen. Assembly, Albany, 1983-86; mem. 100th-103rd Congresses from 30th (now 28th) N.Y. dist., Washington, D.C., 1987—; mem. Ho. Rules com., Ho. Budget com. Del. Dem. Nat. Conv., 1972, 76, 80, 88, 92; mem. Monroe County Pure Water Adminstrn. Bd., Nat. Ctr. for Policy Alternatives Adv. Bd., League of Women Voters, Nat. Women's Polit. Caucus. Office: US Ho of Reps Office of House Mems 2421 Rayburn Washington DC 20515-3228

SLAVIN, ALEXANDRA NADAL, artistic director, educator; b. Port-au-Prince, Haiti, Oct. 26, 1943; came to U.S., 1946; d. Pierre E. and Marie Therese (Clerié) Nadal; m. Eugene Slavin, Dec. 24, 1967; 1 child, Nicholas V. Grad. high sch., Chgo. Dancer Ballet Russe de Monte Carlo, N.Y.C., 1960-61, Chgo. Opera Ballet and N.Y.C. Opera Ballet, 1961-64, Am. Ballet Theatre, N.Y.C., 1965-66, Ballet de Monte Carlo, 1966-67, The Royal Winnipeg (Can.) Ballet, 1967-72; artistic dir. Ballet Austin, Tex., 1972-89; owner, dir. The Slavin Nadal Sch. Ballet, Austin, 1989—. Recipient Achievement in the Arts award Austin chpt. YWCA, 1987. Roman Catholic. Office: Slavin-Nadal Sch Ballet 5521 Burnet Rd Austin TX 78756-1603

SLAVIN, ARLENE, artist; b. N.Y.C., Oct. 26, 1942; d. Louis and Sally (Bryck) Eisenberg; m. Neal Slavin, May 24, 1964 (div. 1979); m. Eric Bregman, Sept. 21, 1980; 1 child, Ethan. BFA, Cooper Union for the Advancement of Sci. and Art, 1964; MFA, Pratt Inst., 1967. One woman exhbns. include Brooke Alexander Gallery, N.Y., 1976, Alexander Milliken Gallery, N.Y.C., 1979, 80, 81, 83, U. Colo., 1981, Pratt Inst., N.Y.C., 1981, Am. Embassy, Belgrad, Yugoslavia, 1984, Heckscher Mus., Huntington, N.Y., 1987, Katherine Rich Perlow Gallery, 1988, Chauncey Gallery, Princeton, N.J., 1990, The Gallery Benjamin N. Cardoza Sch. Law, 1991, Norton Ctr. for Arts, Danville, Ky., 1992, Kavesh Gallery, Ketchum, Idaho, 1993; exhibited in group shows at Bass Mus. Art, Fla., Madison (Wis.) Art Ctr., Santa Barbara (Calif.) Mus., Winnipeg (Can.) Art Gallery, Gensler Assocs., San Francisco, 1986, Eliane Benson Gallery, Bridgehampton, N.Y., 1987, 89, 91, 93, City of N.Y. Parks and Recreation Central Park, N.Y.C. 1989, Benton Gallery, Southampton, N.Y., 1991, Parish Mus., Southampton, 1991, Michele Miller Fine Art, 1993 ; executed murals N.Y. Aquarium, Bklyn., 1982, Pub. Art Fund, N.Y.C., 1983, Albert Einstein Sch. of Medicine, Bronx, N.Y., 1983, Hudson River Mus., Yonkers, N.Y., 1983, Bellevue Hosp. Ctr., N.Y.C., 1986; represented in permanent collections at Met. Mus. of Art, N.Y.C, Bklyn. Mus., Fogg Art Mus., Cambridge, Mass., Hudson River Mus., Yonkers, N.Y., Hecksler Mus., Huntington, N.Y., Cin. Art Mus., Readers' Digest, Pleasantville, N.Y., Guild Hall, East Hampton, N.Y., Allen Meml. Art Mus., Oberlin, Ohio, Norton Mus., Palm Beach, Fla., Portland (Oreg.) Mus., Orlando (Fla.) Mus. Art, Neuburger Mus., Purchase, N.Y.; commd. work iron gates Cathedral St. John the Divine, N.Y.C., 1988, 55' steel fence Henry St Settlement, N.Y., 1992, metal work stairway De Soto Sch., N.Y. Sch. Art, 1994. Grantee Nat. Endowment for Arts, 1977-78, Threshold Found., 1991. Home and Studio: 119 E 18th St New York NY 10003

SLAVIN, JERI BETH, investment banker, art historian; b. Manhasset, N.Y., Sept. 7, 1960; d. Alvin Theodore and Roberta Pearl (Landau) S.; m. Martin M. Gottlieb, Oct. 9, 1988. BA, Brandeis U., 1984; AM, Washington U., 1987; MBA, Harvard U., 1994. Assoc. Barbara Krakow Gallery, Boston, 1987-88; dir. Howard Yezerski Gallery, Boston, 1988-92; founder, pres. Art Savvy Edn. Co., Boston, 1988—; mem. steering com. Visual AIDS New Eng., Boston, 1989-92; acquistions co-chair ARTcetera '92, Boston, 1992; intern external affairs Whitney Mus. Am. Art, N.Y.C., summer 1993; assoc. Goldman, Sachs and Co., N.Y.C., 1994; guest lectr. in field; freelance critic and writer. Alumni Assn. scholar Brandeis U., Waltham, Mass., 1984; Univ. fellow Washington U., St. Louis, 1984-85, Teaching fellow Washington U., 1985-86, summer fellow Harvard Bus. Sch. Non Profit Club, Boston, 1993.

SLAVIN, LESLEY ANNE, clinical psychologist; b. Waterbury, Conn., June 7, 1955; d. Sherman R. and Virginia (Woodbury) S.; m. Paul J. Rupf, May 26, 1990. BA in Psychology, Tufts U., 1977; PhD in Psychology, U. Vt., 1985. Cert. psychologist, N.H. Rsch. assoc. Sidney Farber Cancer Inst., Boston, 1978-80; rsch. asst. dept. psychology U. Vt., Burlington, 1980-81; psychology intern Vt. State Hosp., Waterbury, 1981-82, Behavior Therapy Ctr., Burlington, 1982-83, Lamoille County Mental Health, Morrisville, Vt., 1983-85; asst. prof. Va. Commonwealth U., Richmond, 1985-91; clinician Cen. N.H. Community Mental Health Svcs., Inc., Concord, 1992—. Contbr. articles to profl. jours. Va. Commonwealth U. faculty grantee, 1987. Mem. APA. Democrat.

SLAVIN, ROSANNE SINGER, textile converter; b. N.Y.C., Mar. 24, 1930; d. Lee H. and Rose (Winkler) Singer; student U. Ill.; divorced; children—Laurie Jo, Sharon Lee. Prodn. converter Doucet Fabrics, silk prints, N.Y.C., 1953-57; sales mgr., mdse. mgr. print div. Crown Fabrics, N.Y.C., 1957-65; owner Matisse Fabrics, Inc. printed fabrics (name now Hottmomma Inc.), N.Y.C., 1965—. Recipient Tommy award, 1978, 93; designated ofcl. printed fabric supplier for U.S. Olympic swimteam, 1984. Office: 570 7th Ave New York NY 10018-1602

SLAVINSKA, NONNA, psychoanalyst, psychotherapist; b. Warsaw, Poland; came to U.S., 1953, naturalized, 1958; d. Paul and Nadezda (von Vetter) Slawinski; m. Vaclav L. de P. Holy, Feb. 22, 1970; 1 child, Alexander Levitsky. MS cum laude, L.I. U., 1957; PhD, NYU, 1967; cert. psychoanalysis and psychotheraphy, Postgrad. Ctr. Mental Health, 1971, cert. group psychotherapy, 1974, cert. supervision psychoanalytic process, 1975. Pvt. practice clin. psychology, 1957—; clin. psychologist N.J. Dept. Instns. and Agencies, Trenton, 1957-64; cons. spl. edn. Howell Twp. Bd. Edn., N.J., 1964-66, Monmouth County High Sch., N.J., 1966-68; cons. in psychology Dept. Labor and Industry, Newark, 1970-75; supr. Inst. Mental Health Edn., Englewood, N.J., 1976-80; supr. faculty Payne-Whitney Clinic, N.Y. Hosp., Cornell Med. Ctr., N.Y.C., 1978-82; supr. Psychol. Ctr. CCNY, 1981-82; supr. Psychonanalytic Inst. Postgrad. Ctr. for Mental Health, N.Y.C., 1983—, sr. supr. group therapy dept., 1982—, faculty, 1972—, asst. supr. faculty group therapy dept., 1976—; supr. group and family studies div. Albert Einstein Coll. Medicine, Yeshiva U., N.Y.C., 1987—; founder, chairperson com. on mental health Kosciuszko Found., N.Y.C., 1982-88; founder, chairperson interdisciplinary psychology and mental health sect. Polish Inst. Arts and Scis., N.Y.C., 1984—. Internat. editor GROUP Jour., 1983-86; internat. coord., cons. editor Internat. Jour. Group Psychotherapy, 1984-87. Recipient Five Yr. Service to N.J. award, 1963, Founder's Day award NYU, 1968, Cert. , Am. Group Psychotherapy Assn., 1981. Fellow Am. Psychol. Assn., Am. Group Psychotherapy Assn. (internat. aspects com.); mem. Internat. Assn. Group Psychotherapy (bd. dirs. 198-386, founder, chairperson adv. com. on inquiry and rsch. 1984—), N.J. Psychol. Assn., Internat. Assn. Applied Psychology,Internat Div. 29 Am. Psychol. Assn. (chmn. com. on rsch. 1985—). Home: 29 West Trl Stamford CT 06903-2411 also: 1150 Fifth Ave New York NY 10128 Office: 9 E 96th St # 9B New York NY 10128-0778

SLAYBAUGH, JANET LOUISE, social worker; b. Gettysburg, Pa., Oct. 29, 1942; d. Robert Paul and Ruth Bell (Cook) S. BS, U. Ala., 1963; cert. social work, La. State U., 1966, MSW, 1967; PhD, Union Inst., Cin., 1990. Cert social worker Acad. Cert. Social Workers, bd. cert. social workers, cert. info. systems auditor, CPA. Mem. NASW, AICPA, La. Assn. Cert. Pub. Accts., Electronic Data Processing Auditors Assn. Lutheran. Home: 620 Chippenham Dr Baton Rouge LA 70808-5611 Office: La Dept Social Svcs 755 Riverside St N Ste 232 Baton Rouge LA 70802-5212

SLAYDON, JEANNE MILLER, secondary school educator; b. Kansas City, Mo.; d. Sanderson Staley and Bea Amelia (Hoeger) Miller; m. A. Glynn Slaydon (dec.); children: Kathleen Amelia Slaydon Mayer, Dianne Louise Slaydon Springer. BA, Tex. Christian U.; MEd, U. Houston. Pvt. tutor Midland and Houston, Tex.; elem. tchr. Midland Ind. Sch. Dist.; tchr. sec. social studies Spring Branch Ind. Sch. Dist., Houston, chmn. Social Studies dept., dist. Social Studies coord., 1977-91; pvt. practice social studies cons. Houston, 1991—; cons. So. Assn. Colls. and Univs., 1978—; mem. Tex. State Task Force on Restructuring Social Studies, Grade 1 to 12, 1991-92. Author: (econs. curriculum) Confluent Economic Education, 1979; cons. (textbook) World History, 1982. Mem. Tex. Citizen Bee, Local Close Up, 1985-91; coord. Congl. Dist. 7 Bicentennial Commn.; spkr. Inst. Internat. Edn., Network for Zero Population Growth. Mem. AAUW, SSSA, Inst. for Internat. Edn., Spring Br. Coun. for Social Studies (treas. 1970-73, pres. 1983), Tex. Coun. for Social Studies (v.p. 1986, pres. 1988), Tex. Assn. Advancement of History (bd. dirs.), Tex. State Hist. Assn., Tex. Alliance Geog. Edn., Houston Friends of Geography, Houston Geog. Soc., NAt. Coun. Social Studies, NAt. Coun. Geog. Edn., Alpha Delta Kappa, Alpha Gamma, Phi Delta Kappa (chpt. sec. 1991—). Congregationalist.

SLAYMAN, CAROLYN WALCH, geneticist, educator; b. Portland, Maine, Mar. 11, 1937; d. John Weston and Ruth Dyer (Sanborn) Walch; m. Clifford L. Slayman; children—Andrew, Rachel. B.A. with highest honors, Swarthmore Coll., 1958; Ph.D., Rockefeller U., 1963; D.Sc. (hon.), Bowdoin Coll., 1985. Instr., then asst. prof. Case Western Res. U., Cleve., 1967; from asst. prof. to prof. genetics Yale U. Sch. Medicine, New Haven, 1967—, Sterling prof. genetics, 1991—, chmn. dept. genetics, 1984—; chmn. genetic basis of disease rev. commn. NIH, 1981-85, nat. adv. gen. med. scis. coun., 1989-93; bd. dirs. J. Weston Walch Pub., Portland, Maine, The Perkin-Elmer Corp.; mem. sci. rev. bd. Howard Hughes Med. Inst., 1992—. Mem. editorial bd. Jour. Biol. Chemistry, 1989-94; contbr. articles to sci. jours. Trustee Foote Sch., New Haven, Conn., 1983-89, Hopkins Sch., New Haven, 1988-93; bd. overseers Bowdoin Coll., Brunswick, Maine, 1976-88, trustee, 1988—. Recipient Deborah Morton award Westbrook Coll., 1986. Mem. Am. Soc. Biol. Chemists, Genetics Soc. Am., Soc. Gen. Physiologists, Am. Soc. Microbiology, Phi Beta Kappa. Office: Yale U Sch Medicine Dept Genetics 333 Cedar St New Haven CT 06510-3289

SLEBODNIK, TRESSA ANN, elementary education educator; b. Belle Vernon, Pa., Nov. 11, 1931; d. Michael Ferdinand and Elizabeth (Skruber) Nusser; m. Thomas Patrick Slebodnik, June 6, 1953; children: Thomas, Anita, Eleanor, Edward, Charles, Kathleen, Linda. BS, California (Pa.) State Tchrs. Coll., 1953. Cert. tchr., Pa. Tchr. kindergarten Yough Sch. Dist., West Newton, Pa., 1969-76; tchr. first grade Yough Sch. Dist., Sutersville, Pa., 1976-80, Smithton, Pa., 1980-81; tchr. kindergarten Yough Sch. Dist., Smithton and Ruffsdale, Pa., 1981-82, Ruffsdale, 1982—; devel. Approach to Sci. and Health, Ruffsdale, 1990-93; grade level coord., mentor tchr. and curriculum coun. Pres. curriculum coun. St. Edward Bowling League, Herminie; active Altar-Rosary Soc., Herminie. Mem. NEA, Pa. State Edn. Assn., Keyston State Reading Assn., Yough Edn. Assn. (bldg. rep.), Westmoreland County Reading Coun. Democrat. Roman Catholic. Home: RD 1 Box 200 Irwin PA 15642 Office: Mendon Elem Sch RD 1 Box 680 Ruffs Dale PA 15679

SLEDGE, KAREN PEKLO, retail executive; b. Rocky Mount, N.C., June 1, 1961; d. Joseph William and Marilyn Janelda (Murdoch) Peklo; m. Jon Lowrance Sledge, June 15, 1991. BS in Mktg., U. West Fla., 1987. Dept. mgr. trainee Gayfers, Pensacola, Fla., 1984-88; asst. sr. buyer Gayfers, Mobile, Ala., 1988-89; dept. mgr. and buyer Gayfers, Ridgeland, Miss., 1989-92; dept. mgr. Marshall Fields, Schaumburg, Ill., 1992—. Mem. Jr. League of Jackson, Miss., Univ. West Fla. Alumni Assn. Democrat. Roman Catholic. Home: 1437 Woods Dr # 116 Arlington Heights IL 60004 Office: Marshall Fields 1 Woodfield Mall Schaumburg IL 60173

SLEEPER, PAMELA BOIS, rehabilitation counselor; b. Manchester, N.H., Sept. 19, 1950; d. Maurice Paul and Yeteve Rachel (Vezina) Bois; m. Gordon J. Sleeper, Oct. 27, 1974. BA, Emmanuel Coll., 1972; MS, U. Nev., 1994. From sec./stenographer to reports officer CIA, Washington, 1972-80; assembly attache, com. sec. Nev. State Legis., Carson City, 1981, 82; exec. sec. to pres. Bender Warehouse Co., Reno, Nev., 1981-82; adminstrv. asst. to pres. Restroom Facilities Corp., Reno, Nev., 1982; freelance sec., adminstrv. asst., rsch. & planning Carson City, Reno, Nev., 1983-84; engr. in tng. Reynold's Elec. & Engring. Co., Las Vegas, 1984; from sr. sec. to employee health benefits specialist Clark County, Las Vegas, 1984-86; adminstrv. asst. to welfare benefit trust Clark County Classroom Tchr.'s Assn., Las Vegas, 1986-90; employment specialist State of Nev., North Las Vegas, 1990-93. Mem. Am. Counseling Assn., Am. Rehab. Counseling Assn., Assn. Spiritual, Ethical and Religous Values in Counseling, Nev. Assn. Counseling and Devel., Nat. Assn. Rehab. Profls. in Pvt. Sector (med. facilities sect., Nev. chpt.), Inst. Reality Therapy, Las Vegas Alliance for Mentally Ill, Nev. Vocat. Assn., Delta Soc., Pet Partners Program, Inst. Animal Asst. Therapy, Therapy Dogs Internat., Paws that Serve, Vegas Valley Dog Obedience Club, Agility Club So. Nev., Jackpot Dog Obedience Assn., Nev. Republican. Roman Catholic. Address: PO Box 3097 Detroit MI 48231-3097

SLEWITZKE, CONNIE LEE, retired army officer; b. Mosinee, Wis., Apr. 15, 1931; d. Leo Thomas and Amelia Marie (Hoffman) S. BSN, U. Md., Balt., 1971; MA in Counseling and Guidance, St. Mary's U., San Antonio, 1976. Commd. 1st lt. U.S. Army, 1957, advanced through grades to brig. gen., 1987; ret., 1987; chief dept. nursing Letterman Army Med. Ctr. U.S. Army, San Francisco, 1978-80; asst. chief nurse Army Nurse Corps U.S. Army, Washington, 1980-83; chief brigadier gen. U.S. Army, 1983-87; mem. Va. Adv. Com. on Women Vets. Contbr. articles to profl. jours. Decorated D.S.M., Legion of Merit, Bronze Star medal. Mem. ANA, Va. Nurses Assn., Alumni Assn. U.S. Army War Coll., Assn. U.S. Army, Women in Mil. Svc. for Am. Found. (v.p.), Sigma Theta Tau.

SLICK, JEWEL CHERIE, nurse, consulting service administrator; b. Poplar, Mont., June 13, 1934; d. Ralph and Charity Ruth (Reddoor) Wing; m. Virgil Slick, May 31, 1970; 1 child, Cherie Ann. RN St. Luke's Hosp., Kansas City, Mo., 1955. Pvt. duty nurse, 1958—; advocate for Am. Indians, 1969—; owner Am. Indian Cons. Service, Des Moines, 1980—; mem. Des Moines Human Rights Commn., 1974-77, 82—, Gov. Iowa Interstate Indian Council, 1975-77, Nat. Indian Bd. Alcoholism, 1975-78; bd. dirs. Des Moines YWCA, 1981—; elected to Nat. Regulations Com., 1990—; vice chairperson DSM Human Rights Commn. Recipient Iowa Gov.'s Vol. award, 1987, Proclamation of Recognition award, 1987, Key to the City, 1987. Mem. NAFE, NOW, Iowa Nursing Assn., Nat. Assn. Human Rights Workers, Internat. Human Rights Agencies, Polk Country Charter Commn. Democrat. Address: 3610 Columbia St Des Moines IA 50313-4532

SLIDER, MARGARET ELIZABETH, elementary education educator; b. Spanish Fork, Utah, Nov. 27, 1945; d. Ira Elmo and Aurelia May (Peterson) Johnson; m. Richard Keith Slider, Oct. 25, 1968; children: Thomas Richard, Christopher Alan. AA, Chaffey Coll., 1966; BA, Calif. State U., San Bernardino, 1968, MEd in English as Second Lang., 1993. Cert. elem. tchr., Calif. Tchr. Colton (Calif.) Unified Sch. Dist., 1968—; lead sci. tchr. McKinley Sch., 1994—; mem. kindergarten assessment com. Colton Joint Unified Sch. Dist., Colton, 1988-90, dist. math. curriculum com., 1992-94; trainer Calif. State Dept. Edn. Early Intervention for Sch. Success, 1993—, demonstrator on-site classroom, 1994. Treas. McKinley Sch. PTA, Colton, 1989-91. Mem. NEA, ASCD, AAUW, Calif. Tchrs. Assn., Calif. Elem. Edn. Assn., Calif. Assn. of Tchrs. of English to Students of Other Langs., Calif. Mathematics Coun., Assn. Colton Educators, Pi Lambda Theta. Home: 1628 Waterford Ave Redlands CA 92374-3967 Office: Colton Unified Sch Dist 1212 Valencia Dr Colton CA 92324-1731

SLINDE, ELIZABETH MARY ANNE, county official; b. Detroit, Oct. 17; d. Gifford Norman and Elizabeth (McPike) S. BS, Wayne State U., 1958, MEd, 1960; postgrad., U. Detroit, Mich. State U., Oakland U. Elem. tchr. Beckek Sch., Osage, Mich., 1950-53; elem. tchr. Roseville (Mich.) Cmty. Schs., 1953-63, elem. prin., 1963-86; county commr. Macomb County, Mt. Clemens, Mich., 1976, 79—; fin. chmn. Macomb County Mental Health Com., Mt. Clemens, 1987—; active Macomb County Employees Retirement Commn. Sec. Macomb County Dem. Com., Eastpointe, Mich., 1972—; chmn. United Cmty. Svcs., Warren, Mich., 1989-93; mem. Beautification Commn., Roseville, Mich., 1974—; mem. S.E. Mich. Coun. of Govt., Detroit, 1989-94, vice chmn., 1992-94; mem. Roseville Dem. Com. Recipient Outstanding Achievement in Local Govt. Svc., Mich. Dem. Party, 1989. Mem. Nat. Assn. Counties, Mich. Assn. Counties (Excellence in County Govt. award 1990). Roman Catholic. Home: 26740 Roberta Roseville MI 48066 Office: Office Bd Commrs Macomb County Court Bldg 2nd Fl 40 N Gratiot Mount Clemens MI 48043

SLIVKO, JACQUELINE SUSAN, systems consultant, project manager; b. N.Y.C., Dec. 17, 1950; d. Saul and Seena (Dickman) S. BA in Edn., Hunter Coll., 1971; MBA in Fin., Pace U., 1978; postgrad., Columbia U. Distbn. mgr. Pepsi Cola, Purchase, N.Y., 1978-83; asst. mgr. corp. fin. Gen. Foods, White Plains, N.Y., 1984-86; planning mgr. Port Authority of N.Y. and N.J., N.Y.C., 1986-88; asst. v.p. Chemical Bank, N.Y.C., 1988-91; pvt. practice N.Y.C., 1991-93; systems cons. Personal Fin. Asst., Inc. (subs. N.Y. Life Co.), N.Y.C., 1993-95. Mellon scholar Pace U., 1974-76. Home: 61 Jane St New York NY 10014

SLJAKA, MARY TOMICA, music educator; b. Georgetown, S.C., June 12, 1950; d. Victor John and Sophie (Xanthos) S. BA in Music Edn., CUNY, Flushing, 1972; MA in Music History, L.I. U., 1974; studies with Gertrude Bary. Tchr. music Babylon (N.Y.) Pub. Schs., 1972-74, Brunswick County Pub. Schs., Southport, N.C., 1975—; organizer group piano program South Brunswick Middle Sch. Author numerous music and dance reviews Wilmington Morning Star, 1975-77. Mem. Nat. Guild of Piano Tchrs., Wilmington Concert Assn. (bd. dirs. 1990—), N.C. Music Educators Assn., Cape Fear Astron. Soc., N.C. Music Tchrs. Assn. (chpt. pres. 1987-89), Daus. of Penelope. Home: 2009 E Lake Shore Dr Wilmington NC 28401-6602 Office: S Brunswick Mid Sch Cougar Dr Southport NC 28461

SLOAN, MARY JEAN, media specialist; b. Lakeland, Fla., Nov. 29, 1927; d. Marion Wilder and Elba (Jinks) Sloan. BS, Peabody Coll., Nashville, 1949; MLS, Atlanta U., 1978, S.L.S., 1980. Cert. libr. media specialist. Music dir. Pinecrest Sch., Tampa, Fla., 1949-50, Polk County Schs., Bartow, Fla., 1950-54; pvt. music tchr. Lakeland, 1954-58; tchr. Clayton County Schs., Jonesboro Ga., 1958-59; media specialist Eastualley Sch., Marietta, Ga., 1959—; coord. conf. Ga. Library Media Dept., Jekyll Island, 1982-83, sec., Atlanta, 1982-83, com. chmn. ethnic conf., Atlanta, 1978, pres., 1984-85, state pres., 1985-86; program chmn. Ga. Media Orgns. Conf, Jekyll Island, 1988. Contbr. to bibliographies. Recipient Walter Bell award Ga. Assn. Instructional Tech., 1988, Disting. Svc. award, 1991. Mem. ALA (del. 1984, 85, 90), NEA, Southeastern Library Assn., Am. Assn. Sch. Librarians, Soc. for Sch. Librarians, Internat., Ga. Assn. Educators (polit. action com. 1983), Beta Phi Mu, Phi Delta Kappa. Republican. Methodist. Home: 797 Yorkshire Rd NE Atlanta GA 30306-3264 Office: Eastvalley Elem Sch 2570 Lower Roswell Rd Marietta GA 30068-3635

SLOAN, REBA FAYE, dietitian, consultant; b. South Bend, Ind., Feb. 5, 1955; d. Kenneth and Ruby Faye (Long) Lewis; m. Gilbert Kevin Sloan, May 22, 1976. BS, Harding U., 1976; MPH, Loma Linda U., 1989; Cert. Tng. in Child/Adolescent Obesity, U. Calif., San Francisco. Registered dietitian; lic. dietitian and nutritionist; cert. advanced clin. tng. adolescent obesity. Dietetic intern Vanderbilt U. Med. Ctr., Nashville, 1978, rsch. dietitian, 1979-80; therapeutic dietitian Bapt. Hosp., Nashville, 1981-85; staff dietitian Nautilus Total Fitness Ctrs., Nashville, 1983-86; cons. dietitian Nashville Met. Govt., 1986—, Bapt. Hosp. Ctr. for Health Promotion, Nashville, 1987-91, Parkwest Eating Disorder Clinic, Nashville, 1989-91; nutrition cons. The Nashville Striders, 1979-81; cons. nutritionist; mem. Vanderbilt U. Eating Disorder Com. Vol. Belmont Ch. Ministries, Nashville, 1981—; speaker Am. Heart Assn., Nashville, 1990—. Recipient cert. of appreciation Am. Heart Assn., 1990; Leaders fellow YMCA. Mem. Am. Dietetic Assn., Sports and Cardiovascular Nutritionists, Cons. Nutritionists, Am. Coll. Sports Medicine, Am. Running and Fitness Assn., Nashville Dist. Dietetic Assn. (contbr. diet manual 1984), Nat. Assn. for Chrisian Recovery, Alpha Chi. Home: 1817 Shackleford Rd Nashville TN 37215-3525 Office: 121 21st Ave N Ste 208 Nashville TN 37203-5213

SLOAN, ROSALIND, nurse, military officer; b. New Haven, Apr. 22, 1953; d. Paul and Blanche (Kopp) S. BSN, U. Conn., 1976; M of Ednl. Adminstrn., San Diego State U., 1993. Staff nurse Peter Bent Brigham Hosp., Boston, 1976-79; commd. officer USN, 1979, advanced through grades to comdr., 1988; staff nurse Portsmouth (Va.) Naval Hosp., 1979-83, Charleston (S.C.) Naval Hosp., 1983-85; charge nurse labor and delivery U.S. Naval Hosp., Subic Bay, Philippines, 1985-88; instr. Basic Hosp. Corps Sch.-Naval Sch. Health Scis., San Diego, 1988-90, asst. dir., 1990-91; asst. officer-in-charge, acad. officer Naval Sch. Dental Assisting and Tech., San Diego, 1991-92; dept. head command edn. and tng. Naval Med. Ctr., Oakland, Calif., 1993—. Recipient Naval Commendation medal USN, Subic Day, 1988, Naval Commendation medal Naval Sch. Health Scis., San Diego, 1991. Mem. Nat. Nursing Staff Devel. Orgn., Nat. Holistic Nursing Assn., Bay Area Soc. Health Edn. and Tng., Coun. Coll. and Milit. Educators, Phi Kappa Phi.

SLOAN, SUSAN V., portfolio manager; b. Budapest, Hungary, Jan. 7, 1945; came to U.S., 1949; d. Ernest and Seren (Kasser) Czin; m. Philip R. Sloan; children: Lisa, Michael. BA, Douglass Coll., 1966; postgrad., Pace U., 1980. V.p., portfolio mgr. Merrill Lynch Asset Mgmt., Princeton, N.J., 1966—. Mem. N.J. Women Bus. Owners, N.Y. Soc. Security Analysts. Republican. Home: 51 Hidden Lake Dr N Brunswick NJ 08902-1213 Office: Merrill Lynch Asset Mgmt 800 Scudders Mill Rd Plainsboro NJ 08536-1606

SLOANE, BEVERLY LEBOV, writer, consultant; b. N.Y.C., May 26, 1936; d. Benjamin S. and Anne (Weinberg) LeBov; m. Robert Malcolm Sloane, Sept. 27, 1959; 1 child, Alison Lori Sloane Gaylin. AB, Vassar Coll., 1958; MA, Claremont Grad. Sch., 1975, doctoral study, 1975-76; cert. in exec. mgmt., UCLA Grad. Sch. Mgmt., 1982, grad. exec. program., 1982; grad. profl. pub. course, Stanford U., 1982, 1994; grad. intensive bioethics course Kennedy Inst. Ethics, Georgetown U., 1987, advanced bioethics course, 1988; grad. sem. in Health Care Ethics, U. Wash. Sch. Medicine, Seattle, summer 1988, 89, 90, 94; grad. Summer Bioethics Inst. Loyola Marymount U., summer, 1990; grad. Annual Summer Inst. on Teaching or Writing, Columbia Tchrs. Coll., summer 1990; grad. Annual Summer Inst. on Advanced Teaching of Writing , summer, 1993, Annual Inst. Pub. Health and Human Rights, Harvard U. Sch. Pub. Health, 1994, cert. in ethics corps tng. program, Josephson Inst. of Ethics, 1991; ethics fellow Loma Linda U. Med. Ctr., 1989; cert. clin. intensive biomedical ethics, Loma Linda U., 1989. Circulation librarian Harvard Med. Library, Boston, 1958-59; social worker Conn. State Welfare, New Haven, 1960-61; tchr. English, Hebrew Day Sch., New Haven, 1961-64; instr. creative writing and English lit. Monmouth Coll., West Long Branch, N.J., 1967-69; freelance writer, Arcadia, Calif., 1970—; v.p. council grad. students, Claremont Grad. sch., 1971-72, adj. dir. Writing Ctr. Speaker Series, 1993—; mem. adv. council tech. and profl. writing Dept. English, Calif. State U., Long Beach, 1980-82; mem. adv. bd. Calif. Health Rev., 1982-83; mem. Foothill Health Dist. Adv. Council L.A. County Dept. Health Svcs., 1987-93, pres., 1989-91, immediate past pres., 1991-92. Ann. Key Mem. award, 1990. Author: From Vassar to Kitchen, 1967, A Guide to Health Facilities: Personnel and Management, 1971, 2nd edit. 1977, 3d edit., 1992. Mem. pub. relations bd. Monmouth County Mental Health Assn., 1968-69; chmn. creative writing group Calif. Inst. Tech. Woman's Club, 1975-79; mem. ethics com., human subjects protection com. Jewish Home for the Aging, Reseda, Calif., 1994—, Santa Teresita Hosp., 1994—; mem. task force edn. and cultural activities, City of Duarte, 1987-88; mem. strategic planning task force com., campaign com. for pre-eminence Claremont Grad. Sch., 1986-87, mem. alumni coun., 1993—, bd. dirs., steering com. alumni assn., 1993—, mem. alumni coun., mem. steering com. annual alumni day 1994—, bd. govs. governing com. alumni assn., 1994—, mem. alumni awards com., 1994—, mem. alumni events com., 1994—, mem. vol. deve. com., 1994—; Vassar Coll. Class rep. to Alumnae Assn. Fall Coun. Meeting, 1989,, class corr. Vassar Coll. Quarterly Alumnae Mag., 1993—; co-chmn. Vassar Christmas Showcase New Haven Vassar Club, 1965-66, rep. to Vassar Coll. Alumnae Assn. Fall Coun. Meeting, 1965-66; co-chmn. Vassar Club So. Calif. Annual Book Fair, 1970-71; chmn. creative writing group Yale U. Newcomers, 1965-66, dir. creative writing group Yale U. Women's Orgn., 1966-67; grad. AMA Ann. Health Reporting Conf., 1992, 93; mem. exec. program network UCLA Grad. Sch. Mgmt., 1987—; trustee Ctr. for Improvement of Child Caring, 1981-83; mem. League Crippled Children, 1982—, bd. dirs., 1988-91, treas. for gen. meetings, 1990-91, chair hostesses com., 1988-89, pub. rels. com., 1990-91; bd. dirs. L.A. Commn. on Assaults Against Women, 1983-84; v.p. Temple Beth David, 1983-86; mem. community relations com. Jewish Fedn. Council Greater Los Angeles, 1985-87; del. Task Force on Minorities in Newspaper Bus., 1987-89; community rep. County Health Ctrs. Network Tobacco Control Program, 1991. Recipient cert. of appreciation City of Duarte, 1988, County of L.A., 1988; Coro Found. fellow, 1979; named Calif. Communicator of Achievement, Woman of Yr. Calif. Press Women, 1992. Fellow Am. Med. Writers Assn. (pres. Pacific Southwest chpt. 1987-89, dir. 1980-93, Pacific S.W. del. to nat. bd. 1980-87, 89-91, chmn. various cmn. nat. book awards trade category 1982-83, chmn. Nat. Conv. Networking Luncheon 1983, 84, chmn. freelance and pub. relations coms. Nat. Midyr. Conf. 1983-84, workshop leader ann. conf. 1984-87, 90, 91, 92, nat. chmn. freelance sect. 1984-85, gen. chmn. 1985, Asilomar Western Regional Conf., gen. chmn. 1985, workshop leader 1985, program co-chmn. 1987, speaker 1985, 88-89, program co-chmn. 1989, nat. exec. bd. dirs. 1985-86, nat. adminstr. sects. 1985-86, pres.-elect Pacific S.W. chpt. 1985-87, pres. 1987-89, immediate past pres. 1989-91, bd. dirs., 1991-93, moderator gen. session nat. conf. 1987, chair gen. session nat. conf., 1986-87, chair Walter C. Alvarez Meml. Found. award 1986-87, Appreciation award for outstanding leadership 1989, named to Workshop Leaders Honor Roll 1991); mem. Women in Comm. (dir. 1980-82, 89-90, v.p. community affairs 1981-82, N.E. area rep. 1980-81, chmn. awards banquet 1982, sem. leader, speaker ann. nat. profl. conf., 1985, program adv. com. L.A. chpt. 1987, v.p. activities 1989-90, chmn. Los Angeles chpt. 1st ann. Agnes Underwood Freedom of Info. Awards Banquet 1982, recognition award 1983, nominating com. 1982, 83, com. Women of the Press Awards luncheon 1988, Women in Comm. awards luncheon 1988), Am. Assn. for Higher Edn., AAUW (legis. chmn. Arcadia br. 1976-77, books and plays chmn. Arcadia br. 1973-74, creative writing chmn. 1969-70, 1st v.p. program dir. 1975-76, networking chmn. 1981-82, chmn. task force promoting individual liberties 1987-88, named Woman of Yr., Woman of Achievement award 1986, cert. of appreciation 1987), Coll. English Assn., Am. Pub. Health Assn., Am. Soc. Law and Medicine and Ethics, Calif. Press Women (v.p. programs L.A. chpt. 1982-85, pres. 1985-87, state pres. 1987-89, past immediate past state pres. 1989-91, chmn. state speakers bur. 1989—, del nat. bd. 1989—, moderator ann. spring conv., 1990, 92, chmn. nominating com. 1990-91, Calif. lit. dir. 1990-92, dir. state lit. com. 1990-92, dir. family literary day Calif., 1990, Cert. of Appreciation, 1991, named Calif. Communicator of Achievement 1992), AAUP, Internat. Comm. Assn., N.Y. Acad. Scis., Ind. Writers So. Calif. (bd. dirs. 1989-90, dir. Specialized Groups 1989-90, dir. at large 1989-90, bd. dirs. corp. 1988-89, dir. Speech Writing Group, 1991-92), Hastings Ctr., AAAS, Nat. Fedn. Press Women, (bd. dirs. 1987-93, nat. co-chmn. task force recruitment of minorities 1987-89, del. 1987-89, nat. dir. of speakers bur. 1989-93, editor of speakers bur. directory 1991, cert. of appreciation, 1991, 93, Plenary of Past Pres. state 1989—, workshop leader-speaker ann. nat. conf. 1990, chair state women of achievement com. 1986-87, editor Speakers Bur. Addendum Directory, 1992, editor Speakers Bur. Directory 1991, 92, named 1st runner up Nat. Communicator of Achievement 1992), AAUW (chpt. Woman of Achievement award 1986, chmn. task force promoting individual liberties 1987-88, speaker 1987, Cert. of Appreciation 1987, Woman of Achievement-Woman of Yr. 1986), Internat. Assn. Bus. Communicators, Soc. for Tech. Comm. (workshop leader, 1985, 86), Kennedy Inst. Ethics, Soc. Health and Human Values, Assoc. Writing Programs. Clubs: Women's City (Pasadena), Claremont Colls. Faculty House, Pasadena Athletic, Town Hall of Calif. (vice chair community affairs sect. 1982-87, speaker 1986, faculty-instr. Exec. Breakfast Inst. 1985-86, mem. study sect. council 1986-88). Lodge: Rotary (chair Duarte Rotary mag. 1988-89, mem. dist. friendship exch. com. 1988-89, mem. internat. svc. com. 1989-90, info. svc. com. 1989-90) Home and Office: 1301 N Santa Anita Ave Arcadia CA 91006-2419

SLOAT, BARBARA FURIN, cell biologist, educator; b. Youngstown, Ohio, Jan. 20, 1942; d. Walter and Mary Helen (Maceyko) Furin; m. John Barry Sloat, Nov. 2, 1968; children: John Andrew, Eric Furin. BS, Denison U., 1963; MS, U. Mich., 1966, PhD, 1968. Lab. asst. U. Ghent, Belgium, 1964; teaching fellow, lectr. U. Mich., Ann Arbor, 1964-66, 68-70, asst. rsch. biologist Mental Health Rsch. Inst., 1972-74; vis. asst. prof., lectr. U. Mich., Ann Arbor and Dearborn, 1974-76; dir. women in sci. U. Mich., Ann Arbor, 1980-84, assoc. dir. honors, 1986-87, rsch. scientist, 1976—, lectr. Residential Coll., 1984—; assoc. Inst. Humanities U. Mich., Ann Arbor, 1991—. Author: Laboratory Guide for Zoology, 1979, Summer Internships in the Sciences for High School Women (CASE Silver medal, 1985, Excellence in Edn. award, U. Mich., 1993). Recipient Acad. Women's Caucus award, U. Mich., 1984, Grace Lyon Alumnae Award, Denison U., 1988; grantee NSF, U.S. Dept. Edcn., Warner Lambert Found., others. Mem. AAAS, Am. Soc. Cell Biology, N.Y. Acad. Scis., Nat. Assn. Women Deans, Adminstrs. and Counselors, Assn. for Women in Sci. (councilor 1988-90, pres. elect 1990), Phi Beta Kappa, Sigma Xi. Home: 2010 Hall Ave Ann Arbor MI 48104-4816 Office: U Mich Residential Coll 216 Tyler East Quad Ann Arbor MI 48109-1245

SLOAT, JANE ROBERTS DEGRAFF, government official, civic worker, consultant; b. N.Y.C., Dec. 31, 1939; d. John Wynne and Agnes (Murton) Roberts; m. Elliott Dodd DeGraff, June 28, 1959 (div.); children: Pamela DeGraff Porter, Jill Katherine; m. Jonathan Welsh Sloat, June 19, 1983. Active Hospitality and Info. Svc., Washington, 1964-70, sec. bd., 1971-73; spl. asst. to ambassador-at-large for cultural affairs Dept. State, Washington, 1981; spl. asst. to U.S. coord. refugee affairs, Washington, 1982-85, coord. conf. on Ethical Issues and Moral Principles in U.S. Refugee Policy, 1983; real estate broker Samuel P. Padoe Real Estate, Washington, 1986—. Tour lectr. Corcoran Gallery Art, Washington, 1965-70; vice chmn. UN Concert, Washington, 1971, 50th Jubilee Nat. English Speaking Union, 1971; spl. asst. to chmn. United Givers Fund, Washington, 1971-72; chmn. ball Opera Soc. Washington, 1972; bd. dirs. Jr. League, 1970-71, Nat. Ballet Soc., 1972-74, Washington Performing Arts Soc., 1972-75; mem. D.C. Mayor's Com. on Internat. Visitors, 1972-77; trustee Hosp. for Sick Children, Washington, 1973-76; editor Washington Antiques Show Catalogue, 1972-75; mem. D.C. Rep. Fin. Com., 1972-75; trustee Meridian House Internat. Ctr., Washington, 1964-82, sec. 1974-75, vice chmn. bd., 1976-82; mem. bd. advisers D.C. Lung Assn., 1975—; active fund-raising drive for Washington Cathedral, 1976; bd. dirs. Washington Home for Incurables, 1976-89, Nat. Eye Found., 1976-78, Children's Hosp. Nat. Rsch. Found., 1978-81, D.C. chpt. ARC, 1976-84, Travelers Aid Soc., 1976-90; chmn. Washington Antiques Show, 1976-78, Washington Cathedral Flower Mart; dir. fin. devel. YWCA of Nat. Capital Area, 1979; vice chmn. Reagan Bush Inaugural, Washington, 1981; mem. transition team for Reagan Bush for NEA, 1981; bd. dirs. Family Stress Services, 1981-84; founder, chmn. Entertaining People, 1982-91; bd. dirs. All Hallows Guild, Washington br. English Speaking Union, 1987-90, Woodrow Wilson House, Washington; chmn. Bush-Quayle Inaugural Ball, 1989; fundraiser Ann. Fund kennedy Ctr. Performing Arts, 1987, 90; v.p. bd. Washington Home, 1990-92; appointed mem. Pres.'s Commn. Arts & Humanities, 1990-94. Mem. Million Dollar Club, Sulgrave Club, Chevy Chase Club. Episcopalian. Avocations: art, design, tennis, opera.

SLOATE, SUSAN, writer; b. N.Y.C., June 27, 1957; d. Mortimer and Joyce Ann (Berglas) S. AB, U. So. Calif., 1979. Freelance writer young adult fiction and non-fiction, hist. and contemporary adult fiction, screenplays. Mem. Authors Guild.

SLOBOGIN, KATHY, television producer, news correspondent; b. Washington, July 19, 1952. BA, Yale U., 1974. Asst. to editor N.Y. Review of Books, N.Y.C., 1974-75; asst. to columnist, news clk. N.Y. Times, N.Y.C., 1976-78; prodr. ABC News, N.Y.C., 1978-79, documentary prodr. Closeup, 1979-85; prodr. CBS News, N.Y.C., Washington, 1985-89; prodr., corr. CNN Investigative Unit, Washington, 1990—. Recipient Christopher award Columbus Internat. Film and Video Festival, 1983, Peabody award U. Ga., 1985, Emmy award NATAS, 1985, Joan Shorenstein Barone award Radio and TV Corrs. Assn., 1993, Golden Eagle award Coun. Internat. Non-Theatrical Events, 1993, Westinghouse Sci. Journalism award AAAS-Westinghouse, 1994, Ace award Nat. Acad. Cable Programming, 1995. Mem. Writers Guild Am. East, Inc., Investigative Reporters and Editors. Office: CNN 820 1st St NE Washington DC 20002

SLOCUM, ELIZABETH, newspaper editor; b. Boston, Mar. 21, 1947; d. William and Elizabeth (Dowell) Dulligan; m. James Jackson Slocum, Nov. 21, 1969. B.S. in Journalism, U. Mo., Columbia, 1969. Reporter So. Illinoisan, Carbondale, 1969; reporter, copy editor North Shore Pub. Co., Milw., 1970-72; reporter, copy editor Milw. Jour., 1972-77, asst. mag. editor, 1972-79, mag. editor, 1979-86, Features/Lifestyle editor, 1986-92, Features editor, 1993, asst. mng. editor Features, 1994; editor-in-residence So. Ill. U., Carbondale, 1980, U. Wis, Eau Claire, Wis., 1982, U. So. Fla., Jacksonville, 1983; bd. dirs. Nat. Editorial Bd. for Sunday Mags., N.Y.C., 1983-86. Mem. TEMPO, Milw., 1983—. Recipient best mag. story award Milw. Press Club, 1978, Penney-Mo. award for best Lifestyle sect., 1991. Mem. Milw. Press Club (pres. 1979), Sigma Delta Chi (treas. Milw. chpt. 1977). Office: Milw Jour/Features PO Box 661 Milwaukee WI 53201-0661

SLOCUM, ROSEMARIE R., physician management search consultant; b. Port Arthur, Tex., Dec. 19, 1948; d. Edly and Ella (McNeely) Raccard; m. A.J. Slocum, Jan. 1967; 1 child, Blair Ashton. Student, La. State U., Alexandria, 1966-68; BS, La. State U., Baton Rouge, 1971. Cert. tchr., La. Edn. specialist La. Dept. Occupational Standards, Baton Rouge, 1971-74; account exec. Uarco, Inc., Baton Rouge, 1974-77; owner, broker Rosemarie Slocum Real Estate, Baton Rouge, 1977-91; physician recruiter MSI, New Orleans, 1985-86; assoc. dir. physician recruitment Physician Search, Inc., Fairfax, Va., 1986-88; spl. cons. Caswell/Winters Physician Search Cons., Milw., 1988-89; v.p. U.S. Med. Search, Inc. subs. of Caswell/Winters, Milw., 1988-89; dir. physician recruitment/mktg. East Range Clinics, Ltd., Virginia, Minn., 1989-91; pres. Rosemarie Slocum, Inc., Virginia, Minn., 1991—. Office: Rosemarie Slocum Inc 817 5th Ave S Virginia MN 55792-2804

SLOCUMB, FRANCES GILLIAM, psychoanalyst; b. Shannon, Miss., Aug. 10, 1937; d. Richard Franklin and Evie Lois (Hodges) Gilliam; m. Travis Hugh Slocumb Jr. (div. June 1978); children: Travis Hugh Slocumb III, Stephanie Slocumb Leydig. BS, Old Dominion U., 1969; MA, Coll. William and Mary, 1972; PhD, Va. Commonwealth U., 1982; Diploma, C. G. Jung Inst., Zurich, 1986. Psychology instr. Christopher Newport Coll., Newport News, Va., 1972-75, asst. prof. psychology, 1975-82; assoc. prof. psychology Christopher Newport Coll., 1982-85; pvt. practice Va. Beach, 1986—; asst. prof. psychology Coll. William and Mary, Williamsburg, Va., 1980-81; cons. various pub. and pvt. orgns., U.S. and Switzerland; organizer and leader numerous workshops. Bd. dirs. Planned Parenthood; mem. Women's Internat. League. Mem. Am. Counseling Assn., Am. Psychol. Assn., Am. Bd. Accreditation in Psychoanalysis (bd. dirs.), Nat. Assn. Advancement Psychoanalysis, Inter-Regional Soc. Jungian Analysts, Assn. Grads. in Analytic Psychology. Home and Office: 2356 Bays Edge Ave Virginia Bch VA 23451-1017

SLONE, MARY ELLEN, public relations executive. Pres. Meridian Comm., 1975-93, chmn., CEO. Office: Meridian Comm Goodwin Sq 444 E Main St #200 Lexington KY 40507*

SLONE, SANDI, artist; b. Boston, Oct. 1, 1939; d. Louis and Ida (Spind) Sudikoff; children: Erric Solomon, Jon Solomon. Student, Wheaton Coll., 1957-59, Boston Mus. Fine Arts Sch., 1970-73; BA, Wellesley Coll., 1974. Mem. painting faculty Boston Mus. Fine Arts Sch., 1975-95; instr. grad. program Sch. Visual Art, N.Y.C., 1989-90; lectr. painting Harvard U., Cambridge, Mass., 1982; vis. artist Triangle Artists Workshop, N.Y., 1982, 87, 90; co-founder, dir. Art/Omi Internat. Artists Found., N.Y.C., 1992, 93, 94. One-woman shows include Harcus Krakow Gallery, Boston, 1978, 79, 80, 82, 84, 86, Acquavella Contemporary Art, N.Y., 1977, 79, 80, 82, 84, Stephen Rosenberg Gallery, N.Y., 1988, Levinson Kane Gallery, Boston, 1989, Smith Jariwala Gallery, London, 1990; group shows include at Mus. Fine Arts, Boston, 1977, Corcoran Gallery of Art 35th Biennale, Washington, 1977, Edmonton Art Gallery, 1977, 85, Hayden Gallery MIT, Cambridge, Mass., 1978, New Generation Andre Emmerich Gallery, N.Y., 1980-81, Am. Ctr., Paris, 1980-81, Amerika Haus, Berlin, 1980-81, Carpenter Ctr., Harvard U., Casa de la Caritat, Barcelona, 1987, Federated Union of Black Artists, Johannesburg, South Africa, 1989, Jan Weiss Gallery, N.Y., 1990, Olympia Internat. Art Fairs, London, 1991, Gallery Korea, N.Y., 1992, Klarfeld Perry Gallery, N.Y., 1994, Out of the Blue Gallery, Edinburgh, Scotland, 1994; represented in permanent collections Mus. Modern Art, N.Y.C., Mus. Contemporary Art, Barcelona, Mus. Fine Arts, Boston, Hirshhorn Mus., Washington; artist-in-residence City Hall, Barcelona, 1987, 89. Mus. Fine Arts Boston fellow, 1977, 81; Ford Found. grantee, 1979. Studio: 13 Worth St New York NY 10013

SLONINA, KATHERINE LEE, insurance consultant; b. Chgo., Apr. 14, 1951; d. Henry Rudulph and Patricia June (Gnoske) S.; m. Frank A. Ventresco, July 1973 (div. Jan. 1990). MBA, Roosevelt U., 1993. With Zurich-Am. Ins. Co., Schaumburg, Ill., 1970-82; mgr. tech. svcs. Harco Nat. Ins. Co., Schaumburg, 1982-87; product analyst, product cons., sr. product cons. CNA Ins. Co., Chgo., 1987—. Dir. blood drives, United Way campaigns, Chgo. and Schaumburg; vol. reading instr. Project Literacy U.S., Elk Grove Village, Ill., 1990—; vol. Spl. Olympics, Clearbrook Ctr., Rolling Meadows, Ill., 1987, 88, piano instr., 1991—; poll watcher, election judge Ind. Voters of Ill., Chgo. Mem. Nat. Assn. Ins. Women (cert., Ill. state dir. 1988-90, Ill. state legis. chair 1986-87), Ins. Women of Suburban Chgo. (bd. dirs. 1984-87, pres. 1987-88). Home: 1020 Florida Ln Elk Grove Village IL 60007 Office: CNA Ins Cos 333 S Wabash Chicago IL 60685

SLORAH, PATRICIA PERKINS, anthropologist; b. Williamson, W.Va., Oct. 3, 1940; d. Guy Bennett and Annie Lee (Carlton) Perkins; m. John Brander Slorah III, Apr. 19, 1960; 1 child, Heather Michelle Slorah Newkirk. AA, St. Pete Jr. Coll., Clearwater, Fla., 1969; BA, U. South Fla., 1971, MA, 1988; PhD, %, 1994. Cert. elem. tchr., Fla. Tchr. Belleair Montessorri, Pinellas, Fla., 1964-68, Pinellas Elem. Schs., 1971-80; grad. asst. U. South Fla., Tampa, 1987-88; researcher Case Western Med. Longitudinal Study, Tampa, 1987, Tampa Bay Share, 1991; witness Spl.Com. on Aging, Washington, 1991. V.p., sec. Friends of the Libr., Tarpon Springs, Fla., 1982-86; pres. Local Polit. Club, Tarpon Springs, 1988-90; speaker Congressman Michael Bilirakis Speaker Bur., 9th Dist., 1988—; founder Grandparents Rights Adv. Movement, 1989; mem. adv. bd. Nat. Task Force of Grandparents United for Children's Rights, Madison, Wis., 1991-92; active Nat. Ctr. Sci. Edn., 1993, Fla. Ctr. Children & Youth, 1993—. Mem. AAUW, Am. Antropol. Soc., Gerontol. Soc. Am., Nat. Ctr. Sci. Edn., So. Gerontol. Soc., Soc. Applied Anthropology, Assn. Gerontology and Anthropology, Phi Kappa Phi, Pi Gamma Mu, Phi Mu Sorority (chmn. recomendations com. 1986-88). Presbyterian. Home: 1225 N Florida Ave Tarpon Springs FL 34689-2003

SLOVITER, DOLORES KORMAN, federal judge; b. Phila., Sept. 5, 1932; d. David and Tillie Korman; m. Henry A. Sloviter, Apr. 3, 1969; 1 dau., Vikki Amanda. AB in Econs. with distinction, Temple U., 1953, LHD (hon.), 1986; LLB magna cum laude, U. Pa., 1956; LLD (hon.), The Dickinson Sch. Law, 1984, U. Richmond, 1992; LL.D. (hon.), Widener U., 1994. Bar: Pa. 1957. Assoc., then ptnr. Dilworth, Paxson, Kalish, Kohn & Levy, Phila., 1956-69; mem. firm Harold E. Kohn (P.A.), Phila., 1969-72; assoc. prof., then prof. law Temple U. Law Sch., Phila., 1972-79; judge U.S. Ct. Appeals (3d cir.), Phila., 1979—, chief judge, 1991—; mem. hearing panel Disciplinary Bd. Supreme Ct. Pa., 1978-79. Mem. S.E. region Pa. Gov.'s Conf. on Aging, 1976-79, Com. of 70, 1976-79; trustee Jewish Publ. Soc. Am., 1983-89; Jud. Conf. U.S. com. Bicentennial Constitution, 1987-90, com. on Rules of Practice and Procedure, 1990-93. Recipient Juliette Low medal Girl Scouts Greater Phila., Inc., 1990, Honor award Girls High Alumnae Assn., 1991, Jud. award Pa. Bar Assn., 1994; Disting. Fulbright scholar, Chile, 1990. Mem. ABA, FBA, Fed. Judges Assn., Am. Law Inst., Nat. Assn. Women Judges, Am. Judicature Scc. (bd. dirs.), mem. bd. overseers U. Pa. Law Sch., Phila. Bar Assn. (gov. 1976-78), Order of Coif (pres. U. Pa. chpt. 1975-77), Phi Beta Kappa. Office: US Ct Appeals 18614 US Courthouse 601 Market St Philadelphia PA 19106-1510

SLOWEY, DEBORAH LYNN, artist; b. Syracuse, N.Y., May 1, 1959. 4 Yr. Cert., Pa. Acad. Fine Arts, 1979-83; student, Barnes Found. Sch. Art, 1980-82. Art tchr. Catskill Art, Coll. of Mt. St. Vincent, N.Y.; artist The Printmaking Workshop, 1987—. One-person shows include Chuck Levitan Gallery, 1993; three-person show St. Mary's Coll., 1991, Gilford Gallery, 1991, Pace U., 1992. V.p. Buffalo Colony, 1991-93, com. mem. Nat. Arts Club Benefit for Printmaking Workshop, 1992, Gallery at the Printmaking Workshop, 1993. Home: 329 W 19th St New York NY 10011-3901

SLOWICK COLVIN, CATHERINE ANN, legal administrator; b. Woonsocket, R.I., Sept. 22, 1960; d. Francis Anthony and Isabelle Ann (Dziok) S.; m. J.T. Colvin, Dec. 20, 1985 (div. Sept. 1994); 1 child, Elisabeth. BS in Acctg. and Bus. Adminstrn., Providence Coll., 1982. Acct. Kopp, Koletsky & Berall, Hartford, Conn., 1984-85, Cohen & Channin, Hartford, Conn., 1985-87; adminstr. Mallery & Stern, L.A., 1987-92; adminstr. Wright, Robinson, McCammon, Osthimer & Tatun, L.A., 1992-94, Washington, 1994—. Leader Girl Scouts Am., 1987-94; tchr. rel. edn., L.A., 1991-93.

Recipient Young Women in Bus. in L.A. recognition, City of L.A., 1991. Mem. Am. Legal Adminstrs. Assn. Republican. Roman Catholic. Office: Wright Robinson McCammon Osthimer & Tatum 5335 Wisconsin Ave NW Ste 920 Washington DC 20015

SLOWIK, SHARON A., real estate agent; b. Rochester, N.Y., Apr. 23, 1944; d. Edward and Evelyn (McGillis) Schreiner; m. William G. Slowik, Sept. 12, 1970; children: Heather, Elizabeth, Michael, Matthew. Assoc., Lab. Inst. Mdse., 1964. Agent Carol Paris Brown Realtors, Vienna, Va., 1990—. Mem. Nat. Realtors Assn., Graduate Realtor Inst. (cert.), Cert. Residential Specialist (cert.), No. Va. Bd. Realtors (1993 and 1994 Million Dollar Sales Club, polit. action com. 1991—). Home: 5504 Ashleigh Rd Fairfax VA 22030 Office: Carol Paris Brown Realtors 8230 Boone Blvd Vienna VA 22182

SLOYAN, SISTER STEPHANIE, mathematics educator; b. N.Y.C., Apr. 18, 1918; d. Jerome James and Marie Virginia (Kelley) S. BA, Georgian Ct. Coll., 1945; MA in Math., Cath. U. Am., 1950, PhD, 1952. Asst. prof. math. Georgian Ct. Coll., Lakewood, N.J., 1952-56, assoc. prof., 1956-59, prof., 1959—, coll. pres., 1968-74; lectr. Grad. Sch. Arts and Scis., Cath. U. Am., Washington, 1960-82. Mem. Math. Assn. Am. (bd. govs. 1988-91), Am. Math. Soc., Sigma Xi. Democrat. Roman Catholic. Office: Georgian Ct Coll Dept Math Lakewood NJ 08701

SLOZAK, BETTY JO, mathematics educator; b. Rich Square, N.C., May 21, 1949; d. Walter Edward Bryant and Audrey (Duke) Hargrove; m. Richard Mark Slozak, Jun. 17, 1973; children: Kristopher, Taryn. BS, N.C. Wesleyan Coll., 1971; MA in Math Edn., East Carolina U., Greenville, 1985, MA in Adult Edn., 1991. Math. tchr. Wayne County Schs., Goldsboro, N.C., 1971-81; math. instr. Wayne C.C., Goldsboro, N.C., 1981—; part time math instr. Mt. Olive Coll., 1980, 94, N.C. Wesleyan Coll., 1994—. Bd. dirs. Wayne County Pub. Schs. Found., 1994—; parent mem. Girl Scouts of Am., Goldsboro, 1988—. Mem. N.C. Teachers of Math., N.C. Assn. Math. Teachers, N.C. Wesleyan Alumni Bd. (bd. dirs. 1994—). Home: 209 Glen Oak Dr Goldsboro NC 27534 Office: Wayne Community Coll Goldsboro NC 27530

SLUSHER, RUTH VARNER, banking administrator; b. Harrison County, Ky., June 11, 1945; d. James Edgar and Myrtle Mae (Whitaker) Varner; m. Edward C. Slusher, Dec. 17, 1984; children: Vonda K. Birch Hall, Kevin W. Birch. Ed., Ky. Sch. Bus., Louisville, 1988. Cert. in mgmt. devel., gen. banking, prins. of banking, money and banking. Security officer, br. mgr., teller First Security of Clark County, Winchester, Ky., ops. officer, teller mgr.; client svc. mgr. Bank One, Lexington, Ky.; asst. cashier Ky. Bank. Mem. Lionesses (2d v.p. 1989, Lioness Tamer 1990, pres. 1991-92). Office: 24 W Lexington Ave Winchester KY 40391-1979 also: PO Box 240 Winchester KY 40392-0240

SLUTSKY, LORIE ANN, foundation executive; b. N.Y.C., Jan. 5, 1953; d. Edward and Adele (Moskowitz) S. BA, Colgate U., 1975; MA in Urban Policy and Analysis, New Sch. for Social Rsch., N.Y.C., 1977. Program officer N.Y. Community Trust, N.Y.C., 1977-83, v.p., 1983-87, exec. v.p., 1987-89, pres., chief exec. officer, 1990—; mem., formerly chmn. bd. trustees Coun. on Founds., Inc., Washington, 1986-95. Trustee Colgate U., Hamilton, N.Y., 1989—; bd. dirs. Found. Ctr., Inc., N.Y.C., United Way, N.Y.C. Office: NY Community Trust 2 Park Ave New York NY 10016

SMAIL, ANNETTE KLANG, civic leader, women's rights advocate; b. St. Helena, Calif., July 20, 1920; d. Leon and Victoria Nellie (Hartman) K.; divorced; children: Barry Lee, Karen Smail Poksay. AA, San Francisco Jr. Coll., 1939; AB, U. Calif., Berkeley, 1943; postgrad., U. Chgo., 1945. Cert. adult teaching credential in social studies and English. News reporter Community Newspapers, Chgo., 1945-46; editor textbooks U. Calif., Berkeley, 1948-49; edn. coordinator Econ. Opportunity Council, San Rafael, Calif., 1969-71; cmty. organizer with Saul Alinsky Back of the Yards. Cmty. organizer, co-founder Novato (Calif.) Human Needs Ctr., 1970-72; founder, leader Older Women's Polit. Caucus, 1977-95, Med. Equality for Dependents, 1977; author various resolutions passed by Calif. legis. on med. rights and women's rights; del. White House Conf. on Aging, Washington, 1981; mem. Calif. Task Force on Feminization of Poverty, Sacramento, 1984. Recipient San Francisco Working Woman Achievement award Working Woman mag., 1983, Women Helping Women award Soroptimists, 1979, Marin Martin Luther King Jr. Humanitarian award, 1991, Calif. Legis. Senate Rules Com. commendation, Eleanor Roosevelt Vision award, 1994; named Disting. Woman of Yr. Novato Advance Newspaper, 1979; inducted into Marin Women's Hall of Fame, 1991. Mem. Nat. Women's Polit. Caucus. Democrat.

SMAISTRLA, JEAN ANN, family therapist; b. South Gate, Calif., Oct. 12, 1936; d. Benjamin J. and Janet (Pollock) Craig; m. Charles J. Smaistrla, July 12, 1958; children: Amy Jean, Ben, John. BBA in Mktg., Lamar U., 1958; elec. edn. cert. Tex. Wesleyan Coll., 1963; MEd in Counseling, Tex. Christian U., 1975. Lic. profl. counselor. Tchr. Houston Ind. Schs., 1958-61, Arlington Ind. Schs., Tex., 1961-72; counselor, therapist Arlington Counseling and Cons. Ctr., 1983-85; family therapist Willow Creek Adolescent Ctr., Arlington, 1985-86, dir. edn., 1986-90; therapist, Bob Caprenter PhD and Assoc., 1987-89; pvt. practice Triage Therapist Kaiser Permanente, Ft. Worth, 1989—; owner, founder, chmn. bd. Adolescent Services Arlington, 1981—, founder, owner Mindtime, 1988-90; triage counselor Kaiser Permanente, Ft. Worth, 1991—; cons. Charles J. Smaistrla, D.D.S., Arlington, 1978-85. Vice chmn. bd. Arlington Community Hosp., 1981-85, Willow Creek Adolescent Ctr., 1984-90. Life mem. PTA; bd. dirs. Arlington Art Assn., 1981-85, S. Arlington Med. Ctr., 1987, Ctr. for Well-Being, 1985; chmn. clin. svcs. Parenting Ctr. for Tarrant County, Ft. Worth, 1992—, v.p., 1994-95, pres.-elect, 1994—. Mem. Am. Assn. Marriage and Family Therapy (assoc.), Tarrant County Assn. Marriage and Family Therapy, North Central Tex. Assn. Counseling and Devel., Am. Assn. Counseling and Devel., Alpha Delta Pi. Republican. Roman Catholic. Clubs: Jr. League Arlington, Arlington Women's. Avocations: Sailing; sewing; doll collecting.

SMALARZ, JOAN ANGELA, tax specialist; b. Phila., May 7, 1947; d. Joseph Frank and Josephine Kunegunda (Niedzialek) S. BA, LaSalle U., 1975. Accounts clk. Reliance Ins. Co., Phila., 1965-70; statis. typist Philco Ford, Phila., 1970-71; tchr. 6th grade St. Helena's Parish, Phila., 1971-72; with IRS, Phila., 1972—, tax auditor, 1973-80, revenue agt., 1980—. Vol. St. Josaphat Ch., Manayunk, Phila. Roman Catholic. Home: 1035 Borbeck Ave Philadelphia PA 19111 Office: IRS 801 Old York Rd Jenkintown PA 19046

SMALBEIN, DOROTHY ANN, guidance counselor; b. Rochester, N.Y.; d. Karl Taylor and Virginia (Woodcock) Howard; m. June 27, 1954 (div.); children: William Paul, John Allen. Student, St. Lawrence U., Canton, N.Y., 1952-54; BA, U. Cen. Fla., 1971, MEd in Counseling, 1978. Guidance counselor Pine Trail Elem. Sch., Volusia County Sch. Bd., Fla., 1978—. Recipient Outstanding Svc. award, Volusia County Counselors, 1979. Mem. AACD, Fla. Sch. Counselors Assn., Fla. Assn. for Counseling and Devel. (conv. presenter 1981-88), Volusia Assn. for Counseling and Devel. (sunshine chmn. 1980-81, treas. 1988-90), Volusia County Elementary Counselors Assn. (chmn. 1981-82), Jr. League, Pi Beta Phi. Methodist. Office: Pine Trail Elem Sch 300 Airport Rd Ormond Beach FL 32174-8725

SMALL, ELAINE DOLORES, financial analyst; b. Trenton, N.J., Aug. 18, 1954; d. Moses and Hattie (Mitchell) S.; m. Richmond Akumiah, Dec. 1982 (div. Aug. 27, 1987). BS, Rochester Inst. Technol., 1976; MBA, Atlanta U., 1985. Mktg. rep. Mobil Oil Corp., 1976-77; mfg. analyst Reader's Digest, Pleasantville, N.Y., 1977-80; mgr. fin. instns. Am. Express, N.Y.C., 1980-83; sr. market analyst Ryder Systems Inc., Miami, 1985-86; dir. recruiting Atlanta U., 1986; cons. Consultants & Assocs., Washington, 1987, 88-89; mgr. fin. analysis Blue Cross Blue Shield of Va., Roanoke, 1989-90; dir. group fin. reporting & analysis Blue Cross Blue Shield of Md., Owings Mills, 1990-93; sr. med. group analyst mid-Atlantic states region Kaiser Permanente, Rockville, Md., 1993—. Named IBM scholar, 1983. Mem. NAFE, Md. New Directions (bd. dirs. 1994), Internat. Soc. Strategic Planners, Nat. Assn. MBA Execs. Democrat. Methodist. Home: 6741 Old Waterloo Rd # 107 Columbia MD 21227 Office: Kaiser Permanente Mid Atlantic States Region 2101 E Jefferson St Rockville MD 20849

SMALL, ELISABETH CHAN, psychiatrist, educator; b. Beijing, July 11, 1934; came to U.S., 1937; d. Stanley Hong and Lily Luella (Lum) Chan; m. Donald M. Small, July 8, 1957 (div. 1980); children Geoffrey Brooks, Philip Willard Stanley. Student, Immaculate Heart Coll., Los Angeles, 1951-52; BA in Polit. Sci., UCLA, 1955, MD, 1960. Intern Newton-Wellesley Hosp., Mass., 1960-61; asst. dir. for venereal diseases Mass. Dept. Pub. Health, 1961-63; resident in psychiatry Boston State Hosp., Mattapan, Mass., 1965-66; resident in psychiatry Tufts New Eng. Med. Ctr. Hosps., 1966-69, psychiat. cons. dept. gynecology, 1973-75; asst. clin. prof. psychiatry Sch. Medicine Tufts U., 1973-75, assoc. clin. prof., 1975-82, asst. clin. prof. ob-gyn, 1977-80, assoc. clin. prof. ob-gyn, 1980-82; assoc. prof. psychiatry, ob-gyn U. Nev. Sch. Med., Reno, 1982-85; practice psychiatry specializing in psychological effects of bodily changes on women, 1969—; clin. prof. psychiatry U. Nev. Sch. Medicine, Reno, 1985-86, prof. psychiatry, 1986—, clin. assoc. prof. ob-gyn, 1985—; mem. staff Tufts New Eng. Med. Ctr. Hosps., 1977-82, St. Margaret's Hosps., Boston, 1977-82, Washoe Med. Ctr., Reno, Sparks (Nev.) Family Hosp., Truckee Meadows Hosp., Reno, St. Mary's Hosp., Reno; chief psychiatry svc. Reno VA Med. Ctr., 1989-94; lectr. various univs., 1961—; cons. in psychiatry; mem. psychiatry adv. panel Hosp. Satellite Network; mem. office external peer rev. NIMH, HEW; psychiat. cons. to Boston Redevelopment Authority on Relocation of Chinese Families of South Cove Area, 1968-70; mem. New Eng. Med. Ctr. Hosps. Cancer Ctr. Com., 1979-80, Pain Control Com., 1981-82, Tufts Univ. Sch. Medicine Reproductive System Curriculum Com., 1975-82. Mem. editorial bd. Psychiat. Update Am. (Psychiat. Assn. ann. rev.), 1983-85; reviewer Psychosomatics and Hosp. Community Psychiatry, New Eng. Jour. of Medicine, Am. Jour. of Psychiatry Psychosomatic Medicine; contbr. articles to profl. jours. Immaculate Heart Coll. scholar, 1951-52; Mira Hershey scholar UCLA, 1955; fellow Radcliffe Inst., 1967-70. Mem. AMA, Am. Psychiat. Assn. (rep. to sect. com. AAAS, chmn. ad hoc com. Asian-Am. Psychiatrists 1975, task force 1975-77, task force cost effectiveness in consultation 1984—, caucus chmn. 1981-82, sci. program com. 1982-88, courses subcom. chmn. sci. program com. 1986-88), Nev. Psychiat. Assn., Assn. for Acad. Psychiatry (fellowship com. 1982), Washoe County Med. Assn., Nev. Med. Soc., Am. Coll. Psychiatrists (scientific program com. 1989-96), Ea. Profl. Ski Instrs. Assn. Home: 602 Alley Oop Reno NV 89509 Office: 475 Hill St Reno NV 89511

SMALL, JOYCE GRAHAM, psychiatrist, educator; b. Edmonton, Alberta, Can., June 12, 1931; came to U.S., 1956; d. John Earl and Rachel C. (Redmond) Graham; m. Iver Francis Small, May 26, 1954; children: Michael, Jeffrey. BA, U. Saskatchewan, Can., 1951; MD, U. Manitoba, Can., 1956; MS, U. Mich., 1959. Diplomat Am. Bd. Psychiatry and Neurology, Am. Bd. Electroencephalography. Instr. in psychiatry Neuropsychiat. Inst. U. Mich., Ann Arbor, 1959-60; instr. in psychiatry med. sch. U. Oreg., Portland, 1960-61, asst. prof. in psychiatry med. sch., 1961-62; asst. prof. in psychiatry sch. of medicine Washington U., St. Louis, 1962-65; assoc. prof. in psychiatry sch. of medicine Ind. U., Indpls., 1965-69, prof. psychiatry sch. of medicine, 1969—; mem. initial rev. groups NIMH, Washington, 1972-76, 79-82, 87-91; assoc. mem. Inst. Psychiat. Rsch., Indpls., 1974—. Editorial bd.: Quar. Jour. of Convulsive Therayp, 1984, Clin. Electroencephalography, 1990, and more than 150 publs. in field; contbr. articles to profl. jours. Rsch. grantee NIMH, Portland, Oreg., 1961-62, St. Louis, 1962-64, Indpls., 1967—, Epilepsy Found., Dreyfus Found., Indpls., 1965; recipient Merit award NIMH, Indpls., 1990. Fellow Am. Psychiat. Assn., Am. Electroencephalographic Soc. (councillor 1972-75, 1982); mem. Soc. Biol. Psychiatry, Cen. Assn. Electroencephalographers (sec., treas. 1967-68, pres. 1970, councillor 1971-72), Sigma Xi. Office: Larue D Carter Meml Hosp 1315 W 10th St Indianapolis IN 46202-2885

SMALL, NATALIE SETTIMELLI, pediatric mental health counselor; b. Quincy, Mass., June 2, 1933; d. Joseph Peter and Edmea Natalie (Bagnaschi) Settimelli; m. Parker Adams Small, Jr., Aug. 26, 1956; children: Parker Adams III, Peter McMichael, Carla Edmea. BA, Tufts U., 1955; MA, EdS, U. Fla., 1976; PhD, 1987. Cert. child life specialist. Pediatric counselor U. Fla. Coll. Medicine, Gainesville, 1976-80; pediatric counselor Shands Hosp.-U. Fla., Gainesville, 1980-87, supr. child life dept. social work svcs., 1987—; mem. faculty Ctr. for Coop. Learning for Health and Sci. Edn., Gainesville, 1988—, adminstrv. liaison for self-directed work teams, 1994—; cons. and lectr. in field. Author: Parents Know Best, 1991; co-author team packs series for teaching at risk adolescent health edn. and coop. learning. Bd. dirs. Ronald McDonald House, Gainesville, 1980—, mem. exec. com., 1991—; mem. health profl. adv. com. March of Dimes, Gainesville, 1986—; bd. dirs. Gainesville Assn. Creative Arts, 1994—. Boston Stewart Club scholar, Florence, Italy, 1955; grantee Jessie Ball Du Pont Fund, 1978, Children's Miracle Network, 1990, 92, 93, 94. Mem. ACA, Nat. Bd. Cert. Counselors, Am. Assn. Mental Health Counselors, Assn. for the Care of Children's Health, Fla. Assn. Child Life Profls., Child Life Coun. Roman Catholic. Home: 3454 NW 12th Ave Gainesville FL 32605-4811 Office: Shands Hosp Dept Social Work Svcs PO Box 100306 Gainesville FL 32610

SMALL, REBECCA ELAINE, accountant; b. Meridian, Tex., Apr. 5, 1946; d. James Milford and Rosa Lee Elaine (Berry) Allen; m. Jay Austin Small, Sept. 16, 1964 (div.); children: Lashawn Renee, Jay Austin Jr.; m. Jerry Leon Cooper, Dec. 10, 1983 (div. Sept. 1985). Student Okla. Sch. Bus. and Banking, 1972; BS in Acctg. magna cum laude, Cen. State U., Edmond, Okla., 1977, MA in Exptl. Psychology summa cum laude, 1989; postgrad., U. Okla., 1991—. Staff acct. Robert A. Mosley, CPA, Moore, Okla., 1972-74, Robert Stewart, CPA, Edmond, 1974-75, Lowder & Co., Oklahoma City, 1975-81; pvt. practice acctg., Oklahoma City, 1981—. Fellow Nat. Inst. Mental Health, NIH; recipient Rsch. award Dept. Psychology Cent. State U., 1988. Mem. AICPA, Okla. Woman's Bus. Orgn. (chmn. 1982), Okla. Soc. CPAs, Am. Woman's Soc. CPAs, Nat. Assn. Accts. (hon.), Soc. of Neurosci., Alpha Lambda Delta, Alpha Chi, Psi Chi. Democrat. Avocations: writing poetry, horticulture, bicycling.

SMALL, SARAH MAE, volunteer; b. Salisbury, N.C., Nov. 16, 1923; d. Clint and Lillie Mae (Wilbourn) Evans; m. Jesse Small Sr., May 4, 1941; children: Jesse Jr., Jean Carol Small Bell. Cert., Cortez Bus. Sch., 1948. File clk. gen. acctg. office Fed. Govt., Washington, 1941-47; sec., stenographer CIA, Washington, 1948-52; adminstrv. asst. CIA, McLean, Va., 1952-65; ret. CIA, 1965; elected pres. Energetic Crusaders, Inc., 1993—. Pres. Youth Triumph Ch., Washington, Md., S.C. and Ga., 1965-76, The Energetic Crusaders, Inc., 1993; bd. dirs. ARC, Washington, 1986-87, Children's Edn. Found., Inc., 1989—; mem. adv. bd. D.C. Gen. Hosp., 1985-86. Recipient Outstanding and Dedicated Vol. Svc. award Kiwanis Club of Capital Centre, 1985, Plaque in Recognition of Dedicated and Outstanding Vol. Svc. to the Corps and Washington D.C., Community Jr. Citizen's Corps., 1989, Appreciation award for Outstanding and Dedicated Vol. Svc. to Corps, Jr. Citizens Corps., Inc., 1990, Appreciation award Jr. Citizens Corp., Inc., 1990, Community Svc. award for leadership and youth advocacy Bus. and Profl. Women's League, Inc., 1991, Vol. award achievement excellence svc. youths of Jr. Citizens Corps., Inc., 1992, others. Mem. Jr. Citizens Corps (life, pres. 1985—, Dedicated Community Svc. award 1983, Bus. and Community Svc. award 1986), Bus. and Profl. Women's League (treas. 1982-86), Women in Arts (chartered, pres. 1984—), Nat. Coun. Negro Women, World Affairs Coun. Washington, Agrl. Coun. Am., Exec. Travel Club Riverdale. Democrat. Baptist. Home: 2010 Upshur St NE Washington DC 20018-3244

SMALLEY, PENNY JUDITH, laser nursing consultant; b. Chgo., Feb. 20, 1947; d. Ernest Rich and Muriel L. (Touff) Brown; m. Ivan H. Smalley, Jan. 11, 1972; children: Cherie Ann, Michael John, Geoffry Paul. Grad., Evanston Hosp. Sch. Nursing, Ill., 1980. Cert. Am. Bd. Laser Surgery, 1989. Staff nurse Evanston Hosp., 1979-81, laser coord., 1981-83; office mgr. Women's Health Group, 1981; laser nurse specialist Cooper Lasersonics, various, 1983-86; pres., CEO Laser Concepts Internat., Inc., Chgo., 1986—; lectr., writer Sino Fgn. Laser Conf., People's Republic of China, 1987; bd. dirs. Laser Inst. Am. Contbg. author: Nursing Clinics of North America, 1990; editorial bd. Clin. Laser Monthly, Laser Nursing mag., 1989—, Minimally Invasive Surg. Nursing; contbr. articles to profl. jours. Mem. Am. Soc. Laser Medicine and Surgery (chmn. edn. com. 1987-90, stds. of practice com. 1990, quality assurance com., nursing sect. chmn. 1992-94), Laser Inst. Am. (bd. dirs.), Am. Nat. Stds. Com., Inst. Com. (exec. com.), Z136.3 Lasers in Healthcare (nurse rep.), Brit. Med. Laser Assn. (course dir. first laser nursing conf. in U.K., 1990), AORN (tchr. nat. seminars, spol. comm. on internat. issues), Internat. Soc. Laser Surgery and Medicine (chmn. nursing 1988—). Democrat. Home and Office: 1444 W Farwell Ave Chicago IL 60626-3410

SMALLMAN, GAIL ELIZABETH, entrepreneur; b. Buffalo, N.Y., Mar. 24, 1953; d. Lemuel James and Beverly Ann (Waldron) S.; m. Ronald Hugh Strasser, 1974 (div. 1975). Student, Oreg. State U., 1971-72, Portland State, 1972-74, City U., Seattle, 1979. Word processor Atty. Gen.'s Consumer Protection, Portland, Oreg., 1974-75, Lane Powell Moss & Miller, Seattle, 1978-79; sec. Carney, Probst & Levak, Portland, 1975-76, Jones, Lang, Klein, et al., Portland, 1978; office mgr. Corl & Willis, Corvallis, Oreg., 1976-77; adminstrv. asst. Reed McClure Moceri et al., Seattle, 1978-80; systems mgr. Lane Powell Spears et al., Seattle, 1980-94; owner Sunrise Place Bed & Breakfast, Bainbridge Island, Wash., 1994—; v.p. Wang/Informatics special interest group VS Legal Users' Group, Sacramento, 1990-91. Active Residents Opposed to Aircraft ReRouting, 1991. Scholar Oregon State U., 1971. Mem. Am. Mgmt. Assn., LawNet Inc. (v.p., bd. dirs. 1991-93), Bainbridge Island C. of C., Bainbridge Island Bed & Breakfast Assn., Bremerton/Kitsap County Visitors & Conv. Bur. Democrat. Episcopalian. Home and Office: 10245 NE Sunrise Pl Bainbridge Is WA 98110-1168

SMART, DOROTHY CAROLINE, retired social worker; b. Osborn, Mo.; d. Allen A. and Caroline (Totzke) S. Student, U. Mo., 1929-30; AB, U. Kans., 1937, MSW, 1950; postgrad., U. Chgo., 1963, 65. Advt. copy writer Emery Bird Thayer, Kansas City, Mo., 1937-38; case worker Dept. Pub. Welfare, Kansas City, 1938-44, Jackson County chpt. ARC, Kansas City, 1944-49; disaster rep. Am. Nat. Red Cross, St. Louis, 1950-59, home service rep. area office, 1959-65, regional dir. svc. mil. families, 1965-70, asst. area dir. svc. to mil. families, 1970-76. Mem. Group Action Coun.; bd. dirs. Barnes Hosp. Aux. Mem. Nat. Assn. Social Workers, Nat. Conf. Social Welfare, Acad. Cert. Social Workers, Women in Communications (pres. Kansas City alumni chpt. 1943), Am. Assn. Ret. Persons (pres. 1989, bd. dirs. 1989-92), Pilot Club (St. Louis, pres. 1975-77, Lucy B. Allen Nat. award 1988, Gold medal. Home: 4475 W Pine Blvd Apt 905 Saint Louis MO 63108-2318

SMART, EDITH MERRILL, civic worker; b. N.Y.C., Sept. 10, 1929; d. Edwin Katte and Helen Phelps (Stokes) Merrill; student Smith Coll., 1947-49, Barnard Coll., 1949-50; m. S. Bruce Smart, Jr., Sept. 10, 1949; children—Edith Minturn Smart Moore, William Candler, Charlotte Merrill Smart Rogan, Priscilla Smart Schwarzenbach. Tchr. elem. schs., Gibson Island, Md., 1959-60; guide, instr. Mill River Wetlands Com., Fairfield, Conn., 1967-85; treas. Near and Far Aid Assn., Fairfield, 1970-75, v.p., 1975-77, pres., 1977-79; pres. Nature Ctr. of Environ. Activities, Westport, Conn., chmn., 1981-85; trustee Fairfield Univ., 1987-93; leader No. Cook County council Girl Scouts U.S.A., Kenilworth, Ill., 1962-64; chmn. Southport-Westport Antiques Show, 1974-76; trustee Conn. chpt. Nature Conservancy, 1981-91, Va. chpt., 1992—; guide Nat. Acquarium, 1985-90; dir. Piedmont Child Devel. Ctr., 1994—; vestryman St. Timothy's Ch., Fairfield, 1976-79. Republican. Episcopalian. Clubs: Sasqua Garden (Fairfield), Upperville Garden, Middleburg Tennis, MFH The Fairfax Hunt. Home: 20561 Trappe Rd Upperville VA 22176-9708

SMART, MARRIOTT WIECKHOFF, research librarian consultant, information manager; b. Memphis, Aug. 26, 1935; d. Gerhard Emil and Beatrice (Flanegan) Wieckhoff; m. John A. Smart, May 9, 1959; children: Denise, Holly. B.S. in Geology, U. Tex.-Austin, 1957; M.L.S., U. Pitts., 1976. Geophysicist Mobil Corp., New Orleans, 1957-59; geologist Hanson Oil Co., Roswell, N.Mex., 1959-62; info. specialist Gulf Corp., Pitts., 1977-79, library mgr., Denver, 1979-84, library cons. team, Pitts., 1984; supr. Library-Info. Ctr., Amoco Minerals Co., Englewood, Colo., 1984; dir. Library-Info. Ctr., Cyprus Minerals Co., 1985-92; cons. ask marriott, Littleton, Colo., 1992—. Choir mem. Grace Presbyn. Ch., Littleton, 1979—. Mem. Spl. Libraries Assn. (bull. bus. mgr. 1982, treas. petroleum and energy divsn. 1984-86, chmn. petroleum and energy divsn. 1987-88, pres. Rocky Mountain chpt. 1991-92), Women in Mining, Alpha Chi Omega. Home: 3337 E Easter Pl Littleton CO 80122-1910

SMAYLING, LYDA MOZELLA, speech pathologist; b. Britton, Okla., Apr. 19, 1923; d. Miles and Evelyn (King) Maxwell; m. George F. Smayling, Sept. 12, 1944 (dec. 1985); children: Sally, Michael, Miles. BA magna cum laude, U. Wichita, Wichita, Kans., 1944; MA summa cum laude, U. Wichita, 1947. Dir., cons., assoc. U. Kans. Med. Ctr., Kans. City, 1947-56; cons. Westchester County Cerebral Palsy Assn., Bedford Village, N.Y., 1947-54; asst. dir. Inst. Logopedics, Wichita, 1957-68; instr. Wichita (Kans.) State U., 1957-68; cons. Wichita, 1957-68; pvt. practice Mpls., 1968—. Contbr. articles to profl. jours. V.p. PTA, Wichita, 1957-64, tchr. Unitarian Ch., Wichita, 1959-64;. Mem. Am. Speech-Lang. Hearing Assn., Kans. Speech-Lang. Hearing Assn. (v.p., bd. dirs., treas.). Unitarian Universalist. Home and Office: 3145 Dean Ct # 903 Minneapolis MN 55416-4390

SMEAL, ELEANOR CUTRI, organization executive; b. Ashtabula, Ohio, July 30, 1939; d. Peter Anthony and Josephine E. (Agresti) Cutri; m. Charles R. Smeal, Apr. 27, 1963; children: Tod, Lori. BA, Duke U., 1961, LLD (hon.), 1991; MA, U. Fla., 1963. Mem. bd. Upper St. Clair (Pa.) chpt. LWV, 1968-72, sec.-treas. Allegheny County Council, 1971-72; mem. NOW, 1971—; convenor, 1st pres. S. Hills (Pa.) chpt. NOW, 1971-73, 1st pres., state coordinator, 1972-75; nat. bd. dirs. NOW, 1973-75, chairwoman bd., 1975-77, pres., 1977-82, 85-87, mem. bd. Legal Def. and Edn. Fund, 1975—, chairwoman ERA Strike Force, 1977—; pres. Fund for Feminist Majority, Arlington, Va., 1987—; mem. 1st nominating com., founding conf. Nat. Women's Polit. Caucus, 1971; bd. dirs. Allegheny County Women's Polit. Caucus, 1971-72; co-founder, bd. dirs. S. Hills NOW Day Nursery Sch., 1972—; mem. Nat. Commn., Observance of Internat. Women's Year, 1977; mem. exec. com. Leadership Conf. on Civil Rights, 1979—; mem. Nat. Adv. Com. on Women, 1978. Named One of 25 Most Influential Women in U.S. World Almanac, 1978. Office: Fund For The Feminist Majority 1600 Wilson Blvd Ste 704 Arlington VA 22209-2513*

SMEED, NANCY MCGRATH, lawyer; b. Providence, Feb. 12, 1950; d. William John and Carolyn Ann (O'Sullivan) McGrath; m. Edward Henry Smeed, Oct. 22, 1972. BA, U. R.I., 1971; MBA, Bryant Coll., 1983; JD, New England Sch. Law, 1989. Bar: R.I. 1989, U.S. Dist. Ct. R.I. 1990, Mass. 1992, Fla. 1993. Statistician Mass. Dept. Pub. Welfare, Boston, 1972-73; underwriter Amica Mutual Ins. Co., Providence, 1974-85, sr. underwriter, 1985-87; student intern Atty. Gen.'s Office, Boston, 1989; pvt. practice atty. R.I., 1989—; adj. instr. R.I. Coll., Providence, 1989-91. Mem. NAFE, ABA (trust and property com. 1993), R.I. Bar Assn. (trust and probate com. 1993), Women's Bar Assn.-R.I. Bar Assn., Nat. Acad. Elder Law Attys. Home: PO Box 7672 Warwick RI 02887-7672 Office: 300 Centerville Rd Ste 200 Warwick RI 02886-0200

SMELTZER, DEBRA JEAN, botanist; b. Camden, Ark., Oct. 13, 1953; d. William Dewey and Frankie Jean (Braswell) S.; m. James Richard Ziesler, Sept. 1, 1984. Cert. in interior design, Bauder Fashion Coll., Arlington, Tex., 1973; BA in Botany, U. Tex., 1985. Biol. rsch. asst. U.S. Dept. Interior, Everglades Nat. Park, Fla., 1980; biologist, surveyor Great Lakes Dredge and Dock, Miami Beach, Fla., 1981-82, 1984; biologist, surveyor, drafter Great Lakes Dredge and Dock, Port Everglades, Fla., 1984; biologist, lab. tech. J.B. Reark and Assocs., Miami, 1982-84; fisheries biologist Kathryn Chandler and Assocs., Alexandria, Va., 1981-84; pres. Greensleeves, Inc., Miami and San Juan, P.R., 1985—, San Juan, P.R., 1991—; bd. govs. Nat. Coun. for Interior Hort. Cert., Columbus, Ohio, 1989-92; licensee Interior Landscape Internat. Corp., Dade, Monroe, Caribbean, 1990-92. Active Fairchild Tropical Gardens, Miami, Ch. of the Little Flower. Recipient Best Project award Interiorscape Mag., 1989, State Award of Excellence Fla. Nurserymen and Growers Assn., 1989. Mem. Associated Landscape Contractors Am. (award of Distinction 1989, 91, 92 [2], Grand award 1990), South Fla. Interior Landscape Assn. (ednl. com. 1987-89, bd. dirs. 1986-87, author newsletter articles 1986-89, founder 1986), South Fla. Hort. Soc., Inc., South Fla. Tex. Execs., Coral Gables C. of C. (trustee coun.). Democrat. Office: Greensleeves Inc 9774 SW 60th St Miami FL 33173

SMERLAS, DONNA, foundation director; b. Boston, July 14, 1949; d. Constantine and Betty (Makris) S. BA, Smith Coll., 1971; MA, Boston U., 1977. Tech. writer, editor Raytheon Svc. Co., Burlington, Mass., 1971-72; editor, archivist JFK Presdl. Library & Mus., Boston, 1972-76; meeting and event planner JFK Presdl. Library & Mus., 1976-87; dir. adminstrn. and fin. JFK Presdl. Library & Mus., Boston, 1987-91; dir. ops. John F. Kennedy Libr. Found., Boston, 1991-94; dep. dir. John F. Kennedy Libr. Found., 1994—; ptnr., owner Triangle Assocs., Ltd., Boston, 1989. Editor: Massachusetts Soldiers in the Lexington Alarm, 1976. Dir., Smith Coll. Students for Kennedy for Senate, Northampton, 1970; organizer Paul Tsongas for U.S. Senate, 1978; dir. Mass. local programs Close Up Found., 1982-87; spl. events dir. Greek Orthodox Ch., Watertown, Mass., 1978-84; cons. Mass. Coun. Arts and Humanities, Boston, 1986-88. Nat. Historical Publs. and Records Commn. fellow, 1975. Mem. NOW, Women in Devel., Boston Network for Women in Politics and Govt., Helicon Club (bd. dirs. 1986-88, v.p. 1988-90), Axion Club, Smith Coll. Alumnae Assn. Democratic. Greek Orthodox. Home: 22 Stoneleigh Cir Watertown MA 02172-1330 Office: John F Kennedy Libr Found Columbia Pt Boston MA 02125

SMERNOFF, ANDREA DOROTHY, librarian, technical services consultant; b. Hempstead, N.Y., Mar. 30, 1954; d. Nicholas and Catherine Lillian (Doll) S. BA, Adelphi U., 1976; MSLS, Long Island U., 1978. Lib. pub. libr., sch. libr. media specialist, N.Y. Project coord. Job and Edn. Info. Ctr., Hempstead, 1978-82; audiovisual libr. Hempstead Pub. Libr., 1982-85, tech. svcs. libr., 1985—. Pres., liaison North Ctr. Civic Assn., Hempstead, 1985—. Mem. NOW, Nassau County Libr. Assn. (rec. sec. 1994), Nature Conservancy. Lutheran. Office: Hempstead Pub Libr 115 Nichols Ct Hempstead NY 11550-3101

SMILEY, JANE GRAVES, author, educator; b. L.A., Sept. 26, 1949; d. James La Verne Smiley and Frances (Graves) Nuelle; m. John Whiston, Sept. 4, 1970 (div.); m. William Silag, May 1, 1978 (div.); children: Phoebe Silag, Lucy Silag; m. Stephen Mark Mortensen, July 25, 1987; 1 child, Axel James Mortensen. BA, Vassar Coll., 1971; MFA, U. Iowa, 1976, MA, 1978, PhD, 1978. Asst. prof. Iowa State U., Ames, 1981-84, assoc. prof., 1984-89, prof., 1989-90, Disting. prof., 1992—; vis. asst. prof. U. Iowa, Iowa City, 1981, 87. Author: (fiction) Barn Blind, 1980, At Paradise Gate, 1981 (Friends of American Writers prize 1981), Duplicate Keys, 1984, The Age of Grief, 1987 (Nat. Book Critics Cir. award nomination 1987), The Greenlanders, 1988, Ordinary Love and Goodwill, 1989, A Thousand Acres, 1991 (Pulitzer prize for fiction 1992, Nat. Book Critics Cir. award 1992, Midland Authors award 1992, Amb. award 1992, Heartland prize 1992), Moo: A Novel, 1995; (non-fiction) Catskill Crafts: Artisans of the Catskill Mountains, 1987. Grantee Fulbright U.S. Govt., Iceland, 1976-77, NEA, 1978, 87; recipient O. Henry award, 1982, 85, 88. Mem. Author's Guild, Screenwriters Guild. Office: Iowa State U Dept English 201 Ross Ames IA 50011-1401*

SMILEY, LINDA CASE, financial planner; b. Harrisburg, Pa., Sept. 10, 1958; d. Paul Willis and Olive Blanche Case; m. Edward Barton Smiley, Oct. 20, 1984; children: Danielle Elizabeth, Michelle Lynn, Noelle Elise. Student, Albright Coll., 1975-76; AA, Harrisburg (Pa.) Area C.C., 1982; BS, Elizabethtown Coll., 1989; postgrad., Lebanon Valley Coll., 1993—. CFP. Clk. Pa. Pub. Utility Commn., Harrisburg, 1977-81; nuclear chemistry tech. GPU Nuclear Corp., Middletown, Pa., 1981-89; registered rep. John Hancock, Boston, 1989-90; dist. rep. Luth. Brotherhood, Mpls., 1990—. Mem. AAUW, Nat. Assn. Fraternal Ins. Counselors, Nat. Assn. Life Underwriters, Million Dollar Round Table. Republican. Lutheran. Home: 276 Kokomo Ave Hummelstown PA 17036 Office: Lutheran Brotherhood 276 Kokomo Ave Hummelstown PA 17036

SMILEY, MARILYNN JEAN, musicologist; b. Columbia City, Ind., June 5, 1932; d. Orla Raymond and Mary Jane (Bailey) S. BS (State scholar), Ball State U., 1954; MusM, Northwestern U., 1958; cert., Ecoles d'Art Americaines, Fontainebleau, France, 1959; Ph.D. (Grad. scholar, Delta Kampa Gamma scholar), U. Ill., 1970. Public sch. music tchr. Logansport, Ind., 1954-61; faculty music dept. SUNY-Oswego, 1961—, Disting. Teaching prof., 1974—, chmn. dept., 1976-81; presenter papers at confs. Contbr. articles to profl. jours. Bd. dirs. Oswego Opera Theatre, 1978—, Oswego Orch. Soc., 1978—, Penfield Libr. Assocs., 1985—. SUNY Research Found. fellow, summers 1971, 72, 74. Mem. AAUW (br. coun. rep. dist. III, N.Y. State div. 1986-88, br. coun. coord. N.Y. State div. 1988-90, pres. Oswego br. 1984-86, N.Y. divsn. area interest rep. cultural interests 1990-92, grantee 1984, N.Y. divsn. diversity coord. 1993—), NEH (rsch. grantee 1990-91), Am. Musicological Soc. (chmn. N.Y. chpt. 1975-77, chpt. rep. to AMS Coun. 1993—), Medieval Acad. Am., Music Library Assn., Coll. Music Soc., Renaissance Soc. Am., Sonneck Soc. Am., Oswego County Hist. Soc., Heritage Found. of Oswego, Delta Kappa Gamma, Phi Delta Kappa, Delta Phi Alpha, Pi Kappa Lambda, Sigma Alpha Iota, Sigma Tau Delta, Kappa Delta Pi. Methodist. Office: SUNY Dept Music Oswego NY 13126

SMINK, MARY JANE, graphic communications technology educator; b. Charlotte, N.C., Feb. 19, 1939; d. Arthur Elmore and Louise (Belue) Moore; m. George Thomas Smink Jr.; children: George Thomas III, Karl Frederich. BS, Winthrop Coll., 1959; MA in Indsl. Arts, Appalachian State U., 1970; EdD in Indsl. Arts, N.C. State U., 1983. Cert. technology edn., N.C. Tchr. Columbia (S.C.) City Schs., 1959-61, Mars City/Adams Twp. Schs., Mars, Pa., 1962-63; tchr. Cleveland County Schs., Shelby, N.C., 1964-65, dir. audio visual, 1966-67; coord. adult edn. Wilkes C.C., Wilkesboro, N.C., 1967-70; dir. career exploration Wilkes County Schs., Wilkesboro, N.C., 1970-71; tchr. Wake County Schs., Raleigh, N.C., 1971-79; cons. N.C. Dept. Pub. Instrn., Raleigh, N.C., 1980-90; asst. prof. N.C. A&T State U., Greensboro, 1990—; articulation adv. com. Guilford Tech. C.C., Greensboro, 1990—. Contbr. articles to profl. jours. Organist Milner Meml. Presbyn. Ch., Raleigh, 1971—; leader Boy Scouts Am., Raleigh, 1973-78. Edn. Profl. Devel. Act fellow, 1980; recipient William Warner Rsch. award Epsilon Pi Tau, 1983, Epsilon Pi Tau Laureate citation N.C. State U., 1987, Award of Distinction, Tech. Student Assn., Inc., 1988; named State Supr. of Yr., Internat. Tech. Edn. Assn. Coun. of Suprs., 1986. Mem. S.E. Tech. Edn. Assn., N.C. Tech. Edn. Assn. (pres.-elect 1994-95), Internat. Tech. Edn Assn. (Disting. Tech. Educator award 1991, Meritorious Svc. award 1992, pres. bd. 1988), Tech. Student Assn., Inc. (bd. dirs., pres. bd. 1986-87), Nat. Assn. Indsl. Tech. (jour. rev. bd. 1993—), Phi Delta Kappa (capital area chpt.), Phi Kappa Phi. Home: 5907 S Sharon Dr Raleigh NC 27603-4665 Office: NC A&T State Univ Sch of Technology Greensboro NC 27411

SMITH, ADA L., state legislator; b. Amherst County, Va., Apr. 18, 1945; d. Thomas and Lillian Smith. Grad., CUNY. Dep. clk. N.Y.C.; state senator N.Y. Legislature, Albany, 1988—; mem. various coms. N.Y. Legislature, vice-chairperson mental health and devel. disabilities com., 1994, minority whip; mem. Senate Dem. Task Force Women's Issues, Senate Dem. Task Force Financing Affordable Housing, Senate Dem. Task Force Child Care 2000, Sen. Dem. Task Force Affirmative Action and Econ. Devel., Senate Dem. Task Force Primary Health Care, Senate Minority Puerto Rican and Hispanic Task Force; chair Senate Minority Task Force Preventive Health Care Alcoholic/Substance Abusing Women and Their Children. Bd. visitors Bklyn. Ctr. for the Mentally Retarded and the Developmentally Disabled, 1981, 85; trustee, life dir. Coll. Fund Baruch Coll.; mem. Community I Bd. (chair social svcs. com.); chair. N.Y. Community Scvs. Coalition, Bklyn. Coalition Area Policy Bds.; treas. Bklyn. Pla. Med. Ctr., Friends Lindsay Park Anti-Crime Com.; bd. mgrs. Ea. Dist. YMCA; officer Williamsburg Tenants Assn.; mem. Community Action Bd.; exec. mem. Ctr. for Community Orgns.; mem. adv. bd. Woodhull Hosp.; mem. Area Policy Bd. 4; past pres. Williamsburg/Greenpoint Coalition Community Orgns.; past chair Area Policy Bd. 1; past bd. dirs., pres. Lindsay Park Housing Corp. Recipient Roberto Clemente Community Svc. award, Women of the Yr. award YMCA, Pulaski Community Svc. award, Outstanding Alumni award Baruch Coll., Pres.'s medal, Williamsburg/Greenpoint COCO Community Svc. award, others. Mem. African Am. Clergy and Elected Ofcls., Inc. (treas.), N.Y. State Black and Puerto Rican Legis. Caucus (vice-chair), Baruch Coll. Alumni Assn. (pres., Disting. Svc. award, Outstanding Achievement award). Home: 67 Manhattan Ave Brooklyn NY 11206-3156 Office: NY State Senate Rm 304 Legis Office Bldg Albany NY 12247 also: Queens Dist Office 130-08 Rockaway Blvd South Ozone Park NY 11420 also: Bklyn Dist Office 545 Broadway 4th fl Brooklyn NY 11206

SMITH, AGNES MONROE, history educator; b. Hiram, Ohio, Aug. 8, 1920; d. Bernie Alfred and Joyce (Messenger) Monroe; m. Stanley Blair Smith; children: David, Doris, Darl, Diane. BA, Hiram Coll., 1940; MA, W.Va. U., 1945; PhD, Western Res. U., 1966. Social sci. tchr. Freedom (Ohio) High Sch., 1940-44; instr. of history W.Va. U., Morgantown, 1945; instr. of social sci. Hiram Coll., 1946; inst. history and social sci. Youngstown (Ohio) State U., 1964-66, asst. prof. to prof. of history, 1966-84, prof. history emeritus, 1984—; vis. prof. history Hiram Coll., 1988-90. Co-editor: Bourgeois, San Culottes and other Frenchmen, 1981; contbr. articles to profl. jours. Mem. Ohio Acad. History, Delta Kappa Gamma, Phi Alpha Theta, Pi Gamma Mu. Mem. Christian Ch. (Disciples of Christ). Home: 16759 Main Market Rd West Farmington OH 44491-9608

SMITH, ALICE MURRAY, civic worker, mathematician; b. Buffalo, Apr. 23, 1930; d. Robert Leslie and Alice Emma (Bennett) Murray; m. Robert Crellin Smith, Feb. 21, 1953 (div. 1988); children: William Stewart, Peter Crellin, Edward Bennett. AB, Smith Coll., 1951. Mathematician U.S. Govt., Las Cruces, N.Mex., 1951-52. Contbr. articles to profl. jours. Pres. Phoenix Rep. Women, 1967, Arizonans for Nat. Security, Phoenix, 1983-87, 89-91, Ariz. Coordinating Coun. Rep. Women, 1991-93; mem. Ariz. Rep. Com., 1992—; mem. curriculum com. All Saints Day Sch., Phoenix, 1968-71. Republican.

SMITH, ALLISON LONDON, English language educator, real estate developer; b. Kansas City, Mo., Dec. 1, 1942; d. William Jay Sr. and Emily Ann (Allison) L.; m. Bruce Mitchell Smith, June 5, 1965; children: Travis Mitchell, Chase London. BS, U. Mo., 1964, postgrad., 1992-93; postgrad., S.W. Mo. State U., 1966-68. Educator Overland Park Sch. System, Shawnee Mission, Kans., 1964-66, West Plains Sch. System, West Plains, Mo., 1967-72; legal aid R. Jack Garrett, Atty. at Law, West Plains, Mo., 1972-74; province collegiate dir. Gamma Phi Beta, Mo./Kans., 1974-77; legal aid Howell County Prosecuting Atty., West Plains, Mo., 1978-80; educator Southwest Mo. State Univ., West Plains, Mo., 1981--; v.p. Southern Hills Ctr., Ltd., West Plains, 1979--; sec. treas. K & S Devel., Ltd., Harrison, Ark., 1982--. Pres. Ozark Med. Ctr. Aux., 1971; sec., treas. Country Club Bd. Dirs., 1975; fundraiser Bailey for Congress Campaign, 1980; choreographer People's Park Players & High Sch. Prodns., 1975--. Named Outstanding Young Women Am., 1970; recipient svc. award Gamma Phi Beta, Denver, 1982; Fanfare for Fifty Theta Kappa Phi, Columbia, Mo., 1980. Mem. Nat. Assn. Tchrs. Coll. English, Nat. Soc. Legal Secs., DAR, PEO Sisterhood, Jefferson Club U. Mo., Gamma Phi Beta, Phi Delta Theta Mothers Club. Episcopalian. Home: 8064 County Rd 5010 West Plains MO 65775

SMITH, ALTA MAY, accountant; b. Carthage, Mo., May 24, 1949; d. Bert Walter and Naomi Eve (Card) Nichols; m. Garrett Rayburn Smith, Aug. 9, 1967; children: Regina Eve, Fred William, Garrett Andrew, Richard Emory. BSBA, Mo. So. State Coll., 1986. Cert. mgmt. acct. Receptionist Office of Dr. Naomi Nichols, Carthage, 1967-71; bookkeeper Bert's Truck Stop, Carthage, 1971-73; mgr., bookkeeper Terminal Cab & Cafe, Carthage, 1973-75; billing clk./inventory records Four State Supply Co., Carthage, 1975-80; office mgr., bookkeeper Related Transport Refrigeration Inc., Carthage, 1980-85; divsn. acct. Tamko Roofing Products, Inc., Joplin, Mo., 1985-91, cost analyst, 1991—. Contbr. poems to profl. publs. Mem. Carthage Bus. and Profl. Women Inc. (pres. 1984-85, Woman of Yr. 1986), Inst. Mgmt. Accts. (pres. Joplin Tri-state chpt. 1993-94), Mo. So. State Coll. Alumni Assn., Omicron Delta Epsilon. Home: Rt 6 Box 242 Carthage MO 64836 Office: Tamko Roofing Products Inc PO Box 1404 Joplin MO 64802

SMITH, AMY DIANE, accountant; b. Huntington, W.Va., May 12, 1969; d. Leonard and Patricia Fay (Watts) Napier; m. Timothy Lee Smith, June 8, 1990. BBA, Marshall U., 1991. CPA, W.Va.; cert. mgmt. acct. Staff acct. Rufus & Rufus Acctg. Corp., Huntington, 1991-92; acct. Ashland (Ky.) Petroleum Co., 1992—. Vol. Big Bros./Big Sisters, Huntington, 1993—. Mem. W.Va. Soc. CPAs, Ohio Valley Accts. Assn., Inst. Cert. Mgmt. Accts. Baptist. Home: Rt 1 Box 129A Prichard WV 25555 Office: Ashland Petroleum Co PO Box 391 Ashland KY 41101

SMITH, ANN YOUNGDAHL, museum administrator; b. Alma, Mich., Oct. 7, 1950; d. Russell Charles and Mary Louise (Anderson) Youngdahl; m. Joseph Johnson Smith, Dec. 29, 1973; m. Joel Eric Finn, June 30, 1990. B.A., U. Mich., 1972; M.A., Cooperstown Grad. Program, 1973; JD U. Conn. Law Sch., 1990. Asst. curator Hist. Soc. York County, York, Pa., 1973-74; dir. Lyme Hist. Soc., Old Lyme, Conn., 1974-76; dir. Mattatuck Mus., Waterbury, Conn., 1976—; juror Conn. Commn. for the Arts, Hartford, 1980—; chmn. Conn. Humanities Council, Middletown, 1984-86; adj. fac. U. Conn., 1986—; reviewer NEH, 1989, 90, 92; bd. dirs. Conn. State Libr., 1988-92, Inst. Am. Indian Studies, 1992—; v.p. Waterbury Found., 1989-93. Editor: Metal, Minds & Machines, 1980; Fiddlebacks & Crooked-backs, 1982. Vice pres. Conn. Preservation Action, Hartford, 1980-84; mem. adv. bd. The Banking Ctr., Waterbury, 1980-82; bd. dirs. Waterbury Arts Festival, 1983-85. Recipient Disting. Service award Jaycees/Jaycees Women, 1984. Mem. Conn. Coordinating Commn. for the Promotion of History (treas. 1982-83). Office: Mattatuck Museum 144 W Main St Waterbury CT 06702-1298*

SMITH, ANNA DEAVERE, actress, playwright; b. Baltimore, Sept. 18, 1950; d. Deavere Young and Anna (Young) S. BA, Beaver Coll., Pennsylvania, 1971; MFA, Am. Conservatory Theatre, 1976. Ann O'Day Maples prof. arts and drama Stanford U. Playwright, performer one-woman shows: On the Road: A Search for American Character, 1983, Aye, Aye, Aye, I'm Integrated, 1984, Piano, 1991 (Drama-Logue award), Fires in the Mirror, 1992 (Obie award 1992, Drama Desk award 1992, Pulitzer Prize nomination for drama 1993), Twilight: Los Angeles 1992 (Obie award, 2 Tony award nominations, Drama Critics Cir. Special citation, Outer Critics Cir. award Drama Desk award, Audelco award), 1993; creator with Judith Jamison, performer Hymn, 1993; other appearances include (stage) Horatio, 1974, Alma, the Ghost of Spring Street, 1976, Mother Courage, 1980, Tartuffe, 1983; (television) All My Children, 1983; (film) Soup for One, 1982, Dave, 1993, Philadelphia, 1993. Named one of Women of the Yr., Glamour Mag., 1993; fellow Bunting Inst. Radcliffe Coll. Office: Tantleff Office 375 Greenwich St New York NY 10013 also: Stanford Univ Dept of Drama Memorial Hall Stanford CA 94305

SMITH, ANNA MARIE, retired educator; b. Greenville, S.C., Dec. 22, 1927; d. Albert and Lillie Mae (Donald) Clark; m. Willie T. Smith, Jr., June 9, 1955; 1 child, Willie T. III. AB, Knoxville Coll., 1948; MA, U. Mich., 1957. Tchr. psychology Greenville County Schs., Greenville, 1948-79; ret., 1979; cons. on parenting S.H.A.R.E., Greenville, 1982-84; cons. Sunbelt Human Advancement Resources, 1990-92. Vol. Meals on Wheels, 1984-94; vol. instr. Greenville County Literacy Assn., 1994—; mem. exec. com. Greenville County Dem. Com., 1989—, 1st v.p., 1991—; pres. Coun. Ch. Women, Greenville, 1991-93; v.p., pres.-elect Greenville County Legal Aux., Greenville, 1993—; bd. dirs. YMCA, sec., 1987-88; bd. dirs. March of Dimes, 1969-94, Greenville Alliance for Quality Edn., 1994, Salvation Army Boy's and Girl's Club, Greenville; founder The Greenville Moles, 1990; pres. Piedmont Dist. S.C. Fedn. of Women and Youth Clubs. Recipient cert. of appreciation Solicitor 13th Jud. Cir., 1985, honors March of Dimes, 1985, Citizen of Yr. award Phi Alpha chpt. Omega, 1989, Greenville County Libr., 1989, 93, I Care award gov. of S.C., 1986, Jasamine award Greenville New s Piedmont, 1990, Disting. Svc. award Greenville County Coun., 1991. Mem. Nat. Coun. Negro Women (pres. 1984-86). Presbyterian. Home: 601 Jacobs Rd Greenville SC 29605

SMITH, ANNE BOWMAN, academic administrator, editor; b. Craigsville, Va., Dec. 17, 1934; d. Joseph Benjamin and Louise Frances (Smith) Bowman; m. William Jerry Smith, June 29, 1957; children: Stacey Anne, Joan Elizabeth. Student, Madison Coll., 1951-54, Old Dominion U., 1979-82; BA, Cath. U. Am. Reporter The Richmond (Va.) Times-Dispatch, 1955-56, The Miami (Fla.) Herald, 1965-68, 70-72, The Virginian-Pilot, Norfolk, 1968-70, 72-78; Portsmouth-Chesapeake city editor The Virginian-Pilot, 1978, govt. editor, 1978-80, asst. met. editor, 1980-82; dir. pub. info. Cath. U. Am., Washington, 1982-84, exec. dir. pub. affairs, 1984—; editor in chief Cath. U. Am. mag., 1989—; lectr. journalism, pub. rels. Cath. U. Am., Washington, 1988-92. Editor: Century Ended, Century Begun, 1990. Bd. dirs. Summer Opera Theatre Co., Washington, 1990—. Recipient numerous awards including Va. Press Assn., Va. Press Women, Nat. Fedn. Press Women, Cath. Press Assn. Mem. Soc. Profl. Journalists, Cath. Press Assn., Coun. Advancement and Support of Edn., Assn. Am. Univs., Coll. News Assn. Office: Cath U Am Washington DC 20064

SMITH, ANNE MARIE, accounting educator; b. Joliet, Ill., Sept. 12, 1950; d. Eino Matt and Bertha Mary Tapio; children: Jennifer, Lauren. BS, Ea. Ill. U., 1972; MBA, Ill. Benedictine Coll., 1979; EdD, No. Ill. U., 1992. Cert. mgmt. acct. Acctg. mgr. Kemlite Corp., Joliet, 1972-78; asst. prof. acctg. Coll. of St. Francis, Joliet, 1979-91; assoc. prof. acctg. Grand Canyon U., Phoenix, 1991—. Author logic problems Dell Publs., 1987—. Chair fin. com. St. James Cath. Ch., Phoenix, 1992—. Recipient Cert. of Disting. Performance for Cert. Mgmt. Acct. examination score. Mem. Am. Acctg. Assn., Inst. Mgmt. Accts. (dir. corp. and acad. devel. 1994—), Am. Mensa, Ltd. Office: Grand Canyon U 3300 W Camelback Phoenix AZ 85017

SMITH, BARBARA ANN, gifted education coordinator; b. Oak Park, Ill., Mar. 20, 1950; d. William J. and Mary T. (Barlow) S. BS in Edn., No. Ill. U., 1971, MS in Edn., 1974, cert. advanced study in edn., 1977, EdS, 1988, EdD, 1994; EdD, No. Ill. U., 1994. Cert. tchr., adminstr. gifted edn., verification, Ill.; lic. counselor, Ill. Coord. gifted edn. Dist. 45 Elem. Schs., Villa Park, Ill., 1986—, counselor to group on leadership devel., tchr. Author numerous articles on gifted edn., self-esteem enhancers, sch.-bus. partnerships. Mem. AACD, ASCD, NEA (chpt. sec., treas.), ACA, Ill. West Suburban Reading Coun., AAUW (coord. families facing change group), Delta Kappa Gamma (chpt. pres.), Phi Delta Kappa. Office: Sch Dist 45 255 W Vermont St Villa Park IL 60181-1943

SMITH, BARBARA ANNE, healthcare management company consultant; b. N.Y.C., Oct. 10, 1941; d. John Allen and Lelia Maria (De Silva) Santoro; m. Joseph Newton Smith, Feb. 5, 1961 (div. Sept. 1984); children: J. Michael, Robert Lawrence. Student, Oceanside/Carlsbad Coll. Real estate agt. Routh Robbins, Inc., Washington, 1973-75; gen. mgr. Mall Shops, Inc., Kansas City, Kans., 1975-80; regional mgr. FAO Schwarz, N.Y.C., 1980-84; clin. adminstr. North Denver Med. Ctr., Thornton, Colo., 1984-88; adminstrv. dir. Country Side Ambulatory Surgery Ctr., Leesburg, Va., 1989-91; pres. SCS Healthcare Mgmt. Inc., Washington, 1991—; bd. dirs. Franz Carl Weber Internat., Geneva, 1982-84. Pres. Am. Women Chile, 1968; v.p. Oak Park Assn., Kansas City, 1977-78, pres., 1978-79; vol. Visitor Info. and Assn. Reception Ctr. program Smithsonian Instn., Washington. Mem. NAFE, Network Colo., Profl. Bus. Women Assn., Med. Group Mgmt. Assn., Federated Ambulatory Surgery Assn.

SMITH, BARBARA BARNARD, music educator; b. Ventura, Calif., June 10, 1920; d. Fred W. and Grace (Hobson) S. B.A., Pomona Coll., 1942; Mus.M., U. Rochester, 1943, performer's cert., 1944. Mem. faculty piano and theory Eastman Sch. Music, U. Rochester, 1943-49; mem. faculty U. Hawaii, Honolulu, 1949—; assoc. prof. music U. Hawaii, 1953-62, prof., 1962-82, prof. emeritus, 1982—; sr. fellow East-West Center, 1973; lectr., recitals in Hawaiian and Asian music, U.S., Europe and Asia, 1956—; field researcher Asia, 1956, 60, 66, 71, 80, Micronesia, 1963, 70, 87, 88, 90, 91, Solomon Islands, 1976. Author publs. on ethnomusicology. Mem. Internat. Soc. Music Edn., Internat. Musicol. Soc., Am. Musicol. Soc., Soc. Ethnomusicology, Internat. Coun. for Traditional Music, Asia Soc., Am. Mus. Instrument Soc., Coll. Music Soc., Soc. for Asian Music, Music Educators Nat. Conf., Pacific Sci. Assn., Assn. for Chinese Music Rsch., Phi Beta Kappa, Mu Phi Epsilon. Home: 581 Kamoku St Apt 2004 Honolulu HI 96826-5210

SMITH, BARBARA JEAN, research geologist; b. Garden City, Kans., Feb. 17, 1947; d. Harold Lee and Elva Inez (Smith) Stout; m. Spencer Lee Smith, Aug. 13, 1967; children: Spencer Bruce, Vivien Inelle. BS in Edn., Kans. State U., 1969, BS in Geology, 1975, MS in Geology, 1976. Geologist Kans. Dept. Transp., Manhattan, 1980-81; asst. rsch. geologist Kans. Dept. Transp., Topeka, 1981-88, rsch. geologist, 1988—. Contbr. articles to profl. jours. Mem. Assn. Engring. Geologists (officer various sects. 1982-88, editor directory 1986—). Office: Kans Dept Transp 2300 Van Buren Topeka KS 66611

SMITH, BARBARA JEANNE, library administrator; b. Jersey Shore, Pa., Apr. 14, 1939; d. Moyer Emerson and Mary Kathryn (Ebner) S. BS, Pa. State U., 1961; MS, SUNY, Oswego, 1967; MLS, U. Pitts., 1970; DEd, Pa. State U., 1981. Cert. secondary sch. tchr. Tchr. Binghamton (N.Y.) Sch. Dist., 1961-62, North Syracuse (N.Y.) Cen. Schs., 1962-69; reference librarian Pa. State Libraries, University Park, 1970-75, dept. head, 1975-82, asst. dean., 1982-89; grad. faculty prof. edn. Pa. State U., University Park, 1984-89; regional dir. U.S. Newspaper Project/NEH, University Park, 1985-87; dir. Smithsonian Instn. Libraries, 1989—. Contbr. articles to profl. jours. Life mem. Centre County Hist. Soc., State College, Pa., 1975—; mem. Friends of the Mus., State College, 1975—; bd. dirs. Georgetown Homeowner's Assn., State College, 1975-82; trustee Pitts. Regional Library Ctr., 1978-89. UCLA sr. fellow, 1982. Mem. ALA (coun. mem. 1988-92), Assn. Coll. and Rsch. Librs. (chmn. com. on standards and accreditation 1984-86), Pa. Libr. Assn. (various offices 1976-89), AAUW, D.C. Libr. Assn., U. Pitts. Alumni Assn. (bd. dirs. 1991-94). Republican. Office: NHB22 MRC 154 Smithsonian Inst Librs Washington DC 20560*

SMITH, BARBARA MARTIN, art educator; b. St. Louis, Feb. 3, 1945; d. Charles Landon and Mary Louise (Nolker) Martin; m. Timothy Van Gorder Smith, Nov. 27, 1976; children: Brian Eliot, Marjorie Van Gorder. BA, Lawrence U., 1967; MFA, So. Ill. U., 1975. Cert. tchr., Mo. Art instr. Horton Watkins High Sch., Ladue, Mo., 1968-76; leader Experiment in Internat. Living, Brattleboro, Vt., 1974; art tchr. Michigan City (Ind.) Ctr. for the Arts, 1979-80, Cleve. Mus. of Art, 1981-83; art instr. Villa Duchesne, St. Louis, 1986—; edn. dir. Dunes Art Found., Michigan City, 1979; co-chmn. Internat. Wives Group, Cleve. Coun. on World Affairs, 1982-84; bd. dirs. Webster Groves (Mo.) Sch. Found., 1992. Exhibited in shows at Art Inst. of Chgo., 1979, So. Ill. U. Alumnae Exhibit, 1982, Focus Fiber, Cleve. Mus. of Art, 1982, Nova, Wearable Art, Kuban Gallery, Cleve., 1983, Drawings & Prints, St. Louis Artist's Guild, 1986. Recipient Grad. Fellowship Ann. Grad. award So. Ill. U., 1975; named Artist in Residence/Artist in Schs. Ind. Arts Commn./NEA, 1978-79; named to Honors Seminar for Advancement of Art Edn., R.I. Sch. of Design, 1988, Mem. Art Edn. Delegation to Japan, 1992. Mem. Nat. Art Edn. Assn., Internat. Soc. for Edn. through Art, St. Louis Art Mus., St. Louis Artist Guild. Home: 135 Jefferson Rd Webster Groves MO 63119 Office: Villa Duchesne Oak Hill Sch 801 Spoede Rd Des Peres MO 63131

SMITH, BERNICE LAWSON, librarian; b. Delavan, Wis., May 9, 1917; d. Theodore Hale and Ada Byers S. Student, Northland Coll., 1936-38, U. Wis., 1938-39, Mizen Acad. Art, Chgo., 1939-40. Cert. ct. reporter, Ill. Precision inspector Dodge, Chgo., 1943-45, Ford Aircraft, Chgo., 1951-58, Ordnance Engring. Assocs., Chgo., 1959-60; ct. reporter Chgo. Mcpl. Cts., 1961-76; precision inspector Internat. Harvester, Chgo., 1977-80; libr. John C. Stevenson, Architect, San Diego, Calif., 1991—. Mem. Am. Assn. Individual Investors (life). Home: Apt 4-D 111 W Pennsylvania Ave San Diego CA 92103-4054

SMITH, BERT KRUGER, mental health services professional, consultant; b. Wichita Falls, Tex., Nov. 18, 1915; d. Sam and Fania (Feldman) Kruger; m. Sidney Stewart Smith, Jan. 19, 1936; children: Sheldon Stuart, Jared Burt (dec.), Randy Smith Huke. BJ, U. Mo., 1936; MA, U. Tex., 1949; DHL (hon.), U. Mo., 1985. Soc. and entertainment editor Wichita Falls Post, 1936-37; freelance writer Juneau, Alaska, 1937; assoc. pub. Coleman Daily Dem. Voice, 1950-51; assoc. editor Jr. Coll. Jour., Austin, Tex., 1952-55; spl. cons., exec. Hogg Found. for Mental Health, Austin, 1952—; chmn. bd. Austin Groups for the Elderly, 1985—. Author: No Language But A Cry, 1964, Your Non-Learning Child, 1968, A Teaspoon of Honey, 1970, Insights for Uptights, 1970, Aging in America, 1973, The Pursuit of Dignity, 1977, Looking Forward, 1983; contbr. numerous articles to profl. jours. Bert Kruger Smith professorship Sch. Social Work U. Tex., 1982; recipient Disting. Svc. award City of Austin, 1988, Cert. of Appreciation, Tex. Dept. Human Svcs., 1989, Ann Bert Smith award Sr.'s Respite Svc., 1989, S.W. Found. Founders' Spirit award, 1990, Tex. Leadership award Ann. Tex. Joint Conf. on Aging, 1992, Tex. Leadership award Tex. Dept. on Aging, 1992; named to Tex. Women's Hall of Fame, 1988. Mem. Women in Comm.

(Lifetime Achievement award 1994), Am. Fedn. for Aging Rsch., Adult Svc. Coun. (bd. dirs. 1970—), Family Eldercare (bd. dirs. 1979—), Authors Guild, Nat. Assn. Sci. Writers, Hadassah, B'nai B'rith Women, Delta Kappa Gamma (hon). Jewish. Home: 5818 Westslope Dr Austin TX 78731-3633 Office: Hogg Found Mental Health PO Box 7998 Austin TX 78713-7998 also: U Tex Austin Austin TX 78713

SMITH, BERYL KIRCALDIE, librarian, curator; b. Milw., July 21, 1935; d. William Inglefield and Carol Theresa (Bick) Kircaldie; m. Douglas Wilcox Smith, June 20, 1959; children: Alison Marie Smith Acton, Courtney Ann, Stephanie Leigh. Nursing degree, Mt. Sinai Hosp., 1955; BA in Classics, Douglas Coll., 1982; MLS, Rutgers U., 1983, MA in Art History, 1987. RN. Grad. reference asst. Douglas Coll. Libr., New Brunswick, N.J., 1983-86; art libr. Rutgers U., New Brunswick, N.J., 1986-92, acting head Alexander Libr. Tech. Svcs., 1992-93; art libr. Rutgers U., New Brunswick, 1993—; curator Women Artists Series, Douglas Coll., New Brunswick, 1983-91. Editor: Space Planning for the Art Library, 1990, Art Documentation Art Librs. Soc. N.Am., 1989—; author: The Mary H. Dana Women Artists Series: From Idea to Institution in Jour. Rutgers U. Librs., 1992, Alexander Library: The Past, The Present, The Future in Jour. Rutgers U. Librs., 1993. Bd. dirs. Peters Valley Craft Ctr., Layton, N.J., 1990—; com. chmn. LWV, East Brunswick, N.J., 1966-76. Mem. Art Librs. Soc. North Am. (moderator acad. group 1987-88), Art Librs. Soc. N.J. (chmn. 1987-88), Coll. Art Assn., Women's Caucus for Art, Phi Beta Kappa. Democrat. Office: Rutgers U Art Libr New Brunswick NJ 08903

SMITH, BETSY KEISER, telecommunications company executive; b. Washington, July 31, 1960; d. Henry Bruce and Jessie (Weeks) Keiser; m. Patrick C. Smith, June 2, 1984; 1 child, Alexander Keiser Smith. BA in Fine Arts and Art History, U. Mich., 1984. Account rep. Adam A. Weschler Galleries, Inc., Washington, 1984-85; mgr. customer service Presdl. Airways, Inc., Washington, 1986; merchandise mgr. Burdines Inc., Boynton Beach, Fla., 1986-87; sr. account exec. Cellular One Co., West Palm Beach, Fla., 1987—; cons. Fed. Publs. Inc., Washington, 1981-83, U.S. Telemktg. Inc., Atlanta, 1986—, Lion Internat., London, 1985—, Inst. Paralegal Tng., Phila., 1986—. Mem. DAR, U. Mich. Alumni Assn., U. Mich. Alumni Club, Stuart Corinthian Yacht Club. Home: # A47 2319 Treasure Isle Dr Palm Beach Gardens FL 33410 Office: Cellular One Co 250 S Australian Ave West Palm Beach FL 33401-5012

SMITH, BETTY, writer, nonprofit foundation executive; b. Bonham, Tex., Sept. 16; d. Sim and Gertrude (Dearing) S. Student, Stephens Coll., 1939-40; BJ, U. Tex., 1940-43. Women's editor Daily Texan, 1943; pres. Hope Assocs. Corp., N.Y.C., 1948-50; pres., owner Betty Smith Assocs., N.Y.C., 1950—. Author: A Matter of Heart, 1969. Pres. Melchior Heldentenor Found., N.Y.C., 1987—, Gerda Lissner Found., 1994—; v.p. Herman Lissner Found., 1990—. Mem. Author's Guild. Office: 135 E 55th St New York NY 10022

SMITH, BETTY DENNY, county official, administrator, fashion executive; b. Centralia, Ill., Nov. 12, 1932; d. Otto and Ferne Elizabeth (Beier) Hasenfuss; m. Peter S. Smith, Dec. 5, 1964; children: Carla Kip, Bruce Kimball. Student, U. Ill., 1950-52; student, L.A. City Coll., 1953-57, UCLA, 1965, U. San Francisco, 1982-84. Freelance fashion coordinator L.A., N.Y.C., 1953-58; tchr. fashion Rita LeRoy Internat. Studios, 1959-60; mgr. Mo Nadler Fashion, L.A., 1961-64; showroom dir. Jean of Calif. Fashions, L.A., 1965—; freelance polit. book reviewer for community newspapers, 1961-62; staff writer Valley Citizen News, 1963. Bd. dirs. Pet Assistance Found., 1969-76; founder, pres., dir. Vol. Services to Animals L.A., 1972-76; mem. County Com. To Discuss Animals in Research, 1973-74; mem. blue ribbon com. on animal control L.A. County, 1973-74; dir. L.A. County Animal Care and Control, 1976-82; mem. Calif. Animal Health Technician Exam. Com., 1975-82, chmn., 1979; bd. dirs. L.A. Soc. for Prevention Cruelty to Animals, 1984-94, Calif. Coun. Companions Animal Advocates; dir. West Coast Regional Office, Am. Humane Assn., 1988—; CFO Coalition for Pet Population Control, 1987-92; mem. Calif. Rep. Cen. Com., 1964-72, mem. exec. com., 1971-73; mem. L.A. County Rep. Cen. Com., 1964-70, mem. exec. com., 1966-70; chmn. 29th Congl. Cen. Com., 1969-70; sec. 28th Senatorial Cen. Com., 1967-68, 48th Assembly Dist. Cen. Com., 1965-68; mem. speakers bur. George Murphy for U.S. Senate, 1970; campaign mgr. Los Angeles County for Spencer Williams for Atty. Gen., 1966; mem. adv. com. Moorpark Coll., 1988—. Mem. Internat. Platford Assn., Mannequins Assn. (bd. dirs. 1967-68), Motion Picture and TV Industry Assn. (govt. rels. and pub. affairs com. 1992), Lawyer's Wives San Gabriel Valley (bd. dirs. 1971-74, pres. 1972-73), L.A. Athletic Club, Town Hall, Delta Gamma, Pi Phi Theta. Home: 1766 Bluffhill Dr Monterey Park CA 91754-4533

SMITH, BONNIE BEATRICE, corporate communications executive; b. Dayton, Ohio, July 22, 1948; d. Joseph Edward and Phyllis Jean (Shook) S. BS in Journalism, Ohio U., 1970. Accredited bus. communicator. Reporter Piqua (Ohio) Daily Call, 1970-71; asst. dir. pub. rels. Bethesda Hosps., Cin., 1971-76; dir. communication St. Joseph's Hosp., Ft. Wayne, Ind., 1976-81; publs. editor E. Ohio Gas Co., Cleve., 1981-88, coord. customer communications, 1988-90; mgr. employee communication and wellness programs Picker Internat., Inc., Highland Heights, Ohio, 1990—; speaker, seminar leader various hosps., bus. and profl. orgns., 1975—. Outreach vol. Cleve. Children's Mus., 1986-88, co-chmn. outreach program, mem. speaker's bur., 1988-89, mem. pub. rels. task force, 1989-92. Recipient numerous awards Ohio Hosp. Assn., Ohio Press Women, Acad. Hosp. Pub. Rels., Cin. Editors Assn., also others. Mem. Internat. Assn. Bus. Communicators (dir. mem. svcs. internal communications coun. 1985-88, chmn. directory mktg. coun. 1988-90, dir. examiners accreditation bd. 1986-88), numerous awards 1975—). Home: 1700 E 13th St Apt 22S Cleveland OH 44114-3238 Office: Picker Internat Inc 595 Miner Rd Cleveland OH 44143

SMITH, BRENDA JOYCE, author, editor, social studies educator; b. Washington, Jan. 2, 1946; d. William Eugene and Marjorie (Williams) Young; m. Duane Milton Smith, Aug. 4, 1978. BA in History and Govt. cum laude, Ohio U., 1968, postgrad., 1972, 83; postgrad. in Am. and European History. Tchr. Jr. High Sch., Lancaster, Ohio, 1968-69, Reynoldsburg (Ohio) Mid. Sch. and High Sch., 1970-71; grad. teaching asst. Ohio U., Athens, 1969-70, 71-72; polit. speech writer Legis. Reference Bur., Columbus, Ohio, 1972-74; pub. rels. writer Josephinum Coll., Columbus, 1976-78; social studies editor Merrill Pub. Co., Columbus, 1979-91; freelance author/editor social studies Columbus, 1991—. Project editor: (secondary textbooks) Human Heritage: A World History, 1985, 89, World History: The Human Experience, 1992; author: The Collapse of the Soviet Union, 1994, Egypt: Land of the Pharaohs, 1995; writer of 3 African Am. history series, 5th grade; writer Am. history books. Del. 1st U.S.-Russia Joint Conf. on Edn., 1994. Mem. Nat. Coun. Social Studies, Ohio Coun. Social Studies, Freelance Editorial Assn. Office: 3710 Harborough Dr Gahanna OH 43230

SMITH, BRENDA MARIE, vocational home economics educator; b. Winchester, Tenn., May 28, 1957; d. William Ralph and Mary Elizabeth (Wynne) Hall; m. Kevin Wayne Smith, Mar. 30, 1980; children: Jessica, Andrea. BS in Edn., S.W. Mo. State U., 1979, MS in Edn., 1989. Cert. tchr., home economist, Mo. Tchr. vocat. home econs., advisor Koshkonong (Mo.) Schs., 1979-80, Ava (Mo.) R-1 Sch. Dist., 1980-83, West Plains (Mo.) R-7 Schs., 1983—; advisor Future Homemakers Am., 1979—; adj. faculty S.W. Bapt. U., Mountain View (Mo.) Ctr., 1992-93; mem. WPHS Better Edn. Techniques Team, West Plains, 1987—; mem. adv. bd. Step One Teen Parenting Program, West Plains, 1992—; mem. adv. bd. home econs. dept. S.W. Mo. State U., Springfield, 1983—. Sec., bd. dirs. Friendship Circle Presch., West Plains, 1989-91, chair bd. dirs., 1991-92. Mem. Future Homemakers Am. Alumni Assn., Mo. Home Econs. Tchrs. Assn. (bd. dirs. 1987—, treas. 1989-93, pres.-elect 1993-94, pres. 1994-95), Am. Vocat. Assn., Mo. Vocat. Assn., Am. Home Econs. Assn. (sec. dist. E 1982-83, cert. home economist), Mo. Home Econs. Assn., Mo. State Tchrs. Assn., Cmty. Tchrs. Assn. (pres. 1989-90, 92-93), Bus. and Profl. Women. Methodist. Home: 702 Shuttee St West Plains MO 65775-2916 Office: West Plains Sr High 602 E Olden St West Plains MO 65775-3334

SMITH, BRENDA SUE, psychology educator; b. Grand Rapids, Mich., Dec. 13, 1958. BA, Calvin Coll., 1981; MA, Wayne State U., 1985, PhD, 1991. Asst. prof. Westmont Coll., Santa Barbara, Calif., 1989—, chmn., 1994—; adj. asst. prof. U. Mo., St. Louis, 1986-89. Contbg. author: Knowing and Remembering in Young Children, 1990; contbr. articles to Jour. Exptl. Child Psychology. Recipient Meritorious Svc. award Disabled Student's Union, U. Mo., St. Louis, 1989; faculty devel., Outstanding Tchr. Natural and Behavioral Scis. award, 1992; grantee Westmont Coll., 1991-93. Mem. APA, Western Psychol. Assn., Soc. for Rsch. in Child Devel. Office: Westmont Coll Psychology Dept 955 La Paz Rd Santa Barbara CA 93108-1099

SMITH, BROOKE ELLEN, lawyer; b. Geneva, Ill., Nov. 24, 1956; d. Dale Corwin and Imogene (Henderson) S.; m. Russell W. Ault, June 24, 1988; 1 child, Blair Elizabeth Ault. AB, U. Mo., 1977; JD, Harvard U., 1980. Bar: D.C. 1980, Tex. 1982, U.S. Ct. Appeals (5th cir.) 1982, U.S. Dist. Ct. (so. dist.) Tex. 1982, U.S. Dist. Ct. (we. dist.) Tex. 1984; cert. in bus. bankruptcy law Tex. Bd. legal Specialization. Law clk. to judge U.S. Bankruptcy Ct., Houston, 1980-81; assoc. Ross, Banks, May, Cron & Cavin, Houston, 1981-86, Baker, Brown, Sharman & Parker, Houston, 1986-89, Leonard, Hurt, Terry & Blinn, Houston, 1989—; co-host legal issues talk show Sta. KQQK-FM, Houston, 1988; mediator Tex. Bankruptcy Forum on Lexis Counsel Connect; spkr. in field. Author: Bankruptcy Strategies for Lenders, 2nd edit., 1993. Mem. ABA, Houston Bar Assn., Am. Bankruptcy Inst., State Bar Tex. (bankruptcy com., cert. in bus. bankruptcy law Bd. Legal Specialization 1989), Gulf Coast Mensa (bd. dirs. 1988). Office: Leonard Hurt Terry & Blinn 1221 McKinney Ste 2775 Houston TX 77010-9999

SMITH, CARLA WALSER, elementary school educator; b. Wichita Falls, Tex., Jan. 6, 1953; d. James Carl and Jerry (Sellers) Walser; children: James Rogers, Michael Beau Rogers. AAS in Early Childhood Edn., Vernon Regional Jr. Coll., Wichita Falls, 1983. Tchr. 1st United Meth. Sch., Wichita Falls, 1980-85, Trinity Presbyn. Sch., Wichita Falls, 1981-84; owner, dir. The Playhouse Daycare, Wichita Falls, 1984-86; dir. edn. Boys Clubs of Wichita Falls, 1986—. Mem. United Way of Wichita Falls, 1986—. Mem. Tex. Drug and Alcohol Abuse Counselors, LWV, Assn. Boys and Girls Club Profls. (sec. 1986—, program profl. of yr. 1989). Democrat. Office: Boys Clubs of Wichita Falls 6th And Broad St Wichita Falls TX 76301

SMITH, CAROL JEAN, lawyer; b. Anniston, Ala., Oct. 12, 1947; d. Claudous Sellers and Hester (Ledbetter) S. BS, Jacksonville State U., 1970; JD, U. Ala., 1973. Bar: Ala. 1973, U.S. Dist. Ct. (mid. dist.) Ala. 1974, U.S. Ct. Appeals (5th cir.) 1974, U.S. Supreme Ct. 1977, U.S. Dist. Ct. (no. dist.) Ala. 1981, U.S. Ct. Appeals (11th cir.) 1981, U.S. Dist. Ct. (so. dist.) Ala. 1985. Law clk. to presiding justice Supreme Ct. Ala., Montgomery, 1973-74; asst. atty. gen. State of Ala., Montgomery, 1974—. Named one of Outstanding Young Women Am., 1974, 84, Outstanding Alumna, Jacksonville State U., 1985. Mem. ABA, Ala. Bar Assn., Montgomery County Bar Assn., Farrah Law Soc., Bench and Bar Soc., Am. Assn. Univ. Women, Bama Tip-Off Club (mem. bd. dirs. 1993—), U. Ala. Nat. Alumni Assn. (dist. v.p. 1992-94), League Women Voters (bd. dirs. Montgomery chpt. 1985-89), Phi Alpha Delta (treas. 1972-73), Alpha Xi Delta (pres. 1974-76, nat. fin. v.p. 1978-82, nat. alumnae v.p. 1982-84), Kappa Delta Epsilon, Sigma Tau Delta, Pi Gamma Mu, Rotary (Montgomery chpt.). Democrat. Baptist. Lodge: Zonta (area dir. 1994—). Home: 3141 Fitzgerald Rd Montgomery AL 36106-2628 Office: Office of Atty Gen 11 S Union St Montgomery AL 36130-0001

SMITH, CAROL WOJTOWICZ, curator, archivist, historian; b. Phila., Apr. 29, 1952; d. Edward and Mary Virginia (Hanlon) Wojtowicz; m. Brian Guy Smith, Jan. 2, 1988; children: Jeffrey Robert, Katherine Elizabeth. BA in Am. Civilization, U. Pa., 1974, MA in Material Culture, 1974. Rsch. asst. Phila. Mus. Art, 1975; curator, archivist The Phila. Contributionship, 1976-93, The Mut. Assurance Co., Phila., 1976—; cons. on collections and archival mgmt. and hist. rsch., Haddonfield, N.J.; cons. PSFS, Merc. Beneficial Assn., Phila. Club, 1979; cons., bd. dirs., sec. Phila. Fire Dept. Hist. Corp., 1979. Author: Catalogue of The Green Tree Collection, 1977, The Mutual Assurance Company, 1984, 85; contbg. author: Invisible Philadelphia, 1995; curator exhibits Battle of the Blaze, 1980, Framing the Board: A Look at Corporate Portraiture, 1982. Co-chmn. antiques show Univ. Hosp., Phila., 1980; judge antique fire apparatus in parades and musters, Pa. Mem. Am. Assn. Mus., Soc. Am. Archivists, Acad. Cert. Archivists, Mid-Atlantic Assn. Mus., Mid-Atlantic Regional Archives Conf., Mus. Coun. Phila. and Delaware Valley, Fire Mark Cir. Ams. (bd. dirs., pres. 1988-90). Office: The Mut Assurance Co 414 Walnut St Philadelphia PA 19106

SMITH, CAROLE DIANNE, legal editor, writer; b. Seattle, June 12, 1945; d. Glaude Francis and Elaine Claire (Finkenstein) S.; m. Stephen Bruce Presser, June 18, 1968 (div. June 1987); children: David Carter, Elisabeth Catherine. AB cum laude, Harvard U., Radcliffe Coll., 1968; JD, Georgetown U., 1974. Bar: Pa. 1974. Law clerk to Hon. Judith Jamison Phila., 1974-75; assoc. Gratz, Tate, Spiegel, Ervin & Ruthrouff, Phila., 1975-76; freelance editor, writer Evanston, Ill., 1983-87; editor Ill. Inst. Tech., Chgo., 1987-88; mng. editor LawLetters, Inc., Chgo., 1988-89; editor ABA, Chgo., 1989—. Author: Jour. of Legal Medicine, 1975, Selling and the Law: Advertising and Promotion, 1987, (under pseudonym Sarah Toast) 33 children's books, 1994-95; editor The Brief, 1990—, Criminal Justice 1989-90, 1992-95 (Gen. Excellence award Soc. Nat. Assn. Pubs. 1990), Franchise Law Jour., 1995—. Dir. Radcliffe Club of Chgo., 1990-93. Office: ABA 750 N Lake Shore Dr Chicago IL 60611-4403

SMITH, CAROLYN LORETTA, diversifed financial services company executive, accountant; b. Lakewood, N.J., Nov. 14, 1942; d. Davis Lee and Arline Loretta (Erwin) Knight; widowed; children: Sonia, Angela. BA, Howard U., 1965; MBA, U. Md., 1994. CPA. Sr. assoc., assoc. Coopers & Lybrand, Washington, 1967-71; CFO Nat. Inst. for Comml. Devel., Washington, 1972-73; sr. assoc. Coopers & Lybrand, L.A., 1973-76; mgr. Coopers & Lybrand, Washington, 1976-77; treas. Govt. of D.C., Washington, 1977-79, dir. dept. fin. and revenue, 1979-82; mgr. Coopers & Lybrand, Washington, 1982-86, ptnr., 1986—; fin. analyst United Planning Orgn., Washington, 1965-67. Treas. Women's Nat. Democratic Club. 1992-93; chair D.C. Retirement Bd., Washington, 1990-91; bd. dirs. Young Audiences, Leadership Washington. Mem. D.C. C. of C. (treas.). Democrat. Baptist. Office: Coopers & Lybrand 1800 M St NW Washington DC 20036

SMITH, CATHLEEN LYNNE, psychology educator; b. Salt Lake City, Mar. 17, 1947; d. Dasil Clawson and Melba (Fairbourn) S. BA with honors, U. Utah, 1968, MA, 1972, PhD, 1976. Asst. prof. of psychology Portland (Oreg.) State U., 1975-79, assoc. prof. psychology, 1979-83, prof. psychology, 1983—. Contbr. articles to profl. jours. Chair Portland Foster Grandparent Program Adv. Coun., 1983-86. Mem. APA, Western Psychol. Assn., Gerontol. Soc. Am., Soc. for Rsch. in Child Devel., Oreg. Ethics Commons (bd. dirs.), Phi Beta Kappa, Phi Kappa Phi, Sigma Xi (Portland State U. chpt. pres. 1992-93). Democrat. Home: 2518 SW Vista Portland OR 97201 Office: Dept Psychol Portland State U PO Box 751 Portland OR 97207

SMITH, CATHY DAWN, administrator; b. Northampton, Pa., Feb. 6, 1954; d. Russell W. and Edna (Kleckner) Seidel; m. Ronald James Smith, Nov. 1, 1975; 1 child, Ronald James Jr. Grad. high sch., Slatington, Pa. Fiscal asst. Ctr. for Humanistic Change, Inc., Bath, Pa., 1985—. Sec. Parkland Sch. Dist. Drug Free Schs. Bd., Orefield, Pa., 1989—; mem. community action com. Allert-Partnership of a Drug Free Valley, Lehigh Valley, Pa., 1992-94; program coord. Parkland Alliance for Youth, Pa., 1977-85; explorer advisor Explorers Officer Assn., 1989—; co-pres. Women Guild Grace UCC, 1994—; mem. minsi trails coun. Boy Scouts Am., 1976—; 1st v.p. Catasauqua Suburban North YMCA, 1993. Mem. Chapel of Four Chaplains, Lehigh Valley Kennel Club. Democrat. mem. United Ch. Christ. Office: Ctr for Humanistic Change Inc 7574 Beth Bath Pike Bath PA 18014-8967

SMITH, CECE, venture capitalist; b. Washington, Nov. 16, 1944; d. Linn Charles and Grace Inez (Walker) S.; m. John Ford Lacy, Apr. 22, 1978. B.B.A., U. Mich., 1966; M.L.A., So. Meth. U., 1974. C.P.A., Tex. Staff accountant Arthur Young & Co. (C.P.A.s), Boston, 1966-68; staff accountant, then asst. to controller Wyly Corp., Dallas, 1969-72; controller, treas. sub. Univ. Computing Co., Dallas, 1972-74; controller Steak and Ale Restaurants Am., Inc., Dallas, 1974-76; v.p. fin. Steak and Ale Restaurants Am., Inc., 1976-80, exec. v.p., 1980-81; exec. v.p. Pearle Health Services, Inc.,, 1981-84, pres. Primacare div., 1984-86; gen. ptnr. Phillips-Smith Specialty Retail Group, 1986—; pres. Le Sportsac Dallas, Inc., 1981-87; bd. dirs. A Pea in the Pod, Inc., Henry Silverman Jewelers, Inc., Cheers, Inc., Valley Advisors, Inc., Lil Things, Inc., Hot Topics, Inc.; chmn. Fed. Res. Bank of Dallas, 1994—. Former co-chmn. pres.'s rsch. coun. U. Tex. S.W. Med. Ctr. Dallas; mem. vis. com. U. Mich. Grad. Sch. Bus., former exec. bd. So. Meth. U. Cox Sch. Bus.; former v.p., bd. dirs. Jr. Achievement Dallas, past pres. Charter 100; past. treas. Dallas Assembly; former bd. dirs. Taco Villa, Inc., BizMart, Inc. Mem. Tex. Soc. CPAs (former dir.). Home: 6412 Williams Pky Dallas TX 75205-1717 Office: 5080 Spectrum Dr Ste 700 W Dallas TX 75248-4658

SMITH, CHARLOTTE REED, retired music educator; b. Eubank, Ky., Sept. 15, 1921; d. Joseph Lumpkin and Cornelia Elizabeth (Spenser) Reed; m. Walter Lindsay Smith, Aug. 24, 1949; children—Walter Lindsay IV, Elizabeth Reed. B.A. in Music, Tift Coll., 1941; M.A. in Mus. Theory, Eastman Sch. of Music, 1946; postgrad. Juilliard Sch., 1949. Asst. prof. theory Okla. Bapt. U., 1944-45, Washburn U., 1946-48; prof. music Furman U., Greenville, S.C., 1948-92; chmn. dept. music, 1987-92. Editor: Seven Penitential Psalms with Two Laudate Psalms, 1983; author: Manual of Sixteenth-Century Contrapuntal Style, 1989. Mem. Internat. Musicological Soc., Am. Musicological Soc., Soc. for Music Theory, AAUP (sec.-treas. Furman chpt. 1984-85), Nat. Fedn. Music Clubs, Pi Kappa Lambda. Republican. Baptist.

SMITH, CHARLSIE OPAL, tax specialist, administrator; b. Cullman County, Ala., Oct. 6, 1939; d. Lester Garlington and Annie Lucille (Allen) Farley; m. Gary Donald Smith, June 4, 1957; children: Marvin Lester, Gary Don, Robert Lee, Linda Diane. Diploma, Emma Sansom H.S., Gadsden, Ala., 1957; cert., H&R Block Tax Sch., Gadsden, 1979, cert. tchr., 1987. Tax preparer, office mgr. H&R Block, Gadsden, 1979—. Pres. bd. dirs. Gilchrist Boys & Girls Club, 1984-86, rodeo chmn., 1985-87, sec.-treas., 1987—; sec., office mgr. Boys & Girls Club of N.E. Ala., Gadsden, 1989-92; life mem. Ala. PTA, Gadsden, 1976—.

SMITH, CHERYL IRENE, trust company executive; b. Gunnison, Colo., Dec. 15, 1956; d. William Charles and Joyce Annunciata (Davis) S.; m. Marcellus William Andrews, May 30, 1981 (div. May 1992); 1 child, Isaiah. BS in Fgn. Svc., Georgetown U., 1977; MA in Econs., Yale U., 1979, MPhil, 1980, PhD in Econs., 1984. Rsch. asst. Bd. of Govs. Fed. Reserve, Washington, 1978; teaching asst. Yale U., New Haven, Conn., 1980-81, acting instr., 1981-82; instr., asst. prof. U. Denver, 1982-86; v.p., portfolio mgr. Franklin Rsch. & Devel., Boston, 1987-92, U.S. Trust Co., Boston, 1992—. Dir. Resist!, Somerville, Mass., 1992—; treas. Wellesley (Mass.) A Better Chance, 1987-89. NSF fellow, 1977. Mem. Am. Econs. Assn., New England chpt. Social Investment Forum, Boston Security Analyst Soc., Assn. Investment Mgmt. & Rsch. Roman Catholic. Office: US Trust Co 40 Ct St Boston MA 02108

SMITH, CHRISTINA WEAVER, educator, artist; b. Balt., Oct. 18, 1949; d. Vernon Lloyd and Clara (Fender) W.; m. Joseph H. Smith II, Aug. 18, 1973; children: Rebecca Clare, Duncan Joseph. BA, Wilson Coll., 1971; MFA, George Wash. U., 1976; cert. in tchg., U. Va., 1993. With Union Trust Co., Balt., 1968-79; tchr. Hobby Town, Mt. Airy, Md., 1982-86; tchr. Fauquier County Schs., Warrenton, Va., 1992—, mem. mid. sch. com. arts coun., 1992-93. Leader Girl Scouts USA, Washington, 1986—, mgr., 1987-92. Mem. DAR, Va. Edn. Assn. Presbyterian. Office: Warrenton Mid Sch 244 Waterloo St Warrenton VA 22186

SMITH, CHRISTINE, pharmaceutical executive; b. Bronx, N.Y., Oct. 28, 1958; d. Frank and Virginia (Milone) Michalchuk. AA, Suffolk County C.C., Farmingvale, N.Y., 1978, AS, 1979; BA, SUNY, Stony Brook, 1980. Cert. dental asst., N.Y. Purchasing agt. Ctrl. Dental Supply Co., Hempstead, N.Y., 1981-82; sales mgr. Capital Credit Corp., Hempstead, N.Y., 1982-83; pharm. rep. Bristol Myers, Evansville, Ind., 1983-91, Syntex Labs., Palo Alto, Calif., 1991-93, Abbott Labs., Abbott Park, Ill., 1993—; pres. The Image Consultants, Huntington, N.Y., 1989-91. Mem. Tai-Zen Acad. Self-Def., U.S. Karate Studios. Roman Catholic. Office: Abbott Labs 1 Abbott Park Rd Abbott Park IL 60064-3500

SMITH, CYNTHIA ANN, patient care coordinator; b. Erie, Pa., July 1, 1967; d. Fred Paul and Mary (Norman) Powell; m. Robert Wade Smith, May 28, 1988; 1 child, Ashely Marie. B in Gen. Studies, Valdosta State U., 1992, MPA, 1994. Academic advisor Valdosta (Ga.) State U., 1990—; receptionist USAF Recruting Office, Erie, Pa., summers, 1986, 87, 88. Cofounder parent adv. bd. Child Devel. Ctr., Kingsland, Ga., 1992—. Mem. ASPA. Home: 5840 Sundown Circle #321 Orlando FL 32822 Office: Valdosta State U Ste F2 4303 Vineland Rd Orlando FL 32811

SMITH, CYNTHIA MARLENE, organization planning and training administrator; b. Kansas City, Kans., Mar. 9, 1951; d. James Melvin Johnson and Virgie Lee (Eddy) Edwards; m. Nolan N. Smith, Dec. 18, 1971; children: Tais Kishana, Natalie Marie. BS in Psychology, William Jewell Coll., 1972. Cert. profl. in human resources. Skills instr. Opportunities Industrialization Ctr., Kansas City, 1972-74; job placement specialist Opportunities Industrialization Ctr., Kansas City, Mo., 1974-77; dir. ops. OIC, Kansas City, Mo., 1977-81; asst. exec. dir. O/C, Kansas City, Mo., 1981-82, exec. dir., 1982-83; prodn. supr. Avon Products, Inc., Kansas City, 1983-84, supr. quality assurance, 1984-85; pers. adminstr. Mo. Pub. Svc., Kansas City, 1985-90, sr. human resources adminstr., 1990-93, mgr. orgn. planning and tng., 1993—, sec. polit. action com., 1990—; bus. coord. Inroads, Inc., Kansas City, 1988—. Pres. KCMC Child Devel. Corp., 1986—; mem., chmn. subcom. futures adv. com. Urban League Greater Kansas City, 1991—. Named one of 100 Most Influential Women in Kansas City, Kansas City Globe, 1984, Woman of Yr., Zeta Phi Beta, 1987; recipient Black Achievers in Industry award SCLC, Kansas City, 1988, Greater Kansas City Image award, 1992, awards for excellence Mo. Pub. Svc., 1993. Mem. Human Resources Mgmt. Assn., Black Achievers Soc. (pres. 1990-91). Democrat. Baptist. Office: Mo Pub Svc 10700 E 350th Hwy Kansas City MO 64138

SMITH, DEBBIE JANE, telecommunications manager; b. Fairfield, Ala., Oct. 21, 1957; d. Samuel Adams and Patsy H. (Walker) S. BA in Bus. Adminstrn., Birmingham So. Coll., 1981; MBA, Samford U., 1984. Keypunch operator Mortgage Corp. of the South, Birmingham, Ala., 1976-77, shipping clk., 1977-78; keypunch operator Ala. Power, Birmingham, 1978-79; white page directory clk. South Ctrl. Bell Telephone Co., Birmingham, 1979-83; dispatch clk. BellSouth Advanced Sys., Birmingham, 1983-87, sys. facility adminstr., 1987, supr. telecomm. adminstrn. ctr., 1987-89; staff mgr.-technical support BellSouth Comm. Sys., Birmingham, 1989-93; mgr. telecomm. sys. BellSouth Telecomm., Birmingham, 1993—. Pre-sch. choir dir. 1st Bapt. Ch. Pelham, Ala., 1992-94, 1st Bapt. Ch. Midfield, Ala., 1982-90, coord., worker children's dept., 1990, mem. fin. com., pers. com., benevolence com., 1982-90. Recipient Nat. Cmty. Leadership and Svc. award U.S. Achievement Acad., Lexington, Ky., 1984. Republican. Home: 123 Stratshire Ln Pelham AL 35124 Office: BellSouth Telecomm 3196 US Hwy 280 S Rm 206N Birmingham AL 35243

SMITH, DEBORAH RUTH, lawyer; b. Burnett, Tex., Nov. 19, 1961; d. Hal Ray and Aletta Earlene (Smith) S. BA, Tex. A&M, 1984; JD, St. Mary's U., San Antonio, 1988. Bar: Tex. 1988, U.S. Dist. Ct. (no. dist.) Tex. 1989. Assoc. Ragir & Assocs., Dallas, 1988-89, Jones, Day, Reavis & Pogue, Dallas, 1989-91; with 7th Ct. Appeals, Amarillo, Tex., 1991—; instr. West Tex. State U., 1992, 93-94, 94-95. Contbr. articles to CAI Bull., 1988, 89. Vol. Dallas Ctr. for Ind. Living, 1989-91; active Greater Dallas C. of C. 1990-91; textbook reader North Tex. Taping for the Blind, Dallas, 1988-90; tchr. World Bible Sch., 1991-93. Mem. Tex. State Bar Assn., Am. Bus. Women's Assn., Amarillo Bar Assn., Atwater Group, Rep. Women's Assn., Rotary (Amarillo). Republican. Mem. Ch. of Christ. Office: Ct of Appeals 7th Dist 501 S Fillmore Ste 2A Amarillo TX 79101-2433

SMITH, DEBRA FARWELL, elementary school librarian; b. Lock Haven, Pa., Sept. 9, 1950; d. James Samuel and Betty (Jackson) Farwell; m. James L. Smith, Oct. 4, 1977; children: Jason James, Joshua Jordan. BS, Lock Haven U., 1972. Cert. elem. tchr., libr., early childhood instr. Kindergarten tchr. Follow-Through, Lock Haven, 1972-74; tchr. Keystone Cen. Sch. Dist., Lock

Haven, 1974-83, libr., 1983%. Mem. Pa. State Libr. Assn., Bald Eagle Reading Coun. Republican. Home: 38 Cardinal Dr W Lock Haven PA 17745 Office: Woodward Elem Sch RR 2 Lock Haven PA 17745

SMITH, DEBRA LOUISE, legal assistant, medical transcriptionist; b. Indpls., July 25, 1958; d. Walter W. and Nancy J. (Koehler) S. Grad. high sch., Indpls., 1976; cert. in med. transcription, Ind. U.-Purdue U., Indpls. Legal sec. Burris & Gross, Indpls., 1976-79, Scopelitis & Garvin, Indpls., 1979-92; legal asst. Tabor, Fels & Tabor, Indpls., 1982—. Republican. Home: 1990 Landmark Dr # 511 Indianapolis IN 46260-3011 Office: Tabor Fels & Tabor # 1990 151 N Delaware Indianapolis IN 46204

SMITH, DEIRDRE O'MEARA, lawyer; b. N.Y.C., June 2, 1946; d. Thomas Francis and Mary Veronica (Meehan) O'Meara; children: Thomas Brady Ahr, Andrew Travers Ahr; m. Gerald Monroe Smith, Aug. 15, 1992. BA cum laude, Trinity Coll., 1968; MEd, Va. Commonwealth U., 1976; JD, U. Mo., 1982. Bar: Mo. 1982, U.S. Dist. Ct. (we. dist.) Mo. 1982. Tchr. Prince George's County Schs., Md., 1968-70, St. Michael's Sch., Richmond, Va., 1976-78; staff lawyer Mo. Supreme Ct., Jefferson City, 1982-83; gen. counsel State of Mo. Detention Facilities Commn., Jefferson City, 1983; gen. counsel State of Mo. Jud. Fin. Commn., Jefferson City, 1983-85; clk. of the ct. Mo. Ct. Appeals Eastern Dist., St. Louis, 1985—. Recipient Acad. Excellance award in environ. law U. Mo. Sch. Law, 1981. Mem. ABA, Mo. Bar Assn., St. Louis County Bar Assn., Lawyers Assn. St. Louis, Met. St. Louis Bar Assn. (exec. com. 1988—, pres. 1994—), St. Louis Bar Found. (bd. dirs. 1989—, v.p. 1994—), St. Louis Women Lawyers Assn. (bd. dirs. 1989—, pres. 1992-93), Am. Judicature Soc. (bd. dirs. 1990—, bd. exec. com., 1993—), Nat. Conf. Appellate Ct. Clks. (exec. com. 1990-92), Phi Delta Phi. Roman Catholic. Office: Mo Ct Appeals 111 N 7th St Saint Louis MO 63101-2100

SMITH, DENISE GROLEAU, data processing professional; b. Worcester, Mass., Feb. 7, 1951; d. Edmond Laurence and Audrey Mildred (Paquin) Groleau; m. Wayne Marshall Smith, Apr. 17, 1976; 1 child, Andrew. BSBA, Fitchburg State U., 1983. Bindery worker Atlantic Bus. Forms, Hudson, Mass., 1969-73; proofreader New Eng. Bus., Townsend, Mass., 1974-75; computer operator New Eng. Bus., Groton, Mass., 1975-80, adminstrv. asst. bus. systems, 1980-82, adminstrv. asst. info. ctr., 1982-85; info. ctr. analyst Wright Line Inc., Worcester, 1985-88; personal computer coord. Thom McAn Shoe Co., Worcester, 1988-91; cons. personal computer Buckingham Transp., Groton, 1987-95, Moppet Sch., 1993—. Mem. NAFE. Home: 14 Cedar Cir Townsend MA 01469-1336

SMITH, DIANA MARIE, business educator; b. Des Moines, Oct. 25, 1940; d. Nathan Henry and Helen (Hall) Kitchen; m. Robert Nelson Smith, Jan. 26, 1971; 1 child, Stephen. BA, Drake U., 1968, MA, 1971. Cert. tchr., Iowa. Stenographer Polk County Welfare Dept., Des Moines, 1960-67; typist Polk County Auditor, Des Moines, 1968, Cen. Life Assurance Co., Des Moines, 1976-79; computer oper. IRS, Des Moines, 1988; lead specialist II Norwest Bank, Des Moines, 1978—; sec. Shive-Hattery Engrs., Des Moines, 1976-90; adult edn. instr. Des Moines Ind. Dist., 1969—; tchr. bus., computers Des Moines Pub. Schs., 1968—; ind. computer cons.; instr.-authorized tng. assoc. program for Word Perfect, 1994; Mary Kay beauty cons., 1993—. Chair meml. com. Burns United Meth. Ch., Des Moines, 1988—, Sunday sch. tchr., 1961-83, 92—, sec. adminstrv. bd. Mem. NEA, Nat. Bus. Edn. Assn., Iowa Bus. Edn. Assn., Des Moines Bus. Edn. Assn., Iowa State Edn. Assn., Des Moines Edn. Assn. Democrat. Office: Cen Campus 1800 Grand Ave Des Moines IA 50309

SMITH, DIANNE JEAN, lawyer; b. Elgin, Ill., Mar. 7, 1945; d. Robert Homer and Lucille Helen (Moser) S. BS, U. Wis., 1967, JD, 1982; MA in History, Coll. William & Mary, 1970. Bar: Wis. 1982, D.C. 1983. Assoc. Williams & Connolly, Washington, 1983-90, Office Ind. Counsel, Washington, 1990—; pres., CEO Alfasaga, Inc., Washington, 1989—.

SMITH, DONNA, mayor, small business owner; b. Upper Darby, Pa., July 19, 1954; d. Dave and Theresa (McAleer) Fekay; m. Robert Howard Smith Jr., Dec. 1, 1951; children: Robert H. III, Sean M., Terence J. Grad. high sch., Pomona, Calif., 1970. Mayor City of Pomona, 1987—; owner Pomona Generator Co., 1976—. Pres. Simons Jr. High Sch. PTA, 1983-85; pres., sec. Pomona Youth Sports Com., 1983-85; mem. City Coun. Dist. 3, Pomona, 1985-87; mem. Garey High Sch. Booster Club, 1985—; mem. Hispanic youth task force; mem. econ. and human devel. com. SCAG Community, 1985-87; mem. Pomona Cen. Bus. Dist.; mem. policy com. Rapid Transit Dist.; vice chairperson Tri-City Mental Health; mem. Pomona Valley handicapped and sr. citizens com.; mem. exec. bd. Teen Outreach, ARC; mem. Old Baldy Coun. Boy Scouts Am.; U.S. Olympic torch runner, 1991; mem. U.S. Conf. of Mayors, 1991, chmn. com. disaster preparedness, chair community devel. and housing com., mem. membership com., Lincoln Inst. of Land Policy; mem. adv. bd. Nat. Coalition Against Pornography; mem. U.S. Conf. Mayors; appointed to State of Calif. Rep. Ctrl. Com.; runner U.S. Olympic Torch; hon. chair March of Dimes, Lukemia Soc. Am.; mem. State Rep. Ctrl. Com. Named Women Achiever of 1985, Humanitarian of Yr., 1986, one of Five Outstanding Californians Calif. Jaycees, 1990; recipient PTA Honorary Service award 1985, PTA Honorary Lifetime Service award 1986. Mem. Calif. Elected Women's Assn., Pomona Bus. and Profl. Women's Assn., Pomona Hist. Soc., Pomona C. of C. (legis. action com., edn. com., city affairs com.), Pomona Valley Rep. Women Federated (v.p.), Pomona Jaycees (Disting. Svc. award 1988), Pomona Jaycees (hon. life 1991), Am. Bus. Women's Assn. (hon. life 1991), Nat. League of Cities, League of Calif. Cities (state adminstrv. policy con.), Kiwanis, Fraternal Order of Police, Women of Moose. Mem. Born Again Christian Ch. Office: City of Pomona Office of Mayor 1555 S Palomares St Pomona CA 91766-5312

SMITH, DONNA JEAN, guidance director; b. Springfield, Ill., June 5, 1938; d. Earl W. and Frances Elizabeth (Sanders) Wax; m. Michael Wayne Smith, Aug. 27, 1960; children: Kimberly Ann Smith Hoffmann, Bradley Michael Smith. BS, Ill. State U., 1960; MS, Western Ill. U., 1986. Tchr. 5th grade Higbee Jr. High Sch., Pittsfield, Ill., 1960-61; tchr. home econs. and psychology Pittsfield High Sch., 1965-90, dir. cheerleading squad, 1965-94, dir. pom-pon squad, 1966—, guidance dir., 1990—. Twp. trustee Martinsburg Twp., Pittsfield, 1963—, precinct committeewoman; bd. dirs. Quanada, Pike County, Ill. Ext. Svc., Pike County. Scholar Delta Kappa Gamma, 1983. Mem. NEA (life), Ill. Fedn. Tchrs., Unit 10 Tchrs. Assn. (pres.), Ill. Assn. Coll. Admissions Counselors, Delta Kappa Gamma (legis. chmn.). Office: Pittsfield High Sch 201 E Higbee St Pittsfield IL 62363-1998

SMITH, DONNA LUCILLE, medical/surgical nurse; b. Brattleboro, Vt., Aug. 20, 1943; d. Sidney Proctor and Marion (Greene) S. ADN, So. Vt. Coll., 1991. LPN Brattleboro Meml. Hosp., 1963-91, staff nurse med. unit, 1992—, patient svc. coord., 1994—. Mem. ANA, Vt. Nurses Assn. (Clin. Excellence award 1991). Home: 6 Northfield Box 117 Hinsdale NH 03451 Office: Brattleboro Meml Hosp 9 Belmont Ave Brattleboro VT 05301

SMITH, DORIS CORINNE KEMP, retired nurse; b. Bogalusa, La., Nov. 22, 1919; d. Milton Jones and Maude Maria (Fortenberry) Kemp; m. Joseph William Smith, Oct. 13, 1940 (dec.). BS in Nursing, U. Colo., 1957, MS in Nursing Adminstrn., 1958. RN, Colo. Head nurse Chgo. Bridge & Iron Co., Morgan City, La., 1941-45, Shannon Hosp., San Angelo, Tex., 1945-50; dir. nursing Yoakum County Hosp., Denver City, Tex., 1951-52; hosp. supr. Med. Arts Hosp., Odessa, Tex., 1952-55; dir. insvc. edn. St. Anthony Hosp., Denver, 1961-66; coord. Sch. Vocat. Nursing, Kiamichi Area Vocat.-Tech. Nursing Sch., Wilburton, Okla., 1969-77; supr. non-ambulatory unit Lubbock (Tex.) State Sch., 1978-85, ret., 1985; mem. steering com. Western Interstate Commn. on Higher Edn. for Nurses, Denver, 1963-65; mem. curriculum and materials com. Okla. Bd. Vocat.-Tech. Edn., Stillwater, 1971-76; mem. Invitational Conf. To Plan Nursing for Future, Oklahoma City, 1976-77; mem. survey team to appraise Sch. of Vocat.-Tech. Edn. Schs. for Okla. Dept. Vocat.-Tech. Edn., 1975-76. Author, editor: Survey of Functions Expected of the General Duty Nurse, State of Colorado, 1958; co-editor: Curriculum Guides; contbr. numerous articles to profl. jours. Recipient citation of merit Okla. State U., 1976; named Woman of Yr. Sunrise chpt. Am. Bus. Women's Assn., 1994-95. Mem. AAAS, ANA, AAUW (life), Nat. League for Nursing, Tex. League for Nursing, Tex. Nurses Assn., Dist. 18 Nurses Assn., Tex. Employees Assn. (v.p. 1984-85), U. Colo. Alumni Assn., Am. Bus. Women's Club (pres. Lubbock chpt. 1986-87, rec. sec. 1989-90), Bus. and Profl. Women's Assn. (sec. 1992—), Pi Lambda Theta (sec. local chpt. 1957-58). Republican. Home: 2103 55th St Lubbock TX 79412-2612

SMITH, DORIS VICTORIA, educational agency administrator; b. N.Y.C., July 5, 1937; d. Albin and Victoria (Anderson) Olson; m. Howard R. Smith, Aug. 21, 1960; children: Kurt, Steven, Andrea. BS in Edn., Wagner Coll., 1959; MA in Edn., Kean Coll., 1963, cert., 1980; postgrad., Fairleigh Dickinson U., 1984, Nova U. Cert. adminstr., tchr. elem. edn., N.J. Thorough and efficient coord. East Hanover (N.J.) Twp. Sch. Dist., 1977-79; ednl. specialist N.J. State Dept. Edn., Morristown, 1979—, ednl. planner, 1982-87, ednl. mgr., 1987—; pres. N.E. Coalition Ednl. Leaders, Inc.; founding mem. Morris County Curriculum Network. Author: Affirmative Action—Rules and Regulations, 1982, Supervising Early Childhood Programs, 1984. Past pres. bd. trustees Florham Park Libr.; founding mem. Morris Area Tech. Alliance; founding mem., pres. Calvary Nursery Sch.; bd. of trust office N.J. Coun. Edn.; pres. bd. trustees Madison/Chatham Adult Sch.; trustee Morris County Children's Svcs. Recipient Disting. Svc. award N.E. Coalition Ednl. Leaders, 1991, Disting. Svc. award Morris County Prins. and Suprs. Assn.; tchr. insvc. grantee. Mem. N.J. Coun. Edn., N.J. Schoolmasters Assn., Phi Delta Kappa.

SMITH, DOROTHY BRAND, retired librarian; b. Beaumont, Tex., Oct. 4, 1922; d. Robert and Lula (Jones) Brand; m. William E. Smith, June 15, 1941; children: Wilson B., Lurinda. BS in Social Sci., Lamar U., 1954; MLS, U., Tex., 1971. Tchr., Beaumont Ind. Sch. Dist., 1954-62; tchr. Austin (Tex.) Ind. Sch. Dist., 1962-66; libr. Galindo Elem. Sch., Austin, 1966-94; ret., 1994; cons. Edn. Svc. Ctr., Austin, 1974, 83; workshop leader Austin Ind. Schs., 1980; China del. Citizen Amb. Program People Internat., 1993. Author: Texas in Children's Books, a Bibliography, 1974. Recipient Siddle Joe Johnson award Children's Roundtable of Tex. Library Assn., 1984. Mem. ALA, AAUW, Tex. Libr. Assn. (life), Tex. State Tchrs. Assn. (life), Delta Kappa Gamma, Phi Delta Kappa. Presbyterian. Home: 6108 Mountainclimb Dr Austin TX 78731-3824

SMITH, DOROTHY LOUISE, pharmacy consultant, author; b. Regina, Sask., Can., Apr. 29, 1946; d. William Edward and Edna Irene (Libby) S. BS in Pharmacy, U. Saskatchewan, 1968; PharmD, U. Cin., 1972. Asst. prof. pharmacy U. B.C., Can., 1972-74; assoc. prof. clin. pharmacy U. Toronto, Ont., Can., 1974-80; coord. ambulatory pharmacy care Sunnybrook Med. Ctr., Toronto, 1974-79; dir. clin. affairs Am. Pharm. Assn., Washington, 1980-83; pres. Consumer Health Info. Corp., McLean, Va., 1983—; assoc. clin. prof. Sch. Pharmacy, Med. Coll. Va., 1991—; adj. assoc. prof. community and family medicine Georgetown U., Washington, 1983—. Author several books in field; contbr. articles to profl. jours. Mem. nat. bd. advisors Coll. Pharmacy, Ariz., 1987—. Fellow Am. Coll. Clin. Pharmacy, Am. Coll. Apothecaries; mem. Am. Soc. Hosp. Pharmacists, Am. Pharm. Assn. (chmn. policy com. on pub. affairs), Internat. Order Job's Daughters, Rotary. Presbyterian. Office: Consumer Health Info Corp 8300 Greensboro Dr Ste 1220 Mc Lean VA 22102-3604

SMITH, DOROTHY OTTINGER, jewelry designer, civic leader; b. Indpls.; d. Albert Ellsworth and Leona Aurelia (Waller) Ottinger; student Herron Art Sch. of Purdue U. and Ind. U., 1941-42; m. James Emory Smith, June 25, 1943 (div. 1984); children: Michael Ottinger, Sarah Anne, Theodore Arnold, Lisa Marie. Comml. artist William H. Block Co., Indpls., 1942-43, H.P. Wasson Co., 1943-44; dir. Riverside (Calif.) Art Center, 1963-64; jewelry designer, Riverside, 1970—; numerous design commns. Adviser Riverside chpt. Freedom's Found. of Valley Forge; co-chmn. fund raising com. Riverside Art Ctr. and Mus., 1966-67, bd. dirs. Art Alliance, 1980-81, Art Mus.; mem. Riverside City Hall sculpture selection panel Nat. Endowment Arts, 1974-75; chmn. fund raising benefit Riverside Art Ctr. and Mus., 1973-74, trustee, 1980-84, chmn. permanent collection, 1981-84, co-chmn. fund drive, 1982-84; chmn. Riverside Mcpl. Arts Commn., 1974-76, Silver Anniversary Gala, 1992; juror Riverside Civic Ctr. Purchase Prize Art Show, 1975; mem. pub. bldgs. and grounds subcom., gen. plan citizens com. City of Riverside, 1965-66; mem. Mayor's Commn. on Civic Beauty, Mayor's Commn. on Sister City Sendai, 1965-66; bd. dirs., chmn. spl. events Children's League of Riverside Community Hosp., 1952-53; bd. dirs. Crippled Children's Soc. of Riverside, spl. events chmn., 1952-53; bd. dirs. Jr. League of Riverside, rec. sec., 1960-61; bd. dirs. Nat. Charity League, pres. Riverside chpt., 1965-66; mem. exec. com. of bd. trustees Riverside Arts Found., 1977-91, fund drive chmn., 1978-79, project rev. chmn., 1978-79; juror Gemco Charitable and Scholarship Found., 1977-85; mem. bd. women deacons Calvary Presbyn. Ch., 1978-80, elder, 1989-92; mem. incorporating bd. Inland Empire United Fund for Arts, 1980-81; bd. dirs. Hospice Orgn. Riverside County, 1982-84; Art Awareness chmn. Riverside Arts Found.; mem. Calif. Coun. Humanities, 1982-86. Recipient cert. Riverside City Coun., 1977, plaque Mayor of Riverside, 1977. Mem. Riverside Art Assn. (pres. 1961-63, 1st v.p. 1964-65, 67-68, trustee 1959-70, 80-84, 87-92), Art Alliance of Riverside Art Ctr. and Museum (founder 1964, pres. 1969-70). Recipient Spl. Recognition Riverside Cultural Arts Coun., 1981, Disting. Service plaque Riverside Art Ctr. and Mus., Jr. League Silver Raincross Community Svc. award, 1989, Cert. Appreciation Outstanding Svc. to the Arts Community Riverside Arts Found., 1990. Address: 3979 Chapman Pl Riverside CA 92506-1150

SMITH, EDITH MACNAMARA, artist, educator; b. San Francisco, Apr. 3, 1925; d. Arthur Kingsly and Ann Harriet (Walling) MacNamara; m. Leland Clayton Smith, Feb. 24, 1946; children: Stefanie, Clement, Teresa. BA, U. Calif., Berkeley, 1946, MA, 1947; postgrad., Atelier de Gravure Calevaert, Paris, 1972-74, 80-82. Cert. C.C. tchr., Calif. Lectr. in art U. Calif., Berkeley, 1947-48; instr. of art YMHA, N.Y.C., 1950, Faulkner Sch., Chgo., 1953-55, Art Inst. Chgo., 1955-57, Pacific Art League, Palo Alto, Calif., 1961-64, 67-71, 1981—; instr. of art Foothill Coll., Los Altos Hills, Calif., 1972—; lectr. in humanities U. Chgo., 1956-57; lectr. on computer-assisted printmaking. One woman shows paintings and graphics at Jason Aver Gallery, San Francisco, 1971, Richard Sumner Gallery, Palo Alto, 1974, Dominican Coll., San Rafael, 1976, Palo Alto Civic Ctr., 1977, Galerie Dautzenberg 76, Brussels, 1978, Stanford (Calif.) U., 1980, Ohio State U. Gallery of Fine Art, 1980, Colgate U., N.Y., 1982, Bechtel Internat. Ctr., Stanford U., 1984, Foothill Coll., 1989, Terman Park Libr., Palo Alto, 1991, 92, 93, Inst. for Rsch. on Women and Gender, Stanford U., 1993, numerous others; group exhbns. paintings and graphics 1948— include San Francisco Mus. Modern Art, 1948, 49, 52, 53, (Artists' Coun. Prize 1953), Galerie St. Placide, Paris, 1949, Kootz Gallery, N.Y.C., 1950, Landau Gallery, L.A., 1954, Denver Art Mus., 1955, Art Inst. Chgo., 1956, Whitney Mus. Am. Art, N.Y.C., 1957, Galerie Rene Breheret, Paris, 1972, De Young Mus., San Francisco, 1976, World Print Coun. Gallery, San Francisco, 1982, Pratt Inst., Bklyn., 1987, U. Ind. Gallery Art, 1989, Berkeley Art Ctr., 1992, Calif. State U., Bakersfield, 1993, Syntex Gallery, Palo Alto, Calif., 1993, Koret Gallery, Palo Alto, 1990, 93, Noyes Mus., Oceanville, N.J., 1994, Studio Gallery, Binghampton, N.Y., 1994, Canessa Gallery, San Francisco, 1994; solo exhibits computer-assisted etchings include Jason Aver Gallery, 1974, Pence Gallery, Davis, Calif., 1976, Gallery Dautzenberg, Brussels, 1978, Stanford U., 1980, Ohio State U. Gallery Fine Art, 1980; group exhibits computer-assisted graphics include DeYoung Mus., San Francisco, 1976, World Print Coun. Gallery, 1982, San Jose (Calif.) Inst. Contemporary Art, 1984, Arts Coun. San Mateo, Calif., 1986, Gallery Shoh, Tokyo, 1985, Lawson Gallery, San Francisco, 1987, Pacific Art League, Palo Alto, 1988, Ars Electronica, Linz, Austria, 1989, Brandts Klaede-Fabrik, Odense, Denmark, 1989, Phila. Print Club, 1989, Quincy (Ill.) Art Mus., 1989, U. Ind. Gallery Art, 1989, N.Mex. State U., Las Cruces, 1991, U. Idaho, Boise, 1992, Custer Art Ctr., Mont., 1992, Calif. State U., Bakersfield, 1992, Studio Gallery, 1994, Canessa Gallery, 1994, others. Home and Studio: 3732 Laguna Ave Palo Alto CA 94306

SMITH, EDNA MARIE, editor; b. Mitchell, S.D., Mar. 13, 1932; d. Anton Miller and Nora Levina (Ostrus) Egeland; m. James Douglas Smith, Oct. 29, 1955; children: Scott MacGregor, Shannon Lee. BA, U. S.D., 1953; postgrad., Iowa State U., 1958. Editor Iowa State U., Ames, 1953-59, Tex. A&M Grad. Coll., College Station, 1984-85; project editor Tex. A&M U. Press, College Station, 1985-87; communications specialist Tex. Agrl. Extension Service, 1987—. Editor: Aggies, Moms, and Apple Pie, 1987. Pres. aux. St. Joseph Hosp., Bryan, Tex., 1982, mgr., buyer gift shop, 1985-87; precint judge, alt. Brazos County, 1983-93; precint chair Dem. Com., 1994—; historian Brazoss Valley Symphony Soc., Bryan, College Station. Named Outstanding Woman of Brazos County, 1980. Mem. AAUW (Outstanding mem. 1978), Interant. Assn. Bus. Communicators, Agrl. Communicators in Edn. (Svc. award 1994). Unitarian.

SMITH, ELAINE DIANA, foreign service officer; b. Glencoe, Ill., Sept. 15, 1924; d. John Raymond and Elsie (Gelbard) S. BA, Grinnell Coll., 1946; MA, Johns Hopkins U., 1947; PhD, Am. U., 1959. Commd. fgn. service officer U.S. Dept. State, 1947; assigned to Brussels, 1947-50, Tehran, Iran, 1951-53, Wellington, N.Z., 1954-56; assigned to Dept. State, Washington, 1956-60, Ankara, Turkey, 1960-69, Istanbul, Turkey, 1969-72; assigned to Dept. Commerce Exchange, 1972-73; dep. examiner Fgn. Service Bd. Examiners, 1974-75; Turkish desk officer (Dept. State), Washington, 1975-78; consul gen., Izmir, Turkey, 1978—. Author: Origins of the Kemalist Movement, 1919-1923, 1959. Recipient Alumni award Grinnell Coll., 1957. Mem. U.S. Fgn. Svc. Assn., Phi Beta Kappa. Home: The Plaza 800 25th St NW Apt 306 Washington DC 20037

SMITH, ELAINE E., school system administrator; b. Gooding, Idaho; m. Rich L. Smith, June 8, 1968; children: Camille, Kirk, Brenda. BA in Secondary Edn., Idaho State U. Cert. secondary tchr. Coord. vol. svcs.-bus. and edn. partnerships Sch. Dist. # 25, Pocatello, Idaho, 1985—; coord. Expanding Your Horizons Conf., S.E. Idaho, 1986—. Past pres. Community Svcs. Coun., Pocatello; active Bannock County Youth at Risk, Pocatello, 1988—; mem. Pocatello Area Foster Grandparents Adv., Pocatello, 1989—; bd. dirs. YWCA of Ea. Idaho, 1990—; mem. Idaho West Point Parents Club, 1990-95; active United Way of S.E. Idaho; mem., coord. Portneuf Cropwalk. Recipient Friend of Edn. award Pocatello Edn. Assn., 1990, Disting. Young Woman of Yr. Jaycees, 1980. Mem. AAUW (past state pres.), Nat. Assn. Ptnrs. Edn., Nat. Coalition for Sex Equity Edn., Assn. Vol. Adminstrs., Greater Pocatello C. of C. (K-12 edn. com 1985—, state issues com. 1985—), Soroptimists (Women Helping award 1993 Pocatello chpt.), Alpha Omicron Pi, Delta Kappa Gamma. Office: Sch Dist # 25 3115 Poleline Rd Pocatello ID 83201-6119

SMITH, ELAINE MARIE, human resource professional; b. Syracuse, N.Y., Aug. 6, 1957; d. Issac Junior and Edith Wilma (Sperling) Perry; m. Robert Charles Flanagan, May 20, 1977 (div. 1979); m. John William Smith, June 21, 1980 (div. May 1992). AAS, Onondaga Community Coll., 1977; BBBA, U. North Fla., 1988, MHRM, 1991. Plant personnel mgr. Cargill, Inc., Jacksonville, Fla., 1985-88; dir. human resources Gateway Community Svcs., Jacksonville, 1988-91, Fla. Wire and Cable, Inc., Jacksonville, 1991—. Mem. Jacksonville Cmty. Coun., First Coast Women's Coalition. Mem. Soc. Human Resource Mgrs., First Coast Mfrs. Assn. Republican. Roman Catholic. Office: Florida Wire and Cable Inc 825 N Lane Ave Jacksonville FL 32254

SMITH, ELISE FIBER, international non-profit development agency administrator; b. Detroit, June 14, 1932; d. Guy and Mildred Geneva (Johnson) Fiber; m. James Frederick Smith, Aug. 11, 1956 (div. 1983); children: Gregory Douglas, Guy Charles. BA, U. Mich., 1954; postgrad., U. Strasbourg, France, 1954-55; MA, Case Western Res. U., 1956. Tchr. U.S. Binat. Ctr., Caracas, Venezuela, 1964-66; instr. English Am. U., 1966-68; prof. lang. faculty Catholic U., Lima, Peru, 1968-70; coord. English lang. and culture program, lang. faculty El Rosario U., Bogota, Colombia, 1971-73; lang. specialist, mem. faculty Am. U., English Lang. Inst., 1975-78; exec. dir. OEF Internat. (name formerly Overseas Edn. Fund), Washington, 1978-89, bd. dirs.; dir. Leadership Program, Winrock Internat. Inst. for Agrl. Devel., 1989—; v.p., bd. dirs. Pvt. Agys. Collaborating Together, N.Y.C., 1983-89; trustee Internat. Devel. Conf., Washington, 1983—, mem. exec. com., 1985-90; mem. hon. com. for Global Crossroads Nat. Assembly, Global Perspectives in Edn., Inc. (PACT), N.Y.C., 1984, D.C., 1984-92, mem. gen. assembly, 1992; mem. nat. com. Focus on Hunger '84, L.A.; sec. bd. dirs. U.S. Binat. Sch., Bogota, Colombia, 1971-73; ofcl. observer UN Conf. on Status Women, 1980; mem. mental health adv. com. Dept. State, 1974-76; U.S. del. planning seminar integration women in devel. OAS, 1978; ofcl. observer UN Conf. on Status of Women, Nairobi, Kenya, 1985; participant Women, Law and Devel. Forum; bd. dirs. Interaction (Am. Council for Vol. Internat. Action), 1985-88, mem. exec. com., co-chair commn. advancement women, 1994; bd. dirs. Sudan-Am. Found.; mem. adv. bd. Global Links Devel. Edn., Washington, 1985-86; adv. coun. Global Fund for Women, 1988-93. Co-editor: Toward Internationalism: Readings in Cross-cultural Communication, 1979, 2d edit. 1986. Bd. dirs. Internat. Ctr. Rsch. on Women, 1992—; mem. adv. com. on vol. fgn. aid U.S. AID, 1994—. Rotary Internat. fellow Strasbourg, France, 1954-55; grantee Dept. State, 1975. Mem. Soc. Internat. Devel., Assn. Women in Devel., Soc. Intercultural Edn. Tng. and Rsch., Coalition Women in Internat. Devel. (co-founder 1979, chair 1993—), Pvt. Agys. in Internat. Devel. (co-chmn. 1980-82, pres. 1982-85), Nat. Assn. Fgn. Student Affairs (grantee 1975), U. Mich. Alumni Assn., Women's Fgn. Policy Group. Unitarian. Home: Apt 304 4701 Connecticut Ave NW Washington DC 20008-5617 Office: Winrock Inst Ste 600 1611 N Kent St Arlington VA 22209-2111

SMITH, ELIZA WELLS, photographer, writer; b. N.Y.C., May 30, 1964; d. Richard B. Smith and Mary Wells (Detwiler) Pern. BFA, R.I. Sch. Design, 1986. Printer, asst. Larry Fink, Photographer, Martins Creek, Pa., 1986-87; editor JB Pictures, N.Y.C., 1987-89; printer, darkroom mgr. Magnum Photos, N.Y.C., 1989-91; assoc. photo editor Connoisseur Mag., N.Y.C., 1991-92; asst. photo editor Vanity Fair Mag., N.Y.C., 1992; picture editor The N.Y. Times, N.Y.C., 1992-94; stringer-photographer The N.Y. Times, Santa Fe, 1994—; freelance photographer and writer Santa Fe, 1994—; course dir. Santa Fe Photo Workshops, cons., 1994—; freelance photographer Albuquerque Jour.; photographer, writer New Frontiers of N.Mex., Tijeras, 1994. Exhibited in group shows at Ann. Exhibit Pa. Photographers, 1987 (3 awards). Vol. Animal Shelter, Santa Fe, 1994. Recipient 3 nat. art awards, 1981; scholar French Cultural Attachée, 1981. Mem. Nat. Assn. Black Scuba Divers, Graphic Artists Guild, Nature Conservancy, World Wildlife Fund.

SMITH, ELIZABETH HEGEMAN, mental health therapist, hypnotherapist; b. Mineola, N.Y., Oct. 5, 1942; d. Andrew Burt and Ruth Eliza (Velsor) Hegeman; m. Lloyd W. Smith, June 11, 1966; children: Warren Willits, Lisa Velsor. BA, Adelphi U., 1964; MEd, Temple U., 1969. Cert. tchr., Pa.; registered hypnotherapist. Tchr. health, phys. edn. Friends Acad., Locust Valley, N.Y., 1964-66, Darby (Pa.)-Colwyn Schs., 1966-70; pvt. practice mental health therapy Wallingford, Pa., 1980-85, Charlotte, N.C., 1985—; cons. Dynamic Health Systems, Charlotte, 1989—. Mem. LWV, Wallingford, 1976-85; pres., editor Taxpayers for Quality Edn., Wallingford, 1976-85; chmn. Raintree Archtl. Rev. Com., Charlotte, 1989-91, com. mem., 1987-88; treas. Raintree Homeowners Assn. Mem. Am. Guild Hypnotherapists, Raintree Homeowners Assn. (treas. 1993—). Mem. Soc. Friends. Home and Office: 3609 Windbluff Dr Charlotte NC 28277-9897

SMITH, ELLEN MARGARET, law librarian; b. Sharon, Pa., Nov. 14, 1950; m. Douglas William Smith, Oct. 27, 1973; children: Nathaniel, Christiana. BS in History and Polit. Sci., Bowling Green U., 1972, MA in History, 1973; MLS, Case Western Res. U., 1980. Cert. secondary sch. tchr., Ohio. Head law libr. Thompson, Hine & Flory, Cleve., 1973-80, McDonald, Hopkins, Burke & Haber Co., L.P.A., Cleve., 1984—. Home: 1275 Prince Charles Ave Cleveland OH 44145-2618 Office: McDonald Hopkins Burke & Haber 2100 Bank One Ctr Cleveland OH 44114

SMITH, ELOUISE BEARD, restaurant owner; b. Richmond, Tex., Jan. 8, 1920; d. Lee Roy and Ruby Myrtle (Foy) Beard; m. Omar Smith, Nov. 27, 1940 (dec. July 1981); children: Mary Jean Smith Cherry, Terry Omar, Don Alan. Student, Tex. Womens U., 1937-39. Sec. First Nat. Bank, Rosenberg, Tex., 1939-41; owner Smith Dairy Queen, Bryan, Tex., 1947—. Author: The Haunted House, 1986; editor The College Widow, 1986. Omar and Elouise Beard Smith chair named in her honor Tex. A&M U., College Station, 1983, Elouise Beard Smith Human Performance Labs. named in her honor Tex. A&M U., 1984. Mem. AAUW. Republican. Baptist. Home: 411 Crescent Dr Bryan TX 77801-3712 Office: Metro Ctr 3833 S Texas Ave Bryan TX 77802-4039

SMITH, ELSKE VAN PANHUYS, university administrator; b. Monte Carlo, Monaco, Nov. 9, 1929; came to U.S., 1943; d. Johan Abraham AE and Vera (Craven) van Panhuys; m. Henry J. Smith, Sept. 10, 1950 (dec.

June 1983); children: Ralph A., Kenneth A. BA, Radcliffe U., 1950, MS, 1951, PhD, 1956. Rsch. assoc. Sacramento Peak Observatory, Sunspot, N.Mex., 1955-62; rsch. fellow Joint Inst. for Lab. Astrophysics, Boulder, Colo., 1962-63; assoc. to prof. U. Md., College Park, 1963-80, asst. provost, 1973-78, asst. vice chancellor, 1978-80; dean, coll. humanities and scis. Va. Commonwealth U., Richmond, 1980-92, interim dir. environ. studies, 1992—; cons. NASA, Greenbelt, Md., 1964-76, reviewer, Washington, 1970's, NSF, Washington, 1970's, 86; vis. com. Assn. of Univ.'s for Rsch. in Astronomy, Tucson, 1975-78. Author: (with others) Solar Flares, 1963, Introductory Astronomy and Astrophysics, 1973, 3d edit., 1992; also numerous articles. Mem. various environ. orgns. Rsch. grantee Rsch. Corp., 1956-57, NSF, 1966-69, 90, NIH, 1981-90, NASA, 1974-78; program grantee Va. Found. for Humanities, 1985, NEH, 1987, Assn. Am. Colls., 1987. Fellow AAAS; mem. Am. Astron. Soc. (counselor 1977-80, vis. prof. 1975-78), Internat. Astron. Union (chief U.S. del. 1979, U.S. Nat. com.), Coun. Colls. of Arts and Scis. (bd. dirs. 1989), Phi Beta Kappa. Democrat. Home: 1816 Park Ave Richmond VA 23220-2821 Office: Va Commonwealth U PO Box 3050 Richmond VA 23284-3050

SMITH, ERITHE A., judge; b. L.A., Aug. 28, 1957; d. Sam and Gladys (Alexander) S. BA, Loyola Marymount, 1979; JD, U. Calif., Berkeley, 1982. Bar: Calif. Rsch. atty. Hon. Marcus Kaufman, Calif. Ct. Appeals, San Bernardino, 1982-83, Hon. Peter Elliott, U.S. Bankruptcy Ct., Santa Ana, Calif., 1983-85; assoc. McKittrick, Jackson, DeMarco & Peckempaugh, Newport Beach, Calif., 1985-87; assoc. Label, Winthrop & Broker, Irvine, Calif., 1987-90, ptnr., 1991-94; bankruptcy judge U.S. Bankruptcy Ct. (Calif. central dist.), 9th circuit, 1994—; lectr. Continuing Edn. of Bar, Calif., 1991—. Mem. United Negro Coll. Fund, L.A., 1991, NAACP, Beverly Hills, Calif., 1990. Mem. Nat. Bar Assn., Calif. Women Lawyers, Black WOmen Lawyers L.A. (bd. dirs., historian), Orange County Bankruptcy Forum (bd. dirs., treas.), Orange County Bar Assn., Fin. Lawyers Conf. Roman Catholic. Office: Edward R Roybal Fed Bldg 255 E Temple St Rm 1652 Los Angeles CA 90012*

SMITH, ESTHER THOMAS, editor; b. Jesup, Ga., Mar. 13, 1939; d. Joseph H. and Leslie (McCarthy) Thomas; m. James D. Smith, June 2, 1962; children: Leslie, Amy, James Thomas. BA, Agnes Scott Coll., 1962. Staff writer, Sunday women's editor Atlanta Jour.-Constn., 1961-62; mng. editor Bull. of U. Miami Sch. Medicine, 1965-66; corr. Atlanta Jour.-Constn. and Fla. Times-Union, 1964, 67-68; founding editor Bus. Rev. of Washington, 1978-81; founding editor, gen. mgr. Washington Bus. Jour., 1982; pres., bd. dirs. Tech News, Inc., 1986—; editor-at-large Washington Tech., 1986—, Tech. Transfer Bus. Mag., 1992—; bd. dirs. MIT Enterprise Forum of Washington/Balt., 1981-82; mem. Greater Washington Board of Trade, Internat. Task Force, Women's Forum, Washington, 1981—; mem. exec. com. No. Va. Bus. Round Table; mem. adv. bd. Va. Math Coalition, 1991—; bd. trustees Ctr. for Excellence in Edn., 1993—. Mem. Assn. Tech. Bus. Couns. (chmn. bd. advisors 1989-94), Pres.'s Forum, Mid-Atlantic Venture Assn., No. Va. Tech. Coun. (mem. exec. com.), Suburban Maryland High Tech. Coun. Office: 8500 Leesburg Pike Ste 7500 Vienna VA 22182

SMITH, FAITH MARLENE, academic dean, nursing educator; b. South Connellsville, Pa., July 12, 1936; d. Roy Leonard Geary and Lena Ree (Campbell) Gorton; m. Edward Allan Smith, Mar. 31, 1957; children: Susan Lynne Lybarger, Saundra Lee, Bret Allan. Diploma in nursing, Westmoreland Hosp., Greensburg, Pa., 1957; AS, Connos State Coll., 1972; BSN, U. Tulsa, 1973; MSN, Tex. Women's U., 1978; EdD, Okla. State U., 1985. Staff nurse Connellsville (Pa.) State Hosp., 1957-59; dir. nursing svc. Kingfisher (Okla) Hosp., 1960-67; nursing instr. Bacone Coll., Muskogee, Okla., 1967-69, 73-74, asst. prof., 1976-81, assoc. prof. nursing, 1982-83, acad. v.p., 1983—, liaison acad. com., chairperson acad. com., 1983—; nursing instr. Indian Capital Vo-Tech., Muskogee, Okla., 1969-72. Mem. ANA, Okla. Nurses Assn., Am. Assn. Higher Edn., Am. Women's Bus. Assn., Assn. Study of Higher Edn., Bacone Profls. Assn., Muskogee C. of C. (edn. com. 1993—), Rotary (scholarship com.), Sigma Theta Tau, Delta Kappa Gamma, Phi Delta Kappa, Phi Theta Kappa (advisor Lambda Delta chpt. 1987—, Most Disting. Advisor award 1992, Hall of Honor 1991).

SMITH, FERN M., judge; b. San Francisco, Nov. 7, 1933. AA, Foothill Coll., 1970; BA, Stanford U., 1972, JD, 1975. Bar: Calif. 1975. m. F. Robert Burrows; children: Susan Morgan, Julie. Assoc. firm Bronson, Bronson & McKinnon, San Francisco, 1975-81, ptnr., 1982-86; judge San Francisco County Superior Ct., 1986-88, U.S. Dist. Ct. for Northern Dist. Calif., 1988—; mem. U.S. Jud. Conf., Adv. Com. Rules of Evidence, 1993—; mem. hiring, mgmt. and pers. coms., active recruiting various law schs. Contbr. articles to legal publ. Apptd. by Chief Justice Malcolm Lucas to the Calif. Jud. Coun.'s Adv. Task Force on Gender Bias in the Cts., 1987-89; bd. visitors Law Sch. Stanford U. Mem. ABA, Queen's Bench, Nat. Assn. Women Judges, Calif. Women Lawyers, Women's Forum West/Internat. Women's Forum, Bar Assn. of San Francisco, Fed. Judges Assn., 9th Cir. Dist. Judges Assn., Am. Judicature Soc., Calif. State Fed. Judicial Coun., Phi Beta Kappa.*

SMITH, FRANCES GRAY, vocational technology specialist; b. Wilmington, N.C., Apr. 27, 1954; d. Clayton and Jewell Frances (Sink) S. AAS, Wayne C.C., Goldsboro, N.C., 1974; BA, U. N.C., Wilmington, 1977; MA, George Washington U., 1986, EdS, 1989. Vocat. evaluator Cape Fear Tech. Inst., Wilmington, 1978-84; vocat. assessment coord. Frederick County Pub. Schs., Winchester, Va., 1984-86; vocat. evaluation specialist Fairfax (Va.) County Pub. Schs., 1986-91, vocat. tech. specialist, 1991—; adj. instr. George Washington U., Washington, 1987—, George Mason U., Fairfax, 1992; edn. cons. Vocat. Assessment Consultants, Oakton, Va., 1987—. Contbr. articles to profl. jours. Recipient Rose Mestron award Mid-Atlantic Vocat. Evaluation and Work Adjustment Assn., Washington, 1992. Mem. Vocat. Evaluation and Work Adjustment Assn. (regional rep. 1987-90, bd. mem. 1990-92, Svc. award 1992), The Interdisciplinary Coun. on Vocat. Evaluation/Assessment (chair 1992-94), Commn. on Cert. Work Adjustment and Vocat. Evaluation Specialists (commr., sec. 1993—), Am. Amateur Racquetball Assn. Democrat. Presbyterian. Home: 10222 Bushman Dr # 8121 Oakton VA 22124 Office: Fairfax County Pub Schs Integrated Tech Svcs 2334 Gallows Rd Dunn Loring VA 22027-1116

SMITH, FRANCES HARTER ROBERTS, lawyer, nurse, consultant; b. Columbia, S.C., Oct. 1, 1945; d. Ralph Winfred and Frances Lucille (Harter) Roberts; children: Everett Hudson, Armenta Harter. BS in Biology, U. Ala., 1967; MS in Counseling, Fla. State U., 1970; AA in Nursing, Victoria Coll., Tex., 1978; JD with honors, Jones Sch. Law, Montgomery, Ala., 1986. Bar: Ala. 1987. Staff nurse Citizen's Meml. Hosp., Victoria, Tex., 1978-81, DeTar Hosp., Victoria, Tex., 1981, Bapt. Med. Ctr., Montgomery, 1982-84; adminstr sch. nurse Bloomington (Tex.) Sch. Dist., Montgomery, 1981-82; supr. Humana Hosp., Montgomery, 1985; legal asst. Kaufman, Rothfeder & Blitz, Montgomery, 1985-87; assoc. Powers & Willis, Montgomery, 1987-88; pvt. practice Montgomery, 1988-90; with Office of Atty. Gen., 1990—; adj. prof. U. Houston, Victoria, 1980, Auburn U., Montgomery, 1988-90. Mem. ABA, Montgomery County Bar Assn. Democrat. Methodist. Home: 87 Creek Dr Montgomery AL 36117-4150 Office: Criminal Appeals Divsn 11 S Union St Montgomery AL 36130-0001

SMITH, FREDA JANE, counselor; b. Albany, Ga., June 15, 1953; d. Richard Bruce and Nancy Beatty Smith. AS, Chowan Jr. Coll., Mufreesboro, N.C., 1973; BS, East Carolina U., 1976; MEd, George Mason U., 1989. Lic. profl. counselor, Va. Tchr. Coker-Wimberly Elem. Sch., Rocky Mount, N.C., 1976-77, C.E. Credle Sch., Oxford, N.C., 1977-78; tchr., grade chairperson Carrington Jr. H.S., Durham, N.C., 1978-79; congl. aide L.H. Fountain U.S. Congress, Washington, 1979-80; assoc. editor, assoc. pub. rels. dir., youth tour dir. Nat. Rural Electric Coop. Assn., Washington, 1980-83; pub. rels. dir., contextual therapist, profl. counselor Nat. Ctr. for Treatment of Phobias, Anxiety and Depression, Washington, 1985—; tchg. asst., guest lectr. George Mason U., Fairfax, Va., 1989—; cons., lectr. on anxiety disorders and depression local hosps. and psychiat. groups, Washington, 1989—; expert in panic disorder and phobias on radio and TV shows, 1990—. Contbr. articles to profl. publs. Mem. Am. Counseling Assn., Am. Mental Health Counselors Assn., Internat. Assn. of Marriage and Family Counselors, Specialists in Group Work.

SMITH, FREDA L., retired educator; b. Birds, Ill., Oct. 3, 1923; d. Loney W. and Mattie A. (Perrott) Thomas; m. Lloyd Preston, May 18, 1947 (dec. 1991); 1 child, Thelma. BS, U. Western Ky., 1959. Tchr. Jefferson Sch., Robinson, Ill., 1953-54, Franklin County (Tenn.) Sch., 1954-56, Muhlenberg (Ky.) Pub. Schs., 1956-58, Livingston County Pub. Schs., Salem, Ky., 1958-61, Custer (S.D.) Elem. Sch., 1961-64, Chugwater (Wyo.) Elem. Sch., 1964-87. Vol. Headstart, Wheatland, Wyo., 1991—, Lauback Internat., Kingman, Ariz., 1987-91. With WAVES, 1944-46. Mem. AAUW (pres. 1980-81), NEA, Chugwater Edn. Assn. Episcopalian. Home: PO Box 731 Wheatland WY 82201

SMITH, FREDRICA EMRICH, rheumatologist, internist; b. Princeton, N.J., Apr. 28, 1945; d. Raymond Jay and Carolyn Sarah (Schleicher) Emrich; m. Paul David Smith, June 10, 1967. AB, Bryn Mawr Coll., 1967; MD, Duke U., 1971. Intern, resident U. N.Mex. Affiliated Hsops., 1971-73; fellow U. Va. Hosp., Charlottesville, 1974-75; pvt. practice, Los Alamos, N.Mex., 1975—; chmn. credentials com. Los Alamos Med. Ctr., 1983—, chief staff, 1990; bd. dirs. N.Mex. Physicians Mut. Liability Ins. Co., Albuquerque. Contbr. articles to med. jours. Mem. bass sect. Los Alamos Symphony, 1975—; mem. Los Alamos County Parks and Recreation Bd., 1984-88, 92—, Los Alamos County Med. Indigent Health Care Task Force, 1989—; mem. ops. subcom. Aquatic Ctr., Los Alamos County, 1988—. Fellow ACP, Am. Coll. Rheumatology; mem. N.Mex. Med. Soc., N.Mex. Soc. Internal Medicine (councillor), Friends of Bandelier. Democrat. Office: Los Alamos Med Ctr 3917 West Rd Los Alamos NM 87544

SMITH, GAYNL BEVERLY, hospice director, nurse; b. San Francisco, Nov. 19, 1940; d. Charles Homer and Gladys L. (Harvey) Smith; m. J. Vincent McCann, June 8, 1962 (div. May 1981); children: Kathleen Patricia, Kevin Patrick; m. Paul W. Bachman, Nov. 24, 1989. RN, Johns Hopkins Hosp., 1962; BS, Johns Hopkins U., 1970; MDiv, San Francisco Theol. Sem., 1986. RN, Calif., Md. Asst. dir. nursing Washington Home for Incurables, 1971-73; staff nurse coronary care unit Doctors Hosp., Washington, 1973-74; dir. nursing Washington Home for Incurables, 1974; critical care float Sibley Meml. Hosp., Washington, 1975-82; RN, supr. Hillhaven Victorian Convalescent Hosp., San Francisco, 1984-87; chaplain Hospice, Contra Costa County Health Svcs., Martinez, Calif., 1984-85; nursing dir. and adminstr. Sisters of the Presentation Convent Infirmary, San Francisco, 1987-88; coord. symptom control program Merrithew Meml. Hosp., Martinez, 1988—; mem. Concern for Dying, N.Y.C., 1985—, AIDS Planning Com., Contra Costa County, Martinez, 1988-89, Bereavement Coalition, Contra Costa County, Concord, Calif., 1988—; nursing cons. Sisters of the Presentation Convent Infirmary, San Francisco, 1988—. Vice moderator Golden Gate Assn., United Ch. of Christ, San Francisco, 1986-87, 1st Congl. Ch., San Rafael, Calif., chair pastor search com., 1987-89; active Girl Scouts U.S., San Francisco, 1947—. Mem. Oncology Nursing Soc., Am. Soc. Aging, Nat. Gerontologic Nursing Assn. Democrat. Office: Merrithew Meml Hosp Symptom Control Program 2500 Alhambra Ave Martinez CA 94553-3156

SMITH, GERALDINE FIELD, medical, surgical nurse; b. Talequah, Okla., Dec. 11, 1955; d. Crosslin Field and Glenna E. (Foster) S. BSN, Okla. U., 1982. Staff nurse med./surg. floor Gallup Pub. health Svc., Indian Med. Ctr., Gallup, N.Mex., 1982-83; staff nurse/med./surg./emergency rm. W.W. Hastings Hosp., Talequah, 1983-84; patient instr. W.W. Hastings Hosp., 1983-94, med. quality assurance asst., 1988—. Mem. ANA, Am. Diabetes Assn., Epilepsy Found. Am., Okla. Nurses Assn.

SMITH, GERI GARRETT, nurse, educator; b. Brownsville, Tenn., Nov. 21, 1948; d. F.G. and Willie Mae (Morris) Garrett; m. Lu Smith, Dec. 20, 1967 (dec.); children: Taylor, Alexandra, Amber; m. Tom Jeanes, July 16, 1984; children: Zachary, Garrett. BSN, U. Tenn., Memphis, 1987; MSN, U. Memphis, 1989; MS, Memphis State U., 1978; BS, U. Tenn., Martin, 1970. RN, Tenn.; NCAST instr.; cert. tchr., Fla., Tenn., Tex. Tchr. Aldine Schs., Houston, 1972-74, 1972-74; tchr. Shelby County Schs., Memphis, 1977-85; sch. nurse Memphis Shelby County Health Dept., Memphis, 1987-89, nurse supr. new mothers program, 1989-94; asst. prof. Sch. Nursing Union U., 1993—. Mem. NAACOG, ICEA, Tenn. Nurses Assn., Tenn. Pub. Health Assn., Sigma Theta Tau. Home: 1412 Harbert Ave Memphis TN 38104-4803

SMITH, HARRIET GWENDOLYN GURLEY, educator, writer; b. Goldsboro, N.C., Nov. 14, 1927; d. Charles Harvey and Sadye Reid (Morris) Gurley; m. Albert Goodin Smith, Aug. 29, 1953; children: Susan Reid Smith Erba, Alan English Smith. Grad., St. Mary's Coll., Raleigh, N.C., 1946; BA, U. N.C., 1948; MEd, La. State U., Shreveport, 1982. Cert. tchr., N.C., La. Tchr. English, Journalism, Social Studies Goldsboro City Schs., 1948-49, Rocky Mount (N.C.) City Schs., 1949-51, Durham (N.C.) City Schs., 1951-53, Durham County Schs., 1954-56; realtor assoc. Sam Fullilore and Assocs., Shreveport, 1984-87; contbg. editor, columnist The New Front Gallery Mag., Shreveport, 1988; bridge tchr. Caddo Magnet High Sch., La. State U., Woman's Dept. Club, pvt. groups, 1978—. Pres. Shreveport Med. Soc. Aux., 1985-86, chmn. various coms., 1970—; pres. Faculty Women's Club La. State U. Med. Ctr., 1990; mem. women's bd. dirs. Centenary Coll.; active United Meth. Women, Symphony Guild, Opera Guild, Rep. Women. Mem. Am. Contract Bridge League (life master, cert. tchr.), Am. Bridge Tchrs. Assn. (master tchr.), La. Real Estate Commn., Bull and Bear Stock Club (sec. 1973-74, pres. 1975-76), Kappa Delta Pi. Home: 8502 Rampart Pl Shreveport LA 71106-6226

SMITH, HEATHER LYNN, psychotherapist, recreational therapist,; b. Modesto, Calif., May 31, 1956; d. Gary Fremont and Marilyn Rae (Brown) S. BS, Calif. State U., Fresno, 1979; MA, U. San Francisco, 1989. Lic. marriage, family and child counselor, Calif. Recreational therapist Casa Colina Rehab. Hops., Pomona, Calif., 1979-82; evaluator developmentally delayed, coord. family edn. Cath. Charities, Modesto, 1982-87; bereavement counselor Hospice, Modesto, 1983-87; high risk youth counselor Ctr. Human Svcs., Modesto, 1987-90; pvt. practice, family therapist Modesto, 1993—; program dir. chemically dependent treatment program Stanislaus County Juvenile Hall, 1990—. Named Outstanding Young Woman of Stanislaus County, 1986, Citizen of Yr., Civitan, 1986, Outstanding Individual award Stanislaus County, 1992. Mem. Calif. Assn. Marriage and Family Therapists, Kappa Kappa Gamma. Republican. Episcopalian. Home: 806 Claratina Ave Modesto CA 95356-9610 Office: 11B 250 S Oak Blvd A Ste 2 Oakdale CA 95361 also: 1015 12th Ste 8 Modesto CA 95354

SMITH, HELEN DIBELL, executive assistant; b. Ellwood City, Pa., Apr. 9, 1941; d. Nicholas J. and Helen (Pintea) Savu; m. David L. Dibell, July 8, 1961 (div. 1986); children: Marta, Todd, Troy, Mark; m. Gordon H. Smith, Apr. 9, 1991. Student, Geneva Coll., Beaver Falls, 1959-61, U. Ill., 1962. Payroll acct. Babcock & Wilcox Steel Corp., Beaver Falls, Pa., 1960-62; admininstrv. asst. U. Ill., Urbana, 1962-63, Lockheed Missiles & Space Co., Vandenberg AFB, Calif., 1963-64; acct. tng. Vanda Beauty Counselor, N.Y., 1964-78; adminstrv. asst. Okaloosa Walton Jr. Coll., Niceville, Fla., 1977-78; adminstrv. asst. Tex. Instruments, Va., 1978-79; exec. asst. Allied Signal Bendix Aerospace, Arlington, 1979-89, Orion Group Ltd., Dr. Richard DeLauer and Matra Aerospace Inc., Arlington, 1988-89; asst. to bd. dirs. Fairchild Space and Def. Corp., Germantown, Md., 1989-91; cons. Meridian Strategies, Inc., Fullerton, Calif., 1991-93. Mem. Women Def., Army Assn., Am. Def. Preparedness Assn., Air Force Assn. Republican. Presbyterian. Home and Office: 956 W Rancho Cir Fullerton CA 92635-3337

SMITH, HELEN ELIZABETH, retired military officer; b. San Rafael, Calif., Aug. 11, 1946; d. Jack Dillard and Marian Elizabeth (Miller) S. BA in Geography, Calif. State U., Northridge, 1968; MA in Internat. Rels., Salve Regina, Newport, R.I., 1983; MS in Tech. Comm., Rensselaer Poly. Inst., 1988; postgrad., Naval War Coll., 1982-83. Commd. ensign USN, 1968, advanced through grades to capt., 1989; adminstrv. asst. USN Fighter Squadron 101, Key West, Fla., 1969-70; adminstrv. officer Fleet Operational Tng. Group, Mountain View, Calif., 1970-72; leader human resource team Human Resource Ctr., Rota, Spain, 1977-79; adminstrv. officer Pearl Harbor (Hawaii) Naval Sta., 1979-80; dir. Family Svc. Ctr., Pearl Harbor, 1980-82; officer-in-charge R&D lab. Naval Ocean Systems Ctr., Kaneohe, Hawaii, 1983-85; exec. officer Naval ROTC, assoc. prof. Rensselaer Poly. Inst., Troy, N.Y., 1985-88; comdg. officer Navy Alcohol Rehab. Ctr., Norfolk, Va., 1988-90; faculty mem., commanding officer Naval Adminstrv. Command, dean adminstrv. support, comptr. Armed Forces Staff Coll., Norfolk, Va., 1990-93; ret., 1993. Author: (walking tour) Albany's Historic Pastures, 1987; composer (cantata) Night of Wonder, 1983. Chmn. Hawaii State Childcare Com., Honolulu, 1981-82; coun. mem. Hist. Pastures Neighborhood Assn., Albany, N.Y., 1985-88; mem. working group Mayor's Task Force on Drugs, Norfolk, 1989-90; bd. dirs. Va. Coun. on Alcoholism, 1989-92, Calif. for Drug Free Youth, 1995—; singer North County Baroque Ensemble. Mem. AAUW, Waves (nat. unit 126), Kiwanis. Republican. Presbyterian.

SMITH, HELEN LEE, non-profit association administrator; b. Bogota, Colombia, Aug. 6, 1964; d. William Constant and Theodosia M. (Atchley) S. BS in Journalism, Okla. State U., 1986; M of Liberal Arts, So. Meth. U., 1992. Chpt. coord. Am. Diabetes Assn., Dallas, 1987-88; asst. dir. corp. rels. So. Meth. U., Dallas, 1988-91; devel. dir. Dallas County Heritage Soc., 1991-94; event mgr. LPGA skins game Easter Seals, 1994—. Tutor Adopt-A-Sch. Program, Dallas, 1994—; mem. Arts Dist. Friends, Dallas, 1992—, Dallas Mus. Art, 1993—. Mem. Nat. Soc. Fund Raising Execs. (com. mem. 1993—). Office: Easter Seal Soc 5701 Maple Dallas TX 75235

SMITH, ILEENE ANDREA, book editor; b. N.Y.C., Jan. 21, 1953; d. Norman and Jeanne (Jaffe) S.; m. Howard A. Sobel, June 3, 1979; children: Nathaniel Jacob, Rebecca Julia. BA, Brandeis U., Waltham, Mass., 1975; MA, Columbia U., 1978. Editorial asst. Atheneum Publishers, N.Y.C., 1979-82; sr. editor Summit Books, N.Y.C., 1982-91, lit. editor, 1991-92; edit. cons. The Elie Wiesel Found. for Humanity, 1993; cons. editor Paris Review, N.Y., 1987—. Author introductory scripts for Met. Opera Telecasts, 1987—. Jerusalem fellow, 1987; recipient Tony Godwin Meml. award, 1982, PEN/Roger Klein award for editl. excellence, 1988, Contbg. to Prodn. of Aida cert. NATAS, 1990.

SMITH, JACKLYN ANN, financial analyst; b. San Mateo, Calif., Apr. 14, 1964; d. John Joseph and Phyllis Virginia (Sutliff) S. BA in Polit. Economy, U. Calif., Berkeley, 1986; program on investment appraisal, mgmt., Harvard U., 1993; postgrad., Santa Clara U., 1993-94. Sr. auditor Deloitte & Touche, San Francisco, 1986-91; prin. Toulouse Foods, Inc., San Francisco, 1990-92; fin. mgr., controller Seaboard Mgmt. Co. and Woodson Devel. Co., Redwood City, Calif., 1992-94; dir. consumer/retail divsn. Planter Tech., Mountain View, Calif., 1994—. Author: Brazilian Occidental Pipeline - the Case for Efficiency in Petroleum Products' Transportation, 1994. Bd. dirs. Lighthouse for the Blind and Visually Impaired, San Francisco, 1990— (fin. and devel. coms.). Republican. Roman Catholic. Home: 452 Lake St San Francisco CA 94118-1322 Office: Planter Tech 999 Independence Ave Ste E Mountain View CA 94043

SMITH, JAMESETTA DELORISE, author; b. Chgo., Jan. 26, 1942; d. James Gilbert and Ora Mae (Roberts) Howell; m. Leroy Smith, June 2, 1962; children: Leroy, Darryll Keith. Student, Oxford Bus. Coll., Chgo., 1961-62. Office clerk Justice of the Peace, Gary, Ind., 1966-69; bookkeeper, office mgr. Jones Electric, Gary, Ind., 1971-85. Author: How Strong is Strong, 1988; contbr. articles to profl. jours., newspapers. Treas., bd. dirs. Northwest Ind. Lupus Found., Gary, 1988-92; facilitator Gary Meth. Hosp. for Lupus Found., 1991-92; pastor's aide sec. Greater St. Paul Bapt. Ch., 1990-92, food com. sec., 1994—, ch. trustee, 1994—, bible study leader 1994—. Mem. Jones Electric Gary Ind. (Sec. 1986). Democratic. Baptist.

SMITH, JANE SCHNEBERGER, retired city clerk; b. Chgo., Aug. 9, 1928; d. Frank R. and Marion (Durante) Schneberger; m. Z. Erol Smith, Jr., Oct. 28, 1950 (div. 1974); children: Suzan McCue Kuester, Tracy Smith Cawley, Cameron Farley, Z. Erol III, Kimberly Van Den Elzen, Scott. B.A. in Chemistry, U. Colo., 1950; M.A. in Communication, Mich. State U., 1978, PhD in ednl. adminstrn. Mich. State U., 1987. Chemist, Kellogg Switchboard, Chgo., 1950-51; tchr. Crab Orchard Sch., Palos Heights, Ill., 1969-70; v.p. South Cook County Girl Scouts, Harvey, Ill., 1967-69, (Thanks badge 1972), staff advisor, 1970-72; program and tng. dir. Mich. Capitol coun. Girl Scouts U.S., Lansing, 1972-75; dir. svc. learning ctr. Mich. State U., East Lansing, 1975-81; city clk. City of Ashland, Wis., 1981-89; interim city adminstr., 1989-90, ret. 1990; cons. vol. adminstrn., Mich., Wis., 1975—. Co-editor Looking Backward Moving Forward; Contbr. articles to profl. jours. V.p. Mich. Capitol Girl Scout Council, Lansing, 1976-78 (cert. appreciation 1975); bd. dirs. Lansing RSVP, 1976-81, Ashland Mus., 1985-87, Ptnrs. in Recovery, 1985-87; v.p. Friends of the Libr., 1992—; sec. New Horizons, 1985-90, New Day Shelter, 1990—, v.p., 1993—; pres. LWV of Ashland Bayfield County, 1992-93; sec. No. Wis. History Ctr., 1992-94; commr. Ashland Water & Wastewater Utility, 1993—; mem. Ashland Beautification Com., 1993—. Mem. Internat. Assn. Mcpl. Clks., Wis. Mcpl. Clks. Assn. (dist. dir. 1984-86). Roman Catholic. Club: Am. Bus. Women's Assn. (scholarship chmn. 1985) (Ashland). Lodge: Zonta (pres. 1979-81). Avocations: stained glass, gardening. Home: 700 Macarthur Ave Ashland WI 54806-2903

SMITH, JANET MARIE, professional sports team executive; b. Jackson, Miss., Dec. 13, 1957; d. Thomas Henry and Nellie Brown (Smith) S. BArch, Miss. State U., 1981; MA in Urban Planning, CCNY, 1984. Draftsman Thomas H. Smith and Assocs. Architects, Jackson, 1979; mktg. coord. The Eggers Group, P.C. Architects and Planners, N.Y.C., 1980; program assoc. Ptnrs. for Livable Places, Washington, 1980-82; coord. asst. Lance Jay Brown, Architect and Urban Planner, N.Y.C., 1983-84; coord. architecture and design Battery Park City Authority, N.Y.C., 1982-84; pres., chief exec. officer Pershing Sq. Mgmt. Assn., L.A., 1985-89; v.p. stadium planning and devel. Balt. Orioles Oriole Park at Camden Yard, 1989-94; v.p. sports facilities TBS Properties, Atlanta, 1994—; bd. dirs. Assn. Collegiate Schs. Architecture, Washington, 1979-82, Assn. Student Chpts. AIA, Washington, 1979-82. Guest editor: Urban Design Internat., 1985; assoc. editor: Crit, 1979-82; contbr. articles to profl. jours. Named Disting. Grad., Nat. Assn. State Univs. and Land Grant Colls., 1988, One of Outstanding Young Women of Am., 1982; recipient Spirit of Miss. award, Sta. WLBT, Jackson, 1987. Mem. AIA (assoc.), Urban Land Inst. Democrat. Episcopalian. Office: TBS Properties Inc Ste 275 1 CNN Center Atlanta GA 30303

SMITH, JANET SUE, systems specialist; b. Chgo., Jan. 15, 1945; d. Curtis Edwin and Margaret Louise (Yost) Smith; B.A., Ind. U., 1967. Sales mgr. Marshall Field & Co., Chgo., 1968-70, programmer, 1970-72; sr. programmer, analyst Trailer Train Co., Chgo., 1972-75; mgr. data base and systems devel. Railinc-Assn. Am. R.R., Washington, 1975-85, asst. v.p., corp. sec., 1985-93, asst. v.p. strategic devel., 1994—. Nat. student v.p. YWCA, 1966-67; bd. dirs., v.p. planning and fin. Guide Internat., Friends of the Nat. Zoo; advisor Jr. Achievement. Mem. Am. Council R.R. Women, Ind. U. Alumni Assn. (life), Women's Transp. Seminar. Home: 2000 N St NW Washington DC 20036-2302 Office: 50 F St NW Washington DC 20001-1530

SMITH, JANET SUE, special education educator; b. Kirksville, Mo., Dec. 15, 1964; d. Leland Wayne and Cecille Marie (Magruder) Maize; m. Robert Dale Smith, May 28, 1988; 1 child, Brandon Michael; stepchildren: Dustin Robert, Dana Nicole. BS in Edn., N.E. Mo. State U., 1987. Cert. elem. and secondary tchr., Mo.; cert. learning disabilities and mentally handicapped tchr., Mo. Nurse's asst. Kirksville Manor Care Ctr., 1984-87; tchr. high sch. spl. edn. Beckenridge (Mo.) Sch. Dist. R-1, 1987-89; tchr. high sch. spl. edn. Gallatin (Mo.) Sch. Dist. R-5, 1989—, coord. spl. edn., 1992—. Chairperson Cmty. Appearance Com., Breckenridge, 1989-90; treas. Cmty. Fair Com., Breckenridge, 1990-92. Democrat. Baptist. Office: Gallatin R-5 High Sch 602 S Olive St Gallatin MO 64640-9471

SMITH, JANET VICTORIA, elementary school educator; b. Chgo., July 9, 1946; d. Robert William and Annmarie Victoria (Forslund) S. BA, Northeastern Ill. U., Chgo., 1968; MEd, Nat. Louis U., Evanston, Ill., 1987. Cert. elem. sch. tchr., Ill. Classroom tchr. Bd. Edn., Chgo., 1968—; cons. West Town Arts Project, Chgo., 1993-94; presenter in field. Named Tchr. of Yr., West Town Kiwanis, 1988; recipient Rochelle Lee award, 1993, 94; Chgo. Found. for Edn. grantee, 1988-94. Mem. Am. Fedn. Tchrs., Ill. Coun. for the Social Studies. Office: James Otis Sch 525 N Armour St Chicago IL 60622-6105

SMITH, JEAN CHANDLER, former museum official; b. Phila., Apr. 13, 1918; d. Chandler White and Philena Pennell (Cheetham) S. AB, Bryn

Mawr Coll., 1939; MS, Yale U., 1953; MLS, Cath. U. Am., 1973. Reference librarian D.C. Pub. Library, 1939-43; translator C.Z., 1943-44; librarian Nat. Air Sta., Kaneohe Bay, Oahu, Hawaii, 1944-46; reference librarian, also research asso. Yale U., 1947-58; acting chief acquisitions NIH Library, Bethesda, Md., 1959-63; chief reader services U.S. Dept Interior, Washington, 1964-65; with Smithsonian Instn. Libraries, Washington, 1965-81; asst. dir. instn. services Smithsonian Instn. Libraries, 1972-79, acting dir., 1977-79; research assoc. Smithsonian Instn., 1981-94; ret., 1994; Mem. friends of library com. Bryn Mawr Coll. Compiler: Georges Cuvier, An Annotated Bibliography of his Published Works, 1993. Mem. Conn. Acad. Arts and Scis., Soc. History of Natural History, Bibliog. Soc. Am., History of Sci. Soc.

SMITH, JEAN KENNEDY, ambassador; b. Brookline, Mass., Feb. 20, 1928; d. Joseph P. and Rose Kennedy; m. Stephen E. Smith (dec.); 4 children. BA, Manhattanville Coll. Founder, dir., chair Very Spl. Arts, 1974—; amb. to Ireland Dublin, 1993—. Author: (with George Plimpton) Chronicles of Courage, 1993; contbr. articles on the disabled to profl. jours. Trustee Joseph P. Kennedy, Jr. Found., 1964—, John F. Kennedy Ctr. Performing Arts. Recipient Sec.'s award Dept. Vets. Affairs, Vol. of Yr. award People-to-People Com. Handicapped, Margaret Mead Humanitarian award Coun. Cerebral Palsy Auxs., Jefferson award Am. Inst. Pub. Svc., Spirit of Achievement award Yeshiva U., Humanitarian award Capital Children's Mus. Address: Am Embassy, 42 Elgin Rd, Ballsbridge Dublin Ireland*

SMITH, JEAN WEBB (MRS. WILLIAM FRENCH SMITH), civic worker; b. L.A.; d. James Ellwood and Violet (Hughes) Webb; B.A. summa cum laude, Stanford U., 1940; m. George William Vaughan, Mar. 14, 1942 (dec. Sept. 1963); children: George William, Merry; m. William French Smith, Nov. 6, 1964. Mem. Nat. Vol. Service Adv. Coun. (ACTION), 1973-76, vice chmn., 1974-76; dir. Beneficial Standard Corp., 1976-85. bd. dirs. Community TV So. Calif., 1979-93; mem. Calif. Arts Commn., 1971-74, vice chmn., 1973-74; bd. dirs. The Founders, Music Center, L.A., 1971-74; bd. dirs. costume coun. L.A. County Mus. Art, 1971-73; bd. dirs. United Way, Inc., 1973-80, Hosp. Good Samaritan, 1973-80, L.A. chpt. NCCJ, 1977-80, Nat. Symphony Orch., 1980-85, L.A. World Affairs Coun., 1990, L.A. chpt. ARC, 1994—; bd. fellows Claremont Univ. Ctr. and Grad. Sch., 1987—; bd. dirs. Hosp. Good Samaritan, 1973-80; mem. exec. com., 1975-80; mem. nat. bd. dirs. Boys' Clubs Am., 1977-80; mem. adv. bd. Salvation Army, 1979—; bd. overseers The Hoover Instn. on War, Revolution and Peace; mem. President's Commn. on White House Fellowships, 1980-90, Nat. Coun. on the Humanities, 1987-90; bd. govs. Calif. Community Found., 1990—; bd. regents Children's Hosp. L.A., 1993—. Named Woman of Yr. for community service L.A. Times, 1958; recipient Citizens of Yr. award Boys Clubs Greater L.A., 1982, Life Achievement award Boy Scouts Am., L.A. coun., 1985. Mem. Jr. League of L.A. (pres. 1954-55), Assn. Jr. Leagues of Am. (dir. Region XII, 1956-58, pres. 1958-60), Phi Beta Kappa, Kappa Kappa Gamma. Home: 11718 Wetherby Ln Los Angeles CA 90077

SMITH, JEANNE HICKS (SHERRY SMITH), lawyer; b. L.A., Feb. 19, 1943; d. John Stipp and Virginia Marie (Grace) Hicks; m. Judson Wilmer Smith, Aug. 24, 1963; children: Kimberly Jeanne Schauer, Heather Margaret, Jennifer Lee. Student, Pacific U., 1960-62, U. Calif., Riverside, 1962-63; BA, Calif. State U., L.A., 1964; JD, Northwestern Sch. of Law of Lewis and Clark Coll., 1972. Bar: Oreg. 1972, Tex. 1976, Calif., 1978. Spl. projects coord. local govt. rels. divsn. Exec. Dept., State of Oreg., Salem, 1972-74; staff atty. Gov.'s Commn. Jud. Reform, Salem, 1974-75; founding dir. office continuing legal edn. sch. law So. Meth. U., Dallas, 1975-77; program atty. Continuing Edn. Bar, Berkeley, Calif., 1977—. Editor: (series) Estate Planning, 1992—. trustee Pacific U., Forest Grove, Oreg., 1992—; mem. bd. dirs. KQED, Inc., San Francisco, 1993—, Berkeley Cmty. Chorus & Orch., 1992—, Berkeley LWV Found., 1991—, Berkeley Cmty. Media, Inc., 1993—. Mem. Calif. Women Lawyers (life, charter), Calif. Supreme Ct. Hist. Soc. (charter), Women Lawyers Alameda County (charter), Berkeley-Albany Bar Assn. (bd. dirs., pres. 1991-92), Alumni Assn. Northwestern Sch. Law of Lewis and Clark Coll. (bd. dirs. 1991-95). Democrat. Congregationalist. Office: Continuing Edn Bar 2300 Shattuck Ave Berkeley CA 94704

SMITH, JENNIFER C., insurance company executive; b. Boston, Nov. 3, 1952; d. Herman J. and Margaree L. S.; B.A. in English, Union Coll., 1974; M.A., Fairfield U., 1982. Claim rep. Travelers Ins. Co., Boston, 1974-75, supr., N.J., 1976-78, regional asst., account exec., Hartford, Conn., 1979-81, tng. adminstr., 1981, asst. dir. casualty and property depts., 1981-83, sec. casualty and property depts., 1983-85; personnel dir. City of Hartford, 1984-85, asst. city mgr., 1985-87; dir. mktg. Travelers Cos., 1987; asst. v.p. corp. human resources, Aetna Life and Casualty Co., 1987-88, v.p. pers., 1990, v.p. corp. mktg., 1991; v.p., chief of staff Aetna Health Group, 1992-93; v.p., chief oper. officer Aetna Profl. Mgmt. Co., 1993-94; v.p. Occupl. Managed Care Aetna, 1994—; claim rep. Sentry Ins. Co., N.J., 1975-76. Bd. dirs. Hartford Stage Co., exec. com., nominating com.; bd. dirs. Boys Club Hartford; trustee St. Joseph's Coll., Martin Luther King Jr. Scholarship Fund, U. Conn. Contbr. articles to Conn. Bus. Times. Office: Aetna Life and Casualty Co Aetna Health Plans RE 6K 151 Farmington Ave Hartford CT 06156-0001

SMITH, JUDITH ANN, academic administrator; b. Springfield, Mo., Jan. 1, 1950; d. Harley Jr. and Barbara Jean (Anderson) Cozad; m. Robert Eugene Smith, July 11, 1969. BS in Edn., S.W. Mo. State U., 1973, MA in English, 1976. Cert. tchr. (life), Mo. Tchr. R-12 Schs., Springfield, 1973-83; program/communications mgr. Performing Arts Ctr. Trust, Tulsa, 1983-84; gen. mgr. Springfield Symphony Assn., 1984-86; assoc. dir. devel., dir. planning giving S.W. Mo. State U., 1986-89, dir. devel. alumni rels., 1989—; dir. Summerscape (gifted program), Springfield, 1980-82. Vol. Springfield Symphony Guild, 1986—; vol. fundraising advisor First Night, Springfield, 1993-94; appointee Greene County Hist. Sites Bd., 1994—; bd. dirs. Discovery Ctr. of Springfield, 1994—. Named Outstanding Young Educator Springfield Jaycees, 1976, Mo. Jaycees, 1977. Mem. Coun. for the Advancement and Support of Edn. (com. on women and minorities 1988-90, Merit and Excellence awards 1988, 89, 90), Rotary, Delta Kappa Gamma (past officer Alpha Gamma chpt.). Office: SW Mo State U 901 S National Ave Springfield MO 65804-0027

SMITH, JUDY LYNN, interior designer; b. Myrtle Beach, S.C., May 8, 1965; d. Jesse Therman and Eula Mae (McFadden) Lancaster; m. Edward Jerome Williams III, Aug. 1, 1987 (div. Aug. 17, 1990); m. Calvin Eugene Smith III, Sept. 15, 1992; 1 child, Jessica Lynn Smith. BS in Interior Design, Western Carolina U., 1987. Interior designer The Decorators Inn, Easley, S.C., 1987, Allen Funks Wallpaper, Spartanburg, S.C., 1987-88, Color Tile, Spartanburg, S.C., 1988, Hodge Carpets, Spartanburg, S.C., 1988-89, Hines Lighting, Charlotte, N.C., 1990-91, Henderson Furniture, Greenville, S.C., 1992—; detention officer Spartanburg County Detention Ctr., 1994—; interior designer, Spartanburg, 1987—; in-home consultation, Greenville, 1994—. Recipient Top Performer award Wear Dated Carpet, 1989. Mem. Am. Soc. Interior Designers (pres. 1987—). Baptist. Home: 1756 Memorial Drive Ext Greer SC 29651-8429 Office: Spartanburg County Detention Ctr 1818 N Pleasantburg Dr Spartanburg SC 29651

SMITH, JUDY SERIALE, social services administrator, state legislator; b. Lafayette, La., Mar. 10, 1953; d. Joseph and Vernice (Bellard) S.; m. Sylvester Lee Smith, Jr., Dec. 10, 1974; children: Sylvester Lee Smith III, Joseph Seriale Smith. BA in Social Work, Grambling (La.) State U., 1974. Social svc. coord. Case de Vida, Lake Charles, La., 1976-78; behavioral sci. instr. Family Doctor's Clinic, Lake Charles, 1978-79; caseworker FEMA, Camden, Ark., 1979; community svc. coord. Community Action Authority, Camden, 1980-84; exec. dir. People Are Concerned, Inc., Camden, 1984—; mem. Ark. House of Reps., Little Rock; regional coord. Ark. for Drug Free Youth, Little Rock, 1989—. Trustee Ark. Mus. of Sci. and History, Little Rock, 1991—; mem. Workmen's Comp. Rev. Team, Little Rock, 1993—, Ark. Juvenile Justice Coalition, Little Rock, 1991—; mem. com. on pub. health welfare and labor Ark. Ho. of Reps., 1991—, mgmt. com.; mem. Aging. and Legis. Affairs, Ark., 1991—, Interim Commn. on Children and Youth, Ark., 1993—; vice chair Joint Com. on Children and Youth. Named to Top Ten Legislators Ark., Dem. Gazette, 1993, Ark. Top 15 Women in Leadership, Ark. Bus. Weekly, 1993, Top 100 Women in Ark.; recipient Legislator award Ark. Counselor's Assn., 1992, Cmty. Svc. award Ark. State Press, 1992. Mem. Warren L. Strickland Found., Alpha Kappa Alpha. Democrat. Baptist. Home: 620 Terminal Rd Camden AR 71701-4467 Office: People are Concerned Inc 351 Washington Ste 221 Camden AR 71701*

SMITH, JULIA AMELIA, English language educator; b. San Antonio, Tex., Dec. 25, 1935; d. George Leon and Julia E. (Garcia) S. BA, Our Lady of the Lake, San Antonio, Tex., 1956; MA, U. Tex., 1958; postgrad., Harvard U., 1961; PhD, U. Tex, 1969. Elem. tchr. San Antonio (Tex.) Sch. Dist., 1956-57; instr. Laredo (Tex.) Jr. Coll., 1959-68; asst. prof. English, Tex. A&M U., Kingsville, 1969-72; assoc. prof. Tex. A&I U., Kingsville, 1972-78, prof., 1978—, chmn. dept., 1977-83. Contbr. articles to profl. jours. Organist St. Martin's Ch., Kingsville, Tex. Mem. Modern Language Assn., Nat. Council of Tchrs of English, Conf. of Coll. Tchrs. of English, Tex. Coll English Assn., Music Club of Kingsville, Audubon Soc., Delta Kappa Gamma, Kappa Nu. Democrat. Roman Catholic. Office: Tex A&M PO Box 162 Kingsville TX 78364-0162

SMITH, JULIA LADD, medical oncologist, hospice physician; b. Rochester, N.Y., July 26, 1951; d. John Herbert and Isabel (Walcott) Ladd; m. Stephen Slade Smith; 1 child. BA, Smith Coll., 1973; MD, N.Y. Med. Coll., 1976. Diplomate Am. Bd. Internal Medicine, Am. Bd. Med. Oncology. Intern in medicine N.Y. Med. Coll., N.Y.C., 1976-77; resident in medicine Rochester Gen. Hosp., 1977-79; internist Genesee Valley Group Health, Rochester, 1979-80; oncology fellow U. Rochester, 1980-82, asst. prof. oncology in medicine sch. medicine & dentistry, 1986—; oncologist Med. Ctr. Clinic, Ltd., Pitts., 1982-83; oncologist, internist Rutgers Community Health Plan, New Brunswick, N.J., 1983-86; med. dir. Genesse Region Home Care Assn./Hospice, Rochester, 1988—. Bd. dirs. Am. Cancer Soc., Monroe County, 1988-92. Rsch. grantee Nat. Cancer Inst., 1993—. Mem. ACP, Am. Soc. Clin. Oncology, Acad. Hospice Physicians. Unitarian-Universalist. Address: PO Box 704 601 Elmwood Ave Rochester NY 14642

SMITH, KATHLEEN DANA, principal, consultant; b. Fargo, N.D., June 24, 1947; d. Dana Eugene and Georgia Caroline (Cook) S.; m. Thomas Donald Gash, June 7, 1980; children: Caroline, Kathryn. BA in Polit. Sci. and History, U. Denver, 1969, MA in Counseling and Guidance, 1970; EdD in Leadership and Mgmt., U. No. Colo., 1985. Cert. tchr., Colo.; lic. counselor, Colo. Tchr., counselor Denver Pub. Schs.-East High Sch., 1969-71; counselor, tchr. Cherry Creek Schs.-Cherry Creek High Sch., Englewood, Colo., 1971-77, chair counseling dept., 1977-80, asst. to prin., 1980-81, adminstrv. asst. to dep. supt., 1982-83, dir. of pupil svcs., 1983-88; asst. prin. Cherry Creek Schs./Horizon Mid. Sch., Aurora, Colo., 1988-89, prin., 1989-93; prin. Cherry Creek High Sch., Englewood, Colo., 1993—; presenter in field; cons. in field; mem. faculty U. Phoenix, Denver, 1988—. Mem. Gov.'s Task Force for Better Air, Denver, 1984-86; mem., various chairs Jr. League Denver, 1983—; bd. dirs. Cerebral Palsy Ctr., Denver, 1991—; adv. com. Colo. Bd. Land Commrs., 1992—. Harvard U. fellow, 1989; Colo. Dept. of Edn. grantee, 1987. Fellow Inst. for Devel. Ednl. Activities; mem. ASCD, Nat. Assn. Secondary Sch. Prins., Phi Delta Kappa. Roman Catholic. Office: Cherry Creek High Sch 9300 E Union Englewood CO 80111

SMITH, KATHLEEN TENER, bank executive; b. Pitts., Oct. 19, 1943; d. Edward Harrison Jr. and Barbara Elizabeth (McCormick) Tener; m. Roger Davis Smith, May 30, 1970 (dec.); children: Silas Wheelock, Jocelyn Tener, Luke Ewing Taft. BA summa cum laude, Vassar Coll., 1965; MA in Econs., Harvard U., 1968. Research assoc. Harvard U. Grad. Sch. Bus., Cambridge, Mass., 1967-69; assoc. economist Chase Manhattan Bank, N.Y.C., 1969-70, asst. treas., 1971, 2d v.p., 1972, v.p., 1973—, sec. asset liability mgmt. com., 1985-90, treas. Global Bank, 1990, divsn. exec. structured investment products, 1990-92, global mktg. and comms. exec. Global Risk Mgmt. Sect., 1993-94; global mktg. and comms. exec. Chase Global Markets Sect., 1994—. Trustee Vassar Coll., Poughkeepsie, N.Y., 1979-91, mem. exec. com., 1987-91; mem. subcom. on edn. Chase Manhattan Found., N.Y.C., 1985-90. NSF fellow, 1965-67. Mem. Am. Fin. Assn., Am. Econ. Assn., Yale Club (N.Y.C.), Fin. Mktg. Assn., Phi Beta Kappa. Republican. Episcopalian. Home: 454 Rt 32 N New Paltz NY 12561 Office: Chase Manhattan Bank 1 Chase Manhattan Plz New York NY 10081-0001

SMITH, KATHRYN ANN, advertising executive; b. Harvey, Ill., Mar. 30, 1955; d. Kenneth Charles and Barbara Joan (Wise) Smith; m. Christopher A. Erwin, July 16, 1994; stepchildren: Brian, Courtney, Misty. Student Art Inst. Chgo., 1973. Advt. salesperson Calumet Index, Inc., Riverdale, Ill., 1974-77, Towne & Country Ind., Hammond, 1977-78; owner, sales person Ad-Com, Merrillville, Ind., 1978-92, pres., Crown Point, Ind., 1978-92, corp. pres., chief exec. officer, 1993; pres. Smith-Halcomb Advt., Chgo., 1993; pres., owner Smith-Leonard & Assocs. Advt., Des Plaines, Ill., 1993—. Dir., producer cable TV comml., 1982; dir., producer TV comml., 1987-88. Recipient Silver Microphone award, 1987, 90; named Am. On Line Spl. Interest Forum Leader, 1991. Mem. Advt. Agy. Owners Assn. (chair 1985-88), Merrillville C. of C. Avocations: painting, fishing, antiques, computers, travel.

SMITH, KATHY ANN, educator, state senator; b. Muncie, Ind., Apr. 10, 1944; d. John Francis and H. Emily (Walter) Wallace; m. George Frederick Smith, June 22, 1979; 1 child, Alison Marie Smith. BS in Edn., Ind. U., 1966; postgrad., Ball State U., 1973. Cert. secondary lang. arts tchr., Ind. English tchr. New Albany (Ind.) Floyd Co. Sch. Corp., 1966—; adj. faculty Ind. U. S.E., New Albany, 1977-84. Ind. State senator Ind. Gen. Assembly, Indpls., 1986—; del. Dem. Nat. Conv., N.Y., 1976-80, San Francisco, 1984, Atlanta, 1988, Ind. Dem. State Conv., Indpls., 1980, 82, 84, 86, 88, 90; mem., del. Dem. Nat. Platform Com., Washington, 1984. Mem. New Albany Floyd County Edn. Assn. (legis. chair 1977-86, exec. com. 1979-86), Ind. State Tchrs. Assn. (chair polit. action com. 1978-81, 83-86), NEA (NEA polit. action com. 1978-81, 83-84), Nat. Coun. Tchrs. of English, Pi Lambda Theta (hon., pres. 1986-88), Psi Iota Xi. Democrat. Home: 1214 Beechwood Ave New Albany IN 47150-2521 Office: Ind State Senate State Capital Indianapolis IN 46204*

SMITH, LAUREN, interior designer, writer; b. N.Y.C.; d. Joseph and Rosemary (Griffin) Martin; m. Robert Zane Smith, June 17, 1967. Student, N.Y. Sch. Interior Design, 1968-70. Pres. Lauren Smith, Inc., N.Y.C., 1973—. Author: Your Colors at Home, 1985, Colors for Brides, 1989; editor: Discover Your Decorating Colors, 1987, Discover Your Colors at Home, 1988; spokesperson (TV show) Taste of New York, 1992; cons. Decorating with Wallcovering, 1987. Mem. Am. Soc. Interior Designers (allied). Roman Catholic.

SMITH, LEILA HENTZEN, artist; b. Milw., May 20, 1932; d. Erwin Albert and Marian Leila (Austin) Hentzen; m. Richard Howard Smith, Sept. 12, 1959; 1 child, Jennie. BFA, Miami U., 1955; cert., Famous Artists Schs., 1959. Quilting tchr. Milw. Pub. Schs., 1975-79. Exhibited in two man shows West Bend (Wis.) Gallery of Fine Arts, 1963, George Watts Gallery, Milw., 1965, Mapledale Sch. Gallery, Bayside, Wis., 1981; group shows include Milw. Art Ctr., 1961, Wustum Mus. Art, Racine, Wis., 1966, 77, John Michael Kohler Arts Ctr., Sheboygan, Wis., 1984, 87, 89-94, Ozaukee Art Ctr., Cedarburg, Wis., 1982-86, 93, Artist's World Gallery, Cedarburg, 1975, Cedarburg Cultural Ctr., 1988-95, West Bend (Wis.) Gallery Fine Arts, 1993, Rahr/West Art Mus., Manitowoc, Wis., 1994; represented in permanent collections Milw. County Art Commn. Wheaton Franciscans. Women's aux. vol. salvation Army, Milw. Recipient Honorable Mention for painting Bayshore Merchants Assn, 1969, Delta Gamma Art Fair, 1981, Best of Show for painting John Michael Kohler Arts Ctr., 1988. Mem. AAUW, Cedarburg Artists Guild, Seven Arts Soc. of Milw. (pres. 1967-68, painters group chmn. 1962-63), Wis. Watercolor Soc., DAR (Milw. chpt. Holiday Folk Fair chmn. 1965-76, libr. historian 1974-77, corr. sec. 1977-80, dir. 1983-86, rec. sec. 1992-95, Outstanding Jr. mem. 1966), Wis. Soc. Daus. of Founders and Patriots of Am. (pres. 1964-66, 2d v.p. 1966-68, 70-73, corr. sec. 1976-79), Wis. Ct. Assts. Nat. Soc. Women Descendants Ancient and Hon. Artillery Co. of Boston, Wis. Soc. Mayflower Descendants, Delta Zeta. Congregationalist. Home: 9966 N Corey Ln Mequon WI 53092-6207

SMITH, LINDA A., congresswoman, former state legislator; d. Vern Smith; children: Sheri, Robi. Office mgr.; former mem. Wash. State Ho. of Reps.; mem. Wash. State Senate; congresswoman, Wash. 3rd Dist. U.S. House Reps., Washington, D.C., 1995—. Republican. Home: 10009 NW Ridgecrest Ave Vancouver WA 98685-5159 Office: Senate House Legislative Bldg Olympia WA 98504*

SMITH, LINDA ANN, public relations executive; b. Queens, N.Y., June 1, 1951; d. Edwin Joseph and Elaine A. (Gallo) S. BA, CUNY, 1987. Sec. rsch. Merrill Lynch, N.Y.C., 1965-69; adminstrv. mgr. Doremus Pub. Rels., N.Y.C., 1969-85. Bd. dirs. Make-A-Wish Found. of Met. N.Y. Mem. NAFE, Am. Mgmt. Assn., Publicity Club of N.Y. Office: Gavin Anderson & Co 1633 Broadway New York NY 10019

SMITH, LINDA LOUISE, education director; b. Bronx, N.Y., May 16, 1957; d. John K. and Nellie Noorlander. BS, Nyack Coll., 1982; MS, SUNY, Albany, 1983, D in Ednl. Theory, 1992. Cert. elem. tchr., spl. edn. tchr., sch. adminstr. Rsch. asst. SUNY, Albany, 1983-85, program assoc. Prek program, 1985-88, adminstrv. coord., 1988-90; edn. dir. Pathfinder Village, Edmeston, N.Y., 1992-94; dir. spl. edn. Herkimer (N.Y.) County BOCES, 1994—. Tech. asst. curriculum guide for Devel. Disabilities Coun., 1986. Mem. rep., exec. mem. Capitol Region Preschool Provider Coun., Albany, 1989-92. Mem. Coun. for Exceptional Children. Democrat. Reformed. Home: 18 Lewis St Little Falls NY 13365 Office: Herkimer County BOCES Gros Blvd Herkimer NY 13350

SMITH, LINDA MARIE, economic developer; b. Watkins, Minn., June 7, 1949; d. Daniel Peter and Mildred Margaret (Arens) Christle; m. William Robert Brown Jr., Dec. 10, 1966; children: Anthony R. Brown, Jay Robert Brown; m. 2d Robert James Smith, June 17, 1989. Cert. econ. developer. Adminstrv. asst. Algona (Iowa) C. of C., 1978-86; exec. v.p., CEO Wayne (Nebr.) C. of C./Wayne Industries Inc., 1986-90; pres., CEO, econ. developer Beatrice (Nebr.) C. of C./Gage County Econ. Devel., 1990—; bd. dirs. Am. Econ. Devel. Coun., Chgo., Nebr. Devel. Network, Lincoln, Nebr. C. of C. Execs., Lincoln; mem. adv. bd. Nebr. Tourism Dept., Lincoln, 1991-93; pres. Resource Conservation Devel., Tecumseh, Nebr., 1992—. Author: (book-periodical) The Emerging Role of Higher Education in Rural Economic Development, 1991. Recipient Patsy Dunham award Iowa Jaycee-ettes, 1978, named Outstanding Dir., 1978. Mem. Am. Econ. Developers Coun. (bd. dirs. 1990—), Nebr. Econ. Developers Assn. (v.p., pres. 1986—, bd. dirs.), Nebr. Coun. on Vocat. Edn., Rotary Internat. Home: 1912 S 5th Ave Beatrice NE 68310 Office: Beatrice C of C 226 S 6th St Beatrice NE 68310

SMITH, LINDA MARLENE, pharmacist; b. Rochester, N.Y., Jan. 14, 1948; d. Bernard Edward and Louise Grace (Peck) Smith. BS in Chemistry, Bucknell U., 1969; BS in Pharmacy, U. Conn., 1977. Registered pharmacist, Conn., Mass., Md. Pharmacy intern Arthur Drug, Windsor, Conn., 1977-78; staff pharmacist St. Francis Hosp., Hartford, Conn., 1978-81, Mary Lane Hosp., Ware, Mass., 1982-84; pharmacy mgr. Lemaitre Pharmacy, Ware, Mass., 1982-84; staff pharmacist Amherst (Mass.) Prescription Ctr., 1984-85; staff pharmacist Wash. County Hosp., Hagerstown, Md., 1986-87, IV supr., 1987-89; home IV supr. Antietam Home Infusion, Hagerstown, Md., 1990-92; unit dose supr., co-mgr. Fisher's Pharmacy, Hagerstown, Md., 1992-94; quality team coord. Western Md. Ctr., Hagerstown, Md., 1993-94; guest spkr. Nat. Acad. Scis., Washington, 1987. Editor Wash. County Hosp. pharmacy newsletter, 1986-89; contbr. articles to profl. jours. Mem., chair Bd. of Health, Warren, Mass., 1982-85; apptd. adv. com. Dept. Environ. Mgmt., Boston, 1983; mem. ad hoc steering com. Mass. Hazardous Waste Siting Congress, 1984-85; apptd. mem. Solid Waste Adv. Com., Wash. County, Md., 1991—; mem. Citizens for the Protection of Wash. County, 1991—; mem. campaign Md. for Choice, 1992; mem. steering com. Citizens Ensuring A Safe Environment, 1991-92; spokesperson Stop It, Warren, Mass., 1981-85. Grantee NSF, 1968; recipient citation Mass. State Senate, 1985, Cert. of Appreciation, Gov. State of Md., 1993. Mem. NOW (chpt. v.p., pres. 1989—), Am. Soc. Hosp. Pharmacists. Democrat. Home: 923 View St Hagerstown MD 21742

SMITH, LIZ (MARY ELIZABETH SMITH), newspaper columnist, broadcast journalist; b. Ft. Worth, Feb. 2, 1923; d. Sloan and Sarah Elizabeth (McCall) S. B.J., U. Tex., 1948. Editor Dell Publns., N.Y.C., 1950-53; assoc. producer CBS Radio, 1953-55, NBC-TV, 1955-59; assoc. on Cholly Knickerbocker newspaper column, N.Y.C., 1959-64; film critic Cosmopolitan mag., 1966; columnist Chgo. Tribune-N.Y. Daily News Syndicate (now Tribune Media Services), 1976-91, New York Newsday, L.A. Times Syndicate, 1991—, Family Circle mag., 1993—; TV commentator WNBC-TV, N.Y.C., 1978-91; commentator Fox-TV, N.Y.C., 1991—; freelance mag. writer, also staff writer Sports Illus. mag.; commentator Gossip Show E! Entertainment, 1993—. Author: The Mother Book, 1978. Office: N Y Newsday 2 Park Ave New York NY 10016

SMITH, LORETTA MAE, contracting officer; b. Washington Twp., Pa., May 25, 1939; d. Irvin Calvin and Viola Mary (Deibler) Shambaugh; 1 child, Miriam Estella Smith. B in Humanities, Pa. State U., 1984. Bookkeeper Harrisburg (Pa.) Nat. Bank, 1957-62; contract specialist USN, Mechanicsburg, Pa., 1987—; founder Telecare, Harrisburg, Pa., 1972-82. Active ARC, instr. CPR, 1982—; active Girl Scouts U.S., trainer, 1972—. Recipient Hemlock award Hemlock coun. Girl Scouts U.S., Harrisburg, 1981; Merit scholar Hall Found., 1982. Mem. Nat. Contract Mgmt. Assn., Mensa.

SMITH, LYNN HERSOM, systems analyst; b. Morganton, N.C., Aug. 3, 1949; d. Gifford Pershing and Bertha Mae (Reece) Hersom; m. James T. Smith Jr., Dec. 22, 1970; children: Kathryn Rynee, Michael Benjamyn. BS, Pa. State U., 1971; MA, U. Del., 1987. Tchr. various schs. in Del., Tex. and Pa., 1971-80; profl. U. Del., Newark, 1980-84; tchr., programmer Online Consulting, Wilmington, Del., 1984-87; systems analyst Computer Task Group, Media, Pa., 1987-91, Computer Aid, Inc., Wilmington, 1991—. Contbr. articles to profl. jours. Mem. NRA, Mensa. Home: 105 Fantasia Dr Newark DE 19713

SMITH, DAME MAGGIE, actress; b. Ilford, Eng., Dec. 28, 1934; d. Nathaniel and Margaret (Hutton) S.; m. Robert Stephens, 1967 (div. 1974); m. Beverley Cross, 1974. Grad., Oxford High Sch. Girls; D.Litt. (hon.), St. Andrews, 1971; DLitt (hon.), Oxford U., 1994. dir. United British Artists, 1982—. Stage and film actress, 1952—; stage appearances include: New Faces, debut N.Y.C., 1956, Share My Lettuce, 1957, The Stepmother, 1958, Rhinoceros, 1960, Strip The Willow, 1960, The Rehearsal, 1961, The Private Ear and The Public Eye, 1962, Mary, Mary, 1961; appearances at Old Vic, 1959-60, Nat. Theatre, London, 1963—; productions at Nat. Theatre include Private Lives, 1972, Othello, Hay Fever, Master Builder, Hedda Gabbler, Much Ado About Nothing, Miss Julie, Black Comedy, Stratford Festival, Ont., Can., 1976, 77, 78, 80, Antony and Cleopatra, Macbeth, Three Sisters, Richard III, Night and Day, London and N.Y.C., 1979-80, Virginia, London, 1981, Way of the World, Chichester Festival, London, 1984-85, Interpreters, London, 1985-86, Lettice and Lovage, 1988, also in N.Y., 1990, The Importance of Being Earnest, 1993, Three Tall Women, 1994; films include Othello, 1966, The Honey Pot, 1967, Oh What a Lovely War, 1968, Hot Millions, 1968, The Prime of Miss Jean Brodie, 1968 (Acad. award for best actress), Love and Pain and The Whole Damn Thing, 1971, Travels With My Aunt, 1972, Murder by Death, 1976, Death on the Nile, 1977, California Suite, 1978 (Acad. award for best supporting actress), Quartet, 1978, Clash of the Titans, 1981, Evil under the Sun, 1981, The Missionary, 1982, A Private Function, 1984 (best actress award Brit. Acad. of Film & TV Arts, 1985), Lily in Love, 1985, A Room With a View, 1985, The Lonely Passion of Judith Hearn, 1987 (Brit. Acad. of Film & TV Arts award, 1989), Paris By Night, 1988, Hook, 1991, Sister Act, 1992, The Secret Garden, 1993; TV films include Memento Mori, 1992, Suddenly Last Summer, 1993 (Lead Actress-Miniseries Emmy nominee, 1993); BBC-TV appearance Bed Among the Lentils, 1988. Recipient Best Actress award Eve. Std., 1962, 70, 82, 85, 94, Best Film Actress award Soc. Film and TV Arts U.K., 1968, Film Critics Guild, 1968, Taomina Gold award, 1985, Antoinette Perry award (Tony), 1990, Shakespeare prize, 1991; decorated Dame Brit. Empire, 1989; named Actress of Yr., Variety Club, 1963, 72, Brit. Acad. Best Screen Actress, 1985; Brit. Film Inst. fellow, 1992, Theater Hall of Fame, 1994. Office: Write on Cue, 15 New Row 3d Fl, London WC2N 4LA, England

SMITH, MARA A., small business owner, artist; b. Houston, July 31, 1945; d. Charles Parker and Mary Lee (Langford) S. BS, Tex. Woman's U., 1969, MFA, 1980. Owner, pres. Archtl. Murals in Brick, Seattle, 1977—; lectr. in field. Executed murals in brick Loew's Anatole Hotel, Dallas, 1978, 83, Am. Bank and Trust Co. Bldg., Reading, Pa., 1983, Pacific N.W. Co. Bldg., Reading, 1982, Pacific N.W. Bell Ctr., Seattle, 1985, One Bethesda Ctr., Bethesda, Md., 1986, Dragon Hill Hotel, U.S. Army, Seoul, Republic of Korea, 1989, Tarleton State U. (Tex. A&M U.), Stephenville, Tex., 1994, others; contbr. articles to profl. jours. Mem. NOW (co-director). Named one of Outstanding Young Women of Am., 1978, Disting. Alumna, Tex. Woman's U. Mem. Internat. Sculpture Ctr., Artist Trust. Office: 339 NW 82nd St Seattle WA 98117-4033

SMITH, MARCIA JEAN, accountant, tax specialist, financial consultant; b. Kansas City, Mo., Oct. 19, 1947; d. Eugene Hubert and Marcella Juanita (Greene) S. Student, U. Nebr., 1965-67; BA, Jersey City State Coll., 1971; MBA in Taxation, Golden Gate U., 1976, postgrad., 1976-77; MS in Acctg., Pace U., 1982; Cert. of completion, Cours Commerciaux de Geneve, 1985-86. Legal intern Port Authority, N.Y., N.J., N.Y.C., 1972; legis. aide to Senator Harrison A. Williams Washington, 1973; tax accountant Bechtel Corp., San Francisco, 1974-77; sr. tax accountant Equitable Life Assurance Soc. U.S., N.Y.C., 1977, sec., 1977-79; tax sr. Arthur Andersen & Co., N.Y.C., 1979-82; pres. M.J. Smith Co., N.Y.C., 1983-85; prin. owner MJS Cons. Svcs. Internat. Tax Cons., Boston, Mass., 1988-93; gen. auditor dept. fin. Fulton County Govt., Atlanta, 1993—; cons. U.N., specialized agys., Geneva, 1985-87; asst. sec. Equico Lessors, Inc., Mpls., 1977-78, Equitable Gen. Ins. Group, Ft. Worth, 1977-79, Heritage Life Infield Assurance Co., Toronto, Ont., Can., 1978-79, Informatics, Inc., L.A., 1978-79; sec. Equico Capital Corp., N.Y.C. 1977-79, Equico Personal Credit, Inc., Colorado Springs, Colo., 1978-79, Equico Securites, Inc., N.Y.C., 1977-79, Equitable Environ. Health, Inc., Woodbury, N.Y., 1977-79; tax cons., real estate salesperson. Spl. advisor U.S. Congl. Adv. Bd.; human rights chmn. YWCA, Lincoln, Nebr., 1966-67. Recipient Certificate of Recognition, Central Mo. State Coll., 1965, Unicameral award State Neb., 1967, Mary McLeod Bethune award Jersey City State Coll., 1971. Mem. AAAS, AAUW, NAA (Swiss Romande chpt.), Am. Mgmt. Assn., Nat. Soc. Pub. Accts., Inst. Mgmt. Accts., Am. Acctg. Assn., Internat. Assn. Fin. Planners, Internat. Fin. Mgmt. Assn., Am. Women's Club of Geneva, Nat. Assn. Women Bus. Owners, Am. Assn. Individual Investors, Assn. Gov. Accts., Assn. Cert. Fraud Examiners, Ga. Soc. Cert. Public Accts., Inst. Internal Auditors, N.Y. Acad. Scis., Nat. Hist. Soc., Nat. Assn. Tax Practitioners, Assn. Managerial Economists, Postal Commemorative Soc., Am. Mus. Natural History, Nat. Trust Historic Preservation, Ga. Govt. Fin. Officers Assn., Internat. Tax Inst., Ga. Soc. CPAs, Assn. Cert. Fraud Examiners, Assn. Govt. Accts., Am. Econs. Assn., UN Assn. USA, EDP Auditors Assn., Mass. Soc. Ind. Accts., Acad. Legal Studies in Bus., Am. Bus. Law Assn., Internat. Platform Assn., U.S. Senatorial Club. Office: Fulton County Finance Peachtree Ctr Box 56253 Atlanta GA 30343-0253

SMITH, MARCIA SUE, government official; b. Greenfield, Mass., Feb. 22, 1951; d. Sherman Kenneth and Shirley Fay (Schafer) S. BA, Syracuse U., 1972. Adminstrv. asst., corr. AIAA, Washington, 1973-75; analyst in aerospace and energy tech. Sci. Policy Research div. Congressional Research Service, Library of Congress, Washington, 1975-80, specialist in aerospace and telecommunications systems, 1980-85; exec. dir. Nat. Commn. on Space, Washington, 1985-86; specialist in aerospace policy, Congl. Research Service, Washington, 1986-91, sect. head space and def. techs., 1988-91, specialist sci. and tech. policy, 1991—, acting asst. chief sci. policy rsch. divsn., 1993; mem. com. human exploration space studies bd. U.S. NAS, 1992-93. Mem. editorial bd. Space Policy, Space Commerce; contbg. editor Air & Space mag.; author reports and articles. Fellow Brit. Interplanetary Soc., AIAA (disting. lectr. 1983-88, internat. activities com.); mem. Women in Aerospace (emeritus, founder, pres. 1987, bd. dirs. 1984-90), Internat. Acad. Astronautics (co-chair space activities and soc com. 1991—), Internat. Inst. Space Law, N.Y. Acad. Scis. (life), Washington Acad. Sci. (life), Sigma Xi (life). Office: CRS/SPRD Library of Congress Washington DC 20540-7490

SMITH, MARGARET, state legislator; b. Chgo.; m. Fred J. Smith; 2 sons, (dec.). Student, Tenn. State U. Mem. Ill. Ho. of Reps., 1981-83; mem. Ill. Senate, dist. 12, 1983—. Trustee Chgo. Bapt. Inst. Democrat. Office: State Senate State Capital Springfield IL 62706 Address: 4949 N Melvina Ave Chicago IL 60630-2907*

SMITH, MARGARET ANN, health care executive; b. Marshall, Ark., May 17, 1951; d. Vernon J. and Helen M. (Talbert) Sorensen; m. Rodney J. Smith, Aug. 24, 1969 (div.); children: Shannon Denette, Rodrick Cannon. Cert. patient accounts mgr. Coord. cen. registration Community Gen. Osteo. Hosp., Harrisburg, Pa., 1979-83; supr. patient accounts The Gettysburg (Pa.) Hosp., 1983-84; dir. patient accounts Polyclinic Med. Ctr., Harrisburg, 1984-87; sr. cons. Arthur Young & Co., Washington, 1987-89; asst. v.p. bus. svc. Regional Healthcare Systems, Inc., Brooksville, Fla., 1989—. Mem. Soc. of Patient Accounts Mgmt., Am. Guild of Patient Accounts Mgmt., Nat. Assn. Hosp. Admitting Mgrs., Keystone Assn. Patient Accounts Mgrs. (Outstanding Mem. 1985-87). Republican. Home: 1506 June Ave Brooksville FL 34601-3929 Office: Regional Healthcare Sys Brooksville FL 34601

SMITH, MARGARET BRAND, insurance executive, lawyer; b. Chattanooga, Okla., June 29, 1911; d. William August and Flora May (Davis) Brand; m. Harry Eben Smith, July 24, 1937 (dec. 1970). LLB, Jefferson Sch. Law, Dallas. Pvt. practice, also ins. cos. atty. Dallas, 1937-57; exec. v.p. Union Bankers Ins. Co., Dallas, 1957-62, pres., chief exec. officer, 1962-68, vice chair, 1968-73; pres., chief exec. officer United Gen. Ins. Co., Dallas, 1973-76; chmn. bd. Dallas Gen. Life Ins. Co., Dallas, 1980—. Pres. Dallas Girl Scouts, 1952; bd. dirs., pres. Presbyn. Children's Home, Waxahachie, Tex., 1970-76; elder North Park Presbyn. Ch., Dallas, 1972-76. Recipient Top Hat award Nat. Assn. Bus. and Profl. Women, Chgo., 1963, Award of Excellence Dallas Bus. and Profl. Women, 1964, Mature Woman award Altrusa Club, 1965, Woman of Awareness B'nai B'rith, 1965, Outstanding Svc. award North Dallas Bus. and Profl. Women, 1969. Mem. State Bar of Tex., Dallas Bar Assn. Republican. Presbyterian.

SMITH, MARGARET LACY, counselor; b. Birmingham, Ala., Jan. 25, 1950; d. Harold Bert and Elizabeth Verdeer (Wall) S. BS in Edn., Troy (Ala.) State U., 1972; MS in Sch. Counseling, Troy State U. at Montgomery, 1976. Math. tchr. Dunwoody (Ga.) High Sch.; counselor East Hall High Sch., Gainesville, Ga.; tchr. Gainesville Jr. Coll., Oakwood, Ga.; counselor, tchr. St. James Sch., Montgomery, Ala.; math. tchr. Prattville (Ala.) High Sch.; counselor Stanhope Elmore High Sch., Millbrook, Ala. Mem. Ala. Sch. Counselors Assn. (sec. 1987-88, pres. 1988-89), Ala. Counseling Assn. (pres.-elect 1994—), Civitan Internat. (gov. Ala., West Fla. dist. 1991-92). Office: Stanhope Elmore High Sch 4300 Main St Millbrook AL 36054

SMITH, MARGARET PHYLLIS, editor, consultant; b. Plymouth, Pa., Aug. 24, 1925; d. Harold Dewitt and Mae Elmira (Bittenbender) S. AB magna cum laude, Bucknell U., 1946, AM, 1947; postgrad., U. Pa., summer 1951-54. Instr. English Bucknell U., Lewisburg, Pa., 1947-52, asst. prof., 1952-55; personnel asst. RCA Labs., Princeton, N.J., 1955-58, staff writer pub. affairs dept., 1958-76, adminstr. communications, 1976-87; editor spl. projects David Sarnoff Rsch. Ctr. (formerly RCA Labs.), Princeton, 1987-92, contbg. editor, 1992—; mng. editor Vision mag. David Sarnoff Rsch. Ctr., 1987—, editor UPDATE newsletter, 1969—. Editor: 1942-67 Twenty-five Years at RCA Laboratories, 1968. Mem. corp. communications com. United Way, Princeton, 1976-88. Mem. AAUW, N.J. Press Women (publicity dir. 1985-86), Internat. Assn. Bus. Communicators. Episcopalian. Office: David Sarnoff Rsch Ctr 201 Washington Rd Princeton NJ 08540-6449

SMITH, MARGARET WALKER (MAGGIE SMITH), artist; b. Summerville, S.C., Sept. 10, 1917; d. Lawrence Adams and Margaret Winans (Buswell) Walker; m. Arthur Rockwell Smith, Nov. 23, 1951; children: Margaret McAvoy, Ellen, Lawrence. BS in English, Coll. of Charleston, 1938; student, Art Students League, 1939-41. Textile designer M. Lowenstein & Co., N.Y.C., 1950-51; tchr. art history and studio art South Kent (Conn.) Sch., 1973-79. Work exhibited in various juried shows including Kent Art Assn. 1975—, Housatonic Art League, New Milford, Conn., 1982—. Vol. tchr, adult painting classes Kent Ctr. Sch., 1986—. Recipient Blue ribbon Temple Israel, Waterbury, Conn., 1979. Mem. Nat. Assn. Profl. Artists, Nat. League of Am. Pen Women, Mus. Wowen in the Arts, Kent Art Assn. (mem. bd. dirs. 1980, exhbn. com., sec. 1980,), Washington Art. Assn., Sheffield Art League, Housatonic Art League (many awards 1982-92), Printmakers of Cape Cod, Kent Bridge Gallery. Episcopalian. Home and Office: 38 Studio Hill Kent CT 06757

SMITH, MARGHERITA, writer, editor; b. Chgo., May 24, 1922; d. Henry Christian and Alicia (Koke) Steinhoff; m. Rufus Zartman Smith, June 26, 1943; children: Matthew Benjamin, Timothy Rufus. AB, Ill. Coll., 1943. Proofreader Editorial Experts, Inc., Alexandria, Va., 1974; mgr. proofreading div. Editorial Experts, Inc., Alexandria, 1978-79, mgr. publs. div., 1979-81, asst. to pres., 1980-81; freelance editor, cons. Annandale, Va., 1981—; instr. proofreading and copy editing, George Washington U., Washington, 1978-82; presenter workshops on proofreading for various profl. orgns., 1981—. Author: (as Peggy Smith) Simplified Proofreading, 1980, rev. edit., 1994, Proofreading Manual and Reference Guide, 1981, Proofreading Workbook, 1981, The Proof Is In the Reading: A Comprehensive Guide to Staffing and Management of Typographic Proofreading, 1986, Mark My Words: Instructions and Practice in Proofreading, 1987, rev. edit., 1993; contbr. articles and revs. to various publs. Recipient Best Instrnl. Reporting award Newsletter Assn. Am., 1980, Disting. Achievement award for excellence in ednl. journalism Ednl. Press Assn. Am., 1981, Disting. Citizen award Ill. Coll., 1992. Home and Office: 9120 Belvoir Woods Pky #103 Fort Belvoir VA 22060-2722

SMITH, MARILYN JEAN, management analyst; b. Salt Lake City, June 2, 1968; d. Dee Grant and Janet Irene (Smith) Laws; m. Steve Vernon Smith, Dec. 28, 1985; children: Christopher Grant, Daniel Steven. AS, Coll. Ea. Utah, 1988; BS in Polit. Sci., Weber State U., 1990; postgrad., U. Utah. Legis. intern Utah State Legislature, Salt Lake City, 1989; planning intern Layton (Utah) City Corp., 1989-90; rsch. and planning analyst Salt Lake County Commn., Salt Lake City, 1990-92, mgmt. analyst, 1992-95; adminstrv. analyst Davis County Commn., Farmington, Vt., 1995—. Candidate Utah State House Dist. 11, Weber/Davis Counties, 1994; co-chair Caring for Kids Parent Adv. Bd., Salt Lake City, 1991-94; active Roosevelt PTA, Washington Terrace, Utah, 1992—, Citizen Budget Com., Washington Terrace, 1993. Scholar Mt. Am. CU/UPEA, 1992. Mem. Am. Soc. for Pub. Adminstrs., Am. Polit. Sci. Assn., Weber State Alumni Assn. (exec. coun.), Pi Sigma Alpha, Pi Gamma Mu. Democrat. Mormon. Home: 228 E 5000 S Ogden UT 84405 Office: Salt Lake County Commn # N3003 2001 S State Salt Lake City UT 84190

SMITH, MARILYN LYNNE, small business owner; b. Atlanta, Oct. 15, 1944; d. Odis Madre and Anne Katherine (Luetje) S.; m. Robert H. Jackson, Aug. 21, 1965 (div. 1970); m. William Howard Gamble, July 31, 1970 (div. 1980); children: John Robert Jackson, Benjamin Lewis Gamble. Student, Ga. State U., Atlanta, 1962-65. Bookkeeper Haas, Holland et al, Atlanta, 1963-69; office/bus. mgr. Dr. W. H. Gamble, Jr., Atlanta, 1970-73; placement councillor Amcell div. Norrell, Atlanta, 1973-74; bus. mgr. Dr. W. H. Gamble, Jr., Atlanta, 1974-79; owner Atlanta Document Svc., 1980—; co-owner Atlanta Med. Documents, 1991—. Sponsor Explorer Scout Post, Tucker, Ga., 1987. Named Counsellor of the Yr., Norrell Southeastern Corp., 1974. Mem. Ga. Assn. Personnel Cons. (treas. 1982-84), Women's Commerce Club. Republican. Baptist. Office: Atlanta Document Svcs 1750 Peachtree St NW Atlanta GA 30309-2333

SMITH, MARILYNN JANE, librarian; b. South Bend, Ind., July 30, 1944; d. Lloyd Arthur and Helen Geraldine Gerst (Bryant) Unger; m. Richard Lee Smith, Dec. 19, 1965; children: Charles David, Michael Lee. BA in French, English Edn., Cen. Mich. U., 1966; MA in French, U. S.C., 1969; MS in Libr. Sci., U. Ill., 1974, PhD in Comparative Lit., 1973. Tchr. Fletcher Prep Sch., Barrington, R.I., 1966-67; with U. Ill. Librs., Urbana, 1970-74; ref. bibliographer U. Ala., Birmingham, 1974-77; vis. asst. prof. English Coll. Charleston (S.C.), 1977-79; ref. librarian Bapt. Coll. Libr., Charleston, 1979-80; temp. asst. prof. comparative lit. U. Ga., Athens, 1983-85, instr. comparative lit. evening classes, 1981—; librarian Navy Supply Corps Sch., Athens, 1987—. Contbr. articles to profl. jours.; contbr. to biog. dictionary: Brit. Women Writers, 1988. Recipient Armed Forces Librs. Round Table NewsBank Scholarship award, 1992. Mem. MLA, ALA, Am. Comparative Lit. Assn., Ga. Libr. Assn., Armed Forces Librs. Round Table. Home: 285 Kings Rd Athens GA 30606-3111 Office: Navy Supply Corps Sch Athens GA 30606-5000

SMITH, MARJORIE AILEEN MATTHEWS, museum director; b. Richmond, Va., Aug. 19, 1918; d. Harry Anderson and Adelia Charlotte (Howland) Matthews; m. Robert Woodrow Smith, July 23, 1945 (dec. Mar. 1992). Pilot lic., Taneytown (Md.) Aviation Svc., 1944, cert. ground sch. instr., 1945. Founder, editor, pub. Spinning Wheel, Taneytown, 1945-63; v.p. Antiques Publs., Inc., Taneytown, 1960-68; pres. Prism Inc., Taneytown, 1968-78; mus. dir. Trapshooting Hall of Fame, Vandalia, Ohio, 1976—, sec., 1993—. Co-author: Handbook of Tomorrow's Antiques, 1954; contbr. articles to profl. publs. Sec. Balt. area coun. Girl Scouts USA, 1950. Named to All-Am. Trapshooting team Sports Afield mag., 1960, 61. Mem. Nat. League Am. Pen Women, Amateur Trapshooting Assn. (life), Am. Contract Bridge League, Internat. Assn. Sports Mus. and Halls of Fame (bd. dirs. 1993-94). Lutheran. Office: Trapshooting Hall of Fame 601 W National Rd Vandalia OH 45377

SMITH, MARSHA H., state agency administrator, lawyer; b. Boise, Idaho, Mar. 24, 1950; d. Eugene F. and Joyce (Ross) Hatch; m. Terrell F. Smith, Aug. 29, 1970; 2 children. BS in Biology/Edn., Idaho State U., 1973; MLS, Brigham Young U., 1975; JD, U. Wash., 1980. Dep. atty. gen. Bus./Consumer Protection Divsn., Boise, 1980-81; dep. atty. gen. Idaho Pub. Utilities Commn., Boise, 1981-89, dir. policy and external rels., 1989-91, commr., 1991, pres., 1991—. Legis. dist. chair Ada County Democrats, Idaho, 1986-89. Mem. Nat. Assn. Regulatory Utility Commrs. (vice chair electric strategic issues subcom.), Idaho State Bar, Western Conf. Pub. Svc. Commrs. Office: Idaho Pub Utilities Commn PO Box 83720 Boise ID 83720-0074

SMITH, MARTHA JILL, career development professional, counselor; b. Bryan, Ohio, Dec. 13, 1959; d. Stanley Robert and Wanda Marie (Winter) S. BA in Comm., Bowling Green State U., 1982; MS in Counselor Edn., Ind. U., 1992. Fleet coord., supr. N.Am. Van Lines, Ft. Wayne, Ind., 1983-88; resident dir. Huntington (Ind.) Coll., 1988-91, dir. career devel., 1991—. Mem. Am. Counseling Assn., Ind. Counseling Assn., Nat. Career Devel. Assn. Republican. Office: Huntington Coll 2303 College Ave Huntington IN 46750

SMITH, MARY ALICE See ALICE, MARY

SMITH, MARY ALICE, toxicologist; b. Bowdon, Ga., Jan. 1, 1949; d. Oswell Buren and Ellen Myrtis (Gibbs) Smith; m. Dale Milton Tidwell, Oct. 9, 1971 (div. Nov. 15, 1980); m. Richard Marion Prior, May 16, 1990. BS, Auburn U., 1971; MA in Teaching, Emory U., 1976, MS, 1980; PhD, U. Ark. for Med. Scis., Little Rock, 1990. Registered hazardous substance profl. Tchr. sci. Louisville City Schs., 1971-72; tchr. biology DeKalb County Schs., Decatur, Ga., 1972-77; grad. teaching asst. Emory U., Atlanta, 1977-80, rsch. technician, 1981-85, rsch. assoc., 1989-91; grad. rsch. asst. U. Ark. for Med. Scis., Little Rock, 1985-89; sr. scientist/toxicologist Law Environ., Inc., Atlanta, 1991-93; cons. DynCorp PRI and Pvt., Atlanta, 1993; asst. prof. toxicology U. Ga., Athens, 1993—; cons. in field; adj. asst. prof. Emory U., Atlanta, 1993—. Contbr. articles to profl. jours. Mem. Nat. Dem. Com., Atlanta, 1992-94. Grantee Hoffman LaRouche Found., 1988, Air Force Office Sci. Rsch., 1988. Mem. Teratology Soc., Assn. of Women in Sci. (Atlanta chpt. pres. 1993-94), Soc. of Toxicology (southeastern sect.). Democrat. Unitarian-Universalist. Office: Univ of Georgia 206 Dairy Sci Bldg Athens GA 30602

SMITH, MARY ANN, school administrator; b. Chgo., July 12, 1938; d. Anthony J. and Florence B. (Berendt) Lewandowski; m. Carl Eugene Smith, June 10, 1972. BA, St. Xavier Coll., Chgo., 1960; MEd, Loyola U., Chgo., 1970; Adminstrn. Cert., Northwestern U., Evanston, Ill., 1980. Nat. cert. counselor. Tchr. Visitation High Sch., Chgo., 1960-63; dir. of student activities Mt. Sinai Sch. of Nursing, Chgo., 1963-66; sch. counselor Marywood Sch., Evanston, Ill., 1966-68; sch. counselor Downers Grove (Ill.) South High Sch., 1968-89, dir. guidance, 1989—; cons. Total Community Devel., Downer's Grove, 1993. Contbg. author: Students and Alcohol, 1979. Vol. Health and Human Resources, Downers Grove, 1980-81. Recipient Those Who Excel award State of Ill. Bd. Edn., 1991. Mem. Ill. Assn. Coll. Admission Counselors (bd. dirs., chair various coms. 1980-88), Nat. Assn. Coll. Admission Counselors, Coll. Bd., ASCD, Am. Counselor Assn. Office: Downers Grove South HS 1436 Norfolk St Downers Grove IL 60516-2632

SMITH, MARY ASKEW BACKER, librarian, retired; b. Cin., Jan. 26, 1897; d. Matthew Jackson and Martha Goldsborough (Henry) Askew; m. John William Backer, Sept. 11, 1920 (dec. Feb. 1948); children: Mary Elizabeth Backer Hubbard, John Matthew; m. Russell Evans Smith, Aug. 9, 1969 (dec.). BA, U. Cin., 1918; libr. cert., U. Wis., 1919; MA, John Hopkins U., 1953. Profl. asst. N.Y. Pub. Libr., N.Y.C., 1919-20; br. libr. Enoch Pratt Free Libr., Balt., 1943-64; instr. Catonsville (Md.) Community Coll., 1967-68. Author: (booklet) The College Club-A History of the Baltimore Branch of the American Association of University Women, 1981; contbr. articles to profl. jours. Pres. AAUW Balt. br., 1964-66, Legis. Clearing House of Md., Balt., 1981-82. Mem. Md. Libr. Assn. Republican. Methodist.

SMITH, MARY ELINOR, retired dean, mathematics educator, counselor; b. Louisville, Dec. 18, 1913; d. Harry Robert and Susan Magdalene (Corrigan) S. AA, Sacred Heart Jr. Coll., Louisville, 1933; BA, Nazareth Coll., 1935; postgrad., U. Minn., summers 1937-39; MA, Cath. U. Am., 1951. Tchr. math. Jefferson County Schs., Medora, Ky., 1935-36; substitute tchr. Louisville Pub. Schs., 1936-37, tchr. math., 1937-44; hosp. staff aide ARC, 1944-45; caseworker Jefferson County Children's Home, Louisville, 1946-48; dean women, lectr. Quincy (Ill.) Coll., 1950-52; dean women, lectr. Cath. U., Washington, 1952-71, assoc. dean counseling and svcs., 1971-79; ret., 1979; scholarship evaluator AAUW, Washington, 1975-79, Youth for Understanding, Washington, 1980-86; conf. lectr. Barry U., Miami Shores, Fla., 1990. Chair Task Force on AIDS, Spalding U., Louisville, 1988-89; bd. trustees Ursuline Campus Schs., Inc., Louisville, 1990-92. Recipient Cert. of Appreciation, Black Students of Cath. U., 1977, Frank A. Kunz Alumni award Cath. U., 1978, Outstanding Svc. Appreciation award Undergrad. Student Govt., Cath. U., 1978-79, Citation, Nat. Assn. Women Deans, Adminstrs., Counselors, 1979, Citation, Pres. and Bd. Trustees of Cath. U., 1952-79; Mary Elinor Smith Community Svc. award, 1980—, Caritas award Spalding U., 1985. Mem. APA, Women's Overseas Svc. League (treas. 1991-92), Ky. Ch. Myasthenia Gravis Found., Louisville Geneal. Soc. (city/county chair 1989-90), Spalding U. Alumni Assn., Ursuline Acad. Alumnae Assn., Filson Club. Democrat. Roman Catholic. Home: 2126 Village Dr Apt 2 Louisville KY 40205-1940

SMITH, MARY HOWARD HARDING, business consultant; b. Washington, Jan. 24, 1944; d. John Edward Harding and Sonja (Karlow) Harding Mulroney. AB, Duke U., 1965; MPA, Cen. Mich. U., 1975. With U.S. Army, 1968-91; dir. program mgmt. systems devel. agy. U.S. Army, Washington, 1987-91, dep. dir. program analysis and evaluation, 1987-91; dep. dir. def. info. Office Sec. Def., Arlington, Va., 1991-94; pres. Enterprise Opportunities, Inc., Arlington, Va., 1994—. Contbr. numerous articles to profl. jours. Bd. dirs. Army Family Action Symposiu, Washington, 1982. Mem. Am. Soc. Mil. Comptrollers, NAFE. Home and Office: 1805 24th St S Arlington VA 22202-1534

SMITH, MARY LOU BRAUN, psychiatric-mental health nurse; b. Burlington, Iowa, Oct. 3, 1935; m. Jack E. Smith, Feb. 12, 1966; children: Susan, Michael. Diploma, Mercy Hosp. Sch. Nursing, Davenport, Iowa, 1956; BSN, St. Ambrose Coll., Davenport, 1959; MA in Nursing, U. Iowa, 1971. RN, Iowa; cert. psychiat.-mental health nurse. Asst. prof. nursing U. Iowa, Iowa City, 1972-79; instr. psychiat. nursing Indian Hills Community Coll., Ottumwa, Iowa, 1983-84; clin. supr. psychiatry Burlington Med. Ctr., 1985; surveyor health facilities State of Iowa, Des Moines, 1985—. Contbr. articles to nursing jours. Named Iowa Surveyor of Yr., Iowa Dept. Inspections and Appeals, 1990. Mem. Am. Psychiat. Nurses Assn., Sigma Theta Tau. Home: 2616 Hickory Ave Mount Pleasant IA 52641

SMITH, MARY PERKINS, interior designer; b. Wytheville, Va., July 9, 1949; d. Cooper Kunkel Perkins and Mary Christian (Garth) Gentry; m. Roger Wayne Baiers, Sept. 7, 1968 (div. 1984); children: Christine Leigh, Brian Leslie. Student, LaSalle U., 1977, Rutledge Coll., 1987. Interior decorator Town Sq. Interiors, Radford, Va., 1978-81; mgr. Tupperware Home Parties, Roanoke, Va., 1981-86; patient account analyst Wesley Long Community Hosp., Greensboro, N.C., 1987-90. Mem. Blue Ridge Jr. Womens Club (designer dist. crest 1973), Southwestern Va. Jr. Womens Club (designer dist. crest 1973). Methodist. Office: 5022-4 Hunt Club Rd Wilmington NC 28403

SMITH, MARYA JEAN, writer; b. Youngstown, Ohio, Nov. 12, 1945; d. Cameron Reynolds and Jean Rose (Sause) Argetsinger; m. Arthur Beverly Smith Jr., Dec. 30, 1968; children: Arthur Cameron, Sarah Reynolds. BA, Cornell U., 1967. Editorial asst. Seventeen Mag., N.Y.C., 1967-68; promotion writer U. Chgo. Press, 1968-70; asst. account exec. Drucilla Handy Co., Chgo., 1970-72; feature writer various mags. Chgo., 1972-74; freelance writer Cornell U., Ithaca, N.Y., 1975-76, lectr., 1976-77; playwright Playwrights' Ctr. Prodn., Chgo., 1978; humor columnist various jours. Chgo., 1979-81, freelance writer, 1982—. Author: Across the Creek, 1989, Winter-Broken, 1990, Danish edit., 1991; contbr. poetry Primavera, Ariel VI and VIII, 1974, 87, 89; contbr. articles to mags. and papers, 1984—. Vol. reading tutor Literacy Vols. Western Cook County, Oak Park, Ill., 1988-89, Oak Park Pub. Libr. Reading Program, 1990-94. Recipient 1st Pl. for News Writing Associated Ch. Press, 1986, Poetry award Poets and Patrons, 1986, Triton Coll. Salute to Arts, 1987, 89. Mem. Nat. Writers Union, Soc. Children's Book Writers, Author's Guild, Chgo. Women in Pub., Children's Reading Round Table. Roman Catholic.

SMITH, MAUREEN MCBRIDE, chemist; b. Santa Monica, Calif., Mar. 4, 1952; d. Clayton Laird McBride and Luella (Sullivan) Boudreau; step-father Henry A Boudreau; m. Gary Howard Cothran, July 27, 1974 (div. Apr. 1982); m. Guy Gordon Smith, Feb. 12, 1983; stepchildren: Keri Lynn, Scott Allen. BS magna cum laude, Calif. State Coll., San Bernardino, 1978, MS, 1993. Analytical chemist Chalco Engring., Edwards AFB, Calif., 1978-79, 82; microbiol. lab. tech. AVEK Water Agy., Quartz Hill, Calif., 1979-81, chemist, lab. mgr., 1982—; instr. Antelope Valley Coll., Lancaster Calif., 1980-82. Mem. AAAS, Am. Chem. Soc. Office: Antelope Valley E Kern Water Agy PO Box 3176 Quartz Hill CA 93586-0176

SMITH, MELANIE A., graphic designer, educator; b. Akron, Ohio, Oct. 12, 1963; d. Alfred Russell and Regina Deanne (Morris) S. Grad. in English and Edn., Wittenberg U., 1985; student, Colo. Inst. Art, 1987-88, U. Denver, 1991. Editor Am. Ski Assn., Denver, 1988-91; owner, designer Imeo Design Studio, Denver, 1991—; instr. graphic design Colo. Inst. Art, Denver, 1992—. Designer (book) Stained Glass Rain, 1993, Intelligent Scheduling, 1994, (calendar) 1995 Weather Guide Calendar, 1994, (corp. ID) Cody Brand Sunglasses, 1994. Mem. Art Dirs. Club Denver. Office: Imeo Design Studio 7144 E 4th Ave Denver CO 80220-6134

SMITH, MELINDA RUTH, writer, editor; b. Ponca City, Okla., June 17, 1960; d. Monte Gene and Dorothy Worthington Smith; m. Sanford Marble. BA with high hons., U. Tex., 1984. Mktg. Data Base Publs., Austin, Tex., 1986-87; assoc. editor Austin Area Bus. Women Directory, 1987-88; asst. pub. Travelers' Times, Austin, 1988-89; assoc. editor Tex. Bar Jour., Austin, 1989—; freelance editor, Austin, 1989—. Contbr. articles to newspapers and profl. jours. Mem. comms. com. Tex. Women C. of C., Austin, 1987-89; mem. Nat. Dem. Com., Washingtin, 1992-95, Amnesty Internat., 1992-95. Recipient Gold Quill award of merit Internat. Assn. Bus. Communicators, 1993, Best of Austin 4 Color Mag. award, 1993, 2 awards of merit, 1995, Presdl. Citation, State Bar of Tex., 1993, Nat. Assn. Govt. Communicators award of Honor 4 Color Mag., 1994. Office: Tex Bar Jour/State of Tex 1414 Colorado St Ste 312 Austin TX 78701-1627

SMITH, MELODIE DAWN, marketing professional; b. Albany, Oreg., July 23, 1963; d. Jerome Stafford and Elaine Maureen (Rohde) S. BA in Comm. Scis. and Mktg., U. Conn., 1985. With sales dept. NCR Corp., Richmond, Va., 1985-88; dist. mgr. NCR Corp., Phila., 1989-91; strategic mktg. cons.

AT&T (formerly NCR, Corp.); cons. Arbonne Internat., Portland, 1992—; network mktg. specialist IDN/Nu-Skin Internat., 1994—. Home: 5736 SW Illinois Portland OR 97210 Office: AT&T/NCR 5736 SW Illinois Portland OR 97210

SMITH, MERILYN ROBERTA, art educator; b. Tolley, N.D., July 24, 1933; d. Robert Coleman and Mathilda Marie (Staael) S. BA, Concordia Coll., Minn., 1953; MA, State U. of Iowa, Iowa City, 1956, MFA, 1966. Tchr. Badger (Minn.) High Sch., 1954; instr. in art Valley City (N.D.) State Tchrs. Coll., 1957, 58; instr. in art U. Wis., Oshkosh, 1967, asst. prof. art, 1969, assoc. prof., 1977-91, prof., 1991-93, prof. emeritus, 1993—; represented by Miriam Perlman Gallery, Chgo.; counselor Luth. Student Ctr., U. Iowa, 1959-65, rsch. asst. in printmaking, 1960-65; owner, dir. James House Gallery, Oshkosh, 1972-77; dir. Allen Priebe Gallery, U. Wis., Oshkosh, 1975. Exhibited in group shows at N.W. Printmakers Internat., Seattle and Portland, Oreg., 1964, Ultimate Concerns 6th Nat. Exhbn., Athens, Ohio, 1965, 55th Nat. Exhbn., Springfield, Mass., 1974, 11th An. So. Tier Arts and Crafts, Corning, N.Y., 1974, Soc. of the Four Arts, Palm Beach, Fla., 1974, Appalachian Nat. Drawing Competition, Boone, N.C., 1975, Rutgers Nat. Drawing Exhbn., Camden, N.J., 1975, 8th and 9th Biennial Nat. Art Exhibit, Valley City, N.D., 1973, 75, Clary-Miner Gallery, Buffalo, 1988, Nat. Art Show, Redding, Calif., 1989, Internat. Printmaker, Buffalo, 1990, Westmoreland Nat. Juried Competition, Youngwood, Pa., 1990, Ariel Gallery, Soho, N.Y., 1990, Grand Prix de Paris Internat., Chapelle De La Sorbonne, Paris, 1990, Nat. Juried Exhbn., Rockford, Ill., 1991, Nat. Invitational Exhbn., Buffalo, 1991, East Coast Artists Nat. Invitational Art Exhbn., Havre de Grace, Md., 1991, Ariel Gallery, Soho, N.Y., 1991, N.Y. Art Expo, 1991, Milw. Art for AIDS Auction, 1991, 92, 94. Mem. Winnebago Hist. Soc., Oshkosh, 1987—. Lutheran. Home: 226 High Ave Oshkosh WI 54901-4734 Office: U Wis Dept Art Oshkosh WI 54901

SMITH, MICHELE, lawyer; b. Ogden, Utah, Feb. 12, 1955; d. Max S. and Grace B. (Gerstman) Smith; m. Philip A. Turner, Aug. 25, 1985. BA, SUNY, Buffalo, 1976; JD, U. Chgo., 1979. Law clk. U.S. Ct. Appeals (7th cir.), Chgo., 1979-81; asst. atty. no. dist. U.S. Atty's Office, Chgo., 1981-89; sr. counsel Navistar Internat. Transportation Corp., Chgo., 1989—. Mem. Am. Corp. Counsel Assn., Phi Beta Kappa. Office: Navistar Internat Transp Corp 455 CityFront Plz Dr Chicago IL 60611

SMITH, MILDRED CASSANDRA, systems engineer; b. Rocky Mount, N.C.; d. Naaman and Mildred (Laws) Foster; m. Edward B. Smith III, July 22, 1967 (div. 1976); children: Camille Eileen, Regina Dar. BA, Howard U., 1966; MS, Georgetown U., 1973, PHD, 1979. Cert. computer programmer. Programmer IBM Corp., Gaithersburg, Md., 1966-76; asst. prof. Howard U., Washington, 1976-80; engr./analyst VITRO Corp., Silver Spring, Md., 1980-82; analyst U.S. Dept. Agriculture, Washington, 1983-86; systems engr. MITRE Corp., McLean, Va., 1986—. Contbr. article to Software Reengring. Vol. D.C. Pub. Schs., 1978-80; judge Alice Deal Jr. High Sci. Fair, Washington, 1987; mentor corp. engring. enrichment program T.C. Williams High Sch., 1991. Named one of Outstanding Young Women Am., 1977, 78. Mem. D.C. Assn. for Computing Machinery (chmn. local interest group on mgmt. of data 1989—), Assn. for Computing Machinery, Assn. for Computational Linguistics. Democrat. Presbyterian.

SMITH, NANCY DUVERGNE, editor, writer, educator; b. Meridian, Miss., Mar. 22, 1951; d. Frank Gordin and Edna Henley (Brogan) S.; m. Mark Michael Sirdevan, Oct. 25, 1980; 1 child, Mei Smith Sirdevan. BFA, Tulane U., 1973; M in Liberal Arts, Harvard U., 1989. Newspaper reporter The Meridian (Miss.) Star, 1975-77, 81-82; mng. editor New Age mag., Brookline, Mass., 1978-80; English tchr. Am. Cultural Inst., Alexandria, Egypt, 1981; editorial dir. pub. affairs office Wellesley (Mass.) Coll., 1983—, lectr. writing program, 1989—. Paintings exhibited at Musee des Beaux Arts, 1981; editor NWU Databook, 1988; contbr. articles to mags. Chair adv. bd. Boston Writers Rm., 1990-92; bd. dirs. Artists Found. Mem. AAUP, Women in Communications, Nat. Writers Union (sec.-treas. 1985-89, nat. bd. dirs.), Coun. for Advancement and Support of Edn. (conf. speaker 1988, 89, 92), Nat. Writers United Svcs. Orgn. (sec.-treas.). Democrat. Office: Wellesley Coll 230 Green Wellesley MA 02181

SMITH, NANCY HOHENDORF, sales and marketing executive; b. Detroit, Jan. 30, 1943; d. Donald Gerald and Lucille Marie (Kopp) Hohendorf; m. Richard Harold Smith, Aug. 21, 1978 (div. Jan. 1984). BA, U. Detroit, 1965; MA, Wayne State U., 1969. Customer rep. Xerox Corp., Detroit, 1965-67; mktg. rep. Univ. Microfilms subs. Xerox Corp., Ann Arbor, Mich., 1967-73, mktg. coord., 1973-74, mgr. dir. mktg., 1975-76; mgr. mktg. Xerox Corp., Can., 1976-77; major account mktg. exec. Xerox Corp., Hartford, Conn., 1978-79, New Haven, Conn., 1979-80; account exec. State of N.Y. Xerox Corp., N.Y.C., 1981; N.Y. region mgr. customer support Xerox Corp., Greenwich, Conn., 1982, N.Y. region sales ops. mgr., 1982; State of Ohio account exec. Xerox Corp., Columbus, 1983; new bus. sales mgr. Xerox Corp., Dayton, Ohio, 1983, major accounts sales mgr., 1984; info. systems sales and support mgr., quality specialist Xerox Corp., Detroit, 1985-87, new product launch mgr., ops. quality mgr., 1988, dist. mktg. mgr., 1989-91, major accounts sales mgr., 1992—. Named to Outstanding Young Women of Am., 1968, Outstanding Bus. Woman, Dayton C. of C., 1984, Women's Inner Circle of Achievement, 1990. Mem. NAFE, Am. Mgmt. Assn., Women's Econ. Club Detroit, Detroit Inst. Arts Founders' Soc., Greater Detroit C. of C. Republican. Roman Catholic. Home: 23308 Reynard Dr Southfield MI 48034-6924 Office: Xerox Corp Galleria Officentre Bldg 300 Southfield MI 48034

SMITH, NANCY LYNNE, journalist, real estate agent, public relations consultant; b. San Antonio, July 31, 1947; d. Tillman Louis and Enid Maxine (Woolverton) Brown; m. Allan Roy Jones, Nov. 28, 1969 (div. 1975); 1 dau., Christina Elizabeth Woolverton Jones. BA, So. Meth. U., 1968; postgrad. So. Meth. U., 1969-70, Vanderbilt U., 1964, Ecole Nouvelle de la Suisse Romande, Lausanne, Switzerland, 1962. Tchr. spl. edn. Hot Springs Sch. Dist. (Ark.), 1970-72; reporter, soc. editor Dallas Morning News, 1974-82; soc./celebrity columnist Dallas Times Herald, 1982—; owner, pub. High Soc., Soc. Fax; realtor, Ebby Halliday Realtors; stringer Washington Post, 1978; contbg. editor Ultra mag., Houston, 1981-82, Tex. Woman mag., Dallas, 1979-80, Profl. Woman mag., Dallas, 1979-80; mem. bd. advisors Ultra Mag., 1985—; owner Nancy Smith Pub. Rels. Appeared on TV series Jocelyn's Weekend, Sta. KDFI-TV, 1985. Bd. dirs. TACA arts support orgn., Dallas, 1980—, asst. chmn. custom auction, 1978-83; judge Miss Tex. USA Contest, 1984; bd. dirs. Am. Parkinson Disease Assn. (Dallas chpt.), mem. adv. bd. Cattle Baron's Ball Com., Dallas Symphony Debutante presentations; hon. mem. Dallas Opera Women's Bd., Northwood Inst. Women's Bd., Dallas Symphony League; mem. Friends of Winston Churchill Meml. and Library, Dallas Theatre Ctr. Women's Guild, Childrens' Med. Ctr. Auxiliary; hon. mem. Crystal Charity Ball Com.; mem. Community Council Greater Dallas Community Awareness Goals Com. Impact '88, 1985—; co-chmn. Multiple Sclerosis San Simeon Gala, 1988; celebrity co-chmn. Greer Garson Gala of Hope 1990-91; gala chmn. Greer Garson Gala of Hope for Am. Parkinson's Disease Assn., 1991-93; chmn. gala benefit Northwood U., 1994; co-chmn. star studded stomp Mar. Dimes, 1994; mem. Femmes du Monde com. Dallas Coun. World Affairs. Mem. Soc. Profl. Journalists (v.p. communications 1978-79), Nat. Press Club, Dallas Press Club, DAR, Daus. of Republic of Tex. (registrar 1972), Dallas So. Memorial Assn., Dallas County Heritage Soc., Dallas Mus. Art League, Dallas Opera Guild. Club: Argyle (sec. 1983-84), The 500 (Dallas), Energy. Home: 6324D Bandera Ave Dallas TX 75225-3614 Office: Dallas Times Herald PO Box 2101 Jackson WY 83001-2101

SMITH, NINA MARIA, mental health nurse, administrator, consultant; b. Bethesda, Md., July 15, 1950; d. Albert Henry and Magdalena (Portusach) Geiken; m. Robert John Smith, Nov. 18, 1972; children: Cara Anne, Rachel Marie. ADN, Tarrant County Jr. Coll., 1984; BA in Psychology, U. Md., 1972; MEd, Tex. Christian U., 1990. Charge nurse Psychiat. Inst. Ft. Worth; adolescent program coord. Community Psychiat. Ctr. Oak Bend, Ft. Worth; adminstr. Life Ctrs., Ft. Worth; dir. nursing Community Psychiat. Ctr. Oak Bend, Ft. Worth; adminstr. Total Home Health Care, Ft. Worth; dir. clin. svcs. Mountain Crest Hosp., Ft. Collins, Colo., 1992-94; nat. dir. psychiat. home svcs. Western Med. Svcs., Ft. Collins, 1994—; mem. psychiat. symposium planning com. U. Tex., Arlington. Mem. Am. Psychiat. Nurses Assn., Am. Assn. Partial Hosps., Partial Hosp. Assn. Colo. (pres. 1994-95). Home: 1430 Hilburn Dr Fort Collins CO 80526-3425

SMITH, PAMELA PEARMAN, psychologist; b. Wichita, Kans., Aug. 26, 1958; d. John Bruce and Nancy Lee (Jackson) Pearman; m. David Allen Smith, June 19, 1982; children: Adair, Michael. BA, Duke U., 1980, MEd, 1982, PhD, 1986. Project coord. Model Svcs. program U. N.C., Chapel Hill, 1985-86; coord. child svcs. Johnston County Mental Health Ctr., Smithfield, N.C., 1986-90; prin. Smith & Black Assocs., Durham, N.C., 1990—; cons. psychologist Pride in Carolina, Raleigh, N.C., 1990—. Sec. Johnston County Head Start Policy Coun., Smithfield, 1988-89; sec.-treas. Cmty. Guidance Clinic, Durham, 1990, pres. 1991-94. Recipient cert. of appreciation Durham Jaycees, 1990. Mem. APA, N.C. Psychol. Assn., N.C. Soc. for Clin. Hypnosis, Jr. League (sec. 1994-95), Kappa Delta (pres. alumnae adv. bd. 1980-84). Republican. Presbyterian. Home: 2510 Lanier Pl Durham NC 27705-5006 Office: Smith & Black Assocs 3206 Chapel Hill Rd Ste 200 Durham NC 27707-3606

SMITH, PATRICIA (TRICIA SMITH), state senator; b. Honolulu, 1952; m. Greg Smith; two children. Mem. Oreg. State Senate from 17th dist. Former chairwoman Salem (Oreg.) City Coun. Address: 399 18th St NE Salem OR 97301-4307 Office: Senate House State Capitol Salem OR 97310*

SMITH, PATRICIA ANN, religious organization administrator; b. Strong City, Kans., Oct. 27, 1939; d. Ernest Dale and Zelma Leota (Ziegler) Humbargar; m. David Clarence Smith, Aug. 24, 1958; children: Gregory Allan, Shannon Lynn Smith. Student, Emporia State, 1957-58. Chmn. Christian Women's Club, Overland Park, Kans., 1972-74; chmn. women's ministry Bapt. Women, Overland Park, 1974-76; with Reach Ministry, 1984-86; dir. Second Chance Ministries, Overland Park, 1988—; owner-mgr. The Ark Christian Book Store, Overland Park, 1974-91. Office: Second Chance Ministries PO Box 12265 Shawnee Mission KS 66282-2265

SMITH, PATRICIA ANN, administrative assistant; b. Chattanooga, Sept. 15, 1964; d. Herman Horton and Lula Belle (Brown) Yates; m. Bennie Ray Smith, Sept. 25, 1982; children: Misty Rose, Wendy Ann. Grad., Walker Tech. Inst., 1983. Cert. profl. sec. Sec., receptionist Ctrl. Park Area Office, Chattanooga, 1983-84; wire operator, new accounts clk. E.F. Hutton, Chattanooga, 1984; sec., receptionist Lookout Travel, Chattanooga, 1985-86; sec., transcriptionist Hutcheson Med. Ctr., Ft. Oglethorpe, Ga., 1986-90, adminstrv. asst., 1990—. Mem. Profl. Secs. Internat., Mother of Twins Chattanooga. Baptist. Home: 20 Joe Tike Dr Ringgold GA 30736 Office: Hutcheson Med Ctr 100 Gross Crescent Ft Oglethorpe GA 30742

SMITH, PATRICIA ANN, mental health services professional; b. Dayton, Ohio, Oct. 25, 1950; d. Jerome and Edith A. (Kremer) Brun; m. Douglas K. Smith, Sept. 10, 1971; children: Kristin, Colleen. BA, U. Dayton, 1971; MS, Wright State U., 1978; postgrad., Memphis State U. Nat. cert. counselor; nat. cert. gerontol. counselor. Social worker Montgomery County Welfare Dept., Dayton, 1972; rehab. counselor Ohio Bur. Vocat. Rehab., Dayton, 1972-78, counselor mgr., 1978; geriatric clinician N.E. Community Mental Health Ctr., Memphis, 1987-91, clin. coord., 1991—. Mem. Am. Counseling Assn., Tenn. Counseling Assn., Assn. for Adult Devel. Aging. Home: 8080 Savannah Way Germantown TN 38138 Office: NE Community Mental Health 5515 Shelby Oaks Dr Memphis TN 38134

SMITH, PATRICIA GRACE, government official; b. Tuskegee, Ala., Nov. 10, 1947; d. Douglas and Wilhelmina (Griffin) Jones; m. J. Clay Smith, Jr., June 25, 1983; children—Eugene Douglas, Stager Clay, Michelle L., Michael L. B.A. in English, Tuskegee Inst., 1968; postgrad. Auburn U., 1969-71, Harvard U., 1974, George Washington U., 1983; cert. sr. exec. service 1987; exec. mgmt. tng. devel. assignments Dept. Def., 1986, U.S. Senate Commerce Com., 1987. Instr. Tuskegee Institute, Ala., 1969-71; program mgr. Curber Assocs., Washington, 1971-73; dir. placement Nat. Assn. Broadcasters, Washington, 1973-74, dir. pub. affairs, 1974-77; assoc. producer Group W Broadcasting, Balt., 1977, producer, 1977-78; dir. affiliate relations and programming Sheridan Broadcasting Network, Crystal City, Va., 1978-80; dep. dir. policy, assoc. mng. dir. pub. info. and reference svcs., FCC, Washington, 1992-94, acting assoc. mng. dir., pub. info. and reference svcs., 1994; dep. dir. Office Pub. Affairs, 1994—; assoc. mng. dir. office of coml. space transp., Office of the Sec., U.S. Dept. Transp., 1994—. vice chmn. Nat. Conf. Black Lawyers Task Force on Communications, Washington, 1975-87. Mem. D.C. Donor Project, Nat. Kidney Found., Washington, 1984—; trustee, mem. exec. com., nominating com., youth adv. com. Nat. Urban League, 1976-81; mem. communications com. Cancer Coordinating Council, 1977-84; mem. Braintrust Subcom. on Children's Programming, Congl. Black Caucus, 1976—; mem. adv. bd. Black Arts Celebration, 1978-83; mem. NAACP; mem. journalism and communications adv. council Auburn U., 1976-78; mem. Washington Urban League, 1985—; bd. dirs. Black Film Rev., 1989-91; mem D.C. Commn. on Human Rights, 1986-88, chmn. 1988-91; mem. adv. coun. Nat. Insts. Health, 1992—; mem. bd. advisors The Salvation Army, 1993—. Named Outstanding Young Woman of Yr., Washington, 1975, 78; recipient Sustained Superior Performance award FCC, Washington, 1982-92. Mem. Women in Communications, Inc. (mem. nat. adv. com.), Lambda Iota Tau. Club: Broadcasters (bd. dirs. 1976-77). Democrat. Baptist. Avocations: writing, swimming. Home: 4010 16th St NW Washington DC 20011-7002 Office: DOT/OCST 400 7th St Rm 5415 Washington DC 20590

SMITH, PATRICIA J., educational consultant; b. Chgo., Aug. 19, 1946; d. Joseph Peter and Jean Gloria (Sturmer) S. BA in English, Siena Heights Coll., 1970; MA in Spl. Edn., Eastern Mich. U., 1972. Cert. elem., spl. edn. tchr., Mich. Tchr. St. Theresa Sch., Detroit, 1970-71, Wayne County Child Devel. Ctr., Northville, Mich., 1971-73, Detroit Pub. Schs., 1981-82; tchr., advisor Met. State Hosp., Waltham, Mass., 1973-78; ednl. supr. Children's Friend and Svcs., Warwick, R.I., 1978-81; recruiter Mgmt. Support Svcs., Southfield, Mich., 1982-86; cognitive therapist Rehab. Resources, Inc., Southfield, 1985-86; ednl. coord. Fedn. Girls' Homes, Detroit, 1986-87, Davenport Shelter, Spectrum Youth Svcs., Highland Park, Mich., 1987-92; ednl. cons. Beverly Hills, Mich., 1988—; ednl. cons. Birmingham, Mich., 1988—; tchr. Detroit House of Corrections, Plymouth, Mich., 1971-73. Mem. Mich. Assn. Tchrs. of Emotionally Disturbed Children, Networks of Educators and Therapists Working in Orgns. for Rehab., Corrections and Spl. Edn. (sec. 1989—).

SMITH, PATRICIA JEAN, gifted and talented education educator; b. Dallas, Apr. 23, 1951; d. James M. and Billie Jean (Wyrick) S. BA, U. Tex., Arlington, 1973; MLA, So. Meth. U., 1978. Tchr. social studies Lancaster (Tex.) Mid. Sch., 1973-75; tchr. English and French, Lancaster High Sch., 1975-79; asst. continuing legal edn. dept. So. Meth. U. Sch. Law, Dallas, 1984-86; tchr. English and French, Mabank (Tex.) High Sch., 1980-84, tchr. English, French and Latin, coord. gifted-talented edn., 1986—; mem. accreditation team So. Assn., Austin, 1976-78; sponsor student trips to Europe. Dist. rep. Tex. Gov.'s Inauguration, Austin, 1990; tchr., mem. youth com., musician Clear Creek Bapt. Ch., 1991—. Recipient Outstanding High Sch. Tchr. award Mabank C. of C., 1992, Tex. Excellence award for outstanding high sch. tchr. U. Tex., Austin, 1992. Mem. Tex. Assn. for Gifted and Talented (presenter state conf.), Mabank Fedn. Tchrs. (pres. 1988—). Democrat. Home: RR 3 Box 257B Kemp TX 75143-9573 Office: Mabank High Sch 124 E Market St Mabank TX 75147-8377

SMITH, PATRICIA K., reading educator; b. East Stroudsburg, Pa., Mar. 8, 1934; d. Joseph George and Mabel Lorraine (Repsher) Kuchinski; m. Edwin Raymond Smith, Aug. 18, 1956; children: Timothy E., Steven M., Marianne F. BS in Edn., East Stroudsburg U., 1955; MA, W.Va. U., 1969, EdD, 1975. Elem. tchr. Pleasantdale Elem. Sch., West Orange, N.J., 1955-56, Tuscarora Sch. Dist., Mercersburg, Pa., 1956-59; reading specialist Robert F. Kennedy Ctr., Morgantown, W.Va., 1970-72; asst. prof. W.Va. U., Morgantown, 1975-79, assoc. prof. reading and lang. arts, 1979-86, prof., 1986—, senate faculty sec., 1992—; mem. rev. bd. Prentice-Hall, Inc., Englewood Cliffs, N.J., 1979-91 ; vis. prof. Beijing U. and Beijing Coal Mining Inst., 1991,92; cons. Chpt. 1, Monongalia Pub. Schs., Morgantown, W.Va., 1983-84. Co-author: Keeping Yourself Out of Federal Court, 1980, 2d revision, 1986; mem. editorial bd. Reading Improvement, Chula Vista, Calif., 1983—. Postdoctoral teaching fellow Lilly Endowment, Inc., 1975-76; recipient Outstanding Tchr. award Coll. Human Resources and Edn., Morgantown, W.Va., 1978. Mem. W.Va. State Reading Council (pres. 1979-80), Human Resources and Edn. Alumni Assn. (pres. 1979-80, exec. dir. 1981-85), Kappa Delta Pi, Phi Delta Kappa. Democrat. Roman Catholic. Avocations: traveling, reading. Home: 1456 Dogwood Ave Morgantown WV 26505-2310 Office: WVa U 607 Allen Hall Morgantown WV 26506-6122

SMITH, PAULA MARION, urology and medical/surgical nurse; b. Provincetown, Mass., Apr. 2, 1930; d. Manuel V. and Marion V. (Cabral) Raymond; m. George A. Smith, July 2, 1952; children: Steven, Michael, Elizabeth. Diploma in nursing, Quincy (Mass.) City Hosp., 1951; student, Boston Coll., U. S.C. RN, Tex., Kans., Mass. Operating room nurse Richland County Hosp., El Paso, Tex., 1958-62, Hotel Dieu, El Paso, 1962-64, U.S. Army Hosp., Ft. Riley, Kans., 1967-68; splty. head nurse urology unit Cape Cod Hosp., Hyannis, Mass., 1972—; cons. Urologic Nursing Jour. Recipient H. Harrison Hartwell award. Mem. ANA, Assn. Operating Rm. Nurses, Internat. Acad. Nurse Editors, Am. Urologic Assn. Allied (editor Uro-Gram, award New Eng. chpt. 1988).

SMITH, PEGGY MARIE, government official; b. Balt., Nov. 21, 1940; d. John Weldon and Cecelia Agnes (Goddard) S. Student U. Md., 1978-79, Catonsville Community Coll., 1979-80; Cert. master hypnotist and cert. hypno-anesthesia therapist Nat. Bd. Hypnotherapy and Hypnotic Anaesthesiology. Various secretarial positions, until 1973; adminstrv. officer Health Care Financing Adminstrn., Balt., 1973-80; adminstrv. specialist Social Security Adminstrn., Balt., 1980-85, mgmt. analyst, 1985-87; social ins. claims examiner, 1987—; owner, operator Garamore Hypnosis Ctr., 1987—. Vol. Mercy Hosp., Balt., 1960-62, Baltimore County Gen. Hosp., Balt., 1971; hotline counselor Lighthouse, Inc., Balt., 1975-77; tchr. Salem Lutheran Ch. Sch., Balt., 1962-67. Mem. Nat. Assn. Female Execs., Sierra Club, Nat. Arbor Day Found., Nat. Guild Hypnotists, Maryland Hypnosis Assn., Internat. Assn. Counselors and Therapists, Nat. Authors Registry. Avocations: writing, mainly poetry; reading; psychology; parapsychology; gardening. Office: Social Security Adminstrn 6401 Security Blvd Baltimore MD 21235-0001

SMITH, REBECCA BEACH, federal judge; b. 1949. BA, Coll. William and Mary, 1971; postgrad., U. Va., 1971-73; JD, Coll. William and Mary, 1979. Assoc. Wilcox & Savage, 1980-85; U.S. magistrate Ea. Dist. Va., 1985-89; dist. judge U.S. Dist. Ct. (ea. dist.) Va., Norfolk, 1989—; exec. editor Law Review, 1978-79. Active Chrysler Mus. Norfolk, Jean Outland Chrysler Libr. Assocs., Va. Opera Assn., Friends of the Zoo, Friends of Norfolk Pub. Libr., Ch. of the Good Shepherd. John Marshall Soc. fellow; recipient Acad. Achievement and Leadership award St. George Tucker Soc.; named one of Outstanding Women of Am., 1979. Mem. ABA, Va. State Bar Assn., Fed. Bar Assn. Supreme Ct. Hist. Soc., Fourth Cir. Judicial Conf., The Harbor Club, Order of Coif., Phi Beta Kappa. Office: US Dist Ct US Courthouse 600 Granby St Rm 358 Norfolk VA 23510-1915*

SMITH, REBECCA MCCULLOCH, human relations educator; b. Greensboro, N.C., Feb. 29, 1928; d. David Martin and Virginia Pearl (Woodburn) McCulloch; m. George Clarence Smith Jr., Mar. 30, 1945; 1 child, John Randolph. BS, Woman's Coll., U. N.C., 1947, MS, 1952; PhD, U. N.C., Greensboro, 1967; postgrad., Harvard U., 1989. Tchr. pub. schs., N.C. and S.C., 1947-57; instr. U. N.C., Greensboro, 1958-66, asst. prof. to prof. emeritus human devel. and family studies, 1967-91, adj. prof. emeritus, 1991-94, dir. grad. program, 1975-82; adj. prof. ednl. cons. depts. edn. N.C., S.C., Ind., Ont., Man.; vis. prof. N.W. La. State U., 1965, 67, U. Wash., 1970, Hood Coll., 1976, 86. Named Outstanding Alumna Sch. Home Econs., 1976; recipient Sperry award for service to families N.C. Family Life Coun., 1979. Mem. Am. Home Econs. Assn., Nat. Council Family Rels. (exec. com. 1974-76, treas. 1987-89, Osborne award 1973), U. N.C. at Greensboro Alumni Assn. (chair membership recruitment com. 1994—), Omicron Nu. Author: Teaching About Family Relationships, 1975, Klemer's Marriage and Family Relationships, 2d edit., 1975, Resources for Teaching About Family Life Education, 1976, Family Matters: Concepts in Marriage and Personal Relationships, 1982; co-author: History of the School of Human Environmental Sciences: 1892-1992, 1992, assoc. editor Family Relations (Jour. Applied Family and Child Studies), 1980-90; ednl. cons. Current Life Studies, 1977-84. Home: 1212 Ritters Lake Rd Greensboro NC 27406-7816 Office: U NC Dept Human Devel Sch Human Environ Scis Greensboro NC 27412

SMITH, RHONDA MOORE, security services administrator; b. Demorest, Ga., June 9, 1960; d. Don L. and Miriam Elizabeth (Thompson) Moore; m. Chris D. Smith, May 7, 1988; children: Ethan C., Cody C. BS in Social Work & Psychology, Piedmont Coll., 1983. Sec., adminstrv. asst., security svcs. adminstr. Standard Telephone Co., Cornelia, Ga., 1977—. Active North Habersham PTO. Mem. Kiwanis, H.M. Stewart Sr. Pioneer Club (membership chair 1993-94). Baptist. Office: Standard Telephone Co. PO Box 400 Cornelia GA 30531

SMITH, ROBERTA HAWKINS, plant physiologist; b. Tulare, Calif., May 3, 1945; d. William Brevard and Freda Lois (Kessler) Hawkins; m. James Willie Smith Jr., Sept. 17, 1968; children: James Willie III, Cristine Lois. BS, U. Calif., Riverside, 1967, MS, 1968, PhD, 1970. Postdoctoral fellow dept. plant sci. Tex. A&M U., College Station, 1972-73, asst. prof. dept. plant sci., 1974-79, assoc. prof. dept. plant sci., 1979-85, prof. dept. soil and crop sci., 1985—; asst. prof. Sam Huston State U., Huntsville, Tex., 1973-74. Editorial bd. Biotech. Advances, 1986—, Plant Physiology, 1984—. Mem. Crop Sci. Soc. Am. (chmn. C-7 divsn. 1990-91), Internat. Crops Rsch. Inst. Semi-Arid Tropics (bd. govs. 1989-95), Faculty of Plant Physiology (chmn. 1987-89), Tissue Culture Assn. (chmn. plant divsn. 1983-86, pres. 1994—). Republican. Methodist. Home: RR 1 Box 701 Hearne TX 77859-9734 Office: Tex A&M Univ Dept Soil And Sci College Station TX 77843

SMITH, ROBYN DOYAL, elementary and middle school educator; b. Atlanta, July 12, 1947; d. Buna Eugene and Robyn (Wall) Doyal; m. William Franklin Smith Jr., June 14, 1970; 1 child, William McBrayer. BS in Elem. Edn., Tift Coll., Forsyth, Ga., 1969; MEd, Mercer U., 1973. Tchr. Suder Elem. Sch., Jonesboro, Ga., 1969-73, Mundy's Mill Jr. High Sch., Jonesboro, 1973-82, Pointe South Mid. Sch., Jonesboro, 1982—; owner, mgr. Personalized Imprinting Svc., Fayetteville, Ga.; instr. Tara Driving Improvement Program, Jonesboro, 1985—; adj. faculty Mercer U., 1994. Nominee Honor Tchr. award Atlanta Jour./Constitution, 1987, Ga. Law Educator of Yr. nominee, 1991; recipient Clayton County Tchr. of Yr. award, 1987, Ga. Law Tchr. of Yr. award, 1992, Nat. Law Educator of Yr., 1993. Mem. NEA, Ga. Assn. Educators, Clayton County Assn. Educators, Assn. Driving Sch. Instrs., Ga. Law Consortium. Presbyterian. Home: 165 Essex Cir Fayetteville GA 30214-5333 Office: Pointe South Middle Sch 626 Flint Jonesboro GA 30236-3415

SMITH, ROSEMARY L., human resources specialist; b. Binghamton, N.Y., June 18, 1947; d. Charles Harry and Mary L. (Finlon) Roberts; m. Walter W. Smith; children: Tricia M. Smith, Jennifer R. Assoc. in Retail Bus. Mgmt., Hudson Valley C.C., 1969; BSBA, Franklin U., 1981. Dept. mgr. J.C. Penney, Albany, N.Y., 1963-65; floater Sears, Roebuck and Co., Albany, N.Y., 1965-69, Tucson, 1971-73; dir. human resources O.M. Scott & Sons, Marysville, Ohio, 1973—; bd. dirs. Huntington Bank City Offices. Former v.p., past pres. Union County United Way, 1983-93; vice chair bd. dirs. Meml. Hosp. Union County, 1989—; past pres. Scott Assocs. Credit Union, 1977-82; trustee Health Ohio, 1988-90; chair payor coun. Coalition Cost Effective Health Svcs., 1987-92; active Community Connection for Offender, 1993—. Named Outstanding Young Woman Am., 1980. Mem. Personnel Assn. Ctrl. Ohio, Dublin Women in Bus. and Professions (steering com. 1981—), Soc. Human Resource Mgmt., Kiwanis Marysville. Office: The Scotts Co 14111 Scottslawn Rd Marysville OH 43041

SMITH, RUBY LUCILLE, librarian; b. Nobob, Ky., Sept. 19, 1917; d. James Ira and Myrtie Olive (Crabtree) Jones; AB, Western Ky. State Tchrs. Coll., 1943, MA, 1966; m. Kenneth Cornelius Smith, Dec. 25, 1946; children: Kenneth Cornelius, Corma Ann. Tchr. rural schs., Barren County, Ky., 1941-42; tchr. secondary sch. English, libr. Temple Hill Consol. Sch., Glasgow, Ky., 1943-47, 49-51, 53-56, sch. libr., 1956-83. Sec. Barren County Cancer Soc., 1968-70, Barren County Fair Bd., 1969-70; leader 4-H Club, 1957-72, mem. council Barren County; coord. AARP tax-aide program, 1985—, assoc. dist. dir., 1988—. Trustee Mary Wood Weldon Meml. Libr.,

1964—; trustee Barren County Pub. Libr., 1969—, sec., 1969—. Mem. NEA (life), Ky. Edn. Assn., Ky. Sch. Media Assn. (sec. 1970-71), 3d Dist. Libr. Assn. (pres. 1944, 66), Barren County Edn. Assn. (pres. 1960-62, treas. 1979-80), 3d Dist. Ret. Tchrs. Assn. (pres. 1991—), Ky. Ret. Tchrs Assn. (v.p. 1992—, pres.-elect 1993, pres. 1994—), Ky. Audio Visual Assn., Glasgow-Barren County Ret. Tchrs. Assn. (pres. 1984-86, sec. 1989, treas. 1990), Ky. Libr. Trustee Assn. (bd. dirs. 1985—, pres. 1986-88, 93-94, dir. Barren River region 1985—), Barren County Rep. Women's Club, Monroe Assn. Woman's Missionary Union (dir. 1968-72, 79-83 Monroe Assn. Bapts. (libr. dir. 1972-88, sec. 1985—), Ky. Libr. Assn., Delta Kappa Gamma. Home: 54 E Nobob Rd Summer Shade KY 42166-8405

SMITH, RUTH LILLIAN SCHLUCHTER, librarian; b. Detroit, Oct. 18, 1917; d. Clayton John and Gertrude Katherine (Kastler) Schluchter; m. Thomas Guilford Smith, Sept. 28, 1946; 1 son, Pemberton, III. AB, Wayne State U., Detroit, 1939; AB in Libr. Sci., U. Mich., Ann Arbor, 1942. Libr. Detroit Pub. Libr., 1942-43; rsch. asst. Moore Sch. Elec. Engring. U. Pa., Phila., 1946-47; libr. Bethesda (Md.) Meth. Ch. Libr., 1955-61; reference libr., chief reader svcs. Inst. Def. Analyses, Arlington, Va., 1961-65, chief unclassified libr. sect., 1965-67, head libr., 1967-75, mgr. tech. info. svcs., 1975-81; dir. office customer svcs. Nat. Tech. Info. Svc., 1981-88, cons., 1988—; leader ch. libr. workshops Nat. Tech. Info. Service, 1960—; speaker profl. meetings; founder, chmn. Com. Info. Hang-ups, 1969-86; mem. Depository Libr. Coun. to Pub. Printer, 1975-78, Def. Tech. Info. Ctr. Resource Sharing Adv. Group, 1980-82; chmn. edn. working group Fed. Libr. and Info. Ctr. Com., 1984-88, cons., 1988—. Author: Publicity for a Church Library, 1966, Workshop Planning, 1972, (with Claudia Hannaford) Promotion Planning, 1975, Getting the Books off the Shelves, 1975, rev. edit., 1985, 2nd rev. edit., 1991, Cataloging Made Easy, 1978, rev. edit., 1986, Setting up a Library: How to Begin or Begin Again, 1979, rev. edit., 1987, 2nd rev. edit., 1994, Running a Library, 1982; contbr. articles to library and religious jours. Author: Publicity for a Church Library, 1966, Workshop Plannign, 1972, (with Claudia Hannaford) Promotion Planning, 1975, Getting the Books Off the Shelves, 1975, rev. edit. 1985, rev. edit. 1991, Cataloging Books, Step By Step, 1977, Cataloging Made Easy, 1978, rev. edit. 1986, Setting up a Library; How to Begin of Begin Again, 1979, rev. edit. 1987, 1994, Running a Library, 1982; contbr. articles to library and religious jours. Mem. ALA, Am. Soc. Info. Sci., Ch. and Synagogue Library Assn. (founding mem., life mem., pres. 1967-68), Fedn. Info. Users (v.p. interactive affairs 1973-75), Spl. Libraries Assn. (chmn. aerospace div. 1975-76, chmn. library mgmt. div. 1978-79, chmn. div. cabinet 1980-81, John Cotton Dana award 1979, SLA Fellow award 1987, Hall of Fame award 1988). Republican. Methodist. Home: 5304 Glenwood Rd Bethesda MD 20814-1406

SMITH, SALLY ANN NORTON, bookstore owner; b. Salt Lake City, Dec. 17, 1946; d. Alonzo Ray and Donna Naomi (Borg) Norton; m. Lee Merrill Smith, Mar. 16, 1968; children: Amanda Lee, Scott Norton. BA in English, U. Utah, 1969. Tchr. English N.W. Jr. High Sch., Salt Lake City, 1969-74, Judge Meml. Cath. High Sch., Salt Lake City, 1978-87; bookseller, owner A Woman's Place Bookstore, Salt Lake City, 1987—. Pres. Rowland Hall Home and Sch. Assn., Salt Lake City, 1984-85; trustee Rowland Hall, 1984-85; bd. dirs. Writers at Work Writing Conf., Park City, Utah, 1988-90; mem. devel. adv. bd. Humanities Ctr., U. Utah. Recipient Woman of Courageous Action award NOW, 1993, Woman to Woman award All Women's Day/Evening Festival, 1993, Writers at Work Writing Advocate award, 1994. Mem. Utah Assn. Women Bus. Owners, Intermountain Booksellers Assn. (bd. dirs. 1988-90), Am. Booksellers Assn., Utah NOW. Democrat. Office: A Woman's Place Bookstore 1400 Foothill Dr Salt Lake City UT 84108-2300

SMITH, SALLYE WRYE, librarian; b. Birmingham, Ala., Nov. 11, 1923; d. William Florin and Margaret (Howard) Wrye; m. Stuart Werner Smith, Sept. 20, 1947 (dec. June 1981); children: Carol Ann, Susan Patricia, Michael Christopher, Julie Lynn, Lori Kathleen. BA, U. Ala., 1945; MA, U. Denver, 1969. Psychometrician U.S. Army, Deshon Gen. Hosp., Butler, Pa., 1945-46, U.S. Vet. Adminstrn. Vocat. Guidance, U. Ala., Tuscaloosa, 1946; clin. psychologist U.S. Army, Walter Reed Gen. Hosp., Washington, 1946-47, U.S. Army, Fitzsimons Gen. Hosp., Denver, 1948, U.S. Vets. Adminstrn., Ft. Logan, Colo., 1948-50; head sci.-engring. libr. U. Denver, Colo., 1969-72; instr., reference libr. Penrose Libr., U. Denver, 1972-80, asst. prof., reference libr., 1980-90, interim dir., 1990-92; vis. prof. U. Denver Grad. Sch. Libr. Info. Mgmt., 1975-77, 83; info. broker Colo. Researchers, Denver, 1979—; cons., participant The Indsl. Info. Workshop Inst. de Investigaciones Tecnologicas, Bogota, Colombia, 1979, LIPI-DRI-PDIN workshop on R&D mgmt., Jakarta, Indonesia, 1982; mem. BRS User Adv. Bd., Latham, N.Y., 1983-86. Indexer: Statistical Abstract of Colorado 1976-77, 1977. Recipient Cert. of Recognition, Sigma Xi, U. Denver chpt., 1983. Mem. ALA, Spl. Libr. Assn., Colo. Libr. Assn., Phi Beta Kappa, Beta Phi Mu.

SMITH, SARA ELIZABETH CUSHING, English language educator, writer; b. Richmond, Va., July 7, 1950; d. William Routledge and Sara Margie (Williams) Cushing; m. Bertram Smith, May 18, 1991; stepchildren: David, Susan, Leona, Bernice. BA, Duke U., 1972; MS, SUNY, Cortland, 1978. Cert. tchr. secondary English, N.Y. Adminstrv. asst. Duke Players/Duke Univ., Durham, N.C., 1970-72; substitute tchr. Maine-Endwell and Union Endicott Schs., Endicott and Endwell, N.Y., 1972-73; tchr. English and drama John F. Kennedy High Sch., Richmond, Va., 1973-75; project coord. Alekna Constrn., Endicott, 1975-77; tchr. English Vestal (N.Y.) Sr. High Sch., 1977-78, Greene (N.Y.) Jr.-Sr. High Sch., 1978-88; writer, editor, writing cons., 1981—; instr. English, computer lab. mgr., weekend coord. coll. Piedmont Tech. Coll., Greenwood, S.C., 1988—; rental agt. Drucker and Falk, Richmond, 1974-75; liaison/amb. to Lander Coll., Greenwood, 1990-91, co-chmn. Praxis Conf., 1990-91. Author: (textbook) You, Too, Can Writer, 1990, 3d edit. 1994. Recipient summer seminar stipend NEH, Atlanta, 1984. Mem. South Atlantic MLA, Greene Tchrs. Assn. (pres. 1983-85, mem. negotiating team 1984-86), Nat. Coun. Tchrs. of English, S.C. Tech. Educators Assn. Home: 109 Carriage Ct Saddle Hill Greenwood SC 29649 Office: Piedmont Tech Coll Emerald Rd/Drawer 1467 Greenwood SC 29648

SMITH, SARAH KIM HUEY, training and development consultant; b. Wichita Falls, Tex., Nov. 5, 1952; d. John Thomas Huey and Dovie Maurine (Nash) Huey Murphy; m. Robert Lynn Smith, Apr. 22, 1982. BA summa cum laude, Midwestern State U., 1975; MA, Tex. Tech U., 1976. Prodn. coord. Tex. Instruments, Inc., Lubbock, Tex., 1976-77, tng. mgr., 1977-80, br. tng. mgr., 1980-82; sr. cons. Action Systems, Inc., Dallas, 1982-84; tng. mgr. Aviall, Inc., Dallas, 1984-86; dist. mgr. Devel. Dimensions Internat., Dallas, 1986-90; v.p. DDI Pitts., 1990-91; v.p., gen. mgr. DDI Can., Toronto, 1991-92; v.p. DDI L.A., 1992—; presentor seminars, papers at convs. Vol. tchr. Operation L.I.F.T. (Literacy Instrn. for Texans), Dallas, 1983-84, Big Bros./Big Sisters, 1988-89; mem. Foster Parents Plan, Amnesty Internat., World Wildlife Fund, People for the Ethical Treatment of Animals. Mem. Am. Soc. Tng. and Devel., Alpha Chi Omega, Alpha Psi Omega. Democrat. Avocations: running, music, reading. Office: DDI 6033 W Century Blvd Ste 340 Los Angeles CA 90045-6412

SMITH, SELENA W., community liaison, educator; b. Tuba City, Ariz., Sept. 23, 1956; d. Grover Segani and Zonnie Gai (Selaw) Williams; m. Benjamin C. Smith, Apr. 5, 1980; children: Krystalin, Terrence, Kirkland. AAS, Snow Coll., 1977; student, No. Ariz. U., 1994—. Temporary clk.-typist various orgns., Tuba City, Ariz., 1973-76; sec.-stenographer BIA Housing Devel., Tuba City, 1977-80; clk.-stenographer BIA Law Enforcement, Tuba City, 1981-85; supt., bd. sec. Tuba City Unified Schs., 1985-89, exec. asst., 1989-90, community liaison, 1990-92, community liaison/media ctr. dir., 1992-94; strategic planning team mem. Tuba City Unified Schs., 1991-94, policy rev. com., 1992-94, mem. Meet and Confer Team, 1992-93, Yr.-Round Edn. Com., 1993-94; recorder Senate Bill 1236 Testimonies, 1989. Editor: Coalmine Canyon Rodeo, 1983-85. Sec.-treas. and v.p. Coalmine Mesa (Ariz.) Chpt., 1979-92, Coalmine Canyon Rodeo, 1980-92; sec. Dist. # 3 and Western Navajo Coun., Tuba City, 1983-92, Western Navajo Detention Task Force, Tuba City, 1984-85; voter registrar Navajo Nation and Coconino County, Tuba City, 1989-92; mem. parole rev. bd., Tuba City Dist. Ct., 1993-94; mem. Channel 6 Com., media ctr. dir. 1993-94; sec.-treas., bd. dirs. Diné Beiina' Nahiilnaah Corp. Named to Outstanding Young Women of Am., 1991. Mem. Children's TV Resource Edn. (cert. presenter), Southwest Rodeo Assn. (bd. dirs. 1994), Nat. Sch. Pub. Rels. Assn. Democrat.

SMITH, SELMA MOIDEL, lawyer, composer; b. Warren, Ohio, Apr. 3, 1919; d. Louis and Mary (Oyer) Moidel; 1 child, Mark Lee. Student U. Calif., 1936-39, U. So. Calif., 1939-41; JD, Pacific Coast U., 1942. Bar: Calif. 1943, U.S. Dist. Ct. 1943, U.S. Supreme Ct. 1958. Gen. practice law; mem. firm Moidel, Moidel, Moidel & Smith. Field dir. civilian adv. com. WAC, 1943; mem. nat. bd. Med. Coll. Pa. (formerly Woman's Med. Coll. Pa.), 1953—, exec. bd., 1976-80, pres., 1980-82, chmn. past pres. com., 1990-92. Decorated La Order del Merito Juan Pablo Duarte (Dominican Republic). Mem. ABA, State Bar Calif. (servicemen's legal com., Disting. Svc. award 1993), L.A. Bar Assn. (psychopathic ct. com., Outstanding Svc. award 1993), L.A. Lawyers Club (pub. defenders com.), Nat. Assn. Women Lawyers (chmn. com. unauthorized practice of law, social commn. UN, regional dir. western states, Hawaii 1949-57, mem. jud. adminstrn. com. 1960, nat. chmn. world peace through law com. 1966-67), League of Ams. (dir.), Inter-Am. Bar Assn., So. Calif. Women Lawyers Assn. (pres. 1947, 48), Women Lawyers Assn. L.A. (chmn. Law Day com. 1966, subject of oral hist. project, 1986), State Bar Conf. Com., Coun. Bar Assns. L.A. County (charter sec. 1950), Calif. Bus. Women's Coun. (dir. 1951), L.A. Bus. Women's Coun. (pres. 1952), Calif. Pres.'s Coun. (1st v.p.), Nat. Assn. Composers U.S.A. (dir. 1974-79, ann. luncheon chmn. 1975), Nat. Fedn. Music Clubs (nat. vice chmn. for Western region, 1973-78), Calif. Fedn. Music Clubs (state chmn. Am. Music 1971-75, state conv. chmn. 1972), Docents of L.A. Philharm. (v.p. 1973-83, chmn. Latin Am. community rels. 1972-75, press and pub. rels. 1972-75, cons. coord. 1973-75), Assn. Learning in Retirement Orgns. in West (pres. 1993-94, exec. com. 1994—), Euterpe Opera Club (v.p. 1974-75, chmn. auditions 1972, chmn. awards 1973-75), ASCAP, Iota Tau Tau (dean L.A., supreme treas.), Plato Soc. of UCLA (Toga editor, 1990-93, sec. 1991-92, chmn. colloquium com. 1992-93, discussion leader UCLA Constitution Bicentennial Project, 1985-87, moderator UCLA extension lecture series 1990, Exceptional Leadership award 1994). Composer: Espressivo-Four Piano Pieces (orchestral premiere 1987, performance Nat. Mus. Women in the Arts 1989). Home: 5272 Lindley Ave Encino CA 91316-3518

SMITH, SHARI SUE, human resource specialist; b. Davenport, Iowa, June 21, 1965; d. Larry Dale and Julie Adella (Vn Den Hende) S. AA, Scott C.C., Bettendorf, Iowa, 1986; BSBA in Human Resource Mgmt., Calif. State U., Long Beach, 1994. Salesperson Helzberg Diamonds, Moline, Ill., 1986-87; mgr. Braun's Fashions, Davenport, Iowa, 1987-88; asst.mgr. Belden Jewelers, Moline, 1988-89; mgr. trainee Phoenix Jewelers, Davenport, 1989-90; sales person Merksamer Jewelers, Westminster, Calif., 1990-92, Daniel's Jewelers, Lakewood, Calif., 1992-94; br. coord. Abigail Abbott, Seal Beach, Calif., 1994, staff supr., 1994; human resource specialist Qualex, Inc., Long Beach, Calif., 1995—. Participant City Coun., Long Beach, 1992. Mem. Pers. Indsl. Rels. Assn. (treas. 1993-94, pres. 1994—), scholarship 1994). Home: 4114 Vista St Long Beach CA 90803 Office: Qualex Inc 3400 E 70th St Long Beach CA 90805

SMITH, SHARON LOUISE, state official; b. St. Cloud, Minn., Oct. 25, 1950; d. John Val and Jacquelyn Joyce (Heinen) S. BA, Coll. St. Catherine, 1973; MA, Hamline U., 1990; MPA, U. So. Calif., 1993, DPA, 1994. Tng. officer Emergency Mgmt. divsn. State of Minn., St. Paul, 1973-74, disaster planner, 1974-77, response coord., 1977-79, population planner, 1979-80, comm. officer, 1980-82, adminstrv. dir., 1982-91, power plant planner, 1991—. Ides of March scholar, 1991, 92, Friends of Washington Pub. Affairs Ctr. scholar, 1992. Mem. ASPA, Pi Gamma Mu. Home: 1581 Wheelock Ln # 304 Saint Paul MN 55117-5965

SMITH, SHARRON WILLIAMS, chemistry educator; b. Ashland, Ky., Apr. 3, 1941; d. James Archie and May (Waggoner) Williams; m. William Owen Smith, Jr., Aug. 16, 1964; children: Leslie Dyan, Kevin Andrew. BA, Transylvania U., 1963; PhD, U. Ky., 1975. Chemist, Procter & Gamble, Cin., 1963-64; tchr. sci. Lexington pub. schs., Ky., 1964-67; chemist NIH, Bethesda, Md., 1974-75; asst. prof. chemistry Hood Coll., Frederick, Md., 1975-81, assoc. prof., 1981-87, prof. 1987—, chair dept. chemistry, physics and astronomy, 1982-86, acting dean grad. sch. 1989-91, Whitaker prof. Chemistry, 1993—. NDEA fellow, 1967-70, Dissertation Yr. fellow U. Ky., Lexington, 1970-71; grantee Hood Coll. Bd. Assocs., 1981, 85, 91, Beneficial-Hodson faculty fellow Hood Coll., 1984, 92; grantee NSF, 1986. Mem. AAAS, Am. Chem. Soc., Middle Atlantic Assn. Liberal Arts Chemistry Tchrs. (pres. 1984-85). Democrat. Office: Hood Coll Dept Chemistry Frederick MD 21701

SMITH, SHELAGH ALISON, public health educator; b. Oak Ridge, Tenn., June 3, 1949; d. Nicholas Monroe and Elizabeth (Kimbrough) S.; m. Milton John Axley, 1991; 1 child, Elizabeth Claire. BS in Edn., U. Tenn., 1971, AS in Dental Hygiene, 1974; MPH in Health Svcs. Adminstrn., Johns Hopkins, 1979. Cert. health edn. specialist, 1989. Social sci. rsch. analyst Dept. Health and Human Svcs., Health Care Fin. Adminstrn., Balt., 1980-85; pub. health educator, evaluator Nat. Cancer Inst.-NIH, Bethesda, Md., 1985-90; sr. policy analyst NIMH, Rockville, Md., 1990-92; pub. health advisor Ctr. Mental Health Svcs., Rockville, Md., 1992—; mem. Nat. Commn. Health Credentialing. Recipient adminstr.'s citation Health Care Fin. Adminstrn., 1981, dir.'s spl. act-cash award Nat. Cancer Inst., 1989; Gen. Alumni scholar U. Tenn., 1973. Mem. APHA (pu. health edn. sect., chmn. fin. and reimbursement for prevention svcs. com. 1987-89), Nat. Commn. Health Credentialing, Md. Pub. Health Assn. (membership chmn. 1980, treas. 1981), Md. Women's Health Coalition, Planned Parenthood Md., Soc. Pub. Health Edn. (governing bd. and ho. of dels. 1993-95, nat. capitol area exec. bd./membership chmn. 1986, legis. co-chmn. 1990-91), Phi Kappa Phi. Democrat. Home: 14106 Heathfield Ct Rockville MD 20853 Office: SAMHSA Ctr Mental Health Svc Rm 16C05 Parklawn Bldg 5600 Fishers Ln Rockville MD 20857

SMITH, SHIRLEY, artist; b. Wichita, Kans., Apr. 17, 1929; d. Harold Marvin and Blanche Carrie (Alexander) S. BFA, Kans. State U., 1951; postgrad., Provincetown (Mass.) Workshop, 1962-66. One woman exhbns. 55 Mercer St. Gallery, N.Y.C., 1973, Wichita Art Mus, 1978, Stamford Mus. and Nature Ctr., Conn., 1987, Aaron Gallery, Washington, 1987, 88, Joan Hodgell Gallery, Sarasota, Fla., 1987; group exhbns. include Chrysler Mus., Provincetown, 1964, The Va. Mus., Richmond, 1970, Whitney Mus. Am. Art, 1971, Colo. Springs Fine Art Ctr., 1972, Everson Mus., Syracuse, N.Y., 1976-80, Nat. Acad. Design, N.Y.C., 1986, One Penn Pla., N.Y.C., 1987, 88, Am. Acad., Inst. Arts and Letters, N.Y.C., 1990, 91; permanent collections Whitney Mus. Am. Art, N.Y.C., U. Calif. Art Mus., Berkeley, Phoenix Art Mus., The Aldrich Mus. Contemporary Art, Ridgefield, Conn., Ulrich Mus., Wichita, Everson Mus., Syracuse, South County Bank collection, St. Louis, Prudential Life Ins., Newark, N.J., King Features Syndicate, N.Y.C., Chase Manhattan Bank Collection, N.Y.C., Senator Nancy Kassabaum Russel Senate Bldg., Washington. Recipient Grumbacher Cash award for mixed media New Eng. Exhibition, Silvermine, Conn., 1967, Acad. Inst. award Am. Acad. Arts and Letters, N.Y.C., 1991. Mem. Artist Equity. Democrat. Presbyterian. Home: 141 Wooster St New York NY 10012-3163

SMITH, STEPHANIE ZAHAROUDIS, producer; b. Washington, May 12, 1958; d. Angelo Constantine and Sally (Laliotis) Zaharoudis; m. John Dorrance Smith, Sept. 15, 1990. BS, U. Md., 1980. Asst. editor Bus. Aviation Weekly, Washington, 1980-81; copy aide, free-lance writer Washington Post, 1980-83; assoc. producer Satellite News Channel, Washington, 1982-83; assignment editor, assoc. producer Sta. WJLA-TV, Washington, 1983-84; assoc. producer weekend news Sta. ABC-TV, Washington, 1984-86, producer weekend news, 1986-89, producer Pentagon, 1989-93; producer World News Tonight, 1993—. Recipient Joan Barone award House Radio-TV Gallery, Washington, 1988. Office: ABC News 1717 DeSales St NW Washington DC 20036-4407

SMITH, SUE FRANCES, newspaper editor; b. Lockhart, Tex., July 4, 1940; d. Monroe John Baylor and Myrtle (Krause) Mueck; m. Michael Vogtel Smith, Apr. 20, 1963 (div. July 1977); 1 child, Jordan Meredith. B. Journalism, U. Tex., 1962. Feature writer, photographer Corpus Christi Caller Times, 1962-64; feature writer, editor Chgo. Tribune, 1964-76; features editor Dallas Times Herald, 1976-82; asst. mng. editor for features Denver Post, 1983-84, assoc. editor, 1984-91; asst. mng. editor in charge of Sunday paper Dallas Morning News, 1991-94, asst. mng. editor Lifestyles, 1994—; active Coun. Pres., 1993. Mem. Am. Assn. Sunday and Feature Editors (pres. 1993), Newspaper Features Coun. (bd. dirs.), Delta Gamma. Home: 6060 Jereme Trl Dallas TX 75252-5130 Office: 508 Young St Dallas TX 75202-4808

SMITH, TAMMY MICHELLE GRAY, geriatric, psychiatric, and chemical dependency nurse; b. Waycross, Ga., Apr. 4, 1963; d. Edward Allen and Helen Louise (Terry) Gray. ADN with honors, Chattanooga State Tech. Coll.; BSW, U. Tenn., postgrad. Head nurse geriatrics Greenleaf Ctr. Extended Care Facility, Ft. Oglethorpe, Ga., 1987-93, charge nurse chem. dependency program, house supr., 1993—; also group therapy facilitator, self-esteem tchr. in field. Home: 3 Gala Dr Fort Oglethorpe GA 30742-3913

SMITH, TAMMY SUE, foodservice management professional; b. Tulsa, Feb. 18, 1961; d. Clyde Earnest and Susan Viola (Deckard) S.; children: Jeffrey Clyde Ray, Brandi Sue-Etta. A in Edn., Claremore Jr. Coll., 1981; BS in Edn., Northeastern State U., 1983, MEd in Counseling, 1991. Cert. food svc. sanitation instr., Ill.; cert. home econs. tchr., Okla., Ill.; cert. counselor, Okla., Ill. Vocat. home econs. tchr. Oilton (Okla.) Pub. Sch., 1983-85; asst. mgr. McDonald's Corp., Tulsa, 1985-86; food svc. supr. Tulsa Job Corp, 1986-88; vocat. home econs. tchr. Foyil (Okla.) Pub. Sch., 1988-90, Ft. Gibson (Okla.) Pub. Sch., 1990-91; food svc. tech. instr. MacMurray Coll., Jacksonville, Ill., 1991—; also project connect coord., food svc. instr. MacMurray Coll. Named one of Outstanding Young Women of Am., 1989. Mem. AAUW, Am. Dietetic Assn., Dietary Mgrs. Assn., Assn. for Female Offenders, Am. Sewing Guild, Am. Vocat. Assn., Am. Correctional Food Svc. Assn., Ill. Vocat. Assn., Ill. Restaurant Assn., Nat. Restaurant Assn., Adult Vocat. Edn. Assn., Correctional Edn. Assn., Nat. Jaycees, Ill. Jaycees, Lincoln Jaycees, Jr. Jaycees (co-leader), Kappa Delta Pi, Rho Theta Sigma. Home: 1115 Macon St Lincoln IL 62656-9766 Office: MacMurray Coll c/o Logan Correctional Ctr PO Box 1000 Lincoln IL 62656-8100

SMITH, TERESA MARIE, accountant; b. Davenport, Iowa, Sept. 2, 1964; d. Richard Lee and Jean Marie (Striegel) Duncan; m. Roger Kent Smith, May 5, 1990. BBA in Acctg., U. Iowa, 1986. CPA, Iowa. Acctg. asst. Frances E. Paper, CPA, Davenport, Iowa, 1987; acctg. technician McGladrey & Pullen, Cedar Rapids, Iowa, 1988-89, mem. profl. staff, 1989-93, supr. profl. staff, 1993-94; contr. Hwy. Equipment Co., Cedar Rapids, 1994—. Bd. dirs. YMCA Cedar Rapids and Linn County, 1992—; treas. Profl. Women's Network, 1995—. Mem. AICPA, Iowa Soc. CPAs. Office: Hwy Equipment Co 616 D Ave NW Cedar Rapids IA 52405

SMITH, TERESA MAY, art educator; b. Booneville, Mo., May 10, 1947; d. David Fredrick and Hattie Artibelle (Wren) Berger; m. Ronnie Raymond Smith, Dec. 22, 1969. BS in Art, Sch. Ozarks, Point lookout, Mo., 1970. Lic. tchr. art. Tchr. kindergarten Reeds Spring (Mo.) Pub. Schs., 1969-72, art instr., 1974—; coop. tchr. with future tchrs. Mo. Farmers Assn. scholar, 1965. Mem. NEA, Nat. Art Assn., Reeds Spring Tchrs. Assn. (bldg. rep. 1991—). Home: Box 102 Reeds Spring MO 65737 Office: Reeds Spring Mid Sch Hwy 13 Reeds Spring MO 65737

SMITH, THELMA TINA HARRIETTE, gallery owner, artist; b. Folkston, Ga., May 5, 1938; d. Harry Charles and Malinda Estelle (Kennison) Causey; m. Billy Wayne Smith, July 23, 1955; children: Sherry Yvonne, Susan Marie, Dennis Wayne, Chris Michael. Student, U. Tex., Arlington, 1968-70; studies with various art instrs. Gen. office worker Superior Ins. Corp., Dallas, 1956-57, Zanes-Ewalt Warehouse, Dallas, 1957-67; bookkeeper Atlas Match Co., Arlington, 1967-68; sr. acct. Automated Refrigerated Air Conditioner Mfg. Corp., Arlington, 1968-70; acct. Conn. Gen. Life Ins. Corp., Dallas, 1972-74; freelance artist Denton, Tex., 1974—; gallery owner, custom framer Tina Smith Studio-Gallery, Mabank, Tex., 1983—. Painting in pub. and pvt. collections in numerous states including N.Y., Fla., Ga. and N.D.; editor Cedar Creek Art Soc. Yearbook, 1983—. Treas. Cedar Creek Art Soc., 1987-88, 89—; mem. com. to establish state endorsed Arts Coun. for Cedar Creek Lake Area, Gun Barrel City, Tex. Recipient numerous watercolor and pastel awards Henderson County Art League, Cedar Creek Art Soc., Cmty. Svc. award Mayor Wilson Tippit, Gun Barrel City, Tex., 1986. Mem. Southwestern Watercolor Soc. (Dallas), Pastel Soc. of the S.W. (Dallas), Cedar Creek Art Soc. (Gun Barrel City) (v.p. 1983-86, treas.), Profl. Picture Framers Assn. Baptist. Office: Tina Smith Studio-Gallery 701 S 3D St Mabank TX 75147

SMITH, THOMASINA DENISE, computer programmer analyst, accountant; b. Columbia, S.C., Mar. 20, 1954; d. Tom Smith and Tecora Claratine (Shaw) Drake; m. Jerry Williams, Mar. 15, 1982 (div. Jan. 1983). BS, Winthrop Coll., Rock Hill, S.C., 1974. Computer programmer trainee Blue Cross/Blue Shield, Columbia, S.C., 1974-75; computer operator Kline Iron & Steel Co., Columbia, 1976-78; jr. computer programmer NCR Corp., Dayton, Ohio, 1978-80; systems analyst Bank One, Dayton, 1980-83; programmer analyst Elder Beerman, Dayton, 1984-85, Def. Contract Adminstrn., Columbus, Ohio, 1985-86, U.S. Army, Atlanta, 1986—; owner, operator TDS Enterprises, Atlanta, 1988-91, Columbia, S.C.; seller Safety Plus fire extinguisher, flame retardant and smoke alarms; pub. rels., talent scout Sharp Records; installer computer software and hardware for chs.; tax preparer H&R Block, Columbia; bd. dirs. Shaper Bros., Inc., Atlanta. Vol. Adopt a Sister/Adopt a Brother, Atlanta, 1989, Ben Hill United Meth. Ch. Missionary Soc., Atlanta. Mem. Data Processing Mgmt. Assn., The Phoenix Soc. for Burn Survivors, Endometriosis Assn., Nat. Found. of Ileitis and Colitis. Zeta Phi Beta. Home: 7011 Gavilan Ave Columbia SC 29203-5231 Office: US Hdqrs Forscom FCJ6-PDB Atlanta GA 30330

SMITH, TONI COLETTE, government official, social worker; b. Columbus, Ohio, Oct. 31, 1952. BA, Ohio State U., Columbus, 1974, postgrad., 1975-76; postgrad., Ohio State U., Columbus, 1978-90; MS in Edn., U. Dayton, 1993. Lic. social worker, Ohio. Cons. Ohio Dept. Human Svc., Columbus, 1974-75; mgr. Fisher Body Div., Columbus, 1977-78; with Franklin County Human Svc., Columbus, 1975—, supr., 1979-86, adminstr., 1986-91, asst. dep. dir., 1991—; pub. speaker human svcs. program Franklin County Human Svc., 1988—; instr., human svc. devel. Columbus State C.C., 1990—; grad. United Way Project Diversity Leadership Program. Mem. adv. bd. Columbus City Comprehensive Plan, 1989—, Syntaxis Group Home, Columbus, 1989—; Informed Neighbors Com., 1989—, Berwick Civic Assn., Columbus (v.p. 1990-92, pres. 1992—); trustee Mental Health Assn., Columbus. Mem. AAUW (corr. sec. Columbus chpt. 1988—), NAFE, LWV, Columbus Women's Newtork, Berwick Civic Assn. (pres. 1992). Democrat. Roman Catholic. Home: 2665 Mitzi Dr Columbus OH 43209-3263 Office: Franklin County Dept Human Svc 80 E Fulton St Columbus OH 43215-5127

SMITH, VANGY EDITH, accountant, consultant, writer, artist; b. Saskatoon, Sask., Can., Dec. 17, 1937; d. Wilhelm and Anne Ellen (Hartshorne) Gogel: m. Clifford Wilson, May 12, 1958 (de. Dec. 1978); children: Kenneth, Koral, Kevin, Korey, Kyle; m. Terrence Raymond Smith, Dec. 14, 1979. Student, Saskatoon Tech. Collegiate Inst., 1956, BBA, 1958, MBA, 1987, PhD in English with honors, 1988. Accounts payable clk. Maxwell Labs., Inc., San Diego, 1978; invoice clk. Davies Electric, Saskatoon, 1980-81; office mgr. Ladee Bug Ceramics, Saskatoon, 1981-87, Lazars Investments Corp., Eugene, Oreg., 1987; bookkeeper accounts payable Pop Geer, Eugene, Oreg., 1987; office mgr., bookkeeper Willamette Sports Ctr., Inc., Eugene, Oreg., 1985-89; clk. I Lane C.C., 1992—; self-employed Vangy Enterprises, 1992—; circulation mgr. Nat. WCTU, 1990-92, UN rep. for World WCTUm 1989-91; appointed mem. Parliament for the U. for Peace, Holland, 1991. Contbr. articles to scholarly jours. (recipient doctoral award 1987). Counselor Drug and Rehab. Ctr., Eugene, 1970-88; trustee Children's Farm Home, Corvallis, Oreg., 1989-91, 3d v.p., 1989-90; mem. Found. Christian Living; pres. Oreg. State Christian Temperance Union, 1989-90; mem. pub. safety adv. com. City of Eugene, 1989-90; co-pres. Lane County UN Assn., 1989-90; mem. artist Nat. Bd. Edn., 1989, 90; mem. adv. com. Dept. Pub. Safety for City of Eugene, 1990; exec. dir. H.E.L.P., 1993—; pres. Lane County Coun. of Orgns., 1994; treas. Cascade/Coast chpt. Alzheimers Assn., 1994. Recipient 3d and 4th place artists' awards Lane County Fair, 1987, 1st and 2d place awards Nat. Writing Contest, 1987, 88, 89, 90, 91. Mem. WCTU (life, pres., state bd. dirs. projection methods circulation 1987-90, Appreciation award 1982, Presdl. award 1985, Lane County Euenge Woman of Yr. 1990), Am. Soc. Writers, Alzheimers Assn. (treas. Cascade/Coast chpt. 1994), Rebekkah Juanita Lodge, Lions (sec. 1994). Democrat.

SMITH, VERONICA LATTA, real estate corporation officer; b. Wyandotte, Mich., Jan. 13, 1925; d. Jan August and Helena (Hulak) Latta; m. Stewart Gene Smith, Apr. 12, 1952; children: Stewart Gregory, Patrick Allen, Paul Donald, Alison Veronica, Alisa Margaret Lyons, Glenn Laurence. BA in Sociology, U. Mich., 1948, postgrad., 1948. Tchr. Coral Gables (Fla.) Pub. Sch. System, 1949-50; COO Latta Ins. Agy, Wyandotte, 1950-62; treas. L & S Devel. Co., Grosse Ile, Mich., 1963-84; v.p. Regency Devel., Riverview, Mich., 1984—. Active U. Mich. Bd. Regents, 1985-93, regent emeritus, 1993—; mem., pres. Martha Cook Bd. Govs., U. Mich., 1972-78, 76-78; del. Rep. County Conv., Wayne County, Mich., 1988—, Rep. State Conv., Grand Rapids, Mich., 1985, 87, 89, 91, 92, 94, Detroit, 1986, 88, 90, 92; mem. pres. adv. com. Campaign for Mich., 1992—, mem. campaign steering com., 1992—. Mem. Mich. Lawyers Aux. (treas. 1975, chmn. 1976, 77, 78, 79), Nat. Assn. Ins. Women (cert.), Faculty Women's Club U. Mich. (hon.), Radrick Farms Golf Club (Ann Arbor), Pres.'s Club U. Mich., Investment Club (pres. 1976, sec. 1974-75, treas. 1975-76), Alpha Kappa Delta. Home: 22225 Balmoral Dr Grosse Ile MI 48138

SMITH, VIRGINIA A., media consultant; b. Washington, Oct. 23, 1962; d. Kenneth Ross and Patricia Marcella (Maher) S. BBA, Va. Commonwealth U., 1986; postgrad., George Washington U., 1994—. Pub. rels. coord. Richmond Comedy Club, Va., 1987-90; media coord. Medalist Sports, Richmond, Va., 1991; event coord. ProServ, Washington, 1992; paralegal Law Resources, Washington, 1993-94; cons. MCI, McLean, Va., 1994—; cons., media rels. Va. Internat. Gold Cup, Middleburg, Va., 1993-94, Project Life Animal Rescue, Washington, 1994, The President's Golf Cup, Washington, 1994. Editor: Tour DuPont Mag., 1991. Vol. Octagon Club, Winchester, Va., 1980-81, Senatorial Campaigns, Richmond, 1988, Washington, 1994. Mem. Smithsonian, Nat. Assn. Female Execs. Republican. Roman Catholic. Home: 116 Stonewall Dr Winchester VA 22602

SMITH, VIRGINIA BROWN, classical musician; b. Nashville, July 24, 1954; d. Jordan Stokes and Annie Frances (Sory) Brown; m. Mark Brampton Smith, Feb. 28, 1976 (div. 1986); 1 child, Evelyn Anne. MusB, Eastman Sch. Music, 1976; MusM, U. Mich., 1979. Dir. music Good Shepherd United Meth. Ch., Dearborn, Mich., 1977-81, Westminster Presby. Ch., Ann Arbor, Mich., 1981-84; instr. voice Schoolcraft Coll., Livonia, Mich., 1986-89; pvt. practice voice instr. Ann Arbor, 1976—; adj. instr. Albion (Mich.) Coll., 1991—; solo recitals, performances Ann Arbor, Detroit, Mpls., Nashville, Washington, 1977—. Soprano soloist Christ Ch. Cranbrook, Bloomfield Hills, Mich., 1984—, U. Mich. Early Music Ensemble, 1977-89, Ann Arbor Cantata Singers, 1981-89, Ars Musica Choir, Ann Arbor, 1984-85. Mem. Nat. Assn. Tchrs. Singing (bd. dirs. Mich. chpt.), Music Tchrs. Nat. Assn. (nat. profl. cert. 1989), Acad. for Study and Performance Early Mus. (bd. dirs. and sec. 1994), Early Mus. Am., Mich. Music Tchrs. Assn. (bd. dirs., cert. 1988, state voice chairperson), Ann Arbor Piano Tchrs. Guild (treas. 1983-85), Livonia Area Piano Tchrs. Forum (pres. 1991-93), Detroit Musicians League, Pi Kappa Lambda, Sigma Alpha Iota. Democrat. Episcopalian. Home: 1495 Folkstone Ct Ann Arbor MI 48105-2847

SMITH, VIRGINIA DODD (MRS. HAVEN SMITH), congresswoman; b. Randolph, Iowa, June 30, 1911; d. Clifton Clark and Erville (Reeves) Dodd; m. Haven N. Smith, Aug. 27, 1931. A.B., U. Nebr., 1936; hon. degree, Nebr. U., 1987, Chadron State Coll., 1988. Nat. pres. Am. Country Life Assn., 1951-54; nat. chmn. Am. Farm Bur. Women, 1954-74; dir. Am. Farm Bur. Fedn., 1954-74, Country Women's Council; world dep. pres. Asso. Country Women of World, 1962-68; mem. Dept. Agr. Nat. Home Econs. Research Adv. Com., 1960-65; bd. dirs. Norwest Bank Cmty. Bd., Property Owners and Residents Bd., Sun Health Corp. Bd., Recreation Ctrs. Sun City West, sec., mem. gov. bd. Mem. Crusade for Freedom European inspection tour, 1958; del. Republican Nat. Conv., 1956, 72; bd. govs. Agrl. Hall of Fame, 1959—; mem. Nat. Livestock and Meat Bd., 1955-58, Nat. Commn. Community Health Services, 1963-66; adv. mem. Nebr. Sch. Bds. Assns., 1949; mem. Nebr. Territorial Centennial Commn., 1953, Gov.'s Commn. Status of Women, 1964-66; chmn. Presdl. Task Force on Rural Devel., 1969-70; mem. appropriations com., ranking minority mem. agrl. appropriations subcom., appropriations subcom. on energy and water devel. 94th-101st Congresses from 3d dist. Nebr.; v.p. Farm Film Found., 1964-74, Good Will ambassador to Switzerland, 1950. Apptd. adm. Nebr. Navy; bd. dirs. Shepherd of the Hills Meth. Ch. Recipient award of Merit, DAR, 1956; Disting. Service award U. Nebr., 1956, 60; award for best pub. address on freedom Freedom Found., 1966; Eyes on Nebr. award Nebr. Optometric Assn., 1970; Internat. Service award Midwest Conf. World Affairs, 1970; Woman of Achievement award Nebr. Bus. and Profl. Women, 1971; selected as 1 of 6 U.S. women Govt. France for 3 week goodwill mission to France, 1969; Outstanding 4H Alumni award Iowa State U., 1973, 74; Watchdog of Treasury award, 1976, 78, 80, 82, 83, 84, 86, 88; Guardian of Small Bus. award, 1976, 78, 80, 82, 84, 86, 88; Nebr. Ak-Sar-Ben award, 1983, Agrl. Achievement, Nebr. U., 1987; named Favorite Community Leader, Sun City West, 1994. Mem. AAUW, Delta Kappa Gamma (state hon. mem.), Beta Sigma Phi (internat. hon. mem.), Chi Omega, PEO (past pres.), Eastern Star. Methodist. Club: Business and Professional Women. Address: 13828 Terra Vista Dr Sun City West AZ 85375

SMITH, VIRGINIA WARREN, artist, writer, educator; b. Atlanta, Mar. 7, 1947; d. Ralph Henry and Dorothy Jane (Kubler) S. AB in Philosophy, Ga. State U., 1976, M Visual Art in Art and Photography, 1978. dir. The Upstairs Artspace, Tryon, N.C., 1984-86; mng. editor Art Papers, Atlanta, 1986-88; art critic Atlanta (Ga.) Jour./Constn., Atlanta, 1987-92; adj. faculty Atlanta (Ga.) Coll. Art, 1991—, Ga. State U., Atlanta, 1991—. Author, photographer: Scoring in Heaven: Gravestones and Cemetery Art in the American Sunbelt States, 1991, Alaska: Trail Tails and Eccentric Detours, 1992; exhbns. include Nexus Contemporary Art Ctr., Atlanta, 1986, 87, 91, Sandler Hudson Gallery, Atlanta, 1987, 89, 92, Jackson Fine Art, Atlanta, 1988, 91, 93, Aperture Found., N.Y.C., 1989, MS Found., N.Y.C., 1991, Albany (Ga.) Mus. Art, 1991, Montgomery (Ala.) Mus. Art, 1992, Bernice Steinbaum Gallery, N.Y.C., 1992, others; works in permanent collections including Mus. Modern Art, N.Y.C., Mus. Fine Arts, Boston, High Mus. of Art, Atlanta, New Orleans Mus. Art, Harvard U., Rochester Inst. Tech., N.Y., U. N.Mex., Ctr. for Study of Southern Culture U. Miss., Oxford, Miss. Bd. mem. Art Papers, Atlanta, 1983-88; adv. bd. memd. Arts Festival Atlanta, Ga., 1990-93. Mem. Coll. Art Assn., Soc. for Photographic Edn., Photography Forum of the High Mus. Art (v.p. 1994—). Democrat. Home and Office: 343 Josephine St NE Atlanta GA 30307

SMITH, VME (VERNA MAE EDOM SMITH), sociology educator, freelance writer, photographer; b. Marshfield, Wis., June 19, 1929; d. Clifton Cedric and Vilia Clarissa (Patefield) Edom; children: Teri Freas, Anthony Thomas. AB in Sociology, U. Mo., 1951; MA in Sociology, George Washington, 1965; PhD in Human Devel., U. Md., 1981. Tchr. Alcohol Safety Action Program Fairfax County, Va., 1973-75; instr. sociology No. Va. Community Coll., Manassas, 1975-77, asst. prof., 1977-81, assoc. prof., 1981-84, prof., 1984—, coord. coop. edn., 1983-89; Chancellor's Commonwealth prof. Manassas, 1991-93; freelance writer, editor and photographer, 1965—; asst. producer history of photography program Sta. WETA-TV, Washington, 1965; rsch. and prodn. asst., photographer, publs. editor No. Va. Ednl. TV, Sta. WNVT, 1970-7l; cons. migrant div. Md. Dept. Edn., Balt., summer 1977; researcher, photographer Roundabout presch. high sch. series on Am. Values Sta. WNVT, 1970-71. Author, photographer: Middleburg and Nearby, 1986; co-author: Small Town America, 1993; contbr. photography to various works including Visual Impact in Print (Hurley and McDougall), 1971, Looking Forward to a Career in Education (Moses), 1976, Child Growth and Development (Terry, Sorrentino and Flatter), 1979, Photojournalism (Edom), 1976, 80, Migrant Child Welfare, 1977, (Cavenaugh), Caring for Children, 1973 (5 publs. by L.B. Murphy), Dept. Health, Edn. and Welfare, Nat. Geog., 1961, Head Start Newsletter, 1973-74. Mem. ednl. adv. com. Head Start, Warrenton, Va. Recipient Emmy Ohio State Children's Programming award; Fulbright-Hays Rsch. grantee, 1993. Mem. Va. Assn. Coop. Edn. (com. mem.). Democrat. Office: No Va Community Coll 6901 Sudley Rd Manassas VA 22110-2399

SMITH, WENDY DIANE, accountant; b. Tucker, Ga., Dec. 5, 1971; d. William Allen and Klara Elizabeth (Moser) S. BBA in Acctg., Ga. So. U., 1992. Acct. GTE/Sylvania Lighting, College Park, Ga., 1992-93, Walton C. Bryde & Assocs., Atlanta, 1993—. Office: Walton C Bryde & Assocs 3353 Peachtree Rd Ste 1140 Atlanta GA 30326

SMITH, WENDY HAIMES, federal agency administrator; b. Amarillo, Tex.; d. Ernest A. and Fannie Haimes; m. Jay L. Smith, 1983. BA in Econs., U. Mich., 1972; postgrad., Ohio State U., 1973, Am. U., 1991, Washington Studio Sch., 1993-95. Cert. real estate agt. Office mgr. Haimes Travel Agy., Ohio, 1972-73; mgmt. intern U.S. Dept. Commerce, 1973-75, country specialist for Korea, 1973, spl. asst. to dep. asst. sec. for internat. commerce, 1973-74, project officer, maj. projects divsn., 1974-75, project mgr. indsl. sys., maj. projects divsn., 1975-77, country specialist for Brazil, 1978, project mgr., hydrocarbons and chem. process plants, maj. export projects divsn., 1977-79, exec. asst. to dep. asst. sec. of commerce for export devel. and staff dir. Pres. Export Coun., 1979-81, dir. Pres. Export Coun., 1981-92, acting dir. Office Planning and Coordination, 1988-89, dir. adv. coms. and pvt. sector programs Internat. Trade Adminstrn., 1992—. Author, editor: U.S. Trade in Transition: Maintaining the Gains, 1988; co-author, editor: The Export Imperative, 1980, Coping with the Dynamics of World Trade in the 1980s, 1984. Active Smithsonian Instn., Washington Studio Sch., Washington Opera Guild. Mem. Alpha Epsilon Phi (pres. Pi chpt. 1971). Office: Dept of Commerce Rm H2015B 14th and Constitution Ave NW Washington DC 20230

SMITH, YVONNE CAROLYN, therapist; b. Lockport, N.Y., June 12, 1923; d. William Louis and Bertha (Zoss) S. BA, Valparaiso U., 1948; M in Social Sci. Adminstrn., Case-Western Res. U., Cleve., 1955. Cert. social worker. Caseworker Niagara County Welfare Dept., Lockport, 1950-53, Luth. Children's Aid, Cleve., 1954, Luth. Family Svc., Chgo., 1955-56, Family Svc. Soc., Buffalo, 1956-62; therapist, dir. Child & Family Svcs., Buffalo, 1962-88; ret. Child & Family Svcs., Cheetowaga, N.Y., 1988; field instr. social work SUNY, 1962-80; cons. Genesee County Social Svcs., Batavia, 1975-85, cons. Seneca County Social Svcs. Waterloo, 1988. Bd. dirs. Luth. Svc. Soc., Buffalo, 1979-85, 88-93, mem. family svc. com., 1993—; speaker United Way of Buffalo, 1956-88; mem. edn. com. ea. dist. Luth. Ch. Mo. Synod, 1991—. Mem. AAUW, Internat. Human Learning Resources Network, Nigara County Hist. Soc., Kenmore Art Soc. Republican. Home: 401 Englewood Ave Apt 3 Buffalo NY 14223-2809

SMITHER, GERTRUDE JACKSON, minister; b. Dallas, Oct. 6, 1937; d. John Nelson and Sallie Bell (Gaston) Jackson; m. Robert Bush Smither Jr., Aug. 20, 1960; children: Robert, Sallie, John, Mary Kate. BA, U. Tex., 1959; MDiv, Episcopal Theol. Sem. S.W., Austin, 1985. Ordained to ministry, Episcopal Ch., 1990. Dir. religious edn. Trinity Episcopal Ch., Galveston, Tex., 1979-83; chaplain U. Tex. Med. Br., Galveston, 1985-92; coord. Diocese Dallas Hosp. Chaplaincy and Canon Chaplain St. Matthew's Cathedral, Dallas, 1992—; asst. St. Luke the Physician Episcopal Ch., Galveston, 1985-92; chaplain William Temple Found., Galveston, 1985-92; chaplain U. Tex. Med. Br., 1985-92; pres. St. Vincent's Episcopal House, Galveston, 1987, 88, 91; chmn. Campus Mins., 1987-91; mem. Coun. Religious Ministry, UTMB, 1985-92. Fellow Coll. of Chaplains Inc. (continuing edn. chair Tex. north region), Galveston Ministerial Assn. (pres. 1991). Home: 7854 Caruth Ct Dallas TX 75225 Office: Saint Matthews Cathedral 5100 Ross Ave Dallas TX 75206

SMITH-LEINS, TERRI L., mathematics educator; b. Salina, Kans., Sept. 19, 1950; d. John W. and Myldred M. (Hays) Smith; m. Larry L. Leins, May 26, 1984. BS, Ft. Hays (Kans.) U., 1973, MS, 1976; AA, Stephen Coll., Columbia, Mo., 1970. Math tchr. Scott City (Kans.) Jr. High Sch., Howard (Kans.) Schs.; instr. math. Westark Community Coll., Ft. Smith, Ark. Contbr. articles to profl. jours., chpts. to books. Mem. AADE, ASCD, Nat. Assn. Developmental Edn. (state sec. 1986-88, computer access com. 1980-85), Phi Delta Kappa (Kappan of the Yr. 1985), Delta Kappa Gamma (state chairperson women in art 1993—). Home: PO Box 3572 Fort Smith AR 72913-3572

SMITH REEVE, MINERVA TABITHA, retired university staff member; b. Indpls., June 10, 1907; d. Chaplain Franklin Peter and Deatherage Sophia Pearl (Allen) Smith; m. Keith Graham Reeve, June 9, 1927; children: Patricia Louise Reeve Monroe, Josephine Ann Reeve Savas. Student, U. Ill., Auburn U. Owner Style Shop, Mt. Carmel, Ill., 1939-48; head resident, dean of women's staff Auburn (Ala.) U., 1968-77. Mem. Lee County Hosp. Aux.; philanthropy chair Lee County Nursing Home, 1968-73; pres. PTA, Mt. Carmel, Ill., 1942-44; an organizer Art League Hunstville, pres., 1957; formerly mem. Auburn coun. Girl Scouts U.S.; life mem. Huntsville Art League and Mus., 1957—; active numerous civic orgns. Mem. Nat. Soc. DAR (publicity chair 1971-76, vice regent and program chair 1963-66, 50-Yr. Pin, vice regent Auburn chpt. 1976), Colonial Dames of IVII Century (3d v.p. Capt. Thomas Yale chpt. 1964-66, pres. 1970, state chaplain 1965-66, nat. heealdry com. 1964), Magna Charta Dames (historian Ala. chpt. 1966), Campus Club of Auburn U., Daus. of Am. Colonists, Charlemagne Soc., PEO Sisterhood (organizer, v.p. Huntsville chpt.). Christian. Home: 3905 Richland Dr Huntsville AL 35810

SMITH SIMON, SHIRLEY GRIFFING, social activist; b. Hampton Bays, N.Y.; m. Herbert Smith (dec. 1976); 1 child, Lynne; m. John Simon. Student, Keuka Coll. Host monthly TV program L.I. Cablevision Grown on Long Island. Active Council Overseers of Southampton Campus of L.I. U., Girl Scouts of Am., Cen. Suffolk Hosp. auxs., Suffolk Citizen's Adv. Council, Multiple Sclerosis Soc., Am. Cancer Soc.; chmn. Riverhead Town Landmarks Preservation Commn., ann. L.I. Potato Queen Contest; 1st pres. Hallockville, Inc.; co-organizer Townscape riverfront rehab. project which established Riverhead Country Fair; pres. women's group United Meth. Ch.; sec. L.I. Farm Bur. Women's Com.; bd. dirs. Suffolk Heart Assn., chmn. North Fork unit; contbr., organizer Congl. campaign for Otis Pike. Named Woman of Yr. East End Women's Network, 1987. Address: One Dolphin Way Riverhead NY 11901-1018

SMITHSON, SUSAN MARY, sales executive; b. Evanston, Ill., Apr. 18, 1952; d. Paul Busby and Janet Clara (Baker) S.; m. William Joseph Cherf, Aug. 29, 1987. BSBA in Fin., U. Denver, 1976, MBA in Fin., 1977. Acct. AccounTemps, Denver, 1977; fleet mgr. Carol Buick Co., Evanston, 1977-81; dist. sales mgr. Buick Motor divsn. GM Corp., Cin., Mich., 1981, Newark, 1981-85, Dallas, 1985-87, Flint, Mich., 1987-89, Purchase, N.Y., 1989—. 'Fangette' NFG, 1979—; Ground's Com., Kingsberry Acres Condominium Assn., 1991—.

SMITH-STEVENSON, RUTHIE, curriculum director, secondary education educator; b. Crystal Springs, Miss., May 1, 1947; d. David Dewitt and Pinkie Lee (Powell) Smith; m. Isiah Dotson, Feb. 11, 1968 (div. May 1985); 1 child, Corey Duane Dotson; m. Lee Stevenson, Mar. 12, 1988 (div. Feb. 1994). BS, Jackson State U., 1969, MA, 1976, Edn. Specialist, 1991, PhD, 1994. Cert. English and French tchr., sch. adminstr. Claims rep. trainee Social Security Adminstrn., Elmwood Park, Ill., 1969-70; tchr. Jackson (Miss.) Pub. Schs., 1970-83, curriculum coord., 1983-87, asst. prin., 1983-90, dir. curriculum, 1990—; cons. MRE Ednl. Cons., Jackson, 1985-86, pvt., 1986—. Recipient Achievement award Marino-Jones Br. YWCA, 1989; Rsch. scholar Jackson State U., 1992. Mem. ASCD, NAFE, Nat. Middle Sch. Assn., Am. Assn. Sch. Adminstrs., Miss. Assn. Sch. Adminstrs., Jackson State U. Doctoral Assn. (pres.), Phi Kappa Phi, Pi Lambda Theta. Democrat. Baptist. Office: Canton Pub Schs 403 E Lincoln St Canton MS 39046

SMITH-THOMPSON, PATRICIA ANN, public relations consultant, educator; b. Chgo., June 7, 1933; d. Clarence Richard and Ruth Margaret (Jacobson) Nowack; m. Tyler Thompson, Aug. 1, 1992. Student Cornell U., 1951-52; BA, Centenary Coll., Hackettstown, N.J., 1983. Prodn. asst. Your Hit Parade Batten, Barton, Durstine & Osborne, 1953-54; pvt. practice polit. cons., 1954-66; legal sec., asst. Atty. John C. Cushman, 1966-68; field dep. L.A. County Assessor, 1968-69, pub. info. officer L.A. County Probation Dept., 1969-73; dir. consumer rels. Fireman's Fund, San Francisco, 1973-76; pvt. practice pub. rels. cons., 1976-77; spl. projects officer L.A. County Transp. Commn., 1977-78; tchr. Calif. State U.-Dominguez Hills, 1979-86; editor, writer Jet Propulsion Lab., 1979-80; pub. info. dir. L.A. Bd. Pub. Works, 1980-82; pub. info. cons. City of Pasadena, (Calif.), 1982-84; pub. rels. cons., 1983-90, community rels./Worldport L.A., 1990-92. Contbr. articles to profl. jours. Mem. First United Methodist Ch. Commn. on Missions and Social Concerns, 1983-89; bd. dirs. Depot, 1983-87; mem. devel. com. Pasadena Guidance Clinics, 1984-85. Recipient Pro award L.A. Publicity Club, 1978, Outstanding Achievement award Soc. Consumer Affairs Profls. in Bus., 1976, Disting. Alumni award Centenary Coll., 1992. Mem. Pub. Relations Soc. Am. (accredited mem.; award for consumer program 1977, 2 awards 1984, Joseph Roos Community Service award 1985), Nat. Press Women (pub. relations award 1986), Calif. Press Women (awards 1974, 78, 83, 84, 85, community relations 1stplace winner 1986, 87, 88, 89), Nat. Assn. Mental Health Info. Offices (3 regional awards 1986). Republican.

SMITH-TOOLE, KATRINA RHENEA, school counselor, educator; b. Kingsport, Tenn., Feb. 7, 1963; d. Ralph Taylor and Helen (Johnson) Smith; m. James Matthew Toole, Aug. 7, 1993. BA, Va. Intermont, 1982-85; MEd cum laude, E. Tenn. State, 1990-92. Cert. in elem. edn., sch. counseling; cert. tchr. acad. gifted. Headstart tchr. Scott County Schs., Gate City, Va., 1986-88, tchr. acad. gifted, 1988-90, counselor, 1990—; child-study chairperson, Just Say No club sponsor and parent edn. class instr. Scott County Schs., 1990—, mem. health adv. com., 1992—. Mem. Am. Sch. Counselor Assn., Am. Counselor Assn. Democrat. Methodist. Home: 804 E Holston Ave Johnson City TN 37601-3406 Office: Scott County Sch System 265 E Jackson St Gate City VA 24251-3422

SMITH-WHITSETT, LINDA A., federal agency administrator; b. Aug. 3, 1951; d. Oscar Lynn and Thelma (Gourdine) Smith. BJ, Northwestern U., 1973. Reporter Buffalo Courier-Express Newspaper, 1973-77; writer, then pub. affairs specialist and freedom of info. act officer pub. info. office Occupl. Safety and Health Rev. Commn., Washington, 1980—. Recipient Page One award Newspaper Guild, Buffalo chpt., 1975. Mem. Nat. Assn. Govt. Communicators (commendation), Alpha Kappa Alpha. Office: Occ Safety & Health Review Comm 1 Lafayette Ctr Rm 903 1120 20th St NW Washington DC 20036-3419*

SMITH-YOUNG, ANNE VICTORIA, health services coordinator; b. Long Beach, Calif., Aug. 25, 1947; d. James Warren and Jeanne Anne (Cooney) Wright; m. Lynn Walker Smith, Aug. 11, 1968 (div. Feb. 1980); children: Amy Lyanne and Caroline Walker (twins); m. Stephen Nicholas Young, May 29, 1982. AS, Long Beach City Coll., 1967; BS, Marymount Coll., 1984. Diplomate Am. Bd. Urologic Allied Health Professions. Mgr. office Williams-Brinton Med. Corp., Huntington Beach, Calif., 1975-80; adminstr. Westchester Urol. Assocs., White Plains, N.Y., 1980-82; adminstr. Pediatric Urol. Assocs. Westchester County Med. Ctr., Valhalla, N.Y., 1982-86; clin. coord. urodynamics lab. cystocopy ste. dept. urology Westchester County Med. Ctr., Valhalla, 1986—, chairperson exec. com. employee adv. coun., 1987—; cons. Office Career Svcs., Marymount (N.Y.) Coll., 1984—, Am. Bd. Urologic Allied Health Profls., 1980-87, sec., 1987-93; pres., co-dir. Contineace Restored Inc., 1984—; cons. to mfrs., individuals and healthcare providers on urinary incontinence and urodynamics. Mem. editorial bd. Sex Over Forty; contbr. articles to profl. jours. Mem. NAFE, Am. Urol. Assn. Allied (nat. fundraiser 1980-86, bd. dirs. N.Y. chpt. 1988—, Recognition award 1984), Assn. Urinary Continence Control (bd. dirs. 1988—), Am. Assn. Med. Assts., Nat. Trust for Historic Preservation, Mothers of Twins Club (pres. Long Beach 1974-75), Lions (bd. dirs. White Plains 1989, editor Lions Roar newsletter, pres. 1991-93, zone chmn. 1993-94, region chmn. 1994—, Lion of Month award 1990, Officer of Yr. award 1991). Democrat. Home: 407 Strawberry Hill Ave Stamford CT 06902-2513 Office: Westchester County Med Ctr Dept Urology Macy # 1058 Valhalla NY 10595

SMITS, HELEN LIDA, public adminstrator, physician, educator; b. Long Beach, Calif., Dec. 3, 1936; d. Theodore Richard Smits and Anna Mary Wells; m. Roger LeCompte, Aug. 28, 1976; 1 child, Theodore. BA with honors, Swarthmore Coll., 1958; MA, Yale U., 1961, MD cum laude, 1967. Intern, asst. resident Hosp. U. Pa., 1967-68; fellow Beth Israel Hosp., Boston, 1969-70; chief resident Hosp. U. Pa., 1970-71; chief med. clinic U. Pa., 1971-75; assoc. adminstr. for patient care svcs. U. Pa. Hosp., 1975-77; v.p. med. affairs Community Health Plan Georgetown U., Washington, 1977; dir. health standards and quality bur. Health Care Financing Adminstrn., HHS, Washington, 1977-80; sr. rsch. assoc. The Urban Inst., Washington, 1980-81; assoc. prof. Yale U. Med. Sch., New Haven, 1981-85; assoc. v.p. for health affairs U. Conn. Health Ctr., Farmington, 1985-87; prof. community medicine U. Conn. Sch. Medicine, Farmington, 1985-93; hosp. dir. John Dempsey Hosp., Farmington, 1987-93; dep. administr. Health Care Financing Adminstrn., Washington, 1993—; commr. Joint Com. on Accreditation Hosps., Chgo., 1989-93, chair, 1991-92. Contbr. numerous articles to profl. jours. Bd. dirs. The Ivoryton Playhouse Fedn., Inc., 1990-92, The Connecticut River Mus., 1990-93, Hartford Stage, 1990-93; mem. Dem. Town Com., Essex, Conn., 1982-89. Recipient Superior Svc. award HHS, Washington, 1982; Royal Soc. Medicine Found. fellow, London, 1973; Fulbright scholar, 1959-60. Mem. ACP (master, regent 1984-90), Phi Beta Kappa, Alpha Omega Alpha. Episcopalian. Home: 81 Main St Ivoryton CT 06442-1032 Office: Health Care Fin Adminstrn 200 Independence Ave SW Washington DC 20201

SMOLA, CYNTHIA JANE, mental health nurse; b. Denver, June 12, 1946; d. Franklin B. and Virginia L. (Landrum) Sipes; m. Emery Smola, Dec. 26, 1965. ADN, Cen. Meth. Coll., 1981. RN, Mo. Clin. nurse Fulton (Mo.) State Hosp., 1981-84, nursing supr. psychiat. area, 1984-86, assoc. dir. psychiat. nursing div., 1986-87, unit DON adult psychiat. svcs., 1987-90, dir. nursing edn., 1994—; unit DON Biggs Forensic Ctr., 1991-94. Mem. ANA (cert. mental health nurse). Home: 6103 County Rd 113 Fulton MO 65251-6411

SMOOT, HAZEL LAMPKIN, retired piano teacher, poet; b. Kamiah, Idaho, Oct. 17, 1916; d. Albert Chuning and Cora Benson (Buckland) Weaver; m. Daniel Joseph Smoot, Feb. 18, 1939 (div. 1960); children: Daniel Jerome, David Reed. AA, Sacramento City Coll., 1937; student, Linfield Coll., 1938. Contbr. poetry to anthologies published by World of Poetry, also to Vantage Press and The Golden Treasury of Great Poems, Great American Poetry Anthology. Scholar Linfield Coll.

SMOOT, SKIPI LUNDQUIST, psychologist; b. Aberdeen, Wash., Apr. 10, 1934; d. Warren Duncan and Miriam Stephen (Bishop) Dobbins; m. Harold Richard Lundquist, June 2, 1951 (div. Mar. 1973); children: Kurt Richard, Mark David, Ted Douglas, Blake Donald; m. Edward Lee Smoot, June 14, 1975. BA in Psychology, Coll. of William and Mary, 1978; MA, Pepperdine U., 1980; PhD, Calif. Sch. of Profl., Psychology, San Diego, 1985. Lic. clin. psychologist, Calif.; lic. marriage and family therapist, Calif. Owner, operator McDonald's Restaurants, San Pedro and Torrance, Calif., 1965-76, Williamsburg, Va., 1965-76; psychotherapist Coll. Hosp., Cerritos, Calif., 1979-81, Orange County Child Guidance, Laguna Hills, Calif., 1981-82; psychotherapist Calif. State Police, Costa Mesa, 1982-83, Anaheim, 1983-84; psychologist Orange County Mental Health, Santa Ana, Calif., 1984-85, Psychol. Ctr., Orange and El Toro, Calif., 1985-91; clin. dir. Career Ambitions, Irvine and Laguna Hills, 1991-94, Psychol. Decisions, Irvine-Laguna Hills, Calif., 1991-94; psychol. cons. seminars and workshops for bus., Irvine and Laguna Hills, 1991-94. Mem. APA, Calif. Psychol. Assn., Calif. Assn. Marriage and Family Therapists. Democrat. Office: Psychol Decisions Career Ambitions Unltd 25411 Cabot Rd Ste 105 Laguna Hills CA 92653-5517

SMOTHERMON, REBA MAXINE, elementary education educator; b. Liberal, Kans., July 8, 1933; d. Albert Isaac and Georgia Maxine (Long) Shank; m. Wendell Scott Smothermon, Sept. 6, 1953; children: Jennifer Lynn Smothermon Kirby, Wendell Brent Smothermon. BA in Edn., Wichita State U., 1955; MA in Ednl. Psychology and Guidance, U. No. Colo., 1959. Cert. tchr. Kans., Calif., Colo. Tchr. second grade Unified Sch. Dist. 480/Washington Sch., Liberal, Kans., 1955-57, Adams County Dist. Skyline Vista Sch., Westminster, Colo., 1957-61; elem. tchr. Ventura Unified Santa Ana Sch., Ojai, Calif., 1964-80, Unified Sch. Dist. #480, Southlawn McKinley Schs., Liberal, 1980—; literary coun. mem. Southwest Reading Coun., Liberal, 1985—. Participant devel. sch. curriculum, 1977-79. Sec. to pres. Evergreen Garden Club, Liberal, 1980—; youth sponsor, pres. women's group 1st United Meth. Ch., Liberal, 1945—; mem. Liberal Panhellenic, 1980—; bd. dirs., pres. Community Concerts of Liberal, 1987-91. Mem. AAUW (pres. local chpt. 1980—, Woman of Yr. 1985, state chmn. internat.

rels. com. 1985-90), PEO (various to pres. 1985—), DAR, Ladies' Oriental Shrine N.Am., White Shrine, Delta Kappa Gamma (various to pres. 1981—). Republican. Home: 318 Harvard Ave Liberal KS 67901-3022

SMRCINA, CATHERINE MARIE, nursing administrator, researcher; b. Chgo., June 27, 1952; d. Edward Francis and Helen Marie (Smalarz) S.; B.S. in Nursing, U. Ill., 1974; MS in Nursing Service Adminstrn., U. Ill., 1982. Cert. med./surg. nurse; cert. orthopedic nurse. Nursing asst. Columbus Hosp., Chgo., 1972-74, staff nurse, 1974-77, head nurse orthopedics, 1977-81, clin. supr., 1981-82; nurse assoc. Cabrini Hosp., Chgo., 1983-85; asst. dir. patient and staff edn. and nursing quality assurance Bethany Meth. Hosp., Chgo., 1985-87; assoc. dir. nursing, Meth. Hosp. Chgo., 1987-88, dir. nursing, 1988-89; coord. clinical rsch. Shriners Hosp. for Crippled Children, Chgo, 1989—. Mem. Nat. Assn. Orthopedic Nurses (pres. Chgo. chpt., North Central Dist. rep., Ill. state liaison, nat. pres.), U. Ill. Alumni Assn., Chgo. Nurses Assn., Ill. Nurses Assn., Am. Nurses Assn., Council Cath. Nurses Archdiocese Chgo., Am. Heart Assn., Ill. Coalition of Nursing Orgns. (chmn.), Catholic Order Foresters, Soc. Pediatric Nurses. Office: 2211 N Oak Park Ave Chicago IL 60635-3351

SMUCKER, BARBARA CLAASSEN, former librarian, writer; b. Newton, Kans., Sept. 1, 1915; dual citizen U.S. and Can.; d. Cornelius Walter and Addie (Lander) Claassen; m. Donovan Ebersole Smucker, Jan. 21, 1939; children: Timothy, Thomas, Rebecca. BS, Kans. State U., 1936; postgrad., Rosary Coll., 1963-65; LittD (hon.), U. Waterloo, 1986; DHL (hon.), Bluffton Coll., 1989. English tchr. Harper (Kans.) High Sch., 1937-38; reporter Evening Kansan Republican, Newton, 1939-41; tchr. Ferry Hall Sch., Lake Forest, Ill., 1960-63; children's librarian Kitchener (Ont.) Public Library, 1969-77; reference librarian, head librarian Renison Coll., U. Waterloo, Ont., 1977-82, sr. fellow Renison Coll., 1982—; writer Am. Educator Ency., Lake Bluff, Ill., 1960-63; convocation speaker U. Waterloo, Ont., 1986. Author: Henry's Red Sea, 1955, Cherokee Run, 1957, Wigwam in the City, Susan, 1970, Underground to Canada, 1977, Les Chemins Secrets de la Liberte, 1978, Runaway to Freedom, 1977, June Lilly, 1981, Folge dem Nordstern, 1979, Under Jorden Til Canada, 1977, Days of Terror, 1980, Amish Adventure, 1983, Huida al Canada, 1983, Nubes Negras, 1984, Dagen Van Angst, 1985, White Mist, 1985, Jacob's Little Giant, 1987 (selected as gift to Prince Harry by govt. Ont.), Incredible Jumbo, 1990 (I.O.D.E. award 1991), Race To Freedom, 1994; (oratorio, libretto) The Abiding Place, 1984, Garth and the Mermaid, 1992; (interpretation) Oxford Companion to Canadian Literature, 1985, Michelle Landsberg's Guide to Children's Books, 1986; illustrator (autobiography) Something About the Author, 1991. Recipient prizes Can. Council, 1980, Ruth Schwartz Found., 1980, Disting. Service award Kans. State U., 1980, Brotherhood award NCCJ, 1980; $2000 Vicki Metcalf prize for outstanding contbn. to Can. children's lit. Can. Authors Assn., 1988, Kitchener award, 1990. Mem. AAUW, Canadian Assn. Univ. Women, Canadian Soc. Children's Authors, Illustrators and Performers, Children's Reading Round Table, Chgo. Home: 20 Pinebrook Dr Bluffton OH 45817-1145

SMUTNY, JOAN FRANKLIN, academic director, educator; b. Chgo.; d. Eugene and Mabel (Lind) Franklin; m. Herbert Paul Smutny; 1 child, Cheryl Anne. BS, Northwestern U., MA. Tchr., New Trier High Sch., Winnetka, Ill.; mem. faculty, founder, dir. Nat. High Sch. Inst., Northwestern U. Sch. Edn., Chgo.; mem. faculty, founder dir. high sch. workshop in critical thinking and edn., chmn. dept. communications Nat. Coll. Edn., Evanston, Ill., exec. dir. high sch. workshops, 1970-75, founder, dir. Woman Power Through Edn. Seminar, 1969-74, dir. Right to Read seminar in critical reading, 1973-74, seminar gifted high sch. students, 1973, dir. of Gifted Programs for 6, 7 and 8th graders pub. schs., Evanston, 1978-79, 1st-8th graders, Glenview (both Ill.) 1979—; dir. gifted programs Nat.-Louis U., Evanston, 1980-82, dir. Center for Gifted, 1982—; dir. Bright and Talented and Project 1986—, North Shore Country Day Sch., Winnetka, 1982—; dir. Job Creation Project, 1980-82; dir. New Dimensions for Women, 1973, dir. Thinking for Action in Career Edn. project, 1974-77 , dir. Individualized Career Edn. Program, 1976-79, dir. TACE, dir. Humanities Program for Verbally Precocious Youth, 1978-79; co-dir., instr. seminars in critical thinking Ill. Family Svc., 1972-75 . Writer ednl. filmstrips in Lang. arts and Lit. Soc. for Visual Edn., 1970-74 ; mem. speakers bur. Counc. Fgn. Rels., 1968-69 ; mem. adv. com. edn. professions devel. act U.S. Office Edn., 1969—; mem. state team for gifted, Ill. Office Edn., Office of Gifted, Springfield, Ill., 1977; writer, cons. Radiant Ednl. Corp., 1969-71 ; cons. ALA, 1969-71 , cons., workshop leader and speaker in area of gifted edn., 1971—; coord. of career edn. Nat. Coll. Edn., 1976-78, dir. Project '87, '88, '89, '90, '91, '92, 93, dir. Summer Wonders, 1986—, Creative Children's Acad., bd. dirs., Worlds of Wisdom and Wonder, 1978—; dir. Future Tchrs. Am. Seminar in Coll. and Career, 1970-72; cons. for research and devel. Ill. Dept. Vocat. Edn., 1973—; cons. in career edn. U.S. Office Edn., 1976—; evaluation cons. DAVTE, IOE, Springfield, Ill., 1977, mem. Leadership Tng. Inst. for Gifted, U.S. Office Edn., 1973-74; dir. workshops for high sch. students; cons., speaker in field; dir. Gifted Young Writer's and Young Writer's confs., 1978, 79; dir. Project '92 The White House Conf. on Children and Youth; mem. adv. bd. Educating Able Learners, 1991—; chmn. bd. dirs. Barbereux Sch., Evanston, 1992—; asst. editor and mem. adv. coun. Understanding Our Gifted, 1994—. Mem. AAUP, Nat. Assn. for Gifted Child (nat. membership chmn. 1991—), Nat. Soc. Arts and Letters (nat. bd., 1st and 3d v.p. Evanston chpt., dir. 1983-92, pres. Evanston chpt. 1990-92), Mortar Bd., Outstanding Educators of Am. 1974, Pi Lambda Theta, Phi Delta Kappa (v.p. Evanston chpt., rsch. chmn. 1990-92). Author: (with others) Job Creation: Creative Materials, Activities and Strategies for the classroom, 1982, A Thoughtful Overview of Gifted Education, 1990, Your Gifted Child - How to Recognize and Develop the Special Talents in Your Child from Birth to Age Seven, 1989, paperback, 1991, Education of the Gifted: Programs and Perspectives, 1990; editor, contbr. Maturity in Teaching; writer ednl. filmstrips The Brother's Grimm, How the West Was Won, Mutiny on the Bounty, Dr. Zhivago, Space Odessey 2001, Christmas Around the World; editor Jour. for Gifted, Ill., 1984—, Ill. Coun. Gifted Jour., 1985-93; contbg. editor Roeper Review, 1994—; editor IAGC Jour. for Gifted, 1994—, Potential and Promise: A Collection of Readings on the Gifted Young Child, 1995; contbg. editor numerous books in field; contbr. articles to profl. jours. including Chgo. Parent Mag. Reviewer of Programs for Gifted and Talented, U.S. Office of Edn., 1976-78. Home: 633 Forest Ave Wilmette IL 60091-1713

SMYTHE, SHEILA MARY, academic dean; b. N.Y.C., Nov. 1, 1932; d. Patrick John and Mary Catherine (Gonley) S. Student, Creighton U., 1952; BA, Manhattanville Coll., 1952; MS, Columbia U., N.Y.C., 1956; LHD (hon.), Manhattanville Coll., 1974. From rsch. assoc. to asst. dir. of rsch. and planning Blue Cross Assn., Chgo., 1957-63; exec. assoc. to pres. Empire Blue Cross & Blue Shield, N.Y.C., 1963-72, v.p., 1972-74, sr. v.p., 1974-78, exec. v.p., 1978-82, pres., chief oper. officer, 1982-85; health fin. and mgmt. cons. N.Y.C. and Washington, 1986-87; chief health policy advisor GAO, Washington, 1987—; dean grad. sch. health scis. N.Y. Med. Coll., N.Y.C., 1990—; adj. asst. prof. Grad. Sch. Pub. Health, Columbia U., 1980-86; bd. dirs. Mut. of Am., product & mktg. com. 1991-93, nominating com., 1992-94, audit com., 1993—, strategic planning com., 1994—; bd. dirs. Nat. Health Coun., Inc., mem. fin. com., 1987-94; bd. dirs. Hudson Valley Health Sys. Agy., sec., 1993-94, 1st v.p., 1994-95, pres., 1995—; active N.Y. State Hosp. and Rev. Planning Coun., 1994—. Chmn. of bd. Manhattanville Coll., Purchase, N.Y. 1994—, trustee affairs, acad. affairs, exec coms.; bd. dirs. Cath. Charities-U.S.A., 1989—, mem. exec. pers. coms.; bd. dirs. March of Dimes Birth Defects Found., 1989—, vice chair, mem. fin. com., chair pub affairs com., dir. Greater N.Y. March of Dimes, 1985-89. Recipient Elizabeth Cutter Morrow award YWCA, N.Y., 1977, Disting. Alumni award Manhattanville Coll., 1981, Excellence in Leadership award Greater N.Y. March of Dimes, 1989. Mem. Nat. Arts Club N.Y.C. Roman Catholic. Office: NY Med Coll Grad Sch Health Scis Valhalla NY 10595

SMYTHE-HAITH, MABEL MURPHY, consultant on African economic development, speaker, writer; b. Montgomery, Ala., Apr. 3, 1918; m. Hugh H. Smythe, June 22, 1939 (dec. 1977); 1 child, Karen Pamela; m. Robert Haith, Jr., Oct. 18, 1985. Student, Spelman Coll., 1933-36, LLD (hon.), 1980; BA, Mt. Holyoke Coll., 1937, LHD (hon.), 1977; MA, Northwestern U., 1940; PhD, U. Wis., 1942, LLD (hon.), 1991; LHD (hon.), U. Mass., 1979. Asst. prof. Lincoln U., Mo., 1942-45; prof. Tenn. A. and I. U., 1945-46, Bklyn. Coll., 1946-47; vis. prof. Shiga U., Japan, 1951-53; dep. dir. rsch. for sch. segregation cases NAACP Legal Def. and Edn. Fund, 1953; tchr., prin. New Lincoln High Sch., N.Y.C., 1954-69; with Phelps-Stokes Fund, 1970-77, dir. research and publs., 1970-72, v.p., 1972-77; U.S. amb. to United Republic of Cameroon, Yaounde, 1977-80; U.S. amb. to Equatorial Guinea, 1979-80; dep. asst. sec. for African affairs Dept. State, 1980-81; Melville J. Herskovits prof. African studies Northwestern U., Evanston, Ill., 1981-83; disting. prof. Northwestern U., Evanston, Ill., 1983-85; prof. emeritus Northwestern U., Evanston, Ill., 1985—, co-dir. internat. internship program, 1983-85; co-dir. African seminar Nat. Assn. Equal Opportunity in Higher Edn., 1985; co-dir. Mission to Malawi Women's Commn. for Refugee Women and Children, 1989; mem. Adv. Com. on Ednl. Exchange U.S. Dept. State, 1961-62, Adv. Commn. on Internat. Ednl. and Cultural Affairs, 1962-65; mem. Dept. State adv. coun. on African Affairs, 1962-65; U.S. del. 13th gen. conf. UNESCO, 1964; trustee Conn. Coll., 1964-65, 69-77, Mt. Holyoke Coll., 1971-76, vice chmn., 1975-76, trustee fellow, 1988—, Spelman Coll., 1980-89, life trustee, 1991—, Hampshire Coll., 1971-77, 85-88, vice chair, 1975-76; mem. U.S. Nat. Com. for UNESCO, 1965-70, Nat. Adv. rev. Bd., 1974-77; co-dir. African seminar for pres. black colls., 1971; bd. dirs. Nat. Corp. for Housing Partnerships, 1972-77; scholar-in-residence U.S. Commn. on Civil Rights, 1973-74; U.S. del. Internat. Conf. for Assistance to Refugees in Africa, 1981, So. African Devel. Coordination Conf. II, 1980; guest scholar Woodrow Wilson Internat. Ctr. for Scholars, Smithsonian Instn., Washington, 1982; mem. Aspen Inst. Humanistic Studies Exec. Seminar, 1983; mem. study mission to Japan with Assn. Black Am. Ambassadors, 1984, 85; mem. com. on policy for racial justice Joint Ctr. for Polit. and Econ. Studies, 1983-92; co-leader: Md. Consortium to Togo, Sierra Leone, Senegal, Liberia and Cameroon from 1970; Women's Commn. on Refugee Women and Children, Malawi, 1989; adv. commn. Howard Univ. Patricia Roberts Harris Public Affairs Program, 1989—; adv. bd. Lincoln Univ. (Pa.) Ctr. for Public Policy and Diplomacy, 1991—; bd. dirs. Ralph Bunche Inst. on UN, CUNY, 1986-94; co-chair African-Am. Inst. Del. to observe presdl. elections, Madagascar, Feb., 1993. Author introduction: A Slaver's Log Book or 20 Years Residence in Africa, 1976; co-author: The New Nigerian Elite, 3d edit, 1971, Intensive English Conversation, Vol. I, 1953, Vol. II, 1954; editor: The Black American Reference Book, 1976; co-editor: Curriculum for Understanding, 1965; contbr. chpts. to coop. books, articles to profl. jours. Bd. dirs. Refugee Policy Group, 1983-89, adv. coun., 1989—; cons. African Devel. Found., 1986—; mem. Friends Inst. for Democracy in South Africa (formerly Inst. for a Democratic Alternative in South Africa), 1990—. Decorated grand officer Order of Valor (Cameroon); Grand Dama D'Inore, Order of Royal Crown of Crete (Malta); recipient Top Hat award Pitts. Courier, 1979, Mary McLeod Bethune award, 1981, Decade of Service award Phelps-Stokes Fund, 1982, Ella T. Grasso award Mt. Holyoke Coll., 1982, Northwestern U. Alumna of Year award, 1983, Disting. Service award Nat. Coalition of 100 Black Women, 1984, Disting. Service award USIA, 1986, Am. Bicentennial Presdl. Inaugural award, 1989, Black History Makers award Associated Black Charities, 1990. Mem. Coun. Fgn. Rels., Nat. Coun. Women U.S., Co. Ambassadors, Assn. Black Am. Ambassadors (exec. com.). Address: Watergate South Ste 317 700 New Hampshire Ave NW Washington DC 20037-2406

SNAPP, ELIZABETH, librarian, educator; b. Lubbock, Tex., Mar. 31, 1937; d. William James and Louise (Lanham) Mitchell; BA magna cum laude, North Tex. State U., Denton, 1968, MLS, 1969, MA, 1977; m. Harry Franklin Snapp, June 1, 1956. Asst. to archivist Archive of New Orleans Jazz, Tulane U., 1960-63; catalog librarian Tex. Woman's U., Denton, 1969-71, head acquisitions dept., 1971-74, coordinator readers services, 1974-77, asst. to dean Grad. Sch., 1977-79, instr. library sci., 1977-88, acting Univ. libr., 1979-82, dir. librs., 1982—; chair-elect Tex. Coun. State U. Librs., 1988-90, chmn., 1990-92; mem. adv. com. on library formula Coordinating Bd. Tex. Coll. and Univ. System, 1981-92; del. OCLC Nat. Users Council, 1985-87, mem. by-laws com., 1985-86, com. on less-than-full-services networks, 1986-87; trustee AMIGOS Bibliographic Coun., Inc., 1994—; project dir. NEH consultancy grant on devel. core curriculum for women's studies, 1981-82; chmn. Blue Ribbon com. 1986 Gov.'s Commn. for Women to select 150 outstanding women in Tex. history; project dir. math./sci. anthology project Tex. Found. Women's Resources. Co-sponsor Irish Lecture Series, Denton, 1968, 70, 73, 78. Sec. Denton County Dem. Caucus, 1970. Recipient Ann. Pioneer award Tex. Women's U., 1986. Mem. AAUP, ALA (standards com. 1983-85), Tex. Libr. Assn. (program com. 1978, Dist. VII chmn. 1985-86, archives and oral history com. 1990-92, co-chair program com. Tex. Libr Assn. Ann. Conf. 1994, mem. Tall Texan selection com. 1995), Tex. Hist. Commn. (judge for Farenbach History prize 1990-93), Women's Collecting Group (chmn. ad hoc com. 1984-86), AAUW (legis. br. chmn. 1973-74, br. v.p. 1975-76, br. pres. 1979-80, state historian 1986-88), AAUW Ednl. Found. (rsch. and awards panel 1990-94), So. Conf. Brit. Studies, Tex. Assn. Coll. Tchrs. (pres. Tex. Woman's U. chpt. 1976-77), Alliance Higher Edn. (chair coun. libr. dirs. 1993-95), Woman's Shakespeare Club (pres. 1967-69), Beta Phi Mu (pres. chpt. 1976-78; sec. nat. adv. assembly 1978-79, pres. 1979-80, nat. dir. 1981-83), Alpha Chi, Alpha Lambda Sigma (pres. 1970-71), Pi Delta Phi. Methodist. Club: Soroptimist Internat. (Denton) (pres. 1986-88). Asst. editor Tex. Academe, 1973-76; contbg. author: Women in Special Collections, 1984, Special Collections, 1986; book reviewer Library Resources and Tech. Services, 1973—. Contbr. articles to profl. jours. Home: 1904 N Lake Trl Denton TX 76201-0602 Office: TWU Sta PO Box 24093 Denton TX 76204-2093

SNARSKIS, ELENA A., child services professional; b. Chgo., Apr. 8, 1960; d. Albertas S. and Asta S. BA, Monmouth Coll. Cert. tchr. art and phys. edn. kindergarten-12th grade, Ill. Mem. profl. staff Crystal Lake (Ill.) YMCA, 1982-86, with red cross, 1985-86; day care provider Learning Tree Inc., Algonquin, Ill., 1986-93; pvt. nanny Barrington, Ill., 1993—; supr. summer camp Learning Tree, Inc., 1991-93. Sec. Lithuanian Boy Scouts, Chgo., 1989-93. Home: RR 3 Box 216 Algonquin IL 60102-9689

SNASDELL, SUSAN KATHLEEN, computer company executive; b. St. Louis, July 17, 1948; d. Russell John and Gertrude Burnett (Gassman) S. BA, So. Nazarene U., 1972. Office adminstr. Lake, Van Dyke & Browne Med. Group, Pasadena, Calif., 1972-83; founder, ptnr., adminstr. ComputerEase, Oxnard, Calif., 1984—. Contbr. articles to profl. jours. Mem. Better Bus. Bur., Oxnard C. of C. Office: ComputerEase 1201 Escalon Dr Oxnard CA 93035-2757

SNEAD, ELEANOR LEROY MARKS, secondary school educator; b. Florence, S.C., Oct. 21, 1943; d. Franklin Leroy and Hazel Eleanor (Wallace) Marks; m. Samuel Everette Snead, Aug. 14, 1965; children: Robin Lynne, Ashley Eleanor. BA, Meredith Coll., 1965; MA, U. N.C., Greensboro, 1985. Cert. secondary bus. and marketing tchr., N.C. Tchr. Selma (N.C.) High Sch., 1965, Laurinburg (N.C.) High Sch. (now Scotland High Sch.), 1965-76, 84—, Hoke County High Sch., Raeford, N.C., 1980-84; curriculum writer N.C. Dept. Pub. Instrn., Raleigh, 1985, 90; presenter workshops Mktg. Edn. divsn. Vocat. Edn., N.C. Dept. Pub. Instrn. Named Scotland County Outstanding Young Educator. Mem. NEA, N.C. Assn. Educators, Mktg. Educator's Assn., N.C. Mktg. Educator's Assn. (treas. 1991—, Solid Gold Tchr. 1989, Gold Link Tchr. 1990, Outstanding Mem. of N.C. 1994), Am. Vocat. Assn., N.C. Vocat. Assn., Scotland County Area C. of C., Delta Kappa Gamma (treas. Delta Omicron chpt.), Delta Pi Epsilon. Methodist. Office: Scotland High Sch 1000 W Church St Laurinburg NC 28352

SNEAD, KATHLEEN MARIE, lawyer; b. Steubenville, Ohio, July 1, 1948; d. Donald Lee and Mary Alice (Hobright) O'Dell; m. John Jones Snead, Oct. 14, 1972; 1 child, Megan Marie. BA, Pa. State U., 1970; JD, U. Denver, 1979. Bar: Colo. 1979, U.S. Ct. Appeals (10th cir.) 1980, U.S. Supreme Ct. 1986. Field examiner NLRB, Pitts., 1970-72; freelance photographer Charleston, W.Va., 1973-74; labor relations examiner U.S. Dept. Labor, Denver, 1974-77, labor relations officer, 1978-79; staff atty. Denver & Rio Grande Western R.R., Denver, 1979-81, asst. gen. atty., 1981-84, gen. atty., 1984-92; gen. atty. Southern Pacific Lines, 1992—. Mem. ABA, Denver Bar Assn., Am. Corp. Counsel Assn., Alliance of Profl. Women, Colo. R.R. Assn. (dir. 1982-84). Republican. Roman Catholic. Home: 23 St Devinney St Golden CO 80401-5316 Office: So Pacific Lines One Park Ctr 1515 Arapahoe St Ste 986 Denver CO 80202

SNEDAKER, CATHERINE RAUPAGH (KIT SNEDAKER), editor; b. Fargo, N.D., Apr. 2; d. Paul and Charity (Primmer) Raupagh; B.A., Duke U.; m. William Brooks; children—Eleanor, Peter William; m. 2d, Weldon Snedaker. Pub. relations exec. United Seamen's Service, 1950-57; promotion mgr. sta. WINR-TV and WNBF-TV, Binghamton, N.Y., 1957-60; TV editor, feature writer Binghamton Sun, 1960-68; mem. staff Los Angeles Herald Examiner, 1968—, food editor, 1978—, restaurant critic, 1978-80, food and travel editor, 1980-86; editor The Food Package; columnist Copley News Svc. Author: The Great Convertibles; contbr. numerous articles on food and travel to nat. mags. and newspapers; guest editor Mademoiselle mag., 1942. Recipient 3 awards Los Angeles Press Club, VISTA award, 1979. Mem. Soc. Am. Travel Writers, Travel Journalist's Guild, Internat. PEN U.S.A. Ctr. West. Democrat. Home: 140 San Vicente Blvd Apt A Santa Monica CA 90402-1533

SNEED, MARIE ELEANOR WILKEY, retired educator; b. Dahlgren, Ill., June 12, 1915; d. Charles N. and Hazel (Miller) Wilkey; student U. Ill., 1933-35; B.S., Northwestern U., 1937; postgrad. Wayne State U., 1954-60, U. Mich., 1967; m. John Sneed, Jr., Sept. 18, 1937: children—Suzanne (Mrs. Geoffrey B. Newton), John Corwin. Tchr. English, drama, creative writing Berkley (Mich.) Sch. Dist., 1952-76. Mem. Mich. Statewide Tchr. Edn. Preparation, 1968-72, regional sec. 1969-70; mem. Pleasant Ridge Arts Council, 1982—; mem. Pleasant Ridge Parks and Recreation Commn., 1982-88, sr. citizen cons., 1989—. Mem. NEA, Mich., Berkley (pres. 1961-62, 82-87) edn. assns., Oakland Tchr. Edn. Council (exec. bd. 1973-76), Student Tchr. Planning Com. Berkley (chmn. 1971-72), Farm Bureau Ill., Founder's Soc., Phi Alpha Chi, Pi Lambda Theta, Alpha Delta Kappa, Alpha Omicron Pi. Club: Pleasant Ridge Woman's (pres. 1980-83), Royal Oak Republican Woman's, Nomad's. Home: 21 Norwich Rd Pleasant Ridge MI 48069-1027 also: Heritage Farm Dahlgren IL 62828

SNEIDERMAN, MARILYN SINGER, public school educator; b. Erie, Pa., Jan. 13, 1943; d. Albert E. and Nettie (Levick) Singer; m. Donald G. Sneiderman, Aug. 15, 1965; children: Steven, Russell. BA in Edn., Mercyhurst Coll., 1965. Cert. tchr., Ohio. Substitute tchr. Beachwood (Ohio) Sch. System, 1980-87; tutor Hilltop Sch., Beachwood, 1987-91, instnl. tutor, 1991—. Mem. Greater Cleve. Coun. Tchrs. Math., Phi Delta Kappa. Home: 26200 Fairmount Blvd Beachwood OH 44122

SNELGROVE, ALICE TEMPLE MEDLEY, educator; b. Newberry, S.C., May 17, 1942; d. Ralph Pedigo and Mozelle (Spain) Medley; m. James L. Snelgrove, Sept. 11, 1965; children: Anne Caroline and Sarah Margaret (twins). BA, Tenn. Tech. U., 1964; MA, Ind. U., 1965. Asst. prof. English Coll. DuPage, Glen Ellyn, Ill., 1981-94, assoc. prof., 1994—, coord. honors program, 1992—. Bd. dirs., mem. nominating com. DuPage County coun. Girl Scouts, Naperville, Ill. Mem. AAUW, Nat. Coun. Tchrs. English, Am. Creativity Assn., Nat. Collegiate Honors Coun. Presbyterian. Office: Coll of DuPage 22d St & Lambert Rd Glen Ellyn IL 60137

SNELL, PATRICIA POLDERVAART, librarian, consultant; b. Santa Fe, Apr. 11, 1943; d. Arie and Edna Beryl (Kerchmar) Poldervaart; m. Charles Eliot Snell, June 7, 1966. BA in Edn., U. N.M., 1965; MSLS, U. So. Calif., 1966. Asst. edn. libr. U. So. Calif., L.A., 1966-68; med. libr. Bedford (Mass.) VA Hosp., 1968-69; asst. law libr. U. Miami, Coral Gables, Fla., 1970-71; acquisitions librarian U. N.M., Albuquerque, 1971-72; order libr. Los Angeles County Law Libr., 1972-76, cataloger, 1976-90; libr. Parks Coll., Albuquerque, 1990-92; records technician Technadyne Engrng. Cons. to Sandia Nat. Labs., 1992-93; instr. libr. sci. program Coll. Edn. U. N.Mex., Albuquerque, 1991—, libr. Tireman Learning Materials Ctr., 1993—. Ch. libr.. Beverly Hills Presbyn. Ch., 1974-90, ch. choir libr., 1976-90. Southwestern Library Assn. scholar 1965. Mem. ALA, N.Mex. Libr. Assn., Pi Lambda Theta. Office: U N Mex Coll Edn EM/LS Program Tireman Libr Albuquerque NM 87131

SNELLEN, DEBORAH SUE, training consulting company executive; b. Columbia, Mo., Oct. 23, 1956; d. Howard Earl and Jessie Jewel (Johnson) Durk; m. Steven Wayne Snellen, Jan. 17, 1987; 1 child, Ashlen Dolores. BS in Edn. cum laude, U. Mo., 1979, MA in Speech Communication, 1980. Provider rels. rep. EDS Fed., Columbia, 1981-83; dir. human resources MBS Textbook Exch., Inc., Columbia, 1983-88; pres., owner Business Class, Columbia, 1988—; chmn. adv. bd. for bus. edn. Columbia Adult Edn., 1990-92. Bd. dirs. Advent Enterprises, Inc., Columbia, 1990-92; inaugural participant Greater Mo. Focus on Leadership Program, 1990; participant Tiger Scholarship Fund, Jr. League of Springfield, 1994—; active Springfield Tourism Devel. Task Force, 1994; cert. Herrmann Brain Dominance Instrument Adminstr. and Interpretation, 1994. Honors scholar U. Mo. Mem. ASTD (past pres. Cen. Mo. chpt.), Columbia C. of C. (bd. dirs. 1991-92), Women's Network (pres. 1988-89, amb. 1989-92, strategic planning com. 1990-92). Republican. Presbyterian. Office: Bus Class 2242 E Briar St Springfield MO 65804-7826

SNELLING, BARBARA, state official; b. Fall River, Mass., Mar. 22, 1928; d. Frank Taylor and Hazel (Russell) Weil; m. Richard Arkwright Snelling (five-term Gov. Vt.), June 14, 1947 (wid. Aug. 1991); children: Jacqueline, Mark, Diane, Andrew. AB magna cum laude, Radcliffe Coll., 1950; D of Pub. Svc. (hon.), Norwich U., 1981. V.p. U. Vt., 1974-82; pres. Snelling and Kolb, Inc., 1982—; lieut. gov. State of Vt., 1993—; bd. dirs., chmn. Chittenden Bank Corp. Trustee Radcliffe Coll., 1990—; bd. dirs. Vt. Community Found., 1986—, Shelburne Mus., 1988—; mem. Vt. Ednl. Partnerships, 1992—; v.p. for devel. and external affairs U. Vt., 1974-82; mem. Vt. State Bd. Edn., 1971-77; trustee Champlain Coll., 1971-74; mem. Vt. Alcohol and Drug Rehab. Commn., 1970-73, Shelburne Sch. Bd., 1958-73, chmn. 1965-73; mem. Vt. Edn. Adv. Coun., 1968-71, Vt. Tchr. Edn. Adv. Com., 1968-70, Bd. of Sch. Dirs., Champlain Valley Union High Sch., 1962-69, chmn. 1962-68, others. Recipient Fanny G. Shaw award for Disting. Community Svc., Burlington Community Coun., 1972, Laymen's award Vt. Edn. Assn., 1965. Office: Lieut Gov State House Montpelier VT 05609-0101

SNELLING, NORMA JUNE, retired music educator, English educator; b. Brooten, Minn., June 1, 1928; d. Harold Melvin and Mabel Olga (Markuson) Hellickson; m. Douglas Howard Snelling, June 27, 1953; children: Julie Marie, Mary Merced, Steven Douglas. BA, Concordia Coll., Moorhead, Minn., 1949. Cert. tchr., Minn. Tchr. Wolverton (Minn.) Sch. Dist., 1949-51, Kimball (Minn.) Sch. Dist., 1951-52, Benson (Minn.) Sch. Dist., 1952-53, Belgrade (Minn.) Sch. Dist., 1953-57, Hutchinson (Minn.) Sch. Dist., 1964-66, Litchfield (Minn.) Sch. Dist., 1966-92; mem. staff edn. liaison 2d Congl. Dist. Minn., Litchfield, 1992—. Assoc. chairperson county level, del. Dem. Farmer Labor Party, Minn., 1992—, chair 1994; del. to Dem. Nat. Conv., 1984; co-chairperson Concert Series, Litchfield, 1962, Cancer Dr., Litchfield, 1960; dir. Choralaires, Eden Valley, Minn., 1976—; dir. music Zion Luth. Ch., Litchfield, 1962-85, poet ch. pubs., dedications, etc., also Big Grove Luth. Ch.; speech coach Litchfield Jr. H.S., 1972-77; mem. VFW Aux., Am. Legion Aux. Mem. NEA (congl. contact person 1985-90), Minn. Edn. Assn. (govtl. rels. uniserve chairperson, Leadership award medal 1986), Ret. Educators Minn. (legis. chairperson 1993—), Sons of Norway (pres. 1993—, Bronze medal 1993-94), Gen. Fedn. Women's Study Clubs, Delta Kappa Gamma. Home: 621 W Crescent Ln Litchfield MN 55355-1830

SNELSON, DONNA AYERS, nursing educator; b. Wiles-Barre, Pa., July 5, 1949; m. Alan James, Apr. 8, 1973; children: Ashleigh, Lyndsy. Diploma, Wilkes-Barre Gen. Hosp., 1970; BS in Nursing Edn. cum laude, Wilkes U., 1972; MS in Nursing, U. Pa., postgrad. RN. Nurse clinician Wyo. Valley Hosp., Wilkes-Barre, Pa., 1970-72; educator Mercy Hosp. Sch. Nursing, Wilkes-Barre, 1972-75; from asst. prof. to assoc. prof. nursing Coll. Misericordia, Dallas, Pa., 1975—; dir. nursing and accelerated programs Coll. Misericordia, Dallas, 1988-91; bd. dirs. Mercy Care, Wilkes-Barre, 1986—. Officer PTSA bd. Crestwood High Sch., 1993—; bd. dirs. Rice Elem. PTA, Mountaintop, Pa., 1986-93, Am. Heart Assn., 1994—, chair program com. Recipient USAF Teaching award, 1992. Mem. Pa. Nurses Assn., U. Pa. Greater Wilkes-Barre Club, Wilkes Univ. Gen. Hosp. Alumni Orgn., Sigma Theta Tau (Outstanding Svc. award 1987, Past Pres. Honor 1990, Excellence in Teaching award 1992). Home: 254 Van Ave Mountain Top PA 18707-9103 Office: Coll Misericordia Lake St Dallas PA 18707

SNIBBE, PATRICIA MISCALL, advertising agency executive; b. Hackensack, N.J., June 1, 1932; d. Jack and Margaret Lois (Drake) Miscall; m. Richard Wilson Snibbe, Sept. 8, 1962; stepchildren: John Robinson, Paul Clor. BFA, R.I. Sch. Design, 1954; postgrad., New Sch. for Social Rsch., 1975-80, U. London, 1989. Art dir., film producer Peckham Prodns., N.Y.C., 1960-64; dir. art, ptnr. Stallman and Snibbe, N.Y.C., 1964-66; dir. art Shevlo

Advt., N.Y.C., 1966-72, Bernard Hodes Advt., N.Y.C., 1972-77; owner, creative dir. Designstuff, N.Y.C., 1978-88; creative dir. Archtl. Film Libr., N.Y.C., 1980—; pres. Crommelin and Bliss, Parfumier, 1988—. Author and artist: Feminist Funnies, 1981—. Recipient Golden Cir. award Affiliated Advt. Agys. Internat., 1975-77, Creativity award of Distinction, 1978. Mem. NOW (bd. dirs. N.Y.C. 1983-84), Graphic Artists Guild (steering com. Cartoonists Guild div. 1984-85), NATAS, Archael. Inst. Am. Home: 139 E 18th St New York NY 10003-2470

SNIDER, DEBRA LYNN, academic administrator; b. Paris, Tex., Nov. 9, 1959; d. Travis and Patsy Ann (McHam) Horton; m. Rodney Snider, Nov. 13, 1981; 1 child, Alissa Lynn. AA, York Coll., 1991; B in Profl. Studies, Bellevue Coll., 1992, MA in Mgmt., 1994. Acct. Robert J. Sylvester, CPA, York, Nebr., 1981-86; office mgr. Martin Luther Home, York, 1986-88; with adminstrv. support staff York Coll., 1988—, dir. fin. aids, 1993—. Treas. Larsen Christian Acad., York, 1990—, bd. dirs., 1990—; leader Girl Scouts Am., York, 1990-91; mem. resource coun. City of York, 1986-88. Named one of Outstanding Young Women Am., 1990. Mem. Nebr. Assn. Student Fin. Aid Adminstrs. Republican. Home: 515 Florida Ave York NE 68467-3322 Office: York Coll 9th and Kiplinger York NE 68467

SNIDER, MARIE ANNA, syndicated columnist; b. Croghan, N.Y., Aug. 9, 1927; d. Nicholas and Dorothy (Moser) Gingerich; m. Howard Mervin, Nov. 27, 1954; children: Vada Marie, Conrad Howard. BS, Goshen Coll., 1949; M in Religious Edn., Mennonite Bibl. Sem., 1957; MS, Kans. State U., 1980. High sch. tchr. Rockway Collegiate, Kitchener, Ont., Can., 1949-53; free-lance writer, 1953-54; pub. rels. Goshen Coll., Ind., 1955-57; free-lance writer, homemaker, 1957-67; info. editor Prairie View, Inc., Newton, Kans., 1967-76; dir., pub. info. & edn. Prairie View, Inc., Newton, 1976-85, dir. communications, 1985-91; freelance writer, columnist North Newton, 1991—; syndicated columnist "This Side of 60", 1992—; bd. dirs. Health Systems Agy. of S.E. Kans., 1981-86, v.p., 1986-87; workshop presenter Nat. Coun. of Community Mental Health Ctrs., Atlanta, 1980, N.Y., 1982, 89, Miami, 1987. Editor: Media and Terrorism--The Psychological Impact, 1976; columnist: This Side of 60. pres. City Council, N Newton, 1977-79, pres. 1980. Recipient 1st Pl. MacEachern award Assn. of Hosp. Pub. Rels., 1981, 1st Pl. Media award Nat. Coun. Community Mental Health Ctrs., 1977, 84, runner-up Pub. Rels. award Nat. Assn. Pvt. Psychiat. Hosps., 1980. Mem. NAt. Fedn. Press women, Kans. Press Women. Democrat. Home and Office: PO Box 332 North Newton KS 67117-0332

SNIDER, RUTH ATKINSON, retired counselor; b. Louisville, Jan. 7, 1930; d. Ellis Orrell and Fanola Blanche (Miller) Atkinson; m. Arnold Wills Snider, Feb. 17, 1950; children: Yvonne Marie, Ray Wills, Mark Alan. Student, Centre Coll., 1947-48; BS, Spalding U., 1965, MEd, 1970; rank I, We. Ky. U., 1981. Cert. sch. psychometrist, sch. prin., supr. of instrn. Tchr. Shelby County (Ky.) Bd. Edn., 1949-50, Louisville Pub. Schs., 1956-57; tchr. Jefferson County Pub. Schs., Louisville, 1965-67, counselor, 1967-92; vol. co-chairperson for mentor program Spalding U., Louisville, 1991. Vol. Kyl. Ctr. for Arts, 1989, 90, 91, Actors Theatre of Louisville, 1993-94, 95, Klondike Elem. Sch. Libr., 1994-95. Recipient Caritas award Spalding U., 1994. Mem. ACA (del.), Am. Sch. Counselors Assn. (del. to nat. conf.), Ky. Assn. Counseling Devel., Ky. Sch. Counselor Assn. (conf. chairperson), Klondike PTA, Spalding Soc., Spalding Alumni Assn. (sec. 1994—, Caritas award), Jefferson County Retired Teacher's Assn., Christian Women's Club. Baptist. Home: 2428 Chattesworth Ln Louisville KY 40242

SNIDER, SUZANNE JENNIFER, academic advisor, artist; b. Chgo., Feb. 27, 1947; d. Richard E. and Pauline Una (Nolan) Mette; m. E. Spencer Friedman, June 16, 1968 (div. Apr. 1984); children: Serri J. Friedman, Eric Friedman; m. Marshall A. Snider, Jan. 15, 1989. BA, Metro State U., Denver, 1985; M of Spl. Studies, U. Denver, 1993, M of Environ. Policy and Mgmt., 1993. Cert. in mediation Am. Arbitration Assn.; cert. in advanced studies environ. mgmt. Svc. specialist Ozark Airlines, Peoria, Ill., 1967-68; office asst. French Nat. R.R., Chgo., 1968-70; new accounts teller Greeley (Colo.) Nat. Bank, 1970-72; art/publicity dir. Jewish Community Ctr., Denver, 1985-92; in customer svc. Denver Jet Ctr./Centennial Airport, 1987-88; acad. advisor U. Denver, 1992—. Chair Colo. Lawyers for the Arts, Denver, 1991, 92; performer Schwayder Children's Community Theatre, Denver, 1988, 89; vol. art instr. Denver Pub. Schs., 1992—; vol. conf. program Colo. Hazardous Waste Mgmt. Soc., Denver, 1994—; mem. Colo. Chorale, 1992. Recipient Colo. Scholars award State of Colo., 1982-85; Allied Jewish Fedn. study tour grantee to Israel, 1987. Mem. Nat. Assn. Environ. Communicators (bd. dirs. 1992—), Art Students League, Colo. Ctr. Environ. Mgmt., Women in Arts (charter). Home: 660 York St Denver CO 80206-3746 Office: U Denver Univ Coll 2211 S Josephine St Denver CO 80210-4805

SNIVELY, GLADYS DURBORAW, accountant; b. Chester, Pa.; d. Willis Conover and Florence (Clark) Durboraw; m. James William Snively, Jr., Jan. 29, 1964; children: Florence Durboraw, Gladys Haus. BS with distinction in Elem. Edn., U. Del., 1960; MS in Edn. Adminstrn., U. Pa., 1962. CPA, Pa. Elem. tchr. various sch. dists., Del., Pa., Md., 1960-65; supr. student tchrs. U. Md., College Park, 1965-66; substitute tchr. various sch. dists., Pa., 1979-83; acct. various acctg. firms, Pa., 1985-89; dir. acctg. Community Accts., Phila., 1989-90; owner, mgr. Gladys D. Snively, CPA, Swarthmore, Pa., 1990—. Bd. dirs. Swarthmore Presbyn. Nursery Day Sch., 1968-71, Eagles Mere (Pa.) Park Assn., 1993—; pres. Swarthmore Jr. Woman's Club, 1970-71, Swarthmore Garden Club, 1982-83; treas. Swarthmore Pub. Libr., 1987-92; vol. acct. Cmty. Accts., 1990—; fin. dir. Swarthmore Cmty. Ctr., 1992—. Mem. Inst. Mgmt. Accts. (bd. dirs. 1990-92), Pa. Inst. CPAs (com. on women in acctg. 1993—), Delaware County C. of C., Swarthmore Village Bus. and Profl. Assn. (treas. 1991-93). Home and Office: 243 Ogden Ave Swarthmore PA 19081

SNODDERLY, LOUISE DAVIS, librarian; b. Polk County, Oreg., Feb. 1, 1925; d. Charles Benjamin Franklin and Grace L. (Cassady) Davis; m. Charles Hugh Snodderly, May 19, 1949; 1 son, Lynn Jerome. B.S., E. Tenn. State U., 1946; M.S., U. Tenn., 1962, postgrad., 1979, 82. Tchr., girls' coach Rush Strong High Sch., Strawberry Plains, Tenn., 1946-49, librarian, 1954-62; tchr., girls' coach Cosby High Sch., Tenn., 1949-50; tchr., librarian Maury High Sch., Dandridge, Tenn., 1951-54; cataloger City of Knoxville, Tenn., 1962-67; periodicals librarian Carson-Newman Coll., Jefferson City, Tenn., 1967-90; cons. Jefferson County Librarians, Tenn., 1976—. Sch. commr. Jefferson County, 1976—; com. woman Nat. Fedn. Republican Women, Jefferson County, 1976—. Mem. ALA, Southeastern Library Assn., Tenn. Library Assn., Am. Sch. Bd. Assn., Tenn. Sch. Bd. Assn., PTA, Women's Faculty Club, Les Aimes Club, Order Ea. Star, Pi Lambda Theta. Baptist. Home: 2131 West Highway 11 E Strawberry Plains TN 37871-3546

SNODGRASS, FAYE BIRDWELL, marketing executive; b. Nashville, Apr. 3, 1941; d. Dewey Volner and Eliza Vivian (Price) Birdwell; m. John Christopher Bailey (div. 1967); children: Emily Faye, Sarah Elizabeth; m. William Ramsey Snodgrass, Dec. 29, 1968; 1 child, William Ramsey Jr. BS, Ind. U., 1962. Cert. tchr., Ind., trainer. Tchr. Indpls. Pub. Schs., 1962-65; organizer, dir. Gallatin (Tenn.) Day Care Ctr., 1965-66; asst. to v.p. alumni devel. Vanderbilt U., Nashville, 1966-68; asst. account exec. Holder Kennedy Pub. Relations, Nashville, 1980-82; account exec. Burson, Marstellar, Cohn & Wolfe Pub. Relations, N.Y.C. and Atlanta, 1982-84; pres., chmn. Communications Network, Inc., Nashville, 1984—; v.p. Massmark, Inc., Nashville, 1984-92; v.p. mktg. Med. Mart Internat., Nashville, 1986-91; chmn. Bundles of Joy, Inc., Nashville, 1989—; owner Art and Gift Gallery, Nashville, 1992—. Mem. pres.'s adv. com. Trevecca Coll., Nashville, 1983-90; solicitor Nashville United Way, 1985-86; chmn. parents' fundraising campaign Castle Heights Mil. Acad., Lebanon, Tenn., 1985-86; vol. publicity cons. Parents Anonymous, Operation Chem. Awareness, Nashville, 1986—, Nashville Summer Lights Festival, 1988; bd. dirs. Bethlehem Ctr., Nashville, 1986-89; mem. blue ribbon task force Indigent Care Tenn., Tenn. Hosp. Assn., 1986-87; mem. com. Capitol Restoration Com., Nashville; adv. com. State of Tenn. Dept. Mental Health; mem. adv. bd. Rape and Sexual Abuse Ctr., Nashville, 1991-94; team leader Women for Bredesen for Gov. Campaign. Named Woman of Yr. Bus. Profl. Women, 1986. Mem. NAFE, Nashville Area C. of C. (pres.'s com.), Nashville City Club (social com. 1993—). Democrat. Mem. Christian Ch. Home: 1201 Jefferson Davis Dr Brentwood TN 37027-4123 Office: Communications Network Inc First Am Ctr Ste 110 315 Nashville TN 37238

SNODGRASS, JOAN GAY, psychology educator; b. Pitts., Oct. 4, 1934; d. William Rodney and Grace (Dietrich) S. BS, Pa. State U., 1955; PhD, U. Pa., 1966. Asst. prof. of psychology NYU, N.Y.C., 1966-70, assoc. prof., 1970-83, prof., 1983—. Author: The Numbers Game: Statistics for Psychology, 1977, Human Experimental Psychology, 1985; contbr. articles to Jour. Exptl. Psychology, Jour. Memory and Language, others, also chpts. to books. Grnatee NIMH, 1969-77, NSF, 1985-86, Air Force Office Sci. Rsch., 1989-91. Fellow Am. Psychol. Assn., Am. Psychol. Soc. Office: NYU 6 Washington Pl Rm 857 New York NY 10003-6603

SNOW, JUDITH ROHLETTER, jewelry store executive, gemologist, jeweler; b. Miami, Fla., May 6, 1948; d. Guy Eugene and Mary Evelyn (York) Rohletter; student Miami-Dade Community Coll., 1966-67; cert. in diamond evaluation Gemological Inst. Am., 1979, cert. in colored stones and gem indentification, 1980; grad. Berlitz Sch. Langs., Coral Gables, Fla., 1987; m. Edward Hugh Snow, May 11, 1974; children: Judith Diane, Kelly Michelle, Mary Alice. Office mgr. Ross Printing Corp., Miami, 1965-74; corp. exec., gemologist Snow's Jewelers, Inc., Coral Gables, 1974—, also dir. Active Scott Kelly for Gov. of Fla. Campaign, 1965. Mem. Retail Jewelers Am., Jewelers Security Alliance, Coral Gables C. of C., Miracle Mile Mchts. Assn., Exec. Women Internat., Coral Bay Property Owner's Assn., Ferrari Club Am., Ferrari Owners Club, Zonta, Mus. Patrons. Democrat. Clubs: Ocean Reef, Coral Bay Yacht, Coral Reef Yacht, Fla. Philharm. Prelude, Noteworthy, Progress, Bimini (Bahamas) Big Game, Beach Colony. Office: 299 Miracle Mile Coral Gables FL 33134-5907

SNOW, LURANA S., judge; b. Brooklyn, N.Y., May 10, 1951; d. Lawrence James and Elizabeth Catherine (Luckso) Schling. AB magna cum laude, Radcliffe Coll., 1972; JD, Harvard Law Sch., 1975. Bar: Mass. 1975, Fla. 1977, D.C. 1980. Law clk. to Judge Joe Eaton U.S. Dist. Ct., Miami, 1975-77; asst. fed. public defender Miami, 1977-79; asst. U.S. atty. U.S. Dept. of Justice, Ft. Lauderdale, 1980-86; pvt. practice, 1984; magistrate judge U.S. Dist. Ct. (do. dist.) Fla., Ft. Lauderdale, 1986—. Recipient Spl. Achievement award Drug Enforcement Adminstrn., 1981, 84, 86, U.S. Secret Svc., 1984, U.S. Customs, 1984, Bureau of Alcohol, Tobacco and Firearms, 1984, South Fla. Vice Presidential Task Force, 1984. Mem. Fla. Bar Assn., Mass. Bar Assn., D.C. Bar Assn., Fed. Bar Assn. Office: US Courthouse 299 E Broward Blvd Rm 204 Fort Lauderdale FL 33301-1944*

SNOW, MARINA SEXTON, reference librarian, playwright; b. Boston, Apr. 9, 1937; d. Charles Ernest Snow and Katherine Alice Townsend; m. Richard DeVere Horton, Aug. 30, 1958 (div. 1968); children: Heather Kertchem, James Horton; m. Charles A. Washburn, Jan. 7, 1978 (div. 1979). BA, U. Iowa, 1958; MA in Speech Pathology, N.Mex. State U., 1967; MA in Librarianship, San Jose State U., 1976; MA in Theatre Arts, Calif. State U., Sacramento, 1979. Cert. clin. competence Am. Speech and Hearing Assn. Tchr. ESL Inst. Colombo-Americano, Cali, Colombia, 1958-59; tchr. Las Cruces (N.Mex.) Pub. Schs., 1964-66; speech therapist Sutter County Schs., Yuba City, Calif., 1967-72; reference libr. Calif. State U. Libr., Sacramento, 1976—. Contbr. articles to profl. jours.; author 2 plays: Apricot Coffee, Alkali Flat. Pres. Alkali Flat Neighborhood Assn., Sacramento, 1987—; mem. Sacramento Old City Assn., 1979—. Mem. Calif. Acad. and Rsch. Librs., Calif. State U. Librs., Theatre Libr. Assn., Music Libr. Assn. Office: Calif State U Libr 2000 Jed Smith Dr Sacramento CA 95819-2640

SNOW, MELANIE STRUBLE, finance executive; b. San Mateo, Calif., Oct. 1, 1958; d. Jack Drummond and Margot Gerda (Hamberg) Struble; m. Bruce Reed Snow, Aug. 21, 1982; children: Coburn, Clarke Struble. BSBA, Menlo Coll., 1982; MBA in Internat. Bus., Saint Mary's Coll., Moraga, Calif., 1992. Staff acct. Davy Mckee Internat., San Ramon, Calif., 1982, RJ Builders Inc., San Ramon, Calif., 1984; contr. Laidlaw Transit, Concord, Calif., 1987; v.p. fin. Paramount's Great Am., Santa Clara, Calif., 1991—. Mem. Nat. Accounts Assn., Internat. Mgmt. Accts. Republican.

SNOW, MILDRED ALICE, educational administrator, writer; b. Mpls., Mar. 28, 1937; d. Allen Cinclair Clatworthy and Cora Hazel (Mattice) White; adopted children: Anne DeArden, Linda, Monique, Bryan, Scott, Elizabeth, Marc. BA, U. Minn., 1959. Mgr., dept. head Del Monte Foods, San Francisco, 1959-63; mgr., expense control R.H. Macys, San Francisco, 1963-65; freelance writer Orem, Utah, 1965-82; chmn. bd. dirs., head writer Internat. Comm. Learning Inst., Mpls., 1982—; developer reading program See the Sound/Visual Phonics, 1982—. Author: Yellow Book, 1982, Fonix, 1982, STS/VP Dictionary, 1994. Recipient Rep. Party award for starting women's chpt., 1970; named to 1000 Points of Light, Pres. Bush, 1991. Mem. Sertoma (dist. gov. 1991-92, Svc. to Mankind award 1988). Mem. LDS Ch. Office: Internat Comm Learning Inst 7108 Bristol Blvd Edina MN 55435

SNOW, TERESA LYNN, speech pathologist; b. Owensboro, Ky., Apr. 28, 1962; d. Donald Ray and Nelda Faye (Ambrose) Sinnett; m. James Haven Snow, Mar. 13, 1993. BS in Speech and Comm. Disorders, Western Ky. U., 1985; MA in Speech/Lang. Pathology, U. Tex., 1991. Lic. Speech/Lang. Pathologist. Assoc. speech/lang. pathologist Travis State Sch., Tex. Dept. Mental Health-Mental Retardation, Austin, 1988-90, qualified mental retardation profl., 1990-92, lead speech-lang. pathologist, 1992-93, dir. comm. and visual svcs., 1993—. Vol. income tax asst., IRS, 1994. Mem. Am. Speech-Hearing-Lang. Assn., Inst. Mgmt. Accts. (student). Baptist. Home: 502 A Long Bow Ln Austin TX 78704-5631 Office: Tex Dept Mental Health-Mental Retardation Travis State Sch PO Box 430 Austin TX 78756

SNOWDEN, ALISON, film director. films include: George and Rosemary, 1987, The Boss, 1992, Bob's Birthday, 1994 (Acad. award for Best Animated Short Film 1994). *

SNOWDEN, BERNICE RIVES, former construction company executive; b. Houston, Mar. 21, 1923; d. Charles Samuel and Annie Pearl (Rorex) Rives; grad. Smalley Comml. Coll., 1941; student U. Houston, 1965; m. Walter G. Snowden; 1 dau., Bernice Ann Ogden. With Houston Pipe Line Co., 1944-45; clk.-typist Charles G. Heyne & Co., Inc., Houston, 1951-53, payroll asst., 1953-56, sec. to pres., also office mgr., 1956-62, sec. to pres., also controller, 1962-70, sec.-treas., 1970-77, chief fin. officer, also dir. Mem. Women in Constrn., Nat. Assn. Women in Constrn. (past pres.), San Leon C. of C. Methodist. Club: Lord and Ladies Dance. Home: 6611 Kury Ln Houston TX 77008-5101

SNOWDON, JILL ANN, food technologist; b. Phila., Sept. 23, 1952; d. John James and Anna Elizabeth (Snyder) S. BA, Millersville State U., 1974; MS, U. Wis., 1979, PhD, 1987. Rsch. technician Fels Rsch. Inst., Temple U., Phila., 1974-77; teaching asst. Dept. Food Sci., Madison, 1977-79, rsch. asst., 1979-80; rsch. technician Food Rsch. Inst., Madison, 1980-83, rsch. asst., 1983-87; dir. sci. affairs United Fresh Fruit and Vegetable Assn., Alexandria, Va., 1988-90; cons. SGA Assocs., Silver Spring, Md., 1990—; pres. SGA Assocs., Silver Spring, Md., 1990—. Contbr. articles to profl. jours. Sci. policy analyst polit. campaign for Tex. Agr. Commr., 1990; sci. advisor Proposition 135, Calif., 1990. Mem. Inst. Food Technologists (rsch. com. 1991-93), Am. Soc. Microbiology (com. on agr., food and environ. microbiology 1989—, congl. sci. fellow 1987-88). Presbyterian. Home and Office: 2236 Washington Ave # 301 Silver Spring MD 20910-2640

SNOWE, OLYMPIA J., senator; b. Augusta, Maine, Feb. 21, 1947; d. George John and Georgia G. Bouchles; m. John McKernan. BA, U. Maine, 1969; LLD (hon.), U. Maine, Machias, 1982, Husson Coll., 1981, Bowdoin Coll., 1985. Businesswoman; mem. Maine Ho. of Reps., 1973-76, Maine Senate, 1976-78; mem. 96th-103d Congresses from 2d Maine Dist., 1979-94, mem. fgn. affairs com., mem. budget com.; co-chair Congl. Caucus for Women's Issues; dep. Republican whip, U.S. senator from Maine, 1995—; corporator Mechanics Savs. Bank. Republican. Greek Orthodox. Club: Philoptochos Soc. Office: US Senate 176 Russell Senate Bldg Washington DC 20510-1902

SNOW-WEBB, MARY ALICEN, hospital administrator; b. Jacksonville, Fla., July 7, 1953; d. A.D. and Ruth (Swiney) Snow (both dec.); m. Michael Lynn Webb, Jan. 3, 1981; children: Caitlin Snow, Margaret. BS in Therapeutic Recreation, U. Ga., 1975, postgrad.; postgrad., Ga. Coll., 4 years. Dir. activity therapy College St. Hosp., Macon, Ga., 1975-78, Heritage Park Hosp., Macon, 1979-81, Coliseum Psychiat. Hosp., Macon, 1981—; activity therapy cons. Town and County Nursing Home, Macon, 1982-85, Bloomfield Nursing Home, Macon, 1988-89; instr. therapeutic recreation Ga. Coll. Milledgeville, 1986-87, gubernatorially apptd. master therapeutic recreation specialist rep. Ga. Bd. Recreation Examiners, Atlanta, 1987—, chmn., 1991. Mem. Nat. Assn. Activity Profls. (cert. activity dir.), Nat. Recreation Pks. Assn., Ga. Recreation Pks. Assn. Republican. Episcopalian. Home: 124 Ashford Tracy Ln Macon GA 31210 Office: Coliseum Psychiat Hosp 340 Hospital Dr Macon GA 31201-8002

SNYDER, ALLEGRA FULLER, dance educator; b. Chgo., Aug. 28, 1927; d. R. Buckminster and Anne (Hewlett) Fuller; m. Robert Snyder, June 30, 1951 (div. Apr. 1975, remarried Sept. 1980); children: Alexandra, Jaime. BA in Dance, Bennington Coll., 1951; MA in Dance, UCLA, 1967. Asst. to curator, dance archives Mus. Modern Art, N.Y.C., 1945-47; dancer Ballet Soc. of N.Y.C. Ballet Co., 1945-47; mem. office and prodn. staff Internat. Film Found., N.Y.C., 1950-52; editor, dance films Film News mag., N.Y.C., 1966-72; lectr. dance and film adv., dept. dance UCLA, 1967-73, chmn. dept. dance, 1974-80, 90-91, acting chair, spring 1985, chair of faculty Sch. of the Arts, 1989-91, prof. dance and dance ethnology, 1973-91, prof. emeritus, 1991—; vis. lectr. Calif. Inst. of Arts, Valencia, 1972; co-dir. dance and TV workshop Am. Dance Fest., Conn. Coll., New London, 1973; dir. NEH summer seminar for coll. tchrs. Asian Performing Arts, 1978, 81; coord. Ethnic Arts Intercoll. Interdisciplinary program, 1974-83, acting chmn., 1986; vis. prof. performance studies NYU, 1982-83; hon. vis. prof. U. Surrey, Guildford, Eng., 1983-84; bd. dirs. Buckminster Fuller Inst.; cons. Thyodia Found., Salt Lake City, 1973-74; mem. dance adv. panel Nat. Endowment Arts, 1968-72, Calif. Arts Commn., 1974-91; mem. adv. screening com. Council Internat. Exchange of Scholars, 1979-82; mem. various panels NEH, 1979-85; mem. adv. bd. Los Angeles Dance Alliance, 1978-84; core cons. for Dancing Sta. WNET-TV, 1988—. Dir. film Baroque Dance 1625-1725, in 1977; co-dir. film Gods of Bali, 1952; dir. and wrote film Bayanihan, 1962 (named Best Folkloric Documentary at Bilboa Film Festival, winner Golden Eagle award); asst. dir. and asst. editor film The Bennington Story, 1952; created films Gestures of Sand, 1968, Reflections on Choreography, 1973, When the Fire Dances Between Two Poles, 1982; created film, video loop and text Celebration: A World of Art and Ritual, 1982-83; supr. post-prodn. film Erick Hawkins, 1964, in 1973. Also contbr. articles to profl. jours. and mags. Adv. com. Pacific Asia Mus., 1980-84, Festival of the Mask, Craft and Folk Art Mus., 1979-84; adv. panel Los Angeles Dance Currents II, Mus. Ctr. Dance Assn., 1974-75; bd. dirs. Council Grove Sch. III, Compton, Calif., 1976-81; apptd. mem. Adv. Dance Com., Pasadena (Calif.) Art Mus., 1970-71, Los Angeles Festival of Performing Arts com., Studio Watts, 1970; mem. Technology and Cultural Transformation com., UNESCO, 1977. Fulbright research fellow, 1983-84; grantee Nat. Endowment Arts, 1981, Nat. Endowment Humanities, 1977, 79, 81, UCLA, 1968, 77, 80, 82, 85; recipient Amer. Dance Guild Award for Outstanding Achievement in Dance, 1992. Mem. Am. Dance Therapy Assn., Congress on Research in Dance (bd. dirs. 1970-76, chairperson 1975-77, nat. conf. chair 1972), Council Dance Adminstrs., Am. Dance Guild (chairperson com. awards 1972, Honoree of Yr. 1992), Soc. for Ethnomusicology, Am. Anthropol. Assn., Am. Folklore Soc., Soc. Anthropology of Visual Communication, Soc. Humanistic Anthropology, Calif. Dance Educators Assn. (conf. chair 1972), Los Angeles Area Dance Alliance (adv. bd. 1978-84, selection com. Dance Kaleidoscope project 1979-81), Fulbright Alumni Assn. Home: 15313 Whitfield Ave Pacific Palisades CA 90272-2548 Office: UCLA Dept Dance 124 Dance Bldg Los Angeles CA 90024*

SNYDER, AMY MIDDLETON, accountant; b. Endicott, N.Y., Oct. 27, 1954; d. John A. and Miriam Hazel (Bonear) Middleton; m. Fred H. Snyder III, Aug. 13, 1983. BS in Acctg., Binghamton U., 1976; MBA, Syracuse U., 1982. Cost acct. GTE, Inc., Towanda, Pa., 1977-78, supr. cost control, 1978-82; asst. plant contr. Corning (N.Y.), Inc., 1982-84; budget acct. Brandywine Hosp., Coatesville, Pa., 1985-86; plant acct. Foote Mineral Co., Frazer, Pa., 1986-87; asst. controller Foote Mineral Co., Exton, Pa., 1987-88; acctg. mgr. Cyprus Foote Mineral Co., Malvern, Pa., 1988-92; mgr. budgeting & planning Penn Fuel Gas, Inc., Oxford, 1992—. Mem. AICPA, Pa. Inst. CPA's, Inst. Mgmt. Accts. (Valley Forge chpt. sec. 1993-94, dir. employment 1994-95).

SNYDER, BRENDA LEE, human resources manager; b. Denver, Feb. 27, 1963; d. William Joseph Snyder and Marianne Ethyl (Sweeney) Errebo; m. Scott B. Ladwig, Aug. 10, 1987. BSBA, Regis U., 1990. Adminstrv. mgr. U.S. West Inc., Englewood, Colo., 1983-86, mgr. human resources, 1986-89; mgr. human resources U.S. West Mktg. Resources, Englewood, Colo., 1989—; pres. U.S. West Women, Englewood, 1989-92; workshop leader AISEC, Girls Count, Denver, 1989-93; cons. human resources Eurotel, Prague, Czech Republic, 1994-95. Bd. dirs. Kempe Found., Denver, 1992-94. Recipient Appreciation and Recognition, Girls Count, 1993, Vanguard award Women in Comm., 1994. Mem. Bus. and Profl. Women. Democrat. Home: 1313 Williams St Apt 1203 Denver CO 80218-2674

SNYDER, CAROLYN ANN, university dean, librarian; b. Elgin, Nebr., Nov. 5, 1942; d. Ralph and Florence Wagner; m. Barry Snyder, Apr. 24, 1969. Student, Nebr. Wesleyan U., 1960-61; BS cum laude, Kearney State Coll., 1964; MS in Librarianship, U. Denver, 1965. Asst. libr. sci. and tech. U. Nebr., Lincoln, 1965-67, asst. pub. svc. libr., 1967-68, 70-73; pers. libr. Ind. U. Librs., Bloomington, 1973-76, acting dean of univ. librs., 1980, 88-89, assoc. dean for pub. svcs., 1977-88, 89-91, interim devel. officer, 1989-91; adminstrv. army libr. Spl. Svcs. Agy., Europe, 1968-70; dean libr. affairs So. Ill. U., Carbondale, 1991—; team leader Midwest Univs. Consortium for Internat. Activities-World Bank IX project to develop libr. system and implement automation U. Indonesia, Jakarta, 1984-86; libr. devel. cons. Inst. Tech. MARA/Midwest Univs. Consortium for Internat. Activities Program in Malaysia, 1985. Contbr. chpt. to book and articles to profl. jours. Mem. Humane Assn. Jackson County, 1991—, Carbondale Pub. Libr. Friends, 1991—. Recipient Cooperative Rsch. grant Coun. on Libr. Resources, Washington, 1984. Mem. ALA (councilor 1985-89, Bogle Internat. Travel award 1988, H.W. Wilson Libr. Staff Devel. grantee 1981), Libr. Adminstrn./Mgmt. Assn. (pres. 1981-82), Com. on Instnl. Cooperation/Resource Sharing (chair 1987-91), Coun. Dirs. State Univ. Librs. in Ill. (chair 1992-93), Ill. Assn. Coll. and Rsch. Librs. (chair Ill. Bd. Higher Edn. liaison com. 1993-94), Ill. Network (bd. dirs.), Ind. Libr. Assn. (chair coll./univ. divsn. 1982-83), U.S. Grant Assn. (bd. dirs. 1992—), NetIllinois (bd. dirs.). Office: So Ill U Morris Libr Carbondale IL 62901-6632

SNYDER, JAN LOUISE, administrative aide; b. Warrington Twp., Pa., Sept. 15, 1935; d. Wilbert Adam and Alice (Myers) March; divorced; children: Steven Michael Krone, David Sylvan Snyder. Grad. high sch., York, Pa. Cash audit clk. McCrory Stores Divsn. McCrory Corp., York, 1966; split ticket clk. McCrory Stores divsn. McCrory Corp., York, 1968, pers. sec., 1968-90, co. receptionist exec. buying divsn., 1990—. Active Northwestern region York Hosp. Aux., 1979—, York Symphony Assn., 1990—, membership com., 1992—; active York chpt. Am. Cancer Soc. Am., 1990—, York Chorus, 1988-90; mem. Ch. of the Open Door of Shiloh, 1956—, Dover Twp. Fire Co. Aux. for Women, 1975—, Harrisburg Jr. League Lectr. Series, 1980—. Mem. Am. Bus. Womens Assn. (pres. Colonial York charter chpt. 1986-87, mem. adv. bd. 1980-89). Democrat. Home: 2823 Grandview Ave York PA 17404-3905

SNYDER, JO ANNA W., cartographer, computer graphics designer; b. Atlanta, July 10, 1961; d. Joseph Hans Werner and Ruby Lee (Patty) Horton; m. Edward H. Snyder, Feb. 4, 1992. Grad. high sch., Ooltewah, Tenn., 1979; cert. computer drafting and design specialist, Charter Coll., Anchorage, 1994. Freelance graphics designer; typesetter, artist Printer's Workshop, Anchorage, 1984-85, Pip Printing, Anchorage, 1985-87; computer graphics designer BP Exploration (Alaska) Inc., Anchorage, 1987-92, cartographer, 1990-92; owner desktop pub. firm Graphics Alaska; freelance graphics designer, Wasilla, Alaska, 1989-94; CAD technician, then mktg. specialist New Horizons Telecom., Inc., Palmer, Alaska. Checker Iditarod Trail Sled Dog Assn., Wasilla, 1990-91. Mem. Nat. Computer Graphics Assn., Computer Graphics Network (founder, chmn. 1989-91). Home: HC89 Box 330 Willow AK 99688 Office: New Horizons Telecom Inc PO Box 2409 Palmer AK 99645

SNYDER, JULIA ANN, international trade and coffee company executive; b. Springfield, Mo., May 17, 1950; d. Arthur Jennings and Catheryn Laverna (Gallion) Swain; m. Orville Edward Kelley, Dec. 29, 1968 (div. 1972); 1 child, Adam Wayne; m. Ronald Warren Synder, May 29, 1982. Cert. Graff Vocat. Tech. Ctr., 1974. Sales sec. Paul Mueller Co., Springfield, 1971-73; surg. technician Cox Med. Ctr., Springfield, 1974-76; corp. sec., dir. OR&D, Inc., Springfield, 1979—; v.p., dir. Hey Mon Coffee Ltd., Everton, Mo., 1984—. Active Nat. Republican Com., 1980, Rep. Presdl. Task Force, 1981. Recipient Medal of Merit, Rep. Presdl. Task Force, 1982; named One of Outstanding Young Women of Am., 1984. Mem. Nat. Assn. Female Execs., Am. Notary Assn., Am. Film Inst. Mem. Assembly of God Ch. Avocations: latch hooking, stitchery, collecting depression era glassware, writing poetry, walking. Office: Hey Mon Coffee Ltd 294A Coffee Ln Everton MO 65646

SNYDER, LINDA LEE, elementary educator; b. Amsterdam, N.Y., Aug. 17, 1952; d. Edward Orville and Anna Mae (Parry) S. BA, Elmira Coll., 1974. Cert. tchr., N.Y. Substitute tchr. Stratford (N.Y.) schs., 1974-75; 2d grade and kindergarten tchr. West Canada Valley Sch., Newport, N.Y., 1975-82; sales dir. Mary Kay Cosmetics, Dallas, 1982-85; 3d grade tchr. Niskayuna (N.Y.) Sch. Dist., 1984—; summer program educator San Diego Zoo, 1994. Bd. dirs. Lawrence Ctr. for Ind. Living in the Capital Dist., Inc., Schenectady, N.Y., 1993-94. Mem. NOW, Spinal Cord Soc., Nat. Mus. Women in Arts (charter), Nat. Mus. Native Americans, Sierra Club, Audubon Soc., Nature Conservancy, Sweet Adelines. Presbyterian. Home: 1536 Unadilla St Schenectady NY 12308 Office: Rosedale Elem Sch 2445 Rosendale Rd Niskayuna NY 12309

SNYDER, MARGARET ELIZABETH, assemblywoman, paralegal; b. Elizabethtown, Tenn., Feb. 25, 1940; d. William Clarence Peters and Emma Grace (Elliott) Murphy; m. Melvin Wesley Snyder, Aug. 16, 1968; children: Jonathan L., Jennifer L., David E. Paraglegal cert., Humphreys Coll., 1992. Sec. U.S., Philippines, Germany; assemblywoman State of Calif. Assembly, Sacramento, 1992—. Vol. Family Svc., Philippines, 1962-64, ARC, Germany, 1970-72, bd. dirs., Modesto, Calif., 1981-84; mem. Dem. Ctrl. Com. 1977-86, Stanislaus County Grand Jury, 1978-79; bd. edn. Modesto City Schs., 1985-92; bd. dirs. The Haven, Modesto, 1990-92; mem. Internat. Friendship Com., Modesto, 1988-92. Named Vol. of Yr. Family Svc., Philippines, 1963, ARC, Germany, 1971, Woman of Yr. Stanislaus County Commn. for Women, Modesto, 1992, Woman of Distinction, Soroptomist Internat., Modesto, 1992. Office: 1101 Standiford Ave Ste B5 Modesto CA 95350-0981

SNYDER, MARIAN H., nursing educator and administrator; b. Webster, S.D., June 10, 1942; d. Harry C. and Helen L. (Potter) Walker; 1 child, Susan Marin. BSN, U. Conn., 1964; MS in Nursing, U. Ky., 1977; PhD, Marquette U., 1987. Staff nurse USAF, San Antonio, 1965-67; instr. Norton-Children's Hosp., Louisville, 1967-77; faculty Columbia Coll., Milw., 1977-81; dean, chief exec. officer Carroll-Columbia Coll. Nursing, Milw., 1981—. 1st lt. Nurses Corps, USAF. Mem. ANA, NLN, Sigma Theta Tau. Office: Columbia College 2121 E Newport Ave Milwaukee WI 53211-2952

SNYDER, NANCY MARGARET, translator, language services company executive; b. Detroit, Sept. 24, 1950; d. Estle M. and Noreen V. (Woodruff) S.; m. P. W. Denton, July 15, 1972 (div. Feb. 1980); 1 child, Virginia. BA in German, Mich. State U., 1972; cert. in programming and ops., Control Data Inst., 1984. Office mgr. Detroit Translation Bur., Southfield, Mich., 1980-82; bilingual sec. Volkswagen Am., Troy, Mich., 1984-85, translator, 1985-88; owner, operator Tech. Lang. Svcs., Birmingham, Mich., 1988—; guest speaker Kent State U. Inst. Applied Linguistics, 1992, Ferndale (Mich.) High Sch., 1992. Contbr. articles to profl. jours. Stadium usher Olympic Games, Munich, 1972; mem., worker Cass Corridor Food Coop., Detroit, 1986-90. Mem. S.E. Mich. Translators and Interpreters Network (newsletter editor 1993), Am. Translators Assn. (accredited German to English translator), Chgo. Area Translators Assn., Am. Mensa Ltd., Amherst Block Club. Office: Tech Lang Svcs 600 S Adams Ste 210 Birmingham MI 48009

SNYDER, PEGGY LEE, human resources director; b. Des Moines, Aug. 24, 1947; d. James Willis and Marjorie Lavonne (Nelson) Thompson; m. Joseph John Bastian, June 16, 1967 (div. June 1985); children: Michael Scott Bastian, Bryan John Bastian; m. Robert Eugene Snyder, Dec. 10, 1988. BA in Comm., Wright State U., 1981. Dir. pers. Deloitte Haskins & Sells, Dayton, Ohio, 1979-84, Met. Bank, Lima, Ohio, 1985-90; dir. human resources City of Lima, 1990—. Vol., co-team leader United Way, Dayton and Lima, 1979—; mem. adv. bd. Lima City Schs., 1989—. Mem. Soc. Human Resource Mgmt. (pres., v.p., sec. 1987—), Am. Legion. Home: 3763 Mt Vernon Pl Lima OH 45804 Office: City of Lima 50 Town Sq Lima OH 45801

SNYDER, REBECCA SUE H., small business owner; b. Roanoke, Va., Apr. 9, 1953; d. Wayne Hudson and Iris Jean (Dellis) Norris; m. Warren Chapman Snyder, July 21, 1973. Diploma, Jefferson H.S., Roanoke, Va., 1971. Office ops. Graves Humphreys, Roanoke, Va., 1971-91; bookkeeper Warren Snyder Painting, Roanoke, 1988—; owner, mgr. Valley Sun Tanning Salon, Roanoke, 1991—. Office: Valley Sun Tanning Salon 2838 Orange Ave NE Roanoke VA 24012

SNYDER, SUSAN BROOKE, retired English literature educator; b. Yonkers, N.Y., July 12, 1934; d. John Warren and Virginia Grace (Hartung) S. BA, Hunter Coll., CUNY, 1955; MA, Columbia U., 1958, PhD, 1963. Lectr. Queens Coll., CUNY, N.Y.C., 1961-63; instr. Swarthmore Coll., Pa., 1963-66, asst. prof. English lit., 1966-70, assoc. prof., 1970-75, prof., 1975-93, Eugene M. Lang research prof., 1982-86, Gil and Frank Mustin prof., 1990-93; ret.; prof. emeritus Swarthmore Coll., 1993—; rschr. Folger Shakespeare Libr. Author: The Comic Matrix of Shakespeare's Tragedies, 1979; editor: Divine Weeks and Works of Guillaume de Saluste, Sieur du Bartas, 1979, Othello: Critical Essays, 1988, All's Well that Ends Well, 1993; mem. editl. bd. Shakespeare Quar., 1972—. Folger Library sr. fellow, 1972-73; Nat. Endowment for Humanities fellow, 1967-68; Guggenheim Found. fellow, 1980-81; Huntington Library summer grantee, 1966, 71; Folger Library grantee, 1969; Nat. Endowment for Humanities grantee, 1970; Nat. Endowment for Humanities summer grantee, 1976. Mem. Renaissance Soc. Am. (coun. 1979-81), Shakespeare Assn. Am. (trustee 1980-83).

SNYDERMAN, SELMA ELEANORE, pediatrician, educator; b. Phila., July 22, 1916; d. Harry Samuel and Rose (Koss) S.; m. Joseph Schein, Aug. 4, 1939; children: Roland M. H., Oliver Douglas. AB, U. Pa., 1937, MD, 1940. Diplomate Am. Bd. Pediatrics, Am. Bd. Clin. Nutrition. Intern Einstein Med. Ctr., Phila., 1940-42; resident Bellevue Hosp., 1944-45; fellow NYU Med. Ctr., 1945-46; instr. pediatrics Sch. Medicine NYU, N.Y.C., 1946-50, asst. prof. Sch. Medicine, 1950-57, assoc. prof. Sch. Medicine, 1957-67, prof. Sch. Medicine, 1967—; assoc. prof. Med. Br. U. Tex., Galveston, Tex., 1952-53; attending physician Bellevue Hosp., N.Y.C., 1947—, Tisch Hosp., N.Y.C., 1947—; mem. nutrition study sect. NIH, Bethesda, Md., 1973-77; dir. Pediatric Metabolic Disease Ctr., Bellevue Med. Ctr., N.Y.C., 1965—. Contbr. numerous med. articles to profl. jours. Named career scientist Health Rsch. Coun., 1961-75. Fellow Am. Acad. Pediatrics (Borden award 1975); mem. Am. Pediatric Soc., Soc. for Pediatric Rsch., Am. Soc. Clin. Nutrition, Soc. Inherited Metabolic Disorders (v.p. 1978, pres. 1979, bd. dirs. 1980-83), Soc. Parenteral and Enteral Nutrition, Phi Beta Kappa. Jewish. Office: NYU Med Ctr 550 1st Ave New York NY 10016-6497

SOAVE, ROSEMARY, internist; b. N.Y.C., Jan. 23, 1949. BS, Fordham U., 1970; MD, Cornell Med. Coll., 1976. Diplomate Am. Bd. Internal Medicine, Subspecialty Bd. in Infectious Diseases. Intern, resident N.Y. Hosp., N.Y.C., 1976-79; chief med. resident Meml.-Sloan Kettering Cancer Ctr., N.Y.C., 1979-80; fellow infectious diseases N.Y. Hosp., N.Y.C., 1980-82, asst. prof. medicine, 1982-89, assoc. prof. medicine, 1989—; speaker in field. Contbr. numerous articles to profl. jours., chpts. to books, reviews and abstracts to profl. jours. Recipient Mary Putnam Jacobi fellowship for rsch., 1981-82, Leopold Schepp Rsch. fellowship, 1983-84, Nat. Found. for Infectious Diseases Young Investigator Matching Grant award, 1984-85; NIH grantee, 1986-89, 83-86, 87-90. Mem. AAAS, Am. Fedn. Clin. Rsch., N.Y. Acad. Scis., Infectious Diseases Soc. Am., Am. Soc. for Microbiology, Harvey Soc., Sigma Xi. Office: NY Hosp Cornell Med Ctr 1300 York Ave New York NY 10021-4805

SOBEL, JUDITH CAROL, special education educator; b. Bklyn., Mar. 25, 1939; d. Pincus and Rosalyn (Liphshitz) Weinshenker; m. Stanton Sobel, Dec. 25, 1960; children: Peter, Michael, Nathaniel. BA, CUNY, Bklyn., 1959, MS, 1961; EdS, Ga. State U., 1975. Cert. educator, Ga. Tchr. kindergarten PS 224, Bklyn., 1959-62; tchr. music Silver Lake/Mosely Elem. Sch., Palatka, Fla., 1962-63; instr. music edn. Emory U., Atlanta, 1964-65; asst. dir. kindergarten Cliff Valley Presch., Atlanta, 1967-73; Title X coord. Econ. Opportunity Atlanta, 1976-77; contract cons. Office of Child Devel. HEW, Atlanta, 1977-78; asst. to prin. Harry H. Epstein Sch., Atlanta, 1977-81; tchr. interrelated resources Holcomb Br. Mid. Sch., Atlanta, 1982-92, Lake Windward Elem. Sch., Alpharetta, Ga., 1992-93, New Prospect Elem. Sch., Alpharetta, 1993—; v.p. Bureau Jewish Edn., Atlanta, 1974-81; contract cons. Humanics, Atlanta, 1977-78; supr. Masters level student Ga. State U., Atlanta, 1974-75; music cons. Head Start, Atlanta, 1965-66. Founding mem. Tchr.'s Coun. Fulton County, Ga., 1988-91. Recipient Mid. Sch. Tchr. of Yr. award Fulton County Bd. of Edn., 1987; grantee Fulton County Bd. of Edn., 1989. Mem. Coun. for Exceptional Children (sec. 1982—), Learning Disabilities Assn. Jewish. Home: 6430 Tanacrest Ct NW Atlanta GA 30328 Office: New Prospect Elem Sch 3055 Kimball Br Rd Alpharetta GA 30202

SOBEL, NANCY B., obstetrician/gynecologist, educator; b. Chgo., June 15, 1954; d. Walter Howard and Betty Jane (Debs) S. BA in Chemistry-Biology, Skidmore Coll., 1976; PhD in Pharmacological and Physiol. Scis., U. Chgo., 1982, MD, 1984. Diplomate Am. Bd. Ob-Gyn. Intern, resident in gen. surgery U. Chgo. Hosp. and Clinics, 1984-86; resident in ob-gyn. Yale New Haven (Conn.) Hosp., 1986-89; assoc. Arborway Group St. Margaret's Hosp. for Women, Boston, 1989-91, med. dir. Nurse Midwifery Svc., 1991-92; assoc. staff dept. gynecology Lahey Clinic Med. Ctr., Burlington, Mass., 1992—; asst. prof. ob-gyn. Tufts U. Sch. Medicine, 1989-93; clin. instr. ob-gyn., reproductive biology Harvard Med. Sch., 1992—. Contbr. articles to profl. jours. Active Bus. and Profl. Assn. Chgo. Symphony Orch., 1982—. NIH Gen. Med. Scis. fellow Pharmacological Scis. Rsch. Tng. Program, 1977-81, William Scott Bond fellow Ben May Lab. for Cancer Rsch., 1981; Achievement Rewards for Coll. Scientists scholar, 1983-84. Fellow ACOG (dist. 1 quality assurance com. 1990—, practice com. 1993—), Am. Coll. Surgeons (assoc.); mem. AMA, Mass. Med. Soc., Am. Med. Women's Assn., Am. Soc. Law and Medicine, Assn. Women Surgeons, Achievement Rewards for Coll. Scientists Found. (Boston alumni liaison 1991-92, Boston bd. dirs. 1992—, pres. Boston chpt. 1994—). Office: Lahey Clinic 41 Mall Rd Burlington MA 01805

SOBER, DEBRA E., environmental services administrator; b. Oklahoma City, May 20, 1953; d. Donald E. and Zona E. (Taylor) Tillman; m. Gary L. Sober, May 24, 1980; children: Kara, Jeffrey, Kimberly. BS, Columbia Pacific U. Lic. water and wastewater operator; registered X-ray lab. technician; notary pub. Co-owner UMAS, Inc., Austin, Tex.; chmn. bd. PACE Corp., Austin; gen. mgr. Envir-O-Spec, Inc., Austin; pres., ind. practice Environ. Tng., Inc., Austin. Author numerous textbooks on water and wastewater treatment and operation. Founder ann. Just Fishin Show, Austin, 1989; bd. dirs. Austin Women's Soccer League, 1991-93; bd. dirs., founder Austin Amateur Soccer Assn., 1991; women's commr. Tex. State Soccer Assn. South, 1994—. Mem. Nat. Environ. Tng. Assn., Tex. Water Utilities Assn. (chmn. pub. rels. 1981-85, safety chmn. 1987-88), Okla. Water and Pollution Control Assn., Am. Water Works Assn., Water Pollution Control Fedn., Am. Bus. Women's Assn., N.W. Adult Athletic Assn. (founder and dir. 1986), N.W. Austin Women's Basketball Assn. (founder and pres. 1986), N.W. Austin Women's Soccer Assn. (founder and pres. 1986), Beta Sigma Phi. Baptist. Home: 11807 Highland Oaks Trl Austin TX 78759-2406 Office: 11940 Jollyville Rd Austin TX 78759-2324

SOBERON, PRESENTACION ZABLAN, state bar administrator; b. Cabambangan, Bacolor, Pampanga, Philippines, Feb. 23, 1935; came to U.S., 1977, naturalized, 1984; d. Pioquinto Yalung and Lourdes (David) Zablan; m. Damaso Reyes Soberon, Apr. 2, 1961; children: Shirley,Sherman, Sidney, Sedwin. Office mgmt., stenography, typing cert. East Cen. Colls., Philippines, 1953; profl. sec. diploma, Internat. Corr. Schs., 1971; student Skyline Coll., 1979, LaSalle Ext. U., 1980-82; AA, cert. in Mgt. and Supervision, Diablo Valley Coll. With U.S. Fed. Svc. Naval Base, Subic Bay, Philippines, clerical, stenography and secretarial positions, 1955-73, adminstrv. asst., 1973-77; secretarial positions Mt. Zion Hosp. and Med. Center, San Francisco, 1977, City Hall, Oakland, Calif., 1978; secretarial positions gen. counsel div. and state bar court divsn., State Bar of Calif., San Francisco, 1978-79, adminstrv. asst. fin. and ops. div., 1979-81, office mgr. sects. and coms. dept., profl. and pub. svcs. div., 1981-83, appointment adminstr. office of bar rels., 1983-86; adminstr. state bar sects. bus. law sect., estate planning, trust and probate law sect., labor and employment law section, office of bar rels., 1986-89, adminstr. antitrust and trade regulation law sect., labor and employment law sect., workers' compensation sect., edn. and meeting svcs., 1989—; disc jockey/announcer Philippine radio stas. DZYZ, DZOR and DWHL, 1966-77. Organizer Neighborhood Alert Program, South Catamaran Circle, Pittsburg, Calif., 1979-80. Recipient 13 commendation certs. and outstanding pers. monetary awards U.S. Fed. Svc., 1964-77, 20 Yr. U.S. Fed. Svc. pin and cert., 1975; Nat. 1st prize award for community svc. and achievements Inner Wheel Clubs Philippines, 1975; several plaques and award certs. for community and sch. activities and contbrns. Olongapo City, Philippines. Mem. NAFE, Am. Soc. Assn. Execs., N.Y.C. Olongapo-Subic Bay Assn. No. Calif. (Pittsburg rep. 1982-87, bus. mgr. 1988—, pub. rels. officer 1993-94), Castillejos Assn. of No. Calif. Roman Catholic. Home: 207 S Catamaran Cir Pittsburg CA 94565-3613 Office: State Bar of Calif 555 Franklin St San Francisco CA 94102-4498

SOBOSLAY, DIAN JEAN, secondary education educator; b. Lakewood, Ohio, Mar. 5, 1949; d. Alex Ray and Doris Jean (Sakach) Nemeth; 1 child, Kymberlee Marie Nemeth; m. Richard Ray Soboslay, Jan. 2, 1988. BS, Kent State U., 1971, MEd, 1994. Cert. home econs. tchr., vocat. consumer-homemaking tchr., Ohio. Tchr. vocat. family and consumer scis. Cleve. Bd. Edn., 1972—; piloted modern design fine arts course Cleve. Bd. Edn., 1989-90. Active Tchr.-Leader Inst. and Urban Task Force, 1994-96. Mem. Am. Vocat. Assn., Ohio Vocat. Assn., Greater Cleve. Home Eoncs. Auditor, Am. Assn. of Family and Consumer Scis., Nat. Assn. Vocat. Edn. Spl. Needs Pers., Sigma Sigma Sigma (chpt. adv. bd. 1992, chpt. housing coord. 1992), Kiwanis (dir. 1993-94, sec. 1994-95), Ohio Assn. of Family and Consumer Scis., Omicron Tau Theta. Democrat. Roman Catholic. Home: 8061 Greenwood View Dr Apt 1107 Parma OH 44129

SOCHEN, JUNE, history educator; b. Chgo., Nov. 26, 1937; d. Sam and Ruth (Finkelstein) S. B.A., U. Chgo., 1958; M.A., Northwestern U., 1960, Ph.D., 1967. Project editor Chgo. Superior and Talented Student Project, 1959-60; high sch. tchr. English and history North Shore Country Day Sch., Winnetka, Ill., 1961-64; instr. history Northeastern Ill. U., 1964-67, asst. prof., 1967-69, assoc. prof., 1969-72, prof., 1972—. Author: The New Woman, 1971, Movers and Shakers, 1973, Herstory: A Woman's View of American History, 1975, 2d edit., 1981, Consecrate Every Day: The Public Lives of Jewish American Women, 1981, Enduring Values: Women in Popular Culture, 1987, Cafeteria America: New Identities in Contemporary Life, 1988, Mae West: She Who Laughs Lasts, 1992; editor: Women's Comic Visions, 1991; contbr. articles to profl. jours. Nat. Endowment for Humanities grantee, 1971-72. Mem. Am. Studies Assn. Office: Northeastern Ill U 5500 N Saint Louis Ave Chicago IL 60625-4625

SOCHER, MYRA MALCA, emergency medical service consultant; b. Durban, Natal, South Africa, Feb. 21, 1945; came to U.S., 1975; d. Ivan and Chanalie (Liszanski) Philips; m. Ivan David Socher, July 2, 1963; children: Raoul, Larry. BS in Emergency Mgmt. summa cum laude, George Washington U., 1991. Nationally registered paramedic. Field support mkgt. Computer Advances, Johannesburg, South Africa, 1972-75; recruiter, systems analyst Amadax Corp., Bohemia, N.Y., 1981-82; EMT Medstar Ambulance Svc., Savannah, Ga., 1987; staff support Internat. Assn. Fire Chiefs, Washington, 1989-90; clin. instr. CPR Ctr. Georgetown U. Hosp, Washington, 1991—; adj. instr. emergency medicine George Washington U., Washington, 1989—; dir. ops. Transcare ALS, Washington, 1990-93; founder MMS Assocs., Arlington, Va., 1992—; pres. TriMed Inc., Arlington, 1993—; adj. faculty Children's Hosp., Washington, 1989-93. Vol. firefighter/EMT Southside Fire Dept., Savannah, Ga., 1987; vol. paramedic Dale City (Va.) Vol. Fire Dept., 1989-90; subcom. mem. Am. Heart Assn., Washington, 1992—; vol. paramedic Arlington County Fire/Rescue, 1994. Recipient Exceptional Svc. award Am. Heart Assn., 1993. Mem. Am. Trauma Soc., Coun. on Cardiovascular. Democrat. Jewish. Home: 3926 Georgetown Ct Washington DC 20007 Office: TriMed Inc 2030 Clarendon Blvd # 501 Arlington VA 22201

SOCHET, MARY ALLEN, community organizer, psychotherapist, writer; b. Plattsburgh, N.Y., Feb. 10, 1938; d. Edwin Elisha and Mary Elizabeth (Thomson) Allen; m. Marvin J. Sochet, 1963; children: Melorra, David. BS in Childhood Edn., SUNY, Plattsburgh, 1958; MA in Human Rels., NYU, 1961, PhD in Human Devel., 1963. Tchr. kindergarten L.I. Pub. Schs., 1958-62; tchr. N.Y.C. Pub. Schs., 1962-64; prof. early childhood edn., child devel. and psychology Bklyn. Coll., 1964-71; program dir., acting exec. dir. Newark Pre-Sch. Coun., 1965-66; psychotherapist N.Y.C. Community Guidance Svc., 1966-78; staff cons. Human Resources Inst., 1966—; pvt. practice psychotherapy N.Y.C., 1966—; writer, lectr., ednl. cons. and editorial cons. in field. Author: (with Robert Allen) Toward a Caring Community, 1980; contbr. articles on edn., community orgns., peace and mental health to various jours. Founding mem. Community Loft, 1971-74, Neighbor's Network, 1979—; organizing mem. Children's Free Sch., 1969-81; co-chair Kids Meeting Kids Can Make a Difference, 1982—. NCCJ fellow, 1961-61; recipient Founder's Day award NYU, 1963. Mem. Am. Psychol. Assn., Soc. Psychol. Study Social Issues, Psychologists for Social Responsibility. Home and Office: 380 Riverside Dr New York NY 10025

SODER, DEE A., psychologist; b. Oklahoma City, June 20, 1947; d. Keats Endymion Soder. BS with distinction, U. Okla., 1969, PhD in Psychology, 1976. Sr. rsch. psychologist U.S. Office Pers. Mgmt., Washington, 1974-77, Exec. Office Pres. U.S., Washington, 1978; staffing dir. for D.C., 1979; v.p. human resources devel. Prudential Ins. Co. Am., 1980-84; founder Endymion Co., N.Y.C., 1986—. Author: Job Analysis, An Effective Management Tool, 1983, Breaking Through the Glass Ceiling, Corporate Board, 1993; profiled in Fortune Mag. and numerous other mags. and profl. jours. Founder Pers. Testing Coun. Met. Washington; prin. Ctr. for Excellence in Govt.; bd. dirs. Women's Campaign Fund, Women's Econ. Roundtable, Horse Trails Conservancy. Office: US Endymion Co Inc 50 Rockefeller Ctr New York NY 10020

SODER, SARA LEE, chemist, program administrator; b. Chgo., Nov. 2, 1946; d. Earl Eugene and Alice Katherine (Lien) Soder; m. Thomas Michael Logan, Sept. 8, 1974; stepchildren: Kimberly, Michael. BS in Chemistry Curriculum, U. Ill., 1968; MBA, U. Calif., Berkeley, 1985. Info. specialist Exxon Rsch. and Engring., Linden, N.J., 1968-70; tech. ops. asst. Zoecon Corp., East Palo Alto, Calif., 1973; rsch. analyst, indsl. economist SRI Internat., Menlo Park, Calif., 1971-79, asst. dir. world petrochems. program, 1979-81, dir. world petrochems. program, 1981-85, sr. cons., 1985—, dir. chem. econs. handbook, 1992—; speaker and presenter in field. Mem. Am. Chem. Soc. (chair chem. mktg. and econs. div. 1985-86, program chmn. 1981-84, sec. 1987-88), Chem. Mktg. Rsch. Assn. (meeting chair 1990). Lutheran. Office: SRI Internat 333 Ravenswood Ave Menlo Park CA 94025-3493

SODER-ALDERFER, KAY CHRISTIE, counseling administrator; b. Evanston, Ill., Oct. 25, 1949; d. Earl Eugene and Alice Kathryn (Lien) Soder; m. David Luther Alderfer, May 15, 1976. BSE, No. Ill. U., 1972; postgrad., Luth. Sch. Theology, Phila., 1973; MA, Gov.'s State U., University Park, Ill., 1978; PhD, Walden U., 1985. Consecrated deaconess Luth. Ch., 1974. News reporter Suburban Life Newspaper, La Grange Park, Ill., 1972; counselor various orgns. Ill. & Pa., 1973—; parish worker Luth. Ch., De Kalb, Ill., 1973-74; pub. rels. asst. Luth. Ch. Women, Phila., 1974-76; editor Luth. Ch., Chgo., 1979-93; spiritual dir. Gentle Pathways, Downers Grove, Ill., 1988—, counseling psychologist, 1990—, also bd. dirs.; cons. Evang. Luth. Ch. Am., Chgo., 1988—, LeHigh Valley Hosp. Assn., Allentown, Pa., 1986. Author: Gentle Journeys, 1993, With Those Who Grieve, 1994, editor: (mag.) Entree, 1988-93, (jour.) Multicultural Jour., 1992, 93, 94; graphic designs exhbn. Franklin Mus., Phila., 1981. Spokeswoman Progressive Epilepsy Network, Phila., 1980-85; precinct worker Dem. Party, Ill., 1988—; chair, spiritual life com. Luth. Deaconess Community, Gladwyne, Pa., 1990-92; vol. March of Dimes, Ill., 1991-93; amb. of good will Good Bears of Am., 1993—; sprirtual dir. Synod Evang. Luth. Ch. Am. Recipient Silver award Delaware Valley Neographics Soc., 1981; 50th anniversary scholar Luth. Deaconess Community, 1983. Mem. APA, Assn. for Humanistic Psychology, Religious Pub. Rels. Coun., Internat. Diaconia, Met. Chgo. (appointed). Office: Gentle Pathways 1207 55th St Downers Grove IL 60515-4810

SOECHTIG, JACQUELINE ELIZABETH, telecommunications executive; b. Manhasset, N.Y., Aug. 12, 1949; d. Alvin Hermann and Regina Mary (Murphy) Venzke; m. James Decatur Miller, June 28, 1976 (div. Oct. 1982); M. Clifford Jon Soechtig, Oct. 19, 1983. B.A. cum laude, Coll. of New Rochelle (N.Y.), 1974; M.A. summa cum laude, U. So. Calif., 1978. Computer operator IBM, White Plains, N.Y., 1970-72, ops. job scheduler, 1972-74, various spl. assignments, 1974-75, mktg. rep., Bethesda, Md., 1975-76, Charleston, W. Va., 1979-81, adv. regional mktg. rep. Dallas, 1981-82; dist. mgr. Am. Speedy Printing Co., Dallas, 1982-83, nat. sales devel. mgr., Detroit, 1984; regional mgr. major and nat. accounts MCI Telecommunications, Southfield, Mich., 1984-85, dir. nat. accounts, 1985-86, v.p. nat. accounts, 1987-88, v.p. mktg. and customer svc., 1988-89, v.p. consumer segment, 1989-90; v.p. integrated telecommunications solutions Sprint United, Atlanta, 1990-92; pres., chief exec. officer Precision Systems, 1992—; interviewer, Sergio Segre, Bolonga, Italy, 1977, Radio Free Europe, Brussels, 1978, World Health Program, Rome, 1978, ITT, Brussels, 1977, Franz Josef Strauss, 1978. Recipient Golden Circle Achievement award IBM, 1980, Quar. Recognition award, 1980, 81; named New Bus. Pacesetter, 1980, 81. Republican. Club: German Am. Women's (v.p. Stuttgart, W.Ger. 1977-78). Office: Precision Sys 11800 30th Ct No Saint Petersburg FL 33716

SOETEBER, ELLEN, journalist, newspaper editor; b. East St. Louis, Ill., June 14, 1950; d. Lyle Potter and Norma Elizabeth (Osborn) S.; m. Richard M. Martins, Mar. 16, 1974. BJ, Northwestern U., 1972. Edn. writer, copy editor Chgo. Today, 1972-74; reporter Chgo. Tribune, 1974-76, asst. met. editor, 1976-84, assoc. met. editor, 1984-86, TV and media editor, 1986, met. editor, 1987-89, assoc. mng. editor for met. news, 1989-91, dep. editor editorial page, 1991-94; mng. editor Ft. Lauderdale (Fla.) Sun-Sentinel, 1994—; fellow journalism U. Mich., Ann Arbor, 1986-87. Office: The Sun-Sentinel 200 E Las Olas Blvd Fort Lauderdale FL 33301

SOETH, SARAH LAVERNE REEDY MCMILLAN, psychiatric nurse; b. Amory, Miss., Feb. 20, 1925; d. Samuel Thomas and Bessie Lee (Franklin) Reedy; m. Urshel E. McMillan, Jan. 16, 1944 (dec. 1964); children: David Thomas, Joy Laverne McMillan Keys; m. Glenn Eugene Soeth, Nov. 27, 1976. Student, Miss. State Coll. Women, 1943-44; LPN, Tupelo Sch. Nursing, 1968; MSN, U. Miss., Jackson, 1972. RN, Miss. Pvt. duty nurse Evart, Mich., 1960-64; staff nurse Aberdeen (Miss.) Monroe County Hosp., 1965-72; lic. psychiat. nurse Hinds Gen. Hosp., Jackson, Miss., 1972-78; charge nurse Tigard (Oreg.) Psychiat. Convalescent Hosp., 1978-79; staff nurse VA Med. Ctr., Reno, 1979-80, Glenn County Hosp., Willows, Calif., 1980-81; staff nurse VA Med. Ctr., Martinez, Calif., 1981-91, Fresno, Calif., 1991-93; vol. Mental Health Treatment Ctr. Active Diabetes Assn. Presbyterian.

SOFOS, STEPHANY LOUISE, real estate executive; b. Honolulu, Sept. 16, 1954; d. Thomas A. and Catherine B. (Seros) S. BA in History, U. Hawaii, 1976. Assoc. Chaney Brooks Realty, Inc., Honolulu, 1976-77; supr. property/mgr. shopping ctr. Hawaii Mgmt. Corp., Honolulu, 1977-79; mgr. mktg. and customer relations Kaiser Devel. Co., Honolulu, 1979-82; gen. mgr. Kuhio Mall, Honolulu, 1982-86; pres. SL Sofos and Co., Ltd., Honolulu, 1986—. Mem. Nat. Assn. Realtors, Inst. Real Estate Mgmt. (cert. property mgr., bd. dirs. Hawaii chpt. 1987), Internat. Coun. Shopping Ctrs. (cert. shopping ctr. mgr.), Bldg. Owners and Mgrs. Assn. (real property adminstr.). Greek Orthodox. Clubs: Honolulu, Outrigger Canoe, Oahu Country (Honolulu). Office: 1240 Ala Moana Blvd Ste 305 Honolulu HI 96814

SOHAL, KULVINDER KAUR, systems consultant, accountant; b. Nangal Twp., Punjab, India, Oct. 1, 1957; d. Rajinder Singh and Kuldip Kaur

(Shahi) Grewal; m. Iqbal Singh Sohal, Sept. 12, 1981; children: Jessica, Robinder. BEd, Panjab U., 1977; MS in Computer Sci., Stevens Inst. Tech., 1992. CPA; cert. info. systems auditor. EDP auditor Capital Holding Corp., Louisville, Ky., 1980-82; acct.-systems devel. Purdue U., West Lafayette, Ind., 1983-88; assoc. mgr. Bellcore, Piscataway, N.J., 1989-94; sr. assoc. Coopers and Lybrand, Southfield, Mich., 1994—. Fellow Life Mgmt. Inst. Home: 2210 Carpathian Dr West Bloomfield MI 48322

SOHN, JEANNE, librarian; b. Milton, Pa.; d. Robert Wilson and Juliette Lightner (Hedenberg) Gift; m. Steven Neil Sohn, Nov. 23, 1962. BA, Temple U., 1966; MSLS, Drexel U., 1971. Lit. bibliographer Temple U., Phila., 1971-75, chief of collection devel., 1975-81; asst. dean for collection devel. U. N.Mex., Albuquerque, 1981-86, assoc. dean for libr. svcs., 1986-89; dir. libr. svcs. Cen. Conn. State U., New Britain, 1989—; cons. New Eng. Assn. Schs. and Colls., Winchester, Mass., 1991—. Mem. editorial bd. Collection Mgmt., 1984—; contbr. articles to profl. jours. Mem. Gov.'s Blue Ribbon Commn. on the Future of Libraries, 1994—. Mem. ALA, New Eng. Libr. Assn., Conn. Libr. Assn., Assn. Coll. and Rsch. Librs., Beta Phi Mu. Home: 1820 Boulevard West Hartford CT 06107-2815 Office: Elihu Burritt Libr Cen Conn State U New Britain CT 06050

SOHNEN-MOE, CHERIE MARILYN, business consultant; b. Tucson, Jan. 2, 1956; d. D. Ralph and Angelina Helen (Spiro) Sohnen; m. James Madison Moe, Jr., May 23, 1981. BA, UCLA, 1977. Rsch. asst. UCLA, 1975-77; ind. cons. L.A., 1978-83; cons. Sohnen-Moe Assocs., Tucson, 1984—. Author: Business Mastery, 1988, 2d edit., 1991; contbr. to Compendium mag., 1987-90, Massage Mag., 1992-94, Am. Massage Therapy Assn. Jour., 1989—. Vol. Am. Cancer Soc., Tucson, 1984—; mem. Ariz. Sonora Desert Mus., Tucson; pres. Women in Tucson, 1989. Recipient Outstanding Instr. award Desert Inst. of Healing Arts, 1992. Mem. NOW, ASTD (dir. mem. svcs. 1988, Achievement award 1987, Disting. Svc. award 1988), Internat. Assn. Ind. Pubs., Pubs. Mktg. Assn., New Age Pub. and Retailing Alliance, Sierra Club. Office: Sohnen-Moe Assocs 3906 W Ina Rd # 200-348 Tucson AZ 85741-2295

SOINSKI OPASKAR, GAIL V., secondary school administrator; b. Cleve., May 13, 1948; d. Victor R. and Angela (Penkal) Soinski; m. Frank A. Opaskar, Apr. 13, 1985; 1 child, Amanda. BS, U. Cin., 1971; MS, Cleve. State U., 1977. Tchr. phys. edn. Bolton Elem. Sch., Cleve. Bd. Edn., 1971-72; tchr. phys. edn. and health Jane Addams High Sch., Cleve. Bd. Edn., 1972-89, athletic dir., 1980-89, head coach, volleyball, 1972-87, head track coach, 1972-85; asst. prin. Patrick Henry Intermediate Sch., Cleve., 1989-91, Max Hayes Vocat. High Sch., Cleve., 1991-92, Lincoln West High Sch., Cleve., 1992—. Mem. ASCD, Cleve. Coun. of Adminstrs. and Suprs.

SOJKA, SANDRA KAY, investor; b. Ames, Iowa, Jan. 22, 1942; d. Clyde Burdette and Helen Rae (Daley) Smith; m. Gary Allan Sojka, Aug. 5, 1962; children: Lisa Kay, Dirk Allan. BS in Bus. Mgmt. with acad. honors, Ind. U., 1968, MS in Counseling-Guidance with honors, 1979, MS in Coll. Student Pers. with honors, 1979. Asst. to vet. extension office Purdue U., Lafayette, Ind., 1962-67; CPA asst. Geo. Greene & Co., Bloomington, Ind., 1975-76; office mgr., bldg. supr. Univ. Ministries, 1973-75; counselor, adminstrv. asst. dept. athletics Ind. U., Bloomington, 1977-84; first lady Bucknell U., Lewisburg, 1984—, coord. univ./community activities for the pres.'s office, 1984—, asst. sec. to bd. trustees, 1989—; mem. Susquehanna Valley program adv. com. Pub. TV and Radio Sta. WVIA and FM90, 1994—. Co-author: Job Readiness Training Guide, 1977, Graduate Course Design and Evaluation Module, 1979. Bd. dirs. Evang. Cmty. Hosp., Lewisburg, 1984-91, Bloomsburg Theatre Ensemble, 1986-89; trustee Coe Coll., Cedar Rapids, Iowa, 1988—, chmn. nominating com., 1992—; bd. dirs. Assn. for Arts Bucknell U., 1984—; adv. bd. Four County Mental Health/Mental Retardation Orgn., Danville, Pa., 1986-94, pres. 1991-93; fundraising com. Camp Victory for Disabled Children, Millville, Pa., 1988-91. Recipient Disting. Svc. award Four County Mental Health/Mental Retardation Orgn., 1993. Mem. AAUW (bd. dirs. 1989-90), Bucknell U. Campus Club (pres. 1985-87), Lewisburg Aux. to Evang. Cmty. Hosp., Union County Hist. Soc., Lewisburg Garden Club (chair social program com. 1987-88, 94-95, chair nominations com. 1990-91), Civic Club Lewisburg, Lewisburg Federated Womens Club, Alpha Xi Delta, Beta Gamma Sigma.

SOKALSKI, DEBRA ANN, computer systems developer, programming consultant; b. Paterson, N.J., June 27, 1959; d. John Michael and Cecelia Ann (O'Brien) S. Computer program cert., Electronic Computer Prog.Inst., Paterson, 1978; student, Montclair State Coll., 1988. Programmer trainee Numerax, Inc., Paramus, N.J., 1978-79, programmer, 1979-82, programming supr., 1982-83, mgr. programming, 1983-84, mgr. data processing, 1984-88; dir. system devel. Numerax/McGraw-Hill, Inc., 1989-90; sr. programmer analyst ADP, Roseland, N.J., 1990-92, lead programmer analyst, 1992-93; lead tech. analyst, 1993—; programming cons. Leslie Co., Parsippany, N.J., 1979-80. White House Fellowship nominee, 1994-95. Mem. NAFE. Democrat. Roman Catholic. Home: 174B Main St Little Falls NJ 07424-1411 Office: ADP 1 ADP Blvd # B210 Roseland NJ 07068-1728

SOKELL, GERI ANN, physical therapist; b. Cleve., Nov. 28, 1958; d. Walter John and Mildred Ages (Drensky) Kanieski; m. James Chester Sokell, Mar. 3, 1990. BS in Phys. Therapy magna cum laude, Cleve. State U., 1987, MEd, 1992. Profl. ballet dancer Cleve. Ballet Co., 1978-79, Boston Ballet Co., 1980-81, Ohio Ballet Co., Akron, 1981-82; phys. therapist Cleve. Clinic Found., 1987-89, Winston Salem (N.C.) Convalescent Ctr., 1990-91, Aristocrat Berea Skilled Facility, Parma Therapy Ctr., Cleve., 1991—; cons. Body Sculpting Inc., Cleve., 1991—. Mem. Am. Phys. Therapy Assn. (pub. rels. chmn. 1992-93). Roman Catholic. Home: 7512 Theota Ave Cleveland OH 44129 Office: Aristocrat Bera Skilled Facility 255 Front St Bera OH 44017

SOKOL, SHERRY LYNN, controller; b. Chgo., Sept. 11, 1960; d. Jack and Rita Rose (Miller) Plenner; m. Steven Scott Sokol, June 6, 1982; children: Elizabeth Anne, Jacqueline Sue. BA, Northeastern Ill. U., 1982. CPA, Ill. Staff acct. Laventhol & Horwath, Chgo., 1982-84; supply controller Cooper's Plumbing & Heating, Chgo., 1984—. Mem. Soc. Advancement Mgmt., Am. Inst. CPA's, Ill. CPA Soc. Office: Skokie Plumbing Supply Inc 3714 Oakton St Skokie IL 60076-3407 also: Cooper's Plumbing & Heating Supplies Inc 5239 W Cermak Rd Cicero IL 60650

SOLA, JANET ELAINE, secondary school educator; b. New Britain, Conn., Oct. 23, 1935; d. Walter Andrew and Helen (Mandl) Sinkiewicz; m. Raymond Albert Sola,. BS, Cen. Conn. State U., 1957; MS, So. Conn. State U., 1962; postgrad., U. Conn, 1969. Tchr. bus. Amity Regional High Sch., Woodbridge, Conn., 1957-60; bus. instr. Stone Coll., New Haven, 1962; instr. Manpower Devel. and Tng. Act, New Britain, 1970-74; instr. So. Ctrl. C.C., New Haven, 1977, lectr., 1987; mgmt. lectr. II, Quinnipiac Coll., Hamden, Conn., 1981-87; mayor's aide Town of Hamden, 1987-89, recycling coord., 1989-92; tchr. bus. edn. Hamden High Sch., 1992—, coord. coop. work experience and diversified occupations, 1992—; assessor credit for life Quinn Coll., Hamden, 1986-89. Author: (poetry) Flights of Fancy, 1991, Recycled Thoughts, 1992; contbr. poetry to Contemporary, The Hamden Chronicle, Treasured Poems of Am., Nat. Arts Soc. Campaigner Sola for Town Clk. Com., Hamden, 1981; community liaison Carusone for Mayor Com., Hamden, 1981-87; v.p., Am. Legion Aux. Unit 88, Hamden, 1985—. Mem. ASCD, NAFE, AAUW, Nat. Bus. Educators, Ctrl. Conn. State U. Alumni Assn. (bd. dirs.), Internat. Platform Assn., Soc. Plastics Engrs., Nat. Recycling Coalition, Conn. Recyclers Coalition, Lions (pres. 1994-95). Home: 50 Vernon St Hamden CT 06518-2825 Office: Hamden HS 2040 Dixwell Ave Hamden CT 06514-2479

SOLAUN, HILDA R., real estate broker; b. Habana, Cuba, Jan. 26, 1937; came to U.S., 1961; d. Rene J. and Sara A. (Pelly) Luis; m. Felix M. Solaun, Oct. 26, 1958; children: Maria Teresa, Felix M. and Jose I. (twins), Leticia M. Music Degree, Orbon Conservatory Music, Habana, 1957; Real Estate Cert., Fla. C.C. Jacksonville, 1976. Lic. real estate broker, Fla. Tchr. music Orbon Conservatory Music, Habana, 1957-58; computer operator Xerox Corp., Rochester, N.Y., 1964-65; assoc. realtor Lopez Realty Co., Jacksonville, 1976-79; broker/owner Dahill Internat. Realty Co., Jacksonville, 1979—. Bd. dirs. Equal Bus. Opportunity Adv. Com., City of Jacksonville, 1993—. Mem. Nat. Assn. Realtors (realtor designation), Fla. Assn. Realtors, Hispanic Am. Bus. Assn. (past chair membership com. 1993-94, bd. dirs. 1993—), Cuban Nat. Am. Found., Quien Es Quien in U.S. Commerce (hon.). Office: Dahill Internat Realty Co 2026 University Blvd N Jacksonville FL 32211

SOLBERG, ELIZABETH TRANSOU, public relations executive; b. Dallas, Aug. 10, 1939; d. Ross W. and Josephine V. (Perkins) Transou; m. Frederick M. Solberg, Jr., Mar. 8, 1969; 1 son, Frederick W. BJ, U. Mo., 1961. Reporter, Kansas City (Mo.) Star, 1963-70, asst. city editor, 1970-73; reporter spl. events, documentaries Sta. WDAF-TV, Kansas City, Mo., 1973-74; prof. dept. journalism Park Coll., Kansas City, Mo., 1975-76, advisor, 1976-79; mng. ptnr. Fleishman-Hillard, Inc., Kansas City, Mo., from 1979, now exec. v.p., sr. ptnr., gen. mgr. Kansas City br. Mem. Kansas City Commn. Planned Indsl. Expansion Authority, 1974-91; mem. long-range planning com. Heart of Am. council Boy Scouts Am., 1980-82, bd. dirs., 1986-89; mem. Clay County (Mo.) Devel. Commn., 1979-88; bd. govs. Citizens Assn., 1975—; mem. exec. com. bd. Kansas City Area Devel. Coun.; trustee Pembroke Hill Sch., U. Kansas City. Recipient award for contbn. to mental health Mo. Psychiat. Assn., 1973. Mem. Pub. Relations Soc. Am. (nat. honors and awards com., co-chmn. Silver Anvil com. 1983, Silver Anvil award 1979-82, chair nat. membership com. 1989-91), Counselor's Acad. (exec. com.), Mo. C. of C. Pub. Relations Council, Greater Kans. City C. of C. (vice chair 1994), Pi Beta Phi. Clubs: Jr. League, Kansas City, Carriage, Central Exchange. Office: Fleishman Hillard Inc 2405 Grand Blvd Ste 700 Kansas City MO 64108-2519

SOLBRIG, INGEBORG HILDEGARD, German literature educator, author; b. Weissenfels, Germany, July 31, 1923; came to U.S., 1961, naturalized, 1966; d. Reinhold J. and Hildegard M.A. (Ferchland) S. Grad. in chemistry, U. Halle, Germany, 1948; BA summa cum laude, San Francisco State U., 1964; postgrad., U. Calif., Berkeley, 1964-65; MA, Stanford U., 1966, PhD in Humanities and German, 1969. Asst. prof. U. R.I., 1969-70, U. Tenn., Chattanooga, 1970-72, U. Ky., Lexington, 1972-75; assoc. prof. German U. Iowa, 1975-81, prof., 1981-93, prof. emerita, 1993—; prof. emerita. Author: Hammer-Purgstall und Goethe, 1973; editor: Rilke Heute, Beziehungen und Wirkungen, 1975, Reinhard Goering: Seeschlacht/Seabattle, 1977, Orient-Rezeption, 1995; contbr. numerous articles, revs. and translations to profl. jours., chpts. to books. Mem. Iowa Gov.'s Com. on 300th Anniversary German-Am. Rels. 1683-1983, 1983. Recipient Hammer-Purgstall Gold medal Austria, 1974; named Ky. col., 1975; fellow Austrian Ministry Edn., 1968-69, Stanford U., 1965-66, 68-69; Old Gold fellow Iowa, 1977; Am. Coun. Learned Socs. grantee; German Acad. Exch. Svc. grantee, 1980; sr. faculty rsch. fellow in the humanities, 1983; NEH grantee, 1985; May Brodbeck fellow in the humanities, 1989; numerous summer faculty rsch. grants. Mem. MLA (life), Internat. Verein fur Germanische Sprach und Lit. Wiss., Goethe Gesellschaft, Deutsche Schiller Gesellschaft, Am. Soc. for 18th Century Studies, Can. Soc. for 18th Century Studies, Goethe Soc. N.Am., Inc. (founding), Internat. Herder Soc. Home: 1126 Pine St Iowa City IA 52240-5711

SOLDEVILA-PICO, CONSUELO, physician, gastroenterologist; b. St. Paul, Oct. 11, 1959; d. Manuel Soldevila dn Carmen Pico. BS in Biology, Yale U., 1977-81; MD, U. P.R., 1981-86. Diplomate Am. Bd. Internal Medicine, sub-bd. gastroenterology. Fellow in gastroenterology U. Pitts., 1992-93, Tulane U., 1993—. Mem. ACP, AMA, Am. Assn. Study Liver Disease, Am. Coll. Gastroenterology, Am. Gastroent. Assn., Am. Soc. Gastroent. Endoscopy. Office: Tulane U 1430 Tulane Ave SL35 New Orleans LA 70012

SOLES, ADA LEIGH, former state legislator, government advisor; b. Jacksonville, Fla., May 19, 1937; d. Albert Thomas and Dorothy (Winter) Wall; B.A., Fla. State U., 1959; m. James Ralph Soles, 1959; children—Nancy Beth, Catherine. Mem. New Castle County Library Adv. Bd., 1975-80, chmn., 1975-77; chmn. Del. State Library Adv. Bd., 1975-78; mem. Del. State Ho. Reps., 1980-92; sr. advisor Gov. of Del., 1993-94. Adminstrv. asst. U. Del. Commn. on Status of Women, 1976-77; acad. advisor U. Del. Coll. Arts and Scis., 1977-92. Mem. LWV (state pres. 1978-80), Phi Beta Kappa, Phi Kappa Phi, Mortar Bd., Alpha Chi Omega. Episcopalian.

SOLIS, PATTI, federal official; b. Chgo., Aug. 23, 1965; d. Santiago and Alejandrina (Ortega) S. BA in Comm., Northwestern U., 1990. Asst. to treas. City of Chgo., 1989-91; dir. of scheduling for Hilary Rodham Clinton Clinton-Gore Campaign, Little Rock, 1991-92, Clinton Transition Team, Little Rock, 1992-93; spl. asst. to Pres., dir. of scheduling for First Lady The White House, Washington, 1993—. Roman Catholic. Office: Presdl Scheduling & Advance 1600 Pennsylvania Ave NW Washington DC 20500-0001*

SOLIS-KLEIN, RUTH ELIZABETH, foreign language educator; b. Oberlin, Ohio, July 28, 1935; d. Bertram James and Ruth Langworthy (Brown) Smyth; m. Guillermo Abel Solis-Bonilla, Sept. 14, 1963; children: Roselia Ruth, Bertram Oliver; m. Charles B. Klein, Jr., Nov. 20, 1993. BA, Coll. of Wooster, 1957; MA, U. Kans., 1960; PhD, U. Akron, 1990. Cert. tchr., Kans. Teaching asst. U. Kans., Lawrence, 1957-60; instr. Hiram (Ohio) Coll., 1960-62; asst. instr. Case Western Res. U., Cleve., 1962-64; from. instr. to assoc. prof. fgn. langs. Cuyahoga Community Coll., Cleve., 1964-70, prof. fgn. langs., 1970—; lectrice Ecole de Commerce, Clermont-ferrand, France, 1958-59; dir. courses Inst.-Guatemalteco, Guatemala City, Guatemala, 1979-80. Author: Curriculum Development, 1990; executed sculpture (1st Place award 1961). Deaconess 1st Christian Ch., Hudson, Ohio, 1988—. Recipient Innovator of Yr. award, 1991; Cuyahoga Community Coll. grantee, 1968, 88. Mem. AAUP, AARP, Nat. Inst. of Staff and Orgnl. Devel., Ohio Fgn. Lang. Assn., Akron Univ. Women's Club, Order of Eastern Star, Phi Sigma Iota (pres. 1956-57), Pi Lambda Theta, Phi Delta Kappa. Democrat.

SOLITO, FELICIA ROSE, lawyer; b. Boston, May 9, 1961; d. Gil Lewis. BA in English, San Diego State U., 1986; JD, Calif. Western Sch. Law, 1989. Bar: Calif. 1989, D.C. 1992. Assoc. Sparber, Ferguson, Nauman, Ponder & Ryan, San Diego, 1989-93, McCormick & Mitchell, San Diego, 1993—. Lead articles editor Calif. Western Law Rev., 1988-89. Bd. dirs. San Diego Area Dance Alliance, sec., 1991, pres. 1993. Mem. Calif. Western Sch. Law Alumni Assn. (bd. dirs. 1994—). Office: McCormick & Mitchell 1660 Union St San Diego CA 92101-2990

SOLLID, FAYE EISING, volunteer; b. Milw., Aug. 31, 1913; d. George Walter and Jessie Belle (Davey) Eising; m. Erik Sollid, Aug. 1, 1936 (dec. Mar. 1977); 1 child, Jon Erik. BA in Journalism, U. Wis., 1936; postgrad., U. Denver, 1947. Asst. in basic communications U. Denver, 1947. Editor Am. Hindi cookbook for Am. Woman's Club New Delhi, 1956; mem. Clearwater (Fla.) Libr. Bd., 1981-89, liaison between Libr. Bd. and Friends of Libr. Bd., 1984-89; mem. Clearwater Beautification Com., 1989-92. Recipient Citation of Sincere Appreciation for pub. svc. as mem. libr. bd. 1981-89 Mayor City of Clearwater, 1989. Mem. Internat. Graphoanalysis Soc., AAUW, PACT, Nat. Mus. Women in Arts, Fla. Pub. Interest Rsch. Group, Upper Pinellas African Violet Soc. (v.p. 1973-74, pres. 1974-75), Sovereign Colonial Soc. Ams. Royal Descent, Plantagenet Soc., Soc. Descs. Most Noble Order of Garter, Order of Crown of Charlemagne in U.S.A., Colonial Order of The Crown, Suncoast Magna Charta Dames (rec. sec. 1980-83), Colonial Dames XVII Century (v.p. 1983-85, 89-93).

SOLLIE, DIANN THORNTON, education educator, counselor; b. Jackson, Miss., Sept. 29, 1960; d. Jerry L. Thornton and Helen (Chambers) Taylor; m. William D. Sollie, Apr. 15, 1983; children: Steven, Caitlin. BS, U. So. Miss., 1981; MEd, Miss. State U., 1986; PhD Candidate, U. Ala., 1990—. Lic. profl. counselor, Miss. Field rep. Sigma Sigma Sigma Sorority, Woodstock, Va., 1981-82; police officer Meridian (Miss.) Police Dept., 1982-83; counselor Lauderdale County Juvenile Ctr., Meridian, 1983-86; program coord. Naval Air Sta. Family Svc. Ctr., Meridian, 1987-88; family counselor Laurelwood Ctr., Meridian, 1988-89; assoc. prof. U. So. Miss., Hattiesburg, 1988-92; program dir. Laurelwood Ctr., Meridian, 1992; prof. Meridian C.C., 1992—; cons. Laurelwood Ctr., Meridian, 1989-93; expert witness, Jackson, Miss., 1990-92; cons. Ala. Power, Tuscaloosa, 1991, City of Meridian, 1991. Contbr. articles to profl. jours. Exec. bd. mem. Boy Scouts Am., Meridian, 1992—; bd. dirs. Miss. Juvenile Justice Adv. Bd., State of Miss., 1984-88; faculty advisor Criminal Justice Assn., Meridian C.C., 1990—; faculty sponsor Internat. Studies Program, Meridian C.C., 1993—; faculty senate vice chair Meridian C.C., 1993-96. Mem. Soc. Police and Criminal Psychology (pres. 1992-93, v.p. 1991-92), Am. Counseling Assn., Miss. Criminal Justice Assn., Mid-South Sociol. Assn., Miss. Sociol. Assn., Ala. Sociol. Assn. Office: Meridian Community Coll 910 Hwy 19 North Meridian MS 39301

SOLO, JOYCE R., volunteer; b. Buffalo, N.Y., Feb. 14, 1924; d. Jay Harry and Rose (Maisel) Rubenstein; m. Richard D. Solo, Jan. 6, 1946; children: Harry Jay Solo, Eleanor Solo, Sally Solo. BA, Wellesley Coll., 1945. Pres. LWV, Sarasota County, Fla., 1990-92; healthcare com. chair, 1988-90, 92—; sec. Sarasota County Health Care Coord. Adv. Coun., 1993—; active Planned Approach to Cmty. Health/Healthy Sarasota 2000 (data tracking and rev. com.); sr. adv. com. Sarasota Meml. Hosp.; vol. Reach to Recovery Breast Cancer Task Force, Manatee County Am. Cancer Soc.; ritual chair Beth Israel Women Bd., Temple Beth Israel, numerous other health and civic orgn. activities.

SOLOMON, A. MALAMA, state legislator; b. Honolulu, Mar. 3, 1961; d. Randolph Folau Solomon and Flora Beamer. B.Ed., U. Hawaii-Manoa, 1972, M.A., 1973; B.A., U. Hawaii-Hilo, 1974; Ph.D., Oreg. State U., 1980. Market and sales mgr. beef cattle Kohala Farms, from 1972; lectr. U. Hawaii-Hilo, 1973-75; program coordinator Aloha Week Festivals Inc., 1977-87. Trustee, Office Hawaiian Affairs, 1980-82; mem. Hawaii Senate, Dist. 3, 1983—. Native Am. Ford fellow, 1976-80; recipient Outstanding Community Service award Hilo Coll., 1973-75; Outstanding Leadership award Council Hawaiian Civic Clubs, 1982; named Outstanding Woman of Yr., Hawaii Nat. Women's Week, 1982. Mem. Kohala Community Assn., Dist. Council Hawaiian Civic Clubs. Congregationalist. Office: State Senate State Capitol Honolulu HI 96813 Home: PO Box 219 Kapaau HI 96755-0219*

SOLOMON, ELDRA PEARL BROD, psychologist, educator, biologist, author; b. Phila., Apr. 9, 1940; d. Theodore and Freda Miriam (Warhaftig) Brod; m. Edwin Marshall Solomon, June 28, 1959 (div. Jan. 1985); children: Mical Kenneth, Amy Lynn, Belicia Efros. BS, U. Tampa, 1961; MS, U. Fla., 1963; MA, U. South Fla., 1987, PhD, 1989. Lic. psychologist. Adj. biology prof. Hillsborough Community Coll., Tampa, Fla., 1968-86; biopsychologist Ctr. for Rsch. in Behavioral Medicine, U. South Fla., Tampa, 1985-89; dir. rsch. Advanced Devel. Systems, Tampa, 1989-92; pvt. practice clin. psychologist Tampa, 1990—; clin. dir. Ctr. for Mental Health Edn., Assessment and Therapy, Tampa, Fla., 1992—; expert witness, psychol. expert county and cir. cts., Hillsborough County, Fla., 1989—; health edn. cons. Advanced Devel. Systems, Tampa, 1985-92; adj. prof. U. South Fla., 1992—. Author: Human Anatomy and Physiology, 1990, The World of Biology, 5th edit., 1995, Biology, 4th edit., 1994; author: (with others) Health Psychology: Individual Differences and Stress, 1988; author chpt. in book. Mem. APA, Am. Soc. Criminology, Fla. Psychol. Assn., Internat. Soc. for the Study of Dissociation (chairperson Tampa chpt.). Democrat. Jewish. Office: Ctr Mental Health Edn Assessment & Therapy 2727 W Martin Luther King Blvd Tampa FL 33607-6383

SOLOMON, ELLEN JOAN, business owner, consultant; b. Orange, N.J., Aug. 26, 1943; d. Abram Shrier and Mildred Elizabeth (Berger) S. BA in Psychology, U. N.C., Chapel Hill, 1965; MS in human resource devel. Am. U., 1985. Contract writer Conn. Gen. Life Ins. Co., Bloomfield, 1965-66; mgmt. trainee, asst. buyer G. Fox & Co., Hartford, Conn., 1966-68; account exec. WLAE-FM, Hartford, 1968; sr. analyst Travelers Ins. Co., Hartford, 1968-70; job analyst Conn. Blue Cross, New Haven, 1970-71; sr. ops. auditor Govt. Employees Ins. Co., Washington, 1972-75; employee devel. specialist Employment Standards Adminstrn., U.S. Dept. Labor, Washington, 1975-81, mgmt. analyst, 1981-82, supervisory mgmt. analyst, 1982-87; mgmt. cons. State Maine, 1986-87; program designer, cons. Eastman Kodak Co., Rochester, N.Y., 1987-89, mgr., 1989, sr. orgnl. cons., 1990-93; pres. Strategic Change, Inc., Rochester, N.Y., 1993—. adj. faculty Rochester Inst. Tech., 1993—; conf. speaker; workshop leader; cons. Mem. conf. planning/Program TIA Nat. Conf., 1990-91. Recipient spl. achievement award U.S. Dept. Labor, 1977, 78, 83, 85. Mem. NOW, Am. Soc. Tng. and Devel., OD Network, Gestalt Inst. Cleve., Rochester Women's Network (bd. dirs. 1990-92, v.p. 1991-92, Pres.'s award 1992), U. N.C. Alumni, Soc. for Human Resource Mgmt., Alpha Gamma Delta. Democrat. Jewish. Home: 67 Cornhill Pl Rochester NY 14608-2281 Office: Strategic Change Inc 110 Linden Oaks Ste E Rochester NY 14625

SOLOMON, MARILYN KAY, educator, consultant; b. Marshall, Mo., Oct. 16, 1947; d. John W. and Della M. (Dille) S. BS, Ctrl. Mo. State U., 1969; MS, Ind. U., 1974. Cert. in early childhood and nursery sch. edn., Mo., Ind. Tchr. Indpls. Pub. Schs., 1969-74; dir. Singer Learning Ctrs., Indpls., 1974-78; v.p. ECLC Learning Ctrs., Inc., Indpls., 1978—; mem. OJT tng. task force Dept. Labor, Washington; mem. nat. task force for parenting edn. HEW, Washington; cons. to numerous corps. on corp. child care. Co-author curricula. Founding bd. dirs. Family Support Ctr., Indpls., 1983, pres. bd. dirs., 1985-87; founding bd. dirs Mid City Pioneer, Indpls., 1977. Recipient Outstanding Leadership award Ind. Conf. on Social Concerns, 1975, 76, 77, Children's Mus. Ednl. award, 1975. Mem. Indpls. Mus. Art, Ind. Lic. Child Care Assn. (v.p. 1992, pres. 1974, 75), State of Ind. Quality and Tng. Coun. (chair 1992), Step Ahead-Marion County (rep. for child care 1992—), Ind. Alliance for Better Child Care (bd. dirs. 1992), Order Eastern Star, Indpls. Zool. Soc. (charter). Office: ECLC Learning Ctrs Inc 1315 S Sherman Dr Indianapolis IN 46203-2210

SOLOMON, MARSHA HARRIS, draftsman, artist; b. Tulsa, Oct. 21, 1940; d. Ruel Sutton and Anna May (Fellows) Harris; m. Robert E. Collier, Aug. 13, 1960 (div. Dec. 1968); 1 child, Craig Robert Collier; m. Louis G. Solomon, Sept. 5, 1984. Student, U. Tex., 1958-61; BFA, U. Houston, 1966. Chief draftsman Internat. Paper, Petroleum & Minerals Divsn., Houston, 1985—; artist, ptnr. Archway Gallery, Houston, 1994. Mem. Nat. Mus. Women in Art (charter). Mem. Watercolor Art Soc. Houston (bd. dirs. 1984-91, treas. 1987-89, pres. 1990-91), N.Mex. Watercolor Soc. (signature mem.). Home: 5832 Valley Forge Houston TX 77057

SOLOMON, PENNY GOREN, artist, designer; b. Phila., Mar. 4, 1941; d. Samuel Edward and Frances Lillian (Hellman) Goren; m. Sheldon Dubrow Solomon, June 2, 1963; children: Peter Lindsay, Kenneth Garrett, Jennifer Ann, Emily Lauren. BFA cum laude, BS in Edn., Temple U., 1963. Cert. tchr., Pa., N.J. Art tchr., head dept. art Collingsdale (Pa.) Sch., 1963-65; artist, 1963—, fashion designer, fabric designer, bus. owner, 1990—; curator art show Pavillion Gallery, Mt. Holly, N.J., 1993. One-woman shows include Pavilion Gallery, Mt. Holly, N.J., 1984, 93, Home for Contemporary Theatre and Art, N.Y.C., 1987, Artifacts, Haddonfield, N.J., 1989; two-women shows include DaVinci Soc., Pa., 1985; exhibited in group shows at Stedman Art Gallery, Camden, N.J., 1989, The Noyes Mus., Oceanville, N.J., 1990, Pavilion Gallery, Mt. Holly, 1991, 93 (Dir.'s Choice award 1991), Long Beach Island Art Ctr., Loveladies, N.J., 1991 (Grand prize), Hopkins House Gallery, Haddon Twp., N.J., 1993, Stedman Gallery Rutgers U., 1993, Glouster County Community Coll., Sewell, N.J., 1993, First St. Gallery, N.Y.C., 1993, N.J. Designer Craftsman Gallery, New Brunswick, N.J., 1994, Beaux Arts, Media, Pa., 1994, Westby Art Gallery Rowan Coll., N.J., 1994; TV interviews featured artist: NJN State of the Arts, 1993, PBS State of the Arts, 1994; fashions modeled Phila. Mus. Art, 1993, 94. Bd. dirs. Arthritis Found. South Jersey Art Show, 1984—. Home: 302 Wexford Dr Cherry Hill NJ 08003

SOLOMON, PHYLLIS, executive search firm specialist; b. N.Y.C., May 9, 1935; d. Herman Aaron and Sylvia (Haymes) Kanarick; m. Harvey Charles Solomon, Feb. 5, 1955 (div. Oct. 1976); children: Deborah, William, David. Sec. Scovill Mfg., Montclair, N.J., 1955-56; co-owner, officer mgr. Bloomfield Glass Co., N.J., 1962-75; office mgr. Am. Service, Inc., Bronx, N.Y., 1975-76, PDI, Englewood Cliffs, N.J., 1976-77; pres., owner Phyllis Solomon Exec. Search, Englewood Cliffs, 1977—; Phyllis Temps, Inc., Englewood Cliffs, N.J., 1983—; pres. VIP Med. Personnel, Inc., Englewood Cliffs, 1981. Pres. Women's Am. Orgn. Rehab. Tng., Verona, N.J., 1960-61; chair No. Valley dist. Boy Scouts Am., Sustaining membership enrollment com. Fellow Healthcare Businesswomen's Assn.; mem. Am. Heart Assn. (bd. dirs. northern valley divsn.), N.J. Assn. Staffing Profls., N.J. Assn. Staffing Prof.(pres. 1993-94), Pharm. Advt. Coun., Englewood Cliffs C. of C., Rotary (sec., v.p. Englewood Cliffs chpt., past pres., asst. sec. dist. # 1490, 1994—). Jewish. Avocations: golf, tennis, music, reading. Office: Phyllis Solomon Exec Search PO Box 1563 Englewd Clfs NJ 07632-0563

SOLOMON, PHYLLIS LINDA, social work educator, researcher; b. Hartford, Conn., Dec. 6, 1945; d. Louis Calvin and Annabell Lee (Nitzberg) S. BA in Sociology, Russell Sage Coll., 1968; MA in Sociology, Case Western Res. U., 1970, PhD in Social Welfare, 1978. Lic. social worker, Pa. Rsch. assoc. Inst. Urban Studies Cleve. State U., 1970-71; program evaluator Cleve. State Hosp., 1971-74; project dir. Ohio Mental Health and Mental Retardation Rsch. Ctr., Cleve., 1974-75; rsch. assoc. Psychiat. Rsch. Found. of Cleve., 1975; project dir. Ohio Mental Health and Mental Retardation Rsch. Ctr., 1977-78; rsch. assoc. dirs. rsch. and mental health planning Fedn. for Community Planning, 1978-88; prof. dept. mental health scis., dir. sect. mental health svcs. and systems research Hahnemann U., Phila., 1988-94; prof. Sch. Social Work U. Pa., Phila., 1994—; grant reviewer numerous orgns.; cons. in field; mem. svcs. rsch. rev. com. NIMH, 1992. Author: (with others) Community Services to Discharged Psychiatric Patients, 1984; co-editor: New Developments in Psychiatric Rehabilitation, 1990, Psychiatric Rehabilitation in Practice, 1993; editorial adv. bd. Community Mental Health Jour., 1988—; contbr. articles to profl. jours. Trustee Cleve. Rape Crisis Ctr., 1981-84, CIT Mental Health Svcs., Cleve., 1985-88; mem. citizen's adv. bd. Sagamore Hills (Ohio) Children's Psychiat. Hosp., 1984-88. Named Evaluator of the Yr., Ohio Program Evaluators Group, 1987; recipient Ann. award Cuyahoga County Community Mental Health Bd., 1988. Mem. Internat. Assn. Psychosocial Rehab. Svcs. Jewish. Home: 220 E Mermaid Ln Apt 186 Philadelphia PA 19118-3215 Office: U Pa Sch Social Work 3701 Locust Walk Philadelphia PA 19104

SOLOMON, RISA GREENBERG, video software industry executive; b. N.Y.C., June 22, 1948; d. Nathan and Frances (Guttman) Greenberg; m. Philip Howard Solomon, June 21, 1970; children: Elycia Beth, Cynthia Gayle. BA, NYU, 1969, MA, 1970. Asst. editor Redbook Mag., N.Y.C., 1969-70; assoc. editor Greenwood Press, Westport, Conn., 1970-71; mng. editor Dushkin Pub., Guilford, Conn., 1971-72; freelance editor Yale U. Press, New Haven, 1972-75; v.p. ops. Videoland, Inc., Dallas, 1980-82; v.p. Video Software Dealers Assn., Cherry Hill, N.J. and Dallas, 1981-83; pres. Videodome Enterprises, Dallas, 1983—; cons. Home Recording Rights Coalition, Washington, 1983-84. Contbr. articles to video mags. Bd. dirs. Congregation Anshai Emet, Dallas, 1985-86. Mem. Video Software Dealers Assn. (founder, dir. 1981-82). Democrat. Jewish. Office: Videodome Enterprises 11420 St Michaels Dr Dallas TX 75230-2436

SOLOMON, RUTH, state legislator, teacher; b. Phila., Apr. 16, 1941; d. David and Bella (Azeff) Epstein; m. Arthur Solomon; 1 child, Barry. BA, U. Ariz., 1971. Tchr. Tucson (Ariz.) Unified Sch. Dist., 1971—; mem. Ariz. Legislature; pres. Tucson Edn. Assn., 1983-85; dir. Ariz. Edn. Assn., Phoenix, 1986—. Bd. dirs. Pima County Community Action Agy., Tucson, 1986—, Mayor's Coun. Youth Initiatives, Tucson, 1987—. Mem. Bus. and Profl. Women's Coun., Alpha Delta Kappa, Phi Kappa Phi. Home: 7026 E Kenyon Dr Tucson AZ 85710-4824 Office: Ariz Ho of Reps 1700 W Washington Phoenix AZ 85007*

SOLOWAY, ROSE ANN GOULD, clinical toxicologist; b. Plainfield, N.J., Apr. 19, 1949; d. George Spencer Jr. and Rose Emma (Frank) Gould; m. Irving H. Soloway, Dec. 13, 1979. BSN, Villanova U., 1971; MS in Edn., U. Pa., 1976. Diplomate Am. Bd. Applied Toxicology. Staff nurse Hosp. of U. Pa., Phila., 1971-73; asst. clin. instr. Hosp. of U. Pa. Sch. Nursing, Phila., 1973-77; staff devel. instr. Hosp. of Med. Coll. Pa., Phila., 1977-78; dir. Emergency Nurse Tng. Program Ctr. for Study of Emergency Health Svcs., U. Pa., Phila., 1979-80; edn./comms. coord. Nat. Capital Poison Ctr. Georgetown U. Hosp., Washington, 1980-94; clin. toxicologist Nat. Capital Poison Ctr. George Washington U. Med. Ctr., Washington, 1994—; adminstr. Am. Assn. Poison Control Ctrs., Washington, 1994—; mem. Clin. Toxicology and Substance Abuse Adv. Panel, U.S. Pharmacopeial Conv., Inc., Washington, 1990—; mem. bd. dirs. Am. Bd. Applied Toxicology, 1994—. Contbr. articles to profl. publs. Mem. APHA, Am. Assn. Poison Control Ctrs. (co-chmn. pub. edn. com. 1985-90), Poison Prevention Week Coun. (vice chmn. 1989-91, chair 1991-93). Office: Am Assn Poison Control Ctrs Ste 310 3201 New Mexico Ave NW Washington DC 20016

SOLVAY, PAMELA, elementary education educator; b. Pitts.; d. Theodore P. and Ann (Lesko) Telep; m. Michael J. Solvay. Bachelor's Degree, Waynesburg Coll., 1976; Master's Degree, Duquesne U., 1979; EdD, U. Pitts., 1988. Cert. elem. tchr., elem. prin., Pa.; cert. in coop. edn., Pa. Tchr. Moon Area Sch., Coraopolis, Pa., 1976-81, tchr. gifted and tallented, 1981-83; tchr. Moon Area Schs., Coraopolis, 1983-85, kindergarten tchr., 1985-86, tchr., 1986-93; with Bon Meade Elem. Schs., Coraopolis; coord. sci. fair Bon Meade Elem. Sch., Coraopolis, 1991-93; mem. com. strategic planning Moon Area Schs., 1992-93. Named to Allegheny County Tchrs. and Industry Acad., Allegheny County Commn. Workforce Excellence, 1991-92; recipient A Gift of Time Tribute The Am. Family Inst. at Valley Forge, 1991. Mem. NEA, Pa. State Edn. Assn., Moon Edn. Assn.

SOMAN, SHIRLEY CAMPER, writer, journalist, columnist, consultant, social worker; b. Boston; d. David and Fannie (Apteker) Isenberg; m. Frederic R. Camper (dec.); children: Frederic D., Frances A.; m. Robert O. Soman (dec.). BA, U. Wis.; M in Social Sci., Smith Coll. Sch. social worker Bur. Child Guidance N.Y.C. Bd. Edn.; assoc. editor My Baby mag., Shaws Market News, N.Y.C.; family life cons. Family Svc. Assn. Am., N.Y.C.; v.p., ptnr. Associated Film Cons., N.Y.C.; columnist Springfield (Mass.) Union-News, 1991-93; pres., CEO Acorn to Oak Pub. Co., N.Y.C., 1991—; cons. White House Conf. Children and Youth, Washington, 1980, Child Welfare League Am., Washington, 1989; adj. prof. child advocacy and children's rights CUNY, 1976, 77. Author: How to Get Along With Your Child, Let's Stop Destroying Our Children, 1974, Preparing for Your New Baby, 1982; syndicated columnist; contbr. numerous articles to jours., newspapers. Panelist 1st USA Conf. on Human Rights Amnesty Internat.; founder, chair Parents for Carter-Mondale, N.Y., 1976; bd. dirs. Pub. Action Coalition for Toys, N.Y., 1976-82, Creative Arts Rehab. Ctr., N.Y., 1977-82, Childsavers, Inc., Washington, 1992—; chair First Nat. Child Advocacy Symposium, 1974; founder Fin. Friends, 1994; lectr. social and family issues numerous orgns. Recipient award Women in Communications, 1986. Mem. NATAS, Am. Soc. Journalists and Authors, Nat. Assn. Sci. Writers, Nat. Assn. Social Workers, Acad. Cert. Social Workers (cert. N.Y. State), N.Y. Acad Sci., Soc. Profl. Journalists, Authors Guild and League. Home and Office: 142 West End Ave New York NY 10023

SOMERS, ANNE RAMSAY, medical educator; b. Memphis, Sept. 9, 1913; d. Henry Ashton and Amanda Vick (Woolfolk) Ramsey; m. Herman Miles Somers, Aug. 31, 1946; children: Sara Ramsay, Margaret Ramsay. BA, Vassar Coll., 1935; postgrad., U. N.C., 1939-40; DSc (hon.), Med. Coll. Wis., 1975. Ednl. dir. Internat. Ladies Garment Workers Union, 1937-42; labor economist U.S. Dept. Labor, 1943-46; rsch. assoc. Haverford Coll., 1957-63; rsch. assoc. indsl. rels. sect. Princeton U., 1964-84; prof. U. Medicine and Dentistry of N.J.-R. Wood Johnson Med. Sch. (formerly Rutgers Med. Sch.), 1971-84, adj. prof., 1984—; adj. prof. geriatric medicine U. Pa. Sch. Medicine, 1990—; mem. Nat. Bd. Med. Examiners, 1983-86; cons. in health econs., health edn., geriatrics, gerontology, related areas. Author: Hospital Regulation: The Dilemma of Public Policy, 1969, Health Care in Transition: Directions for the Future, 1971, (with H.M. Somers) Workmen's Compensation: The Prevention, Rehabilitation and Financing of Occupational Disability, 1954, Medicare and the Hospitals, 1967, Doctors, Patients and Health Insurance, 1961, Health and Health Care: Policies in Perspective, 1977, (with N.L. Spears) The Continuing Care Retirement Community: A Significant Option for Long Care?, 1992; editor: (with D.R. Fabian) The Geriatric Imperative: An Introduction to Gerontology and Clinical Geriatrics, 1981. Mem. bd. visitors. Duke U. Med. Ctr., 1972-77, U. Tex. Health Scis. Ctr., Houston, 1980-86. Recipient Elizur Wright award Am. Risk and Ins. Assn., 1962; named to Health Care Hall of Fame, 1993. Fellow Am. Coll. Hosp. Adminstrs. (hon.), Coll. Physicians Phila. (hon.); mem. Inst. Medicine of Nat. Acad. Scis., Am. Pub. Health Assn., Soc. Tchrs. Family Medicine (hon.). Home: Pennswood Vlg # G-205 Newtown PA 18940

SOMERS, MARION, gerontologist, retirement specialist; b. N.Y.C.; d. John Joseph and Lottie (Kramer) Strahl; children: Lynne Caryl, Randy Mass, Craig Caryl; stepchildren: Carolyn Clark, Gail Sun, Matthew Somers. BA, CUNY, 1976; MS, Lehman Coll., 1980; PhD, The Fielding Inst., 1988. Lic. nursing home adminstr., N.Y. Activities dir. Wartburg Luth. Nursing Home, N.Y.C., 1980-82; prof. Lehman Coll., N.Y.C., 1982-84; pres. Marion Somers, Assoc., N.Y.C., 1985—; chief recreation therapist Kingsbrook Jewish Med. Ctr. and Rutland Nursing Home, 1989-91; adminstr. in tng. Hebrew Home for the Aging, Palisades Nursing Home, Riverdale, N.Y., 1991-92; grant reader HHS, Washington, 1980—; observer White House Conf. on Aging, 1982; bd. dirs. Sr. Action in Gray Environ., 1980-84. Author: Viewers Guide for ABC-TV prodn. of The Shell Seekers, Last Wish, The Home, (art jour.) Creative Exit, 1994. Advisor Sen. A. D'Amato, N.Y., 1981-82. Recipient Profl. award Met. Recreation & Pk. Soc., N.Y.C., 1985. Mem. Gerontol. Soc. Am., Nat. Coun. on Aging, Nat. Recreation and Pk. Assn. (Presdl. award 1984), N.Y. State Therapeutic Recreation Soc. (chair 1983-84, pres. 1984-85), Am. Therapeutic Recreation Soc., Nat. Assn. Retirement Profls., Internat. Soc. Retirement Planning.

SOMERSTEIN, AURORA ABRERA, educator; b. Manila, Feb. 17, 1943; d. Bernardo Paez and Rosalia (Sityar) Abrera; m. Jules Leon Somerstein, Dec. 10, 1967; children: Joseph, Sandra, Marc. BA in English, U. Philippines, Manila, 1964; MA in English Edn., NYU, 1978, MA in Elem. Edn., 1987; postgrad., U. Pitts., Oxford (Eng.) U., 1964-66, 86. Cert. tchr., N.Y. Instr. U. Pitts., 1965-66, U. of the East, Manila, 1968-69; tchr. Am. Internat. Sch., Manila, 1966, Domenec High Sch., Pitts., 1967-68; substitute tchr. Lakeland and Peekskill Sch. Dist., N.Y., 1975-77; exec. dir. Internat. Pre-Sch. Ctr., Inc., N.Y.C., 1977—; instr. Bd. Coop. Ednl. Svcs., N.Y.C., 1989-93; exec. sec. Ctr. Ednl. TV, Manila, 1964; sec. NYU, 1973-74, UN, N.Y.C., 1975; producer, interviewer Continental Cablevision, N.Y.C., 1984—; child devel. adviser Westchester County, N.Y.C., 1989—; cons. Hudson Valley Export-Import, Inc., N.Y.C., 1988-92. Vol. Philippine Band of Mercy, Manila, 1963-93. Mem. Nat. Child Care Assn., Nat. Assn. Edn. Young Children, Nat. Coun. Tchrs. English, N.Y. Child Care Assn., Assn. Childhood Edn. Internat., Child Care Coun. Westchester, Manitoga, Peekskill/Cortlandt C. of C. (bd. dirs. 1989-92). Democrat. Office: Internat Pre-Sch Ctr Inc PO Box 187 Buchanan NY 10511-0187

SOMERVILL, CYNTHIA BELLE, lawyer; b. Chgo., July 13, 1959; d. Robert Russell and Anne Currier (Dodge) S.; m. Terrance Alvan Noyes, Mar. 12, 1983; children: Jonathan Currier, Andrew Charters, Taylor Alvan. BA, Rice U., 1980; JD, U. Tex., 1983. Bar: Ga. 1983. Assoc. Ragsdale, Beals, Hooper & Seigler, Atlanta, 1983-85, Decker, Cooper & Hallman, Atlanta, 1985-86, Hurt, Richardson, Garner, Atlanta, 1986-87; corp. counsel, asst. sec. Gerber Alley, Norcross, Ga., 1987-90, v.p., gen. counsel, sec., 1990-92; counsel, asst. sec. First Data Corp.-Health Systems Group, Norcross, Ga., 1992-93; counsel intellectual property First Data Corp, Englewood, Colo., 1994—. Editor Tex. Internat. Law Jour., 1982-83; contbr. articles to profl. jours. Mem. Ga. Bar Assn. (sec. computer law sect. 1987-88, vice chmn. 1988-89), Computer Law Assn., Phi Delta Phi. Democrat. Episcopalian. Home: 795 E Huntington Dr Highlands Ranch CO 80126 Office: First Data Corp Ste 330 6200 S Quebec St Englewood CO 80111

SOMERVILLE, CAROLYN JOHNSON, principal; b. Parkersburg, W.Va., Mar. 11, 1942; d. George Hughes and Nellie Maude (Cather) Johnson; m. Ron D. Somerville, Aug. 22, 1965 (div. 1981); children: Jennifer Nicole Somerville Moon, Ron Dean. BS, Asbury Coll., 1963; MEd, Ohio U., 1966. Cert. elem. prin., Okla. Tchr. jr. high Prince George County Schs., Md., 1963-64; grad. asst. Ohio U., Athens, 1964-65; social worker W.Va. Dept. of Welfare, Huntington, 1965-67; counselor jr. high Wood County Schs., Parkersburg, W.Va., 1972-78, tchr. jr. high, 1979-81; substitute tchr. Yukon (Okla.) Schs., 1982-83; asst. prin. elem. Western Heights Schs., Oklahoma City, 1983-85, Skyview Elem. Sch., 1985—; presenter workshops; cons. in field. Mem. adv. bd. Planned Parenthood, Parkersburg, W.Va., 1974-77; counselor, speaker Gov. Com. on Crime and Delinquency, Parkersburg, 1974-77; tchr. Sunday sch. Trinity Bapt. Ch., Yukon, 1982-83; sponsor Alateen, 1988-93. Mem. ASCD, Okla. Assn. Elem. Sch. Prins. (com.), Coop. Coun. Okla. Sch. Adminstrn., Yukon Curriculum Coun. Home: 113 W Vail Yukon OK 73099 Office: Skyview Elem Sch 2800 Mustang Rd Yukon OK 73099

SOMERVILLE, MARGARET ANNE GANLEY, law educator; b. Adelaide, Australia, Apr. 13, 1942; d. George Patrick and Gertrude Honora (Rowe) Ganley; divorced. A.u.A. (pharm.), U. Adelaide, 1963; LLB (hon. I), U. Sydney, 1973; D.C.L., McGill U., 1978; LLD(hon.), U. Windsor, Ont., 1992; LLD (hon.), Macquarie, NSW, 1993. Registered pharmacist; Bar: Supreme Ct. New South Wales 1975, Quebec 1982. New South Wales; Pharmacist NSW, Australia; atty. Mallesons, Sydney, Australia, 1974-75; cons. Law Reform Com. Can., 1976-85; asst. prof. faculty of law Inst. of Comparative Law, 1978, assoc. prof. faculty of law, 1979, prof. faculty of law, 1984—; prof., faculty law, faculty medicine McGill U., 1984—; founding dir. McGill Ctr. Medicine Ethics & Law, 1986—; Gale prof. law McGill U., 1989—; vis. prof. Sydney U., 1984, 86, 90, Ctr. for Human Bioethics, Monash U., 1985-86; cons. to numerous orgns. Editl. bd. Bioethics, 1986—, Kennedy Inst. Ethics Jour., 1990—, Health and Human Rights, 1993—, Ecosystem Health and Medicine, 1993—; Adv. editor Social Sci. and Medicine, 1988—; reviewer Cmty. Health Studies, Jour. Clin. Epidemiology, Can. Jour. Family Law, Jour. Pharmacy Practice, Jour. AIDS, New Eng. Jour. Medicine, Can. Jour. Law and Soc., Dalhousie Law Jour., Am. Jour. Law, Medicine and Ethics, others; contbr. articles to profl. jours. Clin. ethics com. Royal Victoria Hosp., 1980—; prin. investigator Nat. Health R&D Program, 1986-89; assoc. mem. McGill AIDS Ctr., 1990—, Nat. Adv. Com. on AIDS in Can., 1986-92; chmn. Nat. Rsch. Coun. Can., Ethics Com., 1991. Australian Commonwealth scholar, McGill U., 1975; recipient U. Sydney medal, 1976, Joseph Dainow prize McGill U., 1976, Disting. Svc. award Am. Soc. Law & Medicine, 1985; named to Order of Australia. Fellow Royal Soc. Can.; mem. Am. Soc. Pharm. Law, Inst. Soc., Ethics & Life Sci., Hastings Ctr., Am. Soc. Law & Medicine, Assn. des Prof. de Droit du Que., Can. Bar Assn., Can. Pharm. Assn., World Assn. Med. Law, Can. Law Tchrs. Assn., Soc. Health & Human Values, Internat. Acad. Com. Law. Office: McGill Ctr Medicine Ethics & Law, 3690 Peel St, Montreal, PQ Canada H3A 1W9

SOMERVILLE, MARY ROBINSON, library director; b. Fairfield, Ala., Aug. 16, 1941; d. Edward Bryce Jr. and Margaret Allen (Wallis) Robinson; m. Ormond Somerville Jr., July 10, 1964 (div. Feb. 1976). BA, U. N.C., 1963; MA in English Literature, U. Colo., 1965; MLS, U. Okla., 1971. Reference and documents librarian Lincoln City (Nebr.) Libraries, 1971-73, coord. young people's svcs., 1973-78; mgr. children's svcs., project mgr. Louisville (Ky.) Free Pub. Libr., automation mgr. employee rels., 1978-88; youth svcs. adminstr. Broward County Libr., Ft. Lauderdale, Fla., 1988-90; youth svcs. adminstr. Miami-Dade Pub. Libr., 1990-91, asst. dir. branches and spl. svcs., 1991-93, interim dir., 1993-94, dir., 1994—; cons. U.S. Dept. Edn., Washington, 1988; del. to USSR ALA/ALSC, Moscow, 1989; co-moderator ALSC/YALSA/LAMA Mng. Youth Svcs. Insts. ALA, Chgo., 1988-89; chair nom. com. ALA, Chgo., 1992. Contbr. chpt. to book, articles to profl. jours. Active Jefferson County Cable Commn., 1986; pres. Assn. for Libr. Svc. to Children, 1987-88; mem. exec. bd. SEFLIN, 1993—. Named Miami Today Newsmaker, 1994. Mem. ALA (mem. exec. bd. 1993—, mem. subcom. directions and program review 1993—, 4 John Cotton Dana awards), ALSC (mem. "Born to Read" task force 1994). Roman Catholic. Home: 800 West Ave # 735 Miami Beach FL 33139 Office: Miami-Dade Pub Libr Sys Metro-Dade Cultural Ctr 101 W Flagler St Miami FL 33130

SOMES, JOAN MARIE, emergency nurse; b. St. Paul, Aug. 17, 1952; d. Richard and Jane (Blaiser) Friesen; m. Michael Somes, Nov. 15, 1975. BA in Nursing, Coll. of St. Catherine, St. Paul, 1974; paramedic cert., Inver Hills C.C., Inver Grove Heights, Minn., 1976; MSN, U. Minn., 1989. RN, Minn.; nat. registered EMT-paramedic; cert. ACLS instr., PALS instr.; cert. TNCC instr. Paramedic A.L.F. Ambulance, Apple Valley, Minn., 1987—; charge nurse emergency dept. Divine Redeemer Hosp., South St. Paul, Minn., 1974-94; staff nurse emergency dept. St. Joseph's Hosp., St. Paul, 1994—; instr. numerous local cmty. colls., hosps. and ambulance svcs.; item writer CEN exam., 1994-95. Author nursing home study courses; contbr. articles to profl. jour. Glaxo Pharm. Co. grantee, 1989, Health East Found. grantee, 1991. Mem. Emergency Nurses Assn. (CEN, dir./state coun. liaison Greater Twin Cities chpt., sec.-treas. Minn. state coun., chair state trauma com.).

SOMMA, BEVERLY KATHLEEN, medical and marriage educator; b. Bayonne, N.J., June 13, 1938; d. Leroy and Isabelle (Lysaght) Latourette; m. Louis Anthony Somma, Nov. 24, 1973; children: Francis, Keith. AS, Ocean County Coll., 1973; BA, Georgian Ct., 1977; MAT, Monmouth Coll., 1978; postgrad., U. Pa., 1980-85, 88-89. Nurse's aide Community Meml. Hosp., Toms River, N.J., 1971-72; with marriage coun. dept. psychiatry U. Pa. Sch. Medicine, Phila., 1993—; with Helene Fuld Med. Ctr. Edn., 1993—; ednl. cons. Ctr. for Cognitive Edn., Yardley, Pa., 1990—, tng. program Archdiocese Phila., Penn Found., Inc., 1993; lectr. Marriage Coun. of Phila. dept. psychiatry, sch. medicine U. Pa., 1993—; with Helene Fuld Med. Ctr. Edn., 1993—. Voter svc. chmn. LWV, Toms River, N.J., 1971-72; contact rep. Pro Life Coalition Pa., Phila.; vol. nursing tutor Ocean County Coll., Toms River, 1972; vol. tchr.'s aide St. Michael the Archangel, Levittown, Pa., 1987-88; counselor Bucks County Coun. Alcoholism and Drug Dependence, Inc., 1984-93; vol. VITA; active World Affairs Coun. Phila. All Am. scholar; recipient U.S. Achievement Acad. Nat. award. Mem. Nat. Soc. for Fund Raising Execs., Alumni Assn. Georgian Ct. Coll., Ocean County Coll., Bucks County C.C., Sigma Tau Delta. Republican. Methodist. Home: 1506 Kathy Dr Yardley PA 19067-1717

SOMMER, ALISA BLOCK, architect; b. Miami Beach, Fla., Aug. 9, 1965; d. Michael Jay and Ann Gail (Ruskin) Block; m. Glenn Stuart Sommer, June 15, 1991. BA in Art History, U. Mich., 1987; BArch, U. Miami, 1992, MArch, 1993. Arch. Trelles Archs., Coral Gables, Fla., 1991; arch., rschr. Hector and Lombard, Miami, Fla., 1992-93, Sch. Architecture, U. Miami, 1993; arch., town planner Andres Duany and Elizabeth Plater-Zyberk, Archs., Miami, 1993—. Active Dade Heritage Trust, Miami, 1992—. Mem. Coconut Grove Civic Club. Democrat. Jewish. Home: 2584 Lincoln Ave Coconut Grove FL 33133 Office: Andres Duany and Elizabeth Plater-Zyberk Archs 1023 SW 25 Ave Miami FL 33135

SOMMER, ANNEMARIE, pediatrician; b. Königsberg, Prussia, Federal Republic Germany, Jan. 1, 1932; came to U.S., 1955; d. Heinrich Otto and Maria Magdalena (Kruppa) S. BA, Wittenberg U., Springfield, Ohio, 1960; MD, Ohio State U., 1964. Diplomate Am. Bd. Pediat., Am. Bd. Med. Genetics. Intern Grant Hosp., Columbus, Ohio, 1964-65; resident in pediat. Children's Hosp., Columbus, 1965-67; NIH fellow in med. genetics, 1968-70; asst. prof. pediatrics Coll. Medicine Ohio State U., Columbus, 1975-80, assoc. prof., 1980—, chief genetics div., 1984—; mem. adv. bd. Heinzerling Found., Columbus, 1980—; bd. dirs. Regional Genetics Ctr., Columbus. Contbr. articles to profl. jours. Com. mem. Ohio Prevention MR/DD Coalition, Columbus, 1987; bd. dirs. Franklin County Bd. Health, Columbus, 1985—. Fellow Am. Acad. Pediatrics, Am. Bd. Med. Genetics, Am. Coll. Med. Genetics (founder); mem. Am. Med. Women's Assn., Cen. Ohio Pediatric Soc., Midwest Soc. for Pediatric Research, Dublin (Ohio) Hist. Soc. Lutheran. Home: 4700 Brand Rd Dublin OH 43017-9530 Office: Ohio State Coll of Medicine Chief Sect of Genetics 700 Childrens Dr Columbus OH 43205-2696

SOMMER, VICKI JEAN, business manager; b. Carrington, N.D., Dec. 17, 1949; d. Sherman and Merl Jean (Miller) Montgomery; m. Dale Sommer, Sept. 17, 1968; children: Rhonda Joy, Bobbi Jo. Bookkeeper Holy Family Guest Home, Carrington, 1965-67; sales clk. Borth's, Carrington, 1968-69; bookkeeper Farmers Union Oil, Medina, N.D., 1972-79; bus. mgr. Medina Pub. Sch., 1979—. Office: Medina Pub Sch PO Box 547 Medina ND 58467-0547

SOMMERKAMP, KATHY RITCHELL, product development and marketing executive; b. Mpls., Jan. 5, 1944; d. Edward Clemens and Ann (Gifford) Ritchell; m. H. Jay Sommerkamp, Sept. 6, 1975; children: Sarah Kathlyn, Gifford Scott. BA, Conn. Coll., 1966; Diploma, U. Paris Sorbonne, 1967; MBA, NYU, 1979. Picture editor, rschr. Time-Life Books, Time Inc., N.Y.C., 1967-77; project mgr. W.R. Grace, N.Y.C., 1979-82; asst. v.p. Citicorp, N.Y.C., 1982-86, v.p. bus. devel., 1986-87, v.p. targeting and segmentation, 1988-89, v.p. relationship mktg., 1990-91; dir. product planning and devel. Nat. Geographic Soc., Washington, 1991—. Picture editor: The First Horsemen, 1974, The Celts, 1974, The Metalsmiths, 1974, The Persians, 1975, The Community, 1976; project editor: Audubon Guide to Birds-Western U.S., 1978. Co-chair antiques com. Sidwell Friends Sch., Washington, 1994. Mem. Fin. Women's Assn. Republican. Episcopalian. Office: Nat Geog Soc 1145 17th St NW Washington DC 20036

SOMMERMAN, KATHRYN MARTHA, retired entomologist; b. New Haven, Jan. 11, 1915; d. George VanName and Anna Hilda (Sperling) S. BS, Conn. State Coll., 1937; MS, U. Ill., 1941, PhD, 1945. Instr. botany Wells Coll., Aurora, N.Y., 1945; entomologist Army Med. Ctr. 1948 Alaska Insect Project, Washington, 1946-51, U.S. Dept. Agr., Washington, 1951-53; ind. rschr., cons., 1953-55; rsch. entomologist Arctic Health Rsch. Ctr., USPHS, Anchorage, 1955-67; rsch. entomologist Arctic Health Rsch. Ctr., USPHS, Fairbanks, 1967-73, ind. rsch. entomologist, 1973—; collaborator U.S. Nat. Mus., 1953-58; cons. in field. Author: Airborne Pollen: Father of Lichens and Fungi, 1992; contbr. articles to profl. jours. Recipient Exceptional Civilian Svc. award Dept. of Army, 1950, Sustained Superior Performance award U.S. Dept. HEW, 1960. Fellow Entomol. Soc. Am.; mem. N.Y. Entomol. Soc. Home: SR 76 Box 384 Greenville ME 04441

SOMMERS, KATHRYN M., secondary and elementary education educator; b. Lenawee County, Mich., May 24, 1932; d. F.E. and Gladys E. (Friedly) Densmore; m. Ray B. Sommers, June 26, 1954; children: Judy, Kent, Daniel. BA, Huntington Coll., 1953; MA, Ea. Mich. U., 1962. Cert. tchr., Ind., Mich. Tchr. Union City (Mich.) High Sch., 1953-54; tchr. elem. on-base schs. Ladd AFB, Alaska, 1955; tchr. Morenci (Mich.) High Sch., 1956-57; tchr. elem. sch. Lyons (Ohio) Pub. Schs., 1957-58; tchr. Tecumseh (Mich.) High Sch., 1967-68; tchr. elem. sch. Huntington (Ind.) Pub. Schs., 1969-74; tchr. Huntington Cath. High Sch., 1974-75, 78-79; instr. Huntington Coll., 1975-76; substitute tchr. Concordia High Sch., Ft. Wayne, Ind., 1986-89; tchr. elem. sch. Trinity Luth. Sch., Ft. Wayne, 1989-93; substitute tchr. East Allen County Schs., Allen County, Ind., 1993—, Concordia H.S., 1993—. Author: In All of Life Christ Made the Difference, 1972; contbr. articles to profl. jours. and religious mags. Mem. liturgical arts work area Aldersgate United Meth. Ch., 1992—, mem. United Meth. women, 1992—, mem. adult coun. edn., 1992—.

SOMMI, DEBRA LEE, librarian; b. Tomahawk, Wis., Aug. 10, 1957; d. Roger William and Evelyn Mae (Zeitelhack) S. BS, U. Wis., Stevens Point, 1979; MA in Libr. Sci., U. Wis., Madison, 1983. Tchr. Merrill (Wis.) Area Pub. Schs., 1980-81; rschr. Madison, 1983; project cataloger State Hist. Soc. of Wis., Madison, 1984, asst. newspaper cataloger, 1985-86, project leader U.S. newspaper project, 1986-89; dir. libr. Wis. Dept. Transp., Madison, 1989—. Costume designer Madison Theatre Guild, 1990-91. Mem. Wis. Libr. Assn., Spl. Librs. Assn. Office: Wis Dept Transp 4802 Sheboygan Ave Rm 803 Madison WI 53707

SONDERBY, SUSAN PIERSON, federal bankruptcy judge; b. Chgo., May 15, 1947; d. George W. and Shirley L. (Eckstrom) Pierson; m. James A. De Witt, June 14, 1975 (dec. 1978); m. Peter R. Sonderby, Apr. 7, 1990. AA, Joliet (Ill.) Jr. Coll., 1967; BA, U. Ill., 1969; JD, John Marshall Law Sch., 1973. Bar: Ill. 1973, U.S. Dist. Ct. (cen. and so. dists.) Ill. 1978, U.S. Dist. Ct. (no. dist.) Ill. 1984, U.S. Ct. Appeals (7th Cir.) 1984. Assoc. O'Brien, Garrison, Berard, Kusta and De Witt, Joliet, 1973-75, ptnr., 1975-77; asst. atty. gen. consumer protection div., litigation sect. Office of the Atty. Gen., Chgo., 1977-78; asst. atty. gen., chief consumer protection div. Office of the Atty. Gen., Springfield, Ill., 1978-83; U.S. trustee for no. dist. Ill. Chgo., 1983-86; judge U.S. Bankruptcy Ct. (no. dist.) Ill., Chgo., 1986—; adj. faculty De Paul U. Coll. Law, Chgo., 1986; spl. asst. atty. gen., 1972-78; past mem. U.S. Trustee adv. com., consumer adv. coun. Fed. Res. Bd.; past sec. of State Fraudulent I.D. com., Dept. of Ins. Task Force on Improper Claims Practices. Mem. Fourth Presbyn. Ch., Art Inst. Chgo.; past mem. Westminster Presbyn. Ch., Chgo. Coun. of Fgn. Rels.; past bd. dirs. Land of Lincoln Coun. Girl Scouts U.S.; past mem. individual guarantors com. Goodman Theatre, Chgo.; past chmn. clubs and orgns. Sangamon County United Way Capital campaign; past bd. dirs., chmn. house rules com. and legal subcom. Lake Point Tower; past mem. Family Svc. Ctr., Aid to

Retarded Citizens, Henson Robinson Zoo. Master Abraham Lincoln Marovitz Inn of Ct.; fellow Am. Coll. Bankruptcy; mem. Nat. Conf. Bankruptcy Judges (legis. outreach com.), Am. Bankruptcy Inst., Comml. Law League Am. (exec. coun. bankruptcy and insolvency sect., bankruptcy com., past vice chmn. U.S. Trustee Rev. com., edn. com.), John Marshall Law Sch. Alumni Assn. (bd. dirs., 2d v.p., 1st v.p., chmn. Luncheon Series, chmn. Disting. Svc. Awards com., exec. Long-range Planning com., others), Law Club of Chgo., Legal Club of Chgo. (hon.). Office: US Bankruptcy Ct 219 S Dearborn St Ste 638 Chicago IL 60604-1704

SONDOCK, RUBY KLESS, retired judge; b. Houston, Apr. 26, 1926; d. Herman Lewis and Celia (Juran) Kless; m. Melvin Adolph Sondock, Apr. 22, 1944; children: Marcia Cohen, Sandra Marcus. AA, Cottey Coll., Nevada, Mo., 1944; BS, U. Houston, 1959, LLB, 1961. Bar: Tex. 1961, U.S. Supreme Ct. 1977. Pvt. practice, Houston, 1961-73, 89—; judge Harris County Ct. Domestic Rels. (312th Dist.), 1973-77, 234th Jud. Dist. Ct., Houston, 1977-82, 83-89; justice Tex. Supreme Ct., Austin, 1982; of counsel Weil Gotshal and Manges, 1989-93, Houston Ctr., 1993—. Mem. ABA, Tex. Bar Assn., Houston Bar Assn., Houston Assn. Women Lawyers, Order of Barons, Phi Theta Phi, Kappa Beta Pi, Phi Kappa Phi, Alpha Epsilon Pi. Office: 2650 Two Houston Ctr 909 Fannin Houston TX 77010

SONES, SHARI CAROLYN, counselor, educator; b. Warner Robins, Ga., May 3, 1966; d. Jon Chalmers and Eleanor Jean (Spaulding) Niemeyer. BS, Brenau Coll., 1988; MS, Ga. State U., 1991. Cert. Nat. Bd. for Cert. Counselors, Inc.; lic. profl. counselor. Asst. tchr. Hi Hope, Lawrenceville, Ga., 1988; counselor Anxiety Disorder Inst. Atlanta, Ga., 1991-94; pvt. practice, 1994—; tchr. Oglethorpe U., Atlanta, 1993. Vol. group leader Ga. Counsel on Child Abuse, Atlanta, 1991-92. Mem. ACA, Nat. Assn. Alcoholism and Drug Abuse Counselors. Home: 130 Ashton Ct Roswell GA 30076-1091 Office: Anxiety Disorders Inst of Atlanta 1 Dunwoody Park Ste 112 Atlanta GA 30338-6708

SONI, KUSUM KAPILA, mathematics educator; b. Punjab, India, Nov. 14, 1930; came to U.S., 1959; d. Piare Lal and Sushila Devi (Bajaj) Kapila; m. Raj Pal Soni, Apr. 5, 1958; children: Poonam, Sushma. BA with honors, Punjab U., 1949, MA in Math., 1951; PhD, Oreg. State U., 1964. Lectr. Govt. Colls., Punjab, 1952-59; tchr. asst. Oreg. State U., Corvallis, 1959-64; asst. prof. math. U. Tenn., Knoxville, 1967-70, assoc. prof. math., 1970-83, prof. math., 1983—; vis. asst. prof. Oreg. State U., 1966-67; vis. prof. dept. applied math. Ctr. for Math. and Computer Sci., Amsterdam, 1987, Indian Inst. Sci., Bangalore, India, 1987; vis. mem. U. Dundee (Scotland), 1982; summer mem. Inst. for Advanced Study, Princeton, N.J., 1979; speaker Internat. Symposium, Winnipeg, Can., 1989. Contbr. approximately 40 rsch. articles to profl. jours. Recipient Women of Achievement Rsch. award, U. Tenn., 1983, rsch. and travel grants, 1969, 70, 80, 89. Mem. Am. Math. Soc., Math. Assn. of Am., Sigma Xi. Office: Univ Tenn Dept Math Knoxville TN 37996-1300

SONNE, MAGGIE LEE, sales executive; b. Pasadena, Calif., July 14, 1958; d. Roscoe Newbold Jr. and Ann Miriam (Vierhus) S.; m. Donald Alan Blackburn, Sept. 8, 1979 (div. 1983). AS, Oreg. Inst. Tech., 1981, BS, 1983. Sales trainee NCR Corp., Dayton, Ohio, 1983-84; sales rep. NCR Corp., Portland, Oreg., 1984-86; account mgr. NCR Corp., Seattle, 1986-87; sr. account mgr. NCR Corp., Portland, 1987-88; sr. account rep. Wang Labs., Portland, 1988-91; account exec. Tandem Computers, Portland, 1991—. Active Emily's List, Project Vote Smart, Spl. Olympics, Ams. for Change, Presdl. Task Force, Pres. Coun., Tandem Computers, Inc. Mem. Soc. Advancement Mgmt., Costeau Soc., City Club, Island Sailing Club, Alpha Chi. Home: A33 Surfside Colony PO Box 323 Surfside CA 90743

SONNENFELDT, MARJORIE HECHT, public relations executive, consultant; b. Balt., Feb. 8, 1931; d. Stewart Emanuel and Sylvia (Cahn) Hecht; m. Helmut Sonnenfeldt, Oct. 4, 1953; children: Babette Sonnenfeldt Lubben, Walter H., Stewart H. AB with honors magna cum laude, Smith Coll., 1952. Adminstr. U.S. Dept. State, Washington, 1952-54; rschr./writer Dem. Nat. Com., Washington, 1954-56, Robert L. Spivack, Journalist, Washington, 1956-59; writer, editor Com. Nat. Trade Policy, Washington, 1959-63; freelance writer, cons., editor Washington, 1964-69; mem. coun. staff Montgomery County Coun., Rockville, Md., 1970-71; writer, community rels. adviser Montgomery County Planning Bd., Silver Spring, Md., 1971-73; chmn. Montgomery County Bd. Appeals, Rockville, 1973-81; exec. dir. Consumers World Trade, Washington, 1978-80; dir. internat. govt. affairs, v.p. Hill and Knowlton Inc., Washington, 1981-87; v.p. Fleishman-Hillard, Inc., Washington, 1987—. Bd. dirs. D.C. chpt. Am. Jewish Com., 1982—; bd. dirs. Lourie Ctr. Infants & Young Children, Rockville, 1993—. Office: Fleishman-Hillard Inc 1301 Connecticut Ave NW Washington DC 20036

SONNICHSEN, DOROTHY GRIFFITH, corporation owner and executive; b. Ithaca, N.Y., May 25, 1942; d. Edward Stanley and Grace Louise (Kaltenbach) G.; m. Harold Eric Sonnichsen, Aug. 31, 1968; 1 child, Hans Matthew. Asst. mdse. mgr. Rothschild's Inc., Ithaca, 1964-67; asst. buyer Jordan Marsh Co., Boston, 1967-68; asst. mgr. service to investor program Arthur D. Little Inc., Cambridge, Mass., 1968-71; exec. v.p., owner Test Devices Inc., Stow and Hudson, Mass., 1971—; owner, treas. Griffith Machine, Inc., Hudson, 1979-87, Griffith Balancing Machines, Inc., 1985-89; pres. Griffith Co., Hudson, 1984—. Treas. Stow (Mass.) Rep. Town Com., 1978-90, Stow Hist. Soc., 1979—; treas., trustee Randall Town Fund, 1980—, Randall Relief Fund, Stow, 1980—, Stow Conservation Trust, 1981—; bd. dirs. Stow Community Chest, 1983—, treas. 1983-85. Mem. Assoc. Industries Mass., Stow Bus. Assn. (treas., bd. dirs. 1982-84) Hudson Bus. Assn. Club: Stow Garden (chmn. conservation 1983-85), Concord Piecemakers. Home: 101 Packard Rd Stow MA 01775-1120 Office: Test Devices Inc 6 Loring St Hudson MA 01749-2341

SONS, LINDA RUTH, mathematics educator; b. Chicago Heights, Ill., Oct. 31, 1939; d. Robert and Ruth (Diekelman) S. AB in Math., Ind. U., 1961; MS in Math., Cornell U., 1963, PhD in Math., 1966. Teaching asst. Cornell U., Ithaca, N.Y., 1961-63, instr. math., summer 1963, rsch. asst., 1963-65; asst. prof. No. Ill. U., De Kalb, 1965-70, assoc. prof., 1970-78, prof., 1978—; presdl. tchg. prof. No. Ill. U., DeKalb, 1994—; vis. assoc. prof. U. London, 1970-71; dir. undergrad. studies math. dept. No. Ill. U., 1971-77, exec. sec. univ. coun., 1978-79; chair faculty fund No. Ill. U. Found., De Kalb, 1982—. Author: (with others) A Study Guide for Introduction to Mathematics, 1976, Mathematical Thinking in a Quantitative World, 1990; contbr. articles to profl. jours. Mem. campus ministry com. No. Ill. Dist. Luth. Ch./Mo. Synod, Hillside, 1977—; mem. ch. coun. Immanuel Luth. Ch., De Kalb, 1978-85, 87-89; pres. Luth. Women's Missionary League, 1974-87; bd. dirs., treas. De Kalb County Migrant Ministry, 1967-78. NSF Rsch. grantee, 1970-72, 74-75; recipient 1988 Award for Disting. Svc. of Ill. Sect. of the Math Assn. Am., 1991 Award for Excellence in Coll. Teaching of Ill. Coun. Tchrs. Math. Mem. Am. Math. Soc., Assn. for Women in Math., Math. Assn. Am. (mem. nat. bd. govs. 1989-92, award for disting. svc. to Ill. sect. 1988), Ill. Math. Assn. (v.p. sect., pres.-elect, pres., then past pres. 1982-87, bd. dirs. 1989-92), London Math. Soc., Phi Beta Kappa (pres. No. Ill. assn. 1981-85), Sigma Xi (past. chpt. pres.). Office: No Ill U Dept Math Scis De Kalb IL 60115

SONSTEBY, KRISTI LEE, healthcare consultant; b. Anoka, Minn., Nov. 16, 1958; d. Glenn and Rosella (Rebischke) S. Charge nurse Baylor U. Med. Ctr., Dallas, 1980-81; clin. nurse specialist ARA Living Ctrs., Houston, 1981-86; pres., owner KristiCare Inc., Dallas, 1986-89; healthcare cons. SDG Ent., Inc., Austin, Tex., 1989-90; pres., owner NursePlus Inc., Mpls., 1991—; judge Provider Mag., Washington, 1988; cons. in field; lectr. in field; conductor workshops in field. Patentee in field; author: Handbooks for Nurses, Vols. I-X, 1991; contbr. articles to profl. jours. Vol. to elderly various civic orgns. Office: Nurse Plus Inc 716 Hwy 10 NE Ste 163 Minneapolis MN 55434-2331

SONTAG, SUSAN, writer. Author: (novels) The Benefactor, 1963, Death Kit, 1967, The Volcano Lover: A Romance, 1992; (plays) Alice in Bed: A Play in Eight Scenes, 1993; (stories) I, etcetera, 1978, The Way We Live Now, 1991; (essays) Against Interpretation, 1966, Styles of Radical Will, 1969, On Photography, 1977, Illness as Metaphor, 1978, Under the Sign of Saturn, 1980, AIDS and Its Metaphors, 1989; (anthology) A Susan Sontag Reader, 1982; (film scripts) Duet for Cannibals, 1970, Brother Carl, 1974; editor, author introduction Antonin Artaud: Selected Writings, 1976, A Barthes Reader, 1982; dir.: (films) Duet for Cannibals, 1969, Brother Carl, 1971, Promised Lands, 1974, Unguided Tour, 1983. Guggenheim fellow, 1966, 75, Rockefeller Found. fellow, 1965, 74, MacArthur fellow, 1990-95; recipient Ingram Merrill Found. award in lit. in field of Am. Letters, 1976, Creative Arts award Brandeis U., 1976, prize Nat. Book Critics Cir., 1978, Malaparte prize, 1992; named Officier de l'Ordre des Arts et des Lettres, France, 1984. Mem. Am. Acad. Arts and Scis. (elected 1993), Am. Acad. Inst. Arts and Letters (Arts and Letters award 1976), PEN (pres. Am. Ctr. 1987-89). Office: Wylie Aitken & Stone 250 W 57th St New York NY 10107

SOODHALTER, DEBORAH ANN, private investigator, film producer; b. Davenport, Iowa, Dec. 12, 1948; d. Manuel D. and Esther (Finkel) S. BA, Parsons Coll., Fairfield, Iowa, 1970. Pvt. investigator Miami, Fla., 1970—; producer Gifted Films, Miami, 1990—; v.p. Legendary Concerts, Inc., Miami, 1993—. Producer music video "In 3-D," 1990, "Hit and Run," 1990; co-author music video "Seven Turns," 1990. Mem. Guild of the Greater Miami Opera, 1986—, Ctr. for Fine Arts, Miami, 1985—; vol. United Way of Dade County Fla. Hurricane Andrew Relief Effort. Mem. Nat. Assn. Legal Investigators.

SOPHER, VICKI ELAINE, museum director; b. Streator, Ill., May 22, 1943; d. Donald Bird and Thelma Elsie (Saxton) Watson; m. Terry Ray Sr., Jan. 20, 1962 (div. Aug. 1982); 1 child, Terry Ray Jr. AA, No. Va. Community Coll., 1973; BA, Am. U., 1976; MS, Bank State Coll. Edn., 1986. Adminstrv. asst. Decatur & Wilson House, Washington, 1977-81; asst. dir. Decatur House/Nat. Trust for Hist. Preservation, Washington, 1981-84, dir., 1984—; cons. curator Monmouth Mus., Freehold, N.J., 1978-80; founder, pres. Historic Jouse Mus. Metropolitan Wash. Mem. Am. Assn. Museums, Mid-Atlantic Assn. Museums, Am. Assn. for State and Local History, Victorian Soc. Am. (bd. dirs.). Home: 2621 S 12th St Arlington VA 22204 Office: Decatur Ho Mus 748 Jackson Pl NW Washington DC 20006-4984

SOREL, CLAUDETTE MARGUERITE, pianist; b. Paris; d. Michel M. and Elizabeth S. Grad. with top honors, Juilliard Sch. Music, 1947, postgrad., 1948; student of, Sigismund Stojowski, Sari Biro, Olga Samaroff Stokowski, Mieczyslaw Horszowski, Rudolf Serkin; ensemble with, Felix Salmond; musicology with, Dr. Robert Tangeman; music history with, Marian Bauer; grad., Curtis Inst. Music, 1953; B.S. cum laude in Math., Columbia U., 1954. music faculty, vis. prof. Kans. U., 1961-62; assoc. prof. music Ohio State U., 1962-64; prof. music, head piano dept. SUNY Fredonia, 1964—, Disting. Univ. prof., 1969—, univ. artist, 1969—, faculty exchange scholar, 1976—; mem. internat. jury Van Cliburn Internat. Piano Competition, Tex., 1966, Que. and Ont. Music Festivals, 1967, 75; chmn. music panel Presdl. Scholars in Arts Program, 1979—; juror numerous nat. and internat. music competitions; cons. Ednl. Testing Service, Princeton. Author: Compendium of Piano Technique, 1970, 2d edit., 1987, Japanese edit., 1987, Mind Your Musical Manners - Off and On Stage, 1972, 3d revised edit., 1995, The 24 Magic Keys, 3 vols, 1974, The Three Nocturnes of Rachmaninoff, 1974, 2d edit., 1975, 3d edit. with cassette in compact disc, 1988, Fifteen Smorgasbord Studies for the Piano, 1975, 2d edit., 1995, Arensky Piano Etudes, 1976; spl. editor: Music Insider; painter of oil portraits; contbr. articles to profl. mags.; Compiler: The Modern Music of Today, 1947, Serge Prokofieff - His Life and Works, 1947, The Ornamentations in Mozart's Music, 1948; Debut at, Town Hall, N.Y.C., 1943; since appeared in, leading cities of U.S., performed with, N.Y. Philharmonic, London Philharmonic, Zurich, Boston, San Antonio, Milw., NBC, Phila., New Orleans and Cin. symphony orchs., Youth Orch. of Am., 200 others; appeared at, Aspen, Berkshire, Chautauqua, other festivals, European concert tours, 1956, 57, 58, to, Eng., Sweden, Holland, Germany, Switzerland, France; appeared on various radio, TV programs; made recordings for, R.C.A. Victor Rec. Co., Monitor Records, Musical Heritage.; compact disc MacDowell Piano Concerto #2 with N.Y. Philharmonic Orch., 1993; 2000 solo appearances, U.S. and Europe. Bd. dirs. Olga Samaroff Found.; Jr. com. aux. bd. N.Y. Philharmonic Symphony Orch., N.Y. State Nat. Fedn. Music Clubs; mem. adv. bd. Univ. Library Soc.; pres. Shelton Apartments, Inc. Fulbright fellow, 1951; Ford Found. Concert grantee, 1962; winner Phila. Orch. Youth Auditions, 1950, to appear with orch. under direction of Eugene Ormandy; U.S. Senatorial Bus. Adv. Com. Fulbright scholar, 1951; recipient Harry Rosenberg Meml., Frank Damrosch prizes, 1947, Nat. Fedn. Music Clubs Young Artist award, 1951; citation svc. to Am. music Nat. Fedn. Music Clubs, 1966, citations Nat. Assn. Composers & Condrs., 1967, Mu Phi Epsilon, 1968, Freedom medal U.S. Senatorial Com., 1994; nominated Kyoto Japan Humanitarian award, 1989, 92; Claudette Sorel Scholarship for Women Ctr. in Music created by NYU. Mem. Nat. Music Coun. (dir. 1973—, chmn. performance com.), Nat. Arts Club, Music Critics Assn., Broadcast Music Incorp., Columbia Univ. Club (N.Y.C.), Pi Kappa Lambda, Mu Phi Epsilon (dir. Meml. Found., nat. chmn. Sterling Staff Concert Series, citation 1968). Home: 333 West End Ave New York NY 10023-8131

SORELL, KITTY JULIA, public relations executive; b. Vienna, Austria, Apr. 20, 1937; came to U.S. 1938; d. Bruno Alexander and Ilse (Fischl) Singerman. BA, Syracuse U., 1959. Lic. real estate salesperson. Spl. events coord. Gimbel's, N.Y.C., 1966-69; pub. rels./account exec. Hamra Assocs., N.Y.C., 1969-71; spl. events/pub. rels. dir. Stern Bros., Paramus, N.J., 1972; pub. rels. account exec. Zachary & Front, N.Y.C., 1972-76; dir. pub. rels. RSM&K Advt., N.Y.C., 1976-77; owner Kitty Sorell Pub. Rels., N.Y.C., 1977—; reporter Wisdom's Child, 1981-84, The Villager, 1986-88; lectr. in field. Contbg. editor Mktg. Maker mag., 1976. Fundraiser WNET-TV, N.Y.C., 1974-75; vol. pub. rels. Sheridan Sq. Triangle Assn., N.Y.C., 1984-89; pres. bd. dirs. Apt. House Coop., 1991—; bd. dirs. Greenwich Village Alliance, 1994—. Mem. Am. Soc. Profl. and Exec. Women, Publicity Club. Democrat. Jewish. Office: Kitty Sorell Pub Rels 250 W 57th St New York NY 10107-0001

SOREN, TABITHA L., television newscaster, writer; b. San Antonio, Aug. 19, 1967; d. John Thomas and Mary Jane (Quinn) Sornberger. BA cum laude in Journalism, NYU, 1989. Intern Cable News Network, N.Y.C., Sta. WNBC TV, N.Y.C.; desk asst. ABC TV, N.Y.C.; news anchor, statehouse correspondent ABC Sta. WVNY-TV, Vt.; news reporter, anchor MTV News Dept., N.Y.C., 1991—; contbg. corr. NBC News, N.Y.C., 1992—; columnist N.Y. Times Syndication Sales Corp., N.Y.C.; cons. editor Elle, N.Y.C. Contbr. articles to various periodicals. Recipient Peabody Journalism award U. Ga., 1993, Leadership award Nat. League Women Voters, 1993. Office: MTV News 1515 Broadway New York NY 10036

SORENSEN, ELIZABETH JULIA, cultural administrator; b. Kenora, Ont., Can., Nov. 24, 1934; d. John Frederick and Irene Margaret (Dowd) MacKellar; m. O. Leo P. Sorensen, July 7, 1956 (div. 1963); children: Lianne Kim Sorensen Kruger. BA, Lakehead U., 1970; MA, Brigham Young U., 1972; Assoc. Royal Conservatory, U. Toronto, 1978; Assoc., Mt. Royal Coll., Calgary, AB, 1978. Sec. Canadian Med. Assn. Manitoba div., Winnipeg, 1956-59; legal sec. Filmore, Riley & Co., Winnipeg, 1961-63; tchr. Fort Frances (Ont.) High Sch., 1963-70; instr. drama, speech, English Lethbridge (Alta.) Community Coll., 1972-77; tchr. bus. edn. Henderson Coll. Bus., Lethbridge, 1978-80; supr. cultural programs City Medicine Hat, Alta., 1980—. Mem. Alta. Mcpl. Assn. for Culture (sec. 1982-87, treas. 1982-90, vice-chair 1990-92, chair 1992—), Can. Conf. Arts, World Leisure and Recreation Assn. Mormon. Office: City of Medicine Hat, 580 1 St SE, Medicine Hat, AB Canada T1A 8E6

SORENSEN, JACKI FAYE, aerobic dance company executive, choreographer; b. Oakland, Calif., Dec. 10, 1942; d. Roy C. and Juanita F. (Bullon) Mills; m. Neil A. Sorensen, Jan. 3, 1965. BA, U. Calif., 1964. Cert. tchr., Calif. Ptnr., Big Spring Sch. Dance, 1965; tchr. Pasadena Ave. Sch., Sacramento, 1968; founder, pres., choreographer Jacki's Inc., DeLand, Fla., 1990—; cons., lectr. on phys. fitness. Author: Aerobic Dancing, 1979, Jacki Sorensen's Aerobic Lifestyle Book, 1983; choreographer numerous dance exercises for records and videocassettes. Trustee Women's Sports Found. Recipient Diamond Pin award Am. Heart Assn., 1979, Individual Contbn. award Am. Assn. Fitness Dirs. in Bus. and Industry, 1981, Spl. Olympics Contbn. award, 1982, Contbn. to Women's Fitness award Pres.'s Coun. Phys. Fitness and Sports, 1982, Healthy Am. Fitness Leader award U.S. Jaycees, 1984, Lifetime Achievement award Internat. Dance Exercise Assn., 1985, New Horizons award Caldwell (N.J.) Coll., 1985, Legend of Aerobics award City Sports mag., 1985; Pres. Coun. award Calif. Womens' Leadership Conf., 1986, Hall of Fame award Club Industry mag., 1986, IDEA, 1992. Mem. AAHPERD, AFTRA, Am. Coll. Sports Medicine, Nat. Intramural and Recreation Assn. Office: Jacki's Inc PO Box 289 Deland FL 32721-0289

SORENSEN, MEREDITH JEAN, educator; b. Penn Yan, N.Y., May 23, 1940; d. Kenneth Edwin and Mary (Raiman) S. BA, Ottawa (Kans.) U., 1962; MA, No. Mich. U., 1976; postgrad., New Zealand Whole Lang. Mentorship Program, Hamilton, summer 1989. Cert. elem. tchr., elem. sch. prin. Tchr. Rochester (N.Y.) City Schs., 1962-63, Penfield (N.Y.) Cen. Sch., 1963-67, Marion (N.Y.) Cen. Sch., 1967—. Vol. (correctional facility) Industry (N.Y.) Sch., 1970-83, vis. dir., 1982—; bd. dirs. Ottawa U., 1970-74; mem. N.Y. State Legis. Adv. Com., Albany, 1977-92; bd. dirs. Fairport Apts. for sr. citizens, 1981-83; founder Swinging Singles Western Sq. Dance Club, Rochester, 1967. Named one of Outstanding Young Women Am., 1971. Mem. Am. Fedn. Tchrs., N.Y. State United Tchrs., Marion Tchrs. Assn. (treas., chair legis com. social and sunshine com., negotiations com.), N.Y. State Reading Assn., Genesee Valley Devel. Learning Group, Danish Sisterhood (Penn Yan), Phi Delta Kappa. American Baptist. Office: Marion Cen Sch 3863 N Main St Marion NY 14505-9579

SORENSEN, SHEILA, state senator; b. Chgo., Sept. 20, 1947; d. Martin Thomas Moloney and Elizabeth (Koehr) Paulus; m. Wayne B. Slaughter, May, 1969 (div. 1976); 1 child, Wayne Benjamin III; m. Dean E. Sorensen, Feb. 14, 1977; (stepchildren) Michael, Debbie, Kevin, Dean C. BS, Loretto Heights Coll., Denver, 1965; postgrad. pediatric nurse practicioner, U. Colo., Denver, 1969-70. Pediatric nurse practicioner Pub. Health Dept., Denver, 1970-71, Boise, Idaho, 1971-72; pediatric nurse practicioner Boise (Idaho) Pediatric Group, 1972-74, Pediatric Assocs., Boise, 1974-77; mem. Idaho State Ho. Reps., 1987-92; mem. Idaho Senate, 1992—, chair senate health and welfare com., 1992-94, chair senate majority caucus, vice chair state affairs com. Precinct committeeman Ada County Rep. Cen. Com., Boise, 1982-86, dist. vice-chair, 1985—; polit. chair Idaho Med. Assn. Aux., 1984-87, Ada County Med. Assocs., 1986-87; bd. dirs. Family Practice Residency Program, 1992—, Univ./Comty. Health Sci. Assn., Bishop Kelly Found., 1993—; chair Senate Majority Caucus, 1995, vice-chair state affairs com. Recipient AMA Nathan Davis award for Outstanding State Legislator, 1994. Mem. Nat. Conf. State Legislators, Nat. Orgn. Women Legislators, Am. Legis. Exch. Coun. Roman Catholic.

SORENSON, JOANNE CAROLE, social worker, psychotherapist; b. Harlan, Iowa, Feb. 23, 1950; d. Russell Howard and Helen Shirley (Tippett) S. BA, Doane Coll., 1972; MSW, U. Iowa, 1977. Sch. social worker Miss. Bend Area Edn. Agy., Davenport, Iowa, 1977-78, Adams County 5 Star Sch. Dist., Northglen, Colo., 1978-91; pvt. practice psychotherapist Denver, 1991—; workshop facilitator Wild Women Weekends, Denver, 1993—. Author: 92 Romantic Things To Do in Denver, 1992. Mem. NASW, People Making of Colo. Office: 1777 S Bellaire Ste 415 Denver CO 80222

SORENSON, LIANE BETH MCDOWELL, university administrator, state legislator; b. Chgo., Aug. 13, 1947; d. Harold Davidson McDowell and Frances Elanor (Williams) Daisey; m. Boyd Wayne Sorenson, June 30, 1973; children: Nathan, Matthew, Dana. BS in Edn., U. Del., 1969, M in Counseling with honors, 1986. Tchr. Avon Grove Sch. Dist., West Grove, Pa., 1969-70, Alexis I. duPont Sch. Dist., Wilmington, Del., 1970-73, Barrington (Ill.) Sch. Dist., 1973-75; counseling intern Medill Intensive Learning Ctr.-Christina Sch. Dist., Newark, Del., 1985; counselor Family Violence Shelter CHILD, Inc., Wilmington, 1985, 86-87, dir. parent edn. programs, 1987-88; dir. Office Women's Affairs, exec. dir. Commn. on Status of Women U. Del., Newark, 1988—; mem. Del. Legislature, Dover, 1992—; chair Del. Ho. Edn. Com., 1992—; commr. Edn. Commn. State Del.; mem. tng. com. Nat. Conf. State Legislatures; mem. joint sunset com. Del. Legislature. Presenter papers various meetings & confs. Pres. bd. dirs. Nursing Mothers, Inc., 1980-81; trustee Hockessin Montessori Sch., 1982-84, enrollment chair, 1982-83; trustee Hockessin Pub. Libr., 1982-84, pres. bd., 1982-84; bd. dirs. Del. Coalition for Children, 1986-88; bd. dirs. Children's Bur. Del., 1984-87, sec., 1985-87; pres. Jr. League Wilmington, 1986-87, rsch. coun. v.p., 1985-86; bd. dirs. YWCA New Castle County, 1989-91; pres. Del. Women's Agenda, 1986—; vice chair Women's Leadership Ctr., 1992—; mem. Del. Work Family Coalition. Grantee Del. Dept. Svcs. to Children, Youth and Their Families, 1987-88, 1988, State of Del. Gen. Assembly, 1988. Mem. Am. Assn. for Higher Edn. (chair women's caucus 1991-92, program chair women's caucus 1990-91, pre-conf. workshop coord. women's caucus 1990 Ann Conf.). Republican. Methodist. Office: State of Delaware Legislative Hall Dover DE 19901*

SORENSON, PATRICIA ANN, software engineer; b. Beverly, Mass., Oct. 14, 1955; d. Walter F. and Gloria D. (Mascioli) S. BS in Math., Salem State Coll., 1983. Computer operator Madico, Inc., Woburn, Mass., 1978-80, programmer, 1980-83; cons. Turning Point Systems, Inc., Beverly, 1983-85, project mgr., 1987-91, product mgr., 1991—; programmer/analyst Daly Drug div. Cardinal Health, Peabody, Mass., 1985-87. Mem. Am. Mgmt. Assn., IEEE Computer Soc., Appalachian Mountain Club. Home: 10 Bentley St Salem MA 01970-5213

SORGEN, ELIZABETH ANN, retired educator; b. Ft. Wayne, Ind., Aug. 21, 1931; d. Lee E. and Miriam N. (Bixler) Waller; m. Don DuWayne Sorgen, Mar. 8, 1952; children: Kevin D., Karen Lee Sorgen Hoeppner, Keith Alan. BS in Edn., Ind. U., 1953; MS in Edn., St. Francis Coll., Ft. Wayne, 1967. Tchr. East Allen County Schs., Monroeville, Ind., 1953-94, also bldg. rep. and math. book adoption rep., 1953-94. A founder nursery sch. St. Mark's Luth. Ch., Monroeville, 1960—, mem. choir, 1960—. Recipient Golden Apple award East Allen County Schs., 1976, Monroeville Tchr. of Yr. award, 1993. Mem. AAUW, East Allen County Educators Assn., Buck and Dears Square Dance Club (sec. 1954), Delta Kappa Gamma. Home: 25214 Lincoln Hwy E Monroeville IN 46773

SORGI, DEBORAH BERNADETTE, educational software company executive; b. N.Y.C., May 2, 1955; d. Waldo L. and Maria N. (Santo) S.; m. Philip A. Keith, Dec. 24, 1991. BAin Elem. Edn., St. Francis Coll., 1976; MS in Reading, St. John's U., 1979. Cert. tchr., N.Y. Adminstrv. asst. Will Darrah and Assoc., N.Y.C., 1976-77; classrm. tchr. St. Rita Sch., Bklyn., 1977-80; ednl. cons. Jostens Learning Corp. (formerly, Prescription Learning Corp.), Phoenix, 1980-82, regional dir., 1982-86, regional mktg. mgr., 1986-90, sr. mktg. mgr., 1990-91, area sales mgr., 1991-92; v.p. Simon & Schuster Tech. Group/CCC, Sunnyvale, Calif., 1992; pres. EduStar Am., Inc., Orlando, Fla., 1992-93; gen. mgr. edn. Wang Labs., Inc., Lowell, Mass., 1994—. Republican. Roman Catholic.

SORRENTINO, RENATE MARIA, illustrator; b. Mallnitz, Carinthia, Austria, June 21, 1942; came to the U.S., 1962; d. Johann and Theresia (Kritzer) Weinberger; m. Philip Rosenberg, Nov. 22, 1968 (dec. 1982); m. Francis J. Sorrentino, Sept. 4, 1988. Grad. gold and silversmith artist, Höhere Technische Lehranstalt, Austria, 1961. Draftswoman Elecon Inc., N.Y.C., 1962-65; jr. designer Automatics Metal Prod. Corp., N.Y.C., 1965-70; designer, art dir. Autosplice, Inc., Woodside, N.Y., 1970-90; freelance artist Jupiter, Fla., 1990—. Patentee Quick Disconnect from Continuous Wire, 1977. Home: 2301 Marina Isle Way # 404 Jupiter FL 33477 Office: Autosplice Inc 10121 Barnes Canyon Rd San Diego CA 92121-2725

SORSTOKKE, ELLEN KATHLEEN, marketing executive, educator; b. Seattle, Mar. 31, 1954; d. Harold William and Carrol Jean (Russ) S. MusB with distinction, U. Ariz., 1976; postgrad., UCLA Extension, 1979-83, L.A. Valley Coll., 1984-85, Juilliard Extension, fall 1987, U. Calif. Berkeley Extension, Berkeley Extension, 1992-93, 95—. Cert. music specialist tchr., Ariz. Pvt. practice music tchr. Music Land, Tucson, 1975-77; music tchr. Eloy (Ariz.) Elem. Schs., 1976-77, Whiteriver (Ariz.) Pub. Schs., 1977-78; svc. writer, acting svc. mgr., asst. svc. mgr. Alfa of Santa Monica, Calif., 1978-79; purchasing agt. Advance Machine Corp., L.A., 1979-80; asst. mgr. Atlantic Nuclear Svcs., Gardena, Calif., 1980-81; mgr. Blue Lady's World Music Ctr., L.A., 1981-83; instrument specialist Baxter-Northup Music Co., Sherman Oaks, Calif., 1983-85; dir. mktg. Mandolin Bros., Ltd., S.I., N.Y., 1985-89; product mgr. Gibson Guitar Corp., Nashville, 1989; sales mgr. Saga Musical Instruments, South San Francisco, Calif., 1990-91, mktg. dir., 1991—; freelance mktg. cons., S.I., 1986-89; freelance music tchr., Tucson,

L.A., N.Y.C., 1975-89; music cons. 20th Century Fox, L.A., 1984; freelance music copyist and orchestrator, Tucson, L.A., N.Y.C., 1972-89; freelance graphic designer and advt., Foster City, Calif., 1993—. campaign worker Richard Jones for Supr., Tucson, 1972; mem., program book designer Marina Del Rey-Westchester Symphony Orch., L.A., 1981-83; active Calif. Wind Ensemble, 1992—. Scholar U. Ariz., 1973-76, ASCAP scholar, 1980-81. Mem. Am. Fedn. Musicians, NAFE, Soc. for the Preservation Film Music, Tucson Flute Club (publicity chmn. 1974-75, v.p. 1975-76). Republican. Office: Saga Musical Instruments 429 Littlefield Ave PO Box 2841 South San Francisco CA 94080

SORSTOKKE, SUSAN EILEEN, systems engineer; b. Seattle, May 2, 1955; d. Harold William and Carrol Jean (Russ) S. BS in Systems Engring., U. Ariz., 1976; MBA, U. Wash., Richland, 1983. Warehouse team mgr. Procter and Gamble Paper Products, Modesto, Calif., 1976-78; quality assurance engr. Westinghouse Hanford Co., Richland, Wash., 1978-80; supr. engring. document ctr. Westinghouse Hanford Co., Richland, 1980-81; mgr. data control and adminstrn. Westinghouse Electric Corp., Madison, Pa., 1981-82, mgr. data control and records mgmt., 1982-84; prin. engr. Westinghouse Elevator Co., Morristown, N.J., 1984-87; region adminstrn. mgr. Westinghouse Elevator Co., Arleta, Calif., 1987-90; ops. rsch. analyst Am. Honda Motor Co. Inc., Torrance, Calif., 1990—; adj. prof. U. LaVerne, Calif., 1991-92. Advisor Jr. Achievement, 1982-83; literacy tutor Westmoreland Literacy Coun., 1983-84, host parent EF Found., Saugus, Calif., 1987-88, Am. Edn. Connection, Saugus, 1988-89, 91; instr. Excell, L.A., 1991-92. Mem. Soc. Women Engrs., Am. Inst. Indsl. Engrs., Nat. Coun. Systems Engring., Optimists Charities, Inc. (bd. dirs. Acton, Calif. 1991-94). Republican. Methodist. Home: # 205 2567 Plaza Del Amo Torrance CA 90503 Office: Am Honda Motor Co Inc Dept Parts Quality and Systems 1919 Torrance Blvd Torrance CA 90501-2722

SOTIROPOULOS, LOLA, restauranteur, realtor; b. Haleyville, Ala., Oct. 11, 1950; d. John Rufus and Loysine (Carter) Feltman; m. Constantine Sotiropoulos, Dec. 9, 1975 (dec. Jan. 1993); children: John Oscar, Vanessa Nota. Owner Strawberry Patch Restaurant, Homewood, Ala. Mem. Ala. Symphony Assn., Ladies Philopthochos Soc. Greek Orthodox. Home: 512 Kenilworth Dr Homewood AL 35209-5436 Office: Strawberry Patch Restaurant 1839 28th Ave S Homewood AL 35209

SOTO, RAMONA, training specialist; b. East Chicago, Ind., Apr. 14, 1963; d. Robert Rudy and Antonia (Perez) S. Student, Purdue U., 1982-86, U. Ill., Chgo., 1990, DePaul U., 1992—. Salesperson The Gap, Inc., Ind., 1979-84; asst. mgr. The Gap, Inc., Ind. and Ill., 1984-88; tng. mgr. The Gap, Inc., Ill., 1988-90; tng. specialist Montgomery Ward & Co., Ill., 1990-93; temp. worker The Richard Michael Group, Chgo., 1993, Resort Travel Corp, Oakbrook Terrace, Ill., 1993; ind. tng. cons. Chgo., 1994—; tutor tng. mgr. The Cabrini Green Tutoring Program, Chgo., 1991—, Preparing an Attitude for Learning, Leadership and Success, 1992—. Mem. Am. Soc. Tng. and Devel. (Chgo. chpt. 1990). Home: 3550 N Lake Shore Dr Chicago IL 60657-1916

SOTOMAYOR, SONIA, federal judge; b. N.Y.C., June 25, 1954; d. Juan Luis and Celina (Baez) S.; m. Kevin Edward Noonan, Aug. 14, 1976 (div. 1983). AB, Princeton (N.J.) U., 1976; JD, Yale U., 1979. Bar: N.Y. 1980, U.S. Dist. Ct. (ea. and so. dists.) N.Y. 1984. Asst. dist. atty. Office of Dist. Atty. County of N.Y., N.Y.C., 1979-84; assoc., ptnr. Pavia & Harcourt, N.Y.C., 1984-92; fed. judge U.S. Dist. Ct. (so. dist.) N.Y., N.Y.C., 1992—. Editor Yale U. Law Rev., 1979. Bd. dirs. P.R. Legal Def. and Edn. Fund, N.Y.C., 1980-92, State of N.Y. Mortgage Agy., N.Y.C., 1987-92, N.Y.C. Campaign Fin. Bd., 1988-92; mem. State Adv. Panel on Inter-Group Rels., N.Y.C., 1990-91. Mem. Phi Beta Kappa. Office: US Courthouse Foley Sq New York NY 10007

SOTTILE, JILL ANNE, investment company executive; b. Englewood, N.J., Apr. 13, 1963; d. Michael Ronald and Marjorie Caroline (Ketchum) S. BS in Mgmt., Fairleigh Dickinson U., 1985, MBA in Fin., 1993. Client svc. rep., sales/mktg. rep., asst. supr., mgr. client svcs. Lexington Mgmt., Saddle Brook, N.J., 1986-92; mgr. client svcs., mgr. tng. and adminstrn. Pershing, Jersey City, N.J., 1992-94; v.p.-shareholder/dealer svcs. Sunamerica, Inc., N.Y.C., 1994—. Republican. Office: Sunamerica 733 3d Ave New York NY 10017

SOUDERS, BERYL V., medical/surgical and rehabilitation-detox nurse; b. Pottsville, Pa., Mar. 10, 1938; d. Roy Ralph and Susan Leola (Harding) Dohner; m. Thomas Griffith Souders, Sept. 17, 1960; children: Susan Leith Goold, Miriam Irene Glennon, Martha Lynn Janczewski. Diploma, Allentown (Pa.) Gen. Hosp., 1959. Cert. port-a-cath care and use. Charge nurse night shift Allentown Hosp.; camp nurse East Pa.Boy Scouts, Girl Scouts and Campfire Girls, Marshalls Creek, Phila., Boyertown, Pottstown, Lancaster; oper. rm. nurse Lancaster (Pa.)-St. Joseph Hosp.; staff nurse on med.-surg. trauma unit, part-time detox nurse and rehab. unit nurse. Med. Coll. Hosp., Bucks County Campus, Warminster, Pa.; camp nurse United Ch. of Christ Camps. Active Girl Scouts U.S., 1969-79, Campfire Girls, Inc., 1977-87; assoc. advisor Explorer Post 173, Boy Scouts Am., 1977-85; organist, music dir. St. Mark's United Ch. of Christ, 1974—; past treas., present chaplain Huntingdon Valley Fire Co., Ladies Aux. Home: 525 Welsh Rd Philadelphia PA 19115-1817

SOUESSENBACH, SONJA CHARLOTTE, finance executive; b. Stuttgart, Germany. BA, Northeastern U., 1968; M of Urban Planning, U. Ill., 1972; MBA, U. Houston, 1981. City planner, sr. planner City of Bridgeport, Conn., 1972-77; supt. of prodn. City of Houston Parks Dept., 1977-78; mgr. space planning and spl. svcs. U. Houston, 1978-83, facilities programmer dept. facilities planning and constrn., 1978-83, sr. fin. analyst office of the treas., 1983-85, dir. fin. planning, office of planning and budgeting, 1985-86; fin. cons., 1987-90; dir. pub. sch. facilities funding program Tex. Bond Rev. Bd., 1990—. Richard K. Mellon fellowship, 1969-71. Mem. AICP, Am. Planning Assn. (Tex. chpt.), State Agy. Coun. of the Gov.'s Commn. for Women. Home: 4003 Capistrano Trl Austin TX 78739-4315

SOUKUP, ELOUISE MARILISS, controller; b. Hastings, Nebr., Oct. 15, 1926; d. Robert George and Gretchen Eloise (Guildner) Hoff; m. Leo Soukup Jr., Mar. 22, 1948; children: Leo, Mariliss Suzanne Soukup Erickson. Student, U. So. Calif., 1945-48; BA, U. Nebr., 1973. Co-owner, bus. mgr. Soukup Cleaners, Beatrice, Nebr., 1955—; controller C.D. Hoff, Inc., Hastings, Nebr., 1976—. Curator edn. Nebr. State Hist. Soc., Lincoln, 1974-77; vice-chmn. Gage County Rep. party, 1964; bd. dirs. Beatrice YWCA, 1965-67, Nebr. Gov.'s Commn. on Status of Women, 1977-80. Mem. Am. Hist. Assn., Internat. Fabricare Inst., Nebr. Writers Guild, AAUW, DAR, Women in Laundry and Drycleaning (internat. v.p. 1983-84), Internat. Drycleaning Congress (del. China Exchange 1983), Adams County Hist. Soc., Hastings Area C. of C., Lochland Country Club, Kappa Delta, Pi Alpha Theta. Home: RR 1 Box 22J Doniphan NE 68832-9801 Office: 838 W 2d St PO Box 1141 Hastings NE 68901

SOULE, SALLIE THOMPSON, retired state official; b. Detroit, May 13, 1928; d. Hayward Stone and Elizabeth Robinson Thompson; A.B., Smith Coll., 1950; M.A., U. Vt., Burlington, 1952; m. Gardner Northup Soule, July 26, 1958; stepchildren: Gardner Northup, Nancy Soule Brown; children: Sarah Goodwin, Trumbull Dickson. Sec. trade sales dept. Macmillan Pub. Co., N.Y.C., 1952-57; tech. writer sales svc. div. Eastman Kodak Co., Rochester, N.Y., 1957-58; feature writer Brighton-Pittsford Post, Pittsford, N.Y., 1958-68; v.p., gen. mgr. F. H. Horsford Nursery, Inc., Charlotte, Vt., 1968-76; ptnr., pres. Bygone Books, Inc., Burlington, Vt., 1978—; mem. Vt. Ho. of Reps., 1976-80, mem. ways and means com., 1976-80; mem. Vt. Senate, 1980-84, mem. appropriation com., energy and natural resources com. 1980-84; commr. Vt. Dept. Employment and Tng., Montpelier, 1985-88; chmn. Vt. Employment Security Bd., 1985-88.

SOUSA, CONSUELO MARIA, pediatrician; b. New Bedford, Mass., Aug. 5, 1931; d. Edward Rogers and Candida Helena (Rogers) S.; m. Timothy Leonard Stephens, July 7, 1959; children: Timothy Leonard III, Susan Ellen, Amy Louise. BS, Howard U., Washington, 1953, MD, 1958; MPH, Harvard U., 1962; MBA, Case Western Res. U., Cleve., 1983. Diplomate Am. Bd. Pediatrics. Intern St. Luke's Hosp., New Bedford, 1958; resident pediatrics Freedmen's Hosp., Washington, 1959-61; fellow dept. maternal and child health Harvard Sch. Pub. Health, Boston, 1961-62; instr. preventive medicine Boston U. Sch. Medicine, 1962-63; asst. physician home med. svc. Mass. Meml. Svc. Hosp., 1962-63; pvt. practice, assoc. attending staff St. Luke's Hosp., New Bedford, 1963-66; pediatrician Well Child Conf., Fairhaven, Mass., 1965-66; clin. instr. pediatrics Case Western Res. U., Cleve., 1967-94; mem. pediatric staff Rainbow Babes and Children's Hosp., Cleve., 1967-94; chief pediatrics Hough Norwood Family Health Care Ctr., Cleve., 1967-76; vis. asst. pediatrics Cleve. Met. Gen. Hosp., 1967-91; dir. health svcs. Buckeye Health Plan, Inc., Cleve., 1976-79, acting exec. dir., 1979, med. health svcs. dir., 1979-80; v.p., med. adminstr. Assocs. in Orthopaedics, Inc., Cleve., 1982—, cons., 1980-82; chmn. med. staff Health Hill Hosp., Cleve., 1982-84; mem. Headstart Health Adv. Com., Cleve., 1971-78, chmn., 1977-78. Contbr. articles to profl. jours. Mem. Citizens Adv. Bd. of Juvenile Ct. Cuyahoga County, 1975-90, chmn. bd., 1985-89; appointed commr. Cuyahoga Met. Housing Authority, 1990; mem. bd., founding trustee Harambee Svcs. to Black Families, Cleve., 1979-85; mem. adv. bd. Youth Svcs., Cuyahoga County, 1980-90. Named Outstanding American, Cape Verdean Am. Vets., New Bedford, 1972. Fellow Am. Acad. Pediatrics; mem. AMA, Nat. Med. Assn., No. Ohio Pediatric Soc. Home: 13475 N Park Blvd Cleveland OH 44118-4927 Office: Assocs in Orthopaedics Inc 11201 Shaker Blvd Ste 328 Cleveland OH 44104-3803

SOUTH, MARY ANN, pediatrics educator; b. Portales, N.Mex., May 23, 1933; d. John Anderson and Carrie (Schumpert) S.; m. Allard W. Loutherback, Dec. 29, 1983 (dec. June 1985); children: George Louie, Linda Lee Loutherback Putnam. Student, Baylor U., Waco, Tex., 1951-53; BA, Ea. N.Mex. U., 1955; MD, Baylor U., Houston, 1959. Diplomate Am. Bd. Pediatrics. Intern Presbyn.-St. Luke's Hosp., Chgo., 1959-60, resident in pediatrics, 1960-62; fellow in infectious diseases Baylor U., 1962-64; fellow in immunology, instr. in pediatrics U. Minn., Mpls., 1964-66; asst. prof., assoc. prof. Baylor U. Coll. Medicine, 1966-73; assoc. prof. U. Pa., Phila., 1973-77; prof., chmn. dept. pediatrics Tex. Tech U. Health Scis. Ctr., Lubbock, 1977-79, rsch. prof., 1979-83; med. officer Nat. Inst. Neurol.-Communicative Disorders and Stroke, NIH, Bethesda, Md., 1982-85; vis. scientist Gallaudet Coll., Washington, 1984-85; prof. pediatrics Meharry Med. Coll., Nashville, 1986-89, W.K. Kellogg disting. prof., 1989—. Contbr. over 140 articles to med. jours., chpts. to books. Recipient Disting. Alumnus award Ea. N.Mex. U., 1969, rsch. career devel. award NIH, 1968-73. Fellow Infectious Diseases Soc. Am.; mem. Am. Pediatric Soc., Am. Assn. Immunology, Assn. for Gnotobiology, Am. Med. Women's Assn., Pediatric Infectious Diseases Soc., Alpha Omega Alpha. Home: 6666 Brookmont Ter Nashville TN 37205-4658 Office: Meharry Med Coll 1005 DB Todd Blvd Nashville TN 37208

SOUTH, RUTH EADES, reference librarian; b. Inglewood, Calif., Nov. 23, 1928; d. Ted and Ruth Eden (Houltram) Eades; m. Donald Drager South, Sept. 24, 1950 (dec. Apr. 1985); children: Andrew, Carolyn, Barbara. BA, U. Oreg., 1950, MLS, 1971, MA, 1980. Reference libr. U. Oreg., Eugene, 1973-75, instr. Sch. Librarianship, 1975-78, reference libr., assoc. prof., bibliographer Libr., 1979-94; ret., 1994; part-time traffic petitions officer U. Oreg., 1994—. Author: (bibliography) Citizen Action and the Neighborhood Movement, 1987. Organizer Muscular Dystrophy-Amyotrophic Lateral Sclerosis Support Group, Eugene, 1986; pres. Neighborhood Assn., Eugene, 1990. Mem. Sigma Delta Pi, Beta Phi Mu. Home: 697 Crest Dr Eugene OR 97405 Office: U Oreg Dept Pub Safety Eugene OR 97403

SOUTHARD, PEGGY-DEE ANN, sociologist, anthropologist; b. San Francisco, Jan. 27, 1956; d. Layfette Fate and Wilma May (Trobridge) S. AA in Social Sci., Cen. Oreg. C.C., 1989; BA in Sociology, Anthropology, So. Oreg. State Coll., 1991; postgrad., U. Colo., 1991-92; MS in Sociology, U. Oreg., Eugene, 1993; postgrad., 1993—. Adminstrv. analyst Proteus Adult Tng. Non-Profit Employment and Tng., Visalia, Calif., 1975-83; co-dir. Low Income Families Together, Bend, Oreg., 1984-86; owner, mgr. book store Yesterday's Gone, Bend, 1983-86; spl. collections manuscript processor U. Oreg., Eugene, 1987-88; prof.'s asst. Cen. Oreg. C.C., Bend, 1988-89; tutor sociology, anthropology So. Oreg. State Coll., Ashland, 1989-91; asst. editor, adminstrv. asst. U. Colo., Boulder, 1991-92, teaching asst. sociology, 1991-92; NSF rsch. fellow in sociology U. Oreg., Eugene, 1992—, grad. teaching fellow sociology, 1993—; bus. cons. Pageantry Book Co., Ashland, 1989-91, Eugene, 1992—. Author: Shelters Are for Scum; and I Ain't No Bum, 1992; contbr. to various publs. Bd. dirs. Ctrl. Oreg. Cmty. Action Agy., Bend, 1984-86; mem. Nat. Coalition for the Homeless; coord. Homeless Global Electronic Discussion List. Mem. Am. Sociol. Assn., Sociologists for Women in Soc., So. Oreg. Sociol. Assn. (chair 1989-91), Pacific Sociol. Assn., So. Oreg. Anthropol. Assn., Phi Kappa Phi, Omicron Delta Kappa. Home: PO Box 814 Bend OR 97709-0814

SOUTHER, JEAN LORRAINE, accounting and management educator, accountant; b. North Weymouth, Mass.; d. Herbert Roy and Ruth Agnes (Perry) S. BBA in Acctg., Northeastern U., 1960, MBA, 1968; EdD, U. Mass., 1986. Lic. pub. acct. From acct. to auditor to div. acctg. mgr. to systems mgr. to asst. to contr. Howard Johnson Co., Quincy, Mass., 1949-74; prof. Capd Cod C.C., Barnstable, Mass., 1974-92, prof. emeritus, 1992—; founding dir. Cape Cod Women's Credit Union, Barnstable. Editor: Basic Finance (Gitman), 1987. Chairwoman pers. bd. Town of Eastham, Mass., 1980-84, vice chairwoman fin. bd., 1986-89; pres. Friends of Cape Cod Nat. Sea Shore, bd. dirs. 1991—; mem. Nauset Regional H.S. Coun., 1993—; vol. Lakeland Coll., Sheboygan, Wis., 1994; mem. bd. for homeland ministries United Ch. of Christ. Recipient Merit award Town of Eastham, 1984. Mem. Nat. Soc. Pub. Accts., Am. Soc. Women Accts. (mem. editl. bd. 1980-93), Assn. Sys. Mgmt. Republican. Home: PO Box 326 50 Van Dale Ave Eastham MA 02642-0326

SOUTHERN, EILEEN (MRS. JOSEPH SOUTHERN), music educator; b. Mpls., Feb. 19, 1920; d. Walter Wade and Lilla (Gibson) Jackson; m. Joseph Southern, Aug. 22, 1942; children: April, Edward. A.B., U. Chgo., 1940, M.A., 1941; Ph.D., NYU, 1961; M.A. (hon.), Harvard U., 1976; D.A. (hon.), Columbia Coll., Chgo., 1985. Instr. Prairie View U., Hempstead, Tex., 1941-42; asst. prof. So. U., Baton Rouge, 1943-45, 49-51; tchr. N.Y.C. Bd. Edn., 1954-60; instr. Bklyn. Coll., CUNY, 1960-64, asst. prof., 1964-69; assoc. prof. York Coll., CUNY, 1969-71, prof., 1972-75; prof. music Harvard U., Cambridge, Mass., 1976-87, chmn. dept. Afro-Am. studies, 1976-79, prof. emeritus, 1987—. Concert pianist, 1940-55; author: The Buxheim Organ Book, 1963, The Music of Black Americans: A History, 1971, 2d edit., 1983, Readings in Black American Music, 1971, 2d edit., 1983, Anonymous Chansons in MS El Escorial Biblioteca del Monasterio, IV a 24, 1981, Biographical Dictionary of Afro-American and African Musicians, 1982, African-American Traditions in Song, Sermon, Tale, and Dance, 1630-1920; An Annotated Bibliography, 1990 (with Josephine Wright); editor: The Black Perspective in Music (1973-90), Nineteenth Century African-American Musical Theater, 1994; contbr. articles to profl. jours. Active Girl Scouts U.S.A., 1954-63; chmn. mgmt. com. Queens Area YWCA, 1970-73. Recipient Alumni Achievement award U. Chgo., 1970, Deems Taylor award ASCAP, 1973, Peabody medal Johns Hopkins U., 1991; NEH grantee, 1979-83. Mem. NACCP, Internat. Musicol. Soc., Am. Musicol. Soc. (hon., bd. dirs. 1974-76), Sonneck Am. Music Soc. (bd. dirs. 1986-88), Renaissance Soc., Phi Beta Kappa (hon. Radcliffe Coll.), Alpha Kappa Alpha. Home: PO Drawer 1 Cambria Heights NY 11411 Office: Harvard U Cambridge MA 02138

SOUTHWORTH, JAMIE MACINTYRE, education educator; b. Ironton, Ohio, Oct. 16, 1931; d. Gaylord and Lydia Marcum (Adkins) MacIntyre; m. Horton C. Southworth; children: Jaye, Brad, Alexandra, Sueann, Janet, Jim. BS, Ball State U., 1952, MA, 1961; EdD, U. Pitts., 1981. Cert. adminstr. and tchr., reading specialist, Pa. Instr. Mich. State U., East Lansing, 1964-67; instr., coord. U. Minn., Mpls., 1967-71; rsch. assoc. Pitts. Pub. Schs., 1971-80; assoc. prof. California U. Pa., 1988; prof. edn. California U., Pa., 1993—; state grants educator, 1990-95; univ. faculty devel. comm. mem., 1992—; chancellor State Adv. Com., Calif. Univ. rep., 1994—. Contbr. articles to profl. jours. U.S. Office of Edn. title III & IVC grantee; grantee Pa. Vocat. Tech. State, 1990-91, 93, Bibliotherapy Project California Univ. Pa., 1992, Pa. State, 1993, Pa. Campus Compac, 1993. Mem. Am. Assn. Colls. Tchr. Edn., NEA Young Children, Kappa Delta Pi, Phi Delta Kappa.

SOUTHWORTH, LINDA JEAN, artist, critic, educator; b. Milw., May 11, 1951; d. William Dixon and Violet Elsie (Kuehn) S.; m. David Joseph Roger, Nov. 16, 1985 (div. July 1989). BFA, St. John's U., Queens, N.Y., 1974; MFA, Pratt Inst., Bklyn., 1978. Printmaker, still life and portrait painter, photographer self-employed, N.Y.C., 1974—; art critic Resident Publs., N.Y.C., 1993—; prof. art history St. Francis Coll., Bklyn., 1985—; artist-in-residence Our Saviour's Atonement Luth. Ch., N.Y.C., 1993—. Exhibited in solo shows at Galimaufry, Croton-on-Hudson, N.Y., 1977, Kristen Richards Gallery, N.Y.C., 1982, Gallery 84, N.Y.C., 1990, The Bernhardt Collection, Washington, 1991, The Netherland Club, N.Y.C., 1992; group shows include Union St. Graphics, San Francisco, 1974, Nuance Gallery, Tampa, 1987, 88, Soc. Illustrators Ann. Drawing Show, N.Y.C., 1989, 90, Salmagundi Club, N.Y.C., 1991, 92, Henry Howells Gallery, Soho, 1992, 93, Mus. Gallery, N.Y.C., 1994; artist Christmas card/UNICEF, 1992. Mem. English Speaking Union. Home: 106 Cabrini Blvd 5D New York NY 10033

SOUTHWORTH, PHYLLIS ANNETTE, secondary education educator; b. Tulare, Calif., Aug. 30, 1948; d. Floyd Joseph and Anita Novella (Hale) S. BA, Pt. Loma Coll., 1971. Art and English tchr. Antelope Valley H.S., Lancaster, Calif., 1973-75; house mother, tchr. St. Johns Vianny Home for Troubled Girls, Tulsa, 1975-77; tchr. Lancaster (Calif.) Christian Sch., 1978-81; ch. worker Vineyard Christian Fellowship, Lancaster, 1981-84; occupational therapy tech. Antelope Valley Hosp., Lancaster, 1984-87; jr. high tchr. Art and English Tropico Sch., Rosamond, Calif., 1988—; pvt. art tchr. Exhibited at Lancaster Mus. of Art, pvt. gallery shows. Mus. min. Vineyard Christian Fellowship, Lancaster, 1978—, internat. tchr., 1981—. Recipient numerous art show awards Antelope Valley Fair Assn., Lancaster, 1980-90. Mem. Nat. Tchrs. Assn., Calif. Tchrs. Assn., Allied Arts Assn. Republican. Home: 1501 E Ave I #193 Lancaster CA 93535

SOVDE-PENNELL, BARBARA ANN, sonographer; b. McPherson, Kans., Sept. 27, 1955; d. Benton Ellis and Mary Ann (Ball) Sovde; m. Paul Edwin Pennell, June 5, 1982; 1 child, Eric Louis. AA in Radiologic Tech., Hutchinson Community Jr. Coll., 1977; BS in Radiologic Tech., U. Okla., 1993. Registered diagnostic med. sonographer, radiological technol. Radiographer Hertzler Clinic, Halstead, Kans., 1977-78; radiographer Mercy Health Ctr., Okla. City, 1978-81, sonographer, supr. ultrasound dept., 1981-83; mobile sonographer Sun Med. Systems, Okla. City, 1983-84, Diagnostic Radiology, Edmond, Okla., 1984-87; prin., owner, pres. of corp. Ultrasound Unltd., Inc., Edmond, 1987—; part-time clin. specialist ultrasound Circadian Can. Ultrasound Equipment Co., 1991—. Active neighborhood recycling, Edmond, 1990—; mem. Greenpeace. Named Outstanding Leader in S.W. Nat. Allied Health Assn., 1981; recipient Outstanding Alumnus award U. Okla. Coll. Allied Health, 1990. Mem. Soc. Diagnostic Med. Sonographers (state rep. 1981-87, regional dir., bd. dirs. 1987-90), Okla. Sonographers Soc. (pres. 1982-84, steering com. 1984—). Democrat.

SOVIE, MARGARET DOE, nursing administrator, college dean; b. Ogdensburg, N.Y., July 7, 1934; d. William Gordon and Mary Rose (Bruyere) Doe; m. Alfred L. Sovie, May 8, 1954; 1 child, Scot Marc. Student, U. Rochester, 1950-51; diploma in nursing, St. Lawrence State Hosp. Sch. Nursing, Ogdensburg, 1954; postgrad., St. Lawrence U., 1956-60; BS in Nursing summa cum laude, Syracuse U., 1964, MS in Edn., 1968, PhD in Edn., 1972; DSc (hon.), Health Sci. Ctr. SUNY, Syracuse, 1989. Staff nurse, clin. instr. St. Lawrence State Hosp., Ogdensburg, 1954-55, instr. nursing, 1955-62; staff nurse Good Shepherd Hosp., Syracuse, 1962; nursing supr. SUNY Upstate Med. Ctr., Syracuse, 1963-65, insvc. instr., 1965-66, edn. dir. and coord. nursing svc., 1966-71, asst. dean Coll. Health Related Professions, 1972-84, assoc. prof. nursing, 1973-76, dir. continuing edn. in nursing, 1974-76, assoc. dean and dir. div. continuing edn. Coll. Health Related Professions, 1974-76; spl. assignment in pres.'s office SUNY Upstate Med. Ctr. and Syracuse U., 1972-73; assoc. dean for nursing U. Rochester, N.Y., 1976-88, assoc. prof. nursing, 1976-85, prof., 1985-88; assoc. dir. for nursing Strong Meml. Hosp., U. Rochester Med. Ctr., 1976-88; chief nursing officer, assoc. exec. dir. Hosp. U. Pa., Phila., 1988-94, assoc. dean for nursing practice, Jane Delano prof. nursing adminstrn. Sch. Nursing, 1988, bd. dirs., 1989—, assoc. dep. exec. dir., 1994—; sr. fellow Leonard Davis Inst. Health Econs. U. Pa., Phila., 1992—; trustee U. Pa. Health System, Phila., 1993—; nursing coord. and project dir. Cen. N.Y. Regional Med. Program, Syracuse, 1968-71; mem. edn. dept. State Bd. Nursing, Albany, N.Y., 1974-84, chmn., 1981-83, chmn. practice com., 1975-80, mem. joint practice com., 1975-80, vice chmn., 1980-81; mem. adv. com. to clin. nurse scholars program Robert Wood Johnson Found., Princeton, N.J., 1982-88; adj. assoc. prof. Syracuse U. Sch. Nursing, 1973-76; mem. Gov.'s Health Adv. Panel N.Y. State Health Planning Commn., 1976-82, task force on health manpower policy, 1978, informal support networks sect. steering com., 1980; mem. health manpower tng. and utilization task force State N.Y. Commn. on Health Edn. and Illness Prevention, 1979; mem. task force on nursing personnel N.Y. State Health Adv. Council, 1980; mem. adv. panel on nursing services U.S. Pharm. Conv. Inc., Washington, 1985-90; cons. Nat. Ctr. for Services Research and Health Care Tech. Assessment, Rockville, Md., 1987—; mem. nursing standards task force Joint Commn. Accreditation Health Care Orgns., 1988-90; mem. various other adv. coms.; lectr. in field. Mem. editorial bd. Health Care Supr., 1982-87, Nursing Econs., 1983—, Seminars for Nurse Mgrs., 1994—; manuscript rev. panel Nursing Outlook, 1987-91; contbr. articles to profl. jours., chpts. to books. Mem. bd. visitors Sch. Nursing U. Md., Balt., 1984-89; mem. bd. mgrs. Strong Meml. Hosp., Rochester, 1983-88; bd. dirs. Monroe County Assn. for Hearing, Rochester, 1979-82, Vis. Nurse Svc., Rochester and Monroe County, 1978, Southeastern Pa. chpt. ARC, 1991—. Ann. Margaret D. Sovie lectureship inaugurated Strong Meml. Hosp. U. Rochester, 1989; spl. nurse rsch. fellow NIH, 1971-72; grantee various orgns.; recipient Dean's Outstanding Alumni award Coll. of Nursing, Syracuse U., 1994. Fellow Am. Acad. Nursing (program com. 1980-81, task force on hosp. nursing 1981-83, chair expert panel on quality health 1994—); mem. Inst. Medicine (com. design strategy for quality rev. and assurance in Medicare 1988-90), Am. Nurses Assn. (nat. rev. com. for expanded role programs 1975-78, site visitor to programs requesting accreditation 1976-78, cabinet on nursing svcs. 1986-90, cert. bd. nursing adminstrn. 1983-86, Ad Hoc com. on advanced practice 1992—), Am. Orgn. Nurse Execs. (standards task force 1987), N.Y. State Nurses Assn. (med. surg. nursing group, chmn. edn. com. dist. 4 1974-76, chmn. community planning group for nursing dist. 4 1974-76, coun. on regional planning in nu-76, del. to conv. 1978, Nursing Svc. Adminstrn. award 1985), Sigma Theta Tau, Pi Lambda Theta. Republican. Roman Catholic. Office: U Pa Hosp 21 Penn Tower 3400 Spruce St Philadelphia PA 19104

SOVIERO, DIANA BARBARA, soprano; b. Jersey City, Mar. 19, 1946; d. Amerigo and Angelina Catani; student Juilliard Sch. Music, Hunter Coll. Opera Workshop. Appearances with opera cos. including Tulsa Opera, Houston Grand Opera, San Diego Opera, Ottawa (Ont., Can.) Opera, Zurich Opera, Goldovsky Opera Theatre, Lake George Opera, New Orleans Opera, Hamburg (W.Ger.) Opera, Dallas Opera, Chgo. Opera, Rome Opera, Paris Opera, Nice Opera, Avignon Opera, San Francisco Opera, Montreal (Que., Can.) Opera, Toulouse, France, Caracas, Venezuela, Vienna Opera, Parma Opera, Italy, Munich Opera, W.Ger., Edmonton (Alta., Can.) Opera, Winnipeg (Man., Can.) Opera, Calgary (Alta.) Opera, Madrid Opera, Greater Miami Opera, Bastille Opera, Montreal Opera, Covent Garden, Florence Opera, Opera Pacific at Costa Mesa; with Met. Opera, 1986—, now leading soprano; instr. master classes The Faculty, sch. for actors, Los Angeles. Recipient Richard Tucker award. Mem. AFTRA, Am. Guild Musical Artists, SAG. also: care Royal Opera House-Contracts, Convent Gardens, London WC2, England*

SOVINSKI, SANDRA MARIE, forensic scientist; b. Orlando, Fla., Feb. 23, 1963; d. Frank and Sandra Gail (Safrit) Brauns; m. Douglas Bernard Watson, Dec. 30, 1986 (div. Oct. 1988); m. Paul Richard Sovinski, Apr. 30, 1993. BS, U. Ctrl. Fla., 1986. Forensic scientist/DNA analyst Broward Sheriff's Office, Ft. Lauderdale, Fla., 1987-92, Indpls.-Marion County Forensic Svcs., 1993—. Contbr. articles to profl. jours. Mem. ABA (student), Am. Chem. Soc., Am. Acad. Forensic Scis. Office: Indpls Marion Co Forensic 40 S Alabama St Indianapolis IN 46204

SOWA, GINA MARIE, senior computer consultant; b. Klondike, Tex., June 9, 1965; d. Ernest Edward and Marie (Dudley) Smith; m. Graham Gabriel Sowa, Oct. 23, 1993. BBA, U. North Tex., 1987. Sr analyst Frito-Lay,

Plano, Tex., 1988-91; sr. cons. CSC Consulting, Irving, Tex., 1991—. Mem. NAFE. Office: CSC Cons & Systems 20th Flr 3811 Turtle Creek Blvd Dallas TX 75219

SOWDER, KATHLEEN ADAMS, marketing executive; b. Person County, N.C., Feb. 9, 1951; d. George W. and Mary W. (Woody) A.; BS, Radford Coll., 1976; MBA, Va. Poly. Inst., 1978; m. Angelo R. LoMascolo, Apr. 11, 1980 (div.); 1 child, Mary Jennifer. Asst. product mgr. GTE Sylvania, Waltham, Mass., 1978-79, product mgr. video products, 1979-80; comml. mktg. mgr. Am. Dist. Telegraph, N.Y.C., 1980-87; v.p. mktg. ESL, Hingham, Mass., 1987-91; pres. Q.B. Air dba Falcon Holdings, Summit, N.J., 1991—; exec. v.p. Falcon Detection Techs., Inc., Plymouth, Mass., 1991— Mem. Am. Mktg. Assn., Am. Soc. Indsl. Security (past chair standing com. on phys. security). Republican. Home: PO Box 57 Andes NY 13731-0057 Office: Q B Air dba Falcon Holdings PO Box 675 Summit NJ 07902-0675 also: Falcon Detection Techs Inc 488 State Rd Plymouth MA 02360-5153

SOWERS, MARILYN RAE, librarian; b. Gary, Ind., Jan. 5, 1943; d. Terzo Paul and Mary Saveria (DeNicola) Amidei; m. George Maxton Sowers, Aug. 27, 1966; children: George, Joseph, John, Michael. AB in History, Ind. U., 1964, MAT in Social Studies, 1966, MLS, 1970. Tchr. Gary Pub. Schs., 1966, libr., 1969-70; libr. McIntire Pub. Libr., Charlottesville, Va., 1966-69; reference libr. Indpls. Pub. Libr., 1970; asst. libr. Centerville (Ind.) Pub. Libr., 1976-79; interim libr. Ind. U. East, Richmond, Ind., 1978-79; substitute tchr. Richmond (Ind.) Community Schs., 1984-87; media supervisor Union County Sch. Corp., Liberty, Ind., 1987—; bd. dirs. Ea. Ind. Libr. Svcs. Authority, Ind. Cooperative Libr. Svcs. Authority. Bd. dirs., sec. Wayne Twp. Bd., Richmond, 1985—; mem. Gov.'s Select Commn. for Primary and Secondary Edn., Ind., 1982-84; mem. State Student's Assistance Commn. of Ind., 1988-90. Mem. ALA, Am. Assn. Sch. Librs., ASCD, Ind. State Tchrs. Assn., NEA. Office: Union County High Sch 410 Patriot Blvd Liberty IN 47353

SOYK-SARTY, DEBRA ROBIN, naval officer; b. Ft. Campbell, Ky., Feb. 15, 1956; d. Edward Richard and Norma Francis (Rogers) Soyk; m. Stephen Barry Sarty, June 16, 1987 (div. Nov. 1993). AS in med. lab. tech., C.C. of Air Force, USAF, 1981; BS in Med. Tech., Austin Peay State U., 1986. Lab. tech. USAF, 1976-81, U.S. Army, 1982-89; med. tech. St. Vincent's Med. Ctr., Jacksonville, Fla., 1985-87; assoc. chemist Nichol's Rsch. Inst., San Juan Capistrano, Calif., 1988-89; lab. officer USN, San Diego, 1989-92; dept. head lab. USN, Beaufort, S.C., 1992—. Sec. Women Officers Profl. Orgn., San Diego, 1991—. Sgt. USAF, 1976-81, lt. USN, 1989—. Mem. Am. Soc. Clin. Pathologist, Am. Assn. Blood Banks, Med. Svc. Corps (treas. 1992), Soc. of Armed Forces Mil. Lab. Scientists. Republican. Home: 6091 Vaux Rd Burton SC 29902 Office: Naval Hosp 1 Pinckney Blvd Beaufort SC 29902-6148

SOYSTER, MARGARET BLAIR, lawyer; b. Washington, Aug. 5, 1951; d. Peter and Eliza (Shumaker) S. AB magna cum laude, Smith Coll., 1973; JD, U. Va., 1976. Bar: N.Y. 1977, U.S. Dist. Ct. (so. and ea. dists.) N.Y. 1977, U.S. Ct. Appeals (2nd cir.) 1979, U.S. Supreme Ct. 1981, U.S. Ct. Appeals (4th cir.) 1982, U.S. Ct. Appeals (11th cir.) 1987, U.S. Ct. Appeals (7th cir.) 1991, U.S. Ct. Appeals (3d cir.) 1992. Assoc. Rogers & Wells, N.Y.C., 1976-84, ptnr., 1984—. Mem. ABA, Assn. of Bar of City of N.Y., Nat. Assn. Coll. and Univ. Attys., Phi Beta Kappa. Office: Rogers & Wells 200 Park Ave Ste 5200 New York NY 10166-0005

SPACEK, SISSY (MARY ELIZABETH SPACEK), actress; b. Quitman, Tex., Dec. 25, 1949; d. Edwin S. and Virginia S.; m. Jack Fisk, 1974; children: Schuyler Elizabeth, Virginia Madison. Student, Lee Strasberg Theatrical Inst. Motion picture appearances include Prime Cut, 1972, Ginger in the Morning, 1972, Badlands, 1974, Carrie, 1976 (Acad. award nomination for best actress 1976), Three Women, 1977, Welcome to L.A., 1977, Heartbeat, 1980, Coal Miner's Daughter, 1980 (Acad. award for best actress 1980), Raggedy Man, 1981, Missing, 1982 (Acad. award nomination for best actress), The River, 1984 (Acad. award nomination for best actress), Marie, 1985, 'Night Mother, 1986, Crimes of the Heart, 1986 (Acad. award nomination for best actress), Violets Are Blue, 1986, JFK, 1991, The Long Walk Home, 1990, Hard Promises, 1992, Trading Mom, 1994; TV movie appearances include The Girls of Huntington House, 1973, The Migrants, 1973, Katherine, 1975, Verna: USO Girl, 1978, A Private Matter, 1992, A Place for Annie, 1994, The Good Old Boys, 1995; guest host TV show Saturday Night Live, 1977; appeared in episode TV show The Waltons. Named Best Actress for Carrie, Nat. Soc. Film Critics, 1976, Best Supporting Actress, N.Y. Film Critics, 1977. Office: care Creative Artists 9830 Wilshire Blvd Beverly Hills CA 90212-1825*

SPACKS, PATRICIA MEYER, English educator; b. San Francisco, Nov. 17, 1929; d. Norman B. and Lillian (Talcott) Meyer; 1 child, Judith Elizabeth Spacks. BA, Rollins Coll., Winter Park, Fla., 1949, DHL, 1976; MA, Yale U., 1950; PhD, U. Calif., Berkeley, 1955. Instr. English Ind. U., Bloomington, 1954-56; instr. humanities U. Fla., Gainesville, 1958-59; from instr. to prof. Wellesley Coll., Mass., 1959-79; prof. English Yale U., New Haven, 1979-89, chmn. dept., 1985-88; Edgar F. Shannon prof. English U. Va., 1989—, chmn. dept., 1991—. Author: The Poetry of Vision, 1967, The Female Imagination, 1975, Imagining a Self, 1976, The Adolescent Idea, 1982, Gossip, 1985, Desire and Truth, 1990, Boredom: The Literary History of a State of Mind, 1995. Fellow Guggenheim Found., 1969-70, NEH, 1974, Am. Council Learned Socs., 1978-79, Nat. Humanities Ctr., 1982-83, 89. Mem. MLA (2nd v.p. 1992, 1st v.p. 1993, pres. 1994, mem. adv. com. 1976-80, mem. exec. coun. 1986-89), Am. Acad. Arts and Scis., N.E. Am. Soc. 18th Century Studies (2nd v.p. 1979-80), Am. Coun. Learned Socs. (mem. bd. trustees 1992—, v.p. 1994). Home: 1830 Fendall Ave Charlottesville VA 22903-1614 Office: U of Virginia Dept of English Charlottesville VA 22903

SPAHN BADER, ELLEN, artist, educator; b. Apr. 6, 1953. Student, Ecole des Beaux Arts, Aix-en-Provence, France, 1974; BS in Art Edn., SUNY Coll. at Buffalo, 1975; MA in Studio Art, L.I. U., 1993. Cert. art tchr. K-12, N.Y. Comp artist, mech. artist Constance Kovar Ltd., Manhasset, N.Y., 1980; art dir., studio mgr. 4M Pub., N.Y.C., 1980-82; graphic artist, 1985-92; art instr. After Sch. Program, Port Washington, N.Y., 1992-94; substitute art tchr. Port Washington, Locust Valley, Garden City Sch. Dists., 1994—; art tchr. Sousa Elem. Sch., Port Washington, N.Y., 1994—. One woman show at Nat. West Bank, Port Washington, 1993, 94; exhibited in group shows at Heckscher Mus., 1979, Gallery North, Setauket, N.Y., 1976. Chair art com. Manorhaven Sch. PTA, Port Washington, 1992-93, pride in port float, 1992-94, plant sale fundraiser, 1991-93; scenery designer Childrens Play Troupe, Port Washington, 1993. Mem. NOW, Nat. PTA. Home: 11 Linwood Rd N Port Washington NY 11050-1411

SPAIN, JAYNE BAKER, corporate executive, educator; b. San Francisco; d. Lawrence Ian and Marguerite (Buchanan) Baker; student U. Calif. at Berkeley, 1944-47, Music U. Cin., 1947-50; LL.D., Edgecliff Coll., Cin., 1969; Dr. Pub. Service, George Washington U., 1970; LL.D., U. Cin., 1971, Dumbarton Coll., 1972, Springfield (Mass.) Coll., 1973, Gallaudet Coll., Washington, 1973; L.H.D. Bryant Coll., 1972, Russell Sage Coll., Troy, N.Y., 1973, Loyola Coll., Balt., 1975; m. John A. Spain, July 14, 1952; children—Jeffry Alan, Jon Kimberly. Pres., Alvey-Ferguson Co., Cin., 1952-66, pres. Alvey-Ferguson Operations div. Litton Industries, Inc., 1966-70, also dir. parent co., 1970—; vice chmn. CSC, 1971—; sr. v.p. Gulf Oil Corp., Pitts., from 1975; Disting. vis. prof. and exec.-in-residence George Washington U., Washington, 1979—; dir. Beatrice Foods, Chgo., Ohio Nat. Life Ins., Cin. Vice chmn. Pres.'s Com. on Employment Handicapped, 1966—; participant internat. trade fairs U.S. Depts. State, Commerce, Europe, North Africa, 1961-66, mem. trade and investment mission, India, 1965; mem. U.S. com. Internat. Council Social Welfare; mem. Pres.'s Adv. Com. on Productivity; dir. Pvt. Sector Council, Washington, Dean's Adv. com. Coll. of Bus. U. Cin.; mem. Internat. Soc. Rehab. Disabled; mem. adv. com. sheltered workshops U.S. sec. labor; mem. Ohio Gov.'s Commn. on Status of Women; mem. bldg. com. Children's Med. Center, Cin. Bd. dirs., past pres. Convalescent Hosp. Children, Cin., Greater Cin. Hosp. Council, Children's Neuromuscular Diagnostic Center, Cin., Cin. Sci. Center; bd. dirs. President's Commn. on Personnel Interchange; chmn. bd. trustees Fed. Women's Award; mem. dean's adv. council Coll. Bus. Adminstrn. U. Cin.; chmn. Found. of Ams. for the Handicapped; bd. dirs. Recs. for the Blind. Recipient Distinguished Service award for work overseas blind People Com., Washington, 1965; Migel medal Am. Found. Blind, N.Y., 1966; Golden Plate award industry Acad. Achievement, Dallas, 1967; Top Hat award Bus. and Profl. Women's Clubs. Am., N.Y., 1967; named to Cin. Bus. Hall Fame, 1994. Mem. Conveyor Equipment Mfrs. Assn. (sec., treas., dir. 1960-63), Machinery and Allied Products Inst., Am. Mgmt. Assn. (dir., inducted into Cin. Bus. Hall of Fame, 1994) Internat. Platform Assn. Episcopalian. Contbr. articles to profl. jours.

SPAIN, NETTIE EDWARDS (MRS. FRANK E. SPAIN), civic worker; b. Alexandria, La., Oct. 9, 1918; d. John Henry and Sallie Tamson (Donald) Edwards; student Alexandria Bus. Coll., 1936-37, Birmingham-So. Coll., 1958-59, Nat. Tng. Inst., United Community Funds and Councils Am., 1965-66; m. Frank E. Spain, May 18, 1974. Reporter, Alexandria Daily Town Talk, 1942-45; staff writer Birmingham (Ala.) Post, 1945-49; pub. rels. dir. Community Chest, Birmingham, 1949-53; dir. info. services Pa. United Fund, Phila., 1953-55; asst. exec. dir. Ala. Assn. Mental Health, Birmingham, 1956-57; pub. rels. dir. United Appeal, Birmingham, 1958-68, asst. exec. dir., 1968-71; asst. to pres. for devel. U. Ala., Birmingham, 1971-74, acting dir., 1975. Mem. pub. rels. com. Ala. Heart Assn., Birmingham, 1972-75; bd. dirs. Kate Duncan Smith DAR Sch., Grant, Ala., 1981-82; bd. dirs. Children's Aid Soc., 1971-77, 79, v.p., 1976-77; bd. dirs. Jefferson-Shelby Lung Assn., 1972-75, Vol. Bur. Greater Birmingham, 1973-77, Hale County chpt. ARC, Hale County Library; advisor fin. Hale County Library Bd., 1988; adv. com. Jr. League, 1974-75; exec. com. Historic Hale County Preservation Soc.; hon. mem. president's council U. Ala., Birmingham; bd. dirs. Norton Center Continuing Edn., Birmingham-So. Coll., mem. Edward Lee Norton Bd. Advisers for Mgmt. and Profl. Edn., internat. progam com.; charter mem. bd. Birmingham Children's Theater. Recipient 1st Place awards Nat. Photos for Fedn., 1966-67; citation Pa. United Fund, 1955, citation for service Jefferson-Shelby Lung Assn., 1975, citation Ala. Heart Assn., 1974, Vol. Bur. Greater Birmingham, 1977; award of Merit, Ala. Hist. Commn., 1977, Disting. Svc. award, 1987; Rotary Found. Paul Harris fellow; Benjamin Franklin fellow Royal Soc. Arts, London, U.S.A.; citation Veritas Club, Gt. Am. Citizen of Greensboro, Ala., 1987. Mem. Nat. Pub. Rels. Council of Health and Welfare Services (bd. dir. 1967-69), Birmingham Women's Com. of 100, Pub. Rels. Council Ala. (hon. life), Order of Crown in Am., Ala. Hist. Soc., Nat. Soc. Colonial Dames Am., English Speaking Union, Nat. Trust for Historic Preservation, Met. Opera Guild, Guy E. Snavely Soc. (Birmingham-So. Coll.), Colonial Dames Am., DAR, First Families of Va., Burgess for Ala., Birmingham Astron. Soc. (hon.), Children's Aid Foundation (charter mem). Episcopalian. Clubs: Lakeview Country (Greensboro, Ala.), Mountain Brook Country, The Summit (Birmingham), The Club (Birmingham), Northriver Yacht (Tuscaloosa), Mountain Brook Club (Birmingham). Home: Medley PO Box 400 Greensboro AL 36744-0400

SPALDING, MARY BRANCH, psychologist, psychotherapist; b. Roanoke, Va., Oct. 27, 1938; d. Branch and Mary (Hancock) S.; m. John H. Land, June 13, 1964 (div. 1974); m. Hugh C. Welborn, May 25, 1985; 1 child, Catherine. BA in Art History, Vassar Coll., 1964; MA in Psychology in Edn., Columbia U., 1972, MEd in Counseling Psychology, 1974, EdD in Counseling and Applied Human Devel., 1979. Counselor, research asst. Ruth M. Knight Counseling Service, Manhattan Sch. Music, N.Y.C., 1971-76; psychologist Rockland County Community Mental Health Ctr., Pomona, N.Y., 1975—, supr. group psychotherapy crisis ctr., 1992—; pvt. practice psychotherapy N.Y., 1979—; psychotherapist Eating Disorders Treatment Assocs., Rockland County, N.Y., 1985-87. Poetry pub. in various publs. Fellow Am. Orthopsychiat. Assn.; mem. AACD, APA, Acad. Am. Poets, Nat. Mus. Women in Arts, Met. Mus. Art, Rockland Ctr for Arts, Rockland County Psychol Soc., Poetry Soc. Am. Democrat. Office: 20 Squadron Blvd Ste 630 New City NY 10956-5210

SPALT, STELLA MICKEY, medical nurse, nursing educator; b. Houston, Nov. 24, 1943; d. Morris Elwood and Lena (Borzilleri) Mickey; m. Donald Fredrick Spalt, June 13, 1963; children: Gretchen, Derrick, Heidi. ADN, Marymount Coll., 1978; BA in Humanities, St. Louis U., 1981, BSN summa cum laude, 1987; MS in Adminstrn., Lindenwood Coll., 1985. Staff RN, surg. ICU St. Louis U. Hosp., 1978-79; head nurse, ICU Bethesda Gen. Hosp., 1979-80; staff RN, neonatal ICU U.S. Naval Regional Med. Ctr., Okinawa, Japan, 1981-83; head med. nurse Bethesda Gen. Hosp., St. Louis, 1983-84; staff RN, neonatal ICU St. John's Mercy Med. Ctr., St. Louis, 1984-85, coord. mgmt. devel. instr., level II, 1985-89; mgr., mgmt. devel. ARC St. Louis Bi-State Chpt., 1989-91; dir. employee devel./dir. patient care svcs. Deaconess Health System, St. Louis, 1992-93, dir. patient care svcs., 1993—; pres. Tng. 2000, St. Louis, 1994—. Mem. ASTD (membership com. 1989, pres.-elect 1992, pres. 1993—), Am. Soc. Health Care Edn. Tng. Am. Hosp. Assn., Soc. Human Resources Mgmt., Greater St. Louis Soc. Health Educators Trainers (treas. 1985), Delta Lambda Chpt. Sigma Theta Tau. Republican. Episcopalian. Home: 229 E Argonne Dr Saint Louis MO 63122-4309 Office: Tng 2000 229 E Argonne Dr Saint Louis MO 63122-4309

SPANDORFER, MERLE SUE, artist, educator, author; b. Balt., Sept. 4, 1934; d. Simon Louis and Bernice P. (Jacobson) S.; m. Lester M. Spandorfer, June 17, 1956; children: Cathy, John. Student, Syracuse U., 1952-54; BS, U. Md., 1956. Mem. faculty Cheltenham (Pa.) Sch. Fine Arts, 1969—; instr. printmaking Tyler Sch. Art Temple U., Phila., 1980-84; faculty Pratt Graphics Ctr., N.Y.C., 1985-86. One woman shows include Richard Feigen Gallery, N.Y.C., 1970, U. Pa., 1974, Phila. Coll. Textiles and Sci., 1977, Ericson Gallery, N.Y.C., 1978, 79, R.I. Sch. Design, 1980, Syracuse U., 1981, Marian Locks Gallery, Phila., 1973, 78, 82, Temple U., 1984, Tyler Sch. Art, 1985, University City Sci. Ctr., 1987, Gov.'s Residence, 1988, Wenniger Graphics Gallery, Provincetown, Mass., 1989, Mangel Gallery, Phila., 1992, Widener U. Art Mus., 1995; group shows Bklyn. Mus. Art, 1973, San Francisco Mus. Art, 1973, Balt. Mus. Art, 1970, 71, 74, Phila. Mus. Art, 1972, 77, Fundacio Joan Miro, Barcelona, Spain, 1977, Del. Mus. Art, Wilmington, 1978, Carlsberg Glyptotek Mus., Copenhagen, 1980, Moore Coll. Art, Phila., 1982, Tyler Sch. Art, 1983, William Penn Meml. Mus., Harrisburg, Pa., 1984 Ariz. State U., 1985, Tiajin Fine Arts Coll., China, 1986, Beaver Coll., Phila., 1988, The Port of History Mus., Phila., 1987, Sichuan Fine Arts Inst., Chong Qing, People's Republic China, 1988, Glynn Vivian Mus., Swansea, Wales, 1989, Phila. Mus. Art, 1990, Fgn. Mus., Riga, Latvia, 1995; represented in permanent collections Met. Mus. Art, N.Y.C., Whitney Mus. Am. Art, N.Y.C., Mus. Modern Art, N.Y.C., The Israel Mus., Balt. Mus. (gov's prize and purchase award 1970), Phila. Mus. Art (purchase award 1977), Toyoh Bijutsu Gakko, Tokyo, Library of Congress, Temple U.; commd. works represented in U. Pa. Inst. Contemporary Art, 1991; co- author: Making Art Safely, 1993. Recipient award Balt. Mus. Art/Md. Inst. Art, 1971, Govs. prize and Purchase award Balt. Mus. Art, 1970, Outstanding Art Educators award Pa. Art Edn. Assn., 1982, Purchase award Berman Mus., 1995; grantee Pa. Coun. Arts, 1989. Mem. Am. Color Print Soc., Pa. Art Edn. Assn. Jewish. Studio: 307 E Gowen Ave Philadelphia PA 19119-1023

SPANEL, HARRIET ROSA ALBERTSEN, state senator; b. Audubon, Iowa, Jan. 15, 1939; m. Leslie E. Spanel, June 3, 1961; 3 children. BS in Math., Iowa State U., 1961. Rep. Wash. State, 1987-93, senator, 1993—. Home: 901 Liberty St Bellingham WA 98225-5632 Office: PO Box 40440 Olympia WA 98504-0440

SPANGLER, JUDITH DUNSON, association executive; b. Lexington, Ky., Sept. 16, 1953; . Samuel Sanford and Hazel (Cruse) Dunson; m. Nicholas Dane Spangler, Jan. 2, 1982; children: Ian, Eric, Corinne. BS, Brigham Young U., 1975. Social worker Har-Lin Community Ctr., Erie, Pa., 1983-85; caseworker Office of Children and Youth, Erie, 1985-88; supr. Homeless Case Mgmt. Program, Erie, 1988-90; exec. dir. YWCA, Erie, 1990—; mem. Nat. Fuel Consumer Adv. Coun., 1989-93; cons. LML and Assocs., Erie, 1991—; bd. corporators Hamot, 1992—. Bd. dirs. YWCA, 1988-90, Habitat for Humanity, 1989-94, Experience Children's Mus., 1993—;' mem. nominating com. Penn Lakes coun. Girl Scouts U.S.A., 1993—; bd. dirs. Pa. Downtown Ctr., 1994—. Mem. Nat. Assn. YWCA Execs., Coun. Women's Orgns., The Women's Roundtable (bd. dirs. 1992-93), Women Against Racism (founding member), Pa. Coun. YWCAs, Rotary, Delta Sigma Theta. Office: YWCA of Erie 4247 W Ridge Rd Erie PA 16506-1746

SPANGLER, SABRINA LISA, engineering manager; b. Bethpage, N.Y., Oct. 25, 1961; d. Roman Martin and Lea Alice (Whiteleather) S. BSEE, Rutgers U., 1983; MS in Nuclear Engring., U. Mich., 1984. Svc. engr. Becton Dickinson Immunocytometry, Mountain View, Calif., 1985-86; product specialist Picker Internat., Cleve., 1987-91, installation mgr., 1991-92, ngr. nuclear svc. engring., 1992—. Mem. Soc. Nuclear Medicine. Office: Piker Internat 23060 Miles Rd Bedford Heights OH

SPANGLER, STEPHANIE SUE, obstetrician, gynecologist, university official; b. Lebanon, Pa., Nov. 14, 1951; d. Earl J. and Edna G. (Reid) S.; m. Robert G. Shulman, May 11, 1986. BS, Brown U., 1973, MD, 1976. Diplomate Am. Bd. Ob-Gyn. Internship, residency Yale New Haven Hosp., 1976-80, chief resident, 1979-80; pvt. practice, New Haven, 1980-86; chief ob-gyn. Yale U. Health Svcs., New Haven, 1986-89, acting med. dir., 1989-90, dir., 1990—; mem. bd. univ. health Yale U., 1990—, asst. clin. prof. Sch. Medicine, 1983-93, assoc. clin. prof. Sch. Medicine, 1993—; mem. adv. com. office of healthcare access State of Conn., 1994—. Contbr. articles to med. jours. Mem. adv. bd. Commn. on Infant Health, New Haven Found., 1989-91. Recipient Miller-Meehan award dept. ob-gyn. Yale-New Haven Hosp., 1980. Fellow ACOG; mem. APHA, Am. Coll. Phys. Execs., Am. Coll. Health Assn., Am. Women's Med. Assn., Am. Soc. Medicine, Ethics and Law, Conn. Assn. Bd. Obstetricians and Gynecologists, Assn. Conn. HMO's (sec. 1992-93, treas. 1993-94, pres. 1994—), Sigma Xi (hon. assoc. 1973). Office: Yale U Health Svcs 17 Hillhouse Ave New Haven CT 06520

SPANN, LAURA NASON, data processing executive; b. Columbus, Ga., Aug. 5, 1947; d. Albert Dewey and Edith Maureen (Miller) Nason; m. George William Spann, June 10,1967; children: Tanya Lynne, Stephen William. BA in Math., Ga. State Coll., Atlanta, 1969. Programmer, analyst Coastal States Life Insur. Co., Atlanta, 1969-71, Rollins, Inc., Atlanta, 1972-73, Computech. Systems, Inc., Atlanta, 1975-77; private practice systems programming cons. Atlanta, 1977-81; pres., prin. Exec. Data Systems, Inc., Atlanta, 1981—. Troop leader Girl Scouts U.S., Atlanta, 1982-90; den leader Boy Scouts Am., Atlanta, 1987-92. Mem. Alpha Lambda Delta. Office: Exec Data Systems Inc Bldg 27 1640 Powers Ferry Rd Ste 300 Marietta GA 30067

SPANN, WILMA NADENE, principal; b. Austin, Tex., Apr. 24, 1938; d. Frank Jamison and Nadene (Burns) Jamison Plummer; m. James W. Spann II, Aug. 2, 1958; children: James III, Timothy, Terrance, Kemberly, Kelby, Elverta, Peter, Margo. BA, Marquette U., 1974; MS, U. Wis., 1985. Sec. Spandagle Coop., Milw., 1969-89; tchr. adult basic edn. Milw. area Tech. Coll., Milw., 1975-80; tchr. Milw. Pub. Sch. System, 1975-90, adminstrv. intern, 1990-91; asst. prin. Clara Barton Elem. Sch., Milw., 1992-93; asst. prin. in charge Greenfield Montessori Sch., Milw., 1993-94, 1993-94, prin., 1994—; asst. prin. in charge Cooper Elem. Sch., Milw., 1993. Contbr. articles to profl. jours. Dir. vacation bible sch. Tabernacle Community Bapt. Ch., Milw., 1977-80, bd. dirs. Christian edn., 1981-90; v.p. women's aux. Wis. Gen. Bapt. State Conv., 1986&; instr. Wis. State Congress Christian Edn., 1982—, asst. dean Wis. Gen. Bapt. State Congress Christian Edn., 1985; mem. sr. retreat com. Nat. Bapt. Youth Camp. Recipient cert. of Recognition, women's auxiliary Wis. Gen. Bapt. State Conv., 1986, Bd. Edn. Tabernacle Bapt. Ch., 1990. Mem. NAACP, Internat. Assn. Childhood Edn. (sec. 1990-92), Met. Milw. Alliance Black Sch. Educators, Nat. Bapt. Conv. (life), Marquette U. Alumni Assn., Assn. Childhood Edn. Internat. (sec. 1990-92), Ch. Women United (life), Phi Delta Kappa. Democrat. Home: 1906 W Cherry St Milwaukee WI 53205-2046 Office: Greenfield Montessori Sch 1711 S 35th St Milwaukee WI 53215-2004

SPANNINGER, BETH ANNE, lawyer; b. Bucks County, Pa., July 3, 1950; d. Feryl Louis and Nancy Elizabeth (Hendricks) S. AB magna cum laude, Muhlenberg Coll., 1972; MA, MEd, Lehigh U., 1975; JD, Temple U., 1979. Asst. dist. atty. Phila. Dist. Atty.'s Office, 1979-81; assoc. Bolger, Picker, Hankin & Tannenbaum, Phila., 1981-86, ptnr., 1986-88; sr. counsel SmithKline Beecham Corp., Phila., 1988—. Mem. ABA, Pa. Bar Assn., Phila. Bar Assn., Del. Valley Assn. Corp. Counsel, Animal Health Inst. (law com. 1992—), Phi Beta Kappa.

SPARACINO, LORA LEE, otorhinolaryngology nurse; b. Rochester, N.Y., May 3, 1949; d. Charles Peter and Loretta Barbara (Bletzer) S. BSN, D'Youville Coll., 1971; MSN in Pediatrics, U. Rochester, 1978; cert. pediatric nurse practitioner, 1993. RN, N.Y.; pediat. nurse practitioner. Staff nurse U. Rochester Med. Ctr., 1971-85; staff nurse pediatrics U. Rochester (N.Y.) Med. Ctr., 1972-74, staff nurse pediatric ICU, 1974-78; asst. prof. SUNY, Brockport, 1978-84; nurse practitioner Rochester Otolaryngology P.C., 1984—. CPR instr. ARC, Rochester. Mem. ANA. Assn. Oper. Rm. Nurses, Nat. Assn. Pediatric Nurses Assocs. and Practitioners, Soc. Ear, Nose and Throat Advances in Children, Soc. Otorhinolaryngology and Head and Neck Nurses (bd. dirs., various nat. coms., pres. Upstate N.Y. regional chpt.), Sigma Theta Tau. Roman Catholic. Home: 216 Arbordale Ave Rochester NY 14610 Office: Rochester Otolaryngology 1641 East Ave Rochester NY 14610

SPARKES, CHERYL FLOWERS, accountant; b. Texarkana, Ark., July 31, 1956; d. Charles Glendon and Mary Carolyn (Caldwell) Flowers; m. Jay Bedford Sparkes, July 14, 1984. BSBA, U. Ark., 1978. CPA, Tex., CMA. Staff acct. Ernst & Ernst, Dallas, 1978-80; sr. acct. Ernst & Whinney, Dallas, 1980-82, mgr., 1983-84, sr. mgr., 1984-89; sr. mgr. Ernst & Young, Dallas, 1989-94, fin. adv. svcs. regional dir. human resources, 1993—, ptnr., 1994—. Neighborhood capt. Am. Cancer Soc., Dallas, 1990-92; active Dallas Mus. Art, 1985—, Jr. League Dallas, 1990—. Mem. AICPA, Inst. Mgmt. Accts., Tex. Soc. CPAs, Delta Delta Delta. Home: 4624 S Versailles Dallas TX 75209 Office: Ernst & Young # 500 2121 San Jacinto Dallas TX 75201

SPARKMAN, GLENDA KATHLEEN, librarian, educator; b. Rockwood, Tenn., Sept. 2, 1941; d. James Monroe and Nannie Mae (Ledford) Lawson; m. Clifford Gregory Anderson Jr., June 7, 1966 (dec. 1985); m. Mickey Max Sparkman, Jan. 1, 1987. BA, David Lipscomb U., Nashville, 1963; MLS, George Peabody Coll., 1965. Music librarian David Lipscomb U., Nashville, 1964-67; ref. librarian Ft. Lauderdale (Fla.) Pub. Libr., 1967-68; sch. librarian Phyllis Wheatley Sch., Childersburg, Ala., 1968-69; asst. librarian Harcum Jr. Coll., Bryn Mawr, Pa., 1969-70; head of processing ctr. and cataloger Lower Merion Libr. Assn., Bryn Mawr, Pa., 1970-80; ref. librarian Bala Cynwyd Libr., 1981-82; cataloger, acquisitions librarian Barry U., Miami Shores, Fla., 1982-83, head of tech. svcs., 1983-86; head catalog librarian, asst. prof. Baylor U., Waco, Tex., 1986—. Reviewer books for Libr. Jour., 1989—. Mem. Miami Shores Fine Arts Commn., 1984-86, Historic Waco Found., 1986—. Mem. ALA, Assn. of Coll. and Rsch. Librs., Assn. for Libr. Collections and Tech. Svcs., Tex. Libr. Assn. (Coll. and Univ. Librs. div.), AAUP, AAUW.

SPARKMAN, MARY M., medical, surgical, pediatrics and rehabilitation nurse; b. Ft. Leavenworth, Kans., Jan. 8, 1949; d. Ancil Woodrow and Margaret Louise (Conners) Hopper; m. Paul Aus Sparkman, Oct. 5, 1989; children: Michelle Marie Bingham, Andrea Marlene Bingham. Student, Cameron U., Lawton, Okla., 1980-82; BSN with distinction, U. Okla., 1984. Cert. in chemotherapy, fetal monitoring, arterial blood gases, coronary care, CPR instr. Mem. crisis intervention team Gt. Plains Hosp., Lawton; charge nurse spinal cord unit O'Donoghue Rehab. Inst., Oklahoma City; clin. nurse Lawton Indian Hosp., USPHS; therapy coord. Infusion Svcs., Lawton, Okla.; clin. nurse, charge nurse Reynold's Army Community Hosp., Ft. Sill, Okla. With U.S. Army, 1970-73. Mem. Nat. League Nursing, Okla. Nurses Assn., Golden Key, Phi Kappa Phi. Office: PO Box 2094 Lawton OK 73502-2094

SPARKS, MEREDITH PLEASANT (MRS. WILLIAM J. SPARKS), lawyer; b. Palestine, Ill.; d. John L. and Laura (Bicknell) Pleasant; A.B. with distinction, Ind. U., 1927, A.M., 1928; Ph.D., U. Ill., 1936; J.D., Rutgers U., 1958; m. William J. Sparks, Dec. 31, 1930 (dec.); children—Ruth Sparks Foster, Katherine Sparks Crowl, Charles, John. Tchr. chemistry Rochester (Ind.) High Sch., 1928-29; chemist DuPont Co., Niagara Falls, N.Y., 1929-34, Northam Warren Co., N.Y.C., 1939; chem. patent agt. Am. Cyanamid Co., Bound Brook N.J., 1941-46; bars: Fla. 1958, U.S. Ct. Appeals (fed. cir.), U.S. Dist. Ct. (so. dist.) Fla., U.S. Supreme Ct.; patent agt., 1946-58; patent atty., 1958—; pres. Sparks Innovators, Inc., 1979-84. Recipient Disting. Alumni award Coll. Arts & Scis. Ind. U., 1987. Mem. AAUW (Phoenix award Miami chpt. 1990), ABA, Assn. Ind. U. Chemists (pres. 1950-51), Internat. Bar Assn., Fla. Bar Assn., Coral Gables Bar Assn., Am. Patent Law Assn., N.J. Patent Law Assn., South Fla. Patent Law Assn., Internat. Patent and Trademark Assn., Am. Chem. Soc., Nat. Assn. Women Lawyers (pres. 1981-82), U. Ill. Pres. Council (life, homecoming honoree 1984), Phi Beta Kappa, Sigma Xi, Kappa Delta. Club: Zonta, Riviera Country (Coral Gables). Contbr. articles to profl. jours. Patentee in field. Home: 5129 Granada Blvd Miami FL 33146-2028

SPARLING, MARY LEE, biology educator; b. Ft. Wayne, Ind., May 20, 1934; d. George Hewson and Velmah Evelyn (McClain) S.; m. Albert Alcide Barber, Sept. 1, 1956 (div. Jan. 1975); children: Bonnie Lee Barber, Bradley Paul Barber. BS, U. Miami, Coral Gables, Fla., 1955; MA, Duke U., 1958; PhD, UCLA, 1962. Lectr. UCLA, 1962-63; asst. prof. Calif. State U., Northridge, 1966-72, assoc. prof., 1972-76, prof., 1976—. Contbr. articles to profl. jours. NSF grantee Calif. State U., Northridge, 1971-72, 81-83, 89, NIH grantee Calif. State U., Northridge, 1987-89. Mem. AAUP (pres. 1981-82), Am. Soc. Cell Biology, Soc. for Devel. Biology, Am. Soc. Zoologists, Sigma Xi (bd. dirs. Research Triangle, N.C. 1974-91). Home: 8518 White Oak Ave Northridge CA 91325-3940 Office: Calif State U Biology Dept Northridge CA 91330

SPARR, MARGARET PAULINE, federal agency administrator; b. Binghamton, N.Y., Dec. 23, 1953; d. Henry John and Margaret Ann (Saring) S.; m. Gary Friedman, Dec. 27, 1975 (div. Nov. 1982); m. Steven Michael Fall, Sept. 18, 1992. BA in Comm. Disorders, SUNY, Buffalo, 1975; MS in Edn., State U. Coll., Buffalo, 1978; MPA in Intergovtl. Mgmt., U. Southern Calif., 1982. Cert. tchr. spl. edn., elem. edn., N.Y.; cert. tchr. edn. for the mentally retarded, Mo. Tchr. specialist The Coastal Ctr., Charleston, S.C., 1975-76, coord. individual treatment, 1975-76; unit dir. St. Louis Devel. Disabilities Treatment Ctr., 1978-80, quality assurance officer, 1981-82, 85-86; coord. Medicaid svcs. Divsn. Mental Retardation, Dept. Mental Health, Jefferson City, Mo., 1985-86; sr. program analyst office survey & cert. health stas. Health Care Financing Adminstrn., U.S. Dept. Health Human Svcs., Balt., 1986-91, chief speciality long term care svc. br., 1991—; nat. surveyor Accreditation Coun. Svcs. for People with Devel. Disabilities, Washington, 1982-85; policy analyst The Pre.'s Com. on Mental Retardation, Washington, 1980-81; cons. and speaker in field. Bd. dirs. Coun. Podiatric Med. Edn., Bethesda, Md., 1992—. Mem. Am. Assn. Mental Deficiency, Assn. for Persons with Severe Handicaps. Independent. Office: DHHS Health Care Fin Adminstrn 6300 Security Blvd Baltimore MD 21207

SPARTZ, ALICE ANNE LENORE, retail executive; b. N.Y.C., May 14, 1925; d. John Francis and Alice Philomena (Murray) Rattenbury; m. George Eugene Spartz, Oct. 29, 1949; children: Mary Elizabeth, James, Barbara, Anne, Thomas, William, Michael, John, Matthew, Clare, Robert, Richard. Student, Wright Coll., 1945-47, No. Ill. U., 1950; AA, Triton Coll., 1987. Svc. rep. Ill. Bell Tel., Chgo., 1945-46; stewardess United Airlines, Denver, 1947-49; mgr. Family Life League, Oak Park, Ill., 1987—; bd. dirs. Family Life League, River Forest, Ill., Ill. Pro-Life Coalition, Chgo. Bd. dirs. Cicero (Ill.) Community Coun., 1967-69; mem. Park Dist. Com., Oak Park, 1973-74; active Ill. Right to Life Com., Chgo., 1971—, Com. Pro-Life Cath., Chgo., 1992—; vol. canteen worker ARC, Chgo., 1942-45. Mem. St. Edmunds Womens Club. Democrat. Roman Catholic. Office: Family Life League 1039 South Blvd Oak Park IL 60302

SPATTA, CAROLYN DAVIS, university administrator; b. Gauhati, Assam, India, Jan. 20, 1935; d. Alfred Charles and Lola Mildred (Anderson) Davis; m. John Robert Spatta, June 2, 1957 (div. Feb. 1964); children: Robert Alan, Jennifer Lynn Spatta-Harris; m. S. Peter Karlow, July 25, 1981. AB, U. Calif., Berkeley, 1964; MA, U. Mich., 1968, PhD, 1974. Rsch. asst. U. Calif., Berkeley, 1963-65; instr. Schoolcraft Coll., Livonia, Mich., 1968-74; corp. sec. Oberlin (Ohio) Coll., 1974-78; pres. Damavand Coll., Tehran, Iran, 1978-79; cons. pvt. practice, Washington, 1979-80; v.p., adminstr. E. Mich. U., Ypsilanti, Mich., 1980-81; Dir. Inst. grants programs, and adv. svc. Assn. Am. Colls., Washington, 1982-84; v.p., adminstrn. and bus. affairs Calif. State U., Hayward, 1984-92, prof. geography and eviron. studies, 1992—; vis. lectr. E. Mich. U., Ypsilanti, 1969, 1970; mem. accreditation team Western Assn. Schs. Colls. Contbr. articles to profl. jours. Bd. dirs. Wellness, Inc.; mem. Trinity Parish, Menlo Pk., Calif. (pers., bldg. coms.), U. Mich. Alumni Assn., St. John's Episc. Ch. (pastoral care commn.), Chevy Chase, Md., Oberlin Open Space Com., Tenaya Guild, John Muir Hosp., Walnut Creek, Calif. (pres.), steering com. Ann Arbor Citizens for Good Schs.; trustee Pacific Sch. of Religion, 1992—. Recipient fellowship Nat. Defense Foreign Lang., 1966-68; Fulbright scholar, Malaysia, 1994—. Mem. Am. Assn. Higher Edn., Asian Studies on Pacific Coast, Assn. Asian Studies, Assn. Am. Geographers, Assn. Pacific Coast Geographers. Office: Calif State U Hayward CA 94542

SPEAR, BARBARA L., state legislator; b. Alton, N.H., June 3, 1926; Widow; 4 children. BA, U. N.H., 1948. Ret. tchr. N.H.; mem. N.H. Ho. Reps., 1992—, mem. buget com., parks and recreation com., mem. econ. devel. com., ways and means com., mem. pub. protection com., vets. affairs com. Mem. Womens Club. Republican. Baptist. Office: NH House of Reps State Capitol Concord NH 03301*

SPEAR, KATHLEEN KELLY, lawyer; b. Cinco Bayou, Fla., June 4, 1949; d. John Francis and Alma (Cancian) Kelly; m. Brian Blackburn Spear, June 17, 1972; children: Matthew, Olivia. AB magna cum laude, Smith Coll., 1971; MA, Brown U., 1973; JD cum laude, Northwestern U., 1979. Bar: Ill. 1979, U.S. Ct. Appeals (7th cir.) 1979, U.S. Dist. Ct. (no. dist.) Ill. 1979, U.S. Ct. Appeals (7th cir.) 1980, U.S. Ct. Appeals (8th cir.) 1982, U.S. Ct. Appeals (10th cir.) 1983. Assoc. Kirkland & Ellis, Chgo., 1979-84; antitrust and litigation counsel Kraft Inc., Glenview, Ill., 1984-85; sr. counsel bus. devel. and venture Kraft, Inc., Glenview, Ill., 1985-88, group counsel frozen foods, 1988-92, v.p., dep. gen. counsel, 1992—. Precinct capt. New Trier Dem. Orgn., Wilmette, Ill., 1980-. Mem. ABA, Ill. Bar Assn., Chgo. Bar Assn., Chgo. Council Lawyers, North Shore Smith Club. Roman Catholic. Office: Kraft Gen Foods Inc 3 Lakes Dr Northfield IL 60093*

SPEAR, LAURINDA HOPE, architect. BFA, Brown U., 1972; MArch, Columbia U., 1975. Registered architect, Fla., N.Y., Colo.; cert. Nat. Coun. Archtl. Registration. Founding prin. Arquitectonica, Coral Gables, Fla.; mem. faculty U. Miami; lectr. in field. Prin. works include Pink Ho., Miami, Fla., 1978, The Palace, Miami, 1982 (Honor award Miami chpt. AIA 1982), Overseas Tower (Honor award Fla. chpt. AIA 1982, Honor award Miami chpt. 1982), The Atlantis, Miami, 1982 (Miami chpt. AIA award 1983), The Sq. at Key Biscayne (Honor award Miami chpt. AIA 1982), The Imperial, Miami, 1983, Casa los Andes (Record Hos. award Archtl. Record 1986), North Dade Justice Ctr., Miami, 1987 (Honor award Miami chpt. AIA 1989), Rio, Atlanta, 1988 (Honor award Miami chpt. AIA 1989), Banco de Credito del Peru, Lima, 1988 (Honor award Miami chpt. AIA 1989), The Ctr. Innovative Tech., Herndon, Va., 1988 (Honor award Va. chpt. AIA 1989, Honor award Miami chpt. 1990, Merit award Fairfax, Va., County Exceptional Design Awards Program 1990), Sawgrass Mills (Merit award Miami chpt. AIA 1990, Honor award Fla. chpt. 1991), Miracle Ctr. (Honor award Miami chpt. AIA 1989), Internat. Swimming Hall of Fame, Ft. Lauderdale, Fla., 1991, Banque de Luxembourg, 1993, Disney All-Star Resorts, Orlando, Fla., 1994, Foster City (Calif.) Libr., 1994, U.S. Embassy, Lima, 1994, USCG Family Housing, Bayamon, P.R., 1994, Altamira Ctr., Caracas, Venezuela, 1994. Mem. beaux arts support group Lowe Art Mus., Miami; bd. dirs. Miami Youth Mus. Recipient Design Awards citation Progressive Architecture, 1975, 80, Rome Prize in Architecture, 1978, Award of Excellence, Atlanta Urban Design Commn., 1989. Fellow AIA. Office: Arquitectonica 426 Jefferson Ave Miami Beach FL 33139

SPEARMAN, MAXIE ANN, financial analyst, administrator; b. Piedmont, S.C., Sept. 14, 1942; d. J. Mac and Margaret Cecille (Johnson) S. BS, U. S.C., 1965; postgrad., Ga. State U., 1985; student, U. Ga. Acct. Shell Oil Co., Atlanta, 1965-66; internal auditor Sears, Roebuck & Co., Atlanta, 1966-67; acct. Econ. Opportunity Atlanta, Atlanta, 1967-68; acct. City of Atlanta, 1968-78, fin. analyst, 1978-89, sr. fin. analyst planner, 1989—; investment cons., Atlanta, Conyers, Ga., 1980—. Mem. Rep. Presdl. Task Force, 1985—, U.S. Senatorial Club, Rep. Nat. Com., 1988—, Ga. Rep. Party, 1990—, Atlanta Safety Com., 1985—, Mayor's Spl. Events Task Force, 1990—; charter founder Ronald Reagan Rep. Ctr., 1988; del.-at-large Rep. Platform Planning Com., 1992, 94. Recipient safety award Atlanta City Govt., 1990, Presdl. Commn. Exec. Com. of Republican Party award, 1992. Mem. NAFE, Am. Mgmt. Assn., Ga. Assn. Med. Victims, Inc. (sec., treas. 1985—). Methodist. Home: 1280 Vineyard Dr SE Conyers GA 30208-2466 Office: 55 Trinity Ave SW Ste 1450 Atlanta GA 30303-3531

SPEARMAN, MOLLY M., state legislator. Tchr. S.C.; mem. S.C. Ho. Reps., 1993—. Democrat. Office: SC House of Reps State House Columbia SC 29211*

SPEARS, JAE, state legislator; b. Latonia, Ky.; d. James and Sylvia (Fox) Marshall; m. Lawrence E. Spears; children: Katherine Spears Cooper, Marsha Spears-Duncan, Lawrence M., James W. Student, U. Ky. Reporter Cin. Post, Cin. Enquirer newspapers; research Stas. WLW-WSAI, Cin.; tchr. Jiya Gakuen Sch., Japan; lectr. U.S. Mil. installations East Anglia, Eng.; del. State of W.Va., Charleston, 1974-80, former state senator, 1980-1993; mem. adv. bd. W.Va. Women's Commn., Charleston, 1976—; mem. state visitors com. W.Va. Extension and Continuing Edn., Morgantown, 1977-91, W.Va. U. Sch. of Medicine, 1992—. Chmn. advisory bd. Sta. WNPB, 1992—, congressional liaison Am. Pub. TV Stas. and WNPB-TV, 1992—; mem. coun. W.Va. Autism Task Force, Huntington, 1981—; mem. W.Va. exec. bd. Literacy Vols. Am., 1986-90, 94—, pres. 1990-92; mem. Gov.'s State Literacy Coun., 1991—; bd. dirs. Found. Ind. Colls. W.Va., 1986—; mem. regional adv.com. W.Va. Gov.'s Task Force for Children, Youth and Family, 1989; mem. USS W.Va. Commn., 1989; mem. exec. com. W.Va. Employer Support Group for Guard and Res., 1989, mem. steering com., 1990—. Recipient Susan B. Anthony award NOW, 1982, nat. award Mil. Order Purple Heart, 1984, Edn. award Profl. Educators Assn. W.Va., 1986, Ann. award W.Va. Assn. Ret. Sch. Employees, 1985, Meritorious Service award W.Va. State Vets. Commn., 1984, Vets. Employment and Tng. Service award U.S. Dept. Labor, 1984, award W.Va. Vets. Council, 1984; named Admiral in N.C. Navy, Gov. of N.C., 1982, Hon. Brigadier Gen. W.Va. N.G., 1984. Mem. Bus. and Profl. Women (Woman of Yr. award 1978), Nat. League Am. Pen Women (Pen Woman of Yr. 1984), Nat. Order Women Legislators, DAR, VFW (aux.), Am. Legion (aux.), Delta Kappa Gamma, Alpha Xi Delta. Democrat. Home and Office: PO Box 2088 Elkins WV 26241-2088

SPEARS, MARIAN CADDY, dietetics and institutional management educator; b. East Liverpool, Ohio, Jan. 12, 1921; d. Frederick Louis and Marie (Jerman) Caddy; m. Sholto M. Spears, May 29, 1959. BS, Case Western Res. U., 1942, MS, 1947; PhD, U. Mo., 1971. Chief dietitian Bellefaire Children's Home, Cleve., 1942-53; head dietitian Drs. Hosp., Cleve., 1953-57; assoc. dir. dietetics Barnes Hosp., St. Louis, 1957-59; asst. prof. U. Ark., Fayetteville, 1959-68; assoc. prof. U. Mo., Columbia, 1971-75; prof., head dept. hotel, restaurant, instn. mgmt. and dietetics Kans. State U., Manhattan, 1975-89; cons. dietitian small hosps. and nursing homes; cons. dietetic edn. Author: Foodservice Organizations Textbook, 3d edit., 1995; contbr. articles to profl. jours. Mem. Am. Dietetic Assn. (Copher award 1989), Am. Sch. Foodsvc. Assn., Food Systems Mgmt. Edn. Coun., Soc. Advancement of Foodsvc. Rsch., Nat. Restaurant Assn., Coun. Hotel, Restaurant, Inst. Mgmt. Edn., Manhattan C. of C., Sigma Xi, Gamma Sigma Delta, Omicron Nu, Phi Kappa Phi. Home: 1423 Beechwood Ter Manhattan KS 66502-7435 Office: Kans State U 105 Justin Hall Manhattan KS 66506

SPECCHIO, LISA ANNA, lawyer; b. Reno, May 31, 1963; d. Michael Ronald Specchio and Kathleen Christina (Baldwin) Duncan. BA, U. Nev., 1985; JD, U. Pacific, 1988. Bar: Calif. 1988, U.S. Ct. Appeals (9th cir.) 1989, U.S. Dist. Ct. (ctrl. dist.) Calif. 1989. Assoc. Barton Klugman & Oetting, L.A., 1988-89, Harry Scolinos Law Firm, Pasadena, Calif., 1989-90, Hampton & Wilson, North Hollywood, Calif., 1991-92, Bower & Weiner, Van Nuys, Calif., 1992—. Roman Catholic. Home: 514 Hill Dr Glendale CA 91206-2839 Office: Bower & Weiner 16600 Sherman Way Ste 200 Van Nuys CA 91406-3733

SPECHT, ALICE WILSON, library director; b. Caracus, Venezuela, Apr. 3, 1948; (parents Am. citizens); d. Ned and Helen (Lockwood) Wilson; m. Joe W. Specht, Dec. 30, 1972; 1 child, Mary Helen. BA, U. Pacific, 1969; MLS, Emory U., 1970; MBA, Hardin-Simmons U., 1983. Libr. social scis. North Tex. State U., Denton, 1971-73; reference libr. Lubbock (Tex.) City and County Libr., 1974-75; system coord. Big Country Libr. System, Abilene, Tex., 1975-79; assoc. dir. Hardin-Simmons U., Abilene, 1981-88, dir. univ. librs., 1988—. Author bibliog. instrn. aids, 1981-90; editor; The College Man, For Pilots Eyes Only. Recipient Boss of Yr., Am. Bus. Women's Assn., 1994. Mem. ALA, Tex. Libr. Assn. (chair com. 1978-84, sec.-treas. coll. and univ. librs. divsn. 1993-94, legis. com. 1994—), Abilene Libr. Consortium (chair adminstrv. coun. 1990, 93, coord. nat. conf. 1991, 93), Rotary (chair com. 1989-90). Home: 918 Grand Ave Abilene TX 79605-3233 Office: Hardin-Simmons U 2200 Hickory PO Box 1185 Abilene TX 79698-0001

SPECK, HILDA, retired social services administrator; b. Stalybridge, Cheshire, Eng., Mar. 2, 1916; came to U.S., 1923; d. John Robert and Rose Ethel (Tymns) Smith; m. Willmot Hilton Speck, Sept. 4, 1937 (dec. Jan 1968); foster children: Barbara Ann Beranek Renfrow, Winifred June Beranek Aguilar. Student, Community Coll., Flint, Mich. Lic. social worker, Mich. Founder of Social Svc. Dept. and dir. social svcs. The Salvation Army, Flint, 1945-86; mem. establishing com. 4C Child Care Agy.; life mem. Salvation Army Adv. Bd., Flint, Mich. Active founding safe house for domestic violence victims, Flint, 1976-80; mem. convalescent home com. Ch. Women United; adminstr. clothing distbn. Flint OK; dir. Salvation Army Disaster Rehab. Program; mem. original planning com. Planned Parenthood Orgn.; mem. aux. McLaren Regional Med. Ctr.; mem. Salvation Army, Flint, League of Mercy, Ch. Salvation Army, Centennial Planning Com., Flint; mem. Gensea County Civil Defense. Recipient Hands of Mercy award The Salvation Army, 1967, Centennial Youth award The Salvation Army, 1965, 20 Yr. Svc. award Big. Bros. of Genesee County, award for exceptional svc. The Salvation Army, 1993; named Women of Week local radio sta., 1957. Mem. Coun. Social Agys., Genesee County Commn. on Aging (v.p. 1971—), GLS Counties Health Planning Coun. Bd., Genesee County Emergency Task Force, Zonta. Salvation Army. Home: 1041 Leisure Dr Flint MI 48507

SPECKMAN, JANE ROUDEBUSH, educator; b. Topeka, Nov. 6, 1935; d. Edgar Alton and Eleanor Johanna (Swanson) Roudebush; m. H. Gerald Speckman, May 2, 1964; children: Susan, Stacey. BA in Elem. Edn., U. Colo., 1957. Tchr. Henry Ford Elem. Sch., Redwood City, Calif., 1957-58, Doull Elem. Sch., Denver, 1958-67; substitute tchr. Douglas County, Colo., 1986—. Mem. AAUW (hospitality 1993-94), U. Colo. Alumni, Pi Beta Phi. Home: 19929 S Briarwood Ln Parker CO 80134-3831

SPECKMANN, GAIL ELIZABETH, artist; b. Ft. Dodge, Iowa, Sept. 29, 1951; d. Stanley Charles and Joanne Pearl (Mol) Johnson; m. Richard Thomas Speckmann, Aug. 31, 1974; children: Katherine Linnea, Benjamin Ryan. BA in Fine Arts, Gustavus Adolphus Coll., 1973. With display dept. Wickes Furniture, Mpls., 1973; dept. mgr., asst. buyer Donaldson's Dept. Store, Mpls., 1973-74; shop mgr. European Flower Markets, West St. Paul, Minn., 1974-76, Bachman's Inc., Mpls., 1976-80; asst. store mgr. Bachman's Inc., St. Paul, 1980; watercolor artist St. Paul, 1981-91, Mpls., 1991—; artist Graphique de France, Boston, 1990—. Exhibited in shows at Dakota Ctr. for the Arts, St. Paul, 1983, 86, Inver Hills (Minn.) C.C., 1984, Bloomington (Minn.) Art Ctr., 1989, J. Michaels Galleries, Edina, Minn., 1991, Vern Carver Gallery, Mpls., 1993, others; represented in collections at Midwest Pension & Profit Sharing, Inc., Mpls., Gustavus Adolphus Coll., St. Peter, Minn., IRS, St. Paul, Marquette Bank System, Mpls., Comml. State Bank, St. Paul, numerous others. Mem. City of Maplewood (Minn.) Arts Task Force, 1987. Recipient Grumbacher award Dakota Ctr. for Arts, 1989. Mem. Am. Watercolor Soc. (127th internat. exhbn. 1994), Watercolor West (2d pl. award 1991, Brand Libr. award 1993, juried assoc. 1991—), Minn. Artists' Assn. (Best of Show award 1992, 93), Twin Cities Watercolor Soc. (program chairperson 1994—), Northstar Watercolor Soc. (bd. dirs. 1985-91, program chair 1989-91, Recognition of Svc. award 1991). Democrat. Lutheran.

SPECTOR, ELEANOR RUTH, government executive; b. N.Y.C., Dec. 2, 1943; d. Sidney and Helen (Kirschenbaum) Lebost; m. Mel Alan Spector, Dec. 10, 1966; children: Nancy, Kenneth. BA, Barnard Coll., 1964; postgrad. sch. pub. adminstrn., George Washington U., 1965-67; postgrad sch. edn., Nazareth Coll., 1974. Indsl. investigator N.Y. State Dept. Labor, White Plains, 1964-65; mgmt. intern Navy Dept., Washington, 1965, contract negotiator, 1965-68, contract specialist, 1975-78, contracting officer/br. head, 1978-82, dir. div. cost estimating, 1982-84; dep. asst. sec. def. for procurement Washington, 1984-91; dir. Def. Procurement, Washington, 1991—; advisor Nat. Contract Mgmt. Assn., 1984—. Recipient Def. Meritorious Civilian Svc. medal, 1986, 93, Meritorious Svc. Presdl. award, 1989, 94, Disting. Civilian Svc. Presdl. award, 1990, Def. Disting. Civilian Svc. medal, 1991. Office: Office Under Sec Defense Acqusition & Tech 3060 Def Pentagon Rm 3E144 Washington DC 30301-3060

SPECTOR, JOHANNA LICHTENBERG, ethnomusicologist, former educator; b. Libau, Latvia; came to U.S., 1947, naturalized, 1954; d. Jacob C. and Anna (Meyer) Lichtenberg; m. Robert Spector, Nov. 20, 1939 (dec. Dec. 1941). DHS, Hebrew Union Coll., 1950; MA, Columbia U., 1960. Rsch. fellow Hebrew U., Jerusalem, 1951-53; faculty Jewish Theol. Sem. Am., N.Y.C., 1954—, dir., founder dept. ethnomusicology, 1962-85, assoc. prof. musicology, 1966-70, Sem. prof., 1970-85, prof. emeritus, 1985—. Author: Ghetto-und Kzlieder, 1947, Samaritan Chant, 1965, Musical Tradition and Innovation in Central Asia, 1966, Bridal Songs from Sana Yemen, 1960; documentary film The Samaritans, 1971, Chicago International, 1973, Middle Eastern Music, 1973, About the Jews of India: Cochin, 1976 (Cine Golden Eagle 1979), The Shanwar Telis or Bene Israel of India, 1978 (Cine Golden Eagle 1979), About the Jews of Yemen, A Vanishing Culture, 1986 (Cine Golden Eagle 1986, Blue Ribbon, Am. Film Festival 1986), 2000 Years of Freedom and Honor: The Cochin Jews of India, 1992, Margaret Mead, 1992, Columbus International, 1993; religious and folk recs. number over 10, 000; contbr. articles to encys., various jours.; editorial bd. Asian Music. Fellow Am. Anthrop. Assn.; mem. Am. Ethnol. Soc., Am. Musicol. Soc., Internat. Folks Music Coun., World Assn. Jewish Studies, Yivo, Asian Mus. Soc. (v.p. 1964—, pres. 1974-78), Soc. Ethnomusicology (sec.-treas. N.Y.C. chpt. 1960-64). Home: 400 W 119th St New York NY 10027-7125

SPECTOR, ROSE, state supreme court justice. BA, Columbia U.; JD, St. Mary's Sch. Law, 1965. Judge County Ct. at Law 5, 1974-80, 131st Dist. Ct., 1980-92; justice Tex. Supreme Ct., 1993—. Address: PO Box 12248 Capitol Sta Austin TX 78711 Office: Supreme Ct Bldg Austin TX 78701*

SPEDDING, MICHELLE STEWART, information systems specialist; b. Rockford, Ill., Dec. 1, 1961; d. Chester Lee and Joyce Ann (Schmidt) Stewart; m. Ben S. Spedding, Mar. 6, 1994. BA, Ind. U., 1983; MA, Trenton State Coll., 1991. Sr. media buyer Winner Comm., N.Y.C., 1984-85, Ellentuck & Springer, Princeton, N.J., 1985-86; media mgr. Peterson's Guides, Princeton, 1986-90; v.p. mgmt. info. systems Hibbert Group, Trenton, N.J., 1990—, mem. mgmt. staff, 1993—. Bd. dirs. Nat. Heart Assn., Princeton, 1992. Mem. NAFE, Soc. Info. Mgmt. Office: Hibbert Group 400 Pennington Ave Trenton NJ 08618-3105

SPEED, BILLIE CHENEY (MRS. THOMAS S. SPEED), retired editor, journalist; b. Birmingham, Ala., Feb. 21, 1927; d. John J. and Ruby (Petty) Cheney; m. Thomas S. Speed, July 7, 1968; children: Kathy Lovell Windham, Donna Lovell Adams, Melanie Lovell Wright. Grad., W.Ga. Coll. Reporter, sports writer Birmingham News, 1945; sports writer, gen. assignment reporter, ch. editor Atlanta Jour., 1947-53, with promotion dept., 1955-57, religion editor, 1965-89; feature editor Coach and Athlete Mag., 1958, So. Outdoors, 1958. Recipient Sharp Tack award Cumberland dist. Seventh Day Adventists; Spl. Service award Christian Council of Metro Atlanta, 1974, award for outstanding personal ministry, 1986, personal service award, 1986; Arthur West award for religious feature writing United Meth. Ch., 1977; Alumni Achievement award West Ga. Coll., 1985; Trustee award Protestant Radio & TV Ctr., 1986; Faith & Freedom award Religious Heritage of Am., 1986. Fellow Religious Pub. Relations Council; mem. Nat. Religion Newswriters Assn., Nat. Fedn. Press Women, Theta Sigma Chi. Methodist. Home: 559 Rays Rd Stone Mountain GA 30083-3142

SPEER, MARGARET BAILEY, retired educator, volunteer; b. Englewood, N.J., Nov. 20, 1900; d. Robert Elliott and Emma Doll (Bailey) S. AB, Bryn Mawr Coll., 1922; MA, Columbia U., 1931. Instr. English Sweet Briar (Va.) Coll., 1923-24; instr. then prof. dept of western langs. Yenching (China) U., 1926-41, dean Women's Coll., 1934-41; headmistress The Shipley Sch., Bryn Mawr, Pa., 1944-65. Bd. dirs. YWCA, Phila., 1964-70, Springside Sch., Phila., 1966-70, Buck Lane Day Care Ctr., Haverford, Pa., 1969-90; tutoring program Bryn Mawr Presbyn. Ch., Pa., 1966-82; pres. human rels. coun. Lower Merion Township, 1966-68. Mem. Nat. Assn. Prins. of Schs. for Girls (pres. 1959-61), Haadmistress Assn. of the East (pres. 1950-52). Democrat. Presbyterian.

SPEIER, K. JACQUELINE, state legislator; b. San Francisco, May 14, 1950; m. Steven K. Sierra, 1987; 1 child Jackson Kent. BA, U. Calif., Davis, 1972; JD, U. Calif., 1976. Legal coun., legis. asst. to Leo J. Ryan U.S. Rep. of Calif., 1973-78; mem. San Mateo County Bd. Supr., Calif., 1981-86, chairwomen, 1985; mem. Calif. State Assembly, 1987—, majority wip, 1987—, mem. health commn., mem. judiciary commn., mem. fin. and ins. commn. Mem. Fed. Bar Assn., Calif. Bar Assn., D.C. Bar Assn. Democrat. Roman Catholic. Office: 4140 State Capital Sacramento CA 95814*

SPEIER, KAREN RINARDO, psychologist; b. New Orleans, Aug. 19, 1947; d. William Joseph Rinardo and Shirley Eva (Spreen) Christensen; m. Joe Max Sobotka, Nov. 27, 1970 (div. 1972); m. Anthony Herman Speier, May 29, 1982; children: Anthony Herman III, Austin Clay. Student, Vanderbilt U., 1965-67; BA, La. State U., New Orleans, 1969; MS, U. New Orleans, 1974; PhD, La. State U., 1985. Lic. psychologist, La. Tchr. spl. edn. Huntsville (Ala.) Achievement Sch., 1970-72; instr. neurology La. State U. Med. Ctr., New Orleans, 1972-78; clin. assoc. Dawson Psychol. Assocs., Baton Rouge, 1979-81; tchr. asst. dept. psychology La. State U., Baton Rouge, 1979-81; psychol. examiner La. Sch. for Deaf, Baton Rouge, 1979-80; psychology intern VA Med. Ctr., Martinez, Calif., 1981-82; psychology extern East La. State Hosp., Jackson, 1982-83; clin. assoc. Baton Rouge Psychol. Assocs., 1983-86, pvt. practice clin. psychology, 1986—; sr. neuropsychologist Rehab. Hosp. of Baton Rouge, 1995—; sec. bd. dirs. Baton Rouge Employment Devel. Svcs., 1987-89; mem. psychology cons. com. Meadow Wood Hosp., Baton Rouge, 1987-89; mem. psychology adv. com. Parkland Hosp., Baton Rouge, 1989-92. Contbr. articles to profl. publs. Mem. steering com. Baton Rouge Stepfamily Support Group, 1983-90; tchr. St. James Episcopal Sunday Sch., Baton Rouge, 1984-86, 90-91, 92—. Mem. Orton Dyslexia Soc. (bd. dirs., pres. La. br.), Nat. Head Injury Found., Agenda For Children, Baton Rouge Area Soc. Psychologists, La. Psychol. Assn., Am. Psychology Assn., Internat. Soc. Child Abuse and Neglect, Mental Health Assn. La. Office: Ctr Psychol Resources 4521 Jamestown Ste 2 Baton Rouge LA 70808-3234

SPEIGHT, VELMA RUTH, university administrator; b. Snow Hill, N.C., Nov. 18, 1932; d. John Thomas and Mable Lee (Edwards) S.; m. Howard H. Kennedy, 1953 (div. 1961); 1 child, Chineta. BS, N.C. A&T U., 1953; MEd, U. Md., 1965, PhD, 1976. Cert. counselor, tchr., Md. Tchr. math., French Kennard High Sch., Centreville, Md., 1954-60; counselor Kennard High Sch., Centreville, 1960-66; coord. guidance dept. Queene Anne's County High Sch., Centreville, 1966-69; adv. specialist in civil rights Md. State Dept. Edn., Balt., 1969-72, supr. guidance, 1972-76, dep. asst. state supt., 1976-82, asst. state supt., 1982-86; dir. EEO recruitment U. Md., College Park, 1972; coord. guidance and counseling U. Md. Ea. Shore, Princess Anne, 1986-87; assoc. prof. counselor edn. East Carolina U., Greenville, 1989; chmn. dept. edn., coord. grad. prog. guidance and counseling U. Md., Eastern Shore, Greenville, 1989-93, chmn. dept. edn., 1990-94; dir. alumni affairs N.C. A&T U., Greensboro, 1993—; adj. prof. Loyola U., Balt., 1976-80, Johns Hopkins U., Balt., 1980; cons., 1987—; speaker numerous seminars. Mem. Nat. Coalition for Chpt. 1 Parents, Washington, 1980-87, Human Rights Commn., Howard County, Md., 1987—; chmn. Gov.'s com. Studying Sentencing Alternatives for Women, Annapolis, Md., 1987; founder, chmn. Mothers to Prevent Dropouts, Centreville. Recipient Early Childhood Edn. award Japanese Govt., 1984, Md. State Tchrs'. Assn. Minority award Black Chs. for Excellence in Edn.; Fulbright Hayes scholar, 1991. Mem. Am. Counseling Assn., Nat. Alliance Black Educators, Assn. for Supervision and Curriculum Devel., Assn. Tchr. Edn., Md. Assn. Coll. Tchr. Edn., Md.

Counseling Assn., N.C. A&T U. Alumni Assn. (nat. pres. 197983, Excellence award 1983), Tchr. Edn. and Profl. Standards Bd. Democrat. Presbyterian. Club: Community Action (Centreville). Home: 11 Carissa Ct Greensboro NC 27407-6366 Office: NC A&T State U Greensboro NC 27411

SPEILLER-MORRIS, JOYCE, English composition educator; b. Utica, N.Y., Nov. 11, 1945; d. Arnold Leonard Speiller and Sybil (Sall) McAdam; m. Joseph Raymond Morris, Mar. 17, 1984. BS, Syracuse U., 1968; MA, Columbia U., 1969. Cert. tchr., N.Y., Fla. Chmn. upper sch. social studies dept., tchr. grade 6 social studies and English Cathedral Heights Elem. Sch., N.Y.C., 1969-74; adj. prof. Broward Community Coll., Hollywood, Davie and Pompano, Fla., 1982-90, Biscayne Coll., Miami, Fla., 1983, Miami-Dade Community Coll., 1983, Nova U., Miami and Davie, 1983-84; adj. prof., semester lectr. U. Miami, Coral Gables, 1985—; master tchr. U. Miami, 1990, 92, 94, faculty fellow, 1990-94, mem. curriculum devel., 1991-94; contbr. presentation to Fla. Coll. English Assn., 1991-92, Wyo. Conf. English, 1991; guest spkr. in field of svc.-learning, 1992-94; cons. svc.-learning curriculum design, 1994; acad. advisor U. Miami, 1994. Reviewer textbook McGraw Hill, 1993; contbr. instr.'s manual of textbook, 1994; contbr. poetry to revs., articles to profl. jours. Founder, dir. Meet the Author program, Coral Gables, 1989—. Recipient V.P. award U. Miami, 1992, cert. recognition West Palm Beach, Fla., TV sta., 1992; grantee Fla. Office for Campus Vols., 1992, Dade Community Found., 1992. Mem. MLA, Fla. Coll. English Assn., Coll. English Assn., Nat. Coun. Tchrs. English, Fla. chpt. of Tchrs. of English to Speakers of Other Langs. (speaker conf. 1992), Am. Correctional Assn., Phi Delta Kappa, Phi Lambda Theta. Home: Tower 200 Apt 806 19101 Mystic Point Dr North Miami Beach FL 33180-4512 Office: U Miami Office English Compostion PO Box 248145 Miami FL 33124-8145

SPEIR, MARCIA ANN, accountant; b. Tulsa, Oct. 20, 1935; d. Charles Henry and Pearl Jewell (Palmer) Hall; m. Jack Wesley Speir, June 17, 1955; 1 child, Andrea Renee. Student, Northeastern State Coll., Tahlequah, Okla., 1953-56, Am. River Coll., Sacramento, Calif., 1974-76. Acct. Commonwealth Life Ins. Co., Tulsa, 1953-56, Okla. Natural Gas Co., Tulsa, 1957-62; acct., systems analyst Shell Oil Co., Tulsa, 1962-69; staff acct. Trane Heating and Air Conditioning, Sacramento, 1975-79; owner Arapahoe County Steamway Carpet & Upholstery Cleaning Co., Denver, 1969-74; acct., office mgr. Sureway Corp., Sacramento, 1980-89; on med. leave, 1989—; career counselor Am. River Coll., 1974-76; active in cancer support groups. Mem. NAFE, Sacramento Employer Adv. Group. Republican. Mem. Christian Ch. Home: 5424 Lequel Way Carmichael CA 95608-3063

SPELLMIRE, SANDRA MARIE, systems analyst, programmer; b. San Francisco, Feb. 20, 1950; d. Robert Joseph and Catherine Louise (Sockett) S. BS, Calif. State U., L.A., 1977. Project controls analyst Ralph M. Parsons Co., Pasadena, Calif., 1978-81, C.F. Braun & Co., Alhambra, Calif., 1981-84; configuration mgr. software systems Burroughs Corp., Santa Ana, Calif., 1984-85; sr. scientific analyst, programmer Electronic Data Systems, L.A., 1985, Denver, 1985-87, Mpls., 1987-89; software cons. Shared Resource Mgmt., St. Louis Park, Minn., 1989-91, Shoreview, Minn., 1991-92, TWF & Assocs., Edina, Minn., 1992-93; sr. programmer analyst Harmon Glass, Golden Valley, Minn., 1993-94, Keane Inc., Bloomington, Minn., 1994—.

SPELMAN, MARVA, dancer, writer; b. Sioux City, Iowa, Sept. 19, 1912; d. Max and Lena (Koolish) Jaffe; m. Walter Bernstein, Nov. 1941 (div. 1952); children: Joan, Peter. Student, Sorbonne U., Paris, 1934; grad., Hellerau-Laxemburg Sch. Music, Austria, 1935; BA, New Sch. Social Rsch., 1962; PhD, NYU, N.Y.C., 1966. Prof. choreography New Sch. Social Rsch., N.Y.C., 1955-62; yoga tchr. N.Y.C., 1962-72; prof. English Mills Coll., N.Y.C., 1963-66; prof. comparative lit. SUNY, N.Y.C., 1966-69; prof. dance therapy and dance history grad. students UCLA, 1971-72; prof. yoga UCLA Extension, 1972-82; yoga tchr. Spelman Studio, L.A., 1972—; PhD adviser U. Oriental Studies, L.A., 1977. Solo concert of own choreography at age 15, Goodman Theater, Chgo.; dance ptnr. of Harold Kreutzberg in Salzburg Festspiel (Austria) Jedermann prodns., 1930s; soloist Balleto della Cita di Firenza (Italy) and toured Europe, 1935-36; toured USA with Hanya Holm Dance Group, 1936-41; writer articles and revs. Dance Mag., 1944-54; author: Yoga Transitions, 7 books and audio-casette, 1991. Chosen Yoga Tchr. of Yr. Internat. Samata, L.A., 1989. Democrat. Unitarian. Home and Office: Spelman Studio 936 S Ogden Dr Los Angeles CA 90036

SPELMAN, NANCY LATTING, psychologist, consultant; b. Oklahoma City, Sept. 13, 1945; d. Trimble Baggett and Patience Francelia (Sewell) Latting; m. Douglas Gordon Spelman, June 21, 1970; children: Brooke Patience, Erin Latting. BA in Polit. Sci., Boston U., 1967; MA in Psychology, Bucknell U., 1972; PhD in Psychology, U. Hong Kong, 1987. Cognitive psychologist. Tour guide UN, N.Y.C., summer 1966; tchr. emotionally disturbed and retarded pre-sch. children Mass. Dept. Mental Health, Boston, 1968-70; coord. vols. campaign for mayor Patience Latting, Oklahoma City, 1971; lectr. psychology Petaling Jaya Community Coll., Kuala Lumpur, Malaysia, 1987-88, George Mason U., Fairfax, Va., 1989; interactive skills observer, facilitator mgmt. programs Xerox Corp. Edn. and Tng., Leesburg, Va., 1989-91; pers. officer Am. Inst. in Taiwan, Taipei, 1993—. Bd. dirs. Internat. Sch. Kuala Lumpur, 1986-87, sec., 1987-88; bd. dirs. Golf Course Square Cluster, Reston, Va., 1991; com. mem. Hong Kong Soc. for Disabled, 1976-77. Democrat.

SPENCE, BARBARA E., publishing company executive; b. Bryn Mawr, Pa., July 8, 1921; d. Geoffrey Strange and Mary (Harrington) Earnshaw; m. Kenneth M. Spence Jr., June 29, 1944; children: Kenneth M. III, Christopher E., Hilary B. Grad. high sch. Movie, radio editor Parade Mag., N.Y.C., 1941-45; with Merchandising Group, N.Y.C., 1946-47; exec. dir. Greenfield Hill Congl. Ch., Fairfield, Conn., 1958-74, dir. religious edn., 1968-74; assoc. Ten Eyck-Emerich Antiques, 1974-76; personnel dir. William Morrow & Co., Inc., N.Y.C., 1976-91; ret., 1991. Chmn. pub. relations, bd. dirs. ARC, 1951-56, Family Service Soc., Fairfield, 1956-57, 61-63; chmn. pub. relations Citizens for Eisenhower, 1952, Fairfield Teens Players, 1968-71; bd. dirs. Fairfield Teens, Inc., 1965-70, Planned Parenthood of Greater Bridgeport, 1969-75, chmn. pub. affairs, 1971-72, chmn. personnel, 1972-73, chpt. vice chmn., 1973-75; pres. steering com. Am. Playwrights Festival Theatre, Inc., Fairfield, 1969-70, v.p., bd. dirs., 1971—; bd. govs. Unquowa Sch., Fairfield, 1963-69; bd. dirs. Fairfield U. Playhouse, 1971-73, Downtown Cabaret Theatre, Bridgeport, 1975-76. Mem. AAP (compensation survey com.), Fairfield Women's Exch. (bd. dirs. 1993). Home: 101 Twin Brook Ln Fairfield CT 06430-2834

SPENCE, JANET BLAKE CONLEY (MRS. ALEXANDER PYOTT SPENCE), civic worker; b. Upper Montclair, N.J., Aug. 17, 1915; d. Walter Abbott and Ethel Maud (Blake) Conley; m. Alexander Pyott Spence, June 10, 1939; children: Janet Blake Spence Kerr, Robert Moray, Richard Taylor. Student, Vassar Coll., 1933-35; cert., Katharine Gibbs Sch., 1936. formerly active Jr. League, Neighborhood House, ARC, Girl Scouts U.S.A.; active various community drives; chmn. Darien (Conn.) Assembly, 1955-56; sec., chmn. Wilton Jr. Assembly, 1961-63; subscription chmn. Candlelight Concerts Wilton, Conn., 1963-65; rec. sec. Pub. Health Nursing Assn. Wilton Bd., 1964-67; corr., rec. sec. Royle Sch. Bd., Darien, 1952-55; fund raiser Vassar Class of 1937; mem. Washington Valley Community Assn.; mem. N.J. Symphony Orch. League, treas. Morris County br. 1978-83, corr. sec. 1982-83, pres. 1985-89, acting pres. 1989—, state coun. mem. 1985-89, acting pres. Morris br. 1989-90. Mem. Vassar Alumni Assn., Dobbs Alumni Assn., Jersey Hills Vassar Club, Wilton Garden Club, Washington Valley Cmty. Assn. (life corr. sec. 1977-82, pres. 1982-84, v.p. 1984-85, co-pres. 1985-86, treas. 1988—, chmn. membership com. 1987-89, mem. archives com. 1988—, budget com. 1990—, treas. 1990—), Washington Valley Home Econs. Club. Congregationalist. Home: 168 Washington Valley Rd Morristown NJ 07960-3333

SPENCE, MARTY (MARY EVALINA MARTIN SCANLON SPENCE), psychiatric social worker; b. Balt., Aug. 17, 1946; d. Rea Hammond and Alice (Fitzsimmons) Keech; m. John Scanlon, 1973 (dec. 1978); m. Richard Spence, 1986. RN, Bon Secours Hosp. Sch. Nursing, 1970; BS in Nursing, U. Md., 1984, MSW, 1986. Oper. room nurse Children's Hosp., Balt., 1974-79; nursing supr. pediatrics unit John Hopkins Hosp., Balt., 1979-80, head nurse adolescent unit, 1980-81; child and adolescent family psychotherapist Sheppard and Enoch Pratt Hosp., Balt., 1986-91, 93—; with The Children's Guild, Ellicott City, 1991-92; dir. Day Hosp. for Children, Balt., 1992-93; pvt. practice psychotherapy, 1986—. Author: I'm Mr. Peanut, 1984. Mem. NASW, Balt. Soc. for Psychoanalytic Studies. Home and Office: 103 Seminole Ave Baltimore MD 21228-5640

SPENCE, MARY LEE, historian; b. Kyle, Tex., Aug. 4, 1927; d. Jeremiah Milton and Mary Louise (Hutchison) Nance; m. Clark Christian Spence, Sept. 12, 1953; children: Thomas Christian, Ann Leslie. BA, U. Tex., 1947, MA, 1948; PhD, U. Minn., 1957. Instr., asst. prof. S.W. Tex. State U., San Marcos, 1948-53; lectr. Pa. State U., State College, 1955-58; mem. faculty U. Ill., Urbana-Champaign, 1973—, asst. prof., assoc. prof., 1973-81, 81-89, prof. history, 1989-90, prof. emerita, 1990—. Editor (with Donald Jackson) The Expeditions of John Charles Fremont, 3 vols., 1970-84, (with Clark Spence) Fanny Kelly's Narrative of Her Captivity Among the Sioux Indians, 1990, (with Pamela Herr) The Letters of Jessie Benton Fremont, 1993; contbr. articles to profl. jours. Mem. Children's Theater Bd., Urbana-Champaign, 1965-73. Grantee Nat. Hist. Pub. and Records Commn., Washington, 1977-78, 87-90; recipient Excellent Advisor award Liberal Arts and Sci. Coll., U. Ill., 1986. Mem. Western History Assn. (pres. 1981-82), Orgn. Am. Historians, Phi Beta Kappa (exec. sect. Gamma chpt. 1985-89, pres. 1991-92), Phi Alpha Theta. Episcopalian. Home: 1107 S Foley St Champaign IL 61820-6326 Office: U Ill Dept History 810 S Wright St Urbana IL 61801-3611

SPENCE, SANDRA, association executive; b. McKeesport, Pa., Mar. 25, 1941; d. Cedric Leroy and Suzanne (Haudenshield) S. BA, Allegheny Coll., 1963; MA, Rutgers U., 1964. With Pa. State Govt., Harrisburg, 1964-68, Appalachian Regional Commn., Washington, 1968-75; legis. rep. Nat. Assn. Counties, Washington, 1975-77; fed. rep. Calif. Dept. Transp., Washington, 1977-78; dir. congl. affairs Amtrak, Washington, 1978-81, corp. sec., 1981-83; dir. computer svcs. Nat. R.R. Passenger Corp., Washington, 1983-84; co-owner Parkhurst-Spence Inc., 1985; owner The Spence Group, 1986-90; v.p. Bostrom Corp., Washington, 1990-92; exec. dir. Soc. Glass and Ceramic Decorators, 1992—; chmn. legis. com. Womens Transp. Seminar, 1977-79, dir., 1982-83, v.p., 1983-84, chmn. edn. com., 1982-83; com. on edn. and tng. Transp. Rsch. Bd., 1982-85. Contbr. articles to profl. jours. Dommr., sec. D.C. Commn. for Women, 1983-88; del. Ward III Dem. Com., 1982-90, 1st vice chmn., 1987-88. Fellow Eagleton Inst. Politics, 1963-64; recipient Achievement award Transp. Seminar, 1982, 83. Mem. Greater Washington Soc. Assn. Execs. (vice-chair law and legis. com. 1989-90, chmn. 1990-91, chmn. scholarship com. 1992-93, bd. dirs. 1993—, Rising Star award 1989, Chmn.'s award for Govt. Rels. 1991), Am. Soc. Assn. Execs. (mgmt. cert. 1987), Phi Beta Kappa. Home: 3701 Appleton St NW Washington DC 20016 Office: Soc Glass and Ceramic Decorators 1627 K St NW Ste 800 Washington DC 20006

SPENCE, SHARON STOKES, governmental affairs director; b. Lexington, N.C., Aug. 13, 1958; d. Oscar Barker and Lois Ann (Marley) Stokes; m. Terry Craig Spence, Nov. 1, 1986; children: Jordan Brooke, Brittany Anne. BA in Polit. Sci., U. N.C., 1979; MPA, N.C. State U., 1985. Comml. accounts rep., adminstrv. asst. Am. Refuse Systems, Inc., Sanford, N.C., 1980-82; adminstrv. asst. Triangle Pers. Svc., Raleigh, N.C., 1983, Maupin, Taylor, Ellis & Adams, P.A., Raleigh, 1984; intern Wake County Budget and Fin. Offices, Raleigh, 1985; budget analyst I City of Durham (N.C.) Budget & Fin. Office, 1985-86; budget analyst II Wake County Budget Office, Raleigh, 1986-88; govtl. affairs dir. Wake County Mgrs. Office, Raleigh, 1988—, pub. info. officer, 1990-92. Workplace giving campaign chair United Way, Raleigh, United Arts Fund, Raleigh, 1990-94; mem. Lee County Dem. Women. Mem. Internat. City/County Mgmt. Assn., Am. Soc. for Pub. Adminstrn., Nat. Assn. County Intergovtl. Rels. Officers (v.p., treas. 1993-94, pres. 1995—), Nat. Assn. County Info. Officers, Nat. Assn. Counties Intergovtl. Rels. (steering com. 1992—), Greater Raleigh C. of C. (state govt., local govt. and transp. coms., inter-city visit task force), Sanford Women's League, Pi Alpha Alpha. Methodist. Home: 2605 Wellington Dr Sanford NC 27330 Office: Wake County Mgrs Office 336 Fayetteville St Mall Raleigh NC 27602

SPENCE, SUSAN BATEMAN, counselor; b. Atlanta, Mar. 4, 1947; d. Gregory Wendell and Anne (Chambless) Bateman; m. James E. Spence Jr., Mar. 30, 1985; children: Anna Lee, Katherine Ellen. AB, U. Ga., 1969; MEd, Ga. State U., 1977. Caseworker Richmond County Dept. Family and Children Svcs., Augusta, Ga., 1970-73; vocat. rehab. counselor State of Ga., Atlanta, 1973-77; prof. counselor North DeKalb Mental Health Ctr., Atlanta, 1981—. Mem. Ga. Mental Health Counselors Assn., Alpha Chi Omega (treas. Athens, Ga. chpt. 1967-68), Alpha Lambda Delta. Republican. Baptist. Home: 1105 Oxford Cres NE Atlanta GA 30319-1624 Office: North DeKalb Mental Health Ctr 3300 NE Expressway NE Atlanta GA 30341-3941

SPENCER, ALICIA COCHRAN, accountant; b. Mobile, Ala., Nov. 19, 1963; d. James E. and Joyce (Simmons) Cochran; m. John Ronald Spencer, Aug. 21, 1993. BS in Acctg., U. South Ala., 1986. CPA. Staff auditor Price Waterhouse, New Orleans, 1987-88; sr. auditor KPMG Peat Marwick, Baton Rouge, 1988-90; asst. v.p. AmSouth Bank, Birmingham, Ala., 1990-92; asst. contr. WALA-TV, Mobile, 1992—. Vol. St. John's Episcopal Ch., Mobile, 1993—. Mem. AICPA, Inst. Mgmt. Accts. (v.p. 1993—), Ala. Soc. CPAs, Mobile Chpt. Ala. Soc. CPAs, Alpha Xi Delta, Omicron Delta Kappa. Baptist. Office: WALA TV 210 Government St Mobile AL 36602

SPENCER, CAROL BROWN, association executive; b. Normal, Ill., Aug. 26, 1936; d. Fred William and Sorado (Gross) B.; m. James Calvin Spencer, Dec. 18, 1965 (div. July 1978); children: James Calvin Jr., Anne Elizabeth. BA in English, Calif. State U., Los Angeles, 1964, MA in Pub. Adminstrn., 1986. Cert. secondary edn. tchr., Calif. Corr. Ashland (Ohio) Times Gazette, 1975-78; tchr. English Seneca Vocat. High Sch., Buffalo, 1966-70; pub. info. officer City of Pasadena, Calif., 1979-90, City of Mountain View, Calif., 1990-93; exec. dir. Calif. Assn. for the Gifted, 1993—. Editor: (mcpl. pubs.) Pasadena In Focus, 1984-90, N.W. Bulletin, 1985-90. Sec., bd. dirs. Calif. Music Theatre, 1987-90; bd. dirs. Pasadena Beautiful Found., 1984-90, Pasadena Cultural Festival Found., 1983-86, Palo Alto-Stanford Heritage, 1990-93; mayoral appointee Strategic Planning Adv. Com., Pasadena, 1985-86. Mem. NOW, Pub. Rels. Soc. Am., Calif. Assn. Pub. Info. Ofcls. (exec. bd., Paul Clark Achievment award 1986, award for mktg. 1990), City/County Comms. and Mktg. Assn. (bd. dirs. 1988-90, Savvy award for mktg. 1990), Nat. Assn. for Gifted Children. Democrat. Episcopalian. Home: 426 Escuela Ave Apt 19 Mountain View CA 94040-2022

SPENCER, CAROL DIANE, consulting company executive; b. Pitts., Mar. 12, 1952; d. Louis John and Elinor Edwinna (Clark) Kacinko; m. Dirk Victor Spencer, May 12, 1993; children: Erick Jon Powell, Tiffani Dawn Showalter. AS in Computer Sci., C.C. Allegheny County, 1974; BSBA, U. Pitts., 1979. Data base adminstr. Beckwith Machinery, Murrysville, Pa., 1974-78; systems analyst Mode Inc., Irwin, Pa., 1978-80; supr. data base Tex. Instruments, Dallas, 1980-83, E-Systems Melpar, Falls Church, Va., 1983; dep. dir. Vanguard Techs., Fairfax, Va., 1983-85; mgr. data base Siecor, Hickory, N.C., 1985-86; sr. cons. Computer Task Group, Raleigh, N.C., 1986-88; prin. cons., mgr. Tex. Instruments, 1988-94; pres. Kacinko Consulting, Reston, Va., 1994—; speaker Computer Assocs., Atlanta, 1994. Mem. Digital Users Group, DB2 Users Group. Home and Office: 12608 Bridoon Ln Herndon VA 22071

SPENCER, DOMINA EBERLE, mathematics educator; b. New Castle, Pa., Sept. 26, 1920; d. Andrew Berger and Ina May (Eberle) S.; m. Parry Moon, Aug. 17, 1961; 1 child, Euclid Eberle Moon. SB, MIT, 1939, SM, 1940, PhD, 1942. Asst. prof. physics Am. U., Washington, 1942-43, Tufts Coll., Medford, Mass., 1943-47, Brown U., Providence, 1947-50; assoc. prof. math. U. Conn., Storrs, 1950-60, prof. math., 1960—; cons. Sylvania, Salem, 1953-70, Ainsworth Lighting, L.I., 1943-53, Marlux Corp., Sommerville, Mass., 1948-61, Photo Rsch. Corp., Hollywood, Calif., 1945-58. Author: (with P. Moon) Lighting Design, 1947, Field Theory for Engineers, 1960, Field Theory Handbook, 1960, Foundations of Electrodynamics, 1960, Vectors, 1965, Partial Differential Equations, 1969, The Photic Field, 1981, Theory of Holors, 1986; co-inventor Aperture Lamp. Chmn. concert com. St. Paul's Ch., Brookline, 1988—; pres. Back Bay Manor Tenants Assn., Boston, 1985—. Recipient Disting. Alumna award Friends Select Sch., Phila., 1987. Fellow Illuminating Engring. Soc. (gold medal 1974), Optical Soc. Am.; mem. Am. Math. Soc., Math Assn. Am., Am. Phys. Soc., MIT Nautical Assn. Presbyterian. Home: 75 St Alphonsus St Apt 2101 Boston MA 02120-1676 Office: U Conn U-9 Storrs CT 06268

SPENCER, ELIZABETH, author; b. Carrollton, Miss., 1921; d. James Luther and Mary James (McCain) S.; m. John Arthur Blackwood Rusher, Sept. 29, 1956. BA, Belhaven Coll., 1942; MA, Vanderbilt U., 1943; LittD (hon.), Southwestern U. at Memphis, 1968; LLD (hon.), Concordia U. at Montreal, 1988; LittD (hon.), U. of the South, 1992. Instr. N.W. Miss. Jr. Coll., 1943-44, Ward-Belmont, Nashville, 1944-45; reporter The Nashville Tennessean, 1945-46; instr. U. Miss., Oxford, 1948-51, 52-53; vis. prof. Concordia U., Montreal, Que., Can., 1976-81, adj. prof., 1981-86; vis. prof. U. N.C., Chapel Hill, 1986-92. Author: Fire in the Morning, 1948, This Crooked Way, 1952, The Voice at the Back Door, 1956, The Light in the Piazza, 1960, Knights and Dragons, 1965, No Place for an Angel, 1967, Ship Island and Other Stories, 1968, The Snare, 1972, The Stories of Elizabeth Spencer, 1981, Marilee, 1981, The Salt Line, 1984, Jack of Diamonds and Other Stories, 1988, (play) For Lease or Sale, 1989, On the Gulf, 1991, The Night Travellers, 1991; contbr. short stories to mags. and anthologies. Recipient Women's Democratic Com. award, 1949, recognition award Nat. Inst. Arts and letters, 1952, Richard and Hinda Rosenthal Found. award Am. Acad. Arts and Letters, 1957; Guggenheim Found. fellow, 1953, 1st McGraw-Hill Fiction award, 1960, Henry Bellamann award for creative writing, 1968; Award of Merit medal for the short story Am. Acad. Arts and Letters, 1983, Salem award for lit., 1992, Dos Passos award for fiction, 1992; Kenyon Rev. fellow in fiction, 1957; Bryn Mawr Col. Donnelly fellow, 1962; Nat. Endowment for Arts grantee in lit., 1983, Sr. Arts Award grantee Nat. Endowment for Arts, 1988, N.C. Gov.'s award for lit., 1994. Mem. Am. Acad. Arts and Letters, Fellowship of So. Writers (charter; vice chancellor 1993—). Home: 402 Longleaf Dr Chapel Hill NC 27514-3042

SPENCER, ISABEL BRANNON, editor; b. Tryon, N.C., Nov. 10, 1940; d. George Smith and Isabel (Ducharme) B.; m. F. Gilman Spencer, July 3, 1965; 1 child, Isabel Caroline. BA, Bryn Mawr Coll., 1962. Reporter Main Line Times, 1962, Delaware County Daily News, 1963-65, The Trentonian, 1965-67, The Frentonian, 1969-76, Phila. Inquirer, 1976-77; city editor The News Jour., Wilmington, Del., 1979-84; asst. city editor The Star Ledger, Newark, 1984-88; editor The Daily Jour., Elizabeth, N.J., 1988—. Home: 1133 Race St Denver CO 80206 Office: The Denver Post 1560 Broadway Denver CO 80202*

SPENCER, LAVYRLE, writer; b. Browerville, Minn., Aug. 17, 1943; d. Louis Joseph and Janet Adamek (Baughman) Kulick; m. Daniel F. Spencer, Dec. 10, 1962; children: Amy Elizabeth, Beth Adair. Author: The Fulfillment, 1979, The Endearment, 1982 (Hist. Romance of Yr. award Romance Writers of Am.), Hummingbird, 1983 (Hist. Romance of Yr. award Romance Writers of Am.), Twice Loved, 1984 (Hist. Romance of Yr. award Romance Writers of Am.), Sweet Memories, 1984, The Hellion, 1984, A Heart Speaks, 1986, Tears, 1986, Years, 1986, The Gamble, 1987, Separate Beds, 1987, Vows, 1988, Morning Glory, 1988, Spring Fancy, 1989, Bitter Sweet, 1990, Forgiving, 1991, November of the Heart, 1992, Bygones, 1993, Family Blessings, 1994, Home Song, 1995. Office: 6701 79th Ave Brooklyn Park MN 55445*

SPENCER, MARGARET GILLIAM, lawyer; b. Spokane, Wash., Aug. 30, 1951; d. Jackson Earl and Margaret Kathleen (Hindley) Gilliam; m. John Bernard Spencer, Feb. 21, 1993. BA in Sociology, U. Mont., 1974, MA in Sociology, 1978, JD, 1982. Bar: Mont. 1982, Colo. 1982. Assoc. Holland & Hart, Denver, 1982-84; assoc. Roath & Brega, P.C., Denver, 1984-88, shareholder, dir., 1988-89; spl. counsel Brega & Winters, P.C., Denver, 1989; corp. counsel CH2M Hill, Inc., Denver, 1989—. Democrat. Episcopalian. Office: CH2M Hill Inc PO Box 22508 Denver CO 80222

SPENCER, MARGARET JEAN, public defender; b. Fullerton, Calif., Dec. 9, 1946; d. Donald Earl and Anna Elizabeth (Johnson) S. BA, Whittier Coll., 1968; JD, Citrus Belt Law Sch., 1976. Bar: Calif. 1976. Dep. probation officer Riverside (Calif.) County Probation Dept., 1969-77; dep. pub. defender Riverside County Pub. Defender's Office, 1977-84, supervising dep. pub. defender, 1984-93, chief asst. pub. defender, 1993—. Office: Riverside County Pub Defenders Office 4200 Orange St Riverside CA 92501

SPENCER, MARILYN J., artist; b. Detroit, July 10; d. John and Dorothy Jensen; m. Andrew R. Spencer, July 24, 1948; children: Gary, Linda, James. BA, Wayne State U., 1947. Tchr. Detroit Pub. Schs., 1947-52; sub. tchr. Troy and Birmingham (Mich.) Schs., 1966-76; art instr. Pontiac (Mich.) Art Ctr., 1980, 81. Exhbns. in group shows include various local, state and nat. shows in Mich. and U.S., 1968—; 12 one-woman shows in Mich. galleries; represented in over 300 pvt. and pub. collections. Docent Cranbrook Inst. Sci., Bloomfield Hills, Mich., 1973-76; contbr. paintings Channel 56 Art Auctions, Detroit, Birmingham-Bloomfield Art Assn.; exhbn. art chmn. Birmingham-Bloomfield Art Assn., Pontiac Art Ctr. Recipient numerous awards. Mem. Birmingham Soc. Women Painters, Ariz. Artists Guild, Traverse Area Arts Coun., Detroit Art Inst. (founder soc. 1963—).

SPENCER, MARY MILLER, civic worker; b. Comanche, Tex., May 25, 1924; d. Aaron Gaynor and Alma (Grissom) Miller; 1 child, Mara Lynn. BS, U. North Tex., 1943. Cafeteria dir. Mercedes (Tex.) Pub. Schs., 1943-46; home economist coordinator All-Orange Dessert Contest, Fla. Citrus Commn., Lakeland, 1959-62, 64; tchr. purchasing sch. lunch dept. Fla. Dept. Edn., 1960. Clothing judge Polk County (Fla.) Youth Fair, 1951-68, Polk County Federated Women's Clubs, 1964-66; pres. Dixieland Elem. Sch. PTA, 1955-57, Polk County Council PTA's, 1958-60; chmn. public edn. com. Polk County unit Am. Cancer Soc., 1959-60, bd. dirs., 1962-70; charter mem., bd. dirs. Lakeland YMCA, 1962-72; sec. Greater Lakeland Community Nursing Council, 1965-72; trustee, vice chmn. Polk County Eye Clinic, Inc., 1962-64, pres., 1964-82; bd. dirs. Polk County Scholarship and Loan Fund, 1962-70; mem. exec. com. West Polk County (Fla.) Community Welfare Council, 1960-62, 65-68; mem. budget and audit com. Greater Lakeland United Fund, 1960-62, bd. dirs., 1967-70, residential chmn. fund drive, 1968; mem. adv. bd. Polk County Juvenile and Domestic Relations Ct., 1960-69; worker children's services div. family services Dept. Health and Rehab. Services, State of Fla., 1969-70, social worker, 1970-72, 74-82, social worker OFR unit, 1977-81, with other pers. svcs., 1981-82; supr. OFR unit 1982-83, pub. assistance specialist IV, 1984-89; with other pers. svcs. Emergency Fin. Assistance Housing Program. Mem. exec. com. Suncoast Health Council, 1968-71; mem. Polk County Home Econs. Adv. Com., 1965-71; sec. bd. dirs. Fla. West Coast Ednl. TV, 1960-81; bd. dirs. Lake Region United Way, Winter Haven, 1976-81; mem. Polk County Community Services Council, 1978-88. Mem. Nat. Welfare Fraud Assn., Fla. Congress Parents and Tchrs. (hon. life; pres. dist. 7 1961-63, chmn. pub. relations 1962-66), AAUW (pres. Lakeland br. 1960-61), Polk County Mental Health Assn., Fla. Health and Welfare Council, Fla. Health and Social Service Council, U. North Tex. Alumni Assn. Democrat. Methodist. Lodge: Order of Eastern Star. Home and Office: PO Box 2161 Lakeland FL 33806-2161

SPENCER, SHIRLEY GENEVA, editor; b. Quanah, Tex., July 21, 1941; d. James Bart Weaver and Fanny Mae (McKee) Cross; m. Darrell Dewayne Spencer, Aug. 3, 1957; 1 child, Tanya Arleen. Student, Southwestern Coll., Bethany Nazarene Coll. With edit. dept. Advocate Press, Oklahoma City, 1975—; exec. editor Internat. Pentecostal Holiness Advocate, Oklahoma City, 1980—; editor Sunday sch. lit. Advocate Press, Franklin Springs, Ga., 1991—. Mem. Internat. Pentecostal Press Assn. (sec., treas. 1982—). Republican. Office: Internat Pentecostal Ch PO Box 12609 Oklahoma City OK 73157-2609

SPENCER, SUSAN CRANE, accountant; b. Hartford, Conn.; d. Allen Edward and Wilma Bachmann Crane; m. William Albert Spencer, Nov. 6, 1965 (div. Oct. 1970); 1 child, Sharon Lynn Spencer McCluskey; m. Lawrence N. Spencer, Dec. 7, 1970; children: Lawrence Scott Spencer, Angela Lee Spencer. AS, Mohegan C.C., 1979; BBA, Averett Coll., 1994. Lic. real estate agt., Va. Bookkeeper, acct. Oswalt & Dewitt CPA, Kennewick, Wash., 1979-80; office mgr. Flight Inc., Richland, Wash., 1980-81; cost acct., auditor Bechtel Power Corp., Richland, 1981-85; contr. All-Time Mfg. Co., Inc., Montville, Conn., 1985-90; realtor Century 21 Evelyn Lowe,

Lynchburg, Va., 1991-93; asst. contr. Davis Paint Mfrs. Inc., Lynchburg, 1992—. Mem. Inst. Mgmt. Accts., Beta Sigma Phi. Republican. Methodist. Home: 108 Woodbourne Dr Lynchburg VA 24502-5630 Office: Davis Paint Mfrs Inc PO Box 11405 Lynchburg VA 24506-1405

SPENCER, TRICIA JANE, wholesale manufacturing executive; b. Springfield, Ill., Dec. 8, 1952; d. Frank Edward and LaWanda (Edwards) Bell; m. Mark Edward Spencer, Aug. 21, 1982. Student pub. schs. Instr., Falcons Drum & Bugle Corps, Springfield, 1969-72; concert, stage, TV, film performer, 1970-82, part-time 1982—; guest dir. Sing out Salem, Ohio, 1973; contbg. writer Saddle Tramps Wild West Revue, 1977—; legal sec. to pvt. atty., Tustin, Calif., 1980-82; owner Am. Dream Balloons & Svcs., Orange, Calif., 1982-89; founder, corp. pres. Am. Dream Limousine Svc., Inc., Orange, 1983-90; founder, pres., designer Am. Dream Creations Co., Inc., Irvine, Calif., 1988—; founder Am. Dream Bride's Mus., 1992. Songwriter; designer greeting cards, T-shirts and wedding related gifts; one-of-a-kind automobile; producer, dir. mus. stage shows, 1974-82; author: TIPS - The Server's Guide to Bringing Home the Bacon, 1987, There's a Bunny in the House, 1992, Real Rabbitts Don't Eat Lettuce, 1992. Performer, Up With People, 1972-73; organizer Bicentennial Com. Springfield, 1976; mediator Limousine and Chauffeur Council, Orange County, 1984—; vol. Orange County Performing Arts Soc., 1985—. Recipient Appreciation, Achievement awards Muscular Dystrophy Assn., 1977-79, Transp. Partnership award, 1988, seven songwriting and vocal performance awards Music City Song Festival, 1989, Outstanding Booth Display award Chgo. Gift Show, 1991. Mem. Am. Entrepreneurs Assn., Internat. Platform Assn., Nat. Limousine Assn., So. Calif. Limousine Owners Assn., Nat. Assn. Female Execs., Nat. Bridal Assn., Orange County C. of C., Greenpeace, Doris Day Animal League, People for Ethical Treatment of Animals. Republican. Avocations: guitar, piano, writing. Office: Am Dream Creations Co Inc 634 N Poplar St Ste K Orange CA 92668-1026

SPENCER-DAHLEM, ANITA JOYCE, medical/surgical and critical care nurse; b. Weirton, W.Va., Aug. 26, 1961; d. Carlas A. and Evelyn Faye (Miller) Spencer; m. Terry Dahlem. BS, Alderson-Broaddus Coll., Philippi, W.Va., 1984. Staff nurse, orthopedic unit Charleston (W.Va.) Area Med. Ctr., 1984-86; ICU staff nurse Ohio Valley Hosp., Steubenville, Ohio, 1986—; nurse on cardiac catheterization unit Ohio Valley Hosp., Steubenville, 1994—. Mem. Ohio Nurses Assn.

SPERLING, MINDY TOBY, social sciences and bilingual education educator; b. N.Y.C., Dec. 21, 1954; d. Albert and Jeanette (Klein) Goldweit; m. Jonathan Sperling, June 15, 1980; children: Joshua, Elliot Asher. BS, Cornell U., 1976; MA, New Sch. Social Rsch., 1978; PhD, Yeshiva U., 1989. Rsch. asst. Cornell U., Ithaca, N.Y., 1975; nursery sch. tchr. Women's and Children's Ctr., Pearl River, N.Y., 1976-77; instr. Cen. Colombo-Americano, Medellin, Colombia, 1979; translator Escuela Nacional de Salud Publica, Medellin, 1979; trilingual exec. sec. Bank Leumi Trust Co. N.Y., 1979-82; intern psychol. rsch. pediatrics unit Columbia Presbyn. Hosp., N.Y.C., 1983-84; adj. prof. Internat. Overseas Program, Coll. Edn. U. Ala., Tuscaloosa, 1984-85; instr. Yeshiva U., N.Y.C., 1985-89; program evaluation cons. multicultural edn. Office of Rsch. Evaluation and Assessment, Bklyn., 1990-91, field cons. spl. rsch. div., study on ltd. English proficient students, 1990-91; cons. N.Y.C. Bd. Edn., 1985, program evaluation cons. OREA, 1990, field cons. effective svc. study, 1990; adj. prof. Multicultural Ctr. Jersey City State Coll., summer 1990, bilingual/ESL program, dept. langs. and culture, William Paterson Coll., Wayne, N.J., 1990-91; part time faculty Dept. English/Fgn. Languages Howard C.C., 1993—; presenter LLL of Md./Del./D.C. Area Conf., 1992, 93; bilingual listed leader Collumbia II La Leche League, 1992—, founded La Leche League of Savage/No. Laurel, 1993—; provider instructional svcs. to non-English speaking students, Elkridge (Md.) Elem. Sch., 1992—; rep. N. Am. Conf. Ethiopian Jewry, Beinei'nu (Between Us) project, 1992-93; tchr. hands-on-sci. outreach program Bollman Bridge Elem. Sch., 1993; lectr. U. P.R.; coord. Chaverim Bi' Golah Program Consolidated Religious Sch., Md., 1992-94; part-time faculty, lectr. dept. Spanish and Portugese U. Md., College Park, 1994—, adj. prof. univ. coll., 1994-95; swim instr. Columbia Swim Ctr. Translator Further Studies on Family Formation Patterns and Health, 1981; reviewer in field; contbr. articles to profl. jours. Storyteller, Queensboro Pub. Libr., 1987-88; bilingual leader La Leche League Ctrl.-Queens, N.Y., 1991, Columbia II La Leche League Md./Del./D.C., 1991-92, North Laurel, 1993—; mem. N.Y.C. Storytelling Ctr., 1987-88; bilingual project coord./parent liaison Dual Lang. Enrichment program Brook Ave. Sch., Bay Shore, N.Y., 1990-91; bilingual storyteller Bollman Bridge Elem. Sch., 1991-94; instr. Spanish classes on maternal child health topics for expectant parents Howard County Health Dept., 1994—. Recipient Outstanding Tchr. award Panhellenic Assn. U. Md., 1994-95; U.S. Dept. Edn. fellow, Yeshiva U., 1982-85. Mem. APA, AAAS, Psychology Soc. (chair 1977-78), Soc. Rsch. Child Devel., N.Y. Acad. Scis., Internat. Platform Assn., Nat. Assn. Bilingual Edn., Am. Acad. Polit. and Social Sci, Rockland Coun. for Young Children. Home: 9537 Sea Shadow Columbia MD 21046-2060 Office: U Md Dept Spanish and Portugese 2215B Juan Ramón Jiménez Hall College Park MD 20742 also: University Blvd at Adelphi Rd College Park MD 20742-1660

SPERO, JOAN EDELMAN, multi-service corporation executive; b. Davenport, Iowa, Oct. 2, 1944; d. Samuel and Sylvia (Halpern) Edelman; m. Carl Michael Spero, Nov. 9, 1969; children—Jason, Benjamin. Student, L'Inst. d'Etudes Politiques, Paris, 1964-65; B.A., U. Wis., 1966; M.A., Columbia U., 1968, Ph.D., 1973. Asst. prof. Columbia U., N.Y.C., 1973-79; ambassador of U.S. to UN Econ. and Social Council, N.Y.C., 1980-81; v.p. Am. Express Co., N.Y.C., 1981-83, sr. v.p. internat. corp. affairs, 1983-89; treas., sr. v.p., 1989-91; exec. v.p. corp. affairs and communications Am. Express Co., 1991-93; under sec. for econ., bus. and agrl. affairs Dept. of State, Washington, 1993—; vis. scholar Fed. Res. Bank N.Y , 1976-77; mem. U.S.-Japan Bus. Coun., Washington, 1983—. Author: The Politics of International Economic Relations, 4th edit., 1990, The Failure of the Franklin National Bank, 1980; contbr. articles to profl. jours. Trustee Amherst Coll.; bd. dirs. French-Am. Found.; mem. Coun. Am. Ambassadors. Named to Acad. Women Achievers, YWCA, 1983; named Fin. Woman of Yr., Fin. Women's Assn., 1990; recipient George Washington Disting. Statesperson award, 1994; Woodrow Wilson fellow. Mem. Coun. on Fgn. Rels. (Internat. Affairs fellow), The Trilateral Commn., Svcs. Policy Adv. Com., Phi Beta Kappa. Democrat. Jewish. Office: US Dept State Econ Agt Affairs 2201 C St NW Washington DC 20520-7512

SPERO, MADDALENA ANN, nurse; b. S.I., N.Y., May 27, 1962; d. Albert Joseph and Angela Mary (Carbone) S.; m. Joseph Michael Ruggiero, Sept. 30, 1988; 1 child, Jessie Lynn. Cert. med. asst., Coll. S.I., 1984; diploma in nursing, St. Vincent's Sch. Nursing, S.I., 1986. Cert. BLS, N.Y.; RN, N.Y. Med. asst. S.I. (N.Y.) Med. Group, 1983-84; rehab./phys. medicine staff nurse S.I. (N.Y.) Univ. Hosp., 1986-92; employee health svc. staff nurse, 1992—; nurse, vascular technician, office nurse S.I. (N.Y.) Surg. Assocs., 1986-92, staff nurse, office nurse, 1992—; v.p. student body St. Vincent's Sch. Nursing, S.I., 1984-86. Recipient president's award and svc. award S.I. U. Hosp., 1994. Mem. N.Y. State Nurses Assn., Am. Assn. Office Nurses.

SPERR, JOANNE DOE, educator; b. Jay, Maine, Mar. 8, 1939; d. Walter Henderson and Frances Edla (Lane) Doe; m. William Frederick Sperr, June 21, 1958; children: Bruce Jeffrey, Cheri Lynn, Bonnie Lou. BS summa cum laude, Gordon Coll., 1961; MEd, Northeastern U., 1970. Devel. reading tchr. Mission Ch. High Sch., Roxbury, Mass., 1970-72; reading specialist Dedham (Mass.) Mid. Sch., 1972-82, head reading dept., 1982-93; adminstrv. asst. Mount Ida Coll., Newton Centre, Mass., 1994—; staff devel. leader Dedham Pub. Schs., 1973-79, reading program developer, 1982-90, merit roll coord., 1976-88; workshop presenter Milton (Mass.) Pub. Schs., 1985, New Eng. League Mid. Schs., Hyannis, Mass., 1986, 87. Sunday sch. tchr. 2d Bapt. Ch., Newton Upper Falls, Mass., 1988-93, deaconess, 1991-93; active Needham (Mass.) Hist. Soc., 1978—. Mem. Internat. Reading Assn., Mass. Reading Assn. (mem. parents and reading com. 1988-89), Greater Boston Reading Coun., Dirs. of Reading (chair lit. com. 1989-90), Delta Kappa Gamma (1st v.p. 1993—, scholarship grantee 1992), Phi Alpha Chi, Kappa Delta Pi. Home: 91 Nehoiden St Needham MA 02192-1941

SPERRY, DONNA JEAN, psychologist; b. Port Huron, Mich., June 19, 1960; d. Zina Braden and Betty Lou (Dickens) Bennett; m. George Harold Sperry; children: Ursula Ann, Jasson Lee. BSW, Ctrl. Mich. U., 1982; MA in Clin. Psychology, Mercy Coll., Detroit, 1992. Lic. psychologist; registered social worker. Client svcs. mgr. Ausable Valley Cmty. Mental Clinic, West Branch, Mich., 1982-86; outpatient therapist N.E. Guidance Ctr., Detroit, 1986-89; foster care worker State of Mich., Detroit, 1989-90; specialist State of Mich. Dept. Social Svcs., Detroit, 1990—; child psychologist Eastwood Clinic, East Pointe, Mich., 1992—; developer sch. dropout prevention program Dept. Social Svcs., Detroit, 1990—; presenter sch. dropout prevention program Nat. Sch. Dropout Prevention Network, Tulsa, 1991. Union steward N.E. Guidance Ctr., Detroit, 1986-89, bargaining team mem., 1988; mem. Macomb County Girl Scouts' Bd., 1995—. Recipient Outstanding Profl. and Ethical Svc. award Columbus Mid. Sch., Detroit, 1992. Mem. APA (assoc.), Mich.Women Psychologists. Methodist. Office: State Mich Dept Social Svcs 14050 Maddelein St Detroit MI 48205-2321

SPHAR, GAIL ELLEN, insurance company executive; b. LaPorte, Ind., Mar. 4, 1946; d. Edward R. and Dorothy Mae (Wallace) Trigg; 1 child. BS, U. S.C., 1966, MS, 1972; MBA, U. Ala.-Birmingham, 1984. Instr. U. S.C., Columbia, 1971-73; mgr. tng. and devel. Blue Cross and Blue Shield of S.C., 1973-76; dir. tng. and devel. Blue Cross & Blue Shield of Ala., 1976-79, mgr. dept. human resources, 1979-82, v.p. human resources 1983-87; v.p. administrn. and human resources Blue Cross & Blue Shield of Mo., 1987, sr. v.p. adminstrn., 1988, sr. v.p. corp. and med. adminstrn. 1989-90, sr. v.p. adminstrn. & corp. affairs, 1991-92, regional v.p., COO, 1993—. Chmn. funding and fin. Childcare Task Force, United Way, Birmingham, 1983-84, bd. dirs., chmn. personnel com. Childcare Resources of Jefferson, Shelby and Walker counties, 1984-86, pres., 1987; v.p. membership, pres. FORUM, Birmingham, 1984; mem. adv. bd. Masters in Pub. and Pvt. Mgmt. program Birmingham So. Coll., 1985-87; vice-chmn. pers. com. Confluence St. Louis, 1988-89, chmn., 1990-93, bd. dirs., 1991-93, exec. com., 1992-93; mem. Vol. Svcs. St. Louis chpt. ARC, 1988-93; mem. partnership program com. St. Louis Art Mus., 1992; bd. dirs. The Caring Program Mo., 1988-93, Marshall Coll., 1993, 1st Unitarian Ch., 1991-93, NCCJ, St. Louis Region, 1992-93, Heart of Mo. Girl Scout Coun., 1994; chmn. workforce issues task force Gov. Commn. Mgmt. & Productivity, 1994; mem. adv. bd. St. Louis Regional Quality Inst., 1992-93. Mem. Am. Assn. Indsl. Mgmt. (bd. dirs. 1989-93, St. Louis chpt), Regional AIDS Interfaith Network (bd. dirs. 1993), Vis. Nurses Assn. Ctrl. Mo. (bd. dirs. 1994—), Birmingham C. of C. (bd. dirs. 1987). Avocations: reading, music, astronomy and astrophysics, volleyball. Office: Blue Cross-Blue Shield Mo 1000 W Nifong Columbia MO 65205

SPHEERIS, PENELOPE, film director; b. New Orleans, 1945. MFA, UCLA Film Sch. Producer: TV series of shorts for Saturday Night Live; films include: The Decline of Western Civilization II: The Metal Years, 1988, Real Life, 1979; dir. (documentary) the Decline of Western Civilization, 1981, (films) Suburbia, 1984, (also screenwriter) The Boys Next Door, 1985, Hollywood Vice Squad, 1986, Dudes, 1987, Wayne's World, 1992, The Beverly Hillbillies, 1993, The Little Rascals, 1994;screenwriter: Summer Camp Nightmare, 1987; actress: Wedding Band, 1990; tv films directed include: Prison Stories: Women on the Inside, 1990. Office: The Gersh Agency Inc 232 N Canon Dr Beverly Hills CA 90210*

SPICER, CAROL INGLIS, freelance writer; b. Detroit, June 8, 1907; d. William Inglis and Carolyn (Clay) Rittenhouse; m. Robert Walker Spicer, 1936;1 child, Susan. AB, U. Mich., 1930. Free lancer Ann Arbor, Mich. Contbr. articles to House Beautiful, McCall's, Parents, Yankee, Better Homes and Gardens, Vogue, L.A. Times, Newsday, Boston Globe, Toronto Star, Cleve. Plain Dealer, Washington Post, Saturday Evening Post, others. Mem. Midwest Travel Writers Assn. (Best Mag. Article award 1979, Best Newspaper Article award 1981), Detroit Women Writers. Home: 740 Green Hills Dr Ann Arbor MI 48105-2718

SPICHER, ELIZABETH HERSHBERGER, community health nurse; b. Newton, Kans., Jan. 7, 1923; d. Elmer D. and Amy Elizabeth (Erb) Hershberger; m. Ray S. Spicher, July 20, 1947; children: Jonathan Douglas, Dennis Ray, Ellsworth Doyle, Randall Dean. Diploma, La Junta Mennonite Hosp., 1944; BSN, Goshen Coll., 1949; MSN, Mont. State U., 1969. RN, Kans.; cert. high risk neonate nurse. Staff nurse various hosps., Newton, McPherson, Salina, Kans., 1949-67; nursing instr. U. Kans., Kansas City, 1969-75; community nurse, pre-screener Clinicare Family Health Svc., Kansas City, 1977-86; ret.; part-time pub. health nurse Jefferson County Pub. Health Dept., Oskaloosa, Kans., 1987-93; mem. adv. bd. Nursing Assessment and Mgmt. of Frail Elderly Project. Researcher, contbr. articles to profl. jours. Mem. health and welfare com. Mennonite Ch. Bd. Missions, 1976-81. Recipient Silver Poets award, 1986, 89, 91. Mem. Nat. League Nursing, Kans. State Nurses Assn. (pres. Dist. 2, membership, legis., nominating, resolution coms.), Johnson County Mental Health Assn., Mennonite Nurses Assn. (life mem.), Alumnae Assn. La Junta Mennonite Sch. Nursing, Sigma Theta Tau.

SPICOCHI, ELSA MARIA, nurse; b. Cleve., Nov. 12, 1962; d. Raimond and Norma Leila (Zayas) Liepins; divorced; children: Anthony, Nicolas. BSN, U. N.Mex., 1987. RN; lic. massage therapist. Staff nurse U. N.Mex. Hosp., Albuquerque, 1987-88; assoc. patient care mgr. Tucson Med. Ctr., 1988-89; staff nurse U. Wash. Med. Ctr., Seattle, 1989-93; transport nurse Children's Orthopedic Hosp., Seattle, 1990-92; shift coord. Stevens Meml. Hos., Edmonds, Wash., 1992—, massage therapy coord., 1994—; instr. Neonatal Resuscitation Program. Bd. dirs. North King County Little League, Seattle, 1991-94. Democrat. Christian.

SPIEGEL, BONNIE JOY, artist; b. N.Y.C., Feb. 11, 1945; d. Edward and Rebecca (Figelman) Koenig; m. Stanley Spiegel, Aug. 26, 1965; children: Alisa Kay, Noah Evan. BFA, Cooper Union, 1966; postgrad., Boston U., 1973-75. Book designer Alfred A. Knopf Pub., N.Y.C., 1968-70; freelance artist, graphic designer N.Y.C., Cambridge, Mass., 1972-76; freelance artist, painter, calligrapher, tchr. Portland, Maine, 1976—; tchr. Innovations, Internat. Calligraphy Conf., N.Y.C., 1986, Letter Forum, Washington, 1988. Author: work examples sect.) Lettering Arts in the 80's, 1984, Contemporary Calligraphy, 1986, Sixty Alphabets, 1986, The Creative Stroke, 1992, The Creative Stroke II, 1994. Mem. Portland Dem. City Com., 1993—. Mem. Union Main Visual Artists, Art Dirs. Club, Calligraphers of Maine (pres., founding mem., program chmn., newsletter editor 1981-94). Home: 121 William St Portland ME 04103

SPIEGEL, EVELYN SCLUFER, biology educator, researcher; b. Phila., Mar. 20, 1924; d. George and Helen (Laurantos) Sclufer; m. Melvin Spiegel, Apr. 16, 1955; children: Judith Ellen, Rebecca Ann. BA, Temple U., 1947; MA, Bryn Mawr Coll., 1951; PhD, U. Pa., 1954. Asst. program dir. for regulatory biology NSF, Washington, 1954-55; instr. in biology Colby Coll., Waterville, Maine, 1955-59; rsch. assoc. Dartmouth Coll., Hanover, N.H., 1961-74, rsch. assoc. prof. biology, 1974-78, rsch. prof. biology, 1978-91; rsch. prof. biology emerita, 1991—; vis. scholar Calif. Inst. Tech., Pasadena, 1964-65, U. Calif.-San Diego, La Jolla, 1970, Nat. Inst. for Med. Rsch., Mill Hill, Eng., 1971, NIH, Washington, 1975-76, U. Basel (Switzerland) Biocenter, 1979, 80, 81, 82, 85. Contbr. numerous articles to profl. jours., chpts. to books and book reviews. Mem. Soc. for Devel. Biology, Marine Biol. Lab. Corp. (trustee 1981-86, 88-92). Office: Dartmouth Coll Dept Biol Scis Hanover NH 03755

SPIEGEL, LINDA F., lawyer; b. Bronx, N.Y., Mar. 13, 1953; d. Rubin E. and Edna (Zucker) S.; m. Paul Duboff, June 12, 1983; 1 child, Joshua Michael. AB, Barnard Coll., Columbia U., 1974; JD, Boston U., 1978. Bar: N.J. 1978, U.S. Dist. Ct. N.J. 1978, N.Y. 1980, U.S. Dist. Ct. (so. and ea. dists.) N.Y. 1980, U.S. Supreme Ct. 1982. Tax editor Prentice Hall, Englewood, N.J., 1978; pvt. practice, Hackensack, N.J., 1978-83, 88—; assoc. Friedman, Carney & Wilson, Newark, 1983-84; pvt. practice New Milford, N.J., 1984-85; assoc. LaFianza and Strull, Hackensack, 1985-87, ptnr., 1987-88; instr. Inst. Legal Asst. and Paralegal Tng., Mahwah, N.J., 1978-81. Spkr. Boy Scouts Am., Bergen, N.J., 1980; mem. atty.-acct. divsn. United Jewish Cmty., River Edge, N.J., 1978—; trustee Women's Am. Orgn. Rehab. through Tng., 1987-88; chmn. Jean Robertson Women Lawyers Scholarship Found., Inc., 1987-94. Mem. ABA, Am. Arbitration Assn. (comml. and constrn. arbitator 1989—), N.J. Women Lawyers Assn., N.J. State Bar Assn., Bergen County Bar Assn. (trustee 1989-94, editor-in-chief Bergen Barrister 1991-94), Women Lawyers in Bergen County (pres. 1987-89), B'nai Brith. Democrat. Office: Ste 1 79 Main St Hackensack NJ 07601-7126

SPIEGEL, MARILYN HARRIET, real estate executive; b. Bklyn., Apr. 3, 1935; d. Harry and Sadie (Oscher) Unger; m. Murray Spiegel, June 12, 1954; children: Eric Lawrence, Dana Cheryl, Jay Barry. Grad. high sch., Bklyn. Exec. sec. S & W Paper Co., N.Y.C., 1953-54, Japan Paper Co., N.Y.C., 1954-58; salesperson Red Carpet Realtors, Los Alamitos, Calif., 1974-75, Coll. Park Realtors, Garden Grove, Calif., 1975-79; owner, broker S & S Properties, Los Alamitos, Calif., 1979—. Named Realtor of Yr., 1989. Mem. Calif. Assn. Realtors (bd. dirs. 1984—), West Orange County Bd. Realtors (bd. dirs. 1984—, 1st v.p. 1987, pres. 1988), Million Dollar Sales Club, Long Beach C. of C., Seal Beach C. of C., Orange County C. of C., Summit Orgn., Toastmasters (pres. founders group Garden Grove, Calif. 1990). Home: 4765 Candleberry Ave Seal Beach CA 90740-3035 Office: S & S Properties 3502 Katella Ave Ste 208 Los Alamitos CA 90720-3115

SPIEGEL, PHYLLIS, public relations consultant, journalist; b. Bronx, N.Y.; d. Bernard and Lillian (Horowitz) Finkelberg; m. Stanley Spiegel, Sept. 20, 1959 (div. 1981); children: Mark, Adam. BA, NYU. Feature writer various newspapers, pubs., 1960's-70's; dir. pub. rels. Mort Barish Assocs., Princeton, N.J., 1975-80; account exec. pub. rels. Keyes Martin, Springfield, N.J., 1980-84; pres. Phyllis Spiegel Assocs., Plainsboro, N.J., 1984—. Pub. rels. dir., founder Red Oak Coop. Nursery Sch., Middletown, N.J., 1960's, Matawan, N.J., Student Enrichment Program, 1960's-70's; pub. rels. cons., event organizer New Philharm. of N.J., Morristown, 1991-93; advocate Child Placement Rev. Bd. of Family Ct., Mercer County, N.J., 1994—. Recipient Commendation from Gov. N.J. for U. Med. and Dental of N.J. campaign, 1983, Commendation for N.J. Pharm. Assn. campaign Pub. Rels. News Assn., 1979. Mem. Soc. for Humanistic Judaism (bd. dirs. 1983-85). Office: Phyllis Spiegel Assocs PO Box 243 Plainsboro NJ 08536

SPIEGELBERG, EMMA JO, business education educator; b. Mt. View, Wyo., Nov. 22, 1936; d. Joseph Clyde and Dorcas (Reese) Hatch; BA with honors, U. Wyo., 1958, MEd, 1985; EdD Boston U., 1990; m. James Walter Spiegelberg, June 22, 1957; children: William L., Emory Walter, Joseph John. Tchr. bus. edn. Laramie (Wyo.) High Sch., 1960-61, 65-93, adminstr., 1993—. Bd. dirs. Cathedral Home for Children, Laramie, 1967-70, 72—, pres., 1985-88, Laramie Plains Mus., 1970-79. Author: Branigan's Accounting Simulation, 1986, London & Co. II, 1993; co-author Glencoe Computerized Acctg., 1993, Microcomputer Accounting: Daceasy, 1994, Microcomputer Accounting: Peachtree, 1994, Microcomputer Accounting: Accpac, 1994. Named Wyo. Bus. Tchr. of Yr., 1982. Mem. Am. Vocat. Assn. (policy com. region V 1984-87, region V Tchr. of Yr. 1986), Wyo. Vocat. Assn. (exec. bd. 1978-80, pres. 1981-82, Outstanding Contbns. to Vocat. Edn. award 1983, Tchr. of Yr. 1985, exec. sec. 1986-89), Nat. Bus. Edn. Assn.(bd. dirs. 1987-88, 1991—, Sec. Tchr. of the Yr. 1991), Mt. Plains Bus. Edn. Assn. (Wyo. rep. to bd. dirs. 1982-85, pres. 1987-88, Sec. Tchr. of the Yr. 1991, Leadership award 1992), Internat. Soc. Bus. Edn., Wyo. Bus. Edn. Assn. (pres. 1979-80), NEA, Wyo. Edn. Assn., Albany County Edn. Assn. (sec. 1970-71), Laramie C. of C. (bd. dirs. 1985-88), U. Wyo. Alumni Assn. (bd. dirs. 1985-90pres. 1988-89), Kappa Delta Pi, Phi Delta Kappa, Alpha Delta Kappa (state pres. 1978-82), Chi Omega, Pi Lambda Theta, Delta Pi Epsilon. Mem. United Ch. of Christ. Club: Zonta. Home: 3301 Grays Gable Rd Laramie WY 82070-5031 Office: Laramie High Sch 1275 N 11th St Laramie WY 82070-2206

SPIEGEL-HOPKINS, PHYLLIS MARIE, psychotherapist; b. Chgo., Oct. 28, 1947; d. Joseph Frank and Marie Ann (Hejhal) Spiegel; m. Daniel Mark Hopkins, Jan. 14, 1984. BSE, Chgo. State U., 1968, MA in History, 1972; MA in Clin. Psychology, Ill. Sch. Profl. Psychology, Chgo., 1988; D in Clin. Hypnotherapy, Am. Inst. Hypnotherapy, Santa Ana, Calif., 1991. Cert. tchr., Ill; cert. clin. hypnotherapist. Tchr. Holy Cross Grammar Sch., Chgo., 1968-69, Chgo. Bd. Edn., 1969-81, Mt. Asissi Acad., Lemont, Ill., 1981-82; police officer Chgo. Police Dept., 1981—; psychotherapist pvt. practice Chgo., 1988—. Mem. Am. Bd. Hypnotherapy, Nat. Guild Hypnotists, S.W. Hypnosis Soc., Assn. for Study of Dreams, C.G. Jung Inst. Chgo., Fraternal Order Police, Assn. Past-Life Therapy and Rsch. (life), Assn. Counselors and Therapists (life). Office: P O Box 185 Bedford Park IL 60499

SPIELMAN, BARBARA HELEN NEW, editor, consultant; b. Canton, Ohio, June 28, 1929; d. Arthur Daniel and Helen Barbara (Rickenmann) New; m. David Vernon Spielman, Nov. 24, 1956; children: Daniel Bruce, Linda Barbara. BS in English and History Edn. cum laude, Miami U., Oxford, Ohio, 1951. Cert. tchr., Ohio, Tex. Tchr. Canton Pub. Schs., 1951-53; vets. aide U. Tex., Austin, 1954-57; copy editor, mng. editor U. Tex. Press, Austin, 1964-91; ret., 1991; editorial cons. Chicago Manual of Style, 13th edit., 1975, Amon Carter Mus., Ft. Worth, 1970—, Ctr. for Mex. Am. Studies, Austin, 1980, Archer M. Huntington Art Gallery, Austin, 1975—, 64 Beds Project for Homeless and Hungry, Austin, 1989—; mem. search com. for dir., U. Tex. Press, 1991. Troop leader Girl Scouts Am., Austin, 1970-73; officer PTA, Austin, 1964-73. Mem. AAUW, Am. Assn. Univ. Presses, Smithsonian Instn., Nat. Geog. Soc., Althenoi, Order Eastern Star, Phi Beta Kappa, Kappa Delta Pi, Sigma Sigma Sigma. Democrat. Presbyterian. Home: 3301 Perry Ln Austin TX 78731-5330

SPIER, LUISE EMMA, film editor, director; b. Laramie, Wyo., Aug. 22, 1928; d. Louis Constantine Cames and Vina Jane Cochran; m. John Spier, Sept., 1957 (div. 1962). Student, U. Wyo., 1947, U. Calif., Berkeley, 1948-53. Head news film editor Sta. KRON-TV, San Francisco, 1960-70, film editor, 1980—; freelance film editor, director San Francisco, 1970-80, 83—. Edited and directed numerous news specials and documentaries, including The Lonely Basque, Whaler, The American Way of Eating. Recipient numerous awards for film editing and directing, including Cine Golden Eagle, Best Med. Res. Film award John Muir Med. Found., Chris Statuette, Bronze and Silver Cindy awards Info. Film Producers Am.

SPIES, KAREN BORNEMANN, writer, education consultant; b. Renton, Wash., Sept. 5, 1949; d. William Edward and Aina Jeanette (Johnson) Bornemann; m. Allan Roy Spies, July 18, 1970; children: Karsten, Astrid. BA, Calif. Luth. U., Thousand Oaks, 1970; MEd, U. Wash., 1974. Vice prin., tchr. Lake Washington Sch. Dist., Kirkland, Wash., 1971-79; tchr. various pub. schs. N.J., 1979-82; kindergarten tchr. Mt. Park Sch., Lake Oswego, Oreg., 1982-84; writer, seminar leader, cons. Wash., 1984-87, Oreg., 1984-87, Littleton, Colo., 1987—; lectr. Arapahoe Community Coll., Littleton, 1988—; ski instr. various locations, 1974-87, Copper Mountain Resort, Colo., 1987—; curriculum writer Augsburg-Fortress Pubs.; lectr. in field. Author: Family Activities for the Christmas Season, 1988, Denver, 1988, Raffi: The Children's Voice, 1989, Visiting in the Global Village, Vol. I, 1990, Vol. II, 1991, Vol. III, 1992, Vol. IV, 1993, Vol. V, 1994, Everything You Need to Know About Grieving, 1990, Competitiveness, 1991, Barbara Bush, 1991, George Bush, 1991, Everything You Need to Know About Incest, 1992, Our National Holidays, 1992, Our Money, 1992, The American Family: Can It Survive, 1993, Everything You Need to Know About Diet Fads, 1993, Our Folk Heroes, 1994, Earthquakes, 1994, Our Presidency, 1994, others. Organist Wooden Cross Luth. Ch., 1977-79. Title III grantee, 1974. Mem. AAUW, Soc. Children's Book Writers and Illustrators, Mensa, Profl. Ski Instrs. Am., Pi Lambda Theta. Republican. Lutheran.

SPIES, PHYLLIS BOVA, information services company executive; b. Syracuse, N.Y., Nov. 10, 1949; d. Ralph Anthony and Elizabeth Margaret (Caputo) Bova; m. John William Spies, June 28, 1980; children: Fletcher, Logan. BA in Art History, SUNY, Cortland, 1971; MLS in Libr. and Info. Sci., Syracuse U., 1972. Libr. systems analyst Ohio Coll. Library Ctr., Columbus, 1973-78; mgr. libr. systems analysis OCLC Online Computer Libr. Ctr., Dublin, Ohio, 1978-83, div. v.p., 1983-89, v.p. internat., 1989-92, v.p. mem. svcs., sales and internat., 1992—; v.p. mem. svcs., sales and internat. OCLC Online Computer LIbr. Ctr., Dublin, Ohio, 1994—; trustee Maps Micrographic Preservation Svc., Bethlehem, Pa., 1990—. Contbr. articles to profl. jours. Mem. Columbus Coun. World Affairs. Fellow The Gaylord Co., 1971. Mem. ALA, Internat. Fedn. Libr. Assns., Dublin Women in Bus. Office: OCLC Online Computer Libr Ctr 6565 Frantz Rd Dublin OH 43017-5308

SPIKES, DOLORES R., academic administrator. Vice chancellor acad. affairs So. U. and Agrl. and Mech. Coll., Baton Rouge, until 1987; chancellor So. U., New Orleans, from 1987, Baton Rouge, 1988—. Office: So U & Agrl & Mech Coll System Office of the President Southern Branch PO Baton Rouge LA 70813*

SPILLER, PAT, critical care nurse, educator; b. Wichita Falls, Tex., Nov. 12, 1953; d. William Herman and Frances Euleane (Kimberell) Webb; m. Tommy Spiller, Sept. 3, 1971; children: Patrick Todd, Tara Dyann. ADN, Northwest Community Coll., Phil Campbell, Ala., 1979; BSN, U. Ala., Tuscaloosa, 1985. Asst. coord. spl. care unit Walker Regional Med. Ctr., Jasper, Ala., 1986-87, coor. spl. care unit, 1987-88, coor. spl. care unit/spl. ICU, 1988-89, nursing insvc. coord., 1990—. Author book on Messianic Jewish Festivals; contbg. author profl. reference book. Mem. AACCN, Am. Heart Assn. (nurse edn. com., pres.-elect), Ala. Soc. for Healthcare Edn. and Tng. (speakers bur.), Nat. Nursing Staff Devel. Orgn. Office: Walker Regional Med Ctr Edn and Tng Dept PO Box 3547 Jasper AL 35502-3547

SPILLMAN, JANE SHADEL, curator, researcher, writer; b. Huntsville, Ala., Apr. 30, 1942; d. Marvin and Elizabeth (Russell) Shadel; m. Don Lewis Spillman, Feb. 18, 1973; children: K. Elizabeth, Samuel Shadel. AB, Vassar Coll., 1964; MA, SUNY, 1965. Rsch. asst. Corning (N.Y.) Mus. Glass, 1965-70, asst. curator, 1971-73, assoc. curator Am. glass, 1974-77, curator, 1978—, head of curatorial dept., 1994—; cons. New Bedford (Mass.) Glass Mus., 1986, The White House Curator's Office, Washington, 1987-90. Author: Complete Cut and Engraved Glass of Corning, 1979, Knopf Collectors Guide to Glass, Vol. 1, 1982, Vol. 2, 1983, White House Glassware, 1989, Masterpieces of American Glass, 1990; also 6 other books, numerous articles. Mem. Am. Assn. Mus. (chairperson curators com. 1989-93), Nat. Early Am. Glass Club (bd. dirs. 1989-95), Glass Circle of London. Office: Corning Mus Glass 1 Museum Way Corning NY 14830-2253

SPILLMAN, MARJORIE ROSE, producer, dancer; b. Norfork, Va., Jan. 5; d. William Bert and Rose Marjorie (Naperski) S.; m. David E. Marks, Apr. 4, 1985; children: F. Oscar Marks, Miranda Rose. AS, Mt. Ida Jr. Coll., 1974; CT, Northeastern U., 1975; BS in Nursing, U. Mass., 1977. RN, Mass. Charge nurse VA Med. Ctr., Northampton, Mass., 1977-82; dancer N.E. Am. Ballet, Northampton, 1982, Ballet Theater Sch., Springfield, Mass., 1982-84, Smith Coll., Northampton, 1984—; sales rep. Winthrop Pharm., N.Y.C., 1982-94, Nycomed, N.Y.C., 1994—; prin. dancer Project Opera, Northampton, 1984-86; dancer Polobulus East St. Dance, Hadley, Mass., 1985; dance and theatre reviewer Holyoke T. Telegram, 1991, 92; theater reviewer Daily Hampshire Gazette, 1993—. Dancer, creator part of Carmen in Carmen, 1985, Ruth St. Denis in The House of Ruth Ted and Martha, 1994; dancer, choreographer A Victorian Evening, 1986; dancer Nutcracker Ballet Pioneer Valley Ballet, 1988; creator, prodr. The Halloween House at Sunnyside, 1990, producing dir., 1991, 92; actor, author play Mary P. Wells Smith Narrates, 1987; founder, prodr., dir. Northampton Children's Theatre, 1993—. Democrat. Lutheran.

SPINDEL, CAROL, writer, educator; b. Memphis, Nov. 30, 1954; d. Murray Asher and Christine (Cooper) S.; m. Thomas Joseph Bassett, June 4, 1983; children: Nicholas, Rebecca. BFA, U. Iowa, 1977; MA, U. Ill., 1988. Teaching asst. U. Ill., Urbana-Champaign, 1989—. Author: In the Shadow of the Sacred Grove, 1989 (N.Y. Times Book Review award 1989). Office: U Ill Dept English 70 Allen Hall MC-50 Urbana IL 61801

SPINGOLA, JEANNIE SAUNDRA, counselor, college, special and adult educator; b. San Francisco, June 17; d. Frank and Camella Regina (Mazzaferro) S.; m. Peter William Connolly. BA, San Francisco Coll. Women, 1970; MA, U. San Francisco, 1974; student, Dominican Coll., 1971. Counselor Dept. Store Local 1100, San Francisco; cons. ESL Am. Fgn. Studies, San Francisco; counselor, instr. San Francisco Coll. Dist.; cons. Fgn. Lang. Inst., San Francisco. Composer and vocal performer classical and musical comedy Macy's California. Mem. ASCD, ICF, MEA/OSIA, CABE, Am. Fedn. Tchrs., AMA, CAMP, Nat. Assn. Hist. Preservation, Am. CB Radio Assn., Calif. Psychol. Assn., Friends of J. Paul Libr.

SPINKS, ROBIN HIOTT, marketing professional; b. Greenville, S.C., Nov. 29, 1955; d. David Williams and Jean Carolyn (Rowe) Hiott; m. Lee Anthony Spinks, Nov. 25, 1978 (sep. Oct. 1992). BA in Urban Studies, Furman U., 1977. Lic. real estate broker, N.C. Intern Greenville County Redevel. Authority, 1977; rsch. asst. JE Sirrine Co., 1977-78; planner JE Sirrine Co., Research Triangle Park, N.C., 1978-84; exec. v.p. Edgecombe County Devel. Corp., Tarboro, N.C., 1984-89; mgr., project devel. Cogentrix, Inc., Charlotte, N.C., 1990-93; v.p., indsl. mktg. Cogentrix Energy, Inc., Charlotte, 1993—. Mem. Indsl. Devel. Rsch. Coun., Tech. Assn. Pulp and Paper Industry, Charlotte Area C. of C. (bd. advisors). Presbyterian. Office: Cogentrix Energy Inc 9405 Arrowpoint Blvd Charlotte NC 28273-8110

SPINWEBER, CHERYL LYNN, research psychologist; b. Jersey City, July 26, 1950; d. Stanley A. And Evelyn M. (Pfleger) S.; m. Michael E. Bruich, June 18, 1977; children: Sean Michael Bruich, Gregory Alan Bruich. AB with distinction, Cornell U., 1972; PhD in Exptl. Psychology, Harvard U., 1977. Lic. psychologist, Calif. Asst. prof. psychiatry Tufts U. Sch. Medicine, Medford, Mass., 1977-79; asst. dir. sleep lab. Boston State Hosp., 1973-79; dep. head dept. behavioral psychopharmacology Naval Health Research Ctr., San Diego, 1978-86, head dept. behavioral psychopharmacology, 1986-89; research asst. prof. dept. psychiatry Uniformed Svcs. U. of the Health Scis., Bethesda, Md., 1985—; lectr. workshop instr. U. Calif. San Diego, La Jolla, 1979-81, vis. lectr. 1979-86; assoc. adj. prof. Dept. Psychology, 1989-94, adj. prof., 1994—; courtesy clin. staff oppointee dept. psychiatry Naval Hosp., San Diego, 1984—; clin. dir. Sleep Disorders Ctr. Mercy Hosp., San Diego, 1991—; pediatric sleep specialist Children's Hosp., San Diego, 1992—. Contbr. articles to profl. jours. Scholar Cornell U., Ithaca, N.Y., 1968-72, West Essex Tuition, 1968-72, Cornell U. Fedn. Women, 1917-72, Harvard U., 1972-73, 74-76, NDEA Title IV, 1973-74; postdoctoral associateship Nat. Research Council, 1978-80. Fellow Am. Sleep Disorders Assn., Clin. Sleep Soc., We. Psychol. Assn. (sec.-treas. 1986—); mem. Am. Men and Women of Sci., Sleep Rsch. Soc. (exec. com. 1986-89), Calif. Sleep Soc., Sigma Xi. Office: U Calif San Diego Dept Psychology 0109 La Jolla CA 92093

SPIRE, NANCY WOODSON (MRS. LYMAN SPIRE), civic worker; b. Wausau, Wis., May 6, 1917; d. Aytchmonde Perrin and Leigh (Yawkey) Woodson; B.S., Radcliffe Coll., 1939; postgrad. Syracuse U., 1957—; m. Lyman J. Spire, June 29, 1940; children—Stephen Crittenden Woodson, Abigail Lyman. Vice pres. Woodson Fiduciary Corp., Wilmington, Del. Trustee Aytchmonde Woodson Found., pres., 1963—; trustee Corinthian Found., 1958-63, 68—, Syracuse Child and Family Service, 1957-62; trustee, sec. Crouse-Irving Meml. Hosp., Syracuse; trustee Syracuse Symphony Orch.; mem. exec. com. Syracuse U. Library Assos., 1958-63, trustee, 1958—. Bd. visitors N.Y. State Tng. Sch. for Girls; v.p. bd. dirs. Leigh Yawkey Woodson Art Mus. Mem. Syracuse Symphony Guild (treas. 1958-59), U.S. Trotting Assn. Republican. Universalist (trustee). Club: Virgin Islands Game Fishing. Office: Yawkey Lumber Co PO Box 65 Wausau WI 54402-0065 also: 707 Kimry Moor Fayetteville NY 13066-1834 also: Cowpet Bay W 24 Windward Way Saint Thomas VI 00802

SPIRER, JUNE DALE, marketing executive, clinical psychologist; b. N.Y.C., May 14, 1943; d. Leon and Gloria (Wagner) Spirer; BA, Adelphi U., 1965; MS, Yeshiva U., 1980, PhD in Psychology, 1984, postgrad. NYU, 1988. TV/radio buyer BBD&O, 1965-66, SSC&B, 1966-68; sr. media planner Norman, Craig & Kummel, N.Y.C., 1968-71; assoc. media dir. Ted Bates Co., 1971-72; v.p., account supt. C.T. Clyne Co., N.Y.C., 1972-74; dir. advt. Am. Express, 1974-75; corp. dir. advt. Del Labs., Farmingdale, N.Y., 1975-79; pres. J. Spirer & Assocs., Inc., N.Y.C., 1978—; pres., CEO Media Placement Svcs., Inc., 1985—, Tactics, Inc., 1988—; CEO 75 Main St. Restaurant, Southampton, N.Y., 1990—; Mem. Am. Psychol. Assn. Home: PO Box 490 Southampton NY 11969-0490 Office: 2 Horatio St New York NY 10014

SPIRES, ROBERTA LYNN, court clerk; b. Gary, Ind., Sept. 4, 1952; d. Merle Russell and Kathryn Dias (Felts) Harris; m. Richard John Badovinich, Aug. 16, 1975 (div. 1989); m. Patrick Robert Spires, Mar. 14, 1992; 1 child, Zachary Robert. Grad. high sch., Griffith, Ind. Dep. clk. U.S. Bankruptcy Ct., Gary, 1970-80; chief dep. clk. U.S. Bankruptcy Ct., 1980—. Mem. Fed. Ct. Clks. Assn., Fed. Bar Assn. (lectr., cert. 1984). Democrat. Roman Catholic. Home: 719 N Rueth Dr Griffith IN 46319-3817 Office: US Bankruptcy Ct 610 Connecticut St Gary IN 46402-2549

SPIRN, MICHELE SOBEL, communications professional, writer; b. Newark, Jan. 26, 1943; d. Jack and Sylvia (Cohen) Sobel; m. Steven Frederick Spirn, Jan. 27, 1968; 1 child, Joshua. BA, Syracuse U., 1965. Creative dir. Planned Communications Svcs., N.Y.C., 1966-72, EDL Prodns., N.Y.C., 1972-73; free-lance writer Bklyn., 1973-83; dir. pub. rels. Nat. Coun. Jewish Women, N.Y.C., 1990-95, dir. communications, 1990-95; freelance writer Bklyn., 1995—; adj. lectr. CUNY, Bklyn., 1977-81. Author: The Fast Shoes, 1985, The Boy Who Liked Green, 1985, The Know-Nothings, 1995; co-author: A Man Can Be..., 1981; editor, columnist Children's Entertainment Rev. mag., N.Y.C., 1982; columnist The Phoenix newspaper, Bklyn., 1983. Pres. Tenth St. Block Assn., Bklyn., 1989-91; vol. Model Media Program, Bklyn., 1985—. Recipient Silver medal for pub. svc. film N.Y. Internat. Film and TV Festival, 1972. Mem. Am. Mktg. Assn., Editorial Freelancers Assn.

SPISAK, MAXI, make-up artist; b. Cleve., July 23, 1961; d. Frank Eugene and Mary Louise (Babjak) S. Degree in art, Cleve. Inst. of Art. Pres., founder Make-Up Artists On Wheels, Inc., Cleve., Atlanta; key make-up artist for Metro-Goldwyn-Mayer, TNT Sports, Atlanta, TBS Sports, Atlanta. Make-up artist for feature films It Runs in the Family, Best of the Best 3, Wild Hearts Can't Be Broken, also for numerous cable and network TV programs, including Home Improvement, NBA Playoffs, 1992, 93, Monday Night Football, 1992, 93, Olympic Winter Games, 1992, 94, also indsl. films and print; supervising make-up artist for ABC Sports and TBS Sports at Goodwill Games, St. Petersburg, Russia, 1994. Scholar Cleve. Inst. Art, 1979. Mem. NATAS, Internat. Alliance Theatrical Stage Employees. Byzantine Catholic. Home and Office: 4144 Vezber Dr Seven Hills OH 44131 also: 1185 Collier Rd Ste 18E Atlanta GA 30318

SPISAK, SARA LOUISE, women's apparel retail business owner; b. Parma, Ohio, Mar. 11, 1966; d. Frank Eugene and Mary Louise (Babjak) S. AA in Applied Bus., Mgmt., Mktg., Cuyahoga Community Coll. West, Parma, Ohio, 1985. Exec. fashion buyer, merchandise mgr. Rosenblum's Inc., Cleve., 1986-92; owner Elegance for Less, North Royalton, Ohio, 1994—; adviser Parma 60+ Mall Fashion Shows, 1986-90; fashion coord., model AAA Travel Agy, Cleve. Fashion coord. for Rosenblum's Fashion, Parma Jr. League, 1990, fashion coord., narration writer, Parma Area Fine Arts Coun. Fashion Show, 1991; hon. judge Miss Parma Pageant, 1991. Recipient Scholastic Art awards, Cleve. Inst. Art, 1983. Mem. NAFE, Nat. Assn. Investors Corp., Phi Theta Kappa. Byzantine Catholic. Office: Elegance for Less 12871 State Rd North Royalton OH 44133

SPITTLER, JAYNE ZENATY, advertising executive; b. Chgo., July 24, 1948; d. Ernest Frederick and Mary Winifred (McEvilly) Zenaty; m. Joseph R. Spittler, Aug. 22, 1987; 1 child, Brian Joseph. BA, Clarke Coll., 1971; PhD, Mich. State U., 1980. Asst. dir. pub. rels. Clarke Coll., Dubuque, Iowa, 1974-76; asst. prof. dept. telecommunications Ind. U., Bloomington, 1979-81; supr. media rsch. Leo Burnett Co., Inc., Chgo., 1981-82, mgr. media rsch., 1982-84, v.p., dir. media rsch., 1984—; guest lectr. Northwestern U., Evanston, Il., 1981—. Vol. ARC, McHenry County, Ill.; zoo parent Brookfield (Ill.) Zoo, 1975—. Named to Media Rsch. All Star Team, Media Decisions, N.Y., 1987; recipient Excellence in Teaching award, Mich. State U., 1979, grant broadcast ownership, FCC, 1979, grant VCR Usage, Corp. for Pub. Broadcasting, 1980. Mem. Advt. Rsch. Found. (chair video electronic media coun. 1990-94, media comm. coun. mem. 1986—, radio rsch. coun. 1988—), Chgo. Advt. Fedn. (bd. dirs. 1986-91), Am. Assn. Advt. Agys. (media rsch. com. 1984—), Mich. State U. Alumni Assn. (Disting. Alumna award 1994). Roman Catholic. Office: Leo Burnett Co Inc 17 Bougainvillea Ave Key West FL 33040-6226

SPITZER, JACLYN B. RUBINSON, audiologist; b. Bklyn., July 3, 1951; d. Victor and Elaine (Mendelsohn) Rubinson; m. Jack Spitzer, Aug. 20, 1972; 1 child, Raquel Adina. BA cum laude, Bklyn. Coll., 1972; MS, Tchrs. Coll., 1973, MPhil, 1977; PhD, Columbia U., 1978. Cert. tchr. speech improvement, N.Y.; cert. tchr. speech and hearing handicapped, N.Y; lic. audiologist, Ohio, Conn.; lic. hearing aid dealer, Conn. Substitute tchr. N.Y.C. Bd. Edn., 1973; audiology doctoral stipend trainee Bklyn. VA Hosp., 1973-76; acting dir. audiology dept. Cleve. Hearing and Speech Ctr., 1977-78; instr. dept. speech communication Case Western Res. U., 1977-78, asst. prof. audiology and speech pathology div. otolaryngology and surgery, 1978-79, adj. asst. prof. dept. communication scis., 1980-82; rsch. assoc. Cleve. VA. Med., 1978-79, audiologist, 1980-82; chief audiology and speech pathology svc. West Haven Med. Ctr., 1982—; asst. clin. prof. dept. surgery Yale U., 1982-89, assoc. clin. prof. dept. surgery, 1989—; adj. asst. prof. dept. speech and hearing Cleve. State U., 1980-82; adj. prof. dept. communication disorders So. Conn. State U., 1984—; vis. prof. dept. communication scis. U. Conn., 1985—; presenter in field. Editorial cons. to sci. jours.; contbr. articles and book chpts. to profl. jours. Recipient N.Y. State regent's scholarship. Fellow Am. Acad. Audiology, Am. Speech. and Hearing Assn. (task force on nat. exam. 1978, state coord. for Ea. Ohio, congl. action contact network 1979-82, com. on disorders cen. auditory processing 1980-82, com. on aural rehab. 1986-91, program com. 1986-87, ad hoc com. on advances in audiologic practice 1990—); mem. N.Y. Speech and Hearing Assn., Ohio Speech and Hearing Assn. (audiologic affairs com. 1979, legis. affairs com. 1980-81), Ohio Coun. on Audiology (task force on early identification of hearing loss in infants 1979-81), Acoustical Soc. Am., Am. Auditory Soc., Conn. Speech and Hearing Assn. Home: 1287 Mt Carmel Ave North Haven CT 06473-1048

SPIVEY, SUZAN BROOKS NISBET, association administrator, medical technologist; b. Princeton, Ky., Sept. 19, 1932; d. Dixon Franklin and Eva (Brooks) Nisbet; m. Herman Everette Spivey Jr., June 8, 1953; children: Eva Kathryn Spivey Bridges, Herman Everette III. Student, U. Louisville, 1950; BS, U. Ky., 1954; grad., Inst. Orgnl. Mgmt. U. Ga., 1990; postgrad., U. Ga., 1990—. Registered med. technologist. Med. technologist Madison (Wis.) Gen. Hosp., 1955-58, Fern Creek Clinic, Louisville, 1958-62; med. technologist, cons. Ga. Primary Health Care, Summerville, 1981—, Chattooga County Hosp., Summerville, 1983-86; grad. Inst. for Orgnl. Mgmt. U.S. Chamber U. Ga., 1990; exec. v.p. Chattooga County C. of C., Summerville, 1984—; advisor Inst. for Orgnl. Mgmt. U.S. Chamber U. Ga., 1991. Author: (newsletter) Essentials, 1985—; editor: (book) Becoming a Better Board Member, 1982; columnist You and Your Schs., 1973-80. Pres. memls., dir. Chattooga chpt. Ga. Dist. Field Svc. Am. Cancer Soc., mem., 1964—; mem. Chattooga Bd. Edn., 1972-80, Ga. Assn. Leadership Communities, 1989—, Tri-State Coun., 1989—; bd. dir., advisor Chattooga County Parent/Child Ctr., 1972-92; bd. dirs. Lookout Mountain Pkwy. Assn., 1988—, Job Tng. Ptnrship. Act, Chattooga County, 1985—, 7th Dist. Ga. Sch. Bds. Assn., Atlanta, 1974-80; pres. Bicentennial Com., Chattooga County, 1974-76; producer Hallelujah Players, Summerville, 1976-85; trustee Floyd Coll., 1988—; bd. dirs. Literacy Adv. Com. Walker Tech. Inst., 1991—; mem. 7th dist. Ga. Congl. Adv. Com. on Health Care Reform, 1994. Recipient Excellence award Am. Cancer Soc., 1991; grantee Ga. Bd. Edn., 1990, 91, Ga. Gov.'s Commn., 1991. Mem. Am. Soc. Clin. Pathologists, So. Ind. Devel. Coun., Ga. Ind. Devel. Assn., Am. C. of C., Bus. and Profl. Women (Woman of Achievement award 1984), Ga. Assn. of Chamber Exces., Am. C. of C. Execs. Assn. Democrat. Presbyterian. Office: Chattooga County C of C 4 College Ave Summerville GA 30747-1722

SPOFFORD, SALLY HYSLOP, artist; b. N.Y.C., Aug. 20, 1929; d. George Hall and Esther (McNaull) Hyslop; m. Gavin Spofford, Mar. 11, 1950 (dec. Jan. 1976); children: Lizabeth Spofford Smith, Leslie Spofford Russell. Student, The China Inst., N.Y.C., 1949, The Art Students League, N.Y.C., 1950; BA with high honors, Swarthmore Coll., 1952. Instr. Somerset Art Assn., Peapack, N.J., 1978-85, Hunterdon Art Ctr., Clinton, N.J., 1985-88, chmn. Artists Adv. Coun. and bd. trustees; adv. bd., lectr. Apollo Muses, Inc., Gladstone, N.J.; bd. trustees Artshowcase, Inc. One-man show Riverside Studio, Pottersville, N.J., 1985, Morris Mus., Morristown, N.J. 1989, Schering-Plough Gallery, Madison, N.J., 1989, Phoenix Gallery, N.Y.C., 1990, Robin Hutchins Gallery, Maplewood, N.J., 1992, Berlex Labs. Corp. Office, Wayne, N.J., 1992, Hunterdon Art Ctr., Clinton, N.J., 1993; exhibited in group shows at Hickory (N.C.) Mus., 1983, Purdue U., 1983, Monmouth (N.J.), 1984, Nabisco Brands Gallery, E. Hanover, N.J., 1985, 89, Hunterdon Art Ctr., Clinton, N.J., 1988, 93, Schering-Plough Gallery, Madison, 1988, Morris Mus., Morristown, 1989, Robin Hutchins Gallery, Maplewood, N.J., 1992, Berlex Corp. Office, Wayne, N.J., 1992; represented in permanent collections N.J. State Mus., Trenton, Newark Mus. Painting residency fellow Vt. Studio Ctr., 1992. Mem. Assoc. Artists N.J. (pres. 1985-87), Allied Artists Am., N.J. Watercolor Soc., Federated Art Assns. of N.J. (panel mem. 1985, demonstrator 1991). Home: PO Box 443 Bernardsville NJ 07924-0443

SPOLAR-BLUMER, ANNE MARIE, insurance purchasing specialist; b. Tigerton, Wis., Sept. 2, 1956; d. Anthony R. and Bernadine G. (Donder) Spolar. A in Police Sci., Fox Valley Tech. Inst., Appleton, Wis., 1976; grad., Gemol. Inst. Am., 1989. Cert. gemologist. Salesperson Spolar's Jewelry, Appleton, Wis., 1976-85; asst. mgr. customer svc. Paradise Printing, Madison, Wis., 1985-88; gemology instr. Gemological Inst. Am., Santa Monica, Calif., 1989-93; purchasing specialist State Farm Ins. Co., Bloomington, Ill., 1993—. Mem. NAFE, Am. Gem Soc., Nat. Assn. Watch and Clock Collectors, Women's Jewelry Assn., Gemology Inst. Am. Alumni Assn. Office: State Farm Ins Co 1 State Farm Plz IL3 Bloomington IL 61710

SPONY, EILEEN LOUISE, accountant; b. N.Y.C., Nov. 24, 1949; d. Harold Joseph and Dorothy L. (Saunders) S.; m. Alan G. Glaros, Jan. 26, 1974; children: Christopher Alan Spony Glaros, Alexander William George Glaros. BA, SUNY, Stony Brook, 1971; MBA, NYU, 1977. CPA, Mo., Kans., Fla., Mich. Actuarial asst. Marsh & McLennan, N.Y.C., 1971-74; sr. acct. Arthur Young & Co. (name now Ernst & Young), Detroit, 1974-78; sr. fin. analyst GM, Detroit, 1978-84; contr. Info Tech, Inc., Gainesville, Fla., 1984-88; dir. fin and adminstrn. MTW Corp., Kansas City, Mo., 1989-92; prin. Eileen L. Spony, CPA, Overland Park, Kans., 1993—; adj. instr. acctg. Keller Grad. Sch. Mgmt., Kansas City, 1993; adj. instr. bus. Avila Coll., Kansas City, 1993—. Hon. dir. R.J. Rinehart Found, U. Mo.-Kansas City Sch. Dentistry, 1989-91. Mem. AICPA, Ctrl. Exch. (co-chair Women in Politics Vital Interest Group 1993-94), Am. Woman's Soc. CPAs (pres. Kansas City chpt. 1989-91, dir. 1991-93), Mo. Soc. CPAs (mem. MAP com. 1989—, chair MAP com. Kansas City chpt. 1994—), Fla. Inst. CPAs, Overland Park C. of C. (Pres.' Club 1993-94). Home and Office: 10415 W 126th St Overland Park KS 66213

SPORN, JUDITH BERYL, lawyer; b. N.Y.C., Mar. 3, 1951; d. Milton and Helen Florence (Berman) Shapiro; m. Robert C. Sporn, May 22, 1977; 1 child, David Benjamin. BA magna cum laude, SUNY, Buffalo, 1973; postgrad., Columbia U., 1973-74; JD, Loyola U., L.A., 1979. Bar: N.Y. 1979, Conn. 1982. Atty. firm Cohen & Tucker, N.Y.C., 1980-82, Barst & Mukamal, L.A., 1982-85; sole practice Westport, Conn., 1985—. Vol. atty. Vol. Lawyers for the Arts, N.Y.C., 1980-82, Los Angeles County Bar Pro Bono Immigration Project, L.A., 1983-85; bd. dirs. Women's Crisis Ctr., Norwalk, Conn., 1986. Mem. Fed. Bar Assn., Westport Bar Assn., Fairfield Women's Bar Assn., Am. Immigration Lawyers Assn. Office: 125 Main St Westport CT 06880-3303

SPOTTSVILLE, SHARON ANN, counselor; b. St. Louis; d. Robert F. and Elberta M. (Thompson) Hunter; children: Raymon L., Rodney L. BA, Cleve. State U., 1980, MEd, 1984. Lic. clin. counselor, Ohio. Counselor asst. pvt. practice psychiatry Cleve., 1980-84; counselor, social worker Harambee Svcs. to Black Families, Cleve., 1984-89; coord. parenting devel. rsch. projects Child Guidance Ctr., Cleve., 1989-94; case mgr. supr. Murtis H. Taylor-Multi Svcs. Ctr., Cleve., 1994—; presenter workshops; cons. and trainer in field. Co-author: Parenting Plus. Mem. ACA, Assn. Multi-Cultural Counseling and Devel., Ohio Mental Health Counselors Assn. Home: 2177 Bellfield Ave Cleveland OH 44106-3123 Office: Murtis H Taylor Multi Svcs Ctr 13422 Kinsman Ave Cleveland OH 44120

SPRABERY, CAROL ANN, health facility administrator; b. North Island, Calif., July 6, 1945; d. Thomas Eugene and Dorothy Frances (Grimes) Forister; div.; children: Scott Ellis, Cynthia Anne. BS, U. Miss., 1967; MEd, Miss. State U., 1986, PhD, 1990. Lic. profl. counselor; cert. psychometrist, nat. counselor. Adolescent counselor Laurelwood Psychiat., Meridian, Miss.; counselor Lamar Sch., Meridian; dir. outpatient svcs. Weems Cmty. Mental Health Ctr., Meridian, 1990—; mem. adj. faculty Miss. State U., 1990—. Mem. ACA, Miss. Counselors Assn., Assn. Mental Health Counselors, Assn. Sch. Counselors, Lauderdale County Mental Health Bd.

SPRABERY, PEGGY PEDEN, small business owner and administrator; b. Starkville, Miss., Oct. 21, 1950; d. William Aaron and Genevieve (McGuff) Peden; m. Donald L. Sprabery, Dec. 7, 1985; 1 child, Genevieve Anne. BS, Miss. U. for Women, 1972; MS in Edn. & Psychology, Miss Coll., 1974. Elementary educator Jackson (Miss.) Pub. Schs., 1972-76; English educator Long Beach (Miss.) Pub. Schs., 1976-79; food and beverage adminstr. Frenchman's Reef, St. Thomas, V.I., 1979-82; bus. owner Profl. Dressers, Gulfport, Miss., 1982—, Monograms, Etc., Gulfport, Miss., 1988—. Mem. Auxiliary (impaired phy. chmn. port Miss.), Civic League, Symphony bd. dirs. Home: Oaklawn Plantation Menge Pass Christian MS 39571 Office: Professional Dressers 1900 Pass Rd Gulfport MS 39501-5169

SPRADLEY, DEBBY HAY, advertising executive; b. Dallas, Dec. 8, 1952; d. Jess Thomas and Betty Jo (Peacock) Hay; children: Jessica Kathryn, Rachel Hay. BFA, So. Meth. U., 1975. Vice pres. Dallas Market Ctr., 1975-83; pres. The Hay Agy., Inc., Dallas, 1983—; bd. dirs. Turtle Creek Nat. Bank, New Bus. Devel. Bd. dirs. Dallas Democratic Forum, 1983, TACA, Inc., 1983—, The Family Place, 1985, The Hockaday Sch., 1992—, Dallas Summer Musicals, 1993—; active Jr. League Dallas, 1981—, Dallas Symphony Orch. League, Mental Health Assn.. Mem. Dallas Ad League, Fashion Group, Dallas Mus. Art, Dallas Comm. Coun. Democrat. Methodist. Home: 7226 Desco Dr Dallas TX 75225-2003 Office: The Hay Agy Inc 2121 San Jacinto St Ste 800 Dallas TX 75201-6717

SPRAGGINS, ALETHIA LUCILLE, principal; b. Washington, Oct. 5, 1938; d. Tinsley Lee and Alice (Grant) S.; children: Tracey A. McCauley, Dina R. Headen, Robert J. Headen, Jr. BS, Va. Union U., 1958; MS, Howard U., 1961; PhD, Union Inst., 1992. Rsch. biologist NIH, Bethesda, Md., 1961-62; tchr. Washington Pub. Schs., Washington, 1962-68, asst. prin., 1968-74, dir. curriculum, 1974-77, asst. prin., 1977-86; edn. tchr. Univ. of D.C., Washington, 1985-90; prin. Washington Pub. Schs., Washington, 1986—. Mem. Nat. Assn. Secondary Sch. Prins., Bd. Sr. High Sch. Prins. (treas. 1988—), The Links, Inc. (pres. D.C. chpt. 1991-93), Phi Delta Kappa, Delta Sigma Theta. Democrat. Episcopalian. Home: 10818 Margate Rd Silver Spring MD 20901 Office: Washington Career High Sch 27 O St NW Washington DC 20001

SPRAGUE, JO ANN, state legislator; b. Nashville, Ind., Nov. 3, 1931; m. Warren G. Sprague; 6 children. BA, U. Mass., 1980. Mem. Mass. Ho. of Reps., Boston, mem. capital budget com., 1980—; mem. Walpole Prison Adv. Com., 1990—, Rep. Town Meeting, 1979—. Pres. bd. trustees Walpole Scholar Found., 1990-92. 2d lt. U.S. Army, 1950-53. Mem. Walpole Vis. Nurses Assn. (bd. dirs. 1989-92), Walpole LVW, Norfolk Am. Legion (Post No. 3, adj. 1969-92). Republican. Home: 305 Elm St Walpole MA 02081 Office: Mass Ho of Reps State Capitol Boston MA 02133*

SPRAUER, CYNTHIA CAROL, optometrist; b. Bridgeton, N.J., Apr. 11, 1962; d. Frederick Henry and Edna Catherine (Hepner) S. BS in Biology, Va. Tech., 1984; BS in Visual Sci., Pa. Coll. Optometry, 1988, OD, 1991. Tech. rep. Vineland (N.J.) Chem., 1984-87; optometrist Office of Drs. Klein & Schwab, Mays Landing, N.J., 1991-93, Nu Vision, Northfield, N.J., 1993—. mem. Am. Optometric Assn., N.J. Optometric Assn., Atlantic-Cape May Optometric Soc., Beta Kappa Sigma. Home: 3627 Whitehall Ct Mays Landing NJ 08330

SPRAYBERRY, ROSLYN RAYE, secondary school educator; b. Newnan, Ga., June 29, 1942; d. Henry Ray and Grace (Bernhard) S. BA, Valdosta State Coll., 1964; MA in Teaching, Ga. State U., 1976, EdS in Spanish, 1988; EdD, Nova U., 1993. Cert. tchr., Ga. Tchr. history Griffin (Ga.) High Sch., 1964-65; tchr. 6th grade Beaverbrook Elem Sch., Griffin, 1965-66; tchr. Spanish, chair fgn. lang. dept. Forest Park (Ga.) High Sch., 1966-77; chair fgn. lang. dept. Spanish Forest Park (Ga.) High Sch., 1969-77; tchr. Spanish, chair fgn. lang. dept. Riverdale (Ga.) High Sch., 1977—; correlator Harcourt, Brace, Jovanovich, 1989; adv. bd. So. Conf. Lang. Teaching, 1992—; lectr. and speaker in field. Contbr. articles to The Ednl. Resource Info. Ctr. Clearinghouse on Langs. and Linguistics, Ctr. for Applied

Linguistics, Washington; designed courses for the Gifted, Ga. Dept. of Edn. Cnvener Acad. Alliances-Atlanta II, Clayton County, Ga., 1982—; advisor, workshop leader Ga. Fgn. Lang. Camp, Atlanta, 1983; dir. Clayton County Fgn. Lang. Festival, 1990-91. Recipient STAR Tchr. award Ga. C. of C., 1982; Fulbright-Hays scholar, 1978; NEH grantee, 1977, 84. Mem. NEA, Am. Coun. Tchrs. Fgn. Langs., Am. Assn. Tchrs. Spanish and Portuguese, Ga. Assn. Educators, Fgn. Lang. Assn. Ga. (treas. 1977-85, assoc. editor jour. 1981-86, Tchr. of Yr. award 1976), Clayton County Edn. Assn., So. Conf. Lang. Tchg., KSP Leadership Specialists (co-founder 1993). Methodist. Home: 9261 Brave Ct Jonesboro GA 30236

SPRECHER, SHARON KATHLEEN, government agency administrator; b. Balt., Dec. 23, 1946; d. Edward Purnell and Mara Agnes (Flinn) S.; m. Gerard Clinton Sauter, June 14, 1969 (div. Oct. 1978); children: Charlene Noel Sauter, Joseph Gerard Sauter. AA in Mental Health magna cum laude, Catonsville C.C., 1978; BS magna cum laude, Towson State U., 1980; MSW, U. Md., 1982; cert. in mental health, Sheppard and Enoch Pratt Hosp., 1982; graduate, Integrated Awareness, 1984. Lic. clin. social worker, Md., D.C.; cert. tchr. K-12 learning disabilities, emotional handicaps, mental retardation, EMDR practitioner. Clin. adminstr., social worker USAF, 1984-90; clin. social worker Dept. Vet. Affairs, 1990-91; asst. regional mgr. mid-atlantic region Readjustment Counseling Svc., Balt., 1991—; mental health, 1984—. Mem. Disaster Mental Health Team ARC. Mem. NASW (diplomat), Employee Assistance Profl. Assn., Inc., Music and Imagery Found., Am. Legion Post Women's Aux., Md. Art Therapy Assn. Home: 67 Willow Path Ct Baltimore MD 21236 Office: Readjustment Counseling Svc Dept Vets Affairs Baltimore MD 21236

SPRETNAK, CHARLENE MARIE, writer; b. Pitts., Jan. 30, 1946; d. Joseph William and Donna Rose S.;m. John Paul Merkel, 1970 (div. 1975); 1 child, Lissa Khema; m. Daniel Moses, 1988. BA magna cum laude, St. Louis U., 1968; MA in English and Am. Lit., U. Calif., Berkeley, 1982. Lectr., head writing program U. Calif., Berkeley, 1978-86; scholar-in-residence Schumacher Coll., Totnes, Devon, Eng., 1992; prof. in philosophy and religion Calif. Inst. Integral Studies, San Francisco, 1993—; hon. adv. bd. Soc. for Founding a Peace U., Potsdam, Germany; mem. adv. bd. Elmwood Inst., Berkeley, Calif., 1983-94. Author: Lost Goddesses of Early Greece: A Collection of Pre-Hellenic Myths, 1981, updated edit., 1992, The Spiritual Dimenison of Green Politics, 1986, States of Grace: The Recovery of Meaning in the Postmodern Age, 1991, (with Fritjof Capra) Green Politics: The Global Promise, 1984; editor: The Politics of Women's Spirituality: Essays on the Rise of Spiritual Power Within the Feminist Movement, 1982, updated edit., 1994; contbr. articles to profl. jours. Writer Green Party of Calif., 1991—. Inducted into Ohio Women's Hall of Fame, 1989. Mem. PEN Am., Nat. Writers Union, Am. Philos. Assn., Phi Beta Kappa. Home: PO Box 860 Moss Beach CA 94038 Office: Frances Goldin Lit Agy 305 E 11th St New York NY 10003

SPRINGER, CAROL, state legislator. Mem. Ariz. State Senate from dist. 1. Home: 973 W Gurley St Prescott AZ 86301-2817 Office: Arizona State Senate 1700 W Washington Phoenix AZ 85007

SPRINGER, DEBORAH JEAN, quality engineer; b. Pitts., June 15, 1957; d. Robert Regis and Jean Frederica (Thompson) S.; 1 child, Jackie Lee Martin. BSBA, Robert Morris Coll., Pitts., 1986. Sec. nuclear ops. div. Westinghouse Corp., Pitts., 1979-84, quality engr., 1984-86; systems analyst marine div. Westinghouse Corp., Sunnyvale, Calif., 1986-90, quality engr., 1990-91, supr. quality control, 1991-93, sr. quality engr., 1993-95; sr. quality engr. Coherent Med. Group, Palo Alto, Calif., 1995—. Mem. Am. Soc. Quality Control. Republican. Lutheran.

SPRINGER, MARLENE, university administrator, educator; b. Murfreesboro, Tenn., Nov. 16, 1937; d. Foster V. and Josephine Jones; children: Ann Springer, Rebecca Springer. BA in English & Bus. Adminstrn., Centre Coll., 1959; MA in Am. Lit., Ind. U., 1963, PhD in English Lit., 1969. Chair English dept. U. Mo., Kansas City, 1980-81, acting assoc. dean grad. sch., 1982; Am. Coun. of Edn. Adminstrn. fellow U. Kans., Laurence, 1982-83; dean of grad. sch. U. Mo., Kansas City, 1983-84, assoc. vice chancellor for acad. affairs & grad. studies, 1985-89; vice chancellor for acad. affairs East Carolina U., Greenville, N.C., 1989-94; pres. Coll. Staten Island, 1994—. Author: What Manner of Woman: Essays, 1977, Thomas Hardy's Use of Allusion, 1983, Plains Woman: The Diary of Martha Farnsworth, 1986 (Choice award 1986), Ethan Frome: A Nightmare of Need, 1993. Huntington Libr. fellow, 1988. Mem. Am. Coun. on Edn. (profl. devel. com. 1991—, invited participant Nat. Forum 1984), Am. Assn. State Colls. & Univs. (exec. com. 1992—), Acad. Leadership Acad. (exec. com. 1992—), Assn. Tchr. Educators (chair 1992), Coun. Grad. Schs. (chair 1986-88). Office: Coll Staten Island 2800 Victory Blvd Staten Island NY 10314

SPRINGER, SALLY PEARL, university administrator; b. Bklyn., Mar. 19, 1947; d. Nathaniel Margulies and Fanny (Schoen) S.; m. Hakon Hope; children: Erik Jacob Hope, Mollie Liv Hope. BS, Bklyn. Coll., 1967; PhD, Stanford U., 1971. Postdoctoral fellow Stanford U. Med. Sch., Calif., 1971-73; asst. prof. SUNY-Stony Brook, 1973-78, assoc. provost, 1981-85, assoc. prof., 1978-87; exec. asst. to chancellor U. Calif., Davis, 1987-92; asst chancellor, 1992—. Author (with others): Left Brain, Right Brain, 1981 (Am. Psychol. Found. Disting. Contbr. award 1981), 4th rev. edit., 1993, How to Succeed in College, 1982; contbr. articles to profl. jours. Mem. Internat. Neuropsychol. Soc., Psychonomic Soc. Office: U Calif Office Chancellor Davis CA 95616

SPRINGFIELD, SHERRI LYNNE, sales professional; b. Ft. Worth, Nov. 16, 1960. Student, Baylor U., 1979-83, BBA, 1992. Cert. fair housing Tex.; lic. ins. Tex. Wholesale mktg. sales exec. Dallas Apparel Mart, 1983; mgmt., sales, mktg., leasing exec. Ivest, Inc., Dallas, 1983-84, Johnson Devel. Ltd., Dallas, 1984-87; image and sales cons. BeautiControl Cosmetics, Dallas, 1987-90; ins. consulting and sales profl. LCI Agy., Dallas, 1988-89; property mgmt. and sales exec. Burnett-Gile and Assocs., Dallas, 1992-93; sales rep. PageMart Internat., Inc., Dallas, 1993—. Mem. UN Devel. Fund for Women and Children. Mem. NAFE, Am. Bus. Women's Assn., Results Profl. Ednl. Orgn., Bus. and Profl. Women's Clubs of Dallas, Dallas Women's Found., Dallas C. of C. Home: Ste 431 4606 Cedar Springs Dallas TX 75219 Office: Page Mart 12801 Midway Ste 511 Dallas TX 75244

SPROAT, KEZIA VANMETER, communications executive, writer; b. Chillicothe, Ohio, Nov. 8, 1937; d. Joseph Vause and Helen Rose (Janes) Vanmeter; children: Cornelia Sisson Vanmeter, Eliza Bradford Delano. AB, Vassar Coll., 1959; MA, Ohio State U., 1963, PhD, 1975. Field dir. Miami Valley Campfire Girls, Dayton, Ohio, 1959-60; tchr. English Kingswood Sch. Cranbrook, Bloomfield Hills, Mich., 1960-61; grad. asst. Dept. English Ohio State U., Columbus, 1961-68, lectr. comparative lit., 1968-73, editor ctr. human resource rsch., 1979-85; dir. food for thought Univ. Ctr. Ministries, Columbus, 1978-79; pres. Sproat Comm., Inc., Columbus, 1985—; editor, writer Ross Labs., Columbus, 1987-91; dir. Vanmeter Farm, Inc., Piketon, Ohio, 1993—; pres., founder Highbank Farm Peace Edn. Ctr., Chillicothe, 1994. Author, editor: National Longitudinal Surveys: Bibliography, 1985; editor: Malnutrition: A Hidden Cost, 1993 (2 Addy awards 1994); editor 7 books. Founder, co-chair Community Film Assn., Columbus, 1979—; publicist Peace Grows, Inc., Columbus and Akron, Ohio, 1990—; coord. South Ctrl. Ohio Preservation Soc., 1992—. Recipient Florence Howe award MLA, 1975, Mayor's award for vol. svcs Mayor of Columbus, 1980, Pres. award Abbott Labs., 1988; grantee Ohio Humanities Coun., 1977, 78. Mem. Women Comm., Inc., Physicians Human Rights, Women's Poetry Workshop. Office: Sproat Comm Corp 184 E Oakland Ave Columbus OH 43201

SPROCK, JUNE, psychology educator; b. Paterson, N.J., Sept. 25, 1955; d. Joseph F. and Dorothy (Borden) S. BS in Psychology cum laude, U. Miami, 1976; MS in Clin. Psychology, San Diego State U., 1980; PhD in Clin. Psychology, U. Fla., 1986. Lic. psychologist, health svc. provider in psychology, Ind. Asst. rsch. analyst vol. Passaic (N.J.) Clifton Community Mental Health Ctr., 1975; asst. recreational therapist vol. San Diego (Calif.) Community Mental Health Ctr., 1977-78; grad. rsch. asst. San Diego State U., 1978-79, teaching asst., 1979; rsch. asst. U. Calif., San Diego, 1979-81; grad. rsch. asst. U. Fla., Gainesville, 1981-85; psychology intern VA Med. Ctr., Gainesville, 1985-86; asst. prof. psychology Ind. State U., Terre Haute, 1986-90, assoc. prof., 1990—; dir. Ind. State U. Psychology Clinic, Terre Haute, 1990—; writer exam. item Regents Coll. Exams., SUNY, Albany, 1989. Contbr. articles to profl. jours., chpts. to books. Rsch. grantee Ind. State U., 1988-89, 92. Mem. APA, Midwestern Psychol. Assn., Phi Kappa Phi, Psi Chi. Office: Ind State U Psychology Dept Root Hall Terre Haute IN 47809

SPROULE, BETTY ANN, computer industry market researcher; b. Evanston, Ill., Dec. 30, 1948; d. Harold Fletcher and Lois (Reno) Mathis; m. J. Michael Sproule, Mar. 3, 1973; children: John Harold, Kevin William. BS, Ohio State U., 1969, MS, 1970, PhD, 1972. Mem. tech. staff Bell Telephone Labs., Columbus, Ohio, 1973-74; asst. prof. U. Tex., Odessa, 1974-77; analyst bus. systems Maj. Appliance Bus. div. GE, Louisville, 1977-78; dir. forecasting and analysis Brown and Williamson Tobacco, Louisville, 1978-86; mgr. market rsch. Hewlett-Packard Co., Cupertino, Calif., 1986—. Contbr. articles to profl. jours.; patentee in field. Sr. mem. IEEE, Soc. Women Engrs. Home: 4135 Briarwood Way Palo Alto CA 94306-4610 Office: Hewlett-Packard Co 19111 Pruneridge Ave Santa Clara CA 95052

SPROUSE, CHARLINE HIGGINS, health care facility administrator, educator, family therapist; b. San Angelo, Tex., Jan. 13, 1942; d. Charles Cleophus and Eunice Maxine (Frey) Higgins; m. Marvin Earl Sprouse Jr., July 29, 1988; children: Marvin Earl III, Amber Leigh, Lisa Kauai, Carleen Danielle McGuffy, John Paul, Alicia Denise Slaton, Angela Desiree Cooke, Robin Candi Dione Laster. Student, West Tex. U., 1964-65, 80-81, Columbus (Ga.) Coll., 1978-79, U. Tex. Med. Br., 1981-82; MA, U. Houston, 1988. Internat. lic. drug and alcohol counselor; lic. profl. counselor; cert. hypnobehavioral therapist, neurolinguistic programmer practitioner. Mgr., hostess and waitress Spencecliff Restaurants, Honolulu, 1965-67; office mgr. Polly Grigg Designs, 1966-68; psychiat. occupational therapist, technician N.W. Tex. Psychiat. Pavilion, Amarillo, 1968-74; career placement specialist Snelling & Snelling, Amarillo, 1971-72; psycho-social dysfunction specialist U.S. Army Med. Corps, Ft. Benning, Ga., 1974-78; dispatcher League City (Tex.) Police and Fire Depts., 1981-82; chiropractic trainer, office mgr. Clear Lake, Tex., 1981-82; property mgr. Houston, 1984-88; J.T.P.A. addictions counselor Ed White Youth Ctr., Seabrook, Tex., 1987-88; family addictions therapist, educator, dir. family restoration Chemical Dependency Ctr., Las Cruces, N.Mex., 1990-91; rehab. dir. The Profl. Assessment Ctr., Las Cruces, 1991—; case analyst II TYC Bootcamp Sheffield (Tex.) Youth Leadership Acad., 1995—; presenter N.Mex. Gov.'s Conf., Las Cruces, 1990, Western N.Mex. U., Silver City, 1991; facilitator MVH Community Edn., Las Cruces, 1990-91; addictions counselor, developer family edn. program St. Mary's Hosp., Galveston, 1987-90. Co-author: Human Phallacies, 1988, Streetcar Named Codependency, 1989, Connecting-A Guide to Great Relationship, 1990, Love at the Drive-Through Window, 1991. Provider Support Group Families of Desert Storm Troops, Las Cruces, 1990-91, His Holy Name Cath. Apostolic Ch., Las Cruces, 1990-91. Mem. ACA, NAFE, Soc. Ams. for Recovery Concerned Women for Am., Nat. Assn. Alcohol & Drug Abuse Counselors, Vietnam Vets. Am. (pres. Las Cruces chpt.), Vietnan Vets. War on Drugs (v.p.), Tex. Assn. for Counseling and Devel., Tex. Assn. Alcoholism and Drug Abuse Counselors, N.Mex. Alcohol and Drug Abuse Counselors, N.Mex. Counseling Assn., El Paso Profl. Growth Assocs. Home and Office: PO Box 468-X Sheffield TX 79781 Office: Sheffield Youth Leadership Acad TYC Bootcamp School Rd Sheffield TX 79781

SPROUSE, CHERYL LYNNE, principal; b. Lynchburg, Va., May 29, 1951; d. Elwood Gleason and Essie Ellen (Campbell) S. AS in pre-teaching, Ctrl. Va. C.C., 1971; BS, Radford Coll., 1973; MS, Radford U., 1978. Cert. tchr. Va. 5th and 7th grade tchr. Amherst (Va.) County Pub. Schs., 1973-78; asst. prin., 4th and 5th grade tchr. Amherst Elem. Sch., 1978-79, asst. prin., 1979-80, prin., 1989—; asst. prin. Amelon Elem. Sch., Madison Heights, Va., 1979-80, Monelison Jr. High Sch., Madison Heights, 1980-89; prin. Amherst (Va.) Elem. Sch., 1989-93, Check (Va.) Elem. Sch., 1993—; family life facilitator Amherst County Pub. Schs., 1985-87, family life curriculum Va. Dept. Edn., 1986-87, chpt. 1 adv. bd., 1989-91. Dir. Young Musicians Choir, Grades 1 to 6, Rivermont Ave Bapt. Ch., Lynchburg, Va., 1990—, pres. adult choir, 1991-93; assoc. conductress Order of Eastern Star, Lynchburg chpt. 54; mem. 1st Bapt. Ch., Roanoke, 1994. Mem. ASCD, Va. Assn. Elem. Sch. Prins., Piedmont Assn. Elem. Prins., Radford U. Alumni (pres. 1983-85), Phi Delta Kappa. Republican. Home: 3108K Honeywood Ln Roanoke VA 24014 Office: Check Elem Sch Rte 221 PO Box 8 Check VA 24072

SPROUSE, SUSAN RAE MOORE, human resources specialist; b. Amsterdam, N.Y., Feb. 23, 1948; d. Charles Franklin and Alice Rae (Lawson) Moore; m. Richard D. Sprouse, May 5, 1973; children: Jennifer Lynn, Melinda Rae. BS, U. So. Miss., 1970, MBA, 1971. Spl. non-exempt employee rels. GE Co., Owensboro, Ky., 1972-74; from instr. entry level tng. to spl. profl. rels. and EEO GE Co., Chgo., 1974-78; from employee rels. clk. to material control specialist GE Co., Ft. Smith, Ark., 1978-82; employee rels. rep. Mason Chamberlain Inc., Stennis Space Ctr., Miss., 1982-90; human resource specialist Inst. for Naval Oceanography, Stennis Space Ctr., Miss., 1990-92; program coord. Ctr. for Ocean and Atmospheric Modeling, Stennis Space Ctr., Miss., 1992—; co. rep. Jr. Achievement, Owensboro, 1972-74. Libr., Am. flag chair DAR, Picayune, Miss., 1967-92; bd. dirs. Picayune On Stage, v.p., sec., 1982—. Named Outstanding Jr. Mem. DAR, Picayune, 1970; profiled in Picayune Item, 1988. Mem. Nat. Soc. Magna Charta Dames, Sigma Sigma Sigma, Phi Delta Rho. Republican. Church of Christ. Office: Ctr Ocean & Atmospheric Modeling Bldg 1103 Rm 249 Stennis Sp Ct MS 39529

SPRUILL, LOUISE ELAM, retired secondary educator; b. Mecklenburg County, Va., Aug. 17, 1918; d. William Llewellyn and Lillie Clayton (Puryear) Elam; m. Jacob Sipe Fleming, Aug. 12, 1941 (dec. Nov. 1957); 1 son, James Sipe Fleming; m. Edward Muse Spruill, Nov. 6, 1968; 1 stepdaughter, Florence Spruill Mackie. BA, East Carolina U., 1939, MA, 1961. cert. secondary tchr. Tchr. Washington County Bd. Edn., Plymouth, N.C., 1957-69; chmn. math. dept. Plymouth High Sch., 1965-69; treas. Washington County Hosp. Aux., 1991-93, v.p., 1993—. Mem. Plymouth City Coun., 1980-87; trustee Pettigrew Regional Libr., 1983-88; mem. Washington County Libr. Bd., 1983-92, chmn., 1985-88; mem. Bd. of Adjustments, Plymouth, 1989—; sec. Grace Ch., 1981-84, vestry, 1981-84, 95—. Named Outstanding Woman in Washington County, Washington County Coun. on Status of Women, 1988. Mem. N.C. Ret. Sch. Pers., Washington County Hist. Soc. (bd. dirs. 1987—), Fortnightly Lit. Club of Chase City, Va. (pres. 1978-79), Delta Kappa Gamma (v.p. chpt. 1968-70, corr. sec. chpt. 1986-88). Democrat. Episcopalian.

SPRUNGL, JANICE MARIE, nurse; b. Brooklyn, Ohio, Mar. 9, 1960; d. Donald Edward and Delores Jane (Slys) S. BS in Nursing, U. Akron, 1982. RN, Ohio, Colo. Commd. 2d lt. U.S. Air Force, 1982, advanced through grades to major, 1994; clin. nurse Med. Ctr. Keesler U.S. Air Force, Biloxi, Miss., 1982-86; charge nurse Med. Ctr. Keesler U.S. Air Force, 1986-88; charge nurse U.S. Air Force Acad. Hosp. U.S. Air Force, Colorado Springs, Colo., 1988-91; charge nurse primary care clinic ambulance svcs. Lowry Clinic U.S. Air Force, 1991-94. Vol., Spl. Olympics, Keesler AFB, 1983-87; fundraiser, Biloxi unit Am. Cancer Soc., 1984. Mem. Ohio Nursing Assn., Air Force Assn.

SPRUNGL, KATHERINE LOUISE, nurse; b. Sandusky, Ohio, May 29, 1961; d. Karl William and Patricia Carol (Addy) Steuk; m. Jeffery Alan Sprungl; children: Diana Kristine, Alixandra Marie. AA, Cuyahoga Community Coll., 1982; BS, Bowling Green State U., 1986. RN, Ohio; cert. inpatient obstetric nurse. Med. technician Fairview Gen. Hosp., Cleve., 1983-84; staff nurse labor, delivery Fairview Gen. Hosp., 1984-86; office staff nurse Dr. T. J. Wasserbauer, M.D., Inc., Cleve., 1984-85; counselor, instr. Far West Ctr. Project Find, Westlake, Ohio, 1986—; instr. Am. Heart Assn., Cleve., 1983—, Well Aware, Westlake, Ohio, 1986-88; staff nurse-labor, delivery SW Gen. Hosp., Middleburg Heights, Ohio, 1987, St. Joseph Hosp., Lorain, Ohio, 1988, Cleve. Metrohealth System, 1988—; cons. Well Aware, 1985, Far West Ctr., 1986. Author: Living with Arthritis, 1986, Teen Contact, 1991. Project founder, dir. Teen Contact, 1991. Mem. Assn. Women's Health, Obstetrics and Neonata Nurses. Home: 1545 King Rd Hinckley OH 44233

SPRUNT, JULIA WORTH, broadcast executive; b. Memphis, Oct. 16, 1953; d. Walter Payne and Sue (Joyner) S.; m. William H. Grumbles, Jr., Sept. 2, 1989. BA, U. N.C. Mgr. mktg. Turner Broadcasting, Atlanta, 1981-82, dir. S.E. region TCNS, 1982-86, v.p. we. region Turner Cable Network Sales, 1986-87, sr. v.p., 1987-89, v.p. mktg. TBS Supersta., 1989-90, v.p. corp. mktg. and comm., exec. com., 19,90—. Pres. Children's Mus. Atlanta; bd. dirs. Goodwill Industries; vol. First Presbyn. Ch. Recipient Vanguard award Nat. Cable T.V. Assn., 1993. Mem. Cable T.V. and Mktg. Soc. (bd. dirs.), Women in Cable Found. (trustee, Woman of Yr. award 1992). Office: Turner Broadcasting System 1 CNN Ctr Box 105366 Atlanta GA 30348

SPURLOCK, CYNTHIA MARIE, government official; b. Phoenix, Apr. 27, 1953; d. Charles Elmer and Edith Marie (Duell) S.; m. Michael C. Schouten. BS in Bus., Ariz. State U., 1977, MBA, 1981. Field examiner NLRB, Phoenix, 1976-88, compliance officer, 1988—. Mem. Ariz. Indsl. Rels. Assn., Soroptomists (officer Phoenix 1990—), East Valley Harley Owners Group (HOG) Assn. Republican. Mem. Community Ch. Office: NLRB 234 N Central Ave Ste 440 Phoenix AZ 85004-2212

SPYROPOULOS, SIEGI, export company executive; b. Calw, Fed. Republic Germany; came to U.S., 1966; d. Robert Stoesser and Hildegard Vetter; married, 1958; children: Patricia, Christine, Angelo. BA in Bus. Adminstrn., Fgn. Langs., Vorbeck Inst., Fed. Republic Germany, 1958. Coord. export svcs. & mktg. Am. Hosp. Supply Corp., Glendale, Calif., 1967-79; dir. worldwide purchasing and corp. export control Allergan, Inc., Irvine, Calif., 1979—. Author export manual. Mem. Internat. Mktg. Assn., World Trade Ctr. Assn. Orange County, Women in World Trade. Office: Allergan Inc 2525 Dupont Dr Irvine CA 92715-1599

SQUAZZO, MILDRED KATHERINE (MILDRED KATHERINE OETTING), corporate executive; b. Bklyn., Dec. 22; d. William John and Marie M. (Fromm) Oetting; student L.I. U. Sec.-treas., Stanley Engring., Inc. and v.p. Stanley Chems., Inc., 1960-68; founder, pres. Chem-Dynamics Corp., Scotch Plains, N.J., 1964-68; gen. adminstr., purchasing dir., Richardson Chem. Co., Metuchen, N.J., 1968-69; owner Berkeley Employment Agy. and Berkeley Temp. Help Service, Berkeley Heights, N.J., 1969-91, Berkeley Employment Agy., Morristown, N.J., 1982-91, Bridgewater, N.J., 1987-91; pres. M.K.S. Bus. Group, Inc., Berkeley Heights, 1980-91; mgmt. cons.; personnel fin.; lectr. Served with Nurse Corps, U.S. Army, 1946-47. Mem. Nat. Bus. and Profl. Women's Club. Home and Office: 16 Heather Ln Warren NJ 07059-5258

SQUIBB, SANDRA HILDYARD, special education educator; b. Kansas City, Mo., May 23, 1943; d. Victor Herbert and Vivian Aline (Henderson) Hildyard; children: Jason, Trevor. BA, So. Meth. U., 1966; MS, FHSU, 1984. Cert. early childhood, spl. edn. tchr., Kans., Tex., cert. bldg. adminstr. K-12. Speech pathologist Edinburg (Tex.) Consolidated Sch. Dist., 1971-74; owner, audiologist Northwest Kans. Hearing Svc., Colby, Kans., 1976—; supr. Northwest Kans. Ednl. Svc. Ctr., Colby, 1980-87; coord. Northwest Kans. Ednl. Svc. Ctr., Oakley, Kans., 1987-92; treas. Kans. Div. of Early Childhood, 1987-89. Precinct chmn. Dem. Party, Thomas County, 1980—, party chmn., 1988-90; mem. Parent Adv. Coun., Colby, 1984-87; mem. bd. Alcohol and Drug Abuse Coun.; cmty. rep. Head Start Policy Coun., 1994—. Recipient grants in field. Mem. Coun. for Exceptional Children (award of excellence 1991). Roman Catholic. Home: 425 La Hacienda Dr Colby KS 67701-3912 Office: NW Kans Ednl Svc Ctr Oakley KS 67748

SQUIRE, LAURIE RUBIN, media consultant; b. N.Y.C., Jan. 30, 1953; d. Daniel and Ruth Thelma (Deutsch) Rubin; m. Herbert E. Squire Jr., Aug. 6, 1975; children: Amy Ruth, Julie Wynn. BA cum laude (scholar), Finch Coll., 1974; MA, NYU, 1976; postgrad., Columbia U., 1977—. Actress TV commls., 1960-65; arts editor Finch/Metro newspaper, N.Y.C., 1970-74; co-editor Finch Alumnae mag., 1971-72; intern producer Sta. WBAI-FM, N.Y.C., 1973; music prodn. coord. Ballet Theatre spl. Sta. WNET-TV, 1973; coll. bd. writer Mademoiselle mag., 1973; intern asst. pub. affairs dir. N.Y. Cultural Ctr., 1974; mdse. coord. Sta. WOR-AM, N.Y.C., 1974-76, contbg. writer Bob and Ray's Mary Backstage serial, contbr. nostalgia features Joe Franklin Show, producer Jean Shepherd Show and sydicated markets, 1975-77, producer Bernard Meltzer What's Your Problem, 1977-80; broadcast stage mgr. Texaco Met. Opera, 1976—; dance critic Show Bus., theatre newspaper; bd. dir. publicity and advt. L.I. Playhouse, 1982—; press rep. Great Neck Pla.; writer Chanry Communications. Publicity cons. Nassau County Mus. Fine Art; v.p. pub. rels. United Community Fund. Recipient commendations for Leukemia Radiothons Peabody Broadcasting citation, 1983. Mem. Internat. Radio and TV Soc., Great Neck Hist. Soc. Home and Office: 892 Middle Neck Rd Great Neck NY 11024

SQUIRE, LUCY FRANK, radiology educator; b. Washington, May 10, 1915; d. Leslie Carl and Ethelwyn (Harris) Frank; 1 child, Gordon. MD, Woman's Med. Coll. of Pa., Phila., 1940; DSc, SUNY, Bklyn., 1993. Resident in radiology Mass. Gen. Hosp., Boston, 1942-44; fellow New Eng. Med. Ctr., Boston, 1944-45; lectr. radiology Harvard Med. Sch., 1965—; cons. in tchg. Mass. Gen. Hosp., 1965—; prof. radiology SUNY Health Sci. Ctr., Bklyn., 1970—. Author: (textbook) Fundamentals of Radiology, 1964, 4th edit., 1988; co-author: Living Anatomy, Exercises in Diagnostic Radiology, 1987. Recipient Gold medals Radiol. Soc. N.Am., 1972, Assn. U. Radiologists, 1982. Home: 1 W 72nd St New York NY 10023 Office: SUNY HSCA Bklyn 456 Clarkson Ave Brooklyn NY 11203-2012

SQUIRE, MOLLY ANN, organizational psychologist; b. Highland Park, Mich., Aug. 18; d. George Edward and Dorothy Laura (Molteni) Squirrell; m. Arthur Bruce Hanson, June 23, 1990. AA, NYU, 1978; BS cum laude, U. LaVerne, 1980; MA, Claremont (Calif.) Grad. Sch., 1982; PhD, Pacific-Western U., 1991. Cert. Profl. Cons. to Mgmt. Health svcs. adminstr. health care delivery orgns., 1978-82; nat. dir. Huntington's Disease Rsch. Project, Calif., 1981-82; CEO Claremont Mgmt. Cons. (name now Squire Cons.), Malibu, Calif., 1982—; past statis. analyst to pres. L.A. City Coll.; past part-time instr. L.A. Trade Tech.; part-time instr. Glendale C.C., 1994—; part-time profl. magician. Founding editor LASER; current editor BEACON newsletter; past editor Benezet Gazette, (yearbook) So. Calif. Com. to Combat Huntington's Disease; contbr. articles to profl. jours.; patentee bus. and health care products. Past officer and sci. liaison So. Calif. Huntington's Disease Com.; magic performer various charitable benefits. Decorated knight Templar of Jerusalem, Internat. Br. Netherlands; recipient Cert. of Appreciation City of Ukiah, Calif., 1984, Western Square Dance Assn., 1986, Am. Heart Assn., 1990, So. Calif. Skeptics, 1987, Pacific-Bell, 1990, Achievement award No. Am. Women's Inner Circle, 1991; grad. fellow Claremont Grad. Sch., 1980-82; established Krauthamer & Squire 'Thelma & Louise' Women's Scholarship, L.A. City Coll., 1993. Mem. Nat. Bur. Profl. Cons. to Mgmt., Am. Fedn. Tchrs., Coll. Guild, Soc. Indsl. and Orgnl. Psychologists, Soc. Am. Magicians (Zinger award, Certs. of Appreciation, award of Merit 1991, 94, named Best Character Act 1994, Peller Meml. trophy, 1994), Internat. Brotherhood Magicians (past pres., sec., Best Mentalist trophy 1987, Cert. of Appreciation), Pacific Coast Assn. Magicians (golden circle mem. 1994), Soc. of Am. Magicians (life), Arthurian Soc. Arthuret (hon. life, U.K.), Mensa (proctor). Presbyterian. Office: PO Box 2312 Malibu CA 90265-7312

SQUIRES, BONNIE STEIN, healthcare executive; b. Phila., May 12, 1940; d. Joseph and Lillian (Ponnock) Stein; children: Deborah Rose, David Abram. BE, U. Pa., MA. Various positions Temple U., Phila., 1983-89, exec. dir. capital campaign, 1992-94; asst. exec. dir. Pa. Edn. Assn., Harrisburg, 1989-92; v.p. for devel. Phila. Geriatric Ctr., 1994—. Author: (poetry) New Eden, 1977; editor: (poetry) This Land of Fire, 1988, (student essays, poems and photos) A New Nation, 1976. Mem. Fedn. Jewish Agys., Citizens' Crime Commn., Ctr. UN Reform Edn.; bd. dirs. Phila. com. Am. Jewish Congress, Phila. Mus. Art, Am. Friends Hebrew U., Harrisburg Jewish Community Rels. Coun.; del. Israel's Prime Minister's Solidarity Conf., 1989, Pres. Bush's regional Edn. Summit, 1989. Recipient Torch award and Lillian Alpers award Am. Friends Hebrew U., Louise Waterman award Am. Jewish Congress. Mem. AAUW, LWV. Home: 11 Arthurs Round Table Wynnewood PA 19096-1202

SQUIRES, JOAN H., orchestra executive. Exec. dir. Milwaukee Symphony Orchestra, Wis. Office: Milw Symphony Orch 330 E Kilbourn Ave Ste 900 Milwaukee WI 53202-6623*

SQUIRES, KATHERINE LANDEY, lawyer; b. N.Y.C., Mar. 28, 1959. BA, Clark U., 1980; JD, U. Dayton, 1982; LLM in Tax, Georgetown U., 1983; MDiv, Biola U., 1994. Bar: D.C. 1983, Calif. 1986. Assoc. Kutak, Rock & Campbell, Washington, 1983-85; pres., chief exec. officer Plan Care, Inc., Irvine, Calif., 1985-88; ptnr. Polack & Landey, Irvine, 1985-86, Finley, Kumble, Wagner et.al., Newport Beach, Calif., 1986-88, Sheppard, Mullin, Richter & Hampton, Newport Beach, 1988-89; prin. Law Office of Katherine L. Squires, Irvine, Calif., 1989-92; pres. LawPrep, Inc., LawPrep Press, Inc., 1989—. Contbr. articles on taxation and comml. law to profl. jours. Rep. candidate for U.S. Senate, 1993-94; commr. Workers' Compensation Appeals Bd., 1994—. Mem. ABA (chmn. internat. law com. of gen. practice sect., 1986—), Orange County Bar Assn., Nat. Assn. Women Lawyers (chmn. bankruptcy com., 1983—), Nat. Assn. Women Execs., Newport Beach (Calif.) C. of C. Republican. Club: Dolphins.

SQUIRES, PATRICIA EILEEN COLEMAN, freelance journalist, writer; b. Beaver Falls, Pa., Jan. 28, 1927; d. John Wiley and Helen Marie (Barstow) Purtell; BA in Journalism, Ind. U., 1949; m. Mark B. Squires, Sr., June 30, 1951; children: Sally Regan, Mark B., Susan Barstow. Staff reporter LaPorte (Ind.) Herald-Argus, 1949-51, daily columnist, 1950-51, sect. editor, 1949-51; women's news and feature writer Muskegon (Mich.) bur. Grand Rapids Herald, 1956-57; editor suburban sect. North Shore Line, Chicagoland Mag., Chgo., 1967-69; staff writer Fairpress, Westport, Conn., 1972-73; regular contbr. New Canaan (Conn.) Advertiser, 1975-78, Bridgeport (Conn.) Sunday Post, 1976-78, Soundings, Essex, Conn., 1977-78, N.Y. Times, N.Y.C., 1976-94; tchr. English, journalism, social studies jr. and sr. pub. high schs., Jackson, Mich., 1966-67, Niles Twp., Skokie, Ill., 1967-68; mem. Acad. Sr. Profls. Eckerd Coll.; vol. tutor Social Cultural Ednl. Enrichment Program, Protestant Community Ctr., 1979-86. Public rels., promotion dir. Ella Sharp Mus., Jackson, 1964-66; publicity chmn. New Canaan Soc. for Arts, 1977-78; bd. dirs. Centennial Celebration Com., Winnetka, Ill., 1968-69; Community Coun. New Canaan, 1972-75; New Canaan Bicentennial Com., 1975-76; publicity chmn. parent-tchr. coun. Frost Jr. High Sch., Jackson, 1963-64; active Girl Scouts Am. Mem. Soc. Profl. Journalists, AAUW, Ind. U. Alumni Assn. (assoc. acad. sr. profls. at Eckerd Coll. Fla.), Cedar Point Yacht Club (Westport, Conn.), Lake Mohawk Golf Club (Sparta, N.J.), Isla Del Sol Yacht and Country Club. Presbyterian. Home and Office: 688 W Shore Trl Sparta NJ 07871-1320 also: 5825 Puerta Del Sol Blvd # 466 Saint Petersburg FL 33715

SRINIVASAN, SAMPURNA, psychologist; b. Madras, India, Dec. 4, 1952; came to U.S., 1980; d. T.R.V. and Jayalakshmi (Aiyyar) Murti; m. Cidambi Srinivasan, May 16, 1980; children: Praveen, Priyanka. PhD, Banaras Hindu U., Varanasi, India, 1978. Lic. clin. psychologist, Ky. Lectr. Banaras Hindu U., 1977-80; instr. dept. psychology U. Ky., Lexington, 1989; staff psychologist Comprehensive Care Ctr., Lexington, 1990—. Contbr. rsch. papers to profl. jours. Mem. APA, Indian Assn. Clin. Psychologists (assoc.). Home: 3530 Creekwood Dr Lexington KY 40502 Office: Comprehensive Care Ctr 201 Mechanic St Lexington KY 40507

SRNKA, COLLEEN MAE, accountant; b. Green Bay, Wis., Jan. 12, 1961; d. Norbert J. Kornowske and Shirley M. (Van Den Elzen) Hawley; m. Frank R. Srnka, Aug. 18, 1984; children: Heather Mae, Nicole Lynn. BS in Acctg., U. Wis., La Crosse, 1983; MBA, U. Wis., Oshkosh, 1995. Acct. FMC Corp., Green Bay, 1985-87, cost acct., 1987-90, gen. acct., 1990-91; asst. controller Fox Valley Hosp., Green Bay, 1991-93; acctg. intern Coulee Region Family Planning, La Crosse, 1982-83. Supporter Arthritis Found., 1990—, Wis. Citizen Action, 1993-94. Fellow Inst. Mgmt. Accts. (editor, mem. retention and participation 1986-90, 94); mem. Mgmt. Women, Phi Gamma Nu (alumni). Roman Catholic. Home: 3921 St Croix Cir W Green Bay WI 54301

STABENOW, DEBORAH ANN, state legislator; b. Gladwin, Mich., Apr. 29, 1950; d. Robert Lee and Anna Merle (Hallmark) Greer; children: Todd Dennis, Michelle Deborah. BS magna cum laude, Mich. State U., 1972, MSW magna cum laude, 1975. With spl. svcs. Lansing (Mich.) Sch. Dist., 1972-73; county commr. Ingham County, Mason, Mich., 1975-78; state rep. State of Mich., Lansing, 1979—. Founder Ingham County Women's Commn.; co-founder Council Against Domestic Assault; mem. Dem. Bus. and Profl. Club, Mich. Dem. Women's Polit. Caucus, Grance United Meth. Ch. (past lay leader, chair Social Concerns Task Force, Sunday Sch. music tchr., Lansing Boys' Club, profl. adv. com. Lansing Parents Without Ptnrs., adv. com. Ctr. Handicapped Affairs, Mich. Council Family and Divorce Mediation Adv. Bd., Nat. Council Children's Rights, Big Bros./Big Sisters Greater Lansing Adv. Bd., Mich. Child Study Assn. Bd. Advisors, Mich. Women's Campaign Fund. Recipient Service to Children award Council for Prevention of Child Abuse and Neglect, 1983, Disting. Service to Mich. Families award Mich. Council Family Relations, 1983, Outstanding Leadership award Nat. Council Community Mental Health Ctrs., 1983, Snyder-Kok award Mental Health Assn. Mich., Awareness Leader of Yr. award Awareness Communications Team Developmentally Disabled, 1984, Communicator of Yr. award Woman in Communications, 1984, Lawmaker of Yr. award Nat. Child Support Enforcement Assn., 1985, Disting. Service award Lansing Jaycees, 1985, Disting. Service in Govt. award Retarded Citizens of Mich., 1986; named One of Ten Outstanding Young Ams. Jaycees, 1986. Mem. NAACP, Lansing Regional C. of C., Delta Kappa Gamma. Home: 2709 S Deerfield Ave Lansing MI 48911-1783 Office: Mich State Senate State Capitol Lansing MI 48909-7514*

STABER, DOROTHEE BEATRICE, administrative assistant; b. Frankfurt am Main, Germany, Jan. 19, 1961; came to U.S., 1983; d. Rolf Joachim and Sibylle Dorothee (Grafin von Nostitz) Kundahl; m. Harley Joseph Staber, Dec. 28, 1985; 1 child, Marina Inez. Student, Goethe U., Frankfurt, 1981-83; BBA, U. North Tex., 1987; postgrad., U. Dallas, 1990-93. Sales asst. Xerox Corp., Irving, Tex., 1987-88; asst. mgr. Pioneer Life Ins. Co., Irving, 1988-89; adminstrv. asst. Howard Hughes Med. Inst., Dallas, 1989—. Mem. Women's Advocacy Project, Beta Gamma Sigma. Home: 751 Blue Jay Ln Coppell TX 75019 Office: Howard Hughes Med Inst 5323 Harry Hines Blvd Dallas TX 75235-7200

STABILE, ROSE K. TOWNE (MRS. FRED STABILE), building and management executive, public relations consultant; b. Sunderland, Eng.; d. Stephen and Amelia Bergman; student English schs., Tchrs. Coll., Columbia; m. Wilfred Kernode (dec. Feb. 1934); m. 2d, Arthur Whittlesey Towne, May 29, 1936 (dec. 1954); m. 3d, Norbert Le Veillie, June 10, 1961 (div. Feb. 1969); m. 4th, Fred Stabile, May 30, 1970. Formerly auditor Brit. Govt., Whitehall, London; activities and membership dir. N.Y. League of Girls Clubs, N.Y.C.; real estate exec., now semi-ret. bldg. mgr. State Tower Bldg., Syracuse, N.Y.; cons. public relations, office designer and decorator; lectr. real estate dept. Syracuse U. An initiator Syracuse Peace Council; mem. area sponsoring com. Assn. for Crippled Children and Adults; mem. Met. Mus., N.Y.C., The Met. Opera, N.Y.C. Mem. English Speaking Union (membership com.), Nat. N.Y. Assn. Real Estate Bd., Nat. Assn. Bldg. Owners and Mgrs., Syracuse C. of C., LWV, Assn. UN, Women of Rotary, Bus. and Profl. Women's Clubs, Everson Mus. Art Friends of Reading, Mus. Modern Art (N.Y.C.), Internat. Center of Syracuse, Hist. Soc. Syracuse, Opera Club of Syracuse, Corinthian Club. Unitarian (chmn. service com. 1956-57.). Home: 304 Malverne Dr Syracuse NY 13208-1843

STABILE, SUSAN, nurse; b. East Orange, N.J., Feb. 19, 1960; d. Lawrence and Dorothy (Gargano) S. BSN, Rutgers U., 1984; MSN, Seton Hall U., 1994. RN, N.J.; cert. med.-surg. nurse, CPR instr. Staff nurse St. Mary Hosp., Hoboken, N.J., 1984-85, West Essex Gen. Hosp., Livingston, N.J., 1985, Clara Mass. Health System, Inc., Belleville, N.J., 1985-91; nurse educator Clara Maass Med. Ctr., Belleville, N.J., 1991-92, nurse mgr. same day svcs., 1992—. Mem. NAFE, Am. Soc. Post Anesthesia Nurses, Am. Acad. Ambulatory Care Nursing, Am. Soc. Post Anesthesia Nurses, N.J. State Nurses Assn. (region 3 treas. 1994—, convention com. 1993-96), N.J. League for Nursing, N.J. ONE, Nat. League for Nursing, Federated Ambulatory Surgery Assn., Soc. Ambulatory Care Profls., League of Women Voters, Sigma Theta Tau (Gamma Nu chpt.). Roman Catholic.

STABLER, NANCY RAE, infosystems specialist; b. Elgin, Ill., June 15, 1946; d. Raymond Herman and Eleanora Marie (Gaedke) Redmer, m. Jay Stabler, Mar, 28, 1970; 1 child: Andrea Marie. AAS with honors, Elgin Community Coll., 1982, AA with Honors, 1985. Programmer, analyst Houghton-Mifflin, Geneva, Ill., 1966-77; project leader Kane County, Geneva, 1978-83; systems designer Burgess Norton, Geneva, 1983-87; human resources telecommunication specialist Recon/Optical, Barrington, Ill., 1987-91; MIS project leader, sales and mktg. Advance Transformer, Rosemont, Ill., 1991—; tutor Elgin (Ill.) Community Coll., 1983—. Home: 775 South St Elgin IL 60123-6221 Office: Advance Transformer 10275 W Higgins Rd Rosemont IL 60018-3893

STACEY, KATHLEEN MARY, advertising executive; b. Boston, Jan. 7, 1951; d. John Robert and Catherine Mary (Gray) Young; m. Gary Ronald Stacey, Feb. 10, 1984. BA, Northeastern U., Boston, 1974. Asst. producer WGBH-TV, Boston, 1971-73; asst. editor Arlington (Mass.) Advocate Century Publs., 1973-75; mng. editor New England Pubs., Bradford, Vt., 1975-76; free-lance writer Boston, 1976-81; copywriter Berenson & Isham, Boston, 1981-82; assoc. creative dir. The Interface Group, Needham, Mass., 1983-84; pres. Young Stacey Assocs., Marshfield Hills, Mass., 1984—; pres. West End Designs, Marshfield Hills, Mass., 1992—, Scituate, Mass., 1992—; cons. Bentonwood Café, Copperstone's Ltd., Boston, Music Edn. Collaborative, Monadnock Music, Gift and Gallery. Chair Mass. Radio Reading Day, 1992, Scituate Heritage Days Festival, 1993-94, Festival of Arts, 1994. Mem. North River Arts Soc. (bd. dirs. 1989—, treas. 1994), Scituate C. of C. (bd. dirs. 1992—, treas. 1994), Talking Info. Ctr. (bd. dirs. 1992). Democrat. Roman Catholic. Home: 51 Hampstead Way Marshfield MA 02050-6237 Office: Young Stacey Assocs Inc Box 141 Marshfield Hills MA 02051-0141

STACEY, NORMA ELAINE, farmer, civic worker; b. Roanoke, La., Sept. 13, 1925; d. August and Julie (Ravet) Trahan; m. Louis Brewer, June 10, 1949 (dec. 1978); children: Louis Timothy Brewer, John August Brewer; m. Truman Stacey, Feb. 2, 1980. BA, St. Mary's Dominican Coll., New Orleans, 1946. Acct. Cities Svc. Refining Corp., Lake Charles, La., 1946-49; sec. La. Tchrs. Retirement System, Baton Rouge, 1950-51; bus. mgr. Brewer Studios, Lake Charles, 1951-78; co-owner Ravet Estate, Bell City, La., 1958—, Trahan Farm, Lake Arthur, La., 1969—; co-owner Trahan Ins. Agy., Welsh, La., 1964-72, Trahan Estate, Fenton, La., 1969—. Mem. Lake Charles Messiah Chorus, 1946-52; choir singer Immaculate Conception Ch., 1946-52, chmn. landscaping com., 1975-82; chmn. scrapbook com., mem. ticket com. Lake Charles Community Concerts, 1955—; coordinator Art Assocs., Lake Charles, 1955-58; mem. ticket com. Lake Charles Symphony Auxiliary, 1957—, sec., 1960-61, treas., 1962-64; vol. librarian Landry Meml. High Sch., Lake Charles, 1963-68; active St. Patrick Hosp. Auxiliary, 1965—; sec. Gov. La.'s Program for Gifted Childern McNeese State U., Lake Charles, 1978-80; mem. scholarship com. McNeese State U. Found., 1979—; mem. com. on scouting, vol. sec. and receptionist, chmn. decorating com. Diocese of Lake Charles, 1980—, sec., 1980-84, 90—, mem. Companions of Honor, 1982—; mem. Cath. com. on scouting South Cen. Region, Lake Charles, 1981-88, regional sec., 1985-88; mem. emblems subcom. Nat. Cath. Com. on Scouting, Irving, Tex., 1981-88; mem.-at-large Calcasieu Area council Boy Scouts Am., Lake Charles, 1980—; bd. dirs. Lake Charles Symphony Soc., 1981-87, mem. pops com., 1981, membership co-chmn., 1982-83, chmn., 1983-84, program chmn., 1985-88, mem. endowment com., 1987; patron La. Choral Found., Lake Charles, 1982—. Recipient Nat. Honors award Am. Guild Piano Competitions, 1943-45, Bronze Pelican Emblem award Nat. Cath. Com. on Scouting, 1984; named to Scouting Roll of Honor, Diocese of Lake Charles, 1982; named Dame Equestrian Order of Holy Sepulchre of Jerusalem, 1982, Dame Comdr., 1987, Dame Comdr. with Star, 1992, Dame of Grace, Mil. and Hospitaller Order of St. Lazarus of Jerusalem, 1993, Dame of Merit, Sacred Mil. Constantinian Order of St. George, 1994. Mem. AAUW (treas. pre-sch. program 1954-58), NCCJ (corr. sec. local chpt. 1988-91, sec.), Am. Rose Soc., Lake Charles Rose Soc., Lake Charles Garden Club (treas. 1958-61, sec. 1962-64, chmn. telephone com. 1964-86, cert appreciation 1985), Les Etudientes Book Club, Pioneer Club, Serra Club of Lake Charles (sec. 1992-93). Democrat. Home and Office: 1802 2d Ave Lake Charles LA 70601

STACK, DIANE VIRGINIA, hospital administrator; b. Schenectady, N.Y., June 14, 1958; d. Albert Ross and Irene Anne (Lajeunesse) Musick; m. Robert Michael Stack, June 27, 1981; children: Kelly Irene, Julie Theresa, Tina Marie. BBA in Acctg., U. Mass., 1980. CPA, Mass. Staff acct. Stavisky, Shapiro & Whyte, Boston, 1980-84; asst. controller Joslin Diabetes Ctr., Boston, 1984-88; dir. fin. Marlborough (Mass.) Hosp., 1988—; treas. Marlborough Physician Svc's. Corp., 1992—, The Health Care Mgr. of New Eng., Inc., Marlborough, 1992—; guest lectr. Framingham State Coll. Mem. Am. Hosp. Assn., Mass. Soc. CPA's, Hosp. Fin. Mgmt. Assn. Republican. Home: 106 Cherry St Framingham MA 01701-4499 Office: Marlborough Hosp 57 Union St Marlborough MA 01752-1297

STACK, MAY ELIZABETH, library director; b. Jackson, Miss., Nov. 10, 1940; d. James William and Irene Thelma (Baldwin) Garrett; m. Richard Gardiner, Apr. 15, 1962; children: Elinor, Harley David. BS, Miss. State Coll. for Women, 1962; MBA, Western New Eng. Coll., 1981; MLS, So. Conn. State U., 1989. Clk. Western New Eng. Coll., Springfield, Mass., 1965-66; acquisitions staff Western New Eng. Coll., Springfield, 1966-72, cataloger, 1972-84, asst. dir., 1984-89, acting dir., 1989-90, dir., 1990—; chair Cen./Western Mass. Automated Resource Sharing Collection Devel. Com., Paxton, Mass., 1993—, exec. bd. 1993—. mem. East Longmeadow (Mass.) Hist. Soc., 1989-92. Mem. ALA, Mass. Libr. Assn., Assn. Coll. and Rsch. Librs., Libr. and Mgmt. Assn., Libr. Info. and Technology Assn. Methodist. Office: Western New Eng Coll D'Amour Libr 1215 Wilbraham Rd Springfield MA 01119-2654

STACY, FRANCES H., judge. BA, Baylor Univ., 1977; JD, Baylor Law Sch., 1979. With U.S. Attorney's Office (Tex. so. dist.), criminal div., 1980, U.S. Attorney's Office (Tex. so. dist.), civil rights div., 1980-81, U.S. Attorney's Office (Tex. so. dist.), land and nat. resources div., 1981-86, U.S. Attorney's Office (Tex. so. dist.), civil div., 1986-87, U.S. Attorney's Office (Tex. so. dist.), appellate div., 1987-91; magistrate judge U.S. Dist. Ct. (Tex. so. dist.), 5th circuit, Houston, 1991—. Office: Federal Bldg 515 Rusk St Rm 7525 Houston TX 77002-2600*

STACY, PAULINE FRENCH, writer, artist; b. Pratt, Kans., Feb. 22, 1915; d. Leo Walter and Bessie Rosanna (Branson) French; m. Larcel Romain Stacy, July 21, 1934 (dec. 1994); children: Grace Romaine, Rosanna Pauline. BA, Ariz. State U., 1960; MS, Ft. Hays Kans. State U., 1971. With rentals & air conditioning Phoenix, 1949-62; tchr. Isaac Sch. Dist.High Sch., St. Mary of the Plains Liberty Jr. High Sch., Phoenix, Minneola, Dodge and Pratt, Kans., 1960-71; freelance artist Meade, Kans., 1971—; free lance writer poetry Long Beach, Calif., Phoenix and Meade, 1949—. Author: You Shall Not Want, 1975, As Long As We Both Shall Love, 1975, Ventriloquists: Here's How!, 1976; contbr. articles to profl jours. Vol. in field. Mem. AAUW, Mensa, The Rosicrucian Order. Home and Office: 19008 J Rd Meade KS 67864-9432

STADELMAN, LINDA JEAN, flight attendant, educator; b. Aliquippa, Pa., Feb. 14, 1949; d. Matthew John and Violet Margaret (Yurkovich) Shetek; m. Daniel Leonard Dandrea, Feb. 16, 1982 (div. 1986); children: Nicole Lynn Dandrea; m. Edwin Frederick Stadelman, Oct. 31, 1988. BS in Elem. Edn., Edinboro U., 1971. Cert. tchr., Pa. 2nd grade tchr. Ambridge (Pa.) Sch. Dist., 1971-74; flight attendant Allegheny Airlines, Pitts., 1977-89, U.S. Air (formerly Allegheny Airlines), Pitts., 1989—; instr. flight attendants Allegheny Airlines (now U.S. Air), 1979—; rep. Inter-Airline Confs., 1979-89. Author tng. manuals. Republcan. Roman Catholic. Office: US AIR Pitts Internat Airport Pittsburgh PA 15231

STAEHELIN-SCHULZ, BARBARA REGINA, management consultant; b. Glenridge, N.J., June 28, 1963; d. Fred J. and Roesli (Joos) Schulz; m. Matthias B. Staehelin, 1993. MSc, Swiss Fed. Inst. Tech., Zurich, 1989; MBA, Insead, Fontainebleau, France, 1991. Fellow McKinsey & Co., Inc., Zurich, 1990-91, assoc., 1991-93; assoc. McKinsey & Co., Inc., N.Y.C., 1993—. Author: Ebenso Neu Als Kuehn, 1988. Vice pres. Student Union Eidgenoessische Technische Hochschule, 1985-86; pres. Swiss Nat. Union Students, Berne, Switzerland, 1987. Mem. Swiss Social Dem. Party. Office: McKinsey & Co 55 E 52nd St New York NY 10022

STAFFIER, PAMELA MOORMAN, psychologist; b. Passaic, N.J., Dec. 7, 1942; d. Wynant Clair and Jeannette Frances (Rentzsch) Moorman; B.A., Bucknell U., 1964; M.A. in Psychology, Assumption Coll., Worcester, Mass., 1970, C.A.G.S., 1977; Ph.D., Union Inst., 1978; m. John Staffier, Jr., Apr. 5, 1975; children—M. Anthony, C. Matthew. Psychologist, Westboro (Mass.) State Hosp., 1965, prin. psychologist, also asst. to supt., 1973-76; psychologist Moriarty Mental Health Clinic; psychiat. cons. local gen. hosp.; research psychologist Wrentham (Mass.) State Sch., 1966, Cushing Hosp., Framingham, Mass., 1967; prin. psychologist, also asst. to supt. Grafton (Mass.) State Hosp., 1967-72; dir. Staffier Psychol. Assocs., Inc., 1978—. Mem. Am. Psychol. Assn. (assoc.), Am. Psychol. Practitioners Assn. (founding mem.), Mass. Psychol. Assn., Nat. Register Health Service Providers in Psychology. Research, publs. on state hosp. closings, biochem. basis of Schizophrenia. Home: 68 Adams St PO Box 1103 Westborough MA 01581 Office: 57 E Main St Westborough MA 01581-1464

STAFFORD, BARBARA ROSE, lawyer; b. N.Y.C., July 14, 1949; d. Sol and Theresa (Tenenbaum) S.; m. Robert M. Armstrong. BA, U. Denver, 1971; JD, U. Chgo., 1990. Bar: Ill. 1990, D.C. 1992. Hearing commr. Colo. Dept. Revenue, Denver, 1974-87; assoc. Katten, Muchin & Zavis, Chgo., 1990-91; dep. asst. sec. Internat. Trade Adminstrn., U.S. Dept. Commerce, Washington, 1993—; cons., staff Dem. Nat. Com., Washington, 1992. Author: Caselaw Compendium of Colorado Motor Vehicle Law, 1985. Active Community Econ. Devel. Law Project, Chgo., 1990. Mem. ABA, D.C. Bar Assn., Women's Bar Assn. D.C. Office: 14th and Constitution Washington DC 20030

STAFFORD, EMILY-MAE, former assistant news editor; b. Haverhill, Mass., Dec. 11, 1934; d. Charles Gilbert and Leona May (Stout) S. BS, Tex. Woman's U., 1956; postgrad, U. Tex., 1961-65. News bur. supr. Tex. Woman's Univ., Denton, Tex., 1957-61; researcher/instr. U. Tex., Austin, Tex., 1961-66; asst. news editor Fort Worth Star-Telegram, Ft Worth, 1966-94; ret., 1994. Bd. trustees Shakespeare in the Park, Ft. Worth, 1989—. Mem. Women in Communications, Inc. (newsletter editor 1967—), Tex. Woman's Univ. Alumni Assn. (Denton, bd. dirs. 1986—), Woman's Club Ft. Worth (newsletter editor 1985-87), Woman's Shakespeare Club. Republican. Methodist. Home: 509 Monticello Dr Fort Worth TX 76107

STAFFORD, JOSEPHINE HOWARD, lawyer; b. San Antonio, July 27, 1921; d. Joseph and Olive Maeblume (Goodson) Howard; m. Harry B. Stafford (div. 1958); 1 child, Julie. BA, U. N.C., 1942, LLB, 1952. Bar: N.C. 1952, Fla. 1953, U.S. Dist. Ct. (mid. dist.) Fla. 1954, U.S. Ct. Appeals (11th cir.), U.S. Ct. Appeals (5th cir.); lic. real estate broker; cert. arbitrator, Hillsborough County Cir. Ct. Assoc. Fowler, White, Gillen, Yancey and Humkey, Tampa, Fla., 1952-54; pvt. practice Tampa, 1954-57, 69-72; exec. dir., atty. Legal Aid Bur., Tampa, 1957-69; atty. City of Tampa, 1972—; instr. U. South Fla., Tampa, 1971-72; adj. prof. Hillsborough Community Coll., Tampa, 1980-86; lectr. U. South Fla., Tampa, 1973, U. Tampa, U. Fla., Gainesville, 1959; atty. Housing Authority City of Tampa, 1970-72; substitute judge mcpl. ct., 1958-71, interim mcpl. ct. judge, 1971-72; mem. Grievance Com. "13C". Author: Amendments to Search Warrant Law; Tax Laws, Agencies and Divorce, 1979; author Mayor's Proclamation Commemorating D-Day, 1994. Precinct committeewoman Hillsborough County Dem. Exec. Com., Tampa, 1991, co-chmn., 1970; bd. mem., past pres., chmn. com. Travelers Aid Soc., Tampa, 1971-93; bd. mem., fin. com. Girl Scouts Am., Tampa, 1991—; bd. mem., exec. com., past pres. Police Athletic League, Tampa, 1984-88, 90—; mem. Fla. Commn. on Status of Women; co-chmn. Selective Svc. System, 1971-76; bd. dirs. ARC, Tampa chpt., 1964-79, Am. Cancer Soc., Hillsborough County unit, 1982-84. Recipient Svc. to Mankind award Sertoma Internat., Tampa, 1969, Outstanding Bus. and Profl. Woman of Yr. award Bus. and Profl. Women, Tampa, 1959, 69, Women Helping Women award Soroptimist Club, Tampa, 1979, Excellence award Hillsborough County Dem. Women's Club, 1991. Mem. ABA (Nat. Conf. Lawyers and Social Workers, Nat. Conf. Lawyers and Realtors, Standing Com. on Nat. Conf. Groups), Fla. Bar Assn. (chmn., legal aid com.), Tampa and Hillsborough County Bar Assn. (dir. 1958-63, chmn. elder law com. 1991-93), Nat. Legal Aid and Defender Assn. (nat. bd. dirs.), Fla. Assn. Women Lawyers (pres.), Tampa Assn. Women Lawyers (pres., named Outstanding Women Lawyers of Achievement, 1993), Fla. Fedn. Social Workers (pres. bd. 1969), Fla. Fedn. Social Workers (pres. Hillsborough County chpt. 1964), Tampa Legal Sec. Assn., U.S. Navy League. Democrat. Methodist. Home: 3402 S Gardenia Dr Tampa FL 33629-8208 Office: City of Tampa Legal Dept 315 E Kennedy Blvd Tampa FL 33602-5211

STAFFORD, KATHY ANN, medical technologist, researcher; b. Ypsilanti, Mich., Aug. 5, 1961; d. Robert Blain and Joyce Ann (Neir) S. AAS, Ferris State U., 1982. Nuclear Medicine Tech. Cert. Bd., Am. Registry Radiologic Technologists (Nuclear). Diagnostic nuclear medicine technologist U. Mich. Med. Ctr., Ann Arbor, 1982-89, sr. technologist nuclear cardiology, 1989-90, clin. coord. cardiovascular nuclear medicine, 1990-94; clin. coord. cardiovascular nuclear medicine VA Hosp., Ann Arbor, 1993-94; cons. cardiovascular nuclear medicine Klinikum Rechts der Isar, Munich, 1994. Contbr. articles to profl. jours. Cancer Rsch. grantee U. Mich., 1988. Mem. Soc. Nuclear Medicine (technologist sect., ctrl. chpt., 1st Pl. Sci. Paper award 1986, 88).

STAFFORD, MARY ANN, education consultant, artist; b. Pine Bluff, Ark., Jan. 29, 1933; m. Otis L. Stafford, Sept. 12, 1952; 8 children. BSE, U. Ark., Monticello, 1969; MA, U. Ark., Fayetteville, 1975, EdS, 1982, EdD, 1985. Tchr. Pine Bluff (Ark.) High Sch., 1969-85, asst. prin., 1985-90; program support mgr. Ark. Dept. Edn., Little Rock, 1990-92; staff devel. coord. Ark. Dept. Edn., 1992-93; edn. cons. Stafford & Assocs., Little Rock, 1993—. Exhbns. include Delicious Temptations, Little Rock, Gallery 4, Little Rock, Mother Earth Gallery; contbr. articles to profl. jours. Mem. leadership com. Ark. Acad. for Leadership Tng., Fayetteville, 1993—; Stephen minister Our Lady of Holy Souls Cath. Ch., Little Rock, organist/choir mem. Recipient Recognition award Ark. Dept. Edn., 1986, 87, Ark. Art Educator of the Yr. award Ark. Art Educators, 1985. Mem. ASCD, Mid-South Watercolorists, Ark. League of Artists. Home: 1015 Green Mountain Dr Little Rock AR 72211

STAFFORD, REBECCA, college president, sociologist; b. Topeka, July 9, 1936; d. Frank C. and Anne Elizabeth (Larrick) S. A.B. magna cum laude, Radcliffe Coll., 1958, M.A., 1961; Ph.D., Harvard U., 1964. Lectr. dept. sociology Sch. Edn., Harvard U., Cambridge, Mass., 1964-70, mem. vis. com. bd. overseers, 1973-79; assoc. prof. sociology U. Nev., Reno, 1970-73, prof., 1973-80, chmn. dept. sociology, 1974-77, dean Coll. Arts and Scis., 1977-80; pres. Bemidji (Minn.) State U., 1980-82; exec. v.p. Colo. State U., Ft. Collins, 1982-83; pres. Chatham Coll., Pitts., 1983-91, Monmouth Coll., West Long Branch, N.J., 1993—; bd. dirs. First Fidelity Bancorp, N.J. Contbr. articles to profl. jours. Trustee Monmouth Med. Ctr.; bd. dirs. Univ. Presbyn. Hosp., 1985-93, Pitts. Symphyony, 1984-93, Winchester-Thurston Sch.; chmn. Harvard U. Grad. Soc. Coun., 1987-93. Recipient McCurdy-Rinkle prize for rsch. Eastern Psychiat. Assn., 1970; named Man of Yr. in Edn., City of Pitts., 1986, Woman of Yr. in Edn., YWCA Tribute to Women, 1989; grantee Am. Coun. Edn. Inst. Acad. Deans, 1979, Inst. Ednl. Mgmt., Harvard U., 1984. Mem. Harvard U. Alumni Assn. (bd. dirs. 1985-87), Phi Beta Kappa, Phi Kappa Phi. Address: Monmouth Coll West Long Branch NJ 07764

STAFFORD, TRACY, state legislator; b. Ft. Lauderdale, Fla., Jan. 2, 1948. BA, U. Fla., 1970, JD, 1973. Mem. Fla. Ho. of Reps., 1990—; adminstrv. asst. Broward County Property Appraiser. Councilwoman City of Wilton Manors, 1975-81, adminstr., 1981-82, mayor, 1986-90; asst. to mayor City of Lauderhill, 1982-84. Mem. Fla. Bar Assn., Ft. Lauderdale C. of C. Democrat. Baptist. Home: City Park Mall 128 SE 1st St Fort Lauderdale FL 33301 Office: Fla Ho of Reps State Capitol Tallahassee FL 32301*

STAGE, GINGER ROOKS, psychologist; b. Allentown, Pa., Sept. 23, 1946; d. John Myers Rooks and Catherine Estelle (Graser) Rooks Bistritz; m. Robert Roy Stage, Aug. 23, 1969; 1 child, Stephen. BA in Psychology magna cum laude, Moravian Coll., 1968; MA in Psychology, Temple U., 1969. Lic. psychologist, Pa. Instr. Beaver campus Pa. State U., Monaca, 1969-74; staff psychologist St. Francis Community Mental Health Ctr., Pitts., 1974-83; pvt. practice family therapy Coraopolis, Pa., 1977—; mem. Greenstein Family Therapy Consultation Group, Pitts., 1981—; mem., speaker Human Sexuality Alliance, Pitts., 1989-91; speaker on marital, family and parenting issues. Mem. Am. Psychol. Assn., Greater Pitts. Psychol. Assn., Western Pa. Family Ctr. Episcopalian. Home: 112 Wessex Hills Dr Coraopolis PA 15108-1021 Office: 409 Mill St Coraopolis PA 15108-1607

STAGEN, MARY-PATRICIA HEALY, marketing executive; b. Ridgewood, N.J., Apr. 4, 1955; d. Bernard Patrick and Mary Patricia (O'Connor) Healy; m. Daniel A. Stagen, Oct. 31, 1987. BA in History, lic. in secondary edn.-libr. sci., Elms Coll., Chicopee, Mass., 1977; MBA in Mktg. and Info. Svcs., Rutgers U., 1994. Adminstrv. asst. to meeting dir. Am. Inst. Chem. Engrs., N.Y.C., 1980-81, meetings coord., 1981-84, mgr. spl. projects to exec. dir., 1984-89; v.p. mktg. Wall St. Rsch. Svcs., Inc., Clifton, N.J., 1990-92; salesperson Equifax Svcs., East Rutherford, N.J., 1992—; meeting planner Am. Assn. Engring. Socs., Washington, 1984-85. Mem. NAFE, Assn. of MBA Execs., Am. Mktg. Assn. Republican. Roman Catholic. Home: 86 Boulevard Passaic NJ 07055-4706

STAGG, EVELYN WHEELER, educator, state legislator; b. Waterbury, Vt., Sept. 30, 1916; d. Aiton Grover and Edythe (Boyce) Wheeler; m. David Stagg, May 15, 1942; children: Christie Stagg Austin, Bonnie, Carol Stagg Kevan. BA, Middlebury Coll., 1939; MA, U. Vt., 1971. Assoc. prof. Castleton State Coll., Vt., 1966-82; mem. Vt. Ho. of Reps., 1982-90, chmn. house edn. com., 1982-90, vice chmn. health and welfare com., 1985-86, mem. ways and means com., 1989-90; Commn. of the States, 1987-88; cons. communications projects, Bomoseen, Vt., 1982—. Contbr. articles to profl. jours. Chmn. Women's Legis. Caucus, 1984-88; pres., bd. dirs. Rutland Area Vis. Nurse Assn., 1969-75, 89-92; bd. dirs. Rutland Mental Health Assn., 1986-88; adv. bd. nursing Castleton State Coll.; vol. LUVS for abused children; trustee pub. funds, 1990—, Castle Libr., 1992—; bd. civil authority, 1984-93; justice of peace Town of Castleton, 1984-93; mem. customer adv. coun. U.S. Postal Svc., Naples. Mem. Women's Caucus, Vt. Women's Polit. Caucus of Collier County, Nat. Women's Polit. Caucus, Inst. for Gen. Semantics, Internat. Soc. for Gen. Semantics, Am. Philatelic Soc., Democratic Women's Club of Collier County, Castleton Hist. Soc. Clubs: Women's, Rutland County Stamp. Avocations: stamp and coin collecting, sailing, skiing, traveling. Home: 222 Harbour Dr Naples FL 33940-4022 also: Mason Point Bomoseen VT 05732 Office: Evelyn Stagg Literary Agy Naples FL 33940

STAGG, JUDITH SALKIN, project manager; b. Phila., Oct. 11, 1960; d. Allan George and Arlene Rhea (Goldberg) Salkin; m. Keith Winfield Stagg, Apr. 20, 1986; children: David Jason, Alyssa Francis. BA in Polit. Sci. and Secondary Edn., The Am. U., 1982. Cert. meeting profl. Clk., intern to U.S. Senator Robert Dole Washington, 1980; adminstrv. asst. Manning, Selvage & Lee, Washington, 1983; meeting coord. Nat. Coun. Community Mental Health Ctrs., Rockville, Md., 1984-87; exhibit coord. ACP, Phila., 1987-89; conf. mgr. Anthony J. Jannetti, Inc., Pitman, N.J., 1989-91; sr. project coord. SYMEDCO, Inc., Princeton, N.J., 1992-93; project mgr. Rsch. Data Corp., Haddonfield, N.J., 1993; sr. med. project mgr. McGettigan Corp. Planning Svcs., Phila., 1993—. Author: (jour.) Convene, 1989-90. Active Mt. Laurel (N.J.) Rep. Club, 1987-93. Jewish. Home: 106 Mayfair Ln Mount Laurel NJ 08054

STAGGS, CHARLOTTE MARICIA, therapist, educator, consultant; b. Dickson, Tenn., June 29, 1949; d. Charles and Lenora (Forrester) S. BS, U. Tenn., 1971, MS, 1975; EdS, Vanderbilt U., 1982, EdD, 1988. Lic. profl. counselor, Tenn.; cert. Nat. Bd. Cert. Counselors. Tchr. Hickman County Bd. Edn., Centerville, Tenn., 1972-82, counselor, 1983-84; counselor, instr. Columbia (Tenn.) State Coll., 1987-88; counselor Austin Peay State U., Clarksville, Tenn., 1988-89; clin. therapist, program coord. Columbia Area Mental Health, 1989—. Pres. Fedn. Dem. Women, Hickman County, 1993—; mem. legis. com. Tenn. Fedn. Dem. Women, 1994—, chair ways and means com., 1994-95; mem. adv. bd. Tenn. Nursing Svc. Hospice Program, trainer hospice vols.; past mem. United Way, Hickman County. Laverne Noyes honor scholar Vanderbilt U., 1983-88. Mem. Am. Assn. Adult Devel. & Aging, Am. Counseling Assn., Tenn. Counseling Assn., Chi Sigma Iota. Mem. Ch. of Christ. Home: 3304 Hwy 48 N Nunnelly TN 37137 Office: Family Counseling 1680 Hwy 100 Centerville TN 37033

STAHL, ALICE SLATER, psychiatrist; b. Vienna, Austria, Jan. 28, 1913; came to U.S., 1938; d. Sam and Helen (Bluman) Slater; widowed; chidlren: Kenneth Lee, June Audrey. Baccalaureate, Gymnasium, Vienna, 1932; Med. Dr., U. Vienna Med. Sch., 1938. Intern Williamsport (Pa.) Gen. Hosp., 1939-40; resident in psychiatry Gallinger Mcpl. Hosp., Washington, 1940-41, Independence State Hosp., 1941-42; resident in psychiatry Bellevue Hosp., N.Y.C., 1942-43, attending psychiatry, 1945-48; staff psychiatrist Jewish Bd. of Guardians, N.Y.C., 1943-45; attending psychiatrist Jamaica Hosp., Queens, N.Y., 1948-52; dir. adolescent psychiatry Hillside Hosp., Glen Oaks, N.Y., 1954-62, attending staff psychiatrist, 1962—; supervising psychiatrist Bergen Pines County Hosp., Paramus, N.J.; prof. psychiatry, asst. prof. clin. psychiatry Yeshiva U. Fellow AMA (life), Am. Psychiat. Assn. (life); mem. Am. Psychoanalytic Assn. (life), Am. Soc. for Adolescent Psychiatry (life). Home and Office: 305 Joan Pl Wyckoff NJ 07481-2818

STAHL, FRIEDA AXELROD, physics educator, research physicist; b. Bklyn., May 27, 1922; d. Benjamin and Gertrude (Fagen) Axelrod; m. Joseph I. Stahl, June 19, 1942 (div. 1980); children: Linda Beverly Stahl Rieck, Richard Cary. BA, Hunter Coll., 1942; MA, Hofstra U., 1957; PhD, Claremont Grad. Sch., 1969. Jr. physicist U. S. Army Signal Corps Labs., Belmar, N.J., Mobile, Ala., 1942-44, Petty Geophys. Labs., San Antonio, 1944-46, Hillyer Instrument Co., N.Y.C., 1946-48; from physicist to sr. physicist Sylvania Rsch. Labs., Bayside, N.Y., 1948-52; grad. teaching asst. in physics Hofstra U., Hempstead, N.Y., 1954-56; cons. physicist Gen. Instruments, Jamaica, N.Y., 1956-57; lectr. physics Calif. State U., L.A., 1958-59, asst. prof. physics, 1959-69, assoc prof., 1969-73, prof., 1973-92, prof. emeritus, 1992—, assoc. dean, 1970-75, chmn. Acad. Senate, 1981-83; rsch. assoc. in physics Harvey Mudd Coll., Claremont, Calif., 1969-79, 90-91. Author: Leonardo, 1987; contbr. articles to profl. jours. NSF sci. faculty fellow, 1966-67. Mem. AAUW, Am. Phys. Soc., Am. Assn. Physics Tchrs., Assn. for Women in Sci., Sigma Xi, Phi Kappa Phi. Office: Calif State U LA 5151 State University Dr Los Angeles CA 90032-8206

STAHL, LESLEY R., journalist; b. Lynn, Mass., Dec. 16, 1941; d. Louis and Dorothy J. (Tishler) S.; m. Aaron Latham; 1 dau. B.A. cum laude, Wheaton Coll., Norton, Mass., 1963. Asst. to speechwriter Mayor Lindsay's Office, N.Y.C., 1966-67; researcher N.Y. Election unit London-Huntley Brinkley Report, NBC News, 1967-69; producer, reporter WHDH-TV, Boston, 1970-72; news corr. CBS News, Washington, from 1972; moderator Face the Nation, 1983-91; co-editor, corr. CBS News, 60 Minutes, 1991—. Trustee Wheaton Coll. Recipient Tex. Headliners award, 1973, Dennis Kauff award for lifetime achievement in journalism; named Best White House Corr., Washington Journalism Rev., 1991. Office: CBS News 60 Minutes 555 W 57th St New York NY 10019*

STAHL, MADONNA, lawyer, judge; b. Robinson, Ill., Sept. 26, 1928; d. Lawrence Joy and Inez Lucille (Kennedy) S.; children: Khushro Ghandhi, Rustom Ghandhi, Behram Ghandhi. BS, U. Ill., 1950; JD, Albany Law Sch., 1973. Bar: N.Y. 1974, U.S. Dist. Ct. (no. dist.) N.Y. 1974, U.S. Ct. Apls. (2nd cir.) 1975, U.S. Supreme Ct. 1978. Atty. trainee N.Y. State Dept. Commerce, Albany, 1973-74; atty. Legal Aid Soc., Albany, 1974-76; ptnr. Powers, Stahl & Somers (and predecessor firm Powers & Ghandhi), 1976-89; judge Albany City Ct., part-time, 1984-89, full-time, 1990—; mem. com. on character and fitness N.Y. State Supreme Ct. A.D. 3d Dept., Albany, 1980-86. Lobbyist Com. for Progressive Legislation, Schenectady, 1968-70. Mem. N.Y. State Bar Assn., Albany County Bar Assn., Women's Bar Assn. State N.Y. (Capital dist. pres. 1983-84). Democrat. Unitarian. Office: City Ct Albany Albany City Hall Eagle St Albany NY 12207-1004

STAHL, MARGO SCHNEEBALG, marine biologist; b. Coral Gables, Fla., June 24, 1947; d. Martin and Rose (Osman) Schneebalg; m. Glenn Stahl, Aug. 17, 1969 (div. June 1988); 1 child, Shaina Flori Georgina. BS in Biology, U. Miami, 1969, MS in Marine Biology, 1973. Fish and wildlife aide Calif. Dept. Fish and Game, Long Beach, 1973; assoc. rsch. engr. So. Calif. Edison Co., Rosemead, 1973-75; rsch. assoc. in urban and regional planning U. Hawaii, Honolulu, 1975-76, Hawaii Inst. Marine Biology, Kaneohe, 1975-77, Anuenue Fisheries Rsch. Ctr., Honolulu, 1977-79; aquatic biology Hawaii Dept. Land and Natural Resources, Honolulu, 1979-83; instr. sci. U. Hawaii Windward C.C., Kaneohe, 1985-88; ecologist U.S. Army C.E., Honolulu, 1988-93; supervisory fish and wildlife biologist U.S. Fish and Wildlife Svc., Honolulu, 1993—; pres. Mermaid Aquatic Cons., Honolulu, 1979-81, 84-88; mem. Hawaii Water Quality Tng. Interagy. Com., Honolulu, 1991-93. Contbg. author: Taste of Aloha, 1983 (Jr. League award 1985); contbr. articles to profl. jours. Project mgr. Kokokahi Aquaculture Model, Kaneohe, 1978-80; mem. adv. bd. Windward C.C., 1982-83; hon. coord. RESULTS Hunger Lobby, Honolulu, 1989. Recipient Stoye award in icythyology Am. Soc. Ichtyologists and Herpetologists, 1972, Career Woman award Sierra Mar dist. Calif. Bus. and Profl. Womens Club, 1975, Comdr's award for exceptional performance U.S. Army C.E., Ft. Shafter, Hawaii, 1990. Mem. Nat. Assn. Environ. Profls. (cert. environ. profl., chmn. cert. com. 1992-93, C.E.P. award 1991), Assn. for Women in Sci. (bd. dirs. 1985), Hawaii Assn. Environ. Profls. (bd. dirs. 1991-93, pres.-elect 1993-94), World Mariculture Soc. (bd. dirs. 1981), Am. Fisheries Soc., Western Soc. Naturalists. Home: 46-436 Holopeki St Kaneohe HI 96744-4227 Office: US Fish and Wildlife Svc Honolulu HI 96850

STAHLHUTH, GAYLE SUZANNE, playwright; b. Indpls., Aug. 11, 1950; d. Loyd Judson and Betty Alice (Smith) S.; m. Leon Philip O'Connor III, Nov. 8, 1981. BA in Theatre, U. Indpls., 1972. Actress, dir., playwright various theatres, film, TV, 1972—; bus. mgr. Stage Door Theatre, Charlotte, N.C., 1973-75; assoc. artistic dir. Al Staley's Theatre, Billings, Mont., 1978-79; artist-in-residence N.Y. Found. for the Arts, 1984—, Wyo. Found. for the Arts, 1990—, N.J. State Coun. on the Arts, Utah Arts Coun., 1994—; cons. Bds. of Edn., N.Y., 1986—; guest lectr. schs., elem. through univ. level, 1981—; tchr. Cape May (N.J.) Inst.'s Elderhostel, 1990—; coach one-person shows, N.Y.C., 1989—. Playwright: Lou: The Remarkable Miss Alcott, 1980, The Beast in the Jungle, 1989, others. Mem. Ironbound Assn., N.Y.C., 1986—; sec., pres., treas., v.p. The East Lynne Co., Secaucus, N.J., 1987—; mem. West Cape May (N.J.) Civic Assn., 1993—. Commd. to write plays Pa. Stage Co., Allentown, 1981, Nat. Portrait Gallery, Washington, 1984, Theatreworks/USA, N.Y.C., 1986, 88. Mem. Am. Fedn. TV and Radio Artists, Actors' Equity Assn., Screen Actors Guild, The Dramatists Guild, Internat. Mus. Theatre Alliance, Am. Alliance for Theatre and Edn., Episcopal Actors Guild. Democrat. Home: 121 Madison Ave # 3M New York NY 10016

STALKER, DIANNE SYLVIA, librarian; b. Hudson, N.Y., Feb. 6, 1951; d. Warren Harding and Theresa (Fazio) S.; m. Frederick Charles Blake, June 17, 1980. BA, Hofstra U., 1975; MS in LS, Columbia U., 1982, advanced cert. preservation adminstrn., 1988, Cert. in Advanced Librarianship, 1993. Cert. libr., N.Y. Reference libr. Rockville Centre (N.Y.) Pub. Libr., 1982-83; cataloger Pace U., N.Y.C., 1983-85; supr. retrospective conversion Columbia U., N.Y.C., 1985-87, cataloger Seligman Collection, 1987-88, coll. archivist Barnard Coll., 1988-89; owner, mgr. Dianne Stalker, Bookseller, 1990—; head preservation dept. SUNY, Stony Brook, 1992—; acting head spl. collections dept. SUNY, Stony Brook, 1994—; adj. lectr. bibliographic instrn. Baruch Coll., CUNY, 1989-91. Mem. ALA (rare books and manuscripts, preservation), Soc. Am. Archivists. Home: 45 Seville Ln Stony Brook NY 11790-3329

STALKER, JACQUELINE D'AOUST, academic administrator, educator; b. Penetang, Ont., Can., Oct. 16, 1933; d. Phillip and Rose (Eaton) D'Aoust; m. Robert Stalker; children: Patricia, Lynn, Roberta. Teaching cert., U. Ottawa, 1952; tchr. music, Royal Toronto Conservatory Music, 1952; teaching cert., Lakeshore Tchrs. Coll., 1958; BEd with honors, U. Manitoba, 1977, MEd, 1979; EdD, Nova U., 1985. Cert. tchr. Ont., Man., Can. Adminstr., tchr., prin. various schs., Ont. and Que., 1952-65; area commr. Girl Guides of Can., throughout Europe, 1965-69; administr., tchr. Algonquin Community Coll., Ottawa, Ont., 1970-74; tchr., program devel. Frontenac County Bd. Edn., Kingston, Ont., 1974-75; lectr., faculty advisor dept. curriculum, edn. U. Man., Can., 1977-79; lectr. U. Winnipeg, Man., Can., 1977-79; cons. colls. div. Man. Dept. Edn., 1980-81, sr. cons. programming br., 1981-84, sr. cons. post secondary, adult and continuing edn. div., 1985-88, dir. post secondary career devel. br. and adult and continuing edn. br., 1989; asst. prof. higher edn., coord. grad. program in higher edn. U. Man., 1989-92, assoc. prof., coord. grad. program in higher edn., 1992—; cons. lectures, seminars, workshops throughout Can. Contbr. articles to profl. jours.; mng. editor Can. Jour. of Higher Edn., 1989-93. Mem. U. Man. Senate, 1976-81, 86-89, bd. govs., 1979-82; Can. rep. Internat. Youth Conf., Garmisch, Fed. Republic of Germany, 1968; vol. Can. Cancer Soc.; mem. Assn. RN Accreditation Coun., 1980-85; chair Child Care Accreditation Com., Man., 1983-90; chair Task Force Post-Secondary Accessibility, Man., 1983; vol. United Way Planning and Allocations; provincial dir., mem. nat. bd. Can. Congress for Learning Opportunities for Women. Mem. Can. Soc. Study Higher Edn., Man. Tchrs. Soc., U. Man. Alumni Assn., Women's Legal Edn. and Action Fund, Am. Assn. Study Higher Edn. Home: 261 Baltimore Rd, Winnipeg, MB Canada R3L 1H7 Office: U Manitoba, Faculty Edn, Winnipeg, MB Canada R3T 2N2

STALLARD, G. ANN, printing company executive, association executive; b. Kingsport, Tenn., Nov. 15, 1946; d. James Carter and Helen (McClelland) S. BA in Edn. and Art, U. Ky., 1969. Comml. artist Clarkson-Stallard, Atlanta, 1969-76; with sales dept. Graphic Comm. Corp., Atlanta, 1976-80, v.p., 1980-84, exec. v.p., 1984—; logo and materials designer Women and the Constitution, 1988; cons. Nat. Coop. League, Washington, 1972-74, Artisan's Craft Coop., Chaddsford, Pa., 1974-76; gov.'s com. Post Secondary Edn., 1980; rep. women bus. owners in Ga., SBA Women in Bus. Owners Conf., 1984, 85, 86. Bd. dirs. YWCA of the U.S.A., 1976-88, chair nat. pub. rels. com., 1981-84, chair racial justice com., 1985-88, pres. bd. dirs., 1991—; v.p. Northwest Ga. Girl Scout Coun., Inc., 1988-91; active White House Nat. Initiative on Women's Bus. Ownership Task Force, 1985; founding mem., treas. Vote Choice Ga. Polit. Action Com., 1989—; bd. dirs. United Way of Greater Atlanta, 1993—. Recipient Nat. honor for Display Honoring Hidden Heroines, Girl Scouts U.S., 1977, Willing Svc. award Sta. WSB, Atlanta, 1977, Outstanding Community Svc. award YWCA of Greater Atlanta, 1982, Image Maker award Atlanta Profl. Women's Directory, 1982, Good Guy award Bus. Coun. Ga., 1987, Torchbearer award Women Bus. Owners Atlanta, 1990; named one of ten Outstanding Young Women, Atlanta Jaycees, 1976, Women in Bus. Advocate for Ga., SBA, 1985, Woman of Achievement, Atlanta, 1994; named to Racial Justice Hall of Fame, East Dallas Pub. Schs., 1984;. Mem. Leadership Atlanta (exec. com. 1991—), Atlanta C. of C. (task force on small bus.), Gwinnett C. of C., Women Bus. Owners of Atlanta (bd. dirs. 1981-84, v.p. 1983, pres. 1988-89). Episcopalian. Home: 1231 Fairview Rd NE Atlanta GA 30306-4661 Office: Graphic Comm Corp 394 N Clayton St Lawrenceville GA 30245-4817

STALLER, NATASHA ELENA, art history educator; b. Glencoe, Ill.; d. Norman J. Staller and Florence Levinson; m. Gary Ruvkun, May 24, 1987. BA, Wellesley Coll., 1973; PhD, Harvard U., 1983. Vis. asst. prof. U. Chgo., 1984-86; lectr. Princeton (N.J.) U., 1989-90; asst. prof. art history Amherst (Mass.) Coll., 1992—. Contbr. articles to profl. jours. Soc. Fellows jr. fellow Harvard U. 1978-81, Andrew W. Mellon fellow U. Pa., 198 7-88, J. Paul Getty fellow Yale U. Whitney Humanies Ctr., 1988-89, Mary Ingraham Bunting fellow Radcliffe Coll., 1990-91. Mem. Coll. Art Assn., Phi Beta Kappa (pres. Mass. Beta chpt. 1994—). Office: Amherst Coll Dept Fine Arts 102 Fayerweather Hall Amherst MA 01002

STALLINGS, JAWANNIA HERMENE, surgical nurse; b. Chgo., Jan. 1, 1952; d. John and Elizebeth Miles; m. Roosevelt J. Stallings, Dec. 27, 1973; children: Howard, Jarmaur, Sincerai, Hassan. BSN cum laude, Med. Coll. Ga., 1987. RN, Ga. Staff nurse CCU St. Joseph Hosp., Augusta, Ga., 1987-88; surg.-clin. asst. West Augusta Surg. Assocs., Augusta, 1988—, office bus. mgr., 1988—; developer surg. patient edn. program. With U.S. Army, 1976-79. Mem. NAFE, Richmond County Med. Aux., Stoney Med. Aux., Columbia County C. of C., Richmond County C. of C., Sigma Theta Tau, Chi Eta Phi. Roman Catholic. Office: West Augusta Surg Assocs 1242 Augusta W Pky Augusta GA 30909

STALLINGS, VALERIE AILEEN, councilwoman; b. Chgo., Dec. 23, 1939; d. Jay Sims and Mary Elizabeth (Batson) Spire; adoptive dau. William Mundo Spire; m. John R. Stallings, Sept. 14, 1961 (div. 1970); children: Dana Elizabeth, Marshall Brigg. AA, Palomar (Calif.) Coll., 1978; BA, U. Calif., San Diego, 1980. Rschr., lab. mgr. Salk Inst., La Jolla, Calif., 1970-91; mem. coun. City of San Diego, 1991—; sabbatical rschr. Netherlands Cancer Inst., 1981; city rep. Jack Murphy Stadium Authority, San Diego, 1991—; chmn. pub. facilities and recreation City of San Diego, 1992-95; chmn. fiscal policy San Diego Wastewater, 1993-94; dir. San Diego Area Wastewater Mgmt. Dist., 1993—. Contbr. articles to sci. jours. Pres. Pacific Beach Dem. Club, San Diego; mem. Pacific Beach Planning Commn., San Diego. Named Legislator of Yr., SEIU Svc. Coun., 1992. Mem. Nat. Women's Polit. Caucus, Calif. Elected Women's Assn. for Edn. and Rsch., U. Calif. Alumni Assn. (bd. dirs.). Democrat. Office: Dist 6 202 C St MS 10A San Diego CA 92101

STALLKNECHT-ROBERTS, CLOIS FREDA, publisher, publicist; b. Birmingham, Ala., Dec. 31, 1934; d. August and Sadie Bell (Wisener) Anton; m. Randall Scott Roberts; children: Yvonne Denise, April O'dell, Kurt William. Publicist Ms. Clois Presents, L.A., 1968—; advt. Engineered Magic, Advt., Santa Ana, Calif., 1976, 77, 81; pub. Internat. Printing, L.A., 1981—. Editor: Nostradamus, William Bartram, Apuleious, 1990-92. Home: PO Box 165 Inyokern CA 93527 Office: Engineered Magic 510 De La Estrella San Clemente CA 92672

STALLWORTH, ALMA GRACE, state legislator. Grad., Highland Park Community Coll., 1956; student, Wayne State U., 1956. Mem. Mich. Ho. of Reps., Lansing, 1970-74, 81—; dep. dir. Hist. Dept. City of Detroit, 1975-78, job developer, 1978-79; mem. exec. com. Nat. Conf. State Legislatures, 1986-89. Commr. Wayne County Charter, Detroit, 1978-79, Martin Luther King Commn., Detroit, 1987; chairperson bd. dirs. task force on infant mortality Mich. Legislature, 1987; pres. Nat. Black Child Devel. Inst., Detroit; vol. United Negro Coll. Fund, 1987—; founder, adminstr. Black Caucus Found. of Mich., 1987—. Recipient cert. of appreciation Mich. Dept. Edn., 1986, Advs. award Mich. Health Mothers, Health Babies Coalition, 1987; named Woman Leader in Pub. Health, Mi ch. Assn. Local Pub. Health, 1987, Woman of Yr., Minority Women's Network, 1988. Mem. NAACP, Nat. Conf. State Legislators (exec. commr. 1986), Nat. Black Caucus State Legislators, (sec. women's caucus), Mich. Legis. Black Causus (chair 1987), Alpha Kappa Alpha. Democrat. Clubs: Cameo, Top Ladies of Distinction. Home: PO Box 48825 Oak Park MI 48237-6425 Office: Mich Ho of Reps State Capitol Lansing MI 48909*

STALSBERG, GERALDINE MCEWEN, accountant; b. Springfield, Mo., May 10, 1936; d. Gerald Earl McEwen and Marie LaVerne (Pennington) Plautz; m. Bill Eugene Bottolfson, Mar. 10, 1956 (div. 1978); children: Bill Earl, Robert Edward, Brian Everett, Michelle Marie; m. Arvid Ray Stalsberg, Sept. 21, 1979; stepchildren: Angelite Renae, Neil Ray, Terry Jay. Diploma Hastings Beauty Acad., 1955; cert. in interior design, Cen. Tech. Community Coll., 1975; student Doane Coll., 1982; cert. computer programmer Lincoln Sch. Commerce, Nebr., 1984. Cosmetologist, Marinello Beauty Shop, Hastings, 1955-57; owner Nursery Sch. for Toddlers, 1958-67; acct. grain dept. Morrison-Quirk Elevator, Hastings, Nebr., 1968-69; acct., exec. sec., interior decorator Uerling's Home Furnishings, Hastings, 1970-79; acct., computer programmer, Lincoln Transp., Nebr., 1980-86, systems analyst, 1984-86; tax cons. H&R Block, Lincoln, 1983-86; programmer, tax cons., controller EBKO Industries, Hastings, 1987-90; pvt. practice acctg. and tax cons., 1987—. Emergency radio dispatcher Adams County Civil Def., Hastings, 1973-78; active YWCA, Girl Scouts USA, PTA, 4-H Clubs Am. Recipient Civic Achievement award City of Hastings, 1974. Mem. Nat. Assn. Govt. Employees, Bus. Profl. Women, Library Assn., Nat. Am. Mfrs. Assn., NAFE, Nat. Assn. Mfrs., Soroptimists Internat., Beta Sigma Phi (Woman of Yr. 1978, Order of Rose). Republican. Lutheran. Avocations: reading, bowling, fishing, swimming, jogging. Home and Office: 1602 W 12th St Hastings NE 68901-3745

STAMATAKIS, CAROL MARIE, state legislator, lawyer; b. Canton, Ohio, Apr. 27, 1960; d. Emmanuel Nicholas and Catherine Lucille (Zam) S.; m. Michael Charles Shklar, Mar. 23, 1985. BA in Criminology and Criminal Justice, Ohio State U., 1982; JD, Case Western Res., 1985. Bar: N.H. 1985, U.S. Dist. Ct. N.H. 1985. Atty. Law Office Laurence F. Gardner, Hanover, N.H., 1985-87, Law Office William Howard Dunn, Claremont, N.H., 1987-90, Elliott, Jasper & Stamatakis, Newport, N.H., 1990-93; state rep. N.H. State Legislature, 1988-94; of counsel Law office of Michael C. Sklar, Newport, 1994—; instr. Am. Inst. Banking, Claremont, 1987-88, 91-92, 95. Asst. editor: (jours.) Health Matrix: The Jour. of Health Services Mangement, 1983-85. Treas., mem. Town of Lempster N.H. Conservation Commn., 1987—; bd. dirs. Orion House, Inc., Newport, N.H., 1987-91; vice chair, solid waste chair Sierra Club (upper valley group), Hanover, N.H., 1980—; town chair N.H. Dem. Party, 1987—; mem. Town of Lempster Recycling Com., 1988—, Community Task Force on Drug and alcohol Abuse, 1988. Mem. ABA, N.H. Bar Assn. Home: PO Box 807 Newport NH 03773-0807

STAMATIOU, SANDRA JACQUELINE, dental office manager; b. Perth Amboy, N.J., Feb. 24, 1962; d. Charles Frank and Sonia (Chesner) Messina; m. Stephen Anthony Stamation, June 12, 1986 (div. Apr. 1993); 1 child, Ariana Jacqlyn. AA in Polit. Sci., Middlesex County Coll., Edison, N.J., 1981. Pres., owner Waiter/Waitress Tng. Sch., South Amboy, N.J., 1983-84, Cosmetique, Clifton, N.J., 1986-88; mgr. accounts receivable Office ofDr. Ruderman, Closter, N.J., 1992-94; office mgr. Office of Dr. Boyajian, Little Ferry, N.J., 1994—. Chmn. St. Mary's Parents Guild, Closter, 1993-94. Home: 15 Somers Ave Bergenfield NJ 07621-2655

STAMBERG, SUSAN LEVITT, radio broadcaster; b. Newark, Sept. 7, 1938; d. Robert I. and Anne (Rosenberg) Levitt; m. Louis Collins Stamberg, Apr. 14, 1962; 1 child, Joshua Collins. BA, Barnard Coll, 1959; DHL (hon.), Gettysburg Coll., 1982, Dartmouth Coll., 1984, Knox Coll., U. N.H., SUNY, Brockport. Editorial asst. Daedalus, Cambridge, Mass., 1960-62; editorial asst. The New Republic, Washington, 1962-63; host, producer, mgr., program dir. Sta. WAMU-FM, Washington, 1963-69; host All Things Considered Washington, 1971-86; host Weekend Edition Nat Pub. Radio, Washington, 1987-89; spl. corr. Nat. Pub. Radio, 1990—; bd. dirs. AIA, Washington, 1983-85, PEN/Faulkner Fiction Award Found., 1985—. Author: Every Night at Five, 1982, The Wedding Cake in the Middle of the Road, 1992, Talk: NPR's Susan Stamberg Considers All Things, 1993. Recipient Honor award Ohio U., 1977, Edward R. Murrow award Corp. for Pub. Broadcasting, 1980; named Woman of Yr., Barnard Coll., 1984; fellow Silliman Coll. Yale U., 1984—; inducted Broadcasting Hall of Fame, 1994. Office: Nat Pub Radio 635 Massachusetts Ave NW Washington DC 20001-3753

STAMSTA, JEAN F., artist; b. Sheboygan, Wis., Nov. 2, 1936; d. Herbert R. and Lucile Caroline (Malwitz) Nagel; m. Duane R. Stamsta, Aug. 18, 1956; children: Marc, David. BS, BA, U. Wis., 1958. guest curator Milw. Art Mus., 1986; resident artist Leighton Artist Colony, Banff, Alta., Can., 1987. Solo exhbns. Am. Craft Mus., N.Y.C., 1971, Winona (Minn.) State U., 1986, Lawrence U., Appleton, Wis., 1990, Walkers Point Ctr. Arts, Milw., 1990; group shows include Milw. Art Mus., 1986, 88, Nat. Air & Space Mus. Smithsonian Instn., Washington, 1986, Madison (Wis.) Art Ctr., 1987, 90, Paper Press Gallery, Chgo., 1988, North Arts Ctr., Atlanta, 1990, Dairy Barn Cultural Arts Ctr., Athens, Ohio, 1991, Paper Arts Festival, Appleton, Wis., 1992, Fine Arts Mus., Budapest, Hungary, 1992, Tilburg Textile Mus., The Netherlands, 1993, U. Wis.- Madison Union Gallery, 1994. NEA craftsman fellow, 1974. Home and Studio: 9313 Center Oak Rd Hartland WI 53029

STANAITIS, SANDRA LEE, nurse; b. Chester, Pa., Dec. 27, 1958; d. Leon David and Margaret (Sharpless) S. BA in Psychology, Widener U., 1980; BS in Biology, SUNY, Albany, 1983; postgrad., East Carolina U., 1984; BSN, West Chester U., 1993; student, Delaware County C.C., Media, Pa., 1995. RN Del., N.J., Pa.; cert. in venipuncture, perioperative nursing. Instr. biology lab. East Carolina U., Greenville, N.C., 1987-88, tutor math. and sci., 1986-88, technician biol. lab. Sea Grant Program, 1987, adj. lectr. biology, 1987-88; tutor math. and sci. Vocat. Rehab., Greenville, 1987-88; technician environ. lab. Weyerhauser Pulp Mill, New Bern, N.C., 1987-88; inspector pharmaceutical quality control Burroughs-Wellcome, Greenville, 1988; clin. data asst. Wyeth Labs., Radnor, Pa., 1988-89; rep. customer svc. Met. Pers., Wayne, Pa., 1989-92, Bayada Nurses Home Health Care Specialist, 1994—; staff nurse Genesis Health Ventures Suburban Woods, Norristown, Pa., 1994—. James McDaniel Meml. scholar, 1986-88, Army Nurse Corps scholar, 1991-93, U. N.C., Inst. Nutrition scholar, 1985-87. Mem. U.S. Figure Skating Assn., Nat. League for Nursing, Assn. Oper. Rm. Nurses, Recreational Skating Inst. Am., West Chester U. Nursing Honor Soc., Sigma Xi, Sigma Theta Tau. Office: Bayada Vis Home Nurses 60 Allendale Ct King Of Prussia PA 19406

STANAWAY, ANNE, television producer, writer; b. Elkhart, Ind., Apr. 8, 1931; d. Alfred C. and Ersa S. (Flint) Arbogast; divorced; children: Susan, John, Robin, Sharon. BS, Northwestern U., 1952. Producer Sta. WITF-TV (PBS), Hershey, Pa., 1973-78; exec. producer Sta. WITF-TV, Hershey, Pa., 1978-80; owner, exec. producer Sunlight Prodns., Ltd., Lebanon, Pa., 1980—. Producer, writer documentaries Closing the Gap, 1976 (nat. Emmy nomination), Kids Today, 1982 (Am. Film Festival award), Alzheimer's Disease: You Are Not Alone, 1984 (Retirement Rsch. Found. nat. media award), Happiness and Longevity Club, 1987 (Cine Golden Eagle). Chmn. Ctr. for Study First Ams., Oreg. State U., Corvallis, 1994; bd. dirs., pres., sec.-treas. Arbogast Found. Named NEH fellow U. Mich., 1978-79, Fulbright fellow, Japan, 1985-86, Fulbright fellow, Okinawa, 1991. Office: 91 Valley View Way Boulder CO 80304

STANAWAY, LORETTA SUSAN, small business owner; b. Selfridge AFB, Mich., Jan. 1, 1954; d. Vincent Carl and Carolyn Jane (Grasser) Pizzo; m. Thomas Lee Stanaway, Apr. 23, 1983; stepchildren: Todd Richard, Toni Marie. Student, Ctrl. Mich. U., 1972-75. Intern, reporter Daily Times-News, Mt. Pleasant, Mich., 1974; editorial asst. Bar Jour. Mich., Lansing, 1975-76; with prodn. control dept. Dart Container Corp., Mason, Mich., 1976-80; mgr. Payless Shoes, Lansing, 1980; shift supr. Greyhound Food Mgmt., Lansing, 1980-82; owner, mgr. L.S. Distbg., Lansing, 1982-89, Send Out Svcs. S.O.S., Lansing, 1989—; owner, mgr. lawn care divsn., snow removal divsn. Send Out Svcs., 1993—; mem. focus group on customer svc. Small Bus. Devel. Ctr., Lansing, 1991—. Treas. Mich. Coalition on Smoking or Health, Lansing, 1987-89; bd. dirs. Am. Cancer Soc. Mich., Lansing, 1988-89; mem. custodial svcs. com. Ingham Intermediate Sch. Dist., 1991—; mem. adminstrv. bd., council on ministries, sunday sch. supt., Grovenburg United Meth. Ch., 1994—. Recipient Outstanding Svc. award Am. Cancer Soc. Mich., 1988. Mem. NAFE, Nat. Assn. Self-Employed, Nat. Fedn. Ind. Bus., Internat. Platform Assn. Republican. Methodist. Home and Office: 546 Armstrong Rd Lansing MI 48911-3811

STANCICH, GLORIA VERNON, human rights activist; b. Akron, Ohio, June 12, 1935; d. Clarence Earl and Violet Minerva (Stott) Vernon; children: Christopher, Nicholas. BA in Edn., U. Puget Sound, 1961; MA in Humanities, San Francisco State U., 1964. Cert. tchr. grades K-14. Elem. educator Horace Mann Sch., Tacoma, 1960-62; secondary French tchr. San Marino (Calif.) H.S., 1964-67; social worker Dept. Social and Health Svcs., Tacoma, 1968-74; social svcs. program mgr. Dept. Social and Health Svcs., Olympia, Wash., 1974-82; social svcs. adminstr. Dept. Social and Health Svcs., Olympia and Tacoma, 1982-92; diversity cons. Western Wash. U., Bellingham, Wash., 1992—; pvt. practice polit. activist, lectr., 1992—; adj. faculty Antioch U., 1993—; cons., speaker Child Welfare League Am., 1974-92, Women of Vision, Tacoma, 1991—; cons., presenter Nat. Assn. Homemaker/Home Health Aide Svcs., 1974-80. Contbr. chpt. to manual. Del., spkr. Internat. Women's Conf., Cork, Ireland, 1993; rsch. cons. Womens Forum: Prelude to Bejing, Tacoma, 1994. Mem. NOW (field organizer 1981-82, chpt. devel. com. 1983-85, v.p.), Wash. Women United (bd. dirs.), Women's Internat. League for Peace and Freedom, N.W. Coalition Against Malicious Harassment (conf. com.), Nat. Coalition Bldg. Inst., Parents and Friends of Lesbians and Gays. Home: 9916 90th Ave NW Gig Harbor WA 98332

STANCIL, IRENE MACK., family counselor; b. St. Helena Island, Sept. 29, 1938; d. Rufus and Irene (Wilson) Mack; m. Nesby Stancil, Dec. 29, 1968; 1 child, Steve Lamar. BA, Benedict Coll., 1960, CUNY, 1983; MA, New World Bible Coll., 1984; SSD, United Christian Coll., 1985. Supr. City of New York; tchr. local bd. edn., S.C.

STANDER, NANCY LUCAS, elementary school educator, counselor; b. L.A., July 17, 1945; d. Stephen Earl and Hazel Marie (Lorance) Lucas; m. Thomas Stephen Stander, Aug. 31, 1968 (div. Feb. 1973). BS, Miami U., Oxford, Ohio, 1968; MS summa cum laude, Barry U., 1987. Tchr. Durham Bus. Coll., Corpus Christi, Tex., 1968-69; sales mgr. Rich's, Inc., Atlanta, 1971-76, Felipe Fashions, Miami, Fla., 1977-78; sales exec. Tradewinds, Miami, 1978-80; advt. exec. The Miami Herald, 1980-84, Goodlife Mag., Miami, 1984-85; tchr. Dade County Pub. Schs., Miami, 1986—; counselor Stephen Ministries, Miami, 1989—; clin. supr. Barry U., 1987-90. Mem. ASCD, ACA, Internat. Reading Assn., Barry U. Counseling Assn. Democrat. Presbyterian (elder). Home: 8150 W 9th Ave Hialeah FL 33014-3506 Office: North Carol City Elem Sch 19010 NW 37th Ave Opa Locka FL 33056-2996

STANDFAST, SUSAN J(ANE), state official, research, consultant, educator; b. Callicoon, N.Y., July 2, 1935; m. Theodore P. Wright Jr., 1967; children: Henry S., Margaret S., Catherine B. AB in Biology and Chemistry, Wells Coll., 1957; MD, Columbia U., 1961; MPH In Epidemiology, U. Calif., Berkeley, 1965. Cert. Am. Bd. Preventive Medicine. Intern King County Hosp., Swedish Hosp, Seattle, 1961-62; pediatric resident U. Wash., Seattle, 1963; sr. resident in epidemiology N.Y. State Health Dept., 1965-67; instr. dept. community health Albany (N.Y.) Med. Coll., 1965-67, asst. prof. dept. preventive and community medicine, 1968-72, cons. in epidemiology, 1968-72, adj. asst. prof. preventive and community medicine, 1975-80, adj. assoc. prof., 1980-91, cons. preventive medicine dept. family practice, 1983-91; research physician bur. cancer control, div. epidemiology N.Y. State Dept. Health, Albany, 1975-83, dir. cancer surveillance unit cancer control sect. bur. chronic disease prevention, 1983-85, asst. to dir. div. epidemiology, 1985-86, dir. injury control program div. epidemiology, 1986-90; physician pub. health Albany, 1983—; dir. disability prevention program, 1988-91; cons. epidemiologist div. family health N.Y. State Dept. Health, Albany, 1991—; vis. lectr. G.S. Med. Coll., Bombay, 1969-70, London Sch. Hygiene, 1974-75, Coll. Community Medicine, Lahore, Pakistan, 1991; cons. in epidemiology Bombay Cancer Registry Tata Meml. Hosp., Albany, 1968-72; cons. infectious diseas sect. VA Med. Ctr., Albany, 1979; mem. ad hoc task force on data resource devel. for dir. epidemiology and biometry rsch. program Nat. Inst. Child Health and Human Devel., Bethesda, Md., 1979-80; assoc. prof. epidemiology Sch. Pub. Health, SUNY, 1987—, co-dir. master's pub. health program, 1991—; lectr. in field. Contbr. numerous articles to profl. jours. Mem. med. adv. bd. Hudson-Mohawk chpt. Nat. Founs. SIDS, 1976-84; mem. med. adv. bd. council on human sexuality Planned Parenthood, Albany, 1971-88; mem. Physicians for Social Responsibility, 1984—, Doctors Ought to Care, 1984—, also numerous pub. health task forces and coms. Recipient Disting. Alumnae award Wells Coll., 1994. Fellow Am. Coll. Preventive Medicine, Am. Coll. Epidemiology; mem. APHA, Am. Assn. for Automotive Medicine. Home: 27 Vandenburg Ln Latham NY 12110-1190

STANDIFER, SABRINA, state legislator; m. Brad Barkley. Mem. Kans. Ho. of Reps., 1993—; self-employed computer cons. Democrat. Home: 317 W 41st St N North Wichita KS 67204-3203 Office: Kans Ho of Reps State Capitol Topeka KS 66612*

STANDIFORD, SALLY NEWMAN, technology educator; b. Berkeley, Calif., Dec. 25, 1941; d. Richard Lancaster and Eleanor June (Wagstaff) Newman; m. Jay Cary Standiford, Nov. 21, 1964; children: Barbara, Susan. AB, Georgian Ct. Coll., Lakewood, N.J., 1963; MA in Teaching, The Citadel, 1972; PhD, U. Ill., 1980. Tchr. Goose Creek High Sch., Hanahan, S.C., 1969-73; rsch. and teaching asst. U. Ill., Urbana, 1974-78, rsch. asst. Inst. Aviation, 1979-80, vis. asst. prof., 1980-84; adminstr. City Colls. Chgo., 1978; mgr. Control Data Corp., Champaign, Ill., 1978-79; instrnl. design specialist Control Data Corp., Savoy, Ill., 1979-80; asst. prof. U. St. Thomas, St. Paul, 1984-88; assoc. prof. tech. U. Wis., River Falls, 1988-92, prof., 1992—; dir. Ednl. Tech. Ctr., U. Wis., 1988—; advisor N.W. Instrnl. Broadcast Svc., 1989—; evaluator Wis. Dept. Pub. Instrn., Madison, 1990—; rschr. Saturn Sch. Tomorrow, St. Paul, 1991—; cons. Met. State U., Mpls., 1992—; mem. U. Wis. Sys. Distance Edn. Policy Task Force, 1993—. Author: Computers in English Classroom, 1983; contbg. author: Language Arts Methods, 1987; also numerous articles; designer instrnl. software. Del. Minn. Dem.-Farmer-Labor Conv., Rochester, 1988; computer cons. Women Against Mil. Madness, Mpls., 1988-91; marcher Honeywell Project, Mpls., 1988-91; pres. faculty senate U. Wis., 1992—. Grantee NSF, 1970-71, fellow, 1973-74; ssummer faculty rsch. fellow USAF, 1987. Mem. Nat. Coun. Tchrs. English (instrnl. tech. com. 1983-88, commn. on media 1985-88, cons. 1992—), Assn. Women in Computing, Western Wis. Alliance in Tech. (advisor 1990—), Computer Profls. for Social Responsibility (charter). Office: U Wis A12 Ames River Falls WI 54022

STANDISH, GAVIN, educational administrator; b. Feb. 28, 1946; d. Richard H. and Phyllis E. (Meyers) Black; m. Richard W. Standish, July 5, 1968; children: Richard W., Mary Margaret. BA, Ohio Wesleyan U., 1968; MEd, Salisbury (Md.) State U., 1985; EdD, Wilmington Coll., 1995. Cert. elem. tchr., spl. edn. tchr., reading basic skills specialist, elem. prin., coord. tech., Del. Owner The Tole Patch, Dover, Del., 1979-83; tchr. spl. edn. Lake Forest Sch. Dist., Frederica, Del., 1985-88; tchr. 4th grade Lake Forest Sch. Dist., Felton, Del., 1988-91, coord. instructional tech., 1991—. Mem. ASCD, Internat. Soc. for Tech. in Edn., Diamond State Reading Assn., Del. Assn. Sch. Adminstrs., Del. Coun. Tchrs. math. Office: Lake Forest Sch Dist RD 1 Box 847A Felton DE 19943

STANDLEY-BURT, NANCY VILMA, psychologist, educator; b. Chgo., Aug. 6, 1934; d. Joseph and Anna (Tichna) Pav; m. Fred L. Standley, Sept. 8, 1956 (div. Mar. 1982); m. Jesse W. Burt, Dec. 18, 1982. BS, Northwestern U., 1957; MA, MacMurray Coll., Jacksonville, Ill., 1960; PhD, Fla. State U., 1969. Cert. sch. psychologist and counselor; nat. cert. counselor; lic. psychologist, Fal. Tchr. English Niles Twp. High Sch., Skokie, Ill., 1957-59; counselor, psychologist Maine Twp. High sch., Park Ridge, Ill., 1960-63; instr. English Fla. sTate U., Tallahassee, 1963-65, asst. prof., 1965-70; asst. prof. Fla. A&M U., Tallahassee, 1970-75, prof., 1975—, dir. career devel. ctr., 1973-75, dir. tchr. edn. ctr., 1982-92. Author: (with Fred Standley) James Baldwin : A Reference Guide, 1979, Critical Essays: James Baldwin, 1984; contbr. articles to profl. jours. and monographs. Danforth Found. Assoc. award, 1969, 74; Salley Eckert Stevenson scholar, 1955-57. Mem. ACA, So. Assn. Counselor Edn., Fla. Counseling Assn., Fla. Assn. Counselor Edn., Big Bend Counseling (past pres.), Leon Mental Health Assn., Assn. for Counselor Edn. and Supervision, Psi Chi. Democrat. Methodist. Home: Rt 17 Box 1380 Tallahassee FL 32308 Office: Fla A&M U Coll Edn Tallahassee FL 32307

STANFORD, BEVERLY HARDCASTLE, education educator; b. St. Louis, July 1, 1938; d. Richard Rogers and Jessamine (Hopkins) Hardcastle; m. Clayton Wilson Lewis, Dec. 29, 1958 (div.); children: Jennifer Hopkins Lewis, Daniel Clayton; m. George Richard Stanford, July 4, 1987. Student, Duke U., 1958-59; BA in Elem. Edn., U. Iowa, 1969; postgrad., SUNY, Geneseo, 1972-75; PhD in Human and Child Devel., Ariz. State U., 1981. Cert. elem. tchr., Iowa, N.Y. Elem. tchr. Horace Mann Sch., Iowa City, Iowa, 1969-70, Holcomb Campus Sch., Geneseo, 1971-74, Avon (N.Y.) Ctrl. Sch., 1970-71, 74-79; grad. teaching assoc. Coll. Edn. Ariz. State U., Tempe, 1980-81, instr. Coll. Edn., summer 1981; from asst. to assoc. prof. Dept. Curriculum and Instrn. S.W. Tex. State U., San Marcos, 1981-89; assoc. chair, prof. Dept. Edn. Azusa (Calif.) Pacific U., 1989—; book reviewer Ednl. Forum, Am. Orthopsychiatric Assn. Newsletter; presenter Internat. Human Scis. Rsch. Conf., Edmonton, Alta., Can., 1985, Assn. for Childhood Edn. Internat., 1985, Chgo., 1992, Assn. for Humanistic Edn., Denver, 1989, Brigham Young U., Provo, 1986, Am. Edn. Rsch Assn., New Orleans, 1984, Chgo., 1985, Assn. for the Care of Children's Health, Houston, 1984, Am. Assn. Counseling and Devel., Houston, 1984, Kappa Delta Pi, 1982, among others. Author: Practice in Critical Reading Skills, Books A, B & C, 1975 (with Forrest Parkay) On Becoming a Teacher, 1989, 3d edit., 1995; author chpts. in books; mem. editorial bd. Childhood Edn., 1992—, Ednl. Forum, 1984-87, Kappa Delta Pi Record, 1980-82; columnist Childhood Edn., 1992—; contbr. articles to profl. jours. Grantee Azusa Pacific U., 1992, 94, LBJ Inst. for the Improvement of Teaching and Learning, 1989, S.W. Tex. State U., 1983-86, Ariz. State U., 1979-80. Mem. ASCD, Assn. Childhood Edn. Internat., Am. Ednl. Rsch. Assn., Am. Assn. Higher Edn., Assn. Tchr. Educators (presenter), Kappa Delta Pi. Presbyterian. Home: 1023 Lakeview Terr Azusa CA 91702 Office: Azusa Pacific U Dept Edn 901 E Alosta Ave Box APU Azusa CA 91702-7000

STANGER, ILA, writer, editor; b. N.Y.C., Oct. 13, 1940; d. Jack Simon and Shirley Ruth (Nadelson) S. B.A., Bklyn. Coll., 1961. Feature and travel editor Harpers Bazaar, N.Y.C., 1969-75; exec. editor Travel and Leisure mag., N.Y.C., 1975-85; editor in chief Food and Wine Mag., N.Y.C., 1985-89, Travel and Leisure mag., N.Y.C., 1990-93; contbg. editor Town and Country mag., 1993—; writer on arts, features and travel; consulting editor Saveur mag. Consulting editor Saveur mag. Mem. N.Y. Travel Writers., Am. Soc. Mag. Editors. Home and Office: 115 W 71st St New York NY 10023-3838

STANIAR, LINDA BURTON, insurance company executive; b. Glen Ridge, N.J., July 6, 1948; d. Harold Burton and Helen (Kintzing) Staniar; m. William Glasgow Bergh, Jan. 21, 1978; 1 child, Courtney Christian Bergh. BA, Briarcliff Coll., 1970; MA, NYU, 1974. Pub. rels. asst. N.Y. Life Ins. Co., N.Y.C., 1977-78, pub. rels. assoc., 1978-80, dir., 1981-84, asst. v.p., 1984-86, corp. v.p., 1986-88, v.p. pub. rels. and advt., 1988-93, v.p. corp. comm., 1993—. Mem. Advt. Women of N.Y. Office: NY Life Ins Co 51 Madison Ave New York NY 10010-1603

STANLAKE, KAREN ANN, sales executive, investment advisor; b. Hillsdale, Mich., July 5, 1957; d. Jerry Ward and Donna Jean (Kline) S. BA, Hillsdale Coll., 1984; MA, Mich. State U., 1990. Retail broker various brokerage houses, Denver, 1988-93; instnl. investments Trust Co. of Am., Boulder, 1993-94; sr. sales exec. Nat. Coun. Compensation Ins., Denver, 1994—; pvt. practice investment advisor Highlands Ranch, Colo., 1994—. Mem. Am. Assn. Individual Investors. Home: 5709 S Iris Way Littleton CO 80123 Office: Two Tamarac Sq Ste 613 Denver CO 80231

STANLEY, ELLEN MAY, historian, consultant; b. Dighton, Kans., Feb. 3, 1921; d. Delmar Orange and Lena May (Bobb) Durr; m. Max Neal Stanley, Nov. 5, 1939; children: Ann Y. Stanley Epps, Janet M. Stanley Horsky, Gail L. Stanley Peck, Kenneth D., Neal M., Mary E. Stanley McEniry. BA in English and Journalism, Ft. Hays (Kans.) State U., 1972, MA in History, 1984. Pvt. practice local/state historian, cons., writer local history Dighton, 1973—, cons. genealogy, 1980—; vice chmn. State Preservation Bd. Rev., Kans., 1980-87; area rep. Kans. State Mus. Assn., 1978-84. Author: Early Lane County History: 12,000 B.C. - A.D. 1884, 1993 (cert. of commendation Am. Assn. State and Local History); contbr. articles to profl. jours. Precinct woman com. Alamota Township, Kans., 1962-86; mem. Dem. State Affirmative Action Com., 1975. Recipient hon. mention for photography Ann. Christian Arts Festival, 1974, Artist of Month award Dane G. Hansen Mus., 1975. Mem. Kans. State Hist. Soc. (pres. 1990-91), Lane County Hist. Soc. (sec. 1970-78). Methodist. Home: 100 N 4th Dighton KS 67839 Office: 116 E Long St Dighton KS 67839

STANLEY, KAREN FRANCINE MARY LESNIEWSKI, human resources professional; b. Amsterdam, N.Y., Oct. 10, 1948; d. Francis Raymond and Genievive Mary (Klementowski) Lesniewski; m. Mark Anthony Stanley, Nov. 11, 1972. BA, Alliance Coll., 1970; MA, The Coll. St. Rose, 1976, CAS, 1987. English tchr. Middle Country Sch., Centereach, N.Y., 1970-71; English and social studies tchr. Mt. Carmel, Gloversville, N.Y., 1971-72; English tchr. Bishop Scully H.S., Amsterdam, 1972-80, Shenendehowa Ctrl., Clifton Park, N.Y., 1980-82; English tchr., head dept. Broadalbin (N.Y.) Ctrl. Sch., 1982-86; adminstrv. intern Saratoga Springs (N.Y.) City Sch. Dist., 1986-87, dir. for human resource svcs., 1987—; bd. dirs. N.Y. State Staff Devel. Coun., 1990-92. Mem. Soc. for Human Resource Mgrs., N.Y. State Assn. Women Adminstrs., Nat. Assn. Sch., Colls., and Univs., Nat. Assn. Ednl. Negotiators, Soroptimist Internat. (sec. Saratoga County chpt. 1991-92, del. Dist. I 1992-93, asst. treas. 1994-95), Alumni Adminstrn. Assn./Coll. St Rose (bd. dirs., sec. 1986-89, pres. 1989-92, past pres. 1992-94). Republican. Roman Catholic. Office: Saratoga Springs City Schs 5 Wells St Saratoga Springs NY 12866-9266

STANLEY, LANETT LORRAINE, state legislator; b. Atlanta, Nov. 5, 1962; d. Archie and Ethel Francis (Dixon) S. BS, U. Tenn., 1985; postgrad., Carver Bible Coll., Atlanta, 1991—. Children's reporter Sta. WXIA-TV, Atlanta, 1979-80; model, sales clk. Rich's Dept. Store, Atlanta, 1979-83; copy clk. Knoxville (Tenn.) Jour., 1984-85; reporter Atlanta Daily World, 1986; intern Sta. WTBS-TV, Atlanta, 1986; adminstrv. aide Bd. Commrs. Fulton County, Atlanta, 1986-87; mem. Ga. Ho. of Reps., Atlanta, 1987—; ind. mktg. cons., 1991—; mem. Nat. and Ga. Legis. Black Caucus, 1987. Bd. dirs. West End Med. Ctrs., Inc., 1988—, Southside Youth Athletic Acad. Assn., 1991—. Democrat. Baptist. Office: Ga Gen Assembly Ga State Capitol Atlanta GA 30318*

STANLEY, MARGARET DURETA SEXTON, retired speech therapist; b. Wells County, Ind., Aug. 7, 1931; d. James Helmuth and Bertha Anna (Kizer) Roberts; m. Gale Sexton, Nov. 21, 1950; children: Cregg Alan, Donna Sue, Sheila Rene; m. Charles Stanley, Mar. 24, 1979. BS, Ball State U., 1952, MA, 1963. Speech and hearing clinician Hamilton (Ohio) City Schs., 1955-59, Kettering (Ohio) Pub. Schs., 1959-60; speech, lang. and hearing clinician Muncie (Inc.) Community Schs., 1960-93; asst. prof. speech pathology Ball State U., 1993—; dir. Psi Iota Xi Summer Clinic, Decatur, Ind., 1964, Ball State U., 1965-77, asst. prof., 1993—; supr. clinician Tri-County Hearing Impaired Assn., 1978-81. Compiler, editor curriculum for speech, lang. and hearing clinicians of Muncie Community Schs. Mem. NEA, Am. Speech and Hearting Assn. (cert. clin. competency in speech pathology), Ind. Speech and Hearing Assn., Ind. Edn. Assn., Ind. Coun. Suprs. Speech and Hearing (pres. 1982-84), Adminstrv. Women, Speech and Hearing Area Educators Ind. (founder, 1st pres. 1984-86, Disting. Svc. award 1991, Honors of Assoc. 1992), Delta Kappa Gamma (1st v.p. 1992-94, pres. 1994—). Republican. Methodist. Home: RR 1 Box 99 Parker City IN 47368-9721

STANLEY, MARGARET KING, performing arts administrator; b. San Antonio, Tex., Dec. 11, 1929; d. Creston Alexander and Margaret (Haymore) King; children: Torrey Margaret, Jean Cullen. Student, Mary Baldwin Coll., 1948-50; BA, U. Tex., Austin, 1952; MA, Incarnate Word Coll., 1959. Tchg. cert. 1953. Elem. tchr. San Antonio Ind. Sch. Dist., 1953-54, 55-56, Arlington County Schs., Va., 1954-55, Ft. Sam Houston Schs., San Antonio, 1955-57; art, art history tchr. St. Pius X Sch., San Antonio, 1959-60; tchr. Trinity U., 1963-65; designer-mfr., owner CrisStan Clothes, Inc., San Antonio, 1967-73; founder, exec. dir. San Antonio Performing Arts Assn., 1976-92, founder Arts Council of San Antonio, 1962; founding chmn. Joffrey Workshop, San Antonio, 1979; originator, founding chairwoman Student Music Fair, San Antonio, 1963; radio program host On Stage, San Antonio, 1983—. Originator of the idea for a new ballet created for the City of San Antonio, "Jamboree," commd. from the Joffrey Ballet, world premiere in San Antonio, 1984. Pres. San Antonio Symphony League, 1971-74; v.p. Arts Council of San Antonio, 1975; bd. govs. Artists Alliance of San Antonio, 1982; v.p. San Antonio Opera Guild, 1974-76, founder Early Music Festival, San Antonio, 1990. Recipient Outstanding Tchr. award Arlington County Sch. Dist., 1954, Today's Woman award San Antonio Light Newspaper, 1980, Woman of Yr. in Arts award San Antonio Express News, 1983, Emily Smith award for outstanding alumni Mary Baldwin Coll., 1973, Headliner award Women in Communications Inc., 1982, Erasmus medal The Dutch Consulate, 1992; named to Women's Hall of Fame, San Antonio, 1984; teaching fellow Trinity U., San Antonio, 1964-66. Mem. Internat. Soc. Performing Arts Adminstrs. (regional rep. 1982-85, bd. dirs. 1991—), Met. Opera Nat. Coun., Assn. Performing Arts Presenters, Women in Communications (San Antonio chpt.), Jr. League of San Antonio, Battle of Flowers Assn., S.W. Performing Arts Presenters (chmn. 1988-92). Avocations: traveling, reading.

STANLEY, MARLYSE REED, horse breeder; b. Fairmont, Minn., Sept. 19, 1934; d. Glenn Orson and Lura Mabel (Ross) Reed; m. James Arthur Stapleton, 1956 (div. 1976); 1 child, Elisabeth Katharene; m. John David Stanley, Oct. 22, 1982. BA, U. Minn., 1957. Registered breeder Arabian horses in Spain, 1976—. Chmn. bd. dirs. Sitting Rock Spanish Arabians, Inc., Greensboro, N.C., 1978-81; pres. Sitting Rock Spanish Arabians, Inc., Hollister, Calif., 1981—; bd. dirs. Glenn Reed Tire Co., Fairmont, Minn. Author Arabian hunter/jumper rules Am. Horse Shows Assn.; contbr. articles to horse jours. Named Palomino Queen of Minn., 1951, Miss Fairmont, 1954, Miss Minn., 1955. Mem. Internat. Arabian Assn. (bd. dirs. region 10, Minn. and Wis. 1973-76, nat. chmn. hunter-jumper com. 1976-81), Minn. Arabian Assn. (bd. dirs. 1972-75), Am. Paint Horse Assn. (nat. bd. dirs. 1967-70), Assn. Española de Criadores de Caballos A'rabes (Spain), Alpha Xi Delta. Republican. Episcopalian.

STANLEY, PAMELA AURELIA, state legislator; b. Mar. 13, 1956; 2 children. Student, Ga. Tech., Ga. State. Former clk. U.S. Postal Svc.; mem. Ga. Ho. of Reps., 1992—; mem. indsl. rels., ins. and state planning and cmty. affairs coms. Democrat. Baptist. Home: 706 Foundry St NW Atlanta GA 30314 Office: Ga Ho of Reps 512 Legislative Office Bldg Atlanta GA 30334*

STANLEY, PAMELA MARY, cell biologist; b. Melbourne, Australia, Mar. 25, 1947; came to U.S., 1977; d. John Patrick and Edith Della (Hart) Fetherstonhaugh; m. Evan Richard Stanley, Feb. 6, 1970; children: Damian Alexander, Robert Fenton. BSc with honors, U. Melbourne, 1969, PhD, 1972. Rsch. assoc. U. Toronto, Toronto, Can., 1972-77; asst. prof. Albert Einstein Coll. Medicine, Bronx, 1977-82, assoc. prof., 1982-86, prof. of cell biology, 1986—; mem. study sect. NIH, Bethesda, 1989-93. Editorial bd. Molecular and Cellular Biology, 1980-91, Glycobiology, 1990—, Molecular Biology of the Cell, 1991-93, Jour. Biol. Chemistry, 1995—; contbr. articles to profl. jours. Bd. dirs. Kids Meeting Kids Can Make A Difference, N.Y., 1986—, Alaria Chamber Ensemble, N.Y., 1985—; mem. Educators for Social Responsibility, N.Y., 1985—; mem. review group Am. Cancer Soc., N.Y.C., 1981-85. NSF grantee, 1977, Am. Cancer Soc. grantee, 1978, 80, NIH grantee, 1980, 83, 85, 86, 90, 91. Mem. Am. Soc. for Biochemistry and Molecular Biology, Soc. for Cell Biology, Internat. Assn. Women Biochemists. Office: Albert Einstein Coll Medicine Dept Cell Bio Bronx NY 10461

STANLEY, SHERRY A., lawyer; b. Buffalo, N.Y., Oct. 17, 1955; d. Arthur A. and Irene S.; m. William C. Hearon, Mar. 27, 1987. BA, U. West Fla., 1975; JD, U. Fla., 1978. Bar: Fla. 1978. Assoc. Mahoney, Hadlow & Adams, Miami, Fla., 1978-80; ptnr. Steel, Hector & Davis, Miami, 1980-87, Weil, Gotshal & Manges, Miami, 1987-92; sr. counsel Barnett Banks, Inc., Miami, 1992-94; ptnr. Coll, Davidson, Carter, Smith, Salter & Barkett, P.A., Miami, Fla., 1994—. Mem. Fla. Bar, Order of Coif, Phi Theta Kappa. Republican. Roman Catholic. Office: Barnett Banks Inc 701 Brickell Ave Miami FL 33131

STANLEY, SHERYL LYNN, college administrator; b. Moberly, Mo., Oct. 21, 1952; d. James Melvin and Gloria May (Bagby) S. BS, Coll. of the S.W., Hobbs, N.Mex., 1974. Salesman KHOB Radio, Hobbs, 1973-74; adminstrv. asst. Coll. of the S.W., 1974-80, pub. info. officer, 1980-82, dir. pub. info., 1982-84, dir. pub. affairs, 1984, dir. coll. communications, 1988—; community rels. coord. Lea Regional Hosp., Hobbs, 1985-88. Author, editor, photographer numerous univ. publs. Campaign co-chair United Way of Lea County, Hobbs, 1988. Recipient Excellence in Community Svc. award Hosp. Corp. Am., 1986. Mem. N.Mex. Pres Women, Eastern N.Mex. Rose Soc. (treas. 1986-88, sec. 1988-91). Methodist. Office: Coll of the SW 6610 N Lovington Hwy Hobbs NM 88240-9129

STANLEY, SHIRLEY DAVIS, artist; b. Mt. Vernon, N.Y., Dec. 5, 1929; d. Walter Thompson and Elsie Viola (Lumpp) Davis; m. Charles B. Coble Jr., June 11, 1951 (div. 1968); children: Jennifer Susan Farmer, Charles B. Coble III; m. Marvin M. Stanley, Dec. 18, 1983 (dec.). BA in Home Econs. and Gen. Sci., Greensboro Coll., 1951; grad., Real Estate Inst., 1962. Tchr. Dryher H.S., Columbia, S.C., 1951-52, Haw River (N.C.) Sch., 1954-56, Alexander Wilson Sch., Graham, N.C., 1957-58; guest essayist for news Mebane (N.C.) Enterprise, 1955-56; pres. Shirley, Inc., Burlington, N.C., 1962-94; artist, 1956—. One woman show Art Gallery Originals, Winston-Salem, 1976, Olive Garden Gallery, 21st Century Gallery, Williamsburg, Va., numerous galleries in Fla., N.C. Bd. dirs. Girl Scouts Am., Burlington, 1961, ARC, 1990—; life mem. Rep. Inner Cir., Washington, 1990—; active Salvation Army. Recipient Rep. Medal of Freedom, 1994. Mem. AAUW, Am. Watercolor Soc. (assoc.), Va. Watercolor Soc., Nat. Soc. Amateur Dancers, Sierra Club, Williamsburg Bibliophiles. Episcopalian. Home and Studio: 103 Little John Rd Williamsburg VA 23185-4907

STANLEY, VIRGINIA M. K., accountant; b. Duluth, Minn., May 11, 1953; d. Frank George and Olga Mary (Tasky) S.; m. Joseph Louis Villa, Apr. 1, 1976; 1 child, Adrienne Marie. BA, Coll. St. Teresa, 1974; post-grad., U. N.Mex., 1978-81. CPA, CFP, cert. personal fin. specialist. Prin. Stanley & Assocs., PC, Albuquerque, 1986—. Mem. AICPA (personal fin. planning exec. com. mem. 1993—, personal fin. planning statement responsibilities com. mem. 1993—), Internat. Assn. Fin. Planners, N.Mex. Soc. CPA (chmn. personal fin. planning 1988-89, 93-95, v.p. 1994—), Linc Fee Only Fin. Planners. Republican. Office: Stanley & Assocs PC 1201 Eubank Blvd NE Ste 2 Albuquerque NM 87112-5300

STANLEY-SMITH, LISA ANN, public relations specialist; b. Concord, N.H., Jan. 23, 1965; d. Richard Arnold and Marion Laura (Barrett) S.; m. David A. Smith II, Apr. 29, 1989. BA, Pembroke (N.C.) State U., 1986, M in English Edn., 1990. Asst. mgr. Nautilus Conditioning Ctr., Lumberton, N.C., 1983-86; pub. rels. specialist, bd. dirs. Sta. WECT-TV, Lumberton, 1986-91; legis. producer, reporter N.C. Ctr. for Pub. TV, 1991; mgr., mktg. dir. Biggs Park Mall, 1991—; bd. dirs. Sta. WECT-TV Internship Program, Lumberton; pub. speaker, 1987—. Bd. dirs. ARC, Lumberton, 1988—; lector St. Francis DeSales Ch., Lumberton, 1986-90. Recipient Golden Poet award World of Poetry, 1985, Silver Poet award, 1986. Mem. Zeta Tau Alpha (pres. 1987). Democrat. Roman Catholic. Home: # 14 4900 Independence Blvd Apt 14 Lumberton NC 28358-2319

STANTON, JEANNE FRANCES, retired lawyer; b. Vicksburg, Miss., Jan. 22, 1920; d. John Francis and Hazel (Mitchell) S.; student George Washington U., 1938-39; BA, U. Cin., 1940; JD, Salmon P. Chase Coll. Law, 1954. Admitted to Ohio bar, 1954; chief clk. Selective Svc. Bd., Cin., 1940-43; instr. USAAF Tech. Schs., Biloxi, Miss., 1943-44; with Procter & Gamble, Cin., 1945-84, legal asst., 1952-54, head advt. svcs. sect. legal div., trade practices dept., 1954-73, mgr. advt. svcs., legal div., 1973-84, ret., 1984. Team capt. Community Chest Cin., 1953; mem. ann. meeting com. Archaeol. Inst. Am., 1983; v.p., statutory agt. Friends of Bronze Age Archaeology in the Aegean area, 1987-94, corr. sec., statutory agt., 1994—. Mem. ABA (chmn. subcom. D of com. 307 copyright sect. 1987-88, 89, 90), Ohio Bar Assn. (chmn. uniform state laws com. 1968-70), Cin. Bar Assn. (sec. law day com. 1965-66, chmn. com. on preservation hist. documents 1968-71), Vicksburg and Warren County Hist. Soc, Cin. Hist. Soc., Intercontinental Biog. Assn., Lawyers Club Cin. (exec. com. 1979—, pres. 1983), Cin. Women Lawyers (treas. 1958-59, nominating com. 1976), Terrace Park Country Club. Personal philosophy: Most people are good and honest. If a person does the honorable thing, that is its own reward. Home: 2302 Easthill Ave Cincinnati OH 45208-2608

STANTON, SARA BAUMGARDNER, retired secondary school educator; b. Johnstown, Pa., Sept. 11, 1930; d. Emmanuel Boyd and Ethel Leora (Shaffer) Baumgardner; m. George Welles Stanton, June 20, 1953; children: David Mark, Frederick George. BS in Edn., Bucknell U., 1952. Tchr. Adams-Summerhill High Sch., Sidman, Pa., 1952-53, Waymart (Pa.) High Sch., 1953-55, Honesdale (Pa.) High Sch., 1955-57; substitute tchr. Wayne County Sch. Dist., 1957-77; tchr. Honesdale High Sch., 1977-90; ret., 1990; leadership instr. Pa. Assn. Hosp. Auxs., Harrisburg, Pa., 1976—. Den mother Cub Pack 104, 1965-69; bd. dirs. Health Systems Agy., Wilkes-Barre, Pa., 1983-86, Pa. State U.-Scranton Campus, 1977-85, Wayne County Meml. Hosp., Honesdale, 1974-86, Wayne County Hist. Soc., 1991-92. Recipient Leader's Fellowship award Nat. Bd. YMCA, 1964, B'nai B'rith Citizenship Citation, 1974 (co-recipient with husband). Mem. AAUW (br. pres. 1980-81), Pa. Assn. Hosp. Auxs. (mem. leadership tng. team 1975-80, 91—, chmn. state ann. conv. 1985, pres. 1986-88), Pa. Assn. Sch. Retirees, Hosp. Assn. Pa. (mem. cmty. concerns com. 1974-75, ex officio 1986-88), Wayne County Hist. Soc. (bd. dirs. 1991-92), Woman's Club Honesdale (pres. 1958-60). Republican. Methodist. Home: 1512 West St Honesdale PA 18431-1764

STANTON, SHERRY FRANCES, dermatologist; b. New Haven, Apr. 23, 1950; d. Henry Leopold and Irene Mary (Townsend) Stanton. BA, Wellesley Coll., 1968-72; MD, N.Y. Med. Coll., 1975. Diplomate Am. Bd. Dermatology. Intern medicine Albany (N.Y.) Med. Ctr., 1975-76; resident in dermatology Brown U., Providence, R.I., 1976-79; pvt. practice N.Y.C., 1979—. Fellow Am. Acad. Dermatology; mem. Dermatologic Soc. Greater N.Y., N.Y. State Dermatologic Soc., N.Y. State Med. Soc., Internat. Soc. Dermatology, Women's Dermatologic Soc. Office: 4300 Hylan Blvd Staten Island NY 10312

STANTON, SYLVIA DOUCET, small business owner; b. New Orleans, Sept. 21, 1935; d. Clifton Leo Sr. and Maria Del Vel (Alfonso Swiber) Doucet; m. Robert Elmer Stanton, Jan. 3, 1953; children: Robert, Sylvia, Barbara, Richard, Laura, Cheri. Grad. high sch., New Orleans, 1952. Real estate agt. Century 21, Slidell, La., 1982-88; ptnr. Doucet's Jewelry, Slidell, 1969-82; owner Plantation Antiques, Slidell, 1974-88, Magnolia Plantation, Slidell, 1988—, Doucet-Stanton Ltd., Slidell, 1988—; appraiser jewelry, antiques, real estate, 1969—; artist, painter, 1950—. Founder Le cotillion, Slidell, 1975; founding chmn. Pres. Coun. of Le Cotillion, 1987. Recieved title of nobility Countess De Miron Del Vel, Greece, 1988. Mem. Ozone Camellia Club, Picayune Garden Club, Bayou Liberty Garden Club (sec. 1988—), Albuquerque Art League, World Trade Ctr., Inner Wheel (dist. chmn. 6840 1990-91, founding pres. Slidell 1989). Republican. Roman Catholic. Home: 110 Williamsburg Rd Picayune MS 39466-8415 Office: Doucet-Stanton Ltd 1300 Gause Blvd Slidell LA 70458-3041

STANTON, VIVIAN BRENNAN (MRS. ERNEST STANTON), retired educator; b. Waterbury, Conn.; d. Francis P. and Josephine (Ryan) Brennan; B.A., Albertus Magnus Coll.; M.S., So. Conn. State Coll., 1962, 6th yr. degree, 1965; postgrad. Columbia U.; m. Ernest Stanton, May 31, 1947; children—Pamela L., Bonita F., Kim Ernest. Tchr. English, history, govt. Milford (Conn.) High Sch., 1940-48; tchr. English, history, fgn. Born Night Sch., New Haven, 1948-54, Simon Lake Sch., Milford, 1960-62; guidance counselor, psychol. examiner Jonathan Law High Sch., Milford, 1962-73, Nat. Honor Soc. adv., 1966-73, mem. Curriculum Councils, Graduation Requirement Council, Gifted Child Com., others, 1940-48, 60-73; guidance dir. Foran High Sch., Milford, 1973-79, career center coordinator, 1976-79, ret., 1979. Active various community drives; mem. exec. bd. Ridge Rd PTA, 1956-59; mem. Parent-Tchr. council Hopkins Grammer Sch., New Haven; mem. Human Relations Council, North Haven, 1967-69; vol., patient rep. surg. waiting rm. Fawcett Meml. Hosp., P.C., Sun City Ctr. Emergency Squad, Good Samaritans. Mem. Nat. Assn. Secondary Schs. and Colls. (evaluation com.; chmn. testing com.), AAUW, LWV, Conn. Personnel and Guidance Assn., Conn. Sch. Counselors Assn., Conn. Assn. Sch. Psychol. Personnel, Conn., Milford (pres. 1945-47) edn. assns. Clubs: Univ., Charlotte Harbor Yacht, Sun City Ctr. Golf and Racquet. Home: 307 Thornhill Pl Sun City Center FL 33573

STANTON LANCASTER, MIRIAM RUTH ROSENTRATER, educator; b. Long Beach, Calif., Jan. 11, 1944; d. David Frederick and Olive Wanda (Walter) Rosentrater; m. Larry Robert Stanton, Aug. 21, 1965 (div. Jan. 1986); children: JoLynn Kay, David Clinton; m. Carson Avery Lancaster, Dec. 17, 1994. BA with honors, LeTourneau Coll., 1967; MA in English, U. Tex., Tyler, 1989. Cert. secondary tchr. in English, history, bus. Tchr. Pine Tree Jr. High Sch., Longview, Tex., 1985—. Mem. Ptnrs. in Edn., Longview, 1987—, Longview PTA, 1974—, pres. 1976-77, 82-83, coun. pres. 1978-80. Recipient Danforth award Tex. PTA, 1984; named life mem. Internat. Programs scholar U. Tex. 1988. Mem. Nat. Coun. Tchrs. of English, Tex. Coun. Tchrs. of English, Delta Kappa Gamma, Phi Kappa Delta. Home: 2810 Emerald Dr Longview TX 75605-1949 Office: PO Box 150181 Longview TX 75615-0181

STAPLETON, CAROLYN LOUISE, lawyer, clergywoman; b. West Point, N.Y., July 19, 1947; d. Carl William and Louise Maxine (Starrett) S.; m. J. Peter Jordan, May 18, 1973. BA, Mich. State U., 1969; MTh, So. Meth. U., 1972, D Ministry, 1983; JD, U. Hawaii, 1987. Bar: Hawaii 1987; ordained deacon United Meth. Ch., 1971, ordained elder, 1973. Assoc. min. St. John's United Meth. Ch., Corpus Christi, Tex., 1972-74; Methodist campus min. Emory U., Atlanta, 1974-78; chaplain Punahou Sch., Honolulu, 1978-80; civilian contract chaplain Aliamanu Mil. Housing, Honolulu, 1981; dir. family ministries Naval Sta. Chapel, Pearl Harbor, Hawaii, 1983-84; dep. atty. gen. State of Hawaii, Honolulu, 1987-88, staff atty. labor appeals bd., 1988-89; exec. dir., legal counsel Ethics Commn. City and County of Honolulu, 1989—; staff assoc. for social justice and spiritual concerns Hawaii Coun. Churchs., 1990—; bd. dirs., sec. Spiritual Life Ctr., Honolulu, 1990—; trustee 1st United Meth. Ch., Honolulu, 1988—; mem. Hawaii dist. div. ch. and society United Meth. Ch., 1979-95; mem. nominating com. Coun. on Govtl. Ethics Laws, 1995—. Contbg. author: Called from Within: Early Women Lawyers of Hawaii, 1992; prodr. slide and tape show Womanriver Flowing On: Glimpses of Some Foremothers in the United Methodist Tradition, 1981; contbr. articles to religious jours. Bd. dirs., v.p. Hawaii Lawyers Care, Honolulu, 1990—; bd. dirs. Advs. for Pub. Interest Law, Honolulu, 1986-89; del., com. mem. Hawaii Dem. Conv., 1984, 86, 88, 90, 92, 94; precinct treas. Honolulu Dem. Party, 1986—; mem. Neighborhood Bd. 5, Honolulu, 1983-89; co-founder, bd. dirs. Hawaii Women's Polit. Action League, Honolulu, 1982-85; bd. dirs. Friends Judiciary History Ctr., sec., 1991—; bd. dirs. Interfaith Network Against Domestic Violence, 1990—. Named One of 10 Outstanding Young Women Am., Pres. of U.S., 1974; Laskey scholar women's div. bd. missions United Meth. Ch., 1971; rsch. grantee Women's Studies Coun., So. Meth. U., 1981. Mem. AAUW (bd. dirs., various state and br. offices 1979—), Phi Delta Phi (parliamentarian, historian 1985—), Alpha Delta Pi (chaplain, historian 1966—). Home: 3138 Waialae Ave Apt 1010 Honolulu HI 96816-1544 Office: Ethics Commn City & County Honolulu 715 S King St Ste 211 Honolulu HI 96813-3091

STAPLETON, CLAUDIA ANN, city official; b. Memphis, July 14, 1947; m. Mark Phillip Stapleton, Sept. 18, 1985. Student, Tex. Tech. U., 1976-77, Amarillo Coll., 1989—. Code enforcement officer City of Lubbock, Tex., 1975-85; owner, operator Claudia Stapleton Consulting, Amarillo, Tex., 1985—; code enforcement officer City of Amarillo, 1990—; cons. in field. Mem. NAFE, Nat. Elec. Sign Assn., Tex. Assn. Legal Secs., Tex. Heritage, Am. Bus. Women's Assn., Code Enforcement Assn. of Tex., Beta Sigma Phi. Republican. Methodist. Home: 3321 Lenwood Dr Amarillo TX 79109-3345 Office: City of Amarillo 509 E 7th Ave Amarillo TX 79101-2539

STAPLETON, JEAN (JEANNE MURRAY), actress; b. N.Y.C.; d. Joseph E. and Marie (Stapleton) Murray; m. William H. Putch (dec.); 2 children. Student, Hunter Coll., N.Y.C., Am. Apprentice Theatre, Am. Actors Co., Am. Theatre Wing; student with, Harold Clurman; LHD (hon.), Emerson Coll.; hon. degree, Hood Coll., Monmouth Coll. Opera debut in Candide with Balt. Opera Co.; appeared in The Italian Lesson with Balt. Opera; first N.Y. stage role in The Corn is Green, Equity Library Theatre; starred as mother in Am. Gothic, Circle-in-the-Sq.; Broadway debut with Judith Anderson In The Summer House; also appeared on Broadway in Damn Yankees, Bells Are Ringing, Juno, Rhinoceros and Funny Girl; first major break in comic ingenue role as Myrtle Mae with Frank Fay in Harvey on-tour; played with nat. tour of Come Back, Little Sheba starring Shirley Booth; starred in tour of Morning's at Seven, The Show-Off, Daisy Mayme; appeared in motion pictures including Damn Yankees, 1958, Bells Are Ringin, 1960, Up the Down Staircase, 1967, Cold Turkey, 1971, The Buddy System, 1984, Klute; appeared in numerous TV shows including Studio One, Naked City, Armstrong Circle Theater, The Defenders, Jackie Gleason Show, PBS-TV appearances Grown-ups, Trying Times, The Boss, cable TV appearances Let Me Hear You Whisper, Mother Goose Rock and Rhyme, Faerie Tale Theatre: Cinderella and Jack & The Beanstalk, The Habitation of Dragons, Fee Fi Fo Fum, Mrs. Piggle-Wiggle; starred in the title role of Aunt Mary on Hallmark Hall of Fame, 1979; most famous TV role as Edith Bunker on All In The Family, 1971-79; TV films include Dead Man's Folly, Tail Gunner Joe, 1977, Isabel's Choice, 1981, Angel Dusted, 1981, Eleanor: First Lady of the World, 1982 (Emmy nomination), A Matter of Sex, Grown-Ups, Fire In The Dark, 1991 (CBS-TV), The Parallax Garden, 1993, Ghost Mom, 1993; appeared the Totem Pole Playhouse, Fayetteville, Pa., starred at Kennedy Ctr. in Daisy Mayme, 1978, The Late Christopher Bean, 1982, Bon Appetit; appeared on Broadway in Arsenic and Old Lace (also nat. tour), 1986; mem. nat. tour. co. Drood, 1986, The Birthday Party, 1989, Mountain Language, 1989 (Obie award); in CBS-TV series Bagdad Cafe, 1990, L.A. Opera's Oklahoma, 1990, The Learned Ladies (by Moliere), 1990, Bon Appetit & The Italian Lesson, 1991 (CSC Repertory), (Off-Broadway) The Road to Home U. Va. and N.Y., 1992, Night Seasons. 1993, Bon Appetit (ACT San Francisco), The Learned Ladies (ACT San Francisco), Mrs. Piggle-Wiggle (Showtime), 1994, Romeo and Juliet, The Shakespere Co. D.C., 1994, Night Seasons, Signature Theatre N.Y., 1994. U.S. commr. to Internat. Woman's Yr. Commn. and Nat. Conf. Women, Houston, 1977; bd. dirs. Women's Rsch. and Edn. Inst., Eleanor Roosevelt's Val-Kill; trustee Actors' Fund Am. Recipient Emmy award for best performance in comedy series 1970-71, 71-72, 78, Golden Globe awards Hollywood Fgn. Press Assn. 1972, 73, Obie award, 1990. Mem. Actors Equity Assn. (council 1958-63), Screen Actors Guild, AFTRA. Office: care Bauman & Hiller 5757 Wilshire Blvd Los Angeles CA 90036-3697*

STAPLETON, MAUREEN, actress; b. Troy, N.Y., June 21, 1925; d. John P. and Irene (Walsh) S.; m. Max Allentuck, July 1949 (div. Feb. 1959); children: Daniel, Katharine; m. David Rayfiel, July, 1963 (div.). Student, Siena Coll, 1943. Debut in Playboy of the Western World, 1946; toured with Barretts of Wimpole Street, 1947; plays include Anthony and Cleopatra, 1947, Detective Story, The Bird Cage, Rose Tattoo, 1950-51, The Sea Gull, Orpheus Descending, The Cold Wind and the Warm, 1959, Toys in the Attic, 1960-61, Plaza Suite, 1969, The Gingerbread Lady, 1970 (Tony award 1970), 27 Wagons Full of Cotton, Country Girl, 1972, Secret Affairs of Mildred Wild, 1972, The Gin Game, 1977-78, The Little Foxes, 1981; motion pictures include Lonely Hearts, 1959, The Fugitive Kind, 1960, A View from the Bridge, 1962, Bye Bye Birdie, 1963, Trilogy, 1969, Airport, 1970, Plaza Suite, 1971, Interiors, 1978, The Runner Stumbles, 1979, Reds, 1981 (Oscar award as best supporting actress), The Fan, 1981, On the Right Track, 1981, The Electric Grandmother, 1982, Mother's Day, 1984, Johnny Dangerously, 1984, Cocoon, 1985, The Money Pit, 1986, Nuts, 1987, Made in Heaven, 1987, Cocoon: The Return, 1990, Passed Away, 1992, Trading Mom, 1994; TV films include Tell Me Where It Hurts, 1974, Cat On a Hot Tin Roof, 1976, All the King's Men, 1958, For Whom the Bell Tolls, 1959, Save Me a Place at Forest Lawn, 1966, Mirror, Mirror, Off the Wall, 1969, Queen of the Stardust Ballroom, 1975, The Gathering, 1977, Part II, 1979, Letters From Frank, 1979, Little Gloria ... Happy at Last, 1982, Sentimental Journey, 1984, Private Sessions, 1985, Liberace: Behind the Music, 1988, Last Wish, 1992, Miss Rose White, 1992. Recipient Nat. Inst. Arts and Letters award, 1969. *

STAPP, OLIVIA BREWER, opera singer; b. N.Y.C., May 31, 1940; d. Henry and Jean Brewer; m. Henry Stapp III; 1 child, Henry. BA, Wagner Coll; studied with, Marjorie Mayer Steen, Ettore Campogalliani, Rodolfo Ricci and Oren Brown; Dr. honoris causa, Wagner Coll., 1988. Appeared as leading soprano in Truandot, Idomeno at La Scala, Milano; Tosca, Elektra, Macbeth, Tabarro at Met. Opera, N.Y.C.; Erani, Macbeth, Il Tabarro at Liceo Barcelona; Macbeth, Madame Butterfly, Tosca, Aida, Fanciulla del West, Lohengrin at Deutche Oper Berlin; Vespre Sciciliani at Grand Theater, Geneva; Nabucco, Attila, Macbeth at Zurich Oper; Salome at The Colon Theater, Buenos Aires; Cavalleria Rusticana, Anna Bolena, Tosca, Nabucco at San Francisco; Elektra Cavalleria Rusticana at Vienna Staatsoper; Idameneo at Munich Staatsoper; Carmen, The Consul, Ariadne auf Naxos, Anna Bolena, Roberto Deveraux, Cavalleria Rusticana at City Opera, N.Y.C.; Lady Macbeth, Nabucco, Turandot at Hamburg Staatsoper; Fanciulla el West, Aida, Nabucco, Turandot at the Arena de Verona; Turandot at Seoul, Korea; Turandot in N.H.K. Tokyo; Norma in Winnipeg, Edmonto, Montreal and Vancouver, Can.; Lady Macbeth in Chatelet Theater, Paris, others. Recipient Puccini award Vissi d'Arde, 1991; Fulbright scholar. Address: Artist Mgmt Inc 165 W 57th St New York NY 10019-2201*

STARCK, PATRICIA LEE, academic dean; b. Americus, Ga., Sept. 15, 1938; d. Ernest W. Lee and Margaret Inez (Pilcher) Rush; m. Edward J. Rice, Feb. 11, 1991; children: Jaime Catherine Schier, Patricia Ann Reitz. AA, Ga. Southwestern Coll., 1959; BSN, Emory U., 1960, M in Nursing, 1963; DSN, U. Ala., Birmingham, 1979. RN; cert. logotherapist. Staff nurse Emory U. Hosp., Atlanta, 1959-60; rehab. nursing cons. Liberty Mut. Ins. Co., Atlanta, 1960-61; instr. Grady Meml. Hosp., Atlanta, 1961-62, Ga. Bapt. Hosp., Atlanta, 1963-64; asst. prof. Ga. Southwestern Coll., Americus, 1966, 70-72, 1974-75; tchr. St. Petersburg (Fla.) Jr. Coll., 1972-74; dept. chair nursing Albany (Ga.) State Coll., 1975-77; dean, prof. Troy (Ala.) State U., 1979-84, U. Tex. Health Sci. Ctr., Houston, 1984—; cons. various univs., 1979—; bd. dirs. CURAFLEX Home Health Svc., Houston, 1985-86. Author: The Invisible Dimension of Illness-Human Suffering, 1992; contbr. articles to profl. jours. Mem. Tex. Med. Assn. Task Force, Austin, 1989-90. Mem. Inst. of Logotherapy (diplomate), Nat. League for Nursing (bd. of revs.), Am. Assn. Colls. of Nursing (bd. dirs., chair pub. rels. and resolutions), Coun. Deans, Dirs. Nursing Execs. (chair), Tex. Med. Ctr. Nursing Exec. (chair-elect, Tex. Nurses Assn. (v.p. dist. 9 1991—), Rotary Club Houston (com. mem.). Baptist. Home: 13 Town Oaks Pl Bellaire TX 77401-4237

STARFIELD, BARBARA HELEN, physician, educator; b. Bklyn., Dec. 18, 1932; d. Martin and Eva (Illions) S.; m. Neil A. Holtzman, June 12, 1955; children—Robert, Jon, Steven, Deborah. A.B., Swarthmore Coll., 1954; M.D., SUNY, 1959; M.P.H., Johns Hopkins U., 1963. Teaching asst. in anatomy Downstate Med. Ctr., N.Y.C., 1955-57; intern in pediatrics Johns Hopkins U., 1959-60, resident, 1960-62, dir. pediatric med. care clinic, 1963-66, dir. community staff comprehensive child care project, 1966-67, dir. pediatric clin. scholars program, 1971-76, prof. health policy, head health policy div., joint appointment in pediatrics, 1975—; disting. univ. prof., 1994—; mem. Nat. Com. Vital Stats., 1994—; cons. DHHS; mem. nat. adv. coun. Agy. for Health Care Policy and Rsch., 1990-94. Editorial bd. Med. Care, 1977-79, Pediatrics, 1977-82, Internat. Jour. Health Svcs.,1 978—, Med. Care Rev., 1980-84; contbr. articles to profl. jours. Recipient Dave Luckman Meml. award, 1958; HEW Career Devel. award, 1970-75. Fellow Am. Acad. Pediatrics; mem. Nat. Acad. Sci. Inst. Medicine (governing coun. 1981-83), Am. Pediatric Soc., Soc. Pediatric Rsch., Internat. Epidemiologic Assn., Ambulatory Pediatric Assn. (pres. 1980), Am. Pub. Health Assn., Sigma Xi, Alpha Omega Alpha. Office: Johns Hopkins Sch Hygiene 624 N Broadway Baltimore MD 21205-1901

STARK, DIANA, public relations and promotion executive; b. N.Y.C., July 1; d. Benjamin and Sara (Zelasny) S.; BA, Hunter Coll. Promotion mgr. TV Guide mag., N.Y.C., 1950-61; promotion mgr. Show Bus. Illustrated, N.Y.C., 1961-62; broadcast specialist Young & Rubicam, N.Y.C., 1962-69; pres. Stark Communications, Inc., N.Y.C., 1969-76; pub. svc. publicity account exec. Y & R E, N.Y.C., 1976-77; pres. Stark Communications, Internat., N.Y.C., 1978—; pub. rels. workshop leader Chgo. Econ. Devel. Corp., 1973-76; cons. to Asahi Shimbun for English Language Newsletter. Columnist Host mag., 1960-65; writer, producer programs for women's TV shows, 1962—; coord. We Have Arrived, Portraits at Ellis Island, Augustus Sherman Photographs 1902-1924; book developer Ellis Island: The First Experience With Liberty, 1991. Mem. Pub. Rels. Soc. Am., Nat. Acad. Television Arts and Scis. (trustee 1974-78, publicity com. chmn., chpt. gov. 1972-76, 82—, editor N.Y. TV Directory 1987—), Internat. Radio and TV Soc.

STARK, JOAN SCISM, education educator; b. Hudson, N.Y., Jan. 6, 1937; d. Ormonde F. and Myrtle Margaret (Kirkey) S.; m. William L. Stark, June 28, 1958 (dec.); children: Eugene William, Susan Elizabeth, Linda Anne, Ellen Scism; m. Malcolm A. Lowther, Jan. 31, 1981. B.S., Syracuse U., 1957; M.A. (Hoadly fellow), Columbia U., 1960; Ed.D., SUNY, Albany, 1971. Tchr. Ossining (N.Y.) High Sch., 1957-59; free-lance editor Holt, Rinehart & Winston, Harcourt, Brace & World, 1960-70; lectr. Ulster County Community Coll., Stone Ridge, N.Y., 1968-70; asst. dean Goucher Coll., Balt., 1970-73; asso. dean Goucher Coll., 1973-74; assoc. prof., chmn. dept. higher postsecondary edn. Syracuse (N.Y.) U., 1974-78; dean Sch. Edn. U. Mich., Ann Arbor, 1978-83, prof., 1983—; dir. Nat. Ctr. for Improving Postsecondary Teaching and Learning, 1986-91. Editor: Rev. of Higher Education, 1991—; contbr. articles to various publs. Leader Girl Scouts U.S.A., Cub Scouts Am.; coach girls Little League; dist. officer PTA, intermittently, 1968-80; mem. adv. com. Gerald R. Ford Library, U. Mich., 1980-83; trustee Kalamazoo Coll., 1979-85; mem. exec. com. Inst. Social Research, U. Mich., 1979-81; bd. dirs. Mich. Assn. Colls. Tchr. Edn., 1979-81. Mem. Am. Assn. for Higher Edn., Am. Edn. Rsch. Assn., Assn. Study Higher Edn. (dir. 1977-79, v.p. 1983, pres. 1984, Rsch. Achievement award 1992), Assn. Innovation Higher Edn. (nat. chmn. 1974-75), Assn. Instl. Rsch. (disting. mem.), Assn. Colls. and Schs. Edn. State Univs. and Land Grant Colls. (dir. 1981-83), Acctg. Edn. Change Commn., Phi Beta Kappa, Phi Kappa Phi, Sigma Pi Sigma, Eta Pi Upsilon, Lambda Sigma Sigma, Phi Delta Kappa, Pi Lambda Theta. Office: Univ Mich 2002 Sch of Edn Ann Arbor MI 48109-1259

STARK, MIRIAM JOAN, psychology educator; b. Phila., June 26, 1950. BA in Psychology, King's Coll., 1971; MA in Counseling, Liberty U., 1985; MA in Clin. Psychology, Biola U., 1987, PhD in Clin. Psychology, 1990. Lic. clin. psychologist, Va., Ill. Registrar, asst. to dean Word of Life Bible Inst., Pottersville, N.Y., 1972-83; adminstr. asst. to dean Liberty U., Lynchburg, Va., 1983-85, assoc. prof. counseling Sch. Religion, 1989-93; therapist Friendly Hills Med. Group, La Habra, Calif., 1985-88; clin. intern univ. psychol. svcs. Kent (Ohio) STate U., 1988-89; assoc. prof. dept. pastoral counseling and psychology Trinity Evang. Div. Sch., Deerfield, Ill., 1993—; pvt. practice clin. psychology, 1990—. Contbr. articles to profl. jours. Office: Trinity Evang Div Sch 2065 Half Day Rd Deerfield IL 60015

STARK, NANCY LYNN, critical care nurse; b. Clinton, Ind., July 31, 1956; d. William and Martha Louise (Reed) Gray; m. Matthew Topping Stark, Aug. 4, 1979; children: Matthew Gray, Kyle Reed. BSN, Ind. State U., 1978; MS in Nursing, Ind. U., Indpls., 1985. RN, Ind., Ga. Staff nurse Union Hosp., Terre Haute, Ind., 1978-81, St. Vincent Hosp. and Health Care Ctr., Indpls., 1981-85; head nurse Med. Coll. Ga., Augusta, 1985-86, 91-93, nurse educator, 1986-91, clin. instr. Sch. Nursing, 1990—; acting dir. nursing, critical care divsn. Med. Coll. of Ga., 1992-93, DON critical care divsn., 1993—; cons. on dimensions of critical care nursing, 1989-94. Contbg. author: Nursing Theorists and Their Work, 1989. Mem. AACN (cert., pres. 1990-91), ANA, Am. Trauma Soc., Soc. of Critical Care Medicine, Sigma Theta Tau. Republican. Presbyterian. Home: 595 Country Place Ln Evans GA 30809-8590 Office: Med Coll Ga 15th St B1F-206 Augusta GA 30912-6001

STARK, NELLIE MAY, forest ecology educator; b. Norwich, Conn., Nov. 20, 1933; d. Theodore Benjamin and Dorothy Josephine (Pendleton) Beetham; m. Oscar Elder Stark, Oct. 1962 (dec.). BA, Conn. Coll., 1956; AM, Duke U., 1958, PhD, 1962. Botanist Exptl. Sta., U.S. Forest Svc., Old Strawberry, Calif., 1958-66; botanist, ecologist Desert Rsch. Inst., Reno, Nev., 1966-72; prof. forest ecology Sch. Forestry, U. Mont., Missoula, 1972-92; pvt. cons. Philomath, Oreg.; pres. Camas Analytical Lab., Inc., Missoula, 1987-92. Contbr. articles to profl. jours. Named Disting. Dau. Norwich, Conn., 1985; recipient Conn. award Conn. Coll., 1986, 54 grants. Mem. Ecol. Soc. Am. (chair ethics com. 1974, 76), Bot. Soc. Am., Soc. Am. Foresters (taskforce 1987-88).

STARK, PATRICIA ANN, psychologist; b. Ames, Iowa; d. Keith C. and Mary L. (Johnston) Moore. B.S., So. Ill. U., Edwardsville, 1970, M.S., 1972; Ph.D., St. Louis U., 1976. Counselor to alcoholics Bapt. Rescue Mission, East St. Louis, 1969; researcher alcoholics Gateway Rehab. Center, East St. Louis, 1972; psychologist intern Henry-Stark Counties Spl. Edn. Dist. and Galesburg State Research Hosp., Ill., 1972-73; instr. Lewis and Clark Community Coll., Godfrey, Ill., 1973-76, asst. prof., 1976-84, assoc. prof., 1984, coordinator child care services, 1974-84; mem. staff dept. psychiatry Meml. Hosp., St. Elizabeth's Hosp., 1979—; supr. various workshops in field, 1974—; dir. child and family services Collinsville Counseling Center, 1977-82; clin. dir., owner Empas-Complete Family Psychol. and Hypnosis Services, Collinsville, 1982—; cons. community agys., 1974—; mem. adv. bd. Madison County Council on Alcoholism and Drug Dependency, 1977-80. Mem. Am. Psychol. Assn., Ill. Psychol. Assn., Midwestern Psychol. Assn., Nat. Assn. Sch. Psychologists, Am. Soc. Clin. Hypnosis, Internat. Soc. Hypnosis. Office: 2802 Maryville Rd Collinsville IL 62234-5424

STARKEY, ELIZABETH LARUFFA, accountant; b. Franklin, Ky., May 23, 1947; d. Albert A. and Alma L. (Duer) LaRuffa; m. Jerry L. Starkey, June 14, 1969; children: James, Jonathan. AA, Miami-Dade Jr. Coll., 1967; BS in Math., Fla. State U., 1969; MS in Acctg., U. Houston, 1984. Cert. public acct., math. tchr. Tchr. Dade County, Miami, Fla., 1969-75; mgr. Ernst & Young, Houston, 1984-90; prin. Starkey & Co., Houston, 1990—. Bd. dirs. Am. Cancer Soc., Houston, 1985-87, 90—, chmn. and mem. legacy and planned giving com., 1987—, Tex. divsn. chmn. and mem. legacy and planning giving com., 1990—; mem. Planned Giving Coun. Houston, Houston Estate and Fin. Forum. Mem. AICPAs, Tex. Soc. CPAs (Houston chpt.), Nat. Soc. Tax Profls., Beta Gamma Sigma, Beta Alpha Psi, Omicron Delta Kappa. Roman Catholic. Home: 4410 Merwin St Houston TX 77027-6714 Office: Starkey & Co Ste 358 3000 Weslayan St Houston TX 77027-5753

STARKS, FLORENCE ELIZABETH, special education educator; b. Summit, N.J., Dec. 6, 1932; d. Edward and Winnie (Morris) S. BA, Morgan State U., 1956; MS in Edn., CUNY, 1962; postgrad., Fairleigh Dickinson U., 1962-63, Seton Hall U., 1963, Newark State Coll. Cert. blind and visually handicapped and social studies tchr., N.J. Tchr. adult edn. Newark Bd. of Edn.; tchr. N.Y. Inst. for Edn. of the Blind, Bronx; developer first class for multiple handicapped blind children in pub. sch. system, Newark, 1960; ptnr. World Vision Internat. Mem. ASCD, AFL-CIO, AAUW, Coun. Exceptional Children, Nat. Assn. Negro Bus. and Profl. Women's Club Inc., N.J. Edn. Assn., Newark Tchrs. Assn., Newark Tchrs. Union-Am. Fedn. Tchrs., World Vision Internat. (ptnr.). Home: 4 Park Ave Summit NJ 07901-3942 Office: Newark Bd Edn 2 Cedar St Newark NJ 07102-3015

STARKS, ROSALYN JUNE, physical education and health educator; b. Phoenix, June 17, 1952; d. Ross Owen and Maribel Louise (Barnes) S. BS in Edn., U. Ariz., 1974; MA in Edn., No. Ariz. U., 1991. Tchr. Phys. Edn. K-12, Ariz. Phys. edn. tchr. Santa Cruz Valley Union High Sch., Eloy, Ariz., 1975-84; phys. edn., health tchr. Phoenix Union High Sch. Dist., 1985—; coach Santa Cruz Valley Union H.S. and So. Mountain H.S., Phoenix, 1975—; facilitator student assistance program, 1987—; Phoenix 5A Metro Region Rep. State Softball Adv. Bd., 1990-94; mem. HIV/AIDS articulation com. Phoenix Union H.S. Dist., 1994—. Named Softball Coach of Yr., A Ctrl. Divsn., 1980. Mem. AzAMPERD, AAHPERD, NEA, AEA, Phoenix Union H.S. Dist. Classroom Tchrs. Assn. Home: 4406 N 111th Dr Phoenix AZ 85037-5333 Office: S Mountain High School 5401 S 7th St Phoenix AZ 85040-3199

STARKS-MARTIN, GRETCHEN, dean; b. Muskegon, Mich., Jan. 18, 1947; d. Ernest and Emajean (Krautheim) Lobenherz; m. David Martin, Jan. 2, 1992; 1 child, Joanne Marie Studebaker. BA, U. Mich., 1970; MA, Western Mich. U., 1973; EdD, Syracuse U., 1989. Tchr. English Plymouth (Mich.) Mid. Sch., 1970-71; tchr. reading Whitehall (Mich.) Mid. Sch., 1972-74; dir. Learning Ctr. U. Minn. Tech. Coll., Crookston, 1974-82; dir. devel. studies Finger Lakes C.C., Canadaigua, N.Y., 1982-90, dir. instrnl. and curricular devel., 1990-91; acad. dean Jefferson C.C., Watertown, N.Y., 1992-94; asst. prof. St. Cloud State U., Minn., 1994—; cons. Chisholm Inst. Tech., Melbourne, Australia, 1990, Keuka Coll., Keuka Park, N.Y., 1990, Gilbert Chander C.C., Phoenix, 1992. Editor: (jour.) Forum for Reading, 1986-91. Vol. Minna Anthony Nature Ctr., Wellesley Island, N.Y., 1992—. Recipient Chancellor's award for excellence in profl. svc. State of N.Y., 1989, Cert. of Achievement, Lit. Vols. Am., 1988. Mem. AAUW, Am. Assn. of Women in Community and Jr. Colls., Minn. Reading Assn. (pres. 1981-82), Lit. Vols. of N.Y. State (bd. dirs. 1987-93), N.Y. Coll. Learning Skills Assn. (pres. 1987-88), Assn. of SUNY C.C. Acad. Officers. Lutheran. Office: St Cloud State Univ St Cloud MN 56304

STARLING, JOCELYN CORNELIA, clinical psychologist; b. Detroit, May 27, 1954; d. Joseph Cornelius and Mamie Alberta (Hollingsworth) S. BA, Wayne State U., 1980; MA, Ctrl. Mich. U., 1983. Ltd. lic. psychologist, Mich. Clin. therapist Genesee County Community Mental Health: Child/Adol. Svcs., Flint, Mich., 1983-92; ind. contractor/pvt. practice Auburn Counseling Assocs., Flint, 1989—; psychologist in pvt. practice Flint, 1993—; affiliate Pers. Performance Cons., St. Louis, 1993—. Mem. APA, Mich. Psychol. Assn., Mich. Psychoanalytic Coun., Assn. Black Psychologists. Democrat. African Methodist Episcopal. Office: 2425 S Linden Rd Ste 108 Flint MI 48532

STARN, BARBARA JEAN, nursing administrator; b. Elyria, Ohio, June 1, 1948; d. Andrew and Eugenia Tomoko; m. Richard W. Starn, Feb. 13, 1971; children: Heather, DeAnna, Jennifer. Student, M.B. Johnson Sch. Nursing, 1969, Baldwin Wallace Coll., 1970. RN, Ohio, Mo. Staff nurse Elyria Meml. Hosp.; supr. Medi Ctr. of Am., Springfield, Mo.; asst. dir. nursing Manor Care Nursing Ctr., Olmsted, Ohio; nurse coord. Parkside Health Mgmt. Corp., Middleburg Heights, Ohio; client svc. rep. Parkside Health Mgmt. Corp.; asst. dir. nursing The Oakridge Home, Westlake, Ohio. Zaharas scholar. Home: 1536 Grafton Rd Elyria OH 44035-8108

STARNES, CYNTHIA MARIE, medical transcriptionist, emergency medical technician; b. McCook, Nebr., Nov. 2, 1957; d. Larry A. Reckel and Teresa Jean (Ruda) Johnston; children: Stephanie, Ryan, Jason; m. Mark Wilhelm Starnes, Aug. 17, 1984; 1 child, Patrick. Grad. secretary with legal specialization, Boulder (Colo.) Valley Vo-Tech Ctr., 1982. Cert. EMT. Receptionist Arnold Bros. Ford, Boulder, 1973-75; collections/PBX operator Boulder Cmty. Hosp., 1975-76; nursing asst. Rawlins County Hosp., Atwood, Kans., 1979-80; legal sec. Clarke & Cole, Attys. at Law, Boulder, 1982-85; ind. collection cons. Culpeper, Va., 1985-86; EMT/mgr. Anderson Ambulance, Crozet, Va., 1988-89; med. transcriptionist Martha Jefferson Hosp., Charlottesville, Va., 1989; ind. med. transcriptionist Secretarial Support Svcs., Ruckersville, Va., 1990—. EMT Madison County Rescue, Madison, Va., 1988-89, Greene County Rescue Squad, Stanardsville, Va., 1990—, sec., 1993-94. Roman Catholic.

STARNS, JOY MARIE, federal official; b. Washington, Apr. 15, 1960; d. Charles Edwin and Doris Marie (Fortney) S. BS in Mgmt. and Mktg., George Mason U., 1982. Budget analyst Dept. of State, Washington, 1982—; typist, stenographer Alexandria (Va.) Sch. Bd.; stenographer patent and trademark office Dept. of Commerce, Arlington, Va., insp. gen.'s office Defense Logistics Agy., Alexandria, Dept. of State, Washington. Active Fairlington United Meth. Ch., Alexandria, 1988—, coord. svc., former v.p. singles group, 1992—. Mem. NAFE, Am. Assn. Budget and Program Analysis, Women's Action Orgn., Smithsonian Inst. (resident assocs. program 1994—), Ski Club of Washington DC. Home: 6608 Medinah Ln Alexandria VA 22312-3116 Office: Dept of State 2201 C St NW Washington DC 20520-0004

STARON, VERONICA FRANCES, operating room nurse; b. Davis, W. Va., Aug. 27, 1935; d. Frank and Frances Mary (Zadell) Tekavec; m. Joseph John Staron, Feb. 15, 1958 (div. Nov. 5, 1982); children: Annette Wilson, Cheryl Long, Stephen. Diploma in Nursing, St Mary's Sch. Nursing, Claarksburg, W. Va., 1956; BSN, Wayne State U., 193. Cert. operating room nurse. Staff nurse St. Mary's Hosp., Clarksburg, W. Va., 1956-57; operating room nurse Mt. Carmel Mercy Hosp., Detroit, 1959-78, head nurse operating room, 1979-83, asst. head nurse operating room, 1983-88; mgr. operating room The Toledo (Ohio) Hosp., 1988-89; lt. army reserve 323rd Gen. Hosp., Southfield, Mich., 1988-89; lt. nat. guard W.Va. ARNG, Kingwood, W. Va., 1989-91; capt. nat. guard W.Va. ARNG, Kingwood, 1991—; mgr. operating room W. Va. Univ. Hosp., Morgantown, 1989—. Mem. many edn. and youth rel. orgn. in Redford Mich., 1965-77. Mem. ANA, AORN, St. Mary's Alumni, Sigma Theta Tau. Home: 528 Kennedy Dr Morgantown WV 26505-9040 Office: W Va Univ Hosp Medical Ctr Dr Morgantown WV 26506

STARR, DI, artist; b. Boston, Feb. 23, 1953; d. Harold and Rita S. Student, Marlboro Coll., 1971-72; BFA, U. Mass., 1975. instr. fine arts U. Mass., Amherst, 1982-83; guest lectr. alternative photographic processes Studio One Art Ctr., Oakland, Calif., 1988-89, instr. painted and portrait photographs, 1990-95. Exhbns. include Ariel Gallery, N.Y.C., 1990, 91, Heart Art Gallery St. Mary's Coll., Moraga, Calif., 1990, Helio Gallery, N.Y.C., 1991, Second Story Gallery, Seattle, 1993, Patricia Stewart Gallery, Napa, Calif., 1992, San Francisco Women Artists Gallery, 1994, Agora Gallery, N.Y.C., 1993-94, Photolab Gallery, Berkeley, Calif., 1994, 95. Recipient Landscape Exhbn. Merit award, Photography Exhbn. Merit award San Francisco Women Artists, 1990, Art of Calif. Discovery award Art of Calif. Mag., Napa, 1993. Mem. Berkeley Art Ctr. Assn. Home: PO Box 20174 El Sobrante CA 94820-0174

STARR, ILA MAE, educator; b. La Grande, Oreg., Dec. 27, 1917; d. Samuel Fulmer Andrew and Ida Luella Perry; m. James Marion Starr, Mar. 2, 1940; children: Jacqueline Ann Starr Brandon, James Steven Starr. BA, U. Wash., 1939; BS, Eastern Oreg. Coll., LaGrande, Oreg., 1960, Tchr. Cert. Oreg., 1940. Cert. Wash. 1962, Calif. 1974. Mus. tchr. La Grande (Oreg.) Pub. Schs., 1939-40; girl scout exec. Girl Scouts of Am., Grand Coulee, Wash., 1940-41; Elem. Sch. Tchr. Centralia (Wash.) Pub. Schs., 1954; elem. sch. tchr. Wenatchee (Wash.) Pub. Schs., 1956-64, Lancaster (Calif.) Pub. Schs., 1964-68, Marysville (Calif.) Pub. Schs., 1968-79; pvt. mus. tchr., Seattle, Grand Coulee and Wenatchee, Wash., 1940—. Bd. dirs. Community Concert Assn., Yuba City, Calif., 1986-88; inspiration chmn. Republican Women, Yuba City, 1986-88. Recipient Hon. Pub. Sch. Award, Masonic Lodge 437, Lancaster, 1966; Nominee for Tchr. of Yr., Marysville Pub. Schs., 1978. Mem. Am. Assn. U. Women (program v.p. 1976; Grant Honoree 1977), PTA (hon. life mem. 1965), The Seminar Club (program chmn.), Innerwheel Club (pres. 1985-86). Mem. LDS Ch.

STARR, RHEA F., child care advocate; b. Akron, Ohio; d. Morris and Sarah (Cohen) Axelrod; m. Philip Starr; children: Sonya, Michael, Aviva. BA, U. Mich., 1961; MEd, Millersville U., 1979. Cert. tchr., Ohio, Conn, Pa. Tchr. various sch. systems Ohio, Conn., Pa., 1961-78; dir. nursery sch. City of Hartford (Conn.) Dept. Recreation, 1971-74; dir. child care pub. policy, program coord., interim exec. dir. YWCA, Lancaster, Pa., 1976-87; field specialist YWCA U.S.A., N.Y.C., 1987-92, dir. assn. network svcs., 1992-94, interim asst. exec. dir., 1993-94; child care advocate, 1994—; instr. workshops on child care Pa. State U., 1986—. Past chair negotiating com. Citizens Adv. Bd., Hartford; past chair Family Life Edn. Coun., Lancaster, Cmty. Housing Residency Bd., Fair Housing Com., Lancaster; mgmt. cons., facilitator strategic planning forums YWCA of U.S.A. Recipient Jean Kohr award Women's Coalition, 1983. Home: 512 Bean Blossom Dr Lancaster PA 17603

STARRATT, JEANETTE ELLEN, book store owner; b. San Jose, Calif., Oct. 27, 1943; d. Raymond Walter Huston and Lee Ellen (Smith) Huston-Schwarzbach; m. Norman D. Starratt, Nov. 23, 1962; children: Mark Todd, Wendy Ellen. AA, Foothill Coll., 1974; BA with honors, San Jose State U., 1978. Tchr./tchr. aide Palo Alto (Calif.) Unified Sch. Dist., 1979-87; tchr. Challenger Sch., San Jose, Calif., 1987-88; owner Starratt Enterprises, Los Altos Hills, Calif., 1983—; mgr. Clark's Book Store, Palo Alto, 1988-91; co-owner Secret Staircase Bookshop, Redwood City, Calif., 1992—. Pres. Sequoyah Elem. Sch. PTA, Palo Alto, 1976; co-pres. Wilbur Mid. Sch. PTA, Palo Alto, 1978; rep. Supts. Com. for Sch. Closure, Palo Alto, 1975. Mem. AAUW (mentor), No. Calif. Children's Booksellers Assn. (sec. 1990-91), No. Calif. Ind. Booksellers Assn., Redwood City Merchant's Group (sec. 1993), Hewlett Packard Sailing Club (Posadero award 1983), Assn. of Booksellers for Children, Redwood City San Mateo County C. of C. Home: 11854 Page Mill Rd Los Altos Hills CA 94022-4219 Office: Secret Staircase Bookshop 2223 Broadway St Redwood City CA 94063-1641

STARRATT, PATRICIA ELIZABETH, writer, actress, composer; b. Boston, Nov. 7, 1943; d. Alfred Byron and Anna (Mazur) S.; AB, Smith Coll., 1965; grad. prep. dept. Peabody Conservatory Music, 1961. Teaching asst. Harvard U. Grad. Sch. Bus. Adminstrn., 1965-67; mng. dir. INS Assocs., Washington, 1967-68; adminstrv. asst. George Washington U. Hosp., 1970-71; legal asst. Morgan, Lewis & Bockius, Washington, 1971-72; profl. staff energy analyst Nat. Fuels and Energy Policy Study, U.S. Senate Interior Com., 1972-74; cons., exec. asst. energy resource devel. Fed. Energy Adminstrn., Washington, 1974-75; sr. cons. energy policy Atlantic Richfield Co., 1975-76; energy cons., Alaska, 1977-78; govt. affairs assoc. Sohio Alaska Petroleum Co., Anchorage, 1978-85; legal asst. Hughes, Thorsness, Gantz, Powell and Brudin, Anchorage, 1989—; writer, media specialist corp. affairs Alyeska Pipeline Svc., Co., 1990—; pres. Starratt Monarch Prodns., 1986—; Econ. Devel. Commn., Municipality of Anchorage, 1981; actress/asst. dir. Brattle St. Players, Boston, 1966-67, Washington Theater Club 1967-68, Gene Frankel, Broadway 1968-69; actress Aspen Resident Theater, Colo. 1985-86, Ranyevskya (The Cherry Orchard), Anchorage, 1994-95, Bonfila (Slaus!), Anchorage, 1994-95; writer and assoc. producer Then One Night I Hit Her, 1983; appeared Off-Broadway in To Be Young, Gifted and Black; performed as Mary in Tennessee, Blanche in A Streetcar Named Desire, Stephanie Dickinson in Cactus Flower, Angela in Papa's Wine, Elizabeth Procter in The Crucible, Candida in Candida, Zeuss in J.B., Martha in Who's Afraid of Virginia Woolf, Amy in Dinny and The Witches, as Columbina in Servant of Two Masters, as Singer in Death of Morris Biederman, as Joan in Joan of Lorraine, as Mado in Amadee, as Mrs. Rowlands in Before Breakfast, as the girl in Hello Out There, as Angela in Bedtime Story, as Hannah in Night of the Iguana, as Lavinia in Androcles and the Lion, as Catherine in Great Catherine, as Julie in Lilliom, as First Nurse in Death of Bessie Smith, as Laura in Tea and Sympathy, as Amelia Earheart in Chamber Music; appeared at Detroit Summer Theatre in Oklahoma, Guys and Dolls, Carousel, Brigadoon, Kiss Me Kate, Finnian's Rainbow; asst. to dir. Broadway plays A Cry Of Players, A Way Of Life, Off-Broadway play To Be Young, Gifted, and Black; screenwriter Challenge in Alaska, 1986, Martin Poll Films; asst. dir. Dustin Hoffman, 1974; contbr. articles on natural gas and Alaskan econ. and environ. to profl. jours. Bd. dirs. Anchorage Community Theatre; industry rep. Alaska Eskimo Whaling Commn.; mem. Alaska New Music Forum. Mem. Actors' Equity. Episcopalian. Avocations: skiing, horseback riding, biking, hiking. Home: 1054 W 20th Ave Apt 4 Anchorage AK 99503-1749

STARR-COHEN, NINA K., clinical counselor; b. Greensboro, N.C., Feb. 2, 1942; d. Vernon Wilson and Nell Clifford (Wagoner) Kennedy; m. William B. Starr, Aug. 24, 1964 (div. 1985); 1 child, Renée Lynn Starr; m. Byron Neal Cohen, Dec. 23, 1990; children: Gregory Cohen, Kevin Cohen. BA, U. No. Carolina, 1964, MEd, 1966, EdS, 1980, EdD, 1987. Nat. bd. cert. counselor. Rsch. assoc. U. N.C., Greensboro, 1980-83, assoc. dir. Ctr. Edn. Studies, 1983-87; clin. counselor Counseling Ctr. Greensboro, 1992—; mem. adj. grad. faculty U. N.C., Greensboro, 1987-92; co-dir. Summer Leadership Inst. for Prins. and Tchrs., 1990-92; dist. ct. mediator State Dist. Ct., Salisbury, N.C., 1992-94. Author, co-author proceedings, reports. Bd. trustees, chair The Piedmont Sch., High Point, N.C.; bd. trustees, sec. Guilford Tech. C.C., Jamestown, N.C.; trustee N.C. Arts Coun.; del. White House Conf. on Aging, Washington. Fellow Orthopsychiat. Assn.; mem. ACA, Internat. Alliance Invitational Edn. Office: Counseling Ctr Greensboro Forum VI Ste 604 Greensboro NC 27408

STARRETT, PAMELA ELIZABETH, symphony executive director, violinist, conductor; b. Concord, N.H., July 15, 1962; d. John Frederick and Nancy Elizabeth (Garland) S.; m. John Peter Ingalls, May 14, 1988; children: Hugh Starrett Ingalls, Edmund Starrett Ingalls. B of Mus. Arts, U. Mich., 1984, MusM, MBA, 1988. Orch. mgr. Ann Arbor (Mich.) Symphony Orch., 1987-88, asst. condr., 1988; mktg. dir. Kalamazoo Symphony Orch., 1988-90; music dir. Battle Creek (Mich.) Youth Orch., 1989-91; exec. dir. Battle Creek Symphony Orch., 1990—. Chair young artists competition Kalamazoo Bach Festival, 1989-90. Mem. Mich. Orch. Assn. (trustee 1990-91, 93—). Home: 153 Laurel Dr Battle Creek MI 49017-4666 Office: Battle Creek Symphony Orch 25 Michigan Ave W Ste 1206 Battle Creek MI 49017-7012

STARRS, ELIZABETH ANNE, lawyer; b. Detroit, Jan. 1, 1954; d. John Richard and Mabel Angeline (Gilchrist) S. BA, U. Mich., 1975; JD, Suffolk U., 1980. Bar: Mass. 1980, U.S. Dist. Ct. Mass. 1980, U.S. Ct. Appeals (1st. cir.) 1980, Colo. 1983, U.S. Dist. Ct. Colo. 1983, U.S. Ct. Appeals (10th cir.) 1983. Assoc. Denner & Benjoya P.C., Boston, 1980-83; assoc. Kennedy & Christopher P.C. (formerly Cooper & Kelley P.C.), Denver, 1983-86, ptnr., 1986-94, pres., mng. ptnr., 1994—; instr. bus. law Bay State C.C., Boston, 1981-82. Troop leader Girl Scouts U.S., Denver, 1984-85; pres. CWBA Found., 1992-94. Mem. Colo. Bar Assn. (litigation coun. 1989—, chair 1993-94, profl. liability ins. chair 1991-93), Denver Bar Assn., Colo. Women's bar Assn. (bd. dirs. 1984-85, v.p. 1989-90). Roman Catholic. Office: Kennedy & Christopher PC 1660 Wynkoop St Ste 900 Denver CO 80202-1145

STASHOWER, SARA ELLEN, advertising executive; b. Cleve., Sept. 6, 1954; d. David Lippmann and Sally Carol (Weiss) S. BA cum laude, Macalester Coll., 1976; MEd, Harvard U., 1982. Lower sch. instr., curriculum supr. St. Paul Acad., 1976-81; cons. 3M Co., St. Paul, 1979-81; promotions dir. Robinson Broadcasting, Cleve., 1982-83; account exec. Liggett-Stashower Advt., Cleve., 1984-89, v.p., account supr., 1989-94, sr. v.p., 1994—; sr. v.p., gen. mgr. Liggett Stashower Consulting, Cleve., 1994; cons. Ctr. for Contemporary Art, Cleve., 1993-94. Trustee Playhouse Square Found., Cleve., 1993—, Cleve. Film Soc., 1990—; co-chair Bicentennial Commn. Events, Cleve., 1993—; trustee, com. chair Montefiore Home, Cleve., 1991—; co-founder, co-chair exec. com. Playhouse Square Ptnrs., 1990-93; trustee New Orgn. for Visual Arts, 1991—; Ohio co-chair, alumni rep. Macalester Coll. Alumni Admissions, 1981—. Recipient Achievement award No. Ohio Live Mag., 1992, 93; named one of Outstanding Young Women in Am., 1986. Mem. Cleve. Advt. Club (instr. 1990—), Jr. League Cleve. (community advisor 1990—). Jewish. Home: 16300 Van Aken Blvd Shaker Heights OH 44120 Office: Liggett-Stashower Advt 1228 Euclid Ave Cleveland OH 44106

STASSINOS, GAIL, lawyer; b. N.Y.C., July 6, 1949; d. John and Harriet (Katzen) S. BA in Psychology with honors, San Francisco State U., 1974; MA in Psychology with honors, Calif. State U., Sacramento, 1976; JD, U. Calif., Davis, 1987. Bar: Calif. 1987; Calif. C.C. counseling credential. Counselor Sacramento, 1976; head resident U. Wash., Pullman, 1976-78; pers. dir. Ctrl. Valley Opportunity Ctr., Merced, Calif., 1978-80; field rep. Calif. Sch. Employees Assn., Bakersfield, 1980; pers. analyst III Santa Barbara County, Calif., 1980-84; law clk. Beeson, Tayer, Badine, 1985; assoc. Canelo, Hansen & Wilson, Merced, Calif., 1987-89, Lea, Balavage & Arruti, Sacramento, 1989-90; pvt. practice Carmichael, Calif., 1990—; coord. ann. labor rels. conf. U. Calif., Davis, 1986; instr. U. Calif. Ext., Santa Cruz, 1978; pro tem judge small claims ct., Sacramento County. Author: (orgn. pers. manual) Central Valley Opportunity Center, 1979. Mem. ABA (litigation sect.), Sacramento Social Security Reps. Orgn., NOW (founding mem. Golden Gate chpt. 1968-69), Nat. Orgn. Social Security Reps., Calif. Trial Lawyers Assn., Calif. Women Lawyers, Capitol City Trial Lawyers, Women Lawyers of Sacramento, Bus. and Profl. Women (treas. 1984). Democrat. Jewish. Office: 5740 Windmill Way Carmichael CA 95608

STASSON, SHELLEY ANDREA, lawyer; b. Detroit, Apr. 23, 1953; d. Jerome and Betty (Kowalksy) S. BA in Psychology, U. Mich., 1975; JD, Thomas M. Cooley Law Sch., 1978. Bar: Mich. 1979, D.C. 1983, U.S. Supreme Ct. 1983, U.S. Dist. Ct. (mid. dist.) Pa. 1984, U.S. Ct. Appeals (3d cir.) 1984. Pvt. practice Harrisburg, Pa., 1981-87; pvt. practice, Detroit and West Bloomfield, Mich., 1987—; atty. Legis. Ref. Bur., Harrisburg, 1981-87; guest speaker various interest groups, Pa., 1983—. Contbr. articles to numerous jours. Del. Nat. Conf. State Legislators, Denver, 1983, 84. Republican. Jewish. Home: 5745 W Maple Rd Ste 203 West Bloomfield MI 48322-4412

STATILE, JEANNE GLORIA, accountant, customer service administrator; b. Elizabeth, N.J., Mar. 9, 1950; d. Theodore Edmund and Dorothy (Mullineaux) Sienicki; married, 1972 (div. 1984); children: Annmarie, Melissa, Philip. BA in Math., Caldwell (N.J.) Coll., 1972. Office mgr., bookkeeper IPCO Hosp. Supply, Valhalla, N.Y., 1972-73; govt. contracts mgr. CR Bard Ave, Murray Hill, N.J., 1973-77; acct., bookkeeper Statile & Todd, Inc., Springfield, N.J., 1972-73, LP Statile Inc., Springfield, 1973-82, Ard Appraisal Co., Clark, N.J., 1984-86, Hess, Keeley CPA Firm, Millburn, N.J., 1986-88; acct., office mgr., fin. advisor Dr. Haidri, M.D., Union, N.J., 1987-90, Bodyart Svc. Ctr., Garwood, N.J., 1991—, Belair Instrument, Fanwood, N.J., 1993—. Auditor Deerfield Sch. PTA, Mountainside, N.J., 1986-95; co-chmn., fund raiser Cystic Fibrosis, Secaucus, N.J., 1988-91; bd. dirs. Youth Baseball of Mountainside, 1993—. Roman Catholic. Home: 350 Old Tote Rd Mountainside NJ 07092-1840

STATMAN, JACKIE C., career consultant; b. Kingman, Kansas, June 15, 1936; d. Jack Carl and Dorothy E. (Kendall) Pulliam; m. Jerome Maurice Statman, Dec. 29, 1959; children: David Alan, Susan Gail. BA, U. Kans., 1958. Reg. music therapist Topeka State Hosp., Kans., 1958-59; caseworker Child Welfare, Pensacola, Fla., 1960-61; devel. rsch. tester The Children and Youth Project, Dallas, 1973-74; middle sch. counselor The Hockaday Sch., Dallas, 1981-84; career cons. Career Design Assocs., Inc., Garland, Tex., 1984-86; owner Career Focus Assocs., Plano, Tex., 1987—; pres. Assn. Women Entrepreneurs of Dallas, Inc., 1991-93; mem. career edn. adv. com. Plano Ind. Sch. Dist., 1993—. Author: (newspaper column) "Career Forum", 1991-92. Vice-chair Community Svcs. Commn., City of Plano, 1993—; mem. Leadership Plano Alumnae Assn., 1990—; mem. bd. dirs. Mental Health Assn. in Tex., 1989-93; founding pres. Mental Health Assn. Collin County, 1988-90. Recipient Child Advocacy award Mental Health Assn. of Greater Dallas, 1985, Golden Rule award JC Penney Comp., Inc., 1986, Humanitarian Vo. of the Yr. award Vol. Ctr. Collin County, 1990. Mem. Am. Counseling Assn., Nat. Assn. Women Bus. Owners (mem. Dallas/Ft. Worth bd. dirs. 1992-93), Nat. Career Devel. Assn., Plano C. of C. Office: Career Focus Assocs 1700 Coit Rd Ste 220 Plano TX 75075

STAUB, ANGELA CONRAD, educational specialist, consultant; b. Hanover, Pa., Oct. 31, 1946; d. James Robert and Rosella Philamena (Staub) Conrad; divorced; children: Jodi Aileen, Jeremy Peter, Gabriel Robert. BA in English and Spanish, Marillac Coll., 1970; MA in English and Edn., Nebr. U., 1972; postgrad., Lebanon Valley Coll., 1983-84, Shepphard Pratt Ctr., 1991. Cert. secondary edn. educator. Dir. edn. Divine Savior Sch., Norridge, Ill., 1972-74; junior high tchr. St. Joseph Sch., Cockeysville, Md., 1975-77; dir. edn. St. Elizabeth Parish, Mechanicsburg, Pa., 1979-80; sr. assoc. lectr. Harrisburg (Pa.) Area C.C., 1980-88; asst. dir., coord. Children's Family Ctr., Mechanicsburg, 1990-93; owner, cons. WORDSENSE, Mechanicsburg, 1989—; master tchr. Diocese of Balt. and Harrisburg, 1976-79; ednl. cons. Silver Burdett Pubs., Morristown, N.J., 1973-76. Author: Grade 3 and 4 Silver B Texts, 1976; co-author: (teacher's manual) Separation and Loss/Pre-School Children, 1992, (manual) Teaching Children and Teens about Alzheimer's, 1993; editor-in-chief Dauphin County Prison Policy Manual, 1986. Lay mem. Diocesan Liturgical Commn., Harrisburg, 1970; bd. dirs. St. Elizabeth Steton Ch., Mechanicsburg, 1986, writer, creator of video; cons., nominating chairperson Susquehanna Chorale, Harrisburg, 1990-92; performer for children Mechanicsburg Libr., 1992-93; parent admissions rep. to parent adv. bd. Goucher Coll., 1992—; cons., facilitator Capital Region 2000 Plan for Edn., 1992—. Full Fellowship grantee Nebr. U., 1971-72. Mem. Rotary (chair membership 1993-94, v.p. elect 1994-95, v.p. 1995—), Delta Epsilon Sigma. Democrat. Home and Office: WORDSENSE 17 San Juan Dr Mechanicsburg PA 17055

STAUB, JULIE CADWALLADER, human services administrator; b. Mpls., Mar. 16, 1957. BA in Religious Studies with honors, Earlham Coll., 1979; MSW in Social Policy & Community Organizing, Rutgers U., 1984; postgrad., Bryn Mawr Grad. Sch., 1990-92. Coord. teen advocacy program Mercer area Planned Parenthood Assn., Trenton, N.J., 1981-82; intern asst. to dir. material aids program Am. Friends Svc. Com., Phila., 1983-84, fin. cons. Africa programs, 1984-86; exec. dir. Maternity Care Coalition of Greater Phila., Inc., 1986-88, program assoc., 1992; dir. Vt. Campaign to End Childhood Hunger, Shelburne, 1992—. Vol. polit. campaigns. Danforth Found. grad. fellow, 1980; Roothbert Found. scholar, 1991. Mem. Phi Beta Kappa. Mem. Soc. of Friends. Office: End Childhood Hunger PO Box 866 Shelburne VT 05482-0866

STAUBER, MARILYN JEAN, educator, consultant; b. Duluth, Minn., Feb. 5, 1938; d. Harold Milton and Dorothy Florence (Thompson) Froehlich; children: Kenneth D. and James H. Atkinson; m. Lawrence B. Stauber, Jan. 11, 1991. BS in K-6 Edn., U. Minn., Duluth, 1969, MEd in Math., 1977. Cert. elem. and secondary reading tchr., remedial reading specialist, devel. reading tchr., reading cons. Sec. div. vocat. rehab. State Minn., Duluth, 1956-59; sec. Travelers Ins. Co., Duluth, 1962-66; lead tchr. Chpt. 1 reading and math. Proctor, Minn., 1969—. Mem. choir, comm. coord. Forbes Meth. Ch., Proctor. Mem. NEA, Nat. Reading Assn., Minn. Arrowhead Reading Coun., Elem. Coun. (pres. 1983-84, 86-87), Proctor Fedn. Tchrs. (recert. com. 1980—, treas. 1981-86), Phi Delta Kappa. Home: 6713 Grand Lake Rd Saginaw MN 55779-9782

STAUBS, JOYCE JARRETT, critical care nurse; b. Miami, Fla., May 15, 1947; d. Jones Eli and Maxine (Whitt) Jarrett; m. Ralph Arthur Staubs, Feb. 14, 1976; 1 child, Joel Eli. Diploma, Burge Sch. Nursing, Springfield, Mo., 1974; BA in Edn., Southwest Mo. State U., Springfield, 1971; teaching cert., Bapt. Bible Coll., Springfield, 1971. Staff nurse CCU Prince Georges Hosp. Ctr., Cheverly, Md., 1974-80, staff nurse clin. post anesthetic care unit, 1980-94; staff nurse level IV Dimensions Health Corp., Landover, Md., 1994—. Spl. editor The Recovery Rm. Home: 6908 Barton Rd Hyattsville MD 20784-2502

STAUDENMAIER, MARY LOUISE, banker, lawyer; b. Marinette, Wis., Apr. 13, 1938; d. Louis W. and Hildegarde C. (Schmit) S. BA, Mt. Mary Coll., Milw., 1960; JD, Marquette U., 1971; postgrad. in banking, U. Wis., 1980; postgrad. in bus., Harvard U., 1980. Bar: Wis., 1971. Tchr. math. Milw. High Sch., 1960-66; security analyst 1st Wis. Trust, Milw., 1966-68, trust adminstr., 1968-70; v.p. Am. City Bank & Trust, Milw., 1970-75; trust officer Marine Nat. Exchange Bank, Milw., 1975; v.p., trust officer Heritage Trust Co., Milw., 1975-77; pres., chief exec. officer, trust officer Stephenson Nat. Bank and Trust, Marinette, 1977—, also bd. dirs., chmn.; bd. dirs., chmn.; speaker on estate planning; bd. dirs. TYME Corp. Bd. dirs. Marinette Area Econ. Devel. Corp.; mem. fin. coun. and investment com. Cath. Diocese Green Bay, Wis.; mem. Marinette Downtown Revitalization Com.; past chmn. Marinette Downtown Adv. Com.; past pres. Marinette Voyageurs Com.; chair fin. com. Holy Family Congregation; past bd. dirs. Marinette Area Indsl. Devel. Corp., United Way Marinette and others; bd. dirs. Woolsack Soc. Marquette U. Law Sch. Recipient Touhey award Marinette Cath. Cen. High Sch., 1988, Mary Neville Bielefeld award Marquette U., 1989, Madonna medal for Profl. Excellence, Mount Mary Coll., 1990. Mem. Wis. Bar Assn. (past bd. dirs. corp., banking and bus. law com.), Wis. Bankers Assn. (br. banking task force), Marinette County Bar Assn. (past pres.), Wis. Trustees Assn. (past mem. legis. com.), Ind. Bankers Assn., Marinette Area C. of C. (past bd. dirs.), Marquette U. Law Alumni Assn. (past bd. dirs.), Assn. Marquette U. Women (past bd. dirs.). Home: 2411 Riverside Ave Marinette WI 54143 Office: Stephenson Nat Bank & Trust 1820 Hall Ave Marinette WI 54143

STAUFFER, GWEN LOUISE, horticulturist; b. Reading, Pa., Nov. 30, 1960; d. Curvous Paul Jr. and Elizabeth Louise (Hille) S.; m. Dwain C. Trump, Oct. 9, 1982 (div. 1989). BS in Ornamental Horticulture, Del. Valley Coll. Sci., 1982; MS in Pub. Horticulture Adminstrn., U. Del., 1993. Landscape supr., garden ctr. mgr. Botan. Decorators, Clarksville, Md., 1982-83; maintenance and installation crew supr. Olde English Landscapes, Silver Spring, Md., 1983-84; gardener II Brookside Botan. Gardens, Wheaton, Md., 1984-85; grounds/horticulture supr. Arlington (Va.) Hosp. Assn., 1985-88; landscape specialist Charles E. Smith Mgmt. Inc., Arlington, 1988-91; dir. horticulture Hillwood Mus. and Gardens, Marjorie Merriweather Post Found., Washington, 1993—; lectr. Brookside Gardens, Washington metro. chpt. Landscape Contractors Assn., Montgomery County Men's Garden Club, other garden clubs; cons. to landscape archtl. firms and comml. landscape cos., Washington; mem. selection com. profl. gardener tng. program Longwood Gardens. Recipient Beautification award Arlingtonians for a Clean Environment, 1986. Mem. Am. Assn. Botan. Gardens and Arboreta, Am. Assn. Mus., Nat. Trust for Historic Preservation, Visitor Studies Assn., Am. Hort. Soc., Smithsonian Soc., Profl. Grounds Mgmt. Soc., Am. Landscape Contractors Assn., Sierra Club, Nature Conservancy. Office: Hillwood Mus Post Found 4155 Linnean Ave NW Washington DC 20008-3806

STAUFFER, JOANNE ROGAN, steel company official; b. Coatesville, Pa., Oct. 15, 1956; d. Joseph Chester and Anne Mary (Kauffman) Rogan; m. Robert Lee Marvin Stauffer, Oct. 15, 1988. AS in Bus. Adminstrn., Harrisburg Area Community Coll, 1979, postgrad., 1986—. Store acct. Giant Foods, Harrisburg, Pa., 1977-79; payroll clk. Bethlehem Steel (name changed to Pa. Steel Techs.), Steelton, Pa., 1980-83, material and cost acct., 1983-86, cost analyst, 1986—. Adult vol. River Valley Riders 4H Club. Mem. Internat. Platform Assn., Am. Bus. Women's Assn. (corr. sec. Rainbow Valley charter chpt. 1991-92, v.p. 1992-93, pres. 1993-94), Steelton Plant Engrs. Club (sec. 1982-85, v.p. 1985-86, pres. 1986-87). Republican. Roman Catholic. Home: 401 Sheetz Rd Halifax PA 17032-9695

STAUFFER, LOUISE LEE, retired educator; b. Altoona, Pa., Mar. 31, 1915; d. William Thomas and Mary Hall (Schroyer) Lee; m. John Nissley Stauffer, Aug. 20, 1938 (dec. Sept. 1983); children: Thomas Michael, Nancy Kay, John Lee, Donald David. BA, Juniata Coll., 1936; postgrad., Columbia U., U. Pa., Pa. State U. Tchr. Latin, Middletown (Pa.) High Sch., 1936-41; tchr. English and Latin, Roosevelt Jr. High Sch., Springfield, Ohio, 1949-57; tchr. French, North High Sch., Springfield, 1957-63; ret., 1963. Mem. Moorings Property Owners Assn., Naples, Fla., 1983—; sec. King's Port, Inc., Naples, 1990-94, Emmanuel Luth. Ch., Naples, 1980—; bd. dirs., editor newsletter, membership chmn., rec. sec., corr. sec. Naples Cmty. Hosp. Aux., 1985—. Mem. AAUW, Am. Assn. Ret. Persons, Women's League (Juniata Coll.), Founders Club (Juniata Coll.), Moorings Country Club.

STAUFFER, MARTHA E., pathologist, educator; b. Hagerstown, Md., July 24, 1934; d. Ralph Stanley and Sue Brewer (Craig) S. AB, Vassar Coll., 1956; MD, U. Md., Balt., 1960. Diplomate Am. Bd. Pathology and Clin. Pathology, Am. Bd. Internal Medicine, Am. Bd. Nuclear Medicine. Intern in internal medicine Univ. Hosp. U. Md., 1960-61, fellow in endocrinology, 1962-63, resident in internal medicine, 1963-64; resident in pathology Boston City Hosp., 1961-62; resident in internal medicine U. Wash., Seattle, 1964-65, fellow in endocrinology, 1965-66, resident in pathology, 1970-72; asst. dir. nuclear medicine VA Med. Ctr., Seattle, 1966-70, dir. clin. labs., 1972-77; chief pathology VA Med. Ctr., White River Junction, Vt., 1977—. Author: (with others) Endocrine Pathology, 1982. Fellow Coll. Am. Pathologists (com. mem. 1993—); mem. Alpha Omega Alpha. Office: VA Medical Ctr White River Junction VT 05009

STAUM-KUNIEJ, SONJA, reference librarian; b. St. Joseph, Mich., May 9, 1959; d. Lewis Fredric and Marian Elizabeth (Herrmann) Staum; m. Michael Joseph Kuniej, Aug. 24, 1991; 1 child, Nathaniel Lewis. BA, Ind. U., 1984; MFA, U. Ga., 1986; MLS, Ind. U., 1989. Libr. Mus. Contemporary Art, Chgo., 1989-93; reference libr. Prospect Heights (Ill.) Pub. Libr., 1993—. Mem. ALA, Art Librs. Soc. N.Am. (annual conf. com. 1991-92, space planner roundtable coord. 1989-91, sec.-treas. Midstates chpt. 1990-92, nominating com. 1990), Des Plaines Art Guild, Chgo. Artists Coalition.

STAUTBERG, SUSAN SCHIFFER, communications executive; b. Bryn Mawr, Pa., Nov. 9, 1945; d. Herbert F. and Margaret (Berwind) Schiffer; m. T. Aubrey Stautberg, Jr., Dec. 10, 1979. BA, Wheaton Coll., 1967; MA, George Washington U., 1970. Nat. TV corr., Washington, 1970-74; White House fellow, 1974-75; dir. communications U.S. Consumer Products Safety Commn., Washington, 1976-78, McNeil Consumer Products Co., 1978-80; v.p. Fraser/Assos., Washington, 1980; exec. asst. to pres. Morgan Stanley & Co., N.Y.C., 1980-82; dir. communications Deloitte & Touche, N.Y.C., 1982—. pres. MasterMedia Ltd., 1986—; bd. dirs. States, Inc.; Author: Making It in Less Than an Hour, 1976, Pregnancy Nine to Five: The Career Woman's Guide to Pregnancy and Motherhood, 1985, The Pregnancy and Motherhood Diary: Planning the First Year of your Second Career, 1988, Managing it All, 1989, Balancing Act, 1992. Mem., nat. chmn. adv. coun. Ctr. for Study of the Presidency, 1976—; mem. Phila. Regional Panel for Selection White House Fellows; bd. dirs. Schiffer Pub., The Berwind Found.; mem. Reagan-Bush Presdl. Transition Team; mem. Commn. Presdl. Scholars; State Dept. speaker various countries. Selected as one of Wheaton's 10 Most Outstanding Grads., Alumnae Assn., Wheaton Coll., 1982. Mem. Pub. Rels. Soc. Am. (bd. dirs.), Pub. Affairs Profls., Nat. Soc. Colonial Dames, Acorn Club, City Tavern Club, Cosmopolitan Club, Colony Club, Radnor Hunt Club. Home: 17 E 89th St New York NY 10128-0615 Office: Mastermedia 9 W 57th St Fl 22 New York NY 10019-2600

STAVE, SONDRA ASTOR, adult and community education administrator; b. N.Y.C., Feb. 25, 1941; d. Abraham I. and Faye Ruth (Greif) Astor; m. Bruce Martin Stave, June 16, 1961; 1 child, Channing Matthew Lindsay Stave. BS, CCNY, 1961; MPA, U. Conn., 1977, PhD, 1993. Cert. intermediate adminstr. Tchr. Montour Joint Schs., McKees Rock, Pa., 1962-65, Milford (Conn.) Pub. Schs., 1965-67; dir. Hartford: The City and The Region, Hartford, Conn., 1979-80, Footsteps of History, Storrs, Conn., 1980-82, Eastern Conn. Libr. Assn., Willimantic, 1982-84; instr. Peking U., Beijing, China, 1984-85; scholar-in-residence Manchester (Conn.) High Sch., 1986; dir. Mansfield Adult Edn., Storrs, 1987—. Editor: Hartford: The City and the Region, 1979, 275th Anniversary Cookbook, 1987, Exclusively Rhubarb Cookbook, 1989, Exclusively Pumpkin Cookbook, 1992. Chair Planning and Zoning Commn., Coventry, 1974-77, Bd. of Edn., Coventry, 1981-83, Econ. Devel. Commn., Coventry, 1986—, Inland Wetland Agy., Coventry, 1974-77, 93-94; justice of peace, 1984—. Grantee Nat. Endowment Humanities, 1980. Mem. LWV (bd. dirs., govt. rels. 1993—), Pi Alpha Alpha, Pi Lambda Theta. Democrat. Home: 200 Broad Way Coventry CT 06238-1253 Office: Mansfield Adult Edn 4 S Eagleville Rd Storrs CT 06268-2574

STAVES, SUSAN, English educator; b. N.Y.C., Oct. 5, 1942; d. Henry Tracy and Margaret (McClernon) S. AB, U. Chgo., 1963; MA, U. Va., 1964, PhD, 1967. Woodrow Wilson intern Bennett Coll., Greensboro, N.C., 1965-66; from asst. prof. to prof. Brandeis U., Waltham, Mass., 1967—, Paul Proswimmer prof. of Humanities, 1993—; Clark prof. UCLA, 1989-90. Author: Players' Scepters: Fictions of Authority in the Restoration, 1979, Married Women's Separate Property in England, 1660-1833, 1990; co-author: (with John Brewer) Early Modern Conceptions of Property, 1994; also articles in Modern Philology, 18th-Century Studies, Studies in Eng. Lit., Studies in Eighteenth Century Culture, Law and History. Assoc. mem. Belmont (Mass.) Dem. Town Com.; mem. ACLU, 1967—. Woodrow Wilson fellow, 1963-64, Woodrow Wilson Dissertation fellow, 1966-67, Harward Liberal Arts fellow, 1980-81, John Simon Guggenheim fellow, 1981-82. Mem. MLA (exec. com. div. on late-18th century English lit. 1984-86), Am. Soc. for 18th-Century Studies (exec. bd. 1987-90), Am. Soc. for Legal History, AAUP, English Inst. Episcopalian. Office: Brandeis U Dept English Waltham MA 02254

STAVRAKAKIS, SUSAN MARIE, mortgage banker; b. Hanford, Calif., Dec. 14, 1960; d. James Clark and Sally (Palmer) Gordon; m. Steven George Stavrakakis, Apr. 12, 1986. AS, West Hills C.C., 1981; postgrad., Calif. Poly. State U., 1981-84. Asst. mgr. Morris Plan Co. of Calif., Modesto, 1984-87; asst. v.p. Norwest Mortgage Inc., Modesto, 1987—. Office: Norwest Mortgage Inc 1500 Standiford Ave Ste C-1 Modesto CA 95350

STAVROPOULOS, ROSE MARY GRANT, community activist, volunteer; b. Decatur, Ill.; d. Walter Edwin and Ora Lenore (Kepler) Grant; m. Stan Stavropoulos; children: Becky Ann Stavropoulos Betian, Stephanie Diane. BS, Ea. Ill. U., 1954. Cert. elem. edn. Tchr. 2nd grade Garfield Sch., Decatur, 1954-55; bd. dirs. Wilmot Sch. Bd. PTA, Deerfield, 1971-73, Moraine Girl Scout Coun., Deerfield, 1968-75; also bd. dirs. Moraine Girl Scout Coun., Deerfield, Ill., 1984-89; chmn. Human Rels. Commn., Deerfield, 1975-84; mem. sr. citizen adv. com. Deerfield Park Dist., 1984-89; pres. Lake County (Ill.) LWV, 1979-81; chmn. Deerfield Village Caucus, 1980-82; pres. Caring For Others, Inc., Deerfield, 1986-88, Deerfield Area LWV, 1970-90; bd. mem. Deerfield Area United Way, 1976-93, pres., 1991-93; Mem. Deerfield Village Caucus Adv. Coun., 1980-81, 92—. Recipient Deerfield Human Rels. Humanitarian award, 1984, Lerner Life's Citizen of Month, 1987. Mem. Deerfield Area Hist. Soc., Highland Park Hosp. Aux, Delta Zeta. Home: 1629 Village Green Ct Deerfield IL 60015-2638

STAWNYCHY, ZORIANA MARIA, financial executive; b. N.Y.C., May 31, 1953; d. Walter and Eugenia (Hanusczcak) Salak; m. Yuri Andrij Stawnychy, Oct. 26, 1985. BA, Fordham U., 1975. Cert. fin. planner, registered investment advisor. Fin. planner Cigna, N.Y.C., 1978-83, 85-90; mgr. Bruce Raines Assocs., N.Y.C., 1983-84; sr. fin. counselor Ind. Fin. Services, White Plains, N.Y., 1984-85; owner Stawnychy Fin. Svcs., N.Y.C., 1991—. Mem. Internat. Assn. Fin. Planning, Inst. Cert. Fin. Planners.

STAY, BARBARA, zoologist, educator; b. Cleve., Aug. 31, 1926; d. Theron David and Florence (Finley) S. A.B., Vassar Coll., 1947; M.A., Radcliffe Coll., 1949, Ph.D., 1953. Entomologist Army Research Center, Natick, Mass., 1954-60; vis. asst. prof. Pomona Coll., 1960; asst. prof. biology U. Pa., 1961-67; asso. prof. zoology U. Iowa, Iowa City, 1967-77; prof. U. Iowa, 1977—. Fulbright fellow to Australia, 1953; Lalor fellow Harvard U., 1960. Mem. Am. Soc. Zoologists, Am. Inst. Biol. Scis., Am. Soc. Cell Biology, Entomol. Soc. Am., Iowa Acad. Scis., Sigma Xi. Office: U Iowa Dept Biological Scis Iowa City IA 52242

STEAD, FRANCESCA MANUELA LEWENSTEIN, natural health care consultant, massage therapist; b. Bklyn., May 2, 1949; d. Robert Gottschalk Lewenstein and Shirley Winifred (Goodman) Lewenstein Ozgen; m. Thomas David Stead, May 28, 1975; children: Chandra Dharani, Thomas Robert. Student, Case Western Res. U., 1967-69; BA in Govt. cum laude, Ohio U., 1973; cert. in Massage Therapy, Cen. Ohio Sch. Massage, Columbus, 1978. Lic. massage therapist; cert. sports massage therapist. Youth service coordinator Adams-Brown Community Action Agy., Decatur, Ohio, 1973; child welfare worker Scioto Children's Services, Portsmouth, Ohio, 1975-77; project dir. youth services Scioto County Community Action Agy., Portsmouth, Ohio, 1978-79; co-owner Stead Enterprises, Otway, Ohio, 1978—; self employed massage therapist Portsmouth, Ohio, 1979—; owner Total Health Care Cons., Portsmouth, 1985—; drug and alcohol counselor Coun. on Alcoholism, West Union, Ohio, 1982; instr. Yoga, Cradtal, Shawnee State U., Portsmouth, 1985—; staff mem. Area Psychiatric and Psychotherapy Group, Health Ctr. One, Huntington, W.Va., 1986-90; instr. summer career edn. prog. Shawnee State U., 1986; reimbursement officer Ohio Dept. Mental Health, Columbus, 1982-85; cons. Portsmouth Dept., 1977; cons. drug abuse Aberdeen Sch., Ohio, 1982; Yoga instr. YMCA, Portsmouth, 1979-80, 85-87. Dem. campaign worker Ohio, 1968—; organizer So. Ohio Task Force on Domestic Violence, 1976; organizer campus ministry Shawnee State U., Portsmouth, 1976-77; organizer Portsmouth Food Coop., 1975. Flora Stone Mather scholar Case Western Res. U., 1967. Mem. Portsmouth Area Women's Network (adv. bd. 1988—), Am. Massage Therapy Assn. (govt. affairs com. Nat. Sports Massage Team Ohio chpt. 1990—, Ohio del. nat. conv. 1991, 93, sports massage team strategic planning com. 1995—), Women in Networking, Pi Gamma Mu. Democrat. Kagyupa Buddhist. Home: 4140 Mt Unger Rd Otway OH 45657-9515 Office: Total Health Care Cons PO Box 1586 Portsmouth OH 45662 also: Fitness Express 395 Oliver Rd Minford OH 45653

STEAD LEE, POLLY JAE See LEE, PALI JAE

STEADMAN, LYDIA DUFF, elementary school educator, symphony violinist; b. Hollywood, Calif., Dec. 31, 1934; d. Lewis Marshall and Margaret Seville (Williams) Duff; m. John Gilford Steadman, Apr. 14, 1961 (dec.). Student, Pepperdine U., 1952-55; BA in Music Edn., U. So. Calif., 1957. Cert. spl. secondary music, edn. tchr., Calif. Instrumental music tchr. Lancaster (Calif.) Sch. Dist., 1957-62; instrumental music tchr. Simi Sch. Dist., Simi Valley, Calif., 1962-70, elem. tchr., 1970—; tchr. Polynesian culture, dances, games, 1970—; hist. play wright for elem. grades, organizer elem. sch. dance festivals; dir. All Dist. Orch., Lancaster, Simi Valley Schs., 1957-70; compile Japanese Culture Study Unit for elem. grades Ventura County. 1st violinist San Fernando Valley Symphony, Sherman Oaks, Calif., 1962-75, Conejo Valley Symphony, Thousand Oaks, 1975-81, tour concert mistress, 1980; 2d violinist Ventura County Symphony, 1981-94. Pres. San Fernando Cmty. Concerts, Van Nuys, Calif., 1982-94; free lance with pit orch. Cabrillo Music Theatre, Conejo Players Theater; organizer ann. sch. Jump Rope-a-Thon Am. Heart Assn., Nat. Geog. Geography Bee. Mem. AAUW, NAFE, Bus. and Profl. Women (pres. Golden Triangle chpt. 1988-90, issues and mgmt. chair 1990, ways and means chair Coast chpt. 1990, editor Golden Triangle newsletter 1988-90, treas. 1992-93, sec. 1993-94, v.p. 1994—), Sigma Xi-Sci. Rsch. Soc., Pacific Asia Mus., Armand Hammer Mus. Republican. Mem. Ch. of Christ. Home: 32016 Allenby Ct Westlake Village CA 91361-4001

STEANE, JOANNE ELIZABETH, physician; b. Nuneaton, Warwickshire, Eng., Sept. 30, 1956; came to U.S., 1961; d. Edwin Arthur Steane and Helena Elizabeth (Duckett) Clause; m. Gregory Corradino, May 29, 1982 (div.). BS, U. Wis., 1978; MD, U. Va., 1982. Diplomate Am. Bd. Pediat. Intern Tufts-New Eng. Med. Ctr., Boston, 1982-83, resident in pediatrics, 1983-85; fellow in adolescent medicine U. Md., Balt., 1985-87; asst. dir. Adol Health Svcs. Balt. City Health Dept., 1987-88; physician Am. U., Washington, 1987-88, U. N.C., Chapel Hill, 1988-94; staff physician U. Wyo., Laramie, 1994—. Office: U Wyo Student Health Svc PO Box 3068 Laramie WY 82071-3068

STEARNS, SHEILA MACDONALD, academic administrator; b. Ft. Snelling, Minn., Aug. 30, 1946; d. Colin Alexander and Marie Kristine (Peterson) MacD.; m. Hal Stearns, June 22, 1968; children: Scott, Malin. BA, U. Mont., 1968, MA, 1969, EdD, 1983. English and history tchr. Wiesbaden (West Germany) Jr. High Sch., 1969-72; libr. media specialist Missoula Pub. Schs., 1975-77; dir. alumni rels. U. Mont., Missoula, 1983-87, v.p. univ. rels., 1987-93; chancellor Western Mont. Coll., Dillon, 1993—; legis. liaison Mont. U. System, 1988—; bd. dirs. Bank of Mont. Contbr. articles to profl. publs. Internat. Women's Forum, chair gov. bd. dirs. St. Patrick Hosp., Missoula, 1991-93; mem. Mayor's Adv. Bd., Missoula. Mem. Missoula C. of C. (v.p. exec. com.), Rotary (bd. dirs.) Alpha Phi (Chi chpt.), Phi Delta Kappa. Roman Catholic. Office: U Mont Western Mont Coll 710 S Atlantic Dillon MT 59725

STEARNS, WANDA JUNE, curriculum and instruction director; b. Clarksburg, W.Va., Mar. 14, 1948; d. Walter David and Mary Eleanor (Ashburn) Zeitler; m. Calvin Edward Stearns, July 27, 1973; 1 child, Steven Walter. BS, Eastern Nazarene Coll., Quincy, Mass., 1972; MS, LaVerne U., 1976. Cert. elem. tchr., supr., adminstr. Tchr. Mansfield (Ohio) City Schs., 1970-82; dir. of presch. Sunshine Presch. and Day Care, Mansfield, 1985-86; supr. Mansfield City Schs., 1986-93; dir. curriculum and instrn. Whitehall (Ohio) City Schs., 1993—. Bd. dirs. Sister Cities, Mansfield, 1988-93. Mem. LWV, ASCD, Internat. Reading Assn., Nat. Coun. Tchrs. English, Phi Delta Kappa, Alpha Delta Kappa. Home: 1540 Rosehill Rd Reynoldsburg OH 43068-2916 Office: Whitehall 625 S Yearling Rd Whitehall OH 43213-2861

STEBBINGS, KIM LINKER, sales executive; b. Poughkeepsie, N.Y., Mar. 26, 1955; d. William Landes and Charlotte Louise (Scofield) Linker; m. Russell Edward Hall, Aug. 1977 (div. Mar. 1981); m. George Donald Stebbings, Jr., Apr. 23, 1981. BS in Biology, St. Lawrence U., Canton, N.Y., 1977; postgrad., Ariz. State U., 1983. Biology tchr. John Jay High Sch., Fishkill, N.Y., 1977; employment cons. Snelling & Snelling, Tempe, Ariz., 1977-78, br. mgr., 1978-81; pers. mgr. Cholla Bus. Interiors, Tempe, 1981-83; hosp. account mgr. Boehringer Mannheim Corp., Indpls., 1983-85, regional sales mgr., 1985-91, product mgr., 1991-92, area sales mgr., 1993-94, we. area bus. mgr., 1994—. Mem. Biomed. Mktg. Assn., Am. Assn. Diabetes Educators, Am. Diabetes Assn., Toastmasters (pres., adminstrv. v.p., edn. v.p., treas., sec. 1981-88), Phi Beta Kappa. Republican. Methodist. Home: 9635 Hampton Cir S Indianapolis IN 46256-9747 Office: Boehringer Mannheim Corp 9115 Hague Rd Indianapolis IN 46256-1045

STEBBINS, LOU HIRSCH, health information management educator; b. Los Angeles, Sept. 20, 1930; d. George Knott Reynolds and W. Pauline (Lazenby) Hirsch; m. Edward Jack Stebbins, July 27, 1949 (div. 1975); children: Sherra Lynn Stebbins Naegele, Holly Ann Stebbins Simmons, Scott Edward, Kirk Daniel; m. Douglas Paul Davison, Nov. 25, 1994. AA, Amarillo Jr. Coll., Tex., 1961; BS, Incarnate Word Coll., 1963; MBA, La. Tech. U., 1976, DBA, 1993. Registered record adminstr. Gen. ledger clerk Greenville Ave. Bank, Dallas, 1951-52; bookkeeper H. J. Heinz Co., Dallas, 1952-53; clerical worker Amarillo (Tex.) Osteopathic Hosp., 1958-62, med. records adminstr., 1963-64; asst. med. records adminstr. St. Anthony Hosp., Amarillo, 1964-66, U. Miss. Med. Ctr., Jackson, 1966-67; chief med. record adminstr. Schumpert Meml. Hosp., Shreveport, La., 1967-72; dir. med. records adminstr. program La. Tech. U., Ruston, 1972-82, dept. head, 1982—; mem. panel of accreditation surveyors Am. Health Info. Mgmt. Assn., 1985-93. Mem. La. Health Info. Mgmt. Assn. (pres. 1975, Disting. Mem. award 1990), Am. Health Info. Mgmt. Assn. (coun. on cert. 1981-83), N.E. La. Health Info. Mgmt. Assn. (edn. com. 1988-89), Quota Internat. of Ruston. Republican. Lutheran. Home: 3936 Hwy 818 Ruston LA 71270 Office: PO Box 3171 Tech Station Ruston LA 71272

STEBBINS, VRINA GRIMES, elementary school educator, counselor; b. Columbus, Ohio, Aug. 24, 1939; d. Marion Edward and Vrina Elizabeth (Davis) Grimes; m. Gary Frank Stebbins, Dec. 23, 1959; 1 child, Gregory Gary. Student, Ohio U., 1957-59; BS in Edn., Miami U., Oxford, Ohio, 1965; MS in Edn., St. Francis Coll., 1971; Counseling Endorsement, Ind.-Purdue U., Ft. Wayne, 1988. Cert. elem. educator K-6, sch. counselor, social worker, Ind. 1st grade tchr. Greenville (Ohio) Pub. Schs., 1963-68; elem. educator East Allen County Schs., New Haven, Ind., 1969-84; elem. sch. counselor East Allen County Schs., New Haven, 1984—; presenter at Ind. profl. orgns., 1985-92, 1st Presbyn. Ch., Ft. Wayne, 1984—, Project 2000, Ft. Wayne, 1992—; participant Bus.-Edn. Exchange, Ft. Wayne C. of C., 1993. Mem. ACA, Ind. Counseling Assn. (com. mem. 1992-93, Ind. Elem. Counselor of Yr. 1991), East Allen Educators' Assn. (chair com. 1989—, East Allen County Schs. Educator of Yr. 1989), Arts United, Phi Delta Kappa, Delta Kappa Gamma (participant leadership mgmt. seminar 1993, 1st v.p. Ind. state 1993—). Democrat. Presbyterian. Home: 5712 Sandra Lee Ave Fort Wayne IN 46819-1118 Office: Village Elem Sch 4625 Werling Dr Fort Wayne IN 46806-3493

STECKLER, JESSICA A., continuing nursing education educator; b. York, Pa., June 26, 1941; d. Edward A. and Mary Elizabeth (Hoffman) Debes; divorced; 1 child, Scott Edward. Diploma Sch. Nursing, Bryn Mawr (Pa.) Hosp., 1963; BS in Edn., Millersville State Coll., 1971; MEd, Gannon U., 1979; doctoral candidate in edn., Pa. State U., 1992. Cert. in staff devel., continuing edn., ANA; cert. in med. ethics consultation, U. W.Va. Instr. practical nursing York (Pa.) County Vocat.-Tech., 1966-73; instr. Sch. Nursing Hamot Med. Ctr., Erie, Pa., 1973-75; instr. nursing Behrend Coll. Pa. State U., Erie, 1989-92; assoc. dir. Erie VA Med. Ctr., 1981—, chairperson med. ethics com., 1988—. Mem. adv. com. for elimination of Tb, Erie County Dept. Health, 1991—; chair profl. edn. subcom. Erie County Diabetes Coalition. Recipient Recognition award for promoting excellence in evaluation in edn., Nat. Nursing Staff Devel. Orgn., 1994. Mem. Pa. Nurses Assn. Home: 6124 Washington Ave Erie PA 16509-2726

STECKLER, PHYLLIS BETTY, publishing company executive; b. N.Y.C.; d. Irwin H. and Bertha (Fellner) Schwartzbard; m. Stuart J. Steckler; children: Randall, Sharon Steckler-Slotky. BA, Hunter Coll.; MA, NYU. Editorial dir. R.R. Bowker Co., N.Y.C., Crowell Collier Macmillan Info. Pub. Co., N.Y.C., Holt Rinehart & Winston Info. Systems, N.Y.C.; pres., CEO Oryx Press, Scottsdale, Ariz., 1973-76, Phoenix, 1976—; adj. prof. history Ariz. State U., Tempe. Past chmn. Info. Industry Assn.; pres. Ariz. Ctr. for the Book; past pres. Friends of Librs., U.S.A.; mem. edn. adv. coun. Senator John McCain. Elected to Hunter Coll. Hall of Fame, 1985. Mem. ALA, Spl. Librs. Assn., Am. Soc. Info. Sci., Ariz. Libr. Assn., Phoenix Pub. Libr. Friends (bd. dirs.), Univ. Club of Phoenix (bd. dirs.). Home: 6711 E Camelback Rd Unit 32 Scottsdale AZ 85251-2065 Office: Oryx Press 4041 N Central at Indian School Rd Phoenix AZ 85012

STECKLING, ADRIENNE See ADRI, (ADRIENNE STECKLING)

STEED, RITA DIANA, counselor; b. Electra, Tex., June 22, 1947; d. Raymond J. and Reba Dean (Richardson) Lucas; m. Jack Lee Steed, July 13, 1968; children: William Daniel, Benjamin Joseph. BBA, Midwestern State U., 1969, counselor cert., 1986, mid-mgmt. cert., 1990; MEd, U. North Tex., 1983. Cert. tchr. high sch. bus., high sch. history, vocat. office edn., cert. vocat. supr., cert. counselor, cert. mid-mgmt. adminstr. Tchr. bus., history Byers (Tex.) Ind. Sch. Dist., 1969-78; tchr. vocat. studies Henrietta (Tex.) Ind. Sch. Dist., 1978-87, counselor K-12, 1987-90, counselor K-8, 1990-93, counselor 6-8, 1993—; presenter office edn. workshop, San Antonio, 1980; mem. planning com. essential elements for vocat. edn. HB 246 Curriculum Planning Workshop, Ft. Worth, 1982; mem. tchr. com. Tchr. Edn. Ctr., Midwestern State U., Wichita Falls, Tex., 1984-87; initiator PAL program and acad. intramural program Henrietta Ind. Sch. Dist., 1990, leader parent workshops, 1987, in-svc. presenter, 1986, 93; mem. chpt. 75 essential elements com. Tex. Edn. Agy., Austin, 1987; speaker in field various schs. and orgns. Vol. Wichita Falls State Hosp., 1986; mem. adv. bd. Clay County Outreach Ctr., 1987—, sec./treas.; deaconess, treas. 1st Christian Ch., Henrietta, 1992—. Mem. Tex. State Tchrs. Assn. (pres. Clay County local unit 1977-78, sec. Clay County local unit 1978-80, treas. Clay County local unit 1980-81, 81-82, pres. Clay County local unit 1985-86, 86-87, mem. audit com., profl. rights and responsibilities com. 1982-83), Assn. for Tex. Profl. Educators, Phi Delta Kappa (Texhoma chpt., Wichita Falls chpt.). Office: Henrietta Jr High 308 E Gilbert St Henrietta TX 76365-2802

STEEDMAN, DORIA LYNNE SILBERBERG, advertising agency executive; b. L.A.; d. Mendel B. and Dorothy H. (Howell) Silberberg; m. Richard Cantey Steedman, Feb. 19, 1966; 1 child, Alexandra Loren. BA summa cum laude, UCLA. Producer EUE/Screen Gems, N.Y.C., 1963-66, Jack Tinker & Ptnrs., N.Y.C., 1966-68, Telpac Mgmt., N.Y.C., 1968-72; v.p. broadcast prodn. Geer DuBois Adv., N.Y.C., 1973-78, acctg. mgr., dir. ops., 1979-92; exec. v.p., dir. creative devel. Partnership for a Drug-Free America, N.Y.C.,

1992—. Recipient Andy award Art Dirs. Club, 1968, 71; named one of 100 Best and Brightest Women in Advt., Advt. Age mag., 1988. Mem. Advt. Women N.Y. (pres. 1993-94), Phi Beta Kappa. Office: Partnership for a Drug-Free Am 405 Lexington Ave New York NY 10174-0100

STEEL, DANIELLE FERNANDE, author; b. N.Y.C., Aug. 14, 1947; d. John and Norma (Stone) Schuelein-Steel. Student, Parsons Sch. Design, 1963, NYU, 1963-67. Vice pres. pub. relations and new bus. Supergirls Ltd., N.Y.C., 1968-71; copywriter Grey Advt., San Francisco, 1973-74. Author novels Going Home, 1973, Passion's Promise, 1977, Now and Forever, 1978, The Promise, 1978, Season of Passion, 1979, Summers End, 1979, To Love Again, 1980, The Ring, 1981, Loving, 1980, Love, 1981, Remembrance, 1981, Palomino, 1981, Once in a Lifetime, 1982, Crossings, 1982, A Perfect Stranger, 1982, Thurston House, 1983, Changes, 1983, Full Circle, 1984, (non-fiction) Having A Baby, 1984, Family Album, 1985, Secrets, 1985, Wanderlust, 1986, Fine Things, 1987, Kaleidoscope, 1987, Zoya, 1988, Star, 1988, Daddy, 1989, Message from Nam, 1990, Heartbeat, 1991, No Greater Love, 1991, Jewels, 1992, Mixed Blessings, 1992, Vanished, 1993, Accident, 1994, The Gift, 1994, Wings, 1994; (children's) Martha's Best Friend, Martha's New School, Martha's New Daddy, Max's New Daddy, Max and The Babysitter, Max's Daddy Goes To The Hospital; contbr. poetry to mags., including Cosmopolitan, McCall's, Ladies Home Jour., Good Housekeeping. Home: PO Box 1637 New York NY 10156-1637 Office: 598 Madison Ave New York NY 10022-1614

STEEL, DAWN, motion picture producer; b. N.Y.C., Aug. 19; m. Charles Roven; 1 child, Rebecca. Student in mktg., Boston U., 1964-65, NYU, 1966-67. Sportswriter Major League Baseball Digest and NFL, N.Y.C., 1968-69; editor Penthouse Mag., N.Y.C., 1969-75; pres. Oh Dawn!, Inc., N.Y.C., 1975-78; v.p. merchandising, cons. Playboy mag., N.Y.C., 1978-79; v.p. merchandising Paramount Pictures, N.Y.C., 1979-80; v.p. prodn. Paramount Pictures, L.A., 1980-83, sr. v.p. prodn., 1983-85, pres. prodn., 1985-87; pres. Columbia Pictures, 1987-90; formed Steel Pictures (with Touchstone Pictures and Walt Disney Film & TV), 1990-94, Atlas Entertainment, 1994; mem. dean's adv. bd. UCLA Sch. Theater, Film, TV, 1993. First woman studio pres.; prodns. for Paramount include Flashdance, Footloose, Top Gun, Star Trek III, Beverly Hills Cop II, The Untouchables, The Accused, Fatal Attraction, 1985-87; prodns. for Columbia include Ghostbusters II, Karate Kid III, When Harry Met Sally, Look Who's Talking, Casualties of War, Postcards from the Edge, Flatliners, Awakenings; prodr. Steel Pictures for Disney: Honey, I Blew Up the Kid, 1992, Cool Runnings, 1993, Sister Act 2, 1993; prodr. (benefit concert) For Our Children, Pediatric AIDS Found., 1992; author: They Can Kill You, But They Can't Eat You, 1993. Appointeee Presdl. Commn. Scholars, 1993; mem. L.A. Mayor Richard Riordan's Transition Team, 1993, U.S. Del. to Winter Olympics, 1994; chair Mayor's Entertainment Industry Task Force, 1993; bd. dirs. Hollywood Supports, 1993. Recipient Women Film Crystal award Women in Film, 1989. Mem. Acad. Motion Picture Arts and Scis. Office: Atlas Entertainment 9169 Sunset Blvd Los Angeles CA 90069

STEEL, KUNIKO JUNE, artist; b. San Francisco, June 3, 1929; d. Jirohei and Moriyo (Shiraishi) Nakamura; m. John Schulein-Steel, Jan. 26, 1963 (dec. May 1978). Student, U. Calif., 1948-49; diploma, Am. Acad. Art, Chgo., 1951; student, Academic Julian, Paris, 1952-53, Art Inst. Chgo., 1954-55, Art Students League, N.Y.C., 1959-62, 79-85. Exhibited in group shows at Rafilson Gallery, Chgo., 1954, Arts of N.E., Silvermine, Conn., 1966, 79, 90, 92, Modern Maturity Traveling Exhibit, 1990-92, Schoharie Exhibit, Cobleskill, N.Y., 1993-94, Mus. of Modern Art, Miami, Coral Gables, Fla., 1993, 37th Chautaqua Nat. Exhibit of Am. Art, 1994, Montclair State U., 1994. Vol., crafts tchr. Hosp. for Spl. Surgery, N.Y.C., 1967-84; vol. Japanese Gallery Met. Mus., 1994; past vol. costume conservation Met. Mus., N.Y.C., 1979-94. Recipient scholarship Palo Alto Quota Club, 1948, Art Students League, 1960. Mem. N.Y. Artists Equity.

STEELE, ANA MERCEDES, government official; b. Niagara Falls, N.Y., Jan. 18, 1939; d. Sydney and Mercedes (Hernandez) S.; m. John Hunter Clark, June 2, 1979. AB magna cum laude, Marywood Coll., 1958. Actress, 1959-64; sec. Nat. Endowment for Arts, Washington, 1965-67, dir. budget and research, 1968-75, dir. planning, 1976-78, dir. program coordination, sr. exec. service, 1979-81, assoc. dep. chmn. for programs, dir. program coordination, sr. exec. service, 1982-93, acting chmn., acting sr. dep. chmn., 1993, sr. dep. chmn., sr. exec. svc., 1993—; guest lectr. George Washington U., 1987; trustee Marywood Coll., 1989—. Author, editor report: History of the National Council on the Arts and National Endowment for the Arts During the Johnson Administration, 1968; editor: Museums USA (Fed. Design Council award of Excellence 1975), 1974; National Endowment Arts 1965-1985; A Brief Chronology of Federal Involvement in the Arts, 1985. Former reader Rec. for the Blind, N.Y.C.; former tutor Future for Jimmy, Washington. Named Disting. Grad. in Field of Arts, Marywood Coll., 1976; recipient Sustained Superior Performance award Nat. Endowment for Arts, Washington, 1980, Disting. Service award, 1983, 84, 85, 89, 92. Mem. Actors' Equity Assn., Screen Actors Guild, Delta Epsilon Sigma, Kappa Gamma Pi. Office: Nat Endowment for Arts Nancy Hanks Ctr 1100 Pennsylvania Ave NW Washington DC 20506-0001

STEELE, BRENDA LOU, food service director; b. Lebanon, Pa., July 24, 1950; d. Paul A. Jr. and Edith E. (Birch) Hummel; m. Floyd A. Steele, Jr., Apr. 17, 1971; children: Paul, Dustin, Braden. Diploma, Career Acad., Washington, 1970. Asst. mgr. Wendy's, Lebanon, 1980-87, shift supr., 1991-92; food svc. dir. Svc. Am. Mgmt., Lebanon, 1980-87, Hallmark Mgmt., Lebanon, 1988-89, Pine Grove (Pa.) Area Sch. Dist., 1992—. Jr. choir dir. Zion Evang. Congl. Ch., Annville, Pa., 1990—; chair post prom entrance com. Lebanon High Sch., 1993. Mem. Am. Sch. Food Svc. Assn., PASBO. Democrat. Office: Pine Grove Area Sch Dist School St Pine Grove PA 17963

STEELE, ELIZABETH MEYER, lawyer; b. San Mateo, Calif., Jan. 12, 1952; d. Bailey Robert and Kathryn Steele (Horrigan) Meyer; m. Gene Dee Fowler, Aug. 9, 1975 (div. Apr. 1985); 1 child, Steele Sternberg. BA, Kirkland Coll., 1974; JD, U. N.Mex., 1977. Counsel U.S. Dept. Energy, Los Alamos, N.Mex., 1977-78; law clk. to judge Howard C. Bratton U.S. Dist. Ct., Albuquerque, 1978-80; assoc. Davis, Graham & Stubbs, Denver, 1980-84, ptnr., 1985-87; v.p., gen. counsel Jones Intercable, Inc., Englewood, Colo., 1987—. Office: Jones Intercable Inc 9697 E Mineral Ave Englewood CO 80112-3408

STEELE, HILDA BERNEICE HODGSON, farm manager, retired home economics supervisor; b. Wilmington, Ohio, Mar. 24, 1911; d. George Sanders and Mary Jane (Rolston) Hodgson; m. John C. Steele, Aug. 10, 1963 (dec. Jan. 1973). BS, Wilmington Coll., 1935; MA, Ohio State U., 1941; postgrad., Ohio U., 1954, Miami U., Oxford, Ohio, 1959. Cert. elem. and high sch. gen. tchr. and vocat. supr., Ohio. Part-time tchr. Wilmington Pub. Schs., Midland Elem. Sch., 1931-32; tchr. Brookville (Ohio) Pub. Schs., 1932-37, Dayton (Ohio) Pub. Schs., Lincoln Jr. High Sch., 1937-40; tchr. practical arts, coord. home econs. Dayton Pub. Schs., 1940-45, supr. home econs., 1945-81; mgr. Steele's Farm, Xenia, Ohio, 1972—; mem. home econs. adv. com. Cen. State U., Wilburforce, Ohio, 1941-92, Miami Valley Hosp. Nursing Sch., Dayton, 1951-63; mem. adv. bd. Dayton Sch. Practical Nursing, 1951-92. Mem. adv. com. Montomery County ARC, Dayton, 1940-80; mem. town and country career com. Miami Valley Br. YMCA, Dayton, 1948-59; mem. Ohio Electrification Com., Dayton, 1964-66; mem. corp. com. United Way, Dayton, 1970—; chmn. home econs. adv. com. Ohio Vets. Children Home, 1987—; bd. dirs. Ohio Future Homemakers of Am.-Home Econs. Related Occupations, Columbus, 1979-81. Recipient Outstanding Contbns. award Girls Scouts U.S., 1987, Appreciation award Dayton Practical Nursing Program, 1989; named Ohio Vocat. Educator of the Yr., 1981. Mem. Nat. Ohio Edn. Assn., Am. Home Econs. Assn. (Appreciation award 1990), Am. Vocat. Assn., Ohio Home Econs. Assn. (mem. various com., Friend of Family award 1994), Ohio Vocat. Assn. (life), Ohio Dist. C Home Econs. Assn., Ohio Ret. Tchrs. Assn. (life), Montgomery County Ret. Tchrs. Assn., Dayton Pub. Schs. Adminstrv. Assn., Met. Home Econs. Assn. (pres. 1949-50, 60-61), Greene County Landmark Assn., U.S. C. of C., Phi Upsilon Omicron (hon.), Ea. Star, Zonta (pres. Dayton chpt. 1950-52). Mem. Ch. of Christ. Home: 1443 State Rte 380 Xenia OH 45385-9789

STEELE, JANET FRANCES, mental health services administrator; b. Salt Lake City, Feb. 1, 1947; d. William F. Stockdale and Bernita J. (Beck) Stockdale Fisk; m. Richard L. Baughman, July 12, 1971 (div. Jan. 1978); m. Dorman L. Steele, Nov. 12, 1983; children: Steven C., Christine C. Banks. BBA, U. Calif., Bakersfield, 1968. Asst. mgr. Assn. Gen. Contractors, Fairbanks, Alaska, 1977-86; dir. pers. and risk mgmt. City of Fairbanks, 1986-89; adminstr. Sutter-Yuba Mental Health, Yuba City, Calif., 1989—; v.p. bd. Tanana Valley C.C., Fairbanks, 1983-89. Chmn. Alaska R.R. Labor Rels. Bd., Anchorage, 1984-85; pres. Pvt. Industry Coun., Fairbanks, 1985. Mem. Am. Arbitration Assn., Am. Soc. Safety Engrs. Democrat. Home: 1680 Magnolia Dr Yuba City CA 95991

STEELE, KAREN KIARSIS, state legislator; b. Haverhill, Mass., Sept. 26, 1942; d. Victor and Barbara (McFee) Kiarsis; m. Edward E. Steele, Apr. 16, 1966; children: Shawn Robert, Gretchen Garvey. BA, U. Vt., 1964. Tchr. Waterbury Sch. System, 1964-65, Burlington (Vt.) Sch. System, 1965-67; legislator State of Vt., Montpelier, 1982—. Trustee Cen. Vt. Hosp., Berlin. Mem. Am. Legis. Exch. Coun. (nat. chmn. healthcare task force). Republican. Home: RR 2 Box 796 Waterbury VT 05676-9713 Office: State House Montpelier VT 05602

STEELE, KATHLEEN FRANCES, federal official; b. Kansas City, Mo., Oct. 28, 1960. Admissions counselor N.E. Mo. State U., Kirksville, 1980-83, assoc. dir. admissions, 1983-86, programming coord. dept. pub. svcs., 1986-87; Iowa, N.H. dir. Gephardt for Pres., St. Louis, 1987-88; mem. Mo. Ho. of Reps., Jefferson City, 1988-94; state dir. Clinton for Pres., 1991-92; regional dir. U.S. Dept. Health and Human Svcs., Kansas City, Mo., 1994—; chair Freshman Dem. Caucus, 1989, chair sci., tech. and critical issues com. Bd. dirs. Adair County chpt. ARC, 1987. Recipient Young Careerist award Kirksville Bus. and Profl. Women, 1988. Mem. Nat. Order Women Legislators, Women Legislators of Mo. (pres. 1989-92). Roman Catholic. Home: 6 Nantucket Ct Smithville MO 64089 Office: US Dept Health and Human Svcs 601 E 12th St Room 210 Kansas City MO 64106

STEELE, REBECCA ELIZABETH, insurance company administrator; b. Richlands, Va., May 17, 1949; d. Charlie Shade and Helen Elizabeth (Witt) S. BBA, East Tenn. State U., 1971. Cert. profl. ins. woman Nat. Assn. Ins. Women Internat. Uderwriting trainee State Farm Ins. Co., Charlottesville, Va., 1973-75, underwriter, 1975-77, sr. underwriter, 1977-87, underwriting specialist, 1987-91, personal lines supr., 1991—. Vol. Am. Cancer Soc., Charlottesville and Fredericksburg, Va., 1992, 93, 94, Winter Spl. Olympics, Charlottesville, 1994, Am. Heart Assn., Charlottesville and Fredericksburg, 1992-95; vol. Multiple Sclerosis skiathon Charlottesville, 1991, 92, 93, Ronald McDonald Ho., 1994. Mem. Nat. Assn. Ins. Women (chairperson state pub. rels. 1993-94, 94-95), Ins. Women Charlottesville/Albemerle (pres. pub. rels. 1991-93, Ins. Woman of Yr. award 1993), Ins. Inst. Am., East Tenn. State U. Alumni Club, Va. 4-H All Stars, Toastburners Toastmasters Club (sgt. at arms 1990, Competent Toastmaster award 1994). Republican. Methodist. Office: State Farm Ins Co 1500 State Farm Blvd Chrltsvle VA 22909-0001

STEELE, SANDRA ELAINE NOEL, nursing educator; b. Warren, Pa., May 8, 1939; d. Cecil Harry Johnson and Romaine Mae (Goodwin) Hamblin; children: Lynne Cerise, William Leslie. Diploma in nursing, Allegheny Gen. Hosp., 1961; postgrad., City U., Bellevue, Wash., 1988-89, Bus. Computer Tng. Inst., 1994. RN. Wash.; CNOR. Staff nurse oper. rm. Allegheny Gen. Hosp., Pitts., 1961-62, Dr.'s Hosp., Seattle, 1962-66; staff nurse immunization clinic Snohomish County Health Dept., Everett, Wash., 1969-77; staff nurse oper. rm. Gen. Hosp. Med. Ctr., Everett, 1977-82, clin. educator surg. svcs., 1982-93; patient coord. Cascade Regional Eye Ctr., Marysville, 1993-94; nursing educator Cascade Valley Hosp., Arlington, Wash., 1994—; cons. Reed, McClure, Moceri, Thonn and Moriarty Legal Firm, Seattle, 1989—. Pres. Tulalip Elem. Sch. PTSA, Marysville, Wash., 1974-76, pres. Marysville PTSA Coun., 1976-80; leader Campfire Girls, Marysville, 1972-76; bd. dirs. N.W. Laser Network, Seattle, 1988-90. Recipient Outstanding Svc. award Washington State PTSA, 1974, Goledn Acorn award Marysville PTSA Coun., 1979, People Taking Significant Action award Marysville PTSA, 1978. Mem. Assn. Operating Rm. Nurses. Lutheran. Home: 418 Priest Point Dr NW Marysville WA 98271-6823

STEELMAN, SARA GERLING, state legislator; b. Wichita, Kans., Apr. 24, 1946; d. Paul Henry and Amy (Gessner) Gerling; m. John Henry Steelman; 1 child, Amy. BS in Zoology, U. Chgo., 1967; PhD in Behavior Genetics, Stanford U., 1976. Instr. dept. psychology No. Ill. U., DeKalb, 1974-75; instr. Fullerton (Calif.) Jr. Coll., 1976-80; postdoctoral fellow dept. psychobiology U. Calif., Irvine, 1976-80; asst. prof. dept. biology Skidmore Coll., Saratoga Springs, N.Y., 1980-83; freelance copy editor Saratoga, N.Y., 1983-86; staff writer Saratogian, Saratoga Springs, 1983-86; freelance copy editor Indiana, Pa., 1987-90; contbg. writer Indiana Gazette, 1987-93; elected mem. Pa. Ho. of Reps., Harrisburg, 1990—. Contbr. articles to sci. publs. Co-chair com. on women in politics Pitts. Inst. Politics, 1993—. Rsch. fellow Nat. Inst. Aging, 1979-80. Mem. AAUW (notable Woman 1991), Peace Links Indiana Country (bd. dirs. 1986-91), Indiana Symphony Soc. (bd. dirs. 1992—), Mental Health Assn. (bd. dirs. 1992-93), Pa. Farmers Bur., LWV, Zonta. Democrat. Office: The Atrium 665 Philadelphia St Indiana PA 15701-3929

STEEN, JULIE ANN, medical surgical nurse; b. Findlay, Ohio, Apr. 22, 1953; d. James N. and Martha Jane (Slupe) S. AD, Lourdes Coll., 1977; diploma in nursing with honors, St. Vincent Hosp., 1978; BSN cum laude, U. Toledo, 1983; MSN, Wayne State U., 1990. RN, Mich., Ohio; CCRN, ACLS, CPR instr. Staff nurse maternal child care St. Vincent Med. Ctr., Toledo, Ohio, 1978-79; clin. nurse specialist pulmonary critical care St. Vincent's Med. Ctr., Toledo, 1990-93; staff nurse ICU Providence Hosp., Southfield, Mich., 1979-81; staff nurse Mercy Hosp., Toledo, 1981-87, charge nurse, 1987-89, nurse clinician, project cons., 1989-90; instr. Owens Tech. Coll., Toledo, 1984-86; visiting nurse Caring Cert. Svcs., Toledo, 1986-89; medical-surgical clin. nurse specialist Flower Hosp., Sylvania, Ohio, 1993—; presenter, researcher in field. Vol. Kidney Found. N.W. Ohio, Mercy Hosp. Health Fair, Mercy Hosp. Fair, ARC; del. People to People Internat., Russia and Hungary, 1992. Mem. ANA, AACN (bd. dirs. Greater Toledo Area chpt., pres. 1992-93), Respiratory Nursing Soc., Ohio Nurses Assn., Toledo Dist. Ohio Nurses Assn., Wayne State Alumnae Assn., Med. Coll. of Ohio Alumnae Assn., U. Toledo Alumnae Assn., St. Vincent's Hosp. Sch. Nursing Alumnae Assn., Sigma Theta Tau. Office: Flower Hosp 5200 Hanoun Rd Sylvania OH 43560

STEEN, SARA JANE, editor; b. N.Y.C., Jan. 20, 1963; d. Ivan D. and Gail A. (Cohen) S. BA, NYU, 1985. Assoc. editor Gale Rsch., N.Y.C., 1987-90; editor/mgr. Inst. Internat. Edn., N.Y.C., 1990—. NYU Presdl. scholar, 1981-85. Democrat. Office: Inst Internat Edn 809 United Nations Pla New York NY 10017

STEEN, SUSAN JANE, neurologist; b. Phila., Mar. 9, 1952; d. William James and Mildred (Bean) S.; m. Dominick Joseph Graziano, Oct. 27, 1990; children: Leigh Adrienne, Alexander Gaetano. BS, Fla. State U., 1974; MD, U. Fla., 1978. Resident in internal medicine U. S. Fla., Tampa, 1978-80; resident in neurology U. Fla., Gainesville, 1980-83; pvt. practice Neurology Assocs., Tampa, 1983—; cons. neurologist Tampa Gen. Hosp., St. Joseph's Hosp., Meml. Hosp., Charter Hosp., Women's Hosp. Ethics com. Tampa Gen. Hosp., 1992—. Recipient Barbara McNerney award Epilepsy Found. Am., 1993. Mem. AMA, Am. Acad. Neurology, Am. Women's Med. Assn., So. EEG Soc., Fla. Med. Assn., Hillsborough County Med. Assn. Methodist. Office: Neurology Assocs 2919 W Swann Ave Tampa FL 33609-4038

STEENBURGEN, MARY, actress; b. Newport, Ariz., 1953; m. Malcolm McDowell, 1980 (div.); children: Lilly, Charlie. Student, Neighborhood Playhouse. Films: Goin' South, 1978, Time After Time, 1979, Melvin and Howard, 1980 (Academy Award, Best Supporting Actress), Ragtime, 1981, A Midsummer Night's Sex Comedy, 1982, Cross Creek, 1983, Romantic Comedy, 1983, One Magic Christmas, 1985, Dead of Winter, 1987, End of the Line, 1987 (also exec. prodr.), The Whales of August, 1987, Miss Firecracker, 1989, Parenthood, 1989, Back to the Future III, 1990, The Long Walk Home, 1990 (narrator), The Butcher's Wife, 1991, Philadelphia, 1993, What's Eating Gilbert Grape, 1993, Clifford, 1994, It Runs in the Family, 1994, Pontiac Moon, 1994; appeared in Showtime TV's Faerie Tale Theatre prodn. of Little Red Riding Hood and (miniseries) Tender Is the Night, 1985; TV films: The Attic: The Hiding of Anne Frank, 1988; theater appearances include: Holiday, Old Vic, London, 1987, Candida, Broadway, 1993. Office: William Morris Agy Inc 151 El Camino Beverly Hills CA 90212*

STEENECK, REGINA AULTICE, information systems specialist; d. Albert M. Aultice and Hilda M. (Fields) Smith; m. Lee R. Steeneck; children: Bradley, Darren. BA, Va. Poly. Inst., 1970. Programmer AT&T Long Lines, White Plains, N.Y., 1970-71, So. New Engl. Telephone Co., New Haven, 1971-72; systems specialist Aetna Life and Casualty, Hartford, Conn., 1972-76; systems analyst and programmer Miles Labs., West Haven, Conn., 1976-77; cons. Blue Cross/Blue Shield Conn., North Haven, 1978-79; account mgr. AGS Computers, Inc., Mountainside, N.J., 1977-79; systems cons. Comm. Design Corp., Stamford, Conn., 1986-89; sr. CICS programmer Westinghouse Comm. Software, Stamford, Conn., 1989-90, systems cons., 1990-92; sys. cons. Comware Sys. Inc., Stamford, 1993-94; systems cons. RAS Assocs., Trumbull, Conn., 1979—; co-owner Sunshine Flowers, 1980-81. Bd. dirs., fin. sec., chmn. computer com., vacation Bible Sch. supt., memls. com. chmn., women's soc. sec. Holy Cross Luth. Ch., 1979—. Mem. AAUW, Trumbull Parents Children with Spl. Needs (mem. adv. bd.), Conn. Assn. for Children with Learning Disabilities (bd. dirs., treas.), Fairfield Network Exec. Women (bd. dirs., treas. 1992-94), Assn. Computing Machinery, Trumbull Jr. Woman's Club (bd. dirs. 1980-88, 1st v.p., newspaper editor, other coms.), Conn. Jr. Women's Club (bd. dirs., newsletter editor, Dist. VIII rep.). Lutheran. Home: 211 Putting Green Rd Trumbull CT 06611-2504

STEERE, ANNE BULLIVANT, retired student advisor; b. Phila., July 27, 1921; d. Stuart Lodge and Elizabeth MacCuen (Smith) B.; m. Richard M. H. Harper Jr., Nov. 14, 1942 (div. Oct. 1967); children: Virginia Harper Kliever, Richard M. H. Harper III, Patricia Harper Flint, Stuart Lodge Harper, Lucy Steere, Grace Steere; m. Bruce Middleton Steere, July 5, 1968. BS in Sociology, So. Meth. U., 1978, M in Liberal Arts, 1985. Asst. to dir. Harvard Law Sch. Fund, Cambridge, Mass., 1958-68; advisor to older students So. Meth. U., Dallas, 1976-85. Contbr. articles to profl. jours. Trustee, Pine Manor Coll., Chestnut Hill, Mass., 1983—; bd. dirs. Planned Parenthood, Dallas, 1975-85. Mem. New Eng. Hist. and Geneal. Soc., Alpha Kappa Delta. Episcopalian. Clubs: Chilton (Boston); Jr. League. Avocations: reading, needlepoint, sailing. Home: 1177 N Lake Way Palm Beach FL 33480 also: 44 Snow Inn Rd Harwich Port MA 02646-2414

STEFANE, CLARA JOAN, business education secondary educator; b. Trenton, N.J., Apr. 8; d. Joseph and Rose M. (Bonfanti) Raymond; m. John E. Stefane, July 19, 1975. BS in Bus. Adminstrn., Georgian Ct. Coll., Lakewood, N.J., 1968. Cert. tchr. gen. bus. and secretarial studies, N.J. Tchr. bus. Camden Cath. High Sch., Cherry Hill, N.J., 1960-68, Cathedral High Sch., Trenton, 1970-72; tchr., bus., chair dept. McCorristin Cath. High Sch., Trenton, 1972—; mem. Mercer County Task Force for Bus. Edn., Trenton, 1989-90. Sustaining mem. Rep. Nat. Com.; del. mem. 1992 Presdl. Trust; mem. Rosary Altar Soc., Incarnation Ch. Named Tchr. of Yr., The Cittone Inst., Princeton, N.J., 1991. Mem. ASCD, N.J. Bus. Edn. Assn., Nat. Cath. Edn. Assn., Sisters of Mercy of the Ams. (assoc.). Roman Catholic. Home: 278 Weber Ave Trenton NJ 08638-3638 Office: McCorristin Cath High Sch 175 Leonard Ave Trenton NJ 08610-4807

STEFANICK, PATTI ANN, surgeon; b. Linden, N.J., Sept. 25, 1957; d. John Joseph and Johanna (Breza) S. BA in Biol. Scis., Rutgers U., 1979; DO, U. New England, 1983. Intern Kennedy Meml. Hosps., Stratford, N.J., 1983-84; resident in gen. surgery, chief resident Met. Hosp., Phila., 1984-88; breast cancer fellow Meml. Sloan-Kettering Cancer Ctr., N.Y.C., 1988-89; pvt. practice breast diagnostic surgery Johnstown, Pa., 1989—. Bd. dirs. Cambria County divsn. Am. Cancer Soc., 1993-94, v.p., 1994-96. Named Woman of Yr., Johnstown YWCA, 1994. Mem. AMA, Am. Osteo. Assn., N.J. Assn. Osteo. Physicians and Surgeons (alumni com. 1988-89), Pa. Osteo Med. Assn., Cambria County Med. Soc. (v.p. 1992-93, pres.-elect 1993-94, pres. 1994—), Rutgers Alumni Assn., Rutger's Scarlet R Club. Republican. Roman Catholic. Office: 939 Menoher Blvd Johnstown PA 15905-2838

STEFANICS, ELIZABETH T. (LIZ STEFANICS), state legislator. BA, Eastern Ky. U.; MS, U. Wis.; PhD, U. Minn. Mem. N.Mex. Senate; mem. conservation com., judiciary com., chmn. health and human svcs. com., adminstr. health and human svcs. Democrat. Address: PO Box 1301 Santa Fe NM 87504-6127 Office: N Mex State Senate State Capitol New Mexico State Capitol NM 87503*

STEFANIK, JANET RUTH, realtor; b. Harrisville, W.Va., Apr. 25, 1938; d. John Jackson Jr. and Helen Virginia (Waller) D.; m. Robert John Stefanik, Oct. 13, 1956 (div. Apr. 1977); children: Robert Mark, Deborah Ruth, Perry Wayne, David Lee, Susan Irene. Grad., Midview High Sch., Grafton, Ohio; student, Lorain County Community Coll., Elyria, Ohio, 1982, 85, 90-91. Salesperson Demby Real Estate, Elyria, 1970-71, Schwed Real Estate, Elyria, 1971—; mem. women's coun. Lorain County Bd. Realtors, 1971-74, past pres., 1974. Toll collector Ohio Turnpike Commn., 1975. Mem. Gibson Girls Variety Chorale Group, Nat. Arbor Day Found., AARP. Republican. Roman Catholic. Home: P O Box 1556 Elyria OH 44036

STEFANKO, KAREN ANN, financial analyst; b. Pitts., Mar. 26, 1966; d. Eric Everett and Margaret Mary (Roman) S. BBA in Fin., U. Notre Dame, 1988; MBA in Mktg., Temple U., 1990. Capital analyst McNeil Pharm. divsn. Johnson & Johnson Co., Spring House, Pa., 1988-90; sr. fin. auditor, auditor Johnson & Johnson Co., New Brunswick, N.J., 1990-93; sr. fin. analyst, contract analysis and erosion Ethicon Endo-Surgery divsn. Johnson & Johnson, Blue Ash, Ohio, 1993—. Tutor Adult Literacy Network, Cin., 1993. Mem. Inst. Mgmt. Accts., Inst. Internal Auditors, Mensa. Office: Ethicon Endo-Surgery 4545 Creek Rd Cincinnati OH 45242-2803

STEFANOU, KATERINA, pharmacist; b. N.Y., May 11, 1965; d. George and Nadia (Choroneko) Fedoriw; m. Demos Stefanou, Aug. 19, 1990. BS, St. John's U., 1988. Reg. pharmacist. Clerk Westbridge Pharmacy, Richmond Hill, N.Y., 1982-84, Dale Chemists Pharmacy, Richmond Hill, 1985-86; pharmacy intern Genovese, Glendale, N.Y., 1986-88; pharmacist Genovese, Baldwin, N.Y., 1988-92; supervising pharmacist Genovese, Oceanside, N.Y., 1992—; vol. St. John's Hosp., Rego Park, N.Y., 1979; blood pressure screener Genovese Health Fair, Wantagh, N.Y., 1994, rep. Uniondale, N.Y. TV commercial spokesperson Genovese Drugs, 1994, model cover advertisement, 1994. Home: 18 Euclid Ave Massapequa NY 11758

STEFENSON, EVA, advertising agency executive; b. London, Eng.; d. Julius and Sofia Pietrzak Von Habdank; m. Dana Stefenson, Oct. 27, 1985; 1 child, Audrey Caulfield Stefenson. BA in Advtg. & Graphic Design, Iowa State U.; postgrad. work in Painting, Acad. de Pitta, Florence, Italy. Assoc. art dir. Meredith Pub. Co., Des Moines, Iowa, 1976-81; sr. art dir. Conrans, N.Y.C., 1981-84; art dir. Clinque, N.Y.C., 1984-87; creative dir. Liz Claiborne, N.Y.C., 1987-90; ptnr., pres., creative dir. Calman & Stefenson, N.Y.C., 1990—; cons. art direction Ann Taylor, N.Y.C., 1990-91; design cons. Coach Leatherware, N.Y.C., 1990-91. Editor Fine Arts Calendar, 1993 (Creativity award 1994). Co-chair benefit com. Cancer Rsch. Inst., N.Y.C., 1994—. Recipient Daisy award Seventeen Magazine, 1969, 1st place Student Cosmetic Design, Clairol, N.Y.C., 1969. Fellow Mus. Modern Art; mem. Am. Inst. Graphic Artists (pkg. and corp. identity awards 1990. 91, 93), Internat. Ctr. of Photography. Democrat.

STEFFE, NANCY ELIZABETH, publisher, copywriter, business consultant; b. Mansfield, Mo., Dec. 12, 1959; d. David Louis II and Carolyn Joyce (Padgett) S. Owner Tech. on Paper, Orlando, 1991—; pub. Show Your Stuff, Orlando, 1993—; instr. Knowledge Shop, Winter Park, Fla., 1993—. Author, editor, pub.: Business at Home, 1993, (booklet) In-House Publishing, 1993, Effective Newsletters and Brochures, 1994, (newsletter) Show Your Stuff, 1993—. Mem. Orlando Humane Soc., 1993—, Ctrl. Fla. Zool. Soc., Orlando, 1993—, Wildlife Waystation, 1993—. Recipient Design award Microsoft, 1992. Mem. NAFE, Nat. Assn. Desktop Pubs. (mem. help line 1993—, Honorable Mention Design award 1993), Assn. of Corel Artists and Designers, Windows Prepub. Assn. (charter), Ctrl. Fla. Computer Soc., Greater Orlando C. of C. Republican. Roman Catholic. Office: Tech on Paper 805 W Harvard St Orlando FL 32804-5203

STEFFEN, PAMELA BRAY, secondary school educator; b. Bessemer, Ala., Mar. 9, 1944; d. James Ernest and Margaret Virginia (Parsons) Bray; m. Ted N. Steffen, June 17, 1972; children: Elizabeth, Thor. BA, U. Louisville, 1966; MA, Spalding U., 1975. Cert. tchr., gifted tchr., Ky. Tchr. English and German Louisville (Ky.) Pub. Schs., 1967-73; tchr. English to fgn. students Internat. Ctr., U. Louisville, 1970-78; bookkeeper T.N. Steffen PSC, Louisville, 1978-85; tchr. of adults Jefferson County Pub. Schs., Louisville, 1985-87, tchr. English and German, 1987—; network participant, bd. dirs. Foxfire, Louisville, 1990—; spokesperson Coalition Essential Schs., Providence, 1990—, Ctr. for Leadership in Sch. Reform, Louisville, 1990—; group leader AAUW, Louisville, 1983-88; presenter seminars; 94 AATG summer Austrian Inst. Graz. Bd. dirs. Jefferson County Med. Soc. Aux., Louisville, 1984-88, Highland Community Ministries, Louisville, 1980-87, Highland Ct. Apts. for Elderly, Louisville, 1984-87; nat. v.p. Deafness Rsch. Found. Aux., 1984-88; mem. vestry and rector search com. St. Andrew's Episcopal Ch., Louisville, 1985-88; active Louisville Fund for Arts campaign, 1980-93; Louisville Orch. Assn. fundraiser. Fulbright fellow Goethe Inst., Munich, 1969; grantee Ky. Arts Coun., 1991-92, artist-in-residence, 1992—; grantee Ky. Humanities Coun. CES, 1993, fall forum presenter; named to Ky.'s Commonwealth Inst. Tchrs. and Vis. Tchrs. Inst.; selected for Landeskunde in Österreich, 1994. Mem. ASCD, Nat. Coun. Tchrs. English, Coalition Essential Sch., Nat. Coun. Tchrs. English, Greater Louisville Coun. Tchrs. English, Am. Assn. Tchrs. German. Home: 2404 Park Boundary Rd Louisville KY 40205-1620 Office: Fairdale High Sch 1001 Fairdale Rd Fairdale KY 40118-9744

STEFFEN, TINA MARIE, journalist, home economist; b. Amarillo, Tex., Apr. 10, 1958; d. Lynn Troy and Mary Lou (Odell) Bavousett; m. Gary Edgar Steffen, June 6, 1981; 1 child, Christopher Michael. Student, Sam Houston State U., 1976-78; BS in Home Econs., Tex. Tech U., 1981. Cert. home economist. Lifestyle writer Big Spring (Tex.) Herald, 1981-82, lifestyle editor, 1982-85, dir. creative svcs., 1985-86; reporter edn. beat Daily Ardmoreite, Ardmore, Okla., 1987; freelance writer home econs. reference books and curriculum guides Tex. Edn. Agy. and Tex. Tech U. Home Econs. Curriculum Ctr., Lubbock, Tex., 1987-89; feature writer, fashion editor, Lifestyle writer Lubbock Avalanche-Jour., 1989-91; communications writer Ft. Worth Ind. Sch. Dist., 1991-92; asst. editor spl. features Fort Worth Star-Telegram, 1992—; editor Abode mag. Impact Publs., Ft. Worth, 1993-94. Author: Hospitality Services, 1990; co-author: Apparel and Textiles Production, Management and Services, 1990; contbr. numerous articles to newspapers and mags. Mem. Am. Home Econs. Assn., Soc. Profl. Journalists, Tex. Press Women (treas. dist. 14 1990-91, state scholarship dir. 1991-93, numerous writing awards), Nat. Fedn. Press Women (1st Pl. Writing award 1990), Women in Comms., Inc. (chair freedom of info com. 1990-91, Communicator of Yr. 1991). Mem. Christian Ch. Home: 6316 Whitman Fort Worth TX 76133 Office: Ft Worth Star-Telegram 400 W 7th St Fort Worth TX 76102

STEFFENHAGEN, TERRI LYNN, purchasing executive; b. Madison, Wis., Aug. 12, 1957; d. Arthur Eugene and Barbara Jean (Peterson) S. BS in Bus. Adminstrn., Carroll Coll., 1979. Sr. buyer Allis Chalmers, West Allis, Wis., 1979-84; sr. buyer Waukesha (Wis.) Engine, 1985-90, adv. materials planning analyst, 1991, internat. analyst, 1992-93, internat. facilitator, sr. buyer, 1994—; tchr. quality edn. sys. Waukesha Engine, 1994—. Loan exec. United Way, Waukesha, 1993, mem. allocations bd., 1994. Mem. Milw. World Trade Assn., Milw. Assn. Purchasing Agents. Office: Waukesha Engine Divsn Dresser Industries 1000 W St Paul Ave Waukesha WI 53187

STEFFENS, DOROTHY RUTH, political economist; b. N.Y.C., May 5, 1921; d. Saul M. and Pearl Y. (Reiter) Cantor; m. Jerome Steffens, Nov. 19, 1940; children: Heidi Sue, Nina Ellen. BBA, CCNY, 1941; MEd, Temple U., 1961; PhD, Anthony U., 1981. Economist Nat. War Labor Bd., Washington, 1941-44, United Elec. Radio Machine Workers, Phila., 1944-46; instr. group dynamics Temple U., Phila., 1955-57; seminar program dir. Soc. Friends, Washington, 1958-61; tng. dir. Nat. Coun. Negro Women, Washington, 1967-68; edn. cons. Peace Corps, Nigeria, 1969-70; exec. dir. Women's Internat. League for Peace and Freedom, Phila., 1971-77, Fund for Open Info. and Accountability, Inc., 1978-80; conf. dir. Haverford Coll., 1980-84; exec. sec. Nigerian Women's Com., 1968-69; del. African Women's Seminar UN, Accra, Ghana, 1969; mem. Africa panel Am. Friends Svc. Com., 1976-88, mem. internat. divsn. exec. com., 1977-84; resource lectr. Internat. Women's Seminar, Lillehammer, Norway, 1991. Author: The Day after Summer, 1966; editorial bd. The Churchman, 1977—; mem. nat. bd. Gray Panthers, 1989-91; contbr. articles to profl. jours., newspapers, mags. N.Y. C. of C. scholar, N.Y. State Regents scholar CCNY, 1941. Quaker.

STEFFENS, KAREN LEE MIERS, school counselor; b. Michigan City, Ind., Sept. 26, 1944; d. William August Howard and Pearl Adeline (Parren) Wennerberg; m. Dale Eugene Steffens, June 29, 1974; children: Gabriel Josef, Jesse Catherine. BA, Western Mich. U., 1968; MA, Roosevelt U., 1994. Tchr. Tilton Sch., Chgo., 1969-75; realtor Century 21 Frank Tierney, Lake Zurich, Ill., 1987-89; tchr. Key Sch., Chgo., 1977-80, tchr. gifted edn., coord., 1981-84, head tchr., coord., 1985-87, head fine arts dept., 1989-91, acting counselor, 1991—. Columnist Am. Kennel Gazette, 1985-91, Lake Zurich Courier, 1986-91. Mem. Local Sch. Coun., Chgo., 1991; cheerleader coach Lake Zurich Flames, 1989-90; sec. Lake Zurich Bd. Edn., 1991—; soloist St. Peter United Ch. Christ. Ill. State grantee, 1983. Mem. ASCD, NEA, Nat. Assn. Sch. Bds., Ill. Prin. Assn., Ill. Tchrs. Assn., Ill. Assn. Sch. Bds., Staffordshire Terrier Club Am. (v.p. 1983-89), Greater Chicagoland Staffordshire Terrier Club (pres. 1976-82, editor newsletter 1976-81).

STEFFEY, LELA, state legislator, banker; b. Idaho Falls, Idaho, Aug. 8, 1928; d. Orawell and Mary Ethel (Owen) Gardner; m. Carl A. Hendershott, Jr., Apr. 16, 1949 (div. 1961); children: Barry G., Bradley Carl, Barton P.; m. 2d Warren D. Steffey, July 13, 1973; children: Dean, Wayne, Luann, Scott, Susan. Grad. Am. Inst. Banking, 1972. With Pacific Tel. & Tel., San Diego, 1948-49, Bank of Am., San Diego, 1949-52, Gen. Dynamics/Astro, San Diego, 1960-61; escrow officer, mgr. consumer loans Bank of Am., San Diego, 1961-73; real estate agt. Steffey Realty, Mesa, Ariz., 1978—; mem. Ariz. Ho. of Reps, Phoenix, 1982-86, vice chmn. banking and ins. com., 1982-86, mem. house appropriations, judiciary, counties and municipalities coms., 1986-90, chmn. transp. 1991—, multi-state hwy. transp. commn., 1993-94; chmn. counties and municipalities com., 1987-90. Founder, Citizens Com. Against Domestic Abuse; precinct com. Legis. Dist. 29, 1978—, dep. registrar, 1978—; pres. Mesa Rep. Women, 1980; chmn. Mesa Mus. Adv. bd., 1981-83; del. to Rep. Nat. Conv., Dallas, 1984. Bd. dirs. Mesa Community Coun., 1985—, Ariz. Hist. Soc., Ariz. Life Found., Aide to Women Ctr. Mem. Nat. Order Women Legislators (v.p. 1987-88, pres. 1989-90), Am. Mothers Assn., Nat. Fedn. Rep. Women, Ariz. Fedn. Rep. Women (dir.), Ariz. Assn. of Women (dir.), Am. Legis. Exchange Coun., Pi Beta Phi. Mem. Ch. of Jesus Christ of Latter-Day Saints. Office: Ariz Ho of Reps 1700 W Washington St Phoenix AZ 85007-2812*

STEFFY, MARION NANCY, state agency administrator; b. Fairport Harbor, Ohio, Sept 23, 1937; d. Felix and Anna (Kosaber) Jackopin; 1 child, Christopher C. BA, Ohio State U., 1959; postgrad. Butler U., 1962-65, Ind. U., 1983. Exec. sec. Franklin County Mental Health Assn., Columbus, Ohio, 1959-61; caseworker Marion County Dept. Pub. Welfare, Indpls., 1961-63, supr., 1963-66, asst. chief supr., 1966-73; dir. div. pub. assistance, Ind. Dept. Pub. Welfare, Indpls., 1973-77, asst. adminstr., 1977-85; regional adminstr. Adminstrn. Children and Families Ill. Dept. Health and Human Svcs., Chgo., 1985—; lectr. Ball State U., Lockyear Coll., Ind. U. Grad. Sch. Social Work; mem. Ind. Devel. Disabilities Coun., 1979-81, Ind. Cmty. Svc.s Adv. Coun., 1978-81; Ind. Child Support Adv. Coun., 1976-82, Welfare Svc. League, 1968—; chmn. rules com. Ind. Health Facilities Coun., 1974-81. Chmn. Lawrence Twp. Roundtable, 1983—. Mem. Nat. Assn. State Pub. Welfare Adminstrs., Am. Pub. Welfare Assn., Network of Women in Bus. Roman Catholic. Office: Adminstrn for Children & Families 105 W Adams St Chicago IL 60603-6201

STEFONIK, FERN JOHNSON, retired educator; b. Livingston, Wis., July 29, 1926; d. Albert Walter and Elsie Marie (Gundlach) Johnson; m. Gail Earl Stefonik, June 18, 1949; children: John Reed Stefonik, Susan Jane Stefonik Blount. BS, U. Wis., Madison, 1948, MS, 1971. Cert. tchr., Wis. Educator Wausau (Wis.) High Sch., 1948-50, Rhinelander (Wis.) High Sch., 1964-87. Permanent collections include Rhinelander Telecomm., Inc., Gallery of U. Minn.; also pvt. collections. Active Nicolet Coll. Players Prodns.; co-chair No. Nat. Art Competition, 1987-95; bd. dirs. Nicolet Coll. Found.; Northwood Cmty. Concerts; art com. Rhinelander Hist. Soc. Recipient Vilas award for Outstanding Spkr. of Yr., Purchase award NNAC-Rhinelander Telecomm., Inc., Spl. Merit award No. Arts Coun., 1992. Mem. AAUW (cultural chair Rhinelander br., Outstanding Tchr. of Wis.), Nicolet Coll. Found., Rhinelander Area Libr. Found., Rhinelander Area Retired Educators Assn., No. Arts Coun. (past pres.), Community Concerts Assn., Wis. Pub. Radio and TV Assn. (bd. dirs. 1988-92), U. Wis.-Madison Alumni Assn. (life), Northwoods Alumni Assn. (past pres.), Phi Beta, Delta Sigma Rho. Home: 816 Evergreen Ct Rhinelander WI 54501 also (winter): 1240 W Camino Velasquez Green Valley AZ 85614

STEGALL, DIANE JOYCE, school system administrator; b. Kans. City, Mo., Oct. 12, 1956; d. Dean Edward and Delma June (Veach) Wintermute; m. Thomas Scott Stegall, Nov. 22, 1975; children: Shawn Scott, Shelly Diane, Shey Thomas. BS, East Tex. State U., 1978, MS, 1982. Cert. secondary English tchr., Tex. Tchr. Cooper (Tex.) High Sch., 1978-93; spl. programs coord. Chisum Ind. Sch. Dist., Paris, Tex., 1993—. Adminstr. First United Meth. Ch., Cooper, 1975-93. Mem. ASCD, N.E. Tex. Assn. Supervision and Curriculum Devel. (v.p.), Assn. Tchrs. and Profl. Educators, Vocat. Home Econs. Assn. Tex., Delta Kappa Gamma (corr. sec. 1992-94). Home: 1320 SW 8th St Cooper TX 75432-3714 Office: Chisum Ind Sch Dist 3250 S Church St Paris TX 75462-8909

STEGALL, DOROTHY MCKENZIE, food service director; b. Bay Spring, Miss., Feb. 14, 1940; d. James Lane and Rosie (Upton) McKenzie; m. Mack J. Stegall, July 18, 1970; children: Amanda, Clay, Grant. BS, U. So. Miss., 1961. Assoc. home economist Miss. Extension Svc., Ripley, Wayne County, 1961-64; sch. lunch supr. Miss. Dept. Edn., Jackson, 1965-68, Hattiesburg (Miss.) Schs., 1968-70; sch. lunch supr. Pontotoc (Miss.) County Schs., 1970-94, ret., 1994. Baptist. Home: 10124 Hwy 41 Pontotoc MS 38863

STEGNER, LYNN NADENE, treasurer; b. Bethlehem, Pa., Aug. 20, 1955; d. Edmund Joseph and Evelyn Virginia (Shelbo) S.; m. Frederick Gerald Freitag, Sept. 10, 1977; children: Crescentia Adela Stegner-Freitag, Abigail Amadea Stegner-Freitag, Genevieve Angelica Stegner-Freitag. BBA, U. Wis., 1977; MBA, U. Chgo., 1979. Sr. cons. Arthur Andersen & Co., Cleve., 1979-82; mgr. of fin. Morton Internat. (Morton Thiokol), Chgo., 1982-89; asst. treas. Eclipse, Inc., Rockford, Ill., 1989-90; CFO Bd. of Jewish Edn. and Community Found. for Jewish Edn., 1991—; cons. Diamond Headache Clinic, Chgo., 1989-93. Mem. U. Chgo. Alumni Bd., 1986-88. Recipient Cert. Merit YWCA, Cleve., 1981, Cert. Leadership, Chgo., 1984. Mem. Treasury Mgmt. Assn. (prog. chmn. 1987).

STEHLE, ETHEL GARDINER, corporate secretary; b. Washington, Dec. 21, 1938; d. Francis Espey and Margaret (Burch) Gardiner; m. William N. Stehle, Sept. 29, 1962 (div. 1984); children: Theresa Anne, William N. Jr., Susan Margaret. BS in Edn. cum laude, Towson State U., 1960; postgrad., U. Md., 1991—, Anne Arundel Community Coll., 1993. Elem. tchr. Prince George's County, Md., 1960-61, Anne Arundel County, Md., 1961-63; sec.-treas. Stehle Engrng. Corp., Upper Marlboro, Md., 1972-80; adminstrv. asst. Md. Hist. Trust, Annapolis, 1980-82; exec. asst. U.S. Senate Com. on Fin., Washington, 1982-84; exec. asst., corp. sec. Stoner Broadcasting System, Annapolis, 1984-94; legis. liaison, exec. asst. Dept. Housing & Cmty. Devel. State of Md., Crownsville, Md., 1994—; dir. corp. rels. Stoner Broadcasting System, 1991—; treas. Stoner System Charitable Found., Annapolis, 1984-93; corp. sec. SBS Holding, Inc., Annapolis, 1992-93, KDMI, Inc., Annapolis, 1993, Am. Radio Systems Inc., 1993; project mgr. World Talk, 1987. Editor: 25 Years: Stoner Broadcasting, 1991, (newsletters) Stoner Transmitter, 1984-93, The Sideband, 1991-93, Zonta Zipper, 1989-91. Mem. choir Sacred Heart Ch., Bowie, Md., 1991-92; dir. Davidsonville (Md.) Family Recreation Ctr.; dir., founder Holy Family Sunday Sch., Davidsonville; bd. dirs. Davidsonville Athletic Assn., founder, commr. soccer program; parent rep. to bd. edn., faculty com. for tchrs.' advisory program Ctrl. Middle Sch.; chair fundraising South County Pre-Kindergarten Cooperative. Recipient Edward R. Murrow Brotherhood award B'nai B'rith. Mem. Nat. Assn. Broadcasters, Radio Advt. Bur., Zonta (v.p. Annapolis club 1991, bd. dirs. 1993—), Rotary, Kappa Delta Pi. Home: 138 Spa View Ave Annapolis MD 21401

STEHMAN, BETTY KOHLS, financial and management consultant; b. Glencoe, Minn., Dec. 23, 1952; d. Clarence Otto and Pearl Amelia (Tuman) K.; m. Carl Knottwell Stehman, Feb. 12, 1984; 1 child, Sandra. BA, Winona State U., Minn., 1975. CPA, Md.; cert. internal auditor. Staff auditor Norwest Bank Minn., N.A., Mpls., 1975-78; acctg. mgr. Regan Mgmt., Bloomington, Minn., 1978-79; sr. internal auditor Bemis Co., Inc., Mpls., 1980; internal audit mgr. Hartzell Corp., St. Paul, 1980-82; corp. contr. Ragon Electronics, St. Paul, 1982-85; contr. Gustafson Construction Inc., St. Louis Park, 1985-88; owner Entrepreneurial Fin. Svcs., Inc., Eden Prairie, Minn., 1985-88, Silver Spring, Md., 1988—; independent sales cons. Discovery Toys, Livermore, Calif., 1988-92; cons. in field. Chairperson Immanuel Luth. Ch., Eden Prairie, 1981-84; asst. treas. Berg for Congress Campaign, St. Paul, 1980; vol. acct. Children's Miracle Network Telethon, Mpls., 1984, 85; pres. Citizens Assn., 1991—; treas. St. Stephen Luth. Ch., 1991-94. Mem. NAFE, Inst. Internal Auditors, Am. Assn. Home-Based Businesses (nat. dir., CFO), Nat. Assn. Tax Practitioners, Nat. Soc. Tax Profls., Nat. Soc. Pub. Accts., D.C. Inst. CPAs, Md. Soc. Accts., Kensington Bus. and Profl. Women's Group, Montgomery County Women Bus. Owners. Lutheran.

STEICHEN, JOANNA T(AUB), psychotherapist; b. N.Y.C., Feb. 22, 1933; d. William James and Edna (Notice) Taub; m. Edward Steichen, Mar. 19, 1960 (dec. 1973). BA, Smith Coll., 1954; MS, Columbia U., 1973. Diplomate Am. Bd. Social Work. Copywriter Young & Rubicam, Inc., N.Y.C., 1955-60; asst. social worker Mount Sinai Hosp., N.Y.C., 1970-71; pvt. practice psychotherapy N.Y.C., 1975—; cons. supr. Baltic St. Service, South Beach Psychiatric Ctr., Bklyn., 1976-77; supr. psychotherapy New Hope Guild Ctrs., Bklyn., 1977—, dir. group therapy tng., 1980-88; dir. acad. tng. Ctr. for Advancement Group Studies, 1989-90; faculty, supr. Ctr. for the Advancement of Group Studies, 1989—. Author: Marrying Up: An American Dream-and Reality, 1983; contbr. articles to mags. Mem. task force of schs. self-study Columbia U. Sch. Social Work, N.Y.C., 1972-75; trustee Internat. Mus. Photography, Rochester, N.Y., 1980—; mem. Creative Arts Awards Commn., Brandeis U., 1985-91; bd. dirs. Edward F. Albee Found., Hampton Day Sch., 1994—. Mem. NASW (diplomate), Am. Group Psychotherapy Assn. (Meritorious Contbn. award 1984), N.Y. State Soc. Clin. Social Work Psychotherapists, Am. Acad. Psychotherapists (edtl. bd. Voices 1979-82), Authors Guild, Ea. Group Psychotherapy Soc. (tng. com. 1988-91), Coffee Ho. Club (N.Y.C.). Democrat. Episcopalian. Office: 50 W 29th St #8E New York NY 10001-4205

STEIGER, BETTIE ALEXANDER, information industry specialist; b. Spirit Lake, Idaho, Jan. 27, 1934; d. Walter and Velma Esteline (Williamson) Alexander; m. Donald Wayne Steiger, Nov. 10, 1956; children: Craig Alexander Scott, Ann Alexander Carla. BS in Polit. Sci., Wash. State U., 1956, postgrad., 1957; AMP, Harvard U., 1987. V.p. Gartner Group, Inc., Stamford, Conn., Reference Tech. Inc.; exec. dir. Assn. for Info and Image Mgmt., Silver Spring, Md.; dir. to prin. Worldwide Mktg. Xerox Corp., McLean, Va.; prin. tech. and market devel. v.p. Xerox Graphic Sys., Palo Alto, Calif.; founder online system The Source. Founder Army Family Symposium, 1979; class sec. Harvard Bus. Sch., 1987—; bd. dirs. Internat. Sch. Info. Mgmt. Recipient Outstanding Alumni award Wash. State U., 1988. Mem. Internat. Women's Forum, Army Officers Wives (pres. Greater Washington Area 1976), Wash. State U. Found. (bd. regents), Info. Industry Assn., Videotex Industry Assn. (bd. dirs.), Am. Women's Club (pres. 1971), Pi Beta Phi (pres. alumnae prov. 1965). Republican. Presbyterian. Home: 1370 Trinity Dr Menlo Park CA 94025-6680

STEIGER, JANET DEMPSEY, government official; b. Oshkosh, Wis., June 10, 1939; 1 child, William Raymond. BA, Lawrence Coll., 1961; postgrad., U. Reading, Eng., 1961-62, U. Wis., 1962-63; LLD (hon.), Lawrence U., 1992. Legis. aide Office of Gov., Wis., 1965; v.p. The Work Place, Inc., 1975-80; commr. Postal Rate Commn., Washington, 1980-89, acting chmn., 1981-82, chmn., 1982-89; commr. FTC, Washington, 1989—; U.S. del. OECD, Paris, 1989—. Author: Law Enforcement and Juvenile Justice in Wisconsin, 1965; co-author: To Light One Candle, a Handbook on Organizing, Funding and Maintaining Public Service Projects, 1978, 2d edit., 1980. Chmn. Commn. on Vets. Edn. Policy, 1987-90. Woodrow Wilson scholar; Fulbright scholar, 1961. Mem. Phi Beta Kappa. Office: FTC Office of Chmn 6th & Pennsylvania Ave NW Washington DC 20580-0002*

STEIGER, PATRICIA ANN, community action professional; b. Davenport, Iowa, May 26, 1933; d. Edmunnd John and DeMarys Catherine (McDonnell) Burke; m. James Allen Steiger, Dec. 13, 1958 (dec. Dec. 9, 1990); children: Max, Todd, Dan, Mary. Student, Marycrest, 1951-52; fellowship, UCLA, 1993—. Cert. community action profl. Nat. advt. asst. Davenport (Iowa) Newspaper, 1952-58; advt. asst. Petersen's, Davenport, 1960-61; program dir. Iowa East Ctrl. T.R.A.I.N., Davenport, 1967-69, dep. dir., 1969-71, exec. dir., 1971—. Recipient Robert F. Tyson award Iowa Community Action Assn., 1992, Lyndon Baines Johnson Human Svc. award, 1994. Mem. Iowa Assn. Community Action Dirs. (v.p. 1973), Iowa Assn. Community Action Dirs. (pres. 1974-75), Nat. Assn. Community Action Agencies (1st v.p. 1984-86, pres. 1988-91), Substance Abuse Adv. Coun., Manpower Planning Coun., State Employment and Tng. Coun., United Way Agy. Dirs. Assn., Consumer Adv. Panel, Consumer Advocate (v.p. 1986-89), Davenport C. of C. HNYN: 1325 Hillside Dr Bettendorf IA 52722-3089 Office: Iowa East Ctr TRAIN 2804 Eastern Ave Davenport IA 52803-2012

STEIGERWALDT, DONNA WOLF, clothing manufacturing company executive; b. Chgo., Apr. 2, 1929; d. Harry Hay and Donna (Currey) Wolf; m. William Steigerwaldt, Dec. 31, 1969; children: Debra, Linda. BA, U. Colo., Colo. Springs, 1950, LHD (hon.), 1987. Ins. broker Conn. Mut. Life Ins. Co., Chgo., 1950-53; vice chmn. Jockey Internat., Inc., Kenosha, Wis., 1978-80, chmn., chief exec. officer, 1980—. Pres. Donna Wolf Steigerwaldt Found., Inc.; mem. Infant Welfare Soc., Evanston Hosp.-Glenbrook Hosp. Corp., N.W. Cmty. Hosp. Aux., Aid to Animals No. Ill., Inc.; vice chmn. Carthage Coll., 1982-92, chmn., 1992—; bd. dirs. Century Club Sarasota Meml. Hosp. Paul Harris fellow, Rotary, 1984. Mem. Am. Apparel Mfrs. Assn., Navy League U.S., Glenview Hist. Soc., Exec. Women Internat. (hon.), Rotary (Paul Harris fellow 1984). Republican. Episcopalian. Clubs: North Shore Country, Plaza, Valley Lo Sports; Meadows Country (Sarasota, Fla.). Office: Jockey Internat Inc 2300 60th St Kenosha WI 53140-3889

STEIL, VALERIE GLADYS, interior designer; b. Beloit, Wis., Aug. 18, 1957; d. Melbourne and Dolores Leona (Radtke) S. BS, U. Wis., Stevens Point, 1979. Free lance designer Giltspur Exhibits, Chgo., 1979; prof. interior design Valparaiso (Ind.) U., 1989-90, 94; interior designer Marc T. Nielsen Interiors, Valparaiso, 1980—. Mem. Am. Soc. Interior Designers. Lutheran. Home: 1601 Burlington Beach Rd Valparaiso IN 46383 Office: Marc T Nielsen Interiors Inc 734 N Old Suman Rd Valparaiso IN 46383

STEIN, BELLE WEISS, retired elementary education educator; b. N.Y.C., Aug. 30, 1923; d. Leonard Edwin and Ruth (Scheinzeit) Weiss; m. Henry J. Stein, July 26, 1945; children: Joanne Stein Haiby, Joel, Jacqueline Stein Przytula, Janet Stein, Joyce Stein Schachter. BA, CUNY, 1943; MS, SUNY, New Paltz, 1962. Route mgr. New Manhattan Cleaners, Bklyn., 1942-43; asst. editor Beverage Market Guide, N.Y.C., 1943-45; mil. pers. contact ARC, Bastrop, Tex., 1945; tchr. Unified Free Sch. Dist. 3, North Babylon, N.Y., 1960-86, chmn. reading and social studies, 1968-82; ret., 1986. Contbr. articles to ednl. jours. Sec. Westwood Civic Assn., Babylon, 1950-56, Temple Beth Sholom, Babylon, 1956-58; pres. Sinai Reform Temple, Bay Shore, N.Y., 1992—. Outdoor edn. scholar Cornell U., 1977. Mem. North Babylon Retirees Orgn. (pres. 1989—), North Babylon Tchrs. Orgn. (sec. 1978-86, negotiations team 1974-86), Am. Fedn. Tchrs. (del. 1980—), AAUW, LWV, Hadassah (life). Democrat. Home: 32 Darcy Cir Islip NY 11751-3704

STEIN, CHERYL DENISE, lawyer; b. N.Y.C., Nov. 3, 1953; d. Arthur Earl and Joyce (Weitzman) S. BA magna cum laude, Yale U., 1974; postgrad., U. Chgo., 1974-75; JD, Yale U., 1977. Bar: D.C. 1978, U.S. Dist. Ct. Colo. 1983, U.S. Ct. Appeals (D.C. cir.) 1988, U.S. Dist. Ct. Md. 1995. Atty. advisor CAB, Washington, 1978-79; assoc. Cohn & Marks, Washington, 1979-82; pvt. practice Washington, 1982—. Vol. reader radio reading svc. for the blind Washington Ear, Silver Spring, Md., 1982-91; vol. tutor Friends of Tyler Sch., 1992—. Mem. Nat. Assn. Criminal Def. Lawyers, D.C. Assn. Criminal Def. Lawyers. Democrat. Jewish. Office: 705 8th St SE Ste 100 Washington DC 20003-2856

STEIN, DEBORAH JANE, music educator; b. Balt., Apr. 10, 1946; d. Aaron and Henrietta (Shapiro) S. MusB, U. Mich., 1968, MusM, 1975; PhD, Yale U., 1982. Asst. prof. Eastman Sch. Music, Rochester, N.Y., 1982-89; assoc. prof. New Eng. Conservatory Music, Boston, 1989—; vis. assoc. prof. Harvard U., Cambridge, Mass., 1994—. Author: Hugo Wolf's Lieder, 1985, (with Robert Spillman) Poetry Into Song: Performance and Analysis of Lieder, 1995; contbr. articles to profl. jours. Mellon grantee Andrew Mellon Found., 1987. Mem. New Eng. Conf. Music Theorists, Soc. Music Theory (mem. publ. awards com. 1991-95, chair com. status women 1993-95). Democrat. Jewish. Home: 36 Cerdan Ave Boston MA 02131 Office: New Eng Conservatory 290 Huntington Ave Boston MA 02115

STEIN, ELEANOR BANKOFF, judge; b. N.Y.C., Jan. 24, 1923; d. Jacob and Sarah (Rashkin) Bankoff; m. Frank S. Stein, May 27, 1947; children: Robert B., Joan Jenkins, William M. Student, Barnard Coll., 1940-42; BS in Econs., Columbia U., 1944; LLB, NYU, 1949; grad. Ind. Jud. Coll., 1986. Bar: N.Y. 1950, Ind. 1976, U.S. Supreme Ct. 1980. Atty. Hillis & Button, Kokomo, Ind., 1975-76, Paul Hillis, Kokomo, 1976-78, Bayliff, Harrigan, Kokomo, 1978-80; judge Howard County Ct., Kokomo, 1981-89; ret., 1989; co-juvenile referee Howard County Juvenile Ct., 1976-78. Mem. Republican Women's Assn. Kokomo, 1980—; bd. dirs. Howard County Legal Aid Soc., 1976-80; dir. Howard County Ct. Alcohol and Drug Svcs. Program, 1982-89; bd. advisors St. Joseph Hosp., Kokomo, 1979—; bd. dirs. Kokomo Human Rels. Commn., 1967-70, Howard County Children's Ctr., 1993—. Mem. law rev. bd. NYU Law Rev., 1947-48. Mem. Am. Judicature Soc., Ind. Jud. Assn., Nat. Assn. Women Judges, ABA (apptd. Ind. del. jud. adminstrn. div. 1987), Ind. Bar Assn., Howard County Bar Assn. Jewish. Clubs: Kokomo Country, Altrusa. Home: 3204 Tallyho Dr Kokomo IN 46902-3985

STEIN, MARY KATHERINE, writer, editor, communications executive; b. Denver, Sept. 7, 1944; d. Robert Addison and Minta Mary (MacDonald) Dunlap; m. Lawrence Bronstein, June 29, 1970 (div. 1974); m. Donald L. Stein, Aug. 16, 1982. BS in Journalism, U. Kans., 1966. Sr. editor Am Family Physician mag., Kansas City, Mo., 1967-78; editor-in-chief Current Prescribing mag., Oradell, N.J., 1978-79; sr. editor Diagnosis mag., Oradell, 1979-83; mng. editor Advances in Reproductive Medicine, Bolton, Conn., 1983-85; pres. MD Comm., Coto de Caza, Calif., 1983—. Author: Child Abuse, 1987, Caring for the AIDS Patient, 1987, Lifetime Weight Control, 1988, Substance Abuse, 1988, An Overview of HIV Infections and AIDS, 1989, Cardiovascular Disease: Evaluation and Prevention, 1989; mng. editor: (newsletter) Eating Disorders Rev., 1990—; editor: (newsletter) Nutrition and the M.D., 1992—; contbr. articles to mags. Mem. Women in Communications (pres. Greater Kansas City chpt. 1977-78, pres. Orange County chpt. 1990-91), Am. Med. Writers Assn. Democrat. Lutheran. Office: MD Comm 15 Seacliff Coto De Caza CA 92679

STEIN, PAULA NANCY, psychologist, educator; b. N.Y.C., Aug. 23, 1963; d. Michael and Evelyn (Graber) Stein; m. Andreas Howard Smoller, Sept. 2, 1991; 1 child, Rebecca Leigh Smoller. BA, Skidmore Coll., 1985; MA with distinction, Hofstra U., 1986, PhD, 1989. Lic. clin. psychologist, N.Y.; cert. in sch. psychology, N.Y. Intern NYU Med. Ctr.-Rusk Inst., N.Y.C., 1988-89; instr. Mt. Sinai Med. Ctr., N.Y.C., 1989-93, asst. prof. rehab. medicine, 1993—; chief psychologist Fishkill (N.Y.) Consultation Group, 1991—. Contbr. chpt. to book, articles to profl. jours. Kraewic scholar Skidmore Coll., 1985. Mem. APA, Am. Congress Rehab. Medicine (subcom. on tng.), Assn. for Advancement of Behavior Therapy, Hudson Valley Psychol. Assn.,

Phi Beta Kappa. Jewish. Office: Mt Sinai Med Ctr Box 1240 90 Main St Fishkill NY 12524

STEIN, SANDRA LOU, educational psychologist, educator; b. Freeport, Ill., Oct. 6, 1942; d. William Kenneth and Marien Elizabeth (Dahlgren) S. BS, U. Wis., Madison, 1964; MS in Edn., No. Ill. U., 1967, EdD, 1969. Tchr. English Rockford (Ill.) Sch. Dist., 1964-65; tchr. Russian Jefferson County Sch. Dist., Lakewood, Colo., 1965-66; asst. prof. edn. U. S.C., Columbia, 1969-71, No. Ill. U., DeKalb, 1971-72, Rider U., Lawrenceville, N.J., 1972-75; assoc. prof. edn. Rider Coll., Lawrenceville, N.J., 1975-81, prof. edn., 1981—, dept. chair, 1983-91; cons. on measurement and evaluation, women's edn., 1973—. Contbr. articles to edn. publs. Treas. Lawrenceville Men's Breakfast Club, 1983-85; deacon Presbyn. Ch. Lawrenceville, 1984-87; contest judge N.J. Fedn. Bus. and Profl. Women, 1989; vol. Habitat for Humanity, Trenton, N.J., 1989. Recipient Disting. Teaching award Rider Coll. and Lindback Found., 1981. Mem. AAUP (Outstanding Achievement award Rider Coll. chpt. 1988), Am. Ednl. Rsch. Assn., Am. Psychol. Assn., Phi Delta Kappa (chpt. pres. 1986-87, Svc. Key award 1991, faculty advisor 1994—). Office: Rider U 2083 Lawrenceville Rd Trenton NJ 08648-3099

STEINBACH, INGRID B., critical care nurse; b. Montreal, Apr. 24, 1965; came to the U.S., 1988; d. Ralph Kurt and Brigitti (Blank) S. Diploma in nursing, St. Lawrence Coll., 1987. Cert. ACLS, ACLS instr., CCRN, CEN. Charge nurse ICU/CCU AMI Brownsville (Tex.) Med. Ctr., 1988-92, staff nurse emergency room, alternating charge nurse, 1992—; clin. educator emergency rm. Brownsville (Tex.) Med. Ctr., 1994—; relief call nurse cardiac catheterization lab. AMI Brownsville Med. Ctr., 1989-91; part-time staff nurse, emergency rm. McAllen Med. Ctr., 1994—. Mem. AACN, Emergency Nurses Assn., Ontario Nurses Assn. Lutheran.

STEINBERG, JANET ECKSTEIN, journalist; b. Cin.; d. Charles and Adele (Ehrenfeld) Eckstein; m. Irvin S. Silverstein, Oct. 22, 1988; children: Susan Carole Steinberg Somerstein, Jody Lynn Steinberg Lazarow. BS, U. Cin., 1964. Free-lance writer; guest appearances Braun and Co., Sta.-WLW-TV. Contbr. numerous articles to newspapers, mags. and books, U.S., Can., Singapore, Australia, N.Z.; travel columnist Cin. Post, 1978-86, Ky. Post, 1978-86, Cin. Enquirer, 1986—; travel editor S. Fla. Single Living, 1988-92; contbr. Singles Scene and Cin. Mag., 1980—; contbg. editor Travel Agt., 1986-88, Birnbaum Travel Guides, 1988—, The Writer, 1988—, Entree, 1986—; travel columnist Northeast mag., 1986-88, South Fla. Single Living, 1984-92. Recipient Lowell Thomas travel journalism award, 1985, 86, 91, Henry E. Bradshaw Travel Journalism award, 1st place, best of show, 1988, Buckeye Travel award Ohio Divsn. Travel & Tourism, 1992. Mem. Am. Soc. Journalists and Authors, Soc. Am. Travel Writers (1st place award for best newspaper story 1981, 3d place award for best mag. story 1981, 91, 1st place award for best newspaper article award 1984, 91, best mag. article 1985, 2d place award best pathos article, 1984, 88, 2d place award specific category, 1989), Midwest Travel Writers Assn. (Best Mag. Story award 1981, Best Series award 1981, 94, 84 Cipriani award 1981, 1st place award best article 1989, 2d place award for best article 1982, 83, 84, 89, 3d place award best article 1992, Mark Twain award 1992), Pacific Area Travel Assn., Internat. Food, Wine, and Travel Writers Assn., Losantiville Country Club, Travelers Century Club, Circumnavigators Club. Home: 900 Adams Crossing # 9200 Cincinnati OH 45202-1666

STEINBERG, JOAN EMILY, retired middle school educator; b. San Francisco, Dec. 9, 1932; d. John Emil and Kathleen Helen (Montgomery) S. BA, U. Calif.-Berkeley, 1954; EdD, U. San Francisco, 1981. Tchr., Vallejo (Calif.) Unified Sch. Dist., 1959-61, San Francisco Unified Sch. Dist., 1961-93, tchr. life and phys. sci. jr. high sch., 1978-85, 87-93, sci. cons., 1985-87; lectr. elem. edn. San Francisco State U., 1993-94; ind. sci. edn. cons., 1993—. Contbr. articles to profl. jours. Fulbright scholar U. Sydney (Australia), 1955-56; recipient Calif. Educator award, 1988, Outstanding Educator in Teaching award U. San Francisco Alumni Soc., 1989. Mem. ASCD, San Francisco Zool. Soc., Exploratorium, Nature Conservancy, Astron. Soc. Pacific, Am. Fedn. Tchrs., Calif. Acad. Scis., Calif. Malacozool. Soc., Nat. Sci. Tchrs. Assn., Elem. Sch. Sci. Assn. (sec. 1984-85, pres. 1986-87, newsletter editor 1994—), Calif. Sci. Tchrs. Assn., Sigma Xi. Democrat.

STEINBERG, LINDA ANN, accountant; b. Milw., Mar. 22, 1952. BA in History, U. Wis., 1974, MA in Libr. Sci., 1975; MS in Acctg., U. Wis., Milw., 1986. CPA, Wis. Student asst. U. Wis.-Madison Law Libr., 1974-75; asst. catalog libr. Manitowoc (Wis.) Pub. Libr., 1975-77; libr. asst. West Allis (Wis.) Pub. Libr., 1977-87; tax acct. Wis. Electric, Milw., 1987-94; acct. Wis. Energy Corp., Milw., 1994—. Fellow Wis. Inst. Pub. Accts.; mem. Am. Soc. Women Accts. (pres. Milw. chpt. 1992-93, 93-94), Am. Inst. Pub. Accts., Inst. Mgmt. Accts. Home: 285 N Park Blvd Brookfield WI 53005-6137

STEINBERG, LINDA SUE, interior designer; b. Dallas, Aug. 24, 1945; d. Nathan Charles and Fannie (Rosenbloom) Goidl; m. Lawrence Edward Steinberg, Aug. 31, 1967 (div. 1994); children: Adam Joseph, Ilana Sara. BA, So. Meth. U., 1967; Degree in Interior Design, El Centro Coll., 1987, cert. interior design, 1987. Cert. interior designer, Tex.; cert. NCIDQ. Assoc. Silvergold Interiors, Dallas, 1979-82; owner Linda Steinberg Interiors, Dallas, 1986—; spkr. in field. Mem. Am. Soc. Interior Designers (honor cert. in profl. devel. 1992, Dallas assoc., 1st vice chmn. 1992-93, 2d vice chmn. 1993-94, bd. dirs. Tex. chpt. 1993-95, chair-elect 1994-95), Interior Designers Guild (1st v.p. 1993-94, pres. 1994—), Adventure Investment Club (pres. 1993-95). Jewish.

STEINBERG, LOIS JOYCE RABINOWITZ, psychologist; b. Newark, Dec. 7, 1937; d. Nathan Aaron and Edythe Mary (Kruger) Rabinowitz; m. Richard Mark Steinberg, Dec. 22, 1957; children: Russel Allen, Dina Ann Steinberg Del Amo. BS, Douglass Coll., 1959; postgrad., Seton Hall U., 1959-60; MA, Montclair State Coll., 1973; postgrad., Jersey City State Coll., 1982-83; PhD, Yeshiva U., 1983; advanced cert., CCNY, 1984. Lic. psychologist, N.J., Penn., sch. psychologist, N.J., N.Y., learning disability tchr.-cons., N.J., supr., N.J., tchr. of handicapped, N.J., elem. tchr., N.J. Tchr. Bd. Edn., Elizabeth, N.J., 1959-60; substitute tchr., home instr., supplemental instr. Bd. Edn., various cities, N.J., 1960-72; learning cons. Bd. Edn., Caldwell/West Caldwell, N.J., 1972-73; learning cons., coord. Child Help and Mainstreaming Project, sch. psychologist New Providence (N.J.) Pub. Schs., 1973-85; psychologist, sr. clinician St. Clare's-Riverside Med. Ctr., Denville, N.J., 1986-88; cons. psychologist Assn. for Retarded Citizens of Essex County, Inc., 1988—; pvt. practice Denville and Millburn, N.J., 1985—; adj. faculty Montclair State Coll., Upper Montclair, N.J., 1974; speaker Unitarian House, Summit, N.J., 1993, New Providence Parents of Classified Children, 1991, Parents of Young Children, 1993; mem. adv. com. Family Svcs., Livingston, 1989-92; mem. profl. svcs. coun. N.J. Dept. Edn., 1992—; psychologist Provide Assessments and Consultation to Child Study Team(s), New Providence and Butler, N.J., 1990-94; faciliator, panelist and workshop leader in field. Contbr. articles to profl. jours. Supr. of facilitators Project GRO Self-Help Groups, Nat. Coun. Jewish Women Ctr. for Women, Livingston, 1989—; active Met. Opera Guild, Friends of N.Y. Philharm., Smithsonian Instn., Friends of Zimmerle Art Mus.; mem. adv. com. Am. Cancer Soc., 1994. Mem. NOW, APA, Soc. Psychologists in Pvt. Practice, Assn. for Advancement of Family Therapy in N.J., N.J. Assn. Learning Consultants, N.J. Assn. Women Therapists, N.J. Acad. Psychology (Psychologists Recognition award 1991, 92), N.J. Psychol. Assn. (chair psychology in the schs. com., coun. on legis. affairs, child, youth and family com.), Psi Chi. Office: Ste 204 25 Orchard St Denville NJ 07834

STEINBERG, LOIS SAXELBY, marketing executive; b. New Rochelle, N.Y., Sept. 13, 1926; d. John J. and Ruth (Taussig) Saxelby; m. Jack Steinberg, Nov. 27, 1947 (div. 1980); children: Eric, Mark. BA, Hunter Coll., N.Y.C., 1952; MA, Columbia U., N.Y.C., 1964; PhD, Fordham U., Bronx, 1978. Account exec. The Rowland Co., N.Y.C., 1956-64; rsch. asst. Columbia U., N.Y.C., 1965-67; rsch. assoc. CUNY, 1967-72; staff asst. Community Svc. Soc., N.Y.C., 1972-74; rsch. assoc. Inst. for Responsive Edn., Boston, 1976-77, Designs for Change, Chgo., 1977-78; sr. study dir. Nat. Opinion Rsch. Ctr., U. Chgo., 1979-81; rsch. spr. BBDO, N.Y.C., 1981-82, Marsteller, Inc., Chgo., 1982-83; v.p. Sorkin-Enenstein Rsch. Svc., Inc., Chgo., 1984—. Contbr. articles to profl. jours. Fordham U. fellow, 1974; Columbia U. fellow, 1964. Mem. Am. Sociol. Assn., Am. Assn. for Pub. Opinion Rsch., Am. Mktg. Assn. Office: Sorkin-Enenstein Rsch Svc 500 N Dearborn St Chicago IL 60610-4901

STEINBERG, SUSAN ELIZABETH, minister; b. Phila., Apr. 19, 1963; d. Robert Philip and Doris (Blank) S. BS, Wellesley Coll., 1985; MDiv, Vanderbilt Divinity Sch., 1992. Investigator Christic Inst., Costa Rica & Washington, 1987-89; community organizer United Meth. Urban Ministries, Nashville, 1990-91, Border Com. Women Workers, Edinburg, Tex., summer 1991; supply pastor Spring Creek Presbyn. Ch., Lebanon, Tenn., 1991-92; chaplain Vanderbilt U., Nashville, 1992-93; assoc. pastor Westminster Presbyn. Ch., Charlottesville, Va., 1993—; cons. Gen. Assembly Pres. Ch., Louisville, 1993-94. AIDS buddy Nashville Cares, 1992-93; cons. Tenn. Indsl. Renewal Network, Knoxville & Nashville, 1991-93; bd. dirs. Peidmont Coun. of Arts, Charlottesville, 1994—. Watson Found. fellow, 1985-86, Jonathon Daniels fellow Epsicopal. Divinity Sch., 1991; Hyde scholar Vanderbilt Divinity Sch., 1990-93; recipient Newcomb prize Vanderbilt Divinity Sch., 1992. Mem. NOW, Charlottesville Latin Am. Solidarity Com., Presbyn. Health, Edn. & Welfare Assn., Presbyn. Mins. in Higher Edn., Assn. Religious and Intellectual Life, United Ministry, Nat. Mus. of Women in the Arts. Democrat. Office: Westminster Presbyn Ch 190 Rugby Rd Charlottesville VA 22903

STEINBERG-PODGORNY, JUDY ELLEN, company travel executive; b. Gilroy, Calif.; d. Joseph M. and Eleanor (Gagliardi) Frusetta; m. Victor Serge Podgorny, June 14, 1980. BS, San Francisco State U., 1974. Cert. corp. travel exec. Mgr. transp. E.F. MacDonald Incentive Travel Co., San Francisco, 1974-80; mgr. corp. travel Del Monte Foods, San Francisco, 1980—; bd. dirs. Pan Am. Corp. Adv. Bd., 1990, Holiday Inn Corp. Adv. Bd., 1990. Mem. Nat. Bus. Travel Assn. (dir. 1986-89, treas. 1989-91, bd. dirs. 1991-94), Bay Area Bus. Travel Assn. (sec. 1982-84, pres. 1984-86, chmn. bd. 1986-88), Meeting Planners Internat., Italian Cath. Fedn., Disabled Am. Vets. Aux.

STEINBRUECK, JOANN E., city clerk; b. St. Louis, Feb. 27, 1936; d. Edward F. and Marie E. (Joeckel) Hoffmann; m. Leon E. Steinbrueck, Dec. 29, 1956; children: Randy, David, Debra, Laura. Grad. high sch., St. Louis. With F.W. Woolworth Retail Credit Co., St. Louis, 1950-54; adminstrv. sec. Gen. Am. Life Ins., St. Louis, 1954-58; office mgr. St. John's Luth Ch., Hannibal, Mo., 1967-74; adminstrv. asst. McGraw Edison, Columbia, Mo., 1974-77; owner, office mgr. Dexter (Mo.) Broadcasting (KDEX Radio), 1977-86; city treas. City of Dexter, 1986-90, city clk., 1990—. Treas., v.p. Stoddard County Svc. Orgn., Dexter, 1977—. Mem. Internat. Inst. Mcpl. Clks., Southeast Divsn. Mo. City Clk. & Fin. Officers, State of Mo. City Clks & Fin. Officers. Lutheran. Office: City of Dexter 301 E Stoddard St Dexter MO 63841-1341

STEINEGER, MARGARET LEISY, non-profit organization officer; b. Newton, Kans., Feb. 8, 1926; d. Ernest Erwin and Elva Agnes (Krehbiel) L.; m. John Francis Steineger, Dec. 2, 1949; children: John Steineger III, Cindy Blair, Melissa, Chris. B., So. Meth. U., 1947; M. in Social Work, U. Kans., 1949. County vice-chair United Way, Kansas City, Kans., 1960-61; bd., sec., treas. Wyandotte County Bar Aux., Kans., 1960-63; bd. Jr. League of Kansas City, 1962-66, County Coun. PTA, Wyandotte County, 1963-66, KCK Friends of the Arts, Kansas City, 1974-77; pres. Grinter Place Mus. Friends, Kans., 1977-78; bd. Kaw Valley Arts Coun., Kansas City, 1982-86; commr. Landmarks Commn., Kansas City, 1985-87; bd. Arts with the Handicapped, Wyandotte County, 1986—; bd. dirs. Kans. Arts Adv. Bd., Grinter Place Friends, Kans., Tri-County Tourism Coun., Kans. V.p. Kans. Legis. Wives, Topeka, 1975-76; bd. dirs. KCK Friends of the Libr., Kansas City, 1984—; founder Wyandotte County Libr., 1963-64, Creative Experiences, Kansas City, 1967; commr. Kans. Arts Commn., 1965-85; mem. Kaw Valley Arts and Humanities Bd., 1988-92; mem. adv. bd. Parents as Tchrs., 1992—; mem. KCK Comty. Coll. Endowment Bd., 1989—. Recipient Humanities award Kans. Com. for the Humanities, 1989; named Citizen of Yr. Kansas City, Kans., 1978. Democrat. Methodist. Home: 6400 Valleyview St Kansas City KS 66111-2013 Office: Security Bank Building Ste 600 Kansas City KS 66101

STEINEM, GLORIA, writer, editor, lecturer; b. Toledo, Mar. 25, 1934; d. Leo and Ruth (Nuneviller) S. BA, Smith Coll., 1956; postgrad. (Chester Bowles Asian fellow), India, 1957-58; D. Human Justice, Simmons Coll., 1973. Co-dir., dir. ednl. found. Ind. Rsch. Svc., Cambridge, Mass. and N.Y.C., 1959-60; contbg. editor Glamour Mag., N.Y.C., 1962-69; co-founder, contbg. editor New York Mag., 1968-72; feminist lectr., 1969—; co-founder, editor Ms. Mag., 1971-87, columnist, 1980-87, cons. editor, 1987—; Active various civil rights and peace campaigns including United Farmworkers, Vietnam War Tax Protest, Com. for the Legal Def. of Angela Davis (treas., 1971-72); active polit. campaigns of Adlai Stevenson, Robert Kennedy, Eugene McCarthy, Shirley Chisholm, George McGovern; Co-founder, bd. dirs. Women's Action Alliance, 1970—; convenor, mem. nat. adv. com. Nat. Women's Polit. Caucus, 1971—; co-founder, pres. bd. dirs. Ms. Found. for Women, 1972—; founding mem. Coalition of Labor Union Women, 1974; mem. Internat. Women's Year Commn., 1977; editorial cons., Conde Nast Publications, 1962-69, Curtis Publishing, 1964-65, Random House Publishing, 1988—, McCall Publishing. Author: The Thousand Indias, 1957, The Beach Book, 1963, Wonder Woman, 1972, Outrageous Acts and Everyday Rebellions, 1983, Marilyn: Norma Jeane, 1986, Revolution from Within: A Book of Self-Esteem, 1992, Moving Beyond Words, 1994; contbg. corr. NBC Today Show, 1987-88; contbr. to various anthologies. Pres. Voters for Choice, 1979—. Recipient Penney-Missouri Journalism award, 1970, Ohio Gov.'s award for Journalism, 1972, Bill of Rights award ACLU of So. Calif., 1975; named Woman of the Yr. McCall's mag., 1972; Woodrow Wilson Internat. Ctr. for Scholars fellow, 1977; inducted into Nat. Women's Hall of Fame, 1993. Mem. NOW, AFTRA, Nat. Press Club, Soc. Mag. Writers, Authors' Guild, Phi Beta Kappa. Office: Ms Magazine 230 Park Ave 7th Fl New York NY 10169

STEINER, GLORIA LITWIN, psychologist; b. Newark, Oct. 21, 1922; d. David Milton and Minna (Krasner) Litwin; m. Charles Steiner, Aug. 29, 1942; children: Charles Jr., Susan Steiner Sher, Jeanne. BA, U. Pa., 1944; MS, CCNY, 1956; EdD, Columbia U., 1965. Psychologist St. Michael's Hosp. and Mt. Carmel, Newark, 1956-62; chief psychologist Children's Hosp., Newark, 1965-78; prof. psychology, dir. psychol. svc. Child Study Ctr., Kean Coll., Union, N.J., 1971-78; vis. assoc. prof. grad. sch. applied and profl. psychology Rutgers U., Piscataway, N.J., 1976—; clin. assoc. prof., former dir. psychology tng. U. Medicine and Dentistry N.J.-N.J. Med. Sch., Newark, 1978—; psychology cons. Nat. Pediatric HIV Resource Ctr., 1991-94. Co-author: Traumatic Abuse/Children, 1980; co-editor: Children, Families and HIV/AIDS: Psychosocial and Psychotherapeutic Issues, 1995; contbr. articles to profl. jours.; mem. editl. bd. Jour. Psychotherapy, 1981. Mem. N.J. State Task Force on AIDS, 1986-89, N.J. State Bd. Psychol. Exam., 1978-84, Regional Health Planning Coun., N.J., 1984-85, child adv. com. Mental Health Assn., N.J., 1974-80; trustee, founder N.J. Acad. Psychology, 1978-83, bd. trustees, 1994—. Grantee tng. health care workers Regional AIDS Edn. and Tng. Ctr. U. Medicine and Dentistry N.J., Newark, 1990, Nat. Pediat. HIV Resource Ctr., Newark, 1991-94. Fellow Am. Orthopsychiat. Assn.; mem. N.Y. Acad. Scis., N.J. Assn. for the Advancement Family Therapy (vice-chmn. 1979-81), Am. Psychol. Assn. Home and Office: 35 Sequoia Dr Watchung NJ 07060-6113

STEINER, KAREN RUTH, physician's assistant; b. Milw., Nov. 25, 1953; d. Carl Gustav Martin and Lois Pauline Edna (Koch) S.; m. Christian Joseph Nichols, Sept. 15, 1990. AA in Sci., Glendale Community Coll., 1974; cert. of surg. tech., Maricopa County Tech. Coll., 1976; AA physician asst. pgrm., Essex Community Coll., Balt., 1980. Registered physician asst., Ariz.; lic. phys. asst., Mich.; cert. Nat. Commn. Cert. Physician's Assts. and Nat. Bd. Examiners. Operating room technician Maricopa County Gen. Hosp., Phoenix, 1976-77, Greater Balt. Med. Ctr., 1977-78; resident dept. surgery Franklin Square Hosp., Balt., 1980-811; physician's asst. urgent care unit Ariz. Health Plan, Phoenix, 1981-82; physician's asst. family practice unit CIGNA Healthplan, Tempe, Ariz., 1982-83; physician's asst. cardiac-thoracic surgery dept. Henry Ford Hosp., Detroit, 1983-87, Thoracic Surgeon's Assocs., Grand Rapids, Mich., 1987-88; physician's asst. surg. White Mountain Hosp., 1988-89; physicians asst. Grace Hosp., Detroit, 1989-91, St. John Hosp., 1991—, Women's Health Ctr., Clarkston, Mich., 1993, Livonia (Mich.) Family Physicians, 1994—. Choral Mem. Ariz. State U., Tempe, 1977, 82, Balt. Choral Arts Soc., 1978, White Mtn. Chorale, 1988. Fellow Am. Acad. Physician's Assts., Assn. Physician Assts. in Cardiovascular Surgery, Mich. Acad. Physician Assts. Democrat. Lutheran.

STEINER, SHARI YVONNE, publisher, editor; b. Colorado Springs, Colo., Mar. 3, 1941; d. Evan Keith and Blanche Marie (Ketzner) Montgomery; m. Clyde Lionel Steiner, June 24, 1962; children: Vienna Kay, Marco Romano. BA, Adams State Coll., 1962; cert. in sociology, London Sch. Econs., 1978; postgrad., U. Calif., Berkeley, 1988—. Lic. real estate broker, Calif. Freelance journalist various publs., 1964—; owner, mgr. SREI Group, San Francisco, 1985-87; tng. design developer loan div. 1st Nationwide Bank, San Francisco, 1987—; pub., editor Ind. Info. Publs., San Francisco, 1990—; feature writer Internat. Herald Tribune, Rome, 1964-79; acct. exec. Allen, Ingersol & Weber, Rome, 1970-72; gen. ptnr. Greenhaven Park, Sacramento, 1990—, Port Chicago Indsl., Concord, Calif., 1991—. Author: The Female Factor: A Report on Women in Europe, 1972, 2d edit., 1978, Steiner's Complete How to Move Handbook, 1994; editor The Bottom Line newsletter, 1985—; assoc. editor The Semaphore, 1990—. Coord. urban reforestation Friends of Urban Forest, San Francisco, 1989; co-founder New Sch. for Internat. Elem. Students, Rome, 1970. Recipient internat. journalism award Guida Monaci, 1970, award of merit Lotus Club, N.Y.C., 1975; corr. in archives Am. Heritage Ctr., U. Wyo. Mem. Nat. Assn. Realtors (multiple listing svc. selection com. 1986, 91, investment real estate group 1991), Comml. Real Estate Women (editor, bd. dirs. 1985—), Am. Soc. Journalists and Authors, PEN Internat., Urban Land Inst. (assoc.), Employee Relocation Coun.

STEINER, SHERRY LYNN MEDNICK, artist; b. Bronx, N.Y.. Student, Sch. Visual Arts, N.Y.C., 1968-72. Apprentice Joseph Cornell, Flushing, N.Y., 1969-70; set designer Bill T. Jones/Arnie Zane, Binghamton, N.Y., 1978; gallery owner On Paper, Lenox, Mass., 1982, Gallery Without Walls, Stockbridge, Mass., 1983-85, Le Petit Musee, Housatonic, Mass., 1992—; artist in residence Millay Colony for the Arts, Austerlitz, N.Y., 1978, Cummington (Mass.) Community, 1986, 92, Real Art Ways, Hartford, Conn., 1988. Exhibitions include Arnot Art Mus., Roberson Ctr., Kathryn Markel Perth Gallery, AAG, BCC, On Paper, The Gallery, Berkshire Mus., Five Points, Honey Sharp, Arkos, Fauve, Tokonoma, Sch. Visual Arts; performance pieces include Candlelight Inn, Lenox, 1992, Unitarian Ch., Pittsfield, Mass., 1992, North Adams (Mass.) State Coll., 1992, Ward-Nasse Gallery, N.Y.C., 1992, CW Post, Brookville, N.Y., 1992, Bettes Life and Times, Williamstown, Mass., 1990, Camerata Conservatory, Hartford, 1989; pub. In the Arts, 1991—. Grantee Pittsfield Art Lottery, 1992, 88, 87, N. Berkshire Arts Lottery, 1992, 91, 89, 86, Great Barrington Arts Lottery, 1991, Stockbridge Arts Lottery, 1984. Home: PO Box 556 Housatonic MA 01236-0556

STEINFELS, MARGARET O'BRIEN, editor; b. Chgo., July 28, 1941; m. Peter Steinfels, Aug. 31, 1963; 2 children: Gabrielle, John Melville. BS, Loyola U., Chgo., 1963; MA, NYU, 1971. Editor Hastings Ctr. Report, 1974-80; social sci. editor Basic Books, 1980-81; bus. mgr., later exec. editor Christianity and Crisis, 1981-84; founding editor Church mag., dir. publs. Nat. Pastoral Life Ctr., 1984-87, dir. publications; editor Commonweal mag., 1988—. Author: Who's Minding the Children: The History and Politics of Day Care in America, 1974. Office: Commonweal 15 Dutch St New York NY 10038-3719*

STEINHAUER, GILLIAN, lawyer; b. Aylesbury, Bucks, Eng., Oct. 6, 1938; d. Eric Frederick and Maisie Kathleen (Yeates) Pearson; m. Bruce William Steinhauer, Jan. 2, 1960; children: Alison (Humphrey) Eric, John, Elspeth. AB cum laude, Bryn Mawr (Pa.) Coll., 1959; JD cum laude, U. Mich., 1976. Bar: Mich. 1976, Mass. 1992, U.S. Dist. Ct. (ea. dist.) Mich. 1976, U.S. Ct. Appeals (6th cir.) 1982. Assoc. Miller, Canfield, Paddock & Stone, Detroit, 1976-82, sr. ptnr., 1983-92; dir. Commonwealth of Mass. Workers' Compensation Litigation Unit, Boston, 1992—; mem. Atty. Gen.'s Task Force to Reduce Waste, Fraud and Abuse in the Workers' Compensation System, 1992—. Chancellor Cath. Ch. St. Paul, Detroit, 1976-83, 91; pres. bd. trustees Cath. Cmty. Svcs. Inc., 1989-92; bd. dirs. Spaulding for Children, 1991-92, Davenport House, 1992—; mem. Vestry St. Michael's Ch., Marblehead, Mass., 1994—. Mem. Mich. State Bar Found. (life); mem. State Bar Mich., Fed. Bar Assn., Fed. Jud. Conf. 6th Cir. (life), Women Lawyers Assn., Bryn Mawr Club of Mich. (pres. 1970-91). Home: 510 Hale St Prides Crossing MA 01965 Office: 100 Cambridge St Rm 1801 Boston MA 02202

STEINHAUSER, JANICE MAUREEN, university administrator, artist; b. Oklahoma City, Okla., Apr. 3, 1935; d. Max Charles and Charlotte (Gold) Glass; m. Stuart Z. Hirschman, Dec. 30, 1954 (div. 1965); children: Shayle, David, Susan; m. Sheldon Steinhauser, May 2, 1965; children: Karen, Lisa Steinhauser Hackel. BFA, U. Colo., Denver, 1972; student, U. Mich., 1953-55. Community affairs adminstr. United Bank Denver, 1973-76; dir. visual arts program Western States Arts Found., Denver, 1976-79; exec. dir. Artreach, Inc., Denver, 1980-82; v.p. mktg. Mammoth Gardens, Denver, 1982-83; dir. pub. rels. Denver Ctr. for Performing Arts, 1983-86; founder, pres. Resource Co., Denver, 1986-88; dir. liberal studies div. Univ. Coll. U. Denver, 1992—. Bd. dirs. Met. Denver Arts Alliance, 1982-85, Denver Internat. Film Festival, 1983-86, Colo. Nat. Abortion Rights Action League, 1991-95. Mem. Women's Forum Colo., Colo. New Music Assn. (bd. dirs. 1987-91), Asian Performing Arts Colo. (bd. dirs. 1989—), Art Students League Denver, Phi Beta Kappa, Kappa Delta Phi. Democrat. Jewish.

STEINMAN, LISA MALINOWSKI, English literature educator, writer; b. Willimantic, Conn., Apr. 8, 1950; d. Zenon Stanislaus and Shirley Belle Malinowski; m. James A. Steinman, Apr. 1968 (div. 1980); m. James L. Shugrue, July 23, 1984. BA, Cornell U., 1971, MFA, 1973, PhD, 1976. Asst. prof. English Reed Coll., Portland, Oreg., 1976-82, assoc. prof., 1982-90, prof., 1990—, Kenan prof. English lit. and humanities, 1993—; cons. NEH, Washington, 1984-85. Author: Lost Poems, 1976, Made in America, 1987, All That Comes to Light, 1989, A Book of Other Days, 1992; editor Hubbub Mag., 1983—; editl. bd. Williams Rev., 1991—, Stevens Jour., 1994—; contbr. articles to profl. jours. Fellow Danforth Found., 1971-75, NEH, 1983, Oreg. Arts Commn., 1983-84, Nat. Endowment for Arts, 1984; Rockefeller Found. scholar, 1987-88; recipient Pablo Neruda award, 1987, Oreg. Inst. Literary Arts award, 1993. Mem. MLA, Poets and Writers, PEN (N.W. chpt., co-founder, officer 1989-93). Home: 5344 SE 38th Ave Portland OR 97202-4208 Office: Reed Coll Dept English 3203 SE Woodstock Blvd Portland OR 97202-8199

STEINMAN, LYNNE ANN, psychologist; b. N.Y.C., June 15, 1953; d. Alfred Maurice and Roslyn (Bennett) S. BS, U. Ill., Champaign, 1974; MA, U. So. Calif., 1978, PhD, 1982; postdoctoral, UCLA, 1986-88. lic. clin. psychologist, Calif. Pvt. practice psychology Los Angeles, 1980—; past clin. dir. adult svcs. Ingleside Hosp., Rosemead, Calif. Mem. Am. Psychol. Assn., Phi Kappa Phi. Office: 23504 Lyons Ave Ste 305 Santa Clarita CA 91321-2534

STEINMAN, SHIRLEY PAULINE, registrar; b. Pennsburg, Pa., Oct. 3, 1938; d. Fred and Mary (Fels) Leister. MS in Fin. Svcs., Am. Coll., 1986, MS in Mgmt., 1993. CLU, chartered fin. cons. Registrar, cert. officer Am. Coll. Office: Am Coll 270 S Bryn Mawr Ave Bryn Mawr PA 19010-2110

STEINMETZ, KAYE H., state legislator; m. Bob Steinmetz; children: Mark, Steven, Richard, Stacey. Grad., Columbia Coll.; postgrad., U. Mo. Mem. Mo. Ho. of Reps., chmn. children, youth and families com., mem. social svc. and Medicaid com., edn. com., appropriations com. for social svc. and corrections, others. Alt. del. Nat. Conf. State Legis.; bd. dirs. Nat. Order Women Legislators, Mo. State Jr. Miss Scholar Progam; mem. Gov. Conf. Edn., 1976, Gov. Conf. Children and Youth, White House Conf. Aging, Mo. State Adv. Bd. Sch. Nurses and Parents as 1st Tchrs., Adv. Bd. Ct. App. Spl. Advocates, Planning Coun. United Way Greater St. Louis, Mo. PTA. Recipient Woman of Achievement award, 1975, Dem. Meritorious Svc. award St. Louis Globe; named to 10 Best Legislators List by Mo. Times. Address: 1814 Kilmory Dr Florissant MO 63031-4154 Office: Mo Ho of Reps State Capital Jefferson City MO 65101*

STEIN-NOVACK, PHYLLIS SUSAN, journalist; b. Phila., May 22, 1949; d. Manuel and Berthe (Brucker) Stein; m. Edward Novack, Nov. 8, 1981. BA in English, Temple U., 1971, postgrad., 1974-76. Asst. traveling radio press sec. Senator George McGovern, 1972; grad. student intern, reporter The Evening Bullet, Phila., 1976; freelance journalist The Phila. (Pa.) Inquirer, 1977-85; dance critic The Welcomat, 1983-85; gen. assignment reporter The Courier-Post, Cherry Hill, N.J., 1985-86; monthly food and wine columnist Applause Mag., Phila., 1986-88; contbg. editor Mid-Atlantic Country Mag., Greenbelt, Md., 1988—. Author: Best of the Book and the Cook, 1990; creator, prodr.: (newsletter) The Phila. Dance Alliance, 1988—; editorial cons. Conde Nast Traveler, 1993; contbr. articles to various mags. including The Phila. (Pa.) Daily News, 1982—, The Gourmet Retailer, 1991—, Diversion Mag., 1993. Mem. Les Dames d'Escoffier (bd. mem. 1991—). Home and Office: 230 N 22nd St #11A Philadelphia PA 19103

STEINRAUF, JEAN HAMILTON, biochemistry professor; b. Airdrie, Scotland, Feb. 5, 1938; came to U.S., 1962; d. Alexander Risk and Margaret Shaw Jarvie (Swann) Hamilton; m. Larry King Steinrauf, Nov. 28, 1968; children: Joseph Hamilton, Alexis Willa. BS, Glasgow (Scotland) U., 1959, PhD, 1962. Postdoctoral fellow U. Ill., Urbana, 1962-64; from resident assoc. to prof. sch. medicine Ind. U., Indpls., 1964—. Contbr. articles to profl. jours. Recipient Career Devel. awd. NIH, 1966-70, rsch. grants, NIH, 1966—. Office: Ind U Sch Medicine Dept Biochemistry 635 Barnhill Dr Bldg 450 Indianapolis IN 46202-5126

STEITZ, ELLA EMMA, artist, educator; b. Bklyn.; d. August and Anna (Pimat) Antpusat; m. Alfred C. Steitz; children: Lanning Dennis, Judith Lynn Weis. Art cert., Maironius Art Acad., Kaunas, Lithuania; student, Pratt Inst., Bklyn., Nassau C.C., 1988. Pub. rels. speaker Nat. Bank N.Am., West Hempstead, N.Y., 1962-75; instr. art Village of Lynbrook, N.Y., 1981-85, City of Glen Cove, N.Y., 1987-90, Rockville Centre (N.Y.) Recreation Dept., 1976—; spkr., demonstrator Nat. Coun. State Garden Clubs, 1965—, master flower show judge, 1970—. Author: Pressing Flowers for Fun and Profit, 1970; exhibited in group shows in Southampton (N.Y.) Gallery, 1976, Lever House Gallery, N.Y.C., 1984, Hutchins Gallery, Greenvale, N.Y., 1986; pvt. collections, U.S. Chair Civic Beautificatoin Com., Garden City, N.Y., 1985—; master gardener Cornell Coop. Ext., Plainview, N.Y., 1989—; sec. Salvation Army, Garden City, 1965-82. Recipient Grumbacher award Ind. Art Soc., 1980, Creativity award Federated Garden Clubs, 1985, numerous awards from flower and art shows. Mem. Tri-County Art League (A. Roos Meml. award 1986), Art League Nassau County (Excellence award 1980), Floral Park Art League (Best in Show award 1985, 87), Village Art Club (Winsor and Newton award, Newton award 1986), Village Garden Club (pres. 1973-75, Tri Color award 1965). Home and Studio: 127 Oxford Blvd Garden City NY 11530

STELLA, CONCETTA AMELIA, medical administrator, consultant; b. Bklyn., Nov. 22, 1940; d. Joseph Domenick and Maria (Savino) S. BA in Biology, Bklyn. Coll., 1963; MPH, N.Y. U., 1981; cert. in alcoholism counseling, Marymount Coll., 1989; postgrad., New Sch. for Social Rsch., 1991—. Coord. neurosurgery N.Y. U. Med. Ctr., N.Y.C., 1961-83; adminstr. pediatric primary care St. Lukes-Roosevelt Med. Ctr., N.Y.C., 1983-86; program coord. radiology Coll. Physicians and Surgeons, Neurol. Inst., N.Y.C., 1986-87; mgr. MRI radiology N.Y. U. Med. Ctr., N.Y.C., 1987-88; mgr. KBDI, 1988-89; adminstr., gen. mgr. Corinthian Diagnostic Radiology, N.Y.C., 1989—; cons. Physician Offices for Reimbursement and Coding, N.Y.C., 1990—; lectr. in field; panelist Jr. League Drugs and Alcohol, 1989. Active Planned Parenthood, 1987—, Epicopal Soc. Ministry on Aging, 1988—, Diocese N.Y. commn. on Drug and Alcohol Abuse, 1989—, Partnership for Homeless, 1990—. Mem. Nat. Health Care Radiology Adm., Health Care Fin. Assn. (Advanced standing), Magnetic Resonance Mgrs. Soc., Women's City Club N.Y., N.Y. Fedn. of Alcohol Counselors, N.Y.S. Pub. Health Assn., N.Y.C. Ambulatory Care Assn., Med. Group Mgmt. Assn. (radiology assembly), N.Y.U. Grad Sch. Pub. Adminstr. Alumni. Democrat. Episcopalian. Office: Corinthian Diagnostic Radiology 345 E 37th St Ste 204 New York NY 10016-3217

STELTZLEN, JANELLE HICKS, lawyer; b. Atlanta, Sept. 18, 1937; d. William Duard and Mary Evelyn (Embrey) Hicks; divorced; children: Gerald William III, Christa Diane. BS, Okla. State U., 1958; MS, Kans. State U., 1961; JD, U. Tulsa, 1981. Bar: Okla. 1981, U.S. Dist. Ct. (no., ea. and we. dists.) Okla. 1981, U.S. Tax Ct. 1982, U.S. Ct. Claims 1982, U.S. Ct. Appeals (10th cir.) 1983, U.S. Ct. Appeals (Fed. cir.) 1984, U.S. Supreme Ct. 1986; lic. real estate broker. Pvt. practice, Tulsa, 1981—; lectr. Coll. of DuPage, Glen Ellyn, Ill., 1976, Tulsa Jr. Coll., 1981-88; dietitian, Tulsa; res. dep. for Tulsa County Sheriff's Office. Christian counselor 1st United Meth. Ch., Tulsa, 1986—, coord. legal counseling ministry, 1985—, lay pastor, 1987—; mem. Tulsa County Bd. Equalization and Excise Tax Bd., 1989-90; mem. Leadership Tulsa XX, 1993—; bd. dirs. Sister Cities Tulsa/San Luis Potosi, 1988—, South Peoria Neighborhood Connection Found., 1991—; active Tulsa County Tax Oversight Com., 1994—, Tulsa Home Rule Charter Com., 1994—. Recipient Okla. Sr. Olympics medal. Mem. Okla. Bar Assn., Tulsa County Bar Assn., Vol. Lawyers Assn. (bd. dirs.), Am. Dietetic Assn., Tulsa Dist. Dietetic Assn., Kiwanis Internat., Mensa, DAR, Delta Zeta. Republican. Home: 6636 S Jamestown Pl Tulsa OK 74136-2615 Office: 1150 E 61st St Tulsa OK 74136-0565

STENDER, LINDA DE MILT, county official; b. Fanwood, N.J., July 25, 1951; d. Kenneth E. and Shirley (Lamperti) deMilt; m. Richard Chapman Stender, June 26, 1976; children: Caroline, Niel, Tyler. BA, Am. U., 1973. Councilwoman Borough of Fanwood, 1988-90, mayor, 1992—; freeholder County of Union, Elizabeth, 1994—. Chmn. Fanwood Downtown Commn., 1984-85; mem. Fanwood Planning Bd., 1986; active Fanwood Scotch Plains PTA. Mem. N.J. Elected Women Ofcls., Union County Women's Polit. Caucus (v.p. 1989), Fanwood Scotch Plains Coll. Club. Democrat. Office: Office Bd Chosen Freeholders County Adminstn Bldg Elizabethtown Plaza Elizabeth NJ 07207

STENMARK, JEAN KERR, mathematics educator; b. Davis, Calif., Aug. 25, 1922; d. Norman and Rachel Minerva (Bledsoe) Kerr; m. Roy M., Aug. 24, 1952, (div. July 1975); children: Ruthann, John, Jane. BA, U. Calif., Berkeley, 1942; MS, Calif. State U., Hayward, 1978. Cert. elem. tchr., Calif. With civil svc. U.S. Navy-Aviation Supply, Oakland, Calif., 1942-45; acct. various acctg. firms, San Francisco, 1945-56; tchr. Oakland Unified Sch. Dist., 1969-80; maths. specialist EQUALS and Family Math. Programs U. Calif., Berkeley, 1980—; cons. Calif. Assessment Program, Sacramento, 1975-92; mem. adv. bd. Coop. Math. Project, Danville, Calif., 1987—. Editor: Mathematics Assessment: Myths, Models, Good Questions and Practical Suggestions, 1991, 101 Short Problems, 1995; author: Assessment Alternatives in Mathematics, 1989; co-author: Family Math, 1986, Math for Girls and Other Problem Solvers, 1981; editor: Sharing Resources Newsletter. Mem. Nat. Coun. Tchrs. Maths., Calif. Maths. Coun., Math/Sci. Network, Internat. Orgn. Women in Maths. and Sci., PTA (hon. life mem.). Democrat. Protestant. Home: 1201 Brickyard Way #408 Point Richmond CA 94801-4151 Office: U Calif EQUALS Lawrence Hall of Sci Berkeley CA 94720

STENSLAND, JILL REBECCA, banker; b. Rochester, Minn., Mar. 16, 1960; d. Milton C. and Jacqueline (I.) S.; m. David T. Gilbertson, Sept. 2, 1990. BSBA cum laude, U. Wis., Menomonie, 1982; postgrad., U. St. Thomas, 1993—. With 1st Bank, Austin, Minn., 1980, Vermillion (Minn.) State Bank; Hudsons, Mpls.; officer Met. Fed. Bank, Mpls., 1987-89, area sales mgr., 1989-90, mgr., asst. v.p., 1990-93. Mem. C. of C., N.W. Racquet Club. Lutheran.

STENSLAND, LINDA L., state senator; 3 children. Student, Sioux Falls Coll., Augustana Coll. Mem. S.D. State Senate from 14th dist.; pres. Environ. Consulting Co. Author: Ground Water Protection Act, Comprehensive Recycling Act. Mem. edn. and job tng. com. State Fed. Assembly of Nat. Conf. State Legislatures; bd. dirs. Nat. Recycling Coalition, Washington. Democrat. Lutheran. Home: 1800 E Otonka Rdg Sioux Falls SD 57103-4565 Office: SD Senate Pierre SD 57501*

STEORTS, NANCY HARVEY, international management consultant; b. Syracuse, N.Y., Nov. 28, 1936; d. Frederick William and Josephine Elizabeth (Jones) Harvey; 1 dau., Deborah Joan. BS, Syracuse U., 1959. Asst. buyer, public relations coordinator Woodward & Lothrop, Washington, 1958-61; home economist Washington Gas Light Co., 1961-64; sales assoc. real estate Summit, N.J., 1967-68; survey specialist Dept. Agr., Washington, 1968-69; chmn. Consumer Product Safety Commn., Washington, D.C., 1981-85; pres. Nancy Harvey Steorts & Assocs., Dallas, 1985-88, Nancy Harvey Steorts Internat., Washington and Dallas, 1988—; cons. Exec. Reorgn. Govt., Washington, 1971; nat. dir. women's speakers' bur. Com. Re-elect Pres., Washington, 1971-72; dir. candlelight dinners Presdl. Inaugural Commn., 1972-73, 81; expns. dir. Dept. Commerce, Washington, 1973; spl. asst. for consumer affairs to sec. agr., 1973-77; pres. Nancy Harvey Steorts & Assocs., 1977-81; disting. lectr., Strom Thurmond Inst. Govt. and Pub. Affairs, Clemson U.; mem. adv. coun. to bd. dirs., Adolph Coors Co.; mem. U.S. Dept. of Commerce Nat. Adv. Com. Tex., Nat. Adv. Com., Dist. Export Coun. Tex., Nat. Adv. Com. Export Now; mem. working com. on standards between U.S. and Russia; U.S. del. NAFTA Com. on environ. standards; bd. govs. Nat. Consumers adv. com. Fed. Reserve, 1990-93; U.S. del. to CO-POLCO, Am. Nat. Standards Inst., The Hague, The Netherlands, NAFTA Del. on Environ. Standards; dir. People to People Trade Mission to Spain, 1987; del. Japan-Tex. Trade Mission, Tokyo, Osaka, Japan, Moscow, Kiev, Leningrad, U.S.-Russia Bus. Devel. Com. on Stds.; chmn. Dallas del. to meet with Prince Charles; mem. nat. consumer adv. coun. Fed. Res. Bd.; official U.S. rep. to 4th Pub. Health, Med. Equipment and Drugs Expn. Moscow USSR; speaker U.S. Seminar Soviet Health Care Exhbn., Moscow; bd. dirs., corp. adv. bd. Sch. Mgmt., Syracuse U.; mem. nat. consumer adv. com. Am. Nat. Standards Inst.; bd. dirs. Mission Investment Trust Co., Tuscon; internat. lectr. and keynote speaker in field. Producer, host syndicated TV show spl. Trustee Food Safety Council Conf. Consumer Orgn.; bd. dirs. Women's Inst. Am. U.; bd. advisers Coll. Human Devel., Allumnae Assn., Syracuse U.; commr. Montgomery County Commn. Women; pres. Welcome Wagon Clubs from 1986, Dallas Citizens Council, 1986—; bd. dirs. Council of Better Bus. Burs.; bd. adv. Am. U. Women's Inst.; bd. dirs. Med. Coll. Pa., Tex. Women's Alliance; bd. dirs., vice-chmn. regional devel. Nat. Assn. Women Bus. Owners; mem. internat. com. Com. 2000; bd. dirs. Jr. Achievement, United Way, Dallas, Goals of Dallas, Internat. Mayor's Ball; internat. del. 1st Women's Internat. Trade Mission to Europe for Women Entrepeneurs; chairwoman Trade Mission of Women Leaders to Taiwan, 1988; del. to USSR Internat. Women's Forum Mission; mem. adv. coun. to So. Meth. U. Dept. Economics; co-chmn. fundraising, Dallas Symphony; coord. bicentennial presdl. inaugural dinners, 1989; pres. Dallas Citizens' Coun., 1986-88; chmn. Afternoon with Oprah Winfrey Fundraising Benefit; chmn. Women Leaders Delegation to Taiwan; mem. corp. bd. dirs. Ariz. Rehab. Systems; overseer U.S. Dept. Commerce; mem. Am. Nat. Standards Inst., Nat. Consumer Adv. Coun.; bd. dirs. Nat. Women's Econ. Alliance Found., I Have a Dream Found.; chmn. Dallas Glass Ceiling Commn.; bd. overseers Tex. Quality Bd. Recipient George P. Arents Pioneer medal Syracuse U., 1979, spl. award for consumer concern Nat. Diet Workshop, Malcolm Baldridge award, Bd. of Overseers; named one of five outstanding pub. servants Gallagher Report, 1984. Mem. Nat. Bd. Dirs., Am. Home Econs. Assn., AAUW, Nat. Consumers League, Am. Women in Radio and TV, Exec. Women in Govt. (chmn.), Nat. Conf. Consumer Orgns., Syracuse U. Alumni Assn. (bd. dirs.). Office: 4689 S Versailles Ave Dallas TX 75209-6017

STEPHANI, NANCY JEAN, social worker, journalist; b. Garden City, Mich., Feb. 19, 1955; d. Ernest Helmut Schulz and Margaret Mary Fowler Thompson; m. Edward Jeffrey Stephani, Aug. 29, 1975; children: Edward J., Margaret J., James E. AA, Northwood Inst., Midland, Mich., 1975; student in social work, Boston Coll., 1991; BS summa cum laude, Lourdes Coll., Sylvania, Ohio, 1992; postgrad., Ohio State U., 1993—. Lic. social worker. Profl. facilitator Parents United, Findlay, Ohio, 1989—; contbg. writer Cath. Chronicle, Toledo, 1988—; mem. ministry formation faculty Cath. Diocese of Toledo, 1992—; social work clinician Family Svc. Hancock County, Blanchard Valley Home Health Social Svc.; trustee, bd. dirs. Hope House for the Homeless, Findlay, Ohio, 1990—; adult edn. coord. St. Michael Parish, Findlay, 1986-93, mem. strategic plan core com., 1989-91, v.p. pres. parish coun., 1985-89; program planning com. Cath. Diocese Family Life Conf., 1994-95. Founder Food Coop., MPBA, Findlay, 1981; founding mem. Chopin Hall, Findlay, 1983; mem. Hancock County AIDS Task Force, 1994—. Nat. Inst. Food Svcs. grantee, 1974; Diocese of Toledo grantee, 1991; Ohio State U. Coll. Social Work grantee, 1994. Mem. NOW, NASW, Am. Assn. on Child Abuse, Transpsychol. Assn., Friends of Creation Sprituality, Call to Action, Pax Christi. Home: 2615 Goldenrod Ln Findlay OH 45840-1025

STEPHANICK, CAROL ANN, dentist, consultant; b. South Amboy, N.J., Feb. 5, 1952; d. Edward Eugene and Gladys (Pionkowski) S. BS, Rutgers U., 1974; MS, Med. Coll. Pa., 1980; DMD, Temple U., 1984. Lic. dentist, Pa., N.J., Vt. Med. technologist Jersey Shore Med. Ctr., Neptune, N.J., 1975-76, South Amboy Meml. Hosp., 1976-78, Smith-Kline Clin. Labs., King of Prussia, Pa., 1981; instr. dept. biology St. Peter's Coll., Jersey City, 1976-78; instr., edn. coord. Coll. Allied Health, Hahnemann U., Phila., 1978-80; instr. dept. oral radiology Sch. Dentistry, Temple U., Phila., 1984-87; assoc. dentist Personal Choice Dental Assocs., South Amboy, 1985-86, Marcucci and Marcucci, P.C., Phila., 1986-90, Gwynedd Dental Assocs., Springhouse, Pa., 1990-92; spl. events coord. Liberty Dental Conf., Phila., 1990—. Neighbor patrol Sprague St. Neighbors Town Watch, Phila., 1986-93. Named to Legion of Honor, Chapel of Four Chaplains, 1987. Mem. ADA, Pa. Dental Assn., Philadelphia County Dental Soc. (publicity coord. 1990—, pub. info. coord. 1991, semi-finalist judge sr. smile contest 1990—, com. on concerns of women dentists, select com. 1988—), Delaware Valley Assn. Women Dentists, Am. Assn. for Functional Orthodontics, Am. Soc. Clin. Pathologists (med. technologist), Delta Sigma Delta. Roman Catholic. Home: 14 Colonial Ave Haddonfield NJ 08033 Office: 777 White Horse Pike S Hammonton NJ 08037-2029

STEPHENS, DEBORAH LYNN, health facility executive; b. Newton, Iowa, May 30, 1952; d. Clarence Harry and Nancy Elizabeth (Gass) Wright; m. David K. Brender, Dec. 18, 1971 (div.); m. Michael E. Stephens, May 21, 1988. BS, U. Iowa, 1974; postgrad., U. Wis., Milw., 1978-80, U. Calif., Berkeley, 1987. Asst. to dean of fin. U. Iowa Coll. Medicine, Iowa City, 1975-77; contract audit acct. Miller Brewing Co., Milw., 1977-79; asst. controller Unicare Health Facilities, Milw., 1979-81; v.p. fin. Sacred Heart Rehab. Hosp., Milw., 1981-84; exec. v.p., chief operating officer Sacred Heart Rehab. Hosp., Med. Rehab. Inst., Milw., 1984-88; prin. founding mem., pres., chief exec. officer Behavioral Health Systems, Birmingham, Ala., 1989—, also bd. dirs.; cons. on rehab., corp. planning and zero-base budgeting, Birmingham, 1988; bd. dirs. Rehab. Mgmt. Svc., Inc., Milw., 1986-88, Med. Rehab. Equipment, Inc., Milw., 1986-88; founding mem. Am. Rehab. Network, Inc., Washington, 1986-87; mem. oral exam. bd. City of Milw., 1984-86; mem. prospective payment adv. com. HHS, Washington, 1986; nat. presenter on zero-base budgeting, corp. reorgns., managed care, and planning. Contbr. articles to profl. jours. Mem. healthcare cost containment com. Bus. Coun. Ala., Rotary Club of Birmingham. Mem. Hosp. Fin. Mgmt. Assn. (governing bd. 1981-88), Nat. Forensic League (life), Nat. Assn. Accts., Nat. Assn. Rehab. Facilities (prospective payment adv. bd. 1986-88, com. on med. oriented facilities 1983-88), Birmingham C. of C., Kappa Kappa Gamma Alumnae Assn, Venture Club. Office: Behavioral Health Systems 2 Metroplex Dr Ste 503 Birmingham AL 35209-6827

STEPHENS, DELIA MARIE LUCKY, lawyer; b. Temple, Tex., Aug. 2, 1939; d. James Richard and Mattie (Barfield) Lucky; m. Billy C. Stephens, 1962 (div. 1983); children: William Carl, James Kelley. BA, U. Mary Hardin-Baylor, 1961; JD, Thurgood Marshall Sch. Law, Houston, 1981. Bar: Tex. 1981, U.S. Dist. Ct. (so. dist.) Tex. 1981. Pvt. practice law Houston, 1981—. Writer feature stories The Jour. Newspapers, 1976-79. Elder, trustee Clear Lake Presbyn. Ch., Houston, 1985—; founding dir. East-West Cultural Inst., 1991—; bd. dirs. Palmer Drug Abuse Coun., 1986-90. Mem. AAUW, Tex. State Bar Assn., Houston Bar Assn., Houston Rose Soc., Am. Rose Soc., Houston Mus. Fine Arts, U. Mary Hardin-Baylor Alumni Assn. (nominating com. 1973), Coastal Bend Mary Hardin-Baylor Club (pres. 1972), Clear Lake Area C. of C., Houston Outdoor Nature Club. Democrat. Presbyn. Home: 482 Lost Rock Dr Webster TX 77598-2640 Office: 17000 El Camino Real Ste 104 Houston TX 77058-2632

STEPHENS, GAY, public administrator; b. Aurora, Ill., Sept. 29, 1951; d. Benjamin Mark Jr. and Joyce Audrey (Sinclair) S. BA magna cum laude, George Williams Coll., 1973, MS summa cum laude, 1975. Clin. dir. Village of Downers Grove (Ill.) Dept. Health and Human Svcs., 1975-78; exec. dir. Villages of Bloomingdlae (Ill.) Police Program, 1978-81, Family Support Ctr., Aurora, 1981-83; devel. dir. Family Svc. & Mental Health Ctr. of Oak Park, Ill., 1983-88; mgmt. cons. United Way of Chgo., 1988-89; exec. Office of Inspector Gen. Ill. Dept. Mental Health and Devel. Disabilities, Chgo., 1989—. Mem. Unitarian Ch. of Naperville, 1973—; vol. Girl Scouts U.S. of DuPage County, Naperville, 1973-77; bd. dirs. Horizons, 1991-92. Mem. Nat. Soc. Fundraising Execs., Women in Mgmt., Chgo. Area Runners Assn., Kappa Delta Phi. Democrat.

STEPHENS, LIZETTE, electronics specialist; b. Purcell, Okla., Aug. 29, 1947; d. H.R. and Emma Eudena (Blankenship) S.; m. Ben M. Nance, June 3, 1966 (dec. 1994); children: Kilian Nance, Dawn Nance, Eric Nance. Student, U. Okla., 1965, Ctrl. State U., 1966, 69, Okla. State U., 1983. Bench hand Western Electric, Oklahoma City, 1973-74; field rep. U.S. Census Bur., Denver, 1976; electronic specialist AT&T, Oklahoma City, 1976—. Author 2021 Electrical Worker, 1985-89; editor Elephant Ear, 1974-76. Mem. exec. bd. Ctrl. Okla. Young Reps., Oklahoma City, 1974-76; registrar Oklahoma County Election Bd., 1975; mem. platform com. Oklahoma County Rep. Conv., Oklahoma City, 1975; leader Redlands Coun. Girl Scouts, Oklahoma City, 1981. Named Outstanding Young Rep., Ctrl. Okla. Young Reps., 1975. Mem. Internat. Brotherhood Elec. Workers (coord. 1982-89), Save Work and Time-Total Quality Control (team leader 1992-94). United Methodist. Home: 8529 SW 37th St Oklahoma City OK 73179 Office: AT&T 7725 W Reno Oklahoma City OK 73126

STEPHENS, MARTHA FOSTER, advertising executive; b. Lansing, Mich., Dec. 4, 1961; d. Richard Bailey and Gretchen (Meyer) Foster; m. Mark Burgis Stephens, Apr. 11, 1987; children: Emily Kaitlynn, Matthew Foster. BA in English, Mich. State U., 1984; postgrad., Wayne State U. Mem. editorial staff Better Investing, Royal Oak, Mich., 1986-88; with communications Holtzman and Silverman, Farmington Hills, Mich., 1988-89; tech. writer, intern Unisys, Plymouth, Mich., 1989; dir. corp. svcs. and advt. Nat. Assn. Investors Corp., Royal Oak, 1989—. Mem. Nat. Investor Rels. Inst. (sec. 1991-92, v.p. membership 1992-93, v.p. programs 1993-94, pres. 1994—). Office: Nat Assn Investors Corp PO Box 220 Royal Oak MI 48068

STEPHENS, MARY ANN, real estate broker; b. Claremont, N.H., June 26, 1950; d. Basil and Katherine M. (Burbee) N.; m. Scott Stephens, Jan. 1, 1983 (div. 1988); children: Laura Jeanette, Anthony Inman Pattinson. AA, Northhampton (Mass.) Jr. Coll., 1970. Legal sec. Pinellas County State's Atty., Clearwater, Fla., 1971-73; real estate assoc. Jim Eyster Realty, Crystal River, Fla., 1980-83; real estate broker Citrus Hills, Hernando, Fla., 1983-86, Hampton Square Realty, Hernando, 1986-90, Re/Max Realty One, Crystal River, 1990—. Mem. Crystal River C. of C. (Eagle award 1993). Home: 11939 W Waterwood Loop Crystal River FL 34429-5234 Office: Re/Max Realty One 730 N Suncoast Blvd Crystal River FL 34429-5470

STEPHENS, PATRICIA ANN, marketing professional; b. Gulfport, Miss., Feb. 1, 1945; d. James Marshall and Edna Mathilda (Hogan) S. BA, St. Louis U., 1967; MA, Memphis State U., 1971. Lic. secondary educator speech, theatre, English, religion. Exec. v.p. Prodns. Unltd., Memphis, 1971-73; chairperson speech dept. Southaven (Miss.) High Sch., 1973-77; instr. speech N.W. Jr. Coll., Southaven, 1974-76; pub. rels. dir., instr. St. Agnes Acad., Memphis, 1977-78; religion and English instr. Memphis Cath. High Sch., 1978-82; resource tchr. communications Mobile (Ala.) City Schs., 1982-84; mktg. devel. specialist/mktg. mgr. Prime Health Ala., Mobile, 1984-85; mktg. mgr. Blue Cross Blue Shield Fla./Health Options, Lakeland and Orlando, Fla., 1986-92; ind. agt., 1992-94; nat. mktg. and svc. coord. Delta Care, PMI, Tampa, 1994—. Bd. mem. Red Balloon Players, Memphis, 1971-73, Downtown Dream Machine, Memphis, 1980-82, Cir. Playhouse/Playhouse on the Square, Memphis, 1980-82. Newspaper Fund fellow Wall St. Jour. Newspaper Fund, U. Oreg., 1968, writing fellow Greater Memphis Writing Project, Memphis State U., 1980, part-time masters fellow Memphis State U., 1981-82; recipient Pres.'s Club BCBSF/Health Options Sales Mgr. award Health Options of Polk County, 1987. Democrat. Roman Catholic. Home: 4128 Sunny Land Dr Lakeland FL 33813-3946 Office: Deltacare/Delta Dental Ste 300 8875 Hidden River Pkwy Tampa FL 33637

STEPHENS, SHERYL LYNNE, family practice physician; b. Huntington, W.Va., Dec. 11, 1949; d. William Clayton Stephens and Virginia Eleanor (Hatten) Stephens Terry; 1 child, William Earl Hicks III (dec.); m. Lannie Dale Rowe, Jan. 17, 1981; 1 child, Seton Christopher. BA, U. Ky., 1972; MA, Marshall U., 1982, MD, 1988. Tchr. Wayne County Bd. Edn., Ceredo, W.Va., 1973-83; real estate developer Huntington, 1981-88; resident in family practice Grant Med. Ctr., Columbus, Ohio, 1988-91; gen. practice physician Columbus (Ohio) Health Dept., 1991—; med. dir. Billie Brown Jones Family Health Ctr., 1992—; sch. physician Columbus Bd. Edn., 1994—; sch. physician Columbus Bd. Edn., 1994; chairperson Coll. Health Dept. Com. on Pharmacy and Therapeutics, 1994-95; rschr., 1976-81. Counselor, instr. Contact of Huntington, 1975-88; polit. activist pro choice movement and ratification of equal rights amemdment, 1976-81. Recipient Leadership award Marshall U., 1985. Mem. Am. Assn. Family Practitioners (pres. 1984-85, Leadership award 1985), Am. Med. Women's Assn. (sec. 1985-86), NOW (pres. 1976-78, 79-81, v.p. Huntington 1978-79, sec. 1981-82), Nat. Abortion Rights Action League. Democrat. Home: 703 French Dr Columbus OH 43228-2978 Office: Columbus Health Dept 181 S Washington Ave Columbus OH 43215-5327

STEPHENS, STEVIE MARIE, psychotherapist; b. San Diego, Feb. 24, 1959. Student, Calif. State U., Fullerton, 1978-80; BA in Sociology with distinction, San Diego State U., 1983; M of Social Welfare, U. Calif., Berkeley, 1988. Lic. clin. social worker, Calif. Homefinder Indian Child Welfare Consortium, Escondido, Calif., 1986; alcoholism counselor, social work intern Harriet Street Ctr., San Francisco, 1986-87; social work intern psychiatry dept. San Francisco Gen. Hosp., 1988; social worker Adult Protective Svcs., Inc., San Diego, 1989-90, Naval Hosp., San Diego, 1990-91; psychotherapist, adminstr. in pvt. practice San Diego, 1993—. Vol. Learning Disabilities Assn. of Calif., San Diego, 1992-93, Battered Women's Svcs., San Diego, 1985-86; pres. coll. chpt. Am. Advt. Fedn., 1979; mem. Comms. Student Activities Coun., Fullerton, 1979. Recipient various naval awards; Kappa Kappa Gamma scholar. Mem. NASW, Calif. Soc. for Clin. Social Work, Am. Mensa, Ltd., Alpha Kappa Delta. Address: PO Box 98 La Jolla CA 92038

STEPHENS, SUNNY COURINGTON, special education educator; b. Abilene, Tex., Mar. 13, 1943; d. Samuel Delmar and Delta Ree (Kniffen) Courington; m. Kenneth Edward Stephens, Apr. 6, 1967; 1 child, Lane Bradley. BS, Abilene Christian U., 1965; postgrad., U. Tex., 1972; MEd, Our Lady of the Lake Coll., San Antonio, 1977; PhD, Tex. Woman's U., 1983. Cert. secondary tchr., spl. edn. tchr., supr., bilingual tchr., early childhood tchr. Tchr. Poteet (Tex.) Ind. Sch. Dist., 1965-71, San Antonio Ind. Sch. Dist., 1971-79; tchr. South San Antonio Ind. Sch. Dist., 1979-80, dir. spl. edn., 1991—; prof. Incarnate Word Coll., San Antonio, 1978-93; cons. Advocacy, Inc., Austin, Tex., 1981—, Easter Seal Rehab., San Antonio, 1978—, Children's Hosp., San Antonio, 1978—, Sch. Dists., Tex., Ariz., Colo., Ill., La., 1978—. Author: ABC Cookery, 1980, Curriculum Guide Early Childhood, 1978, (multimedia program) Learning Thru Success, 1980; contbr. articles to profl. jours. Named Outstanding Profl. Nat. Spina Bifida Assn., 1986, Tex. Prof. of Yr. Coun. for Advancement and Support of Edn., 1987, Estee Lauder Knowing Woman, 1988. Mem. Tex. Coun. Exceptional Children (pres. 1980-81), Tex. Spina Bifida Assn. (bd. dirs. 1983-93). Home: RR 1 Box 97 Poteet TX 78065-9742 Office: South San Antonio Sch Dist 2415 W Southcross San Antonio TX 78211

STEPHENS, WANDA BREWER, social services administrator, investor; b. Bolckow, Mo., Nov. 6, 1932; d. Perry Clark and Mary Carolyn (Fisher) Brewer; m. Lloyd Wesley Stephens, June 19, 1954; children: Ruth Ann, Susie Jo, John Allen, Donna Lynn. BS in home econs., U. Ark., 1954, MS, 1958. Cert. secondary edn. Home economics tchr. West Fork (Ark.) High Sch., 1954-58; pres. Devel. Child Care Assn., Fayetteville, Ark., 1971-74; pres., founding bd. Infant Devel. Ctr., Fayetteville, Ark., 1972-75, treas., 1975-81; pres. Am. Assn. Univ. Women, Fayetteville, Ark., 1975-77; edn. chmn., admin. bd. Cen. United Meth. Ch., Fayetteville, Ark., 1976-79; pres. League of Women Voters, Fayetteville, Ark., 1979-83, Nat. Orgn. Women, Fayetteville, Ark., 1983-89; state legis. v.p. NOW, Fayetteville, 1985-90, 93-95;

state pres. Nat. Orgn. Women Ark., Fayetteville, 1991-93; bd. sec., headstart Econ. Opportunity Agy., Fayetteville, 1969-70; treas. Mama's Milk Investment Club, 1970-72. Co-author Bylaws for Economic Opportunities Agy., 1969; co-editor: Washington County, Ark., 1982. Fundraiser United Fun, 1972-75; polit. organizer NOW, 1986; treas. Washington County Dem. Women, 1990-92; organizer/staff/fund Women's Libr., 1982-91; cons./organizer Ctrl. Child Care Ctr., 1977-78. Recipient Internat. 4-H Youth Exch., 1953-54, Infant Devel. Ctr. Founders Plaque Univ. Ark., 1987; named Lay Person of Yr., Ctrl. United Meth. Ch., 1977. Mem. Mental Health Assn. (Community Svc. award 1972), AAUW (Edn. Found. fellowship 1984), ACLU (Susan B. Anthony award 1985), Ark. Women's Polit. Caucus (Uppity Woman award 1987, 92). Democrat. Methodist. Home: 1177 E Ridgeway Dr Fayetteville AR 72701-2612

STEPHENSON, BARBERA WERTZ, lawyer; b. Bryan, Ohio, Dec. 10, 1938; d. Emerson D. and Beryl B. (Barber) Wertz; m. Gerard J. Stephenson Jr., June 22, 1960; 1 child, Thomas. Student, Smith Coll., 1956-57; BSEE, MIT, 1961; JD, U. N.Mex., 1981. Bar: N.Mex. 1981. Electronic engr. Digital Equipment Corp., Maynard, Mass., 1960-66; logic analyst Librascope, Glendale, Calif., 1966; electronic engr. Md. Dept. of Def., Ft. Meade, 1966-68; mem. tech. staff Xerox Data Systems, Rockville, Md., 1968; pvt. practice cons., Silver Spring, Md., 1969-78; pvt. practice law, Albuquerque, 1981—. Author: Financing Your Home Purchase in New Mexico, 1992; patentee analog to digital converter, kitchen calculator. Mem. N.Mex. Bar Assn. Office: 4221 Silver Ave SE Albuquerque NM 87108-2720

STEPHENSON, BETTE MILDRED, physician, former Canadian legislator; b. Aurora, Ont., Can., July 31, 1924; d. Carl Melvin and Clara Mildred (Draper) S.; grad. Earl Haig Coll. Inst.; MD, U. Toronto, 1946; m. Gordon Allan Pengelly, 1948; children: J. Stephen A., Elizabeth Anne A., C. Christopher A., J. Michael A., P. Timothy A., Mary Katharine A. Mem. med. staff Women's Coll. Hosp., 1950-90, chief dept. gen. practice, dir. outpatient dept., 1956-64; mem. med. staff N.Y. Gen. Hosp., 1967-89; elected Ont. Legislature for York Mills, 1975, 77, 81, 85; minister labor, 1975-78; minister edn., minister colls. and univs., 1978-85, treas. and dep. premier, 1985; pres. Gwillimbury Found. Post Secondary Edn.; dir. Can. Inst. Advanced Rsch.; dir. Women's Coll. Hosp.; trustee Recovery Inc. Fellow Coll. Family Physicians Can. (chmn. nat. coordinating com. on edn. 1961-64, chmn. confs. on edn. for gen. practice 1961, 63), Acad. Med. Toronto; mem. Ont. Med. Assn. (dir. 1964-72, pres. 1970-71), Can. Med. Assn. (dir. 1968-75, pres. 1974-75), Art Gallery Ont., Royal Ont. Mus., Order of St. John (officer), Order of Can. (officer).

STEPHENSON, CYNTHIA JO, insurance regulatory specialist; b. Rock Island, Ill., Mar. 27, 1960; d. Richard Gaylen and Emilee Rae (Lewis) S. AS in Liberal Arts, Lincoln Land C.C., 1980; BA in Mgmt., Sangamon State U., 1983, MPA, 1990; postgrad., Loyola U., 1992-93, St. Louis U., 1993—. Methods and procedure advisor Ill. Dept. Pub. Health, Springfield, 1984-85; policy and budget analyst Ill. Bur. of Budget/Exec. Office of Gov., Springfield, 1985-87, 88-90; dir. policy analysis & rsch. Ill. Comprehensive Health Ins. Plan, Springfield, 1990; asst. to dep. dir. fin.-corp. regulatory divsn. Ill. Dept. Ins., Springfield, 1990—. Mem. staff St. Louis U. Pub. Law Rev., 1994—; contbr. articles to profl. jours. Mem. adv. bd., camp vol. COCO Children's Cancer Fund, Springfield, 1989-91; area coord., vol. recruitment com. co-chair 1st Night Springfield, 1989-90. Loyola Law Sch. Merit scholar, 1992-93. Mem. Jr. League Springfield (bd. dirs., chair pub. issues 1992-93). Office: Ill Dept Ins 320 W Washington St Springfield IL 62767

STEPHENSON, IRENE HAMLEN, biorhythm analyst, consultant, editor, educator; b. Chgo., Oct. 7, 1923; d. Charles Martin and Carolyn Hilda (Hilgers) Hamlin; m. Edgar B. Stephenson, Sr., Aug. 16, 1941 (div. 1946); 1 child, Edgar B. Author biorhythm compatibilities column Nat. Singles Register, Norwalk, Calif., 1979-81; instr. biorhythm Learning Tree Open U., Canoga Park, Calif., 1982-83; instr. biorhythm character analysis 1980—; instr. biorhythm compatibility, 1982—; owner, pres. matchmaking svc. Pen Pals Using Biorhythm, Chatsworth, Calif., 1979—; editor newsletter The Truth, 1979-85, Mini Examiner, Chatsworth, 1985—; researcher biorhythm character and compatibility, 1974—, biorhythm columnist Psychic Astrology Horoscope, 1989-94, True Astrology Forecast, 1989-94, Psychic Astrology Predictions, 1990-94; author: Learn Biorhythm Character Analysis, 1980; Do-It-Yourself Biorhythm Compatibilities, 1982; contbr. numerous articles to mags.; frequent guests clubs, radio, TV. Office: PO Box 3893-ww Chatsworth CA 91313

STEPHENSON, LINDA F., public relations executive. With Zigman Joseph Skeen, 1964-69, v.p., 1985-87, exec. v.p., 1987-89; pres., CEO Zigman Joseph Stephenson, 1989—. Office: Zigman Joseph Stephenson 100 E Wisconsin Ave Ste 1000 Milwaukee WI 53202*

STEPHENSON, LINDA JEAN, magazine executive; b. Sacramento, Sept. 26, 1952; d. Homer Nixon and Jean (Hanson) S. BA in Communications, Brigham Young U., 1978. News anchorwoman Sta. KBYU-TV-FM, Provo, Utah, 1977-78; sales rep. Daily Universe, Provo, 1977-78; advt. sales rep. Sawyer Ferguson Walker, N.Y.C., 1978-80; account exec. Gannett Newspaper Advt. Sales, N.Y.C., 1980-84, Ms. mag., N.Y.C., 1985-86; New Eng. mgr. Met. Home mag., N.Y.C., 1984-85, spl. events mgr., 1986-90; spl. events dir. Met. Home, Traditional Home, Country Home mags., N.Y.C., 1990-91; pub. Sunstone mag., Salt Lake City, 1992-93; mgr. The Roof and The Garden Restaurants, Salt Lake City, 1993—. Democrat. Mormon.

STEPHENSON, MARIA I. O'BYRNE, lawyer; b. Cali, Valle, Colombia, Nov. 12, 1951; came to U.S., 1965; d. Alvaro and Maria Teresa (Malvehy) O'Byrne; m. John Edward Stephenson, May 31, 1975; children: Teresa Maria, Phillip David. BA, Tulane U., 1973; JD, U. Houston, 1975. Bar: Tex. 1975, La. 1976. Assoc. Grisbaum & Kleppner, Metairie, La., 1976-78; ptnr. Bryan, Nelson, Allen, Schroeder & Stephenson, New Orleans, 1978-86; pvt. practice New Orleans, 1986—. Active Pan Am. Commn., Baton Rouge, 1993-94; bd. dirs. Shared Housing, New Orleans, 1994—. Recipient Diploma Al Merito, Consulate of Mex., 1994. Mem. La. Bar (bd. dirs. internat. law sect. 1993-94), La.-Mex. Trade Assn. (officer 1991-94), Hispanic Lawyers Assn. (officer 1981-94). Roman Catholic. Office: Law Offices of Maria I O'Byrne Stephenson 905 World Trade Ctr New Orleans LA 70130

STEPNITZ, SUSAN STEPHANIE, special education educator; b. Detroit, Mar. 1, 1948; d. N. Thomas and Dorothy (Richardson) Wagner; m. Kenneth H. Stepnitz Jr., July 25, 1970; children: Joshua, Zachary. BA in Polit. Sci., Olivet Coll., 1970; MA in Spl. Edn., Wayne State U., 1972. Tchr. Traverse Bay Area Intermed. Sch. Dist., Traverse City, Mich., 1973—; negotiator, ednl. profl. and support staff Traverse Bay Area Intermed. Sch. Dist., Travere City, Mich., 1982—; spl. edn. tng. cadre Mich. Edn. Assn., 1990—; spl. edn. adv. com. Mich. Bd. Edn., 1992—; spl. delivery sys. edn. task force Mich. Dept. Edn., 1993-94. Dir. Handicapped Accessibility Awareness Special Kid's Day Nat. Cherry Festival, 1987—. Recipient Anne Sullivan award Mich. Edn. Assn., 1993. Mem. AAUW (pres. Mich. chpt. 1987-89, Outstanding Person in Edn. award 1986, strategic planning com., sub. com. chair 1988). Home: 10729 Wood View Ter Traverse City MI 49684-9203

STEPP, LAURA SESSIONS, journalist; b. Ft. Smith, Ark., July 27, 1951; d. Robert Paul Sessions and M. Rae Barnes; m. Carl Sessions Stepp; children: Ashli, Amber, Jeffrey. BA, Earlham Coll., 1973; MA, Columnia U., 1974. Reporter Palm Beach Times, West Palm Beach, Fla., 1974; investigative reporter, editor The Evening Bull., Phila., 1975; projects editor The Charlotte (N.C.) Observer, 1979-81, asst. editorial page editor, 1981-82; Md. editor The Washington Post, 1982-86, religion editor, 1987-92, writer Style sect., 1992—. Bd. advisors U. Md. Casey Journalism Ctr. Children and Families, College Park. Recipient Nat. Reporting award Religion Writers Am., Feature Writing award AAUW, 1994. Mem. Investigative Reporters and Editors (bd. dirs. 1986-90). Office: Washington Post Co 1150 15th St NW Washington DC 20071-0002

STEPS, BARBARA JILL, lawyer; b. Springfield, Mo., June 19, 1945; d. Louis Edward and Margaret Pearl (Stiver) Bredeman; m. Robert William Steps, Dec. 21, 1968; children: Rebecca Harper, Aaron Andrew, Jessica Anne. BA in Psychology, St. Louis U., 1966; JD, U. Mo., 1969; MBA, U. Conn., 1983. Atty. Ralston Purina Co., St. Louis, 1969; law clerk U.S. Dist. Ct., St. Louis, 1969-72; assoc. Stone, Keck & Staser, Evansville, Ind., 1973-75, Cline & Callahan, Indpls., 1975-77, Law Office, Herbert V. Camp, Ridgefield, Conn., 1978-81; comml. counsel Burndy Corp., Norwalk, Conn., 1981-82, domestic counsel, 1982-86, corp. counsel, 1986-89, corp. counsel, sec., 1989-93, v.p., counsel & sec., 1993—. Mem. ABA, Am. Corp. Counsel Assn., Conn. Bar Assn., Corp. Bar Assn. of Westchester & Fairfield (co-chair bus. & comml. law com. 1990-92, dir. 1993—). Home: 6 Mulberry St Ridgefield CT 06877 Office: Burndy Corp 51 Richards Ave Norwalk CT 06856

STEPTOE, MARY LOU, lawyer; b. Washington, July 15, 1949; d. Philip Pendleton and Irene (Hellen) S.; m. Peter E. Carson, Sept. 1986; children: Elizabeth Maud, Julia Grace. BA, Occidental Coll., 1971; JD, U. Va., 1974. Bar: Va., 1974, Supreme Ct., 1987. Staff atty., Bur. of Competition FTC, Washington, 1974-79, atty. advisor to commr., 1979-86, exec. asst. to chmn., 1988-89, assoc. dir., Bur. of Competition, 1989-90, dep. dir., 1990-92, acting dir., 1992—. Office: FTC Competition Bur 6th & Pennsylvania Ave NW Washington DC 20580-0002

STERCHI, MARY ELIZABETH, social worker; b. Terre Haute, Ind., Jan. 31, 1960; d. Herbert Franklin and Patricia Ann (Lamb) Griffith; m. David Allen Sterchi, Sept. 18, 1982; 1 child, Malcolm Grant. BA, Purdue U., 1982; MSW, Ind. U., 1988. Cert. clin. social worker, sch. social worker, Ind., sch. social work specialist, Nat.; cert. Acad. Cert. Social Workers. Agy. social worker Shelter, Inc., Arlington Heights, Ill., 1983-85; psychiat. social worker Midtown Cmty. Mental Health Ctr., Indpls., 1985-88; sch. outreach program coord. Southside Youth Coun., Indpls., 1988-92; pvt. practice family therapy Family Interventions, Indpls., 1988—; clin. social worker, dir. Greenwood (Ind.) Cmty. Sch. Corp., 1992—; adj. faculty mem. Sch. Social Work, Ind. U., Indpls., 1990-91; peer facilitation advisor Greenwood High Sch., 1992—; cons. Allison Counseling Ctr., Indpls., 1992—. Vol. leader Young Life, Indpls., 1985-90, West Lafayette, Ind., 1979-82; vol. Moselle Sanders Thanksgiving Offering, Indpls., 1988—, Habitat for Humanity, Ky., 1990, Caulk of the Town, Indpls., 1990, 91; deacon Tabernacle Presbyn. Ch., 1985—. Mem. NASW, Alpha Omicron Pi. Republican. Home: 5415 N Carrollton Ave Indianapolis IN 46220 Office: Greenwood Cmty Sch Corp PO Box 218 Greenwood IN 46142

STERIS, CHERYL LYNN, elementary school educator, reading coordinator; b. Denver, Aug. 28, 1948; d. David Hayes Gillard and Vera Agness (Downer) Rubino; children: Kirsten Dianne, Christopher William. BA, Bowling Green State U., 1970; MEd, Ashland U., 1992. Cert. ednl. supr., Ohio. Tchr. U.S. Dependent Schs., Weisbaden, Germany, 1971-73, Berlin-Milan Schs., Milan, Ohio, 1973—; primary reading coord. Milan Elem. Sch., 1979—; cooperating tchr. for Bowling Green State U., Milan, 1983—; mem. Northwest Regional Profl. Devel. Team, 1994-95. Martha Holden Jennings scholar, 1994-95. Mem. NEA, Nat. Coun. Tchrs. of English, Delta Kappa Gamma, Phi Delta Kappa. Home: 4902 Hollyview Dr Vermilion OH 44089-1619 Office: Milan Elem Sch S Main St Milan OH 44846

STERLING, ANN GAYLORD, food products executive; b. Miami Shores, Fla., Dec. 27, 1956; d. Charles Henry and Emilia (Bankowski) Gaylord; m. Alan Sterling (div.). BS in Indsl. Mgmt., Ga. Inst. Tech., 1978; MBA in Mktg., Wake Forest U., 1990. Indsl. engr. Milliken & Co., LaGrange, Ga., 1978-79, PPG Industries, Lexington, N.C., 1978-79; various planning and mfg. positions RJR Tobacco, Winston-Salem, N.C., 1981-91; prodn. mgr. RJR Tobacco, Winston-Salem, 1989-91; mgr. budgets and planning RJR Nabisco, N.Y.C., 1991-92; dir. ops. planning Nabisco Biscuit, East Hanover, N.J., 1992-93; sr. dir. mfg. ops. and support svcs. Nabisco Biscuit, East Hanover, 1993—. Mem. Assn. Jr. Leagues, Winston-Salem, N.C., Scarsdale, N.Y., Montclair, N.J., 1987-93. Mem. Inst. Indsl. Engrs. (treas. 1983). Presbyterian.

STERLING, KENDALL WILLS, medical editor, writer, small business owner; b. Radford, Va., July 22, 1957; d. Willie Blanton and Myrtle Ross (Nolen) Wills; m. William Edward Sterling, Sept. 3, 1983. BA summa cum laude, U. Richmond, 1979; specialty cert. in Pharm. Writing, Am. Med. Writers Assn., 1992. Manuscript editor C.V. Mosby Co., St. Louis, 1980-81; editor, freelance coord. William Byrd Press, Richmond, Va., 1981-89; pres., mng. editor Sterling Comm. Svcs., Richmond, 1989—; cons. Schering-Plough, Madison, N.J., 1993. Editor: (report to U.S. Congress) The Contribution of Pharmaceutical Cos.: What's at Stake for America, 1993; 42 medical or allied health books including: Alzheimer's Disease: Treatment and Management, The Breast: Comprehensive Management of Benign and Malignant Diseases, Atlas of Pediatric Surgery, Cutaneous Surgery, Pediatric Arrhythmias: Electrophysiology and Pacing; article and issue editor: 23 med. and tech. jours including: Jour. Cardiovascular Nursing, Am. Jour. Hosp. Pharmacy, Trauma Quarterly, Am. Journal Occupational Theraphy. Mem. steering com. Campaign for Richmond, U. Richmond, 1991-93. Recipient David E. Howard Journalism scholarship U. Richmond, 1978-79. Mem. Am. Med. Writers Assn., Bd. Editors in Life Scis. (cert. editor in life scis., subcom. on member and pub. rels. 1992—), Coun. Biology Editors (authors editors com. 1993-95), European Assn. Sci. Editors, N.Y. Acad. Scis., Soc. Tech. Comm. Home and Office: Sterling Comm Svcs 2605 Mallards Xing Richmond VA 23233

STERLING, SHIRLEY FRAMPTON, artist, educator; b. L.A., Oct. 9, 1920; d. James Alexander and Elizabeth Mary (Herman) F.; m. Edwin Leigh Sterling, Mar. 26, 1942; children: Michael Leigh, Marianne. BA, Occidental Coll., 1942; postgrad., La. Tech. U., 1979-89. Cert. tchr. Tchr. Glendale, Calif., 1942-45; artist, tchr. Watercolor Art Soc., Houston, Pasadena, Kemah, Tex., 1973—; lectr., demonstrator various art socs. Active as Gray Lady Internat. Red Cross, Wiesbaden, Fed. Republic Germany, 1960-61, Honolulu, 1968-69. Mem. Nat. Watercolor Soc.(elected signature mem.), Knickerbocker Artists, Southwestern Watercolor Soc., Tex. Watercolor Soc. (Patron of Arts award), So. Watercolor Soc., Watercolor Art Soc.-Houston, Western Fedn. Watercolor Soc., Phi Beta Kappa. Republican. Home: 4011 Manorfield Dr Seabrook TX 77586-4209

STERN, GAIL FRIEDA, historical association director; b. Atlantic City, May 18, 1950; d. Herbert and Faith (Beldegreen) Stern; m. Irwin Allen Popowsky (div.); m. Shawn Paul Aubitz, Sept. 20, 1987; 1 child, Jonathan. Student, Brown U., 1972; postgrad., U. Pa., 1973. Asst. in decorative arts Phila. Mus. Art, 1972-75; asst. curator Wheaton Mus. Glass, Millville, N.J., 1973-74; assoc. dir. Pa. Humanities Coun., Phila., 1976-79; mus. curator The Balch Inst. for Ethnic Studies, Phila., 1979-83, mus. dir., 1984-93; dir. Hist. Soc. Princeton, N.J., 1993—; chair State Task Force on Folk Arts and Culture, 1981-82; vice chmn. crafts panel Pa. Coun. on the Arts, Harrisburg, 1988-89; chair cultural conservation com., Pa. Heritage Affairs Commn., Harrisburg, 1990-92; participant Internat. Partnership in Mus., Singapore, 1991. Mem. Mus. Coun. Phila. (v.p. 1982-83), Am. Assn. Mus./Internat. Coun. Mus. (bd. dirs.), N.J. Mus. Assn. (mem. bd. dirs.), Am. Assn. for State and Local History Awards (N.J. chair 1994-95). Home: 131 E Maple Ave Morrisville PA 19067-6235 Office: Hist Soc Princeton 158 Nassau St Princeton NJ 08542-7006

STERN, GERI ELLEN, realtor, nurse; b. Winnipeg, Man., Can., Sept. 24, 1952; d. Maurice and Sara (Angell) S.; m. John A. Monagin, May 13, 1978 (div. Apr. 1988); m. Alan L. Blavins, Sept. 1, 1990; 1 child, Maurissa Monagin. BSN, Calif. State U., Long Beach, 1975; MSN, Tex. Woman's U., 1978. Cert. psychiat. nurse practitioner, Nev. Psychiat. nurse, tchr. nursing and med. students, 1975-87; residential real estate agt. Security Pacific Real Estate, Richmond, Calif., 1988—. Guest author West Contra Costa Times, 1991-92. Capt. Neighborhood Watch Program; bd. dirs. Am. Cancer Soc., West Contra Costa County. Named Outstanding Realtor Active in Politics, Nat. Assn. Realtors; recipient commendation for work on transfer taxes Calif. Assn. Realtors. Mem. West Contra Costa Assn. Realtors (local govt. rels. com. Polit. Action Com. trustee and vice chair 1993-95, bd. dirs., multiple listing svc. pres., Outstanding Svc. award for local govt. rels. 1992), Soroptimist, Million Dollar Club. Office: Security Pacific Real Estate 12411 San Pablo Ave Richmond CA 94805-1996

STERN, GRACE MARY, state legislator; b. Holyoke, Mass., July 10, 1925; d. Frank McLellan and Marguerite M. (Nason) Dain; m. Charles H. Suber, June 21, 1947 (div. 1959); children: Ann, Peter, Thomas, John; m. Herbert L. Stern, May 13, 1962; stepchildren: Gwen, Herbert III, Robert. Student, Wellesley Coll., 1942-45; LLD (hon.), Shimer Coll., 1984. Asst. supr. Deerfield Twp., Lake County, Ill., 1967-70; county clk. Lake County, Ill., 1970-82; mem. Ill. Ho. of Reps., Springfield, 1984-92, Ill. State Senate, 1993—. Author: With a Stern Eye, 1967, Still Stern, 1969. Candidate lt. gov. State of Ill., 1982. Democrat. Presbyterian. Home: 291 Marshman Ave Highland Park IL 60035-4732 Office: 540 Frontage Rd Ste 1000 Northfield IL 60093

STERN, JOAN NAOMI, lawyer; b. Phila., Mar. 7, 1944; d. Clarence J. and Diana D. (Goldberg) S. BA, U. Pa., 1965; JD, Temple U., 1977. Bar: Pa. 1977. Assoc. Blank, Rome, Comisky & McCauley, Phila., 1977-83, ptnr., 1983—, co-chair pub. fin. group, 1983-92, chair pub. fin. group, 1993, co-chair pub. fin. dept., 1994—; cons. counsel Phila. Charter Commn., 1993-94. Contbr. articles to profl. jours. Mem. Sch. Dist. Task Force on Regulatory Reform, Phila., 1987, Tax Policy and Budget Com., Phila., 1989, Phila. Mayor's Fiscal Adv. Com., 1990; chair Sch. Dist. of Phila. Task Force on Alternate Financing Strategies, 1995; bd. mgrs. Moore Coll. Art and Design, Phila., 1993—; bd. dirs. Police Athletic League, Phila., 1994—. Fellow Am. Bar Found.; mem. ABA, Nat. Assn. Bond Lawyers, Phila. Bar Assn., Phila. Bar Assn. (chmn. mcpl. govt. com. 1983—), Pa. Assn. Bond Lawyers. Office: Blank Rome Comisky & McCauley 4 Penn Center Plz Philadelphia PA 19103-2521

STERN, MADELEINE BETTINA, rare books dealer, author; b. N.Y.C., July 1, 1912; d. Moses Roland and Lillie (Mack) S. BA, Barnard Coll., 1932; MA, Columbia U., 1934. Tchr. English N.Y.C. High Schs., 1934-43; ptnr. Leona Rostenberg Rare Books, N.Y.C., 1945—, Leona Rostenberg and Madeleine B. Stern Rare Books, N.Y.C., 1980—; lectr. history of book, feminism, pub. history, lt. Author: The Life of Margaret Fuller, 1942, Louisa May Alcott, 1950, Purple Passage: The Life of Mrs. Frank Leslie, 1953, Imprints on History: Book Publishers and American Frontiers, 1956, We the Women: Career Firsts of Nineteenth Century America, 1962, So Much in a Lifetime: The Story of Dr. Isabel Barrows, 1965, Queen of Publishers' Row: Mrs. Frank Leslie, 1966, The Pantarch: A Biography of Stephen Pearl Andrews, 1968, Heads and Headlines: The Phrenological Fowlers, 1971, Books and Book People in 19th-Century America, 1978, Antiquarian Bookselling in the United States: A History from the Origins to the 1940s, 1985, Nicholas Gouin Dufief of Philadelphia Franco-American Bookseller, 1776-1834, 1988, The Life of Margaret Fuller: A Revised Second Edition, 1991; (with Leona Rostenberg) Old and Rare: Forty Years in the Book Business, 1974, rev. edit. 1988, Between Boards: New Thoughts on Old Books, 1978, Bookman's Quintet: Five Catalogues about Books, 1980, Quest Book-Guest Book: A Biblio-Folly, 1993, Connections: Our Selves-Our Books, 1994; editor: Women on the Move, 4 vols., 1972, Victoria Woodhull Reader, 1974, Louisa's Wonder Book—An Unknown Alcott Juvenile, 1975, Behind a Mask: The Unknown Thrillers of Louisa May Alcott, 1975, Plots and Counterplots: More Unknown Thrillers of Louisa May Alcott, 1976, Publishers for Mass Entertainment in 19th-Century America, 1980, A Phrenological Dictionary of 19th-Century Americans, 1982, Critical Essays on Louisa May Alcott, 1984, A Modern Mephistopheles and Taming a Tartar by Louisa May Alcott, 1987, Louisa May Alcott Unmasked: Collected Thrillers, 1995; co-editor: Selected Letters of Louisa May Alcott, 1987, A Double Life: Newly Discovered Thrillers of Louisa May Alcott, 1988, The Journals of Louisa May Alcott, 1989, Louisa May Alcott: Selected Fiction, 1990, (co-editor) Freaks of Genius: Unknown Thrillers of Louisa May Alcott, 1991, From Jo March's Attic: Newly Discovered Thrillers of L.M. Alcott, 1993 (Victorian Soc. award), We the Women, new edit. 1994. Guggenheim fellow, 1943-45; recipient Medalie award Barnard Coll., 1982, Victorian Soc. award. Mem. Antiquarian Booksellers Assn. Am. (gov. 1966-68, 78-80), Internat. League Antiquarian Booksellers, MLA, Am. Printing History Assn. (co-recipient award 1983), Authors League, Manuscript Soc. (former trustee), Phi Beta Kappa. Jewish. Home: 40 E 88th St New York NY 10128-1176 Office: Rare Books 40 E 88th St New York NY 10128-1176

STERN, MAY C., administrative assistant, executive secretary; b. Evergreen Park, Ill., July 26, 1946; d. John Leonard and Anne (Zoeteman) Ericks; m. William Richard Stern, Sept. 5, 1970; children: Bret Randall, Kevin Richard. BA, Mich. State U., 1968; postgrad., Thornton Jr. Coll., 1969. Cert. profl. seamstress. Typist, gen. sec. Rex Chainbelt Co., Inc., Dolton, Ill., 1964-67 (summers); exec. sec. Kraft Foods Internat., Chgo., 1968-72; telephone operator The Office Answering Svc., Harvey, Ill., 1984-86; bookkeeper, cashier Cub Foods, Lansing, Ill., 1988-89; sec. Bus. One Irwin Pub., Homewood, Ill., 1988-92; exec. sec. Milgram Kagan Shoe Co., Calumet City, Ill., 1992; adminstrv. asst., exec. sec. CFC Internat., Chicago Heights, Ill., 1993—. Named One of Outstanding Young Women of Am., 1980. Mem. Sweet Adelines Internat. (bd. mem. local chpt. 1972-80, editor 1986-94). Republican. Baptist.

STERN, PAULA, international trade advisor; b. Chgo., Mar. 31, 1945; d. Lloyd and Fan (Wener) Stern; m. Paul A. London; children: Gabriel Stern, Genevieve Stern. BA, Goucher Coll., 1967; MA in Middle Eastern Studies, Harvard U., 1969; MA in Internat. Affairs, Fletcher Sch. of Law and Diplomacy, 1970, MA in Law and Diplomacy, 1970, PhD, 1976; D of Comml. Sci. (hon.), Babson Coll., 1985; LLD (hon.), Goucher Coll., 1985. Legis. asst., then sr. legis. asst. U.S. Sen. Gaylord Nelson, Washington, 1972-74, 1976; guest scholar Brookings Inst., Washington, 1975-76; policy analyst Pres. Carter-V.P. Mondale Transition Team, Washington, 1977-78; internat. affairs fellow Council on Fgn. Relations, Washington, 1977-78; commr. Internat. Trade Commn., Washington, 1978-87, chairwoman, 1984-86; sr. assoc. Carnegie Endowment for Internat. Peace, Washington, 1986-88; pres. The Stern Group, 1988—; sr. fellow The Progressive Policy Inst., 1993—; bd. dirs. Scott Paper Co., Westinghouse Corp., Dynatech Corp., Harcourt Gen., Duracell Internat.; sr. adviser to Clinton Campaign.; mem. Pres.'s Adv. Com. for Trade Policy and Negotiations; mem. Trilateral Commn., Comm. for Econ. Devel. Author: Water's Edge--Domestic Politics and the Making of American Foreign Policy, 1979; author numerous articles and chpts. on internat. affairs. Recipient Journalism award Alicia Patterson Found., 1970-71. Mem. Coun. Fgn. Rels., Inter-Am. Found. (bd. dirs. 1980-81). Democrat. Jewish. Office: Progressive Policy Inst 518 C St NE Ste 1000 Washington DC 20002

STERN, ROSLYNE PAIGE, magazine publisher; b. Chgo., May 26, 1926; d. Benjamin Gross and Clara (Sniderman) Roer; m. William E. Weber, May 3, 1944 (div. Mar. 1956); m. Richard S. Paige, June 28, 1958 (div. Apr. 1978); children: Sandra Weber Porr, Barbara Paige Kaplan, Elizabeth Paige (dec.); m. Robert D. Stern, June 5, 1978. Cert., U. Chgo., 1945. Profl. model, singer, 1947-53; account exec. Interstate United, Chgo., 1955-58; sales mgr. Getting To Know You Internat., Great Neck, N.Y., 1963-71, exec. v.p., 1971-78; pub. After Dark Mag., N.Y.C., 1978-82; assoc. pub. Dance Mag., N.Y.C., 1978-85, pub., 1985—; bd. dirs. Rudor Consol. Industries, Inc., N.Y.C., AGC/Sedgwick, Inc., Princeton, N.J. Founding pres. Dance Mag. Found., N.Y.C., 1984-86; life mem. nat. women's com. Brandeis U., Waltham, Mass., 1958—. Mem. Pub. Relations Soc. Am., LWV, Am. Theatre Wing. Democrat. Jewish. Home: 2 Imperial Lndg Westport CT 06880-4934 Office: Dance Mag Inc 33 W 60th St 10th Fl New York NY 10023-7905

STERN, RUTH, business executive, artist; b. Bronx, N.Y., Oct. 14, 1929; d. Albert and Margaret (Karl) Nussbacher; student Hunter Coll., N.Y.C., 1947; cert. writing UCLA, 1988; BFA, Calif. Inst. of Arts, 1994, postgrad., 1995—; m. Martin Szold, Apr. 10, 1949 (div. Sept. 1978); children—Lauren, Terry; m. James C. Stern, Aug. 22, 1982. Exec. legal sec. to sr. partner firm Paul, Weiss, Rifkind, Wharton & Garrison, N.Y.C., 1958-62; asst. to pres. M.E. Green & Co., brokerage co., N.Y.C., 1962-65; demonstrator and cons. for various cosmetic cos., 1965-85; founder, pres. Ruth Szold Promotional Models, N.Y.C., 1968-84, Cosmetic Art, Inc., cosmetic and theatrical workshops, N.Y.C., 1979-85; founder, pres., designer, promoter cosmetic line Cosmetic Art, 1979-85; columnist Fire Island News, Ocean Beach, N.Y., 1985-89; asst. to pres., chief exec. officer Gladden Entertainment, L.A., 1989-90; exec. adminstr. C&O of Cogent Light and Techs., 1990-91; demonstrator-lectr. for TV, also video tapes; condr. cosmetic workshops for N.Y. Salute to Fashion Industries, 1981; chmn. earthquake com. Fountainview Assn., 1989—; cons. in field. Mem. council Girl Scouts U.S.A., 1964-69; bd. dirs. Bleecker Tower Tenants Corp., N.Y.C., 1979-80, chmn. architecture and design com., 1979-80, chmn. maintenance, 1980-85, pres., 1981-82; mem.

Hunger Project, Financial Family; lectr., mem. panel Am. Women's Econ. Devel. Corp., 1981. Recipient Gold medal Deborah Fund Raising Dinner, 1955. Mem. Foragers of Am., Nat. Retail Mchts. Assn., Fragrance Found., Cosmetic Exec. Women. Clubs: Brandeis U., Hadassah. Home: 8455 Fountain Ave Apt 515 Los Angeles CA 90069-2543

STERN, SHARON LYNN, school psychologist; b. Sumter, S.C., Apr. 20, 1961; d. Abraham and Rhea (Edelsberg) S. BA, U. Fla., 1982, MEd, 1986; EdS, 1986. Sch. psychologist Columbia County Sch. Bd., Lake City, Fla., 1987, Alachua County Sch. Bd., Gainesville, Fla., 1987-89, Pinellas County Sch. Bd., Clearwater, Fla., 1989—. Mem. Nat. Assn. Sch. Psychologists, Fla. Assn. Sch. Psychologists. Jewish. Home: 9854 Indian Key Trl Seminole FL 34646 Office: Pinellas County Sch Bd 1960 Druid Rd E Clearwater FL 34624-4722

STERNGLASS, LILA M., advertising agency executive; b. N.Y.C., Aug. 3, 1934; d. Joseph and Sarah (Golden) Kronstadt; m. Arno E. Sternglass, Apr. 20, 1956; children: Adam, Paul. BFA, Cooper Union, 1954. Asst. art dir. Sterling Advt., N.Y.C., 1954-55; art dir. Diamond Barnett Advt., N.Y.C., 1955, I. Miller Shoes, N.Y.C., 1956, Trahey Wolf Advt., N.Y.C., 1969-70; sr. art dir. Sacks & Rosen, N.Y.C., 1970-72; assoc. creative dir. Warwick Advt., N.Y.C., 1972-80, Ketchum Advt., N.Y.C., 1980; creative dir. Rumrill Hoyt Advt., N.Y.C., 1981-88, McCaffrey and McCall Advt., 1988-90; ptnr. Hamilton/Sternglass Inc., Creative Cons., N.Y.C., 1990—. Recipient Merit award Art Dirs. Club, 1954, 56, 69, 70, 71, 74, 82, 85, Merit award Andy Advt. Club, 1971, 72, 82, 83, One Show Merit award, 1983, 84, 85, 88, 89, Clio finalist, 1983-84, 89, Clio award 1985, Internat. Radio Fest award 1984, 85, Internat. Radio Fest finalist 1984, 85, Gold Effies award, 1985, 86, 88, 89, others. Office: 54 W 21st St # 705 New York NY 10010-6908

STERNHAGEN, FRANCES, actress; b. Washington, Jan. 13, 1930. Student, Vassar Coll., Perry-Mansfield Sch. of Theatre; studied with Sanford Meisner, N.Y. Tchr. Milton Acad., Mass.; actress Arena Stage, Washington, 1953-54. Debut Thieves Carnival, N.Y., 1955; plays include The Carefree Tree, The Admirable Bashville (Clarence Derwent award, Obie award), Ulysses in Night Town, Red Eye of Love, Misalliance, The Return of Herbert Bracewell, Laughing Stock, The Displaced Person, The Pinter Plays (Obie award); Broadway shows include The Skin of Our Teeth, Viva Madison Avenue, Great Day in the Morning, The Right Honorable Gentleman, The Cocktail Party, Cock-a-Doodle Dandy, Playboy of the Western World, The Sign in Sidney Brustein's Window, The Good Doctor (Tony award 1973), Equus, Angel, On Golden Pond (Drama League award), The Father, Grownups, Summer, You Can't Take It With You, Home Front, Driving Miss Daisy, Remembrance, A Perfect Ganesh, The Heiress; actress films include Up the Down Staircase, Starting Over, Outland, Independence Day, Romantic Comedy, Bright Lights, Big City, See You in the Morning, Communion, Misery, Doc Hollywood, Raising Cain; (TV series) Love of Life, The Doctors, Secret Storm, Cheers, Golden Years, Under One Roof, The Road Home; (TV movies) Who Will Save Our Children?, Prototype, Resting Place, Follow Your Heart, She Woke Up, Labor of Love: The Arlette Schweitzer Story, Reunion, Tales from the Crypt, Outer Limits.

STETZ, SYLVIA ANN, small business owner; b. Dearborn Heights, Mich., Jan. 3, 1941; d. John and Eleanore Mary (Surma) Hlasny; m. Donald Noel Stetz, Aug. 29, 1964; children: Karyn Elaine, Julie Renee. BS, Wayne State U., Detroit, 1963; postgrad., U. Mich., 1965, Ea. Mich. U., 1987-89; attended, Pfaff Sch. of Creative Sewing, Las Vegas, Nev., 1993. Salesperson Sears Roebuck & Co., Lincoln Park, Mich., 1963; tchr. Crestwood Sch. Dist., Dearborn Hts., Mich., 1964-66; salesperson Saks Fifth Ave., Dearborn, Mich., 1982-84; mgr. maj. accounts Internat. Calculator Sales, Southfield, Mich., 1984-85; personnel coordinator Uniforce Temp. Services, Southfield, 1985-86; office, br. mgr. E.H. Rowley Co., Inc., Detroit, 1986-89; owner, pres. Sylvia Ann, Cedar Falls, Iowa, 1989-93, Pinckney, Mich., 1994—; part-time sewing-sales educator Dralle Bros., Waterloo, Iowa, 1992-93; svc. rep. Manpower, Howell, Mich., 1994—. Trustee, sec. Plymouth Bd. Edn., 1979-83; chairperson Helping Hand Dist. Program, Plymouth-Canton Schs., 1977-82; pres. PTO, Plymouth, 1973-79; rep., v.p. Plymouth-Canton Community Sch. Coun., 1975-79. Recipient Woman of the Yr. award Jaycettes, Plymouth, 1977, Mich. Dist. 30, 1977; first prize in evening wear Vogue-Butterick-Pfaff fashion show contest, 1993. Mem. AAUW (bd. dirs.). Ind. Home and Office: 2279 Sunny Ridge Dr Pinckney MI 48169

STEUART, SYBIL JEAN, elementary school educator; b. New Orleans, Aug. 6, 1954; d. John Thompson and Sybil Rose (Cousans) S. BS in Elem. Edn., Loyola U. of the South, New Orleans, 1976; postgrad., U. So. Miss., William Carey Coll. Cert. elem. sch. tchr., Miss. Tchr. 6th grade St. Rita Elem. Sch., New Orleans; tchr. kindergarten Sacred Heart Elem. Sch., D'Iberville, Miss.; presenter ednl. workshops. Lay mem. Mercy Assocs., St. Louis, 1985—; vol. aide VA Hosp., Biloxi, Miss., 1989, various civic and ch. orgns.; commentator, lectr., kindergarten tchr. Christian doctrine St. Elizabeth Seton Ch., Ocean Springs, Miss., 1982—; commentator, lectr. Sacred Heart Ch., D'Iberville, 1988—; v.p. Friends of Ocean Springs Libr., 1983-91. Recipient Cert. of Appreciation, New Orleans Pub. Schs., 1984, Bishop's Svc. Cross award Diocese of Biloxi, 1985; named Outstanding Young Educator of Biloxi, Jaycees, 1986; named Catechist of Yr. Knights of Columbus, Ocean Springs, 1994, Order of St. Louis, Archdiocese of New Orleans, 1980. Mem. ASCD, Nat. Cath. Educators Assn., Mississippians for Ednl. Broadcasting, Mercy Edn. Assn., St. Elizabeth Seton Altar Soc. (chmn. spiritual com. 1988-92), St. Mary's Dominican High Sch. Alumni Assn. (developer ednl. advancement programs), Loyola U. Alumni Assn. (developer ednl. advancement programs), Sacred Heart Automobile League. Office: Sacred Heart Elem Sch 10482 Lemoyne Blvd Biloxi MS 39532-5911

STEUER, KAREN L., legislative staff member; b. Reading, Pa., Apr. 29, 1953. BA, Goddard Coll., 1989. With Aetna Life & Casualty, Hartford, Conn., 1979-85; prin. investigator, dir. conservation and ednl. programs Ctr. for Coastal Studies, 1991-93; profl. staff mem. com. on merchant marine and fisheries, 1991-93; dep. staff dir. subcom. on environment and natural resources, house com. on merchant marine and fisheries, 1994—. Office: Subcom Environ & Nat Resources 546 Ford House Office Bldg Washington DC 20515*

STEVENS, ALICE MARIE, educational consultant; b. Colorado Springs, Colo., Jan. 18, 1954; d. Charles C. and Gladys Marie (Craft) S. BS, S.W. Bapt. U., 1976; MEd, U. Mo., 1983; postgrad., Purdue U., 1991—. Cert. tchr., Mo. Sci. tchr. Lincoln County R-IV Schs., Winfield, Mo., 1976-78; sci. instr. Ricks Inst., Monrovia, Liberia, West Africa, 1978-79; learning specialist Total Learning Clinic, Columbia, Mo., 1982-89; homebound instr. Rusk Rehab. Ctr., Columbia, Mo., 1988-91; instr. Columbia Coll., Columbia, Mo., 1989, 91; learning disabilities specialist Columbia (Mo.) Pub. Schs., 1989-91; tchr., rsch. asst. Purdue U., West Lafayette, Ind., 1991—; ednl. cons. West Lafayette, Ind., 1991—; instrnl. designer Total Learning Clinic, Columbia, 1985-87. Asst. dir. Cerebral Palsy Assn. Greater Lafayette, 1993-94. Mem. ASCD, Nat. Sci. Tchrs. Assn. (conf. presenter 1993), Coun. for Exceptional Children (conf. presenter tchr. edn. divsn. 1992), Nat. Head Injury Found. Office: Purdue U Liberal Arts And Edn B West Lafayette IN 47907

STEVENS, BRENDA ANITA, psychologist, educator; b. N.Y.C., Oct. 23, 1949; d. Henry Stevens and Frances Marie (Russo) Incorvaia; m. Edwin Randall Trinkle, Feb. 21, 1976 (div. 1987); m. John Alexander Czaja, Sept. 10, 1994; 1 child, Peter A. BS, Boston U., 1971, MEd, 1971, CAGS, 1973; PhD in Edn., U. Tenn., 1991. Nat. cert. sch. psychologist. Sch. adjustment counselor Dedham (Mass.) Pub. Schs., 1972-73; testing specialist Children's Hosp. Med. Ctr., Boston, 1973-74; sch. psychologist North Middlesex Regional Schs., Townsend, Mass., 1974-78; grad. asst. U. Tenn., Knoxville, 1978-79, 89-90, program evaluator, 1983-84, clinic coord., 1989-90; psychology assoc. Cherokee Mental Health Ctr., Morristown, Tenn., 1985; asst. prof. U. Nebr., Kearney, 1990-93, Miami U., Oxford, Ohio, 1993—; psychol. cons. Roane County Pub. Schs., Kingston, Tenn., 1978-89; cons., administrv. intern Knox County Pub. Schs., Knoxville, 1984-85; sch. psychologist Jefferson County Pub. Schs., Dandridge, Tenn., 1986-88, Oak Ridge (Tenn.) Pub. Schs., 1989. Commr.'s appointee Mass. State Coun. for Hearing Impaired, Boston, 1976-78; bd. dirs. Luth. Social Ministries Tenn., Knoxville, 1989; exec. bd. Luth. Community Svcs., Knoxville, 1987-89; cons. Mass. State Dept. Edn., Boston, 1974-78. Head Start grantee, 1991-94, Project One to One grantee Dawson County, 1991; Trustee scholar Boston U., 1968-71; recipient Women of Achievement award Commn. Women, 1983. Mem. Am. Psychol. Assn., Nat. Assn. Sch. Psychologists, Phi Kappa Phi, Pi Lambda Theta, Ohio Sch. Psychologists Assn, Phi Delta Kappa. Office: Miami U Dept Ednl Psychology 201 McGuffey Oxford OH 45056

STEVENS, DOROTHY EMMA, civic worker; b. West Kennebunk, Maine, Oct. 2, 1923; d. Sydney Emery and Emelia (Charette) Towne; m. Maurice William Stevens Jr., May 1, 1922; children: Jacqueline, Sondra, Jeffrey, Scott. Contbr. articles to profl. jours.; guest speaker local radio program Newsmaker, Rochester, N.H., 1993; featured in Down East Mag., 1993. Dist. leader 4-H Club, West Kennebunk, 1954-59; sec. Extension Group, Alewive, Maine, 1954-57; pres. 4-H Leaders Assn., 1955-56; bd. dirs. Pub. Health, Kennebunk, 1975-78, chmn. Planning Bd., 1979-80, sec. Zoning Bd. Appeals, 1977-78, vice chmn. Charter Commn., 1983-84; co-chair Solid Waste Com., 1990—; mem Bd. Selectmen, 1986-87, vice chmn. 1988—; vice chmn. Zoning Re-Write Com., 1986-87; advisor River Study Com., 1986, Cumulative Impact Com., 1986, 87; mem. Civil Emergency Preparedness, 1986, 87, Regional Comprehensive Planning Com., 1989—; coord. Bicentennial Commn. ceremonies, 1987, Meml. Day, Old Home Week, 1987; pres. West Kennebunk Fire Co. Auxiliary, 1987—; sec., treas. Pine Grove Cemetery Corp., West Kennebunk, 1987—, clk., 1989—; steward Land Preservation, 1988—; chmn. Solid Waste Recycling Com., 1986—, Tri-Town Recycling Com., 1991-92; acting chmn. Bd. Selectmen, 1986-87; featured spkr. in field. Recipient Cmty. Svc. award Kennebunk Health Svcs., 1990, Recycling award Town of Kennebunk, 1990; honorable mention Jefferson award Maine Broadcasting System/Am. Inst. Pub. Svc., 1980; named Outstanding 4-H Leader, 1955, Couple of Yr., Maine State Grange, 1957, Master of Alewife Grange, 1957, 58, 59. Mem. Pine Grove Cemetery Assn. (bd. dirs. 1986-87, sec.-treas. 1989—). Democrat. Roman Catholic. Clubs: Athletic Boosters (treas. 1983-85), Women's Softball League (coordinator 1970-87), Women's Bowling League (past pres.). Home: Main St PO Box 453 West Kennebunk ME 04094-0453 Office: Bd of Selectmen 1 Summer St Kennebunk ME 04043-1808

STEVENS, ELISABETH GOSS (MRS. ROBERT SCHLEUSSNER, JR.), writer, journalist; b. Rome, N.Y., Aug. 11, 1929; d. George May and Elisabeth (Stryker) Stevens; m. Robert Schleussner, Jr., Mar. 12, 1966 (dec. 1977); 1 child, Laura Stevens. B.A., Wellesley Coll., 1951; M.A. with high honors, Columbia U., 1956. Editorial assoc. Art News Mag., 1964-65; art critic and reporter Washington Post, Washington, 1965-66; free-lance art critic and reporter Balt., 1966—; contbg. art critic Wall Street Jour., N.Y.C., 1969-72; art critic Trenton Times, N.J., 1974-77; art and architecture critic The Balt. Sun, 1978-86. Author: Elisabeth Stevens' Guide to Baltimore's Inner Harbor, 1981, Fire and Water: Six Short Stories, 1982, Children of Dust: Portraits and Preludes, 1985, Horse and Cart: Stories from the Country, 1990, The Night Lover: Art & Poetry, 1995; contbr. articles, poetry and short stories to jours., nat. newspapers and popular mags. Recipient A.D. Emmart award for journalism, 1980, Critical Writing citation Balt.-Washington Newspaper Guild, 1980, fiction awards Md. Poetry Rev., 1992, 93, 94, 2nd prize Lite Circle, 1994, award Balt. Writers Alliance, 1994, Balt. Writers Alliance Play Writing Contest award, 1994; art critics' fellow NEA, 1973-74, fellow MacDowell Colony, 1981, Vt. Ctr. for Creative Arts, 1982-85, 88-90, 92, 93, Ragdale Found., 1984, 89, Yaddo, 1991; Work-in-Progress grantee for poetry Md. Art Coun., 1986, Creative Devel. grantee for short fiction collection Bapt. Mayor's Com. on Art and Culture, 1986. Mem. Nat. Press Club Washington, Coll. Art Assn., Balt. Bibliophiles, Authors Guild, Am. Studies Assn., Poetry Soc. Am. Home: 6604 Walnutwood Cir Baltimore MD 21212-1213

STEVENS, ELIZABETH, psychotherapist, consultant; b. Evanston, Ill., Jan. 11, 1950; d. Kenneth M. and C. Jane (Reynolds) S.; m. David W. Handy, Oct. 3, 1986. BA in Psychology, U. Fla., 1973; MA in Clin. Psychology, Kent State U., 1976. Lic. prof. counselor, Tex., cert. chem. dependency specialist, lic. marriage and family therapist. Exec. dir. Genesis Women's Shelter, Dallas, 1986-87; dir. outpatient svcs. Green Oaks Hosp., Dallas, 1987-88; mgmt. cons. Houston, 1977—, pvt. practice, 1990—; founder Integrated Clin. Resources, Inc.; Amb. St. Joseph Hosp., also cons., 1977—; co-founder N.E. Hospice, Med. Affiliates, Support N.E. Cancer Workers, Emergency Support System for Police, Fire Dept. and Ambulance Svc., Stevens Counseling Ctrs., The Psychoimmunology Ctr.; cons. to devel. utilization rev. Kelsey-Seybold Clinics, 1992—. Contbr. articles to profl. jours., mags., and newspapers. Vol. Mental Health Assn., Houston and Harris County, bd. dirs., 1988—, chair nominating com., membership com., sec. exec. com.; bd. advisors N.E. Hospice; co-founder Associated Mental Health Group, Inc.; mem. strategic planning team Sisters of Charity; cons. devel. Triage. Named Exceptional Vol. of Yr. Mental Health Assn., Speakers Bur. award. Mem. Walden Country Club. Office: 9810 Fm1960 Ste 205 Humble TX 77338

STEVENS, EMILY FABELLA SILVER, director, theater educator, scriptwriter, producer; b. Mexico, Aug. 10, 1928; d. Raphael Fabella and Leonoa (Hernandez) Silver. Co-founder, co-prodr., actress, designer, production mgr., stage mgr., publicity Circle in the Square, N.Y.C.; co-prodr., actress broadway prodn. Girl on the Via Flaminia, N.Y.C.; co-prodr. 32 prodns. Circle in the Square, Phila.; dir., screen tests Lee Strasberg Actor's Studio; script supr. Universal Studio, Calif.; dialogue dir. Paramount Studio, Calif.; rsch. assoc. Marilyn Monroe Spl., Liberman Prodns.; coord., cons. Ernest Hemingway Spl. Cuba, Bob Banner Prodns.; prodn. mgr. Country Music Spl.; prodrs. asst. South Am./Mex. Culture Exchange, Carousel and Showboat; co-prodr. Oh Boy; co-prodr., designer, co-dir. Blood Wedding Opera; acting workshops Spain, Hollywood, Fla., N.Y.C.; lectr. Spain, N.Y.C., N.C., S.C., Ga., Fla. actress 5 motion pictures. Home: 270 8th & Summit Ave Sea Cliff NY 11579

STEVENS, EUNICE A., accountant; b. Oshkosh, Wis., July 25, 1952; d. Kenneth F. and Margaret P. (Kuntz) Graham; m. Gary Stevens, July 1, 1977 (div. Jan. 1991); children: Neil Shultis, Tina Shultis. A in Acctg., Fox Valley Tech. Coll., 1987. IRS enrolled agt. Owner Stevens Acctg., Wautoma, Wis., 1980—. Coun. mem. Hope Luth. Ch., 1990-92; bd. dirs., treas. Living Environ. Found., 1990—. Mem. Ctrl. Wis. Pvt. Industry Coun. (sec. 1989—), Waushara Area Bus. and Profl. Women (treas. 1984-87), Inst. Mgmt. Accts. Democrat. Office: Stevens Acctg PO Box 588 Wautoma WI 54982

STEVENS, HELEN JEAN, retired elementary school educator, musician; b. Nevada, Iowa, July 11, 1934; d. Paul Ellison and Helen Margaret (Ives) S. MusB, U. So. Calif., L.A., 1956. Cert. secondary music tchr., Calif. Tchr. San Francisco Sch. Dist., 1956-58; prin. oboist Marin Symphony Orch., San Rafael, Calif., 1956-94, Santa Rosa (Calif.) Symphony, 1956-86; tchr. Santa Venetia Mid. Sch., San Rafael, 1958-83; asst. prof. music Sonoma State Coll., Rohnert Park, Calif., 1963-76; tchr. Davidson Mid. Sch., San Rafael, 1984-89; tchr. oboe students; oboist Debut TV Show, L.A., 1954-55, Carmel (Calif.) Bach Festival, 1955-82; prin. oboist Light Opera Curren Theatre, San Francisco, 1966-67, Marin Opera Co., San Rafael, 1980-84. active Sonoma County 4-H Guide Dog Project Leader, Guide Dogs for the Blind, Inc., 1974-87. Recipient Svc. award PTA, 1974, Golden Bell award Marin County Office of Edn., 1984; named Outstanding Tchr., Marin Edn. Found., 1986, Continuing Svc. award Calif. Congress Parents, Tchrs. and Students, Inc, 1989. Mem. German Shepherd Dog Club Am. Democrat. Presbyterian. Home: 8555 Kirk Dr Colorado Springs CO 80909-2910

STEVENS, LEOTA MAE, retired educator; b. Waverly, Kans., Mar. 27, 1921; d. Clinton Ralph and Velma Mae (Kukuk) Chapman; m. James Oliver Stevens, Nov. 7, 1944 (dec.); children: James Harold, Mary Ann Hooker. BA, McPherson Coll., 1954; MS, Emporia U., 1964, postgrad., 1969-77; postgrad., Wichita U., 1977. Educator Pleasant Mound Sch., Waverly, 1940-41; prin. educator Halls Summit Sch., Waverly, 1941-42; educator Waverly Grade Sch., 1942-43, Ellinwood (Kans.) Jr. High, 1943-45, Hutchinson (Kans.) Grade Sch., 1945-48, Lincoln Sch., Darlow, Kans., 1948-49; educator prin. Mitchell-Yaggy Consol. Sch., Hutchinson, 1949-57; educator elem. Hutchinson Sch. Dist. 308, 1957-85, ret., 1985; v.p. Reno County Tchrs. Assn. Hutchinson, 1956-57, pres. Assn. Childhood Edn. Internat., 1978-79. Author of numerous poems; compiler The Alexander-Kukuk Descendants: 1754 to 1990. Mem. Worker ARC Blood Mobile, 1986—, Hutchinson Community Concerts 1970—; ch. sch. tchr. Trinity United Meth. Ch., 1959-71. (attendance chair, 1994); historian Women's Civic Ctr., 1988-92, art com. chmn., 1992—; den mother Cub Scouts, 1963-66, leader Girl Scouts Ellinwood, 1944-45. Mem. AAUW (news reporter 1984-87, legis. chmn. program com. 1991—, 2d v.p., 1994—), Ret. Nation State and Local Edn. Assn., Reno County Tchs. Assn. (v.p. 1956-57), Assn. Childhood Edn. Internat. (pres. 1978-79), Reno County Extension Homemaker Coun. (rep. 1987—), Rainbow Extension Club (pres. 1986-92), Hutchinson Area Ret. Tchrs. Assn., Am. Legion Aux., Friends of Preservation, Delta Kappa Gamma (sec., v.p. 1972-80, grant chmn. 1980-88, publicity com. 1990-93, legis. chmn. 1994—). Republican. Home: 805 W 23rd Ave Hutchinson KS 67502-3765

STEVENS, LINDA GALE BISSON, public utilities executive; 1 child, Teresa Adrienne. BA in History, U. N.H., 1972; MBA, Simmons Coll., Boston, 1980. Cert. utility regulation studies, Mass., Mich. Law sch. admissions dir. Franklin Pierce Law Ctr., Concord, N.H., 1978-79; v.p., co-founder BCI Geonetics, Inc., Santa Barbara, Calif., 1981-87; commr. Pub. Utilities Commn., Concord, N.H., 1987-93; exec. dir. NE Conf. Pub. Utilities Commrs., Inc., Providence, 1993—; adj. faculty bus. Daniel Webster Coll., Nashua, N.H., 1986-91; vice-chmn. Def. Adv. Com. on Women in the Svcs., D.C.; del. 1st Japan-Am. Grassroots Summit; with NARUC; chmn. Com. on Water, subcom. on Conservation. Trustee New Eng. Coll., fin. com.; bd. dirs., chmn. Def. Issues Task Force, WESG; trustee The Nature Conservancy, N.H.; incorporator N.H. Charitable Fund; adv. bd. mem. MIT Energy Lab., NH DRED Econ. Adv. Group; pub. coun. mem. Am. Water Works Assn. Rsch. Found.; admissions coun. mem. Simmons Coll. GSM; mem. U.S.M.C. Scholarship Found. Com.; active numerous nat. and local regulatory agys. RJR Nabisco Fellow Harvard U. Kennedy Sch. Govt.; recipient Rappaport Achievement award Simmons Coll., 1990. Mem. Univ. N.H. Alumni Assn. (nat. pres., bd. dirs.), Rotary Internat., Army and Navy Club, Bald Peak Colony Club, Ida Lewis Yacht Club. Office: NE Conf Pub Utilities Commrs Inc 100 Orange St 2nd fl Providence RI 02903

STEVENS, LINDA LOUISE HALBUR, addiction counselor; b. Huron, S.D., Oct. 28, 1960; d. Alvin LeRoy and Esther Louise (Schroeder) Halbur; m. Lowell Eugene Stevens, July 26, 1980; children: Lowell John Stevens, Tracie Lynn Stevens. BSW, U. N.D., 1991; MEd, N.D. State U., 1993. Lic. social worker, N.D.; lic. addiction counselor, N.D. Tracker Luth. Soc. Svcs., Hillsboro, N.D., 1990-94; addiction counselor Heartland Med. Ctr., Fargo, N.D., 1993-94, S.E. Human Svc. Ctr., Fargo, 1994—. Local/state officer N.D. Women of Today, Hillsboro, 1982-87. Recipient Presdl. award of excellence N.D. women of Today, 1986, 87. Mem. NASW, Am. Counseling Assn. Home: Rte 2 Box 31 Hillsboro ND 58045 Office: SE Human Svc Ctr 2624 9th Ave SW Fargo ND 58103

STEVENS, LINDA TOLLESTRUP, school counselor; b. Salt Lake City, Feb. 7, 1963; d. Garn Alvin and Mary Ann (Cannon) Tollestrup; m. Marshall Le Grand Stevens, Mar. 17, 1982; 1 child, Marli Brynn. BS, U. Utah, 1984, MS, 1989. Cert. sch. counselor, Utah. Tchr. pre-sch. Adventurer's Pre-Sch., Salt Lake City, 1984; adminstr. Headstart program Creative Devel. Ctr., Salt Lake City, 1984-85; vocat. evaluator Utah Div. Rehab. Svcs. Vocat. Evaluation, Salt Lake City, 1985-86; human resource counselor Davis Applied Tech. Ctr., Kaysville, Utah, 1986—; trainee Phoenix Inst., Salt Lake City, 1986, U. No. Colo., Greeley, 1986; instr. Utah State Turning Point, Salt Lake City and Provo, 1992. Mem. Golden Spike Dog Obedience Club, Ogden, Utah, 1986-90, Humane Soc. Utah, 1986—. Mem. NEA, ACA, Am. Vocat. Assn., Am. Bus. Women's Assn. (v.p. 1992), Utah Vocat. Assn. (bldg. fund coord. 1989-90), Utah Fedn. Bus. and Profl. Women (Woman of Achievement award 1991), Golden Key Honor Soc., Delta Soc., Phi Eta Sigma. Mormon. Office: Davis Applied Tech Ctr 550 E 300 St Kaysville UT 84037

STEVENS, LISA GAY, minister, choral director; b. Okla. City, Mar. 30, 1952; d. Charles Alton and Betty Lou (Johnson) Landrum; m. Thomas Lynn Taylor, Dec. 11, 1971 (div. 1983); children: Jason Ryan, Joel Shane; m. James Hervey Stevens Jr., Apr. 29, 1984. Student, Friends U., 1970-72; BA in Music, U. Mo., Kansas City, 1983-87; MDiv with gerontology specialization, St. Paul Sch. Theology, 1987-90. Ordained deacon United Meth. Ch., 1989, elder, 1992. Adminstrv. asst./cashier McLiney and Co., Kansas City, Mo., 1978-80; choral dir. Hickman Mills Christian Community, Kansas City, 1979-82; adminstrv. asst. Hokanson, Lehman & Stevens Creative Planning, Inc., Kansas City, 1981-88; choral dir. Crossroads Reformed Ch., Shawnee Mission, Kans., 1983-84, St. Paul Sch. Theology, Kansas City, 1988-89; chaplain St. Luke's Hosp., Kingswood Manor Health Ctr., Kansas City, 1988; pastor The Belvidere United Meth. Ch., Kansas City, 1988-90, Va./Passaic United Meth. Chs., Butler, Mo., 1990-93; North Cross United Meth. Ch., Kansas City, Mo., 1993—; adj. faculty praxis team leader St. Paul Sch. Theology, 1990-93; mem. fin. and adminstrn. com. Mo. West United Meth. Conf., 1993—, sub-com. health ins. com., 1993—, dist. supts.' salary com., 1994—, Kansas City north dist. supts.' com., 1994—, conf. counseling edler, 1993—; trustee Shepherd's Ctr. of the Northland, 1994—, mem. funding/fin. com., 1994—. Solo flutist Sr. Wichita Youth Orchestra, 1969-70. Pres. Life Ins. Office Mgrs. Assn. Kansas City, 1985, chairperson pub. rels, 1984. Mem. Butler Ministerial Alliance; Butler Chaplains Assn. (chaplain, 1991-93). Methodist. Office: North Cross United Meth Ch 1321 NE Vivion Rd Kansas City MO 64118

STEVENS, LORELEI PATRICIA, brokerage company executive; b. Seattle, Aug. 15, 1950; d. Larry Lawrence Stevens and Patricia Daphne (Crosier) Krenik. BA, Anticoch U., 1991. Pres. Wall Street Brokers, Inc., Seattle, 1973—. Author: Lorelei's Legal Lessons: The Essential Guide for Successful Note Buyers, 1994. Office: Wall Street Brokers Inc 500 Wall St Ste 405 Seattle WA 98121-1577

STEVENS, LORRAINE GERTRUDE, nurse anesthetist; b. Charleston, W.Va., June 12, 1942; d. James Wendel and Edna Mae (Brooks) Bennett; m. Arlen Lee Stevens, Sept. 26, 1964. Grad. in nursing, St. Mary's Hosp., Huntington, W.Va., 1964; BS, U. Cin., 1974, MS, 1976, EdD, 1981. RN, Ohio; registered nurse anesthetist, nurse practitioner ANCC. Nurse VA Hosp., Huntington, 1964-66; didactic and clin. instr. Univ. Hosp., U. Cin. Med. Ctr., 1969-72; mem. bd. admissions for nurse anesthetists Sch. Anesthesia, U. Cin. Med. Ctr., 1970-72; chief nurse anesthetist, dept. mgr. Queen City Anesthesia Assoc., Inc./Providence Hosp., Cin., 1972—; chief nurse 311th Sta. Hosp., USAR, Sharonville, Ohio, 1985-88; mem. adv. bd. nurse anesthetists masters program U. Cin. Coll. Nursing and Health, 1993—. Vol. Pro-Srs. Orgn., Cin., 1990-92. Col. USAR, 1972—. Named Outstanding Black Female in Medicine, NIP mag. Mem. Am. Assn. Nurse Anesthetists, Ophthalmic Anesthesia Assn., Ohio Assn. Nurse Anesthetists, Fla. Nurses Assn. Baptist. Office: Queen City Anesthesia Assoc PO Box 85155 Cincinnati OH 45201

STEVENS, LYDIA HASTINGS, civic worker; b. Highland Park, Ill., Aug. 2, 1918; d. Rolland T.R. and Ruth Shotwell (Beebe) Hastings; m. George Cooke Stevens, Nov. 2, 1940; children: Lydia Stevens Gustin, Priscilla Stevens Goldfarb, Frederick S., Elizabeth Stevens MacLeod, George H., Ruth Stevens Stellard. BA, Vassar Coll., 1939. State rep. 151st Dist. of Conn., Greenwich, 1988-92; cons. Nat. Exec. Svc. Corps, N.Y.C., 1985. Pres. Greenwich YWCA, 1971-74, Greenwich Housing Coalition, 1982-86; v.p. planning Greenwich United Way, 1973-76; sr. warden Greenwich Christ Episcopal Ch., 1981-86; chmn. rev. commn. Episcopal Diocese of Conn., 1985-87; bd. dirs. Greenwich Libr., 1985-93; chmn. Greenwich Commn. Aging, 1986-88; pres., bd. dirs. Greenwich Broadcasting Corp., 1977-79; bd. dirs. Fairfield County Cmty. Found., 1992—. Recipient Golden Rule award J.C. Penney, 1987, President's award Greenwich YWCA, 1992. Republican. Episcopalian.

STEVENS, MARILYN RUTH, editor; b. Wooster, Ohio, May 30, 1943; d. Glenn Willard and Gretchen Elizabeth (Ihrig) Amstutz; BA, Coll. Wooster (Ohio), 1965; MAT, Harvard U., 1966; JD, Suffolk U., 1975; m. Bryan J. Stevens, Oct. 11, 1969; children: Jennifer Marie, Gretchen Anna. Bar: Mass. 1975. Tchr., Lexington (Mass.) Public Schs., 1966-69; in various editorial positions Houghton Mifflin Co., Boston, 1969—, editorial dir. sch. depts., 1978-81, editorial dir. math. and scis. Sch. Div., 1981-84, mng. editor sch. pub., 1984—. Mem. LWV, Mass. Bar Assn. Office: Houghton Mifflin 222 Berkeley St Boston MA 02116

STEVENS, MARRE DANGAR, marketing consultant; b. Atlanta, Mar. 21, 1943; d. Paul Adonaldson and Catherine Eveline (Merritt) Dangar; m. Elmer Cominceola Cowley, June 30, 1968 (div. Jan. 1973); m. 2d John Chenoweth Stevens, Jan. 26, 1973; 1 son, James Chenoweth. Student Oglethorpe U., 1961-63, 73, U. Calif.-San Francisco, 1965. Head directory div. W.R.C. Smith Publs., Atlanta, 1974-75; customer service rep. Visual Graphics Corp., Atlanta, 1974-75; editor Terminus Media, Inc., Atlanta, 1975-76; mktg. mgr. Tech. Analysis Corp., Atlanta, 1976-80; owner Indsl. Mktg. Strategy, Atlanta, 1980-86. Chmn. pub. relation com. Salvation Army Youth Clubs, Atlanta, 1986—. Mem. Am. Mktg. Assn. (bd. dirs., chmn. employee referral com. 1979-80), Southeast Brit. Olympic Assn. (coordinator 1984), atlanta Hist Soc. Democrat. Home and Office: 4093 N Ivy Rd NE Atlanta GA 30342-3909

STEVENS, MARY ANN, state legislator; b. West, Miss.; m. A.J. Stevesn, III; 1 child, Elizabeth Ann. Grad., West H.S. Mem. Miss. Ho. of Reps., 1981—, chmn. ins. com., mem. appropriations com., jud. com., mgmt. and municipalities com.; former banker, landowner; project dir. West Primary Health Care Clinic. Former mayor, former alderman Town of West. Mem. West Garden Club (past pres.), Miss. Women's Club. Democrat. Methodist. Address: PO Box 55 West MS 39192 Office: Miss State Senate State Capital Jackson MS 39201*

STEVENS, PATRICIA ELEANOR, nursing educator; b. Ft. Wayne, Ind., Apr. 13, 1954. BSN, U. Iowa, 1976, MA in Nursing, 1986; PhD in Nursing, U. Calif., San Francisco, 1992, postgrad., 1992-94. RN, Wis., Calif., N.Y., Iowa, D.C. Staff nurse U. Iowa Hosp., Iowa City, 1977-78; sr. staff nurse Cmty. Gen. Hosp., Syracuse, N.Y., 1978-82; primary nurse Psychiat. Inst., Washington, 1982-83; nurse clinician U. Iowa Hosps., Iowa City, 1983-85; primary nurse San Francisco (Calif.) Gen. Hosp., 1986-89; rsch. cons. Lyon-Martin Women's Health Svcs., San Francisco, 1992-94; postdoctoral fellow U. Calif., San Francisco, 1992-94; asst. prof. U. Wis., Milw., 1994—; coord. internat. women's health conf. Internat. Kellogg Found. funding, 1990; rsch. cons. Am. Found. for AIDS Rsch., San Francisco, 1992-94; invited rsch. cons. HIV/AIDS Rsch. in Nursing, NIH, 1993, Improving the Nation's Health with Qualitative Rsch., NIH, 1994; presenter in field. Mem. editorial rev. bd. Advances in Nursing Sci., 1994—, Qualitative Health Rsch., 1994, Western Jour. Nursing Rsch., 1994—; contbr. chpts. to books, articles to profl. jours. Cmty. lectr. in field. Recipient Nat. Rsch. Svc. award predoctoral fellowship NIH, 1989-92, Nat. Rsch. Svc. award postdoctoral fellowship NIH, 1992-94, New Rschr. award Western Soc. for Rsch. in Nursing, 1993. Mem. ANA (coun. nurse rschrs.), APHA (pub. health nursing sect.), Internat. Coun. on Women's Health Issues, Nat. Women's Health Network, Assn. Nurses in AIDS Care, Assn. Cmty. Health Nursing Educators, Sigma Theta Tau. Office: Univ Wis Sch Nursing PO Box 413 Cunningham Bldg Milwaukee WI 53201

STEVENS, PATRICIA MARIE, veterinarian; b. Bala Cynwyd, Pa., Feb. 14, 1962; d. John Mitchell and Marjorie (Jones) S.; m. Robert William Miller, Oct. 13, 1989. BA, Earlham Coll., 1984; VMD, U. Pa., 1988. Assoc. veterinarian Riverside Animal Hosp., Kelso, Wash., 1988-89, Affordable Pet Clinic, Vancouver, Wash., 1989-90, Noah's Ark, Vancouver, 1990-91; owner Timberland Pet Clinic, Woodland, Wash., 1991—. Home: 1112 NW Bolen St La Center WA 98629 Office: Timberland Pet Clinic PO Box 1294 Woodland WA 97674

STEVENS, PHYLISS ELIZABETH, fine art dealer, consultant, publisher, lecturer; b. Balt., Dec. 30, 1953; d. Lawrence and Frances Elizabeth Stevens. BS, Va. Commonwealth U., 1977. Gallery dir. KenWest Gallery, L.A., 1979-84; fine art cons. La Mirage Gallery, L.A., 1984-86; gallery dir. West 43rd St. Gallery, L.A., 1986-89; pres. Vibrant Fine Art, L.A., 1990—; pres., founder, organizer Art in Pub. Places, L.A., 1984-86; creative dir. The Black Child/Art, L.A., 1986-88; art cons. NBC-TV Segment Series, Hill St. Blues, Hollywood, Calif., 1982. Editor Art Forum, 1984, American Black Artists Newsletter, 1988. Recipient Top Cons. Design Workshop award West Coast Art Stars, 1978, Community Involvement In the Arts award Founder's Women Club, 1980. Mem. NAFE, Am. Artist Club (pres. 1986-88). Democrat. Office: Vibrant Fine Art Los Angeles CA 90016

STEVENS, ROSEMARY A., academic dean, public health and social history educator; b. Bourne, Eng.; came to U.S., 1961, naturalized, 1968; d. William Edward and Mary Agnes (Tricks) Wallace; m. Robert B. Stevens, Jan. 28, 1961 (div. 1983); children: Carey, Richard; m. Jack D. Barchas, Aug. 9, 1994. BA, Oxford (Eng.) U., 1957; Diploma in Social Adminstrn., Manchester (Eng.) U., 1959; MPH, Yale U., 1963, PhD, 1968. Various hosp. adminstrv. positions Eng., 1959-61; rsch. assoc. Med. Sch. Yale U., 1962-68, asst. prof. Med. Sch., 1968-71, assoc. prof. Med. Sch., 1971-74, prof. pub. health Med. Sch., 1974-76; master Jonathan Edwards Coll., 1974-75; prof. dept. health systems mgmt. and polit. sci. Tulane U., New Orleans, 1976-78; chmn. dept. health systems mgmt. Tulane U., 1977-78; prof. history and sociology of sci. U. Pa., Phila., 1979—, chmn. dept., 1980-83, 86-91, UPS Found. prof., 1990-91, dean Sch. Arts and Scis., Thomas S. Gates prof., 1991—; vis. lectr. Johns Hopkins U., 1967-68; guest scholar Brookings Instn., Washington, 1967-68; acad. visitor London Sch. Econs., 1962-64, 1973-74. Author: Medical Practice in Modern England: The Impact of Specialization and State Medicine, 1966, American Medicine and the Public Interest, 1971, In Sickness and in Wealth: American Hospitals in the Twentieth Century, 1989, (with others) Foreign Trained Physicians and American Medicine, 1972, Welfare Medicine in America, 1974, Alien-Doctors: Foreign Medical Graduates in American Hospitals, 1978. Bd. dirs. Milbank Meml. Fund. Fellow Am. Acad. Arts and Scis.; mem. Inst. Medicine of Nat. Acad. Sci., History of Sci. Soc., Am. Assn. for History of Medicine, Coll. Physicians of Phila., Cosmopolitan Club. Home: 1900 Rittenhouse Sq # 18 A Philadelphia PA 19103-9999 Office: Office of Dean 116 College Hall U Pa Philadelphia PA 19104-6377

STEVENS, SANDY (AMANDA STEVENSON), document examiner; b. Bklyn., Oct. 24, 1943; d. Haakon and Grace Svendsen; m. James W. Moseley, 1962 (div. 1965); children: Elizabeth B. Moseley, Lawrence Harmon. Grad., Bay Ridge H.S., Bklyn., 1961. Cert. document examiner. Pvt. practice Pitts., 1967—; lectr. Jersey City State Coll., John Jay Coll. of Criminal Justice, N.Y.C., Mcpl. Credit Union, N.Y.C.; cons. numerous lawfirms. Author: How to Make Courtroom Exhibits; co-author: How to Raise an Emotionally Healthy, Happy Child, 1964; designer forms for document examination; composer, librettist (mus.) Nellie Bly. Mem. AEA, Dramatists Guild, Songwriters Guild. Mem. Nat. Bur. Document Examiners. Democrat. Unitarian. Home and Office: 1473 Mervin Ave Pittsburgh PA 15216

STEVENS, TINA WAGNER, writer, editor; b. West Branch, Mich., June 23, 1957; d. Gordon Rodgers and Thelma Lena (Weinberg) Wagner; m. Mike Burgess, Sept. 20, 1975 (div. July 1979); 1 child, Ben Michael Burgess; m. Mark Lester Stevens, Nov. 10, 1980; stepchildren: Jason, Joshua. AA, Delta Coll., 1980; BS, Ea. Mich. U., 1987. Publicity dir. Shoreline Players, Oscoda, Mich., 1980-83; promotion asst. Cen. Bus. Dist. Assn., Detroit, 1983-84; student writer Ea. Mich. U. Alumni Mag., Ypsilanti, 1985-87; asst. editor Gale Rsch. Co., Detroit, 1987-88; mktg. assoc. Ctr. for Entrepreneurship, Ypsilanti, 1988-89; mktg. communications specialist Royal Maccabees Life Ins. Co., Southfield, Mich., 1989-92; freelance writer, 1992—; mktg. cons., Detroit area, 1983—; pub. rels. dir. Sacred Heart Major Sem., Detroit, 1994—; freelance feature and scriptwriter. Recipient 1st Pl. Feature Writing award Women in Communications, 1986. Mem. ASCPA, NAFE, Internat. Asn. Bus. Communicators, Human Soc. U.S., Richard III Soc. Democrat.

STEVENSON, BETTY JEAN, retired teacher and vocational coordinator; b. Raritan, Ill., Jan. 4, 1920; speaker in field.; d. Willis Othal and Reva Marie (Mustain) Adams; m. William Frank Stevenson, Aug. 1, 1937; 1 child, Susan Amelia. BS in Edn., We. Ill. U., 1960; MEd, U. Ill., 1967. Cert. tchr. Insp. Silas Mason Co., Middletown, Iowa, 1952-53; bookkeeper Golden Food Svc. Corp., Middletown, 1954-55; asst. dir. Grote Hall We. Ill. U., Macomb, 1956; elem. tchr. Belmont Elem. Sch. Dist., Little York, Ill., 1957-59; home econs. and gen. sci. tchr. Unit Dist. 103, Media, Ill., 1961-72; tchr., career edn. coord. Unit Dist. 120, Stonghurst, Ill., 1972-77; comprehensive employment and tng. act field rep. Ill. Farmers Union, Galesburg, 1977-78; tchr., vocat. coord. Union Sch. Dist. 115, Biggsville, Ill., 1978-83; speaker in field. Author instructional materials and articles. Mem. Nat. Com. to Preserve Social Security and Medicare, Washington, 1993; bd. dirs. Henderson County Health Dept., 1978-94; pres.; bd. dirs. We. Ill. Area Agy. on Aging, 1990-94; mem. State of Ill. Adv. Coun. on Adult, Vocat. and Tech. Edn., chair, 1978. Mem. Ill. Vocat. Home Econs. Tchrs. Assn. (pres. 1968-69), Ill. Vocat. Asn. (bd. dirs., treas., pres.), Ill. Edn. Assn., Am. Assn. Ret. Persons, Friends of Lane Evans Com.

STEVENSON, CAROL WELLS, secondary education educator; b. Richmond, Va., Feb. 14, 1942; d. Alfred Hatcher and Laura Dowdy (Hobson) Wells; m. James Pendleton Stevenson, June 23, 1962; children: James Brian Stevenson, Anne Pendleton Stevenson. BS in Home Econ. Edn., James Madison U., Harrisonburg, Va., 1962; MA in Adult Edn., Va. Commonwealth U., 1981. Cert. Home Econ., Collegiate Profl. Cert., Va. Home econ. tchr. Patrick Henry High Sch., Ashland, Va., 1962-66, Liberty Middle Sch., Ashland, Va., 1976—. Named Va. Home Econ. Tchr. of Yr., 1988, Tchr. of Yr., Liberty Mid. Sch., 1983-84, 84-85, 85-86, Most Outstanding Home Econs. Tchr. in U.S., Home Baking Assn., 1994; Check Excellence regional winner State Dept. Edn., 1990. Mem. Am. Home Econs. Assn., Va. Home Econ. Tchrs. Assn. (Va. Home Econs. Tchr. of Yr. award 1988), Am. Vocat. Assn., Va. Vocat. Assn., Nat. Assn. Vocat. Home Tchrs., Future Homemakers Am. Found. Episcopalian. Home: 202 Hanover Ave Ashland VA 23005-1815 Office: Liberty Mid Sch RR 3 Box 2500 Ashland VA 23005-9225

STEVENSON, DENISE L., business executive, banking consultant; b. Washington, Sept. 18, 1946; d. Pierre and Alice (Mardrus) D'Auga; m. Walter Henry Stevenson, Oct. 17, 1970 (div. Dec. 1990). AA, Montgomery Coll., 1967; BA in Econs./Bus. Mgmt., N.C. State U., 1983; Cert. in Mgmt. Fin. Women Internat., 1990. Cert. legal asst., Meredith Coll., 1989. Lic. ins. agt. Savs. counselor Perpetual Bldg. Assn. (now Perpetual Savs. Bank), Washington, 1968-70; regional asst. v.p. 1st Fed. Savs., Raleigh, N.C., 1971-83; pres., owner Diversified Learning Services, Raleigh, 1983—; pres., treas. Daily Life Svcs., Inc., Raleigh, 1994—; instr. Inst. Fin. Edn., Raleigh, 1983-89, Am. Inst. Banking, 1986. Mem. Am. Bus. Women's Assn. (woman of yr. award 1982), Fin. Women Internat. (cert. leader 1987, mem. of yr. award 1992, N.C. woman of yr. award 1992), Laurel Hills Women's Club (pres. 1974-75, Raleigh), Omicron Delta Epsilon. Avocation: fishing. Office: Diversified Learning Svcs PO Box 33231 Raleigh NC 27636-3231

STEVENSON, FRANCES KELLOGG, museum program director; b. Boston; d. Charles Summers and Alice deGueldry (Stevens) S.; m. James Richard Wein, 1971 (div. 1989). BA, Wells Coll., Aurora, N.Y., 1967; MA, Oxford U., 1972; MBA, U. Pa., 1992. News editor Sierra Club, San Francisco, 1970-71; copy editor Oxford (United Kingdom) U. Press, 1972-73; from editor to publs. officer Smithsonian Instn., Washington, 1974—. Co-editor: Abroad in America: Visitors to the New Nation, 1976; compiler: (book) National Portrait Gallery Permanent Collection Illustrated Checklist, 1982. James E. Webb fellow Smithsonian Instn., 1988-89. Mem. Sulgrave Club. Home: 2724 Ordway St NW Apt 4 Washington DC 20008-5047 Office: Smithsonian Instn Portrait Gallery 8th and F Sts NW Washington DC 20560

STEVENSON, GALE, librarian; b. Bklyn., Oct. 8, 1942; d. Clifford Edwin and Ruth Helen (Davis) Spates; m. Andrew Kenneth Stevenson Jr., Aug. 28, 1988. BA, Drew U., 1964; MLS, Pratt Inst., 1970. Reference asst. Purdue U., West Lafayette, Ind., 1964-68; libr. Yonkers Pub. Libr., Yonkers, N.Y., 1968-71; adminstrv. svcs. libr. Westchester Community Coll., Valhalla, N.Y., 1971-78; libr. Tompkins County Pub. Libr., Ithaca, N.Y., 1978-88; libr. Bus. Libr., Bklyn. Pub. Libr., Bklyn., 1988—, sr. bus. libr., 1988-93; divsn. chief social scis. Bklyn. Pub. Libr., Bklyn., 1993-94, asst. bus/ libr., 1994—. Office: Bklyn Pub Libr Bus Libr 280 Cadman Plz West Brooklyn NY 11201

STEVENSON, JO ANN C., federal bankruptcy judge; b. 1942. AB, Rutgers U., 1965; JD cum laude, Detroit Coll. Law, 1979. Bar: Mich. 1979. Law clk. to Vincent J. Brennan, Mich. Ct. Appeals, Detroit, 1979; law clk. to Cornelia G. Kenendy, U.S. Ct. Appeals for 6th Cir., Detroit, 1980; assoc. Hertzberg, Jacob & Weingarten, P.C., Detroit, 1980-87; judge U.S. Bankruptcy Ct., Grand Rapids, Mich., 1987—. Office: US Bankruptcy Ct 712 Ford Fed Bldg PO Box 3310 Grand Rapids MI 49503

STEVENSON, JOANNE S., older adults care provider, educator, researcher; b. Steubenville, Ohio, June 8, 1939; d. Joseph A. and Susan (Ploskunak) Sabol; m. Robert J. Stevenson, Aug. 6, 1966; children: James J., Michael J. BS, Ohio State U., 1963, MS, 1964, PhD, 1970. Assoc. prof., dir. Ctr. for Nursing Rsch. Ohio State U. Coll. Nursing, Columbus, prof. dept. adult health and illness. Author books; editor Ann. Rev. of Nursing Rsch.; contbr. articles to profl. jours. NIH predoctoral fellow; recipient Am. Jour. Nursing Book of Yr. award, 1977, 94, others. Fellow AAAS, Am. Acad. Nursing (chmn. knowledge devel. and utilization think tank); mem. AAUP, ANA (cabinet on rsch., coun. nurse researchers), Ohio Nurses Assn., Midwest Nursing Rsch. Soc. (pres. 1991-93), Am. Coll. Sports Medicine, Sigma Theta Tau (chmn. rsch. com.), Alpha Tau Delta, Phi Beta Delta. Home: 4954 Wintersong Ln Westerville OH 43081-4440

STEVENSON, LOIS ANN, marketing specialist; b. Kenton, Ohio, June 28, 1946; d. Charles R. and Edith (Feasel) Sarver; m. Michael B. Stevenson, Sept. 18, 1966 (dec. June 1977); children: Kimberle Stevenson Darst, Tracey, Michelle. Student, Bliss Coll., 1990-92. Ledger clk. United Comml. Travelers, Columbus, Ohio, 1964-65, sec. acctg. dept., 1965-75, sec. pers. dept., 1975-85, adminstrv. asst. to gen. mgr., 1985-92, mktg. specialist, 1992—. Mem. Profl. Secs. Internat. (cert., pres. Delaware, Ohio chpt. 1992—). Home: 201 N Union St Delaware OH 43015-1705 Office: United Comml Travelers 632 N Park St Columbus OH 43215-1627

STEVENSON, SANDRA JEAN, training specialist; b. Butler, Pa., Oct. 5, 1949; d. William Ross and Shirley Elizabeth (Pfaff) S. BA, Carlow Coll., 1975. Lic. pvt. pilot. Gen. mgr. Pa. Liquor Control Bd. Store, Harrisburg, Pa., 1980-82, 87-89; tng. specialist Pa. Liquor Control Bd., Harrisburg, Pa., 1982-87, 89-91, Tng. Sch., Pitts., 1989-91; tng. and employee svcs. mgr. Slippery Rock (Pa.) U., 1991—. Author dramatizations and prototype for conf. on stigma and mental illness 1980. Bd. dirs. County Commrs. Coun. on Drug and Alcohol Programs; office coord., bd. dirs. Lifeline of Southwestern Pa. (Crisis Pregnancy Ctr.), Butler, 1985-90; sec. Mental Health Assn. Pa., Harrisburg, 1981-83, regional v.p., 1979-81; mem. NAACP. Mem. NAFE, Mensa. Democrat. Roman Catholic. Club: Condor Aero. Office: Slippery Rock Univ 205 Old Main St Fl 2 Slippery Rock PA 16057

STEVENSON, TERRIL KAY, geologist; b. Vancouver, Wash., May 25, 1959; d. Jack Clinton and Patricia Ann (Holmberg) S. AS in Geology, Ricks Coll., 1980; BS in Geology, Brigham Young U., 1983. Registered profl. geologist, Idaho. Geologist Bur. of Reclamation U.S. Dept. Interior, Duchesne, Utah, 1980-86, Heber City, Utah, 1986-89; geologist Soil Conservation Svc. USDA, Salt Lake City, 1989, Boise, Idaho, 1989—. Office: USDA Soil Conservation Svc 3244 Elder St Rm 124 Boise ID 83705

STEVOS, JOYCE LOUISE, education director; b. Providence, May 22, 1943; d. Josephus Caldwell and Patricia Anita (Strong) Caldwell Smith; m. Manuel Joseph Stevos, Oct. 22, 1966 (div. Jan. 1981); 1 child, Manuel Joaquim. BEd, R.I. Coll., 1965. Cert. tchr. and prin., R.I. Tchr. Providence Sch. Dept., 1975-76, social studies dept. head, 1971-76, supr. social studies, 1976-80, dir. program and staff devel., 1990-92, dir. strategic planning and profl. devel., 1992—; cons. in field. Author: The Constitution, 1977, 87. Pres. Urban League R.I., Providence, 1983-87. Recipient Never Again award Jewish Fedn. R.I., 1983, Community Svc. award John Hope settlement House, 1987, Edn. award Providence NAACP, 1991, Nat. Educator award Milken Family Found., 1992. Mem. NCCJ (trustee, program com.), DAR, Nat. Coun. for Social Studies (membership com., sec. 1979-80, Carter G. Woodson Book Award com. 1994—), Social Studies Suprs. Assn. (sec. 1979-80), R.I. Black Heritage Soc. (pres. 1989—), Delta Sigma Theta (treas. 1989-91, scholarship). Home: 57 Althea St Providence RI 02907-2801 Office: Providence Sch Dept 797 Westminster St Providence RI 02903-4018

STEWARD, CARY MARIE, association executive; b. Lakeview, Oreg., July 5, 1965; d. Myron Lewis and Judith Anne (Sefert) Steward; m. Terrence John Brewer, June 19, 1993. AA in Bus., Butte Coll., 1985; BS in Bus., Calif. State U., Sacramento, 1990. Asst. mgr. Steward Animal Health, Lakeview, 1982-84; office svcs. tech. Rice Growers Assn., West Sacramento, Calif., 1987; adminstrv. asst. Calif. Probate Referee, Sacramento, 1987-92; asst. mgr. V/ARS Inc., Sacramento, 1990-94; exec. dir. Calif. Assn. Temporary Svcs., Sacramento, 1994—; mentor Calif. State U. Sacramento Sch. Bus. Mentor Program, Sacramento, 1993—. Vol. Red Cross Blood Dr., Bend, Oreg., 1984, Vol. Ctr. for Sacramento United Way, 1987, Crocker Art Mus., 1993—. Mem. Calif. Unemployment Ins. Coun., Sacramento Employers Adv. Coun. (treas. 1993—), Calif. Soc. Assn. Execs., Meeting Profls. Internat., Clan Stewart Soc. Am., Anxiety Disorders Assn. Am., Nat. Trust for Historic Preservation, Smithsonian Assocs. Republican. Roman Catholic. Home: PO Box 19642 Sacramento CA 95819-0642 Office: Calif Assn Temp Svcs 601 Univ Ave Ste 120 Sacramento CA 95825

STEWART, ARLENE JEAN GOLDEN, designer, stylist; b. Chgo., Nov. 26, 1943; d. Alexander Emerald and Nettie (Rosen) Golden; m. Randall Edward Stewart, Nov. 6, 1970; 1 child, Alexis Anne. BFA, Sch. of Art Inst. Chgo., 1966; postgrad., Ox Bow Summer Sch. Painting, Saugatuck, Mich., 1966. Designer, stylist Formica Corp., Cin., 1966-68; with Armstrong World Industries, Inc., Lancaster, Pa., 1968—, interior furnishings analyst, 1974-76, internat. staff project stylist, 1976-78, sr. stylist Corlon flooring, 1979-80, sr. exptl. project stylist, 1980-89, sr. project stylist residential DIY flooring floor div., 1989—, master stylist DIY residential tile, 1992—. Exhibited textiles Art Inst. Chgo., 1966, Ox-Bow Gallery, Saugatuck, Mich., 1966. Home: 114 E Vine St Lancaster PA 17602-3550 Office: Armstrong Innovation Ctr 2500 Columbia Ave Lancaster PA 17603-4117

STEWART, BARBARA ELIZABETH, free-lance magazine editor, artist; b. Ft. Dodge, Iowa, June 26, 1923; d. Warren Wheeler and Christine (Hubbard) Pickett; m. Charles Crombie Stewart, Sept. 2, 1943; 1 child, Charles Crombie IV. Student, Mt. Holyoke Coll., 1940-41, Wayne State U., 1941-42, So. Conn. State U., 1944-45; AA, Mercer County Community Coll., 1970; BA, Trenton State Coll., 1972. Cert, K-12 art tchr. Copywriter Fed. Dept. Stores, Goodwin's, Detroit, 1942-43; dept. coord. Sears, Roebuck & Co., Trenton, N.J., 1944; sec., writer Yale U., New Haven, Conn., 1945, 46; contbg. editor Mercer Bus. Mag., Trenton, 1980—. Oil and acrylic artist. Chmn. Stokes Sch. PTA, Trenton, 1952-58; pres. Rutgers Coop. Extension Mercer County, Trenton, 1970-82; chmn. mem. Hillcrest Civic Assn., Trenton, 1956-83; bd. dirs. Trenton YWCA, 1975-77; chmn. women's fellowship Covenant Presbyn. Ch., Trenton, 1978-88; vol. Art Goes to Sch. program, 1992. Mem. Nat. Art Edn. Assn., N.J. Art Edn. Assn., AAUW (local chmn. 1965, 67), Torch Club (ofcl. del. 1985-88, tchr./vol. Art Goes to Sch. Programs, Pa./N.J. chpt.). Democrat. Home: 31 Clement Ave Trenton NJ 08638-1603

STEWART, BARBARA LYNNE, geriatrics nursing educator; b. Youngstown, Ohio, May 10, 1953; d. Carl Arvid and Margaret (Ashton) Swanson; m. James G. Stewart, Mar. 17, 1973; children: Trevor J., Troy C. AAS, Youngstown State U., 1973, BS, 1982. Cert. gerontol. nurse, ANCC. Asst. dist. office supr. div. health facilities regulation Ohio Dept. Health; supr., dir. nursing svcs. Peaceful Acres Nursing Home, North Lima, Ohio; nurse respondent Health Sci. Ctr. U. Colo., Denver; charge nurse Westwood Rehab. Med. Ctr., Inc., Boardman, Ohio, Park Vista Health Care Ctr., Youngstown, Ohio; dir. nursing Rolling Acres Care Ctr., North Lima, Ohio; primary instr. Alliance (Ohio) Tng. Ctr., Inc.; asst. dist. office supr. Akron dist. office Ohio Dept. Health, Div. Health Facilities Regulation, Akron, Ohio. Former instr. CPR, ARC. Mem. Tri County Dir. Nurses Assn., Youngstown State U. Alumni Assn., Nat. Gerontol. Nursing Assn. (nat. nominating com.).

STEWART, BONNIE JEAN, child development specialist; b. Chgo., Sept. 30, 1961; d. Albert Sr. and Shirley (Luster) Stewart. BS, Ill. State U., 1992; MEd, National-Louis U., 1995. Food mgr. Ill. State U. Child Care Ctr., Normal, Ill., 1990-91; asst. dir. Bell Top Child Care Ctrs., Bloomington, Ill., 1991; presch. tchr. Debra T. Thomas Learning Ctr., Bloomington, Ill., 1992, Beverly Hills Presch., Chgo., 1992; child devel. specialist Head Start, Chgo., 1992-94; early intervention specialist Dept. Mental Health and Devel. Disabilities, Tinley Park, Ill., 1994—; early intervention specialist Dept. Mental Health and D.D., Springfield, Ill. Mem. NAFE, Am. Home Econs. Assn., Nat. Assn. for Edn. Young Childrens, Assn. Childhood Edn. Internat., Kappa Omincron Nu. Democrat. Baptist.

STEWART, CAROL ANN, graphic arts professional; b. Cleve., Oct. 28, 1940; d. Joseph Chapman and Dorothy Jeanne (Page) Bronson; m. Claude Henry Wenner, Apr. 2, 1986 (dec.); m. Robert Ogden Stewart, Sept. 1, 1989. AA in Print Prodn. Mgmt., Graphic Arts Assn. of, Delaware Valley, Phila., 1973; BSBA cum laude, Villanova U., 1980, MBA, 1985. Film libr. Wyeth-Ayerst Labs., Radnor, Pa., 1963-67, prodn. asst., 1967-74, supr. promotion prodn., 1974-86, mgr. graphic arts, 1986—. Sec. Daylesford Hills Civic Assn., Berwyn, Pa., 1973-75; pres. Bear Creek Lakes Civic Assn., Jim Thorpe, Pa., 1985-87, bd. dirs., 1983-88. Recipient Capitol award Nat. Leadership Coun., 1991. Mem. NAFE, Execs. Club Graphic Arts (v.p. 1990-91, pres. 1991-93). Republican. Home: 543 Marietta Ave Swarthmore PA 19081-2416 Office: Wyeth-Ayerst Labs PO Box 8299 Philadelphia PA 19101-0082

STEWART, CAROL JOHNSON, library director; b. Mpls., June 30, 1949; d. William Steele and Constance Harriet (Mattson) Johnson; m. Robert Earl Stewart Jr., May 20, 1983; 1 child, Robert William. BA, Fla. Atlantic U., 1971; MS, Fla. State U., 1972. Br. librarian Memphis/Shelby County Pub. Library, Memphis, 1973-77, DeKalb Library System, Decatur, Ga., 1977-80; library coord. Clayton County Libraries, Jonesboro, Ga., 1980-81; dir. library svcs. Clayton County Library System, Jonesboro, 1981—. Mem. ALA, Southeastern Library Assn., Ga. Library Assn., Avondale Swim and Tennis. Office: Clayton County Libr 865 Battlecreek Rd Jonesboro GA 30236-1919

STEWART, CHARLENE JO, human resources management consultant; b. Norton, Va., Nov. 14, 1946; d. Wiliam Edward and Clarice Hilda (Matz) S.; m. John J. Wegenka Jr., Sept. 19, 1970 (div. Apr. 1987). BSBA, U. Fla., 1969; MBA, Nova U., 1984. Asst. buyer Macy's (Davison's), Atlanta, 1969-70, Wilson's Dept. Store, Gainesville, Fla., 1971; claims clk. Blue Cross/Blue Shield/U. Fla., Gainesville, 1971-72; pers. technician I, II, III U. Fla., Gainesville, 1972-83; mgr. pers. Munroe Regional Med. Ctr., Ocala, Fla., 1983-88; dir. human resources S.W. Fla. Med. Ctr., Ft. Myers, Fla., 1988-90; v.p. Drake Beam Morin, Inc., Tampa, Fla., 1990—; v.p. Munroe Regional Credit Union, Ocala, Fla., 1984-86, pres., 1986-88. Co-dir. Trinity Singles, Gainesville, 1988. Mem. ASTD (bd. mem. Suncoast chpt. 1993-94, mem. rels. dir.), Soc. Human Resource Mgmt. (dist. dir. 1993-94), Human Resources Tampa (bd. mem. 1993). Office: Drake Beam Morin Inc 2502 Rocky Point Dr Ste 350 Tampa FL 33607

STEWART, CLAUDETTE SUZANNE, small business owner, author; b. East Orange, N.J., Jan. 23, 1948; d. Michel Fred and Helen Alberta (Margerum) Mautor; children: Shaun R., Michael B. BS, Rollins Coll., 1980. Bus. mgr. Wometco, Orlando, Fla., 1978-80; acctg. mgr. CNA, Orlando, 1980-81; fin. mgr. Martin Marietta Data Sys., Orlando, 1981-83; owner, operator Yellow Mountain Flower Farm, Leicester, N.C., 1983—; rschr., contbr. Lark Books, Asheville, N.C., 1988, 89, 91; rsch. writer Rodale Press, Emmaus, Pa., 1991. Author: Living with Potpourri, 1988, Everlasting Floral Gifts, 1990, Nature at Ground Level, 1993. Vol. counselor Youth Programs, Inc., Orlando, 1981-83; vol. instr. Jr. Achievement, Orlando, 1981, 82, 83; vol. mountain search and rescue Asheville Area Rescue Squad, 1990-92; vol. firefighter Leicester Vol. Fire Dept., 1990—. Mem. N.C. Herb Assn. Office: Yellow Mountain Flower Farm 57 Davidson Gap Rd Leicester NC 28748

STEWART, DEBORAH RUTH, public relations professional, broadcast executive, television producer and personality; b. Tokyo, May 4, 1954; came to U.S., 1959; d. Eugene M. and Ruth (Somerville) Owens; m. Lorenzo M. Stewart, Apr. 11, 1981 (div. June 1987); 1 child, Lynn M. Student, Hampton Inst., 1972-74; BS in Mass Media, Grand Valley State Colls., 1976. Project dir. Vols. in Probation, Hampton, Va., 1977-78; acting dir. Vols. in Probation City of Hampton, 1978-79; reporter, anchor Stas. WNOR-AM, WNOR-FM99, Norfolk, Va., 1979-80; anchor, dir. pub. svc. Sta. WCMS-AM-FM, Virginia Beach, Va., 1980-81; reporter, anchor Stas. WJNO-

WRMF, West Palm Beach, Fla., 1982-84; asst. info. officer sch. bd. County of Palm Beach, West Palm Beach, 1984-87, pub. rels. planner sch. bd., 1987—; TV host, producer Sta. WPTV, West Palm Beach, 1985—; pres. Owens Broadcasting, Inc., West Palm Beach, 1989—; cons. pub. rels. Hall, Hewko & Leibovitz, P.A., West Palm Beach, 1989—. Sr. editor, contbr. Visions mag., West Palm Beach, 1989—; contbr. to monthly newsletter Insights. Bd. dirs. St. John's Home, Grand Rapids, 1975-76, Am. Cancer Soc., West Palm Beach, 1983-86, Northwood Inst., West Palm Beach, 1986—, Minority Cultural Consortium, West Palm Beach, 1988—; outreach worker Baxter Community Ctr., Grand Rapids, 1974-76; chmn. campaign com. United Way, West Palm Beach, 1987—; vol. Domestic Assault Shelter, 1989—. Recipient Disting. Svc. award St. John's Home, 1976, Urban League PBC, 1986, 87, Outstanding Coverage award in health category for radio news story, UPI, 1981, Appreciation award Alpha Kappa Alpha, 1989; named Community Leader Charmettes, West Palm Beach, 1989. Mem. Women in Communications (pres.), Nat. Sch. Pub. Rels. Assn. Democrat. Baptist. Home: 306 3rd Way West Palm Beach FL 33407-6605 Office: Palm Beach County Sch Bd 3930 R C A Blvd Ste 3004 West Palm Beach FL 33410-4214

STEWART, DOROTHY ANNE, retired meteorologist; b. Beech Grove, Ind., June 2, 1937; d. Thomas Edward and Dorothy Anne (Browne) S.; BS, U. Tampa, 1958; MS, Fla. State U., 1961, PhD, 1966. Tchr. math, sci., high sch., Live Oak, Fla., 1958-59; rsch. physicist U.S. Army Missile Command, Redstone Arsenal, Ala., 1966-89, meteorologist, 1989-93; ret., 1993. Mem. Am. Meteorol. Soc., Am. Geophys. Union, Ala. Acad. Scis., Sigma Xi. Contbr. articles to profl. jours. Home: PO Box 12067 Huntsville AL 35815-2067

STEWART, DORIS MAE, biology educator; b. Sandsprings, Mont., Dec. 12, 1927; d. Virgil E. and Violet M. (Weaver) S.; m. Felix Loren Powell, Oct. 8, 1956; children: Leslie, Loren. BS, Coll. Puget Sound, 1948, MS, 1949; PhD, U. Wash., 1953. Instr. U. Mont., Missoula, 1954-56, asst. prof., 1956-57; asst. prof. U. Puget Sound, Tacoma, 1957-58; head sci. dept. Am. Kiz Lisesi, Istanbul, Turkey, 1958-62; rsch. asst. prof. U. Wash., Seattle, 1963-67, rsch. assoc. prof., 1967-68; assoc. prof. Cen. Mich. U., Mt. Pleasant, 1970-72; assoc. prof. U. Balt., 1973-81, prof., 1981—. Contbr. numerous articles to profl. jours. Mem. Am. Physiol. Soc., Sigma Xi. Home: 1103 Frederick Rd Baltimore MD 21228-5032

STEWART, EILEEN ROSE, real estate broker; b. Indpls., Oct. 20, 1942; d. Burgess Charles and Flora Clara (Schott) S.; m. Richard Michael Grindle, Feb. 12, 1966 (div. 1977). BS, Ind. U., 1965, MS, 1972. Lic. real estate broker, Ind., Fla. Tchr. pub. schs. various locations, Ind., Fla., 1965-72; sales rep. UARCO Bus. Forms, Ft. Lauderdale, Fla., 1972-74; staff trainer Palm Beach County Comprehensive Employment Tng. Act program, West Palm Beach, Fla., 1975-77; pres. Untapped Resources, Inc., West Palm Beach, 1978-80; mgmt. cons. Profl. Mgmt. Assocs., Silver Spring, Md., 1980-82; sales rep. The St. George's Club, Washington, 1983-84; real estate broker Mascari Realty, Indpls., 1985-89; pres. Stewart Manor, Inc., Indpls., 1987-89; sales mgr. Charles Hotel Condominium, Miami Beach, Fla., 1990-92; sales assoc. Infinity Realty, Miami Beach, 1992-93, Real Estate Enterprises, 1993—; gen. mgr. Charles Hotel Condominiums, 1994—; cons. Planned Parenthood, West Palm Beach, 1976-78, Jim Stewart Tire Co., Indpls., 1985-89; chair adv. bd. Palm Beach County Displaced Homemakers Ctr., Lake Worth, 1977-78. Mem. Women's Bus. Initiative, Indpls. Bus. Network, Ind. Bed and Breakfast Assn. (cen. region coord. 1989), NOW (past officer South Palm Beach County chpt., asst. state coord. Fla. sect., 1978, nat. bd. dirs., 1978-79, newsletter editor 1976-77), Women of Miami Beach (pres. 1993—), Miami Beach Devel. Corp. (bd. dirs. 1994—). Democrat. Home: 2457 Collins Ave # 1406 Miami FL 33140 Office: Real Estate Enterprises 1475 Collins Ave PHII Miami Beach FL 33139

STEWART, GEORGIANA LICCIONE, author; b. Mount Vernon, N.Y., May 18, 1973; d. Arthur Alfred and Grace Marie (Zuzzolo) Liccione; m. William Lawrence Stewart, July 18, 1975. BA, Columbia U., 1971; MA, Columbia Tchr.'s Coll., N.Y.C., 1973; MAT, Manhattanville Coll., 1973. Author, cons. Kimbo Ednl., Long Branch, N.J., 1970—; spl. edn. tchr. Tuckahoe (N.Y.) High Sch., 1989—; cons. NAEYC, SACUS, 1975-89, Pres.'s Coun. on Physical Fitness, 1979-81. Author 58 children's books including: Adaptive Motor Learning, 1982, Bean Bag Activities, 1983, Preschool Aerobic Fun, 1989, Children of the World, 1991, Multicultural Rhythm Stick Fun, 1992, Toddlerific, 1993; author musical activity records. Mem. Nat. Assn. for the Edn. of Young Children, So. Assn. for Children Under Six, Am. Assn. Health Phys. Edn. and Recreation, Dance Educators Assn., Assn. Help of Retarded Children, Columbia Club, Women's Nat. Rep. Club. Avocations: after school dance program, organizing local benefit programs. Home: PO Box 625 Bronxville NY 10708-0625 Office: Kimbo Ednl PO Box 477 Long Branch NJ 07740-0477

STEWART, JANICE MAE, judge; b. Medford, Oreg., Feb. 13, 1951; d. Glenn Logan and Eathel Mae (Jones) S.; m. F. Gordon Allen III, Aug. 10, 1975; children—Benjamin Stewart, Rebecca Mae. AB in Econs., Stanford U., 1972; JD, U. Chgo., 1975. Bar: Ill. 1976, Oreg. 1977, U.S. Dist. Ct. Oreg. 1977, U.S. Ct. Appeals (9th cir.) 1978. Assoc. Winston & Strawn, Chgo., 1975-76, McEwen, Gisvold Rankin & Stewart, Portland, Oreg., 1976-81, ptnr., 1981-93; U.S. magistrate judge, Portland, 1993—. Mem. Multnomah County Profl. Responsibility Com., Portland, 1979-82, Oreg. Profl. Responsibility Bd., 1982-85, Oreg. State Bar Practice and Procedure Com., 1985-88, Profl. Liability Fund Def. Panel, Portland, 1985-93, Multnomah County Judicial Selection com., 1985-87, Oreg. State Bar Professionalism Com., 1989-92, Coun. Ct. Procedures, 1991-93, lawyer rep. 9th Cir. Jud. Conf., 1990-93. Mem. ABA, Am. Arbitration Assn. (arbitrator 1990-93), Oreg. Bar Assn., Multnomah County Bar Assn. (dir. 1990-93), Phi Beta Kappa. Democrat. Office: 608 US Courthouse 320 SW Main St Portland OR 97205*

STEWART, JOANNE, secondary school educator; b. Vancouver, Wash., Mar. 10, 1944; d. Edward Charles and Claudine Marie (Meilleur) Spencer; m. William Lemley Stewart, Sept. 2, 1966 (dec. June 1983); children: Amy Diane, Nicholas William. BS, Wash. State U., 1966, MA, 1973. Cert. tchr., Mont., Idaho, Wash., Calif. Tchr. foods Seaside High Sch., Monterey, Calif., 1966-67; tchr. home econs. Marysville (Wash.) High Sch., 1967-68, Palouse (Wash.) High Sch., 1968-73, Ennis (Mont.) High Sch., 1973-76, Genesee (Idaho) High Sch., 1976-77; instr. young family Missoula (Mont.) County High Sch., 1983-84; tchr. home econs. Woodman Sch., Lolo, Mont., 1985-86; travel cons. Travel Masters, Missoula, 1984-87; ticketing mgr. Blue Caboose Travel, Missoula, 1987-91; tchr., chmn. dept. family and consumer scis. Victor (Mont.) High Sch., 1991—. Co-pres. Lolo PTO, 1980-81; v.p. Lolo Community Ctr., 1981; sec. Lolo Mosquito Control Bd., 1988—; mem. telecommunications com. Conrad Burns & Gov. Racicot. Marysville Edn. Assn. scholar, 1962, Future Homemakers Am. scholar, 1962. Mem. AAUW (sec. 1986, program chmn. 1987), Forestry Triangle (pres. 1981, editor cookbook 1982), Future Homemakers Am. (hon. advisor), Am. Family and Consumer Scis. Assn., Mont. Family and Consumer Scis. Assn. (bylaws chair 1994), Mont. Vocat. Tchrs. Assn. (returning Rookie of Yr. 1992), Am. Federated Tchrs., Mont. Vocat. Family and Consumer Scis. Tchrs. (pres. 1994-95). Republican. Methodist. Home: 1200 Lakeside Dr Lolo MT 59847-9705 Office: Victor High Sch Home Econs 425 4th Ave Victor MT 59875-9499

STEWART, JUDITH UNDERWOOD, securities analyst; b. Auburn, N.Y., Aug. 5, 1955; d. Martha (Davenport) Heard; m. Gordon Bennett Stewart III, June 13, 1981; children: Gordon Bennett IV, Charlotte Davenport. BA, Wellesley Coll., 1977; student, MIT, 1975-77; MBA, Wharton Grad. Sch. Bus., 1979. Corp. fin. assoc. Shearson Loeb Rhoades Inc., N.Y.C., 1979-80; asst. treas. Chase Manhattan Bank, N.Y.C., 1980-83; mgr. Citicorp, N.Y.C., 1983-85; rating officer Standard & Poor's Corp., N.Y.C., 1985—. Contbr. writer: Standard & Poor's Structured Finance Criteria, 1988. Mem. Wharton Grad. Bus. Sch. Club N.Y., Jr. League City of N.Y. (chmn. provisional com. winter ball 1984, vice-chmn. and treas. career awareness com. 1985-87), Am. Cancer Soc. N.Y. Div. (jr. com. 1982), French Library (jr. com. 1978), Soc. Mayflower Descendants, Nat. Soc. Colonial Dames, DAR Mary Washington Coll. chpt., New Eng. Soc. City of N.Y., Princeton Club N.Y., Wellesley Coll. Club N.Y., U. Pa. Club N.Y.C.

STEWART, JULIE ANN, energy company executive; b. Los Alamos, N.Mex., Oct. 26, 1961; d. John Neil and Margaret Helen Stewart. BSChemE, U. Calif., Davis, 1983; MBA in Gen. Mgmt., Dartmouth Coll., 1989. Chem. engr. in tng. GE Plastics, Pittsfield, Mass., 1982; project engr. AMFAC Sugar, Honolulu, 1983-87; fin. analyst Combustion Engring., Hartford, Conn., 1988; mem. AVP project fin. staff GE Capital, Stamford, Conn., 1989-93; project devel. mgr. Enserch Devel., Florham Park, N.J., 1993—. Tutor GE Adopt-a-Sch. Program, Stamford, 1991-93; advisor Jr. Achievement, Stamford, 1990; fundraiser Westport (Conn.) YMCA, 1991-94; vol. Children's Ctr. for Learning, 1994. Mem. AIChE, Delta Delta Delta (advisor, mentor 1993-94). Office: Enserch Devel 325 Columbia Turnpike Florham Park NJ 07932

STEWART, LINDA BERENFIELD, librarian; b. Warren, Pa., Oct. 6, 1942; d. Myer and Ida Belle (Samuels) Berenfield; m. Roger H. Stewart, May 23, 1964; children: Sheri Lynne, Michael Lee. BA, U. Mich., 1964; media specialist, Fla. Atlantic U., 1980; MLS, U. South Fla., 1981. Tchr. Garden City, Mich., 1964-66, Charlottesville, Va., 1967-68; libr. cons. Hosp. Librs., Fort Lauderdale, Fla., 1981-82; reference libr. Hebrew Day Sch. Fort Lauderdale, 1982—; reference libr. Pompano Beach (Fla.) Pub. Libr., 1983-85. Active Jewish Fedn. Fort Lauderdale, bd. dirs. women's div., 1990-91. Mem. Broward County Libr. Assn., Fla. Libr. Assn., ALA, Jewish Libr. Assn., Ft. Lauderdale Symphony Soc., Phi Beta Mu. Home: 2350 Sunrise Key Blvd Fort Lauderdale FL 33304-3826 Office: David Posnack Hebrew Day 6511 W Sunrise Blvd Fort Lauderdale FL 33313-6015

STEWART, LUCILLE MARIE, special education program specialist; b. Pittsburgh, Feb. 24; d. William H. and Edna (Hoffman) S. BEd Duquesne U.; MEd, U. Pittsburgh; postgrad. courses Columbia U., U. Calif., Calif. State U. Cert. elem. and secondary tchr., spl. edn. tchr., supr., adminstr. Tchr. Lincoln (Ill). State Sch., 1953; group leader Retarded Education Alliance, N.Y.C., 1954-58; tchr. mentally retarded Ramapo Cen. Sch. Dist., Spring Valley, N.Y., 1958-60, seriously emotionally disturbed, 1960-64; program dir. Pomona (N.Y.) Camp for Retarded, summers 1960-63; tchr. Stockton Sch., San Diego, 1964-65, supr. presch. program for educationally disadvantaged Ramapo Ctrl. Sch. Dist., Spring Valley, N.Y., 1965-67; tchr. Cathdral City (Calif.) Sch., 1967-78; prin. elem. summer schs. Palm Springs (Calif.) Unified Sch. Dist., 1971-72; prin.-tchr. Summer Extended Sch. for Spl. Students, 1979—; mem. exec. com. U. Calif. Extension area adv. com. Mem. NEA, AAUW, Calif. Tchrs. Assn., Palm Springs Tchrs. Assn., Palm Springs Ednl. Leadership Assn., Calif. Assn. Program Specialists, Assn. for Supervision and Curriculum Devel., Am. Assn., Calif. Adminstrs. of Spl. Edn. (Desert community mental health childrens com.), Coun. Exceptional Children (admin., early childhood-learning handicap divsns.), Childhood Edn. Alpha Kappa Alpha, Phi Delta Kappa, Delta Kappa Gamma. Club: Toastmistress. Office: Palm Springs Unified Sch Dist 333 S Farrell Dr Palm Springs CA 92262-7994

STEWART, MARTHA KOSTYRA, caterer, author, lecturer; b. Jersey City; d. Edward and Martha (Ruszkowski) Kostyra; m. Andy Stewart, July 1, 1961 (div. 1990); 1 child, Alexis. BA in European History and Archtl. History, Barnard. Former model; former stockbroker N.Y.C.; profl. caterer; mag. owner, editor-in-chief Martha Stewart Living, 1990—; lifestyle cons. for K-Mart Corp. Author: (with Elizabeth Hawes) Entertaining, 1982, Weddings, 1987; Martha Stewart's Hors d'Oeurvres: The Creation and Presentation of Fabulous Finger Food, 1984, Martha Stewart's Pies and Tarts, 1985, Martha Stewart's Quick Cook Menus: Fifty-two Meals You Can Make in Under an Hour, 1988, The Wedding Planner, 1988, Martha Stewart's Gardening: Month by Month, 1991, Martha Stewarts's New Old House: Restoration, Renovation, Decoration, 1992, Martha Stewart's Christmas, 1993, Martha Stewart's Menus for Entertaining, 1994, Holidays, 1994; appears in weekly cooking segment on Today Show. Office: Martha Stewart Inc 10 Saugatuck Ave Westport CT 06880 also: c/o Susan Magrino Agy 167 E 73rd St New York NY 10021*

STEWART, MARY ANN, educator; b. Decherd, Tenn., Sept. 7, 1936; d. Joseph Francis and Mildred Edrice (Goodman) Knies; m. John Ebb Stewart, Aug. 23, 1969. BS in Bus. Edn., U. Tenn., 1972, MS in Edn., 1976. Cert. profl. sec. Adj. instr. U. Tenn., Chattanooga, 1975-76; assoc. prof. Chattanooga State Tech. Community Coll., 1976—, head bus. admstrn. dept., 1978-82; conductor seminars in field. Editor: Managing for Productivity, 1986. Assoc. probation officer Juvenile Ct., Chattanooga, 1970-72. Recipient Wall St. Jour. award, 1972, Nat. Bus. Edn. award, 1972, Teaching Excellence award Chattanooga State Tech. Community Coll., 1990. Mem. Tenn. Bus. Edn. Ass. (pres. 1982), So. Bus. Edn. Assn., Nat. Bus. Edn. Assn., Profl. Secs. Internat., U. Tenn. Alumni Assn. Avocations: travel, basketball, reading, walking.

STEWART, ORO ROZELLA, retail executive; b. Pendleton, Oreg., July 8, 1917; d. Joseph Allen and Oro Rozella (Overholtzer) Holaday; m. Ivan Stewart, Apr. 4, 1943 (dec.). BE, Oreg. State Coll., 1940; postgrad., Wash. State Coll., 1940-42. Owner, mgr. Stewart's Photo Shop, Anchorage, 1943—; owner Stewart's Jewel Jade Mine, 1970—; instr. TV Sch. Photograhpy; lectr. on Alaskan movies. Writer Alaskan directory on rockhound and internat. locations. Mem. Anchorage Centennial Com., 1967, organizer time capsule to be buried in Juneau; mem. Anchorage Downtown Assn., Fairview Homowners Assn. Recipient various awards at gem and mineral shows. Mem. Alaska Geol. Soc., Alaska Miners Assn., Chugach Gem and Mineral Soc. (chair field trips 1965-78, 81-84, pres. 1967, internat. chair 1967—), Am. Fedn. Lapidary Socs. (internat. relations com. 1977-80), N.W. Fedn. Mineral Socs., Nat. Businesswomens Assn., Anchorage C. of C., Rifleman's Assn., Master Photo Dealers Assn., Profl. Photographers Alaska, Pioneers of Alaska. Democrat. Mem. Soc. of Friends. Clubs: Scottish, Tropical Fish. Lodge: Zonta (v.p. 1971). Home: 840 W 10th Ave Anchorage AK 99501-3402 Office: 531 4th Ave Anchorage AK 99501

STEWART, PAMELA PAQUET, home health administrator, consultant; b. Chgo., June 27, 1948; d. Donald and Lena (Brevard) Paquet; m. Philip James Stewart, Dec. 26, 1969. Diploma, St. Elizabeth Hosp. Sch. Nursing, Chgo., 1969; B. Nursing, Governor State U., 1978. Staff nurse emergency rm. St. Elizabeth's Hosp., Chgo., 1969-72, charge nurse emergency rm., 1973-76; staff nurse trauma Christ Hosp., Oaklawn, Ill., 1972-73; staff nurse SO Suburban Home Health, North Riverside, Ill., 1976-79, supr., 1979, dir., 1979-81; cons. home health HQR, North Riverside, 1981-82; exec. dir. Superior Care, Great Neck, N.Y., 1982—; pres. Health Care Design, Plainfield, Ill., 1984—; cons. Steuben County Pub. Health, BAth, N.Y., 1986-88, Evang. Hosp. Systems, Oakbrook, Ill., 1989-90, Midwest Home Care, Chgo., 1991-92; adv. bd. chmn. Primary Care Svcs., Chgo., 1989—. Author: Nurse, Therapists Notes and Summaries, 1981, Modual Approach, 1984, 87, Computers in Health Care and Home Care Economics, 1992, Documentation for Home Care, 1992. Mem. APHA, Ill. Home Care Coun. (reimbursement com. 1986-88, bd. dirs. and edn. chmn. 1989-91). Office: Health Care Design 1400 N Penny Ln Plainfield IL 60544

STEWART, PATRICIA ANN, bank executive; b. Phoenix, Nov. 3, 1953; d. Travis Delano and Ann Helen (Lopez) Hill. BS, Ariz. State U., 1975. Programmer, analyst Victor Comptometer Corp., Phoenix, 1975-77, Lewis & Roca, Attys., Phoenix, 1977-79; data processing mgr. Central Mgmt. Corp., Phoenix, 1979-80; corp. systems cons. S.W. Forest Industries, Phoenix, 1981-87; human resources system mgr. Western Savs. and Loan, Phoenix, 1987-90; asst. v.p., loan and deposit systems mgr. Bank of Am., Ariz., 1990-91; application mgr. Data Line S.W. div., 1991-93; systems mgr. Bank of Am. Ariz., 1993—; ptnr. Abacus Group, 1981-83. Troop leader, membership registrar Ariz. Catus Pine Girl Scouts Coun. Paradise Vally Neighborhood Girls Scouts U.S.A. Mem. Data Processing Mgmt. Assn. (pres. Phoenix chpt. 1982), Ariz. HP Users Group (mem. dir. 1987). Home: 15849 N 20th Pl Phoenix AZ 85022-3405 Office: Bank of Am Ariz 101 N 1st Ave Phoenix AZ 85003

STEWART, PATRICIA CARRY, foundation administrator; b. Bklyn., May 19, 1928; d. William J. and Eleanor (Murphy) Carry; m. Charles Thorp Stewart, May 30, 1976. Student U. Paris, 1948-49; BA, Cornell U. 1950. Fgn. corr. Irving Trust Co., N.Y.C., 1950-51; with Janeway Rsch. Co., N.Y.C., 1951-60, sec., treas., 1955-60; with Buckner & Co. and successor firms, N.Y.C., 1961-73, ptnr., 1962-70, v.p.-treas., 1970-71, pres.-treas., 1971-73; pres., treas. Knight, Carry, Bliss & Co., Inc., N.Y.C., 1971-73; pres., treas. G. Tsai & Co., Inc., 1973; v.p. Edna McConnell Clark Found. Inc., 1974-92; dir., vice chair Cmty. Found. Palm Beach and Martin Counties; bd. dirs. Melville Corp., Borden Inc., 1976-95, Continental Corp., Bankers Trust Co., Bankers Trust N.Y. Corp., Trans World Airlines, 1973-85, Morton Norivich Inc., 1979-84; allied mem. N.Y. Stock Exch., 1962-73; past mem. nominating com. Am. Stock Exch., N.Y. Stock Exch., N.Y.C. Fin. Svcs. Corp.; dir. emeritus, past chmn. Investor Responsibility Rsch. Ctr. Trustee, vice-chair Cornell U., bd. life overseers Cornell Med. Coll.; vis. com. Grad. Sch. Bus., Harvard U., 1974-80; bd. dirs. NOW Legal Def. and Edn. Fund, 1984-92, Women in Founds./Corp. Philanthropy 1980-86; vice chmn. Community Found. Palm Beach and Martin Counties, 1993—; v.p. fin. com. Women's Forum, 1982-90; vice chmn. CUNY, 1976-80; bd. dirs. United Way of Tri-State, 1977-81, Inst. for Edn. and Rsch. on Women and Work; voting mem. Blue Cross and Blue Shield Greater N.Y., 1975-82; trustee N.Y. State 4-H Found., 1970-76, Internat. Inst. Rural Reconstruction, 1974-79; mem. N.Y.C. panel White House Fellows, 1976-78; mem. bus. adv. coun. The Hosp. Chaplaincy. Recipient Elizabeth Cutter Morrow award YWCA, 1977, Catalyst award Women Dirs. in Corps., 1978, Trustee medal CUNY, 1983, Accomplishment award Wings Club N.Y., 1984, Women's Funding Coalition Innovators for Women$hare award, 1986, Banking Industry Achievement award Nat. Assn. Bank Women, 1987, Cert. Disting. Accomplishments Barnard Coll., 1989; named to YWCA Acad. Women Achievers. Mem. Fin. Women's Assn. N.Y., NOW (bd. dirs.), Coun. Fgn. Rels., Pi Beta Phi. Clubs: University (N.Y.C.); Gullane Golf (Scotland), The Glen (Scotland). Home and Office: 2613 N Ocean Blvd Delray Beach FL 33483 also: Halfland Barns, North Berwick EH395PW, Scotland

STEWART, PENNY MORRIS, secondary education educator; b. Glendale, Calif., Sept. 30, 1949; d. C. Harold and Margaret (Nelson) Morris; m. E. Pierce Stewart, Jr., July 7, 1973 (div. July 1992); children: E. Pierce III, Hailey M. BA in Speech and English, Muskingum Coll., New Concord, Ohio, 1971; MA in Edn., Nat. U., Sacramento, 1991. Cert. multiple and single subject tchr., Calif. Assoc. prod. Alhecama Players, Santa Barbara (Calif.) C.C. Dist., 1972-86; docent Santa Barbara Mus. Art, 1975-86; importer Cambridge Place Corp., Santa Barbara, 1974-86; with promotions and fund raising depts. Stewart-Bergman Assocs., Nevada City, Calif., 1986-89; travel columnist The Union, Grass Valley, Calif., 1987-90; tchr. drama and English Bear River H.S., Grass Valley, 1991—, dept. chair visual and performing arts, 1993—. Art decent coord. Deer Creek Sch., Nevada City, 1986-90, pres. Parent Tchr. Club, 1987-88. Recipient award for valuable contbn. to schs. Nevada City Sch. Dist., 1990. Mem. Ednl. Theatre Assn., Calif. Ednl. Theatre Assn., No. Calif. Ednl. Theatre Assn. Home: 230 Fairmont Dr Grass Valley CA 95945 Office: Bear River HS 11130 Magnolia Rd Grass Valley CA 94949

STEWART, PRISCILLA ANN MABIE, art historian, educator; b. Iowa City, Sept. 21, 1926; d. Edward Charles and Grace Frances (Chase) Mabie; m. Thomas Wilson Stewart, Aug. 28, 1949. BA, U. Iowa, 1948; MA, U. South Fla., 1971; EdS, Fla. Atlantic U., 1983. Coord. elem. art Manatee County (Fla.), 1953-59; prof. art history, intercultural humanities and photography Manatee C.C., Bradenton, Fla., 1959—; organizer, dir. Pelican Perch Wild Bird Hosp., Bradenton, 1953-85. Mem. AAUP, AAUW, Am. Assn. Women in C.Cs. Intertel Soc., Nat. Art Edn. Assn., Fla. Art Edn. Assn., Fla. Assn. C.Cs., Mensa, Sarasota-Manatee Phi Beta Kappa Assn. (pres. 1984-86), Phi Beta Kappa, Alpha Xi Delta, Phi Kappa Phi. Republican. Episcopalian. Home: 2705 Riverview Blvd W Bradenton FL 34205-4335 Office: Manatee Community Coll Dept Art and Humanities Bradenton FL 34207

STEWART, REGINA IDELL, accountant; b. Jersey City, Sept. 12, 1959; d. Ernest and Idell (Brunson) S.; m. Rahmat R. Ghafoor, Jan. 27, 1984; children: Victoria Idell, Stuart Theodore. BA, Upsala Coll., 1981. CPA, N.J. Jr. property acct. B.A.S.F. Wyandotte Corp., Parsippany, N.J., 1979-81; jr. pub. acct. Joseph H. Watson, PA, East Orange, N.J., 1982; sr. supr. pub. acct. Samuel Klein and Co., Newark, 1982-90; sr. internal auditor Johnson & Johnson, New Brunswick, N.J., 1990-94; bus. cons. Ethicon, Inc. Somerville, N.J., 1994—; participant in A Better Chance award Fed. Govt., 1975. Mem. AICPAs, IMA. Home: 293 2C Gemini Dr Somerville NJ 08876

STEWART, RENICE ANN, public relations consultant, writer; b. Milw., Jan. 2, 1947; d. Fredrick and Lucia (Stewart) Fregin; children: Jennifer Jean, Whitney Susan. BA, U. San Diego, 1988, MA, 1990. Pres. Chubby Bumpkins, Inc., Houston, 1980-82; contracts adminstr. Gulf States Computer Svcs., Houston, 1980-82; pres. RAM Prodns., Houston, 1981-82, Pizza Internat., Inc., Houston, 1982-84; contracts adminstr. First Alliance Corp., Houston, 1982-85; freelance pub. rels. cons. San Diego, 1985—. Tutor U. San Diego Writing Ctr., 1987-89; founder, dir. pub. rels.-tng. Montgomery County (Tex.) Crisis Action Line, Houston, 1979-84; founder, v.p., bd. dirs. Montgomery County Rape Crisis Coalition, 1982-84, speaker, 1982-84; speaker Rape Trauma Coalition, 1982-84; mem. prodn. com. Community Women Together, Montgomery County, 1980-82; pres. Living Arts Coun., Houston, 1980-81. Named Woman of Yr. YWCA, 1981, 82. Mem. Am. Assn. Bus. Women (dir. activities Houston chpt. 1983-84), Bus. Women's Forum (bd. dir. community awareness Houston chpt. 1982-83), Assn. Women Bus. Owners, Lions (hon.), Phi Alpha Delta.

STEWART, RITA LYNN, banker; b. Nashville, Oct. 23, 1959; d. Albert Louis and Wilton Lucille (Williams) S.; m. Frank C. Betts, Apr. 27, 1990. BS, La. State U., 1981. Credit analyst Bankers Trust La., New Orleans, 1983-84; asst. v.p. Skaneateles Saving Bank, Syracuse, N.Y., 1986-92; v.p. Savannah (N.Y.) Bank, NA, 1992—. Mem. Town of Savannah Planning Bd.; bd. dirs. Community Action for Self Help, Inc. Mem. Kiwanis. Office: Savannah Bank NA 1565 Main St Savannah NY 13146

STEWART, SALLY BEAL, pilot; b. Englewood, N.J., Apr. 10, 1955; d. Peter Coakley and Betty (Meyer) Van de Water. BS, Northwestern U., 1977. Lic. airline transport pilot, flight engr., flight instr., jumpmaster, skydiving. Sr. tech. rep. Xerox, Milw., 1979-81; flight instr. Capital Aviation, Milw., 1981-82; DC-3 pilot Air Charter/Mr. Douglas, De Leon Springs, Fla., 1982; capt. Mueller Pipeliners, New Berlin, Wis., 1982, Aero Taxi, Rockford, Ill., 1982; skydiver Hi Sky Promotions, Milw., 1980-82; capt., 1st officer Simmons Airlines, Marquette, Mich., 1983-84; capt. Am. Cen. Airlines, Dubuque, Iowa, 1984; first officer Boeing 747-400 Northwest Airlines, Mpls., 1984—; model John Casablancas, Berg Talent Agy., Tampa, Fla., 1991—. Pilot TV spl. Wide World of Sports, 1982; skydiver, interviewee TV spl./video Flight of the Dream Team, 1988. Vol. Univ. Ch. of God, Tampa, 1990-91, choir mem., 1991—; vol. Sr. PGA Tour GTE Suncoast Classic Golf Tournament, Tampa, 1992. Holder world record for 60 woman freefall formation, Deland, Fla., 1986, world record for 120 person freefall formation, Quincy, Ill., 1986. Mem. N.W. Airlines Ski Team, Air Line Pilots Assn., U.S. Parachute Assn., Touch of Country Dance Club, Sky Knights Parachute Club (Pilot of Yr. 1981). Home and Office: 13014 N Dale Mabry Hwy # 260 Tampa FL 33618-2804

STEWART, SALLY E., retired emergency nurse; b. Waynesboro, Miss., Feb. 2, 1932; d. Wm. Grady and Martha Pauline (Grayson) Eldridge; div.; children: Randy, Lou, Ann, Jan. Diploma, Rush Meml. Hosp., Meridian, Miss., 1955; BSN, U. Miss., 1965. Supr., head nurse Univ. Hosp., Jackson, Miss.; head nurse surg. ICU VA Hosp., Jackson, supr., staff nurse. Mem. AACN, ANA, NOVA, Emergency Dept. Nurses Assn. Baptist. Home: PO Box 47 French Camp MS 39745

STEWART, SANDRA ITZEL, language educator; b. Lynwood, Calif., Jan. 18, 1964; d. Lynn Meier and Alicia (Moya) Wolf. BA in Hist. and Polit. Sci., UCLA, 1986; MS in Edn. in Bilingual Curriculum and Instrn., U. So. Calif., 1991; EdM in Lang. and Literacy, Harvard U., 1993; postgrad., U. So. Calif. Bilingual cross-cultural multi subject spl. edn. credential. Spanish tchr., coach Archiodiocese of L.A., Playa Del Rey, Calif., 1987-88; substitute bilingual elem. tchr. L.A. Unified Sch., 1988-89, 92-94; bilingual tchr., 1st grade L.A. Unified Sch. Dist., Wilmington, Calif., 1989-91; bilingual tchr. 5th and 6th grades L.A. Unified Sch. Dist., Wilmington, 1991-92; bilingual math mentor tchr. Mass. Dept. Edn., Boston, 1992-93; rsch. asst. grad. sch. edn. Harvard U., 1992-93; rsch. asst. U. So. Calif., L.A., 1994—, Rockman et al., San Francisco, 1995; organizer and presenter of writing process staff devel. series at Wilmington Pk. Elem. Sch., 1991-92; presenter Eastman Curriculum Design Project Conf., L.A., 1991, survey bilingual edn. Cambridge Coll., Mass., 1992, Parents without Ptnrs., Calif., 1994, sheltered

English methodology and curriculum integration Explorations in Math Project, 1993; spkr. careers in edn. UCLA, 1991; elected faculty rep. office of sec. Wilmington Park Elem. Sch. Local Sch. Leadership Coun., 1991-92; bilingual edn. cons. Merida, Yucatan, Mex., 1994—. Educare scholar Sch. of Edn., U. So. Calif., L.A., 1990; recipient Outstanding Bilingual Tchr. award Accelerated Program, Dept. Edn., U. So. Calif., L.A., 1990; Calif. grad. fellow, 1990-91, title VII fellow U.S. Dept. Edn., 1993—. Mem. Nat. Assn. for Bilingual Edn., Edn. Grad. Orgn. of U. So. Calif., Calif. Assn. for Bilingual Edn., Internat. Reading Assn., Tchrs. English to Spkrs. Other Langs., Am. Ednl. Rsch. Assn., Harvard Alumni Assn., UCLA Alumni Assn., U. So. Calif. Alumni Assn., Phi Delta Kappa. Republican. Roman Catholic.

STEWART, SANDY BROWN, workforce empowerment consultant; b. Buffalo, May 15, 1938; d. Samuel LeRoy and Lula Mae (Gregory) Brown; m. John C. Stewart, Sept. 14, 1955 (div.); children: Gwendolyn, Dawn, A.J., Tracy. Student, Va. State U., 1957, Community Coll. of Balt., 1971-75; Cert. of Mgmt., U. Balt., 1978. Psychiat. nurse attendent Cen. State Hosp., Petersburg, Va., 1959-64; svc. rep. dist. office Social Security Administrn., Petersburg, 1964-69; social ins. claims examiner Social Security Administrn., Balt., 1969-74, social ins. specialist, 1974-81, social ins. mgr., 1981-83; founder, pres. LEADERS Internat., Inc., Balt., 1983-94; exec. dir. Elan Vital Ctr., Owings Mills, Md., 1994—; cons. Dept. of Energy, Fed. Employee Women, New Orleans, 1987-88, Peoples Involvement Corp., Washington, 1987—, Md. State Mgmt. Devel. Ctr., Balt., 1986—, D.C. Dept. of Human Svcs., Washington, 1984-85, US. Dept. Health & Human Svcs.; exec. dir. Elan Vital Ctr., Owings Mills, Md. Author: Taking Control of Your Sandbox, 1988. Bd. dir. Nat Black Women's Health Project, Atlanta, 1988, WMAR-TV Citizen's Adv. Bd., Balt., 1983-88; commn. Balt. City Off-St. Parking, Balt., 1978-82; congrl.candidate 7th Congrl. Dist. of Md., Balt., 1987. Recipient Outstanding svc. Northwood Little League, 1976, Woman of Substance award Glover-Tillman Adult Literacy, 1988, Mayoral Cert. award New Orleans, 1988. Democrat. Office: 10204 Jensen Ln Owings Mills MD 21117

STEWART, SHIRLEY ANNE, assistant principal; b. Bridgeville, Del., June 8, 1957; d. James Elliott and Perline (Jacobs) S. BS in Spl. Edn., U. Del., 1979; MEd in Spl. Edn., Temple U., 1981. Cert. tchr., Del. Spl. edn. tchr. Caesar Rodney Sch. Dist., Camden, Del., 1979; spl. edn. tchr. Indian River Sch. Dist., Frankford, Del., 1980—, bldg. rep. grading com. and health and curriculm com., 1986-87, mem. Curriculum and Instrn. Com., 1987—; tchr. Frankford Elem. Sch., 1980-91, Sussex Cen. Mid. Sch., Millsboro, Del., 1991-94; asst. prin. Woodbridge Elem. Sch., Greenwood, Del., 1994—; mem. Gov.'s Adv. Coun. for Exceptional Citizens, Dover, Del., 1986-91; mem. Coun. Exceptional Children, Dover, 1986—; mem. Statewide Multicultural Com., 1989-90; instr. Del. Tchr. Ctr., 1990; mem. mid. sch. adv. coun. State Del., 1990-91, adv. coun. on multicultural edn., 1991-92, Mid. Sch. Reading Com., 1992, Indian River Sch. Dist. Recruitment/Critical Shortage Com., 1992, instructional materials rev. com. 1993—. Mem. black recruitment com. U. Del., 1987; mem. Minority Action Com., Dover, 1985-87, chmn. Martin L. King Jr. Writing Contest, 1987-88, mem. exec. bd., 1988-89, chmn. black history com., 1986-87, sec. local minority action com., 1985-88; mem. attendance com. Indian River Sch. Dist., 1987-88, recruitment & retention com., 1992, mid. sch. reading com., 1992, mem. materials rev. com., 1993—; chmn. Del. State Edn. Minority Action Com., 1989-90; mem. strategic planning com. Del. State Edn. Assn., 1989-90, issues for the 90's com., 1991; active Dept. Pub. Instrn. Multicultural Inst. Tng., 1989; mem. middle sch. com. State of Del., 1991; mem. Statewide Multicultural Adv. Com., 1991—; vol. Saturday Sch. Com., 1992-93; mem. New Directions Com., 1992-93. Recipient Instructional Profl. Devel. award Minority Action Com., 1987, Del. Tchr. Ctr. Svc. award, 1989, Instructional Profl. Devel. award Del. State Edn. Assn., 1990. Mem. NEA, NAACP, ASCD, Nat. Elem. Sch. Prins. Assn., Del. Assn. Sch. Adminstrs., Del. Elem. Sch. Prins. Assn., Del. State Edn. Assn. (chairperson minority action com. 1988-91, Instrnl. Profl. Devel. award 1991, Human and Civil Rights award 1992), Indian River Edn. Assn. (treas. 1989-91, chairperson minority action com. 1990-93), Adults and Children with Learning Disabilities. Democrat. Pentacostal/Apostolic. Home: 5 Magnolia Dr Millsboro DE 19966-1246

STEWART, SUE STERN, lawyer; b. Casper, Wyo., Oct. 9, 1942; d. Fraizer McVale and Carolyn Eliabeth (Hunt) Stewart; BA, Wellesley Coll., 1964; postgrad. Harvard U. Law Sch., 1964-65; JD, Georgetown U., 1967; m. Arthur L. Stern, III, July 31, 1965 (div.); children—Anne Stewart, Mark Alan; m. John A. Ciampa, Sept. 1, 1985 (div.). Admitted to N.Y. bar, 1968; clk. to Judges Juvenile Ct., Washington, 1967-68; mem. firm Nixon, Hargrave, Devans & Doyle, Rochester, N.Y., 1968-74, ptnr., 1975—; lectr. in field; trustee Found. of Monroe County (N.Y.) Bar, 1976-78. Sec., dir. United Community Chest of Greater Rochester, 1973-87, 92—; trustee, sec. Internat. Museum Photography at George Eastman House, Rochester, 1974—, Genesee Country Mus., Mumford, N.Y., 1976—; bd. dirs. Ctr. for Govtal. Research. Mem. Am. (chmn. task force on charitable giving, exempt orgns. com. tax sect. 1981—), N.Y. State (exec. com. tax sect., 1974-76, chmn. com. exempt orgns. 1975-76), Monroe County Bar Assn. (trustee 1974-75), BNA Portfolio, Pvt. Found. Distbns. Author: Charitable Giving and Solicitation. Office: Nixon Hargrave Devans & Doyle PO Box 1051 Clinton Sq Rochester NY 14603-1051

STEWART-ROACHE, CATHARINE BUCHANAN, minister; b. Oklahoma City, Sept. 17, 1938; d. Frank Wylie Stewart and Gertrude Helen (Buchanan) Stewart; m. Patrick J. Roache, June 1, 1963; children: Amelia, Anne (dec.), Jim, Elizabeth, Emmet. BA, Rosary Coll., 1961; MA, U. Notre Dame, 1962, Webster U.; DMin, Jesuit Sch. of Theology, Berkeley, 1978. Tchr. St. Mary's Acad., South Bend, Ind., 1962, St. Pius High Sch., Albuquerque, 1975-76; mental health counselor Home Counseling Assocs., Albuquerque, 1978-94; chaplain Lovelace Med. Ctr., Albuquerque, 1981-86, Presbyn. Pickard Convalescent Ctr., Albuquerque, 1988-93; core commn. Womens Ordination Conf., 1977-79; convener Sisters of Miriam. Dir. Women Over the Hill Bicycle Tour. Mem. N.Mex. Chaplains Assn. (past pres. 1981, 93-94), N.Mex. Mental Health Counselors Assn. (pres. 1991-92), Coll. of Chaplains (emeritus), Sierra Club, Cousteau Soc. Roman Catholic.

STIBITZ, MARY JO, psychotherapist; b. Muskegon, Mich.; d. Harold Russell and Holly Maxine (Fechner) S. BA, Western Mich. U., 1969; M in Agy. Counseling, Mich. State U., 1989, M in Marriage and Family Therapy, 1991, postgrad. Cert. counselor; limited lic. psychologist. Elem. tchr. Muskegon (Mich.) Pub. Schs., 1969-88; grad. asst., teaching asst. Mich. State U., East Lansing, 1988-93; psychotherapist Mich. Psychotherapy, Lansing, 1991—; cons. Sparrow Hosp., Lansing, 1992-94. Pres., sec., bd. mem., actress Port City Playhouse, Muskegon, 1966-84; bd. mem., actress Civic Theatre, Muskegon, 1985-88. Mem. Assn. Am. Marriage & Family Therapist, Am. Counseling Assn. Home: 633 E Jolly Rd Apt 6 Lansing MI 48910-6803 Office: Mich Psychotherapy 335 Seymour Ave Lansing MI 48933-1114

STICH, THELMA ALLEN, nursing educator; b. Bklyn., Dec. 23, 1958; d. Jack and Vivian (Scherling) Allen; m. Charles Stich, Apr. 4, 1982; 1 child, Justin Sean. BSN, CUNY-Hunter Coll., 1980; MS, Wagner Coll.; postgrad., Rutgers U. RN, N.Y.; cert. community health nurse, specialist med./surg. nurse, diabetes educator, diabetes clin. nurse specialist. Pub. health nurse Vis. Nurse Svc. N.Y., N.Y.C.; home care coord. Cabrini Med. Ctr., N.Y.C.; staff nurse Bayley Seton Hosp., S.I.; diabetes nurse educator Coney Island Hosp., Bklyn.; clin. nurse specialist adult cardiology United Hosps. Med. Ctr.; diabetes clin. nurse specialist SUNY HSCB; mem. Am. Diabetes Assn. patient svcs. and pub. edn. coms. Coney Island Hosp.; mem. adj. faculty NYU; teaching asst., rsch. coord. Rutgers U. Contbg. author: Review of Maternal Infant Nursing, 1991, Maternal-Newborn Nursing, 1992. RN mentor area high sch. program; presenter diabetes edn. various profl. and community groups; participant area health fairs. Fellow Am. Diabetes Assn. Clin. Soc. (coms. pub. edn. and svc.); mem. N.Y. State Nurses Assn., N.J. State Nurses Assn., Am. Assn. Diabetes Educators (cert.), Am. Pub. Health Assn., Sigma Theta Tau (past chair com. pub. rels.). Home: 14 Hampton Grn Staten Island NY 10312-1718

STICK, ALYCE CUSHING, information systems consultant; b. N.J., July 13, 1944; d. George William and Adele Margaret (Wilderotter) Cushing; m. James McAlpin Easter, July, 1970 (div. Aug. 1986); m. T. Howard F. Stick, June, 1989. AA, Colby-Sawyer Coll., 1964; student, Boston U., 1964-65, Johns Hopkins U., 1972-74; cert., Control Data Inst. and Life Office Mgmt. Assn., 1976. Claims investigator Continental Casualty Co., Phila., 1967-69; data processing coord. Chesapeake Life Ins. Co., Balt., 1970-72; sr. systems analyst Comml. Credit Computer Corp., Balt., 1972-80; v.p. Shawmut Computer Systems, Inc., Owings Mills, Md., 1980-85; pres. Computer Relevance, Inc., Gladwyne, Pa., 1985—; cons. Sinai Hosp., Balt., 1982-85, AT&T, Reading, Pa., 1987-88, Dun and Bradstreet, Allentown, Pa., 1988, Arco Chem. Co., Newtown Square, Pa., 1990-91, Rohm and Haas Co., Phila., 1992-94. Designer/author: (computer software systems) Claim-Track, 1977, Property-Profiles, 1979, Stat-Model, 1989; co-designer/author: Patient-Profiles, 1983. Treas. Balt. Mus. Art, Sales and Rental Gallery, 1984. Mem. Assn. for Systems Mgmt., Data Processing Mgmt. Assn., Ind. Computer Cons. Assn., Merion Cricket Club (Haverford, Pa.). Republican. Office: Computer Relevance Inc 1501 Monticello Dr Gladwyne PA 19035-1206

STICKELER, CARL ANN LOUISE, professional parliamentarian; b. Plant City, Fla., Dec. 26, 1930; d. Carl Ulysses and Marian Lucille (Churchill) Sangster; m. Nickolas Joseph Stickeler, May 14, 1949; children: Nickolas J., Juliann E., Carl A., John C., Katherine M. Profl. registered parliamentarian. Bus. mgr. Kendall Automobile Sales, Inc., Miami, 1967-82; parliamentarian Stickeler & Assocs., P.A., Miami, 1982-88, Ocala, Fla., 1988—. Editor: The Answer, 1983-89, The Florida Parliamentarian, 1983-87. Recipient Internat. Woman of Distinction Beta Sigma Phi Internat., 1980, Order of the Rose award Beta Sigma Phi Internat., 1969. Mem. Nat. Assn. Parliamentarians (bd. dirs. 1979-83, 91-93, v.p. 1983-89, pres. 1989-91), Acad. Parliamentary Procedure and Law (bd. dirs. 1979—, pres. 1985-87), Gen. Fedn. Women's Clubs, Fla. Fedn. of Women's Clubs (parliamentarian 1992—), DAR, Beta Sigma Phi. Republican. Roman Catholic. Office: Stickeler & Assocs 102 Almond Rd Ocala FL 32672-8634

STICKNEY, JESSICA, former state legislator; b. Duluth, Minn., May 16, 1929; d. Ralph Emerson and Claudia Alice (Cox) Page; m. Edwin Levi Stickney, June 17, 1951; children: Claudia, Laura, Jeffrey. BA, Macalester Coll., St. Paul, Minn., 1951; PhD (hon), Rocky Mtn. Coll., Billings, Mont., 1986. Rep. State of Mont., 1989-92; mem. Gov.'s Commn. on Post-Sec. Edn., Mont., 1973-75. Mem. Sch. Bd. Trustees, Miles City, Mont., 1968-74; mem., chmn. zoning bd., Miles City, 1975-89; mem. Govt. Study Commn., Miles City, 1974-76, United Ch. Christ Bd. Homeland Ministries, 1975-81; chmn., conf. moderator United Ch. Christ Bd. Mont.-Northern Wyo. Conf., 1980-82; chmn. Town Meeting on the Arts, Mont., 1980; mem., chmn. Miles Community Coll. Bd., 1975-89, chmn. 1978-80. Mem. Mont. Arts Coun. (chmn. 1982-85), Western States Arts Found. (vice chmn. 1984), Nat. Assembly State Arts Agys. (bd. dirs. 1982-88), AAUW (pres. 1964-66). Democrat.

STIDD, LINDA MARIE, rehabilitation nurse; b. Martins Ferry, Ohio, Mar. 20, 1947; d. Stephen George and Helen Jane (Cupryk) Mularcik; m. William Leroy Stidd, May 4, 1968; 1 child, Christopher Alan. Diploma, Ohio Valley Gen. Hosp., 1968; BSN, Ohio U., 1995. CRRN. Staff nurse Ohio Valley Gen. Hosp., Wheeling, W.Va., 1968-69, 73-79; supr. Woodland Acres Nursing Home, St. Clairsville, Ohio, 1971-73; staff nurse Ohio Valley Med. Ctr., Wheeling, 1973-79, head nurse rehab., 1981-91; nurse mgr. OVMC Rehab. at Woodsdale, Wheeling, 1991-92; nurse mgr. for skilled care/rehab. Peterson Rehab. Hosp. and Geriatric Ctr., Wheeling, 1992—. Mem. Assn. Rehab. Nurses, W.Va. Assn. Rehab. Nurses, W.Va. Orgn. Nurse Execs., Nat. Disting. Svc. Registry Med. and Vocat. Rehab. Democrat. Roman Catholic. Office: Peterson Rehab Hosp Homestead Ave Wheeling WV 26003-6697

STIDMAN, EDITH (JANET) SCALES, parliamentarian; b. Balt., Sept. 19; d. Joseph Edward and Edith Morris (Caulk) Scales; m. Herbert Jean Silcox, May 18, 1944 (dec. Mar. 1945); m. John Charles Stidman, Sept. 27, 1947; children: Janet Stidman Eveleth, John Scales Stidman. BS in Instn. Mgmt., U. Md., 1944. Profl. registered parliamentarian. Food svc. supr. Cen. Club for Nurses & Studio Club YWCA, N.Y.C., 1944-45; asst. dietitian Ctrl. Club for Nurses, N.Y.C., 1944-45; dietitian, trouble shooter Studio Club YWCA, N.Y.C., 1944-45; lectr., spkr. and cons. in field. Editor (newsletter) Govans Guidepost, 1959-62, Md. Assn. Capsule Epistle, 1991-93; contbr. articles to profl. jours. Vice-chmn., chmn. Grace United Meth. Ch., bd. dirs., fin., nominating, edn., pastor/parish rels., worships coms., lay mem. to conf.; tchr., jr. dept. supt., counseling tchr., pres. Grace United Meth. Women, 1987-88, 89, 91; recording sec. Md. Congress of Parents & Tchrs., Inc., 1965-68, dist. v.p. 1962-65, bd. dirs., 1960-68; bd. trustees William Lemmel Scholarship Fund and Screening Com., 1960's, The Boy's Latin Sch. Md., 1969-70; charter mem. Jr. Bd. and Sec. Florence Crittenden Home, 1948-50; pack coord. Cub Scout pack Boy Scouts Am.; bd. dirs. Safety Coun. of Md., 1968—, v.p. 3 divsns., 1969-75; pres. Legislative Clearing House of Md., 1971-75; corr. sec. Balt. City PTA Coun. pres. 1959-61; pres. Govans PTA, 1959-61; pres. Northern H.S. PTA, 1965-67; hon. life mem. Md. PTA, Nat. PTA; past pres. Md. Coun. on Edn.; parliamentarian Woman's Club Roland Park, Balt., 1978—, 1st v.p., 1994—; judge parliamentary performance contests h.s. teams statewide for State Dept. Edn., Md., 1993—; bylaws chmn. Union Meml. Hosp. Aux., 1990-92. Recipient Vol. Svc. cert. Balt. City Health Dept. 1957, Generous Svc. and Committment to Bus. Edn. cert. Balt. County Bd. Edn., 1983, Recognition of Svc. to Blue Ridge Region cert. Internat. Toastmistress Orgn., 1983, Appreciation cert. Howard Vocat. Tech. Sch., 1983, Towson State U., Profl. Secs. Internat., Future Bus. Leaders Am., Spl. Mission Recognition award United Meth. Women, 1981. Mem. AAUW (parliamentarian Md. chpt. 1973-75), Nat. Assn. Parliamentarians (pres. 1987-89), Md. Assn. Parliamentarians (pres. 1973-75), Am. Inst. Parliamentarians, Internat. Platform Assn., Nat. League Am. Pen Women (parliamentarian 1992—, 5th v.p. 1994, 4th v.p. 1994—), U. Md. Alumni Assn. (life, reunion com. 1994), Md. Assn. Hosp. Aux. (parliamentarian 1973—), Edith S. Stidman Unit (pres. 1984-87, pres. parliamentary edn. unit 1971-73, pres. M.W. Wheelock unit 1976-79), Md. Registered Parliamentarians (pres. unit 1993-94), Nat. Parks and Conservation Assn., Women's Civic League. Republican. Methodist. Home and Office: 606 Cedarcroft Rd Baltimore MD 21212-2703

STIEBER, TAMAR, writer; b. Bklyn., Sept. 15, 1955; d. Alfred and Florence (Spector) S. Student, Rockland C.C., 1972-75, Rockland C.C., 1972-75, West London (Eng.) Coll., 1973-74; BA in Film cum laude, U. Calif., Berkeley, 1985, postgrad., 1985-86; grad. police reserve academycum laude, Napa Valley Coll., 1988. Office mgr., confidential sec. AP, San Francisco, 1981-83; stringer Daily Californian, Berkeley, Calif., 1983-84; film rsch. teaching asst. U. California, Berkeley, 1984-86; libr. and rsch. asst. Pacific Film Archive, Berkeley, 1984-86; intern San Francisco Examiner, 1984; reporter Sonoma (Calif.) Index-Tribune, 1987-88, Vallejo (Calif.) Times Herald, 1988-89, Albuquerque Journal, 1989-94. Recipient Pulitzer prize for specialized reporting, 1990, first place pub. svc. divsn. N.Mex. Press Assn., 1990, pub. svc. award Albuquerque Press Club, 1990; first place newswriting N.Mex. Press Assn., 1991; honorable mention Assn. Press Managing Editors, 1994. Mem. Soc. Profl. Journalists, Investigative Reporters and Editors, N.M. Found. Open Govt., Phi Beta Kappa.

STIEFEL, SUSAN CAROL, legal services firm human resources executive; b. N.Y.C., Apr. 25, 1945; d. Michael and Judith (Kleinman) Dronsick; m. Lloyd Mark Haffner, Apr. 3, 1966 (div. 1980); children: Jessica Lynn, Meredith Paige; m. Alan Lee Stiefel, Oct. 7, 1984; stepchildren: Suzanne Leigh, Jennifer Lynn. BA in Sociology, SUNY, Binghamton, 1966; MBA with honors, Lake Forest Grad. Sch. Mgmt., 1984. Researcher Child Welfare League Am., N.Y.C., 1966-68; pers. asst. Solo Cup Co., Highland Park, Ill., 1979-80, employment mgr., 1980-83; pers. rep. Denticon/Sybron Corp., Evanston, Ill., 1983-84, mgr. human resources, 1984-86; dir. human resources Medserv Corp., Lake Forest, Ill., 1986-87; v.p. for human resources Medserv Corp., Marietta, Ga., 1988-93; dir. human resources Kilpatrick & Cody, Atlanta, 1993—. Campaign worker Lake County (Ill.) Dem. Cen. Com., 1980. Mem. Soc. for Human Resource Mgmt., NAFE, Lake Forest Grad. Sch. Mgmt. Alumni Assn. (v.p. bd. dirs. 1986-88). Jewish. Office: Kilpatrick & Cody Ste 2800 1100 Peachtree St Atlanta GA 30309

STIEG, CLAUDIA MARGARET, mechanical engineer; b. Hamilton, Ohio, June 25, 1950; d. Fred and Clarissa (Hamilton) S.; m. David W. Fife, May 19, 1984 (div. Aug. 1989). BS in Mech. Engring., U. Utah, 1982; postgrad., Calif. State U., San Bernardino, 1991—. Engring. asst. E-Sys., Salt Lake City, 1973-82, sr. quality engr., 1984-86; quality engr. Thikol, Brigham City, Utah, 1983-84; aerospace engr. Naval Plant Rep. Office, Magna, Utah, 1986-90; sr. quality engr. Ford Aerospace/Loral, Newport Beach, Calif., 1990-91; mech. engr., program integrator Lockheed Aircraft Svc.-Def. Contract Mgmt., Ontario, Calif., 1991—. Josephine Beam Fund scholar, 1981, 82. Republican. Presbyterian. Office: Lockheed Aircraft Svc DCMC PO Box 33 Ontario CA 91761

STIENMIER, SAUNDRA KAY YOUNG, aviation educator; b. Abilene, Kans., Apr. 27, 1938; d. Bruce Waring and Helen E. (Rutz) Young; m. Richard H. Steinmier, Dec. 20, 1958; children: Richard, Susan, Julia, Laura. AA, Colo. Women's Coll., 1957; student, Temple Buell Coll., U. Colo., 1959, 69; ed., Embre Riddle Aviation U., Ramstein, Germany; student, Harriot-Watt U., Edinborough, Scotland. Cert. FAA pilot. Dir. Beaumont Gallery, El Paso, Tex., 1972-77; mem. grad. studies faculty Embre Riddle Aviation U., 1979-80; mgr. Ramstein Aero Club, USAF, 1977-80, Peterson Aero Club, USAF, Peterson AFB, Colo., 1980—. Named Outstanding S.W. Artist. Mem. Internat. Platform Assn., AAUW, Order Eastern Star, Scottish Soc. Pikes' Peak, Scots Heritage Soc., Internat. Women Pilots Assn., Beta Sigma Phi, Delta Psi Omega, Aircraft Owners and Pilots Assn., Nat. Pilots Assn., Colo. PilotsAssn., Soc. Arts and Letters, 99's Club. Office: PO Box 14123 Colorado Springs CO 80914-0123

STIFEL, NELL WARNER, artist; b. N.Y.C., June 25, 1959; d. William Frederick and Carolyn (Graham) S. Cert., Pa. Acad. Fine Arts, 1988; BA in English, Middlebury Coll., 1981. Art dir. Omni Internat. Design, Phila., 1987-89. Set decorator TV, film, and video, N.Y.C., 1982-85; scenic artist TV commls., theater, film and video, 1989—; scenic artist Philadelphia, 1993, Two Bits, 1994, 12 Monkeys, 1995; group shows include Painted Bride Art Ctr., Phila., 1990, Port of History Mus., Phila., 1991. Recipient Toppan prize for drawing Pa. Acad. of Fine Arts, 1988; MacDowell Colony fellow, 1991. Mem. Protean Artists Coop., Highwire Artists Gallery, United Scenic Artists (local 829), Phi Beta Kappa. Home and Office: 3309 Baring St Philadelphia PA 19104-2528

STIGLER, SHIRLEY ANN GENSLER, educator; b. Wichita Falls, Tex., Apr. 28, 1953; d. Alfred and Hulda Evelyn (Jentsch) Gensler; m. Robert Duane Stigler, Aug. 9, 1975. BA, Tex. Tech. U., 1975, MA, 1979. Tchr. Tahoka (Tex.) Ind. Sch. Dist., 1975-76; teaching asst. Tex. Tech. U., Lubbock, 1976-78; tchr. Lubbock Ind. Sch. Dist., 1978—; mem. textbook com. Lubbock Ind. Sch. Dist., 1992—, tech. com., 1991—. Co-author: corr. course for Algebra 2, 1987, Curriculum Guide for Calculus, 1993; author: Curriculum Guide for Calculus, 1989. Mem. Nat. Assn. Secondary Sch. Prins. (Nat. Honor Soc. adviser), Math. Assn. Am. (Edyth M. Sliffe award 1993), Tex. Assn. Profl. Educators. Home: 4803 59th St Lubbock TX 79414-4407 Office: Lubbock High Sch 2004 19th St Lubbock TX 79401-4606

STIGLIANO, STEPHANIE MAHAN, artist; b. Concord, Mass., Oct. 14, 1958; d. Russell P. and Anastasia Mahan; m. Charles Anthony Stigliano, May 29, 1982; 1 child, Angela Mahan. BFA, Phila. Coll. of Art, 1980; MFA, Mass. Coll. of Art, 1988. Exhibited in group shows including Fitchburg (Mass.) Art Mus., 1990, Alchemie Gallery, Boston, 1990, Maliotis Ctr. at the Hellenic Coll., Brookline, Mass., 1991, Space Gallery, Boston, 1991, Ashuah/Irving Gallery, Boston, 1991, 92, Schlesinger Libr., Cambridge, 1992, Ctr. for the Arts at the Chocolate Ch., Bath, Maine, 1992, Boston Pub. Libr., 1993, Newton Pub. Libr., 1993, Houghton Libr., Cambridge, 1993, Barbara Gillman Gallery, Art for Artists, 1994, represented in permanent collections Bank of Boston, Fogg Art Mus., Hougton Libr., Mus. Fine Arts, Boston, William Carlos Williams Estate, Morton Godine Libr., Mass. Coll. Art. Recipient MCA Painting and Printmaking award, 1986, Nashua Corp. award Henley Exhbn., 1984, Honorable mention Fayetteville Mus., 1984, Award Internat. Paper Co., 1983, 2d Pl. Bailey Banks and Biddle Competition, 1980. Mem. Letterpress Guild of New England.

STILES, MARY ANN, lawyer; b. Tampa, Fla., Nov. 16, 1944; d. Ralph A. and Bonnie (Smith) S. AA, Hills Community Coll., 1973; BS, Fla. State U., 1975; JD, Antioch Sch. Law, 1978. Bar: Fla. 1978. Legis. analyst Fla. Ho. of Reps., Tallahassee, 1973-74, 74-75; intern U.S. Senate, Washington, 1977; v.p., gen. counsel Associated Industries Fla., Tallahassee, 1978-81, gen. counsel, 1981-84, spl. counsel, 1986—; assoc. Deschler, Reed & Crichfield, Boca Raton, Fla., 1980-81; founding ptnr. Stiles, Taylor & Metzler, Tampa, Fla., 1982—; shareholder and dir. Stiles Taylor & Metzler, P.A., Six Stars Devel. Co. of Fla., Inc.; shareholder First Comml. Bank of Tampa. Author: Workers' Copmenstaion Law Handbook, 1980-94 edit. Bd. dirs., sec. Hillsborough C.C. Found., Tampa, 1985-87, 94—; bd. dirs. Hillsborough Area Regional Transit Authority, Tampa, 1986-89, Boys and Girls Club of Tampa, 1986—; mem. Bay Area chpt. Nat. Women's Polit. Caucus, 1993—, The Spring, 1992-93, What's My Chance, 1992—; mem. Gov.'s Oversite Bd. on Workers' Compensation, 1989-90, Jud. Nominating Commn. for Workers' Compensation Cts., 1990-93. Mem. ABA, Fla. Bar Assn., Hillsborough County Bar Assn., Hillsborough Assn. Women Lawyers, Fla. Assn. Women Lawyers, Fla. Women's Alliance, Hillsborough County Seminole Boosters (past pres.). Democrat. Baptist. Club: Tiger Bay (Tampa, past pres.). Office: 315 S Plant Ave Tampa FL 33606-2325 also: 111 N Orange Ave Ste 850 Orlando FL 32801 also: 317 N Calhoun St Tallahassee FL 32301 also: 200 E Las Olas Blvd Ste 1760 Fort Lauderdale FL 33301

STILL, LISA STOTSBERY, lawyer; b. North Kingstown, R.I., Dec. 4, 1960; d. Lawrence Edward Stotsbery and Clarice Ann Dudley; m. July, 1992. AA with honors, Pensacola Jr. Coll., 1979; BA with honors, U. West Fla., 1981; JD, U. Fla., 1985. Bar: Fla. 1986, U.S. Dist. Ct. (mid. dist.) Fla. 1986, U.S. Ct. Appeals (11th cir.) 1987, U.S. Tax Ct. 1987, U.S. Supreme Ct. 1993. Tax specialist Coopers & Lybrand, Miami, Fla., 1986, Jacksonville, Fla., 1986-87; pvt. practice Jacksonville, 1987; staff counsel SBA, Jacksonville, 1987—; spl. asst. U.S. atty. No. and Mid. Dists. Fla., 1990—. Mem. ABA (com. enforcement creditors rights and bankruptcy 1990), Fed. Bar Assn. (treas. Jacksonville chpt. 1990-92, v.p. membership 1993, v.p. programs 1994, pres.-elect 1995), Fla. Bar (real property, probate and trust law sect., govt. lawyer sect. 1990-91). Home: 4125 Hidden Branch Dr N Jacksonville FL 32257-7681 Office: SBA 7825 Baymeadows Way Ste 100B Jacksonville FL 32256-7504

STILLE, DARLENE RUTH, editor; b. Chgo., Apr. 17, 1942; d. Theodore E. and Edna L. Stille. BA in English, U. Ill., 1965. Prodn. editor Ency. Britannica, Chgo., 1967-68; staff editor Compton's Ency. and Year Book, Chgo., 1968-71; sr. editor World Book Yearbook, Sci. Year, Chgo., 1971-78; assoc. editor Sci. Year, Chgo., 1978-91; mng. editor World Book Annuals Editl. Dept., Chgo., 1991-94, exec. editor, 1994—. Author: Air Pollution, 1990, Water Pollution, 1990, Soil Erosion and Pollution, 1990, Greenhouse Effect, 1990, Ozone Hole, 1991, Ice Age, 1990, Spacecraft, 1991, Oil Spills, 1991, Extraordinary Women Scientists, 1995. Chair Women Employed, Chgo., 1973-76. Mem. AAAS, NAFE, Nat. Assn. Sci. Writers. Office: World Book Pub 525 W Monroe St Chicago IL 60661-3629

STILLERMAN, ELAINE, massage therapist; b. N.Y.C., June 24, 1950; d. Victor and Belle (Schreiber) S.; m. John Seifert Frey, Aug. 14, 1983 (div. Aug. 1985). BA, Queens Coll., 1972; grad., Swedish Inst. Massage, N.Y.C., 1978. Lic. massage therapist. Pvt. practice N.Y.C., 1978—; tchr. Swedish Inst. Massage, N.Y.C., 1980—, dir. continuing edn., 1992-93; developer bus. practice course Swedish Inst. Massage, N.Y.C., 1985—; instr. profl. workshop Mother Massage: Massage During Pregnancy, 1990—; cons. Time Life Fitness Books, N.Y.C., 1987, 88; instr. basic massage Network for Learning, N.Y.C., 1981-83; instr. Pvt. Shiatsu Workshop, 1980; leader Oriental massage workshop New Eng. Healing Arts Fair, Greenville, N.J., massage workshops Healing Arts Conf., Rincon, P.R., 1980. Author: Mother Massage: A Handbook for Relieving the Discomforts of Pregnancy, 1992; contbr. articles to profl. jours.; featured in various mags.; appeared on radio and TV. Mem. Nat. Assn. Pregnancy Massage Therapy, Internat. Childbirth Edn. Assn., Alliance Massage Therapists (bd. dirs. 1988, sec. 1979-83, v.p. 1983-88), Am. Coll. Sports Medicine. Home and Office: 498 6th Ave New York NY 10011

STILLINGS, IRENE CORDINER, organization executive; b. Boston, Aug. 17, 1918; d. Matthew Wilson and Susan F. (Mason) Cordiner; m. Gordon A. Stillings, May 13, 1945; children: David Gordon, Susan Irene. Student,

Radcliffe Coll., 1936-39; diploma, Burdett Coll., 1941. Sec., bookkeeper Boston Refrigerator Co., 1941-42; sec., tchr. Burdett Coll., 1942-44; sec., bookkeeper Gertrude Rittenburg, Boston, 1944-46. Town chmn. Heart Fund, Woodland, Maine, 1953-61; Brownie leader Girl Scouts U.S., 1954-58; pres. Woodland Woman's Club 1961-63; sec. PTA, 1961-62; chmn. Baileyville Superintending Sch. Com., 1962-64; chmn. women's activities Nat. Found., East Washington County, 1959-61; pres. Hosp. Aid, 1961-63; chmn. Newcomers Coll. group YWCA, 1965-66, chmn. theatre group, 1968-70, pres. Suburbanites, 1970-71; Stamford chmn. Expt. in Internat. Living, 1965-68; bd. dirs. YWCA of Stamford, chmn. devotion, 1970-92, ann. Antique Show benefit, 1970-77. Mem. Mass. Hort. Soc., St. Luke's Guild (treas. 1954-63), Radcliffe Club, Stamford Woman's Club (treas. 1975-79, program com., co-chmn. Am. home dept. 1974, 75, pres. 1981-83, bd. dirs. 1981—, 2d v.p. fin. 1983-85, 87-89, chmn. bldg. investment 1979-81, parliamentarian 1990—, pres., newcomers/suburbanites, 1994—), Theta Alpha Chi. Episcopalian. Home: 277 W Hill Rd Stamford CT 06902-1708

STILLMAN, ANDREA, state legislator; b. N.Y.C.. BA, Calif. State U., Northridge. Mem. Conn. Ho. of Reps., 1993—. Rep. town meeting, 1980-83; mem. Bd. Fin., 1984-92; bd. dirs. Conn. Resource Recovery Authority, 1988-92, Conn. Low Level Radioactive Waste Adv. Coun., 1992; mem. Waterford Dem. Town Com., Waterford Hist. Soc. Democrat. Jewish. Address: 5 Collidge Ct Waterford CT 06385-3309 Office: Conn Ho of Reps State Capitol Hartford CT 06106*

STILLMAN, ANNE WALKER GWATHMEY, fashion designer; b. Amsterdam, The Netherlands, Apr. 15, 1951; came to U.S., 1953; d. Edmund and Mary (Gwathmey) S. Student Barnard Coll., 1968-72. Pres., designer Sofia & Anne, Ltd., Bethel, Conn., Stratford, Conn. and N.Y.C., 1978-90; designer Sofia & Anne Sportknit, 1983-90, Sofia & Anne Children's Wear, 1985-90, Go Cashmere for L'Zinger by Sofia & Anne, 1986; pres., designer Anne Stillman, Ltd., Bethel, Stratford, N.Y.C., 1990—. Dir. pub. rels. Conn. Trust Hist. Preservation, 1994—. Mem. N.Y. Fashion Coun. Office: 940 Whitney Ave Hamden CT 06517

STILLMAN, ELINOR HADLEY, lawyer; b. Kansas City, Mo., Oct. 12, 1938; d. Hugh Gordon and Freda (Brooks) Hadley; m. Richard C. Stillman, June 25, 1965 (div. Apr. 1975). BA, U. Kans., 1960; MA, Yale U., 1961; JD, George Washington U., 1972. Bar: D.C. 1973, U.S. Ct. Appeals (10th cir.) 1975, U.S. Ct. Appeals (9th cir.) 1976, U.S. Ct. Appeals (2d cir.) 1976, U.S. Ct. Appeals (5th cir.) 1983, U.S. Ct. Appeals (4th cir.) 1985, U.S. Supreme Ct. 1976. Lectr. in English CUNY, 1963-65; asst. editor Stanford (Calif.) U. Press., 1967-69; law clk. to judge U.S. Dist. Ct. D.C., Washington, 1972-73; appellate atty. NLRB, Washington, 1973-78; asst. to solicitor gen. U.S. Dept. Justice, Washington, 1978-82; supr. appellate atty. NLRB, Washington, 1982-86, chief counsel to mem. bd., 1986-88, 94—, chief counsel to chmn. bd., 1988-94. Mem. ABA, D.C. Bar Assn., Order of Coif, Phi Beta Kappa. Democrat. Office: Nat Labor Rels Bd 1099 14th St NW Washington DC 20005-3402

STILLMAN, JOYCE L., artist, educator, consultant; b. N.Y.C., Jan. 19, 1943; d. Murray W. and Evelyn (Berger) Stillman. BA, NYU, 1964; student, Art Students League, 1965, Pratt Inst., 1972; MFA, L.I. U., 1975; student, Calif. Inst. Integral Studies, 1994. Tchr. N.Y.C. Pub. Schs., 1964-71; artist Cen. Hall Gallery, Port Washington, N.Y., 1974-76, Louis K. Meisel Gallery, N.Y.C., 1975-84, Tolarno Gallery, Melbourne, Australia, 1976—, Allan Stone Gallery, N.Y.C., 1990—; visiting assoc. prof. Towson State U., 1982; tchr. Women in Art, Tompkins Cortland Community Coll., 1988; lectr. Cornell U., 1990. One-person shows include Cen. Hall Gallery, Port Washington, 1975, Tolarno Gallery, Melbourne, 1976, Louis K. Meisel Gallery, N.Y.C., 1977, 80, 81, 82, Heckscher Mus., Huntington, N.Y., 1980, Holtzman Gallery, Towson (Md.) State U., 1982, Roslyn Oxley Gallery, Sydney, 1976, 82, Tomasulo Gallery, Union College, N.J., 1983, Stages, Keuka Coll., Keuka Park, N.Y., 1985, New Visions, Ithaca, N.Y., 1989, Herr-Chambliss, Hot Springs, Ark., 1990, Artist on the Lake, Hector, N.Y., 1992; designer Mus. Modern Art Christmas Collection, 1978-81, 94, Time-Life Poster, 1978; exhibited in over 50 group shows, corp. and mus. collections. Recipient Flower Painting award Artist's Mag., 1986, Art Dir.'s Club 58th Annual Distinctive Merit award, 1979, N.Y. State Creative Artist's Pub. Svc. grant, 1979. Mem. Nat. Assn. Women Artists, Allan Stone Gallery N.Y.C. Home and Studio: 5120 County Road 4 Burdett NY 14818-9715

STILLMAN, NINA GIDDEN, lawyer; b. N.Y.C., Apr. 3, 1948; d. Melvin and Joyce Audrey (Gidden) S. AB with distinction, Smith Coll., 1970; JD cum laude, Northwestern U., 1973. Bar: Ill. 1973, U.S. Dist. Ct. (no. dist.) Ill. 1973, U.S. Dist. Ct. (ea. dist.) Wis. 1979, U.S. Dist. Ct. (no. dist. trial bar) Ill. 1983, U.S. Ct. Appeals (7th cir.) 1974, U.S. Supreme Ct. 1981. Assoc. Vedder, Price, Kaufman & Kammholz, Chgo., 1973-79, ptnr., 1980—; mem. adv. bd. occupational health and safety tng. program U. Mich., Ann Arbor, 1980-83; adj. faculty Inst. Human Resources and Indsl. Rels., Loyola U., Chgo., 1983-86, mem. bd. advisors, 1986—. Author: (with others) Women, Work, and Health: Challenge to Corporate Policy, 1979, Occupational Health Law: A Guide for Industry, 1981, Employment Discrimination, 1981, Personnel Management: Labor Relations, 1981, Occupational Safety and Health Law, 1988; contbr. articles to profl. jours. Legal advisor, v.p. Planned Parenthood Assn. Chgo., 1979-81; sec. jr. governing bd. Chgo. Symphony Orch., 1983. Mem. ABA (occupational safety and health law com. 1978—), Chgo. Bar Assn. (chmn. labor and employment law com. 1986-87), Human Resources Mgmt. Assn. Chgo. (officer, bd. dirs. 1986-88), Am. Inns of Ct. (v.p. Wigmore chpt. 1988-89), Northwestern U Sch. Law Alumni Assn. (pres. 1991-92), Coun. of 100, Smith Coll. Club Chgo. (pres. 1972), Law Club, Econ. Club Chgo., The Chgo. Com. Office: Vedder Price Kaufman & Kammholz 222 N LaSalle St Chicago IL 60601-1003

STILLWATER, SANDRA, lawyer; b. Winnipeg, Manitoba, Can., Apr. 28, 1942; d. Isaac and Frances (Podhocer) S. BA, U. Calif., Berkeley, 1964; JD, UCLA, 1972. Bar: Calif. Atty. Fischmann Wallerstein, L.A., 1973-75, Bank of Am., L.A., 1975-76; pvt. practice L.A., 1978—; judge protem Santa Monica (Calif.) Mcpl. Ct., 1990-93; arbitrator, AAA, L.A., 1980-93. Bd. govs. Women in Bus., L.A., 1987. Mem. Beverly Hills Bar Assn. (bd. govs. of barristers 1974), County Bar of L.A., South Cen. Bar Assn. Office: 424 S Beverly Dr Beverly Hills CA 90212-4414

STILSON, JOYCE, actress. BA, SUNY, Buffalo, 1986, MA, 1990. Tutor, sub. tchr. Clarence Ctrl. High Sch., 1984—; grad. asst. SUNY, Buffalo, 1988, asst. pub. dir., ticket svcs. mgr., Pfeifer Theatre bldg. mgr., 1988-90; dir. devel. Alleyway Theatre, 1989-92, dramaturg, 1990—, dir. pub. rels., 1992—; instr. acting workshops. Prodn. asst. The Natural, 1983; news dir. WRUB, 1984, 85; news intern WGRZ-TV2, 1985-86; prodr. Vacation Styles, 1986, Intrex, 1986, Lifetime Cable, 1986, Paid TV, 1986, Way-Off Broadway Co., 1983-85, Community Theatre, 1983-85, Offbeat Theatre, 1987-88, Exptl. Theatre, 1987-88; stage mgr. Shakespeare in Delaware Park, 1988, Commedia Pinnochio, 1993; dir. numerous plays Alleyway Theatre, 1991—; actress numerous plays, 1982—. Festival coord. Buffalo Festival of Short Works, 1992, 93, 94, 95; teaching artist Western N.Y. Inst. for Arts in Edn., 1994—. Home: 74 Crescent Ave Buffalo NY 14214 Office: Alleyway Theatre 1 Curtain Up Alley Buffalo NY 14202-1911

STILZ, SUSAN BRUECKNER, accountant; b. Chattanooga, June 20, 1962; d. Robert Davis and Mary Lucile (Sully) Brueckner; m. Charles H. Stilz, June 18, 1994. AS, AAS in Computer Sci., Enterprise State Jr. Coll., 1982; BS in Acctg., Auburn U., 1985. CPA, Tenn. Staff acct. audit dept. Hazelett, Lewis & Bieter, CPAs, Chattanooga, 1985-87; staff acct. tax dept. Joseph Decosimo & Co., CPAs, Chattanooga, 1987-88, sr. acct. tax dept., 1988-91, supr. tax dept., 1991—; chmn. staff devel. com. Joseph Decosimo & Co., CPAs, 1993. Mem. allocations com. United Way, Chattanooga, 1993, fin. chmn. allocations com. resource team, 1994; mem. chancel choir 1st Centenary United Meth. Ch., Chattanooga, 1987—. Mem. AICPA, Tenn. Soc. CPAs (state acctg. careers com. 1993-94), Chattanooga Tax Practitioners, Inst. Mgmt. Accts. (v.p. 1993-94, treas. 1994—). Office: Joseph Decosimo & Co CPAs 2 Union Sq Ste 1100 Chattanooga TN 37402

STIMMEL, JULIE BETH, research scientist; b. Pitts., Apr. 20, 1959; d. Kenneth Lindley and Matilda Delores (Sowko) S. BS, Grove City Coll., 1981; PhD, Purdue U., 1987. Teaching asst. Purdue U., West Lafayette, Ind., 1981-87; postdoctoral fellow UCLA, 1987-90; rsch. scientist Burroughs Wellcome, Research Triangle Park, N.C., 1990—. Contbr. rsch. articles to sci. jours. Mem. Am. Chem. Soc., Phi Lambda Upsilon. Democrat. Methodist. Office: Burroughs Wellcome Co Dept Cell Biology 3030 Cornwallis Research Triangle Park NC 27709

STIMPSON, CATHARINE ROSLYN, English language educator, writer; b. Bellingham, Wash., June 4, 1936; d. Edward Keown and Catharine (Watts) S. A.B., Bryn Mawr Coll., 1958; B.A., Cambridge U., Eng., 1960, M.A., 1960; Ph.D., Columbia U., 1967. Mem. faculty Barnard Coll., N.Y.C., 1963-80; prof. English, dean of grad. sch., vice provost grad. edn. Rutgers U., New Brunswick, N.J., 1980-92, Univ. prof., 1991—; chmn. bd. scholars Ms. Mag., N.Y.C., 1981-92; dir. fellows program MacArthur Found., 1994—. Author: Class Notes, 1979, Where the Meanings Are, 1988; founding editor: Signs: Jour. Women in Culture and Society, 1974-81; book series Women in Culture and Society, 1981; columnist Change Mag., 1992-93. Chmn. N.Y. Council Humanities, 1984-87, Nat. Council Research on Women, 1984-89 ; bd. dirs. Stephens Coll., Columbia, Mo., 1982-85; trustee Bates Coll., 1990—. Hon. fellow Woodrow Wilson Found., 1958; Fulbright fellow, 1958-60; Nat. Humanities Inst. fellow New Haven, 1975-76; Rockefeller Humanities fellow, 1983-84. Mem. MLA (exec. coun., chmn. acad. freedom com., 1st v.p., pres. 1990), PEN, AAUP, NOW, Legal Def. and Edn. Fund (bd. dirs. 1991—), PBS (bd. dirs. 1994—). Democrat. Home: 62 Westervelt Ave Staten Island NY 10301-1432 Office: Rutgers U 172 College Ave New Brunswick NJ 08903-1157

STIMPSON, CYNDI ANN, office manager; b. Lancaster, Pa., Dec. 14, 1949; d. E. Eugene and Gloria E. (Beck) Howell; m. Terry A. Stimpson, Dec. 27, 1969. Student, Pa. State U., 1967-69, Franklin and Marshall Coll., Elizabethtown U. Tour guide dir. Rutt's Tours, Intercourse, Pa., 1973-80; credit and collections supr. Victor F. Weaver Inc., New Holland, Pa., 1980-88; staff acct. Ford New Holland, 1988-89; office mgr. Amelia's Inc., New Holland, 1989—. Bd. dirs., sec. Community Meml. Park, New Holland, 1983-85; mem. Friends of the Libr., New Holland, 1988—. Mem. Am. Bus. Women's Assn. (pres. 1980, Woman of Yr. 1983), Toastmasters Internat. (treas. 1990, v.p. membership 1993, pres. 1994—, Toastmaster of Yr. 1989, 90, 92, Most Active Toastmaster 1991, Toastmaster of Yr. 1993, 94). Methodist. Home: 750 Maple Grove Rd New Holland PA 17557-9314 Office: Amelia's Inc 403 S Custer Ave New Holland PA 17557-9221

STIMSON, HELEN, marketing manager; b. Edinburgh, Scotland, Jan. 5, 1959; came to the U.S., 1975; d. Bernard and Margaret (Reid) Canavan; m. William Stimson, Sept. 24, 1983; children: Laura Elizabeth. BA in Chemistry, Lafayette Coll., 1981. Sales rep. Hewlett Packard, King of Prussia, Pa., 1981-88; dist. svc. mgr. Hewlett Packard, Paramus, N.J., 1988-93; product mgr. Hewlett Packard, Wilmington, Del., 1993-94, chemsta. mktg. mgr., 1994. Office: Hewlett Packard 2850 Centerville Rd Wilmington DE 19808

STIMSON, JUDITH NEMETH, lawyer; b. Hammond, Ind., Oct. 30, 1942; d. John G. and Pearl (Lemish) Nemeth; m. Clare M. Stimson, June 5, 1965 (div. Oct. 1981); children: Justin D., Seth C., Sarah L.; m. John R. Conolly, Dec. 30, 1982. BS, St. Mary of the Woods Coll., Terre Haute, Ind., 1964; MS in Clothing and Textiles, Ind. U., 1968; JD, Ind. U., Indpls., 1981. Bar: Ind. 1982. Tchr. pub. schs. Ind., 1964-79; with Buck, Berry, Landau & Breunig, Indpls., 1982-94, Stimson & Assocs., Indpls., 1994—; instr. Ind. Continuing Legal Edn. Forum, Indpls., 1983—. Named one of Outstanding Young Women in Am., 1974. Fellow Indpls. Bar Assn. (disting., chmn. family law sect. 1985); mem. ABA (exec. mem. continuing legal edn. com. 1986-87), Ind. Bar Assn. (ADR chair 1993-94), Assn. Family and Conciliation Cts. Office: Bank 1 Ctr Tower Ste 3300 111 Monument Cir Indianapolis IN 46204-5133

STINE, ANNA MAE, publishing company executive; b. Monongahela, Pa., Sept. 6, 1938; d. Carlton Lee and Martha Regina (Graham) S.; B.S. in Edn., Calif. State Coll. (Pa.), 1959; elem. prin. cert. Duquesne U., 1962, masters in elem. edn., 1962; cert. reading specialist U. Pitts., 1963, postgrad., 1963-65. Tchr., student tchr. supr. Upper St. Clair Sch. Dist., Pitts., 1959-65; nat. lang. arts cons. Macmillan Pub. Co., N.Y.C., 1965-75, regional mgr., Riverside, N.J., 1975-78; v.p., nat. sales mgr. East of Macmillan Pub. Co., 1978-89, v.p., nat. sales mgr. McGraw Hill Sch. div. East of Macmillan Pub., 1989-92, sr. v.p., 1992—. Recipient Robert Hann award Macmillan Pub. Co., 1965, Donald McGrew award 1967, NJRA award, 1985. Mem. Internat. Reading Assn., NEA, Regional Edn. Service Agy., Keystone Reading Assn., Upper St. Clair Tchrs. Orgn. (pres.). Republican. Roman Catholic. Home: 400 Haddon Ave Unit 215 Haddonfield NJ 08033

STINE, JEANNE M., mayor, educator; b. Detroit, June 18, 1929; d. William Lyle and Eleanor Laura (Abele) Goodwin; m. Cornelius Robert Powers, Oct. 3, 1952 (div. Feb. 1956); 1 child, Sheila Maureen Powers; m. John Follett Stine, Feb. 1962. BS in Edn., Wayne State U., 1960, MA in Edn., 1965. cert. K-8 Elem. edn., K-12 counseling. Telephone operator Mich. Bell, Detroit, 1946-51; clerk typist McGregor Meml. Conf., Detroit, Detroit Pub. Libr., 1950-52; display advertiser Daily Tribune, Royal Oak, Mich., 1952-54; elem. sch. tchr. Guardian Angels Sch., Clawson, Mich., 1958; elem. sch. tchr. Clawson Pub. Schs., 1959-66, middle sch. counselor, 1966-92; sec. Clawson Edn. Assn., 1960-63; pres. Clawson Youth Assist., 1968-74. initiator Troy youth bur. Police Dept., 1977; pres. Troy Youth Svcs. Activities Commn., 1977-80; v.p. Troy Profl. Women's Club, 1978-84, pres. Troy Youth Svcs. Forum, 1980-84, chair Troy Consortium on Drug and Alcohol Abuse; city councilwoman City of Troy, 1976-92; pres. Troy Vol. Firefighters Women's Aux., 1989-92; mayor City of Troy, 1992—. Recipient Dist. Citizen award Troy C. of C., 1985, Community Svc. award Clawson-Troy Elks, 1985. Mem. Nat. League of Cities (mem. transp. steering com. 1978-86, trans. policy com. 1989-92), Am. Legion Aux., Mich. Mcpl. League (chmn. region IV transp. and pub. works 1990, meritorius svc. award 1988), Tri County Mayors Assn. (mem. steering com.), Zontas. Republican. Roman Catholic. Home: 1915 Boulan Troy MI 48084 Office: 500 W Big Beaver Rd Troy MI 48084

STINSON, AVIVA JOCHEBED, psychosocial nurse; b. Jerusalem, Palestine, Mar. 21, 1933; came to U.S., 1957; d. Solomon Isaac and Sarah (Dossik) Ostrovsky; m. Lawrence William Stinson, Jan. 19, 1956; children: Teresa Louise, Lawrence William Jr., John Durant. BS, U. Wash., 1981; MS, U. Alaska, 1987; postgrad., U. Minn., 1990-91. RN, Alaska, Wash., Minn., Ill.; cert. clin. specialist in adult psychiat. and mental health nursing; cert. advanced nurse practitioner. Staff nurse Paxton (Ill.) Gen. Hosp., 1957-58; staff nurse, head nurse Mercy Hosp., Urbana, Ill., 1966-72; staff nurse Guam (Micronesia) Meml. Hosp., 1973-74, Fairbanks (Alaska) Meml. Hosp., 1975-78, Swedish Hosp., Seattle, 1980-81; supr. nurse detox Fairbanks Native Assn., 1981-83; psychosocial nurse, therapist Fairbanks Psychiatric & Neurol. Clinic, Fairbanks, 1985-94; advanced nurse practitioner, psychotherapist Fairbanks, Alaska, 1994—. Bd. dirs. Child Abuse Task Force, Fairbanks, 1982-90, Fairbanks Cmty. Mental Health Ctr., 1985-90, 92-94. Mem. ANA (pres. Dist. IV 1986-89), Alaskan Nurses Assn. Home: 573 Slater Dr Fairbanks AK 99701-3444 Office: Ste 5 250 Cushman St Fairbanks AK 99701

STINSON, MARY FLORENCE, nursing educator; b. Wheeling, W.Va., Feb. 11, 1931; d. Rolland Francis and Mary Angela (Voellinger) Kellogg; m. Charles Walter Stinson, Feb. 12, 1955; children: Kenneth Charles, Karen Marie, Kathryn Anne. BSN, Coll. Mt. St. Joseph, 1953, postgrad., 1983; MEd, Xavier U., Cin., 1967; postgrad. U. Cin., 1981. Staff nurse contagious disease ward Cin. Gen. Hosp., 1953-54, asst. head nurse med. and polio wards, 1955, acting head nurse, clin. instr., 1955-56; instr. St. Francis Hosp. Sch. Practical Nursing, Cin., 1956-57; instr. Good Samaritan Hosp. Sch. Nursing, Cin., 1957-65; instr. refresher courses for nurses Cin. Bd. Edn. and Ohio State Nurses Assn. Dist. 8, 1967-70; coord. sch. health office Coll. Mt. St. Joseph (Ohio), 1969-72, instr. dept. nursing, 1974-79, asst. prof., 1979-89; part-time staff nurse St. Francis/St. George Hosp., Cin., 1988-89; RN assessor Passport program Ohio Coun. on Aging, 1989-90, quality assurance coord., 1990-93; quality assurance supr. Passport and Elderly Svcs. Program, 1993-94; quality assurance mgr. Coun. Aging, Cin., 1995—. Charter mem. Adoptive Parents Assn. St. Joseph Infant and Maternity Home; active Women's Com. for Performing Arts Series, Coll. Mt. St. Joseph; mem. St. Antoninus Rosary Altar Rosary and Sch. Soc., St. Antoninus Athletic Club, com. chmn., 1969-70; bd. dirs. Coll. Mt. St. Joseph Alumnae Assn., 1982-84, sec., 1968-69, v.p., 1969-70, pres., 1970-71, chmn. revision of constn., 1976-77; homecoming chmn. Coll. Mt. St. Joseph, 1970, co-chmn., 1977; mem. Gamble Nippert YMCA. Mem. O.K.I. Gerontol. Nursing Assn. Democrat. Roman Catholic. Club: River Squares (v.p. 1967). Home: 5549 Cleander Dr Cincinnati OH 45238-4266 Office: Coun on Aging of Cin Holiday Office Pk 644 Linn St Cincinnati OH 45203-2477

STINSON, NORMA PERKINS, nurse administrator; b. Bellingham, Mass., Aug. 29, 1929; d. Reginald Harlton and May Dennison (Tyndall) Perkins; m. Wesley Walter Stinson, July 9, 1949; children: Glenn Wesley, David Kim, Brian Matthew, Brenda Diane Eline. AS, Newton (Mass.) Jr. Coll., 1968; BS, R.I. Coll., Providence, 1974; MA, U. R.I., 1979. Clin. specialist in adult psychiatric and mental health nursing. Staff nurse Newport (R.I.) Hosp., 1968-74; team leader, primary therapist Newport County Community Mental Health Ctr., 1974-80; clin. coord. Community Couseling Ctr., Pawtucket, R.I., 1980-81, dir. community support programs, 1981-83, assoc. dir., 1983-85; assoc. dir. nursing Lake Shore Hosp., Manchester, N.H., 1985-87; nurse clinician, case mgr. Dr. Harry Solomon Mental Health Ctr., Lowell, Mass., 1987-88; nurse mgr. Frisbie Meml. Hosp., Rochester, N.H., 1988-91; vol. bereavement counselor Hospice Care of R.I., 1993—; cons. R.I. Assn. Retarded Citizens, 1980-81; substitute nurse tchr. Newport Sch. Dept., 1972-74. Mem. Chaplaincy Dept. R.I. Coun. Churches, Providence, 1978-85; vol. Sen. Bob Kerry presdl. campaign, Dover, N.H., 1991-92. Democrat. United Methodist. Home: 37 Summit Rd Portsmouth RI 02871-5915

STINSON, PHYLES LYNNE, administrative assistant; b. Tyler, Tex., June 11, 1949; d. William Andrew and Juanita (Ford) Smith; m. Stanley Ross Stinson, Aug. 12, 1967 (div. July 1974); children: Michael Shayne, Ginger Lee (dec.). Grad. H.S., Houston. Accts. receivable, payable clk. Stone Supply Co., Houston, 1966-67; ins. verification clk. Meml. Bapt. Hosp. System, Houston, 1969-71; licensing agt. Variable annuity Life Ins. Co., Houston, 1971-74; sec., adminstrv. asst. Brown & Root, Inc., Houston, 1974-80, scheduler, 1980—; scheduler M.W. Kellogg, Houston, 1990. Founder Agape: Good Life Singles, Kingwood, Tex., 1990—; singles ministry leader Kingwood (Tex.) Ch. of Christ, 1991—; hospice vol. N.E. Regional Cancer Ctr., Humble, Tex., 1993. Mem. Church of Christ.

STIRITZ, MARETTE MCCAULEY, English language educator, consultant; b. Center Point, Ark., Dec. 9, 1931; d. Edrie Delos and Lucyle Virginia (Dautrieve) McCauley; m. Charles Wayne Jackson, July 1, 1950 (dec. June 1986); children: Charles, Retta, Shelia; m. John David Stiritz, Dec. 3, 1992. BSE, Ark. State U., 1962; MA, U. Ark., 1965, PhA, 1986. Tchr. elem. Plum Bayou (Ark.) Pub. Schs., 1950-52; tchr. Laura Connor H.S., Augusta, Ark., 1955-59, Swifton (Ark.) Elem. Sch., 1959-60, Swifton H.S., 1962-63; prof. English So. Ark. U., Magnolia, 1965-78, U. Cen. Ark., Conway, 1978—; cons. high schs., Conway, Morrilton, Vilonia, 1983—, Ark. Dept. Edn., Little Rock, 1982, 84; lectr. U. Chile, Santiago, 1989, Moscow Pedagogical U., 1991, 92, Academica Inst. Chileno-Norteamericano, Santiago, 1994; speaker 8th Bi-ann. Conf. Profs. Fgn. Langs., Chile, 1992, 9th Conf., Chile, 1994. Contbr. articles to profl. jours.; book reviewer Ark. Elem. Coun., 1980—. Del. Faulkner County Dems., Conway, 1984; exec. sec., founder Columbia Tchrs. Eng., Magnolia, 1974-78. Mem. Ark. Coun. Tchrs. English (pres. 1979-80, bd. dirs. 1989-93), Ark. Philol. Assn., Nat. Coun. Tchrs. English, Ark. Coll. Tchrs. English (pres. 1992-93), Conway Rotary Internat. Breakfast Club (charter), Alpha Chi (region II v.p. 1992-93. Democrat. Methodist. Home: 3414 Rhonda Ct Conway AR 72032-9168

STIRLING, ELLEN ADAIR, retail executive; b. Chgo., June 21, 1949; d. Volney W. and Ellen Adair (Orr) Foster; m. James P. Stirling, June 6, 1970; children: Elizabeth Ginevra, Diana Leslie, Alexandra Curtiss. Student, U. Chgo., 1970-71; BA, Wheaton Coll., Norton, Mass., 1971; postgrad., U. London, 1974. Pres., CEO, The Lake Forest Shop, 1986—; bd. dirs. Lake Forest Bank and Trust. Founder, v.p. aux. bd. Art Inst. Chgo., 1972-91; dir. Friends of Ryerson Woods, 1992—; mem. women's bd. Lyric Opera, Chgo., 1992—, Lake Forest Coll., 1989—; mem. costume com. Chgo. Hist. Soc. Mem. Onwentsia Club, Racquet Club. Office: The Lake Forest Shop 165 E Market Sq Lake Forest IL 60045

STIRLING, ISABEL ANN, science librarian; b. San Jose, Calif., Dec. 4, 1948; d. James H. and Betty Stirling. BA, U. Calif., Riverside, 1970; MLS, Western Mich. U., 1977. Head bio-agrl. library U. Calif., Riverside, 1977-82; head sci. library, assoc. prof. U. Oreg., Eugene, 1982—. Author: Self-Paced Library Instruction Workbook for the Sciences, 1981; contbr. revs. to jours. Mem. ALA, Assn. Coll. and Research Libraries of ALA (various coms.), Spl. Library Assn., Oreg. Library Assn., Oreg. Online Users Group. Office: U Oreg Sci Libr U Libr Eugene OR 97403-5201*

STITES, ALICE GRAY, editor; b. N.Y.C., Jan. 19, 1965; d. Bowman and Katherine (Condon) Gray; m. James Walker Stites III, Nov. 21, 1992. BA in English, U. Va., 1987; MA in English, Columbia U., 1988. Asst. editor Art & Auction Mag., N.Y.C., 1988-89; assoc. editor Contemporanea Art Mag., N.Y.C., 1989-91; editor Abbeville Press, N.Y.C., 1992—. Author: Ansel Adams: The National Park Service Photographs, 1994; editor: 19th and 20th Century Painting, Living Proof: Courage in the Face of AIDS, and others, 1992-94. Mem. Phi Beta Kappa. Home and Office: 2912 Lilac Way Louisville KY 40206-2913

STITES, BEVERLY R., judge; b. Ft. Smith, Ark., Nov. 26, 1941; d. Floyd Paul and Alice Marie Rickman; children: Scott Douglas, Shane Patton. BA, Ark. Tech. Univ., 1964; BS, Okla. Baptist Univ., 1977; JD, Univ. of Ark., 1981. Bar: Ark. 1981. Law clk. pvt. practice, 1980-81; law clk. to Chief Judge A. Franklin Waters U.S. Dist. Ct. (we. dist.) Ark., 1981, clk. of ct., 1985, magistrate judge, 1987—. Office: US Courthouse PO Box 1525 S 6th St & Rogers Ave Rm 240 Fort Smith AR 72902*

STITES, SUSAN KAY, human resources consultant; b. Colorado Springs, Colo., Sept. 20, 1952; d. William Wallace and Betty Jane (Kosley) Stites; m. Gerald Frederick Simon, Aug. 14, 1988. BA, Wichita State U., 1974; MA, Northwestern U., 1979. Benefits authorizer Social Security Adminstrn., Chgo., 1974-77; trainer Chgo. Urban Skills Inst., 1977-79; human resources mgr. Montgomery Ward, Chgo., 1979-83; mgr. tng. Lands' End, Dodgeville, Wis., 1983-87; dir. human resources Cen. Life Assurance, Madison, Wis., 1988-90; owner Mgmt. Allegories, Madison, Wis., 1987—. Author: Delegating for Results, 1992, Business Communications, 1992, Managing With a Quality Focus, 1994, Training and Orientation for the Small Business, 1994, Powerful Performance Management, 1994, Safety Management Techniques, 1995; contbr. articles to profl. jours. Vol. tutor Japanese Students in English, Evanston, Ill., 1977-80; read to blind Chgo. Coun. for the Blind, 1974-76. Named Outstanding Woman of the Yr. Wichita State U., 1974. Mem. Am. Soc. Tng. and Devel. (chpt. pres. 1988, v.p. membership 1986, region V awards chair 1992), Madison Area Quality Improvement Network, Assn. for Quality and Participation, Rotary (vol. fund raiser), Mendota Yacht Club (treas. 1990—). Home: 3788 Highridge Rd Madison WI 53704-6206 Office: Mgmt Allegories 3788 Highridge Rd Madison WI 53704-6206

STITH, LEAH DRAKE, legislative aide, school system administrator; b. Portsmouth, Va., Nov. 18, 1949; d. Freddie Lee Sr. and Rebecca (Greene) Drake; m. S. DeLacy Stith, Sr., Oct. 20 1979; children: Maisha Kito, S. DeLacy Jr. BS in Polit. Sci., Norfolk State U., 1985, postgrad., 1992—. Substitute tchr. Portsmouth Schs., 1985-90; asst. sr. residential counselor Pines Treatment Facility, Portsmouth, 1986-90; legis. asst. del. Gen. Assembly, Richmond, Va., 1986-90; spl. asst. to lt. gov. Va. State Govt., Richmond, 1990—; mem. sch. bd. Portsmouth Schs., 1991—; mem. adv. bd. WHRO Pub. TV, Portsmouth, 1991—; guest lectr. spl. edn. conf. Norfolk State U., 1994. Sec. Wesley Ctr. Bd., Portsmouth, 1991-92, Portsmouth Dem. Com., 1991-92; coord. Don Beyer for Lt. Gov., Portsmouth, 1989, United Negro Coll. Fund, Portsmouth, 1986. Recipient Disting. Alumnus award Norfolk State U., 1991, Sojourner Truth award Nat. Assn. Black Bus. and Profl. Women, Norfolk, 1992, Woman of Yr. award Black Women's Health Network, 1993, others. Mem. Am. Assn. Sch. Adminstrs., Va. Sch. Bd. Assn. (fin. com., Cert. of Achievement award 1991-92). Episcopalian. Home: 3604 Cedar Ln Portsmouth VA 23703 Office: Office of Lt Gov 101 N 8th St Richmond VA 23219

STITT, DOROTHY JEWETT, journalist; b. Houston, Sept. 4, 1914; d. Harry Berkey and Gladys (Norfleet) Jewett; m. James Wilson Stitt, Feb. 14, 1939; children: James Harry, Thomas Paul. AB, Rice U., 1937; MS, Columbia U., 1938. Reporter Houston Post, 1936-38, asst. city editor, 1938. Editor publs. Jewett Family of Am., Inc., 1971—, bd. dirs., Plaque 1993. Mem. adv. bd., publicity chair Easton Salvation Army, 1956—, bd. chair, 1964, bd. treas., 1981; bd. dirs., publicity chair ARC, 1952-67; organizing mem. bd. dirs., sec., publicity chair Little Stone House Mus. Assn., 1974-91; publicity vol. 1st fund campaign United Way, 1960; bd. dirs. Easton United Cmty. Chest, 1957-60. Recipient Citation, United Way Easton, 1960, Outstanding Svc. award Easton chpt. ARC, 1967, Molly Pitcher Gold Medal of Appreciation, Valley Forge chpt. SAR, 1980, Appreciation award Salvation Army, 1982, 91. Mem. UDC (Jefferson Davis chpt.), DAR (George Taylor chpt. regent 1974-80, 89-95, vice regent 1980-83, historian 1971-74, pub. chmn. 1969—, author and editor The 100th Anniversary Yearbook and History of the George Taylor Chapter, DAR, 1895-1995, 1994), PEO (chpt. AF Houston), Easton Tavern House Assn., Northampton County Hist. and Geneal. Soc. (Outstanding Svc. award 1993), World Affairs Coun. Phila., Northampton Country Club (Niners Golf chmn. 1957-91, Women's Golf Assn. constn. and bylaws chmn., parliamentarian 1960-92), Woman's Club of Easton (pres. 1961-64, bd. dirs. 1959—, publicity chair 1952-68, 70-82, 92—, parliamentarian 1984-92, Gold Medal of Honor and Outstanding Woman of Yr. award 1992). Republican. Episcopalian. Home: 110 Upper Shawnee Ave Easton PA 18042-1377

STITT, PAULINE GEORGE, retired physician and educator; b. Frewsburg, N.Y., May 28, 1909; d. Austin W. and Allene (Davis) S. BS and MD, U. Mich., 1933; MPH cum laude, U. Calif., 1954. Diplomate pediatrics and pub. health. Sr. pediatrician Children's Hosp. East Bay (now Children's Med. Ctr.), Berkeley, 1951-53; asst. health officer Alameda County (Calif.) Health Dept., San Leandro, 1953-54; asst. prof. maternal and child health Harvard Sch. Pub. Health, Boston, 1955-61; assoc. prof. preventive medicine, assoc. prof. pediatrics Boston U. Med. Sch., 1960-62; chief home care svc. Mass. Meml. Hosp. (now Univ. Hosp.), Boston, 1960-62; chief child health studies rsch. div. U.S. Children's Bur., 1962-65, dir. rsch. med. cons., 1965-66; chief home care sect. Health Svcs. and Mental Health Adminstrn., 1966-69; health forums coord. White House Conf. Children, 1969-71; prof. pub. health, chmn. maternal and child health U. Hawaii Sch. Pub. Health, 1972-75, prof. emeritus, 1975—. Home: 1434 Punahou St # 927 Honolulu HI 96822

STOCK, ANITA See SCHERER, ANITA

STOCK, ANN, federal official; m. Stuart C. Stock; 1 child. Grad., Purdue U. Dep. press sec. to V.p. Walter F. Mondale, 1980, 84; regional dir. pub. rels. Bloomingdales Dept. Stores, 1982-85, dir. br. stores, 1986-87, v.p. pub. rels., 1988-93; spl. asst. to Pres. and Social Sec. The White House, Washington, 1993—. Mem. Capital Children's Mus. (co-founder), The Women's Forum, N.Y. Fashion Group (former program chmn.), Washington Woman Roundtable (founder), "Race for the Cure" (co-founder). Office: Office of the First Lady 1600 Pennsylvania Ave NW Washington DC 20500-0001*

STOCK, MARGOT THERESE, nurse, anthropologist, consultant, educator; b. Toronto, Ont., Can., Aug. 10, 1936; Arrived in US 1967.; d. Karl Dwight and Marguerite Anne (Lafitte) K.; m. Philip Anthony, Jan. 11, 1946; children: Dwight, Scott, Kayler, Travis & Anthony (twins) Sean. AAS, Suffolk County Com. Coll., Selden, N.Y., 1981; BS in Nursing, U. S. Fla., Ft. Myers, Fla., 1983; MS in Nursing, U. Tex., 1984; DPhil in Social Anthropology, U. Oxford, England, 1989. Nurse Sarasota Meml. Hosp., Fla., 1981-82, LW Blake Meml. Hosp., Bradenton, Fla., 1982-83, Med. Center Del Oro, Houston, 1983-85, Pitt County Meml. Hosp., Greenville, N.C.; asst. prof. E. Carolina U., Greenville, N.C., 1985-89; Cons. Gerontol. Nursing Network Greensboro N.C. Designer Game and Software (computer), Nursing Math Made Easy, Understanding Mgmt., Teaching Nursing Theory 1984; Author (with others) Book Clinical Pharmacology & Nursing 1987, Poetry Evolution Lycidas Jaso 1980-87. Mem. AAUW, Sigma Theta Tau, Sigma Kappa Found. (Houston Sigma Kappa award), Phi Theta Kappa (pres. 1981). Roman Catholic. Home: 118 Old London Rd Greenville NC 27834-8833 Office: East Carolina U Sch of Nursing Greenville NC 27858-4353

STOCK, PEGGY A(NN), college president, educator; b. Jan. 30, 1936; married; 5 children. BS in Psychology, St. Lawrence U., 1957; MA in Counseling, U. Ky., 1963, EdD, 1969. Lic. psychologist, Ohio. Instr., research asst. dept. psychology and spl. edn. U. Ky., Lexington, 1958-59, 63-67, staff psychologist Med. Ctr., 1964-66; dir. edn. United Cerebral Palsy of the Bluegrass, Lexington, 1959-61; exec. dir. Community Council for Physically Handicapped and Mentally Retarded, Lexington, 1962-64; dir. clin. program No. Ky. Regional Community Mental Health Ctr., Covington, 1969-71; pres. Midwest Inst. Tng. and Edn., Cin., 1971-76; assoc. prof., counseling psychologist Coll. of Edn. Mont. State U., Bozeman, 1975-77, asst. dean Office of Student Affairs and Service, 1977-79; assoc. prof. Coll. of Edn. U. Hartford, Conn., 1980-85, spl. asst. to pres., 1979-80, v.p. adminstrn., 1981-86; prof., pres. Colby-Sawyer Coll., New London, N.H., 1986—; vis. prof. dept. sociology and edn. Thomas Moore Coll., Fort Mitchell, Ky., 1970-71; panelist Nat. Inst. Edn., 1985; cons. and lectr. in field. Contbr. chpts. to books, articles to profl. jours. Mem. coun. N.H. Coll. and Univ.; nat. bd. dirs. Med. Coll. Pa.; mem. New London Bus. Adv. Bd.; active numerous other civic orgns. Recipient Disting. Alumna award St. Lawrence U., 1989; grantee in field, most recent George I. Alden Trust, Helen Fuld Health Trust, Surdna, Cogswell, U.S. Dept. Edn., 1981-89, numerous others; fellow U. Ky., 1966-68, Am. Council Edn., 1979-80, United Jewish Com., 1981. Mem. Am. Coun. on Edn., Am. Assn. for Higher Edn., Advancement Women in Higher Edn. Office: Colby-Sawyer Coll Office of the President New London NH 03257

STOCKAR, HELENA MARIE MAGDALENA, artist; b. Bratislava, Czechoslovakia, Mar. 22, 1933; came to the U.S., 1968; d. Arnost J. and Helena R. (Strakova) Kubasek; m. Ivo J. Stockar, Oct. 31, 1959; children: David, Laura Bates. Diploma, Graficka Skola, Prague, 1952, Music Conservatory, Prague, 1954. Piano tchr. Music Sch., Prague, 1954-68; company pianist State Ballet/Breacrest Sch., R.I., 1968-74; piano tchr. Music Tchr. Assn., R.I., 1968-86. One-woman shows include Warwick Mus., R.I., 1986, Brown U., 1987, The Westerly Art Gallery, R.I., 1987, The Westerly Art Gallery/Morin-Miller, 1988, 89, Galerie Horizon, Paris, 1989, others; exhibited in group shows at The World Congress of the Czechoslovak Soc. of Art and Sci., Washington, 1988, Morin-Miller Internat., N.Y.C., 1989, Ariel Gallery, Soho, N.Y.C., 1989, Art Expo N.Y.C., 1989, others; represented in permanent collections around the world; featured on numerous tv shows. Recipient Second prize Nat. Competition of Children's Book Illustration, Prague, 1965; named finalist Internat. Art Competition, L.A., 1984. Mem. Music Club Providence, Chopin Club Providence, Schubert Club Providence, Chaminade Club Providence. Office: PO Box 7282 Warwick RI 02887

STOCKDALE, GAYLE SUE, wholesale florist, ornamental horticulturalist; b. Crawfordsville, Ind., July 3, 1955; d. Robert Lavern and Faye Louise (Ball) S. Student St. Joseph's Coll., 1973-74, Purdue U., 1974; BS in Tech. Horticulture, Eastern Ky. U., 1977. Reclamation foreman South East Coal Co., Irvine, Ky., 1977-79; asst. mgr., landscape designer Evergreen Garden Ctr., Lexington, Ky., 1979-80; asst. mgr., landscape designer, head grower South Trail Garden Ctr., Ft. Myers, Fla., 1980-82; floral designer Flowers by Jean, Cape Coral, Fla., 1982-83; floral designer, landscape designer Bev's Greenhouse, Owenton, Ky., 1983-84; co-owner Royalty Wholesale, Lexington, 1984-87, Imperial Flowers and Gifts, Lexington, 1988—. Contbr. poetry to anthologies. Sponsor Save the Children, Korea, 1986. Moose lodge scholar, 1973. Mem. NAFE. Democrat. Avocations: reading, movies, exercise, golf, racquetball. Office: Imperial Flowers & Gifts 393 Waller Ave Lexington KY 40504-2914

STOCKER, BEATRICE, speech pathologist; b. N.Y.C., Nov. 20, 1909; d. Tobias and Ida (Weinstein) Klipstein; m. Jule E. Stocker, Mar. 26, 1932; children: Maida Stocker Abrams, Michael. BA, Barnard Coll., 1931; MA, Columbia U., 1937. Adminstrv. asst. Speech and Hearing Ctr. Queens Coll. CUNY, 1949-78, lectr., 1968-78; pvt. practice N.Y.C., 1978—; cons. in field. Author: Stocker Probe Technique for Diagnosis and Treatment of Stuttering in Young Children, 1976, rev. edit., 1980. Axe-Houghton Found. grantee, 1973, CUNY Rsch. Found. grantee, 1971—. Mem. AAUP, Am. Speech, Lang. and Hearing Assn. (cert. clin. competence in speech and audiology), N.Y. State Speech, Lang. and Hearing Assn. (honoree 1994), N.Y.C. Speech, Lang. and Hearing Assn. (honoree 1990). Home and Office: 17 W 54th St New York NY 10019-5412

STOCKER, JOYCE ARLENE, retired secondary education educator; b. West Wyoming, Pa., May 13, 1931; d. Donald Arthur and Elizabeth Mae (Gardner) Saunders; m. Robert Earl Stocker, Nov. 26, 1953; children: Desiree Lee Stocker Stackhouse, Rebecca Lois Stocker Genelow, Joyce Elizabeth Stocker Scrobola. Grad. sum laude, Coll. Misericordia, Dallas, 1991; Master's equivalency diploma, Pa. Dept. Edn., 1991. Cert. tchr., Pa. Tchr. music and lang. arts West Pittston (Pa.) Sch. Dist., 1953-60; tchr. music and choral Wyoming Area Sch. Dist., Exeter, Pa., 1970-78, tchr. English composition, 1978-93, chmn. lang. arts dept., 1982-90, dir. nat. history day activities, 1982-93; state cons. Nat. History Day. Organist, choir dir. United Meth. Ch., Wyo., 1958—; choir dir. Wyo. Centenial Choir, Wyo., 1983; mem. com., sec. Continuing Profl. Devel. Com. Pa., Exeter, 1988-93, Long Range Plan Wyo. Area Sch. Dist., Exeter, 1990-91; tutor, judge Nat. History Day. Recipient DAR Tchr. of Yr. award, 1992-93, Wilkes Univ., 1990; named OutstandingEducator, Times Leader, 1993. Mem. NEA, PMEA, MENC, NCSS, PASR, PSERS, Pa. Edn. Assn., Pa. Coun. Social Studies, Orgn. Am. History, Wyoming Edn. Assn., N.E. Pa. Writing Coun., Nat. Coun. Tchrs. English, Women Educators Internat., Delta Kappa Gamma (recording sec. 1991—), Phi Mu Gamma. Methodist. Office: Wyoming Area Sch Dist 20 Memorial St Exeter PA 18643-2659

STOCKING, JACQUELINE CHERYL, nurse, consultant, entrepreneur; b. Fresno, Calif., May 2, 1967; d. Richard and Hermiline (Vasquez) Hernandez. BA in Biology with honors, U. Calif., Santa Cruz, 1989; ADN, Regents Coll., 1992. Cert. emergency nurse, mobile intensive care nurse, emergency medical technician-paramedic, trauma nurse care course provider, ACLS, pediat. advanced life support provider. RN/ER Saddleback Meml. Med. Ctr., Laguna Hills, Calif., 1989-92; RN Mercy Hosp., San Diego, 1992-94, Emergency Mgmt. Svcs., San Diego, 1993-94; RN/flight nurse Air Evac Inc., San Diego, 1993-94; RN Carson-Tahoe Hosp., Carson City, Nev., 1994—, Washoe Med. Ctr., Reno, Nev., 1994—, St. Mary's Regional Med. Ctr., Reno, 1994—; med.-legal nurse cons., expert witness, Reno, 1994—. Mem. NAFE, Emergency Nurses Assn., Nat. Flight Nurses Assn. Republican. Roman Catholic.

STOCKING, MARION KINGSTON, English language educator, editor; b. Bethlehem, Pa., June 4, 1922; d. William Frank and Louise Anne Kingston; m. David Mackenzie Stocking, Dec. 21, 1955 (dec. 1984); 1 stepchild: Frederick B. AB, Mt. Holyoke Coll., 1943; PhD, Duke U., 1952; LittD (hon.), U. Maine, 1992. Licensed bird bander U.S. Fish and Wildlife Svc., 1960-92. Instr. English U. Maine, Orono, 1946-48, U. Colo., Boulder, 1950-54; from asst. prof. to prof. emerita Beloit (Wis.) Coll., 1954—; faculty assoc. Coll. of the Atlantic, Bar Harbor, Maine, 1985—; publ. The Latona Press, Ellsworth, Maine, 1978—; pres. The Beloit Poetry Jour. Found., 1988—; panelist Maine Community Found., Ellsworth, 1988-93; dir. Freshman English Beloit Coll., 1955-63, dir. Porter Scholars Hons. Program, 1967-69, dir. Underclass Common Course, 1967-70, chairperson Dept. English, 1978-83. Editor: Journals of Claire Clairmont, 1968, The Beloit Poetry Jour., 1955—, (contbg.) Shelley and His Circle, V, 1974, The Clairmont Correspondence, 1995; contbr. profl. publs. Commnr. Maine Arts Commn., Augusta, 1993—, lit. panel, 1984-88, chair, 1987-88; panelist Maine Expansion Arts Program, 1988-93; founder, dir. Wis.-Minn. Poetry Cir.; active Quoddy Regional Land Trust. NEH rsch. fellow, 1979. Mem. AAUW, MLA, Keats-Shelley Assn. Am., Byron Soc., Maine Writers and Publs. Alliance, Sorrento Scientific Soc., Phi Beta Kappa. Home and Office: RR 2 Box 154 Ellsworth ME 04605-9616

STOCKLIN, ALMA KATHERINE, public relations consultant; b. New London, Conn., May 9, 1926; d. Stephen Sullivan and Theresa Catherine (Flynn) Sheehan; m. Philip L. Stocklin, Jan. 28, 1950 (div. 1984); children: Brian, Christopher, Virginia Katherine, Walter, Stephen. Student, U. Conn., 1945-46, Conn. Coll., 1946; cert., Sch. Modern Photography, N.Y.C., 1948; AA, Charter Oak Coll., 1979; BA cum laude, Eastern Conn. State U., 1981. Advt. photographer GE, Bridgeport, Conn., 1948-49; chmn. Conn. State Juvenile Protection, 1959; pub. rels. cons. Norwich and Groton, Conn., 1983-86; asst. to dean Ea. Conn. State U., Willimantic, 1984-91, ret., 1991; adminstr. br. office U.S. Submarine Base Ea. Conn. State U., Groton, 1984-91; pub. rels. cons., 1994—; coord. videotape courses for submarines, New London, 1984-91. Founder, chmn. bd. dirs. Newport (R.I.) Holiday for Sr. Citizens, 1972, Uncas on Thames State Hosp., 1978; mem. Norwich Harbor Day Com., 1982-83, Catchment Area coun. 11 S.E. Conn. Mental Health Bd., 1989-90, Norwich Regional Mental Health Adv. Bd., 1987-90, Norwich State Hosp. Adv. Bd., 1987-89; vice chair Ea. Conn. Regional Mental Health Bd., 1988-89; founder, chmn. Norwich Nuclear Freeze Com., 1982; bd. dirs. Ea. Conn. Symphony Orch., New London, 1984-87, Friend of the Symphony, 1987-90, Laurel Glen, Groton, 1984-91; co-founder, bd. dirs. Newport Ch. Community Housing Corp., 1969-72; founder, chmn. Holiday for Sr. Citizens, Newport, R.I., 1972; chair Conn. State PTA Juvenile Protection, 1957; founder, pres. Cath. Mother's Circle, Dorset, Eng., 1962; exec. sec. Overnight Shelter, Loughborough, Eng., 1973-74; founder, chair Bicycle Paths for Schoolchildren, Loughborough, 1974; bd. dirs. Friends of the Fairfield County Dist. Libr., Lancaster, Ohio, 1994—; mem. St. Bernadette's Parish Coun., 1994—. Recipient award for outstanding svc. in founding the Newport Holiday for Sr. Citizens, City of Newport, 1972, award for outstanding svc. Pres. of Conn. PTAs. Mem. AAUW, Fairfield County (Conn.) Respiratory Disease and TB Assn. (bd. dirs. 1991—) Friends of Libr. Assn. Fairfield County Dist. (bd. dirs. 1994—), Phi Beta Phi, Conn. Alpha Pi Beta Phi. Democrat. Roman Catholic.

STODDARD, ALEXANDRA HOPE, data processing executive, consultant; b. Richmond, Ind., July 23, 1942; d. Willis J. Jr. and Alexandria (Wyte) S.; m. James A. Lohman, Apr. 29, 1967 (div. Nov. 1982); children: Alexandra Catherine, Scott Michael. BS in Math., Loyola U., Chgo., 1966; postgrad., Wright State U., 1983, MIT, 1985. Software engr. Western Electric, Cicero, Ill., 1966-69, IBM, Research Triangle Park, N.C., 1969-72; tech. writer Reynolds & Reynolds, Cin., 1979-82; sr. mem. tech. staff Contel, Dayton, Ohio, 1982-83; project leader Mead Data Cen., Dayton, 1983-87; sr. software engr. Computer Task Group, Orchard Park, N.Y., 1987; prin. WJS Assocs., Downers Grove, Ill., 1987—; cons. Starflo Engring., Cin., 1982, Fed. Sign and Signal, Downers Grove, 1972-75, Amoco, 1987—, AHA (hosp.), Packaging Corp. of Am., Lions Clubs Internat., AT&T Bell Labs, Rockwell Internat., Carlson Mktg. Spenser & Stuart, Andrew Corp. Troop leader Girl Scouts U.S., Cin., 1982-83. Mem. IEEE, Assn. Computing Machinery. Democrat. Home and Office: WJS Assocs 5914 Grand Ave Downers Grove IL 60516

STODDARD, M. ANITA, psychiatric nurse; b. Spartanburg, S.C., July 7, 1946; d. David Dupree and Maudie (Johnson) S. BSN, U. S.C., 1968; MSN, U. N.C., 1972. RN, S.C.; cert. clin. specialist in adult psychiatric and mental health nursing, lic. marriage and family therapist, S.C. Staff nurse in psychiatry S.C. Bapt. Hosp., Columbia, 1968; staff nurse Columbia Area Mental Health Ctr., 1968-70; dir. nursing Spartanburg Area Mental Health Ctr., 1972-87, asst. dir., 1987—; mem. summer faculty U. S.C. Sch. Nursing, Columbia, 1971-72; adj. faculty Mary Black Sch. Nursing, U. S.C., Spartanburg, 1980—; adv. bd. women's program Spartanburg Tech. Coll., 1987—; presenter at profl. meetings. Mem. Spartanburg Symphony Chorus, 1972—, Spartanburg County Emergency Preparedness, 1988—. Mem. ANA (local bd. dirs. 1987-92, pres. 1974-76, Excellence in Practice award 1990), Am. Assn. Marriage and Family Therapy, Sigma Theta Tau. Methodist. Office: Spartanburg Area Mental Health Ctr 149 E Wood St Spartanburg SC 29303

STODDARD, REBA DELL-MARIE (PRAY), medical/surgical nurse; b. New London, Conn., Oct. 15, 1966; d. Robert Edward and Reba Emma (Tiziani) Pray; m. Patrick Frank Stoddard, Sept. 23, 1989; 1 child, Patrick Robert. AS in Nursing, Westbrook Coll., 1986. RN, Conn. Staff nurse Groton (Conn.) Regency Nursing Ctr., 1986-87; orthopedic staff nurse Lawrence and Meml. Hosp., New London, 1987-91; infection control nurse Waterford (Conn.) Health and Rehab. Ctr., 1991-92; shift supr. nursing Pendleton Nursing Facility, Mystic, Conn., 1992—; asst. adminstrv. mgr. UNCAS on Thames Hosp., Nowich, Conn., 1992-93; sch. nurse The Founders Sch., East Haddam, Conn., 1993—. Mem. Nat. League for Nursing, Conn. League Nursing, Westbrook Coll. Alumni Assn. Republican. Methodist. Home: 29 Florida Rd East Haddam CT 06423-1706

STODDARD, SANDOL, writer; b. Birmingham, Ala., Dec. 16, 1927; d. Carlos French and Caroline (Harris) S.; m. Felix M. Warburg (div. 1966); children: Anthony, Peter, Gerald, Jason; m. Peter R. Goethals, May 1, 1984. BA magna cum laude, Bryn Mawr Coll., 1959. Author 24 books including: Growing Time, 1971, The Doubleday Children's Bible, 1983 (Lewis citation 1983), The Hospice Movement: Updated and Expanded Edition, 1992, Prayers, Praises and Thanksgivings, 1992. Bd. dirs., co-founder Hospice of Kona, Kailua-Kona, Hawaii, 1985; co-founder Kona Theol. Inst., 1990; bd. dirs. Choice in Dying, N.Y.C. Recipient Humanitarian Svc. award Forbes Health System, 1979, Notable Book award Am. Libr. Assn., 1964. Mem. AAUW, Nat. Writer's Guild, Cosmpolitan Club. Democrat. Episcopalian. Home and Office: 78-6646 Mamalahoa Hwy Holualoa HI 96725

STODDERT, SANDRA SMITH, media director; b. Easton, Pa., Mar. 12, 1942; d. Harry James and Agnes (Krueger) Smith; m. D. Dale Kleppinger, Aug. 22, 1964 (div. Sept. 1981); children: Eric David, Deborah Ellen; m. Dorwin W. Stoddert, July 15, 1983 (dec. Feb. 1987); stepchildren: Joel Thomas, Jennifer Lea. BS in Edn., Bloomsburg U., 1964; MEd, Lehigh U., 1967. Tchr. Bethlehem (Pa.) Sch. Dist., 1964-67; permanent substitute South Burlington (Vt.) Sch. Dist., 1978-79, media ctr. dir., 1979—. Mem. Nat. ASCD, LWV (pres. 1976-77), Nat. Coun. Social Studies (curriculum devel. com. mem. 1986-88, chair local standards bd. 1991-94), Vt. Ednl. Media Assn., Vt. State Tech. Coun., South Burlington Educators Assn. (bldg. rep. 1984-86, pres. 1987-90, negotiating team mem. 1988-91, grievance chmn. 1991—). Republican. Lutheran. Office: Chamberlin Sch 262 White St South Burlington VT 05403

STOECKEL, JENNIFER J., psychologist, vocational professional; b. Cin., May 10, 1961; d. Joseph Anthony and Mary Ellen (Hubert) S. BS in Psychology, Xavier U., 1983, MA in Clin. Psychology, 1989; PhD in Psychology, Ill. Inst. Tech., 1992. Lic. psychologist, Ohio. Psychology asst. Milcreek Psychiatric Ctr. for Children, Cin., 1984, Longview State Mental Inst., Cin., 1983-85; psychologist, vocational expert Assoc. for Psychol. Resources, Cin., 1985-94; staff psychologist Farrell & Assocs., Cin., 1994—; psychol. cons. U. Cin. Med. Ctr., 1990-92. Mem. APA, Ohio Psychol. Assn. Home: 3537 Jimmar Ct Cincinnati OH 45239

STOECKL, SHELLEY JOAN, marketing professional; b. Buffalo, Feb. 24, 1951; d. Joseph T. and Joan (Carriere) S. AAS in Bus. Adminstrn., Bryant & Stratton, 1978; cert. in gen. banking, Am. Inst. Banking, 1982; cert. in pers. & human resource mgmt., Canisius Coll., 1983; postgrad., Empire State Coll. Cert. profl. sec. Sr. sec. Mfrs. Hanover Trust Co., Buffalo, 1974-79, exec. sec., 1979-82, pers. asst., 1982-84, pers. mgr., 1984-87; account coord. Computer Task Group Direct Mktg. Svcs., Buffalo, 1987-89; project mgr. ANCOR Info. Mgmt., Inc., Buffalo, 1989-91; sr. account coord. IMPCO Direct Response Mktg., Buffalo, 1991—. Co-author: (presentation) Go For the Gold: CPS, 1983—; coord.: 60 Minutes: A Look Inside the Inst. for Certifying Secs., 1991, Marketing Your Credentials to Management, 1992. Co. coord. United Way, Buffalo, 1980-87; vol. Jack Kemp for Congress, Buffalo, 1970. Recipient scholastic award Buffalo Clearing House Assn., 1982. Fellow Cert. Profl. Secs. Acad.; mem. NAFE, Profl. Secs. Internat. (bd. dirs. 1980-82, v.p. 1982-83, corr. sec. 1983-85, pres. 1986-87), Cert. Profl. Secs. Soc. N.Y. State (pres. 1987-88), Inst. for Cert. (rep. N.E. dist. 1988-94), Toastmasters. Conservative. Roman Catholic. Home: 239 Wimbledon Ct Buffalo NY 14224-1955 Office: IMPCO Direct Response Mktg 29 Depot St Buffalo NY 14206-2203

STOECKLE, MARY L., critical care nurse, nursing educator; b. Cin., Nov. 14, 1956; d. Melvin and Margaret Mary (Atkins) S. BSN, Coll. Mt. St. Joseph, Ohio, 1979; MSN, U. Cin., 1988, PhD, 1993. Cert. CCRN, BLS instr., trainer, ACLS instr. Staff nurse St. Francis Hosp., Cin., 1979-81; charge relief nurse Shriners Burns Inst., Cin., 1981-85; staff nurse Univ. Hosp., Cin., 1985; staff, charge nurse St. Elizabeth Med. Ctr., Edgewood, Ky., 1985-88; critical care instr. Mercy Hosp. Anderson, 1988-93; instr. Am. Healthcare Inst., Silver Springs, Md., 1989—; asst. prof. Wright State U., Dayton, Ohio, 1993—; bd. dirs. Kidney Found. of Greater Cin., 1988-94; bd. dirs. Miami Valley chpt. Nat. Kidney Found., 1994—; mem. Organ Donor Awareness Coun., 1988—; mem. ECC task force Am. Heart Assn., 1988-91. Author: (with others) Organ & Tissue Transplantation, 1991; contb'r. of articles to jours. Mem. Ohio Burn Team, 1981-86. Grantee Kidney Found. Greater Cin., 1992, Wright State U., 1994. Mem. AACN, Midwest Nursing Rsch. Soc., Assn. Nurses Endorsing Transplantation, Sigma Theta Tau (rsch. award, Beta Iota Chpt. 1989), Ohio Nurses Assn. Home: 5625 Eula Ave Cincinnati OH 45248 Office: Wright State U Miami Valley Coll Nursing and Health Dayton OH 45435

STOECKLIN, SISTER CAROL ANN, education educator; b. Detroit, July 20, 1953; d. Andrew Charles and Ernestine (Roselli) S. BA, Mercy Coll. of Detroit, 1974; M in theol. studies, St. John's Provincial Sem., 1986; MA, St. Louis U., 1991, PhD, 1993. Joined Religious Sisters of Mercy. Tchr. Bishop Borgess High Sch., Redford, Mich., spring 1976, St. Agatha High Sch., Detroit, 1976-79; adminstrv. asst., campus minister, religion dept. chair Muskegon (Mich.) Cath. Ctrl. High Sch., 1979-84; adminstrv. asst., dir. ministries Nouvel High Sch., Saginaw, Mich., 1984-85; acad. dean, counselor, tchr. St. Joseph's on the Rio Grande High Sch., Albuquerque, 1985-87; tchr. Holy Ghost Elem. Sch., Albuquerque, 1988-89; grad. asst. edn. dept. St. Louis (Mo.) U., 1991-93; asst. prof. edn., dir. student tchrs. U. Detroit Mercy, 1993—; edn. com. mem. Sisters of Mercy, Farmington Hills, Mich., 1990-93; CHRPN, 1993—; literacy program evaluator Macomb County Headstart, Mt. Clemens, Mich., 1990; curriculum cons. St. Mary's H.S., St. Louis, 1991. Co-author: Valuing Our Differences, 9-12, 1992, K-8, 1993. Mem. ASCD, Assn. Univ. Women, Mercy Secondary Edn. Assn., Mercy Elem. Edn. Network, Phi Delta Kappa, Pi Lambda Theta. Roman Catholic.

STOEHR, ISABELLA KASUMI, research analyst; b. N.Y., Dec. 19, 1967; d. Achim A. and Kayoko (Tsutsumi) S. BSc in Bus. Studies, U. Buckingham, England, 1989. Rschr. Dresdner Bank, Germany, 1986; editor (Japanese edit.) Euromoney Publs., England, 1989-91; rsch. analyst Alliance Cap. Mgmt., N.Y., 1992—. Office: Alliance Cap Mgmt 1345 Ave Americas New York NY 10105

STOELTJE, BEVERLY JUNE, liberal studies educator; b. Rotan, Tex., Apr. 1, 1940; d. Roger Caswell and Laura Inez (Kennedy) Smith; children: Gretchen, Rachael; m. Richard Bauman, Nov. 26, 1977; children: Mark, Andrew. BA, U. Tex., 1961, MA, 1975, PhD, 1979. Asst. prof. English U. Tex., Austin, 1983-86; assoc. prof. folklore Ind. U., Bloomington, 1986—, also mem. African studies faculty, women studies faculty, rsch. assoc. in semiotics; cons. S.W. Ednl. Devel. Lab., Austin, 1976, Tex. Women's History Project, San Antonio, 1981; dir. Folk Arts Survey Tex., Austin, 1977, 78; dir. USIA linkage on performance Ind. U. and U. Ghana, 1989-93. Author: Children's Handclaps, 1979; editor (essay collection) Feminist Revision in Folklore Studies, 1988; contbr. articles to profl. jours. and chpts. in books. Fulbright rsch. fellow Ghana, 1989-90; grantee Tex Commn. for Humanities, 1980, Coun. on Internat. Programs, Ind. U., 1988. Mem. African Studies Assn., Am. Folklore Soc. (exec. bd. 1981-84), Am. Anthropol. Assn., Modern Langs. Assn., Semiotic Soc Am. Office: Folklore Inst Ind Univ 504 N Fess Ave Bloomington IN 47408-3890

STOERMER, DAPHNE CAROL, physical therapist, consultant; b. Vancouver, B.C., Feb. 6, 1939; came to the U.S., 1959; d. Douglas William Walker and Thelma Ray (Kelly) Whitelaw; m. Phillip Hilary Stoermer, Apr. 28, 1962; children: Hilary Anne, Mark Andrew, Claire Marie. Student, U. B.C., 1957-59; BSc, cert. in phys. therapy, U. So. Calif., L.A., 1961; lifetime teaching credential, UCLA, 1965. Registered phys. therapist. Staff phys. therapist U. So. Calif. Med. Ctr., L.A., 1962-64, San Gabriel (Calif.) Community Hosp., 1964-72; owner Lafayette (Calif.) Phys. Therapy, 1975—, Orinda (Calif.) Sports Fitness Ctr., 1981-91; cons. Consultation By Design, Lafayette, 1984—; bd. dirs. Phys. Therapy Provider Network Inc., Woodland Hills, Calif. Telephone help worker Contact Care, Lafayette, 1991-92. Mem. Am. Phys. Therapy Assn., N.Am. Back Sch., Internat. Dance Exercise

Assn., Kappa Kappa Gamma (pub. rels. Psi chpt. 1988-90). Office: Lafayette Phys Therapy 895 Moraga Rd # 10 Lafayette CA 94549

STOESSER, SUSAN ALICE (SUSAN ALICE LANGE), librarian, educator, media generalist; b. Milw., May 15, 1947; d. Louis Albert and Ethel (Freeman) Lange; m. Gregory Alan Stoesser, Oct. 17, 1969; children: Matthew Alan, Margaret Alice. BS in Elem. Edn., U. Wis., LaCrosse, 1969, postgrad., 1976-81; postgrad., U. Wis., 1985-91, Hamline U., 1993-94, Alfred Adler Inst., 1994. Cert. elem. edn. tchr. and media generalist, Minn.; cert. sch. media dir., Wis. Libr. Randall Sch., Bassett, Wis., 1971-75, Trevor (Wis.) Sch., 1976-77, Brighton Elem. Sch., Kansasville, Wis., 1976-93, Lincoln Elem. Sch., Robbinsdale, Minn., 1993-94, Meadow Lake Elem. Sch., Robbinsdale, 1994—; bd. dirs. Kenosha County Libr. Bd., 1981-87. Various leadership roles Salem (Wis.) United Meth. Ch., 1975-93; mem. com., bd. dirs. Wis. Conf. United Meth. Ch., Sun Prairie, Wis., 1987-91; pres., mem. Cmty. Libr., Silver Lake, Wis., 1977-82. Named Woman of Yr., Bus. and Profl. Women, 1984. Mem. Minn. Fedn. Tchrs. Home: 12772 210th Cir Elk River MN 55330

STOKELY, JOAN BARBARA, elementary school educator; b. Cleve., May 6, 1945; d. Paul Warner and Florence Leona (Sorensen) S. BS, Lamar U., 1967, M Elem. Edn., 1970. Cert. tchr., adminstr., Tex. 4th grade tchr. Vidor (Tex.) Ind. Sch. Dist., 1967-74, 88-94, 5th grade tchr., 1974-77, 7th and 8th grade tchr., 1979-88, Apple lab. mastery tchr., 1994—; grad. equivalency diploma tchr. Beaumont Ind. Sch. Dist., Vidor, 1977-81; Apple computer and sci. lab. tchr. Vidor (Tex.) Ind. Sch. Dist., 1994—. Pres. Vidor Tchrs. Fed. Credit Union, 1985—; mem. troop com. Boy Scouts Am., Vidor, 1972-83; tchr. Roman Cath. Chs., Beaumont, Tex., 1967-87. Mem. AAUW, DAR, Am. Bus. Women Assn. (Vocat./Woman of Yr., chmn. 1977-78), Tex. State Tchrs. Assn. (pres. Vidor chpt. 1990-94, chmn. uniserv adv. coun. region 15 1991-92, sec. region 15, 1993—), Tex. Computer Edn. Assn. Office: Oak Forest Elem Sch 2400 Highway 12 Vidor TX 77662-3497

STOKEN, JACQUELINE MARIE, physician; b. Beaver Falls, Pa., Sept. 29, 1948; d. Jack Marc and Lillian Marie Stoken; m. John F. Edge, June 2, 1990; children: Randi Elizabeth, Lisa Adrienne, Alexander Joseph. Nursing diploma, Presbyn.-U. Hosp. Sch. Nursing, Pitts., 1970; BS in Biology with honors, Chatham Coll., Pitts., 1986; DO, U. Osteo. Med. & Health Scis., Des Moines, 1990. RN, Pa., Minn., Iowa; cert. ACLS, BCLS. Home care staff nurse South Hills Health System, Pitts., 1976-89; intern internal medicine Des Moines Gen. Hosp., 1990-91; resident physician dept. phys. medicine and rehab. U. Minn., Mpls., 1991-94; lectr. Internat. Rehab. Med. Assn., Des Moines, 1994—; physiatrist Iowa Orthopaedic Ctr., Des Moines, 1994—; guest lectr. dept. phys. therapy U. Minn., Mpls., 1991-94; dept. occupational therapy, 1991-94, U. Osteo. Medicine and Health Sci., Des Moines, 1990; chief resident dept. phys. medicine and rehab. U. Minn., Mpls., 1992-93; mem. Iowa Gov's Task Force on Rural Health, 1989; mgr., seminar leader philosophy corr. course, South Fallsburg, N.Y., 1977-79. Mem. AMA, Am. Assn. Osteo. Postgrad. Physicians (regional chair), Coun. Fed. Health Programs, Am. Acad. Phys. Medicine and Rehab., Am. Osteo. Assn. (sec. coun. student coun. pres. 1988-89), Iowa Osteo. Med. Assn. (student del. ho. of dels. 1987-88, student coun. rep. 1987-88), Am. Med. Women's Assn., Am. Holistic Med. Assn., Am. Acad. Osteopathy, Cranial Acad., Sigma Sigma Phi.

STOKEN, JUDITH DIANE, health education administrator; b. Little Rock, Dec. 9, 1945; d. Obie H. and Lois Bernice (Williams) Echols; children: Kimberly Cheryl, Sean Patrick Jerome. BS, Tex. Women's U., 1968; MEd, cert. of supervision, East Tex. State U., 1981, postgrad., 1982. Classroom tchr. Garland (Tex.) Ind. Sch. Dist., 1967-69, Jefferson County Sch. Dist., Louisville, 1969-76, Texarkana (Tex.) Ind. Sch. Dist., 1976-84; owner, dir. Whispering Hills Sch. Dance, Louisville, 1972-75; adminstr. Sacred Heart Cath. Sch., Texarkana, 1984-87; edn. cons. Thoth Edn. Svcs., Inc., 1987-88; in house pub. rels. developer, sr. svcs. St. Michael Hosp., Texarkana, 1988; dir. Wadley LifeSource/Wadley Regional Med. Ctr., Texarkana, 1988—; owner Great Panes Stain Glass Studio, Texarkana, 1979—; adj. faculty East Tex. State U., Texarkana, 1981-83; state accreditor Tex. Cath. Conf. Edn., Austin, 1984-87; bd. dirs. Am. Heart Assn., Texarkana chpt., Am. Lung Assn., Texarkana chpt., March of Dimes, Texarkana chpt., Cancer Soc., Texarkana chpt., Arthritis Found. Texarkana; mem. Ark.-Tex. Coun. of Govt. HIV/AIDS Consortium. Developer, coord.: (6 video tapes series) Crime Awareness for Children, 1979-80; pub.: Health Texas, 1993; contbr. articles to profl. jours. Mem. Texarkana Unite of Svc., 1978—; bd. dirs., v.p. Ctrl. Mall Mchts. Assn., Texarkana, 1989—; mem. Bowie-Cass Adult Edn. Adv. Coun., 1989—, treas.; mem. Assn. Rsch. and Enlightenment, 1981—; vice-chairperson Texarkana Civil Svc. Commr., 1992—; mem. campaign bd. United Way Texarkana, 1992—, Leadership Texarkana, 1994—. Recipient 6 Addy awards State Tex., 1989. Mem. Tex. Soc. for Hosp. Pub. Rels. and Mktg. (Tesltar award 1994), Texarkana Mus. Systems, East Tex. State U. Alumni Assn. (bd. dirs. 1991—, v.p. 1992, pres. 1993, Tex. Found. bd. vice-chmn. external affairs 1993—, Alumni Achievement award 1993), Quota Internat. (pres. 1991-92), Am. Hosp. Assn. (mgr. hosp. based ctr. 1991—), Texarkana C. of C. (tourism adv. bd. Tang Gang 1989—, Chmn.'s Coun. award 1993), Kiwanis, Alpha Delt Kappa (treas. 1985-86). Office: Wadley LifeSource 57 Central Mall Texarkana TX 75503-2467

STOKES, (GLADYS) ALLISON, pastor, researcher, religion educator; b. Bridgeport, Conn., Aug. 17, 1942; d. Hugh Vincent and Mildred Roberta (Livengood) Allison; m. Jerome Walter Stokes, June 1, 1964 (div. 1977); children: Jonathan Jerome, Anne Jennings. BA, U. N.C., 1964; MPhil, Yale U., 1976, PhD, 1981, MDiv, 1981. Ordained to ministry United Ch. of Christ, 1981. Acting univ. min. Wesleyan U., Middletown, Conn., 1981; assoc. pastor Orange Congl. Ch., Conn., 1981-82; chaplain, asst. prof. religion Vassar Coll., Poughkeepsie, N.Y., 1982-85; assoc. univ. chaplain Yale U., New Haven, 1985-87; pastor Congl. Ch., West Stockbridge, Mass., 1987—; rsch. assoc. Hartford (Conn.) Sem., 1987-92; founding dir. Women's Interfaith Inst. in the Berkshires, 1992—; bd. dirs. Dutchess Interfaith Coun., Pughkeepsie, 1984-85. Author: Ministry after Freud, 1985; co-author: Defecting in Place, 1994, Women Pastors, 1995; contbr. articles to profl. jours. Mem. steering com. Dutchess County Citizens for Safer World, Pughkeepsie, 1982-85. Kanzer Fund Psychoanalysis and Humanities grantee, 1977; AAUW fellow, 1978, Merrill fellow Harvard Div. Sch., 1994. Mem. Am. Acad. Religion, Berkshire Conf. Women Historians, Kiwanis. Home: PO Box 422 Housatonic MA 01236-0422 Office: Congl Ch 45 Main St West Stockbridge MA 01266

STOKES, TEREZE ANN, sales executive; b. Hyannis, Mass., July 30, 1958; d. James Thomas and Arlene Anna (Bourassa) Stokes; m. Curtis Michael Blais, Mar. 19, 1975 (div. June 1977); 1 child, James Brendon Stokes. Student, Rivier Coll., Harvard U. Cert. metallurgy. Sales rep. Diversified Resorts, Burlington, Mass., 1981-88, Edgcomb Metals, Nashua, N.H., 1988-91, Northstar Steel, Manchester, N.H., 1991—, Olympic Steel, Milford, Conn., 1992—. Mem. Nat. Pks. and Conservation Assn., Assn. Women in Metals Industry (publicity chairperson 1992—, editor, pub. newsletter 1993), Exec. Women's Golf League. Office: Olympic Steel 1 Eastern Steel Rd Milford CT 06460

STOKLOSA, JANIS HELENA, psychologist, air safety investigator; b. Panama C.Z., Oct. 13, 1946; d. Joseph Francis and Helena Ann (Wolosz) S. A.B., Emmanuel Coll., 1968; Ph.D., Harvard U., 1976. Teaching fellow, lectr. Harvard U., 1970-77; psychol. cons. spl. edn. program Basics, Inc., Charlestown, Mass., 1977-78; project asst. dir. MIT, 1978-80; engring. psychologist Transp. Systems Ctr., Cambridge, Mass., 1978-80; air. safety investigator Nat. Transp. Safety Bd., Washington, 1980-85; aircraft ops. specialist NASA Hdqrs., Washington, 1985—; lectr. Armed Forces Inst. Pathology, 1984; guest lectr. MIT, 1980; mem. human factors adv. com. Office of Sec., Dept. Transp., 1983. Contbg. mem. Smithsonian Mus., Washington; vol. Boston Symphony Orch., 1980. Recipient spl. service award Nat. Transp. Safety Bd., 1981, 82, 83, 84; New Eng. Psychol. Assn. undergrad. fellow. Mem. Am. Psychol. Assn., Human Factors Soc., Aerospace Med. Assn., Assn. Aviation Psychologists, Women's Transp. Seminar, Boston Mus. Fine Arts, Mass. Fedn. Polish Women, Sigma Xi, Psi Chi, Kappa Gamma Pi. Clubs: Harvard, FAA Flying. Home: 2801 Park Center Dr Alexandria VA 22302-1431 Office: NASA Hdqrs NF 400 Mary Ave Washington DC 20546

STOLL, KATHLEEN HENNESSY, management consultant; b. Boston, July 29, 1936; d. Vincent Lawrence and Mary Louise (Young) Hennessy; m. Myron Saunders Stoll, Aug. 26, 1961; children: Vincent Saunders, Sarah Louise, Heather Anne Wiard Stoll. BA, Smith Coll., 1958; MS, Case Western Res. U., 1960, MBA, 1984. Lic. ind. social worker, Ohio. Social worker Cleve. State Hosp., 1960-62, 64-65, rsch. assoc., 1966-69; aftercare cons., then assoc. dir. Cuyahoga County Mental Health Bd., Cleve., 1970-78; interim dir. mental health Murtis H. Taylor Mental Health Ctr., Cleve., 1978; planning assoc. Univ. Hosps. Cleve., 1978-89; mgmt. cons. Stoll & Assocs., Cleve., 1989—. Chmn. mental health commn. and trustee Fedn. Cmty. Planning; bd. dirs. Aftercare Residential Svcs., Cleve., 1989—; chmn. bd. dirs. Panta Rhei, 1979—. Mem. NASW (Social Worker of the Yr. 1987), Smith Alumnae Assn. (medal com. chair), Smith Club, Rotary (chpt. pres.). Democrat. Office: Stoll & Assocs 2943 S Park Blvd Cleveland OH 44120-1842

STOLL, LOUISE FRANKEL, federal official; b. N.Y.C., June 6, 1939; d. Abraham H. and Ruth C. (Flexo) Frankel; m. Marc H. Monheimer, Dec. 22, 1978; children: Miriam F., Malaika S., Abraham D. BA, MA in Philosophy with honors, U. Chgo., 1961; PhD, U. Calif., Berkeley, 1978. High sch. English tchr. Nairobi, Kenya, 1964-65; trustee Berkeley Unified Sch. Dist., 1971-78; mgr. govt. affairs Clear Water Program San Francisco, 1978-80, budget dir. Pub. Utilities Commn., 1980-85; sr. v.p., No. Calif. regional mgr. O'Brien-Kreitzberg and Assoc., Inc., San Francisco, 1985-93; CFO and asst. sec. budget and programs Office of Sec. Dept. Transp., Washington, 1993—; mem. Nat. Legal Affairs Com., Mid. East. Com. Active Anti-Defamation League of B'nai B'rith. Recipient Mayor's Fiscal Adv. award, City of San Francisco, 1984. Jewish. Office: Office of Sec Dept Transp 400 7th St SW Rm 10101 Washington DC 20590

STOLLDORF, GENEVIEVE SCHWAGER, media specialist; b. Ames, N.Y., July 17, 1943; d. Herbert Blakely and Genevieve Agnes (Alessi) Schwager; m. John G. Stolldorf, June 25, 1972; 1 child, Nathan Schwager. AA, Auburn (N.Y.) C.C., 1963; BS, Murray State U., 1967; MA in Edn., Seton Hall U., 1975. Cert. libr. media specialist, social studies tchr. grades 7-12. Libr. So. Orangetown Schs., Orangeburg, N.Y., 1967-70; libr. media specialist Nanuet (N.Y.) Pub. Schs., 1970-78; tchr. social studies grade 9 Monroe (N.Y.)-Woodbury, 1978-80; libr. media specialist Nyack (N.Y.) Pub. Schs., 1981—. Reviewer Libr. Jour., 1981-90. Kykuit guide Hist. Hudson Valley, 1994—; active Friends of the Nyacks, Nyack. Mem. N.Y. Libr. Assn., N.Y. State United Tchrs., Sch. Libr. Media Specialists Southeastern N.Y., Nyack Tchr. Assn. (editor newsletter 1982-84), Tri-Town League Women Voters, C. of C. of the Nyacks (hon.). Office: Valley Cottage Elem Sch Lake Rd Valley Cottage NY 10989

STOLLER, LINDA A., real estate executive; b. Chgo., Dec. 3, 1954; d. Richard and Arleen E. (Tillisch) S.; m. Marc D. Greenbaum, May 16, 1981. BS in Mgmt., Babson Coll., 1976; JD, Boston Coll., 1979; LLM, Boston U. Bar: Mass., U.S. Dist. Ct.; CPA, Mass. Sr. specialist Coopers & Lybrand, Boston, 1979-82, supr., 1982-84, mgr., 1984-85; v.p., prin. Copley Real Estate Advisors, Boston, 1985-91; dir, ctr. for real estate, co-chair finance divsn. Babson Coll., Wellesley, Mass., 1991—; mem. bd. dirs. Leventhal Sidman Jewish Community Ctr. Housing for the Elderly and Women's Divsn. Combined Jewish Philanthropies. Contbg. editor Real Estate Fin., Boston, 1985—. Mentor Babson Coll., Wellesley, Mass., 1986-87. Mem. ABA. Office: Babson Coll Boston MA 02157

STOLLER, PATRICIA SYPHER, structural engineer; b. Jackson Heights, N.Y., Dec. 16, 1947; d. Carleton Roy and Mildred Vivian (Ferron) Sypher; m. David A. Stoller Sr.; children: Stephanie Jean, Sheri Lynn. BSCE, Washington U., St. Louis, 1975; M in Mgmt., Northwestern U., 1989. R&D engr. Amcar div. ACF Industries, St. Charles, Mo., 1972-79; project engr. Truck Axle div. Rockwell Internat., Troy, Mich., 1979-81; sr. engr. ABB Impell, Norcross, Ga., 1981-83; supervising mgr., client mgr., div. mgr. ABB Impell, Lincolnshire, Ill., 1983—; dir. bus. devel., v.p. VECTRA (formerly ABB Impell), Lincolnshire, 1991-94; pres., CEO ASC Svcs. Co., LLC, Chgo., 1994—; Author computer program Quickpipe, 1983; numerous patents in field. Mem. ASCE, NAFE, Soc. Women Engrs., Am. Nuclear Soc. (exec. bd. Chgo. sect. 1991-93). Office: ASC Svcs Co LLC Ste 200 300 W Washington Chicago IL 60606

STOLLEY, EILEEN CECILIA, school system administrator; b. Pierre, S.D., June 6, 1947; d. Ralph H. and Frances E. (Kotz) Regennitter; m. Richard M. Stolley, Aug. 5, 1967; children: Michael, Gregory. AA, Black Hills State Coll., 1970. Elem. tchr. Belvidere (S.D.) Sch., 1967-69; kindergarten tchr. Kadoka (S.D.) Sch. Dist., 1970, tutor, 1970-72, asst. bus. mgr., 1973-76, bus. mgr., 1976—. Mem. S.D. Assn. Sch. Bus. Ofcls. (bd. dirs. 1982-88), Sch. Adminstrs. S.D. (mem. legis. com. 1987-94, mem. del. assembly 1987—, adminstr. profl. devel. award 1986-94), S.D. Sch. Bus. Ofcls. (treas. 1985-88), Region IV Area Adminstrs., Kadoka Community Betterment Assn. Republican. Roman Catholic. Office: Kadoka Sch Dist 3 Bayberry Kadoka SD 57543-0099

STOLZ, KATHY LYNN, public relations professional; b. Portland, Ind., Mar. 14, 1953; d. Roger Cloyce and Luetta June (Smith) Bowen; m. Dennis Lee Stolz, Aug. 13, 1972; 1 child, Elizabeth Grace. BS, Ind. U., 1975; MA, Ball State U., 1981. Cert. secondary tchr., Ind. Tchr. English/journalism Woodlan High Sch., Woodburn, Ind., 1975-77; co-owner Georgetown Clock Shop, Fort Wayne, Ind., 1975-77; G.E.D. tutor Lockyear Jr. Coll., Indpls., 1977; English tchr. Northview Jr. High Sch., Indpls., 1978; English, journalism tchr. Shelbyville (Ind.) High Sch., 1978-82; dir. alumni & parents rels. Franklin (Ind.) Coll., 1982-88; sales rep. Horace Mann Ins., Springfield, Ind., 1988; info./edn. coord. Meth. Hosp. of Ind. Cancer Ctr., Indpls., 1989-94, program devel. coord. health promotions, 1994—; cons. assoc. Pamela K. Boggs & Assocs., Indpls., 1991—. Sec., mem. City of Franklin Plan Commn., 1989-93; sec., precinct committeeman Johnson County Dem. Ctrl. Com., Franklin, 1988—; vol. Ctrl. Ind. Area Am. Cancer Soc., 1989—, United Way of Ctrl. Ind., 1993—; pres. Johnson County Lit. Coalition, Franklin, 1988, Johnson County Youth Svcs. Bur., Franklin, 1987, 88; mem. Historic Franklin, Inc., 1992—; Sunday sch. tchr. Grace United Meth. Ch., Franklin, 1987—. Recipient Cert. of Merit Cen. Ind. Area Am. Cancer Soc., 1990. Mem. Internat. Assn. of Bus. Communicators, Ind. U. Alumni Assn., Ball State U. Alumni Assn. Democrat. United Methodist. Home: 51 S Edwards St Franklin IN 46131-2503 Office: Meth Hosp of Ind Inc 1701 Senate Blvd Indianapolis IN 46202-1239

STOLZENBERG, PEARL, fashion designer; b. N.Y.C., Oct. 9, 1946; d. Irving and Anna (Shenkman) S. Student, Fashion Inst. Tech., 1964-66. Textile stylist, designer Forum Fabrics Ltd., N.Y.C., 1966-68; freelance ceiling designer Maxwell's Plum, N.Y.C., 1968; dir. styling Beauknit Corp., N.Y.C., 1969-74; stylist, designer Mi-Bru-San Co., Inc., N.Y.C., 1983-84; gen. mgr. Laissez-Faire Inc., N.Y.C., 1984-85; merchandiser prodn. The Clothing Acad. Inc., N.Y.C., 1986-87; v.p. String of Pearls Knitwear, Inc., N.Y.C., 1988—; pres. Pearl's Cutting Ltd., N.Y.C., 1994—; cons. Tam O'Shanter Textile Ltd., Montreal, 1974-79, Mitsui, Osaka, Japan, 1976-79, Sergio Valente English Town Sportswear, N.Y.C., 1980-84; cons. merchandiser The Fashion Acad., Hollywood Crossing, Inc., N.Y.C.; owner Josu Cutting Inc., Bklyn. Democrat. Jewish. Home: 8340 Austin St Apt 1E Jamaica NY 11415-1827 Office: Pearl's Cutting Ltd 410 W 16th St New York NY 10011

STONE, CAROLINE FLEMING, artist; b. N.Y.C., Mar. 26, 1936; d. Ralph Emerson and Elizabeth (Fleming) S.; m. Oakleigh B. Thorne, June 1956 (div. 1969); children: Oakleigh, Henry. Student, Art Students' League, 1954-57, 71-72, Pratt Graphics, 1973-74. One-woman shows include Saginaw (Mich.) Art Mus., 1978, Jesse Besser Mus., Mich, 1979, Washington Art Assn., Conn., Ella Sharp Mus., Mich., 1980, San Diego Pub. Library, Diablo Valley Coll., Calif., 1981, Trustman Gallery Simmons Coll., Boston, 1985, Mary Ryan Gallery, N.Y.C., 1989, Boston Pub. Libr., 1994; two-person shows include Miriam Perlman, Chgo., 1980, U. Mich., 1981, Mary Ryan Gallery, 1985, Katonah Gallery, N.Y., 1986, Davidson Gallery, Seattle, 1990, The Millbrook (N.Y.) Gallery, 1993; juried shows include Silvermine Nat. Printmaking, Conn., 1978, Print Club, Phila., 1981, Trenton State (Nat. Print Exhibn. Purchase award), 1982, Minot State Coll., N.D., 1985, Boston Printmakers (Jurors Commendation), 1986; group shows include Mus. N.Mex., 1984, Wilhelm Gallery, Houston, 1985, De Cordova and Dana Mus., Nat. Acad. Art, N.Y.C., Boston Pub. Library, Mus. Contemporary Hispanic Art, N.Y.C., 1987, World Print Exhbn., San Francisco, Smith Coll. Gallery, Northampton, Mass., Mary Ryan Gallery, 1988, 91, Virginia Lynch Gallery, R.I., 1989, 91, Accent on Paper, Lintas, N.Y., 1991, Women Printmaker's Nat. Touring Show, Boston Pub. Libr.; invitational shows include Abington Ctr., Pa., Printmaking Workshop, N.Y., 1982; represented in permanent collections Art Inst. Chgo., Mid-West Mus. Am. Art, Ind., Mus. N.Mex., Nat. Mus. Am. Art, Saginaw Mus., Boston Pub. Library, U. Chgo., U. Mich., Exxon Corp. Chase Manhattan Bank, IBM, Mellon Bank, The Portland Art Mus.; executed murals Revlon Inc. Mem. The Kitchen & Arden Party (bd. dirs.). Mem. Reformed Church. Home and Office: C Stone Press 80 Wooster St New York NY 10012-4347

STONE, CYNTHIA MARIE BEAVERS, dancing and gymnastics educator; b. Roanoke, Va., Mar. 3, 1952; d. Thomas Lane and Nannie Ruth (Brown) Beavers. BA, Birmingham So. Coll., 1974. Dance dir. Cobb County Parks and Recreation, Marietta, Ga., 1974-77; program dir. Camp Chattoga, Tallulah Falls, Ga., 1974—; dir. Chattooga Sch. of Gymnastics and Dance, Marietta, 1976—; coach Cobb County YMCA, Marietta, 1976; tchr. Peachtree Presbyn. Ch., Atlanta, 1980—; Chattooga dir. Friendship Ambs., Upper Montclair, N.J., 1983, 92. Choreographer opening ceremony Ga. State Games, 1991, 92; internat. choreographer compulsory routines Spl. Olympics, 1991; asst. choreographer closing ceremonies Skate Am., Atlanta, 1992. dir. rhythmic gymnastics competition Ga. Spl. Olympics, 1992—; counselor Camp Sunshine, Atlanta, 1988—, sport chmn. Ga. State Games, Atlanta, 1990—. Mem. U.S. Gymnastics Fedn. (safety cert., level I coach cert., rhythmic state chmn. 1985-91, rhythmic regional chmn. region VIII 1991—), Ga. Gymnastic Coaches Assn. (pres. 1978-80), Ga. Presch. Assn., Mortar Bd., Phi Beta Kappa, Alpha Lambda Delta. Methodist. Home: 3805 Catalina Dr Marietta GA 30066-2813 Office: Chattooga 4005 Canton Rd Marietta GA 30066-2739

STONE, DORIS ZEMURRAY, anthropologist; b. New Orleans, Nov. 19, 1909; d. Samuel and Sarah Zemurray; m. Roger Thayer Stone, Nov. 22, 1930 (dec.); children: Samuel Z., Alison Bixby (dec.). AB, Radcliffe Coll., 1930; LLD (hon.), Tulane U., 1957; DLitt (hon.), Union Coll., 1973; D.Ci. (hon.), Radcliffe Coll., 1994. Assoc. in archaeology Mid. Am. Rsch. Inst. Tulane U., New Orleans, 1930; rsch. assoc. Ctrl. Am. archaeology/ethnology Peabody Mus. Harvard U., Cambridge, Mass., 1954-66, assoc., 1966-71, hon. assoc., 1971-89, hon. curator Ctrl. Am. archaeology/ethnology Peabody Mus., 1989—; reviewer Nat. Endowment for Arts, 1978—; advisor U. San Pedro Sula, Honduras, 1980-82; bd. mgrs. Sch. Am. Rsch., 1978-88, 90—; lectr. in field. Contbr. articles to profl. pubs. Trustee New Orleans Mus. of Art, 1969-74, hon. life trustee, 1976—; mem. Newcomb Nat. Com., 1980—; bd. dirs. Escuela Agricola Panamericana, Honduras, 1942-63, hon. chairwoman emeritus, 1980—; pres. Com. of Indian Protection, Costa Rica, 1945-66; trustee Radcliffe Coll., 1941-53, 68-80, mem. adv. com. Bunting Inst., 1978-83; mem. nat. coun. Mus. of Am. Indian, Heye Found., 1978-80, trustee, 1980-89; bd. visitors Tulane U., 1976-82, pres. coun., 1982—; mem. vis. com. Peabody Mus. Harvard U., 1968-74, 76, 82, 83, 84, 85—; v.p. La. Coun. Music and Performing Arts, Inc., 1980; bd. dirs. New Orleans City Ballet, 1978—, La. Nature and Sci. Ctr., 1990-93, New Orleans Opera Assn., Archaeol. Conservancy, 1985-87, Greater New Orleans Regional Found., Audubon Inst. 1994—. Decorated chevalier Legion of Honor (France); comendador Order of Rubén Dario (Nicaragua), caballero Order of Vasco Nunez de Balboa (Panama); recipient Thomas F. Cunningham award Bd. of Trade, World Trade Ctr., 1993; named Hon. Citizen, Republic of Honduras; hon. fellow Lower Miss. Survey, 1987. Fellow Am. Anthrop. Assn., Soc. for Am. Archaeology (50th Ann. award), Andean Inst., Royal Anthrop. Inst.; mem. Soc. Women Geographers, Soc. Americanists, Soc. Mex. Anthropology, Soc. Geography and History of Honduras. Home: PO Box 295 Madisonville LA 70447 Office: Peabody Mus Harvard U Divinity Ave Cambridge MA 02138

STONE, ELAINE MURRAY, author, composer, television producer; b. N.Y.C., Jan. 22, 1922; d. H. and Catherine (Fairbanks) Murray-Jacoby; m. F. Courtney Stone, May 30, 1944; children: Catherine Rayburn, Pamela Webb, Victoria. Student, Juilliard Sch. Music, 1939-41; diploma, N.Y. Coll. Music, 1942; licentiate in organ, Trinity Coll. Music, London, 1947; student, U. Miami, 1952, Fla. Inst. Tech., 1963; PhD (hon.), World U., 1985. Organist, choir dir. St. Ingatius Episc. Ch., 1940-44; accompanist Strawbridge Ballet on Tour, N.Y.C., 1944; organist All Saints Episc. Ch., Ft. Lauderdale, 1951-54, St. John's Episc. Ch., Melbourne, Fla., 1956-59, First Christian Ch., Melbourne, 1962-63, United Ch. Christ, Melbourne, 1963-65, piano studio, Melbourne, 1955-70; editor-in-chief Cass Inc., 1970-71; dir. continuity radio Sta. WTAI, AM-FM, Melbourne, 1971-74; mem. sales staff Engle Realty Inc., Indialantic, Fla., 1975-78; v.p. pub. relations Consol. Cybertronics Inc., Cocoa Beach, Fla., 1969-70; writer, producer Countdown News, Sta. KXTX-TV, Dallas, 1978-80; assoc. producer Focus News, Dallas, 1980; host, producer TV show, Focus on History, 1982-94, Episc. Digest, 1984—; judge Writer's Contest sponsored Brevard Community Coll., 1987; v.p. Judges Fla. Space Coast Writer's Conf., 1985—, chmn., 1987. Author: The Taming of the Tongue, 1954, Love One Another, 1957, Menéndez de Avilés, 1968, Bedtime Bible Stories, Travel Fun, Sleepytime Tales, Improve Your Spelling for Better Grades, Improve Your Business Spelling, Tranquility Tapes, 1970, The Melbourne Bi-Centennial Book, 1976, Uganda: Fire and Blood, 1977, Tekla and the Lion, 1981 (1st Place award Nat. League Am. PEN Woman), Brevard County: From Cape of the Canes to Space Coast, 1988, Kizito, Boy Saint of Uganda, 1989 (2nd Place award Nat. League Am. PEN Woman 1990), Christopher Columbus: His World, His Faith., His Adventures, 1991 (1st Place award Nat. League Am. PEN Woman 1992), Elizabeth Bayley Seton: An American Saint, 1993 (3d Place award Nat. League Am. PEN Women 1994), Dimples The Dolphin, 1994 (1st Place award Fla. Space Coast Writer's Guild, 1994); composer: Christopher Columbus Suite, 1992 (1st Place award PEN Women Music Awards 1992, 2d Place award 1993), Florida Suite for cello and piano, 1993; contbr. articles to nat. mags., newspapers including N.Y. Herald Tribune, Living Church, Christian Life; space corr. Religious News Service, Kennedy Space Ctr., 1962-78. Mem. exec. bd. Women's Assn., Brevard Symphony, 1967—; mem. heritage com. Melbourne Bicentennial Commn.; mem. Evangelism Commn. Episc. Diocese Cen. Fla., 1985—; v.p. churchwomen group Holy Trinity Episcopal Ch., Melbourne, 1988-89, Stephen minister, 1988—, pres. churchwomen group, 1989—; bd. dirs. Fla. Space Coast Council Internat. Visitors, Fla. Space Coast Philharm., 1989—, Aid for the Arts, 1994. Recipient 1st place for piano Ashley hall, 1935-39, S.C. State Music Contest, 1939, 1st place for piano composition Colonial Suite, Constitution Hall, Washington 1987, 88, 89, 3d place for vocal composition, 1989, honorable mention for article, 1989, 2nd place for piano composition, 1989, award lit. contest Fla. AAUW, 1989, 1st place award Fla. State PEN Women, 1990, 1st Place award Nat. Black History Essay Contest, 1990, Disting. Author of Yr. plaque Fla. Space Coast Writers Guild, 1992; numerous other awards. Mem. AAUW, ASCAP, Nat. League Am. PEN Women (1st place awards Tex. 1979, v.p. Dallas br. 1978-80, organizing pres. Cape Canaveral br. 1969, pres. 1988-90), Women Communications, DAR (Fla. state chmn. music 1962-63), Colonial Dames Am. (organizing pres. Melbourne chpt. 1994), Nat. Soc. DAR (organizing regent Rufus Fairbanks chpt. 1981-85, vice regent 1987—, historian 1989—), Children Am. Revolution (past N.Y. state chaplain), Am. Guild Organists (organizing warden Ft. Lauderdale), Space Pioneers, Fla. Press Episc. Home: 1945 Pineapple Ave Melbourne FL 32935-7656

STONE, ELIZABETH CAECILIA, anthropology educator; b. Oxford, Eng., Feb. 4, 1949; d. Lawrence and Jeanne Cecilia (Fawtier) S.; m. Paul Edmund Zimansky, Nov. 5, 1976. BA, U. Pa., 1971; MA, Harvard U., 1973; PhD, U. Chgo., 1979. Lectr. anthropology SUNY, Stony Brook, 1977-78, asst. prof., 1978-85, assoc. prof., 1985—; participated archaeol. in Eng., Iran, Iraq, Afghanistan; dir. archaeol. projects Ain Dara, Syria,, Tell Abu Duwari, Iraq. Author: Nippur Neighborhoods, 1987; co-author: (monograph) Old Babylonian Contracts from Nippur 1, 1976, Adoption in Old Babylonian Nippur and the archive of Mannum-meshu-lissur, 1991; co-editor: The Cradle of Civilization: Recent Archaeology in Iraq-Biblical Archaeologist, 1992, Velles Paraules: Ancient Near Eastern Studies in Honor of Miguel Cioil on the Occasion of his 65th Birthday, 1991; editorial bd. Bulletin of the Am. Schs. of Oriental Rsch., 1993—; contbr. articles to profl. jours. Assoc. trustee Am. Schs. of Oriental Rsch., 1983-90. Fulbright fellow, 1986-87; rsch. grantee Ford Found., 1974, Nat. Geog. Soc., 1983, 84, 88, 90, Am. Schs. of Oriental Rsch., 1987, 88, NSF, 1989-92, NEH, 1989-93. Office: SUNY Dept Anthropology Stony Brook NY 11794

STONE, ELIZABETH WENGER, retired dean; b. Dayton, Ohio, June 21, 1918; d. Ezra and Anna Bess (Markey) Wenger; m. Thomas A. Stone, Sept. 14, 1939 (dec. Feb. 1987); children: John Howard, Anne Elizabeth, James Alexander. A.B., Stanford U., 1937, M.A., 1938; M.L.S., Catholic U. Am., 1961; Ph.D., Am. U., 1968. Tchr. pub. schs. Fontana, Calif., 1938-39; asst. state statistician State of Conn., 1939-40; libr. New Haven Pub. Librs., 1940-42; dir. pub. relations, asst. to pres. U. Dubuque, Iowa, 1942-46; substitute libr. Pasadena (Calif. Pub. Libr. System), 1953-60; instr. Cath. U. Am., 1962-63, asst. prof., asst. to chmn. dept. libr. sci., 1963-67, assoc. prof., asst. to chmn., 1967-71, prof., asst. to chmn., 1971-72, prof., chmn. dept., 1972-80, dean Sch. Libr. and Info. Scis., 1981-83, prof. and dean emeritus, 1983—, lectr., 1990; libr. cons. U.S. Inst. of Peace, 1988-90; libr. Nat. Presbyn. Ch., Washington, 1991—, archivist, 1994—; founder, exec. dir. Continuing Libr. Edn. Network and Exchange, 1975-79; founder Nat. Rehab. Info. Ctr., 1977, project mgr., 1977-83; co-chmn. 1st World Conf. on Continuing Edn. for the Libr. and Info. Sci. Professions, 1984-85, 2nd World Conf., Barcelona, 1993. Author: Factors Related to the Professional Development of Librarians, 1969, (with James J. Kortendick) Job Dimensions and Educational Needs in Librarianship, 1971, (with R. Patrick and B. Conroy) Continuing Library and Information Science Education, 1974, Continuing Library Education as Viewed in Relation to Other Continuing Professional Movements, 1975, (with F. Peterson and M. Chobot) Motivation: A Vital Force in the Organization, 1977, American Library Development 1600-1899, 1977, (with others) Model Continuing Education Recognition System in Library and Information Science, 1979, (with M.J. Young) A Program for Quality in Continuing Education for Information, Library and Media Personnel, 1980, (with others) Continuing Education for the Library Information Professions, 1985, The Growth of Continuing Education, 1986, Library Education: Continuing Professional Education, 1993, (with others) ALA World Encyclopedia of Library and Information Science, 3d edit., 1993; author, editor: Continuing Professional Education for Library and Information Science Personnel: Papers from Seminar at Matica Slovenska, Martin Czechoslovakia, 1989; editor: D.C. Libraries, 1964-66; contbr. articles to profl. jours. Mem. Pres.'s Com. on Employment of Handicapped, 1972-88, Establishment of Elizabeth W. Stone Lectureship Cath. U. Am., 1990; pres. D.C. chpt. Am. Mothers, Inc., 1984-86, nat. v.p., 1989-91. Recipient Presdl. award Cath. U. Am., 1982, Spl. Librs. Profl. award, 1988, DCLA Ainsworth Rand Spofford Pres's. award, 1990, Alumni Achievement award in libr. and info. sci. Cath. U. Am., 1990; named D.C. Mother of Yr., 1980. Mem. ALA (coun. 1976-83, v.p. 1980-81, pres. 1981-82, chmn. Nat. Libr. Week 1983-85, founder ALA Nat. Ptnrs. for Librs. and Literacy 1984, Lippincott award 1986, Hon. Life award 1986), Assn. Libr. Info. and Sci. Edn. (pres. 1974), Am. Soc. Assn. Execs., Am. Assn. Adult and Continuing Edn., Internat. Fedn. Libr. Assns. and Instns. (chmn. Continuing Profl. Edn. Roundtable 1986—), D.C. Libr. Assn. (hon. life, pres. 1966-67, hon. chair centennial com. 1992-94, hon. life 1994), Spl. Librs. Assn. (hon. life, pres. D.C. chpt. 1973-74), Cath. Libr. Assn. (hon. life), Continuing Profl. Edn. Libr. and Info Sci. Pers., Cosmos Club, Phi Sigma Alpha, Beta Phi Mu, Phi Lambda Theta. Presbyterian. Home: 4000 Cathedral Ave NW # 15B Washington DC 20016-5249 Office: Cath U Am Washington DC 20064

STONE, GAIL SUSAN, gifted/talented education educator; b. Elmhurst, Ill., Aug. 22, 1944; d. Harold Frederick Lopatka and May Anna (Lippert) Lopatka Wickham; m. Ronald Eugene Stone, Dec. 26, 1971; children: Andrew, Susanna. BA in Edn., Elmhurst Coll., 1966; M in Arts/Edn., Nat. Louis U., 1975. Cert. elem. edn. and supr. adminstrn. Tchr. first grade Shc. Dist. 89, Glen Ellyn, Ill., 1966-70; tchr. learning disability and gifted resource, kindergarten Sch. Dist. 94, North Riverside, Ill., 1972-81; gifted program coord. Sch. Dist. 102, La Grange, Ill., 1984-87, Sch. Dist. 96, Riverside, Ill., 1987-88; substitute tchr. Sch. Dist. 181, Hinsdale, Ill., 1988-92; tchr. gifted resources/spl. edn. aide Sch. Dist. 92, Broadview, Ill., 1992-93; coord. gifted program Sch. Dist. 103, Lyons, Ill., 1993—. Mem. Salt Creek Area AAUW (v.p. mem. 1986, v.p. program 1992-94), Ill. Coun. Gifted (v.p. 1979), Nat. Assn. Gifted, Children with Attention Deficit Disorder, Alpha Xi Delta, Phi Delta Kappa. Home: 329 N Stone Ave La Grange Park IL 60525-1818

STONE, GEORGIA GOSSOM, minister; b. St. Louis, Feb. 27, 1939; d. Woodrow Wilson and Georgia Frances (Dalton) Gossom; m. James George Stone, Mar. 2, 1957; children: David Mark, Deana, Larry. BS in Adminstrn. Human Svcs., Met. State Coll., 1984. Sec. Wesley Meth. Ch., Wichita Falls, Tex., 1955-57; sec. St. James Presbyn. Ch., Littleton, Colo., 1974-78, ch. adminstr., 1978-85; ch. adminstr., pres. ministry mgmt. counseling Genesis Presbyn. Ch., Lakewood, Colo., 1985; dir. edn. and program Travis Park United Meth. Ch., 1986-89; pastor McKinley Ave. United Meth. Ch., San Antonio, 1989—. Contbr. articles to profl. jours. Capt. Jefferson County Dem. Com., 1974-76, com. mem., 1974-76, 82-84; pres. bd. dirs. Presa Community Svc. Ctr., 1991—. Named Woman of Yr., Columbine Ind. News, 1975. Mem. Nat. Assn. Ch. Bus. Adminstrs. (v.p. Colo. Mile High chpt. 1981-82, sec. 1983-84), United Meth. Assn. of Ch. Bus. Adminstrs. (pres. San Antonio chpt. 1986-88, nat. bd. dirs. 1987-89). Home: 1607 Hawks Rdg San Antonio TX 78248-1705 Office: McKinley Ave United Meth Ch 2926 S Presa St San Antonio TX 78210-3995

STONE, GLORIA KLEINMANN, accountant; b. Neptune, N.J., June 29, 1959; d. Alfred Emil and Brigitta Gisela (Kuhr) Kleinmann; m. Clarence Ralph Stone, June 17, 1989. BS, Rider Coll., 1981, MBA, 1985. CPA, cert. mgmt. acct. From sr. payroll adminstr. to supr. gen. acctg. Halston Fragrances, Dayton, N.J., 1981-85; from acctg. mgr. to mgr. project & cost mgmt. Integrated Network Corp., Bridgewater, N.J., 1986—. Mem. Inst. Mgmt. Accts. Republican. Roman Catholic. Home: 17 Horseshoe Dr Flemington NJ 08822-3346

STONE, ILEANE GERTRUDE, gerontologist; b. Detroit, Jan. 5, 1933; d. Joseph and Edith (Shecter) Mosten; m. Ted Stone, Dec. 25, 1952; children: Paul, Randall, Howard. BS, Wayne State U., 1954; MA, U. Mich., 1978. Counselor-ex-inst. mentally ill elderly Well Being Svcs., Detroit, 1979-81; dir. social svcs., programs, vol. svc. St. Paul's Manor & Health Ctr., San Diego, 1981-88; dir. programs and spl. projects Villa Pomerado Health Ctr., Poway, Calif., 1988-89; dir. Elderlink adult day care Redwood Sr. Svcs., Escondido, Calif., 1989-90, dir. social svc. activities, vol. svc., 1990—; instr. gerontology Wayne County C.C., Detroit, 1980-81; cons. Nu Age Counseling Svcs., San Diego, 1984—, Dist. Atty. San Diego Spl. Team Cons., 1986-88; lectr. Soc. Clin. Social Work, San Diego, 1987, Svc. Ctr. for Blind, San Diego, 1987, Am. Assn. Homes for Aged, 1987. Author: Success with Seniors, 1989. Charter mem. City of San Diego Coun. on Aging. Mem. Am. Soc. Aging (lectr. 1985, 88), Nat. Coun. on Aging, Am. Bus. Womens Assn. Home: 17790 Fonticello Way San Diego CA 92128-1849 Office: Redwood Terr 710 W 13th Ave Escondido CA 92025-5599

STONE, JANE BUFFINGTON, artist; b. Madison, Wis., Dec. 1, 1942; adopted d. Marshall Buffington and Alvaretta (Smith) Atkinson; 1 child, Anthony Thomas. Student pub. schs., Eau Claire, Wis. Apprentice Karl Haagedorn, St. Paul, 1960-65; art instr. Head Start Program, St. Paul, 1965-67, Walker Art Inst., Mpls., 1967-69; founding mem., instr. Southside Free Sch., Mpls., 1968-69; free-lance artist Minn. and Oreg., 1965-73; art instr. Fairview Tng. Ctr., Salem, Oreg., 1974-77; founder, dir. 3 C's Sch. of Basic Carpentry, Salem, 1978-79; founder, pres. J. Stone Cards, Inc., Silverton, Oreg., 1980—. Author: Curriculum For Basic Carpentry Instruction, 1976. Newsletter editor NAACP, St. Paul, 1965-67, crisis counselor Mpls. Free Clinic, 1968-70, produce coord. Westbank Food Co-op, Mpls., 1968-70, counselor Womanspace, Salem, Oreg., 1978-80. Recipient Louie award Greeting Card Assn., N.Y.C., 1989. Mem. Am. Watercolor Assn., Oreg. Watercolor Assn. Unitarian. Office: J Stone Cards Inc One J Stone Pla Silverton OR 97381

STONE, KAREN RASMUSSEN, clinical psychologist; b. Takoma Pk., Md., Dec. 14, 1948; d. Wayne David and Marion (Fowler) Rasmussen; m. Paul Steven Stone, Sept. 13, 1975 (div. 1990); children: Katie, Kristin, Jesse; m. Michael Lee Waddell, June 26, 1993. AB magna cum laude, Harvard U., 1971; MA, Boston U., 1974, PhD, 1978. lic. psychologist, Mass. Psychology intern Beth Israel Hosp., Boston, 1974-76; teaching fellow Boston U., 1975-77; sch. psychologist Concord (Mass.) Acad., 1976-78; staff psychologist numerous instns., Mass., 1977-91; pvt. practice Marshfield, Mass., 1985-94; dir. psychol. svcs. Women's Health Ctr., Bridgewater, Mass., 1991-94; mentor Radcliffe Mentor Program, 1991-92. Mem. Harvard Schs. and Scholarship com., 1992-94. Mem. APA, Mass. Psychol. Assn. Democrat. Home: 153 Boles Rd Marshfield MA 02050-1765 Office: Women's Health Ctr 110 Main St Bridgewater MA 02324-1409

STONE, MARY ALICE, sales executive; b. Savannah, Ga., Oct. 27, 1940; d. Melvin Theodore and Alice May (Shaw) Pearson; m. Thomas Lanier Stone, Aug. 14, 1960; children: Mary Elizabeth (dec.), Thomas Lanier, Jr., Michael A., Vicki Lynn. Bookkeeper, Radix Microelectronics, Tustin, Calif., 1967-69; owner Smart Set Bookkeeping-Employment Agy., Santa Ana, Calif., 1969-72; cons. Princess House Products, Havelock, N.C., 1973-74, unit organizer, 1974-77, area organizer, New Bern, N.C. and Ga., 1977-82, sr. area organizer, Marietta, Ga., 1982-88, divisional organizer, 1989—. Philanthropic chmn. Cystic Fibrosis Found., Tustin, Calif., 1971-72; vol. Craven Cherry Point Child Devel. Ctr., Havelock, 1972, Spl. Olympics, Marietta, 1983-84; choir dir. Christ Episc. Ch., Havelock, 1973; cookie chmn. Craven Country Council Girl Scouts U.S.; active Mother's March of Dimes, 1989. Mem. NAFE, Am. Soc. Profl. Exec. Women, Beta Sigma Phi (Woman of Yr. Havelock chpt. 1973), Beta Sigma Phi Internat. (life, order of Rose Degree 1979). Avocations: Swimming; reading; dancing. Office: Princess House Products PO Box 965065 Marietta GA 30066-0002

STONE, MARY BETH See FISHTEIN, ELIZABETH

STONE, MARY OVERSTREET, newspaper editor; b. Auburndale, Fla., Mar. 17, 1924; d. LeRoy Blan and Aldah (Myrick) O.; children: Lily Sue, Mary Lou. Student, Orange County Vocat. Sch., Orlando, Fla., 1954-55, Lock Haven Art Inst., Orlando, 1960, U. Tenn., Knoxville, 1979, 89, 90. Owner/operator alteration, drape, slipcover bus., Kissimmee, Fla., 1942-50; retail sales Hunt Bros., Herzbergs, 1950-60; with Martin Marietta Co., Orlando, 1960-70; tchr. adult edn. Monroe County Vocat. Tech., Madisonville, Tenn., 1976-77, Hiwassee Coll., Madisonville, Tenn., 1977-79; corr. The Mountain Press, Sevierville, Tenn., 1981-89, E. Tenn. Bus. Jour., Knoxville, 1981-89, UPI, Knoxville, 1988-90; editor, writer Experienced Living, Sevierville, 1989—; owner, macrame designer Mary's Macrame, Sevierville, 1970-90; owner Inspiration Press, 1993—. Contbr. articles to profl. jours.; author macrame instrn. book; author: Eclectic Verse Mostly Terse, 1993. Mem. Sevier County Geriatric Screening Team, 1986—, Sevier County Coun. on Aging, 1988—. Mem. DAR, LWV, Nat. League Am. Pen Women, Am. Assn. Ret. Persons (women's initi*tive spokesperson 1991—). Republican. Episcopalian. Home: 1870 Sunnydale Dr Sevierville TN 37862-6128 Office: Experienced Living PO Box 4810 Sevierville TN 37864-4810

STONE, MILDRED MARY-ANNE, writer; b. Sturgeon Bay, Wis.; d. Peter John and Catherine (Merget) Simon; m. Grant Clifford Stone, Feb. 7, 1933 (div.); children: Kathleen, K.K. Anderson, Bonnie Melody, Linda, Rebecca. BA in Journalism, U. Wis., 1931, MD, 1938. Pvt. practice medicine and allergy Berlin (Wis.) Hosp., 1939-51; staff physician ARC Blood Bank, Madison, 1951-52; health physician, head allergy clinic VA Hosp., Madison, 1952-60; health officer City of Berlin, 1941-51; chief staff Cuba City (Wis.) Hosp., 1967-80; staff writer Wis. State Jour., Madison, 1932-33. Author: HenMedic, 50 Years in Medicine, 1989; author poetry. Mem. AMA, Wis. Med. Soc., Grant County Med. Soc. (pres. 1972-80), Nat. Assn. Family Physicians (sec.), Metro. Opera, Smithsonian Instn., Women in Communications, Nat. Audubon Soc., Sierra, Theta Sigma Phi. Democrat. Roman Catholic.

STONE, PEGGY ANN, lawyer; b. Trenton, N.J., July 3, 1957; d. Bernard and Beatrice (Mass.) S.; m. Sheldon Sarfan, Jan. 26, 1986; children: Justine Lea, Laurel Danielle. BA, U. Calif., Berkeley, 1979; JD, U. Calif., Davis, 1982. Bar: Calif. 1982. Assoc. Law Office Paul Wolf, Oakland, Calif., 1983-85; dep. pub. defender Contra Costa County, Martinez, Calif., 1985—; cons. Child and Family Therapy Ctr., Concord, Califa., 1992. Mem. Calif. Bar. Assn. Office: Contra Costa Pub Defender 3024 Willow Pass Rd Rm 100 Concord CA 94519-2552

STONE, RUBY R., state legislator; b. Portal, Ga., Feb. 6, 1924; d. Eddie Lee and Della (Taylor) Rocker; widowed; children: Dianne Carolyn Stone Milhollin, Raymond Edward Stone. Office mgr., dental asst. to Dr. Richard W. Collins, 1962-68; asst. to mgr. Am. Machine & Foundry Spl. Missile project Vandenberg AFB, 1959-60; aide to Gov. Don Samuelson, 1970-71; mem. Idaho Ho. Reps., 1971-91, chmn. local govt. com., 1991—. Active ARC, and numerous other cmty. projects and cmty. vol. orgns. Recipient Sportsmanship award Idaho State Women's Amateur Golf Tournament, 1980, Plantation Ladies Golf Assn., Outstanding Woman award, 1992; inducted into Idaho Sports Hall of Fame, 1993, Idaho New Agenda Hall of Fame, 1993. Mem. Nat. Orgn. Women Legislators, U.S. Golf Assn. (mem. jr. girls championship com. 1981), Idaho Golf Assn. (bd. dirs. 1975-87), Plantation Golf Club, Gowen Field Officers Club, Gowen Field Officers Wives Club, Daus. of Nile, El Korah Honored Ladies Club, Elks. Republican. Protestant. Home: 6604 Holiday Dr Boise ID 83709-2022

STONE, SHARON, actress; b. Meadville, Pa., Mar. 10, 1958; d. Joe and Dorothy S; m. Michael Greenburg, 1984 (div. 1987). Student, Edinboro U. Model Eileen Ford Modeling Agy. Appeared in films Stardust Memories, 1980, Deadly Blessing, 1981, Irreconcilable Differences, 1984, King Solomon's Mines, 1985, Allan Quatermain and the Lost City of Gold, 1986, Cold Steel, 1987, Police Academy 4, 1987, Action Jackson, 1988, Above the Law, 1988, Total Recall, 1990, He Said/She Said, 1991, Scissors, 1991, Basic Instinct, 1991, Where Sleeping Dogs Lie, 1992, Sliver, 1993, Intersection, 1994, The Specialist, 1994, Quick and the Dead, 1995; TV appearances include Not Just Another Affair, 1982, Bay City Blues, 1983, Calendar Girl Murders, 1984, The Vegas Strip Wars, 1984, War and Remembrance, 1988, (guest) The Larry Sanders Show, 1994; narrator: Harlow: The Blond Bombshell, 1993. Office: c/o ICM 8942 Wilshire Blvd Beverly Hills CA 90211*

STONE, SUSAN BLANKENSHIP, grants writer, public policy consultant; b. Evansville, Ind., Nov. 1, 1962; d. Sammy Delano and Shirley Elaine (Morlock) B.; m. Lucas Stone, Aug. 11, 1984. BA, Murray State U., 1984; MPA, U. Ky., 1987. Cert. probation officer, Ind. Staff asst. McCloskey for Congress, Bloomington, Ind., 1988; probation officer Monroe County Probation Dept., Bloomington, 1989-91; rsch. asst./assoc. Coun. of State Govts., Lexington, Ky., 1992-93; grants writer MDK Assocs., Inc., Lexington, 1993—; county cons. juvenile jail removal project Monroe County Probation Dept., Bloomington, 1990-91; cons. SBCS, Inc., Mt. Vernon, Ind., 1993—. Contbr. book chpt.: Intermediate Sanctions: Sentencing in the 90s, 1994; co-author: (jour.) Perspectives, 1993, (mag.) Corrections Today, 1993, also papers, tng. manuals and reports. Named Ky. State Epée champion, 1981. Buddhist. Office: MDK Assocs Inc 277 E High St Lexington KY 40507

STONE, SUSAN BROOKS, college arts administrator; b. Cleve., Dec. 10, 1940; d. Sol and Miriam (Kramer) Brooks; m. Harvey Allen Stone, Sept. 13, 1965 (div. Mar. 28, 1984) (dec.); children: Michelle Abra, Jason Adam. BS in Edn., Ohio State U., 1963. Founding mem. co., tchr. Columbus (Ohio) Jr. Theatre of the Arts, 1962; performer cmty. theatre, technician, dir., 1960-90; producer, dir., on-camera host WVIZ-TV (PBS), Cleve., 1972-73; dir. ednl. events, arts adminstr. Cuyahoga C.C., Cleve., 1984—, instr. theatre, 1984; dir. Heights Youth Theatre, Univ. Heights, Ohio, 1964-66; radio/TV voice over announcer, 1963—; freelance advt. promotions Theatre Orgn., Cleve., 1981—; bus. mgr. Cleve. Dancers, 1982-83; mem. adv. bd. Jewish Cmty. Ctr. Visual and Performing Arts, Cleve. Heights, Ohio, 1982-93, spl. events coord. cons. Mng. editor (newsletter) Nat. Assn. Jazz Educators, 1984-89 (Best in Am. 1984, 88). V.p. PTA Cleve. Heights-Univ. Heights Schs., Ohio, 1976-80; office mgr. Congl. Campaign, Cleve., 1981; pres. Heights Singers' Parents Orgn., Cleve. Heights, 1987-88. Named one of 5 disting. women in jazz edn. Arts Midwest, Mpls., 1987; cert. achievement Greater Cleve. Growth Assn., 1994. Mem. Internat. Assn. Jazz Educators. Jewish. Office: Cuyahoga CC Tri C JazzFest TH 11 2900 Community College Ave Cleveland OH 44115

STONE, SUSAN FRANCES, economics educator; b. Norristown, Pa., Mar. 5, 1963; d. James Lewis and Margaret Mary (Mulligan) S.; m. Stephen William Moscatelli, Feb. 11, 1989. Student, U. de Fribourg, Switzerland, 1983-84; BS, Drexel U., 1985, MBA, 1988. Mgmt. asst. Gen. Svcs. Adminstrn., Phila., 1987-88; bus. analyst Fin. Rsch., Inc., Ardmore, Pa., 1988-90; sr. bus. analyst HAAS Bus. Valuation Svc., Haverford, Pa., 1990—; instr. Westchester U., 1994—. Author: Valuation Strategies in Divorce, 1993; contbr. articles to profl. jours. Mem. Am. Econ. Assn., Pa. Econ. Assn., Western Econ. Assn., Am. Soc. Appraisers.

STONE, SUSAN RIDGAWAY, marketing educator; b. Coronado, Calif., Oct. 30, 1950; d. Lester Jay and Marguerite Ridgaway (King) Stone; m. Martin Zachary Sipkoff, Oct. 27, 1984; 1 child, Benjamin. AB, Wilson Coll., 1977; MBA, Shippensburg U., 1980; DBA, George Washington, U., 1992. Assoc. prof. mgmt. and mktg. Shippensburg (Pa.) U., 1983—; dir. mktg. VSP Wastewater Tech., Gettysburg, Pa., 1982; mktg. cons. Svcs. Unltd., Gettysburg, 1975—; lectr. in field. Author: (with Stephen J. Holoviak) Managing Human Productivity: People are Your Best Investment, 1987; contbr. articles to profl. jours.; asst. editor mag. USN Acad. Alumni Assn., 1973-74; pres. Shippensburg U. Press. Former land use chair League of Women Voters, Gettysburg; mem. fund raising com. for local candidates; pers. chair, bd. dirs. Survivors', Inc. Am. Mktg. Assn. fellow, 1986. Mem. Acad. Mktg. Sci., Am. Mktg. Assn., Mensa, Adams County Literacy Coun., Beta Gamma Sigma, Kappa Kappa Gamma. Republican. Episcopalian. Office: Shippensburg Univ Mgmt And Mktg Dept Shippensburg PA 17257

STOODT, BARBARA DERN, education educator, magazine editor; b. Columbus, Ohio, June 12, 1934; d. Millard Fissel and Helen Lucille (Taes) Dern; divorced; children: Linda Stoodt Neu, Susan Stoodt Price. BS in Edn., Ohio U., 1956; MA in Edn., Ohio State U., 1965; PhD, 1970; post-grad., U. Chgo., 1967. Tchr. North Charleston (S.C.) Schs., 1956-57, Cleveland Heights (Ohio) U., 1957-58, Mansfield (Ohio) Bd. Edn., 1958-59, 65-68; dir. reading, 1968; teaching assoc. Ohio State U., 1968-70; prof. edn. U. Akron, Ohio, 1970-77, U. N.C., Greensboro, 1977—. Author: Reading Instruction, 1981, 2d edit., 1989, Teaching Language Arts, 1988; co-author: Secondary School Reading Instruction, 1987, 5th edit., 1994, Riverside Reading Program. U.S. Office Edn. research grantee, 1970. Mem. Nat. Conf. on Research in English, Internat. Reading Assn. (Outstanding Dissertation award), Am. Ednl. Research Assn., Nat. Council Tchrs. English (outstanding research award 1971), Assn. for Supervision and Curriculum Devel., Assn. for Childhood Edn. Internat. Methodist. Home: 5011 Manning Dr Greensboro NC 27410-4310 Office: Learning Mag 1607 Battleground Ave Greensboro NC 27412

STOOP, NORMA MCLAIN, editor, author, photographer; b. Panama, C.Z., July 20, 1910; b. Harry Edward and Gladys (Brandon) McLain; student Penn Hall Jr. Coll., Carnegie Inst. Tech., New Sch., N.Y. U.; m. William J. Stoop, Jr., Sept. 20, 1932. Contbg. editor Dance Mag., N.Y.C., 1969-71, assoc. editor, 1971-79, sr. editor, 1979-91, contbg. editor, 1991-92; sr. editor After Dark, 1978-82, also feature writer; also photographer, theater, ballet and film critic; entertainment editor sr. edit. Sta. WNYC-AM, 1980-83; chief film critic Manhattan Arts, 1983-89, mem. editors panel Antioch U. summer writers workshop, 1988, 89, spl. guest for dialogue sessions, 1990. Mem. Poetry Soc. Am., Acad. Am. Poets, TV Acad. Arts and Scis., Overseas Press Club, Deadline Club, Sigma Delta Chi. Contbr. poems to Tex. Quar., Chgo. Rev., Plains Poetry Jour., Arts in Society, Quest, Atlantic Monthly, Puerto Del Sol, The Quarterly, Md. Poetry Rev., others, short stories to Portland Monthly, others, 1958—, essays to Book Week in N.Y. Herald Tribune; represented in Best Poems of 1973, Exhibit of Dance Photography, Harvard U., Tufts Coll., 1975, featured in 1990 Poet's Market; MacNeil Lehrer News, 1988. Recipient award Dance Tchrs. Club Boston, 1977, Eve of St. Agnes Competition award, 1993

STORB, URSULA BEATE, molecular genetics and cell biology educator; b. Stuttgart, Germany, July 6, 1936; came to U.S., 1966; d. Walter M. Stemmer and Marianne M. (Kämmerer) Nowara. MD, U. Freiburg, Fed. Republic Germany, 1960; Germany. Asst. prof. dept. microbiology U. Wash., Seattle, 1971-75, assoc. prof., 1975-81, prof., 1981-86, head. div. immunology, 1980-86; prof. dept. molecular genetics and cell biology U. Chgo., 1986—. Mem. editorial bd. Ann. Rev. Immunology, Current Opinion in Immunology, Internat. Immunology; contbr. articles to sci. jours. Grantee NIH, NSF, Am. Cancer Soc., 1973—. Fellow Am. Acad. Arts and Scis.; mem. Assn. Women in Sci., Am. Assn. Immunology, Am. Soc. Cell Biology. Office: U Chgo 920 E 58th St Chicago IL 60637-1432

STORCH, BARBARA JEAN, librarian; b. N.Y.C., Jan. 13, 1942; d. Isidore and Ruth (Goldman) Cohen; m. Fred Storch, May 24, 1964; children: Bruce F., Emily S. BA, Bklyn. Coll., 1962; MLS, L.I. Univ., 1981. Cataloger Nassau Libr. System, Uniondale, N.Y., 1981-87; head tech. svcs. West Palm Beach (Fla.) Pub. Libr., 1987—. Pres. Nassau Libr. Sys. Employees Assn., Uniondale, 1986-87; mem. pers. issues and profl. concerns com. Nassau County (N.Y.) Libr. Assn., 1986-87; chair BookFest of the Palm Beaches! Door Prize Com., Palm Beach County, Fla., 1990; mem. Epilepsy Assn. of the Palm Beaches Auction Com. Mem. ALA (new mems. round table, local arrangements com. 1994 ann. conf.), , Palm Beach County Libr. Assn. (sec. 1989-90), Fla. Libr. Assn., Fla. Pub. Libr. Assn. (chair tech. svcs. divsn. 1989-90, chair tech. svcs. civ. 1st conf. program on preservation 1990). Democrat. Jewish. Home: PO Box 3773 Boca Raton FL 33427 Office: West Palm Beach Pub Libr 100 Clematis St West Palm Beach FL 33401-5575

STORCK, LAUREN ELEANOR, psychologist. AB, Barnard Coll., 1966; PhD, CUNY, 1970. Lic. psychologist; cert. health svc. provider; chartered psychologist, U.K. Hosp. and acad. appointments N.Y.C. and London, 1975-87; pvt. practice in profl. psychol. svcs., Harvard Med. Sch., Cambridge and Everett, Mass., 1987—; clin. instr. dept. psychiatry Harvard Med. Sch., Cambridge, 1987—; chmn. continuing edn. com. Northeastern Soc. Group Psychotherapy, Boston, 1992—; cons. Day Treatment Programs, Cambridge Hosp., 1987—; cons. Whidden Hosp., Everett, Mass., 1991—. Office: PO Box 648 Cambridge MA 02238

STORER, MARYRUTH, law librarian; b. Portland, Oreg., July 26, 1953; d. Joseph William and Carol Virginia (Pearson) Storer; m. David Bruce Bailey, Jan. 1, 1981; children: Sarah, Allison. BA in History, Portland State U., 1974; JD, U. Oreg., 1977; M in Law Librarianship, U. Wash., 1978. Bar: Oreg. 1978. Assoc. law librarian U. Tenn., Knoxville, 1978-79; law librarian O'Melveny & Myers, Los Angeles, 1979-88; dir. Orange County Law Library, Santa Ana, Calif., 1988—. Mem. Am. Assn. Law Libraries, So. Calif. Assn. Law Libraries (pres. 1986-87), Coun. Calif. County Law Librs. (sec.-treas. 1990-94, pres. 1994—). Democrat. Episcopalian. Office: Orange County Law Library 515 N Flower St Santa Ana CA 92703-2304

STORM, SANDY LAMM, secondary education educator; b. Shelbyville, Ill., Aug. 6, 1949; d. Raymond Ralph and Hazel Clara (Sands) Lamm; m. David Michael Storm, Aug. 24, 1968; children: Michael Lee, Marc David, Michelle Kimberly. BS in Edn., Eastern Ill. U., 1967-70, MSEd, 1990-91. Cert. tchr. and sch. guidance, Ill. Substitute tchr. Shelby County, Shelbyville, Ill., 1989-90; home econs. tchr. Shelbyville Sch., Shelbyville, 1990—; counselor, sports cons. Human Excellence, Shelbyville, 1991—. Mem. NEA, Am. Counseling Assn., Internat. Assn. Neuro-Linguistical Programming, Ill. Edn. Assn., Phi Delta Kappa. Democrat. Home and Office: P O Box 506 1102 N Long Shelbyville IL 62565

STORRS, ELEANOR EMERETT, research institute consultant; b. Cheshire, Conn., May 3, 1926; d. Benjamin Porter and Alta Hyde (Moss) S.; m. Harry Phineas Burchfield, Jr., Nov. 29, 1963; children: Sarah Storrs, Benjamin Hyde. B.S. with distinction in Botany, U. Conn., 1948; M.S. in Biology, NYU, 1958; Ph.D. in Chemistry, U. Tex., 1967. Asst. biochemist Boyce Thompson Inst. for Plant Research, Yonkers, N.Y., 1948-62; research scientist Clayton Found. Biochem. Inst., U. Tex., Austin, 1962-65; biochemist Pesticides Research Lab., USPHS, Perrine, Fla., 1965-67; dir. dept. biochemistry Gulf South Research Inst., New Iberia, La., 1967-77; adj. prof. chemistry U. Southwestern La., Lafayette, 1974-77; research prof. biology, dir. comparative mammalogy lab. Fla. Inst. Tech., Melbourne, 1977-94, cons. on leprosy-armadillo programs, 1994—, mem. Faculty Senate, 1979-84; cons. in rehab. and prevention deformities leprosy Pan Am. Health Orgn., WHO, Venezuela, Argentina, Brazil, Mex., 1972-90; dep. v.p. Coll. Hansenology in Endemic Countries, 1980-85. Author: (with H.P. Burchfield) Biochemical Applications of Gas Chromatography, 1962, (with Burchfield, D.E. Johnson) Guide to the Analysis of Pesticide Residues, 2 vols, 1965; also articles, book chpts. NIH grantee, 1968—; Center for Disease Control grantee, 1969-73; WHO grantee, 1973-93; leprosy program grantee, 1978-93;

German Leprosy Relief Assn. grantee, 1973-78; Nat. Council Episcopal Ch. grantee, 1975-77; Brit. Leprosy Relief Assn. grantee, 1981-88; recipient plaque La. Health Dept., 1972, Distinguished Alumni award U. Conn., 1975; gold award Am. Coll. Pathologists and Am. Soc. Clin. Pathologists, 1974; Gerard B. Lambert award, spl. recognition, 1975. Fellow AAAS, N.Y. Acad. Scis.; mem. AAUW, Internat. Leprosy Assn., Am. Soc. Mammalogy (legislation and regulations com. 1983—), Am. Assn. Lab. Animal Sci. (Charles A. Griffin award 1975), Wildlife Disease Soc., East Coast Zool. Soc. (bd. dirs. 1989-92), Am. Recorder Soc., Sigma Xi. Episcopalian (vestryman). Clubs: Appalachian (Boston); Green Mountain (Bear Mountain, N.Y.); Mystik Krewe of Iberians (mem. ct. 1972, queen 1974). Home: 72 Riverview Ter Melbourne FL 32903-4640 Office: Fla Inst Tech 150 W University Box 6075 Melbourne FL 32901-6988

STORY, ELLEN, state legislator; m. Ronald Story; 2 children. BA, U. Tex.; attended, U. Wis., SUNY, Stony Brook; MA, Cambridge Coll. Asst. county coord. Family Planning Coun. Western Mass., 1973, county coord., 1974, asst. exec. dir., 1981, assoc. exec. dir., 1984—; mem. Mass. Ho. of Reps., 1992—, mem. criminal justice com., edn. com., ethics com. Founding mem. Hampshire County Human Svcs., Mass., 1974, former mem. prof. adv. com.; organizer Western Mass. Dems. and Independents for Frank Hatch for Gov., 1978; chmn. Barbara Griffith for Amherst Selectbd., 1982; coord. Evelyn Murphy for Lt. Gov., 1982; mem. Amherst Town Meeting, Mass.; former del. Women, Infants and Children Avd. Coun. Mass.; pres., bd. dirs. Hampshire County Coun. Social Agencies, Mass.; bd. dirs. Hampshire Youth 2000 Coalition; charter mem. Friends of Amherst Recreation; co-founder, dir. Concerned Citizens for Quality Edn. Recipient Spl. Recognition award Hampshire County Coun. Social Agencies, 1991. Mem. Amherst Club (sec.). Democrat. Office: Mass Ho of Reps State Capitol Boston MA 02133*

STORY, MONA DEE, artist; b. Woodward, Okla., Dec. 9, 1945; d. Garnett Leroy and Georgia Thurlene (Trego) Frye; m. Keith Leon Story; children: Tray Lee, Stacy Leigh. Grad. high sch.; student, Southwestern Okla. State U., Weatherford, 1964-66, 70-71. Free-lance artist, instr. in field Sharon, Okla., 1974—; owner Country Woodworks, Sharon, 1980—; mgr., buyer Trego's Westwear & Gifts, Woodward, Okla., 1987-93; ladies and men's clothing designer Trego's Westwear, Inc. Mfg., 1987—, v.p. design and product devel., 1993—; designer Artwear "By Mona", 1988—. One woman exhibits in mus., galleries and banks, 1977-94. Mem. Plains Indians and Pioneers Hist. Found., Woodward, 1977—, bd. dirs. 1978-82; co-chmn. Paul Laune Meml. High Sch. Western Art Competition, Woodward, 1979—; co-chmn. Woodward Spring Arts Festival, 1986. Numerous awards art competitions, 1974-86. Mem. Woodward Artisans League (sec., reporter 1976, v.p. 1977, pres. 1978-80). Democrat. Mem. Christian Ch. (Disciples of Christ). Home and Studio: Rte 1 Box 290 Sharon OK 73857

STORY, NANCY ANN, alcohol, drug counselor; b. Freeport, Ill., May 1, 1956; d. Larry Leo Folgate and Julene Helen (Appel) Knouse; children: Catherine H., Margaret A.; m. Tad Story, June, 1994. BS, No. Ill. U., 1978. Cert. drug and alcohol abuse counselor Ill. Profl. Cert. Assn., Freeport Meml. Hosp., Allied Health Profl. Recreational therapist Jane Adams Mental Health, Freeport, Ill., 1980-85; case mgr. Jane Adams Mental Health, Freeport, 1985-88; alcohol and drug abuse counselor Sojourn, Inc., Freeport, 1988-94; dual diagnosis specialist Rock County Human Svcs., Beloit, Wis., 1994—. Bd. dirs., sec. ARC, Freeport, 1991—; bd. dirs. Single Parents Mentor Program of Martin Luther King Ctr., Freeport, 1993—; memtor Project Prosper Freeport Twp., 1992—; active Single Parents in Rewards Affirming Life. Office: Cmty Support Program 504 W Grand Ave Beloit WI 53511

STOTLER, ALICEMARIE HUBER, federal judge; b. Alhambra, Calif., May 29, 1942; d. James R. and Loretta M. Huber; m. James Allen Stotler, Sept. 11, 1971. BA, U. So. Calif., 1964, JD, 1967. Bar: Calif. 1967, U.S. Dist. Ct. (no. dist.) Calif. 1967, U.S. Dist. Ct. (cen. dist.) Calif. 1973, U.S. Supreme Ct., 1976; cert. criminal law specialist. Dep. Orange County Dist. Atty.'s Office, 1967-73; mem. Stotler & Stotler, Santa Ana, Calif., 1973-76, 83-84; judge Orange County Mcpl. Ct., 1976-78, Orange County Superior Ct., 1978-83, U.S. Dist. Ct. (cen. dist.) Calif., L.A., 1984—; assoc. dean Calif. Trial Judges Coll., 1982; lectr., panelist, numerous orgns.; standing com. on rules of practice and procedure U.S. Jud. Conf., 1991—, chair, 1993—; mem. exec. com. 9th Cir. Jud. Conf., 1989-93, Fed. State Jud. Coun., 1989-93, jury com., 1990-92, planning com. for Nat. Conf. on Fed.-State Judicial Relationships, Orlando, 1991-92, planning com for We. Regional Conf. on State-Fed. Judicial Relationships, Stevens, Wash., 1992-93; chair dist. ct. symposium and jury utilization Ctrl. Dist. Calif., 1985, chair atty. liason, 1989-90, chair U.S. Constitution Bicentennial com., 1986-91, chair magistrate judge com.; mem. State Adv. Group. on Juvenile Justice and Delinquency Prevention, 1983-84, Bd. Legal Speciliazations Criminal Law Adv. Commn., 1983-84, victim/witness adv. com. Office Criminal Justice Planning, 1980-83, U. So. Calif. Bd. Councilors, 1993—; active team in tng. Leukemia Soc. Am., 1993. Winner Hale Moot Ct. Competition, State of Calif., 1967; named Judge of Yr., Orange County Trial Lawyers Assn., 1978, Most Outstanding Judge, Orange County Bus. Litigation Sect., 1990; recipient Franklin G. West award Orange County Bar Assn., 1985. Mem. ABA (jud. adminstrn. divsn.and litigation sect. 1984—, nat. conf. fed. trial judges com. on legis. affairs 1990-91), Am. Law Inst., Am. Judicature Soc., Fed. Judges Assn. (bd. dirs. 1989-92), Nat. Assn. Women Judges, U.S. Supreme Ct. Hist. Soc., Ninth Cir. Dist. Judges Assn., Calif. Supreme Ct. Hist. Soc., Orange County Bar Assn. (mem. numerous coms., Franklin G. West award 1984), Calif. Judges Assn. (mem. com. on judicial coll. 1978-80, com. on civil law and procedure 1980-82, Dean's coll. curriculum commn. 1981), Calif. Judges Found. Office: US Dist Ct PO Box 12339 751 W Santa Ana Blvd Santa Ana CA 92701-4509

STOTLER, EDITH ANN, grain company executive; b. Champaign, Ill., Oct. 11, 1946; d. Kenneth Wagner and Mary (Odebrecht) S. Student, Mary Baldwin Coll., 1964-66; BA, U. Ill., 1968. Asst. v.p. Harris Trust and Savs. Bank, Chgo., 1969-83; mgr. Can. Imperial Bank of Commerce, Chgo., 1983, sr. mgr., 1983-85, asst. gen. mgr. group head, 1985-88, v.p., dir. utilities, 1988-90; ptnr. Stotler Grain Co., Champaign, Ill., 1990—; pres. Homer Grain Co., 1990—; bd. dirs., audit com., exec. compensation com., nominating com. Southeastern Mich. Gas Enterprises, Inc. Mem. investment com. 4th Presbyn. Ch.; past pres. liberal arts and scis. constituent bd. U. Ill., mem. pres.' coun. Mem. U. Ill. Found., Champaign Country Club, Art Club. Home: 900 N Lake Shore Dr Apt 2106 Chicago IL 60611-1523

STOTT, DIANA ELLEN, social services advocate; b. Cedarville, Calif., Apr. 14, 1934; d. I.A. and Lois A. (Tyeryar) Barber; m. Norman K. Stott, June 29, 1956; children: Charlotte, Russell. BA, U. Calif., Berkeley, 1956, postgrad. Cert. pre-sch., elem., adult edn. Tchr. Tsuda Sch., Tokyo, 1956, Colegio Americano, Durango, Mex., 1968, Mt. Diablo Schs., Concord, Calif., 1964-74; founder, owner Sunbonnet Sue Templates, Willits, Calif., 1970-89; owner, operator 3T Sheep Ranch, Willits, 1974-89; founder, dir. Animal Crackers PreSch., Willits, 1979-89; outreach advocate CATRL, Kimberling City, Mo., 1992—; co-founder Harbor Lights Shelter Svcs., Stone County, Mo., 1994; mem. com. Mo. Coalition Against Domestic Violence, 1992—; sch./community organizer for drug and alcohol prevention, 1993—. Editor newsletter The Quilting Room, 1974-80. Patron Friends of the Libr., Kimberling City, Mo., 1989-94; legis. chmn. Bus. & Profl. Women, Tri-Lakes Area, 1993-94; publicity chmn. Welcome Wagon, Tri-Lakes Area, 1992. Recipient quilting awards Guild of Quilters, 1975-76, Premium Wool award Mendocino County Fair, 1986-88. Mem. AAUW (founder, chmn. Tri-Lakes 1993-94), Kimberling Area C. of C. (rep. 1993-94), Phi Mu, Pi Lambda Theta. Mem. Unity Ch. Address: PO Box 488 Kimberling City MO 65686 Home: # 6 Stone Edge Rd Kimberling City MO 65686 Office: Christian Assocs of Table Rock Lake Country Club Shopping Ctr Kimberling City MO 65686

STOUDEMIRE, JANICE ANNE, accounting educator, accountant; b. Bloomsburg, Pa., May 9, 1955; d. Thomas H. and Nancy J. (Brunsetter) Anthony; m. Thomas Archie Stoudemire, Aug. 19, 1978; children: Jessica-Anne, Ryan. BS in Accountancy, Va. Commonwealth U., 1980; M in Acctg., U. S.C., 1987. CPA. Auditor Finch, Hamilton, Oxner, CPAs, Columbia, S.C., 1981-85; instr. Midlands Tech. Coll., Columbia, 1985—. Recipient Pres. Achievement award Inst. Mgmt. Accts., 1989, 90, 91, S.C. Ho. of Reps. citation, 1991; named Master Tchr. by Nat. Inst. Staff Orgn. Devel., 1989. Mem. AICPAs, S.C. Assn. CPAs, S.C. Tech. Edn. Assn. (Educator of Yr. 1991-92), Inst. Mgmt. Accts. (dir. acad. rels. 1993-94, treas. 1988-89, v.p. comm. 1987-88). Office: Midlands Tech Coll PO Box 2408 Columbia SC 29202

STOUFER, RUTH HENDRIX, community volunteer; b. Pitts., June 21, 1916; d. Walter Willits and Frances (Ponbeck) Hendrix; m. William Kimball Stoufer, Sept. 8, 1937 (dec.); children: Walter Hendrix, Frances Elizabeth Stoufer Waller. BS, Iowa State U., 1937. Trustee Marcus J. Lawrence Meml. Hosp., 1989—; devel. chairperson Sedona-Verde Valley Am. Heart Assn., 1988-91; mem. adv. bd. L.A. chpt. Freedom's Found., 1965-78; mem. coord. med. adv. bd. U. Ariz., 1986—; founding chairperson Muses of the Mus. No. Ariz., 1984-85, pres., 1986-87, mem. Sinagua Soc., 1983—; bd. dirs. Nat. Charity League, L.A., 1963, Found. for Children, L.A., 1964, 65, 66; pres. Panhellenic adv. bd. U. So. Calif., 1964; key adv. U. So. Calif. chpt. Beta Alpha of Gamma Phi Beta, 1960-63. Named Woman of Yr., Inter-city Coun., Gamma Phi Beta, 1963. Home: 87 Doodlebug Knoll Sedona AZ 86336-6422

STOUFFER, NANCY KATHLEEN, publishing company executive; b. Hershey, Pa., Feb. 14, 1951; d. William Lawrence Sweeny O'Brian and Edna Luttrell; m. David Joel Stouffer, July 19, 1980; children: Jennifer Belle, Vance David. Pres. André Pub. Co., Inc., Camp Hill, Pa., 1985-88; pres., chmn. B.C.I., Camp Hill, Pa., 1988-90; v.p. R & D E.S.P. Inc., N.Y.C., 1989-90; v.p. corp. planning Nu-Tek Labs., Hershey, Pa.; exec. rschr Com. on Advanced Studies in Learning Disabilities Med. and Profl., SPECTRA. Contbr. articles on dyslexia and learning disabilities to popular mags.; author children's books; developer of Reading Genie, EZ read program. Republican.

STOUGHT, CYNTHIA MARIE, psychiatric nurse; b. Connellsville, Pa., Jan. 24, 1953; d. Matthew J. and Veronica Marie (Hertznell) Kremposky; m. Richard C. Stought, Apr. 26, 1975; children: Adam, Jeffrey. Diploma, Shadyside Hosp., 1973; BSN, Lebanon Valley Coll., 1981, student, 1993—. RN, Pa.; cert. psychiat./mental health nurse. Staff nurse Holy Spirit Hosp. Community Mental Health Ctr., Camp Hill, Pa., 1977-94; case mgr. State Employee Assistance Program, 1994—.

STOUT, JUANITA KIDD, judge; b. Wewoka, Okla., Mar. 7, 1919; d. Henry Maynard and Mary Alice (Chandler) Kidd; m. Charles Otis Stout, June 23, 1942. BA, U. Iowa, 1939; JD, Ind. U., 1948, LLM, 1954; LLD (hon.), Ursinus Coll., 1965, Ind. U., 1966, Lebanon Valley Coll., 1969, Drexel U., 1972, Rockford (Ill.) Coll., 1974, U. Md., 1980, Roger Williams Coll., 1984, Morgan State U., 1985, Russell Sage Coll., 1966, Fisk U., 1988, Del. State Coll., 1990. Bar: D.C. 1950, Pa. 1954. Tchr. pub. schs. Seminole and Sand Springs, Okla., 1939-42; tchr. Fla. A&M U., Tallahassee, 1949, Tex. So. U., Houston, 1949; adminstrv. asst. to judge U.S. Ct. Appeals (3d cir.), Phila., 1950-54; pvt. practice law Turner & Stout, Phila., 1954-55; chief of appeals Dist. Atty.'s Office City of Phila., 1955-59, judge mcpl. ct., 1959-69; judge Ct. Common Pleas, Phila., 1969-88, sr. judge, 1989—; justice Supreme Ct. Pa., Phila., 1988-89; sitting as sr. judge Ct. Common Pleas. Recipient Jane Addams medal Rockford Coll., 1966, Disting. Svc. award U. Iowa, 1974, MCP/Gimbel award for humanitarianism, 1988, 89—, John Peter Zenger award John Peter Zenger Soc., 1994; named to Hall of Fame of Okla., Okla Heritage Soc., 1981; named Disting. Dau. of Pa., 1988, Disting. Alumni Svc. award Ind. U., Bloomington, 1992. Mem. ABA, Pa. Bar Assn., Phila. Bar Assn. (Sandra Day O'Connor award 1994), Nat. Assn. Women Judges, Nat. Assn. Women Lawyers. Democrat. Episcopalian. Home: 1919 Chestnut St Apt 2805 Philadelphia PA 19103-3451

STOUT, MAYE ALMA, educator; b. Reliance, S.D., Mar. 3, 1920; d. Jesse Wilbur and Susie Maude (Fletcher) Moulton; m. Dennis William Stout, Jan. 6, 1943; children: Perry Wilbur, David Jay. BA, Dakota Wesleyan U., Mitchell, S.D., 1969. Tchr. Rural Lyman County Sch., Iona/Oacoma, S.D., 1939-42, Vivian (S.D.) Pub. Sch., 1942, Rural Lyman County Sch., Reliance, S.D., 1944-45, Reliance Cons. Dist., 1945-46, 49-51, Ft. Pierre (S.D.) Ind. Sch. Dist., 1954-67, Kadoka (S.D.) Ind. Sch., 1967-82; ret. Asst. editor: Jackson/Washabaugh County History 2, 1989; contbr. articles to publications. Pres. Kadoka Community Betterment Assn., 1987. Mem. Am. Legion Aux. (dist. pres. 1985-89, chmn. com. Dept. Fgn. Rels. 1990-91, dept. chmn. constitution and by-laws com. 1992-93). Republican. Methodist. Address: 6 Poplar St W Po Box 231 Kadoka SD 57543

STOUTENBURG, JANE SUE WILLIAMSON, nursing educator, community health nurse; b. Davenport, Iowa, Mar. 10, 1949; d. George B. and Hazel Elaine (Kline) Williamson; m. Noel Wayne Stoutenburg, Aug. 25, 1979 (div. 1995); 1 child, Karen Elaine. Student, Black Hawk Coll., 1970; BA, Augustana Coll., 1973, BS, 1975; ADN with honors, Elgin (Ill.) Community Coll., 1987. RN, Ill. Rsch. tech. Rush-Preby. St. Luke's Med. Ctr., Chgo., 1974-75; acct. supr., pvt. investigator bodyguard Per Mar Security Inc., Davenport, Iowa, 1975-77; pre-trial release investigator 7th Judicial Ct. Dist., Davenport, Iowa, 1976-77; area med. rep. Bristol Labs., Syracuse, N.Y., 1977-80; dir. safety tng. Zee Med., Irvine, Calif., 1981-83; ednl. specialist Mid-Am. Chpt. ARC, Chgo., 1983-86; tng. safety cons. Lake County Rescue, Barrington, Ill., 1981—; nurse cons., instr., 1st aide, CPR Buehler YMCA, Palatine, Ill., 1985-91; emergency med. svcs. coord. Robbins Vol. Fire Dept., 1985—; camp nurse Boy Scouts Am., Camp Big Timber, Ill. Past bd. dirs. 1st aid program Barrington Area Devel. Coun., Lake County Fire Rescue; leader Girl Scout Troop 369. Recipient Disting. Svc. award ARC, Jaycees; named Ill. Emergency Med. Technician of Yr., 1989-90, Vol. of Yr. N.W. Suburban Chgo. Vol. Bur., 1993. Mem. ASTD, Am. Soc. Safety Engrs., Trauma Soc. Am., Am. Acad. Sci., Internat. Sci. Fire Sci. Instrs., Ill. Acad. Sci., Rescue Emergency Specialists Assn., Ill. Emergency Med. Tech. Assn., Prehosp. Care Providers Ill., Illiana Club Traditional Jazz, PEO, Alpha Phi Omega (Disting. Svc. award), Phi Theta Kappa (Disting. Alumni Key). Office: 618 S Northwest Hwy Ste 213 Barrington IL 60010

STOUT-PIERCE, SUSAN, marketing specialist; b. Denver, June 6, 1954; d. Joseph Edward and Esther Mae (Miller) Hull; m. Jerry Lee Stout, Nov. 3, 1979 (div. Aug. 1984); m. Gary Myron Pierce, Nov. 21, 1987. AS, Denver Community Coll., 1975; BS, Met. State Coll., 1986. Cert. Radiologic Technologist, Calif., Am. Registry Radiologic Technologists. Radiologic technologist The Swedish Med. Ctr., Englewood, Colo., 1975-79, The Minor Emergency Clinic, Lakewood, Colo., 1979-80, The Children's Hosp., Denver, 1980-86, Merit Peralta Med. Ctr., Oakland, Calif., 1986-87, Am. Shared Hosp. Svcs., Oakland, 1987, HCA South Austin (Tex.) Med. Ctr., 1987-88, U. Calif., San Francisco, 1988-89; clin. imaging specialist OEC-Diasonics, Salt Lake City, 1989-92; software applications specialist Cemax, Inc., Fremont, Calif., 1992-93; mktg. specialist ADAC SD & G Healthcare Systems, Inc., Milpitas, Calif., 1993—. Active NOW. Mem. NAFE, Am. Bus. Women's Assn., Am. Soc. Radiologic Technologists. Home: 264 Rachael Pl Pleasanton CA 94566

STOVALL, CARLA JO, state official, lawyer; b. Hardner, Kans., Mar. 18, 1957; d. Carl E. and Juanita Jo (Ford) S. BA, Pittsburg (Kans.) State U., 1979; JD, U. Kans., 1982. Bar: Kans. 1982, U.S. Dist. Ct. Kans. 1982. Pvt. practice, Pittsburg, 1982-85; atty. Crawford County, Pittsburg, 1984-88; gov. Kans. Parole Bd., Topeka, 1988-94; attorney general State of Kansas, Topeka, 1995—; lectr. law Pittsburg State U. 1982-84; pres. Gilston Internat. Mktg., Inc., 1988—. Bd. dirs., sec. Pittsburg Family YMCA, 1983-88. Mem. ABA, Kans. Bar Assn., Crawford County Bar Assn. (sec. 1984-85, v.p. 1985-86, pres. 1986-87), Kans. County and Dist. Attys. Assn., Nat. Coll. Dist. Attys., Pittsburg State U. Alumni Assn. (bd. dirs. 1983-88), Pittsburg Area C. of C. (bd. dirs. 1983-85, Leadership Pitts. 1984), Bus. and Profl. Women Assn. (Young Careerist 1984), Kans. Assn. Commerce and Industry (Leadership Kans. 1983), AAUW (bd. dirs. 1983-87). Republican. Methodist. Home: 3561 SW Mission Ave Topeka KS 66614-3637 Office: Atty Gen Office Jud Bldg 301 W Tenth St Topeka KS 66612-1220

STOVER, ELLEN SIMON, health scientist, psychologist; b. Bklyn., Nov. 21, 1950; d. Ralph and Charlotte (Tulchin) Simon; m. Alan B. Stover, June 3, 1973; children: Elena Randall Simon, Randall Alan Simon, Samantha Anne Simon. BA with honors, U. Wis., 1972; PhD, Catholic U., 1978. Cons. NIMH, Rockville, Md., 1972-74, spl. asst. to assoc. dir. extramural programs, 1976-77, chief, small grants program, 1977-79, asst., acting & chief rsch. resources br., 1980-85, dep. dir., div. basic scis., 1985-88, dir., office of AIDS programs, 1988—; exec. sec., drug abuse rsch. rev. com. Nat. Inst. on Drug Abuse, Rockville, 1974-76. Recipient Superior Svc. award Pub. Health Svc., 1987, 92, 93. Mem. APA, Am. Psychol. Assn., AIDS Rsch. NIH (co-chair Behavioral Coord. com.). Office: NIMH 5600 Fishers Ln # 10-75 Rockville MD 20857-0001

STOWE, CAROL ANN, education educator; b. Evanston, Ill., Nov. 25, 1951; d. Irwin and Albina (Podstupka) Orzech; m. Timothy J. Stowe, July 10, 1971; children: Elspeth Liane, Alyssa Joy, Abaigeal Louise. BA, Nat. Coll. Edn., Evanston, 1983, MSEd, 1987; PhD, Northwestern U., 1994. Cert. elem. tchr., gen. adminstr., early childhood tchr., Ill. Tchr. Ctr. for Life, Palatine, Ill., 1978-83; dir. learning resource ctr. Creative Children's Acad., Arlington Heights, Ill., 1983-84; adminstr. Spectrum Ednl. Ct., Palatine, 1985-87; adj. faculty Ctr. for Gifted, Nat. Coll. Edn., Evanston, 1985-89; asst. dir. ctr. ednl. rsch. and svcs. Nat. Coll. Edn., 1988-90; grad. asst. Northwestern U., Evanston, 1989-91, rsch. asst., 1990-94, mgr. tchr. certification, 1991-92, instr., 1992-94; mem. adj. faculty Nat.-Louis U., Evanston, 1993-94; asst. prof. edn. Nat.-Louis U., Wheeling, Ill., 1994—; advisor Golden Apple Found. for Excellence in Tchg., Chgo., 1990-93; cons. Chgo. Found. for Edn., 1990—. Contbr. articles to profl. jours. Mem. AAUW, ASCD, Am. Ednl. Rsch. Assn., Am. Ednl. Studies Assn., Assn. for Edn. Young Children, Assn. for Childhood Edn. Internat., Soc. for Rsch. in Child Devel., Phi Delta Kappa. Home: 514 W Center Rd Palatine IL 60074-1020 Office: Nat-Louis U Interdisciplinary Studies 1000 Capitol Dr Wheeling IL 60090

STOWE, MADELEINE, actress; b. L.A., Aug. 18, 1958; m. Brian Benben. Films: Stakeout, 1987, Worth Winning, 1989, Revenge, 1990, The Two Jakes, 1990, Closetland, 1991, Unlawful Entry, 1992, The Last of the Mohicans, 1992, Another Stakeout, 1993, Short Cuts, 1993, China Moon, 1993, Blink, 1994, Bad Girls, 1994; TV movies: The Gangster Chronicles: An American Story, The Nativity, Beulah Land, Black Orchid (miniseries). Office: c/o UTA 9560 Wilshire Blvd 5th Floor Beverly Hills CA 90212*

STOWELL, MARGARET CROSS, chemist, ski instructor; b. Evanston, Ill., Aug. 2, 1945; d. Robert Patterson and Harriet Donna (Walker) C.; m. Channing Stowell III, Aug. 19, 1967 (div. Mar. 1985); children: Julia Nash, Channing Werner. BA, Wellesley Coll., 1967; postgrad., Polytechnic Inst. Bklyn., 1967-69; MS in Edn., No. Ill. U., 1983. Cert. level I profl. Ski Instr. Am. Chemistry and math. tchr. Stevenson H.S., Prarie View, Ill., 1983-84; chemistry and phys. sci. tchr. Barrington (Ill.) H.S., 1984-86; chemistry, physics and phys. sci. tchr. Hampshire (Ill.) H.S., 1986-87; chemist Akzo Chems., Inc., McCook, Ill., 1987-90; scientist Sandoz Agro, Inc., Des Plaines, Ill., 1990—. Editor: Density Matrix Theory, 1992. Mem. Am. Chem. Soc. (dir. local Chgo. chpt. 1992-94, house com. 1993-95, membership affairs com. 1991-94), Soc. Applied Spectroscopy, Madison-Chgo.-Milw. Mass. Spectroscopy Discussion Group. Home: 605 S Lill St Barrington IL 60010 Office: Sandoz Agro Inc 1300 E Touhy Ave Des Plaines IL 60018

STOWELL, PENELOPE MARY, nursing administrator, community health nurse; b. Warsaw, N.Y., Aug. 17, 1941; d. Charles Edward and Leona Cecelia (Hawkins) Powers; children: Scott Edward Stowell, Holly Jean Stowell. Diploma in nursing, U. Rochester, 1962; BSN, Fla. So. Coll. Coord. community edn. Mid Fla. Home Health Svcs., Inc., Winter Haven, 1989-90; asst. dir. nursing Meridian Nursing Ctr., Lakeland, Fla., 1990-94, dir. nursing, 1995—.

STOWERS, NELL LOUGENE (GENIE STOWERS), political scientist, educator; b. Huntington, W.Va., May 6, 1957; d. Bernard Lucian and Camille Katherine (Taylor) S. BA in Urban Studies, U. Fla., 1979; MPA in Environ. Growth Mgmt., Fla. Atlantic U., 1980; PhD in Polit. Sci., Fla. State U., 1987. Econ. devel. planning intern Planning Dept., Palm Beach County, Fla., 1980; program analyst HUD, Washington, 1980-81; rsch. assoc. polit. sci. Ariz. State U., 1981-82; rsch. assoc. policy scis. Fla. State U., 1982-86; asst. prof. dept. polit. sci. and pub. affairs U. Ala., Birmingham, 1986-91, dir. Women's Studies Program, 1989-91; asst. prof. pub. adminstrn. San Francisco State U., 1991-93, assoc. prof. pub. adminstrn., 1993—; cons./expert witness State of Fla., others, 1984—; chair exhibits com. S.E. Conf. Pub. Adminstrn., 1988; spl. cons. San Francisco Urban Inst., 1992—, chair colloquia com., 1993—; active San Francisco Urban Inst. Exec. Com., 1993—, sexual harassment com. Co-author: Big City Governing and Fiscal Choices, Big City Politics Revisited, Administration and Social Work, Research in Micropolitics, Vol. 11; author: Ethnic Groups, Public Budgeting and Finance. Bd. dirs., treas., chair fin. and adminstrv. policies com., WOMAN, Inc., 1992-94; mem. personnel com. Am. Friends Svc. Com., Pacific Mountain Region, 1992—; mem. Revenues Enhancement Working Group, Mayor's Task Force on the Fiscal Crisis, 1993; chief acct. Expert Rating Panel, Jefferson County, Ala. Personnel Bd., 1991; analyst United Way Task Force on AIDS survey of Agy. AIDS Policy Efforts, United Way of Cen. Ala., 1991; numerous other panels and coms. Recipient Faculty Affirmative Action grant, San Francisco State U., 1991-92, 93-94, faculty rsch. grant summer stipend, 1992-93, Am. Polit. Sci. Assn. Rsch. Grant award, 1988, grad. assistantships, Fla. State U., 1982-86; named to Outstanding Young Women of Am., 1979, 86; recipient Hubert Humphrey, Jr. Young Dem. of Yr. Community Svc. award, 1979, others. Mem. Am. Soc. Pub. Adminstrn. (nat. coun. 1994—, bd. mem. Bay area chpt. 1992—), Am. Polit. Sci. Assn., U. Fla. Alumnae Assn., Fla. Atlantic U. Alumnae Assn., Fla. State U. Alumnae Assn., Fla. Blue Key, Omicron Delta Kappa, Gamma Sigma Sigma. Democrat. Mem. Soc. of Friends. Office: San Francisco State U Pub Adminstrn Program 1600 Holloway Ave San Francisco CA 94132

STRAAYER, CAROLE KATHLEEN, elementary education educator; b. Jackson, Mich., Jan. 4, 1934; d. Joseph and Maude Vivian (Whitney) Kerr; m. Richard Lee Straayer, Feb. 1, 1958; children: Steven Jay, Susan Kay Straayer Maxson. A, Jackson Community Coll., Mich., 1953; BS, Ea. Mich. u., 1957, MA, 1961. Cert. elem. tchr., Mich. Tchr. Napoleon (Mich.) Sch. Dist., 1954-56, Waterford (Mich.) Twp. Sch. Dist., 1957, Jackson (Mich.) Pub. Schs., 1957—. Mem. choir 1st Presbyn. Ch., Jackson, 1983—. Jackson Citizen Patriot scholar, 1971. Mem. NEA, AAUW (group leader 1989-92), Mich. Assn. Supervision and Curriuclum Devel. (region 3 rep. 1989-90), Mich. Edn. Assn. (ret.), Jackson Edn. Assn. (blg. rep., chairperson tenure com. 1974-80, mem. negotiating team 1995), Jackson/Hillsdale Profl. Devel. (rep. 1988-90), Delta Kappa Gamma (Beta Beta chpt. pres. 1986-88). Home: 2220 Pioneer Dr Jackson MI 49201-8900

STRACHAN, GLADYS, executive director; b. N.Y.C., Dec. 10, 1929; d. Jacob Allen and Annie Mae (Alston) McClendon; m. Eugene S. Callender (div. 1963); 1 child, Renee Denise; m. John R. Strachan (dec. 1982). Student, NYU, 1947-49. Dep. asst. Presbyn. Ch. of East Africa, Nairobi, Kenya, 1964-67; assoc. for women's program Presbyn. Ch. of U.S., N.Y.C., 1970-83; exec. United Presbyn. Women, N.Y.C., 1983—; cons. Peace Corps, Nairobi, 1964-67, Operation Crossroads Africa, Nairobi, 1964-67, Afro-Am. Ednl. Inst., Teaneck, N.J., 1977-79, various women's orgns. in Asia, Australia, Europe, Africa. V.p. Addicts Rehab. Ctr. Bd., N.Y.C., 1957—; mem. N.Y. Coalition of 100 Black Women, N.Y.C., 1972—; sec. Harlem Dowling Children's Svc. Bd., N.Y.C., 1983—; bd. dirs., treas. Bread for the World, Washington, 1983—. Recipient Cert. of citation borough pres. N.Y.C., 1977, Harlem Peacemaking award Harlem Peacemaking Com., 1983. Office: Presbyn Women 100 Witherspoon St Louisville KY 40202-1396

STRACK, ALISON MERWIN, neurobiologist; b. Midland, Mich., Apr. 19, 1963; d. William James and Alice (Armstrong) S. BS, U. Mich., 1985; PhD, Washington U., St. Louis, 1990. Postdoctoral fellow U. Calif.-San Francisco Sch. Medicine, 1990—. Contbr. articles to profl. jours. Postdoctoral grantee Am. Heart Assn., affiliate, 1993. Mem. Soc. Neurosci. Office: U Calif-San Francisco Dept Physiology 513 Parnassus Ave Box 0444 San Francisco CA 94143-0444

STRADA, CHRISTINA BRYSON, educator, librarian; b. Dunoon, Argyll, Scotland; d. Alexander Paul and Margaret (Spencer) Bryson; m. Joseph Anthony Strada; children: Michael, David, Elaine, Mary Margaret. AB, SUNY, Fredonia, 1968, MS, 1970; MLS, U. Buffalo, 1973. Library media specialist. Tchr. English Dunkirk (N.Y.) High Sch., 1969-70, Cardinal Mindzenty High Sch., Dunkirk, 1970-71; tchr. English Lake Shore Cen.

High Sch., Angola, N.Y., 1971-72, librarian, tchr., 1973-77; library dir. Darwin R. Barker Library and Mus., Fredonia, 1977-86; tchr., libr. Cassadaga (N.Y.) Valley Sch. Dist., Fredonia, 1990—; instr. English composition, English lit., libr. rsch. Empire State Coll. N.Y., State Univ. Coll., Fredonia; cons. Friends of Barker Library and Mus., 1986—. Author short stories. Organizer Fredonia Hist. Preservation Soc., 1986—. Mem. N.Y. state Library Assn., N.Y. State Tchr. Assn., AAUW (chmn. telephone and reservations com. 1969—), LWV, Fredonia Shakespeare Club (v.p. 1988-89), Zonta Internat. (corr. sec., membership chmn. 1981-82). Republican. Roman Catholic. Home: 15 Carol Ave Fredonia NY 14063-1207

STRAETER, JANE L., public relations executive; b. St. Louis, Dec. 9, 1919; d. Michael James and Inez Celeste (Howe) Kenney; m. Aug. 18, 1940 (dec. Dec. 1967); children: Terry A., Theodore A. Grad., Miss Hickey's Bus. Sch.; student, Columbia U., Washington U., St. Louis. Model Major Levy Modeling Agy., St. Louis, 1938-42; campaign organizer Muscular Dystrophy Assn., St. Louis, 1950; program dir. Am. Cancer Soc., St. Louis, 1959-63; pub. rels. dir. Goodwill Industries, St. Louis, 1963-67; asst. dir. Mayor's Coun. on Youth, St. Louis, 1967-68; community rels. dir. St. Mary's Health Ctr., St. Louis, 1968-76; coord. St. Louis Variety Club, St. Louis, 1968-89; exec. dir. Lifeline, St. Louis, 1976-78; dir. pub. rels. DePaul Health Ctr., St. Louis, 1978-83; freelance pub. rels. exec. St. Louis, 1990—; instr. workshops Women's Advt. Club, St. Louis, 1964-77; conv. leader Hosp. Assn., Chgo., 1969-79. Contbr. articles to profl. jours. Bd. dirs. Mo. Hosp. Assn. Pub. Rels. Assn., 1970-72, Am. Hosp. Assn. Pub. Rels. Assn., 1974-75, St. Louis Kidney Found., 1977-78, Older Women's League, St. Louis, 1989-90, Met. St. Louis Press Club, sec., 1970-78, UN St. Louis, 1986-90; pres., founder Community Rels. Assn., St. Louis; pres. Hosp. Pub. Rels. Assn. St. Louis, 1973; coord. Cash for Kids St. Louis Variety Club, 1980-85; cons. USO, St. Louis, 1992-94, vol. svc. cons., 1993-94; bd. dirs. Midtown Arts Ctr., 1992-94. Fellow Nat. Assn. Pub. Rels. Dirs. Home: 13018 Geranium Ct Saint Louis MO 63146-4328

STRAHAN, JULIA CELESTINE, electronics company executive; b. Indpls., Feb. 10, 1938; d. Edgar Paul Pauley and Pauline Barbara (Myers) Shawver; m. Norman Strahan, Oct. 2, 1962 (div. 1982); children: Daniel Keven, Natalie Kay. Grad. high sch., Indpls. With EG&G/Energy Measurements, Inc., Las Vegas, Nev., 1967—; sect. head EG&G Co., 1979-83, mgr. electronics dept., 1984—. Recipient award Am. Legion, 1952, Excellence award, 1986. Mem. NAFE, Am. Nuclear Soc. (models and mentors), Internat. Platform Assn. Home: 5222 Stacey Ave Las Vegas NV 89108-3078 Office: EG&G PO Box 1912 Las Vegas NV 89125-1912

STRAHLER, VIOLET RUTH, educational consultant; b. Dayton, Ohio, Sept. 30, 1918; d. Ezra F. and Bertha (Daniels) S. A.B. magna cum laude, Wittenberg U., 1944; M.A., Miami U., Ohio, 1959; Ed.D., Ind. U., 1972; L.H.D. (hon.), Wittenberg U., 1986. Cert. tchr., supt., Ohio. Tchr. Miamisburg Pub. Schs., Ohio, 1944-51; tchr., counselor Dayton Pub. Schs., 1952-66, supr. sci. and math. curriculum, 1967-72, acting asst. supt. curriculum, 1972-73, exec. dir. curriculum services, 1973-85; instr. U. Dayton, Miami U., 1959-74; ednl. cons.; supervisor student tchrs., U. Dayton, 1986—. Author and co-author 23 textbooks, lab. guides; editor newsletter Ohio Jr. Acad. Sci., 1950-52; contbr. articles to profl. jours. Mem. Dayton/Montgomery County Arson Task Force; trustee, life mem. Dayton Mus. Natural History, Honor Seminars of Met. Dayton. Ford Found. fellow, 1952-53; chmn. staff/parish relations com. South Park United Meth. Ch., 1987-90, chair adminstrv. coun., lay leader, 1991-94. Mem. Am. Assn. Sch. Adminstrs., Buckeye Assn. Sch. Adminstrs. (life), Assn. Supervision and Curriculum Devel., Am. Chem. Soc., Nat. Sci. Tchrs. Assn. (life), Altrusa Internat. (pres. DAyton chpt. 1981-83), Engrs. Club of Dayton, Phi Delta Kappa, Delta Kappa Gamma (pres. local chpt. 1983-85). Methodist. Home: 5340 Brendonwood Ln Dayton OH 45415-2831 Office: U Dayton Dept Tchr Edn Chaminade Hall 300 College Park Dayton OH 45469-0001

STRAIN, LUCILLE BREWTON, education educator, researcher; b. Florence, S.C.; d. William O. and Jurheutha (Gibbs) Brewton; m. Winston M. Strain (dec. 1984); 1 child, Rada Ruth Higgins. BA, Benedict Coll., 1943; MEd, Ohio State U., 1954, PhD, 1965. Cert. elem., secondary teaching, adminstrn., supervision. Tchr. Columbus (Ohio) Pub. Schs., 1950-62; prof. various U., 1965-79; policy analyst Nat. Ctr. Edn. Stats., Washington, 1979-83; from coord. to prof. and chmn. dept. edn. Bowie (Md.) State U., 1983-89, prof. edn., coord. grad. reading edn., 1989—; nat. policy fellow Inst. Edn. Leadership, Washington, 1979-80; mem. adv. coun. edn. stats. Nat. Ctr. Edn. Stats., Washington, 1982-85. Author: Accountability in Reading Instruction, 1976; contbr. articles to profl. jours. Recipient grant U.S. Dept. Edn., Washington, 1989, Bowie State U., 1989. Mem. Internat. Reading Assn. (tchrs. rsch. com. 1991-93), Assn. Tchr. Educators (corp. by-laws com. 1990-93), State of Md. Internat. Reading Assn. Coun. (chmn. internat. projects and activities com.). Home: 4701 Willard Ave Apt 1522 Chevy Chase MD 20815-4631

STRAITS, BEVERLY JOAN, gynecologist; b. Aurora, Ill., Jan. 29, 1939; d. Ernest Joseph and Mildred Betty (Shobe) S.; children: Kell Donald, Jill Elizabeth. BA, Carleton Coll., 1961; MD, Northwestern U., 1965. Diplomate in gynecology and obstetrics. Intern Passavant Hosp., Chgo., 1965-66; residency Lutheran Hosp., Milw., 1966-69; pvt. practice Wheat Ridge, Colo., 1969—. Fellow Am. Coll. Obstetrics & Gynecology. Office: 7855 W 38th Ave Wheat Ridge CO 80033-6109

STRAKA, TRACY E., environmental waste management executive; b. Newark, Oct. 16, 1962; d. Murray B. and Linda (Liechenstein) S. BS, George Washington U., 1983; postgrad., Montclair State U., 1989-90. Cert. environ. auditor. Rsch. asst. NSPE, Washington, 1982, Med. Sch., George Washington U., Washington, 1983; asst. sci. Hoffmann-La Roche-Chemotherapy, Nutley, N.J., 1985-87; environ. sci. Environ. Waste Mgmt. Assn., Wayne, N.J., 1987-89, dir. ops., 1989-92, v.p., 1992-94; advisor North Jersey Environ. Edn. and Recycling Coop., 1992—; guest lectr. N.J. Secondary Schs., 1992—; textbook evaluator Prentice Hall, N.Y.C., 1993—, Van Nostrom Rheinhold, N.Y.C., 1993—; environ. advisor Govt. of India, 1993; spkr. World Recycling Conf., Balt., 1993, Nat. Conf. Women Environ. Prof., Washington, 1994, San Francisco, 1995; environ. rep. USDOC. Contbg. editor N.J. Indsl. Jour., 1991—, Tri-State Real Estate Jour., 1992—, N.J. Law Jour., 1993; host, assoc. prodr. TV show Environ. Mother, 1993; contbr. articles to profl. jours. Mem. Nat. Ground Water Assn., Nat. Alliance Women in Waste (nat. co-chairperson 1993—), Commerce & Industry Assn. (amb.), Bus. & Industry Assn., Indsl. Comml. Real Estate Woman, North Jersey Regional C. of C. (bd. dirs.). Home: 1049 Valley Rd Clifton NJ 07013 Office: Creamer Environ Inc 101 Broadway Hackensack NJ 07601

STRAKOSCH, KATHERINE WENTON, executive recruiter; b. N.Y.C., Oct. 4, 1933; d. William J. and Elsie G. (Sullivan) Wenton; m. Raymond D. Strakosch, Nov. 10, 1956 (div. May 1977); children: Joanne, Mark, Gregory, Karen. B.A. cum laude, Coll. Mt. St. Vincent, 1955. Cert. personnel cons. Vice pres. Dunhill of Greater Stamford, Inc., Wilton, Conn., 1976-80, pres., 1980-93; mem. Town of Wilton Personnel Policies Com., 1983-93. Pres. bd. dirs. Wilton Playshop, 1971-73, vice chmn. bd. trustees, 1982-86, chmn. 1986-87; mem. Democratic Town Com., Wilton, 1976-79; pres. Surrey Search Group, 1994—. Mem. Conn. Assn. Personnel Consultants (sec. 1979, mem. ethics com. 1981-93, newsletter editor 1980), Nat. Assn. Pers. Cons., Women in Sales (v.p. membership Fairfield County chpt. 1989-90), Women in Mgmt. (opportunity com. 1991-92). Roman Catholic. Avocations: tennis, travel, reading. Home and Office: Surrey Search Group 60 Surrey Ln East Falmouth MA 02536

STRALEY, RUTH A. STEWART, government administrator, small business owner; b. Tanner, W.Va., May 31, 1949; d. Robert Sherwood Sr. and Reta Virginia (Frymier) Stewart; m. Charles Edward Straley, Aug. 17, 1968. BS magna cum laude, U. Md., 1982. Sec. W.Va. U., Morgantown, 1968-70; certification asst. Prince Georges County Bd. Edn., Upper Marlboro, Md., 1970-71; clerical asst. Def. Intelligence Agy., Washington, 1971-72; budget asst. Naval Weather Svc. Command, Washington, 1972-76; budget analyst Navy Recruiting Exhibit Ctr., Washington, 1976-78, Navy Regional Data Automation Command, Washington, 1978-80; hdqrs. budget officer Naval Facilities Engring. Command, Alexandria, Va., 1980-83; fin. mgr. Naval Res. Readiness Command Region 8, Naval Air Sta., Jacksonville, Fla., 1983-93; owner, pres. Horizons Unltd. Planning Svcs., Orange Park, Fla., 1989—; comptr. Naval Pers. Support Activity Europe, Naples, Italy, 1993-94; comptroller U.S. Naval Sta., San Diego, 1994—. Treas. Eagle Bay Homeowners Assn., Orange Park, 1989-93. Named Woman of Yr., Fed. Women's Program, 1983. Mem. NAFE, Am. Soc. Mil. Comptrs. (sec. 1984-89, v.p. 1990-91, pres. 1989-90, 91-93), Profl. Housing Mgmt. Assn. Republican. Methodist. Home: 432 C Ave Coronado CA 92118 Office: Horizons Unltd Planning Svc 661 Blanding Blvd Ste 338 Orange Park FL 32073-5039

STRAND, MARION DELORES, social service administrator; b. Kansas City, Mo., Dec. 19, 1927; d. Henry Franklin and Julia Twyman (Noland) Pugh; m. Robert Carmen Scipioni, Aug. 2, 1947 (dec. 1984); children: Mark, Brian, Roberta, Laura, Steven, Mary,Angela, Julie, Victor, Robert, Lawrence; m. Donald John Strand, Sept. 1, 1985. BA, U. Kans., 1948; MS, SUNY, Brockport, 1975. Counselor N.Y. Dept. Labor, Rochester, 1971-75, 77-79; regulatory adminstr. N.Y. Dept. Social Svcs., Rochester, 1976-77, 79-81; pres. Greater Rochester Svcs., Inc. (doing bus. as Scribes & Scripts), 1982—. Columnist, local newspaper. Active polit. campaigns for women candidates, 1981—; UN envoy Unitarian Ch., Rochester, 1988-92; fin. chair William Warfield Scholarship Com., Rochester, 1988-90; chair bd. govt. affairs Genesee Valley Arthritis Found., Rochester, 1988-90; mem. parade com. 95/75 Celebration of Monroe County, 1995. Mem. NOW (pres. child care com. Greater Rochester sect. 1987-88, chair family issues task force), AAUW (bd. dirs., cmty. rep. Greater Rochester br.), DAR (mem. Irondequoit chpt.), Greater Rochester C. of C. (legis. com., small bus. coun. 1987—, bd. dirs. women's coun. 1981-91, pres. 1989-90), Susan B. Anthony Rep. Women's Club (program com., 1st v.p. 1994, co-chair Greater Rochester Coalition for Choice 1994-95), Phi Beta Kappa, Psi Chi. Home and Office: Greater Rochester Svcs Inc 105 Elmwood Ter Rochester NY 14620-3703

STRANDBERG, REBECCA NEWMAN, lawyer; b. Ft. Smith, Ark., Apr. 22, 1951; d. Russell Lynn and Doris Jean (Lindsey) Newman; m. Jeffrey Eugene Strandberg, Nov. 23, 1979; children: Lindsey Katherine, Russell Jeffrey. BA, Tex. Christian U., 1973; JD, So. Meth. U., 1976. Bar: Tex. 1976, Md. 1981, D.C. 1983. Field atty. NLRB, New Orleans, 1976-79; legis. asst. Senator Dale Bumpers, Washington, 1979-81; pvt. practice, Montgomery County, Md., 1981-92; ptnr. Carlin & Strandberg PA, Bethesda, Md., 1992—. Vice-pres. bd. dirs. Share-A-Ride Corp., Montgomery County, 1984; dir. children's choir Glenmont Meth. Ch., Silver Spring, Md., 1984; bd. mgrs. Woodside Meth. Ch., 1989-92; mem. Holy Cross Community Hosp Quality Evaluation Com., 1989—; CLE chmn. Montgomery County Bar: Am. Inns of Ct., 1990-92. Named Chmn. of Yr. Montgomery County Bar, 1992-93. Mem. ABA (litigation, labor and employment law sect. 1985—), Md. State Bar (bd. govs. 1992—, spl. com. devel. guidelines for prevention of sexual harassment 1994—), Silver Spring C. of C., Montgomery County Women's Bar Assn. (chmn. membership 1982-83), Md. Women's Bar Assn., Silver Spring Bus. and Profl. Women (pres. 1984-85), SBA Women in Bus. (advocate 1982), Women's Bar D.C. Office: Carlin & Strandberg PA 4405 E West Hwy Ste 603 Bethesda MD 20814-4537

STRANG, MARIAN BOUNDY, librarian; b. Gibson City, Ill., May 5, 1918; d. Ralph Edward and Edna Blackburn (Washburn) Boundy; m. Tom H. Strang, Sept. 27, 1943; children—Terry H., Bruce B., David R. B.A., U. Wis., 1940, M.L.S., 1941. Libr. Richland Center, Wis., 1941-42; children's libr. Dearborn (Mich.) Pub. Libr., 1942-43; asst. libr. Rapides Parish Libr., Alexandria, La., 1943-45, Beloit (Wis.) Pub. Libr., 1945-46, Fort Knox (Ky.) Libr., 1952-54; libr. Sukiran Libr., Okinawa, 1962-64; chief libr. Fort Leonard Wood, Mo., 1964-70; med. libr. U.S. Gen. Wood Army Hosp., Fort Leonard Wood, 1970-88, Med. Libr., Med. Ctr., Independence, Mo., 1989—, VA Med. Ctr. Med. Libr., Kansas City, Mo., 1989—, Independence (Mo.) Regional Health Ctr., 1990—. Mem. ALA, Mo. Library Assn., Fed. Librarian's Assn., Med. Library Assn., AAUN, Bus. and Profl. Women, Delta Zeta. Home: 17711B E 29th St Independence MO 64057-2669

STRANG, RUTH HANCOCK, pediatric educator, pediatric cardiologist, priest; b. Bridgeport, Conn., Mar. 11, 1923; d. Robert Hallock Wright and Ruth (Hancock) S. BA, Wellesley Coll., 1944, postgrad., 1944-45; MD, N.Y. Med. Coll., 1949; MDiv, Seabury Western Theol. Sem., 1993. Diplomate Am. Bd. Pediat.; ordained deacon Episc. Ch., 1993, priest, 1994. Intern Flower and Fifth Ave. Hosp., N.Y.C., 1949-50, resident in pediatrics, 1950-52; mem. faculty N.Y. Med. Coll., N.Y.C., 1952-57; fellow cardiology Babies Hosp., N.Y.C., 1956-57, Harriet Lane Cardiac Clinic, Johns Hopkins Hosp., Balt., 1957-59, Children's Hosp., Boston, 1959-62; mem. faculty U. Mich., Univ. Hosp., Ann Arbor, 1962-89, prof. pediatrics, 1970-89, prof. emeritus, 1989—; priest-in-charge St. Johns Episcopal Ch., Howell, Mich., 1994—; dir. pediatrics Wayne County Gen. Hosp., Westland, Mich, 1965-85; mem. staff U. Mich. Hosps.; mem. med. adv. com. Wayne County chpt. Nat. Cystic Fibrosis Rsch. Found., 1966-80, chmn. med. adv. com. nat. found., Detroit, 1971-78; cons. cardiology Plymouth (Mich.) State Home and Tng. Sch., 1970-81. Author: Clinical Aspects of Operable Heart Disease, 1968; contbr. numerous articles to profl. jours. Mem. citizen's adv. coun. to Juvenile Ct., Ann Arbor, 1968-76; mem. med. adv. bd. Ann Arbor Continuing Edn. Dept., 1968-77; mem. Diocesan Com. for World Relief, Detroit, 1970-72, Am. Heart Assn. Mich. (v.p. 1989, pres. 1991); trustee Episcopal Med. Chaplaincy, Ann Arbor, 1971—; mem. bishop's com. St. Aidan's Episc. Ch., 1966-69, sec., 1966-68, vestry, 1973-76, 78-80, 84-86, 90-91, sr. warden, 1975, 76, 78, 80, 86, 90; del. Episc. Diocesan Conv., 1980, 91; bd. dirs. Livingston Cmty. Hospice, 1995—. Mem. AMA, Am. Acad. Pediatrics, Am. Coll. Cardiology, Mich. Med. Soc., Washtenaw County Med. Soc., N.Y. Acad. Medicine, Am. Heart Assn., Women's Rsch. Club (membership sec. 1966-67), Ambulatory Pediatric Assn., Am. Assn. Child Care in Hosps., Am. Assn. Med. Colls., Assn. Faculties of Pediatric Nurse Assn./Practitioners Programs (pres. 1978-81, exec. com. 1981-84), Episc. Clergy Assn. Mich., Northside Assn. Ministries (pres. 1975, 76, 79-80). Home: 4500 E Huron River Dr Ann Arbor MI 48105-9335

STRANG, SANDRA LEE, airline official; b. Greensboro, N.C., Apr. 22, 1936; d. Charles Edward and Lobelia Mae (Squires) S.; BA in English, U. N.C., 1960; MBA, U. Dallas, 1970. With American Airlines, Inc., 1960—, mgr. career devel. for women, N.Y.C., 1972-73, dir. selection and tng., 1974-75, sr. dir. selection, tng. and affirmative action, 1975-79, sr. dir. compensation and benefits, Dallas/Ft. Worth, Tex., 1979-84, dir. passenger sales tng. and devel., 1984—; regional sales mgr. Rocky Mountain Region, Denver, 1985—; pres. The SLS Group, Inc., (DBAs) Sales Leadership Seminars, Inc., Sr. Leadership Svcs., Inc., Svc. Leadership Seminars, Inc., Speakers, Lectrs., and Seminars, Inc, 1988—. AARP, Mem. Am. Mgmt. Assn., Assn. Advancement of Women into Mgmt., Am. Soc. Tng. and Devel., Am. Compensation Assn., Internat. Platform Assn. Home: 3493 E Euclid Ave Littleton CO 80121-3663

STRANGE, DOUGLAS HART MCKOY, civic worker; b. Wilmington, N.C., Mar. 16, 1929; d. Adair Morey and Katie Reston (Grainger) McKoy; student Hollins Coll., 1946-48; m. Robert Strange, July 16, 1949; children—Robert VI, John Allan, Elizabeth Adair, Katherine Grainger. Fin. chmn. and provisional co-chmn. Knoxville Jr. League; former tchr. Bible class, vestrywoman, pres. ch. women Fox Chapel Episcopal Ch.; former chmn. Fox Chapel House Tour; former chmn. altar guild, mem. worship com. bd. dirs. ch. women, St. John's Episcopal Ch.; altar chmn. Episcopal Diocese of Tenn.; bd. dirs. Dulin Com., Dulin Gallery Art; invitation coordinator Heart Gala Ball, 1985; vol. crisis counselor Contact of Knoxville, Inc.; vol. Fish of Knox County. Recipient cert. of merit Pitts. Heart Fund, 1975, engraved plate Fox Chapel Episcopal Ch., 1976. Mem. Assn. Jr. Leagues Am., Nat. Soc. Colonial Dames Am. (asst. to editor and bus. mgr. newsletter, 1978-79), Knoxville Civic Opera. Republican. Clubs: Cherokee Garden, Nine-o-clock Cotillion, Cherokee Country. Home: 1400 Kenesaw Ave Apt 11G Knoxville TN 37919-7775

STRASSER, ROSE LOUISE, educator; b. Buffalo, Apr. 5, 1907; d. Ferdinand and Louisa (Hermann) S. BS in Edn., U. Mich., 1929, MS, 1933; student, Bennington Sch. Dance, 1939, U. Calif., 1940. Cert. tchr. health, physical edn. Tchr., physical edn. Rochester (Mich.) Pub. Schs., 1929-31; instr., physical edn. Keuka Coll., Keuka Park, N.Y., 1931-33; tchr., elem. physical edn. Buffalo Elem. Schs., 1933-35; tchr., health physical edn. Buffalo High Schs., 1935-46; dance div. health physical edn., recreation SUNY, Brockport, 1946-66; dir. student teaching, health, physical edn., recreation SUNY, chmn., dance dept., 1966-70; lectr. U. Buffalo, 1935—, St. Joseph's Tchrs. Coll., Buffalo, 1938—; vis. prof. NYU, Internat. Dance Camps, 1964-65; sec. Assn. Women Physical Edn., Albany, N.Y., 1939-41, v.p. 1941-42, pres. 1942-43. Contbr. articles to profl. jours. and mags. Dance specialist Internat. Inst., Buffalo, 1944-52; dance cons. N.Y. State Dirs. Health Physical Edn. Recreation, Albany, 1964-66, 68, Girl Scouts Am., Rochester & Monroe County, N.Y., 1962-65; judge square dancing N.Y. State Fair, Syracuse, 1965, 66, 67; judge folk dancing, square dancing Pa. State Fair, Harrisburg, 1967, 68, 69. Recipient Heritage award, 1989; grantee, 1968, 69. Fellow AAHPERD (sec. dance sect. 1964-66, Cert. of Appreciation 1985); mem. AAUP, Nat Dance Assn. (archivist, historian 1973-87), Am. Dance Guild (citation 1974), Am. Assn. Emeritii, N.Y. State Dance Tchrs. Higher Edn., Folk Dance Fedn. Calif., Nat. Folk Orgn. U.S., Soc. Folk Dance History, Arizonans Cultural Devel., We. Monroe Hist. Soc., Congress Rsch. Dance, U. Mich. Alumni Phoenix, Delta Kappa Gamma. Republican. Home: 5060 E Florian Ave Mesa AZ 85206-2830

STRASSMEYER, MARY, newspaper columnist; b. Cleve., Aug. 5, 1929; d. Frederick H. and Katherine (Mullally) S. A.B., Notre Dame Coll., 1951; postgrad., Toledo U., 1952; J.D., Cleve. Marshall Coll. Law, Cleve. State U., 1981. Bar: Ohio 1983. Reporter Cleve. News, 1956-60; contbr. Cleve. Plain Dealer, 1957-60, feature writer, 1960-65, beauty editor, 1963-65, travel writer, 1963—, society editor, 1965-77, 85—; columnist, 1977—; co-creator syndicated cartoon Sneakers; co-owner Gerry's Internat. Travel Agy., Cleve., 1991—. Author: Coco: The Special Delivery Dog, 1979. Mem. Soc. Am. Social Scribes (founder, 1st pres.), Notre Dame Coll. Alumnae Assn., Women in Communications. Club: Press (Cleve.). Home: 2059 Broadview Rd Cleveland OH 44109-4145 Office: The Plain Dealer 1801 Superior Ave E Cleveland OH 44114-2107

STRATAS, TERESA (ANASTASIA STRATAKI), opera singer; b. Toronto, Ont., Can., May 26, 1938. Student of Irene Jessner, 1956-59; grad., Faculty Music, U. Toronto, 1959; LLD (hon.), McMaster U., 1986, U. Toronto, 1994. Winner Met. Opera auditions, 1959; major roles in opera houses throughout world include: Mimi in La Bohème; Tatiana in Eugene Onegin; Susanna in The Marriage of Figaro; Nedda in Pagliacci; Marenka in The Bartered Bride; Three Heroines in Il Trittico; Violetta in La Traviata; title role in Rusalka; Jennie in Mahagonny; created title role in completed version of Lulu (Alban Berg), Paris Grand Opera, 1979; film appearances Kaiser von Atlantis, Seven Deadly Sins; Zefirelli's La Traviata, Salome, Lulu, Paganini, Zarewitsch, Eugene Oregin; creator the role of Marie Antoinette Ghosts of Versailles world premiere Met. Opera, 1992; sang both female leading roles Il Tabarro, Pagliacci double bill opening Met. Opera, 1994. Decorated Order of Can.; recipient 3 Grammy awards, Emmy award, Drama Desk award, 1986, 3 Grammy nominations, Tony nomination, 1986, Tiffany award, 1994; named Performer of Yr., Can. Music Council, 1979. Office: care Met Opera Co Lincoln Center Plz New York NY 10023 also: Vincent & Farrell Associates 157 West 57th St Ste 502 New York NY 10019

STRATOS, KIMARIE ROSE, lawyer, sports agent; b. Miami, Fla., Aug. 24, 1960; d. Jack Sloshower and Charmaine (McDougal) S. BS with high honors, U. Fla., 1981, JD with honors, 1984. Bar: Fla. 1985, U.S. Dist. Ct. (so. and mid. dist.) Fla. 1987. Ptnr. Shutts & Bowen, Miami, 1984-85, 86—; chair sports law dept., law clk. to judge U.S. Dist. Ct. (so. dist.) Fla., Miami, 1985-86; mem. bd. dirs. Fla. Sports Found., 1992—. Co-author, asst. editor: Facility Development and the Sports Authority, Law of Professional and Amateur Sports; asst. editor: Clark Boardmen, 1990; contbr. articles to profl. jours. Mem. ABA, Fla. Bar (bd. govs. young lawyers sect. 1987-93, exec. coun. entertainment, arts and sports law sect. 1988—), Fla. Assn. Women Lawyers, Sports Lawyers Assn. (nat. v.p. 1988-90, 93—, bd. dirs. 1990—). Office: Shutts & Bowen 100 Chopin Plz Ste 1500 Miami FL 33131-2382

STRATTON, CHARLOTTE ETHEL, secondary education educator; b. Kearney, N.J., June 4, 1932; d. Philip Sr. and Ethel (Irwin) Coombe; m. Vernon E. Stratton, June 5, 1954; children: Lynn Stratton McDonald, Vernon Jr., Elaine C. Stratton Iatauro, Laurie. BS, Beaver Coll., 1954. Mem. supts. cabinet TriValley Ctrl., Grahamsville, N.Y., 1989-90; team leader grade 8 Tri-Valley Ctrl. Sch., Grahamsville, N.Y., 1991-93; mem. bldg. leadership team Tri-Valley, Grahamsville, N.Y., 1991—. Recipient Tchr. of Yr. award Tri-Valley Tchrs. Assn., 1990, nominated for Sullivan County Tchr. of Yr., 1993. Home: 697 S Hill Rd Grahamsville NY 12740 Office: Tri Valley Ctr Sch Moore Hill Rd Grahamsville NY 12740

STRATTON, MARIANN, director USN nurse corps; b. Houston, Apr. 6, 1945; d. Max Millard and Beatrice Agnes (Roemer) S.; m. Lawrence Mallory Stickney, nov. 15, 1977 (dec.). BSN, BA in English, Sacred Heart Dominican Coll., 1966; MA in Mgmt., Webster Coll., 1977; MSN, U. Tex., 1981. Cert. adult nurse practitioner. Ensign USN, 1966, advanced through grades to rear adm., 1991; patient care coord. Naval Regional Med. Ctr., Charleston, S.C., 1981-83; nurse corps plans officer Naval Med. Command, Washington, 1983-86; dir. nursing svcs. U.S. Naval Hosp., Naples, Italy, 1986-89, Naval Hosp., San Diego, 1989-91; chief pers. mgmt. Bur. Medicine & Surgery, Washington, 1991-94; dir. USN Nurse Corps, Washington, 1991-94. Decorated Disting. Svc. medal, Meritorious Svc. medal with two stars, Naval Achievement medal. Mem. ANA, Assn. Mil. Surgeons of U.s., Interagy. Inst. of Fed. Health Car Execs.

STRATTON-WHITCRAFT, CATHLEEN SUE, critical care, pediatrics nurse; b. Jackson, Mich., Jan. 14, 1964; d. Ronald Alfred and Shirley Anne (Wickham) Stratton; m. David R. Whitcraft, Aug. 14, 1988. BSN magna cum laude, SUNY, Brockport, 1985. Cert. critical care nurse, ACLS. Student clin. asst. Yale-New Haven Hosp., 1984; charge nurse Walter Reed Army Med. Ctr., Washington, 1990; clin. nurse, critical care med. ICU and pediatric ICU SRT-Med. Staff Agy., Springfield, Va., 1985-88; asst. head nurse Sinai Hosp., Balt., 1988-90; charge nurse surg. SICU ICU VA Med. Ctr., Balt., 1991—. 1st lt. U.S. Army Nurse Corps, 1985-88, Res., 1988-93. Recipient Cert. of Achievement, Elizabeth Dole.

STRAUS, HELEN LORNA PUTTKAMMER, biologist, educator; b. Chgo., Feb. 15, 1933; d. Ernst Wilfred and Helen Louise (Monroe) Puttkammer; m. Francis Howe Straus II, June 11, 1955; children: Francis Howe III, Helen E., Christopher M., Michael W. AB magna cum laude, Radcliffe Coll., 1955; MS in Anatomy, U. Chgo., 1960, PhD in Anatomy, 1962. With U. Chgo., 1964—, asst. prof. anatomy, 1967-73, dean of students, 1971-82, assoc. prof., 1973-87, dean of admissions, 1975-80, prof. anatomy and biol. scis., 1987—. Trustee Radcliffe Coll., Cambridge, Mass., 1973-83. Recipient Quantrell Award for Excellence in teaching, U. Chgo., 1970, 87, Silver medal Case Outstanding Tchr. Program, 1987. Mem. AAAS, NCAA (acad. requirements com. 1986-92, chmn. 1990-92), Nat. Sci. Tchrs. Assn., Am. Assn. Anatomists, Harvard U. Alumni Assn. (bd. dirs. 1980-83), Phi Beta Kappa (sec., treas. U. Chgo. chpt. 1984—). Home: 5642 S Kimbark Ave Chicago IL 60637-1606 Office: U Chgo 5845 S Ellis Ave Chicago IL 60637-1404

STRAUSS, CAROL KAHN, institute executive director, editor, consultant; b. N.Y.C., Sept. 21, 1944; d. Alfred and Lotte (Landau) K.; m. Peter Mathes, Dec. 1977 (div. 1980); m. Peter Strauss, June 1989. BS, Columbia U., 1970; MS, Hunter Coll., 1973. Asst. book editor Council on Fgn. Relations, N.Y.C., 1972-79; sr. editor, dir. pub. affairs Hudson Inst., Indpls., 1984-89; sr. editor, cons. 20th Century Fund, N.Y.C., 1990-94; exec. dir. Leo Baeck Inst., N.Y.C., 1994—; cons., writer, editor Ford Found., 20th Century Fund, Mayoral Task Forces, Kidder Peabody & Co., N.Y. Holocaust Commn. Editor: (books) The Coming Boom, 1982, Thinking About the Unthinkable in the 1980's, 1984; editor, co-author articles for profl. publs. Pres. Congregation Habonim, N.Y.C., 1984-92; trustee Self-Help, Inc., N.Y.C., 1986-93; v.p. Fedn. Jews from Ctrl. Europe, 1990—. Jewish. Club: Atrium (N.Y.C.). Home: 870 Fifth Ave New York NY 10021-4953 Office: Leo Baeck Inst 129 E 73rd St New York NY 10021

STRAUSS, CATHERINE B., lawyer; b. San Francisco, June 11, 1947; d. John Lawrence and Betty (Rosenblatt) Blumlein; m. Jerome Frank Strauss, III, June 21, 1970; children: Jordan Lawrence, Elizabeth Johanna. A.B., Brown U., 1969; M.S.S., Bryn Mawr Coll., 1973; J.D., Temple U., 1976. Bar: Pa. 1976, U.S. Dist. Ct. (ea. dist.) Pa. 1981. Assoc. Drinker Biddle & Reath, Phila., 1976-79; asst. counsel Penn Mut., Phila., 1979-83, dir. acquisitions, 1983-85, asst. v.p. sales, 1985-87, v.p. human resources, 1987—; bd. dirs.

Penn Ins. and Annuity Co., Mutual Assn. Profl. Svcs. Chmn. bd. trustees Women's Law Project, Phila., 1984-89, mem. adv. com., 1989—; bd. dirs. Family Service of Phila., 1978-85, Career Alternatives, Jenkintown, Pa., 1984-85; trustee United Way, Phila., 1982—, officer, 1992-94, exec. com. 1992—; mem. Loma Human Resources Coun., 1990-91; bd. dirs. Penn Ins. and Annuity Co., 1992—. Mem. ABA, MAPS (bd. dirs.), Phila. Bar Assn., Loma Human Resources Exec. Forum. Office: Penn Mut Independence Sq Philadelphia PA 19172

STRAUSS, DOROTHY BRANDFON, marital, family, and sex therapist; b. Bklyn.; d. Marcus and Beatrice (Wilson) Brandfon; widowed; 1 child, Josette E. MacNaughton. BA, Bklyn. Coll., 1932; MA, NYU, 1937, PhD, 1963. Diplomate Am. Bd. Sexology. Instr. Hunter Coll. CUNY, 1960-63; prof. Kean Coll., Union, N.J., 1963-77; pvt. practice and clin. supervision Bklyn. and, N.J., 1970—; clin. assoc. prof. psychiatry Downstate Med. Ctr., SUNY, Bklyn., 1974—; assoc. dir. Ctr. for Human Sexuality, 1974-82; mem. NIMH rsch. team U. Pa., 1973-82. Contbr. articles on gerontology and sexual dysfunctions to profl. jours. Fellow Am. Assn. Clin. Sexologists (founding); mem. Am. Psychol. Assn., Am. Assn. for Marital and Family Therapy (clin. mem. 1971—, supr. 1981), Am. Assn. Sex Therapists, Counselors and Educators (chairperson task force on supervision 1984-86, chairperson supr. cert. com. 1986-93, cert. steering com. 1992—), Kappa Delta Pi. Home and Office: 1401 Ocean Ave Brooklyn NY 11230-3917

STRAUSS, ELAINE G., writer; b. N.Y.C., Aug. 2, 1928; d. Herman and Sylvia (Eilenberg) Greenbaum; m. Ulrich Paul Strauss, Nov. 23, 1950; children: Dorothy, David, Elizabeth, Evelyn. BA in History, Douglass Coll., 1950; MA in Polit. Sci., Rutgers U., 1955; diploma in piano pedagogy, Trinity Coll., London, 1973. Contbr. articles to U.S. 1 Newspaper, 1989—, Clavier, 1994. Pres. LWV, Highland Park, N.J., 1964-67. Mem. Music Educators Assn. (v.p. N.J. chpt. 1989-91), Music Tchrs. Nat. Orgn. Home: 227 Lawrence Ave Highland Park NJ 08904

STRAUSS, HARLEE SUE, environmental consultant; b. New Brunswick, N.J., June 19, 1950; d. Robert Lemuel and Helene (Marcus) S. BA, Smith Coll., 1972; PhD, U. Wis., 1979. Postdoctoral fellow dept. biology MIT, Cambridge, 1979-81; congrl. sci. fellow U.S. House of Reps., Washington, 1981-83; spl. asst. Am. Chem. Soc., Washington, 1983-84; spl. cons. Environ. Corp., Washington, 1984-85; rsch. assoc. Ctr. for Tech., Policy and Indsl. Devel. MIT, Cambridge, 1985-86, rsch. affiliate, 1986—; sr. assoc. Gradient Corp., Cambridge, 1986-88; pres. H. Strauss Assocs., Inc., Natick, Mass., 1988—; pres., exec. dir. Silent Spring Inst., Inc., 1994—; adj. assoc. prof. Sch. of Pub. Health, Boston U., 1990; lectr. Tufts U. Sch. of Medicine, Boston, 1988—; steering com. Boston Risk Assessment Group, 1986—. Co-editor, author: Risk Assessment in Genetic Engineering, 1991; author: Biotechnology Regulations, 1986; author book chpts. in field. Active Instl. Biosafety Com., Army Rsch. Lab., Natick, 1989—, Army Sci. Bd., 1994—. Mem. AAAS, Am. Chem. Soc., Am. Soc. Microbiology, Assn. for Women in Sci. (chmn. com. New Eng. chpt. 1986-88, co-chmn. legis. com. 1985—), Biophys. Soc. (chmn. com. 1983-84, Congl. Sci. fellow 1981-83), Soc. for Risk Analysis (pres. New Eng. chpt. 1991—). Mem. AAAS, Am. Chem. Soc., Am. Soc. Microbiology, Assn. for Women in Sci. (chmn. mem. com. New Eng. chpt. 1986-88, co-chmn. legis. com. 1985—), Biophys. Soc. (chmn. com. 1983-84, Congl. Sci. fellow 1981-83), Soc. for Risk Analysis. Jewish. Office: H Strauss Assocs Inc 21 Bay State Rd Natick MA 01760-2942

STRAUSS, JEANNE H., technical translator, educator; b. Hamburg, Germany, Mar. 5, 1928; came to U.S., 1948, naturalized, 1954; d. Frederic and Julie S. BA, Roosevelt U., 1956; MA, Loyola U., Chgo., 1960; PhD cert. in Spanish and French, U. Wis.-Madison, 1968. Legal sec. Montgomery Ward, Chgo., 1957-60; instr. Creighton U., Omaha, 1961-63; teaching asst. U. Wis., Madison, 1964-65; asst. prof. U. Wis.-Stevens Point, 1965-69, Western Ill. U., Macomb, 1969-71, U. Wis.-Superior, 1973-75; tech. translator, interpreter Phillips Petroleum Co., Bartlesville, Okla., 1975-86; asst. prof. Spanish and French Wayne State Coll., Nebr., 1988-89, Ashland C. C. U. Ky., Ashland, 1989-90; instr. Spanish Auburn (Ala.) U., 1991-92. Mem. Nat. Rep. Congl. Com., 1979-89. Mem. MLA, Am. Assn. Tchrs. French, Am. Assn. Tchrs. Spanish and Portuguese, Am. Translators Assn., Ga. Coun. Internat. Visitors (Internat. Businesswomen's Network), Alliance Francaise of Atlanta. Home: PO Box 48841 Atlanta GA 30362-1841

STRAUSS, PHYLLIS R., biology educator; b. Worcester, Mass., Mar. 19, 1943. BA, Brown U., 1964; PhD, The Rockefeller U., 1971. Rsch. fellow med. sch. Harvard U., Boston, 1971-73; asst. prof. biology Northeastern U., Boston, 1973-78, assoc. prof., 1978-84, prof., 1984—, Matthews Disting. prof., 1987—; sr. scientist Sealy Ctr. Molecular Sci., Galveston, Tex., 1994—; vis. scholar Harvard U., Cambridge, Mass., 1988; reviewer NSF, NIH, Nat. Rsch. Coun., Alberta Heritage Found., U.S. Dept. Agrl. and numerous jours. and books. Author, editor: The Euraryotic Nucleus, 1990; contbr. articles to profl. jours. Grantee Am. Cancer Soc., 1973, NIH, 1977, Office Naval Rsch., 1981, WHO, 1989, 93, 94, also others. Mem. AAAS, Am. Soc. for Cell Biology (coun. 1989-91), Am. Soc. Protozoologists, Am. Soc. Biol. Chemists, Am. Women in Sci. Office: Northeastern U 360 Huntington Ave Boston MA 02115-5096

STRAVALLE-SCHMIDT, ANN ROBERTA, lawyer; b. N.Y.C., Jan. 2, 1957. Grad. cum laude, Phillips Exeter Acad., 1975; student, Occidental Coll., 1975-78, Oxford Coll., Eng., 1976-77; BS cum laude, Boston Coll., 1980; JD, Boston U., 1987. Bar: Conn. 1987, U.S. Dist. Ct. Conn. 1988, U.S. Supreme Ct. 1993. Consulting staff Arthur Andersen, Boston, 1980-82; supr. CID ops. Aetna Life & Casualty, Hartford, Conn., 1982-84; summer intern U.S. Atty.'s Office, Boston, 1985; jud. clk. Hon. Judge Thayer III N.H. Supreme Ct., 1987-88; trial lawyer Day, Berry & Howard, Hartford, 1988-91; sr. lawyer comml. litigation Berman & Sable, Hartford, 1991—. Mem. editl. bd. Conn. Bar Jour., 1990—. Mem. ABA, Conn. Bar Assn. (appellate practice com. of litigation sect.), Hartford BarAssn., Hartford Assn. Women Attys. Home: 515 Elizabeth Dr Hebron CT 06248 Office: Berman & Sable 100 Pearl St Hartford CT 06103

STRAVINSKA, SARAH, dance educator; b. Pitts., Nov. 12, 1940; d. Robert Edwin Williams and Alice Elizabeth Markey Hildeboldt; m. George Lawrence Denton, May 10, 1959 (div. 1973); children: Kathryn, Michael, Laura, David. BFA in Dance, Fla. State U., 1977, MFA in Dance, 1979; Cert. in Ballet, Vaganova Inst., Leningrad, Russia, 1990; Cert., Raoul Gelabert Kinesiology Ins, N.Y.C., 1980. Dancer Ballet Russe, N.Y.C., 1957-58; dance choreographer Dutchess County Ballet, Beacon, N.Y., 1960-65; instr. Brevard C.C., Cocoa, Fla., 1969-73; chair dept. dance Randolph/Macon Woman's Coll., Lynchburg, Va., 1979-84; asst. prof. dance U. So. Miss., Hattiesburg, 1984-86; assoc. prof. and coord. dance U. Southwestern La., Lafayette, 1986—; dir. State of La. Danse Project, Lafayette, 1991-94. Choreographer original dance works: Mama! Stop the Bombs, 1989, The Yellow Wallpaper, 1990; reconstructor of classical ballets: Les Sylphides, 1991, Giselle, 1992, Swan Lake, 1993, Raymonda, Pas de Quatre, 1994. Dir. concerns for children La Danse with Acadiana Arts Coun., Lafayette, 1987-93; mem. Arts in Edn. Program, Lafayette, 1987—. Mellon Found. grantee, 1982, U. So. Miss. faculty devel. grantee, 1986. Mem. Am. Coll. Dance Festival Assn. (bd. dirs., festival coord. 1989-91), Dance History Scholars, Phi Kappa Phi. Episcopalian. Office: Univ of Southwestern La Dept Performing Arts Box 43850 Lafayette LA 70504

STRAWN, FRANCES FREELAND, real estate executive; b. Waynesville, N.C., Nov. 18, 1946; d. Thomas M. and Jimmie (Smith) Freeland; m. David Updegraff Strawn, Aug. 30, 1974; children: Laurel, Kirk, Trisha. AA, Brevard Community Coll., Cocoa, Fla., 1976; postgrad. U. Cen. Fla., 1976-77. acting sr. buyer Brevard County Purchasing Bd. of County Commns., Titusville, Fla., 1971-75; rsch. analyst Brevard Community Coll., Cocoa, 1977-78; realtor assoc., Orlando, Fla., 1979-82; realtor, broker, pres. Advance Am., Inc., Orlando, 1982-89; assoc. Ann Cross, Inc., Winter Park, Fla., 1988—. Contbr. articles to Fla. Realtor, 1993, Communique, 1994. Bd. dirs. Vol. Ctr. of Cen. Fla. (rec. sec. 1989), Cen. Fla. Zool. Pk., 1989-92; co-chmn, fundraiser Black Tie Walk on the Wild Side, 1992; program chmn. Young Rep. Women, Orlando, 1983; coord. Congressman Bill Nelson's Washington Internship Program; co-ticket chmn. Art and Architecture Orlando Regional Hosp.; mem. steering com. Fla. Heritage Homecoming, Orlando, 1987; sec. Mayor's Wife's Campaign Activities, Orlando, 1986-87; vice chmn. Horizon Exec. Bd., 1987-89, chmn., 1989; recording sec. Women's Bus. Edn. Council, 1988, mem. adv. bd. , 1987, bd. dirs. 1988-90; active calendar com. Women's Resource Ctr., bd. dirs. 1989-90; lectr. Jr. Achievement., 1988-93; mem. steering com. scholarship dinner Crummer Bus. Coll. Rollins Coll., 1992. Mem. Orange County Bar Aux. (bd. dirs. 1986-88, corr. sec. 1987), Creative Bus. Ownership for Women (adv. bd. 1986-88, grievance vice chmn. 1989), Nat. Assn. Realtors, Orlando Bd. Realtors (grievance com. 1985-91), Orlando Area Bd. Realtors (membership com. 1980-84, profl. standards com. 1983-84, lectr. Success Series 1988—), Women's Coun. of Realtors, Women's Exec. Coun., Citrus Club (Orlando, social com. 1987-88, bd. dirs 1990—). Episcopalian. Avocations: travel, needlepoint, canoe trips, skiing. Home: 105 NW Ivanhoe Blvd Orlando FL 32804 Office: Ann Cross Inc 233 W Park Ave Winter Park FL 32789-7016

STRAZDON, MAUREEN ELAINE, research and planning director; b. Elizabeth, N.J., Aug. 6, 1948; d. Bruno H. and Leona E.(Sheehan) S.; m. Victor A. Bary, May 17, 1985. BA, Douglass Coll., New Brunswick, N.J., 1970; MLS, Rutgers U., New Brunswick, 1971; MBA, Drexel U., Phila., 1978; CLU, Am. Coll., Bryn Mawr, Pa., 1982. Bus., reference librarian Drexel U., Phila., 1971-78; head librarian Am. Coll., Bryn Mawr, Pa., 1978-82, Pa. State U., Abington, 1982-85; asst. dir. rsch. and devel. Am. Internat. Group, N.Y.C., 1985-93; dir. rsch. and planning CIGNA Property/Casualty, Phila., 1993-94; dir. market analysis Am. Internat. Underwriters, N.Y.C., 1994—. Editor Index, Database Ins. Periodicals Index, 1983—; author contbr. articles in profl. jours. 1979—. Named Outstanding Young Women Am. Mem. Spl. Librs. Assn., Conf. Bd. Market Rsch. Coun., Beta Gamma Sigma. Office: Am Internat Underwriters 15th Fl 70 Pine St New York NY 10270

STRECK, HELEN MARIE, information management consultant; b. Enid, Okla., Sept. 5, 1959; d. Jodie Valentine Sr. and Virginia Mae (Suenram) S.; m. William Christopher Woodard, May 24, 1986; children: Veronica Marie, Michael MacQueen. Assoc. degree, St. Gregorys Coll., 1979; BS in Lab. Tech., U. Okla., 1982. Legal sec. Cooley Godward et al, Palo Alto, Calif., 1983-84; records supr. Cooley Godward et al, Palo Alto, 1984-88; records mgr. County of San Mateo, Redwood City, Calif., 1988-93; info. resource mgr. County of San Mateo, Redwood City, 1993-94; info. mgmt. cons., 1994—. Mem. Assn. Records Mgrs. and Adminstrs. (bd. mem. 1989-90, chpt. pres. 1990-92, past chpt. pres. 1992—, IAC chair 1992-94, Member of Yr. 1988, Pres. award 1992), Assn. Records Suprs. (charity campaign com. 1992), Calif. Law Enforcement, Soc. Calif. Archivist (com. 1990-91). Democrat. Roman Catholic. Home and Office: 2280 Pulgas Ave East Palo Alto CA 94303

STREEP, MERYL (MARY LOUISE STREEP), actress; b. Madison, N.J., June 22, 1949; d. Harry Jr. and Mary W. Streep; m. Donald J. Gummer, 1978. BA, Vassar Coll., 1971; MFA, Yale U., 1975, DFA (hon.), 1983; DFA (hon.), Dartmouth Coll., 1981. Ind. actress stage, screen, 1975—. Appeared with Green Mountain Guild, Woodstock, Vt.; Broadway debut in Trelawny of the Wells, Lincoln Center Beaumont Theater, 1975; N.Y.C. theatrical appearances include 27 Wagons Full of Cotton (Theatre World award), A Memory of Two Mondays, Henry V, Secret Service, The Taming of the Shrew, Measure for Measure, The Cherry Orchard, Happy End, Wonderland, Taken in Marriage, Alice in Concert (Obie award 1981); movie appearances include Julia, 1977, The Deer Hunter, 1978 (Best Supporting Actress award Nat. Soc. Film Critics), Manhattan, 1979, The Seduction of Joe Tynan, 1979, Kramer vs. Kramer, 1979 (N.Y. Film Critics' award, Los Angeles Film Critics' award, both for best actress, Golden Globe award, Acad. award for best supporting actress), The French Lieutenant's Woman, 1981 (Los Angeles Film Critics award for best actress, Brit. Acad. award, Golden Globe award 1981), Sophie's Choice, 1982 (Acad. award for best actress, Los Angeles Film Critics award for best actress, Golden Globe award 1982), Still of the Night, 1982, Silkwood, 1983, Falling in Love, 1984, Plenty, 1985, Out of Africa, 1985 (Los Angeles Film Critics award for best actress 1985), Heartburn, 1986, Ironweed, 1987, A Cry in the Dark, 1988 (named Best Actress N.Y. Film Critics' Circle, 1988, Best Actress Cannes Film Festival, 1989), She-Devil, 1989, Postcards From the Edge, 1990, Defending Your Life, 1991, Death Becomes Her, 1992, The House of the Spirits,1994, The River Wild, 1994; TV film The Deadliest Season, 1977; TV mini-series Holocaust, 1978 (Emmy award); TV dramatic spls. Secret Service, 1977, Uncommon Women and Others, 1978;TV (narrator) The Velveteen Rabbit, 1985, A Vanishing Wilderness, 1990. Recipient Mademoiselle award, 1976, Woman of Yr. award B'nai Brith, 1979, Woman of Yr. award Hasty Pudding Soc., Harvard U., 1980, Best Supporting Actress award Nat. Bd. of Rev., 1979, Best Actress award Nat. Bd. of Rev., 1982, Star of Yr. award Nat. Assn. Theater Owners, 1983, People's Choice award, 1983, 85, 86, 87. Office: Creative Artists Agy 9830 Wilshire Blvd Beverly Hills CA 90212-1825*

STREET, DONNA LEE, accounting educator; b. Johnson City, Tenn., July 3, 1959; d. Roy Lee and Gertrude (Peterson) S.; m. Ashton Coles Bishop, Jr., May 9, 1989. BBA, East Tenn. State U., 1981; M in Acctg., U. Tenn., 1983, PhD, 1987. Assoc. prof. James Madison U., Harrisburg, Va., 1986—. Contbr. articles to profl. jours. KPMG Peat Marwick faculty fellow, 1993-96. Mem. Am. Acctg. Assn., Fedn. Schs. Acctg. (edn. resch. com. 1993—), Acad. Acctg. Historians, Inst. Mgmt. Accts., Beta Alpha Psi (nat. coun. 1992—). Office: James Madison U Sch Acctg Harrisburg VA 22807

STREET, ERICA CATHERINE, lawyer; b. Lansing, Mich., July 5, 1958; d. Cassius English and Helen Joanna (Hoesman) S.; m. Robert John Pratte, Oct. 20, 1984; 1 child, Chelsea Nicole Pratte. BA, Hillsdale Coll., 1979; JD, U. Mich., 1981. Bar: Minn. 1982, U.S. Dist. Ct. Minn. 1982, U.S. Ct. Appeals (8th cir.) 1983. Assoc. Best & Flanagan, Mpls., 1981-85; sr. counsel Fingerhut Corp., Minnetonka, Minn., 1985-89, Target Stores div. Dayton Hudson Corp., Mpls., 1989—. Mem. ABA, Minn. Bar Assn., Hennepin County Bar Assn. Office: Target Stores 33 S 6th St Minneapolis MN 55402-3601

STREET, GLORIA IRENE FORD, music educator; b. Balt., Apr. 2, 1936; d. George Emory and Irene Jones (Marks) Ford; children: Pamela Laureen Street-Ahmed. BS cum laude, Morgan State U., Balt., 1957; M Liberal Arts, Johns Hopkins U., 1970. Cert. advanced profl. in music edn., grades 7-12. Tchr., chmn., dept. head Balt. City Pub. Schs., 1958-90; music resource educator Balt. Pub. Schs., 1990—; travel cons. Parker Travel Assocs., Timonium, Md., 1988—; dean studies United Inst. Bibl. Studies, Balt., 1981-87; organist, choir dir. various chs., Balt., 1960-86. Mem. NEA, Md. State Tchrs.Assn., Music Educators Nat. Conf., Phi Delta Kappa, Alpha Kappa Alpha. Democrat. Home: 4341 Danlou Dr Baltimore MD 21207

STREET, PATRICIA LYNN, educator; b. Lillington, N.C., May 3, 1940; d. William Banks and Vandalia (McLean) S.; m. Col. Robert Gest, June 2, 1962 (div. 1985); children: Robert, Roblyn Renee. BS, Livingstone Coll., 1962; MEd, Salisbury State U., 1974; postgrad., various, 1968—. Tchr. Govt. of Guam Marianas Island, Agana, Guam, 1962-64; sec., typist USAF, Glasgow AFB, Mont., 1964-65, Syracuse (N.Y.) U. AeroSpace Engring., 1966-67; tchr. Syracuse (N.Y.) City Sch. System, 1967-69; lectr. U. of Md., Eastern Shore, Princess Anne, Md., 1970-72; tchr. Prince George's County Pub. Schs., Upper Marlboro, Md., 1973—; instr. U. Guam, Anderson AFB, 1963, U.S. Armed Forces Inst., Anderson AFB, 1963, Yorktowne Bus. Inst., Landover, Md., 1987-90, Cheseapeake Bus. Inst., Clinton, Md., 1983-89; asst. advisor student tchrs. U. Md. Ea. Shore, Princess Anne, 1972; adj. instr. Bowie State U., 1990—; conv. speaker. Mem. AAUW, NEA, ASCD, Am. Vocat. Assn., Md. Bus. Edn. Assn. (pres.-elect 1987-88, pres. 1988-89, Educator of Yr. 1989), Md. Vocat. Assn. (regional rep. 1986-89, audit chmn. 1987-89, Vocat.-Tech. Educator of Yr. 1989), Ea. Bus. Edn. Assn. (co-editor newsletter 1990-91, secondary exec. dir. 1991-94), Md. State Tchrs. Assn., D.C. Bus. Edn. Assn., Nat. Bus. Edn. Assn., Data Processing Mgmt. Assn., Internat. Soc. for Bus. Edn., Md. Bus. Edn. Com., Prince George's County Edn. Assn., New Eng. Bus. Educators Assn. Democrat. Baptist. Home: 8922 Goldfield Pl Clinton MD 20735-2024 Office: Prince George's Pub Sch Upper Marlboro MD 20772

STREET, PICABO, Olympic athlete; b. Triumph, Idaho, 1971. Silver medalist, women's downhill alpine skiing Olympic Games, Lillehammer, Norway, 1994; professional downhill skier, 1994—. Office: US Olympic Com 1750 E Boulder St Colorado Springs CO 80909

STREETER, ANNE PAUL, state senator; b. Phila., July 21, 1926; s. Henry Neill and Marianne (Harris) Paul; m. Ronald Mather Streeter; children—Jean, Deborah, Stephen, Richard, Jonathan. B.A., Smith Coll., 1948. Tchr. Springside Sch., Phila., 1948-1949, Oxford Sch., West Hartford, Conn., 1949-1950; mem. Conn. Senate, Hartford, 1982-87, dep. majority leader, 1985-87. Mem. West Hartford Town Council, 1973-81, mayor, 1975-81. Named Woman of Year, Jr. C. of C., West Hartford, 1979, Hartford, 1981. Mem. LWV (pres. 1966-67, 1969-72). Republican. Congregationalist. Home: 31 Brookmoor Rd West Hartford CT 06107-3104

STREIFF, ARLYNE BASTUNAS, business owner, educator; b. Sacramento, Calif., Nov. 4; d. Peter James and Isabel (Gemnas) Bastunas; children: Peter Joshua, Joshua Gus. BS, U. Nev., 1965; postgrad., U. Calif., Davis, 1965-68, Calif. State U., Chico, 1968, 71. Cert. elem. tchr., Calif., Nev. Tchr. reading, lang. and kindergarten Enterprise Elem. Sch. Dist., Redding, Calif., 1965-95, tchr. kindergarten, 1988-95; owner, pres. Arlyne's Svcs., Redding, Calif., 1990—. Author: Niko and His Friends, 1989, Niko and the Black Rottweiler, 1995, Color-Talk-Spell. Mem. Rep. Women, Five County Labor Coun., Redding, 1976-93, Calif. Labor Fedn., 1974-93, AFL-CIO, 1974-93. Named Tchr. of Yr., Enterprise Sch. Dist., 1969. Mem. AAUW, Am. Fedn. Tchrs., Calif. Tchrs. Assn. (bargaining spokesperson 1968-72, exec. bd. dirs.), United Tchrs. Enterprise (pres. 1979-80, chmn. lang. com.), Calif. Reading Assn., Enterprise Fedn. Tchrs. (pres. 1974), Calif. Fedn. Tchrs. (v.p. 1974-78), Redding C. of C., Women of Moose, Elks. Home: 1468 Benton Dr Redding CA 96003-3116 Office: Arlynes Svcs 1478 Benton Dr Redding CA 96003-3116

STREISAND, BARBRA JOAN, singer, actress, director; b. Bklyn., Apr. 24, 1942; d. Emanuel and Diana (Rosen) S.; m. Elliott Gould, Mar. 1963 (div.); 1 son, Jason Emanuel. Grad. high sch., Bklyn.; student, Yeshiva of Bklyn. N.Y. theatre debut Another Evening with Harry Stoones, 1961; appeared in Broadway musicals I Can Get It for You Wholesale, 1962, Funny Girl, 1964-65; motion pictures include Funny Girl, 1968, Hello Dolly, 1969, On a Clear Day You Can See Forever, 1970, The Owl and the Pussy Cat, 1970, What's Up Doc?, 1972, Up the Sandbox, 1972, The Way We Were, 1973, For Pete's Sake, 1974, Funny Lady, 1975, The Main Event, 1979, All Night Long, 1981, Nuts, 1987; star, prodr. film A Star is Born, 1976; prodr., dir., star Yentl, 1983, The Prince of Tides, 1991; exec. prodr.: (TV movie) Serving in Silence: The Margarethe Cammermeyer Story, 1995; TV spls. include My Name is Barbra, 1965 (5 Emmy awards), Color Me Barbra, 1966; rec. artist on Columbia Records; Gold record albums include People, 1965, My Name is Barbra, 1965, Color Me Barbra, 1966, Barbra Streisand: A Happening in Central Park, 1968, Barbra Streisand: One Voice, Stoney End, 1971, Barbra Joan Streisand, 1972, The Way We Were, 1974, A Star is Born, 1976, Superman, 1977, The Stars Salute Israel at 30, 1978, Wet, 1979, (with Barry Gibb) Guilty, 1980, Emotion, 1984, The Broadway Album, 1986, Til I Loved You, 1989; other albums include: A Collection: Greatest Hits, 1989, Just for the Record, 1991, Back to Broadway, 1993. Recipient Emmy award, CBS-TV spl. (My Name Is Barbra), 1964, Acad. award as best actress (Funny Girl), 1968, Golden Globe award (Funny Girl), 1969, co-recipient Acad. award for best song (Evergreen), 1976, Georgie award AGVA 1977, Grammy awards for best female pop vocalist, 1963, 64, 65, 77, 86, for best song writer (with Paul Williams), 1977, 2 Grammy nominations for Back to Broadway, 1994; Nat. Acad. of Recording Arts & Sciences Lifetime Achievement Award, 1994. Office: Creative Artists Agy care Fred Spector 1888 Century Park E Ste 1400 Los Angeles CA 90067-1718*

STRIBLING, DENISE HOEY, employment specialist; b. Vallejo, Calif.; d. Owen Raymond and Lorraine Theresa (Grossi) Hoey; m. Richard Alan Stribling, Apr. 30, 1988; 1 child, Alison Danielle. AA in Liberal Arts, Solano C.C., Suisun City, Calif., 1974; BA in Psychology, U. Calif., Davis, 1976; MA in Human Resource Mgmt., Marymount U., 1991. Profl. in Human Resources, Human Resource Cert. Inst. Floor mgr. Payless Drug N.W., Oakland, Fresno, Calif., 1976-80; asst. mgr. Payless Drug N.W., Fresno, 1980-86; store mgr. Payless Drug N.W., Concord, Palmdale, Calif., 1986-89; employment specialist Washington Hosp. Ctr., 1989-92, sr. employment specialist, 1992-95, acting dir. employment, 1995—. Mem. ASTD (D.C. metro chpt., mktg. and advt. coord., Spl. Achievement award 1990, Continuous Svc. award 1991), Soc. Human Resources Mgmt., Delta Epsilon Sigma (Delta Kappa chpt.). Democrat. Roman Catholic. Home: 7866 Vervain Ct Springfield VA 22152-3106

STRICK, CYNTHIA LEE, elementary educator; b. Dennison, Ohio, Jan. 15, 1962; d. John Lee and Donna Elaine (Ross) Kilpatrick; m. Thomas Stephen Strick, Dec. 28, 1985; children: Curtis Russell, Victoria Lynn. BS in Edn., Akron U., 1984; postgrad. in Curriculum and Instrn., Ashland U., 1994—. Day care tchr./aide U. Akron, 1980-84; developmentally handicapped tchr. Lorain (Ohio) City Schs., 1984-90, 6th grade tchr., 1990—. Mem. Internat. Reading Assn. Roman Catholic. Home: 212 Moorewood Ave Avon Lake OH 44012 Office: Fairhome Acad Illinois Ave Lorain OH 44052

STRICK, SADIE ELAINE, psychologist; b. Masontown, Pa., May 5, 1929; d. Michael and Mary (Oziemblowski) Wierzbicki; m. John Mackovjak, Aug. 10, 1947 (dec. Mar. 1972); children: Deborah, Susan; m. Ellis Strick, Aug. 11, 1974. BSW, U. Pitts., 1975, MEd, 1977, PhD, 1981. Lic. psychologist; diplomate Am. Bd. Med. Psychotherapists (fellow). Psychologist I Mayview State Hosp., Bridgeville, Pa., 1984-87; owner Counseling & Behavior Specialists, P.C., Pitts., 1981—; mem. C.G. Jung Ednl. Ctr., Pitts., 1980—; guest speaker Compassionate Friends, Pitts., 1986—, Womens Career Conv., Pitts., 1982. Bd. dirs. OAR/Allegheny, Pitts., 1981-82. Fellow Pa. Psychol. Assn.; mem. Am. Psychol. Assn., Pitts. Assn. for Theory and Practice of Psychoanalysis. Home: 2160 Greentree Rd Apt 605 Pittsburgh PA 15220-1437 Office: Counseling and Behavior Specialists PC 429 Forbes Ave Ste 1614 Pittsburgh PA 15219-1604 also: 1 Williamsburg Pl # 230 Warrendale PA 15086-7568

STRICKLAND, ANITA MAURINE, retired business educator, librarian; b. Groom, Tex., Sept. 24, 1923; d. Oliver Austin and Thelma May (Slay) Pool; m. LeRoy Graham Mashburn, Aug. 12, 1945 (dec. Mar. 1977); 1 child, Ronald Gene; m. Reid Strickland, May 27, 1978. BBA, West Tex. State U., 1962, MEd, 1965; postgrad. in library sci., Tex. Women's U., 1970. Cert. tchr., Tex.; cert. librarian. Employment interviewer Douglas Aircraft Co., Oklahoma City, 1942-45; cashier, bookkeeper Southwestern Pub. Services, Groom and Panhandle, Tex., 1950-58; acct. Gen. Motors Outlet, Groom, 1958-62; tchr. bus., lang. arts Groom Pub. Schs., 1962-68; bus. tchr., librarian Amarillo (Tex.) Pub. Schs., 1968-81. Vol. Amarillo Symphony, 1980—, Amarillo Rep. Com., 1981—, Lone Star ballet, 1981-92; docent Amarillo Mus. Art, 1987—, sec. 1987-90, 93—; vol. Amarillo Alliance, 1989—, sec. 1989-90. Mem. AAUW (legis. com. 1986-88, sec. 1989-90, bd. dirs. 1989-91), Amarillo C. of C. (vol. women's divsn. 1981-86), Amarillo Christian Women's Club (asst. prayer advisor 1989-90, treas. 1995—). Baptist. Home: 6513 Roxton Dr Amarillo TX 79109-5120

STRICKLAND, HATTIE DENE, medical, surgical nurse, rehabilitation nurse, home health care nurse; b. Statesville, N.C., Sept. 10, 1944; d. Benton Ozzie and Magdlene (Teague); children: Cindy, Jeffrey. Diploma, Bowman Grey Sch. of Nursing, Winston-Salem, N.C., 1967. RN, N.C.; cert. child devel. nurse. Staff RN, float Rex Hosp., Durham, N.C.; RN, surgical High Point (N.C.) Hosp., Thomasville (N.C.) Hosp.; pvt. duty nurse High Point, 1984—; home health care nurse, owner, operator Strickland Care, High Point, 1995—. Home and Office: 1010 N Rotary Dr High Point NC 27262-3610

STRICKLAND, JILL ANN, product development administrator; b. Toledo, Ohio, Jan. 15, 1951; d. John Floyd and Beatrice Kathryn (Hoye) Wood; m. Guerry Patrick Strickland, June 19, 1982; children: Shana, Lane. BS, U. West Fla., Pensacola, 1973; MS, So. Coll. Tech., Marietta, Ga., 1994. Programmer Gen. Electric, St. Petersburg, Fla., 1973-78; edn. specialist Honeywell, Atlanta, 1978-79; mgr. client conversions Alexander & Alexander, Atlanta, 1979-89; mgr. product devel. Sales Techs., Atlanta, 1989-93; mgr. devel. Systematics, Atlanta, 1993—. Republican. Presbyterian. Office: Systematics Ste 500 219 Perimeter Center Pky NE Atlanta GA 30346-1303

STRICKLAND, NELLIE B., library program director; b. Belmont, Miss., Dec. 12, 1932. BS, Murray State U., 1954; MLS, George Peabody Coll.,

1971. Ref. libr. Murray State Coll., Murray, Ky., 1954; asst. libr. Dept. Army, Ft. Stewart, Ga., 1955-56; field libr. U.S. Army, Japan, 1957-59; area libr. U.S. Army, Europe, 1960-66; staff libr. U.S. Army So. Command, C.Z., 1966-67; area libr. U.S. Army, Vietnam, 1967-68, staff libr., 1971-72; chief libr. U.S. Army, Ft. Benning, Ga., 1970-71; dir. library program U.S. Army Pacific, 1973-74; dir. Army libr. program Washington, 1974-94. Recipient Outstanding Performance award Ft. Benning, 1970, Armed Forces Achievement citation, 1982, 94, Order of the White Plume; Dept. of Army Tng. grantee 1971; Dept. of Addy decoartion for Exceptional Civil Svc., 1994. Mem. ALA, Kappa Delta Phi, Alpha Sigma Alpha. Home: 203 S Yoakum Pky Apt 614 Alexandria VA 22304-3716

STRICKLAND, NORMALIE, library director; b. Effingham, Ill., Jan. 12, 1938; d. Leo J. and Josephine G. (Lidy) Richards; m. Joseph Hubert Strickland, Mar. 20, 1965. BA, Marian Coll., 1960; MLS, U. Ill., 1961. Asst. sci. dept. Enoch Pratt Free Libr., Balt., 1961-63; asst. sci. dept. Phoenix Pub. Libr., 1963-64, head sci. dept., 1964-65; asst. acquisitions dept. U. Okla. Libr., Norman, 1965-66; asst. St. Anthony High Sch. Libr., Effingham, 1966-67; libr. dir. Helen Matthes Libr., Effingham, 1967—. Roman Catholic. Office: Helen Matthes Libr 100 E Market Ave Effingham IL 62401-3472

STRICKLIN, KRISTI ANN, science educator; b. Kingfisher, Okla., Jan. 23, 1956; d. Herman E. and Evelyn J. (Lorenz) Bredel; m. John W. Stricklin, Dec. 26, 1976; children: Brianne, Logan, A. J. BS, Okla. State U., 1978. Cert. tchr. secondary sci. edn., computer sci., math. Tchr. high sch. Strother Pub. Sch., Seminole, Okla., 1978—. Coord. blood dr. Okla. Blood Inst., Strother, 1992-93. Named Blood Dr. Coord. of Yr. Okla. Blood Inst. Mem. Nat. Sci. Tchrs. Assn., Okla. Edn. Assn., Strother Edn. Assn. (pres. 1983-85). Republican. Methodist. Office: Strother Pub Sch Rt 3 Box 265 Seminole OK 74868

STRIEBER, PATTY JO, guidance counselor; b. San Antonio, July 24, 1959; d. Carl Edward Sr. and Mary Alice (Parker) Meeks; m. Bobby Alan Strieber, Nov. 15, 1980; children: Tyler Reed, Maggie Kathryn. BEd, S.W. Tex. State U., San Marcos, 1981; MEd, U. Houston-Victoria, Victoria, Tex., 1988. Cert. guidance counselor, mid-mgmt. adminstr. Tchr. bus. Stroman High Sch., Victoria, Tex., 1981-82, Nordheim (Tex.) High Sch., Tex., 1982-83; elem. libr. Yorktown (Tex.) Elem. Sch., Tex., 1983-84, tchr. 5th grade, 1984-90, elem. counselor, 1990—. Active Yorktown Firemen Ladies' Aux. Mem. ASCD, Tex. Sch. Counseling Assn., LaBahia Counseling Assn., Tex. Assn. for Gifted and Talented. Home: 241 N Gohmert Yorktown TX 78164 Office: Yorktown Elem Sch PO Box 487 Yorktown TX 78164-0487

STRIEFSKY, LINDA A(NN), lawyer; b. Carbondale, Pa., Apr. 27, 1952; d. Leo James and Antoinette Marie (Carachilo) S.; m. James Richard Carlson, Nov. 3, 1984; children: David Carlson, Paul Carlson, Daniel Carlson. BA summa cum laude, Marywood Coll., 1974; JD, Georgetown U., 1977. Bar: Ohio 1977. Assoc., Thompson, Hine and Flory, Cleve., 1977-85, ptnr., 1985—. Loaned exec. United Way of Northeast Ohio, Cleve., 1978; adv. trustee Cleve. Music Sch. Settlement. Mem. Am. Bar Found., ABA (mem. real estate fin. com. 1980—, vice-chair lender liability com. 1993—), Am. Coll. Real Estate Lawyers bd. govs. 1994—), Internat. Coun. of Shopping Centers, Nat. Assn. Office and Indsl. Parks, Ohio State Bar Assn. (bd. govs. real property sect. 1985—), Greater Cleve. Bar Assn. (chmn. bar applicants com. 1983-84, exec. council young lawyers sect. 1982-85, chmn. 1984-85, mem. exec. council real property sect. 1980-84, Merit Svc. award 1983, 85), Pi Gamma Mu. Democrat. Roman Catholic. Home: 2222 Delamere Dr Cleveland OH 44106-3204 Office: Thompson Hine and Flory 1100 Nat City Bank Bldg 629 Euclid Ave Cleveland OH 44114-3070

STRIEGEL, PEGGY SIMSARIAN, advertising executive; b. Phila., July 12, 1941; d. Robert Ernest Samuel and Margaret (Miller) Thompson; m. James P. Simsarian, Sept. 4, 1965 (div. Sept. 1976); children: Catherine Ann, Sheila Thompson; m. Louis E. Striegel, Sept. 14, 1976 (div. June 1984); m. Andrew H. Schmeltz Jr., Dec. 4, 1991. BA, Sarah Lawrence Coll., 1963. Asst. editor Oxford U. Press, N.Y.C., 1963-64; picture editor Western Pub. Co., N.Y.C., 1964-66; art editor Houghton-Mifflin, Inc., Boston, 1966-68; pres. Peggy's Graphics, McLean, Va., 1968-78, Striegel Advt. and Graphics, Inc., Broken Arrow, Okla., 1978—. Lower Merion (Pa.) area coord. Shapp for Congress, Phila., 1970; area coord. and graphic designer Phillips for U.S. Congress, McLean, 1972; pres. bd. dirs. Gatesway Found., Broken Arrow, 1987-89; chmn. Cmty. Playhouse Broken Arrow, 1979-81; mktg. bd. chair Tulsa Philharmonic, 1995-95. Recipient numerous advt. awards including several Addies and citations Tulsa Advt. Club, 1990-91, Gold Quill, 1990, cert. Merit Printing Industries Am., 1983, award of Excellence Am. Inst. Graphic Arts, 1983, Am. Corp. Identity Graphics award, 1994. Mem. Advt. Fedn. Tulsa, Bus. and Profl. Advt. Assn. (Gold Ring award 1986, 87), Women in Communications (prpg. chmn. 1991), Builders Assn. Met. Tulsa, Direct Mktg. Assn., Met. Tulsa C. of C., Broken Arrow C. of C., Bus. Profl. Advt. Assn., Jr. Achievement of Tulsa (bd. dirs. 1990-94). Democrat. Presbyterian. Club: Art Directors. Home: 6110 S 221st East Ave Broken Arrow OK 74014-2017 Office: 716 S Main St Broken Arrow OK 74012-5502

STRIFE, MARY LOUISE, librarian; b. Lowville, N.Y., June 9, 1959; d. Kenneth Francis and Frances Katherine (Linck) S. BA in Biology, SUNY Coll., Potsdam, N.Y., 1981; MLS, SUNY, Buffalo, 1982. Reference libr. Cornell Univ., Ithaca, N.Y., 1982-85; libr. United Technologies Corp., East Hartford, Conn., 1985-86; reference libr. Syracuse (N.Y.) Univ., 1986-86, Univ. Rochester, Rochester, N.Y., 1986-89; coord. of pub. svcs. SUNY Inst. Tech., Utica, N.Y., 1989—. Mem. Upstate N.Y. Spl. Librs. Assn. (treas. 1988-90, v.p./pres.-elect 1990-92), N.Y. Libr. Assn. (Acad. & Spl. Librs. sect. sec., treas. 1988-90), ALA, Spl. Librs. Assn., Gamma Sigma Sigma (exec. sec. 1990-93). Democrat. Roman Catholic. Office: Marcy Campus PO Box 3051 Suny Inst Tech Utica NY 13504

STRINGER, GRETCHEN ENGSTROM, consulting volunteer administrator; b. Pitts., Feb. 25, 1925; d. Birger and Gertrude Anne (Schuchman) Engstrom; m. Loren F. Stringer, Oct. 3, 1953 (dec. Sept. 1992); children: Lizbeth Stringer Coffman, Pamela, William E., Frederick E. BA, Oberlin Coll., 1946; Cert. in Teaching, U. Pitts., 1951, SUNY, Buffalo, 1964; M, SUNY, Buffalo, 1995. Cert. vol. adminstr. Owner, founder, pres. Vol. Cons., Clarence, N.Y., 1979—; Founding pres., bd. dirs. Ctrl. Referral Svc. Author: The Board Manual Workbook, 1980, rev., 1993, The Instructors Guide, 1982, A Magical Formula, 1980; contbr. articles to profl. jours. Exec. dir. Vol. Action Ctr., United Way Buffalo and Erie County, 1978-81; founding vice chair Erie County Commn. on Status of Women, 1989-93; pres. Girl Scout Coun. of Buffalo and Erie County, chair, gen. mgr. cadette encampment; bd. dirs. Clarence Ctrl. Sch. Dist., 1976-86; chair, gen. mgr. Buffalo and Erie County Bicentennial Parade, 1976, Erie County Ski Swap; active Longview Protestant Home for Children Bd., Millard Fillmore Jr. Bd., Preventin is Primary, N.Y. Bd. State Foster Care Youth Ind. Project, others. Recipient Pinny Wilson Vol. award Buffalo and Erie County, 1981, Continuing Svc. award Mass. Mutual, 1987, Girl Scouts Thanks Badge, 1983, Susan Reid Greene Russell award Jr. League of Buffalo, 1994. Mem. N.Y. Assn. Vol. Ctrs. (founding exec. bd.), Vol. Adminstrs. Western N.Y. (founding pres. 1980), Buffalo Ambassadors of C. of C. (bd. dirs.), Jr. League Buffalo, Inc., Assn. Vol. Adminstrn. (chair, gen. mgr. nat. conf. 1986, nat. trainer, re-cert. chair). Office: Vol Cons 9015 Cliffside Dr Clarence NY 14031-1460

STRINGER, MARY EVELYN, art historian, educator; b. Huntsville, Mo., July 31, 1921; d. William Madison and Charity (Rogers) S. A.B., U. Mo., 1942; A.M., U. N.C., Chapel Hill, 1955; Ph.D. (Danforth scholar), Harvard U., 1973. Asst. prof. art Miss. State Coll. for Women (now Miss. U. for Women), Columbus, 1947-58; asso. prof. Miss. State Coll. for Women (now Miss. U. for Women), 1958-73, prof., 1973—; regional dir. for Miss., Census of Stained Glass Windows in Am., 1840-1940. Bd. dirs. Mississippians for Ednl. Broadcasting; mem. Miss. com. Save Outdoor Sculpture, 1992-93. Fulbright scholar W.Ger., 1955-56; Harvard U. travel grantee, 1966-67; NEH summer seminar grantee, 1980. Mem. AAUW, Coll. Art Assn., Southeastern Coll. Art Conf. (dir. 1975-80, 83-89, Disting. Svc. award 1992), Internat. Ctr. Medieval Art, Aubudon Soc., The Nature Conservancy, Sierra Club, Phi Beta Kappa, Phi Kappa Phi. Democrat. Episcopalian. Office: Dept Art Miss U for Women Columbus MS 39701

STRINGER-PAGE, MARTHA, city official; b. Hartford, Conn., Oct. 1, 1950; d. Samuel and Martha (Hawthorn) Harris; divorced; 1 child, Tueré Stringer. BA, Ea. Conn. State U., 1973. Lic. foster parent. EEO asst. U. Conn., Storrs, 1973-78; EEO counselor Old Dominion U., Norfolk, Va., 1979; EEO specialist Castle & Cooke, Inc., San Francisco, 1980-84; tng. coord. YWCA, Hartford, 1984-86; asst. dir. Asylum Hill Organizing Project, Hartford, 1986-88; tng. coord. adolescent parenting program City of Hartford, 1988-93, sr. adminstrv. analyst youth svcs., 1993—. Editor: (videos) Stress Problems of Teen Parenthood, 1992, Young Mothers and Fathers: Where Do We Go from Here, 1993. Office: City of Hartford 2 Holcomb St Hartford CT 06112-1528

STRIPLING, BEVERLY WARREN, association executive; b. Welch, W.Va.; d. Charles Richard and mary Louise (Smootz) Warren; m. Cornelius S. Stripling (div.); children: Anthony E., Anne-Marie. BS, Howard U.; EdD (hon.), Daniel Hale Williams U.; MBA, U. Denver. With Colo. Nat. Bank, Denver; realtor Champion Realty Co., Denver; adminstr. Solar Energy Rsch. Inst., Golden, Colo.; mgr. divsn. adminstrn. and fin. Engring. Info., Inc., N.Y.C.; dir. adminstrn. Mass. Housing Fin. Agy., Boston; pres. Warren Group, Chelsea, Mass.; dir. advicacy and pub. polity, dir. Washington office YWCA of U.S.A., Washington, 1990—. Bd. dirs. Denver YWCA, United Negro Coll. Fund Colo., Inst. Internat. Edn. Colo., Planned Parenthood Colo., Montessori Sch. Denver, Urban League Colo., Religious for Reproductive Choice, 1990—; bd. dirs. Black Women's Agenda, 1991—, sec., 1993—; trustee Internat. Devel. Conf., 1990—; treas. Women for Meaningful Summits, 1990-94, pres.-elect, 1994—; nat. bd. dirs. YWCA, 1976-88; mem. allocations com. Mass Bay United Way, 1985-89; bd. dirs. Boston YMCA, co-chair pub. policy com., 1985-89. Mem. Boston Club. Office: YWCA of USA 624 9th St NW Washington DC 20001-5303

STRISOWER, SUZANNE, clinical hypnotherapist, counselor; b. San Francisco, Oct. 27, 1956; d. Edward Herman and Beverly Gene (Boutell) S. BFA, JFK U., Orinda, Calif., 1988; MA, Pacifica Grad. Inst., 1994. Cert. clin. hypnotherapist; cert. counselor. Wallcovering installer Orinda, Calif., 1974-82; interior designer Lyons, Hill & Ruga Inc., Pleasant Hill, Calif., 1983-85; project mgr. Wayne Ruga Inc., Martinez, Calif., 1985-88; exec. dir. Nat. Symposium for Healthcare Interior Design, Martinez, 1986-88; treatment counselor Youth Homes Inc., Walnut Creek, Calif., 1988-93; clin. hypnotherapist The Inner Journey, Walnut Creek, Calif., 1991—, marriage, family and child counselor, 1994—; tchr. Acalanes Adult Edn. Ctr., Walnut Creek, 1992—; lectr. in field. Child advisor, vice chairperson Contra Costa County Mental Health Commn., 1991-93; pres. Orgn. of Youth Svcs., 1991-94; mem. Juvenile Justice Delinquency Prevention Commn. Contra Costa County, 1988—, mem. family and children's trust com., mem. juvenile sys. planning adv. com. Mem. Am. Coun. Hypnotist Examiners. Home: 542 Center Ave # 285 Martinez CA 94553

STROBEL, SHIRLEY HOLCOMB, magazine editor, educator, non-profit organization writer; b. Hastings, Nebr., May 8, 1929; d. Dent Z. and Helen (Spiegel) Holcomb; m. Howard Austin Strobel, Aug. 26, 1953; children: Paul Austin, Gary Dent, Linda Susan Strobel Helgeson. BS, Northwestern U., 1951; MA, Duke U., 1953. Cert. counselor, N.C.; tchr., N.C. English tchr. Salem Acad., Winston-Salem, N.C., 1952-53; tchr. Durham city schs., N.C., 1954-55, Durham County schs., 1967-90; editor Ch. Tchrs. mag. Nat. Tchrs. Edn. Project, Durham, 1986-89; editor Ch. Tchrs., Harper Collins, San Francisco, 1990-93; part-time instr. Program in Edn. Duke U., Durham, 1991-93; chmn. dept. English Jordan High Sch., Durham, 1967-75; reader Nat. Coun. Tchrs. English, 1969-71; rsch. asst. CUNY, 1973-74; mem. accreditation team Duke U. Edn. Program, 1985; judge mag. competition for Episcopal Communicators Conf., 1992—. Co-author: Advanced Placement English, 1983. Founder, pres. Threshold Clubhouse for Mentally Ill, Durham, 1985, chmn. capital campaign, 1988-91, chmn. ways and means com., 1992—; active Area Bd. Mental Health, Durham, 1990-92; mem. state bd. N.C. Alliance for the Mentally Ill, 1994—. Democrat. Baptist. Home and Office: 1119 Woodburn Rd Durham NC 27705-5737

STRODE, DEBORAH LYNN, English language educator; b. Ft. Dodge, Iowa, June 18, 1948; d. Franklin Max and Helen (Crook) S. BS in Speech and Theater, Parsons Coll., 1971; teaching cert., Boise State U., 1977; MS in Edn., So. Oreg. State U., 1985; adminstrv. cert., U. Alaska, Anchorage, 1986. Cert. tchr. Alaska, cert. adminstr., Nev. Tchr. U.S. Peace Corps., Liberia, West Africa, 1971-73; tchr., adminstr. North Slope Borough Sch. Dist., Barrow, Alaska, 1976-90; adminstr. fed. programs Iditarod Area Sch. Dist., McGrath, Alaska, 1990-91; vis. tchr. English Nishinomiya (Hyogo, Japan) Mcpl. Edn. Bd., 1993—; dir. childrens receiving home North Slope Borough Health Dept., Barrow, summer 1978. Supporting mem. Friends of Liberia, Washington; counselor McLaughlin Youth Detention Ctr., summer 1975; counselor Long and Short House Alaska Children's Svcs., 1974; treas. Barrow PTA; sponsor Internat. Thespian Soc.; active Fairfax County Pub. Access TV. Mem. NEA, Alaska Arts in Edn., Am. Theater Assn., Returned Peace Corps Vol. Assn., North Slope Adminstrn. Assn., North Slope Edn. Assn. (v.p.), Secondary Theater Assn., Childrens Theater Assn. Office: Nishinomiya Hyogo Mcpl Sch Bd, 8-26 Rokutanji-Cho, Nishinomiya 662, Japan

STROHMEYER, LOUISE ANNE, social worker; b. Huntington, N.Y., Nov. 22, 1943; d. John Edward and Lillian (Margraff) Mitskevich; m. George Dewey Strohmeyer, June 05, 1971; children: Donna Anne, Jennifer Sharon. BA, Valparaiso U., 1967. Caseworker Cook County Pub. Aid, Chgo., 1968-69; intake worker Ill. Child and Family Svc., Chgo., 1969-70; billing clk. W.H.S. Lloyd Co., Chgo., 1970-71; activities dir. Sr. Ctr., Springfield, Ill., 1971-72; recreation therapy aide Mediplex, Danbury, Conn., 1989-92. Luth. Peace Corps worker, Prince of Peace Luth. Ctr., Fresno, Calif., 1967-68; vol. Yonkers (N.Y.) Sr. Ctr., 1977-78, Danbury Hosp., 1979-93, Shelter Rock Elem. Sch., Danbury, 1983-90; bd. dirs. Madison (Ohio) Sr. Ctr., 1975-78. Mem. NASW, AAUW (bd. dirs. 1981—). Home: 28 Sunrise Rd Danbury CT 06810-4113

STROMBERG, ANNE B., management consultant, executive recruiter; b. Sidney, Ohio; d. Joseph M. and Mary Louise (Marrs) Bell; children: Steve Stromberg, Anastasia Pflug. Student, Ohio No. U., 1949-50, Ind. U., 1950-51, Miami U., Oxford, Ohio, 1951-52, U. Dayton, 1953-54, Citrus Coll., 1955, U. Nev., 1960-61, Calif. State U., L.A., 1964-65. Tchr. various elem. schs., 1955-65; coord. corp. travel and relocations Mattel, Inc., Hawthorne, Calif., 1966-71; mng. dir. Morgan, Bentley, Bristol, Pasadena, Calif., 1974—; founder L.A. Travel and Transp. Coun., 1969; founder, speaker Careers in Transition Seminars. pub., editor Morgan Plus Four, 1964-65. Dir., mem. adv. bd. Cross Roads/New Life, Hemet, Calif., 1979—; participant Save the Books, L.A., 1986, L.A. Hist. Theater Found., 1989, 90. Named an Outstanding Woman in Bus., Orange County Register, 1976. Mem. DAR, Colonial Dames, Nat. Assn. Exec. Recruiters. Republican. Office: Morgan Bentley Bristol 115 W California Blvd Ste 293 Pasadena CA 91105-3030

STROMBOM, CATHY JEAN, transportation planner, consultant; b. Bremerton, Wash., Nov. 4, 1949; d. Paul D. and Carolyn (Snitman) Powers; m. David Glen Strombom, June 17, 1972; 1 child, Paul Davis. BA summa cum laude, Whitman Coll., 1972; M in City and Regional Planning, Harvard U., 1977; postgrad., U. Wash., 1982-84. Urban planner Harvard Inst. for Internat. Devel., Tehran, Iran, 1977; sr. transp. planner Puget Sound Coun. Govts., Seattle, 1978-84; mgr. transp. planning Parsons Brinckerhoff Quade and Douglas, Inc., Seattle, 1984—; v.p. Women's Transp. Seminar, Seattle, 1988-90 (Woman of Yr. 1989). Contbr. articles to profl. jours. Vol. U.S. Peace Corps, Marrakech, Morocco, 1973-75. Mem. Am. Inst. Cert. Planners (cert.), Am. Planning Assn., Inst. Transp. Engrs., Phi Beta Kappa. Home: 2580 W Viewmont Way W Seattle WA 98199 Office: Parsons Brinckerhoff Quade and Douglas Inc 999 Third Ave Ste 801 Seattle WA 98104

STROMMER, ANNE ELIZABETH RIVARD, librarian; b. Columbus, Ohio, Dec. 24, 1940; d. Edwin Kenneth Rivard and Alda Nathan (Olin) Rivard Willis; m. Mathias Adolf Strommer, Jan. 3, 1965; children: Elisabeth Anne, Mathias Edwin. BA, Kent (Ohio) State U., 1962; MA in Libr. Sci., U. MIch., 1964. Reference libr. Detroit Pub. Libr., 1962-65, Ft. Knox (Ky.) Mil. Libr., 1968-69; reference libr. Houston Pub. Libr., 1978-80, branch mgr., 1980-81; tech. svcs. libr. North Harris County Coll., Houston, 1981-85, coord. tech. svcs., 1985-89, coord. tech. and automation svcs., 1990-93, coord. automated libr. svcs., 1993—. Mem. ALA, NAFE, Tex. Libr. Assn., Freedom to Read Found. Home: 20718 Greymoss Ln Houston TX 77073-3108 Office: N Harris Montgomery Community CollDist 250 N Sam Houston Pky E Houston TX 77060-2000

STRONG, BARBARA JEAN, author, nurse; b. Flushing, N.Y., Mar. 30, 1941; d. James Swen and Laura (Roberto) Anderson; m. widow; children: Annemarie Flores, James Paul Sciortino, Laura Joy Lowe. Student, CUNY, 1958-61, Auburn U., 1962; grad. in nursing, St. Joseph's Hosp. Health Ctr., Syracuse, N.Y., 1982. RN, N.Y. Charge nurse St. Joseph's Hosp. Health Ctr., 1982-84; instr. ARC, Syracuse, 1984-89. Author: Patient's Guide to Bone Marrow Transplant, 1991. Mem. NAFE, Tel. Pioneers Am., Families Against Cancer, St. Joseph's Hosp. Health Ctr. Sch. Nursing Alumni Assn., Nat. Com. To Preserve Social Security and Medicare, Boston Met. Mus. Art. Methodist. Home and Office: 1811 Sabal Palm Dr Apt 408 Fort Lauderdale FL 33324-5934

STRONG, MAYDA NEL, psychologist, educator; b. Albuquerque, May 6, 1942; d. Floyd Samuel and Wanda Christmas (Martin) Strong; 1 child, Robert Allen Willingham. BA in Speech-Theatre cum laude, Tex. Western Coll., 1963; EdM, U. Tex., Austin, 1972, PhD in Counseling Psychology, 1978; lic. clin. psychologist, Colo., 1984; cert. alcohol counselor III, Colo., 1987, nat. addiction counselor II, 1991. Asst. instr. in ednl. psychology U. Tex., Austin, 1974-78; instr. psychology Austin Community Coll., 1974-78, Otero Jr. Coll., La Junta, Colo., 1979-89; dir. outpatient and emergency svcs. S.E. Colo. Family Guidance and Mental Health Ctr., Inc., La Junta, 1978-81; pvt. practice psychol. therapy, La Junta, 1981—; exec. dir. Pathfinders Chem. Dependency program, 1985-94; clin. psychologist Inst. for Forensic Psychiatry, Colo. Mental Health Inst., Pueblo, 1989-94; adj. faculty Adams State Coll., 1992; dir. Allstrong Enterprises, Inc., 1992-94. Del. to County Dem. Conv., 1988. Appeared in The Good Doctor, 1980, On Golden Pond, 1981, Chase Me Comrade, 1989, Plz. Ste., 1987. AAUW fellow, 1974-76. Mem. Bus. and Profl. People (legis. chairperson 1982-83, chmn. news election svc. 1982-88), Colo. Psychol. Assn. (legis. chmn. for dist.), Am. Contract Bridge League. Contbr. articles in field to profl. publs. Author poems in Chinook: Paths through the Puzzle, Decisions, Passion. Home: 500 Holly Ave PO Box 177 Swink CO 81077-0177 Office: 317 W 3rd St Ste 204 La Junta CO 81050

STRONG, SARA DOUGHERTY, psychologist, custody mediator; b. Phila., May 30, 1927; d. Augustus Joseph and Orpha Elizabeth (Dock) Dougherty; m. David Mather Strong, Dec. 21, 1954. BA in Psychology, Pa. State U., 1949; MA in Clin. Psychology, Temple U., 1960, postgrad., 1968-72; cert. in Family Therapy, Family Inst. Phila., 1978. Lic. psychologist, Pa. Med. br. psychologist Family Ct. Phila., 1960-85, asst. chief psychologist, 1985-88, chief psychologist, 1988-92; retired, 1992; pvt. practice Phila., 1992—; cons. St. Joseph's Home for Girls, Phila., 1963-84, Daughters of Charity of St. Vincent De Paul, Albany, N.Y., 1965-90. Mem. APA (assoc.), Am. Assn. Marriage and Family Therapists, Pa. Psychol. Assn., Nat. Register of Health Svc. Providers in Psychology, Family Inst. Phila. Democrat. Home: 1114 N 65th St Philadelphia PA 19151

STRONG, SUSAN CLANCEY, communication consultant; b. Cin., Nov. 10, 1939; d. William Power and Elizabeth (Browne) Clancey; m. Oliver Swigert, 1957 (div. 1972); children: Silvia, David Mack; m. Richard Devon Strong, 1977. BA, Northwestern U., 1965; MA, U. Calif., Berkeley, 1972, PhD, 1979. Tchr. Helen Bush Parkside Sch., Seattle, 1965-66, Taipei (Taiwan) Lang. Inst., 1967-68; acting instr. U. Calif., Berkeley, 1972-78, teaching fellow, 1979, lectr., 1979-84; lectr. St. Mary's Coll., Moraga, Calif., 1982-85; pvt. practice Orinda, Calif., 1985-90; sr. rsch. assoc. Ctr. for Econ. Conversion, 1990—; mem. Contra Costa County Conflict Resolution Panels, Calif., 1987—; affiliate Support Ctr./CTD, San Francisco, 1987—; del. UN Conf. on Econ. Conversion, Moscow, 1990. Author poetry, columnist, book reviewer, 1986—. Mem. Bay Area Global Tomorrow Com., 1986; co-founder Peace Economy Working Group, 1988; co-author Peace Economy Campaign, 1988; mem. Peace Action Nat. Strategy Com., 1989-95, co-chair strategy com., 1992-93; conf. co-chmn. Nat. Sane/Freeze Congress, 1989-90, rep. nat. bd. advisors Nat. Peace Action, Washington, 1989-95; mem. bd. advisors Peace and Environ. Project, San Francisco, 1986-88; chmn. No. Calif. Sane Freeze, San Francisco, 1985-89. Mem. Phi Beta Kappa. Democrat. Episcopalian.

STRONG-CUEVAS, ELIZABETH, sculptor; b. St. Germain en Laye, France, Jan. 22, 1929 (Am. citizen); d. George and Margaret (Strong) de Cuevas; 1 child, Deborah Carmichael. Student, Vassar Coll., 1946-48; AB, Sarah Lawrence Coll., 1952; postgrad., Art Students League, N.Y.C., 1963-68. One-woman shows include Lee Ault Gallery, N.Y.C., 1977-78, Tower Gallery, Southampton, N.Y., 1980, Iolas-Jackson Gallery, N.Y.C., 1983, 85, Guild Hall Mus., East Hampton, N.Y., 1985, Kerr Gallery, N.Y.C., 1988—, Ruth Vered Gallery, East Hampton, 1988; exhibited in group shows at Guild Hall, East Hampton, 1980, Art Students League of N.Y., 1982, Bruce Mus., Greenwich, Conn., 1984, 85, Tower Gallery, N.Y.C., 1984, Andre Zarre Gallery, N.Y.C., 1985, Kouros Gallery, N.Y.C. and Ridgefield, Conn., 1985, Susan Blanchard Gallery, N.Y.C., 1985-86, Ruth Vered Gallery, East Hampton, 1986-87, Benton Gallery, Southampton, 1987—, Kerr Gallery, N.Y.C., 1988—, Elaine Benson Gallery, Bridgehampton, N.Y., 1989, Portico, Inc., Cologne Art Fair, 1990, Feingarten Galleries, N.Y. Art Show, 1990, Marisa del Re Biennale III, Monte Carlo, 1991, Marisa del Re Biennale IV, 1993, Parrish Mus., Southampton, N.Y., 1994, Grounds for Sculpture, Hamilton, N.J., 1994; represented in pvt. collections. Club: Vassar of N.Y.

STRONSKI, ANNA MARIA NIEDŹWIEDZKA, language professional; b. Starachowice, Poland, Aug. 17, 1940; came to U.S., 1954; d. Antoni Niedzwiedzki and Wanda Gluszkiewicz; divorced; 1 child, Alexandra Joanna Paszkowski. BA, Wayne State U., 1963, MA, 1972. Cert. secondary edn. tchr., Mich. Tchr. French and Spanish Ford Mid. Sch., Highland Park, Mich., 1965-66; tchr. fgn. lang. dept. Highland Park Community High Sch., 1966-94, head fgn. lang. dept., 1968-70, 73-78, lang. arts facilitator, 1991-94; owner, founder Horizons-Internat., Grosse Pointe Park, Mich., 1993—; dist.-wide lang. cons./coord. Highland Park Pub. Schs., 1994—; ind. contractor/cons. Langs. and Svcs. Agy., 1993—; judge, field study, tchr. performance lang. arts Nat. Bd. Profl. Teaching Stds., Mich., 1994; scorer writing proficiency assessments Mich. Dept. Edn., 1994-95, trainer of tchrs., 1995. Advisor: (high sch. yearbook) Polar Bear, 1985-86 (Big E award Josten's Printing Div. 1986); editor: (newsletter) Happenings, 1977-79; co-editor (newsletter) Mich. Writing Assessment News, 1994—. Bd. dirs. French Inst. Mich., Southfield, 1985—. Recipient cert. appreciation for participation in Classrooms of Tomorrow program, Mich. Gov., 1990. Mem. Alliance Francaise: Detroit/Grosse Pointe, AAUW. Roman Catholic. Home: 790 Middlesex Blvd Grosse Pointe Park MI 48230 Office: Horizons Internat 790 Middlesex Blvd Grosse Pointe Park MI 48230

STROOCK, ELIZABETH (BETTY STROOCK), consulting geologist and geochemist; b. Casper, Wyo., Oct. 14, 1955. BA in Earth Sci. and Geology cum laude, Dartmouth Coll., 1977; postgrad., Cambridge (Eng.) U., 1983-87. Registered profl. geologist, Wyo. Coal and uranium explorations aid Wold Exploration Co., Casper, 1975; environ. geologist Cold Regions Rsch. and Engring. Lab., U.S. Army C.E., Hanover, N.H., 1977-78; aerial photography analyst Photog. Interpretation Corp., Hanover, 1978; head women's ski coach Mont. State U., Bozeman, 1978-79; NASA geol. rsch. asst. Dartmouth Coll., Hanover, 1979; dist. geologist Bridger Teton Nat. Forest, U.S. Forest Svc., Jackson, Wyo., 1980; landman Stroock, Rogers and Dymond Leasing Corp., Casper, 1981; devel. geologist Can. Hunter Exploration Ltd., Calgary, Alta., 1987-88; founder, propr. Sweetwater Cons., Casper, 1989—. Author: Alpine Tectonics of the South Central Spanish Pyrenees—A Sedimentological, Structural and Geochemical Approach to Thrust Belts Worldwide, 1989; contbr. articles to profl. publs. Bd. dirs. Wyo. Outdoor Coun., Lander, Cowboy State Games, Casper; vol. Big Bros. and Big Sisters Wyo. Mem. Am. Water Resources Assn. (V.p. Wyo. chpt.), Wyo. Geol. Assn. (co-editor guidebook 1992-93), NAFE. Home and Office: 535 W Yellowstone Hwy Casper WY 82601

STROSSEN, NADINE, law educator, human rights activist; b. Jersey City, Aug. 18, 1950; d. Woodrow John and Sylvia (Simicich) S.; m. Eli Michael Noam, Apr. 25, 1980. AB, Harvard U., 1972, JD magna cum laude, 1975. Jud. clk. Minn. Supreme Ct., St. Paul, 1975-76; assoc. Lindquist & Vennum,

Mpls., 1976-78, Sullivan & Cromwell, N.Y.C., 1978-83; prof. clin. law, supervising atty. Civil Rights Clinic, Sch. Law, NYU, 1984-88; prof. law N.Y. Law Sch., N.Y.C., 1988—. Editor Harvard Law Rev., 1975; contbr. book chpts., articles to profl. jours.; author: In Defense of Pornography: Free Speech and the Fight for Women's Rights, 1995. Bd. dirs. The Fund for Free Expression, 1990—. Recipient Outstanding Young Person award Jaycees Internat., 1986, Outstanding Contbn. to Human Rights Jour. Human Rights, N.Y. Law Sch., 1989; named one of Ten Outstanding Young Ams., U.S. Jaycees, 1986. Mem. ACLU (exec. com. 1985—, gen. counsel 1986-91, pres. 1991—), Nat. Coalition Against Censorship (bd. dirs. 1989—), Coalition to Free Soviet Jews (bd. dirs. 1984—), Human Rights Watch (exec. com. 1989-91), Asia Watch (vice chair 1989-91), Mid. East Watch (bd. dirs. 1989-91), Harvard Club (N.Y.C.). Home: 450 Riverside Dr # 51 New York NY 10027-6821 also: Sedgewood Club RD 12 Carmel NY 10512 Office: NY Law Sch 57 Worth St New York NY 10013-2959*

STROTHER, BARBARA ANN, economic development specialist; b. North Kingstown, R.I., Sept. 27, 1949; d. Winfred Green and Margaret E. (Sullivan) S.; m. Daniel J. Crowley, Aug. 25, 1985. BA, Conn. Coll., 1987; postgrad., U. R.I. Cert. paralegal. Med. sec. clin. rsch. Pfizer Inc., Groton, Conn., 1980-81; paralegal Dupont and Tobin, P.C., New London, 1981-83; legis. intern Hartford, Conn., 1984; cons. Strother Cons. Svcs., Mystic, Conn., 1984-87; asst. planner Town of Groton, 1987-91, econ. devel. specialist, 1991—. Mem. Conn. Econ. Devel. Assn., Am. Planning Assn., Conn. Women in Planning and Devel., Phi Beta Kappa. Home: 75 Steamboat Wharf Apt 8 Mystic CT 06355-2548 Office: Town of Groton 45 Fort Hill Rd Groton CT 06340-4332

STROTHER, TILLIE See **WILLIAMS, DALE**

STROUD, DEBRA SUE, medical technologist; b. Jacksonville, Fla., Feb. 15, 1954; d. Albert LeRoy and Jessie Nell (Igou) Brown; m. Stephen Ray Torok (div. 1975); m. Edward Lee Stroud, May 31, 1978. BA, U. North Fla., 1979. Lic. med. tech., Fla.; cert. clin. lab. scientist, clin. lab. specialist in hematology. Office lab. technologist Women's Med. Group, P.A., Jacksonville, 1977-78; hematology and blood bank technologist Meml. Med. Ctr., Jacksonville, 1978-85; hematology supr. Humana Hosp., Orange Park, Fla., 1985—; owner, ptnr. Stroud's Creative Designs, Callahan, Fla., 1990-92; continuing edn. provider, contact person Fla. State Dept. Health and Rehab. Svcs., Orange Park. Vol. Catfish One, Hook Kids in Fishing-Not Drugs, Hilliard-Callahan, Fla., 1991; vol. fundraiser Found for Cheryl Davis, Callahan, 1991. With U.S. Army, 1972-76. Recipient Most Admired Woman of the Decade award, Women of Yr. award, Silver Shield of Valor, 1992, 20th Century award of Achievement; named Internat. Woman of Yr., 1991, 92, Life fellow Am. Biog. Inst., fellow Internat. Biog. Assn. Mem. NAFE, Am. Soc. Clin. Psychologists, Nat. Wildlife Fedn., Internat. Soc. Thrombosis & Haemostasis, NWF Leaders Club. Baptist. Home: RR 2 Box 398 Hilliard FL 32046-9408 Office: Humana Hosp Orange Park 2001 Kingsley Ave Orange Park FL 32073-5111

STROUP, ELIZABETH FAYE, librarian; b. Tulsa, Mar. 25, 1939; d. Milton Earl and Lois (Buhl) S. BA in Philosophy, U. Wash., 1962, MLS, 1964. Intern Libr. of Congress, Washington, 1964-65; asst. dir. North Cen. Regional Libr., Wenatchee, Wash., 1966-69; reference specialist Congl. Reference div. Libr. of Congress, Washington, 1970-71, head nat. collections Div. for the Blind and Physically Handicapped, 1971-73, chief Congl. Reference div., 1973-78, dir. gen. reference, 1978-88; city libr., chief exec. officer Seattle Pub. Libr., 1988—; cons. U.S. Info. Svc., Indonesia, Feb. 1987. Mem. adv. bd. KCTS 9 Pub. TV, Seattle, 1988—; bd. visitors Sch. Librarianship, U. Wash., 1988—; bd. dirs. Wash. Literacy, 1988—. Mem. ALA (pres. reference and adult svcs. div. 1986-87, div. bd. 1985-88), Wash. Libr. Assn., D.C. Libr. Assn. (bd. dirs. 1975-76), City Club, Ranier Club. Office: Seattle Pub Libr 1000 4th Ave Seattle WA 98104-1193

STROUP, KALA MAYS, university president. BA in Speech and Drama, U. Kans., 1959, MS in Psychology, 1964, PhD in Speech Communication and Human Rels., 1974. V.p. acad. affairs Emporia (Kans.) State U., 1978-83; pres. Murray State U., Ky., 1983-90, S.E. Mo. State U., Cape Girardeau, 1990—; pres. Mo. Coun. on Pub. Higher Edn.; mem. pres.'s commn. NCAA. Mem. mem. nat. exploring com., nat. exec. bd., former chair profl. devel. com. Boy Scouts Am.; former chair nat. adv. bd. SBA Devel. Ctrs.; former chair ACE Leadership Commn.; mem. bd. visitors Def. Dept. Air U. ACE fellow. Mem. Am. Assn. State Colls. and Univs. (past bd. dirs., mem. Pres.'s Commn. on Tchr. Edn., Task Force on Labor Force Issues and Implications for the Curriculum), Mortar Board, Phi Beta Kappa, Omicron Delta Kappa, Phi Kappa Phi. Office: SE Mo State U Office of the President 1 University Plz Cape Girardeau MO 63701-4799

STROUP, SHEILA TIERNEY, columnist; b. Aurora, Ill., Nov. 28, 1943; d. Lawrence Clifford and Dorothy (Vilven) Tierney; m. Merwin F. Stroup, Sept. 4, 1965; children: Keegan, Shannon, Claire. BA in Liberal Arts, U. Ill., 1965; MA in English, Southeastern La. U., 1982. Cert. secondary tchr., La. Tchr. English Great Mills (Md.) High Sch., 1966-69; feature writer St. Tammany News, Covington, La., 1974-75; grad. asst. Southeastern La. U., Hammond, 1981-82, instr. English, 1982-85; ednl. cons. Custom Computer Systems, Hammond, 1985-86; tchr. English William Pitcher Jr. High, Covington, 1987; community news writer Times-Picayune, New Orleans, 1988-90; met. page columnist New Orleans Times-Picayune, 1990—; free-lance writer, Covington, La., 1986-88; speaker and workshop leader in field. Author newspaper column Sheila Stroup, 1990 (1st Pl. award La. Press Assn. 1990); author adult and juvenile short stories, 1976-90. Recipient 1st Pl. award Deep South Writers Competition, 1979, 2d Pl. award, 1987-90; 1st Pl. award for column New Orleans Press Club, 1989, 93. Fellow AAUW (bd. dirs. 1978-88, various chairwoman positions); mem. Nat. Soc. Newspaper Columnists (v.p. 1991-93, pres. 1994—). Office: The Times - Picayure 1101 N Highway 190 Covington LA 70433-8963

STROUP, SUSAN ELIZABETH, sales representative; b. Denver City, Tex., Aug. 31, 1959; d. Carl Lee and Robbie Jean (Robinson) S. BSBA, Tex. Tech. U., 1981, postgrad., 1989. Cert. bus. edn. tchr. Tex. Area mgr. Dillards Dept. Store, Lubbock, Tex., 1981-83; asst. mgr. Casual Corner, Lubbock, Tex., 1983-87; sales rep. No Nonsense Hosiery, Lubbock, Tex., 1987-88, RJR Nabisco, Lubbock, Tex., 1988—. Vol. Womens Protective Svcs., Lubbock, 1987; volleyball player City of Lubbock Parks & Recreation, 1993. Mem. NAFE, Tex. Tech. Ex Students Assn. Baptist. Home: 5112 Whisperwood Blvd Lubbock TX 79416 Office: RJR Nabisco 5704 40th St Lubbock TX 79407

STROUPE, CYNTHIA KAY, secondary school counselor, educator; b. Cleve., Dec. 22, 1942; d. Fred Richard and Florence Crockett (Hart) S. BA in History, Queens Coll., 1964; MA in Guidance and Counseling, Rollins Coll., 1982. Cert. tchr., guidance and counseling, history, social sci., Fla. Clerical staff acctg. ops. office IBM Corp.-Cleve., 1964-66; tchr. Andrews Sch. for Girls, Willoughby, Ohio, 1966-67, North Iredell High Sch., Statesville, N.C., 1967-70; tchr. Winter Haven (Fla.) Sch., 1970-82, counselor, 1982—; mem. scholarship selection com. Polk C.C., Winter Haven, 1991—, Polk EDn. Found., Bartow, Fla., 1990—; dir., sec., pres. Polk County Scholarship Fund, Inc., Lakeland, Fla., 1983—. Sec. Rep. Women of Greater Polk, Winter Haven, 1991-93. Mem. NEA, Fla. Edn. Assn., Polk Edn. Assn, Fla. Counseling and Devel. Assn., So. Assn. Coll. Admissions Advisors, Delta Kappa Gamma (2d v.p. 1994—). Presbyterian. Office: Winter Haven High Sch 600 6th St SE Winter Haven FL 33880

STROW, STACY LYNN BURGESS, accountant; b. Paris, Ill., Oct. 22, 1966; d. Connie Lee and Wanda Maxine (Hofmann) Burgess; m. Glenn Richard Strow, June 6, 1986; 1 child, Kirstin Courtney. Student, Ind. State U., 1984-86; BS in Acctg., Mt. Olive Coll., 1988. Acct. Excell Home Fashions, Goldsboro, N.C., 1989-90; staff bookkeeper Fuson Cadillac and Pontiac, Terre Haute, Ind., 1990-92; acctg. mgr. Terrecorp Inc., Clinton, Ind., 1992—. Mem. Inst. Mgmt. Accts., Altrusa Club, Beta Sigma Phi (Chi Theta chpt.). Office: Terrecorp Inc PO Box 369 Clinton IN 47842

STRUBEL, ELLA DOYLE, advertising executive; b. Chgo., Mar. 14, 1940; d. George Floyd and Myrtle (McKnight) D.; m. Richard Craig G'sell, Apr. 26, 1969 (div. 1973); m. Richard Perry Strubel, Oct. 23, 1976; stepchildren: Douglas Arthur, Craig Tollerton. BA magna cum laude, Memphis State U., 1962; MA, U. Ill., 1963. Staff asst. Corinthian Broadcasting Co., N.Y.C., 1963-65; dir. advt.& pub. rels. WANE-TV, Ft. Wayne, Ind., 1965-66; asst. dir. advt. WBBM-TV, Chgo., 1966-67, mgr. sales promotion, 1967-69, dir. advt. sales promotion & info. svcs., 1969-70; pres. Ctr. Pub. Rels., Chgo., 1970-73; dir. pub. rels. Walthaw Watch Co., Chgo., 1973-74; mgr. advt. promotion & pub. rels. WMAQ-TV, Chgo., 1974-76; v.p. corp. rels. Kraft, Inc., Glenview, Ill., 1985-87; sr. v.p. corp. affairs Leo Burnett Co., Inc., Chgo., 1987-92, exec. v.p., 1992—; trustee 231 Funds. Bd. dirs. Rehab. Inst. Chgo., Chgo. Pub. Libr. Found., Leadership Greater Chgo.; pres. Women's Bd. Rehab. Inst., 1982-84; chair Chgo. Network, 1994—. Mem. Northwestern U. Assocs., Casino Club. Democrat. Presbyterian. Home: 55 W Goethe St Chicago IL 60610-2276 Office: Leo Burnett Co Inc 35 W Wacker Chicago IL 60610

STRUBLE, KAREN DENISE, clinical psychologist; b. Dallas, Mar. 25, 1962; d. Homer Allen and Janice Lynn (Robbins) Brown; m. Danny Howard Struble, Oct. 29, 1983; children: Amanda Anne, Benjamin Brown. BA in Psychol. magna cum laude, Baylor U., 1983; MA in Theol., Fuller Theol. Sem., 1989; PhD in Clin. Psychol., Fuller Sem. Grad. Sch. Psychol., 1991. lic. clin. psychol., Calif. Mental health worker Timberlawn Psychiat. Hosp., Dallas, 1982; mental health counselor Southwood Psychiat. Hosp., Chula Vista, Calif., 1983-84; clin. trainee Covenant House (for autistic children), Pasadena, Calif., 1984-85; student clinician The Sycamores Boys' Home, Altadena, Calif., 1985-86, Pasadena Community Counseling Clinic, 1987-89; psychol. clerk L.A. County-USC Med. Ctr., 1987-88; psychol. intern. San Fernando Valley Child Guidance Clinic, Northridge, Calif., 1989-90; reg. psychol. asst. Shepherd's House Counseling Ctr., Van Nuys, Calif., 1988-93; clin. psychol. Pasadena, 1994-95. Contbr. article to profl. jour. Dir. infant-toddler program Vineyard Christian Fellowship, Arcadia, Calif., 1994-95; active Cottage Co-op Nursery Sch., Pasadena, Calif., 1993-95. mem. APA, Baylor U. Alumni Assn., Omicron Delta Kappa, Phi Beta Kappa. Republican. Home: 687 Bellefontaine St Pasadena CA 91105-2440

STRUCK, NORMA JOHANSEN, artist; b. West Englewood, N.J., Feb. 17, 1929; d. Hans Christian and Amanda (Solberg) Johansen; m. H. Walter Struck, Aug. 21, 1955; children: Steven, Laurie. Student, N.Y. Phoenix Sch. Design, 1946-50; Art Students' League, N.Y.C., 1976-77. Staff artist Norcross, Inc., N.Y.C., 1950-60, free-lance artist, 1967-75; artist portraits, prints Scafa-Tornabene, Nyack, N.Y., 1976—; artist portraits, paintings U.S.N., U.S. Coast Guard, Washington, 1976—; com. bd. mem. Navy Art Coop. Liaison, N.Y.C., 1976-80, Coast Guard Art Program, N.Y.C., 1980-. One-woman shows include Nabisco Co., Fairlawn, N.J., 1987; exhibited in group shows Navy Hist. Mus., Washington, 1976, Navy Combat Art Gallery, Washington, World Trade Ctr., 1979, USCG, New Eng. Air Mus., Windsor Locks, Conn., 1984, Fed. Hall, N.Y.C., 1986, 93, 94, Salmagundi Club, N.Y.C., Officers Club, Governor's Island, Hudson Valley Show, White Plains, N.Y.; represented in permanent collections U.S. Pentagon, Washington, Heinie-Onstad Mus., Oslo, World Figure Skating Hall of Fame and Mus., Colo. Springs. Recipient Louis E. Seley award, Navy Art Program, 1979; Grumbacher award, Catherine Lorillard Wolfe, Nat. Arts Club, N.Y.C., 1978; George Gray award Coast Guard Art Program, Governors Island, N.Y., 1983, 89. Mem. Art Students League (life), Hudson Valley Assn. (bd. dirs. 1985-88, M. Dole award 1980), Soc. Illustrators, Salmagundi Club, Am. Artists Profl. League (Pres.'s award 1979). Home: 910 Midland Rd Oradell NJ 07649-1904

STRUNK, BETSY ANN WHITENIGHT, educator; b. Bloomsburg, Pa., May 28, 1942; d. Mathias Clarence and Marianna (Naunas) Whitenight; children: Robert J. Jr., Geoffrey M. BS in Edn., Bloomsburg U., 1964; MEd, West Chester U., 1969; cert. mentally/physically handicapped, Pa. State U., 1981. Cert. elem. edn., spl. edn. Tchr. Faust Sch., Bensalem (Pa.) Twp., 1964, Eddystone (Pa.) Elem. Sch., 1964-66, Lima Elem. Sch., Rose Tree Media Sch. Dist., 1966-69, Rose Tree Media (Pa.) Sch. Dist., 1977—; adj. prof. Wilkes Coll., Wilkes-Barre, Pa., 1981-86; instr. Delaware Community Coll., Media, 1986; instr., dir. ground sch. edn. Brandywine Airport, West Chester, Pa., 1986-88; instr. Drexel U., Phila., 1989—, Performance Learning Systems, Inc., Emerson, N.J., Nevada City, Calif., 1981—; rep. FAA, Phila., 1986-88; spl. edn. resource rm. specialist, tchr. cons. Media Elem. Sch., Rose Tree Media Sch. Dist.; tchr. trainer, designer Performance Learning Systems; curriculum designer pvt. pilot ground sch.; instr. introduction to flying and pilot companion course; chairperson profl. devel. com. Rose Tree Media Sch. Dist., 1992. Inservice Coun. of Del. County, 1992—; cons. ednl. programs, 1988—; keynote presenter, designer, editor, author Performance Learning Systems, Inc., Emerson, N.J., Nevada City, Calif., 1988—; owner, designer Betsy's Belts, Del., N.J., Pa., 1970-74; bd. dirs. Lead Tchr. Ctr. West Chester (Pa.) U., 1992—; presenter State of Pa. Lead Tchr. Conf., 1994; project dir. video documentary Performance Learning Systems, Calif., 1994. Project dir. (video documentary) Anatomy of a Live Event Lesson, 1994; contbr. articles to profl. jours. Mem. Middletown Free Libr. Bd., 1977-79; officer Riddlewood Aux. to Riddle Meml. Hosp., Media, 1973-78; chairperson Lima (Pa.) Christian Nursery Sch., 1973, March of Dimes, Middletown, 1973; pres. Roosevelt PTG (Elem. Sch.), Media, 1982; com. person, v.p. Middletown Twp. Dem. Com., 1974; capt. March of Dimes, Media, 1987-91, Diabetes Assn., Media, 1989-91; mem. Vietnamese refugee com. Media Presbyn. Ch., 1975, mem., 1967—; vol. Tyler Arboretum, Middletown Twp., 1980-82. Recipient 1st pl. Color Divsn. Photography award Pa. Colonial Plantation, PLS 500 Club award; Fine Arts in Spl. Edn. grantee Pa. Dept. Edn., 1993-94. Mem. NEA, ASCD, Pa. ASCD, Rose Tree Media Edn. Assn. (profl. devel. com. chairperson 1992-93, profl. devel. com. rep. 1990-93, Exceptional Svc. award), Pa. State Edn. Assn., Nat. Staff Devel. Coun., Aircraft Owners and Pilots Assn. Democrat. Home: 203 Cohasset Ln West Chester PA 19380 Office: Rose Tree Media Sch Dist Glenwood Elem Sch Pennell Rd Media PA 19063

STRUNK, MARY DOLORES, librarian; b. Colwich, Kans., Aug. 23, 1912; d. Nick and Christina (Albert) S. AB, Mt. St. Scholastica, 1938; AB in Libr. Sci., U. Denver, 1941; MLS, Rosary Coll., River Forest, Ill., 1965. Head libr. Kans. Newman Coll., Wichita, 1940-67, 80-83, asst. libr., 1967-80, head cataloger, asst. libr., 1982—. Recipient Maria de Mattias award Alumna of Kansas Newman Coll., 1986, John Henry Card Newman award, 1991. Democrat. Roman Catholic. Office: Ryan Libr Cataloger 3100 Mccormick St Wichita KS 67213-2008

STRUTHERS, MARGO S., lawyer. BA, Carleton Coll., 1972; JD cum laude, U. Minn., 1976. Atty., shareholder Moss & Barnett, P.A. and predecessor firms, Mpls., 1976-93; ptnr. Oppenheimer Wolff & Donnelly, Mpls., 1993—. Mem. Am. Acad. Hosp. Attys., Nat. Health Lawyers Assn., Minn. State Bar Assn. (bus. law sect., chairperson nonprofit com., former chairperson and governing coun. mem. health law sect.), Minn. Soc. Hosp. Attys. (former pres.). Office: Oppenheimer Wolff & Donnelly Plaza VII 45 South 7th St Ste 3400 Minneapolis MN 55402

STRZYZYNSKI, MARIANNE, sales representative; b. Chgo., Nov. 7, 1961; d. Harry Joseph and Ann Wanda (Popera) S. BA in Bus. Adminstrn. Mktg., U. Ill., Chgo., 1984. Office mgr. Mendheim & Co., Lincolnwood, Ill., 1982-85; real estate sales assoc. AMF, Santa Ana, Calif., 1985-86; sales assoc. Contract Distbrs., Inc., Chgo., 1986-88; telemktg. sales mgr. Minolta Corp., Chgo., 1988-89; sales rep. Assist NEtwork Devel., Chgo., 1989-90, Kent Elecs.-Datacomm Divsn., Elk Grove Village, Ill., 1990—. Fundraiser fashion show Notre Dame High Sch.. for Girls, Chgo., 1989, 90; instr. Cath. edn. Queen Angels, Chgo., 1989-91. Mem. Alumni Assn. Notre Dame High Sch. Republican. Roman Catholic.

STUART, BARBARA FINDLEY, educator; b. Jacksonville, Ill., July 11, 1928; d. Joseph Stilwell and Florence Mary (Nichols) Findley; m. George Warren Stuart, June 17, 1951; children: David Bruce, Ruthann Stuart Kusch. BS in Edn. Music, Ill. State U., 1950, MS in Edn. English, 1968. Tchr. music Mahomet (Ill.) Pub. Schs., 1950-51; tchr. English Downs (Ill.) Jr. Sr. High Sch., 1953-57; tchr. freshman English Ill. State U., Normal, 1958, Ill. Wesleyan U., Bloomington, 1959-61; tchr. music St. Mary's Sch., Bloomington, 1984-89; tchr. piano pvt. practice, Normal, 1958-68, 87—; founder, interim coord. McLean County (Ill.) Community Compact, 1990-94, cons., 1994—. Composer 10 Songs for Special Days, 1991; author, producer (slide/sound presentation) McLean County Govt., 1988. Active mem. justice and pub. safety steering com. Nat. Assn. Counties, 1994—; elected mem. McLean County Bd., 1979—; founder, chair Young Adult Problems Study Group, Bloomington, 1986—; founding pres. Friends of Normal Pub. Libr., 1978; founder, chair Com. to Establish the Corn Belt Libr. System, McLean County, 1972. Mem. Orpheus Club (v.p. 1960-70). Presbyterian.

STUART, DOROTHY MAE, artist; b. Fresno, Calif., Jan. 8, 1933; d. Robert Wesley Williams and Maria Theresa (Gad) Tressler; m. Reginald Ross Stuart, May 18, 1952; children: Doris Lynne Stuart Willis, Darlene Mae Stuart Cavalletto, Sue Anne Stuart Peters. Student, Calif. State U., Fresno, 1951-52, Fresno City Coll., 1962-64. Artist, art judge, presenter demonstrations at schs., fairs and art orgns. Calif., 1962—. Editor, art dir. Fresno High School Centennial 1889-1989, 1989; art advisor Portrait of Fresno, 1885-1985; contbg. artist Heritage Fresno, 1975; exhibited in group shows, including M.H. De Young Mus., San Francisco, 1971, Charles and Emma Frye Mus., Seattle, 1971, Calif. State U.-Fresno tour of China, 1974. Mem. adv. com. Calif. State Ken Maddy Ctrl. Calif. Conf. on Women, 1989-95, Patrons for Cultural Arts, Fresno, 1987-92, bd. dirs., 1991-92. Recipient 53 art awards, 1966-84; nominated Woman of the Yr., Bus./Profl. of Fresno, 1990. Mem. Soc. Western Artists (bd. dirs. 1968-74, v.p. 1968-70), Fresno Womens Trade Club (bd. dirs. 1986-93, pres. 1988-90), Fresno Art Mus., Fresno Met. Mus., Native Daus. Golden West Fresno. Republican. Home and Office: 326 S Linda Ln Fresno CA 93727-5737

STUART, GLORIA MAE, educator; b. Phila., Sept. 29, 1936; d. Herbert Ellsworth and Mathilda Elizabeth (Pangburn) Titus; children: John R. Grissett, David P. Grissett. Diploma, Presby. Hosp., 1957; BSN, U. Pa., 1962; MS in Nursing, U. Ala., Birmingham, 1980. Staff nurse. med. surg. Presby. Hosp., Phila., 1957-62; staff nurse ICU-CCU St. Luke's Hosp., N.Y.C., 1962-65; staff nurse coronary care unit Humana Hosp., Huntsville, Ala., 1970-85; asst. prof. U. Ala, Hunstville, 1980-94, Motlow C.C., Tullahoma, Tenn., 1994—; speaker in field. Author: (with others) Focus on Critical Care Nursing, 1985, contbr. textbooks. Recipient Pa. State scholar, Title II Fed. Nurse traineeship. Mem. ANA (cert. clin. specialist), ACCN, Ala. Heart Assn., Sigma Theta Tau. Office: Motlow CC Tullahoma TN 37388

STUART, JANE ELIZABETH, film and video executive; b. N.Y.C., Dec. 15, 1947; d. Mark Abraham and Melba Rita (Goldstein) Stuart; m. Bernard Schmetterer, Jan. 9, 1972 (div. 1978). Student, Upsala Coll., East Orange, N.J., 1964-66. Lic. real estate broker, N.Y. Reporter The Bergen Record, Hackensack, N.J., 1966-71; polit. speech writer Town of Ramapo, N.Y., 1971-72; pub. rels. specialist Bergen County, N.J., 1972-74; reporter Times Herald Record, Middletown, N.Y., 1974-76; real estate broker, v.p. Elizabeth Gretsch Realty, Monroe, N.Y., 1976-81; v.p., gen. mgr Eventime Inc., N.Y.C., 1981-86; talent mgr. N.Y.C., 1986—; pres., CEO Big Picture Comm., Inc., N.Y.C., 1993—; gen. mgr. The Big Picture, Inc., N.Y.C., 1988—; ptnr. Hwy. Interactive, Inc., N.Y.C., 1994—. Address: 10 Longwoods Ln East Hampton NY 11937 Office: Big Picture Inc 15 W 44th St New York NY 10036

STUART, JOAN MARTHA, fund raising executive; b. Huntington, N.Y., June 2, 1945; d. Ervin Wencil and Flora Janet (Applebaum) S. Student, Boston U., 1963-67. Cert. fund raiser. Prodn. asst. Random House, N.Y.C., 1968-69; book designer Simon & Schuster, N.Y.C., 1969-71; feature writer Palm Beach Post, West Palm Beach, Fla., 1971-72; co-founder, communications dir. Stuart, Gleimer & Assocs., West Palm Beach, 1973-84, pres., 1982—; fin. devel. dir. YWCA Greater Atlanta, 1984-86, Ctr. for the Visually Impaired, Atlanta, 1986-90; ea. divsn. dir. City of Hope, 1990-94; devel. dir. Jewish Family Svcs., Atlanta, 1994—; adj. prof. Kennesaw Coll. Contbr. articles to profl. jours. Mem. crusade com. Am. Cancer Soc. Bd., 1981—; bd. dirs. Theatre Arts Co., 1980-81; community svcs. chmn., bd. dirs. B'nai B'rith Women, 1980-82; chmn. publicity Leukemia Soc. Atlanta Polo Benefit, 1983; com. chmn. Atlanta Zool. Beastly Feast Benefit, 1984; mem. Atlanta Symphony Assocs.; chmn. Salute to Women of Achievement, 1987-90. Recipient Nat. award B'nai B'rith Women, 1978, Regional award, 1979, cert. of merit Big Bros./Big Sisters, 1976. Mem. Nat. Soc. Fund Raising Execs. (cert.), Ga. Exec. Women's Network, Diabetes Assn. (bd. dirs. 1990—), Jerusalem House (bd. dirs. 1991-94), Parent to Parent (bd. dirs. 1993—). Democrat. Jewish. Office: 1605 Peachtree Rd NE Atlanta GA 30309

STUART, JUANITA RYAN, recreation facility executive; b. Cullman, Ala., Aug. 9, 1937; d. Stacy Carlton and Unie Mae (Hopkins) Ryan; m. Roy A. Stuart, Dec. 20, 1962 (div. Sept. 1964); 1 child, Dean Trent. Student, Alverson Draughn, Cleve., 1955-56. Cert. club mgr. Asst. mgr. Vestavia (Ala.) Country Club, 1964-75, Indian Hills Country Club, Tuscaloosa, Ala., 1975-78; gen. mgr. Mountain Brook Club, Birmingham, Ala., 1978—. Chairperson Taste of Birmingham, 1981—. Recipient Deanie Vacalis award Ala. Restaurant and Food Svc. Assn., 1987, Who's Who of Birmingham award C. of C., 1989, 90. Mem. CMAA (Ala. chpt., pres., bd. dirs.), Ala. Restaurant Assn. (pres., bd. dirs., Restauranteur of Yr. 1987, Salut Au Restauranteur of Yr. 1987), Birmingham-Jefferson Restaurant Assn. (pres., bd. dirs.), Ala. Sheriff's Boys and Girls Ranch (bd. dirs.), U. Ala. Alumni Assn. (life). Republican. Baptist. Office: Mountain Brook Club 19 Beechwood Rd Birmingham AL 35213

STUART, LORI AMES, public relations executive; b. Hempstead, N.Y., Oct. 23, 1957; d. Henry Aschner and Janet (Hackel) Goldman; m. John Robert Ames, Jan. 30, 1982 (div. July 1990); 1 child, Robert Walter Ames; m. Robert John Stuart, July 27, 1991. BA, Hofstra U., 1979. Publicist Jane Wesman Pub. Rels., N.Y.C., 1980-84, v.p., 1991—; publicist, publicity mgr. William Morrow & Co., N.Y.C., 1984-89, publicity dir., 1989-90; lectr., mentor NYU, 1994. Jewish. Office: Jane Wesman Pub Rels 928 Broadway # 903 New York NY 10010

STUART, SANDRA JOYCE, computer information scientist; b. Wheatland, Mo., Aug. 15, 1950; d. Asa Maxville and Inez Irene (Wilson) Friedley; m. John Kendall Stuart, Apr. 17, 1971; 1 child, Whitney Renee. Student, Cen. Mo. State U., 1968-69; AA (hon.), Johnson County Community Coll., 1980; BS in Bus. Adminstrn. cum laude, Avila Coll., 1992. Statis. asst. Fed. Crop Ins. Corp., Kansas City, Mo., 1978-83; mgr. Fed. Women's Program, Kansas City, 1979-80; mgmt. asst. Marine Corps Fin. Ctr., Kansas City, 1983-85, analyst computer systems, 1985-88; computer programmer analyst Corps. of Engrs., Kansas City, 1988-91; regional program mgr. FAA, Kansas City, 1991—. Author: The Samuel Walker History, 1983. Asst. supt. Sunday sch. Overland Park (Kans.) Christian Ch., 1979-80, supt., 1980-82. Mem. Wheatland High Sch. Alumni Assn. (pres. 1990-91).

STUART, SANDRA KAPLAN, federal official; b. Greensboro, N.C.; d. Leon and Renee (Myers) Kaplan; children: Jay Jr., Timothy. BA, U. N.C.; JD, Monterey Coll. Law. Chief legis. asst. Rep. Robert Matsui, Washington, 1979-81; legis. dir., assoc. staff Ho. of Appropriations and Budget Coms., Washington, 1981-87; adminstrv. asst. Rep. Vic Fazio, Washington, 1987-89, chief of staff, 1990-93; asst. sec. legis. affairs Dept. Def., The Pentagon, Washington, 1993—. Office: Office Legis Affairs Dept Def The Pentagon Washington DC 20301-1300*

STUBBINS, SARA LOUISE, librarian, library science educator; b. Ann Arbor, Mich., May 29, 1947; d. William Harold and Mary Louise (McCall) S.; m. James Sewell, June 16, 1973 (div. Sept. 1984); children: Debra Louise, Diane Laurel. BA, U. Mich., 1969, AM in LS, 1972. Cert. tchr., Mo., Tex., Mich. Tchr. Plymouth (Mich.) Sch. System, 1969-71; libr. Forest Hills Sch. System, Grand Rapids, Mich., 1972-76; legis. sec. Capitol Bldg., Madison, Wis., 1977-78; pres. Parents Place NE, Madison, 1979-81; chmn. bd. dirs. Work & Play Nursery Coop., Madison, 1981-85; libr. supr. 7 ind. sch. dists., Kerrville, Tex., 1985-88; libr., asst. prof. libr. sci. SW Mo. State U., Springfield, 1988—. Insert editor newsletter La Leche League, Madison, 1978-83; Sunday sch. tchr. 1st and Calvary Presbyn. Ch., Springfield, 1989-93; cons. media ctr. Cowden Elem. Sch., Springfield, 1991; treas. Childrens Lit. Festival of the Ozarks. Music scholar Western Mich. U., 1965. Mem. ALA, Am. Assn. Sch. Librs. (com. chmn., awards com.), Mo. Assn. Sch. Librs. (apptd. liason to Mo. Libr. Assn.), Internat. Reading Assn., Nat. Lab. Sch. Assn., SW Dist. Area Librs. Mo. (workshop leader 1991), Springfield Area Librs. (v.p. 1994), U. Mich. Libr. Sch. Alumni Assn. Home: 1036 E Greenwood Springfield MO 65807 Office: SW Mo State U Greenwood Lab Sch 901 S National Ave Springfield MO 65804-0027

STUBBLEFIELD, KAREN HOLT MCINTOSH, human services administrator; b. Houston, June 2, 1965; d. Thomas Shirley and Audrey (Jean) McIntosh. BA, Tex. A&M U., 1987; cert. in publ. specialization, George Washington U., 1990. Staff asst. Sec. U.S. Senate, Washington, 1987-88; fed. writer Education USA, Arlington, Va., 1988-90; asst. dir. community affairs Mother Frances Hosp., Tyler, Tex., 1990-94, dir. pub. rels., 1994—. Active mem. United Way Tyler/Smith County. Mem. Women in Comm., Tex. Soc. Hosp. Pub. Rels. and Mktg., East Tex. Advt. Fedn., Kappa Alpha Theta. Methodist. Home: 11923 County # 140W Flint TX 75762

STUBBS, JAN DIDRA, travel industry executive; b. Waseca, Minn., June 19, 1937; d. Gordon Everett and Bertha Margaret (Bertsch) Didra; m. James Stewart Stubbs, Nov. 24, 1962; children: Jeffrey Stewart, Jacqueline Didra. BA in Speech/English, U. Minn., 1961; cert. travel counselor, Inst. Cert. Travel Agts., 1988. Sales agt. United Airlines, Mpls., 1961-64; interior decorator Lloyd and Assocs., St. Paul, 1964-66; v.p. Stubbs and Assocs., Textiles, St. Paul, 1966-83; account exec. Twin Cities Mag., Mpls., 1983-85; account exec. Internat. Travel Arrangers, St. Paul, 1985-86, asst. dir. sales, 1986-88; mgr. Dayton's Group Holidays, Mpls., 1988—; writer for Mgmt. Assistance Project. V.p. Jr. Women's Assn. of Minn. Symphony Orch.; chairperson 60th anniversary Jr. League of St. Paul, sec., 1967—, sustaining mem.; deacon Ho. of Hope Presbyn. Ch., St. Paul, 1970. Named Outstanding Alumni, Coll. Liberal Arts, U. Minn., 1995. Mem. AAUW, Inst. Cert. Travel Agts., Am. Soc. Travel Agts., Minn. Exec. Women in Tourism (publicity com. 1987-88, by-laws chmn. 1989-90, sec. 1988-89, 90, fedn. dir. 1990—, v.p., 1993, pres. 1993-94), Internat. Fedn. Women in Travel (alt. gov. Mid-Am. region, standing com. dir. historian, gov. mid-Ams. area I 1994, 95), Jr. Assistance League, St. Paul Pool and Yacht Club, Alpha Omicron Pi (pres. 1958-59, alumni pres. 1962), Whitefish Chain Yacht Club (sec.), U. Minn. Alumni Assn. Republican. Home: 1575 Boardwalk Ct Saint Paul MN 55118-2747 Office: Dayton's Group Holidays 320 Plymouth Bldg 12 S 6th St Minneapolis MN 55402-1508

STUCKART, ROME, artist; b. Sublimity, Oreg., Aug. 29, 1955; d. Robert M. and Cecelia A. (Smith) S.; m. Stephen W. Schultz, Jan. 7, 1984. BA, Gonzaga U., 1977; MA, U. Iowa, 1980, MFA, 1981. Adj. asst. prof. U. Iowa, Iowa City, 1985-88; vis. artist Mont. State U., Bozeman, 1992, U. Oreg., Eugene, 1993; lectr. U. Tex., Austin, 1994. Exhibited in solo shows, including Ariel Gallery, N.Y.C., 1986, Market St. Gallery, Venice, Calif., 1989-90, Beall Park Art Ctr., Bozeman, 1992, U. Idaho, Moscow, 1993, Linda Hodges Gallery, Seattle, 1993; exhibited in groups shows at Boise Art Mus., 1992, We. Wash. U., Bellingham, 1992, Betty Moody Gallery, Houston, 1993. Artist fellowships from NEA, 1993, Guggenheim Found., 1992, Idaho State Arts Commn., 1992. Home and Office: PO Box 323 Hope ID 83836

STUCKEY, HELENJEAN LAUTERBACH, counselor educator; b. Bushnell, Ill., May 17, 1929; d. Edward George and Frances Helen (Simpson) Lauterbach; m. James Dale Stuckey, Sept. 30, 1951; children: Randy Lee, Charles Edward, Beth Ellen. BFA, Ill. Wesleyan U., 1951; MEd, U. Ill., 1969. Cert. art tchr., guidance, psychology instr. Display designer Saks Fifth Ave., Chgo., 1951; interior designer Piper City, Ill., 1953-63; art tchr. Forrest (Ill.)-Strawn-Wing Schs., 1967-68; tchr., counselor Piper City Schs., 1969-74; counselor, art tchr. Ford Cen. Schs., Piper City, 1974-85; psychiatric counselor Community Resource Counseling Ctr., Ford County, Ill., 1985-87; history tchr., counselor Iroquois West High Sch., Gilman, Ill., 1987-88; spl. needs coord. Livingston County Vocat., Pontiac, Ill., 1988-93; ret., 1993. Job skills coord. Livingston Area Edn. for Employment, 1994. Mem. AACD, Am. Vocat. Assn., Ill. Counseling Assn., Ill. Vocat. Assn., Ill. Assn. Vocat. Spl. Needs Pers. (membership com.), Ill. Ret. Tchrs., Delta Kappa Gamma (v.p., sec., program chmn., pres.). Presbyterian. Home: 2667 N 1700E Rd Piper City IL 60959-7032

STUCKY, SUSAN UNRAU, research manager; b. Portland, Oreg., May 22, 1949; d. Walter D. and Wilma Irene (Gilmer) Unrau. BA, Bethel Coll., 1971; MA, U. Kans., 1976; PhD, U. Ill., 1981. Postdoctoral fellow U. Mass., Amherst, 1980-81; postdoctoral fellow Stanford (Calif.) U., 1981-82, vis. scholar, 1982-83; rsch. assoc. CSLI/Stanford U., 1983-87; spl. asst. to dir., rsch. scientist Inst. for Rsch. on Learning, Palo Alto, Calif., 1987-88, asst. dir., 1988-90, assoc. dir., 1990—. Mem. AAAS, Assn. Computational Linguistics, Linguistic Soc. Am., N.Y. Acad. Scis., Cognitive Sci. Soc. Office: Inst for Rsch on Learning 2550 Hanover St Palo Alto CA 94304-1115

STUDLEY, JAMIENNE SHAYNE, lawyer; b. N.Y.C., Apr. 30, 1951; d. Jack Hill and Joy (Cosor) S.; m. Gary J. Smith, July 14, 1984. BA magna cum laude, Barnard Coll., 1972; JD, Harvard U., 1975. Bar: D.C. 1975, U.S. Dist. Ct. D.C. 1978. Assoc. Bergson, Borkland, Margolis & Adler, Washington, 1976-80; spl. asst., sec. U.S. HHS, 1980-81; assoc. Weil, Gotshal & Manges, Washington, 1981-83; assoc. dean law sch. Yale U., New Haven, 1983-87; lectr. law, 1984-87; exec. dir. Nat. Assn. for Law Placement, Washington, 1987-90, Calif. Abortion Rights Action League, 1992-93; dep. gen. counsel U.S. Dept. Edn., 1993—; vis. scholar adj. faculty U. Calif., Berkeley, 1990-93. Pres. Conn. Women's Ednl. and Legal Fund, Hartford, 1986-87; mem. bd. advisors Nat. Assn. Pub. Interest Law Pub. Svc. Challenge. Mem. ABA, D.C. Bar Assn., Bar Assn. San Francisco, Am. Soc. Assn. Execs., Assn. Alumnae Barnard Coll. (bd. dirs. 1978-81), Barnard in Washington (pres. 1977-78), Phi Beta Kappa. Home: 3701 Clay St San Francisco CA 94118-1857 Office: Office of the Gen Coun Dept of Edn 600 Independence Ave SW Washington DC 20202

STUDLEY, MARCIA ANN, insurance company official; b. Sacramento, Jan. 13, 1958; d. George Howard and Lucyle (Weaver) S. AA, Am. River Coll., 1978. Cert. profl. ins. women. Clerical staff Spl. Edn. Resource Network, Sacramento, 1984-86; mem. processing svcs. staff Zurich-Am. Ins., Sacramento, 1986-92, rate technician B, 1992—. Mem., supporter Doris Day Animal League, Performing Animal Welfare Soc., Human Legis. Network, People for the Ethical Treatment of Animals. Mem. Nat. Assn. Ins. Women (com. mem. region 8 1991—), Ins. Women of Sacramento (bd. dirs. 1989-92, sec. 1992-93, Rookie of Yr. 1991). Democrat. Office: Zurich-American Ins PO Box 2070 Rancho Cordova CA 95741-2070

STULL, EMILY RUTH, social worker; b. Holland, Mich., Nov. 13, 1933; d. Andrew Henry and Cora (Laarman) Vinstra; m John W. Stull, May 24, 1958 (div. Apr. 1974); childern: Anneliese, Jonathan Mark, Marietta. Student, Hope Coll., 1951-53; BSN, U. Mich., 1956; MSW, Ohio State U., 1971; MA in Gerontology, Ball State U., 1987. RN, Mich.; lic. social worker, Ohio. Staff hosp. nurse Mich., Conn., Ky., Ind., Ohio, 1956-70; social worker Children's Mental Health Ctr., Columbus, Ohio, 1971-74, adminstrv. dir., 1974-76; clin. social worker, community coord. Five County Human Devel. Ctr., Braham, Minn., 1976-78; clin. dir. St. Vincent Children's Ctr., Columbus, 1978-80, NC Community Mental Health Ctr., Columbus, 1981-82; psychiatric social worker Cen. Ohio Counseling Svc., 1982-85; br. mgr. Dunn Mental Health Ctr., Winchester, Ind., 1985—. Mem. Acad. Cert. Social Workers, Am. Group Psychotherapy Assn. (clin.), Am. Assn. Marriage and Family Therapists (clin.), Nat. Assn. Social Workers (diplomate), Athena Club, Winchester C. of C. (bd. dirs.). Office: Dunn Mental Health Ctr 325 S Oak St Winchester IN 47394-2235

STULTZ, PATRICIA ADKINS, nurse, administrator; b. Wayne County, W.Va.; d. John B. and Gladys (Osburn) Adkins; m. Joseph Stultz; children: Debra, Tammy. AS, Marshall U., 1978, BSN, 1982; MSN, Bellarmine Coll., 1990. Cert. profl. health care quality. Staff nurse St. Mary's Hosp., Huntington, W.Va., nursing supr., nursing care evaluator, nursing performance improvement coord., dir. risk mgmt.

STUMBO, HELEN LUCE, retail executive; b. Macon, Ga., Aug. 7, 1947; d. George Edgar and Willouise (Butts) Luce; m. Edward Paul Coppedge (div. Mar. 1980); 1 child, George Laurence; m. John Ellis Stumbo. BA, Fla. State U., 1969. With Rich's Design Studio, Atlanta, 1970-72; pres. Peachland Consortium, Inc., Ft. Valley, Ga., 1986—, Camellia & Main, Inc., 1987—; bd. dirs. Inst. on Religion and Democracy. Dir. Peach County Hosp. Authority, Ft. Valley, 1986—, also dir. capital campaign com., 1985-88; bd. dirs. Forum for Scriptual Christianity, Wilmore, Ky., 1972—; participant Leadership Ga. program, Bus. Coun. Ga., 1989, Nat. Coalition Against Pornography, 1993—, United Meth. for Faith and Freedom, 1994—; chairwoman, bd. dirs. Enough is Enough!, 1994—. Recipient Athena award Peach County C. of C., Ft. Valley, 1986, Resolution of Commendation Ga. Ho. of Reps., Atlanta, 1987. Methodist. Home and Office: 305 Knoxville St Fort Valley GA 31030-3485

STUMPS, S. JO, counselor; b. Ellsworth, Kans., Jan. 4, 1935; d. Grant and Neita (Pflughoeft) Gwinner; m. Walter John Stumps, Aug. 13, 1955; children: Michael John, Christyn Lynn, Montgomery Jerome, Gretchen Lauri Stumps Donlin. BA in Psychology, Ft. Hays State U., 1988, MS in Counseling, 1991. Editor Holyrood (Kans.) Gazette and Bushton News, 1973-74; owner, trainer Stumps Thoroughbred Stables, Holyrood, 1973-74; sec. Darrel's Electronics, Holyrood, 1986-87; counselor Kanwork Dept. Human Resources, Great Bend, Kans., 1991—; instr. Barton County Community Coll., Great Bend, 1989—. Editor: St. Mary's Catholic Church Centennial Year, 1989. Bd. dirs., St. Mary's Cath. Ch., Holyrood, Kans., 1991—; precinct com. Rep. Party, Valley Twp., 1987-92. Mem. Am. Counseling Assn., Nat. Career Devel. Assn. Home: RR 1 Box 93 Bushton KS 67427-9605 Office: Great Bend Kan Work/DHR 2120 11th St Great Bend KS 67530-4421

STUP, JANET ANITA, delegate state general assembly; b. Washington, Mar. 8, 1945; d. Louis Fillmore Jr. and Janet Lenman (Plummer) Watkins; m. William R. Stup, June 21, 1972; children: Scott Alan, Mark Louis. Student, Montgomery Jr. Coll., Takoma Park, Md., 1963-65; AA (hon.), Frederick Community Coll., 1988. Stewardess United Air Lines, Washington, 1965-66; faculty sec. Columbus Sch. Law, Cath. U. Am., Washington, 1966-68; sec. Univ. Legal Svcs., Washington, 1968; legal sec. Tomes and Spragins, Silver Spring, Md., 1968-70, Jackson Brodsky, Rockville, Md., 1970-74; legal sec., legal asst. Klaven & Mannes, Rockville, 1972-74; office adminstr. Meyers, Wagaman, Corderman & Young, Hagerstown, Md., 1974-75; mem. Bd. County Commrs. for Frederick County, Frederick, Md., 1982-90, pres., 1986-90; del. Md. Gen. Assembly, 1991—. Past mem. various coms. Frederick County Bd. Edn.; past chmn. govt. div. United Way; past mem. adv. bd. Community Commons; past bd. dirs. Arthritis Found.; past pres. Frederick Mid. Sch. PTA; hon. chmn. Big Bros.-Big Sisters; mem. Religious Coalition Frederick County; bd. dirs. Heartly House; mem. steering com. Way Sta., Elephant Club. Mem. Md. Assn. Elected Women, Bus. and Profl. Women, LWV, Frederick County Hist. Soc., DAR, Disabled Citizens Frederick County (life), Phi Theta Kappa. Republican. Lutheran. Home: 587 Pumphouse Rd Frederick MD 21702-6092 Office: 324 Lowe House Office Buil Annapolis MD 21401 Address: 153 W Patrick St Frederick MD 21701-5586

STURGES, GLORIA JUNE, learning disabilities educator; b. Ingallas, Kans., Nov. 10, 1937; d. Donald Nathan and Dorothy Ellen (Whaley) Kitch; m. W.G. Bray, Jan. 22, 1960 (div. Apr. 1978); children—Lori Lynn, William Don; m. Sidney James Sturges. B.S. in Edn., Southeastern State U., 1959; M.A. in Edn., Webster U., 1975; postgrad. U. Kans., 1978-84, cert. learning disabilities specialty, 1984. Cert. tchr. elem. edn., Colo., Mo., reading and learning disabilities specialist, Mo. Tchr., Jefferson County Schs., Denver, 1959-60, Briggsdale, Colo., 1960-63, Colo. Sch. for Deaf and Blind, Colorado Springs, 1963-66, Bertha Heid Sch., Thornton, Colo., 1966-70; reading specialist Center Sch. Dist., Kansas City, Mo., 1970-78, learning disabilities specialist, 1985—; bus. exec. Sturges Co., Independence, Mo., 1982—. Active ARC, 1984—, Nat. Polit. Action, Kansas City, Mo., 1970—. conference presenter Emporia State U. Recipient Excellence in Edn. award ARC, 1984-85; Outstanding Achievement award Colo. for Deaf and Blind, 1963. Mem. Nat. Assn. Females Execs., NEA, Kappa Delta Pi. Republican. Baptist. Avocations: gourmet cooking; tennis; swimming; antiques. Home: 16805 E Cogan Rd Independence MO 64055-2815 Office: Red Bridge Sch 418 E 106th Ter Kansas City MO 64131-4318

STURGES, SHERRY LYNN, recording industry executive; b. Long Beach, Calif., Dec. 11, 1946; d. Howard George and Alice Myrtle (Waymire) Fairbairn; m. Jeffrey Alan Sturges, Dec. 30, 1969; children: Allisun Malinda, Jay. Grad. high sch., Las Vegas, Nev. V.p. Soultime, Inc., Las Vegas, 1968-69, Universe, Inc., Las Vegas, 1971-76; co-developer, owner Fun Trax Music Video and Audio Recording Studios, Westwood, Calif., 1986—; creative cons. John Debella Show, 1990, M.T.V., L.A., 1990, KCET-TV, L.A., 1990, KTLA-TV, L.A., 1991. Officer PTA, Woodland Hills, Calif., 1977-86, pres., 1984-86; vol. Connie Stevens Charity Orgn., Beverly Hills, Calif., 1980-84; vol. Crossroads Sch. for Arts and Sci., Westwood Meth. presch., West L.A. Bapt. Sch., Northridge United Meth. Ch., St. Vincent's Parents Coun., St. Joseph the Worker Sch., Chatsworth H.S., Sepulveda Nursery Sch., Nat. Neurofibromatosis Found., Life Steps Found., Westwood Village Assn. Recipient Outstanding Contribution award L.A. Unified Sch. Dist. Republican. Office: Fun Trax Inc 22270 Del Valle St Woodland Hills CA 91364

STURGIS, EUGENIA FEEMSTER, counselor; b. Rock Hill, S.C., Aug. 16, 1932; d. William Boyd and Willie Thelma (Young) Feemster; m. Leonard David Sturgis Sr. Oct. 6, 1948 (div. Apr. 1980). AA, York Tech. Coll., Rock Hill, 1977, A in Bus., 1987; A in Mgmt., York Tech. Coll., 1987; BA in Music, Winthrop U., 1983, BA in Psychology, 1983. Lic. profl. counselor, S.C.; nat. cert. counselor. Counselor Salvation Army Sister Help, Rock Hill, 1985-89, Winthrop U. Victims Program, Rock Hill, 1989-91, Tri-County Sister Help, Rock Hill, 1991—; ind. piano tchr., Rock Hill, 1970—. Organizer Salvation Army Sister Help, Rock Hill, 1983, Tri-County Sister Help, Rock Hill, 1992. Recipient S.C. State Canning award Clemson (S.C.) Ext. Svc., 1961, AAUW Edn. award AAUW, Rock Hill, 1992. Mem. ACA, S.C. Counseling Assn., S.C. Piano Festival Assn., Rock Hill Piano Tchrs. Forum, Am. Assn. Christian Counselors. Baptist. Home: 275 W Springdale Rd Rock Hill SC 29730-8566 Office: Tri County Sister Help PO Box 686 Rock Hill SC 29731-6686

STURGIS, JOYCE MARIE, accountant, small business owner; b. St. Louis, Jan. 4, 1941; d. William J. and Mary J. (Van Straat) Sturgis; m. Robert L. Brittingham, Dec. 27, 1969 (div. Jan. 5, 1979); 1 child, Paula Therese. BA, Fontbonne Coll., St. Louis, 1963; MA, St. Louis U., 1970; MBA, St. Ambrose U., Davenport, Iowa, 1983. Cert. tchr., Mo., Iowa. Tchr. St. Joseph's Acad., St. Louis, 1963-70; bus. mgr. Quad City Montessori Assn., Davenport, 1976-79; corp. office mgr. Frank Foundries Corp., Moline, Ill., 1979-81; acct. Normoyle-Berg & Assocs., Rock Island, Ill., 1981—; owner Joyce Ent., Davenport. Artist jewelry/handpainted silk; exhibited various invitational art fairs. Mem. Friends of Art, Davenport Mus. Art; trustee, corp. sec. Glynn Fellowship Found., Davenport. Fontbonne Coll. scholar, 1959; St. Ambrose U. mktg. rsch. assistantship, 1980. Mem. AAUW (life, bd. dirs., pres. 1988-89, treas. 1984-88), Left Bank Art League. Democrat. Roman Catholic. Home: 324 N Main St Apt 505 Davenport IA 52801-1418

STURROCK, LOIS CARAWAY, educator, artist; b. Lexington, Tex., Apr. 26, 1915; d. Benjamin Franklin and Sue Etta (Heath) Caraway; m. John Elbert Boedeker, Apr. 12, 1936 (div. May 1944); 1 child, John Caraway; m. Roger Glenn Sturrock, Apr. 21, 1944. AA, Lee Jr. Coll., 1963; BA, U. Houston, 1965, M of Spl. Edn., 1969. Beautician pvt. practice, Houston, 1940-47; tchr. spl. edn. Galena Park (Tex.) Ind. Schs., 1965-78; freelance tchr. art, freelance artist Colmesneil, Tex., 1980—; v.p. Northshore Area Art League, Houston. 1976-77, Jasper (Tex.) Fine Arts League, 1985-86.; pres. Pasadena (Tex.) Art League, 1980-81. Mem. Am. Watercolor Soc. (assoc.), Watercolor Soc. Houston, Water Color U.S.A., Phi Theta Kappa, Phi Kappa Phi, Kappa Delta Pi. Home and Studio: PO Box 555 Colmesneil TX 75938

STURTZ, LAURA G., public relations executive; b. N.Y.C., Apr. 19, 1955. BA in Applied Semiotics, Brown U., 1977. With Young & Rubicam, 1978-81, Burson-Marsteller, 1981-84, Hill and Knowlton, 1985-87, Hill, Holliday, Connors, Cosmopulos, Inc., 1987-88; sr. v.p., dir. creative and bus. devel. Ogilvy & Mather PR, 1989-92; sr. v.p., dir., mktg. group OA&R, 1992-93; mng. dir., mktg. group Ogilvy Adams & Rinehart, N.Y.C., 1993—. Office: Ogilvy Adams & Rinehart 708 Third Ave New York NY 10017*

STUSSY, SUSAN AGNES, lawyer, librarian, history educator; b. Detroit, Apr. 28, 1945; d. Frederick Welter and Lois Eleanor (Amerine) S.; m. H. Carl Markle Jr., Nov. 19, 1966 (div. Oct. 1972). BA in History magna cum laude, Oakland U., Rochester, Mich., 1967; MLS, Wayne State U., 1968; PhD, U. Tenn., Knoxville, 1983; JD, Washburn U., 1994. Bar: Kans. 1994. Asst. cataloger SUNY, Stony Brook, 1969; cataloger St. Peter's Coll., Jersey City, 1970-71, Mt. St. Mary's Coll., Emmitsburg, Md., 1972-78, Converse Coll., Spartanburg, S.C., 1982-83; head librarian Marian Coll., Indpls., 1983-88; libr. dir. St. Norbert Coll., De Pere, Wis., 1988-90; dir. libr. svcs. Barton County C.C., Great Bend, Kans., 1990-91; dir. Internat. Rsch. Libr. Tex. Grad. Sch. Internat. Mgmt., Corpus Christi, 1994-95; supr. ACLU Children's Rights Project, summer 1991; adj. instr. history Kansas City C.C., Leavenworth Center, 1992-93; speaker in field. Author articles on history and libr. sci. Mem. ABA, ALA, Kans. Bar Assn., Am. Hist. Assn., Delta Theta Phi. Republican. Home: 1400 Ocean Dr 201A Corpus Christi TX 78404

STUTER, JANICE CESOLINI, librarian; b. New Bedford, Mass., Oct. 5, 1946; d. Bruno and Irene (Berube) Cesolini; m. Robert Glen Stuter, Aug. 19, 1967; children: Glenn, Ursula. BA, U. Calif., Berkeley, 1971, MLS, 1972. Asst. to librarian Lawrence Hall of Sci., Berkeley, 1971-73; head children's svcs., acting county librarian Yuba County Libr., Marysville, Calif., 1973-76; librarian III, prog. coord. Sacramento Pub. Libr., 1976-77; librarian Preston Sch. Ind. Calif. Youth Authority, Ione, 1977-79; supervising librarian Karl Holton Sch. Libr. Calif. Youth Authority, Stockton, 1979-82; supervising librarian Youth Tng. Sch. Calif. Youth Authority, Chico, 1982-89; prin. librarian Calif. Dept. Corrections, Sacramento, 1989—; chair, rep. SIRCULS Bd., San Bernardino, Calif.; alt. White House Conf. on Libr. and Info. Svcs., 1991; mem. exemplary libr. and media ctr. prog. U.S. Dept. Edn., 1987. Producer, dir. videotape: How to Get a Job: Use Your Library, 1987; co-producer video: Buttestrap, 1973-75; contbr. articles to profl. jours. Bd. sec. Ron Mandella Cmty. Garden, Sacramento, 1993-94, bd. treas., 1994—; vice-chair Libr. Svcs. to Prisoners Forum, 1993-94, chair, 1994—. Queens Coll. grantee, 1973. Mem. ALA (prog. chair 1990—), AAUW (newcomer's chair 1991—), No. Calif. Assn. Law Libraries, Am. Assn. Law Libraries, Inland Herb Soc. Office: Calif Dept Corrections PO Box 942883 Sacramento CA 94283-0001

STUTMAN, VALERIE CARMEL, advertising executive; b. Washington, Sept. 4, 1961; d. David and Antoinette (Skwarek) S. BA, U. Md., 1983. Mktg. rep. Bell Atlantic, Calverton, Md., 1983-84; jr. account exec. Ehrlich Manes Advt., Bethesda, Md., 1984-87; advt. dir. The FASEB Orgn., Bethesda, 1987-88; account exec. Yoder and Assocs., Rockville, Md., 1988—; swim instr. Jewish Community Ctr., Rockville, Md., 1987--; Media Buying Service, Md., 1987--; advt. dir. Potomac Kennels, Md., 1987--. Mem. Defenders of Wildlife, Wash., 1988--. Mem. Advt. Club of Washington, Women's Advt. Nat. Assn. Female Execs., Miniature Pinscher Club, Smithsonian Assn. Democrat. Hebrew.

STUTZMAN, PAMELA SUE, interior designer, jewelry designer; b. Tucson, June 9, 1955; d. Paul Leewell and Winifred Joann (Newlin) S.; m. Robert Frank Madill, Apr. 12, 1975 (div. June 1981). A degree, Delta Coll., University Center, Mich., 1975; grad., Barbizon Modeling Acad., Elmhurst, Ill., 1977. Salesperson Mary Kay Cosmetics, Dallas, 1979-81; beauty advisor Marshall Fields, Bloomingdale, Ill., 1981-84; interior designer PSS Designs, Aurora, Ill., 1984—, jewelry designer, 1991—. Fundraiser Mut. Ground, Inc., 1991-95, med. advocate for victims of sexual assault and domestic violence, 1991-94.

STYER, ANTOINETTE CARDWELL, middle school counselor; b. Martinsville, Va., Apr. 20, 1941; d. John E. Cardwell and I. Lois Cardwell Shelton; children: Yvette D., Christopher P. BA in Liberal Arts, Temple U., 1975; MEd in Elem./Secondary Sch. Counseling, Antioch U., Phila., 1980. cert. sec. prin., 1994. Sec. Edward S. Cooper, M.D., Phila., 1960-66; rsch. asst. Temple U., Phila., 1971-73; confidential sec. Sch. Dist. Phila., 1967-71, sec., 1974-76, social worker Child Care Ctr., 1976-86, sch. counselor elem. edn., 1986-89; secondary edn. counselor Sch. Dist. Phila. Roosevelt Mid. Sch., Phila., 1989—; organizer Project Exposure: Bus.; chaperone student visit to colls., Atlanta; interviewee Nat. Opinion Rsch. Ctr., Phila., 1971-72; mgmt. trainee GSA divsn. U.S. Govt., Phila., 1987; del. leader People to People Student Amb. Programs, Australia, 1993, Russia and the Baltic States, 1994. Past chair 75th anniversary com. Pinn Meml. Bapt. Ch., scholarship com., new mem. com., aides to first lady and women's support group; mem. bd. dirs. Day Care Com.; ann. vol. United Negro Coll. Fund Telethon, mem. small bus. fundraising com. Mem. Nat. Coun. Negro Women, Pa. Sch. Counselors Assn., Delta Sigma Theta (life, chpt. journalist, chair May Week, del. to regional conv., mem. scholarship com.). Home: 925 E Roumfort Rd Philadelphia PA 19150-3215 Office: Sch Dist Phila Roosevelt Mid Sch Washington Ln Musgrave St Philadelphia PA 19144

STYLES, BEVERLY, entertainer; b. Richmond, Va., June 6, 1923; d. John Harry Kenealy and Juanita Russell (Robins) Carpenter; m. Wilbur Cox, Mar. 14, 1942 (div.); m. Robert Marascia, Oct. 5, 1951 (div. Apr. 1964). Studies with Ike Carpenter, Hollywood, Calif., 1965—; student, Am. Nat. Theatre Acad., 1968-69; studies with Paula Raymond, Hollywood, 1969-70; diploma, Masterplan Inst., Anaheim, Calif., 1970. Freelance performer, musician, 1947-81; owner Beverly Styles Music, Joshua Tree, Calif., 1971—; v.p. spl. programs Lawrence Program of Calif., Yucca Valley, Calif. Composer: Joshua Tree, 1975, I'm Thankful, 1978, Wow, Wow, Wow, 1986, Colour Chords (and Moods), Piano Arrangement, 1990, (with lyricist Betty Curtis) The Whispering, 1994; records include The Perpetual Styles Of Beverly, 1978; albums include The Primitive Styles Of Beverly, 1977; author: A Special Plan To Think Upon, the Truth As Seen By A Composer, 1978, A Special Prayer To Think Upon, 1983. Mem. ASCAP (Gold Pin award), Am. Fedn. Musicians, Internat. Platform Assn. Republican. Office: PO Box 615 Joshua Tree CA 92252-0615

STYLES, TERESA JO, producer, educator; b. Atlanta, Oct. 19, 1950; d. Julian English and Jennie Marine (Sims) S. BA, Spelman Coll., 1972; MA, Northwestern U., 1973. Researcher CBS News, N.Y.C., 1975-80, producer, 1980-85; instr. mass communications, English Savannah (Ga.) State Coll., 1985-89, asst. prof. English, 1990; asst. prof. mass comm. and women studies dir. Bennett Coll., Greensboro, N.C., 1990-93; asst. prof. mass comm. N.C. A&T State Univ., Greensboro, 1993—. Researcher documentary CBS Reports: Teddy, 1979 (Emmy cert.); assoc. producer documentaries for CBS Reports: Blacks: America, 1979 (Columbia Dupont cert. 1979), What Shall We Do About Mother?, 1980 (Emmy cert.), The Defense of the U.S., 1980 (Columbia Dupont cert.). Adv. bd. Greensboro Hist. Mus., Eastern Music Festival, Women's Short Film Project. Mem. Writers Guild Am. (bd. dirs. east), Dirs. Guild Am. (bd. dirs. east), African Am. Atelier (Greensboro, N.C. bd. dirs.), Eastern Music Festival (bd. dirs.). Home: 3310 Twin Brook Dr Greensboro NC 27407-6761

STYNES, BARBARA BILELLO, wellness consultant; b. N.Y.C., Apr. 24, 1951; d. Sylvester Francis and Jacqueline Marie (Giardelli) Bilello; m. Frank Joseph Stynes, Aug. 24, 1969; children: Christopher Francis, Jeremy Scott. BA, Rutgers U., 1976; postgrad., Antioch U., 1994—. Mktg. rep. McNeil Consumer Products Co., Fort Washington, Pa., 1979-82, Met Path Inc., Des Plaines, Ill., 1982-85; mktg. coord. Life program Meml. Hosp. and YMCA, Chattanooga, 1986-91; mem. Chattanooga Area Wellness Council, 1986-91, Chattanooga Area Healthcare Coalition, 1986-91; dir. mktg. and comm., met. YMCA, Chattanooga, 1986-91, dir. internat. program, 1989-91; wellness cons., 1992—; fiber sculptor, 1975-77; weaver, 1976-79. Vol. comm. com. Am. Heart Assn., 1972-91, Spl. Olympics, Chgo., 1982-84; speaker Tenn. Safety Belt coalition, 1986-91; clinic leader Am. Lung Assn., Chattanooga, 1986-88, YMCA cert. fitness specialist, 1986, weight mgmt. specialist, 1987; chairperson fundraising, trustee Pine Grove Coop. Sch., New Brunswick, N.J., 1977-78; bd. dirs. Signal Mountain Newcomers Assn., Tenn., 1985-86; mem. sch. bd. Notre Dame High Sch., 1989-91. Mem. NAFE, Am. Bus. Womans Network Chattanooga (chair membership), Fiber Arts Guild, Assn. Profl. Dirs., Kiwanis (chair internat. rels. com. Chattanooga chpt., 1990-91, publicity dir.), Gen. Bd. Newcomers, North Columbus, Sustaining Bd. Choices). Roman Catholic. Avocations: health and wellness, art, music. Home: 7718 Chancel Dr Columbus OH 43235

STYRON, ROSE BURGUNDER, human rights activist, poet; b. Balt., Apr. 4, 1928; d. Benjamin Bernei and Selma (Kann) Burgunder; m. William Styron, May 4, 1953; children: Susanna, Polly, Thomas, Alexandra. BA, Wellesley Coll., 1950; MA, Johns Hopkins U., 1952; LHD (hon.), Briarcliff Coll., 1976, SUNY, Purchase, 1991. Bd. dirs. Amnesty Internat. USA, N.Y.C., 1973-83, chair nat. adv. coun., 1984—. Author: (poems) From Summer to Summer, 1965, Thieves' Afternoon, 1973; co-author, translator: Modern Russian Poetry, 1972; contbr. editorials, profiles, articles, book revs. and poetry to maj. newspapers and mags. Chair, judge Robert F. Kennedy

Meml. Human Rights Award, Washington, 1983-91; mem. adv. bd. Reebok Found. for Human Rights, Boston, 1987—; mem. exec. bd. Human Rights Watch, N.Y.C., 1975—; chmn. adv. coun. Roxbury (Conn.) Libr., 1990—; bd. dirs. N.Y. Found. for Arts, N.Y.C., 1986—, Lawyers Com. for Human Rights, N.Y.C., 1981—, Rainforest Found., N.Y.C., 1989—, Assn. to Benefit Children, Folger Shakespeare Libr.; bd. overseers NYU Faculty of Arts and Scis. Mem. P.E.N. (chair freedom-to-write com. 1983-89, bd. dirs. 1983—), Coun. Fgn. Rels., Vineyard Haven Yacht Club. Democrat. Home: 12 Rucum Rd Roxbury CT 06783

SU, JUDY YA HWA LIN, pharmacologist; b. Hsinchu, Taiwan, Nov. 20, 1938; d. Ferng Nian and Chiu-Chin (Cheng) Lin; m. Michael W. Su; 1 child, Marvin. BS, Nat. Taiwan U., 1961; MS, U. Kans., 1964; PhD, U. Wash., 1968. Asst. prof. dept. biology U. Ala., Huntsville, 1972-73; rsch. assoc. dept. anesthesiology U. Wash., Seattle, 1976-77, acting asst. prof. dept. anesthesia, 1977-78, rsch. asst. prof., 1978-81, rsch. assoc. prof., 1981-89, rsch. prof., 1989—; mem. surg. anesthesiology & trauma study sect. NIH, 1987-91; vis. scientist Max-Planck Inst. Med. Rsch., Heidelberg, West Germany, 1982-83; vis. prof. dept. anesthesiology Mayo Clinic, Rochester, Minn., Med. Coll. Wis., 1988; editorial bd. cons. Jour. Molecular & Cellular Cardiology, London, 1987—, European Jour. Physiology, Berlin, Germany, Muscle & Nerve, Kyoto, Japan, 1989—, Anesthesiology, Phila., 1987—, Molecular Pharmacology, 1988—, Jour. Biol. Chemistry, 1989—, Am. Jour. Physiology, 1990—; mem. rsch. study com. Am. Heart Assn., 1993-95. Contbr. articles to profl. jours. Grantee Wash. Heart Assn., 1976-77, 1985-87, Pharm. Mfrs. Assn. Found., Inc., 1977, Lilly Rsch. Labs, 1986-88, Anaquest, 1987—, NIH, 1978—; recipient Rsch. Career Devel. award NIH, 1982-87; rsch. fellowship San Diego Heart Assn., 1970-72, Max-Planck Inst., 1982-83. Mem. AAAS, Biophys. Soc., Am. Soc. for Pharmacology and Exptl. Therapeutics, Am. Physiol. Soc., Am. Soc. Anesthesiologists. Home: 13110 NE 33rd St Bellevue WA 98005-1318 Office: U Wash Dept Anesthesiology RN-10 Box 356540 Seattle WA 98195-6540

SUAO, ADRIANA CARTAYA, magazine publisher; b. Havana, Cuba, Jan. 20, 1946, came to U.S., 1962; d. Moises Gregorio and Acela Maria (Latour) Cartaya; m. Luis Suao, May 20, 1967; children—Tania Maria, Adriana Elena, Luisa Maria. Student Am. Dominican Acad., Cuba, 1962. Pub. relations staff Kenyon Wiles Advt. Agy., Miami, Fla., 1965, copy editor, 1965-69; gen. mgr., prodn. mgr. Internat. Constrn. Pub. Co., Inc., Miami, 1972—; pres. Cieco, Miami, 1977—; adminstr. BYS Tunnel Forms Co., Miami, 1983—. Republican. Roman Catholic. Avocations: yachting, fishing, cooking. Home: 1401 Lugo Ave Miami FL 33156-6332 Office: Internat Constrn Pub Inc 9500 S Dadeland Blvd Ste 550 Miami FL 33156

SUBAK-SHARPE, GENELL JACKSON, editor, writer; b. Great Falls, Mont.; m. Gerald Subak-Sharpe; children: David, Sarah and Hope (twins). B.A., Butler U., 1959; M.S. in Journalism with honors, Columbia U., 1961. Reporter Indpls. Star, 1958-61; copy editor N.Y. Times, 1962-70; exec. editor Family Health mag. (now Health), 1970-74; editor Med. Opinion mag., 1974-77; v.p., editor Biomed. Info. Corp., 1977-84; pres. G.S. Sharpe Communications Inc., N.Y.C., 1981—. Co-editor: The Physicians' Drug Manual, 1981; editor: The Compendium of Drug Therapy, 1982, The Compendium of Patient Information, 1982, The Physicians' Manual for Patients, 1984, (with Victor Herbert) Mount Sinai School of Medicine Guide to Complete Nutrition, 1990; author: (with Kathryn Schrotenboer) Freedom From Menstrual Cramps, 1981, Living with Diabetes, 1985, Overcomming Breast Cancer, 1987, Breathing Easy, 1988, (with James V. Warren) Frontiers in Medicine series: Surviving Your Heart Attack, 1984, Controlling Hypertension, 1984-87, Living with Diabetes, 1985, (with Joan Ness) The Calcium-Requirement Cookbook, 1985, (with Lois Jovanovic) Hormones: The Woman's Answerbook, 1987, (with Robert Weiss) Columbia University School of Public Health Complete Guide to Health and Well-Being After 50, (with Edward Frohlich) Take Heart, 1990, (with Raul Artal) Exercise and Pregnancy, 1992, (with S.J. Winawer and M. Shike) Cancer Free, 1995; editoral dir.: Columbia University College of Physicians and Surgeons Complete Home Medical Guide, 1985, Columbia University College of Physicians and Surgeons Complete Guide to Pregnancy, 1988, Columbia University College of Physicians and Surgeons Complete Guide to Early Child Care, 1990, Yale University Coll. Medicine Heart Book, 1992, The Good Housekeeping Illustrated Guide to Women's Health, 1995, Disney Encyclopedia of Early Childhood, 1995; founding editor: Being Well Magazine, 1983; Off Hours, 1983; Health and Nutrition Newsletter, 1984, Physicians Lifestyle Magazine, 1989; mng. editor Home Health Handbook, 1988—. Pulitzer Traveling fellow Columbia U., 1961-62; recipient Russell L. Cecil Writing award Arthritis Found., 1972, Mag. Writing award Am. Dental Soc., 1977, Blakeslee award Am. Heart Assn., 1985. Mem. Authors Guild, Women's Press Club, Nat. Assn. Sci. Writers, Newswomens Club N.Y. Avocations: restoration historic houses, antique collecting. Home and Office: 606 W 116th St New York NY 10027-7011

SUBER, ROBIN HALL, former medical/surgical nurse; b. Bethlehem, Pa., Mar. 14, 1952; d. Arthur Albert and Sarah Virginia (Smith) Hall; m. David A. Suber, July 28, 1979; 1 child, Benjamin A. BSN, Ohio State U., 1974. RN, Ariz., Ohio. Formerly staff nurse Desert Samaritan Hosp., Mesa, Ariz. Lt. USN, 1974-80. Mem. ANA, Sigma Theta Tau.

SUBIN, FLORENCE, lawyer; b. N.Y.C., June 5, 1935; d. George and Beatrice (Rodam) Katroser; m. Bert W. Subin, June 6, 1953 (dec.); children: Glen D., Beth Subin Ambler. BA, Herbert H. Lehman Coll., 1972; JD magna cum laude, Bklyn. Law Sch., 1975. Bar: N.Y. 1976, U.S. Dist. Ct. (so. and ea. dists.) N.Y. 1976. Pvt. practice N.Y.C. and Scarsdale, N.Y., 1976—. Mem. Assn. Trial Lawyers City of N.Y. (bd. dirs. 1982-86), Met. Women's Bar Assn. (pres. 1979-81, bd. dirs. 1981—), Bronx Women's Bar Assn. (pres. 1983-85), Bklyn. Law Sch. Alumni Assn. (pres. 1992-94), Phi Beta Kappa. Office: 291 Broadway New York NY 10007-1814

SUBKOWSKY, ELIZABETH, insurance company executive; b. New London, Conn., Feb. 17, 1949; d. Thomas and Matilda (Mastroianni) Logan; m. Robert A. Subkowsky, June 9, 1972. BA with honors and dist., U. Conn., 1971; MBA, DePaul U., Chgo., 1977. Dir. systems CNA Ins., Chgo., 1973—. Bd. dirs. Highland Park (Ill.) Hist. Soc., 1991—, 1st v.p., 1993—. Fellow Life Office Mgmt. Assn. (award 1977); mem. Woman's Club Evanston (aux. officer 1985-87, 79-91). Office: CNA Ins 1 Cna Plz Chicago IL 60604

SUBLETTE, JULIA WRIGHT, music educator, performer, adjudicator; b. Natural Bridge, Va., Sept. 13, 1929; d. Paul Thomas and Annie Belle (Watkins) Wright; m. Richard Ashmore Sublette, Oct. 18, 1952; children: C. Mark, Carey P., Sylvia S. Bennett, Wright D. BA in Music, Furman U., 1951; MusM, Cin. Conservatory, 1954; PhD, Fla. State U., 1993. Ind. piano tchr., 1953—; instr. music and humanities Okaloosa-Walton C.C., Niceville, Fla., 1978—; panelist Music Tchr. Nat. Conv., Milw., 1992. Editor Fla. Music Tchr., 1991—; contbr. articles to profl. music jours. Mem. Music Tchrs. Nat. Assn. (cert., chmn. so. divsn. jr. high sch. piano/instrumental contests 1986-88), Fla. State Music Tchrs. Assn., So. Assn. Women Historians, Southeastern Hist. Keyboard Soc., Friday Morning Music Club, Pi Kappa Lambda. Home: 217 Country Club Rd Shalimar FL 32579

SUBSTAD LOKENSGARD-SCHIMMELPFENNIG, KATHRYN ANN, small business owner, career consultant; b. Mpls., Dec. 4, 1941; d. Arnold Torger and Ardis Louise (Klanderud) Substad; m. Arvid Luther Lokensgard, Nov. 23, 1963 (div. July 1982); children: Sara Kathryn Lokensgard Dickinson, Sigurd Arvid Lokensgard, Laura Ann Lokensgard; m. Wesley Ernest Schimmelpfennig, Mar. 24, 1990. BA, St. Olaf Coll., 1963; postgrad., Pacific Luth. Theol. Sem., 1989. Tchr. Lookout Mountain (Tenn.) Elem. Sch., 1964-66; tchrs. aide Greenvale Elem. Sch., Northfield, Minn., 1974-76; substitute tchr. Inclin Village (Nev.) High Sch., 1978-80, asst. libr., 1980-82; fin. aid dir., fgn. student advisor Sierra Nevada Coll., Incline Village, 1982-85, asst. to pres., 1985-89; mgr., v.p. Paul Bunyan Co., Tahoe Vista, Calif., 1990—; owner Tahoe Christian Bookstore, Tahoe Vista, Calif., 1993—; substitute tchr., career cons., 1990-92; liaison to bd. Sierra Nevada Coll., 1985-88. Bd. dirs. ch. coun. Christ the King Luth. Ch., Tahoe City, 1986-89, local pub. TV sta., 1986-89; vol. tchr. ESL, 1991—; active Nev. Literacy Coalition, 1991—; bd. dirs. North Tahoe Reading Ctr.; deacon Incline Village Community Presbyn. Ch., 1992—. Mem. PEO (social sec. 1988-89), AAUW, C. of C. (bd. dirs. 1988-89, Hospice 1991—, Citizen of Month 1989).

SUCHECKI, LUCY ANNE, elementary education educator; b. East Cleveland, Ohio, May 3, 1945; d. Ben and Adelaide V. (Maneri) Urban; m. Robert K. Suchecki, Aug. 19, 1972. BS, Bowling Green State U., 1967; MA, Oakland U., 1981. Cert. elem. tchr., Mich. Elem. tchr. L'Anse Creuse Pub. Schs., Mt. Clemens, Mich., 1967—; grade cons. (book) Michigan, 1991. Active Immaculate Conception Ch., 1969—, Anchor Bay Women's Pool League, 1972—. Mem. NEA, MEA, MEA-NEA (local 1), L'Anse Creuse Ednl. Assn. (sec. 1968—), New Baltimore Hist. Soc. Roman Catholic. Home: 8504 Anchor Bay Dr Clay MI 48001-3507 Office: Marie C Graham Elem Sch 25555 Crocker Blvd Harrison Township MI 48045-3443

SUCHER, CYNTHIA CLAYTON CRUMB, health company marketing executive; b. Washington, Dec. 19, 1943; d. Francis Paul and Jewell Evangeline (Sheets) Crumb; m. Theodore Richard Sucher III, Sept. 7, 1961 (div. Dec. 1980); children: Theodore Richard IV, Evangeline Leigh Sucher Gabrielson; m. Carlton Wayne Vaught, Dec. 20, 1982; 1 child Clayton Wayne. Student, Stetson U., 1959-61; BA in Communications summa cum laude, U. Cen. Fla., 1975. Reporter, anchorwoman Sta. WFTV-TV, Orlando, Fla., 1974-76, exec. producer, 1977-78; news anchorman Sta. KWTX-TV, Waco, Tex., 1976-77; editor, pub. Dining Out mag., Orlando, 1978-80; pub. info. officer Fla. Dept. Health and Rehabilitative Svcs., Orlando, 1980-82; dir. media communication Orlando Regional Med. Ctr., 1982-85; asst. adminstr. Winter Park (Fla.) Meml. Hosp., 1985-86, v.p. mktg., 1986-92, v.p. customer rels., 1993—; v.p. mktg., devel. Park Health Corp., 1992-93; v.p. customer rels., 1993—; mentor Crummer Sch. Bus., Rollins Coll., Winter Park, 1987-91. Producer/reporter radio documentary Ted Bundy series, 1980 (UPI award). Media coord. Bill Frederick Campaign, Orlando, 1980; bd. dirs. Vol. Ctr. Ctrl. Fla., 1983-87; pres. Winter Park Sidewalk Art Festival, 1985; chmn. Orlando Mayor's Nominating Bd., 1992-93; mem. pres.'s coun. advisors U. Ctrl. Fla., Orlando, 1987—; chmn. ann. rev. com. City of Orlando, 1989. Recipient Healthcare Mktg. Report Merit award, 1986, 89. Mem. Am. Mktg. Assn. (bd. dirs. Cen. Fla. chpt. 1987-88, nat. bd. dirs. 1993—), Acad. Health Svcs. Mktg. (bd. dirs. 1988-91, chmn. nat. symposium 1991, Internat. Mktg. award 1989, Gold and Silver Mktg. awards 1991, Bronze Mktg. award 1991, 92, 93, pres. elect 1993), Soc. Profl. Journalists (pres. Cen. Fla. chpt. 1983), Fla. Exec. Women (pres. Orlando 1985-86), Alliance for Healthcare Strategy and Marketing (nat. pres. 1994—), Orlando C. of C. (chmn. community awards 1987), Winter Park C. of C. (bd. dirs. 1989—, chmn. 1993, v.p. internal affairs 1990, pres.-elect 1991, pres. 1992—), Town and Gown (coun.). Democrat. Methodist. Home: 347 W Palm Valley Dr Oviedo FL 32765 Office: Winter Park Meml Hosp 200 N Lakemont Ave Winter Park FL 32792-3273

SUCHIL, SALLY, lawyer; b. L.A., Mar. 12, 1951; d. Martin Aldana and Catherine (Nicolaides) S. BA, U. So. Calif., L.A., 1975; JD, U. Santa Clara, 1979. Bar: Calif. Staff atty. SEC, L.A., 1979-84; assoc. counsel MGM/UA Entertainment, Culver City, Calif., 1984-86, former v.p., corp. sec., 1986; v.p. corp. legal affairs MGM/UA Comm. Co, Beverly Hills, Calif., 1986-91; sr. v.p. corp. legal affairs MGM/Pathe Comm. Co, Culver City, Calif., 1991—; assoc. gen. counsel Luz Engring. Co., Culver City, 1986; mem. Jud. Nominees Evaluation Commn., San Francsico, 1988, 89. Bd. dirs. Sojourn (battered women and children svcs.), L.A., 1984-1990. Mem. ABA, Am. Soc. Corp. Secs., Inc., Women Lawyers' Assn. L.A. (1st v.p. 1989-90), Mex.-Am. Bar Assn. Democrat. Office: Metro Goldwyn Mayer Inc 2500 Broadway St Santa Monica CA 90404*

SUCHY, SUSANNE N., nursing educator; b. Windsor, Ont., Can., Sept. 20, 1945; d. Hartley Joseph and Helen Viola (Derrick) King; m. Richard Andrew Suchy, June 24, 1967; children: Helen Marie, Hartley Andrew, Michael Derrick. Diploma, St. Joseph Sch. Nursing, Flint, Mich., 1966; BSN, Wayne State U., 1969, MSN, 1971. RN, Mich. Afternoon supr., staff nurse operating and recovery rm. St. John Hosp., Detroit, 1966-70; nursing instr. Henry Ford Community Coll., Dearborn, Mich., 1972—, on leave 1988-90; CNS/case mgr. surg. nursing Harper Hosp., Detroit, 1988-89; CNS case mgr. oncology, 1989—; mem. Detroit Demonstration Site Team for defining and differentiating ADN/BSN competencies, 1983-87. Contbr. articles to profl. jours. Past bd. dirs., pres. St. Pius Sch. Mem. ANA, AACH, N.Am. Nursing Diagnosis Assn. (by-laws com. chair 1992—), Mich. Nursing Diagnosis Assn. (pres. 1987-90, elected by-law chairperson 1991-92, treas. 1993—), NLN, Detroit Dist. Nurses Assn. (past chmn. nominating com., legis. com., sec. 1994—), Oncology Nursing Soc. (gov. rels. chair 1992—, presenter abstract conf. 1991, poster presentations ann. conf. 1991, 92), Daus. of Isabella (internat. dir., past regent, state fin. sec.), Wayne State U. Alumni Assn., Sigma Theta Tau (nominating com. 1991-93). Roman Catholic. Home: 12666 Irene St Southgate MI 48195-1765 Office: Henry Ford CC 5101 Evergreen Rd Dearborn MI 48128-2407

SUCKIEL, ELLEN KAPPY, philosophy educator; b. Bklyn., June 15, 1943; d. Jack and Lilyan (Banchefsky) Kappy; m. Joseph Suckiel, June 22, 1973. A.B., Douglass Coll., 1965; M.A. in Philosophy, U. Wis., 1969, Ph.D. in Philosophy, 1972. Lectr. philosophy U. Wis., Madison, 1969-71; asst. prof. philosophy Fla. State U., Tallahassee, 1972-73; asst. prof. philosophy U. Calif., Santa Cruz, 1973-80, assoc. prof., 1980—, provost Kresge Coll., 1983-89. Author: The Pragmatic Philosophy of William James, 1982, also articles. Mem. Am. Philos. Assn., Soc. for Advancement Am. Philosophy. Office: U Calif Cowell Coll Santa Cruz CA 95064

SUDAK, JANICE, cardiovascular perfusionist; b. Rochester, Pa., Oct. 19, 1958; d. John and Virginia Louise (Alam) S. BS in Biology, Carlow Coll., 1980; grad. cert., Shadyside Hosp. Sch., Cardiovascular Perfusion, 1980. Cert. Am. Bd. Cardiovascular Perfusion, 1982. Staff clin. perfusionist St. Louis (Mo.) U. Dept. Surgery, 1980-83, Clin. Perfusionists, Inc., Annapolis, Md., 1983-89; chief perfusionist Clin. Perfusionists, Inc., Annapolis, 1989—. Vol. spl. events City of Ft. Lauderdale, Fla.; fundraiser Big Bros./Big Sisters Broward County; event co-chair Inaugural HRCF South Fla. black tie awards dinner Dolphin Dem. Club. Mem. NOW, Soc. Extracorporeal Tech., Fla. Perfusion Soc., Broward Women in Network, Nat. Geog. Soc., Lilique Soc. Am., Amnesty Internat., Human Rights Campaign Fund (co-chair So. Fla. inaugural black tie dinner), Broward United Against Discrimination, Greenpeace, Whale Adoption Project. Democrat. Roman Catholic. Home: 810 SE 2nd St # F Fort Lauderdale FL 33301-3614 Office: Clin Perfusionists Inc PO Box 5035 Annapolis MD 21403-7035

SUDANOWICZ, ELAINE MARIE, government executive; b. Dorchester, Mass., Aug. 3, 1956; d. John Anthony and Helen Mary (Budzinski) S. Student, Fontbonne Acad., Milton, Mass., 1974; BA, Boston State Coll., 1978; MPA, Suffolk U., Boston, 1986; grad. Exec. Leadership Devel. Program, Dept. of Def., 1993. Cert. level 2 contractor, and level 3 in program mgmt., notary pub., Mass. Pub. relations office mgr. MacDonald & Evans Inc. Litho., Dorchester, Mass., 1974-78; research asst. Nat. Commn. Neighborhoods, Wash., 1978; pol. cons. Various Nat. State & Local, Pol. Campaigns, 1974-86; telephonist supr., cons. ARC, Boston, 1980-81; adminstrv. asst. Suffolk County Courthouse Commn., Boston, 1981-82; exec. asst. sheriff Suffolk County Sheriff's Office, 1982-86; presl. mgmt. intern ESD/PK Air Force Systems Command, Hanscom AFB, Mass., 1986-89; advanced copper CAP Air Force Systems Command, Andrews AFB, Md., 1989-90; contract negotiatior Hdqrs., Electronic Systems div., Joint STARS Program, Hanscom AFB, Mass., 1990-92; program mgr. Hdqrs., Electronic Sys. Ctr., EN-1, Hanscom AFB, 1992—; asst. program dir. bus. acquisition re-engring. Elec. Sys. Ctr., Hanscom AFB, 1994—. Author: Constitutional Vignette, Separation of Powers and Contracting in the Bureaucrat, 1987; contbr. PMInformer, 1989—; also articles; agt., cons Theatre Arts-Play 1988—. Vol., cons. City & State Pub. Agys.-Pub. Sector, Boston; literacy vol., 1988-89; mem. John F. Kennedy Libr. Recipient Spl. Achievement award U.S. Dept. Transp., 1989, Outstanding Alumnus award Suffolk U., 1990. Mem. Am. Soc. Pub. Adminstrn. (rep. region 1 nat. young profls. forum 1988—), Nat. Contract Mgmt. Assn. (photographer No. Va. chpt. 1989-90, cert. profl. contracts mgr., nat. chair program mgmt. spl. topics com.), Presdl. Mgmt. Alumni Group (nat. bd. dirs. 1989-90, N.E. field bd. dirs. 1990—, Outstanding Alumnus award 1990), Trustees of Reservations Mass., Mass. Audubon Soc., Armed Forces Communications and Electronics Assn., Air Force Assn., Women in Def., Sr. Profl. Women's Assn., Suffolk County Deputy Sheriff's Assn., Boston Network for Women in Govt. and Politics, World Affairs Coun. Boston, Appalachian Mountain Club, Pi Alpha Alpha (pres. Suffolk U. chpt.). Democrat. Roman Catholic. Home: 108 Alban St Dorchester MA 02124-3711 Office: Air Force Materiel Command Hdqs Electronic Systems ESC/AR Shiely Bldg Hanscom AFB MA 01731-2115

SUDBRINK, JANE MARIE, sales and marketing executive; b. Sandusky, Ohio, Jan. 14, 1942; niece of Arthur and Lydia Sudbrink. BS, Bowling Green State U., 1964; postgrad. in cytogenetics Kinderspital-Zurich, Switzerland, 1965. Field rep. Random House and Alfred A. Knopf Inc., Mpls., 1969-72, Ann Arbor, Mich., 1973, regional mgr., Midwest and Can., 1974-79, Can. rep., mgr., 1980-81; psychology and ednl. psychology adminstrv. editor Charles E. Merrill Pub. Co. div. Bell & Howell Corp., Columbus, Ohio, 1982-84; sales and mktg. mgr. trade products Wilson Learning Corp., Eden Prairie, Minn., 1984-85; fin. cons. Merrill Lynch Pierce Fenner & Smith, Edina, 1986-88; sr. editor Gorsuch Scarisbrick Pubs., Scottsdale, Ariz., 1988-89; regional mgr. Worth Publs., Inc., N.Y.C., 1989—. Lutheran. Home and Office: 3801 Mission Hills Rd Northbrook IL 60062-5729

SUDDOCK, FRANCES SUTER THORSON, grief educator, writer; b. Estelline, S.D., Oct. 23, 1914; d. William Henry and Anna Mary (Oakland) Suter; m. Carl Edwin Thorson, July 6, 1941 (dec. Apr. 1976); children: Sarah Thorson Little, Mary Frances; m. Edwin Matthew Suddock, Aug. 7, 1982 (dec. Sept. 1986). BA, Iowa State Tchrs. Coll., 1936; postgrad., Syracuse U., 1940-41, U. Iowa, 1946; MA, Antioch U., San Francisco, 1981. Cert. tchr. Tchr. various high schs., Correctionville and Eagle Grove, Iowa, 1936-38, 38-40, 41-43, 45-47; chief clk. War Price and Rationing Bd., Eagle Grove, 1943-45; instr. (part time) Eagle Grove Jr. Coll., 1953-61; adminstr. Eagle Grove Pub. Library, 1961-77; facilitator Will Schutz Assocs., Muir Beach, Calif., 1987-88. Author: Whither the Widow, 1981. Vol. Nat. Trainer Widowed Persons Svc. Am. Assn. Retired Persons, 1989—, ret. sr. vol. program, Anchorage, 1988—; pres., bd. dirs. Anchorage Widowed Persons Svc., 1992-94; bd. dirs. North Iowa Mental Health Ctr., Mason City, 1959-76, Eagle Grove Cmty. Chest, 1960, Help Line, Inc., Ft. Dodge, Iowa, 1976-77; chmn. Cmty. Mental Health Fund, Eagle Grove, 1966-73; charter pres. Eagle Grove Concerned, Inc., 1973-77; active various civic orgns. Mem. AAUW (charter pres. Eagle Grove br. 1973-75), Am. Soc. on Aging, Alaska Assn. Gerontology (treas. 1992—), Anchorage Woman's Club, P.E.O., Kappa Delta Pi. Home: 333 M St Apt 404 Anchorage AK 99501-1902

SUE, LINDA GAIL, technical illustrator, cartographic technician; b. Oakland, Calif., June 4, 1962; d. Johnson Chee and Darlene Yim (Tom) S. AB, U. Calif., Berkeley, 1985; MA, Calif. State U., Hayward, 1990. Tech. illustrator Kleinfelder, Inc., Pleasanton, Calif., 1987—. Mem. Assn. Am. Geographers, Am. Congress on Surveying and Mapping. Office: Kleinfelder Inc 7133 Koll Center Pky # 100 Pleasanton CA 94566-3101

SUELTENFUSS, SISTER ELIZABETH ANNE, university president; b. San Antonio, Apr. 14, 1921; d. Edward L. and Elizabeth (Amrein) S. BA in Botany and Zoology, Our Lady of Lake Coll., San Antonio, 1944; MS in Biology, U. Notre Dame, 1961, PhD, 1963. Joined Sisters of Divine Providence, Roman Catholic Ch., 1939; tchr. high schs. Okla. and La., 1942-49; mem. summer faculty Our Lady of Lake U. (formerly coll.), 1941-49, mem. full-time faculty, 1949-59, chmn. biology dept., 1963-73, pres., 1978—; mem. adminstrv. staff to superior gen. Congregation Divine Providence, 1973-77. Author articles in field. Bd. dirs. Am. Cancer Soc., Avance-San Antonio, San Antonio chpt. ARC, Mind Sci. Found., YWCA, Alama Pub. Telecom. Bd., S.W. Rsch. Found., I Have a Dream Found., Inst. Ednl. Leadership, Trim and Swim, Cmtys. in Schs., San Antonio Edn. Partnership (pres.), San Antonio Pub. Libr. (pres.); chmn. edn. com. Pvt. Sector United San Antonio; bd. dirs. USO; bd. visitors Air Force Inst. Tech. Recipient Achievement and Leadership awards U. Notre Dame, 1979, Svc. to Community award, 1991, Headliner award Women in Comms., 1980, Good Neighbor award NCCJ, 1982, Brotherhood award, 1992, Today's Woman award San Antonio Light, 1982, Outstanding Women award San Antonio Express-News, 1983, Spirit of Am. Woman award J.C. Penney, 1992, Lifetime Achievement award, 1993, Svc. to Edn. awrd Ford Found., 1993; named to San Antonio Women's Hall of Fame, 1985. Mem. AAUP, AAUW, San Antonio 100 Tex. Women's Forum, San Antonio Women's C. of C., Hispanic Assn. Colls. and Univs., Greater San Antonio C. of C. (former vice chmn.), San Antonio Coun. Pres. (former pres.), San Antonio Women's Hall of Fame (pres.), Zonta. Home and Office: Our Lady of the Lake U Office of Pres 411 SW 24th St San Antonio TX 78207-4617

SUGAR, SANDRA LEE, art consultant; b. Balt., May 18, 1942; d. Harry S. and Edith Sarah (Levin) Pomerantz; children: Gary Lee, Terry Lynn. BS in Edn. and English, Towson State U., 1965; MS in Edn. and Applied Behavioral Scis., Johns Hopkins U., 1986. Chairperson arts exhibit Balt. Arts Festival, 1979; med. interviewer Johns Hopkins Sch. of Hygiene, Balt., 1980-82; copy writer Concepts & Communications, Balt., 1984; instr. art history and world cultures Catonsville Community Coll., Balt., 1981-85; instr. English Community Coll. of Balt., 1981-85; instr. English and math. Info. Processing Tng. Ctr., Balt., 1985; info. specialist Info. of Md. New Directions for Women, Balt., 1986; trainer, job developer Working Solutions, Balt., 1987-88; art gallery dir. Renaissance Fine Arts Gallery, Bethesda, Md., 1988-93; judge nat. high sch. sci. fiction contests. Author poetry collection, juried exhibition, 1979, 80; editor mus. guides' newsletter Guidelines, 1978; painter juried exhibitions, 1979, 80. Docent Balt. Mus. of Art, 1973-86; festival coordinator Internat. Brass Quintet Festival, Balt., 1986; chairperson spl. events Balt. PTA, 1978-82; bd. dirs. Citizens Planning and Housing Assn., Balt., 1980-82; mem. women's com., ctr. stage hand Balt. Ballet, 1979-84, Balt. Symphony, 1979-80. Recipient F.J. Bamberger scholarship, Johns Hopkins U., 1985, Mayoral Vol. of Yr. award Balt. Mus. Art, 1979.

SUGARMAN, ADELAIDE GOODMAN, social services administrator; b. Bklyn., May 5, 1939; d. Solomon and Gertrude (Kaufman) Goodman; m. Robert J. Sugarman, June 12, 1960 (div.); children: Karen Elizabeth, Kenneth; m. Marshall Gary Greenberg, Dec. 7, 1978; stepchildren: David, Paula. BA cum laude, Smith Coll., 1960; MEd, Temple U., 1982. Tchr. elem. sch. Cupertino (Calif.) Sch. Dist., 1960-61; tchr. Lincoln (Mass.) Sch. Dist., 1961-64; program coord., asst. to prin. Miquon (Pa.) Sch., 1964-76; Title IX/Affirmative Action coord. William Penn Sch. Dist., Yeadon, Pa., 1978-81; instr. sex role sterotyping Temple U., Ambler, Pa., 1978-81; trainer in-svc. courses for educators Montgomery County (Pa.) Intermediate Unit, 1978-80; program coord. Multi-Svc. Sr. Ctr., Phila., 1982-85; exec. dir. Ret. Sr. Vol. Program Montgomery County, Pa., 1986-94; cons. and speaker in field, 1978-81. Bd. dirs. Women's Ctr. Montgomery County, 1979-81, Allens Lane Art Ctr., Phila., 1969-76; co-developer Summit Ch. Community After Sch. Program, Phila., 1973; developer pilot adult edn. series Chestnut Hill Community Ctr., Phila., 1973; vol. various polit. campaigns, 1964—. Recipient Leadership award Prudential Found., 1992, Leadership award Kelly Anne Dolan Meml. Fund, 1993. Mem. Nat. Assn. RSVP Dirs., Pa. Assn. RSVP Dirs., Pa. Assn. Vols., Assn. Vol. Adminstrn., Del. Valley Assn. Dirs. Vol. Programs, Women's Ctr. Montgomery County. Home: 1401 Juniper Ave Elkins Park PA 19027

SUGGS, JOSEPHINE GREENWAY, controller; b. Lula, Ga., Dec. 19, 1946; d. Marvin W. and Lucille (Echols) Greenway; m. Ray M. Suggs, May 31, 1969; children: Jeffrey Ray, Martin Ryan. Cert. in computer programming, Lanier Tech. Inst., 1979; AA, Am. Inst. Profl. Bookkeepers, 1989. Contr. Hilb, Rogal & Hamilton Co., Gainesville, Ga., 1988—. Vol. ARC, 1979—, N.E. Ga. Med. Aux., 1993—. Mem. NAFE, Am. Bus. Women, Am. Inst. Profl. Bookkeepers, Nat. Assn. Ins. Women, Ins. Women Gainesville. Baptist. Home: 5906 Homer Hwy Lula GA 30554

SUGINTAS, NORA MARIA, medical sales and marketing executive; b. Evergreen Park, Ill., Mar. 12, 1956; d. George and Mary (Navickas) S. BS in Biol. Scis. with highest distinction, U. Ill., Chgo., 1978; DVM, U. Ill., 1982. Lic. veterinarian, Ill. Profl. hosp. specialist Abbott Labs., Detroit, 1983-87; anesthesia & critical care patient monitoring equipment cons Shiley, Inc., Detroit, 1987-91; anesthesia and critical care monitoring equipment sales exec. and cons. Ohmeda, Detroit, 1991-94; regional mgr. Criticare, Detroit, 1994—. Journalist The Lithuanian World-Wide Daily Newspaper, 1975; author: The Production S-Adenosylmethionine by Saccharomyces cervisiae and Candida utilis. Troop leader Girl Scouts Lithuanian, Chgo., 1972-77, cmap dir., 1977. Recipient Louis Pasteur award for Academic Excellence in the Biol. Scis. and Ind. Rsch. U. Ill., 1978. Mem. NAFE, Econ. Club Detroit, Phi Beta Kappa. Republican. Home and Office: 6284 Aspen Ridge Blvd West Bloomfield MI 48322-4433

SUGIYAMA, TOKU MARY, retired school administrator; b. Sacramento, Sept. 6, 1921; d. Sakae and Kuniko (Kosaka) Koda; m. Yone J. Sugiyama, Apr. 5, 1952; m. George Y. Morishita, Mar. 23, 1942; (dec. Mar. 1949); children: Maeona, Carolyn, George. Jr. cert. U. Calif.-Berkeley, 1941; BA, Towson State U., 1980, MA, 1984. Tchr., Poston Relocation Ctr., Ariz., 1941-44; purchasing agt. U.S. Dept. Def., Tokyo Ordnance Depot, 1952-56; instr. Ikebana Sogetsu Sch., Tokyo, 1956-67, exec. dir. Sogetsu USA, sch. Japanese flower arrangement, 1967-93, ret., 1993. Recipient Mohan Sho, Sogetsu Sch., 1960, Sofu Sho, 1967, Flower Arranger of Yr. award Nat. Council State Garden Clubs, 1979, Sofu Teshigahara Meml. award, 1991, First Sofu Meml. award, 1991. Mem. Md. Fedn. Garden Clubs, Ikebana Internat. (charter), Balt.-Kawasaki Sister City Cultural Com. Home: 959 Ellendale Dr Baltimore MD 21286-1511

SUGRUE, MARY SHARON, epidemiology nurse; b. Detroit; d. James Joseph and Geraldine Grace Sugrue. ADN, Schoolcraft Coll., 1974; BSN, Ea. Mich. U., 1986; MS, Wayne State U., 1992. Staff nurse intensive care Botsford Hosp., Farmington Hills, Mich., 1974-80, infection control coord., 1981-84; infection control practitioner St. Joseph Mercy Hosp., Pontiac, Mich., 1984-86; coord. infection control and employee health Huron Valley Hosp., Milford, Mich., 1986-89, coord. infection control and nursing quality assurance, 1990-91, coord. epidemiology and regulatory compliance, 1991-92; nursing performance improvement coord. Harper Hosp., Detroit, 1992—; premarital counselor AIDS and sexually transmitted diseases Huron Valley Hosp., Milford, 1988-92; cons. infection control and hazardous waste to physician offices, Novi, Mich., 1988—. Contbg. author: Management of Methicillin Resistant Staphylococcus, 1992. Mem. Quality Assurance Nursing Network, Mich. Nursing Assn. (HIV task force), Nat. Nursing Assn., Mich. Soc. for Infection Control Mktg. (program chmn. 1986-89), Assn. for Practitioners in Infection Control. Office: Harper Hosp 3990 John R Detroit MI 48201

SUHR, GERALDINE M., medical/surgical nurse; b. Sumner, Iowa, Mar. 16, 1960; d. Marvin Edward and Peggy Marie (Reiser) S. Diploma, Allen Meml. Luth. Sch. Nursing, Waterloo, Iowa, 1982; student, U. No. Iowa, Cedar Falls, 1979. Sr. ship's nurse Carnival Cruise Lines, Miami, Fla.; emergency room and ICU/CCU nurse New Hampton (Iowa) Community Hosp.; charge nurse Trav Corps, Malden, Mass., Flying Nurses, Dallas, Hosp. Staffing Inc., Fla.; charge nurse, med./telemetry So. Hills Hosp., Nashville.

SUI, ANNA, fashion designer; b. Dearborn Heights, Mich., 1955; d. Paul and Grace S. Grad., Parsons Sch. Design. Founder, designer Anna Sui, 1992—; boutique Macy's Herald Sq., 1992—, N.Y.C.; opened outlet SoHo dist., 1992, N.Y.C. First runway show, 1991. Recipient Perry Ellis award new fashion talent Coun. Fashion Designers Am., 1992. Studio: 214 West 39th St Ste 800 New York NY 10018 also: c/o Keeble Cavaco & Duka Ste 10A 853 7th Ave New York NY 10019*

SUJANSKY, EVA BORSKA, physician, educator; b. Bratislava, Slovak Republic, Feb. 14, 1936; d. Stefan and Terezia (Kaiserova) Borska; m. Eduard Sujansky, Apr. 2, 1960 (dec. 1979); children: Paul, Walter. MD, Comenius U., Bratislava, Czechoslovakia, 1959. Diplomate Am. Bd. Pediats., Am. Bd. Med. Genetics. Resident in pediats. U. Iowa, Iowa City, 1971-73; fellow in human genetics Mt. Sinai Sch. Medicine, N.Y.C., 1973-74; clin. genetist Beth Israel Hosp., N.Y.C., 1973-74; dir. clin. genetics Sch. Medicine, U. Colo., Denver, 1974-90, assoc. prof. pediats., biochemistry, biophysics and genetics, 1981—; co-dir. divsn. genetic svcs. The Children's Hosp., U. Colo., Denver, 1990—. Contbr. articles to profl. jours. Fellow Am. Acad. Pediats., Am. Soc. Human Genetics, Am. Coll. Med. Genetics (founding fellow). Office: U Colo Med Ctr 1056 E 19th Ave Denver CO 80218

SUKHU, PIYANETR, internist; b. Bangkok, Nov. 16, 1946; d. Amnuay and Prachoom (Deva Hasdin) Kohvathana; m. Surin Sukhu, Sept. 7, 1973; children: Peter, Tanya. MD, Mahidol U., Bangkok, 1970. Diplomate Am. Bd. Internal Medicine. Resident internal medicine Med. Coll. Ohio, Toledo, 1972-74; fellow nephrology VA Hines Loyola U., Maywood, Ill., 1974-76; staff physician VA Long Beach, Calif., 1976-80; asst. clin. prof. Med. Sch. U. Calif., Irvine, 1976-80; pvt. practice Laguna Hills, Calif., 1980—. Mem. Am. Soc. Internal Medicine, Orange County Assn. Internal Medicine, Kidney Internat., Thai Physician Assn., Kidney Club. Office: Sukhu Med Group Inc 24953 Paseo De Valencia Ste 14B Laguna Beach CA 92653

SULC, JEAN LUENA (JEAN L. MESTRES), lobbyist; b. Worcester, Mass., Mar. 17, 1939; d. Emilio Beija and Julia (Bulan) Luena; m. Lee Gwynne Mestres, Oct. 9, 1965 (div. Dec. 1973); m. Lawrence Bradley Sulc, Nov. 4, 1983. BS in Psychology, Tufts U., 1961; M in Urban and Regional Planning, U. Colo., 1976. Lic. real estate, Va.; lic. pvt. pilot. Mem. staff U.S. fgn. svc. Dept. State, Washington, 1962-65; intern Adams County Planning Dept., Brighton, Colo., 1974-75; cons. office policy analysis City and County of Denver, 1976; program dir. Coun. Internat. Urban Liaison, Washington, 1976-79; asst., dir. internat. Cities Svc. Oil & Gas Corp., Washington, 1980-81; govt. affairs rep. Cities Svc., OXY USA Inc., Washington, 1982-89; mgr. fed. rels. OXY USA Inc., Washington, 1990—; chmn. govt. affairs com. L.P. Gas Clean Fuel Coalition, Irvine, Calif., 1990-92. Author, editor: (newsletter) Dayton Climate Project, 1979-80; contbr. articles to newsletters. Vol. Reagan/Bush and Bush/Quayle Presdl. Campaigns and Inaugural Coms., Washington, 1984-89; pres. Hale Found., Nathan Hale Inst., Washington, 1984-85; mem. nat. panel consumer arbitrators Better Bus. Burs., Va., 1991—. Recipient Presdl. citation Nat. Propane Gas Assn., 1992; Minority Intern grantee Denver Regional Coun. Govts., 1974-76. Mem. ABA (assoc., arbitration sect.), Am. Petroleum Inst., Am. League Lobbyists (chmn. energy sect., bd. dirs. 1994—), Women Govt. Rels., Psi Chi. Episcopalian. Office: OXY USA Inc (Occidental Oil & Gas Corp) 1747 Pennsylvania Ave NW # 300 Washington DC 20006

SULFARO, JOYCE A., parochial school educator; b. Bklyn., Oct. 23, 1948; d. John Joseph and Mildred Ann (Credidio) Carvelli; m. Guy Sulfaro, Aug. 1, 1971; children: Jacqueline Amber, Kristin Lynn. BA, Molloy Coll., 1970; postgrad. Fla. Atlantic U., 1979-80; MS in Adminstrn. and Supervision, Nova U., 1982. Tutor reading Our Lady of Loretto, Rockville Centre, N.Y., 1969-70; tchr. lang. arts and math. Resurrection Sch., Bklyn., 1970-73; tchr. Annunciation Sch., Hollywood, Fla., 1976-80, prin., 1980-84; tchr. St. Thomas More Sch., 1984-88; writer English curriculum for Jr. High for Archdiocese of Miami, 1979. Author: (with M. Sue Timmins) The Basket, 1980. Travel coord./sec. Rego Park (N.Y.) Met. Youth Orgn., 1969-70. Mem. ASTD, Nat. Council Tchrs. Math., Fla. League Mid. Schs., Cath. Educators Guild Archdiocese of Miami, Nat. Cath. Ednl. Assn. (chair sch.-based com. 1988-91), Am. Mus. Natural History, Rocky Mt. Mental Health Assn. (bd. dirs. 1988-90), IBS Adv. Coun., Prins. and Asst. Prins. Assn. (sec. 1990-91, adminstr. vocat. adv. com. 1990-93, adminstr. media adv. com. 1990-94, sec. 1991-94), Nat. Assn. Secondary Sch. Prins. Home: 1104 Waterloo Ct Rocky Mount NC 27804-8432

SULIK, DOLORES ANN, realtor, marketing professional; b. Cleve., Apr. 11, 1942; d. Howard Anthony and Henrietta (Schulhauser) Nieberding; divorced; children: Jodie Frydl, Rob. Grad. high sch., Euclid, Ohio. Realtor Hilltop Realty, Cleve., 1977-82, residential sales agt., 1982-90; from adminstr. mktg. and sales to dir. devel. mktg. HGM-Hilltop Condominium Assocs., Cleve.; from mktg. mgr. to dir. sales and mktg. new homes dept. Realty One, Cleve.; dir. builder mktg. Smythe Cramer Co., Cleve., 1990—. Mem. Cleve. Bldg. Industry Assn. (chmn. assoc. adv. coun. 1994, chmn. sales and mktg. coun. 1990—, Assoc. of Yr. 1991, 94, Outstanding Mktg. Person of Yr. 1993), Builder Mktg. Soc. (trustee 1992—), Nat. Sales and Mktg. Coun. of Nat. Assn. Home Builders (trustee 1992-94), Inst. Residential Mktg. Roman Catholic. Home: 2250 Par Ln PH7 Willoughby Hills OH 44094 Office: Smythe Cramer Co 5800 Lombardo Ctr # 200 Cleveland OH 44131

SULLENBERGER, ARA BROOCKS, mathematics educator; b. Amarillo, Tex., Jan. 3, 1933; d. Carl Clarence and Ara Frances (Broocks) Cox; m. Hal Joseph Sullenberger, Nov. 2, 1952; children: Hal Joseph Jr., Ara Broocks Sullenberger Switzer. Student, Randolph-Macon Woman's Coll., 1951-52, So. Meth. U., 1952, U. Tex., Arlington, 1953, Amarillo Coll., 1953-54; BA in Math., Tex. Tech. U., 1955, MA, 1958; postgrad., Tex. Christian U., 1963-67, U. N. Tex., 1969-80, Tarrant Jr. Coll., Fort Worth, Tex., 1972-83. Cert. tchr., Tex. Math. tchr. Tom S. Lubbock (Tex.) High Sch., 1955-56; instr. math. Tex. Tech U., Lubbock, 1956-63; teaching fellow math. Tex. Christian U., Ft. Worth, 1963-64; chmn. dept. math. Ft. Worth Country Day Sch., 1964-67; instr. math. Tarrant County Jr. Coll.-South, Ft. Worth, 1967-70, asst. prof. math., 1970-74, assoc. prof. math., 1974—; cons. Project Change, Ft. Worth, 1967-68; math. scis. advisor Coll. Bd., Princeton, N.J., 1979-83; math. book reviewer for various pub. cos. including Prentice-Hall, McGraw Hill West, D.C. Heath, Prindle, Weber & Schmidt, MacMillan, Harcourt, Brace Jovanovich, Wadsworth, Worth Pub., West Pub. Contbr. article, book revs. to profl. publs.; author book supplement to Intermediate Algebra, 1990. Active mem. Jr. League of Ft. Worth, 1954-73, sustaining mem., 1973—; editor newsletter Crestwood Assn., Ft. Worth, 1984, 86, 91, membership sec., 1985, 90, 91, pres., 1988-89, crime patrol capt., 1993, v.p., 1993. Recipient award for excellence in teaching Gen. Dynamics, 1968. Mem. Math. Assn. Am. (life), Nat. Coun. Tchrs. Math. (life), Am. Math. Assn. Two-Yr. Colls. (life), Tex. Math. Assn. Two-Yr. Colls. (charter), Tex. Jr. Coll. Tchrs.' Assn., Pi Beta Phi. Republican. Episcopalian. Home: 600 Eastwood Ave Fort Worth TX 76107 Office: Tarrant County Jr Coll South Campus 5301 Campus Dr Fort Worth TX 76119

SULLIVAN, ANNE ELIZABETH, publishing executive; b. N.Y.C., Oct. 23, 1942; d. Eugene Redmond and Anne (Rigney) S.; m. Alan H. Bomser, Oct. 11, 1984. BA, Newton (Mass.) Coll., 1964; JD, Fordham U., 1980. Bar: N.Y. 1981. With permissions dept. Farrar, Straus & Giroux, N.Y.C., 1967-74, dir. contract and copyright dept., 1988—. Office: Farrar Straus Giroux 19 Union Sq W New York NY 10003-3304

SULLIVAN, ANNIE LUDINGTON, lawyer; b. Midland, Mich., Sept. 21, 1959; d. John Samuel and Dorothy (Lamson) Ludington; m. Patrick Michael Sullivan, Oct. 24, 1987; children: Colin Samuel, Cabriel Patrick. BA, Albion Coll., 1982; JD, Emory U., 1986. Bar: N.C. 1986. Assoc. Alexander & Assocs., Chapel Hill, N.C., 1986-88, Thorp & Assocs., Raleigh, N.C., 1988—; ptnr. Thorp, Sullivan Thorp, Raleigh, N.C., 1992—. Mem. Am. Trial Lawyers Assn., N.C. Acad. Trial Lawyers, N.C. Assn. Women Attys., Order of Coif. Office: Thorp Sullivan Thorp 225 Hillsborough St Raleigh NC 27603

SULLIVAN, CAROL MARY, architect, set designer; b. Bethpage, N.Y., Mar. 18, 1961; d. John Patrick and Henrietta Teresa (Groen) S. BS, Kent State U., 1985. Arch. Ferguson Murray Arch., N.Y.C., 1988-90; set designer Prodn. Design Group, N.Y.C., 1993-94; adminstr. S.D. Goodman Group, N.Y.C., 1995—. Home: 160 E 48th St New York NY 10017

SULLIVAN, CHRISTINE ANNE, creative director; b. Syracuse, N.Y., May 24, 1957; d. Donald Roger and E. Gloria (Stalker) Coffman; m. James Henry Sullivan, Jr., Feb. 16, 1991; 1 child, Madeline Jean. BS in Geography, U. N.H., 1979. Cartographer Butterworth Map Co., West Yarmouth, Mass., 1979-81; chief cartographer Marshall Penn-York Map Co., Syracuse, 1981-86; graphic artist New Channels Corp., Syracuse, 1986-89, creative dir., 1989—. Recycling promoter involved in bus. and community orgns., Syracuse, 1990—. Recipient Telly award Nat. Advt. Profls., 1993, Syracuse Advt. Club awards Regional East Coast Advt. Profls., (1) 1992, (3) 1993, (4) 1994. Mem. Cable TV and Mktg. Soc. (nat. and state mem., MARK award (2) 1990, (1) 1991, (3) 1993), Assoc. Artists of Syracuse, Nat. Mus. of Women in the Arts. Office: NewChannels Corp PO Box 4872 Syracuse NY 13221-4872

SULLIVAN, CLAIRE FERGUSON, marketing educator; b. Pittsburg, Tex., Sept. 28, 1937; d. Almon Lafayette and Mabel Clara (Williams) Potter; m. Richard Wayne Ferguson, Jan. 31, 1959 (div. Jan. 1980); 1 child, Mark Jeffrey Ferguson; m. David Edward Sullivan, Nov. 2, 1984. BBA, U. Tex., 1958, MBA, 1961; PhD, U. North Tex., 1973; grad., Harvard Inst. Ednl. Mgmt., 1991. Instr. So. Meth. U., Dallas, 1965-70; asst. prof. U. Utah, Salt Lake City, 1972-74; assoc. prof. U. Ark., Little Rock, 1974-77, U. Tex., Arlington, 1977-80, Ill. State U., Normal, 1980-84; prof., chmn. mktg. Bentley Coll., Waltham, Mass., 1984-89; dean sch. bus. Met. State Coll. Denver, 1989-92, prof. mktg., 1992—; cons. Denver Partnership, 1989-90, Gen. Tel. Co., Irving, Tex., 1983, McKnight Pub. Co., Bloomington, Ill., 1983, dental practitioner, Bloomington, 1982-83, Olympic Fed., Berwyn, Ill., 1982, Denver Partnership Econ. Devel. Adv. Coun., 1989-91; mem. African-Am. Leadership Inst. Gov. Bd. Contbr. mktg. articles to profl. jours. Direct Mktg. Inst. fellow, 1981; Ill. State U. rsch. grantee, 1981-83. Mem. Am. Mktg. Assn. (faculty fellow 1984-85), So. Mktg. Assn., Southwestern Mktg. Assn., Denver World Trade Ctr., Denver Partnership (econ. devel. adv. bd.), Rotary, Beta Gamma Sigma. Republican. Methodist. Home: 4715 11th St Greeley CO 80634-2318 Office: Met State Coll Dept Mktg MSCD Box 79 PO Box 173362 Denver CO 80217-3362

SULLIVAN, JO BUTLER, banker; b. Rockledge, Fla., Dec. 29, 1952; d. Loran Alburn and Anne (Gettings) Butler; divorced; children: Jocelyn Anne, Julia Leigh. BA in Psychology, U. North Fla., 1974, postgrad. Dir. pers. and pub. rels. Hope Haven Children's Hosp., Jacksonville, Fla., 1974-79; dir. pers. Cape Coral (Fla.) Med. Clinic, 1979-81; dir. human resources Fawcett Meml. Hosp., Port Charlotte, Fla., 1981-88; pers. mgr., asst. v.p. C&S Bank (named changed to NationsBank), Ft. Myers, Fla., 1988—; career continuation cons. Nations Bank, Ft. Myers, 1992—. Mem. exec. bd., vol. chmn. Paint Your Heart Out Lee County, 1992-94; mem. Career Adv. Coun., 1992-94. Named Olympic Hero for Community Vol. Work, 1994. Mem. Soc. for Human Resource Mgmt. (pres. 1992). Republican. Baptist. Home: 1422 SE 28th Ter Cape Coral FL 33904-3917 Office: Nations Bank 1610 Royal Palm Ave Fort Myers FL 33901-2924

SULLIVAN, KAREN LAU, real estate company executive, campaign consultant; b. Honolulu, Jan. 21, 1948; d. Ralph Karn Yee and Beatrice (Loo) Lau; m. Paul Dennis Sullivan, Apr. 24, 1976. BA, Whittier Coll., 1970; MA, U. Hawaii, 1987. Staff asst. to Congresswoman Patsy Mink U.S. Ho. Reps., Washington, 1974, staff asst. subcom. mines and mining, 1975-77, legis. asst. to Congressman Cec. Heftel, 1977-79; spl. asst. to asst. to Pres. for policy and women's affairs The White House, Washington, 1979; spl. asst. office of sec. of transp. U.S. Dept. Transp., Washington, 1979-81; regional dir. mid-Atlantic states Mondale-Ferraro Presdl. Campaign, Washington, 1984; dep. nat. field dir. Paul Simon Presdl. Campaign, Washington, 1987-88; Ill. dir. forum inst. Martin & Glantz Polit. Cons., San Francisco, 1988; regional dir. western states Clinton-Gore Presdl. Campaign, Little Rock, 1992; dep. dir. for public outreach Office of Pres.-Elect Bill Clinton, Little Rock/Washington, 1992-93; v.p. Hoaloha Ventures, Inc., Honolulu, 1981—. Mem. Carter/Mondale Alumni Fund, The Carter Ctr. Home and Office: 810-K N Kalaheo Ave Kailua HI 96734

SULLIVAN, KATHRYN ANN, educator, librarian; b. Elmhurst, Ill., Jan. 22, 1954; d. Joseph Terrence and Rose Marie (Wright) S. Student, Triton Jr. Coll., 1972-73; BA, No. Ill. U., 1975, MLS, 1977; D of Sci. in Info. Sci., Nova U., 1991. Chief periodicals clk. No. Ill. U., Dekalb, 1976-77; periodicals librarian West Chgo. (Ill.) Pub. Library, 1977-78, Winona (Minn.) State U., 1978—. Contbr. articles to profl. jours. Grantee Winona State U., 1986, 88, 92, 94. Mem. ALA, Minn. Libr. Assn., Libr. and Info. Tech. Assn., N.Am. Serials Interest Group. Home: 670 Winona St Winona MN 55987-3353 Office: Winona State U Maxwell Libr Winona MN 55987

SULLIVAN, KATHRYN D., geologist, astronaut; b. Paterson, N.J., Oct. 3, 1951; d. Donald P. and Barbara K. Sullivan. BS in Earth Scis., U. Calif., Santa Cruz, 1973; PhD in Geology, Dalhousie U., Halifax, N.S., Can., 1978; Dr. (hon.), Halhousie, Halifax, N.S., Can., 1985, SUNY, Utica, 1990, Stevens Inst., 1992. Astronaut NASA, 1978-93, mission specialist flight STS-41G, 1984, mission specialist flight STS-31, 1990, payload comdr. flight STS-45, 1992; chief scientist NOAA, Washington, 1993—; adj. prof. Rice U., Houston, 1985-92; mem. Nat. Commn. on Space, 1985-86; mem. exec. panel Chief of Naval Ops., 1988—; first Am. woman to perform extra-vehicular activity. Comdr. USNR. Recipient Space Flight medal NASA, 1984, 90, 92, Exceptional Svc. medal, 1985, 91, Outstanding Leadership medal, 1992, Nat. Air and Space Mus. trophy Smithsonian Instn., 1985, Haley Space Flight award AIAA, 1991, AAS Prather Eva award, 1992, Flight Achievement award, 1990. Mem. AIAA, Geol. Soc. Am., Am. Geophys. Union, Soc. Women Geographers, Explorers Club. Address: 2610 Key Blvd Arlington VA 22201-4002 Office: Dept Commerce NOAA 14th & Constitution Ave NW Washington DC 20230-0002

SULLIVAN, KATHRYN MEARA, telecommunications company executive; b. Schenectady, N.Y., Sept. 20, 1942; d. Vincent Thomas and Agnes (Pendergast) Meara; m. Paul William Sullivan, Feb. 8, 1964; children: Mary Margaret, Paul Hammond, Patricia Eileen. BS in Physics, Bucknell U., 1964; MBA, Fairleigh Dickinson U., 1981. Software developer Gen. Electric Corp., Phila., 1964-65; account exec. Honeywell Corp., Phila., 1975-77; regional sales mgr. Nicolet Instrument Corp., Northvale, N.J., 1977-81; mktg. mgr. AT&T, Basking Ridge, N.J., 1981-83; bus. devel. mgr. AT&T, Berkeley Heights, N.J., 1983-86; pres. AT&T-Pixel Machines, Somerset, N.J., 1986-90; dir. sales ops. and support AT&T Computer Systems, Morristown, N.J., 1990-91; dir. sales transition AT&T Computer Systems, Parisppany, N.J., 1991-92; dir. info. svcs. AT&T Bus. Communications Svcs., Parsippany, N.J., 1992-93; dir. bus. applications and info. svcs. AT&T, Bedminster, N.J., 1993—; mem. charter adv. bd. Rothman Inst. for Entrepreneurial Studies, Fairleigh Dickinson U., 1989—. Chairperson career options for women com. YWCA, Plainfield, N.J., 1989-91. Recipient Anthony Gervino award Fairleigh Dickinson U., 1989, Pinnacle award, 1991. Mem. Nat. Computer Graphics Assn. (treas., exec. com. bd. dirs. 1989—).

SULLIVAN, LAURA PATRICIA, lawyer, insurance company executive; b. Des Moines, Oct. 16, 1947; d. William and Patricia (Kautz) S. BA, Cornell Coll., Iowa, 1971; JD, Drake U., 1972. Bar: Iowa 1972. Various positions Ins. Dept. Iowa, Des Moines, 1972-75; various legal positions State Farm Mut. Auto Ins. Co., Bloomington, Ill., 1975-81, sec. and counsel, 1981-88, v.p., counsel and sec., 1988—; v.p., sec., dir. State Farm Cos. Found., 1985—; sec. State Farm Lloyd's, Inc., 1987—; v.p., counsel and sec. State Farm Fire and Casualty Co., 1988—; v.p., counsel and sec. State Farm Gen. Ins. Co., 1988—, also bd. dirs.; sec., dir. State Farm Life and Accident Assurance Co.; sec. State Farm Annuity and Life Assurance Co., 1991—, State Farm Life Ins. Co., 1992—; bd. dirs. Ins. Inst. for Highway Safety, Nat. Conf. Ins. Guaranty Funds. Trustee John M. Scott Indsl. Sch. Trust, Bloomington, 1983-86; bd. dirs. Scott Ctr., 1983-86, Bloomington-Normal Symphony, 1980-85, YWCA of McLean County, 1993—; chmn. Ins. Inst. for Hwy Safety, 1987-88. Mem. ABA, Iowa State Bar Assn., Am. Corp. Counsel Assn., Am. Soc. Corp. Secs. Office: State Farm Mut Automobile Ins Co 1 State Farm Plz Bloomington IL 61710

SULLIVAN, LYN, psychiatric nurse; b. N.Y.C., July 3, 1943; d. Paul and Anne Jeanne (Urlin) Valente. BA in Psychology, Marymount Manhattan, 1970; MS in Psychiat. Nursing, U. Rochester, 1984. RN. Staff nurse neurosurgery Jacobi Hosp., Bronx, N.Y., 1964-65; med. sec., office nurse Mt. Sinai Hosp., N.Y.C., 1965-66; per diem nurse Rockefeller U. Hosp., James Ewing Hosp., Hosp. Spl. Surgery, N.Y.C., 1966-68; clin. instr. Hosp. for Spl. Surgery Practical Nursing Sch., N.Y.C., 1968-70; pvt. duty nurse Meml. Hosp./Sloan-Kettering Cancer Ctr., N.Y.C., 1970-72; staff nurse, relief supr. Rockefeller Univ. Hosp., N.Y.C., 1972-76; pvt. duty nurse N.Y. Hosp./Cornell Med. Ctr., N.Y.C., 1973-77, 80-82, Rochester (N.Y.) Nurses Registry, 1977-80; staff nurse inpatient psychiat. unit Strong Meml. Hosp., Rochester, 1978-80, Univ. of Tenn., Knoxville, 1980-81; staff nurse inpatient psychiat. unit Mt. Sinai Hosp., N.Y.C., 1981-82; primary therapist Extended Care Clinic, Strong Meml. Hosp., Rochester, 1983, psychiat. emergency rm. nurse, 1982-85; primary individual and group therapist, clin. instr. Rochester Mental Health Ctr., 1985-90; pvt. practice individual and group psychotherapy Rochester, 1988—; primary individual and group therapist Strong Meml. Hosp., 1990—. Mem. ANA, N.Y. State Nurses Assn., Network N.Y. State Clin. Specialists, Rochester Area Group Psychiat. Therapy Soc., Am. Group Psychotherapy Assn. Democrat. Office: 100 Linden Oaks Rochester NY 14625

SULLIVAN, LYNNE ANN, chiropractor; b. San Francisco, Apr. 12, 1961; d. Robert Wayne Fruchtenicht and Barbara Lee (Riedel) Long; m. Frank Alden Sullivan, July 2, 1983; 1 child, Brad Alden. BA in Exercise Physiology, U. Calif., Davis, 1983; D of Chiropractic summa cum laude, Life Chiropractic, San Lorenzo, Calif., 1986. Assoc. dr. Pleasanton (Calif.) Chiropractic, 1986-89; pvt. practice chiropractor, owner Sullivan Chiropractic Health Ctr., Pleasanton, 1989—; found. bd. mem. Valley Care Hosp., Pleasanton and Livermore, 1991—. Bd. mem. Tri-Valley Haven for Women, Livermore, 1989. Mem. AAUW (bd. mem. Alameda county 1988), Am. Chiropractic Assn., Calif. Chiropractic Assn., Alameda County Chiropractic Assn., Pi Tau Delta, Pleasanton C. of C. (amb. 1986-89, small bus. com. 1988), Soroptimist Internat. Pleasanton (bd. mem. 1988). Office: Sullivan Chiropractic 268 Main St Pleasanton CA 94566-7323

SULLIVAN, MARCIA MARIE, chemical company executive; b. Milton, Mass., Apr. 22, 1957; d. Robert John and Barbara Lee (Hain) S. BA in Econs., Mt. Holyoke Coll., 1979. Mfg. supr. Rochester Products div. GM, Rochester, N.Y., 1979-81; order svc. supr. films div. Mobil Chem. Co., Rochester, 1981-83, customer svc. mgr., 1983-85, distbn. analyst, 1985-87; prodn. control mgr. Mobil Chem. Co., Stratford, Conn., 1987-89; distbn. mgr. Plasitc Packaging div. Plastics Packaging div. Mobil Chem. Co., Woodland, Calif., 1989—. Reading tutor Literacy Vols., Rochester and New Haven, 1986-89, Woodland, Calif., 1993—. Roman Catholic. Office: Mobil Chem Co 1351 E Beamer St Woodland CA 95776-6009

SULLIVAN, MARILYN BOBETTE, librarian, consultant; b. Havre, Mont., July 19, 1931; d. Charles Leslie and Alice L. (Wright) Gorman; m. James F. Sullivan, Sept. 25, 1954 (div. Jan. 1983); children: Matthew, Eileen, Andrew. BA, U. Wis., 1953, MLS, 1968. Reference and cataloging libr. med. and dental libr. Marquette U., Milw., 1969-70; head reference libr. Med. Coll. Wis. Librs., Milw., 1970-75, assoc. dir., 1975-81, acting dir., 1982-83; dir. Faculty of Medicine, Kuwait U., Kuwait City, 1981-82, U. Mo. Health Scis. Librs., Kansas City, 1983—; cons. Agy. for Internal Devel., Milw. Area Tech. Coll., 1988; cons. Kuwait U. Faulty of Medicine Med. Libr., Kuwait City, 1991—. Author: (with others) Basic Library Management for Health Sciences Librarians, 1982; contbr. articles to profl. jours. Fulbright fellow to Cairo, Egypt, 1992—. Mem. Med. Libr. Assn. (chair internat. cooperation sect. 1991—), Med. Libr. Assn. (Disting. Mem. of Acad. Health Info. Profls. 1990), Am. Med. Writers Assn., Sierra Club (newsletter editor 1988-90). Home: 6132 Charlotte St Kansas City MO 64110-3310 Office: U Mo 2411 Holmes St Kansas City MO 64108-2741

SULLIVAN, MARY E., state legislator; b. June 29, 1932; m. Charles M. Sullivan; children: Charles M. Jr., Ethel M., Mary E., Kathleen M., Mark C., Ursula M. AB, Regis U., 1954; MA, Boston Coll., 1955. Asst. prof. stats. Bentley Coll., Waltham, Mass., 1966-72; asst. prof., registrar Husson Coll., 1973-79; mem. staff Maine Dept. Manpower Affairs Rsch., 1980-81; math. tchr. John the Baptist Meml. H.S., 1981—; also mem. Maine Ho. of Reps. City councilor City of Bangor, Maine, 1985—, mayor, 1988-89. Mem. Maine Munic Assn. (past pres.). Democrat. Address: 81 Grant St Bangor ME 04401-3821 Office: Maine Ho of Reps State Capitol Augusta ME 04330*

SULLIVAN, MARY JEAN, elementary school educator; b. Cambridge, Mass., May 13, 1956; d. Joseph Leo and Jean Marie (Isaac) S. BA, Flagler Coll., 1978; postgrad., U. No. Fla., 1980—, Fla. State U., 1992, Okla. State U., 1992. Cert. elem. educator, Fla. Tchr. grade 2 St. Agnes Sch., St. Augustine, Fla., 1978-79; tchr. grades 1 through 5 Evelyn Hamblen Elem. Sch., St. Augustine, 1979-91; tchr. grade 5 Osceola Elem. Sch., St. Augustine, 1991—; adv. Sci. Club; chairperson, St. John's County Tchr. Edn. Coun., 1985, SACS Evaluation Team Duval County Schs., 1988, 89, 90; co-chair sch. improvement; rep. tchr. edn. coun.; coord. sch. computers; trainer coll. intern. students. Developer tchr. edn. coun. tng. handbook for State of Fla. Active PTO, past pres., Cub Scouts Am., past asst. program dir., Cathedral-Basilica Ch., United Child Care After Sch. Program, 1988-89; coord. summer recreation Evelyn Hamblen Sch., St. Augustine, 1987-90; dir. tournament Pam Driskell Meml. Paddle Tennis Scholarship Fund, 1986, 87, 88, 89. Recipient Human Rels. award State of Fla., 1992, NEWEST award, 1992, award Geography Summer Inst., 1992; named Kiwanis Tchr. of Yr., 1993; grantee Fla. Coun. Elem. Edn., 1981-82, Fla. Inst. Oceanographers, 1994; Horizons grantee, 1994; Summer Enhancement grantee, 1988, 89. Mem. NEA, Nat. Sci. Tchrs. Assn., Fla. Teaching Profession, Fla. Assn. Staff Devel., Fla. Geographic Alliance, Fla. Assn. Computer Edn., Fla. Assn. Sci. Tchrs., St. John's Educators Assn. Office: Osceola Elem Sch 1605 Osceola Elem Sch Rd Saint Augustine FL 32095

SULLIVAN, MARY MARGARET, state legislator; b. Marlborough, Mass., Sept. 9, 1952; d. Robert Patrick and Eileen Frances (Lawless) S.; m. Donald W. Meals; 1 child. BA in History, Trinity Coll., 1974; MS in Journalism, Boston U., 1979. Legis. asst. Office of Senator Patrick Leahy, Washington, 1975-78; reporter News Tribune, Waltham, Mass., 1979-81; reporter, editor News Limited, Sydney, Australia, 1981-82; copy editor Washington (D.C.) Post, 1982-88; legis. aide Office of Senator Doug Racine, Montpelier, Vt., 1989; writer U. Vt. Office of Pub. Rels., Burlington, 1989-91; comm. dir. Vt. Housing Fin. Agy., Burlington, 1991-92; state rep. Vt. State Legis., 1991—. Chair Chittenden County Dem. Com., 1991—; sec. Dem. State Com., Vt., 1991—; bd. dirs. Burlington (Vt.) Cmty. Land Trust, 1992—. Mem. Amnesty Internat. Home: 368 Flynn Ave Burlington VT 05401

SULLIVAN, NANCY JANE, psychiatric social worker; b. Salem, Oreg., Feb. 11, 1947; d. J. Wesley and Elsie Jane (Brownell) S.; m. Christopher Nicholas Synodis, June 2, 1977; children: Michale Nicholas Synodis, Ana Nicole Synodis. BA, Honors Coll., U. Oreg., 1968; MEd, U. Wash., 1970; MSW, Portland State U., 1972. Cert. bioenergetic therapist. Dir. Chehalem House, Newberg, Oreg., 1973-76; family therapist La Frontera Clinic, Tucson, 1977-79; pediat. cardiology social worker U. Ariz. Health Scis. Ctr., Tucson, 1979-82; neonatal and pediat. social worker U. Wash. Hosp., Seattle, 1984-85; adminstr. N.W. Inst. Acupuncture and Oriental Medicine, Seattle, 1985-88; pvt. practice Olympia, Wash., 1989—; sec., treas. Newberg Human Resources Ctr., 1973-76; sec. Ariz. Soc. for Bioenergetic Analysis, Tucson, 1978-80, Duniway Forum, Olympia, 1991-92. Author: A Child's Eye View of Heart Surgery, 1981. Co-founder Duniway Sch., Olympia, 1992; chair Duniway Sch. Forum, Olympia, 1993-94; mem. staff Mid. Earth Sch., Hood Canal, Wash., 1993-94. Mem. NOW, Ctr. for Sci. in Pub. Interest, Amnesty Internat. Office: Ste 103 1415 W Harrison Olympia WA 98502

SULLIVAN, NELL INKLEBARGER, administrative secretary, counseling assistant; b. Charleston, Ark., Jan. 27, 1932; d. Hubert Huel and Maybelle (Heather) Inklegarger; m. J.W. Miller, June 10, 1950 (div. 1973); children: Allan Evan Miller, Sandy Miller Hays-Lusted, Elizabeth Kay Guyer, Judith Lynelle Miller; m. Nathan Doyal Sullivan Sr., 1973. AA in Journalism, Westark Coll., Ft. Smith, Ark., 1986. Clk. U.S. Postal Svc., Lavaca, Ark., 1959-63; co-owner, operator, photographer Nell Miller Studio, Lavaca, 1960-75; mgr., clk. U.S. Postal Svc., Ft. Smith, 1972-73; computer specialist Westark Coll., Ft. Smith, 1984-86, assoc. editor coll. newspaper, 1985-86; adminstrv. asst. BDM, Inc., Ft. Chaffee, Ark., 1987-89; counseling asst. Ark. Rehab. Svc., Ft. Smith, 1990-94. Recipient journalism scholarship Westark Coll., 1984-86. Mem. YWCA (bd. dirs. Ft. Smith 1986-93), Nat. Rehab. Svc., Ark. State Employees Assn., Nat. Assn. Rehab. Secs., 4-H Alumni Assn. (life), Phi Beta Lambda. Office: Ark Rehab Svc Ste 207 1115 S Waldron Rd Fort Smith AR 72903

SULLIVAN, PATRICIA ANAYA, educational program director; b. Albuquerque, Jan. 10, 1961; d. Jose Miguel and Mary Magdelina (Sandoval) Anaya; m. Robert Patrick Sullivan, May 12, 1984; children: Brendan Patrick, Jordan Christine. BS, N.Mex. State U., 1983. Rsch. tech. SUMMA Med. Corp., Albuquerque, 1983; asst. program coord. N.Mex. State U., Border Rsch. Inst., Las Cruces, 1983-85, program dir., 1985-89, asst. dir., 1989-91, assoc. dir., 1991—; bd. dirs. Enchantment Land Cert. Devel. Corp., Albuquerque. Mem. NAFE, Nat. Assn. Small Bus. Internat. Trade Educators, Border Trade Alliance, N.Mex. Indsl. Devel. Execs. Assns. Democrat. Roman Catholic. Office: NMex State Univ Border Rsch Institute Las Cruces NM 88003

SULLIVAN, SISTER PATRICIA CLARE, hospital administrator; b. Cortland, Nebr., July 2, 1928. R.N. diploma, Mercy Hosp. Sch. Nursing, Denver, 1954; B.S.N., Coll. St. Mary, Omaha, 1955; M.H.A., St. Louis U., 1971, cert. for internal resources for renewal, 1971; cert. in gerontology, U. Nebr., Omaha, 1976. Instr. Mercy Hosp. Sch. Nursing, Des Moines, 1955-58; dir. Mercy Hosp. Sch. Nursing, 1960-64; nursing supr. pediatrics Mercy Hosp., Des Moines, 1955-58; adminstr. Mercy Hosp., 1977—; pres. Mercy Health Ctr. of Central Iowa, 1982—, Mercy Hosp. Med. Ctr., Mercy Found., Mercy Health & Human Services, Mercy Properties, ShareCare Ltd, Mercy Geriatric Services; coordinator rural hosp. nursing, nursing supr. obgyn Mercy Hosp., Durango, Colo., 1958-60, nursing supr., Williston, N.D., 1964-65; adminstr. St. Joseph's Mercy Hosp., Centerville, Iowa, 1965-69; resident Peter Bent Brigham Hosp., Boston, 1970-71; dir. Cen. Nat. Bancshares, First Interstate Bank Corp. Des Moines (formerly Bancshares), 1979—; in organizational renewal Province of Omaha, 1971-74; dir. community relations Archbishop Bergan Mercy Hosp., Omaha, 1974-77; mem. Province of Omaha Health Services Council, 1958—; provincial chpt. del. Province Omaha, 1970-74. Dir. film depicting tornado strike to Archbishop Bergan Mercy Hosp., 1975, numerous showings, including at Congl. hearing at Pentagon. Del. Mercy Gen. Chpt., 1981—; bd. dirs. Mercy Hosp., Devils Lake, N.D., 1972-81, Sub-Area IV, Iowa Health Systems Agy., 1977—, NCCJ, 1979-85, Health System of Mercy, 1979-83, Grand View Coll., Des Moines, 1982-87, Des Moines Better Bus. Bur., 1983-85; regional rep. Diocesan Pastoral Council, 1978-80; mem. Mercy Health Conf., 1979-83, Iowa Network Mercy Hosps. 1979—, IHA Coun. on Profl. Affairs, 1980—; bd. dirs. Convalescent Home for Children, 1980-84, Health System of Midlands, Omaha, 1984-86, Greater Des Moines Com., 1987—; chair Iowa Caucus Project, 1987-88; mem. pres.'s coun. Iowa State U., 1988—. Recipient Leadership award NCCJ, 1984, People of Vision award Iowa Soc. to Prevent Blindness, 1985; named Adminstr. of Yr. Des Moines Consortium of Family Practice Physicians, 1980-81; named to Iowa Women's Hall of Fame Iowa Commn. on Status of Women, 1988, Equestrian Order of Holy Sepulchre of Jerusalem, 1989. Mem. Nat. League for Nursing, Iowa League for Nursing (pres. 1966-69), Iowa Assn. Bus. Industry, Am. Acad. Med. Adminstrs. (pres. Iowa chpt. 1986-87, Adminstr. of Yr. 1984), Omaha League for Nursing (dir. 1976-77), Am. Hosp. Assn., Iowa Hosp. Assn., Soc. Advancement Mgmt., Des Moines C. of C. (bd. dirs.), Cath. Health Assn. (bd. dirs. 1987—), Trendleaders of Ryan Club (advisor to chief exec. officers). Office: Mercy Health Ctr Ctrl Iowa Ste 3265 411 Laurel St Des Moines IA 50314

SULLIVAN, PEGGY (ANNE), library and association consultant; b. Kansas City, Mo., Aug. 12, 1929; d. Michael C. and Ella (O'Donnell) S. A.B., Clarke Coll., 1950; M.S. in L.S, Cath. U. Am., 1953; Ph.D. (Tangley Oaks fellow, Higher Edn. Act Title II fellow), U. Chgo., 1972. Children's public librarian Mo., Md., Va., 1952-61; sch. library specialist Montgomery County (Md.) public schs., 1961-63; dir. Knapp Sch. Libraries Project, ALA, 1963-68, Jr. Coll. Library Info. Ctr., 1968-69; asst. prof. U. Pitts., 1971-73; dir. Office for Library Personnel Resources, ALA, Chgo., 1973-74; dean of students, assoc. prof. Grad. Library Sch., U. Chgo., 1974-77; asst. commr. for extension services Chgo. Public Library, 1977-81; dean Coll. Profl. Studies, No. Ill. U., DeKalb, 1981-90; dir. univ. librs. No. Ill. U., 1990-92; exec. dir. ALA, 1992-94; instr. several grad. libr. edn. programs, 1958-73, UNESCO cons. on sch. librs., Australia, 1970; trustee Clarke Coll., 1969-72; sr. ptnr. Able Cons., 1987-92. Author: The O'Donnells, 1956, Impact: The School Library and the Instructional Program, 1966, Many Names for Eileen, 1969, Problems in School Media Management, 1971, Carl H. Milam and the American Library Association, 1976, Opportunities in Library and Information Science, 1977, Realization: The Final Report of the Knapp School Libraries Project, 1968; (with others) Public Libraries: Smart Practices in Personnel, 1982. Mem. ALA, Cath. Libr. Assn. Roman Catholic. Home and Office: Apt # 816 2800 N Lake Shore Dr Chicago IL 60657

SULLIVAN, PENELOPE DIETZ, computer consulting and software development company executive; b. Roanoke, Va., Dec. 29, 1939; d. Joseph Budding and Katherine (Engart) Dietz; m. Thomas F. Sullivan, Sept. 7, 1963 (div. Mar. 1975); children: Courtney, Todd; m. Paul B. Hill, Mar. 31, 1990. BA, Colby Coll., 1961. Claims examiner Blue Cross/Blue Shield of D.C., Washington, 1961-66; self employed maker slipcovers and upholstery Springfield, Va., 1966-75; ins. sales Met. Life Ins. Co., Arlington, Va., 1975-76, Med. Pers. Pool Inc., Alexandria, Va., 1976-77; mktg. rep. IBM Corp., Washington, 1977-88; program mgr. Advanced Workstations IBM Corp., Somers, N.Y., 1988-92; sales cons. IBM Open Sys., Washington, 1992-93; co-founder Open Sys. Assocs., Inc., Reston, Va., 1993—. Office: Open Sys Assocs Inc Ste 400 1801 Robert Fulton Dr Reston VA 22091-4347

SULLIVAN, PHILIS EVON, retirement facility administrator, consultant; b. Salina, Kans., July 12, 1954; d. Philip H. and Leslie (Knight) Maxey; m. Adam Peter Keidl, Sept. 18, 1973 (div. Apr. 1978); 1 child, Adam Peter Jr.; m. Michael W. Sullivan, Feb. 14, 1991. BA in Acctg., Washburn U., 1973; BBA, McMurry Coll., 1977. Musician ACI Prodns., Nashville, 1970—; owner, operator Philis' Child Care, Abilene, Tex., 1977-79; song writer Nashville Sound, 1978; comptroller, mgr. sales Abilene Linen Supply, 1979-85; mgr. sales Kuy Kendall Bus. Systems, Abilene, 1985-87; adminstr. Wisteria Pl. Retirement Villa, Abilene, 1987-92; gen. sales mgr. Radio Sta. KKHR-Webster Broadcasting, 1992-94; mgr., singer Rumbleseat Show Band, 1992-94; advisor Sta. KACU Radio, Abilene, 1987—. Mem. Mil. Affairs Com., Abilene, 1986—, Say No to Drugs, Abilene; sponsor Abilene Boys Softball; vol. Noah Project Rape Crisis, Abilene, 1990; advisor West Tex. Jr. Miss, 1987-91, Wind Festival, Abliene, 1990—. Recipient Cert. of Appreciation NAFE, 1987, Abilene Bus. Women, 1988-90. Mem. Abilene C. of C. (advisor 1986—, Small Bus. award 1990). Republican. Roman Catholic. Home: RR 8 Box 878S Abilene TX 79601-9750

SULLIVAN, SARAH LOUISE, management and technology consultant; b. Wilmington, Del., Sept. 24, 1954; d. Frederick William III and Ruth (Swavely) S. BS, Bowling Green U., 1975; MS, Ill. Inst. Tech., 1986, PhD, 1990. Programmer Computer Sci. Corp., Langley AFB, Va., 1975-77; sr. systems programmer JPLRCC, Perrysburg, Ohio, 1977-80; sr. systems engr. Kraft Inc., Glenview, Ill., 1980-83; project leader Siemens Gammasonics, Des Plaines, Ill., 1983-85; sect. mgr. Zenith Electronics, Glenview, Ill., 1985; mem. tech. staff AT&T Bell Labs., Naperville, Ill., 1986-87; cons., trainer Sarah L. Sullivan & Assocs., Morton Grove, Ill., 1987-90; instr. Ill. Inst. Tech., Chgo., 1988; asst. prof. dept. computer sci. North Cen. Coll., Naperville, 1988-89, Ind.-Purdue U., Ft. Wayne, 1990-94; pres. Sarah L. Sullivan & Assocs., Ft. Wayne, 1990—; presenter in field. Mem. IEEE, Assn. for Computing Machinery, Oasis Ctr. for Human Potential. Office: Sarah L Sullivan & Assocs Mgmt and Tech Cons 6919 Lake Forest Village Fort Wayne IN 46815

SULLIVAN-BOYLE, KATHLEEN MARIE, association administrator; b. Tulsa, Feb. 9, 1958; d. Thomas Anthony and Jeanne Lee (Agnew) Sullivan; m. Thomas C. Boyle. BS in Polit. Sci., Ariz. State U., 1980; MA in Govt., Coll. William and Mary, 1982. Sec. Ariz. Rep. Party, Phoenix, 1980-81; rsch. asst. Pete Dunn for U.S. Senate Campaign, Phoenix, 1982; adminstra. sec Ariz. Corp. Commn., Phoenix, 1983-84; pub. relations dir. Epoch Univs. Publ., Phoenix, 1984-86; membership dir. Tempe (Ariz.) C. of C., 1986-93; dir. legis. affairs Ariz. Pharmacy Assn., 1994—. Sec., chmn. publicity Cactus Wren Rep. Women, Phoenix, 1983-89, Fiesta Bowl; bd. dirs Tempe Leadership, Tempe YMCA. Mem. Soroptimist (past pres.), Pub. Rels. Soc. Am., Alpha Phi. (chmn. conv.). Republican. Office: Ariz Pharmacy Assn 1845 E Southern Tempe AZ 85282-5831

SULLIVAN-SMOOT, JACQUELINE ANN, secondary school counselor; b. Harrisonburg, Va., Jan. 17, 1952; d. Malcolm Ray Sr. and Marguerite (Whiteside) Sullivan; m. Ronald Leo Smoot, Sept. 1, 1984; children: Malcolm Russell, Patrick Ray. BS in Elem. Edn., Ea. Mennonite Coll., 1974; MEd, U. Va., 1979. Tchr. New Market (Va.) Mid. Sch., 1974-78, 79-81, counselor, tchr., 1981-84; counselor, tchr. Stonewall Jackson H.S., Mt. Jackson, Va., dir. guidance, 1984—. Pres. Beta Nu chpt. Alpha Delta Kappa, Page County, Va., 1992-94. Mem. ACA, NEA, Va. Edn. Assn., Ctrl. Valley Counseling Assn., Phi Delta Kappa, Beta Sigma Phi. Home: 604 S 1st St Shenandoah VA 22849 Office: Stonewall Jackson HS PO Box 385 Mount Jackson VA 22842

SULLO, JOANNE, medical/surgical nurse; b. N.Y.C., May 5, 1961; d. Vincent Joseph and June Anne (O'Donnell) S. AAS in Nursing, Rockland Community Coll., 1982; BSN, Dominican Coll., 1990. Orthopaedic nurse cert. Staff nurse orthopaedics Good Samaritan Hosp., Suffern, N.Y., 1982-88, Nyack (N.Y.) Hosp., 1988-93; head nurse mgr. Nyack Hosp., 1993-94, nurse home care dept., 1994—; mem. nursing practice com. Nyack Hosp., 1991-92. Mem. Nat. Assn. Orthopaedic Nurses, N.Y. State Nurses Assn. (del. 1991, chairperson membership 1991-93, nominating com. 1993-94, bd. dirs. dist. 17 1994—), Sigma Theta Tau. Roman Catholic. Home: 2 Ruby Ct Highland Mills NY 10930-9793 Office: Nyack Hosp Midland Ave Nyack NY 10960

SULTAN, TERRIE FRANCES, curator; b. Asheville, N.C., Oct. 28, 1952; d. Norman and Phyllis Ellen (Galumbeck) Sultan; m. Christopher French, June, 1988. BFA, Syracuse U., 1973; MA, John F. Kennedy U., 1985. Exhbn. dir. Source Gallery, San Francisco, 1982-83; adj. curator Oakland (Calif.) Mus., 1984-85; dir. pub. affairs and pub. programs New Mus. Contemporary Art, N.Y.C., 1986-88; curator contemporary art Corcoran Gallery Art, Washington, 1988—. Author: Representation and Text in the Work of Robert Morris, 1990, Redefining The Terms of Engagement: The Art of Louise Bourgeois, 1944; also exhbn. catalogues. Mem. Am. Assn. Museums, Coll. Art Assn., ArTable. Democrat. Office: The Corcoran Gallery Art 17th St New York Ave N Washington DC 20006

SULVER, EMILY DELOACH, chemist; b. Savannah, Ga., July 25, 1950; d. George A. and Emily Jean (Graham) DeLoach; m. James Charles Sulver, Aug. 21, 1971. BS in Biology, Armstrong State Coll., 1972; student, Ariz. State U., 1972-74. Tchr. sci. St. Martin High sch., Pascagoula, Miss., 1974-75, Kaiserslautern (Germany) High Sch., 1977-80, Moss Point (Miss.) High Sch., 1980-82; chemist Plant Daniel Miss. Power Co., Escatawpa, 1982—. Mem. Am. Chem. Soc., Edison Electric Inst. (chmn. ion chromatography task force 1991-93), Toastmasters. Office: Miss Power Co Plant Daniel PO Box 950 Escatawpa MS 39552

SUMAYLO, SHEILA RUTH, administrator; b. Worcester, Mass., Feb. 3, 1944; d. Walter John and Virginia Clare (Weller) Dulmaine; m. Fereidun Sanjabi, Dec. 19, 1966 (div. 1976); m. Carlos P. Sumaylo, June 21, 1986. BS, Georgetown U., 1965; JD, Am. U., 1980. Bar: Hawaii, D.C. Dir. of profl. programs NACUBO, Washington, 1969-83; dir. fin. St. Louis - Chaminade Edn. Ctr., Honolulu, 1983-85; controller Marine Corps Exch., Kaneohe, Hawaii, 1985-90; dir. support svcs. and comml. activities Morale, Welfare and Recreation, Kaneohe, Hawaii, 1990-92; adminstrv. mgr. Keck Observatory, Kamuela, Hawaii, 1992—.

SUMMERFIELD, ELLEN BETH, college official; b. Hyattsville, Md., Dec. 28, 1949; d. Powell Noah and Helene (Dachslager) S.; m. Phillip J. Pirages. BA, U. Pa., 1970; MA, PhD, U. Conn., 1975. Asst. prof. German, Middlebury (Vt.) Coll., 1975-77, dir. Middlebury Sch. in Mainz, 1977-81; asst. dir. fgn. study Kalamazoo Coll., 1981-84; dir. internat. programs Linfield Coll., McMinnville, Oreg., 1984—. Author: Ingeborg Bachmann, 1976, Crossing Cultures Through Film, 1993; co-author: Forms of Travel: Essential Forms, Documents, and Flyers for Study Abroad Advisers, 1994; translator: History of the German Novel, 1984. Bd. dirs. Ct. Appointed Spl. Advs., 1993—. Mem. Nat. Assn. Fgn. Student Affairs. Democrat. Office: Linfield Coll Office Internat Programs McMinnville OR 97128

SUMMERFIELD, INGRID, hospitality industry professional; b. Stuttgart, Germany, Jan. 12, 1958; came to U.S., 1981; d. Peter and Gerda S. BA in Hotel Mgmt., Lausanne Hotel Sch., 1981; BA in Journalsim, San Francisco State U., 1987. Income auditor Mark Hopkins Intercontinental, San Francisco, 1981-84; sales mgr. Reneson Hotel Group, San Francisco, 1987-90; dir. sales and mktg. Sheehan Hotel, San Francisco, 1990-94; gen. mgr. The Fitzgerald Hotel, San Francisco, 1993-94, The Commodore Hotel, 1994—. Bd. dirs. Better Bus. Bur.; advisor Goodwill Industries, San Francisco. Fellow Hotel Sales and Mktg. Assn., Lausanne Hotel Sch. Alumni, West Coast Alumni (pres.), San Francisco Hotel Assn. (treas.). Democrat. Office: The Commodore Hotel 825 Sutter St San Francisco CA 94109

SUMMERS, AMANDA JANE, computer analyst, small business owner; b. Bury, Lancashire, Eng., Aug. 23, 1965; came to U.S., 1988; d. Albert and Christine (Cockcroft) Slack; m. Michael Laine Summers, Aug. 18, 1990; children: Joshua, Emily. BSc in Computing and Operational Rsch. with honors, Leeds (Eng.) Poly. U., 1987. Computer programmer ICI Plc, Wilmslow, Cheshire, Eng., 1985-87; tech. advisor ICI Plc, Liverpool, Eng., 1987; programmer analyst ICI Plc, Hemel, Hempstead, Eng., 1988; computer analyst Worldwide, Wilmington, Del., 1988-90; sr. programmer analyst Computer People, Inc., Wilmington, Del., 1990; systems specialist Computer Technicians, Inc., Wilmington, Del., 1991—; dep. project mgr. Computer Technicians, Inc., Phila., 1993—; tech. recruiter Computer People, Inc., Wilmington, 1990. Big sister vol. Big Bros./Big Sisters, United Way Am., Wilmington, 1989-91. Mem. NAFE. Episcopalian. Home: 633 Wheatley Rd North East MD 21901-2037

SUMMERS, JANE PFEIFER, realtor; b. Seward, Nebr., Aug. 19, 1951; d. George Henry and Mildred (Jensen) Miller; m. Robert Charles Summers; 1 child, Anthony Grant. MBA, Chadwick U., 1991. Mgr. MIS Lincoln (Nebr.) Tour & Travel, 1973-83; pers. adminstr. Mechanics Wholesale, Denver, 1984-85; v.p. Strategic Mktg. Group, Englewood, Colo., 1985-89; realtor Home Real Estate, Inc., Grand Island, Nebr., 1992—. Field svc. ARC, Conestoga Ter., 1991-92; chmn. womens div. Lincoln C. of C., 1983. Mem. Grand Island Bd. Realtors, Phi Theta Kappa. Home: 2704 Parkview Dr Grand Island NE 68801-7573 Office: Home Real Estate Inc PO Box 5225 1515 N Webb Rd Grand Island NE 68803-2318

SUMMERS, LORRAINE DEY SCHAEFFER, librarian; b. Phila., Dec. 14, 1946; d. Joseph William and Hilda Lorraine (Ritchey) Dey; m. F. William Summers, Jan. 28, 1984. B.A., Fla. State U., 1968, M.S., 1969. Extension dir. Santa Fe Regional Library, Gainesville, 1969-71; pub. library cons. State Library of Fla., Tallahassee, 1971-78, asst. state librarian, 1978-84; dir. adminstrv. services Nat. Assn. for Campus Activities, Columbia, S.C., 1984-85; asst. state librarian State Library of Fla., Tallahassee, 1985—; cons. in field. Contbr. articles to profl. jours. Del. Pres.'s Com. on Mental Retardation Regional Forum, Atlanta. 1975; del. Fla. Gov.'s Conf. on Library and Info. Services, 1978, 90. Mem. ALA (orgn. com. 1979-83, council 1982-84, 93—, resolutions com. 1983-85, mem. legislation com. 1993—), Assn. Specialized and Coop. Library Agys. (dir. 1976-82, chmn. planning and orgn. com. 1976-80, chmn. nominating com., 1980-81, chmn. by laws com. 1985-86, exec. bd. state library agy sect. 1983-86, pres. 1987-88, chmn. standards rev. com. 1990-92), Southeastern Library Assn. (exec. bd. 1976-80, v.p., pres.-elect 1994—), Fla. Library Assn. (sec. 1978-79, dir., 1976-80), Zonta (dir. 1992—). Democrat. Methodist. Office: State Library Fla Ra Gray Bldg Tallahassee FL 32399

SUMMERS, MARLENE BARON, artist; b. Phila., Aug. 27, 1936; d. JAcob Joseph and Elizabeth (Jacobs) Baron; m. Jerry Summers, Mar. 6, 1960; children: Stuart Roger, David Adam. Student, Phila. Coll. Art, 1955-59, Pa. Acad. Fine Arts, 1970-74, Fleisher Art Meml., 1975-80. Freelance visual artist, painter Cherry Hill, N.J., 1975—; instr. visual art Perkins Ctr. for Arts, Moorestown, N.J., 1981-85; master class instr. Fleisher Art Meml., Phila., 1993—; instr. Pub. Coll., Am. Cancer Soc., Atlanta, Am. Mus., Pa. Acad. Fine Arts, Phila., Woodmere Art Mus., Phila., Rosemont (Pa.) Coll., Vets. Home, Paramus, N.J.; east coast v.p. Nat. Orgn. Artist Equity, Inc., Washington, 1982-85, adv., 1983-85; steering com. Vol. Lawyers for Arts N.J., Trenton, 1983-89; adj. instr. fine arts Glassboro (N.J.) State Coll., 1987-90. One-woman show at Rosemont Coll., 1994. N.J. State Coun. Arts fellow, 1991-92, Va. Ctr. for the Creative Arts fellow, 1994; recipient Pa. Acad. Arts Mus. Purchase award, 1991, Woodmere Art Mus. Endowment Fund Meml. award, 1991, Mary Butler award, Phila., 1991. Mem. Fellow Pa. Acad. Fine Arts (co-chair exhibition com. 1993-94). Home and Studio: 3400 Church Rd Cherry Hill NJ 08002-1055

SUMMERS, PATRICIA PRATT, psychology educator, researcher; b. Uniontown, Pa., Jan. 14, 1936; children: William W. Pollock, Marian Pollock Meriwether, Douglas L. Pollock. BA, Marietta Coll., 1976; MA, U. N.C., Greensboro, 1986; PhD, U. Ga., 1989. Lic. profl. counselor. Human rels. cons. Farr Leadership Ctr., Greensboro, 1982-87; rsch. asst. U. Ga., Athens, 1987-89; assoc. prof. Sch. Medicine U. S.C., Columbia, 1990-91; assoc. prof. S.C. State U., 1992—; psychotherapist Counseling Svcs., Columbia, 1993—; pvt. practice cons. in giftedness, Columbia. Bd. dirs. Children's Hosp., Columbia, 1990-93, Wellspring Resource Ctr., 1994—; cons. Young Women at Risk, Columbia; bd. advisors Grace, Inc., 1994—. Mem. APA, Nat. Coun. Family Rels. (cert. life educator), Phi Delta Kappa, Psi Chi. Home: 129 Village Farm Rd Columbia SC 29223

SUMMERS, ROSALIE EVE, real estate agent; b. Detroit, Feb. 11, 1938; d. Eugene Szelag and Veronica Magdalen (Shafranski) Szelag-Scura; m. Eldridge Melvin Summers, Oct. 22, 1955; children: Renee R., Frederick M., Andrea M., Eldridge Michael. BA in Edn., U. New Orleans, 1973. Cert. Grad. Realtors Inst. Tchr. Covington, La., 1973-78; real estate agt. Coldwell Banker Dinning Beard, Wichita, Kans., 1986-88, Coldwell Banker Hancocks, Dodge City, Kans., 1988—. Contbr. articles to profl. jours. V.p. Friends of Gilcrease Mus., 1982; pres. LWV, Tulsa, 1981-82, treas., 1983; pres. Carnegie Art Ctr., Dodge City, 1990, United Way Dodge City, 1990; pres., founder Friendship Force Kans., Wichita, 1983-86; sec. Dodge City Recycling Bd., 1991—, Crimestoppers, 1990—; active Leadership Dodge, 1988. Recipient Outstanding Svc. award Friendship Force Internat., 1984, 86; named Athena Woman of Yr., 1993. Mem. AAUW (pres. 1990-91), New Chance, Inc. (sec. 1991), D.C. Bd. Realtors (edn. chmn. 1990), Women's C. of C. (chmn. city beautification 1989-90, comty. svc. com. 1991), PEO (v.p. 1991), Soroptomists, Leadership Kans., 1993, Kanza Soc. (endowment chair 1993), Kappa Delta Pi. Unitarian. Home: 916 Club View Dr Dodge City KS 67801-2936 Office: Coldwell Banker Hancocks 2300 1st Ave Dodge City KS 67801-2527

SUMMERS, TRACY YVONNE, assistant principal; b. Raymond, Miss., Aug. 12, 1961; d. Neil and Bessie (Christian) S.; divorced, Feb. 1982; 1 child, Shundria Anntawnette. BS in Bus. Edn., Jackson State U., 1985, M in Bus. and Math. Edn., 1988, specialist in sch. adminstrn., 1990; postgrad., U. Miss., 1990-91, Miss. State U., 1993—. Cert. tchr., secondary supr., secondary prin., vocat. dir., Miss. Clk. dept. pers. City of Jackson, Miss., 1978-85; tchr. math. Brinkley Jr. High Sch., Jackson Pub. Sch. Dist., 1985-91; asst. prin. Brinkley Mid. Sch., Jackson Pub. Sch. Dist., 1991—; cheerleading sponsor Brinkley Jr. High Sch., 1986-90. Dir. singles ministry College Hill Bapt. Ch. Edn. Found. Trust co-grantee, 1990-91, 91-92, 92-93; Entergy Corp. grantee, 1990-91. Mem. ASCD, South Ednl. Rsch. Assn., Phi Delta Kappa. Democrat. Baptist. Home: 5334 Sheronn St Jackson MS 39209 Office: Brinkley Mid Sch 3535 Albermarle Rd Jackson MS 39213

SUMMERSELL, FRANCES SHARPLEY, organization worker; b. Birmingham, Ala.; d. Arthur Croft and Thomas O. (Stone) Sharpley; m. Charles Grayson Summersell, Nov. 10, 1934. Student U. Montevallo, Peabody Coll. Ptnr., artist, writer Assoc. Educators, 1959—. Vice chmn. Ft. Morgan Hist. Commn., 1959-63; active DAR, Magna Charta Dames, U. Women's Club (pres. 1957-58), Daus. Am. Colonists (organizing regent Tuscaloosa 1956-63). Recipient Algernon Sidney Sullivan award U. Ala., 1994. Mem. Tuscaloosa County Preservation Soc. (trustee 1965-78, svc. award 1975), Birmingham-Jefferson Hist. Soc., Ala. Hist. Assn. (exec. bd. Ala. Review 1991—), Omicron Delta Kappa, Iota Circle, Anderson Soc. Clubs: University (Tuscaloosa). Co-author: Alabama History Filmstrips, 1961; Florida History Filmstrips, 1963; Texas History Filmstrips, 1965-66; Ohio History Filmstrips, 1967 (Merit award Am. Assn. State and Local History 1968); California History Filmstrips, 1968; Illinois History Filmstrips, 1970. Home: 1411 Caplewood Dr Tuscaloosa AL 35401-1131

SUMMERVILLE, JOYCE WILKINSON, cemetery executive; b. Charlotte, N.C., Nov. 20, 1933; d. Pierce Columbus and Mary Bell (Helms) Wilkinson; m. William Kelly Summerville, June 21, 1952; children: Michael Kelly, Craig Lewis, Emily Beth. Student, Brevard (N.C.) Coll., 1952-53. Lic. cemetarian, N.C. Asst. to dir. coll. extension N.C. State U., Raleigh, 1957-59; asst. to sales mgr. The Pure Oil Co., Charlotte, 1959-64; office mgr. The Forest Lawn Co., Charlotte, 1965-72; v.p., gen. mgr. The Forest Lawn Co., Matthews, N.C., 1972—. Editor, pub. (newsletter) Your North Carolina Cemeterian, 1981-85. Bd. dirs. Valleydale Sch., Charlotte, 1970-71; mem. N.C. citizens Assembly, Charlotte, 1988; co-chmn. Dems. for Gov. Martin Com.; mem. N.C. Cemetery Commn., 1989—, chmn. 1991. Mem. N.C. Cemetery Assn. (bd. dirs. 1972-88, pres. 1986-87), So. Cemetery Assn., Matthews C. of C. (bd. dirs. 1984—, pres. 1986-87, Outstanding Membership Recruiter award 1984, Pres. Appreciation award 1985), Matthews Mcths. Assn. (bd. dirs. 1986-87). Republican. Methodist. Home: 3709 Huntington Dr Matthews NC 28105-7846

SUMMERVILLE, KATIE MAE, elementary education educator; b. Aliceville, Ala., May 11, 1936. BA, Miles Coll., 1961; MA, U. Mich., 1972. Educator Inkster (Mich.) Pub. Schs., 1965-67, Wayne County Community Coll., Detroit, 1967-70, 1972-74, Highland Park (Mich.) Pub. Schs., 1970—. Asst. supt. Carter Met. CME Sun. Sch., Detroit; pres. Detroit chpt. Miles Coll. Alumni, Community Ptnr. Detroit Compact; trustee Miles Coll. Mem. NAACP, Miles Coll. Alumni Assn. (nat. pres.). Methodist. Home: 18309 Snowden St Detroit MI 48235-1462

SUMSKIS, KAREN J., accountant, finance company executive; b. Dayton, Ohio, July 12, 1956; d. Wayne Anthony and Barbara Lee (Scheiner) Blashock; m. Jeff Christopher Sumskis, Sept. 4, 1982 (div. 1992); 1 child, Kolby. BS in Acctg., U. Colo., 1978; MBA, Colo. State U. Acctg. mgr. Ski Times Square Enterprises, Steamboat Springs, Colo., 1984-85; asst. controller Hambleton Inc. dba Sport Stalker, Steamboat Springs, Colo., 1985-86; self-employed acct. Karen Sumskis, Acct., Steamboat Springs, Colo., 1986-88; ptnr. The Gift Basket, Steamboat Springs, Colo., 1988-90; asst. fin. dir. City of Steamboat Springs, 1990—. Mem. Govt. Finance Officer's Assn. of the U.S. and Can. (mem. women's network, 1993-94, cert. of Achievement for Reporting, 1991-92, award of Fin. Reporting Achievement, 1993), Colo. Govt. Finance Officer's Assn. Home: PO Box 773225 1160 Fairview Dr Steamboat Springs CO 80477 Office: City of Steamboat Springs PO Box 775088 137 10th St Steamboat Springs CO 80477

SUN, ALICE LI-LI, banker; b. Taipei, Taiwan, Sept. 27, 1966; came to U.S., 1977; d. Fong-Chuan and Chia-Yao (Lai) S. BA, Barnard Coll., 1989; MA, Columbia U., 1993. Asst. tech. analyst Equico Security, N.Y.C., 1988; asst. officer, fin. contr. Chem. Bank, N.Y.C., 1989-90; sales support Merrill Lynch, N.Y.C., 1992-93; account mgmt. analyst Fed. Res. Bank N.Y., N.Y.C., 1993-94, sr. ops. support analyst fgn. exch. dept., 1994—. Home: 7 Anpell Dr Scarsdale NY 10583

SUN, COSSETTE TSUNG-HUNG WU, law library director; b. Taipei, Taiwan, July 14, 1937; came to U.S., 1960, naturalized, 1972; d. Lin Tsung and Chiu Ching (Wu) Hsieh; m. Stanley Siann-Shyang Sun, Nov. 23, 1961; children: Carol Sun Crowe, Marina Sheree, Olivia Cossette. LLB, Nat. Taiwan U., Taipei, 1960; MA, U. Houston, 1963; MS, Simmons Coll., Boston, 1965. Asst. prof. law, assoc. libr. St. Louis U., 1965-73; assoc. libr.U. Calif.-Berkeley, 1974-75; br. libr. Alameda County Law Libr., Hayward, Calif., 1975-77, law libr. dir., Oakland, 1978—; chmn. law libr. svcs. to instl. residents, 1979-80; pres. Coun. Calif. County Law Librs., 1982-84. Editor: State Ct. County Law Libraries Newsletter, 1979; contbr. articles to law revs. Mem. Castro Valley Mcpl. Adv. Coun., Castro Valley Libr. Adv. Commn. W.H. Anderson scholar, 1966; Matthew Bender scholar, 1971. Mem. Am. Assn. Law Librs. (cert. 1969), Spl. Librs. Assn., Asian-Pacific Libr. Assn., Alameda County Bar Assn. Office: Alameda County Law Libr Courthouse Rm 200 Oakland CA 94612

SUN, EMILY M., economics educator; m. Siao Fang Sun, June 23, 1951; children: Patricia Viane, Caroline Marie, Diana Kate. MA, U. Mich., 1950, PhD, 1957. Prof. econs. Northland Coll., Ashland, Wis., 1957-64; assoc. prof. econs. Manhattan Coll., Riverdale, N.Y., 1964-79, prof. econs., 1979-93, adj. prof. econs., 1993—; cons. Maritime Adminstrn., U.S. Dept. Commerce, 1969-70. Contbr. articles to profl. jours. Rosenthal grantee, 1980; recipient Trustees award, Manhattan Coll., 1987, Bonus et Fidelis medal, 1989. Mem. Am. Econ. Assn., Acad. Internat. Bus. Office: Manhattan Coll Manhattan College Pky Bronx NY 10471-3913

SUN, JING, electrical engineering educator; b. Hefei, Anhui, Peoples Republic of China, Apr. 7, 1961; came to U.S., 1984; d. Hansheng Sun and Xingzhen Xu; m. Bingchang Xu, July 4, 1986; 1 child, Alexander M. Xu. BS in Elec. Engring., U. Sci. and Tech. of China, Heifei, 1982, MS, 1984; PhD, U. So. Calif., 1989. Teaching asst. U. So. Calif., L.A., 1985-87, rsch. asst., 1988-89; asst. prof. elec. engring. Wayne State U., Detroit, 1989—; cons., lectr. Ford Motor Co., Dearborn, Mich., 1991-93, engring. specialist, 1994—. Contbr. articles to profl. jours. Mem. IEEE, Detroit Soc. Engrs., Sigma Xi. Office: Wayne State U 5050 Anthony Wayne Dr Detroit MI 48202

SUN, NORA CHI-JUN, pathologist; b. Shanghai, China, June 16, 1937; came to U.S., 1966; d. K.F. and S.W. Sun; m. David T. Sung; children: Thomas C.K. Lee, Anthony D. Sung. MD, Shanghai 2d Med. Coll., 1960; MS in Pathology, U. Minn., 1973. Demonstrator U. Hong Kong, 1964-66; rsch. biologist A.H. Robins Co., Richmond, Va., 1966-67; clin. teaching asst. Boston U. Sch. Medicine, 1968-70; asst. prof. pathology U. So. Calif., L.A., 1973-76; staff pathologist John Wesley Hosp., L.A., 1973-76; asst. prof. UCLA Sch. Medicine, L.A., 1976-82; staff pathologist, head hematopathology Harbor-UCLA Sch. Medicine, Torrance, Calif., 1976—; assoc. prof. UCLA Sch. Medicine, L.A., 1982-88, prof. pathology, 1988—; lectr. Sargent Coll., Boston U., 1968-70. Teaching fellow Tufts U. Sch. Medicine, Boston, 1969-70; recipient Women Achievement award Delta Kappa Gamma, Rochester, Minn., 1972. Mem. Internat. Assn. Chinese Pathologists (pres.-elect 1991-93, pres. 1993—), Harbor-UCLA Med. Ctr. Faculty Soc. (pres.-elect 1990-91, pres. 1991-92). Home: 548 Chautauqua Blvd Pacific Palisades CA 90272 Office: Harbor UCLA Med Ctr 1000 W Carson St Torrance CA 90509

SUNDAY, LELIA MOUSER, retired educator; b. May 16, 1927; d. Ray Henry and Lelia (Morgan) Mouser; m. Rex Eugene Sunday, Dec. 25, 1950; children: Sara Poling, Nanette Smith. BA, Case Western Res. U., 1949; MLS, U. Mich., 1975. Tchr. English Grover Hill (Ohio) High Sch., 1960-62, Van Wert (Ohio) High Sch., 1962-69; librarian Lincoln View High Sch., Van Wert, 1969-72; media coord. Celina City (Ohio) Schs., 1972-91; cooperative tchr. Wright State U., Dayton, 1973, 75, 78, 88. Elder 1st Presby. Ch., Van Wert, 1983-86, 92-95, also moderator Presbyn. Women; pres. United Presbyn. Women, 1976-77; mem. peacemaking com. Maumee Valley Presbytery, also coord. peace and justice; life mem. Paulding County Hist. Soc., Friends of Libr. NDEA fellow, 1967; COE fellow, 1968. Mem. NEA, Ohio Edn. Assn., Celina Edn. Assn., Ohio Ednl. Library/Media Assn., AAUW, Order Eastern Star, Delta Kappa Gamma. Democrat. Home: 1025 Indian Hills Dr Van Wert OH 45891

SUNDBERG, LORI LYNN, small business owner; b. Galesburg, Ill., June 10, 1958; d. Robert Leroy and Edna Joanne (Jacobs) Smith; m. Rick Eugene Sundberg, Dec. 17, 1952. Grad., Carl Sandburg Cosmetology Sch., Galesburg, Ill., 1976-77, Knox Coll., 1995. Mgr. Glemby Internat., Galesburg, Ill., 1978-86, divisional dir. retail sales, 1984-86; owner The Best Little Hairhouse in Galesburg, 1986—. Bd. mem. Harrington Family Svcs., Galesburg, 1989-92; pres. bd. dirs. Family Planning, Galesburg, 1991-94. Democrat. Home: 1072 Sweetbriar Pl Galesburg IL 61401-2355 Office: The Best Little Hairhouse 155 W Losey St Galesburg IL 61401-2652

SUNDEEN, ANN LESLIE, state official; b. Moline, Ill., May 27, 1960; d. Leslie Alan and Theresa Marie (DeTaeye) Schotka; m. Jace L. Sundeen, Nov. 5, 1988. BA, Augustana Coll., Rock Island, Ill., 1982; MPA, Sangamon State U., Springfield, Ill., 1988. Intern Ill. Dept. Mental Health, Springfield, 1987-88; revenue analyst Ill. Econ. and Fiscal Commn., Springfield, 1989-91, chief revenue unit, 1991—. Author, co-author, editor studies. Vol. Ill. Standardbred Owners and Breeders, Springfield, 1991—; vol., youth sponsor St. John's Luth. Ch., Springfield, 1991—; coord. Children's Miracle Network Racing Fundraiser, Springfield, 1993. Mem. Evang. Lutheran Ch. Office: Ill Econ and Fiscal Commn 703 Stratton Springfield IL 62706

SUNDELL, SUSAN BETH, school system administrator; b. Santa Ana, Calif., Jan. 19, 1941; d. J. Graham and Verda K. (Williamson) Albright; m. Ronald Allen Sundell, Aug. 31, 1985; children: Linda Sue Schmidt, Randall R. Goggin. BA, U. Calif., Riverside, 1967; MA, Calif. State U., San Bernardino, 1987; EdD, U. LaVerne, 1991. Tchr. Chaffey Joint Union H.S. Dist., Ontario, Calif., 1968-87; asst. to supt. Chaffey Joint Union High Sch. Dist., Ontario, Calif., 1987-88, dir. govt. rels., 1988-89, dir. bus. svcs., 1990—. Planning commr. City of Upland, Calif., 1993—. Recipient Hon. Svc. award Upland PTA, 1987. Mem. Calif. Assn. Sch. Bus. Officials, Assn. Calif. Sch. Adminstrs., Montclair C. of C. (pres. 1993-94), Altrusa (Ontario club pres. 1982-83), Rotary. Office: Chaffey Joint Union HS Dist 211 W 5th St Ontario CA 91762-1698

SUNDERLAND, JACKLYN GILES, former college official; b. Corpus Christi, Tex., Oct. 21, 1937; d. Elbert Jackson and Mary Kathryn (Garrett) Giles; m. Joseph Alan MacInnis, Nov. 24, 1963 (div. Feb. 1982); children: Mary Kendall, Jackson Alan; m. Lane Von Sunderland, June 12, 1988. BA, U. Tex., 1960. Editor's asst. House & Garden mag., N.Y.C., 1962; reporter Corpus Christi Caller-Times, 1960, Home Furnishings Daily, Fairchild Publs., N.Y.C., 1961, Houston Post, 1963; writer, rschr. Saudi Press Agy., Washington, 1980; writer/rschr. for V.P. U.S. White House, Washington, 1982-84; dir. pub. affairs President's Com. on Mental Retardation, Washington, 1984-85; dir. speakers bur. Commn. on Bicentennial U.S. Constn., Washington, 1985-87; speechwriter Sec. of HHS, Washington, 1987-88, U.S. Sec. of Labor, Washington, 1989; dir. alumni affairs Knox Coll., Galesburg, Ill., 1990-92. Campaign chmn. Am. Cancer Soc., Corpus Christi, 1961; liaison Am. Embassy, Copenhagen, 1965-68; docent, tchr. art Nat. Gallery and Smithsonian Mus., Washington, 1970-73; vestrywoman Grace Episcopal Ch., Galesburg, 1991; mem. Jr. League Washington, 1963—. Recipient Continental Marine citation for community svc., Camp Pendleton, Calif., 1977. Republican. Home: 185 Park Ln Galesburg IL 61401

SUNDERMAN, DEBORAH ANN, clothing designer and manufacturer; b. Detroit, Feb. 21, 1955; d. Eugene Wayne Sunderman and Nancy May (Reams) Sunderman-Elert. BS magna cum laude, No. Mich. U., 1978. Design instr. Newbury Coll., Boston, 1978-82, 92-93; asst. to designers Clothware, Boston, 1978-82; designer, ptnr. Toute Nue Swimwear, Boston, 1982; designer Mast Industries, The Limited, Woburn, Mass., 1982-83; designer, founder Deborah Mann & Co., Boston, 1983—; instr. fashion Mt. Ida Coll., Newton, Mass., 1991. Designer garment The Fiberarts Design Book, 1980. Organizer Neighborhood Crime Watch Group, Rossmore Rd., Boston, 1989-90. Recipient 2d Pl. award Peter White Art Exhibit, Marquette, Mich., 1978, Fresh Start award Self Mag., Washington, 1985; named one of Boston's Most Interesting Women, Boston Woman Mag., 1990. Mem. Ft. Pointe Arts Comty., Creation: Boston Internat. Assn. Ind. Fashion Designers, Boston Designer's Collaborative. Office: Deborah Mann & Co 1691B Massachusetts Ave Cambridge MA 02138-1842

SUNDGREN, ANN CHRISTINE, physical therapist; b. Manhattan, Kans., July 24, 1962; d. Eldon E. and Beverly (Specht) J. S. BA in Biology, Cornell Coll., 1984; BS in Phys. Therapy, Wichita State U., 1986. Registered phys. therapist. Staff phys. therapist Susan B. Allen Meml. Hosp., El Dorado, Kans., 1986-89; staff phys. therapist Mid-Kans. Therapy, 1989-92; staff PT, clinic mgr. Rehab Clinics, Inc., 1992-94; clinic mgr. Novacare Outpatient Rehab. Divsn., Wichita, 1994—; clin. instr. Wichita State U. Dept. Phys. Therapy, 1987—; ctr. coord. clin. edn. Novacare Outpatient Rehab. Divsn., 1992—. Mem. Am. Phys. Therapy Assn. (Sports Phys. Therapy sect.), Kans. Phys. Therapy Assn (edn. com. chair 1992—). Office: Novacare Outpatient Rehab Divsn 3243 E Murdock Ste 100 Wichita KS 67208

SUNDQUIST, LEAH RENATA, physical education specialist; b. El Paso, Tex., July 22, 1963; d. Dominic Joseph and Patricia Ann (Manley) Bernardi; m. David Curtis Sundquist, June 23, 1990. AA, N.Mex. Mil. Inst., 1983; BS, U. Tex., El Paso, 1986. Field exec. Rio Grande Girl Scout Coun., El Paso, 1983-84; customer teller M-Bank, El Paso, 1984-85; soccer coach St. Clements Sch., El Paso, 1985; substitute tchr. El Paso Sch. Dist., 1986; commd. 2nd lt. U.S. Army, 1983, advanced through grades to capt., 1990-91; plans/exercise officer U.S. Army, Ft. Lewis, Wash., 1990; ops. officer U.S. Army, Ft. Lewis, 1990-1991; dir. Childrens World Learning Ctr., Federal Way, Wash., 1992-94; phys. edn. specialist, tchr. K-6 Kent (Wash.) Elem. Sch., 1994—; image cons. Beauti-Control Cosmetics, Tacoma, Wash. Coord. Nat. Conf. Christians and Jews, El Paso, 1979-81; v.p. Jr. Achievement, El Paso, 1980-81; adult tng. vol., bd. dirs. Girl Scout Coun., 1993—; bd. mem. Jr. League Tacoma, 1993, 94. 3rd Res. Officer Tng. Corps scholar, 1981-83, H.P. Saunder scholar, 1982; recipient Humanitarian Svc. medal Great Fires of Yellowstone, U.S. Army, 1988, Gold award Girl Scouts U.S.A., 1981; decorated Nat. Def. Svc. medal Desert Storm. Mem. NEA, Western Edn. Assn., Assn. U.S. Army, Air Def. Artillery Assn., Zeta Tau Alpha (sec. 1983-85, house mgr. 1984-86), Fellowship of Christian Athletes. Republican. Roman Catholic. Home: 2905 N 14th St Tacoma WA 98406-6905

SUNNESS, KRISTINA EPPINK, educator; b. Lynwood, Calif., Jan. 29, 1949; d. Renaldo Paul and Bertine Othelia (Gilje) Eppink; m. Glenn Alton Sunness, Dec. 26, 1988. BA, Calif. State U., 1971; postgrad., Pepperdine U., 1987. Classroom tchr., demonstration tchr. Porterville (Calif.) Sch. Dist., 1972-85; classroom tchr., mentor L.A. Unified Sch. Dist., 1985—; tchr. math. NSF, L.A., 1993—. Ednl. cons. Rancho San Antonio Boys Town of the West, L.A., 1990—. Julian Virtue fellow Pepperdine U., 1984; Freedom Found. L.A. chpt. scholar, 1990, Calif. State U. scholar, 1990. Mem. AAUW (v.p. membership 1991-92, Project Renewal grantee 1982), Calif. Mentor Tchr. Assn. Episcopalian.

SUNTREE, SUSAN FRANCES, English language educator, poet, playwright; b. L.A., May 19, 1946; d. Edward Francis and Beatrice Madaline (Hays) Stout; m. Philip James Daughtry, May 1, 1972 (div.); children: Sean Philip Daughtry, Califia Selene Suntree. BA in English, U. Ariz., 1968; MA, U. Kent, U.K., 1970. Instr. English La Familia Continuation H.S., Lancaster, Calif., 1970, Modesto (Calif.) C.C., 1970-75; instr. theatre arts Primitive Arts Inst., Grass Valley, Calif., 1976-83; vis. artist UCLA Arts Reach, Westwood, Calif., 1983-85; instr. English Santa Monica (Calif.) Coll., 1984-88, East L.A. Coll., Monterey Park, Calif., 1989—; instr., founder Writers Circle, Santa Monica, 1987—; vis. and resident artist Nev. County Cmty. Workshop, Grass Valley, 1981-82; dir. vis. poet Calif. Poets in Schs., Grass Valley, 1977-82; instr. English Tech. Univ., Helsinki, Finland, 1972; artistic dir. TheatreFlux, Santa Monica, 1985—; co-dir., cons. Simple Path-Arts for the Disabled, Santa Monica, 1982-89. Author: (poetry) Eye of the Womb, 1981, (book) Rita Moreno, 1992, numerous reviews, articles, essays, lectures; plays include: Seed to Snow: Plays for the Seasons, 1978-81, Origins of Praise, 1986, Symphony of Giordano Bruno, 1988, Sacred Sites/Los Angeles, 1992, many others; translator: Tulips (Ana Rossetti); numerous poetry pubs. and readings. Grantee Santa Monica Art Commn. and Santa Monica Art Found., 1986, Calif. Arts Coun., 1976, 78, 79, 80, 83, 84, 85, Ford Found. Cultural Enhancement at Calif. State U.-L.A. Mem. PEN, Dramatists Guild. Zen Buddhist. Home: 1223 11th St Santa Monica CA 90401-2002 Office: East LA Coll 1301 Avenida Cesar Chavez Monterey Park CA 91754

SUPRIANO, SUSAN JEAN, radio producer; b. Evanston, Ill., July 31, 1938; d. Edwin H. Eichler and Carol Jean (McGraw) Root; m. Harold Supriano, Sept. 10, 1966 (div.); 1 child, Gregory. BA, U. Chgo., 1963; MSW, U. Calif., Berkeley, 1976; MPH, U. Hawaii, 1971. With CORE, Berkeley, 1963-64; civic worker, 1965-69; organizer in women's movement Honolulu, 1969-70; therapist, 1976-78; radio producer Pacifica Radio, Berkeley, 1980—, Radio for Peace Internat., San José, Costa Rica, 1987—; coord. San Francisco area anti-war groups; mem. staff Calif. Com. for New Politics; mem. Western Addition Com. Against War in Vietnam, San Francisco. Producer documentaries. Mem. Rigpa Fellowship. Buddhist. Home: 2707 College Ave Apt 109 Berkeley CA 94705-1213

SURBER, REGINA BRAMMELL, early childhood education educator, administrator; b. Grayson, Ky., Apr. 3, 1952; d. Jack D. and Opal (Mullins) Brammell; m. Thomas Jerry Surber, Dec. 18, 1976; 1 child, Jerry David. BA in Elem. Edn., Berea Coll., 1974; MA in Early Childhood Edn., Ea. Ky. U., 1975; MA in Child Care Adminstrn., Nova U. Cert. K-8 grade tchr., ky., Tenn. Kindergarten tchr. Carter County Bd. Edn., Grayson, Ky.; presch. tchr. Oak Ridge Nursery Sch., Tenn.; elem. tchr. Anderson County Bd. Edn., Clinton, Tenn.; dir. daycare Roane State Community Coll., Harriman, Tenn., 1989-94; exec. dir. Knox Assn. on Young Children, Oliver Springs, Tenn., 1994—. Dir. weekday sch. programs 1st Meth. Ch., Oak Ridge. Mem. ASCD, Nat. Assn. for Edn. Young Children, Tenn. Assn. on Young Children, Anderson Area Assn. on Young Children (pres.).

SURESH, NALINA, mathematics educator; b. Tamil Nadu, India, Sept. 5, 1958; d. A. and Bhavani Rajagopalan; m. T.S. Suresh, Sept. 1, 1982 (dec. Oct., 1984). BS in Edn., Lakshmi Coll. Edn., Gandhigram, India, 1981; MS in Math., Madurai (India) U., 1981; MA in Math., U. South Fla., 1988, PhD in Math. and Stats., 1992. Tchr. Freetown, Sierra Leone, 1982-84; teaching asst. U. South Fla., Tampa, 1984-90; asst. prof. U. Wis., Eau Claire, 1990—; mem. Gold Coun. for Excellence, U. South Fla., Tampa, 1989-90; reviewer Quality and Productivity Track, Decision Scis. Inst. meeting, 1993, 94; presenter numerous confs., seminars. Statis. reviewer Am. Jour. Psychiatry; contbr. articles to profl. jours. Mem. IEEE, Am. Statis. Assn., Am. Soc. Quality Control, Am. Math. Soc., Assn. Women in Math., Univ. Women Assn. Eau Claire, Pi Mu Epsilon. Home: 2828 Claudette St # 31 Eau Claire WI 54701-6208 Office: U Wis Eau Claire Dept Math Eau Claire WI 54702

SURGENT, SUSAN PEARL, benefits consultant; b. Binghamton, N.Y., Jan. 6, 1963; d. Victor J. and Joan A. (Linville) Courtney; m. David M. Surgent, Sept. 7, 1985. AAS in Bus., Broome C.C., Binghamton, 1982; BS in Applied Social Sci., Binghamton U., 1993. Notary pub., N.Y. Mktg. asst. Johnson Camping, Inc., Binghamton, 1982-84; employment asst. CAE-Link Corp., Binghamton, 1984-85, adminstr. facility benefits, 1985-90, adminstr. corp. benefits, 1990-94; sr. acct. exec. Prepaid Health Plan, Binghamton, N.Y., 1994—. Vol. educator Sch. and Bus. Alliance, Broome and Tioga counties, 1992—. Mem. Internat. Soc. Employee Benefit Profls., Golden Key, Phi Theta Kappa. Democrat. Episcopalian. Home: 93 Albany Ave Johnson City NY 13790 Office: Prepaid Health Plan 49 Court St Binghamton NY 13901

SURPRISE, JUANEE, chiropractor, nutrition consultant; b. Gary, Ind., Apr. 28, 1944; d. Glenn Mark and Willia Ross (Vasser) Surprise; m. Peter E. Coakley, Feb. 12, 1966 (div. Jan. 1976); children: Thaddeus, Mariah, Darius; m. Robert T.Howell, Feb. 24, 1984. RN, Phila. Gen. Hosp. Sch. Nursing, 1965; DrChiropractic summa cum laude, Life Chiropractic Coll, Marietta, Ga., 1981. Diplomate Nat. Bd. Chiropractic Examiners, Am. Chriopractic Bd. Nutrition, Am. Acad. Pain Mgmt.; cert. in acupuncture, Thompson technique, Nimmo receptor tonus technique. Staff nurse Children's Hosp., Balt., 1966-67; charge nurse Melrose (Mass.)-Wakefield Hosp., 1967-68; hosp. adminstr. Animal Hosp. of Wakefield, Mass., 1967-79; chiropractor Chiropractic Clinic of Greenville, N.C., 1982-84, Howell Chiropractic Clinic, Denton, Tex., 1984—. Mem., chmn. Cmty. Planning Commn., North Reading, Mass., 1976-79; chmn. bldg. com. Immaculate Conception Ch., Denton, 1987-90, parish coun., 1990—. Mem. Am. Chiropractic Assn., ACA Coun. on Nutriton (sec.-treas.), Tex. Chiropractic Assn., Tex. Chiropractic Assn. Coun. on Nutrition (sec.-treas.), Pi Tau Delta. Republican. Roman Catholic. Office: Howell Chiropractic Clinic 1100 Dallas Dr Denton TX 76205

SURYADHARMA, HANDAJANY DEVI, information systems/systems integration consultant; b. Jakarta, Indonesia, Oct. 16, 1968; came to U.S., 1987; d. Juliany (Setiawan) S. BS magna cum laude, U. Calif., Irvine, 1991. Cons. Andersen Cons., L.A., 1991—. Mem. Assn. Computing Machinery, Ind. Profl. Assn., U. Calif. Irvine Alumni Orgn., Golden Key (v.p. chpt. 1990-91), Phi Beta Kappa. Office: 633 W 5th St Los Angeles CA 90071

SUSANKA, SARAH HILLS, architect; b. Bromley, Kent, England, Mar. 21, 1957; d. Brian and Margaret (Hampson) Hills; m. Lawrence A. Susanka, July 4, 1980 (div. May 1984); m. James Robert Larson, Sept. 4, 1988. BArch, U. Oreg., 1978; MArch, U. Minn., 1983. Registered architect. Prin. Mulfinger, Susanka & Mahady (formerly Mulfinger and Susanka), Mpls., 1983—; Contbr. articles to profl. jours. Mem. Minn. Soc. AIA (chmn. publs. com.). Home: 2345 Doswell Ave Saint Paul MN 55108-1630 Office: Mulfinger Susanka & Mahady Archs 43 Main St SE Minneapolis MN 55414

SUSKI, SHERRIE LEIGH, human resources specialist; b. Clearwater, Fla., June 29, 1960; d. H. Mark and Sandy Ann (Tyler) Sherwood; m. Edward Daniel Suski, Apr. 16, 1988. BS in Psychology cum laude, U. Calif., Irvine, 1982; MS in Psychology, Calif. State U., 1985. Human resources positions including staffing, employee rels., tng. and compensation, benefits Silicon Systems, Tustin, Calif., 1983-93; dir. human resources SmartFlex Systems, Tustin, Calif., 1993—; educator Irvine (Calif.) Valley Coll., 1988-89. Mem. ASTD, Pers. and Indsl. Rels. Assn., Am. Compensation Assn., Phi Beta Kappa, Alpha Lambda Delta. Office: SmartFlex Systems 14312 Franklin Ave Tustin CA 92680-7028

SUSKO, CAROL LYNNE, lawyer, accountant; b. Washington, Dec. 5, 1955; d. Frank and Helen Louise (Davis) S. BS in Econs. and Acctg., George Mason U., 1979; JD, Cath. U., 1982; LLM in Taxation, Georgetown U., 1992. Bar: Pa. 1989, D.C. 1990; CPA, Va., Md. Tax acct. Reznick Fedder & Silverman, P.C., Bethesda, Md., 1984-85; sr. tax acct. Pannell Kerr Forster, Alexandria, Va., 1985; tax specialist Coopers & Lybrand, Washington, 1985-87; supervisory tax sr. Frank & Co., McLean, Va., 1987-88; editorial staff Tax Notes Mag., Arlington, Va., 1989-90; adj. faculty Am. U., Washington, 1989—; tax atty. Marriott Corp., Washington, 1993-94; tax mgr. Host Marriott Inc., Washington, 1994—. Mem. ABA, AICPAs, Va. Soc. CPAs, D.C. Soc. CPAs, D.C. Bar Assn., Women's Bar Assn. of D.C., Am. Assn. Atty.-CPAs. Office: Host Marriott Dept 72/92469 10400 Fernwood Rd Washington DC 20058

SUSLOW, JUDITH B., interior designer; b. Pitts., Oct. 3, 1938; d. David D. and Jeannette (Zasloff) Blumenstein; m. Howard G. Suslow, Aug. 26, 1967; children: Steven, Kenneth. BA, U. Mich., 1960. Manhattan dist. mgr. Gidseg, Inc., N.Y., 1979-82; design cons. Berg & Brown, Inc., N.Y., 1983-85; design and sales mgr. Alno Showroom, N.Y., 1985-88; pres. Odyssey Design, Ltd., N.Y., 1988—. Home: 1040 Park Ave New York NY 10028

SUSMAN, KAREN LEE, lawyer; b. Austin, Tex., Oct. 26, 1942; d. Paul and Dorothy (Goudchaux) Hyman; m. Stephen D. Susman, Dec. 26, 1965; children: Stacy M., Harry P. BA, U. Tex., 1964; JD, U. Houston, 1981. Bar: Tex. 1981; bd. cert. in family law 1987. Tchr. high schs. Houston and Washington, 1964-68; realty broker Susman Realty, Houston, 1966-78; assoc. Saccomanno, Clegg, Martin & Kipple, Houston, 1981-83, Marian S. Rosen & Assocs., Houston, 1983-86; of counsel Webb & Zimmerman, Houston, 1986-89; pvt. practice, Houston, 1989—. Editor Internat. Law Jour., 1980-81. Bd. dirs. Downtown YWCA, Houston, 1969-74, pres., 1974; bd. dirs. Tex. Arts Alliance, Houston, 1975-78, Lawyers and Accts. for Arts, Houston, 1985—, Houston Symphony Soc., 1985—, Houston Grand Opera, 1988—, Women's Advocacy Project, 1987-93; bd. dirs. Anti-Defamation League, B'nai Brith, Houston, 1983-86, v.p., 1983—; mem. alumni bd. U. Tex., Houston, 1991—; mem. adv. bd. art dept. U. Houston, 1992—; bd. dirs. NCCJ, 1995—. Fellow Tex. Bar Found., Houston Bar Found.; mem. ABA (chmn. com. on individual and personal rights litigation sect. 1989-92), Tex. Bar Assn., Houston Bar Assn., Gulf Coast Family Law Specialists, U. Houston Alumni Assn. (bd. dirs., v.p., sec. 1983-89), Houston Club, Phi Delta Phi. Home: 10 Shadder Way Houston TX 77019-1416 Office: Post Oak Ctr 14th Fl 1990 Post Oak Blvd Houston TX 77056-3811

SUSON, JODI LYNN, marketing professional; b. Park Ridge, Ill., Oct. 18, 1963; d. Morris and Sharon Barbara Suson. BA, De Paul U., 1990. Dir. mktg. Tech Web, Wheeling, Ill., 1991; owner Creative Odyssey, Barrington, Ill., 1991-93; mgr. mktg. Cash Sta., Inc., Chgo., 1993-94; mgr. debit card products Norwest Card Svcs., Des Moines, 1994—. Vol. Landmark Edn., Chgo., 1991—; bd. dirs. Mitchell Ross Children's Cancer Found., Northbrook, Ill., 1993—. Office: Norwest Card Svcs 7000 Vista Dr West Des Moines IA 50265

SUSSMAN, BONNIE KAUFMAN, art dealer, consultant, interior designer; b. Mpls., Apr. 2, 1932; d. Samuel S. and Marie A. (Green) Kaufman; m. Ross A. Sussman, Dec. 19, 1954 (div. May 1985); children: David, Peter, Marianne. BS in Home Econs., U. Minn., 1954. Designer Jacobson Bus. Furniture, Mpls., 1954-57; owner, designer Contemporary Interiors, Mpls., 1957-70; owner, dir. Peter M. David Gallery, Mpls., 1970—. Mem. mem. Minn. Coun. Chs. Com. on Christian/Jewish Rels., 1991—, co-chair, 1994—; bd. dirs. Goldstein Gallery, U. Minn., 1994—. Mem. Met. Art Dealers Assn. (pres. Mpls.-St. Paul chpt. 1976-85), Phi Upsilon Omicron, Omicron Nu. Home: 3351 Saint Louis Ave Minneapolis MN 55416-4394 Office: Peter M David Gallery 3351 Saint Louis Ave Minneapolis MN 55416-4394

SUSSMAN, CAROL BERGON, insurance broker, estate planner; b. Bklyn.; d. Samuel and Ann (Wiener) Bergon; children: Jill Sussman Rosenberg, Neil Adam. BA, Bklyn. Coll., 1956; postgrad., Am. Coll., 1985—. Mktg. dir. Executrans Internat., Inc., 1973-75; devel. dir. Conf. Bd., N.Y.C., 1975-83; registered investment advisor Holins Group, N.Y.C., 1984-88; estate planner CBS Group, Mamaroneck, N.Y., 1983—; property and casualty broker CBS

Group, Mamaroneck, 1984—; registered investment advisor CBS Group, N.Y.C., 1988—; ins. agt. Home Life Ins. Co., N.Y.C., 1983-88, New Eng. Ins. Co., N.Y.C., 1988—; registered rep. Nathan & Lewis Securities, N.Y.C., 1984—. Mem. Nat. Assn. Life Underwriters. Office: CBS Group PO Box 497 Mamaroneck NY 10543-0497

SUSSMAN, DEBORAH EVELYN, designer, company executive; b. N.Y.C., May 26, 1931; d. Irving and Ruth (Golomb) S.; m. Paul Prejza, June 28, 1972. Student Bard Coll., 1948-50, Inst. Design, Chgo., 1950-53, Black Mountain Coll., 1950, Hochschule für Gestaltung Ulm, Fed. Republic Germany, 1957-58. Art dir. Office of Charles and Ray Eames, Venice, Calif., 1953-57, 61-67; graphic designer Galeries Lafayette, Paris, 1959-60; prin. Deborah Sussman and Co., Santa Monica, Calif., 1968-80; founder, pres. Sussman-Prejza and Co., Inc., Santa Monica, 1980-90, Culver City, Calif., 1990—; speaker, lectr. UCLA Sch. Architecture, Archtl. League N.Y.C., Smithsonian Inst., Stanford Conf. on Design, Am. Inst. Graphic Arts Nat. Conf. at MIT, Design Mgmt. Inst. Conf., Mass.; spl. guest Internat. Design Conf., Aspen, Colo., Fulbright lectr., India, 1976; speaker NEA Adv. Coun., 1985, Internat. Coun. Shopping Ctrs., 1986, USIA Design in Am. seminar, Budapest, Hungary, 1988, participant exhbn., Moscow, 1989, Walker Art Ctr., Mpls., 1989. Mem. editorial adv. bd. Arts and Architecture Mag., 1981-85, Calif. Mag., Architecture Calif. Fulbright grantee Hochschule für Gestaltung Ulm, 1957-58; recipient numerous awards AIA Nat. Inst. Honors, 1985, 88, Am. Inst. Graphic Arts, Calif. Coun. AIA, Communications Arts Soc., L.A. County Bd. Suprs., Vesta award Women's Bldg. L.A. Fellow Soc. Environ. Graphic Design; mem. AIA (hon.), Am. Inst. Graphic Arts (bd. dirs. 1982-85, founder L.A. chpt., chmn., 1983-84, numerous awards), L.A. Art Dirs. Club (bd. dirs., numerous awards), Alliance Graphique Internat. (elect. mem.), Architects, Designers and Planners Social Responsibility, Calif. Women in Environ. Design (adv. bd.), Trusteeship (affiliate Internat. Women's Forum, chmn.'s circle Town Hall), SEGD. Democrat. Jewish. Avocation: photography. Office: Sussman/Prejza & Co Inc 3960 Ince Blvd Culver City CA 90232-2635

SUSSMAN, MONICA HILTON, lawyer; b. N.Y.C., Apr. 2, 1952. BA cum laude, Syracuse U., 1973; JD, Hofstra U., 1977. Bar: Va. 1977, D.C. 1978. Legis. coun. N.Y. State Gov's. Office, Washington, 1977-79; spl. asst. to under sec. U.S. Dept. HUD, Washington, 1979-80, br. chief office State Agy. and Bond Fin. programs, 1980-82, office gen. counsel, 1982-83, also bd. dirs., 1988—, v.p., 1989—, treas. Nat. Housing Conf., 1990—, also programs and regulations dep. gen. counsel; ptnr. McDermott, Will & Emery, Washington; bd. dirs. Nat. Leased Housing Assn. Mem. ABA, Mortgage Bankers Assn. (insured project subcom.), D.C. Bar (govtl. assisted programs for real estate com. 1985—), Va. State Bar. Office: Dept Housing and Urban Devel Office Gen Counsel 451 7th St SW Washington DC 20410*

SUSSMAN, SHARON ANN, art educator; b. Long Beach, Calif., Mar. 2, 1951; d. Martin and Hazel Edna (Sorenson) S.; children: Sebriano, Django, Eric. BA, U. Calif., Santa Cruz, 1978; postgrad., San Jose State U. Prof. U. Calif., Santa Cruz, 1979—, San Jose State U., 1993—; artist IDS, Santa Clara, Calif., 1994; visual interface designer Apple Computer, Inc., Sunnyvale, Calif., 1994—. Elizabeth Greenshields Found. grantee for painting, 1982, art rsch. grantee Daniel Smith, Inc., 1989, art grantee Santa Cruz Arts Coun., 1993. Mem. Internat. Interactive Comm. Soc. Home: 218 Lighthouse Ave Santa Cruz CA 95060

SUSSMAN, SIMMY, management consultant, human resources executive; b. N.Y.C., Dec. 3, 1934; d. Sidney S. and Martha (Kaplan) Schupper; divorced; 1 child, Patricia Anne. Student, Conn. Coll. for Women, 1952-53; AA, Finch Coll., 1954, BA, 1956. Mktg. dir. Carrier Capital, N.Y.C., 1957-61; dir. sales Lancer Enterprises, N.Y.C., 1961-68; v.p., dir. sales Jon Mills Personnel, N.Y.C., 1968-69; pres., owner Simmy Sussman, Inc., N.Y.C., 1969—; pres. Sussman & Morris Assocs., N.Y.C., 1974—; coordinator of Coll. Women of N.Y. Career Confs. Advt., N.Y.C., 1984-86; lectr., dir. Seminars for Media and Mktg. Edn., Los Angeles, N.Y.C., Chgo., Dallas, 1980-88; pres. The Reach Out Network, 1988—, Willow Enterprises. Contbr. articles to profl. jours. Patron Mus. Modern Art. Mem. Advt. Women of N.Y., Advt. Club of N.Y. Office: Simmy Sussman Inc 885 3rd Ave Ste 2900 New York NY 10022-4834

SUSSMAN, STEPHANIE WALLIS, community college administrator; b. N.Y.C., Apr. 20, 1944; d. Alfred Eugene and Sue (Bier) Wallis; m. Stephen Sussman, Dec. 11, 1966; children: David, Adam. BS in Edn., Adelphi U., 1965; MA in Counseling Psychology, Lewis & Clark U., 1982; postgrad., Oreg. State U. Tchr. N.Y. City Sch. Dist., 1965-67, Simi Valley (Calif.) Sch. dist., 1970-72; counselor, pvt. practice Portland, Oreg., 1980-90; dir., youth programs Neighborhood House, Portland, 1976-80; adminstr. Portland C.C., 1980-84; acting asst. commr. for cmty. colls. for state Office of Cmty. Coll. Svcs., Salem, Oreg., 1992; dir. Maywood Park and Centennial Ctrs. Mt. Hood C.C., Gresham, Oreg., 1986—; dir. Oreg. Inst. for Leadership Devel., Portland, 1992—; participant Nat. Inst. for Leadership Devel., Phoenix, 1990, faculty, 1993—; participant Mastering Leadership, Silver Falls, Oreg., 1987; participant Gender Equity Inst., Tempe, Ariz., 1991. Bd. dirs. State of Oreg. Welfare Rev. Bd., Salem, 1993-95. Recipient Fullbright-Hayes scholarship, Washington, 1988. Mem. Am. Assn. Women in C.C., Oreg. Assn. Women in C.C. (bd. mem.-at-large 1989-91, pres. 1993—). Democrat. Jewish. Home: 6514 SW Barnes Rd Portland OR 97225-6104 Office: Mt Hood Community Coll 10100 NE Prescott St Portland OR 97220-3555

SUSSMAN, ZILLA SARAH HOROWITZ, artist, educator; b. Newark, Aug. 4, 1924; d. Robert and Hannah (Malovany) Horowitz; m. Stanley Sussman, Mar. 9, 1945; children: Annette, Susan. BA, Russell Sage Coll., 1944; MA in Fine Arts, Montclair State Coll., 1970; postgrad., Pratt Graphic Ctr., N.Y.C., 1971. Art tchr. Adult Sch., Caldwell, N.J., 1970-82, Fairleigh Dickenson U., Florham Park, N.J., 1970-71, Brookdale C.C., Long Branch, N.J., 1971-76; art tchr. Bd. Edn. Adult Sch., South Orange, N.J., 1982-89, Montclair, N.J., 1989—. One woman shows include West Orange Libr., Summit Art Ctr., County Coll. Morris, State Pavilion Galleries, N.Y.C., Gallery 9, Chatham, N.J., Paper Mill Playhouse, Millburn, N.J., Douglass Coll., New Brunswick, N.J.; exhibited in group shows at Montclair Mus., Newark Mus., Bergen County Mus., Monmouth Coll. Arts Festival, Printmaking Coun. N.J.; represented in permanent collections Newark Pub. Libr., Bristol Myers Squibb, Merck Pharms., Pub. Svc. Elec. and Gas, AT&T, Bell Labs., N.Y. State Divsn. Taxation, N.J. State Libr. for the Deaf, others. Bd. dirs. West Orange LWV, 1980-93; chairperson West Orange Cultural and Heritage Commn., 1976-86. Recipient art awards Summit Art Ctr., Hunterdon Art Ctr., Art Ctr. N.J. Mem. N.J. Ctr. for Visual Arts, Women's Caucus for Art, Artists Equity N.Y. and N.J., Miniature Art Soc. N.J., Printmaking Coun. N.J. Home: 42 Fairview Ave West Orange NJ 07052-3109

SUSTENDAL, DIANE, editor, consultant; b. New Orleans, Aug. 30, 1944; d. George and Mary (Anderson) S. Student, La. State U., 1963-64; cert., John McCrady Sch. Fine Arts, 1966. Asst. art critic Times-Picayune, New Orleans, 1966-68, fashion and beauty editor, 1970-82; asst. mng. editor spl. studies div. Frederick A. Praeger, N.Y.C., 1969; assoc. editor M & Men's Wear mags., Fairchild Publs., N.Y.C., 1982-83; pres. Diane Sustendal & Assocs., Editorial & Creative Svcs., N.Y.C.; cons. Men's Fashions of the Times, N.Y. Times, N.Y.C., 1983-86; fashion and interior design editor N.Y. Daily News, 1990-91; freelance writer, editor. Bd. dirs. New Orleans Ballet, 1971-73. Recipient award La. Press Anns., 1972, Aldo award Men's Fashion Assn. Am., 1985. Mem. Fashion Group N.Y. Republican. Home: Apt 4G 181 E 73rd St New York NY 10021

SUTCLIFFE, MARION SHEA, writer; b. Washington, July 29, 1918; d. James William and Ida (Hewitt) Shea; m. James Montgomery Sutcliffe, Aug. 23, 1941; 1 child, Jill Marion. BMus, Boston Conservatory Music, 1956-60; EdM, Boston State Coll., 1969. Cert. music, English, psychology and reading tchr., Mass. Tchr. Milford (Mass.) Pub. Schs., 1966-70; tchr. music Worcester (Mass.) Pub. Schs., 1970-71; reading tchr. Natick (Mass.) Pub. Schs., 1971-73; real estate developer Sutcliffe Family Trust, South Dennis, Mass., 1969—; developer Delray Beach Club, Dennisport, Mass.; mfr. A&A Assocs., South Dennis, 1989—; dir., sec. bd. mgrs. The Soundings Resort, Dennisport, Mass., 1990—. Songwriter Diablo, 1954. Founder, mgr. Boston Women's Symphony, 1962-66. Fuller grantee New England Conservatory, 1957, grantee State Mass., 1957. Mem. AAUW, Nat. Am. Theatre Organ Soc., Eastern Mass. Am. Theatre Organ Soc. (bd. dirs. 1989-92), Organ-Aires (v.p. 1991—). Episcopalian. Home: 145 Cove Rd South Dennis MA 02660-3515 Office: 60 Macarthur Rd Natick MA 01760-2938

SUTHERLAND, JUDITH LYNNE, humanities educator, artist; b. Waverly, Iowa, Oct. 24, 1939; d. Harry Haven and Melba Sarah (Herman) Cleveland; m. Donald W. Sutherland, Dec. 17, 1961 (dec. Sept. 1986). BA magna cum laude, U. Iowa, 1962, MA in English Lit., 1971, PhD in 19th Century Am. Lit., 1977. Teaching asst. to adj. asst. prof. U. Iowa, Iowa City, 1972-82; program assoc. to the dean of Liberal Arts U. Iowa, 1979-81, program assoc., 1981-82, asst. to the dean Coll. of Liberal Arts, 1982-84; lectr. Shanghai Normal U., Peoples Republic of China, May 1985; Fulbright lectr. in Am. Lit. Northeast Normal U., Changchun, Peoples Republic of China, 1988-89, 90-91; adj. prof. Nanjing U., Peoples Republic of China, 1987-88; Fulbright lectr. in Am. Lit. Srinakharinwirot U., Mahasarakham, Thailand, 1989-90; ind. scholar U. Iowa, 1991-93, adj. assoc. prof. Asian Langs. and Lit., 1993—. Author: The Problematic Fictions of Poe, James and Hawthorne, 1984, book revs., poetry, essays on and works of Chinese calligraphy. Recipient Gladys Romedahl Meml. award Iowa Poetry Assn., 1983, 1st merit Miss. Valley category Miss. Valley Poetry contest, 1982. Mem. Chinese Friendship Assn., Phi Beta Kappa, Alpha Lamda Delta. Democrat. Lutheran. Home: 725 W Benton St Iowa City IA 52246-5903

SUTHERLAND HERNANDEZ, CAMILLE MARIE, mental health center official; b. Woonsocket, R.I., Apr. 9, 1959; d. Omer Albert and Violette Aurora (Sauvageau) S.; B.A. in Biology, Brown U., 1980; M.P.H., Yale U., 1987. Med. abstractor, coder R.I. Health Services Research, Providence, 1980-81, data mgr., 1981-83; research analyst No. R.I. Com. Mental Health, Woonsocket, 1980-81, project coordinator, 1984—; research asst. Monash U., Melbourne, Australia, 1983-84; drug counselor ROADS, Woonsocket, 1984-85; health promotion programs for Johnson & Johnson Health Mgmt. Inc., 1987—. Polit. campaigner for R.I. treasurer, 1984. Recipient Young Career Woman award Bus. and Profl. Women, Woonsocket, 1985; Rotary Club scholar, 1983. Mem. Sigma Xi. Roman Catholic. Club: Brown (Providence). Avocations: water skiing; sailing; aerobics; gourmet cooking. Home: 55 Highland St Woonsocket RI 02895-1814 Office: No RI Community Mental Health Ctr PO Box 1700 Woonsocket RI 02895-0856

SUTLIN, VIVIAN, advertising executive; b. Chgo.; d. Samuel E. and Doris (Weinberg) S. BA, Roosevelt U. V.p. creative group head Grey North Advt., Inc., Chgo.; v.p. creative dir., founder Pilot Products, Inc., Chgo.; TV writer, producer Grey Advt., Inc., N.Y.; sr. writer Young and Rubicam, Inc., N.Y.; v.p. creative dir. Dodge and Delano, N.Y.; pres. Vivian Sutlin Advt., new products and consumer packaged goods specialist with full svc. TV and print, domestic and internat. ops.; creative supr. William Douglas McAdams, Inc., N.Y., Grey Med. Advt., Inc., N.Y.; pres. Vivian Sutlin Comm.; cons. Consumer and Med./Pharm. Advt.; pres. Signature Products East, N.Y.C. Co-author: Industry Women Speak Out. Recipient Chgo. Fedn. Advt. Clubs award, Am. TV Commls. Festival award, TV award Art Dirs. Club Chgo., Triangle award Med. Advt. Print, Internat. Broadcasting award, Best of Decade award RX Club, Guacaipuro TV award.

SUTTER, ELIZABETH HENBY (MRS. RICHARD A. SUTTER), civic leader, management company executive; b. St. Louis, May 15, 1912; d. William Hastings and Alvina (Steinbreder) Henby; AB, Washington U., St. Louis, 1931; m. Richard A. Sutter, June 15, 1935; children: John Richard, Jane Elizabeth, Judith Ann Hinrichs. Sec.-treas. Sutter Mgmt. Co., St. Louis, , until 1985. Chmn. com. on mental health AMA Aux., 1960-62, v.p., 1962-63, 63-64, pres. 1965-66, editor Direct Line newsletter, 1967-74; assoc. editor MD's Wife, 1973-80; mem. adv. bd. Deaconess Hosp. Sch. of Nursing, St. Louis; trustee John Burroughs Sch., 1958-61, v.p. 1959, devel. commn., 1960-61; mem. Hist. Bldgs. Commn. St. Louis County, 1957-91, chmn., 1973-91; bd. dirs. Gamma Phi Beta House Corp. Washington U., St. Louis, 1989-93; chmn. Com. for Preservation Children's Teeth; mem. planning bd. Health, Hosp. Health, Welfare Coun. Met. St. Louis, 1955-64; pres. Aux. Cen. States Soc. Indsl. Medicine and Surgery, 1960-61; pres. St. Louis County Med. Soc. Aux., 1948-49, Mo. Med. Soc. Aux., 1952-53; sec. St. Louis County Health and Hosp. Bd., 1956-61, chmn., 1961; bd. dirs. Am. Lung Assn. Eastern Mo., exec. com., 1956-85, v.p., 1960-61; pres. Tb and Health Soc. of St. Louis, 1962-65; adv. coun.vol. svcs. Nat. Assn. Mental Health, 1962-64; bd. dirs. Am. Cancer Soc., St. Louis, exec. com., 1954-64; bd. dirs. Mental Health Assn. St. Louis, 1960-61; mem. Practical Nursing Edn. Coun., chmn. exec. com., 1959-60; mem. AMA Coun. on Mental Health Planning for Nat. Conf. on Mental Health, 1961; mem. adv. com. on women in svcs. Dept. Def., 1969-72, vice chmn., 1971; participant 24th ann. global strategy discussion U.S. Naval War Coll., 1972; bd. govs. Washington U. Alumni, 1970-71, 75—, vice chmn. 1979-80, chmn., 1980-81; trustee Washington U., 1979-81; pres. Washington U. Arts and Scis. Century Club, 1970-71; bd. dirs. St. Louis Conv. and Tourist Bur., 1975-83, sec., 1980-82; bd. dirs. Health Svcs. Agy., 1975-82; mem. East West Gateway Coordinating Coun. Task Force on Hist. Preservation, 1975-81, U. City Hist. Preservation Commn., 1977-85; bd. dirs. Whitney Beach III Assn., Longboat Key, Fla., 1984-87, 91-94; del. Mo. Rep. Conv., 1972, 76, 80, 84, 88, 92, del. Nat. Rep. Conv., 1984. Named 1 of 10 Women of Achievement in good citizen category St. Louis Globe-Democrat, 1961; Alumna of Yr., Gamma Phi Beta, St. Louis, 1966; recipient St. Louis County Med. Soc. award of merit, 1964; Disting. Alumni citation Washington U., 1968, Disting. Alumni Svc. citation, 1977; Life Style award Eastern Mo. chpt. Am. Lung Assn., 1982; Meritorious Svc. award Am. Park and Recreation Soc., 1985; Endowed Richard A. and Elizabeth H. Sutter chair in Occupational, Industrial and Environ. Med., Washington U., St. Louis, 1993. Mem. Mo. Hist. Soc., St. Louis Symphony Soc., AMA Aux. (hon. life), Mo. Med. Aux. (hon. life), Met. St. Louis Med. Aux. (hon. life), Gamma Phi Beta (bd. found. St. Louis chpt. 1989). Presbyterian. Home: 7215 Greenway Ave Saint Louis MO 63130-4126

SUTTER, NORMA JEAN, mental health counselor; b. Marion, Ind., Dec. 27, 1926; d. H. Nathan and Clara L. (Kenner) Swaim; m. Jack G. Sutter, Aug. 8, 1948; children: John, Joseph, Julia, Janice. BA, Depauw U., 1948; MA, Ball State U., 1974; Adminstrn. Cert., Nova U., 1982. Lic. mental health counselor. Elem. counselor Palm Beach Schs., West Palm Beach, Fla., 1974-90; psychology cons. Presbyn. Day Care Ctr., Marion, Ind., 1971-73; svc. dir. Grant County Crippled Children and Adults Soc., Marion, 1962-65; exec. dir. Grant County Mental Health Assn., Marion, 1967-68; mental health counselor Boynton Beach, Fla., 1974—; guest lectr. Marion Coll., Taylor U., Ball state U., Palm Beach Atlantic U.; lectr. Palm Beach Mental Health Assn. Bd. dirs. Hot-Lure, Inc., Marion, 1969-73; dir. self-devised therapeutic program for emotionally disturbed children, Marion, 1969-71; cons. Grant County Pub. Schs., 1970-74; vol. therapist, S. County mental Health Clinic, Delray, Fla., 1978-79; screener Nat. Depression Awareness Day. Mem. Am. Counseling Assn., Am. Mental Health Counseling Assn., Mental Health Assn. (lectr.), Kappa Kappa Gamma.

SUTTERFIELD, DEBORAH KAY, special education educator; b. Amarillo, Tex., Apr. 22, 1956; d. Gail DeWayne and Esther Jane (Rogge) Quine; m. Thomas Wayne Sutterfield, Dec. 6, 1980; 1 child, Tristan Thomas. AD, Amarillo Jr. Coll., 1976; BS, Tex. Woman's U., 1978. Cert. in spl. edn., elem. edn. Jr. high resource tchr. Dumas (Tex.) Ind. Schs., 1978-80; substitute tchr. Amarillo Ind. Schs., 1980-81, secondary multiple handicapped tchr., 1981—; pvt. tutor, Amarillo, 1988-94. Vol. Vol. Action Ctr., Amarillo, 1991-94; active Boy Scouts Am., 1989—. Mem. CEC, Tex. Assn. for Improvement of Reading, Assn. Tex. Profl. Educators, Tex. Learning Disabilities Assn., Tex. Soc. Augmentative and Alternate Comm. Methodist. Home: 1909 Beech St Amarillo TX 79106-4505

SUTTLES, VIRGINIA GRANT, advertising executive; b. Urbana, Ill., June 13, 1931; d. William Henry and Lenora (Fitzsimmons) Grant; m. John Henry Suttles, Sept. 24, 1977; step-children: Linda Suttles Daniels, Peg Suttles La Croix, Pamela Suttles Diaz, Randall. Grad. pub. schs., Mahomet, Ill. Media estimator and Procter & Gamble budget control Tatham-Laird, Inc., Chgo., 1955-60; media planner, supr. Tracy-Locke Co., Inc., Dallas and Denver, 1961-68; media dir., account exec. Lorie-Lotito, Inc., 1968-72; v.p., media dir. Sam Lusky Assos., Inc., Denver, 1972-86; ind. media buyer, 1984-89; mktg. asst. mktg. dept. Del E. Webb Communities, Inc., Sun City West, Ariz., 1985-88, with telemarketing dept., 1989-90, homeowner coord., 1993—; mktg. coord. asst./media buyer, Del Webb Corp., Phoenix, 1990-93; lectr. sr. journalism class U. Colo., Boulder, 1975-80; condr. class in media seminars Denver Advt. Fedn., 1974, 77; Colo. State U. panelist Broadcast Day, 1978, High Sch. Inst., 1979, 80, 81, 82, 83. Founder, Del E. Webb Meml. Hosp. Found.; patron founder Tree of Life Nat. Kidney Found. of Colo.- Rockies Snow Mountain YMCA Ranch, Winter Park, Colo. Mem. Denver Advt. Fedn. (bd. dir. 1973-75, program chmn. 1974-76, 80-82, exec. bd., v.p. ops. 1980-81, chmn. Alfie awards com. 1980-81, advt. profl. of Yr. 1981-82), Denver Advt. Golf Assn. (v.p. 1976-77, pres. 1977-78), Colo. Broadcasters Assn., Sun City West Bowling Assn. (bd. dirs. 1987-88), Am. Legion Aux., VFW Aux., Air Force Sgt.'s Assn. Aux., Sun City West Women's Social Club. Republican. Congregationalist. Club: Denver Broncos Quarterback. Home: 20002 Greenview Dr Sun City West AZ 85375-4710 Office: Del Webb Communities Inc 13001 Maker Blvd Sun City West AZ 85375

SUTTON, BARBARA POWDERLY, marketing executive, consultant, author; b. Scranton, Pa., Oct. 29, 1940; d. Eugene Thomas and Kathryn Dorothy (Loftus) Powderly. Student, Miami (Fla.)-Dade Jr. Coll., 1960. Ordained minister, 1992. Asst. controller Oak Ridge, Inc., Hialeah, Fla., 1959-63; v.p., media dir. Harold Gardner Assocs., Inc., Miami Beach, Fla., 1963-67; media dir., adminstrv. asst. Stern, Hays & Lang Advt., Inc., Miami, 1967-69; exec. asst. Los Angeles Times, 1969-71; media dir., adminstrv. asst. Greenman Advt., Inc., Hollywood, Fla., 1971-73; asst. to gen. mgr. Sta. WGMA-FM, Hollywood, 1974; with acctg. and settlement dept. Fed. Res. Bank, Miami, 1974-75; bus. mgr. Impart Pub. Corp., Reno, 1975-76; adminstrv. asst., office mgr. Edn. Advancement Inst., Reno, 1976-78; ind. contractor Du-Bar Internat., Reno, 1979-80; pres. Capital Advt., Reno, 1980-81; dir. media Mktg. Systems Internat., Reno, 1981-82; owner Dolphin Secretarial Service, Reno, 1982-88, Dolphin Services, Reno, 1983-88, Powderly Assocs., Reno, 1982—; pres. Bus.-Promotional Services, Inc., Reno, 1986-89; ptnr. Investigative Rsch. Report Svcs., Sedona, Ariz., 1993-94, B & B Graphics, Sedona, 1991-94, Beyond Belief Metaphysical & Spiritual Resources, Sedona, 1991-94, Megatrends Mktg. Assocs., Sedona, 1991-93, Atkinson Fine Artist's Reps., Sedona, 1992-94; adminstrv. asst. U. Colo., Boulder, 1994—; speaker Mktg. Fedn., Inc., N.Y.C., 1986; seminar developer and presenter Advt. and Mktg. for Small Bus., U. Nev. Small Bus. Ctr., 1987-88; editor non-fiction books Atkinson World Pub., Sedona, Longmont, Colo., 1992-94; writer, researcher non-fiction studies Expecting Publication, 1992-95. Bd. dirs. March of Dimes, Reno, 1982; mem. Presdl. Task Force, Washington, 1983-85, Reno Women's Network, 1982-84; appointed commr. Reno Commn. on Status of Women, 1987-88. Named one of 2,000 Women of Achievement, London, 1971. Mem. Entrepreneurial Women of Reno (rec. sec., bd. dirs. 1987-88). Metaphysician.

SUTTON, BEVERLY JEWELL, psychiatrist; b. Rockford, Mich., May 27, 1932; d. Beryl Dewey and Cora Belle (Potes) Jewell; m. Harry Eldon Sutton, July 7, 1962; children: Susan, Caroline. MD, U. Mich., 1957. Diplomate Am. Bd. Pediatrics, Am. Bd. Psychiatry and Neurology. Rotating intern St. Joseph Mercy Hosp., Ann Arbor, Mich., 1958; resident in child psychiatry Hawthorne Ctr., Northville, Mich., 1958-62; resident in pediatrics U. Hosp./U. Mich. Med. Ctr., Ann Arbor, 1959-61; resident in psychiatry Austin (Tex.) State Hosp., 1962-64, dir. children's svc., 1964-89, dir. psychitric residency prof., 1989—; cons. in field. Contbr. articles to profl. jours. Active numerous civic orgns. Recipient Outstanding Achievement award, YWCA, 1989, Jackson Day award, Tex. Soc. Child and Adolescent Psychiatry, 1989, Showcase award, Tex. Dept. Mental Health/Mental Retardation, 1990, Disting. Svc. award, Tex. Soc. Psychiatric Physicians, 1990. Fellow Am. Acad. Child and Adolescent Psychiatry, Am. Psychiatric Soc., Am. Pediatric Assn.; mem. Tex. Soc. Child and Adolescent Psychiatry (pres. 1979-80), Tex. Soc. Psychiatric Physicians, AMA, Tex. Med. Soc., Am. Genetics Soc. Office: Austin State Hospital 4110 Guadalupe St Austin TX 78751-4223

SUTTON, CANDACE ELAINE, educator; b. Reform, Ala., Sept. 19, 1955; d. Lee Vinton and Doris Nell (Alexander) Brown; m. John Chester Sutton III, May 23, 1981; children: Chess, Brandon, Dustin. BS, U. Montevallo, 1977, MA in Teaching, 1980; cert., Livingston U., 1993. Cert. secondary tchr., Ala. Tchr. Pickens Acad., Carrollton, Ala., 1977-92, counselor, 1992—. Recipient Golden Apple award Ala. Power and Sta. WCFT-TV, 1993. Mem. Ala. Assn. Counselors, Ala. Hist. Assn., Ala. Assn. Historians, Gulf Coast Hist. Assn., Delta Kappa Gamma, Kappa Delta Pi. Baptist. Office: Pickens Acad RR 1 Box 10M Carrollton AL 35447-9714

SUTTON, DOLORES, actress, writer; b. N.Y.C.; d. Benjamin Silverstein and Mary Yager; m. Michael Ries, June 15, 1956. BA in Philosophy, NYU. Appeared in plays Man with the Golden Arm, 1956, Career, 1958, Machinal, 1960, Rhinoceros, Liliom, She Stoops to Conquer, Hedda Gabler, Anna Karenina, Eccentricities of a Nightingale, Brecht on Brecht, Young, Gifted and Black, Luv, The Friends, The Web and the Rock, The Seagull, Saturday, Sunday, Monday, The Little Foxes, What's Wrong with This Picture, The Cocktail Hour, My Fair Lady (Broadway revival), 1994, My Fair Lady (nat. tour), 1993-94; films include The Trouble with Angels, Where Angels Go, Trouble Follows, Crossing Delancey, Crimes and Misdemeanors, Tales of the Darkside; TV appearances include Studio One, Hallmark Hall of Fame prodn. Ah Wilderness, Theatre Guild of the Air: Danger, Suspense, Gunsmoke, Valiant Lady, General Hospital, From These Roots, As the World Turns, Edge of Night, F. Scott Fitzgerald in Hollywood, Patty Hearst Story, All in the Family, Bob Newhart Show, All My Children, others; TV writer Lady Doc, The Secret Storm, Loving; playwright: Down at the Old Bull and Bush, The Web and the Rock, Company Comin', 1995. Mem. League of Profl. Theatre Women (bd. dirs.), Ensemble Studio Theatre.

SUTTON, JOYCE ELAINE, medical records director; b. Chillicothe, Mo., Aug. 28, 1946; d. William Stanley and Helen Louise (Ashlock) Henderson; m. Ferold Rodrick Vermilyea, Jr., Feb. 7, 1964 (div. Aug. 1973); m. Ronald Eldon Sutton, Jan. 15, 1978; children: Sherra Wood, Janae Nezerka, Michael Sutton, Brian Sutton, Marcia Sandner. Accredited record technician. Ward clk. Heartland West Hosp. (formerly Meth. Med. Ctr.), St. Joseph, Mo., 1970-73; ward clk. Hedrick Med. Ctr., Chillicothe, 1973-74; med. records clk. Hedrick Med. Ctr., 1974-75, A.R.T. trainee, 1975-77, med. transcriber, 1977-82, asst. supr., 1982-85, med. records supr., 1985-89, med. records dir., 1989—, quality assurance cons., 1989-92, also med. staff sec., treas., coord.; dir. med. records Pershing Meml. Hosp., Pershing Regional Hosp., Brookfield-Marceline, Mo., 1992—; cons. Brookfield (Mo.) Nursing Ctr., 1987—, Excelsior Springs (Mo.) City Hosp., 1988—; dir. outpatient program, Hedrick Med. Ctr., Chillicothe, 1987—, dir. quality assurance/risk mgmt., 1988—. Mem. local civic orgns., Chillicothe, 1987—. Mem. Hedrick Med. Ctr. Aux. (life), Am. Med. Records Assn., Mo. Med. Records Assn., Kansas City Area Med. Records Assn. Republican. Baptist. Home: PO Box 114 Meadville MO 64659-0114 Office: Pershing Meml Hosp 130 E Locklin Brookfield MO 64628

SUTTON, JULIA SUMBERG, musicologist, dance historian; b. Toronto, Ont., Can., July 20, 1928; d. Samuel L. and Anne R. (Rubin) Sumberg. AB summa cum laude, Cornell U., 1949; MA, Colo. Coll., 1952; PhD, U. Rochester, 1962. Instr. music history New Sch. for Social Research, 1962-63; instr. music Queens Coll., CUNY, 1963-66; chmn. dept. music history and musicology New Eng. Conservatory Music, 1971-90, chmn. faculty senate, 1971-73; prof. emerita New England Conservatory Music, 1992; vis. asst. prof. George Peabody Coll. for Tchrs., 1966-67; instr. NYU, summers 1963, 64; pvt. tchr. piano, 1949-65; lectr., rsch. dir. in musicology, music as related to the dance; presenter numerous workshops and summer insts. on Renaissance dance. Dance dir. N.Y. Pro Musica prodn. An Entertainment for Elizabeth, Caramoor, N.Y., Saratoga, N.Y., U. Ariz., Stanford U., UCLA, 1969, nationwide tours, 1970, 71, 72, 73; dance dir. Descent of Rhythm and Harmony, Colorado Springs, Colo., 1970, Renaissance Revisited, Phila., 1972, An Evening of Renaissance Music and Dance, York U., Toronto, 1974; author: Jean Baptiste Besard's Novus Partus 1617, 1962; editor: Thoinot Arbeau: Orchesography 1588, 1967; translator, editor: Fabritio Caroso: Nobiltà di dame 1600, 1986; producer, co-dir. (tng. video) Il Ballarino, 1991; contbr. articles and book revs. to profl. jours. and encys. Mem. Am. Musicological Soc., Coun. of Rsch. in Dance, Soc. of Dance History Scholars, Phi Beta Kappa.

SUTTON, REVONDA LAIL, business educator; b. Morganton, N.C., Sept. 26, 1948; d. Pinkney A. Jr. and Lois (Scott) Lail; m. John Norman Sutton, Mar. 17, 1973; children: John Norman II, Kelly Cheryl. BS, Ark. Tech. U.,

1986; MEd, U. Ark., 1992. Cert. vocat. and bus. edn. tchr., Ark. Sec., receptionist Inmont Corp., Morganton, N.C., 1967-70; acctg. clk. Sigri Gt. Lakes Carbon Corp., Morganton, N.C., 1970-73; sec. Geo. E. Cordell & Assoc., Morganton, N.C., 1979-81; instr. Ark. Valley Tech. Inst., Ozark, 1987; bus. tchr. Ozark H.S., 1987—; adj. instr. Ark. Tech. U., Russellville, 1993—. Edn. leader, trainer LDS Ch., Ft. Smith, Ark., 1986-87, 93—, pub. comms. dir., 1987-90, female media spokesperson, "Know Your Religion" coord./trainer, 1994—; pres. Ozark Elem. PTO, 1981-82; den mother Cub Scout Pack 74, Ozark, 1981-83; mem. com. Troop 74, Boy Scouts Am., Ozark, 1989-92. Named Tandy Tech. Outstanding Tchr., 1993-94. Mem. Am. Vocat. Assn., Ark. Vocat. Assn. (Tchr. of Yr. 1993), Nat. Bus. Edn. Assn., So. Bus. Edn. Assn., Ark. Bus. Edn. Assn. (Bus. Edn. New Tchr. of Yr. 1993), Delta Pi Epsilon (Gamma Pi chpt.), Phi Beta Lambda (finalist Nat. Ms. Future Bus. 1986). Home: Rt 2 Box 308C Ozark AR 72949 Office: Ozark HS 3500 Jeffers Dr Ozark AR 72949

SUTTON, SHARON EGRETTA, architect, educator, artist; b. Cin., Feb. 18, 1941; d. Booker and Egretta (Sutton) Johnson. Student, Manhattan Sch. Music, 1959-62; MusB, U. Hartford, Conn., 1963; postgrad., Parson's Sch. Design, N.Y.C., 1967-69; MArch, Columbia U., 1973; PhM, CUNY, 1981, MA, PhD in Psychology, 1982. Registered architect, N.Y., Mich. Pvt. practice architect N.Y.C. and Dexter, Mich., 1976—; vis. asst. prof. Columbia U., N.Y.C., 1981-82; asst. prof. U. Cin., 1982-84; assoc. prof. U. Mich., Ann Arbor, 1984-94, prof., 1994—; architect-in-residence NEA, N.Y.C., 1978-82; keynote spkr. colls. and profl. meetings. One-woman shows include Nat. Urban League, N.Y.C., 1980, Your Heritage House, Detroit, 1986, June Kelly Gallery, N.Y.C., 1987; exhibited in group shows at Studio Mus., N.Y.C., 1979, U. Mich. Mus. Art, Ann Arbor, 1988, Art-in-Gen. Gallery, Soho, N.Y.C., 1990; represented in permanent collections Mint Mus., Charlotte, N.C., Wadsworth Atheneum, Hartford, Conn., Balt. Mus. Art; Author: Learning Through The Built Environment, 1985; editorial bd. Jour. Archtl. Edn., 1984-87; contbr. articles to profl. jours. Coord. The Urban Network-an urban design program for youth funded by NEA Design Cities Program Kellogg Found., U. Mich., 1988—. Recipient Postbaccalaureate award Danforth Found., 1977-81, Design Rsch. award Nat. Endowment Arts, 1983, Edn. award Am. Planning Assn., 1991, Regents award for disting. pub. svc. U. Mich., 1992; Project Dir. Design Arts grantee Nat. Endowment Arts, 1988-90; W.K. Kellogg Found. fellow, 1986-89. Mem. AIA, APA, Am. Ednl. Rsch. Assn. Democrat. Home: 8071 Main St Dexter MI 48130-1027 Office: Coll Architecture/Urban Planning U Mich Ann Arbor MI 48109

SUYETSUGU, GRACE TAMIKO, nurse; b. San Mateo, Calif., Feb. 16, 1957; d. Frank Takiji and Mitsuka (Shimizu) S. BS magna cum laude in Nursing, San Francisco State U., 1979. RN, Calif. Charge nurse med./surg. unit Peninsula Hosp. and Med. Ctr., Burlingame, Calif., 1979-84, staff nurse ICU, 1984-88, charge nurse ICU, 1988-91, staff nurse endoscopy and ICU, 1991-92, staff nurse recovery rm. and same day surgery, 1992—. Mem. Nat. Nurses Assn., Calif. Nurses Assn., Am. Assn. Critical Care Nurses. Democrat. Buddhist. Avocations: travel, photography, cooking, needlework, sports. Home: 3682 Bobwhite Ter Fremont CA 94555-1524 Office: Peninsula Hosp and Med Ctr 1783 El Camino Real Burlingame CA 94010-3282

SVADLENAK, JEAN HAYDEN, museum administrator, consultant; b. Wilmington, Del., Mar. 4, 1955; d. Marion M. and Ida Jean (Calcagni) Hayden; m. Steven R. Svadlenak, May 26, 1979. BS in Textiles and Clothing, U. Del., 1977; MA in History Mus. Studies, SUNY, Oneonta, 1982; postgrad., U. Calif., Berkeley, 1982. Curatorial asst. The Hagley Mus., Wilmington, 1976-77; curator of costumes and textiles The Kansas City (Mo.) Mus., 1978-82, chief curator, 1982-84, assoc. exec. dir. for collection and exhibits mgmt., 1984-86, interim pres., 1986-87, pres., 1987-89; researcher, guest curator N.Y. State Hist. Assn., Cooperstown, 1980; grant reviewer Inst. for Mus. Svcs., 1985-89; ad hoc faculty U. Kans., 1991—, U. Mo., Kansas City, 1992—. Mem. Am. Assn. Museums (mus. assessment program surveyor 1985-89, accreditation vis. com. 1990—), Am. Assn. Stte and Local History, Costume Soc. Am., Heritage League of Kansas City (bd. dirs. 1987-89), Midwest Mus. Conf. (coun. 1992—), Mo. Mus. Assocs. (pres. 1992-94, com. on mus. profl. tng. 1993—). Home: 624 Romany Rd Kansas City MO 64113-2037

SVARRE, ROBERTA LYNNE, public relations specialist, consultant; b. N.Y.C., Nov. 16, 1935; d. Leonard and Sylvia (Levenson) Smerling; m. Eugene A. Svarre, Nov. 24, 1956; children: Peter, Andrew, Diana. BBA, CCNY, 1956; postgrad., NYU, 1956-57. Account asst. Benjamin Sonnenberg, N.Y.C., 1955-56; staff writer Investor's Reader Mag., N.Y.C., 1956-58; writer CBS-TV, N.Y.C., 1962; dist. mgr. Bergen County (N.J.) decennial census bur. census U.S. Dept. Commerce, N.Y.C., 1980; dir. Bergen County Housing Edn. & Advocacy Program, Hackensack, N.J., 1982; prin. Roberta Svarre Pub. Rels./Pub. Affairs, Ridgewood, N.J., 1976—; pres. Ridgewood Sr. Citizens Housing Corp., Inc., 1974-86. Editor: Where Can I Live in Bergen County: Factors Affecting Housing Supply, 1972. Councilwoman Village of Ridgewood, 1986-94, mayor, 1990-92; chair Environ. Adv. Com., Ridgewood, 1987-94, Ridgewood Centennial Celebration Com.; mem. Planning Bd., Ridgewood; legis. chair Bergen County League Municipalities, 1991-94; dir. Community Resource Coun., Hackensack. Recipient Human Rights award UN Assn., 1984, N.J. Declaration of Excellence, Garden State Games, 1992, Gov.'s Citation, 1994; named Vol. of Yr. by Bergen County Exec., 1994. Mem. LWV (pres. 1974-76, Disting. Svc. award 1979), Rotary (charter, Paul Harris fellow 1994).

SVEC, SANDRA JEAN, state official; b. Evanston, Ill., Dec. 11, 1947; d. Joseph Francis and Martha Marjorie (Randau) Svec; m. Terry L. Yonker, June 28, 1969 (div. 1990). BS in Meteorology, U. Wis., Madison, 1969. Sec., sales asst. Moore Bus. Forms Inc., Lansing, Mich., 1970-72; rsch. asst. Mich. Dept. Social Svcs., Lansing, 1972-74; adminstrv. analyst Mich. Pub. Svc. Commn., Lansing, 1974-79, supr. orgn. devel., 1980-84; program mgr. Gov.'s Energy Awareness Adv. Com., Lansing, 1979-80; labor rels. rep. Mich. Dept. Agr., Lansing, 1984-87, acting personnel dir., 1987-89, asst. to chief dep. dir., 1989-93, dir. EEO/affirmative action office, 1991—. Bd. dirs. Lansing Area Advocates for Choice, 1991-93, Downtown Neighborhood Assn., Lansing, 1990—, v.p., 1992—; vol. reader Radio Talking Book, East Lansing, Mich., 1974-93; active Stratford (Ont., Can.) Shakespearean Festival, 1974—. Mem. Am. Bus. Women's Assn. (chpt. woman of Yr. 1977), Am. Assn. for Affirmative Action, Women in State Govt., State Assn. Accts., Auditors and Bus. Adminstrs., Nat. Wildlife Fedn., Friday Frolics. Home: 617 W Genesee St Lansing MI 48933-1010 Office: Mich Dept Agr PO Box 30017 Lansing MI 48909-7517

SVEINSON, PAMELA J., human resources executive. BA in Sociology, Whitman Coll., 1974; M in Indsl. Rels., U. Minn., 1980. Social worker Mont. State Dept. Social & Rehab. Svcs., 1975-77; behavior therapist Spl. Tng. Exceptional People, Billings, Mont., 1977; asst. mgr. manpower planning Burlington Northern, St. Paul, 1978-80; sr. human resources planner Morrison-Knudsen Co., Inc., Boise, Idaho, 1980-83; asst. v.p. human resources 1st Bank System, 1983-84, v.p., 1984-88, sr. v.p., 1988-90; v.p. human resources Star Tribune and Cowles Media Co., Mpls., 1990—; program chair Human Resources Exec. Coun., 1994—. Mentor Minn. 100; mem. Mpls. Inst. Arts. Mem. Nat. Human Resources Planning Soc., Minn. Human Resources Planning Soc. (bd. dirs.), Horseman's Benevolent & Protective Assn., Park Ave. Meth. Ch. Home: 8537 Eagle Creek Blvd Shakopee MN 55379 Office: Cowles Media Co 329 Portland Ave Minneapolis MN 55415

SVENDSEN, JOYCE ROSE, real estate company executive; b. Bayonne, N.J.; d. Peder and Rita Agnes (Bogert) S.; m. Stephen G. Takach, June 22, 1968; 1 child, Mark Stephen. Lic. real estate broker. Regional investigator Channel Co., Whippany, N.J., 1977-79; pres. Svendsen Studio, Clifton, N.J., 1979-82, Treasures, Sugar Loaf, N.Y., 1982-85; sales dir. M.L. Levine Real Estate, Clifton, 1985-91. Mem. N.J. Assn. Realtors (million dollar sales club 1986-94, Silver award 1993), Passaic County Bd. Realtors (assoc.), Sons of Norway. Republican. Unitarian. Office: Nicholas Real Estate 1624 Main Ave Clifton NJ 07011-2112

SVETLOVA, MARINA, ballerina, choreographer, educator; b. Paris, May 3, 1922; came to U.S. from Australia, 1940; d. Max and Tamara (Andreieff) Hartman. Studies with Vera Trefilova, Paris, 1930-36, studies with L. Egorova and M. Kschessinska, 1936-39; studies with A. Vilzak, N.Y.C., 1940-57; D honoris causa, Fedn. Francaise de Danse, 1988. Ballet dir. So. Vt. Art Ctr., 1959-64; dir. Svetlova Dance Ctr., Dorset, Vt., 1965—; prof. ballet dept. Ind. U., Bloomington, 1969-92, prof. emeritus, 1992—, chmn. dept., 1969-78; choreographer Dallas Civic Opera, 1964-67, Ft. Worth Opera, 1967-83, San Antonio Opera, 1983, Seattle Opera, Houston Opera, Kansas City Performing Arts Found. Ballerina original Ballet Russe de Monte Carlo, 1939-41; guest ballerina Ballet Theatre, 1942, London's Festival Ballet, Teatro dell Opera, Rome, Nat. Opera, Stockholm, Sweden, Suomi Opera, Helsinki, Finland, Het Nederland Ballet, Holland, Cork Irish Ballet, Paris Opera Comique, London Palladium, Teatro Colon, Buenos Aires, others; prima ballerina Met. Opera, 1943-50, N.Y.C. Opera, 1950-52; choreographer: (ballet sequences) The Fairy Queen, 1966, L'Histoire du Soldat, 1968; tours in Far East, Middle East, Europe, S.Am., U.S.; performer various classical ballets Graduation Ball; contbr. articles to Debut, Paris Opera. Mem. Am. Guild Mus. Artists (bd. dirs.), Conf. on Ballet in Higher Edn., Nat. Soc. Arts and Letters (nat. dance chmn.). Office: 2100 E Maxwell Ln Bloomington IN 47401-6119 also: 25 W 54th St New York NY 10019-5411

SVIDOR, RHONA BEVERLY, real estate broker, elementary education educator; b. Boston, May 12, 1934; d. Sydney Z. and Bella (Shapiro) Zonis; m. Leonard Svidor, May 23, 1957; 1 child, Mark Allen. AA, UCLA, 1957; BA, Calif. State U., L.A., 1959, MA in Am. Studies, 1972. Lic. real estate broker; cert. elem. and secondary edn. tchr. Tchr. Rivera Sch. System, 1956-57, Hermosa Beach Sch. System, 1958-59, L.A. City Schs., 1959-88; real estate broker Rhona Realty, San Fernando Valley, Calif., 1977—. Leader art history group Valley U. Women, 1989-94, v.p. of programs, 1994—; bd. dirs. Nat. Bd. Brandeis U. Women's Com., 1993-94; leader Greek World Through Art and French, Brandeis U. Women's Com., 1993—; program chmn. Pacific Asia Mus. Himalyan Arts Counsel, 1993; bd. dirs. Natanya chpt. Na'amat USA, events and theatre chairperson. Mem. Toastmasters (v.p. membership 1993-94, pres. 1994-95, chair 1993-94).

SVIZZERO, ANNA E., state election operations director; b. Niagara Falls, N.Y., June 14, 1954; d. Cesare and Lucia (Spadorcia) S. Student, Niagara U., 1972-76. Computer editor Guardian Bus. Svcs., Boston, 1976-78; office mgr. Ziebart Internat., Niagara Falls, 1978-84; dep. commr. Bd. of Elections, Niagara County, 1985-92; dir. election ops. N.Y. State Bd. of Elections, Albany, N.Y., 1992—. Exec. bd. mem. Niagara County Dem. Com., 1978-92, N.Y. State Dem. Coms., 1990-92.; mem. N.Y. State Dem. Com., 1988-92; campaign coord. Gov. Mario Cuomo, 1982, 86, 90, U.S. Senator Daniel Patrick Moynihan, 1988, Presdl. candidate Walter Mondale, 1984, Michael Dukakis, 1988; regional campaign coord. Pres. Bill Clinton, 1992; affirmative action officer N.Y. State Dem. Com., delegate selection to Nat. Conv., 1984, 88, 92; numerous other campaign mgmt. roles. Mem. NAACP, Niagara Coun. on the Arts, Italian Ams. in Govt. Roman Catholic. Office: NY State Bd of Elections 6 Empire State Plz Ste 201 Albany NY 12223-1650

SVOBODA, DONNA LEE, neonatal nurse; b. St. Clair County, Ill., Aug. 28, 1951; d. James F. Sr. and Pat Lee (Souchek) Durer; m. John R. Svoboda, July 25, 1970; 1 child, Jennifer Lynn. BS in Edn., So. Ill. U., 1973; BSN, So. Ill. U., Edwardsville, 1987. Neonatal staff nurse, parenting skills coord. and educator Anderson Hosp., Maryville, Ill. Recipient Esther Ott Estes award in nursing. Mem. Nat. Assn. Neonatal Nurses, Sigma Theta Tau, Phi Kappa Phi. Home: 106 Dunlap Cove Ct S Edwardsville IL 62025-2491

SVOBODA, PATRICIA HELEN, art historian; b. Washington, Dec. 22, 1950; d. Ladislav Maurice and Marie Martina (Vojta) S. BFA in Graphic Design, U. Wash., 1974, BA in Art History, 1974, MA in Art History, 1980. Graphic artist freelance Seattle, Washington, 1971-86; art history rschr. for exhbns. Collaboration of Seattle Art Mus. & U. Wash., Seattle, 1977-78; graphic artist U. Rsch. Tech. Edn. Ctr., Rockville, Md., 1984; graphic artist, adminstrv. asst. U.S. Dept. Commerce Office Publs. Svc., Washington, 1984-88; art history lectr. Phillips Collection, Washington, 1987—; art history rschr. Smithsonian Instn. Nat. Portrait Gallery, Washington, 1988—; art history lectr. Georgetown U., Washington, 1989—; rep. Art Svcs. Internat., Alexandria, Va., 1990-92; contbr. Inst. for Classical Studies, Prague, Czech Republic, 1993-94. Author: Zoe Dusanne, 1980; interviewer for Northwest Traditions, 1978; prin. work includes Seattle YMCA mural Olympic Race, 1982; contbr. articles to profl. jours. Keyworker Combined Fed. Campaign, Washington, 1985-88. Recipient Nat. Pks. Svc. Purchase Prize award Soc. Illustrators, 1974, Cert. of Performance award Smithsonian Instn., 1989-93. Mem. Coll. Art Assn., Czechoslovak Soc. Arts & Scis., Smithsonian Resident Assoc. Program, Cleve. Pk. Hist. Soc., Alumni of U. Wash. Office: Smithsonian Instn Nat Portrait Gallery F St at Eighth NW Washington DC 20560

SWADOS, ELIZABETH A., composer, director, writer; b. Buffalo, Feb. 5, 1951; d. Robert O. and Sylvia (Maisel) S. B.A., Bennington Coll., 1972. Composer, mus. dir. Peter Brook's Internat. Theatre Group, Paris,, Africa, U.S., 1972-73; composer-in-residence La Mama Exptl. Theater Club, N.Y.C., 1977—; mem. faculty Carnegie-Mellon U., 1974, Bard Coll., 1976-77, Sarah Lawrence Coll., 1976-77. Author: The Girl With the Incredible Feeling, 1976, Runaways, 1979, Lullaby, 1980, Sky Dance, 1980, Listening Out Loud: Becoming a Composer, 1988, The Four of Us, 1991, The Myth Man, 1994; composer theatrical scores: Medea, 1969 (Obie award 1972), Elektra, 1970, Fragments of Trilogy, 1974, The Trojan Women, 1974, The Good Women of Setzuan, 1975, The Cherry Orchard, 1977, As You Like It, 1979, The Sea Gull, 1980, Alice in Concert, 1980, (with Garry Trudeau) Doonesbury, 1983, Jacques and His Master, 1984, Don Juan of Seville, 1989, The Tower of Evil, 1990, The Mermaid Wakes, 1991; composer, dir., adapter, mem. cast: Nightclub Cantata, 1977 (Obie award 1977); composer, adapter (with Andrei Serban) Agamemnon, 1976, The Incredible Feeling Show, 1979, Lullaby and Goodnight, 1980; composer, dir., adapter: Wonderland in Concert, N.Y. Shakespeare Festival, 1978, Dispatches, 1979, Haggadah, 1980, The Beautiful Lady, 1984-86, Swing, 1987, Esther: A Vaudeville Megillah, 1988, The Red Sneaks, 1989, Jonah, 1990; author, composer, dir.: Runaways, 1978 (Tony award nominee for best musical, best musical score, best musical book 1978); adapter: Works of Yehuda Amichi, Book of Jeremiah; composer music for films: Step by Step, 1978, Sky Dance, 1979, Too Far to Go, 1979, OHMS, 1980, Four Friends, 1982, Seize the Day, 1986, A Year in the Life, 1986, Family Sins, 1987; composer music CBS Camera Three shows, 1973-74, PBS short stories, 1979, CBS-TV and NBC-TV spls.; composer: Rap Master Ronnie, 1986; composer, dir. Swing, Bklyn. Acad. Music, 1987; performer: Mark Taper Forum, Los Angeles, 1985, Jerusalem Oratorio, Rome, 1985. Recipient Outer Critics Circle award, 1977; Creative Artists Service Program grantee, 1976; N.Y. State Arts Council playwriting grantee, 1977—; Guggenheim fellow. Mem. Broadcast Music Inc., Actors Equity. Jewish. Home: 112 Waverly Pl New York NY 10011-9109 Office: care Sam Cohn Internat Creative Mgmt Co 40 W 57th St New York NY 10019-4001*

SWAIN, DIANE SCOTT, principal; b. Atlantic City, N.J., July 13, 1946; d. Letha Noble; m. Raymond L. Swain Jr., Dec. 26, 1970; 1 child, Sean Scott Swain. BS, Hampton U., 1968; MEd, Lynchburg Coll., 1978; postgrad., U. Va., 1987—. Tchr. Lynchburg (Va.) City Schs., 1968-86, instructional coord., 1986-87, asst. prin., 1987-89, elem. prin., 1989—. Bd. dirs. Cen. Va. Speech and Hearing Ctr., Va. Bapt. Hosp., Lynchburg, 1990—. Mem. Lynchburg Assn. Elem. Prins. (pres. 1991—), Jack and Jill Inc. (v.p. Lynchburg chpt. 1989-90), Delta Sigma Theta Inc. (pres. Lynchburg alumnae chpt. 1982-84). Baptist. Home: 115 Yorkshire Cir Lynchburg VA 24502-2756 Office: Sheffield Elem Sch 115 Kenwood Pl Lynchburg VA 24502-2119

SWAIN, LAURA TAYLOR, lawyer; b. Bklyn., Nov. 21, 1958; d. Justus E. and Madeline V. (Allgood) Taylor; m. Andrew J. Swain, Oct. 12, 1991. AB, Harvard U., 1979, JD, 1982. Bar: Mass. 1982, N.Y. 1983, U.S. Dist. Ct. (so. and ea. dists.) N.Y. 1983. Law clk to chief judge U.S. Dist. Ct. (so. dist.) N.Y., 1982-83; assoc. Debevoise & Plimpton, N.Y.C., 1983—; mem. N.Y. State Bd. Law Examiners, Albany, 1986—; mem. multistate bar exam. com. Nat. Conf. Bar Examiners, 1987—, mem. testing, R&D devel. com., 1990-94, mem. long range planning com., 1994—. Co-contbr. articles on employee benefits, employee stock ownership plans and acctg. to profl. publs.; contbg. author: New York Insurance Law, 1991. Trustee Diocese of N.Y. (Episcopal), 1991-92; mem. Dessoff Choirs, N.Y.C., 1984-92. Mem. Assn. of Bar of City of N.Y., Met. Black Bar Assn., N.Y. State Bar Assn. Democrat. Episcopalian. Office: Debevoise & Plimpton 875 3d Ave New York NY 10022

SWAJA, VICTORIA LYNN, quality management specialist; b. Rochester, N.Y., Nov. 5, 1963; d. Joseph Bernard and Geraldine Marie (Shipp) S. BA in Sociology, Radford U., 1985; postgrad., Va. Tech. U., 1985-86; MA in Sociology, Miss. State U., 1987; MSW, Ariz. State U., 1994. Cert. clin. sociologist; cert. master social work. Social worker Hope Ctr. for Head Injury, Phoenix, 1988-89; collections clk. Rural/Metro Corp., Scottsdale, Ariz., 1989-90; brief therapy specialist Empact-Suicide Prevention Ctr., Tempe, Ariz., 1990-91; brief therapy/quality assurance specialist Empact-Suicide Prevention Ctr., Tempe, 1991-92, quality assurance specialist, 1992; quality mgmt. specialist Maricopa Clin. Mgmt., Tempe, 1992-93, Community Partnership Behavioral Healthcare, Phoenix, 1993—; mem. community adv. bd. Meridian Point Rehab. Hosp., Scottsdale, 1988-90; bd. dirs. Ariz. Head Injury Found., Casa Grande, Ariz., 1988-89; co-founder S.W. Va. Head Injury Found., Blacksburg, 1985. Bd. dirs. Scottsdale Villa Homeowner Assn., 1990-93; mem. Scottsdale Mayor's Com. on Employment of Persons with Disabilities, 1988-89. Mem. Am. Bus. Women's Assn. (sec. 1989, 94, del. to nat. conv. 1989, Woman of Yr. 1989), Nat. Assn. Social Workers, Sociol. Practice Assn., Alpha Phi Omega. Democrat. Roman Catholic. Home: 10575 E Fanfol Ln Scottsdale AZ 85258 Office: Cmty Partnership in Behavioral Healthcare 4001 N 3d St Ph Phoenix AZ 85021

SWALIN, MAXINE (MARTHA) MCMAHON, musician; b. Waukee, Iowa, May 7, 1903; d. George Thomas and Mary Edith (Wilson) McMahon; m. Benjamin Franklin Swalin, Jan. 1935. BA, U. Iowa, 1932; MA, Radcliffe Coll., 1936. Head music theory dept. Hartford (Conn.) Sch. Music, 1928-30; choral music chapel Hill H.S., Chapel Hill, N.C., 1936-37; asst. to dir., pianist, harpsichordist, accompanist N.C. Symphony Orch., Chapel Hill, 1939-72, ret., 1972; lectr. in field. Author: An Ear to Myself, 1991. Recipient N.C. Pub. Svc. award, 1989. Mem. AAUW. Democrat. Home: 1104 Sourwood Cir Chapel Hill NC 27514

SWAN, ANNA, school nurse; b. Albuquerque, Mar. 14, 1953; d. Robert Stutz and Lupita (Lujan) Swan. BSN, U. N.Mex., 1985. Nurse Pres. Hosp., Albuquerque, Children's Psychiat. Hosp./Heights Psychiat. Hosp., Albuquerque; clin. instr. Albuquerque Tech.-Vocat. Inst.; sch. nurse Los Lunas (N.Mex.) Pub. Schs.; rsch. nurse dept. psychiatry U. N.Mex., Albuquerque; pub. health nurse, Albuquerque, dir. health unit/coord. program Albuquerque Tech.-Vocat. Inst.; mem. nursing practice adv. com. for N.Mex. Bd. of Nursing. Camp nurse Girl Scouts U.S., Albuquerque.

SWAN, BETH ANN, nursing administrator; b. Phila., Nov. 11, 1958; d. John H. and Elizabeth A. Jenkins; m. Eric J. Swan, Apr. 11, 1987. BSN, Holy Family Coll., Phila., 1980; MSN, U. Pa., 1983. Nursing dir. admission evaluation ctr. Hosp. of the Univ. of Pa., Phila. Mem. ANA (cert. adult nurse practitioner), Pa. Nurses' Assn., Am. Acad. Nurse Practitioners, Am. Acad. Ambulatory Nursing Adminstrn., Sigma Theta Tau.

SWAN, JOYCE ANN, comptroller; b. San Antonio, June 11, 1964; d. Richard Bronaugh II and Carolyn Ann (Gerhardt) Harn; m. Jesse G. Swan, June 3, 1983 (div. Dec. 1992). BBA in Acctg., U. Tex., San Antonio, 1986. Bookkeeper Gerhardts Paint and Wallpaper Co., San Antonio, 1976-84, Ike Neumann & Assocs., San Antonio, 1983-86, Patrician Properties, San Antonio, 1984-86; gen. mgr. San Antonio Hermann Sons Home Assn., 1982-86; comptroller Courtesy Chevrolet Co., Phoenix, 1986-91; CFO various orgns., Phoenix, 1992; human resources/customer rels., fin. mgr. Buick Co., Phoenix, 1993; office mgr. World Car Mazda, New Braunfels, Tex., 1993—. Mem. auditor bd. evaluators Valley of Sun United Way, Phoenix, 1988—, Chandler (Ariz.) Planning and Zoning Commn., 1990-92, Valley Forward Assn.; treas. com. re-elect Coy Payne for mayor City of Chandler; precinct com. person dist. 30 Dem. Nat. Com., 1991—, state com. person Ariz. Dem. Com., 1991-92. Mem. Inst. Mgmt. Accts. (bd. dirs. Scottsdale chpt. 1988-89, v.p. edn. 1989-90, pres. 1990-91, mem. nat. contr.'s cound., scholarship sect. com. 1991-92, chmn. nominating com. 1991-92), Am. Soc. Women Accts. (com. Mesa East Valley chpt.), Am. Soc. Assn. Execs., Internat. Credit Assn. Greater Phoenix, Retail Fin. Execs. Ariz., Ariz. Cash Mgmt. Assn., Am. Inst. Individual Investors, Ariz. Automotive Accts. Assn (founding pres., organizer 1991-92), Exec. Bus. and Profl. Women's Club (sec. Phoenix chpt. 1986-88, auditor 1986-87, 88-89, Woman Yr. award 1991, pres. 1991-92), Alamo City Tall Club.

SWAN, MARTHA LOUISE, retired educator; b. Chadron, Nebr., May 6, 1912; d. Neal Watterson and Sarrah Abbie (Brower) Cook; m. Earle Jameson Swan; (dec. 1970); children: Judith Louise, Linda Camille, Calvin Lawrence, Noreen Adell. BA, Conn. Coll. for Women, New London, 1937; MEd, Lewis & Clark Coll., Portland, Oreg., 1964. Tchr. Norwich (Conn.) Free Acad., 1937-38; music-art tchr. Milwaukie (Oreg.) Sch. Dist., 1947-48; music tchr. Skyline Elem. Sch., Washington County, Oreg., 1951-52, Vancouver (Wash.) Sch. Dist., 1952-53, 57-58; tchr. Portland (Oreg.) Sch. Dist., 1958-64, French and Spanish tchr., 1965-72; ret., 1972; pvt. tchr. piano and voice, 1938-92; lectr. on cut glass. Author: (book) American Cut and Engraved Glass: The Brilliant Period in Historical Perspective, 1986, 2d edit., 1994; contbr. articles and poems to numerous pulbs. Winthrop scholar Conn. Coll. for Women, 1936. Mem. AAUW (antiques chpt. Portland), R.I. Honor Soc., Am. Cut Glass Assn., Order Eastern Star (program chair 1938-40), Phi Beta Kappa.

SWANBACK, JEAN KIRK, counselor, administrator; b. Hartford, Conn., Jan. 6, 1936; d. Albert Raleigh and Florence Mattie (Norton) Kirk; m. William Rudolph Swanback; children: Randal, Bradley, Julia. B of Music Edn., Ctrl. Meth. Coll., 1958; MEd in Counseling, Pan Am. U., 1982; MEd in Mid-Mgmt. Adminstrn., S.W. Tex. State U., 1993. Cert. music edutoar (K-12), counselor, administr. (pre-kindergarten-12), Tex., B.C. Classroom, music tchr. Pub. Schs., various, 1959-82; vocat. counselor Pub. Schs., Tex., 1984-90; counselor, adminstr. Hutto (Tex.) Ind. Sch. Dist., 1990—; crisis counselor Vancouver (B.C.) Crisis Ctr., 1983-84. Mem. Am. Counselor Assn., Tex. Counselor Assn., Ctr. Tex. Counselor Assn. Home: 8906 Little Walnut Pky Austin TX 78758-6715

SWANEY, CYNTHIA ANN, sales executive, management consultant; b. Garfield Heights, Ohio, Feb. 25, 1959; d. Peter John and Juanita Catherine (Crowle) Christ; m. C. Keith Swaney, Aug. 4, 1984; children: Jason Scott, Samantha Jean. Grad. high sch., Pepper Pike, Ohio. With Park View Fed. S&L, Cleve., 1975-79; customer svc., teller, trainer Park View Fed. S&L, !977-79; exec. sec., ops. mgr. Majestic Steel Svc., Solon, Ohio, 1979-84; v.p. adminstrn. Datashare Corp., Chagrin Falls, Ohio, 1984-94, pres., 1994—; owner, med. mgmt. cons. Oasis Health Svcs., 1994—; cons. Stenciler's Emporium, Hudson, Ohio, 1988—, Deep Springs Trout Club, Chardon, Ohio, 1988—, Hiram House Camp, Moreland Hills, Ohio, 1990—; numerous med. offices, 1986—. Trustee Hiram House Camp, 1991—. Office: Datashare Corp 17800 Chillicothe Rd Chagrin Falls OH 44022-0743

SWANK, ANNETTE MARIE, software designer; b. Lynn, Mass., Nov. 9, 1953; d. Roland Paterson and Rita Mary (Edwards) S. BSEE and Computer Sci., Vanderbilt U., 1975; postgrad., Pa. State U., 1992—. Lead programmer GE, Phila., 1975-80; system analyst SEI Corp., Wayne, Pa., 1980-82; mgr., designer Premier Systems, Inc., Wayne, Pa., 1982-85, dir., 1985-88, tech. advisor, 1988-90, tech. architect, 1990-92; tech. architect Funds Assocs. Ltd., Wayne, 1992—. Designer: (programming lang. and data dictionary) Vision, 1985. Treas. Master Singers, Plymouth Meeting, Pa., 1987-88. Mem. Assn. for Computing Machinery, Gamma Phi Beta (com. chmn. alumna Phila. 1986-87). Home: 136 Pinecrest Ln King Of Prussia PA 19406-2368 Office: Funds Assocs Ltd 440 E Swedesford Rd Wayne PA 19087-1820

SWANN, LYNETTE MONIQUE, industrial engineer; b. Gary, Ind., Nov. 5, 1964; d. Alonzo Alexander and Margaret Estelle (Ray) S. BS in Indsl. Engring., Purdue U., 1986; MS, Ctrl. Mich. U., 1989. Engr. Consumers Power Co., Jackson, Mich., 1986—. Bd. dirs., sec. Big Bros., Big Sisters, Jackson, 1992—. Fellow Am. Assn. Blacks in Energy. Democrat. Office: Consumers Power Co 212 W Michigan Ave Jackson MI 49201

SWANN, THERESE CATHERINE, artist, curator; b. Port Huron, Mich., Mar. 21, 1960; d. Michael Patrick and Dorothy Josephine (Levitt) Mugan; m. Fred Swann, Oct. 1, 1981. AA, Wayne County C.C., 1981, ASN, 1984; BFA in Painting, Wayne State U., 1992. RN, Mich. RN Henry Ford Hosp., Detroit, 1985; freelance artist, art curator, 1985—; sales cons. Urban Park Gallery, Detroit, 1993-94; vol. teaching asst. Detroit Artist's Market, 1993-94; show coord. A.C.,T. Gallery, Detroit, 1993-94; art curator Mich. Gallery, Detroit, 1994. Mem. Friends of Modern Art, Detroit Artists Market, Paint Creek Ctr. for Arts, Mt. Clemens Art Ctr., Toledo Mus. Art, Concerned Citizens for Arts, Mich. Gallery. Recipient Irish Am. Artist and Civic Leader award Wayn County Coun., 1993. Mem. Detroit Founder's Soc., Birmingham Bloomfield Art Assn., Pewabic Pottery Soc., Nat. Conf. Artists, Mich. Potter's Assn. Home: 50051 Pembroke New Baltimore MI 48047

SWANNER, LINDA ALLEN (LIN SWANNER), artist; b. Burlington, N.C., Dec. 11, 1942; d. Allen Wade Swanner and Mary Jane (Waller) Griffin; m. Eugene Miller Barnes Jr., May 24, 1969. Grad. in Printmaking, Figure Sculpture, Glassell Sch. of Art, Houston, 1979; postgrad., Ecole des Arts Decoratif, Strasbourg, France, 1979-80. Artist, 1981—. Editor (catalogue) The 1984 Show, 1984, The 1985 Show/Self-Image, 1985; artist (cover) Houston Arts Mag., 1982; one-woman shows include Little Egypt Enterprises, Houston, 1981, Meredith Long and Co., Houston, 1986, Lanning Gallery, 1991, 92; exhibited in groups shows at Galveston Art Ctr., 1984, L.A. Gallery Contemporary Art, Calif., 1985, Tex. Art Celebration '86, Houston, 1986, Celebration '87 (3d place award), San Antonio, 1987, Tex. Fine Arts Assn. Traveling Show, 1987-89, Lynn Goode Gallery, Houston, 1989, Transco Gallery (2d place award), Houston, 1991, Pink Floyd, Houston, 1994. Recipient Creative Artist award Cultural Arts Coun. Houston, 1993, Wm. A. Smith Endowment award Glassell Sch. Art, 1979, Carl Jung Sculpture award The Jung Ctr., 1978. Mem. Lawndale Art and Performance Ctr., DiverseWorks, Tex. Accts. and Lawyers for the Arts (chair artist bd. 1992, chair Brush-off 1993, chair fine arts gala 1993, Artist of Yr. 1994), Houston Women's Caucus for Art (pres. 1985, curator "Ex-Officio Exhbn." 1992), Art League Houston. Office: Studio Eleven 1111 East Fwy Houston TX 77002

SWANSEN, DONNA MALONEY, landscape designer, consultant; b. Green Bay, Wis., July 8, 1931; d. Arthur Anthony and Ella Marie Rose (Warner) Maloney; m. Samuel Theodore Swansen, June 27, 1959; children: Jessica Swansen Bonelli, Theodor Arthur Swansen, Christopher Currie Swansen. AS in Integrated Liberal Studies, U. Wis., 1956; AS in Landscape Design, Temple U., 1982. Bridal cons. Richard W. Burnham's, Green Bay, 1951-54, 57-58; asst., buyer Shreve Crump & Low, Boston, 1958-59; buyer Harry S. Manchester, Madison, Wis., 1959-62; ptnr. Corson Borie & Swansen, Ambler, Pa., 1976, Swansen & Borie, Ambler, 1977-82; owner, operator Donna Swansen/Design, Ambler, 1983—; v.p. Energy Islands Internat. Inc., East Troy, Wis., 1963-94. Editor: Internat. Directory Landscape Designers, 1993. Mem. search com. for chair dept. landscape architecture and horticulture Temple U., 1987, curriculum rev. com., 1993; mem. Gwynedd (Pa.) Monthly Meeting of Friends (Quakers), 1974—; Dem. candidate for judge elections, 1988; co-founder Friends of Rising Sun, Ambler, Ambler Area Arts Alliance, 1975-76; founder, 1st pres. Plant Ambler, 1973-83; mem. adv. com. Green Bay Bot. Garden, 1993—; chair Temple U. Exhibit, Do It, Dig It. Recipient Key to the Borough, Borough of Ambler, 1972; winner urban beautification project Roadside Coun. Am., Ambler, 1975; named Best in Show Pa. Hort. Soc., Phila., 1987. Mem. Assn. Profl. Landscape Designers (cert., co-founder, 1st pres. 1989-91; bd. dirs. 1989-95, 1st pres. Landscape Design Network Phila. 1978-85), Pyramid Club, Sigma Lambda Alpha. Home and Office: 221 Morris Rd Ambler PA 19002-5202

SWANSON, ANN ELIZABETH, family counselor; b. Greenfield, Iowa, Dec. 5, 1938; d. John Edred and Jeanette A. (Peck) Don Carlos; m. Eric R. Swanson, June 16, 1967; children: Wendy A., Lorna K. AA, Stephens Coll., 1958; BA, Drake U., 1960; MA in Psychology, U. Iowa, 1963; postgrad., UCLA, UCB, UCSD. Pers. specialist Rike-Kumler Co., Dayton, Ohio, 1960-61; clin. asst. Child Devel. Clinic, SUI, Iowa City, Iowa, 1961-63; counselor, asst. prof. Bakersfield (Calif.) Coll., 1963-67; counselor Grossmont Coll., El Cajon, Calif., 1967-69; pvt. practice individual and family counseling San Diego, 1976-88; individual and family counselor Pt. Loma Counseling Ctr., San Diego, 1988—. Chair Sunset Cliffs Natural Park Recreation Coun., San Diego, 1988-95; mem. coastal area com. San Diego Parks and Recreation Dept., 1978—; 2d v.p. Peninsula Community Planning Bd., San Diego; active, past pres. San Diego City Schs. PTA, 1980's; WSI and canoeing instr. ARC. Mem. ACA, Am. Assn. Marriage and Family Therapists, Calif. Assn. Marriage and Family Therapists, San Diego Assn. Marriage and Family Therapists, Internat. Assn. Marriage and Family Counselors. Home: 3611 Warner St San Diego CA 92106 Office: Point Loma Counseling Ctr Ste D 3725 Talbot St San Diego CA 92106

SWANSON, DARLENE MARIE CARLSON, speech therapist, educator, speaker, writer; b. Boone, Iowa, Aug. 8, 1925; d. Arvid Wilhelm and Edith Marie (Peterson) Carlson; m. Reuben Theodore Swanson, Aug. 8, 1948; children: Conrad T., Joyce Marie Swanson Jobson. BA, Augustana Coll., 1947; postgrad., U. Chgo., 1949, Creighton U., 1972; student, Joslyn Art Mus., Omaha, 1975. Cert. tchr., Ill., Nebr. Speech therapist Rock Island and Rockford (Ill.) Pub. Sch. System, 1946-51, Omaha (Nebr.) Pub. Sch. System, 1963-64; ch. organist Calvary Luth. Ch., Moline, Ill., 1944-46; asst. organist Augustana Luth. Ch., Omaha, 1956-63; mortuary organist Swanson-Golden Mortuary, Omaha, 1956-63; freelance lectr., 1960—; freelance writer, 1960—; chalk artist lectr. and pub. speaker, retreat leader; observer Luth. World Fedn. Assembly, Budapest, Hungary, 1984. Sunday sch. tchr. Kountze Meml. Luth. Ch., Omaha, 1964-74; Sunday sch. supr. St. Andrew's Luth. Ch., West Hempstead, N.Y., 1951-54; sec. Omaha PTA, 1968-70; mem. adv. coun. Cen. High Sch., Omaha, 1971-74, Omaha Pub. Schs., 1971-74; bd. dirs., sec. Luth. Summer Music Program, 1990—; active Met. Opera Guild, 1986-90, Opera Omaha Guild, 1990—, Omaha Symphony Guild, 1990; mem. bd. dirs. Bethpage Mission Great Britain, sec., 1994—. Named Vol. of Yr. Omaha Head Start Program, 1965. Home: 11818 Oakair Plz Box 37448 Omaha NE 68137

SWANSON, EMILY, state legislator; b. Oak Park, Ill., Jan. 12, 1947; m. Tim Swanson; 2 children. BA, Bennington Coll.; MA, U. Calif., Berkeley. Mem. Mont. Ho. of Reps. Home: 1716 S Willson Bozeman MT 59715 Office: Mont Ho of Reps State Capitol Helena MT 59620*

SWANSON, JILL CLUGGISH, small business owner, nurse; b. Newark, Ohio, Sept. 26, 1939; d. Earl Edward and Wanza Marie (Harris) Cluggish; m. Robert Jon Swanson, Dec. 27, 1960 (div. Aug. 1967); 1 child, Eric Jon. Diploma, White Cross Hosp. Sch. Nursing, Columbus, Ohio, 1960. RN, Calif., Tex. Staff nurse Newark Hosp., 1960, Columbus State Hosp., 1961, El Camino Hosp., Mountain View, Calif., 1961-63, Santa Clara County Hosp., San Jose, Calif., 1963-66; staff nurse, asst. head nurse, supr. labor-delivery room San Jose Med. Ctr. Hosp., 1966-92; co-owner, operator, bus. mgr. Antepartum Testing Svc., San Jose, 1985—. Mem. NAACOG (cert. inpatient labor and delivery nurse). Methodist. Home and Office: 4668 Holycon Cir San Jose CA 95136-2313

SWANSON, JOANNE THATCHER, lawyer; b. Washington, Aug. 19, 1932; d. Myron William and Ruth Lucille (Boesel) Thatcher; m. Charles Frances Rawlings, Apr. 12, 1958 (div. Sept. 1973); children: Vance Wayne Rawlings, Joanne Patrice Rawlings Franer. BA, Gustavus Adolphus Coll., 1953; JD, U. Minn., 1977. Bar: Minn. 1977, U.S. Dist. Ct. Minn. 1978, U.S. Ct. Appeals (8th cir.) 1984. Assoc. Grathwol, Oberhauser, Ploetz & Randall, Wayzata, Minn., 1977-81, Wiese & Cox, Mpls., 1981-82; pvt. practice St. Paul, Minn., 1982—; contract adminstr. law judge; mem. com. family ct. procedure Supreme Ct.; speaker in field. Contbr. articles to profl. jours. Mem. planning commn. North St. Paul, 1963-73. Mem. ABA (family law and litigation secs.), Am. Acad. Matrimonial Lawyers (sec. Minn. chpt. 1991-92, bd. govs. 1992-94), Minn. State Bar Assn. (task force on Minn. Ct. Appeals), Hennepin County Bar Assn. (chair family law sect. 1989-90, numerous coms.), Ramsey County Bar Assn. (family law sect.), Jaycees. Democrat. Lutheran. Office: 252 Lowertown Bus Ctr 245 E 6th St Saint Paul MN 55101

SWANSON, KARIN, hospital administrator, consultant; b. New Britain, Conn., Dec. 8, 1942; d. Oake F. and Ingrid Lauren Swanson; m. B. William Dorsey, June 26, 1965 (div. 1974); children: Matthew W., Julie I., Alison K.; m. Sanford H. Low, Oct. 14, 1989. BA in Biology, Middlebury Coll., 1964; MPH, Yale U., 1981. Biology tchr. Kents Hill (Maine) Sch., 1964-66; laboratory instr. Bates Coll., Lewiston, Maine, 1974-78; asst. to gen. dir. Mass. Eye and Ear Infirmary, Boston, 1979-80; v.p. profl. services Portsmouth (N.H.) Hosp., 1981-83; v.p. Health Strategy Assn. Ltd., Chestnut Hill, Mass., 1983-85; v.p. med. affairs Cen. Maine Med. Ctr., Lewiston, 1986-89; health care mgmt. cons. Cambridge, Mass., 1989-91; CEO Hahnemann Hosp., Brighton, Mass., 1991-94; adminstr. Vencor Hosp., Boston, 1994—. Mem. Phi Beta Kappa. Home: 198 Glen St Natick MA 01760-5606

SWANSON, LESLIE KEATING, financial services executive; b. Wilmington, Del., Sept. 27, 1952. BS, U. Del., 1974, student, 1980-83. Registered securities broker and ins. broker. Registered securities broker Merrill Lynch Pierce Fenner & Smith, Wilmington, 1984-89; corp. svcs. specialist Dean Witter Reynolds, Phila., 1989—. Home: PO Box 4046 Wilmington DE 19807 Office: Dean Witter Reynolds Two Logan Sq 18th and Arch Sts Philadelphia PA 19103

SWANSON, LESLIE MORROW, counselor; b. Ft. Wayne, Ind., Nov. 10, 1958; d. Don Stuart and Sharon Kay (Morris) Morrow; 1 child, Emily Kristen Linnea Erwin; m. Paul Oliver Swanson, Jan. 2, 1993. Student, Ind. State U., Evansville, 1979; BS in Psychology, Western Ky. U., 1980; MS in Clin. Psychology, U. Evansville, 1989. Grad. asst. psychology U. Evansville, 1987, rsch. asst. psychology, acad. advisor, 1987-88; vocat. evaluator Assn. for Retarded Citizens, Evansville, 1988; program dir. Work Able, Inc., Evansville, 1988-89; psychol. evaluator Developmental Diagnostics, Inc., Evansville, 1988-89; counselor, mem. disability support svcs. staff U. So. Ind., Evansville, 1989—, mem. enrollment mgmt. team, 1992—, mem. Am. with Disabilities task force, 1992—, mem. adv. com. Children's Ctr., 1991—, mem. disabled student adv. com., 1989—; cons. Henderson (Ky.) Psychol. Assocs., 1988-92. Vol. Evansville State Hosp., 1979; leadership tng. participant Ind. Gov.'s Planning Coun., Indpls., 1992; mem. Cmty. Counseling Resource Com., Evansville, 1992—, Ind. Gov.'s Planning Coun. Com., Evansville, 1992—. Mem. APA (assoc.), Southwestern Ind. Psychol. Assn., Assn. on Higher Edn. and Disability, Ind. Assn. on Higher Edn. and Disability (pres., chair 1993-94). Democrat. Episcopalian. Office: U So Ind Counseling Ctr 8600 University Blvd Evansville IN 47712

SWANSON, LINDA ALDEN, lawyer; b. Chattanooga, May 23, 1941; d. Eric Harry and Dorothy Ruth (Mahoney) Swanson; children: Douglas Graham, Margaret Alden Moody. BA, U. Tenn., 1963; LLB, Columbia U., 1966. Bar: Calif. 1971, U.S. Dist. Ct. (no. dist.) Calif. 1971, U.S. Ct. Appeals (9th cir.) 1971. Rsch. asst. to dir. Am. Law Inst., N.Y.C., 1964-67; assoc. in law Columbia U. Law Sch., N.Y.C., 1966-67; dir. police-cmty. rels. project Lawyers' Com. for Civil Rights under Law and Seattle-King, County Bar Assn., Seattle, 1967-68; legal advisor Seattle Police Dept., 1968-69, Oakland (Calif.) Police Dept., 1969-72; cons. Nat. Commn. on Marihuana and Drug Abuse, Washington, 1972-73; lectr. police law Stanford (Calif.) U. Law Sch., 1973-74; lectr. land use law U. Calif., Berkeley, 1974; founder, chmn., legal counsel Amigos de Diablo, Calif., 1973-77; ptnr. Moody & Moody, Sausalito, Calif., 1986—; project dir. women student intern program The Police Found., Washington, 1972-73. Contbr. articles to legal jours. Trustee, corp. sec. Sierra Club Legal Def. Fund, San Francisco, 1979—; bd. dirs., v.p. Marin Inst. on Alcohol and Other Drug Problems, San Rafael, Calif., 1988—; bd. dirs., corp. sec. The Trauma Found., San Francisco, 1983-88; chmn. legal com. Marin Support Svcs. for Elders, San Rafael, 1988-90; bd. dirs. West Blithedale Canyon Neighborhood Assn., Mill Valley, Calif., 1980—; mem., chmn. Mill Valley Planning Commn., 1985-90; mem. trauma rev. com. Marin Emergency Med. Care Commn., 1988-90. Mem. State Bar Calif., Marin County Bar Assn., Marin County Estate Planning Coun., Am. Law Inst., Nat. Acad. Elder Law Attys., Trust Consultive Group. *. Office: c/o Moody and Moody 62 Princess St Sausalito CA 94965

SWANSON, LORNA ELLEN, physical therapist, athletic trainer, researcher; b. Bridgeport, Conn., July 22, 1954; d. Harold Carl and Marna Ellyn (French) S.; m. James M. Kelley, Oct. 16, 1993. BFA in Dance, So. Meth. U., 1975, MFA in Dance, 1978; BS in Phys. Therapy, U. Tex., Dallas, 1984; PhD in Exercise Sci., U. Tenn., 1994. Lic. phys. therapist, Tenn. Mem. faculty Brookhaven Coll., Dallas, 1982-84; staff therapist St. Mary's Med. Ctr., Knoxville, Tenn., 1984-85, Ft. Sanders Regional Med. Ctr., Knoxville, 1985-86, Knoxville Sports Therapy, 1991-92; program dir., mem. faculty Roane State C.C., Harriman, Tenn., 1987-92; clin. specialist Ft. Sanders Ctr. for Sports Medicine, Knoxville, 1992-93, mgr., 1994—; grad. asst. athletic dept. U. Tenn., Knoxville, 1989-91; reviewer Jour. Orthopedic and Sports Phys. Therapy, 1993, 94; adj. faculty mem. Pellissippi State Tech. C.C., 1994. Contbr. chpt. to book and articles to profl. jours. Ballet mistress Victoria Bolen Dance Theatre, Knoxville, 1986-88. Mem. Am. Phys. Therapy Assn. (bd. content experts 1990-93), Tenn. Phys. Therapy Assn., Nat. Athletic Tng. Assn. (cert. athletic trainer), Tenn. Athletic Tng. Assn., Nat. Strength and Conditioning Assn. (cert. specialist), Neurodevel. Treatment Assn. (nominating com. 1987-89). Democrat. Lutheran. Office: Ft Sanders Ctr Sports Med 270 Ft Sanders West Blvd Knoxville TN 37922

SWANSON, NORMA FRANCES, federal agency administrator; b. Blue Island, Ill., Oct. 24, 1923; d. Arnold Raymond and Bessie Oween (Bewley) Brown; m. George Clair Swanson, Mar. 18, 1948; 1 child, Dane Craig. AB, Asbury Coll., 1946; BS cum laude, Eastern Nazarene Coll., Wollaston, Mass., 1970; MA cum laude, Ind. Christian U., 1986. Confidential asst. dep. undersec. interagy. intergovt. affairs U.S. Dept. Edn., Washington, 1981—; pres. Window to the World, Inc., Schroon Lake, N.Y., 1985—; asst. dir. edn. Commn. Bicentennial U.S. Constn., Washington, 1987—; dir. Horizons Plus Values Program Hampton Roads Va. Detention Homes; dir. Project Fresh Start Washington D.C. Pub. Sch., 1993-94; cons. Conf. Industrialized Nations, Williamsburg, Va., 1982, Nellie Thomas Inst. Learning, Monterey, Calif., 1981-82. Author: Dear Teenager, A Teen's Guide to Correct Social Behavior, 1987, A Constitution Is Born, A Teacher's Guide to Resource Materials, 1987, Sunlights and More, Bright Beginnings, 1993, The Ones that Count and Other Stories with Values to Live By, 1994; editor: (anthology) Horizons Plus; developer ednl. materials; theorem artist Early Am. Life mag., 1974. Bd. regents Ind. Christian U., 1986—; program dir. Tidewater (Va.) Outreach, 1992; dir. project Fresh Start, Washington Pub. Sch., 1993-94; dir. youth outreach with values program U.S. Dept. Juvenile Justice, 1992-93. Recipient J.C. Penny award for volunteerism, 1993. Republican. Baptist. Home: PO Box 308 Schroon Lake NY 12870

SWANSON, PATRICIA K., university official; b. St. Louis, May 8, 1940; d. Emil Louis and Patricia (McNair) Klick; 1 child, Ivan Clatanoff. BS in Edn., U. Mo., 1962; postgrad., Cornell U., 1963; MLS, Simmons Coll., 1967. Reference librarian Simmons Coll., Boston, 1967-68; reference librarian U. Chgo., 1970-79, sr. lectr. Grad. Library Sch., 1974-83, 86-88, head reference service, 1979-83, asst. dir. for sci. libraries, 1983-93, acting asst. dir. for tech. svcs., 1987-88, assoc. provost, 1993—; project dir. Office Mgmt. Svcs., Assn. Rsch. Librs., 1982-83; speaker in field; cons. on libr. mgmt., planning and space. Author: Great is the Gift that Bringeth Knowledge: Highlights from the History of the John Crerar Library, 1989; contbr. articles to profl. jours. Mem. Caxton Club. Office: John Crerar Libr U Chgo 5730 S Ellis Ave Chicago IL 60637-1404

SWANTON, SUSAN IRENE, library director; b. Rochester, N.Y., Nov. 29, 1941; d. Walter Frederick and Irene Wray S.; m. Wayne Holman, Apr. 12, 1969 (div. June 1973); 1 child, Michael; life ptnr. James Donald Lathrop; children: Kathryn, Kristin. AB, Harvard U., 1963; MLS, Columbia U., 1965. Libr. dir. Warsaw (N.Y.) Pub. Libr., 1963-64, Gates Pub. Libr., Rochester, N.Y., 1965—. Pres. Drug and Alcohol Coun., Rocheste,r 1985-91, mem. adv. coun., 1992-94; bd. dirs. Rochester Freenet, 1995—. Named Citizen of Yr., Gates-Chili Coun., 1995. Mem. Rochester Met. C. of C. (pres. Gates-Chili coun. 1982, sec. 1990-94, Citizen of the Yr. 1995), Harvard Club of Rochester (mem. adv. bd.). Office: Gates Pub Libr 1605 Buffalo Rd Rochester NY 14624

SWANTON, VIRGINIA LEE, author, publisher; b. Oak Park, Ill., Feb. 6, 1933; d. Milton Wesley and Eleanor Louise (Linnell) S. BA, Lake Forest (Ill.) Coll., 1954; MA in English Lit., Northwestern U., 1955; cert. in acctg., Coll. of Lake County, Ill., 1984. Editorial asst. Publs. Office, Northwestern U., Evanston, Ill., 1955-58; reporter Lake Forester, Lake Forest, 1959; editor Scott, Foresman & Co., Glenview, Ill., 1959-84; sales assoc. B. Dalton Bookseller, Lake Forest, Ill., 1985—; copy editor, travel coord. McDougal Littell/Houghton Mifflin, Evanston, 1985-94; author, publisher Gold Star Publ. Svcs., Lake Forest, Ill., 1994—; sales assoc. B. Dalton Bookseller, Lake Forest, 1995—; sr. bookseller B. Dalton Booksellers, Market Squ., Lake Forest, Ill., 1985—. Contbr. articles to profl. jours. Mem. bd. deacons First Presbyn. Ch. of Lake Forest; mem., sec. bd. dirs., newsletter editor Career Resource Ctr., Inc., Lake Forest. Mem. Internat. Reading Assn., Deerpath Art League, Chgo. Women in Pub. Presbyterian. Office: Gold Star Publ PO Box 125 Lake Forest IL 60045

SWARTZ, ROSLYN HOLT, real estate investment executive; b. Los Angeles, Dec. 9, 1940; d. Abe Jack and Helen (Canter) Holt; m. Allan Joel Swartz, June 2, 1963. AA, Santa Monica (Calif.) Coll., 1970; BA summa cum laude, UCLA, 1975; MA, Pepperdine U., 1976. Cert. community coll. instr., student-personnel worker, Calif. Mgr. pub. relations Leader Holdings, Inc., L.A., 1968-75, pres., 1991—; sec., treas. Leader Holdings, Inc., North Hollywood, Calif., 1975-81, pres., 1981-91; chief exec. officer Beverly Stanley Investments, L.A., 1979—. Condr. An Oral History of the Elderly Jewish Community of Venice, Calif. at Los Angeles County Planning Dept. Library, 1974. Mem. Hadassah (life), Friends of the Hollywood Bowl; bd. dirs. Am. Friends of Haifa Med. Ctr. L.A., L.A. County Mus. Art, West L.A. Symphony; capital patron Simon Wiesenthal Ctr. Fellow Phi Beta Kappa (bicentennial); mem. NAFE, AAUW, Am. Soc. Profl. and Exec. Women, Am. Pub. Health Assn., Am. Pharm. Assn., Women in Comml. Real Estate, L.A. World Affairs Coun., Town Hall (life), Century City C. of C., UCLA Alumni Assn. (life), UCLA Founders Circle, Women's Coun. Women's Guild Cedars-Sinai Med. Ctr., UCLA Prytanean Alumnae Assn., Santa Monica Coll. Alumni Assn. (life), Phrateres Internat., Order of Eastern Star, Phi Alpha Theta, Alpha Gamma Sigma, Alpha Kappa Delta, Phi Delta Kappa, Pi Gamma Mu. Office: PO Box 241784 Los Angeles CA 90024-9584

SWARTZELL, ANN GARLING, librarian; b. Elkhart, Ind., Jan. 23, 1955; d. Allen Henry and Barbara (Garling) S.; m. Stuart B. Gralnik, June 28, 1989; 1 child, Aaron Samuel. AB, Ind. U., 1977, MLS, 1978. Preservation project libr. Harvard U. Library, Cambridge, Mass., 1978-84; Mellon intern in preservation adminstrn. Yale U. Library, New Haven, 1984; assoc. libr. conservation N.Y. State Libr., Albany, 1985-89; head preservation replacement and photographic svcs. libr. conservation U. Libr. U. Calif., Berkeley, 1989—; mem. adv. com. N.E. Document Conservation Ctr., Andover, Mass., 1985-89. Author: (with others) Preservation of Microfilm: A Guide for Libraries, 1986 (Leland awad 1987); editor Assn. for Libr. Collections & Tech. Svcs. Newsletter, 1989-93. Mem. ALA (vice chair, chair reprodn. library materials sect. 1987-89).

SWATZELL, MARILYN LOUISE, nurse; b. Johnson City, Tenn., July 31, 1942; d. Dallas Fred and Minnie Thelma (Clark) S. BS cum laude, East Tenn. State U., 1966, MS, 1967; BSN, U. Tenn., 1974. Chmn. pediatric nursing Meth. Hosp. Sch. Nursing, Memphis, 1978-80; head nurse Le Bonheur Children's Med. Ctr., Memphis, 1981-83; dir. maternal child nursing Jackson (Tenn.) Madison County Gen. Hosp., 1985-88; staff nurse Vanderbilt U. Hosp., Nashville, 1988-90; supr. Meth. Hosp. Lexington, Tenn., 1990—. Contbr. articles on care plans to profl. jours. Mem. ANA, Tenn. Nurses Assn., Tenn. Orgn. Nurse Execs. Home: 231 Law Ln Lexington TN 38351

SWAZEY, JUDITH POUND, institute president, sociomedical science educator; b. Bronxville, N.Y., Apr. 21, 1939; d. Robert Earl and Louise Titus (Hanson) Pound; m. Peter Woodman Swazey, Nov. 28, 1964; children: Elizabeth, Peter. AB, Wellesley Coll., 1961; PhD, Harvard U., 1966. Rsch. assoc. Harvard U., 1966-71, lectr., 1969-71, rsch. fellow, 1971-72; cons. com. brain scis. NRC, 1971-73; staff scientist neurosci. rsch. program MIT, Cambridge, 1973-74; assoc. prof. dept. socio-med. scis. and community medicine Boston U., 1974-77, prof., 1977-80, adj. prof. Schs. Medicine and Pub. Health, 1980—; exec. dir. Medicine in the Pub. Interest, Inc., Boston and Washington, 1979-82, 89-93; pres. Coll. of the Atlantic, Bar Harbor, Maine, 1982-84, Acadia Inst., Bar Harbor, 1984—; mem. Army Sci. Bd., 1987-92. Author: Reflexes and Motor Integration, the Development of Sherrington's Integrative Action Concept, 1969, (with others) Human Aspects of Biomedical Innovation, 1971, (with R.C. Fox) The Courage to Fail, a Social View of Organ Transplants and Hemodialysis, 1975, rev. edit., 1978 (hon. mention Am. Med. Writers Assn., C. Wright Mills award Am. Sociol. Assn.), Chlorpromazine in Psychiatry, a Study of Therapeutic Innovation, 1974, (with K. Reeds) Today's Medicine, Tomorrow's Science, Essays on Paths of Discovery in the Biomedical Sciences, 1978; editor: (with C. Wong) Dilemmas of Dying, Policies and Procedures for Decisions Not to Treat, 1981, (with F. Worden and G. Adelman) The Neurosciences: Paths of Discovery, 1975, (with R.C. Fox) Spare Parts, Organ Replacement in American Society, 1992; assoc. editor IRB: A Jour. of Human Subjects Rsch., 1979—; contbr. articles to profl. jours. Mem. Maine Dept. Human Svcs. Bioethics Adv. Com. (chair 1991-94). Wellesley Coll. scholar, 1961; Wellesley Coll. Alumnae fellow Harvard U., 1966, NIH predoctoral fellow, 1966, Radcliffe Coll. Coll. grad. fellow, 1966. Mem. AAAS (sci. freedom and responsibility com. 1986-89), Inst. Medicine NAS (mem. health scis. policy bd. 1986-89), Grad. Record Exam. (bd. dirs. 1987-91), Sherrington Soc., Phi Beta Kappa, Sigma Xi. Office: Acadia Inst Bar Harbor ME 04609

SWEASY, JOYCE ELIZABETH, government official, military reserve officer; b. Key West, Fla., Apr. 25, 1948; d. James Alfred and Josephine Mary (Fassel) Messick. BFA, Phila. Coll. Art, 1971; A in Bus. Adminstrn., Howard County Community Coll., 1985; grad., Army Command and Gen. Staff Co, 1988. Commd. 1st lt. U.S. Army, 1978, advanced through grades to maj., 1990; contract specialist U.S. Army, Adelphi, 1978-84, analyst procurement Lab. Command,, 1984-85; appointed command competition adv. Sec. of the Army, Adelphi, 1985-91; dep. chief of staff procurement, 1991-92, div. chief small bus. adminstrn., 1992—; owner, operator Hand Made 'N Ellicott City, Md., 1983—; owner, gen. mgr. Data Solutions. Contbr. numerous articles to profl. jours. Mem. Font Hill Citizens Orgn., Ellicott City, 1987—. Mem. U.S. Army Res. Officers Assn, Nat. Contract Mgrs. Assn., Am. Def. Preparedness Assn. Republican. Roman Catholic. Home: 4008 Arjay Cir Ellicott City MD 21042-5608 Office: SBA Washington DC 20416

SWEDLOW, JUDITH MEYER, volunteer; b. Cin., May 7, 1940; d. Joseph Samuel and Hazel (Gordon) Meyer; m. Gerald Howard Swedlow, Mar. 19, 1961; children: Tracy Ellen, Pamela Jean, Deborah Jane. BFA, Ohio State U., 1990. Acct. exec. Columbus (Ohio) Monthly Mag., 1977-80; owner, v.p. Elja, Unltd., Columbus, 1980-82; mktg. dir. Mentor Techs., Columbus, 1983-85; sales mgr. Target Pub., Columbus, 1986-87. Mem. nat. bd. dirs. women's divsn. United Jewish Appeal, N.Y.C., 1978-94; bd. dirs. Jewish Telegraphic Agy., N.Y.C., 1985—; mem. exec. com., bd. dirs. Am. Israel Pub. Affairs Com., Washington, Columbus (Ohio) Jewish Fedn., 1974—. Recipient Therese Stern Kahn Young Leadership award Columbus Jewish Fedn., 1974, Jewish Welfare Bd. Leadership Recognition award Columbus Jewish Cmty. Ctr., 1976.

SWEENEY, ANNE MARIE, social worker; b. Cambridge, Mass., Aug. 15, 1939; d. Hubert A. and Eleanor F. (Mahoney) Smith; m. Jack R. Sweeney, Oct. 4, 1980. BA, Salve Regina Coll., Newport, R.I., 1961; MSW, Boston Coll., 1963. Social worker Cath. Charities, Salem, Mass., 1963-68; social worker, coord. adoption svc. New Eng. Home for Little Wanderers, Boston, 1968-72; dir. social svc. Malden (Mass.) Hosp., 1972-85; sch. adjustment counselor Medford (Mass.) Pub. Sch., 1987—; pres. Social Work Oncology Group, Boston, 1984-85. Mem. AAUW (pres. Melrose Wakefield br. 1991-93), Nat. Assn. Social Workers, Ctr. for Sch. Counseling Practitioners, Boston Area Educators for Social Responsibility. Home: 22 Dartmouth Rd Melrose MA 02176 Office: Medford Pub Schs Medford MA 02155

SWEENEY, DEIDRE ANN, lawyer; b. Hackensack, N.J., Mar. 17, 1953; d. Thomas Joseph and Robin (Thwaites) S. AB cum laude, Mt. Holyoke Coll., 1975; JD, Fordham U., 1978. Assoc. Curtis, Mallet-Prevost, Colt & Mosle, N.Y.C., 1978-84, Eaton & Van Winkle, N.Y.C., 1984-86; ptnr. Jacobs, Persinger & Parker, N.Y.C., 1986—; adj. instr. Adelphi U., N.Y.C., 1982-86.

Class agt. Mt. Holyoke Coll. Alumni Fund, South Hadley, Mass., 1975-80; chmn. nominating com. Mt. Holyoke Class of 1975, 1990-94; mem. Archdiocese N.Y. Bequests and Planned Gifts Com., 1988—. Mem. Assn. of Bar of City of N.Y. (uniform state laws com. 1982-85), Columbia Golf and Country Club. Democrat. Roman Catholic. Office: Jacobs Persinger & Parker 77 Water St New York NY 10005-4401

SWEENEY, JANICE MAE CONNER, administrator; b. Wilmington, Del., Jan. 30, 1930; d. Walter Jesse and Marjorie Elizabeth (Gentieu) Conner; m. Wayne Glenn Orr, Feb. 9, 1951 (div. Feb. 1956); m. Daniel Joseph Sweeney Jr., Feb. 10, 1956 (div. May 1974); children: Michael H., Diane M. Fowler, Daniel J. III, Christopher M., Victoria Lynn. BS, Beacom Coll., 1949. Sr. sec. Hercules, Inc., Wilmington, Del., 1949-55; sec. to dir. purchasing Marco Beach Resort & Villas, Marco Island, Fla., 1976-80; exec. sec. Marco Beach REalty, Marco Island, Fla., 1981; legal sec. David Skeer, Marco Island, Fla., 1982-86; adminstr. Fla. Adventure Tours, Marco Island, Fla., 1987; office mgr. Admiralty House, Inc., Marco Island, Fla., 1988—. Assoc. editor, contbg. author: The Fever; contbr. editor: Penguin Encyclopedia Popular Music. Mem. Amnesty Internat. (ptnr. conscience), Met. Mus. Modern Art (nat.), Smithsonian Inst. (nat.), Marco Island Art League, Jolly Roger N.Y. Times Crossword Puzzle Club, Quest for Peace, Marco Island Hist. Soc. Methodist. Home and Office: 140 Seaview Ct Apt 104-N Marco Island FL 33937

SWEENEY, JEAN MARIA, lawyer; b. N.Y.C., July 2, 1956; d. John Joseph and Rita Valerie (Colleran) Sweeney; m. David Thomas Maloof, Aug. 11, 1990; 1 child, Julia Jean Maloof. BA in English Lit., Coll. of the Holy Cross, Worcester, Mass., 1978; JD, St. John's U., Jamacia, Queens, 1982. Bar: N.Y. 1983; Supreme Ct. State of N.Y., 1983; U.S. Dist. Ct. (so. dist.) N.Y., 1983. Assoc. atty. First Investers Corp., N.Y.C., 1983-86; assoc. Emmet, Marvin & Martin, N.Y.C., 1986-92; v.p. to first v.p. Shearson Lehman Brothers, N.Y.C., 1992-93; first v.p. Smith Barney, Inc., N.Y.C., 1993—. Democrat. Roman Catholic. Office: Smith Barney Inc 388 Greenwich St New York NY 10013

SWEENEY, JUDITH L., newspaper publishing executive. V.p. L.A. Times. Office: LA Times Times Mirror Sq Los Angeles CA 90012*

SWEENEY, LUCY GRAHAM, psychologist; b. Davenport, Iowa, Nov. 14, 1946; d. B. Graham and Dorothy (Lawson) S.; m. Richard N. Tiedemann, Dec. 2, 1978 (div. 1989); 1 child, Susan Lee. BA with honors, U. Denver, 1968; MA in Devel. Psychology, Columbia U., 1977; PsyD, Rutgers U., 1990. Cert. family therapist. Profl. actress, 1968-73; dir. therapeutic play and recreation program St. Luke's Med. Ctr., N.Y.C., 1973-78; child life coord. St. Francis Hosp., Hartford, Conn., 1978-80; program cons. Child and Family Svcs., Torrington, Conn., 1980-81; clinician Resolve Community Counseling Ctr., Scotch Plains, N.J., 1981-84; staff psychologist women's inpatient unit Lyons (N.J.) VA Med. Ctr., 1990; psychologist women's treatment program Fair Oaks Hosp., Summit, N.J., 1990-92; cons. Kessler Inst. for Rehab., East Orange, N.J., 1992—, Resolve Community Counseling Ctr., Scotch Plains, N.J., 1992—; pvt. practice Westfield, N.J., 1993—; staff psychologist Richard Hall Community Mental Health Ctr., Bridgewater, N.J., , 1990. Contbr. articles to profl. jours. Recipient John Weyandt award for Outstanding Student in Theatre U. Denver, 1968. Mem. APA, N.J. Psychol. Assn., Phi Theta Kappa. Home: 21 Harwich Ct Scotch Plains NJ 07076-3165

SWEENEY, ROSEMARIE, medical association administrator; b. Fall River, Mass., Sept. 2, 1950; d. John Francis and Phyllis (Field) S.; m. Edmund Burke Rice, Feb. 24, 1978; 1 child, Jonathan Field Rice. Student, Hillsdale Coll., 1968-69; BA, Am. U., 1972, MPA, 1978. Profl. staff mem. Office of Rep. Margaret Heckler, Washington, 1972-74; staff assoc. fed. agy. affairs Am. Osteo. Assn., Washington, 1974-78, govt. affairs rep., 1978-79; dir. Washington office Am. Acad. Family Physicians, Washington, 1979-82; v.p. socioeconomic affairs and policy analysis, 1992—; mem. family practice adv. com. George Washington U., Washington, 1990—. Vol. Montgomery County Sexual Assault Svc., Rockville, Md., 1984-93; mem. Glen Echo Fire Dept., Bethesda, Md., 1986-92, Victim Svcs. Adv. Bd., Md., 1987-93; chmn. victim svc. adv. bd. Montgomery County, Md., 1991-93; bd. dirs. Westmoreland Children's Ctr., Bethesda. Recipient Outstanding Svc. award Montgomery County Crisis Ctr., Md., 1986, Outstanding Performance award Montgomery County Sexual Assault Svc., Md., 1987, Recognition award Soc. Tchrs. Family Medicine, Kansas City, Mo., 1990, Govs.' Sixth Annual Victim Assistance award, Balt., 1991. Mem. Women in Govt. Rels. Office: Am Acad Family Physicians 2021 Massachusetts Ave NW Washington DC 20036-1011

SWEENY, RUTH EVANS, psychotherapist; b. Orange, N.J., Jan. 21, 1922; d. Edward Francis and Gertrude (Evans) S.; m. Richard Bender Perkins, Nov. 27, 1970; children: Alexandra E. Johnson, Evan Johnson, Craig E. Johnson, J. Randall Johnson. BA, Smith Coll., 1944; MEd, Rutgers, 1970, EdD, 1981. Lic. marriage and family therapist, N.C.; diplomate Acad. Cert. Clin. Mental Health Counselors. Asst. editor U.S. News, Washington, 1945-46; asst. dir. N.J. Heart Assn., Union, 1967-69; counselor St. Peter's Coll., Jersey City, N.J., 1970-76; dir. women's ctr. St. Peter's Coll., 1974-76; psychotherapist Neuse Ctr., Morehead City, N.C., 1980-88, pvt. practice, Pine Knoll Shores, N.C., 1983—. Pres. Mental Health Assn. Morris County, N.J., 1958-60, Carteret County Coun. for Women, 1982-84, cons. 1991—; dir. Domestic Violence Program Carteret County, 1984-88; fund raiser Habitat for Humanity Carteret County, 1991—; vice chair Mental Health Bd., N.J., 1967-70, chair, pers. com., 1972-74. Recipient Woman of Yr. award Coun. for Women Carteret County, 1987. Mem. APA, Am. Assn. for Sex Educators, Counselors and Therapists, N.C. Assn. for Marriage and Family Therapy (editor newsletter 1987-95), Bogue Banks Country Club, Pine Knoll Shores, Ladies Golf Assn. (pres.). Democrat. Roman Catholic. Office: 115 Dogwood Circle Pine Knoll Shores NC 28512

SWEETERS, KAREN BARBAROSSA, music director; b. Norwich, Conn., Mar. 25, 1950; d. Frederick and Margaret (Dugas) Barbarossa; m. Norman Sweeters Jr., Jan. 30, 1971 (div. Nov. 1985); children: Jakob, Christian. BA, U. Conn., 1971. English tchr. Colchester (Conn.) Pub. Schs., 1971-72, Westport (Conn.) Pub. Schs., 1972-76; title searcher Conn. Abstract, Inc., Greenwich, 1986-93; pres. Conn. Abstract, Inc., Greenwich, Conn., 1994—; dir. Yankeemaid Chorus, Easton, Conn., 1987—; mem. regional faculty Sweet Adelines, Inc., 1994—, coach for visual performance, 1990. Recipient Master Dir. award Sweet Adelines, Internat., 1993, Novice Dir. award, 1989. Mem. Stage Coaches. Roman Catholic. Home: 404 Foxboro Dr Norwalk CT 06851-1148

SWEETING, LINDA MARIE, chemist; b. Toronto, Ont., Can., Dec. 11, 1941; came to U.S., 1965, naturalized, 1979; d. Stanley H. and Mary (Robertson) S. BSc, U. Toronto, 1964, MA, 1965; PhD, UCLA, 1969. Asst. prof. chemistry Occidental Coll., L.A., 1969-70; asst. prof. chemistry Towson (Md.) State U., 1970-75, assoc. prof., 1975-85, prof., 1985—; guest worker NIH, 1976-77; program dir. chem. instrumentation NSF, 1981-82; vis. scholar Harvard U., 1984-85; contractor U.S. Army MRICD, 1991-93. Bd. dirs. Chamber Music Soc. Balt., 1985-91. Mem. Md. Acad. Scis. (mem. sci. council 1975-83, 89-94), Assn. for Women in Sci. (treas. 1977-78, Woman of Yr. 1989), Am. Chem. Soc. (mem. women chemists Com. 1983-89), AAAS, Wilderness Soc. (exec. com. Exptl. NMR Conf. 1985-87), Nature Conservancy, Aircraft Owners and Pilots Assn., Sierra Club, Sigma Xi (sec. TSU Club 1979-81, pres. 1987-88, 91-92, mid-Atlantic nominating com. 1987-90, regional dir. 1988-89, nat. nominating com. 1991-94). Office: Towson State U Dept Chemistry Baltimore MD 21204

SWEETLAND, ANNETTE FLORENCE (ANNIE SWEETLAND), special education educator; b. Dallas; d. George R. and Odessa (Donnhue) S.; children: George William Davison, James Erron Davison; m. Ralph J. Guinn. BS in Edn., U. Okla., 1988, MS in Edn., 1992. Lic. profl. counselor, 1995. Tchr. multi-handicapped students Noble (Okla.) Pub. Sch., 1988-90; child-find S.E.A.R.C.H. coord. and preschool handicap tchr. Shawnee (Okla.) Pub. Sch., 1989-93; regional coord. Sooner Start Okla. Dept. Edn., Norman, 1993-94; case mgr. II Developmental Disabilities Scv. Divsn./DHS, State of Okla., Oklahoma City, 1994—; mgr. group home Able Group Homes, Norman, Okla., 1989-90; dir. returning adult program St. Gregory's Coll., Shawnee, 1990-91. Mem. ARC, Coun. Exceptional Children, Okla. Ednl. Assn. Office: Devel Disabilities Svc 4545 N Lincoln Oklahoma City OK 73142

SWEETSER, SUSAN W., state legislator, lawyer, advocate; b. Dec. 13, 1958; d. Robert Joseph and Lucretia Rose (Donnelly) Williams. BA in Polit. Sci./Environ. Adminstrn. with high honors, Johnson (Vt.) State Coll., 1982; JD magna cum laude, Vt. Law Sch., 1985. Bar: N.Y. 1986, Vt. 1986, U.S. Dist. Ct. Vt. 1989; CLU, ChFC. Confidential law clk. Appellate div. N.Y. Supreme Ct., Albany, 1985-86; assoc. Gravel & Shea, Burlington, Vt., 1986-90; atty. Nat. Life Ins. Co., Montpelier, Vt., 1990—; now mem. Vt. State Senate; victims rights adv. Essex Junction, Vt., 1980—; adj. prof. bus. law St. Michael's Coll., Winooski, Vt., 1991—, Johnson State Coll., 1995—; justice of peace Town of Essex, 1991-95; chair judiciary com.; former mem. Health and Welfare Com.; mem. Housing and Conservation Trust Fund Study Com., Civil Rights Study Com., Adoption Law Reform Study Com., Appropriations Com. Author articles on victims rights. Trustee Vt. State Colls., Waterbury, 1979-81, Univ. Health Ctr., 1992-94; mem. ethics com. Fanny Allen Hosp., Winooski, Vt., 1989-92; v.p. Lyric Theatre, Burlington, 1989—; mem. Vt. Rep. State Com., Montpelier, chmn. Rep. State Conv., 1988, 92; founder, pres. Survivors of Crime, Inc. Recipient Achievement award Vt. Law Enforcement Coordinating Com., 1990, Vt. Ctr. for Prevention and Treatment of Sexual Abuse and The Safer Soc. Program, 1991, Nat. recognition for victims rights work The Giraffe Project, 1991, award Nat. Found. for Improvement of Justice, 1993; named 754th Point of Light by former Pres. George Bush, 1992, Am. Heroine Ladies Home Jour., 1991. Fellow AAUW; mem. Vt. Bar Assn., N.Y. State Bar Assn., Internat. Assn. Fin. Planners (chmn. legis. affairs Greater Vt. chpt. 1988-91). Roman Catholic. Office: Survivors of Crimes Inc PO Box 8304 Essex Junction VT 05451-8304

SWENSON, KATHLEEN SUSAN, music and art teacher; b. Reno, Nev., Oct. 23, 1938; d. Harold Ruthaford McNeil and Hollyce Margaret (Scruggs) McNeil Biggs; m. James Michael Phalan, 1956 (div. 1974); children: David Michael, Jeanine Louise Phalan Lawrence, Gregory Shaun; m. Gerald Allen Swensen, Nov. 1976 (div. 1987); stepchildren: Craig Allen, Sarah Ann, Eric Sander. Student, U. Nev., Reno, 1956-58, Foothill Coll., 1966-68; AA, West Valley Coll.; BA, U. Calif., Santa Cruz, 1983. Concert pianist Nev.,Calif, 1950-64; pvt. piano instr. various locations, 1963—, pvt. art instr., 1970—, pvt. astrology instr., 1973—; founder, pres. AAM Triple Arts, Aptos, Calif., 1974—; founder, owner Aptos (Calif.) Acad. Music, 1993—. Producer, instr. art instrn. videos. Mem. Soc Western Artists, Calif. Piano Tchrs. Assn., Los Gatos Art Assn. (pres. 1985-86), Saratoga Contemporary Artists (v.p. 1984-85), Nat. League Am. Pen Women (honorarian 1985), Soroptimists. Republican. Episcopalian. Home and Office: AAM Triple Arts 3000 Wisteria Way Aptos CA 95003-3318

SWERDA, PATRICIA FINE, artist, author, educator; b. Ft. Worth, Aug. 10, 1916; d. William Emerson and Margaret Ellen (Cull) Fine; B.S. cum laude, Tex. Woman's U., 1941; grad. Ikenobo U., Tokyo, 1965-66, Ikenobo Dojo, Kyoto, Japan, 1976, 77, 81, 83, 85, 87, 91; m. John Swerda, July 7, 1941; children: John Patrick James, Susan Ann Mary Swerda Foss, Margaret Rose Swerda Kownover. Exhibited ikebana in one-woman shows including: Bon Marche, Tacoma, 1966, Seattle, 1967, 85, Gallery Kokoro, Seattle, 1972-78; exhibited in group shows including: Takashimaya Dept. Store, 1965, 76, 77, 83, 85, Matsuzakaya Dept. Store, Tokyo, 1966, Ikenobo Center, Kyoto, 1966, 77, Seattle Art Mus., 1974-80, Sangyo Kaikan, Kyoto, 1976, Burke Mus., U. Wash., ann. Cherry Blossom Festival, Seattle, Bellevue Art Mus., 1984, 85, 87, 89, 90, 91, 92, 93, 94; demonstrations in field for various groups, including Greater Northwest Flower and Garden Show, Japan Week in Bellevue. Master of Ikebana of Ikenobo Ikebana Soc., Kyoto. Pres. Bellevue Sister Cities Assn. 1985; bd. dirs. Washington State Sister Cities Coord. Com. Named Disting. Alumna class of 1941 Tex. Woman's U., 1991. Mem. N.W. Sakura Chpt. of the Ikenobo Ikebana Soc. (pres. 1960-91), Bonsai Clubs Internat., Puget Sound Bonsai Assn., G.O. Philoptochos (Charitable) Soc. Democrat. Greek Orthodox. Author: Japanese Flower Arranging: Practical and Aesthetic Bases of Ikebana, 1969; Creating Japanese Shoka, 1979, Art Deco-Free Style Art Cards, 1990; contbr. articles to mags. in field; creator Ikenobo Gardens, Redmond; numerous radio and TV appearances. Home and Office: 23025 NE 8th St Redmond WA 98053-7230

SWERDLOW, AMY, historian, educator, writer; b. N.Y.C., Jan. 20, 1923; d. Joseph and Esther (Rodner) Galstuck; m. Stanley H. Swerdlow, Nov. 27, 1949 (dec. Sept. 1991); children: Joan Swerdlow-Brandt, Ezra, Lisa Thomas. BA, NYU, 1963; MA, Sarah Lawrence Coll., 1973; PhD, Rutgers U., 1984. Prof. Sarah Lawrence Coll., Bronxville, N.Y., 1981—, dir. grad. studies in women's history, 1983—, dir. women's studies program, 1983—; mem. adv. bd. Feminist Press, 1973—. Editor, co-author: Families in Flux, 1980, reprint, 1989; author: Women Strike for Peace: Traditional Motherhood and Radical Politics in the 1960s, 1993; editor Feminist Perspective on Homework and Childcare, 1978; co-editor: Class, Race and Sex: The Dynamics of Control, 1983; contbr. Sights on the Sixties: Reflections on a Critical Time, Women and Militarism: Essays in History, Politics and Social Theory, Give Peace A Chance, contbr. articles, essays to profl. jours., books. Mem. nat. bd. conf. Pease Rsch. in History. Rutgers U. fellow, 1977-81, Woodrow Wilson Dissertation fellow, 1980. Mem. Am. Hist. Assn., Orgn. Am. Historians (coord. working com. of women in the hist. profession), Berkshire Conf. in Women's History. Home: 2 Hedges Banks Dr East Hampton NY 11937-3505 Office: Sarah Lawrence Coll Bronxville NY 10708

SWERGOLD, MARCELLE MIRIAM, sculptor; b. Antwerp, Belgium, Sept. 6, 1927; came to U.S., 1939, naturalized, 1947; d. Gillel and Sarah (Matuzewitz) Elfenbein; student NYU, Art Students League, Sculptors Workshop; m. Maurice Swergold, June 12, 1949; children—Diane Botnick, Henry, Gary Swergold, Paul Kogan, George Kogan. Sculptor, 1965—; one-woman exhbns. include: Studio 12, N.Y.C., 1980, 82, 86, Nat. Fedn. Temple Sisterhoods, 1984; group exhbns. include Farleigh Dickinson U., Teaneck, N.J., 1972, Audubon Artist Ann., N.Y.C., 1978-86, Internat. Treasury Fine Arts, Plainview, N.Y., 1979, New Britain (Conn.) Mus., 1980, also Cork Gallery, Lincoln Center, N.Y.C., Allied Artists Nat. Acad. Galleries, N.Y.C., U.S. Custom House, N.Y.C., others; represented in permanent collection New Britain Mus. Am. Art Yad Vashem Sculpture Garden, Holocaust Mus., Jerusalem, Monument in the Park of the City of Ma'aleh Adumim, Israel, Sculpture in lobby at Fairlawn (N.J.) Jewish Ctr.; represented in pvt. collection of Master Moshe Castel, Israel. Recipient Best in Show award for Tetons, Women's Art Gallery, N.Y.C., 1977, 1st prize for sculpture Stanley Richter Assn. Arts, 1985, Vincent Glinski Meml. award Audubon Artists, 1986. Mem. N.Y. Soc. Women Artists (pres. 1979-81, exec. v.p. 1981—), Artists Equity, Contemporary Artists Guild. Home: 43 Paul St Danbury CT 06810-8365 Studio: 246 W 80th St New York NY 10024

SWETNAM, RUTH E. DANGLADE, curriculum director; b. Marion, Ind., Jan. 27, 1940; d. Harold Davis and Elizabeth (Lake) Neel; m. James K. Danglade, Sept. 2, 1961 (div. Nov. 1979); children: Annette, John, Douglas, Adam, Matthew; m. Gary L. Swetnam, June 19, 1993. BS, Ball State U., 1961, MA, 1964. Cert. elem., secondary bus., spl. edn. and speech pathology tchr., Ind. Tchr. orthopedically handicapped Muncie (Ind.) Community Schs., 1961-67, tchr. of multiply handicapped, 1969-74, tchr. learning disabled, 1976-79; spl. edn. instr. Ball State U., Muncie, 1974-79; asst. dir. spl. edn. Delaware County Spl. Edn. Coop., Muncie, 1979-91; dir. curriculum Muncie Community Schs., 1991—; sci. curriculum cons. NSF, Muncie, 1976-78; learning disabilities cons. Ball State U., 1974-80. Bd. dirs. Delaware County Easter Seal Soc., 1967—; chairperson adv. coun. Ball State U. Coll. Bus., 1985-90; mem. adminstrv. bd. High St. United Meth. Ch., Muncie, 1984-88, youth coord., 1985-88; bd. dirs. Minnetrista Cultural Found., Inc., 1989—; mem. adv. bd. Delaware County 4-H. Mem. Assn. for Children with Learning Disabilities, Coun. for Exceptional Children (pres. Delaware County chpt. 1977-78), ASCD (Ind. chpt.), Pi Lambda Theta, Phi Delta Kappa, Pi Beta Phi. Methodist. Office: Muncie Community Schs 2501 N Oakwood Ave Muncie IN 47304-2399

SWETT, MARGARET CHRISTINE, finance executive; b. San Francisco, Sept. 14, 1959; d. Benson Payne Swett and Helen Irene (Frey) Iddings. BA in Econ., U. Calif., Santa Barbara, 1981; MBA, San Francisco State U., 1991. Acctg. supr. Geneva Group, Menlo Park, Calif., 1981-83; mgr. acctg. Pearl Cruises, San Francisco, 1983-87; mgr. acctg. and adminstrn. Seabourn Cruise Line, San Francisco, 1987-90, dir. fin. svcs., 1990-93, v.p. fin. and adminstrn., 1993—. Mem. NAFE, Nat. Honor Soc. (life), Beta Gamma Sigma. Avocations: photography, swimming, travel, humanities, literature. Home: 1400 Jones St # 201 San Francisco CA 94109 Office: Seabourn Cruise Line 55 Francisco St # 710 San Francisco CA 94133

SWIATEK, KATHY L., interior designer; b. Racine, Wis., Mar. 8, 1948; d. Leonard C. and Nancy (Matranga) Berchem; m. Harry J. Swiatek, July 8, 1972; children: Tracy, Heather, Gretchen. A in Interior Designing, Kenosha (Wis.) Tech., 1968. Cert. contract designer. Designer Hans Hasen Furniture, Racine, 1966-67, Lathrop Furniture, Racine, 1967-68; designer, buyer Mr. Furniture, Racine, 1968-72; designer Steinhaffles Furniture, Milw., 1972-73, Porter's Furniture, Racine, 1973-79; designer display Landaal Paint & Interiors, Racine, 1979-86; interior designer The Lake Group, Racine, 1986-88; head contract dept. Mrazek-Rudan, Racine, 1988-90; head design dept. Patrick Bus. Interiors, Racine, 1990—; lectr., tchr. Gateway Tech., Kenosha and Racine, 1985-91, Milw. Tech., 1978-79. Author column Racine jour., 1969-71. Pres., v.p. Racine Catholic Jr. League Wis., 1975-88, ways and means dir., philanthropy dir., sec.-treas., 1982-83. Mem. Internat. Interior Design Assn., Am. Soc. Interior Designers (assoc., allied mem.), Inst. Bus. Design. Home: 4900 N Main St Racine WI 53402-2573 Office: Patrick Bus Interiors 1100 Commerce Dr Ste 108 Racine WI 53406-3700

SWICK, MYRA AGNES, accountant; b. Chgo., Dec. 5, 1945; d. Arthur T. and Marcella M. (Pankiewicz) Swick. B.B.A. cum laude, Loyola U.-Chgo., 1967. C.P.A., Ill. Mem. audit staff Ernst & Ernst, Chgo., 1967-72; controller Shorr Paper Products, Aurora, Ill., 1972-73; audit mgr. Otto Hillsman & Co., Ltd., Chgo., 1973-81; audit mgr. Walton, Joplin, Langer & Co., Chgo., 1981-82, ptnr., 1982—; mem. audit com. Loyola U., Chgo., 1977—. Contbr. articles to profl. jours. Mem. Am. Woman's Soc. C.P.A.s (hon., pres. 1976-77), Chgo. Soc. Women C.P.A.s (founder, dir. 1977-80), Am. Soc. Women Accts. (chpt. pres. 1974-75), Chgo. Fin. Exchange (dir. 1984-86), Ill. C.P.A. Soc. (com. mem. 1982-86, 89—, task force chair 1985-86, dir. 1986-88, v.p. 1988-91, 94-95, pres. 95—), Am. Inst. C.P.A.s, Inst. Mgmt. Accts. (chpt. dir. 1972-74), Women's Bd. of Loyola Univ. of Chgo., Beta Alpha Psi, Beta Gamma Sigma. Avocations: travel; reading; crafts. Office: Walton Joplin Langer & Co 122 S Michigan Ave Chicago IL 60603-6107

SWICKARD, PAMELA JOY, accounting clerk; b. Wheeling, W.Va., Oct. 7, 1960; d. Clarence Edward and Deanna Kay (Nelson) Parsons; m. William Michael Swickard, Aug. 28, 1993. Diploma, John Marshall H.S., 1978. Interviewer I W.Va. Dept. of Employment Security, Wheeling, W.Va., 1978-81; cashier, clerk Bethlehem Farm Fresh, Wheeling, W.Va., 1979-82; customer svc. rep. Fed. One Savings and Loan, Wheeling, W.Va., 1982-84; store mgr. Nat. Waterbed Warehouse, Steubenville, Ohio, 1984-89; acctg. clerk Northwood Health Systems, Wheeling, W.Va., 1989—. Democrat. Methodist. Office: Northwood Health Systems 111-19th St Wheeling WV 26003

SWIFT, CATHERINE VAN SCOY, legal search consultant; b. Boston, Sept. 8, 1955; d. H.M. Steel and Catherine Ellen (Dugan) S.; m. Robert F. Montgomery, Nov. 2, 1985 (div. Apr. 1990); 1 child, Spencer. BA, Boston U., 1977. Recruitment coord. Winthrop Stimson, N.Y.C., 1977-80; recruitment dir. Cadwalader Wickersham, N.Y.C., 1980-83, dir. legal staff, 1983-86; pres. Swift & Assocs., Portland, Maine, 1987—; cons. Finley Kumble, N.Y.C., 1986-87. Region coord. Save the Children, Portland, 1992.

SWIFT, DOLORES MONICA MARCINKEVICH, public relations executive; b. Hazleton, Pa., Apr. 3, 1936; d. Adam Martin and Anna Frances (Lizbinski) Marcinkevich; student McCann Coll., 1954-56; m. Morden Leib Swift, Dec. 18, 1966. Pub. rels. coord. Internat. Coun. Shopping Ctrs., N.Y.C., 1957-59, Wendell P. Colton Advt. Agy., N.Y.C., 1959-61, Sydney S. Baron Pub. Rels. Corp., N.Y.C., 1961-65, Robert S. Taplinger Pub. Rels., N.Y.C., 1965-66; prin. Dolores M. Swift, Pub. Rels., Chgo., 1966—. Bd. dirs. Welfare Pub. Rels. Forum, 1971-79, treas., 1975-77; mem. pub. rels. adv. com. Mid-Am. chpt. A.R.C., 1973—; mem. women's com. Mark Twain Meml., 1968-69; pub. rels. dir. N.J. Symphony, Bergen County, 1969-70, mem. pub. rels. and promotion com.; mem. Wadsworth Atheneum, 1968-69; bd. dirs. Youth Guidance, 1972-75, Camp Fire, Met. Chgo. Coun., Inc., 1990-91; mem. NCCJ Labor, Mgmt. and Pub. Interest Conf., 1977-78; mem. pub. rels. com. United Way/Crusade of Mercy, 1979-80, 83, chmn. health svcs. com., 1984, direct mail com. 1985-86. Mem. Pub. Rels. Soc. Am. (accredited, coll. of fellows, Disting. Svc. award 1988, chmn. subcom. Nat. Ctr. for Vol. Action 1971-72, pub. svcs. com. Chgo. chpt. 1971-72, dir. 1975-82, chmn. counselors sect. 1976-77, assembly del. 1976, 79-81, 84-89, sec. 1977-78, v.p. 1978-79, pres.-elect 1979-80, pres. 1980-81, Midwest dist. chmn. 1984, nat. bd. dirs. 1985-89, sec. 1987-89, host chpt. chmn. 1981 conf., chmn. Midwest Dist. Conf. 1983, chmn. ethics awareness com. 1990-92, chmn. sr. forum com. 1993-94, mem. sr. forum com. 1995—, ednl. affairs com. 1990—), Women's Club (publs. chmn. Englewood, N.J., 1970-71), Publicity Club (chmn. pub. info. com. 1975-76). Mem. editorial bd. Public Relations Jour., 1978. Home and Office: 3800 N Lake Shore Dr Chicago IL 60613-3313

SWIFT, EVANGELINE WILSON, lawyer; b. San Antonio, May 2, 1939; d. Raymond E. and Josephine (Woods) Wilson; 1 child, Justin Lee. Student So. Meth. U., 1956-59; LL.B., St. Mary's U., San Antonio, 1963. Bar: Tex. 1963, U.S. Ct. Appeals (5th cir.) 1972, D.C. 1976, U.S. Dist. Ct. D.C. 1976, U.S. Supreme Ct. 1980, U.S. Ct. Appeals (11th cir.) 1981, U.S. Ct. Appeals (10th cir.) 1982, U.S. Ct. Appeals (D.C. cir.) 1982, U.S. Ct. Appeals (fed. cir.) 1983. Atty.-adv. ICC, Washington, 1964-65; staff atty. Headstart Program, OEO, Washington, 1965; exec. legal asst. to chmn., spl. asst. to vice chmn. EEOC, Washington, 1965-71, chief decisions div., 1971-75, asst. gen. counsel, 1975-76; cons. to sec. Employment Standards Adminstrn., Dept. Labor, Washington, 1977-79; ptnr. Swift & Swift, P.C., Washington, 1977-79; gen. counsel Merit Systems Protection Bd., Washington, 1979-86, mng. dir., 1986-87, dir. policy and evaluation, 1987—; bd. govs. U.S. Ct. Appeals (fed. cir.) Bar Assn., 1984-93, treas., 1987-89, sec., 1989-90, pres. elect, 1990; Fed. Cir. Bar Assn. (pres. 1992); guest lectr. Drake U., U. Pa., MIT; mem. U.S. del. 23d Sessions UN Commn. on Status of Women, Geneva, 1970. Recipient Meritorious Service award Fed. Govt., 1967, Fed. Women's award, 1975, Performance award Merit Systems Protection Bd., 1981-86, 92, 93, 94, Gold award 1986, Presdl. CFC award, 1984, 86, 94, EEO award Merit Systems Protection Bd., 1985, 94, Theodore Roosevelt award, 1988, Elmer B. Staats award NCAC, Am. Soc. Pub. Adminstrn., 1994. Methodist. Office: Merit System Protection Bd Office of Policy and Evaluation 1120 Vermont Ave NW Washington DC 20419-0002

SWIFT, ISABEL DAVIDSON, editorial director; b. Tokyo; d. Carleton Byron and Mary Howard (Davidson) S.; m. Steven C. Phillips. BA, Harvard U., 1976. Asst. editor Pocket Books, Simon & Schuster, N.Y.C., 1979-81; assoc. editor, editor, sr. editor, editorial mgr. Silhouette Books, N.Y.C., 1981-91, editorial dir., 1991—; internat. speaker on romance genre. Contbr. articles to profl. jours. Recipient RITA award Romance Writers Am., 1992, 94. Mem. N.Y. Women's Found. Office: Silhouette Books 300 E 42nd St New York NY 10017

SWIFT, JANE MARIA, state senator; b. North Adams, Mass., Feb. 24, 1965; d. John Maynard and Jean Mary (Kent) S.; m. Charles T. Hunt III, Feb. 19, 1994. BA in Am. Studies, Trinity Coll., Hartford, Conn., 1987. Exec. mgmt. trainee G. Fox & Co., Hartford, 1987-88; adminstrv. aide Sen. Peter C. Webber, Boston, 1988-90; mem. Mass. State Senate, Boston, 1991—; 3d asst. minority leader, 1993—. Republican. Roman Catholic. Office: State Senate Rm 407 State House Boston MA 02133

SWIFT, JANET MARGARET BRONSON, library director; b. Boston, Nov. 16, 1947; d. Franklin Chapin and Catherine MacLean (Ross) Bronson; m. Peter Easton Swift, June 28, 1969 (div. Apr. 1981). AB, Brown U., 1969; MS in LS, Columbia U., 1970; MA, Western Conn. State U., 1980. Reference librarian Brown U., Providence, 1970-74; asst. libr. dir. U. Conn., Waterbury, 1975-87, libr. dir., 1987—; pres. Swift Editorial Svcs., Ridgefield, Conn., 1982-93. Co-author: (ann.) Homecomings, 1983-91; contbr. articles to profl. jours., essay to book. Sec. Fox Hill Lake Assn., Ridgefield, 1982—; vol. ranger Ridgefield Conservation Commn., 1982—; mem. Ridgefield Chorale, 1976—; trustee UU Soc. No. Fairfield County, West Redding, Conn., 1984-85; mus. guide Keeler Taver Mus., Ridgefield, 1974-83, mem., 1974—. Mass. Libr. Assn. scholar, 1969-70. Mem. ALA, Assn. Coll. and

Rsch. Librs. (membership chmn. New Eng. chpt. 1981-83, mem.-at-large 1988-90, treas. 1993-95), New Eng. Libr. Assn. (life), Conn. Libr. Assn. (exec. bd. 1980-83, conf. chmn. 1982-83), Beta Phi Mu. Unitarian Universalist. Home: 40 Water's Edge Way Ridgefield CT 06877-2218 Office: U Conn Libr 32 Hillside Ave Waterbury CT 06710-2288

SWIG, ROSELYNE CHROMAN, art advisor; b. Chgo., June 8, 1930; m. Richard Swig, Feb. 5, 1950; children—Richard, Jr., Susan, Marjorie, Carol. Student, U. Calif.-Berkeley, UCLA; MFA with honors, San Francisco Art Inst., 1976, DFA (hon.), 1988. Pres. Roselyne C. Swig Artsource, San Francisco, 1977-94; apptd. by pres. as dir. art in embassies program U.S. Dept. of State, 1994—. Mem. bd. trustees San Francisco Mus. Modern Art, U. Art Mus., Berkeley, Calif., Mills Coll., Oakland, Calif., United Jewish Appeal; ex officio bd. mem. Jewish Mus. San Francisco; bd. dirs. San Francisco Opera, Am. Joint Distbn. Com.; pres., bd. dirs. Jewish Community Fedn. San Francisco, the Peninsula, Marin and Sonoma Counties; past commr. San Francisco Pub. Libr.; past bd. dirs. Am. Coun. for Arts, KQED Broadcasting System; mem. Vail, Colo., Art in Pub. Places Bd.; bd. govs. fine arts adv. panel Fed. Res. System; past pres. Calif. State Summer Sch. Arts, San Francisco Art Inst., San Francisco Arts Commission; past nat. v.p. Am./Israel Pub. Affairs Com.

SWIGER, ELINOR PORTER, lawyer; b. Cleve., Aug. 1, 1927; d. Louie Charles and Mary Isabelle (Shank) Porter; m. Quentin Gilbert Swiger, Feb. 5, 1955; children: Andrew Porter, Calvin Gilbert, Charles Robinson. BA, Ohio State U., 1949, JD, 1951. Bar: Ohio 1951, Ill. 1979. Sr. assoc. Robbins, Schwartz, Nicholas, Lifton & Taylor, Ltd., Chgo., 1979—. Author: Mexico for Kids, 1971, Europe for Young Travelers, 1972, The Law and You, 1973 (Literary Guild award), Careers in the Legal Professions, 1978, Women Lawyers at Work, 1978, Law in Everday Life, 1977. Mem. Northfield Twp. (Ill.) Bd. Edn., 1976-83; mem. Glenview (Ill.) Fire and Police Commn., 1976-86; chmn. Glenview Zoning Bd. Appeals, 1987—. Mem. ABA (chmn. pub. edn. com. urban, state and local govt. sect. 1982-85), Ill. Bar Assn. (chmn. local govt. sect. 1986-87, chmn. legal edn. sect. 1991-92), Ill. Coun. Sch. Attys. (chmn.), Women Bar Assn. Ill., Chgo. Bar Assn. (chmn. legis. exec. com. 1990-92), Soc. Midland Authors. Republican. Home: 1933 Burr Oak Dr Glenview IL 60025 Office: Robbins Schwartz Nicholas Lifton & Taylor 29 S La Salle St Ste 860 Chicago IL 60603-1505

SWIGER, ELIZABETH DAVIS, chemistry educator; b. Morgantown, W.Va., June 27, 1926; d. Hannibal Albert and Tyreeca Elizabeth (Stemple) Davis; m. William Eugene Swiger, June 2, 1948; children: Susan Elizabeth Swiger Knotts, Wayne William. BS in Chemistry, W.Va. U., 1948, MS in Chemistry, 1952, PhD in Chemistry, 1964. Instr. math. Fairmont (W.Va.) State Coll., 1948-49, instr. math. and phys. sci., 1956-57, instr. chemistry, 1957-60, asst. prof. chemistry, 1960-63, assoc. prof. chemistry, 1964-66, prof. chemistry, 1966—, chmn., div. sci., math, and health careers, 1991-92; NSF fellow rsch. W.Va. U., Morgantown, 1963-64; prof. emeritus, 1992; advisor Am. Chem. Soc. student affiliates, 1965-88. Author: Morton Family History, 1984-94, Davis-Winters Family History, 1994, Civil War Letters and Diary of Joshua Winters, 1991; contbr. articles to profl. jours. Bd. dirs. Prickett's Fort Meml. Found., Fairmont, 1988—, chmn. elect, 1990-92, chair., 1992—, Blacks Chapel Meml. Found., 1993—, rep. adv. coun. to Bd. Regents, Fairmont State Coll., Charleston, 1977-78, rep. instl. bd. advisors, Fairmont, 1990-92. NSF grantee, 1963; named Outstanding Prof. W.Va. Legislature, Charleston, 1990. Mem. Am. Chem. Soc. (sec. chmn. North W. Va. 1975, 83), W.Va. Acad. Sci. (pres. 1978-79, exec. com. edn. chmn. 1990-93), The Nature Conservancy (bd. dirs. W.Va. chpt. 1970-86, chmn. 1980-82), AAUW. Republican. Methodist. Home: 1599 Hillcrest Rd Fairmont WV 26554-4807 also: 382 Laird Dr Freeport FL 32439

SWIGERT, DONNA LEE, entrepreneur; b. Logansport, Ind., Oct. 29, 1939; d. Donald L. and Leila J. (Sweet) Kleckner; m. Philip G. Weida, 1957; children: P. Mark, Traci L., Teri L. Weida Folsom; m. Robert G. Swigert, 1989. AA in Bus. Mgmt., Saddleback Coll., 1980; BS, Calif. Coast U., 1992. Sec., bookkeeper K.L.K. Mfg. Co., Logansport, 1957-60, 63-65; sec. Sch. Edn., Mich. State U., 1962-63; sec. Sch. Fine Arts, U. Calif., Irvine, 1966-69; co-founder Plaza Vet. Clinic, Upland, Calif., 1969-70; office mgr. Bob Bondurant Sch. High Performance Driving, Ontario (Calif.) Motor Speedway, 1970-73; mgr., pub. rels. exec. Chuck Jones Racing, Costa Mesa, Calif., 1973; exec. sec. Dana Steel, Newport Beach, Calif., 1974; estimator, acct., corp. treas. Hardy & Harper, Tustin, Calif., 1975-76; contr. Gillen/Kloss Advt., Newport Beach, 1977-78; purchasing adminstr. Butler Housing, Irvine, 1979; contr. XMark Corp., Costa Mesa, 1980-81; adminstrv. mgr. Concept Devel., Costa Mesa, 1981; adminstrv. mgr., corp. sec., co-founder Persyst Inc., Irvine, Calif., 1981-83; founder, owner Numbers & Words, Irvine, 1982-84; Donna Weida Agy., 1984-85; dir. adminstrn. Data Voice Solutions, New Port Beach, 1985; co-owner Fawnview Cabins, Fawnskin, Calif., 1985-89; contr. The Keith French Group, San Clemente, Calif., 1986-87; systems coord. analyst Controls Inc., Logansport, 1987-89; founder, pres. Numbers & Words, Inc., Logansport, 1989—; founder, owner, operator DLS Properties, Logansport, 1989—. Mem. Am. Soc. Women Accts., Nat. Assn. Temporary Svcs. (Ind. chpt.), Am. Inst. Profl. Bookkeepers, Logansport C. of C. (bd. dirs.), Kiwanis (bd. dirs.), Beta Sigma Phi. Republican. Methodist. Home: 625 Lakeview Dr Logansport IN 46947-2202 Office: Numbers & Words Inc 325 Court St Logansport IN 46947-3113

SWINDLER, KATHRYN ELIZABETH, writer; b. Seattle, Nov. 8, 1947; d. Joseph Harrison Pardo and Helmi Gloria (Rantala) Dahl; m. Daris R. Swinder, Nov. 10, 1977. Student, U. Wash., 1967-71. Poet various small presses and anthologies various sml. presses, 1974—; freelance tech. writer Seattle, 1974—; mgr. publs. People's Nat. Bank, Seattle, 1978-80, Seattle First Nat. Bank, 1968-78, Seattle Trust and Savs. Bank, 1980-87; mgr. adminstrv. svcs. Key Bank of Wash., Seattle, 1987-93; writer Edmonds, Wash., 1993—; bd. dirs. Highline Community Coll. Tech. Writing Curriculum Com. Seattle; guest moderator Norwescon 15, 1992. Editor: Soc. for Tech. Communications jour., 1977-79; cons. poet, editor: Olympic View Writers Conf., Everett, Wash., 1991; author: (poetry collections) The Dark Man, 1975, The Brickbuilder, 1976 (Capital Hill Arts on Show award); author numerous poems in sml. presses, 1974—. Mem. Med. Ctr. Coun./Group Health Co-op, Seattle, 1987; vol. Puget Sound Transp. Coun., Seattle, 1989, Am. Cancer So., Seattle, 1980. Recipient award of Achievement Soc. for Tech. Communicators, 1980, award of Excellence, 1978. Mem. Sci. Fiction Poetry Assn., Acad. Am. Poets. Home: 1212 8th Ave N Edmonds WA 98020-2603

SWINGLE, JANE ELIZABETH, curator; b. St. Paul, May 26, 1964; d. Karl Frederick and Rosemary Elizabeth (McSherry) S. BA, U. Minn., 1987. Curator First Bank, Mpls., 1987—; art cons. Dorsey & Whitney Law Firm, Mpls., 1990—, Cosgrove, Flynn, Gaskins & O'Connor Law Firm, Mpls., 1990. Mem. Assn. Corp. Art Curators. Office: First Bank Visual Arts 601 2nd Ave S Minneapolis MN 55402-4301

SWIRE, EDITH WYPLER, music educator, musician, violist, violinist; b. Boston, Feb. 16, 1943; d. Alfred R. Jr. and Frances Glenn (Emery) Wypler; m. James Bennett Swire, June 11, 1965; 1 child, Elizabeth Swire-Falker. BA, Wellesley (Mass.) Coll., 1965; MFA, Sarah Lawrence Coll., Bronxville, N.Y., 1983; postgrad., Coll. of New Rochelle, 1984-85. Tchr. instrumental music, viola, violin The Windsor Sch., Boston, 1965-66; tchr., dir. The Lenox Sch., N.Y.C., 1967-76; music curriculum devel. The Nightingale-Bamford Sch., N.Y.C., 1968-69; head of fine arts dept. The Lenox Sch., N.Y.C., 1976-78, head of instrumental music, 1978-80; founder, dir., tchr. of string sch. Serpentine String Sch., Larchmont, N.Y., 1981—; mem. founding com. Inter Sch. Orch., N.Y.C., 1972, trustee, 1976—; panelist Nat. Assn. Ind. Sch. Conf., N.Y.C., 1977. Mem. music and worship com., Larchmont Ave. Ch., 1978-82, 88. Mem. Westchester Musicians Guild, N.Y. State Music Tchrs. Assn., Music Tchrs. Nat. Assn., Music Tchrs. Coun. Westchester (program com.), Violin Soc. Am., Wellesley in Westchester. Home and Office: 11 Serpentine Trl Larchmont NY 10538-2618

SWIRNOFF, LOIS, artist, educator; b. Bklyn., May 9, 1931; d. Harold and Fannie (Goldstein Swirnoff; m. Richard Boyce (dec.); 1 child, Joshua Avram; m. Jule G. Charney (div.). Cert. of graduation, Cooper Union Art Sch., N.Y.C., 1951; BFA, Yale U., 1954, MFA summa cum laude, 1956. Instr. art Wellesley (Mass.) Coll., 1954-58; asst. prof. UCLA, 1965-68, vis. lectr., 1981-86, assoc. prof., 1986-90, prof. emerita, 1990—; lectr. Harvard U., Cambridge, Mass., 1968-75; assoc. prof., chmn. art dept. Skidmore Coll., Saratoga Springs, N.Y., 1977-81; guest artist Cooper Union Art Sch., 1990-91, assoc. prof., 1992—. Author: Dimensional Color, 1989, paperback edit., 1992; solo shows include Swetzoff Gallery, Boston, Inst. Internat. Edn., N.Y.C., NAS, Washington, Farnsworth Mus., Wellesley Coll., Van Nostrand Reinhold, N.Y.; group show exhbns. including City Art Mus., St. Louis, 1951, Bklyn. Mus., 1951, Munson-Williams Proctor Inst., Utica, N.Y., 1956, Inst. Contemporary Art, Boston, 1961, La Jolla (Calif.) Mus., 1968, Los Angeles County Mus., 1968; represented in permanent collections Addison Gallery Am. Art at Andover, Wellesley Coll., Radcliffe Coll., UCLA, also pvt. collections. Recipient merit award Art Dirs. Club N.Y., 1979; Fulbright fellow, Florence, Italy, 1951-52, Yale-Norfolk summer fellow, 1953, fellow Mary I. Bunting Inst., Radcliffe Coll., 1961-63, Yaddo fellow, 1985, 86; Mellon faculty grantee Skidmore Coll., 1981, grantee Graham Found., 1988. Studio: 80 Monmouth St Brookline MA 02146 Office: Cooper Union Art Sch 41 Cooper Sq New York NY 10003

SWIT, LORETTA, actress; b. N.J., Nov. 4, 1939. Student, Am. Acad. Dramatic Arts, Gene Frankel Repertoire Theatre, N.Y.C. Broadway appearances include Same Time Next Year, Any Wednesday, Mame, The Mystery of Edwin Drood, Shirley Valentine, Chgo. (winner Sarah Siddons award 1990); films include Stand Up and Be Counted, 1972, Freebie and the Bean, 1974, Race with the Devil, 1975, S.O.B, 1980, Beer, 1985, Whoops, 1987, Apocalypse (U.K.), 1987; star TV series M*A*S*H, 1972-83 (Emmy awards for Outstanding Supporting Actress in a Comedy series 1979-81); TV movies include Shirts/Skins, 1973, The Last Day, 1975, Mirror, Mirror, 1979, Valentine, 1979, Friendships, Secrets and Lies, 1979, Cagney and Lacey, 1981, Games Mother Never Taught You, 1982, First Affair, 1983, The Execution, 1985, Dreams of Gold: The Mel Fisher Story, 1986, My Dad Can't Be Crazy, Can He?, Hell Hath No Fury, 1992, A Killer Among Friends, 1993; star on major dramatic shows and musical variety shows, including Bob Hope Christmas Special, Perry Como, The Muppets. Mem. AFTRA, Screen Actors Guild, Actors Equity.

SWITAJ, CARMEN MARIE, administrative assistant; b. Thompson Falls, Mont., Oct. 6, 1948; d. Donald L. Grende and Mary Joeda (Collogan) Brownell; m. Steven Anthony Switaj, Aug. 30, 1975; children: Stephanie Marie, Diana Lee. Grad. high sch., Whitefish, Mont. Typist to cartographers U.S. Army Topographic Command, Washington, 1970-71; sec. dept. installment loan Valley Bank, Kalispell, Mont., 1971-74; typist to civil engr. USAF, Lakeside, Mont., 1974-77; acct. Mel Dutcher, CPA, Caseville, Mich., 1979-80; customer svc. rep. Ann Arbor (Mich.) Trust, 1980-82; with dept. investments Valley Bank, Clarkston, Wash., 1984-86; office mgr. D & S Electric, Inc., Clarkston, 1986-87; mgr. ops. Sta. KLSR-TV, Eugene, Oreg., 1987-90, program dir., 1990-93; administry. asst. engring. dept. Hilton Waikoloa Village, Kamuela, Hawaii, 1994—; facilitator Sta. KLSR-TV, Eugene, 1987-92. Dist. head judge Thanks to Tchrs., Eugene, 1991-93. Mem. Nat. Assn. TV Program Execs., Mu Alpha Theta. Republican. Lutheran. Home: White Sands Vlg # 110 Kailua Kona HI 96740 Office: Hilton Waikoloa Village Engring Dept Kamuela HI 96746

SWITZER, MARY ELIZABETH, insurance account administrator; b. Concord, Calif., Aug. 1, 1954; d. Wallace Bird and Mary Josephine (Shannon) Jameson; m. Michael John Switzer, Aug. 21, 1976; children: Tobias, Nicholas. Student, Diablo Valley Coll., 1972-74, San Francisco State U., 1974-76. Cert. in gen. ins. Ins. Inst. Am., 1991. Ins. clk. Gary & Intersall, Concord, 1972-78, Met. Fed. Savs. & Loan, Seattle, 1978-79; multiline rater Travelers Ins. Co., Seattle, 1978; office mgr. St. Peters Painting, Renton, Wash., 1979-81; acct. adminstr. Sedgwick, Seattle, 1981-83, 88—; customer svc. rep. Dan B. Hauff, Renton, 1985-86, Bell-Anderson, Kent, Wash., 1986-88. Mem. com., rec. sec. ARC/Sedgwick, Seattle, 1993-94; sec. bd. dirs. Wash. chpt. Tourette Assn., Renton, 1993-94; v.p. women's bd. St. Stephen the Martyr Ch., Kent, 1983-84; mem. young women's guild, 1982-84; mem. PTSA, Renton, 1985-94. Recipient Ins. Achievement award Safeco, 1991. Mem. Ins. Women South King County (bd. dirs. 1993-94, treas., cmty. svc. chair, former safety chair), Cert. Profl. Ins. Women. Roman Catholic. Office: Sedgwick 2101 4th Ave Ste 1700 Seattle WA 98121-2344

SWOBE, CARYN COE, advertising executive; b. Reno, Oct. 10, 1960; d. Chester Coe and Janet (Quilici) S. BA in Journalism and Sports Info., U. So. Calif., 1982; postgrad. in bus. adminstrn., U. Nev., 1990—. Cert. accreditation in pub. rels. Asst. dir. news bur. Reno-Sparks C. of C., 1982-84; asst. publicist John Ascuaga's Nugget, Sparks, Nev., 1984; coord. employee communications lst Interstate Bank, Reno, 1984-87, pub. rels. officer, 1987-92; sr. account exec. R:R Advt., Reno, 1992—. Editor First Nevadan, 1984-87. Dir. Nev. Gov.'s Cup Jr. Tennis Tournament, 1987-88; bd. dirs., membership chmn. Sierra Arts Found., Reno, 1990; bd. dirs., treas. Nev. Women's Fund, Reno, 1990; sr. v.p. Jr. Achievement, 1994. Mem. Pub. Rels. Soc. Am. (bd. dirs. 1987-95, v.p. 1990), Reno Tennis Club (bd. dirs. 1983), Lakeridge Tennis Club, Beta Gamma Sigma. Republican. Methodist. Home: 1490 S Arlington Ave Reno NV 89509-2648 Office: R:R Advt 615 Riverside Dr Reno NV 89503

SWOPE, MARILYN FERN MITCHELL, mayor; b. Dresden, Ohio, Nov. 13, 1930; d. Raleigh M. and Eunice F. (Wickham) Mitchell; m. Kenneth W. Swope, July 10, 1948; children: Kenneth W., Vicki, Joan, Thomas, Martha. BS in Edn., Ohio U.; MS in Early/Mid. Childhood, Ohio State U., 1973. Cert. early and mid. childhood tchr., Ohio. Tchr. Zanesville (Ohio) City Schs., 1965-91; owner Quilt Bee; mayor City of Zanesville, 1992—; Bd. dirs. Area Labor-Mgmt. Coop. Coun., Dresden Village Assn. Advisor ACES, Zanesville; past pres. Muskingum County Women's Dem. Club, Y-City Toastmistress, Zanesville. Mem. AAUW, LWV, AARP, NOW, Ohio Edn. Assn., Older Women's League, Mayor's Assn. Ohio, Zanesville C. of C. (bd. dirs. 1992—), Ohio Mid-Eastern Govts. Assn. (bd. dirs. 1992—), Muskingum County Mayor's Assn. (chmn. 1992—). Baptist. Home: 930 Findley Ave Zanesville OH 43701 Office: City of Zanesville 401 Market St Zanesville OH 43701

SWORDS, BETTY EDGEMOND, cartoonist; b. Gilroy, Calif., Aug. 17, 1917; d. John William and Gertrude Catherine (Gahr) Edgemond; m. Henry Leonard Swords, Dec. 12, 1941; children: Richard Allen, Stephen John. BA, U. Calif., Berkeley, 1938; postgrad., Acad. Advt. Art, San Francisco, 1938-39, Fresno State Coll., 1942. Fashion illustrator The Fair, Breuners, Eastern, Sacramento, 1943; instr. U. Denver, 1976, Met. State Coll., Denver, 1977, Arapaho C.C., Littleton,Colo., 1977, U. Colo., Denver, 1985; humor book reviewr Denver Post and KBDI-TV, 1972-85; guest lectr. Nat. Confs. on Violence, Denver, 1975, 76, Federally Employed Women, San Francisco, Denver, 1975, acad., profl., social groups, radio and TV, Denver, 1970—; presenter papers on humor's power internat. confs., 1983, 85. free lance cartoonist Saturday Evening Post, Look, Redbook, Changing Times, Good Housekeeping, Ladies' Home Jour., 1955-74; humor/feature writer McCall's, Christian Sci. Monitor, Denver Post, others, 1960—; illustrator: Making the Most of Every Move, 1957; cartoonist: (Bigelow ads) The New Yorker, 1969; (calendar) Male Chauvinist Pig Calendar, 1974, 1973; author: (chpt.) New Perspectives on Women and Comedy, 1992. Precinct committeewoman Dem. Party, Denver, 1973. Mem. NOW (v.p. 1970, head media, speaker's bur. 1971-76), Colo. Women's Polit. Caucus, Denver Woman's Press Club (awards 1964-90), Colo. Author's League (v.p. 1969, awards 1964—). Home: 2490 S Holly St Denver CO 80222

SWORT, ARLOWAYNE, retired nursing educator and administrator; b. Bartlesville, Okla., Dec. 9, 1922; d. Arlington L. and Clara E. (Church) S. Diploma, St. Luke's Hosp. Sch. Nursing, Kansas City, Mo., 1944; BSN, U. Colo., 1958; MS in Nursing, Cath. U. Am., 1961; EdD, Columbia U., 1973. Dean, prof. Sch. Nursing U. Tex. Health Scis. Ctr., Houston, 1977-83, prof. nursing, 1983-85; prof., assoc. in adminstrn. Johns Hopkins U. Sch. Nursing, Balt., 1985-87; prof., assoc. dean for adminstrn. and grad. acad. affairs Johns Hopkins U. Sch. Nursing, Balt., 1987-89, sr. assoc. dean, 1990-91. Recipient numerous rsrch. grants. Mem. ANA, NLN, APHA, AAUW, Am. Assn. for History of Nursing Soc., Am. Assn. Univ. Adminstrs., Am. Assn. for Higher Edn., Am. Nurses Found.-Century Club, Am. Assn. Nurse Execs., Nat. Gerontol. Nurses Assn., Found. for Nursing of Md., Inc., Sigma Theta Tau, Kappa Delta Pi. Home: 1105 Timber Trail Rd Baltimore MD 21286-1602

SYDNEY, DORIS S., sports touring company executive, interior designer; b. N.Y.C., Feb. 18, 1934; d. Morris and Frances (Terrace) Steinman; m. Herbert P. Sydney, Oct. 20, 1957; children: Madeleine Jane, Peter Samuel. Student, Vassar Coll., 1950-52; BS, Columbia U., 1952-55; postgrad., NYU, 1956-57, N.Y. Sch. Interior Design, 1974. Cert. documentor Equitable Life Ins. Co., N.Y.C., 1955-57; researcher Fairchild Publs., N.Y.C., 1957-58; furniture sales Steinman's Inc., N.Y.C., 1958-60; interior designer, prin. Doris S. Sydney Interiors, Armonk, N.Y., 1975; exec. asst. Tennis Europe Inc., Conn., 1984—. Pres. Coman Hill Sch. PTA, 1971-72, Byram Hills High Sch. PTA, 1977-79, also chmn.; pres. Byram Hills Scholarship Fund, 1980-82, Non-partisan Nominating Com., 1982-84; coun. del. Vassar Coll. Alumni Assn., Poughkeepsie, N.Y., 1973-77; chmn. Fred Caruolo Meml. Fund, 1979-81; pres. bd. trustees North Castle Pub. Libr., 1981-90, bd. Friends North Castle Pub. Libr., 1993—; treas., pres. Armonk Hadassah, 1980—. Republican. Jewish. Home: 65 Windmill Rd Armonk NY 10504-2833

SYDNEY, LAURIN JILL, newscaster; b. N.Y.C., Aug. 6, 1956. BA in Music, Harvard U., 1978. Tchr. music North Miami, 1978-79; host Epcot Mag. Walt Disney Co., 1979-80; hostess quiz show CBS T.V., N.Y.C., 1980-81; weathercaster Sta. WXIA, Atlanta, 1981; spokesperson Showtime Network, N.Y.C., 1982-85; reporter CNN T.V., N.Y.C., 1985-88, anchor Show Biz Today; 1988—. Bd. dirs. N.Y. Host Com., N.Y.C., 1992, Greentrees, N.Y.C., 1994, Crimebusters, N.Y.C., 1994; v.p. E.S.S.A., N.Y.C., 1994; active Make A Wish Found., God's Littlest Angels. Recipient ACE award-T.V. Assn. Cable Executives, 1984, Cambridge Honors, Cambridge Civic Soc., 1978, award CEBA, 1991; fellow John J. McCabe fellow CEBA, 1990. Mem. AFTRA, SAG, Am. Found. AIDS Rsch., Am. Cancer Soc., Am. Heart Assn., Women in Cable. Office: CNN Showbiz Today 5 Penn Plaza 20th Fl New York NY 10001

SYENS, JODI SUE, city official; b. Holland, Mich., July 20, 1953; d. Norman Jay and Shirley Jean (Koning) Japinga; m. Marvin Gene Syens, Aug. 10, 1974; 1 child, Rachel. BA, Hope Coll., Holland, 1975; MPPA, U. Wis., 1978. Cert. mcpl. clk., 1994. Adminstrv. aide City of Holland, 1975-77, 79-80, asst. city mgr., 1980-90, asst. city mgr./city clk., 1990-92, city clk./asst. to the city mgr., 1992—; adminstrv. aide Dept. Health and Social Svcs., State of Wis., Madison, 1978. Dir. Ottawa County Devel. Co., Holland, 1985—; sec. Cable TV Adv. Commn., Holland, 1980—; campaign vol. coord. Greater Holland United Way, 1991. Mem. Internat. City Mgmt. Assn., Mich. City Mgmt. Assn. (dir. 1989-91), Internat. Inst. Mcpl. Clks., Mich. Mcpl. Clks. Assn., Rotary (program chair 1993-94). Ref. Ch. in Am. Office: City of Holland 270 S River Ave Holland MI 49423-3230

SYLKE, LORETTA CLARA, artist; b. Parkston, S.D., Nov. 4, 1926; d. Jacob and Maria Magdelin (Frey) Sprecher; m. Arthur C. Sylke, Apr. 26, 1961; children: Michael Arthur, Patricia, Constance, Sharon, Catherine, Charles (dec.). Grad. H.S., Chgo. Represented by Becca Gallery Berlin, Wis. Works have appeared at N.Mex. Art League, Albuquerque, 1991, El Dorado Gallery, Colorado Springs, Mont. Miniature Show, Billings, The New Eng. Fine Art Inst., The N.E. Trade Ctr., Woburn, Mass., 1993, El Dorado Gallery, Colorado Springs, 1993, others. Recipient Masco award Madison (Wis.) Art Supply, 1982. Mem. Nat. Mus. of Women in the Arts, Soc. Exptl. Artists. Home: N4392 Wicks Landing Rd Princeton WI 54968 Office: 1714 Studio Princeton WI 54968

SYLVESTER, NANCY KATHERINE, speech educator, management consultant; b. Evansville, Ind., July 17, 1947; d. Leonard Nicholas and Marjoire (Moore) Jochim; m. James Andrew Sylvester, Aug. 21, 1971; children: Marcy Dee, Holly Nicole. BS, Ind. State U., 1969; MA, U. Mich., 1970. Registered profl. parliamentarian; cert. prof. parliamentarian; team/meeting mgmt. specialist. Assoc. prof. speech Rock Valley Coll., Rockford, Ill., 1970—. Author: Basics of Parliamentory Procedure, 1983, Handbook for Effective Meetings, 1993; contbr. articles to profl. jours. Bd. dirs. Jr. League Rockford, 1974-78, Rock River coun. Girl Scouts U.S., 1979-81, Rock River Homeowners Assn., 1990-91; pres. Children's Devel. Ctr. Aux. Bd., Rockford, 1984-85; parliamentarian Winnebago County Dem. Caucus, 1991; vice-chmn. Commn. on Am. Parliamentary Practice, 1989-90, chmn., 1990-91. Recipient Jardene medal Inst. State U., 1969, RVC Faculty of Yr. award, 1994; Rackham scholar U. Mich., 1969-70. Mem. Am. Inst. Parliamentarians, Am. Soc. Women Accts. (parliamentarian 1980—), Am. Women Soc. CPAs (parliamentarian 1991—), Nat. Coun. State Bds. Nursing (parliamentarian 1992—), Ill. Assn. Parliamentarians, Nat. Assn. Ins. Women (parliamentarian 1983-91), Nat. Assn. Parliamentarians, Assn. Quality and Participation, Speech Comm. Assn., Coun. Better Bus. Burs. (parliamentarian 1993), Rockford C. of C. (ex-officio bd. dirs.), Phi Rho Pi (Region 4 v.p. 1972-73, nat. v.p. 1973-74). Roman Catholic. Home: 4826 River Bluff Ct Rockford IL 61111-5836

SYMCHOWICZ-LIPPER, BEATRICE ANITA, radiologist; b. Orange, N.J., Dec. 6, 1958; d. Samson and Sarah Rachel (Nussbaum) Symchowicz; m. Jeffrey Mark Lipper, Dec. 14, 1986; children: Jaimie Shira, Seth Joseph, Erica Amanda. BA in Biology and Psychology with honors, SUNY, Binghamton, 1980; MD, Sackler Sch. Medicine, Tel Aviv, 1984. Diplomate Am. Bd. Radiology. Intern in pediatrics Northshore U. Hosp., Manhasset, N.Y., 1984-85; resident in radiology Overlook Hosp., Summit, N.J., 1985-89, chief resident, 1987-88, 88-89; assoc. Freehold (N.J.) Radiology Group, 1989—. Co-author: Pharmacology, Biochemistry & Behavior, 1981. Mem. Am. Coll. Radiology, Radiol. Soc. N.Am., Ocean County Med. Soc., N.J. Med. Soc. Home: 1634 McLean Ct Toms River NJ 08755 Office: Freehold Radiology Group 1001 W Main St Ste C Freehold NJ 07728

SYMENS, MAXINE CORRINE, restaurant owner; b. Primghar, Iowa, June 12, 1930; d. George Herman and Irene Marie (Dahnke) Brinkert; m. Jack Frederiksen Tanner, Dec. 28, 1950 (dec. Oct. 1976); m. Delbert Glenn Symens, Sept. 26, 1981. BS magna cum laude, Westmar Coll., 1970. Cert. tchr., Iowa. Elem. tchr. Rural Sch. O'Brien Co., Primghar, 1949-54, Gaza (Iowa) Com. Sch., 1954-60; secondary tchr. Primghar Com. Sch., 1960-81; fitness salon owner Slim 'N' Trim, George, Rock Rapids, Iowa, 1982-87; restaurant owner George Cafe, 1985-90, Pizza Ranch, 1988—. Pres. Primghar Edn. Assn., 1970-71. Mem. George C. of C., George Kiwanis Club (sec. 1991—), Delta Kappa Gamma. Lutheran. Home: 307 Dell St NE George IA 51237-1030

SYMONDS, JOHNNIE PIRKLE, retired pscyhologist; b. Wynnewood, Okla., Apr. 5, 1900; d. John Thomas and Lillie Belle (Driver) Pirkle; m. Percival Mallon Symonds, Dec. 25, 1922. BA, U. Tex., 1920, MA, 1921; postgrad. Columbia U., 1921-22, 26-27, 28-29, 30-31, NYU, 1975. Asst. dept. psychology U. Tex., Austin, 1919-21; rsch. assoc. Inst. Ednl. Rsch. Tchrs. Coll. Columbia U., N.Y.C., 1921-22; psychologist Family Svc. Soc., Yonkers, N.Y., 1937-46; ret., 1960. Editor: Jour. Cons. Psychology, 1937-47; contbr. articles to profl. jours. Mem. Columbia Com. for Community Svc., 1972—; active English in action program, English speaking union Riverside Ch., N.Y.C., 1974-75, honored 50th anniversary mem., 1979. Named disting. grad. Tchrs. Coll. Columbia U. Trustees, 1990. Mem. AAAS, AAUW, APA, N.Y. Acad. of Sci., N.Y. State Psychol. Assn., Am. Assn. Applied Psychology, Ednl. Press Assn., World Fedn. Mental Health, Pi Lambda Theta, Kappa Delta Pi, Appalachian Mountain Club (Honor award 50th anniversary mem. 1981). Home: 106 Morningside Dr Apt 71 New York NY 10027-6011

SYMS, HELEN MAKSYM, educator; b. Wilkes Barre, Pa., Nov. 12, 1918; d. Walter and Anna (Kowalewski) Maksym; m. Louis Harold Syms, Aug. 16, 1947; children: Harold Edward, Robert Louis. BA, Hunter Coll., 1941; MS, Columbia U., 1947; teaching credentials, Calif. State U., Northridge, 1964. Statis. clk. McGraw Hill Pub. Co., N.Y.C., 1941-42; acct. Flexpansion Corp., N.Y.C., 1943-47, Oliver Wellington & Co., N.Y.C., 1947-48, Broadcast Measurement Bur., N.Y.C., 1948-51; tchr. Calif. State U., Northridge, 1964, Burbank (Calif.) Unified Sch. Dist., 1964-79; chmn. bus. edn. dept. Burbank High Sch., 1974-79; docent, acct. arts coun. Calif. State U., Northridge, 1979—; tchr. M.E.N.D. (Meet Each Need with Dignity) Learning Ctr., Pacoima, Calif., 1987-89, assoc. dir., 1989—. Mem. Phi Beta Kappa, Delta Kappa Gamma (pres. 1972-74, treas. Xi chpt. 1982-90, treas. area IX 1975-78). Home: 9219 Whitaker Ave Northridge CA 91343-3538 Office: MEND 13460 Van Nuys Blvd Pacoima CA 91331-3058

SYNNOTT, MARCIA GRAHAM, history educator; b. Camden, N.J., July 4, 1939; d. Thomas Whitney and Beatrice Adelaide (Colby) S.; m. William

Edwin Sharp, June 16, 1979; children: Willard William Sharp, Laurel Beth Sharp. AB, Radcliffe Coll., 1961; MA, Brown U., 1964; PhD, U. Mass., 1974. History tchr. MacDuffie Sch., Springfield, Mass., 1963-68; instr. U. S.C., Columbia, 1972-74, asst. prof., 1974-79, assoc. prof. history, 1979—, dir. grad. studies history dept., 1990-92. Author: The Half-Opened Door, 1979; contbr. essays to books. Fulbright scholar, 1988; Am. Coun. Learned Socs. grantee, 1981. Mem. Am. Hist. Assn., So. Hist. Assn., Orgn. Am. Historians (membership com. 1990-93). Office: U SC Dept History Columbia SC 29208

SYPHERS, MARY FRANCES, music educator; b. Floresville, Tex., Sept. 26, 1912; d. Little Fleming and Lillian Frances (Herrington) Spruce; m. Ansel James Syphers, July 23, 1959 (dec. 1972). BA in English, U. Tex., 1938; MEd, So. Meth. U., Dallas, 1950; studied voice with Dr. Wilcox, 1947, studied composition with Roy Harris, 1947. Cert. high sch. music tchr., cert. elem. tchr., Tex. Tchr. music Ehlers Country Sch., Poth, Tex., 1931-35, Poth Ind. Sch. Dist., 1936-40, Sinton (Tex.) Ind. Sch. Dist., 1941, Stephen J. Hay Sch., Dallas, 1942-50, Alamo Sch., Dallas, 1951—, Edwin J. Kiest Sch., Dallas, 1955—, Lakewood Elem., Dallas, 1976-81; voice, drama tchr. Poth Ind. Sch. dist., 1936-40. Contbg. author: New England To Texas, 1986. Choir dir. 1st Meth. Ch., Sinton, Tex., 1941-42; soloist, jr. choir dir. Oaklawn Meth. Ch., Dallas, 1942-43; soloist 1st Presbyn. Ch., Dallas, 1943-46, Highland Park Presbyn. Ch., Dallas, 1946-47; symphony chorus Dallas Music Staff, 1944-60; mem. choir St. Michael and All Angels Episocpal Ch., Dallas, 1949-91; organizer jr. female vols. USO, Dallas, 1960-70, coordinator jr. female vols. anniversary celebration, Dallas, 1966; mem. publicity com. So. Meml. Assn., Dallas, 1981; life mem. PTA; mem. Shakespeare Study Club. Recipient Citation as member of concert choir Am. Culture and Lang. Ctr., Salzburg, Austria, 1987. Mem. New Eng. Women (pres. Tex. chpt. 1985-87), Dallas Coun. World Affairs, Dallas Inst. Humanities (sponsor), Buckland Hist. Soc. (life), Nat. Soc. Colonial Dames (chmn. 1981-90), DAR (Jane Douglas chpt.), Standard Club Dallas (recreation sec. 1981-91), Delta Kappa Gamma (Epsilon chpt.). Republican. Episcopalian. Home: 5106 Stanford Ave Dallas TX 75209-3322

SYRETT, ELENA FRANGAKIS, history educator; b. Assiout, Egypt, June 11, 1954; came to U.S., 1985; d. Stephen Anthony and Catherine (Ioannou) Frangakis; m. David Syrett, July 10, 1986. BA in Modern History with honors, London U., 1976, PhD in Econ. History, 1985. Lectr. Inner London Ednl. Authority Insts., Kensington, Marylebone, 1977-79; rsch. asst. geography dept. Southampton U., Eng., 1979-81; asst. prof. history dept. CUNY, 1985-90, assoc. prof. history dept., 1991—. Author: The Commerce of Smyrna in the Eighteenth Century, 1700-1820, 1992; contbr. numerous articles, notes, revs. and papers to profl. jours. Recipient PSC-CUNY Rsch. award, 1991-92, 92-93, 93-94, 94-95, NEH Travel to Collections grant, 1992, Faculty in Residence award CUNY, 1986-87, 89-90, 94—, Agrl. Bank of Greece Rsch. grant, 1984-85, Ronald Burrows studentship, London U., 1983-84, French Govt. Rsch. scholarship, 1981-82, Ronald Burrows Meml. prize, London U., 1976-79. Home: 329 Sylvan Ave Leonia NJ 07605-2026 Office: Queens Coll CUNY History Dept 65-30 Kissena Blvd Flushing NY 11367-0704

SYTEK, DONNA P., state legislator; b. Haverhill, Mass., Dec. 14, 1944; m. John Sytek; 1 child. AB, Regis Coll., 1966, MA. Mem. rules com., chmn. corrections & criminal justice com. N.H. State Senate, Concord; chmn. N.H. Rep. Com., 1982-84; pres. Nat. Rep. Legislators Assn., 1992-93; del. to Rep. Nat. Conv., 1980, 84, 88, 84 Const. Conv., Assembly on the Legislature, chmn., 1991-92; mem. exec. com. NCSL, 1990—, Coun. State Govt., 1989-92. Mem. Salem-BPW Club (pres. 1978-79), Crimeline (bd. dirs. 1985—), Dist. Nursing Assn. (bd. dirs. 1989—), Boys and Girls Club (bd. dirs. 1989—). Roman Catholic. Home: 9 Garrison Rd Salem NH 03079-3911 Office: NH State Senate State Capital Concord NH 03301*

SZANTAI, LINDA MARIE, speech and language therapist; b. Phila., Dec. 21, 1957; d. Richard George Reckeweg and Eileen Theresa (Wrenn) Renders; m. Paul Matthew Vidunas, July 22, 1978 (div. Dec. 1987); m. Stephen Michael Szantai, Sept. 16, 1989. BS, Trenton State Coll., 1986. Cert. in speech correction, N.J. Speech/lang. therapist Dept. Corrections, State of N.J., Skillman, 1986-89, Ventnor (N.J.) Sch. Dist., 1989—, Port Republic (N.J.) Sch., 1989-92. Mem. Kappa Delta Pi (pres. Greater Trenton chpt. 1985-86, recognition award 1986), Phi Kappa Phi (Outstanding Freshman Achievement award 1983).

SZARO, JUDITH SALOMEA, advertising executive, artist, political worker; b. Elizabeth, N.J., Aug. 2, 1952; d. Albert Stanley and Mary Stella (Turon) S. BA, Douglass Coll., 1974; MBA, Rutgers U., 1989; cert. in art, Albert Pels Sch. Art, 1980. Mktg. researcher Phila. Mftr. Mut. Ins. Co., N.Y.C., 1976-78; advt. bd. artist Spiros Assocs., N.Y.C., 1980-82; freelance comml. artist, polit. fundraiser N.J., 1982-85; advt. exec. Grey Advt., Inc., N.Y.C., 1985-91; mktg. mgr. Western Industries, Inc., Parsippany, N.J., 1991—. Corr. sec. Greater Elizabeth Dem. Club, Union County, N.J., 1982-85; local fundraiser, campaign promoter Raymond J. Lesniak for N.J. State Senator, 1982-85, fin. sec., 1982-85. Democrat. Roman Catholic. Office: Western Industries Inc 30 Lanidex Plz W Parsippany NJ 07054-2717

SZCZECHOWICZ, GRETCHEN, medical surgical nurse; b. Middletown, Conn., Apr. 13, 1939; d. Norman and Ellen G. (Green) Wilson; m. Fred Szczechowicz, Oct. 3, 1968; 1 child, Christopher. Diploma, Salem Hosp. Sch. Nursing, 1959; student, Boston U., Emmanuel Coll., St. Joseph's Coll. Cert. coll. health nurse, ANCC. Staff nurse Salem Hosp., Mass., supr., med. surg.; health svc. coord. Salem State Coll., Mass. Recipient Mass. Commonwealth Citation for Outstanding Performance, Merit awards. Mem. APHA, Am. Coll. Health Assocs., New Eng. Coll. Health Assn.

SZEGO, CLARA MARIAN, cell biologist, educator; b. Budapest, Hungary, Mar. 23, 1916; came to U.S., 1921, naturalized, 1927; d. Paul S. and Helen (Elek) S.; m. Sidney Roberts, Sept. 14, 1943. A.B., Hunter Coll., 1937; M.S. (Garvan fellow), U. Minn., 1939, Ph.D., 1942. Instr. physiology U. Minn., 1942-43; Minn. Cancer Research Inst. fellow, 1943-44; rsch. assoc. OSRD, Nat. Bur. Standards, 1944-45, Worcester Found. Exptl. Biology, 1945-47; rsch. instr. physiol. chemistry Yale U. Sch. Medicine, 1947-48; mem. faculty UCLA, 1948—, prof. biology, 1960—. Named Woman of Year in Sci. Los Angeles Times, 1957-58; Guggenheim fellow, 1956; named to Hunter Coll. Hall of Fame, 1987. Fellow AAAS; mem. Am. Physiol. Soc., Am. Soc. Cell Biology, Endocrine Soc. (CIBA award 1953), Soc. for Endocrinology (Gt. Britain), Biochem. Soc. (Gt. Britain), Internat. Soc. Rsch. Reprodn., Phi Beta Kappa (pres. UCLA chpt. 1973-74), Sigma Xi (pres. UCLA chpt. 1976-77). Home: 1371 Marinette Rd Pacific Palisades CA 90272-2627 Office: U Calif Dept Biology Los Angeles CA 90024-1606

SZEKERES, AGNES VERONICA, endocrinologist; b. Budapest, Hungary, June 14, 1942; came to U.S., 1966; d. Jozsef and Maria (Szalai) Gervai; m. Gabor Laszlo Szekeres, Sept. 4, 1966; children: David Leslie, Jeffrey Philip. Med. Technologist, Fodor Jozsef Sch., Budapest, 1962; BS, Semmelweis Med. Sch., Budapest, 1966; MD, SUNY, Buffalo, 1970. Diplomate Am. Bd. Internal Medicine, Am. Bd. Endocrinology, Am. Bd. Geriatrics. Intern Buffalo Gen. Hosp., 1970-71; resident in internal medicine Orange County Med. Ctr., Orange, Calif., 1971-73; fellow in endocrinology U. Calif. Med. Ctr., Orange, 1980-82; mem. staff Kaiser Permanente Med. Group, Bellflower, Calif., 1973-80, So. Calif. Permanente Med. Group, Bellflower, Calif., 1982—; vol. attending staff U. Calif. Med. Ctr., Orange, 1974—. Mem. ACP. Democrat. Jewish. Home: 18082 Dorchester Cir Villa Park CA 92667-4502 Office: 12500 Hoxie Ave Norwalk CA 90650

SZEREMETA-BROWAR, TAISA LYDIA, endodontist; b. Geneva, N.Y., Mar. 21, 1957; d. Swiatoslaw Bohdan and Stefania (Melnyk) Szeremeta; m. Andrew Wolodymyr Browar, Sept. 19, 1981. BS in Dentistry, Case Western Res. U., 1978, DDS, 1980; cert. specialty endodontics magna cum laude, U. Ill., Chgo., 1982. Pvt. practice Hinsdale (Ill.) Periodontics and Endodontics, 1982—; asst. clin. prof. Northwestern U. Dental Sch., Chgo., 1986—. Counselor, mem. Plast-Ukrainian Scouting, 1963—; presenting team Worldwide Marriage Encounter, Chgo., 1985-94; mem. parish coun. Sts. Volodymyr and Olha, Chgo., 1985-94. E. Wach rsch. grantee U. Ill., Chgo., 1980. Mem. ADA, Am. Assn. Endodontists, Am. Coll. Stomatologic Surgeons, Ukrainian Med. Assn. (chair membership 1983-88), Ill. Assn. Endodontists (pres. 1990-91), Ill. State Dental Soc., Chgo. Dental Soc. (sec. table clinic 1990, vice chair 1991, chair 1992), Hinsdale C. of C. Ukrainian Catholic. Office: Hinsdale Periodontics and Endodontics 40 S Clay St Ste 111W Hinsdale IL 60521-3257

SZIGETHY, NANCY SUE, accountant; b. Dallas, May 7, 1968; d. John William and Judy Ann (Jones) Smith; m. Stephen Michael Szigethy, May 18, 1991. AA, North Harris Coll., 1992; student, U. Houston, 1990-91, 92-93. Tax acct. Stewart & Stevenson, Houston, 1987-93; clk. cash receipts Reiss Media Enterprises, Englewood, Colo., 1994—. Mem. Inst. Mgmt. Accts. (dir. attendence 1988-93, award for 100% attendence 1988, 90, 92). Home: 11458 Settlers Dr Parker CO 80134

SZIGETI, MICHELLE MARIE, critical care nurse; b. South Bend, Ind., Mar. 21, 1954; d. Eugene Peter and Patricia Joyce (May) S. RN, Meml. Hosp., South Bend, 1976; BS, St. Francis Coll., Joliet, Ill., 1990. Cert. critical care nurse. Charge nurse cardiac intermediate care Meml. Hosp., South Bend, 1976-83, charge nurse cardio vascular intensive care, 1983—; tchr. cardiovasular intensive care Meml. Hosp. of South Bend, 1991—. Mem. AACN. Home: 112 S Mccombs St South Bend IN 46637-3330

SZILAGYI, SHERRY ANN, psychotherapist, paralegal; b. Cheverly, Md.; d. John Alex and Mary Ann (Mazzola) S. BA in Edn.-Social Work Psychology magna cum laude, U. Md., Catonsville, 1989; MSW summa cum laude, U. Md., Balt., 1990, postgrad., 1991—. Lic. cert. social worker, clin.; cert. health ins. analyst; lic. child rights advocate, daycare provider, Md. Dir. Teen and Community Ctr., Crofton, Md., 1987-89; social worker Dept. Social Svcs. and Child Protection, Hyattsville, Md., 1988-89; clin. therapist Mental Health Ctr., Annapolis, Md., 1989-90; pvt. practice, Columbia, 1990—; clin. therapist Sexual Assault Crisis Ctr., Annapolis, Md., 1990—; tutor, rschr. U.Md., College Park, 1989—; comty. chair Balt. Domestic Violence Advocacy Project, 1994—. Scholar State of Md., 1988. Mem. ABA, APA, AACD, NASW, NOW, Women's Bar Assn., Psi Chi, Phi Kappa Phi. Office: ACPC Ste B 6535 Huntshire Dr Baltimore MD 21227-6165

SZPORN, RENEE MARLA, religious studies educator; b. N.Y.C., Sept. 6, 1956; d. Bernard and Charlotte Lee (Kustich) Siegal; m. Michael Szporn, Oct. 12, 1980; 1 child, Ari David. BA in Music with honors, CCNY, 1977; postgrad., Pa. State U., 1977-78, NYU, 1978-82. Cert. tchr. Credit analyst Lord & Taylor, N.Y.C., 1975-77; instr. Pa. State U., Univ. Park, 1977-78; estimator Medicus Communications, N.Y.C., 1978-80; fin. coord. Sudler & Hennessey, N.Y.C., 1980-87; tchr. Beth El Synagogue, 1988-90, Temple Beth Shalom, Manalapan, N.J., 1990—. Mem. Nat. C. of C. for Women, Am. Philatelic Soc., Soc. Israel Philatelists, CCNY Alumni Assn. Republican.

SZRAMA, LUCY THERESA, financial executive; b. Buffalo, Sept. 10, 1938; d. John Jerome and Victoria Appelonia (Gielinski) Mikulski; m. Bernard Leo Szrama, Aug. 9, 1958; children: Elaine Szrama Moore, Peter, James. With Erie County Dept. Health, Buffalo, 1956-61, Cheektowaga (N.Y.) Libr. Bd., 1966-73; CCD coord. Our Lady Help of Christians Parish, Cheektowaga, 1973-74; bus. mgr. R. Chmiel DDS, A. Shapiro DDS, Cheektowaga, 1974-84; reimbursement coord. Am. ContinueCare, Amherst, N.Y., 1984; reimbursement specialist Caremark, Amherst, 1985; reimbursement mgr. Caremark Homecare, Amherst, 1988-93; br. mgr. Advanced Home Care of W. N.Y., 1993—; area reimbursement liaison Caremark, 1994—. Past pres. and other offices Chapel Parents Guild, Buffalo; counselor Boy Scouts Am. 1973-84, cons. Maryvale Dist. on Bus. Reorgn., Cheektowaga, 1980; eucharistic minister Our Lady Help of Christians. Recipient Caremark Cornerstone award, Master Performer, 1989-92. Mem. NAFE, Cheektowaga Hist. Soc., Polish Nat. Alliance. Office: Caremark 375 N French Rd Buffalo NY 14228-2009

SZTO, MARY CHRISTINE, law educator; b. N.Y.C., Oct. 12, 1960; d. Paul Chu-Hsuen and Clarice Mui-jung (Huang) S. BA in English, Wellesley Coll., 1981; postgrad., Chinese U., Hong Kong, 1981-82; MA in Religion, Westminster Sem., 1983; JD, Columbia U., 1986. Bar: N.Y. 1987. Atty. Citibank, N.Y.C., 1989-92; chmn. Jubilee Legal Svcs., N.Y.C., 1990-93; assoc. prof. law Pepperdine U. Sch. of Law, Malibu, Calif., 1994—. Atty. del. Christian Reformed Ch. World Relief Com., 1993—. Rotary fellow, 1981-82. Mem. Christian Legal Soc. (bd. dirs. 1989—). Office: Pepperdine Law Sch 24255 Pacific Coast Hwy Malibu CA 90263

SZWED, BERYL J., school system administrator, mathematics educator; b. Bklyn., Mar. 21, 1948; d. Jules and Bertha (Dlugash) Cooper; m. Joseph Szwed, May 28, 1970; children: Nissa, Rory, Joshua. BS in Elem. Edn., SUNY, Cortland, 1970; MS in Guidance, Counseling, Tex. A and I U., 1973; postgrad, SUNY, Oswego; postgrad., U. N.H. Cert. elem. tchr. K-6 perm., Math. secondary 7-12. Guidance counselor, test dist. coord. Cato-Meridian Sch. Dist., N.Y.; test administr. Fed. Correctional Inst., Raybrook, N.Y.; remedial Math. specialist, cons. Lake Placid (N.Y.) Schs.; adj. instr. math. North Country C.C., Saranac Lake, N.Y.; math. cons.; coordinating mentor N.Y. State Elem. Math. Mentors; mem. Mid. Sch. MATHLINE. Editor (newsletter to parents); creator Pamper Your Child With Math program; contbr. rsch. to profl. jours.; presenter workshops in field. Area staff devel. com., vice chmn. Instructional TV Sch. Svc. com. WCFE, Plattsburgh, N.Y.; coord., chmn. scholarship com. Adirondack Festival Am. Music; sec., grant writer Adirondack Singers; chair Messiah Sing-In; sec. Town Hall Players; co-chair Saranac Lake Winter Carnival Skating Race. Grantee Adirondack Tchr. Ctr., 1988, 89, NYSACE, 1989, Mathematics into the 21st Century, 1990, NSF Leadership Network, 1991-93. Mem. ASCD (assoc.), Nat. Coun. Tchrs. Math., N.Y. State Assn. Math. Suprs., Assn. Math. Tchrs. N.Y. State (Essex County chmn., Hamilton County chmn., elem. rep. exec. bd., rec. sec., presenter various functions), N.Y. State Assn. Compensatory Educators, Delta Kappa Gamma (treas. Beta Mu chpt.). Home: 64 Riverside Dr Saranac Lake NY 12983-2319

SZYMANSKI, EDNA MORA, rehabilitation psychology and special education educator; b. Caracas, Venezuela, Mar. 19, 1952; came to U.S., 1952; d. José Angel and Helen Adele (McHugh) Mora; m. Michael Bernard, Mar. 30, 1973. BS, Rensselaer Poly. Inst., 1972; MS, U. Scranton, 1974; PhD, U. Tex., 1988. Cert. rehab. counselor. Vocat. evaluator Mohawk Valley Workshop, Utica, N.Y., 1974-75; vocat. rehab. counselor N.Y. State Office Vocat. Rehab., Utica, N.Y., 1975-80; sr. vocat. rehab. counselor N.Y. State Office Vocat. Rehab., Utica, 1980-87; rsch. assoc. U. Tex., Austin, 1988-89; asst. prof. U. Wis., Madison, 1989-91, assoc. prof., 1991-93, assoc. dean sch. edn., 1993—, dir. rehab. rsch. and tng. ctr., 1993—, prof. rehab. psychology and spl. edn., 1993—; cons. Rsch. Assocs. Syracuse, N.Y., 1988-90. Co-author various book chpts.; co-editor: Rehabilitation Counseling Basics and Beyond, 1992; co-editor bull. Rehab. Counseling, 1994—; contbr. numerous articles to profl. jours. Mem. Pres.'s Com. on Employment of People with Disabilities, Washington, 1987—. Recipient Rsch. awards Am. Assn. for Counseling and Devel., 1990, Am. Assn. Counselor Edn. and Supr., 1991; named Rehab. Edn. Rschr. of Yr., Nat. Coun. Rehab. Edn., 1993. Mem. ACA (chair rsch. com. 1992-94, Rsch. award 1993), Am. Rehab. Counseling Assn. (pres. 1985-86, Rsch. award 1989), Coun. on Rehab. Edn. (chair rsch. com. 1990—, v.p. 1993—). Office: U Wis Dept Rehab Psychology and Spl Edn 432 N Murray St Madison WI 53706

SZYMANSKI, JOYCE ANN, publicist; b. Oak Lawn, Ill., Aug. 25, 1964; d. Donald Daniel and Sylvia Ann (Grzyb) S. BA in Comm., Wash. State U., 1986. Reporter West Seattle Herald, Seattle, 1986; asst. cmty. rels. Seattle Mariners, 1980-86; intern pub. rels. Seattle Super Sonics, 1986-87; asst. media svcs. Chgo. Bulls, 1987-94; dir. pub. rels. Harlem Globetrotters, Alhambra, Calif., 1994—. Mem. Women Comm. Office: Harlem Globetrotters 1000 S Fremont Ave Alhambra CA 91803-1349

SZYMONIAK, ELAINE EISFELDER, state senator; b. Boscobel, Wis., May 24, 1920; d. Hugo Adolph and Pauline (Vig) Eisfelder; Casimir Donald Szymoniak, Dec. 7, 1943; children: Kathryn, Peter, John, Mary, Thomas. BS, U. Wis., 1941; MS, Iowa State U., 1977. Speech clinician Waukesha (Wis.) Pub. Sch., 1941-43, Rochester (N.Y.) Pub. Sch., 1943-44; rehab. aide U.S. Army, Chickasha, Okla., 1944-46; audiologist U. Wis., Madison, 1946-48; speech clinician Buffalo Pub. Sch., 1948-49, Sch. for Handicapped, Salina, Kans., 1951-52; speech pathologist, audiologist, counselor, resource mgr. Vocat. Rehab. State Iowa, Des Moines, 1956-85; mem. Iowa Senate, Des Moines, 1989—. Mem. Des Moines City Coun., 1978-88; bd. dirs. Nat. League Cities, Washington, 1982-84, Girl Scouts U.S., Civic Ctr., House of Mercy, Westminster House, Iowa Leadership Consortium, Coun. on Internat. Understanding, Iowa Commn. on Status of Women, Young Women's Christian Assn.; chairperson Greater Des Moines Coun. for Internat. Understanding, United Way, 1987-88. Named Woman of Achievement YWCA, 1982, Visionary Woman, Young Women's Resource Ctr. Mem. Am. Speech Lang. and Hearing Assn., Iowa Speech Lang. and Hearing Assn. (pres. 1977-78), Nat. Coun. State Legislators, Women's Polit. Caucus, Nexus (pres. 1981-82). Home: 2116 44th St Des Moines IA 50310-3011 Office: State Senate State Capitol Des Moines IA 50319

TABANDERA, KATHLYNN ROSEMARY, secondary education educator; b. Honolulu, Aug. 6, 1960; d. William Fernandez and Sakae Sandra (Shibata) Rosa; m. Russell Takao Tabandera, Dec. 24, 1979 (separated); children: Tiffany Nohelani, Christine Lei, Angela Nani, Nicole Ku'ulei, Ricky William Kanaina. BA in Psychology, U. Hawaii, Hilo, 1988, BA in Econs., 1988, BBA in Bus. Adminstrn., 1988, Tchr. Edn. Program, 1988, Profl. Edn. Program, 1989, Natural Sci. Certificate Program, 1994. Profl. cert. secondary educator, Hawaii. Adminstr. Tabandera Fishing Co., Hilo, Hawaii, 1980-85; realtor assoc. Ala Kai Realty Inc., Hilo, Hawaii, 1985—; owner Tracks Enterprises, Hilo, Hawaii, 1985—; tchr. Kohala High Sch. Alternative Learning Ctr., 1989-91; social studies tchr. Honoka'a High Sch., 1991-92; real estate appraiser Hilo, 1992; tchr. Hilo High Sch. Alternative Learning Ctr., 1992-94, Waiakea High Sch., 1994—; mentor, tutor Kamehameha Schs. Talent Search, 1993-94. Named to Dean's List, U. Hawaii, 1985-88. Mem. AAUW, NEA, NAFE, Am. Soc. Profl. Appraisers, Hawaii Island Bd. Realtors, Hawaii Assn. Realtors, Nat. Assn. Realtors, Hawaii State Tchrs. Assn., Assn. Supervision and Curriculum Devel., Adminstrn. of Justice.

TABER, CAROL A., magazine publisher. AA, Green Mountain Coll., 1965. Network mgr. Media Networks, Inc., 1970-74; N.Y. advt. mgr. Ladies' Home Jour., 1974-79; assoc. pub., advt. dir. Working Woman, N.Y.C., 1979-83, pub., 1984-94; pub. Working Mother, N.Y.C., 1994—; exec. v.p., group pub. Working Woman and Working Mother mags., 1989. Office: Working Mother 230 Park Ave 7th fl New York NY 10169*

TABLER, SHIRLEY MAY, retired librarian, artist; b. Washington, Mar. 18, 1936; d. Howard Leon and Ella May (Miles) Bosley; m. Edward Charles Sepelak, July 30, 1954 (div. 1965); children: David Edward, Linda May, William Bryan; m. Carlton Byard Tabler, June 27, 1968 (dec. May 1993); stepchildren: Roger Byard, Charlotte Virginia. BS in Art Edn., U. Md., 1977, BA in Libr. Sci., 1978, MA in Art Edn., 1981, MLS, 1990. Sec. Nat. Capital Housing Authority, Washington, 1954-55; clk. Vitro Corp., Silver Spring, Md., 1956-57; hostess, cashier Hot Shoppes, Wheaton, Md., 1960-63; new accounts sec. State Nat. Bank, Bethesda, Md., 1966-68; media aide, art tchr. Montgomery County Pub. Schs., Rockville, Md., 1968-86, libr., cataloguer, computer tech., 1986-93. Exhibited works in numerous group shows including Arts Club, Washington, 1990, 91, 92, 93, Rockville Mcpl. Gallery, 1992, 93, Sugar & Fricht Gallery, 1994, Ten Oaks Gallery-Clarksville, 1994, Town Ctr. Gallery, 1994; exhibited works in numerous one-person shows including Rockville Mcpl. Gallery, 1989, Landon Gallery, Bethesda, Md., 1990, Washington Printmakers Gallery, 1994. Leader, advisor Girl Scouts Am., Rockville, Md., 1964-82. Mem. ALA, Soc. Sch. Librs. Internat., Am. Art League, Nat. League Am. Penwomen Chevy Chase (pres.), Miniature Painters, Sculptors and Gravers Soc. D.C., Fla. Miniature Soc., Cider Painters Am., The Art League, Olney Art Assn. (newsletter editor 1984-91, show chmn. 1993, libr. show chmn. 1992—, Phi Kappa Phi. Democrat. Methodist. Home and Studio: 123 Charles St Rockville MD 20850-1510 Office: Genevieve Roberts Studio 17521 Shenandoah Ct Ashton MD 20861

TABNER, MARY FRANCES, educator; b. Rochester, N.Y., Dec. 11, 1918; d. William Herman and Mary Frances (Willenbacher) Arndt; m. James Gordon Tabner, June 27, 1942; 1 child, Barbara Jean. BA, SUNY, Albany, 1940, MA, 1959; postgrad., U. Rochester, N.Y., 1944, 45, Northwestern U. (John Hay fellow), 1963-64, U. Manchester (Eng.), 1971-72. Tchr. history pub. schs. Mattituck, N.Y., 1940-43, Gorham, N.Y., 1943-46; tchr. pub. schs. Waterford, N.Y., 1949-55; tchr. social studies Shaker High Sch., Latham, N.Y., 1959-83, also dir., 1959-83, ret., 1983; tchr. ch. history Our Lady of Assumption Ch., Latham; dir. seminar in Russian Studies. Author bibliographies on Russian history, Am. studies. Mem. Citizens Exch. Coun. N.Y. State Regents independent study grantee, 1966. Mem. AAUW, Nat. Coun. Social Studies, N.Y. State United Tchrs. Assn., Advancement Slavic Studies, SUNY Albany Alumni Assn., Albany Inst. History and Art, Capital Dist. Coun. Social Studies, Shaker Heritage Soc. (trustee, guide, tchr.), Nat. Trust Historic Preservation, English Speaking Union, Am. Assn. Retired Persons. Republican. Roman Catholic. Home: 557 Columbia St Cohoes NY 12047-3807

TABOR, BEVERLY ANN, elementary school educator; b. Dallas, Feb. 12, 1943; m. Charles W. Tabor, Aug. 22, 1964; children: Shawn, Josh. BS in Edn., U. N. Tex., 1964, MEd in Guidance, Counseling, 1970. Cert. tchr. elem. art, guidance and counseling, supr., Tex. Elem. tchr. Ft. Davis (Tex.) Ind. Sch. Dist., 1964-65, Mesquite (Tex.) Ind. Sch. Dist., 1965-69, '71—; counselor Amarillo (Tex.) Ind. Sch. Dist., 1970-71; mem. ins. adv. com. Tchr. Retirement Sys. of Tex., Austin, 1986—; chmn. site based mgmt. com. Tosch Elem. Sch., Mesquite, 1992-94, mentor for new tchrs., student tchrs., H.S. students considering the tchg. profession. Life mem. Tosch Elem. PTA, 1985—. Named to Apple Corps, 1995. Mem. Tex. State Tchrs. Assn. (life), Mesquite Edn. Assn., Alpha Delta Kappa (past pres. Mesquite). Home: 5321 Meadowside Dr Garland TX 75043-2733 Office: Tosch Elem Sch 2424 Larchmont Dr Mesquite TX 75150-5233

TABOR, MARY BRITT WELLFORD, journalist; b. Phila., Oct. 4, 1964; d. Owen Britt and Margaret Walker (Wellford) T.; m. Robert Andrew Engel, Oct. 23, 1993. BA, Princeton U., 1986. Staff editor, reporter The Christian Sci. Monitor, Boston, 1986-88; contbg. reporter The Boston Globe, 1989; news asst. The N.Y. Times, Boston, 1990-91; reporter The N.Y. Times, N.Y.C., 1991—. Office: The NY Times 229 W 43d St 3d fl New York NY 10036

TABOR, MARY LEEBA, oil trade association executive; b. Balt., Mar. 3, 1946; d. Gerson and Freda (Roseman) T.; m. Ardell Louis Persinger, Sept. 16, 1984; children: Benjamin George Hammerschlag, Sarah Esther Hammerschlag. BA with high honors, U. Md., 1966; MA in Teaching, Oberlin Coll., 1967; postgrad., U. Chgo., 1988. Tchr. Towson (Md.) High Sch., 1967-70; employment profl. Ctr. for Naval Analyses, Alexandria, Va., 1970-71; tchr. adult edn. Montgomery County (Md.) Bd. Edn., 1975-80; editor pub. affairs Am. Petroleum Inst., Washington, 1980-83, writer, editor-in-chief, 1983-86, mgr. environ., health and pub. affairs, 1986-89, dir. pub. affairs writing, 1989—; advisor on high sch. sci. curriculum reform NSTA, Washington, 1991—. Debate judge Nat. Cath. Forensic High Sch. League, Bethesda (Md.)-Chevy Chase High Sch., 1991—; bd. dirs. Bethesda Jewish Congregation, 1993—. Mem. Nat. Press Club, Phi Beta Kappa, Phi Kappa Phi, Alpha Lambda Delta. Office: Am Petroleum Inst 1220 L St NW Washington DC 20005-4018

TABORN, JEANNETTE ANN, real estate investor; b. Cleve., June 9, 1926; d. Ralph Mason and Catherine MArie (Mitchell) Tyler; m. Albert Lorenzo Taborn, Oct. 4, 1947; children: Wesley Orren, Annette Loren, KAren Faye, Albert Lorenzo II, Thomas Tyler. Student, Ohio State U., 1944-47. Real estate agt. and investor Cleve., 1947-61; tech. proofreader Sass-Widder Tech Writers, Port Hueneme, Calif., 1961-66, Upjohn Co., Kalamazoo, Mich., 1966-84; mktg. rep. pvt. practice, Kalamazoo, Mich., 1984—; regional mgr. Primerica, 1994. Pres. Kalamazoo County Parent Tchr. Student Assn., 1975; active YWCA, 1981, NAACP, 1983; Kalamazoo Pub. Sch. bd., 1978; Greater Kalamazoo Arts Coun., 1979, Mich. sch. bd. vocat./Edn., Liberty com. C. of Com.; pres. Loy Norrix Trustee Fund, 1983; trustee Kalamazoo Intermediate Sch.; regional mgr. Al Williams. Recipient Cmty. Medal of Arts. Mem. Delta Sigma Theta (Mary McLeod Bethune award). Mem. Bahai Faith. Office: Taborn Realty 3872 Greenleaf Cir Kalamazoo MI 49008-2509

TABRISKY, PHYLLIS PAGE, physiatrist, educator; b. Newton, Mass., Aug. 28, 1930; d. Joseph Westley and Alice Florence (Wainwright) Page; m.

Joseph Tabrisky, Apr. 23, 1955; children: Joseph Page, Elizabeth Ann, William Page. BS, Douglass Coll., 1952; MD, Tufts U., 1956. Cert. phys. medicine and rehab. Intern U. Ill. Hosp., Chgo., 1956-57; phys. medicine and rehab. residency U. Colo. Sch. Medicine, Denver, 1958-60; gen. med. officer dept. pediatrics and medicine Coco Solo Hosp., Panama Canal Zone, 1961-62; staff physician dept. pediatrics Ft. Hood (Tex.) Army Hosp., 1963; instr. dept. rehab. medicine Boston (Mass.) U. Sch. Medicine, 1964-66; asst. prof. phys. medicine and rehab. U. Colo. Sch. Medicine, Denver, 1966-68; staff physician VA Med. Ctr., Long Beach, Calif., 1968-71; acting chief phys. medicine and rehab. VA Med. Ctr., Long Beach, 1971-73, asst. chief rehab. med. svcs., 1973-91, chief phys. medicine & rehab. svc., 1992—; asst. clin. prof. phys. medicine and rehab. U. Calif. Coll. Medicine, Irvine, 1970-75, assoc. clin. prof., 1975-80, prof., 1980—, vice chair dept. phys. medicine and rehab., 1985—, dir. residency tng., 1982—. Fellow Am. Acad. Phys. Medicine and Rehab.; mem. Am. Congress Rehab. Medicine, Assn. Acad. Physiatrists, Alpha Omega Alpha. Republican. Episcopalian. Office: VA Med Ctr 5901 E 7th St Long Beach CA 90822

TACHA, DEANELL REECE, federal judge; b. Jan. 26, 1946. BA, U. Kans., 1968; JD, U. Mich., 1971. Spl. asst. to U.S. Sec. of Labor, Washington, 1971-72; assoc. Hogan & Hartson, Washington, 1973, Thomas J. Pitner, Concordia, Kans., 1973-74; dir. Douglas County Legal Aid Clinic, Lawrence, Kans., 1974-77; assoc. prof. law U. Kans., Lawrence, 1974-77, prof., 1977-85, assoc. dean, 1977-79, assoc. vice chancellor, 1979-81, vice chancellor, 1981-85; judge U.S. Ct. Appeals (10th cir.), Denver, 1985—. Office: US Ct Appeals 10th Cir 4830 W 15th St Ste 100 Lawrence KS 66049-3846

TACK, THERESA ROSE, women's health nurse; b. Lunenburg, Vt., Nov. 10, 1940; d. Gustave L. and Blanche Rose Fournier; m. Dennis M. Tack, Sept. 2, 1961; children: Lynelle Dannecker, Karyn Terry, LeAnn Gemperline. Diploma, Cen. Maine Gen. Hosp., 1961. Cert. ACLS, neonatal resuscitation Am. Heart Assn. Staff nurse neurosurgery unit Hillcrest Med. Ctr., Tulsa, 1961-62; staff nurse cardiovascular unit Meth. Hosp., Houston, 1962-65; staff nurse St. John's Hosp., Red Wing, Minn., 1979-85, Wasatch County Hosp., Heber City, Utah, 1985—. columnist, Nurses Notes in Wasatch Wave, Heber City, Utah, 1990—.

TACKI, BERNADETTE SUSAN, principal; b. Kenosha, Wis., Oct. 21, 1913; d. Peter Frank and Anna (Rathke) T. BS in Edn., Dominican Coll., 1952; MA in Edn., Northwestern U., 1958. Tchr. Whitley Sch., Brighton Twp., Wis., 1932-33, Highland Sch., Pleasant Prairie, Wis., 1933-41, Victory Sch., Pleasant Prairie, 1941-47, Paris (Wis.) Consol. Sch., 1947-53, Southport Sch., Kenosha, 1953-61; prin. Harvey Sch., Kenosha, 1961-80; tchr. St. Casimir, Kenosha, 1983-93, vol. tchr. part-time, 1983—. Pres. Kenosha County Hist. Soc., 1985-89, St. James Parish Coun., Kenosha, 1975-89. Recipient Disting. Svc. award Wis. State Dept., 1980. Mem. Ret. Tchrs. Assn., AAUW, PTA, Kenosha County Tchrs. Assn. (past pres.), Kenosha Edn. Assn. (past pres.), Schubert Club, Delta Kappa Gamma (past pres.). Republican. Roman Catholic. Home: 7527 37th Ave Kenosha WI 53142-7217

TACKWELL, ELIZABETH MILLER, social worker; b. Caney, Kans., Mar. 14, 1923; d. Jesse Winfield and Mattie (Shuler) Miller; m. Joseph J. Tackwell, Dec. 13, 1946 (dec. Mar. 1988); children: Steven, Tiana Tackwell David, Christy Tackwell Reyner. BA, U. Okla., 1953, MSW, 1962. Bd. cert. diplomate Am. Bd. Examiners in Clin. Social Work; lic. social worker, Okla. Social worker Dept. Pub. Welfare, Tulsa and Cleve. Counties, Okla., 1958-59; med. social analyst Dept. Pub. Welfare, Okla., 1960-61; assoc. John Massey M.D. Clinic, Oklahoma City, 1964-69; clin. asst. prof. Okla. U. Sch. Social Work, Oklahoma City, 1964-84; asst. prof., clin. instr. dept. psychiatry/behavioral scis. Okla. U. Health Scis. Ctr., Oklahoma City, 1963—; psychiat. social worker VA Med. Ctr., Oklahoma City, 1961—, chief mental health sect., 1976—, adminstrv. dir. day treatment ctr., 1993—; pvt. practice Oklahoma City, 1971—; psychiat. surveyor Health Care Fin. Adminstrn., Dept. Human Svcs., Washington, 1985—. Recipient Svc. Commendation award DAV, 1980, Chi Omega Scholastic award, Awards Am. Ex-Prisoners of War, 1994. Mem. NASW (diplomate in clin. social work, pres. Okla. chpt. 1971-73, Social Worker of the Yr. Western Okla. chpt. 1975), Acad. Cert. Social Workers, Okla. Health and Welfare Assn. (conf. chmn. 1975—), Pi Gamma Mu. Home: 1328 Tarman Cir Norman OK 73071-4846 Office: Vets Affairs Med Ctr 921 NE 13th St Oklahoma City OK 73104-5028

TADA, KIM GOBETZ, chemistry educator; b. Massapequa, N.Y., Mar. 24, 1963; d. Henry Paul and Susan (Spund) Gobetz; m. Hiroomi Tada, June 26, 1993. BS, Va. Tech., Blacksburg, 1985; MS, U. Pa., Phila., 1987. Cert. tchr. chemistry, biology, math. and gen. sci. Tchr. biology Friends Select Sch., Phila., 1987-92; tchr. chemistry Penncrest High Sch., Media, Pa., 1992-94; tchr. chemistry, biology and math. Strath Haven H.S., Wallingford, Pa., 1994—. Softball coach Friends Select Sch., Phila., 1988; SADD advisor Penncrest High Sch., Media, 1993—. Home: 834 N Taylor St Philadelphia PA 19130-1928 Office: Strath Haven HS 200 S Providence Rd Wallingford PA 19086-3817

TAESCHLER, DEBRA ANN, advertising executive; b. Jersey City, Jan. 7, 1953; d. Edward George and Marion Madeline (Naas) Miller; m. John Paul Taeschler, June 24, 1978. BA summa cum laude, Rutgers U., 1975. With mech. arts dept. Vornado, Inc., Garfield, N.J., 1975-76; asst. account exec. Clifton (N.J.) Graphix Assn., 1976-77; advt. mgr. Davis Printing Corp., Carlstadt, N.J., 1977-80; v.p. account mgr. Landmark Assocs., Whippany, N.J., 1980-85; account mgr. R.Z.A. Advt., Inc., Park Ridge, N.J., 1985-86; pres. Grafica, Inc., Chester, N.J., 1986—. Mem. Phi Beta Kappa. Roman Catholic. Office: Grafica Inc 50 Main St Chester NJ 07930-2535

TAFT, PATRICIA EARLENE, state official; b. Marysville, Kans., July 20, 1945; d. Earl William and Winifred Beulah (Lundblade) Kohlmeyer; m. Elvon Arvis Taft, Aug. 23, 1970; children: Candace Renee, Ryan Wade. BA in Social Welfare, U. Nebr., 1970. Caseworker Nebr. Dept. Social Svcs., Lincoln, 1974-80, tng. specialist, 1980-84, dir. vol. svcs., 1984—, adminstr. for community resource devel., 1985—; cons./trainer Patton Cons. Svcs., South Hampton, Mass., 1988—. Bd. dirs. United Way of Lincoln/Lancaster County, Human Svcs. Planning Coun., Lincoln; chmn. United Way Vol. Ctr., Lincoln, 1989-90. Recipient Dedicated Svc. award Jaycee Women, 1982. Mem. nat. Mgmt. Assn. (v.p. 1986-87, Pres.'s award 1988), Assn. for Vol. Adminstrn., Gov.'s Coun. on Volunteerism, Nebr. Orgn. of Vol. Leaders (pres. 1987-89), Jaycees (life). Home: 5448 S 31st St Ct Lincoln NE 68516

TAGER, ALISA DEBORAH, writer, producer; b. L.A., Aug. 29, 1965; d. Robert Michael and Gail Sandra (Reuben) T.; m. David Michael Pagel, Mar. 12, 1994. BA in History, U. Calif., Berkeley, 1987; MA in Internat. Rels., Yale U., 1989. Free-lance writer/producer N.Y.C., 1989-94, Buenos Aires and Madrid, 1989-94, L.A., 1994—. Contbg. author: Art of the Americas: The Argentine Project, 1992; (exhbn. catalog) Leave the Balcony Open, 1992, The Space of Time, 1993; contbg. screenwriter: I'm Your Man. U. Calif.-Berkeley Alumni scholar, 1983-84. Mem. Phi Beta Kappa. Democrat.

TAGGART, LINDA DIANE, women's health nurse; b. Balt., June 14, 1940; d. Louis and Annie Helena (Heertje) Glick; divorced; 1 child, Keri Anne. AS in Nursing, Pensacola Jr. Coll., 1967; BA, U. West Fla., 1970; postgrad., St. Joseph's Coll., 1976-78. RN, Fla., Ala. Staff nurse Bapt. Hosp., Pensacola, Fla., 1967-70, head nurse, 1970-72; dir. in-svc. edn. Baycrest, Inc. Extended Care Facility, Pensacola, 1973, DON, 1973-74; DON Medica Media, Pensacola, 1974, clinic adminstr., 1974—; dir. Sex and Health Edn., Pensacola, 1974—; regional dir. Medica Media, ea. U.S., 1990; testified before Jud. com. U.S. Ho. of Reps., 1994. Contbr. articles to popular mags. Bd. dirs. Rape Crisis Ctr., Pensacola, 1976-91, chair, 1980, 84, 89 (Addie Brooks award 1984); mem. exec. com. Lakeview Community Mental Health Ctr., Pensacola, 1989 (Expression of Appreciation award 1980-91). Recipient Pioneer/Heroe award Fla. Abortion Coun., 1989. Mem. NOW (Woman of Yr. award 1985, Women's Equity Day award 1986), NAFE, LWV, Am. Assn. Sex Educators, Counselors and Therapists (cert. sex educator), Religious Coalition for Abortion Rights, People for Am. Way. Democrat. Presbyterian. Office: Medica Media 6770 N 9th Ave Pensacola FL 32504-7346

TAGGART, SALLIE TYSON, training/development director; b. Waco, Tex., Jan. 16, 1953; d. Patrick Ewing and Ruth Lee (Young) T. BA, Baylor U., 1975, MA, 1977. Reporter, feature writer Waco Tribune-Herald, 1971-77; mgmt. trainee Montgomery Ward, Ft. Worth, 1972-81; mgr. mgmt. devel. Montgomery Ward, Chgo., 1981-85; ptnr. Key Mgmt. Strategies, Phila., 1985-86; mgr. human resources devel. ARA Svcs., Inc., Phila., 1986-87; dir. tng. Nutrisystem, Inc., Phila., 1987-91; v.p. corp. tng. and devel. Novacare, Inc., Phila., 1991—. Recipient 1st pl. award enterprise reporting UPI, Tex., 1977. Mem. ASTD. Office: Novacare Inc 1016 W 9th Ave King of Prussia PA 19126

TAGGART, SONDRA, financial planner, investment advisor; b. N.Y.C., July 22, 1934; d. Louis and Rose (Birnbaum) Hamov; children: Eric, Karen. BA, Hunter Coll., 1955. Cert. fin. planner; registered investment advisor; registered prin. Nat. Assn. Securities Dealers. Founder, dir., officer Copyright Svc. Bur., Ltd., N.Y.C., 1957-69; dir., officer Maclen Music, Inc., N.Y.C., 1964-69, The Beatles Ltd., 1964-69; pres. Westshore, Inc., Mill Valley, Calif., 1969-82; investment advisor, securities broker, chief exec. officer The Taggart Co. Ltd., 1982—. Editor: The Red Tapes: Commentaries on Doing Business With The Russians and East Europeans, 1978. Mem. Internat. Assn. Fin. Planners, Registry Fin. Planning Practitioners. Republican. Club: Bankers. Office: 9720 Wilshire Blvd Ste 205 Beverly Hills CA 90212-2006

TAGGE, ANNE KATHERINE, not-for-profit organization administrator; b. Waltham, Mass.; d. Raymond Carl and Anne (Weller) T. BA, Wellesley Coll., 1977. Pres., founder Susan Lee Campbell Inst., Wellesley, Mass., 1986—; participant confs. (Alpbach); speaker (Exchange Series); lectr. Contbr. to newspapers, mags., jours. and books. Pres. Fulbright Assn., Mass.; chair Lake Waban League; establisher Friends of Martha's Vineyard. Fellow Salzburg Seminar; Fulbright scholar Romania; French Min. Fgn. Affairs grantee; recipient US/UNEP Achievement award; honoree Rolex Awards for Enterprise; named Town of Wellesley scholar. Mem. Explorers Club. Office: Campbell Inst 37 Avon Rd Wellesley MA 02181-4618

TAGIURI, CONSUELO KELLER, child psychiatrist, educator; b. San Francisco; d. Cornelius H. and Adela (Rios) Keller; m. Renato Tagiuri; children: Robert, Peter, John. BA, U. Calif.-Berkeley; MD, U. Calif.-San Francisco. Diplomate Am. Bd. Psychiatry and Neurology. Resident psychiatry Mass. Gen. Hosp., Boston; staff psychiatrist Children's Hosp., Boston, 1951-59; med. dir. Gifford Sch., Weston, Mass., 1965-85; chief psychiatrist Cambridge (Mass.) Guidance Ctr., 1961-84; mem. faculty dept. psychiatry Harvard Med. Sch., Cambridge, 1965—; cons. early childhood program Children's Hosp., 1985—. Contbr. articles in field to books. Fellow Am. Orth. psychiat. Assn., Mass. Med. Soc., New Eng. Council Child Psychiatry.

TAGLIARINI, PATRICIA ROSE, elementary school educator; b. Schenectady, N.Y., Sept. 12, 1952; d. Charles B. and Ruth Maybell (Stevens) Harris; m. John Alden Tagliarini, Apr. 21, 1973; children: Jennifer, Gianna. AA, Polk Community, 1976; BA, Tusculum Coll., 1981. Cert. elem. tchr., Tenn., N.C., Ky. Title I math. tchr. Polk County Sch., Lakeland, Fla., 1976-78; 1st and 2nd grade tchr. Towering Oaks Sch., Greeneville, Tenn., 1982-84; reading specialist Murphy (N.C.) Elem. Sch., 1985-86; 2nd grade tchr. Martins Creek Elem. Sch., Murphy, 1986—; chmn. Martins Creek Self Study Math. com. for So. Assn. Colls. and Sch., 1989-90, com. mem. Martins Creek Self Study Sci. com., 1989-90; chmn. Martins Creek Sch. Tech. com., 1993; com. mem. Reading com. for adoption of lang. arts program, 1988-89; instr. Martins Creek Elem. Computer Camp, 1986; com. mem. Cherokee County Sch. Found., 1992; com. mem. Comer project, 1991-94. Author Mailbox Jour., 1990. Dir. youth Sunday sch. Murphy 1st Bapt. Ch., 1988-91, dir. missions, 1989-91, puppet dir., 1990—; com. mem. Cherokee County Sch. Found., 1992; chmn. Martins Creek Sch. Tech. Com., 1993—; com. mem. Comer Project, 1991-94. Mem. N.C. Assn. Educators, N.C. Wildlife Resources Commn. Home: 104 Gilbert St Murphy NC 28906-3206 Office: Martins Creek Sch RR 2 Murphy NC 28906-9802

TAGLIENTI, JOSEPHINE MARLENE, artist; b. Chisholm, Minn., Nov. 23, 1939; d. Joseph and Carmela (DeLuca) T.; m. Wayne W. Brown, May 28, 1960 (div. 1972); children: Michael Anthony, Troy Taglienti, Roben Taglienti, Angela Monique, Ninon Terese, Anina Maria (dec.). Student, Mpls. Coll. Art and Design, 1957-59, Mankato State Coll., 1966, Kansas City Art Inst., 1972; MFA, U. Guanajuato, Mex., 1974. artist-in-residence Jewish Cmty. Ctr., Wilmington, 1969; illustration chairperson, mem. faculty Ray Coll. of Design, Chgo., 1980-87. One-woman exhbn. Natalini Gallery, Chgo., 1986; group exhbns. include Windbell Gallery, Wilmington, Del., Newark (Del.) Gallery, Galeria San Miguel, Mex., Galeria Osman, Mex., Galeria Condor, Mex., Torres Gallery, Albuquerque, Dartmouth Gallery, Albuquerque, Edith Lampert Gallery, Santa Fe, La Luna Nueva, Santa Fe, Artesimo Gallery, Scottsdale, Ariz., Del. Art Mus., Wilmington, others; also pvt. and pub. permanent collections; illustrations published in books; poetry published in anthologies; inventor garden products, office implements, exercise equipment, others. Vol. art educator St. Anne's Intercity, Wilmington, 1967-68, Recreation Intercity, Chgo., 1978-79; cultural advocate for homeless Cultural Labor Party, Chgo., 1980-87, cultural advocate for minority concerns, 1985-88. Recipient Fine Art award Artist's Guild of Chgo., 1977, Print Drawing award, 1978, Educator/Svcs. award Sauk Area Career Ctr., 1984. Mem. Nat. Mus. Women in Arts, The Drawing Soc., Affiliated Inventor's Found. Social Democrat. Studio: The Cliffs at North Canyon Phoenix AZ 85024

TAHIR, MARY ELIZABETH, retail marketing and management consultant; b. Greenwood, Miss., Dec. 14, 1933; d. Mahmoud Ibrahim and Mary Constance (Ollie) T. Student, U. Miss., 1951-53. Cert. Profl. Cons., Acad. Profl. Cons. and Advisors. Mgmt. trainee Neiman-Marcus Co., Dallas, 1954-56; asst. buyer D.H. Holmes Co. Ltd., New Orleans, 1956-58, buyer, 1958-65, assoc. divisional mdse. mgr., 1965-67, divisional v.p., 1969-79, corp. v.p., gen. mdse. mgr., 1979-89; pres. Liz Tahir & Assocs., New Orleans, 1990—. Author: Mexico's Cosmetic and Fragrance Market: Past, Present and Future Opportunities, 1991, The Changing World of Mexican Retail Opportunities, 1991, Mexico: Window of Opportunity, 1991, Art of Negotiating, 1993, Negotiating More Profitable with Your Suppliers, Customers and Employees, 1994. Bd. dirs. Vieux Carre Property Owners Assn., New Orleans, 1990. Recipient Role Model award YWCA, 1990. Mem. Women's Profl. Coun. (chmn. New Choices 1989), World Trade Ctr., Fashion Group Internat. (Alpha award 1987-88, Lifetime Achievement award 1993), Nat. Spkrs. Assn., Am. Mktg. Assn., Am. Assn. Profl. Cons., Am. Mgmt. Assn., Fgn. Rels. Assn. (bd. dirs. 1992—, pres. bd. dirs. 1994—). Home: 817 Esplanade Ave New Orleans LA 70116-1940 Office: Liz Tahir & Assocs 201 St Charles Ave # 2500 New Orleans LA 70170-0001

TAI, JULIA CHOW, chemistry educator; b. Shanghai, China, Dec. 15, 1935; came to U.S., 1957; d. Fei-chen and Jean-tson (Liao) Chow; m. Hung-Chao Tai, Aug. 14, 1960; children: Eve, Helen, Michael. BS in Chemistry, Nat. Taiwan U., 1957; MS in Chemistry, U. Okla., 1959; PhD in Chemistry, U. Ill., 1963. Rsch. assoc. Wayne State U., Detroit, 1963-66, 67-68; vis. assoc. prof. Nat. Taiwan U., Taipei, Republic of China, 1968-69; asst. prof. U. Mich., Dearborn, 1969-73, assoc. prof., 1973-79, prof. chemistry, 1979—. Contbr. articles to sci. jours. Mem. Am. Chem. Soc., Quantum Chemistry Program Exch., Mich. Coll. Chemistry Tchrs. Assn. Office: Univ Mich Dearborn 4901 Evergreen Rd Dearborn MI 48128-1491

TAJON, ENCARNACION FONTECHA (CONNIE TAJON), retired educator, association executive; b. San Narciso, Zambales, Philippines, Mar. 25, 1920; came to U.S., 1948; d. Espiridion Maggay and Gregoria (Labrador) Fontecha; m. Felix B. Tajon, Nov. 17, 1948; children: Ruth F., Edward F. Teacher's cert., Philippine Normal Coll., 1941; BEd, Far Eastern U., Manila, 1947; MEd, Seattle Pacific U., 1976. Cert. tchr., Philippines. Tchr. pub. schs. San Narciso and Manila, 1941-47; coll. educator Union Coll. Manila, 1947-48; tchr. Auburn (Wash.) Sch. Dist., 1956-58, Renton (Wash.) Sch. Dist., 1958-78; owner, operator Manila-Zambales Internat. Grill, Seattle, 1980-81, Connie's Lumpia House Internat. Restaurant, Seattle, 1981-84; founder, pres. Tajon-Fontecha, Inc., Renton, 1980—, United Friends of Filipinos in Am. Found., Renton, 1985—; founder Labrador Fontecha and Baldovi-Tajon Permanent Scholarship Fund of The Philippine Normal U., 1990; bd. mem. World Div. of the Gen. Bd. of Global Ministries of the United Meth. Ch., 1982-84, Ch. Women United Seattle Chapt.; mem. advisory bd Univ. Wash. Burke Mus., 1991—; mem. King TV Asian Am. Adv. Forum, 1993. Editor bull. Renton 1st United Meth. Ch., 1994. Bd. dirs. women's div. Gen. Bd. Global Ministries United Meth. Ch., 1982-84, Renton Area Youth Svcs., 1980-85, Girls' Club of Puget Sound, Ethnic Heritage Coun. of Pacific N.W., 1989—; mem. Mcpl. Arts Commn. Renton, 1980—; chair fundraising steering com. Washington State Women's Polit. Caucus, 1985-89; governing mem. nat. steering com. Nat. Women's Polit. Caucus Wash. State Coun., 1990—, mem. vol. action, 1990 Goodwill Games, Seattle, vol. worker Native Am. Urban Ministries, 1990—; adv. bd. Renton Community Housing Devel.; community adv. bd. U. Wash. Thomas Burke Meml. Mus., 1990—; mem. program com. UN, 1992—, Asian Pacific Task Force of Ch. Coun. Greater Seattle, 1993—; ch. women coord. United Ecumenical World Community Day Celebration, 1994. Recipient spl. cert. of award Project Hope, 1976, U.S. Bicentennial Commn., 1976, UNICEF, 1977, Spirit of Liberty award Ethnic Heritage Coun. Pacific Northwest, 1991; named Parent of Yr. Filipino Community of Seattle, Inc., 1984, One of 500 Seattle Pacific U. Centennial "Alumni of a Growing Vision", 1991. Mem. NEA, Wash. State Edn. Assn. (bd. dirs. 1990-92), Am. Assn. Ret. Persons, Nat. Ret. Tchrs. Assn., Renton Ret. Tchrs. Assn., U. Wash. Alumni Assn. (life), U. Wash. Filipino Alumni Assn. (pres. Wash. state chpt. 1985-87), Renton Hist. Mus. (life), Internat. Platform Assn., United Meth. Women, Pres.'s Forum, Alpha Sigma, Delta Kappa Gamma. Democrat. Home and Office: 2033 Harrington Pl NE Renton WA 98056-2303

TAKASE, NAOMI, banker; b. Nagoya, Japan, Feb. 16, 1960; d. Shozo and Kazuko (Moriya) Obara; m. Naohiko Takase, June 7, 1986. BA, Sophia U., Tokyo, 1983; MBA, Boston Coll., 1990. Producing coord. Nagoya Broadcasting Network, Tokyo, 1982-84; mgr. Mitsui O.S.K. (Am.) Inc., N.Y.C., 1991-92; leasing officer The Indsl. Bank of Japan, N.Y.C., 1992—. Home: 401 E 34th St # S19 New York NY 10016-4914

TALALAY, KATHRYN MARGUERITE, librarian; b. New Haven, Oct. 29, 1949; d. Anselm and Marjorie Ruth (Freedman) T.; m. Frank James Ponzio III, Sept. 16, 1989. Student, Bennington Coll., 1967-69; BA in Classics, NYU, 1971; MA in Musicology, MLS, Case Western Res. U., 1975. Asst. reference and rsch. libr. Ind. U. Sch. Music, Bloomington, 1975-90; asst. libr., researcher Am. Acad. of Arts and Letters, N.Y.C., 1990—. Author: Scores by Women Composers, 1988, Composition in Black and White, 1995; author: (with others) Notable Black American Women, 1992; translator: A Literal Translation of Joseph Haydn's Cantata, Applausus, 1977, (comic opera) The Deserter, 1980; contbr. articles to profl. jours. Grantee Ind. U., summer 1977, fall, 1980, 82-83; Rockefeller Found. scholar, 1988-89. Mem. Music Libr. Assn., Am. Musicological Soc., Ctr. for Black Music Rsch. Office: Am Acad Arts and Letters 633 W 155th St New York NY 10032-7501

TALAMANTES, JOY ELAINE, interior designer; b. Cin., Aug. 29, 1938; d. Francis Joseph and Doris Mae (Lamping) Suttman; m. Simon Garcia Talamantes; children: Francis, Laurie, Richard, Ronald, Timothy, Lutterbie. Student, Cin. Acad. Comml. Art, 1956-58. Sales rep. Olsten Temporary Svcs., Cin.; sales, producer WCPO-Scripps Howard Broadcasting, Lighthouse Prodns., Cin., 1979-81; owner, founder CAJOinc, design svcs., Cin., 1983. Recipient Homearama Design awards Cin. Home Builders Assn. Mem. Am. Soc. Interior Design (Disting. Svc. award). Office: CAJO Inc PO Box 31133 Cincinnati OH 45231-0133

TALARICO, MARIA THERESA, tax accountant; b. Chgo., July 11, 1960; d. Alfredo and Maria Rose (Altomari) T. BS in Commerce, DePaul U., Chgo., 1982, MS in Taxation, 1988. CPA, Ill. Jr. tax acct. Harris Trust and Savs. Bank, Chgo., 1982-86, tax acct., 1986-87, sr. tax acct., 1988-89; tax supr. Aon Corp., Chgo., 1989-91; sr. tax. cons. Arthur Andersen & Co., Chgo., 1991-92, experienced sr. tax cons., 1992-94, asst. tax mgr., 1994—. Mem. AICPA, Ill. Soc. CPAs.

TALBERT, FRANCES SUZANNE, counseling psychologist, educator; b. Oxford, Miss.. BA, U. Miss., 1971; M of Human Devel. and Learning, U. N.C., Charlotte, 1983; PhD, Auburn U., 1989. Lic. psychologist, Ga. Reporter Comml. Dispatch, Columbus, Miss., 1971-72; copy editor Evansville (Ind.) Press, 1972-75; journalist Charlotte (N.C.) News, 1975-82; teaching asst. U. N.C., Charlotte, 1982-83, Auburn (Ala.) U., 1984-88; counseling psychology intern U. Ga., Athens, 1988-89; counseling psychologist Augusta (Ga.) Coll., 1989-90; dir., Learning Support Ctr. Med. Coll. of Ga., Augusta, 1989-90; psychologist VA Med. Ctr., Augusta, 1990—; asst. prof. Med. Coll. Ga., Augusta, 1990—. Contbr. articles to profl. jours. Recipient Disting. Alumna award Women in Comm., U. Miss., 1979. Mem. APA.

TALBOT, ARDITH ANN, editor; b. Superior, Nebr., Mar. 11, 1933; d. Charles Howard and Dollie Eunice (Ryan) Snell; m. Richard Charles Talbot, Oct. 17, 1954; children: Richard Daryl, Robert Charles. BA in Edn., U. Nebr., 1956. Recorded Friends min., 1993. Tchr. high sch. Pub. Schs., Juniata, Nebr., 1957-59, Hudson, Iowa, 1962-68, New Providence, Iowa, 1968-71; owner Retail Bookstore, Sutherland, Iowa, 1971-72, Marshalltown, Iowa, 1972-74, Mason City, Iowa, 1974-89; mgr. book store Friends United Mktg., Richmond, Ind., 1986-89; mgr., editor Friends United Press, Richmond, Ind., 1989—. Republican. Home: PO Box 343 Lynn IN 47355-0343 Office: Friends United Meeting 101 Quaker Hill Dr Richmond IN 47374-1926

TALBOT, CARMEN V., county official; b. Highland Park, Mich., July 18; d. Albert Kennedy and Verda Muriel Bowers Carter; children: Jeffery Thomas, Cheryl Lynn Ellis. Newspaper reporter Southfield (Mich.) Sun Newspaper, 1970-73; adminstrv. asst. Charter Twsp. of Highland, Mich., 1980-84; legal sec. Willis C. Bullard, Jr., Milford, Mich., 1987-89; exec. sec. mktg. and pub. rels. Jervis B. Webb Co., Farmington Hills, Mich., 1985-88, prodn. coord. mktg. dept., 1988-89; exec. sec. Barbier & Tolleson, P.C., Troy, Mich., 1989-90, Patterson, Potter, Carniak & Anderson, Auburn Hills, Mich., 1990-92; transition team dir. L. Brooks Patterson, Oakland County Exec.-Elect, Pontiac, Mich., 1992; state govt. liaison County of Oakland, Pontiac, 1993—. Campaign coord. Willis C. Bullard Jr., 1982-86; Rep. precinct del. for Highland Twsp., 1982-92; Rep. conv. del. Highland Twsp. to Mich. State Rep. Convs., 1985-92; sec. 6th dist. Mich. 6th Congl. Dist. Exec. Bd., 1986-88; mem. exec. com. Oakland County Rep. Exec. Com., 1984-92, sec., 1989-92; regional coord. Oakland County 6th Dist. George Bush for Pres., 1986-88; polit. advisor David Galloway for State Rep., 1992, 94; scheduler L. Brooks Patterson for Oakland County Exec., 1992; trustee Highland Twsp., Mich., 1984-92. Lutheran. Office: County of Oakland Dept 409 1200 N Telegraph Pontiac MI 48341

TALBOT, DOROTHY MCCOMB, public health nurse and consultant; b. Hurley, N.Mex., Aug. 18, 1918; d. Parker Deems and Mildred (Willcox) McComb; m. Raymond James Talbot, Aug. 1, 1940 (dec. Apr. 1991); children: Raymond James Jr., Patricia Martin, Betty Sue. BSN, Tex. Women's U., 1945; MA, Columbia U., 1958; MPH, Tulane U., 1964; PhD, 1970. RN, N.C. Sch. nurse Tex. Women's U., Denton, 1939-40; dir. nursing Ruston (La.) Hosp., 1946-50; pub. health nurse Lincoln County, Ruston, 1952-57; instr. La. State U., New Orleans, 1958-62; chair pub. health nursing Tulane U., New Orleans, 1962-74; chair pub. health U. N.C., Chapel Hill, 1974-84; cons. throughout U.S.; leader overseas workshops Profl. Seminar Cons., U. N.Mex., 1982, 85, 88. Mem. adv. bd. Greenways Commn. and Orange County Med., N.C. Recipient Meritorious award La. Pub. Health Assn., 1973, So. Health Assn., 1978. Fellow APHA (Disting. Pub. Health Nurse award 1984), Am. Acad. Nursing; mem. ANA, Sigma Theta Tau. Democrat. Episcopalian. Home: 437 14300 W Bell Rd Surprise AZ 85374

TALBOT, KATHLEEN MARY, elementary education educator; b. Lansdowne, Pa., Apr. 11, 1944; d. Bernard Lawrence and Kathleen T. (Fleck) T. BS, Chestnut Hill Coll., 1971; MEd, Kutztown U., 1980. Cert. elem. tchr., Pa., Del. Tchr. elem. schs. Archdiocese of Phila., 1965-83, 1986—, Diocese of Wilmington (Del.), 1983-85, Garnet Valley Sch. Dist., Concordville, Pa., 1986—; co-chairperson middle states evaluation, Drexel Hill, Pa., 1979-81; adj. prof. Chestnut Hill Coll., Phila., 1980-91; coord. math. curriculum Garnet Valley Sch. Dist., Corcordsville, 1991—; mem. strategic planning steering com., 1994. Grantee Impact Ptnrs. in Edn., 1989, Garnet Valley Sch. Dist., 1992. Mem. NEA, ASCD, Nat. Coun. Tchrs. Math., Pa.

Edn. Assn., Chester County Reading Assn., Garnet Valley Edn. Assn. (mem. negotiating team 1992-93). Democrat. Roman Catholic.

TALBOT, SUSAN ANDERSON, French language educator; b. Madison, Wis., Oct. 15, 1930; d. Donald Wells and Florence (Aitken) Anderson; m. John Talbot, July 15, 1952; children: Peter W., Deborah M. Talbot Frandsen. BA, Radcliffe U., 1952; MA, U. Mont., 1980. Tchr. French Ea. Mont. Coll., Billings, 1967-70, sr. high sch., Billings, 1968, Hellgate High Sch., Missoula, Mont., 1977-79. Chair Youth Homes Bd., Missoula, 1981-83, United Way Campaign, Missoula, 1986-87, Mont. Arts Coun., 1984-89, Mont. Community Found., 1991—. Recipient "George" award Missoula C. of C., 1986, Silver Achievement award YWCA, 1987; co-recipient Gov.'s award for arts, 1994. Mem. Internat. Women's Forum. Episcopalian. Home: 11 Greenbrier Dr Missoula MT 59802-3353

TALBOT-KOEHL, LINDA ANN, dancer, ballet studio owner; b. Fremont, Ohio, July 22, 1956; d. Donald Ray and Doris Ann (Opperman) Talbot; m. James G. Koehl, July 30, 1983. Student, U. Akron, 1974-76; BA in Psychology, Heidelberg Coll., 1984. Owner, instr. BalleTiffin, Inc., Tiffin, Ohio, 1987—; choreographer Heidelberg Summer Theater, Tiffin, 1986, Singing Collegians, 1993; choreographer Calvert H.S. Theater, Tiffin, 1986-88, Swing Choir, 1987-89, 91-92. Appeared (ednl. film) Rights on the Job, State of Ohio Dept. Edn., 1986. Mem. Dance Masters of Am., Nat. Multiple Sclerosis Soc., The Ritz Players (choreographer 1985, 88-89, make-up designer, advisor 1989-92, sound booth operator 1993—). Home and Office: BalleTiffin Inc 449 Melmore St Tiffin OH 44883-3628

TALBOTT, MARTHA WILD, department store executive; b. Buffalo, Nov. 29, 1951; d. Ralph Edward and Betty V. (Mann) Wild. AS, Cazenovia Coll., 1971; BS, Skidmore Coll., 1973. Mgmt. trainee Consol. Millinery Co., Chgo., 1975-77; asst. buyer Carlisle Retailers, Inc., Ashtabula, Ohio, 1977-78; buyer Carlisle Allen Co., Ashtabula, Ohio, 1978-79, May Co., Cleve., 1979-83; buyer Bealls Dept. Stores, Bradenton, Fla., 1983-85, div. mdse. mgr., 1985—. Mem. United Way Pathfinders Club, Bradenton, 1989—; bd. dirs. Womens Resource Ctr. Manatee, Inc., Bradenton, 1990—, treas., 1991—; past mem. bd. dirs. Pine Bay Forest Condominium Assn., Bradenton, sec., 1989. Mem. Manatee Symphony Assn. and Guild, Altrusa. Lutheran. Office: Bealls Dept Stores 1806 38th Ave E Bradenton FL 34208-4700

TALESE, NAN AHEARN, publishing company executive; b. N.Y.C., Dec. 19, 1933; d. Thomas James and Suzanne Sherman (Russell) Ahearn; m. Gay Talese, June 10, 1959; children: Pamela Frances, Catherine Gay. B.A., Manhattanville Coll. of Sacred Heart, 1955. Fgn. exchange student 1st Nat. City Bank, London and Paris, 1956; editorial asst. Am. Eugenics Soc., N.Y.C., 1957-58, Vogue mag., N.Y.C., 1958-59; copy editor Random House Pub., N.Y.C., 1959-64; assoc. editor Random House Pub., 1964-67, sr. editor, 1967-73; sr. editor Simon & Schuster Pubs., N.Y.C., 1974-81; v.p. Simon & Schuster Pubs., 1979-81; exec. editor, v.p. Houghton Mifflin Co., N.Y.C., 1981-83, v.p., editor-in-chief, 1984-86, v.p., pub., editor-in-chief, 1986-88; sr. v.p. Doubleday & Co., N.Y.C., 1988-90; pres., pub., editorial dir. Nan A. Talese Books, 1990—. Home: 109 E 61st St New York NY 10021-8101

TALIAFERRO, NANCY ELLEN TAYLOR, artist; b. Richmond, Va., Feb. 16, 1937; d. Samuel Beryl and Nancy Loomis (Brinton) Taylor; m. Charles Mitchell Taliaferro, July 3, 1958; children: Chester Parsons, Nancy Brinton. BFA, Va. Commonwealth U., 1959. Comml. artist, illustrator, 1959-63, drawings, pastel portraits, 1963—, oil paintings, 1978—. Exhbns. include The Chrysler Mus., Norfolk, Va., 1994, Du Pont Art Gallery, Washington and Lee U., Lexington, Va., 1993, Uptown Gallery, Richmond, 1992, 93, 94, The Art Gallery, Ashland, Va., 1992, 93, 94, Va. Gen. Assembly and State Capitol Bldgs., 1989, 91, 93, Jacob Javits Fed. Bldg., N.Y.C., 1986, Women's Resource Ctr., U. Richmond, 1985. Recipient award The Artists Mag., 1992. Mem. Nat. Assn. Women Artists, Uptown Gallery (charter mem.), James River Art League, U. Painters. Republican. Methodist. Home: 6724 Forest Hill Ave Richmond VA 23225 Studio: 8413 Forest Hill Ave Richmond VA 23235

TALLCHIEF, MARIA, ballerina; b. Fairfax, Okla., Jan. 24, 1925; d. Alexander Joseph and Ruth Mary (Porter) T.; m. Henry Paschen, Jr., June 3, 1956; 1 child, Elise. DFA (hon.), Lake Forest (Ill.) Coll., Colby Coll., Waterville, Maine, 1968, Ripon Coll., 1973, Boston Coll., Smith Coll., 1981, Northwestern U., Evanston, Ill., 1982, Yale U., 1984, St. Mary-of-the-Woods (Ind.) Coll., 1984, Dartmouth Coll., 1985, St. Xavier Coll., 1989. Ballerina Ballet Russe de Monte Carlo, 1942-47; with N.Y.C. Ballet Co., 1947-65, prima ballerina, 1947-60; founder Chgo. City Ballet, 1979—; now artistic dir. Lyric Opera Ballet; prima ballerina Am. Ballet Theatre, 1960; founder Sch. Chgo. Ballet. Guest star, Paris Opera, 1947, Royal Danish Ballet, 1961; created roles in Danses Concertantes, 1944, Night Shadow, 1946, Four Temperaments, 1946, Orpheus, 1948, The Firebird, 1949, Bourée Fantastique, 1949, Capriccio Brillante, 1951, À la Françaix, 1951, Swan Lake, 1951, Caracole, 1952, Scotch Symphony, 1952, The Nutcracker, 1954, Allegro Brillante, 1956, The Gounod Symphony, 1958; appeared in films Presenting Lily Mais, 1943, Million Dollar Mermaid, 1953. Named Hon. Princess Osage Indian Tribe, 1953; recipient Disting. Service award U. Okla., 1972, award Dance mag., 1960, Jane Addams Humanitarian award Rockford Coll., 1973, Bravo award Rosary Coll., 1983, award Dance Educators Am., 1956, Achievement award Women's Nat. Press Club, 1953, Capezio award, 1965, Leadership for Freedom award Roosevelt U. Scholarship Assn., 1986. Mem. Nat. Soc. Arts and Letters. *

TALLET, MARGARET ANNE, fundraising and marketing communications executive; b. Binghamton, N.Y., Feb. 14, 1953; d. George Francis and Wilma Ann (Wagner) T.; m. Peter A., Myks, July 6, 1991. BA, St. Mary's Coll., 1975; MBA, SUNY, 1979. Asst. dir. Parrish Art Mus., Southampton, N.Y., 1979-87; assoc. dir. devel. Detroit Inst. Arts Founders Soc., 1981-92; v.p. Franco Pub. Rels. Group, Detroit, 1992—. Bd. dirs. Aid for AIDS Rsch., 1987-92, Detroiters at Heart, 1992—; mktg. com. Mich. Career Found., Detroit, 1992—. Mem. Pub. Rels. Soc. Am. Roman Catholic. Office: Franco Pub Rels Group 400 Renaissance Ctr # 600 Detroit MI 48243

TALLEY, PAT LOUREA, corporate librarian; b. Abilene, Tex., Sept. 13, 1947; d. Herman Lee and Elsie Lourea (Alexander) T.; m. Terry Hair (div. 1984); 1 child, Desel Lourea Hair. BS in Edn., Midwestern U., 1969; MLS, Tex. Women's U., 1978. Pub. welfare worker I Tex. State Dept. Pub. Welfare, Wichita Falls, Tex., 1969-72, pub. welfare worker II, 1974-77; media libr. Farmers Br. (Tex.) Pub. Libr., 1978-80; asst. libr. McKinsey & Co., Dallas, 1980-82; supv. libr. svcs. Fed. Home Loan Bank Dallas, 1983—. Author: The Savings and Loan Crisis: An Annotated Bibliography, 1993; contbr. articles, revs. to profl. jours. Libr. First Meth. Ch., Lewisville, Tex., 1978-83; leader Girl Scout Troop, Lewisville, 1976-82; dir., stage mgr., Lewisville, 1983-85; historian PTA, Lewisville, 1982; sec. bd. dirs. North Tex. Coun. Am. Youth Hostel Assn., Dallas, 1991-94; active Mus. Bicentennial Com., Lewisville, 1975-76. Mem. ALA, Tex. Libr. Assn. (spl. librs. chpt. sec./treas. 1987-88), Spl. Libr. Assn. (mem. Tex. chpt. pub. affairs chair 1991-93, DFW divsn. newsletter chair 1993-94, ann. conf. pub. rels. chair 1991), Dallas Assn. Law Librs., Soc. Children's Book Writers, Native Plant Soc. Tex., Dallas Paleontology Soc., Dallas Trekkers, Beta Phi Mu. Office: Fed Home Loan Bank Dallas 5605 N Macarthur Blvd Irving TX 75038-2617

TALLEY, RUTH ELIZABETH, small business owner, association executive; b. Pitts., Aug. 20, 1948; d. Randall Earl Talley, Jr. and Ruth Minnie (Hayden) Nickeson; m. Jan Richter, Mar. 10, 1984. BA, Elmhurst Coll., 1970; MA, Duquesne U., 1975. Reading specialist Hempfield Area Sch. Dist., Greensburg, Pa., 1975-80; med. staff coord. Santa Monica (Calif.) Hosp., 1980-83; owner Make Believe, Inc., Santa Monica, 1983—. Pres. So. Calif. coun. YWCA, 1993—; pres. Santa Monica YWCA, 1991-93. Recipient Geoffrey Costume Design award Morgan-Wixson Theatre, 1990, 93. Mem. Santa Monica C. of C. Office: Make Believe Inc 3240 Pico Blvd Santa Monica CA 90405-2114

TALLY, LURA SELF, state legislator; b. Statesville, N.C., Dec. 9, 1921; d. Robert Ottis and Sara (Cowles) Self; A.B., Duke U., 1942; M.A., N.C. State U., Raleigh, 1970; m. J.O. Tally, Jr., Jan. 30, 1943 (div. 1970); children: Robert Taylor, John Cowles. Tchr., former guidance counselor Fayetteville (N.C.) city schs.; mem. N.C. Ho. of Reps. from 20th Dist., 1971-83, chmn. com. higher edn., from 1975, also 1980-83, vice chmn. com. appropriations for edn., 1973-86; state senator from 12th Dist. N.C., 1983-94; chmn. N.C. Senate Com. of Natural Resources, Community Devel. and Wildlife, 1987, Environment and Natural Resources, 1989-94. Past pres. Cumberland County Mental Health Assn., N.C. Historic Preservation Soc.; trustee Fayetteville Tech. Inst., 1981-94; mem. Legis. Research com. Mem. Am. Personnel and Guidance Assn., Fayetteville Bus. and Profl. Women's Club, Kappa Delta, Delta Kappa Gamma. Methodist. Club: Fayetteville Woman's (past pres.). Office: W Jones St Raleigh NC 27601

TALMADGE, MARY CHRISTINE, nursing educator; b. Monticello, Ga., Nov. 6, 1940; d. Herbert Pope and Margaret (Allen) T.; m. Larry Benson, Aug. 10, 1962 (div. 1975). Diploma, Crawford W. Long Hosp. Sch. of Nursing, Atlanta, 1961; BSN, U. Dayton, 1966; MPH, U. Hawaii, 1971, PhD, 1989. RN; cert. Family Life Edn. Staff charge nurse Crawford W. Long Hosp., Atlanta, 1961-62; instr. LPN program Dayton (Ohio) Bd. Edn., 1963-66; instr. Miami Valley Hosp. Sch. of Nursing, Dayton, 1967-69; clin. nurse specialist Hawaii State Hosp., Kaneohe, 1970-77, dir. nursing, 1978-80; adminstrv. asst. to dir. health Hawaii State Dept. of Health, Honolulu, 1977-78; clin. nurse specialist Windward Community Counseling Ctr., Kaneohe, 1980-83; asst. prof. U. Hawaii, 1983-85; assoc. prof., assoc. program dir. Hawaii Loa Coll., Kaneohe, 1987-89; assoc. prof., acting dept. head Ga. So. U., Statesboro, 1990-93; prof., chair dept. nursing Calif. State U., Long Beach, 1993—; cons. Tokyo Women's Med. Coll. Sch. of Nursing, 1988-90; local and internat. healthcare orgns. Sec., mem. Gov.'s Commn. on Mental Health and Criminal Justice, Honolulu, 1978-80; mem., chmn. Windward Oahu Svc. Area Bd. on Mental Health and Substance Abuse, Honolulu, 1985-86; candidate Neighborhood Bd. Kaneohe, 1988; bd. dirs. New Beginnings for Children; chair nursing task force, health com. Statesboro C. of C. Recipient Cmty. Svc. award African-Am. Caucus, Ga. So. U., 1993. Mem. NLN, Sigma Theta Tau. Democrat. Methodist. Home: 105 Lancaster Pt Statesboro GA 30458-6238 Office: Calif State Univ Long Beach CA 90802

TALMADGE-LUFTGLASS, NAOMI, real estate agent, public relations consultant; b. Morristown, N.J., Jan. 30, 1932; d. Abraham and Diana (Bieley) Stessel; m. Murray A. Luftglass, Sept. 14, 1952 (div. Feb. 1987); children: Paula Jean, Bryan Keith, Robert Andrew, Richard Eric. Student, Bklyn. Coll.; BA, UCLA, 1956. Tchr. emotionally disturbed and neurologically handicapped Sunny Hill Children's Ctr., Greenwich, Conn., 1969-72; social researcher U. Chgo., N.Y.C., 1972-84; owner N.S.L. Rsch. Svcs., Bedford, N.Y., 1979-88; dir. pub. rels. R.R. Ragetté Inc. Realtors, Eastchester, N.Y., 1984-88; sales rep. R.R. Ragetté Inc. Realtors, Bedford, 1988-91, Coldwell Banker-Schlott Realtors, Bedford, 1991-92; sales rep Bayswater Realty Brokerage, Katonah, N.Y., 1992—; pub. rels. cons., Westchester, N.Y., 1984-91. Mem. Nat. Assn. Realtors (grad. Realtors Inst. 1990, cert. residential specialist 1991, Women's Coun. 1991), Westchester County Bd. Realtors, Phi Beta Kappa. Democrat. Jewish. Home: Hickory Pass Bedford NY 10506 Office: Bayswater Realty Brokerage Katonah Ave Katonah NY 10536

TAM, MARILYN HAY-LIT, health and beauty company executive; b. Hong Kong, Oct. 16; d. Chak Lam and Rosalind Yeungkui (Yeung) T. BS, Oreg. State U., 1972, MS, 1974. Buyer May Co. Calif., Calif., 1974-78, merchandise mgr., 1981-84; gen. merchandise mgr. Brittania Sportswear, Seattle, 1978-81, Miller's Outpost, Ontario, Calif., 1984-87; v.p. apparel Nike Inc., Beaverton, Oreg., 1987-88; pres. MTA Inc., Long Beach, Calif., 1988-90; pres. apparel and retail Reebok Internat. Ltd., Stoughton, Mass., 1990-93; CEO Aveda Corp., Mpls., Minn., 1993—; also bd. dirs. Aveda Corp., Blaine, Minn. Bd. dirs. Reebok Human Rights Counf., Stoughton, 1991—, Give to the Earth, Blaine, 1993—.

TAMAREN, MICHELE CAROL, special education educator; b. Hartford, Conn., Aug. 2, 1947; d. Herman Harold and Betty (Leavitt) Liss; m. David Stephen Tamaren, June 8, 1968; 1 child, Scott. BS in Elem. Edn., U. Conn., 1969; MA in Spl. Edn., St. Joseph Coll., West Hartford, Conn., 1976. Cert. elem. and spl. edn. tchr., Conn., Mass. Tchr. N.Y. Inst. for Spl. Edn., Bronx, 1971-74; ednl. cons. Renbrook Sch., West Hartford, 1975-78; grad. instr. St. Joseph Coll., 1978; elem. tchr. Acton (Mass.) Pub. Schs., 1969-70, tchr. spl. edn., 1978—; ednl. cons. to schs., parents, orgns., pubs., 1980—; internat. and nat. lectr. on bldg. self-esteem in classroom, 1988—. Author: I Make a Difference!, 1992; also articles. Horace Mann grantee Mass. Dept. Edn., 1987, 88, Mass. Gov.'s Alliance Against Drugs, 1992. Mem. Coun. for Exceptional Children, Learning Disabilities Assn., Orton Dyslexia Soc., Nat. Ctr. Learning Disabilities, Phi Kappa Phi, Kappa Delta Pi. Home: 15 Willis Holden Dr Acton MA 01720

TAMBURELLO, VIVIAN ANN, psychologist; b. Denville, N.J., Sept. 27, 1960; d. Anthony Charles and Doris Claire (Beaulieu) T.; m. Khaled Ahmad Darres, May 26, 1990. BA in Elem. Edn., Glassboro State Coll., 1982; MEd in Sch. Psychology, Southwest Tex. State U., 1986; PhD in Counseling Psychology, Tex. A&M U., 1992. LIc. psychologist; cert. tchr. K-8, Tex., N.J. Tchr. Austin (Tex.) Ind. Sch. dist., 1982-87; counselor Job Tng. Partnership Act, Hearne, Tex., 1987-88; asst. clin. coord. Counseling and Assessment Clinic, College Station, Tex., 1988-89; therapist U. Pediatrics Assn., Bryan, Tex., 1989-90; doctoral intern Towson (Md.) State U., 1990-91; psychology assoc. Charles County Health Dept., La Plata, Md., 1991-93; psychologist Johns Hopkins U., Balt., 1993—; therapist Children of Separation and Divorce Ctr., Columbia, Md., 1991—; program svcs. com. Sexual Assault Recovery Ctr., Balt., 1992—; cons. Phoebe's Home: Shelter for Battered Women, College Station, Tex., 1988-90. Co-author: (treatment manual) ACHEVE: Adults and Children Helping Eliminate Violent Endings, 1993. Mgr. girls' softball, Columbia Youth Baseball Assn., Columbia, 1994. Mem. APA, Md. Psychol. Assn., Nat. Coalition Against Domestic Violence, Kappa Delta Pi, Pi Delta Phi, Psi Chi, Phi Kappa Phi. Home: 4730 Leyden Way Ellicott City MD 21042 Office: Counseling Ctr Johns Hopkins U 3400 North Charles St Baltimore MD 21218

TAMEN, HARRIET, lawyer; b. Yonkers, N.Y., May 17, 1947; d. Saul and Lily (Balglau) T. A.B., Bryn Mawr Coll., 1969; J.D., George Washington U., Washington, 1973. Bar: N.Y. 1974, U.S. Dist. Ct. (so. dist.) N.Y. 1975. Atty., W.T. Grant, N.Y.C., 1974-76; atty. City of N.Y. Office Econ. Devel., Div. Real Property, N.Y.C., 1977-81; atty. Credit Lyonnais Bank, N.Y.C., 1981-86, Chase Manhattan Bank, 1986-89; v.p., counsel internat. corp. fin. Citibank, 1989-92, partner, Claugus Tamen & Orenstein, 1992-93; pvt. practice, N.Y.C., 1994—. Bd. dirs. Dromenon Theatre, N.Y., 1980-86, Nat. Dance Inst., N.Y., 1982, chmn. bd. dirs., 1984-87; chmn. bd. dirs. Theatre & Dance Alliance, 1989-90; del. exch. program Women in Law, South Am., 1987—; mem. campaign staff Ed Koch for Mayor, N.Y.C., 1977, steering com. Soviet Am. Banking Law Working Group, 1991—; guest lectr. Moscow Conf. on Banking, 1992, Ulaan Baatar, Mongolia, 1993-94, Harriman Inst. of Columbia U., 1994. Mem. ABA, Bar of Assn. of City of N.Y.

TAMI, MARY E., visiting nurse; b. St. Marys, Pa., July 7, 1959; d. Robert Sr. and Elizabeth (Lanzel) Cotter; children: Justin, Amanda. AS magna cum laude, U. Pitts., St. Marys, 1990. RN, Pa. Formerly oper. rm. nurse Bradford (Pa.) Regional Med. Ctr., St. Marys; now vis. nurse Community Nurses of Elk and Cameron Counties, St. Marys. Home: PO Box 1027 Saint Marys PA 15857-5027

TAMM, ELEANOR RUTH, retired accountant; b. Hansell, Iowa, July 20, 1921; d. Horace Gerald and Sibyl (Armstrong) Wells; m. Roy C. Tamm, Oct. 18, 1941 (dec. Jan. 1980); children: Larry LeRoy, Marilyn Ruth Tamm-Schmitt. Grad., Am. Soc. Travel Agts., Inc., 1970; student, Iowa Cen. C.C., 1983, 85; grad., Inst. Children's Lit., 1994. Tchr. Howard County Rural Sch., Riceville, 1939-41; bookkeeper, cashier Cen. States Power and Light Co., Elma, Iowa, 1941-42; office supr. J.C. Penney Co., Goldsboro, N.C., 1942-44; bookkeeper J.C. Penney Co., West Palm Beach, Fla., 1945; head teller Iowa State Bank, Clarksville, Iowa, 1955-69; office and group mgr. Allen Travel Agy., Charles City, Iowa, 1969-81; tour conductor, tour organizer and planner Allen Travel Agy., Charles City, 1971-81; office mgr. Arora Clinics, P.C., Fonda, Iowa, 1986-90; freelance collaborator on children's books Clarksville, 1989—. Leader Girl Scouts U.S.A., Clarksville, 1946-47; tchr. St. John Luth. Ch., Clarksville, 1946-66, ch. sec., 1954-66, sec.-treas. Altar Guild, 1993-94; United Fund sec.-treas. Clarksville Cmty. Fund, 1956-66; sec.-treas. Clarksville Band Boosters, 1964-66. Lutheran. Home: 408 E 3d St Fonda IA 50540

TAMULEVICH, JOAN FRANCES, substance abuse therapist; b. Worcester, Mass., July 27, 1940; d. Anthony and Constance (Kucewicz) T. AS in Mech. Engrng., Worcester Jr. Coll., 1978; BS, Worcester State Coll., 1989; MA, Framingham State Coll., 1990. Lic. mental health counselor, rehab. counselor, Mass. Mech. draftsperson Norton Co., Worcester, 1962-69, Morgan Constrn. Co., Worcester, 1973-87; substance abuse/intervention counselor Adcare Hosp., Worcester, 1987-88; substance abuse counselor Longwood Treatment Ctr., Jamaica Plain, Mass., 1989-90; word processor Fenwall Safety Systems, Marlboro, Mass., 1990; instr. driver alcohol edn. program G. B. Wells Human Svcs. Ctr., Southbridge, Mass., 1988-93; group co-leader Women's Recovery Group, Framingham, 1990-91; with mech. drafting svcs. TBV Inc., Sutton, Mass., 1990-91; substance abuse therapist Together, Inc., Marlboro, 1990-92; counselor, trainer employee assistance svcs. Family Svcs. Ctrl. Mass., Worcester, Mass., 1992-94; pvt. practice therapy, Shrewsbury, Mass., 1992—; emergency svcs. clinician North Ctrl. Human Svcs., Gardner, Mass., 1993-94; internat. trade and mktg. cons., Shrewsbury, 1993—; program coord. Women's Hope Ctr. for Wellness and Recovery, Mass. Correctional Inst., Farmingham, 1994—. Candidate for selectman, Leicester, 1982; v.p. Belmont Home Cmty. Assn., Worcester, 1990. Recipient scholarship to the New Eng. Inst. of Addiction Studies, The Commonwealth of Mass. Div. of Substance Abuse Svcs., Brown Univ., Providence, 1991. Mem. ACA, Mass. Mental Health Counselors Assn.

TAN, AMY RUTH, writer; b. Oakland, Calif., Feb. 19, 1952; d. John Yuehhan and Daisy Ching (Tu) T.; m. Louis M. DeMattei, Apr. 6, 1974. BA in Linguistics and English, San Jose (Calif.) State U., 1973, MA in Linguistics, 1974; LHD (hon.), Dominican Coll. San Rafael, 1991. Specialist lang. devel. Alameda County Assn. for Mentally Retarded, Oakland, 1976-80; project dir. M.O.R.E. Project, San Francisco, 1980-81; free-lance writer, 1981-88. Author: The Joy Luck Club, 1989 (Nat. Book Critics Circle award for best novel nomination 1989, L.A. Times Book award nomination 1989, Gold award for fiction Commonwealth Club 1990, Bay Area Book Reviewers award for best fiction 1990), The Kitchen God's Wife, 1991, The Moon Lady, 1992, The Chinese Siamese Cat, 1994; also numerous short stories and essays; screenwriter, prodr.: (film) The Joy Luck Club, 1993. Recipient Best Am. Essays award, 1991. *

TAN, COLLEEN WOO, communications educator; b. San Francisco, May 6, 1923; d. Mr. and Mrs. S.H. Nq Quinn; m. Lawrence K.J. Tan; children: Lawrence L., Lance C. BA in English/Am. Lit., Ind. U., 1950, MA in English, 1952; MA in Speech Arts, Whittier Coll., 1972; postgrad., U. Calif. Berkeley, 1952-53. Cert. secondary edn. tchr., K-12, community coll., Calif. Tchng. aide English U. Calif., Berkeley, 1952-53; tchr. English and Social Studies Whittier (Calif.) High Sch., 1957-60; prof. speech comms. Mt. San Antonio Coll., Walnut, Calif., 1960-94; dir. forensics, 1969-80; sen. acad. senate Mt. San Antonio Coll., Walnut, Calif., 1982-90, faculty rep., 1990—; mem. numerous collegiate coms., campus advisor to Chinese Club and Asian Students Assn. Named Outstanding Prof. Emeritus, Mt. San Antonio Coll. Found., 1994. Mem. AAUW (pres. Whittier Br. 1982; cultural interests chair Calif. state divsn. 1985-87, Fellowship award 1973-74), Calif. Asian-Am. Faculty Assn., Delta Kappa Gamma, Phi Beta Kappa (Outstanding Educator of Am. award 1972, Las Distinguidas award 1992). Roman Catholic. Home: 13724 E Sunrise Dr Whittier CA 90602 Office: Mt San Antonio 1100 N Grand Ave Walnut CA 91789

TAN, LI-SU LIN, accountant, insurance executive; b. Keelung, Taiwan, Republic of China, Mar. 7, 1956; came to U.S. 1985; d. I-Chang and Sung-Mei (Chen) Lin; m. Bert T. Tan, Aug. 19, 1985; children: Patricia Tan, Peter Puwen Tan, Lotus Tan. BBA, Nat. Taiwan U., 1978; MBA, Ill. Inst. Tech., 1991. CPA, Ill., Taiwan; lic. ins. agt., Ill. Asst. mgr. Arthur Anderson, Taipei, 1978-85; practitioner Li-Su Lin, CPA, Taipei, 1981-85, Li-Su Lin Tan, CPA, Naperville, Ill., 1988-90; pres. Lisu L. Tan & Co., Ltd., CPAs, Naperville, Ill., 1990—; agt. Mut. of Omaha Co., Lombard, Ill., 1991-94, Met. Life and Affiliated Cos., Bloomingdale, Ill., 1993—. Chair family Naperville Chinese Assn., 1990. Mem. AICPA (tax div., quality control program), Ill. Soc. CPAs, Taipei First Girls High Alumni Assn. (treas. 1990—). Buddhist. Office: Lisu L Tan & Co Ltd CPAs 620 Bakewell Ln Naperville IL 60565

TAN, REGINA, internist; b. Ujungpandang, Indonesia, June 4, 1961; came to U.S., 1973.; d. Johannes and Joen (Bong) T. BA summa cum laude, St. Scholastica, 1983; MD, U. Minn., 1988. Intern, then resident Med. Coll. Va., Richmond, Va., 1988-91; physician in gen. internal medicine Internal Medicine of Chesapeake, Va., 1991—; mem. med. records audit com. Chesapeake Gen. Hosp., 1991-92, quality assurance com., 1991-93, infectious disease com., 1992-93; vol., physician Chesapeake Care, 1991—. Mem. ACP. Roman Catholic. Office: Internal Medicine of Chesapeake 1015 Eden Way N Ste E Chesapeake VA 23320

TAN, VERONICA Y., psychiatrist; b. Manila, The Philippines, Oct. 8, 1944; came to U.S., 1970; children: Terrence, Kristine. MD, U. St. Thomas, Manila, 1969. Intern U. Ill. Hosp., Chgo., 1970-71; resident Lafayette Clinic & Children's Hosp., Detroit; child, adolescent psychiatrist Bon Secours Hosp., Grosse Pointe, Mich., 1993—. Author: The Gifted Child, 1970.

TANAKA, LEILA CHIYAKO, lawyer; b. Honolulu, Mar. 11, 1954; d. Masami and Bernice Kiyoko (Nakamura) T. B Arts and Scis. with distinction in Japanese Lang. and Am. Studies, U. Hawaii, Manoa, 1977; JD, U. Santa Clara, 1980. Bar: Hawaii 1980, U.S. Dist. Ct. Hawaii 1980. Pvt. practice Honolulu, 1980-81; law clk. to judge Hawaii State Cir. Ct. (2d cir.), Wailuku, Maui, 1981-82; spl. dep. atty. gen. Dept. of Atty. Gen., Hawaii, 1983, dep. atty. gen., 1983-88; housing unit supr., 1987-88; eviction hearings trial examiner Hawaii Housing Authority, 1986-88; mgr. departmental liability Dept. Transp., Hawaii, 1988-94; boating regulation officer Office of Transp., Hawaii, 1994—. Mem. motor vehicle industry licensing bd. Dept. Commerce and Consumer Affairs, Hawaii, 1991—; mem. bd. Pacific Inst. Chem. Dependency, 1993—. Mem. Am. Judicature Soc., Smithsonian Instn., Hawaii Bar Assn., Soroptimist Internat. (v.p. Honolulu chpt.), Plaza Club, Phi Kappa Phi. Buddhist. Office: Hawaii Dept Transp 79 S Nimitz Hwy Honolulu HI 96813

TANCREDI, TERRY, social worker; b. Bronx, N.Y., Mar. 2, 1947; d. Max and Gussie (Kfare) Stengel; divorced; 1 child, Daniel. AA, Queensborough C.C., 1966; AB, CUNY, 1969; MSW, Adelphi U., 1978. Cert. social worker N.Y.; Diplomate Clin. Social Worker; Cert. Sch. Social Worker, Specialist Mental Retardation Profl. Employment interviewer N.Y. State Dept. Labor, N.Y.C., 1969-76; social worker sheltered workshop United Cerebral Palsy Assn. of N.Y.C., S.I., N.Y., 1978-80; sch. social worker N.Y.C. Bd. Edn., S.I., 1980-84; svc. provider, social worker N.Y.C. Bd. Edn., Bklyn., 1985-89; social worker N.Y.C. Bd. Edn., S.I., 1989—; cons. ACRMD Group Home, S.I., 1989-91, N.Y. State Dept. Determination and Disability, N.Y.C., 1991—; pvt. practice psychotherapy, S.I., 1985—. Mem. NASW. Democrat. Jewish.

TANDY, JEAN CONKEY, art educator; b. Reese, Mich., May 17, 1931; d. Samuel Hall and Christine Margaret (Walker) Conkey; m. Norman Edward Tandy, Jan. 25, 1952; children: Michelle Tandy Ryan, Kristen, Peter Spence. BA, Mich. State U., 1962, MA in Fine Arts, 1965. Instr. French Bath (Mich.) Community Schs., 1961-62, designer program art curriculum, instr., 1962-65; instr. art Mahar Regional Schs., Orange, Mass., 1966-67, Athol (Mass.)-Royalston Regional Schs., 1967-68; invited designer & developer art curriculum Mt. Wachusett C.C., Gardner, Mass., 1968, chair art dept., 1968—, prof. art, 1968—. Watercolors and clay exhibited in various shows, 1950—. Mt. Wachusett C.C. grantee, 1970-94, Fed. Govt. grantee, 1968. Mem. Am. Crafts Coun., Mass. C.C. Coun., Women in Arts, Teaching Faculty Assn. (v.p. 1979-80, pres. 1980-81, grievance officer 1981-82). Independent. Home: 539 Whipple Hill Rd PO Box 2 Winchester NH 03470

TANENBAUM, JILL NANCY, graphic designer; b. Glen Cove, N.Y., Dec. 18, 1954; d. Joseph and Barbara Sally (Kosberg) W.; m. Alan Lloyd T. BA in Studio Arts, SUCO, Oneonta, 1976; MA in Publ. Design, U. Balt., 1981. Asst. art dir. John Wine Design, Washington, 1981-82; pres. art dir. Jill Tanenbaum Graphic Design and Advt., Inc., Bethesda, Md., 1982—. Work included in S.D. Warren Idea Exchange and Promotional Services Library, Logobook, The Best of Business Card Design, 1994, The Best of Brochure Design, 1994. Recipient Cert. Excellence Strathmore Graphics Gallery, Westfield, Mass., 1984, Excellence award Hopper Paper Co., 1994, Beckett Paper Co., 1994. Mem. Am. Inst. Graphic Arts (bd. dirs. 1992-94), Direct Mktg. Assn. of Washington (bd. dirs.), Gaithersbury C. of C. Office: 4701 Sangamore Rd Bethesda MD 20816-2508

TANESE, NAOKO, educator; b. Tokyo, Nov. 18, 1959; came to U.S., 1976; d. Tomio and Ritsuko (Tsunemura) T. BA, U. Chgo., 1981; MA, Columbia U., 1984, MPhil, 1985, PhD, 1988. Rsch. technician U. Chgo., 1981-82; postdoctoral rsch. scientist U. Calif., Berkeley, 1988-93; asst. prof. NYU Med. Ctr., 1993—. Contbr. articles to profl. jours. Postdoctoral fellowship Am. Cancer Soc., Calif. Divsn., Inc., 1990-92; rsch. grant Am. Cancer Soc. Office: Dept Microbiology NYU Med Ctr 550 1st Ave New York NY 10016-6497

TANG, DEBBY TSENG, counselor; b. Taichung, Taiwan, Aug. 20, 1956; m. Almon Tang, Aug. 21, 1979. MS, Purdue U., 1980, PhD, 1984. Nat. cert. counselor and career counselor; lic. profl. counselor, Mich. Counselor Purdue U., West Lafayette, Ind., 1981-84; oranizational cons. U. Mich., Ann Arbor, 1984-86; counselor Wayne State U., Detroit, 1987—; mem. facutly Ea. Mich. U., Ypsilanti, 1989-93. Named Counselor of Yr., Mich. Minority Women's Network, 1989. Mem. ACA, AAUP (Wayne State chpt. chair academic staff steering com. 1989-90), Mich. Coll. Pers. Assn. (pres. 1993-94, editor newsletter 1989-91), Phi Kappa Phi. Home: 8122 Sandpiper St Canton MI 48187-1738 Office: Wayne State U 573 Student Ctr Detroit MI 48202

TANG, ROSA ANA, ophthalmologist; b. Lima, Peru, Aug. 23, 1948; came to U.S., 1974; d. Carlos Alberto and Rosa Zayda (Tanjun) T. MD, U. Peruana Cayetano Heredia, Lima, 1974. Diplomate Am. Bd. Ophthalmology. Intern, resident ophthalmology Georgetown U., Washington, 1976-79; fellow neuro-ophthalmology Baylor Coll. Medicine, Houston; clin. prof. dept. ophthalmology U. Tex., Houston, 1980—, clin. assoc. prof. dept. neurology, 1980—, clin. assoc. prof. dept. neuro-surgery, 1981—; clin. assoc. surgeon, clin. assoc. U. Ted. M.D. Anderson, Houston, 1981—; clin. prof. dept. ophthalmology U. Tex. Med. Br., Galveston, 1991—, clin. prof. dept. neurology, 1992—; dir. neuro-ophthalmology U. Tex. Med. Sch., Houston, 1980—, U. Tex. Med. Br., Galveston, 1991—; mem. dir. outpatient svc., 1993—; chairwoman Minority Adv. Com. for Women's Health Initiative, houston, 1993—. Office: Houston Eye Assocs 2855 Gramercy Houston TX 77025

TANGUY, NICOLE RENEE, lawyer; b. Houston, June 16, 1950; d. Denis Rene and Mary Jane (McNair) T. AB, Mt. Holyoke Coll., 1972; JD, Fordham U., 1978; LLM, NYU, 1984. Bar: N.Y. 1979. Tax assoc. Hawkins, Delafield & Wood, N.Y.C., 1978-82, Shearman & Sterling, N.Y.C., 1982-84; v.p. Salomon Bros., Inc., N.Y.C., 1984—. Stern scholar NYU. Mem. Securities Industry Assn. (mem. tech. tax com. 1986—), Wall St. Tax Assn. Home: 77 7th Ave Apt 10H New York NY 10011-6625 Office: Salomon Bros Inc 7 World Trade Ctr New York NY 10048

TANIGUCHI, DIANE FUMIE, sales executive; b. Honolulu, May 31, 1948; d. Hitoshi and Taeko (Hoshiwara) T. BA, U. Wash., 1970. Sec. (dept. head/inventory control to exec.) various cos., Seattle, 1970-88; volleyball coach, 1988—; designer garments and crafts Pen 'n Pins, Seattle, 1988—; project asst. Westin Hotel Co., Seattle, 1979—. Former chair and pres. Aux. Ways and Means, Children's Hosp. of Cedar Park; adv. bd. Women's Sports Found.; local volleyball ofcl.; pub. educator on ovarian cancer and death/dying. Mem. U.S. Volleyball Assn. (commr. Evergreen region).

TANNEN, DEBORAH FRANCES, writer, linguist; b. Bklyn., June 7, 1945; d. Eli S. and Dorothy (Rosen) T. BA, SUNY, Binghamton, 1966; MA, Wayne State U., 1970, U. Calif., Berkeley, 1976; PhD, U. Calif., 1979. Instr. Greek-Am. Cultural Inst., Herakleion, Greece, 1966-67; instr. in English as fgn. lang. Hellenic Am. Union, Athens, Greece, 1967-68; English instr. Detroit Inst. Tech., 1969, Mercer County C.C., Trenton, N.J., 1970-71; lectr. in acad. skills CUNY, Bronx, N.Y., 1971-74; asst. prof. Georgetown U., Washington, 1979-85, assoc. prof. linguistics, 1985-90; univ. prof., 1991—; McGraw disting. lectr. in writing Coun. for Humanities and dept. anthropology Princeton U., fall 1991; visitor Inst. for Advanced Study, Princeton, spring 1992. Author: Lilika Nakos, 1983, Conversational Style: Analyzing Talk Among Friends, 1984, That's Not What I Meant!: How Conversational Style Makes or Breaks Your Relations With Others, 1984, Talking Voices: Repetition, Dialogue and Imagery in Conversational Discourse, 1989, You Just Don't Understand: Women and Men in Conversation, 1990, Gender and Discourse, 1994, Talking From 9 to 5: How Women's and Men's Conversational Styles Affect Who Gets Heard, Who Gets Credit, and What Gets Done at Work, 1994; editor: Analyzing Discourse: Text and Talk, 1982, Spoken and Written Language: Exploring Orality and Literacy, 1982, Coherence in Spoken and Written Discourse, 1984, Perspectives on Silence, 1985, Linguistics in Context, 1986, Gender and Conversational Interaction, 1993, Framing In Discourse, 1993; editor: Linguistics in Context: Connecting Observation and Understanding, 1988. Rockefeller Humanities fellow, 1982-83, Ctr. Advanced Study Behavioral Scis. fellow, Stanford, Calif., 1992-93; grantee NEH, 1980, 85, 86; recipient Elizabeth Mills Crothers prize U. Calif., 1976, Dorothy Rosenberg Meml. prize U. Calif., 1977, Joan Lee Yang Meml. Poetry prize U. Calif., 1977, Shrout Short Story prize, 1978, Emily Chamberlain Cook prize, 1978. Office: Georgetown U Linguistics Dept Washington DC 20057

TANNENWALD, LESLIE KEITER, educational administrator; b. Boston, May 5, 1949; d. Irving Jules and Barbara June (Caplan) Keiter; m. Robert Tannenwald. BA, Brandeis U., 1971, MA, 1976; MAT in Social Studies, Simmons Coll., Boston, 1972. Cert. Social Worker, Tchr., Mass. Sr. assoc. Combined Jewish Philanthropies of Greater Boston, 1977-84; interim dir., asst. dir. Cambridge (Mass.) Community Svcs., 1984-85; ednl. cons. Bur. Jewish Edn., Boston, 1985-87; ednl. dir. Congregation Shalom Emeth, Burlington, Mass., 1987-92, Congregation Temple Aliyah, Needham, Mass., 1992-93; religious sch. dir. Falmouth (Mass.) Jewish Congregation, 1993—; cons. Selected Ednl. Orgns. Boston 1972. Author: Curriculum, Male and Female, 1979 (Honors award 1971), Understanding the Holocaust, 1990. Officer, bd. dirs. Combined Jewish Philantropies of Greater Boston 1972—; mem. Am. Jewish Congress, Boston 1976—. Recipient Leadership award Inst. Leadership Devel. and Fund Raising. Mem. Nat. Alliance Profl. & Exec. Women, Alumni Assn. Benjamin S. Hornstein Program of Jewish Communal Svc., Assn. Jewish Community Personnel. Democrat. Home: 6 Clifton Rd Newton MA 02159-3147

TANNER, GLORIA GERALDINE, state legislator; b. Atlanta, July 16, 1935; d. Marcellus and Blanche Arnold Travis; m. Theodore Ralph Tanner, 1955 (dec.); children: Terrance Ralph, Tanvis Renee, Tracey Lynne. BA, Met. State Coll., 1974; MUA, U. Colo., 1976. Office mgr. Great Western Mfg. Co., Denver, 1965-67; writer Rage mag., 1969-70; reporter, feature writer Denver Weekly News, 1970-75; dir. East Denver Cmty. Office, 1974—; also real estate agt.; mem. Colo. Ho. of Reps., 1985—; minority caucus chairwoman; mem. appropriations, bus. affairs, labor coms. Dist. capt. Denver Dem. Com., Colo., 1973-75; chairwoman Senatorial Dist. 3 Dem. Com., 1974-82; adminstrv. aide Colo. State Senator Regis Groff, Denver, 1974-82; alt. del. Dem. Nat. Conv., 1976, del., 1980; commr. Colo. Status of Women, 1977—; chairwoman Colo. Black Women for Polit. Action, 1977—; exec. asst. to Lt. Gov., 1978-79; mem. adv. bd. United Negro Coll. Fund, Colo. State Treas. Served USAF, 1952-55. Recipient Outstanding Cmty. Leadership award Scott's Meth. Ch., 1974, Tribute to Black Women award, 1980; named Woman of Yr., Colo. Black Women Caucus, 1974. Mem. Colo. Black Media Assn. (pub. dir. 1972—), Reginas' Civic Club (founder, first pres. 1959—, Outstanding Woman of Yr. 1975), Nat. Assn. Real Estate Brokers. Roman Catholic. Democrat. Home: 2150 Monaco Pky Denver CO 80207-3951 Office: Colo Ho of Reps State Capital Denver CO 80203*

TANNER, HELEN HORNBECK, historian; b. Northfield, Minn., July 5, 1916; d. John Wesley and Frances Cornelia (Wolfe) Hornbeck; m. Wilson P. Tanner, Jr., Nov. 22, 1940 (dec. 1977); children—Frances, Margaret Tanner Tewson, Wilson P., Robert (dec. 1983). A.B. with honors, Swarthmore Coll., 1937; M.A., U. Fla., 1949; Ph.D., U. Mich., 1961. Asst. to dir. pub. rels. Kalamazoo Pub. Schs., 1937-39; with sales dept. Am. Airlines Inc., N.Y.C., 1940-43; teaching fellow, then teaching asst. U. Mich., Ann Arbor, 1949-53, 57-60, lectr. extension svc., 1961-74, asst. dir. Ctr. Continuing Edn. for Women, 1964-68; project dir. Newberry Libr., Chgo., 1976-81, rsch. assoc., 1981—; dir. D'Arcy McNickle Ctr. for Indian History, 1984-85; cons., expert witness Indian treaties; mem. Mich. Commn. Indian Affairs, 1966-70. Author: Zespedes in East Florida 1784-1790, 1963, 89, General Green Visits St. Augustine, 1964, The Greeneville Treaty, 1974, The Territory of the Caddo Tribe of Oklahoma, 1974, The Ojibwas, 1992; editor: Atlas of Great Lakes Indian History, 1987. NEH grantee, 1976, fellow, 1989; ACLS grantee, 1990. Mem. Am. Soc. Ethnohistory (pres. 1982-83), Am. Hist. Assn., Conf. Latin Am. History, Soc. History Discoveries, Orgn. Am. Historians, Chgo. Map Soc., Fla. Hist. Soc. Home: 5178 Crystal Dr Beulah MI 49617-9618 Office: The Newberry Libr 60 W Walton St Chicago IL 60610-3305

TANNER, JACQUI DIAN, chemist, information scientist; b. Indpls., Feb. 2, 1946; d. Richard O. and Norris (Shane) Tanner; divorced; children: Patrick Mahaffey, David Bridgeforth, Regina Easley, Darla Smith, Mark Young. BS, Marian Coll., 1970; MS, Ball State U., 1982. With Union Carbide, Indpls., 1965-68; with Eli Lilly & Co., Indpls., 1968-85, sr. patent specialist, 1978-85; group leader chem. and patents groups Ayerst Research Labs, Princeton, N.J., 1985-88; sr. info. scientist, mgr. chem. and patent info. sect. R.W. Johnson Pharm. Rsch. Inst., divsn. of Ortho Pharm. Co., Raritan, N.J., 1988-89; mgr. Proprietary Info. Mgmt., 1990-91, asst. dir., 1992—. Bd. dirs., hosp. counselor Marion County Victims Advocates Program, 1978—; bd. dirs. Big Bros./Big Sisters Somerset County, 1990-91; mem. youth adv. bd. Ctr. for Leadership Devel., 1979-85; mem. adv. bd. Walker Career Ctr., 1981-86; mem. Warren Twp. (Ind.) Sch. Improvement Council, 1980-86; mem. Warren Twp. curriculum study steering com., 1982-86; founder, exec. dir. Found. for the Success of Unwed Parents, 1986—; bd. dirs. Martin Luther King Youth Ctr., Bridgewater, N.J., 1992—. Mem. ALA, AAAS, Am. Statis. Assn., Assn. Imaging and Info. Mgrs., Assn. Info. Mgrs., Am. Soc. Info. Sci., Spl. Libr. Assn., N.Y. Acad. Sci., Am. Chem. Soc. Roman Catholic. Office: RW Johnson-Pharm Rsch Inst PO Box 300 1000 Us Highway 202 Raritan NJ 08869-1425

TANNER, LAUREL NAN, education educator; b. Detroit, Feb. 16, 1929; d. Howard Nicholas and Celia (Solvich) Jacobson; m. Daniel Tanner, July 11, 1948; m. Kenneth J. Rehage, Nov. 25, 1989. BS in Social Sci, Mich. State U., 1949, MA in Edn., 1953; EdD, Columbia U., 1967. Pub. sch. tchr., 1950-64; instr. tchr. edn. Hunter Coll., 1964-66, asst. prof., 1967-69; supr. Milw. Pub. Schs., 1966-67; mem. faculty Temple U., Phila., 1969—; prof. edn. Temple U., 1974-89, U. Houston, 1989—; vis. professorial scholar U. London Inst. Edn., 1974-75; vis. scholar Stanford U., 1984-85, U. Chgo., 1988-89; curriculum cons., 1969—; disting. vis. prof. San Francisco State U., 1987. Author: Classroom Discipline for Effective Teaching and Learning, 1978, La Disciplina en la enseñanza y el Aprendizaje, 1980; co-author: Classroom Teaching and Learning, 1971, Curriculum Development: Theory into Practice, 1975, 3d edit., 1995, Supervision in Education: Problems and Practices, 1987, (with Daniel Tanner) History of the School Curriculum, 1990; editor Nat. Soc. Study Edn. Critical Issues in Curriculum, 87th yearbook, part 1, 1988. Faculty rsch. fellow Temple U., 1970, 80, 81; recipient John Dewey Rsch. award, 1981-82, Rsch. Excellence award U. Houston, 1992; Spencer Found. rsch. grantee, 1992. Mem. ASCD (dir. 1982-84), Soc. Study Curriculum History (founder, 1st pres. 1978-79), Am. Edn. Rsch. Assn. (com. on role and status of women in ednl. R & D 1994—), Profs. Curriculum Assn. (Facotum 1983-84, chair membership com. 1994-95), Am. Ednl. Studies Assn., John Dewey Soc. (bd. dirs. 1989-91), Alumni Coun. Tchrs. Coll. Columbia U.

TANNER, MARISA ANN, army officer; b. Germany, Mar. 16, 1959; (parents Am. citizens); d. Francis Alphonse and Ann Louise (Wiggin) Ianni; m. William Frederick Tanner, Jr., May 20, 1985. AA in Art, Salem (W.Va.) Coll., 1979; BSBA, Goldey Beacom Coll., Wilmington, Del., 1984; postgrad., Joint Mil. Intelligence Coll., Washington, 1994—. Commd. 2d lt. U.S. Army, 1983, advanced through grades to maj., 1994; asst. sec. to gen. staff 2d Inf. Div., Republic of Korea, 1984, electronic counter measures platoon leader, 1984-85; strategic intelligence officer Intelligence Security Command (Airborne), Ft. Bragg, N.C., 1985-87, intelligence officer 9th psychol. ops. bn.(Airborne), 1987-88; chief order of battle 1st Republic of Korea Army, 1989; asst. ops. officer 14th Mil. Intelligence Bn., Ft. Lewis, Wash., 1990, comdr. Bravo co., 1991; brigade intelligence officer 210th Field Artillery Brigade, Ft. Lewis, 1992-93; sr. intelligence officer Joint Readiness Tng. Ctr. (Airborne), Ft. Polk, La., 1994—. Mem. U.S. Field Artillery Assn., U.S. Army Polo Team, Assn. U.S. Army. Republican. Roman Catholic. Home: # 35 Briarwood Manor Deridder LA 70634 Office: Def Intelligence Agy Joint Mil Intelligence Coll Washington DC 20340-5485

TANNER, TERESA L., medical nurse; b. Lancaster, Pa., Nov. 21, 1968; d. Donald G. and Roxie B. Wood. AS, Odessa (Tex.) Coll., 1990, postgrad., 1990—. TN, Tex.; ACLS; advanced EKG cert. Former oncology/telemetry charge nurse; now staff nurse med. floor Mother Frances Hosp., Tyler, charge nurse med./telemetry; staff nurse Akron (Ohio) City Hosp. Vol. ARC, Lancaster.

TANUR, JUDITH MARK, sociologist, educator; b. Jersey City, Aug. 12, 1935; d. Edward Mark and Libbie (Berman) Mark; m. Michael Isaac Tanur, June 2, 1957; children: Rachel Dorothy, Marcia Valerie. BS, Columbia U., 1957, MA, 1963; PhD, SUNY, Stony Brook, 1972. Analyst Biometrics Rsch., N.Y.C., 1955-67; lectr. SUNY, Stony Brook, 1967-71, from asst. prof. to prof. sociology, 1971-94, disting. teaching prof., 1994—; cons. NBC, N.Y.C., 1976-89, Lang. of Data Project, Los Altos, Calif., 1980-89; mem. Com. on Nat. Stats. of Nat. Acad. of Scis., 1980-87; trustee NORC, U. Chgo., 1987—. Editor: Statistics: A Guide to the Unknown, 1972, Internat. Encyclopedia of Statistics, 1978, Cognitive Aspects of Survey Methodology, 1984, Questions About Questions, 1991; editor Internat. Ency. of Social Scis., N.Y.C., 1963-67; contbr. articles to sci., statis. and social sci. jours. Bd. dirs. Vis. Nurse Svc., Great Neck, N.Y., 1970—; bd. govs. Gen. Soc. Survey, Chgo., 1989-92. Sr. rsch. fellow, Am. Statis. Assn./NSF/Bur. Labor Statistics, 1988-89. Fellow, AAAS, Am. Statis. Assn.; mem. Internat. Statis. Inst., Phi Beta Kappa. Home: 17 Longview Pl Great Neck NY 11021-2508 Office: SUNY Dept Sociology Stony Brook NY 11794

TANZMAN-BOCK, MAXINE M., psychotherapist, hypnotherapist, consultant; b. New Brunswick, N.J., Mar. 30, 1957. BA is Sociology, Rutgers U., 1980; MSW, Fordham U., 1984. Cert. hypnotherapist, hypno-anaesthesia therapist, social worker; registered hypnotherapist; qualified clin. social worker; lic. clin. social worker. Therapist Van Ost Inst. for Family Living, Englewood, N.J.; pvt. practice Wayne, N.J., 1986—; ptnr. To the Maxx; cons. Union City Schs., N.J., Physicians Weight Loss Ctr., Wayne; psychotherapist Cath. Cmty. Svcs., Paramus, N.J.; with Family Svcs. Bergen Couny, N.J.; vol. probation counselor, residence counselor Serv Ctrs., N.J.; social worker st. Lawrence Rehab. Ctr., N.J.; ptnr. To The Maxx Firm; designer and presenter workshops. Featured cable TV 1990; host weekly call in therapy show on radio, 1991-92. Mem. NASW, Acad. Cert. Social Workers, Am. Assn. Behavioral Therapists, Am. Assn. Profl. Hypnotherapists. Office: 25 Packanack Lake Rd Wayne NJ 07470-5809

TAPER, GERI, artist, educator; b. Pitts., Dec. 5, 1929; d. William and Fannye (Goldman) T.; children: Ronald, Richard, David. BS, U. Pitts., 1951; postgrad., Carnegie-Mellon U., Pitts., 1970-72. Tchr. Pitts. Pub. Schs., 1951-54; art instr. Art Inst. Pitts., 1970-73, U. Pitts., 1970-71, Duquesne U., Pitts., 1970-71, Met. Mus. Art, N.Y.C., 1983-84; environ. artist N.Y.C. and Phila., 1980-90; cons. Arts And The Handicappped, N.Y.C., 1983-85, environ. artist La Guardia Coll., N.Y.C., 1988-89. One-woman shows include Sculpted Painting Accessible to the Blind and Visually-Impaired, N.Y.C., 1984, Transformation of Large Indsl. Bldgs. into Visual Experiences, N.Y.C., 1980-90, Center Bldg., L.I. City, N.Y., Redstone Rocket Bldg., L.I. City, Falchi Bldg., L.I. City, 1990; creator banner sculpture transit program Met. Transp. Authority Arts, L.I., N.Y., 1989, Celebrating the Boroughs Van Project, Bronx C.C., N.Y.C., 1990; cmty. mural project, Sunnyside Cmty. Svcs. Early Childhood Ctr., N.Y.C., 1991. Mem. Arts and the Handicapped (charter), Found. for the Community of Artists, Artists Equity, Mus. Modern Art, New Mus. Contemporary Art, Whitney Mus. Art. Home and Studio: 458 Broome St New York NY 10013-2611

TAPP, JUNE LOUIN, psychology educator; b. N.Y.C.; d. R.B. Louin and Ann Revier-Wacholder. B.A. magna cum laude in Sociology, U. So. Calif., 1951; M.S. in Ednl. Psychology, 1952; Ph.D. in Psychology, Syracuse U., 1963. Registered psychologist, Ill. Instr. ednl. psychology and psychology St. Lawrence U., Canton, N.Y., 1952-55; adminstrv. asst. to dean Moran Crime Inst., 1954-60; asst. instr. in citizenship Maxwell Grad. Sch., Syracuse U., N.Y., 1955-56; tutor in psychology and sociology Albert Schweitzer Coll., Churwalden, Switzerland, 1957-58; asst. prof. psychology Harvey Mudd Coll., Claremont, Calif., 1961-64; organizer behavioral scis. program, 1961-64; lectr., cons. Indian Coll. Youth Project, U. Poona, India, 1963-64; asst. prof., research assoc. com. on human devel. U. Chgo., 1964-67; assoc. prof., research assoc. com. on human devel., 1964-67, assoc. prof. in social scis., 1968-72; co-investigator, project adminstr. Children's Socialization into Compliance Systems, 1965-70; sr. research social scientist Am. Bar Found., Chgo., 1967-72; affiliated scholar, 1972-74; fellow in law and psychology Harvard U. Law Sch., Cambridge, Mass., 1971-72; prof. psychology U. Calif.-San Diego, La Jolla, 1976-78; provost Revelle Coll., 1976-78; chmn. humanities program, 1976-77, chmn. law and society program, 1977-78; prof. child psychology and criminal justice studies, adj. prof. law, adj. prof. family studies U. Minn., Mpls., 1972—; participant U. Calif.-Irvine Mgmt. Inst., 1977; cons. in field; lectr. profl. confs. and symposia. Author: (with F. Krinsky) Ambivalent America: A Psycho-political Dialogue, 1971; (with F.J. Levine) Law, Justice and Individual in Society, 1977. Mem. numerous editorial bds. of profl. jours. Manuscript reviewer for numerous profl. jours. Contbr. articles to profl. jours., chpts. to books. Mem. numerous civic, govtl. and profl. orgns. Recipient numerous civic and profl. awards; grantee in psychology and law from numerous profl. and govtl. agys. and orgns. Fellow Am. Psychol. Assn. (council 1981-84); mem. Am. Psychology-Law Soc. (pres. 1972-73), Soc. Psychol. Study Social Issues (pres. 1978-79), Soc. Research Child Devel., Internat. Assn. Polit. Psychology (council 1979-82), Assn. Advancement Psychology (trustee 1980-84), Interam. Soc. Psychology (v.p. 1985—), Internat. Assn. Cross-Cultural Psychology, Internat. Assn. Philosophy (exec. com. 1974-75), Law and Soc. Assn. (sec. 1973-74, trustee 1980-82), Soc. Exptl. Social Psychology (mem. forum White House Conf. on Children 1970). Address: Inst Child Devel 51 E River Rd U Minn Minneapolis MN 55455

TAPPER, JOAN JUDITH, magazine editor; b. Chgo., June 12, 1947; d. Samuel Jack and Anna (Swoiskin) T.; m. Steven Richard Siegel, Oct. 15, 1971. BA, U. Chgo., 1968; MA, Harvard U., 1969. Editor manuscripts Chelsea House, N.Y.C., 1969-71, Scribners, N.Y.C., 1971; editor books Nat. Acad. Scis., Washington, 1972-73; assoc. editor Praeger Pubs., Washington, 1973-74; editor New Rep. Books, Washington, 1974-79; mng. editor spl. pubs. Nat. Geog. Soc., Washington, 1979-83; editor Nat. Geog. Traveler, Washington, 1984-88; editor-in-chief Islands (internat. mag.), Santa Barbara, Calif., 1989—. Mem. Am. Soc. Mag. Editors, Soc. Am. Travel Writers (editors' coun.), Channel City Club. Democrat. Jewish. Home: 603 Island View Dr Santa Barbara CA 93109-1508 Office: Islands Mag 3886 State St Santa Barbara CA 93105-3112

TARANOW, GERDA, English language educator, researcher, author; b. N.Y.C.; d. Samuel and Sabina (Ostro) T. B.A., NYU, 1952, M.A., 1955; Ph.D., Yale U., 1961, postdoctoral studies, 1962-63. Instr. English, U. Ky., Lexington, 1963-65, asst. prof., 1965-66, Syracuse U., N.Y., 1966-67; asst. prof. Conn. Coll., New London, 1967-70, assoc. prof., 1970-76, prof., 1976—; referee NEH, Washington, 1972—. Author: Sarah Bernhardt: The Art Within the Legend, 1972. Yale U. fellow, 1962-63, NEH fellow, 1980-81. Mem. MLA, Am. Soc. Theatre Research, Soc. for Theatre Research (England), Internat. Fedn. for Theatre Research, Société, d'Histoire du théâtre (France). Avocations: opera; theatre; ballet. Office: Conn Coll PO Box 5567 New London CT 06320

TARANTO, MARIA ANTOINETTE, psychology researcher and educator; b. Framingham, Mass., Dec. 28, 1941; d. Gaetano (Tom) Peter and Rose Marie (Busceme) T.; m. John Curtis Mahon, June 5, 1988. BA in Psychology, Bennington Coll., 1965; MA in Psychology, George Peabody Coll., 1968; M Philosophy in Psychology, Columbia U., 1981, PhD, 1985. Tchr. Head Start Pub Sch. System, Pitts., 1966-67; rsch. assoc. Hofstra U., Hempstead, N.Y., 1968-69; instr. Hofstra U., Hempstead, 1969-72; co-dir. Inst. for Piagetian Studies, Hempstead, 1972-76; instr. Nassau Community Coll., Garden City, N.Y., 1976-78; asst. prof. Nassau Community Coll., Garden City, 1978-85, assoc. prof. psychology, 1985—; jour. reviewer Baywood Pub. Co., Long Island, N.Y., 1989, Karger, Basel, Switzerland, 1989. Co-author: (monographs) A Study of Number..., 1972, Liquid Conservation, 1976; contbr. articles to profl. jours and govt. pubs. Mem. Union of Concerned Scientists, 1981—, Amnesty Internat., 1987—; sponsor Pearl S. Buck Found., 1984—. Recipient Mellon fellowship CUNY, N.Y.C., 1987. Mem. Am. Psychol. Assn., Jean Piaget Soc., Gerontol. Soc., New Eng. Psychol. Assn. Office: Nassau CC Stewart Ave Garden City NY 11530-2200

TARASKO, ALEXANDRA, nursing educator; b. Austria, Jan. 15, 1949; came to U.S., 1955; d. Peter Stephen and Alexandra (Narizna) Bazylewsky; m. Basil Paul Tarasko, Aug. 15, 1970; children: Andrei, Michael. BSN, Hunter Coll., 1973; MA in Nursing Edn., NYU, 1980. Psychiat. nurse Roosevelt Hosp., N.Y.C., 1974-76, head nurse, 1976-78; assoc. prof. Queensborough C.C., Bayside, N.Y., 1981—; recruiter nursing dept. Queensborough C.C., 1986-90; adj. lectr. NYU, N.Y.C., 1980; coord. Older Adults: Health Care '90's, Bayside, 1990, AIDS Conf., Bayside, 1991; participant TV and radio appearances, 1989, 91. Apptd. mem. Health Careers Task Force, N.Y.C., 1991, CUNY Health Professions Task Force, Psychosocial Svcs., 1994—; leader Health Explorer post Boy Scouts Am., Queensborough C.C., 1988-90. Mem. Nat. League for Nursing. Home: 36-46 212 St Bayside NY 11361 Office: Queensborough CC Springfield Blvd And 5 Ave Flushing NY 11364

TARBELL, JANET ROGERS, accountant, auditor; b. Washington, June 18, 1955; d. Robert John and Ruth (Parish) Rogers; m. Richard Goldon Tarbell, June 11, 1988 (div. Mar. 1991). BBA, S.W. Tex. State U., 1976, MBA, 1978. CPA, Tex.; lic. real estate broker, Tex. Acct. Brown & Root, Inc., Houston, 1978-81; sr. auditor Skytop Brewster Co., Houston, 1981-83; controller Jewel Foliage Co., San Antonio, 1983-85; internal audit mgr. Church's Fried Chicken, Inc., San Antonio, 1985-89; asst. state auditor Tex. State Auditor's Office, Austin, 1992—. Vol. Jr. League of Austin, 1991-93, San Antonio Conservation Soc., 1985-93. Mem. ASCPAs, Tex. Soc. CPAs. Office: State Auditors Office 206 E 9th St Ste 1900 Austin TX 78701-2516

TARBOX, RUTH RUNNING, art gallery executive; b. Toronto, Ont., Can., Sept. 25, 1916; came to U.S., 1951, naturalized, 1958; d. Claude William and Dorothy Victoria (Hartman) Running; m. John William Tarbox, Mar. 11, 1946. Student, U. Toronto. Reporter Globe and Mail newspaper, Toronto, 1936-42; fin. advisor nat. war fin. com. Govt. of Can., Ottawa, Ont., 1942-46; copy writer McLaren Advt. Agy., Toronto, 1946-48, John D. Hoel Advt., Pasadena, Calif., 1953-55; pub. rels. ofcl. Sascha Brastoff, L.A., 1955-57; owner, mgr. Tarbox Gallery, L.A., 1957-71, La Jolla, Calif., 1971-83, San Diego, 1983—. Republican. Episcopalian. Office: Tarbox Gallery 1202 Kettner Blvd San Diego CA 92101

TARBOX, SUSAN WEBER, filmmaker; b. Fulton, N.Y., Aug. 17, 1955; d. Duward Marshall and Ruth (Freeman) Tarbox. BS, SUNY, Brockport, 1977; MFA, N.Y.U., 1982. Dir. photography IATSE, N.Y., 1990. Home: 41-37 Parsons Blvd #1B Flushing NY 11355

TARLOW, JANE RAE, community health nurse; b. Glasgow, Ky., Oct. 22, 1948. BA in Psychology, Washington U., St. Louis, 1970; BSN, U. Ala., Birmingham, 1974; MSN in Community Health summa cum laude, Emory U., 1979. RN, Ala., Fla.; cert. cmty. health clin. specialist; cert. BLS. Psychiat. recreational therapist Renard Hosp., St. Louis, 1970-72; program coord. hypertension control Ala. Dept. Pub. Health, Montgomery, 1975-76; pub. health nurse Montgomery County Health Dept., 1976-78; psychiat. nurse, group leader River Oaks Hosp., New Orleans, 1978; instr. Sch.

Nursing Auburn U., Montgomery, 1979-83; area dir. nursing, then perinatal coord. Ala. Dept. Pub. Health, Pelham, 1983-90; coord. obstet. complications clinic U. Ala., Birmingham, 1990-91; case mgmt. dir. Children's Hosp. Ala., Birmingham, 1991-94; dir. collaborative care Sarasota Meml. Hosp., 1994—; health cons. Southeast region Head Start Program, Atlanta, 1987-94; wellness cons. Southeast Health Plan HMO, Birmingham, 1988-89; bd. dirs., treas. Child Care Resources, Birmingham, 1988-94; childbirth educator Jefferson County Dept. health, Birmingham, 1991-94; regional bd. dirs. Ala. Perinatal Adv. Com., Birmingham, 1986-94; bd. dirs. March of Dimes Adv. Com., Birmingham, 1989-94, bd. dirs. cen. dist. Ala. chpt. Am. Lung Assn., 1982-88. Contbr. articles, revs. to profl. publs. Named Outstanding Vol. Ala. chpt. Am. Lung Assn., 1982. Mem. ANA (mem. various state and county coms. and bds.), APHA, Ind. Case Mgmt. Assn., Zonta, Sigma Theta Tau. Office: Sarasota Meml Hosp Childrens Hosp Ala 1700 S Tamiami Tr Sarasota FL 34239-3555

TARNOW, MALVA MAY WESCOE, post anesthesia care nurse; b. Allentown, Pa., July 27, 1942; d. Frederick H. and Malva M. (Tharp) Wescoe; m. Donald F. Tarnow, Aug. 5, 1967; children: Dean, Elizabeth. Diploma, Bellevue Sch. Nursing, N.Y.C., 1963; BS in Hosp. Mgmt., Pacific Christian Coll., 1978. Cert. post anesthesia nurse. Staff nurse recovery rm. Bellevue Hosp., N.Y.C., 1963-66; charge nurse recovery rm. Los Angeles County Gen. Hosp., L.A., 1966-68; staff nurse post anesthesia care unit Los Robles Regional Med. Ctr., Thousand Oaks, Calif., 1968-70, 73-93; staff nurse ICU and CCU Ventura County Gen. Hosp., Ventura, Calif., 1970; staff nurse post anesthesia care unit Granada Hills (Calif.) Community Hosp., 1989—. Mem. Am. Soc. Post Anesthesia Nurses (Calif. alt. dir. 1990-93), Post Anesthesia Nurses Assn. Calif. (dist. bd. dirs. 1980-84, treas. 1984-86, pres.-elect 1986-87, pres. 1987-88). Home: 2769 Redondo Cir Camarillo CA 93012-8229

TARQUINIO, ANTOINETTE CAMILLE, handicapped education educator; b. Pitts., June 13, 1956; d. Edythe Marie Tarquinio. BS in Edn., Calif. U. Pa., 1993. Merchandising asst. Wetterau Inc., Belle Vernon, Pa., 1979-91; pvt. tutor Monessen, Pa., 1991-93; devel. specialist Early Intervention, Monessen, 1994—, Diversified Human Svcs., Monessen, 1994—; residential program worker community living arrangements Diversified Human Svcs., Monessen, 1991-93. Choir dir. Epiphany of Our Lord Ch., Monessen, 1990—. Named All Am. Scholar, 1993; recipient Nat. Collegiate award U.S. Achievement Acad., 1991, 93. Mem. Coun. for Exceptional Children, Sigma Pi Epsilon Delta, Kappa Delta Pi. Democrat. Roman Catholic. Home and Office: 144 Meadowview Dr Canonsburg PA 15317

TARR, KATHLEEN ROSE ROSS, mortgage company executive; b. Boston, Apr. 17, 1949; d. David Tebbutt and Pauline Claire (Brooks) Peck; m. Raymond Kimball Tarr Jr., Dec. 30, 1987. BS, Boston U., 1971; postgrad., MacQuarie U., Sydney, Australia, 1976-79. Cert. of tng., Nat. Assn. Mortgage Brokers. Tchr. N.S.W. Dept. Edn., Sydney, 1976-80; mgr. mortgage Chilton Credit Reporting, Boston, 1980-86; mortgage cons. Farragut Mortgage Co., Boston, 1986-87; v.p. Comfed Mortgage Co., Wakefield, Mass., 1987-90; pres., founder Homestead Mortgage Corp., North Reading, Mass., 1990—. Author children's story: A Duck out of Water, 1976. Instr. Bentley Coll., Waltham, Mass. Named Credit Women of Yr., Credit Women Internat., Boston, 1983, Cert. of Appreciation Ea. Middlesex Bd. Realtors, 1987. Mem. Ea. Middlesex Bd. Realtors, Women's Coun. Realtors, Mass. Assn. Mortgage Brokers and Corr. Lenders (v.p., chmn. edn. com.), North Reading Bus. Assn. (sec.). Home: 14 Boardman St Haverhill MA 01830-6401 Office: Homestead Mortgage Corp 50 Main St North Reading MA 01864-2281

TARR-WHELAN, LINDA JANE, political organization administrator; b. Springfield, Mass., May 24, 1940; d. Albert and Jane Zack; m. Keith Tarr-Whelan; children: Scott, Melinda. BSN, Johns Hopkins U., 1963; MS, U. Md., 1967. Program dir. AFSCME AFL-CIO, Washington, 1968-74, union area dir., 1974-76; adminstrn. dir. N.Y. State Labor Dept., Albany, N.Y., 1976-79; dep. asst. to pres. Carter White House, Washington, 1979-80; dir. govt. rels. NEA, Washington, 1980-86; exec. dir., pres. Ctr. for Policy Alternatives, Washington, 1986—. Bd. dirs. Fannie Mae Nat. Adv. Com., Benton Found., Advocacy Inst., Voters for Choice, State Issues Forum, Nat. Consumers League, Ctr. for Policy Alternatives, Washington, 1985—. Named Japan Leadership Fellow Japan Soc., 1987-88, Disting. Grad. Johns Hopkins U., 1981. Democrat. Home: 3466 Roberts Ln N Arlington VA 22207 Office: Ctr for Policy Alternatives 1875 Connecticut Ave NW Washington DC 20009-5728

TARTAGLIONE, BARBARA LEE, career development consultant and trainer; b. Cleve., May 27, 1947; d. Frank A. and Bertha M. Taranto; m. John A. Tartaglione, May 31, 1968; children: Tracey, Michael, Jennifer. BS in Edn., Ill. Benedictine Coll., 1982; MS in Counselor Edn., No. Ill. U., 1987. Nat. bd. cert. career counselor. Career ctr. coord. Lisle (Ill.) Sr. High Sch., 1985-87; career cons., pres. Career Connection, Naperville, Ill., 1986—; gender equity cons. Career Transition Ctr., Bus. and Profl. Inst., Coll. DuPage, Glen Ellyn, Ill., 1988; cons. Ill. State Bd. Edn., Springfield, 1989-91; career cons., pres. Career Connection, Naperville, 1986—; dir. career svcs. The Mgmt. Assn. of Ill., 1994—; intern, cons. The Tabbert Group, Naperville and Chgo., 1987; instr., teaching asst. No. Ill. U., Dekalb, 1986-88; mem. Career Edn. Adv. Coun. Mem. ASTD, ACA (state conv. com. 1990—), Internat. Assn. Outplacement Profls. (charter mem.), Nat. Career Devel. (membership chair 1990). Democrat. Roman Catholic. Office: Career Connection 1755 Park St #200 Naperville IL 60563

TARVER, ALICE MAGEE, marketing professional; b. Natchez, Miss., Aug. 31, 1945; d. Thomas Louis and Ethel Odie (Burr) Magee; m. Daniel Howard Tarver, Oct. 6, 1963; 1 child, Paul Howard. Grad. high sch., Natchez. Cert. gen. ins. Pianist, soloists, trio Congrl. Fellowship Ch., Jackson, Miss., 1975—. Mem. Nat. Assn. Ins. Women (cert.), Ins. Women of Jackson (chmn. com. 1987—, bd. dirs. 1991-92), DAR. Home: 677 Woody Dr Jackson MS 39212

TASHJEAN, CATHERINE RICHARDSON, librarian; b. St. Paul; d. James A. and Katherine D. (Connolly) Richardson; m. John Tashjean, June 2, 1962. BS in Library Sci., Coll. St. Catherine, St. Paul, 1949. Asst. cataloguer Loyola U., Chgo., 1949-50; jr. libr. sch. engring. U. Minn., Mpls., 1950-51, cataloguer law sch., 1951-53, libr. sch. journalism, 1953-62; reference libr. FHA, Washington, 1966; acquisitions libr. Canisius Coll., Buffalo, 1966-71; staff libr. Manhattanville Coll., Purchase, N.Y., 1972-73, acting dir., 1974-75, dir., 1975-78; libr. U.S. Office Personnel Mgmt., Washington, 1978-84, dir. libr., 1984—. Office: US Office Personnel Mgmt 1900 E St NW Washington DC 20415-0001*

TASKA, EILEEN RUTH, therapist, sculptor; b. Bklyn., May 22, 1932; d. Henry Austin and Mildred Elinore (Deisseroth) Johnson; m. Frederick Anton Taska, May 27, 1956 (Jan. 1974); children: Lynn Suzanne, Todd Walker, Heidi Gaye, Gretel Nell. Student, The Cooper Union, N.Y.C., 1954, 55; studies with mem. of Nat. Sculpture Soc., N.Y.C., 1969-72; student, Yale U., 1972-74; BA, Goddard Coll., 1973; MS, Coll. New Rochelle, 1974; PhD, Union Grad. Sch., Cin., 1975. Free-lance graphic artist Greenwich, Conn., 1956-68; pvt. practice psycho-ednl. therapist Greenwich, 1975—; lectr., presenter of workshops and numerous demonstrations in field, Tex., Chgo., N.Y., N.J., Vt., Mass., Wis., 1975—. Exhibited in shows in Vt., Conn., Mass., N.Y., 1971-80; represented in numerous pvt. collections; inventor in field. Club: Midday (Stamford, Conn.). Home and Office: 1035 North St Greenwich CT 06831-2701

TASSANI, SALLY MARIE, communications executive, marketing consultant; b. Teaneck, N.J., Dec. 30, 1948; d. Peter R. and Marie Irene (Sorbello) T. BA, Am. U., 1970. Elem. sch. tchr., Washington, 1970-73; asst. prodn. and promotion mgr. First Nat. Bank of Chgo., 1973-74; exec. dir. Jack O'Grady Graphics, Inc., Chgo., 1974-76; creative dir. Dimensional Mktg., Inc., Chgo., 1976-78; CEO, founder Tassani & Paglia, Inc. (formerly Tassani Comm., Nexus, Inc.), Chgo., 1978—; mem. adv. bd. Heizer Entrepreneurship Rsch. Ctr. Northwestern U. J.L. Kellogg Grad. Sch. Mgmt., U.Ill. Urbana-Champaign Coll. Commerce and Bus. Adminstrn. Elected to Com. of 200; hon. bd. dirs. Girl Scouts Chgo. Named one of Ad Age's Best and Brightest Women in Advt., Top Women Entrepreneur Crain's Chgo. Bus., Top Entrepreneurs poll USA Today, Who's Who in Chgo. Bus. 1990-93, Top Woman-Owned Firms 1990-92, Entrepreneur of Yr. women's category INC, 1990; named to Nat. Women's Hall Fame. Mem. Alliance, The Art Inst. Chgo., Chgo. Coun. on Fgn. Rels. (Chgo. com.), Old Town Triangle Assn, Entrepreneur of Yr. Inst., Internat. Assn. of Bus. Communicators (Spectra award 1987, guest speaker 1988), Women's Advt. Club of Chgo. (hon., bd. dirs., Advt. Woman of Yr. 1994), Young Pres.' Orgn., Econ. Club, Chgo. Advt. Fedn., The Chgo. Network, The Execs. Club Chgo. Avocations: power walking, sailing, photography, American crafts, graphic design. Home: 1735 N Orleans St Chicago IL 60614-5719 Office: Tassani & Paglia Inc 515 N State St Chicago IL 60610-4320

TASSINARI, MELISSA SHERMAN, toxicologist; b. Lawrence, Mass., Sept. 26, 1953; m. R. Peter Tassinari; children: Michael, Emily, Sara. AB, Mt. Holyoke Coll., 1975; postgrad., U. St. Andrews, Scotland, 1973-74; Phd, Med. Coll. Wis., 1979. Rsch. asst. in orthopedic surgery., Lab. Human Biochemistry Children's Hosp. Med. Ctr., Boston, 1981-83; rsch. affiliate in toxicology Toxicology Dept. Forsyth Dental Ctr., Boston, 1983-86, staff assoc., 1986-89; asst. prof. cell biology U. Mass. Med. Ctr., Worcester, 1989-91; mgr. reproductive toxicology Pfizer Ctrl. Rsch., Groton, Conn., 1991—; rsch. fellow oral biology Harvard Sch. Dental Medicine, Boston, 1978-81, instr. oral biology and pathophysiology, 1981-83; asst. prof. biol. scis. Wellesley Coll., Mass., 1983-86, cons. teratology Arthur D. Little, Inc., Cambridge, Mass., 1985-91; asst. prof. biology Simmons Coll., Boston, 1986-87. Contbr. abstracts, articles to profl. jours. Mem. Teratology Soc., Neurobehavioral Teratology Soc., Mid Atlantic Soc. Toxicology, Mid Atlantic Reproduction and Teratology Assn. (steering com. 1994), Sigma Xi. Office: Pfizer Central Research Eastern Point Rd Groton CT 06340

TASSONE, GELSOMINA (GESSIE TASSONE), metal processing executive; b. N.Y.C., July 8, 1944; d. Enrico and A. Cira (Petriccione) Gargiulo; children: Ann Marie, Margaret, Theresa, Christine; m. Armando Tassone, Mar. 20, 1978. Student, Orange County Community Coll., 1975-79, Iona Coll., 1980—. Head bookkeeper Gargiulo Bros. Builders, N.Y.C., 1968-72; pres., owner A&T Iron Works, Inc., New Rochelle, N.Y., 1973—. Recipient Profl. Image award Contractors Coun. Greater N.Y.C., 1986; named Businesswoman of Yr., Contractors Coun. Greater N.Y.C., 1985, N.Y. State Small Bus. Person of Yr., 1988, Entrepreneur of Yr. Inc. mag., 1990; company named a Successful Small Bus. Co. Westchester County C. of C./BSBA, 1986-88. Mem. Nat. Ornamental and Miscellaneous Metal Assn., Builders Inst. Westchester and Putnam County, Westchester Assn. Women Bus. Owners, Profl. Women in Constrn., Westchester C. of C. Office: A&T Iron Works Inc 25 Cliff St New Rochelle NY 10801-6803

TASTO, COLLEEN MARIE, Spanish language educator; b. Mpls., Oct. 5, 1950; d. Richard Stafford and Shirley Margurite (Gorman) Cassady; m. Jerome Jenry Tasto, Nov. 18, 1972; children: Joseph, David, Thomas, Michael, John. BA in Spanish Philosophy, Theology, Loretto Hts. Coll., 1972; MA in Liberal Studies, Hamline U., 1995. Tchr. religion Sacred Heart Sch., Robbinsdale, Minn., 1972—; dir. religious edn. St. Michael's Parish, Madison, Minn., 1975-76; farmer Tasto Farm, Madison, Minn., 1975-85; tchr. Spanish New Ulm (Minn.) Pub. Schs., 1985—. AAUW grantee; named Borwn County Hist. Soc. Woman of Yr., 1991, Tchr. of Yr., New Ulm Edn. Assn., 1991. Mem. NEA, Minn. Edn. Assn., Am. Assn. Tchrs. Spanish, MCTFL.

TATE, BARBARA MARIE, art director; b. Canton, Ohio, Jan. 13, 1958; d. John Lawrence and Dolores Magaret (Hill) T.; m. Charles Allan Kerecz, May 25, 1985. Student, Kent State U., 1975-79, Sch. Visual Arts, N.Y.C., 1979-80. Assoc. art dir. All in Style Mag., N.Y.C., 1975-81; art dir. Macy's, N.Y.C., 1981-83, Direct Mktg. Group, N.Y.C., 1983, Avon, N.Y.C., 1983-84; design dir. Tateworks, N.Y.C., 1984—. Office: 24 W 30th St Fl 6 New York NY 10001-4410

TATE, EVELYN RUTH, real estate broker; b. Ottumwa, Iowa, Sept. 21; d. Frank Edward and Ella Belle (Smith) Ross; student public schs., Huntington Park, Calif.; m. William Tate (dec.); 1 son, William. Owner, mgr. Evelyn R. Tate Realty Co., Sherman Oaks, Calif., 1943-53, Beverly Hills, Calif., 1942—; owner, mgr. Evelyn Tate Fine Arts, San Francisco, 1976—; mgr. Beverly Hills Galleries, Hyatt Regency Hotel, San Francisco, 1979—; mgr. art gallery Fairmont Hotel; owner, mgr. Tate Gallery, St. Francis Hotel, San Francisco, Hyatt Regency Hotel San Francisco, Fairmont Hotel, Dallas, Ritz Carlton Hotel, San Francisco. Home: 999 Green St Apt 1003 San Francisco CA 94133

TATE, JOAN C., state legislator; b. Nashua, N.H., Feb. 6, 1946; m. Richard Tate; 5 children. Grad., St. Louis H.S., Nashua, 1964. Mem. N.H. Ho. of Reps., mem. edn. com.; ret. bookkeeper. Republican. Roman Catholic. Home: 104 Pelham Rd Hudson NH 03051 Office: NH Ho of Reps State Capitol Concord NH 03301*

TATE, KAREN GRIFFIN, quality assurance professional, consultant; b. Springfield, Ohio, Sept. 8, 1951; d. Juddy Wayne and Betty Jean (Springer) Griffin; m. Andrew Lee Tate, May 20, 1978; children: James, Jordan. Student of Engring., Vanderbilt U., 1969-71; student of Bus., U. Louisville, 1971-74; BS in Fin., Bloomsburg U., 1985; postgrad. in Bus. Adminstrn., Xavier U., 1991-94. Registered engr. in tng., Ky. Designer GE, Louisville, Gainesville, Ky., Fla., 1969-71; systems designer Hueblein, Ky. Fried Chicken, Louisville, 1976-77; engr. Bechtel Petroleum, Louisville, 1977-82; sr. constrn. engr. Bechtel Power, Berwick, Pa., 1982-85, Huntsville, Ala., 1985-86; project mgr. Belcan Engring. Group, Inc., Cin., 1986-91, mgr. corp. quality, 1991—; cons. Xavier U., Ctr. for Mgmt. and Profl. Devel., Cin., 1991. Mem. planning commn. Sycamore Community Schs., Cin., 1987-91, Am. Lung Assn. S.W. Ohio Camp Superkids; cons. Jr. Achievement Project. Mem. Soc. Womens Engrs., Project Mgmt. Inst. (cert. project mgmt. profl.), Assn. for Quality and Productivity, Ohio Quality and Productivity Forum, GOAL/QPC (cert. instr.). Home: 11830 Loganfield Ct Cincinnati OH 45249-1771 Office: Belcan Engring Group BGP Svcs 650 Northland Blvd Cincinnati OH 45240

TATE, SHARON SUE, special events and catering executive; b. Gainesville, Tex., Sept. 21, 1949; d. Lucien Harvey and Ollie Pauline (Insel) T. AA, Cooke County Coll., 1972; postgrad., U. North Tex., 1973-74, So. Meth. U., 1984. Credit collections cons. J.C. Penney, Dallas, 1978-80; exec. v.p. Orville McDonald Assocs., Dallas, 1980-86; conf. coord. Plaza Ams. Hotel, Dallas, 1986-92; spl. events and catering mgr. dani' Foods at the Dallas Mus. Art, 1992-95; pres. Orville McDonald Assocs., Dallas, 1995—. Republican. Home: 8780 Park Ln Apt 1017 Dallas TX 75231-5504 Office: Orville McDonald Assocs PO Box 823185 Dallas TX 75382

TATE, SHEILA ANN, trust officer; b. Omaha, Mar. 22, 1964; d. Lee Willie and Elaine Marie (Finn) T. BS in Acctg., U. Nebr., 1986. CPA. Staff acct. Arthur Andersen & Co., Omaha, 1986-88; trust officer Firstar Bank, Council Bluffs, Iowa, 1988-92, FirsTier Bank, Omaha, 1992—. Mem. AICPA, Nebr. Soc. CPAs. Roman Catholic. Office: FirsTier Bank 1700 Farnam St Omaha NE 68102-2005

TATE, SHEILA BURKE, public relations executive; b. Washington, Mar. 3, 1942; d. Eugene L. and Mary J. (Doherty) Burke; m. William J. Tate, May 2, 1981; children: Hager Burke Patton, Courtney Paige Patton. BA in Journalism, Duquesne U., 1964; postgrad. in mass communications, U. Denver, 1975-76. former chairperson bd. dirs. Corp. for Pub. Broadcasting. Rsch. asst. Westinghouse Air Brake Co.; asst. account exec. Falhgren and Assos.; copywriter Ketchum, MacLeod and Grove, 1964-66; account exec. Burson-Marsteller Assocs., Pitts., 1967; sr. v.p. Burson-Marsteller Assocs., Washington, 1985-87; public rels. mgr. Colo. Nat. Bank, Denver, 1967-71; account exec. Hill and Knowlton, Inc., Houston, 1977-78; v.p. Hill and Knowlton, Inc., Washington, 1978-81; dep. to the chmn. Hill and Knowlton Inc., Washington, 1987-88; press sec. to First Lady White House, Washington, 1981-85; press sec. George Bush for Pres. Campaign, 1988; press sec. to Pres.-elect George Bush, 1988-89; vice chmn. Cassidy and Assocs. Pub. Affairs, Washington, 1989-91; pres. Powell Tate, Washington, 1991—; bd. dirs. Corp. for Pub. Broadcasting, chmn., 1991-94. Mem. civilian pub. affairs adv. bd. U.S. Mil. Acad.; mem. adv. bd. Ronald Reagan Inst. Emergency Medicine, George Washington U. Hosp., Washington. Mem. Nat. Press Club, Nat. Press Found. (bd. dirs.). Republican. Clubs: Duquesne U. Century, F Street, Washington Golf and Country. Office: Powell Tate 700 13th St NW # 1000 Washington DC 20005

TATELBAUM, BRENDA LOEW, publisher; b. Boston, Apr. 1, 1951; d. Kenneth F. and Florence (Rosoff) Loew; m. Ira R. Tatelbaum, Aug. 1970 (div. May 1983); children: Laura Rani, Max Loew. BA, Boston U., 1971, postgrad., 1980-83; MA, Brown U., 1973; Hon. Cultural Doctorate Internat. Comm., World U., 1992. Cert. English, speech tchr., Mass. Library asst. John D. Rockefeller Library, Providence, 1973; speech therapist Dartmouth (Mass.) Pub. Schs., 1974-79; pub., editor Eidos mag., Boston, 1984—; pres., treas., bd. dirs. Brush Hill Press, Inc., Boston, 1984-88; founder and pub. Tatelbaum Assn. Pub. Rels. & Fund Raising, Boston, 1987; active fundraising and pub. rels. Bill Baird AIDS Awareness Fund, 1987, Boston U. Ad Hoc Com. for Reproductive Freedom, Boston, 1987; chairperson Bill Baird Pro-Choice Def. League, Boston, 1989—; participant numerous radio, TV, news broadcasts. Author: Eden Poems, 1982, Life Evolves From Living, 1983; short stories; editor: Boston Collection of Women's Poetry, 1983; editor (newspaper) Eidos; contbr. articles to profl. jours. Media coordinator Emerson Coll. Polit. Awareness Orgn.-Safer Sex March, Boston, 1987; dir. Nat. AIDS Telethon, Boston, 1987; mem. Nat. Coalition Agaist Censorship. Recipient The Lifestyle award, 1993. Fellow World Lit. Acad., Internat. Biog. Assn.; mem. Hadassah, Nat. Kidney Found., Am. Biog. Inst. Rsch. Assn. (dep. gov., hon. advisor 1987), Internat. Platform Assn. (speaker). Libertarian. Office: EIDOS PO Box 96 Boston MA 02137-0096

TATHAM, ELIZABETH TERESA, association executive; b. Timisoara, Banat, Romania, Aug. 10, 1935; came to U.S., 1949; d. Julius Convad and Elizabeth Theisz; married; children: Richard, Susan Crotts. BA in Sociology, Fairleigh Dickinson U., 1976; postgrad., Fordham U., 1976; cert., Nat. YWCA Tng. Exec. Dirs., 1978. Owner Floral Art, Paramus, N.J., 1962-64; tchr. H.S. Adult Edn. Program, Paramus, 1965-75; exec. dir. YWCA Hackensack, N.J., 1973-76, YWCA Salt Lake City, 1976-85; adminstrv. asst. health and social svcs. Gov. of Utah, 1985-87; adminstr. Utah Dept. Social Svcs., Salt Lake City, 1987-91; exec. dir. YWCA Bucks County, Trevose, Pa., 1992—; presenter nat. and local confs. on domestic violence, Calif., Colo., Md., N.Y., 1977-85. Chair citizen com. to build Community Ctr., Paramus, 1971-76; co-chair citizen com. to improve Children's Ctr., Bergen County, N.J., 1970-72; co-chair Salt Lake Commn. Youth, Salt Lake City, 1978-86, Salt Lake County Blue Ribbon Task Force City Jail, 1980-81; chair Utah Task Force Domestic Violence, Salt Lake City, 1981-82, Salt Lake County Task Force on Child Abuse, 1983-85, Legis. Task Force Revamp Utah's Guardianship Laws, 1988-89, Bucks County Commn. Counseling and Employment Tng. Homeless, Langhorne, 1993-94; mem. Utah Legis. Task Force Victim Comp., 1984-85, Bucks County Sunset Rev. Com., 1992, Bucks County Com. Health Promotion and Disease Prevention, 1994; conf. coord. 1st Utah Conf. Family, 1988; active Martin Luther King Birthday Celebration Com. Recipient Woman of Achievement award Utah Bus. and Profl. Women's Club, 1983, Book of Golden Deeds award Exch. Club West Valley City, 1983, Area Community Svc. award, 1988, commendation Bucks County Commrs., 1993; named Spirit of Am. Woman, J.C. Penney Co., 1989. Mem. Pa. Coun. YWCAs, Bucks County Women Exec. Dirs., Bus. Women's Assn. Bucks County. Home: 79 Old Mill Ln Holland PA 18966

TATHAM, JULIE CAMPBELL, writer; b. N.Y.C., June 1, 1908; d. Archibald and Julia deFres (Sample) Campbell; student pvt. schs., N.Y.C.; m. Charles Tatham, Mar. 30, 1933; children—Charles III, Campbell. Author more than 30 juvenile books including: The Mongrel of Merryway Farm, 1952; The World Book of Dogs, 1953; To Nick from Jan, 1957; author Trixie Belden series, 1946—, Ginny Gordon series, 1946—; co-author Cherry Ames and Vicki Barr series, 1947—; author: The Old Testament Made Easy, 1985; many series books transl. into fgn. langs.; contbr. numerous mag. stories and articles to popular publs., 1935—; free-lance writer, 1935—; contbr. numerous articles to Christian Sci. publs., including Christian Sci. Monitor, 1960—. Address: 1202 S Washington St Apt 814 Alexandria VA 22314-4446

TATZ SHERMAN, GLORIA JANE, physician assistant; b. Huntington, N.Y., May 14, 1964; d. Sherman Joseph and Margaret Louise (Strehan) Tatz; m. Thomas W. Sherman Jr., Sept. 10, 1994. BA in Psychology, Oberlin Coll., 1986; M in Health Professions, Northeastern U., 1990. Cert. physician asst. Physician asst. Norfolk (Mass.) State Correctional Facility, 1990-91, Waltham (Mass.) Weston Hosp., 1991—. Active Dedham (Mass.) Choral Soc. Mem. Am. Assn. Physician Assts., Mass. Assn. Physician Assts. Home: 73 Broadway 2nd fl Arlington MA 02174 Office: Waltham Weston Hosp Hope Ave Waltham MA 02254

TAU, MARI SUZANNE, accountant, educator; b. Quincy, Fla., Oct. 22, 1964; d. Gareth Devon and Patricia (Lewis) Harper. AA in Acctg., Pensacola (Fla.) Jr. Coll., 1984; BA in Acctg. Info. Systems, U. W. Fla., 1985, MA in Acctg., 1988. CPA, Fla. Contr. Robert Tau Auto Svc., Pensacola, Fla., 1982-94; grad. asst. U. W. Fla., Pensacola, 1986-88, adj. fin. instr., 1988-89; tax semi-sr. O'Sullivan, Patton, Jacobi, Thornton & Bloomer CPA's, Pensacola, 1988-90; project leader tax support Fenimore Software Group, Inc., Pensacola, 1990-92; owner, prin. Mari Suzanne Tau, CPA, Pensacola, 1990-93; supr. pension and deferred compensation plans Saltmarsh, Cleaveland & Gund, CPAs, Pensacola, 1993; asst. dept. head Coll. Bus., Pensacola (Fla.) Jr. Coll., 1994—; adj. acctg. instr. Troy State U., Hurlburt AFB, Fla., 1991-94; fin. mgr. Contract Resources, 1992. Office: 100 College Blvd Pensacola FL 32504

TAUB, KATHY SPERLING, lawyer; b. N.Y.C., Mar. 30, 1955; d. Philip Elwood and Florence Ruth (Cohen) Sperling; m. Bruce Fraser Taub, Sept. 7, 1985. BA in Polit. Sci. and Sociology, Duke U., 1977; JD, U. Md., 1980. Bar: Md. 1980. Assoc. Shapiro & Olander, Balt., 1980-84; v.p., gen. counsel Clark Enterprises, Inc., Bethesda, Md., 1984—. Co-editor: Design/Build Contracting Handbook, 1992. Trustee, mem. exec. com., chmn. bldg. com. Balt. City Life Mus., 1989—. Recipient Profl. Leadership award Profl. Women in Constrn., 1993. Mem. ABA, Cattail Creek Country Club (bd. dirs.). Office: Clark Enterprises Inc 7500 Old Georgetown Rd Bethesda MD 20814

TAUBIN, ROBIN LIVINGSTON, lawyer; b. N.Y., June 20, 1952; d. Edgar Alan and Arlene (Caro) L.; m. Michael Jay Taubin, Aug. 8, 1976; children: Ian Lloyd, Lance Harris. BA in History, Russel Sage Coll., 1974; JD, Hofstra U. Law Sch., 1977. Nat. underwriting atty. Chgo. Title Ins. Co., N.Y., 1977-80; sr. counsel Paramount Comm., Inc., N.Y., 1981—; v.p., counsel real estate Viacom Inc., N.Y., 1994—; pro-bono counsel N.Y. Landmarks Conservancy, N.Y., 1984—. Mem. N.Y. State Bar Assn., Comml. Real Estate Women (v.p. 1994-95). Office: Viacom Inc 1515 Broadway New York NY 10036

TAUBMAN, JANE ANDELMAN, Russian literature educator; b. Boston, Oct. 23, 1942; d. Hyman M. and Esther (Rosenthal) Andelman; m. William Chase Taubman; children: Alexander, Phoebe. BA, Radcliffe Coll., 1964; MA, Yale U., 1968, PhD, 1972. Instr. Russian Smith Coll., Northampton, Mass., 1968-72; asst. prof. Russian Amherst (Mass.) Coll., 1973-83, assoc. prof. Russian, 1983-89, prof. Russian, 1989—. Author: A Life Through Poetry: Marina Tsvetaeva's Lyric Diary, 1989; co-author: Moscow Spring, 1989; co-editor: Marina Tsvetaeva: One Hundred Years, 1994; contbr. articles to profl. jours. Woodrow Wilson Found. fellow, 1964—, Am. Coun. Learned Socs.-SSRC, 1974; trustee-faculty fellow Amherst Coll., 1978, fellow Nat. Def. Title VI, 1965-68; grantee Am. Philos. Soc., 1975, Amherst Coll., 1991, 94, IREX grantee USSR, 1988. Mem. AAUP, Modern Langs. Assn., Am. Assn. Tchrs. Slavic and East European Langs., Am. Assn. Slavic Studies, Am. Coun. Tchrs. of Russian, Am. Assn. Tchrs. of Slavic and East European Langs. Office: Amherst Coll Dept Russian Amherst MA 01002

TAUBY, DIANA MARIE, marketing executive; b. Bay Shore, N.Y., Sept. 13, 1965; d. Charles A. and Lorraine Marion (Sersen) T. AA in Mktg., U. Ala., 1986. Asst. mgr. Health and Tennis Corp. Am., Melville, N.Y., 1986-88; proposal coord. Support Systems Assoc., Inc., Hauppauge, N.Y., 1988-90; mktg. coord. Daniel, Mann, Johnson & Mendenhall, N.Y.C., 1990—; Mem. NAFE, Soc. Mktg. Profl. Svcs. Home: 1116 Reilly St Bay Shore NY 11706-2620 Office: Daniel Mann Johnson & Mendenhall 300 E 42nd St New York NY 10017-5947

TAUNTON, KATHRYN JAYNE, accountant; b. Thomaston, Ga., Nov. 3, 1953; d. Mack Doudal and Martha Jayne (Goolsby) T. AA, Cypress Coll., 1973; BA in Accounting, Calif. State U., 1977. Circulation clk. Buena Park Library Dist., Buena Park, Calif., 1973-76; account supr. ORCO State Employees Credit Union, Santa Ana, Calif., 1977-78, Santa Ana City Credit Union, 1978-79; self employed Reliable Credit Union Service, Buena Park, 1979—.

TAUNTON, ROMA LEE, nurse educator. Diploma, Ida V. Moffett Sch. Nursing, 1959; BS In Nursing, U. Ala., 1963; M in Nursing, Emory U., 1965; PhD in Ednl. Psychology, U. Kans., 1983. Chief nurse children & youth project U. Ala. Med. Ctr., Birmingham, Ala., 1967-68; coord. children & youth project U. Ark. Med. Ctr., Little Rock, 1968-69; coord. pediatric nursing Grady Meml. Hosp., Atlanta, 1970-74; dir. pediatric nurse practitioner project Am. Nurses Assn., 1974-76; dir. nursing practice dept. Am. Nurses Assn., Kansas City, Mo., 1976-79; assoc. prof. Sch. of Nursing U. Kans. Med. Ctr., Kansas City, Kans., 1983—; cons. in field. Contbr. numerous articles to profl. jours. Recipient Investigator Recognition award U. Kans. Med. Ctr., 1989, Dean's Rsch. award U. Kans. Sch. Nursing, 1989, Am. Jour. Nursing Books of the Yr. award, 1986, 88, 89, Mable Korsell award, 1975, Outstanding Young Women Am. award, 1974, Cert. Outstanding Svc. in Nursing and Health Programs Met. chpt. ARC, 1973, Chancellor's award for Outstanding Teaching, 1992; rsch. grantee Am. Nurses Found., NIH. Mem. ANA, ANA Coun. Nurse Researchers, Midwest Nursing Rsch. Soc., Acad. Mgmt., Assn. for Health Svcs. Rsch., Coun. for Grad. Edn. for Adminstrn. in Nursing, Am. Orgn. Nurse Execs, Sigma Theta Tau (rsch. grantee). Home: 4417 Wyoming St Kansas City MO 64111-4370 Office: U Kans Med Ctr 39th Rainbow Blvd Kansas City KS 66103

TAVON, MARY E., public relations, marketing and communications executive; b. Montreal, Apr. 4, 1958. Student, Marianopolis Coll. Lit. and Langs., 1977; BA in English, Theatre and Film, McGill U., 1980. Mktg. analyst Korea Trade Promotion Assn., 1980-82; advt., pub. rels. asst. Ann Taylor, 1983-84; acct. exec. Michael Klepper Assocs., N.Y.C., 1984-86; acct. supr. Michael Klepper & Assocs., N.Y.C., 1986-88; v.p. Michael Klepper Assocs., N.Y.C., 1988-89, pres., exec. prodr., 1989. Recipient cert. merit Chgo. Internat. Film Festival, 1990. Office: Michael Klepper Assoc Inc 805 3d Ave New York NY 10022

TAYLOR, ADRIENNE ELIZABETH, nurse, administrator; b. Orange, N.J., Nov. 12, 1956; d. William Ernest and Madelyn Louise (Ruso) T. BS in Nursing, Georgetown U., 1978; MPH, Columbia U., 1986; postgrad., NYU, 1990—. RN, N.Y. Staff nurse Lenox Hill Hosp., N.Y.C., 1978-80, sr. staff nurse, 1980-82, asst. patient care coordinator, 1982-83, quality assurance coordinator, 1983-86, asst. v.p. nursing, 1986—. Recipient Advil Fitness of Yr. award, 1990. Mem. Am. Hosp. Assn., N.Y. State Nurses Assn., N.Y. Women in Health Mgmt., Georgetown U. Alumni Assn., N.Y. Road Runners Club, Sigma Theta Tau. Democrat. Roman Catholic. Home: 460 E 79th St Apt 12F New York NY 10021-1445 Office: Lenox Hill Hosp 100 E 77th St New York NY 10021-1882

TAYLOR, ANGELA LYNN, critical care nurse; b. Harriman, Tenn., Oct. 18, 1967; d. Marshall and Wilma (Griffith) T. ASN, Lincoln Meml. U., 1988, BSN, 1993. Nurse East Tenn. Bapt. Hosp., Knoxville; staff nurse St. Mary's Med. Ctr., Knoxville. Mem. AACN, Am. Soc. Post-Anesthesia Nurses, Tenn. Soc. Post-Anesthesia Nurses, East Tenn. Soc. Post-Anesthesia Nurses. Home: 6818 Lindal Rd Knoxville TN 37931-3635

TAYLOR, ANN LOUISE, marketing executive; b. Fairmont, Minn., Aug. 8, 1937; d. Eugene and Celia Ethel (Fulton) Lundahl; m. James Harold Taylor, May 23, 1959; children: Kimberly Taylor Locey, Jayme K. BA in Edn., U. Minn., 1959; postgrad., Am. Inst. Banking, 1985-87. Tchr. Nokomis Jr. High Sch., Mpls., 1959-61, Helen Keller Mid. Sch., Easton, Conn., 1973-75; photojournalist Suburban & Wayne Times, Berwyn, Pa., 1975-80; cons. pub. relations Fla. Internat. Bank, Miami, Fla., 1981-84; v.p. Fla. Internat. Bank, Miami, 1984-94; employee rels. mgr. Am. Bankers Ins. Group, Miami, 1994—. Contbr. articles to profl. jours. Mem. women's adv. coun. Bapt. Hosp. of Miami, 1991—. Mem. Women in Comms. (pres. Greater Miami chpt. 1987-88, v.p. so. region 1989-92, v.p. fin. 1993-94, nat. pres. elect 1994-95), Greater South Dade-South Miami C. of C. (bd. dirs. 1987—, pres.-elect 1989—, chmn. 1991-92), Founders of South Dade (pres. 1987-88). Republican. Presbyterian. Office: Am Bankers Ins Group 11222 Quail Roost Dr Miami FL 33157

TAYLOR, ANNA DIGGS, federal judge; b. Washington, Dec. 9, 1932; d. Virginius Douglass and Hazel (Bramlette) Johnston; m. S. Martin Taylor, May 22, 1976; children: Douglass Johnston Diggs, Carla Cecile Diggs. BA, Barnard Coll., 1954; LLB, Yale U., 1957. Bar: D.C. 1957, Mich. 1961. Atty. Office Solicitor, Dept. Labor, W, 1957-60; asst. prosecutor Wayne County, Mich., 1961-62; asst. U.S. atty. Eastern Dist. of Mich., 1966; ptnr. Zwerdling, Maurer, Diggs & Papp, Detroit, 1970-75; asst. corp. counsel City of Detroit, 1975-79; U.S. dist. judge Eastern Dist. Mich. Detroit, 1979—. Trustee Detroit Symphony, United Found., Cmty. Found., SE Mich. Found. Soc., Detroit Inst. Arts, Greater Detroit Health Coun., Eastern Region Henry Ford Health Sys.; co-chair, vol. Leadership Coun. for SE Mich. Mem. Fed. Bar Assn., State Bar Mich., Wolverine Bar Assn. (v.p.), Yale Law Assn. Episcopalian. Office: US Dist Ct 740 US Courthouse 231 W Lafayette Blvd Detroit MI 48226-2719

TAYLOR, BARBARA ANN, insurance company executive; b. Newark, Feb. 19, 1950; d. Walter B. and Alice (Schwarz) Blumberg; m. C.W. Taylor Jr., Jan. 24, 1988. BS cum laude, Ohio U., 1972. Trainer, writer Am. States Ins., Indpls., 1976-79, tng. devel. supr., 1979-81, quality commitment cons., 1981-86, quality commitment mgr., 1986—, asst. v.p., 1987-94; asst. v.p., dir. employee devel. Lincol Nat. Corp., Fort Wayne, 1994—; instr. in ins. Am. States Ins., Indpls., 1979-86; ins. textbook reviewer Ins. Inst. Am., Malvern, Pa., 1985, 90. Big sister Big Sisters of Indpls., 1980-82; tchr. adult literacy Greater Indpls. Literacy League, 1985—; bd. dirs. Arts Ind., Inc., Indpls., 1988—, Friends of Herron Gallery and Sch. Art, Indpls., 1990—, Greater Indpls. Literacy League, 1993—.. Mem. ASTD, Human Resource Planning Soc., Assn. Quality and Participation, Quality and Productivity Mgmt. Assn. Office: Lincoln Nat Corp 1300 S Clinton St Fort Wayne IN 46801

TAYLOR, BARBARA ANN, records and publishing company executive; b. Wichita, Kans., Feb. 6, 1947; d. Waverly W. and Edith V. (Murphy) Zimmerman; m. Robert Taylor, July 12, 1969. MusB in Oboe Performance, Fla. State U., 1969; MusM in Musicology, U. Fla., 1977; postgrad., Inst. Paralegal Tng., Atlanta, 1984. Oboist Jacksonville (Fla.) Symphony Orch., 1969-77; high sch. band dir. Alachua County Schs., Gainesville, Fla., 1969-79; high sch. orch. dir. DeKalb County Schs., Atlanta, 1979-83; v.p., paralegal Nat. Legal Svcs., Atlanta, 1983-92; founder, pres. Rising Star Records and Pubs., Atlanta, 1987—; condr. Alachua youth orchs. U. Fla., Gainesville, 1976-79; guest speaker S.E. Music Conf. Editor: National Directory of Record Labels and Music Publishers, 1-4th edits., International Directory of Print Music Publishers, 1993, How To Submit Your Music to Record Labels and Music Publishers, 1993; composer Waterlilly Waltz, Sea of Tranquility. Bd. dirs. Atlanta Women's Fall Tennis Classic, 1988-89. Mem. Nat. Acad. Recording Arts and Sci., Music Educators Nat. Conf., Nat. Assn. Indie Record Distbrs. (chmn. new age div. 1993), Nat. Music Pubs. Assn., Ga. Music Educators Assn. (orch. chmn. 1980-83), Atlanta Songwriters Assn. (bd. dirs. 1990—, v.p. 1992-94, organizer bus. and craft of songwriting workshop), Atlanta Soc. Audio Profls. (Olympic Games liaison 1994), Atlanta Jazz Soc., Nat. Assn. Ind. Record Distbrs. (judge Indie awards, organizing chmn. new age meeting), Sigma Alpha Iota, Pi Kappa Lambda. Republican. Office: Rising Star Records & Pubs 710 Lakeview Ave NE Atlanta GA 30308

TAYLOR, BARBARA JO ANNE HARRIS, government official, librarian, educator, civic and political worker; b. Providence, Sept. 9, 1936; d. Ross Cameron and Anita (Coia) Harris; m. Richard Powell Taylor, Dec. 19, 1959; 1 child, Douglas Howard. Student, Tex. Christian U., 1952, Salve Regina Coll., 1952-53; Student, Our Lady of the Lake Coll. and Convent, 1953-54, St. Mary's U., 1954, Incarnate Word Coll., 1954-55, Georgetown U., 1956-59, 62-63; BS cum laude, Georgetown U., 1963. Adminstrv. asst. profl. devel. and welfare NEA, Washington, 1956-59; asst. to dir. Georgetown U., Washington, 1956-59; exec. asst. All Am. Conf. to Combat Communism, Washington, 1960; spl. legis. asst. mil. affairs to chmn. mil. R & D subcom. U.S. Senate Armed Svcs. Com., 1971-72; U.S. nat. commr. UNESCO, 1982—, mem. exec. com. U.S. nat. commn., 1983—, sr. advisor 22d gen. conf., 1983. Del. numerous internat. confs.; U.S. commr. Nat. Commn. Librs. and Info. Sci., 1985—, mem. various coms.; gen. chmn. George Bush for Pres. Md. State Steering Com., 1987-88; co-chmn. Md. del. Rep. Nat. Conv., 1988, 92; dep. chmn. Md. Victory '88, Bush-Quayle Campaign; mem. Nat. Fin. Com. Reagan for Pres., 1980, Reagan-Bush, 1984; state fin. chmn. Md. Rep. Party, 1980; mem. Nat. Rep. Club; mem. exec. bd. Salvation Army Aux., Washington, 1967-75, chmn. membership com., 1969-70, chmn. fund-raising com., 1968-69, mem. exec. com. of exec. bd., 1970-75, treas., mem. fin. com., 1970-71, v.p., 1971-72, historian, 1972-73, editor newsletter, 1968-69, chmn. nominating com., 1974-75, spl. awards. for exceptional vol. svc., 1969, 72; mem. exec. bd. Welcome to Washington Internat., 1969-74, bd. advisers, 1969-74, dir. workshop, 1969-74; exec. bd. Am. Opera Sch. Soc., Washington, 1970—, v.p., 1974—; mem. Episc. Ch. Home for Aged Women's Aux., 1970-75, Episc. Ctr. for Emotionally Disturbed Children Women's Aux., 1970-75; exec. bd. St. David's Episc. Ch. Aux., 1970-72, 73-74; bd. dirs., treas. Spanish-Portuguese Study Group, 1970-72; mem. exec. bd. League Rep. Women D.C., 1964-67, 75-77, treas., 1964-67; mem. nat. coun. Women's Nat. Rep. Club, N.Y.C., 1969—, chmn. Washington-Md.-Va. legis. com., 1970-75; mem. Nat. Fedn. Rep. Women, 1964—; mem. nat. fin. com. Reagan for Pres., 1979-80; mem. governing bd. Capital Speakers Club, 1973-75, chmn. by-laws com., 1973-74; mem. exec. bd. Nat. Vols. in Action, 1975-77; mem. adv. com. Rock Creek Found. Mental Health, 1982-87; mem. 50th anniversary com. Save the Children; mem. fund-raising com. Washington Choral Arts Soc., 1982-84; state fin. chmn. Reagan-Bush campaign Md. Rep. Com., 1980; Md. coord. Nat. Inaugural Com., 1981, 85; trustee Crossnore Sch., Inc., N.C., 1983—, vice chmn. bd; trustee Kate Duncan Smith DAR Sch., Grant, Ala., 1983-86, Tamassee (S.C.) DAR Sch., 1983-86; adviser Bacone Am. Indian Coll., Inc., Muscogee, Okla., 1983-88. Mem. ALA, Spl. Librs. Assn., Coun. on Libr. Resources (commn. on preservation and access), Am. Libr. Trustees Assn., Libr. Adminstrn. and Mgmt. Assn., Assn. Coll. and Rsch. Librs., Am. Antiquarian Soc., Internat. Platform Assn., Spanish-Portuguese Study Group, Nat. Lawyers' Wives, Nat. Capital Law League, DAR (chmn. nat. resolutions com. 1980-83, chmn. nat. DAR sch. com. 1983-86; state historian 1978-80, mem. state bd. mgmt., 1973—, libr. gen., mem. exec. com. 1986-89, chmn. nat. commemorative events com. 1992—, numerous other offices), Nat. Soc. Children Am. Revolution (sr. nat. asst. registrar 1978-80, mem. sr. nat. bd. mgmt. 1978-80, sr. nat. exec. com. 1978-80), Nat. Assn. Parliamentarians, World Affairs Council, League of Rep. Women, Md. Fedn. Rep. Women, WNRC, Nat. Fed. Rep. Women, Commn. on Preservation and Access, Lit. Vols. Am. (Washington Met. area affiliate), Exec. Women in Govt., Am. News Women's Club, Internat. Club, Capitol Hill Club, Washington Club, Congl. Country Club (Potomac, Md.).

TAYLOR, BARBARA O., educational consultant; b. St. Louis, Feb. 8, 1933; d. Spencer Truman and Ann Amelia (Whitney) Olin; m. F. Morgan Taylor Jr., Apr. 5, 1954; children: Frederick M. III, Spencer O., James W., John F. AB, Smith Coll., 1954; M of Mgmt., Northwestern U., 1978, PhD, 1984; LHD, U. New Haven, 1995. Mem. faculty Hamden (Conn.) Hall Country Day Sch., 1972-74; cons. Booz, Allen & Hamilton, Inc., Chgo., 1979; program assoc. Northwestern U., Evanston, Ill., 1982; co-founder, exec. dir. Nat. Ctr. Effective Schs. Rsch. & Devel., Okemos, Mich., 1986-89, rsch. assoc., 1987; cons. on effective schs. rsch. and reform Nat. Ctr. Effective Schs. R&D, U. Wis., Madison, 1990—; mem. exec. com. Hudson Inst., New Am. Schs. Devel. Corp. Design Team, 1990—; Danforth Disting. lectr. U. Nebr., Omaha, 1993. Co-author: Making School Reform Happen, 1993, Keepers of the Dream, 1994; editor Case Studies in Effective Schools Research, 1990; contbr. articles to profl. jours. Pres. Jr. League of New Haven, 1967-69; pres. NCCJ, New Haven, 1971-73; co-chair Coalition Housing and Human Resources, Hartford-New Haven, 1970-73; co-chair steering com. Day Care Conn., Hartford, 1971-73; bd. dirs. U. New Haven, 1961-71, Smith Coll., Northampton, Mass., 1984-90. Recipient Humanitarian award Mt. Calvary Bapt. Ch., 1988, Outstanding Alumna award John Burroughs Sch., 1994. Mem. ASCD, Nat. Commn. Citizens Edn. (bd. dirs. 1980-86), Nat. Staff Devel. Coun., Phi Delta Kappa. Episcopalian. Office: Nat Ctr Effective Schs Rsch & Devel 222 E Wisconsin Ave # 301 Lake Forest IL 60045

TAYLOR, BEVERLY LACY, stringed instrument restorer, classical guitarist; b. Denver, Mar. 1, 1928; d. Frederick Thurlow and Ruth (Rogers) Lacy; m. Arthur D. Taylor, Mar. 18, 1967. BA, Wheaton Coll., 1949; postgrad., U. Denver, 1951-53, U. Colo., 1953. Scene designer, tech. dir. Piper Players, Idaho Springs, Colo., 1949-51; art instr. Denver Art Mus., 1952; craft and speech instr. Wallace Sch., Denver, 1953; illustrator dept. native art Denver Art Mus., 1954-56; designer, owner The Art Studio, Santa Fe, 1956-58; instr., owner Classic Guitar Studio, Santa Fe, 1959—; instr. classical guitar Santa Fe Conservatory of Music, 1966-67, Coll. Sante Fe, 1971-72; stringed instrument restorer Lacy Taylor Studio, Santa Fe, 1967—. One-woman shows include Mus. N.Mex., Santa Fe, 1959; exhibited in group shows at Mus. New Mex., 1962, 63; executed mosaic panels Denver Art Mus. Recipient Miriam Carpenter Art prize Wheaton Coll., 1949, prize N.Mex. State Fair, 1959, 61. Mem. Guild Am. Luthiers, Assn. String Instrument Artisans. Home: 1210 Canyon Rd Santa Fe NM 87501-6128

TAYLOR, BRENDA CAROL, computer specialist; b. Kansas City, Kans., July 27, 1956; d. Collis Billy and Lela V. (Caldwell) T. AS, Community Coll. in Kansas City, 1976; BS in Computer Sci., Kansas State U., 1978. Fin. ops. asst., programmer United Telecom Computer Group, Overland Park, Kans., 1979-81; asst. data processing mgr., systems analyst Truman Nat. Life Ins. Co., Kansas City, Mo., 1981-82; computer programmer analyst Boilermarkers' Nat. Funds Office, Kansas City, Kans., 1982-84, USDA/ASCS, Kansas City, Mo., 1984-88; computer systems programmer, computer specialist Nat. Computer Ctr./OIRM/USDA, Kansas City, Mo., 1988—. Vice chmn. Fed. Women's Program Com., 1988-92). Mem. NAFE, Federally Employed Women (v.p. Heart of Am. local chpt. 1992-93, pres. 1993-94), Am. Bus. Women's Assn., Blacks in Govt., Alpha Kappa Alpha Sorority Inc., Phi Theta Kappa (hon. frat. 1975-77, pres. 1977). Home: 2827 N 55th St Kansas City KS 66104

TAYLOR, CAROLE JAN HUDSON, insurance company administrator; b. Port Arthur, Tex., May 17, 1949; d. Henry and Vivian Corine (Duncan) Hudson. BBA, Stephen F. Austin U., 1971. Claim rep. The Travelers Ins. Co., Houston, 1971-73, asst. supr., 1973-78, sr. rep., 1978-87, regional gen. adjuster, 1987-93, exec. gen. adjuster, 1993—. Author software program Business Interruption, 1988. Mem. Women for Reagan, Houston, 1983. Recipient cert. of achievement Am. Ednl. Inst., 1974, G.A.B. Bus. Interruption, 1988. Mem. NAFE, Ford's of 50's (treas. 1981-82). Republican. Baptist. Office: Travelers Ins Co 10800 Richmond Houston TX 77042

TAYLOR, CELIANNA I., information systems specialist; b. Youngstown, Ohio; d. Paul Thornton and Florence (Jacobs) Isley; m. (div.); children: Polly, Jerry, Jim. Bachelors degree, Denison U., 1939; MLS, Western Res. U., 1942. Worked in several pub. librs. and u. librs., 1939-50; head Libr. Cataloging Dept. Battelle Mem. Inst., Columbus, Ohio, 1951-53; head Personnel Office and assoc. prof. of Libr. Adminstrn. Ohio State U. Librs., Columbus, Ohio, 1954-65; coord. Info. Svcs. and Assoc. Prof. of Libr. Adminstrn. Nat. Ctr. for Research in Vocat. Edn., Ohio State U., Columbus, 1966-70; sr. research assoc., adminstrv. assoc., assoc. prof. libr. adminstrn. Dept. of Computer and Info. Sci. Ohio State U., Columbus, 1970-86, retired assoc. prof. emeritus Univ. Librs., 1986—; mem. Task Force on a Spl. Collections Database, Ohio State U. Librs., Columbus, 1988-89, comm. systems and recs. coord. Ohio State U. Retirees Assn., Columbus, 1992-93; cons. for several profl. orgns. including Ernst & Ernst CPA's and Oreg. State Systems of Higher Edn., 1961-82. Author: (with J. Magisos) book, Guide for State Voc-Tech Edn. Dissemination Systems 1971, (with A.E. Petrarca, and R.S. Kohn) book, Info. Interaction 1982; several articles for profl. jours.; designer: info. systems, CALL System, 1977-82, Channel 2000 Proj. Home Info. Svc., 1980-81, Continuing Education Info. Ctr., 1989-90, Human Resources (HUR) System, 1976-77,1979-82, DECOS, 1975-86, Computer-asst. libr. System, Optical Scan System, 1972-73, ERIC Clearinghouse for vocat. edn., 1966-70. Bd. dirs. Columbus Reg. Info. Svc., 1974-78, Community Info. Referral Svc., Inc. 1975-81; chmn. Subcom. on Design, Info. and Ref. Com. Columbus United Community Council, 1972-73; dir. Computer Utility for Pub. Info. Columbus, 1975-81. Mem. ALA, ACM, Am. Soc. for Info. Sci., Assn. Faculty and Profl. Women Ohio State U., Columbus Metro Club, Coun. for Ethics in Econs., Olympic Indoor Tennis Club. Home: 3471 Greenbank Ct Columbus OH 43221-4724

TAYLOR, CHERYL ANN, museum administrator; b. Hattiesburg, Miss., Apr. 28, 1955; d. Harold Landon and Bessie Mae (Kennedy) Taylor; m. William L. Fox, Sept. 9, 1987 (div. Jan. 1991). BA, U. So. Miss., 1978; MA, U. Nev., Reno, 1991. Archaeologist Miss. Dept. Archives & History, Jackson, 1980-81, historian, 1981-85; asst. dir. Nev. Hist. Soc., Reno, 1985-91; dir. Desert Caballeros Western Mus., Wickenburg, Ariz., 1991—. Editor Nev. Hist. Soc. Quar., 1985-91; coantbr. articles to profl. jours. Mem. Mus. Assn. Ariz. (sec. 1991-93), Western Mus. Assn. (bd. dirs. 1993—), Rotary (membership chair 1993—). Democrat. Home: PO Box 341 Wickenburg AZ 85358 Office: Desert Caballeros We Mus PO Box 1446 Wickenburg AZ 85358

TAYLOR, CLAUDIA ANN, psychotherapist, nurse; b. Knoxville, Tenn., May 22, 1946; d. Darlene M. Moore; m. Kendryl S. Taylor (div. 1974). RN, Grady Nursing Sch., 1966; BSN, Ga. State U., 1979, MEd, 1982. Acting head nurse Grady Meml. Hosp., Atlanta, 1966, psychiatric clin. coordinator, 1969—; instr. in counseling Barbara King Sch. of Ministry, Atlanta, 1982-83; workshop, seminar coordinator and facilitator Atlanta, 1977—; pvt. practice psychotherapist, cons. C. Ann Taylor & Assocs., Atlanta, 1983—; assoc. trainer, counselor The Inst. for Effective Living, Trinidad, 1983—; producer Relationships on Cable Atlanta, 1984—; founder, CEO Inst. for Psychotherapy and Rsch. for HIV-Positive Women and, 1994—; cons. Ga. Inst. Tech., Atlanta, 1985-87, Psychiatric Inst. Atlanta, 1986-87, AT&T, Atlanta, 1988, IRS, Atlanta, 1988. Bd. dirs. Community Friendship, Inc., Atlanta; group leader Dept. Offender Rehab., Atlanta, 1980. Lt. col. USAFR, 1976—. Mem. NAFE, ASTD, Assn. Black Psychologists (chmn. 1986-88), Mental Health Assn., Ga. Nurses Assn., Res. Officers Assn., Internat. Transactional Analysis Assn., Nat. Coun. Negro Women (chmn. Atlanta 1983—, award of appreciation 1985, 87), Delta Sigma Theta (award of appreciation 1986). Democrat. Home: 410 Mary Erna Dr Fairburn GA 30213-2720 Office: Peachtree Psychol Svcs 600 W Peachtree St NW Ste 1430 Atlanta GA 30308-3609

TAYLOR, CONSTANCE ELAINE, botany educator, researcher; b. Washington, Nov. 14, 1937; d. Connie Virgil and Opal Ann (Johnson) Southern; m. Raymond John Taylor, Aug. 8, 1959; children: Kathryn Elaine, Brian William, Kimberly Ann. BS, U. Okla., 1959, MS, 1961, PhD, 1975. Asst. to Bebb Herbarium U. Okla., Norman, 1957-59, Okla. Biological Survey, Norman, 1959-61; tchr. Okla. Pub. Sch. System, Okla. City, 1963-64; prof. botany Southeastern Okla. State U., Durant, 1970—. Recipient Educator of the Year award Okla. Wildlife Fedn., 1975, Women of the Year award Bus. and Profl. Women's Club, Durant, Okla., 1986, Burlington Northern award Southeastern Okla. State Univ., Durant, Okla., 1990, Scientist of the Year award Okla. Acad. Sci., 1993. Mem. Am. Assn. Univ. Women, Okla. Native Plant Soc. (pres. 1994-95), Okla. Acad. Sci. (pres.-elect, biology chair., 1994), Okla. Orrithological Soc. (pres. 1975-77), Sierra Club (conservation chair 1972-74), Okla. Garden Club. Democrat. Mem. United Methodist Ch. Office: Southeastern Okla State Univ PO Box 4027 Durant OK 74701-0609

TAYLOR, CYNTHIA RENA, real estate credit and collections director; b. Bklyn., Sept. 6, 1951; d. Raymond Ward and Hazel McDonald Lovett; m. Charles D. Taylor, Aug. 31, 1974 (div.); children: Charles, Chanay, Candejah. BBA, Bernard M. Baruch Coll., N.Y.C., 1983. Lic. real estate salesperson. Mortgage modification corr. Met. Life Ins. Co., N.Y.C., 1972-79, examiner and approver mortgages, 1979-81, leasing adminstr., 1981-83; lease compliance auditor Helmsley-Spear Inc., N.Y.C., 1983-85; dir. lease compliance Helmsley-Spear Nat. Inc., N.Y.C., 1985-89; br. commn. credit mgr. Helmsley-Spear, Inc., N.Y.C., 1990-91, credit/collection mgr., 1991—; office mgr., personnel liaison dir. Empire State Bldg, N.Y.C., 1993—; spl. project coord. Helmsley-Spear Inc., 1990—. Mem. Sigma Alpha Delta. Democrat. Roman Catholic.

TAYLOR, DARLA JEAN, nurse; b. L.A., Feb. 21, 1959; d. Samuel and Darlene Taylor. AS, Compton Community Coll., 1983. Pediatric nurse Harbor UCLA Med. Ctr., Torrance, Calif., 1983-86; pediatric nurse U. So. Calif., L.A., 1986-89, recovery rm. nurse, 1989-91, health facilities evaluator I, 1991—. Author, editor: (video) Living With Illness as a Teenager, 1985. author: (manuel) Medications Policy and Procedures, 1986. Mem. Black Nurses Assn. Office: 600 S Commonwealth Ave Ste 800 Los Angeles CA 90005-4018

TAYLOR, DEBRA ANN, manufacturing company executive; b. Pekin, Ill., Apr. 10, 1960; d. Robert Harold and Mary Ann (Witovec) T. BS in Metall. Engrng., U. Ill., 1982; MBA, Lake Erie Coll., Painesville, Ohio, 1990. Devel. engr. The Lincoln Elec. Co., Cleve., 1982-85; R&D engr. PCC Airfoils, Inc., Cleve., 1985-91; dept. head supplier devel. Teledyne CAE, Toledo, Ohio, 1991-93; dir. supplier quality Teledyne Continental Motors, Mobile, Ala., 1993—; grad. tchr. Lake Erie Coll., 1991. Cert. vol. instr. ARC, Toledo, 1993. Mem. NAFE, ASM (chpt. sec. 1992-93), Nat. Mgmt. Assn., Teledyne Continental Mgmt. Assn. (program dir. 1994-95), U. Ill. Alumni Assn. Home: 103 Betty Cir Daphne AL 36526-7761 Office: Teledyne Continental Motors PO Box 90 Mobile AL 36601-0090

TAYLOR, DEBRA THOMAS, education trainer; b. New Orleans, June 4, 1957; d. Jesse L. and Flora L. (Derozin) Thomas; m. Christopher E. Taylor, Apr. 17, 1987; 1 child, Amanda. BS in Edn., So. U., Baton Rouge, 1979. Br. mgr. Pelican Homestead & Savs., Baton Rouge, 1981-84, tng. mgr., 1984-91; career devel. specialist FDIC/Resolution Trust Corp., Baton Rouge, 1991-92; edn. and tng. mgr. La. Workers Compensation Corp., Baton Rouge, 1993—. Sec. Delmont Gardens Civic Assn., Baton Rouge, 1991—; mem. Spl. Edn. Adv. Coun., Baton Rouge, 1993—; bd. dirs. New Hope Devel. Corp. Mem. ASTD (v.p. 1994—). Democrat. Baptist. Office: La Workers Compensation Co 2237 S Acadian Thruway Baton Rouge LA 70808

TAYLOR, DONNA BLOYD, vocational rehabilitation consultant; b. Louisville, Ky., July 15, 1958; d. Donald Ray Bloyd and Georgia Carmen (Bryant) Whitehead; 1 child, Stephanie Micah Taylor; m. Douglas A. Garner, June 6, 1992. BS, U. Louisville, 1981, MEd, 1982. Lic. profl. counselor, qualified rehab. provider, Ohio; cert. rehab. counselor U.S. Dept. Labor; qualified rehab. coord., Ky.; cert. ins. rehab. specialist; cert. case mgr., vocat. evaluator, nat. counselor; diplomate Am. Bd. Vocat. Experts; qualified mental retardation profl. Program coord. Hazelwood ICF-MR, Louisville, 1981-83; lead vocat. therapist Rehab. Ctr. Southeastern Ind., Clarksville, 1983-85; regional supr., vocat. cons. Rehab. Coords., Inc., Louisville, 1985; asst. mgr., rehab. cons. Nat. Rehab. Cons., Cin., 1985-88; dist. mgr., vocat. cons. Recovery Unlimited, Inc., Cin., 1988-92; pvt. practice Cin., 1992—; vocat. expert Social Security Adminstrn. Co-author: (with Timothy Field and others) The Cancun Study Guide to the CIRS Exam, The St. Thomas Resource on Cert., Ethics and Training for Private Sector Rehab., The Maui Study Guide for the CCM Guide. Vol. Am. Cancer Soc., mem. Rape Crisis Intervention Team. Mem. Nat. Assn. Rehab. Profls. in Pvt. Sector (past pres. Ky. chpt., SCRB com.), Nat. Rehab. Assn., Nat. Forensic Ctr., Nat. Disting. Svc. Registry, Individual Case Mgmt. Assn., U. Louisville Alumni Assn., Disability Network Ohio-Solidarity, Rehab. Referral Network, Phi Kappa Phi. Democrat. Methodist. Office: 1500 Chiquita Ctr 250 E 5th St Cincinnati OH 45202

TAYLOR, DONNA LYNNE, coordinator adult education; b. Balt., July 1, 1944; d. Noel Leroy and Dorothy Anna (Henry) Welsh; 1 child, Tom A., Jr. BS, Okla. State U., 1965, EdD, 1992; MS, Phillips U., 1984. Cert. vocat. bus. and trade and indsl. edn. tchr., prin., supt. retail sales. Retail sales Tulsa, 1961-62; secretary Okla. State U. Coop. Extension Svc., Stillwater, 1965-67; secondary instr. social studies Waller Jr. High, Enid, Okla., 1967-69; substitute instr. Autry Tech. Ctr., Enid, 1971-78; instr. vocat. bus. part-time Autry Tech., Enid, 1978-84, instr. vocat. bus. full time, 1984-94; small bus. owner Lynne's Country Crafts, Enid, 1975-85; adult educator Sch. Continuing Edn., Enid, 1981-85; mem. strategic planning com. and policy and procedures com. Staff Devel. Affirmative Action, Enid, 1989—; presenter ann. confs. and meetings Okla. State Dept. Vocat. Tech., Stillwater, 1991-92; coord., chair Articulation Agreement Com., Enid, 1991—; advisor FBLA/Phi Beta Lambda, Enid, 1990-94; mem. North Ctrl. Accreditation

Steering Com., 1992-93, staff devel. chair, 1993-94. Bd. dirs. Sch. Continuing Edn., Enid, 1975-85; mem., vol. YWCA, March of Dimes, Am. Heart Assn., Multiple Sclerosis Soc., Am. Diabetes Assn., Enid Art Assn., 1985—; deacon Christian Ch., Enid, 1986-88, elder, 1988-92, 94—; active Leadership Greater Enid; mem. LWV. Recipient Women of Achievement award March of Dimes, 1992; named Okla. Bus. Tchr. of Yr., 1994. Mem. ASCD, Am. Vocat. Assn., Okla Vocat. Assn., Mountain Plains Bus. Edn. Assn., Okla. Bus. Edn. Assn., Nat. Bus. Edn. Assn., Nat. Assn. Classroom Bus. Educators, Vocat. Bus. and Office Edn., Enid C. of C. (edn. com. 1991-92), Phi Delta Kappa (sec. 1992—), PEO. Republican. Home: 2110 Appomattox Enid OK 73703 Office: Autry Tech Ctr 1201 W Willow Enid OK 73703

TAYLOR, EILEEN TUROWSKI, civil engineer, tree farmer; b. Waukegan, Ill., Sept. 6, 1949; d. Eugene Anthony and Dolores Constance (Jarosewicz) Turowski; m. Flynn Anthony Taylor, Sept. 13, 1970 (div. June 1992). BCE, McNeese State U. Cert. engring. in tng. Respiratory therapist Firmin Desloge Hosp., St. Louis, 1970-72; biochemistry rsch. asst. Sch. Medicine St. Louis U., 1972-74; respiratory therapist Beauregard Meml. Hosp., De Ridder, La., 1979-80; surveying instr. McNeese State U., Lake Charles, La., 1990-92; owner, mgr. E & F Tree Farms, De Ridder, 1984-91; owner Taylor Grown Trees, Port Arthur, Tex., 1991—; grad. engr. Arceneaux & Gates Cons. Engrs., Inc., Port Arthur, 1992—; asst. to dist. engr. Park Ctrl. Mcpl. Utility Dist., Port Arthur, 1992—; project engr. Pleasure Island Beach Park, Port Arthur, 1992—. Mem. allocation bd. dirs. United Way, Lake Charles, 1989—; bd. dirs. Beauregard Cmty. Concerns, De Ridder, 1984-89; pres., mem. De Ridder Jr. Women's Club, 1982-90. Recipient Outstanding Gordon P. Boutwell Achievement award Soil Testing Engrs., Inc., 1992. Mem. La. Forestry Assn. (bd. dirs. 1987—, Dist. Tree Farmer of Yr. 1986), Project Mgmt. Inst. (membership dir. 1994—), Propeller Club of U.S. (Port of Lake Charles chpt.). Home: 7201 Lake Arthur Dr # 215 Port Arthur TX 77642-8142 Office: Arceneaux & Gates Cons Engr 3501 Turtle Creek Ste 102 Port Arthur TX 77642-8075

TAYLOR, ELINOR ZIMMERMAN, state legislator; b. Norristown, Pa., Apr. 18, 1921; d. Harold I. and Ruth A. (Rahn) Zimmerman; m. William M. Taylor, 1947; 1 child, Barbara. BS, West Chester State Tchrs. Coll., 1943; student, Columbia U., 1944, U. Del., 1955; MEd, Temple U., 1958. Tchr. Ridley Park (Pa.) H.S., 1943-46, West Chester (Pa.) H.S., 1946-50; prof. West Chester State Coll., 1955-68, adminstr., 1968-76, now. prof. emeritus; mem. Pa. Ho. of Reps., 1977—; chmn. subcom. on higher edn.; bd. dirs. Pa. Higher Edn. Assistance Agy., Pa. Edn. Seminar; active Gov. Commn. on Funding Higher Edn., Women; in Politics and Polit. Action Com.; mem. adv. bd. Pa. Conservative Union; Rep. chmn. Health and Welfare Com.; trustee Charles S. Swope Found.; founding trustee Bd. Chester County Edn. Found. Councilwoman Borough of West Chester, Pa., 1974-77, mem. recreation com., 1974-77; active Big Bros./Big Sisters, United Way, ARC (bd. dirs.). Recipient Hon. award Pa. State Assn. for Health, Phys. Edn. and Recreation, 1962, Hon. Umpires award U.S. Field Hockey Assn., 1967, Disting. Alumni award West Chester State Coll., 1977, Alumni award Temple U., 1982, Love of Children of Greater West Chester Golden Heart award, Achievement cert. Pa. Fedn. of Bus. and Profl. Women's Club, George Washington Honor award Valley Forge Freedom Found., 1990. Mem. AAUW (former pres.), Nat. Assn. Women Legislators, Chester County Art Assn. Republican. Presbyterian. Home: 404 Price St West Chester PA 19382-3531 also: 13 W Miner St West Chester PA 19382 Office: Pa Ho of Reps State Capitol Harrisburg PA 17120*

TAYLOR, ELISABETH COLER, educator; b. N.Y.C., Jan. 24, 1942; d. Gerhard Helmut and Judith (Horowitz) C.; m. Billie Wesley Taylor II, Jan. 27, 1960; children: Letitia Rose, Billie Albert. Student, Wilmington Coll., 1959-60; BS, Wayne State U., Detroit, 1969; MS, The Ohio State U., 1980; postgrad., Wright State U., Dayton, Ohio, 1989—. Cert. home economist. Tchr. home econs., computer literacy, lang. arts Dayton (Ohio) City Schs., 1972—. Bd. mem. Camp Fire Girls, 1970-71, vol. Detroit Mus. of Art, 1970-71, group leader Camp Fire Girls, Boy Scouts, Detroit, 1968-74. Mem. AAUW, NEA, Ohio Edn. Assn., Dayton Edn. Assn., Mensa. Home: 131 Snow Hill Ave Dayton OH 45429-1705

TAYLOR, ELIZABETH JANE, investment consultant, real estate and international marketing executive; b. Tiffin, Ohio, Oct. 27, 1941; d. Albert Joseph Lucas and Mary Jane Siebenaller-Swander; m. Gaylen Lloyd Taylor, July 11, 1977. Student, Heidelberg Coll., 1961, Austin Community Coll., Tex., 1983-84; grad. Real Estate Edn. Ctr., 1984, Inst. Real Estate, 1988, Real Estate Inst., 1989, Tex. Realtors Inst., 1989; student Rockhurst Coll., 1991-92. Cons., Hypnosis Conn., Ohio and Tex., 1967—; dir. regional mktg. Sibrow, Inc., Ottawa, Can., 1981-83; realtor assoc. Alliance Sales, Austin, 1985-88; assoc. Broadway Comml. Investments, 1988-91; prin., Taylor & Assocs., Internat. Mktg. & Bus. Devel., Hong Kong, U.S., 1980—; tchr. mktg. and bus. develop., 1980—. Author: profl. column Austin Women Mag., 1984-86; (poetry) Letters from Home, 1986, Best New Poets of 1986, American Poetry Anthology, vol. VI., #3, 1986. V.p. Am. Congress on Real Estate, 1982-83; arbitrator Better Bus. Bur., 1984-89, sr. arbitrator, 1989—; mem. speakers bur. Austin Woman's Ctr., 1985-88; v.p. Austin World Affairs Coun., 1984-94; mem. adv. panel Austin Woman Mag., 1984-86. Nominated to Tex. Womens Hall of Fame, 1984. Mem. NAFE (network dir. 1980-88), Am. Biog. Inst. Rsch. (hon., bd. advisers 1988). Avocations: writing, behavior research. Home: 1414 Cardinal Hill Dr Austin TX 78758-2705

TAYLOR, ELIZABETH ROSEMOND, actress; b. London, Feb. 27, 1932; d. Francis and Sara (Sothern) T. Student, Byron House, Hawthorne Sch., Metro-Goldwyn-Mayer Sch. Motion pictures include There's One Born Every Minute, 1942, Lassie Come Home, 1943, The White Cliffs of Dover, 1944, Jane Eyre, 1944, National Velvet, 1944, Courage of Lassie, 1946, Cynthia, 1947, Life with Father, 1947, A Date with Judy, 1948, Julia Misbehaves, 1948, Little Women, 1950, Conspirator, 1950, The Big Hangover, 1950, Father of the Bride, 1950, Father's Little Dividend, 1951, A Place in the Sun, 1951, Callaway Went Thataway, 1951, Love Is Better Than Ever, 1952, Ivanhoe, 1952, The Girl Who Had Everything, 1953, Elephant Walk, 1954, Rhapsody, 1954, Beau Brummel, 1954, The Last Time I Saw Paris, 1954, Giant, 1956, Raintree County, 1957, Cat on a Hot Tin Roof, 1958, Suddenly Last Summer, 1959, Scent of Mystery, 1960, Butterfield 8, 1960 (Acad. award best actress), Cleopatra, 1963, The V.I.P.'s, 1963, The Sandpiper, 1965, Who's Afraid of Virginia Woolf?, 1966 (Acad. award best actress), The Taming of the Shrew, 1967, The Comedians, 1967, Reflections in a Golden Eye, 1967, Dr. Faustus, 1967, Boom!, 1968, Secret Ceremony, 1968, The Only Game in Town, 1970, Under Milkwood, 1971, X, Y and Zee, 1972, Hammersmith Is Out, 1972, Night Watch, 1973, Ash Wednesday, 1973, That's Entertainment, 1974 (guest star), The Driver's Seat, 1974, Blue Bird, 1975, Winter Kills, 1977, A Little Night Music, 1977, The Mirror Crack'd, 1980, Young Toscanini, 1988, The Flintstones, 1994; TV appearances include Divorce His/Divorce Hers, 1973, Victory at Entebbe, 1977, Return Engagement, 1979, Between Friends, 1982, Hotel (series), 1984, Malice in Wonderland, 1986, North and South (miniseries), 1986, There Must Be a Pony, 1986, Poker Alice, 1987, Sweet Bird of Youth, 1989; theatre appearances in The Little Foxes, 1981 (Broadway debut), Private Lives, 1983; narrator film documentary Genocide, 1981; author: (with Richard Burton) World Enough and Time, poetry reading, 1964, Elizabeth Taylor, 1965, Elizabeth Taylor Takes Off: On Weight Gain, Weight Loss, Self Esteem and Self Image, 1988; lics. (fragrances) Elizabeth Taylor's Passion, Passion for Men, White Diamonds/Elizabeth Taylor, Elizabeth Taylor's Diamonds & Emeralds, Diamonds & Rubies, Diamonds & Sapphires, (jewelry) The Elizabeth Taylor Fashion Jewelry Collection for Avon. Active philanthropic, relief, charitable causes internationally, including Israeli War Victims Fund for the Chaim Sheba Hosp., 1976, UNICEF, Variety Children's Hosps., med. clinics in Botswana; initiated Ben Gurion U.-Elizabeth Taylor Fund for Children of the Negev, 1982; supporter AIDS Project L.A., 1985; founder, nat. chmn. Am. Found. for AIDS Rsch. (AmFAR), 1985—, internat. fund, 1985—; founder Elizabeth Taylor AIDS Found., 1991—. Named Comdr. Arts Letters (France), 1985; recipient Legion of Honor (France), 1987 (for work with AmFAR), Aristotle S. Onassis Found. award, 1988, Jean Hersholt Humanitarian Academy award, 1993 (for work as AIDS advocate), Life Achievement award Am. Film Inst., 1993; honored with dedication of Elizabeth Taylor Med. Ctr. Whitman-Walker Clinic, Washington, 1993. Address: care Chen Sam & Assocs Inc 506 E 74th St ste 3E New York NY 10021-3486

TAYLOR, ELLEN BORDEN BROADHURST, civic worker; b. Goldsboro, N.C., Jan. 18, 1913; d. Jack Johnson and Mabel Moran (Borden) Broadhurst; student Converse Coll., 1930-32; m. Marvin Edward Taylor, June 13, 1936; children: Marvin Edward, Jack Borden, William Lambert. Bd. govs. Elizabethan Garden, Manteo, N.C., 1964-74; mem. Gov. Robert Scott's Adv. Com. on Beautification, N.C., 1971-73; mem. ACE nat. action com. for environ. Nat. Coun. State Garden Clubs, 1973-75; bd. dirs. Keep N.C. Beautiful, 1973-85; mem. steering com., charter mem. bd. dirs. Keep Johnston County (N.C.) Beautiful, 1977-92; life judge roses Am. Rose Soc.; chmn. local com. that published jointly with N.C. Dept. Cultural Resources: An Inventory of Historic Architecture, Smithfield, N.C., 1977; co-chmn. local com. to survey and publish jointly with N.C. Div. Archives and History: Historical Resources of Johnston County, 1980-91; charter life mem. N.C. Mus. History Assocs., 1994; charter mem. founder's circle New Mus. History Bldg., Raleigh, 1994. Mem. Nat. Coun. State Garden Clubs (life; master judge flower shows), Johnston County Hist. Soc. (charter), Johnston County Arts Coun. (Spl. award for 1987 projects of Pub. Libr. Johnston County & Smithfield 1965-87), N.C. Geneal. Soc. (charter), Johnston County Geneal. Soc. (charter), Hist. Preservation Soc. N.C. (life), N.C. Art Soc. (life). Democrat. Episcopalian. Clubs: Smithfield (N.C.) Garden (charter; pres. 1969-71), Smithfield Woman's (v.p. 1976), DAR (organizing vice-regent chpt. 1976), Gen. Soc. Mayflower Descs. (life), Descs. of Richard Warren, Nat. Soc. New Eng. Women (charter mem. Carolina Capital chpt.), Colonial Dames Am. (life), Magna Charta Dames, Nat. Soc. Daus. of Founders and Patriots Am. Home: 616 Hancock St Smithfield NC 27577-4008

TAYLOR, ELOUISE CHRISTINE, artist; b. Berkeley, Calif., Sept. 17, 1923; d. Charles Vincent and Lola Lucile (Felder) T.; m. P.S. Carnohan, Sept. 8, 1947 (div. 1982); children: Marcus Jay, Max Todd, Cecilia Ann. Grad. high sch., Hollywood, Calif., 1941. Featured skater Sonja Henie Hollywood Ice Revue, 1941-51, Ctr. Theater, N.Y.; artist Reno, Nev.; instr. figure skating and painting. Oil paintings featured in numerous group and one-woman shows; portrait of Sonja Henie and several others in permanent collection at World Figure Skating Hall of Fame and Mus., Colorado Springs, Colo.; paintings exhibited local shows Los Altos, Calif., 1970-74, Santa Rosa, 1974-79, also Half Moon Bay-Shoreline Sta. Gallery & art shows, 1981, 82, Parklane Mall, Reno, Nev., 1993; numerous commd. paintings. Mem. Sports West Athletic Club, Reno. Home: 420 Shady Ln Ct Reno NV 89509

TAYLOR, FANNIE TURNBULL, social education and arts administration educator; b. Kansas City, Mo., Sept. 11, 1913; d. Henry King and Fannie Elizabeth (Sills) Turnbull; m. Robert Taylor, Dec. 2, 1938 (div. 1974); children: Kathleen Muir Taylor Isaacs, Anne Kingston Taylor Wadsack. BA, U. Wis., 1938; LHD (hon.), Buena Vista Coll., Storm Lake, Iowa, 1975. Mem. faculty U. Wis., Madison, 1941—, prof. social edn., 1949—, emeritus, 1979—, dir. Wis. Union Theater, 1946-66, coord. univ. systems arts council, 1967-70, assoc. dir. Ctr. Arts Adminstrn., 1970-72, coord. Consortium for Arts, 1976-84; cons. in field. Author: The Arts at a New Frontier, Wisconsin Union Theater: Fifty Golden Years; contbr. articles to profl. jours. Program dir. music Nat. Endowment Arts, 1966-67, program info. dir., 1972-76; bd. dirs. Wis. Arts Council, 1964-72, Wis. Found. Arts, 1976-91, Madison Civic Music Assn., 1976-84, Madison Children's Mus., 1983—, Elvehjem Mus. Art Coun., 1976—; chair, 1983-86; active Madison Civic Ctr. Found., 1981-94; hon. chair Wis. Union Theater Program Endowment Fund, 1985—; bd. dirs. Wis. chpt. Nature Conservancy, 1963-84, chmn., 1976-77; bd. dirs. Shorewood Hills Found., 1976—, pres., 1976-81. Recipient Oak Leaf award Nature Conservancy, 1981, Wis. Gov.'s award in Support of the Arts, 92; named Women of Distinction, Madison YMCA, 1994. Fellow Wis. Acad. Scis., Arts and Letters; mem. Assn. Performing Arts Presenters (founder, exec. dir. 1970-72, Fannie Taylor award 1972), Am. Assn. Dance Cos. (bd. dirs. 1967-72), Nat. Assn. Regional Ballet (bd. dirs. 1975-77), Nat. Guild Community Schs. Arts (bd. dirs. 1977-80), Women in Communications (Writers' Cup 1980), U. Wis. Alumni Assn. (Disting. Svc. award 1979, Madison Civics Club (pres. 1969-70), Madison Club, Univ. Club (pres. 1982-85), Blackhawk Club. Home: 1213 Sweetbriar Rd Madison WI 53705-2227

TAYLOR, GRACE ELIZABETH WOODALL (BETTY TAYLOR), lawyer, educator, law library administrator; b. Butler, N.J., June 14, 1926; d. Frank E. and Grace (Carlyon) Woodall; m. Edwin S. Taylor, Feb. 4, 1951 (dec.); children: Carol Lynn Taylor Crespo, Nancy Ann Filer. AB, Fla. State U., 1949, MA, 1950; JD, U. Fla., 1962. Instr. asst. librarian U. Fla., 1950-56; asst. law librarian Univ. Libraries, U. Fla., 1956-62; dir. Legal Info. Ctr., 1962—, prof. law, 1976—; Clarence J. TeSelle prof. of law U. Fla., 1994—; trustee Nat. Ctr.for Automated Rsch., N.Y.C., 1978—; past chmn. joint com. on LAWNET, Am. Assn. Law Librs., Am. Assn. Law Schs. and ABA, 1978-86; cons. to law librs., 1975—; mem. adv. com. N.E. Regional Data Ctr., U. Fla.1990—. Co-author: American Law School, 1986, 21st Century: Technology's Impact, 1988; also articles. Recipient 1st Disting. Aluni award Fla. State U. Libr. Sch., 1983; Lewis Scholar Fla. Legislature, 1949-50; Grantee NEH,1981-82, Coun. Libr. Resources, 1984-86. Mem. ABA (Law Libr. Congress facilities com. 1991—), Am. Assn. Law Librs. (exec. bd. 1981-84), Am. Assn. Law Schs. (accreidtation com. 1978-81), OCLC Users COun. (pres. 1983-86), Phi Beta Kappa (v.p. U. Fla. chpt. 1994-95), Beta Phi Mu. Democrat. Methodist. Office: U Fla Legal Info Ctr Gainesville FL 32611

TAYLOR, JANET MAY, gifted/talented education educator; b. Florence, Ala.; d. Granvile and Ila (Haddock) May; J. Mark Taylor, June 6, 1970; children: Josh, Molly. Student, U. Ala., 1967-69; BS in Secondary Edn., Auburn U., 1971, MEd, 1976; postgrad., U. Fla., 1972. Cert. tchr., Colo. Reading specialist Lee County Schs., Opelika, Ala., 1973-76; tchr. 6th grade Bryan (Tex.) Sch. Dist., 1977-79; resource tchr. gifted/talented Auburn (Ala.) City Schs., 1979-81, 84-88, Tuscaloosa (Ala.) City Schs., 1988-91, Cherry Creek Schs., Englewood, Colo., 1991—; adj. prof. Auburn U., 1982; mem. Cherry Creek Gifted/Talented Adv. Bd., 1991-93. Active Cherry Creek Gifted/Talented Parent Assn. Mem. Nat. Soc. Geographic Edn. (Cram award 1992), Nat. Assn. for Gifted, Assn. for Edn. of Underachieving Gifted Students, Kappa Delta Alumnae Assn. (sec. 1981-85, alumni adv. bd. 1983-88, 88-91, pres. 1985-88). Methodist. Home: 6277 E Jamison Dr Englewood CO 80112 Office: Polton Elem Sch 2985 S Oakland St Aurora CO 80014

TAYLOR, JANICE KEITH, librarian; b. Vicksburg, Miss., Dec. 27, 1945; d. John Franklin and Venie (Cannon) Keith; m. James Ronald Taylor, July 16, 1967; 1 child, James Lloyd. BSE, Delta State U., Cleveland, Miss., 1967; MLS, U. Miss., 1980. Tchr. Senatobia (Miss.) Jr. High Sch., 1967-70; libr. media specialist Coldwater (Miss.) High Sch., 1970-78, Senatobia Mid. Sch., 1978—. Dir. Friends of Senatobia Pub. Libr., 1993-95. Mem. Miss. Libr. Assn., Coterie Club (v.p. 1993-95). Baptist. Office: Senatobia Mid Sch 303 College St Senatobia MS 38668-2126

TAYLOR, JERRY LYNN, microbiologist, educator; b. Warrenton, Mo., Jan. 12, 1947; d. Albert Marcus and Naomi Azalee (Greer) Hafner; m. William Carl Taylor, June 12, 1971. BA in Microbiology, U. Mo., Columbia, 1969, MA in Botany, 1971; PhD in Microbiology, So. Ill. U., 1976. Asst. prof. microbiology Calif. State U., Long Beach, 1976-77; postdoctoral fellow Med. Coll. Wis., Milw., 1977-79, instr., 1979-80, asst. prof. microbiology, 1980-81, asst. prof. microbiology, ophthalmology, 1981-84, assoc. prof. microbiology and ophthalmology, 1984-90, prof., 1990—, vice-chmn. microbiology, 1988—. Contbr. sci. papers to jours. Mem. AAAS, Am. Soc. Microbiology, Am. Soc. Virology, Internat. Assn. Antiviral Rsch., Internat. Assn. Interferon and Cytokine Rsch., Assn. Rsch. in Vision and Ophthalmology, Phi Beta Kappa, Sigma Xi. Office: Med Coll Wis Dept Microbiology 8701 W Watertown Plank Rd Milwaukee WI 53226-3548

TAYLOR, J(OCELYN) MARY, museum administrator, zoologist, educator; b. Portland, Oreg., May 30, 1931; d. Arnold Llewellyn and Kathleen Mary (Yorke) T.; m. Joseph William Kamp, Mar. 18, 1972 (dec.). B.A., Smith Coll., 1952; M.A., U. Calif., Berkeley, 1953, Ph.D., 1959. Instr. zoology Wellesley Coll., 1959-61, asst. prof. zoology, 1961-65; assoc. prof. zoology U. B.C., 1965-74; dir. Cowan Vertebrate Mus., 1965-82, prof. dept. zoology, 1974-82; collaborative scientist Oreg. Regional Primate Research Ctr., 1983-87; prof. (courtesy) dept. fisheries and wildlife Oreg. State U., 1984—; dir. Cleve. Mus. Nat. History, 1987—; adj. prof. dept. biology Case Western Res. U., 1987—. Assoc. editor Jour. Mammalogy, 1981-82. Contbr. numerous articles to sci. jours. Trustee Benjamin Rose Inst., 1988-93, Western Res. Acad., 1989-94, U. Circle, Inc., 1987—, The Cleve. Aquarium, 1990-93, Cleve. Access to the Arts, 1992—; corp. bd. Holden Arboretum, 1988—. Fulbright scholar, 1954-55; Lalor Found. grantee, 1962-63; NSF grantee, 1963-71; NRC Can. grantee, 1966-84; Killam Sr. Research fellow, 1978-79. Mem. Soc. Woman Geographer's, Am. Soc. Mammalogists (1st v.p. 1978-82, pres. 1982-84, Hartley T. Jackson award 1993), Australian Mammal Soc., Cooper Ornithol., Assn. Sci. Mus. Dirs. (v.p. 1990-93), Rodent Specialist Group of Species Survival Commn. (chmn. 1989-93), Sigma Xi. Episcopalian. Office: Cleve Mus Natural History 1 Wade Oval Dr Cleveland OH 44106-1701

TAYLOR, JUDITH ANN, sales executive; b. Sheridan, Wyo., July 9, 1944; d. Milo G. and Eleanor M. (Wood) Rinker; m. George I. Taylor, Sept. 15, 1962; children: Monte G., Bret A. Fashion dept. mgr. Montgomery Ward, Sheridan, 1968-73; pers. mgr., asst. mgr. Dan's Ranchwear, Sheridan, 1973-80; sales/prodn. coord. KWYO Radio, Sheridan, 1981-83; sales mgr., promotions coord. KROE Radio, Sheridan, 1984—; mng. editor BOUNTY Publ., 1993—; notary pub. State of Wyo., 1985—; lectr., instr. BSA Merit U.; lectr. acad. achievement LVA Adv. Bd., 1993—. mng. editor BOUNTY Publ., 1993—. Sec.-treas. Sheridan County Centennial Com., 1986-89; local sec.-treas. Wyo. Centennial Com., Sheridan, 1986-90; exec. dir. Sheridan-Wyo. Rodeo Bd., 1983—; bd. dirs. Sheridan County Fair Bd., 1991—, treas., 1995—; bd. dirs. "Christmas in April" Sheridan County, 1992—; mem. WJTP Coun., Cheyenne, 1990-92; mem. adv. coun. Tutor-Literacy Vols. of Am., 1993—; Mrs. Santa Claus for local groups; vol. coord. AIDS Quilt. Mem. Wyo. Assn. Broadcasters, S.C. C. of C. (dir. 1988—, pres. 1989-91), UMWA Aux. (pres. 1982-89), Kiwanis (v.p. 1992—, pres.-elect 1993, pres. 1994). Democrat. Christian Ch. Home: 98 Decker Rd Sheridan WY 82801 Office: KROE AM PO Box 5086 Sheridan WY 82801-1386

TAYLOR, JUDITH ANNE, librarian; b. Bklyn., July 21, 1937; d. Edward S. and Ida (Osterland) Weber; m. Arnold H. Taylor, July 17, 1960; children: Beth Allison, Lynn Erica. BA, Barnard Coll., 1959; MS, Columbia U., 1960, postgrad., 1960-62; postgrad., L.I. U., 1970-72, U. Colo., 1980, 81. Cert. tchr., N.Y.; pub. libr., N.Y. Reference libr. CUNY, 1960-61; rsch. libr. Barnard Coll., N.Y.C., 1961-63; edn. libr. CUNY, Flushing, 1963-68; reference libr. Plainview (N.Y.)-Old Bethpage Pub. Libr., 1968-70; libr. media specialist Plainview-Old Bethpage Schs., 1970-72, Manhasset (N.Y.) Jr. High Sch., 1972—; bd. dirs. tchr. Resource Ctr., Manhasset Schs., 1986-90, dist.-wide and county wide tech. coms.; presenter workshops ALA, N.Y., LA. Author: Great Paperback Contest, 1980, newsletter Link Up, 1988-90; contbr. articles to profl. jours. Triviathon organizer, participant United Cerebral Palsy, Roosevelt, N.Y., 1989—; bd. trustees Internat. Brotherhood Elec. Workers Scholarship Alumnae, 1985—. Mem. ALA, N.Y. Libr. Assn. (sch. libr. media sect.), N.Y. State United Tchrs., L.I. Sch. Media Assn., Nassau Sch. Libr. Assn. (rep. sys. coun. 1989-92, cluster leader 1987-92, liaison 1988—), Manhasset Edn. Assn., Barnard Coll. Alumnae Assn. (class corr. 1984-89, coun. mem. 1984-89). Jewish. Home: 90 Virginia Ave Plainview NY 11803-3626 Office: Manhasset Schs 200 Memorial Pl Manhasset NY 11030-2300

TAYLOR, JUDITH CAROLINE, entrepreneur; b. Quincy, Ill., June 23, 1948; d. Earl George and Caroline Clara (Knuffman) Schenk; m. Richard Odell Taylor, Nov. 28, 1970; children: Alexander James and Nicholas James (twins). BA, Quincy (Ill.) U., 1985. Resident mgr. Landing Heights Apts., Brighton, N.Y., 1973-75; facilitator adult student program Quincy U., 1983-85; dist. mgr. Creative Expressions, 1981-85; mgr. mem. svcs. Quincy Conv. and Visitors Bur., 1985; sales dir. Motor Inn Hotel, Quincy, 1986; entrepreneur Taylor Enterprises, Quincy, 1985—; exec. dir. The Kensington, Quincy, 1987-90; mgr., salesperson, cons. Taylor's Fine Furniture & Gifts, Quincy, 1990—; cons., freelance designer. Designed, marketed series I and II Quincy Postcards, 1987, 90; photo show John Wood C.C., 1993. House tour chairperson Quincy Perserves Bd., 1989; pres. Quincy Newcomers Club, 1980; pres. Great Rivers Mothers of Twins, Quincy, 1979. Recipient Americanism award VFW, Quincy, 1966. Mem. AAUW, Older Womens League (pres. 1988), The Atlantis Study Group, Quincy Conv. and Visitors Bur., Altrusa Club. Mem. Unity Ch. Home: 1461 Maine St Quincy IL 62301-4260 Office: Taylors Fine Furniture & Gifts 123 N 4th St Quincy IL 62301-2913

TAYLOR, JULIA H., association executive; b. Windfall, Ind., Oct. 31, 1954; 1 child, Lea. BA in English and Philosophy, Ball State U. Area mktg. rep. McDonalds Corp., Saginaw, Mich., 1976-79; regional dir. Am. Lung Assn. Mich., 1979-80; exec. dir. YWCA, Bay County, Mich., 1980-86; exec. dir., CEO YWCA Greater Milw., 1986—. Active Bay City Sch. Bd., Profl. Adv. Coun. United Way Greater Milw., Kenwood Meth. Ch., Wis. Meth. Conf. Coun. Fin and Adminstrn.; bd. dirs. Bay City Med. Ctr. Regional Hosp., Women's Bus. Initiative Corp.; mem. 6th Ward City Commn. Named one of Five Outstanding Young Women, Mich. Jaycees, 1984, Ninety for the 90's, Milw. Jour., 1989, Top 40 Under 40, Bus. Jour., 1992. Mem. Nat. Assn. YWCA Execs. (bd. dirs. 1985—, past co-chair 1st nat. conf., past treas., past pres., 1st Edith Lerrago award 1991, Nat. Exec. Excellence award 1993), Profl. Dimensions (Sacajawea award 1993), Tech. Electronic Mgmt. Planning Orgn., Milw. Assn. in Urban Devel. (bd. dirs., Community Achievement award 1989), Rotary. Office: YWCA Greater Milw 3112 W Highland Blvd Milwaukee WI 53208-3250

TAYLOR, JUNE RUTH, minister; b. Annapolis, Md., June 27, 1932; d. Benjamin and Naomi Medora (Dill) Michaelson; m. Thomas Wayne Taylor, Mar. 20, 1954; children: Rebecca Susan Taylor DeLameter, Michael Steven. AB, Goucher Coll., 1952; MRE, Presbyn. Sch. of Christian Edn., Richmond, Va., 1954; MDiv., McCormick Theol. Sem., 1978. Ordained to ministry Presbyn. Ch. (U.S.A.), 1976. Min. Christian Edn. Congl. United Ch. of Christ, Arlington Heights, Ill., 1974-79; dir. pastoral svcs. Presbyn. U. Hosp., Pitts., 1979-89; dir. chaplaincy svcs. Ephrata (Pa.) Community Hosp., 1991—; chaplain Rush-Presbyn. St. Luke's Med. Ctr., Chgo., 1976-78; chair exec. com., pres. Assn. Specialized Pastoral Ministries, Louisville, 1987-89. Book reviewer in field. Fellow Coll. Chaplains (sec. exec. com. 1985-87); mem. Soc. Chaplains, Hosp. Assn. Pa. (pres. 1983), Assn. Mental Health Clergy, Assn. for Clin. Pastoral Edn. (clin.), Rotary (liaison to Boys and Girls Club S.W. Pitts. chpt. 1990-91), Gamma Phi Beta Alumnae Club (pres. 1990-91).

TAYLOR, KAREN ANNETTE, mental health nurse; b. Kinston, N.C., Oct. 7, 1952; d. Emmett Green and Polly Ann (Taylor) Tyndall; m. Paul Othell Taylor Jr., June 24, 1979; 1 child, Clarissa Anne. AA, Lenoir C.C., Kinston, 1972; Diploma, Lenoir Meml. Hosp. Sch. of, Nursing, 1984; student, St. Joseph's Coll., Windham, Maine, 1993-94. RN, N.C. Staff nurse Lenoir Meml. Hosp., 1984-86; staff nurse, relief patient care dir. Brynn Marr Hosp., Jacksonville, N.C., 1987-90; staff nurse, quality assurance Naval Hosp., Camp Lejeune, N.C., 1990-92. Recipient Meritorious Unit Commendation Am. Fedn. of Govt. Employees, 1992. Baptist.

TAYLOR, KAREN MARIE, education educator; b. Batavia, N.Y., June 15, 1961; d. Francis Edward and Barbara (Kearney) Dyrbala; m. Kenneth Douglas Taylor, July 3, 1992; 1 child, Kyle. AS, Genesee Community Coll., 1982; BS, Utah State U., 1984; MS, Nazareth Coll., 1991. Cert. tchr., N.Y., Ark. Reading coord. Genesee-Wyoming BOCES, Batavia, N.Y., 1985; secondary English educator Penn Yan (N.Y.) Acad., 1985-92, alternative edn. tchr., 1987-88; instr. TESOL Hobart Coll., Geneva, N.Y., 1991; adj. instr. English BOCES, Genesee Valley, N.Y., 1993—; class advisor Penn Yan Acad., 1986-89, drug free schs. mem., 1989-90, student coun. advisor, 1989-92, coord. natural helpers, 1990-92; vis. lectr. English Ark. Tech. U., Russellville, Ark., 1992-93; TESOL instr. Genesee Valley BOCES, 1993—. Author: (poetry) A Child's World, 1985 (Honorable Mention 1985), Always: A Vilanelle, 1985 (Honorable Mention 1985), You, 1985 (Honorable Mention 1985), The American Flag, 1986 (Honorable Mention 1986). Mem. Assn. Sch. Curriculum and Design, Nat. Coun. Tchrs. English. Democrat. Roman Catholic. Home: 751 Creek Rd Attica NY 14011

TAYLOR, LAVONNE TROY, editor; b. Riverside, Calif., May 20, 1941; d. Troy Virgil Bradstreet and R. Victoria (Freeman) Chambers; m. Robert Martin Taylor, May 15, 1958 (div. 1975); children: Dana Freeman, Timothy Rene; m. Herman Pickell, Feb. 14, 1985; children: Marianne, Barry,

David. Reporter Thousand Oaks (Calif.) Chronicle; with prodn. News Chronicle, Thousand Oaks, prodn. supr., 1979-81; with prodn. Ind. Jour., Thousand Oaks, Herald Examiner, L.A., L.A. Times; asst. mgr. Publ. Typography, Agoura, Calif., 1981-85; owner Excellence Enterprises, L.A., 1982—; sr. editor arts Glencoe/McGraw-Hill Sch. Pub., Mission Hills, Calif., 1987—; speaker various writers clubs. Editor, pub. L.A. My Way, 1991, On the Wings of Song, 1994; mng. editor The BookWoman, 1991-93. Mem. pub. rels. com. Conejo Players Theatre, Thousand Oaks, 1970-75, Betty Mann for 38th Assembly Dist., Agoura, 1975-76. Mem. NAFE, Nat. Writers Club (pres. 1990-91, Merit Svc. award 1991), Women's Nat. Book Assn. (pres. 1992-93, newsletter editor, bd. dirs.), L.A. County Art Mus., Huntington Mus., Nat. Mus. of Women in the Arts, Pub. Mktg. Assn., Soc. of Children's Book Writers, L.A. Book Publicist's Assn., Calif. Writer's Club, Bookbuilders West, Rosarian Soc. Am. Office: Glencoe/McGraw-Hill Sch Pub 15319 Chatsworth St Mission Hills CA 91345-2040

TAYLOR, LESLI ANN, pediatric surgery educator; b. N.Y.C., Mar. 2, 1953; d. Charles Vincent Taylor and Valene Patricia (Blake) Garfield. BFA, Boston U., 1975; MD, Johns Hopkins U., 1981. Diplomate Am. Bd. Surgery. Surg. resident Beth Israel Hosp., Boston, 1981-88; rsch. fellow Pediatric Rsch. Lab. Mass. Gen. Hosp., Boston, 1984-86; fellow pediatric surgery Children's Hosp. of Phila., Phila., 1988-90; asst. prof. pediatric surgery U. N.C., Chapel Hill, 1990—. Author: (booklet) Think Twice: The Medical Effects of Physical Punishment, 1985. Recipient Nat. Rsch. Svc. award NIH, 1984-86. Fellow Am. Coll. Surgeons; mem. AMA.

TAYLOR, LINDA RATHBUN, investment banker; b. Rochester, N.Y., May 25, 1946; d. Lewis Standish and Elizabeth Florence (Hunt) Rathbun; m. Donald Gordon Taylor, Mar. 1, 1975; children: Alexander Standish, Abigail Elizabeth, Elizabeth Downing. BA, Vassar Coll., 1968; MBA, Harvard U., 1973. Chartered fin. analyst, D.C. Assoc. corp. fin. Donaldson, Lufkin & Jenrette, N.Y.C., 1973-75; cons. World Bank, Washington, 1975; fin. analyst U.S. Treas. Dept., Washington, 1976-78; chief investment officer United Mine Workers Fund, 1978-85; investment mgr. Cen. Pension Fund of Internat. Union Oper. Engrs., Washington, 1985-86; investment banker The Saranow Co., 1986-89; pvt. investor, 1990—, pres. Pony Prodns., Inc. Bd. dirs. Fluid Mgmt., Inc., 1987-93; trustee Montgomery County Md. Employees' Retirement System, 1987-93; com. mem. Vassar Coll. Endowment Fund, 1992—; elder Bradley Hills Presbyn. Ch., 1992—. Contbr. articles to profl. jours. Mem. Jr. League Washington. Mem. Washington Soc. Investment Analysts (bd. dirs. 1984-85), Fin. Analyst Fedn. Republican. Presbyterian.

TAYLOR, LINDAJEAN THORTON, information systems executive; b. Cambridge, Mass., Apr. 16, 1942; d. Ferdinand and Hazel Irene (Towne) Karamanoukian; m. John Robert Thornton, Jan. 21, 1961; 1 child, John Robert; m. F. Jason Gaskell, Nov. 30, 1978. AA in Bus. Adminstrn., West L.A. Coll., 1976; BS, West Coast U., 1978, MS in Bus. and Info. Scis., 1980. Cert. quality analyst, computing profl. Asst. to chief indsl. engr. Pitts. Plate Glass Co., Boston, 1960-64; corp. sec., gen. mgr. Seaboard Planning Corp., Boston, 1967-69, L.A., 1969-72; prin. Tay-Kara Mgmt., L.A., 1972-73; chief systems adminstrn. Comp-La, L.A., 1973-74; mgr. systems analysis Trans Tech Inc., L.A., 1974-77; mgr. software engring. and tech. audit depts. System Devel. Corp., L.A., 1977-81; v.p. Gaskell and Taylor Engring., Inc., L.A., 1981-86; pres. Taylor and Zeno Systems, Inc., 1986—; mem. faculty, sr. lectr. West Coast U., L.A., 1980-93; vis. lectr. sr. seminar Calif. Poly. U., Pomona, 1978, 87-89, 90; del. 11th World Computing Congress, San Francisco, 1989, Internat. Fedn. Info. Processing, del. 12th World Computing Congress, Madrid, 1992, speaker security conf. '90 Internat. Fedn. Info. Processing, Helsinki, Finland, del. to 10th World Computer Congress, Dublin, Ireland, 1986; invited speaker 13th World Computer Congress, Hamburg, Germany, 1994; leader ednl. exch. del to People's Republic China, 1987; del. to 10th World Computing Congress; keynote speaker Hong Kong Computer Soc., Hong Kong Assn. for Advancement Sci. and Tech., 1987, NEC Inc. Software Engring. Lab., Tokyo, 1987, Tarleton State U., 1992. Appeared in 12 episodes of The New Literacy: An Introduction to Computers, Pub. Broadcasting System; mem. editorial bd.: Data Processing Quality jour. Chmn. bus. and profl. women's com. Calif. Rep. Cen. Com., 1974; mem. White House Com. on Workers Compensation, 1976; mem. fiscal adv. com. Santa Monica Unified Sch. Bd. Edn., 1979-81. Recipient Pub. Svc. award West L.A. C. of C., 1974. Mem. Assn. Women in Computing (pres. 1980-84, v.p. L.A. chpt. 1979-80), Nat. Computer Conf. (vice chmn., program com. 1980, mem. adv. com. 1983), Data Processing Mgmt. Assn. (v.p. South Bay chpt. 1979-80, bd. dirs. L.A. chpt. 1984, chmn. program com., media rels. com. 1984 internat. conf., pres. L.A. chpt. 1992, chmn. internat. conf. 1990, Individual Performance awards), IEEE (software engring. terminology task force 1980), Am. Def. Preparedness Assn. (congl. legis. adv. com. 1991-94), Assn. Systems Mgmt. (sec. local chpt. 1974-75), EDP Auditors Assn., Assn. for Computing Machinery, Nat. Assn. Women Bus. Owners, Internat. Fedn. for Information Processing (delegate security conf. Toronto 1993), Inst. for Cert. of Computing Profls. (bd. dirs., v.p. 1992, 93, pres. 94).

TAYLOR, MARETTA MITCHELL, state legislator; b. Columbus, Ga., Jan. 25, 1935. BS, Albany State, 1957; MS, Ind. U., 1966. Mem. Ga. Ho. of Reps., 1991-92, 93—; mem. edn., retirement, state planning and cmty. affairs coms.; co-owner, mgr. Designers Ltd., 1987—. Democrat. Baptist. Home: 1203 Bunker Hill Rd Columbus GA 31907-6718 Office: Ga House of Reps State Capitol Atlanta GA 30334*

TAYLOR, MARGARET ALEXANDER, newspaper publisher; b. Magnolia, Ark., June 12, 1926; d. Sam Pickering and Louie Maye (Falkner) Alexander; m. Joe Wayne Taylor, Sept. 12, 1948 (dec. Feb. 1978); children: Deborah Ann Taylor Starks, Timothy Wayne. AA, Magnolia A&M Coll., 1946; BS in Home Economics, Oklahoma A&M Coll., 1948. d. Sam Pickering and Louie Maye (Falkner) Alexander; m. Joe Wayne Taylor, Sept. 12, 1948 (dec. Feb. 1978); children: Deborah Ann Taylor Sparks, Timothy Wayne. Pub./editor The Davis News, Davis, Okla., 1978-92; retired, 1992. Mem. Okla. Press Assn. (bd. dirs. 1983-92, pres. 1990-91), Order of Eastern Star, Akomda Club. Democrat. Baptist. Office: The Davis News Inc 1008 S 5th St Davis OK 73030-3317

TAYLOR, MARGARET TURNER, clothing designer, economist, writer, planner; b. Wilmington, N.C., May 7, 1944. A.B. in Econs., Smith Coll., 1966; M.A. in Econ. History, U. Pa., 1970, now Ph.D. candidate in City and Regional Planning. Tchr. Jefferson Jr. High Sch., New Orleans, 1966-69; instr. econs. U. Tex.-El Paso, 1974-75; adj. prof. econs., Salisbury State U., Md., 1976-78; prin. mgr., designer Margaret Norriss, women's clothing, Salisbury, Md., 1980—; planner at Wharton Ctr. Applied Research, Phila., 1985-86; planning cons., writer.

TAYLOR, MARGARET WISCHMEYER, retired English language and journalism educator; b. Terre Haute, Ind., Aug. 5, 1920; d. Carl and Grace (Riehle) Wischmeyer; m. John Edward Taylor, Sept. 5, 1942 (dec. 1988); children: Deborah Ann, Tobin Edward, Mary Leesa. BA magna cum laude, Duke U., Durham, 1941; MA, John Carroll U., Cleve., 1973. Feature writer Dayton Daily News, Dayton, 1945-53; freelance writer Cleve., 1953—; asst. to Dr. Joseph B. Rhine Duke U. Parapsychology Lab., Durham, 1941; asst. prof. English and journalism Ea. Campus, Cuyahoga C.C., Cleve., 1973-92, prof. emeritus, 1992—, advisor campus newspaper, 1973-84, dir. Writers Conf., 1975-90; writing cons., editor various cos. and pubs., Cleve., 1973—; founder, operator Grammar Hot Line, 1987-92. Author: Crystal Lake Reflections, 1985, English 101 Can Be Fun, 1991, The Basic English Handbook, 1995. Recipient top state honors Ohio Newspaper Women's Assn., 1947, award for best ednl., best overall stories Am. Heart Assn., 1970, Besse award for teaching excellence, 1980, Nat. Teaching Excellence award Coun. for Advancement and Support of Edn., 1989; named Ohio Outstanding Citizen, Ohio Ho. Reps., 1987, 89, Innovator of Yr., League for Innovations in C.C.s, 1988. Mem. Mensa, Phi Beta Kappa. Presbyterian. Home: 27900 Fairmount Blvd Cleveland OH 44124-4616

TAYLOR, MARIAN ALECIA, assembly, quality engineer; b. Kansas City, Mo., Apr. 26, 1961; d. M.A. and Ellen Ardena (Hume) Nossaman; m. Michael Keith Taylor, July 26, 1986; 1 child, Alecia Ellen. AA, Johnson County C.C., 1989; BSME, BS in Bus., U. Kans., 1993. Dental asst. SE Brotherson DDS, Kansas City, Kans., 1983-85; dental instr. Kansas City Coll. of Med. and Dental Careers, Overland Park, 1985-86; math tutor Overland Park, 1988-91; tech. writer ArComm, Lenexa, Kans., 1991-92; total quality mgmt. rschr. U. Kans., Lawrence, 1992-93; process engr. NCR microelectronics products AT&T Global Info. Solutions, Ft. Collins, Colo., 1993—; sec. Hilltop Child Devel. Ctr., Lawrence, 1991-93. Contbr. articles to profl. jours. Student senator U. Kans. Student Senate, Lawrence, 1992-93; com. mem. Kans. U. Child Care Com., Lawrence, 1991-93, work and family com., 1991-92. Recipient U. Kans. Hilltopper award, 1993. Mem. ASME (treas. 1992-93), Oaks Nontraditional Students Orgn. (pres. 1991-92, treas. 1990-91, editor 1990-92), Tau Beta Pi, Pi Tau Simga. Home: 2707 Adobe Fort Collins CO 80525

TAYLOR, MARILYN GAIL, music educator, organist; b. Medford, Oreg., July 19, 1952; d. Leo L. and Helen Louise (Power) T.; m. Doremus Platt Scudder III, July 29, 1978 (div.); m. Thomas Miller Whitmore, June 20, 1993. BS in Mus. Edn./Piano Performance cum laude, So. Oreg. State Coll., 1978; MusM in Piano Performance, U. Tex., 1988. Tchr. music K-12 Ashland (Oreg.) Pub. Schs., 1978-81; accompanist, pianist Rogue Valley Chorales, Medford and Ashland, 1980-85; pvt. tchr. piano, accompanist Medford, 1981-85; festival pianist, harpsichordist Britt Music Festival, Jacksonville, Oreg., 1983-85; grad. asst. piano U. Tex., San Antonio, 1985-88, faculty, 1989; pvt. tchr. piano San Antonio, 1985—; organist, music dir. Alamo United Meth. Ch., San Antonio, 1987-93; organist, choirmaster Madison Sq. Presbyn. Ch., San Antonio, 1993—; accompanist, instrumental and vocal coach, San Antonio, 1985—, So. Oreg. State Coll., Ashland, 1975-85. Composer: (piano piece) Inaugural Rag, 1992, (organ piece) Dedication - For All the Saints, 1993. Mem. recycling com. Sierra Club, San Antonio, 1989—; active Common Cause, 1992—; block leader Recycle San Antonio, 1993. Mem. Nat. Guild Piano Tchrs., Tex. Music Tchr.'s Assn., San Antonio Music Tchr.'s Assn. Home: 4123 Goshen Pass San Antonio TX 78230

TAYLOR, MARTHA SUE, librarian; b. Sweetwater, Tex., Aug. 16, 1947; d. John Neville Shipley and Erma Hall Shipley Neeper; m. Linn Bryant Taylor, May 22, 1981; children: Mark Bryant, Melissa Anne. BA in English and Govt., Tex. Tech U., 1969, MA in English, 1971; postgrad., U. Tex., 1973. Tchr. English Sweetwater Ind. Sch. Dist., 1971-73, supr. elem. libr., 1973-78, tchr. govt. and English, 1978-83, libr. high sch., 1983—; mem. dist. improvement coun. Sweetwater Ind. Sch. Dist., 1991-94, sec. 1993-94, mem. H.S. campus improvement com., 1991—; instr. govt. Western Tex. Coll., Snyder, 1983-88. Sec. adminstrv. bd. 1st United Meth. Ch., 1978-83, organist, 1979—. Mem. AAUW (pres. 1971-73, 1st v.p. 1985-87, treas. 1989-90), Tex. State Tchrs. Assn. (pres. 1987-88), Tex. Libr. Assn. Methodist. Home: 1632 Morris Ave Sweetwater TX 79556-2646 Office: Sweetwater High Sch 1205 Ragland St Sweetwater TX 79556-2438

TAYLOR, MARY ANNE, public relations executive; b. Detroit, June 20, 1948; d. Robert George and Elizabeth A. (Murphy) Klein; m. Alexander Lindsay Taylor III, Apr. 21, 1983; children: Alexander, Madeleine. BS in Mktg., Wayne State U., 1972; BA in English, Fordham U., N.Y.C., 1983. Officer tng. prog. City Nat. Bank, Detroit, 1971-72; mgr. pub. rels. City Nat. Bank, 1972-73, dir. pub. rels., 1973-75, asst. v.p. pub. affairs, 1975-78; dir. invester rels. The Pittston Co., Greenwich, Conn., 1978-83; mgr. communications Philip Morris Cos., Inc., N.Y.C., 1983-86; dir. communications Philip Morris Cos., Inc., 1986-89, dir. spl. projects, 1989-91; v.p. pub. affairs Avon, 1992-93; sr. v.p. mktg. support and comm. Home Ins. Co. divsn. of Home Holdings, N.Y.C., 1993—. Contbr. articles to profl. jours. Bd. dir. Nat. Found. of Reconstructive Surgery. Mem. Civitas. Office: Home Insurance 59 Maiden Lane New York NY 10038

TAYLOR, MARY ELIZABETH, dietitian, educator; b. Medina, N.Y., Dec. 10, 1933; d. Glenn Aaron and Viola Hazel (Lansill) Grimes; m. Wilbur Alvin Fredlund, Apr. 12, 1952 (div. Jan. 1980); 1 child, Wilbur Jr.; m. Frederick Herbert Taylor, Mar. 15, 1981; children: Martha Dayton, Jean Grout, Beth Stern, Cindy Hey, Carol McLellan, Cheryl, Robert. BS in Food and Nutrition, SUCB, Buffalo, 1973; MEd in Health Sci. Edn. and Evaluation, SUNY, 1978. Registered dietitian, 1977. Diet cook Niagara Sanitorium, Lockport, N.Y., 1953-56; cook Mount View Hosp., Lockport, N.Y., 1956-60, asst. dietitian, 1960-73, dietitian, food svc. dir., 1973-79, cons. dietitian, 1979-81; instr. Erie Community Coll., Williamsville, N.Y., 1979-81; sch. lunch coord. Nye County Sch. Dist., Tonopah, Nev., 1970-93; retired Nye County Sch. Dist., 1993; food svc. mgmt. cons., fin. mgmt. advisor pvt. practice, 1994—; activity dir. PEC RU Resort, Pahrump, Nev., 1993—; cons. dietitian Nye Gen. Hosp., Tonopah, 1983-88; adj. instr. Erie Community Coll., Williamsville, 1978-79; nutrition instr. for coop. extension Clark County Community Coll., 1990—; cons. Group Purchasing Western N.Y. Hosp. Adminstrs., Buffalo, 1975-79, vice-chmn. adv. com., 1976-78; cons. BOCES, Lockport, 1979-81. Nutrition counselor Migrant Workers Clinic, Lockports, 1974-80; mem. Western N.Y. Soc. for Hosp. Food Svc. Adminstrn., 1974-81; nutritionist Niagara County Nutrition Adv. Com., 1977-81. Recipient Outstanding Woman of the Yr., YWCA-UAW Lockport, 1981, Disting. Health Care Food Adminstrn. Recognition award Am. Soc. for Hosp. Food Svc. Adminstrs., 1979, USDA award Outstanding Lunch Program in Nev. and Western Region, 1986, 91. Mem. Am. Assn. Ret. Persons, Am. Sch. Food Svc. Assn. (bd. dirs. 1987, 92-93, cert. dir. II 1987, 5-yr. planning com. 1990, mem. ann. confs. 1988-93), Am. Dietetic Assn. (nat. referral system for registered dietitians 1992-93), So. Nev. Dietetic Assn. (pres. 1985-86), Nev. Food Svc. Assn. (participant ann. meetings 1990-93), Nutrition Today Soc., Nev. Sch. Food Svcs. Assn. (dietary guidelines com. 1991-93). Republican. Baptist. Home: 481 N Murphy PO Box 656 Pahrump NV 89041-0656

TAYLOR, MARY HODGE, education administrator; b. Jackson, Tenn., Dec. 8, 1959; d. James Nelson and Barbara (Taylor) Hodge; 1 child, Amanda Leigh. BS, U. Tenn., 1981, MPA, 1983. Fin. coord. U. Tenn. Residence Halls, Knoxville, 1983-85; bus. asst. U. Tenn. Inst. Pub. Svc., Knoxville, 1985-87, asst. to exec. dir., 1987-89, asst. to v.p., 1989-91; asst. dir. U. Tenn. Ctr. Govt. Tng., Nashville, 1991-93; dir. U. Tenn. Inst. Pub. Svc., Knoxville, 1993—. Fund raiser United Way, Knoxville, 1983—; mem. Rep. Presdl. Task Force. U. Tenn. Valedictorian scholar, Knoxville, 1977; recipient Upperclassman award U. Tenn., 1978; named Outstanding Young Women Am., Knoxville, 1981. Mem. Am. Soc. Pub. Adminstrn. Presbyterian. Home: 10009 Eastshire Ln Knoxville TN 37922 Office: U Tenn Inst Pub Svc 105 Student Svcs Bldg Knoxville TN 37996

TAYLOR, MARY KAY, geriatrics nurse; b. Knoxville, Iowa, Jan. 26, 1954; d. Wendell Shawver and Margery Ethel (Beebe) Kubli; m. Gregory Taylor, Sept. 4, 1993. ADN, Indian Hills Community Coll., 1979; BSN, Teikyo Marycrest U., 1993. RN, Iowa. Staff nurse Mercy Hosp., Des Moines, 1979-81, Knoxville Area Community Hosp., 1981-83, VA Med. Ctr., Knoxville, 1983—. Home: PO Box 646 Knoxville IA 50138-0646

TAYLOR, MARY SUE, musician, educator; b. Toccoa, Ga., Dec. 4, 1934; d. A. Oliver and Mary Ruth (Snelson) Humphries; 1 child. Student, Shorter Coll., 1954, Ga. State Coll., 1955, 56. Pianist, orchestral leader Mary Sue Taylor Bands, Atlanta, 1958—; staff pianist Atlanta Pops Orch., 1980-93; pvt. tchr. Atlanta Art Ctrs., 1984—; pianist Atlanta Symphony, 1960, Democratic Conv., Atlanta, 1989. Mem. Atlanta Fedn. of Musicians. Baptist. Home and Office: 280 Holly Berry Ln Roswell GA 30076

TAYLOR, MINNA, lawyer; b. Washington, Jan. 25, 1947; d. Morris P. and Anne (Williams) Glushien; m. Charles Ellett Taylor, June 22, 1969; 1 child, Amy Caroline. BA, SUNY, Stony Brook, 1969; MA, SUNY, 1973; JD, U. So. Calif., 1977. Bar: Calif. 1977, U.S. Dist. Ct. (cen. dist.) Calif. 1978. Extern to presiding justice Calif. Supreme Ct., 1977; field atty. NLRB, L.A., 1977-82; dir. employee rels., legal svcs. Paramount Pictures Corp., L.A., 1982-85, v.p. employee rels. legal svcs., 1985-89; dir. bus. and legal affairs Wilshire Ct. Prodns., L.A., 1989-91; sr. counsel Fox Broadcasting Co., L.A., 1991-92, v.p. legal affairs, 1992—. Editor notes and articles: U. So. Calif. Law Rev., 1976-77. Mentor MOSTE, L.A., 1986-87, 88-89; pres. Beverly Hills chpt. ACLU, L.A., 1985. Fellow ABA, L.A. County Bar Assn.; mem. Beverly Hills Bar Assn., L.A. Bead Soc. (membership sec. 1992-94, mem. bd. dirs. 1994—), Order of Coif. Office: Fox Broadcasting Co 10201 W Pico Blvd Los Angeles CA 90035

TAYLOR, PATRICIA ELSIE, epidemiologist; b. Ayr, Queensland, Australia, Mar. 20, 1929; d. Ernest Howard and Mayzie Lucy (Kwong) Lee; m. Kenneth Douglas Taylor, Oct. 1, 1960; 1 child, Douglas Craig. BS, U. Queensland, 1952, postgrad., 1954; PhD, U. Calif., Berkeley, 1964; LLD (hon.), St. Francis Xavier U., N.S., Can., 1981. Mem. rsch. staff Queensland Inst. Med. Rsch., Brisbane, 1949-58; assoc. in epidemiology Sch. Pub. Health U. Calif., Berkeley, 1958-60; grad. rsch. fellow Inst. Nutrition for Cen. Am. and Panama, Guatemala, 1960-63; rsch. fellow Child Rsch. Ctr. of Mich., Detroit, 1965-66; sr. rsch. assoc. London Sch. Hygiene and Tropical Medicine, 1967-71; rsch. scientist Dept. Nat. Health and Welfare, Ottawa, Ont., Can., 1972-78; sr. cons. in virology and sci. rsch. Iranian Nat. Blood Transfusion Svc., Pasteur Inst., Tehran, 1978-80; epidemiologist Lindsley F. Kimball Rsch. Inst., N.Y. Blood Ctr., N.Y.C., 1981—; prin. dancer Queensland Ballet Theatre, 1956-58; solo dancer Guatemalan Nat. Ballet, 1960-63; mem. various U.S. Fed. Adv. Panels for infectious disease and AIDS. Author more than 100 sci. publs. Trustee Cathedral of St. John the Divine, N.Y., 1981. Named Woman of Yr., Can. Women's Club of N.Y., 1992; Paul Harris fellow, 1983, Internat. fellow AAUW, 1954-55; grantee Fulbright Found., 1954-55, Rockefeller Found., 1955. Mem. Royal Acad. Dancing, West Point Soc. N.Y. (hon.), Order of Can. (hon.). Home: 146 W 57th St # 61T New York NY 10019-3323 Office: NY Blood Ctr Lindsley F Kimball Rsch Inst 310 E 67th St New York NY 10021-6204

TAYLOR, RENITA WIMBERLY, chemist; b. Pine Bluff, Ark., June 28, 1958; d. Gale Elbert and Luvenia (Creggett) Wimberly; m. Clifton P. Taylor, Aug. 14, 1993; children: Jarvis, Kamilah, Jadice. BS, U. Ark., Pine Bluff, 1981; MS, Tex. So. U., Houston, 1988. Technologist Exxon, Houston, 1981-86; analytical chemist Gen. Mills, Covington, Ga., 1989-92; process chemist E.I. DuPont, Mobile, Ala., 1991-92; staff scientist Johnson & Johnson, Milltown, N.J., 1992—. Tchr. Ebenezer Bapt. Ch., Atlanta, 1989-91; troop leader Girl Scouts U.S., Atlanta, 1989-91. Mem. Am. Soc. Quality Control (quality engr.), Soc. Plastic Engrs., Nat. Orgn. Black Chemists and Chem. Engrs., Am. Chem. Soc., Delta Sigma Theta (mentor Single Parents Project 1989). Home: 240 Glenn Ave Lawrenceville NJ 08648-3744 Office: Johnson & Johnson 1 Van Liew Ave Milltown NJ 08850-1120

TAYLOR, ROSE PERRIN, social worker; b. Lander, Wyo., Feb. 11, 1916; d. Wilbur Rexford Perrin and Agatha Catherine (Hartman) Perrin DeMars; m. Louis Kempf Kugland, Sept. 1942 (div. 1951); children: Mary Louise, Carolyn Kugland McElhany; m. Wilfred Taylor, Oct. 13, 1962 (dec. 1991). AB, U. Mich., 1937; MSW, U. Denver, 1956; student, Columbia U., 1936, Santa Rosa Jr. Coll., 1974-93; Coll. of Marin, 1994. Group worker Dodge Community House, Detroit, 1937-38; case worker Detroit Welfare Dept., Detroit, 1938-40; child welfare worker Fremont County Welfare Dept., Lander, Wyo., 1940-42; worker children's svcs. Laramie County Welfare Dept., Cheyenne, Wyo., 1951-57, dir., 1957-58; supr. San Mateo (Calif.) County Health & Welfare, 1958-74; dir. Fed. Day Care Project, San Mateo, 1964—; tchr. Sch. Pub. Health Nursing, U. Wyo., 1951-55; tchr. Sch. Social Work, U. Calif., San Jose, 1962-63; workshop leader NIMH, Prescott, Ariz., 1961, Ariz. State U., Phoenix, 1962, Oreg. State Welfare Dept., Otter Crest, 1973; cons. day care workshops. Contbr. articles to profl. jours. Bd. dirs. YMCA, Sonoma County, Calif., 1980-84. Recipient Resolution of Commendation, Calif. State Senate, 1974; Annual Rose Taylor award San Mateo Child Care Coordinating Coun., 1982. Mem. NASW. Democrat. Mem. United Ch. of Christ. Home: 500 Lincoln Village Ctr 128 Larkspur CA 94939

TAYLOR, ROSEMARY, artist; b. Joseph, Oreg.; d. Theodore and Sarah A. (Lambright) Resch; student Cleve. Inst. Art, 1937-40, NYU, 1947; m. Robert Hull Taylor; children: Barbara Taylor Ryalls, Robert H. Tchr. pottery Rahway (N.J.) Art Center, 1950-55; one-woman shows: Paterson (N.J.) Coll., 1964, Westchester (Pa.) Coll., 1970, Gallery 100, Princeton, N.J., 1967, George Jensen's, N.Y.C., 1972, Artisan Gallery, Princeton, 1974, Am. Crafts (Ohio), 1979-94, Guild Gallery, 1986-91, Little Art Gallery, N.C., 1985-94, Olde Queens Gallery (N.J.), 1987, N.J. Designer Craftsmen, 1990 (bd. dirs. 1986-87, standard chmn., 1994), Creative Hands, Princeton, 1994; group shows include: Mus. Natural History, N.Y.C., Newark Mus., Trenton (N.J.) Mus., Montclair (N.J.) Mus., Phila. Art Alliance, Pa. Horticulture Soc., 1988, Nat. Design Center, N.Y.C.; represented in permanent collection Westchester Coll.; pottery cons. McCalls Mag., 1962-72. Bd. dirs. Solebury Community Sch.; mem. Fulbright award com., 1982, 83. Mem. LWV (pres. Plainfield, N.J. chpt.). Mem. Am. Craft Council, N.J. Designer-Craftsmen, Phila. Craft Group, Bucks County (Pa.) C. of C., Visual Artists and Galleries Assn., Nat. Assn. Am. Penwoman, Women in the Arts (charter). Democrat. Unitarian. Home: PO Box 46 Lumberville PA 18933-0046 Office: PO Box 282 Stockton NJ 08559-0282

TAYLOR, RUTH MUELLER, artist; b. Atchison, Kans., Jan. 31, 1934; d. Alfred Christian and Emma (Kautz) Mueller; m. Thomas Elbert Taylor, Mar. 21, 1970; children: Marilyn Diane Campbell, Robert Douglas Hegarty. Student, Kansas City Art Inst., 1980; student, Naples Art Inst., 1994. Asst. mgr. Kansas City Fiberglas Fed. Credit Union, 1962-80; rental mgr. various locations, 1972-90; profl. artist Mo. and Fla., 1982—; treas. Ozark Brush and Palette, Camdenton, Mo., 1986-89, workshop coord., 1986-87 (Artist of Yr. 1989). Mem. Mich. Guild Artists, Columbia Art League, Art League Mareo Island, Naples Art Assn. Republican. Roman Catholic. Office: Ruth Mueller Taylor Studio and Gallery 3754 Arnold Ave Naples FL 33942

TAYLOR, SANDRA ORTIZ, artist, educator; b. L.A., Apr. 27, 1936; d. John Santry and Juanita Loretta (Shrode) T. BA in Art, UCLA, 1958; MA in Art, State U. Iowa, 1962. Instr. art State U. Iowa, Iowa City, 1961-62, Indian Valley Colls, Marin County, Calif., 1973-74, San Francisco C.C., 1966—; seminar guest speaker Nat. Book Conf., 1991; chair all-media nat exhibit Fine Arts Gallery Broward C.C., Davie, Fla., 1994, Humanities Art Gallery Palm Beach C.C. Exhibited in group shows Calif. Mus. Art, Santa Rosa, 1991, 92, 93, Falkirk Ctr., San Rafael, Calif., 1992, 93, Gallery Route One, Point Reyes Station, Calif., 1993, San Jose (Calif.) Inst. Contemporary Art, 1993-94, San Francisco Airport Com. & Corp. of Fine Arts Mus. of San Francisco, 1994, San Mateo County Arts Coun., Belmont, Calif., San Francisco Women Artists Gallery, San Jose Contemporary Art & Performance Gallery; commd. for grad. program Chicano and Latino studies U. Calif., Irvine, 1992; work reviewed in various publs. Recipient jurors award Calif. Mus. Art, 1992; scholar Anderson Ranch Art Ctr., Snow Mass, Colo., 1991. Home and Office: Ephemera Studio 2854 Harrison St San Francisco CA 94110-4117

TAYLOR, STEPHANIE DENISE, organization administrator; b. Tulsa, Sept. 19, 1961; d. Richard Harvey and Judith Carol (Holtzinger) Welcher; m. Jeffery Lee Taylor, June 16, 1990 (div. July 1992). BS, Okla. State U., 1983; MA, U. Okla., 1994. Reporter The Daily O'collegian, Stillwater, Okla., 1980-83; news anchor KOSU-FM, Stillwater, 1981, KRXO-FM, Stillwater, 1982; asst. producer KTVY-TV, Oklahoma City, 1983-84; anchor/reporter KTEN, Ada, Okla., 1985-86; producer America's Shopping Channel, Oklahoma City, 1987; pub. rels. coordinator S.W. Med. Ctr. Okla., Oklahoma City, 1988-89, pub. rels. assoc., 1990-91, mgr. pub. rels. and devel., 1991-93; exec. dir., CEO, Neighborhood Alliance, Oklahoma City, 1994—; cons. on brochure, Women to Woman, 1990. Mem. comms. com. United Way, Oklahoma City, 1989-90; bd. dirs. Nat. Clown and Laughter Hall of Fame, 1989—; bd. dirs. HUGS. Recipient Good Guy award, KTVY-TV, 1988, 89. Mem. Women in Comms. (v.p. 1981-82), Am. Hosp. Assn., Okla. Hosp. Assn., Am. Soc. Health Care Mktg. and Pub. Rels., PRSA, Oklahoma City C. of C., South Oklahoma City C. of C., Lions Internat., Am. Bus. Clubs (bd. dirs.). Methodist. Office: Neighborhood Alliance 1236 NW 36th St Oklahoma City OK 73118

TAYLOR, SYLVIA PINDLE, educational entrepreneur; b. Macon, Ga.; d. Arthur Jackson Sr. and Beatrice (Williams) Pindle; m. John Benjamin Taylor III, June 14, 1969 (div. 1976). BA, Spelman Coll., 1965; postgrad., Howard U., 1966-69, 72-73, Am. U., 1975, 76; MA, Fayetteville State U., 1987. Cert. tchr., N.C., adult counselor, D.C. Tchr. D.C. Pub. Schs., 1966-68; staff asst. U.S. Congresswoman Shirley Chisholm, Washington, 1970-72; adult counselor D.C. Skills Ctr. (Pub. Schs.), Washington, 1972-75; asst. to v.p. for student life Am. U., Washington, 1975-76; staff aide White House Press Office (Main), Washington, 1977-78; editorial asst. Assn. for the Study of Afro-Am. Life and History, Washington, 1980-82; adminstrv. asst. Operation Sickle Cell, Inc., Fayetteville, 1985-86; cert. substitute tchr. Cumberland County Pub. Sch., Fayetteville, 1987-90; owner, CEO, founder Nat. Coll.

Svc., Inc., Fayetteville, 1987—; counselor Neighborhood Youth Corps, Inc. Washington, 1968-70; vol. cons. Conv. Planning, Inc., Washington, 1978, Ofield Dukes & Assocs., Inc., Washington, 1969-78, Nat. Urban League, Julius A. Thomas Vol. Soc., N.Y.C., 1979. Co-author: The Handbook of Information for International Students, 1976. Mem. NAACP, Fayetteville, 1987-89. Acad. scholar Coll. Entrance Exam. Bd., 1959, 61. Mem. ASCD, The Links Inc., Teen Involvement Project Inc., Alpha Kappa Alpha, Kappa Delta Pi, Alpha Kappa Mu. Episcopalian. Home and Office: Nat Coll Svc Inc PO Box 2056 3105 Mars Pl Fayetteville NC 28302-2056

TAYLOR, TERRY, editor, educator; b. Valley Forge, Pa., Oct. 4, 1952; d. Thomas R. and Anna P. (Bystrek) T. BA in Journalism, Temple U., 1974. Reporter gen. assignments, sch. news Charlotte (N.C.) News, 1974-77; supr., writer AP, Phila., 1977-81; supr., writer sports desk AP, N.Y.C., 1981-85, asst. editor sports, 1985-87, dep. editor sports, 1987-91, asst. chief bur., 1991-92, editor sports, 1992—; asst. editor sports N.Y. Times, 1991; assoc. in journalism Columbia U., N.Y.C., 1991—. Roman Catholic. Office: AP Sports 50 Rockefeller Plz New York NY 10020-1666

TAYLOR, THERESA EVERETH, registered nurse, artist; b. Carthage, N.Y., Aug. 9, 1938; d. Michael Patrick and Angelina (Cerroni) Evereth; m. James Edgar Taylor II, Mar. 12, 1966; children: Britt, Priscilla, Blackwell. Diploma in nursing, House of God Samaritan Sch. Nursing, Watertown, N.Y., 1959; BFA summa cum laude, Ursuline Coll., 1992. RN, N.Y., Ohio. Office mgr. Design Mgmt. Inc., Cleve., 1981—; clin. nurse Ohio Clinic for Aesthetic and Plastic Surgery, Westlake, Ohio, 1993—; home health care nurse A.C. Home Nursing, Akron, Ohio, 1994—. Exhbns. in group shows. Pres. Wasmer Gallery Coun., Pepper Pike, Ohio, 1992-94; clk. vestry St. Christophers by the River, Gates Mills, 1979-81; treas. Welcome Wagon, Chesterland, Ohio, 1984-85: vol. artist Cleve. Ctr. Contemporary Art, 1993—. Home: 12060 Caves Rd Chesterland OH 44026-2104 Office: 21711 Tungsten Rd Cleveland OH 44117

TAYLOR, THERESA TULLEY, financial consultant; b. Methuen, Mass., May 25, 1965; d. Raymond Dennis and Anna Maria (Manzi) Tulley; m. Gregory Paul Taylor, Oct. 9, 1988; 1 child, Gregory Paul Jr. BS in Acctg., Merrimack Coll., 1988. Auditor Peat Marwick, Boston, 1988-90; fin. analyst Bronner, Slosberg Humphrey, Boston, 1990-93; MIS cons. Cowan, Bolduc & Co., Andover, Mass., 1993—. Mem. Nat. Assn. Accts. Republican. Roman Catholic. Home: 144 Castle Hill Rd Windham NH 03087-1746 Office: Cowan Bolduc & Co 300 Brickstone Sq Andover MA 01810-1486

TAYLOR, VESTA FISK, real estate broker, educator; b. Ottawa County, Okla., July 15, 1917; d. Ira Sylvester and Judie Maude (Garman) Fisk; m. George E. Taylor, Aug. 17, 1957 (dec. Oct. 1963); stepchildren: Joyce, Jean, Luther. AA, Northeastern Okla. A&M, 1931; BA, N.E. State U., Tahlequah, Okla., 1937; MA, Okla. State U., 1942. Life cert. Spanish, English, history, elem. Tchr. rural sch. grades 1-4 Ottawa County, Okla., 1931-33; tchr. rural sch. grades 1-8 Ottawa County, 1933-38; tchr. H.S. Spanish, English Wyandotte, Okla., 1938-42; tchr. H.S. Spanish, English, math. Miami, Okla., 1942-57; tchr. H.S. Spanish Jacksonville, Ill., 1960-65; tchr. H.S. Spanish, English Miami, 1965-79; owner, broker First Lady Realty, Miami, 1979—; tchr. real estate for licensing N.E. Okla. Vocat.-Tech., Afton, 1980—; radio spellmaster weekly-county groups Coleman Theater Stage, 1954-57, radio program weekly 4-H, Miami, 1953-57. Author: (poem) The Country School, 1994. Sec. Ottawa County Senior's Ctr., 1993—; restoration com. Friends of Theater, 1993—. Named Outstanding Coach Ottawa County 4-H Clubs, Miami, 1955, 67, Outstanding Alumnus All Yrs. H.S. Reunion, Wyandotte, Okla., 1992, Champion Speller N.E. Okla. Retirees, Oklahoma City, 1991. Mem. AAUW (pres. 1978-80), Ottawa County Retired Educators (treas. 1990—), Spanish Study Club (pres., instr. 1962-63), Miami Classroom Tchrs. (v.p. 1973-77), Tri-State Travel Club (purser 1989—), Kappa Kappa Iota. Democrat. Baptist. Home: 821 Jefferson Blvd Miami OK 74354 Office: First Lady Realty 206 A St NW Miami OK 74354

TAYLOR, VIRGINIA S., lawyer; b. Quitman, Ga.; d. Allen Candler and Anne (Sanderson) Smith; divorced; children: Anne Taylor Hendry, Thomas Fielding. AB, Smith Coll., 1961; JD with distinction, Emory U., 1977. Bar: Ga. 1977, U.S. Dist. Ct. (no. dist.) Ga. 1977, U.S. Dist. Ct. (mid. dist.) Ga. 1979, U.S Dist. Ct. (ea. dist.) Mich. 1988, U.S. Ct. Appeals (5th and 11th cirs.) 181, U.S. Ct. Appeals (fed. cir.) 1982, U.S. Supreme Ct. 1981. Assoc. Kilpatrick & Cody, Atlanta, 1977-83, ptnr., 1983—. V.p. Olmstead Parks Soc., Atlanta, 1985-93; bd. dirs. Piedmont Park Conservancy, Atlanta, 1991—, YWCA Metro. Atlanta, 1989-92, Leadership Atlanta, 1990. Mem. Ga. State Bar (chair patent, trademark and copyright sect. 1985-86), Order of Coif, Lawyer's Club Atlanta, Internat. Trademark Assn. (chair internat. forums subcom. 1992—, bd. dirs. 1991-93, chair pub. com. 1988-90). Democrat. Methodist. Office: Kilpatrick & Cody 1100 Peachtree St Ste 2800 Atlanta GA 30309

TAYLOR, WENDY HALL, auditor; b. Cohasset, Mass., Oct. 1, 1959; d. Robert Sterling and Barbara Ruth (Sparks) Hall; m. James Allen Taylor, Nov. 28, 1986. Student, Salem Coll., 1977-79; BS in Acctg., U. N.C., Greensboro, 1987. CPA, N.C. Staff auditor Deloitte & Touche, Greensboro, N.C., 1987-90; sr. auditor Deloitte & Touche, Winston Salem, N.C., 1990-93, audit mgr., 1993—. Dir. fin. Steeplechase at Tanglewood, Winston-Salem, 1993, 94, Vantage Championship, Winston-Salem, 1994. Mem. AICPA, Inst. Mgmt. Accts. (bd. dirs., sec. 1993-94, dir. newsletter 1994—), Profl. Women Winston-Salem. Democrat. Episcopalian. Home: 328 Vintage Ave Winston Salem NC 27127 Office: Deloitte & Touche 500 W 5th St Ste 1401 Winston Salem NC 27120

TAYLOR-MEARHOFF, CHERYL LYNN, school administrator; b. Phila., Dec. 28, 1962; d. Charles L. and Carol A. (Janeika) Taylor; m. Richard A. Mearhoff, June 29, 1985; children: Richard, Charles. BA, Pa. State U., 1983, guidance/crisis counselor, 1984. Cert. prevention specialist. Guidance counselor Stroudsburg (Pa.) High Sch., 1984-85; guidance, crisis counselor Phoenixville (Pa.) High Sch., 1985-88; chmn. dependency counseling instr. Pa. State U., Berks County, Pa., 1990—; coord student assistance programs Owen J. Roberts Sch. Dist., Pottstown, Pa., 1988—; tng. cons. Pa. Dept. Edn., 1983—; pvt. practice counselor Innovative Counseling, Pottstown, 1988-90. Producer parent edn. series, 1991-93; contbr. articles to profl. jours. Mem. Pa. State Commn. for Women, Bright Light Early Learning Ctr., Pa. Assn. of Student Assistance Profls., Pi Lambda Theta. Office: Owen J Roberts Sch Dist RR 1 Pottstown PA 19464-9801

TAYLOR-YOUNG, LEIGH, actress; b. Washington, DC, Jan. 25, 1945. films include: I Love You, Alice B. Tolkas, 1968, The Big Bounce, 1969, The Games, 1970, The Buttercup Chain, 1970, The Adventurers, 1970, The Horsemen, 1971, The Gang That Couldn't Shoot Straight, 1971, Soylent Green, 1973, Can't Stop the Music, 1980, Looker, 1981, Secret Admirer, 1985, Jagged Edge, 1985, Honeymoon Academy, 1990; TV appearances include: (series) Peyton Place, 1964-69, The Devlin Connection, 1982, The Hamptons, 1983, Dallas, 1987-88, Picket Fences, 1994— (Emmy award Best Supporting Actress - Drama, 1994); (movies) Marathon, 1980, Napoleon and Josephine: A Love Story, 1987, Perry Mason: The Case of the Sinister Spirit, 1987, Who Gets the Friends?, 1988. Office: Don Buchwald & Associates 9229 Sunset Blvd Suite 710 Los Angeles CA 90069*

TAYMOR, BETTY, political science educator; b. Balt., Mar. 22, 1921; d. William and Tillie (Blum) Bernstein; m. Melvin Lester Taymor, June 7, 1942; children; Michael, Laurie, Julie. AB, Goucher Coll., 1942; MA in Am. Govt., Boston U., 1967. Dir. program for women in politics and govt. Boston Coll., 1970-92; instr. in govt. Northeastern U., Boston, 1969-71; cons. office of pres. U. Mass., Boston, 1973-74; instr. MA in Urban Affairs program Boston U., 1967-68; instr. in politics & govt. McCormack Inst., Boston, 1973-92; coord. Boston Network for Women in Politics & Govt. U. Mass.-Boston, 1992-94; dir. spl. projects Ctr. for Women in Politics & Pub. Policy U. Mass.-Boston, 1992—. State committeewoman Dem. State Com., Boston, 1956-92, nat. committeewoman, Washington, 1976—; mem. U.S. nat. commn. UNESCO, 1966; bd. dirs. Univ. Hosp., boston, 1989-91; mem. New Eng. Bd. Higher Edn., 1985-89; mem. adv. com. John F. Kennedy Libr. Elizabeth King Ellicott fellow Goucher Coll., 1959-60; recipient Abigail Adams award Mass. Women's Polit. Caucus, 1989. Home: 14 Eliot Memorial Rd Newton MA 02158

TCHAIKOVSKY, LESLIE J., judge; b. 1943. BA, Calif. State Univ., Hayward, 1967; JD, Univ. of Calif., Berkeley, 1976. Law clk. to Hon. John Mowbray Nev. Supreme Ct., 1976-77; with Dinkelspiel, Steefel, Leavitt & Weiss, 1977-80, Gordon, Peitzman & Lopez, 1981, Dinkelspiel, Donovan & Reder, 1981-88; bankruptcy judge U.S. Bankruptcy Ct. (Calif. no. dist.), 9th circuit, Oakland, 1988—. Office: US Courthouse 1300 Clay St Oakland CA 94604-2070*

TCHERKASSKY, MARIANNA ALEXSAVENA, ballerina; b. Glen Cove, N.Y., Oct. 28, 1952; d. Alexis and Lillian (Oka) T.; m. Terrence S. Orr. Student, Washington Sch. Ballet (scholar), 1965-67, Sch. Am. Ballet and Profl. Children's Sch., 1967-70; pupil of Edward Caton. Appeared with Bolshoi Ballet in Ballet Sch., 1961, 62, N.Y.C. Ballet in A Midsummer Night's Dream, 1963; profl. debut with Andre Eglevsky Ballet Co., 1968; mem., Am. Ballet Theatre, 1970—, soloist, 1972-76, prin. dancer, 1976—, guest appearances throughout U.S. and in Europe, also on TV; roles include The Nutcracker, La Bayadere, Bruch Violin Concerto No. 1, Coppelia, Giselle, Etudes, Les Liaisons Dangereuses, Romeo and Juliet, The Sleeping Beauty, La Sylphide, Les Sylphides, The Leaves are Fading. Winner Nat. Soc. Arts and Letters competition, 1967; Ford Found. scholar, 1967-70. Office: care Am Ballet Theatre 890 Broadway New York NY 10003-1211*

TEACH, JOAN KRAUSS, school administrator; b. Norristown, Pa., Jan. 19, 1939; d. Alton L. and Eva L. (Fleck) Krauss; m. Richard D. Teach, July 2, 1980; children: Brett David, Danette Suzanne, Alian Diahanne, Kurt Jarred. BS, Wittenberg U., 1960; MS, Purdue U., 1966; PhD, Ga. State U., 1978. Cert. tchr., Ga. Tchr. Columbus (Ohio) Pub. Schs., 1960-61, Romney (Ind.) Pub. Schs., 1961-63; adminstrv. asst. Newell C. Kephart Achievement Ctr. for Children, 1963-66; instr. Practicum in Programming and Educating the Slow Learner, 1964-66; cons. Bd. Cooperative Ednl. Services, N.Y. Spl. Edn. Dept., Buffalo, 1968-70; instr. Ga. State U., Atlanta, 1975-76; diagnostic specialist Howard Sch., Atlanta, 1974-79; dir. Lullwater Sch., Decatur, Ga., 1979—; program coordinator Project ACTION, Atlanta, 1976-79; hearing officer City Schs. Decatur, 1977-79; seminar leader, Decatur, 1986, 87. Contbr. profl. jours., books, 1969—; speaker numerous profl. orgns., 1977—. Developer child service program Christ United Presbyn. Ch., 1978-80, elder, 1978-80; mem. Decatur Devel. Authority, Decatur Area Network. Mem. Inst. Devel. Ednl. Activities, Assn. Individually Guided Edn., Child Advocacy Coalition, Coun. for Exceptional Children (Ga. rep. 1979-81, pres. Ga. divsn. for learning disabilities 1980-82), Nat. Assn. Edn. Young Children, Decatur Bus. and Profl. Women, Atlanta Women's C. of C., Bus. and Profl. Women's Club (v.p. 1991-93, state woman achievement chmn. north ctrl. dist. dir., state sec. 1991-92, 1st v.p. 1992-93, pres.-elect 1993-94, pres. 1994-95), Atlanta Area Computer Educators, Pi Lambda Theta (pres. 1993—), Chi Omega. Office: Lullwater Sch 705 S Candler St Decatur GA 30030-4457

TEACHEY, TERESA JOLLEY, manufacturing representative, marketing consultant; b. Shelby, N.C., July 27, 1948; d. Timothy Harlan and Reba (Odom) Jolley; m. Gary Russell Sugg, Feb. 14, 1970 (div. Jan. 1981); children: Thomas, Heather; m. James Timothy Teachey, June 21, 1987. MusB, U. N.C., Greensboro, 1970; BA, U. N.C., Charlotte, 1982. Music tchr. Chatham County Schs., Pittsboro, N.C., 1971-74; proofreader Ernst and Whinney, Charlotte, 1981; sales asst. IBM, Charlotte, 1982; sales rep. Otis Elevator, United Techs., Charlotte, Miami (Fla.), 1983-88; mfrs.' rep. DSA Group, Roswell, Ga., Apex, N.C., 1989—. Soloist Gastonia (N.C.) Choral Soc., 1976-77, Charlotte Oratorio Soc., 1980-83. Scholar U. N.C., Greensboro, 1966. Mem. Am. Mktg. Assn., Networkers Club, Mu Phi Epsilon, Pi Kappa Lambda. Home and Office: 5517 Brushy Meadows Dr Fuquay Varina NC 27526

TEAGUE, JANE LORENE, lay worker; b. Brainerd, Miss., May 27, 1918; d. Willis Ernest and Ellenora Christine (Yde) Lively; m. Jasper Uriah Teague, Nov. 26, 1939; children: Jack, James, Janet. Grad., high sch. Pres. Women's Aux., L.A. Bapt. City Mission Soc., 1968-69; leadership devel. chairperson Am. Bapt. Women, 1969-70, conf. chairperson, 1971-75, v.p., program chmn., 1975-77, pres. Pacific S.W. region, 1980-83, pres. local ch., 1983-85; pres. Am. Bapt. Chs. of Pacific S.W., 1973, bd. mgrs., exec. com., chmn. bd. edn., 1975-76, also mem. nominating and camping coms., reps. from L.A. Bapt. Assn.; mem. gen. bd. Am. Bapt. Chs. in U.S.A., 1974—; moderator L.A. Assn., 1974—, mem. bd. nat. housing ministries, 1985—; mem. com. local arrangements, women's dept. Bapt. World Alliance, 1983-85; chairperson bd. edn. 1st Bapt. Ch., North Hollywood, Calif., 1985-95; mem. Prayer Task Force Am. Bapt. Chs. of Pacific S.W., 1990—, bd. mgrs., 1990—; program chairperson Children's Bapt. Home Aux., 1968-69; bd. dirs. Atherton Bapt. Homes, exec. search com., 1994; bd. dirs. Am. Bapt. Homes of West, Children's Bapt. Home, Inglewood, Calif.; White Cross chairperson L.A. Valley Assn., 1989-92. Address: 1030 E Valencia Ave Burbank CA 91501-1551

TEAGUE, MARY ELIZABETH, small business owner; b. Mt. Vernon, Tex., Aug. 18, 1928; d. Jodie Felter and Martha Willie (Crafts) T. AAS, C.C. of Air Force, 1987. Advanced through grades to chief master sgt. USAF, 1950, retired, 1988. Mem. San Antonio Computer Soc., Internat. Platform Assn. Lutheran. Home: 4027 Waterwood Pass Dr Elmendorf TX 78112-6024

TEAGUE, MARY KAY, realtor; b. Troy, Ohio, May 15, 1925; d. Carl Joseph and Laura Mae (Jones) Wack; m. Roger A. Teague, Apr. 29, 1944 (dec. Nov. 1980); children: Margaret Colleen, Barbara Lynn, Roger A. Jr., Mary P., Betty A., Howard J. Realtor Teague Real Estate, Hitchcock, Tex., 1962—. Chmn. Hitchcock Planning Bd., 1987-93; dir. Hitchcock Indsl. Devel. Bd., 1983—. Mem. Nat. Assoc. Realtors, Tex. Assn. Realtors, Texas City-LaMarque Bd. Realtors (dir. 1974-78, 81-87, sec. 1979, pres. 1980, 88, Realtor of Yr. award 1986), Women's Coun. Realtors (sec. 1988, pres. 1991, Golden Rule award 1983), Hitchcock C. of C. (bd. dirs. 1984-91). Republican. Roman Catholic. Home: 301 Greenwood Dr Hitchcock TX 77563 Office: Teague Real Estate PO Box 21 Hitchcock TX 77563

TEAGUE, SHARON BEASLEY, state legislator; b. Feb. 15, 1952; widowed. AA, Ind. Coll. Bus. and Tech. Mem. Ga. Ho. of Reps., 1992—, mem. motor vehicles com., regulated beverages and state inst. and property com.; realtor. Cmty. activist. Baptist. Democrat. Home: 1107 Pine Tree Trail Atlanta GA 30349 Office: Ga House of Reps 512 Legis Office Bldg Atlanta GA 30334*

TEAL, ELIZABETH JENRETTE, organization executive; b. Myrtle Beach, S.C., June 4, 1962; d. John Wilson Jenrette Jr. and Sara (Jordan) Floyd; m. Ralph R. Teal Jr., Dec. 20, 1986; children: R. R. Teal III, B. B. Teal III. Student, Coll. of Charleston, 1980-82; BA in Polit. Sci., Coastal Carolina Coll., 1986. Sales rep. North Myrtle Beach (S.C.) Times, 1985-86; dir. activities Beach Cove Hotel, North Myrtle Beach, 1986-88; mgr. sales Radisson Resort/Kingston Plantation, Myrtle Beach, 1988-89; exec. dir. Little River (S.C.) C. of C., 1989—, Kids Voting-Horry County, 1994; chmn. charities bd. Golf. Mag. Sr. Tour Com. Bd. dirs. St. Patrick's Day Festival, North Myrtle Beach, 1988—, Horry (S.C.) Human Rels. Coun., 1990—, Children's Mus. S.C.; adminstr. Kids Vote, Horry County; mem. Horry Cultural Arts Coun., 1989—, N. Strand Coun. C. of C.; mgr. Blue Crab Festival, Little River, 1990—; chmn. Christmas com. Am. Cancer Soc., North Myrtle Beach, 1990; mem. children's com. and svc. com. Myrtle Beach 1st Presbyn. Ch.; grad. Leadership Grand Strand, 1989. Mem. S.C. Festival Assn., N.C.-S.C. Chamber Execs., Assn. Membership Execs., North Myrtle Beach Woman's Club (chmn. ways and means com. 1989—), Anything Grows Garden Club, Zeta Tau Alpha. Democrat. Home: Dunes Cove 9503 Lake Dr Myrtle Beach SC 29572 Office: Little River C of C PO Box 400 Little River SC 29566-0400

TEANEY, CAROL RUTH, law librarian; b. Alton, Ill., May 17, 1950; d. Darrel Francis and Lelia Ruth (Springman) T. BA, Ea. Ill. U., 1972; MS in Edn., So. Ill. U., Edwardsville, 1983. High sch. libr. Marquette High Sch., Alton, 1972-81; law libr. Lashly & Baer, St. Louis, 1981—. Mem. Am. Assn. Law Librs., ALA, Mid-Am. Assn. Law Librs., Southwestern Assn. Law Librs. Office: Lashly & Baer PC 714 Locust St Saint Louis MO 63101

TEASLEY, ANNA DELORES, corporate executive, engineer; b. Detroit, July 20, 1949; d. Pete Turner and Ruth Roberta Teasley. AS, Wayne County Community Coll., 1974; postgrad., Oakland U., 1976. Lic. engr., Mich. Water plant operator City of Detroit, 1977-79; power plant operator State of Mich., Pontiac, 1979-80; stationary engr. U.S. Postal Svc., Detroit, 1984; mech. maintenance specialist Mich. Consol. Gas Co., Detroit, 1983-88; bldg. engr. Detroit Bd. of Edn., 1980-90; pres. Home Search Insps., Inc., Detroit, 1987—. Contbr. articles to profl. jours. Mem. Nat. Polit. Congress Black Women, Detroit, 1988. Mem. Am. Soc. Home Insps., Am. Inst. Home Insps. (cert.), Nat. Assn. Home Insps., Nat. Assn. Women Bus. Owners, Inc. (chair membership com. 1990), Mich. Assn. Housing Ofcls. Office: Home Search Insps Inc PO Box 27132 Detroit MI 48227-0132

TEATER, DOROTHY SEATH, county official; b. Manhattan, Kans., Feb. 11, 1931; d. Dwight Moody and Martha (Stahnke) Seath; m. Robert Woodson Teater, May 24, 1952; children: David Dwight, James Stanley, Donald Robert, Andrew Scott. BS, U. Ky., 1951; MS, Ohio State U., 1954. Home econs. tchr. Georgetown (Ky.) City Schs., 1951-53; extension specialist Ohio Coop. Extension, Columbus, 1967-73; consumer affairs adminstr. City of Columbus, 1974-79, Bank One Columbus NA, 1980-85; councilmember Columbus City Coun., 1980-85; commr. Franklin County, Columbus, Ohio, 1985—; active Ohio Cmty. Corrections Adv. Bd., Columbus, Columbus Met. Area Cmty. Action Orgn. Cons. Land Policy & Boom Bust, Real Estate Markets, 1994, Lincoln Inst. Land Policy. Bd. dirs. BBB; mem. hon. adv. bd. Girl Scouts. Recipient Outstanding Alumnus award U. Ky., 1989, Women of Achievement award YWCA, 1995; named Disting. Alumni, Ohio State U., 1977. Mem. County Commrs. Assn. Ohio (pres. 1994), Columbus Met. Club. Republican. Methodist. Office: Franklin County Commrs 373 S High St Columbus OH 43215

TEBEDO, MARYANNE, state legislator; b. Oct. 30, 1936; m. Don Tebedo; children: Kevin, Ronald, Linda, Thomas, Christine. Former mem. Colo. Ho. of Reps.; now mem. Colo. Senate; profl. parliamentarian. Republican. Office: Colorado State Senate State Capitol Bldg Denver CO 80203*

TECCE, JACQUELINE, real estate administrator; b. N.Y.C., Apr. 23, 1956; d. Sam L. and Lee M. (Malandri) T.; children: Samantha Nicole, Nicholas Alexander, Max Anthony. BA in Pychology St. Francis Coll., Bklyn., 1978, AAS in Bus Adminstrn., 1978. Lic. real estate sales agent. Asst. dir. lease adminstrn. Brooks Fashion Stores, N.Y.C., 1979-81; coordinator info. services Richard Kove Assocs., N.Y.C., 1981-87; systems cons. J.T.F. Word Pros, 1988-92; real estate adminstr. Lysaght, Lysaght & Kramer, 1992—. Mem. Anti-Vivisection Soc., 1978—, Save Our Strays, Bklyn., 1978—; vol. Rusk Inst., N.Y.C., 1982; mem. Citizens to Replace LILCO, 1985—. Mem. NAFE, Ill. Mgmt. and Exec. Search Cons., Parent Resource Ctr., Psi Chi, Chi Beta Phi. Republican. Roman Catholic. Home: 3 Oak Valley Dr Glen Head NY 11545-1728 Office: Lysaght Lysaght & Kramer PC Ste C100 1983 Marcus Ave Lake Success NY 11042

TEDDER, JANE ANN, portfolio manager; b. Stillwater, Okla., Oct. 1, 1942; d. Robert M. and Guila M. (Harp) Pyle; children: Troy, Jay, Kira. B in Music Edn., Okla. State U., 1964; diploma in trust banking, Northwestern U., 1979; diploma in sr. mgmt. banking, Rutgers U., 1982. Chartered fin. analyst. Asst. trust officer Douglas County Bank, Lawrence, Kans., 1975-76, trust officer, 1976-83, v.p., 1978-83; portfolio mgr. Security Mgmt. Co., Topeka, 1983-91, sr. portfolio mgr., 1991—; vis. lectr. Kans. U., Lawrence, 1986-87. Trustee Plymouth Congl. Ch., Lawrence, 1981-83, moderator, 1984; bd. trustees Plymouth Endowment, 1986—, chair, 1989; dir. Ecumenical Christian Ministries Kans. U., Lawrence, 1984-88. Fellow Life Mgmt. Inst., Assn. of Investment Mgmt. and Rsch., Fin. Analysts' Fedn. Office: Security Mgmt Co 700 SW Harrison St Topeka KS 66636-0001

TEDERS, ELLA GROVE, financial planner, nurse; b. Brownsville, Tex., Oct. 8, 1931; d. Philip Wayne and Alberta Wilma (White) Grove; m. Kenneth Joseph Teders, July 14, 1951; children: Mark Alan, Clark Owen. Diploma in nursing, U. Okla., 1954, BS in Nursing, 1968. RN, Okla.; CFP; registered investment advisor, health underwriter, fin. cons.; cert. investment specialist. DON Enid (Okla.) State Sch., 1954; head nurse St. Mary's Hosp., Enid, 1955; pub. health nurse Payne Co. Health Dept., Stillwater, Okla., 1955-59; nursing service adminstr. Stillwater Health Ctr., 1959-68; med. cons., 1960—; nursing service adminstr. Bass Meml. Bapt. Hosp., Enid, 1968-76; agt. Prudential Ins. Cos. Am., Enid, 1976—; owner, operator Ella Teders Fin. Ctr., Enid, 1977—, Teders Fin. Ctr. Expansion Br. Office, Oklahoma City, 1993—; co-adminstr. Garfield County Eldercare, Enid, 1980-91; instr. Francis Tuttle Vo-Tech. Sch.; med.-legal cons., 1960—. Author: Nursing Service Procedures, 1966, 70. Bd. dirs. Crossroads Counseling, 1993-94, chmn. elect, 1994. Mem. AAUW (polished Diamond award 1986, Outstanding Women Achievement in Bus. 1987), CFPs, Nat. Assn. Health Underwriters (bd. dirs. 1980-86, 90, Leader Producers Roundtable 1980-91), Nat. Assn. Life Underwriters (local nat. committeeman 1985-88), N.W. Okla. Life Underwriters (pres. 1983-84), Internat. Assn. Fin. Planners, Internat. Assn. Registered Fin. Planners, Mariners Club. Presbyterian. Office: Teders Fin Ctr PO Box 3006 Enid OK 73702-3006 also: 3904 NW 10th St Oklahoma City OK 73107-6037

TEDESCO, SUSAN MARY, pharmacy technician; b. Chgo., Sept. 22, 1954; d. Edmund L. and Viola M. (Cote) T. BA, U. St. Thomas, Houston, 1976. Cert. pharmacy technician, Ill. Sr. pharmacy technician, intravenous specialist Children's Meml. Hosp., Chgo., 1978—; pres., cons. Aseptech, Inc., Chgo., 1989—; instr., pharmacy technician educator South Suburban Coll., 1993—. Mem. Ill. Coun. Hosp. Pharmacists (rep. bd. dirs. 1984-88, voting mem. bd. dirs. 1990-92, Pres.'s award 1987). Home: 2245 N Magnolia Ave Chicago IL 60614-3103 Office: Children's Meml Med Ctr 2300 N Childrens Plz Chicago IL 60614-3318

TEDFORD, DONNA LEE ROBINSON, geriatrics nurse; b. Salem, Ky., July 14, 1959; d. James Harold and Helen Majorie (Croft) Robinson; m. John Paul Tedford, June 30, 1990; 1 child, James Willard. BSA, Murray State U., 1981; ADN, Paducah Community Coll., 1983. Staff nurse Crittenden County Hosp., Marion, Ky., 1983-84, Salem (Ky.) Nursing Home, 1984-86, Livingston County Hosp., Salem, 1986-89, Regional Med. Ctr., Madisonville, Ky., 1989; supr. weekends Salem Nursing Home, 1989-91, 92—, Hill-Top Nursing Home, Kuttawa, Ky., 1991-92; nurse Salem Nursing Home, 1993—. Home: 6330 SR 297 Marion KY 42064

TEDFORD, TERRI ANN, small business owner; b. Woodland, Calif., Nov. 3, 1947; d. John Frank Seno and Frankie Joann (Smith) McMichael; m. John B. Minor, Feb. 29, 1992; 1 child, Richard David. BBA, U. Tex., 1985. Sales mgr. Frank Green Enterprises, Odessa, Tex., 1975-82; mgr. Meek & Mancom, Odessa, 1982-85; mgr., owner Computer Tech. Assocs., Odessa, 1985—. Mem. Big Bend Rifle and Pistol Club (sec., treas.), Chatham Bridge Club (sec., v.p.). Republican.

TEELE, CYNTHIA LOMBARD, lawyer; b. Boston, Oct. 11, 1961; d. John Hughes and Patricia Jeanne (Linder) T. AB in Urban Studies magna cum laude, Brown U., 1983; JD, U. Va., 1986. Bar: Calif. 1986. Assoc. Lillick McHose & Charles, L.A., 1986-87, Wyman Bautzer Kuchel & Silbert, L.A., 1987-91; sr. atty. Paramount Pictures Corp.-TV Divsn., Hollywood, Calif., 1991-92, dir., legal, 1992-94, v.p., legal, 1994—. Office: Paramount Pictures Corp 5555 Melrose Ave Los Angeles CA 90038

TEER, KAY STOLTZ, museum director; b. Southern Pines, N.C., July 30, 1947; d. John Wesley and Ellen (Kathrine (Wheeless) Stoltz; m. William Stewart Teer, June 2, 1968; children: John Stewart, Marguerite Kathrine. BS, East Carolina U., 1969; postgrad., U. S.C., 1971-89, U. N.C., 1983. Tchr. English Sch. Dist. 17, Sumter, S.C., 1969-73; exec. dir. Sumter Gallery of Art, 1982-88; grants writer S.C. Arts Commn., Columbia, 1988-89; advocacy coord. S.C. Arts Alliance, Columbia, 1988-89; exec. dir. Sumter County Mus., 1989—. Bd. dirs. Sumter Sch. Dist. 17, 1978-94, S.C. Arts Alliance, 1985-88, Fine Arts Coun., Sumter, 1986-93. Mem. Am. Assn. Mus., S.C. Fedn. Mus. (sec. 1994—), Southeastern Mus. Conf., Sumter C. of C. (bd. dirs. 1979-81, 90-92). Methodist. Home: 11 Snowden St Sumter SC 29150-3224 Office: Sumter County Mus PO Box 1456 Sumter SC 29151-1456

TEETERS, NANCY HAYS, economist; b. Marion, Ind., July 29, 1930; d. S. Edgar and Mabel (Drake) Hays; m. Robert Duane Teeters, June 7, 1952; children: Ann, James, John. A.B. in Econs., Oberlin Coll., 1952, LL.D. (hon.), 1979; M.A. in Econs., U. Mich., 1954, postgrad., 1956-57, LL.D. (hon.), 1983; LL.D. (hon.), Bates Coll., 1981, Mt. Holyoke Coll., 1983. Teaching fellow U. Mich., 1954-55, instr., 1956-57; instr. U. Md. Overseas, Germany, 1955-56; staff economist govt. fin. sect. Bd. Govs. of FRS, Washington, 1957-66; mem. bd. Bd. Govs. of FRS, 1978-84; economist (on loan) Coun. Econ. Advs., 1962-63; economist Bur. Budget, 1966-70; sr. fellow Brookings Instn., 1970-73; sr. specialist Congl. Rsch. Svc., Library of Congress, Washington, 1973-74; asst. dir., chief economist Ho. of Reps. Com. on the Budget, 1974-78; v.p., chief economist IBM, Armonk, N.Y., 1984-90; bd. dirs., trustee Prudential Mut. Funds, 1985—; bd. dirs. Inland Steel Industries; mem. Coun. on Fgn. Rels., Forum for World Affairs, Women in Mgmt. Author: (with others) Setting National Priorities: The 1972 Budget, 1971, Setting National Priorities: The 1973 Budget, 1972, Setting National Priorities: The 1974 Budget, 1973; contbr. articles to profl. publs. Recipient Comfort Starr award in econs. Oberlin Coll., 1952; Disting. Alumnus award U. Mich., 1980. Mem. Nat. Economists Club (v.p. 1973-74, pres. 1974-75, chmn. bd. 1975-76, gov. 1976-79), Am. Econ. Assn. (com. on status of women 1975-78), Am. Fin. Assn. (dir. 1969-71). Democrat. Home: 243 Willowbrook Ave Stamford CT 06902-7020

TEICH, PEGGY LYNN, librarian, educator; b. N.Y.C., Nov. 28, 1955; d. Rudolph H. and Marion D. (Dann) Weiner; m. Steven A. Teich, Oct. 14, 1990. BA, Clark U., 1977; MS, Pratt Inst., 1982. Libr. asst. Found. Ctr., N.Y.C., 1978-80; from reference trainee to head ref. libr. J. Walter Thompson CO., N.Y.C., 1980-87; sr. reference libr. 1st Boston Corp., N.Y.C., 1987-91; libr. mgr., v.p. Citibank Rsch. Libr., N.Y.C., 1991—; instr. bus., econ., statis. sources Rutgers U. Sch. Comm., Info., Libr. Studies, New Brunswick, N.J., 1987; vis. prof. bus., econ., statis. sources, online bus. database searching Sch. Libr. and Info. Sci. Pratt Inst., Bklyn., 1987—; lectr. bus. and econ. lit. Sch. Libr. Svc. Columbia U., N.Y.C., 1988-92; spkr., lectr. in field. Mem. Spl. Libr. Assn. (spkr. NE Regional Conf. 1993, chmn. advt. and mktg. group 1987-88, mem. editorial bd. newsletter 1987), Pratt Inst. Alumni Assn. (v.p. 1982-87). Office: Citibank Rsch Libr 399 Park Ave New York NY 10043

TEICHMAN, EVELYN, antiques appraiser, educator, estate liquidator; b. N.Y.C., Mar. 13, 1929; d. Bernard and Minnie (Goldenberg) Mensch; m. Milton Teichman, Jan. 16, 1949; children: David, Jeb, Sondra. Student, CUNY, 1946-49. Tchr. Bergen County Adult Schs., N.J., 1976—; freelance appraiser Paramus, N.J., 1978—; house contents and estate sale coord. Home: 56 Bush Pl Paramus NJ 07652-4004

TEIXEIRA, LISA MARIE, veterinarian; b. Worcester, Mass., Aug. 25, 1963; d. Anthony Augustus and Rose Marie Helen (Pascarelli) T. BA, Mt. Holyoke Coll., 1985; DVM, Tufts U., 1989. Veterinarian Hanson (Mass.) Animal Hosp., 1989—. Mem. AVMA, NOW, Nat. Mus. Women (assoc.), World Wildlife Found. Roman Catholic. Office: 1 Harvest View Dr Carver MA 02330

TELANDER, MARCIE ANN, psychotherapist, writer; b. Chgo., Mar. 30, 1947; d. H. Richard and Jeanne Forster (Overstolz) T. BA in English, Ind. U., 1969; MA in Lit. and Writing, Northeastern Ill. U., 1981. Sr. writer, creative dir. Calico Advt. Agy., Chgo., 1970-75; founding and artistic dir. Acting Up! Theatre Co., Skokie, Ill., 1975-78; dir., co-prodr. arts, editor film and video Eyes Prodns., Chgo., 1976-87; dir., psychotherapist East River Counseling and Comm. Svcs., Crested Butte, Colo., 1985—; expressive and narrative therapy specialist Urban Gateways Arts Edn., Chgo., 1975-83; writer, theatre artist-in-residence state arts couns. Ill., Colo., Mont., S.C., Wash., 1976-87; exec. dir., arts educator Crested Butte Mountain Arts Workshops, 1979-80; founding and artistic dir. Vision Circle Festival Theatre, Chgo., 1980-83, Vinotok Storytelling and Cultural Festival, Crested Butte, 1985—; pvt. practice psychotherapy, Chgo. and Boulder, Colo., 1980-85; lectr. throughout U.S., 1974; others. Co-prodr., dir. film Acting Up!, 1981, author book, 1983; contbg. editor Fiction Internat., 1975-77; feature editor Crested Butte Pilot newspaper, 1978-82; editor-in-chief Touts arts and fashion jour., 1984-86. Founding mem. Internat. Ctr. for Celebration, 1991—. Recipient Elizabeth Enwright award for short fiction Ind. U., 1974, award for journalism Women's Almanac, 1977; Ind. U. awarrd and grant for fiction Ind. U. Writers' Conf., 1975, film grantee HEW, 1977. Mem. ACA, Colo. Counseling Assn., Assn. for Humanistic Psychology, Am. Mental Health Counselors Assn., Colo. Psychotherapists Assn., Northlands Storytelling Network (founding, western regional rep. 1980-91). Office: East River Counseling and Comm Svcs PO Box 1101 Crested Butte CO 81224-1101

TELBAN, SHARON GRACE, nursing educator; b. Pittston, Pa., May 10, 1944; d. Joseph F. Telban and Grace (Love) Jones. BS in Nursing Edn., Wilkes Coll., Wilkes-Barre, Pa., 1969, MS in Edn., 1979; MS in Nursing, Pa. State U., 1980; EdD in Higher Edn., Pa. State U., University Park, 1994. Cert. gerontologic nurse. Staff nurse Moses Taylor Hosp., Scranton, Pa., 1964-66, asst. head nurse, 1966-68; instr. Bryn Mawr (Pa.) Hosp. Sch. Nursing, 1969-74; instr., asst. prof. Wilkes U., Wilkes-Barre, 1974-87, assoc. prof., 1987—; lectr. continuing edn. Pa. State U., University Park, 1985—; mem. task force older adult ministry Presbytery of Lackawanna, Scranton, Pa., 1989—; USPHS trainee, 1976, 78-79. Elder Presbyn. Ch., Moosic, Pa., 1979-85, 86-89, 92—. Mem. Pa. Nurses Assn. (pres. dist. 3, 1986-88, bd. dirs. 1989-91, 92-94), Sigma Theta Tau (faculty advisor Zeta Psi chpt. 1989-93, exec. com. 1982, 89—, v.p. 1993-95, Excellence in Leadership award 1990), Phi Delta Kappa, Pi Lambda Theta. Presbyterian. Office: Wilkes U Wilkes Barre PA 18766

TELESHA, MEREDITH CAROL, writer, employment specialist/procedures analyst; b. Hershey, Pa., Oct. 24, 1948; d. Carl Eugene and Ada Kann (Wagner) Cope; m. Edward A. Telesha, Feb. 14, 1987. Cert., York Thompson Bus. Coll., 1967; student, Pa. State U., 1972, Elizabethtown Coll., 1978. Sec. Milton S. Hershey Med. Ctr. of Pa. State U., Hershey, 1967-74, pers. asst., 1975-80, employment specialist, 1980-81, employment specialist, training coordinator, 1981-87, employmnet specialist procedures analyst, 1987-93; speaker at high schs., bus. schs.; conductor of in-house tng. programs. Author: Krista's Treasure: A Legacy of Freedom, 1994. Mem. Bus. Adv. Com., Hershey, 1978-92; sec. Employee Safety Com., Hershey, 1981-90; mem. Com. for the Disabled, Hershey, 1986-90; cons. Right-to-Know Task Force, Hershey, 1987-93; mem. Presdl. task force 1980-86, Nat. Rep. Com., Pa. Rep. Com.; Integrated Bus. Info. System trainer and task force mem., 1989-93. Recipient Problems of Democracy study award Am. Legion, 1965, Cert. of Merit Gov. of Pa., 1965. Mem. Leadership Found., U.S. Senatorial Club, Am. Bus. Women's Assn. (recording sec. 1979-80, 82-83, v.p. 1980-81, pres. 1981-82, treas. fall frolics 1982), Nat. Secs. Assn., Am. Soc. Personnel Amdminstrn. Lutheran. Lodges: Women's Auxillary to Elks, Order Rainbow. Home: 2267 E Harrisburg Pike Middletown PA 17057-3937

TELFER, MARGARET CLARE, internist, hematologist; b. Manila, The Philippines, Apr. 9, 1939; came to U.S., 1941; d. James Gavin and Margaret Adele (Baldwin) T. BA, Stanford U., 1961; MD, Washington U., St. Louis, 1965. Diplomate Am. Bd. Internal Medicine, Am. Bd. Hematology, Am. Bd. Oncology; lic. Ill., Mo. Resident in medicine Michael Reese Hosp., Chgo., 1968, fellow in hematology and oncology, 1970, assoc. attending physician, 1970-72, dir. Hemophilia Ctr., 1971—, interim dir. div. hematology and oncology, 1971-74, 81-84, 89—, attending physician, 1972—; asst. prof. medicine U. Chgo., 1975-80, assoc. prof. medicine, 1980-85, assoc. prof. clin. medicine, 1985-89; assoc. prof. clin. medicine U. Ill., Chgo., 1990—; mem. med. adv. bd. Hemophilia Found. Ill., 1971, chmn., 1972-83, lectr. annual symposium, 1978-84; mem. med. adv. bd. State of Ill. Hemophilia Program; dir. hematology-oncology fellowship program Michael Reese Hosp., 1971-75, 81-84, lectr. and mem. numerous coms.; lectr. Cook County Grad. Sch. Medicine, 1980-85, U. Chgo., ARC. Contbr. articles to profl. jours. Fellow ACP; mem. Am. Soc. Clin. Oncology, Am. Assn. Med. Colls., Am. Soc. Hematology, World Fedn. Hemophilia, Blood Club (Chgo.), Thrombosis Club (Chgo.). Office: Michael Reese Hosp 294 & Ellis Rm 1200 RC Chicago IL 60616

TELLEM, SUSAN MARY, public relations executive; b. N.Y.C., May 23, 1945; d. John F. and Rita C. (Lietz) Cain; m. Marshall R.B. Thompson; children: Tori, John, Daniel. BS, Mt. St. Mary's Coll., L.A., 1967. Cert. pub. health nurse; RN. Pres. Tellem Pub. Rels. Agy., Marina del Rey, Calif., 1977-80, Rowland Grody Tellem, L.A., 1980-90; chmn. The Rowland Co., L.A., 1990—; pres., CEO Tellem, Inc., L.A., 1992-93; instr. UCLA Extension, 1983—; speaker numerous seminars and confs. on pub. rels. Editor: Sports Medicine for the '80s, Sports Medicine Digest, 1982-84. Bd. dirs. Marymount High Sch., 1984-87, pres., 1984-86; bd. dirs. L.A. Police Dept. Booster Assn., 1984-87; mem. Cath. Press Coun.; mem. pres.'s coun. Mus. Sci. and Industry. Mem. Am. Soc. Hosp. Mktg. and Pub. Rels., Healthcare Mktg. and Pub. Rels. Assn., Pub. Rels. Soc. Am. (bd. dirs. 1994—), L.A. Counselors, PETA, Am. Lung Assn. (chair comm. com. L.A. chpt.) Soc. for Prevention of Cruelty to Animals (chair PetSet), Sports Club (L.A.). Roman Catholic. Office: Tellem Inc Museum Sq 5757 Wilshire Blvd Ste 655 Los Angeles CA 90036

TELLES, MARELYN V. TAYLOR, psychiatric clinical nurse specialist; b. N.Y.C., July 30; d. Edward J. and Mary J. (Byrnes) Taylor; 1 child, James T. III. Diploma, St. Mary's Hosp., Waterbury, Conn., 1963; AA in Psychology, San Diego Mesa Coll., 1980; BSN magna cum laude, U. San Diego, 1982, MSN, 1984. ARNP, N.H.; cert. adult psychiat. and mental health clin. nurse specialist ANCC. Psychiat. clin. nurse specialist VA Med. Ctr., San Diego, 1985-86, Manchester, N.H., 1986—; clin. adj. faculty Rivier Coll., Nashua, N.H. Grantee NIMH, 1982-83; recipient award for disting. govt. svc. N.H. Fed. Execs. Assn., 1990. Mem. ANA, N.H. Nurses Assn. (past bd. dirs. Hillsborough County chpt., editorial adv. bd. Nursing News), Sigma Theta Tau. Home: 512 Bodwell Rd Manchester NH 03109-5007 Office: 718 Smyth Rd Manchester NH 03104

TEMELKOFF, VONDA LEE, counselor, therapist; b. Sharon, Pa., July 12, 1937; d. Edward Hopkins and Alberta (Hall; m. Thomas B. Temelkoff, Nov. 10, 1956; children: Linda Temelkoff Schuller, Thomas C., Timothy B., Todd A. BS in Edn., Youngstown State U., 1970, MS in Edn., 1986; postgrad., Kent State U., 1981, 90, 92, Akron State U., 1981, Mt. St. Joseph, Cin., 1987, Bowling Green State U., 1989, Ashland Coll., 1990, Drake U., 1990. Cert. sch. counselor, Ohio, tchr., Ohio; nat. bd. cert. counselor, 1986; lic. profl. counselor, Ohio, 1991. Tchr. elem. Woodside Elem. Sch., Austintown, Ohio, 1971-84; tchr. Am. history Austintown Middle Sch., 1984-85; tchr. math. and sci. Frank Ohl Middle Sch., Austintown, 1986-87; guidance counselor five elem. schs. Austintown, 1987—; children's therapist Regional Assocs. in Counseling, Canfield, Ohio, 1987-91; presenter, trainer parent workshop Austintown Elem. Sch., winter 1989, 91; speaker Rotary and Kiwanis, 1987, 89; presentor, facillitator, speaker parenting and drug free schs. programs Communtiy Orgns. and Ohio Sch. Confs.; intern NEOUCOM Cancer Rsch. Ctr., Rootstown, summer 1986. Writer, prodr. (video) It's Your Choice, 1986. Youngstown State U. scholar, 1985-86, Jennings scholar, 1993-94. Mem. AACN, AAUW (bd. dirs. 1987, program v.p. 1988), NEA, Ohio Edn. Assn., Austintown Edn. Assn. (bldg. rep. 1978), Am. Counseling Assn., Ohio Assn. for Counseling and Devel., Internat. Reading Assn. (bd. dirs. membership com. 1989), Friends of Am. Art, Chi Sigma Iota, Delta Kappa Gamma Soc. Republican. Episcopalian. Home: 235 Topaz Cir Canfield OH 44406-9676

TEMIN, DAVIA BETH, marketing executive; b. Cleve., June 5, 1952; d. J.T. and Sylvia (Black) Temin; m. Walter T. Kicinski, Aug. 10, 1991. BA, Swarthmore Pa./Coll., 1974; MA, Columbia U., 1976. Community svcs. specialist Commonwealth Mass., Boston, 1975; editor-in-chief, founder Hermes mag. Columbia U. Bus. Sch., N.Y.C., 1976-79, dir. publ. affairs, 1979-83; v.p., dir. mktg. Citicorp Global Investment Bank, N.Y.C., 1983-86; v.p., dir. corp. mktg. Scudder, Stevens & Clark, N.Y.C., 1986-89; pres. The Temin Group, 1989-90; v.p., dir. mktg. Wertheim Schroder & Co., Inc., 1990—; exec. prodr. The Night & The Music Prodns., 1994—. Chmn., bd. dirs. Mark Taylor Dance Co., 1987—, chmn.; bd. dirs. Motio Dance Found., N.Y.C., 1982—, Overseas Ednl. Fund, 1982-91, The Fin. Comm. Soc., 1994—; advisor to pres. Swarthmore Coll., 1994—, trustee, 1995—. Recipient Nat. Sch. Pub. Rels. award, 1978, numerous Printing Industries of N.Y. awards, 1979— , Meritorious Svc. award Commonwealth of Mass., 1976. Mem. Fgn. Policy Assn., Internat. Assn. Bus. Communicators, Fin. Communications Soc. (bd. dirs.), Pub. Relations Soc. (exec. com.), Women in Communications, Fin. Women's Assn., Columbia Bus. Sch. Club, Swarthmore Club. Home: 530 E 90th St Apt 5K New York NY 10128-7860 Office: Wertheim Schroder 787 7th Ave New York NY 10019-6018

TEMKIN, ELAINE BAKER, education educator; b. Boston, June 7, 1925; d. Max and Edith (Leavitt) Baker; m. David Temkin, June 19, 1949; children: Nancy, Elizabeth. BA, Cornell U., 1947; MA in Teaching, R.I. Coll., 1966; LHD (hon.), Brown U., 1991. Tchr., head dept. Nathan Bishop Jr. H.S., Providence, 1966-70; tchr. Classical H.S., Providence, 1970-90; supr., coord. student tchrs. Brown U., Providence, 1990—; pres., ednl. cons. Elaine Temkin Assoc., Inc., Providence, 1991—; liaison Coalition of Essential Schs., Providence and Four Seasons Project, Columbia U., N.Y.C., 1992-93; mem. com. for devel. of disting. merit program R.I. Dept. Edn., 1985; mem. bd. overseers Regional Lab. for Ednl. Improvement for N.E. and the Islands, 1986-89. Mem. Gov.'s Commn. on Women, R.I., 1980's; mem. Probe cmty. wide assessment of Providence Pub. Schs., 1992. Recipient Intellectual Freedom award, N.E. Regional Conf. for Social Studies, Boston, 1983, Presdl. Scholars Cert. of Excellence in Tchg., Washington, 1987. Mem. R.I. Social Studies Assn. (exec. bd. 1977-87, pres. 1981-82), New Eng. Assn. Schs. and Colls., Inc. (commn. on pub. schs., adv. com. on stds. for 90's 1986-88, evaluator, mem. com. 1975-87). Jewish.

TEMKIN, TERRIE CHARLENE, professional non-profit administrator, educator; b. Milw., June 6, 1950; d. Blair Huntley and Leah Dahlia (Sigman) T. BS in Communication, Ohio U., 1971; MA, U. Ill., 1972; EdS, U. Wis., Milw., 1976; PhD, U. Okla., 1984. Dir. spl. programs B'nai B'rith Youth Orgn., Milw., 1972-73; speech comm. specialist Alverno Coll., Milw., 1973-75; tng. and devel. specialist pvt. practice San Diego, 1975-78; fundraiser Am. Heart Assn., L.A., 1978-80; mgmt. cons. Hosp. Learning Ctrs., L.A., 1980-84; exec. dir. Women's Am. ORT, Hallandale, Fla., 1985-94; adj. prof. Nova U., Ft. Lauderdale, Fla., 1989—; pres. Nonprofit Mgmt. Solutions, Inc., Hollywood, Fla., 1994—; chair pub. info. com. Fla. Edn. and Employment Coun. for Women and Girls, 1991-94. Contbr. articles to profl. jours. Co-chair edn. com. Bus. Vols. for Arts, Miami, Fla., 1985-87; bd. dirs. Bridge Theater, Miami, 1985-89; mem. adv. com. Single Parent/Displaced Homemaker Program, Broward County, Fla., 1987-88; NDEA fellow, 1972. Named one of Outstanding Young Women of Am., 1982. Mem. Soc. for Nonprofit Mgmt., Nat. Soc. for Profl. Fund Raisers, Dirs. of Vol. Svcs., B'nai B'rith Youth Orgn. (v.p. adult bd. 1989—), Bus. and Profl. Women's Network (co-chair 1987-89), Women's Am. Orgn. for Rehab. through Tng. (life), B'nai B'rith Women (life), Hadassah (life). Jewish.

TEMPCZYK, ANNA MARIA, chemist, researcher; b. Malbork, Poland, Mar. 25, 1951; came to the U.S., 1989; d. Stanislaw and Janina (Block) Pulter; m. Boleslaw Piotr Tempczyk, July 27, 1972; children: Aleksandra, Magdalena. MS in Chemistry, U. Gdansk, Poland, 1974, PhD in Phys. Chemistry, 1983. Sr. assoc. rschr. U. Gdansk, Poland, 1975-84; assoc. prof. U. Gdansk, 1984-88; rsch. assoc. Columbia U., N.Y.C., 1988-89, Biosym Technologies, San Diego, 1989-91; rschr. Park-Davis Warner-Lambert, Ann Arbor, Mich., 1991-92; staff scientist Cytel corp., San Diego, 1992-93; sr. staff scientist Agouron Pharms., San Diego, 1994—. Contbr. articles to profl. jours. Home: 7699 Palmilla Dr #3414 San Diego CA 92122

TEMPLE, ROCHELLE LARNE, sales executive; b. West Chester, Pa., Mar. 23, 1957; d. Robert Richard and Carolyn Adaline (Wright) T.; m. Curtis Lee Grogan, Oct. 13, 1979 (div. June 1985); 1 child, Elkanah Hays. Student, Averett Coll., 1975-77. Cert. horsemaster, riding instr. Horse trainer, riding instr. West Chester, Pa., 1979-84; account exec. Frame's Motor Freight, Inc., West Chester, 1984-87, asst. sec.- treas., 1987-91, v.p. sales, 1991—; bd. dirs. Nat. Motor Freight Traffic Assn., Alexandria, Va. Bd. dirs. Delaware Valley Combined Tng. Assn., Inc., West Chester, 1988-91, v.p., 1992, pres., 1993—; event dir. Dressage at Devon (Pa.) Horse Show, 1987, 88, 91, 92, breeding show chmn., 1994. Mem. United Parachute Club, 1993—. Republican. Mem. Soc. of Friends. Office: Frames Motor Freight Inc Box 1600 West Chester PA 19380

TEMPLETON, BARBARA ANN, civil engineering technologist; b. Miller, S.D., Aug. 26, 1954; d. Edward Eugene and Helen Roxanne (Siegling) Labor; m. David James Templeton Jr., Aug. 7, 1976; 1 child, Brian James. AS, U. S.D., 1974. Staff asst. S.D. Dept. Water, Pierre, 1978-81; civil engring. tech. U.S. Army C.E., Pierre, 1981—. Active area PTA. Mem. ACLU, NOW, Nat. Abortion Rights Action League. Democrat. Lutheran. Home: 1701 Flag Mountain Dr Pierre SD 57501-2316

TENER, CAROL JOAN, educator; b. Cleve., Feb. 10, 1935; d. Peter Paul and Mamie Christine (Dombrowski) Manusack; m. Dale Keith Tener, Feb. 13, 1958 (div. Aug. 1991); children: Dean Robert, Susan Dawn. BS in Edn. cum laude, Kent State U., 1957; MS in Supervision, Akron U., 1974; postgrad., Kent State U., 1964, 81, 88-90, Akron U., 1975, 79, John Carroll U., 1982, 83, 85-86, Ohio U., 1987, Baldwin Wallace Coll., 1989. Cert. permanent K-12 tchr., Ohio. Stenographer Equitable Life Iowa, Cleve., 1953-54; tchr. elem. art Cuyahoga Falls (Ohio) Bd. Edn., 1957-58, 62-63, 1965-68, jr. high sch. tchr., 1968-69; high sch. tchr. Brecksville (Ohio)-Broadview Heights Sch. Dist., 1969-94; chmn. dept. art Brecksville-Broadview Heights (Ohio) H.S., 1979-94; ret., chmn. curriculum devel., 1982, 89; advisor, prodr. cmtry. svc. in art Brecksville Broadview Heights Bd. of Edn., 1969-94; former tchr. recreation and adult art edn. City of Cuyahoga Falls; com. mem. North Ctrl. Evaluation Com., Nordonia City, Ohio, 1978, Solon City, Ohio, 1989; chmn. north ctrl. evaluation com. Garfield Heights High Sch., 1991; mem. curriculum devel. com. in art/econs. Brecksville-Broadview Heights High Sch., 1985, 86. Contbr. articles to newspapers, brochures, magazines. Chmn. Artmart Invitational Exhibit, PTA, 1982—. Recipient Ohio Coun. on Econ. Edn. award, 1985-86, Teaching Excellence award Brecksville-Broadview Heights High Sch., 1st Pl. State, 2d Pl. State; named Tchr. of Yr., Brecksville-Broadview Heights High Sch., 1988; President's scholar Kent State U., 1954-57; Credit-Mem. Dist. Total Quality Mgmt. Deployment Team/Recognition, 1993-94. Mem. NEA, ASCD, Nat. Art Edn. Assn., Ohio Edn. Assn., Ohio Ret. Tchrs. Assn., Brecksville Edn. Assn., Acad. econ. Edn., Cleve. Mus. Art, Phi Delta Kappa Pi. Roman Catholic. Home: 7301 Sagamore Dr Parma OH 44134-5732

TENG, JULIET, artist; d. Teng Lenten and Waiyu Ho; children: Brendan, Trish, Jamie, Stacy, Phaeleau. B Commerce, U. Rangoon. Programmer First Boston Corp., N.Y.C.; systems programmer Chase Manhattan, N.Y.C., Merrill Lynch, Pierce, Fenner & Smith, Inc., N.Y.C.; artist/painter, 1976—. Exhbns. include Nat. Arts Club, N.Y.C., Pastel Soc. Am., N.Y.C., Audubon Artists Soc., N.Y.C., Catherine Lorrilard Wolf Art Club, N.Y.C., Painters and Sculptors Soc. N.J., N.Y.C., Knickerbocker Artists Am. Soc., N.Y.C., Keene-Mason Galleries, N.Y.C., Nat. Art Ctr., N.Y.C., Hudson Valley Art Assn., Westchester, N.Y., Manchester Art Ctr., Vt., Five Point Gallery, East Chatham, N.Y., Connoisseur Gallery, Rhinebeck, N.Y., Ridgewood Art Inst., N.J., The New England Fine Art Inst., Boston, numerous others. Mem. Nat. Arts Club, Art Students League. Home: Ford Rd Old Chatham NY 12136

TENNEY, LISA CHRISTINE GRAY, health care administrator; b. Pitts., Feb. 5, 1952; d. Elmer Burtt and Elizabeth (Scharding) Gray; m. Robert Howard Tenney, Mar. 8, 1972; children: Brian, David, Michael. BSN, W.Va. U., 1974. Cert. emergency nursing, advanced cardiac life support. Staff nurse Suburban Hosp., Bethesda, Md.; pvt. practice nursing Gaithersburg, Md.; staff nurse Holy Cross Hosp., Silver Spring, Md.; co-founder, assoc. dir. Md. Profl. Staffing Svcs., Bethesda; asst. nurse mgr. emergency dept. Holy Cross Hosp., Silver Spring, Md.; speaker in field. Contbr. articles to profl. jours. CPR instr. ARC, Am. Heart Assn. Mem. Emergency Nurses Assn., Sigma Theta Tau. Home: 9226 Bluebird Terr Gaithersburg MD 20879-1739

TENNEY, RUTH DAWN, medical/surgical nurse; b. Saginaw, Mich., Oct. 16, 1940; d. Grover L. and Nora L. (Schlappi) Wolfgang; m. Jay Beach Tenney, Dec. 4, 1979; children: Gary Lee Seibert, Floyd Eric Seibert, Rodney Grover Seibert, Steven J. Tenney, John J. Tenney, Barbara Luongo, Julie Tenney. ADN, Delta Coll., 1974; BS in Mgmt., Ctrl. Mich. U., 1994. Cert. med.-surg. nurse, cert. gerontol. nurse. Staff nurse med.-surg., instr., unit edn. coord. VA Hosp., Saginaw, 1974-78, 87—; charge nurse obstetrics, prenatal instr. Saginaw Osteo. Hosp., 1978-86.

TENNYSON, CATHY LEE, legal assistant, musician; b. Washington, Apr. 12, 1954; d. Robert Lee and Barbara Mae (Gill) Kanak; m. Robert Scott Tennyson, Aug. 16, 1980 (div. Apr. 1986); children: Tracy Linn, Sokhoeun Kay. AA in Humanities, Montgomery Coll., 1976; BS in Bus. and English cum laude, U. Md., 1984, BS in Paralegal Studies, 1989. Office mgr. Herschel Shosteck Assocs., Silver Spring, Md., 1979-86; paralegal Law Office of David A. Splitt, Washington, 1986-91; spl. asst. to gen. counsel U. D.C., Washington, 1991—; profl. singer, 1982—; performing mem. Choral Arts Soc. of Washington, 1983-89, Richard Crittenden Opera Workshop, 1989-92, British Embassy Players, 1993—; notary public, Washington, 1990—; catalog photographer, D.C. Sch. of Law, 1991-93. Recipient 2nd through 6th Place awards for photography and home arts Montgomery County Fair, 1986—, 1st Place awards in needlework and cooking, 1990—. Mem. Am. Fedn. TV and Radio Artists, Alpha Sigma Lambda, Phi Kappa Phi. Democrat. Episcopalian. Home: 10115 McKenney Ave # 302 Silver Spring MD 20902 Office: U DC 4200 Connecticut Ave NW Washington DC 20008

TENOPYR, MARY LOUISE WELSH (MRS. JOSEPH TENOPYR), psychologist; b. Youngstown, Ohio, Oct. 18, 1929; d. Roy Henry and Olive (Donegan) Welsh; AB, Ohio U., 1951, MA, 1951; PhD, U. So. Calif., 1966; m. Joseph Tenopyr, Oct. 30, 1955. Psychometrist, Ohio U., Athens, 1951-52, also housemother Sigma Kappa; personnel technician to research psychologist USAF, 1953-55, Dayton, Ohio, 1952-53, Hempstead, N.Y.; indsl. research analyst to mgr. employee evaluation N.Am. Rockwell Corp., El Segundo, Calif., 1956-70; asso. prof. Calif. State Coll.-Los Angeles, 1966-70; assoc. research educationist UCLA, 1970-71; program dir. U.S. CSC, 1971-72; dir. selection and testing AT&T, N.Y.C., 1972—; lectr. U. So. Calif., Los Angeles, 1967-70; vice chmn. research com. Tech. Adv. Com. on Testing, Fair Employment Practice Commn. Calif., 1966-70; adviser on testing Office Fed. Contract Compliance, U.S. Dept. Labor, Washington, 1967-73. Pres., ASPA Found., 1985-87; mem. Army Sci. Bd. Fellow Am. Psychol. Assn. (bd. prof. affairs, edn. and training bd., mem. council reps., pres. div. indsl. organizational psychology, pres. divsn. evaluation, measurement and stats.); mem. Am. Psychol. Assn. (pres. divsn. evaluation, measurement, statistics 1994—), Eastern Psychol. Assn., Am. Soc. Personnel Adminstrn. (bd. dirs. 1984-87), Nat. Acad. Sci. (coms. on ability testing, math. and sci. edn., panel on secondary edn.), Soc. Indsl. and Organizational Psychology (pres. 1979-80, Profl. Practices award 1984), Nat. Council Measurement in Edn., Psychometric Soc., Met. N.Y. Assn. Applied Psychology, Am. Ednl. Research Assn., Sigma Xi, Sigma Kappa, Psi Chi, Alpha Lambda Delta, Kappa Phi. Editorial bd. Jour. Applied Psychology, 1972-87, Jour. Vocat. Behavior; assoc. editor Am. Psychologist, Jour. Applied Psychology; contbr. chpts. to books and articles to profl. jours. Home: 557 Lyme Rock Rd Bridgewater NJ 08807-1604 Office: 100 Southgate Pky Morristown NJ 07962-1955

TENUTA, JEAN LOUISE, sports reporter, medical technologist; b. Kenosha, Wis., Apr. 12, 1958; d. Fred and Lucy Ann (Taylor) Tenuta; m. Robert Louis Bennett, Nov. 22, 1989. BS in Biology, U.Wis., 1979; BA in Journalism, Marquette U., 1983; MS in Print Journalism, Northwestern U., 1989. Sports reporter Kenosha News, 1978-84, Washington Post, 1984-86, Jour. Messenger, Manassas, Va., 1986, Jour. Times, Racine, Wis., 1988-89; med. technologist St. Therese Med. Ctr., Waukegan, Ill., 1980-83, 86-87, Suburban Hosp., Bethesda, Md., 1985-86, Group Health Assn., Washington, 1985-86, St. Francis Hosp., Milw., 1988-89; sports reporter Jour.-Gazette, Ft. Wayne, Ind., 1989-90; med. technologist Columbia Hosp., Milw., 1991; tech. assoc. Coll. Am. Pathologists, 1991—. Recipient 1st place in sports writing Capital Press Women, 1986, 87, Women's Press Club of Ind., 1990, 91, Nat. Fedn. Press Women, 1986, 91. Mem. Assn. Women in Sports Media (Midwest region coord 1990—), Nat. Fedn. Press Women (treas. Capital area 1985-87, 1st pl. in sports writing 1986, 91), Soc. Profl. Journalists, Women in Comms. (v.p., sec. Milw. chpt.), Nat. Writers Club. Democrat. Home: 9110 32d Ave Kenosha WI 53142 Office: Coll Am Pathologists 325 Waukegan Rd Northfield IL 60093-2719

TEPE, ANN SILCOTT, library services trainer; b. Parkersburg, W.Va., Nov. 7, 1946; d. Jesse Delbert and Imogene Kathryn (Lewis) Silcott; children: Dirk S., Chana B. BA, Marietta (Ohio) Coll., 1968; MEd, Ohio U., 1973. Cert. libr./media, reading, computer and English tchr., Ohio. Tchr. Marietta City Schs., 1968-69, Ft. Frye Schs., Beverly, Ohio, 1969-73; libr. supr. Warren Local Schs., Vincent, Ohio, 1973-75, Fort Frye Schs., 1975-84, Wolf Creek Schs., Waterford, Ohio, 1984-92; mgr. of edn. and tng. Follett Software Co., McHenry, Ill., 1992—; cons. edn. dept. Marietta Coll., 1981-85; del. People to People, People's Republic of China, 1985, People to People, Russia and Poland, 1992; adj. prof. Ashland (Ohio) U., 1988-92; presenter in field. Recipient Merit award Ohio Ednl. Libr. Media, 1991. Mem. ALA, Am. Assn. Sch. Librs., Libr. Media Assn. (pres. 1981-82), Phi Delta Kappa. Office: Follett Software Co 1391 Corporate Dr McHenry IL 60050

TEPE, VICTORIA, research psychologist, women's health care advocate; b. Chgo., May 5, 1961; d. Donald James and Lillian Gloria (Hagberg) T.; m. Erik Torgny Nasman, Sept. 27, 1984 (div. Mar. 1994). BA in Psychology, Saginaw Valley State U., 1983; Grad. Diploma in Social Sci., U. Stockholm, 1984; MS in Psychology, Northwestern U., 1987, PhD in Psychology, 1988. Rsch. assoc., grad. student summer rsch. program Air Force Office Sci. Rsch., Brooks AFB, Tex., 1986, 87; instr. psychology univ. coll. Northwestern U., Evanston, Ill., 1987-88; rsch. assoc. Chgo. Inst. Neurosurgery & Neuroresearch, 1989-90, Nat. Rsch. Coun./NAS, Washington and Wright-Patterson AFB, Ohio, 1990-92; coord. vol. svcs. Dayton (Ohio) Women's Ctr., 1991—; sr. human factors engr. Logicon Tech. Svcs., Inc., Dayton, 1992—; rsch. psychologist, cons. ProActive Rsch., Kettering, Ohio, 1994—; with community outreach/rsch./media Dayton Women's Ctr., 1991-94. Author, editor Choice Mail Internet Newsletter, 1992—; contbr. articles to profl. jours. and newspapers. Pres. Miami Valley Voters Legal Abortion, Dayton, 1994. Benton J. Underwood Grad. fellow Northwestern U., 1988; Univ. scholar Northwestern U., 1984. Mem. APA, Nat. Abortion Fedn., Soc. Psychophysiological Rsch. Democrat. Office: ProActive Rsch PO Box 292645 Kettering OH 45429

TEPPER, AMANDA, bank executive; b. N.Y.C., July 17, 1963; d. Ronald and Nancy (Boxley) T.; m. Jeffrey David Kiker, Feb. 14, 1993. BA, Brown U., 1985; MBA, U. Pa., 1991. Music dir. Sta. WPLR-FM, New Haven, 1985-86; corp. bond marketer Mabon, Nugent & Co., N.Y.C., 1986-89; with sect. banking and fin. Chem. Bank, N.Y.C., 1991-92, banking and corporate fin. assoc., 1992-94, v.p. banking and corporate fin., 1995—. Fishman-Davidson Ctr. Grant fellow Fishman-Davidson Ctr., U. Pa., 1990-91. Mem. Banking and corp. Fin. Assn., Phi Beta Kappa. Home: 21 West End Ave Summit NJ 07901 Office: Chem Bank 270 Park Ave 10th fl New York NY 10172

TEPPER, LYNN MARSHA, gerontology educator; b. N.Y.C., Mar. 16, 1946; d. Jack Mortimer and Ida (Golembe) Drukatz; m. William Chester Tepper, Aug. 27, 1967; children: Sharon Joy, Michelle Dawn. BS, SUNY, Buffalo, 1967; MA, Wayne State U., 1971; MS, Columbia U., 1977, EdM, 1978, EdD, 1980. Instr. John F. Kennedy Sch., Berlin, 1967-68, ednl. counselor, 1968-69; ednl. coordinator Army Edn. Ctr., Berlin, 1969-71; psychologist U.S. Dept. Def., Berlin, 1971-73; prof. Gerontology L.I. U., Dobbs Ferry, N.Y., 1979—, Columbia U., N.Y.C., 1982—; cons. NATO, Belgium, Naples, Italy, 1969-71, numerous nursing homes, N.Y.C., 1978—, Found. for Long Term Care, 1992—; prof. gerontology Mercy Coll., Dobbs Ferry, 1979—; dir. Gerontology Resource Ctr., Ctr. for Geriatrics and Gerontology, Columbia U., N.Y.C., 1980-85, dir. divsn. behavioral sci., 1982—; del. White House Conf. on Aging, 1980. Author: (textbooks) Long Term Care, 1993, Respite Care, 1993; contbr. articles to profl. jours. and textbooks. Advisor Office on Aging, State of N.Y., Albany, 1980—; dir. Mercy Coll., Inst. Gerontology, 1990—; trustee St. Cabrini Nursing Home, 1991—. Brookdale Inst. on Aging fellow, 1983. Fellow Gerontol. Soc. Am.; mem. Northeastern Gerontol. Soc., N.Y. Assn. Gerontol. Edn., Am. Psychol. Assn. Home: 50 Burnside Dr Hastings Hdsn NY 10706-3013 Office: Columbia U Med Campus Box 20 630 W 168th St New York NY 10032

TERHORST, CHERYL ANN, journalist; b. Buffalo, Aug. 3, 1960; d. Paul Bernard and Mary Jean (McNab) terH.; m. Burt W. Constable, Mar. 26, 1988. BS in Journalism, U. Ill., 1982. Editorial asst. Woman;s Day mag., N.Y.C., 1982-84; city reporter Daily Herald, Arlington Heights, Ill., 1984-85, edn. reporter, 1985-86, feature writer, 1987—. Vol. Community Response, Oak Park, Ill., 1992-94. Recipient Peter Lisagor award Soc. Profl. Journalists, 1991, 94. Office: Daily Herald 217 W Campbell St Arlington Heights IL 60005

TERHUNE, JANE HOWELL, legal assistant, educator; b. Newark, June 8, 1932; d. Charles Edwin and Audrey L. (Rogers) Howell; m. Richard N. Terhune, Dec. 22, 1951 (div. 1980); children: Richard C., Susan J., Carolyn A. Cert., Katherine Gibbs Sch., 1951. cert. legal asst. specialist, civil litigation. Legal sec. Howell, Kirby, et al, Jacksonville, Fla., 1954-56, Bidwell Adam, Gulfport, Miss., 1962-63; legal asst. Sinkler Gibbs & Simons, Charleston, S.C., 1963-77; sr. legal asst. Hall, Estill, Hardwick, Gable, Golden & Nelson, P.C., Tulsa, Okla., 1977—; adv. com. to legal asst. com. ABA, Chgo., 1978-85; adv. com. legal asst. program Tulsa Jr. Coll., 1978-85; trustee Okla. Sinfonia, Inc., Tulsa, 1984-92; speaker/faculty Cert. Legal Asst. Short Course, 1986—. Contbr. articles to profl. jours.; seminar speaker in field. Mem. Nat. Assn. Legal Assts. (charter pres. 1975-77, chmn. certifying bd. 1977-80, parl. 1988-90), Tulsa Assn. Legal Assts. (parl. 1987-89). Republican. Presbyterian. Home: 3164 S 101st East Ave Tulsa OK 74146-1437 Office: Hall Estill Hardwick Gable Golden & Nelson PC 320 South Boston Ste 400 Tulsa OK 74103

TERMINI, ROSEANN BRIDGET, lawyer; b. Phila., Feb. 2, 1953; d. Vincent James and Bridget (Marano) T. BS magna cum laude, Drexel U., 1975; MEd, Temple U., 1979, JD, 1985. Bar: Pa. 1985, U.S. Dist. Ct. (ea. dist.) Pa. 1985, D.C. 1986. Jud. clk. Superior Ct. of Pa., Allentown, 1985-86; atty. Pa. Power & Light Co., Allentown, 1986-87; corp. counsel food and drug law Lemmon Co., Sellersville, Pa., 1987-88; sr. dep. atty. bur. consumer protection plain lang. law Office of Atty. Gen., Harrisburg, Pa., 1988—, sr. dep. atty. gen. bur. consumer protection; instr. Del. County C.C., Media, Pa., 1983-85, adminstr., 1979-83; adj. prof. Dickinson Sch. Law, 1992, food and drug law, legal writing, Widener Sch. Law, 1993—. Contbr. articles to profl. jours, law revs.; speaker environ. conf. Active in Sr. Citizens Project Outreach, Hospice, 1986—; mem. St. Thomas More Law Bd. Named Outstanding Young Women of Yr., Dauphin County Bar Assn., 1987; Edn. fellow Temple U., 1978-79. Mem. ABA (various coms.), Bar Assn. D.C., Pa. Bar Assn. (ethics and environ. sects.), Temple U. Law Alumni Assn., Drexel U. Alumni Assn., Omicron Nu, Phi Alpha Delta. Home: 5533 Partridge Ct Harrisburg PA 17111-3769 Office: Office Atty Gen Harrisburg PA 17120

TERNBERG, JESSIE LAMOIN, pediatric surgeon; b. Corning, Calif., May 28, 1924; d. Eric G. and Alta M. (Jones) T. A.B., Grinnell Coll., 1946, Sc.D. (hon.), 1972; Ph.D., U. Tex., 1950; M.D., Washington U., St. Louis, 1953; Sc.D. (hon.), U. Mo., St. Louis, 1981. Diplomate: Am. Bd. Surgery. Intern Boston City Hosp., 1953-54; asst. resident in surgery Barnes Hosp., St. Louis, 1954-57; resident in surgery Barnes Hosp., 1958-59; research fellow Washington U. (Sch. Medicine), 1957-58; practice medicine specializing in pediatric surgery St. Louis, 1966—; instr., trainee in surgery Washington U., 1959-62, asst. prof. surgery, 1962-65, assoc. prof., 1965-71, prof. surgery in pediatrics, 1975—, prof. surgery, 1971—, chief div. pediatric surgery, 1972-90; mem. staff Barnes Hosp., 1974-90, pediatric surgeon in chief, 1974-90, mem. operating room com., 1971—, mem. med. adv. com., 1975—; mem. staff Children's Hosp., dir. pediatric surgery, 1972-90. Contbr. numerous articles on pediatric surgery to profl. jours. Trustee Grinnell Coll., 1984—. Recipient Alumni award Grinnell Coll., 1966, Faculty/Alumni award Washington U. Sch. Medicine, 1991, 1st Aphrodite Jannopaulo Hofsommer award, 1993. Fellow ACS; mem. AAAS, SIOP, Am. Pediatric Surg. Assn., Western Surg. Assn. (2d v.p. 1984-85), St. Louis Med. Soc., Soc. Surgery of the Alimentary Tract, Am. Acad. Pediatrics, Soc. Pelvic Surgeons (v.p. 1991-92), Brit. Assn. Paediatric Surgeons, Mo. State Surg. Soc., St. Louis Surg. Soc. (pres. 1980-81), St. Louis Pediatric Soc., Soc. Surg. Oncology, Pediatric Oncology Group (chmn. surg. discipline 1983—), St. Louis Childrens Hosp. Soc. (pres. 1979-80), Barnes Hosp. Soc., Phi Beta Kappa, Sigma Xi, Iota Sigma Pi, Alpha Omega Alpha. Office: St Louis Childrens Hosp 1 Childrens Pl Saint Louis MO 63110

TERNUS, JEAN ANN, nursing educator; b. Columbus, Nebr., Feb. 29, 1944; d. Maurice Henry and Marcella (Huntemer) T. BS in Nursing, Mt. Marty Coll., 1966; MS, Kans. State U., 1977. RN Kans., Mo., Nebr. Staff nurse Brian Meml. Hosp., Lincoln, Nebr., 1966-67; staff nurse VA Hosp., Milw., 1967-69, Kansas City, Mo., 1969-72; nursing instr. Kansas City (Kans.) Community Coll., 1973—; cardiovascular nurse specialist Meth. Hosp., Houston, 1973. Mem. AAUW, NEA, AACN, Kans. State Nurses Assn. (pres. dist. II 1980-82, chair dist. newsletter 1980—, 2d v.p. 1986-90, 1st v.p. 1990-92, sect. dist. II 1993—, v.p. 1993—), Nat. League Nursing, Gerontol. Nurses Assn., Kans. Nurses' Found. (bd. dirs. 1990-91, sec. 1992—), Sigma Theta Tau, Delta Kappa Gamma. Democrat. Roman Catholic. Home: 5342 Juniper Dr Shawnee Mission KS 66205-2225 Office: Kansas City CC 7250 State Ave Kansas City KS 66112-3003

TERPINSKI, EVA ANTONINA, pharmaceutical company executive; b. Warsaw, Poland, Jan. 17, 1946; came to U.S. 1983; d. Stanislaw and Marianna (Lis) Zajaczkowski; m. Jacek Terpinski, Jan. 22, 1972; children: Peter, Agatha. MSc in Chemistry, Poly. U., Warsaw, 1969, MSc in Chem. Engring., 1969, PhD in Chemistry, 1977. Asst. Poly. U., Warsaw, 1969-73, sr. asst., 1973-78, asst. prof., 1978-83; lectr. Rutgers U., New Brunswick, N.J., 1983-84; sr. scientist Nat. Patent Co., New Brunswick, N.J., 1984-88; mgr. Nat. Patent Co., New Brunswick, 1988-90, dir., 1990—. Contbr. articles to profl. jours.; editor 5 books; patentee in field. Instr. Girl Scouts U.S.A., Perth Amboy, N.J., 1988—. Mem. AAAS, Am. Assn. Pharm. Scientists, Internat. Soc. Magnetic Resonance, Am. Chem. Soc. Office: Nat Patent Devel Co 783 Jersey Ave New Brunswick NJ 08901-3605

TERR, LENORE CAGEN, psychiatrist, writer; b. N.Y.C., Mar. 27, 1936; d. Samuel Lawrence Cagen and Esther (Hirsh) Cagen Raiken; m. Abba I. Terr; children: David, Julia. AB magna cum laude, Case Western Res. U., 1957; MD with honors, U. Mich., 1961. Diplomate Am. Bd. Psychiatry and Neurology. Intern Med. Ctr. U. Mich., Ann Arbor, 1961-62, resident Neuropsychiat. Inst., 1962-64, fellow Children's Psychiat. Hosp., 1964-66; from instr. to asst. prof. Med. Sch. Case Western Res. U., Cleve., 1966-71; pvt. practice Terr Med. Corp., San Francisco, 1971—; from asst. clin. prof. to clin. prof. psychiatry Sch. Medicine U. Calif., San Francisco, 1971—; lectr. law, psychiatry U. Calif., Berkeley, 1971—, U. Calif., Davis, 1974—; bd. dirs. Am. Bd. Psychiatry and Neurology, Deerfield, Ill., 1988—. Author: Too Scared to Cry, 1990, Unchained Memories, 1994; contbr. articles to profl. jours. Rockefeller Found. scholar-in-residence, Italy, 1981, 88; project grantee Rosenberg Found., 1977, 80-81, William T. Grant Found., 1986-87; recipient Career Tchr. award NIMH, 1967-69, Child Advocacy award, APA, 1994. Fellow Am. Psychiat. Assn. (Child Psychiatry Rsch. award 1984, Clin. Rsch. award 1987), Am. Coll. Psychiatrists (program chair 1991-92), Am. Acad. Child and Adolescent Psychiatry (coun. 1984-87); mem. Group for Advancement Psychiatry (bd. dirs. 1986-88), Phi Beta Kappa, Alpha Omega Alpha. Office: Terr Med Corp 450 Sutter St Rm 2534 San Francisco CA 94108-4204

TERRACUSO-DONLON, RENA, public relations executive. BA, Fairfield U. Mgr. nat. press media rels. dept. CBS Entertainment, N.Y.C.; publicist ABC News Prime Time Live, N.Y.C.; sr. publicist ABC News; dir. press and pub. rels. Donahue Show, N.Y.C., 1993—. Office: Donahue Show 30 Rockefeller Plz # 827 New York NY 10112*

TERRAS, AUDREY ANNE, mathematics educator; b. Washington, Sept. 10, 1942; d. Stephen Decatur and Maude Mae (Murphy) Bowdoin. BS with high honors in Math., U. Md., 1964; MA, Yale U, 1966, PhD, 1970. Instr. U. Ill., Urbana, 1968-70; asst. prof. U. P.R., Mayaguez, 1970-71; asst. prof. Bklyn. Coll., CUNY, 1971-72; asst. prof. math. U. Calif.-San Diego, La Jolla, 1972-76, assoc. prof., 1976-83, prof., 1983—, vis. positions MIT, fall 1977, 83, U. Bonn (W.Ger.), spring 1977, Inst. Mittag-Leffler, Stockholm, winter, 1978, Inst. for Advanced Study, spring 1984, Math. Scis. Rsch. Inst., Berkeley, Calif., winter 1992; dir. West Coast Number Theory Conf., U. Calif.-San Diego, 1976, AMS joint summer research conf., 1984; lectr. in field. Author: Harmonic Analysis on Symmetric Spaces and Applications, Vol. I, 1985, Vol. II, 1988. Contbr. articles and chpts. to profl. publs. Woodrow Wilson fellow, 1964; NSF fellow, 1964-68; NSF grantee Summer Inst. in Number Theory, Ann Arbor, Mich., 1973; prin. investigator NSF, 1974-88. Fellow AAAS; mem. AAAS (nominating com. math. sect. project 2061), Am. Math. Soc. (com. employment and ednl. policy com. on coms., council, transactions editor, com. for the yr. 2000), Math. Assn. Am. (program com. for nat. meeting 1988-90, chair joint com. Am. Math. Soc. and Math. Assn. Am. 1991), Soc. Indsl. and Applied Math., Assn. for Women in Math., Assn. for Women in Sci. Research in harmonic analysis on symmetric spaces and number theory. Office: U Calif San Diego Dept Math La Jolla CA 92093-0112

TERREBONNE, ANNIE MARIE, medical technologist, educator, clinical laboratory scientist; b. Isola, Miss., Mar. 17, 1932; d. Tommy and Alpha (Whitfield) Patterson; m. Frank Paul Terrebonne, May 7, 1960. A.A., Co-Lin Jr. Coll., 1950; B.S., Miss. State U., 1952; grad. Knoxville Gen. Hosp. Sch. Med. Tech., 1953. Cert. Nat. Cert. Agy. Med. Lab. Personnel. Med., x-ray and EKG technician Layman-Saffold Clinic, Knoxville, Tenn., 1952-55; med. technologist in bacteriology St. Dominic's Hosp., Jackson, Miss., 1956-58; parasitologist Oschner's Clinic and Hosp., New Orleans, 1959-65; asst. supr., med. technologist II spl. hematology dept. U. Tex. Med. Br., Galveston, 1969-91 , supr. med. technologist III Lab, 1991—; mem. research and devel. staff, 1974—, instr. med. tech. students, 1981-86, instr. med. students, residents, and hematology fellows, 1987—. Contbr. articles to profl. jours. Mem. Nat. Certification Agy. for Med. Technologists, Am. Assn. Med. Technologists, Assn. Advancement of Sci., Galveston Dist. Soc. Med. Technologists, Tex. Soc. Med. Technologists, Am. Soc. Clin. Pathologists (cert.), Miss. State U. Alumni Assn. Democrat. Methodist. Clubs: Loyalty, Found. for Christian Living, Bayou Vista Recreation, Positive Thinkers'. Lodge: Order of Eastern Star, Grand 1894 Opera House. Home: 353 Ling St Hitchcock TX 77563-2601 Office: U Tex Med Br Spl Hematology Dept 424 Clin Sci Bldg Galveston TX 77550

TERRELL, DOMINIQUE LARA, dramatic soprano, actress, real estate and marketing executive; b. South Bend, Ind., Apr. 26; d. Harold J. Metzler and Margaret Terrell (Whiteman) Metzler Fogarty. BA, Ithaca Coll., 1960; diploma, Brown's Bus. Coll., Decatur, Ill., 1960; postgrad. in real estate sales, NYU, 1984. Lic. securities dealer, real estate salesperson. Exec. legal asst. Carb Luria Glassner Cook & Kufeld, N.Y.C., 1962-64; Exec. legal asst. Graubard Moskovitz McGoldrick Dannett & Horowitz, N.Y.C., 1964-79; opera and concert singer N.Y.C., 1964—; real estate salesperson Rosemary Edwards Realty, N.Y.C., 1985, Kenneth D. Laub & Co., Inc., N.Y.C., 1987-89, GSW Realty, Inc., N.Y.C., 1990-91, Kuzmuk Realty, Inc., 1992-94, Gala 72 Realty, Inc., 1994—; bd. dirs., singer Broadway-Grand Opera, 1992—; pres. Terrell Internat., Mystique of Dominique, Whiteman and Stewart Prodns., TS Assocs., TS Enterprises, DharMacduff Publs.; corr. sec., bd. dirs. Community Opera, Inc., N.Y.C., 1984—. Mem. internat. affairs com. and other coms. Women's Nat. Rep. Club, N.Y.C., 1968-82; active Rep. County Vols., N.Y.C., 1976-82; mem. nominating com. Ivy Rep. Club, N.Y.C., 1983-87; bd. dirs. Am. Landmark Festivals, 1986—. Named Female Singer of Yr., Internat. Beaux Arts, Inc., 1978-79, Princess Nightingale, Allied Indian Tribes N.Am. Continent-Cherokee Nation, 1985. Mem. Wagner Internat. Instn. (dir. pub. rels. 1982-84), Navy League U.S. (life, mem. N.Y. coun.), Assn. Former Intelligence Officers (assoc.), Friends of Spanish Opera (bd. dirs. 1982—), Finlandia Found., Inc. (life), The Bohemians, Nat. Arts Club (music com. 1983-87), N.Y. Opera Club.

TERRELL, JANICE S., mortgage company executive; b. St. Louis, Mo., Oct. 13, 1958; d. William and Addie Marjorie Terrell. BS in Psychology, UCLA, 1980; A. in Fin. Mgmt., Chgo. Inst. Fin., 1985. Ops. supr. First Pacific Bank, Beverly Hills, Calif., 1979-83; br. supr. Mo. Savs., St. Louis, 1983-85; mortgage loan officer Germania Fin. Corp., St. Charles, Mo., 1985-89; mortgage systems analyst Citicorp Mortgage, Inc., St. Louis, 1987; loan compliance contr. Landmark Bank, St. Charles, Mo., 1989-92; mortgage loan officer Magna Bank (formerly Landmark Bank), O'Fallon, Mo., 1992—. Mem. Bd. Realtors, St. Charles C. of C., St. Charles Home Builders Assn., Women's Council, Hist. Soc., St. Louis Charity Horse Show Assn., Horse Protection Assn. Democrat. Office: Magna Bank 1201 Hwyk O Fallon MO 63366

TERRELL, NATALIE DORETHEA, educational instruction specialist, consultant; b. Norfolk, Va., Mar. 11, 1959; d. Louis Smith Sr. and Rosia Lee (Little) T.; m. Hakim Ben Adjoua, June 20, 1983 (div. May 1986). BBA in Bus. Mgmt., Ea. Mich. U., 1983; MS in Instnl. Tech., Ga. State U., 1994. Cert. tchr., Ga. Sr. tax examiner, trainer IRS, Chamblee, Ga., 1985-88; tchr. bus. edn. DeKalb County Bd. Edn., Decatur, Ga., 1988-92; ednl. instrn. specialist EduQuest--An IBM Co., Atlanta, 1992—; tax cons. Terrell Bookkeeping Svcs., Decatur, 1991-93. Recipient Nat. Commemorative Cert. U.S. Achievement Acad., 1988. Mem. Nat. Soc. Performance and Instrn., Assn. for Ednl. Comms. and Tech., Nat. Bus. Edn. Assn., NEA, NAFE. Home: 3510 Shepherds Path Decatur GA 30034-5043

TERRIQUEZ-KASEY, LAURA MARIE, critical care nurse; b. Bronx, N.Y., May 12, 1950; d. Gilbert Manuel and Elizabeth (Areuena) Terriquez; m. William Kasey, July 23, 1988. AAS, SUNY, Morrisville, 1971; BSN, Long Island U., 1980; MSN, CUNY, 1985. RN, N.Y., Tex. Commd. 2d lt. AUS, 1974, advanced through grades to major, 1990—; staff nurse emergency svc. Bellevue Hosp. Ctr., N.Y.C., 1971-73, head nurse emergency svc., 1973-81, nursing supr., 1981-84; clin. nurse coord. South Nassan Community Hosp., Oceanside, N.Y., 1984-85; staff nurse Brooke Mgmt. Ctr., San Antonio, 1985-86, head nurse vascular surg. ward, 1987-89, charge nurse, EMT, head nurse PACU, 1987-89; staff nurse med. ICU William Beaumont Army Med. Ctr., Ft. Bliss/El Paso, Tex., 1985-90, staff nurse trauma unit, 1990-91, head nurse trauma unit, 1991-93; nurse mgr. emergency svcs. Bassett Health Care Systems, Cooperstown, N.Y., 1993—; instr. U.S. Army, El Paso, 1991-92; mem. com. nursing adv. Southwest Organbank, El Paso, 1992—; adj. instr. U. Tex. Dept. Nursing, El Paso, 1992. Recipient Meritorious Svc. award San Antonio Police Dept., 1988, Svc. award ARC, 1980, cert. Appreciation N.Y. Emergency Med. Svcs., 1984. Mem. Emergency Nurses Assn., Res. Officers Assn., Adrondock Regional Adv. Emergency Med. System. Home: RR 4 Box 340 Park Dr Angel Heights Oneonta NY 13820 Office: Bassett Health Care Systems 1 Atwell Rd Cooperstown NY 13866

TERRIS, LILLIAN DICK, psychologist, association executive; b. Bloomfield, N.J., May 5, 1914; d. Alexander Blaikie and Herminia (Doscher) Dick; BA, Barnard Coll., 1935; PhD, Columbia U., 1941; m. Louis Long, Apr. 22, 1935 (dec. Sept. 1968), 1 son, Alexander Blaikie Long; m. Milton Terris, Feb. 6, 1971. Instr. psychology Sara Lawrence Coll., Bronxville, N.Y., 1937-40; jr. pers. tech. SSA, Washington, 1941; sr. pers. clk. OWI, N.Y.C., 1941-43; dir. profl. examination svc. Am. Pub. Health Assn., N.Y.C., 1943-70, pres., 1970-79, pres. emeritus, 1979—. Assoc. editor Jour. Pub. Health Policy, 1979—. Life mem., bd. dirs. Profl. Exam. Svc.; chair bd. VNA Chittenden County, Vt., 1989, mem. hon. bd., 1993—. Recipient Nat. Environ. Health Assn. award, 1976, Cert. of Svc. award Am. Bd. Preventive Medicine, 1979. Diplomate Am. Bd. Examiners in Profl. Psychology. Fellow Am. Psychol. Assn.; mem. Am. Pub. Health Assn., N.Y. State Psychol. Assn., Am. Coll. Hosp. Adminstrs. (hon. fellow), Phi Beta Kappa, Sigma Xi. Contbr. articles in field to profl. jours. Home: 208 Meadowood Dr South Burlington VT 05403-7401 Office: 475 Riverside Dr New York NY 10027

TERRY, ELIZABETH HAYS, needlepoint designer; b. Bryn Mawr, Pa., July 29, 1935; d. James Franklin and Mary Ellen (Carmichael) Hays; m. Charles L. Terry, III, Feb. 8, 1958; children: Elizabeth Harllee Carmichael Terry Littlefield, Charles L. IV. AB, Smith Coll., 1957. Asst. to profs. Harvard U., Cambridge, Mass., 1957-58; art tchr. Exeter (N.H.) Day Sch., 1968-72; asst. editor Phillips Exeter Acad. Alumni Quarterly, 1972-75, dir. alumni records, 1975-85; owner Elizabeth Terry, Needlepoint Design, North Hampton, N.H., 1980—; tchr. needlepoint Guild of Strawbery Banke, Portsmouth, N.H., 1985—. Dir. for Town of Exeter-Save Our Shores, 1972. Mem. Smith Coll. Class of 1957 (class fund agt. 1972-77, alumnae fund com. 1977-80, class bequest chair 1982—, com. on deferred giving 1990—), N.H. Colonial Dames (pres. 1989-92, nat. historian 1992-94, nat. v.p. 1994—). Episcopalian. Home: 76 Exeter Rd North Hampton NH 03862-2004 Office: Nat Soc Colonial Dames Am Moffatt Ladd House 154 Market St Portsmouth NH 03801-3730

TERRY, JULIE WESTBROOK, controller; b. Tunica, Miss., Nov. 28, 1962; d. Bobby Joe and Donna Elaine (Selph) Westbrook; m. Jefferson Shelton Terry, Oct. 17, 1987; 1 child, Brooke Elana Terry. BS in Acctg., Christian Brothers U., Memphis, 1984. CPA. Sr. acct. Arthur Anderson, Memphis, 1984-89; mgr. fin. reporting Smith and Nephew Richards, Memphis, 1989-91, group mgr., budgets forecasting, 1991-94, support contr. orthopaedic divsn., 1994—. Mem. AICPA, Am. Mgt. Assn. Republican. Methodist.

TERRY, KAY ADELL, management consultant and sales training executive; b. Portland, Oreg., July 11, 1939; d. Langdon Alcott and Emma Francis (Meyer) Howard; m. Frank F. Terry, Aug. 31, 1963 (div. Mar. 1988); 1 child, Kimberly Sue. CPC, CIPC. Office mgr. Merck Sharp & Dohme, Portland, 1959-63; asst. dir. admissions Seattle Pacific U., Seattle, 1963-66; owner United Personnel Svc., Seattle, 1966-86; pres., chief exec. officer Ram Force Cos., Seattle, 1986-91; pres. N.W. region Robert Half Internat., Seattle, 1991-93; pres., CEO Terry & Assocs., Seattle, 1993—; bd. dirs. Ram Force Cos., Seattle Acctg. Force, Inc., Seattle, Office Force, Inc., Seattle, Data Force, Inc., Seattle. Contbr. articles to profl. jours. Mem. Seattle C. of C., 1989; vol. Spl. Olympics, Seattle. Fellow Seattle Pacific U., 1989. Mem. Women Bus. Owners, Nat. Assn. Accts. (bd. dirs. 1985-87, Mem. Achievement award 1987, Disting. Svc. award 1987), Nat. Assn. Pers. Svcs. (vice chmn. 1993), Nat. Assn. Temp. Svcs., Pacific N.W. Pers. Mgmt. Assn., Wash. Athletic Club. Republican.

TERRY, MEGAN, playwright, performer , photographer; b. Seattle, July 22, 1932; d. Harold Joseph and Marguerite Cecelia (Henry) Duffy. Student, Banff Sch. Fine Arts, summers, 1950-52, 56, U. Alta., Edmondton, Can., 1952-53; B.Ed., U. Wash., 1956. Founding mem. Open Theater, N.Y.C., 1963; ABC fellow Yale U., 1966-67; founding mem., v.p. N.Y. Theatre Strategy, 1971; adj. prof. theatre U. Nebr., Omaha, until 1977; Hill prof. fine arts U. Minn.-Duluth, spring 1983; Bingham prof. humanities U. Louisville, 1981; mem. theatre panel, mem. overview panel Nat. Endowment Arts, 1976-86, mem. opera/music theatre panel, 1985, mem. advancement panel, 1987; mem. theatre panel Rockefeller Found., 1977-85; mem. performing arts panel Nebr. State Council for Arts, 1977; mem. Nebr. Com. for Humanities, 1983-86; mem. Gov.'s Com. on Film and Telecommunications, 1985-86; founding mem. N.Y. Open Theatre, 1963-73; judge playwriting competition Mass., Wis., Ohio, Oreg. states, So. Playwrights Competition; Nat. Endowment Arts vis. artist in residence U. Iowa, 1992. Dir. Cornish Players, Cornish Sch. Allied Arts, Seattle, 1954-56, founding dir. playwrights workshop, Open Theatre, N.Y.C., 1963-68, playwright-in-residence, literary mgr. Omaha Magic Theatre, 1974—; author plays including: Kegger, Comings and Goings, The Magic Realists, Sanibel & Captiva, The People vs. Ranchman, Kepp Tightly Closed in a Cool Dry Place, The Gloaming Oh My Darling, Approaching Simone, Viet Rock, Massachussetts Trust, The Tommy Allen Show, Calm Down Mother, Sleazing Toward Athens, Babes in the Big House, Ex Miss Copper Queen, Mollie Bailey's Traveling Family Circus, Goona-Goona, Retro, Hothouse, Dinner's in the Blender, Objective Love, Katmandu, Fifteen Million Fifteen Year Olds, Fireworks, The Trees Blew Down, Choose a Spot on the Floor, Future Soap, Brazil Fado, Pro Game., Amtrak, Headlights, Breakfast Serial, Do You See What I'm Saying?, The Snow Queen, India Plays, I Forgot How Much I Like You; editor, writer: plays including Sea of Forms, Nightwalk, 1001 Horror Stories of The Plains, Running Gag, Couplings and Groupings, Walking Through Walls, Babes Unchained, Cancel That Last Thought; or See The 270 Foot Woman in Spandex, X-Raydiate: E-Motion in Action, Body Leaks, Sound Fields, Belches on Couches, Star Path Moonstop; photographer/editor: Right Brain Vacation Photos: Production Photographs of Omaha Magic Theatre Productions, 1972-92; mem. performance ensemble Omaha Magic Theatre nat. and internat. performance tours Body Leaks, 1991, Body Leaks, 1992, Sound Fields, 1993, 94, Belches on Couches, 1993, 94; contbr. articles in field to profl. jours. Mem. Nebr. Artist-in-the Schs., 1987—. Recipient Stanley Drama award, 1965, Office of Advanced Drama Rsch. award, 1965, Obie award, 1970, Disting. Contbrn. To and Svc. in Am. Theatre Silver medal Amoco Oil Co., 1977; Dramatists Guild Com. of Women Ann. award, 1983,

Nebr. Artist of Yr. 1992; Gov. award Nebr., 1992; Rockefeller grantee, 1968, 87; NEA Lit. fellow, 1973; Guggenheim fellow, 1978; NEA playwriting fellow, 1989, Lifetime Am. Theatre fellow, 1994. Mem. NEA (reporter and panelist for theatre program, 1975-85), Women's Theatre Coun. (founding 1971), Women's Forum (charter), Am. Theatre Assn. (co-chmn. playwriting program 1977, chmn. playwrights project com. 1978-79, C. Crawford playwriting judge of 1987), Theatre Comm. Group (bd. dirs. 1988-92), New Dramatists (alumni, judge nat. playwriting competition 1987-88), ASSISTEJ-USA (bd. dirs. 1986-91). Home: 2309 Hanscom Blvd Omaha NE 68105-3143 Office: E Marton Agy Rm 612 One Union Sq New York NY 10003-3303

TERRY, MIRIAM JANICE, minister; b. Aliceville, Ala., May 4, 1956; d. Ernest Lee Jr. and Nolie (Lee) T. Student, U. Tex., Arlington, 1974-75, Am. Banking Sch., Tampa, Fla., 1978; BA in Bibl. Studies, Living Word Coll. and Sem., St. Louis, 1991, MRE, 1993, postgrad., 1993—. Ordained to ministry Life Anew Missionary Fellowship, 1987. Children's pastor Brandonville (Fla.) Christian Ch., 1975, Oxford (Ala.) Ch. of God, 1980-81; dir. children's ministries Newark Heights Ch. of God, Newark, Ohio, 1982-83, Life Christian Ctr., Madisonville, Ky., 1984—; dir. promotions Life Anew Ministries, Inc./Sta. WLCN-TV, Madisonville, 1984—; dir. edn. Life Christian Acad., Madisonville, 1990—; dir. day care Life Ctr. Day Care Plus, Madisonville, 1991—. Dir., producer seasonal dramas and musicals, 1989—; contbr. articles to religious jours. Vol. Regional Med. Ctr., Madisonville, 1984—, mem. laughter therapy com., 1990-91; vol. St. Jude's Children's Hosp., 1991—; vol. pediatric chaplain to various hosps.; dir ann. Summer Camp for children, 1988—. Recipient Outstanding Svc. award Regional Med. Ctr., 1986. Republican. Office: Life Anew Ministries Inc 721 Princeton Pike PO Box 1087 Madisonville KY 42431-1087

TERRY, SHERRIE LYNN, marketing executive; b. Portland, Oreg., Nov. 21, 1957; d. Milton Dee and Jennie Lee (Gillman) Kingsland; m. Randall Keith Terry, May 14, 1983. BBA, Lewis & Clark Coll., 1980; MBA in Mktg., Memphis State U., 1984. With Dr. Scholl's Footcare, Memphis, 1980-86, assoc. product mgr., 1983, product mgr., 1984-85, sr. product mgr., 1985-86; sr. product mgr. ConAgra Frozen Foods, St. Louis, 1986-87; product mgr. Vlasic Foods, Inc., Farmington Hills, Mich., 1987-88, sr. product mgr., 1988-89, dir. mktg., 1989-91, sr. dir. mktg., 1991-92; dir. new product devel. Chiquita Brands Internat., Cin., 1992-93; dir. mktg. Chiquita Brands N.Am., Cin., 1993—. Mem. NAFE, Am. Mktg. Assn., Beta Gamma Sigma, Alpha Nu Alpha, Phi Kappa Phi, Delta Mu Delta. Home: 11740 Park Ct Loveland OH 45140

TERWILLEGAR, LINDA S., administrative assistant; b. West Fork, Ind., Aug. 26, 1956; adopted d. Paul Arthur and Leona (Andres) Lawson; m. Kent Wilson Dodge, Aug. 31, 1974 (div. Aug. 1987); children: Beverly Lynn Dodge Bewley, Mark Wilson Dodge (dec.); m. LeRoy J. Terwillegar, Feb. 6, 1988. Grad. high sch., New Albany, Ind. Asst. to pres. Jer-L-Lee, Inc. dba Papeno's Pizza, Restaurant, Video, Tanning Salon, Greenville, Ind., 1984—. Home: PO Box 337 8969 Hwy 150 Greenville IN 47124 Office: Jer-L-Lee Inc PO Box 337 Greenville IN 47124

TESORO, GIULIANA CAVAGLIERI, chemistry research educator, consultant; b. Venice, Italy, June 1, 1921; came to U.S., 1939; d. Gino and Margherita (Maroni) Cavaglieri; m. Victor Tesoro, Apr. 17, 1943; children: Claudia, Andrew. PhD, Yale U., 1943. Rsch. chemist Am. Cyanamid Co., Boundbrook, N.J., 1943-44; asst. dir. rsch. Onyx Chem. Co., Jersey City, 1944-58, J. P. Stevens & Co., Inc., Garfield, N.J., 1958-68; dir. chem. rsch. Burlington Industries, Greenboro, N.C., 1968-72; sr. scientist, adj. prof. MIT, Cambridge, 1973-82; rsch. prof. Poly. U., Bklyn., 1982—; Mem. nat. materials adv. bd. NRC, Washington, 1979-82. Contbr. numerous articles to profl. publs.; patentee in field. Recipient Am. Dyestuff Reporter award, 1959, Achievement award Soc. Women Engrs., 1978. Fellow Textile Inst. Gt. Britain; mem. AAAS (co-chmn. polymer combustion and fire retardance conf. 1977), Am. Assn. Textile Chemists and Colorists (Olney medal 1963), Am. Chem. Soc., Am. Inst. Chemists, Info. Coun. Fabric flammability, N.Y. Acad. Sci., Textile Rsch. Inst. (editorial bd.jours.), Fiber Soc. (pres. 1974-75). Democrat. Home: 278 Clinton Ave Dobbs Ferry NY 10522-3007 Office: Poly U 333 Jay St Brooklyn NY 11201-2907

TESSMAN, CORINNE LEE, elementary school principal; b. Milw., Nov. 22, 1941; d. Walter Henry and Viola Emma (Kautza) Umaske; children: Timothy Jon, Tina Marie. BS, U. Wis., La Crosse, 1964; MS, U. Colo., 1968, Ind. U., Ft. Wayne, 1989. Cert. tchr. (life) Ind., adminstrn., supr. elem. sch. Tchr. Rockford (Ill.) Cmty. Schs., 1964-67, Ft. Wayne (Ind.) Cmty. Schs., 1967-69; tchr. Diocese Ft. Wayne, South Bend, Ft. Wayne, 1980-93, prin., 1993—. Mem. Kappa Delta Pi, Alpha Omicron Pi.

TESTA, MARIA, psychologist, researcher; b. Buffalo, N.Y., Feb. 15, 1961; d. Jospeh S. and Mary Ann (Vullo) T.; m. Thomas D. Petrocelli, Aug. 3, 1985; 1 child, John Testa Petrocelli. BA in English and Psychology, SUNY, Buffalo, 1983, MA in Psychology, 1986, PhD in Social Psychology, 1989. Instr. Millard Fillmore Coll. SUNY, Buffalo, 1986-89; rsch. scientist Rsch. Inst. on Addictions, Buffalo, 1989—. Author: (with others) Social Comparison, 1991; contbr. articles to profl. jours. Grantee Nat. Inst. on Alcohol Abuse and Alcoholism, 1992—. Mem. APA, Rsch. Soc. on Alcoholism, Soc. for Personality and Social Psychology. Office: Rsch Inst on Addictions 1021 Main St Buffalo NY 14203-1016

TETELMAN, ALICE FRAN, city government official; b. N.Y.C., Apr. 15, 1941; d. Harry and Leah (Markovitz) T.; m. Martin A. Wenick, Dec. 7, 1980. BA, Mt. Holyoke Coll., South Hadley, Mass., 1962. Rsch. and info. asst. Edn. and World Affairs, N.Y.C., 1963-67; legis. asst. U.S. Sen. Charles Goodell, Washington, 1968-70; land use and energy specialist Citizens Adv. Com. on Environ. Quality, Washington, 1973-74; sr. assoc. prog. mgr. Linton & Co., Washington, 1971-73, 75-76; pub policy cons. Washington, 1977-78; adminstrv. asst. U.S. Congressman Bill Green (N.Y.), Washington, 1978-81; cons. The Precious Legacy Project, Prague, Czechoslovakia, 1982-83; Rep. staff dir. Select Com. on Hunger, U.S. Ho. of Reps., Washington, 1984-85; dir. State of N.J. Washington Office, 1986-90; exec. dir. Coun. of Gov/'s Policy Advisors, Washington, 1991-94; dir. Washington Office The City of N.Y., 1994—. Bd. mem. Republican Women's Task Force, Nat. Women's Polit. Caucus, 1976-80. European Community grantee, 1975. Mem. Ripon Soc. (nat. exec. com. 1971-73). Republican. Office: City of NY Washington Office 555 New Jersey Ave NW Washington DC 20001

TETENMAN, ALISON, public relations executive; b. L.A., Sept. 19, 1964; d. Henry Aaron and Arlene Sylvia (Hoffberg); m. Robert Lee, Jan. 10, 1987 (div). BA in Journalism, Humboldt State U., Arcata, 1987. Communications specialist Nat. Environ. Tng. Assn., Scottsdale, Ariz., 1987-88; mktg., publs. asst. Internat. Assn. Mgrs. Inc., Scottsdale, Ariz., 1988-89; promotions coordinator ARC, L.A., 1990-92; mktg. adminstrn. coord. CareAm 65 Plus, Woodland Hills, Calif., 1992—. Mem. NAFE, So. Calif. Ventura Publishers Users Group. Home: 3830 Aztec Ct Simi Valley CA 93063

TETERYCZ, BARBARA ANN, entrepreneur, advertising executive; b. Chgo., Jan. 23, 1952; d. Sylvester and Anne (Deutsch) T.; m. Robert Nathan Estes, Oct. 13, 1984. BA, U. Ill., 1974; postgrad. Parkland Coll., 1975-76, U. Ill., 1976-77; grad. Second City Tng. Ctr., 1991. Teller First Fed. of Champaign, Ill., 1974-75; cashier Kroger Co., Champaign, 1975-77; merchandise rep. RustCraft Greeting Cards, Champaign, 1977-78; sales rep. Hockenberg-Rubin, Champaign, 1978, John Morrell & Co., Champaign, 1978-80; account exec. Sta. WICD TV, Champaign, 1981-86; owner Left-Handed Compliments, Champaign; creator 1987, 88 left-handed calendar; now actress, singer/songwriter; active Sta. WEFT Radio Theater, 1991. Contbg. editor mag. Champaign County Bus. Reports, 1986; singer/songwriter I Want to be a Country Music Star, Highway 57; writer, dir. and prodr. Rappin'zel - A 90s Fairy Tale radio Sta. WEFT, 1992, Rumplestiltskin - A Tale of Love and Politics, 1993; inventor Left-Behind Sweat Pants and Shorts. Vol. Am. Cancer Soc., 1985, Ill. Radio Readers for the Visually Impaired, U. Ill. Alumni Assn., 1985-88, Mercy Hosp. Aux., coms. to Elect and Re-elect Beth Beauchamp to City Coun., Champaign, 1984, 87. Ill. State scholar, 1970-74; grad. players workshop of Second City, 1989, grad. Second City Tng. Ctr., 1991. Mem. NAFE, Ad Club of Champaign (finalist several copywriting contests), Internat. Platform Assn., Entrepreneurs Roundtable (founding), Women's Bus. Coun., Urbana C. of C., Champaign C. of C. (pub. rels. com., pres.'s club), Alpha Omega. Roman Catholic. Avocations: reading, writing, bicycling, bodybuilding. Home: 1615 Harbor Point Dr PO Box 873 Champaign IL 61824

TETTEGAH, SHARON YVONNE, educator; b. Wichita Falls, Tex., Jan. 14, 1956; d. Lawrence Guice and Doris Jean (Leak) Oliver; 1 child, Tandra Ainsworth; m. Joseph Miller Zangai, Dec. 22, 1978 (div. 1983); 1 child, Tonia Manjay Zengai; m. George Tettegah, Apr. 28, 1989; 1 child, Nicole Jennifer Tettegah. AA, Coll. Alameda, 1985; BA, U. Calif., Davis, 1988, teaching cert., 1989, MA, 1991; postgrad., U. Calif., Santa Barbara. Cert. elem. tchr., Calif. Clk. II Alameda County Mcpl. Ct., Oakland, Calif., 1976-77; acct. clk. Alameda County Social Svcs., Oakland, 1977-78, eligibility technician, 1978-82; supervising clk. Alameda County Health Care Svcs., Oakland, 1982-84; tchr. Davis (Calif.) Joint Unified Sch. Dist., 1988-89, L.A. Unified Schs., L.A., 1990-92; tchr. Oakland Unified Sch. Dist., Oakland, 1992—, tchr. sci. mentor, 1993—; teaching asst. U. Calif., Santa Barbara, 1993-94; adminstrv. intern Oxnard Unified Sch. Dist., 1994, U. Calif. Cultural Awareness Program, Santa Barbara, 1994—; cons. U. Calif., Davis, 1988-89, multicultural cons. Davis Unified Sch. Dist., 1988-89; edn. cons. Ednl. Testing Svc., Emeryville, Calif., 1994. Pres. African-Am. Grad. and Profl. Student's Orgn., Davis, 1988-89. Recipient Charlene Richardson Acad. Honors award Coll. Alameda, 1985; Calif. State Acad. fellow, 1989-91, Grad. Opportunity Acad. Excellence fellow, 1994—. Mem. Am. Ednl. Researchers Assn., Calif. Sci. Tchrs. Assn., Calif. Advocacy for Math and Sci., Calif. Tchrs. Assn., Calif. Media Libr. Educators Assn., PTA, Multicultural Curriculum Assn., Supervision and Curriculum Leadership Assn., Bay Area Sci. and Tech. Educators Corsortium, Pan-African Students Assn.,. Address: PO Box 1782 Santa Barbara CA 93116 Office: U Calif Santa Barbara Sch Edn/Ednl Psychology Santa Barbara CA 93106

TETZLAFF, KAREN MARIE, state official; b. Florence, Oreg., Mar. 9, 1950; d. Chester Arthur and Martha Jane (Howell) Mitchell; m. Sterling Franklin Tetzlaff, July 16, 1988; children: Michelle René Reece, André Scott Matney, Derrick Anthony. Diploma, Chemeketa C.C., Salem, Oreg., 1981. Notary pub., Oreg. Sec. Oreg. Corrections div., Madras, 1977-78; intake-release data clk. community corrections Oreg. Corrections div., Salem, 1979-80, correctional officer, 1980-83, records mgr., 1983—, instr., 1990—; facilitator, trainer breaking barriers Gordon Graham & Co., Salem, 1992—, developing capable people, Salem, 1993—; instr., law enforcement data system rep. Oreg. Women's Correctional Ctr., Salem, 1984—, facilitator, 1993—. Head usher John Jacobs Evangelistic Assn., Salem, Medford, Redmond, Oreg., 1990-92; youth worship leader South Salem Foursquare Ch., Salem, 1990—; vol. Driving Under Influence Tng. Task Force, Salem, 1992—. Recipient 5-yr. outstanding svc. award Law Enforcement Data System, 1990, traffic safety award Oreg. Dept. Transp., 1993, Employee of Quarter award Oreg. Women's Correctionala Ctr., 1993. Mem. Am. Correctional Assn., Oreg. Corrections Assn., Nat. Notary Assn., Cognitive Restructuring Network (letter of appreciation 1993). Republican. Office: Oreg Women's Correctional Ctr 2809 State St Salem OR 97310-1307

TEUTON, LUELLA BOSMAN, library director; b. Saginaw, Mich., Feb. 22, 1946; d. William and Ella (Anderson) Bosman; divorced. BS, Ctrl. Mich. U., 1967; MA in Libr. Sci., U. Mich., 1972; PhD, Nova U., 1991. H.s. libr. Westwood Hgts. Schs., Flint, Mich., 1967-72; head of cataloging Ctrl. Fla. C.C., Ocala, 1972-77; mgr. travel agy. Wyo., Fla., 1978-87; head reference Ocala Pub. Libr., 1987; adult svcs. libr. Citrus County Libr. Sys., Crystal River, Fla., 1987-88; dir. libr. svcs. South Fla. C.C., Avon Park, 1988—; cons. Springdale Coll., Birmingham, Eng., 1993—; mem. Coll. Ctr. Libr. Automation Adv. Bd., 1990—; mem. vis. com. So. Assn. Colls. and Schs., 1992—; mem. Small Libr. Product Adv. Bd., 1992-94; mem. adv. bd. Highlands County Law Libr., 1993-94; spkr. in field. Contbr. articles to profl. jours. Mem. ALA, Assn. Coll. and Rsch. Librs., Fla. Assn. C.C. (pres. local chpt. 1993), Fla. Libr. Assn. (chair cmty./jr. coll caucus 1992-93). Office: S Fla CC 600 W College Dr Avon Park FL 33825

TEWHEY, KAREN MARIE, special education and mental health administrator; b. Cambridge, Mass., Nov. 21, 1949; d. John Richard and Alice (Smith) Donovan; m. James Richard Tewhey, Feb. 18, 1981; children: Katherine Michaela, James Allyn Tripoli. BA, Simmons Coll., Boston, 1971; MA, Lesley Coll., Cambridge, 1976. Cert. tchr., prin., Mass. Spl. edn. tchr. Krebs Sch., Lexington, Mass., 1976-79, Judge Baker Guidance Clinic, Boston, 1979-80; coord. Hampshire Collaborative, Northampton, Mass., 1980-81; therapeutic tchr. Amherst (Mass.) Elem. Schs., 1985-86; coord. Amherst Alternative High Sch., 1981-85; prin. Mass. Migrant Edn., Holyoke, 1986; edn. specialist Dept. Edn., Boston, 1987-88; spl. edn./mental health adminstr. ABCD Head Start, Boston, 1988—; adj. faculty Urban Coll., Boston, 1990-94, Lesley Coll., 1988-90. Mem. Coun. for Exceptional Children (div. early childhood). Office: ABCD Head Start 178 Tremont St Boston MA 02111-1017

TEWKESBURY, JOAN F., film director, writer; b. Redlands, Calif., Apr. 8, 1936; d. Walter S. and Frances M. (Stevenson) T.; m. Robert F. Maguire, III, Nov. 30, 1960 (div.); children: Robin Tewkesbury, Peter Harlan. Student, Am. Sch. Dance, 1947-54, Mt. San Antonio Jr. Coll., Walnut, Calif., 1956-58; drama scholar, U. So. Calif., 1958-60. Dancer in: film Unfinished Dance, 1946; dancer, flying understudy Peter Pan, LosAngeles and N.Y.C., 1954-55; choreographer film, Los Angeles, 1958-70, tchr. dance and drama, U. So. Calif., 1966-69, Immaculate Heart Coll., Los Angeles, 1960-63, Am. Sch. Dance, Los Angeles, 1959-69; tchr. film writing UCLA, 1986; choreographer, dir., actress, U. So. Calif. Repetory Co., 1965-68, London and Edinburgh (Scotland) Festival, 1965-68; scriptgirl: film McCabe and Mrs. Miller, 1970; author: screenplays Thieves Like Us, 1974, Nashville, 1975 (Los Angeles Critics Best Screenplay award), A Night in Heaven, 1983; playwright, dir. Cowboy Jack Street, 1978; dir. film Old Boyfriends, 1979; film writer, dir. TV 10th Month, 1979, The Acorn People, 1981; dir. film documentary Anna Freud, 1976; writer, dir. (TV show) Alfred Hitchcock Presents, from 1986, (TV movie for TNT) Cold Sassy Tree, 1989; screenwriter, dir., scriptwriter, co-exec. producer TV pilot Elysian Fields, 1988; dir. (Time-Life cable TV film) Sudie and Simpson; scriptwriter, dir.(TV) Shannon's Deal; dir. (TV movie) Wild Texas Wind, 1991, The Stranger (HBO), 1992; dir. (TV episodes) Northern Exposure, 1992, Picket Fences, 1992, Doogie Hauser, 1992; dir.(theater) Chippy, 1993; dir. (TV movie Disney Cable) On Promised Land, 1993. Mem. Literacy Vols. Am. Mem. Writers Guild Am., Dirs. Guild Am., ACLU, Nat. Abortion Rights Action League, Calif. Abortion Rights Action League. Office: care Jane Sindell Creative Artists Agy 1888 Century Park E Ste 1400 Los Angeles CA 90067-1718*

THACKER, CHERYL LYNN, development officer, fund raiser; b. Orange City, Iowa, Mar. 1, 1960; d. Donald Dale and Morla Glee (Essman) Baker; m. Jeffrey Walter Thacker, July 7, 1990; children: Christopher Allen, Craig Thomas; 1 stepchild, Casey Anne. BA in Social Scis. and English, Sioux Falls Coll., 1982. Prodn. asst. KELO-TV, Sioux Falls, S.D., 1980-83; announcer, news dir. KELO-FM Radio, Sioux Falls, S.D., 1980-83, KLQL-KQAD, Luverne, Minn., 1983-84; pub. rels., devel. dir. Ga. Bapt. Children's Homes and Family Ministries, Inc., Atlanta, 1984-91; dir. annual scholar fund Sioux Falls Coll., 1991-94; dir. mktg., pub. rels. and devel. Family Svc., Inc., Sioux Falls, 1994—. Playwright: Bethlehem and Beyond, 1986. Supt. Sunday sch. Community Reformed Ch., Sioux Falls, 1993-94. Named Nat. Merit finalist, 1978. Mem. Nat. Soc. Fund-Raising Execs. (state program coun. 1993-94). Republican. Home: 2517 S Norton Sioux Falls SD 57105

THALER, NANCY REGINA, state agency administrator; b. Kingston, Pa., Apr. 2, 1949; d. Walter Raymond and Dolores Bernadette (Gitautis) Kuzma; m. Karl Williams, Dec. 26, 1970; 1 child, Aaron Richards. BA in Music, Coll. Misericordia, Dallas, Pa., 1971; MA in Human Sci., Villanova U., 1989. Special edn. tchr. Lacawanna Intermediate, Scranton, Pa., 1971-72; childcare aid Ken Crest Svcs., Plymouth Meeting, Pa., 1972-74, houseparent in group home, 1974-78, dir. residential scvs., 1978-87; dir. bur. community programs Dept. Pub. Welfare, Commonwealth of Pa., Harrisburg, Pa., 1987-92; dep. sec. Office of Mental Retardation, Dept. Pub. Welfare, Commonwealth of Pa., Harrisburg, Pa., 1992—. Recipient Positive Approaches award Assn. Persons with Severe Handicaps, San Francisco, 1993. Office: Office Mental Retardation Rm 512 Health Welfare Bldg Harrisburg PA 17105-2675

THARP, KAREN ANN, insurance agent; b. Montpelier, Ohio, Sept. 24, 1944; d. Howard Wesley and Thelma (Myers) Skiles; children: Pamela Lyn Tharp Grasso, James Alan, Jennifer Ann. Grad. high sch., Edon, Ohio. Sales agt. Equitable Life, Delray Beach, Fla., 1978-79; owner, pres. Fin. Profiles, Inc., Coral Springs, Fla., 1980—. Mem. Nat. Assn. Life Underwriters, Million Dollar Round Table. Republican. Home: 10992 NW 13th Ct Pompano Beach FL 33071-8211 Office: Fin Profiles Inc 10101A W Sample Rd Pompano Beach FL 33065-3997

THARP, TWYLA, dancer, choreographer; b. Portland, Ind., July 1, 1941; m. Peter Young (div.); m. Robert Huot (div.); 1 child, Jesse. Student, Pomona Coll.; BA in Art History, Barnard Coll., 1963; D of Performing Arts (hon.), Calif. Inst. Arts, 1978, Brown U., 1981, Bard Coll., 1981; LHD, Ind. U., 1987; DFA, Pomona Coll., 1987; studied with Richard Thomas, Merce Cunningham, Igor Schwezoff, Louis Mattox, Paul Taylor, Margaet Craske, Erick Hawkins. With Paul Taylor Dance Co., 1963-65; freelance choreographer with own modern dance troupe and various other cos. including Joffrey Ballet and Am. Ballet Theatre, 1965-87; founder Twyla Tharp Dance Found., N.Y.C., 1965-87; artistic assoc. Am. Ballet Theatre, N.Y.C., 1988-91; teaching residencies various colls. and univs. including U. Mass., Oberlin Coll., Walker Art Ctr., Boston U.; choreographer White Oak Dance Project. Choreographer: Tank Dive, 1965, Re-Moves, 1966, One Two Three, 1966, Forevermore, 1967, Generation, 1968, Medley, 1969, After Suite, 1969, Dancing in the Streets of London and Paris, 1969, The One Hundreds, 1970, The Fugue, 1971, The Big Pieces, 1971, Eight Jelly Rolls, 1971, The Raggedy Dances, 1972, Deuce Coupe, 1973, As Time Goes By, 1974, Sue's Leg, 1975, Ocean's Motion, 1975, Push Comes to Shove, 1976, Once More Frank, 1976, Mud, 1977, Baker's Dozen, 1979, When We Were Very Young, 1980, The Catherine Wheel, 1981 (Emmy award nom. Outstanding Choreography, 1982), Bach Partita, 1984, The Little Ballet, 1984, In the Upper Room, 1987, Everlast, 1989, Quartet, 1989, Bum's Rush, 1989, The Rules of the Game, 1990, The Men's Piece, 1991, (with Mikhail Baryshnikov) Cutting Up, 1992-93, Demeter and Persephone, 1993, Waterbaby Bagatelles, 1994, Demeter and Persephone, 1994, Red, White & Blues, 1995; (film) Hair, 1979, Ragtime, 1981, Amadeus, 1984, White Nights, 1985; (video spls.) Making Television Dance, 1977, CBS Cable Confessions of a Corner Maker, 1980; (Broadway shows) Sorrow Floats, 1985, Singin' In The Rain, 1985; (TV) Baryshnikov by Tharp (Emmy award Outstanding Choreography, 1985, Emmy award Outstanding Writing of Classical Music/Dance Programming, 1985, Emmy award Outstanding Directing of Classical Music/Dance Programming, 1985), The Catherine Wheel; author (autobiography): When Push Comes to Shove, 1992. MacArthur Found. Chgo. fellow, 1992; recipient Creative Arts award Brandeis U., 1972, Dance mag. award, 1981, Univ. Excellence medal Columbia U., 1987, Lions of the Performing Arts award N.Y. Pub. Libr., 1989, Samuel M. Scripps award Am. Dance Festival, 1990. Office: Twyla Tharp Dance Found care MPL Productions 170 W 74th St New York NY 10023-2350 Office: care PMX 1776 Broody 8th Fl New York NY 10019*

THAYER, EDNA LOUISE, service executive, nurse; b. Madelia, Minn., May 21, 1936; d. Walter William Arthur and Hilda Engel Emily Ann (Geistfeld) Wilke; m. David LeRoy Thayer, Aug. 30, 1958; children: Scott, Tamara, Brenda. Diploma in nursing, Bethesda Luth., 1956; BS in Nursing Edn., U. Minn., 1960; MSN, Washington U., St. Louis, 1966; MS in Counseling, Mankato (Minn.) State U., 1972. Cert. nursing adminstr. advanced ANA. Nurse Bethesda Luth. Hosp., St. Paul, 1956-58, U. Minn. Hosp., Mpls., 1958; from nurse to asst. head nurse supr., edn. dir. Fairmont (Minn.) Community Hosp., 1959-63; instr. Alton (Ill.) Meml. Hosp., 1963-66; from nursing instr. to assoc. prof. and dean Sch. Nursing Mankato State U., 1966-77; asst. adminstr. Rice County Dist. One Hosp., Faribault, Minn., 1977-89; RN, adminstrv. supr. St. Peter (Minn.) Regional Treatment Ctr., 1990—; nurse surveyor Minn. Dept. Tech. Edn., St. Paul, 1980-93; mem. adv. co. LPN and MA programs Tech. Inst., Faribault, 1977—. Mem. Rice County Ext. Bd., Faribault, 1986-91, adult leader 4-H Club, Rice County and St. Paul, 1971—; advisor Med. Explorers, Faribault, 1977-89; mem. Rep. Rodosovich Health Com., Faribault, 1984-94; coun. mem. Our Savior's Luth. Ch., Faribault, 1984-87. Recipient Alumni award Nat. 4-H Club, 1983. Mem. Minn. Orgn. Nurse Execs. (bd. dirs. 1987-89), Dist. F Nursing Svc. Adminstrs. (pres. 1980-82), Minn. Nurses Assn. (bd. dirs. 1982-87, Pres.'s award 1983, pres. 5th dist. 1974, 75, pres. 13th dist. 1984-86), AAUW, Sigma Theta Tau, Delta Kappa Gamma (pres. Pi chptr. 1982-84, Woman of Achievement award 1985), Hosp. Aux. Republican. Home: RR 1 Box 7B Elysian MN 56028-9801 Office: Saint Peter Regional Treatment Ctr 100 Freeman Dr Saint Peter MN 56082-1599

THAYER, JANE See WOOLLEY, CATHERINE

THAYER, MARTHA ANN, small business owner; b. Santa Fe, N.Mex., May 8, 1936; d. Duren Howard and Lena Odessa (Fox) Shields; m. Norman S. Thayer Jr., Jan. 30, 1960; children: Murray Norman, Tanya Noelle. BS, U. N.Mex., 1960. Child welfare worker State of N.Mex., Farmington and Santa Fe, 1961-63; owner Baskets by Thayer, Albuquerque, 1975-83, Noelle's, Albuquerque, 1985-89; ptnr., co-owner Indian Originals, Albuquerque, 1989-94; co-owner S.W. Originals, 1995—; crafts instr. Village Wool, Continuing Edn., Albuquerque, 1975-78; trustee Shields Trust, 1994—; treas. DHS Properties, Inc., 1994—. Contbr. articles, revs. to craft publs.; juried show, Mus. of Internat. Folk Arts, 1975; baskets exhibited in group shows at N.Mex. State Fair, 1980 (1st place award), Women's Show, 1983 (1st place award). Campaign mgr. Dem. Candidate for State Supreme Ct., Bernalillo County, N.Mex., 1970; founding mem. Women's Polit. Caucus, Bernalillo County; chmn. Mother's March of Dimes, Bernalillo County, 1974. Mem. AAUW, Hist. Preservation Soc., Petroleum Club, Genealogy Club of Albuquerque Pub. Libr., Albuquerque Tennis Club. Office: SW Originals 1516 Plaza Encantada NW Albuquerque NM 87107

THEISEN, MARIBETH, psychotherapist; b. Anchorage, May 15, 1956; d. Emmett John and Mabel Adele (Bubb) T.; m. Mark Randall Dreher, Aug. 15, 1981 (div. Dec. 1989); m. Jeffrey Bruce Weinrach, July 9, 1994. BA in Psychology & Social Work, Oral Roberts U., 1977; MSW, La. State U., 1982; postgrad., Our Lady of the Shining Star, 1994—. Lic. ind. social worker N.Mex., advanced clin. practitioner, Tex. Psychiat. social worker State of La., Jackson, 1982-84; foster care worker State of La., Baton Rouge, 1984; tchr. broadcast copywriting, scriptwriting U. North Tex., Denton, 1988-90; pvt. investigator Equifax Svcs., Dallas, 1988; med. social worker Dallas Hospice Care, 1990-91; program therapist Twin Lakes Hosp., Denton, 1991-92; clin. case mgr. Preferred Health Care, Dallas, 1992; employee assistance counselor Sandia Nat. Labs., Albuquerque, 1992-93; psychotherapist pvt. practice, Albuquerque, 1992—; prof., career counselor Our Lady of Shining Star Sem., Gallup, N.Mex., 1994—. Writer, vocalist (record) A Secret Place, 1977; documentary videographer. Recipient Honorable Mention, Assn. Visual Communicators, 1989. Mem. NASW. Office: 6020 Acad NE Ste 204 Albuquerque NM 87109

THELIAN, LORRAINE, public relations executive; b. N.Y.C., Jan. 13, 1948; d. Anthony G. and Inez (Gelfo) Bufano. BA, Molloy Coll., 1969. Account coordinator Basford Pub. Rels., N.Y.C., 1969-71; from asst. account exec. through v.p. Paluszek & Leslie Assoc., N.Y.C., 1971-74; sr. v.p., assoc. dir. Ketchum Pub. Rels., Washington, 1985-91, exec. v.p., dir., 1991—, mem. pub. affairs coun., 1990—; bd. dirs. Ketchum Comm., Inc., Washington, 1994—; mem. Pub. Affairs Coun., 1990—; mem. Washington Bd. Trade, 1987—; bd. dirs. Ketchum Comm., Inc. Mem. Pub. Rels. Soc. Am. (accredited, chmn. accreditation com. Washington chpt. 1987), Washington Comms. Assn., Women in Pub. Rels. (adv. panel 1994, honoree Pub. Rels. Woman of Yr. 1993). Roman Catholic. Office: Ketchum Pub Rels 1201 Connecticut Ave NW # 300 Washington DC 20036-2605

THEVENET, PATRICIA CONFREY, social studies educator; b. Norwich, Conn., Apr. 16, 1924; d. John George and Gertrude Pauline (Doolittle) Confrey; m. Rubén Thevenet, Dec. 15, 1945 (dec. Mar. 1983); children: Susanne, Gregory, Richard, R. James. BS, U. Conn., 1944; AM, U. Chgo., 1945; EdM, Columbia U., 1992, EdD, 1994. Cert. elem. tchr., N.J. Counselor testing and guidance U. Chgo., 1945; home economist Western Mass. Electric Co., Pittsfield, 1946; tchr. Unquowa Sch., Fairfield, Conn., 1950-53, Alpine (N.J.) Sch., 1958-86; program asst. soc. studies Tchrs. Coll. Columbia U., N.Y.C., 1987-93; ret., 1993; historian Borough Northvale, N.J., 1987-94; participant summer seminar Smithsonian Instn., Washington, 1984. Del 2d dist. rep. Town Mtg., Trumbull, Conn., 1954-56; pres., trustee Northvale Pub. Libr. Assn., 1957-63; trustee Northvale Bd. Edn., 1963-72, pres. Northvale Bd. Edn., 1969-70; exec. bd. dirs. Bergen County (N.J.) County Bds. Edn., 1965-72; mem. Evening Sch. Comm. No. Valley Regional Dist., Bergen County, 1976-83. Mem. AAUW, Am. Hist. Assn., Nat. Coun. Social Studies, Alumni Coun. Tchrs. Coll., Columbia U. Home: 88 B North Shore Rd Voluntown CT 06384

THIBAUDEAU, MAY MURPHY, writer; b. Nasboro, Wis., May 8, 1908; d. Hugh Isadore and Laura (Brown) Murphy; m. Raymond Joseph Thibaudeau, June 16, 1941; children: Adele, Yvonne, Clairese, Camille, Valerie, Marguerete, Hugh. BS, U. Wis., Milw., 1973. Lic. tchr., Wis. Tchr. rural state graded Fond du Lac County, Wis., 1927-34; tchr. city graded City of Peshtigo (Wis.), 1934-42; tchr. grade 3 St. Mary's Parish, South Milwaukee, Wis., 1956-75; writer South Milwaukee, 1976—. Author: Life and Times of Frederick Layton, 1984, I Shall Not Die I Shall Live on in You, 1990 (State Assembly citation 1990), The Donkey Stayed in Ireland, 1980. Pres. Fond du Lac County Tchrs. Assn., 1933-34; mem. Wis. Edn. Assn., Madison, 1935-42, Nat. Cath. Edn. Assn., Washington, 1956-75, Common Cause, Washington, 1975—, LWV, Washington, 1985-90; leader Girl Scouts U.S., Milw., 1955-62. Mem. Wis. Regional Writers, Writers Ink, AAUW (Edn. Found. Name grantee 1990). Democrat. Roman Catholic. Home: 1212 N Chicago Ave South Milwaukee WI 53172-1633

THIBAUDEAUX, MARY FRANCES, cultural organization administrator; b. Anaconda, Mont., Dec. 6, 1943; d. Frank Albert and Mary (May) T.; m. Alex W. Wells, Jr.; 1 child, Christopher. BA magna cum laude, U. Washington, Seattle, 1969. Therapist, counselor Thibaudeaux and Assocs., Atlanta, 1976-88; chmn. Vietnam Reconciliation Bus. Group, Atlanta, 1988—; cons. Ga. Vets. Leadership Program, Atlanta, 1994. Exec. prodr. (documentary) Vietnam: The Final Healing, 1991; co-author, editor (screenplay) Perfume River, 1995. Exchange dir. Friendship Force Internat., Atlanta, 1993-94. Named Ga. Outstanding Citizen, Ga. Sec. State, 1994. Mem. Atlanta Vets. Assn. (hon.). Home: 185 Softwood Cir Roswell GA 30076

THIBODEAU, JUDITH ANN, physical therapist; b. New London, Conn., Oct. 1, 1963; d. Richard Michael and Evelyn Joyce (Chambliss) Silva; m. Peter Paul Thibodeau, Oct. 1, 1988; children: Kaylee Marie, Matthew Alan, Richard Norman. BS, U. Conn., 1985. Staff phys. therapist Youville Rehab. Ctr., Cambridge, Mass., 1986-87, Middlesex Meml. Hosp., Middletown, Conn., 1987-88; phys. therapist II Seaside Regional Ctr., Dept. Mental Retardation, Waterford, Conn., 1987-89; phys. therapist Phys. Therapy Svcs. of New London, 1989-90; area rehab. coord. Nutmeg Pavilion Healthcare, New London, 1989-92; phys. therapist Bride Brook Rehab. Ctr., East Lyme, Conn., 1992—; home care phys. therapist Groton (Conn.) Pub. Health Nursing Ctr., 1992—, Waterford (Conn.) Pub. Health Nursing Svc., 1992—; contract phys. therapist Waterford Pub. Schs. Spl. Svcs., 1993-94. Democrat. Roman Catholic. Home: 2 Rosemarie Ct Ledyard CT 06339-1221

THIBODEAU, ROBIN ANN, mail carrier, union official; b. Southington, Conn., Oct. 27, 1956; d. Robert Edward and Irene Josephine (Bendott) Dunbar; m. Roland Leo Thibodeau, Feb. 25, 1978 (div. Aug. 1983); children: Christina Ann Thibodeau, Desilyn Joanne Nelson. Grad. high sch., Southington; grad., Porter & Chester Auto. Inst. Sec. Bd. of Edn., Southington, 1974-75; cashier, clk. Cumberland Farms, Plantsville, Conn., 1974; acctg. clk. to contr. Waterbury Farrel, Mfg., Cheshire, Conn., 1975-76; machinist Supreme Lake Mfg., Plantsville, 1976-77; auto transmission re-builder Transmission Works, Hartford, Conn., 1978-79; rural carrier substitute Southington Post Office, 1979-81, Terryville (Conn.) Post Office, 1980; regular rural carrier Plainville (Conn.) Post Office, 1981-84, Farmington (Conn.) Post Office, 1984—; local union steward Plainville Post Office, 1981-84; local/area steward Farmington Post Office, 1985-94. Democrat. Home: 17 Spruce St Plainville CT 06062 Office: Conn Rural Letter Carrier Assn 210 Main St Farmington CT 06032

THIEL, RUTH ELEANOR, real estate broker; b. Chgo., June 11, 1930; d. Frank A. and Lucille L. (Bromm) Dell; m. Joseph Donald Thiel, Sept. 30, 1950; children: Michael F., Jeffrey D., Patti Thiel Pavey, Mary Beth Thiel Davies, Tracy J. Thiel Carroll. Grad. Evanston Twp. Community Coll., 1950, Realtors Inst., 1972. Sales assoc. Indian Hill Realty, Winnetka, Ill., 1967; v.p., mgr. Mitchell Bros. Realtors, Northbrook, Ill., 1972-75; exec. v.p., gen. mgr. Century 21 Mitchell Bros., Evanston, Ill., 1975-82; v.p. Koenig & Strey Realtors, 1982-87; sr. v.p., 1987—. Mem. State of Ill. Real Estate Disciplinary Bd., 1977—, Evanston Econ. Devel. Com., 1979; treas. North Shore Assn. Retarded, 1977-79; mem. instl. rev. com. St. Francis Hosp., 1981—; mem. Evanston Zoning Bd., 1983-85; pres. Evanston Library Friends, 1984-86; alderman 2d Ward, City of Evanston, 1985-86. Recipient Ill. Women's Council of Realtors Woman of the Year award, 1979, 93; Service award City of Hope, North Shore Assn. for Retarded, 1977. Mem. Nat. Assn. Realtors (bd. dirs. 1978-91), Ill. Assn. Realtors (exec. com. 1979, bd. dirs. 1977-85, Realtor of Yr. award 1984), North Shore Bd. Realtors (dir. 1970-80), Evanston North Shore Bd. Realtors (pres. 1978), Women's Council Realtors (state pres. 1977), Women in Real Estate (award 1980). Clubs: Woman of Evanston, Million Dollar, Zonta Club of Evanston (pres. 1994—), Kiwanis (pres. Glenview-Northbrook chpts. 1990-91). Office: Koenig & Strey Realtors 2528 Green Bay Rd Evanston IL 60201

THIEL, THELMA KING, foundation executive; b. East Orange, N.J., Feb. 12, 1926; d. Thaddeus and Elizabeth Clara (Fickert) King; m. Charles T. Thiel, Mar. 25, 1954 (div. 1976); children: Mark Douglas, Donna Kalani, Dean Alan (dec.). B.A. in Health Edn. and Sch. Nursing, Jersey City State Coll., 1973. Cert. health educator, N.J. Exec. dir. Am. Council for Healthful Living, East Orange, 1973-79; commr. Nat. Com. of Digestive Diseases, Bethesda, Md., 1977-79; founder, chair Dean Thiel Found., Cedar Grove, N.J., 1971—; vice chmn, exec. dir. Am. Liver Found., Cedar Grove, N.J., 1979-84, pres., COO, 1984-94; founder, chair, CEO Hepatitis Found. Internat., 1994—. active Nat. Digestive Diseases Adv. Bd.; advisor Nat. Digestive Diseases Edn. and Info. Clearinghouse; charter mem. Rutgers U. Sch. Communication, Info. and Library Studies Bd. of Adv. Assocs. Author: Foundation for Decision Making, 1978. Mem. AAUW, Digestive Diseases Nat. Coalition (chmn. 1985-90, chmn. Nat. Health Coun., nom. com. 1989-91), Am. Nursing Assn., Soroptimist Internat., Am. Assn. Occupational Health Nurses, Nat. Soc. Fund Raising Execs. Presbyterian (elder). Office: 30 Sunrise Terr Cedar Grove NJ 07009-1423

THIELE, GLORIA DAY, retired librarian, small business owner; b. Los Angeles, Sept. 4, 1931; d. Russell Day Plummer and Dorothy Ruby (Day) Plummer Thi.; m. Donald Edward Cools, June 13, 1953 (div.); children: Michael, Ramona, Naomi, Lawrence, Nancy, Rebecca, Eugene, Maria, Charles. MusB, Mt. St. Mary's Coll., L.A., 1953. Libr. asst. Anaheim (Calif.) Pub. Libr., 1970-73, head Biblioteca de la Comunidad, 1973-74, children's libr. asst., 1974-76, children's br. specialist, 1976-78, children's libr., 1978-81; head children's svcs. Santa Maria (Calif.) Pub. Libr., 1981-85; cons. Literature Continuum, Santa Maria Sch. Dist., 1981-85; cons. Organizational Ch.-Sch. Libr., L.A., 1980; guest lectr. children's lit. Allan Hancock Coll., Santa Maria, 1981-85; owner, founder Discovery Garden, Grass Valley, Calif., 1989-93. Libr. liaison Casa Amistad Community Svc. Group, Anaheim, 1973-74; mem. outreach com. Santiago Libr. System, Orange County, 1973-74, mem. children's svcs. com., 1971-81; mem. Community Svcs. Coordinating Council, Santa Maria, 1982-85; chairperson children's svcs. com. Black Gold Libr. System, 1983-84; cons. children's libr. programs, 1986—; profl. storyteller, 1989—. Contbr. poems to Amherst Soc.'s Am. Poetry Ann., 1988. Mem. So. Calif. Council Lit. for Children and Young People, Kiwanis, Delta Epsilon Sigma. Republican. Roman Catholic.

THIELEN, CYNTHIA HENRY, lawyer, state legislator. Student, Stanford U., 1951-52, UCLA, 1952-53; BA with high honors, U. Hawaii, 1975, JD, 1978. Staff atty. Legal Aid Soc. Hawaii, 1979-84; staff atty. planning and zoning com. Honolulu City Coun., 1984-85; sr. litigation assoc. Brown, Johnston & Day, 1985-88; pvt. practice Honolulu, 1988-93; ptnr. Gerson Grekin Wynhoff & Thielen, Honolulu, 1994—. Editor Windward Community Newspaper, 1969-71. Mem. State Ho. of Reps., 1990—, minority floor leader, 1992—; mem. State Hwy Safety Coun., 1977-81, State Environ. Coun., 1984-87, Nature Conservancy, Hist. Hawai'i; bd. dirs. Hanahauoli Sch., 1976-86, Hawaii Women's Polit. Action League, 1987; candidate for lt. gov., Hawaii, 1986; v.p. State Helicopter and Tour Aircraft Adv. Bd., 1986-88, Kailua Neighborhood Bd., 1987-89; pres. Hawaii Children's Mus. Arts, Sci. and Tech., 1987-88, mem., 1987-90; chair Mayor's Adv. Task Force on the Environ., 1989-90. Sixth generation direct descendant of Patrick Henry. Mem. LWV, ABA, Hawaii Bar Assn., Hawaii Women Lawyers (chartered), Orgn. Women Leaders, Stanford Club. Office: State Capitol 235 S Beretania St Rm 1107 Honolulu HI 96813-2437

THIER, MARIAN JOYCE, management consultant, writer; b. Allentown, Pa., May 5, 1939; d. Isadore Rapoport and Libbie (Cooper) Twining; m. Jerome M. Thier, Aug. 6, 1962 (div. 1982); children: Whitney, Antony Michael, J. Alexander. BS in Drama, Skidmore Coll., 1961; MA in Adult Devel., Temple U., 1980. Tchr. creative writing Abington Heights Sch. Dist., Clarks Summit, Pa., 1961-64; producer, writer, moderator Sta. WVIA-TV, Plains, Pa., 1965-72; course developer Internat. Corr., Scranton, Pa., 1972-74; coordinator acad. support services Keystone Coll., La Plume, Pa., 1974-85; v.p. The Communication Link, Florham Park, N.J., 1985-87; prin. Marian Thier & Assocs., N.Y.C., 1987—, Expanding Thought, Boulder, Colo., 1993—. Inventor (game) Think Tank: The Game of Creative Problem Solving, 1986; author: The Journey, A Fable; co-developer: The Genesis Creativity Audit; contbr. articles to profl. jours. Mem. Assn. Tng. and Devel., The Friday Group, Nat. Soc. Performance and Instrn., Assn. Quality and Productivity, Skidmore Coll. Alumnae Assn. Office: Expanding Thought 3180 Westwood Ct Boulder CO 80304

THIERYUNG, KAREN JEAN, accountant; b. Bklyn., Dec. 18, 1967; d. Nikolaus and Ruth (Denzer) T. AA with honors, Pasco-Hernando C.C., 1991; BS in Acctg. summa cum laude, Tampa Coll., 1993. Gen. office clk. Marsha's Dept. Store, Huntington, N.Y., 1984; bookkeeper Hernando Egg Producers, Masaryktown, Fla., 1985-88; acct. U. Med. Svc. Assn. Dept. Psychiatry U. South Fla., Tampa, Fla., 1993—. Mem. Inst. Mgmt. Accts., Phi Theta Kappa. Office: U South Fla Dept Psychiatry 3515 E Fletcher Ave Tampa FL 33613

THIESSEN, LAURA JANE, secondary education educator; b. Clinton, Okla., Oct. 22, 1964; d. Abe Curt and Kathrine Marie (Hornsby) T. BS in Office Adminstrn., Southwestern Okla. State U., 1986, BS in Bus. Edn., 1986, MEd, 1987. Cert. secodary tchr., Okla. Educator Felt (Okla.) Pub. Sch., 1987-89, Hydro (Okla.) Pub. Sch., 1989—. Democrat.

THIMSEN-WHITAKER, KATHI, nursing administrator; b. Red Bud, Ill., Sept. 18, 1953; d. Udell S. and Dolores M. (Hauser) Thimsen; m. Jeffrey D. Whitaker, July 4, 1987; children: Justin, Chad, Randi, Andrea. BSN, Webster U., 1992, postgrad., 1993—. Bd. cert. E.T. nursing. E.T. nurse Meml. Hosp., Belleville, Ill., 1979-85; corp. tng. dir. Roho, Inc., Belleville, 1987-89, profl. rels. dir.; dir. E.T. nursing Jewish Hosp., St. Louis, 1989-90; pres. Whitaker Care Cons., 1991—; v.p. Pathways to Empowerment, LLC, 1990; mem. steering com. Hospice So. Ill.; intern Nurse in Wash., 1988. Contbr. articles to profl. jours. Elder Peace Luth. Ch. Recipient Humanitarian award Hosp. Assn. St. Louis, Elks Leadership award. Mem. WOCN (profl. rels., midwest regional v.p., govt. affairs, scholar), ANA, INA, WCET. Home: 35 Metcalf Dr Belleville IL 62223-1917

THODE, MARY JOAN, educational program coordinator; b. Ashland, Wis., July 28, 1952; d. Walter David and Anne Isabel (Gima) Stadler; m. Thomas Alan Thode, Aug. 2, 1979. BS, U. Minn., 1974; MA, No. Ariz. U., 1982; MA in Spanish, U. Ariz., 1993. Cert. tchr., Ariz. Bilingual counselor Behavioral Health Svcs., Yuma, Ariz., 1975-81; guidance counselor Kofa High Sch., Yuma, 1981-91; program coord. Crane Elem. Sch. Dist., Yuma, 1991—; part-time tchr. Spanish Ariz. Western Coll., Yuma, 1978-93. Bd. dirs. Rainbow Ctr. for Exceptional Children, Yuma, 1982-93; chair edn. com. Yuma County/San Luis Commn., Yuma, 1992-93. Recipient award Ariz. Minority Access and Achievement Coop., 1991, Golden Bell award Ariz. State Sch. Bd. Assn., 1993. Mem. Yuma County C. of C., Delta Kappa Gamma. Democrat. Roman Catholic. Office: Pueblo Sch Migrant Even Start Program 2803 W 20th St Yuma AZ 85364-5059

THOEN, CYNTHIA NIBLOCK, educator; b. Lansing, Mich., June 11, 1957; d. James Franklin and Helen (Beall) Niblock; m. Lawrence Edward Egly, Aug. 4, 1979 (div. June 1991); m. Randall Craig Thoen, Oct. 16, 1992. BA in Elem. and Spl. Edn., Mich. State U., 1978, MA in Spl. Edn., 1981. Spl. edn. tchr. Doris Klaussen Devel. Ctr., Battle Creek, Mich., 1978, Laurel (Nebr.) Elem. Sch., 1978-79, Moose Lake (Minn.) Pub. Schs., 1979-80; spl. edn. tchr. Esko (Minn.) Pub. Schs., 1980-84, K-12 coord. gifted/talented, 1982-84; spl. edn. and reading tchr. Anoka (Minn.)-Hennepin Schs., 1984-86; behavior analyst Anoka (Minn.)-Hennepin Schs., Coon Rapids, Minn., 1986-88; spl. edn. tchr. Anoka (Minn.)-Hennepin Schs., Andover, Minn., 1988—. Lutheran.

THOLE, MARY ELIZABETH, insurance company executive; b. Salt Lake City, July 29, 1950; d. John Bernard and Emily Josephine T. BA, U. Hawaii, Hilo, 1984, paralegal cert. cum laude, 1989; postgrad., U. Hawaii, Manoa, 1985-86. Lic. ins. agt. Hawaii, Calif., Fla., N.C. Regional rep. Lightolier, Inc., Salt Lake City, 1978-80; group sales rep. FHP/Utah, Salt Lake City, 1980-81; health net rep. Blue Cross Corp., L.A., 1981-82; v.p. fin. Bus. Support Systems, Hilo, 1983-89; rep. Prudential Ins. and Fin. Svcs., Hilo, 1989—; registered rep. Pruco Securities Corp., 1989—. Docent Lyman House, 1984-85, L.A. County Mus. of Art, 1980-81, S.L.C. Art Mus., 1970-80; bd. dirs. YWCA, Hawaii Island, 1980-91, 1st v.p., 1988. Recipient Nat. Quality award 1991, 92, 93, Nat. Sales Achievement award 1992, 93; named YWCA Vol. of Yr., 1991. Fellow Life Underwriters Tng. Coun.; mem. AAUW (fundraiser chair Kona chpt. 1992, bd. dirs. Hilo chpt. 1987-89, cmty. area rep. 1989), Am. Bus. Women's Assn. (cmty. svc. chair 1993-95, audit com. chair Kanoelani chpt. 1992, program chair Hilo chpt. 1985, expansion com. Hilo Lehua chpt. 1985, Steven Bufton grantee 1985, ways and means com. 1984, membership chair Lehua chpt. 1983), Nat. Assn. Life Underwriters (legis. rep. West Hawaii 1989—), Million Dollar Round Table (qualifying mem. 1992, 93, 94). Roman Catholic. Home: Prudential Ins Co Am PO Box 4638 Hilo HI 96720

THOMA, MARTA RUTH, artist; b. Lincoln, Nebr., Nov. 25, 1951; d. Clemens Berandt and Evelyn Clair (Butler) Thoman; m. Michael Hodges, Dec. 21, 1974; children: Michelle, Nicole, Heidi. BFA, U. Calif., Berkeley, 1973; MFA, San Francisco State U., 1975. with Norcal Artist-in-Residence Program, San Francisco. One person show includes J. Claramunt Gallery, N.Y., 1974-94, Works Gallery, San Jose, Calif., U. Oreg. Mus. Art; group exhibits include San Francisco Mus. Art, Portland Mus. Art, L.A. Mus. Art; contbr. detail arts to profl. jours. Arts Coun. Santa Clara fellow, 1992. Mem. South Bay Area Women's Caucus for Art (pres. 1989-92, v.p. 1992-94). Unitarian. Office: Cubberly Art Ctr 4000 Middlefield Rd # E5 Palo Alto CA 94303-4739

THOMAN, MARY E., rancher, vocational and secondary educator; b. Kemmerer, Wyo., Sept. 14, 1949; d. William J. and Mary A. (Ferentchak) T. AA, Western Wyo. C.C., Rock Springs, 1970; BS in Bus., U. Wyo., 1972; MEd in Mktg., Colo. State U., 1978, PhD in Secondary/Vocat. Adminstrn., 1981. Profl. Teaching Cert., Wyo. Bus. edn. Green River (Wyo.) High Sch., 1972-75; part time bus. and mktg. instr. Western Wyo. C.C., Green River, 1972-77, Rock Springs, Wyo., 1972-80, Kemmerer, Wyo., 1983—; mktg. and coop. educator Green River (Wyo.) High Sch., 1975-77; asst. dir. Nev. St. Coun. on Vocat. Edn., Carson City, Nev., 1977; exec. dir. Mont. St. Coun. on Vocat. Edn., Helena, Mont., 1981-82; owner Wyo. Cattle/Sheep Ranch, Kemmerer, 1981—; sr. sales dir. Mary Kay Cosmetics, Kemmerer, Wyo., 1988—; ednl. cons. past chair Wyo. St. Coun. on Vocat. Edn., Cheyenne, 1984-92; bus. cons. Western Wyo. Coll., Rock Springs, 1983—; edn. cons. Kemmerer Sch. Dist., 1993—; mem. Agr. in the Classroom, Douglas, Wyo., 1992-94. Fellow Ednl./Profl. Devel. Act, 1977-78, Grad. Leadership Devel. award, 1978-81. Mem. C. of C. Edn. Com., Kemmerer, Wyo. (bd. dirs. 1992—, active in western range issues, testified on range reform hearings), Cumberland Allotment Coordinated Resource Mgmt. Team. Roman Catholic. Home: PO Box 146 Green River WY 82935

THOMAS, ANNE J., retired educator, association executive; b. Denver, Aug. 12, 1911; d. Howard and Nell (Poage) Jenkins; m. Earl D. Thomas, Sept. 4, 1942 (dec. 1986). BA, U. Denver, 1932; MA, Northwestern U., 1936. Tchr., counselor Kansas City (Mo.) Sch. Bd., 1937-41. Pres. YWCA, Kansas City, 1949-51; nat. bd. dirs. YWCA of U.S.A., N.Y.C., 1955-75; mem. exec. com. World YWCA, Geneva, Switzerland, 1961-75; bd. dirs. Panel of Am. Women, Kansas City, 1961-71, ARC, Kansas City, 1968-69, Metro C.Cs., Kansas City, 1969-71, Continuing Edn. U. Mo., Kansas City, 1970-72. Recipient Disting. Citizen award NCCJ, 1964. Home: 333 Meyer W # 708 Kansas City MO 64113-1713

THOMAS, BARBARA ANN, record company executive; b. Bklyn., Feb. 5, 1958; d. Wilfred Godfrey and Violet Rose (Howell) Swaby; m. Ronald L. Hannah (div.). Adminstrv. asst. Million Dollar Record Poll, College Park, Ga., 1985-86, Points East Records, College Park, 1986-87, Greer Booking Agy., Atlanta, 1986-87; pres. Gunsmoke Records, College Park, 1988—; v.p. Toroy Mercedes Records, 1994—; mgr. Jesse James, 1983—. Mem. NAFE, Blues Found., Atlanta Top Star Awards, Nat. Young Black Programmers (bd. dirs.). Democrat. Roman Catholic. Office: Gunsmoke Records 2523 Roosevelt Hwy Ste 3D Atlanta GA 30337-6244

THOMAS, BARBARA DEE STEEN, women's health nurse; b. New Kensington, Pa., Feb. 10, 1963; d. Walter and Idella Lorraine (Mitchell) Steen; m. Steven Douglas Thomas, Sept. 14, 1985; 1 child, Justin Drew. BSN, Indiana U. of Pa., 1985. RN, N.C. Staff nurse John F. Kennedy Med. Ctr.; primary nurse Moses Cone Meml. Hosp., Greensboro, N.C. Mem. Sigma Theta Tau.

THOMAS, BARBARA SINGER, lawyer; b. N.Y.C., Dec. 28, 1946; d. Jules H. and Marcia (Bosniak) Singer; m. Allen Lloyd Thomas, Mar. 12, 1978; 1 child, Allen Lloyd Jr. B.A. cum laude, U. Pa., 1966; J.D. cum laude (John Norton Pomeroy scholar 1968-69, editor law rev. 1968-69, Jefferson Davis prize public law 1969), NYU, 1969. Bar: N.Y. 1969. Assoc. Paul, Weiss, Rifkind, Wharton & Garrison, N.Y.C., 1969-78; assoc. Kaye, Scholar, Fierman, Hayes & Handler, N.Y.C., 1973-77, ptnr., 1978-80; commr. SEC, Washington, 1980-83; pres. Samuel Montagu Holdings Inc., N.Y.C., 1984-86; regional dir. Asia Pacific Samuel Montagu Ltd., London, 1984-86; sr. v.p., group head The Internat. Pvt. Bank, Bankers Trust Co., N.Y.C., 1986-90; pres. The Geneva Capital Mgmt. Corp., N.Y.C., 1990-92; dir. bus. and legal affairs News Internat., London, 1993—; bd. dirs. United Asset Mgmt., Astro Comms., Inc., Watson Philip PLC. Mem. adv. coun. Women's Econ. Roundtable; mem. internat. adv. bd. Am. U.; mem. Women's Forum, London and N.Y.C.; bd. dirs. N.Y.C. Opera; bd. govs. U. Pa. Joseph H. Lauder Inst. Mgmt. and Internat. Studies; mem. bd. overseers Sch. Arts and Scis.; trustee Youth for Understanding, U. Pa. Alumni Assn., Wahsington Opera, Fin. Women's Assn., N.Y. Law Rev. Alumni Assn., Internat. House; mem. adv. com. Nat. Mus. Women's Art; mem. internat. com. N.Y.C. Ballet. Recipient award for outstanding service in govt. Fin. Mktg. Council Greater Washington, 1982, Woman of Achievement award WETA-FM, 1983; named one of Outstanding Young Women in Am., 1981, mem. of Men and Women Under 40 Changing Am., Esquire Mag., 1984, Baylor U. Woman of Yr., 1987. Mem. ABA, NAFE (bd. dirs.), Young Pres.' Orgn., Washington Bar Assn. (sect. on corp., banking and bus. law), N.Y. State Bar Assn., Internat. Bar Assn., Assn. Bar City of N.Y. (chmn. corp. law com. 1979-80), Global Econ. Action Inst., Coun. on Fgn. Rels., Order of Coif, Econ. Club N.Y., Cosmopolitan Club, River Club, The Reform Club (London), Hong Kong Club. Office: News Internat PLC, PO Box 495 1 Virginia St, London E1 9XY, England

THOMAS, BERTHA SOPHIA, office manager, paralegal; b. Chgo., May 18, 1959; d. James Winston, Jr. and Juanita (Smith) T.; 1 child, Kamarya Lynell. Cert., Am. Inst. Paralegal Studies, 1988; student, Nat. Coll. Edn., 1988—. Supr. filing systems Susan E. Loggans & Assocs., Chgo., 1979-81; legal sec. Harth, Stroger, Boarman & Blue, Chgo., 1982-83, Lidov & Block, Chgo., 1984-86; paralegal, office mgr. Law Office Mary L. Sfasciotti, Chgo., 1987-89; paralegal, personal injury specialist Neal B. Strom and Assocs., Ltd., Chgo., 1988-90; office mgr., paralegal Spencer W. Schwartz & Assocs., P.C., Chgo., 1990-93; co-owner B&B Paralegal Svc., Chgo., 1994—. Mem. NAFE, PHA, Ill. Notary Assn., Order Eastern Star, Heroines of Jericho, Daughters of Isis, Omega Pearl, Omega Psi Phi. Democrat. Roman Catholic. Home: 11329 S Peoria St Chicago IL 60643-4611 Office: B&B Paralegal Svc 11329 S Peoria Chicago IL 60643

THOMAS, BETH EILEEN WOOD (MRS. RAYMOND O. THOMAS), editor; b. North Vernon, Ind., May 12, 1916; d. Fayette J. and Emma J. (Ream) Wood; m. Raymond O. Thomas, Feb. 28, 1941; 1 son, Stephen W. Comml. diploma, Bedford High Sch., 1934; student, Lockyear Bus. Coll., 1936. Sec. WPA, Vincennes, Ind., 1935-36, Evansville, Ind., 1937-38, Indpls., 1939-41; sec. to adj. AAF Storage Depot, Indpls., 1941-44; sec. Coll. Life Ins., Indpls., 1957-58, Indpls. Sch. Bd., 1958-59; classified office mgr. North Side Topics Newspaper, Indpls., 1960-67. Editor: Child Life mag., 1967-71, Brownie Reader, 1971-73, Children's Playmate mag., 1968-91; editorial assoc. Saturday Evening Post, 1971; exec. editorial dir. Jack and Jill mag., 1971-91, Young World mag., 1971-79, Child Life mag., 1971-91, Design mag., 1977-80, Turtle mag. for Presch. Kids, 1979-91, Humpty Dumpty's mag., 1980-91, Children's Digest, 1980-91; editor emeritus juvenile mags., Children's Better Health Inst., 1991—. Mem. Women in Communications, Indpls. Press Club, Soc. Children's Book Writers. Club: Thetis. Home: 3831 Rue Voltaire Indianapolis IN 46220-1541 Office: Children's Better Health Inst Box 567 1100 Waterway Blvd Indianapolis IN 46202-2156

THOMAS, BETTY, actress; b. St. Louis. BFA, Ohio U. Former sch. tchr.; co-star Hill St. Blues, from 1981; joined Second City Workshop, Chgo.; appeared on Second City TV, 1984; appeared in after sch. spl. The Gift of Love, 1985, Prison of Children, 1986. Appeared in The Fun Factory game show, 1976; film: Troop Beverly Hills, 1989; in TV film Outside Chance, 1978, Nashville Grab, 1981, When Your Lover Leaves, 1983; star TV series Hill Street Blues, 1981-87 (Emmy nominations 1981, 82, 83); dir.: (TV) Dream On: "For Peter's Sake" (Emmy award, Outstanding Individual Achievement in Directing in a Comedy Series, 1993), 1993, (film) The Brady Bunch Movie, 1995. Emmy Best Supporting Actress, 1985. Office: care Internat Creative Mgmt 3100 N Damon Way Burbank CA 91505-1015*

THOMAS, BETTY RAE, nurse; b. Galveston, Tex., May 16, 1935; d. Dewey and Viola (Brown) Mosley; m. Lonnie K. Watkins, Feb. 10, 1954 (div. 1965); children: Lonnnitta, Denis, Mario, Danny; m. Edward Guidry Jr., 1968 (dec.); m. James Eddie Thomas, June 16, 1978 (dec. 1986); children: Letitia, James R. LVN, U. Tex. Med. Br., 1963; Cert. Inhalation Therapist, Lamar U., 1972; AAS, Galveston Coll., 1980; Cert. Counselor, Coll. of the Mainland, Texas City, Tex., 1992; student, Galveston Coll., 1994—. Staff nurse U. Tex. Med. Br., 1962-64; pvt. duty nurse Galveston, 1965—; charge nurse/relief supr. Moody House Inc., 1974-86; counselor intern Gulf Coast Ctr., Galveston, 1992—; substitute tchr. Galveston Ind. Sch. Dist., 1983-91; caregiver Alzeheimer's Assn., Houston, 1993—; case mgr. HIV, 1994—. Author poetry. Bears facilitator for Children's Yeager Ctr.; math. tutor Galveston Ind. Sch. Dist., 1994. Mem. ABWA, Order of Ea. Star (worthy matron 1992—, family group counselor 1994), Heroines of Jericho. Democrat. African Meth. Episcopal. Home: 3207 N 1/2 Galveston TX 77550

THOMAS, CHRISTINE LEE, human resources administrator; b. L.A., Mar. 11, 1956; d. Milan Francis and Barbara Ann (Holt) Ford Wallmark; m. David Allen Thomas, Aug. 9, 1980 (div. Oct. 1988). BS in Bus. Adminstrn. magna cum laude, Calif. State U., Hayward, 1987, MBA, 1988. Pers. asst. Verbatim Corp., Sunnyvale, Calif., 1982-83; pers. specialist VisiCorp, San Jose, Calif., 1983-84; account mgr. AmeriComm, Santa Clara, Calif., 1987-88; sr. human resources rep. U.S. Adminstrs., Inc., L.A., 1988-89; corp. pers. mgr. AME, Inc., Burbank, Calif., 1989; dir. human resources Musicians Inst., Inc., Hollywood, Calif., 1989—. Mem. Soc. for Human Resource Mgmt., Pers. Indsl. Rels. Assn. Office: Musicians Inst Inc 1655 N McCadden Pl Hollywood CA 90028-6157

THOMAS, CLARA MCCANDLESS, retired English language educator, biographer; b. Strathroy, Ont., Can., May 22, 1919; d. Basil and Mabel (Sullivan) McCandless; m. Morley Keith Thomas, May 23, 1942; children: Stephen, John. B.A., U. Western Ont., London, 1941, M.A., 1944; Ph.D., U. Toronto, 1962; DLitt (hon.) York U., 1986, Trent U., 1991; LLD (hon.), Brock U., 1992. Instr. English U. Western Ont., London, 1947-61, U.

Toronto, 1958-61; asst. prof. English York U., Toronto, 1961-68; prof. York U., 1969-84, prof. emeritus, 1984—; acad. adv. panel Social Scis. and Humanities Research Council, 1981-84; mem. Killam Awards Selection Bd., 1978-81. Author biography of Anna Jameson, 1967, of Egerton Ryerson, 1969, of Margaret Laurence, 1969, 75, of William Arthur Deacon, 1982; Literary criticism (Can.), 1946, 72, 94; mem. editl. bd. Literary History of Can., 1980—, Collected Works of Northrop Frye, 1993—. Recipient Internat. Coun. of Can. Studies prize No. Telecom, 1989; grantee Can. Coun., 1967, 73, Social Sci. and Humanities Rsch. Coun. Can., 1978-80. Fellow Royal Soc. Can.; mem. Assn. Can. Univs., Tchrs. English (pres. 1971-72), Assn. Can. and Que. Lit., Bus. and Profl. Women's Club, Assn. for Can. Studies. New Democratic. Office: York U 305 Scott Libr, 4700 Keele St, Downsview, ON Canada M3J 1P3

THOMAS, CYNTHIA ELIZABETH, advanced practice nurse; b. Highland, Ind., Sept. 3, 1958; d. James William and Naomi Elizabeth (Rice) T. BS in Animal Sci., Purdue U., 1980; ADN, Purdue U. Calumet, 1986, BSN, 1988, MSN, 1990. RN, Ind., Ill.; cert. adult nurse practioner, family nurse practitioner, clin. specialist in med.-surg. nursing, clin. nurse specialist in adult health, ACLS, CPR, Mantoux adminstrn. Med.-surg./ICU/CCU staff nurse Porter Meml. Hosp., Valparaiso, Ind., 1986-94; advanced practice nurse Cmty. Health Ctr., North Judson, Ind., 1994—. Mem. AACCN, Ceres, Alpha Zeta. Office: Community Health Ctr North Judson 108 W State St North Judson IN 46366

THOMAS, CYNTHIA GAIL, public policy research executive; b. Tulsa, Jan. 26, 1956; d. Jack Marcy and Dorothy (Bergfors) T. BS summa cum laude, U. Minn., 1978, MA, 1981. Analyst Met. Coun., St. Paul, 1978; rsch. analyst Common Cause Minn., St. Paul, 1979, lobbyist, 1980, rsch. cons., 1982; adminstr. NBC, N.Y.C., 1980; researcher Minn. State Sen., St. Paul, 1983-85, rsch. dir., 1985-86; owner Thomas Rsch., Roseville, Minn., 1986—; pub. policy adv. Rep. Party, Mpls., 1986—; commr Roseville Planning Commn., 1991—. Contbr. articles to profl. publs. Vol. Little Bros. of Poor, Mpls., 1987—, YWCA, St. Paul, 1989-90; softball coach Girls Age 10-12 Team, St. Paul, 1988. Mem. Nature Conservancy, Amnesty Internat., Fraser Inst., Sierra Club. Republican. Home and Office: Thomas Rsch 1127 Oakcrest Ave Saint Paul MN 55113-3219

THOMAS, DEBORAH ELIZABETH, environmental municipal engineer; b. Mt. Kisco, N.Y., Dec. 18, 1966; d. Dennis James and Deborah Ann (Howley) Malanchuk; m. John A. Thomas, Oct. 9, 1993. B of Civil Engring., The Cooper Union, 1988; postgrad., Pace U., 1989—. EIT, N.Y. Civil engring. intern sources N.Y.C. Dept. Environ. Protection, Corona, 1988-89, asst. civil engr. sources, 1989-91, project mgr. planning and programs, 1991-94, project mgr. strategic planning and devel., 1994—. Chair young alumni The Cooper Union, N.Y.C., 1992-94; spkr. instr. grant program for minority women in engring. edn. NASA/Soc. Women Engrs., N.Y.C., 1989-93; leader Girl Scouts Am., Westchester, N.Y., 1989-91. Named Young Govt. Civil Engr. of Yr., N.Y. met. sect. ASCE, 1992. Mem. Am. Water Works Assn. (conf. com. 1994, N.Y. sect. membership chair and strategic planning vice-chair), N.Y. Soc. Women Engrs. (conv. com. 1990, pres. 1991, 94, Outstanding New Mem. 1989), Met. Engring. Socs. Coun. (sec. 1990-93), Mcpl. Engrs. of City of N.Y. (bd. dirs. 1991—). Roman Catholic. Office: NYC Dept Environ Protection 59-17 Junction Blvd Corona NY 11368

THOMAS, DOROTHY WITT, school counselor; b. High Springs, Fla., Nov. 15, 1940; d. Joseph Leroy and Hazel Dorothea Witt; m. Donald Robert Thomas, June 23, 1963. BS in Phys. Edn., U. Fla., 1963, MEd, 1968, EdS, 1979, PhD, 1987. Lic. mental health counselor, Fla. Tchr. phys. edn. Stephen Foster Elem. Sch., Gainesville, Fla., 1963-64, Santa Fe H.S., Alachua, Fla., 1964-68; sch. counselor Newberry (Fla.) Jr.-Sr. H.S., 1968-70, Spring Hill Mid. Sch., High Springs, 1970-90, Westwood Mid. Sch., Gainesville, 1990-93, Horizon Ctr. and New Pathways, Gainesville, 1993—; ednl. cons. various sch. dists., 1970—; mental health counselor, Gainesville, 1994—. Contbr. articles to profl. jours. and newsletters. Mem., officer High Springs Jr. Women's Club. Recipient merit award Alachua County Sch. Bd., 1983. Mem. ACA (governing bd. 1983-86, pres.-elect 1987), Am. Sch. Counselor Assn. (pres. 1984-85), Am. Mental Health Counselors Assn., So. Assn. for Counselor Educators and Suprs., Fla. Counseling Assn. (governing bd. 1980-83, Paul Fitzgerald Outstanding Mem. award 1990), Fla. Sch. Counselors Assn. (past pres.), Fla. Mental Health Counselors Assn., Nat. Mid. Sch. Assn., Alachua County Edn. Assn. (bldg. rep.), LWV, Phi Delta Kappa, Chi Sigma Iota (Wittmer Profl. Svc. award 1991). Democrat. Methodist. Home: 2056 NW 55th Blvd Apt C-1 Gainesville FL 32653

THOMAS, ELIZABETH IRENE, city official, small business owner; b. Pasadena, Calif., May 15, 1951; d. William Klein and Laurie Louise (Aslin) Reif; m. Ahmad Dehghan, July 19, 1972 (div. Feb. 1979); children: Mehrdad Dehghan, Nader Dehghan; m. Rodger H. Thomas, Dec. 31, 1988. AA, Allen Hancock Coll., 1977; BS, Calif. State U., L.A., 1980. Cert. recycling facility operator N.Mex., 1994. Owner, mgr. Lizzy's Computer Help, Portales, N.Mex., 1980—, Strawberry Patch, Portales, 1980-82; dir. of instrn. Acropolis Info. Sys., Ada, Okla., 1982-84; mgr. Radioshack, Oklahoma City, 1984-85; mgr. Radioshack, Clovis, N.Mex., 1985-91, saleswoman, 1987-91; mapping specialist dept. pub. works City of Clovis, 1987—, recycling coord., 1991—. Exec. coord. Beautiful Clovis!, 1992—; active Keep N.Mex. Beautiful, 1991-94, N.Mex. Recycling Coalition, 1993, sec. 94-95; vol. Master Recycler Environ. Shopper, 1994. Recipient Environ. Leadership award Gov. of N.Mex., 1992. Mem. NAFE, Solid Waste Assn. North Am. Office: City of Clovis PO Box 760 Clovis NM 88102

THOMAS, ELLEN LOUISE, private school administrator; b. Doylestown, Pa., Nov. 30, 1940; d. Edward Martin and Evelyn Graham (Axenroth) Happ; m. Eugene Greene Leffever, June 30, 1963 (dec. Nov. 1978); children: Eugene Greene II, Jeanette Ellen Dellaripa; m. William Dewey Thomas, Sept. 15, 1981; 1 child, Jeremiah David. BA in Edn., Immaculata (Pa.) Coll., 1962; postgrad., Pa. State U., 1962-67. Pvt. practice tutor Doylestown, 1958-65; tchr. Cen. Bucks Sch. System, Doylestown, 1962-65; adminstr. The Curiosity Shoppe, Doylestown, 1965—, The Toddler Ctr., Doylestown, 1979—; exec. dir. Camp Curiosity, Doylestown, 1984—, Thomas Lea Equestrian Ctr., Doylestown, 1988—; tchr. trainer Confortunity of Christian Doctrine, Doylestown, 1965-78; cons. early childhood Am. Sch. in Hong Kong, 1981-84; lectr. in early childhood Bucks County Community Ctr., Newtown, Pa., 1978-90; workshop facilitator Head Start, Phila., 1990; cons. day care Cen. Bucks C. of C., Doylestown, 1989-90; ednl. coord. Forest Grove Presbyn. Ch., 1984-90. Mem. U.S. C. of C., Washington, Bucks County C. of C., Doylestown, Nat. Fedn. of Ind. Bus., Washington. Mem. ASCD, Assn. for Childhood Edn. Internat., United Pvt. Acad. Schs. Assn., Bucks County Assn. Edn. Young Children (pres. 1974-78). Home: 4425 Landisville Rd Doylestown PA 18901-1134 Office: The Curiosity Shoppe 4425 Landisville Rd Doylestown PA 18901-1134

THOMAS, EMILY ANN, feature writer, songwriter, composer; b. Warsaw, Ind., Dec. 21, 1952; d. Dester and Myrtle Joann (Bohnstedt) Bell; m. Daryl Eldon Thomas, June 12, 1976; children: Amanda Eilleen, Schaya Jennifer. Grad. high sch., Syracuse, Ind., 1971. Feature writer The Mail-Jour., Milford, Ind., 1983—, The Paper, Milford, 1983—, Warsaw Times Union, 1986—, Indpls. Star. Writer, composer song and lyrics: Hometown Feelin', 1985 (Gov. Commn. recognition), No Deposit, No Return, 1986, Tennessee Pride, 1986, The Circuit Rider, 1986, Time-Forgotten Treasures, 1986, Mama Said, 1986, God's Recipe, 1987, Another Lost Sheep, 1987, Too Many Pieces (In the Puzzle), 1987, Evening Star, 1988, Strut-Street Blues, 1988, When the Flame Rekindled, 1988, Willy Worm's Walk, 1988, The Message, 1988, Seeds, 1991, Hidden Treasures, 1994, On My Own, 1994, Grandpa's Little Book, 1994, The Country Church, 1994, Pray for the World, 1994, God's Voice, 1994, The Great I Am, 1994, East of the Pulpit, 1994, Wishing Star, 1994, The State of the Heart Collection, 1994; contbr. poems to mags. Charter mem. Statue of Liberty Ellis Island Found., N.Y.C., 1984—; mem. Rep. Nat. Com., Washington, 1982—; bd. dirs. Internat. Palace of Sports Found. Recipient Medal of Merit Internat. Assn. of Lions Clubs, 1989, Sagamore of the Wabash State of Ind., 1989, Recognition award Carnegie Hero Fund Commn., 1989. Mem. ASCAP (assoc.), Gospel Music Assn. (assoc.). Home and Office: 7161 E 800 N North Webster IN 46555

THOMAS, ESTHER MERLENE, educator; b. San Diego, Oct. 16, 1945; d. Merton Alfred and Nellie Lida (Von Pilz) T. AA with honors, Grossmont Coll., 1966; BA with honors, San Diego State U., 1969; MA, U. Redlands, 1977. Cert. elem. and adult edn. tchr. Tchr. Cajon Valley Union Sch. Dist., El Cajon, 1969—; sci. fair coord. Flying Hills Sch.; tchr. Hopi and Navajo Native Americans, Ariz, Calif., Utah, 1964-74, Goose and Gander Nursery School, Lakeside, Calif., 1964-66; dir., supt. Bible and Sunday schs. various chs., Lakeside, 1961-87; mem. sci. com., math coun. Cajon Valley Union Sch. Dist., 1990-91. Author: Individualized Curriculum in the Affective Domain; contbg. author: Campbell County, The Treasured Years, 1990, Legends of Lakeside; conbtr. articles to profl. jours. and newspapers. Mem. U.S. Senatorial Club, Washington, 1984—, Conservative Caucus, Inc., Washington, 1988—, Ronald Reagan Presdl. Found., Ronald Reagan Rep. Ctr., 1988, Rep. Presdl. Citizen's Adv. Commn., 1989—, Rep. Platform Planning Com., Calif., 1992, at-large del. representing dist. #45, Lakeside, Calif., 1992, Am. Security Coun., Washington, 1994, Congressman Hunter's Off Road Adv. Coun., El Cajon, Calif., 1994, Century Club, San Diego Rep. Party, 1995; mem. health articulation com. project AIDS, Cajon Valley Union Sch. Dist., 1988—, Concerned Women Am., Washington, Recruit Depot Hist. Mus., San Diego, 1989—, Citizen's Drug Free Am., Calif., 1989—, The Heritage Found., 1988—; charter mem. Marine Corps; mem. Lakeside Centennial Com., 1985-86; hon. mem. Rep. Presl. Task Force, Washington, 1986; del. Calif. Rep. Senatorial Mid-Term Conv., Washington, 1994; mus. curator Lakeside Hist. Soc., 1992-93. Recipient Outstanding Svc. award PTA, 1972-74; recognized for various contbns. Commdg. Post Gen., San Diego Bd. Edn., 1989. Mem. Tchrs. Assn., Calif. Tchrs. Assn., Nat. Trust for Hist. Preservation, Cajon Valley Educators Assn. (faculty advisor, rep. 1980-82, 84-86, 87-88), Christian Bus. and Profl. Women, Lakeside Hist. Soc. (mus. curator 1992), Capitol Hill Women's Club, Am. Ctr. for Law and Justice, Internat. Christian Women's Club (Christian amb. to Taiwan, Korea, 1974). Republican. Home: 13594 Highway 8 Business Apt 3 Lakeside CA 92040-5235 Office: Flying Hills Elem Sch 1251 Finch St El Cajon CA 92020-1433

THOMAS, FAYE EVELYN J., elementary school educator; b. Summerfield, La., Aug. 3, 1933; d. Reginald Felton and Altee (Hunter) Johnson; B.A., So. U., 1954; student Tuskegee Inst., 1958, 69, U. Detroit, summers, 1961, 62, 63, Central Mich. U., summer 1965; M.S., U. Central Ark., 1971; M.S., Cleve. State U., 1979; m. Archie Taylor Thomas, Sept. 8, 1960; 1 son, Dwayne Andre. Tchr., Cullen (La.) Elem. Sch., 1957; tchr. English and social studies Charles Brown High Sch., Springhill, La., 1957-70; tchr. English, Upward Bound Program, Grambling State U., 1968; tchr. English, Springhill (La.) High Sch., 1970; elem. intermediate tchr. Riveredge Elem. Sch., Berea, Ohio, 1971-93; tchr. 7th grade English Ford Middle Sch., 1993-94; tchr. asst. elem. council curriculum and instrn. Berea Sch. Dist., 1984-85. Trustee Charles Brown Soc. Orgn., Christian Forum of N.Y., Inc., 1988—. EPDA grantee, 1970-71; Internat. Paper Found. grantee, summers 1958, 60; NDEA grantee, summer 1965; Martha Holden Jennings scholar, 1984-85. Mem. NEA, Ohio Edn. Assn., Berea Edn. Assn. (2d v.p. 1992-93), N.E. Ohio Tchrs. Assn., Assn. for Supervision and Curriculum Devel., Charles Brown Soc. Orgn. (trustee 1984—), People United to Save Humanity, Black Caucus Nat. Edn. Assn., Ohio Motorists Assn, Order Eastern Star, Midpark Toastmaster Club. Democrat. Baptist. Home: 19353 Bagley Rd Cleveland OH 44130-3317 Office: 17001 Holland Rd Brookpark OH 44142-3523

THOMAS, FLORENCE KATHLEEN, retired military officer; b. Torrington, Conn., June 20, 1945; d. James Dudley and Nova Lee (Campbell) T. BA in Mass Comm., U. Tex.-El Paso, 1970; MA in Adminstrn. of Justice, Wichita State U., 1984.. Commd. 2d lt. U.S. Army, 1969, advanced through grades to lt. col., 1990; chief ops. tng. devels. U.S. Mil. Police Sch., Ft. McClellan, Ala., 1979-80; exec. officer criminal investigation div. Kaiserslautern, Germany, 1980-82; comdr. criminal investigation div. Nuernberg Field Office, Fed. Republic Germany, 1982-83; corrections officer Forces Command, Provost Marshal, Ft. McPherson, Ga., 1985; chief law enforcement mgmt. div., 1985-87, chief evaluations, exercise div., dir. ops., 1987-88; chief force deployment br. plans div. office of dir. for ops. HQ USAREUR & 7A, Heidelberg, Germany, 1988-92, ret., 1992; with K & S Custom Framing, El Paso, Tex., 1992—. mil. cons. law enforcement activities, 1977—. Mem. NAFE, Assn. U.S. Army, U.S. Golf Assn., Sun Country Golf Assn., Horizon Women's Golf Assn., Internat. Women's Vet's. Golf Assn., Internat. Women's Golf Assn., Border Golf. Avocation: golf, fishing. Home: 15000 Ashford St Apt 12 El Paso TX 79927-6413

THOMAS, GEORGIE A., state official. B.A., Cornell U., 1965; M.B.A., Columbia U., 1973. Asst. portfolio mgr. Money Mgmt. dept. R.W. Pressprich & Co. Inc., N.Y.C., 1968-71; portfolio analyst Bache & Co., N.Y.C., 1971-72; with Exxon Corp., N.Y.C., 1973-76, consolidation analyst Treas. dept., 1975-76; treas. Penntech Papers Inc., N.Y.C., 1976-79; budget dir. Yankee Publishing Inc., Dublin, N.H., 1982-85; treas. State of N.H., Concord, 1985—; mem. econ. growth and productivity and tech. coms. Bus. Research Adv. Council of Bur. Labor Statistics, 1978-79; mem. alumni counseling bd. Columbia U. Bus. Sch., 1973-79. Editor: Jour. World Bus., Columbia Bus. Sch. Mem. Fin. Women's Assn. N.Y. (mem. exec. bd. 1977-78), Womens Econ. Roundtable. Club: Cornell of Fairfield County (Conn.). Home: Ashley Rd Antrim NH 03440 Office: State NH State House Annex Rm 121 Concord NH 03301*

THOMAS, GERALDINE P., personnel executive; b. Atlanta, Dec. 10, 1951; d. Arthur and Vivian (Spence) Perrimon; m. Ronald Floyd Thomas, June 21, 1970; children: Erinn Danielle, Erich Perrimon. BS in Human Resources, Ga. State U., 1985. Coord. NationBank, Atlanta, mgr. recruitment, mgr. employee rels., mgr. payroll, cons. human resources, mgr. personnel, 1989—, now sr. v.p., state pers. exec.; exec. com. Fin. Employee Rels. Study Group, Wharton Sch. Bus., Phila. Mem. NAACP. Named Best and Brightest Bus. Woman Dollars & Sense, Chgo., 1991; Outstanding Woman in Banking Success Guide, 1992. Mem. Am. Bankers Assn. (exec. com. human resources com.), Am. Inst. Banking (bd. dirs., Nat. Bankers Assn. (bd. dirs., pres., Trailblazer award), Atlanta Inst. Banking (bd. dirs.), Atlanta Urban League, Alpha Kappa Alpha. Baptist. *

THOMAS, HELEN A. (MRS. DOUGLAS B. CORNELL), newspaper bureau executive; b. Winchester, Ky., Aug. 4, 1920; d. George and Mary (Thomas) T.; m. Douglas B. Cornell. BA, Wayne U., 1942; LLD, Eastern Mich. State U., 1972, Ferris State Coll., 1978, Brown U., 1986; LHD, Wayne State U., 1974, U. Detroit, 1979; LLD, St. Bonaventure U., 1988, Franklin Marshall U., 1989, No. Michigan U., 1989, Skidmore Coll., 1992; Susquehanna U., 1993, Sage Coll., 1994, U. Mo., 1994. With UPI, 1943—; wire svc. reporter UPI, Washington, 1943-74; White House bur. chief UPI, 1974—. Author: Dateline White House. Recipient Woman of Yr. in Comm. award Ladies Home Jour., 1975, 4th Estate award Nat. press Club, 1984; Journalism award U. Mo., Dean of Sch. Journalism award, Al Newharth award, 1990, Ralph McGill award, 1995. Mem. Women's Nat. Press Club (pres. 1959-60, William Allen White Journalism award), Am. Newspaper Women's Club (past v.p.), White House Corrs. Assn. (pres. 1976), Gridiron Club (pres. 1993), Sigma Delta Chi (fellow, Hall of Fame), Delta Sigma Phi (hon.). Home: 2501 Calvert St NW Washington DC 20008-2620 Office: UPI World Hdqrs 1400 I St NW Washington DC 20005-2208

THOMAS, HILARY BRYN, telecommunications executive, interactivist, writer; b. Brignorth, U.K., Jan. 31, 1943; came to U.S., 1985; parents, Kenneth Bryn and Nancy Barbara Tench (Cullum) T. BSc with honors, U. Wales, 1965. Instr. U. Victoria, B.C., Can., 1967-73; rsch. asst. Communications Studies Group Univ. Coll., London, 1975-76; cons. Communications Studies & Planning, Ltd., London, 1976-80; v.p. CSP Internat., Inc., London and N.Y.C., 1980-82, Aregon Internat., London and N.Y.C., 1982-85, Videodial, Inc., N.Y.C., 1985-88; pres. Minitel USA, Inc., N.Y.C., 1988-92; pres., bd. dirs. Minitel Holdings, Inc., Del.; chmn. bd. dirs. Minitel Svcs. Co., 1988-92; pres. Interactive Telecommunications Svcs. Inc., Mountain Lakes, N.J., 1992—; pres., founder ISED Corp., Howell, N.J., 1992—. Contbr. articles to industry publs. Mem. Interactive Svcs. Assn. (bd. dirs. 1985—, chmn. 1987-89; Disting. Svc. award 1989), Internat. Inst. Comm., World Inst. on Disability (bus. adv. coun.). Office: 420 The Blvd Ste 101 Mountain Lakes NJ 07046

THOMAS, JACQUELYN MAY, librarian; b. Mechanicsburg, Pa., Jan. 26, 1932; d. William John and Gladys Elizabeth (Warren) Harvey; m. David Edward Thomas, Aug. 28, 1954; children: Lesley J., Courtenay J., Hilary A. BA summa cum laude, Gettysburg Coll., 1954; student U. N.C., 1969; MEd, U. N.H., 1971. Libr., Phillips Exeter Acad., Exeter, N.H., 1971-77, acad. libr., 1977—, chair governing bd. Child Care Ctr., 1987-91; chair Com. to Enhance Status of Women, Exeter, 1981-84; chair Loewenstein Com., Exeter, 1982—; pres. Cum Laude Soc., Exeter, 1984-86; James H. Ottaway Jr. prof., 1990—. Editor: The Design of the Libr.: A Guide to Sources of Information, 1981, Rarities of Our Time: The Special Collections of the Phillips Exeter Academy Libr. Trustee, treas. Exeter Day Sch., 1965-69; mem. bd. Exeter Hosp. Vols., 1954-59; mem. Exeter Hosp. Corp., 1978—; mem. bldg. com. Exeter Pub. Libr., 1986-88; chair No. New Eng., Coun. for Women in Ind. Schs., 1985-87; chmn. Lamont Poetry Program, Exeter, 1984-86; dir. Greater Portsmouth Community Found, 1990—. N.H. Coun. for Humanities grantee, 1981-82; NEH grantee, 1982; recipient Lillian Radford Trust award, 1989. Mem. ALA, New Eng. Libr. Assn., N.H. Ednl. Media Assn., New Eng. Assn. Ind. Sch. Librs., Am. Assn. Sch. Librs. (chmn. non-pub. sch. sect., program com. 1985—), Phi Beta Kappa. Home: 16 Elm St Exeter NH 03833 Office: Acad Libr Phillips Exeter Acad 20 Main St Exeter NH 03833-2460

THOMAS, JANET VERLINE, counselor; b. Caldwell, Idaho, June 14, 1936; d. Lougene and Josephine Connaway (Hill) Andersen; m. Carol Lloyd Thomas, May 10, 1956 (div. 1965); children: Gary Lee, Michael Louis. BA, Coll. Idaho, 1958, MEd, 1968; EdD, U. Nev., 1994. Cert. counselor; lic. profl. counselor, cert. sch. counselor, Idaho. Tchr. Wilder (Idaho) Elem. Sch., 1958-59, Ill. Elem. Sch., Park Forest, 1960-67; counselor Marsing (Idaho) Schs., 1968-72; career guidance specialist Canyon-Owyhee Sch. Svc. Agy., Caldwell, Idaho, 1972-74; elem. sch. counselor Boise Schs., 1974—; grad. asst. instr. U. Nev., Reno, 1991-93; spl. lectr. Boise State U., 1978—; adj. faculty Albertson Coll. Idaho, Caldwell, 1988—. Contbr. articles and columns to profl. newsletters. Mem. N.Am. Soc. Adlerian Psychologists, Idaho Soc. Individual Psychology (Significant Adlerian Contbr. 1987, pres. 1982-83, Am. Counseling Assn. (APGA senator 1979-82, Outstanding Svc. award 1982), Idaho Counseling Assn. (pres. 1977-78, Disting. Svc. award 1979), Am. Sch. Counselors Assn. (regional elem. coord. 1976-77), Idaho Sch. Counselor Assn. (pres. 1975-76), Phi Delta Kappa, Phi Kappa Phi. Home: 4007 Northbridge Way Boise ID 83706 Office: Boise Ind Sch Dist 1207 Fort Boise ID 83702

THOMAS, JANICE NORINE RAGON, media coordinator, school librarian; b. Ft. Wayne, Ind., Nov. 19, 1930; d. Leroy Willard and Nora Winifred (Nall) Ragon; m. Larry Clifford Thomas, Feb. 14, 1959; children: Lyndon Mark, Lori Norine. BA, Marion (Ind.) Coll., 1953; MLS, Kent (Ohio) State U., 1960. High sch. tchr. York Local Schs., Van Wert, Ohio, 1953-55; middle sch. tchr. Van Buren (Ind.) Schs., 1955-57; sch. librarian Perry Local Schs., Massillon, Ohio, 1957-60; libr., media coord. Manchester Local Schs., Akron, Ohio, 1960-93. Editor newsletter, 1979. Bd. dirs., pres. Coventry Local Schs., Akron, 1986—. Mem. Ohio Ednl. Libr. Media Assn. (pres.-elect 1992-93, pres. 1993—, award of merit 1988), Manchester Edn. Assn. (pres. 1980-82), Delta Kappa Gamma (pres. 1976-78), Phi Delta Gamma. Mem. Apostolic Faith Assembly. Home: 3549 Malley Ave Akron OH 44319-2229 Office: Manchester Local Schs 437 W Nimisila Rd Akron OH 44319-4964

THOMAS, JEANETTE MAE, accountant; b. Winona, Minn., Dec. 19, 1946; d. Herbert and Arline (Shank) Harmon; m. Gerald F. Thomas, Aug. 9, 1969; children: Bradley, Christopher. BS, Winona State U., 1968; postgrad., Colo. State U.; CFP, Coll. for Fin. Planning, Denver, 1985. Enrolled agt.; cert. fin. planner; registered rep. NASD; registered investment advisor; accredited tax advisor. Tchr. pub. schs. systems Colo., N.Mex., Mich., 1968-72; adminstrv. asst. Bus. Men's Svcs., Ft. Collins, Colo., 1974-75; tax cons. Tax Corp. Am., Ft. Collins, Colo., 1972-80; chief acct. Jayland Electric, La Porte, Colo., 1981-90; pres., CEO Thomas Fin. Svcs. Inc., Ft. Collins, 1980—. Contbr. articles to newspapers and profl. newsletters. Bd. dirs. local PTO, 1984-85; treas. Boy Scouts Am., 1985-88; master food safety advisor coop. ext. Colo. State U., 1988—; spkr., mem. steering com. AARP Women's Fin. Info. Program, 1988—; chair adv. bd. Larimer County Coop. Ext., Colo. State U.; mem. quality rev. com. Poudre R-1 Schs. Mem. Internat. Assn. Fin. Planning (past officer), Am. Soc. Women Accts. (bd. dirs. 1984-86), Pvt. Industry Coun. (chair 1994-95), Nat. Soc. Pub. Accts., Inst. CFPs, Am. Notary Assn., Ft. Collins C. of C. (red carpet com. bus. assistance coun. 1989—). Home: PO Box 370 Laporte CO 80535-0370 Office: 400 S Howes St Ste 2 Fort Collins CO 80521-2802

THOMAS, JOYCE MOFFETT, secondary education educator; b. Hobart, Ind., July 29, 1935; d. Walter and Ruby (Stephenson) Moffett; m. John James Thomas, Oct. 18, 1958; children: Amy Carrell, Sarah Smith. BA in English, Ind. U., 1971; MA in English, Purdue U., 1977. Tchr. Andrean H.S., Merrillville, Ind., 1971—; instr. North Ctrl. Purdue U., Westville, Ind., 1989-93. Contbr. articles to various publs. Named Outstanding Chgo. Area Tchr., U. Chgo., 1984, Tchr. of Yr., Inland-Ryerson Fedn., 1989. Mem. Nat. Coun. Tchrs. English, Nat. Cath. Edn. Assn. Democrat. Episcopalian. Home: 748 Memory Ln Hobart IN 46342

THOMAS, JUDITH BECKER, financial services executive; b. Chgo., July 24, 1943; d. Charles Peter and Pearl Jean (Woodrich) B. BSBA, Roosevelt U., Chgo., 1978; MBA, Northwestern U., 1981. Dir. human resources, indsl. relations GE Railcar Svc. Corp., Chgo., 1966-80, v.p. pers. and indsl. relations, 1980-81, v.p. adminstrn., 1981-82, v.p. adminstrn. and regional ops., 1982-84; v.p. human resources Haworth, Inc., Grand Rapids, Mich., 1984-88; v.p. human resources, labor Cowles Media Co., Star Tribune, Mpls., 1988-90; v.p. adminstrn. Greyrock Capital Group, Stamford, Conn., 1990-94, sr. v.p. adminstrn., 1994—. Mem. Pres. Commn. on Employment of Handicapped, Chgo., 1981; bd. dirs. Community Coordinated Child Care, Holland, 1988. Mem. Ill. Mfrs. Assn. (indsl. relations com. 1984), Am. Soc. Pers. Adminstrn., Human Resources Mgmt. Assn. (bd. dirs. 1982), LWV (fin. advisor Chgo. chpt. 1988), Univ. Club Chgo. Office: Greyrock Capital Group 1 Canterbury Green Stamford CT 06901

THOMAS, JULIA DESSERY, planner; b. Riverside, Calif., Dec. 4, 1938; d. Floyd Gordon and Myrtle (Thomas) Dessery; m. David B. Thomas, Nov. 30, 1963 (div.); 1 child, Leslie; m. Michael Lawrence Bobrow, Mar. 24, 1980; stepchildren—Elizabeth, Erica, David. B.A., Calif. State U.-San Francisco, 1963; M.A., Sch. Architecture and Urban Planning, UCLA, 1974. Dir. communications William L. Pereira Assocs., Los Angeles, 1972-73; sr. assoc. Bobrow/Thomas and Assocs., Los Angeles, 1973-78, pres., 1978-84, chmn. bd., chief exec. officer, 1984-92, pres., CEO, 1992—; guest lectr. U. So. Calif., Los Angeles, UCLA, Scripps Coll., Claremont, Calif., Calif. Poly. U., Pomona; mem. exec. com., dean's council UCLA Sch. Architecture and Urban Planning, 1982—; mem. design award jury Progressive Architecture, Stamford, Conn., 1983; adv. dir., mem. pub. policy com. Blue Cross Calif. Prin. works include: Merle Norman Pavilion, Shriners Hosps. for Crippled Children, Los Angeles, Shreveport, Santa Monica Hosp. Med. Ctr., UCLA Arroyo Bridge, Mus. Cultural History; restoration of adminstrn. bldg. Calif. Inst. Tech., Pasadena; Motion Picture and TV Hosp. and Country Home, Woodland Hills, Calif.; Kings Road Housing for Elderly, Hollywood, Calif. (Los Angeles chpt. AIA award 1981), Natividad Med. Ctr., U. Ariz. Cancer Ctr., Cook County Hosp. Replacement Plan, Stanford Psychiatry/Behavioral Scis. Acsd. Clinic, San Bernardino City Replacement Hosp., St. Luke's Med. Ctr. Milw., City of Hope, VA Outpatient Clinic, L.A./Hong Kong Hosp. Authority. Contbr. articles to profl. publs. Recipient Los Angeles Conservancy award, 1984, Alumni award for Excellence Profl. Achievement UCLA, 1988, AIA, NAVFAC award of merit, Spl. award for Energy Conservation for Med. Clinic, Kaneohe, Hawaii. Trustee UCLA Found., 1985—; bd. vis. UCLA Grad. Sch. Mgmt., 1985—; past vice chmn. Calif. Council for Humanities, San Francisco, 1980-83; mem. Nat. Women's Forum, Urban Land Inst. Task Force; co-conferree Bobrow-Thomas fellowship, UCLA; past pres. Com. of 200, 1984-85; bd. regents Mt. St. Mary's Coll. Leadership award Calif. Chpt. Am. Planning Assn., 1986, Design Excellence award U.S. Dept. Def. for Naval Med. Clinic, Mem. L.A. Area C. of C., Am. Inst. Cert. Planners, Am. Inst. Planners, Tech. Corridor Assn., Regency (Los Angeles). Office: Bobrow/Thomas and Assoc Ste 1600 15301 Valley Vista Blvd Sherman Oaks CA 91403-3932

THOMAS, KAREN P., composer, conductor; b. Seattle, Sept. 17, 1957. BA in Composition, Cornish Inst., 1979; MusM in Composition,

Conducting, U. Wash., 1985. Condr. The Contemporary Group, 1981-85; condr., music dir. Wash. Composers Forum, 1984-86; condr. Seattle Summer Concert Band, 1985-87; artistic dir., condr. Seattle Pro Musica, 1987—. Conducting debut Seattle, 1983; composer: Four Delineations of Curtmantle for trombone or cello, 1982, Metamorphoses on a Machaut Kyrie for string orch. or quartet, 1983, Stabat Mater for Mezzo, choir, orch., 1984, Cowboy Songs for voice and piano, 1985, There Must be a Lone Ranger for soprano and chamber ensemble, 1987, Brass Quintet, 1987, Four Lewis Carroll Songs for choir, 1989, (music/dance/theater) Boxiana, 1990, Elementi for clarinet and percussion, 1991, (one-act children's opera) Coyote's Tail, 1991, Clarion Dances for brass ensemble, 1993, Roundup for sax quartet, 1993, Three Medieval Lyrics for choir, 1992, Sopravvento for wind quintet and percussion, 1994, numerous others. Recipient Composers Forum award N.W. Chamber Orch., 1984, King County Arts Commn., 1987, 90, Artist Trust, 1988, 93, Seattle Arts Commn., 1988, 91, 93, New Langton Arts, 1988, Delius Festival, 1993; fellow Wash. State Arts Commn., 1991; Charles E. Ives scholar AAAL. Mem. Broadcast Music, Inc., Am. Music Ctr., Internat. League Women Composers, Soc. of Composers Inc., Chorus America.

THOMAS, LAURA MARLENE, artist, private antique dealer; b. Chico, Calif., Apr. 29, 1936; d. Boyd Stanley Beck and Lois Velma (Behrke) Lyons; m. Charles Rex Thomas; children: Tracy Loraine, Jeffory Norris. AA in Fine Arts, Sacramento City Coll., 1978; BA in Fine Arts, Calif. State U., 1981. Tchrs. asst. Hanford Elem. Sch., Hanford, Calif., 1963-68; asst. dir. RSVP: Retired Sr. Vol. Program, Hanford, 1971-74; dir. of Art Bank Sacramento City Coll., Sacramento, 1976-78; pub. asst. Student Activities Calif. State Univ., Sacramento, 1978-81; antique dealer pvt. practice, Sacramento, 1981--, arts and crafts bus., 1976--; social worker Cath. Social Svcs., Sacramento, 1985--. Artist: weaving, Double Image, 1977, 2nd Place 1977; ceramic sculptor, Bird. Charter mem. YWCA, Sacramento, 1972, Folsum Hist. Soc., 1988. Cert. of appreciation, Carmellia City Ctr. Adv. Council, Sacramento, 1986. Mem. Statue of Liberty-Ellis Island Found., 1985, North Shore Animal League (Benefactors award 1985), Calif. State U. Alumni Assn., Hanford Sportsman Club (v.p. 1963-68). Republican. Protestant. Home: 2719 I St #4 Sacramento CA 95816

THOMAS, LEONA MARLENE, health information educator; b. Rock Springs, Wyo., Jan. 15, 1933; d. Leonard H. and Opal (Wright) Francis; m. Craig L. Thomas, Feb. 22, 1955; (div. Sept. 1978); children: Peter, Paul, Patrick, Alexis. BA, Govs. State U., 1982, MHS, 1986; cert. med. records adminstrn., U. Colo., 1954. Dir. med. records dept. Meml. Hosp. Sweetwater County, Rock Springs, Wyo., 1954-57; staff assoc. Am. Med. Records Assn., Chgo., 1972-77, asst. editor, 1979-81; statistician Westlake Hosp., Melrose Park, Ill., 1982-84; asst. prof. Chgo. State U., 1984—, acting dir. health info. adminstrn. program, 1991-92, 94—; acting coord. health info. program Internat. Coll., 1994—; chairperson Coll. Allied Health Pers., 1986-88; mem. rev. bd. network Newsletter of the Assembly on Edn.; acting dir. health info. Internat. Coll., Naples, Fla., 1994. Co-pres. Ill. Dist. 60 PTA, Westmont; liaison Ill. Trauma Registry, 1991. Mem. Assembly on Edn., Am. Health Info. Mgmt. Assn., Am. Pub. Health Assn., Ill. Pub. Health Assn., Chgo. and Vicinity Med. Records Assn. (publicity com. 1989-90), Ill. Assn. Allied Health Profls., Gov.'s State Alumni Assn. Democrat. Methodist. Home: 6340 Americana Dr Apt 1101 Clarendon Hills IL 60514-2249 Office: Chgo State U Coll Nursin & Allied Health 95th at King Dr Chicago IL 60628

THOMAS, LINDA JOYCE, English composition and literature educator; b. Glasgow, Ky., Mar. 13, 1944; d. Dennis Cloyd and Mary Dorothy (Cary) T. BA in English, French and Secondary Edn., Western Ky. U., 1966, MA in English, 1968; postgrad., Beaver Coll., 1982-83, U. Ky. Cert. tchr., Ky. Grad. asst. to dean women Western Ky. U., Bowling Green, 1966-68, asst. to dean students, 1968-69; instr. English Butler High Sch., Louisville, 1969-70; tchr. writing and lit. Pinkerton High Sch., Midway, Ky., 1970-73; prof. writing and lit. Midway Coll., 1970—; dir. Writing Across the Curriculum, Midway Coll., 1982-84, 90—, chairperson arts and humanities divsn., 1983-86, apptd. faculty rep. to pres.'s instl. planning com., 1992—, strategic planning; mem. Internat. Book Project, Lexington, 1988-90; mem. Nat. English Lang. Standards Project Task Force, 1992—. Mem. adv. com. Writer's Voice YMCA Ctrl. Ky., Lexington, 1992—, co-chair, 1994—; mem. Writer's Voice YMCA of Am.; friend Ky. Ednl. TV; supporter Ky. Humanities Coun. Grantee NEH, 1982, 93, 94, Ky. Humanities Coun., 1985-86. Mem. NEA, MLA, Nat. Coun. Tchrs. English, Nat. Mus. Women Artists (charter), Conf. on Coll. Composition and Comm., Ky. Coun. Tchrs. English/Lang. Arts (sec. exec. bd. 1992-94, 94—), Ky. Edn. Assn. (faculty advisor student programs 1975-93, Outstanding Svc. award 1992, 93, 94), Smithsonian Assocs., Western Ky. Alumni Assn., Chi Omega, Phi Theta Kappa (hon., faculty advisor, Horizon Svc. award 1992). Democrat. Mem. Ch. Christ. Home: 3708 Cottage Circle Lexington KY 40513 Office: Midway Coll 512 E Stephens St Midway KY 40347

THOMAS, LYDIA WATERS, research and development executive; b. Norfolk, Va., Oct. 13, 1944; d. William Emerson and Lillie Ruth (Roberts) Waters; m. James Carter Thomas (div. 1970); 1 child, Denee Marrielle. BS in Zoology, Howard U., 1965, PhD in Cytology, 1973; MS in Microbiology, Am. U., 1971. Sr. v.p., gen. mgr. The MITRE Corp., McLean, Va., 1973-94, 1994—; affiliate Ctr. Sci. and Internat. Affairs, Harvard U., Cambridge, Mass., 1990—; bd. dirs. Cabot Corp.; mem. Draper Labs., Inc. Author: Automation Impacts on Industry, 1983. Mem. Environ. Adv. Bd., U.S. C.E., 1980-82; expert witness, Senate, U.S. govt. pub. hearings, Washington, 1985; mem. adv. bd. INFORM, N.Y.C., George Wash. U. Va. Campus; mem. Supt.'s Bus./Industry Adv. Coun. Fairfax County Pub. Schs. Recipient Tribute to Women in Internat. Industry YMCA, 1986, EBONE Image award Coalition of 100 Black Women, 1990, Dean's award Black Engineer of the Year, 1991. Mem. AAAS, AIAA, Am. Def. Preparedness Assn., Am. Mgmt. Assn., Am. Soc. Toxicology, Am. Astronautical Soc., Nat. Energy Resources Orgn., Nat. Security Indsl. Assn., Soc. Macro-Engring., Teratology Soc., U.S. Energy Assn., African Sci. Inst., Women in Aerospace, Nat. Space Club, Sigma Xi (steering com.), Alpha Kappa Alpha. Office: The MITRE Corporation 7525 Colshire Dr Mc Lean VA 22102

THOMAS, MABLE, communications company executive, former state legislator; b. Atlanta, Nov. 8, 1957; d. Bernard and Madie Thomas. BS in Pub. Adminstrn., Ga. State U., 1982, postgrad., 1983—. With acctg. dept. Trust Co. Bank, Atlanta, 1977; recreation supr. Sutton Community Sch., Atlanta, 1977-78; data transcriber Ga. Dept. Natural Resources, Atlanta, 1978-79; clk. U.S. Census Bur., Atlanta, 1980; laborer City of Atlanta Parks and Recreation, 1980-81; student asst. Ga. State U., Atlanta, 1981-82; state rep. Ga. House Reps., Atlanta, 1984-94; pres. Master Comms. Inc., Atlanta, 1994—; mem. exec. com. Ga. Legis. Black Census, Atlanta, 1985—. Mem. adv. youth council Salvation Army Bellwood Club, 1975; founder Vine City Community Improvement Assn., Atlanta, 1985; mem. Neighborhood Planning Unit, Ga. State U. Adv. Bd. of Comprehensive Youth Services, 1988—, Nat. Black Woman's Health Project, Ga. Housing Coalition; actively involved in Say No to Drugs Program; bd. dirs. Am. Cancer Soc., 1988—. Recipient Bronze Jubilee award City of Atlanta Cultural Affairs, 1984, Disting. Service award Grady Hosp., 1985, Human Service award for community and political leadership for disadvantaged, 1986, Exceptional Service award Young Community Leaders, 1986, Citizenship award Salvation Army Club; named Outstanding Freshman Legislator, 1986, one of Outstanding Young People of Atlanta, 1987. Mem. Ga. Assn. Black Elected Officials (mem. housing and econ. devel. com.), Conf. Minority Pub. Adminstrn. (Outstanding Service award), Nat. Polit. Congress Black Women (bd. dirs.). Democrat. Methodist. Home: PO Box 573 Atlanta GA 30301-0573

THOMAS, MARGARET JEAN, clergywoman, religious research consultant; b. Detroit, Dec. 24, 1943; d. Robert Elcana and Purcella Margaret (Hartness) T. BS, Mich. State U., 1964; MDiv, Union Theol. Sem., Va., 1971; DMin, San Francisco Theol. Sem., 1991. Ordained to ministry United Presbyn. Ch., 1971. Dir. rsch. bd. Christian edn. Presbyn. Ch. U.S., Richmond, Va., 1965-71; dir. rsch. gen. coun. Presbyn. Ch. U.S., Atlanta, 1972-73; mng. dir. rsch. div. support agy. United Presbyn. Ch. U.S.A., N.Y.C., 1974-76; dep. exec. dir. gen. assembly mission coun. United Presbyn. Ch. U.S.A., 1977-83; dir. N.Y. coordination Presbyn. Ch. (U.S.A.), 1983-85; exec. dir. Minn. Coun. Chs., Mpls., 1985-95; synod exec. Synod of Lakes and Prairies Presbyn. Ch. (U.S.A.), Bloomington, Minn., 1995—; mem. Permant Jud. Commn., Presbyn. Ch. (U.S.A.), 1985-91, moderator, 1989-91, mem. adv. com. on constn., 1992—; sec. com. on ministry Twin Cities Area Presbytery, Mpls., 1985-91, vice moderator, 1991-92, moderator, 1992-93; mem. joint religious legis. coalition, 1985—; mem. Commn. on Regional and Local Ecumenism Nat. Coun. Chs., 1988-91, officer Ecumenical Networks, 1992—, mem. Unity and Rels. unit, 1992-93; mem. nat. planning com. Nat. Workshop on Christian Unity, 1992—; bd. dirs. Franklin Nat. Bank, Mpls., 1987—. Contbr. articles to profl. jours. Mem. adv. panel crime victims svcs. Hennepin County Atty.'s Office, 1985-86, Police and Community Rels. Task Force, St. Paul, 1986; mem. adv. panel Hennepin County Crime Victim Coun., 1990-93, chmn., 1990-93; bd. dirs. Minn. Foodshare, 1985-95, Minn. Coalition on Health, 1986-92, Minn. Black-on-Black Crime Task Force, 1988, Twin Cities Coalition Affordable Health Care, 1986-87; co-chmn. Minn. Interreligious Com., 1988-95; bd. dirs. Abbott Northwestern Pastoral Counseling Ctr., 1988-91, chmn., 1990-91. Recipient Human Rels. award Jewish Community Rels. Coun./Anti-Defamation League, 1989, Gov.'s Cert. of Commendation for Women's Leadership, 1993. Mem. Nat. Assn. Ecumenical Staff, N.Am. Acad. Ecumenists, Religious Edn. Assn. (sec. 1974-76), NOW (Outstanding Woman of Minn. 1986), Amnesty Internat. Mem. Democrat-Farm-Labor Party. Office: Synod of Lakes and Prairies Presbyn Ch USA 8012 Cedar Ave S Bloomington MN 55425

THOMAS, MARIANNE GREGORY, school psychologist; b. N.Y.C., Dec. 10, 1945. BS, U. Conn., 1985; MS, So. Conn. State U., 1987. Cert. sch. psychologist, Conn., N.Y. Sch. psychology intern Greenwich (Conn.) Pub. Schs., 1986-87; sch. psychologist Hawthorne (N.Y.)-Cedar Knolls, U.F.S.D., 1987-88, Darien (Conn.) Pub. Schs., 1988—. Mem. AAUW, NASP (cert.), Conn. Assn. Sch. Psychologists. Home: 154 Indian Rock Rd New Canaan CT 06840-3117

THOMAS, MARILYN JANE, insurance company executive; b. Fremont, Ohio, Dec. 11, 1944; d. Myron Elwood and Elvira Evelyn (Plagman) Magsig; m. William E. Thomas, Jr., Nov. 7, 1992; stepchildren: Dana Lauren Thomas, Keira Anne Schwartz. BS in Edn., Capital U., Columbus, 1966; postgrad., U. Calif., Irvine, Fullerton, 1969-70. Tchr. pub. schs., Ohio, Calif., La., 1966-71; underwriter Tenn. Life Ins. Co., Houston, Tex., 1971-73; supr., mgr. contracts adminstrn. Phila. Life Ins. Co. (merger with Tenn. Life Ins. Co.), Houston, 1973-80; systems analyst Phila. Life Ins. Co., Houston, 1980-84; dir. market research/product devel. Phila. Am. Life Ins. Co. (merger Phila. Life Ins. Co.), Houston, 1984-87; 2d v.p. mktg. Phila. Am. Life Ins., Houston, 1987—. Vol. Spl. Olympics, Houston; tchr. Project Business, 1981. Recipient Outstanding Woman award, Houston YWCA, 1984. Mem. Am. Bus. Women's Assn. (chmn. edn. com. 1987-88), Soc. Group Contract Analysts (chmn. com. 1977-80), Houston Assn. Health Underwriters. Republican. Lutheran. Office: Phila Am Life Ins 3121 Buffalo Speedway Houston TX 77098-1805

THOMAS, MARLO (MARGARET JULIA THOMAS), actress; b. Detroit, Nov. 21, 1943; d. Danny and Rose Marie (Cassanti) T.; m. Phil Donahue, May 21, 1980. Ed., U. So. Calif. Theatrical appearances in Thieves, Broadway, 1974, Barefoot in the Park, London, Social Security, Broadway, 1986, The Shadow Box, Broadway, 1994; star: TV series That Girl, 1966-71 (Golden Globe award Best TV actress, 1967); appeared in TV films: The Body Human: Facts for Girls (Emmy award Best Performer Children's Program), 1981, The Last Honor of Kathryn Beck, 1984 (also exec. prodr.), Consenting Adults, 1985, Nobody's Child, 1986 (Emmy Best Dramatic Actress), Held Hostage: The Sis and Jerry Levin Story, 1991, Ultimate Betrayal, 1994, Reunion, 1994; conceived book and record, starred in TV spl. Free to Be. . . You and Me, 1974 (Emmy for best children's show); films include Thieves, 1977, In the Spirit, 1991, Jenny, 1963; conceived book, record and TV spl. Free to Be A Family (Emmy Best Children's Show). Recipient 4 Emmys, Golden Globe award, George Foster Peabody award, Tom Paine award Nat. Emergency Civil Liberties Com. Mem. Ms. Found., Nat. Women's Polit. Caucus. Office: CAA 9830 Wilshire Blvd Beverly Hills CA 90210*

THOMAS, NADINE, nurse, legislator, state official; b. Fort Myers, Fla., May 14, 1952; d. Marvin Lee and Carrie Lee (North) Dixon; m. Jolivet Aurelious Thomas, Jan. 15, 1977 (div. 1982); children: Nadia Joli, Doris Silas, Dorothy Silas. A, Edison Community Coll., 1974; student, Ga. State U., 1978-82. RN, Ga. Nursing unit coord. Crawford Long Hosp., Atlanta, 1977-90; nursing supr. S.W. Hosp. and Med. Ctr., Atlanta, 1990—; chmn. Changed Living Recovery, Decatur, Ga., 1991-92; bd. dirs. Ctr. for Drug Rehab. Mem. DeKalb Dem. Party Exec. Com., Decatur, 1988-90; pres. Brookwood and Knollwood Community Assn., Atlanta, 1988-92; state rep. Ga. Ho. Reps., Atlanta, 1990-92; co-pres. Sky Haven Pres. PTA, Atlanta, 1991-92. Mem. ANA, Ga. Nurses Assn. (Nurse Excellence award 1991). Home: 1375 Town Country Dr SE Atlanta GA 30316-3919 Office: Ga Ho Reps Capitol Ave Atlanta GA 30334*

THOMAS, PATRICIA ANNE, retired law librarian; b. Cleve., Aug. 21, 1927; d. Richard Joseph and Marietta Bernadette (Teevans) T.; BA, Case Western Res. U., 1949, JD, 1951. Admitted to Ohio bar, 1951, U.S. Supreme Ct. bar, 1980; librarian Arter & Hadden, Cleve., 1951-62; asst. librarian, then librarian IRS, Washington, 1962-78; library dir. Adminstrv. Office, U.S. Cts., 1978-93; ret. 1993. Mem. Am. Assn. Law Libraries, Law Librarians Soc. D.C. (pres. 1967-69).

THOMAS, PATRICIA ANNE, counselor; b. New Orleans, July 6, 1943; d. Charles Gerald and Ruth Mary (Hebert) T. BS, Webster U., 1966; MA, U. Colo., 1975; PhD, U. New Orleans, 1983. Lic. profl. counselor; nat. cert. counselor. Sci. tchr. St. Francis/Aloysius High Sch., Vicksburg, Miss., 1966-70, St. Joseph Sch., Springfield, Mo., 1970-71, Mercy High Sch., St. Louis, 1971-72; neighborhood worker Hope House, Inc., New Orleans, 1972-74; houseparent Mercita Hall, St. Louis, 1974-75; counselor New Orleans Pub. Schs., 1975—. Bd. dirs. Kingsley House, New Orleans, 1983-91. Mem. La. Sch. Counselors Assn. (pres. 1993-94), La. Counseling Assn., Am. Counseling Assn., Am. Sch. Counselors Assn., Assn. Multicultural Edn. and Devel., Am. Holistic Counselors Assn. (treas., newsletter editor 1984-90). Home: 7827 Sycamore New Orleans LA 70118 Office: McMain Magnet Sch 5712 S Claiborne New Orleans LA 70125

THOMAS, PATRICIA GRAFTON, secondary school educator; b. Michigan City, Ind., Sept. 30, 1921; d. Robert Wadsworth and Elinda (Oppermann) Grafton; student Stephens Coll., 1936-39, Purdue U., summer 1938; BEd magna cum laude, U. Toledo, 1966; postgrad. (fellow) Bowling Green U., 1968; m. Lewis Edward Thomas, Dec. 21, 1939; children: Linda T., Stephanie A. (Mrs. Andrew M. Pawuk), I. Kathryn (Mrs. James N. Ramsey), Deborah (Mrs. Edward Preissler). Tchr., Toledo Bd. Edn., 1959-81, tchr. lang. arts Byrnedale Sch., 1976-81. Dist. capt. Planned Parenthood, 1952-53, ARC, 1954-55; mem. lang. arts curriculum com. Toledo Bd. Edn., 1969, mem. grammar curriculum com., 1974; bd. dirs. Anthony Wayne Nursery Sch., 1983—; bd. dirs. Toledo Women's Symphony Orch. League, 1983—, sec., 1985—; co-chmn. Showcase of the Arts, 1990-92. Mem. AAUW, Toledo Soc. Profl. Engrs. Aux., Helen Kreps Guild, Toledo Artists' Club, Spectrum, Friends of Arts (bd. dirs. 1989—), Phi Kappa Phi, Phi Delta Kappa, Kappa Delta Pi, Pi Lambda Theta (chpt. pres. 1978-80), Delta Kappa Gamma (chpt. pres. 1976-78, area membership chmn. 1978-80, 1st place award for exhbn. 1985). Republican. Episcopalian. Home: 4148 Deepwood Ln Toledo OH 43614-5512

THOMAS, PHYLLIS EUNICE, elementary coordinator, educator; b. Pt. Austin, Mich., Feb. 2, 1933; d. Enoch S. and Gertrude (Inda) Horetski; m. Robert Harold Thomas, Aug. 17, 1957; children: Kevin G., Tammie M. BA, Madonna U., 1957; MAT in Reading, Oakland U., 1971; postgrad., Saginaw Valley U., 1990. Tchr. grades. K-4 Rosevile (Mich.) Community Schs., 1956-80, tchr. chtp. 1, 1980-93, coord. elem. testing, 1988—, parenting coord. chpt. 1, 1990—, coord. chpt. 1, 1992—; chair dist. testing com. Roseville Schs., 1990-94; mem. Roseville Early Childhood Com., 1992-94. Active parent adv. bd. Warren (Mich.) Schs., 1973. Recipient Cert. of Appreciation, Gov. of Mich., 1990. Mem. ACA, Internat. Reading Assn., Mich. Assn. for Edn. of Young Children, Macomb Area Assn. of State and Fed. Program Specialists (pres.-elect 1993-94, pres. 1993-94), Macomb Reading Coun. (treas. 1993—). Home: 31471 Pinto Dr Warren MI 48093-7624 Office: Roseville Community Sc Roseville MI 48066

THOMAS, RHONDA CHURCHILL, lawyer; b. 1947; m. J. Regan Thomas; children: Ryan, Aaron, Evan. BA, Drury Coll., 1969; JD, U. Mo., 1972, Yale U., 1973. Bar: Mo. 1973. Newswoman Sta. KFRU Radio, Columbia, Mo., 1969-70; law clk. to Hon. Robert E. Seiler Supreme Ct. of Mo., Jefferson City, 1973-74; asst. city counselor City of Columbia, 1974-76, city counselor, chief legal advisor to city coun., dept. heads, 1976-79; assoc. prof. law U. Mo., 1979-82; assoc., then ptnr. Gaar & Bell, St. Louis, 1982-85; ptnr. Thompson & Mitchell, St. Louis, 1985—; past chmn. franchise com. Nat. Inst. Mcpl. Law Officers. Contbr. articles to profl. jours. Past chmn. Boone County Home Rule Charter Commn.; past pres. Boone County Indsl. Devel. Authority. Mem. ABA (local govt. law sect., taxation sect.), Mo. Bar Assn. (mem. edn. law com., mem. local govt. law com., mem. med.-legal rels. com., past mem. spl. com. on quality and methods of practice), St. Louis Bar Assn., Nat. Assn. Bond Lawyers, Mo. Mcpl. Attys. Assn. (past pres.). Office: Thompson & Mitchell 1 Mercantile Ctr Ste 3400 Saint Louis MO 63101-1623

THOMAS, RHONDA ROBBINS, marketing executive, consultant; b. Houston, Dec. 15, 1958; d. George B. and Barbara (Lillich) R.; m. Fred Holt Thomas, Aug. 22, 1981 (div. 1991); children: Brian P., Paige A. BA, U. Tex., 1980; MBA, So. Meth. U., 1989; PhD, U. Tex., Arlington, 1994. Profl. interior designer. Pres., CEO Design Austin, Tex., 1984-90; pres. Denova, Austin, 1988-93; prin. MarketShare Consulting, 1993—; vis. asst. prof. mktg. U. Tex. Arlington, 1990—; adj. mktg. faculty mem. Cox Sch. So. Meth. U., 1993—. Bd. dirs. Children's Cancer Ctr., Austin, 1987-88, Dallas Mus. Art, 1990—. Lester Johnson Grad. fellow Inst. Bus. Designers Found., 1990, Lakawanna Leather fellow, 1991. Mem. DAR, Am. Soc. Interior Designers (Design Excellence award 1985, 87, 88), Inst. Bus. Designers, Austin C. of C. Home: 7409 Turtle Creek Blvd Dallas TX 75225 Office: U Tex Arlington Dept Mktg Arlington TX 76019

THOMAS, ROSE LORRAINE CROSSETT, federal government secretary; b. Little Rock, May 6, 1921; d. Jesse Hawkins and Agnes Rose (Dowden) Crossett; m. Gordon Ward Thomas, Sept. 10, 1943 (dec. Oct. 1989); 1 child, Rose Elizabeth Thomas Camp. Student, Stanford (Calif.) U., 1946-47, Lake Forest (Ill.) Coll., 1960-62; AA, Rockford (Ill.) Coll., 1965; BA, U. Ark., 1979. Sec. Senator John L. McClellan, Little Rock, 1942; mgr. mail order Sears, Roebuck & Co., Little Rock, 1943; sec. War Assets Adminstrn., Willow Run, Mich., 1947-48; adminstrv. asst. U. Mich., Ann Arbor, 1948-51; fiscal acct. 9th Naval Dist., Great Lakes, Ill., 1951-52; sec. admissions office Lake Forest Coll., 1959-62, Rockford Coll., 1963-66; budget analyst U.S. Army, Ft. Sheridan, Ill., 1967-72; budget analyst U.S. Army, Ft. Sam Houston, Tex., 1967-72, army community svc. asst., 1972-73; sec. Housing Referral Office, Little Rock Air Force Base, 1974-80, U.S. Army Info. Systems Command, Ft. McPherson, Ga., 1982-85; counselor Equal Opportunity Office, Ft. McPherson, 1981-85; sec./adminstr. Alcohol and Drug Abuse Program, Ft. McPherson, 1985-91. Author: (with others) The David Lowe Family, 1976. Mem. Rep. Women, Newnan, Ga., 1980-83, Federally Employed Women, Atlanta, 1984-86. Mem. AAUW (v.p. 1985-90), United Daus. of the Confederacy, DAR, The Ark. Pioneers, Officers Wives Club, U. Ark. Alumni Club. Republican. Presbyterian. Home: PO Box 712 Newnan GA 30264-0712 Office: Alcohol & Drug Abuse Prevention and Control Bldg 171 Fort McPherson GA 30330

THOMAS, RUTH EICKELBERG, preschool educator, medical assistant; b. Fairmont, Minn., Nov. 29, 1940; d. Elmer William and Emma Lillian (Hansen) Eickelberg; m. John Henson Thomas, Aug. 5, 1962; children: John David, Mark Evan. BS in Home Econs. cum laude, Ohio State U., 1962. Cert. home economist, Ohio. Tchr. home econs. Whitehall (Ohio) Yearling High Sch., 1962-63; chmn. home econs. dept. Chillicothe (Ohio) High Sch., 1963-66; program dir. Falls Church (Va.) City Presch., 1976—; med. asst. Dr. Eric Lauf, Falls Church, 1989—; product cons. SP Demonstrations, Gt. Falls, Va., 1987—. Den mother, com. chmn. Boy Scouts Am., 1976-82; v.p., treas. PTA, 1978; pres. Jr. Women's Club, 1974-75; elder Presbyn. Ch., 1981-85; chmn. session records rev. Nat. Capital Presbytery, 1984-87; mem. ecclesiastical com. Synod of Piedmont, 1986-87; clk. of session Lewinsville Presbyn. Ch., 1982-85, vol. coord., 1989-94. Mem. Nat. Assn. for Edn. Young Children, Phi Upsilon Omicron, Omicron Nu. Home: 6702 Moly Dr Falls Church VA 22046-1834

THOMAS, SANDRA ANN, songwriter, lyricist; b. Dayton, Ohio, Oct. 14; d. Joseph Burghard and Mary Josephine (Bogie) T. AA, Palm Beach Community Coll., Lake Worth, Fla.; BA, Fla. Atlantic U. Cert. English tchr. V.p. Lady Sabre Recording and Prodn. Co., Inc., Delray Beach, Fla., 1989-90; pres. Lady Sabre Publishing Co., Inc., Delray Beach, 1989—. Lyricist, singer (albums) Under a Strange Spell, 1988, , Sandra Thomas Sings Folk Music, 1989, Enchanted, 1990; composer (documentary soundtrack) First Breath, 1971, Life and Breath, 1990; singer, guitarist Fla. Atlantic U., 1971. Nat. dir. pub. edn. Iron Overload Diseases Assn., Inc., West Palm Beach, Fla., 1991; mem. Gulf Stream (Fla.) Rep. Club, 1991, Jr. League Boca Raton. Recipient Awards for Composition Music City Song Festival, 1988-91. Mem. ASCAP (award for lyrics 1991), AFTRA, AAUW, SAG, Am. Guild Variety Artists, Actors Equity Assn., DAR (2nd v.p.), Ladies Oriental Shrine North Am., Boca Raton and Fla. Atlantic U. Alumnae Assn., Order Ea. Star, Alpha Omicron Pi. Office: Lady Sabre Pub Co Inc PO Box 6906 Delray Beach FL 33484-0906

THOMAS, SHARYN LEE, elementary education educator; b. Springfield, Mass., Nov. 6, 1948; d. John H. and Meta L. (Postell) T. BFA, U. Mass. at Amherst, 1974; MEd, Springfield Coll., 1980; postgrad. in Spanish, Worcester State Coll., Am. Internat. Coll.; postgrad., Our Lady of Elms Coll., Anna Maria Coll., 1990, Fitchburg State Coll., 1994. Cert. elem. educator K-8, Mass., art educator K-12, Mass. Classroom tchr. Springfield (Mass.) Pub. Schs., 1980-83, tchr. K-4 FLES/Spanish, art and art appreciation, 1983-88, tchr. grades 5 and 6, 1988-91, tchr. 3rd grade, 1991—; tchr. tng. task force Springfield Coll., 1993. Recipient Dept. Edn. Bd. Edn. Citation Merit for Exemplary Ednl. Program, 1986, Springfield Edn. Fund Mini-Grant, 1986. Mem. Mass. Fgn. Lang. Assn., Am. Assn. Tchrs. Spanish and Portuguese, Mass. Tchrs. Assn., Springfield Edn. Assn. Home: PO Box 90598 Springfield MA 01139-0598

THOMAS, SHERIDEN ETOILE, educator; b. Los Alamos, N.Mex., Jan. 31, 1949; s. Paulus Powell and Lillian Catherine (Emmich) T. BFA, U. N.Mex., 1971; MFA, U. Minn., 1974. Actor Garrett County Playhouse, Md., summers 1968/69, Nebr. Repertory Co., Lincoln, Nebr., summers 1970/71, Guthrie Theatre, Mpls., 1972-74; tchr. Wright State U., Dayton, Ohio, 1987; actor/tchr. Cin. Playhouse, Ohio, 1988; dir./tchr. Gov.'s Magnet Sch. for the Arts, Norfolk, Va., 1990; artist-in-residence Cornell U., Ithaca, 1991-93; actor Dallas Theatre Ctr., Tex., 1994; asst. prof. So. Meth. U., Dallas, 1993—. Actor: King Lear, 1993, Who's Afraid of Virginia Woolf?, 1991; dir. The Triumph of Love, 1994, Women Beware Women, 1993, The Triumph of Love, 1994. Founding bd. dirs. Women in Theatre, L.A., 1978-80. Recipient Recognition award Women in Theatre, L.A., 1980; Bronze medal Nat. Am. Coll. Theatre Festival, Washington, 1973; Bush fellow U. Minn., 1971-74. Mem. Actors Equity Assn., Assn. for Theatre in Higher Edn., Women in Theatre Program. Democrat. Office: So Methodist Univ Meadows Sch of the Arts Dallas TX 75275

THOMAS, SHIRLEY, author, educator, business executive; b. Glendale, Calif.; d. Oscar Miller and Ruby (Thomas) Annis; m. W. White, Feb. 22, 1949 (div. June 1952)); m. William C. Perkins, Oct. 24, 1969. BA in Modern Lit., U. Sussex, Eng., 1960, PhD in Comm., 1967. Actress, writer, producer, dir. numerous radio and TV stas., 1942-46; v.p. Commodore Prodns., Hollywood, Calif., 1946-52; pres. Annis & Thomas, Inc., Hollywood, 1952—; prof. technical writing U. So. Calif., L.A., 1975—; Hollywood corr. NBC, 1952-56; editor motion pictures CBS, Hollywood, 1956-58; corr. Voice of Am., 1958-59; now free lance writer; cons. biol. scis. communication project George Washington U., 1965-66; cons. Stanford Rsch. Inst., 1967-68, Jet Propulsion Lab., 1969-70. Author: Men of Space vols. 1-8, 1960-68, Spanish trans., 1961, Italian, 1962; Space Tracking Facilities, 1963, Computers: Their History, Present Applications and Future, 1965; The Book of Diets, 1974. Organizer, chmn. City of L.A. Space Adv. Com., 1964-73, Women's Space Symposia, 1962-73; foudner, chmn. aerospace hist. com. Calif. Mus. Sci. and Industry; chmn. Theodore von Karman Postage Stamp Com., 1965—, stamp issued 1992. Recipient Aerospace Excellence award Calif. Mus. Found. 1991, Nat. Medal Honor DAR, 1992. Fellow Brit. Interplanetary Soc.;

mem. AIAA, AAAS, Internat. Soc. Aviation Writers, Air Force Assn. (Airpower Arts and Letters award 1961), Internat. Acad. Astronautics, Nat. Aero. Assn., Nat. Asn. Sci. Writers, Soc. for Tech. Communications, Am. Astronautical Soc., Nat. Geog. Soc., Am. Soc. Pub. Adminstrn. (sci. and tech. in govt. com. 1972—), Achievement Awards for Coll. Scientists, Muses of Calif., Theta Sigma Phi, Phi Beta. Home: 8027 Hollywood Blvd Los Angeles CA 90046-2510 Office: U So Calif Profl Writing Program University Park Waite-Phillips Hall 404 Los Angeles CA 90089-4034

THOMAS, SUZANNE WARD, college official, communications educator; b. Akron, Ohio, Sept. 21, 1954; d. Kendall Kramer and Margaret Ann (Owen) Ward; m. James Michael Thomas, Oct. 20, 1980; children: Seth Evin, James Kendall. BS in Edn., Miami U., Oxford, Ohio, 1977; MA in Communications, Regent U., Virginia Beach, Va., 1980. Writer, producer Sta. WVIZ, PBS, Cleve., 1980-82; dir. pub. rels. Sta. WOAC-TV, Canton, Ohio, 1982-83, hostess children's show, 1982-84; v.p. Thomas Video Prodns., Canal Fulton, Ohio, 1987-90; dir. pub. rels., instr. communications Malone Coll., Canton, 1990—, editor Horizon, 1990—. Author: (children's book) The Miracles of Jesus, 1991, also manuals. Hostess pub. affairs program Community TV Consortium, Canton, 1987; subcom. chmn. Govt. Day, Leadership Canton, 1987; v.p. Right to Life Ednl. Found., Canton, 1990; chmn. pub. rels. Jr. League Canton, 1986-87, rec. sec., 1987-88; bd. dirs. PTO, 1989-90. Recipient Sparkler award Jr. League Canton, 1986, Pub. Rels. award, 1987, Addy awards Canton Advt. Club, 1992. Mem. Sales and Mktg. Execs. (bd. dirs. Stark County chpt. 1989), Assn. Jr. Leagues Internat. Republican. Office: Malone Coll 515 25th St NW Canton OH 44709-3897

THOMAS, TERESA ANN, microbiologist, educator; b. Wilkes-Barre, Pa., Oct. 17, 1939; d. Sam Charles and Edna Grace T. BS cum laude, Coll. Misericordia, 1961; MS in Biology, Am. U. Beirut, 1965; MS in Microbiology, U. So. Calif., 1973. Tchr., sci. supr., curriculum coord. Meyers High Sch., Wilkes-Barre, 1962-64, Wilkes-Barre Area Public Schs., 1961-66; rsch. assoc. Proctor Found. for Rsch. in Ophthalmology U. Calif. Med. Ctr., San Francisco, 1966-68; instr. Robert Coll. of Istanbul (Turkey), 1968-71, Am. Edn. in Luxembourg, 1971-72, Bosco Tech. Inst., Rosemead, Calif., 1973-74, San Diego Community Coll. Dist., 1974-80; prof. math.-sci. div. Southwestern Coll., Chula Vista, Calif., 1980—, pres. acad. senate, 1984-85, del., 1986-89; chmn., coord., steering com. project Cultural Rsch. Educational and Trade Exchange, 1991—, Southwestern Coll.-Shanghai Inst. Fgn. Trade; coord. Southwestern Coll. Great Teaching Seminar, 1987, 88, 89, coord. scholars program, 1988-90; mem. exec. com. Acad. Senate for Calif. C.Cs., 1985-86, Chancellor of Calif. C.Cs. Adv. and Rev. Council Fund for Instrnl. Improvement, 1984-86; coord. So. Calif. Biotech Edn. Consortium, 1993—; adj. asst. prof. Chapman Coll., San Diego, 1974-83; asst. prof. San Diego State U., 1977-79; chmn. Am. Colls. Istanbul Sci. Week, 1969-71; mem. adv. bd. Chapman Coll. Community Center, 1979-80; cons. sci. curriculum Calif. Dept. Edn., 1986—; pres. Internat. Relations Club 1959-61; mem. San Francisco World Affairs Coun., 1966-68, San Diego World Affairs Coun., 1992—; v.p. Palomar Palace Estates Home Owners Assn., 1983-85, pres. 1994—. mem. editorial rev. bd. Jour. of Coll. Sci. Teaching, NSTA, 1988-92; bd. dirs. San Diego-Leon Sister Cities Soc., 1991-94. Mem. Chula Vista Nature Interpretive Ctr. (life), Internat. Friendship Commn., Chula Vista, 1985—, vice chmn. 1989-90, chmn. 1990-92, Chula Vista, Calif., 1987—; mem. U.S.-Mex. Sister Cities Assn., nat. bd. dirs., 1992-94, gen. chair 30th nat. conv., 1993. NSF fellow, 1965; USPHS fellow, 1972-73; recipient Nat. Teaching Excellence award Nat. Inst. Staff and Orgnl. Devel., 1989; recognized at Internat. Conf. Teaching Excellence, Austin, 1989; Pa. Heart Assn. research grantee, 1962; named Southwestern Coll. Woman of Distinction, 1987. Mem. Am. Soc. Microbiology, Nat. Sci. Tchrs. Assn. (life, internat. com., coord. internat. honors exchange lectr. competition sponsored with Assn. Sci Educators Great Britain, 1986), Nat. Assn. Biology Tchrs. (life), Soc. Coll. Sci. Tchrs. (life), S.D. Zool. Soc., Calif. Tchrs. Assn., NEA, Am. Assn. Community and Jr. Colls., Giraffes, Am.-Lebanese Assn. San Diego (chmn. scholarship com., pres. 1988-93), Am. U. of Beirut Alumni and Friends of San Diego (1st v.p. 1984-91), Lions Internat. (S.W. San Diego County chpt. 1994—, bull. editor 1991-93, best bull. award 1992, 93, 2nd v.p. 1992-93, 1st v.p. 1993-94, editor Roaring Times Newsletter 1993-94, pres. 1994-95, chmn. dist. internat. rels. and cooperations com. 1993-95), Kappa Gamma Pi (pres. Wilkes-Barre chpt. 1963-64, San Francisco chpt. 1967-68), Sigma Phi Sigma, Phi Theta Kappa (hon. mem. 1994—), Alpha Pi Epsilon (advisor Southwestern Coll. chpt. 1989-90). Club: Am. Lebanese Syrian Ladies (pres. 1982-83). Office: Southwestern Coll 900 Otay Lakes Rd Chula Vista CA 91910

THOMAS, TERRA L., human services institute executive, psychologist; b. Easton, Md., Oct. 16, 1947; d. Clarence S. and Betty (Leatherberry) T.; children: Brooks, Rheaves and Nia (triplets). BS in Exptl. Psychology cum laude, Morgan State U., Balt., 1969; MA in Counselor Edn., NYU, 1971; MA in Clin. Psychology, Adelphi U., 1973, PhD in Clin. and Sch. Psychology, 1982; MBA, Northwestern U., 1991. Acting dean women Bloomingfield (N.J.) Coll., 1969-71; psychol. cons. Brownville Child Devel., Inc., Bklyn., 1972-74, Ebony Mgmt. Assocs., Bklyn., 1976-77; cons., program coord. children's div. Ada S. McKinley, Inc., Bklyn., 1976-78; with Human Resources Devel. Inst., Inc., Chgo., 1978—; v.p. Office Employee Devel., Assistance and Tng. Human Resources Devel. Inst., Inc., 1987-88, sr. v.p. Office Clin. Profl. Svcs., 1988-89, sr. v.p. Office Program Ops., 1989—, sr. v.p. Office Community and Support Svcs., 1990—, exec. v.p. Tech. Resources and Tng. Ctr., Inc., 1984—; assoc. mem. faculty Northwestern U. Med. Sch., Chgo., 1983—; adj. prof. Lewis Nati Coll. Edn., Chgo., 1982-83; mental health specialist Bobby Wright Comprehensive Mental Health Ctr., Chgo., 1975-77; sr. cons. Bakeman and Assoc., Chgo., 1983-87; presenter in field; trainer V.I. Dept. Health, 1988, Nat. Forum for Black Pub. Adminstrs., Chgo., 1990; instr. Jackson (Miss.) State U., summer 1988—; cons. Midwest AIDS Tng. Ctr., U. Ill., Chgo., 1987—, Nat. Inst. on Drug Abuse, 1987—; also others. Bd. dirs.-at-large Nat. Black Alcoholism Coun., 1984—; mem. Ill. Gov.'s Task Force on Consolidation, 1983-84; bd. dirs. Ill. Cert. Bds., Inc., 1985—, AIDS Found. Chgo., 1986-89; co-chmn. internal AIDS adv. panel Chgo. Dept. Health, 1987-88; mem. prevention communication adv. com. Ill. Dept. Alcoholism and Drug Abuse, 1988-89; mem. instl. rev. bd. Addiction Rsch. Inst., 1988—; bd. dirs. Nat. AIDS Network, 1988-90; mem. Ill. AIDS Adv. Coun., 1988—; also others. Recipient mayor's cert. of merit City of Chgo., 1985, Outstanding Alumni award Nat. Assn. for Equal Opportunity in Higher Edn., 1988, recognition award AIDS Found. Chgo., 1989; named One of 10 Outstanding Young Citizens, Chgo. Jr. Assn. Commerce and Industry, 1986. Mem. Assn. Black Psychologists (pres. 1976), Ill. Alcoholism and Drug Dependence Assn. (Prevention Leadership award 1987), NAACP (bd. dirs., edn. com. Chgo. chpt. 1988—), Psi Chi, Alpha Kappa Alpha. Home: 2008 S 7th St Camden NJ 08104

THOMAS, VIOLETA DE LOS ANGELES, real estate broker; b. Buenos Aires, Dec. 21, 1941; came to U.S., 1962; d. Angel and Lola (Andino) de Rios; m. Jess Thomas, Dec. 23, 1974; 1 child, Victor Justin. Student, Harvard U. and U. Buenos Aires, 1967-73. Mgr. book div. Time-Life, N.Y.C., 1967-73; real estate broker First Marin Realty, Inc., Mill Valley, Calif., 1985—. Bd. dirs. City of Tiburon, Calif., 1987-93, Art and Heritage Commn., Tiburon. Named Woman of Yr. City of Buenos Aires, 1977, Ageny of Yr. Marin County and San Francisco, 1987-92. Home: PO Box 6608 Town & Country MO 63006

THOMAS, VIRGINIA ANN, village clerk; b. Fife Lake, Mich., July 8, 1938; d. Floyd Elery and Lorraine Sybil (Birgy) Williams; m. Duane L. Thomas, Sept. 22, 1956; children: James Duane, Royce Dale. Student, Kirtland Coll., Roscommon, Mich., 1975, Northwestern Coll., Traverse City, Mich., 1976. Sec. Wayne Wire Cloth Products, Kalkaska, Mich., 1955-56, 65-70; typist, newswriter Leader & Kalkaskian, 1960-65; office mgr., village clk. Village of Kalkaska, 1970—; dep. clk. Kalkaska Twp., 1980—. Sec. RSVP Park Bd., Kalkaska, 1993—. Named Outstanding Elected Ofcl. for Kalkaska County, Traverse City C. of C., 1977. Mem. Mich. Mcpl. League, Mich. Mcpl. Clk.'s Assn., Sunshine Guild. Republican. Home: 710 4th St Kalkaska MI 49646-9506 Office: Village of Kalkaska 109 Fourth St Kalkaska MI 49646

THOMAS, VIRGINIA M., state legislator; married; 2 children. BS, Fairleigh Dickinson U., 1962; MSW, Rutgers U., 1965, ACSW, 1967. Mem. Howard County Coun., 1974-82, chmn., 1975-76; mem. Md. Ho. of Dels., 1983—, mem. coms. environ. matters, spl. drug & alcohol abuse, spl. joint mem. asst. program, subcom. long-term care, govt. commn. health care policy & fin.; psychiat. social worker. Bd. dirs. Grassroots; past bd. dirs. Howard County Sexual Assault Ctr.; trustee Howard County Gen. Hosp. Capital Fund, 1985—; mentor Howard County Sch. Sys., 1985-87. Mem. Howard County C. of C. (mentor 1985-87), Patuxent Bus. and Profl. Womens Club (bd. dirs.). Democrat. Home: 6153 Forty Winks Way Columbia MD 21045 Office: Md State Senate State Capital Annapolis MD 21401*

THOMAS, WENDY MARIE, lawyer; b. San Bernardino, Calif., June 6, 1960; d. Raymond E. and Cora G. Pecsar; m. Kelly Thomas, Sept. 25, 1982 (div. Oct. 1988). BA, U. Calif., Berkeley, 1981; JD, San Francisco Law Sch., 1986. Bar: Calif. 1989. Paralegal Office of City Atty., San Francisco, 1981-84, Fisher & Hurst, San Francisco, 1984-86; paralegal Selby Law Offices, San Francisco, 1986-89, assoc., 1989-90; ptnr. Gibson & Thomas, Novato, Calif., 1990—. Mem. ABA, ATLA, San Francisco Bar Assn., Sweet Adelines, Bel Marin Keys Yacht Club (rear commodore). Home: 284 Montego Key Novato CA 94949-5354 Office: Ste 3 394 Bel Marin Keys Blvd Novato CA 94949

THOMAS, YVONNE LINDER, psychological assistant; b. L.A., Jan. 6, 1962; d. Gerald Seymour and Lorraine Faye Linder; m. Morgan Edward Thomas, June 26, 1988. BA in Psychology cum laude, Calif. State U., Northridge, 1986; MA in Psychology, Calif. State U., L.A., 1987; PhD in Clin. Psychology, Calif. Grad. Inst., L.A., 1992. Registered psychol. asst. Psychol. intern The Counseling Ctr. West Los Angeles, Calif., 1988-92; psychol. asst. The Beverly Hills (Calif.) Counseling Ctr., 1992—; guest radio therapist KIEV-870 AM Radio, Glendale, Calif., 1993. Regular performer American Bandstand, 1981-84. Mem. APA, Calif. Psychol. Assn., Golden Key, Psi Chi. Office: The Beverly Hills Counseling Ctr 8383 Wilshire Blvd Ste 401 Beverly Hills CA 90211

THOMAS, YVONNE SHIREY, family and consumer science educator; b. Jenner Cross Roads, Pa., Dec. 1, 1938; d. Edward Merle and Orphabel (Shaffer) Shirey; m. William Edward Thomas, Dec. 23, 1961; children: Scott Forrest, Matthew David. BS, Indiana U. of Pa., 1960; MS, Hood Coll., 1987. Home econs. educator Bristol (Pa.) Jr. Sr. High Sch., 1960-64; elem. educator Barbers Point Elem. Sch., Ewa Beach, Hawaii, 1964-65; guidance counselor Workman Jr. High Sch., Pensacola, Fla., 1966-68; middle sch. educator Broadfording Christian Acad., Hagerstown, Md., 1973-76; home econs. educator Hancock (Md.) Jr. Sr. High Sch., 1986-88, Springfield Middle Sch., Williamsport, Md., 1988—; consumer affairs intern Citicorp Credit Svcs., Inc, Hagerstown, 1986; career day coord. Springfield Middle Sch., Williamsport, 1988-92. Bd. mem. Washington County Commn. for Women, Hagerstown, 1989-96, Cedar Ridge Ministeries, Hagerstown, 1990—. Recipient Judith Ruchkin Rsch. award Md. ASCD, Balt., 1987; named Washington County Home Econs. Tchr. of Yr., Md. Home Econs. Assn., Hagerstown, 1989, Women-on-the-Move, The Herald Mail Co., Hagerstown, 1991. Mem. AAUW (chair edn. fund 1989-90, v.p. membership 1990-92, grant 1992, pres. elect 1992-93, pres. 1993-94, grantee 1994, chair Md. state edn. fund 1990-92), Am. Assn. Family and Consumer Scis. (cert. family and consumer scientist 1986-96), Nat. Coun. on Family Rels. (cert. family life educator 1990-98), Delta Zeta (pres. 1959-60). Republican. Grace Brethren. Home: 8134 Mountain Laurel Rd Boonsboro MD 21713-1830

THOMAS-HARRIS, YVONNE ANITA, writer, poet; b. Millington, Tenn., Aug. 27, 1964; d. William Albert and Romelia Louise (Rich) Thomas; m. Gregory Harris; children: Antonio Dewayne James, Trishanna Renea, Chantell S. Harris. Cert., Morris & McDaniel Sch., Memphis, 1987, ITT Career Tng. Ctr., Millington, Tenn., 1991; diploma, Jefferson Bus. Coll., Memphis, 1988. Security guard Ringling Bros. and Barnum Bailey, Washington, 1986; mental health tech. S.E. Mental Health Ctr., Memphis, 1987; nursing asst. St. Peters Villa, Memphis, 1987; profl. model Memphis, 1990; housekeeper Econo Inn, Millington, 1990; med. asst. Primary Med. Care, Inc., Memphis, 1991; receptionist/supr. H & R Block, Memphis, Tenn., 1991—. Contbr. poems to World Treasury of Golden Poems, 1990, Poetic Voices of America, 1992; songwriter Cream High Records, Blue Time Blues, 1986. Sec. Project Amos, Memphis, 1989; vol. Dept. Human Svcs., Memphis, 1988. Democrat. Home and Office: 3815 Kerr Rd Millington TN 38053-4312

THOMASSEN, PAULINE F., medical/surgical nurse; b. Cleve., Jan. 19, 1939; d. Henry Clifford and Mabel Pauline (Hill) Nichols; m. Ruben Thomassen, Nov. 10, 1979; children: Rhonda, Terry, Diana, Philipp, Jody, Barbara. AA in Nursing, So. Colo. State Coll., 1974, BA in Psychology with distinction, 1975; BSN magna cum laude, Seattle Pacific U., 1986. RN, Wash. Staff nurse III orthopedic unit, preceptor orientation RNs and student RNs Swedish Hosp. Med. Ctr., Seattle, 1975—. Contbr. articles to nursing jours.

THOMAS TOPP, MARGARET ANN, art educator; b. Waukesha, Wis., June 19, 1951; d. Melvin Michael and Elizabeth (Brewer) T.; 1 child, James Michael; m. Joel David Topp, May 24, 1991. BA in Art Edn., Beloit Coll., 1974; MA in Art, U. Wis., Whitewater, 1981, MA in Ednl. Psychology, 1985; postgrad., U. Wis., 1987. Cert. K-12 art tchr., Wiss. Tchr. art Beloit (Wis.) Pub. Schs., 1974—; mem. staff Beloit Coll., 1992-93; muralist instr. Beloit Coll., summers, 1985-91, adj. prof., 1993—; adj. prof. Nat. Louis U., 1994—. Author: Effective Teachers; Effective Schools, 1989; contbr. articles to profl. jours. Bd. dirs. Wis.-Gate Found., 1985-87, Wis. Racquetball Assn., 1986-87, Wis. Future Problem Solving, 1986-87; pres. bd. dirs. YWCA, 1987-91; dir. Beloit and Vicinity Art Show, Beloit Coll., 1982-84, Rock Prairie Showcase Festival; founder Summer Explorers Beloit Coll. Mem. Wis. Coun. for Gifted and Talented (bd. dirs. 1984-87, v.p. 1985-86, pres. 1986-87). Home: 901 Bluecrest Dr Rockford IL 61107-3705

THOMI, LOIS JOY, social services administrator; b. Wichita, Kans., July 16, 1927; d. Arthur Glen and Frances Lenora (Hume) Shultz; m. Glenn Earl Thomi, Apr. 13, 1947; 1 child, Diana Kay. Student, Wichita State U., 1989-90. Various mgmt. positions Montgomery Ward, Kans., N.Mex., Tex, 1950-62; office mgr. Union Rescue Mission, Wichita, Kans., 1966-86; founder, exec. dir. Victory in the Valley, Inc., Wichita, Kans., 1983—; speaker various civic and ch. orgns. Recipient Matrix award Women in Communications, Inc., 1988, 1st Citizen award 1st Nat. Bank, 1988, Good Neighbor award Vulcan Chem. and KFDI Radio, 1988; named to 10 Who Care KAKE TV, 1985, State Disting. Internat. Acad. of Noble Achievement Epsilon Sigma Alpha, 1986; appointed 471st Daily Point of Light Pres. Bush, 1991. Mem. Am. Bus. Women's Assn., Prairie Pilot Club, Nat. Soc. Fund Raising Execs. Republican. Baptist. Office: Victory in the Valley Inc 917 N Market St PO Box 2210 Wichita KS 67214-3521

THOMPSON, ALICE ROXANA (ANN THOMPSON), labor researcher; b. Washington, Jan. 16, 1940; d. Brittain Bragunier and Clara Mildred (Green) Robinson; m. Raymond Edward Thompson, Jan. 11, 1975. BA in Economics, Am. U., Washington, 1971; MSLS, Cath. U. Am., 1975; MS in Labor Studies, U. D.C., 1990. Tchr. Dacca (Bangladesh) Am. Sch., 1959-60; mortgage collections acct. Fed. Credit Svc., Washington, 1960-61; libr. Internat. Brotherhood of Teamsters, Washington, 1962-77, asst. dir. rsch. and edn., 1978-81, assoc. dir. rsch. and edn., 1982, dir. info., 1983-90; dir. rsch. Spl. Librs. Assn., Washington, 1991-92; dep. corp. accountability rsch. Internat. Bros of Teamsters, Washington, 1992—; U.S. del. to UN Decade for Women, Nairobi, Kenya, 1986. Author: Teamsters All, 1976. Mem. adv. bd. Assn. for Progressive Stewardship, Northumberland County, Va., 1989—; mem. adv. coun. U.S. Peace Corps, Washington, 1985-89. NEH labor history fellow/grantee, U. Calif., Davis, 1977. Mem. Indsl. Rels. Rsch. Assn., Coalition for Labor Union Women. Home: 7710 Falstaff Rd Mc Lean VA 22102-2723 Office: IBT 25 LA Ave NW Washington DC 20001

THOMPSON, ANGELA COLEMAN, nurse, educator; b. Miami, Fla., July 14, 1949; d. William Carl Sr. and Roberta (Demmons) Coleman; m. Rodney David Thompson Sr., Sept. 13, 1969; children: Rodney David, Catrece Dionne. AA in Nursing, Miami Dade Med. Ctr., 1975; BA, Fla. A&M U., 1970. RN, Fla. Charge nurse Humana Hosp. Biscayne, Miami, 1975-91; supr. nursing Pines Rehab. Ctr., Miami, 1990-91; dir. edn. Concorde Career Inst., Miami, 1991—. Mem. AMA, Black Nurses Assn. Democrat. Methodist. Home: 17330 NW 16th Ave Miami FL 33169

THOMPSON, ANNE ELISE, federal judge; b. Phila., July 8, 1934; d. Leroy Henry and Mary Elise (Jackson) Jenkins; m. William H. Thompson, June 19, 1965; children: William H., Sharon A. BA, Howard U., 1955, LLB, 1964; MA, Temple U., 1957. Bar: D.C. bar 1964, N.J. bar 1966. Staff atty. Office of Solicitor, Dept. Labor, Chgo., 1964-65; asst. dep. public defender Trenton, N.J., 1967-70; mcpl. prosecutor Lawrence Twp., Lawrenceville, N.J., 1970-72; mcpl. ct. judge Trenton, 1972-75; prosecutor Mercer County, Mercer County, Trenton, 1975-79; judge U.S. Dist. Ct. N.J., Trenton, 1979—, now chief judge; vice chmn. Mercer County Criminal Justice Planning Com., 1972; mem. com. criminal practice N.J. Supreme Ct., 1975-79, mem. com. mcpl. cts., 1972-75; v.p. N.J. County Prosecutors Assn., 1978-79; chmn. juvenile justice com. Nat. Dist. Attys. Assn., 1978-79. Del. Democratic Nat. Conv., 1972. Recipient Assn. Black Women Lawyers award, 1976, Disting. Service award Nat. Dist. Attys. Assn., 1979, Gene Carte Meml. award Am. Criminal Justice Assn., 1980, Outstanding Leadership award N.J. County Prosecutors Assn., 1980, John Mercer Langston Outstanding Alumnus award Howard U. Law Sch., 1981; also various service awards; certs. of appreciation. Mem. Am. Bar Assn., Fed. Bar Assn., N.J. Bar Assn., Mercer County Bar Assn. Office: US District Court 343 US Courthouse 402 E State St Trenton NJ 08608-1507*

THOMPSON, ANNE MARIE, newspaper publisher; b. Des Moines, Feb. 7, 1920; d. George Horace and Esther Mayer Sheely; m. J. Ross Thompson, July 31, 1949; children: Annette McCracken, James Ross. BA, U. Iowa, 1940; postgrad. U. Colo., 1971. Co-pub. Baca County Banner, Springfield, Colo., 1951-54, Rocky Ford (Colo.) Daily Gazette, 1954-82, pub., 1982—. Editor Toastmasters, 1983-94. Mem. Otero Jr. Coll. Coun., 1987-93, Colo. Ho. of Reps., 1957-61; Colo. presdl. elector, 1972; chmn. Colo. adv. com. SBA, 1979-81. Recipient Community Service award Rocky Ford C. of C., 1975; named Colo. Woman of Achievement in Journalism, 1959, Colo. Bus. Person of Yr., Future Bus. Leaders of Am., 1981; elected to Colo. Community Journalism Hall of Fame, 1981. Mem. Nat. Fedn. Press Women (dir. 1971-81), Nat. Newspaper Assn. (Emma C. McKinney award 1984), Colo. Press Assn. (dir. 1981-83, Golden Make-Up award 1991) , Colo. Press Women, PEO, Bus. and Profl. Women's Club. Republican. Methodist.

THOMPSON, ANNIE FIGUEROA, academic director, educator; b. Río Piedras, P.R., June 7, 1941; d. Antonio Figueroa-Colón and Ana Isabel Laugier; m. Donald P. Thompson, Jan. 23, 1972; 1 child, John Anthony. BA, Baylor U., 1962; MSLS, U. So. Calif., 1965; M, Fla. State U., 1978, PhD, 1980. Educator Mayan Sch., Guatemala City, Guatemala, 1962-63; cataloger libr. system U. P.R., Río Piedras, 1965-67, head music libr., 1967-81, assoc. prof. librarianship, 1981-85; dir. grad. sch. libr. info. sci. U. P.R., Rio Piedras, 1986-93; prof. U. P.R., Río Piedras, 1986—. Author: An Annotated Bibliography About Music in Puerto Rico, 1975; co-author: Music and Dance in Puerto Rico from the Age of Columbus to Modern Times, An Annotated Bibliography, 1991; contbr. articles to profl. jours.; performed song recitals Inst. of P.R. Culture and U. P.R. Artist Series, 1974-78; soloist with P.R. Symphony Orch., San Juan, 1978; performed in opera, on radio and TV, San Juan, 1968-81;. sec. P.R. Symphony Orch. League, San Juan, 1982-84; mem. pub. libr. adv. com. Adminstrn. for Devel. of Arts and Culture, P.R., 1982-84, Pub. Libr. Adv. Bd., 1989—. Recipient Lauro a la Instrucción Bibliotecaria Sociedad de Bibliotecarios de P.R., 1985, Lauro a la Bibliografía Puertorriqueña, 1993. Mem. ALA, Assn. Coll. and Rsch. Librs., Am. Musicological Soc., Assn. for Libr. and Info. Sch. Edn., Soc. Bibliotecarios de P.R. (pres. 1994—), Music Libr. Assn., San Juan Rotary Club, Sigma Delta Kappa, Mu Phi Epsilon, Beta Phi Mu. Episcopalian. Home: N-64 Acadia St Park Gardens Rio Piedras San Juan PR 00926 Office: Grad Sch Library & Info Sci U of PR PO Box 21906 Rio Piedras San Juan PR 00931-1906

THOMPSON, ARLENE RITA, nursing educator; b. Yakima, Wash., May 17, 1933; d. Paul James and Esther Margaret (Danroth) T. BS in Nursing, U. Wash., 1966, Masters in Nursing, 1970, postgrad., 1982—. Staff nurse Univ. Teaching Hosp., Seattle, 1966-69; mem. nursing faculty U. Wash. Sch. Nurses, Seattle, 1971-73; critical care nurse Virginia Mason Hosp., Seattle, 1973—; educator Seattle Pacific U. Sch. Nursing, 1981—; nurse legal cons. nursing edn., critical care nurse. Contbr. articles to profl. jours. USPHS grantee, 1969; nursing scholar Virginia Mason Hosp., 1965. Mem. Am. Assn. Critical Care Nurses (cert.), Am. Nurses Assn., Am. Heart Assn., Nat. League Nursing, Sigma Theta Tau, Alpha Tau Omega. Republican. Presbyterian. Home: 2320 W Newton St Seattle WA 98199-4115 Office: Seattle Pacific U 3307 3rd Ave W Seattle WA 98119-1997

THOMPSON, BELINDA SUE, veterinarian; b. Oceanside, N.Y., May 10, 1955; d. William Henry and Gloria Dorothy (Boyd) T. BS in Animal Sci., Cornell U., 1977; DVM, N.Y. State Coll., 1981. Assoc. vet. Pine City (N.Y.) Vet. Clinic, 1981-84, ptnr. vet., 1984—. Agrl. issues com. Chemung County Coop. Extension, 1989—, adult issues com. 1991—. Mem. Am. Farmland Trust, N.Y. Pride Agenda, Nat. Gay and Lesbian Task Force (leadership coun.). Office: Pine City Vet Clinic 1384 Pennsylvania Ave Pine City NY 14871-9202

THOMPSON, BERTHA BOYA, retired educator; b. New Castle, Pa., Jan. 31, 1917; d. Frank L. and Kathryn Belle (Park) Boya; m. John L. Thompson, Mar. 27, 1942; children: Kay Lynn Thompson Koolage, Scott McClain. BS in Elem. & Secondary Edn., Slippery Rock State Coll., 1940; MA in Geography and History, Miami U., 1954; EdD, Ind. U., 1961. Cert. elem. and secondary edn. tchr. Elem. tchr., reading specialist New Castle (Pa.) Sch. System, 1940-45; tchr., chmn. social studies Talawanda Sch. System, Oxford, Ohio, 1954-63; assoc. prof. psychology and geography, chair edn. dept. Western Coll. for Women, Oxford, 1963-74; assoc. prof. edn., reading clinic Miami U., Oxford, 1974-78, prof. emeritus, 1978—; pvt. antique dealer, appraiser Oxford, 1978—. Contbr. articles to profl. jours. Mem. folk art com. Miami U. Art Mus., Oxford, 1974-76; mem. adv. com. Smith libr., Oxford Pub. Libr., 1978-81. Mem. AAUP, Nat. Coun. Geographic Edn. (exec. bd. dirs. 1966-69), Nat. Soc. for Study Edn., Assn. Am. Geographers, Soc. Women Geographers, Nat. Coun. for the Social Studies, Pi Lambda Theta, Zeta Tau Alpha, Pi Gamma Mu, Gamma Theta Upsilon, Kappa Delta Pi. Home: 6073 Contreras Rd Oxford OH 45056-9708

THOMPSON, BETTY JANE, small business owner; b. Ladysmith, Wis., Nov. 18, 1923; d. Edward Thomas and Mayme Selma (Kratwell) Potter; m. Frederick Sturdee Thompson, Apr. 19, 1945 (div. Apr. 1973); children: Denise Alana, Kent Marshall; m. J.R. Critchfield, Feb. 14, 1977 (div. 1989). Student, Jamestown (N.D.) Coll., 1946-47, U. Calif., Long Beach, 1964-69; AA, Orange Coast Coll., 1976; postgrad., Monterey Peninsula Coll., 1979-80; SBA Cert., Hartnell Coll., 1982. Cert. fashion cons. Owner, mgr., buyer Goodview (Minn.) Food Mart, 1947-50; dist. mgr. Beauty Counselor of Minn., Winona County, 1951-61; Boy Scout liaison J.C. Penney Co., Newport Beach, Calif., 1969-72; dept. mgr. and buyer boyswear At Ease, Newport Beach, 1972-77; mgr. Top Notch Boys Wear, Carmel, Calif., 1977-83, buyer, 1984-88; owner, mgr. Top Notch Watch, Sun City, Ariz., 1989—; v.p., chmn. Don Loper Fashion Show, 1967, pres., 1968, bd. dirs., 1969. Co-editor Aux. Antics mag., 1965. Vol. fundraising leadership Family Svc. Assn., Orange County, Calif., 1962-68, other orgns.; chmn. publicity, study group, Sunday sch. tchr., Congl. Ch., Winona, Minn., 1956-58, fellowship pres., Santa Ana, Calif., 1963-65; pres. Goodview Civic Club, 1948. Recipient Athena award Panhellenic Assn. Orange City, Calif., 1968, El Camino Real Dist. Svc. award Orange Empire coun. Boy Scouts Am., Baden-Powell award, Outstanding Leadership award, El Camino Real Dist., Calif., 1972J. Ringling North award, 1949; named Outstanding Svc. Vol. Family Svc. Assn., 1969. Mem. Carmel Bus. Assn. Home and Office: 10048 W Hawthorn Dr Sun City AZ 85351-2829

THOMPSON, CAROL ANN, artist, educator; b. Dodge City, Kans., July 8, 1940; d. Donald Lyle and Carol (Challman) Dayton; children: Kenneth Rodman, Jon Christopher, Wendy Fredenberg, Becky Stephens. BA cum laude, U. Calif., San Diego, 1977; MFA, U. Calif., 1980. C.C. lifetime credential. Gallery asst. Palomar Coll., San Marcos, Calif., 1981-84; program dir. Columbia Coll., Pleasanton, Calif., 1990-91; adj. prof. Miramar Coll., San Diego, 1981-84, Palomar Coll., San Marcos, 1981-87, Chapman U., Orange, Calif., 1981—; cons., artist Alameda County Office of Edn., Hayward, Calif., 1992, Bay Farm Christian Fellowship, Alameda, 1994. Performance art exhbns. at L.A. County Mus., La Jolla Mus.; one-woman shows include Mandeville Gallery, U. Calif., San Diego; represented in permanent collections at Women's Mus., San Francisco. Cmty. svcs. commr. City of Escondido, Calif., 1977-85; founding pres. Felicita Found., Escondido, 1983; docent, mus. asst. Alameda (Calif.) Hist. Mus. Recipient Order of Merit, Boy Scouts Am., 1982. Home: 2050 B Alameda Ave Alameda CA 94501

THOMPSON, CAROL FETTERLY, manufacturing executive; b. Columbia, S.C., Apr. 14, 1948; d. Orville Dale and Gwendolyn Elizabeth (Spratlin) Fetterly; children: Robert Julian, Michael Dale. BA in Anthropology, U. S.C., 1974; MA in Sociology, U. Tenn., 1982. Case worker Dept. Social Svcs., Lexington, S.C., 1973-75; rsch. assoc. Oak Ridge (Tenn.) Associated Univs., 1980-82; coord. maintenance tng. Goodyear Atomic, Piketon, Ohio, 1982-84; designer tng. program Goodyear Tire & Rubber Co., Akron, Ohio, 1984-86; mgr. mfg. & support tng. Goodyear Tire & Rubber Co., Akron, 1991-93; mgr. EEO and govtl. pers. rels. Goodyear Tire & Rubber Co., Lawton, Okla., 1986-88; mgr. prodn. bus. ctr. Goodyear Tire & Rubber Co., Lawton, 1988-90, Danville, Va., 1990-91; plant mgr. Goodyear Tire & Rubber Co., Spartanburg, S.C., 1993—. Bd. dirs. United Way of Spartanburg, 1994; active exec. selection com. Girl Scouts, Spartanburg, 1994. Office: Goodyear Tire & Rubber Co 1095 Simuel Rd Spartanburg SC 29301

THOMPSON, CAROL LUFKIN, computer sales company executive; b. Gloucester, Mass., Aug. 18, 1941; d. Henry Lee and Naomi (Shoares) Lufkin; m. Lawrence F. Thompson, Oct. 9, 1965; children: Jeffrey, Maureen. Student, U. Mass., 1959-61; BSN, Cornell U., 1964; postgrad., U. Calif., Riverside, 1968-69. RN, Mass., Ariz., Calif. Pub. health nurse Maricopa County Health Dept., Phoenix, 1964-65, Riverside County Health Dept., Riverside, 1966-72; mgr. Collector's Showcase, Orange, Calif., 1972-80; pres. Computer Craft, Austin, Tex., 1980-85, Advance Computer Rentals, Austin, 1985—; chief exec. officer Computerland, Austin, 1985-91; v.p. Computerland Tex., Austin, 1991-93; pres. The Thompson Group, Austin, 1993—; owner, mgr. Lufkin's, Austin, 1972—; mem. adv. bd. U. Tex. Sch. Nursing, Austin, Ronald McDonald House, Austin; Tex. del. White House Conf. on Small Bus., 1986. Contbr. numerous articles to various publs. Bd. dirs. Fed. Res. Bd. San Antonio, Ctr. for Battered Women, 1980-82, Better Bus. Bur., 1987-90, Jr. Achievement, 1989, Austin Tech. Incubator; mem. adv. bd. Travis County Minority and Women Bus. Enterprises, 1989-90, Buy Greater Austin; mem. Jr. League Austin, Leadership Tex., 1990-91. Named Bus. and Profl. Person of Yr., YWCA, Austin, 19899, Female Entrepreneur of Yr., Nat. Bus. League, 1989. Mem. AAUW, Tex. Computer Industry Coun., Austin Purchasing Mgrs. Assn. (bd. dirs.), Nat. Assn. Women Bus. Owners, Austin Quality Coun. (dir. 1992-93), A+ Coalition-New Generation Schs. (pres. elect), Greater Austin C. of C. (vice chmn. small bus. div. 1988-89, chmn. econ. devel. assocs. 1990, chmn. 1992—, Vol. of Yr. award 1987), Women's C. of C. Tex. (chmn. bd. dirs. 1989), Rotary. Presbyterian. Home: 4301 Cat Mountain Dr Austin TX 78731-3706 Office: 100 Congress Ave Ste 1100 Austin TX 78701-4042

THOMPSON, CAROLINE WARNER, film director, screenwriter; b. Washington, Apr. 23, 1956; d. Thomas Carlton Jr. and Bettie Marshall (Warner) T.; m. Alfred Henry Bromell, Aug. 28, 1982 (div. 1985). BA summa cum laude, Amherst Coll., 1978. Author: First Born, 1983; screenwriter: (films) Edward Scissorhands, 1990, The Addams Family, 1991, Homeward Bound: The Incredible Journey, 1993, The Secret Garden, 1993, Tim Burton's The Nightmare Before Christmas, 1993; screenwriter, dir.: Black Beauty, 1994. Mem. Phi Beta Kappa. Office: William Morris Agency Inc 151 S El Camino Dr Beverly Hills CA 90212-2775*

THOMPSON, DARLA J., county officiala; b. Tulsa, Aug. 21, 1962; d. Darvell H. and Alice Joy (Myers) Roberts; 1 child, Justin Weaver; m. Jeff E. Thompson, May 22, 1985; 1 child, Ashley. BS in bus. mgmt., Rogers State Coll., Claremore, Okla., 1990. Cert. word processor II. Exec. sec. TNT Drilling & Exploration, Pryor, Okla., 1983-85; integration analyst Philip Morris Svc. Co., Claremore, 1985-87; customer rep. Farmers Ins. Co., Pryor, 1987-88; coord. eldercare intake Mayes County Health Dept., Pryor, 1988—; programs mgr. Okla. Dept. Health, Pryor, graphics technician, 1992. Founder, area coord. Mayes County Cancer Support Group, 1988—; pres. I Can Cope cancer survivorship, Pryor, 1988—; adminstrv. Reach to Recovery, Pryor, 1991—, Look Good Feel Better, Pryor, 1993—; elected bd. dirs. Am. Cancer Soc., Okla., 1994. Recipient Third Ear award for outstanding achievement, State of Okla., 1990, gov.'s citation, 1993, Outstanding Achievement award LaFortune Cancer Ctr., Tulsa, 1993, Outstanding Svc. award Am. Cancer Soc., 1994. Mem. Mayes County Resource Coun. (pub. rels. com. 1991), Pryor C. of C. (sr. citizens com. 1991). Democrat. Mem. Assembly of God. Home: PO Box 344 Pryor OK 74362-0344

THOMPSON, DAYLE ANN, aerospace company executive; b. Grand Forks, N.D., Jan. 6, 1954; d. Duane Theodore and anna Mae (Desautel) T.; m. Michael Gary Sciulla, Aug. 6, 1977 (div. Sept. 1980); m. Manfred Hans von Ehrenfried II, June 11, 1982. Secretarial degree, Aaker's Bus. Coll., Grand Forks, 1973; cert. of completion mgmt., George Washington U., 1979, postgrad. in Project Mgmt., Cert. in Contracting for Project Mgrs., 1993, 94. Receptionist U.S. Rep. Norman F. Lent U.S. Ho. of Reps., Washington, 1973-74; office mgr., personal sec. U.S. Rep. Les AuCoin, U.S. Ho. of Reps., Washington, 1975-78; bus. mgr., bookkeeper Virgin Islands POST, St.Thomas, USVI, 1978; office and pers. mgr. Internat. Energy Assocs. Ltd., Washington, 1978-82; program support mgr. MSI Svcs. Inc., Washington, 1982-84; pres., treas., chief exec. officer Tech. and Adminstrv. Svcs. Corp., Washington, 1984—; Hosp. vol. ARC, Arlington, Va., 1987. Recipient Group Achievement award NASA, 1984, 93, Commendation Letter, NASA, 1985, 87, 88, 91, 93, 94, Small Bus. Prime Contractor of Yr. award Small Bus. Adminstrn. Region 3, 1994. Mem. Washington Space Bus. Roundtable (sponsor-benefactor 1990-92), Women in Aerospace, Capital Yacht Club. Republican. Roman Catholic. Home: 4250 42d Ave S Saint Petersburg FL 33711 Office: TADCORPS 300 7th St SW Ste 110 Washington DC 20024-2511

THOMPSON, DIDI CASTLE (MARY BENNETT), writer, editor; b. Terre Haute, Ind., Feb. 7, 1918; d. Robert Langley Bennett and Marjorie Rose (Tyler) Castle; student U. Ill., Champaign, 1935-36, U. Ky., 1936-39; m. Jamie Campbell Thompson, Jr., June 24, 1939; children—Jamie III, Julia King Balko, Langley Stewart Ruede. News editor Glen-Echoes, Glencoe, Ill., 1930; columnist Ky. Kernel, U. Ky., Lexington, 1937-39; radio script writer Modern Am. Music, 1940-42; asst. pub. relations dir. Salem Coll., Winston-Salem, N.C., 1945; pub. relations chmn. Barrington (Ill.) Horse Show, 1959-67; staff writer, columnist Barrington Press Newspapers, 1958-84; editor ECHO, Defenders of the Fox River, Inc. newsletter, 1970-80; travel editor Barrington Press Newspapers, 1973-84; columnist The Daily Herald, Paddock Publs., 1984-86; columnist Rapid City (S.D.) Journal, 1990—; freelance writer, 1943—. Past bd. mem. Barrington chpt. Lyric Opera Guild Chgo., Barrington Sr. Center, Infant Welfare Soc. Chgo., Art Inst. Chgo., Barrington Assos.; elected trustee Village of Barrington Hills, 1969-73, health, pub. relations chmn., 1969-73; mem. Barrington Hills Plan Commn., 1986. Mem. Women in Communications (past dir.), Citizens for Conservation (past dir.), Barrington Countryside Assn. (past dir.), Barrington Hist. Soc., Spring Creek Basset Hounds Club, Barrington Hills Riding Club (past dir.), Pan Hellenic Council, DAR, Chgo. Press Club, Chi Omega. Episcopalian. Address: 1827 Princess Ct North Naples FL 33942

THOMPSON, DOREEN, public relations executive; b. Somerville, Mass., Mar. 26, 1955; 2 children. BA in Mass. Comm., U. N.H., 1977; MA in Speech Comm., Emerson Coll., 1982. Account exec. Arnold Pub. Rels., Boston, 1984-85; account exec., account supr., v.p. Ingalls, Quinn & Johnson Pub. Rels., Boston, 1985-88; v.p., then sr. v.p. The Weber Group, Cambridge, Mass., 1988—. Trustee Lasell Coll., Newton, Mass., 1990—; pro bono work Gang Peace, Boston, 1994. Recipient Regional award CIPPRA, 1993, Bellringer award Publicity Club, 1994. Office: The Weber Group 101 Main St Cambridge MA 02142

THOMPSON, DOROTHY BARNARD, elementary school educator; b. Flushing, N.Y., Aug. 14, 1933; d. Henry Clay and Cecelia Minnie Theresa (La Pardo) Barnard; m. Norman Earl Thompson, Aug. 12, 1956; children: Greg, Scot, Henry, Marc, Matthew. BSEd, SUNY, New Paltz, 1953; MS, Hofstra U., 1984. Cert. elem. tchr. K-6th grades, reading specialist K-12th grades, N.Y. Adjunct prof. Suffolk Community Coll., Brentwood, N.Y., 1987—, Nassau Community Coll., Uniondale, N.Y., 1986—; adjunct prof., instr. Ctr. for Acad. Achievement Long Island U., Greenvale, N.Y., 1984-92; tchr. reading, K-5th grades Long Beach (N.Y.) Pub. Schs., 1988—; mem. founding group Parent/Tchr., The Learning Tree, Garden City, N.Y., 1971; founder parent coop. Happy Day Nursery Sch., Bellmore, N.Y., 1975; parent-tchr. Commonwealth Sch., Bay Shore, Oakdale, 1976-82. Mem. NEA, Nassau Reading Coun., N.Y. State Tchrs. Assn., Assn. for Supervision and Curriculum Devel. Home: 2385 Warren Ave Bellmore NY 11710-2545 Office: 456 Neptune Blvd Long Beach NY 11561-2425

THOMPSON, DOROTHY BROWN, writer; b. Springfield, Ill., May 14, 1896; d. William Joseph and Harriet (Gardner) Brown; m. Dale Moore Thompson, July 2, 1921 (dec. 1990); 1 child, William B. (dec. 1978). AB., U. Kans., 1919. Began writing professionally, 1931; published more than 2000 poems to nat. mags. and newspapers including Saturday Rev., Saturday Evening Post, Va. Quar. Rev., Poetry, Commonweal, Good Housekeeping and others, author research articles for various hist. jours.; poems reprinted in over 200 collections, textbooks and anthologies in England, Canada, Australia, New Zealand, Malaysia, Sweden; 25 in Braille. Author: (poetry) Subject to Change, 1973, (book) Near View, 1991—. Leader poetry sect. Writers' Conf., U. Kans., 1953-55, McKendree Coll., 1961, 63, Creighton U., Omaha, 1966; lectr. writers' conf. U. Kans., 1965, Am. Poets Series, Kansas City, Mo., 1973; mem. staff Poets Workshop, Cen. Mo. State U., 1974; poet-in-schs. residency for Mo. State Council of Arts, 1974. Recipient Mo. Writers' Guild Award, 1941, Poetry Soc. Am., nat. and local awards. Mem. Diversifiers, Poetry Soc. Am., Nat. Soc. Colonial Dames, First Families of Va. Mem. Christian Ch. Clubs: Woman's City, Filson (Louisville). Address: 221 W 48th St Apt 1402 Kansas City MO 64112

THOMPSON, DOROTHY MAE, school system administrator, real estate manager; b. Idaho, Ohio, Jan. 10, 1932; d. Sanford M. and Elizabeth (Smith) Williams; m. Robert D. Van Meter, Sept. 27, 1957 (dec. 1974); children: Carmen, Lois, Holly; m. Charles Thompson, Jan. 18, 1977. Student, Ohio U., 1957-60; BS in Edn., Rio Grande Coll., 1965; MS in Ednl. Adminstrn., Xavier U., 1968, MS in Pupil Pers., 1969. Elem. tchr. Pike County Schs., Piketon, Ohio, 1959-69; guidance counselor Piketon High Sch., 1971-73; coord. spl. edn. Waverly (Ohio) City Schs., 1969-71, elem. supr., 1973-79, asst. supt., 1979-81; mgr. personal real estate New Smyrna Beach, Fla., 1982-90; farm mgr. Abbeville, S.C., 1990—. Mem. AAUW, Delta Kappa Gamma (v.p.). Methodist. Home and Office: RR 1 Box 232 Abbeville SC 29620-9723

THOMPSON, DOROTHY PERRY, English language educator; b. Orangeburg City, S.C., June 24, 1944; d. Joe Roger Perry and Lessie Mae (Corbitt) Whaley; m. Johnnie Clifton Thompson, Jr., Jan. 14, 1965; children: Johnnie III, Danya, Jene. BA, Allen U., 1968; MA in Edn., U. S.C., 1974, PhD, 1987. English tchr. Riverside High Sch., Saluda, S.C., 1968-69, Webber High Sch., Eastover, S.C., 1969-70, Lower Richland High Sch., Hopkins, S.C., 1970-80, 85, Dreher High Sch., Columbia, S.C., 1983-84; tchr. composition U. S.C., Columbia, S.C., 1980-83; instr. English Allen U., Columbia, S.C.; assoc. prof. English Winthrop U., Rock Hill, S.C., 1985—, coord. African Am. studies, 1992—; cons. U. S.C. Inst. Internats., 1984—, State Supt. Arts Program, 1988—; chair Multi Ethnic Lit. of U.S. Conf., 1994. Author: (poetry anthology) The Ninety Six Sampler, 1994; contbr. to profl. jours. Bd. mem. Booker T. Washing Found., Columbia, 1974—; bd. govs. S.C. Acad. Authors, Charleston, S.C., 1988—; panelist lit arts S.C. Arts Commn., Columbia, 1988-90; performer Trustus Theatre, Columbia, 1994. Recipient Sandhill Poetry award Sandhill Writer's Conf., 1992. Mem. Philological Assn. of the Carolinas, Modern Lang. Assn. (chair MELUS 1994—), S.C. Black Arts Coalition (bd. dirs., treas.), Delta Sigma Theta. Office: Winthrop U English Dept Rock Hill SC 29733

THOMPSON, ELAINE KOPECKY, optometrist; b. Bklyn., Jan. 8, 1953; d. Walter John and Anna Theresa (Dzezynska) Kopecky; m. Joseph John Hyduke, June 19, 1976 (div. Aug. 1984); m. Lee Roy Thompson, Oct. 25, 1986; 1 child, Shane. BS, U. Miami, 1975; OD, Centro Escolar U., Manila, 1980, Ind. U., 1984. Practice optometry St. Louis, 1984-86, Birmingham, Ala., 1986—. Named Crimson Classic Body Bldg. Champion, 1990, Peach State Body Bldg. Champion, 1990, Ala. State Body Bldg. Champion, 2d lightweight divsn., 1990, Masters Nat. Body Bldg. Middleweight Champion, 1991, Ea. Seaboard Body Bldg. Middleweight Champion, 1991; recipient Best Tech. Article So. Jour. Optometry, 1990. Mem. Am. Optometric Assn. (gen. and contact lens sect.), Ala. Optometric Assn.

THOMPSON, ELEANOR DUMONT, nurse; b. Derry, N.H., May 26, 1935; d. Louis Arthur and Florence Berthae (Gendreau) D.; m. Carl Hugh Thompson, Aug. 22, 1959; children: Justine, Julie. Student, Dartmouth Hitchcock Nur. Sch., 1956; BA, New Eng. Coll., 1977; MS, Drake U., 1984. Registered art therapist. Pediatric instr. Hanover (N.H.) Sch. Practical Nursing, 1958-61; pub. W.B. Sanders Co., Phila., 1962—; pediatric instr. St. Joseph Hosp., Nashua, N.H., 1978-81; cert. clin. nurse specialist Mercy Hosp. Med. Ctr., Des Moines, 1987-90; clin. nurse specialist HCA Portsmouth (N.H.) Regional Hosp., 1991—; pvt. practice Silverman & Assoc., Inc., 1991-93; puppeteer St. Joseph's Hosp. Sch. Nursing, Nashua, 1981-82; created and conducted shows on hospitalization for children; nursing cons. Hospice Cen. Iowa, Des Moines, 1982-89. Author: Pediatric Nursing An Introductory Text, 1965, 6th edit., 1992, Introduction to Maternity and Pediatric Nursing, 1990, 2d edit., 1995. Vol. nurse Vietnam Vets. Ctr., Des Moines, 1985-87, Camp Apanda Childrens Cancer Camp Boone, Iowa, 1984-86; organist Holy Trinity Ch. Des Moines, 1982, St. Pius Ch., Des Moines, 1982. Fellow Am. Acad. Pain Mgmt.; mem. ANA, Am. Psychiat. Nurses Assn., Am. Art Therapy Assn., N.H. Art Therapy Assn., Drake Alumnae Assn., N.H. Nurses Assn. Republican. Roman Catholic. Home: 13 Sherman Ave Brentwood NH 03833-6225

THOMPSON, ELIZABETH JANE, small business owner; b. Ithaca, N.Y., Jan. 11, 1927; d. Merle Godley and Nellie Gray (Trowbridge) T. AB, Syracuse U., 1948, MA, 1962, PhD, 1971. Writer, editor Cornell U., Ithaca, N.Y., 1950-53; dir. pub. rels. Taylor Ward Advt., Ithaca, 1953-54; account exec. Doug Johnson Assocs., Syracuse, N.Y., 1954-58; assoc. in community rels., Youth Devel. Ctr. Syracuse U., 1958-66, grad. asst., 1967-68; from asst. prof. to prof. sociology Shippensburg (Pa.) U., 1968-90, dir. Fashion Archives, 1980-90; owner Timelines & Hemlines Cons. Svc., Shippensburg, 1991—; lectr. on costume, fashion and sociology of dress to numerous civic and ednl. groups. Co-editor: Among the People: Studies of the Urban Poor, 1968; contbr. articles on sociology of dress to numerous publs. Mem. Costume Soc. Am., Am. Sociol. Soc. Dutch Reform. Home and Office: 19 S Prince St Shippensburg PA 17257-1919

THOMPSON, ELLEN ANN, elementary education educator; b. Newton, Mass., Mar. 23, 1955; d. Arthur Malachi and Eva Louise (Harris) T.; m. John A. Rasys, Nov. 30, 1980 (div. Apr. 1987); 1 child, Christopher Michael Rasys. BS in Edn., U. Vt., 1977, MEd, 1986, postgrad. Cert. elem. tchr., spl. edn. tchr., Vt. Title I tchr. remedial reading grades 1-3 Colchester (Vt.) Sch. Dist., 1977-78; title I readiness rm. tchr. Union Meml Sch., Colchester, 1978-79, tchr. grade 2 transitional grade, 1979-81, classroom tchr. grades 1-3 multiage, 1981—; adj. instr. dept. grad. edn. U. Vt., Burlington, 1987—; adj. instr. undergrad. edn. program Trinity Coll., Burlington, 1992—; presenter N.E. Whole Lang. Conf., Johnson (Vt.) State Coll., 1987; resource agt. tchr. insvc. programs Vt. Dept. Edn., 1988—, resource cons. Vt. Writing Portfolio Assessment Program, 1990—, network leader # 16, 1991—; conf. presenter, adj. instr. Am. Inst. for Creative Edn., Augusta, Maine, 1988—; art cons. Within the Forest, Sci. Rsch. Assocs., 1991—; ednl. cons., presenter Soc. for Devel. Edn., Peterborough, N.H.; teaching fellow regional lab. Rural Small Sch. Network, 1991-92. Author: (videos) The Nuts and Bolts of Multiage Classrooms, 1994, How to Teach i a Multiage Classroom, 1994. Recipient State Teacher of the Yr. award., Vermont, Coun. of Chief State School Offices, 1993. Mem. ASCD, Nat. Coun. Tchrs. English (presenter 1991, 92), Internat. Reading Assn. (presenter annual conf. 1991, Leaders of Readers award 1990), Vt. Coun. on Reading (newsletter editor and conf. presenter 1988—, pres. 1991-92), Vt. Tchrs. Applying Whole Lang., Colchester Edn. Assn. (internal newsletter 1987-89, newsletter editor 1988-89), Phi Delta Kappa. Home: 3 Justin Morgan Dr Colchester VT 05446-1189 Office: Union Meml Sch 29 Main St Colchester VT 05446-1156

THOMPSON, ELLEN KUBACKI, microbiologist, medical writer, consultant; b. Bethesda, Md., July 21, 1950; d. Edward Leonard and Ellen Angelina (Battaglia) Kubacki; AB, Miami U., Oxford, Ohio, 1972; m. Richard Kent Thompson, Jan. 25, 1975; 1 son, James Edward. Asst. microbiologist Hoffmann-La Roche Inc., Nutley, N.J., 1972-77, med. writer, 1977-79; freelance writer and cons., 1979-91; v.p. Princeton Trading Internat., Inc., 1991—. Elected Rep. committeewoman South Brunswick Twp. (dist. 3), 1983-89; pres. Chapin Sch. Parents' Assn., 1987-88; mem. Bd. Health South Brunswick Twp., 1985-91, vice chair , 1989-90, chair, 1990-91. Mem. Am. Soc. for Microbiology, Am. Med. Writers Assn., Theobald Smith Soc., Miami U. Alumni Assn. No. N.J. (trustee 1972—), Sigma Xi (treas. Roche research chpt. 1977, sec. 1978), Sigma Kappa. Home: 35 Fairfield Rd Princeton NJ 08540-9577

THOMPSON, G. GAYE, lawyer; b. Greensboro, N.C., Sept. 15, 1945; d. O.C. and Jean (Esterak) T.; m. Alvis Layton Barrier, Jr., Aug. 28, 1965 (div. 1988); children: Breton Foster, Amé Rebecca. BA, Southwestern U., 1967; JD, St. mary's U., 1987. Bar: Tex. 1987, U.S. Ct. Appeals (5th cir.) 1991, U.S. Supreme Ct. 1992. Psychiat. caseworker Austin (Tex.) State Hosp., 1967-68; counselor, acting dir. counseling Meth. Mission Home Tex., San Antonio, 1968-70; co-therapist sex and marital therapy J. Franklin Stokes, M.D., San Antonio, 1976-78; pvt. practice sex therapy, marital counseling Seguin, Tex., 1978-89; assoc. Irvine & Dial, P.C., Attys. at Law, Seguin, 1987; 1st asst. county atty. Guadalupe County, Seguin, 1987-90; ptnr. Thompson & Tiemann, Attys. at Law, Austin, 1991—; sex therapist Am. Assn. Sex Educators, Counselors and Therapists, Washington, 1978-91; sex educator Am. Bd. Sexology, Washington, 1990-93. V.p., bd. dir. Marywood Child and Family Svcs., Palmer Drug Abuse Program, Sequin, 1982; organizer, dir. Helping Hand program Seguin PTA, 1980; presenter sexuality workshops for teens and parents, various chs., Seguin, 1981-82; bd. dir. Family Eldercare. Fellow Am. Coll. Sexologists, Internat. Coun. Sex Edn. and Parenthood; mem. AAUW, Am. Bd. Sexology (diplomate), Am. Assn. Sex Educators, Counselors and Therapists, State Tex. Bar Assn., Travis County Bar Assn., Tex. Dist. and County Attys. Assn., Tex. Guardianship Assn. (bd. dirs.), Old Bakery and Emporium Bd. and Guild (pres.), Family Eldercare (bd. dirs.), Mary Wood (v.p. bd. dirs.), Delta Delta Delta. Episcopalian. Home: PO Box 5459 Austin TX 78763-5459 Office: Thompson & Tiemann Attys at Law 1206 S Congress Ave Austin TX 78704-2422

THOMPSON, GENEVA FLORENCE, medical technologist, cytotechnologist; b. Zionsville, Ind., Apr. 5, 1915; d. Alfred Seymour and Grace Viola (Kutz) T. Cert. in cytotechnology, Ohio State U., 1964; BA, Ind. U./Purdue U., Indpls., 1972. Cert. Am. Soc. Clin. Pathologists. Med. technician Noblesville (Ind.) Hosp., 1948-52; med. technician Riverview Hosp., Noblesville, 1952-56, med. technologist, 1956-60; med. technologist Office of Robert Harris, M.D., Noblesville, 1960-64; cytotechnologist Office of Thornton, Haymond, Costin, Buehl & Bolinger, M.D., Indpls., 1965-78; ret., 1978. Active with local church; served with U.S. Army W.A.C., 1944-46. Mem. AAUW (chmn. literature study group), Ind. U. Women's Club of Indpls., Am. Soc. Clin. Pathologists, Noblesville Tourist Club (sec.), Sr. Citizens Orgn., Inc. Republican.

THOMPSON, JANE JOHNSON, retail executive; b. Charleston, W.Va., July 13, 1951; d. Robert Paul and Phyllis Jane (Judson) Johnson; m. T. Stephen Thompson, Aug. 28, 1976; children: Robert Baker, Catherine Brooke. BBA, U. Cin., 1973; MBA, Harvard Coll., 1978. Brand mgr. Procter & Gamble, Cin., 1973-77; prin., ptnr. McKinsey & Co., Inc., Chgo., 1978-88; v.p. Sears Specialty Merchandising div. Sears Roebuck & Co., Chgo., 1988-89; v.p. planning Sears Roebuck & Co., Chgo., 1989-90, v.p. corp. and mdse. group planning, mem. corp. mgmt. com., 1990-93; exec. v.p. credit, gen. mgr., mem. exec. com. Sears Merchandise Group, 1993—; bd. dirs. ConAgra, Inc. Bd. dirs. Lincoln Park Zoo Soc. Aux., 1988—; bd. dirs., exec. com., head strategic planning com. Boys and Girls Club of Chgo., 1992—. Baker scholar Harvard U., 1978. Mem. Chgo. Network, Econ. Club Chgo., Nat. Retail Fedn. (credit. coun., bd. dirs.), Internat. Credit Assn. (bd. dirs.). Office: Sears Mdse Group B6-133A 3333 Beverly Rd Hoffman Estates IL 60179

THOMPSON, JEAN TANNER, retired librarian; b. San Luis Obispo, Calif., June 15, 1929; d. Chester Corey and Mildred (Orr) T.; 1 child, Anne Marie Miller. Student, Whitworth Coll., Spokane, Wash., 1946-49; A.B., Boston U., 1951; postgrad., U. Wis., Eau Claire, 1964-67; M.S.L.S., Columbia U., 1973; Ed.M., U. Va., Charlottesville, 1978. Asst. social sci. librarian Univ. Libraries Va. Polytechnic Inst. and State U., Blacksburg, 1973-77, head social sci. dept. Univ. Libraries, 1977-83; head reference dept. Meml. Library U. Wis., Madison, 1983-86, asst. dir. reference and info. svcs., 1986-91, ret. Contbg. editor: ALA Guide to Information Access, 1994; mem. editorial bd. RQ, 1984-89. Mem. ALA, Assn. Coll. and Research Libraries (edn. and behavioral sci. sect. vice chmn. 1985-86, chmn. 1986-87), Wis. Library Assn., Wis. Assn. of Acad. Librarians. Methodist. Home: 103 S Hunter Ln Troy AL 36081-8206

THOMPSON, JOSIE, nursing administrator; b. Ark., Apr. 16, 1949; d. James Andrew and Oneda Fay (Watson) Rhoads; m. Mark O. Thompson, Feb. 14, 1980. Diploma, Lake View Sch. Nursing, 1970; student, Danville Community Coll., 1974-75, St. Petersburg Jr. Coll., 1979. RN, Ill., Wyo. Staff nurse St. Elizabeth Hosp., Danville, Ill., 1970-78, Osteopathetic Hosp., St. Petersburg, Fla., 1980-81, Wyo. State Hosp., Evanston, 1981-83; staff nurse Wyo. Home Health Care, Rock Springs, 1984—, adminstr., 1986—; pres. Home Health Care Alliance Wyo., 1991-92. Mem. nursing program adv. bd. Western Wyo. Community Coll.; mem. Coalition for the Elderly, Spl. Needs Com. Sweetwater County, 1992-93. Home: PO Box 1154 1207 McCabe Rock Springs WY 82902

THOMPSON, JOYCE ELIZABETH, arts management educator; b. Pasadena, Tex., Aug. 15, 1951; d. James Little and Ruth Lake (Skinner) Wilkison; divorced; children: Christine Joy, Cassidy Jane. BA in Psychology, David Lipscomb Coll., 1974; MA in Speech, Theater, Murray State U., 1976; postgrad., U. Tex., 1978; MA in Arts Adminstrn., Ind. U., 1981. Asst. prof. speech Vincennes (Ind.) U., 1976-79; asst. dir. mktg. Hartford (Conn.) Ballet, 1981-82; touring dir. Hartford Ballet/Conn. Opera, 1982-84; exec. dir. Wyo. Arts Coun., Cheyenne, 1984-91, South Snohomish County Arts Coun., Lynwood, Wash., 1991-92; asst. prof. arts mgmt. Sangamon State U., Springfield, Ill., 1992—; adj. instr., Manchester (Conn.) Community Coll., 1982-84, Chapman Coll., 1990—, Edmonds Community Coll., 1992—; mem. selection com. Coca-Cola Scholars Found., 1989, 90, 91. Mem. adv. bd. Cheyenne Little Theatre Players, 1986, Cheyenne Civic Ctr., 1987-88. Mem. Assn. Arts Adminstrn. Educators (sec.), Assn. Performing Arts Producers, Speech Communication Assn., Western States Arts Fedn. (bd. dirs. 1984-91, chair performing arts com. 1985-87). Democrat. Home: 854 S Glenwood Springfield IL 62704 Office: Sangamon State Univ PAC 370 Springfield IL 62794-9243

THOMPSON, JOYCE ELIZABETH, retired state education official; b. Pearson, Okla., Nov. 22, 1929; d. Walter Samuel and Clara Gertrude (Davis) T.; m. Gordon Pybas, May 22, 1989. BS, Okla. State U., 1951; M in Home Econs., Okla. U., 1974. Cert. vocat. and gen. home econs., Okla. Home econs. tchr. Wister (Okla.) High Sch., 1951-55, Tishomingo (Okla.) High Sch., 1955-56, Wilson (Okla.) High Sch., 1956-67, Konawa (Okla.) High Sch., 1967-71; dist. supr. State Dept. of Vo-Tech., Oklahoma City, 1971-80; state supr. State Dept. of Vo-Tech., Stillwater, Okla., 1980-88; ret., 1988; mem. adv. com. Future Homemakers Am., Oklahoma City, 1961-68; treas. Nat. Assn. State Suprs., Washington, 1983-87; advisor Nat. Assn. Vocat. Home Econs. Tchrs., Washington, 1986-87. Chairperson Okla. Home Econs. Legis. Network, Stillwater, 1984; mem. fin. com. Wes Watkins for Gov., Stillwater, 1988-90. Named Tchr. of Yr. Ancient Free and Accepted Masons, Wilson, 1960, 65; recipient Grand Cross of Colors, Internat. Order of Rainbow, Wilson, 1964, Hon. membership Future Homemakers of Am., Oklahoma City, 1976, Young Homemakers of Okla., Oklahoma City, 1977, Spl. award of merit Nat. Assn. Vocat. Home Econs. Tchrs., Washington, 1986. Mem. Am. Vocat. Assn. (life mem., membership chair 1981-84), Okla. Vocat. Assn. (life mem., v.p. 1965), Am. Legion Aux., Order Ea. Star. Democrat. Mem. Church of Christ. Home: RR 2 Box 113 Wanette OK 74878-9725

THOMPSON, JOYCE LURINE, information systems specialist; b. White Oak Twp., Mich., Mar. 5, 1931; d. Orla Jacob and Ethel Inita (Thayer) Sheathelm; m. Robert E. Thompson, Dec. 10, 1949 (div. 1972); children: Wendy, Robin, Kristen. Student, Mich. State U., 1972-78, Lansing (Mich.) Community Coll, 1976-77. Programmer, analyst Mich. State U., East Lansing, 1966-73; tech. programmer Mich. State Police, East Lansing, 1973-77; database coord. Mich. Dept. Treasury, Lansing, 1977-79; systems engr. 4-Phase Systems, Grand Rapids, Mich., 1979-81; mktg. rep. Motorola, Grand Rapids, 1981-84; data analyst Whirlpool Corp., Benton Harbor, Mich., 1984-88, data adminstr., 1988—; owner, propr. Thompson House, South Haven, Mich., 1994—. Activity chmn. Girl Scouts U.S.A., East Lansing; leader 4-H Clubs, East Lansing; vol. Stepping Stones South Haven, ADA Com., Lake Mich. Maritime Mus. Mildred Erickson fellow Mich. State U., EAst Lansing, 1974-78. Mem. Assn. Systems Mgmt. (sec. 1984), Data Adminstrn. Mgmt. Assn. Office: Whirlpool Corp 2000 N M 63 Hwy Benton Harbor MI 49022

THOMPSON, JUDITH ANN, quality control professional, graphic artist; b. Ridgway, Pa., Nov. 28, 1954; d. John Robert Sr. and Marie Anne (Merat) Miller; m. William James Thompson Sr., May 11, 1985: stepchildren: William Jr., Brandy May. AA in Specialized Tech., Art Inst. Pitts., 1972-74. Cert. stats. process control, Pa. Artist and printer Al's Sign Svc., Erie, Pa., 1974-77; printer Silk Screen Unlimited, Erie, 1977-79; quality control insp. Exotic Metals, Inc., Ridgway, 1979—. Editor EMI ECHO, Ridgway, 1990-94.

THOMPSON, JUDITH KASTRUP, nursing researcher; b. Marstal, Denmark, Oct. 1, 1933; came to the U.S., 1951; d. Edward Kastrup and Anna Hansa (Knudsen) Pedersen; m. Richard Frederick Thompson, May 22, 1960; children: Kathryn Marr, Elizabeth Kastrup, Virginia St. Claire. BS, RN, U. Oreg., 1958, MSN, 1963. RN, Calif., Oreg. Staff nurse U. Oreg. Med. Sch., Eugene, 1957-58; staff nurse U. Oreg. Med. Sch., Portland, 1958-61, head staff nurse, 1960-61; instr. psychiat. nursing U. Oreg. Sch. Nursing, Portland, 1963-64; rsch. asst. U. Oreg. Med. Sch., Portland, 1964-65, U. Calif., Irvine, 1971-72; rsch. assoc. Stanford (Calif.) U., 1982-87; rsch. asst. Harvard U., Cambridge, Mass., 1973-74; rsch. assoc. U. So. Calif., L.A., 1987—. Contbg. author: Behavioral Control and Role of Sensory Biofeedback, 1976; contbr. articles to profl. jours. Treas. LWV, Newport Beach, Calif., 1970-74; scout leader Girl Scouts Am., Newport Beach, 1970-78. Named Citizen of Yr. State of Oreg., 1966. Mem. Soc. for Neurosci., Am. Psychol. Soc. (charter), ANA, Oreg. Nurses Assn. Republican. Lutheran. Home: 28 Sky Sail Dr Corona Del Mar CA 92625-1436 Office: U So Calif University Park Los Angeles CA 90089-2520

THOMPSON, JULIA ANN, physicist, educator; b. Little Rock, Mar. 13, 1943; d. Erwin Arthur and Ruth Evelyn (Johnston) T.; m. Patrick A. Thompson, Mar. 22, 1964 (div. 1974); 1 child, Diane E.; m. David E. Kraus, Jr., June 22, 1976; children: Vincent Szewczyk, Larry Lynch. B.A., Cornell Coll., Mt. Vernon, Iowa, 1964; M.A., Yale U., 1966, Ph.D., 1969. Research assoc. Brookhaven Lab., Upton, N.Y., 1969-71; research assoc./assoc. instr. U. Utah, Salt Lake City, 1971-72; asst. prof. physics U. Pitts., 1972-78, assoc. prof., 1978-85, prof., 1986—; mem. users coms. Brookhaven Nat. Lab., 1983-86; condr. expts. Inst. Nuclear Physics, Novosibirsk, USSR, Ctr. Europeene Recherche Nucleaire, Switzerland, Brookhaven Natl. Lab., L.I.; spokesperson hyperon decay expt BNL, 1972-80. Contbr. articles to profl. jours. Bd. dirs. 1st Unitarian Ch., Pitts., 1980-83; zone councillor Soc. Physics Students, 1986-88; with Nat. Acad. Sci. Exch. to USSR, 1989-90. Woodrow Wilson fellow, 1964-65. Mem. Am. Phys. Soc. (com. on status of women in physics 1983-86, exec. com. forum on physics and soc. 1990—). Democrat. Unitarian. Avocations: promoting effective science education, hiking, reading, music. Achievements include research with W.E. Cleland and D.E. Kraus in optical triggering; with the collaboration with AFS and HELIOS expt. in direct photon and lepton production, leading to modified understanding of the gluon function, and limits on anomalous electron production; studies of rare and semi-rare kaon decays.

THOMPSON, KATHERINE GENEVIEVE, lawyer; b. Bklyn., May 11, 1945; d. George Otway and Marie (Burke) T. BS, Good Counsel Coll., 1966; JD, Bklyn. Law Sch., 1970; LLM, NYU, 1981. Bar: N.Y. 1971, U.S. Dist. Ct. (so. and ea. dists.) N.Y. 1978, U.S. Supreme Ct. 1981. Editor Matthew Bender Pub. Co., N.Y.C., 1970-71; atty. juvenile rights div. Legal Aid Soc., N.Y.C., 1971-76, asst. atty. in charge juvenile rights div. N.Y. County office, 1976-77; sole practice N.Y.C., 1977-78; ptnr. Rothenberg, Sherman, Thompson & Halpin, N.Y.C., 1978-84, Sherman, Thompson & Halpin, N.Y.C., 1984-87, Beldock, Levine & Hoffman, N.Y.C., 1987—; mem. appellate div. 1st Dept. Screening Panel, 1981-82, appellate div. 1st Dept. Family Ct. Adv. Com., 1983-90, chmn., 1986-89. Co-author: Adoption Law and Practice, 1988; contbg. editor: Bender's Federal Practice Forms, 1971, Bender's Forms of Discovery, 1971. Bd. dirs. August Aichorn Resdl. Ctr., N.Y.C., 1979-94. Fellow Am. Bar Found., N.Y. State Bar Found.; mem. ABA (family law sect.) N.Y. State Bar Assn. (spl. com. on juvenile justice 1980-87, family law sect. 1980—), Assn. of Bar of City of N.Y. (family ct. and family law com. 1977-80, chmn. 1980-83, lectures and continuing edn. com. 1984-85, matrimonial law com. 1985-88), Womens Bar Assn., N.Y. County Lawyers Assn. (family ct. com. 1978-79). Office: Beldock Levine & Hoffman 99 Park Ave New York NY 10016-1508

THOMPSON, KAY FRANCIS, dentist; b. Pitts.; d. Lony C. and Betha E. (Porter) T.; m. Ralph P. Krichbaum, Jan. 10, 1959. BS, U. Pitts., 1951, DDS, 1953. Pvt. practice dentistry Pitts., 1953—; assoc. prof. U. Pitts., Behavioral Sci., Dentistry, Pitts., 1970-80, W.Va. U. Sch. Dentistry, Morgantown, 1980—; dentist for handicapped Robinson Devel. Ctr., McKees Rocks, Pa., 1976—; cons. NIH, Washington, 1975-90, VA Hosp., Pitts., 1978—; lectr., educator various med., dental and psychol. assns. Contbr. articles to profl. jours. Chmn. Dental Legis. Fund Pa., Pitts., 1981-83; mem. World Affairs Coun., Pitts., 1980—, Pa. Dental Polit. Action Com., Harrisburg; bd. dirs. Am. Dental Polit. Action Com., Washington, 1985-90; trustee U. Pitts., 1988-91; mem. Amdental Assoc. Govt. Svcs., 1990-93. Recipient Erickson award De Nederlands Bereniging voor Hypnotherapie, 1983, Bicentennial Medallion of Distinction, U. Pitts., 1988, Alumnae of Yr., 1991, Erickson Found. Lifetime Achievement award, 1992. Fellow ADA (trustee 1993), Am. Coll. Dentists, Internat. Coll. Dentists, Am. Soc. Clin. Hypnosis (pres. 1972-73, scientific 1970), Soc. Clin. and Exptl. Hypnosis (exec. bd. 1976-80), Pierre Fauchard Acad.; mem. Am. Assn. Women Dentists (trustee 1982—, Pres.'s award 1986), Pa. Dental Assn. (sec. 1984-88, pres. 1989-90), U. Pitts. Dental Alumni Assn. (pres. 1988-91). Lutheran. Office: PO Box 16152 Pittsburgh PA 15242-0141

THOMPSON, LAURA REESE, psychology educator; b. Danville, Va., Nov. 28, 1950; d. Leon White Thompson and Eleanor (Sanford) Spencer; m. Robert Morris Smith, Feb. 17, 1990 (dec. April 1993); stepchildren: Katherine, Jacqueline, Robert. BA, U. N.C., Greensboro, 1973; MS, Peabody Coll., 1975; PhD, Vanderbilt U., 1980. Lic. nursing home adminstr. Unit dir. Midlands Ctr., Columbia, S.C., 1980-84; program dir. Alston Wilkes Soc., Columbia, S.C., 1984-85; unit dir. Dept. Mental Health, State of S.C., Columbia, S.C., 1985-88, psychologist, 1988-91; prof. Midlands Tech. Coll., Columbia, S.C., 1991—; cons. Allen U., Columbia, S.C., 1991-93, Dept. Mental Health, State of S.C., 1992-93. Author: (manual) Behavior Management, 1985. Mem. of vestry Good Shepherd Episcopal Ch., Columbia, S.C., 1991-94. Mental Retardation Tgn. fellow NICHHD, 1977-80; Profl. Devel. grant Midlands Tech. Coll., 1994. Mem. NAFE, Am. Assn. Mental Retardation, Am. Psychol. Soc., Assn. Advancement of Retarded Citizens, Nat. Assn. Advancement of Colored People, Nat. Assn. Univ. Women. Episcopalian. Home: 21 Constable Lane Columbia SC 29223-5305

THOMPSON, LAVERNE ELIZABETH THOMAS, English language educator; b. Bklyn., July 17, 1945; d. Roscoe Lee and Mary Elizabeth (Blackwell) Thomas; m. Robert Louis Thompson, Sept. 28, 1968. BA in English, Bluffton Coll., 1967; MS in Ednl. Adminstrn./Supervision, U. Dayton, 1977; PhD in Higher Edn., U. Toledo, 1991. Cert. sch. prin., Ohio; cert. secondary sch. supr., Ohio; cert. realtor, Ohio; cert. notary public, Ohio. Instr. English, speech Piqua (Ohio) Cen. High Sch., 1967-68; instr. Lima (Ohio) Sr. High Sch., 1968-77, Shawnee High Sch., Lima, 1977-86; grad. asst. U. Toledo, 1986-91, interim counselor/adminstr. Student Support Svcs., 1989, interim adminstrv. asst. Multicultural Student Devel., 1990; real estate agt. Alberta Lee Realty, Lima, Ohio, 1978-82, Slonaker Realty, Lima, 1982-84, Gooding Co., Lima, 1985-90. Editor Higher Edn. newsletter, 1987. Bd. dirs. Lima YWCA, 1971; co-chair Brotherhood Dinner Sr. High Sch., Lima, 1976; participant 17th annual Nat. Conf. on Citizenship, Washington, 1962. Mem. NAFE, Va. Assn. New Homemakers Am. (state pres. 1962, nat. pres. 1963), Blackwell Family Assn., M.I. Hummel Club, Lladro Collectors Soc., Internat. Platform Assn., Duncan Royale Collectors' Club, All God's Children Collectors' Club, Belleek Collectors' Internat. Soc., Gartland USA Collectors League, Lalique Soc. Am., G. Armani Soc., Sarah's Attic Forever Friends Collectors; Club, Walt Disney Collectors' Soc., Phi Delta Kappa, others. Home: 1038 Valley Grove Dr Maumee OH 43537-3203

THOMPSON, LILLIAN HURLBURT, communications company executive; b. Bennington, Vt., Apr. 27, 1947; d. Paul Rhodes and Evelyn Arlene (Lockhart) Hurlburt; m. Wayne Wray Thompson, June 28, 1969. BS, Skidmore Coll., 1969; MS, U. So. Miss., 1975; MBA, George Washington U., 1994. Comm. cons. Southwestern Bell Telephone, San Antonio, 1978-80; acct. exec. C&P Telephone, Washington, 1980-82, Am. Bell, Washington, 1983; staff mgr. AT&T Info. Systems, Rosslyn, Va., 1984; mgr. sales intermediary mktg. dept. Bell Atlantic Corp., Silver Spring, Md., 1984-89, mgr. product line mgmt. dept., 1989-92, mgr. product profitability system fin. dept., 1992-93; mgr. market planning and strategies large bus. svcs. dept. Bell Atlantic Internat. Inc., Arlington, Va., 1993-94; dir. Bell Atlantic Internat., Inc., Arlington, Va., 1994—. Home: 9203 St Marks Pl Fairfax VA 22031-3045 Office: Bell Atlantic 1310 N Court House Rd Arlington VA 22201-2501

THOMPSON, LOIS JEAN HEIDKE ORE, industrial psychologist; b. Chgo., Feb. 22, 1933; d. Harold William and Ethel Rose (Neumann) Heidke; m. Henry Thomas Ore, Aug. 28, 1954 (div. May 1972); children: Christopher, Douglas; m. Joseph Lippard Thompson, Aug. 3, 1972; children: Scott, Les, Melanie. BA, Cornell Coll., Mt. Vernon, Iowa, 1955; MA, Idaho State U., 1964, EdD, 1981. Lic. psychologist, N.Mex. Tchr. pub. schs. various locations, 1956-67; tchr., instr. Idaho State U., Pocatello, 1967-72; employee/orgn. devel. specialist Los Alamos (N.Mex.) Nat. Lab., 1981-84, tng. specialist, 1984-89, sect. leader, 1989-93; pvt. practice Los Alamos, 1988—; sec. Cornell Coll. Alumni Office, 1954-55, also other orgns.; bd. dirs. Parent Edn. Ctr., Idaho State U., 1980; counselor, Los Alamos, 1981-88. Editor newsletter LWV, Laramie, Wyo., 1957; contbr. articles to profl. jours. Pres. Newcomers Club, Pocatello, 1967, Faculty Womens Club, Pocatello, 1968; chmn. edn. com. AAUW, Pocatello, 1969. Mem. APA, ACA, N.Mex. Psychol. Assn. (bd. dirs. div. II, 1990, sec. 1988-90, chmn. 1990), N.Am. Soc. Adlerian Psychology, N.Mex. Soc. Adlerian Psychology (pres. 1990, treas. 1991-94), Soc. Indsl. and Orgnl. Psychology, Nat. Career Counseling Assn. Mem. LDS Ch. Home: 340 Aragon Ave Los Alamos NM 87544-3505 Office: Thompson Counseling & Cons 340 Aragon Ave Los Alamos NM 87544-3505

THOMPSON, MARCIA SLONE, choral director, educator; b. Ary, Ky., June 30, 1959; d. Ray and Wevena (Hall) Slone; m. Randall C. Thompson, Sept. 22, 1979; children: Tiffany, Ashley, Brittany, Alicia, Jessica. B in Music Edn., Pikeville Coll., 1981; M in Secondary Edn., Morehead State U., 1985. Cert. Rank I supervision, music edn. tchr. with endorsement, grades K-12. Guitarist Slone Family Band, 1970-77; pvt. practice Hindman, Ky., 1977-93; band, choral dir. Pike County Bd. Edn., Pikeville, Ky., 1981-82, Floyd County Bd. Edn., Eastern, Ky., 1982-87; choral dir. Knott County Bd. Edn., Hindman, 1987—, Knott County Central High, Hindman, Ky, 1993—; piano instr. guitar instr., Upward Bound program Pikeville Coll., Hindman, 1977. Albums include Appalachian Bluegrass, 1972, Ramblin' Round with Slone Family, 1977; appeared on the Grand Ole Opry, 1976. Band conductor jr. high divsn. Pike County All-County Festival, Pikeville, 1981; music chair Red White Blue Festival, Martin, Ky., 1982; music judge Floyd County All-County Band, Prestonsburg, Ky., 1982-87; band dir. Ky. Derby Festival Parade, Louisville, 1985; piano accompanist choir 1st Bapt. Ch., Hindman, 1990-91, nursery asst., 1990-93, dir. youth choir, 1992, choral dir. music makers (children's music), 1994, Bapt. young women's hospitality officer, 1995, mem. sch. com.; performer Senator Benny Bailey Salute, Prestonsburg, 1991, Gingerbread Festival, Hindman, 1992-93; active Bapt. Young Women, 1993; co-founder Knott County Fine Arts Day Celebration, 1992—. Mem. Nat. Educators Assn., Am. Choral Dirs. Assn., Ky. Educators Assn., Ky. Music Educators. Democrat. Home: PO Box 15 Hindman KY 41822-0015 Office: Knott County Ctrl High Sch Hindman KY 41822

THOMPSON, MARGARET ELLIS, business educator; b. Detroit, Mar. 26, 1948; d. Carl Langford and Vodel (Garrison) Ellis; m. Charles C. Thompson, Oct. 6, 1972 (dec. July 1991); children: Bonnie, Clay. BS in Secondary Edn., David Lipscomb U., 1970. Cert. tchr., Tenn. Sec. Third Nat. Bank, Nashville, 1970-71; student svcs. sec. Nashville Tech. Inst., 1971-74; tchr. adult edn. program Met. Schs. Nashville, 1971-72; bus. tchr. and devel. coord. Friendship Christian Sch., Lebanon, Tenn., 1983—; banquet coord. Friendship Christian Sch., Lebanon, 1984—. Mem. Alpha Delta Kappa. Mem. Ch. of Christ. Home: 1616 Hickory Valley Rd Lebanon TN 37087 Office: Friendship Christian Sch 5400 Coles Ferry Pike Lebanon TN 37087

THOMPSON, MARGUERITE MYRTLE GRAMING (MRS. RALPH B. THOMPSON), librarian; b. Orangeburg, S.C., Apr. 23, 1912; d. Thomas Laurie and Rosa Lee (Stroman) Graming; m. Ralph B. Thompson, Sept. 17, 1949 (dec. Oct. 1960). BA in English cum laude, U. S.C., 1932, postgrad., 1937; BLS, Emory U., 1943. Tchr. English pub. high schs., S.C., 1932-43; libr. Rockingham (N.C.) High Sch., 1943-45, Randolph County (N.C.) Libr., Asheboro, 1945-48, Colleton County (S.C.) Libr., Walterboro, 1948-61; dir. Florence (S.C.) County Libr., 1961-78. Sec. com. community facilities, svcs. and instns. Florence County Resources Devel. Com., 1964-67; vice chmn. Florence County Coun. on Aging, 1968-70, exec. bd. 1968-82, bd. treas., 1973-75, bd. sec., 1976-77, bd. v.p., 1979; mem. Florence County Bicentennial Planning Com., 1975-76; mem. rels. and allocations com. United Way, 1979-80. Named Boss of Yr. Nat. Secs. Assn., 1971. Mem. ALA (coun. 1964-72), Southeastern Libr. Assn., S.C. Libr. Assn. (pres. 1960, chmn. assn. handbook revision com. 1967-69, 80, sect. co-chmn. com. standards for S.C. pub. librs. 1966-75, fed. rels. coord. 1972-73, planning com. 1976-78), Greater Florence C. of C. (women's div. chmn. 1969-70, bd. dirs. 1975-77), S.E. Regional Conf. Women in C. of C. (bd. dir. 1970-71), Florence Bus. and Profl. Women's Club (2d v.p. 1975-76, Career Woman of Yr. 1974, parliamentarian 1980-81, chmn. scholarship com. 1981-82), Delta Kappa Gamma (county chpt. charter pres. 1963-65, treas. 1966-70, chmn. com. on expansion 1977-80, 82-84, state chpt. chmn. state scholarship com. 1967-73, state 2d v.p. 1971-73, state 1st v.p. 1973-75, state pres. 1975-77, chmn. policy manual 1977-81, chmn. adv. coun. 1978-85, chmn. fin. com. 1981-83, parliamentarian 1987-91, adminstrv. bd. 1987—, chmn. nominations com. 1989-91, dir. S.E. Region 1978-80, coord. S.E. Regional Golden Anniversary Conf. 1979, internat. scholarship com. 1970-74, internat. exec. bd. 1975-77, 78-80, internat. adminstrv. bd. 1978-80, internat. constn. com. 1980-82, internat. achievement award com., 1986-88), Florence Literary Club (sec. 1964-66, 79-82, pres. 1970-72). Methodist (chmn. ch. libr. com. 1965-71, chmn. com. ch. history, 1968-69, sec. adminstrv. bd. 1979-82). Home: 1000 Live Oaks Dr SW # 8B Orangeburg SC 29115-9600

THOMPSON, MARI HILDENBRAND, medical staff services operations coordinator; b. Washington, Apr. 26, 1951; d. Emil John Christopher Hildenbrand and Ada Lythe (Conklin) Hildenbrand-Kammer; m. R. Marshall Thompson, Sept. 27, 1970 (div. June 1981); 1 child, Jeremy Marshall. BA in Secondary Edn., Am. U., 1976, BA in Performing Arts, 1976. Cert. med. staff coord. Employment interviewer Scripps Meml. Hosp., La Jolla, Calif., 1977-81; office mgr. Jacksina & Freedman Press Office, N.Y.C., 1982-83; staffing coord., med. staff asst. Am. Med. Internat. Clairemont Hosp., San Diego, 1983-85; adminstrv. asst. Am. Med. Internat. Valley Med. Ctr., El Cajon, Calif., 1985-88; med. staff coord. Sharp Meml. Hosp., San Diego, 1988-92; adminstrv. asst. Grossmont Hosp., La Mesa, Calif., 1992-93, coord. Sharp family practice residency program, 1993-94; ops. coord. Sharp Meml. Hosp. med. staff svcs., San Diego, 1994—; wardrobe mistress various community theatres, San Diego, 1978-79, actress, San Diego, 1979-81. Appeared N.Y.C. (N.Y.) Playreaders Group, 1981-83, N.J. Shakespeare Theatre, Madison, 1982, Good Humor Improv Co., N.Y.C., 1982-83. Mem. World Wildlife Fedn., Calif., 1991, Greenpeace, Calif., 1991, Sierra Club, Calif., 1991, 92, Audubon Soc., Calif., 1991, 92, Internat. Wildlife Fedn., 1992, Smithsonian, 1993, 94. Included in Outstanding Young Women of Am., 1986. Mem. NAFE, AFTRA, Nat. Assn. Med. Staff Svcs., Calif. Assn. Med. Staff Svcs., San Diego Assn. Med. Staff, Nat. Assn. Health Care Quality, Assn. Family Practice Adminstrs. Democrat. Lutheran. Home: 7951 Beaver Lake Dr San Diego CA 92119-2610

THOMPSON, MARY DAVIS, lawyer; b. Boston, June 15, 1951; d. Ralph and Beatric (Levy) Davis; children: Sam, Benjamin. BA cum laude, Brandeis U., 1973; MEd, Goucher Coll., 1974-75; JD, U. N.C., 1988. Bar: N.C. 1989; cert. elem. tchr. Rsch. asst. U. N.C., Chapel Hill, 1987-88; clk. to hon. judge S. Gerald Arnold N.C. Ct. of Appeals, 1988-89; com. counsel N.C. Gen. Assembly, Raleigh, 1990—. Pres. Midtown Atlanta Neighborhood Assn., 1981-82; bd. dirs., pers. chair Chapel Hill Day Care, 1983-85; bd. dirs. Lake Forest Neighborhood Assn., 1990. Edn. Policy fellow, 1991-92. Mem. N.C. Bar Assn. (editor newsletter 1992), N.C. Assn. Women Attys. (editor newsheet 1988-89), Southeastern Regional Vision for Edn. Legis. Staff Network, Coun. State Edn. Attys. Democrat. Jewish. Home: 2540 Booker Creek Rd Chapel Hill NC 27514-5120 Office: NC Gen Assembly 545 Lob 300 N Salisbury Raleigh NC 27603

THOMPSON, MARY EILEEN, chemistry educator; b. Mpls., Dec. 21, 1928; d. Albert C. and Blanche (McAvoy) T. B.A., Coll. St. Catherine, 1953; M.S., U. Minn., 1958; Ph.D., U. Calif.-Berkeley, 1964. Math. and sci. tchr. Derham Hall High Sch., St. Paul, 1953-58; faculty Coll. St. Catherine, St. Paul, 1964—, prof., chmn. dept. chemistry, 1969-90; project dir. Women in Chemistry, 1984—. Contbr. articles to profl. jours. Mem. Am. Chem. Soc. (chair women chemists com. 1992-94), Coun. Undergrad. Rsch. (councilor 1991—), N.Y. Acad. Sci., Chem. Soc. London, AAAS, Sigma Xi, Phi Beta Kappa. Democrat. Roman Catholic. Achievements include research interests in Cr(III) hydrolytic polymers, kinetics of inorganic complexes, Co(III) peroxo/superoxo complexes. Office: Coll St Catherine 2004 Randolph Ave Saint Paul MN 55105-1789

THOMPSON, MARY KOLETA, sculptor, non-profit organization director; b. Portsmouth, Va., Dec. 27, 1938; m. James Burton Thompson, May 5, 1957; children: Burt, Suzan, Kate, Jon. BFA, U. Tex., 1982; postgrad., Boston U. Cert. fund raising exec. Pres. The Planning Resource People, Austin, Tex., 1990—; Tex. fin. devel. specialist Am. Red Cross Tex., 1994—; devel. dir. Very Spl. Arts Tex., 1991-92; dir. devel. Centex chpt. Am. Red Cross, Austin, 1992—; dir. Tex. Children's Mus., Fredericksburg, 1987-88, Internat. Hdqrs. SHAPE Command Arts and Crafts Ctr., 1985-86; com. chmn. Symposium for Encouragement Women in Math. and Natural Sci., U. Tex., Austin, 1990. Sculptor portrait busts. Bd. dirs. Teenage Parent Coun., Austin, 1990-92. Named U.S. Vol. of Yr., Belgium, 1986; grantee NEA, 1988. Mem. AAUW (life, pres. 1990-92), Women in Comm. (co-chmn. S.W. regional conf.), U. Tex. Ex-Student Assn. (life), Tex. Hist. Found. (life), Leadership Tex. (life), Leadership Tex. Alumnae Assn. (bd. dirs.), Raleigh Tavern Soc. (founder), Austin Antiques Forum (founder 1990). Office: San Antonio Area Chpt ARC 3642 E Houston St San Antonio TX 78219-3830

THOMPSON, NANCY JEAN, home furnishings executive; b. Stillwater, Okla., July 25, 1954; d. Ramon D. and Jean (Ward) Prohaska; m. Noel David Thompson, Sept. 1, 1976; children: Alexander, Maximilian. BFA, Skidmore Coll., 1976. Exec. trainee Saks Fifth Ave., N.Y.C., 1976-78; mgr. Saks Fifth Ave., Chgo., 1978-79; buyer Wieboldt's, Chgo., 1979-81, Marine Corps Exchange Svc., Quantico, Va., 1981-82; sales mgr. mil. and spl. markets Loew's Corp./Bulova, Woodside, N.Y., 1982-88; v.p. home div. R.C. Staff/Milan, N.Y.C., 1988-90; buyer Lynn Hollyn Madison Ave.-Itokin/Japan-Space Creation, N.Y.C., 1990-91; product devel. Am. Pacfic, Enterprise, N.Y.C., 1991; prin. Nancy Thompson, Design, Licensing & Mktg., Ltd., N.Y.C., 1992—; cons. to textile, furniture, retail industries in product devel. and licensing. Group leader Ridgewood-Glen Rock Coun. Boy Scouts Am. Mem. NAFE, I.H.F.D.A., Hoboken Creative Alliance, Fashion Group N.Y.C. Episcopalian.

THOMPSON, PATRICIA CHELL, information systems specialist; b. Balt., Dec. 11, 1947; d. Raymond Neal and Norma Sophia (Hauswald) Chell; m. Dale Edward Thompson, April 1, 1984; children: Erin, Carl. BS cum laude, U. Md., 1982. Cert. clin. lab. scientist, 1980. Clin. lab. technologist Clinical Lab., Pa., 1968-77, Md., 1977-81; systems analyst Georgetown U. Hosp., Washington, 1982-83, project leader, 1983-84, asst. dir., hosp. info. systems, 1984-86; mgr., distributed info. systems Geisinger Health Sys., Danville, Pa., 1986-87, adminstrv. dir., info. mgmt., 1987-93, v.p., info. systems, 1993-94, v.p. info. svcs., chief info. officer, 1994—. Active mem. long range planning com. Danville Sch. Dist., Pa. 1988-89, mem. tech. coun., 1994—; bd. dir. Danville Child Devel. Ctr., Pa. 1989-92, exec. com. sec., 1992; chmn. bldg. com. Danville Alliance Ch., Pa., 1990. Mem. Pa. Healthcare Info. and Mgmt. Systems Soc. (sec/treas. 1989-90, pres. 1990-91), Hosp. Assn. Pa. (systems ad hoc com. 1991, work group 1992-94), Computer Based Patient Record Inst. (security workgroup 1992—, bd. dirs. 1994—), Coll. Healthcare Info. Mgmt. Execs. Office: Geisinger Health Sys 100 N Academy Ave Danville PA 17822-3301

THOMPSON, PATRICIA EILEEN, clinical psychologist; b. Lawrence, Kans., Mar. 17, 1945; d. Leslie Foy and Mavis Eileen (Richardson) T. BA, U. Vt., 1966; MA, Mich. State U., 1973, PhD, 1980. Lic. psychologist, Mich. Mental health therapist St. Lawrence Mental Health Ctr., Lansing, Mich., 1971-85; psychologist Adrian (Mich.) Psychotherapy Assocs., 1983—; pvt. practice Ann Arbor, Mich., 1988—; adj. instr. dept. psychiatry Mich. State U., East Lansing, 1975-76; community rep. Listening Ear Crisis Intervention Ctr., East Lansing, 1975-76. Mem. Am. Psychol. Assn., Mich. Psychoanalytic Coun., Mich. Psychol. Assn., Mich. Soc. for Psychoanalytic Psychology, Mich. Women Psychologists (continuing edn. com. 1991-92). Home: 839 W Huron Ann Arbor MI 48103 Office: Adrian Psychotherapy Assocs 604 N Main St Adrian MI 49221

THOMPSON, POLLY, artist; b. Orange, N.J., Mar. 13, 1952; d. Albert Rackenberg and Nina Nichy; m. Julian Francis Thompson, Aug. 11, 1978. AB, Oberlin Coll., 1974. Tchr. Changes, Inc., East Orange, N.J., 1976-78. Exhibited in group shows at The Hyde Collection, Glens Falls, N.Y., 1986, Silvermine Galleries, New Canaan, Conn., 1989, Stratton Arts Festival, Stratton Mountain, Vt., 1988, 90, 91, 92, Mus. of Fine Arts, Springfield, Mass., 1993 (J.D. Ayers Art award 1993), Cheekwood Mus., Nashville, 1993. Mem. Women's Caucus for the Arts. Democrat. Home: PO Box 138 West Rupert VT 05776 Office: 347 S Winooski Ave Burlington VT 05401

THOMPSON, RONELLE KAY HILDEBRANDT, library director; b. Brookings, S.D., Apr. 21, 1954; d. Earl E. and Maxine R. (Taplin) Hildebrandt; m. Harry Floyd Thompson II, Dec. 24, 1976; children: Clarissa, Harry III. BA in Humanities magna cum laude, Houghton Coll., 1976; MLS, Syracuse U., 1976; postgrad., U. Rochester, 1980, 81; cert., Miami U., 1990. Libr. asst. Norwalk (Conn.) Pub. Libr., 1977; elem. libr. Moriah Cen. Schs., Port Henry, N.Y., 1977-78; div. coord. pediatric gastroenterology and nutrition U. Rochester (N.Y.) Med. Ctr., 1978-81, cons., mem. pediatric housestaff libr. com., 1980-81; dir. Medford Libr. U. S.C., Lancaster, 1981-83; dir. Mikkelsen Libr., libr. assocs., Ctr. for Western Studies, mem. acad. computing com., libr. com. Augustana Coll., Sioux Falls, S.D., 1983—, mem. adminstrv. pers. coun., 1989—; presenter in field. Contbr. articles to profl. jours. Mem. adv. com. S.D. Libr. Network, 1986—, chair, 1989-91, 94—; mem. Sioux Falls Community Playhouse, S.D. Symphony, Sioux Falls Civic Fine Arts Assn.; advisor Minnehana County Libr., pers. dept. City of Sioux Falls. Named one of Outstanding Young Women Am., 1983; Syracuse U. Gaylord Co. scholar, 1976; recipient YWCA leader award, 1991. Mem. ALA, AAUW, Assn. Coll. and Rsch. Librs. (nat. adv. coun. coll. librs. sect. 1987—), Mountain Plains Libr. Assn. (chair acad. sect., nominating com. 1988, pres. 1993-94), S.D. Libr. Assn. (chair interlibr. cooperation task force 1986-87, pres. 1987-88, chair recommended minimum salary task force 1988, chair local arrangements com. 1989-90), S.D. Libr. Network (adv. coun. 1986—, exec. com. 1992—). Office: Augustana Coll Mikkelsen Libr 29th & Summit Sioux Falls SD 57197

THOMPSON, SALLY ANN, newspaper editor; b. Hillsboro, N.D., Apr. 10, 1943; d. C. Hilman and Blanche E. (Bjerkan) Swenson; m. Arthur G. Thompson, July 1, 1965 (dec. Mar. 1990); 1 child, Laurie Kate

Beth. Student, Concordia Coll., Moorhead, Minn., 1961-65. Reporter The Valley Journal, Halstad, Minn., 1979-84; contbg. editor Prairie West Publs., Wahpeton, N.D., 1982-84; editor Hillsboro Banner, Hillsboro, N.D., 1984—; lectr. Career Day Mayville State U., N.D., 1985-92. Mem. commns. com. Eastern N.D. Synod ELCA, 1990-93; bd. dirs. Traill County Hist. Soc., 1979—, Hillsboro Forestry Bd., 1990-93. Recipient numerous journalism awards. Lutheran. Home: 1001 44th St SW # 301 Fargo ND 58103 Office: Hillsboro Banner 20 W Caledonia Ave Hillsboro ND 58045-4205

THOMPSON, SALLY ANNE MARGARET, librarian; b. Chgo., Jan. 7, 1934; m. William Richard Thompson; children: Deborah, William, Susan, Michael, Robin. AA in Edn., Felician Coll.; BA, Ariz. State U.; MEd, Lesley Coll. With Immaculate Conception Sch., Chgo., 1964-70, St. Theresa Sch., Phoenix, Ariz., 1972-79, Orangedale Sch., Phoenix, 1981—; mem. adv. bd. Librs. Ltd., Phoenix, 1988—, Notable Books for Children com., 1993-97, chair, 1995—; mem. print media award com. IRA, 1992-94. Editor: There's a Fly in My Soup, 1991; contbr. articles to profl. jours.; co-editor: Achieving Excellence in Library Instruction, 1988; book reviewer, co-editor: Cath. Libr. World, 1985—. Treas. Orangedale PTA, 1990-91; v.p. Orangedale Parent-Tchr.-Student Orgn., 1993-94. World book grantee Cath. Libr. Assn., 1987. Mem. ALA (Caldecott award com. 1991-93), Cath. Libr. Assn. (Regina medal chmn. 1977-79, exec. bd. 1983-85), Balsz Fedn. Tchrs. (pres. 1992—), Phi Delta Kappa. Roman Catholic. Office: Orangedale Sch 5048 E Oak St Phoenix AZ 85008

THOMPSON, SALLY ENGSTROM, state official; b. Spokane, Wash., Feb. 17, 1940; d. Logan C. and Ava Leigh (Phillips) Engstrom; m. Donald Edward Colcun, 1981; children: Lauri Thompson, Tom Thompson, Tami Thompson, Sheri Colcun Trumpfheller. BS magna cum laude, U. Colo., 1975. CPA, Colo. 1976, Kans. 1986. Audit mgr. and mgmt. cons. Touche Ross & Co., Denver, 1975-82; v.p., mgr. planning and fin. analysis United Bank, Denver, 1982-85; pres., chief oper. officer Shawnee Fed. Svgs., Topeka, 1985-90; treas. State of Kans., 1990—. Past editorial advisor New Accountant mag. Bd. dirs. Everywoman's Resource Ctr., Topeka, 1988-92, Community Svc. Found. Kans., Kids Voting Kans. (hon.); v.p., bd. dirs. Downtown Topeka Inc., YWCA, Topeka, 1986-93, Woman of Achievement award, 1984; mem. fin. com. Girl Scouts U.S., Kaw Valley, various coms., United Way of Greater Topeka; chmn. art auction com. KTWU-TV, summer concert, Topeka Civic Theatre. Recipient Disting. Community Leadership award Topeka Pub. Schs., 1989, Disting. Leadership award Nat. Assn. Community Leadership, 1991, 1991 Class Leadership Kans. Mem. AICPAs, Am. Soc. Women Accts., Kans. Soc. CPAs, Kansas C. of C. and Industry, Greater Topeka C. of C. (bd. dirs. 1989-92), Emporia State U. Bus. Sch. Adv. Bd., Nat. Assn. State Auditors, Controllers and Treas., Nat. Assn. State Treas. (v.p., Midwest regional chair), Women Execs. in Govt., Beta Alpha Psi. Democrat. Offices: Office State Treasurer Landon State Office Bldg 900 SW Jackson St Ste 201N Topeka KS 66612-1220*

THOMPSON, SANDRA ROMAINE, corporate facility nurse; b. West Grove, Pa., Mar. 6, 1938; d. Thomas Walter and Florence Elizabeth (Mahan) T. Diploma in nursing, Del. Hosp., 1959. Cert. HIV infection and AIDS, N.Y. State Dept. Health, 1991, cert. HIV counselor, 1991. Staff nurse and charge nurse Mt. View Hosp., Lockport, N.Y., 1960-67; dir. nurses Newfane (N.Y.) Nursing Home, 1967-72; staff nurse Harrison Radiator Div., GM, Lockport, 1972—. Vol. AIDS Community Svcs., Buffalo, 1987-94, Ea. Niagra County divsn. Am. Heart Assn., Buffalo, 1987-94, bd. dirs., 1989-94, v.p. bd. dirs., 1991-92, pres. 1992-94; bd. dirs. western N.Y. region, 1991-94, program com., 1989-92; active Niagra Falls chpt. Am. Cancer Soc., 1987, 90-94, bd. dirs. 1990-94; charter mem. Niagra County Healthy Heart Program, 1988-94, mem. task force on smoking cessation and obesity. Recipient Smoking Cessation Achievement award Lakeside Pharm. Co., Lockport, 1988, Program award of Excellence Ea. Niagra County div. Am. Heart Assn., 1988, 89, 90, Program Vol. Yr. award Western N.Y. Region, 1991, 93, Pub. Edn. Life Saver's award Niagra chpt. Am. Cancer Soc., 1988, Pub. Edn. award Am. Cancer Soc., 1989, Vol. award United Way, 1990, Community Svc. award Lockport Community Cable, 1991. Mem. Am. Assn. Occupational Health Nurses, Western N.Y. Assn. Occupational Health Nurses, N.Y. State Occupational Health Nurses, N.Y. State Am. Heart Assn. (profl. mem.). Liberal. Roman Catholic.

THOMPSON, SHAWNA MARGARET, lawyer; b. Glen Cove, N.Y., Sept. 4, 1961; d. Vincent John and Margaret Catherine (Kelly) Haley; m. John Arthur Thompson, April 30, 1994. BA in Bus., U. Ariz., 1981; JD cum laude, U. San Diego, 1986. Assoc. Lee & Holbrook, Redondo Beach, Calif., 1987-89; sr. staff CSL Litigation Northrop Grumman Corp., L.A., 1989—; arbitrator Superior Ct., L.A., 1993-94; mem. Sr. Women in Aerospace, L.A., 1994. Mem. ABA, Calif. Bar Assn., L.A. Bar Assn., Century City Bar Assn. Office: Northrop Grumman Corp 1840 Century Park E Los Angeles CA 90067-2199

THOMPSON, SHIRLEY J., public relations executive. Co-founder Carl Thompson Assocs., Boulder, Colo., 1985, sr. account exec., 1989-90, v.p., 1990-91, sr. v.p., 1991, pres., 1991—. Recipient Golden Quill award IABC. Mem. NIRI. Office: Carl Thompson Assocs 75 Manhattan Dr Ste 205 Boulder CO 80303*

THOMPSON, SUE WANDA, small business owner; b. Azle, Tex., Nov. 26, 1935; d. Weldon W. Beasley and Eula Mae Hardee; m. William Henry Clark, Feb. 20, 1952 (div. 1959); children: Gloria, Russ, Bonnie; m. Robert L. Thompson Jr., Sept. 20, 1963; stepchildren: Christene, Lee. Nurse Harris Hosp., Ft. Worth, 1960-62, Denton State Sch., 1962-63; owner, v.p. Dalworth Med. Labs., Ft. Worth, 1963-68; sales leader, trainer Home Interior and Gifts, Dallas, 1970-80; owner, pres. Thompson Enterprises, 1980—; mgr., trainer Jafra Cosmetics, West Lake Village, Calif., 1981-84, Jewels by Park Lane, Chgo., 1984-89, Just Am., Rutlerfordton, N.C., 1989-91; with sales Dyna Tech Nutritionals, Willston Park, N.Y., 1993-94. Dir. parks and recreation City Forest Hills, Tex., 1970. Mem. Beta Sigma Phi (treas. Eta Lambda chpt. 1971-72, pres. 1972-73, Girl of Yr. 1974). Republican. Mem. Ch. Nazarene. Home: 4717 Applewood Rd Fort Worth TX 76133

THOMPSON, SUSAN COLE, middle school educator; b. Trion, Ga., Nov. 19, 1957; d. Edwin Coleman Sr. and Yvonne (McCullough) T. BS in Elem. Edn., West Ga. Coll., 1979, M in Elem. Edn., 1980. Substitute tchr. Menlo (Ga.) Elem. Sch., 1975-79; grad. asst. dept. elem. edn. West Ga. Coll., Carrollton, 1979-80, media asst. tchrs. materials ctr., 1981, 82; banquet stewardess Ramada Inn, Carrollton, 1988; sales clk. Designer's Touch, Carrollton, 1989-90; tour escort Lakeland Tours, Inc., Washington, 1990—; 6th grade math. tchr. Ctrl. Middle Sch., Carrollton, 1980—; pvt. tutor, Carrollton, 1985—. Mem. Carroll County Leadership Acad., Carrollton, 1993. Mem. Profl. Assn. Ga. Educators, Nat. Trust for Hist. Preservation. Home: 110D Waverly Way Carrollton GA 30116-4455 Office: Ctrl Middle Sch 155 Whooping Creek Rd Carrollton GA 30116-8999

THOMPSON, TARA DENISE, illustrator, writer, career counselor; b. Borger, Tex., June 7, 1962; d. Sammy Jo and Jeannean (Johansen) T. AA, Tex. State Tech. Inst., 1982; AAS, Richland Coll., 1991; BA, U. Tex., Dallas, 1993; MA in Counseling, Amber U., 1995. Art dir. Dalco Athletic Lettering, Garland, Tex., 1983-85; office mgr. Jean West Enterprises, Dallas, 1985-86; dept. adminstr. Dean Witter Reynolds, Inc., Dallas, 1986-87; info. specialist, pub. relations asst. Anderson Fischel Thompson Advt., Dallas, 1986-87, office mgr., 1987-89, traffic mgr., 1989-90; illustrator, writer Garland, Tex., 1990—; intern Richland Coll., Dallas, 1994—. Vol. listener Dallas Ind. Sch. Dist., 1991-92; CTM competent toastmaster, 1993. Mem. Am. Counseling Assn., Nat. Employment Counseling Assn., Nat. Career Devel. Assn., Undergrad. Psychology Assn. U. Tex. (treas. 1992), Speaking Scholars Toastmasters (pres. 1992-93), People for the Ethical Treatment of Animals. Office: 2618 Centennial Dr Garland TX 75042-5604

THOMPSON, TINA LEWIS CHRYAR, publisher; b. Houston, Dec. 31, 1929; d. Joshua and Mary Christine (Brown) Thompson; m. Joseph Chryar, May 25, 1943; 1 child, Joseph Jr. Cosmotologist, Franklin Coll., Houston, 1950; student, Crenshaw Coll., L.A., 1961. Pubr., composer, author B.M.I., N.Y.C., 1964-74; pubr. ASCAP, N.Y.C., 1974-86, The Fox Agy., N.Y.C., 1986—, Tech. World, L.A., 1990—; v.p. music Asset Records, L.A., 1978—; music dir., v.p. Roach Records, L.A., 1968; music dir. Rendezvous Records, Hollywood, 1950; v.p. Assoc. Internat., L.A., 1973; pres. Cling Music Pub., Soprano Music; pub. processor music catalogs Broadcast Music Inc. Author: Soprano Poems, 1985; creator/designer Baby Napin brand form-fitting, no-leak, no pins baby diaper, 1967, Saver Belt, 1993; patentee/pub. Letter's Tech in Word, used by TV stas. to advertise, 1972. Recipient recognition award IBC, Cambridge, Eng., 1991, cert. of proclamation Internat. Woman of Yr., 1991-92, Merit award Pres. Ronald Reagan, 1986; named Most Admired Woman of Decade, ABI, 1993. Mem. AAUW, NARAS, Am. Soc. Authors and Composers, Nat. Mus. Pubs. Assn., Song-writers Guild Am., Am. Fedn. Label Co. Unions, Am. Theatre Assn. Broadcast Music Inc. (pres. Soprano Music Publ. 1968), Rec. Acad. Country Music Acad., Internat. Platform Assn., L.A. Women in Music. Home: PO Box 7731 Beverly Hills CA 90212-7731

THOMPSON, VIRGINIA LOU, agricultural products supplier and importer; b. Malcolm, Iowa, July 15, 1928; d. Isaac Cleveland and Viola (Montgomery) Griffin; m. Alfred Thompson, Mar. 1, 1946 (dec. March 1992); children: Michael Duane, Cathryn Lynn, Steven Curtis, Laura Lue; m. David Hartman Rud, Sept. 5, 1993. Student Phoenix Coll., 1962, Phoenix-Scottsdale Jr. Coll., 1973-74. With sales dept. Trend House, Phoenix, 1962-67; importer World Wide Imports, Ft. Collins, Colo., 1974-79; owner, mgr. Windsor Elevator Inc. (Colo.), 1979-89; participant in trade shows, seminars. Pres. Am. Luth. Ch. Women, 1973-74. Mem. Nat. Grain and Feed Assn., Colo. Grain and Feed Assn., Rocky Mountain Bean Dealers, Colo. Cattle Feeders Assn., Western U.S. Agrl. Assn., Rice Millers Assn. Democrat. Lutheran. Clubs: Christian Women (Greeley, Colo.); Order of Eastern Star (Iowa). Home: 3331 Riva Ridge Dr Fort Collins CO 80526-2887

THOMPSON, WYNELLE DOGGETT, chemistry educator; b. Birmingham, Ala., May 25, 1914; d. William Edward and Dollie Odessa (Ferguson) Doggett; m. Davis Hunt Thompson, Sept. 17, 1938; children: Carolyn Wynelle, Helen Hunt, Cynthia Carle, Davis Hunt, jr. BS summa cum laude, Birmingham Southern, 1934, MS, 1935; MS, U. Ala., 1956, PhD, 1960. From grad. lab. asst. to instr. chemistry Birmingham (Ala.) Southern Coll., 1934-36,39-44; tchr. Bd. Edn., Sheffield, Ala., 1936-37; jr. chemist Bur. Home Econs. USDA, Washington, 1937-38; instr. chemistry U. Ala. extension ctr., Birmingham, 1950-54; grad. asst. biochemistry U. Ala. Med. Coll., Birmingham, 1954-55; from asst. prof. chemistry to prof. emerita Birmingham (Ala.) Southern Coll., 1955-76; rsch. assoc. U. Ala. Dept. Biochemistry, Birmingham, 1965, 1968, 1969, Dept. Biophysics, 1976-78; adj. prof. chemistry New Coll. Tuscaloosa, Ala., 1980—. Contbr. articles to profl. jours. Bd. dirs. Cahaba Coun. Girl Scouts U.S. (vol. chmn. troop orgn., camping.). Grantee NSF, Appleton, Wis., Emory U., Atlanta; recipient disting. alumna award Birmingham So. Coll., 1976, medal of svc. award, 1994. Fellow Am. Inst. Chemists; mem. AAUW (bd. dirs., treas.), Am. Chem. Soc. (sec. 1942-44, 72-73, chmn.-elect 1966-67, chmn. 1967-68, 50-Yr. Mem. award 1992), Ala. Acad. Sci. (chmn. edn. sect. 1960-62), Phi Beta Kappa, Sigma Xi (sec. 1970-72), Theta Chi Delta, Delta Phi Alpha, Theta Sigma Lambda, Kappa Delta Epsilon, Delta Kappa Gamma, Kappa Mu Epsilon. Republican. Methodist. Home: 1237 Berwick Rd Hoover AL 35242-7124

THOMPSON-ACKERMAN, ELIZABETH ANN, marketing and advertising executive; b. Jersey City, Jan. 25, 1944; d. Adolf and Elizabeth Ann (Serry) Hept; children from previous marriage: Dawn Elizabeth, Joseph Patrick; m. Irwin Ackerman, July 31, 1992 (div. July 1993). AA, Bergen C.C., Paramus, N.J., 1989. Adminstrv. asst. brokerage divsn. Hanover Bank, N.Y.C., 1961-65; sales and mktg. mgr. Greene Uniform Co., Inc., Hackensack, N.J., 1978-87; asst. v.p. sales and mktg. Essex Chem. Co., Clifton, N.J., 1987-90; mktg. and advt. mgr. Ultra Additives, Inc., Paterson, N.J., 1990—. Mem. NAFE, Soc. Tribologists and Lubrication Engrs. (historian 1992-93). Roman Catholic. Home: 639 Blue Ridge Ln Mahwah NJ 07430 Office: Ultra Additives Inc 460 Straight St Paterson NJ 07501

THOMPSON-JURICH, SUSAN KAYE, therapist, addictions consultant; b. Pueblo, Colo., Feb. 20, 1953; d. Everett Frederick and Lila Lee (Faust) Thompson; m. Peter L. Jurich, Oct. 13, 1982 9div. Mar. 1985); children: Andrew Merek Starfinder, Michelle Sunshine Raven. BA in Sociology magna cum laude, Seattle Pacific U., 1989; MA in Ednl. Counseling, Seattle U., 1992-94; doct. student, U. Wash., 1994—. Founder, dir. Homeskills Workshop, Bellingham, Wash., 1976-85; owner, mgr. Harvest Yarns, Seattle, 1985-89; probation counselor King County Dist. Ct., Seattle, 1987-93; co-founder, co-dir., therapist N.W. Network for Christian Recovery, Lynnwood, Wash., 1989-93; co-dir. Sonora Ctr., Lynnwood, Wash., 1993—; cons. Shoreline Family Care, Seattle, 1989—, Bethesda House Shelter, Seattle, 1989-90; trainer King County Probation Dept., Seattle, 1991; dir. SMART, Seattle, 1989—. Author tng. manuals. Mem. AACD, Christian Assn. for Psychol. Studies, Am. Assn. for Christian Counselors, Nat. Assn. for Christian Recovery (N.W. regional rep. 1991—, co-chair N.W. Regional Conf., vice chair nat. bd.). Home: 3233 180th Pl SW Lynnwood WA 98037 Office: Sonora Ctr 20016 Cedar Valley Rd Ste 104 Lynnwood WA 98036

THOMPSON-KOWBEL, JOANN, artist; b. Mt. Vernon, Ill., Dec. 8, 1956; d. Phillip Edwin and Marjorie Pauline (Carnes) Thompson; m. Witold Kowbel, Oct. 18, 1985. AA, Rend Lake Coll., 1978; BA, So. Ill. U., 1981. artist in residence Atelier Neo-Medeci, Paris, 1981. One-woman shows include Vergette Gallery, 1980, The Park Dist., 1984; group shows include So. Ill. Open Competition, 1982, Sheila Cheek Interior and Accessories, 1989; exhibitor Associated Artists Gallery, Carbondale, 1987. Participant Bible Study, Auburn, Ala., 1987-92. Home: 8880 E Broadway Apt 146 Tucson AZ 85710-4043

THOMS, BONNIE ANNE, elementary school educator; b. Vancouver, B.C., Can., Dec. 6, 1952; d. Arthur and Irna T. AA, Flathead Valley Community Coll, Kalispell, Mont., 1973; BS, Dickinson State U., 1975; MA, Lesley Coll., 1986; postgrad., Walden U., 1993—. Cert. phys. fitness specialist, helath promotion dir. Coach, instr. Bozeman (Mont.) Sch. Dist.; instr. health, phys. edn., driver's edn. Campbell County Sch. Dist., Gillette, Wyo.; tchr. gifted & talented Campbell County Sch. Dist., Gillette; active in TESA, Wellness, & Curriculum programs; cons. tech. & wellness. State and regional volleyball ofcl., 1986-94; local coord. United Blood Svc. Drive; bd. dirs. ARC, Am. Heart Assn. Recipient Wyo. Gov.'s Innovative grant 1991-92; nat. finalist Profl. Best 1990 Educator; named Young Educator of Yr., Jaycees, 1990. Mem. AAHPERD, NEA, AHA, ASA, Wyo. Edn. Assn., Nat. Coaches Assn., Campbell County Edn. Assn., NAESP, Epsilon Sigma Alpha, Alpha Sigma Alpha. Home: 916 Fairway Dr Gillette WY 82718-7608

THOMSON, GRACE MARIE, nurse, minister; b. Pecos, Tex., Mar. 30, 1932; d. William McKinley and Elzora (Wilson) Olliff; m. Radford Chaplin, Nov. 3, 1952; children: Deborah C., William Earnest. Assoc. Applied Sci., Odessa Coll., 1965; extension student U. Pa. Sch. Nursing, U. Calif., Irvine, Golden West Coll. RN, Calif., Okla., Ariz., Md., Tex. Dir. nursing Grays Nursing Home, Odessa, Tex., 1965; supr. nursing Med. Hill, Oakland, Calif.; charge nurse pediatrics Med. Ctr., Odessa; dir. nursing Elmwood Extended Care, Berkeley, Calif.; surg. nurse Childrens Hosp., Berkeley; med./surg. charge nurse Merritt Hosp., Oakland, Calif.; adminstr. Grace and Assocs.; advocate for emotionally abused children; active Watchtower and Bible Tract Soc.; evangelist for Jehovah's Witnesses, 1954—.

THOMSON, IRENE TAVISS, sociologist; b. N.Y.C., Dec. 10, 1941; d. David and Ruth (Geller) Taviss; m. Michael G. R. Thomson, Feb. 8, 1974; children: Kenneth, Janet. BA, Bklyn. Coll., 1962; PhD, Harvard U., 1967. Rsch. assoc. Harvard U. Program on Tech. and Soc., Cambridge, Mass., 1966-72; lectr. dept. sociology Harvard U., Cambridge, 1972-74; cons. Am. Acad. Arts & Scis., Cambridge, 1974-75, Harvard U. Program on Info. Resources Policy, Cambridge, 1974-75, Ctr. for Policy Rsch., N.Y.C., 1974-75; asst. prof. to full prof. sociology Fairleigh Dickinson U., Madison, N.J., 1975-89; prof. sociology Fairleigh Dickinson U., Teaneck, N.J., 1989—. Editor: The Computer Impact, 1970; co-editor: Human Aspects of Biomedical Innovation, 1971; author: Our Tool-Making Society, 1972; contbr. articles to profl. jours. Recipient Nat. fellowship Woodrow Wilson Found., Princeton, N.J., 1962-63. Mem. Am. Sociol. Assn., Ea. Sociol. Soc., Phi Beta Kappa. Home: 54 Cedar Hill Rd Bedford NY 10506 Office: Fairleigh Dickinson Univ Dept Sociology Teaneck NJ 07666

THOMSON, JOAN ALBERTA, retired English educator; b. Chgo., July 6, 1912; d. Mark Hopkins and Ellen (Crandall) Place; m. Sam Swadesh, 1937 (div. 1942); m. Godfrey Edward Thomson, Nov. 20, 1948 (dec. Feb. 1974); children: Alice Ellen Thomson Jutras, George Edward; m. Epeli Ratambathatha, 1980 (div. 1984). BA cum laude, Milton Coll.; MA in English, Colo. Coll. Asst. prof. English U. So. Colo., Pueblo, 1965-73; Peace Corps lectr. in English U. South Pacific, Suva, Fiji, 1976-80; founder Beulah Melodrama, 1953. Group shows include USC Student Art Show, 1993, 94, Pueblo Art Guild Spring Show, 1994 (honorable mention); Author: Winnowings: An Autobiography in Verse, 1993; founding editor U. South Pacific Bull., 1977—; editor H.O.P.E. Alive (Helping Orgn. for Pueblo's Empowerment), 1991—. Cand. for alderman Chgo. City Coun., 1943; active Communist Party U.S.A., 1937-52; convener Causes and Cures Nat. Teleconf. on Narcotics Epidemic, Pueblo, 1991; social concerns chair Unitarian Fellowship Pueblo, 1990; chair nuclear weapons freeze campaign Pueblo. Mem. NAACP, AAUP, AAUW, Women's Internat. League Peace and Freedom, U.S. Peace Coun., Christic Inst., Am. Assn. Ret. Persons. Democrat. Unitarian. Home: 8957 Grand Ave PO Box 303 Beulah CO 81023

THOMSON, MABEL AMELIA, retired elementary school educator; b. Lancaster, Minn., Oct. 28, 1910; d. Ernest R. and Sophie Olinda (Rotert) Poore; m. Robert John Thomson, June 20, 1936; children: James Robert, William John. BS, U. Ill., 1933; MEd, Steven F. Austin Coll., Nacogdoches, Tex., 1959. Tchr. La Harpe (Ill.) Sch. Dist., 1930, Scotland (Ill.) Sch. Dist., 1934, Washburn (Ill.) Sch. Dist., 1935-36, Tyler (Tex.) Ind. Sch. Dist., 1959-76; ret., 1976; substitute tchr. Tyler (Tex.) Ind. Sch. Dist., 1976-86. Past pres. Woman's Soc. Christian Svc. of local Meth. Ch. Mem. AAUW (pres. Tyler chpt. 1947-48), Am. Childhood Edn. (pres. 1960-61), Alpha Delta Kappa (charter Tyler br.), Phi Mu (life). Republican. Methodist.

THOMSON, MARJORIE BELLE, sociology educator, consultant; b. Topeka, Dec. 4, 1921; d. Roy John and Bessie Margaret (Knarr) Anderson; m. John Whitner Thomson, Jan. 4, 1952 (div. June 9, 1963); 1 child, John Coe. Diploma hostess, Trans World Airlines, 1945; diploma, U.Saltillo, Mex., 1945; BS, Butler U., 1957; MS, Ft. Hays Kans. State U., 1966; postgrad., U. Calif., Santa Barbara, 1968, Kans. State U., 1972-73, Kans. U., 1973. Cert. elem. tchr., Calif., Colo., Ind., Kans., jr. coll. tchr. Tech. libr. N.Am. Aviation, Dallas, 1944-45; flight attendant TWA, Kansas City, Mo., 1945-50; recreation dir. U.S. Govt., Ft. Carson, Colo., 1951-52; elem. tchr. Indpls. Pub. Schs., 1954-57; jr. high tchr. Cheyenne County Schs., Cheyenne Wells, Colo., 1958-59; elem. tchr. Sherman County Schs., Goodland, Kans., 1961-62; lectr. Calif. Luth. U., Thousand Oaks, 1967-69; instr. Ft. Hays Kans. State U., 1969-71; dir. HeadStart Kans. Coun. of Agrl. Workers and Low Income Families, Inc., Goodland, 1971-72; supr. U.S. Govt. Manpower Devel. Programs, Plainville, Kans., 1972-74; bilingual counselor Kans. Dept. Human Resources, Goodland, 1975-82; leader trainee Expt. in Internat. Living, Brattleboro, Vt., 1967-71; cons. M. Anderson & Co., Lakewood, Colo., 1982—; participant Internat. Peace Walk, Moscow to Archangel, Russia, 1991, N.Am. Conf. on Ecology and the Soviet Save Peace and Nature Ecol. Collective, Russia, 1992; amb. Internat. Friendship Force, Tiblisi, Republic of Georgia, 1991; presenter State Convention AAUW, Aurora, Colo., 1992, nat. conv. Am. Acad. Audiology, Denver, 1992; cons. Gov.'s Conf. in Libr. and Info. Svc., Vail, 1992—. Docent Colo. Gallery of the Arts, Littleton, 1989; spkr., state resource chairperson Internat. Self Help for Hard of Hearing, Inc., Denver, 1990—; mem. Denver Deaf and Hard of Hearing Access Com., 1991—; spkr. Ret. Sr. Vol. Program, Denver, 1992—; dir. Holiday Project, Denver, 1992. Grantee NSF, 1970, 71. Mem. AAUW (life), AARP (pres. Denver-Grandview chpt. 1994), VFW Aux. (life), Sociologists for Women in Soc., Bus. and Profl. Women's Club, Internat. Peace Walkers, Spellbinders, Denver Press Club, Lakewood Women's Club, TWA Internat. Clipped Wings (cert.), Mile High Wings, Pi Gamma Mu, Alpha Sigma Alpha (life), Order of Ea. Star, Sons of Norway. Democrat. Presbyterian. Home: 12313 W Louisiana Ave Lakewood CO 80228 Office: M Anderson & Co 6941 W 13 Ave G Lakewood CO 80215

THOMSON, SHIRLEY LAVINIA, museum director; b. Wakerville, Ont., Can., Feb. 19, 1930; d. Walter T. and Edith May (MacKenzie) Cull. BA in History with honors, U. Western Ont., 1952; MA in Art History, U. Md., 1974; PhD in Art History, McGill U., 1981; PhD (hon.), Ottawa U., 1988; Doctorat honoris causa, McGill U., 1989, Mt. Allison U., 1990, U. Western Ont., 1990. Editor, conf. NATO, Paris, 1956-60; asst. sec. gen. World Univs. Svc. Can., Toronto, Ont., 1960-63; asst. sec. gen. Can. Commn. for UNESCO, Ottawa, 1964-67, sec., gen. dir., 1985-87; dir., dep. commn. UNESCO Pavilion at Man and His World, Montreal, 1978-80; rsch. coord., writer Memoirs of Sen. Thérèse Casgrain, 1968-70; spl. coord. Largillière Exhbn., Mus. Fine Arts, Montreal, 1981; dir. McCord Mus., Montreal, 1982-85, Nat. Gallery Can., Ottawa, 1987—. Decorated Chevalier des Arts et Lettres (France), officer Order of Can.; fellow Can. Coun., 1977-78, doctoral awardee, 1978-79. Mem. Can. Soc. Decorative Arts (coun.), Can. Mus. Assn. (dir.). Office: Nat Gallery, 380 Sussex Dr, Ottawa, ON Canada K1N 9N4

THOMSON, THYRA GODFREY, former state official; b. Florence, Colo., July 30, 1916; d. John and Rosalie (Altman) Godfrey; m. Keith Thomson, Aug. 6, 1939 (dec. Dec. 1960); children—William John, Bruce Godfrey, Keith Coffey. B.A. cum laude, U. Wyo., 1939. With dept. agronomy and agrl. econs. U. Wyo., 1938-39; writer weekly column Watching Washington pub. in 14 papers, Wyo., 1955-60; planning chmn. Nat. Fedn. Republican Women, Washington, 1961; sec. state Wyo. Cheyenne, 1962-86; mem. Marshall Scholarships Com. for Pacific region, 1964-68; del. 72d Wilton Park Conf., Eng., 1965; mem. youth commn. UNESCO, 1970-71, Allied Health Professions Council HEW, 1971-72; del. U.S.-Republic of China Trade Conf., Taipei, Taiwan, 1983; mem. lt. gov.'s trade and fact-finding mission to Saudi Arabia, Jordan, and Egypt, 1985. Bd. dirs. Buffalo Bill Mus., Cody, Wyo., 1987—; adv. bd. Coll. Arts and Scis., U. Wyo., 1989, Cheyenne Symphony Orch. Found., 1990—. Recipient Disting. Alumni award U. Wyo., 1969, Disting. U. Wyo. Arts and Scis. Alumna award, 1987; named Internat. Woman of Distinction, Alpha Delta Kappa; recipient citation Omicron Delta Epsilon, 1965, citation Beta Gamma Sigma, 1968, citation Delta Kappa Gamma, 1973, citation Wyo. Commn. Women, 1986. Mem. N.Am. Securities Adminstrs. (pres. 1973-74), Nat. Assn. Secs. of State, Council State Govts. (chmn. natural resources com. Western states 1966-68), Nat. Conf. Lt. Govs. (exec. com. 1976-79). Home: 3102 Sunrise Rd Cheyenne WY 82001-6136

THON, PATRICIA FRANCES, pediatrics nurse, medical/surgical nurse; b. Portland, Oreg., Sept. 25, 1959; d. Anthony William and Catherine Mary (Scully) Brenneis; m. Eric Phillip Thon, Apr. 30, 1988. AS, Johnson County C.C., 1980; BSN, U. Kans., Kans. City, 1982; MA, Webster U., 1992; postgrad., Portland State U., 1977; grad., St. Louis U., 1994. Staff nurse in pediatrics and oncology St. Luke's Hosp., Kansas City, Mo., 1982-84; commd. nurse officer USAF, 1984, advanced through grades to maj., 1988; staff nurse USAF, Scott AFB, Ill., 1984-88; flight nurse USAF, Scott AFB, 1988-91, sr. staff nurse in pediatrics and orthopedics, 1992; head nurse, chief maternal/child health flight Pediatric Clinic, Altus AFB, Okla., 1994—. Office: 97 MDG/SGOB 301 N 1st St Altus AFB OK 73523-5005

THOR, LINDA MARIA, college president; b. L.A., Feb. 21, 1950; d. Karl Gustav and Mildred Dorrine (Hofius) T.; m. Robert Paul Huntsinger, Nov. 22, 1974; children: Erik, Marie. BA, Pepperdine U., 1971, EdD, 1986; MPA, Calif. State U., Los Angeles, 1980. Dir. pub. info. Pepperdine U., Los Angeles, 1971-73; pub. info. officer L.A. C.C. Dist., 1974-75, dir. comm., 1975-81, dir. edn. svcs., 1981-82, dir. high tech., 1982-83, sr. dir. occupl. and tech. edn., 1983-86; pres. West Los Angeles Coll., Culver City, Calif., 1986-90, Rio Salado C.C., Phoenix, 1990—; bd. dirs. Coun. for Adult and Experiential Learning, Tech. Exch. Ctr., Greater Phoenix Econ. Coun. Editor: Curriculum Design and Development for Effective Learning, 1973; author: (with others) Effective Media Relations, 1982, Performance Contracting, 1987. Active Am. Assn. C.Cs. Commn. Urban C.C., 1992—, Publs./Pub. Rels. Commn., 1993—, Continuous Quality Improvement Network for C.Cs., 1991—; mem. Ariz. Gov.'s Adv. Coun. on Quality, 199—; pres.-elect Ariz. C.C. Pres.'s Coun., 1994-95. Recipient Delores award Pepperdine U., 1986, Alumni Medal of Honor, 1987, Outstanding Achievement award Women's Bus. Network, 1989; named Woman of the Yr., Culver City Bus. and Profl. Women, 1988. Office: 640 N First Ave Phoenix AZ 85003

THORELL, MARGARET, English language educator, writer; b. N.Y.C., Mar. 13, 1946; d. Algot F. and Margaret (McCarron) Thorell; m. John J. Murray, Sept. 14, 1963 (div. 1983); children: Margaret Anne, John Thomas, Christopher Thorell. BS in Psychology and Journalism, SUNY, Albany, 1979; postgrad., Temple U., 1981-84, U. Pa., 1984-87, Temple U., 1988-89. Cert. secondary tchr., Pa. Tech. writer SEI Corp., Valley Forge, Pa., 1974-76; asst. to dir. Paoli (Pa.) Meml. Hosp. Addictions Ctr., 1976-77; free lance journalist Bulletin, Phila., 1978-80; instr. Community Coll. of Phila., 1981-83, Temple U., Phila., 1981-86; editorial asst. U. Pa., Phila., 1984-87, forum coord., 1983-87; asst. prof. English Temple U., Phila., 1988, assoc. dir. Writing Ctr., 1989, dir. English Lang. Enrichment Ctr., 1989-94; test development staff Ednl. Testing Svc., 1994—; cons. Phila. Internat. Programs, 1985, U. Pa.-Writing Across the Curriculum, 1987, Chestnut Hill Devel. Group, 1986, Paoli Meml. Hosp. Hospice, 1983; bd. dirs. Weavers Way Co-op Fed. Credit Union. Author: Rittenhouse Square, 1980; contbr. articles to profl. jours.; reviewer Holt Rinehart Jour. Multilingual and Multicultural Dev., Houghton Millflin, Longman Press Anthropology and Edn. Q., Harcourt Brace Jovanovitch. Recipient teaching award Coll. Arts and Scis. Temple U., 1991, ESL Conf. grant Pa. Humanities Coun., 1991, NEH grant, 1990, Hambridge Ctr. for Creative Arts & Scis. fellowship, 1988, Pa. Coun. for the Humanities grant, 1985. Mem. Pa. TESOL East., Assn. for Teaching ESL, Nat. Coun. Tchrs. of English, Jungian Soc. of Phila., NOW (pres. Greensburg chpt. 1979-81).

THORELLI, SARAH, economist, researcher; b. Atlanta, Dec. 30, 1922; m. Hans B. Thorelli; children: Irene, Tom. AB, U. Ga., 1944; MA, U. Ala., 1945; Ph.Lic., U. Stockholm, 1954. Free-lance researcher and scholar; assoc. Heartland Assocs.; cons. FTC, NSF, Washington, Sears, Roebuck and Co.; ofcl. translator legal documents Swedish Fgn. Office, Stockholm; intelligence rsch. analyst U.S. Dept. State; overseas rep. Equifax Co.; account exec. J. Walter Thompson Advt. Agy., N.Y.C.; bd. dirs. INTOPIA, Inc. Co-author: Consumer Information Handbook: Europe and North America, Consumer Information Systems and Consumer Policy; contbr. articles to profl. jours. Mem. Ind. U. Women's Club, AAUW, Network Career Women, Local Coun. Women, Psi Iota Xi. Home and Office: 2604 E 2nd St Apt F Bloomington IN 47401-5351

THOREN-PEDEN, DEBORAH SUZANNE, lawyer; b. Rockford, Ill., Mar. 28, 1958; d. Robert Roy and Marguerite Natalie (Geoghegan) Thoren; m. Steven E. Peden, Aug. 10, 1985. BA in Philosophy, Polit. Sci./Psychology, U. Mich., 1978; JD, U. So. Calif., 1982. Bar: Calif. 1982. Assoc. Bushkin, Gaines & Gaims, L.A., 1982-84, Rutan & Tucker, Costa Mesa, Calif., 1984-86; counsel First Interstate Bancorp, L.A., 1986—; lectr. on Bank Secrecy Act and Ethics. Supervising editor U. So. Calif. Entertainment Law Jour., 1982-83, Entertainment Publishing and the Arts Handbook, 1983-84. Mem. ABA (retail investment task force, regulatory compliance com.), Calif. Bankers Assn. (regulatory compliance com., co-chair regulatory compliance conf., ex-officio mem state govt. rels. com.). Office: First Interstate Bancorp 633 W 5th St T7 10 Los Angeles CA 90017

THORLAKSON-BELL, ROSEMARY AHEARN, trauma nurse clinician, nursing administrator; b. Columbus, Ohio, July 12, 1947; d. Joseph Edmond and Elizabeth Sabrina (Morse) Ahearn; children: AmySue, Stephen; m. Gary Lee Bell. AAS in Nursing, Gemanna Community Coll., Locust Grove, Va., 1975; BS in Nursing, U. Va., 1976, MEd, 1986. RN; cert. instr. ACLS/BCLS, medicolegal death investigator, critical care nurse, emergency care nurse, trauma nurse instr., others. Emergency rm. supr. Carbon County Meml. Hosp., Rawlins, Wyo., 1979-80; with Minidoka Meml. Hosp., Rupert, Idaho, supr. emergency dept., 1989-91; nurse Life Flight, Wyo., Va.; contract trauma nurse in Calif., Wyo., Colo., Va., Idaho, N.C., Tex., Wash., Wis., S.C., Oreg., Washington, Tenn., Mont., Mich., N.Y., N.J. Contbr. articles to profl. jours. Community educator CPR, First Aid, Water Safety. Mem. AACN, Women in Mil. Svc. for Am., Am. Trauma Soc., Emergency Nurses Assn., Nat. Assn. Underwater Rescue and Recovery, Am. Legion, VFW, Vietnam Vets. Am., Beta Sigma Phi (Xi Omega chpt.). Democrat. Roman Catholic. Office: PO Box 45 Rupert ID 83350-0045

THORN, ROSEMARY KOST, librarian; b. N.Y.C., Dec. 15, 1954; d. Stephen John and Henrietta (Rosso) K.; m. Michael Thorn; children: Russell, Stephen. BA in Anthropology, Rutgers U., 1977; MLS, U. N.C., 1980. Head libr. U.S. EPA, Research Triangle Park, N.C., 1980—; EPA. Office: EPA Libr Svcs Mail Drop 35 Durham NC 27711

THORNE, BONNIE BAKER, education educator; b. Houston, Feb. 22, 1928; d. George Hall Baker and Idabelle (Anderson) Hazlett; m. Oscar Lee Thorne, Dec. 21, 1946; 1 child, Oscar Lee, Jr. (dec.). AA in Bus., Lon Morris Jr. Coll., Jacksonville, Tex., 1947; BS in Libr. Sci./English, Sam Houston State U., 1960; MA in Libr. Sci., Tex. Woman's U., 1964; PhD, 1975. Libr. Sam Houston State U., Huntsville, Tex., 1961-72, dir. pub. svcs., 1970-71, asst. prof. Sch. Libr. Sci., 1972-77, acting dir. Sch. Libr. Sci., 1977, 80, 84-88, assoc. prof. to prof. Sch. Libr. Sci., 1988-93, ret., 1993; instr. workshop, 1994; conductor study tours abroad. Author: The History of Sam Houston State Teachers College as Reflected in the Library and the Library Science Department, 1964, Elbert Hubbard and the Publications of the Roycroft Shop, 1893-1915, 1975, others; contbr. articles to profl. jours. Friend, vol. Huntsville Pub. Libr., 1969-80, Libr. First Bapt. Ch. of Huntsville, 1975—; patron Sam Houston State Meml. Mus., 1983-90; vol. United Way, Walker County, 1989, county chmn., others. Recipient Beatrice Craig Libr. Sci. award, 1959; nominated for Minnie Fisher Piper award, 1990. Mem. AAUW (various offices, named Outstanding Woman of 1979, Huntsville br.), AAUP, ALA (life), Am. Assn. Sch. Librs., Am. Assn. Libr. Schs., Assn. Coll. and Rsch. Librs., Assn. Libr. and Info. Sci., Southwestern Archivists (charter), Beta Phi Mu, Delta Kappa Gamma, numerous others. Baptist. Home: 147 Sunset Lake Dr Huntsville TX 77340-9715

THORNE, ELIZABETH, psychologist, psychoanalyst, lawyer; b. Evanston, Ill., Apr. 14, 1919; d. Clifford and Ruth (Latta) T. AB, Vassar Coll., 1940; JD, U. Mich., 1943; PhD, NYU, 1967. Lic. psychologist, N.Y. Lawyer Dewey, Ballantine, N.Y.C., 1943-52; pvt. practice N.Y.C., 1952—, psychoanalyst pvt. practice, 1963—, psychologist pvt. practice, 1969—. Editor: Psychoanalysis Today: A Case Book, 1993. Mem. ABA, APA, Nat. Assn. Advancement Psychoanalysis (pres. 1985-88), Nat. Psychol. Assn. for Psychoanalysis (cert., pres. 1977-80, 88-90), Cosmopolitan Club. Democrat. Office: 265 E 66th St New York NY 10021-6404

THORNE, JOYE HOLLEY, special education administrator; b. Shreveport, La., Jan. 4, 1933; d. Lockett Beecher and A. Irene (McWilliams) Holley; m. Michael S. Thorne, July 24, 1953; 1 child, Michael S. Jr. BS, Centenary Coll., 1954; MEd, U. Houston, 1969, EdD, 1974. Cert. tchr., Tex. Tchr. Aldine Ind. Sch. Dist., Houston, 1959-66, curriculum cons., 1966-69, dir. spl. edn., 1969—; adj. prof. U. Houston, Clear Lake, Tex., 1974-83; spl. edn. specialist Dept. Def. Dependent Schs., Washington, 1983-84. Recipient Pres.'s award Gulf Coast chpt. Coun. Exceptional Children, Austin, Tex., 1980. Mem. Coun. Exceptional Children (pres. Gulf Coast chpt. 1976-77, pres. Tex. fedn. 1982-83, Pres.'s award 1980), Tex. Coun. Adminstrs. Spl. Edn. (pres. 1985-86, Dir. of Yr. award 1993). Republican. Methodist. Office: Aldine Ind Sch Dist 1617 Lauder Rd Houston TX 77039-3096

THORNE, ROSEMARY ELAINE, library administrator; b. San Luis Obispo, Calif., Jan. 7, 1941; d. Dan and Gladys Marie (Walker) T. BS in Edn. with honors, Calif. State Poly. Coll., 1963; MA in Librarianship, U. Denver, 1964; postgrad., San Jose State U. Reference libr. music reading room San Jose (Calif.) State Coll., 1964-65, reference libr. humanities reading room, 1965-70, acting head humanities reading room, 1970-73, head humanities reading room, 1973-79; head gen. ref. dept. San Jose State U., 1979-82, head reference dept., 1982-84, 85-90, acting head user svcs. & collection devel. div., 1984-85, interim assoc. libr. dir. user svcs. & collection devel., 1990—; mem. numerous univ. & libr. coms. San Jose State U., 1970—; presenter in field. Co-author: (with Eileen Keim) Colorado Private Presses, 1966; editor: California Intellectual Freedom Handbook, 1992. Recipient Ralph H. Lutz Meml. rsch. grant San Jose State U., 1982, faculty devel. travel grant, 1987. Mem. ALA (reference & adult svcs. div.), Assn. Coll. & Rsch. Librs., Calif. Libr. Assn. (intellectual freedom com. 1989—com. chair 1990, chair nomination com. Calif. State Univ. Librs. chpt. 1982), Calif. Acad. & Rsch. Librs. (campus liaison coord. No. Calif. 1988—), No. Calif. State Univ. Reference & Pub. Svc. Heads, Calif. Acad. Reference Librs. Discussion Interest Group, No. Calif. State Univ. Librs. Computerized Reference Search Svc. Coords.' Group. Home: 95 Hobson St Apt 14-B San Jose CA 95110

THORNQUIST, MARY HULDA, psychologist; b. Milw., Mar. 3, 1962; d. William Robert and Mary Jane (McCabe) T. BS with distinction, U. Wis., 1985; MA, U. Del., 1990, PhD, 1993. Lectr. U. Del., Newark, 1989; psychology intern VA Hosp., Perry Point, Md., 1989-90, Fed. Correctional Instn., Fairton, N.J., 1990-92, U. Medicine and Dentistry N.J., Piscataway, 1992-93; staff psychologist Therapeutic Alternatives, Woodbury, N.J., 1993-94; sr. staff psychologist Sch. Medicine, Johns Hopkins U., Balt., 1995—. Contbr. articles to profl. jours. Crisis counselor, trainer, educator SOS-Sexual Assault Support Svcs., Newark, 1990-92. Tuition scholar U. Del., 1989-90.

THORNTON, ELAINE SERETHA, oncology nurse; b. N.Y.C., Mar. 25, 1967; d. Jerry Richard and Shelia (Beckford) T. BS, Syracuse U., 1990. Cert. in gerontology. Staff nruse, clin. nurse I New Rochelle (N.Y.) Hosp. Med. Ctr., 1990-92, staff nurse, clin. nurse II, 1993—; RN lab. asst. Sch. Nursing Coll. New Rochelle, 1992—; adj. prof. Coll. New Rochelle; vol. Am. Cancer Soc. Vol. Cancer Info. Svc., N.Y.C., 1991-92, Liz Holzman for Senate, N.Y.C., 1992, Clinton/Gore Presdl. campaign, 1992; vol. providing cancer screening, blood pressure screening Pelham (N.Y.) Sr. Ctr., 1992; pub. info. rep. to economically disadvantaged Am. Cancer Soc.; bd. dirs. Westchester div. Am. Cancer Soc., 1993—. Recipient Orthobiotech. Quality of Life award. Mem. ANA, Oncology Nursing Soc. (Hudson Valley chpt., nominating com. 1992-93, treas. 1993-94), Black Nurses Assn., Am. Psychiat. Nurses Assn., Oncology Nursing Soc. (corr.), CTME, St. Thomas More Found. Democrat. Home: 50 Guion Pl Apt 5K New Rochelle NY 10801-5517

THORNTON, GLENDA ANN, librarian; b. Chickasha, Okla., Aug. 11, 1949; d. G. Van and Clara Maude (Lister) Long; m. Phillip Wynn Thornton, Sept. 18, 1970; children: Edward D., Jonathan C. BA, U. Okla., 1971, MLS, 1973; PhD, U. North Tex., 1993. Reference libr. Aurora (Colo.) Pub. Libr., 1974-75; tech. svcs. libr. Admas State Coll., Alamosa, Colo., 1975-80; collection devel. libr. Henderson State U., Arkadelphia, Ark., 1980-85, acting dir. libr., 1984; head material acquisitions libr. U. North Tex., Denton, 1985-91; assoc. dir. libr. svc. Auraria Libr. U. Colo., Denver, 1991—. Co-author: AHE Vendor Directory, 1988; contbr. articles to profl. jours. Mem. ALA, LAMA, ACRL, N.Am. Serials Interest Group, Colo. Libr. Assn., Beta Phi Mu. Office: Auraria Libr Lawrence at 11th Denver CO 80204

THORNTON, KATHRYN C., physicist, astronaut; b. Montgomery, Ala., Aug. 17, 1952; d. William C. and Elsie Cordell; m. Stephen T. Thornton; children: Carol Elizabeth, Laura Lee, Susan Annette; stepchildren: Kenneth, Michael. BS in Physics, Auburn U., 1974; MS in Physics, U. Va., 1977, PhD, 1979. Physicist U.S. Army Fgn. Sci. & Tech. Ctr., Charlottesville, Va., 1980-84; with NASA, 1984—; astronaut Lyndon B. Johnson Space Ctr. NASA, Houston, 1985—, mission specialist Space Shuttle Discovery flight STS-33, 1989; aboard maiden flight Space Shuttle Endeavor, 1992. Nato post-doctoral fellow Max Planck Inst. Nuclear Physics, 1979-80. Mem. AAAS, Am. Phys. Soc., Sigma Xi, Phi Kappa Phi. Address: NASA Johnson Space Ctr CB Astronaut Office Houston TX 77058*

THORNTON, MARIA ANGELA, interpreter, translator, educator, civic worker; b. Hampton, Va., Mar. 15, 1949; d. James Otis and Caterina Maria (Quarri) T. Assoc. Applied Arts, Bauder Coll.; BA, U. Akron, 1971; postgrad., U. Tex., Arlington, 1983, Am. U., Barcelona, Spain. Cert. tchr., Tex. Tchr. Benedict Sch. of Langs., Barcelona, Spain, 1972-73; interpreter, translator, assoc. v.p. adminstrn. O.S.V. di Ermanno Arbizzi, Modena, Italy, 1973-78; fgn. officer Autogru P.M., Modena, 1978-81; asst. pers. dir. Am. Marazzi Tile Co., Sunnyvale, Tex., 1984-89; Amnesty program coord.-dir. Ctr. for English Lang., Dallas, 1989-91; ESL tchr., freelance cons. Dallas, 1989—; tutor, lang. tchr., Italy, France, Spain, 1972-81. Vol. Dallas Com. for Fgn. Visitors, Dallas Pers. Assn., N.E. Dallas Pers. Assn., Animal Rehab. Ctr., Midlothian, Tex., 1989—, People for the Ethical Treatment of Animals, Washington, 1989—, Acad. Achievement Assn., Dallas, 1989—, Union Gospel Mission, Dallas, 1990—, Walden Inst. Human Potential Resource Ctr., Dallas, 1992. Recipient achievement award for outstanding mus. study Music Tchr.'s Assn. Ala. Mem. Am. Literary Translators assn., Italian Am. Coun. for Commerce and Culture, Internat. Women's Club Dallas, Soc. d'Honneur Francaise (alumni, v.p.), Soc. Nacional Hispanica (life), Dallas So. Meml. Assn., Dallas Genealogical Soc., Rosicrucian Order AMORC, DAR (Ellis Island restoration chpt. chmn. 1988-91, Americanism and DAR manual for citizenship chpt. chmn. Farmer's Branch, Tex. 1990-91, organizing mem. Peter's Colony chpt. 1990-91, chmn. motion picture, radio , TV, pub. rels. 1992), United Daus. Confederacy (adopt-a-momument com.), Kappa Delta Pi. Mem. Unity Ch. Home: 9628 Park Highland Dr Dallas TX 75238 Office: 5759 Pineland Ste 1104 Dallas TX 75231

THORNTON, MARY ELIZABETH, education educator; b. Ft. Belvoir, Va., Mar. 2, 1920; d. Alexander Palmer and Rose Giovanni (Perry) Kelly; m. Robert Lee Thornton, Dec. 6, 1941; children: Mary Elizabeth, Alix Lee, John Kelly, Sally Fredrick. AB, Goucher Coll., 1941; AM, U. Mich., 1951, U. Mich., 1967; PhD, Fla. State U., 1972. Asst. prof. Miami U., Oxford, Ohio, 1975-82, 1982-89, prof., 1989—. Co-author: Building Programs of the Julio-Claudian Emperors, 1989; contbr. articles to profl. jours. Office: Miami U Oxford OH 45056

THORPE, ANDREA LEE, librarian; b. Exeter, N.H., Jan. 19, 1952; d. Harry Andrew and Emma Marie (Thulin) T.; m. Lee Evans Topham, Aug. 25, 1973; children: James, Caitlin. BA in English, Bates Coll., 1973; MSLS, Simmons Coll., 1988. Tchr. Kennedy Jr. High Sch., Randolph, Mass., 1974-75; libr. asst. Dartmouth Coll., Hanover, N.H., 1978, 86-88; libr. Etna Libr., Hanover, N.H., 1984-88, Gates Meml. Libr., White River Junction, Vt., 1985-87; libr. dir. Richards Free Libr., Newport, N.H., 1988—. Contbr. to book: The History of the Richards Free Library, 1993. Mem. Rotary (pres. 1993-94). Unitarian. Office: Richards Free Libr 58 N Main St Newport NH 03773

THORPE, JANET CLAIRE, lawyer; b. Bklyn., Dec. 8, 1953; d. Burton Walter and Phyllis Claire (Read) T.; m. David Frank Palmer, Aug. 26, 1978 (div. Aug. 1988); children—Katherine Elaine, Jennifer Claire; m. James Francis Box, June 29, 1991; children: Melissa Richelle, Maergrethe Cashel. Student, Boston U., 1972-74; A.B. in Polit. Sci. and History with honors, Union Coll., 1975; postgrad. Western New Eng. Sch. Law, 1975-76; J.D., Emory U., 1978. Bar: Ga. 1978, U.S. Dist. Ct. (no. dist.) Ga. 1978, U.S. Ct. Appeals (5th and 11th cirs.) 1978, 80, Fla. 1987, U.S. Dist. Ct. (mid. dist.) Fla. 1987. Comptroller's asst. Boston U., 1974-75; law librarian Western New Eng. Coll., Springfield, Mass., 1976; law clk. to judge U.S. Dist. Ct., Atlanta, 1978; regional atty. Comptroller of Currency, Atlanta, 1978-80; assoc. corp. counsel Trust Co. Ga., Atlanta, 1980-86 ; dir. Trusco Properties, Inc., Atlanta 1981-86; gen. counsel, corp. sec. Sun Banks, Inc., 1986—, sr. v.p., 1986; bd. mem., corp. sec. SunTrust Bank Card N.A.; gen. counsel Sun Bank, N.A., 1986—; group v.p. SunTrust Banks, Inc., 1995. Mem. Council on Battered Women, Atlanta, 1983-86, bd. dirs., 1986; bd. visitors Cornell Mus. Fine Art, Rollins Coll., 1988—. Mem. Ga. Bar Assn. (banking and corp. sect.), Fla. Bar Assn., Assn. Bank Holding Cos. (lawyers com. 1983—), Am. Corp. Counsel Assn. (bd. dirs. ctrl. Fla. chpt. 1991-94), Am. Diabetes Assn. (bd. dirs. Fla. chpt. 1989—), Atlanta Arts Alliance, 1985. Democrat. Episcopalian. Avocations: gardening; child rearing; house renovation; photography. Office: Sun Bank NA 200 S Orange Ave Orlando FL 32801-3410

THORPE, JUDITH MOSIER, communication educator; b. Ft. Wayne, Ind., Mar. 19, 1941; d. James Earl Mosier and Betty Izetta (Carder) Mosier Sipe; m. Charles R. Thorpe, July 27, 1968 (dec. Dec. 1980). BA, Ball State U., 1963, MS, 1978; PhD, Ohio State U., 1986. Dir. guest rels. Edison Inst.: Henry Ford Mus. and Greenfield Village, Dearborn, Mich., 1963-67; tchr. Birmingham (Mich.) Pub. Schs., 1965-73; dir. debate Tates Creek H.S., Lexington, Ky., 1973-74, Ball State U., Muncie, Ind., 1979-84; dir. forensics Jay County H.S., Portland, Ind., 1974-79; grad. asst. Ohio State U., Columbus, 1984-86; asst. prof. comm. U. Tenn., Knoxville, 1986-87; assoc. prof. comm. U. Wis., Oshkosh, 1987—; cons. City of Kenosha, Wis., 1989, Paine Art Ctr., Oshkosh, 1992-93, Bergstrom Art Mus., Neenah, Wis., 1992-93; media cons. Christine Ann Ctr., Oshkosh, 1994. Author: (with Scodari) Media Criticism Journeys in Interpretation; contbg. author: Rhetorical Studies Honoring James L. Golden, 1986; contbr. articles to profl. jours. Faculty adviser Sigma Sigma Sigma sorority. C-Span fellow, 1990; U. Wis.-Oshkosh faculty devel. grantee; recipient Faculty award Acad. TV Arts and Scis., 1992. Mem. AAUW (state bd. dirs. 1976, 90 grantee 1993), Wis. Comm. Assn., Speech Comm. Assn. (v.p. 1994-95), Wis. Broadcasters Assn. (ednl. com. 1993-94), Phi Beta Kappa, Delta Sigma Rho, Tau Kappa Alpha. Lutheran. Office: U Wis Oshkosh Algoma Blvd Oshkosh WI 54901

THORSEN, MARIE KRISTIN, radiologist, educator; b. Milw., Aug. 1, 1947; d. Charles Christian and Margaret Josephine (Little) T.; m. James Lawrence Troy, Jan. 7, 1978; children: Katherine Marie, Megan Elizabeth. B.A., U. Wis., 1969; M.B.A., George Washington U., 1971; M.D., Columbia U., 1977. Diplomate Am. Bd. Radiology. Intern, Columbia-Presbyn. Med. Ctr., N.Y.C., 1977-78, resident dept. radiology, 1978-81; fellow computed body tomography Med. Coll. Wis., Milw., 1981-82; asst. prof. radiology, 1982-87, assoc. prof., 1987-94, prof., 1994—; staff radiologist John L. Doyne Hosp., Froedtert Luth. Meml. Hosp. Contbr. articles to profl. jours. Mem. Am. Coll. Radiology, Radiol. Soc. N.Am.

THORSEN, NANCY DAIN, real estate broker; b. Edwardsville, Ill., June 23, 1944; d. Clifford Earl and Suzanne Eleanor (Kribs) Dain; m. David Massie, 1968 (div. 1975); 1 child, Suzanne Dain Massie; m. James Hugh Thorsen, May 30, 1980. BSc in Mktg., So. Ill. U., 1968, MSc in Bus. Edn., 1975; grad. Realtor Inst., Idaho, 1983. Cert. resdl. and investment specialist, fin. instr.; accredited buyer rep. Personnel officer J.H. Little & Co. Ltd., London, 1969-72; instr. in bus. edn. Spl. Sch. Dist. St. Louis, 1974-77; mgr. mktg./ops. Isis Foods, Inc., St. Louis, 1978-80; asst. mgr. store Stix, Baer & Fuller, St. Louis, 1980; assoc. broker Century 21 Sayer Realty, Inc., Idaho Falls, Idaho, 1981-88, RE/MAX Homestead Realty, 1989—; speaker RE/MAX Internat. Conv., 1990, 94, RE/MAX Stars Cruise, 1993, RE/MAX Pacific N.W. Conv., 1994; real estate fin. instr. State of Idaho Real Estate Commn., 1994. Bd. dirs. Idaho Vol., Boise, 1981-84, Idaho Falls Symphony, 1982; pres. Friends of Idaho Falls Library, 1981-83; chmn. Idaho Falls Mayor's Com. for Vol. Coordination, 1981-84; power leader Power Program, 1995. Recipient Idaho Gov.'s award, 1982, cert. appreciation City of Idaho Falls/Mayor Campbell, 1982, 87, Civitan Disting. Pres. award, 1990; named to Two Million Dollar Club, Three Million Dollar Club, 1987, 88, Four Million Dollar Club, 1989, 90, Top Investment Sales Person for Eastern Idaho, 1985, Realtor of Yr. Idaho Falls Bd. Realtors, 1990, Outstanding Realtors Active in Politics, Mem. of Yr. Idaho Assn. Realtors, 1991, Women of Yr. Am. Biog. Inst., 1991, Profiles of Top Producers award Real Estate Edn. Assn. Mem. Idaho Falls Bd. Realtors (chmn. orientation 1982-83, chmn. edn. 1983, chmn. legis. com. 1989, chmn. program com. 1990, 91), Idaho Assn. Realtors (pres. Million Dollar Club 1988—, edn. com. 1990-93), So. Ill. U. Alumni Assn., Idaho Falls C. of C., Newcomers Club, Civitan (pres. Idaho Falls chpt. 1988-89, Civitan of Yr. 1986, 87, outstanding pres. award 1990), Real Estate Educators Assn. Office: RE/MAX Homestead Inc 1301 E 17th St Ste 1 Idaho Falls ID 83404-6273

THORSON, LINDA CHRISTINE, clinical psychologist; b. Honolulu, Jan. 29, 1952; d. Duane Theodore and Betty Irene (Dayton) T.; m. Sandor Ross Schoichet, May 5, 1978; 1 child, Nicholas Nathan. MS in Edn., U. So. Calif., 1976; PhD, Calif. Sch. Profl. Psychology, 1986. Lic. clin. psychologist. Tchr. spl. edn. Calif. Sch. for the Deaf, Riverside, 1976-77, Beverly (Mass.) Sch. for the Deaf, 1977-79, Boston Sch. for the Deaf, Randolph, Mass., 1979-82; pvt. practice San Francisco, 1986—; prodr. pub. & profl. seminars, 1994—; seminar leader women in transition Alumnae Resources, San Francisco, 1990-93. Mem. APA, Calif. Psychol. Assn., San Francisco Acad. Hypnosis. Office: 220 Montgomery St Ste 640 San Francisco CA 94104-3415

THORSON, MARCELYN MARIE, applied art educator; b. Houston, Dec. 18, 1927; d. Oliver Herbert and Helene Marie (Brown) Fritts; m. Edward L. Thorson, June 16, 1956. BS, Pratt Inst., N.Y.C., 1950. Cert. home economist, tech. tchr. Apparel designer Dallas Sportswear Co., 1954-64, Srader Sportswear Co., Dallas, 1964-65; instr., coordinator apparel design program and pattern design program El Centro Coll., Dallas, 1966-88; cons. computer research Camsco, Inc., Richardson, Tex., summer 1976-77; project devel. coordinator state grant Fashion Design Series, North Tex. State U., summer 1978-79, instr. Indsl. Tng. Lab., summer 1978. Instr. Adult Christian Edn. Found., Bethel Bible Series, Luth. Ch., 1965-80. Mem. Costume Soc. Am., Am. Home Econs. Assn., Cert. Home Economist, Dallas Met. Home Economists in Home and Community, The FAshion Group (edn. com. 1975-90, scholarsip chmn. 1975-85, bd. dirs. fashion mus. 1963-65, Silver Tray award 1965). Republican. Home: 11229 Lanewood Cir Dallas TX 75218-1908

THOYER, JUDITH REINHARDT, lawyer; b. Mt. Vernon, N.Y., July 29, 1940; d. Edgar Allen and Florence (Mayer) Reinhardt; m. Michael E. Thoyer, June 30, 1963; children: Erinn, Michael John. AB with honors, U. Mich., 1961; LLB summa cum laude, Columbia U., 1965. Bar: N.Y. 1966, D.C. 1984. Law libr. U. Ghana, Accra, Africa, 1963-64; assoc. Paul, Weiss, Rifkind, Wharton & Garrison, N.Y.C., 1966-75, ptnr., 1975—. Bd. dirs. Women's Action Alliance, N.Y.C., 1975-89, pro bono counsel, 1975—; mem. bd. visitors Columbia Law Sch., N.Y.C., 1991—. Mem. N.Y. County Lawyers Assn. (securities and exchs. com.), Assn. of the Bar of the City N.Y. (securities regulation com. 1976-79, recruitment of lawyers com. 1980-82), Women's Coun. Democratic Senatorial (campaign com. 1993—). Home: 1115 5th Ave Apt 3B New York NY 10128-0100 Office: Paul Weiss Rifkind Wharton & Garrison 1285 Avenue Of The Americas New York NY 10019-6064

THRAILKILL, FRANCIS MARIE, college president; b. San Antonio, Sept. 21, 1937; d. Franklin E. and Myrtle M. (Huggins) T. B.A. cum laude, Coll. New Rochelle, N.Y., 1961; M.A., Marquette U., Milw., 1969; Ed.D., Nova U., Ft. Lauderdale, Fla., 1975. Joined Ursuline Order of Sisters, Roman Catholic Ch., 1955; tchr. Ursuline Acad., Dallas, 1961-64; prin. Ursuline Acad., 1970-77; vice prin. Ursuline Acad., New Orleans, 1965-70; pres. Springfield (Ill.) Coll., 1978-87, Coll. of Mt. St. Joseph, Ohio, 1987—. Trustee Community, Found. Ind. Colls., Little Miami Inc.; mem. Leadership Cin.; mem. edn. com. Cin. At Mus.; bd. dirs. Dan Beard Coun., Ursuline Acad., Cin. Assn. for Blind, Coun. Ind. Colls., Summit Country Day, Joy Outdoor Edn. Ctr., Community Mut. Blue Cross/Blue Shield. Mem. Assn. Cath. Colls. and Univs., Assn. Governing Bds. of Colls. and Univs., Assn. Ind. Colls. and Univs., Greater Cin. Corsortium Colls., Nat. Assn. Ind. Colls. and Univs., Ohio Bd. Regents, Council Ind. Colls. Office: Coll of Mt St Joseph Office of the President 5701 Delhi Rd Cincinnati OH 45233-1672*

THRASHER, DIANNE ELIZABETH, mathematics educator, computer consultant; b. Brockton, Mass., July 11, 1945; m. George Thomas Thrasher, Jan. 28, 1967; children: Kimberly Elizabeth, Noelle Elizabeth. BA in Math., Bridgewater State Coll., 1967, postgrad. in computer sci., 1984-87. Cert. secondary math. and history tchr., Mass. Tchr. math. Plymouth/Carver Regional Schs., Plymouth, Mass., 1976-78, Alden Sch., Duxbury, Mass., 1980-82, Marshfield (Mass.) High Sch., 1982-84; computer cons. TC2I-Thrasher Computer Cons. and Instrn., Duxbury, Mass., 1988—; dir., owner Duxbury Math. Ctr., 1991—; owner K-Adult Ednl. Ctr. Active U.S. Figure Skating Assn., Colorado Springs, 1978-85; 2d reader First Ch. Christ Scientist, Plymouth, 1971-73; bd. govs. Skating Club of Hingham, Mass., 1978-85, pres., 1983-85, dir. Learn to Skate program, 1983-85; mem. First Ch. Christ Scientist, Boston, 1964—; charter mem. Nat. Adv. Coun. of the U.S. Navy Meml. Found., 1992. Nominated for Presdl. award for Excellence in Math. Teaching, NSF, 1992. Mem. NAFE, AAUW, Nat. Coun. Tchrs. Math., Boston Computer Soc., New Eng. Duxbury Bus. Assn. Home: 140 Toby Garden St Duxbury MA 02332-4945

THRASHER, ROSE MARIE, critical care and community health nurse; b. Urbana, Ohio, Jan. 19, 1948; d. Jesse and Anna Frances (Clark) T. Student, Mercy Med. Ctr. Sch. Med. Tech., 1966-67, Wittenberg U., 1969-70; BSN, Ohio State U., 1974, postgrad., 1985—. RN, Ohio; CCRN; cert. community health nurse, BCLS, ACLS. Pub. health nurse Columbus (Ohio) Health Dept.; critical care nurse VA Med. Ctr., San Francisco, Staff Builders Health Care Svc., Oakland, Calif.; supr. and staff mem. home health nurse passport program and intermittent care program Interim Health Care (formerly Med.

Pers. Pool), Columbus. Recipient numerous acad. scholarships Wittenberg U. and Ohio State U. Mem. AACN, ANA (coun. community health nursing), AAUW, Ohio Nurses Assn., Acad. Med.-Surg. Nurses, Intravenous Nurses Soc., Ohio State U. Alumni Assn.

THREADGILL, MAE ELLEN, educational administrator; b. Stroud, Okla., Apr. 25, 1938; d. Edward Allen Cupp and Lucy Mae (Burns) Cupp Pickens; m. John Douglas Threadgill, Dec. 2, 1958 (div. 1969); children: Naudja Mijanou, John Arthur, John Allen. BA in Elem. Edn., San Francisco State U., 1961, MA in Elem. Sch. ADminstrn., 1966. Tchr. Redding Sch. and Twin Peaks Annex, San Francisco, 1961-66; community tchr. various schs., San Francisco, 1966-67; coord. San Francisco Unified Sch. Dist. Berkeley Program, 1967-68; asst. prin. various schs., San Francisco, 1968-74; prin. Bret Harte Sch. and Fairmount Sch., San Francisco, 1974-84, El Dorado Sch., San Francisco, 1985—. Mem. exec. com. San Francisco chpt. Am. Heart Assn., 1991-92, bd. dirs., 1990-92, chmn. Heart in Black Comty., 1990-94; participant Coro Found. City Focus Leadership Tng. program, 1992-93. Recipient Educator award Top Ladies of Distinction, San Francisco, 1991, Outstanding Svc. award Am. Heart Assn., 1992. Mem. United Adminstrs. San Francisco, Delta Sigma Theta. Democrat. African Methodist Episcopal. Office: El Dorado Elem Sch 70 Delta St San Francisco CA 94134

THRIFT, JULIANNE STILL, academic administrator; b. Barnwell, S.C.; m. Ashley Ormand Thrift; children: Lindsay, Laura. BA, U. S.C., MEd; PhD in Pub. Policy, George Washington U. Formerly asst. exec. dir. Nat. Assn. Coll. and Univ. Attys.; ombudsman U. S.C.; exec. dir. Nat. Inst. Ind. Colls. and Univs., 1982-88; exec. v.p. Nat. Assn. Ind. Colls. and Univs., Washington, 1988-91; pres. Salem Acad. and Coll., Winston-Salem, N.C., 1991—. Office: Salem Coll Office of the President Winston Salem NC 27108-0548

THROCKMORTON, JOAN HELEN, advertising agency executive; b. Evanston, Ill., Apr. 11, 1931; d. Sydney L. and Anita H. (Pusheck) T.; m. Sheldon Burton Satin, June 26, 1982. B.A. with honors, Smith Coll., 1953. Mktg. exec. Lawrence Chait & Co., N.Y.C., 1965; mktg. exec. Cowles Communications, Inc., N.Y.C., 1968-69; founder, chief exec. officer Throckmorton Assocs., Inc., N.Y.C., 1970-83; pres. Joan Throckmorton, Inc., N.Y.C., 1983—; lectr. in field; instr. Direct Mktg. Assn., Sch. Continuing Edn., NYU, N.Y.C., 1985. Author: Winning Direct Response Advertising, 1986. Bd. dirs. Halle Ravine Com. Nature Conservancy, 1985; mem. expedition com. Outward Bound, 1980-83. Named Direct Mktg. Woman of Yr., 1986. Mem. Women's Dir. Response Group (founding mem.), Dir. Mktg. Assn. (bd. dirs. 1971-77, exec. com. 1972-77, mem. long-range planning com. 1977-78), Women's Forum, Dir. Mktg. Idea Exchange, Dir. Mktg. Creative Guild (bd. dirs. 1984-85), Jr. League Mexico City, Jr. League N.Y.C., Phi Beta Kappa. Office: Joan Throckmorton Inc PO Box 452 Pound Ridge NY 10576-0452

THRONE, MARILYN ELIZABETH, English educator; b. Cleve., Oct. 24, 1939; d. Charles George and Clara Elizabeth (Kieffer) T.; m. James R. Woodworth. AB, Miami U. in Oxford, 1961, MA, 1962; PhD, Miami U. in Oxford, Ohio State, 1969. Instr. Miami U., Oxford, Ohio, 1964-69; asst. prof. Miami U., Oxford, 1969-79, assoc. prof., 1979-90, prof., 1990—. Author: Walter Havighurst: Novelist of the Heartland, 1979. Office: Miami U English Dept Oxford OH 45056

THRONE, ROBIN M., secondary education educator; b. Bklyn., May 5, 1954; d. Lawrence Harold and Pearl Janet (Small) T. AB, U. Ill., 1976; MA, U. Mich., 1978. Cert. tchr., N.Y. Spanish instr. U. Richmond, Va., 1978-81; spanish tchr. Elisabeth Irwin H.S., N.Y.C., 1981-82, N.Y.C. Bd. Edn., 1985-89, Herricks H.S., New Hyde Park, N.Y., 1989—; account exec. Font and Vaamonde Inc., N.Y.C., 1982-83, Smith, Greenland Inc., N.Y.C., 1983-85; translator, interpreter N.Y.C. Bd. Edn., Bklyn., 1985-89, freelance translator, Queens, N.Y., 1985—. Fellow NEH, 1992, 94. Mem. Am. Assn. Tchrs. Spanish and Portugese, N.Y. State Assn. Lang. Tchrs., Phi Beta Kappa, Phi Kappa Phi, Sigma Delta Pi. Democrat.

THROWER, ELLEN, academic administrator. BS in Bus. Adminstn., U. N.C., Greensboro, 1975, MBA, 1978; PhD, Ga. State U., 1981; postgrad., Harvard U., 1988. Instr. dept. risk mgmt. Ga. State U., Atlanta, 1978-80; asst. prof. ins. and risk mgmt. dept. ins., real estate, and law Fla. State U., Talahassee, 1981-84; assoc. prof. ins. dept. ins., actuarial sci. and stats. Drake U., Des Moines, 1984-88, dir. ins. ctr., 1985-88; pres., CEO The Coll. of Ins., N.Y.C., 1988—; dir. Profl. Ins. Agts. Nat. Ins. Sch., Oberlin, Ohio and Chico, Calif., 1983-87; mem. adv. bd. Nat Ins. Ind. Assn., 1990—; bd. dirs. Pa. Nat. Ins. Cos., 1990—; editorial adv. bd. Insurance Review, 1990-92, Risk Management, 1992. Author: (with kathy Mohr) Iowa Ins. Fact Book, 1988; (with Lisa Gardener) The Status of Insurance Education at American Colleges and Universities, 1989; contbr. numerous publs. to profl. jours. Bd. dirs. N.Y.C. Coun. on Econ. Edn., 1992, N.C. Ins. Edn. Found., 1989—, Ins. Edn. Found., 1988—, PIA Ins. Found.; active Griffith Found. Grantee Nat. Assn. Mut. Ins. Cos., 1988, 90, 91, 92, Aetna Life and Casualty Co., 1987, State of Iowa Dept. Econ. Devel., 1987, James F. Kemper Found., 1987; Rsch. grantee Fla. State Found., 1983, Fla. State U., 1982. Mem. Internat. Ins. Soc., Am. Risk and Ins. Assn. (bd. dirs.), Am. Mgmt. Assn., Risk and Ins. Mgmt. Soc., Soc. for Ins. Rsch., So. Risk and Ins. Assn. (bd. dirs.), We. Risk and Ins. Soc., Fin. Womens Assn. N.Y., Consortium. Office: The Coll of Ins 101 Murray St New York NY 10007*

THULIN, ADELAIDE ANN, design company executive, interior designer; b. Chgo., Nov. 15, 1925; d. Martin Evold and Kathleen Marie (Glennon) Peterson; m. Frederick Adolph Thulin, Jr., Aug. 18, 1945; children: Frederick, Kristin, Mary, Margaret, Francis, Peter, Andrea, Charles, Joseph, Kathleen, James, Suzanne, Patricia. Student Northwestern U., 1943-46; AA in Interior Design, Harper Coll., 1977. Asst. production mgr. Cruttenden & Eger, Chgo., 1946; editor Mt. Prospect (Ill.) Independent, 1960; real estate salesperson Homefinders, Northwest Chgo. suburbs, 1965, 69-70; asst. v.p. advt. Littelfuse, Des Plaines, Ill., 1966-67; owner, pres. Applied Design Assocs., Mt. Prospect, 1977—; ptnr., sec. Applied Design Internat. Ltd., Mt. Prospect, 1992—; career day speaker local high schs., 1982—; bd. dirs. Works subs. Pvt. Industry Council. Author, editor monthly newsletter Women's Archtl. League, 1983-85, The Binnacle, CYC, 1979-81. Organizer, Mother's March of Dimes, Mt. Prospect, 1953-54, Vols. for Stevenson, 1952, 56, Citizens for Douglas, 1954, Citizens for Kennedy, 1960; mem. Fair Review Council, Chgo., 1983-84; mem. 13th Congl. Dist. Dem. Women's Club, publicity chmn. 1957-58; mem. Chgo. Symphony Orchestra Chorus, 1972; del. Ill. Statehouse Conf. on Small Bus., 1984, 85; bd. dirs. Arts Coun. of Mt. Prospect, 1986-93; organizer Mt. Prospect chpt. Internat. Sister Cities Program; chmn. Mt. Prospect Sign Rev. Bd.; mem. renovation com. Mt. Prospect Hist. Soc.; pres. community edn. coun. High Sch. Dist. 214; bd. dirs. Community Edn. Found. Mem. AIA (profl. affiliate Chgo. chpt.), Am. Women Internat. Understanding, Nat. Small Bus. United (bd. dirs., v.p. state govt. affairs), Ill. Coalition for N.Am. Free Trade Agreement, Women's Archtl. League (publicity chmn. 1964-65), Mt. Prospect C. of C., Gamma Alpha Chi. Roman Catholic. Avocations: reading for print-handicapped on CRIS radio, 1982-92; choral singing. Home: 4 S Owen St Mount Prospect IL 60056-3309 Office: Applied Design Assocs Ltd 200 E Evergreen Ave Mount Prospect IL 60056-3240

THULIN, JOANN HART, adult medicine nurse practitioner; b. Montevideo, Minn., Nov. 12, 1934; d. Leonard Leslie and Violet (Potter) Hart (dec.); m. Robert Duane Thulin, Aug. 20, 1956; children: Margaret, Susan, Robert H., Jonathan. Diploma, RN, Northwestern Hosp., Sch. Nursing, 1955; adult medicine nurse practitioner, Hartford (Conn.) Hosp., 1981. Obstet. nurse U. Minn. Hosp., Mpls., 1955-57; emergency dept. nurse Manchester (Conn.) Meml. Hosp., 1957-76; sch. nurse, instr. Illing Jr. High Sch., Manchester, 1976-80; supr. Oak Hill Sch. for Handicapped, Hartford, 1981-83; med. supr. SNE dist. UPS, Hartford, 1983—; mem. adv. bd. heart and work task force Am. Heart Assn., Meriden, Conn., 1988—. Trustee South United Meth. Ch., Manchester, 1989-92. Mem. Hartford Occupational Health Nurses Assn. (v.p. 1989-91, pres. 1992—, cert.). Republican. Home: 211 Carter St Manchester CT 06040 Office: UPS 90 Locust St Hartford CT 06114

THUM, GLADYS ETHEL, retired English language educator; b. St. Louis, Nov. 9, 1920; d. Frank and Louise (Holle) T. BA in Journalism, Washington U., 1948, MA in English, 1950; postgrad., U. Calif., Berkeley, 1952; PhD in Comm. Edn., St. Louis U., 1975. Info. specialist, info. officer U.S. Govt. Civil Svc., various cities in Asia, 1950-64; English prof., dept. and divsn. chair St. Louis (Mo.) C.C., 1965-86; ret., 1986. Co-author: The Persuaders, 1974, Persuasion and Propaganda, 1976, Exploring Military America, 1982, Airlift, 1986; contbr. articles to profl. jours. With USAF, 1944-46. Named David Underwood lectr. St. Louis (Mo.) C.C., 1978. Mem. St. Louis Writers Guild. Home: 6507 Gramond Dr Saint Louis MO 63123-2601

THUREAU, LANI CAROLE, speech and language pathologist; b. Jacksonville, Fla., Sept. 23, 1948; d. Samuel Howard and Joan (Miller) Zeigler; m. Donald Douglas Thureau, June 14, 1969; 1 adopted child, Christina Marie. BA, U. Miami, 1970; MA, Kent State U., 1979; postgrad. in Neurodevel. Treatment Tng., Johns Hopkins Hosp. and John F. Kennedy Inst., 1982. Cert. clin. competence Am. Speech-Lang. Assn.; cert. tchr., Del.; lic. speech-lang. pathologist, Del. Speech therapist Vanguard Sch., Miami, Fla., 1970-71, Marian Ctr., Opa-Locka, Fla., 1971-73; speech-lang. pathologist Beechwood Sch., Wilmington, Del., 1979-80; speech-lang. pathologist, supr. Del. Curative Workshop, Wilmington, Del., 1980-86; speech-lang. pathologist Pilot Sch., Inc., Wilmington, Del., 1986—; cons. Del. Curative Workshop, 1986-88, Pilot Sch., 1986—. Co-author, advisor (film) Del.: A Place to be Somebody, 1990. Exec. chmn. United Way, Wilmington, 1986-94; host mother Au Pair Home Stay, 1993-95. Recipient Adult Ice Dance Silver level U.S. Figure Skating Assn., 1990, Pres.'s award, 1994. Mem. Am. Speech-Lang.-Hearing Assn., Del. Speech, Lang. and Hearing Assn. (exec. coun., chair job bank), Skating Club of Wilmington (Gold mem. level 10 badge improvement 1985, improvement award 1988), Jewish Comty. Ctr., Endometriosis Assn., Delta Gamma. Home: 1605 Shipley Rd Wilmington DE 19803-3266

THURMAN, KAREN L., congresswoman; b. Rapid City, S.D., Jan. 12, 1951; d. Lee Searle and Donna (Altfillisch) Loveland; m. John Patrick Thurman, 1973; children: McLin Searl and Liberty Lee. BA, U. Fla., 1973. Mem. Dunnellon City Council (Fla.), 1974-82; mayor of Dunnellon, 1979-81; mem. Monroe Regional Med. Ctr. Governancy Com.; mem. Comprehensive Plan Tech. Adv. Com.; del. Fla. Dem. Conv.; Dem. Nat. Conv., 1980; mem. Regional Energy Action com.; mem. Fla. State Senate, 1982-1992; mem. 103rd Congress from 5th Fla. dist., 1993—. Recipient Svc. Above Self award Dunnellon C. of C., 1980; Regional Planning Coun. Appreciation for Svc. award. Mem. Dunnellon C. of C. (dir.), Fla. Horseman's Children's Soc. (charter). Episcopalian. Office: US Ho of Reps 130 Cannon House Office Bldg Washington DC 20515-0905

THURMAN, UMA KARUNA, actress; b. Boston, Apr. 29, 1970; d. Robert and Nena (von Schlebrugge) T.; m. Gary Oldman (div.). Appeared in films Kiss Daddy Good Night, 1987, Johnny Be Good, 1988, Dangerous Liaisons, 1988, The Adventures of Baron Munchausen, 1989, Where the Heart Is, 1990, Henry and June, 1990, Final Analysis, 1992, Jennifer Eight, 1992, Mad Dog and Glory, 1993, Even Cowgirls Get the Blues, 1993, Pulp Fiction, 1994 (Acad. award nom. Best Supporting Actress); TV movies include Robin Hood, 1991. Office: 9057 Nemo St # A Los Angeles CA 90069*

THURMON, JUDY A., sales manager; b. Memphis, Jan. 8, 1960; d. James Braxton Cason Sr. and Constance Anita (Gage) Waldrop; m. Earl P. Donald Jr., Nov. 20, 1968 (div. Mar. 1993); m. Ted A. Thurmon, May 28, 1994. BBA, U. Memphis, 1982. Nat. accounts mgr. Ft. Howard Paper, Green Bay, Wis., 1984-87, Scott Paper Co., Phila., 1987—; distbr. trainer Scott Paper Co., Memphis, 1987-92, office budget sales specialist, 1988-91; nat. accounts sales mgr. Ctrl. divsn. Scott paper Co., 1991—. Home: 8725 Hunter's Run Olive Branch MS 38654

THURSTON, ALICE JANET, former college president; b. Milw., Mar. 20, 1916; d. Karl J. and Nellie Ann (Smith) Stouffer; children: Anne, Robert. B.A., Denison U., 1937; MA, Northwestern U., 1938; PhD, George Washington U., 1960. Mem. faculty dept. psychology, counselor, dean students Montgomery Coll., Takoma Park, Md., 1950-65; dir. counseling Met. Campus, Cuyahoga Community Coll., Cleve., 1965-66; dean of students Western Campus, Cuyahoga Community Coll., 1966-67; vis. lectr. U. Ill., 1968-69; dir. Inst. Research and Student Services Met. Jr. Coll. Dist., Kansas City, Mo., 1969-71; pres. Garland Jr. Coll., Boston, 1971-75, Los Angeles Valley Coll., Van Nuys, Calif., 1975-81; lectr. Pepperdine U., L.A., 1978-81, Calif. State U., Worthridge, 1984-95; mem. adv. com. grad. program student affairs Calif. State U., Northridge. Author works in field. Bd. dirs. New Dir. for Youth, Van Nuys, Calif.; mem. ministerial search com. Unitarian Ch., Studio City, Calif., 1991-92, chair caring com., 1994—. Recipient Disting. Alumnae award Denison U., 1987, Humanitarian award Juvenile Justice Connection Project, 1987. Mem. Kappa Alpha Theta, Mortar Bd. Democrat. Unitarian. Home: 13156 Crewe St North Hollywood CA 91605-4727

THUSS, MARIAN BRIGID, telecommunications company executive; b. Reading, Pa., Apr. 19, 1966; d. Leonard Charles and Bridget Ann (Edwards) McDevitt; m. Jeffrey Paul Thuss, June 16, 1990. BA in English/Comm., Chestnut Hill Coll., Phila., 1988. Tng. specialist AT&T Microelectronics, Reading, Pa., 1988-90, quality cons., 1990-91, mktg. comm. mgr., 1991—. Active pub. rels. Reading/Berks United Way Campaign, 1994. Roman Catholic.

TIBBS, MARTHA JANE PULLEN, civic worker; b. Memphis, Feb. 12, 1932; d. John Thomas Jr. and Martha Frances (Gragg) Pullen; m. Eugene Edward Tibbs; children: Martha Katherine, Eugene Edward Jr. BSBA, U. Tenn., 1953; MA in Edn., Memphis State U., 1958. Cert. tchr., social worker, Tenn. Tchr. Lausanne Sch., Memphis, Tenn., 1954-55, Millington High Sch., Memphis, 1955-56, Presbyterian Day Sch., Memphis, 1956-57, St. Mary's Episcopal Sch., Memphis, 1958-60; social worker Tenn. Dept. Pub. Welfare, Memphis, 1962-63. Author genealogical works. Mem. Memphis Vol. Svc. Bd., 1963-64; commr. Shelby County Hist. Commn., Memphis, 1983—; block worker Cancer, Kidney and Heart Fund, Memphis, 1984—. Mem. NEA, AAUW, Tenn. Tchrs. Assn., Tenn. Geneal. Soc., Tenn. Founders and Patriots of Am. (state registrar), Early Settlers Shelby County (sec. 1984—, registrar 1988, bd. dirs. 1992—), Nineteenth Century Club (sec. 1993—, newsletter editor 1985-88), Cleve. Jr. Aux., Cleve. Med. Aux. (sec./treas.), West Tenn. Hist. Soc, Univ. Club Memphis, Racquet Club, DAR (past chpt. regent, sec.-treas. regents coun.), Chicasaw Dist. DAR Sch. (Tenn. state vice chmn., parliamentarian, chmn. Zachariah Davies chpt.), Cleve. Garden Club (past pres.), Cleve. Woman's Club, Nat. Soc. Magna Charta Dames (Memphis chpt.), Nat. Soc. Daus. of Founders and Patriots of Am. (Tenn. chpt.), Tenn. State Registrar Founders and Patriots, Nat. Soc. Colonial Dames (Memphis Chucaqua chpt.), Nat. Soc. So. Dames Am. (Memphis chpt.), Colonial Order of Crown (descendants of Charlemagne), The Sovereign Colonial Soc. Ams. Royal Descent, Memphis Scottish Soc., Family of Bruce Soc., Alpha Omega Pi (alumnae pres., advisor collegiate chpt. Rhodes Coll.). Republican. Presbyterian. Home: 2008 Massey Rd Memphis TN 38119-6404

TICE, CAROL HOFF, educator, consultant; b. Ashville, N.C., Oct. 6, 1931; d. Amos H. and Fern (Irvin) Hoff; m. (div.); children: Karin E., Jonathan H. BS, Manchester Coll., North Manchester, Ind., 1954; MEd, Cornell U., 1955. Cert. tchr., Mich., N.Y., N.J. Tchr. Princeton (N.J.) Schs., 1955-60; tchr. Ann Arbor (Mich.) Schs., 1964—; dir. intergenerational programs Inst. for Study Children and Families Eastern Mich. U., Ypsilanti, 1985—; founder, pres. Lifespan Resources, Inc., Ann Arbor, 1979—; commr. U.S. Nat. Commn. Internat. Yr. of the Child, Washington, 1979-81. Innovator; program, Tch. Learning Intergenerational Communities, 1971; author: Guide Books and articles, Community of Caring, 1980; co-producer, Film, What We Have, 1976 (award, Milan, Italy Film Festival 1982). Mem. Democratic Party, Ann Arbor; trustee Blue Lake Fine Arts Camp, Twin Lake, Mich., 1975—. Recipient Program Innovation award Mich. Dept. Edn., 1974-80, C.S. Mott Found. award, 1982, Nat. Found. Improvement in Edn. award, Washington, 1986, Disting. Alumni award Manchester Coll., 1979, A+ Break the Mold award U.S. Sec. of Edn., 1992; Ford Found. fellow, Ithaca, N.Y., 1955. Mem. Am. Soc. of Curriculum Devel., Am. Assn. U. Women (Agt. 1979), Generations United (Pioneer Award 1989), Optimist Club. Democrat. Presbyterian. Office: Scarlett MS 3300 Lorraine St Ann Arbor MI 48108-1970

TICER, TERRI JEAN, sales executive; b. Childress, Tex., Apr. 15, 1955; d. Jerry H. and J. Colene (Eudey) T. AA, Clarendon Jr. Coll., 1977; BS, W. Tex. State U., 1979. Human svcs. dir. S. Plains Coll., Plainview, Tex., 1979-81; sales rep. Avon Products, N.Y.C., 1981—. Contbr. articles to profl. jours. Vol. Hospice of Plains, Plainview, 1985—; mem. Faith in Sharing House, 1985-89, Friends of Libr., Plainview, 1986-91, Humane Soc., Plainview, 1987-92; bd. dirs. Big Bros./Big Sisters, 1987-88; chmn. Youth Group Reunion, 1990-91. Mem. AAUW (membership v.p. 1987-89, chmn. edn. found. 1989-92, hosp. aux. 1992—). Home: 2503 W 13th St Apt 5 Plainview TX 79072-4869

TICHAUER, GAYLE MARLENE, counselor, consultant; b. Omaha, Oct. 25, 1949; d. George and Lillian (Weise) Lerman; m. Carl Joseph Tichauer, June 14, 1970; children: Cory, Jayme. BS in Spl. Edn., U. Nebr., Omaha, 1975, MS in Counseling and Guidance, 1986, postgrad. Exec. reviewer Mut. Protective Ins. Co., Omaha, 1973-78; rsch. asst. Boystown, Boystown, Nebr., 1979-80; sales cons. Newton Mfg. Co., Newton, Iowa, 1980-86; vocat. evaluator Eischen Rehab. Svcs., Inc., Omaha, 1986-88; sr. vocat. cons. Eischen Rehab. Svcs., Inc., 1988-90, regional dir. vocat. evaluation, 1990-91; pres., chief vocat. cons. Vocat. Assessment Svcs., Inc., Omaha, 1991—; cons. Social Security Adminstrn., Omaha. Ways and means chmn. Women's League, Omaha, 1993-94, v.p., program chmn., 1994-95. Mem. Nat. Assn. Rehab. Profls. in Pvt. Sector (treas. 1993—), Women's Am. Orgn. for Rehab. (program chmn. 1993-94), Nebr. Profl. Counselors' Assn., Am. Assn. Counseling and Devel., Nebr. Assn. Counseling and Devel., Nat. Career Devel. Assn., Nebr. Career Devel. Assn., Nat. Rehab. Assn., Rehab. Assn. of Nebr., Vocat. Evaluation and Work Adjustment Assn., Human Resources Assn. of the Midlands, Phi Delta Gamma. Office: Vocat Assessment Svcs 10730 Pacific St #27 Omaha NE 68114

TIDBALL, M. ELIZABETH PETERS, educator, author; b. Anderson, Ind., Oct. 15, 1929; d. John Winton and Beatrice (Ryan) Peters; m. Charles S. Tidball, Oct. 25, 1952. BA, Mt. Holyoke Coll., 1951, LHD, 1976; MS, U. Wis., 1955, PhD, 1959; MTS summa cum laude, Wesley Theol. Sem., 1990; ScD (hon.), Wilson Coll., 1973; DSc (hon.), Trinity Coll., 1974, Cedar Crest Coll., 1977; ScD (hon.), U. of South, 1978, Goucher Coll., 1979; DSc (hon.), St. Mary-of-The-Woods Coll., 1986; LittD (hon.), Regis Coll., 1980, Coll. St. Catherine, 1980, Alverno Coll., 1989; HHD (hon.), St. Mary's Coll., 1977, Hood Coll., 1982; LLD (hon.), St. Joseph Coll., 1983; LHD (hon.), Skidmore Coll., 1984, Marymount Coll., 1985, Converse Coll., 1985, Mt. Vernon Coll., 1986. Teaching asst. physiology dept. U. Wis., 1952-55, 58-59; research asst. anatomy dept. U. Chgo., 1955-56, research asst. physiology dept., 1956-58; USPHS postdoctoral fellow NIH, Bethesda, Md., 1959-61; staff pharmacologist Hazleton Labs., Falls Church, Va., 1961; assoc. in physiology George Washington U. Med. Ctr., 1960-62; cons. Hazleton Labs., 1962; asst. research prof. dept. pharmacology George Washington U. Med. Ctr., 1962-64, assoc. research prof. dept. physiology, 1964-70, research prof., 1970-71, prof., 1971-94, prof. emeritus, 1994—; disting. rsch. scholar Hood Coll., Frederick, Md., 1994—; asst. dir. M of Theol. Studies program Wesley Theol. Sem., 1993-94; co-dir. Tidball Ctr. for Study of Ednl. Environments Hood Coll., 1994—; Lucie Stern Disting. vis. prof. natural scis. Mills Coll., 1980; scholar in residence Coll. Preachers, 1984, Salem Coll., 1985, Wesley Theol. Sem., 1992; Disting. scholar in residence So. Meth. U., 1985; cons. FDA, 1966-67, assoc. sci. coordinator sci. assocs. tng. program, 1966-67; mem. com. on NIH tng. programs and fellowships Nat. Acad. Scis., 1972-75; faculty summer confs. Am. Youth Found., 1967-78; founder, dir. Summer Seminars for Women Am. Youth Found., 1987-95; cons. for instl. research Wellesley Coll., 1974-75; exec. sec. com. on edn. and employment women in sci. and engring. Commn. on Human Resources, NRC/NAS, 1974-75, vice chmn., 1977-82; cons., staff officer NRC/Nat. Acad. Scis., 1974-75; cons. Woodrow Wilson Nat. Fellowship Found., 1975-94, NSF, 1974-91 ; bd. mentor Assn. Governing Bds. of Univs. and Colls., 1991—, Gale Fund for the study of Trusteeship Adv. Comm., 1992—; cons. Assn. Am. Colls. Women's Coll. Coalition Rsch. Adv. Com., 1992—; Single Gender Schooling Working Group., U.S. Dept. Edn., 1992-94; rep. to D.C. Commn. on Status of Women, 1972-75; nat. panelist Am. Coun. on Edn., 1983-90; panel mem. Congl. Office of Tech. Assessment, 1986-87; mem. fellows selection com., fellows mentor Coll. Preachers, 1992—; vis. trustee prof. Skidmore Coll., 1995. Columnist Trusteeship, 1993—; mem. editorial bd. Jour. Higher Edn., 1979-84, cons. editor, 1984—; mem. editorial adv. bd. Religion and Intellectual Life, 1983; contbr. sci. articles and rsch. on edn. of women to profl. jours. Trustee Mt. Holyoke Coll., 1968-73, vice-chmn., 1972-73, trustee fellow, 1988—; trustee Hood Coll., 1972-84, 86-92, exec. com., 1974-84, 89-92; overseer Sweet Briar Coll., 1978-85; trustee Cathedral Choral Soc., 1976-90, pres. bd. trustees, 1982-84, hon. trustee, 1991—; trustee Skidmore Coll., 1988—, mem. exec. com., 1993—; trustee Coll. of Preachers, 1979-85, chmn., 1983-85; mem. governing bd. Washington Cathedral Found., 1983-85, mem. exec. com. 1983-85; bd. vis. Salem Coll., 1986-93; ctr. assoc. Nat. Resource Ctr., Girls Clubs Am., 1983—. Shattuck fellow, 1955-56; Mary E. Woolley fellow Mt. Holyoke Coll., 1958-59; USPHS postdoctoral fellow, 1959-61; recipient Alumnae Medal of Honor Mt. Holyoke Coll., 1971, Award for Valuable Contbns. Gen. Alumni Assn. George Washington U., 1982, 87, Chestnut Hill Medal for Outstanding Achievement Chestnut Hill Coll., Phila., 1987; named Outstanding Grad. The Penn Hall Sch., 1988. Mem. AAAS, Am. Physiol. Soc. (chmn. task force on women in physiology 197coms. 1977-80, mem. emeritus 1994—), Am. Assn. Higher Edn., Mt. Holyoke Alumnae Assn. (dir. 1966-70, 76-77), Histamine Club, Sigma Delta Epsilon, Sigma Xi. Episcopalian. Home: 4100 Cathedral Ave NW Washington DC 20016-3584

TIDWELL, ENID EUGENIE, sculptor, advocate; b. Farmington, N.Mex., Sept. 20, 1944; d. James Eugene and Eleanor Pynchon (Davenport) MacDonald; m. Thomas Russell Walker, May 12, 1963 (div. 1968); 1 child, Thomas Shawn; m. Roy Mc Tidwell, June 19, 1969; 1 child, Michael Eric. BA in English, Teaching cum laude, U. Ala., Huntsville, 1975. Sec. U. N.Mex., Albuquerque, 1964-66, Sandia Labs., Albuquerque, 1966-69; office mgr. Stanford Rsch. Inst., Kuwait, 1977-78; artist Calif., Va., 1978—; chmn., treas. Gallery House, Palo Alto, Calif., 1979-80. Exhibited in one person shows including Stanford U. Faculty Club, Palo Alto, Calif., 1979, Dominican Coll. Gallery, San Rafael, Calif., 1980; group shows include Quadrangle Devel. Corp., Washington, 1990, Artists Equity 3d Annual Memberhip Awards Exhibit, Washington, 1988, Allied Artists Am. 74th Annual Exhbn., N.Y.C., 1987, Hudson Valley '86, Poughkeepsie, N.Y., 1986, Washington Women's Art Ctr. Sculpture Show, 1982, 85, 86, Allied Artists Am. 71st Annual Exbn., N.Y.C., 1984, City Art 1981, Washington, 4th Annual Open Juried Non-Member Exbn. The Salmagundi Club, N.Y., 1981, Nat. Small Sculpture and Drawing Open Juried Competition Westwood Ctr. the Arts, L.A., 1981, numerous others; represented in permanent collections including Ingersoll & Block, Walker Wire, Centennial Devel. Corp., Signet Bank, Fisher Group, others. Mem. Fairfax County (Va.) Cultural Facility Task Force, 1989-90; treas. Bluffs of Wolftrap Homeowners Assn., Vienna, Va., 1985-88; pres. Monte Sano Homeowners Assn., Huntsville, Ala., 1975-76; bd. dirs. Monte Sano Elem. PTA, Huntsville, 1970-72; active PTA, Ala., Calif., Va., 1969-89, Boy Scouts Am., Ala., Va., 1971-89. Mem. AAUW (pres. McLean br. 1988-90, Ednl. Found. grantee 1986, 91, program v.p. N.Mex. chpt. 1994—), Allied Artists Am., Sigma Tau Delta. Home and Office: 5 Sunflower Cir Santa Fe NM 87501

TIDWELL, MARY ELLEN, risk/insurance coordinator; b. Liberty, S.C., June 25, 1940; d. William Robert and Ruby Irene (Trammell) Murphy; m. Howard Eugene Anderson, Sept. 8, 1956 (div. Jan. 1987); children: Howard Eugene Jr., Sterling Craig; m. Lear Tidwell, July 9, 1989. AS in Office Mgmt., Polk C.C., 1993. Sec. H. Lamar Stewart Ins. Agy, Frostproof, Fla., 1962-64; accounts payable clk. Ben Hill Griffin, Inc., Frostproof, 1964-65; agt. Bullard Ins. Agy., Inc., Lake Wales, Fla., 1966-79; risk/ins. coordinator Coca-Cola Foods, Auburndale, Fla., 1979—; dir. Fla. Girls State, Inc., Orlando, 1988-93. City chmn. March of Dimes, Frostproof, 1964; campaign worker Tom Wheeler for Sheriff, Winter Haven, Fla., 1988. Mem. Risk and Ins. Mgmt. Soc., Am. Legion, Order of Eastern Star. Democrat. Baptist. Office: Coca-Cola Foods PO Box 247 Auburndale FL 33823-0247

TIEDEMANN, RUTH ELIZABETH FULTON, writer, educator; b. Knoxville, Tenn., Aug. 27, 1935; d. Frank Keene and Ruth Almeda

(McConnell) Fulton; m. Herbert Allen Tiedemann, Sept. 3, 1955; children: Ruth Patten, Keene Fulton, Melvin John (dec.), Herbert Allen Jr. Student, U. Tenn., 1953-56; cert. in real estate, U. Md., 1976, cert. appraiser, 1977; student, U. Okla., 1983-84. Mgr. Corbin Co. Realtors, Bartlesville, Okla., 1977-80; legal document analyst Phillips Petroleum Co., Bartlesville, 1980-84; columnist Bartlesville Examiner-Enterprise, 1984-94; pres. Pens and Lens, Bartlesville, 1985—; book columnist The Bartlesville Times, 1994—; CEO Phoenix Media, 1994—; contemporary books editor Rave Revs. Mag., N.Y.C., 1987-89; publicity dir. Okla. Mozart Internat. Festival, Bartlesville, 1988; adj. prof. Bartlesville Wesleyan Coll., 1990—; teacher creative writing Tri-County Vocat. Tech. Contbr. articles to profl. jours. and newspapers. Co-founder Bartlesville Compassionate Friends, 1979—; developer libr. Creative Writing Contest. Mem. Women's Coun. Realtors, Bartlesville Writers Fedn. (Creative Writing award 1987, 89, 92), Nat. Book Critics Circle, Sisters in Crime, Bartlesville WordWeavers (prs. 1991-92), Tulsa Nightwriters, Okla. Ctr. for the Book (bd. dirs.), Delta Delta Delta. Republican. Presbyterian. Home: 1609 S Dewey Bartlesville OK 74003

TIEFEL, VIRGINIA MAY, librarian; b. Detroit, May 20, 1926; d. Karl and June Garland (Young) Brenkert; m. Paul Martin Tiefel, Jan. 25, 1947; children: Paul Martin Jr., Mark Gregory. B.A. in Elem. Edn., Wayne State U., 1962; M.A. in Library Sci., U. Mich., 1968. Librarian Birmingham Schs., Mich., 1967-68; librarian S. Euclid-Lyndhurst Schs., Cleve., 1968-69; acquisitions-reference librarian Hiram Coll., Ohio, 1969-77; head undergrad. libraries Ohio State U., Columbus, 1977-84; dir. library user edn. Ohio State U., 1978—. Contbr. articles to profl. jours. Recipient Disting. Alumnus award U. Mich. Sch. Info. and Libr. Studies, 1993. Mem. ALA (v.p. Ohio sect. 1973-74, pres. 1974-75, Miriam Dudley Bibliographic Instrn. Librarian of Yr. 1986), Acad. Library Assn. Ohio (Outstanding Ohio Acad. Librarian 1984), Assn. Coll. and Research Libraries (chmn. bibliographic instrn. sect. com. on research 1983-84, chmn. com. on performance measures 1984-90). Lutheran. Home: 4956 Smoketalk Ln Westerville OH 43081-4433 Office: Ohio State U Libraries 1858 Neil Ave Columbus OH 43210-1286

TIEFENTHAL, MARGUERITE AURAND, school social worker; b. Battle Creek, Mich., July 23, 1919; d. Charles Henry and Elisabeth Dirk (Hoekstra) Aurand; m. Harlan E. Tiefenthal, Nov. 26, 1942; children: Susan Ann, Daniel E., Elisabeth Amber, Carol Aurand. BS, Western Mich. U., 1941; MSW, U. Mich., 1950; postgrad., Coll. of DuPage, Ill., 1988-90. Tchr. No. High Sch., Flint, Mich., 1941-44, Cen. High Sch., Kalamazoo, 1944-45; acct. Upjohn Co., Kalamazoo, 1945-48; social worker Family Svc. Agy., Lansing, Mich., 1948-50, Pitts., 1950-55; sch. social worker Gower Sch. Dist., Hinsdale, Ill., 1962-70; sch. social worker Hinsdale (Ill.) Dist. 181, 1970-89, cons., 1989—; sch. social worker Villa Park (Ill.) Sch. Dist. 45, 1989; addictions counselor Mercy Hosp., 1990-92; asst. prof. sch. social work, liaison to pub. schs. Loyola U., Chgo., 1990—; field instr. social work interns U. Ill., 1979-88; impartial due process hearing officer; mem. adv. com. sch. social work Ill. State Bd. Edn. approved programs U. Ill. and George Williams Coll.; speaker Nat. Conf. Sch. Social Work, Denver, U. Tex. Joint Conf. Sch. Social Work in Ill.; founder Marguerite Tiefenthal Symposium for Ill. Sch. Social Work Interns. Co-editor The School Social Worker and the Handicapped Child: Making P.L. 94-142 Work; sect. editor: Sch. Social Work Quarterly, 1979. Sec. All Village Caucus Village of Western Springs, Ill., mem. village disaster com.; deacon Presbyn. Ch. Western Springs, Sunday sch. tchr., mem. choir; instr. Parent Effectiveness, Teacher Effectiveness, STEP; trainer Widowed Persons Service Tng. Program for Vol. Aides AARP. Recipient Ill. Sch. Social Worker of Yr., 1982. Mem. Nat. Assn. Social Workers (chmn. exec. council on social work in schs.), Ill. Assn. Sch. Social Workers (past pres., past conf. chmn., conf. program chmn.), Sch. Social Workers Supervisors Group (del. to Ill. Commn. on Children), Programs. for Licensure of Social Work Practice in Ill., LWV, DKG, PEO. Home: 4544 Grand Ave Western Springs IL 60558-1545

TIEGS, CHERYL, model, designer; d. Theodore and Phyllis T. Student, Calif. State U., Los Angeles. Profl. model, appearing in nat. mags., including, Time, Life, Bazaar, Sports Illustrated, Glamour; appeared weekly on ABC's Good Morning America; also appearing in TV commls., Cheryl Tiegs line of sportswear, Cheryl Tiegs nationally-distributed line of women's eyeglass frames, Cheryl Tiegs Collection of 14k Gold Jewelry, Fashion Watches, Shoes and Hosiery; author: The Way to Natural Beauty, 1980; Sports Illustrated video Aerobic Interval Training with Cheryl Tiegs. Address: care Barbara Shapiro 2 Greenwich Plz Ste 100 Greenwich CT 06830-6353

TIEMAN, SUZANNAH BLISS, neurobiologist; b. Washington, Oct. 10, 1943; d. John Alden and Winifred Texas (Bell) Bliss; m. David George Tieman, Dec. 19, 1969. AB with honors, Cornell U., 1965; postgrad., MIT, 1965-66, Calif. Inst. Tech., 1971-72; PhD, Stanford U., 1974. Postdoctoral fellow dept. anatomy U. Calif., San Francisco, 1974-77; rsch. assoc. Neurobiology Rsch. Ctr. SUNY, Albany, 1977-90; sr. rsch. assoc., 1990—; rsch. assoc. prof. dept. biol. scis. SUNY, Albany, 1984-90, rsch. prof., 1990—, sr. rsch. assoc., 1990—; adj. asst. prof. dept. biol. scis., SUNY, Albany, 1977-84. Contbr. articles to profl. jours., chpts. to books in field. Recipient predoctoral fellowship NSF, NIH, Stanford U., 1970-73,73-74, postdoctoral fellowship Nat. Eye Inst., U. Calif., San Francisco, 1974-77, rsch. grant SUNY, Albany, 1979-83, NSF, SUNY, 1983-86, '88-92, '92-95. Mem. AAAS, Soc. for Neurosci. (steering com. Hudson Berkshire chpt. 1980-81, pres. 1991-93), Assn. Rsch. in Vision and Ophthalmology, Am. Assn. Anatomists, Assn. Women in Sci., Women In Neurosci., Nat. Audubon Soc., Nature Conservancy. Office: SUNY Neurobiology Rsch Ctr 1400 Washington Ave Albany NY 12222-0001

TIEMANN, RUTH CAROL, art educator; b. San Antonio, Jan. 5, 1938; d. Philip Leroy McGuire and Frances Ruth (Fuhrmann) McGuire Caldwell; m. Robert Eugene Tiemann, Sept. 7, 1958 (div. Nov. 1971); children: John, Michael, Marc, Paul, Kathleen. BFA, U. Tex., 1958; MFA, U. Tex., San Antonio, 1978. Art tchr. Northeast Ind. Sch. Dist., San Antonio, 1971—; part time art instr. Incarnate Word Coll., San Antonio, 1982—, St. Mary's U., San Antonio, 1994—; tchr. Gifted and Talented Acad., San Antonio, 1990; mem. textbook curriculum guide revision adoption com., San Antonio, 1989, 91. Contbr. How Art Works, 1989; author: (with others) Art Education Book, 1989; contbr. articles, illustrations to profl. jours. Organizer Fiesta Estrella Azul, Blue Star Art Complex, 1992, 93; contbr. Share Project, San Antonio, 1990—; state evaluator San Antonio Mus. Children's Program, 1988; active Target 90s Mayor's Art and Edn. Task Force, San Antonio, 1990, Tex. Commn. on the Arts; dir. student ceramic mural NCCJ, San Antonio, 1989; judge Tex. high schs. Nat. Art Honor Soc. Competition, 1991. Mem. NEA, Nat. Art Edn. Assn. (multicultural register 1995), Northeast Tchrs. Assn. (rep. 1991-93, Tchr. of Yr. 1982), Tex. State Edn. Assn., Tex. State Art Edn. Assn. (presentor state conv. 1992), San Antonio Art Edn. Assn. (tchr., contbr., judge Youth Art Month Exhibit 1990—, sec. 1991-94), Delta Kappa Gamma (lectr. program com. 1987—). Democrat. Home: 630 Tuxedo San Antonio TX 78209 Office: Northeast Ind Sch Dist Garner Mid Sch 4302 Harry Wurzbach San Antonio TX 78209

TIEMEYER, HOPE ELIZABETH JOHNSON, retired advertising company executive, civic worker; b. Ft. Wayne, Ind., May 20, 1908; d. Edward Tibbens and Burton (Meyers) Johnson; m. Edwin H. Tiemeyer, Oct. 30, 1929 (dec. Apr. 1955); children: Ann Elizabeth (Mrs. G. L. Lewin, Jr.), Edwin Houghton (dec.). BA, U. Cin., 1932. Pres., owner Mail-Way Advt. Co., Cin., pres., 1955-87. Regent, Cin. chpt. D.A.R., 1956-58, chmn. nat. sch. survey com., 1961-62, nat. vice chmn. Americanism Manual for Citizenship, 1962-65, Continental Congress program com., 1962-65, Congress Marshall Com., 1966-68, mem. Congress hostess com., 1969-77; rec. sec. Nat. Chmn.'s Assn., 1969-71, pres. Ohio State Officers Club, 1975-77; sr. nat. membership chmn. Children Am. Revolution, 1958-60, sr. nat. rec. sec., 1960-62, nat. chmn. Mountain Sch., 1962-64, hon. sr. nat. v.p., 1963-64, sr. nat. 1st v.p. 1964-66, sr. nat. pres., 1966-68, hon. nat. life pres., 1970—, 1st v.p. Nat. Officers Club, 1965-69, pres., 1970-73, hon. sr. life pres. Ohio soc.; hon. life mem. Ohio Congress PTA, treas., 1957-62, v.p., dir. dept. health, 1962-63; hon. life mem. Nat. Congress PTA; life mem. Kappa Alpha Theta Mothers Club, pres., 1958-59; v.p. women's com. Cin. Symphony Orch., 1964-65; pres. U. Cin. Parents Club, 1959-61, v.p., 1963-64; area chmn. State House Conf. on Edn., 1953; dir. AAUW, 1963-64; mem. Cin. Social Health Bd., 1950—, exec. com., 1965-70, v.p., 1973-75, treas., 1975-78, life trustee, 1978—; pres. Singleton's of Cin. Club, 1969-71, 73-76, mem. travel bd., 1973—, pres., 1973-74, art com., 1971-88, mem. membership com., 1973-78; pres. Newtown Garden Club, 1947-49, City Panhellenic Assn., 1951-52, Ohio Hobby Club, 1958-59, Sigma Nu Mothers Club, 1963-65, pres. Alumnae chpt. Alpha Omicron Pi, 1930-32, nat. admissions com., 1933-35; life mem. Craftshops for Handicapped; chmn. Amelia Earhart Fellowship com. Zonta Club, Cin., 1963-64, program chmn., 1964-65, orientation chmn., 1965-67, internat. relations chmn., 1967-68, dir., 1969-74, mem. exec. com., 1969-74, mem. nat. nominating com., 1970-74, v.p., 1971-73; mem. music com., mem. tea room com. Cin. Woman's Club, 1969-72; treas. Queen City chpt. Nat. Assn. Parliamentarians, 1965-69; v.p. Greater Cin. area women's chpt. Freedoms Found. at Valley Forge, 1975-77, sec. 1977-79, pres., 1978-80, bd. dirs. 1987—; bd. dirs. Covington-Cin. Suspension Bridge com., 1987—. Mem. Nat. Platform Assn. (com. bd. 1987—), Nat. Gavel Assn., English Speaking Union. Recipient Jonathon Moore citation and award Ind. Soc. S.A.R., 1967; Good Citizenship medal Nat. Soc., 1967; named Ky. col., Ohio commodore, 1990. Club: Cin. Women's, Town. Home: 2786 Little Dry Run Rd Cincinnati OH 45244-2846

TIERNAN, BERNADETTE BRUNHUBER, management consultant; b. Rego Park, N.Y., Oct. 30, 1951; d. William Ernest and Mary Regina (Fitzpatrick) Brunhuber; m. William Clark Tiernan Jr., July 27, 1974; children: Katherine, Billy, Caroline. BA in Psychology, Merrimack Coll., 1973; Cert. in Human Factors Engring., U. Mich., 1976; MA in Indsl. Psychology, Fairleigh Dickinson U., 1979. Human factors engr. Long Lines div. AT&T, White Plains, N.Y., 1973-79, info. systems mgr. Data Svcs. div., 1979-81; dir. mgmt. devel. program Human Resources div. AT&T, Bedminster, N.Y., 1981-84; v.p. Human Resources Assocs., Englewood Cliffs, N.J., 1984-86; pres. Tiernan Assocs., Ridgewood, N.J., 1986—; instr. Bergen Community Coll., Paramus, N.J. Author: Segues: Smooth Transitions for the 90's, 1990, The Complete Homebased Business Sourcebook. Publicist Valley Hosp. Auxiliary, Ridgewood, N.J., 1989-91, Coll. Club of Ridgewood, 1990-91. Named Bus. Woman of the Yr. Bergen chpt. N.J. Assn. Women Bus. Owners, 1994. Mem. APA, Nat. Assn. Women Bus. Owners (program v.p. 1989-91), N.J. Assn. Women Bus. Owners (bd. dirs. 1986—, pres. 1991-93, pres. no. region 1994—). Roman Catholic. Office: PO Box 1382 Ridgewood NJ 07451-1382

TIERNEY, SUSAN FALLOWS, federal official; married; 2 children. BA, Scripps Coll., 1973; student, L'Institut d'Etudes Politiques, Paris; MA, Cornell U., 1976, PhD, 1980; LLD (hon.), Regis Coll. Asst. prof. U. Calif., Irvine, 1978-82; sr. economist Mass. Exec. Office Energy Resources, 1983-84; exec. dir. Mass. Energy Facilities Siting Coun., 1984-88; commr. Dept. Pub. Utilities, 1988-90, sec. environ. affairs, resources authority, 1991-93; asst. sec. energy, office of policy, planning and program evaluation Dept. Energy, Washington, 1993—; chmn. transmission task force New Eng. Gov.'s Conf. Power Planning Com.; mem. Keystone Project Electric Transmission Ind. Power Prodrs. Contbr. articles to profl. jours. Mem. New Eng. Conf. Public Utility Commrs., Nat. Assn. Regulatory Utility Commrs. (energy conservation gas com.), Electric Power Rsch. (adv. com.). Office: Dept Energy Policy 1000 Independence Ave SW Washington DC 20585

TIETZE, PHYLLIS SOMERVILLE, media specialist; b. Bklyn., Aug. 5, 1941; d. Samuel Clark and Norma Helen (Vanderbeck) Somerville; m. Robert Morse Tietze, Dec. 22, 1962; children: Kevin North, Andrea Kristina. BS, U. Miami, 1962; ML, U. S.C., 1989. Rsch. asst. U. Miami Inst. Marine Sci., 1962-65; media specialist Pendleton (S.C.) High Sch., 1989—. Mem. ALA, S.C. Assn. Sch. Librs., Anderson County Libr. Assn. Presbyterian. Home: 226 Weaver Rd Pendleton SC 29670 Office: Pendleton High Sch Hwy 187 Box 218 Pendleton SC 29670

TIFFANY, SANDRA L., state legislator; b. Spokane, Wash., June 30, 1949; m. Ross M. Tonkens; 1 child, Courtney. Student, U. Calif. Mem. Nev. Assembly, 1993—. Mem. Nev. Rep. Women's Club, Green Valley Cmty. Assn. Home: 75 Quail Run Rd Henderson NV 89014 Office: Nev Assembly State Capitol Carson City NV 89710*

TIGHE-MOORE, BARBARA JEANNE, electronics executive; b. Wadsworth, Ohio, Jan. 12, 1961; d. Norton Raymond and Laura Alida (Frank) T.; m. Derek William Moore, June 26, 1982. AS in Electronic Engring. summa cum laude, Hocking Tech. Coll., 1981; AS in Electronic Data Processing magna cum laude, Sinclair Coll., 1986; BBA Honors Coll. magna cum laude, Kent State U., 1988. Lic. amateur radio operator. Tech. writer computer dept. Sinclair Coll., Dayton, Ohio, 1983; project mgr. O'Neil & Assocs., Dayton, 1983-84; biomed., bio-acoustic real-time flight simulation tempest developer Systems Rsch. Labs., Dayton, 1984-86; owner, pres. Lida Ray Techs., Dayton, 1978—; computer specialist Kent State U. Press, 1987-88; mgmt. analyst Electronic Warfare Frontier Engring. Inc., 1988-89; supr. small computer tech. svcs. Frontier Engring., Inc., 1989-90, project engr., 1990-92; ptnr. MKCC, Dayton, 1990—; sr. program mgr. C.E.T.A., Dayton, 1992-93; ptnr., bd. dirs. SDCC, Dayton, 1992—; pres. Lida Ray Techs., Dayton; user, regional mgr. Tech. Assocs., Dayton; mem. graphics steering com., mem. sanctioned UNIX software adv. team Aero. Systems Divsn.; program chair IEEE Internat. Wireless LAN Conf.; mem. Engring. Application Support Environ. Security Working Group; bd. dirs. MKCC, SDCC; spkr. Govt. Land Mobile Comm. Conf., 1993, Internat. Engring. Mgmt. Cons., 1994, Wireless '93, Calgary, Alta., Nat. Aero. & Electronics Conf., Dayton, Ohio, 1993. Author: Job Search Strategies for the 90's, 1993; editor: Graphics Directions, 1990-91, Team Advisor; pub. SDCC Cleaning Times, IEEE Update; contbr. papers, articles to profl. jours. Counselor Kwam's Kinder Kamp; tchr. Bible Sch.; cook Meals on Wheels; organizer/cook funeral Svcs. Dinners. Recipient Vol. Citizen award Wadsworth C. of C, 1979, Ohio Essayist award, 1979, Virginia Perryman award, 1979, Disting. Leadership award, 1990, 91. Mem. IEEE (former treas.), Computer Soc. of IEEE (sec. 1991-92, vice chmn. 1992—), Engring. Mgmt. Soc. of IEEE, Tech. and Soc. of IEEE, Data Processing Mgmt. Assn., Assn. Computer Machinery, Assn. Internat. Students Econs. & Commerce (pres. 1986-87), Internat. Film Soc. (pres. 1986-88), Armed Forces Communications and Electronics Assn. (judge sci. fair we. dist. 1992—), Equestrian Team (point rider 1987-88), Fencing Club, Phi Theta Kappa, Mortar Bd., Omnicron Delta Kappa, Beta Gamma Sigma. Home: 3125 Glen Rock Rd Dayton OH 45420-1900

TIGS, PATRICIA DELORES, municipal official; b. Annapolis, Md., Oct. 13, 1943; d. Morris and Margaret Jane (Parker) Peters; m. Willie James Tigs, Jan. 19, 1963 (div. Dec. 1979); children: Dwayne, Darryl, Ivette, Derick, Dewitt, Demond. BBA, Sojorner-Douglass Coll., 1987. Clerk Anne Arundel County, Annapolis, 1976-79; aide Ho. of Dels., Annapolis, 1987; sec. City of Annapolis, 1979-90, ops. asst., 1990—. Contbr. articles to newsletters. Instr. Anne Arundel County Health Dept., Annapolis, 1979-89; counselor Youth Svc. Bur., Annapolis, 1979-82; sec. Kiva House, Severna Park, Md., 1992-93; pub. rels. Women of Color, Annapolis. Mem. NAFE. Democrat. Methodist. Home: 1976 Dominoe Rd Annapolis MD 21401 Office: Annapolis Transportation 160 Duke of Gloucester St Annapolis MD 21401

TILBERIS, ELIZABETH, editor-in-chief; m. Andrew Tilberis, 1971. Student, Jacob Kramer Coll. Arts, Leeds, England; BA, Leicester (Eng.) Poly. Fashion asst. British Vogue, 1970, fashion editor, 1974, exec. fashion editor, 1984, sr. fashion editor, 1986, editor-in-chief, 1987; dir. Conde Nast Pubs., 1989; editor-in-chief Harper's Bazaar, N.Y.C., 1992—. Recipient 2 Nat. Mag. awards for design, photography, 1993, Coun. Fashion Designers of Am. award, 1994. Office: Harper's Bazaar 1700 Broadway New York NY 10019-5905 also: care Susan Magrino Susan Magrino Agency 167 East 73rd St New York NY 10019

TILDEN, ANNE LINCOLN, archivist; b. South Weymouth, Mass., Mar. 2, 1949; d. Nathaniel and Lydia (Haller) T.; m. Wayne Albert Mills, Dec. 2, 1973 (div. Mar. 1985); 1 child, Thalia Tilden Mills. BA, U. Wis., 1972; cert. elem. edn., U. South Fla., 1977-78; MS, Ga. State U., 1989. Cert. tchr. elem. edn., Mass., cert. archivist. Archival asst. Ga. State U., Atlanta, 1989—. Mng. editor Provenance, 1994—. V.p., sec. Emory Garden Condominium Assn., Decatur, Ga., 1987-94; coord. United Way, Pullen Libr., Ga. State U., Atlanta, 1992, 93. Mem. Soc. Am. Archivists, Acad. Cert. Archivists, Soc. Ga. Archivists, Soc. Ala. Archivists, So. Archives Conf., Atlanta Adlerian Soc., Kappa Delta Pi. Home: K5 1111 Clairmont Ave # K5 Decatur GA 30030 Office: Ga State U Spl Collections Pullen Libr 100 Decatur St SE Atlanta GA 30303-3202

TILGER, JUSTINE THARP, research director; b. New Point, Ind., Sept. 11, 1931; d. Joseph Riley and Marcella Lorene (King) Tharp; m. Clarence A. Tilger II, Aug. 22, 1959 (div. Nov. 1972); children: Evelyn Mary, Clarence Arthur III, Joseph Thomas. AB, U. Chgo., 1951; BA, St. Mary's Coll., Notre Dame, Ind., 1954; MA, Ind. U., 1962, PhD, 1971. Mem. Sisters of the Holy Cross, Notre Dame, 1954-58; teaching fellow Ind. U., Bloomington, 1959-61; asst. editor Ind. Mag. History, Bloomington, 1962-64; bookkeeper Touche Ross, Boston, 1974-77; mgr. account services Harvard U., Cambridge, Mass., 1977-81; dir. research and records Bentley Coll., Waltham, Mass., 1982-84; dir. support services Sta. WGBH-TV, Boston, 1985; dir. research Tufts U., Medford, Mass., 1986—; cons. Laduke Assocs., Framingham, Mass., 1972-74, New Eng. Ballet, Sudbury, Mass., 1981-82. v.p. Potter Rd. Sch. Assn., Framingham, 1968-69; chmn. vols. St. Anselm's, Sudbury, 1970-71. Mem. Coun. for Advancement and Support Edn., New Eng. Online User's Group, Am. Prospect Rsch. Assn., New Eng. Devel. Rsch. Assn., Mass. Bus. and Profl. Women (sec. 1981-82), Mensa. Roman Catholic. Home: 15 Auburn St # 6 Framingham MA 01701-4844 Office: Tufts U Packard Hall Medford MA 02155

TILLEMANS, PATRICIA LOUISE, clinical psychologist, psychiatric social worker; b. Milbank, S.D., June 12, 1937; d. Patrick Henry and Gwendolyn Faye (Schultz) T. BA, Mt. St. Mary's Coll., Los Angeles, 1966; MSW, U. So. Calif., 1978; PhD in Clin. Psychology, Cambridge Grad. Sch. Psychology, Los Angeles, 1991. Cert. teacher, Calif.; lic. clin. social worker, Calif.; diplomate clin. social work. Social worker Good Shepherd Residence, San Francisco, Los Angeles, Chgo., 1967-75; coordinator Status Offender Detention Alternative Program, Los Angeles, 1976; clin. social worker Long Beach (Calif.) Neuropsychiat. Inst., 1978-81; supr. Gateways Conditional Release Program, Los Angeles, 1981-85; dir. Gateways Mentally Ill Offender Program, Los Angeles, 1985-90; clin. psychologist Juvenile Hall Svcs. L.A. County Dept. Mental Health, 1991—; pvt. practice, 1981—; mem. legis. com. Mental Health Council, Los Angeles, 1982-84. Mem. Fellowship of Reconciliation, Los Angeles, 1981—. Mem. APA, NASW (cert., steering com. 1982-84), Forensic Mental Health Assn., Calif. Psychol. Assn., L.A. County Psychol. Assn., Ventura County Psychol. Assn., Pax Christi U.S.A., Amnesty Internat. Democrat. Roman Catholic.

TILLER, MARTHA RUSSELL, public relations executive, consultant; b. Temple, Tex., Jan. 20, 1940; d. John Lafayette and Cleo (Davidson) Russell; m. David Clyde Tiller, Nov. 26, 1966; 1 child, John Russell. BFA cum laude, U. Tex., 1961; postgrad. Nat. U. Mex., 1962, Piaget Inst. of Tex. Christian U., 1970. With radio-TV prodns. dept. U. Tex. and Sta. KTBC-TV, Austin, 1959-61; asst. to producer CBS TV, N.Y.C., 1961-64; with Goodson Todman Prodns., N.Y.C., 1964-66; dir. publs. Tex. Fine Arts Commn., Austin, 1967-69; press and social sec. to Mrs. Lyndon B. Johnson, Austin, 1973-76, also spl. asst. to Pres. Lyndon B. Johnson, Office of the Former Pres., Austin, 1972; dir. pub. info. S.W. Ednl. Devel. Lab., Austin, 1976, media specialist, 1969-72, writer, 1967; dir. pub. affairs Glenn, Bozell & Jacobs, Inc., Dallas, 1977-78; dir. pub. affairs U.S. Dept. HEW Region XII, 1978-79; dir. pub. rels. Pla. of Ams. Hotel, Dallas, 1979-82; chmn., chief exec. officer Martha Tiller & Co. Pub. Rels. Counselors, Dallas, 1982—. Creator, producer award-winning video Basic Steps to Fire Safety, 1981. Mem. cultural activities task force Goals for Dallas; mem. Sta. KLRN-TV, Austin, Austin Symphony Orch. Soc., Town Lake Beautification Com. of Austin, Laguna Gloria Art Mus. and Guild, Austin; vice chmn. 8 Arts Ball, TACA Assn., 1981-82, bd. dirs., 1987-88; nat. gifts chmn. Worldwide USO Gala, 1985; vice chmn. James K. Wilson Luncheon, 1982; bd. dirs. Dallas Symphony Orch. League, 1986—, Grand Heritage Ball Commn., 1986, Dallas Opera Women, 1984, Girls Club of Dallas, 1987-89; mem. March of Dimes Women's Aux., Friends of LBJ Libr. (life), women's com. Dallas Civic Opera; bd. govs. Dallas Ballet, 1987-88, Dallas Opera, 1988—; mem. adv. coun. Austin Coll. Communications U. Tex., 1989—. Recipient Golden Key Pub. Rels. award Am. Hotel/Motel Assn., 1982; named Nation's Top Broadcasting Coed, Am. Women Radio and TV, 1959. Mem. Pub. Rels. Soc. Am., Tex. Pub. Rels., Internat. Women's Forum (mem. adv. coun. coll. of communicatoin found. U. Tex. at Austin), Tex. Pub. Rels. Assn. (Best of Tex. award 1981), Women in Communications, Austin Natural Sci. Assn., Mortar Bd., Alpha Epsilon Rho. Office: Martha Tiller & Co 2811 Mckinney Ave Ste 209 Dallas TX 75204-2530

TILLER, OLIVE MARIE, retired church worker; b. St. Paul, Dec. 13, 1920; d. Otto William and Myrtle Alice (Brougham) Foerster; m. Carl William Tiller, June 21, 1940; children: Robert W., Jeanne L. Peterson. BS, U. Minn., 1940. Spl. edn. tchr. Prince Georges County, Md., 1955-63; spl. asst. for profl. svcs. Kendall Demonstration Elem. Sch., Gallaudet Coll., Washington, 1971-78; spl. asst. for program Ch. Women United, N.Y.C., 1979-80; exec. asst. to gen. sec. Nat. Coun. Chs. of Christ in U.S.A., N.Y.C., 1981-87; dep. gen. sec. for coop. Christianity Am. Bapt. Chs. of U.S.A., Valley Forge, Pa., 1987-88. Author: (with Carl W. Tiller) At Calvary, 1994. Mem. Human Rels. Commn., Prince George's County, 1967-73; v.p. Am. Bapt. Chs. U.S.A., Valley Forge, 1976-77; bd. dirs. Am. Leprosy Missions, Greenville, S.C., 1981—, Bapt. Peace Fellowship of N.Am., Memphis, 1984—; mem. Nat. Interreligious Svc. Bd. for Conscientious Objectors, 1991—, treas., 1994—. Recipient Dahlberg Peace award Am. Bapt. Chs., 1991, Valiant Woman award Ch. Women United, 1978, Meeker award Ottawa U., 1995. Baptist. Home: 100 Norman Dr Apt 283 Cranberry Township PA 16066-4235

TILLEY, CAROLYN BITTNER, information manager, technical information specialist; b. Washington, July 29, 1947; d. Klaud Kay and Margaret Louise (Hanson) Bittner; m. Frederick Edwin Dudley, June 18, 1985. B.S., Am. U., 1975; M.L.S., U. Md., 1976. With NIH, 1965-71; statis. research asst. Health Manpower Edn., Bethesda, Md., 1971-72; tech. info. specialist Nat. Library Medicine, Bethesda, Md., 1972-81, head medlars (med. lit. analysis and retrieval system) mgmt. sect., 1981—. Mem. editorial bd.: Med. Reference Services Quar. Mem. CENDI User Edn. Com., Nat. Fed. Abstracting and Info. Svc. Pub. Com. Recipient Merit award NIH, 1984, Rogers award Nat. Libr. Medicine, 1991. Mem. Med. Library Assn. Presbyterian. Office: Nat Libr Medicine 8600 Rockville Pike Bethesda MD 20894-0001

TILLINGHAST, META IONE, civic worker; b. Newark, Nov. 14; d. Ralph Vincent and Florence Virginia (MacDonald) Muldoon; m. Frederick William Tillinghast; children: Anne (Mrs. Robert Riley). Student, Leland Powers Sch. of Spoken Word, Boston. Bd. dirs. Balt. chpt. ARC, 1955-58, chmn. Queen Anne's chpt. 1964-66, nat. bd. govs., 1966-69, Md. state fund chmn., 1969-71, Delmarva div. chmn. mems., funds, 1971-73, vols., 1971-74, coord. community relations Eastern area, 1975-76; chmn. vols. nat. field office (now Eastern field office) ARC, Alexandria, Va., 1976-83, regional chmn. Eastern ops., 1983-86, chmn. vols. Del. chpt., 1986-88, chmn. vols. Nat. Hist. Resources, 1986—, mem. nat. hist. resource com.; dir. ch. plays; chmn. United Fund Baltimore County (Md.) Women's div., 1950. Named vol. of year Md., ARC, 1965; recipient award Gen. Fedn. Women's Clubs, 1952. Mem. Md. No. Dist. Fedn. Women's Clubs (pres. 1953-55), Women's Glyndon Club (pres. 1949-51), Talbot County Women's Club (pres. 1962-64), Women's Ten Hills Club (pres. 1940-42). Home: 500 Nesbit Rd Queenstown MD 21658-0024

TILLMAN, ELIZABETH CARLOTTA, nurse, educator; b. Md., Aug. 31, 1929; d. Walter Monroe and Mozelle Virginia (Shugars) Brown; m. Lloyd A. Tillman, Apr. 16, 1949; children: Lloyd A. Jr., William L., Susan E. Tillman Chaires. Diploma, Md. Gen. Hosp. Sch. Nursing, 1950; student, Towson State U., U. Md., Loyola Coll., Balt., Howard C.C. RN. Psychiatric nurse Spring Grove Hosp. Ctr., Catonsville, Md., 1950; pvt. duty home health nurse Md., 1951-60; dir., tchr., nurse Doughoregan Manor Day Sch., Ellicott City, Md., 1960-80; med.-surg. nurse Woman's Hosp., Balt., 1964, Md. Gen. Hosp., Balt., 1980; nursing instr. Howard County Dept. Edn., Ellicott City, 1981-91; nursing educator Howard County Sch. Tech., 1981-91, Howard County Gen. Hosp., 1981-91; geriatric nurse Lorien Columbia (Md.) Nursing & Rehab. Ctr., 1981-91; home health nurse Md., 1992—. Mem. NEA, Md. State Tchrs. Assn., Md. Gen. Hosp. Alumni Assn., Am. Vocat. Assn., Health Occupations Educators, Md. Vocat. Assn., Phi Eta Sigma, Iota Lambda Sigma.

TILLMAN, KAY HEIDT, real estate executive, commodity broker; b. Tampa, Fla., Jan. 24, 1945; d. Clarence Eugene and Doris (Tyson) Heidt; m. Thomas E. Barnes, Mar. 18, 1967 (div. 1972); children: Britton H., William H.; m. Herbert A. Tillman, Oct. 7, 1988. BA with honors, Rollins Coll., 1975, MS with honors, 1979. Lic. real estate sales person, Fla. Tchr. art Orange County Sch. Bd., Orlando, Fla., 1976-79; pres., owner Internat. Handcraft Ctr., Winter Garden, Fla., 1980-83, Decors Internat., Inc., Winter Garden, Fla., 1980-83, Mohamad & Barnes Investment Co., Orlando, Fla., 1983-89, Eagle Investment Properties, Orlando, 1985-89, Eagle-One Internat., Winter Garden, 1986—; pres., ptnr. Eagle Mktg. Group, Inc., Winter Garden, 1989—; cons. Nigerian Govt., Lagos, Nigeria, 1987-88, 93-94, Mid-East Investment Group, Orlando, Fla., 1986-89, 93-94. Pres. coun. Orlando C. of C., 1987-88; active recreation coun. Bapt. Ch., 1994; founder Loving Hands Outreach to Homeless, 1994. Miss. Fla., Am. Beauty Pageant, Long Beach, Calif., 1975. Mem. Am. Soc. Ind. Sec., Orlando Bd. Realtors, Alpha Chi Omega (v.p. 1966). Republican. Baptist. Home: 215 Valencia Shores Dr Winter Garden FL 34787-2619 Office: Eagle One Internat PO Box 770397 Winter Garden FL 34777-0397

TILLMAN, LINDA D., clinical psychologist; b. Nashville, Nov. 22, 1948; d. Clifford and Sarah Ann (Gardner) T.; m. James F. Bycott, Aug. 26, 1972 (div. 1985); children: Sarah, Rebecca, Valerie; m. Albert W. Bauer, May 5, 1990; stepchildren: Bret, Sarah. BA, Vanderbilt U., 1970, MS, 1978, PhD, 1980. Lic. psychologist, Ga. Asst. dir. Counseling Ctr., Emory U., Atlanta, 1984-86; instr. Atlanta, 1986—; staff psychologist Ga. Regional Hosp., Atlanta, 1986-88; pvt. practice, Atlanta, 1986—. Contbr. articles to newspaper. Leader Girl Scouts U.S.A., Atlanta, 1982-90; active Sierra Club, 1988, 89; chmn. fundraiser North Atlanta High Sch. Parents, Tchr. and Students Assn. Fellow Ga. Psychol. Assn. (membership chmn.); mem. APA. Episcopalian. Home: 3089 Marne Dr NW Atlanta GA 30305-1929 Office: 2004 Cliff Valley Way NE Atlanta GA 30329-2423

TILLOTSON, CAROLYN, state legislator; m. John C. Tillotson. Mem. Kans. Senate, 1993—. Republican. Home: 1606 Westwood Dr Leavenworth KS 66048 Office: Kans State Senate State Capitol Topeka KS 66612*

TILLY, JENNIFER, actress. TV series include: Shaping Up, 1984, Bodyguard, 1990, Key West, 1993; TV movies include: Heads, 1994; films include: No Small Affair, 1984, Moving Violations, 1985, He's My Girl, 1987, Inside Out, 1987, Rented Lips, 1988, High Spirits, 1988, Johnny Be Good, 1988, Remote Control, 1988, The Fabulous Baker Boys, 1989, Let It Ride, 1989, Far From Home, 1989, Scorchers, 1991, Shadow of the Wolf, 1992, Made in America, 1993, At Home With the Webbers, 1993, Double Cross, 1994, Bullets Over Broadway, 1994 (Acad. Awd. nom., Best Supporting Actress), The Getaway, 1994. Office: Agency for the Performing Arts 9000 Sunset Blvd Ste 1200 Los Angeles CA 90069*

TILLY, LOUISE AUDINO, history and sociology educator; b. Orange, N.J., Dec. 13, 1930; d. Hector and Piera (Roffino) Audino; m. Charles Tilly, Aug. 15, 1953; children: Christopher, Kathryn, Laura, Sarah. BA, Rutgers U., 1952; MA, Boston U., 1955; PhD, U. Toronto, 1974. From instr. to asst. prof. Mich. State U., East Lansing, 1972-75; from asst. prof. to prof. U. Mich., Ann Arbor, 1975-84; Michael E. Gellert prof. history and sociology New Sch. for Social Rsch., N.Y.C., 1984-94, chair com. hist. studies, 1984—, Michael E. Gellert prof. history and sociology, 1994—; assoc. dir. studies Ecole des Hautes Etudes en Scis. Sociales, Paris, 1979, 80, 88; fellow Shelby Cullom Davis Ctr., Princeton (N.J.) U., 1978; vis. mem. Inst. for Advanced Study, Princeton, 1987-88; fellow Ctr. for Advanced Studies Behavioral Scis., 1991-92; vis. scholar Russell Sage Found., 1994-95; bd. dirs. Social Scis. Rsch. Coun., N.Y.C., 1983-86. Author: Politics and Class in Milan, 1881-1901, 1992; co-author: The Rebellious Century, 1975, Women, Work and Family, 1978, rev. edit., 1987; co-editor, co-author: Class Conflict and Collective Action, 1981, Women, Politics and Change, 1990; co-editor: The European Experience of Declining Fertility: The Quiet Revolution, 1992; also articles. Active com. on women's employment and related social issues Nat. Acad. Scis., 1981-86, chmn., co-editor report Panel on Tech. and Women's Employment, 1984-86. Grantee Rockefeller Found., 1974-76, Am. Philos. Soc., 1977-78, 85-86, Russell Sage Found., 1985-86; Guggenheim Found. fellow, 1991-92. Mem. Am. Hist. Assn. (coun. 1985-87, pres. elect. 1992, pres. 1993), Social Sci. History Assn.(pres. 1981-82), Coun. on European Studies (exec. com. 1980-83), Berkshire Conf. Women Historians. Democrat. Home: 5 E 22nd St Apt 5K New York NY 10010 Office: Com on Hist Studies 64 University Pl New York NY 10003-4520

TILMAN, FRANCES HARDY, accountant; b. Dinwiddie, Va., July 25, 1932; d. William Daniel Hardy and Clarinda (Campbell) Richardson; m. Samuel Cole Tilman, May 19, 1962; 1 child, Mary Novella. Dataprocessing systems analyst Commonwealth of Va., Richmond, 1949-72; kindergarten aide Powhatan (Va.) Sch. System, 1977-81; eligibility Powhatan DSS, 1982-84; fiscal officer VA compensation, Richmond, 1984—. Sunday sch. tchr. Poole Ch., Church Road, Va., 1945-49, Highland Park Ch., Richmond, 1955-62, Mau Meml. Ch., Powhatan, 1965-75. Mem. Nat. Machine Accts. Assn., Garden Club. Home: PO Box 134 Powhatan VA 23139-0134 Office: Compensation Bd PO Box 710 Richmond VA 23206-0710

TILSON, DOROTHY RUTH, word processing executive; b. Bloomsburg, Pa., Mar. 24, 1918; d. Roy Earl and Mary Etta (Masteller) Derr; m. Irving Tilson, Sept. 1949. BS, Bloomsburg U., 1940. Tchr. Madison Consol. Sch., Jerseytown, Pa., 1940-42; gage checker Phila. Ordinance Gage Lab., 1942-43; tabulating asst. Remington Rand, Phila., N.Y.C., 1943-46; copy writer Sears Roebuck, Phila., N.Y.C., 1946-48; statis. asst. Ford Internat., N.Y.C., 1949-56; word processing adminstrv. asst. Coopers & Lybrand, N.Y.C., 1956-91. Life mem. Rep. Senatorial Inner Circle, Washington, 1987—. Mem. Am. Movement for World Govt. (sec. 1991—), N.Y. Theosophical Soc. (libr. 1969—), UN Assn.-USA (mem. global policy project which includes internat. econ. governance and human rights). Office: Coopers & Lybrand 1301 Ave Of The Americas New York NY 10019-6022

TILSON, VEANN, school system administrator; b. Hugo, Okla., Sept. 19, 1954; d. Lowell and Noveline (Martin) Burgess; m. Jay Tilson, Aug. 4, 1972; children: Lynn Tilson Conway, Sandra Lea. AA, Hillsdale Coll., 1976; BS in Elem. Edn., Southeastern Okla. State U., 1977; MA in Reading, U. Okla., 1980; MA in Adminstrn., U. Mo., St. Louis, 1992. Cert. elem. tchr., reading specialist, elem. adminstr., Mo. Tchr. Hugo Pub. Schs., 1977-78, Pleasant Grove Sch., Shawnee, Okla., 1978-80; tchr., adminstr. Lonedell (Mo.) R-14 Sch., 1981—; grant reader Dept. Elem. and Secondary Edn., Jefferson City, Mo., 1988—. Contbr.: Tem, 1985-93. Grantee Dept. Elem. and Secondary Edn., Jefferson City, 1988-91, 88-90, 91-94. Mem. NEA, ASCD, Delta Kappa Gamma. Baptist. Office: Lonedell R-14 Sch HC62 Box 14 Lonedell MO 63060

TILTON, BERNICE SHEPPARD (MRS. EARLE BARTON TILTON), civic worker; b. Chgo.; d. Samuel Charles and Elizabeth (Keith) Sheppard; Mus.B., Wis. Coll. Music, 1954; m. Earle Barton Tilton, Mar. 12, 1940. Performed as soloist and two-piano team for orgns., Ill., Wis., Fla., 1947—. Pres., Symphony Club, Clearwater, Fla., 1958-60; founder Mus. Arts Soc., Clearwater, 1960, pres., 1960-62, 81-83; chpt. pres. Delta Omicron, 1964-66, Fla. chmn. alumnae-at-large, 1965-67, internat. v.p. alumnae, internat. bd. dirs., 1967-71; pres. Fla. West Coast Panhellenic Assn., 1967-68, chpt. adv. bd., 1968—. Bd. dirs. Clearwater Community Concert Assn., 1963-74. Recipient Gold Star Delta Omicron, 1967, Recognition award, 1971. Mem. Nat. Soc. Arts and Letters (local sec., v.p. 1972-73), Henry Solomon Lehr Soc. (life), Tampa Bay Rsch. Inst. (bd. dirs. 1991—), Delta Omicron (alumnae chpt. pres. 1973-74, 81-84, rec. sec. 1985-88). Home: 510 13th Ave NW Largo FL 34640

TILTON, KATHLEEN JOAN, English language educator; b. Denver, Feb. 14, 1953; d. Warren deBlois and Virginia (Haught) T. BA, Adams State Coll., 1974; MA, Colo. State U., 1982. Elem. tchr. various schs., 1974-88; instr. Colo. State U., Ft. Collins., 1982-83, Regis Coll., Denver, 1983-85, Aurora (Colo.) Community Coll., 1985-87, L.A. Pierce Community Coll., 1990, Mission Community Coll., Santa Clara, Calif., 1990—, West Valley Community Coll., Saratoga, Calif., 1990—, Skyline Coll., San Mateo, Calif.; owner Tilton Typesetting Co., Denver, 1985-89; mgr. Graphic Concepts, Denver, 1990; office mgr. Lovewell, Palo Alto, Calif., 1990—. Asst. editor Colo. State Review, 1980-82; editor: Genesis Adams State Coll., 1973, Tilton House; contbr. numerous poems and short stories to literary mags. and jours. Mem. Jr. League. Mem. AAUW. Republican.

TIMBERS, ROSEANN S., association executive; b. Solomon, Alaska, June 2, 1952; d. Lloyd H. and Adrienne (Newcomb) Tarpenning; m. Bryan P. Timbers, Aug. 3, 1974; children: Gregory P., Kirsten M. AA in Acctg., Bryant & Stratton, San Jose, Calif., 1972; student, U. Alaska, 1972, 80-81. Pres. Solomon Native Corp., Nome, Alaska, 1980—, Solomon Trad. Coun., Nome, Alaska, %. Chairperson Western Alaska Coun., Nome, 1992—; treas. North Northwest Mayors Conf., Nome, 1993—; bd. dirs. Alaska Fedn. Natives, Anchorage, 1990—; v.p. Kawerak, Inc., Nome, 1986—; bd. dirs. Bering Straits Native Corp., Nome, 1986—; del. Inuit Circumpolar Conf., Anchorage, 1986—; mem. State of Alaska Gov.'s Task Force on Govt. Roles, 1990-92, Gov.'s Commn. for Adminstrn. of Justice, 1980-84. Address: PO Box 243 Nome AK 99762

TIMINS, BONITA LEA, home health care administrator, curator; b. Scranton, Pa., Nov. 26, 1951; d. Edward Joseph and Mary Loretta (Lake) T. BS in Art Edn., Kutztown U., 1973; MA in Art Edn. magna cum laude, Marywood Coll., 1976, MA in Psychology magna cum laude, 1990; PhD in Metaphysics, Am. Internat. U., 1994. Art tchr. Scranton Sch. Dist., 1974-77; prodn. asst. Garan, Inc., N.Y.C., 1977-78, Marty Gutmacher, Inc., N.Y.C., 1979-81, R.R.J. Industries, N.Y.C., 1981-82; prodn. mgr. Double Dutch Sportswear, N.Y.C., 1982-84; MR/CLA supr. Allied Svcs., Scranton, 1984-86; home health care coord. Scranton, 1986—; ind. curator, Scranton, 1992—; chemistry tutor U. Scranton, 1994—. Com. woman Dem. Party, Scranton, 1994; fundraiser Am. Cancer Soc., Scranton, 1993; participant group study exchange to Brazil, Rotary Internat., 1994; pub. rels. chair Hook O'Malley Race Against Cancer, Am. Cancer Soc., 1994. Mem. Art Student's League N.Y.C. (life), Psi Chi, Kappa Pi. Roman Catholic. Home: 2108 Jackson St Scranton PA 18504-1610

TIMKO, MARY CATHERINE, medical social worker, nurse; b. Hazleton, Pa., Mar. 7, 1949; d. John and Anna (Felock) T. Diploma in Nursing, Sacred Heart Hosp., Allentown, Pa., 1970; BA in Psychology, Ea. Coll., 1980; MSW, Marywood Coll., 1990. Cert. bereavement counselor. Staff nurse Sacred Heart Hosp., 1970-74, Lehigh Valley Hosp., Allentown, 1974-81, 83-84; staff nurse Lehigh Valley Vis. Nurses Assn., Allentown, 1984-90, med. social worker, 1990—; mem. adv. bd. Lehigh Valley Brain Tumor Support Group, Allentown, 1992—. Vol. Trinidarian Missions, DeLisle, Miss., 1981-83; mem. adv. bd. Lehigh County Office Drug and Alcohol Abuse, Allentown, 1993—, chair allocations com., 1994—; bd. dirs. Am. Cancer Soc., Allentown, 1993—, chair svc./rehab. com., 1994—. Mem. NASW, Lehigh Valley Assn. Home Health Social Workers. Roman Catholic. Home: 1703 S Albert St Apt 7 Allentown PA 18103

TIMM, DEBORAH A., critical care nurse; b. Sandusky, Ohio, Nov. 8, 1953; d. Eugene and Shirley F. (Lane) Lentz; m. Thomas R. Timm, June 17, 1973; children: Dawn Marie, Rebecca Lynn. AA in Bus., Bowling Green State U., Huron, Ohio, 1974; lic. practical nurse, Sandusky Sch. Practical Nursing, 1978; diploma, Providence Hosp. Sch. Nursing, Sandusky, 1990. RN, Ohio; cert. basic trauma life support, advanced cardiac life support. Emergency room nurse Providence Hosp.; pediatric advanced life support, contingency Bellevue Hosp. Mem. AACN (nat. and local chpt.), Providence Hosp. Sch. Nursing Alumni Assn.

TIMME, KATHRYN PEARL, secondary education educator; b. Houston, Feb. 15, 1934; d. William Emil and Neoma Leila (Harvey) T. BA, Rice U., 1956; MA, U. Houston, 1965. Cert. secondary tchr., Tex. Tchr. Houston Ind. Sch. Dist., 1956—; rsch. fellow Houston Maths. and Sci. Consortium, 1986-87. Author: Horticultural Chemistry, 1976, Chemistry of The Sea, 1977, Textile Chemistry, 1978, Geochemistry, 1982, Exploring Electrolytes, 1987. Grantee NSF, 1970, 72, Houston Bus. Com., 1987, Impact II, 1989. Mem. Am. Chem. Soc., Phi Beta Kappa (Rice chpt.), Phi Alpha Theta. Episcopalian. Office: Robert E Lee High Sch 6529 Beverlyhill St Houston TX 77057-6499

TIMMER, BARBARA, lawyer; b. Holland, Mich., Dec. 13, 1946; d. John Norman and Barbara Dee (Folensbee) T. BA, Hope Coll., Holland, Mich., 1969; JD, U. Mich., 1975. Bar: Mich. 1975, U.S. Supreme Ct. Assoc. McCrosky, Libner, VanLeuven, Muskegon, Mich., 1975-78; apptd. to Mich. Women Commn. by Gov., 1976-79; staff counsel subcom. commerce, consumer & monetary affairs Ho. Govt. Ops. Com., 1979-82, 85-86; exec. v.p. NOW, 1982-84; legis. asst. to Rep. Geraldine Ferraro, 1984; atty. Office Gen. Counsel Fed. Home Loan Bank Bd., 1986-89; gen. counsel Com. on Banking, Fin. and Urban affairs U.S. Ho. of Reps., Washington, 1989-92; asst. gen. counsel, dir. govt. affairs ITT Corp., Washington, 1992—; bd. dirs. ITT Fed. Bank, San Francisco. Recipient Affordable Housing award Nat. Assn. Real Estate Brokers, 1990, Acad. of Women Achievers, YWCA, 1993. Mem. ABA (bus. law, exec. coun. adminstrv. law and regulatory practice sects.), Mich. Bar Assn., Fed. Bar Assn. (exec. coun. of banking law com.), Women in Housing and Fin. (bd. dirs. 1992-94, gen. counsel 1994—), Supreme Ct. Hist. Soc. Episcopalian. Office: ITT Corp 1600 M St NW Washington DC 20036

TIMMER, MARGARET LOUISE (PEG TIMMER), educator; b. Osmond, Nebr., July 4, 1942; d. John Henry and Julia Adeline (Schilling) Borgmann; m. Charles B. Timmer, May 23, 1964 (div. June 1990); children: Jill Marie, Mark Jon. AA, N.E. Community Coll., Norfolk, Nebr., 1987; BA in Edn., K-12 art endorsement, Wayne (Nebr.) State U., 1988; MEd, Bank Street Coll./Parsons Sch. Design, N.Y.C., 1992. Cert. tchr., Nebr. Bookkeeper Goeres Electric, Osmond, 1960-61; tel. operator Northwestern Bell, Norfolk, 1961-64; with want advt. dept. Washington Post, 1964-65; saleswoman Jeannes Fashion Fabrics, Norfolk, 1970-72, Tripps, Norfolk, 1986-87; office and fin. mgr. Tim's Plumbing & Heating Inc., Norfolk, 1972-86; tchr. art Norfolk Cath. Schs., 1988—, mem. bd., 1985-88; instr. art history N.E. Community Coll., 1992—; mem. youth art bd. Norfolk Art Ctr., 1988—. One-woman show Uptown Restaurant, Norfolk, 1993; exhibited in group shows Sioux City (Iowa) Art Ctr., 1988, Columbus (Nebr.) Art Ctr., 1993. Mem. choir St. Mary's Cath. Ch., Norfolk, 1991—; mem. Norfolk Community Choir, 1991; bd. dirs. Norfolk Community Concerts Assn., 1984-87; treas. Norfolk Cath. Booster Club, 1985-86; leader 4-H, Madison County, 1973-78; judge art show Laurel (Nebr.) Women's Club, 1988. Mem. Nat. Art Edn. Assn. (presenter 1987), Nebr. Art Edn. Assn. (3d place award 1988). Home: Box 239 83729 Warnerville Dr Norfolk NE 68701-9758 Office: Norfolk Cath Schs 2300 Madison Ave Norfolk NE 68701-4535

TIMMONS, ANDREA CARROLL, publisher, public relations professional, paralegal, photographer, author; b. Lockesburg, Ark., Jan. 8, 1945; d. Jake Charles and Lola Evelyn (Hale) Carroll; m. Ronald William Jackson, Dec. 23, 1967 (div. Jan. 1978); m. Franklin Wayne Timmons, Aug. 3, 1991. B.S. in Edn., Henderson State U., 1967; postgrad. in journalism La. State U., 1981-82. Phys. edn. tchr. Lamar Consol. Schs., Ark., 1967-68; field advisor Ark. Post coun. Girl Scouts U.S., Pine Bluff, 1969-74, pub. rels. dir. Ouachita coun., Little Rock, 1974-79; program and pub. rels. dir. Baton Rouge Area YWCA, 1979-81; editor Bayou Country Publs., Plaquemine, La., 1981-83; communications dir. Am. Lung Assn. of Ark., Little Rock, 1984-91; former owner, operator TLC Pet Care Svc.; owner, pub., author Pinnacle-Mission Press, Charlo, Mont., 1993—; editor: (tng. manual) Safe Homes Project for Battered Women, 1981; Ark. Women's Rights OURS newspaper, 1985-86, Ark. chpt. Sierra Club newspaper, 1988-90. Recipient Excellence in color slide photography awards Ouachita Girl Scout Coun. and Girl Scouts U.S., 1978, Feature Writing award Am. Pen Women, 1992; Outstanding Svc. award Baton Rouge Area YWCA, 1980. Mem. COSMEP (Internat. Assn. Ind. Pub.), Ark. Press Women (feature writing awards, 2 in 1982, 3 in 1983, 2 interview awards 1984, 2 broadcast awards 1984, 87, writing editing and interviewing, 1985, 86), Internat. Platform Assn., Authors of Flathead. Avocations: movies, hiking, travel. Author: Concerned Citizens' Guide: How to Use the Media to Affect Public Opinion, 1991, Book Promotion Kit for Authors, 1993. Office: Pinnacle-Mission Press PO Box 190 Charlo MT 59824

TIMMONS, ANN ELIZABETH, school system administrator; b. Bridgeton, N.J., Jan. 17, 1940; d. Elwood Merton Getsinger and Mary Ellen (Hickman) Getsinger Lore; m. James A. Timmons Sr., July 17, 1959; children: James Albert Jr., Gregory Alan, David Austin, Christopher Andrew. BA, Rowan Coll., 1976, MA, 1985; EdD, Nova U., 1993. 1st grade tchr. Maurice River Twp. Bd. Edn., Port Elizabeth, N.J., 1976-82, basic skills coord., 1982-84, adminstrv. asst., 1984-85, sch. bus. adminstr., sec. bd., 1985—. Music dir. Port Elizabeth United Meth. Ch., 1974—. Mem. N.J. Sch. Bus. Officers (so. trustee 1991-94, 2d v.p. 1994). Office: Maurice River Twp Sch Dist Drawer D Port Elizabeth NJ 08348

TIMMONS, BARBARA ALICE, geriatrics nurse; b. Muncie, Ind., Dec. 11, 1932; d. John and Audrey Muriel (Halleck) Schumacher; m. Jerry Alyn Timmons, Apr. 7, 1951; children: Gary Alyn, Karen, Benjamin. Diploma in nursing, Muncie Sch. Practical Nursing, 1983. LPN. Charge nurse Maple Village Nursing Home, Middletown, Ind., 1983-84, Millers Merry Manor, Middletown, Ind., 1984-85, Sylvesters Nursing Home, Muncie, 1985-87; dir. nursing Countryside Healthcare, Muncie, 1987-90, med. records, 1990-91; nursing adminstrn. Liberty Village, Muncie, 1991—. Mem. Ind. Health Care Assn. Dirs. Nursing (legis. lobbying com. 1989-90).

TIMMONS, DONNA FRANCES, music educator; b. Rockville Centre, N.Y.; d. Donald Francis and Eudrice Lorraine (Hacket) T. MusB, The Julliard Sch.; MusM, The Juilliard Sch.; postgrad., Adelphi U. Cert. music tchr., K-12. Music dir. Cathedral Sch. of St. Mary, Garden City, N.Y., 1984-86; music tchr. Berkeley County Schs., Moncks Corner, S.C., 1986-91; choral dir. Woodstock (Va.) Mid. Sch., 1991—, Central High Sch., Woodstock, 1991—; conductor Garden City Community Orchestra, 1980-81; organist, choir dir. Pinopolis (S.C.) United Meth. Ch., 1987-91; musical dir. Cen. High Sch. Musical Prodns., Woodstock, 1992—; owner, pres. Four Ten Pub./Prodns., Harrisonburg, Va., 1988—. Exec. producer, composer, lyricist: (album) Don't Be a Fool, Stay in School, 1988, Voices of the Heart, 1991; writer/composer: (TV comml.) several including Save the Turtles, 1991 (Gold Addy award 1991), Stay in School, 1989 (Bronze Addy award 1989); co-creator/composer: (TV film) Synchronize, Let's Come Together, 1990. Internat. Exch. student to Italy, 1970; recipient scholarships Juilliard Pre-Coll. Div., N.Y.C., 1962-71, Juilliard Sch., 1972-77, grad. fellowship, 1975-77, piano pedagogy asst., 1975-76; grantee S.C. Commn. on Alcohol and Drug Abuse, 1990-91; recipient Outstanding Contbn. Sch. Prevention award Berkeley County Commn. on Alcohol and Drug Abuse, 1990, Magic Tchr. award S.C. Mid. Sch. Assn., 1988. Mem. Am. Assn. Composers, Authors and Pubs., Va. Edn. Assn., Va. Music Edn. Assn., Music Educators Nat. Conf., Shenandoah County Edn. Assn. (Outstanding Svc. award 1993), Delta Kappa Gamma.

TIMMONS, NATALIE EVE, public relations executive, marketing professional; b. Atlanta, June 9, 1962; d. George Emile and Linda Eve (Cloutier) Marquis; m. William A. Timmons Jr., June 23, 1984; 1 child, George Marquis. BA, U. N.H., 1984. V.p., gen. mgr. Merrill Assocs., Inc., Kingston, N.H., 1983-89; community rels. dir. Home Health VNA, Haverhill, Mass., 1989-93; prin. Comms. Coach, Kingston, 1993—; freelance comms. cons. and copywriter, 1987-93; mem. Plaistow Area Commerce Exch. Mem. GFWC Kingston Area Jr. Women's Club, 1983-87; vol. dispatcher Kingston Fire Dept., 1987-89; chair Haverhill br. Am. Heart Assn., 1989-92; mem. Kingston Mcpl. Budget Com., 1989-92; co-chair Haverhill Community Health Network, 1992-93; pres., bd. dirs. Haverhill YWCA. Mem. Pub. Rels. Soc. Am. (mem. Yankee chpt.), Greater Haverhill C. of C., Haverhill Exch. Club, Haverhill Quota Club. Home: 96 New Boston Rd Kingston NH 03848-3323 Office: Communications Coach 96 New Boston Rd Kingston NH 03848-3323

TIMMONS, SHIRLEY M., nursing administrator, consultant; b. Pamplico, S.C., Mar. 14, 1956; d. Roy and Eva (Hyman) T.; 1 child, Eve Nichole Bowers. BSN, U. S.C., 1978, M of Nursing, 1988. Occupl. health cons. Allied Fibers, Columbia, S.C., 1980-82; health svcs. adminstr. Westinghouse NFD, Columbia, 1982-85; PRN staff nurse Lexington Med. Ctr., West Columbia, S.C., 1985-86; home health nurse Tri-County Home Health, Lexington, S.C., 1986-88; coord. nursing edn. Midlands Area Health Edn. Ctr., Columbia, 1988-94; assoc. dir. S.C. Healthcare Recruitment and Retention Ctr., Columbia, 1994—; staff nurse Richland Meml. Hosp., Columbia, 1978-79; PRN staff nurse Bapt. Med. Ctr., Columbia, 1979-80; mem. adj. faculty coll. nursing U. S.C., 1988—; mem. S.C. Tuberculosis Task Force, 1993—, S.C. Health Occupations Edn. Adv. Com., 1994—. Bd. dirs. blood svcs. ARC, Columbia, 1994—. Mem. Am. Soc. Healthcare Edn. & Tng., S.C. Nurses' Assn., S.C. Hosp. Assn. (mem. soc. educators 1988—, edn. counselor project LINC ladders in nursing and allied health careers 1994—), S.C. C. of C., S.C. Women's Consortium, Columbia C. of C. Home: 454 Forest Grove Cir Columbia SC 29210 Office: SC Healthcare Recruitment & Retention Ctr 1331 Elmwood Ave Ste 160 Columbia SC 29202

TIMPANO, ANNE, museum director, art historian; b. Osaka, Japan, June 17, 1950; d. A.J. and Margaret (Smith) T. BA, Coll. William and Mary, 1972; MA, George Washington U., 1983. Program mgmt. asst. Nat. Mus. Am. Art, Washington, 1977-86; dir. The Columbus (Ga.) Mus., 1986-93, DAAP Galleries, U. Cin., 1993—; grant reviewer Inst. Mus. Svcs., Washington, 1988—, Ga. Coun. for Arts, Atlanta, 1988-91. Mem. 1992 Quincentenary Commn., Columbus, 1987-92. Recipient David Lloyd Kreeger award George Washington U., 1980. Mem. Am. Assn. Mus. (surveyor mus. assessment program), Assn. of Coll. and Univ. Mus. and Galleries, Coll. Art Assn., Midwest Mus. Conf. Roman Catholic. Home: 30 Bent Tree Dr Fairfield OH 45014 Office: U Cin PO Box 210016 Cincinnati OH 45221-0016

TIMPTE, SHANNON TALBERT, public relations executive; b. Bristol, Va., Feb. 11, 1942; d. Harry Irvin and Isabella Lois (Calhoun) Talbert; m. John Chandler Hopkins, Sept. 19, 1964 (div. Dec. 1981); children: John Chandler, David Calhoun, Nancy Talbert; m. Rudolph Gerhardt Timpte, Nov. 7, 1987. BA, Fla. State U., 1963; MA in Comm. Studies, St. Mary's U., 1993. Accredited pub. rels. profl. Legal sec. Smith, Swift, Currie McGhee Hancock, Atlanta, 1964-65; mgr. proxy dept., adminstrv. asst. Courts and Co., Atlanta, 1965-68; adminstrv. asst. customer complaints Budget Rent-a-Car, San Antonio, 1968-82; sec. nuclear medicine computed tonogora div. Univ. Tex. Health Sci. Ctr., San Antonio, 1981-82; mgr. pub. rels. dept., adminstrv. asst. Barshop Enterprises, Inc., San Antonio, 1983-85; spl. asst., fundraiser legal staff State Sen. Cyndi Krier, San Antonio, 1985; with news bur., spl. programs, community rels. comm./mktg., property and casualty claims comm., bus. process integration United Svcs. Automobile Assn., San Antonio, 1985—; mem. United Svcs. Automobile Assn. Spkrs. Bur. and mentor program. Mistress of ceremonies Channel 12 TV, 1959; contbr. articles to profl. jours. Bd. dirs., newsletter editor, mem. spl. events com., image brochures and ads com., stategic plans, bench marking, comm. audits/surveys United Way, 1986-87; co-chmn. Arneson River Restoration Commn., 1985-86; bd. dirs. San Antonio Coun. on Alcoholism, 1986-87; mem. fundraising com. San Antonio Symphony; mem. illiteracy prevention com. San Antonio Target 90; active Heart of Gold Dinner Am. Heart Assn., 1994. Recipient Friend of Edn. award Northside Ind. Tchrs. Assn., 1979-80. Mem. PRSA (sec. bd. 1988-90, v.p. programs 1993, v.p. membership 1994, pres. 1995), No. San Antonio and C. of C. (chmn. task force, chair bus. book libr. campaign, chair image com.), Women in Comm. (v.p. bd. 1989-90), Internat. Assn. Bus. Communicators, NAFE, Am. Mktg. Assn., Toastmasters Internat. (area gov. dist. 56 1994-95). Republican. Methodist. Office: USAA 9800 Fredericksburg Rd San Antonio TX 78288-0002

TINCHER, BARBARA JEAN, not for profit fund-raiser; b. Shawano, Wis., June 9, 1963; d. George William and Phyllis Jean (Albrecht) T. Student, Ripon Coll., 1983-84; BA, U. Minn., 1988. Cert. theatre adminstrn. Artistic and gen. adminstrv. asst. Pepsico Internat. Performing Arts Festival, Purchase, N.Y., 1986; programming and press asst. Riverside Studios, Hammersmith, England, 1987; club coord. Guthrie Theater, Mpls., 1986-88; devel. assoc. Huntington Theatre Co., Boston, 1988-89, annual fund coord., 1989-90; annual fund mgr. L.A. (Calif.) Theatre Ctr., 1990, dir. devel., 1991; ind. fund raising cons. L.A., 1991; bd. devel. specialist AIDS Project L.A., Calif., 1991-94, dir. bd. relations, 1994—; mem. Women in Devel. Greater Boston, 1989-90; del. Conf. About Vols. Regional Theatres, Milw., 1990; participant fall fund raising day Nat. Soc. Fund Raising Execs., L.A., 1990, Non-Profit Mgmt. Inst. Bd. Devel. Tng., San Diego, 1992, Nat. Ctr. for Non-Profit Bds. Annual Conf., 1994. Guest panelist AIDS Vision Cable Show, 1992. Mem. Alpha Xi Delta. Methodist. Home: 422 Western Ave Glendale CA 91201-2838 Office: AIDS Project Los Angeles 1313 N Vine St Los Angeles CA 90028

TINER, DONNA TOWNSEND, nurse; b. Memphis, Dec. 14, 1947; d. Jack Edwin and Anne Coolidge (Burleigh) Townsend; m. Clinton William Matson, Aug. 30, 1969 (div. 1976); m. Dow David Tiner, Apr. 15, 1978; children: Jeffrey David, Cynthia Leigh, Catherine Renee. Grad., Bapt. Meml. Hosp. Sch. Nursing, Memphis, 1969. RN, Ark.; cert. ACLS. Nurse Bapt. Meml. Hosp.,, Memphis, 1969, New Bern (N.C.) Surgical Assocs., 1970-71, Bapt. Meml. Hosp, 1971-72, Meml. Hosp., North Little Rock, Ark., 1972-73, Bapt. Med. Ctr., North Little Rock, Ark., 1974-87; practice nursing specializing in post-anesthesia care Little Rock, 1987-89; post-anesthesia care specialist Little Rock Surgery Ctr. (formerly Freeway Surgery Ctr.), 1989—. Instr., ARC, 1975—; leader Park Hill Bapt. Ch., 1986—. 1st. lt. U.S. Army Med. Unit 1976-79. Mem. Am. Soc. Post Anesthesia Nurses (chartered), Ark. Post Anesthesia Care Nurses, Alumnae Assn. Bapt. Hosp. Sch. Nursing. Republican. Home: 12 Knights Bridge Rd North Little Rock AR 72116-6535

TING, HELENA MARIA, management consultant, educator; b. Hong Kong, July 24, 1954; came to U.S., 1966; d. K.W. and P.K. (Lou) Wong; m. Alan Ting, Mar. 20, 1990. BA, San Francisco State U., 1978, MA, 1983; D in Orgn., U. San Francisco, 1991. Edn. dir. Presbyn. Ch., San Francisco, 1982-86; prodn. mgr. Integrated Device Tech., Santa Clara, Calif., 1986-91; orgnl. devel. cons. Nat. Semiconductor, Santa Clara, Calif., 1991—; cons. Bay Area Sch. Dist., 1994—. Trustee Pacific Grad. Sch. of Psychology, Palo Alto, Calif., 1992—; mem. Bay Area Orgn. Devel., 1989. Mem. ASTD, Art Mus. Soc. Home: 1473 Parkwood Dr San Mateo CA 94403

TINGLE, KATHY CARTWRIGHT, school administrator; b. Lexington, Ky., May 25, 1961; d. Kenneth Cartwright and Marietta (Canter) Martin; m. M. Keith Tingle, July 12, 1980; children: Marshal Keith, Alexander Kenneth. BS, Georgetown Coll., 1984, MA in Edn., 1987; Adminstrv. Endorsement, Morehead State U., 1992. Cert. instrnl supr. elem. and secondary schs. Elem. tchr. Grant County Schs., Williamstown, Ky., 1984-89; early childhood tchr. Bath County Sch., Owingsville, Ky., 1990-92, dir. spl. edn. and early childhood programs, 1992—; task force cert. of early childhood, Ky. Dept. Edn., Frankfort, 1993, assoc. Regional Svc. Ctr., 1993, early childhood cons., 1992—. Mem. Coun. for the Arts, Owingsville, 1991, Owingsville Homemakers, 1991; dir. Owingsville Community Choir, 1991—. Mem. Ky. Early Childhood Assn., So. Early Childhood Assn., ASCD, Nat. Mid. Sch. Assn., Ky. Assn. Sch. Adminstrs., Phi Delta Kappa. Democrat. Baptist. Home: 181 Sherman Ct Owingsville KY 40360 Office: Bath County Bd Edn 459 W Main St Owingsville KY 40360

TINGLEY, JUDITH CLARK, psychologist; b. Norwich, Conn., Nov. 18, 1938; d. John Kinney Tingley and Regina (Fenton) Burleson; m. Theodore G. Dodenhoff, June 18, 1960 (div. May 1977); children: James, Steven, David, Sara; m. Michael Fairchild Killion, Mar. 23, 1985. BSN, U. Mich., 1960; MSN, U. Wash., 1962; PhD, Ariz. State U., 1978. Lic. psychologist, Ariz. Asst. prof. nursing U. Mich., Ann Arbor, 1967-69; clin. specialist St. Joseph's Hosp., Phoenix, 1970-73; grad. rsch. asst. Ariz. State U., Tempe, 1973-78, adj. faculty mem., 1978-81; pvt. practice Ctr. for Brief Psychotherapy, Phoenix, 1978—; corp. cons. on comm., 1985—. Author: Genderflex, 1993; contbr. articles to profl. publs. Bd. dirs. Valley Big Sisters, Phoenix, 1982-85, Phoenix City Club, 1985-88. Mem. ASTD (treas. 1994—), Nat. Speakers Assn. (bd. dirs. 1989-90), Toastmasters. Democrat. Roman Catholic. Office: 727 E Bethany Home Rd C-102 Phoenix AZ 85014

TINKLE, CAROLYN J., state legislative staff member; b. Henderson, Ky., Oct. 27, 1940; d. Frank Mason and Hazel LaVerne (Potts) Ploch; m. Charles Everman Tinkle II, Feb. 11, 1961; children: Charles Everman III, Christopher Mason, Amanda Lynn Tinkle Rowe. Student in Bus., Ind. U., 1958-60. Legal sec. King, Deep & Branaman, Henderson, Ky., 1960-61; sec. Jewell Tea Co., Chgo., 1961-73; sec. to state chmn. Rep. Nat. Com., Indpls., 1973-80; sec. to chmn. majority caucus Ind. State Senate, Indpls., 1980-82, sec. supr., 1982-83, legis. asst. to pres. pro tempore, 1983-85, prin. sec., 1985—. Editor: (newsletter) Reaching Out; editor, pub.: (newsletter) The Legislative Administrator, 1988. Recipient Sagamore of Wabash State Ind., 1989; named to Hon. Order Ky. Colonels, 1987. Mem. Am. Soc. Legis. Clks. and Secs. (editor, pub. Roster 1987, sec.-treas. 1989-90, v.p. 1990-91, pres. nat. orgn. 1991-92). Home: 404 Beech Park Dr Greenwood IN 46142 Office: Ind State Senate 200 W Washington Indianapolis IN 46204

TINNEL MATHENY, BETTY JENNETTE, office systems educator; b. Gauley Bridge, W.Va., Dec. 26, 1937; d. Eugene Craig and M. Sybil (Murphy) Tinnel; m. John Erwin Matheny, Aug. 5, 1960; children: Melinda Sue, Jonathan Eric. BS in Bus. Edn., W.Va. Inst. Tech., 1959; MA in Bus. Edn., Marshall U., 1965; postgrad., Va. Poly. Inst. and State U., 1975. Cert. tchr. bus. edn., Va., W.Va. Tchr. bus. Nicholas County High Sch., Summersville, W.Va., 1959-60; sec. Autonetics div. North Am. Aviation, Cape Canaveral, Fla., 1960-61; tchr. bus. Ripley (W.Va.) High Sch., 1961-62, Richwood (W.Va.) High Sch., 1963-68; assoc. prof. office systems tech. Wytheville (Va.) Community Coll., 1969—. Contbr. articles to profl. jours. Fin. sec. Wytheville Bapt. Ch., 1972-93, treas. women's missionary union, 1984-87, bd. dirs. 1987-94; leader Troop 625 Girl Scouts U.S., Wytheville, 1974-76, 1974-76; bd. dirs. United Way of Wythe County, 1981-87, treas. 1981-88, sec. Mem. AAUW (treas. Wytheville chpt. 1978-85), Nat. Bus. Edn. Assn. Profl. Secs. Internat. (sponsor Wytheville Community Coll. collegiate secs. internat. chpt. 1982—), So. Bus. Edn. Assn. (sec., v.p., pres. jr. community coll. div. 1987, Honor award 1985), Va. Bus. Edn. Assn. (sec. 1983-85, treas. 1985-87, Outstanding Contbn. award 1986), Va. Community Coll. Assn. (chmn. instructional affairs com. subject matter 1984-85), Wytheville Community Coll. Govt. Assn. (sec., treas.), Alpha Delta Kappa (pres. 1990-92), Delta Kappa Gamma (treas. 1987—). Office: Wytheville Community Coll 1000 E Main St Wytheville VA 24382-3308

TINNER, FRANZISKA PAULA, social worker, artist, designer; b. Zurich, Switzerland, Sept. 18, 1944; came to U.S., 1969; d. Siegfied Albin and Gertrude Emilie (Sigg) Maier; m. Rolf Christian Tinner, Dec. 19, 1976; 1 child, Eric Francis. Student, U. Del., 1973-74, Va. Commonwealth U., 1974; BFA, U. Tenn., 1984; BA of Arts, U. Ark., Little Rock, 1991, postgrad. Lic. real estate broker. Dominican nun Ilanz, Switzerland, 1961-67; waitress London, 1968-69; governess Bryn Mawr, Pa., 1969; model, 1983; artist, designer Made For You, Kerrville, Tex. and Milw., 1984—; realtor Century 21, Milw., 1987—; intern Birch Community Ctr., 1992-93. Designer softsculptor doll Texas Cactus Blossom, 1984. Ombudsman Action 10 Consumerline, Knoxville, Tenn., 1983-84; foster mother, Powhatan, Va., 1976-81; vol. ARC, Knoxville, 1979, Va. Home for Permanently Disabled, 1975; tchr. pager/achiving host on Am. On Line; vol. Interactive Ednl. Svc. Recipient Art Display award U. Knoxville, 1983, Prof. Choice of Yr. award, 1983, Outstanding Achievemnt award TV Channel 10, Knoxville, 1984, 1st place award for paintings and crafts State Fair Va., Tenn., 1st place award Nat. Dollmakers, 1985, finalist Best of Coll. Photography, 1991, Achievement award Coll. Scholar of Am., 1991, Cert. of Achievement Technique of Anger Therapy, 1993. Mem. Nat. Assn. of Social Workers, Milw. Bd. Realtors, Homemakers Club (pres. 1979-80), Newcomers Club, Bowlers Club (v.p.), NAFE.

TINOCO, JUDITH MARSHALL, food service executive; b. Copaigue, N.Y., June 18, 1959; d. Kenneth Clinton and Nancy (Rasmusson) Marshall; m. Porfirio Francisco Tinoco, Apr. 29, 1984 (div. 1990); children: Robert William, Angelina J. Student, Fla. Internat. U., 1983-86; degree in culinary arts, Inst. of South, 1987. Chef, gen. mgr. Maxfields of Boca Raton, Fla., 1974-81; mgr. Alfredo l'Originale di Roma, Lake Buena Vista, Fla., Bistro Internat. Inc., Miami, Fla., 1981-86; dir. ops. Bistro Internat. Inc., Miami, 1986-89; dir. career svcs. Restaurant Sch., Phila., 1989-91; dir. food svc. ops. Union League Club Phila., 1991-92; dir. ops. corp. foodsvc. div. Univest Corp., Washington, 1992-94; dir. Natcher Conf. Ctr., NIH, 1995—; culinary instr. Main Line Sch. Night, Radnor, Pa., 1989-91; speaker in field. Vol. supr. Show Our Strength to Feed the Homeless, Phila., 1989-91; mem. community rels. bd. Bally's Grand, Atlantic City, N.J., 1989-91. Mem. Nat. Restaurant Assn., Phila./Del. Valley Restaurant Assn., NAFE, Womens Foodservice Forum, Roundtable for Women in Foodservice (bd. dirs. 1990—), Greater Phila. Restaurant and Purveyors Assn. (edn. com. 1991—), Pa. Restaurant Assn. Republican. Episcopalian.

TINSLEY, ADRIAN, college president; b. N.Y.C., July 6, 1937; d. Theodore A. and Mary Ethel (White) T. AB, Bryn Mawr Coll., 1958; MA, U. Wash., 1962; PhD, Cornell U., 1969. Asst. prof. English U. Md., College Park, 1968-72; dean William James Coll., Grand Valley State, Allendale, Mich., 1972-80; assoc. vice chancellor acad. affairs Minn. State U., St. Paul, 1982-85; exec. v.p., provost Glassboro (N.J.) State Coll., 1985-89; pres. Bridgewater (Mass.) State Coll., 1989—; coord. women higher edn. adminstrn. Bryn Mawr (Pa.) & Hers Summer Inst., 1977—. Editor: Women in Higher Education Administration, 1984. Office: Bridgewater State Coll Office of Pres Bridgewater MA 02325

TINSLEY, DIANE JOHNSON, psychologist, educator; b. Hibbing, Minn., Jan. 22, 1944; d. Frank Gustav and Evelyn Loretta (Dahlner) Johnson; m. Howard E.A. Tinsley, Dec. 16, 1967; children: Kelly Anne, Laurel Jeanne. BA, U. Pa., 1966; PhD, U. Minn., 1972. Lic. clin. psychologist; diplomate Am. Bd. Vocat. Experts. Intern Macalester Coll. and U. Minn., Mpls., 1968-70; vocat. counselor, then rsch. psychologist U. Oreg., Eugene, 1972-73; coord. career counseling So. Ill. U., Carbondale, 1973-78, adj. prof. psychology, 1977—; postdoctoral intern U. Tex., Austin, 1979-80; counseling psychologist So. Ill. U., Carbondale, 1980—; vis. fellow U. Minn., Mpls., 1987-88; cons. VA, Ill., 1973-78, St. Louis U., 1976, APA, 1976—; edit. cons. Am. Counseling Assn., APA, 1976—. Mem. ACA, APA (chmn. 1987-89), Bus. & Profl. Women (chmn. 1985-87, 89-92, State award 1986, 87), Am. Coll. Pers. Assn. (chmn. 1976-78, Rsch. award 1990). Home: 100 S Parrish Ln Carbondale IL 62901-2028 Office: So Ill U Dept Psychology Carbondale IL 62901

TINSMAN, MARGARET NEIR, state senator; b. Moline, Ill., July 14, 1936; d. Francis Earl and Elizabeth (Lourie) Neir; m. Robert Hovey Tinsman Jr., Feb. 21, 1959; children: Robert Hovey III, Heidi Elizabeth, Bruce MacAlister. BA in Sociology, U. Colo., 1958; MSW, U. Iowa, 1974. Health care coord. Community Health Care, Inc., Davenport, Iowa, 1975-77; assoc. dir. Scott County Info., Referal, and Assistance Svc., Davenport, Iowa, 1977-79; county supr. Scott County Bd. Suprs., Davenport, Iowa, 1978-89; senate State of Iowa, Des Moines, 1989—; asst. minority leader Iowa Senate, coms. appropriations, edn., human resources, appropriations subcom., ranking mem. health and human rights, 1989—; chair Iowa adv. commn. on inter-govt. rels., 1982-84; U.S. county rep. to the German-Am. Symposium German Marshall Plan, 1983; commr. Iowa Dept. Elder Affairs, Des Moines, 1983-89. Chairperson Planning Com. Quad City United Way, Davenport; bd. dirs. Bi-State Met. Planning Commn., Davenport, 1981-89, Quad City Devel. Group, Davenport, 1988-90. Named Iowa Social Worker of Yr., NASW, 1978. Mem. Am. Lung Assn. (bd. dirs. 1989—), Davenport C. of C. (local/state govt. com. 1989—), Nat. Assn. Legislators, Nat. Assn. of Counties (bd. dirs. 1984-89, pres. Women Ofcl. 1984-89), Iowa State Assn. of Counties (bd. dirs. 1983-89, chair), Jr. League (sustaining mem. 1989), Vol. Action Ctr. (pres. 1989). Republican. Episcopalian. Home: 3055 Red Wing Ct Bettendorf IA 52722 Office: c/o Twin State 3541 E Kimberly Rd Davenport IA 52807-2551

TIONGSON, MARYLOU MALIGAYA, critical care nurse; b. Manila, July 29, 1960; came to U.S., 1965; d. Antonio C. and Cornelia (Maligaya) T. BA, U. Vt., 1983; BFA, Rochester Inst. Tech., 1986; BSN, U. South Fla., 1993. RN, Fla. Nursing asst. Bon Air Nursing Home, Auburn, Maine, 1983-84; photo asst. Dick Zimmerman Studios, L.A., 1986; prodn. mgr. Premiere Merchandising, Inc., Inglewood, Calif., 1988-89; critical care nurse Bayfront Med. Ctr., St. Petersburg, Fla., 1994—. Co-pres. JR Vols. St. Mary's Gen. Hosp., Lewiston, Maine, 1976-76; eucharistic min. Prince of Peace Cath. Ch., Sun City Ctr., Fla., 1992-94. Named for clin. excellence in nursing Rotary Club, 1994. Mem. Sigma Theta Tau. Republican. Home: 1617 E Del Webb Blvd Ruskin FL 33573 Office: Bayfront Med Ctr 701 6th St S Saint Petersburg FL 33701

TIPP, KAREN LYNN WAGNER, school psychologist; b. Chgo., Feb. 15, 1947; d. Harry and Sarah (Damask) Wagner; m. Michael Harvey, Dec. 30, 1973; children: Brenda Alyse, Brandon Philip. BA in Gen. High Sch. Edn., Roosevelt U., 1971; B of Jewish Studies, Spertus Coll., 1973, cert. in sch. psychology, 1981, MS in Jewish Studies, 1993; MS in Ednl. Theory, Nat. Louis U., 1974, CAS, 1981. Cert. psychologist, Ill.; nat. cert. sch. psychologist. Tchr. Niles Twp. High Sch., Skokie, Ill., 1971-72; mgr. travel agy. Chgo., 1983-85; tchr. spl. edn. No. Cook County, Ill., 1972-90; tchr. Hebrew Chgo. Bd. Jewish Edn., 1969-90, interim prin. religious sch., 1989-90; sch. psychologist Chgo. Pub. Schs., 1990—; ind. ednl. therapist, Chgo., 1973-91; contract psychologist, N.W. Suburban Chgo., 1981-90; cons. learning disabled Chgo. Bd. Jewish Edn., 1983-90; mem. adv. bd. Tchr.'s Task Force, 1993-94. Pres. Truman Coll. Coun., 1993-95, City Coll. Chgo., 1985-87, nom. chair, 1990—; exec. sec. North Town Community Coun., Chgo., 1984-86, pres., 1989-91, v.p., 1991-93, treas. 1993—; pres. dist. 2 coun. Chgo. Bd. Edn., 1987-89, spl. ed. chair, 1990-92; exec. sec. North Town Civic League, 1978-80, pres., 1981-84; mem. coop. extension youth coun. U. Ill., sec., 1985-91, exec. coun., 1990-91; charter mem. Hild Culture Ctr., membership chair; beat rep. Chgo. Police Dept.; vice-chair Head Start, Salvation Army; corresponding sec. Day Care Ctr. Bd.-Evanston, 1978-81, Rogers Park Mental Health Coun.; vice chair Dewey Day Care Evanston, 1972-75, Rogers Park Montessori Sch., 1979-80; youth chair Indian Boundary Playground Bldg., 1986-89; mem. steering com. Rogers Park Centennial, 1991-93; mem. state coms. 4-H, 1982-88, Chgo./Cook County 4-H Coun., 1984-90. Master Tchr. grantee Jewish Bd. Edn., Chgo., 1981-89, 20 Yr. award, 1990; recipient Community Leadership award Dept. Human Svcs., Chgo., 1985, North Town-Dorothy LeRoy Community Svc. award, 1992. Fellow Am. Orthopsychiat. Assn.; mem. NASP, Coun. Exceptional Chldren (liaison 1972-86), Ill. Psychol. Assn. (Sch. Psychologist of Yr. 1991), Family Resource Ctr. on Disabilities (spl. edn. com. 1990—, bd. dirs. 1993—), Profls. in Learning Disabilties (legis. chair 1987—), Children with Attention Deficit Disorder, Learning Disabilities Assn., Ill. Sch. Psychologists Assn. (Practitioner of Yr. 1991, child study com.), Chgo. Assn. Sch. Psychologists, Greater Uptown Youth Network, Family Resource Handicapped (spl. edn. com.), Family Resource (bd. dirs. 1993-94), Ill. 4-H Found., Edn. Therapists. Home: 6730 N Maplewood Ave Chicago IL 60645-4620

TIRRO, IRMA JACOBS, aerospace transportation executive; b. Miami Shores, Fla., July 3, 1935; d. Virgil Ellis and Mollie Estelle (Faircloth) Goodson; m. Jesse F. Jacobs, July, 1953 (div. 1979); 1 child, Brian Jay Jacobs; m. A.J. Tirro, Aug. 23, 1986. BA, Barry U., Miami, Fla., 1985; MA in Mgmt., Webster U., Orlando, Fla., 1994. Judicial asst. State of Fla., Titusville, Fla., 1967-81; exec. asst. to pres. Heritage Real Estate and Devel. Co., Cocoa Beach, Fla., 1981-83; various Lockheed Space Ops. Co., Titusville, Fla., 1983—; prin. Life Mgmt. Strategies, Melbourne, Fla.; motivational trainer and speaker. Recipient Manned Flight Awareness award NASA, 1991. Mem. NAFE, ASTD, Nat. Mgmt. Assn. Home: 508 Crystal Lake Dr Melbourne FL 32940-1935

TIRSCHWELL, KATHY ANN, event production company executive; b. Hudson, Wis., Jan. 8, 1961; d. Walter Haskell and Doris Hilda (Dornfeld) T. DDS (hon.), Roth/Williams Ctr., 1993. Traffic dir. Sta. KRKC, King City, Calif., 1978-79; office mgr. Cable TV of King City/Greenfield, 1979-82; lead cashier Del Webb's High Sierra Hotel & Casino, Lake Tahoe, Nev., 1982-84; acctg. analyst Hyatt Hotels, Burlinghame, Calif., 1984-87; v.p., owner Computer Diagnostic Info Inc., Burlingame, Calif., 1987-93; exec. dir. Roth/Williams Ctr., Burlingame, Calif., 1990-93; event support mgr. Stuart Rental Co., Sunnyvale, Calif., 1994—. Pres. Jr. Fairboard, Salinas Valley Fair, King City, Calif., 1979-80. Jewish. Office: Stuart Rental Co 521 E Weddell Dr Sunnyvale CA 94089-2164

TISE, REBECCA JANE, sales training consultant; b. Winston-Salem, N.C., June 5, 1957; d. Banner Franklin and Billie Jane (Perrell) T.; m. Douglas Wayne Comer, Nov. 4, 1984 (div. July 1986). BA in English, Appalachian State U., 1980. Court reporter Arthur Jordan & Assoc., Kernersville, N.C., 1980-81; engring. asst. Arco Oil & Gas, Houston, 1981-83; tng. asst. R.J. Reynolds Industries, Winston-Salem, 1983; sales edn. cons. Digital Equipment, Winston-Salem, 1984—. Vol. Vantage Championship, Winston-Salem, 1988-94. Mem. ASTD, Triad Investment Club (rec. sec. 1993—). Democrat. Methodist. Office: Digital Equipment Corp 7820 N Point Blvd # 100 Winston Salem NC 27106

TISINGER, CATHERINE ANNE, college dean; b. Winchester, Va., Apr. 6, 1936; d. Richard Martin and Irma Regina (Ohl) T. BA, Coll. Wooster, 1958; MA, U. Pa., 1962, PhD, 1970; LLD (hon.), Coll. of Elms, 1985. Provost Callison Coll., U. of Pacific, Stockton, Calif., 1971-72; v.p. Met. State U., St. Paul, 1972-75; v.p. acad. affairs S.W. State U., Marshall, Minn., 1975-76, interim pres., 1976-77; dir. Ctr. for Econ. Edn., R.I. Coll., Providence, 1979-80; v.p. acad. affairs Cen. Mo. State U., Warrensburg, Mo., 1980-84; pres. North Adams State Coll., Mass., 1984-91; dean arts and scis. Shenandoah U., Winchester, Va., 1991—; cons. North Cen. Assn. Colls. and Schs., 1980-84, New Eng. Assn. Schs. and Colls., 1978-79, 85—, Minn. Acad. Family Physicians, 1973-77; mem. adv. bd. First Agrl. Bank, North Adams, 1985-91; pres. No. Berkshire Cooperating Colls., 1986-91; v.p. Coll. Consortium for Internat. Studies, 1989-90. V.p. Med. Simulation Found., 1986-88; bd. dirs. Williamstown Concerts, 1988-91, Shawnee coun. Girl Scouts U.S., 1992-93. Mem. No. Berkshire C. of C. (bd. dirs. 1984-89, v.p. 1986-89). Avocations: fiber and textile arts, photography. Office: Shenandoah U 1460 College Dr Winchester VA 22601

TISON-BRAUN, MICHELINE LUCIE, French language educator; b. Arras, France, Apr. 7, 1913; came to U.S., 1947, naturalized, 1964; d. Eugène and Lucie (Duchat) T.; m. Lev Braun, Apr. 1, 1948. Agregée ès lettres, 1937, Docteur ès lettres, 1972. Prof. French Education Nationale, London, 1938-47; translator BBC, London, 1941-45; translator, précis writer UN, N.Y.C., 1947-54; prof. French Lycée N.Y., City U. N.Y. Grad. Ctr. and Hunter Coll., 1961-81. Author: La Crise de l'Humanisme, vol. I, 1957, rev. edit., 1963, vol. II, 1968, Nathalie Sarraute la Recherche de l'Authenticitè, 1971, Dada et le Surreálisme, 1975, Tristan Tzara, 1977, Poetique du Paysage, 1980, L'Introuvable Origine, 1981, Ce Monstre Incomparable, A. Malraux et le Probleme de la Personnalite (Prix Jouvenel), 1982, Marguerite Duras, 1983, Le Moi décapité Lang, 1989. Decorated Palmes Academiques; Guggenheim fellow, 1978-79. Mem. MLA, Am. Assn. Tchrs. French, Pen Club, Gens de Lettres, Société d'Histoire littéraire de la France. Home: 50 Central Park W New York NY 10023

TITCOMB, BONNIE L., state legislator; m. Fred Titcomb; 3 children. Mem. Maine State Senate. Democrat. Office: Maine State Senate State Capital Augusta ME 04330*

TITILOYE, VICTORIA MOJIRAYO, pediatrics nurse; b. Okemesi Ekiti, Nigeria, Nov. 17, 1955; d. Ezekiel Ajiboye and Julianah Oyindaola (Atitebi) T. Diploma, Lagos U. Teaching Hosp., 1977; BS, SUNY, Bklyn., 1981; MA, NYU, 1983, PhD valedictory rep., 1988. Cert. occupational therapist, Nigerian nurse, RN. Asst. nursing supt. Wesley Guild Hosp., Unife-Complex, Ilesha, Oyo; sr. occupational therapist United Cerebral Palsy, Bklyn.; occupational therapist con., Sch. for Multiply Handicapped Children, Vis. Therapist Assocs., Bklyn.; rsch. assoc. NYU, N.Y.C.; asst. dir. occupational therapy Cobble Hill Nursing Home, Bklyn.; dir. occupational therapy dept. Sts. Joachim and Ann Residence, Bklyn.; cons. drs. office occupational therapy dept. U. Medicine and Dentistry N.J.; clin. and rsch. cons. League Therapeutic Ctr., Bklyn.; rsch. cons. Kessler Inst. Rehab., East Orange, N.J.; adj. asst. prof. dept. life scis. N.Y. Inst. Tech.; asst. prof. occupational therapy program SUNY Health Sci. Ctr., Bklyn.; food coord. Food Program for the Homeless, Sts. Ann and George, Bklyn. Contbr. articles to profl. jours. Recipient scholarships Nigerian govt., NYU Grad. Sch., Downstate Acad. Achievement. Mem. ANA, Am. Occupational Therapy Assn., Am. Soc. on Aging, N.Y. Acad. Scis., Nigerian Nurses Assn., MEDART Internat.

TITO, MAUREEN LOUISE, educational administrator; b. Long Beach, Calif., Mar. 14, 1946; d. Francis Bowen and Marie Louise (Hogan) Barrett; m. Jose D. Tito, July 4, 1971; children: Yvonne, Russell, Daryl, Nathan. AB in Polit. Sci., Holy Name Coll., Oakland, Calif., 1969; MA in Linguistics, Ateneo de Manila, Philippines, 1985. English lang. cons. Lang. Internat., Manila, 1979-85; English dept. coord. Maryknoll Coll. High Sch., Manila, 1981-85; edn. specialist Farrington Community Sch., Honolulu, 1985-91; English lang. cons. Job Preparation Program, Honolulu, 1990-91; project trainer U. Hawaii, Honolulu, 1989-90; edn. dir. Dept. of Pub. Safety, Honolulu, 1990-91, state dir. correctional edn., 1991—. Contbr. articles to profl. jours. Trainer AIDS for ARC, 1991—. Mem. AAUW, NAFE, Am. Assn. Adult and Continuing Edn., Hawaii Assn. Counseling and Devel., Correctional Edn. Assn., Nat. Assn. State Correctional Edn. Dirs. Home: PO Box 11958 Honolulu HI 96828-0958 Office: Dept Pub Safety 919 Ala Moana Blvd Honolulu HI 96814

TITTLE, CAROLE JEAN, computer programmer; b. Temple, Tex., June 5, 1959; d. Lloyd Melvin Johnson and Shirley Faye (Bruss) Druley; m. Jerry Allen Tittle, Oct. 1, 1977; 1 child, James Adam. AA, NE Wis. Tech. Coll., 1988. Bookkeeper, sec. White House Music, Waukesha, Wis., 1976-77; acct. Lamplight Farms, Brookfield, Wis., 1979; prodn. clk. W.A. Krueger, Brookfield, Wis., 1979-80; data processing asst. Video Images, West Allis, Wis., 1980-85; adminstrn. asst. Jones Intercable, Brookfield, 1985; computer programmer Anamax Corp., Green Bay, Wis., 1988-89; quality assurance analyst Nielsen Mktg. Rsch., Green Bay, Wis., 1989; applications programmer N.E. Wis. Tech. Coll., Green Bay, 1990; programmer/analyst Saranac, Green Bay, 1995. Democrat. Roman Catholic. Office: NWTC 2740 W Mason St Green Bay WI 54303-4966

TITUS, ALICE CESTANDINA (DINA TITUS), state legislator; b. Thomasville, Ga., May 23, 1950. AB, Coll. William and Mary, 1970; MA, U. Ga., 1973; PhD, Fla. State U., 1976. Prof. polit. sci. U. Nev., Las Vegas; mem. Nev. Senate, 1989—; alt. mem. legis. commn., 1989-91, mem., 1991-93; minority floor leader, 1993—; chmn. Nev. Humanities Com., 1984-86; mem. Eldorado Basin adv. group to Colo. River Commn.; active Gov. Commn. Bicentennial of U.S. Constn.; former mem. Gov. Commn. on Aging. Author: Bombs in the Backyard: Atomic Testing and American Politics, 1986, Battle Born: Federal-State Relations in Nevada during the 20th Century, 1989. Mem. Western Polit. Sci. Assn., Clark County Women's Dem. Club. Greek Orthodox. Home: 1637 Travois Cir Las Vegas NV 89119-6283 Office: Nev State Senate State Capitol Carson City NV 89710*

TITUS, AMY JEAN, librarian, computer consultant; b. Washington, Aug. 5, 1958; d. Joseph Sylvanus and Norma Jean (Mulder) T.; m. Robert Hoag Rawlings Jr., June 4, 1990; 1 child, Romeo Maximillion Titus Rawlings. BA, U. Mass., 1985; MS, Simmons Coll., 1987. Libr. Lasell Coll., Newton, Mass., 1986-89, U. San Francisco, 1989-90, San Bruno (Calif.) Pub. Libr., 1990-94, Skyline Coll. Libr., San Bruno, 1995—; database cons. Minuteman Libr. Network, Natick, Mass., 1988-89; computer cons., San Francisco, 1991—. Sponsor Childreach, San Francisco, 1990—. Mem. ACLU, Amnesty Internat. Democrat. Home: 158 Santa Clara St Brisbane CA 94005-1737 Office: Skyline Coll Libr San Bruno CA 94066

TITUS, CHRISTINA MARIA, lawyer; b. Phila., Oct. 31, 1950; d. George Herman and Frieda Anna (Szuchy) T.; m. Richard Christopher Daddario, Jan. 19, 1980; children: Alexandra Daddario, Matthew Daddario, Catharine Daddario. BA, NYU, 1972; JD, Georgetown U., 1977. Bar: N.Y. 1978, U.S. Dist. Ct. N.Y. (so. and ea. dists.) 1979. Assoc. Trubin Sillcocks Edelman & Knapp, N.Y.C., 1977-80; v.p., co-gen. counsel Merrill Lynch, Hubbard, Inc., N.Y.C., 1980—. Recipient 1st prize Drexel Keyboard Competition, 1968. Mem. ABA, N.Y. State Bar Assn. (mem. com. on real estate financing and liens real property law sect.), Assn. of Bar of City of N.Y. Lutheran.

TOADVINE, JOANNE ELIZABETH, physical therapy foundation executive; b. Covington, Ky., Nov. 29, 1933; d. Ralph and Myrtle (Wasson) Bailer; children: Daniel, Michael, Patrick, Michell, Joseph. Student, St. Benedict Coll. Bus. Sch., 1948; PhD, U. for Humanistic Studies, Las Vegas, Nev., 1986. Cert. rehab. technician in functional elec. stimulation, Nev. Founder, pres. Help Them Walk Again Found., Inc., Las Vegas, 1976—. Contbr. articles to profl. jours. Mem. State of Nev. Dem. Cen. Com., Clark Clunty (Nev.) Dem. Cen. Com. Recipient Humanitarian award Chiropractic Assn. of Ariz., Channel 3 Spirit award, Humanitarian award Dr. Otto Kestler, Spl. Congl. recognition, 1992; named to Honorable Order Ky. Cols., Mother of Yr. Clark County, 1988, Disting. Women of So. Nev., 1989, 90, 91, 92, 93, 94; recognized in The Congl. Recorder, 1980. Mem. Am. Acad. of Neurol. Orthopedic Surgeons (nat. coordinating council on spinal cord injury), Nat. Coordinating Coun. on Spinal Cord Injury, Las Vegas C. of C. (Women's Achievement award in health care), VFW, NAFE, The Pilot Club Internat. Office: Help Them Walk Again Found 5300 W Charleston Blvd Las Vegas NV 89102-1307

TOAL, JEAN HOEFER, lawyer, state supreme court justice; b. Columbia, S.C., Aug. 11, 1943; d. Herbert W. and Lilla (Farrell) Hoefer; m. William Thomas Toal; children: Jean Hoefer, Lilla Patrick. BA in Philosophy, Agnes Scott Coll., 1965; JD, U. S.C., 1968; LHD (hon.), Coll. Charleston, 1991; LLD (hon.), Columbia Coll., 1992. Bar: S.C. Assoc. Haynsworth, Perry, Bryant, Marion & Johnstone, 1968-70; ptnr. Belser, Baker, Barwick, Ravenel, Toal & Bender, Columbia, 1970-88; assoc. justice S.C. Supreme Ct., 1988—; mem. S.C. Human Affairs Commn., 1972-74; mem. S.C. Ho. of Reps., 1975-88, chmn. house rules com., constitutional laws subcom. house judiciary com.; mem. parish coun. and lector St. Joseph's Cath. Ch.; chair S.C. Juvenile Justice Task Force, 1992-94; chair S.C. Rhodes Scholar Selection Com., 1994. Mng. editor S.C. Law Rev., 1967-68. Mem. bd. visitors Clemson U., 1978; trustee Columbia Mus. Art; chair S.C. Juvenile Justice Task Force, 1992-94; chair S.C. Rhodes Scholar Selection Com., 1994. Named Legislator of Yr. Greenville News, Woman of Yr., U. S.C.; recipient Disting. Svc. award S.C. Mcpl. Assn., Univ. Notre Dame award, 1991, Algernon Sydney Sullivan award U. S.C., 1991. Mem. John Belton O'Neill Inn of Ct., Phi Alpha Delta. Office: Supreme Ct SC PO Box 12456 Columbia SC 29211

TOBACH, ETHEL, retired curator; b. Miaskovka, USSR, Nov. 7, 1921; came to U.S., 1923; d. Ralph Wiener and Fanny (Schechterman) Wiener Idels; m. Charles Tobach, 1947 (dec. 1969). BA, Hunter Coll., 1949; MA, NYU, 1952, PhD, 1957; DSc (hon.), L.I. Univ., 1975. Lic. psychologist, N.Y. Rsch. fellow Am. Mus. Natural History, N.Y.C., 1958-61, assoc. curator, 1964-69, curator, 1969-90, emerita curator; rsch. fellow NYU, N.Y.C., 1961-64; adj. prof. psychology CUNY, N.Y.C., 1964—. Co-editor: (series) T.C. Schneirla Conference Series, 1981, Genes & Gender, 1975; editor: Informational Jour. Comparative Psychology, 1987-93; assoc. editor: Peace and Conflict: Jour. of Peace Psychology, 1994—. Recipient Disting. Sci. Career, Assn. Women in Sci., 1974, Disting. Sci. Publ., Assn. for Women in Psychology, 1982, Kurt Lewin award Soc. for Psychol. Study of Social Issues, 1993. Fellow APA (pres. comparative psychology div. 1985); mem. Internat. Soc. Comparative Psychology (pres. 1984-86, sec. 1988-92), Ea. Psychol. Assn. (pres. 1987), N.Y. Acad. Scis. (v.p. behavioral scis. 1973-76). Office: Am Mus Natural History Central Pkwy 79th St New York NY 10024-5192

TOBIAS, JUDY, university development executive; b. Pitts.; d. Saul Albert Landau and Bess (Previn) Kurzman; m. Seth Tobias (dec. May 1983); children: Stephen Frederic, Andrew Previn; m. Lewis F. Davis, 1990. Student Silvermine Artists Guild, 1951-55. Art cons. Westchester Mental Health Assn., White Plains, N.Y., 1968-69; cons. sch. social work NYU, 1973-74, devel. exec. 1976—; conf. coord. Today's Family: Implications for the Future, N.Y.C., 1974-75; cons. Playschools, Inc., N.Y.C., 1975; majority counsel mem. Emily's List, 1991—. Mem. Gov.'s Commn. on Continuing Edn., Albany, N.Y., 1968-70, Nat. Coun. on Children and Youth, Washington, 1974-75, Manhattan Inter-Hosp. Group on Child Abuse, 1975-76; chmn. N.Y. met. com. for UNICEF, 1976-77; mem. exec. com. Town Hall Found., N.Y.C., 1979—, vice chmn., 1986-90; founder, bd. dirs. N.Y. chpt. WAIF, Inc., 1961—, nat. pres., 1978-82, nat. bd. dirs. 1978—; pres. emeritus, 1993—; bd. dirs. Citizen's Com. for Children, City of N.Y., 1975—, v.p., 1983-90; bd. dirs. Am. br. Internat. Social Svc., 1965-80; bd. dirs. Andrew Glover Youth Program, 1986-89, mem. adv. coun. 1989—; bd. dirs. Goddard Riverside Community Svcs., 1985—, Dance Mag. Found., 1986-92, St. John's Place Family Ctr., 1987-93, Capitol Hall Preservation Corp., 1989-93. Recipient Nat. Humanitarian award WAIF, 1990. Mem. Child Study Assn. Am. (bd. dirs. 1963-71, pres. 1969-71, bd. dirs. Wel-Met Inc. 1972-85). Democrat.

TOBIAS, SHEILA, writer, educator; b. N.Y., Apr. 26, 1935; d. Paul Jay and Rose (Steinberger) Tobias; m. Carlos Stern, Oct. 11, 1970 (div. 1982); m. Carl T. Tomizuka, Dec. 16, 1987. BA, Harvard Radcliffe U., 1957; MA, Columbia U., 1961, MPhil, 1974; PhD (hon.), Drury Coll., 1994. Journalist W. Germany, U.S. and Fed. Republic Germany, 1957-65; lect. in history C.C.N.Y., N.Y.C., 1965-67; univ. adminstr. Cornell U., Wesleyan U., 1967-78; lect. in women's studies U. Calif., San Diego, 1985-92; lect. in war, peace studies U. So. Calif., 1985-88. Author: Overcoming Math Anxiety, 1978, rev. edit., 1994, Succeed with Math, 1987, Revitalizing Undergraduate Science: Why Some Things Work and Most Don't, 1992, Science as a Career: Perceptions and Realities, 1995; co-author: The People's Guide to National Defense, 1982, Women, Militarism and War, 1987, They're Not Dumb, They're Different, 1990, (with Carl T. Tomizuka) Breaking the Science Barrier, 1992. Chmn. bd. dirs. The Clarion newspaper. Mem. Coll. Sci. Tchrs. Assn., Nat. Women's Studies Assn., Phi Beta Kappa.

TOBIN, ILONA LINES, psychologist, marriage and family counselor, educator, consultant; b. Trenton, Mich., Apr. 15, 1943; d. Frank John and Marjorie Cathalean (Lines) Kotyuk; m. Roger Lee Tobin, Aug. 20, 1966. BA, Ea. Mich. U., 1965; MA, 1968; MA, Mich. State U., 1975; EdD, Wayne State U., 1978. Diplomate Am. Bd. of Sexology; cert. marriage, family counselor; cert. sex educator and counselor; cert. sex therapist. Tchr., counselor Willow Run Pub. Schs., Ypsilanti, Mich., 1966-72; prof. Macomb County Community Coll., Mt. Clemens, Mich., 1974-79; psychotherapist Identity Ctr., Inc., Mt. Clemens, 1974-79; dir. treatment Alternative Lifestyles, Inc., Orchard Lake, Mich., 1979-80; psychologist Profl. Psychotherapy and Counseling Ctr., Farmington Hills, Mich., 1980-83; pvt. practice clin. psychology, Birmingham, Mich., 1983—; lectr. Wayne State U., Detroit, 1977-88; tchr., lectr. med. edn. St. Joseph's Hosp., Pontiac, Mich., 1993—; recruitment dir. Upward Bound Ea. Mich. U., Ypsilanti, 1969-72. Creator Doc's Dolls. Co-chmn. Birmingham Families in Action, 1982-83; bd. dirs. HAVEN-Oakland County's Phys. and Sexual Abuse Ctr. and Oakland Area Counselors Assn., 1984-85; mem. exec. bd., v.p. pres. Birmingham Community Women's Ctr., 1984-85, also bd. dirs.; mem. adv. bd. Woodside Med. Ctr. for Chemically Dependent Women, 1984-86. NIMH fellow, 1976-78; Wayne State U. scholar, 1976-78. Mem. Am. Psychol. Assn., Mich. Psychol. Assn. (mem. crisis intervention network, legis. com. 1992-94), Am. Assn. Sex Educators, Counselors and Therapists, Am. Assn. for Counseling and Devel., Pi Lambda Theta, Phi Delta Kappa. Jewish.

TOBIN, JOAN ADELE, writer; b. N.Y.C., Nov. 24, 1930; d. William and Helen (Steinis) Butler; m. Oct. 15, 1950; children: Patricia, Michael, Eileen. Freelance editor Suffield, Conn., 1980-85; owner, pub. Paper Works, Suffield, Conn., 1984-92. Contbr. over 80 articles to Internat. Mensa Jour., OWL Nat. News, N.Y. Times, N.Y. Mensa, and others. Mem. Am. Mensa, NOW, Universalist-Unitarian Womens Fedn., Writers Group Mensa. Home: 32 Harmon Dr Suffield CT 06078

TOBIN, JUDITH MARIE, mental health counselor; b. Paterson, N.J.; d. James Vincent and Maria Judith (Baldino) Parlegreco; m. George Shelley, June 7, 1963 (div.); m. David L. Tobin, June 3, 1974. BS, U. Miami, 1972, MEd, 1987; postgrad., Miami Inst. of Psychiatry, 1987-89. Legal sec. Tobin, Bayer, Miami, 1985-87; milieu therapist Grant Ctr. Hosp., Miami, 1989-90; cons. Asilomar Psychiatr. Svc., Coral Gables, Fla., 1990, Dr. Gary Schwartz, Miami, 1991-92; psychotherapist Anxiety and Stress Mgmt. Ctr., Miami, 1993—; substitute tchr. Dade County Sch. System, Miami, 1973-75; co-owner Franchise Restaurant, 1978-82; cert. family mediator Nova U., Ft. Lauderdale, 1992. Fundraiser Big Bros./Big Sisters, Miami, 1983-85, The Villages, Miami, 1983-85, Theatre Arts League, Miami, 1983-85. Mem. ACA, Am. Psychol. Assn., Am. Mental Health Counselors Assn., Epsilon Tau Lambda, Pi Sigma Alpha, Psi Chi. Home: 8646 SW 94th St Miami FL 33156-7311

TOBIN, KAREN MARIE, librarian; b. Framingham, Mass., Apr. 18, 1958; d. Thomas Francis and Doris Marie (Neuhaus) T. BA in English, Bridgewater State Coll., 1980. Libr. page Marlborough (Mass.) Pub. Libr., 1974-80, libr. technician, 1976-80, circulation staff, 1980-82, govt. documents libr., 1980-81, govt. and documents libr., 1982-84, cataloguer, 1984-93, tech. svcs. libr., 1993-95, head of circulation, 1995—. Bd. dirs. Worcester Community Cable Access, 1992—; chair worship/celebration com. Unitarian Universalist Ch. of Worcester, 1993—. Recipient Romeo Gibbons Pub. Svc. award City of Marlborough, 1992. Mem. Mass. Libr. Assn. (co-chair intellectual freedom com. 1993—, exec. bd. 1993—). Office: Marlborough Pub Libr 35 W Main St Marlborough MA 01752-5515

TOBIN, LOIS MOORE, home economist, educator, retired; b. Johnstown, Pa., Oct. 8, 1928; d. William B and Ida L. (Diehl) Moore; m. Warner E. Tobin, June 7, 1953 (dec.); children: Brian W., Robert E. BS, Ind. (Pa.) State Tchrs. Coll., 1951; postgrad., U. Pitts., 1952, U. Colo., 1953; MEd, Pa. State U., 1967; postgrad., Ind. U. of Pa., 1977-85. Tchr. Allegheny Valley Joint Sch. Dist., Springdale, Pa., 1951-53, Kittanning (Pa.) Sch. Dist., 1953-55, Carlisle (Pa.) Joint Sch. Dist., 1964-66, State Coll. (Pa.) Sch. Dist., 1967-73; mem. faculty Dept. Food/Nut Ind. U. of Pa., 1974, 76-77, mem. faculty Home Econs. Edn., 1979-82, coord. Single Parent-Homemaker Svc. Ctr. Vocat. Pers. Prep., 1984-91; mem. adv. com. Ind. Area Vocat.-Tech. Sch., 1981—; presenter Pa. Vocat. Edn. Conf., Seven Springs, 1985, Lancaster, 1991. Author: (booklet) Home Economics Education Bibliography on Special Needs, 1982, Teaching Special Needs Individuals in Home Economics, 1982; contbr. articles to profl. newsletters. Sec. Ind. County Human Svcs. Coun., 1990-91; vol. Bloodmobile, 1986—; tour guide Breezedale Restoration, 1986—; pres. Calvary Ch. Women's Club, 1975-76, Ind. County Newcomer's Club, 1974, 75. Grantee Dept. Edn. Bur. of Vocat. Edn., 1980-82, 86-91, Human Svcs. Devel. Fund, 1989-91. Mem. Am. Vocat. Assn., Pa. Vocat. Assn., Nat. Trust for Hist. Preservation. Home: 896 White Farm Rd Indiana PA 15701-1254

TOBIN, PATRICIA KAYE, trust banker; b. Milw., Nov. 30, 1962; d. Robert James and Shirley (Coppersmith) T. BA, U. Wis., 1985, MS, 1990. Registered rep. series 7 and 63 and securities prin. series 24. Securities tech. Valley Trust Co., Madison, 1985-87; registered bond rep. Midwest Stock Exchange, Chgo., 1987-88; staff cons. Fin. Acctg. Svcs., N.Y.C., Chgo. office, 1988-89; mgmt. trainee Firstar Bancorp., Milw., 1991-93; retail distbn. Firstar Trust-Portico Funds, Milw., 1993-94; with employee benefits new bus. Firstar Trust, Milw., 1994—. Mission vol. La Parroquia, San Lucas and Tolimon, Guatemala, 1988; loaned exec. United Way of Greater Milw., 1991; loan exec. lender Milw. Econ. Devel., 1992; vol. Wis. Pub. Radio; mem. Future Milw. Mem. Inst. World Affairs, Milw. World Trade Assn., Beta Gamma Sigma. Office: Firstar Trust Portico Funds 615 E Michigan St Milwaukee WI 53202-5207

TOBIN, SHIRLEY ANN, elementary school educator; b. Elko, S.C., Aug. 29, 1953; d. Norman Hunter and Ruth Tobin. BS in Elementary Edn., Voorhees Coll., 1975; MEd, S.C. State Coll., 1981. Cert. tchr., S.C., APT observer, S.C. Tchr. 1st grade Blackville (S.C.) Pub. Schs., 1976—, homebound instr., 1979-84, coordinator drug and alcohol abuse program, 1987—; pper evaluator, tchr. evaluation com. Blackville (S.C.) Pub. Schs., 1989. Vol. tchr. Barnwell County Headstart, Blackville, 1967-69, Summer Sch. Program for Ch., Elko, 1983; del. Williston (S.C.) Dem. Party, 1984; co-chairperson St. Jude Children's Hosp. Bikeathon, 1985-87. Recipient Service award Cancer Drive, 1977, Cystic Fybrosis Drive, 1978, St. Jude Children's Hosp., Columbia, 1985-86. Mem. Nat. Tchrs. Assn. (faculty rep. 1982-85), S.C. Edn. Assn. (faculty rep. 1982-85, Cert. Appreciation 1982-85), Blackville Edn. Assn. (faculty rep. 1982-85), AAUW (chmn. com. 1982-83), Council for Exceptional Children, Delta Sigma Theta (chmn. com. 1984—). Democrat. Baptist. Club: Please (sec. 1985-88) (Blackville). Home: PO Box 126 Elko SC 29826-0126 Office: Blackville Pub Schs PO Box 185 Blackville SC 29817-0185

TOCKLIN, ADRIAN MARTHA, insurance company executive, lawyer; b. Coral Gables, Fla., Aug. 4, 1951; d. Kelso Hampton and Patricia Jane (Crook) Cook Atkins; m. Gary Michael Tocklin, Nov. 23, 1974. BA, George Washington U., 1972; JD, Seton Hall U., 1994. Regional claim examiner Interstate Nat. Corp., St. Petersburg, Fla., 1973-74; branch supr. Underwriter's Adjusting Co. subs. Continental Corp., Tampa, Fla., 1974-77, asst. dir. edn. tng. adminstrn., N.Y.C., 1977, asst. regional mgr. adminstrn. ops., Livingston, N.J., 1977-78, br. mgr., Paramus, N.J., 1978-80, sr. v.p. mktg., N.Y.C., Piscataway, N.J., 1980-84, regional v.p., mgr., Livingston, N.J., 1984-86, exec. v.p., 1986-88, also bd. dirs.; sr. v.p. Continental Corp., 1988-92, exec. v.p. 1992-94, pres., N.Y.C., 1994—; pres. bd. dirs. U.S. Protection Indemnity Agy., Inc., N.Y.C.; bd. dirs. Underwriters Adjusting Co., Arbitration Forums, Inc., Tarrytown, N.Y., Continental Ins. Co., Sonat Corp.; v.p. Continental Risk Services, Inc., Hamilton, Bermuda, 1983-86; editor-in-chief Profl. Ins. Bulletin Update, N.Y.C., 1977-79. Mem. YWCA Acad. Women Achievers. Mem. Nat. Assn. Ins. Women (Outstanding Ins. Woman in N.Y.C.), NOW. Democrat. Lutheran. Office: Continental Corp 180 Maiden Ln New York NY 10038-4925

TODARO, ARLEEN, nurse; b. Elizabeth, N.J., June 6, 1959; d. Joseph and Jean (Forberger) Bent; m. Antonio J. Todaro, July 7, 1985; 1 child, Nancy Christina. AAS, Middlesex County Coll., Edison, N.J., 1979; BSN, Kean Coll., 1985; MS, Ga. State U., 1987. RN; clin. nurse specialist. RN, asst. head nurse Newark Beth Israel Med. Ctr., 1979-85, med.-surg. nurse educator, 1988-93; grad. student rsch. asst. Ga. State U., 1987; RN, charge nurse Kennestone Hosp. at Windy Hill, Marietta, Ga., 1985-87. Contbr. articles to profl. jours. Mem. Sigma Theta Tau. Roman Catholic. Home: 1280 Westfield Ave Rahway NJ 07065

TODARO, PATRICIA ANNE, sculptor, painter; b. Rockville Centre, N.Y., Feb. 24, 1933; d. Russell Norman and Grace Ruth (Eyerman) Sheidow; m. Raymond Ashman, Feb. 6, 1958 (div.); children: Robert Ashman, Richard Ashman, Kathryn Ashman. Student, Sullins Coll., 1950-51, Art Students League, 1954, Susquehanna U., 1952-54, Coll. of William and Mary, 1982-84. With programming dept. ABC, 1954-55; with travel dept. Rand, Santa Monica, Calif., 1955-56; pres. Seltzer Gallery, N.Y.C., 1986, 87. One-woman shows include Seltzer Coll., 1985-87, Phoenix Visual Arts Ctr., 1988, Kerr Cultural Ctr., Scottsdale, Ariz., 1989, Williamsburg Duke of Glouster Show, 1984, Albert Einstein Med. Ctr., N.Y.C., 1987, Seltzer Gallery; represented in pvt. collections Abbi-France, 1986, Leo House, N.Y.C., 1986-87, Shanti-AIDS Home, Phoenix, Ariz., 1988, Unipas Gallery, N.Y.C., 1991. Recipient Silver medal Salon D'Automne, Albi, France, 1986; scholar Am. Theatre Wing, 1954-58. Mem. Am. Fedn. Musicians.

TODD, DEBORAH ELIZABETH, practice development manager; b. Tuscaloosa, Ala., May 8, 1965. BA in Psychology, Randolph-Macon Woman's Coll., 1987. Mgmt. intern Compass Bank (formerly named Ctrl. Bank of the South), Birmingham, Ala., 1987; investment supr. Compass Bank (formerly named Ctrl. Bank of the South), Birmingham, 1987-88, product mgr. consumer loans, 1988-90, mktg. dir. U.S. banking, 1990-91; mgr. ladies dept. Jos. A. Banks Clothiers, Birmingham, 1991; practice devel. mgr. Balch & Bingham, Birmingham, 1991—; mktg. budget mgmt., tng., client svc. program cons., spl. events coord., Birmingham, 1993—. Vol. Birmingham Family Ct., 1988-89; coord. Legal Assistance to Homeless Women and Children, Birmingham, 1992—; group V.I.P. United Cerebral Palsy, Birmingham, 1989-91. Mem. Am. Mktg. Assn. (asst. v.p. ops. 1991-92), Nat. Law Firm Mktg. Assn. (conf. com. 1992, mem. svcs. com. 1993, boot camp chair and panelist 1993). Office: Balch & Bingham Attys & Counslrs 1710 6th Ave N Birmingham AL 35203

TODD, FRANCES EILEEN, pediatrics nurse; b. Hawthorne, Calif., Aug. 20, 1950; d. James Clark and Jean Eleanor (McGinty) Nailen; m. Steven Charles Todd, Oct. 25, 1975; 1 child, Amanda Kathryn. ASN, El Camino Jr. Coll., 1974; BSN, Calif. State Coll., Long Beach, 1982, postgrad. RN, Calif.; cert. nurse practitioner, pub. health nurse, Calif.; cert. pediatric nurse practitioner; cert. pediatric advanced life support Am. Heart Assn. Nursing attendant St. Earne's Nursing Home, Inglewood, Calif., 1973; clinic nurse I Harbor-UCLA Med. Ctr., Torrance, Calif., 1974-77, evening shift relief charge nurse, clinic nurse II, 1977-85, pediatric liaison nurse, 1984-90, pediatric nurse practitioner, 1985—; steward Local Union 660, 1995—; tutor Compton (Calif.) C.C., 1988, clin. instr., 1987-88; lectr. faculty dept. pediatrics UCLA Sch. Medicine, 1980—; lectr. in field. Contbr. articles to profl. jours. Co-chair parent support group Sherrie's Schs., Lomita, Calif. Mem. Nat. Assn. Pediatric Nurse Assocs. and Practitioners, L.A. Pediatric Soc., Emergency Nurses Assn., Local 660 (shop steward), Peruvian Paso Horse Registry N.Am. (co-chair judge's accreditation com. 1989—). Avocations: Peruvian Paso horses, orchids. Office: Harbor UCLA Med Ctr 1000 W Carson St PO Box 14-7W Torrance CA 90509

TODD, IMO KELLAM, insurance association executive; b. Mobile, Ala., Dec. 26, 1943; d. Claude Moore and Minnie (Barth) Kellam; m. Jordan A.M. Todd, Sept. 29, 1962 (Div. 1972); 1 child, Shannon Elise. BA, Wesley U., 1963; BS, U. Montevallo, 1966; MBA, U. Ga., 1974. Exec. asst. Baumhauer-Croom Ins., Mobile, Ala., 1963-73; v.p. acct. exec. Haas & Dodd Ins., Atlanta, 1973-78; asst. prof. U. Ga., 1973-79; v.p. acct. exec. Fickling & Walker Ins. Agy., Atlanta, 1978-81; exec. v.p. Profl. Ins. Agts. Ga., Atlanta, 1981-91, Profl. Ins. Agts., Fla., 1991—, Profl. Ins. Agts. Ala., S.C., 1992—; pres. Assn. Profls. of the South, Inc., 1990—; dir. southeastern ins. conf. U. Greensboro, 1984-87; lectr. in field. Author: How to-of Education, 1984; editor monthly ins. mag.; contbr. articles to profl. mags. Campaign mgr. Cystic Fibrosis, Atlanta, 1975; chmn. annual fund raisers Spl. Olympics, 1983—. Named Speaker of Yr., Speakers Unltd., 1979, Atlanta's One in 100 Women, City of Atlanta, 1984, Cobb County Top 10 Women, 1991, Nat. Exec. of Yr., 1990. Mem. Am. Soc. Assn. Execs., Nat. Soc. Execs., U.S. Women's C. of C., Nat. Assn. Ins. Women (Ins. Woman of Yr. 1973-74, Exec. of Yr. 1989). Republican. Office: Assoc Profls of South Inc 3101 Roswell Rd Ste N-149 Marietta GA 30062

TODD, JAN THERESA, counselor; b. Mobile, Ala., Mar. 20, 1961; d. Joseph Thomas and Lessie Grey (Sullivan) T. BA, U. Tex., San Antonio, 1983, MA, 1992. Cert. profl. counselor; cert. provisional tchr. English tchr. Bandera (Tex.) High Sch.-Bandera (Tex.) Ind. Sch. Dist., 1987-91; counselor Yorktown (Tex.) High Sch.-Yorktown (Tex.) Ind. Sch. Dist., 1992-93, John F. Kennedy High Sch.-Edgewood Ind. Sch. Dist., San Antonio, 1993—. Mem. ACA, Tex. Counselors Assn., South Tex. Counselors Assn., Edgewood Counselors Assn., San Antonio Area Women Deans, Adminstrs. and Counselors. Home: 9415 De Sapin San Antonio TX 78250 Office: John F Kennedy High Sch 1922 S General McMullen San Antonio TX 78226

TODD, JUANITA, artist, educator; b. Winchester, Ky., July 26, 1929; d. Hugh B. and Geneva Reynolds T. AB, Georgetown Coll., 1951; MA, U. Ky., 1956; postgrad., Ind. U., 1961, 64. Art tchr. Lexington (Ky.) Jr. High Sch., 1954-60; prof. art Ea. Ky. U., Richmond, 1960-88, prof. emeritus, 1988—. Selected exhibits include: Exhbn. 280/Regl. Exhbn., Huntington, W. Va., 1981, 82, 88, Miss. Corridors Regl. Exhbn., Davenport, Iowa, 1980, W.& J. Nat. Painting Show, Washington, Pa., 1981, 88, Evansville Mus. Arts Mid-States Exhbn., 1983, 84, 88, Nat. Painting Show, Butler Inst. Am. Art, Youngstown, Ohio, 1983, 89, Nat. 2-D Art Exhbn., E. Tenn. U., Johnson City, 1988, LaGrange (Ga.) Nat., 1985, Burke Arts Coun., So. Appalachia Regl., Morganton, N.C. (grand prize 1985, cash award 1986), others. Mus. Purchase award Mid-America Biennial, Owensboro (Ky.) Mu., 1988.

TODD, KATHLEEN GAIL, physician; b. Portland, Oreg., Aug. 31, 1951; d. Horace Edward and Lois Marie (Messing) T.; m. Andrew Richard Embick, March 31, 1980; children: Elizabeth Todd Embick, Margaret Todd Embick. BA, Pomona Coll., 1972; MD, Washington U., St. Louis, 1976. Diplomate Am. Bd. Family Practice. Resident U. Wash. Affiliated Hosps., Seattle, 1976-79; pvt. practice Valdez (Alaska) Med. Clinic, 1980—; chief of staff Valdez Community Hosp., 1986—. Mem. AMA, AAFP, Am. Acad. Family Practice, Alaska State Med. Assn. (counselor-at-large 1986-87). Democrat. Episcopalian. Office: Valdez Med Clinic Box 1829 Valdez AK 99686

TODD, LINDA MARIE, air traffic-weather advisor, financial consultant; b. L.A., Mar. 30, 1948; d. Ithel Everette and Janet Marie (Zito) Fredricks; m. William MacKenzie Cook, Jan. 11, 1982 (div. Oct. 1989); m. Robert Oswald Todd, Apr. 8, 1990; 1 child, Jesse MacKenzie Todd. BA in Psychology and Sociology, U. Colo., 1969; student Psychology Grad. work, U. No. Colo., 1970. Pilot lic., weather cert., FCC lic., Calif. life ins. lic., coll. teaching credential; registered with Nat. Assn. Securities Dealers. Counselor Jeffco Juvenile Detention Ctr., Golden, Colo., 1969-71; communications Elan Vital, Denver, 1971-81; legal sec. Fredman, Silverberg & Lewis, San Diego, 1980-82; escrow supr. Performance Mktg. Concepts, Olympic Valley, Calif., 1982-85; mgmt. commn. instr. Sierra Coll., Truckee, Calif., 1986-87; regional mgr. Primerica Fin. Svcs., Reno, 1987-91; air traffic, weather advisor Truckee (Calif.) Tahoe Airport Dist., 1986—; student tour leader, air show organizer Truckee (Calif.) Tahoe Airport; fin. cons. Primerica Fin. Svcs., Truckee, Calif., 1987-91; gen. agt. TTS Fin., 1992—. Editor: (newsletter) Communications, 1975. Sec. gen. High Sch. Model UN, Arapahoe, Littleton, Colo., 1965; del. State Model UN, Colo., 1966; conv. del. Elan Vital, The Ninety-Nines, Inc. Recipient Univ. scholarship Littleton (Colo.) Edn. Assn., 1966, flight scholarship The Ninety-Nines Inc., Reno, 1990; named Recruiter of Month, Al Williams Primerica, Reno, 1987. Mem. Plane Talkers, The Ninety Nines, Elan Vital, Planetary Soc. Home and Office: PO Box 1303 Truckee CA 96160-1303

TODD, LISA ANDERSON, administrative judge, lawyer; b. Summit, N.J., Mar. 2, 1942; d. Carl Magnus and Ida (Johnson) Anderson; m. David C. Todd, Sept. 6, 1986. BA, Cornell U., 1964; LLB, Stanford U., 1967. Bar: Calif. 1968, D.C. 1968, U.S. Ct. Claims 1970, U.S. Supreme Ct. 1973. Staff atty. United Planning Orgn., Washington, 1967-69; assoc. vomBaur, Coburn, Simmons & Turtle, Washington, 1970-73, Morgan, Lewis & Bockius, Washington, 1973-79; sole practice, Washington, 1979-83; adminstrv. judge, bd. contract appeals NASA, Washington, 1983-93, vice chmn., 1990-93, chmn., 1993; adminstrv. judge, Armed Svcs. Bd. of Contract Appeals, 1993—. Mem. ABA, Fed. Bar Assn., Bd. Contract Appeals Judges Assn. (bd. dirs. 1991-92, 94—), Nat. Assn. Women Judges (treas. 1987-88). Democrat. Lutheran. Home: 3811 Fulton St NW Washington DC 20007-1345 Office: 5109 Leesburg Pike Falls Church VA 22041-3201

TODD, MARGARET LOUISE, retired secondary education educator; b. Newport News, Va., Nov. 27, 1919; d. Preson Curtis and Lydia Emos (Diggs) Watson; m. Jesse Emerson Todd, Sr., Apr. 5, 1947; children: Frances Diggs, Jesse Emerson Jr. AB, Coll. William & Mary, Williamsburg, Va., 1943; MA, Hampton U., 1978. Elem. tchr. Newport News (Va.) Sch. System, 1943-45; newspaper reporter Times-herald, 1945-46; tchr. English Goerge Wythe Jr. High, 1946-47; tchr. English Bethel High Sch., Hampton, 1970-82, ret., 1982; speaker in field and tchr. workshops. Author: (with others) Hampton From the Sea to the Stars, 1985; author: (biograph) C. Alton Lindsay: Educator and Community Leader, 1994; contbr. articles to profl. jours. Lay speaker United Meth. Ch., Peninsula, 1970s-92; judge Va. Forensics Debate, 1970s-91; debate coach Bethe High Sch., Hampton, 1971-82. Mem. AAUW (life), Va. Ret. Tchrs. Assn. (trustee Va. conf. UM Hist. Soc.), Nat. Assn. Parliamentarians, Great Books Group, Planned Parenthood (pres. 1967-68), Hampton Hist. Found. Home: 909 Todds Ln Hampton VA 23666-1842

TODD, NORMA JEAN ROSS, retired government official; b. Butler, Pa., Oct. 3, 1920; d. William Bryson and Doris Mae (Ferguson) Ross; m. Alden Frank Miller, Jr., Apr. 16, 1940 (dec. Feb. 1975); 1 child, Alden Frank III; m. Jack R. Todd, Dec. 23, 1977 (dec. Sept. 1990). Student, Pa. State U., 1944-46, Yale U., 1954-57. Exec. mgr. Donora (Pa.) C. of C., 1950-57, Donora Community Chest, 1950-57; office mgr. Donora Golden Jubilee, 1951; staff writer Herald-Am., Donora, 1957, city editor, 1957-70; assoc. editor Daily Herald, Donora, 1970-73; svc. rep. Pitts. Teleservice Ctr., Social Security Adminstrn., HHS, 1977-83. Mem. Mayor's Adv. Council, Donora, 1965-69, Citizens' Adv. Council, Donora, 1965-69; mem. Donora Bd. Edn., 1954-60, pres., 1960; mem. Donora Borough Council, 1970-72; bd. dirs. Mon Valley chpt. ARC, 1964—, sec. bd., 1966—; bd. dirs. Washington County Tourism Agy., 1970-90, sec., 1972-90; bd. dirs. Washington County History and Landmarks Found. 1971-80, 91-92, sec., 1975-80, 91-92; bd. dirs. Mon Valley council Camp Fire Girls, 1965-79, Mon Valley Drug and Alcoholism Council, 1971-78; hon. life mem. Pa. Congress PTAs; bd. dirs. United Way Mon Valley, 1973-82, chmn. pub. rels., 1973-74. Recipient Fine Arts Festival of Pa. Poetry first prize award Fedn. of Women's Clubs, 1987, 1st and 2nd pl. awards for photography Washington County Fine Arts Festival, County Fedn. of Women's Club, 1990. Mem. Pa. Soc. Newspaper Editors, Pitts. Press Club, Donora C. of C. (pres. 1971-72), DAR (regent Monongahela Valley chpt. 1974-77, treas. 1992—), Internat. Platform Assn., World Poetry Soc. Internat., Washington County Poetry Soc. (pres. 1967-69), Donora Hist. Soc. (curator 1990—), Family of Bruce Soc. (descendants of King Robert the Bruce of Scotland 1987—), Washington County Fedn. Women's Clubs (rec. sec. 1964-66, pub. rels. chmn. 1990-92). Clubs: Order Ea. Star (worthy matron 1966-67, treas. 1986-94), White Shrine of Jerusalem (high priestess 1973-74), Order of Amaranth (royal matron 1966, dist. dep. 3 times, grand rep. W.Va. 1979-80), Donora Forecast (pres. 1962-63), Donora Unidon (pres. 1965-66, 56-57). Avocation: genealogy. Home: Overlook Ter Donora PA 15033 also: 1310 Mckean Ave Donora PA 15033-2200

TODD, RAE ANN, writer, editor; b. Denver, May 20, 1952; d. Dick Todd and Paige Louise Todd Love; divorced, Mar. 1981. Student, U. No. Colo.,

1970-71; AA in Visual Comm. and Design, Aims Jr. Coll., 1990; student in Tech. Journalism and Pub. Rels., Colo. State U., 1991—. Abstractor, rschr., legal typist Security Abstract/Stewart Title, Greeley, Colo., 1970-74; technician, land surveyor in tng. Miner and Miner Consulting Engrs., Greeley, 1974-81; clk. typist Platte River Power Authority, Ft. Collins, Colo., 1982, drafting technician, 1982-84, drafting designer, 1984-88, drafting supr., 1988-92, writer/editor, 1992—; owner Todd Enterprises. Author: From the Silence of My Mind, 1976. Zoo parent Denver Zoo, 1988—; mem. Landmark Preservation Commn., Ft. Collins, 1990-92; active Paint-A-thon 1st Interstate Bank, Ft. Collins, 1990-94, Adopt-A-Hwy, Wellington, Colo., 1990-94; reading tutor Poudre R-1 Sch. Dist., Ft. Collins, 1992-93; mktg. chair Taste of Fort Collins Tast of the Nation, 1993—. Recipient Honorable Mention in Lyric Writing Am. Song Festival, 1977, Honorable Mention in Photography Canon Nat. Photo Contest, 1985-86, 1st Place, Honorable Mention and Purchase awards Poudre Valley Art League, Ft. Collins, 1989, 1st Place print, 2d Place color Nat. Employees Svc. and Recreation Assn., 1990. Mem. Internat. Assn. Bus. Communicators, Platte River Power Employees' Assn.(treas. 1988-94, pres. 1994), Colo. Balloon Club (newsletter editor 1981-83, Pres. award 1981, Don Ida Spirit Ballooning award 1983), Golden Key Nat. Honor Soc. Home: 1924 B Langshire Dr Fort Collins CO 80526

TODD, SHIRLEY ANN, school system administrator; b. Botetourt County, Va., May 23, 1935; d. William Leonard and Margaret Judy (Simmons) Brown; m. Thomas Byron Todd, July 7, 1962 (dec. July 1977). B.S. in Edn., Madison Coll., 1956; M.Ed., U. Va., 1971. Cert. tchr., Va. Elem. tchr. Fairfax County Sch. Bd., Fairfax, Va., 1956-66, 8th grade history tchr., 1966-71, guidance counselor James F. Cooper Mid. Sch., McLean, Va., 1971-88, dir. guidance, 1988—; chmn. mktg. Lake Anne Joint Venture, Falls Church, Va., 1979-82, mng. ptnr., 1980-82. Del. Fairfax County Republican Conv., 1985. Fellow Fairfax Edn. Assn. (mem. profl. rights and responsibilities commn. 1970-72, bd. dirs. 1968-70), Va. Edn. Assn. (mem. state com. on local assns. and urban affairs 1969-70), NEA, No. Va. Counselors Assn. (hospitality and social chmn., exec. bd. 1982-83), Va. Counselors Assn. (exec. com. 1987), Va. Sch. Counselors Assn., Am. Assn. for Counseling and Devel., Chantilly Nat. Golf and Country Club (v.p. social 1981-82, Centreville, Va.). Baptist. Avocations: golf, tennis. Home: 6543 Bay Tree Ct Falls Church VA 22041-1001 Office: James F Cooper Mid Sch 977 Balls Hill Rd Mc Lean VA 22101-2099

TOENSING, VICTORIA, lawyer; b. Colon, Panama, Oct. 16, 1941; d. Philip William and Victoria (Brady) Long; m. Trent David Toensing, Oct. 29, 1962 (div. 1976); children: Todd Robert, Brady Cronon, Amy Victoriana; m. Joseph E. diGenova, June 27, 1981. BS in Edn., Ind. U., 1962; JD cum laude, U. Detroit, 1975. Bar: Mich. 1976, D.C. 1978. Tchr. English Milw., 1965-66; law clk. to presiding justice U.S. Ct. Appeals, Detroit, 1975-76; asst. U.S. atty. U.S. Atty.'s Office, Detroit, 1976-81; chief counsel U.S. Senate Intelligence Com., Washington, 1981-84; dep. asst. atty. gen. criminal div. Dept. Justice, Washington, 1984-88; spl. counsel Hughes Hubbard & Reed, Washington, 1988-90; ptnr. Cooter and Gell, Washington, 1990-91; ptnr., co-chmn. nat. white collar group Manatt, Phelps and Phillips, Washington, 1991—; mem. U.S. Sentencing Commn. Working Group on Corp. Sanctions, 1988-89; co-chair Coalition for Women's Appts. Justice Judiciary Task Force, 1988-92. Author: Bringing Sanity to the Insanity Defense, 1983, Mens Rea: Insanity by Another Name, 1984; contbg. author: Fighting Back: Winning The War Against Terrorism, Desk Book on White Collar Crime, 1991; contbr. articles to profl. jours. Founder, chmn. Women's Orgn. To Meet Existing Needs, Mich., 1975-79; chmn. Republican Women's Task Force, 1979-81; bd. dirs. Project on Equal Edn. Rights, Mich., 1980-81, Nat. Hist. Intelligence Mus., 1987—. Recipient spl. commendation Office U.S. Atty. Gen., 1980, agy. seal medallion CIA, 1986, award of achievement Alpha Chi Omega, 1992; featured on cover N.Y. Time Mag. for anti-terrorism work, April 1991. Mem. ABA (standing com. on law and nat. security, council criminal justice sect., adv. bd. com. complex crimes and litigation, vice chmn. white collar crime com., chmn. subcom. on corp. criminal liability), U. Detroit Law Sch. Alumnae (bd. dirs.).

TOEPFER, SUSAN JILL, editor; b. Rochester, Minn., Mar. 9, 1948; d. John Bernard and Helen Esther (Chapple) T.; m. Lorenzo Gabriel Carcaterra, May 16, 1981; children: Katherine Marie, Nicholas Gabriel. BA, Bennington Coll., 1970. Mng. editor Photoplay Mag., N.Y.C., 1971-72; freelance writer, N.Y.C., 1972-78; TV week editor N.Y. Daily News, N.Y.C., 1978-79, leisure editor, 1979-82, features editor, 1982-84, arts and entertainment editor, 1984-86, exec. mag. editor, 1986-87; sr. writer People Mag., 1987-89, sr. editor, 1989-91, asst. mng. editor, 1991-94, exec. editor, 1994—. Democrat. Presbyterian. Office: People Mag Time-Life Bldg Rockefeller Ctr New York NY 10020

TOFFEY, CYNTHIA GENN, artist; b. San Francisco, Feb. 10, 1953; d. Vernon Chathburton and Nancy Anne (Thompson) Genn; m. Kyle Akin Toffey, July 1, 1983; children: Akina Ruth, Kyra Judith. Student, Sonoma State Coll., Rohnert Park, Calif., 1971-73, Calif. Inst. Arts, Valencia, 1973-74; BFA in Painting, San Francisco Art Inst., 1977. One-woman show United Meth. Ch. Gallery, Red Bank, N.J., 1985, 88, Red Bank (N.J.) Pub. Libr., 1985, 89, Little Silver (N.J.) Pub. Libr., 1990, Thompson Park, N.J., 1992, Monmouth County Arts Coun., Red Bank, 1992, Gallery Kerygma, Ridgewood, N.J., 1992, Laughing Bean Art Cafe, Red Bank, 1993; group shows include San Francisco Art Inst. Gallery, 1977, The Glass Garden, N.Y.C., 1979, 84, Guild of Creative Art, Shrewsbury, N.J., 1984, 86, 88, Art Alliance Monmouth County, Red Bank, N.J., 1984-87, 91, Monmouth Mus., Lincroft, N.J., 1987, 91, N.Y. Ctr. for Visual Arts, Summit, N.J., 1989, 91, Helio Galleries, N.Y.C., 1990, Kerygma Gallery, Ridgewood, N.J., 1993, Decor Gallery, Rockville, Md., 1993, Internat. Assn. Contemporary Artists, Kyoto, Japan, 1993, numerous others; sculptures executed N.Y. Exptl. Glass Workshop, N.Y.C., 1979-80. Asst. Little Silver Com. for Safe Power, 1989—; community leader Woman's Fedn. for World Peace, N.Y.C., 1991—. Mem. Art Alliance Monmouth County, Internat. Assn. Contemporary Artists (Kyoto, Japan), Women's Caucus for Art (N.Y.C. chpt.), Orgn. Ind. Artists (N.Y.C.). Home and Studio: 68 Rumson Rd Little Silver NJ 07739-1334

TOFT, PAM CHENEY, marketing executive; b. Springfield, Mo., July 2, 1959; d. David Raymond and Patricia Anne (Snow) C.; m. Thomas Andrew Toft, Feb. 7, 1980 (div. June 1984); 1 child, Alaric Anthony; m. William Stephen Michael Mutschler, Feb. 14, 1987. BA magna cum laude, U. Toledo, 1983; postgrad., NYU, 1983-84. Account mgr. TPS Inc., Edison, N.J., 1983-84; documentation specialist Geostar Corp., Princeton, N.J., 1984-85; account mgr. The Clark Group, Trenton, N.J., 1985-87; media dir., asst. account exec. Sardi & Bleecker, Princeton, 1987-89; mktg. mgr. Megamation Inc., Princeton, 1989-91; v.p., gen. mgr. Videos Comm. & Multimedia, Cranbury, N.J., 1991-94; ind. prodr. corp. indsl. video Videos Comm. & Multimedia, 1994—. Grad. fellow NYU, 1983-84; recipient Citation for Outstanding Achievement in Bus. Bus. Profl. Women's Assn., 1990. NAFE, Bus. and Profl. Advt. Assn. (cert. bus. communicator), Desktop Pub. Users Group of Cen. N.J. (sec., treas. 1990-92, media rels. team leader), N.J. Communications Advt. and Mktg. Assn., Women in Communications, Mensa. Office: Videos Comm & Multimedia 2670 South River Rd Cranbury NJ 08512

TOFT, THELMA MARILYN, secondary educator; b. Balt., Sept. 15, 1943; d. George Edward and Thelma Iola (Smith) Trageser; m. Ronald Harry Toft, Aug. 27, 1966; 1 child, Joanna Lynn. BS in Med. Tech., Mt. St. Agnes Coll., Balt., 1965; BSE, Coll. Notre Dame, Balt., 1972; MEd, Pa. State U., 1983. Recreation dir. Villa Maria, Balt., 1961-65; blood bank supr. Wayman Park NIH, Balt., 1965-68; tchr. Sacred Heart, St. Mary's Govan's, Balt., 1968-74, Lincoln Intermediate Unit # 12, Adams County, Pa., 1979-80, York (Pa.) City Sch. Dist., 1980—; curriculum dir. M.O.E.S.T. Pa. State U.; curriculum dir. M.O.E.S.T., Pa. State U., 1991-93; mem. Md. State Consortium-Pa. Team for Improving Math & Scis.; grant writer, speaker in field; writer sch. to work curriculum. Active Girl Scouts USA, Hanover, 1988-92, leader, 1984-87; mgmt. bd. Agrl. Indsl. Mus. Mem. ASCD, AAUW, Nat. Ptnrs. in Edn., Am. Bus. Womens Assn. (edn. com. 1992, sec. 1993, Women of Yr. 1994), Phi Delta Kappa. Democrat. Roman Catholic. Home: 30 Panther Dr Hanover PA 17331-8888

TOKER, KAREN HARKAVY, physician; b. New Haven, Conn., Oct. 23, 1942; d. Victor M. and Nedra (Israel) Harkavy; m. Cyril Toker, Sept. 1, 1968; children: David Edward, Rachel Lee. BS in Chemistry, Coll. William and Mary, 1963; MD, Yale U., 1967. Diplomate Am. Bd. Pediatrics, 1974. Intern dept. pediatrics Bronx Mcpl. Hosp. Ctr., Albert Einstein Coll. Medicine, N.Y., 1967-68, asst. resident dept. pediatrics, 1968-69, sr. resident dept. pediatrics, 1969, 70-71, attending pediatrician, 1971-72, 73-76; pediatrician Montgomery Health Dept., Silver Springs, Md., 1976-83; pediatric cons. Head Start Program Montgomery County Pub. Schs., Rockville, Md., 1976-83; pvt. practice gen. pediatrics Rockville, 1983-89; pediatrician Nemours Children's Clinic, Jacksonville, Fla., 1991—; instr. pediatrics Albert Einstein Coll. Medicine, N.Y., 1971-74, asst. prof. pediatrics, 1974-76. Exec. bd. sec. Congregation Har Shalom, Potomac, 1989-91. Fellow Am. Acad. Pediatrics; mem. Fla. Med. Assn., Duval County Med. Soc., Ambulatory Pediatric Assn. Democrat. Jewish. Home: 6030 Oakbrook Ct Ponte Vedra Beach FL 32082 Office: Nemours Child Clinic 5220-24 Pearl St Pearl Plz Jacksonville FL 32208

TOKOLY, MARY ANDREE, microbiologist; b. Manila, Dec. 4, 1940; (parents Am. citizens) d. Robert Francis Tokoly and Ruby Waunita (Shriner) Kaderli. BS, Tex. Woman's U., 1962, MS, 1964, PhD, 1974. Instr Victoria (Tex.) Coll., 1964-66; asst. prof. Kans. State Coll., Pittsburg, 1966-68, Kans. Newman Coll., Wichita, 1974-75; grad. teaching asst. Tex. Woman's U., Denton, 1968-74; microbiologist Nix Hosp., San Antonio, 1975-77, Met. Hosp., San Antonio, 1977—. Sec. Bexar County chpt. Czech Heritage Soc. Tex., San Antonio, 1988-92; mem. See the Sea, 1985—. Robert A. Welch Found. grantee, 1971, 72. Mem. Am. Soc. Clin. Pathologists (registered microbiologist), Am. Soc. Microbiology, Tex. Soc. Microbiology, South Tex. Assn. Microbiology Profls., Am. Soc. Med. Tech., N.Y. Acad. Scis., AAUW, S.W. Assn. Clin. Microbiologists, Sigma Xi. Roman Catholic. Office: Met Hosp 1310 McCullough Ave San Antonio TX 78212-5699

TOLAN, MARY C., pediatric nurse practitioner, educator; b. Mendota, Ill., Apr. 20, 1949; d. Robert John and Anne (Oklesen) T. BSN, U. Ill., Chgo., 1971; postgrad., Ill. Benedictine Coll., 1993—. RN, Ill.; cert. CPR, pediatric nurse practitioner. Staff nurse in surg. ICU U. Ill. Hosp., Chgo., 1971-72; pub. health nurse Mile Sq. Health Ctr., Chgo., 1972-73; PNP DuPage Health Dept., Wheaton, Ill., 1973-78, U. Chgo. Hosp., 1978-80; Sudden Infant Death Syndrome regional cons. Loyola U. Med. Ctr., Maywood, Ill., 1980-82; Apnea clinician Ctrl. DuPage Hosp., Winfield, Ill., 1982-86; PNP Michael Reese HMO, Chgo., 1986-90; Sudden Infant Death Syndrome regional counselor Ill. Dept. Pub. Health, Springfield, Ill., 1990—; cons. Lisle Youth Coun., Lisle, Ill. 1973-78. Fellow Nat. Assn. of Pediatric Nurse Assocs. and Practitioners (cert. CPNP); mem. Am. Coll. of Sports Medicine, Nordic Fox Ski Club (v.p. 1985-86), Banana Belt Cross-Country Ski Racing Club, Ill. Paddling Coun. Roman Catholic. Home: 1660 N La Salle Dr Apt 508 Chicago IL 60614-6008 Office: Ill Dept of Pub Health 4212 Saint Charles Rd Bellwood IL 60104-1146

TOLAND, JOY E., marketing professional; b. Newark, Apr. 8, 1965; d. William D. Cartwright; m. Mark E. Toland, Sept. 10, 1988. BS, Montclair State Coll., 1987. Staff acct., acctg. clk., billing clk. Delta Dental Plan of N.J., Parsippany; product mgr., territory mgr., product specialist, mktg. support specialist PyMaH Corp, Somerville, N.J.; dir. mktg. Am. Multi-Svcs. Unltd., Inc., Manville, N.J. Mem. NAFE, N.J. Healthcare Cen. Svc. Assn., N.Y.C. Assn. for Cen. Svc. and Materials Mgmt. Pers., L.I. Intercounty chpt. Cen. Svc. Pers., Kiwanis (treas. Circle K 1983-84).

TOLBERT, LINDLEY AMANDA, advertising executive; b. Ozark, Ark., Apr. 26, 1968; d. Paul Samuel and Sharon Lavonne (Ramsey) T. BSBA, William Woods U., 1990. Asst. mgr. Michael's Arts & Crafts, Jacksonville, Fla., 1990-91; sales mgr. First Coast Entertainer, Jacksonville, Fla., 1992, Stas. WAPE-WFYV, Jacksonville, Fla., 1993—. Chmn. fundraising ball Big Bros./Big Sisters, Jacksonville, 1993, 94; dir. pub. rels. Art of the Eye Exhibit Cummer Art Mus., Jacksonville, 1994, 95; mem. E'Sprit D'Corps Hospice, Jacksonville, 1993, 94, 95. Mem. Advt. Fedn. Republican. Home: 111 Rose Pl Neptune Beach FL 32266-6042

TOLCHIN, JOAN GUBIN, psychiatrist, educator; b. N.Y.C., Mar. 10, 1944; d. Harold and Bella (Newman) Gubin; m. Matthew Armin Tolchin, Sept. 1, 1966; 1 child, Benjamin. AB, Vassar Coll., 1964; MD, NYU, 1972. Diplomate Am. Bd. Gen. Psychiatry, Am. Bd. Child Psychiatry. Rsch. asst. Albert Einstein Coll. Medicine, N.Y.C., 1964-68; instr. psychiatry med. coll. Cornell U., N.Y.C., 1977-78, clin. instr., 1978-86, clin. asst. prof., 1986—. Contbr. articles to profl. jours. Fellow Am. Acad. Child and Adolescent Psychiatry; mem. APA, Am. Acad. Psychoanalysis, N.Y. Coun. Child and Adolescent Psychiatry (bd. dirs. 1992—, pres. 1994-95), Alpha Omega Alpha. Office: 35 E 84th St New York NY 10028

TOLCHIN, SUSAN JANE, public administration educator, writer; b. N.Y.C., Jan. 14, 1941; d. Jacob Nathan and Dorothy Ann (Markowitz) Goldsmith; m. Martin Tolchin, Dec. 23, 1965; children: Charles Peter, Karen Rebecca. B.A., Bryn Mawr Coll., 1961; M.A., U. Chgo., 1962; Ph.D., N.Y.U., 1968. Lectr. in polit. sci. City Coll., N.Y.C., 1963-65, Bklyn. Coll., 1965-71; adj. asst. prof. polit. sci. Seton Hall U., South Orange, N.J., 1971-73; assoc. prof. polit. sci., dir. Inst. for Women and Politics, Mt. Vernon Coll., Washington, 1975-78; prof. pub. adminstrn. George Washington U., Washington, 1978—. disting. lectr. Industrial Coll. of the Armed Forces, 1994. Co-author (with Martin Tolchin): To The Victor: Political Patronage from the Clubhouse to the White House, 1971, Clout-Womanpower and Politics, 1974, Dismantling America-The Rush to Deregulate, 1983, Buying Into America-How Foreign Money Is Changing the Face of Our Nation, 1988, Selling Our Security-The Erosion of America's Assets, 1992. Bd. dirs. Cystic Fibrosis Foun., 1982—; county committeewoman Dem. Party, Montclair, N.J., 1969-73. Dilthey fellow George Washington U., 1983, Aspen Inst. fellow, 1979; named Tchr. of Yr., Mt. Vernon Coll., 1978; recipient Founder's Day award NYU, 1968. Fellow Nat. Acad. Pub. Adminstrn.; mem. Am. Polit. Sci. Assn. (pres. Women's Caucus for Polit. Sci. 1977-78), Am. Soc. Pub. Adminstrn. (chairperson sect. Natural Resources and Environ. Adminstrn. 1982-83). Democrat. Jewish. Office: George Washington U Dept Pub Adminstrn Washington DC 20052

TOLER, ANN PATRICK, public relations executive; b. Washington, Oct. 7, 1948; d. William A. and Marie Violet (Tyer) Patrick; m. Ronald Aubrey Toler, July 4, 1970; 1 child, Bradley Neal. Student, East Carolina U., 1966-68; cert. bank mktg, U. Colo., 1989. Admiting clk. Beaufort County Hosp., Washington, N.C., 1966-69; receptionist then exec. sec. Flanders Filters, Washington, 1969-81; adminstrv. sec. Bank of Va., Richmond, 1981-85, personal svc. assoc., 1985-87; mktg. coord. Signet Bank, Richmond, 1987-89, mktg. officer, 1989-90, asst. v.p., 1990-93, regional pub. rels. exec., 1993—. Dir. tournament Signet Open Va., Richmond, 1986—; bd. dirs. Easter Seal Soc., Richmond, 1989—; co-chair spl. events com. United Way, Richmond, 1991, chair 1992 ; chair regional conf. Am. Heart Assn., Richmond, 1991. Mem. Bank Mktg. Assn., Va. Bankers Assn. (Group II 1989—), Fin. Women Internat. Methodist. Office: Signet Bank 701 E Franklin St Richmond VA 23219-2512

TOLIA, VASUNDHARA K., pediatric gastroenterologist; b. Calcutta, India; came to U.S., 1975; d. Rasiklal and Saroj (Kothari) Doshi; m. Kirit Tolia, May 30, 1975; children: Vinay, Sanjay. MBBS, Calcutta U., 1968-75. Intern, resident Children's Hosp. Mich., Detroit, 1976-79, fellow, 1979-81; asst. prof. Wayne State U., Detroit, 1983-91, assoc. prof., 1991—; dir. pediat. endoscopy unit Children's Hosp. of Mich., Detroit, 1984-90, dir. pediat. gastroenterology and nutrition, 1990—; instr. pediatrics Wayne State U., 1981-83. Contbr. articles to profl. jours. Named Woman of Distinction, Mich. chpt. Crohn's and Colitis Found. Am., 1991. Fellow Am. Coll. Gastroenterology, Am. Acad. Pediats.; mem. Am. Gastroenterology Assn., N.Am. Soc. Pediat. Gastroenterology & Nutrition, Soc. Pediat. Rsch. Office: Children's Hosp of Mich 3901 Beaubien St Detroit MI 48201-2119

TOLINO, ARLENE BECENTI, elementary education educator; b. Crownpoint, N.Mex., Dec. 26, 1942; d. Little Billie and Mary (Arviso) Becenti; m. Albert Ray Tolino, Nov. 23, 1963; children: Adrian, Nathaniel Ray, Bryan. BS, U. N.Mex., 1977; MA, No. Ariz. U., 1984. Cert. elem. tchr., N.Mex. Ednl. aide Bur. Ind. Affairs Ea. Agy., Crownpoint, 1966-77; elem. tchr. Bur. Ind. Affairs Ea. Agy., Mariano Lake, N.Mex., 1977-79; elem. tchr. Bur. Ind. Affairs Ea. Agy., Crownpoint, 1979—, adult edn. tchr., summer 1988; sch. curriculum trainer BeautyWay curriculum Navajo Tribe, Crownpoint, 1989; computer tchr. Crownpoint Community Sch., 1988-89; site coord. pilot project ICON, Crownpoint, 1986-87; mem. com., tutor Gifted and Talented Program, Crownpoint, 1989-91. Sch. coord. Girl Scouts Am., 1977-79; sec. Navajo Nation Chpt. Officers, Crownpoint, 1983-86; mem. St. Paul Parish Coun., Crownpoint, 1982—, sec., 1992—, chairperson edn. com. 1992—; pres. Crownpoint Community Sch. Staff Assn., 1992—. Recipient Appreciation award Chaparral coun. Girl Scouts U.S.A., 1978, Title I Outstanding Tchr. award Crownpoint Community Sch. Parent Action Com., 1981, Ea. Navajo Coun., 1988. Mem. Ea. Navajo Agy. Tchrs. (sch. rep. 1987-88). Democrat. Roman Catholic. Home: PO Box 344 Crownpoint NM 87313-0344 Office: Crownpoint Community PO Box Drawer H Crownpoint NM 87313

TOLL, PAMELA KAY, school counselor; b. Columbus, Ind., Aug. 27, 1964; d. Ralph Edward and Barbara Ella (Trent) B.; m. David William Toll, May 27, 1989; children: Shelby Elizabeth, Sawyer William. Cert., Ind. U.-Purdue U., Indpls., 1984, BS in Psychology, 1987. Program specialist Human Svcs., Greenwood, Ind., 1987-88; home sch. ptnr. Bartholomew Cons. Sch. Corp., Columbus, 1988-89; at-risk coord./counselor Flat Rock-Hawcreek Sch. Corp., Hope, Ind., 1990—.

TOLL, ROBERTA DARLENE (MRS. SHELDON S. TOLL), clinical psychologist; b. Detroit, May 14, 1944; d. David and Blanche (Fischer) Pollack; married, Aug. 11, 1968; children: Candice, John, Kevin. B.A., U. Mich., 1966; M.S.W., U. Pa., 1971; PhD, 1990. Dir. counselors Phila. Family Planning, Inc., 1971-72; psychologist Lafayette Clinic, Detroit, 1972-73; social worker Project Headline, Detroit, 1973-75; pvt. practice clin. psychology, Bloomfield Hills, Mich., 1975—; adj. prof. U. Detroit, Oakland Community Coll. Past bd. dirs. Detroit chpt. Nat. Council on Alcoholism. Cert. social worker, Mich. Fellow Masters and Johnson Inst.; mem. APA, Nat. Assn. Social Workers. Democrat. Club: Franklin Hills Country. Home and Office: 640 Lone Pine Hl Bloomfield Hills MI 48304-2822

TOLLE, BRENDA KAY, secondary school educator, computer consultant; b. Xenia, Ohio, Nov. 30, 1942; d. Charles Wilbur and Agnes Geneva (Blakely) Massie; m. Richard William Davenport, May 16, 1963 (div. June 1965); 1 child, Lee A.; m. Glenn Walker Tolle, Apr. 11, 1970. BS in Edn., Ctrl. State U., 1971; MEd, Wright State U., 1976. Clk., sec. Ctrl. State U., Wilberforce, Ohio, 1964-70; tchr., educator Ohio Soldiers and Sailors Orphans Home, Xenia, 1970-72, Cedarville (Ohio) H.S., 1972—; owner, operator Brenda's Computer Svc., Xenia, 1986—; tech. coord. Cedar Cliffs Schs., Cedarville, 1992—. Contbr. articles to profl. jours. Bd. dirs. Future Bus. Leaders Am., Ohio, 1976-87; sec. Greene County Uni-Serv/Ohio Edn. Assn., 1988-90. With U.S. Army, 1962-63. Mem. NEA, Ohio Edn. Assn., Ohio Bus. Tchrs. Assn., Cedarville Area C. of C. (sec. 1991—), Cedarville Edn. Assn. (pres. 1985-91). Republican. Baptist. Home: 3160 Jasper Rd Xenia OH 45385

TOLLE, PAT MINA, artist; b. Ann Arbor, Mich., Jan. 17, 1948; d. Charles B. Tolle and Charlene J. (Vallet) Snow; m. Dennis A. Bohn, Aug. 12, 1986; children: Koshtra B. Tolle, Kira Bohn. Student, Brooks Art Inst., Santa Barbara, Calif., 1969-72, Chouinard Art Inst., L.A., 1968. One-woman shows include Kauai (Hawaii) Regional Libr., 1978, Casa-U-Betcha, Seattle, 1991, Jackson Street Gallery, Seattle, 1992, King County Arts Commn. Gallery Program, Seattle, 1992, Julia's, Wallingford, Seattle, 1992, Cafe Forza, Seattle, 1992, Phinney Ctr. Gallery, Seattle, 1992, Gunnar Nordstrom Gallery, Kirkland, Wash., 1993—, Lynnwood Arts Coun., 1995; represented in group shows at Santa Barbara Art Mus., 1966, The Artists' Own Gallery, Santa Barbara, 1973, Hawaii Artists League, 1978, Kauai Women's Art Show, 1978, Art Kauai '79, 1979 (3 1st Pl. awards), Arts Coun. Snohomish County Gallery, Everett, Wash., 1987, Eileen Enck Gallery, Bellevue, Wash., 1987, Snohomish (Wash.) Invitational Show, 1988, Artworks Gallery, Santa Barbara, 1988, Alligator Gallery, San Francisco, 1988, A New Space Gallery, Seattle, 1988, Prima Gallery Edmonds (Wash.) Coll., 1989, Seattle Art Mus., 1989, Cheney Cowles Mus., Spokane, Wash., 1990, Pacific N.W. Arts & Crafts Fair, Bellevue, Wash., 1991, Ea. Wash. U. Gallery, Cheney, 1992, Santa Barbara Art Co., 1993, 1994 N.W. Poets and Artists Calendar Exhbn., Bainbridge Island, Wash., 1993, Arts Coun. Snohomish, Monte Cristo, Everett, Wash., 1994, Ea. Wash. U. Gallery, Cheney, 1995; represented in The Calif. Art Review, 2d edit., 1989, The Encyclopedia of Living Artists, 4th edit., 1989, Limited Ink, 1st edit., 1991. Home: 10111 Marine View Dr Mukilteo WA 98275

TOLLEFSON, JO M., nursing administrator; b. Minn., Apr. 30, 1938; d. William and Anne J. (Steen) Jensen; m. Dean R. Tollefson, Jan. 9, 1960; children: Jon, Kristi, Kari, Jodi. BSN, Gustavus Adolphus Coll., 1960. RN, Minn. Staff nurse Bethesda Hosp., St. Paul; nursing coord. Mercy Hosp., Coon Rapids, Minn.; nursing supr. Anoka (Minn.) County Community Health and Environ. Svc. Mem. Minn. Home Care Assn., N. Metro Continuity of Care, Minn. League Nursing. Home: 2531 Wexford Heights Ln New Brighton MN 55112-3153

TOLLES, ANNE LOUISE, biochemical company executive; b. Long Beach, Calif., Sept. 24, 1955; d. Peter Franklin and Phyllis Arlene (Lothe) T.; m. Frank Roy Sanchez, Sept. 21, 1985; children: Shelby Anne, Tessa Francesca, Ariel Elizabeth. BS, Calif. State U., 1980, MS, 1984. Cert. tchr. jr. coll., Calif. Student dietician Woodruff Cmty. Hosp., Long Beach, 1975-76; med. technician St. Mary Med. Ctr., Long Beach, 1977-79; rsch. assoc. Specialty Labs., Santa Monica, Calif., 1980-83, City of Hope, Duarte, Calif., 1984-85; mng. dir. Advanced ImmunoChem., Inc., Long Beach, 1986-89, pres., CEO, 1990—; cons. Cosmo Bio Co., Ltd., Tokyo, 1993—, Bio-Trade, Vienna, 1993—, Cambridge (U.K.) Biosci., 1993—, CliniSci. P.H. Stehelin & Cie AG, Basel, Switzerland, 1993—, Canadian BioClinical, Ontario, 1993—, D.B.A., Italia, Milan, 1993—, Kormed Corp., Seoul, 1994—. Author: (book) An Enzyme-Limited Immunosorbent Assay for Anti-Histone Abs. Recipient fellowship Specialty Labs,, Santa Monica, Calif., 1980. Mem. AAAS, DAR, Daughters of Colonial Wars, Sigma Xi. Democrat. Roman Catholic. Office: Advanced ImmunoChem Inc 105 Claremont Ave Long Beach CA 90803

TOLLETT, GLENNA BELLE, accountant, mobile home park operator; b. Graham, Ariz., Dec. 17, 1913; d. Charles Harry and Myrtle (Stapley) Spafford; m. John W. Tollett, Nov. 28, 1928; 1 child, Jackie J., 1 adopted child, Beverly Mae Malgren. Bus. cert., Lamson Coll. Office mgr. Hurley Meat Packing Co., Phoenix, 1938-42; co-owner, sec., treas. A.B.C. Enterprises, Inc., Seattle, 1942—; ptnr. Bella Investment Co., Seattle, 1962—, Four Square Investment Co., Seattle, 1969—, Warehouses Ltd., Seattle, 1970—, Tri State Partnership, Wash., Idaho, Tex., 1972—; pres. Halycon Mobile Home Park, Inc., Seattle, 1979—; co-owner, operator Martha Lake Mobile Home Park, Lynwood, Wash., 1962-73. Mem. com. Wash. Planning and Community Affairs Agy., Olympia, 1981-82, Wash. Mfg. Housing Assn. Relations Com., Olympia, 1980-84; appointed by Gov. Wash. to Mobile Home and RV Adv. Bd., 1973-79. Named to RV/Mobile Home Hall of Fame, 1980. Mem. Wash. Mobile Park Owners Assn. (legisl. chmn., lobbyist 1976-85, cons. 1984, pres. 1978-79, exec. dir. 1976-84, This is Your Life award 1979), Wash. Soc. of Assn. Execs. (Exec. Dir. Service award 1983), Mobile Home Old Timers Assn., Mobile Home Owners of Am. (sec. 1972-76, Appreciation award 1976), Nat Fire Protection Assn. (com. 1979-86), Aurora Pkwy. North C. of C. (sec. 1976-80), Fremont C. of C. Republican. Mormon. Home: 18261 Springdale Ct NW Seattle WA 98177-3228 Office: ABC Enterprises Inc 3524 Stone Way N Seattle WA 98103-8924

TOLLIVER, EDITH CATHERINE, educator; b. Greenup, Ky., Sept. 6, 1925; d. Reece Madison and Nancy Elizabeth (Knipp) Bowling; m. Homer Tolliver, May 4, 1949 (dec. Nov. 1987); children: Gary M., Rodney D., James C., William H.; m. Robert O. Hutchins, July 7, 1990. BA, Morehead (Ky.) U., 1960; MA, Calif. State U., 1990. Cert. elem. tchr., Calif., Ky.; cert. reading specialist, Calif. Tchr. Fleming County Schs., Flemingsburg, Ky., 1943-48; factory worker Ecorse, Mich., 1948-49; tchr. Greenup County Schs., 1953-54, Carter County Schs., Olive Hill, Ky., 1954-62; 1st grade tchr. San Jacinto (Calif.) Elem. Sch., 1963-68, 72-87, mentor tchr., 1987-90; reading specialist Hyatt Elem., San Jacinto, 1968-72; 1 st grade tchr. DeAnza Elem., San Jacinto, 1987—. Named Tchr. of Yr. San Jacinto Elem. Sch., 1982, 85.

Mem. NEA, Calif. Tchrs. Assn., San Jacinto Tchrs. Assn. (sec. 1972, v.p. 1985), Delta Kappa Gamma. Republican. Southern Baptist. Home: 26032 Amy Ln Hemet CA 92544-6230

TOLLIVER, URSULA DENISE, home improvement contractor, consultant; b. Balt., July 12, 1962; d. James Howard and Jennie Velma (Givan) T. BS, Morgan State U., Balt., 1984. Cert. med. lab. technician, Md. Sales assoc. AT&T IS, Balt., 1984-86; mgr. Tandy Corp., Balt., 1986-88; staff painter Community Realty Co., Beltsville, Md., 1988-90; propr. Ursa Major Enterprises, Balt., 1990—; maintenance cons. People Encouraging People, Balt., 1991—. Mem. Tau Beta Sigma.

TOMA, DONNA M., psychologist, researcher; b. Belleville, N.J., Sept. 8, 1962; d. David and Patricia (D'Amore) T. BA, U. N.C., Charlotte, 1984; MA, Seton Hall U., 1986, Yeshiva U., 1990; PhD, Yeshiva U., 1993. Cert. instr. crisis/suicide. Liaison, therapist Union County Psychiat. Clinic, Plainfield, N.J., 1986-88; therapist individuals, families Sch. Based Youth Svc. Program, Plainfield, 1988-90; psychologist Spofford Maximum Security Facility Juvenile Offenders, Bronx, N.Y., 1990-91, Alliance for Recovery, Belleville, 1991—, Bergen County Spl. Svcs., Ridgewood, N.J., 1991-94, Contemporary Counseling Psychotherapy Inst., Teaneck, N.J., 1994—; cons. substance abuse Da-Tom Enterprises, Clark, N.J., 1986-93, consulting psychologist, 1988—. Contbr. articles to profl. jours. Vol. Children's Aid Soc., N.Y.C., 1992—, Gay Men's Health Crisis, N.Y./N.J., 1993—. Mem. APA, NOW, Menninger Found., Orthopsychiatric (N.Y.C.), Kappa Delta Pi.

TOMACCI, TONI, multicultural programs specialist; b. San Jose, Calif., June 16, 1952; d. Peter and Rose Mary (Calamello) T. BA in Liberal Studies, San Jose State U., 1975; MEd, Coll. Notre Dame, Belmont, Calif., 1976; postgrad., U. San Francisco, 1979. Cert. Montessori tchr. Dir. MIU Children's Sch., Fairfield, Iowa, 1977-78; tchr. Campbell (Calif.) Montessori, 1978-80; head tchr. Montessori Children's House, San Mateo, Calif., 1980-81; rsch. asst. Stanford Rsch. Inst., Menlo Park, Calif., 1981-83; software licensing adminstr. Apple Computer, Cupertino, Calif., 1983-84, specialist in customer rels., 1984-85, supr. developer rels., 1985-86, mgr. customer rels., 1986-89, specialist in multicultural programs, 1989—; trustee, mem. student affairs com. and strategic planning com. Pacific Grad. Sch. of Psychology, Palo Alto, Calif., 1993—; mem. adv. bd. Kid One, Inc., Mill Valley, Calif., 1993—. Co-author: Vacations and Weekends Learning Guide, 1983. Mem. AAUW, Bay Area OD Network, Internat. Network of Women in Tech., No. Calif. Diversity Bus. Forum, World Bus. Acad. Office: Apple Computer Inc 20525 Mariani Ave MS 38MC Cupertino CA 95014

TOMAN, MARY ANN, federal official; b. Pasadena, Calif., Mar. 31, 1954; d. John James and Mary Ann Zajec T.; m. Milton Allen Miller, Sept. 10, 1988; 1 child, Mary Ann III. BA with honors, Stanford U., 1976; MBA, Harvard U., 1981. Mgmt. cons. Bain and Co., Boston, 1976-77; brand mgr. Procter & Gamble Co., Cin., 1977-79; summer assoc. E.F. Hutton, N.Y.C., 1980; head corp. planning The Burton Group, PLC, London, 1981-84; pres., founder Glendair Ltd., London, 1984-86; pres. London Cons. Group, London, Beverly Hills, Calif., 1987-88; mem. U.S. Presdl. Transition Team, Bus. and Fin., 1988-89; dep. asst. sec. commerce, automotive affairs, consumer goods U.S. Dept. Commerce, Washington, 1989-93; commr., chmn. L.A. Indsl. Devel. Authority, 1993-95; dep. treas. State of Calif., Sacramento, 1995—; bd. dirs. U.S. Coun. of Devel. Fin. Agencies, 1994—. Founder, chair Stanford U. Fundraising, London, 1983-88; chair Reps. Abroad Absentee Voter Registration, London, 1983-88; bd. dirs. Harvard Bus. Sch. Assn., London, 1984-87; vol. Bush-Quayle Campaign, 1988; trustee Bath Coll., Eng., 1988—; apptd. by Gov. Wilson to State of Calif. Econ. Devel. Adv. Coun., 1994—; bd. dirs. U.S. Coun. Devel. Fin. Agys., 1994—. Mem. Stanford Club U.K. (pres. 1983-88), Harvard Club N.Y., Harvard Club Washington. Roman Catholic. Home: 604 N Elm Dr Beverly Hills CA 90210 Office: State Treasurers Office 915 Capitol Mall Rm 110 Sacramento CA 95814

TOMASEVICZ, AMY JOAN, art educator; b. Guide Rock, Nebr., May 2, 1949; d. Neal Bryant and Irene (Hesford) Zimmerman; m. Dennis Lee Tomasevicz, July 18, 1973; children: Curtis Lee, Jonathan Ross. BFA in Edn., U. Nebr., 1971, MEd in Art, 1977. Registered profl. educator, Nebr. Educator art Osceola (Nebr.) Pub. Schs., 1971-74, Shelby (Nebr.) Pub. Schs., 1974—. City coun. chairperson Nebr. Cmty. Improvement Program, Shelby, 1980-84; mem. C. of C., Shelby, 1980—. Named Outstanding Edn. nominee Shelby Edn. Assn., 1978; Perkins grantee Consortium for Vocat. Edn., 1994, Lifetouch Enrichment grantee. Mem. NEA, Nebr. State Edn. Assn., Shelby Edn. Assn. (pres. 1974—), Nebr. Art Tchrs. Assn., PALS, Phi Delta Kappa. Republican. Roman Catholic. Home: 201 2nd Ave Shelby NE 68662

TOMASULO, VIRGINIA MERRILLS, retired lawyer; b. Belleville, Ill., Feb. 10, 1919; d. Frederick Emerson and Mary Eckert (Turner) Merrills; m. Nicholas Angelo Tomasulo, Sept. 30, 1952; m. Harrison I. Anthes, March 5, 1988. BA, Wellesley Coll., 1940; LLB (now JD), Washington U., St. Louis, 1943. Bar: Mo. 1942, U.S. Ct. Appeals (D.C. cir.) 1958, Mich. 1974, U.S. Dist. Ct. (ea. dist.) Mo. 1943, U.S. Supreme Ct. 1954, U.S. Tax Ct. 1974, U.S. Ct. Appeals (6th cir.) 1976. Atty. Dept. of Agr., St. Louis and Washington, 1943-48, Office of Solicitor, Chief Counsel's Office, IRS, Washington and Detroit, 1949-75; assoc. Baker & Hostetler, Washington, 1977-82, ptnr., 1982-89, of counsel, 1989, ret., 1989. Sec., S.W. Day Care Assn., Washington, 1971-73; mem. fin. com. Residents Assn. Village on the Green, Longwood, Fla. Mem. ABA, Mo. Bar, Fed. Bar, Village on the Green Residents Assn. (fin. com.), Wellesley Club (Ctrl. Fla.). Episcopalian. Home: 570 Village Pl Apt 300 Longwood FL 32779-6037

TOMASZESKI, JOSEPHINE GALLAS, retired nursing educator; b. Manchouli, Manchuria, China, Jan. 18, 1919; d. Paul Fedorovich Kislitzin and Barbara Matveevna (Borodeev) Kislitzin-Meisel; m. John Joseph Gallas, Jan. 22, 1953 (dec. Feb. 1966); m. Julian Stephen Tomaszeski, June 10, 1972; stepchildren: Julie Ann, Mary Jane, Wayne Michael, John William. Student, Mary Washington Coll., 1937; diploma, St. Mary's Coll. Nursing, 1941; BS in Pub. Health Nursing, Cath. U. Am., 1943; MSN, U. Calif., Berkeley and San Francisco, 1960. RN, Calif.; cert. pub. health nurse, tchr., Calif. Nurse, charge nurse Children's Hosp., Washington, 1941-43; pub. health nurse Dept. Pub. Health, Washington, 1943-45; dir. outpatient clinic, nurse instr. Mary's Help Hosp., San Francisco, 1946-49; nurse, pub. health nurse, nurse instr. VA Med. Ctr. and Gen. Clinics, San Francisco, 1949-54; nurse instr. St. Mary's Hosp., San Francisco, 1954-55; asst. prof. nursing U. San Francisco, 1954-72; medicine and treatment nurse Schutz Am. Sch., Alexandria, Egypt, 1972-73; newspaper corr. Representative, Calmar, Alta., Can., 1975-81; medicine and treatment nurse Hillhaven Convalescent Hosp., San Rafael, Calif., 1982. Vol. nurse County Health Dept., Sausalito, Calif., 1956-63; vol. pollworker City of Sausalito, 1962-65; vol. city coun. campaigns, SAusalito, 1962-65. Fed. Nursing grantee Cath. U. Am., 1942-43; Fed. scholar U. Calif., Berkeley, 1959-60. Mem. ANA, AAUP, Nursing Alumni Bd. U. San Francisco (voting vol. 1982—), Nat. League Nursing (sec. 1956-60), Sigma Theta Tau, Alpha Phi Sigma. Republican. Roman Catholic. Home: 61 Labrea Way San Rafael CA 94903-3065 Also: 5114 49th Ave, PO Box 444, Calmar, AB Canada T0C 0V0

TOMBERS, EVELYN CHARLOTTE, lawyer; b. Phila., Nov. 7, 1956; d. Gerold G. and Margot (Ort) Knauerhase; m. Peter C. Tombers. AS, Temple U., 1976, BA, 1977; JD, Thomas M. Cooley Law Sch., 1991. Bar: Mich. 1991. Dist. intake counselor Fla. Dept. Health Rehab. Svc., Naples, 1985-87; satellite dir. Youth Shelter S.W. Fla., Naples, 1987-88; adj. prof. Thomas M. Cooley Law Sch., Lansing, Mich., 1991-92; jud. law clk. to Justice Patricia J. Boyle Mich. Supreme Ct., Detroit, 1992-94; assoc. Harvey, Kruse, Westen and Milan, Troy, Mich., 1994—. Named one of Outstanding Women Grads., Women Lawyers Am., 1991. Home: 726 Englewood Ave Royal Oak MI 48073-2833 Office: Harvey Kruse Westen Milan 1050 Wilshire Dr Ste 320 Troy MI 48084-1526

TOMCISIN, THERESA ANN, public relations executive; b. Cleve., Jan. 12, 1960; d. George Tomcisin and Miyoko Oka; m. James D. Rosenthal, May 29, 1988. BA in Polit. Sci. cum laude, U. Dayton, 1982. Asst., corp. communications Playboy Enterprises, Inc., Chgo., 1984-85, coord., corp. communications, 1985-86, adminstr., corp. communications, 1986-88, mgr., corp. communications, 1988-90, dir., corp. communications, 1990—. Recipient acad. scholarship Univ. Dayton, 1978-82, Wright-Patterson Officers' Wives acad. scholarship, 1978. Mem. Nat. Investor Relations Inst., Chgo. Advt. Fedn., Internat. Assn. Bus. Communicators (Spectra award 1987, 90, Gold Quill Merit award 1991), Publicity Club of Chgo. (Silver Trumpet award 1987, 90, bd. dirs. arts bridge). Office: Playboy Enterprises Inc 680 N Lake Shore Dr Chicago IL 60611-4402

TOMEI, MARISA, actress; b. Bklyn., Dec. 4, 1964. TV appearances include (series) A Different World, 1987, (films) Parker Kane, 1990; film appearances include: The Flamingo Kid, 1984, Playing for Keeps, 1986, Oscar, 1991, Zandalee, 1991, My Cousin Vinny, 1992 (Acad. award best supporting actress 1993), Chaplin, 1992, Untamed Heart, 1993, Equinox, 1993, The Paper, 1994, Only You, 1994, The Perez Family, 1994; theatre appearances include Slavs! Thinking About the Longstanding Problems of Virtue and Happiness, 1994. Office: William Morris Agy 151 S El Camino Dr Beverly Hills CA 90212-2704*

TOMHAVE, BEVERLY KORSTAD, corporate executive; b. St. Paul, Feb. 17, 1947; d. William Bernard and Dorothy Ann (Danielson) Korstad; m. Jonathan F. Tomhave, Oct. 15, 1977; children: Anna M., William D. Stefan. BA, Grinnell Coll., 1969; postgrad., U. Minn., 1974-76; student, various schs., India, Japan, Thailand, Ethiopia. Researcher Devel. Rsch. Corp., Mpls., 1965-66; researcher dept. biology Grinnell (Iowa) Coll., 1966-69; with dist. office Northwestern Bell, St. Paul, 1969-72; dist. traffic inst. Northwestern Bell, Mpls., 1972-74; v.p., pres. Jonathan Studios, Plymouth, Minn., 1974—; treas. Korridor Capital Investment, Mpls., 1986—, bd. dirs; founder Jardin Ltd., 1994—. Active Human Rights Commn., St. Paul, 1969, United Fund Commn., St. Paul, 1972; adviser Jr. Achievement, St. Paul, 1973. Recipient Spectrum award Ceramic Tile Distbrs. Assn., 1988. Mem. Minn. State Hist. Soc., Greene County Hist. Soc., Clan Douglas Soc. North Am., Minn. Bus. and Profl. Women. Office: Jonathan Studios 1882 Berkshire Ln N Minneapolis MN 55441-3723

TOMIC, CHARLOTTE FRENKEL, communications administrator; b. Paris, June 7, 1949; came to U.S., 1952; d. Salo and Hilda Lockspeiser Frenkel. BA, Queens Coll., 1971; MBA, St. John's U., 1982. Asst. editor Simon and Schuster Inc., N.Y.C., 1971-75; chief copywriter Barron's Edn. Series, Woodbury, N.Y., 1975-76; staff writer Direct Mail/Mktg. Assn., N.Y.C., 1976-77; asst. v.p. communications St. John's U., N.Y.C., 1977—. Chair, Queens Tobacco Control Task Force, Am. Cancer Soc.; bd. dirs. Women in Comms., Inc., Am. Lung Assn., Youth Women's Agenda, Bread-and-Life Soup Kitchen, Svcs. for the Under Served. Home: 67-15 190 Lane J RR 1 Box 17 # J Woodbourne NY 12788-9712 Office: St Johns U Grand Cen Utopia Pky Jamaica NY 11439

TOMICH, LILLIAN, lawyer; b. L.A., Mar. 28, 1935; d. Peter S. and Yovanka P. (Ivanovic) T. AA, Pasadena City Coll., 1954; BA in Polit. Sci., UCLA, 1956, cert. secondary teaching, 1957, MA, 1958; JD, U. So. Calif., 1961. Bar: Calif. Sole practice, 1961-66; house counsel Mfrs. Bank, Los Angeles, 1966; assoc. Hurley, Shaw & Tomich, San Marino, Calif., 1968-76; assoc. Driscoll & Tomich, San Marino, 1976—; dir. Continental Culture Specialists Inc., Glendale, Calif. Trustee, St. Sava Serbian Orthodox Ch., San Gabriel, Calif. Charles Fletcher Scott fellow, 1957; U. So. Calif. Law Sch. scholar, 1958. Mem. ABA, Calif. Bar Assn., Los Angeles County Bar Assn., Women Lawyers Assn., San Marino C. of C., UCLA Alumni Assn., Town Hall and World Affairs Council, Order Mast and Dagger, Iota Tau Tau, Alpha Gamma Sigma. Office: 2460 Huntington Dr San Marino CA 91108-2643

TOMKIEL, JUDITH IRENE, small business owner; b. St. Louis, Nov. 4, 1949; d. Melvin Charles William and Mildred Neva (Kayhart) Linders; m. William George Tomkiel, Dec. 15, 1972; children: Soteara, William, Kimberli, Jennifer, Christopher. Order filler Baker & Taylor Co., Sommerville, N.J., 1972-74; owner, founder The Idea Shoppe, Garden Grove, 1983-90; seamstress, crafts person Cloth World, Anaheim, Calif., 1987-89; mgr. S.M.T. Dental Lab., San Clemente, Calif., 1990-94, pres., 1994—; Vol. Reading Is Fundamental Program, Garden Grove, 1988-89; freedom writer Amnesty Internat., Garden Grove, 1988-91. Author numerous poems; pub., editor (newsletter) Shoppe Talk, 1987-90; pub. Fakatale, 1988. Fellow World Literary Acad.; mem. NAFE, Nat. Writer's Club, Soc. Scholarly Pub., Dental LAb Owners Assn. (pres. S.M.T. Dental Lab., Inc. 1994).

TOMKINS, JOANNE KARK, health physicist, educator; b. Newark, Sept. 18, 1953; d. Jon Joseph and Anna Rose (Peters) Kark; m. Robert Norton McVey, Mar. 24, 1979 (div. Apr. 1980); m. Robin Joseph Tomkins, Mar. 6, 1992. BS, Villanova U., 1975; postgrad., Colo. State U., 1984-85. Cert. nuclear medicine technologist. Analytical chemistry technician SpectroChem Labs., Inc., Franklin Lakes, N.J., 1976-77; nuclear medicine technologist Albert Einstein Med. Ctr., Phila., 1977-79; biol. technician Oak Ridge (Tenn.) Nat. Lab., 1979-81, radiol. technician, 1981-84; nuclear safety health physicist Ill. Dept. Nuclear Safety, Glen Ellyn, 1986—; instr. radiation safety Oakton C.C., Des Plaines, Ill., 1989-91. Contbr. articles to profl. jours. Recipient program cert. of appreciation Suburban Bldg. Ofcls. Conf., 1988. Mem. Soc. Nuclear Medicine (assoc.), Health Physics Soc. (plenary treas. Midwest chpt. 1989, pub. info. com. 1989-92, chmn. legis. com. 1990-92). Roman Catholic. Office: Ill Dept Nuclear Safety 800 Roosevelt Rd Ste 200 Glen Ellyn IL 60137-5839

TOMKINSON, NORMA SUE, marketing professional; b. Ft. Wayne, Ind., May 9, 1950; d. Stanley Everest and Almeda (Miller) T. BS, Ball State U., 1972. Various positions Ft. Wayne Marriott, 1972-77; relocation/tng. dir. Rousseau Realtors, Ft. Wayne, 1977-80; sales mgr. Marriot, Chgo., 1980-81, Marriott's Lincolnshire (Ill.) Resort, 1981-82; dir. sales Miami Airport Marriott, 1982-84; dir. mktg. Greensboro (N.C.)-High Point Marriott, 1984-87, Marriott's Hunt Valley (Md.) Inn, 1987-89, J.W. Marriott at Century City, L.A., 1989-92, Santa Clara (Calif) Marriott, 1993—. Republican. Office: Santa Clara Marriott Hotel 2700 Mission College Blvd Santa Clara CA 95052-8181

TOMLIN, LILY, actress; b. Detroit, 1939. Student, Wayne State U.; studied mime with Paul Curtis, studied acting with Peggy Feury. Appearances in concerts and colls. throughout U.S.; TV appearances include Lily Tomlin, CBS Spls., 1973, 81, 82; 2 ABC Spls., 1975, Edithann Animated Specials, ABC, 1994; formerly cast mem. The Music Scene, Laugh In; motion picture debut in Nashville, 1975 (N.Y. Film Critics award); also appeared in The Late Show, 1977, Moment by Moment, 1978, The Incredible Shrinking Woman, 1981, Nine to Five, 1980, All of Me, 1984, Big Business, 1987, Shadows and Fog, 1992, The Player, 1992, Short Cuts, 1993, The Beverly Hillbillies, 1993, And the Band Played On, HBO, 1993 (Best Supporting Actress Emmy nominee - Special, 1994); one-woman Broadway show Appearing Nitely, 1977 (Spl. Tony award), The Search for Signs of Intelligent Life in the Universe, 1985 (Drama Desk award, Outer Critics Circle award, Tony award 1986); recs. include This is a Recording, And That's The Truth, Modern Scream, On Stage. Recipient Grammy award 1971, 5 Emmy awards for CBS Spl. 1973, 81, Emmy award for ABC Spl. 1975.

TOMLIN-HOUSTON, LISA, educational director; b. Bklyn., Apr. 6, 1965; d. George L. and Joan J. (Hill) Tomlin; m. Anthony Houston, Feb. 2, 1991. BA in Psychology, Oberlin Coll., Ohio, 1987; MEd in Counseling Psychology, Rutgers U., 1990. Career counselor U. Pa., Phila., 1990-93; dir. career svcs. H. John Heinz III Sch. of Public Policy and Mgmt., Carnegie Mellon U., Pitts., Pa., 1993—. Mem. Middle Atlantic Placement Assn. (com. mem. profl. devel. commn. 1990-91, chairperson new profl. com. 1991-92). Office: Carnegie Mellon U The Heinz Sch 5000 Forbes Ave Pittsburgh PA 15213

TOMLINSON-KEASEY, CAROL ANN, university administrator; b. Washington, Oct. 15, 1942; d. Robert Bruce and Geraldine (Howe) Tomlinson; m. Charles Blake Keasey, June 13, 1964; children: Kai Linson, Amber Lynn. BS, Pa. State U., 1964; MS, Iowa State U., 1966; PhD, U. Calif., Berkeley, 1970. Lic. psychologist, Calif. Asst. prof. psychology Trenton (N.J.) State Coll., 1969-70, Rutgers U., New Brunswick, N.J., 1970-72; prof. U. Nebr., Lincoln, 1972-77; prof. U. Calif., Riverside, 1977-92, acting dean Coll. Humanities and Social Scis., 1986-88, chmn. dept. psychology, 1989-92; vice provost for faculty rels. U. Calif., Davis, 1992—. Author: Child's Eye View, 1980, Child Development, 1985; also numerous chpts. to books; articles to profl. jours. Recipient Disting. Tchr. award U. Calif., 1986. Mem. APA, Soc. Rsch. in Child Devel., Riverside Aquatics Assn. (pres.). Office: Office of Provost U Calif Davis Davis CA 95616

TOMLJANOVICH, ESTHER M., judge; b. Galt, Iowa, Nov. 1, 1931; d. Chester William and Thelma L. (Brooks) Moellering; m. William S. Tomljanovich, Dec. 26, 1957; 1 child, William Brooks. AA, Itasca Jr. Coll., 1951; BSL, St. Paul Coll. Law, 1953, LLB, 1955. Bar: Minn. 1955, U.S. Dist. Ct. Minn. 1958. Asst. revisor of statutes State of Minn., St. Paul, 1957-66, revisor of statutes, 1974-77; dist. ct. judge State of Minn., Stillwater, 1977-90; assoc. justice Minn. Supreme Ct., St. Paul, 1990—. Former mem. North St. Paul Bd. Edn., Maplewood Bd. Edn., Lake Elmo Planning Commn; bd. trustees William Mitchell Coll. Law, 1995—. Mem. Minn. State Bar Assn., Bus. and Profl. Women's Assn. St. Paul (former pres.). Office: Supreme Ct MN MN Judicial Ctr Rm 423 25 Constitution Ave Saint Paul MN 55155-1500

TOMOEDA, CHERYL KUNIKO, academic researcher; b. Honolulu, Sept. 24, 1958; d. Charles Kunio and Doris Masue (Takehara) T. BS, U. Hawaii, 1980; MS, U. Ariz., 1982. Cert. speech-lang. pathology. Speech pathologist Amphitheater Pub. Schs., Tucson, 1983-84; rsch. asst. U. Ariz., Tucson, 1982-83, rsch. asst. II, 1984-86, rsch. coord., 1985-91, sr. rsch. specialist, 1991—. Author: (test) Ariz. Battery for Comm. Disorders of Dementia, 1991, The Functional Linguistic Communication Inventory, 1994, (book) The ABC/s of Dementia, 1993; prodr. videoconf. series Telerounds. Mem. Acad. Neurologic Communication Disorders and Scis. (acting sec. 1991, sec. 1992-93), Internat. Neuropsychol. Soc., Am. Speech-Lang.-Hearing Assn. Office: U Ariz Nat Ctr Neurogenic Comm Disorders Dept Speech & Hearing Scis Tucson AZ 85721

TOMPKINS, EILEEN, state legislator; m. Patrick Tompkins; 9 children. Attended, Inver Hills C.C., U. Minn., Coll. of St. Thomas. Mem. Minn. Ho. of Reps., 1984—; mem. health and human svcs. com., mem. local govt. com., mem. met. affairs com., mem. transp. and transit com. Home: 7734 133rd St W Apple Valley MN 55124 Office: Minn Ho of Reps State Capitol Saint Paul MN 55155 also: 245 State Office Bldg Saint Paul MN 55155*

TOMPSON, MARIAN LEONARD, association executive; b. Chgo., Dec. 5, 1929; d. Charles Clark and Marie Christine (Bernardini) Leonard; m. Clement R. Tompson, May 7, 1949 (dec. 1981); children: Melanie Tompson Kandler, Deborah Tompson Mikolajczak, Allison Tompson Fagerholm, Laurel Tompson Davies, Sheila Tompson Dorsey, Brian, Philip. Student public and parochial schs., Chgo. and Franklin Park, Ill. Co-founder La Leche League (Internat.), Franklin Park, 1956; pres. La Leche League (Internat.), 1956-80, dir., 1956—, pres. emeritus, 1990—; exec. dir. Alternative Birth Crisis Coalition, 1981-85; cons. WHO; bd. dirs. North Am. Soc. Psychosomatic Ob-Gyn, Natural Birth and Natural Parenting, 1981-83; mem. adv. bd. Nat. Assn. Parents and Profls. for Safe Alternatives in Childbirth, Am. Acad. Husband-Coached Childbirth; mem. adv. bd. Fellowship of Christian Midwives; mem. profl. adv. bd. Home Oriented Maternity Experience; guest lectr. Harvard U. Med. Sch., UCLA Sch. Public Health, U. Antioquia Med. Sch., Medellín, Columbia, U. Ill. Sch. Medicine, Chgo., U. W.I., Jamaica, U. N.C., Nat. Coll. of Chiropractic, Am. Coll. Nurse Midwives, U. Parma, Italy, Inst. Psychology, Rome, Rockford (Ill.) Sch. Medicine, Northwestern U. Sch. Medicine; mem. family com. Ill. Commn. on Status of Women, 1976-85; mem. perinatal adv. com. Ill. Dept. Pub. Health, 1980-83; mem. adv. bd. Internat. Nutrition Communication Service, 1980—; bd. cons. We Can, 1984—; exec. adv. bd. United Resources for Family Health and Support, 1985-86. Author: (with others) Safe Alternatives in Childbirth, 1976, 21st Century Obstetrics Now!, 1977, The Womanly Art of Breastfeeding, 3d edit., 1981, Five Standards for Safe Childbearing, 1981, But Doctor, About That Shot..., 1988, Breast Feeding, 5th edit., 1991; author prefaces and forwards in 10 books; columnist La Leche League News, 1958-80; columnist People's Doctor Newsletter, 1977-88, mem. adv. bd., cons., 1988-92; assoc. editor Child and Family Quar., 1967—; mem. med. adv. bd. East West Jour., 1980—; also articles. Recipient Gold medal of honor Centro de Rehabilitacao Nossa Senhora da Gloria, 1975, Night of 100 Stars III Achiever award Actors Fund Am., 1990. Office: 1400 N Meacham Rd Schaumburg IL 60173-4840

TOMS, KATHLEEN MOORE, nurse; b. San Francisco, Dec. 31, 1943; d. William Moore and Phyllis Josephine (Barry) Stewart. RN, AA, City Coll. San Francisco, 1963; BPS in Nursing Edn., Elizabethtown (Pa.) Coll., 1973; MS in Edn., Temple U., 1977; MS in Nursing, Gwynedd Mercy Coll. 1988; m. Benjamin Peskoff; children from previous marriage: Kathleen Marie Toms Myers, Kelly Terese Toms. Med.-surg. nurse St. Joseph Hosp., Fairbanks, Alaska, 1963-65; emergency room nurse St. Joseph Hosp., Lancaster, Pa., 1965-69, blood, plasm and components nurse, 1969-71; pres. F.E. Barry Co., Lancaster, 1971—; dir. inservice edn. Lancaster Osteo. Hosp., 1971-75; coord. practical nursing program Vocat. Tech. Sch., Coatesville, Pa., 1976-77; dir. nursing Pocopson Home, West Chester, Pa., 1978-80, Riverside Hosp., Wilmington, Del., 1980-83; assoc. Coatesville VA Hosp., 1983-89; chief Nurse, 1984-89; with VA Cen. Office; supr. psychiat. nursing Martinez (Calif.) VA Med. Ctr., 1989-94; assoc. chief nursing svc. edn. VA No. Calif. Sys. Clinics, Pleasant Hill, Calif., 1994—; trainee assoc. chief Nursing Home Care Unit, Washington; mem. Pa. Gov.'s Council on Alcoholism and Drug Abuse, 1974-76; mem. Del. Health Council Med.-Surg. Task Force, 1981-83; dir. Lancaster Community Health Ctr., 1973-76; lectr. in field. Lt. col. Nurse Corps, USAR, 1973-94, col., 1994—, apptd. chief nurse, 1992. Decorated Army Commendation medals (5), Meritorious Svc. medal XI; recipient Community Service award Citizens United for Better Public Relations, 1974; award Sertoma, Lancaster, 1974; Outstanding Citizen award Sta. WGAL-TV, 1975; U.S. Army Achievement award, 1983. Mem. Elizabethtown, Temple U. Alumni Assns., Pa. Nurses' Assn. (dir.), Sigma Theta Tau, Beta Gamma. Inventor auto-infuser for blood or blood components, 1971. Home: 208 Sea Mist Dr Vallejo CA 94591-7748 Office: VA No Calif System of Clinics 2350 Contra Costa Blvd Pleasant Hill CA 94523

TOMSHINSKY, IDA, librarian; b. Riga, Latvia, Russia, Aug. 2, 1953; came to U.S. 1989; d. Abram and Zelda (Helman) Milman; m. Jan. 7, 1977; children: Sabina, Yardy. MLS, Latvia State U.; student, U. S. Fla. Main librarian State Sci. & Tech. Libr., Riga, Latvia, USSR, 1970-89; bookkeeper Hour House Conf. Tapes, Miami, Fla., 1989-90; libr. asst. Hebrew Acad., Miami Beach, Fla., 1990-91; main librarian Internat. Fine Arts Coll., Miami, 1991—. Author: Library Science Social Management, 1970-76, 1980, How to Write a Bibliography of Books, 1986. Mem. Assn. Soviet Jews of S. Fla. (treas. 1991—). Office: Internat Fine Arts Coll 1737 N Bayshore Dr Miami FL 33132-1121

TONAY, VERONICA KATHERINE, psychology educator; b. LaJolla, Calif., Mar. 28, 1960. BA with honors, U. Calif., Santa Cruz, 1985; MA, U. Calif., Berkeley, 1988, PhD, 1993. Teaching asst. U. Calif.-Berkeley, U. Calif.-Santa Cruz, 1985-88; psychology intern Family Svcs. Assn., Santa Cruz, 1989-90; lectr. psychology U. Calif., Santa Cruz, 1989—, Berkeley, 1992-94; psychology intern Santa Cruz County Children's Mental Health, 1994-95; dir. Psychology Field Study Program U. Calif., Santa Cruz, 1994—; counselor, rschr., Santa Cruz. Contbr. articles to profl. jours. Fellow State of Calif., 1985-89. Mem. APA (program chmn. div. 32 1989-90), Assn. for Study of Dreams (conf. organizer 1987-88, 91-92). Office: U Calif Psychology Dept Santa Cruz CA 95064

TONELLI, GIOVANNA MARIE, professional development consultant, social worker; b. Phila., Nov. 13, 1951; d. Peter Paul and Mary Rita (Campagna) T. AAS, Community Coll. of Phila., 1972; B of Social Work, Temple U., 1974, MSW, 1981. Lic. social worker, Pa. Med. social worker Bio-Med. Applications, Phila., 1976-79; with foster care program Tabor Children's Svcs., Doylestown, Pa., 1981; with adoption program, cons. Tabor Children's Svcs., Doylestown, 1982; social worker City of Phila., 1982; program dir. Italian Home for Children, Boston, 1983-87; trainer, cons. Temple U., Phila., 1987; social worker Support Ctr. for Child Advocates, Phila., 1987-88; trainer/ cons. profl. devel. Becoming, Phila., 1987—; mem. exec. bd. Today's Child, Boston, 1985-87 ; mem. network speakers USA, Inc., Pigeon Forge, Tenn., 1991; convenor Gathering Bus. Women in South

Phila., 1991—. Vol. Boston Dept. Social Svcs., 1986-87; adv. Nat. Abortion Rights Action League, Phila. and Boston, 1974-89. Recipient Achiever award Success Motivation Inst., Inc., Waco, Tex., 1988. Mem. Nat. Assn. Social Workers (mem. child welfare task force 1984-87), NAFE, Bus. Women's Network. Home and Office: Becoming 905 Mountain St Philadelphia PA 19148-1117

TONELLO-STUART, ENRICA MARIA, political economist; b. Monza, Italy; d. Alessandro P. and Maddalena M. (Marangoni) Tonello; m. Albert E. Smith; m. Charles L. Stuart. BA in Internat. Affairs, Econs., U. Colo., 1961; MA, Claremont Grad. Sch., 1966, PhD, 1971. Sales mgr. Met. Life Ins. Co., 1974-79; pres. E.T.S. Rsch. and Devel., Inc., 1977—; dean internat. studies program Union U., L.A. and Tokyo; lectr. internat. affairs and mktg. UCLA Ext., Union U.; CEO, ETS Internat. Investments and ETS Publs., Inc., 1986—. Pub., editor Tomorrow Outline Jour., 1963—, The Monitor, 1988; pub. World Regionalism-An Ecological Analysis, 1971, A Proposal for the Reorganization of the United Nations, 1966, The Persuasion Technocracy, Its Forms, Techniques and Potentials, 1966, The Role of the Multinationals in the Emerging Globalism, 1978; developed the theory of social ecology and econsociometry. Organized first family assistance program Langley AFB Tactical Air Command Commandation, 1956-58. Recipient vol. svc. award VA, 1956-58, ARC svc. award, 1950-58. Mem. Corp. Planners Assn. (treas. 1974-79), Investigative Reporters and Editors, World Future Soc. (pres. 1974—), U.S.-China Journalists Fellowship Assn., Asian Bus. League, Chinese Am. Assn. (life), Japan Am. Assn., Fgn. Trade Assn., World Trade Assn., Palos Verdes C. of C. (legis. com.), L.A. Press Club (bd. dirs.), L.A. World Trade Ctr., Zonta (chmn. internat. com. South Bay), Pi Sigma Alpha.

TONG, MARY POWDERLY, retired mathematician, educator; b. N.Y.C., May 24, 1924; d. William Joseph and Katherine Colwell Powderly; m. Hing Tong, Aug. 19, 1956; children: Christopher, Mary Elizabeth, William, Jane Frances, James. BA, St. Joseph's Coll., 1950; MA, Columbia U., 1951, PhD, 1969. Instr. math. St. Joseph's Coll., Bklyn., 1951-54, Columbia Univ., N.Y.C., 1954-60; asst. prof. math. Univ. Conn., Storrs, 1960-66; assoc. prof. math. Fairfield (Conn.) Univ., 1966-70; prof. math. William Paterson Coll., Wayne, N.J., 1970-81; ret., 1981. Contbr. articles to profl. jours. Trustee South Bergen Mental Health Ctr., Lyndhurst, N.J., 1988—, pres., 1994—. Recipient fellowship NSF, Washington, 1959-60. Mem. Am. Math. Soc., Math. Assn. Am., Am. Phys. Soc., N.Y. Acad. Scis., Delta Epsilon Sigma. Roman Catholic. Home: 725 Cooper Ave Oradell NJ 07649-2334

TONJES, MARIAN JEANNETTE BENTON, education educator; b. Rockville Center, N.Y., Feb. 16, 1929; d. Millard Warren and Felicia E. (Tyler) Benton; m. Charles F. Tonjes (div. 1965); children: Jeffrey Charles, Kenneth Warren. BA, U. N.Mex., 1951, cert., 1966, MA, 1969; EdD, U. Miami, 1975. Dir. recreation Stuyvesant Town Housing Project, N.Y.C., 1951-53; tchr. music., phys. edn. Sunset Mesa Day Sch., Albuquerque, 1953-54; tchr. remedial reading Zia Elem. Sch., Albuquerque, 1965-67; tchr. secondary devel. reading Rio Grande High Sch., Albuquerque, 1967-69; rsch. asst. reading Southwestern Coop. Ednl. Lab., Albuquerque, 1969-71; assoc. dir., vis. instr. Fla. Ctr. Tchr. Tng. Materials U. Miami, 1971-72; asst. prof. U.S. Internat. U., San Diego, 1972-75; prof. edn. Western Wash. U., Bellingham, 1975-94, prof. emeritus, 1994—, dir. summer study at Oxford (Eng.) U., 1975-94; vis. prof. adult edn. Palomar (Calif.) Jr. Coll., 1974; reading supr. Manzanita Ctr. U. N.Mex., Albuquerque, 1968; vis. prof. U. Guam, Mangilao, 1989-90; speaker, cons. in field; invited guest Russian Reading Assn., Moscow, 1992. Author: (with Miles V. Zintz) Teaching Reading/Thinking Study Skills in Content Classrooms, 3d edit., 1992, Secondary Reading, Writing and Learning, 1991; contbr. articles to profl. jours. Tng. Tchr. Trainers grantee, 1975; NDEA fellow Okla. State U., 1969. Mem. Am. Reading Forum (chmn. bd. dirs. 1983-85), Internat. Reading Assn. (mem. travel, interchange and study tours com. 1984-86, mem. non-print media and reading com. 1980-83, workshop dir. S.W. regional conf. 1982, mem. com. internat. devel. N.Am. 1991-95, Outstanding Tchr. Educator 1988-90), U.K. Reading Assn. (speaker 1977-93), European Conf. Reading, Berlin, Edinburgh, Malmo and Budapest (speaker), World Congress in Reading Buenos Aires (speaker 1994), PEO (past chpt. pres.), Phi Delta Kappa, Delta Delta Delta.

TONKENS, REBECCA A., obstetrical-gynecological nurse, chemical dependency and adolescent psychology nurse; b. Searcy, Ark., Dec. 17, 1943; d. William T. and Velda M. (Goodloe) McAfee; m. Richard E. Morris, June 24, 1960 (div. Nov. 1980); children: Terri L. Morris Bomar, Toni L. Morris Carroll; m. Solvin W. Tonkens, Dec. 22, 1986. LPN, Area Vocat. Tech. Sch., 1973; ADN, Kansas City (Kans.) C.C., 1980; BSN, Webster U., 1992. RN, Kans., Mo. Staff nurse Providence-St. Margaret Hosp., Kansas City, 1973-80; indsl. nurse, office mgr. Kansas City Indsl. Clinic, 1980-81; staff nurse Bethany Med. Ctr., Kansas City, 1981—; active community rels. diabetes unit Bethany Med. Ctr., 1983-86. Officer, v.p., bd. dirs. Cambridge Townhouse Assn., Leawood, Kans., 1989-92; chaperone Rose Bud (Ark.) Band at Presdl. Inauguration, Washington, 1992; vol. Habitat for Humanity, Salvation Army, others. Recipient Cert. of Appreciation, Salvation Army, 1994. Mem. ANA, Am. Coll. Occupational and Environ. Medicine (aux.). Episcopalian. Home and Office: 12861 Cambridge Ter Leawood KS 66209

TONNIES, JUDITH ANN, learning disabilities educator, director; b. Macon, Mo., Jan. 16, 1953; d. Harold William and Georgia Rose (Gaier) Threlkeld; m. Richard Keith Tonnies, Jan. 22, 1972; children: Ryan Keith, Brandon Seth, Shelby Michael. BSE, N.E. Mo. State U., 1974. Cert. spl. edn. tchr. learning disabilities, emotionally disturbed/behavior disordered, educationally mentally handicapped, K-12; cert. in spl. edn. adminstrn. EMR tchr. Monroe City (Mo.) Jr. High, 1974-75, Marion County R-II Schs., Phila., 1975-77, Hannibal (Mo.) Pub. Schs., 1977-78; elem./jr. h.s. learning disabilities tchr. Shelby County C-I Schs., Shelbyville, Mo., 1978—, spl. svcs. dir., 1978—; dir. spl. programs Shelby County C-I North Shelby, Shelbyville, 1980-93, dir. spl. svcs, 1993—. Mem. Local Adminstrs. of Spl. Edn. (N.E. Mo. chpt. treas 1980-84), Mo. Learning Disabilities Assn. (Profl. of Yr. award 1994). Home: 411 W Main Shelbyville MO 63469 Office: Shelby County C-I North Shelby Rt 2 Box 142 Shelbyville MO 63469

TONSO, CHERYL JACKSON, retired secondary education educator; b. Denver, Jan. 12, 1934; d. James Homer and Virginia Isabelle (Anderson) Jackson; m. Jerome Peter Tonso, Mar. 2, 1957 (dec. May 1977); children: Tawlys Grace Tonso Kaufman, Trynis Marie Tonso Bradley. AA, Cottey Coll., 1954; BA, U. Colo., 1956. Classroom tchr. Mesa Valley Schs., Grand Junction, Colo., 1956-58; classroom tchr. Boulder (Colo.) Valley Pub. Schs., 1965-77, 80-87, organizational specialist, 1977-80, dean of students, 1987-95; pvt. bus. owner; real estate, property devel. specialist Colo., 1992—; cons. Denver Pub. Schs., 1979-80, Elizabeth (Colo.) Pub. Sch., 1979-80. Collaborative author: Organization Development, 1977-90, Boulder Schools English Curriculum, 1987-89, Boulder Schools Junior High School Curriculum, 1969-73. Mem. NEA, PDK, PEO, AAUW (pres. 1969-71), Colo. Edn. Assn., Boulder Valley Edn. Assn. (several offices), Colo. North Ctrl. Assn. (state com. 1981-95, chmn. 1990-91), Delta Kappa Gamma (pres. 1977-79). Democrat. Home: 1690 Dogwood Ln Boulder CO 80304-1525

TOOHEY, CYNTHIA D., state legislator; b. N.Y.C., Apr. 16, 1934; widowed; children: Camden, Sean, Kate. ADN, U. Alaska-Anchorage C.C., 1974. Co-owner, operator Crow Creek Mine, 1970—; mem. Alaska House of Reps., Anchorage, 1992—. Trustee Alaska Regional Hosp.; bd. dirs. Anchorage Conv. & Visitors Bur.; past mem. Girdwood Bd. Suprs. Office: The House of Representatives 2642 Forest Park Dr Anchorage AK 99517-1326*

TOOMEY, BEVERLY GUELLA, social work educator; b. Cleve., Aug. 8, 1940; d. Fred John and Frances (Sutkowy) Guella; m. Rickard S. Toomey, Jr., Oct. 6, 1962 (div. Sept. 1981); children: Rickard S. III, A. Katherine; m. Richard J. First, Jan. 4, 1985. BA cum laude, Miami U., 1962; MSW, Ohio State U., 1974, PhD, 1977. Lic. ind. social worker. Asst. prof. Ohio State U., Columbus, 1977-81, assoc. prof., 1981-90, prof., 1990—; acting dean Coll. of Social Work, 1993-94; mem. Ohio State U. Acad. of Teaching, Columbus, 1993—; chmn. Panel on Breakup of Family Commn. Interprofl. Edn., Columbus, 1987-89. Author: Practice Focused Research, 1985; author, editor: Mentally Ill Offenders and the Criminal Justice System, 1979; editor: Social Work in the 1980's, 1981; reviewer NIMH, Washington, 1982-86; contbr. over 40 articles to profl. jours. Mem. Ohio Hunger Task Force, Columbus, 1991; bd. dirs. Friends of Homeless, Columbus, 1985-89, YWCA, Columbus, 1989—; evaluation com. United Way, Columbus, 1988-90. Rural homelessness grantee NIMH, 1989-92. Mem. NASW (Social Worker of Yr. 1989), Coun. Social Work Edn., Nat. Women's Studies Assn., Am. Evaluation Assn., Phi Beta Kappa, Alpha Delta Mu. Office: Ohio State Univ 1947 N College Rd Columbus OH 43210-1123

TOOMEY, KATHRYN W., state legislator; b. Nashua, N.H., Feb. 3, 1942. Student, Nashua Bus. Coll. Mem. corrections & criminal justice com. N.H. Ho. of Reps., Concord. Democrat. Roman Catholic. Home: 10 Lantern Ln Nashua NH 03062 Office: NH Ho of Reps State Capitol Concord NH 03301*

TOOTE, GLORIA E. A., developer, lawyer, columnist; b. N.Y.C.; d. Frederick A. and Lillie M. (Tooks) Toote. Student, Howard U., 1949-51; J.D., NYU, 1954; LL.M., Columbia U., 1956. Bar: N.Y. 1955, U.S. Dist. Ct. (so. and ea. dists.) N.Y. 1956, U.S. Supreme Ct. 1956. With firm Greenbaum, Wolff & Ernst, 1957; mem. editorial staff Time mag., 1957-58; asst. gen. counsel N.Y. State Workmen's Compensation Bd., 1958-64; pres. Toote Town Pub. Co. and Town Sound Studios, Inc., 1966-70; asst. dir. Action Agy., 1971-73; asst. sec. Dept. HUD, 1973-75; vice chmn. Pres.'s Adv. Council on Pvt. Sector Initiatives, 1983-85; housing developer, 1976—; pres. Trea Estates and Enterprises, Inc.; newspaper columnist; chairperson The Policy Coun. Former bd. dirs. Citizens for the Republic, Nat. Black United Fund, Exec. Women in Govt., Am. Arbitration Assn., Consumer Alert; bd. overseers Hoover Inst., 1985—; vice chair Nat. Polit. Congress of Black Women, 1984-92; former mem. Coun. Econ. Affairs, Rep. Nat. Com.; pres. N.Y.C. Black Rep. Coun.; exec. trustee Polit. Action Com. for Equality. Recipient citations Nat. Bus. League, Alpha Kappa Alpha, U.S. C. of C., Nat. Assn. Black Women Attys. Mem. N.Y. Fedn. Civil Svc. Orgns., Nat. Assn. Real Estate Brokers, Nat. Fed. Mortgage Assn. (bd. dirs. 1992), Nat. Citizens Participation Coun., Nat. Bar Assn.,Delta Sigma Theta, others. Address: 282 W 137th St New York NY 10030-2439

TOPELIUS, KATHLEEN E., lawyer; b. July 15, 1948. BA, U. Conn., 1970; JD, Cath. U. Am., 1978. Bar: D.C. 1978, U.S. Supreme Ct. 1988. Atty. office of gen. counsel Fed. Home Loan Bank Bd., 1978-80; ptnr. Morgan, Lewis & Bockius, Washington, 1985-93, Bryan Cave, Washington, 1993—. Office: Bryan Cave 700 13th St NW Washington DC 20005-3960

TOPHAM, SALLY JANE, ballet educator; b. N.Y.C., June 2, 1933; d. William Holroyd Topham and Marian Phyllis (Thomas) Topham Halligan; m. Joseph Vincent Ferrara, Dec. 27, 1958 (div. 1977); children: Gregory Paul, Mark Edward. Student Ballet Theatre Sch., Royal Acad. Dancing, London; trained in Europe. Free-lance profl. dancer ballet, opera ballet, summer stock, 1956-59; founder, dir. Monmouth Sch. Ballet, N.J., 1963-83, 85—; founder Central Jersey Acad. Ballet, Red Bank, N.J., 1983-85 , also dir.; dir. Westfield sch. Ballet, N.J., 1976-77; tchr., dir. Mount Allison U. Summer Sch., New Brunswick, Can., 1973-77; prof. ballet Monmouth Coll., West Long Branch, N.J., 1981-83. Choreographer (ballet) Coppelia, 1981, 83; Shubert Songs, 1980; Homage to Bournonville, 1977; Nutcracker, 1985, Cinderella, 1988; staged many ballets and opera ballets. Bd. dirs. Monmouth Arts Found., Red Bank, 1972—, Shore Ballet Co., Red Bank, 1976—; founder, bd. dirs. Monmouth Civic Ballet, Red Bank, 1972-75. Mem. Royal Acad. Dancing (assoc., advanced tchr's. cert. 1979), English Speaking Union. Avocations: sailing, theater, music, books. Office: Shore Ballet Theater Sch 25 Broad St Red Bank NJ 07701-1901

TOPINKA, JUDY BAAR, state official; b. Riverside, Ill., Jan. 16, 1944; d. William Daniel and Lillian Mary (Shuss) Baar; 1 child, Joseph Baar. BS, Northwestern U., 1966. Features editor, reporter, columnist Life Newspapers, Berwyn and LaGrange, Ill., 1966-77; with Forest Park (Ill.) Rev. and Westchester News, 1976-77; coord. spl. events dept. fedn. comm., AMA, 1978-80; rsch. analyst Senator Leonard Becker, 1978-79; mem. Ill. Ho. of Reps., 1981-84; mem. Ill. Senate, 1985-94; treas. State of Ill., Springfield, 1995—; former mem. judiciary com., former chmn. senate health and welfare com.; former mem. fin. instn. com.; former co-chmn. Citizens Coun. on Econ. Devel.; former co-chmn. U.S. Commn. for Preservation of Am.'s Heritage Abroad, serves on legis. ref. bur.; former mem. minority bus. resource ctr. adv. com. U.S. Dept. Transp.; former mem. adv. bd. Nat. Inst. Justice. Founder, pres., bd. dirs. West Suburban Exec. Breakfast Club, from 1976; chmn. Ill. Ethnics for Reagan-Bush, 1984, Bush-Quayle 1988; spokesman Nat. Coun. State Legislatures Health Com.; former mem nat. adv. coun. health professions edn. HHS; mem., GOP chairwoman Legis. Audit Commn. of Cook County; chmn. Riverside Twp. Regular Republican Orgn., 1994—. Recipient Outstanding Civilian Svc. medal, Molly Pitcher award, Abraham Lincoln award, Silver Eagle award U.S. Army and N.G. Office: JR Thompson Ctr 100 W Randolph Ste 15-600 Chicago IL 60601

TOPLIFF, CONNIE LYNN, physician; b. Las Cruces, N.Mex., Jan. 11, 1961; d. Lewis Henry Topliff and Irene (Statz) Hafen. BS, U. Ariz., 1985; MD, U. Kans., 1993. Utilization rev. coord. Stormont Vail Regional Med. Ctr., Topeka, Kans., 1980-81; emergency med. technician Kords Ambulance Svc., Tucson, Ariz., 1982-85; med. asst. Drs. Sufi & Challa, Topeka, 1988-89; house staff physician Trinity Luth. Hosp., Kansas City, Mo., 1993—; vol. Kansas City Free Health Clinic, 1993—. Supporter Am. Mus. for Women in the Arts, Washington, 1991—, Am. Indian Coll. Fund, N.Y.C., 1993—, Nat. Mental Health Assn., Alexandria, Va., 1994—. Supporter Am. Mus. for Women in the Arts, Washington, 1991—, Am. Indian Coll. Fund, N.Y.C., 1993—, Nat. Mental Health Assn., Alexandria, Va., 1994—; vol. Kansas City Free Health Clinic, 1993—. Mem. AAUW, Am. Acad. Family Physicians, Am. Assn. Physicians for Human Rights. Office: Trinity Lutheran Hosp Family Medicine Ctr 2900 Baltimore Ste 400 Kansas City MO 64108

TOPOL, ROBIN APRIL LEVITT, lawyer; b. N.Y.C., Apr. 2; d. Anatole Roy and Phyllis Patricia (Redman) Levitt; m. Clifford Miles Topol, Oct. 23, 1982. Student, Stanford U., Eng., 1974; BA, Barnard Coll., 1976; JD, NYU, 1979; postgrad. exec. mgmt. program, Yale U., 1987. Bar: N.Y. 1980, Fla. 1981. Assoc. Dreyer & Traub, N.Y.C., 1980-84, Willkie, Farr & Gallagher, N.Y.C., 1985-87; ptnr., real estate dept., specializing in coml. real estate, leasing, and sales Davis & Gilbert, N.Y.C., 1988—. Trustee alumni bd. dirs. Yale U. Sch. Mgmt., 1987-88. Mem. ABA (vice chmn. real property com. 1986—), N.Y. County Bar Assn. (real estate com. 1986—), Women's Bar Assn. (chmn. real estate com. 1980—). Office: Davis & Gilbert 1740 Broadway New York NY 10019-4315

TOPPAN, CLARA ANNA RAAB (MRS. FREDERICK WILLCOX TOPPAN), accountant; b. Cheyenne, Wyo., Nov. 9, 1910; d. Cornelius Emil and Gizella (Marczelly) Raab; m. Frederick Willcox Toppan, July 23, 1949 (dec. Nov. 1966). BS, U. Wyo., 1931. CPA, Wyo., D.C. Sec. Yellowstone Nat. Park, 1934, Nat. Park Svc., Washington, 1934-37; chief clk. Grand Teton Nat. Park, Moose, Wyo., 1937-42; acct. Cordle Raab & Roush CPA, Casper, Wyo., 1942-45; owner Clara Raab Toppan CPA, Jackson, Wyo., 1945-53; ind. part-time acct., 1954—; instr. acctg. U. Wyo., 1967. Treas. Community Bldg. Fund, Jackson, 1952-54, Teton County Libr. Fund, Jackson, 1950-53. Clara Raab Toppan Day proclaimed by Gov. of Wyo., 1990. Mem. AICPA (hon.), AAUW, Am. Women's Soc. CPA's, Wyo. Soc. CPA's (hon. life), Bus. and Profl. Women (organizer Jackson Hole), Jackson Hole C. of C. (an organizer), U. Wyo Alumni Assn., Jackson Hole Trap Club, Jackson Hole Golf and Country Club, Bradenton Country Club, Phi Gamma Nu. Republican. Home: 3605 Sun Eagle Ln Bradenton FL 34210-4235 Home: 4525 N Fish Creek Rd Wilson WY 83014

TOPPING, EVA CATAFYGIOTU, writer; b. Fredericksburg, Va., Aug. 23, 1920; d. Themistocles John and Katherine (Polizou) Catafygiotu; m. Peter Topping, June 20, 1951; 1 child, John T. BA, Mary Washington Coll., 1941; MA, Radcliffe Coll., 1943; postgrad., U. Athens, 1950-51. trustee Greek Orthodox Ch. of Fredericksburg, 1990—; bd. dirs. Orthodox Christian Laity, Chgo., 1988-92; exec. coun. Ch. Women United, N.Y.C., 1981-85. Author: Sacred Stories from Byzantium, 1977, Holy Mothers of Orthodoxy, 1987, Saints and Sisterhood, 1990; contbg. editor: The Greek American, N.Y.C.; contbr. articles to profl. jours. Exec. bd. Greek Am. Women's Network, N.Y.C., 1990-94; adv. com. Athenaeum Univ. Club, Washington, 1982-94, Helen Z. Papanikolas Trust, Salt Lake City, 1989—. Recipient Am. Hellenic Achievement award Hellenic Spirit Found., 1992, Lifetime Achievement award Am. Hellenic Inst., 1993; Fulbright scholar U.S. Ednl. Found., N.Y.C., 1950. Mem. NOW, Philoptochos Women's Soc., Women's Ordination Conf., Orthodox Christian Assn. of Medicine, Psychology and Religion, Women's Alliance for Theology, Ethics and Rituals, Phi Beta Kappa. Democrat. Home: 1823 Rupert St Mc Lean VA 22101-5434

TORAN, KAY DEAN, social services administrator; b. Birmingham, Ala., Nov. 21, 1942; d. Benjamin and Mary Rose Dean; children: Traci Rossi, John D. Toran. BA, U. Portland, 1964; MSW, Portland State U., 1970. Asst. prof. social work Portland (Oreg.) State U., 1971-76; mgr. Adult and Family Svcs., Salem, Oreg., 1976-79; asst. gov. Office of Gov., Salem, 1979-87; adminstr. purchasing divsn. Dept. Gen. Svcs., Salem, 1987-90; regional adminstr. Children's Svcs. Divsn., Portland, 1991-94, adminstr., 1994—; pres. Walker Inst., Portland, 1990-94, Portland chapter Links, Inc., 1990-92. Bd. trustees Catlin Gabel Sch., Portland, 1980-84, Portland State U. Found., 1980-87; bd. dirs. Oreg. Law Found., 1990-93. Office: Childrens Svcs Divsn 500 Summer St NE Salem OR 97310

TORANSKA, TERESA, journalist; b. Wolkowysk, Poland, Jan. 1, 1946; came to U.S., 1989; m. Leszek Sankowski, Dec. 15, 1945. Student law sch., Warsaw U., 1969, journalist sch., 1972; postgrad., Harvard U., 1989. Editor Kultura, Warsaw, 1974-81, Solidarnosc, Warsaw, 1980-89; freelance journalist, 1982—. Author: View from the Bottom, 1979, Them, 1986, We, 1994. Mem. Internat. Fedn. Journalists. Home: 10204B Willow Mist Ct Oakton VA 22124 Office: Tor-Press, Zywnego 12/102, 02701 Warsaw Poland

TORDIFF, HAZEL MIDGLEY, education director; b. Columbia Station, Ohio, Sept. 24, 1920; d. Joseph and Mary Ceclia (Vitovec) Midgley; m. Joseph F. Tordiff, Nov. 13, 1946; children: Cathy, Joseph F. Jr., John C. BS, Kent State U., 1942; student, U. Va., 1968, Catholic U., 1975. Instr. Warren (Ohio) Bus. Coll., 1942-44; exec. sec. to plant mgr. GE, Warren, 1943-44; adminstrv. asst. Fgn. Svc., Dept. State, and Am. Embassy, Stockholm and Lisbon, Portugal, 1947-52; dir. tng. Washington Bus. Sch., Vienna, Va., 1969—. Leader Girls Scouts U.S., Bonn, Fed. Republic of Germany, 1960-64, den mother Cub Scouts Am., Bonn, 1962-66; scorekeeper Little League Baseball, Bonn and Vienna, 1960-70. Sgt. WAC, U.S. Army, 1944-47. Named Outstanding Bus. Tchr. in U.S., Assn. Ind. Schs. and Colls., 1984. Mem. Prof. Secs. Internat. (faculty sponsor 1981-84). Home: 1302 Ross Dr SW Vienna VA 22180-6724 Office: Washington Bus Sch 1980 Gallows Rd Vienna VA 22182-3913

TORGHELE, SALLY JANE DAVIDSON, jeweler, appraiser; b. Trinidad, Colo., Apr. 14, 1947; d. Paul Benjamin and Julia Ann (Dobesh) Davidson; m. John Bradford Torghele, Mar. 19, 1977 (dec. Jan. 1983). Student, Kearney (Nebr.) State Coll., 1965-67; diploma, Kearney Vocat. Sch. Practical Nursing, 1967; cert., U. Calif., San Diego, 1972, Gemological Inst. Am., 1980. Practical nurse Good Samaritan Hosp., Kearney, 1967-70, Palomar Hosp., Escondido, Calif., 1970-72, Hastings (Nebr.) Regional Ctr., 1973-75; jeweler, appraiser Davidson's Jewelry, Kearney, 1976—. Co-founder Ft. Kearney Humane Soc., 1980—. Mem. Am. Gemological Soc. (registered jeweler), Jewelers of Am. (bd. dirs. 1981), Nebr. and S.D. Jewelers Assn. (v.p. 1985—), Gemological Inst. Am. Alumni Assn., Buffalo County Bus. and Profl. Women's Assn., Under Water Soc. Am., Gt. Plains Dive Council (sec. 1982-85). Republican. Roman Catholic. Club: Kearney Aqua Lords (treas. 1981-83). Office: Davidson's Jewelry Inc 2311 Central Ave Kearney NE 68847-5348

TORIELLO, TRACEY LYNN, anesthetist nurse; b. Balt., Oct. 10, 1965; d. Dominic O. and Kathleen F. (Huebner) T. AA in Nursing, Harford Community Coll., Bel Air, Md., 1985; BSN, U. Md. Baltimore County, 1987; M in Health Sci. Nurse Anesthesia, LaRoche Coll., 1989. Cert. RN anesthetist. Staff nurse Franklin Square Hosp., Balt., 1986-87; staff nurse anesthetist Shadyside Hosp., Pitts., 1989—. Mem. Am. Assn. Nurse Anesthetist, Md. Nurses Assn., Phi Kappa Phi, Sigma Theta Tau, Phi Theta Kappa. Office: Akien Anesthesia Assoc Centre Ave Pittsburgh PA 15213

TORKELSON, LUCILE EMMA, writer; b. Fond du Lac, Wis., Sept. 24, 1915; d. Joseph Michael Julka and Matilda (Elz) Pickart; m. Ivar John Torkelson, Sept. 24, 1945; children: Jean, David. PhB in Journalism, Marquette U., 1938; postgrad., U. Minn., 1950s. Reporter Fond du Lac Reporter, 1938-41, Milw. Jour., 1941-45; movie critic South Bend (Ind.) Tribune, 1945; editor LWV Mag., Mpls., 1961-62; office mgr. Midwest Bearing Corp., Milw., 1963-89; book features writer Milw. Sentinel, 1963-75, book reviewer, 1963—; freelance writer Wauwatosa, Wis., 1990—. Contbr. articles to popular jours., mags. Active LWV, Mpls., 1957-62. Mem. Women in Communications (50 Years of Svc. cert. 1988), Great Books Assn., Theta Sigma Phi. Republican. Roman Catholic. Home: 6511 Washington Cir Milwaukee WI 53213-2459

TORME, MARGARET ANNE, public relations executive, communications consultant; b. Indpls., Apr. 5, 1943; d. Ira G. and Margaret Joy (Wright) Barker; children—Karen Anne, Leah Vanessa. Student Coll. San Mateo, 1961-65. Pub. rels. mgr. Hoefer, Dieterich & Brown (now Chiat-Day), San Francisco, 1964-73; v.p., co-founder, creative dir. Lowry & Ptnrs., San Francisco, 1975-83; pres., founder Torme & Co. (now Torme & Kenney), San Francisco, 1983—; cons. in communications. Mem. Pub. Rels. Soc. Am., San Francisco Advt. Club, North Bay Advt. Club, San Francisco C. of C. (outstanding achievement award for women entrepreneurs 1987), Jr. League (adv. bd.) Office: 545 Sansome St San Francisco CA 94111-1708

TORNATORE-MORSE, KATHLEEN MARY, pharmacist, educator; b. Oneida, N.Y., Feb. 25, 1955; d. James Joseph and Concetta Barbara (Crimi) T.; 2 children. BS in Pharmacy, Union U., 1978; PharmD, SUNY, Buffalo, 1981. Registered pharmacist, N.Y. Hosp. pharmacy residency U. Nebr. Med. Ctr., Omaha, 1978-79; pharmacist Health Care Plan, West Seneca, N.Y., 1979-80; lab. instr. Profl. Practice Lab. Sch. of Pharmacy SUNY, Buffalo, 1979-80, instr. in pharmacology nurse practitioner program, 1982-85, 87-91, clin. instr. Sch. of Pharmacy, 1981-83, rsch. asst. prof. pharmacy Sch. of Pharmacy, 1985-87, asst. prof. pharmacy, 1987-90, clin. asst. prof. pharmacy, 1990-91, asst. prof. pharmacy, 1991—; lectr. and presenter in field; pharmacokinetics cons. VA Med. Ctr., Buffalo, 1986-91; curriculum com. mem. Sch. of Pharmacy, SUNY, Buffalo, 1990-91, mem. Ctr. for Clin. Pharmacy Rsch., 1989—, mem. substance abuse com., 1990—, mem. Doctor of Pharmacy Student Rsch. com., 1987—, mem. curriculum com. Doctor of Pharmacy program, 1984-86, mem. policy and implementation com., 1984-86; quality assurance com. Buffalo Gen. Hosp. Corp., 1981-82, investigational rev. bd., 1982-83. Contbr. chpts. to Textbook of Pharmacology, 1991; contbr. numerous articles to profl. jours. Mem. PTA, Williamsville, N.Y., 1993-94; vol. Parent Vol.-Kindergarten Program, N. Forest Elem. Sch., Williamsville, 1993-94. Recipient Outstanding Young Women of Am. award, 1984, Achievement award Albany Coll. Pharmacy, 1984, Bd. Trustees Honor scholarship, 1976-78, Bigelow Scholarship award, 1976-78; grantee Upjohn, 1984-86, 88, 90-91, 93. Mem. AAAS, Am. Coll. Clin. Pharmacy (membership com. 1992-93, 91-93, N.Y. State chpt. mem., devel. and steering com. mem. 1990-91), Am. Soc. Hosp. Pharmacists, Am. Assn. Colls. of Pharmacy, Am. Fedn. Aging Rsch. Office: SUNY Sch of Pharmacy Dept Pharmacy Practice 313 Cooke Hall Buffalo NY 14260-1200

TORNEDEN, CONNIE JEAN, bank executive; b. Tonganoxie, Kans., Sept. 14, 1955; d. Byron Calvin and Edna Jeannette (Keck) Swain; m. Lawrence Dale Torneden, Sept. 18, 1976; 1 child, James Milton. Bus. cert., Kansas City C.C., Kans., 1974; student, Nat. Compliance Sch., Norman, Okla., 1984. Adminstrv. sec. to chmn. of bd., pres. First State Bank and Trust, Tonganoxie, 1974-80, asst. cashier, 1981-83, asst. v.p. and compliance officer, 1984—, bank security officer, 1989—. Lobbyist, treas. 24-40 Hwy. Task Force, Leavenworth, Kans., 1989-91; bd. dirs., sec. Reno Cemetary Assn., Tonganoxie, 1986—; sec.-treas. Maple Grove Cemetary Assn., Tonganoxie, 1988—; co-founder Tonganoxie Days, chmn., 1986, 88-93, 95; grad. So. Leavenworth County Leadership Devel., 1991. Mem. Am. Bus. Women's Assn. (treas. 1986-87, Twilight chpt. Woman of Yr. 1994), Mid-Am. Dairymen Assn. (sec. 1978-80), Nat. Assn. Old West Gunfighter Teams (Nat. Champions 1989, 90), Linwood Grange (5th and 6th degrees 1978), Tonganoxie C. of C. (sec. 1983-86, chamber sec. 1983-86, 92-94, pres. 1986, 88, 89, Mem. of Yr. 1990, 92), Tonganoxie Jaycees (sec. 1991). Democrat.

Mem. Soc. of Friends. Office: First State Bank and Trust 4th and Bury PO Box 219 Tonganoxie KS 66086

TORNESE, JUDITH M., financial institution executive; b. Pitts., Aug. 26, 1942; d. Ilario and Rose Mary (Ali) T.; m. Jerrry E. Winters. Student, U. Pitts. CPCU. Various positions Transam Corp., San Francisco, 1971-81; dir. risk mgmt. TransAm. Corp., San Francisco, 1981-87, v.p. risk mgmt., 1987—. Dir. San Francisco Suicide Prevention, 1984-90; mem. Earthquake Ins. and Recovery Fin. Com. of Seismic Safety Commn., 1988-91. Named Risk Mgr. of Yr. Bus. Ins. Mag., 1992. Mem. Risk and Ins. Mgmt. Soc. (soc. dir. 1981—, chair nominating com. 1987-92), Mfr.'s Alliance Productivity anb Innovation (risk mgmt. coun. 1981—). Office: Transam Corp 600 Montgomery St San Francisco CA 94111-2702

TORNEY-PURTA, JUDITH VOLLMAR, developmental psychologist; b. Oakland, Calif., Oct. 2, 1937; d. Ralph C. and Anne (Flournoy) Vollmar; m. E. Keith Torney, Sept. 10, 1960 (div. 1978); children: Elizabeth A., Katherine D.; m. Paul P. Purta, Oct. 18, 1980. AB in Psychology, Stanford U., 1959; postgrad., Harvard U., 1959-60; MA in Human Devel., U. Chgo., 1962, PhD in Human Devel., 1965. Asst. prof. psychology Ill. Inst. Tech., Chgo., 1967-69; asst. prof. edn. U. Ill., Chgo., 1969-70, assoc. prof. psychology and edn., 1970-77, prof., vice chmn. psychology dept., 1977-81; prof. human devel., asst. chmn. dept. U. Md., College Park, 1981—, affiliate prof. psychology dept., 1981—; vis. prof. Stanford (Calif.) U. Sch. Edn., 1988, 91; evaluator Internat. Communication Negotiations Simulation, College Park, 1983—; mem. bd. on internat. studies in edn. NRC, NAS, Washington, 1988—; mem. task force on youth devel. Carnegie Corp., N.Y.C., 1990-92. Co-author: Development of Political Attitudes, 1967 (award NEA 1967), Civic Education in Ten Countries, 1975, Development of Political Understanding, 1992; contbr. chpts. to books, articles to profl. jours. Mem. U.S. Nat. Commn. for UNESCO, Washington, 1976-82, 83-85; cons. on civic edn. Govt. of Can., Ottawa, 1990, 94. Recipient career rsch. award Nat. Coun. for Social Studies, 1977, Global Apple award Am. Forum for Edn., 1988. Fellow APA, Am. Psychol. Soc.; mem. Am. Ednl. Rsch. assn. (chmn. book award com. 1991-92), Soc. for Rsch. in Child Devel. (chmn. internat. com. 1991-93), Comparative and Internat. Edn. Soc. (editorial bd. 1990-92), Internat. Assn. Evaluation Ednl. Achievement (civic edn. com. 1971-80, 93—, sci. and math. com. 1991—), Internat. Soc. for Polit. Psychology, Phi Beta Kappa, Sigma Xi. Office: U Md Dept Human Devel College Park MD 20742-1131

TORO, AMALIA MARIA, lawyer; b. Hartford, Conn., Nov. 6, 1920; d. Frederick and Maria (Casale) T. BA, U. Conn., 1942; JD, Yale U., 1944. Bar: Conn. 1944. Assoc. Wiggin & Dana, New Haven, 1944-46; atty., dir., chief elections div. Office Sec. of State, Conn., 1946-75; judge Ct. Common Pleas State of Conn., 1975; pvt. practice Hartford, Conn., 1975—; alt. pub. mem. Conn. State Bd. Mediation and Arbitration, 1993—. Corporator St. Francis Hosp. & Med. Ctr., Hartford, 1984—; former mem. Ford Found Com. on Voting and Election Systems; mem. State Employees' Retirement Commn., 1956-75, past vice-chmn.; Conn. Fedn. BPW rep. Conn. Commn. on Status of Women, 1990—. Named Woman of Yr., 1969; recipient AMITA award, 1970, Humanitarian award Columbus Day Celebration Com., 1986. Greater Hartford Bus. & Profl. Women (pres. 1989-91, legis. chairperson, counsellor), Conn. Bar Assn. (Merit award), Conn. State Employees Assn., Conn. Assn. Mcpl. Attys. (past pres.), Greater Hartford U. Conn. Alumni Assn. (past pres.). Office: 234 Pearl St Hartford CT 06103-2113

TOROK, MARGARET LOUISE, insurance company executive; b. Detroit, June 22, 1922; d. Perl Edward Ensor and Mary (Seggie) Armstrong; m. Leslie A. Torok, Aug. 14, 1952; 1 child, Margaret Mary Ryan. Lic. Ins. Agy. Ins. agy. Grendel-Wittbold Ins., Southgate, Mich., 1961-68, corp. officer, 1968-72; pres. of corp. Grendel-Wittbold Ins., Southgate, 1972--; bd. dirs. Ind. Ins. Agts. of Mich., Lansing, 1984-92, Ind. Ins. Agts. of Wayne County, Dearborn, 1979—, pres. 1978. Bd. dirs. So. Wayne County C. of C., Taylor, 1975, 2d vice chair 1995; leadership chmn. YMCA, Wyandotte, 1980—, Downriver Cmty. Alliance; lay chmn. Cath. Svc. Appeal for Archdiocese of Detroit, 1989; co-chair fundraiser Sacred Heart Ch.; chmn. MESC Employers Com., 1991—. Recipient Capital award Ind. Ins. Agents of Mich., 1988, Amb. award, 1994, Woman of Yr. AAUW, 1994, Salute to Excellence award Downriver Coun. of Arts, 1993-94, Chmn. of Yr. award MESC Job Svc. Employers Com., 1991, Robert Stewart award Wyandotte Svc. Club Coun., 1994. Mem. Wyandotte Yacht Club, Soroptimist Club of Wyandotte (2nd vice chair 1995, Advancing Status Women award 1988, sgt., Soroptimist of Yr. award 1993-94). Roman Catholic. Office: Grendel Wittbold Agy Inc 12850 Eureka Rd Southgate MI 48195-1344

TORR, ANN M., state legislator; b. Rochester, N.H., Feb. 11, 1935; m. Franklin Torr; 3 children. RN, Notre Dame Sch. Nursing, Manchester, N.H., 1955; BA, New Eng. Coll., 1977. RN, N.H. Real estate agt. and nurse; mem. N.H. Ho. of Reps., 1985—; mem. legis. adminstrv. and ruls coms.; trustee Westworth Douglass Hosp., chmn., 1982—; vice chmn. bd. dirs. Health Cir. Inc. Del. N.H. Constnl. Conv., 1984; active Stafford County Exec. Com., 1984-90. mem. Stafford County Cmty. Action (bd. dirs., vice chmn. 1985-92), Northam Colonists Hist. Soc., C. of C., Dover Bus. and Profl. Women's Found. Republican. Roman Catholic. Home: One Old Littleworth Rd Dover NH 03820-4311 Office: NH Ho of Reps State Capitol Concord NH 03301*

TORRENS, PEGGY JEAN, technical school coordinator; b. El Dorado, Kans., Oct. 7, 1952; d. Wayne E. and Evelyn M. (Hornbostel) Clark; m. Dennis L. Torrens, May 3, 1975; children: Jason L., Jennifer L. BS in Edn., Emporia State U., 1974, MS, 1975. Cert. secondary tchr., Kans. Instr. reading Burlington (Kans.) High Sch., 1974-75, Lowther Mid. Sch., Emporia, Kans., 1975-76; coord. resouce ctr., tech. prep coord. Flint Hills Tech. Sch., Emporia, Kans., 1976—; mem., chairperson Profl. Devel. Coun., Emporia, Kans., 1990—, applied curriculum inservice presenter. Author software programs; reviewer workbook Modern Reading, 1982. Community leader Lyon County 4-H, Emporia, 1988—. Mem. NEA, Am. Vocat. Assn. Democrat. Lutheran. Office: Flint Hills Tech Sch 3301 W 18th Ave Emporia KS 66801-5957

TORRES, CYNTHIA ANN, banker; b. Glendale, Calif., Sept. 24, 1958; d. Adolph and Ruth Ann (Smith) T.; m. Michael Victor Gisser, Mar. 11, 1989; 1 chld, Spencer Williams Gisser. AB, Harvard U., 1980, MBA, 1984. Research assoc. Bain & Co., Boston, 1980-82; assoc. Goldman, Sachs & Co., N.Y.C., 1984-88, v.p., 1988; v.p. First Interstate Bancorp, L.A., 1989-92; dir. Fidelity Investments Mgmt. (H.K.) Ltd., Hong Kong, 1993—. Mem. judiciary rev. bd. Bus. Sch. Harvard U., Boston, 1983-84. Rockefeller Found. scholar, 1976; Harvard U. Ctr. for Internat. Affairs fellow, 1979-80; recipient Leadership award Johnson and Johnson, 1980; by Council for Opportunity in Grad. Mgmt. Edn. fellow, 1982-84. Mem. Acad. Polit. Sci., Asia Soc., Fin. Women's Assn. Hong Kong (bd. dirs.), Harvard Club of Hong Kong (bd. dirs.). Office: Fidelity Investments Mgmt, 16/F Citibank Tower 3 Garden Rd, Hong Kong Hong Kong

TORRES, LIZABETH GOSLEE, Spanish educator; b. New London, Ohio, Mar. 18, 1948; d. James Robert and Elsie (Evans) Goslee; m. Armando A. Torres, June 14, 1970 (div. July 1978); children: Alexandra C., Anthony A. BA in Psychology, La Universidad de las Ams., Mexico City, 1970; BS in Spanish Edn., Ohio State U., 1979; MA in Curriculum and Devel. magna cum laude, Ashland U., 1994. Spanish tchr. Columbus (Ohio) Pub. Schs., 1979—, East H.S., Columbus, 1981—, U. Tenn., Knoxville, 1994—; student advisor Columbus Educators of Tomorrow, 1990—. Cons., author future tchr.'s handbook for Ohio State U., 1990. Mem. NEA, Columbus Edn. Assn., Phi Delta Kappa. Home: 206 Geya Ln Loudon TN 37774

TORRES, RENEÉ FINEBERG, elementary school educator; b. Buffalo, N.Y., July 27, 1939; d. Ester (Lerner) Fineberg; divorced; 1 child, Karin Alicia Torres. B degree, CUNY, 1963, M degree, 1966. Cert. tchr., N.Y. Tchr. common brs. N.Y.C. Bd. Edn., 1963—, coord. sch. fundraising for sr. classes. Mem. holiday feeding program for city's homeless, Goddard-Riverside, N.Y.C., 1994—. Mem. United Fedn. Tchrs., N.Y. State United Tchrs., Am. Fedn. Tchrs. Democrat. Jewish. Home: 35 W 81st St New York NY 10024-6045

TORRES, SUNNY, relief agency administrator; b. Thomaston, Maine, Oct. 4, 1939; d. Wilbert and Bertha (Kent) Mull; m. Edward Torres, July 11, 1959; children: Debra, Dale, David. BS, Bridgewater Coll., 1974; MEd, R.I. Coll., 1980; postgrad., U. So. Maine, 1980—. Spl. edn. specialist L.G. Nourse Sch., Norton, Mass., 1974-80; dir. spl. edn. Sch. dist. 39, Sumner, Maine, 1980-81; instr., cons. U. So. Maine, Gorham, 1981-85; dir. spl. edn. Sch. Union 29, Poland, Maine, 1982-83; pres., dir. Therapy Edn. Assn., North Conway, N.H., 1983-86; headmaster Elan Sch., Poland Spring, Maine, 1986—; owner, dir. Profl. Health Care Services, Naples, Maine, 1987—; ednl. supr., Jackson Brook Inst., Portland, Maine, 1988—; ednl. cons., U. So. Maine, 1980—. Mem. Nat. Assn. Female Execs. Home: PO Box 334 Naples ME 04055-0334

TORRES, VIRNA LIZZETTE, nurse; b. Guatemala, Mar. 27, 1969; came to U.S., 1979; d. Bernarda Torres. ADN, Kettering Coll. Med. Arts, 1991. RN, Ohio. Charge nurse Kettering (Ohio) Hosp., 1991—. Democrat. Home: 412 E Dorothy Ln Kettering OH 45419-1801

TORRES-ULLAURI, MARIÁ ISABEL, banker; b. Valencia, Spain; d. José Manuel and Vicenta (Soriano) Mazás; m. Modesto Ignacio Torres-Ullauri. Student, U. Madrid; cert., Cambridge (Eng.) U.; BA, NYU; MBA, Adelphi U., 1977. Mgr. corp. banking Royal Bank Can., N.Y.C., 1975-85; v.p., rep. N.Am. Banque de la Soc. Financiere Europeenne, N.Y.C., 1986-90; v.p. pvt. banking Swiss Bank Corp., N.Y.C., 1990-93, dir., 1993—. Bd. dirs. Kennedy Child Study Ctr., N.Y.C., 1984-87; lectr. St. Patrick's Cathedral, N.Y.C., 1985—. Mem. Am. Mgmt. Assn., Univ. Club. Office: Swiss Bank Corp 10 E 50th St New York NY 10022-6831

TORREY, BARBARA BOYLE, research council administrator; b. Pensacola, Fla., Nov. 27, 1941; d. Peter F. and Elsie (Hansen) Boyle; m. E. Fuller Torrey, Mar. 23, 1968; children: Michael, Martha. BA, Stanford U., 1963, MS, 1970. Vol. Peace Corps, Tanzania, 1963-65; fiscal economist Office Mgmt. and Budget, Washington, 1970-80; dept. asst. sec. HHS, Washington, 1980-81; dir. Ctr. for Internat. Rsch., Census Bur., Washington, 1984-92; pres. Population Reference Bur., Washington, 1992-93; exec. dir. Commn. on Behavioral and Social Scis. and Edn., NRC, NAS, Washington, 1993—; bd. dirs. Luxembourg Income Study, 1984—. Co-editor: The Vulnerable, 1987, Population and Land Use, 1992; contbr. articles to profl. jours. Mem. Population Assn. Am. (bd. dirs. 1993—). Office: NRC 2101 Constitution Ave NW Washington DC 20418-0007

TORREY, CLAUDIA OLIVIA, lawyer; b. Nashville, June 10, 1958; d. Claude Adolphus and Rubye Mayette (Prigmore) T. BA in Econ., Syracuse U., 1980; JD, N.Y. Law Sch., 1985. Bar: N.Y. State 1988. Legal intern Costello, Cooney & Fearon, Syracuse, N.Y., 1979; legal clk. First Am. Corp., Nashville, 1981; legal asst. James I. Meyerson, N.Y.C., 1982-85; jud. law clk. N.Y. State Supreme Ct., N.Y.C., 1985; interim project supr., legal asst. CUNY Ctrl. Office, 1985-86; legal analyst Rosenman & Colin Law Firm, N.Y.C., 1986-87; asst. counsel N.Y. State Legis., Albany, 1988-90; atty., cons. pvt. practice, Nashville, Cookeville, Tenn., 1991—; bd. mem. Children's Corner Day Care Ctr., Albany, N.Y., 1989-90. Ch. rep. FOCUS exec. coun. Westminster Presbyn. Ch., Albany, 1990; v.p. dormitory coun., flr. rep. Syracuse U., 1977-79. Mem. ABA, N.Y. State Bar Assn., Alpha Kappa Alpha (Syracuse U. chpt. treas. 1977-78, pres. 1979). Home and Office: PO Box 150234 Nashville TN 37215-0234

TORREZ, NAOMI ELIZABETH, copyright review editor, librarian; b. Scranton, Pa., July 3, 1939; d. Sterling E. and Naomi (Reynolds) Hess; m. Lupe F. Torrez, Dec. 23, 1961; children: Sterling Edward, Stanley Marshall. BA, U. Ariz., 1961; MA, U. Calif., Berkeley, 1964, MLS, 1970; DRE, Golden State Sch. Theology, Oakland, Calif., 1988; cert. in travel industry, Vista C.C., 1993. Libr. asst. Oakland Pub. Libr., 1966-67, U. Calif. Libr., Berkeley, 1967-70; tutor, couns. Sonoma State Hosp., Eldridge, Calif., 1973-77, libr. tech. asst., 1977-79; health scis. libr. Kaiser Hosp., Vallejo, Calif., 1979-87; copyright rev. editor Kaiser Dept. Med. Editing, Oakland, 1987—; participant Statewide Latino Congress, 1994. Author: Not in My Pew, 1990, GSST Research Manual, 1990. Mem. Albany 75th Anniversary Com., 1983. Woodrow Wilson fellow, 1961; winner Nat. Spelling Bee, 1953. Mem. Kaiser Permanente Latino Assn., Kaiser Affirmative Action Com., Kaiser Health Edn. Com., K.P. Regional Libr.'s Group (chair 1988), Internat. Platform Assn., Phi Beta Kappa, Phi Kappa Phi. Baptist. Home: 829 Jackson St Albany CA 94706 Office: Kaiser Dept Med Editing 1800 Harrison 16th Fl Oakland CA 94612

TORRIE, R. ELAINE, human resources professional; b. Columbus, Ohio, Sept. 3, 1961; d. James Clarence and Dolores Evelyn (Brown) Torrie. BA in English, Ohio State U., 1982, MA in Journalism, 1989. Script- and copywriter ICOM, Inc., Columbus, 1985; pub. rels. cons. Columbus, Ohio, 1984-86; news bur. specialist Battelle Meml. Inst., Columbus, 1986-88; mgr. communication svcs. Mt. Carmel Health, Columbus, 1988-89; communications specialist Borden, Inc., Columbus, 1990-94, mgr. human resources policies & programs, 1994-95, mgr. human resources, 1995—. Mem. communcations com. St. Johns Episc. Ch., Worthington, Ohio, 1986—. Mem. NAFE, Pub. Rels. Soc. Am. (publicity chmn. Columbus chpt. 1987-88, bd. dirs.), Am. Mgmt. Assn., Kappa Tau Alpha, Phi Kappa Phi. Democrat. Office: Borden Inc 180 E Broad St Columbus OH 43215-3707

TORRINGTON, MARY CHRISTINE, photographer; b. Denver, July 20, 1949; d. Warren Rene and Inez Marie (Alexander) T.; B.S. in Zoology, Duke U., 1971; M.A., U.S. Internat. U., 1973, Ph.D. in Clin. Psychology, 1976. Postdoctoral fellow in psychology Devereux Found., Santa Barbara, Calif., 1976-77; psychol. cons. Alysan Ctr., Santa Clara, Calif., 1979; counselor/cons. employee assistance program Wells Fargo Bank, San Francisco, 1980; participant, intern Johnson Inst., Mpls., 1980; internat. tng. cons., employee assistance program Standard Oil of Calif., San Francisco, 1980-81; pres. M. Christine Torrington Photography, San Francisco, 1981—; ofcl. No. Calif. chpt. profl. photographer various profl. orgns. Mem. Am. Soc. Assn. Execs., Nat. Assn. Women Bus. Owners, Nat. Assn. Catering Execs., No. Calif. Soc. Assn. Execs., Bay Area Assn. Cov. Ops. Mgrs., San Francisco Conv. & Visitors Bur., San Francisco C. of C., Women Comm. Internat., Meeting Planners Internat., Hospitality Sales & Mktg. Assn. Internat., Soc. Incentive Travel Execs., Internat. Assn. Exposition Mgrs., Internat. Spl. Events Soc., World Affairs Council, Internat. Visitors Ctr., Commonwealth No. Calif. Club, City Club, Bay Area Publicity Club. Home: 2200 Sacramento St Apt 1505 San Francisco CA 94115-2354 Office: 209 Post St Ste 812 San Francisco CA 94108-5210

TOSELLO, COLLEEN FRANCIS, real estate agent; b. Chicago Heights, Ill., Apr. 9, 1962; d. David Glen Colen and Jeannine Ann (Scully) Chapman; m. Paul Alan Tosello, July 12, 1985. Lic. real estate agt. Real estate sales counselor Coldwell Banker Paul Stringer, Realtors, Hurst, Tex., 1991—. Col. Care Corps, N.E. Tarrant County, Tex., 1993-94; mentor Grapevine (Tex.) H.S., 1994. Mem. NAFE, Nat. Assn. Realtors, Tex. Assn. Realtors, N.E. Tarrant County Realtors. Home: PO Box 1004 Colleyville TX 76034 Office: Coldwell Banker Paul Stringer 714 Grapevine Hwy Hurst TX 76054

TOSTI-VASEY, JOANNE LOUISE, human development research analyst; b. N.Y.C., Aug. 8, 1953; d. Louis Peter and Martha Magdaline (Bowery) Tosti; m. Joseph John Vasey, Jr., July 13, 1975. BS with distinction, Va. Poly. Inst. and State U., 1974, MS, 1977; postgrad., Radford U., 1979-81; PhD, Pa. State U., 1987. Teaching asst. Va. Poly. Inst. and State U., Blacksburg, 1974-75; co-counselor Marriage & Family Consultation Ctr., Blacksburg, 1975-76; instr. Ohio State U. Coop. Extension Svc., Woodsfield, 1976-77; social worker Mental Health Svcs. of New River Valley, Blacksburg, 1978-81; teaching asst. Pa. State U., University Park, 1981-83, rsch. asst., 1981-87, instr., 1982-85; rsch. assoc. Hubbard & Revo-Cohen, Inc., Reston, Va., 1987-88; pvt. practice Bellefonte, Pa., 1988—; asst. prof. Pa. State U., University Park, 1991; rsch. assoc. human devel. and family studies Pa. State U., 1992-95; dept. rep. Grad. Student Assn. Pa. State U., 1985-87, adminstrv. aide Ctr. Women Students, 1986-87, dir. Sisterhood is Global conf., 1987. Author: (with others) Maintaining Professional Competence: Approaches to Career Enhancement, Vitality and Success Throughout a Work Life, 1990; editorial asst. Jour. of Gerontology: Psychol. Scis., 1991-92; contbr. articles to profl. jours. Mem. Centre County Pa. adv. Coun. Pa. Human Rels. Commn.; elected Dem. State Com., 1994—. Mem. NOW (chpt. pres. 1980-91, state policy coun. 1980-81, state bd. dels. 1991-93, chpt. coord. 1991-92, state treas. 1994-95, coord. Mid-Atlantic region Biennial Conf. 1992), APA, Assn. Women in Psychology, Gerontol. Soc. Am., Bellefonte Hist. and Cultural Assn., Mortar Bd., Phi Kappa Phi, Omicron Nu, Phi Upsilon Omicron. Democrat.

TOTAH, MICHELLE SHARLEEN, association administrator; b. Kemmerer, Wyo., Mar. 28, 1965; d. Raymond Joseph and Sharleen Kay (Hayden) Kominsky; m. John E. Totah, June 14, 1991. Student, U. Wyo., 1983-85; BA in Econs./Govt. and Politics, U. Md., 1988; postgrad., U. Del., 1992—. Rsch. analyst U.S. Dept. Justice, Washington, 1988, Club Mgrs. Assn. Am., Alexandria, Va., 1988-89; assoc. dir. legis. and pub. affairs U.S. C. of C., Washington, 1989-92, assoc. legis. and grassroots publs., 1992-93; dir. state and community rels. Am. Wholesale Marketers Assn., Washington, 1993—. Editor: Congressional Handbook, 1989-93, A Guide to Communicating with Members of Congress, 1991. Mem. NAFE, Nat. Mus. Women in Arts, Coun. State Govts. (assoc.), Women in Govt. Rels. Roman Catholic. Home: 313 N Alfred St Apt B Alexandria VA 22314-2422 Office: Am Wholesale Marketers Assn 1128 16th St NW Washington DC 20036-4802

TOTER, KIMBERLY MROWIEC, nurse; b. Chgo., Apr. 22, 1956; d. A. Kenneth and Megan Dawson (Schiefer) Mrowiec; m. William Frank Toter, Dec. 16, 1978; children: William Kenneth, Kimberly Helen, Tod Frank, Matthew Jonathan, Haley Victoria, Toria Megan. BS in Biology, Millikin U., 1978; cert. sch. nursing, Decatur (Ill.) Meml. Hosp., 1978. RN, Ill.; cert. operating room nurse. Oper. room nurse Riddle Meml. Hosp., Media, Pa., 1979-89; pres., chief exec. officer Towic Med., Inc., Park Ridge, Ill., 1986—; staff nurse oper. room Luth. Gen. Hosp., Park Ridge, 1991; perioperative nurse, 1991—; instr. Delaware Community Coll., Media, 1986; reviewer, cons. Perioperative Nursing Care Planning; speaker laparoscopy seminar Luth. Gen. Hosp., 1992, 93. Contbg. author: Decision Making in Perioperative Nursing, 1987; also articles; patentee gastric drainage system. Cheerleading coach St. Paul of the Cross, 1993—. Recipient Young Alumnus of Yr. award Millikin U., 1991. Mem. Assn. Operat. Rm. Nurses (v.p. Southeast Pa. chpt. 1983-85, pres.-elect 1985-86, pres. 1986-87, ednl. chmn. 1983-85, chmn. bylaw and policy com. 1987—, bd. dirs. 1983-89, chmn. 1987-89), Pa. Coun. Oper. Rm. Nurses, Am. Tech Mgmt. (bd. dirs. 1989—), Am. Reprographics Mgmt. (bd. dirs. 1989—), Pi Beta Phi. Roman Catholic.

TOTH, ELIZABETH LEVAY, retired educational organization executive, lawyer; b. Woodbridge Twp., N.J.; d. Nicholas and Elizabeth (Nagy) Levay; m. Frederick Louis Toth; children: Frederick Albert, Thomas Franklin. BA, Rutgers U., 1970; JD, Seton Hall U., 1973; LLM, NYU, 1980. Bar: N.J. 1973. Mgr., dispatcher, prin. Tri-R-Bus Svc., Inc., Metuchen, N.J., 1959-71; arbitration atty. Robert J. Casulli, East Orange, N.J., 1973; mediator, hearing officer N.J. Pub. Employment Relations Commn., Trenton, 1974-75; assoc. dir. employee relations Woodbridge (N.J.) Twp. Pub. Schs., 1975-81; dir. govt. and community relations Ariz. Sch. Bd. Assn., Phoenix, 1981-85; exec. dir. Greater Phoenix Ednl. Mgmt. Coun., 1985-92; ret., 1992; completed Insts. for Orgnl. Mgmt., San Jose (Calif.) State U. and Stanford U., Calif., 1985-90. Mem. community adv. bd. Sta. KAET-TV, Ariz. State U., Tempe, 1985-91; bd. dirs. North Community Behavioral Health Ctr. (merged into Terros Community Mental Health Orgn. 1988), Phoenix, 1984-88, Ariz. Partnership, 1988-92, Ariz. Alliance Sci., Math. & Tech., 1989-92; sr. arbitrator Better Bus. Bur., Phoenix, 1987—; judge Acad. Decathlon, 1988-92. Recipient plaque and pub. recognition North Community Behavioral Health Ctr., 1987. Mem. Am. Arbitration Assn. (arbitrator), Nat. Panel Mediators, Am. Soc. Assn. Execs., Ariz. Soc. Assn. Execs. (life, bd. dirs. 1987-88, Exec. of Yr. 1987), Soc. Profls. in Dispute Resolution), Pub. Affairs Profls. Ariz., Rutgers U. Alumni Club (pres. 1992-93), Ariz. State U. West Alumni Assn. (sec. 1990-92), Phi Alpha Delta, Alpha Sigma Lambda. Home: 1731 E Alameda Dr Tempe AZ 85282

TOTH, PATRICIA ANN, critical care nurse, educator; b. Phila., May 31, 1956; d. J. Paul and Helen E. (McKeever) T. Diploma in nursing, Abington Meml. Hosp., 1977; BSN, LaSalle U., 1989; MSN, Widener U., 1990, postgrad., 1992—. Cert. BLS, ACLS, med.-surg. nurse. Staff nurse, preceptor, clin. leader Abington (Pa.) Meml. Hosp., 1977-86; staff nurse R.N. Temp., Inc., Blue Bell, Pa., 1986-89; traveling nurse Med. Recruiters of Am., Ft. Lauderdale, Fla., 1987-88; critical care instr. Germantown Hosp. and Med. Ctr. Sch. Nursing, Phila., 1989—. Vol. Am. Cancer Soc., Am. Heart Assn., Phila. Mayor's Commn. on Literacy. Mem. AACN, Nurses Assn. for Tchr. Edn. (pres. Phila. chpt. 1992—), Sigma Theta Tau. Home: 209 Mews Dr Sellersville PA 18960 Office: Germantown Hosp and Med Ctr Sch Nursing 3 Penn Blvd Philadelphia PA 19144

TOTH, SARAH ANN, physician assistant, child health associate; b. Santa Monica, Calif., Sept. 19, 1962; d. Joseph Michael Jr. and Ann Todd (Carlton) T. BS, U. Colo., 1984; MS, U. Colo., Denver, 1986. Cert. physician asst. Physician asst. Lactation Program at AMI-St. Luke's Hosp., Denver, 1986-87, Porter Meml. Hosp, Denver, 1986-89, Baylor Coll. Medicine, Houston, 1991, Tex. Children's Hosp., Houston, 1991—. Contbr. articles to profl. jours. Vol. Hospice Care Inc., Houston, 1989; instr., vol. Safesitter Inc., Houston, 1991—. Mem. Tex. Acad. Physician Assts. (bd. dirs. 1993—), Tex. Gulf Coast Physician Asst. Aassn. (v.p. 1993, pres. 1993-94), Am. Acad. Physician Assts. (com. chair 1993). Episcopalian. Home: 7979 Westheimer Rd Apt 403 Houston TX 77063-4500

TOTTEN, GLORIA JEAN (DOLLY TOTTEN), real estate executive, financial consultant; b. Port Huron, Mich., Sept. 23, 1943; d. Lewis Elmer and Inez Eugenia (Houston) King; m. Donald Ray Totten, Feb. 5, 1961 (div. Apr. 1981); children: D. Erik, Angela J. Totten Sales, Kymberly D. Totten DiVita. Student, Patricia Stevens Sch., Detroit, 1976-79, Gold Coast Sch., West Palm Beach, Fla., 1988; degree in mktg., St. Clair County Coll., Port Huron, Mich., 1979. Lic. real estate saleswoman, Fla., Mich. Demonstrator, saleswoman Hoover Co., 1969-75; instr., promoter Port Huron Sch. Bus., 1973-75; real estate borker Select Realty, Port Huron, 1979-81, Earn Keim Realty, Port Huron, 1981-83, Schweitzer's Better Homes and Gardens, Marysville, Mich., 1983-86, Coldwell Banker Property Concepts Corp., North Palm Beach, Fla., 1986-94; pres., broker, owner Dolly Totten Real Estate Inc., West Palm Beach, Fla., 1994—; model, instr. Patricia Stevens Modeling Sch., Troy, Mich., 1972-75; beauty cons. Mary Ky Cosmetics, 1982—. Grantee Mich. State U., 1972. Mem. Nat. Assn. Realtors, North Palm Beach Bd. Realtors, Million Dollar Club, Womens Coun. of Realtors (co-founder). Home: 4923 Tortuga Dr West Palm Beach FL 33407-1731

TOTTEN, MARY ANNE, internist; b. Topeka, May 22, 1946; d. Frederick Eugene Totten and Mildred Roberta (Johnson) Black. BA in Microbiology, U. Kans., 1968, MD, 1972; MPH, Boston U., 1984. Am. Bd. Internal Medicine, Nat. Bd. Med. Examiners. Intern in internal medicine Hosp. of St. Raphael, New Haven, 1972-73; resident New Eng. Deaconess Hosp., Boston, 1973-75; fellow in endocrinology and metabolism Lahey Clinic Found., Burlington, Mass., 1975-76; fellow in diabetes Joslin Clinic, Boston, 1976-77; instr. medicine Boston U. Med. Ctr., 1977-83, asst. clin. prof., 1983-84; staff physician in gen. internal medicine Boston City Hosp., 1977-80; staff physician endocrinology Boston Hosp., 1977-84; dir. diabetes treatment and rehab. unit Mattapan (Mass.) Hosp., 1982-84; staff physician St. Joseph's Hosp., Parkersburg, W.Va., 1984—, chmn. dept. internal medicine, 1989-91, med. dir. skilled nursing unit, 1992—, pres. med. staff, 1995-96; staff physician Camden Clark Meml. Hosp., Parkersburg, 1984—, chair diabetes mgmt. com., 1990-93; pres.-elect med. staff St. Joseph's Hosp., Parkersburg, 1994-95, physician liaison advisor to Diabetes Care Task Force, 1994—, sec. to med. staff, 1994-95; mem. del. diabetes educators People to People Tour, USSR and People's Republic China, 1987. Author, editor: Case Studies for Nurses and Nurse Practitioners, 1990; contbr. articles to med. jours. Bd. dirs., mem. YWCA, Parkersburg, 1986-87; mem. League of Women's Voters., Parkersburg. Recipient Physician Recognition award AMA, 1987, 90, Trailblazing Women of the Yr award YWCA and Altrusa, 1988, Leadership Devel. award Parkersburg C. of C., 1990. Fellow ACP (mem. Gov.'s Coun. W. Va. 1990-91); mem. Am. Diabetes Assn. (bd. dirs. W.Va. 1987-89), W.Va. Med. Assn., Parkersburg Area Diabetes Assn. (pres. 1988-90, bd. dirs. 1991—), Parkersburg Acad. Medicine. Methodist. Office: Primary Health Care Inc 600 18th St Ste 303 Parkersburg WV 26101

TOUBORG, MARGARET EARLEY BOWERS, non-profit executive; b. Rome, N.Y., Aug. 12, 1941; d. George Thomas and Margaret Earley

(Brown) Bowers; m. Jens Touborg, Sept. 9, 1961 (div. 1985); children: Margaret Earley, Anne Monroe, Sarah Friis, Peter Nicolai. AB magna cum laude, Radcliffe Coll., 1965; MEd, Harvard U., 1984. Asst. to pres. Radcliffe Coll., Cambridge, Mass., 1984-86, exec. asst. to pres., 1986-87, dir. corp. and found. relations, 1988-89; pres. U. Cape Town Fund, Inc., N.Y.C., 1989—; sr. project dir. Open Soc. Scholars Fund, N.Y.C., 1989—; bd. dirs. Technoserve. Trustee The Trinity Sch., N.Y.C., 1994—, Bemis Lectr. Series, Lincoln, Mass., 1982-85; nat. cons. Schlesinger Libr. on History of Women in Am., mem. adv. bd. 1988-94; assoc. chmn. edn. div. United Way Mass., 1986; mem. South African adv. com. New Eng. Bd. Higher Edn., 1987—. Mem. Harvard Club N.Y.C., Phi Beta Kappa (chmn. com. hon. membership 1976—). Episcopalian. Office: 441 Lexington Ave Ste 405 New York NY 10017-3910

TOUCHET, ALICE FAYE, enrolled agent; b. Lafayette, La., Jan. 4, 1959; d. Lauris and Evadelle (Trosclair) T. A in Bus. Admintrn., U. Southwestern La., 1979. Acct. Harry J. Clostio & Co., CPAs, Lafayette, La., 1981-92, Arsement, Redd & Morella, CPAs, Lafayette, 1992; ptnr. Touchet & Pontiff, Lafayette, 1992—. Mem. Nat. Assn. Enrolled Agts., La. Soc. Enrolled Agts. (v.p.). Democrat. Roman Catholic. Office: Touchet & Pontiff PO Box 80157 3108 W Pinhook Ste 201 Lafayette LA 70508

TOUCHY, DEBORAH K. P., lawyer, accountant; b. Pasadena, Tex., Dec. 9, 1957; d. Donald Carl and Bobbie Jo (Jackson) Putzka; m. Harry Roy Touchy, Jr., Feb. 23, 1980. BBA, Baylor U., 1979; JD, U. Houston, 1988. Bar: Tex. 1989; CPA, Tex.; cert. in estate planning and probate law Tex. Bd. Legal Specialization. Sr. mgr. tax KMPG Peat Marwick, Houston, 1980-86; assoc. Fizer Beck Webster & Bentley, Houston, 1989-90; pvt. practice law and acctg. Houston, 1990—. Editor Houston Law Rev., 1988-89, Jr. League Houston, 1988-89. Chmn. ticket sales incentives Chi Omega, Houston, 1985; active ticket sales Mus. of Fine Arts, Houston, 1984; facilities chmn. Woodland Trails West Civic Orgn., Houston, 1982-83; pres. Women Attys. in Tax & Probate, 1994-95. Mem. ABA (mem. estate-probate sect. 1989—, vice chmn. commn. property com. 1994—), AICPA (taxation sect., estate and gift tax com. 1992—), Tex. Soc. CPAs (bd. dirs., tax inst. com. 1986—, estate planning com. 1990—), Houston Chpt. CPAs (chmn. taxpayer edn. 1985-86, chmn. membership com. 1992-93, v.p. 1993-94, chmn. tax forums 1994—), Houston Bar Assn. (estate-probate sect. 1989—), State Bar Tex. (estate-probate sect. 1989—, mem. elder law com. 1991—), Houston Estate and Fin. Forum, Baylor U. Women's Assn. (treas. 1993-94, chmn. fin. com. 1994—), Chief Justice-Advocates, Tex. Bd. Legal Specializations (cert. estate planning, probate law, 1994), Order of Coif, Omicron Delta Kappa, Phi Delta Phi. Office: 2932 Plumb St Houston TX 77005-3058

TOUHILL, BLANCHE MARIE, university chancellor, history-education educator; b. St. Louis, Mo., July 1, 1931; d. Robert and Margaret (Walsh) Van Dillen; m. Joseph M. Touhill, Aug. 29, 1959. BA in History, St. Louis U., 1953, MA in Geography, 1954, PhD in History, 1962. Prof. history and edn. U. Mo., St. Louis, 1965-73, assoc. dean faculties, 1974-76, assoc. vice chancellor for acad. affairs, 1976-87, vice chancellor, 1987-90, chancellor, 1991—; bd. dirs. Boatmen's Nat. Bank of St. Louis, Barnes-Jewish Christian Health Hosps. Conglomerate. Author: William Smith O'Brien and His Irish Revolutionary Companions in Penal Exile, 1981, The Emerging University UM-St. Louis, 1963-83, 1985; editor: Readings in American History, 1970, Varieties of Ireland, 1976; adv. editor Victorian Periodicals Rev. Bd. dirs. Sister City Internat., Am. Coun. Fgn. Rels., St. Louis Forum, Network Bd., Mo. State Hist. Soc., 1989—, Mo. Bot. Garden, 1980, St. Louis Symphony Soc., 1993—. Named Outstanding Educator St. Louis chpt. Urban League, 1976; recipient Leadership award St. Louis YWCA, 1986. Mem. Nat. Assn. State Univs. and Land Grant Colls. (exec. com. 1988—), Am. Com. on Irish Studies (pres. 1991—), Phi Kappa Phi, Alpha Sigma Lambda. Office: U Mo Office of the Chancellor 8001 Natural Bridge Rd Saint Louis MO 63121-4499

TOURTILLOTT, ELEANOR ALICE, nurse, educational consultant; b. North Hampton, N.H., Mar. 28, 1909; d. Herbert Shaw and Sarah (Fife) T. Diploma Melrose Hosp. Sch. Nursing, Melrose, Mass., 1930; BS, Columbia U., 1948, MA, 1949; edn. specialist Wayne State U., 1962. RN. Gen. pvt. duty nurse, Melrose, Mass., 1930-35; obstet. supr. Samaritan Hosp., Troy, N.Y., 1935-36, Meml. Hosp., Niagara Falls, N.Y., 1937-38, Lawrence Meml. Hosp., New London, Conn., 1939-42, New Eng. Hosp. for Women and Children, Boston, 1942-43; dir. H. W. Smith Sch. Practical Nursing, Syracuse, N.Y., 1949-53; founder, dir. assoc. degree nursing program Henry Ford Community Coll., Dearborn, Mich., 1953-74; dir. pioneering use of learning techs. via mixed media USPHS, 1966-71; prin. cons., initial coord. Wayne State U. Coll. Nursing, Detroit, 1975-78; cons. curriculum design, modular devel., instructional media Tourtillott Cons., Inc., Dearborn, Mich., 1974—; condr. numerous workshops on curriculum design, instructional media at various colls., 1966—; mem. Mich. Bd. Nursing, 1966-73, chmn., 1970-72, mem. rev. com. for constrn. nurse tng. facilities, div. nursing USPHS, 1967-70, mem. nat. adv. coun. on nurse tng., Dept. Health Edn. and Welfare, 1972-76. Author: Commitment-A Lost Characteristic, 1982; contbg. co-author: Patient Assessment-History and Physical Examination, 1975-78; contbr. chpts., articles, speeches to profl. publs. Served to capt. Nurse Corps, U.S. Army, 1943-47; ETO. Recipient Disting. Alumnae award Tchrs. Coll. Columbia U., 1974, Spl. tribute 77th Legislature Mich., 1974, Disting. Alumnae award Wayne State U., 1975, Disting. Service award Henry Ford Community Coll., 1982; established and endowed Eleanor Tourtillott Outstanding Student Nurse of Yr. award at Henry Ford C.C., 1993. Mem. ANA, Nat. League Nursing (chmn. steering com. dept. assoc. degree programs 1965-67, bd. dirs. 1965-67, 71-73, mem. assembly constituent leagues 1971-73, council assoc. degree programs citation 1974, Mildred Montag Excellence in Leadership award coun. assoc. degree programs 1994), Mich. League for Nursing (pres. 1969-71), Mich. Acad. Sci., Arts and Letters, Am. Legion, Tchrs. Coll. Alumnae Assn., Wayne State U. Alumnae Assn., Phi Lambda Theta, Kappa Delta Pi.

TOUSLEY, REBECCA PERKINS, librarian; b. Columbus, Miss., Mar. 28, 1926; d. Mosey Miles and Virginia Susan (Shelton) Perkins; m. Jasper Clayton Tousley Jr., Aug. 11, 1946; children: Judith Ann, Roger Clayton, Susan Elizabeth. Student, Trevecca Nazarene Coll., 1947-48; BS in Libr. Sci., Miss. Univ. for Women, 1974, MA in English Lit., 1981. Asst. to serials libr. Fant Libr., Miss. Univ. for Women, Columbus, 1966-74, asst. serials libr., govt. publs. libr., 1974-80, govt. publs. libr., 1980-90, ret., 1990; treas. Miss. Govt. Documents Roundtable, 1978; libr. Ch. of the Nazarene, Columbus, 1975—. Author: History of the Columbus Mississippi Church of the Nazarene, 1978; co-author Libr. Info. Bull., 1983-84. Mem. AAUW (publicity chmn. 1990-91), Miss. Univ. for Women Alumni Assn., Phi Kappa Phi (sec.-treas. 1980-82, 84-86). Home: 415 Highway 373 Columbus MS 39701-9345

TOUSSIENG, YOLANDA, make-up artist. television work includes: (movies) Fallen Angel, 1981, Blue de Ville, 1986, (series) Pee-wee's Playhouse, 1986, (mini-series) North and South, Book II, 1986; films include: Blue City, 1986, No Man's Land, 1987, Beetlejuice, 1988, Gross Anatomy, 1989, Three Fugitives, 1989, Farewell to the King, 1989, Edward Scissorhands, 1990, Flatliners, 1990, Everybody Wins, 1990, Hoffa, 1992, Batman Returns, 1992, Mrs. Doubtfire, 1993, Rising Sun, 1993, Ed Wood, 1994 (Acad. award for Best Make-up 1994), Being Human, 1994, Junior, 1994. Office: IATSE Local 706 11519 Chandler Blvd North Hollywood CA 91601*

TOVAR, CAROLE L., real estate management administrator; b. Toppenish, Wash., May 19, 1940; d. Harold Max and Gertrude Louisa (Spicer) Smith; m. Duane E. Clark, Aug. 1959 (div. 1963); 1 child, David Allen; m. Vance William Gribble, May 19, 1966 (div. 1989), m. Conrad T. Tovar, June 25, 1992. Student, Seattle Pacific Coll. With B.F. Shearer, Seattle, 1959-60, Standard Oil, Seattle, 1960-62, Seattle Platen Co., 1962-70; ptnr. West Coast Platen, Los Angeles, 1970-87, Waldorf Towers Apts., Seattle, 1970—, Cascade Golf Course, North Bend, Wash., 1970-88; co-owner Pacific Wholesale Office Equipment, Seattle and L.A., 1972-87; owner Pacific Wholesale Office Equip., Seattle, L.A. and San Pablo, Calif., 1988-92, Pac Electronic Service Ctr., Commerce and San Pablo, Calif., 1988-90, Waldorf Mgmt. Co. dba Tovar Mgmt. Co., 1988—; Tovar Properties, 1993—. Mem. Nat. Ctr. Housing Mgmt. (cert. occupancy specialist), Assisted Housing Mgmt. Assn. (nat. cert., Wash. bd. dirs.). Methodist. Office: 706 Pike St Seattle WA 98101-2301

TOWE, A. RUTH, museum director; b. Circle, Mont., Mar. 4, 1938; d. David and Anna Marie (Pedersen) James; m. Thomas E. Towe, Aug. 21, 1960; children: James Thomas, Kristofer Edward. BA, U. Mont., 1960, MA, 1970. Bookkeeper, copywriter Sta. KGVO, Missoula, Mont., 1960-61; grad. asst. Sch. of Journalism U. Mont., Missoula, 1961-62; editorial asst. Phi Gamma Delta mag., Washington, 1964; reporter The Chelsea (Mich.) Standard, 1965-66; bookkeeper, legal sec. Thomas E. Towe, Atty. of Law, Billings, Mont., 1967-68; mus. exec. dir. The Moss Mansion Mus., Billings, 1988—. Pres. Mont. Assn. of Symphony Orchs., 1987-88; sheriff Yellowstone Corral of Westerners, Billings, 1993; v.p. Yellowstone Hist. Soc.; vice-chmn. Yellowstone Dem. Ctrl. Com., Billings, 1983-84; judge flower show Nat. Coun. State Garden Clubs. Mem. AAUW, NAFE, PEO, Mus. Assn. Mont. (pres. 1990-92, bd. dirs. 1989—), Jr. League. Democrat. Mem. Soc. of Friends. Office: The Moss Mus 914 Division St Billings MT 59101

TOWER, ANN PALMER, artist; b. Glen Cove, N.Y., Jan. 26, 1951; d. Albert Kneeland and Lina (Johnson) Tower; m. Robert Holm Tharsing, Dec. 8, 1973; 1 child, Lina Tower Tharsing. BA, U. Ky., 1973, MFA, 1975. Dir. Barnhart Gallery, U. Ky., Lexington, 1973-74; painting instr. Living Arts and Sci. Ctr., Lexington, 1975-77; curator Crossroads Mus. Art, Lexington, Ky., 1978-79; vis. instr. Dept. Art, U. Ky., Lexington, 1979-82; dir. Ctr. for Contemporary Art, U. Ky., Lexington, 1981-83; art critic Lexington Herald-Leader, Lexington, 1983-91; curator of exhbns. Community Bank, Lexington, 1989—. One-woman shows include Ctrl. Bank Gallery, Lexington, 1989, Yvonne Rapp Gallery, Louisville, 1990, Community Bank, Lexington, 1991; exhibited in group shows at Ky. State U. Gallery, Frankfort, 1988, Houston North Gallery, Lunenburg, N.S., Can., 1989, Yvonne Rapp Gallery, 1993, ArtsPlace, Lexington, 1994; represented in pub. collections at U. Ky. Art Mus., Lexington. Bd. dirs. Northside Neighborhood Assn., Lexington, 1991-93. Lexington Arts and Cultural Coun. grantee, 1989; U. Ky. Art Dept. grad. teaching asst., 1973-75. Mem. Nat. Mus. of Women in the Arts. Home: 419 Davidson Ct Lexington KY 40508-1454

TOWER, RONI BETH, psychologist; b. Akron, Ohio, Dec. 11, 1943; d. Arnold Edward Weinstein and Elva Hermoine (Gross) MacRae; children: Jennifer, Daniel. BA, Barnard Coll., N.Y.C., 1964; MS, Yale U., 1977, M in Philosphy, 1979, PhD, 1980. Lic. in clin. psychology, Conn., Maine; diplomate Clin. Psychology Am. Bd. Profl. Psychology. Psychologist Silver Hill Found., New Canaan, Conn., 1979-81; pvt. practice Westport, Conn., 1981—; co-founder, dir. rsch. Clarity Cons. Corp., Westport, 1990-94; lectr. in psychology Yale U., New Haven, 1981-89, Am. Bd. Profl. Psychology seminar, Washington, 1990; cons. in field. Cons. editor Jour. of Imagination Cognition and Personality, 1983—; contbr. numerous articles to profl. jours. Active Yale Alumni Fund Bd. Recipient Traineeship award USPHS, 1979-80; postdoctoral fellow Yale Sch. Epidemiology and Pub. Health, 1992-95. Mem. LWV, Am. Assn. for Study of Mental Imagery (pres. 1988-89, conf. organizer New Haven 1988), Am. Psychol. Assn., Am. Psychol. Soc., Conn. Psychol. Assn., Sigma Xi. Office: Yale Univ Dept Epidemiology 60 College St New Haven CT 06510-3210

TOWERS, MARSHA CAROL, commercial attache; b. N.Y.C., Nov. 4, 1945; d. Abner A. Towers and Marica (Cok) Miller; m. William Baer Endictor, Dec. 27, 1975 (div.). AB, Randolph-Macon Women's Coll., 1967; diplome superior, Sorbonne U., Paris, 1971; MBA, Ga. State U., 1978. Exec. trainee Macy's Dept. Store, Atlanta, 1967-70; clk. Orgn. for Econ. Coop. and Devel., Paris, 1971; sales rep. World Airways, Atlanta, 1972-75; dist. mgr. sales Overseas Nat. Airways, Atlanta, 1975, The Davis Agy., Atlanta, 1976; comml. attache Govt. of Quebec (Can.), Atlanta, 1979—. Active Paul Coverdell for Senator campaign, Atlanta, 1968-70. Mem. Can.-Am. Soc. (bd. dirs.), Atlanta Women in Internat. Trade (pres. 1992-93), Atlanta Women's Network, World Trade Club Atlanta (sec. bd. dirs. 1991-92), Randolpha-Macon Women's Coll. Alumni Assn. (Atlanta chpt.). Episcopalian. Office: Govt Quebec Can 245 Peachtree Ctr Ave Atlanta GA 30303

TOWGOOD, JEAN MARGARET, artist, arts administrator; b. Vancouver, B.C., Can., Jan. 8, 1938; came to U.S., 1964; d. Victor and Marjorie Winnifred (Moss) Haggart; m. Dennis Arthur Towgood, May 21, 1960; children: Gary Thomas, Kenneth Victor, David Arthur. BA in Painting and Drawing, Calif. State U., Fullerton, 1982. Founder, mem. Gallery 318, L.A., 1983-87; artist, artists cons., 1982—; exhbns. dir. SITE, Culver City, Calif., 1988, projects and funding cons., 1989. Supporter Huntington Beach (Calif.) Arts Ctr., 1992—; mem. fundraising com. Orange County Ctr. for Contemporary Art, Santa Ana, Calif., 1994. Mem. AAUW, Coll. Art Assn., Women's Caucus for Art (pres., bd. dirs. 1992-94, bd. dirs. 1990—, So. Calif. chpt. pres., bd. dirs. 1988-90, bd. dirs. 1986-92), Nat. Assn. Arts Orgns., Nat. Mus. Women in Arts (charter). Home: 17611 San Roque Ln Huntington Beach CA 92647 Office: Towgood Studio 652 Moulton Ave Los Angeles CA 90031

TOWNE, KATHLEEN DUGAN, counselor, educator; b. Brockton, Mass., June 14, 1947; d. Kastanter Julius and Alice Lucy (Nevitt) Dugan; m. Stephen Burrows Dates, June 17, 1967 (div. 1981); children: Carrie D. Dates, Liza D. Dates, S. MacDonald Dates; m. Bruce Gene Towne, Aug. 21, 1981; 1 child, M. Schuyler Littlefield. BA in English, U. Vt., 1969, MEd in Counseling, 1971; MEd in Gifted Edn., Johnson State Coll., 1983, MEd in Adminstrn., 1988. Cert. tchr., counselor, prin., Vt. Tchr. Westford (Vt.) Elem. Sch., 1969-70; tchr., acting dir. Renhen Presch., Essex, Vt., 1970-71; real estate broker Riddell Assocs., Burlington, Vt., 1974-78; aide, coach Burlington High Sch., 1980-81; assoc. prof. Champlain Coll., Burlington, 1981-87; counselor Fairfax (Vt.) Pub. Sch. Dist., 1987-88; gifted coord. Montpelier (Vt.) Pub. Sch. Dist., 1988-90; counselor Milton (Vt.) Pub. Sch. Dist., 1990-92, coord. adminstrv. svcs., 1992—; bd. dirs. Vt. Coun. for Gifted Edn., pres., 1989-91; co-founder, presenter Project All Resources Combined, Milton, 1990—; coord. Drug/Alcohol Super Team, Milton, 1991—; co-founder, dir. Connect Through Communication-Conflict Mediation, Milton, 1990—. Co-author: I Am Not Feeling Too Good About This War, 1991. Justice of the Peace, State of Vt., 1987—; bd. civil authority Town of Colchester, Vt., 1987—, sch. bd., 1987-88; trustee Burnham Meml. Libr., Colchester, 1983-85; chmn. Cemetery Commn., Colchester, 1981-82. Named Outstanding Young Woman of Am., 1980. Mem. AACD, AAUW, Vt. Counseling Assn.

TOWNSEND, ALAIR ANE, city official; b. Rochester, N.Y., Feb. 15, 1942; d. Harold Eugene and Dorothy (Sharpe) T.; m. Robert Harris, Dec. 31, 1970 (div. 1994). BS, Elmira Coll., 1962; MS, U. Wis., 1964; postgrad. Columbia U., 1970-71. Assoc. dir. budget priorities Com. on Budget, U.S. Ho. of Reps., Washington, 1975-79; dep. asst. sec. for budget HEW, Washington, 1979-80, asst. sec. for mgmt. and budget, 1980-81; dir. N.Y.C. Office Mgmt. and Budget, 1981-85; dep. mayor for fin. and econ. devel. City of N.Y., 1985-89; pub. Crain's N.Y. Bus., N.Y.C., 1989—; former vice chmn., trustee Elmira Coll.; former mem. Coun. on Fgn. Rels.; bd. govs. Am. Stock Exchange; chmn. Am. Woman's Econ. Devel. Corp.; bd. dir. Fay's Inc.; former chmn. N.Y.C. Sports Commn.; bd. dirs. Lincoln Ctr. Mem. Women's Forum, Fin. Women's Assn. N.Y., Advt. Women N.Y., N.Y.C. Partnership, N.Y. State Bus. Coun. (vice chmn.), N.Y. C. of C. and Industry (bd. dirs.). Office: Crain's NY Bus 220 E 42nd St New York NY 10017-5806

TOWNSEND, ANN VAN DEVANTER, foundation administrator, art historian; b. Washington, June 20, 1936; d. John Ward and Ellen Keys (Ramsey) Cutler; m. Willis Van Devanter, Dec. 27, 1958 (div. May 1974); 1 child, Susan Earling Van Devanter (Mrs. John Philip Newell); m. Lewis Raynham Townsend, Dec. 10, 1983. BA, Brown U., 1958; MA, George Washington U., 1975. Grantsmanship ctr. cert. Guest curator Balt. Mus. Art, 1971-77; dir. cultural affairs Chevy Chase (Md.) Savs. & Loan, Inc., 1978-81; dir. spl. partnership projects NEA, Washington, 1982-83; founding pres. The Trust for Mus. Exhbns., Washington, 1984—; organizer over 60 nat. and internat. mus. exhbns. for more than 200 mus. Co-author: Self-Portraits of American Artists, 1670-1973, 1974; author: Anywhere So Long As There Be Freedom, 1975, Two Hundred Years of American Painting, 1976; contbr. articles to mags. U.S. commr. Cagnes-Sur-Mer Internat. Arts Festival, France, 1977, 78; mem. women's com. Washington Opera, 1993—; bd. dirs. Friends of Corcoran Gallery of Art, Washington, 1975-76, Strathmore Hall Arts Ctr., Rockville, Md., 1978-80, Am. Swedish Hist. Mus., Phila., 1987-89. Acad. grad. fellow Johns Hopkins Sch. Advanced Internat. Studies, 1958. Mem. Nat. Soc. Arts & Letters, Am. News Women's Club, Soc. Women Goegraphers, Sulgrave Club. Episcopalian. Office: The Trust for Mus Exhbns 1424 16th St NW Ste 502 Washington DC 20036

TOWNSEND, BARBARA, actress; b. Oakland, Calif.; d. Charles Edward and Anna Woodworth (Kalkman) T.; m. John Jackson Shaffer III, June 25, 1938 (dec. 1944); 1 child, Sandra Shaffer Van Doren; m. William Louis Wheeler Jr., May 27, 1958 (dec. 1969). BA, U. Calif., Berkeley; student, Am. Acad. Dramatic Arts, N.Y.C. tchr. Sch. of Drama, Nairobi, Kenya, 1970-75. Actress appearing in feature films Hard to Kill, Say Anything, Motel Vacancy, Good Cop, (TV shows) Star Trek, Divorce Court, Nikki and Alexander, After Mash, Murder She Wrote, Aaron's Way, Hunter, St. Elsewhere, Mr. Belvedere, Highway to Heaven, Remington Steele, Little House on the Prairie, Streets of San Francisco, As the World Turns, Guiding Light, Quantum Leap, Civil Wars, Northern Exposure, Sisters, (Broadway shows) The Rose Tatoo, Best of Spirits, As You Like It, (theatre) Children's World Theatre, Am. Theatre Wing, Orpheus Descending, Ann of Green Gables, Taper II. Vol. recorder Braille Inst., L.A., 1978—; vol. Bedside Network, N.Y.C., 1960-69. Researcher Spl. Women's Auxiliary of Navy, Washington, 1941-44. Mem. Actors Equity Assn., Screen Actors Guild, Am. Fedn. Radio and TV Artists. Democrat. Office: Artists Group Inc 10100 Santa Monica Blvd # 2490 Los Angeles CA 90067-4115

TOWNSEND, HEATHER MARIE, critical care nurse; b. Waukegan, Ill., Apr. 9, 1963; d. Henry Delano and Geneva May (Mitchell) Overby; m. Robert E. Townsend, Aug. 8, 1988; 1 child, Robert E. II. BSN magna cum laude, Columbus Coll., 1991; student, Emory U., 1994—. RN, BLS, ACLS. Supr. Columbus (Ga.) Emergency Ctr., 1986-89; postgrad. Doctors Hosp., Columbus, 1994—; intern in internal medicine Martin Army Cmty. Hosp., Ft. Benning, Ga.; cons. Nat. Student Nurses Assn., 1990-91, Alcohol and Drug Panel, Columbus, 1990. Active Concerned Citizens Columbus, 1989-91; chair Code 99 (Blue) Com., 1993—. Recipient Spirit of Nursing award Army Nurse Corps, 1991. Mem. AACN, Columbus Coll. Nursing Honor Soc., Phi Kappa Phi, Phi Eta Sigma. Home: 2935 Hatcher Dr Columbus GA 31907-2157 Office: Doctors Hosp 616 19th St Columbus GA 31901-1528

TOWNSEND, IRENE FOGLEMAN, accountant, tax specialist; b. Birmingham, Ala., May 29, 1932; d. James Woods and Virginia (Martin) Fogleman; m. Kenneth Ross Townsend, Mar. 18, 1951; children: Marietta Irene, Martha Shapard, Kenneth Ross Jr., Elizabeth Buchanan. BSBA, East Carolina U., 1980. CPA, N.C., Va. Acct. Norwood P. Whitehurst & Assocs., Greenville, N.C., 1981-86; tax dir. Nat. Med. Enterprises, Inc., Fairfax, Va., 1986—. Fellow AICPA, N.C. Assn. CPA's, D.C. Inst. CPA's; mem. DAR, N.C. Soc. Daughters of the Colonial Wars, Colonial Dames 17th Century. Democrat. Episcopalian (lay reader, chalice bearer). Home: 2521 Paxton St Lakeridge VA 22192-3414 Office: Nat Med Enterprises Inc 3060 Williams Dr Fairfax VA 22031-4628

TOWNSEND, JANE KALTENBACH, zoologist, educator; b. Chgo., Dec. 21, 1922; B.S., Beloit Coll., 1944; M.A., U. Wis., 1946; Ph.D., U. Iowa, 1950; m. 1966. Asst. in zoology U. Wis., 1944-47; asst., instr. U. Iowa, 1948-50; asst., project assoc. in pathology U. Wis., 1950-53; Am. Cancer Soc. research fellow Wenner-Grens Inst., Stockholm, 1953-56; asst. prof. zoology Northwestern U., 1956-58; asst. prof. to assoc. prof. zoology Mt. Holyoke Coll., South Hadley, Mass., 1958-70, prof., 1970-93, chmn. biol. scis., 1980-86, prof. emeritus, 1993—. Fellow AAAS (sec. sect. biol. sci. 1974-78); mem. Am. Assn. Anatomists, Am. Inst. Biol. Scis., Am. Soc. Zoologists, Soc. Experimental Biology and Medicine, Soc. Devel. Biology, Corp. of Marine Biol. Lab., Sigma Xi, Phi Beta Kappa. Office: Mount Holyoke Coll Dept Biology South Hadley MA 01075

TOWNSEND, KATHLEEN KENNEDY, state official; m. David Townsend; children:Meaghan, Meave, Kate, Kerry. BA cum laude, Harvard U.; JD, U. N.Mex. Former program dir. U.S. Peace Corps; former dep. asst. atty. gen. U.S. Dept. Justice, Washington; lt. gov. State of Md., 1994—; tchr. U. Md., Balt. County, Essex. C.C., Dundalk C.C., U. Pa.; past exec. dir. Md. Student Svcs. Alliance. Editor U. N.Mex. Law Rev. Founder Robert F. Kennedy Human Rights award. Recipient 4 hon. degrees. Office: Lt Govs Office State House 100 State Circle Annapolis MD 21401*

TOWNSEND, LINDA LADD, mental health nurse; b. Louisville, Apr. 26, 1948; d. Samuel Clyde and Mary Elizabeth (Denton) Ladd; m. Stanley Allen Oliver, June 7, 1970 (div. 1978); 1 child, Aaron; m. Warren Terry Townsend Jr., Jan. 1, 1979; children: Mark, Amy, Sarah. Student, Catherine Spalding Coll., 1966-67; BSN, Murray State U., 1970; MS in Psychiat./Mental Health Nursing, Tex. Woman's U., 1976. RN, Tex., Ky.; lic. advanced nurse practitioner, profl. counselor, marriage and family therapist, Tex. Charge nurse med. and pediatric units Murray (Ky.)-Calloway County Hosp., 1970-71; team leader surg./renal transplant unit VA Hosp., Nashville, 1971-73; team leader, charge nurse gen. med.-surg. unit Providence Hosp., Waco, Tex., 1973-74; outpatient therapist Mental Hygiene Clinic, Ft. Hood, Tex., 1975-76; outpatient nurse therapist Ctrl. Counties Ctr. for Mental Health/Mental Retardation, Copperas Cove & Lampasas, Tex., 1977-80; psychiat. nurse clin. specialist, marriage/family therapist Profl. Counseling Svc., Copperas Cove, 1979—; cons. Metroplex Hosp. and Pavilion, Killeen, Tex., 1980—, Woods Psychiat. Inst., Killeen, 1987—. Founding mem. Family Outreach of Coryell County, Copperas Cove, 1986—, also past pres. and past sec.; founding mem. Partnership for a Drug and Violence-Free Copperas Cove. Recipient Mary M. Roberts Writing award Am. Jour. of Nursing, 1970; named Mem. of Yr.-Vol., Family Outreach of Coryell County. Mem. ANA (cert. clin. specialist in adult psychiat. and mental health nursing, cert. clin. specialist in child and adolescent psychiat. and mental health nursing, Coun. Psychiat. and Mental Health Nursing), AAUW (past bd. dirs., sec.-treas.), Tex. Nurses Assn., Am. Group Psychotherapy Assn., Learning Disabilities Assn., Inst. for Humanities at Salado, Sigma Theta Tau. Democrat. Methodist. Home: Rt 1 Box 253 D Kempner TX 76539 Office: Profl Counseling Svc 806 East Ave D Ste F Copperas Cove TX 76522

TOWNSEND, MARILYN MORAN, video production company executive; b. Seminole, Okla., Sept. 12, 1954; d. Melvin R. and Jasmine L. (Birchell) Moran; m. Bill Dean Townsend, July 31, 1976; children—Allison, Julie. B.A., Purdue U., 1976. Announcer Sta. KWSH, Seminole, Okla., 1973; news/weather anchorwoman Sta. WLFI TV, West Lafayette, Ind., 1973-76, Sta. WBBH, Ft. Myers, Fla., 1976-77, Sta. WKJG-TV Ft. Wayne, Ind., 1977-81; owner, mgr. Custom Video Corp., Ft. Wayne, 1981—; dir. Pvt. Industry Council Ft. Wayne, 1983-87, vice chmn., 1986; chmn. Small Bus. Council, Ft. Wayne, 1983-87; TV producer, series Heartbeat, 1982-84. Chmn. 1990 fund drive Ft. Wayne Fine Arts Found., 1990; active Parkview Hospice, 1978-80; chmn. United Way of Allen County, 1994-95, co-chmn. Human Svcs. Panel on Youth and Violence, 1994—. Recipient 1st place award for news documentary AP, Ind., 1979, for med. documentary Ind. Med. Assn., 1978-79, Ind. Women Entrepreneur of the Yr. award Inc. Mag. and Ernest and Young, 1988, Ind. Small Bus. Owner of the Yr. award Small Bus. Assn., 198, Bus. Women of the Yr. award Foellinger Found, 1990; Named Ind. Women Bus. Owners Advocate of Yr., SBA, 1985. Mem. Women in Communications (past pres.; numerous awards), Women Bus. Owners Assn. (founding mem.), Nat. Assn. Female Execs., Ft. Wayne C. of C. (dir. 1983—), Ind. C. of C. (vice chair 1994-95). Home: 5131 Binford Ln Fort Wayne IN 46804-6503 Office: Custom Video Corp 811 Lawrence Dr Fort Wayne IN 46804

TOWNSEND, SANDRA LYNNETTE, nurse; b. Boise, Idaho, Nov. 16, 1957; d. Edward Elmo and Betty Jean (Maus) Letney; m. Richard Wayne Townsend, Apr. 2, 1982; 1 child, Mallory Jean. BSN, Boise State U., 1992. CNA. From claims approver to internal auditor, asst. supr. John Hancock Ins. Co., 1978-88; RN III on oncology/BMT unit. Singer-dancer Mayors and Minors, Nampa, Idaho, 1988. Mem. Nat. Student Nurses Assn. (treas. 1991-92, western dir. 1991-92), Idaho Nurses Assn. (membership dir. 1993, treas. 1994—). Republican. Home: 11101 Hummingbird Dr Boise ID 83709-1371

TOWNSEND, SUSAN ELAINE, social service institute administrator, hostage survival consultant; b. Phila., Sept. 5, 1946; d. William Harrison and Eleanor Irene (Fox) Rogers; m. John Holt Townsend, May 1, 1976. BS in Secondary Edn., West Chester State U., 1968; MBA, Nat. U., 1978; PhD in Human Behavior, La Jolla U., 1984. Biology tchr. Methacton Sch. Dist., Fairview Village, Pa., 1968-70; bus. mgr., analyst profl. La Jolla Research Corp., San Diego, 1977-79; pastoral asst. Christ Ctr. Bible Therapy, San Diego, 1980-82, also bd. dirs.; v.p., pub. relations World Outreach Ctr. of Faith, San Diego, 1981-82, also bd. dirs.; owner, pres., cons. Townsend Research Inst., San Diego, 1983-89; teaching assoc. La Jolla U. Continuing Edn., 1985-86, adminstr., assoc. registrar, adj. faculty, 1990. Author: Hostage Survival-Resisting the Dynamics of Captivity, 1983; contbr. articles to profl. jours. Instr. USN Advanced Survival Evasion Resistance Escape Sch., 1986-89; security officer Shield Security, San Diego, 1991-92; bd. dirs. Christ Fellowship Ch. of San Diego, 1987—, music dir., 1992—; religious vol. Met. Correctional Ctr., San Diego, 1983-89, San Diego County Jail Ministries, 1978—, scheduling coord., 1993—. Served to comdr. USN, 1970-76, USNR, 1976—. Mem. Naval Res. Assn. (life), Res. Officers Assn. (Outstanding Jr. Officer of Yr. Calif. chpt. 1982), Navy League U.S. (life), West Chester U. Alumni Assn., Nat. U. Alumni Assn. (life), La Jolla U. Alumni Assn., Gen. Fedn. Women's Clubs (pres. Peninsula club 1983-85, pres. Parliamentary law club 1984-86, Past Pres.' Assn.), Calif. Fedn. Women's Clubs (v.p.-at-large San Diego dist. 25 1982-84).

TOWNSEND, TERRY, publishing executive; b. Camden, N.J., Dec. 14, 1920; d. Anthony and Rose DeMarco; BA, Duke U., 1942; LHD (hon.) Dowling Coll., 1991; m. Paul Brorstrom Townsend, Dec. 8, 1961; 1 son, Kim. Pub. rels. dir. North Shore Univ. Hosp., Manhasset, N.Y., 1955-68; pres. Theatre Soc. L.I., 1968-70; pres. Townsend Comm. Bur., Ronkonkoma, N.Y., 1970—, L.I. Communicating Service, Ronkonkoma, 1977—; columnist, writer L.I./Bus., Ronkonkoma, 1970-75; pub. L.I. Bus. News, 1978—; v.p. Parr Meadows Racetrack, Yaphank, N.Y., 1977. Assoc. trustee North Shore U. Hosp., 1968—; bd. govs. Adelphi U. Friends Fin. Edn., 1978-85; chmn. ann. archtl. awards competition N.Y. Inst. Tech., 1970-83; trustee, vice chair Dowling Coll., 1994—, trustee L.I. Fine Arts Mus., 1984-85; pub. broadcasting Sta. WLIW TV, Garden City, L.I., N.Y., 1990-93; bd. dirs. Family Svc. Assn. Nassau County, 1982-92; dinner chmn. L.I. 400 Ball, 1987; vice chmn. bd. trustees Dowling Coll., 1994—; trustee Mus. at Stony Brook, 1994—. Recipient Media award 110 Center Bus. and Profl. Women, 1977, Enterprise award Friends of Fin. Edn., 1981, L.I. Loves Bus. Showcase Salute, 1982, Community Svc. award N.Y. Diabetes Assn., 1983, Disting. Long Islander in Communications award L.I. United Epilepsy Assn., 1984, Spl. award Dowling Coll. Spring Tribute, 1989, Disting. Svc. award Episcopal Health Svcs., 1989, Disting. Citizen award Dowling Coll., 1991, Gilbert Tilles award Nat. Assn. Fundraising Execs., 1994; named First Lady of L.I., L.I. Public Relations Assn., 1973, L.I. Woman of Yr. L.I. Assn. Action Com., 1989. Office: LI Bus News 2150 Smithtown Ave Ronkonkoma NY 11779-7348

TRABAN, BARBARA GERALYN, controller; b. New Bedford, Mass., Oct. 16, 1954; d. Frank and Frances (Borowicz) T. BS, U. Mass., 1976; MBA, U. Mass., Dartmouth, 1989. Contr. Calvin Clothing, New Bedford, Mass., 1976—. Home: 46 Winthrop St New Bedford MA 02744 Office: Calvin Clothing 64 Conduit St New Bedford MA 02745

TRABERT, JUDITH ANNE, human resources specialist; b. Rochester, N.Y., Apr. 14, 1949; d. Carl Frederick and Ruth Marie (Leimberger) T.; m. J. Joseph Pia, May 30, 1972. Student, St. Michael's Coll./U. Toronto, 1967-69; BA magna cum laude, Syracuse U., 1971, MA, 1976, PhD, 1986. Assoc. Devel. and Evaluation Assocs., Inc., Syracuse, N.Y., 1977-84; prin. Bus. Fitness, Syracuse, 1980-84; mgr. selection and devel. City of Rochester, 1987—; co-founder, dir. Pers. Testing Coun. of Upstate N.Y., Rochester, 1991—. Mem. Internt. Pers. Mgmt. Assn. Assessment Coun. (dir. 1992—). Office: City of Rochester 103A City Hall Rochester NY 14614-1280

TRACEY, MARGARET, dancer; b. Pueblo, Colo.. Student, Sch. Am. Ballet, 1982. With corps de ballet N.Y.C. Ballet, 1986-88, soloist, 1989-91, prin., 1991. Featured in ballets (Balanchine) Ivesiana, Tarantella, The Nutcracker, Symphony in C, Jewels, Square Dance, Tschaikovsky Pas de Deux, Tschaikovsky Suite No. 3, Vienna Waltzes, Apollo, Ballo Della Regina, Divertimento No. 15, Donizetti Variations, Harlequinade, A Midsummer Night's Dream, Sonatine, La Source, Stars and Stripes, Symphony in Three Movements, Valse Fantaisie, Western Symphony, Who Cares?, (Robbins) Afternoon of a Faun, The Four Seasons, The Goldberg Variations, (Martins) Les Petits Riens, Mozart Serenade, Fearful Symmetries, Zakouski, Sleeping Beauty, (Anderson) Baroque Variations; also appeared in N.Y.C. Ballet's Blanchine Celebration, 1993; toured in Europe, Asia. Recipient U.S.A. award Princess Grace Found., 1985-86; scholar Atlantic Richfield Found., 1982-85. Office: NYC Ballet NY State Theater Lincoln Ctr Plaza New York NY 10023*

TRACHEVSKI, LISA ANN, human resources executive; b. Columbus, Ohio, Nov. 15, 1956; d. Donald Henry and Joan Mary (Morbitzer) Bryant; m. George Joseph Trachevski, Mar. 16, 1979. Student, Ohio State U., 1977. Cert. temporary staffing specialist. File/payroll clk. Olsten of Columbus, Inc., 1974-75, placement coord., 1975-78, office supr., 1978-80, office mgr., 1980-84, v.p. ops., 1984-88, v.p. adminstrn., 1991—; v.p., bd. dirs. Olsten Health Care Svcs., Columbus; cons. Intensive Office Edn., Grove City, Ohio, 1986—; facility security officer Olsten of Columbus, 1979—. Mem. Nat. Assn. Personnel Cons., Ohio Temporary Svc. Assn. (sec. 1992—), Workforce Basics Consortium (advisor 1991). Roman Catholic. Home: 6306 Home Rd Delaware OH 43015 Office: Olsten of Columbus Inc 88 E Broad St 630 Columbus OH 43215

TRACHTA, PAMELA HALE, consulting executive; b. Sacramento, May 10, 1943; d. James Struthers and Mary Wilder (Richards) Lochhead; m. Robert Louis Weaver, June 18, 1966 (div. Oct. 1988); children: Laura Michelle, Erin Hale; m. S. Jon Trachta, June 24, 1989. BA, Stanford U., 1965; MA, Columbia U., 1966. Tchr. N.Y.C. (N.Y.) Pub. Schs., 1966-68; paraprofl. counselor Pasadena (Calif.) Mental Health Ctr., 1970-73; asst. dir. U. So. Calif. Ctr. for Health Svcs. Rsch., L.A., 1973; freelance writer, photographer, 1973—; founder, dir., ednl. cons. Images (Ednl. Photography), So. Pasadena, Calif., 1978-85; dir. of devel. Friends of the Jr. Arts Ctr., L.A., 1985-87; assoc. dir. of devel. Stanford U., So. Calif. Office, L.A., 1987-89; dir. of devel. U. Heart Ctr., U. Ariz., Tucson, 1990-94; cons. L.A. Pub. Schs., So. Pasadena Pub. Schs., Calif. Poly. Pomona, Pacific Oaks Coll., pvt. schs., youth assns., 1978-85; dir. Phototherapy Assn., 1980-84; artist-in-residence Calif. Arts Coun., So. Pasadena, 1982, 83, 84. Artist, photographer various one-woman and group exhibits, 1973-84; co-editor: Phototherapy Jour., 1973-84. Dir. Pasadena (Calif.) Mental Health Ctr., 1973-76, Tucson Symphony Orgn., 1991-93, Planned Parenthood So., Ariz., Tucson, 1990—, Tucson/Pima Arts Coun., 1992—, sec.; pres. bd. Stanford Alumni of So. Ariz., 1992-93; mem. Ariz.-Mexico commn.; dir. Tucson Pima Arts Coun., 1993—. Democrat. Episcopalian. Office: Univ Ariz Univ Heart Ctr Tucson AZ 85724

TRACY, ALOISE See SHOENIGHT, PAULINE ALOISE SOUERS

TRACY, BARBARA MARIE, lawyer; b. Mpls., Oct. 13, 1945; d. Thomas A. and Ruth C. (Roby) T. BA, U. Minn., 1971; JD, U. Okla., 1980. Bar: Okla. 1980, U.S. Dist. Ct. (we. dist.) Okla. 1980, U.S. Dist. Ct. (no. dist.) Tex. 1991, U.S. Supreme Ct. 1988. Assoc. Pierce, Couch, Hendrickson, Johnston & Baysinger, Oklahoma City, 1980-82; ptnr. Rizley & Tracy, Sayre, Okla., 1982-84; pvt. practice Oklahoma City, 1984-90; gen. atty. U.S. Army Corps Engrs., Ft. Worth, 1991—. Mem. citizens adv. bd. O'Donoghue Rehab. Inst., Oklahoma City. Mem. ABA, Okla. Bar Assn., Internat. Tng. in Commn. (pres. Ace Club chpt.). Democrat. Roman Catholic. Office: 819 Taylor St Fort Worth TX 76102-6114

TRACY, CHRISTINA L., secondary school educator; b. Marshall, Ill., June 12, 1942; d. Lawrence and Kathryn (Setzer) Goekler; m. Darrell M. Tracy, Nov. 28, 1964; children: Lawrence, Melissa, Melanie, Megan, Mynda. BS in Edn., Ea. Ill. U., 1964; postgrad., Ill. State U. Cert. secondary chemistry, math., physics, computer edn. tchr., Ill. Chemistry, physics, computer, and math. tchr. Arcola (Ill.) High Sch., 1964-65, Rossville (Ill.)-Alvin High Sch., 1966—; state student advisor Ill. Jr. Acad. Sci., 1985—. Leader 4-H Club, Rossville, 1966-91; pres. Rossville Jr. Women's Club, 1971; pres., trustee Vermilion County Conservation Dist., Danville, Ill., 1980-89. Recipient Rsch. Sci. Tchr. award Sigma Xi, 1991. Office: Rossville-Alvin High Sch 350 N Chicago St Rossville IL 60963

TRACY, DOROTHY SHEA, financial planner; b. Pitts., Oct. 4, 1920; d. Thomas Francis and Frances Marie (Gilhouse) Shea; widow; children: Patrick, Thomas, Nancy, Christine, Michael, Kathleen. BBA in Econs., Ga. State U., 1967. Tchr. Ga. Continuing Edn., Atlanta, 1978-85; fin. planner Atlanta, 1980—; lobbyist Coun. for Children, Atlanta, 1979-81; rep. Legislex, Washington, 1980-81; legis. aide to Rep. Eleanor Richardson, Ga. Gen. Assembly, Atlanta, 1983-90. Author: ABC's of School Finance in Georgia, 1983. Mem. Atlanta Civil Svc. Rev. Bd., 9185-94; bd. dirs. Atlanta Regional Commn. Task Force on Elderly, 1988—. Recipient Outstanding Cath. Woman award Archdiocese of Ga. Coun., 1977, community svc. award Atlanta Women's C. of C., 1984, Gov.'s commendation State of Ga., 1988; co-author: Study of Georgia's Lottery. Mem. LWV (task force for tax study Ga. 1987-88, task force for marital property study 1988, co-author Ga.'s Lottery 1992, Eudora Rogers award for outstanding svc. 1992), AAUW (legis. chmn. Ga. and Atlanta 1983-87), Am. Assn. Ret. Persons (nat. econ. issues team, vice chmn. state legis. com.). Democrat. Home and Office: 3037 Slaton Dr NW Atlanta GA 30305-2006

TRACY, JANET RUTH, legal educator, librarian; b. Denison, Iowa, July 16, 1941; d. L. M. and Grace (Harvey) T.; m. Rodd Mc Cormick Reynolds, Feb. 15, 1975 (dec. June 1993); children: Alexander, Lee. BA, U. Oreg., 1963; ML, U. Wash., 1964; JD, Harvard U., 1969. Bar: N.Y. 1970. Reference libr. Harvard Coll. Librs., Cambridge, Mass., 1964-66; assoc. Kelley Drye & Warren, N.Y.C., 1969-71; dir. data base design Mead Data Ctrl., Inc., N.Y.C., 1971-75; dir. rsch. Mvpl. Employees Legal Svc. Fund, N.Y.C., 1975-76; from asst. to assoc. prof. N.Y. Law Sch., N.Y.C., 1976-82; asst. libr. dir. Law Libr. Columbia U., N.Y.C., 1982-86; prof., law libr. dir. Fordham U., N.Y.C., 1986—; chmn. Conf. Law Librs. Jesuit Univs., 1988-89. Co-author: Professional Staffing and Job Security in Academic Law Libraries, 1989. Recipient Catalog Automation award Winston Found., 1990, 91, 92. Home: 285 Riverside Dr New York NY 10025 Office: Fordham U Sch of Law 140 W 62nd St New York NY 10023

TRACY, MARGARET LYNNE, small business owner; b. Chgo., Sept. 24, 1955; d. Leo P. and Eleanor (Jankowski) Karolewski; m. Richard J. Tracy, Oct. 24, 1981; children: Christopher, Elizabeth. BA, Mundelein Coll., 1977; MBA, Loyola U., Chgo., 1981. Acct. Walter E. Heller & Co., Chgo., 1974-82; investment advisor Insight Fin. Planning, Barrington, Ill., 1982-84, Strategic Fin. Cons., Bensenville, Ill., 1984-86; owner Priority Planning, Wheaton, Ill., 1986—; adj. faculty Coll. Fin. Planning, Denver, 1984—. Mem. Internat. Assn. Fin. Planning, Inst. Cert. Fin. Planners, Nat. Assn. Tax Practitioners, Registry Fin. Planning Practitioners. Office: Priority Planning 520 W Roosevelt Rd Ste 301 Wheaton IL 60187-5084

TRACY, SUSAN M., state legislator. BA, Boston Coll. Mem. Mass. Ho. of Reps.; vice chmn. com. on natural resources and agr.; mem. ways and means, and ethics coms. Home: 24 Adair Rd Boston MA 02135 Office: Mass Ho of Reps State Capitol Boston MA 02133*

TRADEWELL-VEGA, CAREY, mental health, alcohol and drug educator; b. Antigo, Wis., June 4, 1948; d. James Bennett and Rosemary (Wall) Tradewell; m. William H. Frackelton, Jan. 27, 1968 (div. 1974); children—Bill, Damion Clayton; m. Daniel Paul Vega, Feb. 15, 1986. B.S.W., U. Wis.-Milw., 1974, postgrad. in social work, 1978—. Cert. alcohol and other drug abuse counselor. Social worker Planned Parenthood, Milw., 1974-77, coordinator social services, 1977-82; family program coordinator Kettle Moraine Hosp., Oconomowoc, Wis., 1982-84, dir. tng. and edn., 1984—; therapist Catalyst Counseling, Milw., part-time 1984—; field instr. U. Wis.-Milw., 1982—; field advisor, bd. dirs. U. Wis.-Whitewater, 1985—; cons. woman and family psychotherapy services, Waukesha, Wis., 1986—; mem. subcom. on sexual abuse and assault Wis. Ho. of Reps., 1980-81. Vol. Parents Anonymous, Milw., 1977-82; vol. speaker Alcoholics Anonymous and Alanon, Milw., Waukesha, 1982—; vol. cons. Mental Health Clinic, Milw., 1977—. Mem. Am. Assn. for Marriage and Family Therapy, Nat. Assn. Social Workers, Wis. Family Relations Council, Wis. Alcohol and Other Drug Abuse Council. Democrat. Mem. United Ch. of Christ. Avocations: travel; reading; family activities. Home: 4313 N Maryland Ave Milwaukee WI 53211-1650 Office: Kettle Moraine Hospital 4839 N Hewitts Point Rd Oconomowoc WI 53086

TRAFELI, MARJORIE A., social services administrator; b. Phila., Apr. 19, 1932; d. Charles Henry and Amelia Elizabeth (Fox) Busch; m. Mario Marcello Trafeli, Feb. 19, 1955; children: Barbara Fenton, Janet Urich, Robert, John Paul, Mark. A of Dental Hygiene, U. Detroit, 1953, BS in Dental Hygiene, 1977. Registered dental hygienist. Dental hygienist various dentist's offices Mich., 1953-75; dental hygienist State of Mich.-WC Dental Prior Approval Rev., Detroit, 1975-82; forms analyst State of Mich.-WC Sys. and Tech. Svcs., Detroit, 1982—; publs. adv. bd. State of Mich. dept. Social Svcs., Detroit. Artist, designer, print specialist posters, pamphlets and forms Dept. Social Svcs. Initiator employee action flower planting state bldg. Mem. Bus. Forms Mgmt. Assn. Republican. Roman Catholic.

TRAG, ARVILLA L., regulatory affairs professional; b. Gt. Barrington, Mass., Apr. 5, 1955; d. William Willard and Susan Louise (Williams) T. BA in Biology and Chemistry, Coll. St. Rose, 1986. Lab. technician N.Y. State Dept. Health, Albany, 1986-92; regulatory affairs mgr. Virogenetics, Troy, N.Y., 1992-94; dir. regulatory affairs, quality assurance, quality control Am. Biogenetic Scis., South Bend, Ind., 1994; sr. regulatory affairs assoc. Biopure, Boston, 1994—. Vol. Planned Parenthood, Albany, 1992-93. Mem. Regulatory Affairs Profl. Soc., Parenteral Drug Assn.

TRAHAN, MARGARET FRITCHEY (PEGGY TRAHAN), mayor; b. Harrisburg, Pa.; d. John Augustus and Dorotha Amy (Warren) Fritchey; m. Henry Voltaire Trahan, Jr., Sept. 29, 1956 (dec. July, 1991); children: Henry Voltaire III, Randall Scott. BS in Bus. Edn., Cedar Crest Coll., 1955; BE in Curriculum & Instrn., Fla. Atlantic U., 1971. Corr. course writer Acad. Health Scis., U.S. Army, San Antonio, 1976-77, team chief, individual analysis and design. br., 1977-80, dep. chief individual tng. analysis and design br., 1980-81; satellite TV program dir. U.S. Army Health Svcs. Command, San Antonio, 1981-84; chief individual tng. in forces br. Acad. of Health Scis., U.S. Army, San Antonio, 1984-85; co-owner, operator Circle T Farms, San Antonio, 1985-89; presdl. gen. elections Tex. Sec. of State Insp., 1988; vol. worker Army Community Svcs., 1966-67, ARC, 1966-74, South Padre Island Visitor and Conv. Bur., 1991-92; dir. South Padre Island Econ. Devel. Corp., 1993—; pres. sr. state officer club, 1980-81, sr. 1st v.p. Tex. soc. Children of the Am. Revolution, 1979-81, sr. nat. v.p. south cent. region, 1978-80, sr. nat. historian, nat. conv. vice chmn., 1980-82, hon. sr. nat. v.p. nat. soc., 1982-85, sr. Nat. Officers' Club, 1977—; sr. organizing pres. Rio Grande Soc., 1988-89, sr. pres., 1989-91, Denny Anderson Soc., 1976-78; sr. state chmn. awards and presentations Tex. Soc. C.A.R., 1989-90; v.p. Laguna Madre Rep. Club, 1988-89, pres. 1989-91; coord. Gulf Coast area Cameron County Rep. Exec. Com., 1989-90; coord. Gulf Coast and Mid-County Primary Elections, 1989-90; mem. Brownsville Rep. Club, 1989—, Hidalgo Rep. Women's Club, 1989-91, Cameron County Rep. Women's Club, 1990—; exec. dir. Cameron County Rep. Exec. Com., 1990-92; clerk South Padre Island Municipal Elections, 1989, alternate judge, 1990, judge, 1991; mem. beautification com. South Padre Island, 1990-91; mayor South Padre Island, 1992—; mem. adv. bd. South Padre Island Conv. and Visitor's Bur., 1991-92; bd. dirs. Rio Grande Valley Internat. Music Festival, 1990—, mem. bi-nat. com., 1993-94, Lower Rio Grande Valley Devel. Coun., 1992—; bd. dir., chair Cameron County Airport Zoning Commn., 1992—; mem. small cities adv. coun. Tex. Mcpl. League, 1992—, vice chair, 1995—, mem. legis. com. fin. and adminstrn. ann. conv., 1994—, annual conf. planning com., 1994, 2d v.p. region 12 elected official assn., 1994; chmn. Citizen's Exec. Adv. Coun., Rio Grande State Ctr. Mental Health and Retardation, 1993—, vice chmn. 1992-93; mem. grand opening com. South Padre Island Conv. Ctr., 1992; mem. South Padre Island Community Chorus; chmn. welcoming com. Miss U.S.A. Pageant, 1993—; chmn. Pirate Days Festival, 1993—; mem. Rio Grande Valley Emergency Mgmt. Coun., 1994—. Recipient Outstanding Performance award Acad. of Health Scis. and Sec. of Army, 1958, 79, 80, commendation cert. ARC, 1967, U.S. Army Community Svcs., 1974, Nat. Soc. Children Am. Revolution, 1980, Spl. Act award Acad. Health Scis. U.S. Army, 1977, Exceptional Performance award U.S. Army Health Svcs. Command and Acad. of Health Scis., 1981, 83, 84, Comdr.'s award for civilian svc. Dept. Army, 1985, medal of appreciation Nat. Soc. Sons of the Am. Revolution, 1989, Outstanding Performance award Cameron Rep. Party, 1991; named one of Notable Women of Tex., 1983-84. Mem. AAUW, BPW, Fed. Ednl. Tech. Assn., Assn. Edn. and Communication Tech., Armed Forces Pub. Affairs Coun., Dept. of Army Nutrition Com., NAFE, Am. Mgmt. Assn., Tex. Fedn. Rep. Women, Lower Rio Grande Valley City Ofcls. Assn. (2d v.p. 1994—), Hilton Sea Island Tower Assn. (v.p., bd. govs. 1987-89), Nat. Fedn. of Rep. Women, DAR (rec. sec. Alamo chpt. 1975-76), DuBois-Hite chapter (corr., sec. 1989-91), Radisson Sea Island Tower Assn. (v.p. 1989—, bd. govs.), Hidalgo County Rep. Women's Club, Laguna Madre Bus. and Profl. Women's Assn., Cameron County Rep. Women's Club, South Padre Island C. of C. (bd. dirs. 1991-93, chmn. cultural arts com., Islanders, liaison com.), U.S. Army Theater Support Communicatio Club (pres. 1968-69), Comm. Zone Europe Army Officers' Wives (v.p. 1968), Ladies of the Shrine. Republican. Lutheran. Avocations: tennis, seashells, swimming, needlework, Mahjongg, modeling. Home: PO Box 2576 South Padre Island TX 78597-2576

TRAIGIS, MARY ELIZABETH, nurse; b. Mt. Holly, N.J., Feb. 15, 1963; d. William Peter and Mary (Frankovich) T.; m. John A. McCormac (div.). ADN summa cum laude, Walters State Community Coll., Morristown, Tenn., 1989; cert. EMT, State Tech. Inst., Knoxville, Tenn., 1983. RN, Tenn., Fla. Firefighter, emergency med. technician, comm. supr. Rural Metro Fire Dept., Knoxville, 1981-87; emergency med. dispatcher Knox County Govt., Knoxville, 1983-86; nurse extern, monitor technician St. Mary's Hosp., Knoxville, 1987-89; staff nurse U. Tenn. Hosp., Knoxville, 1989-90; staff nurse coronary care unit Washington Hosp. Ctr., 1990-92; staff nurse CCU surgery Bayfront Med. Ctr., St. Petersburg, Fla., 1992-93; with Criticare Nursing Svc., 1993—; quality mgmt. supr. HIP health Plan of Fla., St. Petersburg, 1994—; mem. dive rescue team, leader dispatch team, Jr. squad advisor, sec., historian Knoxville Vol. Rescue Squad, 1983-85; basic life support instr. Am. Heart Assn., Knoxville, 1987-92, 93—; nursing del. People to People, People's Republic of China, 1990. Mem. ANA, AACN, Nat. League for Nursing, Nat. Assn. for Healthcare Quality, Fla. Nurses Assn. Roman Catholic. Home: 1200 102nd Ave N # 2-210 Saint Petersburg FL 33716

TRAIL, MARGARET ANN, employee benefits company executive; b. Bryan, Tex., July 17, 1941; d. Louis Milton and Margaret (Stromberg) Thompson; m. Robert A. Rosemier, Aug. 25, 1962 (div. Feb. 1973); 1 child: Gretchen Elisabeth; m. Newt Shands Trail, Dec. 4, 1989. BS in Nursing, U. Iowa, 1963; MS, No. Ill. U., 1971. Instr. Cooley Dickinson Hosp., Northampton, Mass., 1964-65; dir. nursing De Kalb (Ill.) Pub. Hosp., Kishwaukee Community Hosp., 1972-76, Terre Haute (Ind.) Regional Hosp., 1976-78; from mgr. clin. systems to dir. spl. projects Hosp. Corp. Am., Nashville, 1978-86; from dir. med. mgmt. to v.p. Equicor, Nashville, 1986-90; divsn. v.p. The Travelers Ins. Co., Hartford, Conn., 1990-93; mgr. health svcs. quality mgmt. Aetna Health Plans, Hartford, 1993—. Mem. LWV (pres. DeKalb chpt. 1970-72), Nat. League Nursing, Group Health Assn., Am. Managed Care and Rev. Assn. Office: Aetna 151 Farmington Ave Hartford CT 06156-0001

TRAIL, MARY JO, physical therapist; b. Bartlesville, Okla., Jan. 28, 1937; d. Norman Maurice and Virginia Pearl (Ehly) Weaver; m. George Arthur Trail, Sept. 1, 1961 (div. 1984); children: Regina, Angela, George, Amy. BS in Phys. Therapy, U. Kans., 1958. Lic. in phys. therapy. Staff phys. therapist Rancho Los Amigos Rehab. and Respiratory Hosp., Downey, Calif., 1958-60, Queen's Hosp., Honolulu, 1960-61, Meth. Hosp., Houston, 1964-65; phys. therapist supr. Manor Care Nursing Ctr., Arlington, Va., 1984-86, N. Med. Head Injury Sys., Wauchula, Fla., 1987-88; phys. therapist Home Health Svcs. of Manatee, Bradenton, Fla., 1990-94, Profl. Health Care Svcs., Tampa, Fla., 1995—. Active Dem. Party of Manatee County, Bradenton, Fla., 1994. Mem. AAUW, Am. Phys. Therapy Assn. (pres. Hawaii chpt. 1961). Presbyterian. Home: 6604 29th Ave W Bradenton FL 34209

TRAINOR-SMITH, SHARON, marketing professional; b. Dearborn, Mich., July 1, 1954; d. George Edward and Agnes Jane (Epple) Trainor; m. David Scott Smith, Aug. 6, 1977; children: Ryan G., Kathleen R. BA in English with honors, U. Va., 1976; MBA, Dartmouth Coll., 1982. Adminstrv. asst. David C. Wilson Psychiat. Hosp., Charlottesville, Va., 1976-78; part-time copy writer Decker, Decker & Desandro, Charlottesville, 1977-78; assoc. dir. Va. Trial Lawyers Assn., Charlottesville, 1978-80; part-time v.p. client svc. Word Merchants Ltd., Charlottesville, 1978-80; mgr. mktg. Swanson Divsn.-Campbell Soup, Camden, N.J., 1982-85, acting dir. new products, 1985-87; nat. mktg. dir. Ben & Jerry's Ice Cream, Waterbury, Vt., 1988; cons. mktg., new products Boston, N.Y.C., N.H., Vt., 1988-93; sr. v.p. client svc. ASI Market Rsch. Inc., Stamford, Conn., 1994—. Recipient 1st Place award Va. Graphic Design and Copy Writing Assn., 1980, David Ogilvy Award for Mktg. Excellence, 1984-85; Tuck scholar. Mem. New Products Devel. and Mktg. Assn., NARAL, Bus. & Profl. Women. Office: ASI Market Rsch Inc 1 Stamford Plz 263 Tresser Blvd Stamford CT 06901

TRANSOU, LYNDA LEW, advertising art administrator; b. Atlanta, Dec. 11, 1949; d. Lewis Cole Transou and Ann Lynette (Taylor) Putnam; m. Lue Gregg Loso, Oct. 25, 1991. B.F.A. cum laude, U. Tex.-Austin, 1971. Art dir., The Pitluk Group, San Antonio, 1971, Campbell, McQuien & Lawson, Dallas, 1973-74, Bozell & Jacobs, Dallas, 1974-75; art dir., ptnr. The Assocs., Dallas, 1975-77; art dir. Belo Broadcasting, Dallas, 1977-80; creative dir., v.p. Allday & Assocs., Dallas, 1980-85; owner Lynda Transou Advt. & Design, 1986—. Recipient Merit award N.Y. Art Dirs. Show, 1980; Gold award Dallas Ad League, 1980, Silver award, 1980, Bronze award, 1981, 82, 2 Merit awards Houston Art Dirs. Club, 1978-86; Merit award Broadcast Designers Assn., 1980, 82; Merit awards Dallas Ad League, 1978, 87; Silver award Houston Art Dirs. Show; Gold award Tex. Pub. Relations Assn., 1982, 85; Gold award N.Y. One Show, 1982, Creativity award Art Direction mag., 1986, Print award Regional Design Annual, 1988, Telly Finalist, 1987. Mem. Am. Inst. Graphic Arts, Dallas Soc. Visual Communications (Bronze award 1980, Merit awards, 1978-86), Delta Gamma (historian 1969-70).

TRANUM, JEAN LORRAINE, freelance writer; b. Staten Island, N.Y., Apr. 8, 1935; d. William Frederik and Jennie Marguerite (Nye) Stuart; m. John Emil Tranum Sr., June 5, 1954; children: John Emil Jr., Karen Jean Yeisley, William Karl, Jeannette Aileen Zaza. Grad. high sch., Staten Island, N.Y., 1953. Freelance writer Sacramento, Calif., 1968—; guest speaker for schs. on writing, 1988; rsch. on book in Denmark for biography on John Tranum, stuntman for movies including Wings, Hell's Angels, 1990. Author: (with Gladys Stuart Pucillo) The Winant House (pseudonym Billie Stuart). Active in PTA, Sacramento, 1968-72, Nat. Endowment of the Arts, 1989. Mem. Writers Critique Group Freelancers, Sisters in Crime Orgn., Sacramento Suburban Writers. Democrat. Methodist. Home: 168 Redondo Ave Sacramento CA 95815-1031

TRAPNELL, CHRISTINE, county official; b. Tientsin, China, Feb. 4, 1945; came to U.S., 1947; d. Wallace Hamilton and Irene Renée (Teodoro) Robinson; m. Gordon Robins Trapnell, Oct. 8, 1966; children: Andrea Renée, William Todd. BS in Fgn. Svc., Georgetown U., 1966. Dir. Sleepy Hollow Sr. Ctr., 1979-83; adminstrv. asst. Fairfax County Bd. Suprs., 1984-90, Mason dist. mem., 1992—. Pres. Lake Barcroft Civic Assn., Falls Church, Va., 1984-86, Mason Dist. Coun., Annandale, Va., 1988-90; commr. No. Va. Planning Dist. Commn., 1993—; mem. bd. advisors USA-Asian Bus. Coun., 1994; bd. dirs. Savation Army Alcoholic Rehab. Ctr. Adv. Coun., Annandale, 1992—, No. Va. Dental Clinic, Bailey's Crossroads, 1994. Mem. Rotary Internat. (bd. dirs. 1991), Lake Barcroft Womens Club (pres. 1988), Greater Falls Ch. Rep. Womens Club. Office: Mason Dist Govt Ctr 6507 Columbia Pike Annandale VA 22003

TRASK, BETTY M., journalist; b. Laconia, N.H., Jan. 28, 1928; d. James Edwin and Clemency (Anstey) Burbank; m. Allison Keith Trask, June 28, 1947; children: Frank Edwin, Michael Thomas, Rory Scott, Allison Keith Jr. Women's editor Laconia Evening Citizen, 1966-70, county editor, 1970-89, life style editor, 1989-93, travel columnist, 1981-93, retired Laconia Evening Citizen, 1993; freelancing, 1993—. mem. adv. bd. N.H. Vocat.-Tech.

Coll., Laconia, 1972-78; treas. N.H. Commn. on Status of Women, Concord, 1974-76; mem. state adv. bd. N.H. Vocat.-Tech. Coll. and Inst., Concord, 1981-84. Bd. dirs. Laconia Salvation Army, 1973-89, 1993—, aux. 1984-90, Belknap Easter Seals, 1980-92; trustee Gilford Village Knolls, Inc., N.H., 1985-90; mem. task force on alcohol and drug abuse N.H. Gov.'s Commn. on Criminal Adminstrn. and Juvenile Delinquency, 1969-71; former mem. adv. bd. Lakes Region YMCA, Belknap County Unit Am. Cancer Soc., Lake Region Community Concert Assn., Child and Family Svcs., N.H. Orgn. for Drug Abuse Control. Recipient Recognition award Laconia Lions Club, 1977, Am. Legion Aux. (Recognition award), 1993, VFW Aux., 1993, Lakes Region Citizenship award N.H. Vocat. Tech. Coll., 1978; named Woman of the Year AARP, 1993; Betty Trask Day observed in her honor by Laconia Elders Friendship Club, 1993. Mem. Internat. Platform Assn., Laconia Altrusa Club (past pres., dist. pub. rels. chmn.,), Laconia Bus. and Profl. Women's Club (past pres., dist. dir.), Soc. Profl. Journalists. Republican. Avocations: travel, photography. Home and Office: 120 Liberty Hill Rd Gilford NH 03246

TRAUB, MARSHA LYNN, software engineer; b. Ridley Park, Pa., Aug. 3, 1953; d. David Walther and Naomi Hope (Hilditch) T. BA, U. Maine, 1975; MS, West Chester U., 1985. Sales rep. Typewriter Svcs. and Equipment, Aberdeen, Scotland, 1976-80, Tri-State Office Systems, Secane, Pa., 1981; test engr. Unisys Corp., Downington, Pa., 1986; software engr. Unisys Corp., Malvern, Pa., 1987—. Trustee Meth. ch. Mem. U. Maine Alumni Assn. (alumni amb.), Garnet Valley H.S. Alumni Assn., Wilmington, Del. Alumnae Panhellenic, Phi Alpha Theta, Pi Sigma Alpha, Sigma Kappa (pres. No. Delaware chpt. 1990—, alumnae expansion coord. 1990-94, dist. dir. 1994—). Home: 305 Meadow Ct Glen Mills PA 19342 Office: Unisys Corp 70 E Swedesford Rd Malvern PA 19355

TRAUBE, VICTORIA G., lawyer; b. Los Angeles, Sept. 3, 1946; d. Shepard and Mildred (Gilbert) T. BA, Radcliffe Coll., 1968; MA, Harvard U., 1970; JD, U. Pa., 1974. Bar: N.Y. 1975, U.S. Dist. Ct. (so. dist.) N.Y. 1975, U.S. Ct. Appeals (2d cir.) 1975. Assoc. Paul, Weiss, Rifkind, Wheaton & Garrison, N.Y.C., 1974-81; assoc. counsel Home Box Office Inc., N.Y.C., 1981-82, dir. bus. affairs, 1981-85; counsel Stults & Marshall, N.Y.C., 1985-86; v.p. bus. affairs Reeves Entertainment Group, Los Angeles, 1986-87, Internat. Creative Mgmt., N.Y.C., 1987—; adj. prof. Cardozo Law Sch., N.Y.C., 1986. Office: Internat Creative Mgmt 40 W 57th St New York NY 10019-4001

TRAUDT, MARY B., elementary education educator; b. Chgo., Jan. 1, 1930; d. Lloyd Andrews Haldeman and Adele Eleanor (MacKinnon) Haldeman-Oliver; m. Eugene Peter Traudt, Dec. 6, 1952 (dec.); 1 child, Victoria Jean. BS, Cen. Mich. U., 1951; MA, Roosevelt U., 1978; postgrad., U. Ill., 1982. Asst. editor Commerce Clearing House, Chgo., 1951-53; tchr. Cleve. Elem. Sch., 1954-56, Chgo. Sch. System, 1956-57, Community Consolidated # 54, Hoffman Estates, Ill., 1957-64, Avoca Elem. Sch., Wilmette, Ill., 1964—; ret., 1995. Recipient Computer award Apple Computer Co. Mem. Avoca Edn. Assn. (v.p. 1986-91), Alpha Psi Omega. Presbyterian. Home: 107 Lincoln St Glenview IL 60025-4916 Office: Avoca Elem Sch 235 Beech Dr Glenview IL 60025-3274

TRAUGER, ALETA ARTHUR, judge. BA in English magna cum laude, Cornell Coll., Iowa, 1968; MA, Vanderbilt Univ., Tenn., 1972; JD, Vanderbilt Univ. Law Sch., Tenn., 1976. Tchr. Tenn., Eng., 1970-73; assoc. law clk. Barrett, Brandt & Barrett, P.C., Nashville, 1974-77; first asst., chief of Criminal Div. U.S. Dist. Ct. (no. dist.) Ill., 1979-80; asst. U.S. atty. U.S. Dist. Ct. (mid. dist.) Tenn., 1977-82; assoc. Hollins, Wagster & Yarbrough, P.C., Nashville, 1983-84; legal counsel Coll. of Charleston, S.C., 1984-85; ptnr. Wyatt, Tarrant, Combs, Gilbert & Milom, Nashville, 1985-91; judge Tenn. Ct. of the Judiciary, 1987-93; chief of staff Tenn. Mayor's Office, Nashville, 1991-92; bankruptcy judge U.S. Bankruptcy Ct. (mid. dist.) Tenn., Nashville, 1993—; bd. dirs. Nashville Bar Assn., 1984, 89-91, Tenn. Lawyers' Assn. for Women, 1988-89, 90-91, Marion Griffin Chpt. Lawyers' Assn. for Women, 1983-84, 86-88, Nashville Inst. for the Arts, 1992—; mem. hearing panel Tenn. Supreme Ct. Bd. of Profl. Responsibility, 1983-84; lectr. Vanderbilt Univ. Sch. of Law, 1986-88, mem. alumni bd., 1989-92; mem. Tenn. Supreme Ct. Advisory Commn. on Rules of Civil and Appellate Procedure, 1989—; master of bench Harry Phillips Am. Inn of Ct., 1990-94; mem. Internat. Women's Forum, 1993—, Nat. Conf. of Bankruptcy Judges, 1994—. Mem. Fed. Bar Assn. (v.p. 1983-84, 85-86), Tenn. Lawyers' Assn. for Women (v.p. 1988-89, pres. 1989-90), Tenn. Bar Found. (fellow 1990—); Nashville Bar Found. (fellow 1991—), Am. Bar Found. (fellow 1992—), Nat. Assn. of Women Judges. Office: Customs House 701 Broadway 2nd Fl Nashville TN 37203*

TRAUGOTT, ELIZABETH CLOSS, linguistics educator and researcher; b. Bristol, Eng., Apr. 9, 1939; d. August and Hannah M.M. (Priebsch) Closs; m. John L. Traugott, Sept. 26, 1967; 1 dau., Isabel. BA in English, Oxford U., Eng., 1960; PhD in English lang., U. Calif., Berkeley, 1964. Asst. prof. English U. Calif., Berkeley, 1964-70; lectr. U. East Africa, Tanzania, 1965-66, U. York, Eng., 1966-67; lectr., then assoc. prof. linguistics and English Stanford U., Calif., 1970-77, prof., 1977—, chmn. linguistics dept., 1980-85; vice provost, dean grad. studies Stanford U., 1985-91, mem. grad. record examinations bd., 1989-93, mem. test of English as a fgn. lang. bd., 1989-91, chmn. test of English as a fgn. lang. bd., 1991-92. Author: A History of English Syntax, 1972, (with Mary Pratt) Linguistics for Students of Literature, 1980, (with Paul Hopper) Grammaticalization, 1993; editor: (with ter Meulen, Reilly, Ferguson) On Conditionals, 1986, (with Heine) Approaches to Grammaticalization, 2 vols., 1991; contbr. numerous articles to profl. jours. Am. Coun. Learned Socs. fellow, 1975-76, Guggenheim fellow, 1983-84, Ctr. Advanced Study of Behavioral Scis. fellow, 1983-84. Mem. MLA, AAUP, AAUW, Linguistics Soc. Am. (pres. 1987, sec.-treas. 1994), Internat. Soc. Hist. Linguistics (pres. 1979-81). Office: Stanford Univ Dept Linguistics Bldg 460 Stanford CA 94305

TRAUGOTT, LEAH SCHNEIDER, artist and educator; b. Cin., Jan. 16, 1924; d. Joseph Henri and Rose Schneider; m. Harry Joseph Traugott, June 27, 1946; children: Joseph Henri, Dale Ellen. Grad., Ind. U. One woman shows include Indpls. Mus. of Art Rental Gallery, Indpls. Mus. Art, Indpls. Art League Found., Brown County Art Guild, Nashville, Ind., Ind. Repertory Theatre, Indpls., Jewish Cmty. Ctr., Indpls., U. Indpls., Kokomo (Ind.) Pub. Libr., others; works in collections in Evansville (Ind.) Mus. Arts and Sci., Franklin Coll., Wabash Coll., Kokomo Pub. Libr., Indpls. Mus. Art, Ind. State Mus., Radisson Hotel, Orlando, Fla., Lilly Endowment, Meth. Hosp., Indpls., Indpls. Life Ins. Co., others. Group shows include Indpls. Mus. Art, South Bend (Ind.) Art Ctr., Ind. State U., 1975, 78, 79, 80, Ind. Printmakers, Indpls., Butler Inst. of Am. Art, Youngstown, Ohio, Springfield (Mo.) Mus. Art, Marietta (Ohio) Coll., Pastel Soc. Am., N.Y.C., Ky. Watercolor Soc., Louisville, 1981, 86, Frankfort, 1982, Cin. Mus. Ntural History, Nat. Miniature Art Show, Nutley, N.J., 1978, Sculptors and Gravers Soc. of Washington, others. Sec. Women's com. Ind. State Symphony Commn.; bd. dirs. Indpls. Art League Found.; visual artist panelist Ind. Arts Commn. Recipient art awards Ind. Artist Show, Indpls. Mus. Art, 1983, Ky. Watercolor Soc., Frankfort, 1981, Hoosier Salon, Indpls., 1980, 86, 88, 89, Anderson (Ind.) Watercolor and Print Show, 1982, 88, 93, Ind. State Fair Profl. Show, 1980, 85, 87, 88, 89, 91, 92, 94, Ind. Artist Club Exhbn., 1980, 82, 85, 86, 89, 90, 92, 93, Ind. State Art Exhbn., 1981, 83, Ind. Watercolor Soc., 1983, 84, 88, 89, Women's Alternative Competition, Anderson, 1988, Ind. Heritage Ann. Exhbn., 1992, others. Mem. Ind. Artists (past pres.), Ind. Watercolor Soc. Home: 220 W 81st St Indianapolis IN 46260

TRAUNERO, DEBRA ANN, social worker; b. Tiffin, Ohio, July 30, 1959; d. William Louis and Betty Jane (Suttner) T. BS in Social Worker, Ohio State U., 1981, MSW, 1988. Lic. ind. social worker, Ohio. Caseworker Marion County Children Svcs. Bd., Marion, Ohio, 1981-90; therapist Network Enrichment Ctr., Marion, 1990; social worker, adminstr. Delwood, Delaware, Ohio, 1990—; women's program coord. Turning Point, Marion, Ohio, 1992-93; mental health therapist Sandusky Valley Ctr., Tiffin, Ohio, 1993—. Vol. Big Bros.-Big Sisters, 1982. Mem. NASW. Republican. Roman Catholic. Office: Sandusky Valley Ctr 304 N Main St Fostoria OH 44830

TRAVALINE, MARJORIE D., music librarian; b. Mt. Holly, N.J., Aug. 13, 1947; d. Galan W. and Frances W. (Welsh) Demuth; separated; children: Gabriella, Katharine. BA cum laude, U. Pa., 1969; MS, Drexel U., 1971. Assoc. libr. Phila. Mus. Acad., 1969-71; music libr. Glassboro (N.J.) State Coll./Rowan Coll., 1972—; oboist Haddonfield (N.J.) Symphony, 1964-78; exec. mem. Am. Fedn. of Tchrs. Local 2373, 1977—; faculty founder, advisor Voice for Choice, Rowan Coll., 1990—. Mem. NOW, Nat. Abortion Rights Action League of N.J., Music Libr. Assn. Democrat. Home: 6 Winterberry Ct Glassboro NJ 08028-2800 Office: Roman Coll of NJ 201 Mullica Hill Rd Glassboro NJ 08028-1701

TRAVER, PHYLLIS ANNE, food products company executive; b. N.Y.C., Mar. 31, 1952; d. Harold August and Barbara Lucille (Seifert) T.; m. C. Carl Muscari, June 30, 1979 (div. Nov. 1982). BA, Northwestern U., 1974; MBA, Harvard U., 1978. Dir. rsch. Staub, Warmbold and Assocs., N.Y.C., 1974-75; dir. rsch., assoc. cons. Coopers and Lybrand, N.Y.C., 1975-76; asst. product mgr. Nestle Food Corp., White Plains, N.Y., 1978-79, product mgr., mktg. mgr., 1979-83; bus. dir. Nestle Food Corp., Purchase, N.Y., 1983-90; pres. PT Ventures, 1990—, Barrier Systems, Inc., Greenwich, Conn., 1991-92; v.p. mktg. Homeview, Inc., Needham, Mass., 1992-94, Continental Cablevision, Inc., Boston, 1995—. Contbr. articles to mktg. jours. Named to Acad. Women Achievers YWCA. Mem. Harvard U. Bus. Sch. Club. Republican. Episcopalian. Home: 133 Washington St Duxbury MA 02332

TRAVERS, JUDITH LYNNETTE, human resources executive; b. Buffalo, Feb. 25, 1950; d. Harold Elwin and Dorothy (Helsel) Howes; m. David Jon Travers, Oct. 21, 1972; 1 child, Heather Lynne. BA in Psychology, Barrington Coll., 1972; cert. in paralegal course, St. Mary's Coll., Moraga, Calif., 1983; postgrad., Southland U., 1982-84. Exec. sec. Sherman C. Weeks, P.A., Derry, N.H., 1973-75; legal asst. Mason-McDuffie Co., Berkeley, Calif., 1975-82; paralegal asst. Blum, Kay, Merkle & Kauftheil, Oakland, Calif., 1982-83; CEO, bd. dirs. Dela Pers. Svcs. Inc., Concord, Calif., 1983—; pres. All Ages Sitters Agy., Concord, 1986—; CEO Guardian Security Agy., 1992—; bd. dirs. Guardian Security Agy., Concord, Calif. Vocalist record album The Loved Ones, 1978. vol. local Congl. campaign, 1980, Circle of Friends, Children's Hosp. No. Calif., Oakland, 1987—; mem. Alameda County Sheriff's Mounted Posse, 1989, Contra Costa Child Abuse Prevention Coun., 1989; employer adv. coun. Ctrl. Contra Costa County, 1993—. Mem. NAFE, Am. Assn. Respiratory Therapy, Soc. for Human Resource Mgmt., Am. Mgmt. Assn., Gospel Music Assn., Palomino Horse Breeders Am., DAR, Barrington Oratorio Soc., Commonwealth Club Calif., Nat. Trust Hist. Preservation, Alpha Theta Sigma. Republican. Baptist. Home: 3900 Brown Rd Oakley CA 94561-2532 Office: Delta Pers Svcs Inc 1820 Galindo St Ste 225 Concord CA 94520-2447

TRAVIS, JO MARLENE, anesthesiologist; b. Raleigh, N.C., Feb. 14, 1958; d. James Stokes and Ruby Allene (Ferrell) T.; m. Henry Kasimir Godek, Oct. 19, 1991. BS in Pharmacy, U. N.C., 1981, MD, 1986. Diplomate Am. Bd. Anesthesiology, Am. Bd. Pain Mgmt. Asst. prof. Sch. Medicine, Yale U., New Haven, 1990-93; pvt. anesthesiologist Mississippi Delta Gen. Anesthesiology Svcs., Greenville, Miss., 1993—. Mem. Am. Soc. Anesthesiology.

TRAVIS, MARLENE O., healthcare management executive; b. Edmonton, Alta., Can.; Came to U.S. 1959.; d. LeRoy David and Della Jessie (Campbell) T.; m. Gary T. McIlroy, Aug. 20, 1962; children: Jennifer Renee, Montgomery Travis. Student (mass comms.), St. Cloud State U., 1974-76; exec. edn., U. Pa., Stanford U., 1989-92. Cert. exec. edn. Owner Travis Communications, Brainerd, Minn., 1975-77; mgr., sec.-treas, dir. Upper Miss. Pathologists, Brainerd, 1973-80; co-founder, operating officer Midwest Lab. Assoc., Mpls., 1977-80; dir., corp. v.p. Meidinger-HRM (MHRM), Mpls., 1981-83; co-founder, exec. v.p., bd. dirs. Health Risk Mgmt. Inc., Mpls., 1977—, dir., pres., COO, 1986—; chair of bd., CEO HRM Ltd. (Can.), 1989—; founder, chair CEO Inst. Healthcare Quality, Mpls., 1991—; vice-chair Med. Alley, 1994—, bd. dirs. Co-author Self Health Guide to Laboratory Tests, 1982. Chmn. Minn. Task Force on Battered Women, 1977-79; bd. dirs. Minn. Task Force on Sexual Assault, 1974-76; co-founder, chair Mid Minn. Women's Ctr. Brainerd, 1975; founder, chair Crow Wing County Task Force on Sexual Assault, Brainerd, 1974-77; founder Crow Wing County Task Force to Support Battered Women, 1974; mem. Minn. Commr. of Edn.'s Task Force to Eliminate Sexism in Edn., 1973-74; mem. leadership group Amnesty Internat., 1990—, mem. exec. com., 1990—, com. of 200, 1991—. Named Cornerstone Leader in Giving United Way Mpls., 1992, 93. Mem. AAUW, NOW (convenor Marshfield, Wis. chpt. 1972, Brainerd area chpt. 1974), C-200 Found. (mentor contbr.), Can. Coll. Health Svc. Execs., Internat. Platform Assn., Nat. Assn. Corp. Dirs., Toastmasters (sponsor 1988), Phi Beta Gamma. Office: Health Risk Mgmt Inc 8000 W 78th St Minneapolis MN 55439-2534

TRAVIS, SUSAN FRANCES, pediatrician, educator; b. Bklyn., Dec. 10, 1940; d. Abraham and Mina (Bebrowsky) T.; widowed; children: Andrew Grossman, Sandra Grossman. AB, Syracuse U., 1961; MD, NYU, 1965. Diplomate Am. Bd. Pediatrics, Am. Bd. Pediatric Hematology/Oncology. Teaching asst. pediatrics NYU, Bellevue Med. Ctr., N.Y.C., 1967-69; teaching asst. hematology U. Phila., Children's Hosp. Phila., 1969-71; instr. pediatrics, assoc. hematology Children's Hosp. Phila., 1971-72; asst. prof. pediatrics Thomas Jefferson U., Cardeza Found., Phila., 1973-79, assoc. prof., 1979-85, dir. pediatric hematology, 1973-85; assoc. prof. U. Medicine and Dentistry N.J.-Robert Wood Johnson Med. Sch., Camden, 1985—; cons. Our Lady of Lourdes Hosp., Camden, 1975-91, 94—, West Jersey Health System, Camden, 1993—; coord. clin. svcs. divsn. pediatric hematology/oncology Cooper Hosp./Univ. Med. Ctr., Camden, 1985—, dir. So. N.J. Regional Sickle Cell Ctr. Children, 1990—, dir. Regional Comprehensive Hemophilia Care & Treatment Ctr., 1992—; mem. sickle cell adv. com., spl. child health svcs., N.J. Dept. Health, mem. patient care subcom. Contbr. articles to profl. jours. Recipient Physician's Recognition award AMA, 1992—. Fellow Am. Acad. Pediatrics; mem. Am. Soc. Pediatric Hematology/Oncology, Am. Soc. Hematology, Hemophilia Assn. N.J. (mem. med. adv. bd.), Phi Beta Kappa, Alpha Epsilon Delta, Phi Sigma Phi. Office: Cooper Hosp/Univ Med Ctr 3 Cooper Plz Ste 309 Camden NJ 08103

TRAVIS-JASPERING, MARGARET ROSE, artist, educator; b. St. Louis, Dec. 1, 1950; d. George Thomas and Margaret Lina (Black) Travis; 1 child from previous marriage, Jo Anne Urian; m. Richard W. Jaspering, Jan. 31, 1989; children: Wendy E., Mandy E., Sarah M., Chloe K. BFA, Lindenwood Coll., 1980, postgrad., 1981; postgrad., U. Mo., St. Louis, 1980, U. Mo., Columbia, 1981. Cert. art edn. tchr. K-12. Tchr. Troy and Winfield (Mo.) Schs., 1979-80, Silex (Mo.) Schs., 1980-81, Wentzville (Mo.) Schs., 1981-86, Wright City (Mo.) Schs., 1984-90; artist, tchr., owner Jasmar Studios and Gallery, Foristell, Mo., 1987—; instr. adult painting workshops, 1985—. Exhibited in group shows at Harry Henderson Gallery, Lindenwood Colls., 1976-80, Grand Gallery South, Belleville Ceramic Show, 1987 (Best of Show, 4 1st pl. awards), Internat. Ceramic Conv. and Show, 1988 (Best of Show, Best of Category, 5 1st pl. awards), Greater St. Louis Ceramic Assn. Show, 1988 (Best of Show, 1st pl. award), 76th Ann. Sculpture and Fine Crafts, 1989, Black and White Show, 1989, U. Mo., Chancellor's Residence, 1988-90, St. Charles Artists Guild, 1989 (Best of Show), Nat. Invitational of Am. Contemporary Art, 1993. Organizer Art for Animals fundraiser Animal Welfare Assn., Warren City, Mo., 1993; active St. Charles Artists Guild, 1987-89. Dept. scholar in art Lindenwood Colls., 1976-80, art scholar Dept. Exhbn., 1965-67-69. Mem. St. Louis Artists Coalition (3d divsn.), Art St. Louis. Roman Catholic. Office: Jasmar Studios and Gallery PO Box 147 Archer Rd Foristell MO 63348-0147

TRAXLER, EVA MARIA, marketing executive; b. Phorzheim, Germany, June 1, 1955; d. Wayne Delmar and Ruth Lydia (Mischak) Frasure; m. Richard John Traxler, Mar. 25, 1986. BS, U. Minn., 1980; MBA, U. St. Thomas, 1987. Ops. control planner Gen. Mills, Mpls., 1981; asst. prodn. planner Pillsbury, Mpls., 1982-87, planning specialist, 1987-88; new products planner Land O'Lakes, Mpls., 1988-89, mktg. asst., 1989-90; sr. product mgr., mgr. mdse. svcs. Anchor Hocking Plastics, St. Paul, 1990-94, product mgr. USA direct, 1994; product mktg. mgr. Novus Inc., Mpls., 1994—. Big sister Big Bros./Big Sisters, St. Paul, 1982-89, bd. mem., 1986-92. Mem. Am. Mgmt. Assn., Color Mktg. Group. Office: Novus Inc 10425 Hampshire Ave S Minneapolis MN 55438

TRAYLOR, ANGELIKA, stained glass artist; b. Munich, Bavaria, Fed. Republic of Germany, Aug. 24, 1942; came to U.S., 1959; d. Walther Artur Ferdinand and Berta Kreszentia (Boeck) Klau; m. Lindsay Montgomery Donaldson, June 10, 1959 (div. 1970); 1 child, Cameron Maria Greta; m. Samuel William Traylor III, June 12, 1970. Student, Pvt. Handelsschule Morawetz Jr. Coll., Munich, 1958. came to U.S., 1959;. Freelance artist, 1980—. Works featured in profl. jours. including The Daylily Jour., 1987, Design Jour., South Korea, 1989, The Traveler's Guide to American Crafts, 1990, Florida Mag., 1991, Florida TODAY, 1993, Melbourne Times, 1994. Recipient Fragile Art award Glass Art Mag., 1982, 1st Yr. Exhibitor award Stained Glass Assn. Am., 1984, 2d pl. Non-figurative Composition award Vitraux des USA, 1985, Best of Show, Stained Glass Assn. Am., 1989, 3d pl., 1989, Merit award George Plimpton All-Star Space Coast Art Open, 1994; named Hist. Woman of Brevard by Brevard Cultural Alliance, 1991, one of 200 Best Am. Craftsmen, Early Am. Life Mag., 1994. Home and Office: 100 Poinciana Dr Indian Harbor Beach FL 32937-4437

TRAYLOR, CLAIRE GUTHRIE, state senator; b. Kansas City, Mo., Jan. 18, 1931; d. Frank and Janet Guthrie; m. Frank A. Traylor, 1954; children: Nancy, Frank, Susan, David. BS, Northwestern U., 1952; MA, Washington U., St. Louis, 1955. Primary sch. tchr., 1955-57; mem. Colo. Ho. of Reps., 1978-82, majority caucus chmn., 1980-82; mem. Colo. State Senate, 1987—, chair bus. affairs and labor, 1985—, capital devel. com., 1988; mem. health, environ. and insts., audit coms., 1987—; mem. Colo. Commn. on Aging, Colo. Commn. on Children and Families, Colo. Housing Fin. Authority Bd., Colo. Guaranteed Student Loan Bd., Colo. Indsl. Commn. Adv. Com., Colo. Internat. Trade Adv. Commn., Colo. Capital Complex Commn., Wheat Ridge, Golden, Arvada, Lakewood, Jefferson County, Rep. Cen. Coms., del. rules com. Rep. Nat. Com., 1988; Jr. League, Clear Creek (Colo.) Valley Med. Aux., pres. bd. Highland West-Highland So. (Colo.). Presbyterian. Mem. Lakewood C. of C., Nat. Conf. State Legislators (dir. western region), Women's Network (chair Human Svcs. com. 1988-89), vice chair internat. trade com.). Office: Colo State Senate State Capitol Bldg Rm 259 Denver CO 80203*

TRAYNOR, BARBARA MARY, school system administrator; b. Somerset, Mass., May 1, 1935; d. Joseph Chadwick and Ivah Helene (Richardson) T. BA in Music Edn., Syracuse (N.Y.) U., 1957; cert., Calvin Coolidge Coll., 1958, Bridgewater (Mass.) State Coll, 1959; MEd in Guidance and Counseling, U. Va., 1963; postgrad., Ithaca Coll., 1959, U. Md., Loyola U., Balt., Bowie State Coll. Asst. supr. elem. music New Bedford (Mass.) Pub. Schs., 1957-59; supr. vocal music Swansea (Mass.) Pub. Schs., 1959-60, 60-61; guidance counselor jr. high Prince Georges County Pub. Schs., Upper Marlboro, Md., 1963-64, 64-65, guidance counselor sr. high, 1965-68, pupil pers. worker, 1969-73, coord. student transfer desegregation, 1973-74, 84-85, supr. student transfer and records, 1985-86, 94-95; student records cons. Records Rights, Responsibilities, Inc., Md. and D.C., 1981-94. Author: (manual) Student Records Guidelines, 1983. Fin. supporter Capitol Hill Arts Workshop, Washington, 1981-94; violinist Annapolis (Md.) Symphony Orch., 1963-67; singer Paul Hill Chorale, Takoma Park, Md., 1979-81. Mem. Am. Pers. Guidance Assn., Internat. Assn. Pupil Pers. Workers, Orton Dyslexia Soc., Kappa Delta Pi. Republican. Home: 644 E St SE Washington DC 20003-2712 Office: Prince George County Pub Sch 14201 School Ln Upper Marlboro MD 20772-2866

TREACY, SANDRA JOANNE PRATT, art educator, artist; b. New Haven, Aug. 5, 1934; d. Willis Hadley Jr. and Gladys May (Gell) P.; m. Gillette van Nuyse, Aug. 27, 1955; 1 child, Jonathan Todd. BFA, R.I. Sch. Design, 1956. Cert. elem. and secondary tchr., N.J. Tchr. art and music Pkwy. Christian Ch., Ft. Lauderdale, Fla., 1964-66; developer Pequannock Twp. Bd. of Edn., Pompton Plains, N.J., 1970-72, tchr. art, 1972-76; vol. art tchr. Person County Bd. of Edn., Roxboro, N.C., 1978-80, tchr. art, 1980-91; tchr. art So. Jr. High Sch., Roxboro, 1989-91, Woodland Elem. Sch., Roxboro, 1989-93; tchr. Helena Elem. Sch., Timberlake, N.C., 1991-93; tchr. elem. art, mem. faculty Bethel Hill Sch., Roxboro, 1974-79; tchr. basic art, vol. all elem. schs. Person County, Roxboro, 1981; tchr. arts and crafts, summers 1981-882; tchr. art home sch. So. Mid. Sch., 1993—, Person H.S., 1993-94. Artist, illustrator. Mem. Roxboro EMTs, 1979-81; bd. dirs. Person County Arts Coun., 1980-81, 93-95, pres., 1981-82; piano and organ choir accompanist Concord United Meth. Ch., 1981—; leader Morgan Trotters, 1992-94, asst. dir., 1993-94, bd. dirs.; mem. Roxboro Community Choir, 1993-94. Mem. NEA, Nat. Mus. of Women in the Arts (continuing charter), Smithsonian Assocs., N.C. Assn. Arts Edn., N.C. Assn. Educators, N.C. Art Soc. Mus. of Art, Internat. Platform Assn., Womans Club (tchr. Pompton Plains chpt. 1974-79), Person County Saddle Club (rec. sec. 1981-84), Puddingston Pony Club (dist. sec. 1974-75), Roxboro Garden Club (continuing, commr. 1980-82, pres. 1982-84, 87—, sec. 1993-94, v.p. 1993-95, pres. 1995—), Roxboro Woman's Club (arts dept.). Republican. Home: 1345 Kelly Brewer Rd Leasburg NC 27291-9720

TREADWAY-DILLMON, LINDA LEE, athletic trainer, actress; b. Woodbury, N.J., June 4, 1950; d. Leo Elmer and Ona Lee (Wyckoff) Treadway; m. Randall Kenneth Dillmon, June 19, 1982. BS in Health, Phys. Edn. & Recreation, West Chester State Coll., 1972, MS in Health and Phys. Edn., 1975; postgrad., Ctrl. Mich. U., 1978; Police Officer Stds. Tng. cert. complaint dispatcher, Goldenwest Coll., 1982. Cert. in safety edn. West Chester State Coll.; cert. EMT, Am. Acad. Orthopaedic Surgeons. Grad. asst., instr., asst. athletic trainer West Chester (Pa.) State Coll., 1972-76; asst. prof., program dir., asst. athletic trainer Ctrl. Mich. U., Mt. Pleasant, 1976-80; police dispatcher City of Westminster, Calif., 1980-89; oncology unit sec. Children's Hosp. Orange County, Orange, Calif., 1989—. Stuntwoman, actress United Stunt Artists, SAG, L.A., 1982—; dancer Disneyland, Anaheim, Calif., 1988—; contbr. articles to profl. jours. Athletic trainer U.S. Olympic Women's Track and Field Trials, Frederick, Md., 1972, AAU Jr. World Wrestling Championships, Mt. Pleasant, Mich., 1977, Mich. Spl. Olympics, Mt. Pleasant, 1977, 78, 79. Named Outstanding Phys. Educator, Delta Psi Kappa, Ctrl. Mich. U., 1980, Outstanding Young Woman of Am., 1984. Mem. SAG, Nat. Athletic Trainers Assn. (cert., women and athletic tng. ad hoc com. 1974-75, placement com. 1974-79, program dirs. coun. 1976-80, ethics com. 1977-80, visitation team 1978-80), U.S. Field Hockey Assn. (player), Pacific S.W. Field Hockey Assn. (player, Nat. Champion 1980, 81, 82), L.A. Field Hockey Assn. (player), Swing Shift Dance Team (dancer). Presbyterian. Home: 15400 Belgrade #152 Westminster CA 92683 Office: Childrens Hosp Orange County 455 S Main St Orange CA 92668

TREAS, JUDITH KAY, sociology educator; b. Phoenix, Jan. 2, 1947; d. John Joseph and Hope Catherine (Thomas) Jennings; m. Benjamin C. Treas II, May 14, 1969; children: Stella, Evan. BA, Pitzer Coll., Claremont, Calif., 1969; MA, UCLA, 1972, PhD, 1976. Instr. U. So. Calif., L.A., 1974-75, asst. prof., 1975-81, assoc. prof., 1981-87, dept. chair, 1984-89, prof., 1987-89; prof. U. Calif., Irvine, 1989, dept. chair, 1989-94; bd. overseers Gen. Social Survey, 1986-88; cons. social sci. and population study sect. NIH, 1989-92. Contbr. articles to profl. jours. Trustee Pitzer Coll., 1977-79. Recipient Rsch. award NSF, 1978-81, 84-91, NIH, 1979-81; Univ. scholar U. So. Calif., 1982-83. Fellow Gerontological Assn. Am.; mem. Golden Key (hon.), Am. Sociol. Assn., Population Assn. Am., Internat. Union for Sci. Study Population. Office: U Calif-Irvine Dept Sociology Irvine CA 92717

TREAT, SHARON ANGLIN, state legislator; b. Brattleboro, Vt., Jan. 30, 1956; d. Robert Sherman and Mary Lou (Strassburger) T. AB, Princeton U., 1978; JD cum laude, Georgetown U., 1982. Bar: Maine, N.J. Asst. dep. pub. adv. N.J. Dept. of the Pub. Adv., Trenton, 1982-85; assoc. atty. Ball, Livingston & Tykulsker, Newark, 1985-86; staff atty. Natural Resources Coun. Maine, Augusta, 1986-90; state rep. Maine State Legis., Augusta, 1991—; pvt. practice Hallowell, Maine, 1991—; leader Ctr. for Policy Alternatives, Washington, 1992—. Bd. dirs. N.J. Environ. Lobby, Trenton, 1984-86, Maine People's Resource Ctr., Augusta, 1991—, N.E. Citizen Action Resource Ctr., Hartford, Conn., 1992—; co-founder, dir. Alliance, Portland, Maine, 1987; trustee Class of 1978 Found., White Plains, N.Y., 1988—; mem. adv. bd. Augusta Area Rape Crisis Ctr., 1992—; mem. Natural Resources Coun. Maine, Maine Women's Lobby. Mem. Rotary. Democrat. Office: 222 Water St Hallowell ME 04347-1391 also: Maine Ho of Reps State House Augusta ME 04330*

TREESE, LISA MAUREEN, deaf educator; b. Chgo., Apr. 15, 1963; d. Robert James and Mary Elyse (Ziegler) Doyle; m. Randy William Treese, Aug. 3, 1985; 1 child, Timothy Charles. BS, Indiana U. Pa., 1985. Cert. tchr., Pa., S.C. Substitute tchr. Meyersdale (Pa.) Area Sch. Dist., 1986-87; itinerant tchr. of hearing handicapped students Horry County Sch. Dist., Conway, S.C., 1987-88; tchr. of mentally handicapped students Conway Mid. Sch., 1988-90, tchr. of hearing handicapped students, 1990-91; tchr. of hearing handicapped students Whittemore Park Mid. Sch., Conway, 1991—; staff devel. chair Strategic Planning Tact Team. Instr. Sunday sch. St. James Cath. Ch., Conway, 1991—, chair family com. ladies guild, 1992; team mem. Worldwide Marriage Encounter, Conway, 1992—. Mem. Am. Sign Lang. Tchrs. Orgn., Conv. Am. Instrs. Deaf, S.C. Edn. Assn., Horry County Coun. Exceptional Children (v.p. 1991-92), S.C. Assn. of Deaf, Sunshine Coastal Assn. of Deaf. Democrat. Roman Catholic. Home: 802 Berrywood Ct Myrtle Beach SC 29577-8800

TREFZ, LINDA MARIE, writer, editor video arts; b. Bridgeport, Conn., Mar. 13, 1959; d. Ernest Christian and Joan Marie (Frisk) T. BS in Mag. Journalism, Syracuse U., 1981. Editorial asst. McCall's Mag., McCall's Working Mother Mag., N.Y.C., 1979; asst. editor Millimeter Mag., N.Y.C., 1981-83; free lance writer Millimeter Mag., Back Stage, Am. Cinematographer, Virtual Reality Report, CyberEdge Jour., others, 1983—. Mem. Soc. Profl. Journalists, Internat. Interactive Comm. Soc., Artists Using Sci. and Tech., Art & Sci. Collaborations, NYC ACM/SIGGRAPH.

TREGAY, SUSAN WEBB, artist, educator; b. Concord, N.H., Nov. 12, 1946; d. Reuel W. and Natalie (Stevens) Webb; m. George W. Tregay, Sept. 9, 1967; children: Steven W., Sarah B. BS in Edn., Wheelock Coll., 1968; MS, SUNY, Buffalo, 1975. Artist Buffalo, 1982—, pvt. art educator, 1987—. Paintings exhibited in solo shows including SUNY, Buffalo, 1985, Mazur Gallery, Buffalo, 1986, Klienhan's Music Hall, Buffalo, 1987, Peopleart/Buffalo Gallery, 1988, Gallery in the Square, Snyder, N.Y., 1989, Unique Gallery, Amherst, N.Y., 1989, Artisan's Alley, Niagara Falls, N.Y., 1990, Art Dialogue Gallery, Buffalo, 1991, Impact Gallery, Buffalo, 1994; group shows include Hallwalls Gallery, Buffalo, 1982, 94, Jr. League Showhouse Gallery, Buffalo, 1987, Herdman's Gallery, Buffalo, 1988, Niagara Coun. of Arts, 1989, Roberta Wood Gallery, Syracuse, N.Y., 1993, Anderson Gallery, Buffalo, 1994; cover art included in Buffalo Philharm. Programs, 1986-87; contbr. articles to art mags. Recipient numerous First Place and Best of Show awards, Puget Sound award N.W. Watercolor Soc. Nat. Exhbn., 1993, NEWS award N.Am. Open Exhbn., 1994. Mem. Midwest Watercolor Soc. (assoc., Dillman Creative Workshop award 1993), Watercolor West (assoc., Arches and Rives Paper award 1993), Niagara Frontier Watercolor Soc. (signature mem., Napa Valley award 1994). Home and Studio: Webb Tregay Studio 470 Berryman Snyder NY 14226

TREGELLAS, PATRICIA, musical director, composer; b. Kans., Feb. 22, 1936; d. Clarence and Lena T.; BMus in Edn., U. Denver, 1959; scholar, Trossingen, Germany, 1960-61; MA in Teaching Music, CUNY, 1985. Concert artist, chamber musician, condr.; music supr. Prowers County (Colo.) High Sch. Band and Chorus, 1962-65; accordionist and orch. leader USO tours abroad, 1966-69; mem. orch., asst. condr. Hal Prince musicals on nat. tours, 1969-71; freelance musician, N.Y.C., 1972—; mus. dir., condr. N.Y. Concerto Orch., 1979—; condr. workshops, Tokyo, London, N.Y.C.; performed in premier performances of new music. Bd. dirs. The Music Educators of N.Y.C., 1990—. Recipient cert. appreciation Gen. Westmoreland and others for work in Vietnam with USO; fellow Conducting Inst. S.C., 1994. Methodist. Mem. Am. Accordionists Assn. (bd. dirs. 1994—). Home: 817 W End Ave Apt 3aa New York NY 10025-5323 also: 2372 S Clayton St Denver CO 80210-5418

TREICHEL, JEANIE NIERI, computer company executive; b. South San Francisco, May 23, 1931; d. Robert Tancredi and Lena Marie (Borelli) Nieri; m. Georg Treichel, Mar. 14, 1955; children: Carl Stanford, Tiffany (dec.), Todd (dec.), Jennifer (dec.), David (dec.). BA, San Jose State U., 1952, MA, 1955; MBA, Golden Gate U., 1983. Tchr. San Mateo (Calif.) City Sch. Dist., 1952-55; research assoc. The Conservation Found., Africa, 1956-58; from research sec. to systems doc., administrn. Xerox Palo Alto (Calif.) Research Cnt., 1974-82; asst. treas. Sutherland, Sproull & Assoc., Menlo Park, Calif., 1982-90; mgr. lab. ops. Sun Microsys. Labs. Inc., Mountainview, Calif., 1990—. Mem. Assn. Computing Machinery, Alpine Hills Tennis Club, Sequoia Yacht Club. Republican. Roman Catholic. Office: Sun Microsystems Labs Inc 2550 Garcia Ave Mountain View CA 94043-1100

TREINAVICZ, KATHRYN MARY, software engineer; b. Brockton, Mass., Nov. 25, 1957; d. Ralph Clement and Frances Elizabeth (O'Leary) T. BS, Salem State Coll., Mass., 1980. Tchr., Brockton Pub. Schs., 1980-81; instr. Quincy CETA Inc., Mass., 1981-82; programmer Systems Architects Inc., Randolph, Mass., 1982, programmer analyst, Dayton, Ohio, 1982-84; sr. programmer analyst System Devel. Corp., Dayton, 1984-86; project mgr. Unisys Inc., Dayton, 1986-87; software engr. Computer Scis. Corp. (formerly Systems and Applied Scis. Corp. 1988), 1987-89, project mgr. Computer Scis Corp. (formerly Atlantic Rsch. Corp. 1994), Fairborn, Ohio, 1989—. Mem. NAFE. Democrat. Roman Catholic. Avocations: Steven King novels, needlepoint, knitting, crocheting.

TREKELL, SHARON ELIZABETH, marriage and family counselor; b. Piqua, Ohio, Nov. 9, 1944; d. Vonus Lee and Alma Elizabeth (Manson) Ellis; m. Howard Rudolph Otto, July 23, 1966 (div. Dec. 1986); children: Gustave, Clinton, Hans, Nikolaus, Josef; m. Leslie Winston Trekell, Aug. 14, 1987. AA in Liberal Arts, Sinclair C.C., 1986; BA in Comm. Arts, Coll. Mt. St. Joseph, Cin., 1988; MS in Counseling, Wright State U., 1992; postgrad., Union Inst., 1993—. Dir. pub. rels. Internat. Childbirth Edn. Assn., Milw., 1977-79; columnist Star Free Press, Springboro, Ohio, 1981-83; marriage and family counselor Mental Health Svcs. N.W., Cin., 1991-92, New Creations Care Ctr., Vandalia, Ohio, 1992-93; marriage and family counselor Dayton Inst. Family Therapy and Wellness, Centerville, Ohio, 1993—, stress mgmt. and wellness cons., 1993—. Editor newsletter Forum, 1977-79. Pres. Dayton Childbirth Edn. Assn., 1975-76. Named Outstanding Woman of Yr., Dayton Childbirth Edn. Assn., 1976. Mem. ACA, Am. Assn. Marriage and Family Therapy, Chi Sigma Iota. Home: 1042 Beaver Valley Rd Beavercreek OH 45434 Office: Dayton Inst Fam Therapy Wellness 65 W Franklin St Centerville OH 45459

TREMBLY, CRISTY, television executive; b. Oakland, Md., July 11, 1958; d. Charles Dee and Mary Louise (Cassidy) T. BA in Russian, German and Linguistics cum laude, W.Va. U., 1978, BS in Journalism, 1978, MS in Broadcast Journalism, 1979; advanced cert. travel, West L.A. Coll., 1982; advanced cert. recording engring., Soundmaster Schs., North Hollywood, Calif., 1985. Videotape engr. Sta. WWVU-TV, Morgantown, W.Va., 1976-80; announcer, engr. Sta. WVVW Radio, Grafton, W.Va., 1979; tech. dir., videotape supr. Sta. KMEX-TV, L.A., 1980-85; broadcast supr. Sta. KADY-TV, Oxnard, Calif., 1988-89; news tech. dir. Sta. KVEA-TV, Glendale, Calif., 1985-89; asst. editor, videotape technician CBS TV Network, Hollywood, Calif., 1989-90; videotape supr. Sta. KCBS-TV, Hollywood, 1990-91, mgr. electronic news gathering ops., 1991-92; studio mgr., engr.-in-charge CBS TV Network, Hollywood, 1992—; radio operator KJ6BX Malibu Disaster Comm., 1987—. Producer (TV show) The Mountain Scene, 1976-78. Sr. org. pres. Children of the Am. Revolution, Malibu, Calif., 1992—; sec., adv. com. Tamassee (S.C.) Sch., 1992—; vol. Ch. Coun., LA Riot Rebuilding, Homeless shelter work, VA Hosps., Mus. docent; chair adminstrv. coun. Malibu United Meth. Ch., 1994—; sponsor 3 overseas foster children. Recipient Outstanding Young Woman of Am., 1988, Asst. editor Emmy award Young and the Restless, 1989-90, Golden Mike award Radio/TV News assn., 1991, 92. Mem. DAR (state chmn. jr. membership 1987-88, state chmn. scholarships 1992-94, state chmn. jr. contest 1994—, others, organizing regent Malibu chpt. 1991, chpt. regent 1988-90, 91-94, state chmn. motion pictures radio and TV Calif., 1988-90, Mex. 1990—, Nat. Outstanding Jr. 1993), Am. Women in Radio and TV (so. Calif. bd. 1984-85, 93-95, pres. elect 1995—), Soc. Profl. Journalist, Women in Comm., Travelers Century Club (life, program chmn. 1987—), Mensa (life), Beta Sigma Phi. Democrat. Methodist. Home: 2901 Sea Ridge Dr Malibu CA 90265-2969 Office: CBS TV City 7800 Beverly Blvd Los Angeles CA 90036-2165

TREMONTE SPIGONARDO, ADA MARY, interior architect; b. Phila., Jan. 15, 1959; d. John Robert and Anne Rita (Di Carlo) Tremonte; m. Giuliano Spigonardo, Sept. 17, 1983; children: Ariella, Gianna, Vincenzo. BS, Drexel U., 1980. Design asst. Daroff Design Inc., Phila., 1978-80; project mgr. Curtis, Cox, Kennerly, Phila., 1980-85; project dir. The Design Partnership, Phila., 1985-87; assoc. Space Design, Phila., 1985-87; founding ptnr. AI-FIVE inc., Phila., 1987—; tchr. Architecture in Schs. program Phila. Pub. Schs., 1984-89. Active Unite of United Way, Darby, Pa., 1991. Mem. Found. for Architecture, Omicron Nu. Republican. Roman Catholic. Office: AI-FIVE Inc 1712 Walnut St # 2 Philadelphia PA 19103-6101

TREMPER, CAROL BORDEN, educator; b. Atlanta, Dec. 26, 1942; d. Linvent Henry and Frances Lucille (Newman) Borden; m. Howard Dupont Tremper, Aug. 25, 1962; children: David, Christopher. BA in Gen. Elem. Edn., William Paterson Coll., 1976; MEd, Widener U., 1987. Cert. tchr., supr., N.J. Tchr. Jefferson Twp. (N.J.) Mid. Sch., 1976; Tchr. McKeown Sch., Hampton Twp., N.J., 1976—, coord. , tchr. gifted program, 1978—; cons. in field. Author: Createatraption: To Find and Encourage The Innovative, 1984, Creative challenges for Cognetics: Aerie Lands, 1987, Atomic Cafeteria, 1988, Maglevity, 1991; editor: Gifted and Talented Educator's Resource Directory, 1991. Recipient Presdl. award NSF, 1992; named Tchr. of Yr. Gov.'s Tchr. Recognition, N.J., 1988, Best in Show Dover (N.J.) Art Assn., 1978. Mem. ASCD, N.J. Assn. Gifted Children (v.p. 1993—, editor), N.J. Commn. Edn. Adv. Coun. Gifted and Talented Children, Sussex County Arts and Heritage Coun. Methodist. Home: 128 Mary Jones Rd Newton NJ 07860-6466 Office: McKeown Sch One School Rd Newton NJ 07860

TRENCH, ANNE HOLBROOK, drug development research administrator; b. Washington, Oct. 2, 1949; d. Francis Irvine and Dorothy Louise (Schwartz) Holbrook; m. John Durand Trench, June 12, 1971; children: Sarah, Durand, David. BA, U. Md., 1971. Tech. editor Bell Labs., Whippany, N.J., 1971-72; med. editor Ciba-Geigy, Summit, N.J., 1972-77; cons. various clients including Triton Bioscis., Ciba-Geigy, physicians, researchers, 1977-87; asst. dir. clin. adminstrn. Berlex Labs. (formerly Triton Bioscis.), Richmond, Calif., 1987-92; asst. dir. clin. rsch. Immunex Corp., Seattle, 1992—. Editor drug license application. Vol. Habitat for Humanity, Contra Costa County, Calif., 1990-92. Mem. Drug Info. Assn. (invited speaker 1993), Washington State Biotech. Assn. Office: Immunex Corp 51 University St Seattle WA 98101

TRENERY, MARY ELLEN, librarian; b. Conran, Mo., Jan. 10, 1939; d. John Herman and Stella Cecelia (Durbin) Hulshof; m. Frank E. Trenery, June 10, 1967. BA in Classics, Coll. New Rochelle, 1962; MALS, Rosary Coll., River Forest, Ill., 1966; postgrad., Fla. Atlantic U., 1986-89. Tchr. grades 6, 8 Archdiocesan Sch. System, St. Louis, 1962-64; serials and acquisition libr. U. Ill., Chgo., 1966-69; acquisitions, circulation and cataloging libr. Rosary Coll., River Forest, Ill., 1964-66, 70-72; libr. media specialist St. Coleman Cath. Sch., Pompano Beach, Fla., 1973-94; coord. for self study St. Coleman Schs., 1982, 83, 89, 90; cons. Pompano Beach City Libr. Author: Policies and Procedures for School Libraries, 1976, UICC Call Number (founding editor), 1967-68, NIUCLA Newsletter (editor 1969-72). Fed. Funding liaison with Broward County Sch. Bd., 1974-94. Mem. Ill. Libr. Assn. (rsch. and tech. svcs. div. chair 1967-69), Cath. Libr. Assn. (No. Ill. unit chair, sec. 1969-72). Office: St Coleman Sch 2250 SE 12th St Pompano Beach FL 33062-7098

TRENSE, SHARON, state legislator; b. Nov. 23, 1939; m. Charles Trense; 2 children. Student, Northwestern U. Owner Sharons of Dunwoody; mem. Ga. Ho. of Reps., 1992—; mem. edn., human rels. and aging coms., mem. state inst. and property coms. Republican. Methodist. Home: 135 Classic Cove Atlanta GA 30350 Office: Ga Ho of Reps State Capitol Atlanta GA 30334*

TRENT, BEVERLY ANN, business manager; b. La Junta, Colo., Apr. 21, 1942; d. Zach Adin and Helen Marie (Rodighero) Palmer; m. William Dale Allen, Apr. 20, 1962 (div.); children: Willidea Renee Allen Hansen, Zach David Allen; m. James William Trent, Mar. 18, 1983. AA, Lamar C.C., 1962; BA, Loretto Heights Coll., 1985; postgrad., Colo. State Bd. C.C.s, 1991—. Multi-line ins. agt. Otero Savs. & Loan, La Junta, 1968-74; sr. acct. East Otero Sch. Dist. R-1, La Junta, 1974-80; office mgr., owner B & B Trucking, La Junta, 1980-82; office mgr. La Junta Tribune Dem., 1982-83; sr. acct. East Otero Sch. Dist. R-1, La Junta, 1983-90; bus. mgr. Cheraw (Colo.) Consol. Sch. # 31, 1990-91, Fremont Sch. Dist. Re-2, Florence, Colo., 1991—. Chair Safety Pers. Com., Florence, 1992—; fundraising chair Otero County Hospice, 1988-90; active Rep. Women's Orgn., Otero County, Colo., 1989-90, Colo. Agriculture Program, Denver, 1990-92; trustee 1st Bapt. Ch., La Junta, 1991—; leader 4-H Club, 1976-82. Mem. Nat. Mgmt. Assn., Colo. Assn. Bus. Ofcls. Home: 1625 Chestnut St Lot 4 Canon City CO 81212-5147 Office: Fremont Sch Dist Re-2 403 W 5th St Florence CO 81226-1103

TRENT, JOYCE MILLER, librarian; b. Dayton, Ohio, Dec. 7, 1946; d. Fielding Leo and Joyce (Henry) Miller; m. Robert Cody Trent, Mar. 17, 1973; children—Michael Frederick Cody, Paul Templeton, Mark Fielding. B.A., Stephen F. Austin State U., 1969; M.L.S., U. Tex., Austin, 1975. Pub. service librarian Deer Park Pub. Library, Tex., 1969-73; system interlibrary loan librarian San Antonio Pub. Library, 1975-76; dir. system, county librarian Atascosa County Library System, Jourdanton, Tex., 1976-81; library dir. Leon Valley (Tex.) Pub. Library, 1981—. Biweekly columnist N.W. Leader, 1981—. Pres. parish council St. Brigid's Ch., San Antonio, 1980-81; del. Met. Congl. Alliance, San Antonio, 1982—; mem. civic affairs com. Tex. Sesquicentennial Com., Leon Valley, 1984—. Mem. ALA, Tex. Library Assn. (treas. dist. 10, vice chair-elect, then chair), Leon Valley Bus. and Profl. Assn., San Antonio Geneal. Hist. Soc. (sec. 1977-78). Democrat. Roman Catholic. Home: 5903 Forest Rim St San Antonio TX 78240-3218 Office: Leon Valley Pub Library 6425 Evers Rd San Antonio TX 78238-1453

TRENTHAM, MAXINE DELORES, human resources professional; b. St. Paul, Feb. 16, 1946; d. Arnold Gerdesmeier and Hazel Marie (Madden) Reed; m. Ronald Maurice Trentham, Oct. 11, 1969. BS, U. Md., 1980; MS, Am. U., 1985. Staffing asst. Adminstrv. Office US Ct., Washington, 1974-78; human resources adminstr. Internat. Food Policy Rsch. Inst., Washington, 1979-80; human resources dir. Am. Pharm. Assn., Washington, 1980-83; mgr. employment svc. Edison Electric Inst., Washington, 1983-88; corp. human resource mgr. Systemhouse Inc., Arlington, Va., 1988-91; human resources dir. CTA Inc., Rockville, Md., 1991-93, Svc. Employees Internat. Union, Washington, 1993—. Vol. Friendly Instant Sympathic Help, Reston, Va. Mem. Soc. Human Resource Mgmt. Republican. Roman Catholic. Office: Svc Employees Intl Union 1313 L St NW Washington DC 20005-4101

TRENT-OTA, JANE SUZANNE, elementary school educator; b. Long Beach, Calif., June 10, 1935; d. George Lionel and Jennie Bolton (Rundio) Heap; children from previous marriage: Katharine Trent, Cecily Finegan; m. William T. Ota, Sept. 27, 1991; stepchildren: William N. Ota, Douglas W. Ota. BA, Mary Washington Coll., Fredericsburg, Va., 1957; MA in Edn., Azua-Pacific U., 1978; cert. K-8, Calif. Western-USIU, San Diego, 1970; cert. in master gardening, U. Calif., 1994. Cert. elem. tchr. K-8, Calif., Level I Orff-Schulwerk nat. cert.; cert. master gardener. Tchr. 5th and 6th grades Chula Vista (Calif.) Elem. Sch. Dist., kindergarten tchr., ret., 1991; cons. bargaining team Chula Vista Edn. Assn. Vol. with U. Calif. Cooperative Extension/U.S. Dept. Agr. Vol. numerous civic orgns. Recipient Instruction grant, ORFF Instrumentarium, We Honor Ours award San Diego county svc. ctr. coun. Calif. Tchrs. Assn., 1991. Mem. Calif. Ret. Tchrs. Assn., NSF Math. Inst. Univ. Calif. San Diego, Am. ORFF-Schulwerk Assn. (bd. sec. San Diego chpt. 1991-93), Delta Kappa Gamma (chpt. exec. bd., chmn. scholarship). Home: 620 First St Coronado CA 92118

TREPEL, MINDY J., county official, lawyer; b. N.Y.C., Dec. 20, 1955; d. Jerome and Anita Lee (Kalish) Trepel; m. Ronald F. Harnisch, Apr. 12, 1986; 1 child, Matthew Charles. BA, SUNY, Stony Brook, 1977; JD, Vt. Law Sch., 1980. Law asst. Queens County Civil Ct., Kew Gardens, N.Y., 1982-83; prin. law clk. to surrogate Queens County Surrogate's Ct., Jamaica, N.Y., 1984-91; pub. adminstr. Queens County, Jamaica, 1992—. Mem. Queens County Bar Assn., Queens County Women's Bar Assn. (pres. 1994—). Home: 153 Beach 131 St Belle Harbor NY 11694 Office: Queens County Office Pub Adminstr 88-11 Sutphin Blvd Jamaica NY 11435

TREPPLER, IRENE ESTHER, state senator; b. St. Louis County, Mo., Oct. 13, 1926; d. Martin H. and Julia C. (Bender) Hagemann; student Meramec Community Coll., 1972; m. Walter J. Treppler, Aug. 18, 1950; children: John M., Steven A., Diane V. Anderson, Walter W. Payroll chief USAF Aero. Chart Plant, 1943-51; enumerator U.S. Census Bur., St. Louis, 1960, crew leader, 1970; mem. Mo. Ho. of Reps., Jefferson City, 1972-84; mem. Mo. Senate, Jefferson City, 1985—; chmn. Minority Caucus, 1991-92. ActiveGravois Twp. Rep. Club, Concord Twp. Rep. Club; alt. del. Rep. Nat. Conv., 1976, 84. Recipient Spirit Enterprise award Mo. C. of C., 1992, Appreciation award Mo. State Med. Assn., Nat. Otto Nuttli Earthquake Hazard Mitigation award, 1993; named Concord Twp. Rep. of Yr., 1992. Mem. Nat. Order Women Legislators (rec. sec. 1981-82, pres. 1985), Nat. Fedn. Rep. Women. Mem. Evangelical Ch. Office: Mo State Senate Rm 433 Jefferson City MO 65101

TRESCOTT, SARA LOU, water resources engineer; b. Frederick, Md., Nov. 17, 1954; d. Norton James and Mabel Elizabeth (Hall) T.; m. R. Jeffrey Franklin, Oct. 8, 1983. AA, Catonsville C.C., Balt., 1974; BA in Biol. Sci., U. Md., Balt., 1980. Sanitarian Md. Dept. Health & Mental Hygiene, Greenbelt, 1982; indsl. hygienist Md. Dept. Licensing & Regualtion, Balt., 1982-85; from water resources engr. to chief dredging div. Md. Dept. Natural Resources, Annapolis, 1985-92; chief navigation div. Md. Dept. Natural Resources, Stevensville, 1992—; chair adv. bd. EEO, Annapolis, 1990-92; tech. com. Nat. Mgmt. Info. Systems, Balt., 1983. Contbr. articles to profl. jours. Mem. ASCE, County Engrs. Assn. Md. Democrat. Home: PO Box 22 Woodbine MD 21797 Office: DNR Navigation div 305 Marine Academy Dr Stevensville MD 21666

TRESMONTAN-STITT, OLYMPIA DAVIS, marriage and family counselor, psychotherapy educator, consultant; b. Boston, Nov. 27, 1925; d. Peter Konstantin and Mary (Hazimanolis) Davis; B.S., Simmons Coll., 1946; M.A., Wayne State U., 1960; Ph.D. (Schaefer Found. grantee), U. Calif., Berkeley, 1971; m. Dion Marc Tresmontan, Sept. 15, 1957 (dec. Mar. 1961); m. 2d, Robert Baker Stitt, Mar. 21, 1974. Child welfare worker San Francisco Dept. Social Service, 1964-66; sensitivity tng. NSF Sci. Curriculum Improvement Study, U. Calif., Berkeley, 1967-68; individual practice psychol. counseling, San Francisco, 1971-92; dir. Studio Ten Services, San Francisco, Promise for Children, San Francisco, 1981-88; tchr. U. Calif. extension at San Francisco, 1971-72, Chapman Coll. Grad. Program in Counseling, Travis AFB, 1971-74; clin. cons. Childworth Learning Ctr., San Francisco, 1976-80; cons. project rape response Queen's Bench Found., San Francisco, 1977; adjunct instr. Unity Coll., Maine, 1992; adv. bd. Childrens' Multicultural Mus., San Francisco, 1988-92. Active Women's Heritage Mus., Palo Alto, Calif., 1991-92, Friends of Belfast (Maine) Free Libr., 1993—, Friends of the San Francisco Pub. Libr., 1971-92; bd. dirs. Childworth Learning Center, 1976-80. Mem. Am. Psychol. Assn., Am. Orthopsychiat. Assn., Calif. Assn. Marriage, Family and Child Therapists. Author: (with J. Morris) The Evaluation of A Compensatory Education Program, 1967; (Karplus edit.) What is Curriculum Evaluation, Six Answers, 1968. Home: RR 1 Box 632 Morrill ME 04952-9709

TREXLER, SUZANNE FRANCES, geriatrics nurse; b. Harrisburg, Pa., Feb. 8, 1963; d. Walter Richard and Catherine Frances (Mourawski) Markham; m. Barry Kenneth Trexler, Nov. 9, 1991; children: William Chester, Brittany Nancy, Katye Iona. LPN, Harrisburg Stelton Highs, Sch. Practical Nursing, 1984; ADN, Harrisburg (Pa.) Area C.C., 1984; student, Gracelan Coll., 1988—; BA in Long Term Care Adminstrn., St. Joseph Coll., 1994, postgrad., 1994—. Nurse ICU and critical care unit Meml. Hosp., York, Pa., 1987-88; staff nurse emergency dept. Polyclinic Med. Ctr., Harrisburg, 1988-91; assoc. prof. Nat. Edn. Ctr.-Jr. Coll., Harrisburg, 1991; dir. nursing Camp Hill (Pa.) Care Ctr., 1991-92; resident assessment supr. Susquehanna Ctr., Harrisburg, 1992-94; dir. nursing Susquehanna Luth. Village, Millersburg, Pa., 1994; asst. administr. Dauphin Manor, Harrisburg; ACLS, CPR instr. Am. Heart Assn., Harrisburg, 1989—; BCLS, CPR instr. ARC, Harrisburg, 1992—; RN, paramedic Lebanon (Pa.) County First Aide and Safety Patrol, 1992—. Sec. Little People PTA, Harrisburg, 1991-92; pres. Student Human Resource Mgmt. Club, York (Pa.) Coll., 1992—. Recipient Nurse of Hope award Am. Cancer Soc., Dauphin County, Harrisburg, 1983-84. Mem. AACN, Pa. Nurses Assn., Pa. Dir. Nursing Assn. for Long Term Care, PANPHA (advocate). Roman Catholic. Office: Dauphin Manor Paxton St Harrisburg PA 17111

TREXLER, WYNN RIDENHOUR, paralegal; b. Salisbury, N.C., Sept. 15, 1941; d. Lee R. and Olena (Ludwig) Ridenhour; m. Frederick C.D. Trexler, June 14, 1959; children: Dale, Wendy, Chris, Matt. Grad. high sch., Salisbury. Legal sec. Woodson & Woodson and successor firm Woodson, Hudson & Busby, Salisbury, 1959-60, 64-67; teller Home Savs. & Loan Assn., Salisbury, 1961-63; legal sec. Burke, Donaldson & Holshouser, Salisbury, 1968-77, Carlton, Rhodes & Wallace, Salisbury, 1977-81; paralega Mona Lisa Wallace, Salisbury, 1981-86; freelance paralegal Pidmont Paralegal Svc., Salisbury, 1986—. Mem. Nat. Assn. Legal Assts. (cert.), Nat Assn. Legal Secs. (cert.), N.C. Paralegal Assn. (charter, bd. dirs. 1980-86, liaison), N.C. Acad. Trial Lawyers (assco., legal assts. sect., edn. com. 1984—), Profl. Legal Assts. Democrat. Lutheran. Home: PO Box 275 Faith NC 28041-0275 Office: Piedmont Paralegal Svc 2450 Artz Rd Salisbury NC 28146-1164

TREYBIG, EDWINA HALL, sales executive; b. Ft. Worth, Dec. 12, 1949; d. George Edward and Lillian Wanita (Herring) Hall; m. Jerry Kenneth Treybig, Sept. 20, 1980; children: Allison Lindsey, Gifford Carl, Brick Edward. BS in Home Econs., Tex. Tech U., 1972. Office mgr. Am. Internat. Rent-A-Car, Dallas, 1973, gen. mgr., 1973-74; sales rep. Martinez Mud Co., Denver, 1977-80, Am. Mud Co., Denver, 1980-83, Robinson Construction Co., Denver, 1983-87, Dig-It, Inc., N.Y.C., 1987-88; sales rep., corp. sec. Treybig Enterprises, Littleton, Colo., 1984—. Organizer Mile High Golf Tournament, Denver, 1980-84; mem. subcom. Colo. Devel. Disabilities Planning coun., Denver, 1989-90; mem. Coalition to Insure the Uninsurable, Denver, 1989-90. Mem. Soc. Petroleum Engrs. (organizer golf tournament), Internat. Assn. Drilling Contractors, Ind. Producers Assn. Mountain States, Assn. Retarded Citizens, Denver Petroleum Club (organizer golf tournament), Alpha Chi Omega (social chmn. 1970-72). Republican. Mem. Ch. of Christ. Home and Office: 7397 S Fillmore Cir Littleton CO 80122-1942

TRIANA, GLADYS, artist; b. Camaguey, Cuba, Nov. 17, 1937; came to U.S., 1974; d. Jose Daniel Triana and Francisca Maria (Perez) Valdez; m. Manuel Angel Malleiro, Apr. 11, 1974. Student, Oriente U., Santiago de Cuba, 1957; B in Art summa cum laude, Mercy Coll., 1976; MEd, L.I. U., 1977. Art educator N.Y.C. Bd. Edn., 1978—; exhbn. cons. Salute to Bklyn.'s Creative Youth Exhbn., The Bklyn. Art Coun., Children's Gallery at Bklyn. Mus., 1986—; created and implemented Children Expressions Mural Program at Cmty. Sch. Bd. Dist. #2, N.Y.C., 1987—. One women shows include Lyceum Gallery, Havana, Cuba, 1962, 63, Tramontana Gallery, 1971, Intar Gallery, 1975, Cuban Mus. Art and Culture, Miami, Fla., 1988, Mus. Contemporary Hispanic Art, N.Y., 1990, Mus. Modern Art, Santo Domingo, 1991, Nader Gallery Fine Arts, Santo Domingo; exhibited in group shows at Palacio de Bellas Artes Mus., 1962, 91, Sala de Arte Gallery, Madrid, 1971, Mus. Sci., Chgo., 1975, Inst. de Cultura Puertorriquena, Museo de Ponce, P.R., 1976, 92, Queens Coll., 1979, Meeting Point Gallery, Miami, 1982, Todd Capp Gallery, N.Y., 1986, Mus. Contemporary Hispanic Art, N.Y., 1988, Warehouse Gallery, N.Y.C., 1989, Stratus Gallery, N.Y.C., 1989, L.I. U., 1989, Mus. Contemporary Art, Caracas, Venezuela, 1990, Discovery Mus., Bridgeport, Conn., 1990, Modern Art Latin Am., Washington, 1990, Humphrey Gallery, N.Y.C., 1992, Paine Weber Art Gallery, N.Y.C., 1992, Artspace, New Haven, Conn., 1992, Adriana Landon Gallery, N.Y.C., 1993, Sotavento Gallery, Caracas, 1993, Insights Gallery, Seattle, 1993, Ceres Gallery, N.Y.C., 1994, Henry St. Settlement, N.Y.C., 1994, Art in Gen., N.Y.C., 1994, Luigi Marrozini Gallery, P.R., 1994, others; contbr. articles to profl. publs.; illustrator in field. Mem. Mus. of Women, Washington, 1990—, Women of Caucus, N.Y.C., 1992—, Ctr. for Books of Art, N.Y.C., 1993—. Recipient Art Competition 3rd prize Ateneo de Marianao Gallery, Havana, Cuba, 1964, Ednl. scholarship Nat. Clairol Loving Care Art Program, 1974, Hon. mention Mus. of Sci., Chgo.,

1975, Spl. mention The N.Y.C. Bd. Edn. Masters and Apprentices Exhibit, 1990, Outstanding Achievement in Visual Arts award The Queens Borough Pres. of City of N.Y., 1990, Cintas fellowship, 1993. Mem. NOW, Mus. Modern Art, Met. Mus. Studio: 450 W 31st St 4F New York NY 10001

TRIBETT, BRENDA DIANE BELL, religious organization administrator; b. Richmond, Va., Oct. 3, 1947; d. Ervin George Jr. and Claudia (Miller) Bell; m. Louis Tribett Jr., Sept. 2, 1967 (div. 1973); 1 child, Diondrea Nichelle. BS in Juvenile Justice, Va. Commonwealth U., 1978; MA in Legal Studies, Antioch Sch. Law, 1981; MA in Christian Edn., Presbyn. Sch. Christian Edn., 1991, EdS in Christian Edn., 1992. Ch. sec., youth coord. Mt. Olive Bapt. Ch., Richmond, 1973-89; acad. skills coord. Va. Union U., Richmond, 1987-89; ESL/adult basic edn. tchr. Richmond Pub. Schs., 1982-92; dir. Joseph Nash Multicultural Ctr., Richmond, 1990-92; exec. dir. Christian edn. Prog. Nat. Bapt. Conv., Washington, 1992—; workshop facilitator Bapt. Gen. Conv., Richmond, 1974-92, mem. leadership team, 1980-92; cons. Commonwealth Girl Scouts, Richmond, 1988; tchr. Adult Basic Edn., 1991-92. Named one of 100 Most Influential Black Women, Koinonia Ind. Meth. Ch., 1993; Educator's fellow Ecumenical Resource Ctr. Mem. Nat. Coun. Chs., Religious Edn. Assn. Democrat. Office: Prog Nat Bapt Conv Inc Dept of Christian Edn 601 50th St NE Washington DC 20019-5499

TRICHEL, MARY LYDIA, education educator; b. Rosenberg, Tex., Feb. 2, 1957; d. Henry John and Henrietta (Jurek) Pavlicek; m. Keith Trichel, Aug. 8, 1981; children: Daniel, Nicholas. BS cum laude, Tex. A & M U., 1980. Cert. tchr., Tex. Social studies tchr. grades 6, 7 and 8 St. Francis de Sales, Houston, 1980-81; English tchr. grades 7 and 8 Dean Morgan Jr. High, Casper, Wyo., 1983-86; English and journalism tchr. grades 9 and 11 Tecumseh (Okla.) High Sch., 1987; English tchr. grade 6 Christa McAuliffe Middle Sch., Houston, 1988-92; tchr. Tex. history grade 7, journalism grade 8 Lake Olympia Middle Sch., Missouri City, Tex., 1991-92; tchr. social studies 6th grade Lake Olympia Mid. Sch. Ft. Bend Ind. Sch. Dist., 1993—. Recipient teaching awards. Mem. Nat. Coun. Tchrs. English, Nat. Coun. Tchrs. Social Studies, Am. Fedn. Tchrs. Home: 3707 Pin Oak Ct Missouri City TX 77459-7018

TRICK, ANN LOUISE, accountant; b. Jefferson Parish, La.; d. Claybourne and Avis Margaret (Middleton) Waldrop; m. Joseph Michael Trick, Dec. 28, 1982 (div.); children: Philip Michael, Justin Anthony, Kristen Alicia. BA, Tex. Tech. U., 1979; M of Profl. Acctg., U. Tex., Arlington, 1992. CPA. Acct. exec., office mgr. DBG & H, Dallas, 1979-80; bus. mgr. Creative Microsystems, Inc., Dayton, Ohio, 1980-81; office mgr. Sinclair & Rush, Inc., Arlington, 1981-83, Norand Corp., Arlington, 1983-84; acct. Price Waterhouse, Ft. Worth, 1992—. SERVA vol. Arlington Ind. Sch. Dist., 1990-91; den leader Cub Scout Pack 389, Arlington, 1992-93; mem. bd. fin. All Saints Luth. Ch. Recipient Scholarship Cert. of Merit, Inst. Cert. Mgmt. Accts., 1991; scholar Am. Women's Soc. CPAs, 1991, Mid Cities Assn. CPAs, 1991. Mem. Am. Soc. Women Accts., Tex. Soc. CPAs, Inst. Mgmt. Accts. (assoc. dir. acad. rels. 1991-92, dir. acad. rels. 1992-93), Beta Alpha Psi, Beta Gamma Sigma. Office: Price Waterhouse 1700 City Ctr Tower III 301 Commerce St Fort Worth TX 76102

TRICKLER, SALLY JO, technical illustrator; b. Burlington, Iowa, Jan. 7, 1948; d. Frank Joseph and Florence Christina (Hein) Koehler; m. James Edward Trickler, Nov. 4, 1967 (div.); 1 child, Brenda Jo. AA, Southeastern Community Coll., West Burlington, Iowa, 1976; BA, Western Ill. U., 1988. Draftsman Iowa Army Ammunition Plant, Middletown, 1967-73; sr. tech. illustrator J.I. Case Co., Burlington, 1973—; representer tech. illustrating Burlington Community High Sch. Career Day ann. event, 1985-91. Mem. pub. relations com. United Way, Burlington, 1975, chmn. pub. relations 1976-77, art designer, 1987. Mem. Burlington Engrs. Club (v.p. 1974-75, pres. 1975-76, chmn. high sch. counseling com. on career days, 1977-80), Allegro Motor Home Club Iowa, Phi Kappa Phi. Roman Catholic. Club: Good Sam (Big River Sams, Iowa) (sec./treas. 1985-87). Home: 11904 44th St Burlington IA 52601 Office: JI Case Co 1930 Des Moines Ave Burlington IA 52601

TRIFOLI-CUNNIFF, LAURA CATHERINE, psychologist, consultant; b. L.I., N.Y., June 8, 1958; d. Peter Nicholas and Susan Maria (Graziano) T.; m. John Kevin Cunniff, June 6, 1992; 1 child, James Peter. BA, Hofstra U., Uniondale, N.Y., 1980, MA, 1982, PhD, 1986. Founder, prin. Quality Cons., West Islip, N.Y., 1980-87; sr. tng. officer Norstar Bank, Garden City, N.Y., 1985-87; asst. v.p. mgmt. devel. First Boston Corp., N.Y.C., 1986-90; mgr. exec. devel. Merrill Lynch, N.Y.C., 1990-91; pres. The Exec. Process, 1991—; cons. Am. Mgmt. Assn., N.Y.C., 1981-83, AT&T, Basking Ridge, N.H., 1982-83, The First Boston Corp., 1991—, Goldman Sachs, 1991—, Merrill Lynch & Co., 1991—, Union Bank of Switzerland, 1991—, Sanford C. Bernstein & Co., 1992—, Alexander & Alexander, 1993—, S.G. Warburg, 1994; instr. dept. psychology Hofstra U., 1983-85. Author: Vietnam Veterans: Post Traumatic Stress and its Effects, 1986; contbr. articles to profl. publs. Shift coord. Islip Hotline, 1976-78; eucharistic min. Hofstra U. Cath. Soc., 1980-85, Good Samaritan Hosp., West Islip, N.Y., 1988—. Scholar, Hofstra U., 1978-81, fellow, 1980, 81. Mem. Am. Psychol. Assn., Am. Soc. Tng. and Devel., Nat. Psychol. Honor Soc., Internat. Platform Soc. Roman Catholic. Office: 2906 Bree Hill Rd Oakton VA 22124-1212

TRIGERE, PAULINE, fashion designer; b. Paris, Nov. 4, 1912; came to U.S., 1937, naturalized, 1942; d. Alexandre and Cecile (Coriene) Trigere; children: Jean-Pierre, Philippe Radley. Student, Victor Hugo Coll., Paris. Began career at Martial et Armand, Paris, 1937; became asst. designer at Hattie Carnegie, N.Y.C.; started House of Trigere, N.Y.C., 1942. Recipient Coty Am. Fashion Critics award, 1949, Return award, 1951, Neiman-Marcus award, 1950, Cotton award Nat. Cotton Coun., 1959, award Filene's, 1959, Coty Hall of Fame award, 1959, Silver medal City of Paris, 1972, medal of Vermeil City of Paris, 1982, Lifetime Achievement award, 1992, Nat. Arts Club award, 1993; celebrated 50 yrs. in the bus. at Fashion Inst. Tech., 1992. Office: Trigere Inc 498 7th Ave New York NY 10018 also: Trigere Inc 550 7th Ave New York NY 10018*

TRILIOURIS, ANA MARIA, dentist; b. Buenos Aires, Dec. 7, 1949; came to U.S., 1970; d. Juan and Purificacion (Grana) Martinez; m. George Alexander Triliouris, Aug. 20, 1973; children: Evangelina, Alexander Juan. BS cum laude, Pace U., 1974; DDS, NYU, 1976. Pvt. practice Merrick, N.Y., 1976—. Mem. ADA, Acad. Gen. Dentistry, Acad. Laser Dentistry (editor, bd. dirs.), Greater N.Y. Acad. Laser Dentistry (bd. dirs.), NOW, MADD. Democrat. Greek Orthodox. Office: 56 Merrick Ave N Merrick NY 11566-3431

TRILL, VALERIE LINDA, personnel executive; b. Bklyn., Nov. 24, 1955; d. Raymond Allen and Lois Beverly (Lebwith) T.; 1 child, Cory James. AAS, Rio Salado C.C., 1993; BA in Pub. Adminstrn., Ottawa Univ., 1994. Cert. pub. mgr.; cert. tchr. in mgmt./supervision. Adminstrv. sec. Ariz. Dept. of Liquor Lics. and Control, 1980-84, adminstrv. asst., 1984-86; adminstrv. svc. officer Ariz. Dept. of Water Resources, 1987—. Mem. Ariz. Soc. of Cert. Pub. Mgrs., Inc. (bd. dirs. 1991—). Home: 7748 N 13th Pl Phoenix AZ 85020-4203 Office: Ariz State Dept Water Resources 500 N 3d St Phoenix AZ 85004

TRIMARCHI, RUTH ELLEN, educator, researcher, community activist; b. Adams, Mass., Jan. 9, 1954; d. Anthony Rocco and Millicent June (Brimmer) T.; m. David Wayne Miller, Sept. 17, 1981; children: Eliot, Jacob. BA in Biology, Vassar Coll., 1978; MEd, U. Mass., 1993. Cert. tchr., Mass. Rsch. asst. U. Ghent (Belgium), 1978-79, Harvard U., Cambridge, Mass., 1980-81; tchr. sci. Amherst (Mass.) Regional H.S., 1994—. Bd. dirs. LWV, Amherst, Mass., 1991-93; mem. adv. com. Children's Svcs. Dept., Amherst, 1990-93; fund raiser Abortion Rights Fund of Western Mass., Amherst, 1989—. Mem. Phi Delta Kappa. Office: Amherst Regional HS 22 Mattoon St Amherst MA 01002

TRIMBLE, LYNDA KAYE, health care executive; b. Amarillo, Tex., July 24, 1947; d. Willis Otto and Ella Pauline (Owens) Hendrick; m. Charles Richard Trimble, Nov. 25, 1965; 1 child, Jody Lynn Trimble Thrasher. Grad., Hereford (Tex.) High Sch., 1965. Med. sec. William L. Reed, M.D., Plainview, Tex., 1965-70, Russell K. Williams, M.D., Plainview, Tex., 1971-72; office mgr. Kiser Auto Parts, Plainview, Tex., 1975-78, KKYN Radio Sta., Plainview, Tex., 1981-85; gen. mgr. Am. HomePatient, Inc., Plainview, Tex., 1985—. Mem. Jr. Svc. League (pres. 1981-82). Republican. Presbyterian. Home: 309 Mesa Cir Plainview TX 79072-6508 Office: Healthstar Med Inc 605 Garland St Plainview TX 79072-6635

TRIMMER, BRENDA KAY, pharmacist; b. Carlisle, Pa., May 26, 1955; d. Harold Gleim and Mary Martha (McKinney) T. BS in Sci., Morehead State U., 1977; BSc in Pharmacy cum laude, Phila. Coll. Pharmacy and Sci., 1981; postgrad., Northwestern U., 1990. Lic. pharmacist, Pa., Ga., Tenn., Ala. Grad. intern Thomas Jefferson U. Hosp., Phila., 1981; dir. pharmacy Geriat. Pharmacy Sys., Chambersburg, Pa., 1981-83, Harrisburg, Pa., 1983-85; itinerant pharmacist Geriat. Pharmacy Sys., Pottsville, Pa., 1986-88; nutritional support pharmacist, cons. Polyclinic Med. Ctr., Harrisburg, 1985—; dir. pharmacokinetics Instnl. Pharmacy Cons., Griffin, Ga., 1988-93; cons. pharmacist Phila., Wilkes-Barre, and Harrisburg regions Pharmacy Corp. Am., 1993—; clin. pharmacist Pa. Med. Soc., Harrisburg, 1994—; chmn. Acad. Long Term Care, Pa., 1987-89. Mem. Am. Diabetes Assn., First Ch. of Brethren. Named Outstanding Young Women of Am., 1981. Fellow Am. Soc. Cons. Pharmacists; mem. Am. Pharm. Assn., Am. Assn. Diabetes Educators, Pa. Pharm. Assn. (mem. exec. coun. 1987-89). Democrat. Home: 960 Innsbruck Dr Hummelstown PA 17036-9749 Office: 777 East Park Dr Harrisburg PA 17111

TRINDER, RACHEL BANDELE, lawyer; b. Ibadan, Nigeria, Feb. 21, 1955; came to U.S., 1977; d. Victor William John and Margaret (Almond) T. BA with honors, Oxford U., 1977, MA, 1994; LLM, U. Va., 1978. Bar: D.C. 1979, U.S. Dist. Ct. 1979, U.S. Ct. Appeals (D.C. cir.) 1980, U.S. Supreme Ct. 1986. Assoc. Zuckert, Scoutt & Rasenberger, Washington, 1978-85, ptnr., 1985—; v.p. aviation spl. interest chpt. Transp. Rsch. Forum, 1988-90, exec. v.p., 1990-91, gen. counsel, 1989-91; mem. bd. advisors 3d Ann. Symposium on Law and Outer Space, 1991, program dir., mem. bd. advisors, 4th Ann., 1991-92. Contbr. articles to legal jours. Bd. govs. Internat. Student House, 1986-93, mem. exec. com., asst. treas., 1987-88. Fellow English Speaking Union, 1977. Mem. Fed. Bar Assn. (chair space law com. 1990-94, chair internat. law sect. 1994—), Internat. Bar Assn., Inter-Pacific Bar Assn., Internat. Inst. Space Law (life), Internat. Inst. Air and Space Law (mem. bd. govs. exec. com. 1992—), Internat. Aviation Club (bd. govs. 1984-86, pres. 1986), Aero Club (bd. govs. 1993—, chair legal com. 1993). Home: 1266 Dartmouth Ct Alexandria VA 22314-4784 Office: Zuckert Scoutt & Rasenberger 888 17th St NW Washington DC 20006-3939

TRINER, ALMA, public relations executive; b. N.Y.C., Feb. 17, 1925; d. Abraham and Frances (Tennenbaum) T.; children: Susan, Kim. BA, Bklyn. Coll., 1944. With Daniel J. Edelman, Inc., Chgo., N.Y.C., 1953-62; dir. pub. relations, gen. pub. Macmillan, Inc., N.Y.C., 1963-67, asst. v.p. corp. pub. relations, 1967-74; v.p. pub. relations Arthur D. Little, Inc., Cambridge, Mass., 1975-88; mng. dir. Corporate Initiatives, Boston, 1988-91, Triner Comm., Belmont, Mass., 1991—; mem. adv. bd. Pub. Rels. News, N.Y.C., 1982-88. Bd. dirs. Nat. Hair Techs.; trustee Endicott Coll., Beverly, Mass., 1982—. Recipient Matrix award Women in Communications, Boston, 1981. Mem. Pub. Relations Soc. Am., Pub. Affairs Council. Office: Triner Comm 150 Radcliffe Rd Belmont MA 02178-2650

TRINH, NGOC-DUNG, program analyst; b. Moncay, Vietnam, Oct. 28, 1936; came to the U.S., 1975; d. Mau V. and Tuong T. (Nguyen) T. Elem. tchg. degree, Saigon (Vietnam) Normal Sch., 1963; BA in Pedagogy, Saigon (Vietnam) U., 1972; AAS, North Va. C.C., 1979; BA in Human Svcs./MA in Human Resource, George Washington U., 1980, 82. Elem. tchr. Ministry of Edn. Vietnam, 1958, secondary tchr., 1961; tchr. Vinh Long Tchrs. Coll., Hamlet Tchr. Tng., Vinh Long Province, Vietnam, 1963; ednl. specialist U.S. Agy. for Internat. Devel., U.S. Edn. Divsn., 1963-75; refugee concerns specialist Dept. State, Washington, 1975-76; with refugee program Dept. Health and Edn. and Welfare, Washington, 1976-87; with office refugee resettlement Dept. Health and Human Svcs., Washington, 1987—, mgr. unaccompanied minors program, 1987—, comptr. budget and grants funding, 1987—. Founding Arlington (Va.) Sr. Citizen Assn., 1976; sec. gen. Families of Vietnam Polit. Prisoners Assn., 1984-89, adv. bd. mem., 1989—; active Mindful Meditation Group, Va., 1990—. Recipient Pres.'s Vol. Action award, 1994. Home: 3223 S Utah St Arlington VA 22206-1907

TRINKOFF, ELAINE, librarian; b. N.Y.C., Aug. 10, 1930; d. Herman and Sadye (Hommel) Waxman; m. Stuart Trinkoff, June 19, 1949; children: Harold Eliot, Paul David. BA cum laude, Bklyn. Coll., 1951; MLS, Queens (N.Y.) Coll., 1970; MA with distinction, Hofstra U., 1976. Cert. tchr., N.Y. Libr. Great Neck (N.Y.) Sch. Dist., 1966-70; ref. libr. York Coll., CUNY, Queens, 1970-75; art ref. libr. various art galleries, N.Y.C., 1980-82; ref. libr. Great Neck Libr., 1974—; cons. in field. Compiler, artist, editor bibliographies Am. Indian, Then and Now, 1973, The Two Faces of Narcotics, 1974; reviewer books. Mem. Am. Assn. Ret. Persons, Women's Am. ORT, Womanspace, Lake Success Civic Assn., B'nai B'rith Women, Beta Phi Mu (pres. Beta Alpha chpt. 1972-74). Democrat. Jewish. Home: 38 Olive St Great Neck NY 11020 Office: Great Neck Libr Bayview Ave Great Neck NY 11024

TRIPLETT, ARLENE ANN, travel company executive; b. Portland, Oreg., Jan. 21, 1942; d. Vincent Michael and Lorraine Catherine (Starr) Jakovich; m. William Karrol Triplett, Jan. 27, 1962; children: Stephen Michael, Patricia Ann. B.A. in Bus. Adminstrn., U. Calif., Berkeley, 1963. Budgets and reports analyst Cutter Labs., Berkeley, 1963-66; controller Citizens for Reagan, 1975-76; dir. adminstrn. Republican. Nat. Com., 1977-80; asst. sec. Dept. Commerce, Washington, 1981-83; assoc. dir. mgmt. Office Mgmt. and Budget, Exec. Office of Pres., Washington, 1983-85; prin. assoc. McManis Assocs., Inc., 1985-87, v.p., 1987-89, sr. v.p., 1989-93; v.p. Am. Tours Internat., Inc., L.A., 1993—, exec. v.p., 1994—. Roman Catholic. Office: Am Tours Internat Inc 6053 W Century Blvd Los Angeles CA 90045-6430

TRIPLETT, CAROLYN ROBERTA, counselor; b. Grosse Pointe, Mich., Jan. 14, 1955; d. Charles Robert and Betty Lou (Ping) Nash; m. John Charles Boasen, Feb. 14, 1975 (div. 1984); children: Jared Franklin, Laura Shannon; m. Mark B. Triplett, June 20, 1987. BA in Social Scis. summa cum laude, Wash. State U., 1991, MEd in Counseling Psychology, 1993. Registered profl. counselor. Counselor intern Pasco (Wash.) Sch. Dist., 1992; therapist Christian Counseling Svc., Richland, Wash., 1993—. Pres., bd. dirs. Sexual Assault Response Ctr., Richland, 1992, v.p., 1991. Mem. Am. Assn. Christian Counselors, Am. Counseling Assn., Wash. Counseling Assn., Wash. Mental Health Counselors Assn., Am. Mental Health Counselors Assn., Am. Sch. Counseling Assn., Tri-Cities Counseling Assn., Phi Beta Kappa, Phi Kappa Phi. Democrat. Christian Ch. Office: Christian Counseling Svc 1124 Stevens Dr Richland WA 99352

TRIPP, KAREN BRYANT, lawyer; b. Rocky Mount, N.C., Sept. 2, 1955; d. Bryant and Katherine Rebecca (Watkins) Tripp; m. Robert Mark Burleson, June 25, 1977 (div. 1995). BA, U. N.C., 1976; JD, U. Ala., 1981. Bar: Tex. 1981, U.S. Dist. Ct. (so. dist.) Tex. 1982, U.S. Dist. Ct. (ea. dist.) Tex. 1991, U.S. Ct. Appeals (fed. cir.) 1983, U.S. Supreme Ct. 1994. Law clk. Tucker, Gray & Espy, Tuscaloosa, Ala., 1978-81, to presiding justice Ala. Supreme Ct., Montgomery, summer 1980; atty. Exxon Prodn. Rsch. Co., Houston, 1981-86, coord. tech. transfer, 1986-87; assoc. Arnold, White and Durkee, Attys. at Law, Houston, 1988-93, shareholder, 1994—. Contbr. articles to profl. jours. Recipient Am. Jurisprudence award U. Ala., 1980, Dean's award, 1981. Mem. ABA (intellectual property law section, ethics com. 1992-95), Houston Bar Assn. (interprofl. rels. com. 1988-90), Houston Intellectual Property Lawyers Assn. (mem. outstanding inventor com. 1982-84, chmn. 1994-95, chmn. student edn. com. 1986, sec. 1987-88, chmn. awards com. 1988-89, chmn. program com. 1988-91, treas. 1991-92, bd. dirs. 1992-94, nominations com. 1993), Tex. Bar Assn. (antitrust law com. 1984-85, chmn. Internat. Law com. of Intellectual Property Law Sect. 1987-88, internat. transfer tech. com. 1983-84), Am. Intellectual Property Lawyers Assn., Women in Tech. (founder), Phi Alpha Delta (clk. 1980). Democrat. Episcopalian. Office: Arnold White & Durkee PO Box 4433 Houston TX 77210-4433

TRIPP, MARIAN BARLOW LOOFE, public relations company executive; b. Lodge Pole, Nebr., July 26; d. Lewis Rockwell and Cora Dee (Davis) Barlow; m. James Edward Tripp, Feb. 9, 1957; children: Brendan Michael, Kevin Mark. BS, Iowa State U., 1944. Writer Dairy Record, St. Paul, 1944-45; head, product promotion div., pub. rels. dept. Swift & Co., Chgo., 1945-55; mgmt. supr., v.p. pub. rels. J. Walter Thompson Co., N.Y.C. and Chgo., 1956-74; v.p. consumer affairs, Chgo., 1974-76; pres. Marian Tripp Communications Inc., Chgo., 1976-94. Mem. Pub. Rels. Soc. Am., Am. Inst. Wine and Food, Les Dames d'Escoffier, Chgo. Network, Fortnightly Club, Confriere de la Chaine des Rotisseriers (officer Chgo. chpt.) Episcopalian. Office: 100 E Bellsvue Pl Chicago IL 60611

TRIPP, RUTH ENDERS, actress, writer; b. Hackensack, N.J., May 10, 1920; d. Howard Crosby and Ada Beatrice (Jursch) Enders; m. Paul Tripp, Aug. 8, 1943; children: Suzanne Tripp Jurmain, David Enders. Student, John Drew Theatre Sch., 1935-37, Thorndike Drama Sch., 1938. speech tchr. of retarded children, N.Y.C., 1941-62; tchr. Am. Acad. Dramatic Art, N.Y.C., 1958-61; pres. Fantasy Music Pub., N.Y.C., 1955-65. Broadway debut in The American Way, 1939, appeared in Twelfth Night, 1951; one woman nat. tours, 1940-46; TV appearances include Mr. I Magination, 1949-53 (Look award 1951), On the Carousel, 1954-60 (Ohio State and Emmy awards 1955), Birthday House, 1963-69, Verdict is Yours, 1960-63, numerous others; film appearances include The Christmas That Almost Wasn't, 1966; writer N.Y. Daily News, 1943-46, (theater) Sackful of Dreams, 1974. Mem. SAG, AFTRA, Acad. TV Arts and Scis., Actors Equity. Office: Silverstone & Rosenthal 230 Park Ave New York NY 10169-0004

TRIPP, SUSAN GERWE, museum director; b. Balt., Dec. 28, 1945; d. Earl Joseph and Maria Elizabeth (Wise) Gerwe; m. David Enders Tripp, June 9, 1977. BS, U. Md., 1967. Home econs. tchr. Balt. County Pub. Sch. Sys., 1967-74; curator of art Johns Hopkins U., Balt., 1974-76; curator of art, archivist Johns Hopkins U., 1976-78, instr. evening coll., 1978-84, dir. univ. collections, 1979-91; supr., instr. art history Goucher Coll., Notre Dame U., Balt., 1977-86; dir. docent tng. Homewood Mus., Balt., 1987-89; exec. dir. Old Westbury (N.Y.) Gardens, 1992—; dir. Homewood Restoration Adv. Com., 1983-92, Evergreen Restoration Adv. Com., 1988-92; lectr. in field. Co-author: The Garrett Collection of Japanese Art, 1993 (NEA Grant 1980), Contbr. articles to profl. jours. Recipient Hist. Preservation award Balt. Heritage, Inc., 1988, 91, Rsch. award Am. Soc. Interior Designers, 1991. Mem. Am. Assn. Bot. Gardens and Arboreta, Netsuke Kenkyokai Japanese Cir. of Art, Oreintal Ceramic Soc., Balt. Mus. Art, Oreintal Ceramic Soc. Hong Kong, Assn. of Frick Art Ref. Libr. So. Garden Hist. Soc., Furniture History Soc., N.Y. Zool. Soc., Am. Assn. Mus. John Hopkins U. Falcuty Club., Omicron Nu. Office: PO Box 283 60 Old Post Rd Old Westbury NY 11568

TRIPP, SUSAN LYNN, small business owner; b. Long Beach, Calif., May 1, 1953; d. Fred Robert and Marion Mary (Swales) Mulker; m. Gary Elliot Wolf, July 3, 1977 (div. Aug. 1986); 1 child, Daniel Gary; m. Robert Rolan Tripp, Mar.22, 1987. BA in Liberal Arts, San Jose State U., 1976. Cert. tchr., Calif. Dir.. San Jose (Calif.) State Housing, 1975-77; dir. Wonderland Presch., San Jose, 1978; tchr. Hillbrook Sch., Los Gatos, Calif., 1979-87; owner, mgr. TeleVet, San Jose, 1987-90; mgr. La Mirada Animal Hosp., Santa Fe Springs, Calif., 1989-90, owner, mgr., 1990—; spkr. Vet. Mgmt. Co., Ft. Collins, Colo., 1992, Ebell Club, La Mirada, 1993; cons., 1993; TV appearances include La Mirada Cable, 1993. Author: Sex is Good, Abuse is Wrong, 1986-93. Pub. safety commr. La Mirada, Calif., 1993—; campaign chair Sch. Bd. candidate, 1993; coord. Neighborhood Watch Program, La Mirada, 1993; chair Com. to Elect Pat Ruiz, La Mirada, 1993; mem. La Mirada Gang Task Force, 1993-94, La Mirada Disaster Steering Com., 1993-94; elder Cmty. Presbyn. Ch., La Mirada, 1994. Mem. La Mirada C. of C. Office: La Mirada Animal Hosp 13914 E Rosecrans Ave Santa Fe Springs CA 90670

TRIPPET, SUSAN E., nursing educator; b. Princeton, Ind., Nov. 3, 1946; d. Charles Kightly and Isabel (Key) T. AA, Ind. U., Indpls., 1971, MS in Nursing, 1983; DS in Nursing, U. Ala., Birmingham, 1988. Lectr. Ind. U., Indpls., asst. prof.; CNS perinatal div. U. Hosps., Birmingham; asst., then assoc. prof. U. So. Miss., Hattiesurg; pres. D.J.S. Resources P.A.; various presentations on older women, relationship issues, mothers & daughters, and therapeutic use of music. Mem. Am. Nursing Assn., So. Nursing Rsch. Soc., Internat. Coun. Women's Health Issues, Sigma Theta Tau, Sigma Tau Delta.

TRITTIPO, JANE KNECHT, publishing executive; b. Rapid City, S.D., Oct. 24, 1933; d. Ronald Clem and Ruth Irene (Slocumb) Knecht; m. Thomas Twineham Trittipo, Oct. 6, 1956; children: Karen Ann Trittipo Freedman, Lynn Diane Trittipo Segundo. BS in Med. Tech., U. Colo., 1956. Med. technologist Children's Hosp., Honolulu, 1956-59; pvt. practice med. technologist No. Calif., 1959-88; author, pub., speaker Creative Cookery, Alamo, Calif., 1988—. Author, pub.: The Everyday Gourmet-Fast and Fabulous Microwave Recipes, 1988. Treasurer Round Hill Property Owners Assn., Alamo, 1983-86; vestry Episcopal Ch., 1966-90; pres. Lyra chpt. Easter Seals Soc., 1985-86. Mem. AAUW (treas. 1988-89, prse. 1994-95), P.E.O., Am. Soc. Clin. Pathologists, San Francisco Profl. Food Soc., San Francisco Conv. Bur., Chi Omega. Republican. Office: Creative Cookery PO Box 437 Alamo CA 94507-0437

TRIVISON, DONNA RAE, library director, mathematics and science educator; b. Lakewood, Ohio, Sept. 4, 1951; d. Lee Michael and Joyce Irene (Perry) T. BS, Grove City Coll., 1973; MS Libr. Sci., Case Western Res. U., 1979, PhD, 1986. Asst. libr. Lake Erie Coll., Painesville, Ohio, 1979-83; dir. libr. Dyke Coll., Cleve., 1986—, asst. prof. math. and sci., 1986—; chmn. ednl. TV com. Cleve. Commn. on Higher Edn., 1989-91. Mem. Am. Soc. for Info. Sci. (chmn. no. Ohio chpt. 1990), Acad. Libr. Assn. Ohio, Downtown Cleve. Christian Bus. and Profl. Women (treas. 1991—), Beta Phi Mu. Office: Dyke Coll 112 Prospect Ave SE Cleveland OH 44115

TROCKMAN, RACHEL W., pediatrician; b. Mpls., Jan. 22, 1942; d. Phillip J. and Bernice Weiner; m. Mitchell D. Trockman, July 1, 1962; children: Mark Alan, Daniel Gary, Steven Jay. BA in Liberal Arts magna cum laude, U. Minn., 1962, BS in Med. Sci., 1964, MD, 1966. Diplomate Am. Bd. Pediatrics. Rotating intern Hennepin County Gen. Hosp., Mpls., 1967; pediatric resident U. Minn., Mpls., 1970, fellow pediatric neurology, 1971; asst. prof. pediatrics and pub. health U. Minn., 1972—; dir. Child Behavior & Learning Clinic Hennepin County Med. Ctr., Mpls., 1971—, program dir., clinician, staff pediatrician, clin. tchr., 1971—. Recipient Top award Antique Porcelain Doll Reprodns., 1992-94. Mem. N.W. Pediatric Soc., Phi Beta Kappa. Office: Hennepin County Med Ctr 701 Park Ave S Minneapolis MN 55415

TROEDEL, LOWELL JEAN, anesthesiologist, nurse; b. Jamestown, N.Y., Apr. 28, 1937; d. Walter Stanley and Mary Jane (Lowers) Barker; (div. Dec. 1987); 1 child, Stephanie Liane. Diploma in nursing, Gowanda Sch. of Nursing, Helmuth, N.Y., 1958; cert. nurse anesthetist, S.W. Mo. Sch. Anesthesia, 1961; BS, St. Joseph's Coll., Windham, Maine, 1985. RN, N.Y., Tex. Asst. head nurse Gowanda State Hosp., Helmuth, 1958-59; evening supr. Osteo. Hosp., Springfield, Mo., 1960-61; staff anesthetist N.Y. Hosp. Cornell Med. Ctr., N.Y.C. and Manhattan, N.Y., 1961-63; instr. anesthesiology Project Hope, Ecuador, S. Am., 1963-64; staff anesthetist Jackson Meml. Hosp., Miami, Fla., 1965-66; contract anesthetist St. Anthony & N.W. Tex. Hosp., Amarillo, Tex., 1970-75; dir. dept. anesthesiology Cen. Plains Regional Hosp., Plainview, Tex., 1975-84; pvt. practice anesthetist Tex., 1984—; chairperson ann. sem. Ednl. Dist. IV, 1977-84. Capt. USAF, 1966-70. Mem. Am. Assn. Nurse Anesthetists, Tex. Assn. Nurse Anesthetists (pres. edn. dist. IV, 1977-84, govt. and pub. rels. coms. 1984-86), MENSA (sec. Amarillo chpt. 1972-75). Home: 2502 Itasca St Plainview TX 79072-1618

TROJAN, VERA MARIA, investment company executive; b. N.Y.C., Sept. 5, 1960; d. Myroslaw and Nadia (Perehinsky) T.; m. Mark Carthy, Aug. 26, 1989; children: Lydia Trojan Carthy, Natalie Alexandra Carthy. AB in Econs., Princeton U., 1982; MBA, Harvard U., 1987. Econs. educator U. East Asia, Macau, 1982-83; analyst First Boston Corp./CSFB, N.Y.C., 1983-85; asst. to Robert V. Roosa Brown Brothers Harriman & Co., N.Y.C., 1987-89; v.p. Wellington Mgmt. Co., Boston, 1989—. Econs. editorial The Jour. of Commerce, 1988, 89, 90. Mem. Boston Com. on Fgn. Rels. Office: Wellington Mgmt Co Boston MA 02109

TROLANDER, JUDITH ANN, historian, educator; b. Mpls., May 31, 1942; d. Everett William and Harriett Dawn Trolander. BA, U. Minn., 1964; MSLS, Case Western Res. U., 1966, MS, 1969, PhD, 1972. Caseworker St. Louis County Welfare Dept., Virginia, Minn., 1964-65; libr. L.A. County Pub. Libr., 1966-67; instr. U. Akron, Ohio, 1971; asst. prof. Western Ill. U., Macomb, 1971-75; assoc. prof. U. Minn., Duluth, 1975-87, prof., 1987—; lectr. Cleve. State U., 1971. Author: Settlement Houses and the Great Depression, 1975, Professionalism and Social Change: From the Settlement House Movement to Neighborhood Centers, 1886 to the Present, 1987. Precinct chair Dem. Farmer Labor Party, Duluth, 1992-94, dir., 1994—. Recipient Collections of St. Louis Co. Hist. Soc. award NEH, 1979-81, Oral History award Minn. Hist. Soc., 1979-81, History Component of Midwest Settlement House Centennial award Minn. Humanities Commn., 1986. Office: U Minn Duluth MN 55812

TROMBLEY, FITTERER See ST. ANDREWS, BARBARA

TRONVOLD, LINDA JEAN, occupational therapist; b. Yankton, S.D., Dec. 8, 1950; m. Marvis D. Tronvold, July 7, 1976; children: Marcie, Tami, Kristi, Bradley, Cindy. Student, Mt. Marty Coll., 1989; AS, Kirkwood Community Coll., Cedar Rapids, Iowa, 1989; BS, Creighton U., 1991. Registered occupl. therapist, S.D., Neb., Iowa. Psychiatric aide S.D. Human Svcs. Ctr., Yankton, 1969-74, mental health technician, 1974-85, occpul. therapist asst., 1985-89, occupl. therapist, 1991-92; mem. edn. svc. unit Human Svcs. Ctr., Yankton, 1991-93; asst. program dir. occupl. therapy Western Iowa Tech. C.C., Dakota Dunes, S.D., 1993—; dir. occupl. therapy Nova Care, Inc., 1993—; guest speaker Creighton U., Omaha, U. S.D., Vermillion; mem. student staff Upward Bound, Omaha, 1989-91,. Scout leader Boy Scouts Am., Hartington, Nebr., 1977-80, Girl Scouts USA, Yankton, 1986-89; Sunday sch. tchr. United Ch. of Christ, Yankton, 1984-88; mem. spl. populations staff YWCA, Cedar Rapids, Iowa, 1987-88. Mem. Am. Occupl. Therapy Assn., S.D. Occupl. Therapy Assn., Nebr. Occupl. Therapy Assn., Iowa Occupl. Therapy Assn., Creighton U. Student Occupl. Therapy Assn., VFW Aux., Sq. Dance Club (pres. 1979-81), Alpha Tri Ota Club. Home: 705 Broadway St Yankton SD 57078-3923 Office: 350 W Anchor Dr Ste 500 Dakota Dunes SD 57049

TROPPER, SANDRA JAY, art dealer and appraiser; b. Amityville, N.Y., Oct. 11, 1951; d. Julius and Gladys Margaret (Anderson) Schwartz; m. Peter Tropper, Aug. 25, 1974. BA, Sweet Briar Coll., 1973; MA in Internat. Studies, Johns Hopkins U., 1975; MA in Art History, George Washington U., 1986. Rschr. Rep. Rsch. Com., Washington, 1975-76; writer and editor Nat. Ctr. for Cmty. Action, Washington, 1976-78; publ. cons. ATI, Washington, 1978-79; cons. Art Source, Columbia, Md., 1980-83; cons., owner Art Source, Washington, 1984-89; art dealer and appraiser, owner Artemis, Inc., Washington, Bethesda, D.C., Md., 1990—. Mem. Am. Soc. Appraisers, Coll. Art Assn. Home and Office: 4715 Crescent St Bethesda MD 20816-1720

TROST, EILEEN BANNON, lawyer; b. Teaneck, N.J., Jan. 9, 1951; d. William Eugene and Marie Thelma (Finlayson) Bannon; m. Lawrence Peter Trost Jr., Aug. 27, 1977; children: Lawrence Peter III, William Patrick, Timothy Alexander. BA with great distinction, Shimer Coll., 1972; JD cum laude, U. Minn., 1976. Bar: Ill. 1976, U.S. Dist. Ct. (no. dist.) Ill. 1976, Minn. 1978, U.S. Tax Ct. 1978, U.S. Supreme Ct. 1981. Assoc. McDermott, Will & Emery, Chgo., 1976-82, ptnr., 1982-93; v.p. No. Trust Bank Ariz. N.A., Phoenix, 1993—. Mem. Minn. Bar Assn., Internat. Acad. Estate and Trust Law. Roman Catholic. Office: Northern Trust Bank Ariz NA 2398 E Camelback Rd Phoenix AZ 85016-9001

TROSTLE, MARY PAT, judge; b. Wilmington, Del., Dec. 15, 1951; d. Robert Eyer and Loretta Carolyn (Grane) Albert; m. Keith Allen Trostle, Aug. 16, 1974. B.S., Miami U., Oxford, Ohio, 1972; J.D., Ohio No. U., 1975; postgrad. Temple Sch. Law, 1979-80. Bar: Del. 1976. Assoc., Biggs & Battaglia, Wilmington, Del., 1975-89; mng. lawyer White and Williams, 1989-92; seminar lectr. Palmer Assocs., Aurora, Ill., 1981-89; magistrate judge U.S. Dist. Ct. Del., Wilmington, Del., 1992—. Mem. ABA, Del. State Bar Assn. (treas. 1979-81, chmn. med.-legal, dental-legal com. 1985-92, bd. dirs. 1986-93; nominating com., 1984-90, v.p.-at-large 1990-92), Wilmington Women in Bus. (co-editor WWB News 1985-89, mem. bd. dirs. 1982-89), Defense Council Del. (v.p. 1988-90, pres. elect 1990-92). Republican. Roman Catholic. Home: 321 Hampton Rd Wilmington DE 19803-2425 also: Caleb Boggs Fed Bldg 844 King St Rm 6309 Wilmington DE 19801*

TROSTRUD-WHITE, CHERYL NANCY, artist; b. Chgo., Oct. 23, 1946; d. Earl John and Lillian Charlotte (Carlsen) Trostrud; m. Bob F. Ellis, July 13, 1968 (div. 1972); 1 child, Amie Elizabeth Ellis-White; m. William Luther White II, Dec. 16, 1981; stepchildren: Suzan R. White, Brent W. White. Student, Sch. of the Art Inst., Chgo., 1966, 82; student, U. Oslo, Norway, 1967; BA in Art Edn., Monmouth Coll., Monmouth, Ill., 1968; design program, UCLA Ext., 1986-88. Elem. sch. tchr. Monmouth Pub. Schs., 1968-70; tchr. grade 4 Arlington Heights (Ill.) Pub. Schs., 1972-74; art tchr. K-6 Northfield, Glencoe and Highland Park (Ill.) Schs., 1974-76, Glenview (Ill.) Pub. Schs., 1976-84; tchr., lectr., 1987—; founder, pres., editor newsletter Wearable Art Connection, 1991—; tchr., lectr. in field. Author: (mag.) American Quilter, 1993—. Work displayed in numerous exhbns. including New England Quilt Mus., Lowell, Mass., 1991, Yeiser Art Ctr., Paducah, Ky., 1991, Am. Quilter's Soc. Fashion Show, Paducah, 1991, Am. Quilter's Soc. 5th Ann. Quilt Show, Paducah, 1991, Fabric Festival Bazaar del Mundo, Old Town San Diego, Calif., 1991 (1st Pl. award), Nat. Quilting Assn., Lincoln, Nebr., 1991 (Most Innovative Design award), Glass City Quilt Commn., Toledo, 1991, Houston Internat. Quilt Market and Festival, 1991, 94, City of Quilts Fashion Show, San Francisco, 1992, Internat. Fedn. Univ. Women, Palo Alto, Calif., 1992, Mid. Atlantic Quilt Festival III, Williamsburg, Va., 1992, Pacific Internat. Quilt Festival, Burlingame, Calif., 1992, Mus. Am. Quilters' Soc., Paducah, 1992, Oreg. Sch. Arts and Crafts, Portland, 1992, Quilt Expo Europa III, The Hague, Holland, 1992, Convergence, Washington, 1992, 5th Ann. Ky. Fall Festival Quilts, Louisville, 1992, Houston Quilt Festival, 1992, Sulky of Am. Traveling Exbhn., 1993, Fairfield/Concord Fashion Show, Nihon Vogue Quilt Salon, Tokyo, 1993, Houston Quilt Market, 1993, Houston Spring Quilt Market, 1993, Boston Quilt Market, 1993, European Quilt Market, 1993, Quilt Expo Acad. I, Brussels, 1993, Nat. Quilting Assn., Inc., 1994, Convergence, Mpls., 1994. Contbr. articles to various publs. Coord. inner city group quilt Quilt of Common Dreams, presented to VA Med. Ctr., 1991; formed Clothes for Kids. Recipient numerous awards for quilting excellence. Mem. San Fernando Valley Quilt Assn. (v.p. programs 1988-90, 1990-92), Wearable Art Connection (pres., editor newletter 1992-93), Pi Beta Phi. Lutheran. Home and Studio: 23344 Park Hacienda Calabasas CA 91302-1715

TROTTA, MARCIA MARIE, librarian, consultant, education educator; b. Meriden, Conn., Nov. 12, 1949; d. Salvatore Dominic and Teresa Stella (Fuda) Marando; m. Carmine Joseph Trotta, Oct. 23, 1971; 1 child, Christopher Michael. AB, Albertus Mangus Coll., 1971; MLS, So. Conn. State U., 1979. Tchr. St. Mary's Sch., Meriden, 1971-73; circulation libr. Meriden Pub. Libr., 1973-74, asst. children's libr., 1974-76, reference libr., 1976-81, dir. children's libr., 1981-91, asst. dir., 1992—, dir., 1994—; adj. prof. So. Conn. State U., New Haven, 1987—; cons. Pfizer Metall. Libr., Wallingford, Conn., 1987, Woodbridge Town Libr., 1987-89, Conn. Assocs. for Counseling, Wilton, 1988—. Author: (books) Managing Outreach Programs, 1992, Successful Staff Development and Special Events Program, 1995; editor: CDA Manual, Outreach Services for Children and Youth, 1992. Mem. coun. Day Care Adv. Com. Meriden, 1990—, coun. Student Drug and Alcohol Abuse Prevention, Meriden, 1990-94; pres. Conn. Jaycee Women, 1984-85. Named one of Outstanding Women of Am., U.S. Jaycee Women, 1983, recipient Steve Little award, 1986. Mem. ALA, Conn. Libr. Assn. (pres. 1991—, Outstanding Libr. 1986, 93), New Eng. Libr. Assn., Rotary Internat. (Rotarian of Yr. 1994). Democrat. Roman Catholic. Home: 28 Goff St Meriden CT 06451-2838 Office: Meriden Pub Libr 105 Miller St Meriden CT 06450-4213

TROTTER, FRANKIE, public school administrator; b. Lamesa, Tex., Aug. 23, 1932; d. Charley Hargus and Sarah Katherine (Kirk) Scott; m. James Henry Trotter, June 19, 1950; children: James Richard, Joy Annell, Rodney Harell, Roger Jeffery. BS in Edn., Tex. Tech. U., 1975, MEd, 1980; MEd, Sul Ross State U., 1989. Cert. mid-mgmt. adminstr., supr., ednl. diagnostician, grade 1-8, early childhood handicapped tchr., kindergarten, elem. educator, mentally retarded, lang. and/or learning disabilities. Resource tchr. HONDA Coop-New Deal Elem., New Deal Ind. Sch. Dist., Abernathy, Tex., 1976-81; ednl. diagnosistician MetroCountry Spl. Svcs., Frenship Ind. Sch. Dist., Wolfforth, Tex., 1981-89; adminstrv. asst., curriculum coord. Shallowater Ind. (Tex.) Sch. Dist., 1989—; coord. Parents Adv. Coun. for MetroCountry Spl. Svcs., Wolfforth, 1985-87; developer thematic units using life skills to teach math, reading and lang. to handicapped children, 1979. Coord. United Way, Shallowater Schs., 1992; coord. Drug Free Schs. and Communities/At-Risk Adv. Coun., Shallowater, 1990—; pre-sch. coord. Trinity Bapt. Ch., 1975-88. Mem. ASCD, Assn. for Compensatory Educators of Tex., Coun. for Exceptional Children, Phi Delta Kappa, Kappa Delta Pi (historian 1975-76), Phi Delta Pi. Home: 4818 7th St Lubbock TX 79416 Office: Shallowater Ind Sch Dist 1009 Ave L PO Box 220 Shallowater TX 79363

TROUPE, MARILYN KAY, education educator; b. Tulsa, Sept. 30, 1945; d. Ernest Robinson and Lucille (Andrew) Troupe. BA in Social Sci., Langston U., Okla., 1967; MA in History, Okla. State U., 1976; EdD Okla. State U., 1993; Lic. in Cosmetology, Troupe's Beauty Sch., 1970. Cert. tchr. Okla. Tchr. social studies Margaret Hudson Program, Tulsa, 1969-81, tutor Tulsa Indian Youth, 1971-72; instr. cosmetology McLain-Tulsa Pub. Schs., 1982-94; instrnl. devel. specialist Okla. Dept. Vocat. and Tech. Edn., Stillwater, 1987-94; asst. prof., coord. tchr. preparation program Lane Coll., Jackson, Tenn., 1995—; vis. lectr. Okla. State U., 1980-81; cons., lectr. cosmetology; bd. dirs., adv. bd. Stillwater Park & Recreation, Stillwater Community Relations and Fair Housing, 1991-94; bd. dirs Adult Day Care Center, 1990-94; v.p. Okla. Recreation and Park Soc., 1994; judge Okla. Sch. Sci. and Math., 1994; mem. Leadership Stillwater, 1990; vol. Special Olympics State Games, Meals on Wheels, United Way. Roman Catholic Ch., Tulsa, 1985-86. Recipient numerous awards for profl. and civic contbns. including Woman of Yr., Zeta Phi Beta, 1985; Salute award Gov. Okla., 1985; Outstanding Community Service Cert., WomenFest, 1985. Mem. ASCD, Okla. Assn. Advancement of Black Ams. in Vocat. Edn. (Golden Torch award 1994), Vocat. Indsl. Clubs Am. (dist. advisor 1985-86, Appreciation award 1985), Am. Vocat. Assn., Okla. Vocat. Assn., Okla. State Beauty Culturalists League (pres. 1979-85, Outstanding Service award 1985), Nat. Assn. Bus. and Profl. Women's Club (charter mem., past pres.), Stillwater C. of C. (bd. dirs.), Langston Alumni Assn., Phi Alpha Theta, Theta Nu Sigma, Alpha Kappa Alpha (Soror of Yr. 1993), Iota Lambda Sigma, Phi Delta Kappa. Democrat. Roman Catholic. Clubs: Tulsa Links, Cath. Daus. Am. Avocations: travel, reading, collecting antiques, volunteer work, shopping. Home: 18 Rachel Dr # 10 Jackson TN 38305

TROUT, DEBORAH LEE, clinical psychologist, managed behavioral healthcare executive; b. Manistee, Mich., May 8, 1953; d. Paul Eugene and Rosemary Ruth (Beebe) T.; m. Curtis Lee Harris, June 5, 1982; 1 child, Sarah Elizabeth. AB cum laude, Bucknell U., 1975; MA in Clin. Psychology, U. Kans., 1978, PhD in Clin. Psychology, 1980. Lic. psychologist, Minn. Intern U. Minn., Mpls., 1979-80; psychotherapist, dept. psychiatry Ramsey Clinic, St. Paul, 1980-82, psychologist, 1983-86, dir. prepaid psychiatry, 1986-88, dir. managed care and off campus ops., 1988-90; dir. utilization review and network programs United Behavioral Systems, Inc., 1990-91; ops. dir., 1991-92, v.p. clin. systems, 1992-94, v.p. ops., 1994—; psychotherapist Washington Co. Human Svcs., Inc., Oakdale, Minn., 1981-83. Mem. Am. Psychol. Assn., Minn. Psychol. Assn. (chmn. prepaid-managed care subcom. on ins. com. 1988-90), Assn. Mental Health Adminstrs., Nat. Register Health Svc. Providers in Psychology, Nat. Women's Polit. Caucus, Women's Health Leadership Trust, Minn. 100, Phi Beta Kappa, Alpha Lambda Delta, Psi Chi. Office: United Behavioral Systems Inc Mail Rt MN06-0210 PO Box 1459 Minneapolis MN 55440-1459

TROUT, LINDA COPPLE, judge; b. Tokyo, Sept. 1, 1951. BA, U. Idaho, 1973, JD, 1977. Bar: Idaho 1977. Judge magistrate divsn. Idaho Dist. Ct. (2d jud. divsn.), 1983-90; dist. judge Idaho Dist. Ct. (2d jud. divsn.), Lewiston, 1991-92; acting trial ct. adminstr. Idaho Dist. Ct. (2d jud. divsn.), 1987-91; justice Idaho Supreme Ct., 1992—; instr. coll. law U. Idaho, 1983, 88. Mem. Idaho State Bar Assn., Clearwater Bar Assn. (pres. 1980-81).

TROUTNER, JOANNE JOHNSON, computer resource educator, consultant; b. Muncie, Ind., Sept. 9, 1952; d. Donal Russel and Lois Vivian (Hicks) Johnson; m. Lary William Troutner, May 17, 1975. BA in Media and English, Purdue U., 1974, MS in Edn., 1976. Media specialist Lafayette (Ind.) Sch. Corp., 1974-77, 81-83, computer resource tchr., 1983-84; media specialist, Tippecanoe Sch. Corp., Lafayette, 1984-85, ednl. computer coord., 1985-87, coord. instrl. support, 1988-94, dir. tech. and media, 1994—; instrnl. specialist edn. IBM, 1987-88; tchr. English, Minot Pub. Schs. (N.D.), 1978-79, media specialist, 1979-81; vis. prof. continuing edn. U. S.C., Columbia, summer 1983; instr. Purdue U., West Lafayette; vis. prof. continuing edn. U. N.D.; bd. dirs. Tippecanoe County Pub. Libr., pres., 1994, 95. Author: The Media Specialist, The Microcomputer and the Curriculum, 1983,; software selector Elementary Sch. Libr. Collection; contbr. materials rev. column Sch. Libr. Media Quar.; computer literacy columnist Jour. Computers in Math. and Sci. Teaching; computer software columnist Emergency Libr.; pub. Computers and the Gifted Student; editor newsletter Indiana Computer Educators. Active Greater Lafayette Leadership Acad. Alumni Group, 1983—; bd. dirs. Lafayette Family Svc. Agy., 1987-89; mem. dean's adv. coun. Sch. Edn. Purdue U. Mem. ALA, Ind. Assn. Media Educators (chmn. computer div. 1982-84), Am. Assn. Sch. Librarians (sec. 1983-84, 2d v.p. 1985-86), Internat. Coun. for Computers in Edn. (interactive video spl. interest group newsletter editor 1986-87), Ind. Computer Educators (bd. dirs. 1986-92, pres. 1990-91), Internat. Soc. Tech. Educators, Assn. Supr. and Curriculum Devel., Phi Beta Kappa, Kappa Delta Gamma, Phi Delta Kappa (v.p. programs 1987-88, v.p. memberships 1988-89, pres. 1989-90). Home: 4001 Penny Packers Mill Rd Lafayette IN 47905-3557 Office: Tippecanoe Sch Corp 21 Elston Rd Lafayette IN 47905-2899

TROUTWINE-BRAUN, CHARLOTTE TEMPERLEY, psychologist, educator, writer; b. Newton, Mass., Nov. 27, 1906; d. Joseph and Libbie (Kempton) Temperley; m. Arklay S. Richards, Nov. 28, 1928 (div. 1942); children: Whitman Albin, Lincoln Kempton, Sylvia Caroline; m. Harry Troutwine, May 3, 1945 (div. 1954); m. Charles E. McCrum, 1961 (div. 1965); m. Lester Lewis Walsh, Feb. 16, 1968 (div. Feb. 1972); m. George Braun, Feb. 6, 1975 (dec. Oct. 1975). BS, Simmons Coll., 1927; postgrad. Boston U., 1947-49; MA, Northeastern U., 1966; BES, Internat. Ch. Ageless Wisdom, 1981. Pvt. sec. pres. Hygrade Sylvania Electric Corp. Salem, Mass., 1927-28; pvt. and dept. exec. sec. Dr. Stanley Cobb, Bullard prof. neuropathology Harvard U. Med. Sch., 1928-31; part-time caseworker Friends of Framingham Reformatory, 1928-31, others, 1931-51; organizer, exec. dir. Postgrad. Med. Inst., 1951-57; mgr. Postgrad. Information Services, Lederle Labs. div. Am. Cyanamid Co., Pearl River, N.Y., 1957-61; exec. dir. postgrad. med. edn., Hahnemann Med. Coll. and Hosp. also exec. dir. Mary Bailey Inst. Cardiovascular Research, 1961; counselor, tchr. psychology Holliston High Sch., 1965-66. Counselor Falmouth (Mass.) High Sch., 1966-74; psychotherapist Hallgarth Clinic, 1974-75. Speaker for Am. Epilepsy League. Mem. Mass. Tchrs. Assn. (life), Spiritual Frontiers Assn. (life), N.E.A. (life), Nat. Ret. Tchrs. Assn. (life), Nat. Assn. Sch. Counselors (charter, life), Assn. Research Enlightenment, Soc. Mayflower Descs. (life), Simmons Coll. Alumnae Assn., AAUW, Med. Soc. Execs. Assn. (emeritus), Am. Soc. Psychical Research, States Med. Postgrad. Assn. (past sec.), Mass. Psychol. Assn. (life), Spiritual Frontiers Fellowship (life), World Fedn. Healers (healer mem.), Mass. Healers Assn. Author: Practicing the Silence, 1978, 5th edit., 1992, Open Windows, 1994; contbr. numerous articles in med., spiritual and psychol. fields. Mem. Soc. of Friends. Home: 83 Falmouth Ct Bedford MA 01730-2912

TROW, JO ANNE JOHNSON, university official; b. Youngstown, Ohio, Feb. 10, 1931; d. Raymond Leonard Johnson and Mary Belle Beede; m. Clifford W. Trow, Oct. 10, 1969. BA, Denison U., 1953; MA, Ind. U., 1956; PhD, Mich. State U., 1965. Case worker Office Pub. Assistance, Cleve., 1953-54; asst. dean women Denison U., Granville, Ohio, 1956-59, Wash. State U., Pullman, 1959-63; asst. dir. resident program Mich. State U., East Lansing, 1964; dean women Oreg. State U., Corvallis, 1965-69, assoc. dean students, 1969-83, v.p. student affairs, 1983—, program dir., 1972-83; presenter, speaker in field. Contbr. articles to profl. jours. Bd. dirs. Benton County Mental Health Assn., 1975-79, United Way Benton County, 1977—, United Way Oreg., 1977-80; mem. adv. bd. Old Mill Sch., 1979—, chmn., 1983, 94-95; mem. Oreg. Cmty. Corrections Adv. Bd., 1988—; moderator 1st Congl. Ch., 1977, trustee, 1979-83, 91—; mem. Oreg. Gov.'s Com. on Status of Women, 1972-78, vice chmn., 1976-77; mem. fund campaign Good Samaritan Hosp. Found. Cancer Care Ctr., 1982-83. Recipient Corvallis Woman of Achievement award, 1974, Boss of Yr. award Oreg. State U. Office Personnel Assn., 1979, White Rose award March of Dimes, 1987, Elizabeth A Greenleaf Disting. Alumna award Ind. U., 1987, Scott Goodnight award, 1989, Disting. Alumni Citation, Denison U., 1993, Coun. Woman of Distinction award Oreg. State U. Meml. Union Program, 1993. Mem. Nat. Assn. Women Deans, Adminstrs. and Counselors (pres. 1981-82), Am. Coll. Personnel Assn. (sec. 1969-70), Nat. Assn. Student Personnel Adminstrs., Am. Coun. on Edn., N.W. Assn. Schs. and Colls. (comn. on colls., 1989—), Am. Assn. for Higher Edn., N.W. Coll. Personnel Assn. (life, pres. 1969-70), Assn. Oreg. Faculties, AAUW (state and local bd. dirs.), LWV (bd. dirs., v.p. Corvallis 1966-69, 79-80), Corvallis Area C. of C. (bd. dirs. 1972-74, 78-80), Mortar Bd., Phi Delta Kappa, Phi Kappa Phi, Alpha Lambda Delta. Democrat. Office: Oreg State U Ads A632 Corvallis OR 97331

TROWBRIDGE, LAURA A., controller; b. Cleve., Jan. 7, 1964; d. John P. and Marjorie A. (Sked) Zaremba; m. Richard K. Trowbridge, May 31, 1986; children: Ryan, Alexander. BBA, U. Mich., 1985. Sr. cons. Peterson Cons., N.Y.C., 1985-88; mgr. fin. SNET Systems, New Haven, 1989-91; contr. SNET Real Estate, New Haven, 1991—; treas. SNET Real Estate Inc., New Haven, 1991-93. Mem. Orange Jr. C. of C. (treas.). Republican. Congregational. Home: 584 Orange Center Rd Orange CT 06477-2956 Office: SNET Real Estate Inc 13th Fl 555 Long Wharf Dr Fl 13 New Haven CT 06511-5989

TROWBRIDGE, LYNN CARTER, accountant; b. Gary, Ind., Apr. 2, 1942; d. Frank L. and Harriet M. (Nash) Carter; m. Richard J. Bunn, Nov. 25, 1960 (div.); m. Philip A. Trowbridge, Sept. 11, 1970. BS in Acctg., Ball State U., 1982. CPA, Ind., Ga. Staff acct. Colley & Kise, P.C., Tucker, Ga., 1982-86, Simmons & Co., Muncie, Ind., 1986-88; prin. Lynn C. Trowbridge, CPA, Albany, Ind., 1988—. Vol. cons., spkr. East Central Ind. Small Bus. Devel. Ctr., Muncie, Ind., 1990—; vol. treas. Unitarian Universalist Ch., Muncie, 1988-91. Mem. AICPA, Ind. CPA Soc., Inst. Mgmt. Accts. (dir. newsletter 1989-92). Office: Lynn C Trowbridge CPA 9510 N County Rd 425E Albany IN 47320

TROXCLAIR, DEBRA ANN, gifted education educator; b. New Orleans, Jan. 29, 1953; d. Richard Joseph and Joyce Marie (Braud) Troxclair; divorced; 1 child, Christopher Richard Pinner. BA, U. New Orleans, 1976, MEd, 1989; postgrad., U. So. Miss., 1991—. Cert. edn. 4th grade tchr. Laurel Elem. Sch., New Orleans, 1977; 2d grade tchr. St. Frances Cabrini Elem., New Orleans, 1977-80; 1st grade tchr. St. Joseph Sch., Gretna, La., 1982-83; kindergarten tchr. Lake Castle Pvt. Sch., New Orleans, 1983-84; libr. St. Frances Cabrini, New Orleans, 1984-85; 3d grade tchr. Abney Elem. Sch., Slidell, La., 1985-89; gifted resource tchr. Little Oak Elem., Slidell, 1989—; instr. Delgado C.C., Slidell, 1991—; cons. St. Tammany Parish Schs., Slidell, 1988-89, 90-91; presenter La. State Dept. Edn. Superconference, 1993, La. Assn. Gifted Students, Mar. 1993. Elder Northminster Presbyn. Ch., Pearl River, La. Mem. AAUW (newsletter editor Slidell br. 1985-86), Northshore Reading Coun., Assn. Gifted and Talented Students, Nat. Assn. Gifted Children (conv. presenter 1993), Phi Delta Kappa (pres. St. Tammany Parish 1991). Presbyterian. Office: Little Oak Elem 59241 Rebel Dr Slidell LA 70461-3732

TROXEL, LISA SUSAN STARR, data processing specialist, educator; b. Centerville, Iowa, Oct. 28, 1962; d. George Trenton and Marilyn Joanne (Crawford) Starr; m. Jack Curtis Troxel, Sept. 6, 1992. AAS, Indian Hills C.C., Ottumwa, Iowa, 1983. Computer operator WII, Des Moines, 1983-85; programmer We. Internat. Inc., Des Moines, 1986-88; programmer analyst Fin. Info. Trust, West Des Moines, Iowa, 1988-89, State of Iowa Dept. Commerce, Ankeny, 1989-90; programmer analyst State of Iowa Dept. Gen. Svcs., Des Moines, 1990-91, data processing specialist, 1991—. Chair Fellowship Bapt. Property Com., chair, 1993—; leader Fellowship Bapt. Youth. Mem. Toastmasters. Home: 1100 Sunset Dr Carlisle IA 50047-9768 Office: State of Iowa Gen Svcs Hoover State Office Bu Des Moines IA 50319

TROXELL, CAROLYN BARRETT, bank executive, association administrator; b. L.I. City, N.Y., Dec. 10, 1941; d. Joseph Theodore and Mary Carolyn (Grossmann) Barrett; m. Lawrence A North, 1961 (div. 1972); children: Mary C. Schwentker, Roger A. Troxell, Lawrence A. North; m. Frank Vollmer Troxell, 1976. Student, Marywood Coll., 1959-61, Hunter Coll., 1962-63. Advt. asst. Union Carbide Corp., N.Y.C., 1961; bus. rep. Bell Telephone, N.Y.C., 1962; consumer correspondent Lever Bros., N.Y.C., 1963; v.p., mktg. mgr. Mellon Bank, Harrisburg, Pa., 1971—; co-owner boarding stable Westwynd Farm, Hummelstown, Pa. Mem. social ministry com. St. Mark's Luth. ch., 1985—, chair 1987-89, mutual min. com. 1989-94, chair 1992-94; bd. dirs. YWCA Greater Harrisburg, 1992—, tri-county chpt. Am. Diabetes Assn., 1992—, pres., 1994-95; sec. environ. adv. com. East Hanover Twp., 1992, 93, pres. 1992—. Recipient Disting. Svc. award Kidney Found. Ctrl. Pa., 1982, Twin award YWCA Greater Harrisburg, 1990, Outstanding Svc. award Tri-County chpt. Am. Diabetes Assn., 1992. Mem. Am. Mktg. Assn. (treas. ctrl. Pa. chpt. 1973), U.S. Pony Club (dist. commr. Manada Creek Pony Club 1980-86, 95). Democrat. Lutheran. Home: Westwynd Farm RD 2 Box 238G Hummelstown PA 17036 Office: Mellon Bank 10 S Market Sq Harrisburg PA 17101

TROXELL, LUCY DAVIS, consulting firm executive; b. Cambridge, Mass., Apr. 25, 1932; d. Ellsworth and Mildred (Enneking) Davis; m. Charles DeGroat Bader, June 13, 1952 (div. Aug. 1974); children: Christie P. Walker, Mary Ellsworth Bader, Charles D. Bader Jr., Davis Bradford Bader; m. Victor Daniel Shirer Troxell, Aug. 1974. BA, Smith Coll., Northampton, Mass., 1952. Cert. paralegal, employee benefit specialist, assoc. in risk mgmt. Paralegal O'Melveny & Myers, L.A., 1976-77; account exec. Olanie Hurst & Hemrich, L.A., 1977-78; asst. to trustee Oxford Ins. Mgmt., L.A., 1978-80; dir. corp. svcs., asst. corp. sec. Consolidated Elec. Distbrs., Inc., Westlake Village, Calif., 1980-93; pres. MONMAK LDT, Westlake Village, 1993—. Sustaining mem., bd. dirs. Jr. League, Hartford, Conn., L.A., 1952—; clk. St. Mathew's Parish Vestry, Pacific Palisades, Calif., 1988, sr. warden, 1989-90; bd. dirs. Smith Coll. Club, Hartford, L.A., 1952—, Nat. Charity League, L.A., 1964-68; lic. lay eucharistic minister Episcopal Ch. Sophia Smith scholar. Fellow Internat. Soc. Cert. Employee Benefit Specialists (charter mem., bd. dirs., sec., treas. 1988-89, pres. 1989-90, edn. chmn. 1986-88 L.A. chpt.), Risk and Ins. Mgmt. Soc. (program chmn. L.A. chpt. 1985-86), Theatre Palisades (bd. dirs. 1960-74). Republican. Home: 450 Puerto Del Mar Pacific Palisades CA 90272-4233 Office: MONMAK LDT 31220 La Baya Dr # 319 Westlake Vlg CA 91362-4008

TROXELL-GURKA, MARY THERESA (TERRY TROXELL-GURKA), geriatrics services professional; b. Syracuse, N.Y., Aug. 29, 1950; d. Henry and Mary (McDermott) Flynn; m. Richard Gurka, Apr. 2, 1994; 1 child, Melissa Lee. BSN, U. Pa., 1971. Cert. quality improvement specialist; cert. gerontol. nurse specialist. Supr. neonatal ICU St. Joe's, Syracuse, 1976-79; dir. nursing Hillhaven, Phoenix, 1979-81; quality assurance nurse long term care Maricopa County, Phoenix, 1981-83; dir. nursing Desert Haven Nursing Home, Phoenix, 1983-84; team leader, surveyor health care licensure State of Ariz., Phoenix, 1985-87, program mgr. long term care licensure and certification, 1987-89, program mgr. enforcement and compliance licensure and cert., 1989-91; dir. profl. svcs. SunQuest Healthcare, Phoenix, 1991-94, v.p. clin. ops., 1994—. Author: (manuals) Licensure Procedures, 1990, Quality Improvement, Restorative Nursing: A Key to Quality, 1992, Director of Nursing Manual, 1993. Developer legislation for adult care homes, health care licensure laws State of Ariz., 1990. Mem. Ariz. Health Care Assn. (chair legis. com. 1992-94, chair devel./revision nursing facility laws 1992-94), Am. Health Care Assn. (nat. facility stds. com. 1992-94, nat. multifacility com. 1993-94, LTC nurses coun. 1995), Quality Improvement Nurses Assn. Home: 3608 E Woodland Dr Phoenix AZ 85044 Office: Sunquest Health Care 7272 E Indian School Rd Ste 214 Scottsdale AZ 85251

TROYER, LISA LYNN, marketing and activities director; b. Washington, Mar. 26, 1964; d. Jarnot DeVere and Virginia Mae (Holmes) T. AA in

Mktg. Mgmt., Prince George's Community Coll, 1985; B in Gen. Studies, U. Md., 1987; postgrad., Abilene Christian U., 1993—. Staff asst. U.S. House Reps., Washington, 1987-88; adminstrv. coord. Nuclear Info. & Resource Svc., Washington, 1988-89; residential child devel. specialist Country Acres, Gilsum, N.H., 1989-90; program asst. NSF, Washington, 1990-92; mktg. and activities dir. Springvale Ter., Silver Spring, Md., 1992-93; grad. asst. Tex. Del. of the White House Conf. on Aging, 1994—; mission team mem. S.E. Asia Global Campaign Project, summer 1994; bd. dirs. Employees Assn.; prin. rep. EEO Coun., Washington, 1991; sch. outreach vol. NSF Rep., Washington, 1991. Assoc. editor: Children of the American Revolution National Magazine, 1981-82, nat. pubs. chmn., 1982-83. bd. dirs. Prince George's County Chpt. ARC, Hyattsville, 1981-82; polit. intern Gary Hart's Pres. Campaign, 1983-84; del. Md. Young Democrats, Largo, 1984-85; pres. student program bd. Prince George's Community Coll., Largo, 1984-85, bd. trustees mem., 1985-86; active City's Human Resource League Com., Bowie, Md., 1987-89; coord. Laotian refugee camp rescue mission Ch. of Christ, Silver Spring, Md., 1989, youth coord.; vol. Silver Spring Soup Kitchen. Mem. NAFE, U. Md. Alumni Assn., Prince George's Community Coll. Alumni Assn. (v.p., 1985-86, bd. dirs., 1985-91), Alpha Delta Pi Alumni Assn. Democrat. Home: ACU Station PO Box 6374 Abilene TX 79699 Office: Abilene Christian U Abilene TX 79699

TRUB, ALEXANDRA BRINTNALL, non-profit organization administrator; b. Glen Ridge, N.J., June 20, 1960; d. Richard G. and Patricia A. Trub. BS in Studio Art, Skidmore Coll., 1982; MA in Visual Arts Adminstrn., NYU, 1995. Gallery dir. Jane Hartsook Gallery - Greenwich House Pottery, N.Y.C., 1985-88; pres., bd. trustees Watershed Ctr. for the Ceramic Arts, Edgecomb, Maine, 1989—; cons. Contemporary Porcelain, N.Y.C., 1990-93; guest curator Wheeler-Seider Gallery, N.Y.C., 1991. Co-author: The Handbook for Ceramic Artists, 1989; exec. prodr. video documentary: Watershed AIDS Project, 1991. Mem. Coll. Art Assn., Nat. Coun. for Ceramic Arts (group moderator 1992, lectr.-coord. 1989, 91).

TRUBISKY, KATHY KRAMER, social service administrator; b. Cleve., Oct. 4, 1958; d. Archibald Charles and Katherine Faith (Porter) K.; m. David Allen Trubisky, June 13, 1987; 1 child, Nicholas Charles. BA, Kent State U., 1980, MEd, 1981, EdS, Specialist, 1982. Lic. profl. counselor, Ohio. Career counselor Kent (Ohio) State U., 1981-82; dir. YMCA Big Bros./Big Sisters YMCA-Canton (Ohio) Area, 1982—; assoc. exec. Downtown YMCA, Canton, 1992—; field isntr. Malone Coll., Canton, 1983—, Kent State U., 1993—, Walsh U., 1993—. Editor: (manual) Child Sexual Abuse Prevention, 1990-91. Recipient YMCA Dist. award of Achievement, 1986. Mem. Am. Counseling Assn., Assn. for Specialists in Group Work, Citizen's Rev. Bd.-Stark County Family Ct., Community and Vol. Svcs. Coun. Democrat. Roman Catholic. Office: YMCA-Canton Area 405 Second St NW Canton OH 44702

TRUCKENBROD, JOAN RUTH, artist, educator; b. Greensboro, N.C., Sept. 18, 1945; d. John Mills and Edith Olive (Chambers) Sharman; 1 child, Emily Mills Truckenbrod. BA, Beloit Coll., 1967; MA, No. Ill. U., 1973; MFA, Sch. Art Inst., Chgo., 1979. lectr. Lafayette (Ind.) Mus. Art, 1993, Inst. Contemporary Art, London, 1994; juror La Cite des Arts and Nouvelle Techs., Montreal, 1993; invited curator Pa. State U., 1994. Asst. prof. No. Ill. U., DeKalb, 1973-81; assoc. prof., chair time arts dept. The Sch. of the Art Inst., Chgo., 1981—. Author: Creative Computer Imaging, 1988; works have appeared in one-person show, Chgo., 1993; various group shows. Fellow Am. Scandinavian Found., Denmark, 1994. Mem. Internat. Soc. for Art, Sci. and Tech., Soc. for Photographic Educators, Coll. Art Assn., Chgo. Artists Coalition. Office: Sch of the Art Inst 37 S Wabash Chicago IL 60603

TRUCKSIS, THERESA A., library director; b. Hubbard, Ohio, Sept. 1, 1924; d. Peter and Carmella (DiSilverio) Pagliasotti; m. Robert C. Trucksis, May 29, 1948 (dec. May 1980); children: M. Laura, Anne, Michele, Patricia, David, Robert, Claire, Peter; m. Philip P. Hickey, Oct. 19, 1985 (dec. May 1993). BS in Edn., Youngstown Coll., 1945; postgrad., Youngstown State U., 1968-71; MLS, Kent State U., 1972. Psychometrist Youngstown (Ohio) Coll., 1946-49; instr. ltd. svc. Youngstown State U., 1968-71; libr. Pub. Libr. Youngstown & Mahoning County, Youngstown, 1972-73, asst. dept. head, 1973-74, asst. dir., 1985-89, dir., 1989—; dir. NOLA Regional Libr. System, Youngstown, 1974-85. Contbr. articles to profl. jours. Mem. bd. Hubbard Sch. Dist., 1980-85. Mem. ALA, Ohio Libr. Assn. (bd. dirs. 1979-81), Pub. Libr. Assn. Office: Pub Libr Youngstown & Mahoning Co 305 Wick Ave Youngstown OH 44503-1079

TRUE, JEAN DURLAND, entrepreneur, oil company executive; b. Olney, Ill., Nov. 27, 1915; d. Clyde Earl and Harriet Louise (Brayton) Durland; m. Henry Alfonso True, Jr., Mar. 20, 1938; children: Tamma Jean (Mrs. Donald G. Hatten), Henry Alfonso III, Diemer Durland, David Lanmon. Student, Mont. State U., 1935-36. Ptnr. True Drilling Co., Casper, Wyo., 1951—, True Oil Co., Casper, 1951-94, Eighty-Eight Oil Co., 1955-94, True Geothermal Energy Co., 1980—, True Ranches, 1981-94; officer, dir. White Stallion Ranch, Inc., Tucson, Smokey Oil Co., Casper; officer Toolpushers Supply Co., Belle Fourche Pipeline Co., Black Hills Trucking, True Geothermal Drilling Co., Casper. Mem. steering com. YMCA, Casper, 1954-55, bd. dirs., 1956-58; mem. bd. dirs. Gottsche Rehab. Ctr., Thermopolis, Wyo., 1966-93, mem. exec. bd. 1966-93, v.p., 1973-90; mem. adv. bd. for adult edn. U. Wyo., 1966-68; mem. Ft. Casper Commn., Casper, 1973-79; bd. dirs. Mus. of Rockies, Bozeman, Mont., 1983-87, bd. dirs. Nicolaysen Art Mus., 1988-93; mem. Nat. Fedn. Rep. Women's Clubs; del. Rep. nat. conv., 1972. Mem. Rocky Mountain Oil and Gas Assn., Casper Area C. of C., Alpha Gamma Delta, Casper Country Club, Petroleum Women's Club (Casper). Episcopalian. Office: Rivercross Rd PO Box 2360 Casper WY 82602-2360

TRUEBLOOD, EMILY HERRICK, artist, librarian; b. Alexandria, Va., Aug. 13, 1942; d. Lorman Chancellor and Helen Julia (Smith) Trueblood; m. Ernest Theodore Patrikis, Mar. 18, 1972. Student, Beloit (Wis.) Coll., 1960-62; BA, U. Wis., 1965; MS, Columbia U., 1969. Libr. Fed. Res. Bank of N.Y., N.Y.C., 1969-75, sr. libr., 1975-83, asst. chief libr., 1983-85, chief libr., 1985—; works in permanent collects including The Newark Pub. Libr., Trenton State Coll., Mus. of Modern Art, Haifa, Israel, Portland Mus. Art. One-woman shows include Loho Gallery, Louisville, 1985, Lumen Winter Gallery, New Rochelle Pub. Libr., N.Y., 1986, New Sch. Social Rsch., 1994; exhibited in group shows at Susan Teller Gallery, N.Y.C., 1991, Kanagawa, Japan, 1992, New Pub. Libr., Newark, 1994; represented in permenant collections at The Newark Pub. Libr., Trenton State Coll., Mus. of Modern Art, Haifa, Israel, Portland Mus. of Art. Recipient Hugh P. Botts award Salmagundi Club, N.Y.C., 1993, Solo award Pen and Brush, 1992, E. Weyhe Gallery award Soc. Am. Graphic Artists, 1991, Purchase prize Trenton State Coll., 1982, Am. Artist award Audubon Artists, 1995. Mem. Soc. Am. Graphic Artists (treas. 1988—), The Pen and Brush Inc. (graphics chair 1988—), Nat. Arts Club, Nat. Assn. Women Artists, Spl. Libr. Assn., Salmagundi Club. Home: 20 E 9th St New York NY 10003-5944

TRUGLIA, CHRISTEL, state legislator; m. Anthony D. Truglia (dec.); 3 children. Student, Darien (Conn.) H.S. Mem. Conn. Ho. of Reps., 1973-84, 88—, Conn. Senate, 1984-87; mem. appropriations, human svcs., substance abuse prevention coms, L.I. task force, children at risk task force and gray haired caucus; mem. Dem. Leadership Coun., 1991—, Nat. Order of Women Legislators, 1991—, Lower Fairfield County Conf./Exhbn. Authority, 1992—, Com. on Edn. Excellence, 1992—. Vice chmn. Stamford (Conn.) Dem. City Com., 1976-78; bd. dirs. Com. on Tng. and Employment, 1990—; mem. exec. com. Lower Fairfield County Action Against Chem. Dependency, 1991—; active Coun. on Probate Jud. Conduct, 1976-88, Stamford Com. on Aging, 1978-88, Child Care Ctr. of Stamford, Family Re-entry, Inc., 1990—, Aide for Retarded Inc. Aux. Recipient Hannah G. Solomon Cmty. Svc. award Nat. Coun. Jewish Women, 1987, Spl. award Family Re-entry, 1990, Friend of Edn. award Conn. Coun. for Am. Pvt. Edn., 1991, Adv. Leadership award, 1991, Appreciation cert. Conn. Acad. Physicians Assts., 1991, Cmty. Svc. award Coun. Chs. and Synagogues, 1991, Law Day Liberty Bell award Stamford-Norwalk Regional Bar Assn., 1992, United Srs. in Action award Conn. Gen. Assembly, 1992, Child Adv. Legis. Leadership award Conn. Coalition for Children, 1992, Spl. Recognition award Coalition of 100 Black Women of Lower Fairfield County, 1992, Bd. dirs. Jewish Home for Elderly, 1992; named Child Adv. Legislator, State Coalition for Children and State Commn. on Children, 1990, Legis. Advisor of Yr., Conn. Youth Svcs. Assn., 1990. Mem. Rippowan Bus. and Profl. Women's Club (Woman of Yr. 1991). Democrat. Home: 7 Gypsy Moth Landing Stamford CT 06902*

TRUHLAR, DORIS BROADDUS, lawyer; b. Oklahoma City, Sept. 18, 1946; d. Elbridge Sidney and Doris Mary (Prock) Broaddus; div.; children: Samara Taryle, Brett Taryle (dec.); m. Robert John Truhlar, June 234, 1978; children: Ivy, Holly. B in journalism, U. Mo., 1967; MA, U. Denver, 1976, JD, 1980. Bar: Colo. 1981, U.S. Dist. Ct. Colo. 1981, U.S. Ct. Appeals (10th cir.) 1981. Law clk. to Hon. Robert H. McWilliams, Jr. U.S. Ct. Appeals (10th cir.), Denver, 1980-81; assoc. Holme, Roberts & Owen, Denver; corp. sec., gen. counsel Hart Exploration and Prodn. Co., Englewood, Colo.; ptnr. Truhlar & Truhlar, Littleton, Colo., 1985—; adj. prof. U. Denver Coll. Law, 1986-88, 90-91, mem. adv. com. advocacy skills program, 1990; speaker Continuing Legal Edn. Programs; expert witness regarding attys. fees; bd. dirs. Colo. Foster Care Tng. Inst., 1991-93. Trainer attys. and vols. who work with abused and neglected children; active various vol. programs; mem. vestry bd. Good Shepherd Episcopal Ch., 1992—. Recipient Woman of Achievement, Entreprneur of Yr. award Met. YWCA of Denver, 1993, Denver Gridiron award, 1st pl. Editorial Writing award Nat. Edn. Writers Assn., also several Mo. Press Assn. awards and newspaper writing awards. Mem: ABA, Am. Trial Lawyers Assn., Denver Bar Assn. (Vol. Atty. of Yr. award), Colo. Bar Assn. (organizer, tchr. pro se div. clinics, ethics com. 1984-91, calling com.), Colo. Trial Lawyers Assn. (chmn. Torts Involving Children 1990), Arapahoe County Bar Assn. (Community Svc. award, Pro Bono Atty. 1992). Office: 1901 W Littleton Blvd Littleton CO 80120-2058

TRUITT, SUZANNE, real estate broker; b. Lewes, Del., Aug. 20, 1943; d. James Shockley and Dorothy Virginia (Shockley) T. Student, U. Del., 1961-62; AA, Goldey Beacom Coll., 1964; grad., Realtors Inst., 1988. Cert. in real estate brokerage mgmt., real estate appraiser, residential specialist;. Notary public State of Del., Dover, 1976—; property and casualty ins. agt. J. A. Montgomery Inc., Wilmington, 1984—; real estate broker C-21/Mann Moore Assocs., Inc., Rehoboth Beach, Del., 1988—; mktg. mgr. Long Neck Village, Millsboro, Del., 1991; broker of record, mgr. Gull Point, Patterson Schwartz Real Estate, Millsboro, 1991-93; with C-21/Mann Moore Assocs., Inc., Rehoboth Beach, Del., 1993—, Atlantic Appraisal, Rehoboth Beach, 1993—, ECN Appraisals, Rehoboth Beach, 1994—. Mem. NAFE (life), Am. Soc. Notaries, Ins. Women Sussex County, Women's Coun. Realtors. Republican. Methodist. Home: 8 Sheffield Rd, RBYCE Rehoboth Beach DE 19971-1400 Office: C21 Mann Moore Assocs Inc Atlantic Appraisal 4343 Hwy One Rehoboth Beach DE 19971-1147 also: Atlantic Appraisal 8 Sheffield Rd Rehoboth Beach DE 19971-1400

TRUMAN, MARGARET, author; b. Independence, Mo., Feb. 17, 1924; d. Harry S. (32nd Pres. U.S.) and Bess (Wallace) T.; m. E. Clifton Daniel Jr., Apr. 21, 1956; children: Clifton T., William, Harrison, Thomas. LHD, Wake Forest U., 1972; HHD, Rockhurst Coll., 1976. Concert singer, 1947-54, actress, broadcaster, author, 1954—; author: Souvenir, 1956, White House Pets, 1969, Harry S. Truman, 1973, Women of Courage, 1976, Murder in the White House, 1980, Murder on Capitol Hill, 1981, Letters from Father, 1981, Murder in the Supreme Court, 1982, Murder in the Smithsonian, 1983, Murder on Embassy Row, 1985, Murder at the FBI, 1985, Murder in Georgetown, 1986, Bess W. Truman, 1986, Murder in the CIA, 1987, Murder at the Kennedy Center, 1989, Murder in the National Cathedral, 1990, Murder at the Pentagon, 1992, Murder on the Potomac, 1994; editor: Where the Buck Stops: The Personal and Private Writings of Harry S. Truman, 1989. Trustee and v.p. Harry S. Truman Inst.; sec. bd. trustees Harry S. Truman Found.

TRUMBLE, BEVERLY JANE, artist; b. Milw., Oct. 31, 1934; d. Harvey George and Rachel Rebecca (Wagner) Bowers; m. Henry Esser; children: Gail Lorraine, Deann Loreen; m. Morris M. Trumble, July 28, 1968. Student, Colo. U., 1960, Arts Students League, 1976-83, Daniel Green Workshop, 1984. Sec. bd. dirs. West Side Arts Coalition, N.Y.C., 1985-87, co-chair visuals, 1987-88, speaker, moderator, 1988-89, dir. studio, 1988-90; co-chair pastel sect. Pen & Brush, Inc., N.Y.C., 1989-91; bd. dirs. com. Summit County Arts Coun., Breckenridge, Colo., 1993. One-woman shows include The Pen and Brush, 1987, Internat. House, 1989, Pleiades Gallery, N.Y.C., 1993, U. Denver, 1993; exhibited in numerous group art exhbns. Dir. studio tours various civic orgns., N.Y.C., 1988-90; speaker Littleton Pub. Sch., Littleton, Colo., 1992. Recipient merit scholarship Art Students, N.Y.C., 1982, Solo Exhibit award The Pen and Brush, 1985, Artists Guild award Mamaroneck (N.Y.) Artists Guild, 1988, Salmagundi award Salmagundi Club, 1989. Mem. Pastel Soc. Am., Soc. Layerists in Multi-Media, Art Students League N.Y. (Life), New York Artists Equity Assn. Inc. (nominating com. 1987), Taos Art Assn. Home: 6946 NCDBU Taos NM 87571

TRUMBO, CYNTHIA L., counselor educator; b. Dallas, Aug. 9, 1955; d. John Reinhardt and Carolyn Harvey (Herbert) Taylor; m. Dana Andrew Bulter, June, 4, 1977 (div. June 1979); m. Floyd Michael Trumbo, Feb. 13, 1988; 1 daughter, Jennifer Lynn. BS, Kans. State U., 1977; MS, Iowa State U., 1982, PhD, 1987. Nat. cert. counselor. Asst. program coord. Lubbock (Tex.) Regional Mental Health/Retardation Ctr., 1979, program coord., 1979-81; counseling grad. asst. Iowa State U., 1982-83, adminstrv. grad. asst., 1983-87; asst. prof. Western Ky. U., Bowling Green, 1987-89, part-time prof., 1989-91, adj. prof., 1991—; pvt. cons., 1990. Mem. Ky. Assn. Counselors, Am. Assn. for Marriage and Family Therapy. Republican. Baptist.

TRUPP, ROBIN JEAN, nursing administrator; b. Cin., Dec. 19, 1953; d. Jack Raymond and Barbara Jean (Huff) Shaw; m. Robert W. Trupp; children: Robert J., Amanda E. RN, Jewish Hosp. Sch. Nursing, Cin., 1975; BSN, Miami U., Oxford, Ohio, 1991. RN, Ohio, Ind.; CCRN. Staff nurse Providence Hosp., Cin., 1975-79; RN cardiac catheterization lab Deaconess Hosp., Cin., 1983-88; ICU staff nurse Mercy Fairfield (Ohio) Hosp., 1979-83, dir. cardiac catheterization lab., 1988-91; nat. account exec. McFaul & Lyons, Inc., 1992-94; dir. critical care Deaconess Hosp., Cin., 1994—. Advanced cardiac life support instr. Am. Heart Assn., 1988—. Mem. Am. Nurses Assn., Ohio Nurses Assn., Am. Assn. Critical Care Nurses, Am. Assn. Cardiovascular Adminstrs., Am. Coll. Cardiovascular Invasive Specialists. Home: 5281 Cherry Mill Ct Fairfield OH 45014-3251

TRUSCOTT, JUDITH FARREN, church education administrator; b. Parkersburg, W.Va., Mar. 20, 1939; d. Oran Bearl and Marjorie Elizabeth (Bergen) Farren; m. Frederick G. Truscott Jr., Aug. 25, 1961; children: Lisa Kay Truscott Wiggins, Tina Diane Truscott Strautman, Lynne Noelle. BA, Marietta Coll., 1961; MA, U. West Fla., 1981. Cert. Christian educator, 1989. Dir. Christian edn. Grace Presbyn. Ch., Lakewood, Ohio, 1973-76, elder, 1973—; dir. Christian edn. 1st Presbyn. Ch., Pensacola, Fla., 1977-83, John Knox Presbyn. Kirk, Kansas City, Mo., 1983-91, Westover Hills Presbyn. Ch., Little Rock, 1991—; moderator, mem. Ecumenical Ch. Resource Ctr., Kansas City, 1986-91; cert. educator, advisor Heartland Presbytery, Kansas City, 1989-91, edn. cons., 1984-91; mem. Christian edn. com. Presbytery of Cleve.; cert. educator, adv. Ark. Presbytery, 1992; mem., moderator, adv. coun. Presbytery Resource Ctr., 1993—. Mem., treas. Presbytery PTA, Lakewood, 1966-70; mem., sec. PTA, Lakewood, 1970-76; mem. Ch. Women United Speaker's Bur., Cleve., 1970-76; mem. PTO, Pensacola, 1976-83, Girls Volleyball, Basketball Boosters, Shawnee, Kans., 1989-91; elder Presbyn. Ch., 1973. Mem. Mid-Cen. Assn. Presbyn. Ch. Educators (cabinet 1990-91), Heartland Presbyn. Assn. Christian Educators (steering com. 1984-88, cert. advocate 1989-91, Heartland Presbytery cert. educator advisor), Assn. Presbyn. Ch. Educators, Chi Omega Alumni Assn. Republican. Office: Westover Hills Presbyn Ch Little Rock AR 72207

TRUSKOSKI, ELAINE BARBARA, executive secretary; b. Torrington, Conn., July 19, 1947; d. Edward John and Wanda Mary (Tokarz) Drenzyk; m. Mark Lucian Truskoski, June 6, 1970; children: Ryan Thomas, Jason Todd. Student, Cambridge Sch. Bus./Broadcast, Boston. Prodn. asst. ESPN, Bristol, Conn., 1981, exec. sec., 1982-87, 1993—. Active Coalition to Stop Gun Violence, Washington, 1992. Named to 20 Great Am. Women, McCall's Mag., 1993. Mem. Conn. NOW (Alice-Paul award 1992), Nat. NOW. Roman Catholic. Home: 205 Wildcat Hill Rd Harwinton CT 06791 Office: ESPN 935 Middle St Bristol CT 06010

TRUTA, MARIANNE PATRICIA, oral and maxillofacial surgeon, educator, author; b. N.Y.C., Apr. 28, 1951; d. John J. and Helen Patricia (Donnelly) T.; m. William Christopher Donlon, May 28, 1983; 1 child Sean Liam Riobard Donlon. BS, St. John's U., 1974; DMD, SUNY, Stonybrook, 1977. Intern The Mt. Sinai Med. Ctr., N.Y.C., 1977-78, resident, 1978-80, chief resident, 1980-81; asst. prof. U. of the Pacific, San Francisco, 1983-85, clin. asst. prof., 1985—; asst. dir. Facial Pain Rsch. Ctr., San Francisco, 1986-92; pvt. practice oral and maxillofacial surgery Peninsula Maxillofacial Surgery, South San Francisco, Calif., 1985—, Burlingame, Calif., 1988—, Menlo Park & Redwood City, Calif., 1990—. Contbr. articles to profl. jours., chpts. to textbooks. Mem. Am. Assn. Oral Maxillofacial Surgeons, Am. Dental Soc. Anesthesiology, Am. Soc. Cosmetic Surgery, Am. Assn. Women Dentists, Western Soc. Oral Maxillofacial Surgeons, No. Calif. Soc. Oral Maxillofacial Surgeons, San Mateo County Dental Soc. (bd. dirs 1995). Office: Peninsula Maxillofacial Surgery 1860 El Camino Real Ste 300 Burlingame CA 94010-3114

TRYBAN, ESTHER ELIZABETH, lawyer; b. Chgo., Aug. 14, 1958; d. Chester Joseph and Lottie Elizabeth (Napora) T. AAS with high honors, Elgin (Ill.) Community Coll., 1977, AS with high honors, 1982; BS with honors, Roosevelt U., Chgo., 1986; JD, U. Chgo., 1989. Bar: Ill. 1989, U.S. Dist. Ct. (no. dist.) Ill. 1989, U.S. Ct. Appeals (7th cir.) 1990. Supr. adminstrv. svcs. law dept. Motorola, Inc., Schaumburg, Ill., 1977-86; staff law clk. U.S. Bankruptcy Ct., No. Dist. Ill., Chgo., 1989-90; asst. corp. counsel City of Chgo., 1990—. Mem. ABA, Nat. Lawyers Guild (mem. exec. bd. 1990—), Assn. Former Bankruptcy Law Clerks, Ill. State Bar Assn., Chgo. Bar Assn. Roman Catholic. Office: City Chgo Dept Law 121 N La Salle St Ste 610 Chicago IL 60602-2503

TRYGESTAD, JOANN CAROL, secondary education educator; b. Mpls., Feb. 11, 1950; d. Harvey Oscar and Frances Anne (Libera) T. BS, U. Minn., 1972, MEd, 1983. Cert. tchr. social studies, history, English, Minn. Tchr. Sch. Dist. 742, St. Cloud, Minn., 1973-77, Sch. Dist. 196, Rosemount, Minn., 1977—; grad. asst. U. Minn., Mpls., 1988-90; adj. instr. Hamline U., St. Paul, 1987-90; steering com. mem. Alliance for Geography, St. Paul, 1988—; cons. in field. Contbr. articles to profl. jours. Mem. Nat. Coun. for Social Studies, Nat. Coun. for Geog. Edn., Am. Ednl. Rsch. Assn. Home: 4133 Arbor Ln Eagan MN 55122-2869 Office: Rosemount Sch Dist 14445 Diamond Path Rosemount MN 55060

TRZETRZELEWSKA, BASIA See BASIA

TSAI, MAVIS, clinical psychologist; b. Kowloon, Hong Kong, Sept. 30, 1954; came to U.S. 1966; d. Edwin Fang-Chin and Emily (Tseng) Tsai; m. Robert Joseph Kohlenberg, June 22, 1980; 1 child, Jeremy Tsai Kohlenberg. BA magna cum laude, UCLA, 1976; PhD, U. Wash., 1982. Undergrad. teaching asst. UCLA, 1975-76; teaching asst., predoctoral instr. U. Wash., Seattle, 1977-79; predoctoral lectr., psychology fellow Langley Parker Psychiat. Inst., San Francisco, 1980-81; predoctoral lectr. U. Wash., Seattle, 1981-82, ext. lectr., 1982-88; clin. psychologist in pvt. practice Seattle, 1982—; clin. supr. grad. students U. Wash., Seattle, 1989—. Co-author: Functional Analytic Psychotherapy, 1991; contbr. articles to profl. jours. Bd. dirs. Asian Counseling and Referral Svc., Seattle, 1984-85, Gifted Women's Conf., U. Wash., 1986-87. Calif. State scholar, 1972-76; recipient APA Minority fellowship, 1977-82, Danforth fellowship honorable mention, 1977. Mem. APA, Wash. Psychol. Assn., Asian Am. Psychol. Assn., Phi Beta Kappa. Office: 3245 Fairview Ave E Ste 303 Seattle WA 98102-3053

TSAMIS, DONNA ROBIN, lawyer; b. Yonkers, N.Y., Sept. 26, 1957; d. Donald Charles and Lenore Angela (Boccia) Lanza; m. Vasili Tsamis, June 18, 1983; children: Niki Alexandra, Victoria Angela. BA summa cum laude, Fordham U., 1979, JD, 1982. Bar: N.Y. 1983, U.S. Dist. Ct. (so. and ea. dist.) N.Y., U.S. Supreme Ct. 1993. Assoc. Jackson, Lewis, Schnitzler & Krupman, N.Y.C., 1982-86, White Plains, N.Y., 1986-89; ptnr. Jackson, Lewis, Schnitzler & Krupman, 1990—. Vice chmn. ann. luncheon com. Girl Scouts U.S.A., Westchester, 1989-92. Mem. Westchester Women's Bar Assn. (chmn. Forum on Alternative Work Schedules for Atty. 1989, bd. dirs. 1990, 92, chmn. lawyering parenting com. 1989-91), Westchester Assn. Women Bus. Owners, Columbian Lawyers Assn. (bd. dirs. 1990-94). Office: Jackson Lewis Schnitzler & Krupman 1 N Broadway # 1502 White Plains NY 10601-2310

TSCHETTER, PATRICIA LINN BARRETT, investor, oil producer; b. Denver, May 9, 1960; d. Arthur Eames Wright Barrett and Patricia Ruth Pickens; m. Robert Alan Tschetter, Jan. 9, 1988. BBA, BA, So. Meth. U., 1982; MBA, U. Dallas, 1984; MS, Tex. Woman's U., 1993. Investor, ind. oil prodr. Houston and Dallas, 1981—; interpreter Automatic Radius Mgmt., Dallas, 1984; exec. asst. Pickens Energy Corp., Dallas, 1984-87; artist, designer Moroch & Assocs., Dallas, 1988; staff therapist Galaxy Ctr., Garland, Tex., 1991-93; pres. Krazy Karrot, Inc., Dallas, 1993—, Tschetter Properties, Ltd., 1993—; student therapist Marriage and Family Clinic, Tex. Woman's U., Denton, 1990; student intern Galaxy Ctr., Garland, 1990-91. Author: Comparative Analysis of Marital Satisfaction Between Alcoholic and Nonalcoholic Couples, 1993, (design) Theta Kat, 1982. Ct. advocate The Family Place, Dallas, 1988-91. Mem. Nat. Soc. Magna Charta Dames, Nat. Soc. Daughters of the Am. Revolution, 1993—, Soc. of Colonial Dames of XVII Century, Metroplex Early Birds, Classic Thunderbird Club Internat., Sigma Iota Epsilon, Sigma Delta Pi (v.p. 1980), Delta Sigma Pi.

TSCHINKEL, SHEILA LERNER, banker, economist; b. N.Y.C., Nov. 21, 1940; d. Abraham and Mira (Nevelova) Lerner. BA, Hunter Coll., 1961; MA, Yale U., 1963, postgrad., 1967-68; grad. advanced mgmt. program, Harvard Bus. Sch., 1988. Asst. prof. U. Alaska, Fairbanks, 1963-65, U. Conn., Storrs, 1967-68; instr. Yale U., New Haven, 1968-69; asst. v.p. Fed. Res. Bank, N.Y.C., 1970-79; v.p., dir. global asset mgmt. Chase Manhattan Bank, N.Y.C., 1979-81; exec. v.p. MPH Commodities Corp., N.Y.C., 1982-83; sr. v.p., dir. research Fed. Res. Bank Atlanta, 1984—. Active Com. on Future of the South, 1986, 92; trustee Literacy Action, Inc.; bd. dirs. Atlanta Symphony Orch., also treas.; mem. exec. bd. Boy Scouts Am. Yale U. fellow, 1961-63; Ossabaw Island Project fellow, Ga., 1977. Mem. Am. Econ. Assn., So. Econ. Assn., So. Fin. Assn., Money Marketeers N.Y. (bd. govs. 1979-82), Internat. Women's Forum, Rotary, Phi Beta Kappa. Office: Fed Res Bank of Atlanta 104 Marietta St NW Atlanta GA 30303-2706

TSCHUMY, FREDA COFFING, artist, educator; b. Danville, Ill., Mar. 18, 1939; d. Frederick Winfield and Minnie Isabelle (Buck) Coffing; m. William Edward Tschumy, Jr., June 17, 1967; 1 child, William Coffing. BA, Vassar Coll., 1961; postgrad., Art Students' League N.Y., 1961-63, Accademia di Belli Arti, Rome, 1963; MFA, U. Miami, 1990. Instr. art Miami (Fla.) Fine Arts Conservatory, 1968; instr. ceramics Grove House, Coconut Grove, Fla., summer 1970; instr. sculpture Upstairs Gallery, Miami Beach, 1971, Continuum Gallery, Miami Beach, 1972-73; instr. painting Barry Coll., Miami, fall 1974; instr. sculpture Met. Mus. Sch., Coral Gables, Fla., 1980-89, Bass Mus. Sch., Miami Beach, 1989-92; teaching asst. U. Miami, Coral Gables, 1988-90, lectr. sculpture, 1991—; lectr. sculpture U. Miami; pres. founding mem. Continuum Gallery, Miami Beach, 1971-75, treas. 1975-83; treas. The Gallery at Mayfair, Coconut Grove, 1982-83, pres., 1983-84; artist in residence Hawaii Sch. for Girls, Honolulu, 1987; founding dir. Foundry Guild, U. Miami, Coral Gables, 1993—. Prin. works include sculptures at Dade Metrorail Univ. Sta., Melbourne (Fla.) Libr.; traveling exhbn. various colls., Miami. Mem. Tropical Audubon Soc., Miami, 1975—, Fla. Conservation Found., 1978—, Fla. Pub. Interest Rsch. Group, 1986—, Fla. Abortion Rights Action League, 1985—. Recipient Excellence award, Sculptors Fla. 1972, Fine Art Achievement award Binney & Smith, 1990; grantee Posey Found., 1989. Mem. Am. Foundryman's Soc., Womens Caucus Art (1st v.p. local chpt. 1981-86, bd. dirs. 1980-91, nat. bd. dirs. 1982-85), Internat. Sculpture Ctr. Studio: 3610 Bayview Rd Miami FL 33133-6503

TSENG, JOAN LIU, librarian; b. Chengtu, China, Jan. 5, 1939; came to U.S., 1963, naturalized, 1973; d. Yi-chiang and Chin-feen (Chou) Liu; m. Gan-tai Tseng, Sept. 5, 1965; children—Carol, Michelle. B.A., Nat. Taiwan U., Taipei, 1961; M.L.S., Tex. Woman's U., 1965. Children's libr. San Mateo County (Calif.) Libr., 1965-66; periodical libr. Loyola Maymount U., L.A., 1966-70, cataloging libr., 1977-80; catalog libr. Palos Verdes (Calif.) Libr. Dist., 1980-84, asst. supr. tech. svcs., 1984-86, supr. cataloging svcs., 1986-87; libr.The Charles C. Lauritsen Libr., The Aerospace Corp., L.A.,

1987-88 reference libr., 1988-89, lit. rsch. analyst, 1989—. Vol., Maurice Hawks Sch., Princeton Junction, N.J., 1975-77, Montemalaga Elem. Sch., Palos Verdes Estates, Calif., 1977. Scholar Nat. Taiwan U., 1957-61. Mem. ALA, Calif. Libr. Assn. (councilor 1983-85), Chinese-Am. Librs. Assn.Librs. Assn. Office: Charles Lauritsen Library Aerospace Corp Mail Sta M/199 PO Box 92957 Los Angeles CA 90009-2957

TSIRANTONAKIS, MARGARET, artist, curator; b. Chania, Crete, Greece, Mar. 9, 1958; came to U.S., 1959; d. Thomas and Katina (Philipakis) T.; m. Hugh McBirney Bareiss, June 16, 1990; children: Tassos Conrad, Molly Katina. BFA, Parsons Sch. Design, N.Y.C., 1980. Arts adminstr., curator N.Y.C. Dept. Parks and Recreation, 1983-91; guest curator Sch. Visual Arts, N.Y.C., 1986; curator Noah's Art, N.Y.C., 1989. One-woman show Philip Bareiss Contemporary Exhbns., TAos, N.Mex., 1992, Burnham Libr., Bridgewater, Conn., 1994—; exhibited in group shows Studio K Gallery, Long Island City, N.Y., 1987, Stamford (Conn.) Hist. Soc., 1991, Stamford Mus., 1992, Mayor's Gallery, Stamford, 1993, NYU Washington Square East Galleries, N.Y.C., 1993; represented in numerous pvt. collections throughout the U.S. and Europe. Recipient Winsor and Newton award Stamford Art Assn., 1991. Mem. Stamford Loft Artists Assn.

TSUI, ELLEN CHUN-KWOK, psychologist; b. Hong Kong, 1957; d. S. and Y. Tsui. BS, Chinese U. of Hong Kong, 1979; MS in Edn., U. Wis., 1983; PhD, NYU, 1989. Applied behaviour psychologist Assn. of Children with Retarded Mental Devel., Bklyn., 1989; staff psychologist Maimonides Med. Ctr., Bklyn., 1990-92, Luth. Med. Ctr., Bklyn., 1992—; cons. psychologist Bd. Edn. of City of N.Y., 1992—. Mem. Am. Psychologist Assn., Assn. Advancement of Behavioral Therapy, Assn. for Play Therapy.

TSUI, SOO HING, research consultant; b. Hong Kong, Aug. 2, 1959; came to U.S., 1985; d. Sik Tin and Yuk Kam (Cheung) T. BSW cum laude, Nat. Taiwan U., 1983; MSW cum laude, Columbua U., 1987, PhD, 1992. Cert. social worker, N.Y. Dir. community handicapped ctr., Taipei, Taiwan, 1983-85, youth recreational program, N.Y., 1986; social work dept. supr. St. Margaret's House, N.Y.C., 1987-89; chief bilingual sch. social work N.Y.C. Bd. Edn., 1990-93, rsch. cons., 1993—; chief rsch. cons. N.Y.C. Dept. Transp., 1993—. Union social work regional rep. N.Y.C. Bd. Edn., 1990—, citywide bilingual social work rep., 1991-93, citywide social work budget allocation comms. rep., 1992—; mem. planning com. social work bd. Asian Am. Comms., N.Y.C., 1991—; mem. conf. planning com. bd. Ambassador For Christ, Boston, 1991-93; coord. doctoral colloquial com. bd. Scholarship Coun. Social Work Edn., Columbia U., N.Y.C., 1992-94, mem. nat. minority awards, 1992—. Nat. Rsch. fellow Sch. Coun. Social Work Edn., Columbia U.; Nat. Acad. scholar, 1988-87; recipient Nat. Acad. award 1979-83. Mem. Nat. Assn. Asian/ Am. Edn. (bilingual social worker). Home: 507 W 113th St Apt 22 New York NY 10025

TSUNG, CHRISTINE CHAI-YI, chief financial officer, treasuruer; b. Nanking, China, Mar. 23, 1948; came to U.S., 1970; d. Chi-Huang Tsung and Siao-Tuan Huang; m. Icheng Wu, Aug. 14, 1971 (div. Dec. 1989); m. Jerome Chen, Aug. 10, 1990; children: Jonathan, Julia. BBA, Nat. Taiwan U., Taipei, 1970; postgrad., Washington U., St. Louis, 1970-71; MBA, U. Mo., 1973. Acct. Capital Land Co., St. Louis, 1972-74; chief acct. Servis Equipment Co., Inc., Dallas, 1974-75; acctg. supr. Calif. Microwave, Sunnyale, 1975-76; budget and sales mgr. Columbia Pictures TV Internat., Burbank, Calif., 1976-77; acctg. mgr. Husquarna, San Diego, 1977-82; sr. acct. City of Poway, Calif., 1982-88, fin. mgr., 1988—; pres., treas. Jade Poly Investment, San Diego, 1989—; cons. assoc. Metro Properties, San Diego, 1989—. Tchr. San Diego North County Chinese Sch., 1985-86; v.p. San Diego Chinese Culture Assn., 1982-86, bd. dirs., 1988-90, 93-94. Mem. Govt. Fin. Officers Assn. (Cert. of Achievement 1988-94), Calif. Soc. Mcpl. Fin. Officers (standing com. membership devel., Cert. of Award 1988-94), Mcpl. Treas. Assn. U.S. and Can., Taiwanese C. of C. of N.Am. (bd. dirs. 1994-95). Home: 18766 Aceituno St San Diego CA 92128-1564 Office: City of Poway 13325 Civic Center Dr Poway CA 92064-5755

TU, SUSAN, retired librarian; b. Taipei, Taiwan, Republic of China, June 10, 1923; arrived in U.S., 1961, naturalized, 1976; d. Tsungming Tu and Sonsui Lin; children: Helene Lin, Andy Lin, Jean Lin, Charlyn Lin. Student, Surugadai Girl's Jr. Coll., Tokyo, 1942, Taihoku Imperial U., Taiwan, 1944, U. Calif., Berkeley, 1961; BA, Utah State U., 1965; MA, U. Utah, 1971; MSLS, La. State U., 1973, cert. of med. librarianship, 1975, MEd, 1977, postgrad., 1976-77. Tchr. Taipei (Taiwan) Mcpl. Girls' High Sch., 1958-61; chief libr. Saints Coll., Lexington, Miss., 1974-76; hosp. libr. U.S. Army, Ft. Polk, La., 1977-79; dist. libr. Rock Island (Ill.) dist. U.S. Army Corps Engrs., 1979-83; div. libr. North Atlantic div. U.S. Army Corps Engrs., N.Y.C., 1984-88; dist. libr. N.Y. Dist., N.Y.C., 1988-90. Co-producer various videos, slide prodns., TV program. Mem. Spl. Librs. Assn., Chinese-Am. Librs. Assn., Photographic Soc. Am.

TUAN, DEBBIE FU-TAI, chemistry educator; b. Kiangsu, China, Feb. 2, 1930; came to U.S., 1958; d. Shiau-gien and Chen (Lee) T.; m. John W. Reed, Aug. 15, 1987. BS in Chemistry, Nat. Taiwan U., Taipei, 1954, MS in Chemistry, 1958; MS in Chemistry, Yale U., 1960, PhD in Chemistry, 1961. Rsch. fellow Yale U., New Haven, 1961-64; rsch. assoc. U. Wis., Madison, 1964-65; asst. prof. Kent (Ohio) State U., 1965-70, assoc. prof., 1970-73, prof., 1973—; rsch. fellow Harvard U., Cambridge, 1969-70; vis. scientist SRI Internat., Menlo Park, Calif., 1981; rsch. assoc. Cornell U., Ithica, N.Y., 1983; vis. prof. Yeshiva U., N.Y.C., 1966, Academia Sinica of China, Nat. Taiwan U. and Nat. Tsing-Hwa U., summer 1967, Ohio State U., 1993, 95. Contbr. articles to profl. jours. Recipient NSF Career Advanced award, 1994—; U. Grad. fellow Nat. Taiwan U., 1955-58, F.W. Heyl-Anon F fellow Yale U., 1960-61, U. Faculty Rsch. fellow Kent State U., 1966, 68, 71, 85; Pres. Chiang's scholar Chinese Women Assn., 1954, 58, Grad. scholar in humanity and scis. China Found., 1955. Mem. Am. Chem. Soc., Am. Phys. Soc., Sigma Xi. Office: Kent State U Chemistry Dept Williams Hall Kent OH 44242

TUBBS, JOAN ROSE, accountant; b. Brownwood, Tex., May 25, 1943; d. Carl Russell and Alva Mae (Rose) Stanley; m. Thomas Milton Cole, June 1, 1963 (div. Feb. 1965); 1 child, Stanley Milton; m. James Arthur Tubbs, Mar. 22, 1979. Student, Howard Payne U., 1974-82, BBA cum laude, 1992; student, U. Tex. Permian Basin, Odessa, 1985-92. CPA. Sec., bookkeeper J.W. Fisher, P.A., Brownwood, 1962-68; cashier, bookkeeper Weakley-Watson Hardware, Brownwood, 1968-76; acct.'s asst. Leanco Corp., Brownwood, 1976-81; accounts payable clk. FMC Corp., Brownwood, 1981-82; chief acct. asst. Williamson Petroleum, Midland, Tex., 1982-84; full-charge bookkeeper Baytech, Inc., Midland, 1984-86; staff acct. EnClean, Inc., Odessa, 1986-93; controller Permian Petroleum Corp., Midland, Tex., 1994—. Scholar Petroleum Accts. Soc., 1990. Mem. U. Tex. Permian Basin Acctg. ASsn., Am. Bus. Women's Assn. (pres. 1982, Bluebonnet award 1981). Home: 6747 N Dixie Blvd Odessa TX 79763 Office: Permian Petroleum Corp 125 N Ft Worth Midland TX 79702

TUCCERI, CLIVE KNOWLES, science writer and educator, educational consultant; b. Bryn Mawr, Pa., Apr. 20, 1953; d. William Henry and Clive Ellis (Knowles) Hulick; m. Eugene Angelo Tucceri, Sept. 1, 1984 (div. Nov. 1991); 1 child, Clive Edna. BA in Geology, Williams Coll., 1975; MS in Coastal Geology, Boston Coll., 1982. Head sci. dept. Stuart Hall Sch., Staunton, Va., 1975-77; mem. sci. faculty William Penn Charter Sch., Phila., 1977-79, Tower Sch., Marblehead, Mass., 1982-86, Bentley Coll., Waltham, Mass., 1986-88; adminstrv. dir., co-founder Stout Aquatic Libr. Nat. Marine and Aquatic Edn. Resource Ctr., Wakefield, R.I., 1982-89; mem. sci. faculty Mabelle B. Avery Sch., Somers, Conn., 1989-90; mem. faculty, head sci. dept. MacDuffie Sch., Springfield, Mass., 1992-93; mem. sci. faculty East Hampton (Conn.) Middle Sch., 1993—; cons. Longmeadow (Mass.) Pub. Schs., 1989-94, Addison-Wesley Pub. Co., Menlo Prk, Calif., 1986—; cons., freelance writer Prentice-Hall Inc., Needham, Mass., 1991. Bd. dirs. People against Rape, Staunton, 1976-77. Mem. AAUW (bd. dirs., br. pres.-elect 1975-77, v.p. 1985-86, sec. 1986-87), NSTA, Nat. Marine Edn. Assn. (sec. 1986-87, chpt. rep. 1987—), Mass. Marine Educators (pres. 1987-89, bd. dirs. 1983—, editor Flotsem and Jetsem newsletter 1991—), Cousteau Soc., Oceanic Soc., Woods Hole Oceanographic Found., Mass. Environ. Edn. Soc. (bd. dirs. 1985-88), Sigma Xi. Episcopalian. Home: 12 Birchwood Dr East Hampton CT 06424-1312

TUCCERI, ELLEN LEE, retail executive; b. Boston, Feb. 7, 1945; d. Martin and Natalie (Green) Weiner; m. Anthony Tucceri, June 17, 1988 (dec. Mar. 1993). Student Boston U. Sch. Edn., 1967-68; B.S. in Bus. Edn., U. Mich., 1969; postgrad. in edn. NYU, 1973-74; M.B.A. in Mktg., Fordham U., 1983. Circulation mgr. McGraw Hill Publs. Co., N.Y.C., 1973-76, mgr. distbn. research McGraw Hill Info. Systems Co., 1976-80, distbn. mgr., 1980-85, mgr. market adminstrn., 1985-87, dir. mkt. adminstrn., 1987-88; owner, operator The Golden Pearl, Ogunquit, Maine, 1989—. Cons. Arts and Bus. Council, N.Y.C., 1979-80, 84-88. Bd. dirs. Fairmont Tenant's Corp., 1986-88, Dunelawn Condominium Assn., 1990—, pres. 1994—; mem. bd. selectman Town of Ogunquit, 1990—, chmn. bd. selectman, 1991; chmn. budget com. Town of Ogunquit, 1989. Mem. Ogunquit Women's Club (v.p. 1991-92).

TUCCI, JANIS A(NN), infection control practitioner; b. Columbus, Ohio, Nov. 20, 1947; d. John Anthony and Mildred Frances (Frazier) Tucci; m. William Allen Law, May 18, 1974 (div.); 1 child, Jennifer Erin. Diploma, Mt. Carmel Sch. Nursing, 1968; student, Ohio State U., Columbus, 1969-72, 80; MA in Health Care Adminstrn., Norwich U., 1993. RN, Ohio, Fla.; cert. infection control. Asst. clin. instr. Mt. Carmel Sch. Nursing, Columbus, 1969-70; staff educator Mt. Carmel Med. Ctr., Columbus, 1974-75; head nurse orthopedics unit Ohio State U. Hosps., Columbus, 1977-79; evening asst. clin. mgr. Humana Women's Hosp., Tampa, Fla., 1986-90; head nurse med. unit Centurion Hosp. Carrollwood, Tampa, 1990-92; dir. epidemiology, pers. health and nursing edn. Centurion Hosp. Carrollwood, 1992-93; infection control practitioner Univ. Community Hosp.-Carrollwood, Tampa, Fla., 1993—. Mem. Am. Assn. Profls. in Infection Control (cert.), Fla. Profls. in Infection Control, Tampa Bay Profls. in Infection Control. Home: 9331 Pontiac Dr Tampa FL 33626-2955

TUCK, AMY, state senator, lawyer; b. Starkville, Miss., July 8, 1963; d. Grady William and Mary (Boykin) Tuck. BA in Polit. Sci., Miss. State U., Starkville, 1985; postgrad., Miss. State U., Miss. State U., Starkville, 1992—; JD, Miss. Coll., 1989. Legal asst. Ben. F. Hilburn Jr., Atty. at Law, Starkville, Miss., 1984-85; grad. asst. dept. polit. sci. Miss. State U., Starkville, 1986-87; law clk. Minor Buchanan, Jackson, Miss., 1987-88, Deposit Guaranty Nat. Bank, Jackson, 1988-89; state senator dist. 15 State of Miss., Jackson, 1990—; adj. prof. Wood Jr. Coll., Mathiston, Miss., 1990—. Mem. Oktibbeha County Voter Re-Registration Com., Oktibbeha County Fedn. Dem. Women; bd. dirs. Oktibbeha County Am. Cancer Soc., 1991-92; mem. local rels. com. Children and Family Svcs.; assoc. mem. Nat. Mus. Women in the Arts, 1992-93. Mem. NAFE, Am. Legis. Exch. Com., Am. Soc. Pub. Adminstrs., Nat. Conf. State Legislature, Nat. Order Women Legislators, Miss. State U. Alumni Assn., Starkville Area Bus. and Profl. Women's Club, Oktibbeha County C. of C., Gamma Beta Phi, Pi Sigma Alpha, Omicron Delta Kappa, Phi Delta Phi (vice-magister 1988, historian 1988-89). Methodist. Home: 2004 Pinoak Dr Starkville MS 39759-3534 Office: Miss State Senate New Capitol Jackson MS 39205*

TUCK, DOLETTA SUE, lawyer, exempt organization specialist; b. Hugo, Okla., June 18, 1966; d. Benny Doyle and Tommie Marie (Cousins) T. AS, Murray State Coll., Tishomingo, Okla., 1986; BS magna cum laude, S.E. Okla. State U., 1988; JD with highest honors, U. Okla., 1991. Bar: Okla. 1991, U.S. Dist. Ct. (we., ea., and no. dists.), U.S. Ct. Appeals (10th cir.). Summer assoc. Andrews Davis, Oklahoma City, 1989-90; instr. in legal rsch, writing and oral advocacy U. Okla., Norman, 1989-91; assoc. Crowe & Dunlevy, Oklahoma City, 1991-93, Tulsa, Okla., 1993-94; pvt. practice Antlers, Okla., 1994; exempt orgn. specialist IRS, Oklahoma City, Okla., 1994—. Contbg. author, editor: Oklahoma Environmental Law Practitioner's Handbook, 1992. Firm com. mem., participant Harvest Food Dr., Oklahoma City, 1991; chairperson Okla. Young Lawyers Rape Victims Assistance Com., 1992-94; bd. dirs. Okla. County Young Lawyers Divsn., 1993; participant, vol. Legal Aide of Western Okla., 1991. Named Miss Murray State Coll., Student Senate Pres., Tishomingo, Okla., 1986-86, Order of Coif U. Okla., Norman, Okla., 1991, Okla. Law Review U. Okla., Norman, 1991. Mem. Okla. Bar Assn. (bd. dirs. young lawyers divsn. 1994—, mock trial com. 1994-95, liaison mental health com. 1994-95), Okla. County Bar Assn., Tulsa County Bar Assn., Am. Agrl. Law Assn., Phi Delta Phi, Phi Kappa Phi. Democrat. Baptist. Home: 850 Brookwood Dr #105 Oklahoma City OK 73139 Office: IRS MC 4900 OKC 55 N Robinson Oklahoma City OK 73101

TUCK, JUDITH MCVAUGH, family therapist; b. Wilmington, Del., Aug. 8, 1945; d. John Burgess and Roberta Elizabeth (MacMillan) McVaugh; m. Robert Wayne Bramble, July 21, 1968 (div. Jan. 1980); m.l Howard Kline Tuck, May 12, 1983; 1 child, Alyson Darlene. BS, U. Del., 1967; MA, W.Va. Coll. Grad. Studies, Institute, 1985. Cert. social worker; lic. profl. counselor, W.Va. Formerly family therapist Family Svcs. Netowrk, Parkersburg, W.Va.; family therapist Abraxas of W.Va., Parkersburg, 1994—. V.p. Lioness Club, Oxford, Pa., 1978-80; advisor Kiwanis Internat., Wilmington, Del., 1981-82. Mem. ACA, W.Va. Counseling Assn., W.Va. Mental Health, Counselors Assn. Republican. Presbyterian. Home: 2902 Avery St Parkersburg WV 26104-2426 Office: Abraxas of WVa 1318 12th St Parkersburg WV 26101

TUCK, MARY BETH, nutritionist, educator; b. Point, Tex., Dec. 9, 1930; d. Basil Barney and Daisy (Morris) Rabb; divorced; 1 child, William Kenneth. BS, East Tex. State U., 1952, MEd, 1966; PhD, Tex. Woman's U., 1970. Lic. dietitian, Tex. Tchr. Longview (Tex.) Pub. Schs., 1952-64; instr. nutrition Stephen F. Austin U., Nacogdoches, Tex., 1966-69; assoc. prof. East Tex. State U., Commerce, Tex., 1970—; cons. Women, Infants and Children Program, Hunt County, Tex., 1989, East Tex. State U. Wellness Program, Commerce, 1989—, Selvaggi Med. Clinic, Commerce, 1989—; nutrition del. People to People Citizen Amb. Program, USSR, 1990; lectr. in field. Reviewer, editor textbooks; contbr. articles to profl. jours. Bd. dirs. Commerce div. Am. Heart Assn., 1994—. Mem. Am. Dietetic Assn., Tex. Dietetic Assn., Afflatus Culture Club (pres. 1988-91), Louise Drake Garden Club (v.p. 1991-92, pres. 1992-94), Commerce Area Alumni Assn. (1st v.p. 1993-94), Delta Kappa (sec. 1988-92, 94—). Office: East Tex State U Dept Health And Edn Commerce TX 75429

TUCKER, ANNETTE LA VERNE, nursing home administrator; b. N.Y.C.; d. Roy L. and Gwendolyn (Cush) Tucker; 1 child, Aaron Nathaniel. Diploma in Nursing, Misericordia Sch. Nursing, 1976; BS in Health Care Adminstrn. with distinction, Iona Coll., 1984; M in Profl. Studies, New Sch. for Social Research, 1988; postgrad., LaSalle U., 1995—. Cert. long term care mgmt., 1988. Charge nurse Jacobi Hosp., 1976-77; charge nurse pediatrics Bronx (N.Y.) Mcpl. Hosp., 1977-78, asst. head nurse neonatal ICU, 1978-83, coord. utilization rev., 1983-84; charge nurse hematology Van Etten Hosp., Bronx, 1984-85; asst. dir. Salem Home Care, N.Y.C., 1985-87, dir., 1987-90. Fellow Hunter-Brookdale Coll. on Aging; mem. Am. Assn. Homes for the Aging (assoc.), Am. Coll. Health Care Adminstrs., Nat. Caucus and Ctr. on Black Aged.

TUCKER, BEVERLY SCALES, lawyer; b. Detroit, Mar. 24, 1949; m. Benjamin Fredrick Tucker, 1977 (div. 1981); 1 child, Azizi. BA, Wayne State U., 1971; JD, U. Calif., Berkeley, 1976. Bar: Calif. 1976, Mich., 1984, U.S. Supreme Ct. Atty. Found. Advancement of Minority Enterprise, Oakland, Calif., 1976-78, Bay Area Rapid Transit Dist., Oakland, 1978-79; staff atty. Calif. Dept. Fair Employment Housing, San Francisco, 1979-83; asst. gen. counsel United Auto Workers, Detroit, 1983-86; dep. atty. gen. Calif. Dept. Justice, San Francisco, 1986-88; chief counsel, assoc. exec. dir. Calif. Tchrs. Assn., Burlingame, 1988—. Bd. dirs. Legal Aid Soc. San Francisco, 1988-93, ACLU, 1988-93. Mem. Charles Houston Bar Assn., Calif. Women Lawyers Assn. (bd. dirs. 1987-88). Democrat. Home: 4080 Sequoyah Rd Oakland CA 94605 Office: Calif Tchr Assn 1705 Murchison Dr Burlingame CA 94010

TUCKER, BEVERLY SOWERS, information specialist; b. Trenton, N.J., Dec. 1, 1936; d. Eldon Jones and Verbeda Eleanor (Roberts) Sowers; m. Harvey Richard Tucker, Dec. 27, 1958 (div. Nov. 1983); children: Randall Richard, Brian Alan. BS in Chemistry with distinction, Purdue U., 1958; MS in Geology, No. Ill. U., 1985; MA in Library and Info. Sci., Rosary Coll., 1989. Asst. rsch. librarian CPC Internat., Argo, Ill., 1958-62; chem. patent searcher Chgo., 1962-66; info. specialist C. Berger & Co., Wheaton, Ill., 1986, Amoco Corp., Naperville, Ill., 1987—; faculty Coll. Du Page, Glen Ellyn, Ill., 1989—. Mem. Spl. Libraries Assn., Ill. Fedn. Women's Club (treas. 5th dist. 1979-81, Outstanding Jr. Clubwoman award 1979-80), Garden Club Council Wheaton (pres. 1981-82), Wheaton Jr. Woman's Club (pres. 1977-78, Single Parent scholar 1984), Gardens Etc. Club (pres. 1978-79), Alpha Lambda Delta, Delta Rho Kappa, Theta Sigma Phi, Alpha Chi Omega (grantee 1985). Republican. Presbyterian. Home: 1507 Paula Ave Wheaton IL 60187-6135 Office: Amoco Corp PO Box 3083 Warrenville Rd and Mill St Naperville IL 60566

TUCKER, FRANCES LAUGHRIDGE, civic worker; b. Anderson, S.C., Dec. 4, 1916; d. John Franklin and Sallie V. (Cowart) Laughridge; m. Russell Hatch Tucker, Aug. 30, 1946 (dec. Aug. 1977); children—Russell Hatch, Pamela Tucker (dec.). Student U. Conn., 1970, Sacred Heart U., Fairfield, Conn., 1977, 79, Fairfield U., 1978, U. S.C., 1984. Sec. to atty., Asheville, N.C., 1935-37; sec. to gen. mgr. Ga. Talc Mining & Mfg., Asheville, 1937-42; sec. engring. dept. E.I. duPont de Nemours, Wilmington, Del., 1942-46. Chmn. radio com. D.C. chpt. ARC, 1947-48, bd. dirs., chmn. pub. rels. Westport-Weston Ct. chpt., 1968-73, mem. adv. coun. ARC Ct. Divsn., 1973-80, chmn. pub. rels., Hilton Head Island, S.C., 1981-84, 89-92, chmn. pub. rels. bloodmobile, Hilton Head Island, 1984-89; bd. dirs., mem. pub. relations com. United Fund, Westport-Weston, Conn., 1968-69, bd. dirs. Beaufort County chpt., 1982-87, 89-92; mem. media communications St. Luke's Episcopal Ch., Hilton Head Island, 1980-94; with Hilton Head Hosp. Aux., 1984-89. Mem. Sea Pines Country Club. Home: 13 Willow Oak Rd Hilton Head Island SC 29928-5926

TUCKER, JANET PIKE, employment agency owner; b. Mercedes, Tex., Aug. 21, 1944; d. Herbert McDowell and Marjorie Evelyn (Hale) Pike; m. Edwin Hal Tucker, Sept. 28, 1966; children: Stephanie Anne, Gregory McDowell. BA, Trinity U., San Antonio, 1966. Cert. tchr., Tex., N.Mex. Tchr. San Antonio Ind. Sch. Dist., 1966, Weslaco (Tex.) Ind. Sch. Dist., 1968-69, Farmington (N.Mex.) Ind. Sch. Dist., 1978-82; exec. dir. San Juan United Way, Farmington, 1982-83; co-owner Horizons Travel, Farmington, 1983-84; owner, pres. Temporarily Yours, Inc., Farmington, 1984—. Bd. dirs., v.p. Four Corners Opera Assn., Farmington, 1978-82; bd. dirs., div. head San Juan United Way, Farmington, 1984-85; bd. dirs. San Juan Coll. Found., Farmington, 1985—; pres. Anasazi Pageant Found., Farmington, 1988—; bd. dirs. FIDS/San Juan Econ. Devel. Svcs., 1986—; mem. N.Mex. Pvt. Industry Coun., 1987-92; bd. dirs. Assn. of Commerce and Industry. Named Citizen of Yr. C. of C., 1990. Mem. N.Mex. Assn. Pers. Cons., Nat. Assn. Pers. Cons., Nat. Assn. Temp. Svcs., Assn. Commerce and Industry, Nat. Fedn. Ind. Bus., Rotary (bd. dirs. Farmington chpt. 1989—). Republican. Methodist. Office: Temporarily Yours Inc 111 N Behrend Ave Farmington NM 87401-8413

TUCKER, JO-VON, marketing executive; b. Dallas, Feb. 7, 1937; d. Worley Charles and Julia Allene (Mayo) Jones; m. George Richard Tucker, Mar. 1, 1958 (div. July 1977); 1 child, Tracy Lynn Tucker Rolsten. Student, Tex. U., 1955-58. Art asst. Bud Biggs Studio, Dallas, 1958-59; illustrator Ed Bearden Art Studio, Dallas, 1959-62; art dir. The Bloom Agy., Dallas, 1962-63, Glenn Advt., Dallas, 1963-66; pres. Unltd. Concepts, Dallas, 1966-73; v.p., creative dir. The Horchow Collection, Dallas, 1973-75; pres. JVT Direct Mktg., 1975—; owner/chmn. Clambake Celebrations, Orleans, Mass., 1990—; internat. cons. P.J. Carroll & Co., Dublin, Ireland, 1988-90; direct mktg. cons. Walt Disney Co., Anaheim, Calif., 1986-87, Neiman-Marcus, Dallas, 1965-71; trustee Direct Mktg. Ednl. Found., N.Y.C., 1986-93. Author, photographer: Perspectives, 1981; contbg. author: Successful Direct Marketing Methods, 1985, 87, 89, Ed Nash on Direct Marketing, 1987, 91; contbr. articles to profl. jours. Mem. Orleans Selectmen's Com. on Disabilities, 1992—; bd. dirs. Southeastern Mass. Am. Lung Assn.; founder, coord. for people with disease Cape Chronic Obstructive Pulmonary Disease (C.O.P.D.) Support Group. Named Advt. Woman of Yr., Women in Communications, Dallas, 1978, Direct Marketer of Yr., Direct Mktg. Assn. North Tex., 1985, Direct Mktg. Woman of Yr., Women's Direct Response Group, N.Y.C., 1988; recipient graphic awards nat. and internat. groups. Mem. Direct Mktg. Assn. (bd. mem. 1979-85, bd. sec., exec. com. 1984, Echo award 1973, 75, 80, 83, 85), Direct Mktg. Ednl. Found. (trustee 1986-93), Direct Mktg. Idea Exch. (bd. mem. 1980-90), Creative Guild. Republican. Office: Clambake Celebrations 6 West Rd at Skaket Corners Orleans MA 02653

TUCKER, KIM ELISABETH, secretary, graphic artist; b. Phila., Sept. 27, 1957; d. Frank Lemmon Tucker and Susan Idella (Black) Ford. AS, Harcum Jr. Coll., Bryn Mawr, Pa., 1978; student, Chestnut Hill Coll., 1994—. Data entry clk., market rsch. profl. Chilton Pub., Radnor, Pa., 1975-77; vet. tech. Wyncote Dog and Cat Hosp., Phila., 1977-86; clk., vet. technician Pa. Soc. Cruelty Animals, Phila., 1986-88; sec., graphic artist Chestnut Hill Coll., Phila., 1988—, cons., vol. African-Am. Awareness Soc., 1992—. Supporter, vol. Sisters of St. Joseph, Phila., 1988—; vol. Sta. WRTI-FM Radio, Phila., 1990—, Jazz 3 Scholarships for the Young, Phila., 1985-92; mem. Pa. Soc. for Prevention of Cruelty to Animals, 1986—; mem. People Interested in People to Feed the Needy, 1990—. Mem. Tri-State Jazz Soc., Phila. Clef Club, Psi Chi. Lutheran. Home: 13 W Upsal St Philadelphia PA 19119-2712

TUCKER, MARCIA, museum director, curator; b. N.Y.C., Apr. 11, 1940; d. Emanuel and Dorothy (Wald) Silverman; student Ecole du Louvre, Paris, 1959-60; BA, Conn. Coll., New London, 1961; MA, Inst. Fine Arts, N.Y. U., 1969; hon. doctorate San Francisco Art Inst. Curator, William N. Copley Collection, N.Y.C., 1963-66; editorial asso. Art News mag., N.Y.C., 1965-69; collection cataloger Alfred H. Barr, Jr., N.Y.C., 1966-67, catalog raisonée Howald Collection Am. Art, Ford Found., Columbus (Ohio) Gallery Fine Arts, 1966-69; curator painting and drawing Whitney Mus. Am. Art, N.Y.C., 1969-77; dir./founder The New Museum, N.Y.C., 1977—; faculty U. R.I., Kingston, 1966-68, City U. N.Y., 1967-68, Sch. Visual Arts, 1969-73, Columbia U. Sch. Arts and Scis., N.Y.C., 1977; guest lectr. San Francisco Art Inst., Yale U., Balt. Mus. Art, Art Inst. Chgo., Smithsonian Instn., Princeton U.; U.S. commr. 1984 Venice Biennale Mem. Coll. Art Assn., Am. Assn. Mus. (dir.), Phi Beta Kappa. Author: Anti-Illusion: Procedures/Materials, 1969; Catalogue of Ferdinand Howald Collection, 1969; Robert Morris, 1970; The Structure of Color, 1971; James Rosenquist, 1972; Bruce Nauman, 1973; Al Held, 1974; Richard Tuttle, 1975; Early Work by 5 Contemporary Artists, 1977; Bad Painting, 1978; Barry Le Va, 1979; John Baldessari, 1981; Not Just For Laughs: The Art of Subversion, 1981; Earl Staley: 1973-83, 1984; Paradise Lost/Paradise Regained catalog for Am. exhbn. at Venice Biennale, commr., 1984; Series editor: Art After Modernism: Rethinking Representation, 1984; Choices: Making An Art Out of Everyday Life, 1986, Pat Steir, Self Portrait: An Installation, 1987; Blasted Allegories: An Anthology of Writings by Contemporary Artists, 1987; Markus Raetz: In the Realm of the Possible, 1988; Out There: Marginalization & Contemporary Cultures, 1990; Discourse: Conversations In Postmodern Art & Culture, 1992; Bad Girls, 1994; catalog for Am. exhbn. at Venice Biennale; also articles. Office: New Mus Contemporary Art 583 Broadway New York NY 10012-3228

TUCKER, MAUREEN ANN, musician; b. Jackson Heights, N.Y., Aug. 26, 1944; d. James Thomas and Margaret Mary (Daly) T.; divorced; children: Kerry, Keith, Austen, Kate, Richard. Grad., Levittown (N.Y.) Meml. H.S., 1962. Drummer Velvet Underground, 1965-71; guitarist, songwriter, singer Moe Tucker Band, 1989—. Recordings include (singer, guitarist, songwriter) Playin Possum, 1981, Life in Exile After Abdication, 1986, (prodr., arranger) I Spent a Week There The Other Night, 1990, Dogs Under Stress, 1993; drummer Lou Reed Band, Japan, 1990, European tours with Velvet Underground, 1993, Moe Tucker Band, 1989—. Tchr. English St. Pauls Hispanic Ministry, Douglas, Ga., 1990—. Roman Catholic. Office: Maureen Tucker Music PO Box 2357 Douglas GA 31533

TUCKER, SHIRLEY LOIS COTTER, botany educator, researcher; b. St. Paul, Apr. 4, 1927; d. Ralph U. and Myra C. (Knutson) Cotter; m. Kenneth W. Tucker, Aug. 22, 1953. BA, U. Minn., 1949, MS, 1951; PhD, U. Calif., Davis, 1956. Asst. prof. botany La. State U., Baton Rouge, 1967-71, assoc. prof., 1971-76, prof., 1976-82, Boyd prof., 1982—. Co-editor: Aspects of Floral Development, 1988, Advances in Legume Systematics, Vol. 6, 1994; Contbr. more than 90 articles on plant devel. to profl. jours. Fellow Linnean Soc., London, 1975—; Fulbright fellow Eng., 1952-53. Mem. Bot. Soc. Am. (v.p. 1979, program chmn. 1975-78, pres.-elect 1986-87, pres. 1987-88, Merit award 1989), Am. Bryological and Lichenological Soc., Brit. Lichenological Soc., Am. Inst. Biol. Scis., Am. Soc. Plant Taxonomists (pres.-elect 1995, pres. 1995), Phi Beta Kappa, Sigma Xi. Home: 1022 Baird Dr Baton Rouge LA 70808-5922 Office: La State U Dept Botany Baton Rouge LA 70803

TUCKER, TANYA DENISE, singer; b. Seminole, Tex., Oct. 10, 1958; d. Boe and Juanita Tucker; 2 children, Presley, Beau. Regular on Lew King Show; rec. artist formerly with Columbia Records, MCA Records, Capitol Records; albums include Tear Me Apart, Changes, Delta Dawn, Dreamlovers, Here's Some Love, TNT, Girls Like Me, Greatest Hits, 1989, Greatest Hits (1972-1975), Greatest Hits Encore, 1990, Greatest Country Hits, 1991, Greatest Hits 1990-92, 1993, Love Me Like You Use To, 1987, Strong Enough to Bend, 1988, Tanya Tucker Live, Tennessee Woman, 1990, What Do I Do With Me, 1991, (with Delbert McClinton) Can't Run From Yourself, 1992, Soon, 1993; TV appearances include A Country Christmas, 1979, The Georgia Peaches, 1980; actress: (mini-series) The Rebels, 1979, (film) Jeremiah Johnson, 1968. Recipient: Country Music Assn. award, 1991, female vocalist of the year; 2 Grammy nominations, 1994. Office: care Chapple Fin Svcs Inc 5200 Maryland Way Ste 103 Brentwood TN 37027-5018*

TUCKER-KETO, CLAUDIA A., academic administrator; b. Phila., Jan. 24, 1948; d. Arthur and Erma (Miller) Tucker; m. Clement T. Keto (div. 1993); children: Victor Lefa, James Lefanyana (twins). BA, Temple U., 1982. With adminstrv. office Pa. Supreme Ct., Phila.; coll. adminstr., family resource specialist Camden County Coll., Blackwood, N.J.; coord. women's programs Camden County Dept. Health and Human Svcs., Camden, N.J. mem. ethics com. Dist. IV Supreme Ct., 1993-95. Legis. chairwoman N.J. Fed. Dem. Women, Trenton, N.J.; mem. planning com. U.S. Dept. Labor Women's Bur. Region II, N.Y.; commr. N.J. Martin Luther King Jr. Organization, Trenton; bd. dir. N.J. Women's Summit, Sicklerville, N.J.; chairwomen Camden County Commn. on Women, N.J. Recipient Women in Bus. award Nat. Hookup of Black Women, 1992, Outstanding Svc. to Women award African Am. Women's Network, 1994. Mem. AAUW. Baptist. Home: 3211 Arborwood III Lindenwold NJ 08021 also: Commission on Women 2101 Ferry Ave 4th fl Camden NJ 08104

TUCKERMAN, SUSAN, information broker, librarian; b. Bklyn., Mar. 13, 1948; d. Samuel and Norma (Zitch) Joseph; 1 child, Rachel. BA, SUNY, 1970; MLS, U. Mich., 1971. Cert. prof. libr. N.Y., Va. Reference libr. Free Libr. of Phila., 1971-77, Fairfax County Pub. Libr., Alexandria, Va., 1979-80, Mercy Coll., Dobbs Ferry, N.Y., 1980-81, Westchester Community Coll., Valhalla, N.Y., 1981-86, Scarsdale (N.Y.) Pub. Libr., 1992—; pres. Infolink, Montrose, N.Y., 1986—. Mem. Assn. Ind. Info. Profls., Spl. Librs. Assn., Westchester Libr. Assn. Office: Infolink P O Box 306 Montrose NY 10548

TUCKER-MCFARLAND, THERESA LYLA, psychologist; b. Barre City, Vt., June 7, 1953; d. Lee Clyde and Vivian Irene (Lyon) Tucker; m. LeRoy Everett Adams, June 1977 (div. 1980); m. David Eugene Frazier Jr., May 1985 (div. Aug. 1988); m. David Layne McFarland, Aug. 7, 1993. ADN, U. Vt., 1973; BA, Hawthorne Coll., 1982; PhD, U. Tenn., 1991. Lic. psychologist, Oreg., Tenn.; RN, Tenn. Staff nurse VA Adminstrn. Hosp., White River Junction, Vt., 1973-75, 78-83, psychology technician, 1983-85; staff nurse Hale Hosp., Haverhill, Mass., 1975; staff nurse, relief supr. Cookeville (Tenn.) Gen. Hosp., 1975-77, evening supr., 1977; sr. clin. psychologist Ridgeview Psychiat. Hosp., Oak Ridge, Tenn., 1991-93; pvt. practice Knoxville, 1991-93, Klamath Falls, Oreg., 1993—; cons. Luth. Family Svcs., Klamath Falls, 1993. Mem. APA. Office: 905 Main St Ste 602 Klamath Falls OR 97602

TUCKSON, CONCHETTA CHERETTY, control analyst; b. Meridan, Miss., July 13, 1962; d. McKinley and Barbara Ann (Taylor) T. BS, U. Tenn., 1984; MBA, Bristol U., 1992. Cert. info. systems auditor. Claims adjuster Allstate Ins. Co., Nashville, 1985; programmer Computer Scis. Corp., Tullahoma, Tenn., 1985-86; programmer, analyst Provident Life & Accident, Chattanooga, 1985-87, TVA, Hollywood, Ala., 1987-89; control analyst TVA, Knoxville, 1989-93, sr. control analyst, 1994. Bd. dirs. Matrix, Knoxville, 1993-94. Mem. Am. Govtl. Accts., Inst. Internal Auditors, Info. Systems Audit and Control Assn., Blacks in Govt., Jazz Exch., Optimist Club.

TUDOR, JEAN ELIZABETH, artist, educator; b. Tacoma, Wash., Dec. 2, 1933; d. Donald Irving and Katharine (Harvey) Cameron; m. William Ellis Tudor, June 9, 1956; children: Elizabeth Cameron, Andrew John. BA, U. Puget Sound, 1956; postgrad., Penland (N.C.) Sch. Crafts, 1970-71, 73; BFA, Wayne State U., 1982. Enamel instr. adult edn. Newport News (Va.) Pub. Schs., 1973-78; enamel instr. Indpls. Art League, 1984-94, enamel instr., dept. head metals, 1987-94. One-person shows include Indpls. Mus. Art, Long Gallery, 1987, Peninsula Fine Arts Ctr., Newport News, 1988, 89, D'Art, Norfolk, Va., 1989, Shircliff Gallery, Vincennes (Ind.) U., 1992, Stagedoor Gallery, Tacoma, Wash., 1993, Chatham Gallery, Indpls., 1994; two-person shows Richmond Art Mus., 1989, Am. States Ins. Gallery, Indpls., 1989; exhibited in group shows at U. Md. Gallery, 1975, Torpedo Factory, Alexandria, Va., 1978, Long Beach (Calif.) Mus. Art, 1985, Sarah Squeri Gallery, Cin., 1987, Espace Fauré, Limoges, France, 1988, 9th Biennale Internat., Limoges, 1988, Carnegie Art Ctr., Covington, Ky., 1989, Enamelist Soc. Juried Show, 1991, Junko Takao Gallery, N.Y.C., 1992, Vale Craft Gallery, Chgo., 1993, Indpls. Art League, 1993, Clay and Glass Gallery, Waterloo, Ont., Can., 1994; author: Vitreous Enamels: A Bibliography of Processes, Objects and Enamelists, 1994. Grantee Indpls. Art Commn., 1991. Mem. Enamelist Soc. (pres. 1991-95), Am. Crafts Coun., Soc. N.Am. Goldsmiths. Democrat. Episcopalian. Office: 546 S Meridian Studio 707 Indianapolis IN 46225

TUDRYN, JOYCE MARIE, professional society administrator; b. Holyoke, Mass., July 27, 1959; d. Edward William and Frances Katherine (Bajor) T.; m. William Wallace Friberger III, Sept. 18, 1982; 1 child, Kristen. BS in Comm., Syracuse U., 1981. Asst. editor Nat. Assn. Broadcasters, Washington, 1981-83; dir. programs Internat. Radio and TV Soc. Found., N.Y.C., 1983-87; assoc. exec. dir. Internat. Radio and TV Soc., N.Y.C., 1988-94, exec. dir., 1994—; spkr. in field; nat. adv. bd. Alpha Epsilon Rho Broadcasting Soc., 1988-91, 93-94, hon. trustee, 1994—; v.p. Corp. for Ednl. Radio and TV, 1988-94. Editor-in-chief IRTS News, 1983—; columnist TV Facts, Figures and Film mag., 1983-88. Recipient Mass. Kodak Photography award, 1977; S.I. Newhouse scholar Syracuse U., 1980-81. Mem. N.Y. Media Roundtable, Gamma Phi Beta. Home: 602 Bennington Dr Union NJ 07083-9104 Office: Internat Radio and TV Found 420 Lexington Ave Ste 1714 New York NY 10170-0001

TUETING, PATRICIA ANN, neuroscientist, researcher; b. Owatonna, Minn., Jan. 26, 1941; d. Thomas Christian and Lucille Evelyn (Basness) Peterson; m. William Francis Tueting, June 10, 1966; children: Jonathan Leif, Sarah Kirsten. BA magna cum laude, St. Olaf Coll., 1963; PhD, Columbia U., 1968. Postdoctoral fellow Columbia U., N.Y.C., 1968-69; asst. prof. CUNY, N.Y.C., 1969-71; rsch. scientist N.Y. State Psychiat. Inst., N.Y.C., 1969-77; asst. prof. St. John's U., N.Y.C., 1976-77; cons. NIMH, Washington, 1977-78; asst. prof. U. Md., Md. State Psychiat. Inst., Balt., 1978-79; rsch. scientist Psychiat. Inst., Chgo., 1979-94; asst. prof. U. Chgo., 1994—. Editor: Event Related Brain Potentials in Man, 1978, Brain and Information, 1984; author Annals of the N.Y. Acad. Sci., 1992. MacArthur Found. grantee, 1982-84; Scottish Rite Schizophrenia Found. grantee, 1993. Mem. AAAS, APA, Soc. for Neurosci., Soc. for Psychophysiol. Rsch., N.Y. Acad. Sci., Am. Psychol. Soc., Phi Beta Kappa, Sigma Xi. Republican. Episcopalian. Home: 488 Ash St Winnetka IL 60093-2604 Office: The Psychiat Inst UIC/UC 1601 W Taylor St Chicago IL 60612

TUFT, MARY ANN, former association executive; b. Easton, Pa., Oct. 11, 1934; d. Ben and Elizabeth (Reibman) T. B.S., West Chester (Pa.) State Coll., 1956; M.A., Lehigh U., 1960. Cert. assn. exec. Nat. trainer Girl Scouts U.S.A., N.Y.C., 1965-68; cons. Nat. League for Nursing, N.Y.C., 1968-69; exec. dir. Nat. Student Nurses Assn., N.Y.C., 1970-85; mem. Commn. on Dietetic Registration, Am. Dietetic Assn., 1981-85; pres. Specialized Cons. Ltd., 1983-85; exec. dir. Radiol. Soc. N.Am., Oak Brook, Ill., 1985-88; prin. Tuft & Assocs., 1989—. Bd. dirs. Nurses House, Inc., 1981-85; bd. dirs. Chgo. Sinai Cong., 1987-91, v.p., 1988. Mary Ann Tuft Scholarship Fund named in her honor Found. Nat. Student Nurses Assn.; Kepner-Tregoe scholar, 1966. Mem. ALA (pub. mem. com. on accreditation 1993-95), Am. Soc. Assn. Execs. (bd dirs. 1980-83, trustee for cert. 1980-83, vice chmn. 1983-84), N.Y. Soc. Assn. Execs. (pres. 1978-79, bd. dirs. 1975-78, 1st Outstanding Exec. award 1982), Continuing Care Accreditation Assn. (bd. dirs. 1983-85), Specialized Cons. in Nursing (faculty).

TUFTON, JANIE LEE (JANE TUFTON), dental hygienist, animal rights lobbyist, activist; b. Allentown, Pa., Jan. 6, 1949; d. Robert Harry and Jean Lorraine (Seng) T. BS in Edn., Indiana U. Pa., 1979; postgrad. in English, 1979-82. Registered dental hygienist, Pa., N.J., Calif.; cert. tchr., Pa. Dental hygientist pvt. dental practices, Pa., N.J., Calif., 1976-90. Author bd. game for dental health edn., 1974. Lobbyist, activist for animal rights; bd. dirs. Lehigh Valley Animal Rights Coalition, 1984-93; active civil rights movement, cultural events, literacy programs, detoxification units for drug and alcohol abuse, venereal disease clinics, practical-life workshops for the cognitively impaired, suicide hotlines, YWCA, Girl Scouts U.S. Recipient recognition Pa. Dental Hygienists Assn., 1974; named Internat. Woman of Yr., Internat. Biog. Ctr., 1992-93, Internat. Profl. and Bus. Women's Hall of Fame, Am. Biog. Inst., Inc., 1994, Woman of Yr., Am. Biographical Inst., Inc., 1994. Mem. Am. Anti-Vivisect. Soc., Nat. Humane Edn. Soc., Nat. Alliance for Animals, Internat. Soc. for Animal Rights, Physicians Com. for Responsible Medicine, Culture and Animals Found., Animal Legal Def. Fund, People for the Ethical Treatment of Animals, Farm Animal Reform Movement, Farm Sanctuary, Com. to Abolish Sport Hunting, Animal Rights Mobilization, In Def. of Animals, United Animal Nations, Internat. Platform Assn. Home: 2102 S Lehigh Ave Whitehall PA 18052-5532

TUGAEFF, BARBARA TRASK LAWRIE, art director; b. Waltham, Mass., June 15, 1955; d. Richard Warner and Eleanor Birchard (Cox) Lawrie; m. Gary Lamar Tugaeff, Mar. 12, 1983. Grad. high sch., Phoenix. Art dir. S&K Linear Products, Phoenix, 1974-76; pasteup/layout artist Cape Codder News, Orleans, Mass., 1976-78; designer Chateau de Ville, Framingham, Mass., 1978; detail draftswoman Polaroid Corp., Waltham, Mass., 1978-80; designer The Vail (Colo.) Trail, 1980-82; prodn. mgr. Avon (Colo.)-Beaver Creek Times, 1982-83; art dir. Pacific Coast Quarter Horse Assn., Sacramento, Calif., 1984-89, Animal Protection Inst., Sacramento, 1990—; ptnr. Creative Counterparts, Sacramento, 1992-93. Recipient 1st pl. award Two/Three Color Advertisement Am. Horse Publs., 1989, 2nd pl. Black and White Editorial Design, 1988. Republican. Epsicopalian. Home: 8607 Elaine Dr Sacramento CA 95828

TULL, THERESA ANNE, ambassador; b. Runnemede, N.J., Oct. 2, 1936; d. John James and Anna Cecelia (Paull) T. B.A., U. Md., 1972; M.A., U. Mich., 1973; postgrad., Nat. War Coll., Washington, 1980. Fgn. svc. officer Dept. State, Washington, 1963, Brussels, 1965-67, Saigon, 1968-70; dep. prin. officer Am. Consulate General, Danang, Vietnam, 1973-75; prin. officer Cebu, Philippines, 1977-79; dir. office human rights, 1980-83; charge d'affaires Am. Embassy, Vientiane, Laos, 1983-86; Dept. State Senior Seminar, 1986-87; ambassador to Guyana, 1987-90; diplomat-in-residence Lincoln U., Pa., 1990-91; dir. office regional affairs, bur. East Asian & Pacific affairs Dept. State, Washington, 1991-93; amb. to Brunei Bandar Seri Begawan, 1993—. Recipient Civilian Service award Dept. of State, 1970, Superior Honor award, 1977. Mem. Am. Fgn. Svc. Assn. Home: care Waldis 416 N Washington Ave Moorestown NJ 08057-2411 Office: Am Embassy Box B APO AP 96440 also: Am Embassy, Bandar Seri Begawan, Brunei Darussalam

TULLEY, MONICA ELAINE, marketing professional; b. Jacksonville, Fla., Feb. 12, 1953; d. Douglas Campbell and Lucy (Balestrini) T. BA, U. North Fla., 1976; MBA, U. Calif., Irvine, 1991. Mktg. exec. Am. Hosp. Supply, Cin., 1977-79; mgr. nat. account programs Gen. Electric Med. Systems, Milw., 1979-85; mgr. mktg. svcs. Internat. Imaging, Chgo., 1985-88; mgr. strategic mktg. Toshiba Am. Med. Systems, Tustin, Calif., 1988-91; mgr. CT Products Picker Internat., Cleve., 1993—. Office: 595 Miner Rd Carmel IN 46033

TULLOCH-REID, ELMA DEEN, nurse, consultant; b. Erie, Pa., June 27, 1938; d. Theodore and Roberta (Hicks) Carlisle; B.S., N.C. Agrl. and Tech. State U., 1960; M.A., Calif. State U., 1977; Ed.D., Nova U., 1981; children: Robynne and Stacey (twins). Staff nurse Michael Reese Hosp., Chgo., 1960-62; instr. Cook County Sch. Nursing, Chgo., 1962-64; tchr. St. Joseph Convent, Trinidad, West Indies, 1964-66; med./surg. coordinator St. Vincent Coll. Nursing, Los Angeles, 1966-68, med./surg. coordinator, 1968-69; charge nurse Century City Hosp., Los Angeles, 1971-72; tchr. Los Angeles Unified Schs., 1972-75; instr. inservice dept. St. Vincent Med. Center, Los Angeles, 1972-75; dir. edn. and tng. Imperial Hosp., Inglewood, Calif., 1977-79; pres. Elma Tulloch-Reid Assocs., Los Angeles, 1981—; asst. prof. dept. continuing edn. Calif. State U., Long Beach, 1977-81, asso. prof., 1982—; instr. Pilot Program in Health Occupations, Culver City Unified Sch. Dist., 1985—; DON edn. and rsch. King Drew Med. Ctr., L.A., 1991—; clin. performance examiner Regent's Coll. NYU; provider Advanced Life Support in Cardiopulmonary Resuscitation, Am. Heart Assn., 1982-84. Community instr. certified basic life support Los Angeles Cardio-Pulmonary Resuscitation Consortium, 1981-82. Recipient commendation City of Los Angeles XXIII Olympiad, 1984. Mem. Nat. Orgn. Mothers of Twins, NAFE, Am. Nurses Found., Am. Coll. Healthcare Execs., N.C. Agrl. and Tech. State U. Alumni Assn., AAUW, Assn. for psychological Type, Nat. Nursing Staff Devel. Orgn., Phi Kappa Phi. Club: Westside Mothers Twins (pres. 1971-73) (Los Angeles). Home: 1056 S Cochran Ave Los Angeles CA 90019-2857 Office: 5350 Wilshire Blvd Los Angeles CA 90036

TULLY, CHERYL ANNE, marketing professional, consultant; b. Cambridge, Mass., Apr. 10, 1962; d. James Michael and Carol Ann (Martin) T. BA in Econs., Framingham (Mass.) State Coll., 1986; MBA, Bentley Coll., Waltham, Mass., 1988. Cable TV producer Community Cablevision, Framingham, 1979-81; grad. rsch. asst. Bentley Coll., 1986-88; media cons. Mass. Commn. Against Discrimination, Bostson, 1985-88; mktg. mgr. Lord Pub., Inc., Natick, Mass., 1988-89; mktg. and media cons. Framingham, 1989-92; account mgr. Computer Currents and I.D.G. Publ., Framingham, 1991-92; direct mktg. mgr. Motorola Codex Corp., Mansfield, Mass., 1993-94; channel mktg. mgr. Motorola Corp., Mansfield, 1994—; cons. to pvt. clients, 1985—; mentor Bentley Coll. Mentor Program. Author newspaper articles on civic and polit. topics. Mem. Dem. Town Co., Framingham, 1982-94; mem Framingham Youth Commn., 1984-86, 91-93; chmn. Alliance for a Better Framingham, 1989-93. Mem. Direct Mktg. Assn., New Eng. Direct Mktg. Assn. (publicity com.), Bentley Grad. Sch. Bus. Alumni Assn. Home: 20 Claudette Dr Apt 7 Milford MA 01757-1474 Office: Motorola Corp 20 Cabot Blvd Mansfield MA 02048-1153

TUMELAIRE, JUANITA HEAD, artist; b. Louisville, July 8, 1944; d. William Russell and Juanita Mildred (Hazenbuhler) Head; m. Theodorus M. Tumelaire, May 20, 1972. BA, U. Louisville, 1966; ME in Edn., SUNY, Buffalo, 1973; postgrad., Decordova Mus. Sch., 1984-90. Vol. Peace Corps, Lemery, Batangas, P.I., 1966-68; media buyer Stern-Frank Advt., Boston, 1969-71; tchr. SUCB Grad. Program, Buffalo, 1972-74, Language House Internat., Esfahan, Iran, 1974-76, U.S.I.A., Kathmandu, Nepal, 1976-78; tchr. Walnut Hill Sch., Natick, Mass., 1979-81, dean, 1981-90; freelance artist Signal Mountain, Tenn., 1990—; freelance instr. printmaking Tenn. & Ga., 1990—; v.p. arts bd. Assn. Visual Artists, Chattanooga, 1991-94; mktg. dir. Intown Gallery, Chattanooga, 1991-94; cons. in field. Illustrator: (book) AVA Newsletter, 1993. Tenn. Arts Commn. fellow, 1993-94; recipient Merit award Creative Arts Guild, Dalton, Ga., 1993. Mem. So. Graphics. Home: 1909 E Brow Rd Signal Mountain TN 37377

TUNG, ROSALIE LAM, educator, consultant; b. Shanghai, China, Dec. 2, 1948; came to U.S., 1975; d. Andrew Yan-Fu and Pauline Wai-Kam (Cheung) Lam. BA (Univ. scholar), York U., 1972; MBA, U. B.C., 1974, PhD in Bus. Adminstrn. (Univ. fellow, Seagram Bus. fellow, H.R. MacMillan Family fellow), 1977; m. Byron Poon-Yan Tung, June 17, 1972; 1 child, Michele Christine. Lectr. diploma div. U. B.C., 1975, lectr. exec. devel. program, 1975; asst. prof. mgmt. grad. sch. mgmt. U. Oreg., Eugene, 1977-80; assoc. prof. U. Pa. , Phila. 1981-86; prof., dir. internat. bus. ctr. U. Wis., Milw., 1986-90; endowed chaired prof. Simon Fraser U., 1991—; vis. scholar U. Manchester (Eng.) Inst. Sci. and Tech., 1980; vis. prof. UCLA, 1981, Harvard U., 1988; Wis. disting. prof. U. Wis. System, 1988-90, Ming and Stella Wong chair in internat. bus., 1991—. Mem. Acad. Internat. Bus. (mem. exec. bd., treas. 1985-86), Acad. Mgmt. (bd. govs. 1987-89), Internat. Assn. Applied Psychology, Am. Arbitration Assn. (comml. panel arbitrators). Author: Management Practices in China, 1980, U.S.-China Trade Negotiations, 1982, Chinese Industrial Society After Mao, 1982, Business Negotiations with the Japanese, 1984, Key to Japan's Economic Strength: Human Power, 1984, The New Expatriates: Managing Human Resources Abroad, 1988; editor: Strategic Management in the U.S. and Japan, 1987, International Management in International Library of Business and Management Series, 1994. Oppehheimer Bros. Found. fellow, 1973-74, U. B.C. fellow, 1974-75, H.R. MacMillan Found. fellow, 1975-77; named Wis. Disting. Prof., 1988, Ming and Stella Wong Prof., 1991. Roman Catholic; recipient Leonore Rowe Williams award U. Pa., 1990, U. B.C. Alumni 75th Anniversary award, 1990. Avocation: creative writing. Office: Simon Fraser U, Faculty Bus Adminstrn, Burnaby, BC Canada V5A 1S6

TUNICK, CAROL KAPLIN, marketing communications consultant; b. Norwalk, Conn., Sept. 19, 1949; d. Hyman and Fannie (Ruttenberg) Kaplin; m. Edward J. Tunick, May 6, 1979. AS, Quinnipiac Coll., 1969. Cert. Bus. Communicator, Conn. Advt. mgr. Wilks Sci. Corp., South Norwalk, 1974-77; communications mgr. The Foxboro Co., South Norwalk, 1977-90; marketing communications cons. Carol Tunick Assocs., East Norwalk, Conn., 1990—. Mem. Bus. Profl. Advt. Assn. Norwalk (So. Conn. chpt. pres. 1983-84), Bus. Mktg. Assn. (Chgo. v.p. 1986-92). Republican. Office: Carol Tunick Assocs 1 Island Dr Apt 12 Norwalk CT 06855-2718

TUNISON, ELIZABETH LAMB, education educator; b. Belfast, Northern Ireland, Jan. 7, 1922; came to U.S., 1923; d. Richard Ernest and Ruby (Hill) Lamb; m. Ralph W. Tunison, Jan. 24, 1947 (dec. Apr. 1984); children: Eric Arthur, Christine Wait, Dana Paul. BA, Whittier Coll., 1943, MEd, 1963. Tchr. Whittier (Calif.) Schs., 1943-59; tchr. T.V. Stas. TV Channels 13 and 28, So. Calif. Counties, 1960-75; dir. curriculum Bassett (Calif.) Schs., 1962-65; elem. sch. prin. Rowland Unified Schs., Rowland Heights, Calif., 1965-68; assoc. prof. edn. Calif. State Poly. U., Pomona, 1968-71; prof. Whittier Coll., 1968-88, prof. emerita, 1988—. Bd. dirs. Presbyn. Intercommunity Hosp. Found. Recipient Whittier Coll. Alumni Achievement award 1975; Helen Hefernan scholar 1963. Mem. AAUP, Assn. Calif. Sch. Adminstrs. (state bd., chmn. higher edn. com. 1983-86, region pres. 1981-83, Wilson Grace award 1983), PEO (pres. 1990-92), Assistance League of Whittier (v.p. 1994—), Delta Kappa Gamma. Home: 5636 Ben Alder Ave Whittier CA 90601-2111

TUNNELL, CLIDA DIANE, air transportation specialist; b. Durham, N.C., Nov. 20, 1946; d. Kermit Wilbur and Roberta (Brantley) T. BS cum laude, Atlantic Christian Coll., 1968; pvt. pilot rating, instr. rating, Air Care, Inc., 1971, 83. Cert. tchr. Tchr. Colegio Karl C. Parrish, Barranquilla, Colombia, 1968-69, Nash County Schs., Nashville, N.C., 1969-86; ground sch. instr. Nash. Tech. Coll., Nashville, 1984-85; specialist Am. Airlines, Dallas-Ft. Worth Airport, Tex., 1987—, A300 lead developer in flight tng. program devel., 1988-89, with flight ops. procedures flight ops. tech., 1990—, F100-fleet specialist flight ops. tech., 1992—; ednl. cons., Euless, Tex., 1989—; profl. artist. State Tchrs. Scholar N.C., 1964-68, Bus. and Profl. Women Scholar, 1980-81. Mem. 99, Internat. Orgn. Women Pilots (various offices), AMR Mgmt. Club. Home: PO Box 234 Euless TX 76039-0234

TUNSTALL, SHARON SUE, advertising executive; b. Houston, Oct. 19, 1949; d. O. Ray and Etta Mae (Stodghill) T. BA, U. Houston, 1973, MA, 1977, PhD, 1981. Tchr. Dulles High Sch., Stafford, Tex., 1974-77; asst. prof. Oakland U., Rochester, Mich., 1980-85; v.p., dir. human resources D'Arcy Masius Benton & Bowles, Bloomfield Hills, Mich., 1985-91, dir. corp. tng. N.Am. div., 1986-90; v.p., dir. human resources B.H. and Corp, Tng., 1990-91; sr. v.p., dir. human resources N.Am. and Corp. Tng. Worldwide, 1991—; polit. cons. U. Houston; guest speaker Advt. Ednl. Found., N.Y.C., 1988—. Mem. Am. Soc. Tng. and Devel., Am. Mgmt. Assn. Democrat. Office: 1725 N Woodward PO Box 811 Bloomfield Hills MI 48303-0811

TUOHY, MARY VIRGINIA, oil company executive; b. Chgo., Dec. 8, 1963; d. John O'Connor and Irena Helena (Frydrych) T. BS in Elec. Engring., Marquette U., 1987; MBA, DePaul U., Chgo., 1992. Engr. coop. Motorola, Inc., Schaumburg, Ill., 1984-87; account rep. Otis Elevator Co., Columbus, Ohio, 1987-88, Alsip, Ill., 1988-90; account mgr. Otis Elevator Co., Chgo., 1990-93; nat. account mgr. Amoco Oil Co., Oak Brook, Ill., 1993—. Tutor St. Malachy's Sch., Chgo., 1989-90, Mercy Boys Home, Chgo., 1993; vol. Old St. Patrick's Ch., Chgo., 1989-91; active in Chgo. polit. campaigns. DePaul U. Grad. Sch. Bus. Alumni Club (bd. dirs. 1992—), Marquette U. Alumni Club (bd. dirs. 1988-91). Roman Catholic. Office: Amoco Oil Co 2021 Spring Rd Ste 500 Oak Brook IL 60521-1859

TUPLER, HARRIET, television producer; b. Bronx, N.Y., Dec. 10, 1935; d. Louis and Rose (Cohen) Harris; m. Dec. 17, 1956 (div. 1976); children: Larry N., Anne T., Diana L. AA, U. Fla, 1955; B in Edn., U. Miami, 1959; postgrad., Fla. Atlantic U., 1978. Cert. tchr., early childhood and elem. edn., Fla.; cert. in journalism. Tchr. Dade County Sch. Bd., Miami, 1959-64, Alachua County Sch. Bd., Tallahassee, 1964-65, Broward County Sch. Bd., Ft. Lauderdale, 1970-72, 75-77, 89, Temple Beth Torah, Tamarac, Fla., 1983-88; co-owner, dir. Discovery Preschool, Ft. Lauderdale, 1968-69; coord. handicapped program Fla. Internat. U., Miami, 1977-78, Miami Herald, Hollywood, Fla., 1979—; co-owner, co-producer Changing Directions, Inc., Ft. Lauderdale, 1990—; co-producer, co-host TV show on handicapped concerns, Ft. Lauderdale, 1990. Author: Legal Rights of the Handicapped, 1978. Foster parent Seed Drug and Alcohol Abuse Ctr., Ft. Lauderdale, 1974-75; sec. Broward Ostomy Assn., Hollywood, Fla., 1974-75; mem. Gov.'s Com. on Employment of the Handicapped, Tallahassee, 1977-82. Named Outstanding Woman of Yr., Women in Communications, 1989; recipient Pres.'s award Plantation Kiwanis Clubs, 1989. Mem. Pompano Ostomy Assn., Against All Odds (chair 1989), Quota Club of Plantation (charter mem., program chair 1989), Kiwanis Club of Deaf. Democrat. Jewish. Home: 430 Commodore Dr Apt 314 Fort Lauderdale FL 33325-2162 Office: Changing Directions Inc PO Box 25082 Fort Lauderdale FL 33320-5082

TURCHIN, CAROLYN, judge; m. Marc Turchin. Grad., U. Calif., Berkeley, 1967; JD, Loyola U., 1978. Tchr. pub. sch., 1967-77; formerly with Santa Monica (Calif.) City Atty.'s Office, U.S. Atty.'s Office, L.A.; magistrate judge U.S. Dist. Ct. (ctrl. dist.) Calif., L.A., 1991—. Office: US Courthouse 312 N Spring St Rm 1031 Los Angeles CA 90012*

TURCOT, MARGUERITE HOGAN, innkeeper, medical researcher; b. White Plains, N.Y., May 19, 1934; d. Joseph William (dec.) and Marguerite Alice (dec.) Barrett) Hogan; children: Michael J., Susan A. Turcot, William R. Student, Syracuse U., 1951-54; BS in Nursing, U. Bridgeport, 1968. RN, Conn., N.C. Staff nurse Park City Hosp., Bridgeport, Conn., 1968-69, Meml. Mission Hosp., Asheville, N.C., 1969-70; instr. St. Joseph's Hosp., Asheville, 1970-71; oper. rm. nurse St. Joseph's Hosp., 1973-77, charge nurse urology-cystoscopy, 1977-85; tchr. Asheville-Buncombe Tech. Coll., Asheville, 1971-72, Buncombe County Child Devel., Asheville, 1972-73; researcher VA Med. Ctr., Asheville, 1988—; owner Reed House Bed & Breakfast, Asheville, 1985; bd. dirs. RiverLink. Charter mem. French Broad River Planning Com., Asheville, 1987—, Biltmore Village Hist. Mus.; mem. Asheville Bicentennial Commn., 1990-93. Faculty scholar Syracuse U., 1951-54, U. Bridgeport, 1967-68. Mem. Am. Urology Assn. (presenter VA urology workshop Asheville chpt. 1981, nat. meeting allied), Am. Bd. Urologic Allied Health Profls., Nat. Trust for Hist. Preservation, Preservation Found. N.C., Blue Ridge Pkwy. Assn., Preservation Soc. Asheville and Buncombe County (past pres.), Asheville Newcomers Club (founder, 1st pres.), Earthwatch, Friends of Blue Ridge Pkwy. Inc. Republican. Roman Catholic. Home: 119 Dodge St Asheville NC 28803-2731 Office: VA Med Ctr Tunnel Rd Asheville NC 28805-1233

TURCZYN-TOLES, DOREEN MARIE, pharmaceutical consultant; b. Chelsea, Mass., Aug. 5, 1958; d. Francis Henry and Rosalie (Lomba) Turczyn; m. Ronald Eugene Toles, Oct. 19, 1986. BA cum laude, Boston U., 1981; MA, U. Chgo., 1984. Programming subcontr. Abbott Labs., Abbott Park, Ill., 1983-84; programmer, analyst Nat. Opinion Research Ctr., Chgo., 1984-88; statis. computing analyst G.D. Searle & Co., Skokie, Ill., 1988-90; supr. Parke-Davis Pharms., Ann Arbor, Mich., 1990-92; mgr. applications programming Univax Biologics, Inc., Rockville, Md., 1993—. Mem. Nat. Assn. Female Execs., NOW. Democrat. Roman Catholic.

TURECK, ROSALYN, concert artist, author, editor, educator; b. Chgo., Dec. 14, 1914; d. Samuel Tureck and Mary (Lipson) Tureck-Wise; (w. 1964). Studies with Sophia Brilliant-Liven, 1925-29, with Jan Chiapusso, 1929-31, with Gavin Williamson, 1931-32; BA cum laude, The Juilliard Sch. Music, 1935; studies with Olga Samaroff; MusD (hon.), Colby Coll., 1964, Roosevelt U., 1968, Wilson Coll., 1968, Oxford U., Eng., 1977, Music and Arts Inst., San Francisco, 1987. Mem. faculty Phila. Conservatory Music, 1935-42, Mannes Sch., N.Y.C., 1940-44, Juilliard Sch. Music, N.Y.C., 1943-55, Columbia U., N.Y.C., 1953-55; prof. music, lectr. U. Calif., San Diego, 1966-72; vis. prof. Washington U., St. Louis, 1963-64, U. Md., 1981-85, Yale U., 1991-93; vis. fellow St. Hilda's Coll., Oxford (Eng.) U., 1974, hon. life fellow, 1974—; vis. fellow Wolfson Coll., Oxford, 1975—; lectr. numerous ednl. instns., U.S., Eng., Spain, Denmark, Holland, Can., Israel, Brazil, Argentina, Chile; lectr. Royal Inst. Great Britain, 1993, Boston U., 1993, 94, Smithsonian Instn., 1994, Rockefeller U., 1994, U. Calif., Santa Barbara, 1995; hon. mem. adv. coun. Ams. for Music Libr., Hebrew U., Israel., Royal Inst. Great Britain, London, U. Southampton, Oxford U., 1993, 10th Internat. Congress Logic, Methodology and Philosophy Sci., 1995; bd. dirs., founder Internat. Bach Soc., Inst. for Bach Studies; founder Composers of Today, 1949-53, Tureck Bach Players, 1955, London, 1981, New York, Tureck Bach Inst., Inc., 1981, Symposia 1983, 84, 86—; 1st woman invited to conduct N.Y. Philharm., 1958, San Antonio Symphony, Okla. Symphony, 1962, World Tour, U.S., Eng., Holland, Turkey, Israel, 1985-86; soloist at White House State Dinner for Can. Prime Minister, 1986, Casals Festival Tour Italy, 1991; conv. organizer Symposium on Structure, U. Internat. Menendez Pelayo, Spain, 1990. Debut 2 solo recitals, Chgo., 1924; soloist Chgo. Symphony Orch., 1926, 2 all-Bach recitals, Chgo., 1930; N.Y.C. debut Carnegie Hall with Phila. Orch., 1936; series 6 all-Bach recitals, Town Hall, N.Y.C., 1937, ann. U.S.-Can. tours, 1937—, ann. series 3 all-Bach recitals, N.Y.C., 1944-54, 59—; European debut Copenhagen, 1947; organizer, dir. soc. for performance internat. contemporary music, Composers of Today, Inc, 1951-55; extensive European tours, 1947—; condr., soloist, London Philharmonia, 1958; founder, dir. Tureck Bach Players, London, 1957, N.Y.C., 1981, Bach festivals cities, Eng., Ireland, Spain, 1959—, Carnegie Hall Ann. Series, N.Y.C., 1975—; TV series Well-Tempered Clavier, Book I, Granada TV, Eng., 1961; BBC series Well-Tempered Clavier, Books 1 and 2, 1976; numerous TV appearances, U.S., 1961—, including Wm. F. Buckley's Firing Line, 1970, 85, 87, 89, Today Show, Camera Three, Bach recitals on piano, harpsichord, clavichord, antique and electronic instruments, 1963—; concert Teatro Colon, Buenos Aires, 1992, Rome, Florence, Imola, Italy, Sevilla and Alicante, Spain, 1993, 94; concert tour, recitals, master classes in Spain, Italy, Switzerland, Eng., S.Am., 1994; world tours in Far East, India, Australia, Europe, 1971, S.Am., 1986, 87, 88, 89, Europe, Israel, Turkey, Spain, 1986, 90, Argentina, Chile, 1989, 90, 91, 92, Casals Festival, 1991, Italy, 1991, 92, Eng., Italy, Spain, 1992-93; N.Y.C. series, Met. Mus. Art and Carnegie Hall, 1969—; appeared with leading orchs. U.S., Can., Europe, South Africa, S.Am., Israel; recs. for HMV, Odeon, Decca, Columbia Masterworks., Everest, Allegro, Classical Music, Inc; condr., soloist N.Y. Philharmon., 1960, London Philharmon. Orch., 1959—, Tureck Bach Players, London, 1960-72, Israel Philharmon., Tel Aviv, Haifa and Kol Israel orchs., 1963, Israel Festival, Internat. Bach Soc. Orchs., 1967, 69, 70, Washington Nat. Symphony, 1970, Madrid Chamber Orch., 1970, Carnegie Hall, N.Y., 1975-86, N.Y. 1981, 84, 85; numerous solo recitals including U. Kansas, 1992, N.Y.C., 1992; author: Introduction to the Performance of Bach, 3 vols., 1960, Video Artists Internat.eo Teatro Color CD's, 1992—, Authenticity, 1994; contbr. articles to various mags.; editor Bach-Sarabande, C minor, 1960, Tureck Bach Urtext Series: Italian Concerto, Schirmer Music, Inc., 1983, 2d edit., 1991, Lute Suite, E minor, 1984, C minor, 1985, Carl Fischer Paginini-Tureck: Moto Perpetuo, A. Scarlatti: Air and Gavotte, Bach and Tureck at Home series, 1990; films: Fantasy and Fugue: Rosalyn Tureck Plays Bach, 1972, Rosalyn Tureck plays on Harpsichord and Organ, 1977, Joy of Bach, 1978, Camera 3: Bach on the Frontier of the Future, CBS film, Ephesus, Turkey, 1985. Decorated Officers Cross of the Order of Merit, Fed. Republic Germany, 1979; recipient 1st prize Greater Chgo. Piano Playing Tournament, 1928, 1st Town Hall Endowment award, 1937, Phi Beta award, 1946; named Schubert Meml. Contest winner, 1935, Nat. Fedn. Music Clubs Competition winner, 1935, Musician of Yr., Music Tchrs. Nat. Assn., 1987; NEH grantee. Fellow Guildhall Sch. Music and Drama (hon.); mem. Royal Mus. Assn. London, Am. Musicological Soc., Inc. Soc. Musicians (London), Royal Philharmonic Soc. London, Sebastian Bach de Belgique (hon.), Am. Bach Soc., Oxford Soc. Clubs: Century (N.Y.C., Oxford and Cambridge, London), Bohemians (N.Y.C.) (hon.). Office: care Christa Phelps, Lies Askonas Ltd 6 Henrietta St, London WC2 EALA, England also: Tureck Bach Inst 215 E 68th St New York NY 10021

TUREK, SONIA FAY, journalist; b. N.Y.C., Aug. 2, 1949; d. Louis and Julia (Liebson) T. BA in English, CCNY, 1970; MSLS, Drexel U., 1972; MS in Journalism, Boston U., 1979. Children's libr. Wissahickon Valley Pub. Libr., Ambler, Pa., 1973; supr. children's svcs. Somerville Pub. Libr., 1973-78; stringer The Watertown (Mass.) Sun, 1979, The Bedford (Mass.) Minuteman, 1979; reporter The Middlesex News, Framingham, Mass., 1979-82, county bur. chief, 1982-83; reporter The Boston Herald, 1983, asst. city editor, city editor, 1985-86, asst. mng. editor features, 1986-89, asst. mng. editor Sunday, 1989-93, dep. mng. editor, arts and features, 1993—; tchr. Cambridge (Mass.) Ctr. for Adult Edn., 1982, 83; adj. prof. Boston U., 1986; travel writer The Boston Herald, 1984-88, wine columnist, 1984—. Office: The Boston Herald One Herald Sq Boston MA 02106

TUREL, JOAN MARIE, religious program director; b. Kingston, Pa.; d. John Alexander and Anna (Kornova) T. MusB, Marywood Coll., 1964; MA, NYU, 1970, Notre Dame U., 1994. Cert. in music edn., Pa., N.Y. Chairperson music dept. St. Patrick's H.S., Scranton, Pa., 1967-69; music cons. Immaculata, St. Alphonsus, St. Stephen's High Schs., N.Y.C., 1969-72; chairperson music dept. Bishop Hoban High Sch., Wilkes-Barre, Pa., 1971-76; choral dir. Kings Coll., Wilkes-Barre, 1978-86; dir. music St. Aloysius Parish, Wilkes-Barre, 1983—; dir. worship Roman Cath. Diocese Scranton, Pa., 1986—; guest condr. Pa. Music Educators Assn., 1978, Nat. Shrine Immaculate Conception, Washington, 1982, Disneyworld, Orlando, Fla., 1983, 84. Editor: (jour.) The Assembly Celebrates, 1987—. State rep. Pa. Music Educators Assn., 1977; founder/condr. Annual Children's Charities Concerts, Wilkes-Barre, 1981-86. Recipient Senatorial commendation Pa. Legis., 1973. Mem. Nat. Assn. Pastoral Musicians (program dir., 1986—, dir. music div., 1988—, chairperson nat. convention, 1987), Fedn. Diocesan Liturgical Com. (nat. bd. dirs., 1991—), Religious Edn. Inst. Bd. (bd. mem., 1988—), Scranton Commn. on Ecumenism, N.Am. Forum (chairperson two nat. institutes, 1989, 91). Roman Catholic. Office: Diocese of Scranton 300 Wyoming Ave Edwardsville PA 18503-1279

TUREN, BARBARA ELLEN, lawyer; b. Newark, Nov. 4, 1951; d. Samuel and Elaine (Goldfarb) T.; m. Leonard Paul Caplan, May 22, 1982 (div. June 1987); 1 child, Andrew. BA with distinction, George Washington U., Washington, 1973; MA with honors, London U., 1974; JD magna cum laude, Seton Hall U., 1990. Bar: N.J. 1990, U.S. Dist. Ct. N.J. 1990, U.S. Ct. Appeals (3d cir.) 1991. Fundraiser Am. Pl. Theatre, N.Y.C., 1978-79; lit. scout Warner Theatre Prodns., N.Y.C., 1979-80; lit. cons. Theatre Now, Inc., N.Y.C., 1980-82; lit. and talent agt. Don Buchwald & Assocs., N.Y.C., 1982-85; assoc. Hannoch Weisman, Roseland, N.J., 1990-92, Vogel, Chait, Schwartz and Collins, Morristown, N.J., 1992-93; dep. atty. gen. Divsn. Law and Pub. Safety, State of N.J., Newark, 1994—; adj. prof. law Seton Hall U. Sch. Law, Newark, 1994—. Pre-sch. vol. Head Start, Washington, 1970-73; lit. vol. N.Y.C. Sch. System, 1978-85. Recipient Cert. of Membership Seton Hall Constl. Law Jour., Newark, 1989-90. Mem. ABA, N.J. Bar Assn., Essex County Bar Assn., Morris County Bar Assn., Phi Alpha Delta. Jewish. Office: Office of Atty Gen Divsn Law and Pub Safety Newark NJ 07101

TURETSKY, JUDITH, librarian, researcher; b. Bklyn., Jan. 19, 1944; d. Samuel and Ruth (Moskowitz) Turetsky. BS, Boston U., 1965; MS, Long Island U., 1969. Tchr. Trumbull (Conn.) Bd. Edn., 1965-66; libr. Darien (Conn.) Bd. Edn., 1968-69, Albert Einstein Coll., Bronx, 1969-74; researcher Koskoff, Koskoff & Bieder, Bridgeport, Conn., 1977-86. Author:(book and micro film), The History and Development of the D. Samuel Gottesman Library of Albert Eistein College of Medicine. Mem. Med. Library Assn., Conn. Assn. Health Sci. Libraries, N. Atlantic. Democrat. Home and Office: 62 Gate Ridge Rd Fairfield CT 06432

TURKUS-WORKMAN, CAROL ANN, educator; b. Balt., Nov. 12, 1946; d. Stanley Phillip and Catherine Anna (Koppleman) Turkus; m. William Thomas Workman, Apr. 23, 1973 (div. 1983); children: Devin Thomas, Timothy Michael. BA in History, Calif. State U., Long Beach, 1969; spl. cert. classroom mgmt., Centralia Sch. Dist., 1980, crosscultural devel. and acad. devel. cert., 1994; BS, Commr. Coll., 1992. Cert. crosscultural lang. and acad. devel. Educator Centralia Sch. Dist., Buena Park, Calif., 1970—; ednl. tech. Centralia Sch. Dist., Buena Park, 1986—; cons. U. Sch.-Space Sci. Acad., Cleve., 1991. Unit commr. Boy Scouts Am., Orange County Coun., 1989—; co. systems officer Starfleet Bulletin Bd. System, Long Beach, 1990-94; life mem. PTA, Buena Park. Recipient Gold Leaf, PTA Nat., 1991, Woodbadge Beads, Boy Scouts Am., 1991. Mem. Computer Using Educators, Order of Arrow, Kappa Delta Pi. Republican. Roman Catholic. Office: Centralia Sch Dist 6215 San Rolando Way Buena Park CA 90620-3635

TURLEY-MOORE, SUSAN GWEN, minister; b. Boston, June 19, 1952; d. Calvin Earl and Marilyn (Anderson) Turley; m. Clifford Jesse Moore, Jr., Jan. 7, 1978; 1 child, Keith Jesse. BA in Sociology, Urbana (Ohio) U.; MEd, Suffolk U. Lic. cert. social worker, Mass.; ordained to ministry Swedenborgian Ch. Pvt. practice as pastoral psychotherapist Turley and Assocs., Newton, Mass., 1979-81; pastor Swedenborgian Ch., Portland, Maine, 1981-84; pastor on ministerial team Wayfarer's Chapel, L.A., 1984-87; founder, dir. Swedenborgian Social Action Concerns Com., 1987-92; guidance counselor Fairbanks Elem. Sch., Sacramento, Calif., 1987-89; interim assoc. pastor Swedenborgian Ch., San Francisco, 1989-90; chaplain and pastoral staff New Ch. Youth League West Coast, 1990-92; founding exec. dir. of living waters HIV ministry Swedenborgian Ch., San Francisco, 1992—. Mem. ACA, Nat. Coun. of Chs. (counseling com. 1977—),. Home: 94 Midcrest Way San Francisco CA 94131 Office: Swedenborgian Ch Living Waters PO Box 460388 San Francisco CA 94146

TURLINGTON, CHRISTY, model; b. Walnut Creek, Calif., Jan. 2, 1969; d. Dwain and Elizabeth T. With Ford Models, Inc., 1985; model Calvin Klein, 1986; face of Calvin Klein's Eternity Fragrance, 1988—; with Maybelline Cosmetics, 1992; rep. (abroad) Ford Models, Paris; beauty spread with Vogue, 1987; has worked with Herb Ritts, Patrick Demarchelier, Steven Meisel; has worked for Anne Klein, Michael Kors, Chanel, Perry Ellis; appeared in George Michael's "Freedom" video. Office: Ford Models Inc 344 E 59th St New York NY 10022

TURNAGE, JEAN A., state supreme court chief justice; b. St. Ignatius, Mont., Mar. 10, 1926. JD, Mont. State U., 1951. Bar: Mont. 1951, U.S. Supreme Ct. 1963. Formerly ptnr. Turnage, McNeil & Mercer, Polson, Mont.; formerly Mont. State senator from 13th Dist.; pres. Mont. State Senate, 1981-83; chief justice Supreme Ct. Mont., 1985—. Mem. Mont. State Bar Assn., Nat. Conf. Chief Justices (past pres.), Nat. Ctr. State Courts (past chair). Office: Mont Supreme Ct 215 N Sanders St Helena MT 59601-4522*

TURNBULL, VERNONA HARMSEN, retired residence counselor; b. Teeds Grove, Iowa, Dec. 6, 1916; d. Henry Ferdinand and Ida Amelia (Dohrmann) Harmsen; m. Alexander Turnbull, Oct. 12, 1961. BA, Cornell Coll., Mt. Vernon, Iowa, 1939; MEd, U. Colo., Boulder, 1947, profl. cert. edn., 1955. Cert. secondary and high sch. tchr. Tchr. English, Latin and phys. edn. Winslow (Ill.) High Sch., 1939-45; dir. women's activities, instr. Trinidad (Colo.) State Jr. Coll., 1947-53; counselor women, assoc. prof. edn. Western State Coll., Gunnison, Colo., 1953-54; instr., residence counselor Stephens Coll., Columbia, Mo., 1955-61. Active Salvation Army Aux. Mem. AAUW, Am. Assn. Ret. Persons (corr. sec. 1986-87), Kena Kampers Camping Club.

TURNER, BERNICE HILBURN, recording industry executive; b. Black Rock, Ark., Jan. 13, 1937; d. Floyd W. and Clementime (Higgins) Hilburn; m. Doyle Turner, Feb. 28, 1957 (div. Jan. 1980); children: Johnny, P.J., Danny, Jill, Robby. PhD in Applied Psychology, 1974. Musician Hank Williams Sr., Nashville and Montgomery, Ala., 1950-52, 1952-76; owner Onyx Recording Studio, Memphis, 1985—, Turner Limousine Svc., Memphis, 1988—. Named Pioneer in Country Music, United Music Heritage of Tenn., 1989. Mem. Unity Ch. Home: 1646 Bonnie Dr Memphis TN 38116-5732

TURNER, BONESE COLLINS, artist, educator; b. Abilene, Kans.; d. Paul Edwin and Ruby (Seybold) Collins; m. Glenn E. Turner; 1 child, Craig Collins. BS in Edn., U. Idaho, MEd; MA, Calif. State U., Northridge, 1974. Instr. art L.A. Pierce Coll., Woodland Hills, Calif., 1964—; prof. art Calif. State U., Northridge, 1986-87; art instr. L.A. Valley Coll., Van Nuys, 1987-89, Moorpark (Calif.) Coll., 1988—; advisor Coll. Art and Architecture U. Idaho, 1988—; juror for numerous art exhibitions including Nat. Watercolor Soc., 1980, 91, San Diego Art Inst., Brand Nat. Watermedia Exhibition prin. gallery Orlando Gallery, Sherman Oaks, Calif. Prin. works exhibited in The White House, 1984, 85, Smithsonian Inst., 1984, 85, Olympic Arts Festival, L.A., 1984; one woman shows include Angel's Gate Gallery, San Pedro, Calif., 1989, Art Store Gallery, Studio City, Calif., 1988, L.A. Pierce Coll. Gallery, 1988, Brand Art Gallery, Glendale, Calif., 1988, 93, Coos (Oreg.) Art Mus., 1988, U. Nev., 1987, Orlando Gallery, Sherman Oaks, Calif., 1993, others; prin. works represented in pub. collections including Smithsonian Inst., Hartung Performing Arts Ctr., Moscow, Idaho, Home Savs. and Loan, San Bernardino Sun Telegram Newspapers, Oreg. Coun. for the Arts, Newport, Nebr. Pub. Librs., Lincoln (Nebr.) Indsl. Tile Corp. Recipient awards Springfield (Mo.) Art Mus., 1989, Butler Art Inst., 1989. Mem. Nat. Mortar Bd. Soc., Nat. Watercolor Soc. (life, past pres., Purchase prize 1979), Watercolor U.S.A. Honor Soc. (award), Watercolor West.

TURNER, CAROL ANNE, prevention specialist, nurse, counselor; b. Ft. Dodge, Iowa, Sept. 26, 1941; d. Francis Lawrence and Evelyn Gladys (Steinman) Erpelding; m. Michael R. Turner, May 29, 1971 (div. 1993); children: Kristen, Sue Anne. RN, Mercy Sch. Nursing, 1962; BSN, U. Colo., 1969; MA in Counseling, U. N.Mex., 1991. Cert. pediatric nurse. Infectious control nurse Penrose Hosp., Colorado Spring, Colo., 1972-75; head nurse Cmty. Hosp., Colorado Spring, 1975; instr. pediatric nursing Coll. Santa Fe, 1976-77, 79; pediatric nurse clinician Los Alamos (N.Mex.) Vis. Nurse Svc., 1980-84; head nurse pediatrics Los Alamos Med. Ctr., 1984-86, infection control coord., 1985-87; sch. nurse Los Alamos Schs., 1987-91, sch. counselor, 1991-92, prevention specialist, 1992—. Bd. dirs. Los Alamos Cmty. Partnership, 1992—, Family Coun., Los Alamos, 1993—, Ret. Sr. Vols. Program, Los Alamos, 1993—; active Los Alamos Coalition for Svc. Providers, 1992—, Los Alamos Coalition for Prevention of Child Abuse, 1992—. Mem. ANA (Search for Excellence award 1994). Home: 1795 Camino Redondo Los Alamos NM 87544 Office: Los Alamos Schs PO Box 90 Los Alamos NM 87544

TURNER, CATHY, Olympic athlete; b. Apr. 10, 1962. BS in Computer Sys. Gold medal 500 meter short-track speedskating Albertville Olympic Games, 1992, also silver medal 3000 meters relay, 1992; Star made in Am. tour Ice Capades, 1992-93; Gold medalist 500 meter speedskating Winter Olympics, Lillehammer, Norway, 1994, Bronze medalist 3000 meter relay, 1994; owner, pres. Cathy Turner's Empire Fitness; spkr. in field. Address: US Olympic Committee 1750 E Boulder St Colorado Springs CO 80909

TURNER, CHERI ANNE, financial executive; b. Spring City, Pa., Apr. 7, 1949; d. Harold William and Evelyn Virginia (Wagner) T. Student Syracuse U., 1967-69; Cert. fin. paraplanner, fin. planner, Coll. Fin. Planning, Denver, 1986. Pub. relations mediator Don Poindexter & Assocs., St. Petersburg, Fla., 1969-72; exec. sec. Honeywell Inc., Largo, Fla., 1972-75; sec., design coordinator SCM Design Ctr., Syracuse, N.Y., 1975-76; personnel dir. Jay Galbraith's Penthouse, St. Petersburg, 1977-79; cert. fin. paraplanner R. A. Siebern & Assocs., St. Petersburg, 1982-87, pres. C.A. Turner Services, 1987-93; real estate sales rep. Corwin Realty Inc., St. Petersburg 1988-90; registered rep. gen. securities Mut. Benefit Fin. Service Co. Inc., Tampa, Fla., 1985-89; assest technician Resolution Trust Corp., 1991-93; adminstr, acting comm. officer S. Fla. Water Mgmt. Dist., 1993—; music dir. Capt. Anderson Cruises, Clearwater, Fla., 1982-88; pres. CA Turner Services, Inc., Marathon, Fla., 1987; pvt. practice music tchr., Marathon, Fla., 1964—. Composer, illustrator children's music book: Ditties for Kiddies, 1980 (RTC Spl. Achievement award, 1992). Mem. Nat. Assn. Female Execs., Inst. Cert. Fin. Planners (soc. adminstr. 1988-89), Am. Soc. Notaries, Hospitality Industry Assn. Inc., Nat. Assn. Security Dealers, Internat. Assn. Reg. Fin. Planners, U.S. Figure Skating Assn. (preliminary test judge 1975—), Sun Coast Figure Skating Club. Avocations: figure skating, music, fishing, gemology, rock hounding. Office: CA Turner Svcs PO Box 522536 Marathon Shores FL 33052-2536

TURNER, ELIZABETH ADAMS NOBLE (BETTY TURNER), business and strategic planning executive, former mayor; b. Yonkers, N.Y., May 18, 1931; d. James Kendrick and Orrel (Baldwin) Noble; m. Jack Rice Turner, July 11, 1953; children: Jay Kendrick, Randall Ray. BA, Vassar Coll., 1953; MA, Tex. A&I U., 1964. Ednl. cons. Noble & Noble Pub. Co., N.Y.C., 1956-67; psychometrist Corpus Christi Guidance Ctr., 1967-70; psychologist Corpus Christi State Sch., 1970-72, dir. programs, asst. supt., 1972, dir. devel. and vol. svc., 1972-76, dir. rsch. and tng., 1977-79, psychologist Tex. Mental Health and Mental Retardation, 1970-79; pres. Turner Co., 1979—; program cons. Tex. Dept. Mental Health and Mental Retardation, 1979-85; v.p. bus. and govt. rels. Columbia/HCA Healthcare Corp. in Tex., 1985—. Dir. alumni Corpus Christi State U., 1976-77; coord. vols. Summer Head Start Program, Corpus Christi, 1967; chmn. spl. gifts coml United Way, Corpus Christi, 1970; mem. Corpus Christi City Coun., 1979-91; mayor pro tem Corpus Christi, 1981-85, mayor, 1987-91; family founded Barnes and Noble, N.Y.C.; with Leadership Corpus Christi II; founder Com. of 100 and Goals for Corpus Christi; pres. USO; bd. dirs. Coastal Bends Coun. Govts., Corpus Christi Mus., Harbor Playhouse, Communities in Schs., Del Mar Coll. Found., Pres.' Coun., Food Bank, Salvation Army, Jr. League; bd. govs. Southside Community Hosp., 1987-93, Gulfway Nat. Bank, 1985-92, Bayview Hosp., 1992—, strategic planning com. Meml. Hosp., 1992, Bayview Psychiatric Hosp., 1993—, Tex. Capital Network Bd., 1992—, Humana Hosp., Rehab. Hosp. South Tex., Admiral Tex. Navy; apptd. Gov.'s Commn. for Women, 1984-85, Leadership Tex. Class I; founder Goals for Corpus Christi, Bay Area Sports Assn., Assn. Coastal Bend Mayor's Alliance; founder Mayor's Commn. on the Disabled, Mayor's Task Force on the Homeless; active Port Arkansas Cmty. Ch. Recipient Love award YWCA, 1970, Y's Women and Men in Careers award, 1988, Commander's Award for Pub. Svc. U.S. Army, Scroll of Honor award Navy League, award Tex. Hwy. Dept., Road Hand award Tex. Hwy. Commn., 1989; named Corpus Christi Newsmaker of Yr., 1987. Mem. Tex. Psychol. Assn. (pres., mem. exec. bd.), Psychol. Assn. (pres., founder), Tex. Mcpl. League (bd. dir.), Corpus Christi C. of C. (pres., CEO), Jr. League Corpus Christi, Tex. Bookman's Assn., Tex. Assn. Realtors, Kappa Kappa Gamma, Corpus Christi Town Club, Corpus Christi Yacht Club, Jr. Cotillion Club. Home: 4600 Ocean Dr Apt 801 Corpus Christi TX 78412-2542

TURNER, ELIZABETH ROBINSON, junior high educator; b. Madison, Wis., Feb. 19, 1946; d. Elbert Elden and Elva Esther (Miller) Robinson; m. William John Turner, Mar. 10, 1990; 1 child, Ian Elbert Robinson. BS in English edn. with honors, U. Wis., 1968; MS, No. Ill. U., 1972. Lic. tchr. high sch., Social Emotional Disorders/Learning Disabilities, Ill. English tchr. E.G. Kromrey Jr. High Sch., Middleton, Wis., 1968-69, Addison (Ill.) Trail High Sch., 1969-70; tchr. severe emotionally disturbed Larkin Home for Children, Elgin, Ill., 1976-84; tchr. primary diagnostic Davis Elem. Sch. Dist. 303, St. Charles, Ill., 1984-87; tchr. trainer/cons. N.W. Suburban Spl. Edn. Orgn., Palatine, Ill., 1987-89; spl. edn. cons. Keystone Area Edn. Agy. # 1, Dubuque, Iowa, 1989-90; 6th grade tchr. Haines Jr. High Sch. Dist. 303, St. Charles, 1990—; cons. various sch. dists. and schs., Ill., Iowa, Wis., 1987—. Recipient Kane County Disting. Educator award Kane County Edn. Region, 1986. Mem. Assn. Ill. Mid. Schs., Ill. Reading Coun., Delta Kappa Gamma, Phi Delta Kappa.

TURNER, FELICIA ANN, computer specialist; b. Syracuse, N.Y., Sept. 24, 1955; d. Frederick Dewitt and M. Patricia (Murphy) Renz; m. George W. Turner III, Oct. 20, 1979. BS, SUNY, Binghamton, 1976. Auditor U.S. Gen. Acctg. Office, Chgo., 1976-80; evaluator U.S. Gen. Acctg. Office, Atlanta, 1980-83; computer specialist U.S. Gen. Acctg. Office, Atlanta and Denver, 1983-86; sr. computer specialist U.S. Gen. Acctg. Office, Denver, 1986—. Named Outstanding Profl./Adminstr., Denver Fed. Exec. Bd., 1990. Office: US Gen Acctg Office 1244 Speer Blvd Ste 800 Denver CO 80204

TURNER, FLORENCE FRANCES, ceramist; b. Detroit, Mar. 9, 1926; d. Paul Pokrywka and Catherine Gagal; m. Dwight Robert Turner, Oct. 23, 1948; children: Thomas Michael, Nancy Louise, Richard Scott, Garry Robert. Student, Oakland C.C., Royal Oak, Mich., 1975-85, U. Ariz., Yuma, 1985, U. Las Vegas, 1989—. Pres., founder Nev. Clay Guild, Henderson, 1990-94, mem. adv. bd., 1994—; workshop leader Greenfield Village, Dearborn, Mich., 1977-78, Plymouth (Mich.) Hist. Soc., 1979, Las Vegas Sch. System, 1989-90, Detroit Met. area, 1977-85. Bd. dirs. Las Vegas Art Mus., 1987-91; corr. sec. So. Nev. Creative Art Ctr., Las Vegas, 1990-94. Mem. Las Vegas Gem Club, Nev. Camera Club, Golden Key, Phi Kappa Phi. Office: Nev Clay Guild PO Box 50004 Henderson NV 89016

TURNER, FRANCES BERNADETTE, minister, lecturer, author; b. Superior, Wis., June 28, 1903; d. Fyler Bedell and Eleanor Dolores (Donaly) Rainsford; m. Delos Ashley Turner, Dec. 8, 1936. BS in Edn., U. Minn., 1926; MA in Sociology, Northwestern U., 1938; postgrad. social service adminstrn., U. Chgo., 1941-44; PhD in Sociology and Social Work, Washington U., St. Louis, 1948. Ordained to ministry Episcopal Ch. as deacon, 1986, as priest, 1990. Tchr. high sch. Bessemer, Mich., 1924-28; field rep. nat. staff ARC, 1929-36, chpt. exec. sec. Kans., Wash., Nev., 1929-36; psychiat. social worker Chgo. State Hosp. and Ill. Inst. Research, 1938-41; chief social service Dixon (Ill.) State Hosp., 1945; assoc. prof. sociology and social work Ariz. State Coll., Tempe, 1946-56; student counselor nursing schs. Good Samaritan Meml. Hosps., Phoenix, 1946-56; ordained minister Divine Sci. Ch., 1965; founder Divine Sci. Ctr., Evanston, Ill., 1965; pastor Divine Sci. Ch., Roanoke and Evanston, Ill., 1971-72; conducted chapel service Carrillo Hotel, Santa Barbara, Calif., 1979-80; resident counselor Retirement Home, Wichita, Kans., 1974-76; instr. div. continuing edn. Marquette U., 1976, 81-82, Calif. State U., 1976; chaplain Hillcrest Retirement Home, Boise, Idaho, 1986-87, North Shore Retirement Hotel, Evanston, Ill., 1988-90; pastoral care ministry St. John's Episcopal Ch., Roanoke, Va., 1989-90; chaplain, lectr. Park Grove Retirement Home, Roanoke, Va., 1990-91; assisting priest St. Paul's Episcopal Ch., Milw., 1991—; host radio program Pages from My Notebook, Sta. KTAR, Phoenix, Sta. KYND, Tempe, Ariz., Stas. WEAW and WRSV, Chgo. area, Sta. WFIR, Roanoke, Sta. KICT, Wichita, Kans., Stas. WTMJ and MYMS, Milw., Sta. KSUL, Long Beach, Calif., Sta. KRUZ, Santa Barbara, Calif., radio program Growing Older Graciously, Sta. WRIS, Roanoke, 1990-91. Author: Happy Is the Man, 1965, God-centered Therapy, 1968, Faith of Little Creatures, 1972, Prosperity and the Healing Power of Prayer, 1984; contbr. articles and poetry to newspapers and mags. Bd. dirs. Maricopa council Campfire Girls, Phoenix, 1955-61. Fellow Am. Sociol. Assn.; mem. Nat. Assn. Social Workers, Assn. Cert. Social Workers, Am. Assn. Marriage Counselors, Internat. Assn. Women Ministers, Am. Assn. Pastoral Counselors (affiliate), Nat. League Am. Pen Women, Kans. Authors Club, World Poetry Soc., Internat. New Thought Alliance, Ret. Officers Assn. (aux.), St. Hilda's Guild, St. Michael's Episcopal Cathedral, Channel City Women's Forum, Santa Barbara, Calif., Daus. of Nile, Aviation Pioneers. Home: 924 E Juneau Ave Apt 404 Milwaukee WI 53202-2748

TURNER, GLORIA LOUISE, quality improvement and risk management professional; b. Jersey City, N.J., Jan. 28, 1951; d. Luther Porter Sr. and Bessie Louise (Mallisham) T. BA, Glassboro State Coll., 1973. Cert. tchr., N.J. English tchr. Frank H. Morrell High Sch., Irvington, N.J., 1973-81; spl. agt. Prudential Ins. Co., West Orange, N.J., 1981-83; customer svc. rep. Blue Cross & Blue Shield of N.J., Newark, 1984-85, training analyst, 1985-87, asst. mgr., 1987-89, mgmt. devel. specialist, 1989—; cert. instr. The Forum Corp., Boston, 1989—. Corp. vol. Boys and Girls Club, Newark, 1990-92; bd. dirs. First Wesleyan Ch., Jersey City, 1981-82, head ch. teller, 1976—, Sunday sch. tchr., 1991—; workshop leader Inroads of No. N.J., 1991—, mem. tng. adv. com., 1994—; advisor Irvington H.S. Student Coun., 1977-81; mem. Newark Mus. Named one of Outstanding Young Women of Am., 1981, 83. Mem. AAUW, ASTD, Network for Blue Cross and Blue Shield of N.J. Inc. Employees (pres. 1990-92, exec. bd. dirs. 1992—, celebrity read program 1992—), Minority Interchange (No. N.J. chpt. conf. facilitator

1993). Office: Blue Cross Blue Shield NJ 3 Penn Plz E Newark NJ 07105-2200

TURNER, JANE ANN, federal agent; b. Rapid City, S.D., Aug. 26, 1951; d. John Owen and Wilma Veona (Thompson) T.; 1 child, Victoria Thompson. BA, Carroll Coll., 1973; student forensic psychology, John Jay Sch. Criminal Justice, N.Y.C., 1985-87. Spl. agt. FBI, Seattle and N.Y.C., 1978-87; sr. resident spl. agt. FBI, Minot, N.D., 1987—; spkr., instr. FBI, Seattle, N.Y.C. and Minot, 1978—, Psychol. Profiler, 1983—. Mem. Minot Commn. on the Status of Women, 1991-93. Mem. Gen. Fedn. Women's Clubs (v.p. 1992-93), Women in Law Enforcement, N.D. Peace Officer Assn., Optimist Club. Office: FBI PO Box 968 Fed Bldg Minot ND 58701

TURNER, JANET SULLIVAN, painter; b. Gardiner, Maine, Nov. 15, 1935; d. Clayton Jefferson and Frances (Leighton) Sullivan; m. Terry Turner, Oct. 6, 1956; children: Lisa Turner Reid, Michael Ross, Jonathan Brett. BA cum laude, Mich. State U., 1956; student, Haystack Mountain Sch. lectr. student cultural exch. program Pa. State U., Harrisburg, 1985; rep. Am. Women in Art, UN World Conf. on Women, Nairobi, Kenya, 1985. One-artist shows include San Diego Art Inst., 1971, Villanova (Pa.) U. Gallery, 1982, Pa. State U. Gallery, Middletown, 1985, Temple U. Gallery, 1986, Widener U. Art Mus., Chester, Pa., 1987, Suzanne Gross Gallery, Phila., 1986-89, Trenton City Mus., 1990, Gloucester Coll., 1990; group shows include Del. Art Mus., Wilmington, 1978, Woodmere Art Mus., Phila., 1980, Port of History Museum, Phila., 1984, Allentown Art Mus., 1984, Trenton City Mus. Ellarslie Open VIII, Trenton, N.J., 1989, Ammo Gallery, Bklyn., 1989, Pa. State Mus., Harrisburg, 1990, 91, Galeria Mesa, Mesa, Ariz., 1991, Del. Ctr. for Contemporary Arts, Wilmington, 1992, Holter Mus., Helena, Mont., 1992, S.W. Tex. State U., San Marcos, Tex., 1993, Fla. State U. Mus., Tallahassee, 1993, Newark Mus., 1993, U. Del., 1994, 1st St. Gallery, N.Y.C., 1994; represented in permanent collections Nat. Mus. Women in Arts, Washington, Mich. State U., East Lansing, ARA Services Inc., Phila., Blue Cross/Blue Shield, Phila, Am. Nat. Bank and Trust Co., Rockford, Ill., Burroughs Corp., Lisle, Ill., State Mus. Pa., Harrisburg, Bryn Mawr (Pa.) Coll.; contbg. writer and art critic Art Matters, Phila., 1987; artists of the 1990's series featured in Manhattan Arts mag., N.Y.C., 1990. Bd. dirs. Rittenhouse Sq. Fine Arts Ann., Phila., 1984-86. Recipient 2d pl. award San Diego Art Inst. 19th Ann. Exhbn., 1971, award of merit Pavilion Gallery, Mt. Holly, N.J., 1991, 3d pl. Art of State of Pa. Katonah Mus. of Art, N.Y., 1992. Mem. Artists Equity (bd. dirs. 1985-86, 1st v.p. Phila. 1986-87, newsletter editor 1985-86, pres. 1987-88), Phila. Watercolor Club, Delta Phi Delta. Democrat. Roman Catholic. Home and Studio: 88 Cambridge Dr Glen Mills PA 19342

TURNER, JANINE, actress; b. Lincoln, Nebr., Dec. 6, 1963; d. Janice Gaunt. Appearences include (TV) Behind the Screen, 1981-82, General Hospital, 1982-83, Norther Exposure, 1990— (Hollywood Fgn. Press Assn. award 1992, Emmy award nominee 1993), (films) Young Doctors in Love, 1982, Knights of the City, 1985, Tai-Pan, 1986, Monkey Shines: An Experiment in Fear, 1988, Steel Magnolias, 1988, The Ambulance, 1990, Cliffhanger, 1993. Office: CAA 9830 Wilshire Blvd Beverly Hills CA 90212*

TURNER, JEAN-LOUISE, public relations executive; b. Washington, Sept. 29, 1942; d. Fletcher Wood and Mary Louise (Gant) T.; student Howard U., 1959-62; B.A., Fed. City Coll., 1970; M.A., 1972; children—Nathaniel Anthony Landry, Mark Andrew Landry. Coordinator public relations Sta. WRC-TV, Washington, 1969; adminstr. prodn., 1970-72; mgmt. trainee NBC, Washington, 1972; producer spls. Sta. WRC-TV, 1972-76, asso. producer documentaries, 1972-76; mgr. community affairs and public affairs, host Sta. WRC/WKYS, Washington, 1976-78, producer WRC 1978-79; media rep. PEPCO, Washington, 1979-81; press aide D.C. City Council, 1981-82; dir. pub. relations LaMancha, Inc., 1983-84; v.p. Talisman Assocs., 1984—. cons. Jafra Skin Care, 1994; Judge Gabriel awards; mem. media panel D.C. Arts and Humanities Commn.; bd. dirs. Epilepsy Found. Am.; pres. parish coun. St. Francis de Sales Roman Cath. Ch., 1993, 94—; career role model St. Anthony's High Sch. Recipient Hallmark award Jr. Achievement, 1976, Public Service award Washington Area Council Alcoholism and Drug Abuse, 1977; Public Interest award Council Better Bus. Burs. Inc., 1977. Mem. Capital Press Club, Washington Assn. Black Journalists, Nat. Acad. TV Arts and Scis., Nat. Assn. Public Continuing Adult Edn., Anchor Mental Health Assn. (bd. dirs., chmn. 1992-94, Award of Appreciation 1994), Washington Women's Forum (charter), Alpha Kappa Alpha. Roman Catholic. Editorial bd. NAPCAE Exchange, 1979-81. Home: 2715 31st Pl NE Washington DC 20018-1601 Office: 4005 20th St NE Washington DC 20018

TURNER, KAREN ELAINE, pastor; b. Chgo., Jan. 29, 1953; d. Washington Sylvester and Geraldine (Price) T. BA, Ill. Wesleyan U., 1974. Ordained to Ch. of God ministry; cert. tchr., Ill. Ins. agt. Washington Nat., Evanston, Ill., 1977-79; group ins. exec. sales Bankers Life, Des Moines, 1979-81; tchr. St. James Acad., Chgo., 1984, Chgo. Bd. Edn., 1989-91; tchr., office adminstr. Ahead Christian Ctr., Chgo., 1989—; pastor Ch. of God Ch., Chgo., 1990—. Coord. Ahead Adult Literacy Program, Chgo., 1991—. Mem. NAFE, internat. Platform Assn. Office: Ch of God Ch 1459 E 69th St Chicago IL 60637-4863

TURNER, KATHLEEN, actress; b. Springfield, Mo., June 19, 1954; m. Jay Weiss, 1984; 1 child, Rachel Ann. Student, Cen. Sch. of Speech and Drama, London, Southwest Mo. State U.; BFA, U. Md. various theater roles, Broadway debut: Gemini, 1978, Cat on a Hot Tin Roof, 1990; appeared in TV series The Doctors, 1977; films include Body Heat, 1981, A Breed Apart, 1982, The Man With Two Brains, 1983, Crimes of Passion, 1984, Romancing the Stone, 1984, Prizzi's Honor (Golden Globe award for best actress), 1985, The Jewel of the Nile, 1985, Peggy Sue Got Married, (D.W. Griffith award for best actress, Oscar nomination for best actress) 1986, Julia and Julia, 1988, Switching Channels, 1988, Who Framed Roger Rabbit, 1988, Accidental Tourist, 1988, The War of the Roses, 1989. V.I. Warshawski, 1991, Undercover Blues, 1993, House of Cards, 1993, Serial Mom, 1994, Naked in New York, 1994; dir. (Showtime Cable movie) Leslie's Folly, 1994; also performed in radio shows with the BBC, 1992, 93. Office: ICM 8899 Beverly Blvd Los Angeles CA 90048*

TURNER, KIMBERLY ANN, marketing professional, research center administrator; b. Salem, Ohio, May 31, 1957; d. James Lester and Lola Mae (Jones) Boone; m. Marvin Turner, Dec. 3, 1986 (div. Oct. 1994); children: Brittany Lauren, Erika Nikki. BA, Morgan State U., 1980. Contracts adminstr. HITCO, Gardena, Calif., 1981-82; cost analyst N.Am. Rockwell, El Segundo, Calif., 1982-84; fin. planning analyst Northrop Electronics, Hawthorne, Calif., 1984-86; project mgr. Northrop Aircraft, Hawthorne, 1986-89, fin. adminstr., 1989-94; supr. ctr. survey rsch. U. Nev., Las Vegas, 1994—; asst. rsch. cons. Downey Rsch. Assoc., Las Vegas, 1994—; trainer Total Quality Mgmt., Hawthorne, 1991; cons. Dept. Aviation, Las Vegas, 1994, Boulevard Mall, Las Vegas, 1994; coord. rsch. Wait & Schaffer, Reno, 1994. Coord. United Way, Hawthorne, 1987. Grantee Morgan State U., 1975; scholar Morgan State U., 1975. Fellow Am. Mgmt. Assn. (cert. 1987), Performance Mgmt. Assn., Mgmt. & Profl. Devel. (cert. 1990). Republican. Home: 2371 Moorpark Way Henderson NV 89014 Office: Downey Rsch Assocs PO Box 19136 Las Vegas NV 89132

TURNER, LA FERRIA MARIA, business consultant, financial planner; b. Chgo., Oct. 7, 1962; d. James and Erma (Thomas) T. Student, Coll. Fin. Planning, Denver. Data processor Acad. Gen. Dentistry, Chgo., 1986-87; exec. officer adminstr. Alpha Kappa Alpha, Chgo., 1986; computer cons. Ellis & Ellis Realty, Chgo., 1987; tax cons. IRS, Chgo., 1987-90, L. Turner Fin. Svcs., Chgo., 1990—. Cert. Appreciation Chgo. Dist. Electronic Filing Program Implementation. Fellow NAFE (chairperson membership bd.), Am. Soc. Women Accts., Am. Mgmt. Assn., Nat. Coun. on Pay Equity, Assn. Info. Systems Profls. Democrat. Home: 8011 S Union Ave # G Chicago IL 60620-2538 Office: L Turner Fin Svcs 400 N Wells St 338 Chicago IL 60610-4521

TURNER, LANA (JULIA JEAN MILDRED FRANCES TURNER), actress; b. Wallace, Idaho, Feb. 8, 1921; d. Virgil and Mildred T.; m. Artie Shaw, Feb. 8, 1940 (div.); m. Steven Crane, 1942 (div.); m. Bob Topping (div.); m. Lex Barker (div.); m. Fred May, Nov. 27, 1960 (div.); m. Robert Eaton (div.); m. Ronald Dante. Ed. pub. schs., Presentation Convent, San Francisco. Motion picture actress 1937—; appeared in motion pictures including Love Finds Andy Hardy, 1938, Dramatic School, 1938, Calling Dr. Kildare, Those Glamour Girls, Dancing Co-ed, 1939, Two Girls on Broadway, We Who Are Young, 1940, Ziegfeld Girl, Dr. Jekyll and Mr. Hyde, Honky Tonk, Johnny Eager, 1941, Somewhere I'll Find You, Slightly Dangerous, 1942, Marriage Is a Private Affair, Women's Army, 1944, Keep Your Powder Dry, Week End at the Waldorf, Cass Timberlane, Homecoming, 1947, The Merry Widow, 1951, The Bad and the Beautiful, 1952, Latin Lovers, Flame and the Flesh, Betrayed, The Sea Chase, The Prodigal, Rains of Ranchipur, Another Time, 1958, Imitation of Life, 1959, By Love Possessed, 1961, Bachelor in Paradise, Who's Got the Action, Love Has Many Faces, Madame X, The Big Cube, Persecution, Portrait in Black, Bittersweet Love, 1976; appeared in TV series The Survivors, 1969, Falcon Crest, 1982-83; also numerous theatrical appearances. Author: The Lady, The Legend, The Truth, 1983.

TURNER, LESLIE MARIE, federal official; b. Neptune, N.J., Oct. 2, 1957. BS, NYU, 1980; JD, Georgetown U., 1985. Law clk. Cole, Raywid & Braverman, Washington, 1984-85; jud. clk. to Hon. William C. Pryor U.S. Ct. Appeals (D.C. cir.), Washington, 1985-86; assoc. Akin, Gump, Strauss, Hauer & Feld, L.L.P., Washington, 1986-93; asst. sec. for territorial and internat. affairs Dept. Interior, Washington, 1993—. Office: Dept Interior Territorial & Internat Affairs 1849 C St NW Washington DC 20240

TURNER, LETITIA RHODES, artist; b. Media, Pa., Aug. 17, 1923; d. Samuel Noblit and Letitia (Eves) Rhodes; m. Ellwood Jackson Turner Jr., Aug. 1, 1942; children: Rue Baronsky, Letitia Mayo, Elizabeth Rorke. Sec., treas. Rose Tree Realty Inc., Media, Pa., 1961-81; dance tchr., 1939, 40, 41. Portrait painter (Portrait of Mary 3d pl. 1990, Portrait of Brett 2d pl. 1987). Pres. Am. Legion Aux., Media, 1991, 92, photographer, 1992, sec., 1993-94; 1st v.p. Woman's Aux. Media Presbyn. Ch., Media, 1963; mem. D.A.R.E., Media, 1983-91, 92, 93-94. Mem. Artist Guild Del. County, Art League Del. County. Republican. Home and Office: 321 Dash Ave Media PA 19063-1307

TURNER, LILLIAN ERNA, nurse; b. Coalmont, Colo., Apr. 22, 1918; d. Harvey Oliver and Erna Lena (Wackwitz) T. BS, Colo. State U., 1940, Columbia U., 1945; cert. physician asst., U. Utah, 1978. Commd. 2d lt. Nurse Corps, U.S. Army, 1945; advanced through grades to lt. comdr. USPHS, 1964; 1st lt. U.S. Army, 1945-46; U.S. Pub. Health Svc., 1964-69; dean of women U. Alaska, Fairbanks, 1948-50; head nurse Group Health Hosp., Seattle, 1950-53; adviser to chief nurse Hosp. Am. Samoa, Pago Pago, 1954-60; head nurse Meml. Hosp., Twin Falls, Idaho, 1960-61; shift supr. Hosp. Lago Oil and Transport, Siero Colorado, Aruba, 1961-63; nurse adv. Province Hosp., Danang, South Vietnam, 1964-69, Cho Quan Hosp., South Vietnam, 1970-72; chief nurse, advisor Truk Hosp., Moen, Ea. Caroline Islands, 1972-74; nurse advisor Children's Med. Relief Internat., South Vietnam, 1975; physician's asst. U. Utah, 1976-78, Wagon Circle Med. Clinic, Rawlins, Wyo., 1978-89, Energy Basin Clinic Carbon County Meml. Hosp., Hanna, Wyo., 1989—. Named Nat. Humanitarian Pa. of Yr., 1993, Wyo. Pa. of Yr., 1992. Mem. Wyo. Acad. Physician Assts. (bd. dirs. 1982-83), Am. Acad. Physician Assts., Nat. Assn. Physician Assts. Home: PO Box 337 Hanna WY 82327-0337

TURNER, LISA HILL, county official; b. Rexburg, Idaho, Sept. 11, 1959; d. Dale A. and Betty Jean (Owens) Hill; m. Rick I. Turner, June 10, 1979; 1 child, Keith D. Staff mem. Fremont County Herald-Chronicle, St. Anthony, Idaho, 1977-93, editor, 1985-93; chief dep. treas. Fremont County, St. Anthony, 1994—. Dir. Foster Grandparents, Fremont Gen. Hosp. Found., St. Anthony, Idaho. Named Most Respected Citizen, Free Fisherman's Breakfast, 1991, Hon. Chef, 1987; recipient Cert. of Appreciation, Idaho Gov. Cecil Andrus, 1990. Mem. So. Fremont C. of C. (sec. 1985-88, dir. 1986-89). Mem. LDS Ch.

TURNER, LISA JOYCE, paint manufacturing company executive; b. Galveston, Tex., June 1, 1959; d. Carlton and Dorothy Lee (McPeters) Pappas Kelly; m. E.D. Turner. Student N. Tex. State U., 1977, Richland Coll., 1978, U. Ark.-Little Rock, 1980, IBM Continuing Edn., 1981-82. Mktg. asst. Membership Services, Irving, Tex., 1978, tech. support asst., 1980; programmer, analyst Mail Mktg. Services, Little Rock, 1980-82; bus. broker VR Bus. Brokers, Longview, Tex., 1982-85; mgr., v.p. Creative Coatings Inc., Kilgore, Tex., 1985—, also bd. dirs. Mem. Mothers Against Drunk Drivers, Longview, Tex., 1985-86, v.p. Gregg County chpt.; sec. East Tex. Area Parkinsonism Soc., 1987—. Mem. Data Processing Mgrs. Assn. Baptist. Avocations: skiing, traveling. Home: 3715 Ben Hogan Dr Longview TX 75605 Office: Creative Coatings Inc 428 N Longview St Kilgore TX 75662-5899

TURNER, LISA PHILLIPS, human resources executive; b. Waltham, Mass., Apr. 10, 1951; d. James Sinclair and Virginia (Heathcote) T. BA in Edn. and Philosophy magna cum laude, Washington Coll., Chestertown, Md., 1974; AS in Electronics Tech., AA in Engring., Palm Beach Jr. Coll., 1982; MBA, Nova U., 1986, DSc, 1989; PhD, Kennedy Western U., 1990. Cert. pers. adminstr., quality engr., human resource profl.; lic. USCG capt. Founder, pres. Turner's Bicycle Svc., Inc., Delray Beach, Fla., 1975-80; electronics engr., quality engr. Audio Engring. and Video Arts, Boca Raton, 1980-81; tech. writing instr. Palm Beach Jr. Coll., Lake Worth, Fla., 1981-82; adminstr. tng. and devel. Mitel Inc., Boca Raton, 1982-88; mgr. communications and employee rels. Modular Computer Systems, Inc., Ft. Lauderdale, Fla., 1988-89; U.S. mktg. project mgr. Mitel, Inc., Boca Raton, Fla., 1990-91; v.p. human resources Connectronics, Inc., Ft. Lauderdale, Fla., 1991-93; mgr. human resources Sensormatic Electronics Corp., Boca Raton, Fla., 1993—. With USCG Aux. Mem. ASTD, Am. Soc. for Pers. Adminstrn., Internat. Assn. Quality Circles, Am. Soc. Quality Control, Fla. Employment Mgmt. Assn., Am. Acad. Mgmt., Employment Assn. Fla., Am. Capts. Assn., Citizens Police Acad. Home: PO Box 4687 Boynton Beach FL 33424-4687 Office: Sensormatic Electronics Corp 6600 Congress Ave Boca Raton FL 33487

TURNER, MARGERY AUSTIN, government agency administrator; b. Ithaca, N.Y., July 10, 1955; d. William Weaver and Elizabeth Jane (Hallstrum) Austin; m. James Charles Turner, Aug. 26, 1979; children: James Austin, Benjamin Phillip. BA, Cornell U., 1977; M Urban Planning, George Washington U., 1984. Rschr. Urban Inst., Washington, 1977-88, dir. housing rsch., 1988-93, 1988-93; dep. asst. sec. for rsch. U.S. Dept. HUD, Washington, 1993—. Author: Housing Market Impacts of Rent Control, 1990; co-author: Urban Housing in the 1980's, 1985, Future U.S. Housing Policy, 1987, Opportunities Denied, Opportunities Diminished, 1991, Housing Markets and Residential Mobility, 1993. Mem., coach Boys and Girls Club, Camp Springs, Md., 1990—. Mem. Lambda Alpha.

TURNER, MARGUERITE ROSE COWLES, library administrator; b. Port Sulphur, La., June 21, 1941; d. John Clinton and Marguerite Eileen (Slaybaugh) Cowles; B.A., U. New Orleans, 1963; M.L.S., La. State U., 1966; M.A. in History, U. So. Miss., 1970; divorced; 1 son, Jeffrey Jason. Reference librarian edn. div. U. So. Miss., 1966-70; librarian Pascagoula (Miss.) Jr. High Sch., 1970-71, Irwin County High Sch., Ocilla, Ga., 1971-72; dir. Fitzgerald (Ga.) Carnegie Library, 1974-80; adminstrv. librarian Assumption Parish Library, Napoleonville, La., 1980-83; dir. Jacob S. Mauney Meml. Library, Kings Mountain, N.C., 1983—. Author poems, short stories; writer weekly column Kings Mountain Herald, Shelby Star; contbr. articles to profl. jours. Sunday sch. tchr., First Baptist Ch., librarian, 1975—, Fitzgerald, 1978-80, Napoleonville, 1980-83. Mem. ALA, N.C. Library Assn., Broad River Libr. Assn. Democrat. Office: 100 S Piedmont Ave Kings Mountain NC 28086-3414

TURNER, MARJORIE CLAIRE BONHAJO, retired graphic artist, educator; b. Bay City, Mich., Apr. 14, 1926; d. George Henry and Marjorie Rebekah (Vreeland) Bonhajo; m. Connell Lewis Davis, May 1949 (div. Jan. 1956); m. Edwin Charles Turner, Sept. 21, 1961; 1 child, Tailyn Lee Turner McNeal. Student, Bradley U., 1947-48; BFA, Sch. Art Inst. Chgo., 1948; postgrad., Am. Acad. Art, Chgo., 1954-56, Cranbrook Acad. Art, Bloomfield Hills, Mich., 1957-58; MA in Art, Wayne State U., 1960. Illustrator Treasure Trails, Spenser Press, Chgo., 1956; layout artist Detroit Free Press, 1960-61; art dir., artist Delta Advt., Bay City, 1961-64; adj. instr. painting and comml. art Delta Coll., Saginaw, Mich., 1965-67; art dir., layout artist T&B Advt., Columbia, Md., 1975-79; comml. artist Impressions in Ink, Columbia, 1979-81; graphic artist UCF-Image Link, Orlando, Fla., 1984-94; ret., 1994; instr. painting Visual Arts Ctr., Antioch Coll., Columbia, 1975-79; adj. prof. graphic design UU. Ctrl. Fla., Orlando, 1991—. One-woman shows include Brevard Art Ctr., Melbourne, Fla., 1983, Rainy River C.C., Internat. Falls, Minn., 1993; group shows include U. Mich., 1962-64, Mich. Watercolor Soc., Detroit, 1961-67, Peale Mus., Balt., 1968, 69, 26th Street Gallery, 1968-72, Jerry Gilden Gallery, Pikesville, Md., 1969, Balt. Mus., 1973, Balt. Arts Tower, 1973, 76, Slaton House, Columbia, 1977, 79, Balt. Arts Festival, 1973, 77, 78; represented in numerous pvt. collections. Recipient award Midland Mus., 1966, Saginaw Mus., 1966, Mich. Watercolor Soc., 1967, Peale Mus., 1968. Mem. Daus. Am. Colonists, Soc. Mayflower Descs. (colony gov.-elect Orlando 1994, colony gov. 1995). Democrat. Presbyterian. Home: 933 Millshore Dr Chuluota FL 32766 Office: U Ctrl Fla Graphic Design Dept Orlando FL 32816

TURNER, MARTA DAWN, youth program specialist; b. Morgantown, W.V., Oct. 7, 1954; d. Trubie Lemard and Dorothy Genevieve (Helmick) T.; m. David Michael Dunning, Mar. 1, 1980. Student, Royal Acad. Dramatic Art, London, 1975; BA with honors, Chatham Coll., 1976; grad. cert. in arts adminstrn., Adelphi U., 1982; MA Devel. Drama, Hunter Coll., 1988. Cert. video prodn. specialist. Asst. dir. Riverside Communications, N.Y.C., 1985-88; dir. drama, video youth environ. group Water Proof, Cornell Coop. Extension, 1989-91; playwright, dir. Awareness Players, The Disabled Theatre of Maine, 1993—. Exec. prodr. video projects including Hispanic City Sounds, Time for Peace, Home, Home in Inwood, 1985—; asst. dir., dir. video series Riverside at Worship, 1985-88. Bd. dirs. Trinity Presbyn. Ch., N.Y.C., 1980-90, Am. Diabetes Assn., 1986-87. Home and Office: 818 Ohio St Apt 90 Bangor ME 04401-3859

TURNER, MARYALICE BOWER, employee education and development manager; b. Columbus, Ohio, Dec. 27; d. Jack Leslie and Sylvia Ann (Llewelyn) Bower; m. Don William Turner, July 25, 1981; children: Joshua W., Jessica B. BS in Indsl. Tech. Edn., Ohio State U., 1982; MEd in Ednl. Adminstrn. summa cum laude, Ashland U., 1993. Cert. elem. prin, Ohio, indsl. tech. educator K-12, Ohio; authorized gender/ethnic expectation and student achievement facilitator. Instr. indsl. tech. Ctr. for Effective Learning, Virginia Beach, Va., 1982-85; ednl. cons. Discovery Toys, Martinez, Calif., 1984-87; regional mgr. Flash Video, Granville, Ohio, 1989-92; instr., coord. Licking County Joint Vocat. Sch., Newark, Ohio, 1989-92; employee edn. and devel. mgr. Communicolor, Newark, 1992—; cons. Master Svcs. Group, Granville, 1992—. Bd. dirs. Am. Heart Assn. Mem. AAUW, NAFE, ASTD, Soc. Human Resource Mgrs., Am. Vocat. Assn., Pers. Mgrs. Assn., Ohio State U. Alumni Assn., Epsilon Pi Tau. Home: 1950 Hallie Ln Granville OH 43023-9517

TURNER, MILDRED EDITH, day care owner; b. Winnebago, Wis., Jan. 11, 1926; d. Jewet Candfield and Angeline Mary (Long) T. BS, State Tchrs. Coll., 1949; MS of Edn., U. Wis., Milw., 1962; postgrad., U. Wis., Oshkosh, 1965-70. Cert. tchr., Wis. Tchr. Winnebago County, Omro, Wis., 1945-47, Plymouth (Wis.) Pub. Schs., 1949-51, Ripon (Wis.) Pub. Schs., 1951-53, Omro Pub. Schs., 1953-88; instr. U. Wis., Oshkosh, 1971, supervising tchr. of student tchrs., 1970-91; owner, operator Wee Care Children's Ctr., Omro, 1974—. Contbr. articles to newspapers and profl. publs. Acolyte coord. Algoma Blvd. United Meth. Ch.; supt. Sunday sch., pianist, choir dir., ch. music dir. Eureka/Waukau United Meth. Ch.; sub-dist. children's dir. Watertown sub-dist. United Meth. Ch. Mem. Ret. Tchrs. Assn. Winnebago County, Ret. Tchrs. Assn. Omro, Fox Valley Assn. for Edn. of Young Children, Word and Pen Christian Writers (sec., treas.), Alumni Assn. U. Wis. Oshkosh (treas.), Alumni Assn. Omro, Odd Fellows (past noble grand Rebekah lodge), Omro Study Club (past. pres.). Home and Office: Wee Care Childrens Ctr 305 E Scott St Omro WI 54963-1707

TURNER, PEGGY ANN, graphic designer, visual artist; b. Memphis, Jan. 17, 1951; d. James Patrick and Margaret Helen (Brastock) T. BFA, U. Tenn., 1974, MFA summa cum laude, 1992. Art dir. Turner Design, Knoxville, 1972-84; designer, illustrator Creative Displays, Knoxville, 1974-75; designer alumni affairs U. Tenn., Knoxville, 1975-81; sr. art dir. Whittle Comm., Knoxville, 1982-85; creative dir., sr. art dir. Sullivan-St. Clair Advt., Mobile, Ala., 1985-89; grad. teaching asst. dept. art U. Tenn., Knoxville, 1989-91; prof. graphic design Savannah (Ga.) Coll. Art and Design, 1991-92; asst. prof. graphic design Va. Polytechnic Inst. and State U., 1992—. One-woman shows include: Ewing Gallery, Savannah, 1993, 94, Armory Art Gallery, Va., Poly. Inst., 1993, Gallery 303, Ga. So. U., 1994; group exhbns. include: Women's Art Works III, Rochester, N.Y. (jury prize), Nat. Expos II, Chgo., 1993, Current Works '93, Kansas City, Mo., Visual Voices: The Female, U. W. Fla., 1994, Paper Stars, San Francisco, 1994, Nat. Exposures, Winston Salem, N.C. and others. Recipient Coun. for the Advancement of Edn. Nat. Citation award, 1981, Warren Paper Co. award, 1984; named Outstanding Young Woman of Am., 1988; grantee Arts and Sci./Va. Poly. Inst. Pilot Creative Arts, 1992, Va. Poly. Inst. Creative/Match grantee Women's Rsch. Inst., 1993; Fred M. Roddy scholar, 1970, Blinn scholar for fgn. study, 1991. Mem. Am. Inst. Graphic Arts, Coll. Art Assn., Alpha Lambda Delta. Democrat. Episcopalian. Home: 1726 Emerald St Blacksburg VA 24060-5806 Office: Va Polytechnic Inst/State U Dept Art and Art History 201 Draper Rd Blacksburg VA 24061-0103

TURNER, REGINA ANN, sales associate; b. Hobgood, N.C., Mar. 21, 1950; d. Milton Zakerize and Mamie Etheline (White) Anthony; m. Lawrence Elton Turner, June 29, 1974; children: Shenesa Reneé, Lawrence Elton Jr. Grad. high sch., Scotland Neck, N.C. Sec. Boy Scouts Office, Waterbury, Conn., 1974-76; tchr.'s asst. Community Assocs., Waterbury, Conn., 1983-88; day care worker Honey Bear Hideaway, Waterbury, Conn., 1988-89; with Sears, Waterbury, Conn., 1989-92; sales assoc. Bradless, Waterbury, Conn., 1993-94; with Siemer Co., Watertown, 1995—. Named Mother of Yr. 1st Assembly of God, Waterbury, 1989, 93, Sunday Sch. Tchr. of Yr., 1985. Home: 150 Manhan St Waterbury CT 06710

TURNER, SHIRLEY BROADHEAD, court office administrator; b. Brewer, Miss., May 11, 1940; d. Samuel Elzie and Virdie Matilda (Cox) Broadhead; m. Jerome Turner, Oct. 18, 1969 (div. July 1986); children: Alexandra Cox, Christian Annette; m. Jerry Wayman Hamilton, Jan. 14, 1995. BS, U. Miss., 1961; MEd, Memphis State U., 1968. Cert. tchr. secondary edn., splty. in retardation. Exec. sec. Shelby County Gen. Sessions Ct., Memphis, 1989-91, ct. adminstr., 1991—; past living ads chmn. Les Passees, Inc. Past founder, pres. County Polit. Club; past bd. dirs. Memphis Symphony; active Opera Guild, Ennead Carnival, 2d Bapt. Ch., Memphis/Shelby County Assn. for Retarded People Assn.; past mem. curriculum com. Memphis City Schs., 1963, 64. Mem. Le Bonheur Club, Inc. (past bd. dirs.), Duration Club, Inc. (past bd. dirs.). Office: Shelby County Gen Session Judge's Office LL56 201 Poplar Ave Memphis TN 38103-1947

TURNER-MCCANN, ROBIN LEE, child analyst; b. Spokane, Wash., Sept. 27, 1945; d. Robert Allen McCann and Mary Lavelle Wilson; m. C. F. Turner, Sept. 10, 1975. BA, U. Mont., 1967; MSW, Wash. U., 1969; cert. child-adolescent psychoanalysis, Hampstead Ctr., London, Eng., 1979. Asst. clin. prof., child and adolescent medicine St. Louis U. Med. Sch., 1984—, Cardinal Glennon Children's Hosp., 1984—; pvt. practice; mem. faculty St. Louis Psychoanalytic Inst., 1982—, chmn. child study group, 1994—, dir. child devel. project, 1994—; mem. ho. of dels. U. Mont., Missoula, 1990—. Mem. APA, Assn. Child Psychoanalysis. Office: 141 N Meramec Ave Ste 208-209 Clayton MO 63105

TURO, JOANN K., psychoanalyst, psychotherapist, consultant; b. Westerly, R.I., Feb. 13, 1938; d. Angelo and Anna Josephine (Drew) T. BS in Biology and Chemistry, U. R.I., 1959; MA in Human Rels. and Psychology, Ohio U., 1964; postgrad., NYU, 1966-71, N.Y. Freudian Inst., N.Y.C., 1977-85, Mental Health Inst., N.Y.C., 1977-80. Rsch. asst. biochemistry studies on schizophrenia Harvard U. Med. Sch., Boston, 1959-60; indsl. psychology asst. studies on managerial success N.Y. Telephone Co., N.Y.C., 1964-66; staff psychologist Testing and Advisement Ctr. NYU, 1966-70; staff psychologist M.D.C. Psychol. Svcs., N.Y.C., 1971-72; clin. dir. Greenwich House Substance Abuse Clinic, N.Y.C., 1973-76; cons. psychotherapist Mental Health Consultation Ctr., N.Y.C., 1977-82; pvt. practice psychoanlysis and psychotherapy N.Y.C., 1981—; mental health cons. Bklyn. Ctr. for Psychotherapy, 1976-78; with Psychoanaltyic Consultation Svcs., 1994—;

presenter in field. Mem. Internat. Psychoanalytic Assn. (cert.), Soc. for Personality Assessment (cert.), N.Y. Freudian Soc. (cert., co-chmn. grad. com. 1985-86, mem. continuing edn. com. 1986—, pub. rels. com. 1992-93, psychoanalytic consult svc. 1994—), N.Y. Coun. Psychoanalytic Psychotherapists (cert.), Met. Assn. for Coll. Mental Health Practitioners (cert.). Office: 15 W 12th St Apt 12D New York NY 10011-8556

TUROCI, MARSHA MAY, county official; b. East Chicago, Ind., Mar. 21, 1940; d. Marshall W. and Georgia May Burrell; m. Les Turoci, Aug. 6, 1960 (div. 1994). Field rep. San Bernardino (Calif.) County, mem. bd. suprs., 1988—; chmn. Victor Valley Econ. Devel. Authority; active Mojave Desert Air Quality Control Bd., Southwestern Low Level Radiation Waste Commn. Active Calif. State Rep. Ctrl. Com. Recipient Law Enforcement award Optimists Club, 1985, Disting. Citizen award Boy Scouts Am., 1993; named Hesperian of Yr., Hesperia C. of C., 1981, Woman of Achievement, Victor Valley Bus. and Profl. Women, 1989. Mem. Nat. Assn. Counties (mem. pub. lands com.), So. Calif. Regional Assn. County Suprs., So. Calif. Associated Govts., Calif. State Assn. Counties, Calif. Elected Women's Assn. for Edn. and Rsch. Office: San Bernardino County Bd Suprs 385 N Arrowhead Ave San Bernardino CA 92415-0110

TUROCK, BETTY JANE, library and information science educator, educational association administrator; b. Scranton, Pa., June 12; d. David and Ruth Carolyn (Sweetser) Argust; BA magna cum laude (Charles Weston scholar), Syracuse U., 1955; postgrad. (scholar) U. Pa., 1956; MLS, Rutgers U., 1970, PhD, 1981; m. Frank M. Turock, June 16, 1956; children: David L., B. Drew. Library and materials coordinator Holmdel (N.J.) Public Schs., 1963-65; story-teller Wheaton (Ill.) Public Library, 1965-67; ednl. media specialist Alhambra Public Sch., Phoenix, 1967-70; br. librarian, area librarian, head extension service Forsyth County Public Library System, Winston-Salem, N.C., 1970-73; asst. dir. Montclair (N.J.) Public Library, 1973-75, dir., 1975-77; asst. dir. Monroe County Library System, Rochester, N.Y., 1978-81; asst. prof. Rutgers U. Grad. Sch. Communications, Info. and Library Studies, 1981-87, assoc. prof. 1987-93, prof. 1994—, dept. chair, 1989—, dir. MLS program, 1990—; vis. prof. Rutgers U. Grad. Sch. Library and Info. Studies, 1980-81; adviser U.S. Dept. Edn. Office of Libr. Programs, 1988-89. Trustee, Raritan Twp. (N.J.) Public Library, 1961-62, Keystone Jr. Coll., 1991—, Freedom to Read Found; mem. Bd. Edn. Raritan Twp., 1962-66; mem. Title VII Adv. Bd., Montclair Public Schs., 1975-77; ALA coord. Task Force on Women, 1978-84, mem. action coun.; treas. Social Responsibilities Round Table, 1978-84. Recipient N.J. Libr. Leadership award, 1994; named Woman of Yr., Raritan-Holmdel Woman's Club, 1975. Mem. AAUP, Am. Soc. Info. Assn., Assn. Libr. and Info. Sci. Edn., Am. Libr. Assn. (pres.-elect 1994—, exec. bd. 1991—, coun. 1988—), Rutgers U. Grad. Sch. Library and Info. Studies Alumni Assn. (pres. 1977-78, Disting. Alumni award 1994), Phi Theta Kappa, Psi Chi, Beta Phi Mu, Pi Beta Phi. Unitarian. Author: Serving Older Adults, 1983, Creating a Financial Plan, 1992; editor: The Bottom Line, 1984—; contbr. articles to profl. jours. Home: 39 Highwood Rd Somerset NJ 08873 Office: Rutgers U 4 Huntington St New Brunswick NJ 08901-1071

TUROCK, JANE PARSICK, nutritionist; b. Peckville, Pa., Apr. 15, 1947; d. Paul Charles and Elizabeth Dorothy (Mistysyn) Parsick; m. Michael John, July 12, 1968; children: Eric Matthew, Nathan Andrew, J. Seth, Melanie Kay. BS, Marywood Coll., Scranton, 1969; MS, Marywood Coll., 1982. Registered dietitian; cert. nutrition specialist. Registered dietitian Jane P. Turock, Scranton, Pa., 1985--; founder and chief dietitian Gastric Bubble, Scranton, Pa., 1986--; prof. Penn State Coll., Scranton, Pa., 1987--; dietitian & presenter WNEP TV Healthwatch, Avoca, Pa., 1988--; dir. & chief dietitian Vascular Inst. of Northeast Pa., Pa., 1989--; owner, mgr. Nutrition...Plus/Fitness Unlimited, Scranton, Pa., 1991—; cons. Home Health Care Assn., Clarks Summit, 1985—; dietitian Clarks Summit, 1985—; founder Nat. Nutrition Month Bakeoff; dir. Camp Jane. Treas. Lackawanna County Med. Soc. Aux., 1974-76, pres., 1979-80, bd. dirs., 1980-81; allocations com. United Way Lackawanna County, 1990—. Mem. Am. Dietic Assn., Northeast Dist. Pa. Dietic Diet Therapy, Consulting Nutritionists in Pvt. Practice, Am. Diabetic Assn., Northeast Womens Network, Allied Wedding Firm. Republican. Roman Catholic. Office: Nutrition Plus Fitness Unltd 815 Smith St Scranton PA 18504-3150 also: Abington Family Svcs 211 N State St Clarks Summit PA 18411-1087 also: Lady Jane Inc Chesterbrook Plz Wayne PA 19087

TURRI, LINDA, secondary education educator; b. Rochester, N.Y., June 11, 1947; d. Clarence C. and Elsie (Smith) Monahan; m. Robert Turri, June 21, 1974 (dec. Aug. 1992). BS, N.Y. State Coll. at Cortland, 1969. Tchr. sci. Geneva (N.Y.) High Sch., 1969—. Mentor Human Genome Project. Mem. NEA, N.Y. Sci. Tchrs. Assn., N.Y. State Tchrs. Assn. Home: 124 Cayuga St Seneca Falls NY 13148 Office: Geneva High Sch Carter Rd Geneva NY 14456

TURRI, SUSAN TESTA, writer, editor, researcher; b. Manchester, N.H., Aug. 29, 1946; d. Michael P. and Christine (Holscher) Testa; m. Joseph A. Turri, Dec. 27, 1975; 1 child, Michael. Cert. interpreting, U. Lisbon, 1962-64; BA, NYU, 1969; postgrad., Cimade Inst., Paris, 1971-73. Freelance writer, 1975—; U.S. corr. narcotics and substance abuse Interdépendances, Paris, 1992—. Author: 150 Years (Banks), 1978; contbr. articles to AGORA (French med. ethics jour.), numerous others. Trustee Met. Forum, Rochester, N.Y., 1993; mem. women's coun. Meml. Art Gallery, Rochester, 1990—; founding mem., treas. Thousand Island Park Landmark Soc., Thousand Island Park, N.Y., 1983—; participant edn. project Cimade/UNESCO, Algeria, 1973; advisor preservation bd. Thousand Island Park, N.Y., 1994—. Home: 110 Merriman St Rochester NY 14607

TUTT, GLORIA J. RUTHERFORD, insurance company executive; b. Texarkana, Ark., Sept. 1, 1945; d. William Thomas and Lois Elizabeth (Vick) Rutherford; m. F. David Tutt, Nov. 27, 1964; children: David Wayne, Danny Ray, Darryl Wilson. Student, Texarkana Jr. Coll., 1962-63. Agy. adminstr. Nat. Found. Life Ins., Oklahoma City, 1973-77; office mgr. NFC Assocs., Little Rock, 1977-78; owner, corp. sec. So. Capitol Enterprises, Baton Rouge, 1980—; exec. sec. Ins. Mgmt. & Assocs., 1989—; exec. v.p., chief oper. officer Southern Capitol Enterprises, Inc., Baton Rouge, 1990—; sec. Ins. Mgmt. Consultants, 1991—. Scoutmaster Boy Scouts Am., Baton Rouge, 1977-78; officer PTA, Bethany, Okla., 1971-74; PTF v.p. Parkview Bapt. Sch., Baton Rouge, 1989-90; corp. sponsor, bd. dirs. Baton Rouge chpt. Am. Heart Assn., 1991-92, 93. Democrat. Baptist. Office: So Capitol Enterprises 10915 Perkins Rd Baton Rouge LA 70810-3003

TUTT, LINDA MARIE, counselor; b. Wellington, Tex., Jan. 30, 1947; d. William Leonard and Vada Marie (Hall) Karnes; m. Floyd Wayne Tutt, Mov. 2, 1974; children: Tracy, Terry. BBA, West Tex. State U., 1968; MA, Tex. Western U., 1983. Cert. tchr., counselor, Tex. Tchr. Coppell (Tex.) Ind. Sch. Dist., 1970-75; tchr., counselor Sanger (Tex.) Ind. Sch. Dist., 1981—; counselor trainer, supr. Upward Bound, Denton, Tex., 1991—. Mem. Assn. of Tchrs. and Profl. Educators.

TUTT, LOUISE THOMPSON, lawyer; b. Centerville, Iowa, Nov. 10, 1937; d. Lawrence Eugene and Alice Helen (Thompson) T. B.A., U. Ariz., 1963, J.D., 1969. Bar: Calif. 1972, U.S. Dist. Ct. (so. dist.) Calif. 1972, Mo. 1976. Practice law, San Diego and LaJolla, Calif., 1972-75; appeals referee Div. Employment Security, Jefferson City, Mo., 1977-79; counsel Labor and Indsl. Rels. Commn., Jefferson City, Mo., 1979-80; legal adviser Div. Workers Compensation, Jefferson City, 1980—. Bd. dirs. LaJolla Sinfonia, 1975. Democrat. Home: 6445 Nottingham 2 West Saint Louis MO 63109 Office: 11 N 7th St Rm 250 Saint Louis MO 63101

TUTT, NANCY JEAN, physical therapist; b. Washington, July 4; d. Lewis Jackson and Louise Monroe (Abbott) T. BS, U. Ky., 1947; MA, Columbia U., 1951, Cert. in Phys. Therapy, 1952. Staff Columbia-Presbyn. Med. Ctr., N.Y.C., 1952-54, 56-57; sr. phys. therapist St. Vincent's Hosp., N.Y.C., 1957-60; staff Hans Kraus, M.D., N.Y.C., 1955-56; pvt. practice N.Y.C., 1955-63; phys. therapist James Ewing Hosp., N.Y.C., 1962-63; sr. phys. therapist Inst. Phys Rehab., N.Y.C., 1963-66, Mt. Sinai Hosp./Elmhurst City Hosp., N.Y., 1966-68; asst. dir. phys. rehab. U. N.C. at Dix Hosp., Raleigh, 1968-70, Medictr., Raleigh, 1970-71; pres. Therapeutic Home Care Assocs., Inc., Raleigh, 1970-72, Tammy Lynn Ctr., Raleigh, 1971-72. Vol. VA Hosp., Durham, N.C., 1980-82, Rex Hosp., Raleigh, 1983-84, Duke Inst. for Learning in Retirement, Durham, 1985—. With WAC, 1943-45. Named Ky. Col.; March of Dimes scholar, 1951-52. Mem. AAUW, DAV, NOW, Am. Soc. on Aging, Am. Phys. Therapy Assn. Home: PO Box 51536 Durham NC 27717-1536

TUTTLE, LAURA SHIVE, health care educator, administrator; b. Morristown, N.J., Nov. 19, 1962; d. Richard Byron and Patricia (Butler) Shive; m. Richard Lawrence Tuttle, Dec. 15, 1984; 1 child, Marissa Lynn. BSN, Skidmore Coll., 1984; postgrad., Northeastern U., 1992—. RN. Pub. health nurse Navy Relief Vis. Nurse, San Diego, 1985-86; home health nurse Trend Home Health, San Diego, 1986-87, Scripps Home Health Care, San Diego, 1987, Community Health and Counseling Svcs., Bangor, Maine, 1988-89; clin. svcs. coord. Bangor Dist. Nursing Assn., 1989-91; clin. supr. Spl. Care Home Health Svcs., Woburn, Mass., 1991; br. dir. Spl. Care Home Health Svcs., Quincy, Mass., 1991-92; founder, pres. Career Visions, Inc., Brockton, Mass., 1992—; nursing instr. Eastern Maine Tech. Coll., Bangor, 1988-89; pub. speaker Maine Vets. Homes, Augusta, 1991, Bangor Dist. Nursing Assn., 1990-91. Co-author: Clinical Care of the Geriatric Patient, 1991. Mem. NAFE, Prof. Ski Instrs. Assn. (cert. 1982). Republican.

TUTTLE, LESLIE WOEHR, clinical psychologist, management consultant; b. Haddonfield, N.J., Aug. 20, 1957; d. Harry J. and Mindell (Small) Woehr; m. Robert Bruce Tuttle, Aug. 21, 1977; children: Alexander, Robert Nicholas. BA, Syracuse U., 1977; D in Psychology, Hahnemann U., 1983. Clin. coord. T.R.I.S. Children's Crisis Intervention Ctr., Sicklerville, N.J., 1983-85; pvt. practice Haddonfield, N.J., 1983—; ptnr. Woehr Assocs., Haddonfield, 1984—; adj. prof. Widener U., Chester, Pa., 1993. Mem. APA, Phila. Assn. of Psychoanalytic Psychology (treas. 1987-88). Democrat. Home: 14 S Shirley Ave Moorestown NJ 08057 Office: 38 N Haddon Ave Haddonfield NJ 08033

TUTTLE, M(ARGARET) DIANE, infosystems executive; b. Kansas City, Mo., Aug. 11, 1945; d. Allen T. and Vernia Margaret (Pugh) Ashbaugh; m. Robert Stephen Tuttle; 1 child, Robert Stephen II. BBA, Baker U. Supr. bus. officer South Cen. Bell Tel. Co., 1975-80, supr. network adminstrn., 1980-81, project mgr. billing adminstrn. and contracts, 1981-83, mgr. data telecommunications data systems, 1983-85; sr. mgr. telecommunications, mgmt. infosystems Fed. Express, Memphis, 1985—. Active Alcohol and Drug Coun., Memphis, 1987. Fellow Data Processing Mgmt. Assn.; mem. Christian Bus. Women's Club. Republican. Baptist. Home: 1402 E Rolling Oaks Dr Memphis TN 38119-5930 Office: Fed Express 2828 Business Park Dr Memphis TN 38118-1515

TUTTLE, MARTHA BENEDICT, artist; b. Cin., Feb. 4, 1916; d. Harris Miller and Florence Stevens (McCrea) Benedict; m. Richard Salway Tuttle, June 3, 1939; children: Richard, Jr., McCrea Benedict (dec.), Martha (dec.), Elisabeth Hall. Grad. high sch., Cin. V.p. Barg Bottling Co., Inc., Cin., 1948-80. One-woman shows include KKAE Gallery, 1963, Univ. Club, 1967, Miller Gallery, 1971, St. Clements, N.Y., 1973, Livingston Lodge, 1974, Holly Hill Antiques, 1979, Peterson Gallery, 1983, Art Acad. Cin., 1984, Closson Gallery, 1986, Camargo Gallery, 1992; represented in permanent collection Cin. Art Mus. Tchr. Sunday sch. Grace Episcopal Ch. and Indian Hill Ch., Cin., 1953-75; shareholder Cin. Art Mus.; founder partnership to save the William and Phebe Betts House; donor with partnership to The Nat. Soc. Colonial Dames of Am. the William and Phebe Betts House for establishing a Rsch. Ctr. Recipient Ross Sloneker Collection award. Mem. Soc. Colonial Dames Am. (bd. dirs. 1976-89), Camargo Club. Republican. Home: 5825 Drewry Farm Ln Cincinnati OH 45243

TUTTLE, VIOLET MYREL, elementary school educator; b. Grassy Meadows, W.Va., Aug. 28, 1938; d. Alva Huston and Ila Myrel (Bowles) Fitzwater; m. Donald Silas Tuttle, Sept. 16, 1956; children: Donna Hope McCase, Donald Marion. AS, W.Va. State Coll., 1973, BS, 1975; postgrad., W.Va. U., 1985-92, MEd, 1983. Cert. elem. and secondary sch. tchr., W.Va. Tchr. aide Mary Ingles Sch. Kanawha County Schs., Tad, W.Va., 1969-75; tchr. Chelyan (W.Va.) Sch. Kanawha County Schs., 1975-86, tchr. Belle (W.Va.) Sch., 1986-94, v.p. PTA, 1991-92, computer specialist, 1987-93; tchr. evaluation com. Kanawha County Schs., Charleston, 1985, Elk Elem. ctr., Charleston, 1994—. Mem. Christian edn. bd. dirs. Judson Bapt. Ch., 1986-87, vacation Bible sch. dir., 1986-88. Mem. Belle Women's Club (historian 1994—), Alpha Delta Kappa (v.p. Theta chpt. 1990-91, pres. 1992-94, corr. sec. 1994—, Kanawha dist. coun. v.p. 1994—), Kanawha Coun. Tchrs. Math. Home: 786 Campbells Creek Dr Charleston WV 25306-6735 Office: Elk Elem Ctr 3320 Pennsylvania Ave Charleston WV 25302-4632

TUTTON, BETTY JANE, humanities educator; b. Buffalo, N.Y., June 16, 1924; d. George W. and Beatrice (Hosken) T. AB, Houghton Coll., 1947; EdM, U. Buffalo, 1951; Phd, U. Minn., 1979. Dir. youth and music Princeton (W.Va.) Presbyn. Ch., 1947-48; asst. to assoc. prof. English Bob Jones U., Greenville, S.C., 1950-55; bible tchr. Beaver High Sch., Bluefield, W.Va., 1955-57; asst. prof. English, acting dean of women Agl.-Tech. Inst. SUNY, Alfred, N.Y., 1957-59; assoc. prof. English Taylor U., Upland, Ind., 1959-60; teaching asst. English U. Minn., Mpls., 1960-61; assoc. prof. to prof. English Bethel Coll., St. Paul, 1961-66; prof. humanities St. Petersburg Jr. Coll., Clearwater, Fla., 1966—; chmn. humanities dept. St. Petersburg Jr. Coll., Clearwater, 1986-88; bd. dirs. Samaritan Counseling Ctr., Clearwater, 1991—; exec. com. Clearwater (Fla.) Pub. Libr. Found., 1993—; cons. art edn. Manatee County Pub. Schs., Bradenton and Sarasota, Fla., 1987-88. Ruling elder Trinity Presbyn. Ch., Clearwater, 1981-84; edn. work in area chs., 1966—. Recipient rsch. grant, assistantship U. Minn., Mpls., 1967-69, Excellence in Teaching Alfred and Lisl Schick award, Clearwater, 1980. Mem. Community Coll. Humanities Assn., Nat. Coun. for Excellence in Teaching of Critical Thinking, Pi Lambda Theta. Democrat. Home: 406 N Mars Ave Clearwater FL 34615 Office: St Petersburg Jr Coll Drew St Clearwater FL 34625

TUTWILER, MARGARET DEBARDELEBEN, communications executive; b. Birmingham, Ala., Dec. 28, 1950; d. Temple Wilson and Margaret (DeBardeleben) Tutwiler, II. Student, Finch Coll., 1969-71; B.A., U. Ala., 1973. Sec. Ala. Rep. Party, Birmingham, 1974; scheduler Pres. Ford Com., Birmingham, 1975-78; exec. dir. Pres. Ford Com. Ala., Birmingham, 1976; pub. rels. rep. Nat. Assn. Mfrs. for Ala. and Miss., Birmingham and Washington, 1977-78; dir. scheduling George Bush for Pres. Com., Houston and Washington, 1978-80; spl. asst. to Pres. Reagan and exec. to Chief of Staff The White House, Washington, 1981-85; asst. sec. Dept. Treasury, 1985-88; sr. advisor transition team U.S. Dept. State, Washington, 1988-89, asst. sec. pub. affairs, spokesman, 1989-92; ptnr. Fitzwater & Tutwiler, Inc., Washington, 1993—; dep. chmn. Bush-Quayle '88, Washington, 1988. Recipient Woman of Yr. award Wake Forest U., 1986, Alexander Hamilton award, 1988, Am. Ctr. for Internat. Leadership's Marshall award for outstanding leadership Birmingham Sothern's GALA 10, 1991. Republican. Episcopalian.

TWAROG, SOPHIA NORA, economist; b. Columbus, Ohio, Nov. 29, 1964; d. Leon I. and Katherine (Foster) T.; m. Alberto Klaas, July 2, 1993. BA in Economics magna cum laude, U. Notre Dame, Ind., 1987; MA in Economics, Ohio State U., 1989, PhD in Economics, 1993. Intern Ctr. of Concern, Washington; vol. in Ctr. America Sisters of the Assumption, Phila., 1987-88; vol. in India Christian Found. for Children & Aging, Kansas City, Mo., 1988; rsch. cons. Nat. Bur. Econ. Rsch., Cambridge, Mass., 1990; grad. teaching assoc. Ohio State U., Columbus, 1989-91; econ. affairs officer UN Conf. on Trade and Devel., Geneva, 1993—; contbr. UN Internat. Symposium on Trade Efficiency, Columbus, OH, 1994. Contbr. articles to books. Founder, pres. Overseas Devel. Network-U. Notre Dame, 1986-87; chmn. First Ann. Great Hunger Clean-up, South Bend, Ind., 1987; chmn., co-chmn. Third World Awareness Week, U. Notre Dame, 1986, 87. Recipient Glenna R. Joyce scholarship Joyce Found., 1983-87, John W. Gardner Leadership award U. Notre Dame, 1987, U. Multi-Yr. fellow Ohio State U., 1988, 92, Rsch. fellowship Rheinische Friedrich-Wilhelms U., Bonn, 1990-91, Dice fellowship Ohio State U., 1993. Mem. Am. Econ. Assn., Phi Beta Kappa, Phi Kappa Phi. Home: 182 Oakland Park Ave Columbus OH 43214-4122 Office: UN Conf on Trade & Devel, Palais Des Nations, Ch 1211 Geneva 10, Switzerland

TWEDDLE, JENNIFER LYNNE, academic mental health counselor; b. Toronto, Ont., July 15, 1963; d. Allan Stanley Tweddle and Beth Margaret (Gerry) Smith. Student, U. London, 1983; BA, Calif. State U., Hayward, 1986; MA, Gallaudet U., 1988. Lifeguard Sierra Madre (Calif.) Aquatic Program, 1979-85, instr. water safety, 1980-85, asst. mgr., 1982-85, dir. adapted aquatics, 1984-86; info. asst. Nat. Info. Ctr. on Deafness, Washington, 1986-87; rsch. asst. Gallaudet Rsch. Inst., Washington, 1987; mental health counselor Phoenix Day Sch. for Deaf, 1988-93; counselor Calif. Sch. for Deaf, Riverside, 1993—; speaker, guest Minn. Found. for Better Speech and Hearing, Mpls., 1988; speaker Breakout Conf., Washington, 1992, Calif. Edn. Conf., Sacramento, 1994; conf. coord. Drug Free Schs. Ariz. State U., 1993. Mem. ACD, Am. Sch. Counselor Assn. (speaker 1990), Kappa Delta Pi (speaker, guest 1987). Episcopalian. Office: Calif Sch for Deaf 3044 Horace St Riverside CA 92506-4499

TWINEM, MARY R., psychotherapist, physical therapist; b. Newark, Ohio, June 9, 1941; d. William Way and Thelma Clarendon (George) T.; m. David M. Hopkins, Aug. 17, 1963 (div. 1973); children: Kelly Crabtree, Tarik Hopkins. BA in Psychology, Miami U., 1963; MS in Rehab. Counseling, Syracuse U., 1973; PhD in Psychol. Counseling, U. No. Colo., 1990. Lic. psychotherapist; lic. phys. therapist. Phys. therapist Upstate Med. Ctr., Syracuse, N.Y., 1969-71; counselor Syracuse (N.Y.) Health Ctr., 1973-75; coord. edn. grant Onon Assn. for Retarded, Syracuse, 1975-76; phys. therapist cons. Seguin Cmty. Svcs., Syracuse, 1976-77; sch. psychologist Pueblo (Colo.) Dist. # 60, 1977-91; pvt. practice Lake Point Ctr., Evergreen, Colo., 1991-92; psychotherapist Park Area Family Counseling, Pueblo, 1992-93; head dept. phys. therapy Northridge Care Ctr., New Hope, Minn., 1993—; Denver regional mgr. Cheyenne Mountain Therapy, 1994—; mem. adv. com. Pueblo PTA program Pueblo (Colo.) C.C., 1990-91. Mem. Am. Assn. Counseling & Devel., Am. Phys. Therapy Assn. Office: 245 S Benton # 205 Lakewood CO 80226

TWINING, BEVERLY A., critical care nurse; b. Glen Cove, N.Y., May 10, 1944; d. Harold C. and Lois (Linton) T. RN, Meth. Hosp. of Bklyn., 1965; student in nursing, SUNY, Stony Brook, 1993. Charge nurse Winthrop Hosp., Mineola, N.Y., Cen. Gen. Hosp., Plainview, N.Y., Mather Meml. Hosp., Port Jefferson, N.Y., Sunrest Nursing Home, Port Jefferson; pvt. duty nurse CNR Agy., L.I. Mem. ACCN, N.Y. State Nurses Assn. Address: 31 Birch Hill Rd Mount Sinai NY 11766

TWINING, LYNNE DIANNE, psychotherapist, researcher, writer; b. Midland, Mich., Aug. 14, 1951; d. James and Dorothy Twining; m. Alan Howard Mass. BA in Psychology, Oakland U., 1974; MSW, Wayne State U., 1977; MA in Psychology, Yeshiva U., 1993. Diplomate Am. Bd. Clin. Social Work; cert. Bklyn. Inst. Psychotherapy and Psychoanalysis. Social work supr. non-profit orgn., Detroit, 1977-83; co-founder, co-dir. Women Psychotherapists Bklyn., 1986—; pvt. practice Bklyn. and N.Y.C., 1987—; psychotherapy rschr. Beth Israel Med. Ctr., N.Y.C., 1992—. Author: (with other) Metro Detroit Guide, 1975; contbg. editor: Detroit Guide, 1983; asst. prodr. docudrama Home; columnist Bklyn. Woman; contbr. articles to profl. jours., papers to profl. confs. Bd. dirs. Progressive Artists and Educators Coalition, Detroit, 1977-79. Fellow Am. Orthopsychiat. Assn.; mem. NASW (diplomate), ACLU (sec. exec. bd. Mich. chpt. 1982-83), Internat. Fedn. Psychoanalytical Edn., N.Y. Acad. Scis., Soc. for Psychotherapy Rsch., Nat. Trust for Hist. Preservation, Tng. Inst. Mental Health Practitioners, Nat. Assn. Advancement Psychoanalysis (affiliate), Women Psychotherapists Bklyn. (founding mem.), Amnesty Internat. (freedom writer), Acad. Cert. Social Workers, Bklyn. Inst. Psychotherapy and Psychoanalysis Grad. Assn (mem. steering com.). Office: 55 Eastern Pky Apt 3A Brooklyn NY 11238-5913

TWITTY, MYRTIS JOLENE, medical, surgical nurse, psychiatric nurse; b. Kershaw, S.C., May 21, 1938; d. Minor and Madge Myrtis (Johnson) Sullivan; m. Francis Warren Twitty, Aug. 28, 1958; children: William Joseph, Cindy Darlene, Tony Warren, Larry Wayne, Danny Calvin. ADN, U. S.C., Lancaster, 1982. RN, S.C. Med-surg. nurse Elliot White Meml. Hosp., Lancaster, 1982-84; mem. IV team Chesterfield (S.C.) Gen. Hosp., 1984-85; nurse in residence St. Francis Hosp., Greenville, S.C., 1990; mental health nurse Chestnut Hill Psychiat. Hosp., Travelers Rest, S.C., 1990-91; primary care/med.-surg. nurse St. Francis Hosp., Greenville, S.C., 1990-93; primary neuro/surg. nurse Gaston Meml. Hosp., Gastonia, N.C., 1993-94; home health nurse Total Care, Inc., Monroe, N.C., 1994—; dialysis nurse B.M.A. Tri-County Dialysis Ctr., Chester, S.C., 1994. Den mother Boy Scouts Am., McAllen, Tex., 1964-66. Mem. S.C. Nurses Assn., UDC. Republican. Baptist.

TWOHEY, JERILOU COSSACK, labor arbitrator, mediator; b. Detroit, Apr. 11, 1944; d. Charles Minot and Betty Louise (Weber) Hollis; m. Donald E. Twohey, Dec. 30, 1977 (div. Aug. 1990); children: Paul Kenneth, Rebecca Jean. BA, UCLA, 1965, MS, 1969. Rsch. asst. Inst. of Indsl. Rels., L.A., 1966-68; asst. to pres. Engrs. and Scientst Guild, Burbank, Calif., 1968-69; field examiner region 31 Nat. Labor Rels. Bd., L.A., 1969-73, supr., 1973-76; mem. Calif. Pub. Employment Rels. Bd., Sacramento, 1976-79; arbitrator, mediator Lafayette, Calif., 1979—; lectr. Calif. State U., Hayward, 1993, Chabot C.C., Livermore, 1979-81, U. Louvain, Belgium, 1970; cons. on loan Calif. Agrl. Labor Rels. Bd., Sacramento, 1975. Co-chair Com. to Re-elect Joe Grodin, Contra-Costa County; mem. Com. to Evaluate Sch. Site Usage, Lafayette, 1982-83; chair Springhill Auction Solicitation, Lafeyette, 1989-90. Mem. Am. Arbitration Assn., Indsl. Rels. Rsch. Assn., Soc. of Pofls. in Dispute Resolution, San Francisco Bar Assn. (labor and employment law sect.), Calif. Bar Assn. (membership chair, labor and employment law sect.). Democrat. Presbyterian. Home: 3231 Quandt Rd Lafayette CA 94549

TWOMEY, ELIZABETH M., education commissioner; b. Lynn, Mass.; d. Hugh E. and Theresa A. (Callahan) Molloy; children: Ann, Paula, Charles. AB, Emmanuel Coll., 1959; MEd, Mass. State Coll., 1964; EdD, Boston Coll., 1982; LLB (hon.), Notre Dame, Manchester, N.H., 1984. Elem. sch. tchr. Lynn (Mass.) Pub. Schs., 1959-63; English tchr. Reading (Mass.) Pub. Schs., 1973-75, prin., 1975-81, vice prin., 1981-82; supt. Lincoln (Mass.) Pub. Schs., 1982-88; assoc. commr. Dept. Edn., Quincy, Mass., 1988-92; dep. commr. Dept. Edn., Concord, N.H., 1992-94, commr., 1994—. Trustee Emmanuel Coll., Boston, 1975-85, U. N.H., Durham, 1994—. Recipient Disting. Alumni award Emmanuel Coll. Office: Dept Edn 101 Pleasant St Concord NH 03301

TWOMEY, MARY REGINA, women's rights activist, writer; b. Trenton, N.J., Oct. 11, 1941; d. Anthony James and Mary Beatrice (Burns) Moran; div.; children: Moira, William III, Kathleen. Student, Trenton Jr. Coll., 1960, U. N.H., 1984, McIntosh Coll., Dover, N.H., 1992—. Engrs.' asst. U.S. Govt., Burlington, Mass., 1961-62; ptnr. nursing home business various orgns., Mass., 1969—; tchr. Sacred Heart Sch., Amesbury, Mass., 1974-75; sports writer Rockingham County Newspapers, Hampton, N.H., 1986-88; exec. planning com. Women in Sports Conf., New Agenda/Northeast, 1987—; runner NOW/NAGWS Run for Equality, Washington to Phila., 1986. Del. N.H. Dem. Convs., 1988, 90, 92; cand. for N.H. State Legis., 1990; del. Dem. Nat. Convs., 1964-86; mem. Lobbyist Epilepsy Found. Am., Landover, Md., 1970—. Inducted into New Agenda/Northeast Sports Hall of Fame, 1990. Mem. AAUW, NOW (past state and local v.p. N.H. pres., local publicity chmn., named 1st Woman of Yr. 1990), Dem. Alliance for Women in N.H. (founding mem.), N.H. Women's Lobby, Women's Sports Found. (lobbyist, N.H. chmn. Nat. Women's Sports Day 1989, 90), Assn. for Women in Sports Media, N.H. Common Cause, Paralegal Assn. N.H., N.H. Commn. of Sports Equity for Women. Democrat. Roman Catholic. Home: 7 Hedman Ave Hampton NH 03842-4022

TYAU, GAYLORE CHOY YEN, business educator; b. Honolulu, May 13, 1934; d. Moses M.F. and Bessie (Amana) T. BS, U. Calif., Berkeley, 1956, MBA, 1959. Cert. bus. tchr., instr., C.C. supervision credential, Calif. Tchr. bus. Richmond (Calif.) Union High Sch., 1959-64, Westmoor High Sch., Daly City, Calif., 1964-89; instr. bus. City Coll. San Francisco, 1978-87, 88—; office mgr. P.F. Freytag Assocs., San Francisco, 1978-86. Coordinator Pacific Telephone Co.'s Adopt-a-Sch. Program, Colma, Calif, 1987. Grantee Bechtel Corp., 1983. Mem. Nat. Bus. Edn. Assn., Calif. Bus. Assn. (chairperson program com. 1979, mem. program com. 1981-82, Pacific Bell contract edn. grantee 1989), Calif. Bus. Educatos Assn. (co-chair exec. bd. Bay sect. 1994—), Am. Vocat. Assn., ASCD, Western Bus. Edn. Assn., Internat. Soc. for Bus. Edn., City Coll. Faculty Assn., Jefferson Union High Sch. Dist. Tchrs. Assn., Commonwealth Club of Calif., Beta Phi Gamma.

Republican. Episcopalian. Home: 4050 17th St # 1 San Francisco CA 94114-1903

TYLER, ANNE (MRS. TAGHI M. MODARRESSI), author; b. Mpls., Oct. 25, 1941; d. Lloyd Parry and Phyllis (Mahon) T.; m. Taghi M. Modarressi, May 3, 1963; children: Tezh, Mitra. B.A., Duke U., 1961; postgrad., Columbia U., 1962. Author: If Morning Ever Comes, 1964, The Tin Can Tree, 1965, A Slipping-Down Life, 1970, The Clock Winder, 1972, Celestial Navigation, 1974, Searching for Caleb, 1976, Earthly Possessions, 1977, Morgan's Passing, 1980, Dinner at the Homesick Restaurant, 1982, The Accidental Tourist, 1985, Breathing Lessons, 1988 (Pulitzer Prize for fiction 1989), Saint Maybe, 1991, (juvenile) Tumble Tower, 1993, Ladder of Years, 1995; contbr. short stories to nat. mags. Home: 222 Tunbridge Rd Baltimore MD 21212-3422

TYLER, CAROLYN SMITH, librarian; b. Culverton, Ga., Jan. 30, 1923; d. Marvin Henry and Emmie Frank (Waller) Smith; m. Josie Lee Tyler, Jr., Aug. 31, 1954; 1 child, Josie Lee III. AB, Ga. State Coll. for Women, Milledgeville, 1944; AB in Libr. Sci., Emory U., 1945. Libr. Emory U. Libr. Sch. Libr., Atlanta, 1945-56; serials cataloger William R. Perkins Libr., Duke U., Durham, N.C., 1956-57; part-time cataloger Colleton County Meml. Libr., Walterboro, S.C., 1957-58; edn. libr. Edn. Libr., U. S.C., Columbia, 1960-76; edn. libr. Thomas Cooper Libr., Columbia, 1976-91, ref. libr., 1991-94. Mem. AAUW (v.p. Columbia Br. program 1986-90), ALA, S.C. Libr. Assn., Thomas Cooper Soc. Democrat. Methodist. Home: 1100 Eastminster Dr Columbia SC 29204-3309

TYLER, DARLENE JASMER, dietitian; b. Watford City, N.D., Jan. 26, 1939; d. Edwin Arthur and Leola Irene (Walker) Jasmer; BS, Oreg. State U., 1961; m. Richard G. Tyler, Aug. 26, 1977 (dec.); children: Ronald, Eric, Scott. Clin. dietitian Salem (Oreg.) Hosp., 1965-73; sales supr. Sysco Northwest, Tigard, Oreg., 1975-77; clin. dietitian Physicians & Surgeons Hosp., Portland, Oreg., 1977-79; food svc. dir. Meridian Park Hosp., Tualatin, Oreg., 1979—. Registered dietitian. Mem. Am. Dietetic Assn., Oreg. Dietetic Assn., Portland Dietetic Assn., Am. Soc. Hosp. Food Svc. Adminstrs. Episcopalian. Home: 9472 SW Hume Ct Tualatin OR 97062-9039 Office: 19300 SW 65th St Tualatin OR 97062

TYLER, GAIL MADELEINE, nurse; b. Dhahran, Saudi Arabia, Nov. 21, 1953 (parents Am. citizens); d. Louis Rogers and Nona Jean (Henderson) Tyler; m. Alan J. Moore, Sept. 29, 1990; 1 child, Sean James. AS, Front Range Community Coll., Westminster, Colo., 1979; BS in Nursing, U. Wyo., 1989. RN. Ward sec. Valley View Hosp., Thornton, Colo., 1975-79; nurse Scott and White Hosp., Temple, Tex., 1979-83, Meml. Hosp. Laramie County, Cheyenne, Wyo., 1983-89; dir. DePaul Home Health, 1989-91; field staff nurse Poudre Valley Hosp. Home Care, 1991—. Avocations: collecting internat. dolls, sewing, reading, travel.

TYLER, PRISCILLA, retired English language and education educator; b. Cleve., Oct. 23, 1908; d. Ralph Sargent and Alice Lorraine (Campbell) T. BA in Latin and Greek, Radcliffe Coll., 1932; MA in Edn., Case Western Res. U., 1934, PhD in English, 1953; LLD (hon.), Carleton U., Ottawa, Ont., Can., 1993. Parole officer, case worker Cleve. Sch. for Girls, 1934-35; tchr. English, Latin and French Cleveland Heights (Ohio) Pub. Schs., 1935-45; instr. to asst. prof. English Flora Stone Mather Coll., Cleve., 1945-59, asst. dean, 1957-59; asst. prof. edn., head dept. English Sch. of Edn. Harvard U., Cambridge, Mass., 1959-63; assoc. prof. English, U. Ill., Champaign-Urbana, 1963-67, dir. freshman rhetoric, 1966-67; prof. edn. and English U. Mo., Kansas City, 1967-78, prof. emeritus, 1978—; instr. N.S. (Can.) Dept. Edn., Halifax, summers 1972-73; condr. numerous seminars; former lectr. U. Calif., Berkeley, U. Chgo., Purdue U., U. Mo., Columbia, U. Nebr., Emory U., Fresno State U., Calif. State U., Hayward, San Jose State Coll., Mills Coll., Ala., Tift Coll., Ga., Va. Poly. Inst. and Midwestern U., Tex. Editor: Harpers Modern Classics, 19 vols., 1963, Writers the Other Side of the Horizon, 1964, (with Maree Brooks) Inupiat Paitot, 1974, Sevukakmet, Ways of Life on St. Lawrence Island (Helen Slwooko Carius), 1979; interviewed authors, Jan Carew, Guyana, George Lamming, Barbados, Christopher Okigbo, Nigeria; also articles. Mem. Ohio Gov.'s Com. on Employment of Physically Handicapped, 1957; mem. Friends of Art of Carleton U., Nelson Atkins Mus. Art, Kansas City, Ottawa (Kans.) Art Gallery, Friends of Libr., Ottawa. Recipient Outstanding Achievement and Contbns. in Field of Edn. award Western Res. U., 1962, Disting. Alumna award Laurel Sch., Cleve., 1994; Priscilla Tyler Endowment Fund named in her honor Case Western Res. U., 1980. Mem. MLA, NEA, Archaeol. Inst. Am., Nat. Coun. Tchrs. English (v.p. 1963, mem. com. on history of the profession 1965-68, Commn. on Composition 1968-71, trustee Rsch. Found. 1970-78, Disting. Svc. award 1978), Conf. on Coll. Composition and Comm. (pres. 1963), Arctic Inst. N.Am., Inuit Art Found., Franklin County Hist. Assn., Calif. Assn. Tchrs. English (hon.. Curriculum Commn. Ctrl. Calif.), Delta Kappa Gamma (pres. Upsilon chpt. 1950-52). Democrat. Presbyterian. Home: 4213 Kentucky Ter Ottawa KS 66067-8715

TYLER, SUZANNE M., stage manager; b. Sacramento, Dec. 16, 1964; d. Spencer H. and Lily S. (Serebrakian) T. AA, Sacramento City Coll., 1984; BA, Calif. State U., Sacramento, 1986; MFA, Calif. Inst. of Arts, 1988. Stage mgr. Colo. Shakespeare Festival, Boulder, 1988, Sacramento Theatre Co., 1988—. Democrat. Office: Sacramento Theatre Co 1419 H St Sacramento CA 95814-1901

TYNDALL, MARGARET, association executive; b. Detroit, July 22, 1942; d. Alfred and Annie Catherine (Abey) T.; m. William Wesley Armstrong, July 9, 1988. BS, Wayne State U., Detroit, 1963, MA, 1968; MEd, U. Pitts., 1972, PhD, 1985. Coord. retail retraining U. Ctr. for Adult Edn., Detroit, 1964-65; asst. dir. conf. and inst. Wayne State U., Detroit, 1965-68; dir. adult and continuing edn. Robert Morris Coll., Pitts., 1968-74; dir. career planning Chatham Coll., Pitts., 1974-77; CEO YWCA of Greater Pitts., 1977—. V.p. Women's Leadership Assembly, Pitts., 1991-93, Women's Ctr. & Shelter, Pitts., 1993—; mem. adv. bd. Forbes Fund Com., Pitts., 1983—; bd. dirs. Greater Pitts. Commn. for Women, 1987-91. Mem. Nat. Assn. of YWCA Execs. (pres. 1985-88). Presbyterian. Office: YWCA of Greater Pittsburgh 305 Wood St Pittsburgh PA 15222-1982

TYNES, PAMELA ANNE, federal judge; b. Natchitoches, La., Dec. 3, 1958; d. Robert Jerrell and Carol Ann (Murphy) T.; m. Joseph Henderson Hidalgo, Aug. 8, 1988. BA, Northwestern State U., Natchitoches, 1978; JD, La. State U., 1983. Law clk. U.S. Dist. Ct. (we. dist.) La., Opelousas, 1983-85; assoc. Hunter & Plattsmier, Morgan City, La., 1985-86, Paul Guilliot, Lafayette, La.; pvt. practice Lafayette; U.S. magistrate U.S. Dist. Ct. (we. dist.) La., Lafayette, 1988—. Mem. Nat. Assn. Women Judges, Am. Inns of Ct., La. Bar Found., La. Bar Assn., Lafayette Parish Bar Assn., Acadiana Assn. Women Attys. Republican. Office: US District Court 705 Jefferson St St 178 Lafayette LA 70501-7059*

TYNG, ANNE GRISWOLD, architect; b. Kuling, Kiangsi, China, July 14, 1920; d. Walworth and Ethel Atkinson (Arens) T. (parents Am. citizens); 1 child, Alexandra Stevens. AB, Radcliffe Coll., 1942; M of Architecture, Harvard U., 1944; PhD, U. Pa., 1975. Assoc. Stonorov & Kahn, Architects, 1945-47; assoc. Louis I. Kahn Architect, 1947-73; pvt. practice architecture Phila., 1973—; adj. assoc. prof. architecture U. Pa. Grad. Sch. Fine Arts, 1968—; assoc. cons. architect Phila. Planning Commn. and Phila. Redevel. Authority, 1952-54, Mill Creek Redevel. Plan, 1954; vis. disting. prof. Pratt Inst., 1979-81, vis. critic architecture, 1969; vis. critic architecture Rensselaer Poly. Inst., 1969, 78, Carnegie Mellon U., 1970, Drexel U., 1972-73, Cooper Union, 1974-75, U. Tex., Austin, 1976; lectr. Archtl. Assn., London, Xian U., China, Bath U., Eng., Mexico City, Hong Kong U., 1989, Baltic Summer Sch. Architecture and Planning, Tallinn, Estonia, Parnu, Estonia, 1993; panel speaker Nat. Conv. Am. Inst. Architects, N.Y.C., 1988, also numerous univs. throughout U.S. and Can.; asst. leader People to People Archtl. del. to China, 1983. Subject of films Anne G. Tyng at Parsons School of Design, 1972, Anne G. Tyne at University of Minnesota, 1974, Connecting, 1976, Forming the Future, 1977; work included in Smithsonian Travelling Exhbn., 1979-81, 82, work included in travelling exhbn. Louis I. Kahn: In the Realm of Architecture 1990-94; contbr. articles to profl. publs.; prin. works include: Walworth Tyng Farmhouse (Hon. mention award Phila. chpt. AIA 1953); builder (with G. Yanchenko) Probability Pyramid. Fellow Graham Found. for Advanced Study in Fine Arts, 1965, 79-81. Fellow AIA (Brunner grantee N.Y. chpt. 1964, 83, dir., mem. exec. bd. dirs. Phila. chpt. 1976-78, John Harbeson Disting. Svc. award Phila. chpt. 1991); mem. Nat. Acad. Design (nat. academician), C.G. Jung Ctr. Phila. (planning com. 1979—), Form Forum (co-founder, planning com. 1978—). Democrat. Episcopalian. Home: 2511 Waverly St Philadelphia PA 19146-1049 Office: Univ Pa Dept Architecture Grad Sch Fine Arts Philadelphia PA 19107

TYRRELL, KARINE, documentation analyst; b. Saarbrucken, Germany, Nov. 4, 1940; came to U.S., 1968, naturalized, 1978; d. Eduard and Charlotte (Faber) Ambrosius; BA, McMaster U., Can., 1964; MA, So. Ill. U., 1972, PhD, 1984; m. James Tyrrell, Aug. 27, 1964 (div. 1979); 1 child, Dalton. Tchr., Hamilton (Ont., Can.) Sch. Bd., 1964-65, Ottawa (Ont., Can.) Sch. Bd., 1966-68; research asst. U.S. Grant Assos., So. Ill. U., Carbondale, 1973-74, teaching asst. 1974-77, dissertation fellow, 1977-78; tech. writer Action Data Services, St. Louis, 1979-80, Boeing Computer Services, Wichita, Kans., 1980-90; various contract assignments including Sprint Comm., No. Telecom., and MCI. Home: 210 W 100th Ter Apt 307 Kansas City MO 64114-4435

TYSER, CLAIRE SIPPIL, former secondary education educator; b. Chgo., Aug. 8, 1927; d. Richard and Dorothy (Saperstone) Sippil; m. Alwyn N. Tyser, Apr. 15, 1950; children: Patricia, Pamela Tyser Bartlett. BS, Skidmore Coll., 1949; postgrad., Rochester Inst. Tech., 1968-72. Cert. art tchr. K-12, N.Y. Art layout and ad worker Neisner Bros., Rochester, N.Y., 1949; tchr. art Brighton High Sch., Rochester, 1968-91, ret., 1991; tchr. painting adult edn., Pittsford, N.Y., Penfield, N.Y., 1964-67; substitute tchr. grades 1-12 local Rochester and suburban schs., 1964-68. Author, illustrator: (children's book) Poofy, 1954. Vol. Genesse Hosp., 1991—. Mem. Irondiquoit Country Club. Home: 1906 Elmwood Ave Rochester NY 14620

TYSON, ANNE ELIZABETH DODGE, theologian; b. Phila., May 10, 1959; d. Harold Stuart and Anne (Zillger) Dodge; m. John Horton Tyson, Jan. 6, 1990. BA, U. Calif., 1981; MDiv, Gordon Conwell Theol. Sem., 1986; STM, Yale U., 1987; PhD, U. Edinburgh, 1993. Sr. rsch. assoc. World Vision, Internat., Monrovia, Calif., 1987-88; program dir. Trinity United Meth. Ch., Jacksonville, N.C., 1991-93; dir. Christian Edn. Haymount United Meth. Ch., Fayetteville, N.C., 1993—. Scholarship Leighton F.S. Ford Found., 1985. Republican. Home: PO Box 64132 Fayetteville NC 28306 Office: Haymount United Meth Ch 1700 Ft Bragg Rd Fayetteville NC 28303

TYSON, CHARLOTTE ROSE, storage systems development manager; b. San Mateo, Calif., Aug. 14, 1954; d. Herbert Parry and Rose (Goldner) T.; m. Edward Philip Sejud, Aug. 11, 1979; children: Laura Rose, Elizabeth Ann. AA in Physics, DeAnza Coll., 1974; BS in Elec. Engring., U. Calif.-Berkeley, 1976; MS in Computer Info. Systems, U. Denver, 1992. Engr. IBM, Boulder, Colo., 1976-82, project engr. mgr., 1982-84, devel. engr. mgr., 1984-91, staff to lab. dir., 1986-87, 3820 program mgr., 1987-89, project office mgr. 3825, 1988-89, mgr. svc. process support, 1990-92, mgr. software mfg. ops., 1992-93; systems devel. and program mgr. Storage Tek, Louisville, Colo., 1993—. Leader Mountain Prairie Coun. Girl Scouts U.S., 1992-94; fund raiser Longmont Symphony Guild, 1994. Mem. Soc. Women Engrs. (life), IEEE (Debt of Gratitude award 1981, 82, 83, chmn. Denver sect. 1982-83), Electromagnetic Compatability Soc. (chmn. Boulder chpt. 1979-91, registration chmn. EMC internat. symposium 1981, bd. dirs. 1985-90, awards and membership chmn. 1986-90). Office: Storage Tek 2270 S 88th St Louisville CO 80028

TYSON, CICELY, actress; b. N.Y.C., Dec. 19, 1933; d. William and Theodosia Tyson; m. Miles Davis, 1981 (div.). Student, N.Y. U., Actors Studio; hon. doctorates, Atlanta U., Loyola U., Lincoln U. Former sec., model; co-founder Dance Theatre of Harlem; bd. dirs. Urban Gateways. Stage appearances include: The Blacks, 1961-63, off-Broadway, Moon on a Rainbow Shawl, 1962-63, Tiger, Tiger, Burning Bright, Broadway; films include: Twelve Angry Men, 1957, Odds Against Tomorrow, 1959, The Last Angry Man, 1959, A Man Called Adam, 1966, The Comedians, 1967, The Heart is a Lonely Hunter, 1968, Sounder, 1972 (Best Actress, Atlanta Film Festival, Nat. Soc. Film Critics, Acad. award nominee, Best Actress, Emmy award, Best Actress in a spl., 1973), The Blue Bird, 1976, The River Niger, 1976, A Hero Ain't Nothin' but a Sandwich, 1978, The Concorde-Airport 79, 1979, Bustin' Loose, 1981, Fried Green Tomatoes, 1991; TV appearances include: (series) East Side, West Side, 1963, Sweet Justice, 1994—; (films) Marriage: Year One, 1971, The Autobiography of Miss Jane Pittman, 1974, Just an Old Sweet Song, 1976, Wilma, 1977, Roots, 1977, A Woman Called Moses, 1978, King, 1978, The Marva Collins Story, 1981, Benny's Place, 1982, Playing With Fire, 1985, Samaritan: The Mitch Snyder Story, 1986, Acceptable Risks, 1986, Intimate Encounters, 1986, The Women of Brewster Place, 1989, Heat Wave, 1990, Winner Takes All, 1990, The Kid Who Loved Christmas, 1990, When No One Would Listen, 1992, Duplicates, 1993, House of Secrets, 1993, Oldest Living Confederate Widow Tells All, 1994 (Emmy Awd., Best Supporting Actress - Miniseries); other appearances include: Wednesday Night Out, 1972, Marlo Thomas and Friends in Free to Be...You and Me, 1974, CBS: On the Air, 1978, Liberty Weekend, 1986, The Blessings of Liberty, 1987, Without Borders, 1989, Visions of Freedom: A Time Television Special, 1990, Clippers, 1991, A Century of Women, 1994. Trustee Human Family Inst.; trustee Am. Film Inst. Recipient Vernon Price award, 1962; also awards NAACP Nat. Council Negro Women; Capitol Press award. Address: care CAA 9830 WIlshire Blvd Beverly Hills CA 90212*

TYSON, CYNTHIA HALDENBY, college president; b. Scunthorpe, Lincolnshire, Eng., July 2, 1937; came to U.S., 1959; d. Frederick and Florence Edna (Stacey) Haldenby; children: Marcus James, Alexandra Elizabeth. BA, U. Leeds, Eng., 1958, MA, 1959, PhD, 1971. Lectr. Brit. Council, Leeds, 1959; faculty U. Tenn., Knoxville, 1959-60, Seton Hall U., South Orange, N.J., 1963-69; faculty, v.p. Queens Coll., Charlotte, N.C., 1969-85; pres. Mary Baldwin Coll., Staunton, Va., 1985—; bd. dirs. Am. Coun. on Edn./Commn. on Higher Edn. and Adult Learning, Washington, 1981-85. Contbr. articles to profl. jours. Mem. Va. Internat. Trade Commn., Richmond, 1987; bd. dirs. Am. Frontier Culture Mus., Va., United Way, Staunton, 1986—; mem. Va. Lottery Bd.; trustee Woodrow Wilson Birthplace Found., Staunton, 1985—; ruling elder Presbyn. Ch.; mem. gov.'s adv. coun. on self determination & federalism, 1995—. Fulbright scholar, 1959; Ford Found. grantee Harvard U., 1981; Shell Oil scholar Harvard U., 1982. Fellow Soc. for Values in Higher Edn.; mem. Operation Enterprise Coun. of Am. Mgmt. Assn., So. Assn. Colls. for Women (pres. 1980-81). Republican. Office: Mary Baldwin Coll Office of the President Staunton VA 24401

TYSON, HELEN FLYNN, civic leader; b. Wilmington, N.C.; d. Walter Thomas and Fannie Elizabeth (Smith) Flynn; Student Guilford Coll., Am. U., Washington; m. James Franklin Tyson, Dec. 25, 1940 (dec.). U.S. Civil Svc. auditor, Disbursing Office, AUS, Ft. Bragg, N.C., 1935-46, chief clerical asst. Disbursing Office, Pope AFB, N.C., 1946-49, asst. budget and acctg. officer, 1949-55, supervisory budget officer hdqrs. Mil. Transport Command, USAF, 1955-57, budget analyst Hdqrs. USAF, Washington, 1957-74, ret. Active Arlington Com. 100, Ft. Belvoir, Salvation Army Women's Aux., Inter-Svc. Club Coun. of Arlington. Recipient awards U.S. Treasury, 1945, 46, U.S. State Dept., 1970, Good Neighbor award Ft. Belvoir Civilian-Mil. Adv. Coun., 1978; awards U.S. First Army, 1973, ARC, 1977; named Arlington Woman of Yr., 1975; recipient Cert. of Recognition, 1981, Vol. Activists award Greater Washington Met. Area, 1981. Mem. NAFE, Nat. Fedn. Bus. and Profl. Women's Clubs, Am. Assn. Ret. Fed. Employees (hon.), Am. Soc. Mil. Comptrs. (hon., Outstanding Mem. award Washington chpt. 1988), Am. Inst. Parliamentarians, Guilford Coll. Alumni Assn., N.C. Soc. Washington, Altrusa Internat. Home: 3909 Rosedale Dr Brandon FL 33511-7910

TYSON, LAURA D'ANDREA, economist, government adviser, educator; b. Bayonne, N.J., June 28, 1947; m. Erik Tarloff; 1 child, Elliot. BA, Smith Coll., 1969; Ph.D., Mass. Inst. Tech., 1974. Prof. econ. and bus. adm. Univ. of Calif., Berkeley, 1978—; chmn. President's Coun. Econ. Advisors, Washington, 1993—; dir. Inst. of Internat. Studies and Research, Univ. of Calif., Berkeley Roundtable on the Internat. Economics, Univ. of Calif.; visiting scholar Inst. for Internat. Economics; Subcom. on a global Economic Strategy for the U.S.. Editor: (with John Zysman) American Industry in International Competition, 1983, (with Ellen Comisso) Power, Purpose and Collective Choice: Economic Strategy in Socialist States, 1986, (with William Dickens and John Zysman) The Dynamics of Trade, 1988, (with Chalmers Johnson and John Zysman) Politics and Productivity: The Real Story of How Japan Works, 1989, Who's Bashing Whom? Trade Conflict in High Technology Industries, 1992. Office: President's Coun Economic Advs Old Exec Office Bldg Rm 314 17th St and Pennsylvania Ave NW Washington DC 20500*

TYSON, LUCILLE A., administrator. AS, Middlesex County Coll.; BA, Wheaton Coll.; MSW, Rutgers U. Cert. gerontol. nurse. Dir. N.J. Parkinson Info. & Referral Ctr. Robert Wood Johnson U. Hosp., New Brunswick, N.J.; human svcs. planner Middlesex County Dept. Human Svcs., New Brunswick; dir., right ro know regulations Roosevelt Hosp., Edison, N.J.; dir., quality assurance Cen. N.J. Jewish Home for Aged, Somerset, N.J. Mem. Piscataway (N.J.) Twp. Coun., 1990—; mem. rev./appeals com. Middlesex County Office: Human Svcs., 1992—; bd. dirs. Metlar Ho. Found.; mcpl. dir. Piscataway Rep. Orgn., 1995—; county committeewoman Middlesex County Rep. Orgn., 1995—. Mem. ANA, NASW, N.J. Nurses Assn., Assn. Quality Assurance Profls. N.J., Geriatric Inst. N.J.

TYTLER, LINDA JEAN, communications and public affairs executive, state legislator; b. Rochester, N.Y., Aug. 31, 1947; d. Frederick Easton and Marian Elizabeth (Allen) T.; m. George Stephen Dragnich, May 2, 1970 (div. July 1976); m. James Douglas Fisher, Oct. 7, 1994. AS, So. Sem., Buena Vista, Va., 1967; student U. Va., 1973; student in pub. adminstrn. U. N. Mex., 1981-82. Spl. asst. to Congressman John Buchanan, Washington, 1971-75; legis. analyst U.S. Senator Robert Griffin, Washington, 1975-77; ops. supr. Pres. Ford Com., Washington, 1976; office mgr. U.S. Senator Pete Domenici Re-election, Albuquerque, 1977; pub. info. officer S.W. Community Health Service, Albuquerque, 1978-83; cons. pub. relations and mktg., Albuquerque, 1983-84; account exec. Rick Johnson & Co., Inc., Albuquerque, 1983-84; dir. mktg. and communications St. Joseph Healthcare Corp., 1984-88; mktg. and bus. devel. cons., 1987-90; mgr. communications and pub. affairs Def. Avionics Systems div., Honeywell Inc., 1990—; sgt. N.Mex. Mounted Patrol, 1993—; mem. N.Mex. Ho. of Reps., Santa Fe, 1983-95, ret. 1995, vice chmn. appropriations and fin. com., 1985-86, interim com. on children and youth, 1985-86, mem. consumer and pub. affairs com., transp. com., 1992-95; chmn. Rep. Caucus, 1985-88; chmn. legis. campaign com. Rep. Com.; del. to Republic of China, Am. Council of Young Polit. Leaders, 1988. Bd. dirs. N. Mex. chpt. ARC, Albuquerque, 1984. Recipient award N.Mex. Advt. Fedn., Albuquerque, 1981, 82, 85, 86, 87. Mem. Am. Soc. Hosp. Pub. Relations (cert.), Nat. Advt. Fedn., Soc. Hosp. Planning and Mktg., Am. Mktg. Assn. Republican. Baptist.

TZAVELLAS, CHRISTINA ELEFTHERIOU, meeting planner; b. New Orleans, Dec. 28, 1952; d. Eleftherios C. and Mary (Kleamenakis) T. BA, Ariz. State U., 1978. Cert. meeting planner. Adminstrv. asst. Hi-Health, Inc., Scottsdale, Ariz., 1978-79; personnel asst. Doubletree Inn, Scottsdale, Ariz., 1979-80; mktg. support rep. Hughes-Calihan/3M, Phoenix, 1981-85; spl. projects Scottsdale Conf. Ctr., 1985-87; meeting planning mgr. Nat. Assn. Purchasing Mgmt., Tempe, Ariz., 1987—; assoc. faculty Ariz. State U., Tempe, 1994—. Recipient Conf. Mgmt. award Am. Soc. Assn. Execs. Mem. Meeting Planners Internat. Home: 821 N Los Feliz Dr Chandler AZ 85226

UBBING, MINA HAMILTON, accountant; b. Wheeling, W.Va., Mar. 21, 1949; d. Clifton Devere and Madelyne Bloch (Scharf) Hamilton; m. James W. Creighton (div. Oct. 1989); m. Robert E. Ubbing, Jan. 5, 1990. BSBA, Wheeling Coll., 1977; MBA in Exec. Mgmt., Ashland Coll., 1983. Internal auditor Mansfield (Ohio) Gen. Hosp., 1979-84, contr., 1984-86; acctg. mgr. Lancaster (Ohio)-Fairfield Community Hosp., 1986-87, v.p. fin., 1987—. Bd. dirs. Fairfield Industries, Lancaster, 1992-94; treas. United Way of Fairfield County, Lancaster, 1993-94. Recipient Tribute to Women in Industry, YWCA, 1985-86. Fellow Healthcare Fin. Mgmt. Assn. (bd. dirs. 1988-91, treas. 1991-92, sec. 1992-93, chpt. v.p. 1993-94, Follmer award 1989, Reeves award 1991). Office: Lancaster-Fairfield Hosp 401 N Ewing St Lancaster OH 43130

UBOSI, ANGIE NONYGLUM, nutrition center executive, consultant; b. Enugu, Nigeria, Aug. 12, 1952; came to U.S., 1978, naturalized, 1978; d. Thomas and Nwaobonne (Ukagi) U.; m. Williams Clearame, Nov. 8, 1984. BS, U. Ark., 1982; BA in Bus., McNeese State U., 1983; postgrad., Donsbech U., 1984—. Registered nutrition cons. Officer, Dept. Customs, Nigeria, 1973-78; mgr. Nutrition, Little Rock, 1978-82; pres. Angie Internat. Nutrition Ctr., Inc., Lake Charles, La., 1982-86, Nutritional Motivation, Lake Charles, 1983—. Author poetry. Pres. Lake Charles chpt. Am. Cancer Soc., 1982—; vol. Edn. Therapy Ctr., Lake Charles, 1986. Mem. NAFE (network dir. 1983-85), Am. Nutritional Med. Assn., Internat. Trade Orgn., Nat. Health Assn. (pres. Lake Charles chpt. 1983—). Home: 1421 Rauch Pl Decatur GA 30035 Office: Angie Internat Nutrition Ctr Inc PO Box 930216 Norcross GA 30093-0216

UCELLI, LORETTA MARIA, communications executive; b. Staten Island, N.Y., Mar. 10, 1954; d. Luke A. and Florence (Bocchino) U. BS in Journalism, W.Va. U., 1976. News anchor, news dir. Sta. WCLG-Radio, Morgantown, W.Va., 1976-79; news editor Sta. KDKA-Radio, Pitts., 1979-80; asst. to pres. Am. Fedn. Govt. Employees, Washington, 1981-84, dir. communications, 1984-86; regional press sec. Mondale-Ferraro Campaign, Washington, 1984; v.p. pub. affairs and communications Nat. Assn. Broadcasters, Washington, 1986-88; with Dukakis-Bentsen Campaign, Boston, 1988; dir. communications Nat. Abortion Rights Action League, Washington, 1989-92; assoc. adminstr. U.S. EPA, Office of Comm., Edn. and Public Affairs, Washington, 1992—. Mem. Nat. Press Club, Am. Coun. Young Polit. Leaders. Democrat. Roman Catholic. Office: US EPA 401 M St SW Washington DC 20460

UCHELLO, PATRICIA MILLER, artist, educator; b. New Orleans, Apr. 19, 1954; d. Albert John and Patricia (Shields) Miller-Di George; m. Carlo Anthony Uchello, June 2, 1979; children: Virginia Leigh, Jean-Pierre Christophe. BFA, Tulane U., 1976; MFA, Pratt Inst., 1978. Instr. art Pratt Inst., N.Y.C., 1978; instr. art summer sch. De La Salle High Sch., New Orleans, 1979-82; instr. art Acad. Sacred Heart, New Orleans, 1982-83; pvt. instr. art Alexandria, Va., 1986-94; instr. art No. Va. C.C., Alexandria, 1995—; artist erl originals, inc., Winston-Salem, N.C., 1993-95, Galleria Fenice, Venice, Italy, 1983-95; Pratt Inst. asst., N.Y.C., 1977. Illustrator Seaport Savouries, 1994. Mem. The Twig of Alexandria (Va.) Hosp., 1991—; visual arts panelist Alexandria Arts Commn., 1989-92. Recipient 1st Pl. award Fed. Bus. Assn., New Orleans, 1979, Extempo Contest Purchase award 1st Pl. Am.-Italian Renaissance Found., New Orleans, 1982. Mem. Nat. Mus. Women in the Arts, Art League (Equal Merit awards 1988-93), Historic Alexandria Docent, The Lyceum. Democrat. Roman Catholic. Studio: 2001 Shiver Dr Alexandria VA 22307

UEHLING, BARBARA STANER, academic administrator; b. Wichita, Kans., June 12, 1932; d. Roy W. and Mary Elizabeth (Hilt) Staner; children: Jeffrey Steven, David Edward. B.A., U. Wichita, 1954; M.A., Northwestern U., 1956, Ph.D., 1958; hon. degree, Drury Coll., 1978; LLD (hon.), Ohio State U., 1980. Mem. psychology faculty Oglethorpe U., Atlanta, 1959-64, Emory U., Atlanta, 1966-69; adj. prof. U. R.I., Kingston, 1970-72; dean Roger Williams Coll., Bristol, R.I., 1972-74; dean arts scis. Ill. State U., Normal, 1974-76; provost U. Okla., Norman, 1976-78; chancellor U. Mo.-Columbia, 1978-86, U. Calif., Santa Barbara, 1987-94; sr. vis. fellow Am. Council Edn., 1987-94; interim dir. bus./higher edn. forum, 1994—; mem. Pacific Rim Pub. U. Pres. Conf., 1990—; interim dir. Bus.-Higher Edn. Forum, Washington, 1994—; cons. North Ctrl. Accreditation Assn., 1974-86; mem. nat. educator adv. com. to Compt. Gen. of U.S., 1978-79; mem. Commn. on Mil.-Higher Edn. Rels., Am. Coun. on Edn., 1978-86, bd. dirs. 1979-83, treas., 1982-83, mem. Bus.-Higher Edn. Forum, 1980-94, exec. com. 1991-94; Commn. on Internat. Edn., 1992-94, vice chair 1993; bd. dirs. Coun. on Postsecondary Edn., 1986-87, 90-93, Meredith Corp., 1980—; mem. Transatlantic Dialogue, PEW Found., 1991-93. Author: Women in Academe: Steps to Greater Equality, 1979; editorial bd. Jour. Higher Edn. Mgmt., 1986—; contbr. articles to profl. jours. Bd. dirs., chmn. Nat. Ctr. Higher Edn. Mgmt. Sys., 1977-80; trustee Carnegie Found. for Advancement of Teaching, 1980-86, Santa Barbara Med. Found. Clinic, 1989-94; bd. dirs. Resources for the Futrue, 1985-94; mem. select com. on athletics NCAA, 1983-84, also mem. presdl. commn.; mem. Nat. Coun. on Edn. Rsch., 1980-82. Social Sci. Research Council fellow, 1954-55; NSF fellow, 1956-57; NIMH postdoctoral research fellow, 1964-67; named one of 100 Young Leaders of Acad. Change Mag. and ACE, 1978; recipient Alumni Achievement award Wichita State U., 1978, Alumnae award Northwestern U., 1985, Excellence in Edn. award Pi Lambda Theta, 1989. Mem. Am. Assn. Higher Edn. (bd. dirs. 1974-77, pres. 1977-78), Western Coll. Assn. (pres.-elect 1988-89,k pres. 1990-92), Golden Key, Sigma Xi. Office: Bus-Higher Edn Forum One Dupont Cir Ste 250 Washington DC 20036

UFFELMAN-ANDREWS, MARY EVELYN, ophthalmologist; b. Port Arthur, Tex., July 14, 1945; d. Harry Walter and Heloise Cecile (Morrow) Uffelman; m. Kenneth Earl Andrews, July 2, 1972 (div. Feb. 1989). BS, La. State U., Baton Rouge, 1965; MD, La. State U., New Orleans, 1969. Diplomate Am. Bd. Ophthalmology. Intern Confederate Meml. Med. Ctr., Shreveport, La., 1969-70, resident in ophthalmology, 1970-73; pvt. practice, Longview, Tex., 1973—; mem. staff Good Shepherd Hosp., Longview, 1973—; mem. active med. staff Longview Regional Hosp., 1982—. Bd. dirs. Women's Ctr. East Tex., Longview, 1988-93, Longview Opera Repertory Co., 1992—. Mem. Women in Ophthalmology, La. State U. East Tex. Alumni Assn. (pres. 1991-93). Office: 804 Medical Circle Dr Ste I Longview TX 75601

UGGAMS, LESLIE, entertainer; b. N.Y.C., May 25, 1943; d. Harolde Coyden and Juanita Ernestine (Smith) U.; m. Grahame John Kelvin-Pratt, Oct. 16, 1965; children: Danielle Nicole Pratt, Jason Harolde John Kelvin-Pratt. Student, Juillard Sch. Music, 1961-63; degree (hon.), Jarvis Coll., Tyler, Tex., Wilberforce (Ohio) U. Appeared on TV show Beulah, 1949; featured on Sing Along with Mitch, 1961-64; starred in Broadway play Hallelujah Baby, 1967 (Tony award 1968), Her First Roman Broadway Musical, 1968; star of weekly TV variety show The Leslie Uggams Show, 1969; appearances in nightclubs, top TV mus. variety shows; appeared in film Skyjacked, 1972, 2 Weeks in Another Town, ABC-TV film Roots, 1977 (Critics Choice award as best supporting actress 1977); star Broadway musicals Blues in the Night, 1982, Jerry's Girls, 1985, Anything Goes, 1987; star in TV mini-series Backstairs at the White House, 1979; co-host Fantasy TV, 1982-83 (Emmy award 1983); author: The Leslie Uggams Beauty Book, 1966. Founding mem. BRAVO chpt. City of Hope, Los Angeles, 1969, treas. 1969-79. Chosen best singer on TV, 1962, 63; recipient Drama Critics award Newspaper and TV critics, 1968, Tony award 1968, Emmy award 1983. Mem. AFTRA, Nat. Acad. Recording Arts and Scis., Screen Actors Guild, Actors' Equity Assn. Democrat. Presbyterian. Office: William Morris Agy care Glen Rigberg 151 S El Camino Dr Beverly Hills CA 90212-2775

UGUR, HUBERTA GOWEN WOLF, non-profit foundation administrator; b. Phila., Oct. 8, 1943; d. Richard O'Shea and Huberta Horan (Gowen) Wolf; m. Serafettin Ugur; 1 child, Kemal. BS in Sociology, Daemen Coll., 1967; MS in Counseling, U. Ariz., 1969; MEd in Ednl. Leadership, Bank Street Coll., 1994. Lic. prin., asst. prin., adminstr., supr., notary pub., N.Y.; cert. infant massage educator. Rehab. counselor Fountain House, Inc., Rockland State Hosp., N.Y.C., 1969-72; tchr. of the deaf N.Y.C. Bd. of Edn., Hearing Edn. Svcs., 1974—; tchr. Mid. Coll. High Sch., LaGuardia Community Coll., Queens, N.Y., 1991—; exec. dir. N.Y. Ctr. for Law and the Deaf, N.Y.C., 1980—; cons. St. Joseph Sch. for the Deaf, Bronx, N.Y., 1978-82; mem. nat. adv. com. The Captions Ctr., 1987—. Exec. producer TV video series, New York Connection, 1987—. Chairperson N.Y. Deaf Women, 1981; adv. bd. N.Y.C. Mayor's Office for Handicapped, 1984—. Recipient Durfee award for enhancing human dignity Durfee Found., 1987. Mem. ASCD, NAFE, Lexington Mental Health Ctr. for the Deaf (adv. bd.) Am. Women Econ. Devel. Democrat. Roman Catholic. Office: NY Ctr for Law and the Deaf 309 W 57th St New York NY 10019-3113

UHLENBECK, KAREN KESKULLA, mathematician, educator; b. Cleve., Aug. 24, 1942; d. Arnold Edward and Carolyn Elizabeth (Windeler) Keskulla; m. Olke Cornelis, June 12, 1965 (div.). B.S. in Math., U. Mich., 1964; Ph.D. in Math., Brandeis U., 1968. Instr. math. MIT, Cambridge, 1968-69; lectr. U. Calif.-Berkeley, 1969-71; asst. prof., then assoc. prof. U. Ill., Urbana, 1971-76; assoc. prof., then prof. U. Ill., Chgo., 1977-83; prof. U. Chgo., 1983-88; Sid W. Richardson Found. Regents' Chair in Math. U. Tex., 1988—; speaker plenary address Internat. Congress Maths., 1990; mem. com. women on sci. and engring. Nat. Rsch. Coun., 1992-94; mem. steering com., dir. mentoring program for women IAS/PCMI. Author: Instantons and Four Manifolds, 1984. Contbr. articles to profl. jours. NSF Grad. fellow, 1964-68, Sloan Found. fellow, 1974-76, MacArthur Found. fellow, 1983-88; recipient Alumni Achievement award Brandeis U., 1988. Mem. AAAS, NAS, Alumni Assn. U. Mich. (Alumnae of Yr. 1984), Am. Math. Soc., Assn. Women in Math., Phi Beta Kappa. Office: U Tex Dept Math Austin TX 78712

UHLIR, LINDA MARIE, accountant; b. Berwyn, Ill., Jan. 8, 1961; d. Charles Eugene and Patricia Jean U. BS, No. Ill. U., 1983; M in Acctg. Scis., U. Ill., 1988. CPA; cert. mgmt. acct. Cash office supr. The Right Price, Wood Dale, Ill., 1983-84; acct. Cray Kaiser Ltd., Oakbrook Terrace, Ill., 1984-86, sr. acct., 1991—; tax cons. Price Waterhouse, Chgo., 1988-91. Mem. Am. Mensa, Am. Coaster Enthusiasts, Beta Sigma Phi (treas.), Phi Kappa Phi, Beta Gamma Sigma, Beta Alpha Psi. Office: Cray Kaiser Ltd One Trans Am Plaze # 460 Oakbrook Terrace IL 60181

UHLMAN, HELENE CLARE, health administrator; b. Lorain, Ohio, July 11; d. Nick and Ida (Toth) Dullos; m. Howard Uhlman; 1 child, Melody. Registered environ. health specialist. Health adminstr. Gary (Ind.) Health Dept., 1977-79, environ. dir., 1980-82, health tchr., 1983-86; health coord. Calumet Region Milk Sanitation, Hammond, Ind., 1987-91; health dir. Am. Stop Smoking Intervention Study, Ind. State Health Dept., Gary, 1992-94; pub. health adminstr. Hammond (Ind.) Health Dept., 1994—; liaison to State of Ind. Health Officers Assn. Pres. Lake County AIDS Task Force, Ind.; coord. Mayors Health Bd., Health Officers Lake County; mem. gov. commn. Drug-Free Ind.; active Black and Minority Health Coalition, Black Expo Steering Com. Mem. Internat. Assn. Milk, Food and Environ. Health (nat. del.), Ind. Environ. Health Assn. (mem. exec. bd.). Lutheran. Office: Hammond Health Dept Hammond IN 46320

UHRMAN, CELIA, artist, poet; b. New London, Conn., May 14, 1927; d. David Aaron and Pauline (Schwartz) U. BA, Bklyn. Coll., 1948, MA, 1953; PhD, U. Danzig, 1977; postgrad. Tchrs. Coll., Columbia U., 1961, CUNY, 1966, Bklyn. Mus. Art Sch., 1956-57, PhD (hon.), LittD, 1973; cert. Koret Living Library U. of San Francisco, 1982. One-woman shows: Leffert Jr. High Sch., Bklyn., 1958, Flatbush C. of C., N.Y.C., 1963, Conn. C. of C., New London, 1962; exhibited in group shows: Smithsonian Instn., Washington, 1958, Springfield (Mass.) Mus. Fine Arts, 1959, Bklyn. Mus., 1959, Old Mystic (Conn.) Art Center, 1959, Carnegie Endowment Internat. Center, N.Y.C., 1959, Lyman Allyn Mus., New London, 1960, Palacio de La Virrelna, Barcelona, Spain, 1961, YMCA, Bklyn., 1962, UFT Art Exhibit, N.Y.C., 1963, Soc. of 4 Arts, Palm Beach, Fla., 1964, Perspective 68, Monte-Carlo, Monaco, 1968, George W. Wingate High sch., Bklyn., 1967, Premier Salon Internat., Charleroi, Belgium, 1968, Palme d'or Beaux Arts, Monte-Carlo, 1970, 72, Dibuix-Joan Miro Premi Internacional, Barcelona, 1970; N.Y. Art Festival, 1970, Internat. Platform Assn. Art Show, Washington, 1971, 73, Ovar Mus., Portugal, 1974, others; represented in permanent collections: Bklyn. Coll., Ch. of Evangel, Bklyn.; tchr. N.Y.C. Sch. System, 1948-82; ptnr. Uhrman Studio, 1973-83; hon. rep. U.S., Centro Studi E Scambi Internazionali, Rome, mem. Internat. Com., 1969. Hon. life mem. World Poetry Day Com., Inc. and Nat. Poetry Day Com., 1977. Recipient award Freedoms Found., George Washington medal of honor, 1964, Diplome d'Honneur Palme d'Or des Beaux Arts Exhbn., Monaco, 1969, 72, Diploma and Gold medal, Centro Studi E Scambi Internazionali, 1972; decorated Order of Gandhi Award of Honour, Knight Grand Cross, 1972; personal poetry certificate WEFG Stereo, 1970; Gold Laurel award Esposizione Internazionale D'Art Contemporain, Paris, 1974; named Poetry Translator Laureate World Acad. Lang. and Lit., 1972, Poet of Mankind Acad. Philosophy, 1972; cert. of appreciation Bd. Edn. of N.Y.C., 1982. Fellow World Lit. Academy Eng.; mem. Internat. Arts Guild (comdr. 1966—), World Poetry Soc. Intercontinental (rep. at large 1969—), Internat. Acad. Poets (founding fellow). Author: Poetic Ponderances, 1969, A Pause for Poetry, 1970, Poetic Love Fancies, 1970, A Pause for Poetry for Children, 1973, The Chimps Are Coming, 1975, Love Fancies, 1987. Home: 1655 Flatbush Ave Apt 106C Brooklyn NY 11210-3271

UHRMAN, ESTHER, artist, writer, retired social worker; b. New London, Conn., July 7, 1921; d. David Aaron and Pauline (Schwartz) U. Grad. Traphagen Sch. Fashion, 1955; Diploma Di Benemerenza, Centro Studi E Scambi Internat., Rome, 1972, Diploma Academia Leonardo Da Vinci, 1980; A.A., N.Y.C. Community Coll., 1974; cert. in labor relations Cornell U., 1976, cert. unemployment ins. advocate, 1984; Ph.D., Danzig U., Poland, 1977; Ph.D. (hon.) World Acad. Langs. and Lit., 1977. Self-employed writer, artist, Bklyn., 1954—; social worker N.Y. State, Bklyn., N.Y.C., 1959-76; ptnr. Uhrman Studio, Bklyn., 1973-83. Author: Gypsy Logic, 1970, From Canarsie to Masada, 1978, Mitras II, 1988; (radio play) Holland 2067, 1971 (Golden Windmill award 1970); asst. editor: Inside Detective, 1977; contbr. articles to profl. jours.; two-man art shows include Ligoa Duncan Gallery, N.Y.C., 1960, New London C. of C., 1962, Flatbush C. of C., 1963, Uhrman Studio, 1973-83; exhibited in group shows at Traphagen Sch. Fashion, N.Y.C., 1954-55, Carnegie Endowment Internat. Ctr., N.Y.C., 1959, Exposcion De Obras, Palacio De La Virreina, Barcelona, Spain, 1961, Smithsonian Inst., Washington, 1962, Cape May (N.J.) County Lighthouse, 1965, N.Y. Art Festival, 1970, Premier Internacional Dibuix, Barcelona, 1970, Internat. Platform Assn., Washington, 1972-73. Recipient Civilian Service award U.S. Army, 1944, five N.Y. State awards, 1962-65, Silver medal Verso Mexico, 1968, cert. Stamp Designs, 1968, cert. Merit Rassegna Internazionale D'Arte Grafica, Ovar Mus., Portugal, 1974, cert. Merit 26th Exposition D'Arte Contemporain, Luxemborg, 1974. Fellow World Literary Acad., Internat. Acad. Poets (co-founder). Mem. AFL-CIO, Internat. Arts Guild (commandeur, Diplome D'Honneur award 1976), World Poetry Soc. Intercontinental, CSEA Retirees. Avocations: walking, theatre, anthropology. Home and Office: 1655 Flatbush Ave Apt 106C Brooklyn NY 11210-3271

UILKEMA, GAYLE BURNS, mayor, councilwoman, business educator; b. Detroit, Sept. 2, 1938; d. Joseph A. and Pearl (Rasmussen) Burns; children: Lynn, Sharon. BS in Edn., U. Mich., 1959; MPA, Calif. State U., Hayward, 1987. Instr. bus. edn. and mgmt. subjects Heald Coll., Oakland, Calif., 1961-62; tchr. bus. edn. dept. Oakland High Sch., 1962-66; lectr. Calif. State U. Grad. Sch. Pub. Adminstrn., Hayward; mem. coun. City of Lafayette, 1978—, mayor, 1981-84, 90-91, 94-95; lectr. in field; cons. U. Calif. Ext., Berkeley; adj. prof. John F. Kennedy U. Sch. of Mgmt., Orinda, Calif., 1989—. Mem. Contra Costa Local Agy. Formation Commn., 1986—, commr., former chair, 1986, 95; mem. exec. bd. dirs. state bd. Calif. Assn. Local Agy. Formation Commn.; Lafayette dir., former chair, bd. dirs. Ctrl. Contra Costa Transit Authority, 1980-94, chmn. fin. com., 1981-85, 94, chmn. ops. and scheduling, 1986, dir. ops. and scheduling com., 1987, chmn., 1989, bd. dirs., 1990—. Recipient award Met. Transp. Commn. Bay Area, 1981. Mem. AAUW (bd. dirs. 1971-78, pres. 1972-73, state bd. dirs. 1974-76, nat. rep. 1977-78, Disting. Woman award 1978), Soroptimists Internat. Republican. Roman Catholic. Home: 670 Sky Hy Cir Lafayette CA 94549-5228 Office: City of Lafayette PO Box 1968 Lafayette CA 94549-4342

ULASEWICZ, MARGARET MCGOVERN, special education educator; b. Bklyn., July 3, 1950; d. Joseph Leo and Margaret Joan (Cashin) McG.; m. Richard John Ulasewicz, Sept. 3, 1972; children: Brian Michael, Michael Joseph. BA, St. Bonaventure U., 1972, MS, 1974, advanced cert., 1989. Cert. tchr. elem. edn., N.Y., secondary social studies, spl. edn., cert. sch. adminstr. Curriculum specialist Bd. Coop. Edn. Svcs., Olean, N.Y., 1973-74, tchr. learning disabled students primary grades, 1974-77, tchr. learning disabled students secondary grades, 1978-83; resource rm. tchr., chair dept. Olean City Schs., 1984—; bd. dirs. Olean Tchrs. Fed. Credit Union; varsity tennis coach Olean City Sch. System, 1990—, corp. cup capt., 1988-92. Mem. N.Y. State Staff Devel. Assn. Republican. Roman Catholic. Office: Olean City Schs Olean Mid Sch 410 N 7th St Olean NY 14760-2330

ULERY, SHARI LEE, lawyer; b. Marshalltown, Iowa, July 13, 1953; d. Kenneth Eugene and Edith Viola (Harding) U.; m. Steven Bernard Nelson (div. 1987); children: Benjamin, Christopher. BS, Iowa State U., 1975; JD, Drake U., 1980. Bar: Iowa 1980, Colo. 1981. Staff atty. Geico Fin. Svcs., Denver, 1985-87, asst. gen. counsel, 1987-89, v.p., gen. counsel, 1989—. Mem. ABA, Am. Assn. Corp. Counsel, Colo. Bar Assn., Colo. Womens Bar Assn. Office: Geico Fin Svcs Inc 7551 W Alameda Ave Lakewood CO 80226-3205

ULLERY, PATRICIA ANNE, marketing professional; b. Casper, Wyo., July 13, 1949; d. Warren James and Nella Marie (Hammack) U.; m. Royce Edward Gilpatric, Apr. 1, 1968 (div. 1992); children: Royce Edward Gilpatric II, Eric Wynn Gilpatric. AA, Oakland C.C., Auburn Hills, Mich., 1978; student, Oakland U., 1979; BS in Internat. Bus. and Econs., Regis U., 1992; postgrad., U. Colo., 1994—. Divsn. editor Richardson Vick, Inc., Phila., 1979-81; dir. mktg. Rocky Mountain region Flack & Kurtz, Denver, 1982-86; dir. mktg. western region M.A. Mortenson Co,, Denver, 1986-88; dir. mktg. Associated Gen. Contractors Colo., Denver, 1990-91; mgr. comml. devel. Cybercon Corp., Denver, 1992—; mem. real estate coun. U. Colo.; bd. dirs. Lower Downtown Dist., Inc., mktg. com., 1993-94. Mem. steering com. Great City Symposium '84, Urban Design Forum, Met. Denver's Great Neighborhoods, 1985, Parks and Pub. Spaces, 1986, bd. dirs. 1986-89; chair New Denver Airport design conf., 1987; mem. mktg. and mgmt. com. lower downtown task force Downtown Plan, 1986; mem. comprehensive plan land use/urban design task force City of Denver, 1987-88; bd. dirs. Community Housing Svcs., 1994; mem. Downtown Denver, Inc., 1982—. Recipient Outstanding Bus. Comm. Merit award Internat. Assn. Bus. Communicators, 1982, Fifty for Colo. award Colo. Assn. for Commerce and Industry, 1988, Ace Constrn. Excellence award Associated Gen. Contractors Colo., 1988, 91, Bus. in Arts award COlo. Bus. Com. for Arts, 1991. Mem. Soc. for Mktg. Profl. Svcs. (publicity chair Colo. chpt. 1984, v.p. 1985, pres. 1986, chair editorial com. Marketer, 1986-87, nat. bd. dirs. 1987-90, Leonardo award 1986), Ctrl. City Opera House Assn. (bd. dirs., pres. OperaPros 1993-94). Republican. Methodist. Home: 7880 W Woodward Dr Denver CO 80227 Office: Cybercon Corp 1050 17th St Ste 1800 Denver CO 80265

ULLMAN, NELLY SZABO, statistican, educator; b. Vienna, Austria, Aug. 11, 1925; came to U.S., 1939; d. Viktor and Elizabeth (Rosenberg) Szabo; m. Robert Ullman, Mar. 20, 1947 (dec.); children: Buddy, Wiliiam John, Martha Ann, Daniel Howard. BA, Hunter Coll., 1945; MA, Columbia U., 1948; PhD, U. Mich., 1969. Rsch. assoc. MIT Radiation Lab, Cambridge, Mass., 1945; instr. Polytechnic Inst. of Bklyn., 1945-63; asst. prof. to prof. Ea. Mich. U., Ypsilanti, 1963—. Author: Study Guide To Actuarial Exam, 1978; contbr. articles to profl. jours. Mem. Am. Math. Assn., Am. Stat. Assn., Biometric Soc., Am. Assn. Univ. Profs. Office: Ea Mich Univ Dept Math Ypsilanti MI 48197

ULLMAN, TRACEY, actress, singer; b. Slough, Eng., Dec. 30, 1959; m. Allan McKeown, 1984; children: Mabel Ellen, John Albert Victor. Student, Itaia Conti Stage Sch., London. Appeared in plays Gigi, Elvis, Grease, The Rocky Horror Show, Four in a Million, 1981 (London Theatre Critics award), The Taming of the Shrew, 1990, The Big Love, (one-woman stage show) 1991; films include The Young Visitors, 1984, Give My Regards to Broad Street, 1984, Plenty, 1985, Jumpin' Jack Flash, 1986, I Love You To Death, 1990, Household Saints, 1993, I'll Do Anything, 1994, Bullets over Broadway, 1994, Ready to Wear (Prêt-à-Porter), 1994; Brit. TV shows include Three of a Kind, A Kick Up the Eighties, Girls on Top; actress TV series: The Tracey Ullman Show, from 1987-90 (Emmy award Best Performance, Outstanding Writing, 1990, Golden Globe award Best Actress, 1987); album You Broke My Heart in Seventeen Places (Gold album). Recipient Brit. Acad. award, 1983, Am. Comedy award, 1988, 90, 91, Emmy award for Best Performance in a Variety/Music Series for "Tracey Ullman Takes on New York", 1994. Office: Creative Artists Agy Inc 9830 Wilshire Blvd Beverly Hills CA 90212*

ULLOM, BRIGITTE LORRAINE, travel agency owner; b. Washington, Pa., May 7, 1957; d. Edwin Charles and Janine (Roland) U. BA, Bucknell U., 1980. Dir. pub. rels. Sheraton Inn East, Harrisburg, Pa., 1980-81; mgr. The Plum, Harrisburg, 1981-82; employment coord. The Byrnes Group, Camp Hill, Pa., 1982-84; pres. First World Travel, 1984—. Mem. Am. Soc. Travel Agts., SKAL of Ctrl. Pa., Exch. Club of Harrisburg (dir. 1992-94), Profl. Investment Club (presiding ptnr. 1993-94). Office: First World Profl Travel 1800 Linglestown Rd Ste 106 Harrisburg PA 17110

ULLRICH, ROXIE ANN, special education educator; b. Ft. Dodge, Iowa, Nov. 10, 1951; d. Rocco William and Mary Veronica (Casady) Jackowell; m. Thomas Earl Ullrich, Aug. 10, 1974; children: Holly Ann, Anthony Joseph. BA, Creighton U., 1973; MA in Teaching, Morningside Coll., 1991. Cert. tchr., Iowa. Tchr. Corpus Christi Sch., Ft. Dodge, Iowa, 1973-74, Westwood Community Schs., Sloan, Iowa, 1974-80, Sioux City Community Schs., 1987—. Cert. judge Iowa High Sch. Speech Assn., Des Moines, 1975—. Mem. Am. Paint Horse Assn., Am. Quarter Horse Assn., Sioux City Hist. Assn., M.I. Hummel Club. Home: 819 Brown St Sloan IA 51055

ULMER, FRAN, state official; m. Bill Council; children: Amy, Louis. B in Econs. and Polit. Sci., U. Wis.; JD with honors, Wis. Sch. Law. Polit. advisor Gov. Jay Hammond, Alaska, 1973-83; former mayor City of Juneau, Alaska; mem. 4 terms, minority leader Alaska Ho. Reps.; lt. gov. State of Alaska, 1995—. Home: 1700 Angus Way Juneau AK 99801-1411 Office: State Capitol PO Box 110015 Juneau AK 99811*

ULRICH, GLADYS MARJORIE, printing company executive; b. Chgo., Dec. 18, 1932; d. Harry Pikal and Rose Barbara (Vojta) Albert; m. William John Ulrich, Dec. 4, 1954; children: Valerie Lynn, Mark Robert, Laura Ann. Student, Gregg Coll., 1950-52. Owner, CEO Insty-Prints, Arlington Heights, Ill., 1978—; pres., owner Insty-Prints, Elk Grove Village, Ill., 1986—; mem. pres. coun. Insty-Prints, Mpls., 1987-90, nat. adv. governing com., 1987—. Organizer blood drive ARC/Cancer Soc., Elk Grove Village, 1970. Mem. Women's Resource Assn. (pres. 1988-89), Bus. & Profl. Women Assn. Republican. Office: Insty-Prints 2355 E Oakton St Arlington Heights IL 60005-4817

ULRICH, LAUREL THATCHER, historian, educator; b. Sugar City, Idaho, July 11, 1938; d. John Kenneth and Alice (Siddoway) Thatcher; m. Gael Dennis Ulrich, Sept. 22, 1958; children: Karl, Melinda, Nathan, Thatcher, Amy. BA in English, U. Utah, 1960; MA in English, Simmons Coll., 1971; PhD in History, U. N.H., 1980. Asst. prof. humanities U. N.H., Durham, 1980-84, asst. prof. history, 1985-88, assoc. prof. history, 1988-91, prof. history, 1991-95; prof. history and woman's studies Harvard U., Cambridge, Mass., 1995—; audiocourse cons. Annenberg Found.; cons., participating humanist numerous exhibits, pub. programs, other projects; project humanist Warner (N.H.) Women's Oral History Project; bd. editors William & Mary Quar., 1989-91, Winterthur Portfolio, 1991—. Author: Good Wives: Image and Reality in the Lives of Women in Northern New England, 1650-1750, 1982, A Midwife's Tale: The Life of Martha Ballard Based on Her Diary, 1785-1812, 1990 (Pulitzer Prize for History 1991); contbr. articles, abstracts, essays and revs. to profl. publs. Coun. mem. Inst. Early Am. History and Culture, 1989-91; trustee Strawberry Banke Mus., 1987-93. John Simon Guggenheim fellow, 1991-92, NEH fellow, 1982, 84-85; women's studies rsch. grantee Woodrow Wilson Fellowship Found., 1979; co-recipient Best Book award Berkshire Conf. Women's Historians, 1990; recipient Best Book award Soc. for History of Early Republic, 1990, John S. Dunning prize and Joan Kelly Meml. prize Am. Hist. Assn., 1990, Bancroft Prize for Am. History, 1991. Mem. Orgn. Am. Historians (nominating com. 1992—, ABC-Clio award com. 1989), Am. Hist. Assn. (rsch. coun. 1993-96). Office: Harvard U Dept History Cambridge MA 02138

UMMEL, TAMRA KAY, special education director; b. VanWert, Ohio, May 9, 1957; d. John J. and Darlene M. (Noll) Schimmoller; m. Gregory A. Ummel, Aug. 7, 1981; children: Aislinn Marie, Jason Ross. BS in Edn., Bowling Green State U., 1979, MEd, 1981; postgrad., Ind. U., 1987—. Tchr. Trenton (Mich.) Pub. Schs., 1979-80, Warsaw (Ind.) Community Schs., 1981-84, Wawasee Community Schs., Syracuse, Ind., 1984-85; ednl. cons. N. Cen. Ind. Spl. Edn. Co-op., Warsaw, 1986-90, supr. spl. edn., 1990-91, asst. dir. spl. edn., 1991—. Mem. ASCD, AAUW (sec. 1990-92), Am. Assn. Sch. Adminstrs., Ind. Coun. Adminstrs. in Spl. Edn., Coun. Exceptional Children. Home: 112 Ems T 36 Ln Leesburg IN 46538

UNDERHILL, ANNE BARBARA, astrophysicist; b. Vancouver, B.C., Can., June 12, 1920; d. Frederic Clare and Irene Anna (Creery) U. BA, U. B.C., 1942, MA, 1944, DSc (hon.), 1992; PhD, U. Chgo., 1948; DSc (hon.), York U., Toronto, Ont., 1969. Sci. officer Dominion Astrophys. Obs., Victoria, B.C., 1949-62; prof. astrophysics U. Utrecht, The Netherlands, 1962-70; lab chief Goddard Space Flight Ctr./NASA, Greenbelt, Md., 1970-77, sr. scientist, 1978-85; hon. prof. U. B.C., Vancouver, 1985—. Author: The Early-type Stars, 1966; author/editor: B Stars with and without Emission Lines, 1982, O, Of and Wolf-Rayet Stars, 1988; contbr. articles to profl. jours. Fellow NRC, 1948, Can. Fedn. Univ. Women, 1944, 47. Fellow Royal Soc. Can., Royal Astron. Soc.; mem. Internat. Astron. Union (pres. commn. #36 1963-66), Am. Astron. Soc., Can. Astron. Soc. Anglican. Office: U BC, Dept Geophysics & Astronomy, Vancouver, BC Canada V6T 1Z4

UNDERWOOD, BRENDA S., microbiologist, grants administrator; b. Oak Ridge, Tenn., Mar. 19, 1948; d. William Henry Hensley and Maudell (Walker) Townsend; m. Thomas L. Janiszewski, Feb. 14, 1984; 1 child, Thomas Zachary Janiszewski. BS, U. Tenn., 1970; MS, Hood Coll., 1980; MBA, Mt. St. Mary's Coll., 1993. Scientist I chem. carcinogenesis Frederick (Md.) Cancer Rsch. Ctr., 1977-84; microbiologist NCI/NIH, Bethesda, Md., 1984-86; sci. tech. writer Engring. and Econs. Rsch., Germantown, Md., 1987-88; spl. asst. to assoc. dir., program dir. grants div. Cancer Biology Diagnosis Ctrs., NCI/NIH, Bethesda, 1988-91; indexer, div. extramural activities Rsch. Analysis and Evaluation br. NCI/NIH, Bethesda, 1991—. Leader Riding for the Handicapped, Frederick, 1990-91; mem., recreational sec. Capital Hill Equestrian Soc., Washington, 1988. Mem. AAAS, Am. Soc. for Microbiology, Am. Assn. for Cancer Rsch., Women in Cancer Rsch., Federally Employed Women. Office: NCI/NIH RAEB Divsn Extramural Activ Bethesda MD 20892

UNDERWOOD, JANE ANGELINE, counselor; b. Thomaston, Ga., May 11, 1941; d. Claude Milton and Thelma (Salter) Adams; m. Emory Marvin Underwood, Jan. 30, 1963; 1 child, John N. BA, Auburn U., 1970, MEd, 1976; EdS, Troy State U., 1985. Lic. profl. counselor. Rehab. counselor Vocat. Rehab. Svc., Montgomery, 1976-88; asst. dir., various staff positions Montgomery Therapeutic Foster Home Program, Montgomery, 1990—; counselor Montgomery Counselor Ctr., Montgomery, 1992—; pres. Montgomery area Inter-agy. Coun., Montgomery, 1988—. Treas. Civitan Internat., Montgomery, 1987-88. Mem. League of Women Voters (pres. 1989, sec. 1990, bd. dirs.). Office: Montgomery Counseling Ctr 2900 McGehee Rd Montgomery AL 36111

UNDERWOOD, JOANNA DEHAVEN, environmental research and education organizations president; b. N.Y.C., May 25, 1940; d. Louis Ivan and Helen (Guiterman) U.; m. Saul Lambert, July 31, 1982; stepchildren: Jonathan Whitty, Katherine Aviva. B.A., Bryn Mawr Coll., 1962; Diplome d'etudes de Civilisation francaise with honors, Sorbonne U., Paris, 1965. Audio-visual dir. Planned Parenthood World Population, N.Y.C., 1968-70; co-dir. Council on Econ. Priorities, N.Y.C., 1970-73; pres. INFORM, Inc., N.Y.C., 1973—; bd. dirs. N.Y. State Energy R&D Authority, Albany, Hampshire Rsch. Inst., Clean Sites, Rocky Mountain Inst.; mem. Dow Environ. Adv. Coun., 1992—; awards com. Pres.'s Coun. on Environ. Quality, 1991. Author (with others) Voices from the Environmental Movement: Perspectives for a New Era, 1991; co-author: Paper Profits, 1971; editor: The Price of Power, 1972; contbr. articles to profl. jours. Bd. dirs. Planned Parenthood of N.Y.C., 1985-92. Recipient U.S. EPA Environ. Achievement award, 1987, 92. Home: 138 E 13th St New York NY 10003-5306 Office: Inform Inc 120 Wall St 16th Fl New York NY 10005

UNDERWOOD, MARTHA JANE MENKE, artist, educator; b. Quincy, Ill., Nov. 28, 1934; d. Francis Norman Menke and Ruth Rosemary (Wells) Zoller; divorced; children: Leslie, Stephen. BA, Scripps Coll., 1956; MFA, Otis Art Inst., 1958. Cert. adult edn. and post secondary tchr. Designer staineglass windows Wallis-Wiley Studio, Pasadena, Calif., 1959-60; mural asst., designer Millard Sheets Murals, Inc., Claremont, Calif., 1960-68; art instr. adult edn. Monrovia, Pomona and Claremont Sch. Dists., Calif., 1967-69; prof. art Chaffey C.C., Alta Loma, Calif., 1970—; free lance illustrator Claremont, 1975—, watercolorist, 1970—; lectr. and demonstrator in field. Contbr. photographs to: How to Create Your Own Designs, 1968, Weaving Without Loom, 1969; illustrator: Opening a Can of Words, 1994; contbr. illustrations to Wayfarers Jour. Active Citizens for Saving Bonelli Park, San Dimas, Calif., 1991. Recipient Strathmore award, 1985, Grumbacher award, 1990, 92; Faculty Initiated Projects Program grantee, 1991-92. Mem. Associated Artists, Riverside Art Alliance, Soc. Children's Book Writers and Illustrators. Office: Chaffey Coll 5885 Haven Ave Alta Loma CA 91701

UNDERWOOD, SHIRLEY ANN, business administrator; b. Washington, Aug. 2, 1958; d. George Albert Jr. and Shirley Mae (Simms) U. AS, No. Va. Community Coll., 1983; diploma, Temple Bus. Sch., Alexandria, 1981, Cappa Chell Modeling Sch., 1983; student, Strayer Coll., 1993—. Staff asst. U.S. Senator, adminstrv. asst., staff asst.; exec. asst., adminstrv. asst. BDM Corp.; support coord. Systems Mgmt. Am. Corp. Contbr. atricles to newsletters and mags. Sec.-treas. Alexandria Bowling Ctr., 1989; mem. budget and fin. com. Saxony Square Condominium, Alexandria, 1990, chairperson Ad Hoc com. on mgmt. rev., 1990, chairperson covenants com., 1987-88; pres. Seminary Fair Lanes, 1986-87; participant Super Cities Walk Multiple Sclerosis Soc., 1990; sponsor Kennedy Center Stars John F. Kennedy Ctr. for Performing Arts, 1993—. Mem. NAFE, Profl. Secs. Internat. (NOVA chpt.), Henson Creek Golf Club (Oxon Hill, Md.) (named Most Improved Female Golfer 1989, winner Women's Longest Drive 1989, Pres's. Cup 3d Low Gross 1989), Robindale Country Club (Brandywine, Md.). Home: 3510 Bath Ct Woodbridge VA 22193 Office: TRW Environ Safety Systems 2650 Park Tower Dr Vienna VA 22180

UNGACTA, MALISSA SUMAGAYSAY, software engineer; b. Agana, Guam, July 3, 1967; d. Renerio Ong and Irene Acfalle (Salas) S. BS in Info. Sci., U. Hawaii, 1989; MS in Info. Tech. Mgmt., Johns Hopkins U., 1992. Programmer, analyst Facilities Mgmt. Office, Honolulu, 1987-89, Data House Inc., Honolulu, 1989-90, ANSTEC Inc., Fairfax, Md., 1990-93; software specialist, project leader HJ Ford Assocs. Inc., Crystal City, Va., 1993-94; software cons. McDonnell Douglas Tech. Svcs., 1994—. Mem. NAFE. Home: PO Box 1546 Agana GU 96910 Office: McDonnell Douglas 77 West Port Plz Ste # 219 Saint Louis MO 63146 Address: 4554 Laclede Ave 107 Saint Louis MO 63108

UNGAR, CAROLE WILSON, public relations executive; b. Bklyn., Nov. 7, 1933; d. Morris and Frances (Michaelson) Beckerman; m. Lloyd Diehl Wilson, July 3, 1952 (div. 1965); m. Benjamin Andrew Ungar, Aug. 15, 1972; 1 child, Kimberly Jo Wilson Figueroa. BFA, U. Cin., 1991. Weather girl WNHC-TV, New Haven, 1962-64; actress various orgns., N.Y.C., 1965-72; anchor WLWT-TV, Cin., 1973-86; sr. acct. exec. Judith Bogart Assocs., Cin., 1986-90; pres./owner Carole Wilson Pub. Rels., Inc., Cin., 1991—. Prodr., writer TV documentaries Battered Women, 1979, Women on the Move, 1979; TV program Women USA!, 1980. Bd. dirs. Alice Paul House for Battered Women, Cin., 1980, YWCA, 1978-81; chmn. Career Women of Achievement Project, 1981. Recipient Walter Bartlett award Multimedia Broadcasting, 1989. Mem. Pub. Rels. Soc. Am. (Prism award, Cin. chpt. 1992), Women in Comm. (named Outstanding Woman in Comm., Cin . chpt. 1980). Republican. Office: Carole Wilson Pub Rels Inc Whitehall Office Park 8041 Hosbrook Rd Cincinnati OH 45236

UNGAR, MANYA SHAYON, volunteer, education consultant; b. N.Y.C., May 30, 1928; d. Samuel and Ethel M. (Liese) Shayon; m. Harry Fireman Ungar, June 25, 1950; children: Paul Benedict, Michael Shayon. BA, Mills Coll., 1950. Actress TV and radio NBC, CBS, N.Y.C., 1950-58; founder chpt. AFS, Scotch Plains-Fanwood, N.J., 1958-60; vol. project dir. Boy Scouts Am., Plainfield, N.J., 1958-61; founder, co-dir. Summer Theater Workshop, Scotch Plains, 1967-78; legis. v.p. N.J. State PTA, 1977-79, pres., 1979-81; legis. v.p. Nat. PTA, Chgo., 1981-85, 1st v.p., 1985-87, pres., 1987-89; Mem. arts edn. adv. panel Nat. Endowment Arts, Washington, 1988-91, panel Nat. Inst. Work and Learning, 1988-91; adv. coun. Nat. Panel Drug Free Schs., Washington, 1989-91, edn. adv. bd. NBC, 1988-92, PBS, 1988-91, Scholastic, Inc., 1990-94; bd. dirs. Math. Sci. Edn. Bd., 1988-92. Trustee N.J. Children's Specialized Hosp., 1990—, N.J. Pub. Edn. Inst., 1987—; mem. adv. coun. Natural Resources Def. Coun., Mothers and Others, 1990—; mem. geography assessment adv. coun. Nat. Assessment Edn. Progress, 1991-92, mem. nat. oversite commn. on geog. standards, 1992-94; mem. N.J. Basic Skills Coun., 1990-94; chmn. N.J. Math. Coalition, 1994—; mem. accreditation com. APA, 1992—; mem. tchr. programs adv. panel Ednl. Testing Svc., 1990-94; mem. external rev. com. Ctr. Disease Control Preventing Risk Behaviors in Adolescents, 1993; dir. N.J. LWV, 1995—; bd. dirs. Washington Rock Girl Scout Coun., 1995—. Manya Shayon Ungar Scholarship and Auditorium named in her honor, 1989; named Outstanding Citizen N.J. Jaycees, 1979, Scotch Plains Twp., 1989, 92, State of N.J., 1987, Bd. of Freeholders, 1987; named life mem. nat. PTA, 45 state PTAs. Mem. LWV (chmn. voter svc. Westfield area 1991, mem. N.J. voters svc. com. 1994—). Home: 10 Brandywine Ct Scotch Plains NJ 07076-2550

UNGARO, SUSAN KELLIHER, magazine editor. Editor-in-chief Family Circle mag., N.Y.C. Office: Family Circle 110 Fifth Ave New York NY 10011*

UNGARO-BENAGES, URSULA MANCUSI, federal judge; b. Miami Beach, Fla., Jan. 29, 1951; d. Ludivico Mancusi-Ungaro and Ursula Berliner; m. Michael A. Benages, Mar., 1988. Student, Smith Coll., 1968-70; BA in English Lit., U. Miami, 1973; JD, U. Fla., 1975. Bar: Fla. 1975. Assoc. Frates, Floyd, Pearson et al, Miami, 1976-78, Blackwell, Walker, Gray et al, Miami, 1978-80, Finley, Kumble, Heine et al, Miami, 1980-85, Sparber, Shevin, Shapo et al, Miami, 1985-87; cir. judge State of Fla., Miami, 1987-92; U.S. dist. judge Miami, 1992—; mem. Fla. Supreme Ct. Race & Ethnic & Racial Bias Study Commn., Fla., 1989-92, St. Thomas U. Inns of Ct., Miami, 1991-92. Bd. dirs. United Family & Children's Svcs., Miami, 1981-82; mem. City of Miami Task Force, 1991-92. Mem. ABA, Fed. Judges Assn., Fla. Assn. Women Lawyers, Dade County Bar Assn. Office: US Dist Ct 300 NE 1st Ave Rm 243 Miami FL 33132-2126*

UNGER, HELEN JOAN, industrial real estate broker; b. Queens, N.Y., June 2, 1932; d. Maurice and Rose (Ludmerer) Grayson; m. Howard Unger, Sept. 19, 1954; children: Diane Yorkmark, Lawrence Unger. BA Speech and Dramatic Arts, Adelphi Coll., 1953; postgrad., Columbia U., 1954-56. Capts. lic. U.S. Coast Guard. Copywriter various TV stas., N.Y.C., 1953-72; pres. Unger Indsl. Realty Co., Inc., Great Neck, N.Y., 1975—; owner, rep. marine cons. Capt. Unger, Great Neck, 1960—. Mem. Temple Emanuel, Great Neck, 1970—, Hadassah, Great Neck, 1970—. Mem. Shelter Bay Yacht Club (1st woman commodore 1980-84), Great Neck Power Sq. (port capt. 1989), Ioreba, Nat. Bd. Realtors. Democrat. Jewish. Home: 80 Beach Rd Great Neck NY 11023

UNGER, LAURA S., lawyer; b. N.Y.C., Jan. 8, 1961; d. Raymond and Susan Marie (Vopata) Simone; m. Peter Van Buren Unger, June 29, 1991. BA in Rhetoric, U. Calif., Berkeley, 1983; JD, N.Y. Law Sch., 1987. Bar: Conn. 1987, N.Y. 1988. Staff atty. divsn. enforcement SEC, 1988-90; legis. counsel to Sen. Alfonse M. D'Amato, 1990-91; minority counsel Senate com. banking, housing and urban affairs, 1991-95, counsel, 1995—. Recipient Performance award SEC, N.Y., 1988, D.C., 1989. Mem. ABA, Fed. Bar Assn., Jr. League Washington, Decade Soc., Women in Housing and Fin. Roman Catholic. Office: Banking Housing & Urban Affairs 534 Sen Dirksen Office Bldg Washington DC 20510*

UNGER, MARIANNE LOUISE, computer graphics artist, consultant; b. Reading, Pa., June 8, 1957; d. Paul Richard and Virginia Ruth (Moyer) U. BS in Art Edn., Kutztown U., 1982. Art tchr. 7 local sch. dists., Reading, 1982-83; sec. Berks Cable, Reading, 1983-84, project asst. new bus. devel., 1984-85; art educator Reading Area Community Coll., 1983-87; pres. Unger Computer Graphics, Reading, 1985—; cons. in field, video and multi-image producer, dir., animator; dir. Christian Edn. Zion's UCC, Pottstown, Pa. Grantee NET Ben Franklin Advanced Tech. Ctr., 1986-87. Mem. Nat. Computer Graphics Assn., Berks Women's Network, Berks County C. of C. Office: 38 Aldine Ave Reading PA 19606-1002

UNITHAN, DOLLY, visual artist; came to U.S., 1976; BFA, Hornsey Coll. Art, 1975; MFA, Pratt Inst., 1978; postgrad., Brit. Coun. Fine Arts Exch., 1974, Ecole Nationale des Beaux Arts de Nancy, France, 1974. Summer intern Guggenheim Mus., N.Y.C., 1976; panelist, artist in residence Asian Am. Arts Ctr., N.Y.C., 1993; lectr. in field. One-person shows include Internat. Art Ctr., London, 1975, Am. Assn. State Colls. and Univs., Orlando, Fla., 1977, Sloan Gallery, Lock Haven State Coll., Pa., 1978, Permanent Mission of Malaysia to UN, N.Y.C., 1987, Kerr Gallery, N.Y.C., 1987, Lyman Allyn Art Mus., New London, Conn., 1990, Secretariat Bldg UN, N.Y.C., 1991, Gracie Mansion, N.Y.C., 1994; exhibited in group shows including Palace of Westminster, Hos. of Parliament, London, 1978, City Mus. and Art Gallery, Gloucester, Eng., 1978, Mus. Art, Hove, Eng., 1978, Contemporary Gallery, Warsaw, 1978, Arts Coun. Gallery, Belfast, No. Ireland, 1978, Parrish Art Mus., Southampton, N.Y., 1979, Modern Art Ctr., Guadalajara, Mex., 1979, Alternative Mus., N.Y.C., 1981, Nat. Mus. Fine Arts, Havana, Cuba, 1986, Hillwood Art Mus., Brookville, N.Y., 1988, PS 1 Mus., N.Y.C., 1990, Nat. Art Gallery, Kuala Lumpur, 1991-92, League of Nations Archives, Palais des Nations, Geneva, 1993, Jewish Mus., Vienna, Austria, 1993, Peace Mus., Remagen, Germany, Westbeth Galleries, N.Y.C., Tweed Courthouse Gallery, N.Y.C., 1994; represented in permanent collections including Lock Haven State Coll., Pa., Alternative Mus., N.Y.C., Am. Assn. State Colls. and Univs., Washington, Permanent Mission of Malaysia to UN, Wilfredo Lam Ctr., Havana, Malaysian Embassy, Washington, Spirit Found., N.Y.C., Asian Am. Arts Ctr., N.Y.C.; artwork included in (jours.) Multicultural Edn., 1994, Artspiral, 1994, (book) Sculpture. Technique, Form, Content. Recipient Artist award Rainbow Art Found., N.Y.C., 1985, Art award ArtQuest '88 Internat. Art Competition, Calif., 1988; named to Archives of Contemporary Arts Venice Biennale, 1990; grantee Lee Found., Singapore, 1972, 76, Pollock-Krasner Found., 1991-92; grad. scholar MARA, Malaysia, 1976-78.

UNO, ANNE QUAN, financial planner; b. Ukiah, Calif., Feb. 27, 1942; d. Dock and Chew (Ying) Quan; divorced; children: Kiri, Marili. BS, UCLA, 1964; MEd, Tex. A&M U., 1972; cert., Coll. Fin. Planning, Denver, 1983. CFP; enrolled agt. Tchr. Waco (Tex.) Ind. Sch. Dist., 1969-76; rep. Investors Diversified, Mpls., 1977-79, Cardell & Assocs., Morristown, N.J., 1979-81, Mut. Svc. Corp., Palm Beach, Fla., 1982—; fin. planner Fin. Assocs., Arlington, Va., 1982—. Author: Aesthetic Activities for Exceptional Children, 1975. Mem. Nat. Assn. Investors Corp. (nat. assoc. dir. Met. Washington coun. 1987—), Inst. Cert. Fin. Planners, Nat. Assn. Tax Practioners, Md. Soc. Accts., Nat. Soc. Tax Profls., Am. Assn. Individual Investors, Orgn. Pan Asian Am. Women, Hui 5 Club. Office: Fin Assocs No Va Soc Cert Fin Planners 933 N Kenmore St Ste 217 Arlington VA 22201

UNTERBERGER, BETTY MILLER, history educator, writer; b. Glasgow, Scotland, Dec. 27, 1923; d. Joseph C. and Leah Miller; m. Robert Ruppe, July 29, 1944; children: Glen, Gail, Gregg. B.A., Syracuse U., N.Y., 1943; M.A., Harvard U., 1946; Ph.D., Duke U., 1950. Asst. prof. E. Carolina U., Greenville, 1948-50; assoc. prof., dir. liberal arts ctr. Whittier Coll., Calif., 1954-61; assoc. prof. Calif. State U.-Fullerton, 1961-65, prof., chmn. grad. studies, 1965-68; prof. Tex. A&M U., College Station, 1968—; vis. prof. U. Hawaii, Honolulu, summer 1967, Peking U., Beijing, 1988; vis. disting. prof. U. Calif., Irvine, 1987—, Patricia and Bookman Peters prof. history, 1991—; vis. prof. Charles U., Prague, Czechoslovakia, summer 1992; mem. adv. com. fgn. rels. U.S. Dept. State, 1977-81, chair, 1981; mem. hist. adv. com. U.S. Dept. Army, 1980-82, USN, 1991—; mem. Nat. Hist. Publs. and Records Commn., 1980-84. Author: America's Siberian Expedition 1918-1920: A Study of National Policy, 1956, 69 (Pacific Coast award Am. Hist. Assn. 1956); editor: American Intervention in the Russian Civil War, 1969, Intervention Against Communism: Did the U.S. Try to Overthrow the Soviet Government, 1918-20, 1986, The United States, Revolutionary Russia and the Rise of Czechoslovakia, 1989; contbr.: Woodrow Wilson and Revolutionary World, 1982; editorial adv. bd.: The Papers of Woodrow Wilson, Princeton U., 1982-92; bd. editors: Diplomatic History, 1981-84, Red River Valley Hist. Rev., 1975-84. Trustee Am. Inst. Pakistan Studies, Villanova U., Pa., 1981—, sec., 1989-92; mem. League of Women Voters. Fellow Woodrow Wilson Found., 1979; named Disting. Univ. Teacher State of Calif. Legislature, 1966; recipient All-Univ. Disting. Teaching award Tex. A&M U., 1975. Mem. LWV, NOW, AAUW, Am. Hist. Assn. (chair 1982-83, nominating com. 1980-83), Orgn. Am. Historians (govt. relations com.), Soc. Historians of Am. Fgn. Relations (exec. council 1978-81, 86-89, govt. relations com. 1982-84, v.p. 1985, pres. 1986, co-winner Myrna F. Bernath prize 1991), Am. Soc. for Advancement Slavic Studies, Coordinating Com. on Women in Hist. Profession, Rocky Mountain Assn. Slavic Studies (program chair 1973, v.p. 1973-74), So. Hist. Assn., Asian Studies Assn., Assn. Third World Studies, Czechoslovak Soc. Arts and Scis., Czechoslovak History Conf., Women's Fgn. Policy Coun., Beyond War, Peace History Soc., Sierra Club, Phi Beta Kappa, Phi Beta Delta. Office: Tex A&M U College Station TX 77843

UPBIN, SHARI, theatrical producer, director, agent, educator; b. N.Y.C.; m. Hal J. Upbin, May 29, 1960; children: Edward, Elyse, Danielle. Master tap instr. Talent mgr. Goldstar Talent Mgmt., Inc., N.Y.C., 1989-91; guest tchr. Total Theatre Lab., N.Y.C.; faculty Nat. Shakespeare Conservatory, N.Y. Asst. dir. 1st Black-Hispanic Shakespeare prodn. Julius Caesar, Coriolanus at Pub. Theatre, N.Y., 1979; dir., choreographer Matter of Opinion, Players Theatre, N.Y., 1980, Side by Side, Sondheim Forum Theatre, N.J., 1981 (Nominated Best Dir. of Season N.J. Theatre Critics); producer, dir. Vincent, The Passions of Van Gogh, N.Y., 1981; producer Bojangles, The Life of Bill Robinson, Broadway, 1984, Captain America, nat. Am. tour; dir. Fiddler on the Roof, Cabaret, Life with Father, Roar of the Grease Paint, regional theatre, 1979-82; co-producer One Mo' Time, Village Gate, N.Y., nat. and internat. tour.; producer/dir. off-Broadway musical Flypaper, 1991-92, Women on Their Own, Things My Mother Never Told Me, Theatre East, N.Y. Founded Queens Playhouse, N.Y., Children's Theatre, Flushing, N.Y.; mem. Willy Mays' Found. Drug Abused Children. Recipient Jaycees Service award Jr. Miss Pageants Franklin Twp., N.J., 1976. Mem. League Profl. Theatre Women (pres.), Soc. Stage Dirs. and Choreographers, Actors Equity Assn., Villagers Barn Theatre (1st woman pres.), N.Y. Womens Agenda, Faculty Nat. Shakespeare Conservatory (N.Y.). Address: Shari Upbin Prodns 45 E 89th St New York NY 10128

UPCHURCH, PEGGY GUPTON, councilwoman; b. Louisburg, N.C., Oct. 23, 1945; d. E. Buckley and Ada Ruth (Boyd) Gupton; m. Harold R. Moore, Dec. 3, 1965 (div. July 1974); 1 child, Michelle P.; m. Frank Jefferson Upchurch Jr., Dec. 11, 1976; children: Frank Jefferson III, Nathaniel Buckley. Student, Louisburg Jr. Coll., 1966, N.C. State U., 1973, Winthrop U., 1979-81. Owner Careers Coordinated, Henderson, N.C., 1973-76; councilwoman York County, S.C., 1985—. Co-founer Carolinas Counties Coalition, Charlotte, N.C., 1987-90, vice-chmn., 1987—; mem. S.C. Adv. Commn. on Intergovtl. Rels., 1988—; chmn. Carolinas Transp. Compact, Charlotte, 1989-94, Police Athletic League, 1989-92. Recipient Cert. of Achievement, AAUW, 1988, Cert. of Appreciaiton, York County Police Athletic League, 1989, Cert. of Honor, S.C. Gen. Assembly, 1990. Mem. Nat. Assn. Counties Transp. (sub-com. 1992—), S.C. Assn. Counties (chmn. sub-com. 1992-94), Lake Wylie C. of C. (bd. dirs., Cert. of Appreciation 1990), Clover Women's Club (pres. 1988-92), Clover/Lake Wylie Rep. Women (charter). Baptist. Home: 12 Sandy Cove Rd Lake Wylie SC 29710-8930 Office: York County PO Box 66 York SC 29745-0066

UPDEGRAFF SPLETH, ANN L., church executive, pastor; b. Newark, Ohio, Sept. 15, 1949; d. John C. and Lela V. (Mervine) Updegraff; m. Randall Alan Spleth; children: Andrew Alan, Claire Campbell. BA, Transylvania Coll., 1971; MDiv, Vanderbilt U., 1974; DMin, Claremont Sch. Theology, 1985. Ordained min. Christian Ch., 1973. Assoc. min. First Christian Ch., New Castle, Ind., 1974-75, Sacramento, 1975-78; sr. assoc. regional min. Pacific S.W. region Christian Ch., L.A., 1978-85; exec. v.p. Divsn. Homeland Ministries, Indpls., 1985-89, pres., 1990—. Author: Youth Ministry Manual, 1980; co-author: Congregation: Sign of Hope, 1989, Worship and Spiritual Life, 1992; editor Vanguard, 1990—; contbr. articles to profl. jours. Founding mem. Profl. Women's Forum, L.A., 1978-85. Mem. Ind. Soc. Democrat. Home: 8961 Sawmill Ct Indianapolis IN 46236-9171 Office: Divsn Homeland Ministries PO Box 1986 Indianapolis IN 46206

UPHAM, JOYCE HARRIS, library director; b. Johnstown, Pa., Aug. 28, 1935; d. William Henry Jr. and Frieda Mae (Miller) Harris; m. Donald Bassett Upham, Oct. 19, 1963; children: Harris William, Margaret Weston. BS in Edn., Towson State U., 1957; MSLS, U. N.C., 1963. Cert. Mass. Bd. Libr. Commrs., Mass. Bd. Edn. Elem. tchr. Prince George's County, Adelphi, Md., 1957-60, Dept. Army, Machinato, Okinawa, 1960-61; secondary sch. libr. Durham (N.C.) Schs., 1961-66, Orange County Schs., Chapel Hill, N.C., 1966-67; libr. Fairbanks North Star Borough Libr., Fairbanks, Alaska, 1970-71; tutor/developer Tanana Valley Coop., Fairbanks, 1974-78; dir. Carver (Mass.) Pub. Libr., 1988—. Researcher/developer Plate Tectonic Program, 1982, Fairbanks History Program, 1983. Facilitator/researcher Elmer Rasmusson Libr., University, Alaska, 1977; docent U. Alaska Mus., Fairbanks, 1980-85, Art Complex Mus., Duxbury, Mass., 1987-88. Recipient Outstanding Sci. Tchr. NSF, Washington, 1956. Mem. AAUW (life, br. pres., gift recipient 1986), Mass. Libr. Assn. Methodist. Office: Carver Pub Libr 106 Main St Carver MA 02330-1301

UPHOLD, MARGARET BROADWATER (MARGE UPHOLD), bank officer; b. Keyser, W.Va., Oct. 27, 1948; m. Rodger Lee Uphold, May 19, 1968; 1 child, Teresa. AA, Allegany Community Coll., Cumberland, Md., 1982; BS, Frostburg (Md.) State U., 1984, postgrad., 1990. Sec. USDA, Hyattsville, Md., 1966-68; bank teller 1st Nat. Bank, Oakland, Md., 1968-69; freelance transcriber, editor Oakland, 1969-77; adminstrv. sec. Sacred Heart Hosp., Cumberland, 1977-80, staff writer, 1984-85, staff asst., 1985-87; dir. mktg. and community rels. Frostburg (Md.) Community Hosp., 1987-92; sales rep. Fidelity Bank, Frostburg, 1992—; vol. Whitewater Internat., McHenry, Md., 1989-92. Author poetry. Bd. dirs. Am. Lung Assn., 1989-92, Am. Heart Assn., 1991—, Arthritis Found., 1992—. Mem. Frostburg Bus. and Profl. Assn., Lions Club, Beta Sigma Phi (sec. Cumberland chpt. 1991-92, v.p. 1989-90, 94-95). Republican. Methodist. Home: 18621 Woodlawn Dr Rawlings MD 21557-1027 Office: Fidelity Bank PO Box 50 Frostburg MD 21532-0050

UPJOHN, LISA HATHERLY, artist; b. Grand Rapids, Mich., Mar. 1, 1962; d. Harold Irvin Hatherly and Yvonne Joan (Aquilina) Maloney; m. Henry L. Upjohn II, Aug. 6, 1983. BA, Western Mich. U., 1986. Exhbns. include Mary Bell Gallery, Chgo., Malton Gallery, Cin., Gallery ZZ, Bloomfield Hills, Mich., Joan Bowers Gallery, Kalamazoo, Mich., Joyce Pelter Gallery, Saugatuck, Mich., 1988. Bd. dirs. Kalamazoo Nature Ctr. Home: 4120 Lake Forest Ln Portage MI 49008-3380

UPRIGHT, DIANE WARNER, auction house executive; b. Cleve.; d. Rodney Upright and Shirley (Warner) Lavine. Student, Wellesley Coll., 1965-67; BA, U. Pitts., 1969; MA, U. Mich., 1973, PhD, 1976. Asst. prof. U. Va., Charlottesville, 1976-78; assoc. prof. Harvard U., Cambridge, Mass., 1978-83; sr. curator Ft. Worth Art Mus., 1984-86; dir. Jan Krugier Gallery, N.Y.C., 1986-90; sr. v.p., head contemporary art dept. Christie's, N.Y.C., 1990—. Author: Morris Louis: The Complete Paintings, 1979, Ellsworth Kelly: Works on Paper, 1987, various exhbn. catalogues; contbr. articles to art jours. Mem. Coll. Art Assn., Art Table, Inc. Office: Christies 502 Park Ave New York NY 10022-1108

UPSHAW, LISA GAYE, business computer systems analyst; b. Alamogordo, N.Mex., June 27, 1959; d. James Leroy Upshaw and Margaret (Shackelford) Carrell; m. Michael J. Zamora, Nov. 3, 1976 (div. July 1983); 1 child, Jeremy Brandon; m. Eddie Gonzalez, Mar. 19, 1984 (div. 1989). BS in Bus. Computer Systems, U. N.Mex., 1983. Govt. and large account system analyst Office Systems, Alburquerque, 1982-84; sr. system analyst, nat. accounts mgr. Bell Atlantic/CompuShop, Houston, 1984-89; nat. account mgr. CompuCom Systems, Inc., Houston, 1988—, mem. president's coun., 1988-89; br. mgr. CompuCom Systems, Inc., Atlanta, 1990-93, nat. sales mgt., 1993—; cons. Bell Atlantic President's Club, Dallas, 1986-87, 88, Bell Atlantic Leaders Club, 1986-89. Chmn. publicity Ronald McDonald House, Alburquerque, 1982, chairwoman spl. events, 1983; chairwoman Rep. Vol. Community, Houston, 1986; sponsor Houston Ballet, Theatre of Arts, Fundraising Heart Assn. Mem. NAFE (network dir. 1987-88), Assn. Info. System Profls., Houston Area League Personal Computer Specialists, NOW, VFW, CompuCom Leaders Club. Home: 3551 Robinson Rd Marietta GA 30068-2445 Office: CompuCom Systems 2580 Cumberland Pkwy # 400 Atlanta GA 30339

UPTON, KATHRYN ANN, emergency trauma nurse; b. Ft. Smith, Ark., Dec. 13, 1955; d. William A. and Kathryn (Derrickson) U. BSN, U. Tex., Arlington, 1986. Cert. CEN, ACLS, BLS, PALS, trauma nurse core certification. Commd. ensign USN, 1987-89, advanced through grades to lt., 1989-90; staff nurse med.-surg. USN San Diego Balboa, 1987-88, relief charge/staff emergency rm., 1988-90; staff nurse neonatal ICU USN Bethesda (Md.) Nat. Naval Med. Ctr., 1990-91; staff nurse burn ICU/emergency rm. USNS Comfort-Persian Gulf, 1990-91; asst. charge nurse USN Nat. Naval Med. Ctr., Bethesda, 1991-92; ret. USN, Ft. Lauderdale, Fla., 1992; trauma nurse Broward Gen. Trauma Ctr., Ft. Lauderdale, Fla., 1992-94; nurse mgr. ambulatory care Miami Vets. Adminstn. Hosp., Miami, 1994—. Decorated Meritorious Unit Commendation, Navy Commendation medal, Nat. Def. medal, SW Asia medal, Kuwait Liberation medal, Sea Svc. medal, Combat Action ribbon, Battle "E" ribbon.

URATO, BARBRA CASALE, entrepreneur; b. Newark, Oct. 10, 1941; d. Dominick Anthony and Concetta (Castrichini) Casale; m. John Joseph Urato, June 20, 1965; children: Concetta U. Graves, Gina E., Joseph D. Student, Seton Hall U., 1961-63. File clk. Martin Gelber Esquire, Newark, 1956-58; policy typist Aetna Casualty Ins., Newark, 1959-61; sec. to dean Seton Hall U., South Orange, N.J., 1961-63; paralegal sec. Judge Robert A. McKinley, Newark, 1963-65, Joseph Garrubbo, Esquire, Newark, 1965-66; office mgr. Valiant I.M.C., Hackensack, N.J., 1971-73; asst. pers. mgr. Degussa Inc., Teterboro, N.J., 1975-78; night mgr. The Ferryboat Restaurant, River Edge, N.J., 1976-78; mgr. Fratello's and Ventilini's, Hilton Head, S.C., 1978-80; day mgr. Ramada Inn Restaurant, Paramus, N.J., 1980-81; mgr. Gottlieb's Bakery, Hilton Head, 1982-83; asst. mgr. closing dept. Hilton Head Mortgage Co., 1983-84; owner, mgr. All Cleaning Svc., Hilton Head, 1984—; owner Hilton Head Investigations, 1990-93, Hilton Head Island, 1990-92; owner Aaction Investigators, 1992—. Mem. NAFE, Profl. Women of Hilton Head, Assn. for Rsch. and Enlightenment, Preferred Bus. Assn., Rosicrucian Order, Low Country Property Mgmt. Roman Catholic.

URBACH, SUSAN KAY, small business development administrator; b. York, Nebr., June 30, 1956; d. James Floyd and Mary Jane (Schwab) U. B. Mus., Oklahoma City U., 1978, M in Mus., 1980. Comml. loan asst., sec. Citizens Nat. Bank, Oklahoma City, 1983-86; loan svc. asst. SBA, Oklahoma City, 1986-88; dir. Small Bus. Devel. Ctr. Univ. Cen. Okla., Edmond, Okla., 1988—; mem. adv. bd. Okla. Home Based Bus. Assn.; mem. steering com. Gov.'s Conf. on Small Bus. Editor: (songbook) Sigma Alpha Iota Songbook Supplement vols. I and II, 1981, 84. Mem., choir dir. Chapel-Tinker AFB, Midwest City, Okla., 1982-88, St. Francis Assisi Cath. Ch., Oklahoma City, 1988-92; mem. Gatewood Neighborhood Bd., 1990. Mem. Edmond C. of C., Oklahoma City C. of C., Sigma Alpha Iota. Republican. Episcopalian. Home: 2012 NW 13th St Oklahoma City OK 73106-1606 Office: Univ Cen Okla Ctr 100 N University Dr Edmond OK 73034-5209

URBAN, CATHLEEN ANDREA, software developer; b. Elizabeth, N.J., June 7, 1947; d. Emil Martin and Susan (Rahoche) Cupec; m. Walter Robert Urban, Nov. 5, 1966; children: Karen Louise, Kimberly Ann. Student, Rutgers U., 1965-66, 91—; AS in Computer Info. Systems, Raritan Valley Community Coll., North Branch, N.J., 1990, AAS in Computer Programming, 1990. Office mgr. K-Mart Corp., Somerville, N.J., 1987-90; software developer Bell Communications Rsch., Piscataway, N.J., 1990-93, sys. tech. support cons., 1993-94; software developer Bell Comm. Rsch., Piscataway, 1994—. Leader Somerset County 4-H Program, Bridgewater, 1978-87. Mem. NAFE, AAUW, Nat. Space Soc., Internat. Platform Assn., Internat. Guild Candle Artisans, Golden Key Honor Soc., Phi Theta Kappa. Roman Catholic. Home: 570 Amwell Rd Neshanic Station NJ 08853-3404 Office: Bell Comm Rsch 444 Hoes Ln Piscataway NJ 08854-4182

URBAN, JO ELLEN, federal agency administrator; b. Fairfax, Va., Aug. 7, 1964; d. Al and Joan E. (Nicaise) U. BA in Polit. Sci., Villanova U., 1986; MBA, Marymount U., 1988. Dir. house staff task force on trade and competitiveness, chief legis. asst. econs. and internat. trade, various other positions Staff of House Majority Leader Richard Gephardt, 1986-91; legis.

asst. to Senator Donald W. Riegle, Jr. Senate Com. on Finance, 1991-93; dir. office legis./intergovtl. affairs, policy staff mem. office under sec. internat. trade adminstrn. Dept. of Commerce, Washington, 1993—. European Cmty. Visitors Programme scholar, 1992. Mem. Trade Policy Forum. Office: Office of the Under Sec Dept of Commerce Rm 3424 14th St & Independence Ave NW Washington DC 20230*

URBAN, NATALIE LERO, educator; b. Providence, Mar. 16, 1948; d. William Paul and Josephine Marie (Loscalzo) Lero; m. James Robert Urban Jr., Sept. 14, 1975; 1 child, James III. BA cum laude, U. R.I., 1969; MA, Middlebury Coll., 1971; postgrad., New HAven Coll., 1973-74. Tchr. Bristol (R.I.) High Sch., 1969-70, West Haven (Conn.) Sch. System, 1971-77; tchr., sec. Italo-Am. Med. Edn. Found., Perugia, Italy, 1977-78; tchr. Oxford Inst., Milan, Italy, 1978-79; tchr., interpreter Gondwana Spa, Milan, Italy, 1979-81; adminstrv. asst. Continental Bank Chg., Milan, Italy, 1981-84; tchr. Centro Pilota, Rome, Italy, 1984-86; adminstrv. asst. Cable News Network, Rome, Italy, 1986; tchr. Ctrl. Falls (R.I.) High Sch., 1986-87; tchr. Italian and Spanish Cranston (R.I.) High Sch. West, 1987—. Vol. Linden Pl. Spl. Events, Bristol, 1991-92. Mem. R.I. Fgn. Langs. Assn., R.I. Tchrs. of Italian, Phi Kappa Phi, Kappa Delta Pi. Roman Catholic. Home: 59 Aaron Ave Bristol RI 02809-1518 Office: Cranston High Sch West 29 Metropolitan Ave Cranston RI 02920

URBAS, ELSIE JOAN, educational diagnostician; b. N.Y.C., Mar. 14, 1931; d. Edward and Elsie (Zittel) Steudtner; m. Walter Urbas, Sept. 8, 1950; children: Lance and Layne (twins), Don. BA, Hunter Coll., N.Y.C., 1962; MS, Adelphi U., 1967; PhD, Hofstra U., 1971. Tchr. Sea Cliff and Franklin Sq. Schs., L.I., N.Y., 1962-71; asst. prin. Harborfield Schs., Greenlawn, N.Y., 1971-73; prin. Willis Ave. Sch., Mineola, N.Y., 1973-76, Covert Ave. Sch., Elmont, N.Y., 1976-88; instr. C.W. Post Coll./L.I. U., Brookville, N.Y., 1988-89; computer program facilitator Balt. Schs./Johns Hopkins, 1989-90; ednl. diagnostician Hannah More Sch., Reisterstown, Md., 1990—; mem. Adaptive Learning Environments Model N.E. site Temple U.-C.W. Post Coll.-L.I. U., 1985-88. Sec., Anne Arundel County LWV, Annapolis, Md., 1993—, vice chmn. nominating conv. com., 1990-93; docent Walters Art Gallery, Balt. Recipient Sisterhood award NOW, 1986. Mem. Coun. of Adminstrs., Suprs. (Nassau County dir. 1985-89), Nassau County Elem. Sch. Prin. Assn. (pres. 1980-81, Arthur E. Hamalanien Educator award 1988). Democrat. Christian Science. Home: 881 New London Harbour Pasadena MD 21122-6504 Office: Hannah More Sch 12305 Reisterstown Rd Reisterstown MD 21136-0249

URDANG, ALEXANDRA, book publishing executive; b. N.Y.C., June 29, 1956; d. Laurence Urdang and Irena (Ehrlich) Urdang de Tour. BA in English Lit., U. Conn., 1977. Customer svc. and fulfillment mgr. Universe Books, N.Y.C., 1978-79, sales mgr., assoc. mktg. mgr., 1980-82; asst. v.p., dir. spl. sales Macmillan Pub. Co., N.Y.C., 1982-88; v.p. new markets Warner Books, Inc., N.Y.C., 1988—. Office: Warner Books Inc Time and Life Bldg 1271 Avenue Of The Americas New York NY 10020-1300

UREEL, PATRICIA LOIS, retired manufacturing company executive; b. Detroit, Nov. 29, 1923; d. Peter Walter and Ethel Estelle (Stewart) Murphy; grad. Detroit Bus. Inst., 1941; student Wayne State U., 1942, U. Detroit, 1943, U. Miami, 1945-46; m. Joseph Ralph Ureel, Jan. 4, 1947; children—Mary Patricia, Ronald Joseph. Exec. sec. to chmn. bd. and pres. Detroit Ball Bearing Co. of Mich., 1965-67; exec. sec. to partner charge Mich. dist. Ernst & Ernst, Detroit, 1967-71, Clubs of Inverrary, Lauderhill, Fla., 1971-72, partner charge of group Coopers & Lybrand, Miami, Fla., 1972-74; corp. sec., personnel mgr. Sanford Industries, Inc. and 4 subsidiaries, Pompano Beach, Fla., 1974-81; corp. sec., asso. Asphalt Assos., Ft. Lauderdale, 1982-86. Named Sec. of Yr. for City of Detroit, 1966; cert. profl. sec. Mem. Nat. Secs. Assn., Women's Econ. Club Detroit, Moose, Zeta Tau Alpha Sorority (Gamma Alpha chpt). Republican. Roman Catholic. Home: 16250 S Pacific Hwy # 65 Lake Oswego OR 97034

URIBE, JENNIE ANN, elementary school educator; b. National City, Calif., Apr. 17, 1958; d. Robert and Alice (Packard) U. BA, San Diego State U., 1981, cert. teacher, 1982. Tchr. Langdon Ave. Sch., L.A. Unified Sch. Dist., Sepulveda, Calif., 1984-94, tchr. potentially gifted students class, 1987-94; tchr. Spreckels Elem. Sch., San Diego City Schs., 1994—; tchr./advisor for student govt., 1987-93. Home: 1109 Palm Ave National City CA 91950 Office: Spreckels Elem Sch 6033 Stadium St San Diego CA 92122

URMAN-KLEIN, PHYLLIS, psychologist; b. Newark, N.J., Nov. 11, 1942; m. Peter Klein, June 23, 1976; children: Nadia, Alexis. BA, Boston U., 1964; MS, Columbia U., 1968; PhD, Union Inst., 1983. Clin. social worker adult psychiat. clinic Jacobi Hosp., 1968-72, chief social worker, 1972-80; assoc. dept. psychiatry Albert Einstein Coll. Medicine, 1975-85; lectr. in psychiatry Cornell U. Med. Coll., 1985—; pvt. practice, 1972—; presenter in field; appraiser and evaluator of teaching materials Assn. Am. Med. Colls., 1979-80. Contbr. articles to profl. jours. Fellow Am. Orthopsychiatry Assn.; mem. Am. Psychol. Assn., State Psychol. Divsn. Psychoanalysis, Am. Family Therapy Assn., Nat. Coun. on Women's Health, NYU Psychoanalytic Soc. Office: Cornell U Med Coll 56 E 87th St New York NY 10128-1036

URMER, DIANE HEDDA, management firm executive, financial officer; b. Bklyn., Dec. 15, 1934; d. Leo and Helen Sarah (Perlman) Leverant; m. Albert Heinz Urmer, Sept. 2, 1952; children: Michelle, Cynthia, Carl. Student U. Tex., 1951-52, Washington U., St. Louis, 1962-63; BA in Psychology, Calif. State U.-Northridge, 1969. Asst. auditor Tex. State Bank, Austin, 1952-55; v.p., controller Enki Corp., Sepulveda, Calif., 1966-70, also dir., 1987—; v.p., fin. Cambia Way Hosp., Walnut Creek, Calif., 1973-78; v.p., controller Enki Health & Research Systems, Inc., Reseda, Calif., 1978—, also dir. Contbr. articles to profl. jours. Pres. Northridge PTA, 1971; chmn. Northridge Citizens Adv. Council, 1972-73. Mem. Women in Mgmt. Club: Tex. Execs. Avocations: bowling, sailing, handcrafts, golf. Office: Enki Health and Rsch Systems Inc 21601 Devonshire St Chatsworth CA 91311

URQUHART, SALLY ANN, environmental scientist, chemist; b. Omaha, June 8, 1946; d. Howard E. and Mary Josephine (Johnson) Lee; m. Henry O. Urquhart, July 31, 1968; children: Mary L., Andrew L. BS in Chemistry, U. Tex., Arlington, 1968; MS in Environ. Scis., U. Tex., Dallas, 1986. Registered environ. mgr.; lic. asbestos mgmt. planner, Tex. Rsch. asst. U. Tex. Dallas, Richardson, 1980-82; substitute sci. tchr. Dallas Ind. Sch. Dist., 1982; high sch. sci. tchr. Allen (Tex.) Ind. Sch. Dist., 1983-87; hazardous materials specialist Dallas Area Rapid Transit, 1987-90, environ. compliance officer, 1990-94; environmental compliance coordination officer, 1994—. Pres. Beacon Sunday Sch. Spring Valley United Meth. Ch., Dallas, 1987, adminstrv. bd. dirs., 1989, com. status and role of women, 1992. Scholar Richardson (Tex.) Br. AAUW, 1980. Mem. An. Inst. Chemists, Am. Chem. Soc., Am. Soc. Safety Engrs., Am. Indsl. Hygiene Assn., Am. Conf. Govtl. Indsl. Hygienists (assoc.), Nat. Registry Environ. Profls., Soc. Tex. Environ. Profls. (sec./treas. Dallas chpt. 1994), U. Tex.-Dallas Alumnae Assn. (com. 1992-94). Home: 310 Sallie Cir Richardson TX 75081-4229 Office: Dallas Area Rapid Transit PO Box 660163 Dallas TX 75266-0163

USELMANN, CATHERINE ROSE, small business owner, behavioral research and finance consultant; b. Madison, Wis., Sept. 17, 1960; d. Richard Lewis and Evelyn Mae (Parr) U. BA in Sociology, U. Wis., 1984, MA in Rsch. and Analysis, 1985; DD (hon.), Charter Ecumenical Ministries Internat., 1994. Pub. utility rate analyst Pub. Svc. Commn. Wis., Madison, 1986-89; rsch. mgr. Wis. Lottery, Madison, 1989-90; energy cons. HBRS, Inc., Madison, 1990-91; sr. cons., project mgr. XENERGY, Inc., Burlington, Mass., 1991-93; pres. CRU Prodns., Madison, 1993—; speaker Nat. Assn. Regulatory Utility Commrs., 1987-89; contbg. mem., speaker Assn. for Demand-Side Mgmt. Profls., 1991-93. Univ. rep. operating com. Mall/Concourse, Madison, 1982-84; lobbyist Inst. for Rsch. Poverty, Madison, 1984; activist, mem. People for Ethical Treatment Animals, Washington, 1989—. Mem. Fin. Independence Assn., U. Wis. Alumni Assn., Badger Quarter Horse Assn. (life), Sierra Club. Lakota. Home and Office: 3753 Robin Hood Way Madison WI 53704-6243

USHER, LAURIE EDITH, environmental educator; b. West Chester, Pa., Nov. 1, 1956; d. Hallan Joseph and Ida Arvilla (Reynolds) U. BS in Recreation and Parks, Pa. State U., 1979, cert. in marine sci., 1979; MS, Ohio State U., 1985. Program developer Project C.A.P.E. Marine Edn., Manteo, N.C., 1979-80; rsch. assoc. info. dissemination project EPA, Columbus, Ohio; dir. marine sci. camp Pacific Sci. Ctr., Seattle, 1985; founder., co-dir. Adopt-A-Beach, Seattle, 1985-86; recreation supr. Bainbridge Island (Wash.) Park Dist., 1987-90; owner Enviro-Ed, Bainbridge Island, 1989—; water quality educator coop. extension Wash. State U., Olympia, 1990-91; girls lacrosse coach, founder Bainbridge High Sch., 1987—; freelance women's sports photographer, 1974—; project coord. Bainbridge Island Watershed Edn., 1994, Snohomish County Watershed Edn., Everett, Wash., 1993-94. Named Outstanding Women's Sports Photographer, Women Sports Mag., 1976. Mem. N.W. Aquatic and Marine Educators (bd. dirs. 1989-94, Outstanding Aquatic Cons. 1992), Bainbridge Island Land Trust (bd. dirs., edn. chair 1991-94), Nat. Marine Educators Assn. (N.W. chpt. rep. 1992—), Environ. Educators Assn. Wash., N.Am. Assn. Environ. En., Wash. Schoolgirls Lacrosse League (pres. 1994—). Home and Office: 9730 Manitou Pl NE Bainbridge Is WA 98110-1327

USHIJIMA, JEAN M., retired city official; b. San Francisco, Feb. 14, 1933; d. Toyoharu George and Frances Fujiko (Misumi) Miwa; m. Tad E. Ushijima; 1 child, Carol M. BS, U. San Francisco, 1981. City clk. City of Beverly Hills, Calif., 1973-94. Bd. dirs. West L.A. Japanese Am. Citizens League, 1979—, pres., 1988-81, also chmn. bd.; bd. dirs. Leadership Edn. for Asian Pacifics, 1985-90. Mem. Acad. Advanced Edn., City Clks. Assn. Calif. (pres. 1986, City Clerk of Yr. award 1989), Calif. Women in Govt. (program chmn. 1978-79), Beverly Hills C. of C. (Employee of Yr. award 1990), Leadership Edn. for Asian Pacific (chmn. bd. 1987), League Calif. Cities (adminstrv. svcs. com. 1982-86, 93—), Internat. Inst. Mcpl. Clks. (bd dirs. 1988-91). Avocations: reading, Japanese dancing. Office: City Clk 455 N Rexford Dr # 190 Beverly Hills CA 90210-4817

USINGER, MARTHA PUTNAM, educator; b. Pitts., Dec. 10, 1912; d. Milo Boone and Christiana (Haberstroh) Putnam; m. Robert Leslie Usinger, June 24, 1938 (dec. Oct. 1968); children: Roberta Christine, Richard Putnam. AB cum laude, U. Calif., Berkeley, 1934; postgrad., Oreg. State U., 1935, U. Ghana, 1970, Coll. Nairobi, 1970. Tchr. Oakland (Calif.) Pub. Schs., 1936-38; tchr. Berkeley (Calif.) Pub. Schs., 1954-57, dean West Campus, counselor, 1957-78; lectr., photographer in field. Author: Ration Books and Christmas Crackers, 1989. Mem. adv. coun. Lifespan Alta Bates Hosp. Mem. DAR, Berkeley Ret. Tchrs., U. Calif. Emeriti Assn., U. Calif. Alumnae Assn., Prytanean Alumnae Assn. (pres. 1952-54), Mortar Bd., Delta Kappa Gamma. Congregationalist.

USRY, JANA PRIVETTE, special education educator; b. Richmond, Va., Oct. 23, 1943; d. Millard Due and Dorothy (Daneman) Privette; m. David Page Usry, Feb. 5, 1972 (dec. Sept. 1975); 1 stepchild, Stephanie Page Usry. BA in Psychology, Mary Washington Coll.; MEd in Spl. Edn., U. Va.; postgrad., Va. Commonwealth U., 1984. Cert. tchr. psychology, spl. edn. tchr., spl. edn. supr., prin. elem. & secondary. Tchr. emotionally disturbed Va. Treatment Ctr. for Children, summer 1966; program cons. Va. Soc. for Prevention of Blindness, Inc., 1966-67; tchr. emotionally disturbed, intermediate and self-contained Henrico County Pub. Schs., 1967-70; tchr. emotionally disturbed and learning disabled The Learning Ctr., St. Joseph's Villa, 1971-73; ednl. cons., tchr. dept. pediatrics, adolescent unit Med. Coll. of Va., 1973-74; spl. edn. tchr. Albert Hill Mid. Sch./Richmond Pub. Schs., 1974-78, Thomas Jefferson High Sch./Richmond Pub. Schs., 1978-86, United Meth. Family Svcs., 1986-87, Monacan High Sch., Chesterfield County, 1987-88, Higland Springs High Sch./Henrico County Pub. Schs., 1988-93; tchr. Henrico Juvenile Detention Home, Richmond, Va., 1993—; organizer learning disabilities workshop Supt.'s Sch. for the Gifted, 1980; condr. workshops and state convs. for learning disabled youth Va. Assn. for Children with Learning Disabilities, 1980, 81; condr. in-svc. workshop fgn. lang. tchrs. City of Richmond, 1982-83; participant learning disabilities workshop Va. State Dept. of Spl. Edn., Lynchburg, 1983; condr. learning disabilities workshops Richmond Pub. Schs., spring 1983; mem. com. on permanent records for exceptional edn. Richmond Pub. Schs., 1984, sponsor cheerleaders, pep club, other extra-curricular activities; mem. spl. edn. curriculum task force Learning Disabilities Sect. Henrico County Pub. Schs., 1989-90; mem. leadership team, faculty trainer Highland Springs High Sch. Moving Up Project, 1989-90, 90-91; guest speaker Found. for Dyslexia, 1991. Member Westhampton Jr. Woman's Club, Richmond, 1967-71, Women's Com. of Richmond Symphony, 1971-78, Va. Mus. of Fine Arts, Richmond, 1967-78, Richmond Symphony Chorus, 1991—. Mem. NEA, ASCD, Va. Edn. Assn., Learning Disability Assn. Va., Learning Disbility Assn. Richmond, Henrico Edn. Assn., Orton Dyslexia Soc., Coun. for Exceptional Children (past treas. state unit devel. com., past del. assembly Nat. Conv.), Learning Disabilities Assn., Richmond Jazz Soc., U. Va. Alumni Assn., Mary Washington Coll. Alumni Assn. (class agt., past pres. Richmond chpt.), Mu Phi Epsilon. Home: 1512 Confederate Ave Richmond VA 23227-4406

UTLEY, ROSE, nursing educator and researcher; b. Broken Arrow, Okla., Aug. 31, 1953; d. Reuben D. and Margie B. (Hudson) U. ADN, Rochester Community Coll., Minn., 1976; BSN, U. Minn., 1981, MS, 1985; postgrad., Wayne State U. RN, N.D., Mich.; CEN. Staff nurse emergency dept. Fairview Community Hosp., Mpls., 1979-86; instr. nursing U. N.D., Grand Forks, 1985-87, U. Mich., Ann Arbor, 1987-90; emergency rm. staff nurse Saratoga Hosp., 1991—. Contbr. articles to profl. jours. Mem. AACCN, Emergency Nurses Assn., Sigma Theta. Home: 2700 Shimmons Rd Lot 144 Auburn Hills MI 48326-2047

UTTAL, SUSAN E., legal professional; b. N.Y.C., Oct. 8, 1954; d. Sheldon and Jane Louise (Kaufmann) Uttal. BA, Clark U., 1976; cert. paralegal, Inst. Paralegal Tng., Phila., 1978. Legal asst. Winthrop, Stimson, Putnam & Roberts, N.Y.C., 1978-80; legal coordinator Schroder Real Estate Corp., N.Y.C., 1980-83; legal asst. supr. real estate services sect. Cravath, Swaine & Moore, N.Y.C., 1983-89; sr. legal asst. real estate dept. Rackemann, Sawyer & Brewster, Boston, 1989-90; sr. legal asst. leasing and real estate depts. Goulston & Storrs, Boston, 1990—. Mem. Clark U. N.Y. Young Alumni Assn. (steering com.). Democrat. Jewish. Office: Goulston & Storrs 400 Atlantic Ave Boston MA 02110-3338

UTTERBACK, BETTY HARRIS, writer; b. Coalmont, Ind., July 30; d. Earl Daniel and Esther Jane (Bosley) Harris; student in journalism Ind. U., 1945-47; BA in Cultural Studies, Empire State Coll., 1988; m. Max Gene Utterback, Aug. 10, 1947; children: Pamela Kim Utterback Tyminski, Max Andrew. Pub. relations ofcl. Purdue U., 1947-50; free lance writer, 1950-69, 84—; with Gannett Rochester (N.Y.) Newspapers, 1969-84, TV editor, 1973-80, feature writer, 1980-84, columnist Gannett News Service, 1973-80. Co-author: (with John Robertson) Suddenly Single, 1986. Bd. dirs. Literacy Vols. Am., Rochester, 1984-87. Recipient 1st prize for feature N.Y. State AP, 1977. Republican. Presbyterian. Home: 80 E Jefferson Rd Pittsford NY 14534-2320

UYENO, LANI AKEMI, education educator; b. Wahiawa, Hawaii, Apr. 4, 1954; d. Gilbert Kenichi and Tomoyo (Imura) Yuruki; m. Kenneth Akira Uyeno, May 6, 1978; children: Julie Masako, Joy Hiromi. BEd, U. Hawaii, 1976, MEd, 1977. Cert. tchr., Hawaii. Tchr. Kapiolani C.C., Honolulu, 1977-85; asst. prof. Leeward C.C., Pearl City, Hawaii, 1977—; mem. adv. bd. Hawaii Writing Project, Honolulu, 1991—, co-dir., 1991. Contbr. articles, short stories to profl. publs. Buddhist. Office: Leeward CC 96-045 Ala Ike St Pearl City HI 96782

UZSOY, PATRICIA J., nursing educator and administrator; b. Corning, Ark.; m. Namik K. Diploma, Mo. Bapt. Hosp. Sch. Nursing, St. Louis, 1960; BSN, Washington U., St. Louis, 1962; MEd, Lynchburg Coll., 1977, EdS, 1981; MS in Nursing, U. Va., 1987. RN, Va. Dir. sch. nursing Lynchburg (Va.) Gen. Hosp., dir. Mem. ANA, NLN, Va. Nurses Assn. (Nurse of Yr. dist. III 1987).

UZZELL-BAGGETT, KARON LYNETTE, air force officer; b. Goldsboro, N.C., Apr. 28, 1964; d. Jesse Lee and Ernestine Smith (Merriweathers) Uzzell; m. Ronald Walter Baggett, July 26, 1990; stepchildren: Christina, Brian, Adam. BS, U. N.C., 1986; postgrad., U. Md., 1993—. Commd. 2d lt. USAF, 1986, advanced through grades to capt., 1990; exec. officer 6ACCS USAF, Langley AFB, Va., 1986-88; ops. tng. officer 7393MUNSS USAF, Murted AFD, Turkey, 1988-89; command and control officer 52FW USAF, Spangdahlem AB, Germany, 1989-92; SENEX mission dir. 89AW USAF, Andrews AFB, Md., 1992—, exec. officer 89OSS, 1993-94. Emergency med. technician Orange County Rescue Squad, Hillsborough, N.C., 1985-86; treas. Melwood PTA, Upper Marlboro, Md., 1994—; meml. vol. Women in Mil. Svc., Washington, 1993—; entitlements vol. Whitman Walker Clinic, Washington, 1993—. Mem. NOW, Women in Mil. Svc. for Am., U.S. Holocaust Meml. Democrat. Baptist. Home: 10704 Tyrone Dr Upper Marlboro MD 20772-4631

VACCA, DOROTHY MARY, psychologist; b. Boston, Aug. 17, 1941; d. Milanino Emilio and Rosaria (Guarino) V. BS, Framingham State Coll.; MEd, Northeastern U., Boston, 1968, EdD, 1986; MA, Boston Coll., 1980; Cert. Advanced Grad. Study, Northeastern U., Boston, 1980. Lic. psychologist, Mass. sch. psychologist; cert. sch. counselor. Tchr. Milton (Mass.) Pub. Schs., 1963-68, Dept. Def. Dependents Sch., Libya, Italy, 1968-70; tchr. Needham (Mass.) Pub. Schs., 1970-78, sch. counselor, 1980-84, sch. psychologist, 1985-86, counseling psychologist, workshop presenter, 1986—; pvt. practice Waltham, Mass., 1986—; cons. Fitzgerald & Assocs., Waltham, 1989—; workshop presenter Lexington (Mass.) Adult Edn., 1990; asst. prof. adj. Northeaster U.; lectr. in field, 1989. Contbr. articles to profl. jours. V.p. Northeast Coalition Ednl. Leaders, 1993—. Horace Mann grant, State Mass., 1987, 90. Mem. NEA, APA, NASP, Mass. Edn. Assn., Needham Edn. Assn., Mass. Assn. Guardians Ad Litem. Home: 64 Bishops Forest Dr Waltham MA 02154-8802 Office: Needham Pub Schs Highland Ave Needham MA 02192

VACCARIELLO, PAULA ANN, librarian, consultant; b. Cin., Aug. 20, 1967; d. Paul John Vaccariello and Doris Naomi (Basham) Johnston. BLS, Ohio Dominican Coll., 1989. Cert. libr. media tchr., Ohio. Libr. asst. Am. Electric Power Svc. Corp., Columbus, Ohio, 1989-91; libr. Southern Engring. Co., Atlanta, 1991—; cons. NB Prodns., Columbus, 1989—. Mem. Spl. Libs. Assn. Republican. Roman Catholic. Office: Southern Engring Co 1800 Peachtree St NE Atlanta GA 30367

VADER, LINDA ANDERSON, ophthalmic nurse; b. Grand Rapids, Mich., June 29, 1949; d. Stuart Edward and Margaret Sophia (Peterson) Anderson; m. Robert Elden Vader, July 10, 1970. Diploma, Butterworth Hosp. Sch. Nursing, 1970; BS, Eastern Mich. U., 1983. RN. Staff nurse Sparrow Hosp., Lansing, Mich., 1970-71, asst. head nurse, 1971-76; asst. head nurse U. Mich., Ann Arbor, 1976-77; head nurse Kellogg Eye Ctr., Ann Arbor, 1977—. Contbr. articles to profl. jours. and chpt. to book. Mem. Am. Soc. Ophthalmic RN's (pres. Great Lakes chpt. 1983-87), Am. Soc. Ophthalmic RN's (sec. 1986-88, pres. 1990-91), Natl. Certifying Bd. for Ophthalmic Registered Nurses (pres. 1988-90, 1994—), Sigma Theta Tau (Excellence in Nursing award 1987). Home: 2848 N Maple Rd Ann Arbor MI 48103-2161 Office: U Mich Kellogg Eye Ctr 1000 Wall St Ann Arbor MI 48105-1912

VADUS, GLORIA A., document examiner; b. Forrestville, Pa.. Diploma, Cole Sch. Graphology, Calif., 1978; BA in Psychology Counseling, Columbia Pacific U., 1981, MA in Psychology, 1982; diploma handwriting expert, Edith Eisenberg, Bethesda, Md., 1991. Cert. Am. Acad. Graphology, Washington, tchr. Coun. Graphological Socs., 1980; ct. qualified document examiner; registered graphologist; cert. behavioral profiling and cert. questioned documents, diplomate Am. Bd. Forensic Examiners, 1993. Pres., owner Graphinc, Inc., 1976—; accredited instr. graphology Montgomery County Schs., Md., 1978; instr. Psychogram Centre, 1978-85; testifier superior and probate cts. Author numerous studies, papers, articles in field. Chmn. Letter of Hope for POW's; vol. Montgomery County, 1987-88. Recipient Gold Nib Analyst of Yr. award, 1982, Dancing Fan award IEEE, 1990, Marine Tech. Soc., Japan, 1991, Spl. award U.S./Japan Marine Facilities Panel, 1978-84; named Woman of Yr. Japanese Panel UJNR/MFP, 1994. Fellow Am. Bd. Forensic Examiners (cert.); mem. Am. Handwriting Analysis Found. (cert., pres. 1982-84, chmn. rsch. com. , adv. bd. 1981-86, chmn. nominations com. 1985-86, officiator 1986, mem. policy planning and ethics com. 1986-91, ethics chmn. 1989-91, chmn., past pres. adv. bd. 1989-91), Nat. Forensic Ctr., Nat. Assn. Document Examiners (ethics hearing bd. 1986, chmn. nominations com. 1987-88, elections chmn. 1988, parliamentarian 1988—), Internat. Platform Assn., Soc. Francaise de Graphologie, Nat. Writers Club, Meninnger Found., Soroptimist Interant. (v.p.), Nat. Capital Jaguars Club Am. (judge 1976-86), Henry Hicks Garden Club (v.p., judge, chmn. flower shows), Sierra Club. Home: 8500 Timber Hill Ln Potomac MD 20854

VAIA, CHERYL LYNN, consultant; b. Newark, Ohio, Sept. 13, 1955; d. James Lee V. and Barbara N. (Barber) Canter; m. Herbert S. Bresler, Aug. 1, 1982; children: Reuben, Marika. BA, Capital U., 1977; MS, Wright State U., 1980. Economist Dept. Energy, Columbus, Ohio, 1979-80; econ. analyst Energy & Environ. Analysis, Arlington, Va., 1980-83; analyst, sys. analyst, mgr., dir., v.p. Orkand Corp., Silver Spring, Md., 1983-93; dir. fed. sys. KCM Cons., Inc., Greenbelt, Md., 1993-94; ind. cons., 1994—; instr. Capital U., Columbus, 1980. Pres. Crofton (Md.) Meadows Home Owners Assn., 1984-85, sec., 1983. Mem. APHA, Am. Statis. Assn., Am. Mgmt. Contractors Assn., Women in Technology. Democrat. Jewish. Home and Office: 10009 Brookmoor Dr Silver Spring MD 20901

VAIL, MARY BARBARA, museum consultant; b. Kingsville, Tex., Apr. 24, 1956; d. Fred G. and Nora J. (Smith) Leon; m. David L. Vail, Mar. 30, 1980; children: Sean Kristofer, Ashley Noel. Student, Tex. A&I U.; BS, U. Hawaii, 1982; postgrad., Hawaii Pacific U., 1991—. Display specialist Linda's, Kingsville, 1986-87; membership dir. Malibu (Calif.) Riding and Tennis Club, 1990-91; mktg. dir. Pacific Aerospace Mus., Honolulu, 1991-93; pres. Vail Media, Inc. (Scarlett Mktg. & Promotions), Aiea, Hawaii, 1993—. Vol. fundraiser AOWC, Point Mugu, Calif., 1990-91; vol. Laguna Vista Elem. Sch., Camarillo, Calif., 1990, Barbers Point (Hawaii) Elem. Sch., 1992—; vol., mil. liaison 1st Night Honolulu, 1991; co-chmn. Aloha Family Festival, Pearl Harbor, Hawaii, 1991, Fly Thru Time, 1992, 93, 94, Mugu Air Show, Chinese C. of C. Fashion Show, 1994, Narcissus Festival; Ho'Okipa Aloha, HIA Hospitality Tng. Coun. Mem. Pub. Rels. Soc. Am., Pub. Rels. Soc. Hawaii, CINCPAC Fleet Officers Wives Club, U. Hawaii Alumni Assn., Food Science and Numan Nutrition Alumni Assn. Home and Office: 15 Honu St PO Box 998 Aiea HI 96701

VAIL, PATRICIA, lawyer; b. Worcester, Mass., Apr. 7, 1941; d. Jeremiah Hamilton and Gladys (Conner) V.; children: Nathan, Norman. BA, Wilson Coll., 1963; JD, Cleve. Marshall Law Sch., 1977; MBA, Jacksonville U., 1987. Bar: Ohio 1977, Fla. 1988, U.S. Dist. Ct. Ohio (south dist.) 1978, U.S. Dist. Ct. Ohio (north dist.) 1981, U.S. Dist. Ct. (mid. dist.) Fla., U.S. Dist. Ct. Fla. (north dist.) 1993, U.S. Ct. Appeals (6th, 7th, 11th cirs.). Staff atty. Ohio Atty. Gen. Office, Columbus, Ohio, 1977-80, C&O R.R., Cleve., 1980-83, Seaboard System R.R., Jacksonville, Fla., 1983-86; sr. counsel CSX Transp., Jacksonville, 1986—. Bd. dirs. Jacksonville Area Legal Aid, 1990—, pres. 1995, Uptown Civitan, Jacksonville, 1988-90, Pine Castle, Inc., Jacksonville, 1989-90, Planned Parenthood NE Fla., 1993—. Mem. Jacksonville Coalition for Visual Arts (officer 1988-89), Jacksonville Women Lawyer's Assn. (pres. 1989-91), Fla. Assn. Women Lawyers (sec. 1991—). Home: 5709 St Isabel Dr Jacksonville FL 32277 Office: CSX Transp 500 Water St J-150 Jacksonville FL 32202-4420

VAITUKAITIS, JUDITH LOUISE, medical research administrator; b. Hartford, Conn., Aug. 29, 1940; d. Albert George and Julia Joan (Vaznikaitis) V. BS, Tufts U., 1962; MD, Boston U., 1966. Investigator, med. officer reproductive rsch. Nat. Inst. Child Health and Human Devel., NIH, Bethesda, Md., 1971-74; assoc. dir. clin. rsch. Nat. Ctr. Rsch. Resources NIH, Bethesda, Md., 1986-91, dir. gen. clin. rsch. ctr., 1986-91, dep. dir. extramural rsch., 1991; acting dir. Nat. Ctr. Rsch. Resources NIH, Bethesda, 1991-92, dir., 1993—; from assoc. prof. to prof. medicine Sch. Medicine Boston U., 1974-86, assoc. prof. physiology, 1975-80, assoc. prof. ob-gyn., 1977-80, program. dir. gen. clin. rsch. ctr., 1977-86, prof. physiology, 1980-86; head sect. endocrinology and metabolism Boston City Hosp., 1974-86. Mem. editorial bd. Jour. Clin. Endocrin. and Metabolism, 1973-80, Proc. Soc. Exptl. Biol. and Medicine, 1978-87, Endocrine Rsch., 1984-88. Author: Clinical Reproductive Neuroendocrinology, 1982; contbr. articles to profl. jours. Recipient Disting. Alumna award Sch. Medicine, Boston U.,

1983, Mallincrodt award for Inv. Rsch. Clin. Radiossay Soc., 1980. Mem. Am. Fedn. Clin. Rsch., Endocrine Soc., Am. Soc. Clin. Rsch., Soc. Exptl. Biology and Medicine, Assn. Am. Physicians, Soc. for Study of Reproduction, Am. Soc. Andrology. Office: Nat Ctr Rsch Resources NIH Bldg 12A Rm 4007 12 South Dr MSC 5660 Bethesda MD 20892-5660

VALANCE, MARSHA JEANNE, library director, story teller; b. Evanston, Ill., Aug. 2, 1946; d. Edward James Jr. and Jeanne Lois (Skinner) Leonard; m. William George Valance, Dec. 27, 1966 (div. 1976); 1 child, Marguerite Jeanne. Student Northwestern U., 1964-66; AB, UCLA, 1968; MLS, U. R.I., 1973; cert. in Profl. Devel., U. Wis., Madison, 1991. Children's libr. trainee N.Y. Pub. Libr., N.Y.C., 1968-69; reference libr. Action Meml. Pub. Libr. (Mass.), 1969-70; mgr. The Footnote, Cedar Rapids, Iowa, 1976-78; assoc. editor William C. Brown, Dubuque, Iowa, 1978-79; dir. Dubuque County Libr., Dubuque, 1979-81, G.B. Dedrick Pub. Libr., Geneseo, Ill., 1981-84, dir. Grand Rapids (Minn.) Pub. Libr., 1984-89; mgmt. libr., Wis. Regional Libr. for Blind and Physically Handicapped, 1989—; workshop coord., participant, sect. chmn. profl. confs.; LSCA grant reviewer U.S. Dept. Edn., 1989—. Author: (with others) Mystery, Value and Awareness, 1979; Pluralism, Similarities and Contrast, 1979; contbr. articles to pubis. Troop leader Miss. Valley Coun. Girl Scouts U.S., Cedar Rapids, 1976-78; mem. liturgy com. St. Malachy's Roman Cath. Ch., Geneseo, 1983; com. judging clinic 4-H, Moline, Ill., 1984; trustee KAXE No. Community Radio, 1986-89, ICTV, 1988-90; sec. Grand Rapids Community Svcs. Coun., 1986; coach Itasca County 4-H Horse Bowl Team, 1987; dir. Grand Rapids Storyfest, 1987-89; program chmn. Spotlight on Books Conf., 1989; bd. dirs., trustee Vols. in Svc. to the Visually Handicapped, 1989—; audio describer Artreach, Milw., 1991—. Recipient Weavers award Telephone Pioneers, 1992; Iowa Humanities Bd. grantee, 1981, Minn. Libr. Found. grantee, 1985, 86, 87, Blandin Found. grantee, 1986, Arrowhead Regional Arts Coun. grantee, 1987, 89, Ms. Soc. grantee, 1989. Mem. ALA, Wis. Libr. Assn., Iowa Librs. of Medium Size (sec. 1981), Northlands Storytelling Network (bd. dirs. 1988-94, v.p. 1989, pres. 1990, editor Grapevine, 1991-94), Nat. Assn. Preservation and Perpetuation Storytelling, Alliance Info. and Referral Svcs., DAR (constn. chmn. 1983-84), Miss. Valley Morgan Horse Club, Wis. Morgan Horse Club (newsletter editor 1994—, sec. 1995), Am. Morgan Horse Assn., Mid States Morgan Horse Club, Geneseo Jr. Women's Club (internat. chmn. 1983-84), UCLA Club Wis. (pres. 1990-91), Alpha Gamma Delta. Home: 6639 W Dodge Pl Milwaukee WI 53220-1329 Office: Wis Regional Libr Blind & Physically Handicapped 813 W Wells St Milwaukee WI 53233-1436

VALCIC, SUSAN JOAN, lawyer; b. N.Y.C., Mar. 23, 1956; d. Joseph and Eve Manderville; m. Alexander C. Valcic, July 28, 1979. BA magna cum laude, Columbia U., 1983; JD, Cardozo Sch. Law, 1986. Assoc. attorney Bailey, Marshall & Hoeniger, N.Y.C., 1986-87, Zalkin, Rodin & Goodman, N.Y.C., 1987-89; pvt. practice N.Y.C., 1989—. Apptd. adminstrv. law judge, N.Y., 1990. Mem. Assn. Bar City N.Y., N.Y. County Lawyers Assn., N.Y. State Bar. Assn., Fed. Bar. Assn., Columbia Club, Phi Beta Kappa.

VALDES-DAPENA, MARIE AGNES, pediatric pathologist, educator; b. Pottsville, Pa., July 14, 1921; d. Edgar Daniel and Marie Agnes (Rettig) Brown; m. Antonio M. Valdes-Dapena, Apr. 6, 1945 (div. Oct. 1980); children: Victoria Maria Valdes-Dapena Dead, Deborah Anne Valdes-Dapena Malle, Maria Cristina, Andres Antonio, Antonio Edgardo, Carlos Roberto, Marcos Antonio, Ricardo Daniel, Carmen Patricia Valdés-Dapena Fater, Catalina Inez Valdés-Dapena Amram, Pedro Pablo. BS, Immaculata Coll., 1941; MD, Temple U., 1944. Diplomate: Am. Bd. Pathology (spl. qualification-pediatric pathology 1990). Intern Phila. Gen. Hosp., 1944-45, resident in pathology, 1945-49; asst. pathologist Fitzgerald Mercy Hosp., Darby, Pa., 1949-51; dir. labs. Woman's Med. Coll. Pa., Phila., 1951-55; instr. pathology Woman's Med. Coll. Pa., 1947-51, asst. prof., 1951-55, assoc. prof., 1955-59; assoc. pathologist St. Christopher's Hosp. for Children, Phila., 1959-76; dir. sect. pediatric pathology U. Miami (Fla.)-Jackson Meml. Hosp., 1976-81, pediatric pathologist, dir. div. edn. in pathology, 1981-93, co.-dir. edn. in pathology, 1993—; cons., lectr. U.S. Naval Hosp., Phila., 1972-76; instr. pathology Sch. Medicine U. Pa., 1945-49; instr. Sch. Medicine U. Pa. (Sch. Dentistry), 1947, Sch. Medicine U. Pa. (Grad. Sch. Medicine), 1948-55, vis. lectr., 1960-62; asst. prof. Temple U. Med. Sch., 1959-63, assoc. prof., 1963-67, prof. pathology and pediatrics, 1967-76; prof. pathology and pediatrics U., Miami, 1976-93, prof. emeritus pathology and pediatrics, 1993—; cons. pediatric pathology div. med. examiner Dept. Pub. Health Phila., 1967-70; mem. perinatal biology and infant mortality research and tng. com. Nat. Inst. Child Health and Human Devel., NIH, 1971-73; mem. sci. adv. bd. Armed Forces Inst. Pathology, 1976-82; assoc. med. examiner, Dade County, Fla., 1976—; chmn. med. bd. Nat. Sudden Infant Death Syndrome Found., 1961-81, 87-91, pres., 1984-87, chmn. bd., 1985-88; mem. med. and sci. adv. coun. The SIDS Alliance, 1990—. Contbr. articles to profl. jours. NIH grantee. Mem. U.S. and Can. Acad. Pathology, Coll. Physicians Phila., Internat. Assn. Pediatric Pathology, Soc. for Pediatric Pathology (pres. 1980-81), Alpha Omega Alpha. Roman Catholic. Home: 179 Morningside Dr Miami FL 33166-5240 Office: Dept Pathology U Miami Sch Medicine PO Box 016960 Miami FL 33101-6960

VALDÉS-ZACKY, DOLORES, advertising executive; b. Mexico City, Sept. 22, 1947; came to U.S., 1976; d. German and Dolores (Menendez) Valdes; children: Lorena, Daphne. BA in Spanish and Latin Am. Studies, U. of the Ams., Mexico City, 1970; postgrad., Inst. Latin Am. Studies, London, 1970-71; MA in Spanish with distinction, UCLA, 1978. Producer McCann Erickson, Mexico City, 1971-72; copywriter Manin Display Internat., Mexico City, 1972-74; prof. lit. Colegio Columbia, Mexico City, 1974-76; account exec. Latmark Advt., Los Angeles, 1980-81; assoc. creative dir. Bermudez and Assocs., Los Angeles, 1981-82; v.p., creative dir. J. Walter Thompson/ Hispania, Los Angeles, 1982-87; pres., creative dir. Valdes Zacky Assocs., Inc., Los Angeles, 1987—. Creative dir. (TV commls.) Nature, 1987 (Don Belding award), Te Quiero Mucho, 1987 (Don Belding award 1987); featured in the L.A. Times as one of So. Calif.'s Rising Stars, 1989. Recipient Se Habla Espanol awards, 1990; named one of 4 top women in advt. Adweek mag., 1986. Republican. Roman Catholic. Office: Valdes Zacky Assocs Inc 1925 Century Park E 19th Fl Los Angeles CA 90067

VALDEZ, LORRAINE PAT, sales executive; b. Shreveport, La., May 19, 1958; d. Lawrence T. Walker and Catherine E. (Marksberry) Michael. Student, Ariz. State U., Tempe, 1982-84. From receptionist to asst. underwriter Marlar, Johnson & Allen Ins. Agy., Phoenix, 1977-81; ins. agt. Ins. West, Inc., Phoenix, 1981-83, Alliance Ins. Agy., Phoenix, 1983-84, Anderson, Reeve & Assocs., Scottsdale, Ariz., 1984-86; employee benefits adminstr. Fidelity Nat. Title Ins. Co., Scottsdale, 1986-89; v.p., dir. human resources South Coast Title Co., Santa Ana, Calif., 1989—, sales rep.; arbitrator Maricopa County Arbitration Bd., Phoenix, 1988-89; health ins. advisor Discovery Rsch., Irvine, Calif., 1989—. Vol. Maricopa County Crisis Nursery, Phoenix, 1988-89, Coaltion Against Illiteracy, Phoenix, 1989. Democrat.

VALE, MARGO ROSE, physician; b. Balt., June 16, 1950; d. Henry and Pauline Esther (Koplow) Hausdorff; m. Michael Allen Vale, Aug. 22, 1971; children: Edward, Judith. BA magna cum laude, Brandeis U., 1971; MD, Albert Einstein Coll. Medicine, 1975. Diplomate Am. Bd. Dermatology. Resident in internal medicine and dermatology NYU, N.Y.C., 1975-79, Bellevue Hosp., N.Y.C., 1975-79, VA Hosp., N.Y.C., 1975-79; staff physician HIP Greater N.Y., Bay Shore, 1979-81; pvt. practice medicine Huntington, N.Y., 1981—; cons. in dermatology Huntington Hosp., 1981—, Gurwin Jewish Geriatric Ctr., Commack, N.Y., 1990—. Contbr. articles to profl. jours. Mem. Am. Acad. Dermatology, Med. Soc. State N.Y., Long Island Dermatology Soc., Suffolk County Med. Soc., Suffolk Dermatology Soc. (pres. 1990-92), Phi Beta Kappa. Office: 205 E Main St Huntington NY 11743-2923

VALENCIA, SANDRA DENISE, company executive; b. Pasadena, Tex., Mar. 5, 1967; d. James Edward Simpson and Sheryl Lee Robinson Grenier; m. Octavio Valencia, Nov. 4, 1984 (div. Aug. 22, 1990). Collector Ctrl. Frt. Lines, Houston, 1988-89; customer svc. staff Pers. Pool, Cerritos, Calif., 1989-90; front office mgr. Stemmons Neck & Back, Dallas, 1990-91; switchboard operator Red Bird Chrysler, Duncanville, Tex., 1990-91, Lingard, Fivestar Ford, Hurst, Tex., 1991-92; switchboard/cashier John Roberts BMW, Dallas, 1991-92; br. mgr. Backlog of North Tex., Dallas, 1991—. Mem. Huntington Disease Soc. Office: Backlog of North Tex 8035 E RL Thornton #112 Dallas TX 75228

VALENSTEIN, SUZANNE GEBHART, art historian; b. Balt., July 17, 1928; d. Jerome J. and Lonnie Cooper Gebhart; m. Murray A. Valenstein, Mar. 31, 1951. With dept. Asian Art Met. Mus. Art, N.Y.C., 1965—; rsch. curator Asian Art. Author: Ming Porcelains: A Retrospective, 1970, A Handbook of Chinese Ceramics, 1975, rev. and enlarged, 1989, Highlights of Chinese Ceramics, 1975, (with others) Oriental Ceramics: The World's Great Collections: The Metropolitan Museum, 1977, rev., 1983, The Herzman Collection of Chinese Ceramics, 1992. Mem. Oriental Ceramic Soc. (London), Oriental Ceramic Soc. (Hong Kong). Office: Met Mus Art Dept Asian Art Fifth Ave at 82nd St New York NY 10028

VALENTI-HEIN, DENISE CARMELLA, psychologist; b. Milw., Oct. 9, 1956; d. John Joseph and Frances May (Ponick) Valenti; m. Charles Duane Hein, Aug. 1, 1980; children: Lisa Marie, Gabrielle Leigh. BS, U. Wis., Milw., 1978; MA, U. Ill., Chgo., 1984, PhD, 1988. Lic. psychologist, Wis., Ill. Teaching asst. U. Wis., Milw., 1979-80, ad hoc instr., 1989-90, clin. asst. prof., 1992-93; teaching asst. U. Ill., Chgo., 1980-82, ad hoc instr., 1985-91, clin. asst. prof., 1991—; adj. asst. prof. U. Wis., Parkside, 1985-88; presenter continuing edn. series Inst. for Study of Devel. Disabilities, 1983—, rsch. coord. Mental Health Program, 1991—, clin. rsch. fellow, 1988-91, clin. asst., 1982-84; pvt. practice, 1989—; psychology intern Zablocki VA Hosp., 1986-87. Cons. editor: Mental Retardation; guest reviewer: Clin. Psychology Rev., Am. Jour. Mental Retardation, Joseph P. Kennedy Jr. Found.; contbr. articles to profl. jours. Kemper Knapp scholar, 1975-77; recipient Outstanding Student Achievement award U. Ill. Chgo. Dept. Psychology, 1983-84; grantee Assn. for Retarded Citizens, 1994—, McCormick Tribune Found., 1992-93, Donnelley Found., 1989-91, U. Ill. Chgo., 1984. Mem. Am. Psychol. Assn., Am. Assn. on Mental Retardation, Nat. Assn. Dual Diagnosis, Am. Prof. Soc. on Abuse of Children, Psi Chi, Phi Eta Sigma. Office: U Ill Inst Study Develop 3090 BSB Box 4348 m/c 285 Chicago IL 60680

VALENTINE, SUZANNE NOEL, biostatistician; b. Pitts., Jan. 2, 1967; d. Maurice William and Janet Elinor (Wetzig) Collins; m. John David Valentine, May 26, 1991. BA in Applied Math., U. Calif. San Diego, La Jolla, 1989; postgrad., Mich. State U., 1989-90; MS in Biostatistics, U. Mich., 1992. Computing libr. San Diego Supercomputer, La Jolla, Calif., 1987-89; program intern San Diego Supercomputer, La Jolla, 1989; teaching asst. Mich. State U., East Lansing, 1989-90; graphics programmer, cons. U. Mich., Ann Arbor, 1990-91, rsch. asst., 1990-92, rsch. assoc., 1992-93; assoc. scientist Procter & Gamble, Cin., 1993—; rsch. asst. Los Alamos (N.Mex.) Nat. Lab., summers, 1988-89; mem. Women in Sci. Program, U. Mich., Ann Arbor, 1991-92. Flautist La Jolla (Calif.) Civic Symphony, spring 1988, Ypsilanti (Mich.) Community Band, 1992-93. Mem. Am. Statis. Assn., U. Mich. Alumni Assn. Democrat. Methodist. Home: 1269 Ida St Cincinnati OH 45202-1525 Office: Procter & Gamble 11262 Cornell Park Dr Ste C Cincinnati OH 45242-1812

VALESKIE-HAMNER, GAIL YVONNE, infosystems specialist; b. San Francisco, May 16, 1953; d. John Benjamin and Vera Caroline (Granstrand) Valeskie; m. David Bryan Hamner, May 21, 1983. Student, Music Conservatory, Valencia, Spain, 1973, U. Valencia, 1973; BA magna cum laude, Lone Mountain Coll., 1973, MA, 1976. Fgn. exchange broker trainee Fgn. Exchange Ltd., San Francisco, 1978-79; fgn. exchange remittance supr. Security Pacific Nat. Bank, San Francisco, 1979-81; exec. sec. Bank of Am., San Francisco, 1981-83, fgn. exchange ops. supr, 1983-84; word processing specialist Wolborg-Michelson, San Francisco, 1984-86; office mgr. U.S. Leasing Corp., San Francisco, 1986-88; cons. Valeskie Data/Word Processing, San Francisco, 1987-89, pres., 1989—. Sec. chmn., mem. mission edn. com. Luth. Women's Missionary League, Vallejo, Calif., 1986-94; vol. Luth. Braille Workers, Vallejo, 1987; organist Shepherd of Hills Luth. Ch., San Francisco, 1988—. Mem. NAFE, Profl. Assn. Secretarial Svcs. (pres. 1993—), Am. Guild Organists, Am. Choral Dirs. Assn.

VALETTE, REBECCA MARIANNE, Romance languages educator; b. N.Y.C., Dec. 21, 1938; d. Gerhard and Ruth Adelgunde (Bischoff) Loose; m. Jean-Paul Valette, Aug. 6, 1959; children: Jean-Michel, Nathalie, Pierre. BA, Mt. Holyoke Coll., 1959, LHD (hon.), 1974; PhD, U. Colo., 1963. Instr., examiner in French and German U. So. Fla., 1961-63; instr. NATO Def. Coll., Paris, 1963-64, Wellesley Coll., 1964-65; asst. prof. Romance Langs. Boston Coll., 1965-68, assoc., 1968-73, prof., 1973—; lectr., cons. fgn. lang. pedagogy; Fulbright sr. lectr., Germany, 1974; Am. Council on Edn. fellow in acad. adminstrn., 1976-77. Author: Modern Language Testing, 1967, rev. edit., 1977, French for Mastery, 1975, rev. edit., 1988, Contacts, 1976, rev. edit., 1993, C'est Comme Ça, 1978, Rev. edit., 1986, Spanish for Mastery, 1980, rev. edit., 1989, 94, Album: Cuento del Mundo Hispanico, 1984, rev. edit., 1992, French for Fluency, 1985, Situations, 1988, rev. edit., 1994, Discovering French, 1994, A votre tour, 1995; contbr. articles to fgn. lang. pedagogy and lit. publs. Decorated Palmes académiques (France). Mem. Modern Lang. Assn. (chmn. div. on teaching of lang. 1980-81), Am. Coun. on Teaching Fgn. Langs., Am. Assn. Tchrs. French (v.p. 1980-86, pres. 1992-94), Am. Assn. Tchrs. German, Phi Beta Kappa, Alpha Sigma Nu, Palmes Academiques. Home: 16 Mt Alvernia Rd Chestnut Hill MA 02167-1019 Office: Boston Coll Lyons 311 Chestnut Hill MA 02167

VALIGRA, LORI, journalist; b. Kingston, Pa., July 16, 1954; d. Matthew Bartholomew and Irmgard Anna (Fortig) V. BS in Med. Writing, U. Pitts., 1975; MS in Sci. Jour., Boston U., 1978. Sr. news editor Cahners Pub., Boston, 1980-85; fgn. editor Computer Industry Daily, N.Y.C., 1985; journalist, cons. N.Y.C., 1985-87; Tokyo Bur. chief IDG News Svc., Boston, 1987-92; MIT Knight fellow MIT, Cambridge, 1992-93; journalist Cambridge, 1993—; sci./tech. corr. Reuters, Nikkei Electronics Asia, Asian Bus., among others; co-organizer Sci. Writers' Group, MIT, Cambridge, 1993—. Freelance contbr. to numerous publs. including N.Y. Times, Wall St. Jour., The Fin. Times, Asian Bus., Sci., others; editor No. 1 Shimbun, Fgn. Corrs. Club of Japan, 1990-92. Bd. dirs. Fgn. Corrs. Club of Japan, 1990-91. Recipient Excellence in Writing award Am. Soc. Bus. Press Editors, Boston, 1980. Mem. Japan Soc., Nat. Geographic Soc., World Wildlife Fund, Boston Computer Soc., Mortar Bd.

VALLBONA, RIMA-GRETEL ROTHE, foreign language educator, writer; b. San Jose, Costa Rica, Mar. 15, 1931; d. Ferdinand Hermann and Emilia (Strassburger) Rothe; m. Carlos Vallbona, Dec. 26, 1956; children: Rima-Nuri, Carlos-Fernando, Maria-Teresa, Maria-Luisa. BA/BS, Colegio Superior de Senoritas, San Jose, 1948; diploma, U. Paris, 1953; diploma in Spanish Philology, U. Salamanca, Spain, 1954; MA, U. Costa Rica, 1962; D in Modern Langs., Middlebury Coll., 1981. Tchr. Liceo J.J. Vargas Calvo, Costa Rica, 1955-56; faculty U. St. Thomas, Houston, 1964—, prof. Spanish, 1978—, Cullen Found. prof. Spanish, 1989, head dept. Spanish, 1966-71, chmn. dept. modern fgn. lang., 1978-80; vis. prof. U. Houston, 1975-76, Rice U., 1980-83, U. St. Thomas, Argentina, 1972, vis. prof. U. St. Thomas Merida program, 1987-91; vis. prof. Rice U. program in Spain, 1974. Author: Noche en Vela, 1968, Yolanda Oreamuno, 1972, La Obra en Prosa de Eunice Odio, 1981, Baraja de Soledades, Las Sombras que Perseguimos, 1983, Polvo del Camino, 1972, La Salamandra Rosada, 1979, Mujeres y Agonias, 1982, Cosecha de Pecadores, 1988, El arcangel del perdon, 1990, Mundo, demonio y mujer, 1991, Los infiernos de la mujer y algo mas, 1992, Vida i sucesos de la Monja Alférez, critical edition, 1992, Flowering Inferno-Tales of Sinking Hearts, 1994; mem. editorial bd. Letras Femeninas, Alba de America, U.S.; co-dir. Foro Literario, Uruguay, 1987-89; contbg. editor The Americas Review, 1989—; contbr. numerous articles and short stories to lit. mags. Mem. scholarship com. Inst. Hispanic Culture, 1978-79, 88, 91, chmn., 1979, bd. dirs., 1974-76, 88-89, 91-92, chmn. cultural activities, 1979, 80, 85, 88-89; bd. dirs. Houston Pub. Libr., 1984-86; bd. dirs. Cultural Arts Coun. of Houston, 1991-92. Recipient Aquileo J. Echeverria Novel prize, 1968, Agripina Montes del Valle Novel prize, 1978, Jorge Luis Borges Short Story prize, Argentina, 1977, Lit. award S.W. Conf. Latin Am. Studies, 1982; Constantin Found. grantee for rsch. U. St. Thomas, 1981; Ancora Lit. award, Costa Rica, 1984, Civil Merit award King Juan Carlos I of Spain, 1989. Mem. MLA, Am. Assn. Tchrs. Spanish and Portuguese, Houston Area Tchrs. of Fgn. Langs., South Cen. MLA, S.W. conf. Orgn. Latin Am. Studies, Latin Am. Studies Assn., Inst. Internat. de Lit. Iberoam., Latin Am. Writers Assn. of Costa Rica, Inst. Hispanic Culture of Houston, Casa Argentina de Houston, Inst. Lit. y Cultural Hispanico, Phi Sigma Iota, Sigma Delta Pi (hon.), Nat. Writers Assn. Roman Catholic. Home: 3706 Lake St Houston TX 77098-5522 Office: 3800 Montrose Blvd Houston TX 77006

VALLEE, JUDITH DELANEY, environmentalist, fundraiser; b. N.Y.C., Mar. 14, 1948; d. Victor and Sally Hammer; m. John Delaney, Apr. 9, 1974 (div. 1978); m. Henry Richard Vallee, May 15, 1987. BA, CUNY, 1976. Exec. dir. Save the Manatee Club, Maitland, Fla., 1985—; mem. U.S. Manatee Recovery Plan Team, Jacksonville, Fla., 1988—, Fla. Manatee Tech. Adv. Coun., Tallahassee, 1989—, Save the Manatee Com., Orlando, Fla., 1985-92; advisor Save the Wildlife Inc., Chuluota, Fla., 1992-93. Lobbyist Save the Manatee Club, 1989; vol. Broward County Audubon Soc., Ft. Lauderdale, 1983, 84, Wild Bird Care Ctr., Ft. Lauderdale, 1984. Recipient Refuge Support award Chassahowitzka Nat. Wildlife Refuge, 1989. Mem. Coop. Am., Fla. Coalition for Peace and Justice, People for Ethical Treatment of Animals, Carrying Capacity Networkk. Democrat. Office: Save the Manatee Club Inc 500 N Maitland Ave Maitland FL 32751-4482

VALLERY, JANET ALANE, industrial hygienist; b. Lincoln, Nebr., Apr. 4, 1948; d. Gerald William and Lois Florence (Robertson) V.; BS, U. Nebr., Lincoln, 1970; diploma Bryan Meml. Sch. Med. Tech., Lincoln, 1971. Med. technologist Lincoln Gen. Hosp., 1971-72; congressional sec., 1973; lab. scientist Nebr. Dept. Health, 1973-79; sr. indsl. hygienist Nebr. Dept. Labor, 1979-85; indsl. hygienist U.S. Dept. Labor OSHA, 1985-89; indsl. hygienist VA Med. Ctr., Omaha, Nebr., 1989—. Mem. Am. Conf. Govt. Indsl. Hygienists, Am. Soc. Clin. Pathologists (assoc.), Arabian Horse Assn. Nebr., Nebr. Dressage Assn., Am. Indsl. Hygiene Assn., Am. Legion Aux. Republican. Methodist. Home: 4900 S 30th St Lincoln NE 68516-1603 Office: VA Med Ctr 4101 Woolworth Ave Omaha NE 68105-1873

VALLES, CHRISTINE ANITA, state official; b. L.A., Jan. 10, 1953; d. Rudy Estrada and Evelyn Mary (Rosa) V.; m. Robert William Heath, June 26, 12983. BA in Anthropology, U. Calif., Berkeley, 1978. Evaluator Nomos Inst., Berkeley and Honolulu, 1974-84; rschr. Office Hawaiian Affairs, Honolulu, 1984-87, grants specialist, 1987-90, planning officer, 1990—; sec.-treas. Nomos Inst., Honolulu, 1981—; proposal reviewer U.S. Adminstrn. for Native Ams., Washington, 1988—. Mem. Alii Pauahi Hawaiian Civic Club, Honolulu, 1988—; bd. dirs. Hawaii Advs. for Children and Youth. Mem. AAUW. Home: 2350 10th Ave Honolulu HI 96816 Office: Office of Hawaiian Affairs 711 Kapiolani Blvd Ste # 500 Honolulu HI 96813

VALLONE, JOYCE ANN, educational administrator; b. Gowanda, N.Y., Apr. 2, 1947; d. Elinor Carol (Hancock) Thompson; m. Dino Jerome Vallone, Dec. 18, 1976; children: James Christopher, Anne Michelle. BA, Roberts Wesleyan Coll., 1969; MA in Teaching C.C. English, Wayne State U., 1977. Cert. tchr., Mich. Classroom tchr. Thomas C. Armstrong Mid. Sch., Ontario Center, N.Y., 1969-72; grad. asst. Wayne State U., Detroit, 1973-74, instr. project 350, 1974; vocat. reading and math. coord. Oakland Tech. Ctr., Wixom, Mich., 1974-80; pvt. practice cons. various sch. dists. and county orgns., Mich., 1980-81; coord. gifted program Romeo (Mich.) Community Schs., 1988—. Organizer neighborhood walkathon Muscular Dystrophy Assn., Mt. Clemens, Mich. 1993; mem. choir Mt. Zion Temple, Clarkston, Mich., 1991-93. Recipient Eisenhower Exemplary and Demonstration Project grant in Math., 1994. Mem. ASCD, Mich. Assn. Computer-Related Tech. Users in Learning, Mich. Alliance for Gifted Edn. Office: Romeo Community Schs 316 N Main St Romeo MI 48065

VALO, MARTHA ANN, hospital dietary executive, consultant; b. West Aliquippa, Pa., Apr. 6, 1938; d. George and Susan Helen (Pollak) V.; m. John Daniel Dempsey, Dec. 17, 1974. B.S., Carlow Coll., 1960; MS, U. Pa., 1991. Registered dietitian; disting. health care food svd. adminstr. Food service mgr. Stouffer's Mgmt. Co., Phila., 1960-76; restaurant mgr. Strawbridge & Clothier, Phila., 1976-78; food service dir. Saunders House, Phila., 1978-80; dir. food/nutrition svcs. U. Med. Ctr., Stratford, N.J., 1980-93, adminstrv. dir. supply svcs., 1993—; adj. faculty Camden County Coll., Blackwood, N.J., 1985—. Mem. Am. Soc. for Hosp. Food Service Adminstrs., Am. Coll. Health Care Execs., Nat. Soc. Healt Care Food Svcs. Mgrs., So. N.J. Nutritional Coun., N.J. Dietetic Assn., Phila. Dietetic Assn. Home: 135 Fenway Ave Atco NJ 08004-3016 Office: Kennedy Meml Hosps Univ Med Ctr 18 E Laurel Rd Stratford NJ 08084

VALVO, BARBARA-ANN, lawyer, surgeon; b. Elizabeth, N.J., June 7, 1949; d. Robert Richad and Vera (Kovach) V. BA in Biology, Hofsta U., 1971; MD, Pa. State U., 1975; JD, Loyola Sch. Law, 1993. Diplomate Am. Bd. Surgery; Bar: La. 1993. Surg. intern Nassau County Med. Ctr., East Meadow, N.Y., 1975-76; resident gen. surgery Allentown-Sacred Heart Med. Ctr., Allentown, Pa., 1976-80; asst. chief surgery USPHS, New Orleans, 1980-81; pvt. practice gen. surgery New Orleans, 1981-89, pvt. practice law, 1995—. Upjohn scholar, 1975. Fellow ACS; mem. ABA, FBA, La. Bar Assn., La. Trial Lawyers Assn. Republican. Home and Office: PO Box 640217 Kenner LA 70064

VAN ALLEN, KATRINA FRANCES, painter; b. Phoenix, Ariz., Feb. 18, 1933; d. Benjamin Cecile Sherrill and Magdalen Mary (Thomas) Adams; m. Ray C. Bennett II, Dec. 31, 1950 (div. 1956); m. William Allen Van Allen, Mar. 15, 1963 (dec. Mar. 1971); m. Donovan Wyatt Jacobs, Apr. 22, 1972; children: Ray Crawford Bennett III, Sherri Lou Bennett Maraney. Student, Stanford U., 1950, 51, 52, Torrance C.C., 1962, 63; MA, U. Tabriz, Iran, 1978; studied with Martin Lubner, Jerold Burchman, John Lepper, L.A.; student, Otis Art Inst., Immaculate Heart Coll.; studied with Russa Graeme. Office mgr. H.P. Adams Constrn. Co., Yuma, Ariz., 1952-59; nurse Moss-Hathaway Med. Clin., Torrance, Calif., 1962-63; interviewer for various assns. N.Y.C., 1964-70. Solo shows include: Zella 9 Gallery, London, 1972, Hambleton Gallery, Maiden Newton, Eng., 1974, Intercontinental Gallery, Teheran, Iran, 1976, USIA Gallery, Teheran, 1977, 78, Coos Art Mus., Coos Bay, Oreg., 1993; exhibited in group shows at La Cienega Gallery, L.A., 1970, 80, 81, 82, Design Ctr. Gallery, Tucson, 1985, Coos Art Mus., 1992, 93, 94; represented in permanent collections at Bankers Trust Bd. Rm., London, Mfrs. Hanover Bank, London, U. Iowa Med. Sch., Iowa City, Bank of Am., Teheran, and numerous pvt. collections. Bd. dirs. Inst. for Cancer and Leukemia Rsch., 1966-67. Recipient Five City Tour and Honorarium, Iran Am. Soc., 1977. Mem. Nat. Women in the Arts, L.A. Art Assn., Coos Bay Art Assn., Coos Bay Power Squadron. Home and Studio: 3693 Cape Arago Coos Bay OR 97420-9604

VAN ALSTYNE, JUDITH STURGES, English language educator; b. Columbus, Ohio, June 9, 1934; d. Rexford Leland and Wilma Irene (Styan) Van A.; m. Dan C. Duckham (div. 1964); children: Kenton Leland, Jeffrey Clarke. BA, Miami U., Oxford, Ohio, 1956; MEd, Fla. Atlantic U., 1967. Sr. prof. Broward C.C., Ft. Lauderdale, Fla., 1967-93, ret., 1993; spl. asst. for women's affairs Broward C.C., 1972-93, dir. cmty. svcs., 1973-74, dir. cultural affairs, 1974-75, dir. Broward C.C. Found., Inc., 1973-89; spkr., cons. Malaysian Coll., 1984; ednl. travel group tour guide, 1992—; v.p., ptnr. travel agy., 1994—. Author: Professional and Technical Writing Strategies, 3d edit., 1994, Write it Right, 1980; freelance writer travel articles; contbr. articles to profl. jours. Active Sister Cities/People to People, Ft. Lauderdale, 1988—; docent Ft. Lauderdale Mus. Art, 1988—; officer Friends of Mus., Ft. Lauderdale, 1992—; bd. dirs. Broward Friends of the Libr., 1994—, Broward Friends of Miami City Ballet, 1994—. Recipient Award of Achievement Soc. for Tech. Communication, 1986, Award of Distinction Fla. Soc. for Tech. Communication, 1986. Mem. English-Speaking Union (bd. dirs. 1984-89). Democrat. Episcopalian. Home: 1688 S Ocean Ln # 265 Fort Lauderdale FL 33316-3346

VAN ANTWERPEN, REGINA LANE, underwriter, insurance company executive; b. Milw., Aug. 16, 1939; d. Joseph F. Gagliano and Sophia B. (Johannik) Wolfe; widowed; children: Thomas II, Victoria. Student, U. Wis., Milw., 1954-57. Office mgr. Gardner Bender Inc., Milw., 1972-80; mfg. rep. Rosenbloom & Co., Chgo., 1980-81; spl. agt. Northwestern Mut. Life Equities Inc., Milw., 1981-88, registered rep., 1985-88; account rep. Fin. Instn. Mktg. Co., Milw., 1988-93; investment specialist Fimco Securities Group, Inc., Milw., 1993—; pres. Anvers Ltd., 1990—, 1990—. Author: (poetry) One More Time Its Christmas, 1978, True Friendship, 1979, Beautiful Brown Eyes, 1990 (award 1992). Mgr. Sch. Bd. Elections, Fox Point,

1969; v.p. Suburban Rep. Women's CLub, Milw., 1968-72; vol. tchr. St. Eugene Sch., Milw., 1968-72. Mem. AAUW, Milw. Life Underwriters, Women's Life Underwriters (v.p. 1982-83), Legis. Orgn. Life Underwriters, Nat. Assn. Securities Dealers (lic.), Investment Club (sec. 1989-90, pres. 1990—). Republican. Roman Catholic. Office: Fin Instn Mktg Co 111 E Kilbourn Ave Ste 1850 Milwaukee WI 53202-6611

VAN ARK, JOAN, actress; d. Carroll and Dorothy Jean (Hemenway) Van A.; m. John Marshall, Feb. 1, 1966; 1 child, Vanessa Jeanne. Student, Yale Sch. Drama. Appeared at Tyrone Guthrie Theatre, Washington Arena Stage, in London, on Broadway; appeared in plays: Barefoot in the Park, 1965, School for Wives, 1971, Rules of the Game, 1974, Cyrano de Bergerac, Ring Round the Moon; appeared on TV series: Temperatures Rising, 1972-73, We've Got Each Other, 1977-78, Dallas, 1978-81, Knots Landing, 1979-92 (dir. episodes Letting Go, Hints and Evasions); motion pictures for TV: The Judge and Jake Wyler, 1972, Big Rose, 1974, Shell Game, 1975, The Last Dinosaur, 1977, Red Flag, 1981, Shakedown on the Sunset Strip, 1988, My First Love, 1989, Murder at the PTA, 1990, To Cast a Shadow, 1990, Grand Central Murders, 1992, Tainted Blood, 1992, Someone's Watching, 1993: TV miniseries Testimony of Two Men, 1978; dir., star TV spl. ABC Afterschool Spl. Boys Will Be Boys, 1993. Recipient Theatre World award, 1970-71, L.A. Drama Critics Circle award, 1973, Outstanding Actress award Soap Opera Digest, 1986, 89. Mem. AFTRA, SAG, Actors Equity Assn., San Fernando Valley Track Club. Address: care William Morris Agy Inc 151 S El Camino Dr Beverly Hills CA 90212-2704 also: 1350 Avenue Of The Americas New York NY 10019-4701

VANARSDALE, DIANA CORT, social worker; b. N.Y.C., Oct. 27, 1934; d. Arthur and Augusta Deutsch; B.S., N.Y.U., 1955; M.S.W., Columbia U., 1957; m. Leonard Van Arsdale, Sept. 17, 1978; children by previous marriage—Hayley, Daniel. Clinician, Payne Whitney Clinic, N.Y. Hosp., N.Y.C., 1957-59, psychiat. clinic Jewish Bd. Guardians, N.Y.C., 1959-61; founder, pres. Big Six Towers Nursery Sch., N.Y.C., 1962-67; dir. intake and social service L.I. Consultation Center, Forest Hills, N.Y., 1966-84, clin. dir., coordinator clin. services, 1984-86; supr., faculty mem. L.I. Inst. Mental Health, 1973-86; cons. in social work Bergen Ctr. for Child Devel., 1981-87; dir. Seniors Option Service, Allendale, N.J., 1980-90. Author: Transitions A Woman's Guide to Successful Retirement, 1991. Mem. Nat. Assn. Social Workers, N.Y. Soc. Clin. Social Workers. Home: 47-30 61st St Woodside NY 11377

VANAUKER, LANA LEE, recreational therapist, educator; b. Youngstown, Ohio, Sept. 19, 1949; d. William Marshall and Joanne Norma (Kimmel) Speece; m. Dwight Edward VanAuker, Mar. 16, 1969 (div. 1976); 1 child, Heidi. BS in Edn. cum laude, Kent (Ohio) State U., 1974; MS in Edn., Youngstown (Ohio) U., 1989. Cert. tchr., Ohio; nat. cert. activity cons. Phys. edn. instr. St. Joseph Sch., Campbell, Ohio, 1973-75; program dir. YWCA, Youngstown, 1975-85; exercise technician Youngstown State U., 1985-86; health educator Park Vista Retirement Ctr., Youngstown, 1986-87; sch. tchr. Salem (Ohio) City Sch., 1987-88; recreational therapist Trumbull Meml. Hosp., Warren, Ohio, 1988—; activity cons. Mahoning/Trumbull Nursing Homes, Warren, 1990-92. Producer chair exercise sr. video Exercise is the Fountain of Youth, 1993; photographer, choreographer. Youngstown State U. scholar, 1986-89. Mem. AAHPERD, Youngstown Camera Club (social chair 1989-90), Resident Activity Coords. Assn. (sec. 1988-91, pres. 1993-94), Pa. Activity Profl. Assn., Kappa Delta Pi. Democrat. Presbyterian. Home: 385 N Broad St Canfield OH 44406-1256 Office: Trumbull Meml Hosp 1350 E Market St Warren OH 44483-6628

VAN BLARCOM, ELIZABETH ANNE, agricultural products executive; b. Trenton, Mo., Dec. 9, 1960; d. Lewis Leon Griffin and Nellie Ruth (Yates) Bobenhouse; m. Don Lee Schafer, Oct. 23, 1982 (div. Apr., 1989); 1 child, Stacie Elizabeth; m. David James Van Blarcom, July 10, 1993. Student, Drake U., 1979, U. Ark., 1980. Sec. Pioneer Hi-Bred Internat., Inc., Des Moines, 1981, air freight specialist, 1981-82; documentation specialist, ocean freight Pioneer Hi-Bred Internat., Inc., Johnston, Ia., 1982-86; sec. microbial products dept. Pioneer Hi-Bred Internat., Inc., Johnston, 1986-87; internat. documentation and traffic coord. Pioneer Hi-Bred Internat., Inc., West Des Moines, Iowa, 1987—. Mem. Profl. Women in Trans. (corr. sec. Des Moines chpt. 1992-94, historian 1994—). Republican. Roman Catholic. Home: 4012 51st St Des Moines IA 50310-1844 Office: Pioneer Hi-Bred Internat Inc 4601 Westown Pky Ste 120 West Des Moines IA 50266-1071

VAN BLARCOM KUROWSKI, ANNE, artist, educator; b. Glen Ridge, N.J., Jan. 22, 1940; d. Gerald and Thelma Aurora (Lawless) Van Blarcom; m. Robert John Kurowski, Sept. 8, 1962; children: Robin Anne, Evan Jon, Jaime Lara. BA, Montclair State Coll., 1962, MA, 1971. Art tchr. New Brunswick, N.J., 1967-68, Matawan, N.J., 1969-71; art tchr. Woodbridge (N.J.) Twp., 1987—, substitute tchr., 1989—; ind. artist Edison, N.J., 1987—; dir. life classes Barron Arts Ctr., Woodbridge, 1985—. Author, designer, illustrator (book) Have Fun. Recipient Beth Born Meml. Portrait award N.J. Ctr. Visual Arts, 1989, Gold medal Barron Arts Ctr., 1990, Degas Pastel award Pastel Soc. Am., 1994. Mem. N.J. Watercolor Soc. (assoc.; Henry Gasser Meml. award 1993), N.J. Ctr. Visual Arts, Garden State Watercolor Soc. (assoc.), Art Educators N.J. (artist/tchr. network). Unitarian. Home: 16 1st St Edison NJ 08837

VAN BLARICUM, AMY JOAN, perioperative nurse; b. Englewood, N.J., Sept. 23, 1963; d. Julius Herbert Jr. and Mildred Doris Van Blaricum. BSN, Widener U., Chester, Pa., 1987. RN, Pa.; cert. in chemotherapy adminstrn., venipuncture, 1987. Nurse med.-surg. unit Mercy Cath. Med. Ctr., Darby, Pa., 1987, nurse oncology unit, 1988, nurse operating room, 1989. Mem. Assn. Operating Room Nurses.

VAN BRUNT, MARCIA ADELE, social worker; b. Chgo., Oct. 21, 1937; d. Dean Frederick and Faye Lila (Greim) Slauson; student Moline (Ill.) Pub. Hosp. Sch. Nursing, 1955-57; B.A. with distinguished scholastic record, U. Wis., Madison, 1972, M.S.W. (Fed. tng. grantee), 1973; M.O.E. Bartholomew; children—Suzanne, Christine, David. Social worker div. community services Wis. Dept. Health Social Services, Rhinelander, 1973, regional adoption coordinator, 1973-79, chief adoption and permanent planning no. region, 1979-83, asst. chief direct services and regulation no. region, 1983-84, adminstr., clin. social worker No. Family Services, Inc., 1984—; counselor, public speaker, cons. in field of clin. social work. Home: 5264 Forest Ln Rt 1 Rhinelander WI 54501 Office: PO Box 237 Rhinelander WI 54501-0237

VAN BUREN, ABIGAIL (PAULINE FRIEDMAN PHILLIPS), columnist, author, writer, lecturer; b. Sioux City, Iowa, July 4, 1918; d. Abraham and Rebecca (Rushall) Friedman; m. Morton Phillips, July 2, 1939; children: Edward Jay, Jeanne. Student, Morningside Coll., Sioux City, 1936-39; Litt.D. (hon.), Morningside Coll., 1965; L.H.D. (hon.), U. Jacksonville, Fla., 1984. Vol. worker for causes of better mental health Nat. Found. Infantile Paralysis; tng. Gray Ladies, ARC, 1939-56; pres. Minn.-Wis. council B'nai B'rith Aux., 1945-49; columnist Dear Abby San Francisco Chronicle, 1956, McNaught Syndicate, 1956-74, Chgo. Tribune Syndicate, 1974-80, Universal Press Syndicate, 1980—; syndicated U.S., Brazil, Mex., Japan, Philippines, Fed. Republic Germany, India, Holland, Denmark, Can., Korea, Thailand, Italy, Hong Kong, Taiwan, Ireland, Saudi Arabia, Greece, France, Dominican Republic, P.R., Costa Rica, U.S. Virgin Islands, Bermuda, Guam; host radio program The Dear Abby Show, CBS, 1963-75; life-time cons. Group for Advancement Psychiatry, 1985—. Author: Dear Abby, 1957 (also translated into Japanese, Dutch, German, Spanish, Danish, Italian, Finnish), Dear Teen Ager, 1959, Dear Abby on Marriage, 1962, The Best of Dear Abby, 1981, reissued, 1989, Dear Abby on Planning Your Wedding, 1988, Where Were You When President Kennedy Was Shot?: Memories and Tributes to a Slain President as Told to Dear Abby, 1993. Mem. nat. adv. council on aging NIH, HEW, 1978-81; hon. chairwoman 1st Nat. Women's Conf. on Cancer, Am. Cancer Soc., Los Angeles, 1979; mem. public adv. council Center for Study Multiple Gestation, 1981; trustee, mem. adv. bd. Westside Community for Ind. Living, 1981; bd. dirs. Guthrie Theatre, Mpls., 1970-74; charter mem. Franz Alexander Research Found., Los Angeles; charter trustee Armand Hammer United World Coll. of Am. West; bd. dirs. Am. Fedn. for Aging Research Inc.; mem. nat. bd. Goodwill Industries, 1968-75; nat. chmn. Crippled Children Soc., 1962; founding mem. The Amazing Blue Ribbon 400; hon. chmn. Easter Seal campaign Nat. Soc. Crippled Children and Adults, Washington, 1963; del. to Democratic Nat. Conf. from Calif., 1964; Calif. del. White House Conf. on Children and Youth, 1974; non. life mem. Concern for Dying-Am. Ednl. Council; mem. White House Conf. on Physically Handicapped, 1976, NIH, 1976; mem. adv. council Suicide Prevention Ctr., Los Angeles, 1977; mem. com. on aging HHS, 1977-82; council sponsor Assn. Vol. Sterilization, 1981; mem. Women's Trusteeship, 1980; sponsor Mayo Found., Rochester, 1982; bd. dirs. Lupus Found. Am., 1983; mem. adv. com. Ams. for Substance Abuse Prevention, 1984; participant XIII Internat. Congress Gerontology, N.Y.C., 1985; mem. adv. bd. Young Writer's Contest Found., 1985; bd. dirs. Am. Found. for AIDS Research, 1985—; mem. adv. bd. Nat. Council for Children's Rights, Washington, 1988; mem. adv. bd. San Diego Hospice, 1990; mem. adv. bd. Rhonda Fleming Mann Clinic for Women's Comprehensive Care, 1991; mem. Scripps Rsch. Coun. Recipient Times Mother of Yr. award, Los Angeles, 1958; Golden Kidney award, Los Angeles, 1960; Sarah Coventry award, Miami, 1961; Woman of Yr. award Internat. Rotary Club, Rome, 1965; award NCCJ, St. Louis, 1968; award for disting. service to sightless Internat. Lions Club, Dallas, 1972; Disting. Service award Suicide Prevention Center, San Mateo, Calif., 1975; Good Samaritan award Salvation Army, San Francisco, 1970; Margaret Sanger award Nat. Planned Parenthood, 1974; award for outstanding services in mental health So. Psychiat. Assn., 1974; Robert T. Morse writer's award Am. Psychiat. Assn., 1977; Tex. Gov.'s award in recognition of exceptional service to youth of Am. for Ops. Peace of Mind, 1979; Humanitarian award Gay Acad. Union, Los Angeles, 1979, Braille Inst. So. Calif., 1981, Gay and Lesbian Community Services Ctr., 1984; pub. Awardness trophy for Living Will, Soc. for Right to Die, 1983; citation of commendation Simon Weisenthal Found., 1984; Internat. Image in Media award Gay Fathers Coalition, 1985; 1st ann. Woman of Yr. Humanitarian award Rainbow Guild of Amy Karen Children's Cancer Clinic, Cedars-Sinai Med. Ctr., Los Angeles, 1985; Pub. Service award Nat. Kidney Found., 1985, John Rock award Ctr. Population Options, 1986, Serve Am. award Ladies Auxiliary to the VFW, 1986, Genesis award Fund for Animals, 1986, Disting. Service award Inst. Studies Destructive Behavior and Suicide Prevention Ctr., 1986, Citizen of Yr. award Beverly Hills, Calif. C. of C., 1988, Humanitarian award Nat. Council on Alcoholism, 1988, Helen B. Taussig medal Internat. Socs. for the Right to Die with Dignity, 1988, Media award So. Psychiat. Soc., 1988; named Hon. Dir. Found. for Craniofacial Deformities, 1988; Disting. Achievement award Nat. Assn. to Advance Fat Acceptance, 1988, Hand to Hand award Episc. Charities San Francisco, 1989; Nat. Media award for print Nat. Down Syndrome Congress, 1991; Sec.'s award for excellence in communication HHS, 1992; Dove award Assn. Retarded Citizens, 1992. Mem. Women in Communications (hon.), Am. Coll. Psychiatrists (hon. life mem.), Nat. Council Jewish Women (hon. life mem.), Newspapers Features Council, Soc. Profl. Journalists, Nat. Orgn. Women, "Women For", Nat. Com. Preserve Social Security and Medicare, Korean War Vets. Assn. (hon.), Sigma Delta Chi. Office: Phillips-Van Buren Inc 9200 W Sunset Blvd Ste 1003 West Hollywood CA 90069-3605

VANBUREN, DENISE DORING, media relations executive; b. Troy, N.Y., May 15, 1961; d. James L. and Eunice A. (Myers) Doring; m. Steven Paul VanBuren, Apr. 1, 1989; children: Schuyler Paul, Troy James Doring VanBuren. BA in Mass Comm. magna cum laude, St. Bonaventure U., 1983; postgrad., Mount St. Mary Coll. Reporter, news anchor Sta. WGNY-AM-FM, Newburgh, N.Y., 1984; news dir., anchor NewsCtr. 6, Dutchess County, N.Y., 1985-90; dir. media rels. Ctrl. Hudson Gas & Electric, Poughkeepsie, 1993—; bd. dirs. Gateway Industries, Beacon, N.Y. City councilwoman City of Beacon, 1992-93; pres. Beacon Hist. Soc., 1989-94. Recipient Salute to Women in Bus. & Industry award D.C. YWCA, 1990. Mem. Nat. Soc. DAR (Melzingan chpt., trustee 1990—). Republican. Roman Catholic. Home: 37 Deerfield Pl Beacon NY 12508 Office: Ctrl Hudson Gas & Electric Corp 284 South Ave Poughkeepsie NY 12601

VAN BUREN, PHYLLIS EILEEN, Spanish and German language educator; b. Montevideo, Minn., June 4, 1947; d. Helge Thorfin and Alice Lillian (Johnsrud) Goulson; m. Barry Redmond Van Buren, Apr. 4, 1970; children: Priscila Victoria Princesa, Barry Redmond Barón. Student, Escuela de Bellas Artes, Guadalajara, Mex., 1968; BS, St. Cloud (Minn.) State U., 1969, MS, 1976; postgrad., Goethe Inst., Mannheim, West Germany, 1984, U. Costa Rica, 1989; PhD, The Union Inst., Cin., 1992. Instr. in Spanish Red Wing (Minn.) Pub. Schs., 1969-70; instr. in Spanish and German St. Cloud Pub. Schs., 1970-80; prof. foreign lang. edn., German and Spanish St. Cloud State U., 1975, 79—; advanced placement reader Ednl. Testing Svcs., Princeton, N.J., 1987—; translator in field; mem. Cen. State Adv. Bd. Contbr. articles to El Noticiero, Minn. Lang. Rev., Hispania; textbook reviewer. Coord. children's programs St. Cloud, 1970—; vol. ELS instr. St. Cloud Community, 1973—; reviewer St. Cloud Pub. Schs., 1985-89. U.S. Dept. Def. fellow, 1969, Goethe Inst. fellow, 1983; grantee N.W. Area Found., 1985-86, Bush Found., 1986, FIPSE/NEH, 1993-96. Mem. AAUW (exec. bd. 1988-92, grantee Minn. Internat. AR 1992), ASCD, MLA, Am. Assn. Tchrs. Spanish and Portuguese, Am. Assn. Tchrs. German, Am. Coun. Tchg. Fgn. Langs. (tester 1989—), Minn. Coun. Tchg. Fgn. Langs. (exec. bd.), Phi Kappa Phi (pres.-elect 1991-92, pres. 1992-93), Sigma Delta Pi, Delta Kappa Gamma, Delta Phi Alpha. Republican. Lutheran. Home: 3001 County Rd # 146 Clearwater MN 55320-1405 Office: St Cloud State U 720 4th Ave S Saint Cloud MN 56301-4498

VANBURKALOW, ANASTASIA, retired geography educator; b. Buchanan, N.Y., Mar. 16, 1911; d. James Turley and Mabel Ritchie (Ramsay) VanB. BA, Hunter Coll., 1931; MA, Columbia U., 1933, PhD, 1944. Rsch. asst. in geomorphology Columbia U., N.Y.C., 1934-37; from tutor to prof. geography Hunter Coll. CUNY, 1938-45, 48-75; rsch. and editorial asst. Am. Geog. Soc., N.Y.C., 1945-48; prof. Hunter Coll. CUNY, 1961-75, prof. emeritus Hunter Coll., 1975—; cons. geologist E.I. DuPont deNemours & Co., Wilmington, Del., 1945-59. Editor: Megalopolis (Jean Gottman), 1961, Geol. Edn., 1954-56; contbg. editor Geog. Rev., 1949-72; contbr. articles to profl. jours.; composer hymns. Bd. dirs. United Meth. City Soc., N.Y.C., 1972—, Bethany Deaconess Soc., 1982—, N.Y. Deaconess Assn., 1984—, Five Points Mission, N.Y.C., 1979-89; trustee John Street United Meth. Ch., N.Y.C., 1972-84. Kemp fellow, 1937-38. Fellow AAAS, N.Y. Acad. Scis. (sec. geology sect. 1957-58), Geol. Soc. Am., Hymn Soc. of Am. (recording sec. 1974-80); mem. Assn. Am. Geographers, Am. Geophys. Union, Am. Guild Organists, Soc. Woman Geographers (mem. exec. com. 1978-80, 83-85), Phi Beta Kappa, Sigma Xi. Home: 160 E 95th St New York NY 10128-2511

VAN CASPEL, VENITA WALKER, financial planner; b. Sweetwater, Okla.; d. Leonard Rankin and Ella Belle (Jarnagin) Walker; m. Lyttleton T. Harris IV, Dec. 26, 1987. Student, Duke, 1944-46; B.A., U. Colo., 1948, postgrad., 1949-51; postgrad., N.Y. Inst. Fin., 1962. Cert. fin. planner. Stockbroker Rauscher Pierce & Co., Houston, 1962-65, A.G. Edwards & Sons, Houston, 1965-68; founder, pres., owner Van Caspel & Co., Inc., Houston, 1968—, Van Caspel Wealth Mgmt.; owner, mgr. Van Caspel Planning Service, Van Caspel Advt. Agy.; sr. v.p. investments Raymond James and Assocs.; owner Diamond V Ranch; moderator PBS TV show The Money Makers and Profiles of Success, 1980; 1st women mem. Pacific Stock Exchange. Author: Money Dynamics, 1978, Money Dynamics of the 1980's, 1980, The Power of Money Dynamics, Money Dynamics for the 1990's, 1988; editor: Money Dynamics Letter. Bd. dirs. Boy Scouts Am., Horatio Alger Assn., Robert Schuller Ministries. Recipient Matrix award Theta Sigma Phi, 1969, Horatio Alger award for Disting. Americans, 1982, Disting. Woman's medal, Northwood Univ., 1988, Georgia Norlin award U. Colo. Alumni Assn., 1987. Mem. Internat. Assn. Fin. Planners, Inst. Cert. Fin. Planners, Phi Gamma Mu, Phi Beta Kappa. Methodist. Office: Raymond James & Assocs Inc 2700 Post Oak Blvd Ste 2325 Houston TX 77056-5705

VANCE, BETH KUNTZ, legislative staff director; b. July 29, 1953; d. Donald C. and Karin (Ericson) K.; m. B. Wayne Vance. AA, BA, U. Fla., 1975, JD, 1978. Bar: Fla., 1979, D.C., 1986; U.S. Supreme Ct., 1986. Asst. counsel Ho. Com. on Ways and Means, Washington, 1978-84, staff dir. subcom. on oversight, 1985—. Mem. Delta Delta Delta, Fla. Blue Key, Omicron Delta Kappa. Office: Ho Com on Ways & Means 1135 Longworth House Office Bldg Washington DC 20515*

VANCE, CYNTHIA LYNN, psychology educator; b. Norwalk, Calif., Mar. 31, 1960; d. Dennis Keith and Donna Kay (Harryman) V. BS, U. Oreg., 1982; MS, U. Wis., Milw., 1987, PhD, 1991. Teaching asst. U. Wis., Milw., 1983-89; computer graphics mgr. Montgomery Media, Inc., Milw., 1987-92; asst. prof. Cardinal Stritch Coll., Milw., 1992-93, Piedmont Coll., Demorest, Ga., 1993—. Contbr. articles to profl. jours. Vol. Dunwoody (Ga.)-DeKalb Kiwanis Club, 1993-94. Mem. AAUP, APA, Assn. Women in Psychology, S.E. Psychol. Assn., Am. Psychol. Soc. Office: Piedmont Coll PO Box 10 Demorest GA 30535

VANCE, SARAH S., federal judge; b. 1950. BA, La. State Univ., 1971; JD, Tulane Univ. Sch. of Law, 1978. With Stone, Pigman, Walther, Wittmann & Hutchinson, New Orleans, 1978-94; district judge U.S. Dist. Ct. (La. ea. dist.), 5th circuit, New Orleans, 1994—. Recipient Phi Beta Kappa Faculty Group award. Mem. Am. Bar Assn., La. State Bar Assn., Fed. Bar Assn., New Orleans Bar Assn., Bar Assn. of the Fed. Fifth Circuit, Nat. Assn. of Health Lawyers, Fed. Energy Bar Assn., La. Assn. of Women Attys. Address: US Courthouse 500 Camp St Rm C-255 New Orleans LA 70130*

VANCE, ZINNA BARTH, artist, writer; b. Phila., Sept. 28, 1917; d. Carl Paul Rudolph Barth and Dorothy Ellice (Wilson) Hart; m. Nathan E. Curry (div. 1959); m. Samuel Therrel Vance, Dec. 2, 1960; children: Barry, Scott Hart. BS in Edn. summa cum laude, Southwestern U., Georgetown, Tex., 1965; MA in Communications, U. Tex., 1969. Cert. in teaching langs., Tex. Freelance writer various publs., 1946-56; assoc. editor, newspaper Canacao Clipper, Philippines, 1956-58; dir. Region One Tex. Fine Arts Assn., Austin, 1962-63; curricular cons. U. Tex. Curricular Conf., 1966; sec. Tex. Fgn. Langs. Assn., 1967; publicity dir. Burnet (Tex.) Creative Arts, 1983—; freelance portrait artist, Liberty Hill, Tex.; owner Gallery Zinna Portrait Studio, Liberty Hill, Tex., 1978—; artist registry Hill Country Arts Found., Ingram, Tex., 1984—; art columnist two newspapers Burnet, 1983—. Contbr. numerous articles to profl. jours.; exhibited in pvt. and corp. collections; illustrator children's books; numerous one-woman shows. Active Hill Country Arts Found., 1978—, Burnet Creative Arts, 1980—, Hill Country Council of Arts, 1986—. Named one of Tex. Emerging Artists, Hill Country Arts Found., 1985; featured as Cover Story Philippines Internat. mag., 1957, featured in book Artists of Texas, 1989, 94. Mem. Nat. Mus. Women in Arts (charter mem.), Nat. Portrait Inst., Alpha Chi, Phi Kappa Phi. Republican. Episcopalian. Home: RR 2 Box 135 Liberty Hill TX 78642-9501

VANCE-HUNT, FLORENCE (F. V. HUNT), former state official; b. Cleve.; d. Harold Alexander and Mathilda Emile (Vance) Hunt. BA in Sociology, St. Xavier Coll., Chgo., 1945; postgrad., U. Chgo., 1943, NYU, 1952-53. With Pharm. Advt. Assocs., N.Y.C., 1957; pharm. copywriter Wm. Douglas McAdams, 1958-59; dir. sta. promotion, pub. mcpl. broadcasting WNYC Radio & TV, N.Y.C., 1960-62; with N.Y.C. Commn. Human Rights, 1962-66; dir. communications N.Y. State Dept. Mental Hygiene, 1970-72; pub. rels. staff N.Y.C. Health Svc. Adminstrn., 1973-74; dir. pub. info. N.Y.C. Employment Tng. Planning Coun., 1976-83; developer spl. prog. initiatives N.Y. State Ct. System, N.Y.C., 1984-92; cons. C.A.P.S., N.Y.C., 1983-84; playwright-in-residence Northeastern U., Boston, 1973-75. Prodr. 12 plays off-off Broadway; prodr. (one act plays) Dough, 1992, Andrgyny, 1992 (full length plays) Bird in Flight, Some Family Values; one woman sculpture show Chgo. Art Inst., 1947, New Sch., N.Y.C., 1952; group shows include Guggenheim Mus., 1951-52; represented Lincoln Ctr. Play Collection, Heritage Collection, U. Wyo., O'Neill's Am. Playwrights series, 2 vols., Anthology Women in Am. Theatre, 2 vols.; reviews of plays in N.Y. Times, Village Voice, Time Mag., Herald Tribune, Boston, Playboy Mag., Daily News, Show Biz. Recipient Brotherhood award, Nat. Assn. Christians and Jews, 1962-65; Guggenheim grantee, 1951; Va. Ctr. for Arts fellow, Edward MacDowgal Colony fellow. Mem. Dramatist Guild, PEN Am., Authors League of Am. Democrat. Episcopalian.

VANCE SIEBRASSE, KATHY ANN, newspaper publishing executive; b. Kansas City, Kans., Oct. 28, 1954; d. Donald Herbert Vance and Barbara June (Boris) Vance-Young; m. Charles Richard Siebrasse, Mar. 8, 1980; 1 stepson, Michael; 1 child, Bradley. BS in Journalism, No. Ill. U., 1976. Reporter Des Plaines (Ill.) Suburban Times and Park Ridge Herald, 1974-75, DeKalb (Ill.) Daily Chronicle, 1976-78; stringer Rockford (Ill.) Register Star, 1978; editor The MidWeek Newspaper, DeKalb, 1978-81, owner and pub., 1982—. Active No. Ill. U. Found., 1992—, mem. exec. bd., 1994—, chair bus. and industry for No. Ill. U. campaign, 1993-94; chair Kishwaukee Hosp. Health Coun., 1984-92, DeKalb County Partnership for a Substance Abuse Free Environment, 1990—; bd. dirs. DeKalb Edn. Found., sec., 1987-89, pres., 1989-93, active, 1987-94; sponsor Big Bros./Big Sisters Bowl-a-Thon. Recipient Comty. Svc. award Nat. Assn. of Advt. Pubs., 1980, Athena award Oldsmobile, DeKalb C. of C., 1990, Bus. of Yr., 1994. Mem. Ill. Press Assn., No. Ill. Newspaper Assn., Ind. Free Papers Am. (Community Svc. award 1992-93), Free Papers of Am., DeKalb County Farm Bur., DeKalb and Sycamore C. of C. (editor Sycamore newsletter 1994—, mem. Dekalb Athena award com., Dekalb bd. dirs.). Office: The MidWeek Newspaper 121 Industrial Dr De Kalb IL 60115-3977

VAN CLEAVE, KIRSTIN DEAN (KIT VAN CLEAVE), martial arts educator, writer, educator, publishing executive; b. Ft. Worth, Jan. 9, 1940; d. Henry Shibley and Lola Kathryn (Wimberly) van C. BA in Journalism, North Tex. State U., 1961; MA in English, U. Houston, 1972; DL in English, London Inst., 1973. Cert. self-defense instr. Tex. Commn. Law Enforcement Officer Standards and Edn., 1992, Nat. Women's Martial Arts Fedn., 1994. Reporter Associated Gen. Contractors News Svc., Houston, 1961-62; dir. pub. rels. Diboll Advt. Agy., Tex., 1963-64; writer Goodwin, Dannenbaum, Littman and Wingfield Advt. Agy., Houston, 1964-65; reporter Houston Tribune, 1965-68; copywriter sales promotion dept. Gulf Pub. Co., 1968-70; Houston editor, then mng. editor Metrobeat, Dallas, 1970; editor publs., dir. pub. rels., press rep. Baroid div. NL Industries, Inc., Houston, 1973-74; presdl. speechwriter Gulf Oil Co., 1974-76; chief exec. officer Inner-View Pub. Co., Houston, 1980-88; instr. self-def. Houston Area Women's Ctr., 1989—, Harris County Sheriff's Dept., 1991—; past mem. faculty U. Houston, Coll. of Mainland, Texas City, Tex., St. Agnes Acad., Houston. Author: They Still Do, 1973, Folklore of Texas Cultures, 1975, (poetry) Day of Love (set into a song cycle which was nominated for Pulitzer prize in Mus. Composition), 1978, Amourette, 1979, Laurels, 1980; librettist: Four Songs (composer Thomas Pasatieri), 1980; editor Inner-View mag., Houston; columnist: Houston Home & Garden, Houston Guide, Scene mag., In Houston, Billboard; contbr. articles to mags. Regional coord. South and S.W. region, leader Houston chpt. Guardian Angels, 1986-90. Recipient Mayor's Vol. award City of Houston, 1988, Excellence in Journalism award Houston Exec. Adv. Council, 1986, 1st Place award Harris County Med. Soc., 1986, Clean Houston Pub. Service award, 1986-87, Presdl. Sports award, 1994; named one of fifty Most Interesting Houstonians, City Mag., 1985, Goodwill Amb. City of Houston, 1994. Mem. S.W. C. of C., Houston C. of C., AAUP, Music Critics Assn., Internat. Assn. Bus. Communicators, Am. Soc. Authors and Journalists, World Tae Kwon Do Fedn., Cha Yon Ryu Black Belt Assn., Nat. Women's Martial Arts Fedn., Pacific Assn. Women Martial Artists, Am.-Ireland Martial Arts Assn. (pres. 1992—). Home: PO Box 66127 Houston TX 77266-6127

VAN CLEVE, SANDRA ROSE, retired nursing educator; b. Olney, Ill., Aug. 31, 1938; d. Muriel William and Marjorie May (Houchin) Cutshall; m. Charles Chadwick, June 14, 1958 (dec. Mar. 1988); children: Rosemarie Finley, Gilbert, Kent. Diploma, Union Hosp. Sch. Nursing, 1960; BA, Ea. Ill. U., 1974; MS in Edn., So. Ill. U., 1980. RN, Ill. Med./surg. staff nurse Good Samaritan Hosp., Mt. Vernon, Ill., 1960-61; staff nurse obstetrics Meml. Hosp., Carbondale, Ill., 1961-62; surg. staff nurse St. Mary's Hosp., Centraila, Ill., 1963-64; staff nurse obstetrics St. Mary's Hosp., Centralia, Ill., 1969-70; nursing asst. instr. Centralia Jr. Coll., 1964-65; practical nursing instr. Mt. Vernon C.C., 1965-69; practical nursing instr. Rend Lake Coll., Ina, Ill., 1970-94, ret., 1994; textbook reviewer W. B. Saunders Co., Orlando, Fla., 1990. Pres. Centralia Bus. and Profl. Woman's Club, 1990-91; mem. Centralia Little Theater Players, Centralia Choral Soc. Recipient Outstanding Faculty award Rend Lake Coll. Found., 1986, Outstanding Community Coll. Faculty Mem. award Ill. Community Coll. Trustees Assn., 1986. Mem. ANA, AAUW, Ill. Nurses Assn. (bd. dirs. 10th dist. 1975-84), Delta Kappa Gamma. Democrat. Methodist. Home: 18 Crestview Dr PO Box 309 Irvington IL 62848

VAN CURA, JOYCE BENNETT, librarian; b. Madison, Wis., Mar. 25, 1944; d. Ralph Eugene and Florence Marie (Cramer) Bennett; m. E. Jay Van

Cura, July 5, 1986. BA in Liberal Arts (scholar), Bradley U., 1966; MLS, U. Ill., 1971. Library asst. rsch. library Caterpillar Tractor Co., Peoria, Ill., 1966-67; reference librarian, instr. library tech. Ill. Central Coll., East Peoria, 1967-73; asst. prof. Sangamon State U., Springfield, Ill., 1973-80, assoc. prof., 1980-86; head library ref. and info. svcs. dept. Ill. Inst. Tech., 1987-90; dir. Learning Resources Ctr. Morton Coll., 1990—; convenor Coun. II, Ill. Clearinghouse for Acad. Library Instrn., 1978; presentor 7th Ann. Conf. Acad. Library Instrn., 1977, Nat. Women's Studies Assn., 1983, others; participant Gt. Lakes Women's Studies Summer Inst., 1981. Dem. precinct Committeewoman, 1982-85 . Pres., Springfield chpt. NOW, 1978-79. Ill. state scholar, 1962-66; recipient Am. Legion citizenship award, 1962; cert. of recognition Ill. Bicentennial Commn., 1974; invited Susan B. Anthony luncheon, 1978, 79, vice-moderator Fourth Presbyn. Women, 1989-90; elder Riverside (Ill.) Presbyn. Ch., 1992—; mem. adv. bd. Suburban Libr. System, 1992-94, Nat. Commn. Learning Resources; v.p. membership Riverside chpt. Lyric Opera Chgo., 1994—; active Riverside (Ill.) Arts Ctr. Mem. ALA, Ill. Library Assn. (presentor 1984) Ill. Assn. Coll. and Rsch. Libraries (bibliog. instrn. com.), Spl. Libraries Assn., No. Ill. Learning Resources Consortium Bd., Am. Mgmt. Assn., Women in Mgmt., AAUW (chmn. standing com. on women Springfield br., mem. com. on women Ill. state divsn., bd. dirs. Riverside br., 1992-94), Nat. Women's Studies Assn. (presentor 1983, 84, 85), No. Ill. Learning Resources Coop. (del. 1990—), Springfield Art Assn., Nat. Trust Historic Preservation, Women in Mgmt., Beta Phi Mu. Reviewer Library Jour., Am. Reference Books Ann. Contbr. article in field to publ. Home: 181 Scottswood Rd Riverside IL 60546-2221 Office: Morton Coll Learning Resources Ctr 3801 S Central Ave Chicago IL 60650-4306

VANDEL, DIANA GEIS, management consultant; b. San Antonio, Apr. 2, 1947; d. John George and Elma Ruth (Triplett) Geis; m. Jerry Dean Vandel, Apr. 17, 1976; 1 child, Jeremy Kyle. MusB, U. Tex., 1969. Cert. tchr., Tex.; lic. nursing home adminstr., Tex. Tchr. music Zilker Elem. Pub. Sch., Austin, Tex., 1969-70, Isely Sch., Austin, 1986; asst. adminstr. Hillside Manor Nursing Home, Inc., San Antonio, 1970-76, cons. to nursing homes, 1976-78, asst. adminstr., 1978-79, cons. adminstr., 1979-91, adminstr., 1988; mgmt. cons. Promoting Excellence Consultation, Austin, 1991—; owner, facilitator creative music and relaxation in motion classes, workshops and retreats, San Antonio, 1982-84; fine arts facilitator Cedar Creek Elem. Sch., Austin, 1988-91; seminar leader Movement Spiritual Inner Awareness, Austin, 1986—, min., 1989—. Austin rep. Peace Theol. Sem., L.A., 1988-93; mem. exec. bd. Cedar Creek Booster Club, 1989-91. Mem. NAFE, Inst. Individual and World Peace, South Tex. Profl. Spkrs. Assn., Nat. Spkrs. Assn. Home: 916 Terrace Mountain Dr Austin TX 78746-2732 Office: Promoting Excellence 916 Calithea Austin TX 78746-2732

VANDELINDER, DEBRA LOU, art educator; b. Troy, Pa., Nov. 9, 1961; d. Harry L. and Betty L. (Christopher) VanD. BA, Mansfield State Coll., 1983; MEd, Mansfield U., 1986. Cert. art tchr., N.Y. Freelance graphic designer VanDelinder Graphic Design, Millerton, Pa., 1983-86; art tchr. West Perry Sch. Dist., New Bloomfield, Pa., 1986, Newfield Ctrl. Sch. Dist., Newfield, N.Y., 1987, Elmira (N.Y.) City Sch. Dist., 1987—. Artist, illustrator: Chemistry for Children, 1985. Decorated Gold medal Women's Olympic Lifting 56.0 kg divsn. Empire State Games, 1988; named Women's Powerlifting Champion 114 lb. divsn. N.Y.S., 1988. Mem. Elmira Tchrs. Assn., Lupus Found. Am. Office: Elmira City Sch Dist Pine City Sch Pennsylvania Ave Pine City NY 14871

VANDELL, DEBORAH LOWE, educational psychology educator; b. Bryan, Tex., June 5, 1949; d. Charles Ray and Janice (Durrett) Lowe; m. Kerry Dean Vandell, May 16, 1970; children: Colin Buckner, Ashley Elizabeth. AB, Rice U., 1971; EdM, Harvard U., 1972; PhD, Boston U., 1977. Tchr. Walpole (Mass.) Pub. Schs., 1972-73; rschr. Ralph Nader Congress Project, Washington, 1972; asst. prof. U. Tex., Dallas, 1976-81, assoc. prof., 1981-89; prof. ednl. psychology U. Wis., Madison, 1989—; vis. scholar MacArthur Rsch. Network, Cambridge, Mass., 1985-86, U. Calif., Berkeley, 1988-89; mem. steering com. NICHD Study of Early Child Care. Assoc. editor Child Devel., 1993-95; mem. editl. bd. Child Devel., 1980-93, Jour. Family Issues, 1983-89, Devel. Psychology, 1989-93; co-author books; contbr. articles to profl. jours. Mem. bd. Infant Mental Health Assn., 1988-89, Community Coord. Child Care, Madison, Wis., 1990-93, chair, 1991-93; Sunday sch. tchr. Ch. of the Epiphany, Richardson, Tex., 1990—; mem. altar guild St. Andrew's Ch., also vestry, 1992-95. Named Outstanding Young Scholar, Found. for Child Devel., 1982; grantee infant child and family processes NIH, 1989. Mem. Am. Psychol. Assn. (exec. com. div. 7 1985-88), Southwestern Soc. Rsch. in Human Devel. (pres. 1988-90), Am. Psychol. Soc., Soc. for Rsch. in Child Devel., Phi Beta Kappa. Episcopalian. Office: U Wis Dept Ednl Psychology 1025 W Johnson St Madison WI 53706-1706

VANDEMARK, MICHELLE VOLIN, critical care, neuroscience nurse; b. Sioux Falls, S.D., Feb. 14, 1962; d. Verlynne V. and Suzanne (Cronin) Volin; m. Richard E. VanDemark, June 5, 1982; children: Andrew Porter, Hannah Elizabeth. BA in Biology, Lake Forest (Ill.) Coll., 1984; BSN, Northwestern U., Chgo., 1986; MS in Nursing, Loyola U., Chgo., 1990. RN, Ill.; cert. neurosci. nursing. Mem. ANA, Am. Assn. Neurosci. Nurses, Sigma Theta Tau, Alpha Sigma Nu.

VAN DEMARK, RUTH ELAINE, lawyer; b. Santa Fe, N. Mex., May 16, 1944; d. Robert Eugene and Bertha Marie (Thompson) Van D.; m. Leland Wilkinson, June 23, 1967; children: Anne Marie, Caroline Cook. AB, Vassar Coll., 1966; MTS, Harvard U., 1969; JD with honors, U. Conn., 1976. Bar: Conn. 1976, U.S. Dist. Ct. Conn. 1976, Ill. 1977, U.S. Dist. Ct. (no. dist.) Ill. 1977, U.S. Supreme Ct. 1983, U.S. Ct. Appeals (7th cir.) 1984. Instr. legal research and writing Loyola U. Sch. Law, Chgo., 1976-79; assoc. Wildman, Harrold, Allen & Dixon, Chgo., 1977-84, ptnr., 1985-94; prin. Law Offices of Ruth E. Van Demark, Chgo., 1995—; bd. dirs., sec. Systat, Inc., Evanston, Ill., 1984-94. Assoc. editor Conn. Law Rev., 1975-76. Mem. adv. bd. Horizon Hospice, Chgo., 1978—; del.-at-large White House Conf. on Families, Los Angeles, 1980; mem. adv. bd. YWCA Battered Women's Shelter, Evanston, Ill., 1982-86; mem. alumni coun. Harvard Divinity Sch., 1988-91; vol. atty. Pro Bono Advocates, Chgo., 1982-92, bd. dirs. 1993—, chair devel. com., 1993; bd. dirs. Friends of Pro Bono Advocates Orgn., 1987-89, New Voice Prodns., 1984-86, Byrne Piven Theater Workshop, 1987-90; founder, bd. dirs. Friends of Battered Women and their Children, 1986-87; chair 175th Reunion Fund Harvard U. Div. Sch., 1992. Mem. ABA, Ill. Bar Assn., Conn. Bar Assn., Chgo. Bar Assn., Appellate Lawyers Assn. Ill. (bd. dirs. 1985-87, treas. 1989-90, sec. 1990-91, v.p. 1991-92, pres. 1992-93), Women's Bar Assn. Ill., AAUW, Jr. League Evanston (chair State Pub. Affairs Com. 1987-88, Vol. of Yr. 1983-84). Clubs: Chgo. Vassar (pres. 1979-81), Cosmopolitan (N.Y.C.). Home: 1127 Asbury Ave Evanston IL 60202-1136

VAN DEN AKKER, KOOS, fashion designer; b. The Hague, Netherlands, Mar. 16, 1939; came to U.S., 1968, naturalized, 1982; Student, Royal Acad. Arts, The Hague, 1956-58, Ecole Guerre Lavigne, Paris, 1961. Apprentice designer Christian Dior Fashion House, Paris, 1963-65; freelance designer, est. custom fashion boutique The Hague, 1965-68; designer Eve Stillman lingerie co., N.Y.C., 1969-70; freelance designer, est. boutique, 1971—, freelance designer, est. showroom, 1978—. Works include: collaged fur coat range, Ben Kahn Furs, 1981—, handbag range, Meyers Manufacturing, 1986-88; couture lingerie collections, La Lingerie stores, 1987—; collaged upholstery furniture ranges James II Galleries, 1988—. Recipient Gold Coast award, 1978, Tommy award Am. Painted Fabrics Coun., 1982. Office: 550 7th Ave Fl 18 New York NY 10018-3203*

VAN DENBURGH, PEGGY SUE, chiropractor; b. Gary, Ind., Dec. 15, 1959; d. George William and Phyllis Jean (Manwaring) Van D. B in Biology, Franklin Coll., 1982; D of Chiropractic, Palmer Coll., 1985; grad., Dale Carnegie Course, 1993-94. Diplomate Nat. Bd. Chiropractic Examiners, BioEnergetic Synchronization Technique. Clin. teaching resident Palmer Coll. Chiropractic, Devenport, Iowa, 1986, instr. of clinics, 1987; instr. Lumsdon Chiropractic, Franklin, Ind., 1987; owner Pyramid Chiropractic, Indpls., 1988-92; owner, CEO Psuvan Enterprises, P.C., Indpls., 1993—; facilitor Altitudral Healing, Indpls., 1994. Fund raiser Julian Ctr. for Domestic Violence, Indpls., 1992—, Ind. Cares AIDS, Indpls., 1992-94; vol. Reach to Recovery Am. Cancer Soc., Indpls., 1994—. Mem. Am. Chiropractic Assn., Ind. State Chiropractic Assn. (legis. com. 1994). Democrat. Roman Catholic. Office: Psuvan Enterprises PC 8648 Purdue Rd Indianapolis IN 46268

VANDENDORPE, MARY MOORE, social scientist, educator; b. Chgo., June 2, 1947; d. Era William and Mary Desales (Dobis) M.; m. James Edward Vandendorpe, Aug. 16, 1969; children: Laura Marie, David Lucien. AB, St. Louis U., 1969; MS, Ill. Inst. Tech., 1975, PhD, 1980. Copywriter, Spiegel Inc., Chgo., 1969-72; adj. instr. Lewis U., Romeoville, Ill., 1976-79, asst. prof., 1980-85, assoc. prof., 1985-89, prof., 1989—, dept. chairperson, 1985—. Mem. APA, Am. Psychol. Soc., Assn. Colls. Chgo. Area (chair psychology 1992—), Gerontol Soc., Chgo. Psychol. Assn. (dir. 1979—, pres. 1982—), Naperville Heritage Soc., Psi Chi. Office: Lewis U 213 Science Romeoville IL 60441

VAN DE PUTTE, LETICIA, pharmacist, state official; b. Tacoma, Dec. 6, 1954; d. Daniel and Isabel (Aguilar) San Miguel; m. Henry P. Van de Putte, Jr., Oct. 223, 1977; children: Nichole, Vanessa, Henry, Gregory, Isabella, Paul. Student, St. Mary's U., San Antonio, 1973-74, U. Houston, 1975, 76-77, U. Tex., 1979; cert. JFK sch. exec. program, Harvard U., 1993. Registered pharmacist, Tex. Supr. MHMR T. L. Vordenbaument and Assocs., San Antonio, 1971-82; pharmacist in charge Botica Guadalupana, San Antonio, 1982-85; owner Loma Park Pharmacy, San Antonio, 1985—; panelist Eil Lilly & Co. Pham. Adv. Panel, 1989—. Mem. St. Josephs Cath. Ch., 1977—; mem. YWCA, 1983—, bd. dirs., 1983-86; appointee City Coun. Commn. on Status of Women, San Antonio, 1985; sec. Mex.-Am. Legis. Caucus; mem. Tex. Ho. of Reps. Labor and Employment Commn. and Human Svcs. Commn., 1991—; mem. Alamo Area Coun. Govts., 1992—; chair Interagency Child Abuse Network Com. Recipient Mother and Leader award LULAC, 1992, Mujeres Project award Mex.-Am. Unity Coun., 1992; Kellogg Fellow Havard/JFK Exec. Elected Ofcls. program, 1993; named Young Career Woman of Yr., Mex.-Am. Profl. Women's Club, 1983, Outstanding Women in Politics, San Antonio Express News, 1992. Mem. Market Sq. Assn. (sec. 1985-86), Tex. Pharm. Assn. (coun. mem. 1987-90), Bexar County Pharm. Assn., Nat. Assn. Retail Druggists, Women of the Moose. Democrat. Office: 3718A Blanco Rd Ste 2 San Antonio TX 78212-1308

VANDERBEKE, PATRICIA K., architect; b. Detroit, Apr. 3, 1963; d. B. H. and Dolores I. VanderBeke. BS in Architecture, U. Mich., 1985, MArch, 1987. Registered architect, Ill. Archtl. intern Hobbs & Black, Assocs., Ann Arbor, Mich., 1984-86, Fry Assocs., Ann Arbor, 1988; architect Decker & Kemp Architecture/Urban Design, Chgo., 1989-92; prin., founder P. K. VanderBeke, Architect, Chgo., 1992—. Contbr. photographs and articles to Inland Architect mag.; contbr. photographs to AIA calendar. Chair recycling com. Lake Point Tower Condo. Assn., Chgo., 1990T, chair. ops. com., 1993. George S. Booth travelling fellow, 1992. Mem. AIA (1st place photog. contest award 1992, hon. mention 1994), Chgo. Archtl. Club. Office: P K VanderBeke Architect 505 N Lake Shore Dr Apt 808 Chicago IL 60611-3402

VANDERBILT, GLORIA MORGAN, artist, actress, fashion designer; b. N.Y.C., Feb. 20, 1924; d. Reginald Claypoole and Gloria (Morgan) V.; m. Pasquale di Cicco (div.); m. Leopold Stokowski, 1945 (div. 1955); children—Stanislaus, Christopher; m. Sidney Lumet, 1956 (div.); m. Wyatt Emory Cooper, 1963; children—Carter V. (dec.), Anderson H. Attended, Mary C. Wheeler, Miss Porter's schs.; studied acting with, dir. Sanford Meisner, beginning 1955. Exhibited in one-man shows at Rabun Studio, N.Y.C., 1948, Bertha Shaeffer Gallery, N.Y.C., 1954, Juster Gallery, N.Y.C., 1956, Hammer Gallery, N.Y.C., 1966, 68, Cord Gallery, N.Y.C., 1966, Washington Gallery Art, 1968, Neiman-Marcus, Dallas, 1968, Vestart Gallery, N.Y.C., 1969, Parish Museum, Southampton, N.Y., also in Nantucket, Mass., Houston, Reading, Pa., Monterey, Calif., Nashville; exhibited in group shows, Washington Gallery Art, 1967, Hoover Gallery, San Francisco, 1971, stage career; acted in summer stock prodn. The Swan; made Broadway debut in The Time of Your Life, 1955; other stage appearances include Picnic, 1955, The Spa, 1956, Peter Pan, 1958, The Green Hat; made TV debut in Tonight At 8:30; other TV appearances include Colgate Comedy Hour, 1955, Flint and Fire on U.S. Steel Hour, 1958, Family Happiness on U.S. Steel Hour, 1959, Very Important People; appeared in film Johnny Concho, 1955; dir. design film, Riegel Textile Corp., N.Y.C., from 1970; designer stationary and greeting cards, Hallmark Co., fabrics, Bloomcraft Co., bed linens, Martex Co., table linens, Peacock Co., Gloria Vanderbilt jeans; also china, glassware, scarves. Recipient Sylvania award 1959, Fashion award Neiman-Marcus 1969. Author: Love Poems, 1955, (with Alfred Allen Lewis) Gloria Vanderbilt Book of Collage, 1970, Woman to Woman, 1979, Once Upon a Time: A True Story, 1985, novel Never Say Good-Bye, 1989, The Memory Book of Starr Faithfull, 1994; author: (with Alfred Allen Lewis) play Three by Two, early 1960's, Black White, White Knight, 1987; poems and short stories. Mem. Actors Equity, Screen Actors Guild, AFTRA, Authors League Am., Am. Fedn. Arts. *

VANDERBURG, KATHLEEN, surgical nurse; b. Milw., Feb. 2, 1951; d. Raymond Lawrence and Louise Mary (Jelich) Ksobiech; m. Richard John, July 27, 1975. Diploma, Mt. Sinai Hosp. Sch. Nursing, 1972; BS, Chapman Coll., 1979; BS in Nursing, McKendree Coll., 1988; MS, Health Sci. Chapman Coll., 1981. RN, Miss. Supr. oper. room svcs. USAF, Langley AFB, Va., 1991-93; commd. USAF, 1974, advanced through grades to col., 1994; dir. oper. rm. and c.s.s. svcs. USAF, Keesler AFB, Miss., 1994—. Decorated Meritorious Svc. medal (4), Commendation medal (3). Mem. Air Force Assn., Assn. Operating Rm. Nurses. Home: 14001 Solano Cir Ocean Springs MS 39564-2557 Office: USAF Keesler Med Ctr Biloxi MS 39534

VANDERGRIFF, CHRISTINA RAI, purchasing agent; b. Prineville, Oreg., Nov. 13, 1964; d. Marvin Ronald and Virginia Lucille (Warren) Craig; m. Kenneth Wayne Vandergriff, Aug. 23, 1987. Cert. legal adminstrn. with honors, Trend Coll., Eugene, Oreg., 1989; student, Morrison Coll., Reno, 1993—. Shipper, asst. loan processor Centennial Mortgage Co., Inc., Eugene, 1989-90; asst. acct. Kimwood Corp., Cottage Grove, Oreg., 1990-91; sec., asst. Bill Vollendorff Appraisal, Walla Walla, Wash., 1991-92; inventory supr., purchaser Sierra Office Concepts/Nev. Copy Systems, Reno, 1992—, mem. employee adv. com., 1993—. Active Adopt-A-Sch. Program, Reno, 1992;-co-sponsor Nev. Women's Fund, Reno, 1993. Democrat. Baptist. Office: Sierra Office Concepts/ Nev Copy Systems 1301 Corporate Blvd Reno NV 89502-7120

VANDERGRIFF, LINDA JOYCE, engineering physicist; b. Sugar Creek, Mo., July 20, 1956; d. Ronald and Joyce (Smart) Dawbarn; m. Glenn Reid Vandergriff, Dec. 11, 1976. BS in Engring. Physics, U. Tenn., 1979; postgrad., U. Tenn., Tullahoma, 1979-80, U. Mich., 1981, U. Calif., Los Angeles, 1982, Ga. Inst. Tech., 1982; MS in Engring. Electro-Optics, Southeastern Inst. Tech., 1986, postgrad., 1988—. Asst. librarian Coffee County Pub. Library, Manchester, Tenn., 1973-74; coop. engr. Sverdrup/ARO Inc., Tullahoma, 1974-78, jr. engr., 1979-81; asst. instr. U. Tenn., Knoxville, 1978-79; jr. engr. Calspan, Tullahoma, 1981; mem. tech. staff Gen. Research Corp., Ft. Walton Beach, Fla., 1981-83, Huntsville, Ala., 1983-86; engring. physicist Sparta Inc., Huntsville, 1986-88; sr. systems engr. GE Aerospace, Blue Bell, Pa., 1988-93; dir. electro-optics rsch. ctr. Sci. Applications Internat. Corp., Torrance, Calif., 1993—; sub-chair tracking panel Strategic Defense Initiative Orgn., 1992-93. Contbr. articles to profl. jours. Dir. youth camp Reorganized Ch. of Jesus Christ of LDS, Tenn. and Ky. Dists., 1986-87, dir. Family Camp, 1988-89, historian, solicitor, 1987-89, elder, 1988—; pastor Phila. Congregation, 1993, L.A. Pastoral Unit. Mem. NAFE, Am. Def. Preparedness Assn., Optical Soc. Am., Internat. Soc. for Optical Engring., Sigma Pi Sigma. Home: 12520 Montecito Rd Seal Beach CA 90740-2724

VANDERHEYDEN, MIRNA-MAR, resort management and services executive; b. Freeport, Ill., Oct. 8, 1932; d. Orville Ray and Frances Elmira (Miller) Van Brocklin; m. Roger Eugene Vanderheyden, Dec. 23, 1950 (div. 1983); children: Romayne Lee, Adana Dawn, Grayling Dwayne, Willow B., Tiffany LaMarr. Cert., Brown's Bus. Coll., Freeport, Ill., 1949; BA, Milliken U., 1953. Paralegal various locations, 1953-93; pres. Carlin Bay Corp., Coeur d'Alene, Idaho, 1981—. Lobbyist PTA, Springfield, Ill., 1972. Home: 609 W Apple Dr Delta CO 81416 Office: Carlin Bay Svcs 609 W Apple Dr Delta CO 81416

VANDERHORN, SHEILA ANN, human resources specialist, consultant; b. Redfield, S.D., May 25, 1949; d. Charles Lindberg and Lois Helen (Luxton) Robertson; m. Steven John VanderHorn, Aug. 2, 1969 (div. June 1986); children: Lori, Stephani. Student, Marycrest Coll., 1967-69; BE, St. Ambrose U., 1983. Customer svc. mgr. Thoms-Proestler Co., Davenport, Iowa, 1984-86; asst. student svcs. mgr. Hamilton Tech. Coll., Davenport, 1986-87; br. mgr. Interim Employment Svcs., Milw., 1987-91; regional mgr. (midwest) LTW Mgmt. Svcs., Inc., Milw., 1991—. Telephone counselor Women's Crisis Line, Milw., 1987-91; pers. advisor First Unitarian Ch., Milw., 1992—. Mem. Nat. Human Resources Assn. (sec. 1989-91, Milw. chpt. affiliate pres. 1992-93, v.p.- fin. 1993—). Unitarian Universalist. Office: LTW Mgmt Svcs Inc 1223 N Prospect Milwaukee WI 53202

VANDERHOST, LEONETTE LOUISE, psychologist; b. Phila., June 11, 1924; d. Charles and Pauline (McGhaney) V. BA, CUNY, 1945; MA, NYU, 1949, PhD, 1966. Lic. psychologist, N.Y. Intern staff Lincoln (Ill.) State Sch., 1951-52; staff Evansville (Ind.) State Hosp., 1953-54, Children's Guidance Ctr., Dayton, Ohio, 1954-56; psychotherapist Hempstead (N.Y.) Consultation Services, 1963-66; staff, sr. psychologist Hillside Hosp., Glen Oaks, N.Y., 1957-64; sr. psychologist, chief West Nassau Mental Health Ctr., Franklin Sq., N.Y., 1959-63; pvt. practice psychologist N.Y.C., 1959—; cons. Big Sisters, N.Y., 1960-62, Health Ins. Planning, N.Y., 1962-64, Head Start, N.Y., 1967-73. Mem. Am. Psychol. Assn., Am. Orthopsychiatric Assn.

VANDERKOLK, MARIA ELIZABETH, marketing professional; b. Mpls., Dec. 20, 1964; d. Clarence Michael and Louise Elizabeth (Kurtzman) Lederhos; m. Michael James VanderKolk, Nov. 28, 1987. BS, U. Colo., 1986, BA, 1986; MPA, Calif. Lutheran U., 1994. Mktg. coord. MiniScribe Corp., Longmont, Colo., 1986-88; sr. mktg. coord. EEsof, Inc., Westlake Village, Calif., 1988-89; product mgr. Applause, Inc., Woodland Hills, Calif., 1989-90. mem. Ventura County Bd. Suprs., 1991—; mem. Ventura County Med. Ctr. Bd. Trustees; mem. bd. dirs. Santa Monica Mtns. Cons. Mem. Beta Gamma Sigma. Republican. Roman Catholic. Office: Office Bd County Suprs County Govt Ctr Adminstn Bldg 800 S Victoria Ave 4th Fl Ventura CA 93009

VAN DER LEUN, PATRICIA ELLEN, literary agency executive; b. N.Y.C.; d. Gerald Herzfeld and Mildred (Halbreich) Katleman; 1 child, Justine Van Der Leun. MA, San Francisco Art Inst. Pres. Van der Leun & Assocs., Easton, Conn.

VANDERLINDEN, CAMILLA DENICE DUNN, telecommunications industry manager; b. Dayton, July 21, 1950; d. Joseph Stanley and Virginia Danley (Martin) Dunn; m. David Henry VanderLinden; Oct. 10, 1980; 1 child, Michael Christopher. Student, U. de Valencia, Spain, 1969; BA in Spanish and Secondary Edn. cum laude, U. Utah, 1972, MS in Human Resource Econs., 1985. Asst. dir. Davis County Community Action Program, Farmington, Utah, 1973-76; dir. South County Community Action Program, Midvale, Utah, 1976-79; supr. customer service Ideal Nat. Life Ins. Co., Salt Lake City, 1979-80; mgr. customer service Utah Farm Bur. Mutual Ins., Salt Lake City, 1980-82; quality assurance analyst Am. Express Co., Salt Lake City, 1983-86, quality assurance and human resource specialist, 1986-88; mgr. quality assurance and engring. Am. Express Co., Denver, 1988-91; mgr. customer svc. Tel. Express Co., Colorado Springs, Colo., 1991—; mem. adj. faculty Westminster Coll., Salt Lake City, 1987-88. mem. adj. faculty, mem. quality adv. bd. Red Rocks Community Coll., 1990-91. Vol. translator Latin Am. community; vol. naturalist Roxborough State Park; internat. exch. coord. EF Fgn. Exch. Program. Christian. Home: 10857 W Snow Cloud Trl Littleton CO 80125-9210

VANDER PLATE-HELD, ELAINE, organist, choir director, music educator; b. Paterson, N.J., Dec. 15, 1946; d. Louis and Doris (Gnade) Vander Plate; m. Timothy Lee Seitz, Aug. 24, 1969 (div. 1984); children: Derek Stefan, Kirsten Leigh; m. Richard William Held, July 18, 1988. B in Music Edn., Westminster Choir Coll., 1969, M in Ch. Music, 1992. Organist, choir dir. Unitarian Ch., Princeton, N.J., 1969-71, Unitarian Fellowship, Morristown, N.J., 1973-86, First Presbyn., Springfield, N.J., 1987-88, Reformed Ch., North Brunswick, N.J., 1988-90, Emanuel Luth., New Brunswick, N.J., 1990—; owner and tchr. piano, organ, voice The Music Store, Morris Plains, 1971-81; pvt. tchr., Morristown, N.J., 1973-88; gen. music tchr. Myschool, Mt. Freedom, N.J., 1976-79; pvt. organ, piano, voice Emanuel Luth. Ch., New Brunswick, 1990—. Condr.: (childrens choirs) Chorister's Guild Festival, 1993, 94; performer of various organ recitals. Mem. Am. Choral Dirs. Assn., Assn. Luth. Ch. Musicians, Am. Guild Organists, Choristers Guild.

VANDERSTEEN, BARBARA SHERYL, oil company executive; b. Pittsburg, Calif., June 13, 1951; d. J.M. and Annette E. (Berry) Monroe; divorced; 1 child, Robert S. Ford. BS in Human Devel., Calif. State U., Hayward, 1973. With Shell Oil Co., 1973—; office asst. Shell Chem. Co., Walnut Creek, Calif., 1973-78; analyst Shell Oil Co., San Ramon, Calif., 1979-83; salary sta. mgr. Shell Oil Co., East Bay, Calif., 1983-85; ter. sales rep. Shell Oil Co., San Francisco, 1985-86, sales devel. rep., 1986-87, ter. mgr. for So. Calif., 1987-88; mktg. rep. Shell Oil Co., Houston, 1988-90, sr. mktg. rep., 1990-93, mgr. store standards, 1993-94, mgr. franchise bus. devel., 1994—; mem. adv. bd. Gatorade, 1993-94. Active boosters club, parents assn. FSU. Mem. Nat. Assn. Convenience Stores, Laurel Soc., Kelliwood Women's Club, Willowfork Women's Club. Republican. Office: Shell Oil Co 900 Louisiana Osp # 2634 Houston TX 77002

VANDERSYPEN, RITA DEBONA, guidance counselor; b. Alexandria, La., Sept. 13, 1953; d. Sam S. and Myrtle (Genova) DeBona; m. Robert Louis Vandersypen, Aug. 17, 1974; children: Regina Marie, Ryan Matthew. BA summa cum laude, La. Coll., 1975; MEd, La. State U., 1980, postgrad., 1982; EdS, Northwestern State U., Natchitoches, La., 1993. Eligibility worker Rapides Parish Office Family Svcs., Alexandria, 1975-78; welfare social worker Rapides Parish Foster Care Svcs., Alexandria, 1978-79; tchr. A. Wettermark High Sch., Boyce, La., 1979-84; tchr. English English Alexandria Sr. High Sch., 1984-92, guidance counselor, 1992—. Contbr. to handbook and curriculum guide. Sponsor Future Voters Am. Club, 1984-89, 4-H Club, 1988—. Mem. AAUW, Rapides Parish Guidance Counselors Assn., Rapides Fedn. Tchrs., L.A. Sch. Counselor Assn., Rapides Livestock Club, Belguam-Am. Club, Am. Quarter Horse Assn., Phi Kappa Phi, Kappa Delta Pi. Roman Catholic. Office: Peabody Magnet High Sch 2727 Jones Ave Alexandria LA 71302

VANDER WEIDE, MICHELLE ELAINE, educator; b. Grand Rapids, Mich., Oct. 30, 1961; d. Daryl Jay and Maris Elaine (Hager) Vander Kooi; m. Paul Allan Vander Weide, June 24, 1983; children: Jessica Kelly, Brandon Lyn (dec.), Lindsey Renae, Shannon Rose; foster children: Melissa, David, Aaron Sandbulte. BA, Dordt Coll., 1983, postgrad., 1990-91. Cert. elem. tchr., Iowa. 3d grade tchr. Netherlands Reformed Christian Sch., Rock Valley, Iowa, 1983-85; kindergarten through 8th grade art and 7th grade Bible tchr. Rock Valley Christian Sch., 1991—. Sunday sch., catechism and vacation Bible sch. tchr., Sioux Center, Iowa and Rock Valley chs.; counselor Calvinettes of Carmel, Rock Valley. Office: Rock Valley Christian Sch 1405 17th Rock Valley IA 51247

VANDERWERKEN, KAREN BAURLE, financial services educator; b. Lafayette, Ind., Apr. 3, 1947; d. Dwight Lee Mood and Rachel Maurine (Deich) Good; m. Alan Harry Baurle, Aug. 8, 1970 (dec. Sept. 1975); 1 child, Shari Michele; m. David Leon Vanderwerken, Aug. 1, 1981; children: Brian Randall, Eric Leon. BA in English and Psychology, Milligan Coll., 1969; MA in English and Edn., Ball State U., 1974. Cert. secondary tchr., Ind. Intermediate English tchr. Marion (Ind.) Pub. Schs., 1969-76; instr. writing Tarrant County Jr. Coll., Ft. Worth, Tex., 1977-80, Tex. Christian Univ., Ft. Worth, 1979-84; exec. dir. Am. Inst. Banking, Ft. Worth, 1984—; cons. Holt Reading Program, Marion, 1971-74, Programmed Instrn., Fort Worth, 1980-84. Author: Imagery, 1972. Chmn. Unlimited Potential Gifted Students Program, Marion, 1972-76. Named Outstanding Tchr. Tex. Christian U., 1984. Mem. Nat. assn. Bank Women (cert. instr. editor, chmn. tng. 1986-87), am. Bankers Assn. (Chpt. of Excellence awards 1985-94, Joseph E. Chapman award 1987, 94), Coll. Eng. Assn., Coll. Coun. Tchrs. English, ASAE, LERN, Alpha Delta Kappa (v.p. 1981-83). Democrat. Home: 2825 Princeton St Fort Worth TX 76109-1763 Office: Am Inst Banking 6100 Western Pl Ste 540 Fort Worth TX 76107

VANDERWOUDE, CAROL ANN, sleep disorders technician; b. Plainfield, N.J., Aug. 14, 1951; d. John Raphael and Catherine Barbara (Stebor) V. AA, Brevard C.C., Cocoa, Fla., 1971; BS, U. Ctrl. Fla., 1973. Registered respiratory therapist. Respiratory therapist Orange Meml. Hosp., Orlando, Fla., 1971-74; asst. dept. dir. Gen. Hosp., Ft. Walton Beach, Fla., 1974-76; shift supr. Children's Hosp., Denver, 1976-78; shift supr. Providence Hosp., Everett, Wash., 1978-87, sleep technician, supr., 1987—; coord. A.W.A.K.E. Support Group, Everett, 1991—. Inventor infant chest percussor, 1979; contbr. articles to mags. Mem. Pacific NW Polysomnography Group. Democrat. Roman Catholic. Home: 21309 52d Ave W # D221 Mountlake Terrace WA 98043 Office: Providence Gen Med Ctr 916 Pacific Ave Everett WA 98201

VAN DEUSEN, JENIFER, educational consultant; b. Rockville Centre, N.Y., Feb. 24, 1952; d. James A. and Glays E. (Rinderman) V.D.; m. John A. Henkel, June 21, 1980 (div. 1991); children: Marissa Jane, Monica Rose. BS in Edn., Lesley Coll., 1975; postgrad., Sonoma State U., 1983; MEd in Ednl. Adminstrn., U. South Maine, 1992. Cert. prin., curriculum coord., tchr., Maine; cert. tchr., Mass. Therapeutic caregiver Creative Playmates, Inc., Arlington, Mass., 1971-73; with Mus. Transp., Brookline, Mass., 1974-75; tchr. Beginning Sch., Marin City, Calif., 1975-77; ungraded primary tchr. West Marin Sch., Pt. Reyes Station, Calif., 1977-84, chair sch. site coun., 1981-83; early edn. specialist Maine Dept. Edn., Augusta, 1985-93, mgr. divsn. curriculum, 1986-93; coord. Project SEED Maine Ctr. for Ednl. Svcs., Auburn, 1993—; mem. restructuring cadre Maine Ctr. for Ednl. Svcs., 1991—; founding dir. Maine Child & Family Enterprise, Augusta, 1992—; cons. Waterville (Maine) Regional Vocat. Ctr., 1993—; mem. Spl. Commn. Early Edn. & Care, Augusta, 1988-89; chair delegation Surgeon Gen.'s Conf. on Healthy Children, Augusta, 1992. Co-author: Beyond Tinkering to Transformation, 1992, Big Book for Educators, 1988. Organizer children's programs Peace Action Nat. Congress, Portland, 1994—; bd. dirs. New Beginnings, Inc., Lewiston, Maine, 1994—, Trout Found., 1994—; active Puente de Amor, Durham, Maine, 1994—. Mem. New England Coun. Ednl. Leaders, Maine Assn. Supervision and Curriculum Devel., Nat. Assn. for Edn. Young Children, Durham Monthly Meeting. Democrat. Quaker. Home: Rt 2 Box 4650 Bowdoinham ME 04008 Office: Maine Ctr Ednl Svcs 223 Main St Auburn ME 04212

VANDEVELDE, AGNES ANN, tax preparer; b. Carleton, Mich., Feb. 1, 1931; d. August John and Lena Eliza (Rivard) Wickenheiser; m. Oscar Maurice Vandevelde, May 1, 1954; children: Irene M., Edward J., Amy T., Nancy C., Martin G., Dennis J., Charles A., William P. Student, various tax insts. Bookkeeping clk. Monroe (Mich.) Pub. Co., 1950-54, 78-87; tax vol. Monroe Sr. Citizens, 1988—; tax preparer in pvt. practice, Monroe, 1990—. Vol., Ret. Srs. Vol. Program, Monroe, 1987—. Mem. Belgian-Am. Club, Monroe Sr. Citizens (pres. 1989-90). Democrat. Roman Catholic. Home: 3293 N Otter Creek Rd Monroe MI 48161-9576

VAN DEVELDE, CAROLYN, special education educator; b. Morristown, N.J., July 27, 1962; d. William Ray and Sophie (Morgello) Van D. BA in Spl. Edn., Kean Coll., 1984. Cert. tchr. of the handicapped, N.J. Tchr. resource rm. Red Bank (N.J.) Mid. Sch., 1984-85, tchr. self contained NI, 1985-87; tchr. Sandy Hook Residential Group Ctr., Divsn. Juvenile Svcs. N.J. Dept. Human Svcs., Ft. Hancock, 1987—; coach tournament of champions Red Bank Mid. Sch., 1984-87, home instrn. tchr., 1985-86. Mem. Comm. Worker Am. Home: 34 Steven Ave Eatontown NJ 07724 Office: Sandy Hook Residential Group Ctr 119 Hartshorne Dr Fort Hancock NJ 07732

VANDEVENDER, BARBARA JEWELL, elementary education educator, farmer; b. Trenton, Mo., Dec. 4, 1929; d. Raleigh Leon and Rose Rea (Dryer) S.; m. Delbert Lyle Vandevender, Aug. 15, 1948; children: Lyle Gail, James R. BS, N.E. Mo. State U., 1971, MA, 1973. Elem. tchr. Williams Sch., Spickard, Mo., 1948-49; reading specialist Spikard R-2 Sch., 1971-74, Princeton (Mo.) R-5 Sch., 1974-89; spkr. Mo. State Coun. of IRA, Columbia, 1987-89, Plains area IRA, 1988; mem. ad hoc com. Mo. State Dept. Edn., Jefferson City, 1994. Dir., writer Children's Drama, 1964-72, Comedy, 1967-68. Pres. Spickard PTA, 1963-64, Women's Ext. Club, Galt, Mo.; foster mother Family Svcs., Trenton, Mo., 1972-79. Recipient Mo. State Conservation award Goodyear Tire Co., Akron, Ohio, 1972, Balanced Farming award Gulf Oil Co., N.Y.C., 1972, Mo. State Farming award Kansas City C. of C., 1974, FHA State Farming award, Jefferson City, Mo., 1974, Outstanding Leadership Mo. U., Columbia, 1976, Ednl. Leadership award MSTA, Columbia, 1984, Outstanding Contbn. to Internat. Reading Assn., Newark, Del., 1988. Mem. Internat. Reading Assn. (pres. North Ctrl. coun. 1985-86). Republican. Baptist.

VANDEVENDER, DEBORAH ANN, critical care nurse; b. Syracuse, N.Y., Nov. 24, 1954; d. Charles Arthur and Patricia Ann (McGreevy) Kieffer; m. Robert Vandevender II, Sept. 26, 1992. BA in Biology, U. Toledo, 1980, BS in Nursing, 1983. RN, Ohio, N.Y., Pa., Ill., Calif.; cert. CCRN. Critical care nurse clinician III Toledo Hosp., 1977-89, St. Joseph Hosp., Syracuse, N.Y., 1989-91; critical care nurse II Brandywine Hosp., Coatsville, Pa., 1991; critical care nurse St. Therese Med. Ctr., Waukegan, Ill., 1991-93, Rush Northshore Med. Ctr., Skokie, Ill., 1993-94, St. Lukes Hosp., Davenport, Iowa., 1994—, Rush Northshore Med. Ctr., Skokie, Ill., 1994—. Nurse ARC, Toledo, 1988-89. With USN, 1972-77; lt. USNR, 1977—. Mem. AACN, Fractional Currency Collectors Bd., Smithsonian Inst. (assoc.), Nat. Trust for Hist. Preservation.

VAN DE WORKEEN, PRISCILLA TOWNSEND, small business owner and executive; b. Denver, July 9, 1946; d. Reginald and Ruth (Poor) Townsend; m. Melvin Charles Van de Workeen, Oct. 27, 1973. BA in Chinese History, Wheaton Coll., Norton, Mass., 1968; postgrad., Cornell U., 1965. Asst. dir. Nat. Info. Bur., N.Y.C., 1969-73; dep. dir. Harkness Fellowships, N.Y.C. and London, 1973-83; owner, mgr. Vernalwood Enterprises, Splty. and Custom Crafts, Dudley, Mass., 1984-93; co-owner, mgr. Vernalwood Bed & Breakfast, Dudley, 1989-93, Folkstone Bed & Breakfast Reservation Svc., Dudley, 1989-94; co-founder, chairperson Vernalwood Conceptual Enhancements, Dudley, 1991—. Tchr. quilting and needlework Chester Corbin Libr., Webster, Mass.; bd. dirs. Hubbard Regional Hosp. Guild, Webster, 1986-91, Internat. Ctr., Worcester, Mass., 1989-90; chair bd. trustees Pearle L. Crawford Libr., Town of Dudley, 1993—; coord. Nat. Coun. Internat. Visitors, Washington, 1989-90; founder, chmn. The Concordia Found., Dudley, 1992—. Mem. Tri-Cmty. Area C. of C., Webster Dudley Garden Club (bd. dirs.), The Tuesday Club (pres. 1994—). Democrat. Home and Office: Vernalwood Darling Rd Dudley MA 01571

VAN DEWOSTINE, KAREN LEE, accountant; b. Geneseo, Ill., Jan. 4, 1962; d. Melvin Carl and Lila Jean (Lambert) Becker; m. Denny Ray Van DeWostine, Sept. 25, 1981; children: Heather Marie, Logan Michael. AS, Sauk Valley Coll., 1986; BS in Acctg., No. Ill. U., 1988. CPA, Ill., Iowa. Paraprofl. Dennis Jokerst, CPA, Sterlins, Ill., 1986-88; sr. tax cons. Deloitte & Touche, Davenport, Iowa, 1988—. Mem. AICPA, Inst. Mgmt. Accts., Ill. CPA Soc. (membership chair Western chpt. 1991, 92, pub. rels. chair Western chpt. 1993). Lutheran. Home: 53 Rainbow Dr Bettendorf IA 52722 Office: Deloitte & Touche 101 W 2d St Davenport IA 52801

VANDIVER, PAMELA BOWREN, research scientist; b. Santa Monica, Calif., Jan. 12, 1946; d. Roy King and Patricia (Woolard) Evans; m. J. Kim Vandiver, Aug., 1968 (div. 1984); 1 child, Amy. BA in Humanities and Asian Studies, Scripps Coll., 1967; postgrad., U. Calif., Berkeley, 1968; MA in Art, Pacific Luth. U., 1971; MS in Ceramic Sci., MIT, 1983, PhD in Materials Sci. and Near Eastern Archeology, 1985. Instr. in glass and ceramics Mass. Coll. of Art, Boston, 1972; lectr. MIT, Cambridge, 1973-78, rsch. assoc., 1978-85; rsch. phys. scientist Conservation Analytical Lab., Washington, 1985-89; sr. scientist in ceramics C.A.L. Smithsonian Instn., Washington, 1989—; bd. dirs. Rolatape Corp., Spokane, Wash.; guest researcher Nat. Inst. Standards & Tech., Gaithersburg, Md., 1989-91. Co-author: Ceramic Masterpieces, 1986; co-editor: Materials Issues in Art and Archaeology, 1988, 2d edit., 1991, 3d edit., 1992; bd. editors Archeomaterials, 1986-93; contbr. numerous articles to profl. jours. Advisor Lexington (Mass.) Montessori Sch., 1980; camping leader Girl Scouts U.S., Alexandria, Va., 1985-88; sponsor mentorship program Thomas Jefferson High Sch. of Sci. and Tech., Alexandria, 1992. Recipient Disting. Alumna Achievement award Scripps Coll., 1993. Mem. AAAS, Am. Inst. Archeology, Soc. Am. Archeology, Internat. Inst. of Conservation, Soc. for History of Tech., Am. Ceramics Soc. (ancient ceramics com. 1978—), Materials Rsch. Soc. (guest editor bull. 1992), Am. Chem. Soc., Cosmos Club, Sigma Xi. Office: Smithsonian Inst Conservation Analytical Lab Washington DC 20560

VAN DOVER, KAREN, elementary school educator, curriculum consultant, language arts specialist; b. Astoria, N.Y.; d. Frederick A. and Frances L. (Thomas) Van D. BA, CUNY, 1969; MALS, SUNY, Stony Brook, 1973; postgrad., St. John's U., Jamaica, N.Y., 1992—. Cert. permanent N-6 tchr., art tchr. K-12, sch. adminstr., supr., N.Y. Tchr. St. James (N.Y.) Elem. Sch., 1969-77; tchr. Nesaquake Intermediate Sch., St. James, 1977-92, lead tchr. English, 1984-92; lead tchr. English Smithtown Mid Sch., St. James, 1992-93, curriculum specialist, 1993—; leader staff devel. and curriculum devel. workshops Smithtown Sch. Dist., 1984—, mem. supt.'s adv. com. for gifted and talented, mem. textbook selection coms., site-based mgmt. team, 1994—, mem. supt. adv. bd. for lang. arts assessment, 1994; mem. master tchr. bd. Prentice Hall, Englewood Cliffs, N.J., 1990—. Contbg. author: Prentice Hall Literature Copper, 1991. Corr. sec. Yaphank Taxpayers and Civic Assn., 1984-86, Nesaquake Sch. PTA, 1990-91, active, 1977-92. Mem. ASCD, Am. Ednl. Rsch. Assn., Am. Fedn. Sch. Adminstrs., Nat. Assn. Secondary Sch. Prins., Nat. Assn. Elem. Sch. Prins., Nat. Coun. Tchrs. English, Internat. Reading Assn., Nat. Middle Schs. Assn., N.Y. State English Coun., Phi Delta Kappa. Home: 8 Penn Commons Yaphank NY 11980-2025 Office: Smithtown Mid Sch 10 School Rd Saint James NY 11780

VAN DUSEN, DONNA BAYNE, corporate communication training consultant, researcher, educator; b. Phila., Apr. 21, 1949; d. John Culbertson and Evelyn Gertrude (Godfrey) Bayne; m. David William Van Dusen, Nov. 30, 1968 (div. Dec. 1989); children: Heather, James. BA, Temple U., 1984, MA, 1986, PhD, 1993. Instr. Kutztown (Pa.) U., 1986-87, Ursinus Coll., Collegeville, Pa., 1987-93; cons., rschr. Comm. Rsch. Assoc., Valley Forge, Pa., 1993—; rschr. Fox Chase Cancer Ctr., Pila., 1985-86; adj. faculty Temple U. Law Sch., 1994—, LaSalle U., 1994—, Wharton Sch., U. Pa., 1994—. Mem. NOW, Speech Comm. Assn., Ea. Comm. Assn. Home: 15 Shirley Rd Narberth PA 19072

VAN DUSEN, LANI MARIE, psychologist; b. Alexandria, Va., July 23, 1960; d. Arthur Ellsworth and Ann Marie (Brennan) Van D. BS magna cum laude, U. Ga., 1982, MS, 1985, PhD, 1988. Cert. secondary tchr., Ga. Tchr. Henry County Sch. System, McDonough, Ga., 1982-83; rsch. psychologist Metrica Inc., Bryan, Tex., 1988; asst. prof. psychology U. Ga., Athens, 1988-89, chmn. Conf. for Behavioral Scis., 1987; assoc. prof. psychology Utah State U., Logan, 1989—; cons. Western Inst. for rsch. and Evaluation, Logan, 1990—; bd. dirs. Human Learrning Clinic, Logan, 1990—; reviewer William C. Brown Pubs., 1990, Dushkin Pub. Group Inc., 1990-91. Contbr. articles to profl. jours. Fellow Menninger Found.; mem. APA, Psychonomic Soc., Am. Ednl. Rsch. Assn., AAUP, ASCD. Republican. Home: 435 E 1200 N Logan UT 84321-2421 Office: Utah State U Dept Psychology UMN 2810 Logan UT 84322-2810

VAN DUYN, MONA JANE, poet; b. Waterloo, Iowa, May 9, 1921; d. Earl George and Lora G. (Kramer) Van D.; m. Jarvis A. Thurston, Aug. 31, 1943. B.A., U. No. Iowa, 1942; M.A., U. Iowa, 1943; D.Litt. (hon.), Washington U., St. Louis, 1971, Cornell Coll., Iowa, 1972, U. No. Iowa, 1991, U. of the South, Sewanee, Tenn., 1993, George Wash. U., 1993; LHD, Georgetown U., 1993. Instr. in English U. Iowa, Iowa City, 1943-46; instr. in English U. Louisville, 1946-50; lectr. English Univ. Coll., Washington U., 1950-67; poetry editor, co-pub. Perspective, A Quar. of Lit., 1947-67; lectr. Salzburg (Austria) Seminar Am. Studies, 1973; adj. prof. poetry workshop Washington U., Spring 1983; vis. Hurst prof., 1987; poet-in-residence Sewanee Writers Conf., 1990, Breadloaf Writing Conf., Mass., 1974. Author: Valentines to the Wide World, 1959, A Time of Bees, 1964, To See, To Take, 1970, Bedtime Stories, 1972, Merciful Disguises, 1973, Letters from a Father and Other Poems, 1983, Near Changes, 1990 (Pulitzer Prize in poetry 1991), Firefall, 1993, If It Be Not I, 1993. Recipient Eunice Tietjens award, 1956, Helen Bullis prize, 1964, 76, Harriet Monroe award, 1968, Hart Crane Meml. award, 1968, Borestone Mountains 1st prize, 1968, Bollingen prize, 1970, Nat. Book award, 1971, Sandburg prize Cornell Coll., 1982, Shelley Meml. prize Poetry Soc. Am., 1987, Lilly prize for poetry, 1989, Mo. Arts award, 1990, Golden Plate award Am. Acad. Achievement, 1992, Arts and Edn. Coun. St. Louis award, 1994; named U.S. Poet Laureate, 1992-93; grantee Nat. Coun. Arts, 1967, NEA, 1985; Guggenheim fellow, 1972. Fellow Acad. Am. Poets (chancellor 1985); mem. Nat. Acad. Arts and Letters (Loines prize 1976).

VAN DYCK, WENDY, dancer; b. Tokyo. Student, San Francisco Ballet Sch. With San Francisco Ballet, 1979—, prin. dancer, 1987—. Performances include Forgotten Land, The Sons of Horus, The Wonderer Fantasy, Romeo and Juliet, The Sleeping Beauty, Swan Lake, Concerto in d: Poulenc, Handel-a Celebration, Menuetto, Intimate Voices, Hamlet and Ophelia pas de deux, Connotations, Sunset, Rodin, In the Night, The Dream: pas de deux, La Sylphide, Beauty and the Beast, Variations de Ballet, Nutcracker, The Comfort Zone, Dreams of Harmony, Rodeo, Duo Concertant, Who Cares; performed at Reykjavik Arts Festival, Iceland, 1990, The 88th Conf. of the Internat. Olympic Com., L.A., 1984, with Kozlov and Co. Concord Pavilion; guest artist performing role Swan Lake (Act II), San Antonio Ballet, 1985, Giselle, Shreveport Met. Ballet, 1994; featured in the TV broadcast of Suite by Smuin. Office: San Francisco Ballet 455 Franklin St San Francisco CA 94102-4471*

VAN DYNE, MICHELE MILEY, information engineer; b. Harrisburg, Pa., Sept. 8, 1959; d. Joseph Lawrence Miley and Tina Theresa (Dudash) Smollack; m. David Franklin Buck, Aug. 8, 1981 (div. July 1984); m. David George Van Dyne, Sept. 9, 1989. BA in Psychology, U. Mont., 1981, MS in Computer Sci., 1985; postgrad., U. Kans., 1992—. Div. sr. tech. programmer, analyst Allied-Signal Aerospace, Kansas City, Mo., 1985-89; knowledge engr. United Data Svcs., Inc., United Telecom, Overland Park, Kans., 1989-90; pres. IntelliDyne, Inc., Kansas City, Mo., 1990—; cons. Comprehensive Devel. Ctr., Missoula, Mont., 1984; speaker Sigart, Kansas City, 1988; chmn. Expert-Systems-Kans. and Mo. (ESKaMo), 1990-92. Vol. Planned Parenthood Greater Kansas City, 1986. United Bldg. Ctrs. scholar, 1976. Mem. IEEE Computer Soc., Am. Assn. for Artificial Intelligence, Internat. Neural Network Soc., Instrnl. Tech. Network (steering com. 1990-92), Women in Tech. Network (steering com. 1990-91, chmn. pub. rels. com. 1991-92), Alpha Lambda Delta. Democrat. Episcopalian. Home and Office: 6040 Wornall Rd Kansas City MO 64113-1418

VANE, SYLVIA BRAKKE, anthropologist, cultural resource management company executive; b. Fillmore County, Minn., Feb. 28, 1918; d. John T. and Hulda Christina (Marburger) Brakke; m. Arthur Bayard Vane, May 17, 1942; children: Ronald Arthur, Linda, Laura Vane Ames. AA, Rochester Jr. Coll., 1937; BS with distinction, U. Minn., 1939; postgrad., Radcliffe U., 1944; MA, Calif. State U., Hayward, 1975. Med. technologist Dr. Frost and Hodapp, Willmar, Minn., 1939-41; head labs. Corvallis Gen. Hosp., Oreg., 1941-42; dir. lab. Cambridge Gen. Hosp., Mass., 1942-43, Peninsula Clinic, Redwood City, Calif., 1947-49; v.p. Cultural Systems Rsch., Inc., Menlo Park, Calif., 1978—; pres. Ballena Press, Menlo Park, 1981—; cons. cultural resource mgmt. So. Calif. Edison Co., Rosemead, 1978-81, San Diego Gas and Elec. Co., 1980-83, Pacific Gas and Elec. Co., San Francisco, 1982-83, Wender, Murase & White, Washington, 1983-87, Yosemite Indians, Mariposa, Calif., 1982-91, San Luis Rey Band of Mission Indians, Escondido, Calif., 1986-89, U.S. Ecology, Newport Beach, Calif., 1986-89, Riverside County Flood Control and Water Conservation Dist., 1985-95, Infotec, Inc., 1989-91, Alexander & Karshmer, Berkeley, Calif., 1989-92, Desert Water Agy., Palm Springs, Calif., 1989-90, Metropolitan Water Dist., Nat. Park Svc., 1992—. Author: (with L.J. Bean), California Indians, Primary Resources, 1977, rev. edit., 1990, The Cahuilla and the Santa Rosa Mountains, 1981, The Cahuilla Landscape, 1991; contbr. chpts. to several books. Bd. dirs. Sequoia Area coun. Girl Scouts U.S., 1954-61; bd. dirs., v.p., pres. LWV, S. San Mateo County, Calif., 1960-65. Fellow Soc. Applied Anthropology, Am. Anthropology Assn.; mem. Southwestern Anthrop. Assn. (program chmn. 1976-78, newsletter editor 1976-79), Soc. for Am. Archaeology. Mem. United Ch. of Christ. Office: Ballena Press 823 Valparaiso Ave Menlo Park CA 94025-4206

VAN EGMOND, CORALEE ANN, chiropractor, consultant; b. Grand Rapids, Mich., Jan. 30, 1955; d. Elmer Eugene and Margorie Grace (Steketee) Van E. BA, Smith Coll., 1977; D of Chiropractic, Palmer Coll., 1986. Cert. chiropractic examiner, Ky. Pub. info. coord., asst. editor Am. Running and Fitness Assn., Washington, 1978-81; crisis counselor Families and Children in Trouble (Parents Anonymous), Washington, 1978-80; editor-in-chief Beacon Alumni and Student Newspaper, Davenport, Iowa, 1984-85; rsch. work asst. diagnosis/pathology dept. Palmer Coll., Davenport, Iowa, 1984-86; faculty instr. Palmer Sch. Chiropractic Technicians, Davenport, Iowa, 1985-86; intern Strang Chiropractic Clinic, Davenport, Iowa, 1985-86; assoc. dr. Chiropractic Assocs. Ark., Little Rock, 1986-87, Darnall Chiropractic Offices, Stockton, Calif., 1987-88, Goben Chiropractic Offices, Louisville, 1989-93; staff dr. Sports and Performance Rehab. Facility, Louisville, 1993—; cons. to health ins. cos., Louisville, 1989—; bd. dirs. Ky. State Bd. of Chiropractic Examiners, 1994—. Author: Chiropractic in the Prevention and Management of Drug and Alcohol Abuse, 1993; contbr. rsch. papers to profl. confs. Pres. Kentuckiana Women's Network, Louisville, 199-94; bd. dirs., program com. chair S.W. YMCA, Louisville, 1993—. Named Hon. Order of Ky. Cols., 1994. Mem. Ky. Chiropractic Soc. (congrl. del. 1989-93, Pres.'s award 1991), Internat. Chiropractors Assn. (charter mem. pediatrics coun. 1992-93, exec. com. coun. sports and fitness health sci.), Am. Running and Fitness Coun. Clinic Advisors, Kiwanis Internat. (bd. dirs. 1989-93, pres. 1990-91), Delta Delta Alumni Assn. (v.p. 1991-93). Office: Breuer Sports & Perf Rehab 1810 Sils Ave Louisville KY 40205-2159

VANELLA, LISA A., public relations executive, business owner; b. Queens, N.Y., May 29, 1965; d. James Robert and Lucille Clair (Menna) Van Casteren; m. Anthony S. Vanella, Aug. 17, 1990. BS, St. John's U., Jamaica, N.Y., 1987. V.p. Robert Marston & Assocs., Inc., N.Y.C., 1987—; co-owner A & L Distbrs., Middle Village, N.Y., 1992—. Republican. Roman Catholic. Home: 62-48 Dry Harbor Rd Flushing NY 11379 Office: Robert Marston & Assocs Inc 485 Madison Ave New York NY 10022

VAN ESSEN, DENISE MARIE, psychologist; b. Balt., Dec. 6, 1955; d. Garrett John and Pauline Marie (Kantz) Van E. BA, Towson State U., 1978; MS, Johns Hopkins U., 1985; PhD in Clin. Psychology, Union Inst., 1990. Lic. clin. psychologist, N.C. Police agt. Balt. City Police Dept., 1979-88; mental health therapist Sexual Assault Recovery Ctr., Balt., 1987-91, Montgomery County Police Dept., Md., 1988-90; psychology assoc. Ea. Cmty. Mental Health, Balt., 1990-94; staff psychologist Roanoke-Chowan Human Svcs. Ctr., Ahoskie, N.C., 1994—; adj. faculty psychology instr. Essex C.C., Balt., 1994. Mem. APA. Democrat. Methodist. Office: Essex C C 7201 Rossville Blvd Baltimore MD 21237

VAN ETTEN, EDYTHE AUGUSTA, occupational health nurse; b. Arthur, N.D., Oct. 13, 1921; d. Lacy Edward and Emma Erna (Mundt) Roach; m. Robert Scott Van Etten, Feb. 12, 1944; children: Ronald, Cynthia Czernysz, Martin, Roger, Randall, Janet K. Diploma, Mt. Sinai Hosp. Sch. Nursing, Chgo., 1945; AS, Waubonsee Community Coll., Sugar Grove, Ill., 1978; BSN, No. Ill. U., 1981. Cert. occupational health nurse; RN, Ill. Occupation health relief nurse Barber-Greene Co., Aurora, Ill., 1965-82; occupational health relief nurse No. Ill. Gas Co., Naperville, Ill., 1983-85; supr. or staff nurse Michealsen Health Ctr., Batavia, Ill., 1982-93; occupational health relief nurse The Dial Corp., Montgomery, Ill., 1982—; occupational health nurse cons. AT&T Svc. Ctr., West Chicago, Ill., 1988—. Mem. adminstrv. bd. Ch. of the Good Shepherd Meth., Oswego, Ill., 1988—; active Fox Bend Ladies Golf League, United Meth. Women; mem. Lyric Opera of Chgo. Mem. Suburban Chgo. Assn. Occupational Health Nurses, Dist. 2 Ill. Nurses Assn. (del. state conv. 1985, Award for Excellence in Nursing Practice 1993), Sr. Svcs. Assn. Inc. (adv. 1983-87, Humanitarian award 1985), Oswegoland Women's Civic Club (bd. dirs. 1985—). Republican. Home: 427 S Madison St PO Box 1 Oswego IL 60543 Office: The Dial Corp 2000 Aucutt Rd Montgomery IL 60538

VAN FLEET, SHARON KAY, psychiatric nurse; b. Denver, Dec. 16, 1960. Student, Coe Coll., 1979-80; BS cum laude, U. Colo., Denver, 1984; MS in Psychiat.-Mental Health Nursing, U. Mich., 1990. Cert. psychiat.-mental health nurse. Staff nurse U. Chgo. Hosps., 1984-89; clin. nurse specialist psychiat. sect. M.D. Anderson Cancer Ctr., Houston, 1991—. Recipient Edith Galt Morgan Meml. award for outstanding grad. rsch. U. Mich., 1991; dean's fellowship, 1989-90. Mem. ANA, Tex. Nurses Assn., Oncology Nursing Soc., Alpha Omicron Pi. Home: 1800 El Paseo St Apt 1210 Houston TX 77054-3013 Office: MD Anderson Cancer Ctr Box 100 Dept Neuro-Oncology 1515 Holcombe Blvd Houston TX 77030-4009

VAN GASSE, JANICE MARTHA, school counselor; b. N.Y.C., May 1, 1951; d. Walter Thomas and mary Rebecca (Brookes) Porter; m. Randall Mark Van Gasse, July 14, 1984; children: Kristen Anne, Michael Porter. AB, U. Mich., 1973; MA, Ea. Mich. U., 1979. Lic. profl. elem. and secondary counselor, Mich. Tchr. Clinton (Mich.) Community Schs., 1973-90, counselor, peer advisor, testing coord., teenage inst. advisor, 1986—. Contbr. articles to profl. jours. Parent rep. Parent Adv. Com. ofr Spl. Edn., Adrian, Mich., 1991—. Named Counselor of Yr., Lenawee County Counselors Assn., 1991, Peer Advisor of Yr., Mich. South Ctrl. Substance Abuse Commn., 1991. Mem. Am. Sch. Counselors Assn. (assembly rep. 1994), Mich. Sch. Counselors Assn. (ethics chair 1989—, Mich. Counselor of Year award 1992), Mich. Counseling Assn. (ethics chair 1993—), Phi Delta Kappa. Home: 2559 Wilmoth Hwy Adrian MI 49221 Office: Clinton Community Schs 341 E Michigan Clinton MI 49236

VAN GELDER, TERESA ANN, insurance agency executive; b. Eau Claire, Wis., Jan. 19, 1946; d. Fred Harrison and Geneva (Cook) King; m. Richard Allen Van Gelder, Sept. 4, 1965; children: Stacy L., R. Aric. Student, Ins. Inst. Am., 1971-75. Sec. Eau Claire Ins. Agy., 1964-74, mgr., 1974-85; owner Van Gelder Ins. Agy., Inc., Eau Claire, 1985-94, Gustaveson-Van Gelder Assocs., Eau Claire, 1994—; mem. agts. adv. com. Fireman's Fund, 1977-80, Integrity's Agts. Adv. Coun., 1990-93, small bus. adv. com. to U.S. Congressman, Wis., 1981-91; mem. woman's fin. coun. Charter Bank, 1990—. Active 4-H, Eau Claire, 1979-84; pres. Eau Claire Child Passenger Safety Com., 1981-85. Mem. Ind. Ins. Agts., Ins. Women of Eau Claire (named Ins. Woman of Yr. 1982), Ind. Ins. Agts. of Wis. (named Com. Chairperson of Yr. 1985, Ins. Agt. of Yr. 1990, sec.-treas. 1993-94), Nat. Assn. Ins. Women. Republican. Lutheran. Home: RR 2 Box 127 Eau Claire WI 54703-9506 Office: Gustaveson Van Gelder Assoc PO Box 65 2645 Harlem St Eau Claire WI 54702

VAN GILDER, BARBARA JANE DIXON, interior designer, consultant; b. South Bend, Ind., Dec. 6, 1938; d. Vincent Alan and Wanda Anita (Rapell) Dixon Van Gilder; student Mich. State U.; postgrad. St. Mary's Coll., N.Y. Sch. Design, 1956-58; m. Erwin Delton Van Gilder, May 25, 1959; children: Eric Dalton, Marc David. Factory color cons. Smith-Alsop Paint Co., Terre Haute, Ind.; archtl. design cons., Mishawaka, Ind., 1956-58; residential-comml. designer, South Bend, Chgo., 1958-63; designer industrialized housing industry, Ga., Fla., Ind., Mich., Calif., 1962—; speaker seminars on career mitivation; design cons. Skyline Corp., Ind., Calif., Pa., 1962-66; v.p. design Treasure Chest Corp., Sturgis, Mich., 1969, also dir.; pres., dir. Sandpiper Art, Inc.; v.p. T.C.I. Ltd.; design cons. C.O. Smith Ind. Peachtree Housing, Moultrie, Ga., Nobility Homes, Ocala, Fla.; head merchandising and design Sandpiper Originals, clothing boutique, 1978-87; pres., owner mktg. design firm, 1987—; placement dir. specialized design mktg. STS Corp., South Bend, 1989—; currently pub. relations ofcl. Am. Mktg. Assn., adj. tchr. Lakeshore Sch. System. also coordinator trade show displays; nat. advt. rep. Studebaker-Packard Corp., Mercedes Benz, Clark Equipment, 1959-63; writer series on decorating for 2 Mich. newspapers, 1961-63; participant TV show Know Your Decorator, Calif. and Maine, 1962, 77. Officer Shoreham Village (Mich.) Bd. Zoning, 1960-63; presenter sales mktg. seminars McBride Assocs.; pres. Design Mktg. Assocs., 1992—. cons. Internat. Housing and Internat. Univ. Exchange Program, London, Amsterdam, 1993-94. Named Woman of Yr., Profl. Model's Club; recipient 1st pl. furniture design hardwoods Nat. Hardwoods Assn., 1956; 1st pl. Best in Show award, Louisville, Atlanta, 1964-65, 66, 69, 70-74, 76; others. Mem. Design Council Industrialized Housing (award 1974), Nat. Soc. Interior Designers, Mich. State U. Alumni Assn., Internat. Platform Assn., Internat. Biog. Assn., Berrien Art Guild. Contbg. editor Skyliner mag., 1962-66; permanent guest editor, contbr. Today's Home mag., 1974—. Home: 3630 S

Lakeshore Dr Saint Joseph MI 49085-9260 Office: PO Box 244 Stevensville MI 49127-0244 also: PO Box 1100 Dunedin FL 34697-1100

VAN HORN, LECIA JOSEPH, legal secretary; b. L.A., Jan. 19, 1963; d. McKinley Joe and Opal Geneva (Ivie) Joseph; m. Philip Dale Van Horn, Apr. 19, 1986; children: Kari Christine, Brandon Joseph. BA in Journalism, U. Southern Calif., 1984. News reporter Sta. KSCR Radio, L.A., 1983; consumer news researcher Sta. KCBS-TV, L.A., 1983, Sta. KABC-TV, L.A., 1983-84; newswriter Headline News, Atlanta, 1984-85; editorial asst., newswriter, field producer Sta. KNBC-TV, Burbank, Calif., 1985-86; newswriter, assoc. producer Sta. WYFF-TV, Greenville, S.C., 1986; freelance newswriter, assoc. producer Sta. WSB-TV, Atlanta, 1987-88; newswriter CNN, Atlanta, 1987-94; legal sec. Columbia Heights, Minn., 1994—. Author: Thoughts and Inspirational Sayings, 1985; contbr. poetry and articles to newspapers. Mem. U. So. Calif. Alumni. Mem. Science of Mind.

VAN HOUSE, NANCY ANITA, library educator; b. Ogden, Utah, Aug. 3, 1950. AB, U. Calif., Berkeley, 1971, MLS, 1972, PhD, 1979. Reference libr. San Mateo County Libr., Belmont, Calif., 1972-75; coord. East Bay Info. Svc., Oakland, Calif., 1975-76; sr. rsch. assoc. King Rsch., Inc., Rockville, Md., 1979-81; asst. prof. U. Calif., Berkeley, 1981-87, assoc. prof., 1987-93, prof., 1993—, acting dean, 1991—. Author: Public Library User Fees, 1983; co-author: Output Measures for Public Libraries, 1987, Planning and Role-Setting for Public Libraries, 1987, Measuring Academic Library Performance, 1990, What's Good, 1993, Public Library Effectiveness Study, 1993; contbr. articles to profl. jours. Recipient Young Investigators award NSF; grantee NSF, 1984, U.S. Dept. Edn., 1987-88, 92-93. Mem. ALA, Assn. for Libr. and Info. Sci. Edn. (rsch. award 1983, 84). Office: U Calif Sch Libr & Info Studies Berkeley CA 94720-4600

VAN HOUTEN, ELIZABETH ANN, corporate communications executive; b. Washington, Feb. 22, 1945; d. Raymond R. and Marian Edna (Hovemann) Van H. BA, Mary Washington Coll., 1966. Analyst U.S. Gov., Washington, 1966-68; dep. chief of publs. Found. for Coop. Housing, Washington, 1968-72; editor Nat. League of Savs. Inst., Washington, 1972-76; dir. pub. relations Fed. Nat. Mortgage Assn., Washington, 1976-83; v.p. communications & investor relations Sallie Mae (Student Loan Mktg. Assn.), Washington, 1983-93; v.p. corp. and investor rels. Sallie Mae, Washington, 1993—. Apptd. by city coun. to Master Plan Task Force, Alexandria, Va., 1987-92; chmn. emeritus Liz Lerman Dance Exch.; mem. campaign com. for Del Pepper, Alexandria, 1987; bd. dirs. Watergate of Alexandria, 1984-89, pres., 1988-89. Mem. Nat. Assn. Real Estate Editors (bd. dirs. 1970). Office: Student Loan Mktg Assn 1050 Thomas Jefferson St NW Washington DC 20007-3837

VAN HOVEN, MRS. JAY See VOIGHT, NANCY LEE

VAN HOWE, ANNETTE EVELYN, real estate agent; b. Chgo., Feb. 16, 1921; d. Frank and Susan (Linstra) Van Howe; m. Edward L. Nezelek, Apr. 3, 1961. BA in History magna cum laude, Hofstra U., 1952; MA in Am. History, SUNY-Binghamton, 1966. Editorial asst. Salute Mag., N.Y.C., 1946-48; assoc. editor Med. Econs., Oradell, N.J., 1952-56; nat. mag. publicist Nat. Mental Health Assn., N.Y.C., 1956-60; exec. dir. Diabetes Assn. So. Calif., L.A., 1960-61; corp. sec., v.p., editor, pub. rels. dir. Edward L. Nezelek, Inc., Johnson City, N.Y., 1961-82; realtor, broker, Ft. Lauderdale, 1980—; mgr. condominium, Fort Lauderdale, Fla., 1982-83; dir. Sky Harbour East Condo, 1983-88; substitute tchr. high schs., Binghamton, N.Y., 1961-63. Editor newsletters Mental Health Assn., 1965-68, Unitarian-Universalist Ch. Weekly Newsletter, 1967-71. Bd. dirs. Broome County Mental Health Assn., 1961-65, Fine Arts Soc., Roberson Ctr. for Arts and Scis., 1968-70, Found. Wilson Meml. Hosp., Johnson City, 1972-81, White-Willis Theatre, 1988—, Found. SUNY, Binghamton, mem., 1991—; mem. Fla. Women's Alliance, 1989—; v.p. Fla. Women's Polit. Caucus, 1989-92; chair Women's History Coalition, Broward County, 1986—; pres. Fla. Women's Consortium, 1989-92; trustee Broome Community Coll., 1973-78; v.p. Broward County Commn. on Status of Women, 1982-93; bd. dirs. Ft. Lauderdale Women's Coun. of Realtors, 1986-88, Broward Arts Guild, 1986; grad. Leadership Broward Class III, 1985, Leadership Am., 1988; trustee Unitarian-Universalist Ch. of Ft. Lauderdale, 1982-89; mem. adv. bd. Planned Parenthood, 1991-93; pres. Broward Alliance of Planned Parenthood, 1993-94; sec. Nat. Women's Conf. Com., 1994—; bd. dirs. Nat. Women's Party, 1987-93. Named Feminist of Yr., Broward County, 1987; Women's Hall of Fame, Broward County, 1992. Mem. AAUW (legis. chair Fla. divsn. 1986-87, chair women's issues 1989-94), NAFE, Am. Med. Writers Assn., LWV (bd. dir. Broome County 1969-70), Alumni Assn. SUNY Binghamton (bd. dir. 1970-73), Fla. Bar Assn. (grievance com. 1991-94), Am. Acad. Polit. and Social Sci.Broward Women's Alliance, Broward County Voice for Choice (v.p.), Am. Heritage Soc., Nature Conservancy, Nat. Hist. Soc., Symphony Soc., Pacers, Zonta, Alpha Theta Beta, Phi Alpha Theta, Phi Gamma Mu, Binghamton Garden Club, Binghamton Monday Afternoon Club, Acacia Garden Club (pres.), 110 Tower Club, Tower Forum Club (bd. dirs. 1989—), Downtown Coun., Ft. Lauderdale Woman's Club. Home: 2100 S Ocean Dr Fort Lauderdale FL 33316-3806 Office: 1010 E Las Olas Blvd Fort Lauderdale FL 33301-2314

VANIMAN, JEAN ANN, manufacturing executive; b. Huntsville, Ala., Dec. 3, 1960; d. Jerold L. and Janis (Taylor) V. BSChemE, U. Ala., Tuscaloosa, 1984; MBA, Utah State U., 1989. Rsch. analyst dept. chem. engring. U. Ala., 1983-84; process engr. Rsch. & Devel. Lab. Morton Thiokol Corp., Brigham City, Utah, 1984-86; program mgr. Trident Strategic Programs, 1986-88; program mgr. advanced launch vehicle ops. Morton Thiokol, Inc., Brigham City, Utah, 1988-89; program mgr. space shuttle program Thiokol Corp., Huntsville, 1989-91; participant exec. Leadership Program Thiokol Corp., Brigham City, Utah, 1991-94; program mgr. Thiokol Yellow Creek Nozzle Divsn., Iuka, Miss., 1994—; dir. Thiokol Recreation Coun., 1989—. Vol. counselor Huntsville Crisis Line; vol. Utah Mus. Natural History, 1992—. Mem. NAFE, Am. Inst. Chem. Engrs., Capstone Engring. Soc. (bd. dirs.), Am. Mgmt. Assn., Soc. Women Engrs., Tau Beta Pi Alumni Assn., Chi Omega Alumni Assn. Home: 211 Meadowcrest Dr Florence AL 35630 Office: Thiokol Corp Nozzle Divsn 1 NASA Dr Bldg 1000 Luka MS 38852

VANLEEUWEN, LIZ SUSAN (ELIZABETH VANLEEUWEN), state legislator, farmer; b. Lakeview, Oreg., Nov. 5, 1925; d. Charles Arthur and Mary Delphia (Hartzog) Nelson; B.S., Oreg. State U., 1947; m. George VanLeeuwen, June 15, 1947; children—Charles, Mary, James, Timothy. Secondary sch. and adult tchr., 1947-70; news reporter, feature writer The Times, Brownsville, Oreg., 1949—; co-mgr. VanLeeuwen Farm, Halsey, Oreg.; mem. Oreg. Ho. of Reps., 1981—; mem. Western States Forestry Legis. Task Force, Pacific Northwest Econ. Region; weekly radio commentator, 1973-81. Mem. E.R. Jackman Found., PTA, sch. adv. com.; precinct committeewoman; founder, apptd. spl. advs. Linn County Ct.; mem. regional strategies bd. Linn County Commn. on Children and Families. Recipient Outstanding Service award Oreg. Farm Bur., 1975, Oreg. Farm Family of Yr. award, 1983; Chevron Agrl. Spokesman of Yr. award, 1975. Mem. Oreg. Women for Agr. (pres.), Oreg. Women for Timber, Linn-Benton Women for Agr. (pres.), Linn County Farm Bur., Am. Legion (aux.), Linn County Econ. Devel. Com., Grange, Am. Agri-Women. Republican. Office: H-291 Capitol Bldg Salem OR 97310

VAN LONE-TRIESCHMAN, JANET ANNE, art educator; b. Huntington, N.Y., Oct. 27, 1963; d. Ross Bowering and Anne Katherine (Feder) Van L. BA, Purdue U., 1985; MFA in Graphic Design, Ind. U., 1991. Graphic designer Boehringer Mannheim Diagnostics, Indpls., 1985; freelance graphic designer Indpls., 1985-91, IMS/Visions, Indpls., 1985-86, Matrix Photographic Labs., Indpls., 1986-90; grad. asst. Ind. U., Bloomington, 1988-90, grad. instr., 1990-91; asst. prof. Art Acad. of Cin., 1991-94, Md. Coll. Art and Design, 1994—; design editor Incliner Mag., 1991-94; dir. Acad. Design Svc., 1992-93. Active student exhibit Indpls. Art League, 1989, MFA Exhibit, Bloomington, 1990, Women Artist's Invitational, Bloomington, 1990-91, Evansville Mus. Art & Sci., 1991; mem. Cin. Art Mus., Coll. Art Assn., Fig-Fiber Interest Group, Cin. Letterpress Group. Rosenthal scholar, 1990; recipient Potlatch Award of Excellence, 1994, 9th Ann. Admissions Advt. award, 1994. Mem. Soc. Typographic Artists, Graphic Design Edn. Assn., Nat. Soc. Arts and Letters, Smithsonian Instn., Graphic Design Club (treas. Bloomington chpt. 1988-89), Alpha Delta Pi (corr. sec. 1984-85). Home: 1010 Broderick Ct Crofton MD 21114 Office: Md Coll Art and Design 10500 Georgia Ave Silver Springs MD 20902

VAN MATRE, JOYCE DIANNE, rehabilitation nurse; b. Bklyn., June 1, 1943; d. Gerard Thibault and Helene Clara (Wright) Hair; m. Richard Givens Van Matre, Aug. 27, 1965; children: Kimberly, Karyn, Richard. Diploma in Nursing, Gordon Keller Sch. Nursing, 1964; BS in Health Arts, Coll. of St. Francis, 1990. Cert. ins. rehab. specialist, Fla., rehab. svc. provider, Ga., rehab. provider; cert. case mgr. Case supr. rehab. Vocat. Placement Svcs., Tampa, Fla., 1980-81; RN mgr. Always Care Nursing Svc., Tampa, 1981-82; staff nurse Vis. Nurse's Assn., Tampa, 1983-84; rehab. coord. Underwriter's Adjusting Co., Tampa, 1984-85; pres. of corp., case mgr., supr., bus. owner Ind. Group Consultants, Inc., Brandon, Fla., 1985-90; case mgr. Sullivan Health & Rehab. Mgmt., Inc., St. Petersburg, Fla., 1991-92; rehab. nurse Liberty Mut. Ins. Co., Tampa, 1992—. Recipient Disting. Acad. Achievement award Coll. of St. Francis, 1991. Mem. ANA, Assn. Rehab. Nurses, West Coast Regional Case Mgr. Assn. Office: Liberty Mut Ins Co 3350 Buschwood Park Dr Tampa FL 33618-4451

VANMEER, MARY ANN, publisher, writer, researcher; b. Mt. Clemens, Mich., Nov. 22; d. Leo Harold and Rose Emma (Gulden) VanM.; stepmother Ruth (Meek) VanM. Student Mich. State U., 1965-66, 67-68, Sorbonne U., Paris, 1968; BA in Edn., U. Fla., 1970. Pres. VanMeer Tutoring and Translating, N.Y.C., 1970-72; freelance writer, 1973-79; pres. VanMeer Publs., Inc., Clearwater, Fla., 1980-88, VanMeer Media Advt., Inc., Clearwater, 1980-88; exec. dir., founder Nat. Ctrs. for Health and Med. Info., Inc., Clearwater, 1987-88, Nat. Health and Med. Info. Ctr., Palm Beach, Fla., 1990-93; pres., CEO Traveling Free Publs., Inc., 1993—. Author: Traveling with Your Dog, U.S.A., 1976, How to Set Up A Home Typing Business, 1978, Freelance Photographer's Handbook, 1979; See America Free, 1981, Free Campgrounds, U.S.A., 1982, Free Attractions, U.S.A., 1982, VanMeer's Guide to Free Attractions, U.S.A., 1984, VanMeer's Guide to Free Campgrounds, 1984, The How to Get Publicity for Your Business Handbook, 1987, Asthma: The Ultimate Treatment Guide, 1991, Allergies: The Ultimate Treatment Guide, 1992, Cancer: The Ultimate Treatment Guide, 1993, The Thrifty Traveler, 1995; pub. Nat. Health and Med. Trends Mag., 1986-88, Thrifty Traveler Newsletter, 1993—. Pub. info. chairperson, bd. dirs. Pinellas County chpt. Am. Cancer Soc., Clearwater, 1983-84, 86-88; mem. fin. devel. com. ARC, Palm Beach County, 1990-92. Mem. Am. Booksellers Assn., PACT (Performing Arts, Concert, and Theatre), Author's Guild. Office: Traveling Free Publs Inc PO Box 8168 Clearwater FL 34618

VANMETER, VANDELIA L., library director; b. Seibert, Colo., July 17, 1934; d. G.W. and A. Pearl Klockenteger; m. Victor M. VanMeter, Jan. 21, 1954; children: Allison C., Kristopher C. BA, Kansas Wesleyan U., 1957; MLS, Emporia State U., 1970; PhD, Tex. Woman's U., 1986. Cert. libr. media specialist. Tchr. Ottawa County Rural Sch., Kans., 1954-55; social scis. tchr. McClave (Colo.) High Sch., 1957-58, Ellsworth (Kans.) Jr. High Sch., 1959-68; libr., media specialist Ellsworth (Kans.) High Sch., 1968-84; asst. prof. libr. sci. U. So. Miss., Hattiesburg, 1986-90; chair dept. libr./info. sci. Spalding U., Louisville, 1990—, libr. dir., 1991—; cons. to sch., pub. and spl. librs., Kans., Miss., Ky., 1970—; mem. Ky. NCATE Bd. Examiners. Author: American History for Children and Young Adults, 1990, World History for Children and Young Adults, 1992; editor: Mississippi Library Media Specialist Staff Development Modules, 1988, Library Lane Newsletter, 1991—; contbr. chpts. to books; contbr. articles to profl. jours. Active City Coun., Ellsworth, Kans., 1975-79, Park Bd., Ellsworth, 1975-79; bd. dirs. Robbins Meml. Libr., 1977-79. Grantee Kans. Demonstration Sch. Libr., 1970-72, Miss. Power Found., 1989; named Women of Yr. Bus. and Profl. Women of Ellsworth, Kans., 1976. Mem. ALA, Am. Assn. Sch. Librs., Nat. Assn. State Ednl. Media Profls., Assn. Coll. & Rsch. Librs., Ky. Libr. Assn., Ky. Sch. Media Assn., Ky. Assn. Tchrs. Educators, Assn. for Libr. and Info. Sci. Educators. Office: Spalding U Libr 851 S 4th St Louisville KY 40203-2115

VAN NESS, LOTTYE GRAY, author, genealogist; b. Clarksville, Tenn., Nov. 14, 1925; d. Charles Robert and Willie (Murphy) Gray; m. Robert Parmelee Van Ness, Jan. 3, 1947; 1 child, Marc Robert. Student, Austin Peay State U., 1946, Murray State U., 1963. Civilian sec. U.S. Army, 1944-48; mgr. Associated Underwriters, Inc., Louisville, 1948-51; exec. sec. to the pricing dir. Reynolds Metals Co., Louisville, 1951-53; instr. classes on genealogy, Paducah, Ky., 1962-64, Louisville, 1970. Author: The Van Ness Heritage and Allied Genealogies, 1960, The Cookie Connection, 13th rev. edition, 1992; newspaper poetry columnist, 1947-48. Cookbook judge various orgns., Louisville, 1986. Named to hon. Ky. Col., 1978. Mem. Nat. Soc. So. Dames of Am., Northfield Garden Club (v.p. 1976-77, various chairmanships), Filson Hist. Club, United Daus. of Confederacy, Beta Sigma Phi. Republican. Episcopalian. Home: 6644 Foxdale Cir Colorado Springs CO 80919-1778

VAN NESS, PATRICIA CATHELINE, composer, violinist; b. Seattle, June 25, 1951; d. C. Charles and Marjorie Mae (Dexter) Van N.; m. Wendell James Ketcham, Dec. 16, 1972 (div. 1977); m. Adam Sherman, June 26, 1983. Student in music, Wheaton (Ill.) Coll., 1969-70; student, Gordon Coll., 1972. Composer: ballet score for Beth Soll, 1985, 87, 94, for Monica Levy, 1988, for Boston Ballet, 1988, 90, for Charleston Ballet Theatre, 1994; music scored for voices and early instruments; text translated into Latin for Evensong, 1991, Five Meditations, 1993, Cor Mei Cordis, 1994, Lament, 1995; various scores, 1985, 86, 87, 88; rec. violinist A&M Records, Private Lightning. Grantee Mass. Cultural Coun., 1993, New Eng. Biolabs. Found., 1989, Mass. Arts Lottery Coun., 1988; recipient Spl. Recognition award Barlow Internat. Composition for Evensong, 1993. Mem. Am. Women Composers, Am. Music Ctr.

VAN NIMAN, CYNTHIA MARIE, family physician, artist; b. Cin., Feb. 5, 1958; d. Kempton Charles and Colette Catherine (Ast) Van N.; m. Daniel John Wissel, July 27, 1980 (div. Oct. 1985); children: Catherine Marie, Stephanie Ann. Diploma in German studies, U. Vienna, Ströbl, Austria, 1978; BA summa cum laude, Edgecliff Coll., Cin., 1980; MA in Art Therapy, Wright State U., 1983, MD, 1991. Diplomate Am. Bd. Med. Examiners, Am. Bd. Family Practice; cert. ACLS, pediatric advanced life support, ATR. Reservationist Gogo Tours, Cin., 1975-81; primary tchr. German, St. Agnes Sch., Cin., 1977-78; asst. counselor Living Arrangements for Developmentally Disabled, Cin., 1977-78; art therapist U. Cin. Med. Ctr., 1983-87, Millcreek Psychiat. Ctr. for Children, Cin., 1987; resident in family practice St. Elizabeth Med. Ctr., Dayton, Ohio, 1991-94; mem. staff Clinton Meml. Hosp., Wilmington, Ohio, 1994-95; pvt. practice Beavercreek, Ohio, 1995—; pvt. practice Ohio Valley Family Physicians, Hillsboro, Ohio, Sabina, Ohio; keynote speaker Assn. for Edn. Young Children, Cin., 1987. One-woman show Emery Art Gallery, Cin., 1980. Judge Montgomery County Sci. Fair, 1988. Acad. presdl. and German studies scholar, 1976, activity scholar Edgecliff Coll., 1978, grad. scholar Wright State U., 1982, Cornaro scholar, 1990. Mem. Am. Acad. Family Practice, Ohio Med. Assn., Montgomery County Med. Assn., Chi Sigma Iota, Kappa Gamma Pi, Psi Chi. Roman Catholic. Office: Forest View Family Practice 1911 N Fairfield Rd Dayton OH 45432

VAN NORTWICK, BARBARA LOUISE, librarian, social science educator; b. Johnson City, N.Y., Jan. 3, 1940; d. Joseph John and Mary Louise (Hamzik) Goodwin; m. David Harry Van Nortwick, Nov. 17, 1962; children: Kimberly Lynn, Craig Michael. BA, Harpur Coll., 1961; MLS, State U. N.Y. at Albany, 1976; DA Info./Library Adminstrn. (U.S. Govt. Title II B fellow in library adminstrn.), Simmons Coll., Boston, 1986. Coord. ednl. facilities Maine-Endwell H.S., Endwell, N.Y., 1961-64; tchr. English, Guilderland H.S. (N.Y.), 1965-66; audiovisual libr. So. Colonie (N.Y.) H.S., 1974-76; head libr. Westfield (Mass.) H.S., 1976-78, Columbia H.S., East Greenbush, N.Y., 1978-79; libr. dir. N.Y. State Nurses Assn., 1979-84; dir. Com. Aging and Subcom. librs. N.Y. State Senate, 1983-84, dir. Select Com. Interstate Coop., 1985-89; assoc. prof. govt. documents and social scis. Skidmore Coll., Saratoga Springs, N.Y., 1989-94; libr. New Lebanon (N.Y.) Jr./Sr. High Sch., 1994—; del. Mass. Gov.'s Conf. Libraries and Info. Services, 1978-79; trustee Capital Dist. Libr. Coun., 1990—; cons. HEW grant on self-directed continuing edn. for nurses; prof. Sch. Library and Info. Sci., SUNY-Albany, 1983-84; mem. editorial bd. Coll. and Undergrad. Librs. Jour., 1992-94. Mem. ALA, N.Y. Libr. Assn., Med. Libr. Assn. Methodist. Home: RR 1 Box 292 Nassau NY 12123-9723 Office: Skidmore Coll Lucy Scribner Libr Saratoga Springs NY 12866

VAN NOSTRAND, CATHARINE MARIE HERR, human resources development executive, writer; b. Dubuque, Iowa, June 17, 1937; d. King George and Julia Marie (Hansen) Herr; m. David Michael Van Nostrand, July 16, 1960; children: Laura Susan Van Nostrand Caviani, Catharine Louise, Maren Thyra. Student, Grinnell (Iowa) Coll., 1955-57; BA in Music Edn., U. Iowa, 1959; MA in Human Devel., St. Mary's Coll. of Minn., Winona, 1989. Music specialist Bound Brook, N.J. and Brookline, Mass., 1959-62; coord. music and worship First United Meth. Ch., St. Cloud, Minn., 1970-75; founder, prin. cons. Catharine Van Nostrand & Assocs., St. Cloud, 1975—; guest lectr., author-in-residence nat. colls. and univs., regional, statewide, nat. and internat. acad. symposia, 1975—; tng. and devel. cons. numerous bus., govt., health and ednl. orgns., 1975—; keynote speaker and workshop facilitator regional and nat. confs. and convs., 1987—. Author: Gender-Responsible Leadership: Detecting Bias, Implementing Interventions, 1993; contbr. articles to profl. jours. Capt. prof. div. fundraising for area family YMCA, St. Cloud, 1975; founding bd. dirs. St. Cloud Civic Orch.; vol. radio interviewer Minn. Pub. Radio and WJON Radio, Collegeville/St. Cloud, 1976-77. Mem. AAUW, Forum Exec. Women, Nat. Spkrs. Assn., Minn. Spkrs. Assn., St. Cloud Area Tng. and Devel. Group, St. Cloud Area C. of C. Democrat. Methodist. Home: 36854 Winnebago Rd Saint Cloud MN 56303-9657 Office: 14 7th Ave N Saint Cloud MN 56303-4766

VAN NOTTEN, HENRIETTE DIGNA ALBERTINA WINTHROP, diplomat; b. N.Y.C., Aug. 10, 1962; came to U.S., 1992; d. Marinus Michiel and Henriette Albertina (van Roijen) van N.; m. Reindert Carl Francis Eduard Houben, Aug. 28, 1993. BA, Georgetown U., 1984; MA, U. Leiden, The Netherlands, 1988. Staff mem. bd. Leiden U., 1988; press agt. European Parliament Netherlands Info. Office, The Hague, 1989; staff mem. Ministry of Fgn. Affairs, The Hague, 1990-92; second sec. Netherlands Embassy, Washington, 1992—. Home: 5542 Nevada Ave NW Washington DC 20015 Office: Netherlands Embassy 4200 Linnean Ave Washington DC 20008

VAN NOY, CHRISTINE ANN, executive assistant; b. Oakland, CA, Mar. 25, 1948; d. Julio Ceaser and Bernice Thelma (Rose) Lucchesi; m. David Craik Van Noy, July 10, 1971; children: James Allan, Joseph Julio. Student, U. Calif., Berkeley, 1971-73, U. Phoenix, 1994—. Exec. sec. Kaiser Permanente Med. Care Program, Oakland, 1966-76; owner Secret Closet Boutique, Moraga, Calif., 1972-82; owner, operator The Wordshop, Moraga, 1976-86; owner, cons. Van Noy & Assocs., Moraga, 1979—; exec. sec. to sr. v.p., regional mgr. Kaiser Permanente Med. Care Program, 1986-88, chmn., CEO, 1988—; instr. U. Calif., Santa Cruz, 1983-84, Diablo Valley Coll., Concord, Calif., 1984; cons. Nat. Alliance Homebased Businesswomen, San Francisco, 1981-84. Author: Homebased Business Guide, 1982, (with others) Women Working Home, 1982. Mem. bd. Joaquis Moraga Sch. Dist., 1983-84, Calif. Federated Jr. Women's Clubs, 1972-77; bd. dirs. Orinda/Moraga Recreational Swimming Assn., 1984-85, St. Mark's United Methodist Ch., Moraga, 1983-84; pres. bd. Protect Our Nation's Youth Baseball Assn., 1987-90; dir. Ctr. for Living Skills, 1990—. Mem. Women Health Care Execs. Democrat. Roman Catholic. Home: 181 Paseo Del Rio Moraga CA 94556-1641 Office: Kaiser Permanente Med Program 1 Kaiser Plz Oakland CA 94612-3610

VANOCHTEN, MARJORIE MAE, lawyer, educator; b. Essexville, Mich., Feb. 6, 1944; d. Norbert Henry Sr. and Dorothy Esther (Wainwright) VanO.; 1 child, Andrew Martin Roth. BA in high distinction, U. Mich., 1968, JD, 1975. Bar: Mich. 1975. Staff atty. Legal Aid & Defender Assn., Grand Rapids, Mich., 1975-76; hearings officer Mich. Dept. State, Lansing, 1976-78; hearings adminstr. Mich. Dept. Corrections, Lansing, 1980-88, adminstr. Office Policy & Hearings, 1988—. Mem. editorial bd.: Correctional Law Reporter, 1989—; contbr. articles to profl. jours. Mem. Women Lawyers Assn. Mich., State Bar Prisons and Corrections Com., Phi Beta Kappa. Office: Mich Dept Corrections PO Box 30003 Lansing MI 48909-7503

VAN ORDEN, AMANDA KAY MITCHELL, insurance consultant; b. McAlester, Okla., Feb. 11, 1953; d. Fane LeRoy and Norma Evelyn (Magruder) Mitchell. BA magna cum laude, U. Utah, 1975. Registered health underwriter. V.p. Nirvana, Inc., Phoenix, 1978—. Vol. PHX Open, 1980—; vol. reader Sun Sounds, Phoenix, 1987—; pledge dr. vol. PBS, Tempe, Ariz., 1988—; vol. Spl. Olympics, Phoenix, 1988—; co-leader Daisy coun. Girl Scouts U.S.A., 1993. Mem. Health Care Choic Coalition (membership dir. 1993), Women Life Underwriters, Ariz. Employee Benefit Assn., Greater Phoenix Assn. Health Underwriters, Greater Phoenix Assn. Life Underwriters, Jr. League of Phoenix, Christian Bus. Women's Assn., Southwestern Women's Conf. (treas. 1991—), Phoenix Art Mus., U. Utah Alumnae (founding mem.), Chi Omega (treas. 1985-92). Republican. Mem. ChristianCh. Home: 10624 N 7th Pl Phoenix AZ 85020-5816 Office: Nirvana Inc 1240 E Missouri Ave Phoenix AZ 85014-2920

VAN ORMAN, JEANNE, planning consultant; b. N.Y.C., Apr. 9, 1939; d. Wayne and Jean (O'Gara) Van O.; m. Robert F. Brown, May 25, 1963 (div. 1975); children: Frank Van Orman Brown, Virginia Corbin Brown. BA, Smith Coll., 1961; M in City Planning, Harvard U., 1974. Land use planner Mass. Exec. Office of Communities and Devel., Boston, 1979-83, mgr. planning grants program, 1984-85, dir. strategic planning program, 1985-87; prin. Van Orman & Assocs., Easton, Mass., 1987—. Contbr. articles to profl. jours. Mem. Easton Charter Commn., 1971-72, mem. fin. com., 1982-83, libr. com., 1984-86, selectman, 1973-75, Mass. DPW Privitization Com. 1991—; bd. overseers Moses Brown Sch., Providence. Mass. Housing Partnership grantee, 1987, NEA grantee, 1981; recipient Disting. Svc. award, Jaycees, 1973. Mem. Am. Planning Assn. (exec. bd. Mass. sect.). Mem. Soc. of Friends. Home: 479 Bay Rd South Easton MA 02375-1424 Office: Harvard U Unit for Housing and Urbanization 48 Quincy St Cambridge MA 02138

VAN PATTEN, JOYCE BENIGNIA, actress; b. Bklyn.; d. Richard Byron and Josephine (Acerno) Van P.; divorced; children: T. Casey King, Talia Balsam. Appeared in Broadway plays including Loves Old Sweet Song, 1941, Tomorrow the World, 1943, The Perfect Marriage, 1944, Wind is Ninety, 1945, Desk Set, 1956, Hole in the Head, 1957, Same Time Next Year, 1975, Murder at the Howard Johnson, 1978, The Supporting Cast, Rumors, Brighton Beach Memoirs, I Ought To Be In Pictures, Jake's Women (with daughter Talia Balsam), 1992, L.A. prodn., 1993, (off Broadway plays) Ivanov, The Seagull, All My Sons, (films) Trust Me, Monkey Shines, St. Elmo's Fire, Falcon and the Snowman, Billy Galvin, Mame, Blind Date, Infinity (TV shows) The Haunted, Sirens, Under The Influence, Malice In Wonderland, First Lady of the World; (TV movie) Breathing Lessons; (TV series) Unhappily Ever After; writer (play) Donuts, (screenplay) Would You Show Us Your Legs Please?. Co-founder The Workshop Theatre West; fund raiser AIDS Project L.A., West Hollywood, 1989, 90. Mem. Am. Film Inst.

VAN PELT, FRANCES EVELYN, management consultant; b. Oregon, Ill., Aug. 25, 1937; d. Henry Benjamin and Bessie May (Himes) Ulferts; m. R. Richard Van Pelt, Oct. 28, 1953; children: R. Richard Jr., Robin F. Van Pelt Dobbs, Raymond Scott, Ronda Jean. Student, Waubonsee Coll., Sugar Grove, Ill., 1971-75. Adminstrv. asst. Sears, Roebuck & Co., Aurora, Ill., 1960-73; owner, mgr., pres. Outdoor World, Inc., Aurora, 1973-87; 20 group dir. Spader Mgmt. Groups, Inc., Sioux Falls, S.D., 1988—; bd. dirs. RV Consumer Care Commn., Fairfax, Va., 1985-88. Contbr. articles to profl. jours. Bd. dirs. Breaking Free, Aurora, 1988-90; cellist Fox Valley Symphony, Aurora, 1961-81. Mem. Aurora C. of C. Recrational Vehicle Dealers Assn. (bd. dirs. 1978-79, exec. bd. 1980-82, pres. 1983, chmn. bd. dirs. 1984), Ill. RV Dealers Assn. (pres., bd. dirs. 1978-79, exec. bd. 1980-82, pres. 1983, chmn. bd. dirs. 1984). Republican. Roman Catholic. Home: 1273 Colorado Ave Aurora IL 60506-2044 Office: PO Box M Sioux Falls SD 57101-1937

VAN PELT, JANET RUTH, insurance executive; b. Baltimore, Md., Jan. 28, 1948; d. John Francis and Helen Janet V. BA, Fla. State U., 1969, MA, 1972. Instr. Wayne State U., Detroit, Mich., 1971-72; promotion asst. Actors Theatre of Louisville, Ky., 1972-73; lecturer Towson State U., Towson, Md., 1973-75; workers' compensation Harry T. Campbell Sons'

Co., Towson, 1973-74; claims representative Atlantic Mutual Companies, Hunt Vly., Md., 1974-78; claims supr. Atlantic Mut. Cos., N.Y., 1978-79; home office claims examiner Atlantic Mutual Co., N.Y., 1979-88; supr. home office excess claims Am. Home Assurance Co., East Orange, N.J., 1988, sr. supr. home office excess claims, 1989-90; claims mgr. GRE Ins. Group, Princeton, N.J., 1990-92, Elliston, Inc., New Hope, Pa., 1992—. Mem. Assn. of Research and Enlightment, Holistic Health Assn. Democratic. Episcopalian. Office: Elliston Inc Buckingham House 9 Reeder Rd New Hope PA 18938-1015

VAN PELT, MEREDITH ALDEN, general and vascular surgeon; b. Lake Preston, S.D., June 22, 1923; s. Herman Earl and Pearl Glenn (Williams) Van P.; m. Margaret E. Springs, Nov. 9, 1947 (div. Feb. 1969); children: Gregory Alden, Sharman Louise Van Pelt Halloran, Susan Lee Van Pelt Lockett, Stephanie Lane Van Pelt Stemmark; m. Sheila Mae Kimball, July 19, 1969; 1 child, Stephen. BA, U. Iowa, 1943, MD, 1946; postgrad., U. Vienna, 1948. Diplomate Am. Bd. Surgery. Intern Good Samaritan Hosp., Cin., 1946-47; resident in surgery Swedish Med. Ctr., Seattle, 1949-53; asst. chief surgery VA Hosp., Fresno, Calif., 1953-55; pvt. practice gen. and vascular surgery San Rafael, Calif., 1955-92; surgeon, cons. San Quentin State Prison, San Rafael, 1989—; chief of surgery San Rafael Gen. Hosp., 1962-65, Terra Linda Valley Hosp., San Rafael, 1962-68; chief of gen. surgery Ross (Calif.) Gen. Hosp., 1987-88, Marin Gen. Hosp., San Rafael, 1964-65; commr. Calif. State Bd. Med. Examiners 1992—; instr. vascular surg. clinic U. Calif., San Francisco, 1957-69; civilian cons. in surgery U.S. Air Force, Hamilton Field, Calif., 1960-65. Capt. M.C., U.S. Army, 1947-49. Fellow ACS, Am. Coll. Angiology, Internat. Coll. Angiology; mem. AMA, Calif. Med. Assn., Marin Med. Soc., San Francisco Yacht Club (life). Episcopalian. Home: 14 Eucalyptus Belvedere CA 94920

VAN REENEN, JANE SMITH, speech-language pathologist; b. Baton Rouge, Sept. 16, 1949; d. William Robert and Mary Jane (Laidlaw) Smith; m. Dirk Andries van Reenen, Mar. 3, 1973; children: Andrea Lee, Erika Lynn. BS in Speech Pathology, La. State U., 1971; MEd in Speech Pathology, Ga. State U., 1984. Cert. clin. competence Am. Speech-Lang.-Hearing Assn.; lic. Ga.; cert. tchr. Ga. Speech-lang. pathologist Livingston Parish Schs., La., 1971-73, Gwinnett County (Ga.) Schs., 1973-75; pvt. practice speech-lang. pathology Norcross, Ga., 1995—; speech-lang. pathologist Nova Care, Atlanta, 1990—; grad. asst. Ga. State U., Atlanta, 1983-84, substitute clin. supr., 1988-90, interim clinic coord., 1991; speech-lang. pathologist Americana Nursing Home, Decatur, 1984; chairperson Atlanta (Ga.) Orofacial Myology Study Group, 1987-89; adv. com. Comm. Disorders Program, Atlanta, 1990-94; mem. Ga. Supervision Network, 1991—; mem. Cognitive Remediation Interest Group, Atlanta, 1993. Mng. editor: Internat. Jour. Orofacial Myology, 1989-91; contbr. articles to profl. jours. Ruling elder Northminster Presbyn. Ch., Roswell, Ga., 1981; mem. local sch. adv. com. Pinckneyville Middle Sch., Norcross, 1987-92, co-founder sch. based drug/alchol abuse prevention program, 1988; v.p. Parent Tchr. Student Assn. Norcross High Sch., 1990-91; pres. River Valley Estates Homeowners Assn., Norcross, 1991; local sch. adv. com. Norcross High Sch., 1993—, AIDS rep. PTSA, 1993—, drug/alcohol abuse rep., 1993—, care team, 1993—. Recipient Positive Parenting awards Ga. State Supt. of Schs., Atlanta, 1987-88, 88-89; named Outstanding Sch. Vol., Gwinnet County Bd. Edn., Lawrenceville, Ga., 1989-90. Mem. Am. Speech-Lang.-Hearing Assn. (congl. action contact com. 1991—), Ga. Speech-Lang.-Hearing Assn. (honors and ethics com. 1989-91), Internat. Assn. Orofacial Myology (mng. editor 1989-91). Republican. Home and Office: 3992 Gunnin Rd Norcross GA 30092

VANSANT, JOANNE FRANCES, academic administrator; b. Morehead, Ky., Dec. 29, 1924; d. Lewis L. and Dorothy (Greene) VanS. BA, Denison U., Granville, Ohio; MA, The Ohio State U.; postgrad., U. Colo. and The Ohio State U.; LLD (hon.), Albright Coll., 1975. Tchr., health and phys. edn. Mayfield, Kentucky High Sch., 1946-48; instr. Denison U., Granville, Ohio, 1948; instr. women's phys. edn. Otterbein Coll., Westerville, Ohio, 1948-52, assoc. prof., 1955-62, dept. chmn., 1950-62, chmn. div. profl. studies, 1961-65, dean of women, 1952-60, 62-64, dean of students, 1964-93, v.p. student affairs, 1968-93; v.p., dean student affairs emeritus, 1993—, cons. Instnl. Advancement, 1993—. Co-pres. Directions for Youth, 1983-84, pres., 1984-85; bd. dirs. North Area Mental Health; trustee Westerville Civic Symphony at Otterbein Coll., 1983-88; active numerous other community orgns.; ordained elder Presbyn. Ch., 1967. Named to hon. Order of Ky. Cols., 1957; recipient Focus on Youth award Columbus Dispath, 1983, Vol. of the Yr. award North Area Mental Health Svcs., 1982. Mem. Am. Assn. Counseling and Devel., Ohio Personnel and Guidance Assn., Ohio Assn. Women Deans, Adminstrs., Counselors (treas., exec. bd. 1972-73), Nat. Assn. Student Personnel Adminstrs., Ohio Coll. Personnel Assn., Mortar Bd. (hon.), Zonta Internat. (pres. Columbus, Ohio club 1984-85, dist. gov. 1988-90), Vocal Arts Resource Network (chair bd. dirs. 1994-96), Cap and Dagger Club, Torch and Key Hon., Order Omega, Alpha Lambda Delta, Theta Alpha Phi, others. Home: 9100 Oakwood Pt Westerville OH 43081-9643 Office: Otterbein Coll Instnl Advancement Westerville OH 43081

VAN SICE, PAMELA RAE, marriage, family, and child therapist; b. Burlington, Iowa, Feb. 23, 1951; d. Raymond King and Harriett Marie (Westfall) Sheldon; children: Jonathan Edward, Janette Marie. MusB, U. Arizona, 1973; MA in Marriage, Family and Child Counseling, Pacific Christian Coll., 1989. Lic. marriage, family, and child therapist. Tchr. music Mansfield Jr. High Sch., Tucson, 1974-77, Lake Havasa Jr. High Sch., Lake Havasa City, Ariz., 1981-85; marriage, family and child counselor, speaker Genesis Counseling Svc., San Bernardino, Calif., 1989-94, Riverside County Dept. Pub. Social Svcs. Author: Genesis Counseling Training Manual for Interns, 1994. Recipient 1st Pl. London Bridge Talent Contest, Lake Havasa City, 1984. Mem. Am. Assn. Christian Counselors, Calif. Assn. Marriage, Family and Child Counselors, Sigma Alpha Iota. Republican. Home: PO Box 4446 Crestline CA 92325-4446

VANSTROM, MARILYN JUNE, retired elementary education educator; b. Mpls., June 10, 1924; d. Harry Clifford and Myrtle Agnes (Hagland) Christensen; m. Reginald Earl Vanstrom, Mar. 20, 1948; children: Gary Alan, Kathryn June Vanstrom Marinello. AA, U. Minn., 1943, BS, 1946. Cert. elem. tchr., N.Y., Ill. Tchr. Pub. Sch., St. Louis Park, Minn., 1946-47, Deephaven, Minn., 1947-50, Chicago Heights, Ill., 1950-52, Steger, Ill., 1964; substitute tchr. Pub. Sch., Dobbs Ferry, N.Y., 1965-72, Yonkers, N.Y., 1965-92. Mem. Ch. Women, Dobbs Ferry Luth. Ch.; election supr. Town of Greenburgh, Elmsford, N.Y.; vol. Children's Village, Dobbs Ferry. Mem. AAUW (life, pres. 1988-90, Ednl. Found. award 1990), Westchester County Fedn. Women's Clubs Inc., Past Pres.'s Club of Westchester, Yonkers Fedn. Tchrs., U. Minn. Alumni Assn. Democrat. Home: 12300 Marion Ln W Apt 2105 Minnetonka MN 55305-1317

VAN SUETENDAEL, NANCY JEAN, physicist; b. Plainfield, N.J., Dec. 13, 1957; d. Robert Frederick and Jean Beck Malone; m. Richard Lee Van Suetendael, Apr. 20, 1984. BA, Albright Coll., 1980; MA, Montclair State Coll., 1985; AS in Physics, Brookdale C.C., Lincroft, N.J., 1989; BS in Applied Physics, Math., Richard Stockton State Coll. N.J. Cert. secondary edn. tchr. Engring. technician Sanders and Thomas, Inc., Jackson, N.J., 1983-85; quality assurance mgr. Orbiting Astron. Observatory, Inc., Lincroft, N.J., 1985-86; scientific researcher, writer Bell Comms. Rsch., Lincroft, 1986-87; software analyst, tester Concurrent Computer Corp., Lincroft, 1987-90; sr. ops. analyst, sr. mem. tech. staff, project mgr. Computer Resource Mgmt., Inc., Atlantic City, N.J., 1990—; tech. cons. FAA Task Force, Dallas-Ft. Worth Airport Capacity Design Team, Dallas-Ft. Worth and Atlantic City, 1991-92; field analyst, Windsor, Conn., 1989. Author: Software Quality Metrics, 1991, Parallel Processing Using E/SP, 1990, Stepping Through An E/SP Session Tutorials, 1990, others. Participant March of Dimes Walkathon, Freehold, N.J., 1972-76; del. Harlaxton Coll., Community Affairs, Grantham, Eng., 1978-79. Recipient grad. assistantship Montclair U., Upper Montclair, 1980-81, Outstanding Tech. Publ. award, Soc. Tech. Communicators, 1990. Mem. Am. Inst. Physics, FAA Flying Club, The Nature Conservancy. Home: 97 Water St Barnegat NJ 08005-2454 Office: Computer Resource Mgmt Inc FAA Tech Ctr Bldg 270 Atlantic City Internat Airport Atlantic City NJ 08405

VAN TUYL, KATHRYN URSULA LEACH, retired secondary educator; b. New Bethlehem, Pa., Jan. 10, 1909; d. Alonzo and Catherine (Hoelzel) Leach; m. George Henry Van Tuyl Jr., Aug. 10, 1933; children: George Henry III, John Steelman. BA, Bucknell U., 1930; postgrad., Columbia U., 1932. Permanent teaching cert. Tchr. Summerville (Pa.) High Sch., 1930-33; part time teaching various high schs., Pa., N.Y., 1946-55; part time substitute tchr. various high schs., Garden City, N.Y., 1955-65; real estate sales person Garden City (N.Y.) Realty, 1965-72; high sch. drama coach, newspaper coach, Pa., N.Y.; founder English in Action fgn. student group Adelphi U., Garden City. Sunday sch. tchr. McKeesport, Pa., Garden City, 1940-80. Recipient scholarship Bucknell U., Lewisburg, Pa., 1926. Mem. AAUW (various positions), PEO. Republican. Methodist. Home: 221 North Ave Lehigh Acres FL 33936-5143

VAN UMMERSEN, CLAIRE A(NN), university president, biologist, educator; b. Chelsea, Mass., July 28, 1935; d. George and Catherine (Courtovich); m. Frank Van Ummersen, June 7, 1958; children: Lynn, Scott. BS, Tufts U., 1957, MS, 1960, PhD, 1963; DSc (hon.), U. Mass., 1988, U. Maine, 1991. Rsch. asst. Tufts U., 1957-60, 60-67, grad. asst. in embryology, 1962, postdoctoral teaching asst., 1963-66, lectr. in biology, 1967-68; asst. prof. biology U. Mass., Boston, 1968-74; assoc. prof. U. Mass., 1974-86, assoc. dean acad. affairs, 1975-76, assoc. vice chancellor acad. affairs, 1976-78, chancellor, 1978-79, dir. Environ. Sci. Ctr., 1980-82; assoc. vice chancellor acad. affairs Mass. Bd. Regents for Higher Edn., 1982-85, vice chancellor for mgmt. systems and telecommunications, 1985-86; chancellor Univ. System N.H., Durham, 1986-92; sr. fellow New Eng. Bd. Higher Edn., 1992-93; sr. fellow New Eng. Resource Ctr. Higher Edn. U. Mass., 1992-93; pres. Cleve. (Ohio) State U., 1993—; cons. Mass. Bd. Regents, 1981-82, AGB, 1992—, Kuwait U., 1992-93; asst. Lancaster Course in Ophthalmology, Mass. Eye. and Ear Infirmary, 1962-69, lectr., 1970-93, also coord.; reviewer HEW; mem. rsch. team which established safety stds. for exposure to microwave radiation, 1958-65; participant Leadership Am. program, 1992-93. Mem. N.H. Ct. Systems Rev. Task Force, 1989-90; mem. New Eng. Bd. Higher Edn., 1986-92, mem. exec. com., 1989-92, N.H. adv. coun., 1990-92; chair Rhodes Scholarship Selection Com., 1986-91; bd. dirs. N.H. Bus. and Industry Assn., 1987-90, 90-93; governing bd. N.H. Math. Coalition, 1991-92; exec. com. 21st Century Learning Community, 1992-93; state panelist N.H. Women in Higher Edn., 1986-93; bd. dirs. Urban League Greater Cleve., 1993—, Great Lakes Sci. & Tech. Mus., 1993—, Cleve. Playhouse, 1994—, Greater Cleve. Growth Assn., Sci. & Tech. Coun. Cleve. Tomorrow, Ohio Aerospace; mem. Leadership Am. Class '93, Leadership Cleve. Class '95. Recipient Disting. Svc. medal U. Mass., 1979, Am. Cancer Soc. grantee Tufts U., 1960. Mem. Am. Coun. on Edn. (com. on self-regulation 1987-91), State Higher Exec. Officers (fed. rels. com., cost accountability task force, exec. com. 1990-92), Nat. Assn. System Heads (exec. com. 1990-92), Nat. Ctr. for Edn. Stats. (network adv. com. 1989-92, chair accreditation teams 1988—), New Eng. Assn. Schs. and Colls. (commn. on higher edn. 1990-93), Am. Soc. Zoologists, Soc. Devel. Biology, Greater Cleve. Round Table (bd. dirs.), 1986-92, Greater Cleve. Growth Assn. (mem. bd. dirs. 1993—), mem. Leadership Am. Class of '93, Cleve. Playhouse bd. trustees, 1994—, Phi Beta Kappa, Sigma Xi. Office: Cleve State Univ Rhodes Tower Euclid Ave at E 24th St Cleveland OH 44115

VAN VLEET, SUSAN ELLEN BASH, management consultant; b. Trenton, N.J., Dec. 10, 1946; d. Albert and Marion Bash; m. John Tyler Van Vleet, Feb. 10, 1979; children: Charles Tyler, Adam Joshua. BA in Sociology, Fairleigh Dickinson U., 1968; MSW, Rutgers U., 1974. Social worker Div. Youth and Family Svcs., Trenton, 1968-76; dir. govt. rels. Effectiveness Tng. Inc., Solano Beach, Calif., 1976-79; pres. Susan Van Vleet Cons., Inc., Denver, 1979—, V2 Cons., Inc., Englewood, Colo., 1992—. Mem. Calif. State Com. for Children and Youth, Sacramento, 1978-79; mem. pers. com. Temple Sinai, 1990-92; del. Women's Coalition Denver, 1991-92.. Mem. NASW, Nat. Foster Parent Assn., Nat. Coun. Jewish Women (life, bd. dirs. 1979—). Republican. Jewish. Office: Susan Van Vleet Cons Inc 6093 S Quebec St Ste 102 Englewood CO 80111-4543

VAN WAGNER, ELLEN, lawyer, educator; b. Chgo., Dec. 10, 1942; d. Paul David and Eleanor (Sullivan) Van W.; m. Burton Neal Genda, Mar. 27, 1964 (div.); children: Kevin Paul, Kelly Elan. BA, U. Ariz., 1964; MA, Calif. State U., L.A., 1971; JD, U. La Verne, 1984. Bar: Calif. 1984, U.S. Dist. Ct. (cen. dist.) Calif. 1985, U.S. Ct. Appeals (9th cir.) 1985. Tchr., adminstr. Baldwin Park (Calif.) Sch. Dist., 1965-81; ptnr. Rose, Klein & Marias, Pomona, Calif., 1985-94; prof. U. La Verne (Calif.) Coll. Law, 1987—. Writer, asst. editor U. La Verne Law Rev., 1981-83, editor-in-chief, 1983-84. Chmn. youth activities commn. City of Baldwin Park, 1971-81. Recipient Humanitarian and Svc. awards L.A. Human Rels. Commn., 1976, 77. Mem. Calif. Bar Assn., L.A. County Bar Assn., Ea. County Bar Assn., Phi Delta Theta. Home: PO Box 351 Blue Jay CA 92317-0351 Office: Law Offices Ellen Van Wagner 12490 Central Ave Ste 104 Chino CA 91710

VAN WAGNER, NANCY LEE, retired educator; b. Bklyn., Aug. 8, 1938; d. Antonio and Julia Kathryn (Frieri) Mercaldo; m. Arthur L. Van Wagner (div. 1979); 1 child, Anthony Burton. Student, Pine Crest Bible Inst., 1959-62; BA, Roberts Wesleyan Coll., 1964; MEd, Mich. State U., 1970; diploma in legal assistance, Oakland U., 1984. Elem. tchr. Holly (Mich.) Sch. Dist., 1966-69; elem. tchr. Clarkston (Mich.) Sch. Dist., 1969-94, ret., 1994; legal asst. intern George Dovas, Southfield, Mich., summer 1984; mem. 1st task force to establish requirements for spl. edn., Mich., 1970-71; mem. sch. improvement com. Pine Knob Elem. Sch., Clarkston, 1994-95; sec. to bd. dirs. WE Restaurant Corp., 1989-90; established Van Wagner Pub. Co., 1992. Precinct del., 1984-92, mem. exec. com. Oakland County Dem. Com., 1986-92, Sunday Sch. leader Brightmoor Tabernacle. Recipient Presdl. Fitness award for walking, 1991. Mem. NEA , Mich. Edn. Assn., Clarkston Edn. Assn. (regional rep. 1988-94, del.-at-large to NEA conf. 1990). Home: 8564 Elzabeth Lake Rd PO Box 402 Union Lake MI 48387

VAN WHY, REBECCA RIVERA, guidance counselor; b. Casa Blanca, N.Mex., Sept. 14, 1932; d. Charles and Doris (Thompson) Rivera; m. Raymond Richard Van Why, Aug. 27, 1955; children: Raymond R., Ronald R., Randall R. BS, U. N.Mex., 1959. Tchr. Bur. of Indian Affairs, Albuquerque, 1960-62, guidance counselor, 1969-94, tchr., supr., 1973-74, acting dir. student life, 1987, ret., 1994; head tchr. Laguna (N.Mex.) Headstart OEO, 1967-69, acting dir., 1969. Appt. N.Mex. Youth Conservation Corps Commn., 1992-95. Recipient Cert. of Recognition, Sec. of Interior, 1975, Cert. of Appreciation, State of N.Mex., 1986, N.Mex. Commn. on the Status of Women, 1993; named honoree Internat. Women's Day, U. N.Mex., 1987. Republican. Home: 14417 Central Ave NW Albuquerque NM 87121

VAN WORMER, KATHERINE STUART, sociology educator; b. New Orleans, July 24, 1944; d. Rupert Alison and Elise (Talmage) Lieb; m. Robert Potter van Wormer, Sept. 1, 1972; children: Flora Talmage, Rupert Talmage. BA, U. N.C., 1966; diploma in edn., Queen's U., Belfast, Northern Ireland, 1967; PhD in Sociology, U. Ga., 1976; MSSW, U. Tenn., Nashville, 1984. Instr. Livingstone Coll., Salisbury, N.C., 1976-77; asst. prof. Kent (Ohio) State U., 1978-83, Winona (Minn.) State U., 1985-86; alcoholism counselor Community Alcohol Ctr., Longview, Wash., 1983-85; program dir. Vangseter Treatment, Hamar, Norway, 1988-90; asst. prof. U. No. Iowa, Cedar Falls, 1990-92, assoc. prof., 1992—. Author: Alcoholism Treatment: A Social Work Perspective, 1995; contbr. articles to profl. publs. Bd. dirs. N.E. Coun. on Substance Abuse, Waterloo, Iowa, 1990—. Mem. NASW, NOW, Nordmanns-Forbundet, Friends in Higher Edn. Socialist. Mem. Soc. of Friends. Home: 610 Tremont St Cedar Falls IA 50613-2927 Office: U No Iowa Dept Social Work 33 Sabin Hall Cedar Falls IA 50614

VAN WYCK, JEAN D., caterer; b. Phila., May 23, 1952; d. William Earl and Dorothy Ruth (Tegeler) Deuber; m. Timothy Frank Caruso, June 7, 1975 (div. July 1988); m. Edward Gerth Van Wyck, June 19, 1993. Cert., Taylor Bus. Inst., Plainfield, N.J., 1971. Human resource & adminstrv. asst. Pharmacia Inc., Piscataway, N.J., 1976-83; owner, pres. Culinary Hearts Specialties, Inc., Warren, N.J., 1982-87; exec. sec. U.S. Golf Assn., Far Hills, N.J., 1986-87; adminstrv. asst. Adidas USA, Warren, 1987-88; human resources specialist Bristol-Myers Products, Somerville, 1989-90; owner Queen of Hearts Desserts Ltd., Warren, 1990—; dept. head sec. Beneficial Data Processing Corp., 1991—; tchr. dessert class Green Brook (N.J.) Adult Sch., 1986. Contbr. recipes to book: The New Carryout Cuisine, 1988. Episcopalian. Home: 1010 Sunset Dr Basking Ridge NJ 07920

VAN WYK, BETTY VICHA, financial planner, township clerk; b. Berwyn, Ill., Apr. 12, 1939; d. Louis J. and Vlasta Marie (Topinka) Vicha; m. Paul Herbert Van Wyk, June 4, 1960 (div. June 1977); children: Laura Elizabeth, Mark Paul. BA magna cum laude, Hope Coll., 1961; postgrad., No. Ill. U., 1976-80. Cert. fin. planner, Ill. Reporter, columnist Pioneer Press Newspapers, Oak Park, Ill., 1970-75; freelance pub. relations cons. Oak Park, 1975-88; dir. communications Oak Park-River Forest High Sch., Oak Park, 1975-88; fin. planner, investment advisor Van Wyk Fin. Svcs., Oak Park, Ill., 1988—; workshop presenter, panelist speaker Ill. Assn. Sch. Bds.; clk. Oak Park Twp., 1985—. Trustee Oak Park Twp., 1981-85; commr. Oak Park Community Relations Commn., 1979-81. Recipient Faculty Honors Mortar Bd., Hope Coll. Mem. Publicity Club Chgo., Nat. Sch. Pub. Rels. Assn., Ill. Sch. Pub. Rels. Assn. (bd. dirs. 1982-88, various awards), LWV, Oak Park C. of C. (task force 1985-88), Zonta (bd. dirs. Oak Park 1988-91). Unitarian. Office: Van Wyk Fin Svcs 632 Gunderson Ave Oak Park IL 60304-1422

VANZANT, RACHEL GENE, controller; b. Girard, Kans., Oct. 7, 1967; d. Leonard Joseph and Wanda Lee (McColm) Westhoff; m. John R. Vanzant, June 26, 1993. BBA in Acctg., Pittsburg State U., 1990. CPA, Kans. Sr. acct. Baird, Kurtz & Dobson, Joplin, Mo., 1991-93; contr. Pitsco, Inc., Pittsburg, Kans., 1993—. Mem. adv. bd. Kelce Sch. Bus., 1993—; active YMCA, 1993—. Mem. AICPA, Inst. Mgmt. Accts., Pittsburg State U. Alumni Assn. Roman Catholic. Home: 525 E Madison Pittsburg KS 66762 Office: Pitsco Inc 915 E Jefferson Pittsburg KS 66762

VAN ZANTE, SHIRLEY M(AE), magazine editor; b. Elma, Iowa; d. Vernon E. and Georgene (Woodmansee) Borland; m. Dirk C. Van Zante. AA, Grandview Coll., 1950; BA, Drake U., 1952. Assoc. editor Mchts. Trade Jour., Des Moines, 1952-55; copywriter Meredith Pub. Co., Des Moines, 1955-60, book editor, 1960-67; home furnishings editor Better Homes and Gardens Spl. Interest Publs., Meredith Corp., 1967-74; home furnishing and design editor Better Homes and Gardens mag., 1974-89; writer, editl. cons., 1989—. Named Advt. Woman of Yr. in Des Moines, 1961; recipient Dorothy Dawe award, 1971, 73, 75, 76, 77, Dallas Market Ctr. award, 1983, So. Furniture Market Writer's award, 1984. Mem. Am. Soc. Interior Designers (press affiliate), Alpha Xi Delta. Address: 1905 74th St Des Moines IA 50322

VARALLO, DEBORAH GARR, marketing executive; b. Nashville, Feb. 14, 1952; d. August Anthony and Kathleen Marie (Baltz) Garr; m. James Edward Varallo, May 6, 1978. BS in Secondary Edn., Baylor U., 1976. With pub. relations dept. Hermitage (Tenn.) Landing, 1976-77; salesperson Elm Hill Meats, Nashville, 1977-78; asst. dir. ARC, Nashville, 1978-81; sales mgr. Varallo Foods, Inc., Nashville, 1981-85; salesperson Mid. Tenn. Equipment, Nashville, 1985-86, Garr Equipment Co., Mt. Juliet, Tenn., 1986-89, Scott Bolt & Screw, Nashville, 1989-90; owner, pres. Varallo & Assocs., Nashville, 1990—. Mem. adv. com. Hemophilia Adv. Bd. Tenn. Health and Environment, 1986-90; chmn. Mid-Cumberland chpt. Hemophilia Found., 1986-88, treas., 1989-90; chairperson fund raiser, 1988; co-chair, Bus. Expo, 1988, bd. dirs. 1989-91, mem. chairperson 1989; rep. Metro Airport Wilson County, 1988; bd. dirs. Combined Health Appeal, 1988-90; bd. dirs. Cumberland Valley Girl Scouts Coun., 1993—, nominating chair 1994 Cookie Sculpture chair, 1993; speechcraft dir., mem. blood recruitment bd. for Tenn. ARC, blood svcs. bd. dirs., 1992—, vice chair 1994—, chair blood recruitment com., Clara Barton charter mem., mem. blood svcs. task force, 1994; bd. dirs., publicity chair Our Kids, 1991—; mem. Nashville region membership recruitment Music City C. of C., 1991—; active First Tuesday Rep. Group, 1992—, 1st v.p., 1992-93, v.p. publicity, 1993-94, Women in the Nineties, 1993, 94, Leadership Nashville, 1993-94, co-chair, 1994-95; mem. Wilson County # 911 Bd., 1994—; publicity chair Habitat for Humanity, 1995. Recipient Outstanding Vol. award Mid-Cumberland Chpt. Hemophilia Found., 1985, Vols. award Metro Council Dirs. Nashville, 1987, Nat. Outstanding Leadership award Hemophilia Found., 1987, Humanitarian award Jan Van Eys 1988, Finalist award Athena, 1991; named to Davidson County Women of Yr., 1991. Mem. NAFE, Nat. Assn. Profl. Saleswomen (adv. bd. 1986-89, v.p. Nashville chpt. 1986-87, pres. 1987-89, chair nat. com. for membership retention 1987—, chair nat. task com. 1988, nat. publicity chairperson 1989-90, Pres.'s Cup 1989), Nashville Assn. Mfrs. Reps. (pres. 1979-81), Assn. Builders and Contractors (program dir. Tenn. chpt. 1986-87, membership com.), Am. Rental Assn., Wilson County Home Builders Assn. (membership com. 1988, bd. dirs. 1994—), Mt. Juliet West Wilson C. of C. (co-chairperson Mt. Juliet Expo '88, bd. dirs. 1988—, membership chairperson 1989, coun. dir. econ. devel. 1990, joint econ. and devel. bd. 1991—), Nashville C. of C. (mem. task force 1993, chair bus. Expo Promotions 1994, Vol. of Yr. award 1994), Nashville Assn. Profl. Saleswomen Toastmasters (v.p. 1988, Competent Toastmaster Designation 1990, dist. sec. 1990-91), Brentwood Early Risers Toastmasters (v.p. publicity 1993), Nashville Women's Breakfast Club (sec. 1993-94). Club: Toastmasters (Nashville) (charter, pres. 1986-87). Home: 425 Beacon Hill Dr Mount Juliet TN 37122-2084

VARELLAS, SANDRA MOTTE, judge; b. Anderson, S.C., Oct. 17, 1946; d. James E. and Helen Lucille (Gilliam) Motte; m. James John Varellas, July 3, 1971; children: James John III, David Todd. BA, Winthrop Coll., 1968; MA, U. Ky., 1970, JD, 1975. Bar: Ky. 1975, Fla. 1976, U.S. Dist. Ct. (ea. dist.) Ky. 1975, U.S. Ct. Appeals (6th cir.) 1976, U.S. Supreme Ct. 1978. Instr. Midway Coll., Ky., 1970-72; adj. prof. U. Ky. Coll. Law, Lexington, 1976-78; instr. dept. bus. adminstrn. U. Ky., Lexington, 1976-78; atty. Varellas, Pratt & Cooley, Lexington, 1975-93; atty. Varellas & Pratt, Lexington, 1993—; Fayette County judge exec., Ky., 1980—; hearing officer Ky. Natural Resources and Environ. Protection Cabinet, Frankfort, 1984-88. Committeewoman Ky. Young Dems., Frankfort, 1977-80; pres. Fayette County Young Dems., Lexington, 1977; bd. dirs. Ky. Dem. Women's Club, Frankfort, 1980-84; grad. Leadership Lexington, 1981; chairwoman Profl. Women's Forum, Lexington, Ky., 1985-86, bd. dirs., 1984-87, Aequum award com, 1989-92; mem. devel. coun. Midway Coll., 1990-92; co-chair Gift Club Com., 1992. Named Outstanding Young Dem. Woman, Ky. Young Dems., Frankfort, 1977, Outstanding Former Young Dem., Ky. Young Dems., 1983. Mem. Ky. Bar Assn. (treas. young lawyers div. 1978-79, long range planning com., 1988-89), Fla. Bar, Fayette County Bar Assn. (treas. 1977-78, bd. govs. 1978-80), LWV (nominating com 1984-85), Greater Lexington C. of C. (legis. affairs com. 1994—, bd. dirs. coun. smaller enterprises 1992—, legis. affairs com., 1994—). Club: The Lexington Forum, Lexington Philharm. Guild (bd. dirs. 1979-81, 86—), Nat. Assn. Women Bus. Owners (chmn. community liaison/govtl. affairs com. 1992-93), Lexington Forum (sec. 1994—). Office: Varellas & Pratt 167 W Main St Lexington KY 40507-1713

VARGA, CAROLYN ANN, computer company executive; b. Rockford, Ill., Jan. 5, 1950; d. Robert B. and Marie (Pekel) Graff; m. Andrew Varga; children: Charles Kerwin, Robert Kerwin. BS, U. Wis., 1972; MBA, U. Detroit, 1980. Engr. Burroughs, Plymouth, Mich., 1973-81; engring. mgr. Burroughs, Coral Springs, Fla., 1981-84, mgr. product support, 1984-85; mgr. product support Burroughs, Livingston, Scotland, 1985-86; mgr. engring. adminstrn. Unisys, Detroit, 1986-87, mgr. configuration mgmt., 1987-89, mgr. adv. mfg. engring., 1989-90, mgr. new products releases, 1990-93, mgr. media mfg., 1993—. Mem. DAR (regent 1991-92, chmn. state jr. membership 1987-91, chmn. credentials 1991-93, Outstanding Jr. mem. 1983, state vice-regent 1994—), Women in Engring. (guest lectr. 1983-86, OPCON speaker 1994). Roman Catholic. Office: Unisys 13250 N Haggerty Rd Plymouth MI 48170-4208

VARGA, JOAN R(ITA), marketing professional; b. Stamford, Conn., June 12, 1956; d. John MacDonald and Rita May (Barney) Robertson; m. Stephen Daniel Varga, Apr. 17, 1982; children: Cheryl Lynn, Theodore John, Joseph Vass. BBA in Mktg., Western Conn. State U., 1979, postgrad. Sales coord. Duracell USA, Bethel, Conn., 1979-80, ops. analyst, 1980-82; proposal specialist, mktg. comm. PHH Homequity, Danbury, Conn., 1982-84, assoc. cons., home sale, 1984-85, cons. and resale specialist, 1985-92, home mktg. specialist, 1992—. Recipient Wall St. Jour. Achievement award, 1978. Mem. Delta Mu Delta. Home: 299 W Flat Hill Rd Southbury CT 06488-1128

VARGAS, PATTIE LEE, author, editor; b. Spencer, S.D., Feb. 4, 1941; d. Gilbert Helmuth and Carol Maxine (Winans) Bohlman; m. Richard D. Gulling Sr., July 17, 1960 (div. 1977); children: Richard D. Jr., David M., Toni

C.; m. Allen H. Vargas, May 9, 1979 (dec. 1993). BS in Secondary Edn. cum laude, Miami U., 1969; MA in English, U. Dayton, 1972. Tchr. Kettering (Ohio) City Schs., 1972-83; editor Gurney's Gardening News, Yankton, S.D., 1984-88; dir. pub. relations Gurney Seed and Nursery Co., Yankton, 1985-89; creative supr. catalogs Dakota Advt. div. Gurney Seed and Nursery Co., Yankton, 1986-89; v.p. A.H. Vargas Assocs., Vermillion, S.D., 1987-93; editl. project mgr. Mazer Corp., Dayton, Ohio, 1993—; v.p. A.H. Vargas Assocs. Mktg. and Comm. Cons., Vermillion, S.D., 1987-93; pub. rels. cons. Cath. Conf. of Ohio, Columbus, 1975-76. Author: Country Wines, 1991, Stay Well Without Gaining Broke, 1993; writer (movie): Planning Cath. Schs. Week, 1975, (multi-media show) Tribute to the Bicentennial, 1976. Mem. Miamisburg (Ohio) Sch. Bond Steering Com., 1980. Mem. Nat. Fedn. of Press Women (recipient Editorial Writing award, 1986, 87, 88), S.D. Press Women (recipient Sweepstakes award 1987, 1988, Catalog award 1988), Nat. Garden Writing Assn.

VARLEY, KATHLEEN LYDON, writer, psychologist; b. Malden, Mass., Aug. 25, 1951; d. John Thomas and Evelyn Ruth (Carli) Lydon; m. Thomas Arthur Varley, Aug. 23, 1986; children: Maureen Evelyn, John Thomas. BA, Clark U., 1973; MS, U. Pa., 1977, PhD, 1982. Lic. psychologist, Pa. Psychology intern Benjamin Rush Ctr. for Mental Health/Mental Retardation, Phila., 1978-79; psychologist Devereux Found., Devon, Pa., 1979-87, clin. dir., 1986-87; writer Swarthmore, Pa., 1965—; psychologist with admitting privileges Phila. Psychiat. Ctr., 1984-86; storyteller Patchwork, Phila., 1984—. Author: Gingko Fruit, 1990, Off Center, 1992, Pot Luck, 1994, Requiem for a Pagan, 1994. Vol. Wallingford Swarthmore Schs., 1993-94, Wallingford Co-op Nursery Sch., 1993-94, Suburban Music Sch., Media, Pa., 1991—, Notre Dame de Lourdes Sch., 1994—. Recipient award for best children's story Phila. Writers Conf., 1993, advanced short story, 1994. Mem. Sisters in Crime. Home: 640 Magill Rd Swarthmore PA 19081-1003

VARMA, ASHA, civilian military administrator, researcher; b. Bareilly, India, Mar. 19, 1942; came to U.S., 1966; d. Gulzari Mall and Javitri Devi Varma; m. Vinod Shanker Agarwala, Feb. 14, 1967; children: Veena V., Vinay. BSc, Agra U., Bareilly, 1958, MSc, 1960; PhD, Banaras Hindu U., Varanasi, India, 1963; exec. mgmt. diploma, Office Pers. Mgmt., 1988. Rsch. fellow Banaras Hindu U., 1960-64, Nat. Rsch. Lab, Poona, India, 1964-66; asst. dir. Forensic Sci. Lab., Sagar, India, 1966-68; sci. officer Coun. Sci. and Indsl. Rsch., Kanpur, 1969-70; rsch. assoc. U. Conn., Storrs, 1973-76; rsch. scientist U. Pa., Phila., 1977-82; rsch. chemist Naval Air Devel. Ctr., Warminster, Pa., 1983-88, dep. dir., 1988-92; acting dir. Office Sci. and Tech., Naval Air Warfare Ctr., Warminster, 1992-94; chmn. Navy R&D Info. Exch. Conf., Washington, 1990—. Author: Handbook of Atomic Absorption Spectroscopy, Vols. I and II, 1984, Handbook of Furnace Atomic Absorption, 1990, Handbook of Inductively Coupled Plasma Spectroscopy, 1991; editor CRC Press Inc., 1982-83, 89-91; contbr. over 80 articles to profl. jours. Past mem. Indo-U.S. Orgn., Phila.; commr. Nat. Cert. Commn., A.I.C., 1991—; vol. judge sci. fairs at local schs. Recipient Performance awards, 1977-94, Appreciation award Office Pers. Mgmt., 1988; scholar Govt. of India, 1954-66; Govt. fellow, 1963-75. Fellow Am. Inst. Chemists; mem. AAAS, Am. Chem. Soc., Navy Civilian Mgrs. Assn. (v.p. 1991-93, pres. 1994), Federally Employed Women (pres. Buxmont chpt. 1986-87, chairperson fed. women's program com. 1988-89), Internat. Union of Pure and Applied Chemistry, Coblentz Soc., Am. Mus. Natural History, Nat. Wildlife Fedn., Internat. Wildlife Fedn., Women in Sci. Engring. Home: 1006 Marian Rd Warminster PA 18974-2728 Office: Naval Air Warfare Ctr Aircraft Div PO Box 5152 Warminster PA 18974

VARNER, CHARLEEN LAVERNE MCCLANAHAN (MRS. ROBERT B. VARNER), nutritionist, educator, administrator, dietitian; b. Alba, Mo., Aug. 28, 1931; d. Roy Calvin and Lela Ruhama (Smith) McClanahan; student Joplin (Mo.) Jr. Coll., 1949-51; B.S. in Edn., Kans. State Coll. Pittsburg, 1953; M.S., U. Ark., 1958; Ph.D., Tex. Woman's U. 1966; postgrad. Mich. State U., summer, 1955, U. Mo., summer 1962; m. Robert Bernard Varner, July 4, 1953. Apprentice county home agt. U. Mo., summer 1952; tchr. Ferry Pass Sch., Escambia County, Fla., 1953-54; tchr. biology, home econs. Joplin Sr. High Sch., 1954-59; instr. home econs. Kans. State Coll., Pittsburg, 1959-63; lectr. foods, nutrition Coll. Household Arts and Scis., Tex. Woman's U., 1963-64, research asst. NASA grant, 1964-66; assoc. prof. home econs. Central Mo. State U., Warrensburg, 1966-70, adviser to Colhecon, 1966-70, adviser to Alpha Sigma Alpha, 1967-70, 72, mem. bd. advisers Honors Group, 1967-70; prof., head dept. home econs. Kans. State Tchrs. Coll., Emporia, 1970-73; prof., chmn. dept. home econs. Benedictine Coll., Atchison, Kans., 1973-74; prof., chmn. dept. home econs. Baker U., Baldwin City, Kans., 1974-75; owner, operator Diet-Con Dietary Cons. Enterprises, cons. dietitian, 1973—, Home-Con Cons. Enterprises. Mem. Joplin Little Theater, 1956-60. Mem. NEA, Mo., Kans. state tchrs. assns., AAUW, Am., Mo., Kans. dietetics assns., Am., Mo., Kans. home econs. assns., Mo. Acad. Scis., AAUP, U. Ark. Alumni Assn., Alumni Assn. Kans. State Coll. of Pittsburg, Am. Vocat. Assn., Assn. Edn. Young Children, Sigma Xi, Beta Sigma Phi, Beta Beta Beta, Alpha Sigma Alpha, Delta Kappa Gamma, Kappa Kappa Iota, Phi Upsilon Omicron, Theta Alpha Pi. Methodist (organist). Home: Main PO Box 1009 Topeka KS 66601

VARNER, JOYCE EHRHARDT, librarian; b. Quincy, Ill., Sept. 13, 1938; d. Wilbur John and Florence Elizabeth (Mast) Ehrhardt; m. Donald Giles Varner, Sept. 12, 1959; children: Amy, Janice, Christian, Matthew, Nadine. BA, Northeastern Okla. State U., 1980; MLS, U. Okla., 1984. Lab. analyst Gardner Denver Co., Quincy, 1956-60; sales rep. Morrisonville, Ill., 1963-69; libr. clk. U. Ill., Urbana, 1973-75; libr. tech. asst. Northeastern Okla. State U., Tahlequah, 1976-86; asst. reference libr. Muskogee (Okla.) Pub. Libr., 1986-90; libr. Jess Dunn Correctional Ctr., Taft, Okla., 1990—. Editor Indian Nations Audubon Nature Notes, 1977-81; contbr. articles to newspaper. Vol. Lake-Wood coun. Girl Scouts U.S.A., 1975—, bd. dirs. 1992—, pres., 1995—; sec.-treas. Cherokee County Rural Water Dist. 7, 1987—; edn. chmn. Indian Nations chpt. Nat. Audubon Soc., 1989—. Recipient Thanks Badge, Lake-Wood coun. Girl Scouts U.S.A., 1990. Mem. ALA, AAUW, Okla. Libr. Assn. (nominating com. 1989), Okla. Acad. Sci., Okla. Ornithol. Soc. (chmn. libr. com. 1978-88, Award of Merit 1990, pres.-elect 1994, pres. 1995—), Am. Correctional Assn., Okla. Correctional Assn., Alpha Chi, Beta Beta Beta, Phi Delta Kappa (Found. rep. 1984-86, historian 1992—). Home: RR 1 Box 1 Welling OK 74471-9701 Office: Jess Dunn Correctional Ctr Leisure Libr PO Box 316 Taft OK 74463-0316

VARNER, ROSE CHRISTIANNA, career counselor; b. Newark, Jan. 13, 1965; d. John and Christianna Rees (Kearsley) Pappas; m. Paul Aaron Varner, Dec. 23, 1989; 1 child, Erin. BA in Anthropology/Sociology, Upsala Coll., 1987, MS in Counseling, 1989. Asst. to placement dir. Upsala Coll., East Orange, N.J., 1986-89; counseling intern West Point (N.Y.) Mil. Acad., 1989-90; counselor The Safe House, Bloomfield, N.J., 1989-90; transition svcs. coord. Domestic Violence Shelter, Xenia, Ohio, 1990; vol. supr. Army Cmty. Svc., Germany, 1990-91; transition specialist Army Career & Alumni Program, Germany, 1991-92; transition analyst Army Career & Alumni Program, Alexandria, Va., 1993; vol. mgr. USAF, Washington, 1994. Fellow Am. Counseling Assn., Mil. Educators and Counselors Assn. Home: 700 Willow Brook Charles Town WV 25414

VARNEY, SUZANNE GLAAB, health facility administrator; b. Ft. Meade, Md., Dec. 17, 1951; d. Lawrence Harold and G. Sue (Strain) Glaab; m. Richard Alan Varney, Dec. 31, 1983; children: Alysen Suzanne, Judson Dietrich. Student, Ohio U., Lancaster, 1969. Cert. med. staff coord. Transp. asst. U.S. Army, Seoul, 1979-81; pers. specialist U.S. Army Hosp., Ft. Knox, Ky., 1982-84, credentials specialist, 1984-86; adminstrv. asst. Brooke Army Med. Ctr., Ft. Sam Houston, Tex., 1987, adminstr. credentials program, 1988-90; credential programs adminstr. Walter Reed Army Med. Ctr., Washington, 1990-92; med. staff coord. Fairfield Med. Ctr., Lancaster, Ohio, 1992—; seminar leader office basic course Army Med. Dept., Ft. Sam Houston, 1988-90. Rep. Brookwood Neighborhood Assn., San Antonio, 1987-90; mem. N.E. Ind. Sch. Dist. PTA, San Antonio, 1986-90; den leader Cub Scouts/Boy Scouts Am., San Antonio, 1986-90. Mem. NAFE, Nat. Assn. Med. Staff Coords., Tex. Hosp. Assn., Tex. Soc. Med. Staff Svcs., Ohio Assn. Med. Staff Coords. Home: 1025 E 5th Ave Lancaster OH 43130 Office: Fairfield Med Ctr Lancaster OH 43130

VARNHAGEN, MICHELE L., legislative staff director, counsel. BA in Econs. and Math., N.Y.U., 1982; JD, Catholic U., 1985. Bar: N.Y. Law clerk Ctr. for Nat. Policy Review, 1983-84, Teamsters Rank and File Edn. Fund, 1984-88; counsel subcom. on labor mgmt. rels., house com. on edn. and labor, 1989-93, 1993—; staff dir., chief counsel subcom. on labor, senate com. on labor and human resources, 1993—. Office: Subcommittee on Labor 608 Senate Hart Office Bldg Washington DC 20510*

VARRO, BARBARA JOAN, editor; b. East Chicago, Ind., Jan. 25, 1938; d. Alexander R. and Lottie R. (Bess) V. B.A., Duquesne U., 1959. Feature reporter, asst. fashion editor Chgo. Sun-Times, 1959-64, fashion editor, 1964-76, feature writer, 1976-84; v.p. pub. rels. Daniel J. Edelman Inc., Chgo., 1984-85; v.p. PRB/Needham Porter Novelli, Chgo., 1985-86; editor Am. Hosp. Assn. News, Chgo., 1987-94; asst. editor spl. sects. Chgo. Tribune, 1995—. Recipient awards for feature writing Ill. AP, 1978, 79, 80. Mem. AAAS, Chgo. Council on Fgn. Relations. Office: Chgo Tribune 435 N Michigan Ave Chicago IL 60611

VARTANIAN, ISABEL SYLVIA, dietitian; b. Duquesne, Pa.; d. Apel and Mary (Kasparian) V. BS, U. Ala., 1957; MS, Columbia U., 1962. Registered dietitian. Dietetic N.Y. Hosp./Cornell Med. Ctr., N.Y.C., 1957-58; therapeutic dietitian Vets. Affairs Med. Ctr., Bronx, N.Y., 1958-60, adminstrv. dietitian, 1960-62, nutrition clinic dietitian, 1962-63; rsch. and nutrition clinic dietitian Vets. Affairs Med. Ctr., Coral Gables, Fla., 1963; nutrition clinic dietitian Vets. Affairs Med. Ctr., Richmond, Va., 1963-66, chief nutritional therapy edn. and rsch. sect., 1966-83, nutrition support dietitian, 1983—. Bd. dirs. Richmond Cmty. Action Program, 1978-83; adv. com. Social Svcs., Hopewell, Va., 1991—. Recipient Outstanding award, Vets. Affairs Med. Ctr., Performance award, Outstanding award. Mem. Richmond Dietetic Assn. (chairwoman diet therapy sect. 1966-67, pres. elect 1967-68, pres. 1968-70, chairwoman Dial-A-Dietitian 1972-74, chairwoman pub. rels. 1973-74, 78-81, chairwoman Division of Community Dietetics 1983-85, chairwoman program planning com. 1985), Va. Dietetic Assn. (chairwoman career guidance com. 1963-65, ednl. exhibits, 1967, chairwoman Dial-A-Dietitian 1972-74, pub. rels. 1982-84, visibility campaign, 1984, exhibit com. 1984, program planning com. 1989, divsn. community dietetic 1989-91), Va. Soc. Parenteral and Enteral Nutrition (chairwoman program planning com. 1988-89, membership com. 1990), Am. Dietetic Assn. (life), Nat. Kidney Found. (renal nutrition sect.), Am. Soc. Parenteral and Enteral Nutrition. Home: 2005 Jackson St Hopewell VA 23860 Office: VA Med Ctr 1201 Broad Rock Blvd Richmond VA 23249

VARY, EVA MAROS, chemical company executive; b. Kecskemet, Hungary, Apr. 13, 1933; came to U.S., 1958; d. Anthony and Kathleen (Czencz) Maros; m. Eugen Szent-Vary, June 13, 1956 (div. 1958); 1 child, Susan Marie. Chem. engring. diploma, Tech. U. Budapest (Hungary), 1956; PhD in Phys. Chemistry, UCLA, 1966. Chem. engring. area supr. Ujpesti Textile Plant, Budapest, 1956-57; chemist geology dept. UCLA, 1958-65; rsch. chemist, staff chemist Fabrics and Finishes Dept. Dupont, Phila., 1966-71, rsch. supr., 1971-79; tech. area supt. Fabrics and Finishes Dept. Dupont, Parlin, N.J., 1979-80; asst. plant mgr. Fabrics and Finishes Dept. Dupont, Parlin, Toledo, 1980-85; product supt. mng. Tedlar plant Dupont Fabricated Products, Buffalo, 1985-87; environ. cons. Dupont Fabricated Products, Wilmington, Del., 1987-90; dir. product safety, regulatory affairs pigments div. Ciba-Geigy Corp., Newport, Del., 1990—. Inventor, patentee release coatings. Com. chair Zonta Internat., Toledo, 1984, Buffalo, 1987. Mem. Am. Chem. Soc. Roman Catholic. Home: 1100 Lovering Ave Apt 1508 Wilmington DE 19806 Office: Ciba Geigy Corp Pigments Div 315 Water St Newport DE 19804

VASILAKI, LINDA BOOZER, music educator; b. Grand Rapids, Mich., Jan. 2, 1949; d. Gordon and Dianne (Demmon) Boozer; m. Yuri G. Vasilaki, Sept. 29, 1979; children: Camilla Dianne, Andrew Alten, Maria Demmon. BMus in Edn., Mich. State U., 1971; MFA, U. Iowa, 1973. Cert. kindergarten-12 music tchr., 7-8 all subjects tchr., Mich., Fla.; cert. Orff, Level 1. Kindergarten-6 music cons. Grand Rapids (Mich.) Pub. Schs., 1973-75; tchr., founder Suzuki violin program Grand Rapids Bd. Edn., 1976-80; tchr. violin Nat. Music Camp, Interlochen, Mich., 1981, 82; tchr. music, choir dir. Out of Door Acad., Sarasota, Fla., 1983—; founder, dir. Encore Fine Arts Program, Sarasota, Fla., 1988—; tchr. viola Blue Lake Fine Arts Camp, Muskegon, 1973; violist Fla. West Coast Symphony, Sarasota, 1982—; mem. Grand Rapids Symphony, 1973-80; tchr. Suzuki Assn. Am., Sarasota, 1976—; former viola tchr. Hope Coll., Grand Valley State Coll. Author: Music Lovers' Cookbook, 1983, Symbol of Liberty, 1985; editor: Out of Door Academy Cuisine, 1983; contbr. articles to profl. jours. Counselor, music therapist Indian Trails Camp for the Phys. Handicapped, Grand Rapids, 1968-69; violist Venice (Fla.) Symphony, 1991-92; recruiter, vol. New Eng. Music Camp. Recipient scholarships New Coll. Music Festival, 1971, Lenox String Quartet Seminar, 1971, Banff (Can.) Centre-Fine Arts String Quartet Seminar, 1972, U. Iowa, 1972-73. Mem. Phi Beta Kappa, Kappa Alpha Theta, Delta Omicron (pres. 1971), Delta Kappa Gamma. Home: 3341 Bougainvillea St Sarasota FL 34239

VASLEF, IRENE, historian, librarian; b. Budapest, Hungary, Mar. 23, 1934; came to U.S., 1956, naturalized, 1960; d. Imre and Ilona (Selyebi-Kovats) Szabo; m. Nicholas P. Vaslef, Sept. 22, 1956; children—Suzanne, Steven. B.A., San Jose (Calif.) State U., 1960; M.S., Simmons Grad. Sch. Library Sci., Boston, 1963; postgrad., Columbia U., 1968, U. Colo., 1961-62, U. Munich, 1967-68; Ph.D., Catholic U. Am., 1984. Librarian Cambridge, Mass., 1962-64; librarian Colorado Springs (Colo.) Sch. System, 1964-67; head catalog librarian Colo. Coll., Colorado Springs, 1968-72; librarian Dumbarton Oaks Rsch. Libr., Trustees for Harvard U., 1972—. Editor/compiler Am. Byzantine Bibliography in Byzantine studies/Etudes Byzantines, 1979—, Classica et Mediaevalia, 1986, Leyden: Brill, 1986; contbr. articles to profl. jours. Mem. Spl. Libraries Assn., Art Libraries Assn. N.Am., Phi Gamma Mu. Home: 1405 Grady Randall Ct Mc Lean VA 22101-2512 Office: Harvard U Dumbarton Oaks Rsch Libr 1703 32nd St NW Washington DC 20007-2934

VÁSQUEZ, MARY SUZANNA, foreign language educator; b. Bronxville, N.Y., Oct. 16, 1942; d. Jerrold Walfrid and Gladys Maud (Summy) Lundale; m. Angel M. Vásquez, Aug. 16, 1976 (div. 1990); children: Suzanna Teresa, Anamaría Belén. BA with honors in Spanish magna cum laude, Fla. State U., 1964; MA in Spanish, U. Wash., 1966, PhD in Romance Langs. and Lits., 1972. Instr. Spanish Kendall Coll., Evanston, Ill., 1970-72; asst. prof. Spanish, coord. basic Spanish Fla. State U., Tallahassee, Fla., 1973-75; asst. prof. Spanish Ariz. State U., Tempe, 1975-81, assoc. prof., 1981-89; assoc. prof. Spanish Mich. U., East Lansing, 1989-91, prof., 1991—; dir. adminstrv. ctr. State of Fla. Migration Child Compensation Program, 1975. Author, co-editor: Homenaje a Rosario Castellanos, 1980, Homenaja a Ramón Sender, 1987, The Sea of Becoming: Approaches to the Fiction of Esther Tusquets; founding editor: Letras peninsulares, 1988—; editorial bd. Letras Femeninas, 1990—; contbr. articles to profl. jours. Recipient Faculty Achievement award Burlington No. Found., 1987. Mem. MLA (exec. com. 18th and 19th century Spanish lit. 1994—), Am. Assn. Tchrs. of Spanish and Portuguese, Mich. Fgn. Lang. Assn. (Univ. Fgn. Lang. Tchr. of Yr. 1994), Conf. Editors Learned Jours., Asociación de Letras Femeninas, Phi Beta Kappa. Democrat. Home: 1341 Bayshore Dr Haslett MI 48840-9731 Office: Mich State U Dept Romance & Classical Langs East Lansing MI 48824-1112

VASS, ELLEN LORRAINE, community health nurse; b. Bronx, N.Y., Apr. 14, 1945; d. Charles and Florence (McGowan) O'Neill; m. Jeffrey Arthur Vass, July 3, 1965; children: Elizabeth Anne, Charlene Ellen. AAS, Dutchess Community Coll., 1981. Head nurse Eded Park Nursing Home, Cobleskill, N.Y., supr., in-svc. coord. edn.; primary community nurse Schoharie County Dept. Health, Schoharie, N.Y. Home: RR 1 Sloansville NY 12160-9801

VASS, JOAN, fashion designer; b. N.Y.C., May 19, 1925; d. Max S. and Rose L.; children by previous marriage: Richard, Sara, Jason. Student Vassar Coll., 1941; BA, U. Wis., 1946. Pres., Joan Vass Inc., N.Y.C., 1977—, Vass-Ludacer, N.Y.C., 1993—. Recipient Prix de Cachet, Prince Machiabelli, 1980, Coty award, 1979, Disting. Woman in Fashion award Smithsonian Instn., 1980. Office: Joan Vass Inc 117 E 29th St New York NY 10016-8022 also: 485 7th Ave Ste 510 New York NY 10018-6804

VASSALLI, SHORTY See COLLINGS, CELESTE LOUISE

VASSBERG, C. SHERE, organization official; b. Newark, July 15, 1937; d. George G. and Julia (Kittick) Sundra; m. Charles John Vassberg, Sept. 15, 1957; children: John Charles, Eric Dale, Brian George. AB in Math. and Physics, Upsala Coll., 1962; MA in Math. and Physics, Tex. A&I U., 1973, adminstr.'s cert., 1976. Cert. fraternal ins. counselor, life underwriter tng. coun. fellow; registered health underwriter. Tchr. math. and physics Raymondville (Tex.) Ind. Sch. Dist., 1962-65; tchr. advanced math. Harlingen (Tex.) Ind. Sch. Dist., 1966-75; computer analyst Harlingen High Sch., 1976-85; dist. rep. Aid Assn. for Luths., Lyford, Tex., 1985—. Pres. adv. com. Luth. Social Svcs., McAllen, Tex., 1985—, Rio Grande Valley Cluster for Women of Evang. Luth. Ch. in Am., 1991-93; bd. dirs. La. Synodical Unit of Luth. Ch. Women, 1980-88; mem. Bethel Luth. Ch., Lyford, Tex. Recipient recognition Nat. Symposium Health Underwriters, 1993; also aware from cmty. groups for fraternal activities. Mem. Tex. Assn. Health Underwriters (bd. dirs. 1991-92), Tex. Leaders Round Table, Valley Assn. Health Underwriters (pres. 1991-93), Aid Assn. for Luths. (exec. conf. 1990-91), Valley Assn. Life Underwriters (bd. dirs. 1988—, treas. v.p., pres.-elect and pres., Over and Beyond Call of Duty award 1988, Dubin award for Pub. Svc. 1989, Most Outstanding Bd. Mem. award 1990, Nat. Health Ins. Quality award 1991, Agt. of Yr. award 1992), Tex. Assn. Life Underwriters, Nat. Assn. Life Underwriters (Nat.

VASSILOPOULOU-SELLIN, RENA, medical educator; b. Dec. 29, 1949. MD, Albert Einstein Coll. Medicine, 1974. Resident Montefiore Hosp., Bronx, 1974-77; fellow Northwestern U., Chgo., 1977-80; assoc. prof. Univ. Tex., Houston, 1980—. Fellow ACP; mem. AAAS, AMA, Am. Soc. Bone and Mineral Rsch., Am. Diabetes Assn., Am. Soc. Clin. Oncology, Endo Soc. Office: Anderson Cancer Ctr 1515 Holcombe Blvd #15 Houston TX 77030-4009

VASWANI, SHEILA ANN, secondary education educator; b. N.Y.C., Feb. 27, 1948; d. Elwood Stanley and Zulia Zita (Sullivan) Kent; m. A. N. Vaswani; 1 child, Neela. BA in Asian Studies and Eurasian History, Hofstra U., 1972; MA in Chinese Studies, St. John's U., Jamacia, N.Y., 1977. Mng. editor County Weekly, Vt., 1979-80; secondary social studies tchr. Babylon (N.Y.) H.S., 1984—; co-organizer adv. program Babylon (N.Y.) H.S., 1991-94, mem. middle states evaluation com., 1991-92, mem. human rels. seventh grade coms., 1993-94; presenter in field. Contbr. articles to profl. jours. Advisor Babylon (N.Y.) H.S. chpt. Nat. Honor Soc., 1989—, Home Econ. Club, Babylon, 1989—; v.p. Parents Tchrs. and Students Together, Babylon, 1994—. Mem. Nat. Coun. for Social Studies, L.I. Coun. for Social Studies. Office: Babylon High Sch 50 RR Ave Babylon NY 11746

VATHIS, ALMA CHRISTINE, librarian, educator; b. Phila., Oct. 24, 1948; d. James and Joyce Crouthamel (Beer) V. BS in Edn., Shippensburg State U., 1970; MA in Librarianship, U. Denver, 1972; cert. in advanced studies Drexel U., 1982. Tchr., librarian Bensalem (Pa.) Sch. Dist., 1970-71, 72-87, coordinator K-12 library, 1984-87; vis. asst. librarian Ariz. State U., Tempe, 1987-90; info. specialist Intel Corp. Libr. Info. Svcs., Chandler, Ariz., 1990—. Editor: Learning and Media Jour., 1982-87; contbr. articles to profl. jours. Mem. ALA, Am. Assn. Sch. Librarians, Pa. Sch. Librarians' Assn. (editor 1982-87), Bucks County Sch. Librarians Assn. (v.p. 1981-82), Assn. State Library Agys., NEA, Pa. State Edn. Assn., Bensalem Twp. Edn. Assn. (treas. 1981-82). Club: Liberty Divers (Levittown, Pa.) (pres. 1976). Home: 4702 E Winston Dr Phoenix AZ 85044 Office: Intel Corp Libr Info Svcs 5000 W Chandler Blvd CH-92 Chandler AZ 85226

VAUCLAIR, MARGUERITE RENÉE, public relations and sales promotion executive; b. Englewood, N.J., Jan. 26, 1945; d. Maurice Joseph and Yvonne Jeanne (Reynaud) V.; m. William Augustus Peeples II, (div. 1986). BS in Journalism, Bowling Green State U., 1967. Asst. promotion mgr. Internat. Herald Tribune, Paris, 1967-70; Europe promotion mgr. Vision-The European Bus. Mag., London, 1971; dir. programs and promotion Am. C. of C. in France, Paris, 1973-76; promotion and rsch. mgr. Johnston Internat. Pubs., N.Y.C., 1977-80; prin. Marguerite Vauclair Promotion-Pub. Rels.-Advt., 1981—; promotion mgr. L.A. Times Syndicate, 1985-88; advt. promotions and spl. sects. mgr. Soundings Publs. Inc., Essex, Conn., 1990. Collaborator on books, author: (guide) Guest Houses, Bed-and-Breakfasts, Inns and Hotels in Newport, R.I., 1982; contbr. travel articles and photographs to mags. and newspapers. Mem. Pub. Rels. Soc. Am. (Prisms awards com. L.A. 1988), Overseas Press Club Am., Women in Comm. (bd. dirs. L.A. 1987-89), French-Am. C. of C. in U.S., Inc. (publs. com. 1993—), World Trade Club of Westchester, Advt. Club of Westchester (bd. dirs. 1994—), Fairfield County Pub. Rels. Assn., Conn. Press Club, Kappa Delta (bd. dirs. UCLA chpt. 1986-88, U. Conn. 1990-91). Office: 131 Purchase St Rye NY 10580

VAUGHAN, ALICE FELICIE, accountant, real estate executive, tax consultant; b. Laredo, TX, July 14, 1937; d. Wilfred John and Mayme Alice (Mitchell) Peck; m. Sam J. Vaughan, Feb. 27, 1960; children: Nicole Pam, Bonnie Kay, Kimberly Ann, Linda Marie. AS, AA, Del Mar Coll., 1981; BBA, Corpus Christi State U., 1982, MBA, 1983. Staff acct. Robin Perrone, CPA, Corpus Christi, Tex., 1985-86; owner Alice Vaughan Realty, Corpus Christi, 1982—; mgr. Country Club Estates Parks, Inc., Corpus Christi, 1986-89; tax acct. Jon Hurt, CPA, Corpus Christi, Tex., 1989—; v.p., sec., treas. Sa-Gu Corp., 1989—; bus. tchr. Incarnate Word Acad. High Sch., Corpus Christi, 1988. Aquatic instr. YMCA, Corpus Christi, 1986-88; water safety instr. ARC, Corpus Christi (20 Yr. Svc. award, 1991). Mem. Tex. Assn. Realtors, Nat. Assn. Realtors, Country Club Civic Assn. Republican. Roman Catholic. Home and Office: 6410 Coral Gables Dr Corpus Christi TX 78413-2612

VAUGHAN, DORIS CELESTINE WALKER, former librarian, educator; b. Lawrenceville, Va., Aug. 21, 1930; d. Warner L. and Otelia R. (Collier) Walker; m. Clyde Wilson Vaughan Sr., Nov. 6, 1954 (dec.); children: Sharon Maria, Clyde Wilson Jr., Gregory Andre. BS, St. Paul's Coll., Lawrenceville, 1952; MLS, U. Mich., 1979. Tchr. Loudoun County Sch. System, Leesburg, Va., 1953-54, Nottoway (Va.) County Sch. System, 1954-55, Brunswick County Sch. System, Lawrenceville, 1956-70; libr. asst. Cen. State U., Wilberforce, Ohio, 1971-80, libr. reference and gifts, adj. instr., 1980-92; ret.; libr., archivist Letterkenny Army Depot, Chambersburg, Pa., summers 1986-87. U. Mich. fellow, 1978. Mem. AAUP, Southwestern Ohio Coun. for Higher Edn., Alpha Kappa Alpha. Democrat. Home: 1062 Frederick Dr Xenia OH 45385-1649

VAUGHAN, MARGARET EVELYN, psychologist, consultant; b. Mpls., Nov. 9, 1948; d. Robert Bergh and Evelyn (Glockner) Cedergren; m. William Vaughan Jr., July 30, 1981. BA, St. Cloud (Minn.) State U., 1972; MA, Western Mich. U., 1977, PhD, 1980. Lic. psychologist, Mass. Asst. prof. psychology Kalamazoo (Mich.) Coll., 1979-81; postdoctoral fellow Harvard U., Cambridge, Mass., 1981-82, rsch. assoc., 1982-83, rsch. assoc. Sch. of Bus., 1983-84; asst. prof. psychology Salem (Mass.) State Coll., 1984-88, assoc. prof. psychology, 1988-93, prof., 1994—; cons. Shore Ednl. Collaborative, Medford, Mass., 1984—; bd. dirs. B.F. Skinner Found., Cambridge. Author: (with B.F. Skinner) Enjoy Old Age, 1983; editor-elect The Behavior Analyst Jour., 1991-93, editor, 1993—. Mem. APA, Assn. for Behavior Analysis, Phi Kappa Phi, Psi Chi, Alpha Lambda Delta. Office: Salem State Coll Dept Psychology Salem MA 01970

VAUGHAN, MARTHA, biochemist; b. Dodgeville, Wis., Aug. 4, 1926; d. John Anthony and Luciel (Ellingen) V.; m. Jack Orloff, Aug. 4, 1951 (dec. Dec. 1988); children: Jonathan Michael, David Geoffrey, Gregory Joshua. Ph.B., U. Chgo., 1944; M.D., Yale U., 1949. Intern New Haven Hosp., Conn., 1950-51; research fellow U. Pa., Phila., 1951-52; research fellow Nat. Heart Inst., Bethesda, Md., 1952-54, mem. research staff, 1954-68; head metabolism sect. Nat. Heart and Lung Inst., Bethesda, 1968-74; acting chief molecular disease br. Nat. Heart, Lung and Blood Inst., Bethesda, 1974-76, chief cell metabolism lab., 1974-94; dep. chief pulmonary and critical care medicine br. Nat. Heart, Lung, and Blood Inst., Bethesda, 1994—; mem. metabolism study sect. NIH, 1965-68; mem. bd. sci. counselors Nat. Inst. Alcohol Abuse and Alcoholism, 1988-91. Mem. editl. bd.: Jour. Biol. Chemistry, 1971-76, 80-83, 88-90, assoc. editor, 1992—; editl. adv. bd.: Molecular Pharmacology, 1972-80, Biochemistry, 1989-94; ditor: Biochemistry and Biophysics Rsch. Comms., 1990-91; contbr. articles to profl. jours., chpts. to books. Bd. dirs. Found. Advanced Edn. in Scis., Inc., Bethesda, 1979-92, exec. com., 1980-92, treas., 1984-86, v.p., 1986-88, pres., 1988-90; mem. Yale U. Coun. com. med. affairs, New Haven, 1974-80. Recipient Meritorious Service medal HEW, 1974, Disting. Service medal HEW, 1979, Commd. Officer award USPHS, 1982. Mem. NAS, Am. Acad. Arts and Scis., Am. Soc. Biol. Chemists (chmn. pub. com. 1984-86), Assn. Am. Physicians, Am. Soc. Clin. Investigation. Home: 11608 W Hill Dr Rockville MD 20852-3751 Office: Nat Heart Lung & Blood Inst NIH Bldg 10 Rm 5N-307 Bethesda MD 20892

VAUGHAN, MARTHA LOUISE, agency administrator; b. Shreveport, La., Aug. 14, 1944; d. Thomas Worth and Martha Louise (Shepherd) V. BS in Edn., Centenary Coll., 1966; MA in Sociology, Stephen F. Austin State U., 1974. Cert. EMT. High sch. tchr. Airline High Sch., Bossier City, La., 1966-68; grad. asst. Stephen F. Austin State U., Nacogdoches, Tex., 1969; camp dir. YWCA of Greenville, S.C., 1970-74, exec. dir., 1974-83; asst. dir. Alston Wilkes Soc., 1985-86, facility dir., 1986—; therapist Holder and Assocs., 1991-92. Hospice vol. Greenville Hosp. System, 1992—; mem. coms. ARC, Greenville, 1970—; team mem. S.C. Crisis Response Team, 1987; vice chair Women's Task Force, 1993-94; safety officer River Falls Fire Dept., 1986—; mem. Nova Nat. Crisis Response Team, 1990—; sec./treas. Greenville Homeless Coalition, 1991-92. Recipient Clara Barton award Greenville chpt. ARC, 1989, Disting. Svc. award Greenville chpt. ARC, 1990, Parker Eualt award S.C. Assn. Community Residential Programs, 1988, Boss of Yr. award Am. Bus. Women's Assn., 1978. Mem. AID Upstate (pres. 1991-93), Nat. Fire Protection Assn. Democrat. Home: 2351 Farm Rd 134 Box 141 Jonesville TX 75659 Office: Alston Wilkes Soc 614 Pendleton St Greenville SC 29601

VAUGHAN, OLIVE ELIZABETH, marketing and industrial specialist, educator; b. Bridgeport, Conn., Oct. 23, 1925; d. Joseph Jackson and Olive Elizabeth (Sears) V. BA, Mt. Holyoke Coll., 1947, MA, 1949; PhD in Econs., Columbia U., 1973. Price economist U.S. Bur. Labor Stats., N.Y.C., 1949-50; econ. researcher, chief price sect. The Conf. Bd., N.Y.C., 1951-58; research analyst Gen. Electric Co., N.Y.C., 1958-66; asst. prof. C.W. Post Coll., Greenvale, N.Y., 1967-73, Fordham U., Bronx, N.Y., 1973-76; staff specialist, planning So. New Eng. Telephone, New Haven, Conn., 1977-89; planning cons. Gen. Electric Co. N.Y.C., 1973-74. Contbr. articles to bus. publs. Mem. Nat. Assn. Bus. Economists, Am. Econ. Assn., Am. Mktg. Assn., Am. Statis. Assn. Home: 153 Bull Hill Ln West Haven CT 06516-3928

VAUGHAN, STEPHANIE RUTH, water aerobics business owner, consultant; b. Winchester, Va., Feb. 27, 1956; d. Robert Hall Sr. and Peggy (Owen) Hahn; m. Ward Pierman Vaughan, Nov. 29, 1980; children: Carol Owen, Eva Virginia, Robert Alexander. BS in Biology, Shenandoah U., 1983, MBA, 1985. Sales rep., cashier Best Products, Roanoke, Va., 1977-78; dir. Peg-Ell Sch. Modeling, Winchester, 1978-79; mgr. purchasing and metal fabrication materials Fabritek Co., Inc., Winchester, 1979-84, sec. bd. dirs., 1980—; CEO, owner Splash Co. of Va., Winchester, 1991—; presenter in field; tennis instr. Camp Camelot, Wilmington, N.C., summer 1978; cons. Fabritek Co., Inc., 1993—; membership dir. Stonebrook Swim and Raquet Club, Winchester, 1992-93, corp. fitness dir., 1993; instr. Workout in Water class Crooked Run Fitness and Racquet Club, Front Royal, Va., 1992—, Winchester Parks and Recreation Dept., 1991-92; instr., designer Children's Water Fitness Classes Winchester Country Club, Va., 1993, Stonebrook Country Club, 1994. Author: Water Exercises for Physicians, Physical Therapists and Water Fitness Instructors, 1994 (award); contbr. articles to profl. jours. Mem. AAHPERD, NAFE, AAUW, Va. Assn. Health, Phys. Edn., Recreation and Dance (conf. presenter, chair aquatic coun. 1994-95), Va. Recreation and Parks Soc. (conf. presenter), U.S. Water Fitness Assn. (adv. bd., chair tech. com. 1993—, mem. nat. tech. com. 1992—, C. Carson Conrad Top Water Fitness Leader for Va. award 1993, Deep Water Running Champion 1993, BEMA Nat. Water Fitness Champion 1993, cert. pool coord., cert. instr., nat. conf. aquatic fashion show dir. 1992, 93, 94, conf. presenter, leader 1st nat. aquatic summit, Washington, Team Water Aerobics champion 1994), United Daus. of Confederacy, Aquatic Exercise Assn. (conf. presenter, regional rep. 1994-95), U.S. Synchronized Swimming, Shenandoah U. Alumni Assn. (bd. dirs.). Home: 115 Old Forest Cir Winchester VA 22602

VAUGHAN KROEKER, NADINE, psychologist; b. Tampa, Fla., Aug. 30, 1947; d. Joseph Marcus and Velna Pearl (Jones) Williams; m. E.L. Vaughan III, 1966 (div. Aug. 1976); children: E.L. Vaughan, Heather Vaughan Oyarzun; m. Dennis Wayne Kroeker, Apr. 9, 1982 (div. Jan. 1994); 1 child, Melanie Sage. BA in Criminal Justice, U. South Fla., 1974, MA with honors in Rehab. Counseling, 1975; PhD in Psychology, Saybrook Inst., 1990. Lic. mental health counselor, Fla., lic. clin. psychologist, Calif. Co-founder Women's Resource Ctr., Tampa, Fla., 1973—; exec. dir. Vocare Found., Oakland, Calif., 1976-78; community and organizational devel. specialist STate of Calif., Berkeley, Sacramento, 1978-82; cons., trainer N. Vaughan Kroeker, PhD, Profl. Svcs., 1982—, APA Hope Program, 1994—; adj. faculty psychology Sierra Coll., Rocklin, Calif., 1990-94; exec. dir. Women's Resource Ctr. No. Calif., Nevada City, 1990-92. Mem. Nevada County (Calif.) Task Force on Drug/Alcohol Abuse, 1990; bd. dirs. Foothill Theatre Co., Nevada City, 1988-89; prodr., dir. The Living Theatre Co., Port Townsend, Wash. Mem. Am. Psychol. Assn., Assn. Humanistic Psychology. Democrat.

VAUGHN, ELEANOR, state legislator; b. Troy, Idaho, Nov. 12, 1922; m. Benjamin Vaughn Sr.; 3 children. Grad., Kinman Bus. U. Mem. Mont. Senate. Democrat. Home: 251 Mahoney Rd PO Box 45 Libby MT 59923-2819 Office: Mont Senate State Capitol Helena MT 59620-0001*

VAUGHN, JOANN WOLFE, emergency department nurse; b. Knoxville, Tenn., Mar. 4, 1947; d. Paul Albert and Elizabeth (Umburger) Wolfe; m. Neville Dewayne VAughn, Nov. 8, 1985. Diploma, Johnston Meml. Hosp., Abingdon, Va., 1968; BSN, East Tenn. State U., Johnson City, 1981. Cert. emergency nurse, ACLS. Staff nurse Bristol (Tenn.) Meml. Hosp., 1968-70, Med. Coll. Va., Richmond, 1970-72; staff nurse ICU/CCU Chippenham Hosp., Richmond, 1972-73; staff nurse Bristol Regional Med. Ctr., 1973-92, asst. nurse mgr. emergency dept., 1992—. Mem. Emergency Nurses Assn. (pres. Appalachian chpt. 1983-84), Sigma Theta Tau. Republican. Lutheran. Home: PO Box 201 Bristol VA 24203-0201 Office: Bristol Regional Med Ctr Emergency Dept 1 Medical Park Blvd Bristol TN 37620

VAUGHN, LISA FINGER, lawyer; b. Lincolnton, N.C., Oct. 5, 1962; d. Charles Reid and Jessie Juanita (Farmer) Finger; m. David Farmer Vaughn, Apr. 24, 1993. BA in Govt., Campbell U., 1984, JD, 1987. Bar: N.C. 1987. Atty. Duke Power Co., Charlotte, N.C., 1987-90, sr. atty., 1990-93, dir. fed. govtl. affairs, 1993—. Bd. dirs. Travelers Aid Soc., Charlotte, 1991-93; vol. lawyer Children's Law Ctr., Charlotte, 1992—; mem. facilities com. Ctrl. YMCA, Charlotte. Mem. ABA, Mecklenburg County Bar (mem. spl. projects com. 1993—), N.C. State Bar. Office: Duke Power Co 422 S Church St Charlotte NC 28242

VAUGHT, WILMA L., foundation executive, retired air force officer; b. Pontiac, Mich., Mar. 15, 1930; d. Willard L. and Margaret J. (Pierce) V. BS, U. Ill., 1952; MBA, U. Ala., 1968; postgrad., Indsl. Coll. Armed Forces, 1972-73; D Pub. Affairs (hon.), Columbia Coll., 1992. Cert. cost acct. Commd. 2d lt. USAF, 1957, advanced through grades to brig. gen., 1980; chief data services div. 306th Combat Support Group USAF, McCoy AFB, Fla., 1963-67; mgmt. analyst Office Dep. Chief of Staff, comptroller Mil. Assistance Command USAF, Saigon, Vietnam, 1968-69; chief advanced logistics systems plans and mgmt. group Air Force Logistics Command USAF, Wright-Patterson AFB, Ohio, 1969-72; chief cost factors br., chief security assistance br. USAF, Washington, 1973-75, Directorate Mgmt. Analysis, Office of Comptroller, 1973-75; dir. program and budget Office Dep. Chief of Staff, comptroller Hdqrs. Air Force Systems Command USAF, Andrews AFB, Md., 1980-82; comdr. U.S. Mil. Entrance Processing Command USAF, North Chicago, Ill., 1982-85; ret. USAF, 1985; pres. Women in Mil. Svc. Meml. Found., Arlington, Va., 1987—; pres. bd. dirs. Pentagon Fed. Credit Union, 1975-82; bd. regents Inst. Cost Analysis, 1979-83; Air Force sr. mil. rep. Def. Adv. Com. on Women in Services, 1982-85; chmn. Com. on Women in Armed Forces, NATO, Brussels, 1984-85. Bd. dirs. Air Force Retired Officer Community, 1986-90; mem. adv. bd. Jane Addams Conf.; mem. bd. trustees The Teller Found. Decorated Bronze Star medal, Def. Disting. Service medal, U.S. Air Force Disting. Service medal; recipient Ill. Achievement award U. Ill., 1983. Mem. Chgo. Network, Internat. Women's Forum. Methodist. Home: 6658 Van Winkle Dr Falls Church VA 22044-1010 Office: Women in Mil Svc Meml Found 5510 Columbia Pike Ste 302 Arlington VA 22204

VAUX, DORA LOUISE, sperm bank official, consultant; b. White Pine, Mont., Aug. 8, 1922; d. Martin Tinus and Edna Ruth (Pyatt) Palmlund; m. Robert Glenn Vaux, Oct. 25, 1941; children: Jacqueline, Cheryl, Richard, Jeanette. Grad. high sch., Bothell, Wash. Photographer Busco-Nestor Studios, San Diego, 1961-68; owner, mgr. Vaux Floors & Interiors, San Diego, 1968-82; cons., mgr. Repository for Germinal Choice, Escondido, Calif., 1983-91; adminstr. Found. for the Continuity of Mankind, Spokane, 1991—. Republican. Home: 605 S Liberty Lake Rd Liberty Lake WA 99019-9739 Office: Found Continuity of Mankind 1209 W 1st Ave Spokane WA 99204-0601

VAWTER, NANCY VANDEGRIFF, educator; b. Henning, Tenn., May 26, 1941; d. Wilmer Montell and Ruby May (Pittman) Vandegriff; m. Bartlett Chester Durham III, Feb. 23, 1965 (div. Aug. 1976); children: Colin Sanford Durham, Blair Pierson Durham; m. William Franklin Vawter, Oct. 28, 1989. BS in Edn. magna cum laude, U. Tenn., Nashville, 1975; MS in Biology magna cum laude, Peabody/Vanderbilt U., 1976; postgrad., U. Calif., Berkeley, 1987. Tchr. sci. Hillwood High Sch., Nashville, 1975-76, Bellevue High Sch., Nashville, 1976-78; tchr., rschr. Pelham (Ala.) High Sch., 1978-79; tchr.-in-residence Ala. Power Co., Birmingham, 1987-89; ednl. cons. in pvt. practice N. Vawter & Assocs., Montgomery, Ala., 1990-93; with Troy (Ala.) State U., 1989-90, project dir. Ctr. for Environ. Rsch. and Svc., 1993—; chmn. bd. ALA-NEED, Ala. Dept. Econ. and Cmty. Affairs, Montgomery, 1991-94; mem. team Global Environ. Conf./Washington Press Club, Washington. Grant writer; book reviewer. Advisor Ala. Power Co./So. Ctrl. Bell, statewide, 1989-94; trustee Gorgas Foud., Birmingham, 1993-94. Mem. AAAS, NEA, ASCD, Ala. Acad. Sci., N.Y. Acad. Sci., Assn. for Presdl. Award Winners in Sci. Teaching (nat.-dir.-at-large), Nat. Sci. Tchrs. Assn., Ala. Sci. Tchrs. Assn. (gen. chair 1988-90), Ala. Edn. Assn., Coalition for Better Edn., Montbomery C. of C. (chmn. task force 1992-93), Capitol City Club. Republican. Methodist. Home: 532 Wakefield Dr Montgomery AL 36109

VAZIRANI-FALES, HEEA, legislative staff member; b. Calcutta, India, Apr. 1, 1938; d. Sunder J. Vazirani; m. John Fales Jr., 1978; children: Deepika, Reetika, Ashish, Monika, Jyotika, Denise. AB, Guilford Coll., 1959; JD, Howard U., 1979. Legis. dir. Montgomery County Del, Gen. Assembly of Md., 1981-87; staff asst. for sub-coms. on civil svc. and compensation and employee benefits Ho. Com. on Post Office and Civil Svc., Washington, 1987—. Mem. Phi Delta Phi. Presbyterian. Office: Ho Com on Post Office & Civil Svc 602 O'Neill House Office Bldg Washington DC 20515*

VAZQUEZ, MARTHA ALICIA, judge; b. Santa Barbara, Calif., Feb. 21, 1953; d. Remigio and Consuelo (Mendez) V.; m. Frank Mathew, Aug. 7, 1976; children: Cristina Vazquez Matthew, Nicholas Vazquez Matthew, Nathan Vazquez Matthew. BA in Govt., U. Notre Dame, 1975, JD, 1978. Bar: N.Mex. 1979, U.S. Dist. Ct. (we. dist.) N.Mex. 1979. Atty. Pub. Defender's Office, Santa Fe, 1979-81; ptnr. Jones, Snead, Wertheim, Rodriguez & Wentworth, Santa Fe, 1981-93; judge U.S. District Ct., 10th Circuit, Santa Fe, 1993—. Chmn. City Santa Fe Grievance Bd. Mem. N.Mex. Bar Assn. (fee arbitration com., chmn. trial practice sect. 1984-85, mem. task force on minority involvement in bar activities), Santa Fe Bar Assn. (jud. liasion com.), Nat. Assn. Criminal Def. Lawyers, Assn. Trial Lawyers Am., N.Mex. Trial Lawyers Assn. Democrat. Roman Catholic. Office: US Courthouse PO Box 2710 Santa Fe NM 87504-2710*

VAZQUEZ, SUE ELLEN, elementary education educator; b. Rome, N.Y., Aug. 2, 1951; d. Louis Frank and Eileen Louella (Hayes) Mercurio; m. Gordon Orlin Jock, June 29, 1974 (div. Oct. 1985); children: Katie, Kristin; m. Kermith Vazquez, Feb. 17, 1995. AA, Mater Dei Coll., 1971; BA in Elem. Edn. and Sociology, SUNY, Potsdam, 1973, MS in Edn. and Learning Disabilities, 1987. Cert. in elem. education (nursery through grade 6), N.Y. Elem. tchr. Twin Rivers Elem. Sch., Massena, N.Y., 1973-88, Nightengale Elem. Sch., Massena, N.Y., 1988—; curriculum writer, rschr. Massena Ctrl. Schs., 1980—, AIDS adv. coun., 1987-91, student assistance program, 1994—, sci. curriculum, media coord., 1986. Co-author: (curriculum) Life Education for Children, 1980, Sexual Abuse Awareness for Educators, 1985, AIDS Awareness for Children, 1987; co-editor Immaculatan, 1970-71. Mem. NEA, Massena Tchrs. Fedn. (bldg. rep. 1978-80), Am. Fedn. Tchrs., Sci. Tchrs. Assn. of N.Y. State, North Country Colls. Internat. Reading Assn., Coll. Club of Massena, Massena Home Bur. (sec. 1975-77). Roman Catholic. Home: 11 Sharon Dr Massena NY 13662-1601 Office: Massena Ctrl Schs 290 Main St Massena NY 13662-1999

VEACO, KRISTINA, lawyer; b. Sacramento, Calif., Mar. 4, 1948; d. Robert Glenn and Lelia (McCain) V.; m. William H. Heinemann, June 23, 1984 (div. Aug. 1991). BA, U. Calif., Davis, 1978; JD, Hastings Coll. of the Law, 1981. Legal adv. to commr. William T. Bagley Calif. Public Utilities Commn., San Francisco, Calif., 1981-86; sr. counsel Pacific Telesis Group, San Francisco, Calif., 1986-94; sr. counsel corp. and securities and pol. law Air Touch Communication, San Francisco, 1994—. Mem. ABA, Calif. Women Lawyers, San Francisco Bar Assn., Am. Soc. Corp. Secs., Phi Beta Kappa. Democrat. Episcopalian. Office: Air Touch Coms 1 California St Rm 2108 San Francisco CA 94105

VEATCH, BARBARA GENE, artist, customer service manager; b. Columbus, Ohio, Sept. 2, 1949; d. Eugene Augustus and Edith Bertha (Hudson) Lohmann; m. Ellis Robert Veatch, II, Jan. 22, 1972; children: Brian, Cara. BFA, Ohio State U., 1972, MFA with honors, 1987. Creative arts therapist Wesley Glen Retirement Ctr., Columbus, 1979-85; activities coord. Heritage Tower, Columbus, 1984-85; grad. teaching assoc. Ohio State U., Columbus, 1985-87; field supr. Vols. Am., Denver, 1988-89; rental/leasing mgr. Ashtech, Inc., Sunnyvale, Calif., 1989-93; customer svc. mgr. Total Sound, Inc., San Jose, Calif., 1994—; instr. art Creative Arts Ctr., Sunnyvale, Calif., 1994—; juror Lane Sq. Arts Festival, Lancaster, Ohio, 1984, Morrow County Art League, Mt. Gilead, Ohio, 1985, lectr., 1985; cons. Arts Partnership Program, Columbus, 1987-88. One-person shows include Ohio State U., 1987, Worthington Arts Coun., 1988, Columbus Parks and Recreation Dept., 1988, 91; exhibited in group shows at Art for Springfield City Bldg., Ohio, 1979, Nationwide Gallery, 1980, 83, Gallery 200, Columbus, 1981, Columbus Mus. Art, 1984, 87, 88, Govs. Residence, Columbus, 1984, Franklin U., Columbus, 1984, Estevez Vilas Gallery, Cin., 1985, Leo Yassenoff Jewish Ctr., Columbus, 1986, Ohio State Fair, 1986, Battelle Meml. Inst., Columbus, 1987, Upper Arlington Mcpl. Bldg., 1989, Santa Cruz (Calif.) Art League, 1991, San Jose Art League, 1991, 93, Allegra Gallery, San Jose, 1991, San Jose Mus. Art, 1992, Los Gatos Mus. Art, 1994, others; represented in permanent collections Columbus Mus. Art, Springfield City Bldg., Shoe Corp. Am., Columbus, 3M Co., Mpls., Wesley Glen Retirement Ctr., Columbus, others, numerous pvt. collections. Recipient First Place award Art of Alaskan Women, 1976, Purchase award Greater Columbus Art Coun., 1977, 79, Art for City Bldg., 1979, Ohio State Fair, 1980, 81, Dollar Savs. award Columbus Art League Exhbn., 1983, Painting award Santa Clara County Fair, 1991, 92, 94, Edith Fergus Gilmore Materials Fund grantee Ohio State U., 1987. Mem. Coll. Art Assn., Columbus Art League, Pacific Art League Palo Alto, Phi Kappa Phi. Home: 4035 Pearl Ave San Jose CA 95136 Office: Total Sound Inc 1752 Junction Ave San Jose CA 95112

VEATCH, DIANE LYNN, aircraft assembler; b. Riverside, Calif., Oct. 5, 1957; d. Cecil Max and Mildred Clair (Miller) V. Student, Riverside (Calif.) City Coll., 1976-77. Gal Friday Ferguson Mgmt. Exchange, Riverside, 1973-76; pep squad coach Riverside (Calif.) Unified Sch. Dist., 1976-77; sales person Sears & Roebuck, Riverside, 1976-77; typist Serco Internat., Garden Grove, Calif., 1977-78; aircraft assembler Rohr Industries, Riverside, 1979—. Author of poetry. Mem. Job's Daus. #35, Riverside, 1974; chpt. princess Riverside (Calif.) Chpt. DeMolay, 1974, chpt. sweetheart, 1974-77. Recipient Cert. merit Miss Drill Team USA Pagent, 1976, Lamp of Knowledge, Internat. Supreme Coun., Order of DeMolay, 1975, Golden Poet award World of Poetry, 1985.

VEATCH, JEAN LOUISE CORTY, telemetry nurse; b. Farmer City, Ill., June 4, 1932; d. Eugene Louis and Mary Violette (Mounce) Corty; m. July 23, 1955 (div.); children: Irvin, Ronald, Steven, Julie, James, Jeffery. Diploma, Holy Cross Cen. Sch. Nursing, 1954; BS, Coll. St. Francis, 1984; student, Valparaiso U. Cert. ACLS. Obstetrics nurse Holy Family Hosp., LaPorte, Ind., 1954-64; office nurse Dr. McDonald, Gulfport, Miss.; office nurse Dr. Jack Cartwright, LaPorte, med./telemetry unit nurse, 1977-95, diabetic resource nurse, 1987—; staff nurse level III LaPorte Hosp., 1988—, charge nurse, preceptor, 1979—. Mem. Am. Assn. Diabetic Educators, Am. Heart Assn. Home: 4409 Campbell St Valparaiso IN 46383-1303

VEATCH, SHEILA WILLIAMSON, counselor; b. Fitchburg, Mass., Jan. 10, 1950; d. William Robert Barse, Jr. and Joan Jessie (Tothill) Williamson; m. Michael Alan Veatch, July 3, 1993; children: Michael, Katie. BSEd, U. Ga., 1971; MEd in Counseling, West Ga. Coll., 1991, EdS in Counseling, 1992. Nat. bd. cert. counselor; lic. profl. counselor. Tchr. Cobb County Schs., Marietta, Ga., 1971-73, 86-91, counselor, 1991—; instr. Cobb Staff Devel., Marietta, 1992-93; workshop leader Kennesaw (Ga.) Student Educators, 1993; presenter Cobb Mega Conf., 1992. Co-author: Manners Mania, 1993 (rsch. grantee 1992). Rsch. grantee social skills program Cobb County, 1991-92, 92-93. Mem. Am. Counseling Assn., Ga. Sch. Counselors Assn. (presenter 1993), Am. Sch. Counseling Assn., Cobb Sch. Counselor Assn., Atlanta Adlerian Soc., PTA (hon., life). Home: 3146 Due West Ct Dallas GA 30132 Office: Cobb County Sch System Glover St Marietta GA 30060

VEAZEY, DORIS ANNE, field office administrator; b. Dawson Spring, Ky., Feb. 16, 1935; d. Bradley Basil and Lucy Mable (Hamby) Sisk; m. Herman Veazey Jr., Aug. 15, 1964 (dec. Sept. 1987); 1 child, Vickie Dianne Veazey Kicinski. Student, Murray State U., 1952-54. Unemployment ins. examiner Dept. for Employment Svcs., Madisonville, Ky., 1954-73, unemployment ins. supr., 1973-85, field office mgr., 1985—; bd. dirs., adv. bd. region II Vocat. Tech. Schs., Madisonville, 1988-92. Mem. Mayor's Work Force Devel. Com., 1993—, Ky. Indsl. Devel. Com., 1992—. Mem. Internat. Assn. of Personnel in Employment Svcs., Southeastern Employment and Tng. Assn., Tenure, Greater Madisonville C. of C. (dir. leadership 1988-93). Baptist. Office: Dept Employment Svcs 56 Federal St # 1226 Madisonville KY 42431-1226

VEBLEN, MARTHANNA ELVIDGE, retired librarian, retirement consultant; b. Seattle, Oct. 3, 1920; d. Ford Quint and Anita Emily (Miller) Elvidge; m. John Veblen, Oct. 24, 1942; children: John Elvidge, Christopher Ford. BA, U. Wash., 1942, MLS, 1959. Rsch. cons. Wash. State Gov.'s Coun. on Aging, Olympia, 1959-61; asst. librarian Seattle Pacific Coll., 1960-65, head librarian, 1965-66; regional supr. King County Library System, Seattle, 1969-72; coordinator book mobile ext. King County Library System, 1972-75, govt. documents librarian, 1975-82; retirement cons., pres. Creative Retirement Cons., Inc., Seattle, 1980-86. Author: Aging in the State of Washington, 1961, Giant Strides Since Andrew Carnegie, 1975, Aging-Where to Turn in Washington State, 1976; contbr. articles to profl. jours. Mem. Wash. State Coun. on Aging, 1967-71; trustee Seattle-King County Coun. on Aging, 1968-74, chmn., 1973-76; mem. Wash. Adv. Com. on Depository Standards, 1975-79; mem. libr. com. Found. for Preservation Gov.'s Mansion, Olympia, 1975-77; mem. health svcs. panel United Way King County, 1977-80; trustee Women's Heritage Ctr., Seattle, 1983-85; chmn. Commn. on Aging, Episcopal Diocese of Olympia, 1975-78; chmn. bd. dirs. Retirement Homes Western Wash., 1978-91. Mem. N.W. Coll. Assn. (chmn. 1964), Pacific N.W. Libr. Assn. (sec. ednl. div. 1964-66), Washington Libr. Assn. (fed. rels. coord. 1973-77), Women's Profl. Managerial Network, Internat. Soc. Pre-Retirement Planners, U. Wash. Grad Sch. Sci. and Info., DAR, Nat. League Am. Pen Women, Daus. Soc. Calif. Pioneers, Nat. Soc. Colonial Dames Am. in Wash., Women's Univ. Club, City Club Seattle, Sunset Club, Kappa Kappa Gamma, Beta Phi Mu, Alpha Delta Kappa. Home: 6720 E Green Lake Way N Seattle WA 98103-5420

VECCHIONE, JANE F., school nurse; b. Phila., Jan. 25, 1946; d. Frank M. and Jane (Brophy) V. Diploma, Chestnut Hill Hosp., Phila., 1984; BSN magna cum laude, LaSalle U., 1987; M in Health Edn., St. Joseph's U., 1991. Cert. sch. nurse, Pa. Staff nurse Chestnut Hill Hosp., Abington (Pa.) Meml. Hosp.; sch. nurse Phila. Sch. Dist. Recipient Martins Sci. award, Med./Surgical Nursing award, others, LaSalle U. and Chestnut Hill Hosp. Fellow The Nightingale Soc.; mem. Phila. Pub. Sch. Nurses Assn., Nat. Sch. Nurse Assn., Sigma Theta Tau.

VECCHIOTTI, RACHEL IRENE, management consultant; b. St. Louis, Nov. 14, 1968; d. Robert Anthony and Dorothea Irene (Hoban) V. Student, London Sch. Econs./Polit. Sci., 1988-89; BA in Econs. cum laude with honors, Wellesley Coll., 1990; postgrad., Claremont Coll., 1994—. Asst. to contr. Fenster Steel, St. Louis, summer 1987-89; rsch. asst. Nat. Bur. Econ. Rsch., Cambridge, Mass., 1987-88; rsch. assoc. Kuczmarski & Assocs., Inc., Chgo., 1990-92, cons., 1992-94; summer intern Monsant Co., St. Louis, summer 1988. Contbr. articles to mgmt. handbooks. Jr. bd. dirs. Lawrence Hall Youth Svc., Chgo., 1990—.

VEECK, LUCINDA LEIGH, embryologist, researcher; b. Jacksonville, Ill., Aug. 9, 1950; d. Edgar Allen Burrows and Phyllis Leigh Pleasant Gibson; children: Alan, Jason. MLT, Norfolk Gen. Hosp., 1979; DSc, Eastern Va. Med. Sch., Norfolk, 1993. Cytogenetics assoc. Eastern Va. Med. Sch., Norfolk, 1979-82; lab. dir. IVF program Jones Inst. for Reproductive Medicine, Norfolk, 1980—; lectr. dept. ob-gyn. Med. Coll. of Hampton Roads, Norfolk, 1984—; cons. Luth. Gen. Hosp., Chgo., 1988—; lectr. in U.S. and abroad. Author: Atlas of the Human Oocyte and Early Conceptus, Vol. 1, 1986, Vol. 2, 1991; ad hoc reviewer for various jours. Mem. Am. Fertility Soc., Hampton Roads Fertility Soc. (dir. 1992—), Soc. for Assisted Reproductive Tech. (dir. 1991-93), Reproductive Lab. Tech. Study Group (chair 1992-94), Reproductive Biology Study Group. Episcopalian. Home: 829 Botetourt Gardens Norfolk VA 23507

VEEDER, DONNA CLARK, artist; b. Nashville, Feb. 7, 1933; d. Harry Gribsby and Thelma Clayton (Black) Clark; m. Nicholas Schermerhorn Veeder, Aug. 24, 1957; children: Kristen Black Veeder Walker and Katrina Bradt Veeder Polito (twins). BFA, U. Ga., 1958; student in figure and portrait painting, Munson Williams Procter Sch. Art, Utica, N.Y., 1973-91. Tchr. art N.Y. Pub. Schs., Mohawk, 1960-63; portrait artist Van Hornesville, N.Y., 1976—; tchr. painting Mohawk Valley Ctr. for Arts, Little Falls, N.Y., 1985—; art tchr. Owen D. Young Sch., Van Hornesville, N.Y., 1984-87; tchr. portrait painting Herkimer (N.Y.) County C.C., 1982-83; coord. portrait/figure class Munson Williams Proctor Sch. art, Utica, N.Y., 1988-91, curator class show, 1990; tchr. portrait and figure study Ctrl. Inst. Fine Arts, Beijing, Mohawk Valley Ctr. Arts, Little Falls, 1991, 94, Gallery 53, Cooperstown, N.Y., 1992, 94, Picture Perfect Gallery, Canajoharie, N.Y., 1992; curator Van Hornesville Artists Show, Van Hornesville Cmty. Corp., 1989, 91, 93, 95. Co-author: (illustrated poetry) Rare Friends, 1975. Mem. United Meth. Ch. Van Hornesville, 1965—, Van Hornesville Community Corp., 1989—. Recipient 1st Pl. award Canal Celebration, Little Falls, 1989, award of Excellence, 1991, 1st Pl. in oil award Tri-County SUNY Utica/Rome, 1990, 1st Pl. in oil award 42nd Ann. Ctrl. Adirondack Old Forge, 1994. Mem. Cooperstown Art Assn., Mohawk Valley Ctr. for Arts (com. exhbns.), Van Hornesville Artists Group (chair 1989-95), Kirkland Art Ctr., Upper Catskill Cmty. Coun. of the Arts.

VEGA, MARYLOIS PURDY, journalist; b. Chgo., Nov. 4, 1914; d. William Thomas and Mary Helene (Buggy) Purdy; m. Carlos Juan Vega, Sept. 4, 1965. B.A., U. Wis., Madison, 1935. With Time mag., N.Y.C., 1942-84; chief Letters to the Editor, 1951-67, chief editl. rsch., 1967-76, assoc. editor, 1976-84. Roman Catholic. Club: Overseas Press. Home: 140 West End Ave New York NY 10023-6131 also: Sand Hill Rd Gardiner NY 12525

VEGA, SUZANNE, singer, songwriter; b. Santa Monica, Calif., July 11, 1959. Grad., Barnard Coll., 1982. Singer, songwriter, concert performer, 1975—. Began performing in Greenwich Village coffeehouses, N.Y.C., 1975; albums include Suzanne Vega, 1985, Solitude Standing, 1987, Days of Open

Hand, 1990, 99.9 F, 1992; songs include Cracking, Marlene on the Wall, Tom's Diner, Luka, Solitude Standing, (song for Pretty in Pink soundtrack) Left of Center; concert tours of U.S., Can., Europe and Far East, 1987. Buddhist. Office: care A&M Records 825 Eighth Ave 27th Fl New York NY 10019 also: care AGF Entertainment Ltd PO Box 2036 Old Chelsea Station New York NY 10113*

VEHMAS, LISA A., federal and state government lawyer; b. Plainfield, N.J., Mar. 23, 1959; d. Olavi E. and Eleanor (Miller) V.; m. Mark Miller, Aug. 31, 1991. BA in Polit. Sci. and Environ. Studies, Hood Coll., 1981; JD, Georgetown U., 1992. Environ. analyst, office environ. project review Dept. Interior, Washington, 1981; legis. and regulatory asst. Am. Mining Congress, Washington, 1982-85; minerals cons., sub-com. on mining and natural resources House Com. on Interior and Insular Affairs, Washington, 1985-87; counsel Senate Com. on Energy and Natural Resources, Washington, 1987—. Office: Com on Energy & Nat Resources 362 Senate Dirksen Office Bldg Washington DC 20510*

VEIT, CLAIRICE GENE TIPTON, measurement psychologist; b. Monterey Park, Calif., Feb. 20, 1939; d. Albert Vern and Gene (Bunning) Tipton; children: Steven Jay, Barbara Gene, Laurette Henry, Catherine Swanky. BA, UCLA, 1969, MA, 1970, PhD, 1974. Asst. prof. psychology Calif. State U., L.A., 1974-76, assoc. prof. psychology, 1975-80; rsch. psychologist The Rand Corp., Santa Monica, Calif., 1977—; rsch. cons. NATO Tech. Ctr., The Hague, The Netherlands, 1980-81; faculty Rand Grad Sch., Santa Monica, 1993—. Invented subjective transfer function (SFT) method to complex sys. analysis. Mem. LWV, ACLU, NOW, Mil. Ops. Rsch. Soc. Am., Inst. Mgmt. Sci., Soc. Med. Decision-Making, Soc. for Judgment and Decision-Making, L.A. Opera League. Office: The Rand Corp 1700 Main St Santa Monica CA 90401-3208

VEITH, MARY ROTH, assistant dean; b. Middletown, Conn., Feb. 7, 1931; d. John Stephen and Margaret (Healey) Roth; children: Richard, Frank, Margaret, Katherine. BS, U. Conn., 1952; MBA, Iona Coll., 1975. Registered dietitian. Asst. head dietitian St. Francis Hosp., Hartford, Conn., 1954-55; dietitian Quality Control Lab A&P Corp., N.Y.C., 1955-56; head dietitian Cabrini Hosp., N.Y.C., 1956; homemaker, 1957-75; instr. mgmt. Coll. New Rochelle, N.Y., 1975; instr. mktg. Iona Coll., New Rochelle, N.Y., 1975-78, asst. prof., 1979—; asst. dean Hagan Sch. of Bus., Iona Coll., New Rochelle, N.Y., 1985—; treas. Advt. Club Westchester, N.Y. Mem. Am. Dietetic Assn., N.Y. Dietetic Assn., Am. Mktg. Assn., World Trade Club (Westchester). Office: Hagan Sch Business Iona College 715 North Ave New Rochelle NY 10801

VEITH, NANCY ANN, lawyer, consultant, lecturer; b. Englewood, N.J., July 15, 1949; d. Harold Charles and Anita Mae (Scanlon) V.; m. Leslie J. Fenyves, Jan. 16, 1993. BA, Gettysburg (Pa.) Coll., 1971; MAT, Northwestern U., 1972; JD, U. San Francisco, 1979. Bar: Calif. 1979. Atty. Pillsbury, Nagel & Atcheson, San Francisco, 1980-83, Bell Rosenberg & Hughes, Oakland, Calif., 1983-87; sole practitioner Larkspur, Calif., 1987—; bd. dirs. James Moore & Assocs., San Francisco; treas. Franklin Groves, Inc., Zolfo Springs, Fla., 1987—; vice chair Nomellinc, San Francisco, 1993. Comments editor U. San Francisco Law Rev., 1978-79. Bd. dirs. Ctr. for Attitudinal Healing, Tiburon, Calif., 1987-91, v.p., 1990-91. Mem. Marin County Bar Assn., San Francisco Bar Assn., Marin County Women Lawyers, Bus. Execs. Assn. Marin, Sausalito C. of C. Office: 700 Larkspur Landing Cir Larkspur CA 94939-1715

VEJSICKY, CATHLEEN LYNN, management executive, educator; b. Columbus, Ohio, June 25, 1958; d. Eugene Joseph and Jane Ann (Thomas) V. BS, U. So. Calif., L.A., 1981, MBA, 1987. Cert. tchr., bus. mgmt. and mktg. tchr., C.C. tchr., Calif. Sr. product mgr. Dataproducts Corp., Woodland Hills, Calif., 1980-86; product mktg. mgr. Light Signatures, Century City, Calif., 1987-88; mgr., mgmt. cons. KPMG Peat Marwick, L.A., 1988-92; dealer bus. cons. Steelcase Inc., Tustin, Calif., 1992-93; v.p. Stranberg & Assocs., Newport Beach, Calif., 1993—; substitute tchr. Long Beach (Calif.) Unified Sch. Dist., 1993—, Anaheim (Calif.) City Sch. Dist., 1994—; guest mktg. lectr. U. So. Calif., 1986—; developer, leader U. So. Calif. Western Europe's Grad. Bus. Exch. Program, 1987. Polit. campaign vol., Long Beach, Calif., 1989—. Mem. Am. Prodn. and Inventory Control Soc., Town and Gown. Republican. Presbyterian. Home: 7001 E Seaside Walk Long Beach CA 90803

VELAZQUEZ, ANABEL, sales executive; b. Havana, Cuba, July 26, 1958; came to U.S, 1966; d. Joel Velazquez and Elsa (Miranda) V.; m. Richard P. DiBacco; 1 child, Alexandra Chloe. BS in Nursing, Fla. Internat. U., 1987; AS, So. Coll., Collegedale, Tenn., 1979. RN, Fla.; CRRN, CEN; cert. ins. rehab. specialist; cert. case mgr. Staff nurse Hialeah (Fla.) Hosp., 1980-85; home care supr. Med. Pers. Pool, Miami, 1985-88; regional mgr. Peninsular Rehab. Assocs., Winter Park, Fla., 1988-89; med. sales specialist Bristol Myers-Squibb, Evansville, Ind., 1989-91; clin. sales specialist, sr. hosp. sales rep. Fujisawa Pharm. Co., Ill., 1990-92; rehab. specialist dir. Workers Rehab. Inc., Winter Park, Fla., 1993—. Recipient award Am. Legion. Mem. Coun. on Future of Nurses, Assn. Rehab. Nurses, Case Mgr. Assn. Home: 229 Crooked Stick Ct Orlando FL 32828-8831 Office: Workers Rehab Inc PO Box 2464 Goldenrod FL 32733

VELAZQUEZ, NYDIA, congresswoman. Mem. 103rd Congress from 12th N.Y. dist., Washington, D.C., 1993—. Office: US Ho of Reps 132 Cannon Washington DC 20515

VELÁZQUEZ DE CANCEL, LOURDES, religious organization executive, educator, interpreter, translator, poet; b. Santurce, P.R., Jan. 28, 1941; d. Manuel Velázquez-Conde and Ramonita Torres-Marrero; m. Eduardo Cancel-Rodriguez, June 3, 1961; children: Lourdes Isabel, Eduardo Juan, Daniel Eduardo. Grad., Inst. Children's Lit., West Redding, Conn., 1993. Pres., founder Ralvec Ministries, Carolina, 1991—. Author: A Crisis of Faith, 1986, Does Anyone Care? 1991, My Secret Garden, 1991, On Love and Power, 1991, On a Daily Basis, 1991, A Question of Integrity, 1991, Amidst Deep Waters, 1991, No One is So Great or So Small, 1994, The Tree of Life, 1994, Erotika-Poems, Proverbs and Undiluted Thoughts, 1994, His Way, 1992, Tulip Woman, 1993, Erotika, 1994, It is not Enough to Beg, 1994, The Money Value of Man, 1994, Come Home, Mother Come Home, 1994, The Signet, The Shield, The Pair of Keys, 1994; author numerous hymns, psalms, poems and short stories; editor Resurrection Life Mag., 1991. Translator ARC, San Juan, P.R., 1989-90. Recipient Merit award Internat. Soc. Poets, 1992. Mem. Soc. Tech. Communicators. Office: Ralvec Ministries PO Box 9466 Plaza Carolina Sta Carolina PR 00628

VELDE, JANE DOOLITTLE, French tutor, artist, interior designer; b. Aurora, Ill., June 17, 1934; d. John Russell and Janet (Snook) Doolittle; m. Karl Herget Velde, Oct. 8, 1960 (div. July 1991); children: Janet Velde Paine, Mary-Helen Velde Black, Ty. A degree, Bradford (Mass.) Jr. Coll., 1954; cert., Ecole des Louvre, Paris, 1955, Ecole des Beaux Arts, Paris, 1993. Travel agt. Am. Express, Paris, 1956-58, Clara Laughlin Travel Svc., Chgo., 1959-62, Murphy Travel Svc., Winnetka, Ill., 1967-72; French tutor Chgo., 1991—; apprentice interior designer Sandcastle Interiors, Winnetka. Vol. Winnetka caucus, Ill. Coun. Against Handgun Violence, 1992-94; women's bd. dirs. Northwestern Meml. Hosp., Chgo., 1953-94. Recipient Cmty. Svc. award Caucus of Village of Winnetka, 1988-90. Episcopalian. Home: 1212 N Lake Shore Dr Chicago IL 60610-2371

VÉLEZ, EILEEN MCLELLAN DE, social worker; b. Boston, Apr. 26, 1955; d. Robert Francis and Mary Joan (McNulty) McLellan; m. Luis Arnaldo Vélez-Cortés. Bachelor in Journalism, Suffolk U., 1977; BS in Journalism. Cert. in cultural understanding in child welfare, substance abuse and family violence. Eligibility worker Dept. Pub. Welfare, Quincy, Mass., 1977-78; adminstrv. asst. Dept. Pub. Welfare, Quincy, 1978-80; sr. interviewer Div. Employment Security, Boston, 1980; social work tech. Dept. Social Services, Quincy, 1980-81, social worker III, 1981—, supr. B of Social Work student interns, 1990—; hotline counselor Survival Crisis Lines, Quincy, 1978-80. Vol. spl. events, cmty. outreach coord. for fundraising AIDS Action Com., Boston, 1988—, asst. dir. of acquisitions Acad. Awards Night Fundraiser, 1992; mem. com. women's concerns, libr., eucharistic minster Dignity-Boston, exec. bd., sec., 1993—; active Greater Boston Bus. Coun., 1992, 500 Club-Walk for Life, 1991-92, Greenpeace, 1994-95. Named Social Worker of Yr., Mass. Foster Parent Assn., 1989. Mem. NOW, Parents and Friends Lesbians and Gays, Dignity-Boston, Suffolk U. Alumni Ambs., Gamma Sigma Sigma. Democrat. Roman Catholic. Home: 1153 Hyde Park Ave Hyde Park MA 02136-2808 Office: Dept Social Svcs 541 Main St Weymouth MA 02190-1845

VELICER, JANET SCHAFBUCH, elementary school educator; b. Cedar Rapids, Iowa, Aug. 27, 1941; d. Allan J. and Geraldine Frances (Stuart) Schafbuch; m. Leland Frank Velicer, Aug. 17, 1963; children: Mark Allan, Gregory Jon, Daniel James. BS, Iowa State U., 1963, MS, 1966; cert. Elem. Edn., Mich. State U., 1976. Tchr. chemistry Prendergast High Sch., Upper Darby, Pa., 1964-65; tchr. home econs. Cardinal O'Hara High Sch., Springfield, Pa., 1965-66; substitute tchr. Pa., Mich., 1967-76; elem. tchr. Winans Elem. Sch., Waverly, Mich., 1976-78, Wardcliff Elem. Sch., Okemos, Mich., 1978-94; tchr. gifted and talented alternative program grades 4 and 5 Hiawatha Elem. Sch., Okemos, 1994—; computer coord., Great Books coord.; dist. com. mem. math, computer, substance abuse, cable TV, evaluation revision Okemos Pub. Schs., Instructional Coun. Author: (video) Wardcliff School Documentary, 1982, The Integrated Arts Program of the Okemos Elementary Schools, 1983. Citizens adv. com. to develop a five-yr. plan, 1982-83, Bldg. utilization adv. com., 1983-84, Community use of schs. adv. com., 1984-85, Strategic planning steering com., 1989-90, Taking our schs. into tomorrow com., 1990-91, Bonding election steering com., 1991; chmn. wellness com. Okemos Pub. Schs., 1993—. Recipient Classrooms of Tomorrow Tchr. award Mich. Dept. Edn., 1990. Mem. NEA, Mich. Edn. Assn., Okemos Edn. Assn., Phi Kappa Phi, Omicron Nu, Iota Sigma Pi. Democrat. Home: 2678 Blue Haven Ct East Lansing MI 48823-3804 Office: Okemos Pub Schs 4406 Okemos Rd Okemos MI 48864-2553

VELLENGA, KATHLEEN OSBORNE, former state legislator; b. Alliance, Nebr., Aug. 5, 1938; d. Howard Benson and Marjorie (Menke) Osborne; m. James Alan Vellenga, Aug. 9, 1959; children: Thomas, Charlotte Vellenga Landreau, Carolyn. BA, Macalester Coll., 1959. Tchr. St. Paul Pub. Schs., 1959-60, Children's Ctr. Montessori, St. Paul, 1973-74, Children's House Montessori, St. Paul, 1974-79; mem. Minn. Ho. of Reps., St. Paul, 1980-94, mem. health and human svcs. com., 1987-92, mem. tax. com., rules com., chmn. judiciary com., 1991—, chmn. St. Paul del., 1985-89, chmn. criminal justice div., 1989-90, chmn. crime and family law div., 1987-88, mem. Dem. steering com., 1987—; chmn. judiciary Minn. Ho. of Reps., 1991, 92, chmn. edn. fin., 1992-93, 93-94; mem. Gov.'s Council on Youth, St. Paul, 1983-86, St. Paul Family Svcs. Bd., 1994-95; coord. St. Paul, Ramsey County Children's Initiative, 1994—. Mem. steering com. Alliance for Sci., St. Paul, 1982-84, 89; bd. dirs. Landmark Ctr., St. Paul, 1985-87; chmn. Healthstart, St. Paul, 1987-91. Mem. LWV (v.p. St. Paul chpt. 1979), Minn. Women Elected Ofcls. (vice chair 1994). Democrat. Presbyterian. Office: A H Wilder 919 La Fond Saint Paul MN 55104

VENDLER, HELEN HENNESSY, literature educator, poetry critic; b. Boston, Mass., Apr. 30, 1933; d. George and Helen (Conway) Hennessy; 1 son, David. A.B., Emmanuel Coll., 1954; Ph.D., Harvard U., 1960; Ph.D. (hon.), U. Oslo; D.Litt. (hon.), Smith Coll., Kenyon Coll., U. Hartford, Union Coll., Columbia U., George Washington U., Marlboro Coll., St. Louis; DHL (hon.), Dartmouth Coll., U. Mass., Bates Coll., U. Toronto, Ont., Can., Trinity Coll., Dublin, Ireland. Instr. Cornell U., Ithaca, N.Y., 1960-63; lectr. Swarthmore (Pa.) Coll. and Haverford (Pa.) Coll., 1963-64; asst. prof. Smith Coll., Northampton, Mass., 1964-66; asso. prof. Boston U., 1966-68, prof., 1968-85;, $D; Fulbright lectr. U. Bordeaux, France, 1968-69; vis. prof. Harvard U., 1981-85, Kenan prof., 1985—, Porter U. prof., 1990—, assoc. acad. dean, 1987-92, sr. fellow Harvard Soc. Fellows, 1981-93; poetry critic New Yorker, 1978—; mem. edn1. adv. bd. Guggenheim Found., 1991—, Pulitzer Prize Bd., 1991—. Author: Yeat's Vision and the Later Plays, 1963, On Extended Wings: Wallace Stevens' Longer Poems, 1969, The Poetry of George Herbert, 1975, Part of Nature, Part of Us, 1980, The Odes of John Keats, 1983, Wallace Stevens: Words Chosen Out of Desire, 1985, Harvard Book of Contemporary Am. Poetry, 1985; editor: Voices and Visions: The Poet in America, 1987, The Music of What Happens, 1988, Soul Says, 1995, The Given and the Made, 1995, The Breaking of Style, 1995. Fulbright fellow, 1954, AAUW fellow, 1959, Guggenheim fellow, 1971-72, Am. Coun. Learned Socs. fellow, 1971-72, NEH fellow, 1980, 85, 94, Overseas fellow Churchill Coll., Cambridge, 1980, Charles Stewart Parnell fellow Magdalene Coll., 1995; recipient Lowell prize 1969, Explicator prize, 1969, award Nat. Inst. Arts and Letters, 1975, Radcliffe Grad. Soc. medal, 1978, Nat. Book Critics award, 1980, Keats-Shelley Assn. award, 1994. Mem. MLA (exec. coun. 1972-75, pres. 1980), English Inst. (trustee 1977-85), Am. Acad. Arts and Scis (v.p. 1992—), Norwegian Acad. Letters and Sci., Nat. Humanities Ctr. (bd. dirs. 1989-93), Am. Acad. Arts and Letters, Am. Philos. Soc., Phi Beta Kappa. Home: 54 Trowbridge St # 2 Cambridge MA 02138 also: Harvard U Dept English 8 Prescott St Cambridge MA 02138

VENEZIA, JOYCE ANN, journalist; b. Englewood, N.J., Sept. 26, 1960; d. Rocco Peter and Maria L. (Matera) V.; m. Sherwin Alan Suss, Mar. 3, 1990. BA in Journalism and Am. Studies, Pa. State U., 1982. News. clk. Asbury Pk. (N.J.) Press, 1982; copy editor Montgomery County Record, Jenkintown, Pa., 1982-83; newswoman AP, Augusta, Maine and Hartford, Conn., 1983-85; corr. AP, Evansville, Ind., 1985-86, Atlantic City, 1986-89; reporter The Star-Ledger, Newark, 1989—. Roman Catholic. Home: 438 Overbrook Rd Ridgewood NJ 07450-3417 Office: The Star Ledger Press Rm Bergen County Courthouse Hackensack NJ 07601

VENEZIA, LINDA CRISTA, nurse midwife; b. Bklyn., Apr. 14, 1961; d. Nicholas Cosimo and Emily Marie (Romani) Gaglioti. BSN, Adelphi U., 1983, MSN magna cum laude, 1992; post master's cert. in nurse midwifery, Columbia U., 1994. RN, N.Y.; cert. childbirth educator, BLS. Student nurse technician Luth. Med. Ctr., Bklyn., 1982-83; staff nurse gynecology, surgery Luth. Med. Ctr., 1983-85, staff nurse labor and delivery, 1985-89, asst. nursing care coord. labor and delivery, 1989-94; staff nurse, midwife Maimonides Med. Ctr., 1994—. Mem. ANA (cert.), AWHONN (cert.), Am. Coll. Nurse-Midwives, Coun. Childbirth Edn. Specialists, N.Y. State Perinatal Assn., Sea Gate Assn., Sigma Theta Tau. Republican. Roman Catholic. Home: 4923 Beach 49 St Brooklyn NY 11224

VENNE, PIERRETTE, general elector, lawyer; b. Beauharnois, Quebec, Can., Aug. 8, 1945; d. Lucien Venne and Marcelle Laberge; m. Jean-Marc Perron. Student, U. Sherbrooke, U. Aix-En-Provence, U. Winnipeg, Cegep du Vieux Montréal. Elector, Saint-Hubert Ho. of Commons, 1988—; lawyer, 1976—. Active YMCA Feminist Action Com. Mem. East-Ctrl. Montreal Notaries' Assn. (former pres.), Chamber Notaries, U. Sherbrooke Law Faculty Alumni Assn. Mem. Bloc Québecois. Office: House Commons Legis Office, Confederation Bldg Rm 286, Ottawa, ON Canada K1A 0A6 also: 5440 Chemin Chambly # 110, Saint-Hubert, PQ Canada

VENNERI, DOREEN AGATHA, dentist; b. Hatboro, Pa., Dec. 2, 1961; d. A. Joseph and Rosanna Margaret (Yanni) V. BS in Biology, St. Joseph's U., Phila., 1983; DMD, Temple U., 1987. Dentist Venneri Dental Assocs., Hatboro, 1987—; com. chairperson Ann. Dental Conf. at Valley Forge, King of Prussia, Pa., 1989—. Bd. govs. St. Joseph's U., 1991—. Mem. ADA, Pa. Dental Assn., Phila. County Dental Soc., Acad. Gen. Dentistry, Montgomery Bucks Dental Soc., St. Joseph's U. Med. Alumni Assn. (officer, treas. 1993—).

VENTIMIGLIA, KATHARINE JANE GARVER, education educator; b. Muncie, Ind., Sept. 1, 1949; d. Edwin Gilmore and Sybil Marie (Daughtry) Garver; m. Joseph John Ventimiglia, June 17, 1972; children: Joseph Marc, Robert Edwin, Jeffrey Peter, Matthew Patrick. BA in Edn., NE La. U., 1971; MEd, Dowling Coll., 1991; postgrd., Hofstra U. Cert. nursery and elem. tchr., Ill., N.Y. Tchr. Archdiocese of Chgo., 1971-72, Diocese of Bklyn., 1972-74; adj. asst. prof. coll. reading Suffolk Community Coll., Selden, N.Y., 1986-91, prof. reading, 1991—; asst. to dir. program learning disabled Dowling Coll., Oakdale, N.Y., 1991—; reading/writing specialist student support svcs. Dowling Coll., Oakdale, 1993—, adj. lectr. edn., 1994—; pvt. practicereading clinic; reading/learning disabilities specialist Dowling Coll., Oakdale, 1989—. Author: (with others) Successful Strategies for Learning Disabled College Students: Reading, Writing and Reasoning, 1991. Treas. Sagamore Jr. High Sch. PTA, Holtsville, N.Y., 1987-88, bd. dirs. 1986-89; treas. Gatelot Ave. PTA, Lake Ronkonkoma, N.Y., 1983-92, mem. exec. bd. 1979-92, project coord. Reading Is Fundamental, 1989-92. Mem. AAUW, DAR, Internat. Reading Assn., Orton Dyslexia Soc., Kappa Delta Pi, Alpha Upsilon Alpha. Office: Dowling Coll Student Support Svcs Fortunoff Hall Rm 007 Oakdale NY 11769 also: Suffolk Community Coll Sagtikos Bldg Crooked Hill Rd Rm 201 Brentwood NY 11717

VENTRES, JUDITH MARTIN, lawyer; b. Ann Arbor, Mich., Feb. 10, 1943; d. D. Lawrence and Donna E. (Webb) Moran; children: Laura C. Martin, Paul M. Martin, A. Lindsay Martin; m. Daniel B. Ventres Jr., Dec. 27, 1984. BA, U. Mich., 1963; postgrad., Universite de Jean Moulin, Institut du Droit, Lyon, France, 1981; JD, U. Minn., 1982. Bar: Minn. 1982, Fla. 1991, Colo. 1994, U.S. Tax Ct. 1989, U.S. Dist. Ct. Minn. 1989, U.S. Ct. Appeals (8th cir.) 1989. Tax supr., dir. fin. planning, asst. nat. dir. Coopers & Lybrand, Mpls., 1981-84; dir. fin. planning Investors Diversified Services subs. Am. Express, Mpls. and N.Y.C., 1984-85; sr. tax mgr., dir. fin. planning KPMG Peat Marwick Main & Co., Mpls., 1985-89; prin. Martin & Assocs., P.A., Mpls., Minn., 1989—; faculty Minn. CLE, 1994. owner Alternatax, Inc. Mem. Mpls. C. of C. Campaign, Downtown Coun. Coms., Mpls., 1982-84, Metro Tax Planning Group, 1984-86, Mpls. Estate Planning Coun., 1985—, Planned Giving Coun.; class chmn. fundraising campaign U. Minn. Law Sch., Mpls., 1985; usher Christ Presbyn. Ch., Edina, Minn., 1983—; mem. adv. coun. on planned giving ARC. Mem. ABA (task force on legal fin. planning), Minn. Bar Assn., Hennepin County Bar Assn., Fla. Bar Assn., Minn. Soc. CPAs (instr. continuing legal edn. 1983-84, continuing profl. edn. 1982-86, individual, trust and estate provisions Tax Reform Act 1986, continuing legal edn.- estate planning 1994), Am. Assn. Ind. Investors (speaker), Am. Soc. CLUs, Minn. Soc. CLUs, Minn. Women Lawyers, Fla. Women Lawyers, Lex Alumnae, U. Mich. Alumni Assn. (coun. govs. 1989—, pres.- elect, scholarship chmn.), U. Minn. Alumni Club (coun. govs. 1988—, pres., treas., membership com.), Minn. World Trade Assn., Internat. Assn. Fin. Planners, Colo. Bar Assn., Edina C. of C., Interlachen Club, Coun. Women Lawyers, Athletic Club, Lafayette Club, U. Minn. Alumni Assn. Bd. (mem. univ. issues com.). Home: 1355 Vine Pl Mound MN 55364-9635 Office: Martin & Assocs PA 1650 W 82d St Ste 1460 Minneapolis MN 55431

VENTRY, CATHERINE VALERIE, lawyer; b. Bronxville, N.Y., Feb. 19, 1949; d. Victor and Catherine Regina (Dillon) V. AB in Logic and Philosophy, Vassar Coll., 1971; postgrad., Boston U., 1972; JD, N.Y. Law Sch., 1978. Bar: N.Y. 1979, U.S. Dist. Ct. (so. and ea. dists.) N.Y. 1979. Adj. asst. prof. John Jay Coll. of Criminal Justice, N.Y.C., 1978-80; adj. asst. prof. bus. law Coll. Mount St. Vincent Lehman Coll., N.Y.C., 1978-82; staff atty. City of N.Y. Dept. Housing Preservation and Devel. Litigation Bureau, N.Y.C., 1981-84; pvt. practice N.Y., 1984—; Tax editor Prentice-Hall Pub. Co., Englewood Cliffs, N.J., 1980-81. Mem. N.Y. State Bar, Rockland County Women's Bar, Rockland County Bar Assn., MENSA. Office: 873 Union Ave New Windsor NY 12553-5034

VENUTO, DONNA FRANCINE, nurse, quality assurance manager; b. Stowe, Pa., Mar. 27, 1949; d. Frank Anthony Jacketti and Ruth Elaine (Schoch) Cecchi; m. Anthony Robert Venuto, Mar. 11, 1972; children: Cristianna, Frank. RN diploma, St. Joseph's Hosp., Reading, Pa., 1970; student, Phila. Coll. Textiles & Sci., 1992—. RN, Pa. Staff nurse critical care St. Joseph's Hosp., Reading, 1970-71, Children's Hosp., Phila., 1971-75; charge nurse critical care Arcadia (Calif.) Meth. Hosp., 1976-80; charge nurse pediatric rehab. Children's Seashore House, Phila., 1980-85; staff nurse blood collections ARC, Phila., 1986-88, staff educator, 1988-90, quality assurance specialist, 1990-91, quality assurance mgr., 1991—; chief safety officer ARC, Phila., 1990—, co-developer seminar, 1990. Co-author: (tng. manual) ARC Biosafety Tng. Manual, 1991. Mem. ARC, 1991. Mem. Am. Assn. Blood Banks. Republican. Roman Catholic. Home: 1 Samuel Ct Sewell NJ 08080 Office: ARC Penn-Jersey 23rd & Chestnut Sts Philadelphia PA 19103

VEON, DOROTHY HELENE, education educator; b. Oxford, Nebr., May 31, 1924; d. John B. and Ella (Robertson) V. BSc, U. Nebr., 1945; MA, George Washington U., 1949; EdD, Columbia U., 1957; M. Med. Sci., Tulane U., 1969. Asst. prof. edn. George Washington U., Washington, 1945-50; prof. edn. Pa. State U., University Park, 1950-66; asst. dir. Sch. of Nursing Thomas Jefferson U., Phila., 1966-68; vis. prof. Ariz. State U., 1959-60, Drexel U., Phila., 1973-74, Temple U., Phila., 1974-75, U. Vt., 1966; Bradley U., 1962, U. Oreg., 1964; ednl. and bus. cons. Phila., 1988—; prof., dir. div. econs. and bus. adminstrn. C.C. Phila., 1970-88, NIH Schs., 1968-69. Editor Am. Bus. Edn. U.S. del. to World Congress of Women, Moscow, 1987; organizer, spkr. UN Decade for Women Conf., Nairobi, Kenya, 1985, UN Fourth World Conf. for Women, Beijing, 1995, NGO Forum for Women, Beijing, 1995; keynote spkr. Wilton Park Conf. NATO, West Sussex, Eng., 1994; mem. confs. Internat. Fedn. Univ. Women, Mexico City, 1965, Karlsruhe, Germany, 1968, Phila., 1971, Tokyo and Kyoto, 1974, Stirling, Scotland, 1977, Vancouver, B.C., Can., 1980, Groningen, The Netherlands, 1983, Christchurch, N.Z., 1986, Helsinki, 1989, Stanford U., 1992, Trinity Coll., Dublin, Oxford U., Yokojama, Japan, 1995; bd. dirs. Virginia Gildersleeve Internat. Fund for Univ. Women, 1982-92. Recipient Internat. Disting. Svc. award Status of Women, 1986; Radcliffe Rsch. scholar, 1988-90; named Internat. Woman of Yr., Internat. Biog. Ctr., Cambridge, Eng., 1993-94. Mem. NAFE, AAUW (nat. grantee 1968, 84, 93, v.p. Pa. divsn. 1964-66, Disting. award 1985, pres. Phila. br. 1983-85, Nat. 50 Yr. honoree 1992), Am. Acad. Natural Scis., Am. Mgmt. Assn., Am. Mktg. Assn., Am. Bus. Comm. Assn. (v.p. 1962-65, nat. fellow 1970), Internat. Soc. Bus. Edn. (pres. 1958-60), Am. Econ. Assn., Am. Acctg. Assn., Am. Assn. Natural History, World Affairs Coun. Phila., Fgn. Policy Rsch. Inst., Phila. Mus. Art, Nat. Space Soc., Pa. Acad. Fine Art, Mt. Vernon Soc. George Washington U. (hon.), Emerald Soc. (hon.), Kappa Delta (province pres. 1948-50, 62-64, 70-72), Phi Delta Gamma, Pi Omega Pi, Delta Pi Epsilon (nat. pres. 1960-62, Nat. Rsch. award 1949), Pi Lambda Theta (nat. treas. 1960-64). Republican. Episcopalian. Home: 1700 Benjamin Franklin Pky Philadelphia PA 19103

VERBA, BETTY LOU, real estate executive; b. Cleve., Sept. 22, 1933; d. Albert Roy and Philomena (Weigel) Short; m. James Richard Verba, Sept. 11, 1954; children: Marilyn Danko, Christine Adkins, Patricia Zore. Student, Miami U., Oxford, Ohio, 1952, Bowling Green State U., 1953. Lic. realtor, Ohio. Owner B&J Properties, 1963—; trustee Holiday Lakes Property Owners Assn., Willard, Ohio, 1973-77; realtor Realty One (formerly HGM/Hilltop), Parma Heights, Ohio, 1977-94, Century 21 DePiero & Assocs., 1994—. Geneaologist (family history book) Short Family History, 1823-1973, Update, 1974-85. Mem. grand jury Cuyahoga County, 1990. Mem. Parma Genealogy Club (v.p.). Democrat. Roman Catholic. Home: 8800 Banner Ln Parma OH 44129-6072 Office: Century 21 De Piero and Assoc 5581 Ridge Parma OH 44130 Office: 5581 Ridge Parma OH 44130

VERBAGE-LANE, KATHRYN ELEANOR, special education educator, consultant; b. Huntington, W.Va., Mar. 6, 1952; d. Thomas J. and Betty E. (Caverlee) Verbage; m. Michael G. Lane, Feb. 1991; 1 child, Rebecca. BA in Elem. Edn. and Mental Retardation, Marshall U., 1974; MA in Learning Disabilities, W.Va. U., 1980. Cert. spl. edn. tchr., W.Va., Va. Ward clk. ICU St. Mary's Hosp., Huntington, 1970-72; recreation dir. Green Acres Regional Ctr. for Mental Retardation, LeSage, W.Va., 1972-74, tchr. mentally retarded, summer 1975; tchr. learning disabilities Ritchie County Schs., Harrisville, W.Va., 1974-77; tchr. learning disabilities Mercer County Schs., Princeton, W.Va., 1977-79, spl. edn. specialist, 1979-89; substitute tchr. Roanoke (Va.) County, Salem City, and Franklin County Schs., 1989—; homebound tchr. spl. edn. students, pvt. tutor Franklin County (Va.) Schs., 1994; instr. W.Va. Coll. Grad. Studies, Institute, summer 1981; participant standard profl. edn., Austin, Tex., spring 1983; examiner hearing impaired outreach project Brescia Coll., Owensboro, Ky., 1981, Chapel Hill (n.C.) Tng./Outreach, 1983; trainer Woodcock-Johnson by Dr. R. Woodcock, Balt., 1981. Author poetry. Goodwill amb. Mercer County Sheriff's Dept., Princeton, 1984; children's pastor. Recipient Cert. of Appreciation, Green Acres Ctr. for Mental Retardation, 1973, Mercer County Schs., 1982. Mem. Coun. for Exceptional Children, Assn. for Retarded Children (sponsor jr. orgn.), Bibl. Archeology Soc., Smithsonian Assocs., Assn. for Children with Learning Disabilities, W.Va. Edn. Assn., Civitan, Phi Delta Kappa (membership com.). Home: RR 1 Box 887 Boones Mill VA 24065-9789

VERBURG, JOANN, artist, photography educator; b. Summit, N.J., June 9, 1950; d. Robert Martin and Jane Carol Verburg; m. James McConaughy Moore, July 21, 1984. BA, Ohio Wesleyan U., 1972; MFA, Rochester Inst. Tech., 1977. Coord. spl. events The Phila. (Pa.) Mus. Art, 1972-74; exhbn. curator, rschr. Internat. Mus. Photography, Rochester, N.Y., 1974-77; photographer, rsch. coord. The Rephotographic Survey Project, Breckenridge, Colo., 1977-83; artist liaison Polaroid Corp., Cambridge, Mass., 1978-81; photography vis. artist The Colo. Coll., Colorado Springs, Colo., 1984—; photography MA in Liberal Arts program MALS Program, Hamline U., St. Paul, 1989—; critic dept. photography Yale Sch. Art, 1994. Author: Second View: A Rephotographic Survey, 1984; artist: (catalog) Robert Wilson's Knee Plays, 1984, (book/exhbn. catalog) Pleasures and Terrors of Domestic Comfort, 1991; exhbns. include Pace/MacGill Gallery, N.Y.C., 1993, Mus. of Modern Art, N.Y.C., 1990, Light Gallery, N.Y.C., 1985. Artist fellow Guggenheim Found., N.Y.C., 1986, McKnight Found., Mpls., 1988, Bush Found., St. Paul, 1993-94.

VERCIGLIO, TINA MARIA, publishing executive, consultant; b. Birmingham, Ala., Sept. 20, 1955; d. Norman Frank and Katherine (Zaden) V. BS in Edn., U. Ala., 1977. Cert. elem. tchr.; lic. life ins. agt. Tchr. early childhood Pasco County Bd. Edn., Dade City, Fla., 1977-80; specialist child devel. Emma Pendleton Hosp., Providence, 1980-81; tchr. early childhood Jefferson County Bd. Edn., Birmingham, 1981-83; pub., editor Birmingham Bus. Jour., 1983—; pub. Ala. Health News, Birmingham, 1988—, Shoppers Guide and News, Birmingham, 1989—; pub. cons., Birmingham, 1988—. Bd. dirs. Magic City Art Connection, Birmingham, 1988—. Mem. Women's Network. Office: Birmingham Bus Jour 2101 Magnolia Ave S Ste 400 Birmingham AL 35205-2852

VERDERAIME, MARIA KIMBERLY, nurse; b. Balt., July 23, 1965; d. Earl Stuart and Charlene Barbara (Randall) Oxley; m. Bruce Robert Verderaine, Dec. 8, 1993; children: Seth Jordan, Samantha Christine. AA, Essex C.C., Balt., 1992. Nurse Shock Trauma, Balt., 1992, Spring Grove, Balt., 1992-93, Favorite Nurses, Silver Spring, Md., 1993—. EMT, mem. Fire Dept., Carroll County, Md., 1994—. Roman Catholic. Home: 6805 Runkles Rd Mount Airy MD 21771-7319 Office: Favorite Nurses Fenton St Silver Spring MD

VERDUIN, BERT M., real estate executive; b. Benton, Ark., Feb. 9, 1947; d. Elvis Lee and Helen Lee (McBride) Moses; m. Michael Hankins Verduin, May 23, 1970; children—Valerie Ann, Clinton Logan. A.A.S., Brookhaven Coll., 1982; grad. real estate designation George Leonard Sch. Real Estate. Lic. real estate broker. Acct., Realty Devel. Corp., Dallas, 1970-77; owner, mgr. Tax Service, Dallas, 1977-83; sr. v.p., contr. Realty Devel. Corp., Dallas, 1983-87; pres. Strobe Mgmt. Svcs., Inc., Dallas, Tyler, 1987—. East Tex. Women's Resource Coun., Apt. Assn. Greater Dallas, Tyler Exec. Women's Network, Tyler Apt. Assn., Zonta Club. Republican. Mem. Ch. of Christ. Avocations: reading; crafts. Office: Strobe Mgmt Svcs Inc 2102 Montclair Ln Lewisville TX 75067-6148

VERED, RUTH, art gallery director; b. Tel Aviv, Sept. 26, 1940; d. Abraham and Helen (Psisuska) Rosenblum; children: Sharon, Oren. BA in Art Hisotry with honors, Bezalel U., Jerusalem, 1964. Freelance art cons., Israel and N.Y.C., 1965-75; dir. Vered Gallery, East Hampton, N.Y., 1977—. Sgt. paratroops Israeli Army, 1958-60. Home: 891 Park Ave New York NY 10021-0326 Office: Vered Gallery East Hampton NY 11937

VERGAMINI, JUDITH SHARON ENGEL, counselor, educator; b. Milw., May 21, 1941; d. Max E. and Rose (Ladish) Engel; m. Jerome Carl Vergamini, May 1, 1965; children: Michael David, Beth Allison, Daniel Carl. BS, U. Wis., 1963, postgrad., 1964, 66-76; MS, U. Oreg., 1978, postgrad., 1980—. Nat. cert. counselor; lic. tchr., sch. counselor, profl. lic. counselor, marriage and family therapist. Elem. tchr. Crestwood Elem. Sch., Northbrook, Ill., 1963-64, Odana Elem. Sch., Madison, Wis., 1964-65, Fitzmorris Elem. Sch., Arvada, Colo., 1965-66; tchr. Headstart, Madison, Wis., 1966; coord., founder parent vols. program Alternate Sch., Eugene, Oreg., 1976-77; pvt. practice counselor Eugene, 1978—; instr. Lane C.C., Eugene, Oreg., 1978—; lectr. Addictions Treatment Hosp. Program, 1989-92; mental health specialist Headstart of Lane County, Oreg., 1993-94; resource counselor Newman Ctr. U. Oreg., Eugene, 1979—, adj. prof., 1994—; presenter in field. Recipient Appreciation award Eugene Edn. Assn., 1980, Svc. to Edn. award, Oreg. Edn. Assn., 1980, Dedication and Performance award Nat. Disting. Svc. Registry, 1990, Outstanding Merit award Nat. Bd. Cert. Counselors, 1991. Fellow Am. Orthopsychiatric Assn.; mem. AACD, Am. Assn. for Marriage and Family Therapy (clin.), Am. Mental Health Counselors Assn., Oreg. Counseling Assn. Home: 1047 Brookside Dr Eugene OR 97405-4913 Office: 1508 Oak St Eugene OR 97401-4042

VERGANO, LYNN (MARILYNN BETTE VERGANO), artist; b. N.Y.C., Nov. 14; d. George and Helainesis (Haas) Anagnostis; children: Scott, Stephen, Sandy, Sefton. Student, Pratt Inst., 1959-60; BA, NYU, Heights, 1963; MA, NYU, 1964. Lectr. art Morris County Coll., 1982; lectr. in field; judge, art juror. Author/illustrator: (book) Paintings, 1980; one-woman shows include Papermill Playhouse, N.J., 1976, 79, 83, Fairleigh Dickinson U., N.J., 1977, Drew U., N.J., 1977, Rutgers U., N.J., 1978, 79, Hong Kong Arts Ctr., 1980, Am. Univ. Alumni, Bangkok, Thailand, 1980, Caldwell Coll., N.J., 1980, União Cultural Brasil-Estados Unidos, São Paulo, Brazil, 1982, Galleria Fenice, Venice, Italy, 1985, St. Sophia Mus., Istanbul, Turkey, 1988, Nat. Arts Club, N.Y.C., 1989, Centreplace, Hamilton, New Zealand, 1990; exhibited in group shows Monmouth Mus., Lincroft, N.J., 1976, 77, 82, Morris Mus., Morristown, N.J., 1977, 78, N.J. State Capital Mus., Trenton, 1979, Macculloch Hall Historical Mus., N.J., Morristown, 1984, 87, 89, 92, Nat. Audubon Artists, N.Y.C., 1981, Salmagundi Club, N.Y.C., 1981, World Trade Ctr., N.Y., 1981, Nat. Arts Club, N.Y.C., 1981-94, Bergen Mus., Paramus, N.J., 1983, Lincoln Ctr., N.Y.C., 1987, Bklyn. Botanic Gardens, N.Y., 1987, many others. Pres., chpt. and hon. mem. Welcome Wagon Club Randolph, N.J., 1969-70. Recipient UN 25th Anniversary Creative Writing award, 1970, John H. Miller award Morris County Coll., 1979, Grumbacher gold medallion, 1984, Torch award NYU, 1993. Mem. AAUW, Am. Watercolor Soc. (assoc.), Nat. Arts Club (exhibiting), Nat. Soc. Arts and Letters (exec. bd. N.J. chpt. 1979—), Federated Art Assns. N.J. (trustee 1982—, pres., chmn. bd. dirs. 1982-88, Heritage plaque 1989), Morris County Art Assn., Dover Art Assn. (bd. dirs. 1975-88), Kenilworth Art Assn. (hon.), Millburn-Short Hills Arts Ctr. Home: 16 Bragman Rd Randolph NJ 07869 also: 229 Van Cortlandt Park Ave Yonkers NY 10705

VERGERONT, SUSAN BOWERS, state legislator, public relations consultant; b. Milw., Nov. 30, 1945; d. Arthur William and Mary (Oberly) Bowers; m. David J. Vergeront, May 2, 1945; children: Margaret, John W., David E. BS, U. Wis., 1967; postgrad., Trinity Evang. Divinity Sch. Research assoc. Wis. Legis. Council, Madison, 1967-70; exec. dir. Grafton (Wis.) C. of C., 1978-80; account exec. Vollrath & Assocs., Cedarburg, Wis., 1981-84; mem. Wis. Assembly, 1984—; dir. Rep. Assembly Campaign Com., sec. 1989-92; chmn. Wis. State Bd. Am. Legis. Exch. Coun., Madison, 1985-87, Ozaukee Econ. Devel. Corp, 1989—. Bd. dirs. Women's Bus. Initiatives Corp., Milw., 1987-91, Manitou Council Girl Scouts U.S.A., Manitowic, Wis., 1984-87, Ozaukee Council on Alcohol and Drug Abuse. Named Outstanding Young Woman, Grafton Jaycettes, Outstanding Young Wisconsinite, Wis. Jaycees, 1981, Legislator of Yr., Wis. Am. Legion, 1987, 93, Outstanding Leader Am. Legis. Exch. Coun., 1991. Mem. Nat. Conf. State Legislators (nat. com.), Am. Legis. Exch. Coun. (chair task force on empowerment 1992), Wis. Women's Coun. (chmn. 1988-89), U.S. Jaycees (life), Grafton C. of C. (v.p. 1980-81). Presbyterian. Office: Wis State Legislature PO Box 8953 Madison WI 53708-8953

VERHESEN, ANNA MARIA HUBERTINA, counselor; b. Heerenveen, Friesland, Netherland, Dec. 6, 1932; came to U.S., 1968; d. Hendrikus H. and Henrika C. (Kluessjen) V. BS, Mercy Coll. of Detroit, 1981; MA, Sienna Height, Adrian, Mich., 1992. Childcare worker Schiedam, Netherland, 1952-54; social worker Rotterdam Halfweg, Netherland, 1954-59; childcare worker Mt. St. Ann's Home, Worcester and Lawrence, Mass., 1968-70; chem. dependency social worker St. Vincent Med. Ctr., Toledo, Ohio, 1970-75; social worker St. Joseph Hosp., Nashua, N.H., 1975-78; vocation dir. Grey Nuns, Lexington, Mass., 1978-79; coord. community svcs. St. Vincents Med. Ctr., Toledo, 1981-91; pvt. practice clin. therapist Sylvania, Ohio, 1992—; alcohol/drug addiction/mental health counselor for ex-prisoners; founder St. Vincent Med. Ctr. Alcoholism Detox and Rehab. Unit, Toledo, 1970-75. Co-founder Transitional Residences for the Homeless, Toledo, 1981-90, Ohio Coalition for the Homeless, Columbus, 1982-89; co-founder of a home for persons with AIDS; co-chair City of Toledo Housing Policy, 1985-90; coord. Housing Now, Toledo, 1988-90. Recipient Woman of Achievement award Women in Communication, Toledo, 1986, Spirit of '87 award N.W. Ordinance and U.S. Constn. Bicentennial Commn., Toledo, 1987, Gov.'s Spl. Recognition award, 1988, Man for Others award St. John's High Sch., 1991; named Woman of Toledo, St. Vincent Med. Ctr. Aux., 1988, Ohio Ho. of Reps., 1987; featured in various mags. Roman Catholic. Home: 219 Page St Toledo OH 43620-1400 Office: Elliott and Assocs Inc 5600 Monroe St Sylvania OH 43560

VERHOEK, SUSAN ELIZABETH, botany educator; b. Columbus, Ohio, 1942; m. S.E. Williams. Student, Carleton Coll., 1960-62; BA, Ohio Wesleyan U., 1964; MA, Ind. U., 1966; PhD, Cornell U., 1975. Herbarium supr. Mo. Bot. Garden, St. Louis, 1966-70; asst. prof. Lebanon Valley Coll., Annville, Pa., 1974-82, assoc. prof., 1982-85, prof., 1985—; vis. researcher Cornell U., Ithaca, N.Y., 1982-83; content cons. Merrill Pub. Co., 1987-89; vis. profl. Chgo. Bot. Garden, 1991. Author: How to Know the Spring Flowers, 1982; contbr. articles to profl. jours., newspapers, and bulls. Bd. trustees Lebanon Valley Coll., Annville, 1979-82, 84-90, 92-95. Named one of Outstanding Young Women of Am., 1976. Mem. Soc. for Econ. Botany (pres. 1985-86), Bot. Soc. Am., Am. Soc. Plant Taxonomists, Am. Assn. Bot. Gardens and Arboreta. Office: Lebanon Valley Coll Pa Annville PA 17003

VERLICH, JEAN ELAINE, writer, public relations consultant; b. McKeesport, Pa., July 5, 1950; d. Matthew Louis and Irene (Tomko) V.; m. S(tanley) Wayne Wright, Sept. 29, 1979 (div. June 1988). Student, Bucknell U., 1968-69; BA, U. Pitts., 1971. Press sec. Com. to Re-elect President, S.W. Pa., 1972; adminstrv. asst. Pa. Rep. James B. Kelly III, 1972-73; reporter Beaver (Pa.) County Times, 1973-74; proofreader Ketchum, MacLeod & Grove, Pitts., 1975-76; community rels. specialist, PPG Industries, Pitts., 1976-77, editor PPG News, 1977-79, sr. staff writer, 1979-84, comm. coord., 1984-85; pub. rels. assoc. Glass Group, 1986-87; mgr. pub. rels. Glass Group PPG Industries, 1987-92; account mgr. Maddigan Comm., Pitts., 1992-93; owner JV Comm., Pitts., 1993—. Mem. Internat. Assn. Bus. Communicators (bd. dir. Pitts. chpt. 1981, v.p. pub. rels. Pitts. chpt. 1982, v.p. programs Pitts. chpt. 1985, pres. Pitts. chpt. 1986), Travelers Aid Soc. Pitts. (bd. dirs., v.p. 1994—), Phi Beta Kappa, Delta Zeta. Office: JV Comm 3 Gateway Ctr Ste 1526 Pittsburgh PA 15222

VERMEER, MAUREEN DOROTHY, sales executive; b. Bronxville, N.Y., Mar. 21, 1945; d. Albert Casey and Helen (Valentine Casey) Vermeer; m. John R. Fassnacht, Feb. 11, 1966 (div. 1975); m. George M. Dallas Peltz IV, Oct. 26, 1985. Grad., NYU Real Estate Inst., 1976. Lic. real estate broker, notary pub., N.Y. With Douglas Elliman, N.Y.C., 1965-74, mgmt. supr., 1974-78, v.p., 1978-83; real estate broker Rachmani Corp., N.Y.C., 1983-84; v.p. sales and mktg. Carol Mgmt. Corp., N.Y.C., 1984-90; v.p. mktg. The Sunshine Group, N.Y.C., 1990; v.p., sec., bd. dirs. H.J. Kalikow & Co., N.Y.C., 1991—; bd. dirs. Ascot Owners, Inc., N.Y.C.; speaker in field. Mem. Real Estate Bd. N.Y., Assn. Real Estate Women. Republican. Presbyterian. Home: 206 County Rd Demarest NJ 07627-2202 Office: H J Kalikow & Co 101 Park Ave New York NY 10178-0001

VERMEER, WANDA BETH, health care consultant; b. Orange City, Iowa, Dec. 9, 1954; d. Bernard E. and Wilminia (Vander Schaaf) V. BSN, Augustana Coll., 1977; MBA, Ariz. State U., 1985. Head nurse Good Samaritan Med. Ctr., Phoenix, 1980-86; spl. projects dir. Good Samaritan Regional Med. Ctr., Phoenix, 1987-88; physician hosp. orgn. project mgr. Iowa Meth. Health System, Des Moines, 1989-92; dir. bus. devel. Tokos Med. Corp./Matrys Health Ptnrs., Phoenix, 1992—. Home: 2406 E Mountain Vista Dr Phoenix AZ 85048-4216 Office: Tokos Med Corp/Matryx Health Ptnrs 1821 E Dyer Rd Santa Ana CA 92705

VERMETT, ELIZABETH, realtor; b. Ann Arbor, Mich., June 7, 1953; d. Rudolph Joseph and Verna Florence (Conger) V.; 1 child, Emma Elizabeth. A in Criminal Justice, Washtenaw C.C., 1974. State trooper Mich. Dept. State Police, 1978-83; realtor Mich. Group Realtors, Ann Arbor, 1983-93; asst. mgr. Spear & Assocs., Inc. Realtors, Ann Arbor, 1994—; orientation instr. Ann Arbor Area Bd. Realtors, 1989—. Pub. Women's Yellow Pages of Washtenaw County, 1983-87. Mem. Nat. Assn. Realtors, NOW (Ann Arbor co-chair ERA task force 1981-82, bd. dirs. 1981-83, pres. 1983), Ann Arbor Bd. Realtors, Mich. Assn. Realtors. Home: 2415 Faye Dr Ann Arbor MI 48103 Office: Spear & Assocs Inc Realtors 1915 Pauline Plz Ann Arbor MI 48103

VERMEULE, EMILY TOWNSEND (MRS. CORNELIUS C. VERMEULE, III), classicist, educator; b. N.Y.C., Aug. 11, 1928; d. Clinton Blake and Eleanor (Meneely) Townsend; m. Cornelius C. Vermeule III, Feb. 2, 1957; children: Emily Dickinson Blake, Cornelius Adrian Comstock. AB, Bryn Mawr Coll., 1950; student, Am. Sch. Classical Studies, Athens, 1950-51, St. Anne's Coll., Oxford U., 1953; MA, Harvard, 1954; PhD, Bryn Mawr Coll., 1956; DLitt, Douglass Coll.; D. Litt., Rutgers U., 1968, Tufts U., 1980, U. Pitts., 1983, Bates Coll., 1983, U. Miami, Oxford, Ohio, 1986; LL.D., Regis Coll., 1971; D. Fine Arts, U. Mass, Amherst, 1971; D.Litt., Smith Coll., 1972, Wheaton Coll., 1973, Trinity Coll., 1974; LHD, Emmanuel Coll., 1980, Princeton U., 1989, Bard Coll., 1994. Instr. Greek lang. Bryn Mawr Coll., 1956-57; instr. Wellesley (Mass.) Coll., 1957-58, prof. art and Greek, 1965-70, chmn. dept. art, 1966-67; asst. prof. classics Boston U., 1958-61, assoc. prof. classics, 1961-65; fellow for research Boston Mus. Fine Arts, 1965—; James C. Loeb vis. prof. classical philology Harvard, 1969; dir. univ. Cyprus expdn. Harvard U., 1971—, Samuel and Doris Zemurray Stone-Radcliffe prof., 1970-94; Sather prof. U. Calif., Berkeley, 1975; Geddes-Harrower prof. Greek art and archaeology U. Aberdeen, 1980-81; Bernhard vis. prof. Williams Coll., 1986; excavations in Greece, Turkey, Libya, Cyprus. Author: Euripides v. Electra, 1959, Greece in the Bronze Age, 1964, The Trojan War in Greek Art, 1964, Götterkult, 1974, Toumba tou Skourou, The Mound of Darkness, 1975, Death in Early Greek Art and Poetry, Mycenaean Pictorial Vase-Painting (with U. Karageorghis), 1982, Toumba tou Skourou, A Bronze Age Potters' Quarter on Morphou Bay in Cyprus (with F.Z. Wolsky), 1990; contbr. articles to scholarly pubs. Judge Nat. Book Award, 1977; bd. dirs. Humanities Rsch. Inst., U. Calif., 1988-91, bd. govs., 1988-90; trustee Isabella Stewart Gardner Mus., 1988—. Recipient Gold medal for disting. achievement Radcliffe Coll. Grad. Soc., 1968; Guggenheim fellow, 1964-65. Fellow Soc. Antiquaries, Brit. Acad. (corr.), German Archaeol. Inst. (corr.); mem. AAAS, Am. Inst. Archaeology, Am. Philos. Soc. (v.p. 1978-81), Am. Philol. Assn. (Charles J. Goodwin award 1980, pres.-elect 1994), Smithsonian Coun. (bd. scholars 1983-89), Hellenic Soc. Office: Harvard U Widener Libr 215 Cambridge MA 02138

VERMYLEN, DEBRA MAE SINGLETON, sales executive; b. Tulsa, May 7, 1955; d. George Monroe and Jacqueline Romaine (Redman-Williams) Singleton; m. Patrick Roger Guy Vermylen, July 21, 1984; children: Nathan Christopher, Nicholas Patrick. AA, Erie Community Coll., Williamsville, N.Y., 1976; BS, SUNY, Buffalo, 1978. Sales rep. Kraft Inc., Columbia, Md., 1979-80, key sales rep., 1980-81, account mgr., 1981-82, sales supr. for Balt., 1982-84, sales supr. for Washington, 1984, supr. mil. sales, 1984-89; unit mgr. Kraft Gen. Foods, Columbia, 1989-90, sales mgr. ops., 1990-91; sales mgr. Kraft Gen. Foods, Houston, San Antonio, Rio Grande Valley, Austin, 1991-94, Fleming Co., Houston, 1993—, Randall's Food Mkts., Houston, 1993—. Coord. Children's Time Presch., Columbia, 1990; aide The Learning Tree Sch., Humble, Tex., 1994-95. Republican. Baptist. Home: 6007 Matt Rd Humble TX 77346-2758 Office: Kraft Gen Foods 14900 Woodham Dr Ste 125 Houston TX 77073-6009

VERNERDER, GLORIA JEAN, librarian; b. Ft. Wayne, Ind., June 2, 1930; d. John Otto and Vergie W. (Geiger) Krieg; m. Carl Penrod Vernerder, Dec. 25, 1952 (dec. Sept. 1984); children: Carla Jeanne Vernerder Kelly, Nina Marie Vernerder Anderson. Grad., Midway (Ky.) Coll.; student, Ind. U., Ft. Wayne, U. Ky. Br. libr. Pub. Libr. of Ft. Wayne and Allen County, 1950-52; children's libr. La Grange (Ill.) Pub. Libr., 1952-59; children's libr. Hinsdale (Ill.) Pub. Libr., 1961-68, head of youth svcs., 1969—. Editor: Sunlight and Shadows, 1983, 87, 90, 92; contbr. articles to profl. jours. Adminstrv. bd. First United Meth. Ch., LaGrange, 1986-88, Stephen Ministry, 1986—. Mem. ALA, Ill. Library Assn., Library Adminstrs. Conf. of No. Ill. (treas. 1969). Republican. Methodist. Home: 732 7th Ave La Grange IL 60525-6706 Office: Hinsdale Pub Library 20 E Maple St Hinsdale IL 60521-3490

VERNIERO, JOAN EVANS, special education educator; b. Wilkes-Barre, Pa., Nov. 30, 1937; d. Raymond Roth and Cary Hazel (Casano) Evans; m. Daniel Eugene Verniero Jr., Jan. 7, 1956; children: Daniel Eugene III, Raymond Evans. BA, Kean Coll., 1971; MS in Edn. Adminstrn., Monmouth Coll., West Long Branch, N.J., 1974; postgrad., Calif. Coast U., 1986-92. Cert. elem. sch. tchr., spl. edn. tchr., sch. adminstr., N.J., N.Mex., Colo.; nat. registered emergency med. technician. Tchr. Children's Psychiat. Ctr., Eatontown, N.J., 1965-69; tchr. Arthur Brisbane Child Treatment Ctr., Farmingdale, N.J., 1969-71, prin., 1971-75; prin. S.A. Wilson Ctr., Colorado Springs, Colo., 1976-82; tchr. pub. schs. Aurora, Colo., 1982-93; retired, 1993; edn. rep. Aurora Pub. Schs. Crew leader Black Forest (Colo.) Rescue Squad 1979-85, treas., bd. dirs. Fire Protection Dist., 1980-85; evaluator Arson divsn. Aurora (Colo.) Fire Dept., 1993—. Mem. Phi Delta Kappa. Republican. Presbyterian. Home: 671 S Paris St Aurora CO 80012-2315

VERNON, LILLIAN, mail order company executive; b. Leipzig, Germany; d. Herman and Erna Menasche; children: Fred, David. DCS (hon.), Mercy Coll., Dobbs Ferry, N.Y., 1984, Coll. New Rochelle, DSc in Bus. Adminstrn. (hon.), Bryant Coll., LLD (hon.), Baruch Coll., LHD (hon.), Old Dominion U., DCS (hon.) Mercy Coll., DCS (hon.) Coll. New Rochelle; D in Bus. Adminstrn. (hon.) Bryant Coll., LLD (hon.) Baruch Coll. CEOLillian Vernon, New Rochelle, N.Y., 1951—; lectr. in field. Contbr. articles to profl. jours. Bd. dirs. Westchester County Assn., N.Y., Mental Health Assn. Westchester County, Ctr. Preventive Psychiatry, Va. Opera, Children's Mus. Arts, Retinitis Pigmentosa Found.; trustee Coll. Human Svcs., Bryant Coll.; mem. adv. bd. Giraffe Project, Girl Scout Coun. Tidewater, Women's News; mem. bd. overseers Columbia U. Bus. Sch., NYU; mem. adv. com. Citizen Amb. Program; mem. bus. com. Met. Mus. Art; bd. govs. The Forum; mem. nat. com. The Kennedy Ctr. for Performing Arts, Washington; active The Ellis Island Reopening Com., Women's News Bd. Advisors; bd. govs. The Forum. Recipient Dist. Achievement award Lab. Inst. Merchandising, Entrepreneurial award Women's Bus. Owners of N.Y., 1983, Bravo award YWCA, Woman of Achievement award Woman's News, Nat. Hero award Big Bros./Big Sisters, Legend in Leadership award Emory U., A Woman Who Has Made A Difference award Inter. Womens Forum, medal of honor Ellis Island, Bus. Leadership award Gannett Newspapers, Outstanding Bus. Leader award Northwood Inst., Congl. Record Commendation award, Crystal award Coll. Human Svcs., City of Peace award Bonds of Israel, Svc. award Sr. Placement Bur., Excellence award Westchester Assn. Women Bus. Owners, Commendation in Congl. Record, Magnificent Seven award Bus. and Profl. Women, Woman of Distinction award Birmingham So. Coll.; named Va. Press Women Newsmaker of Yr., Woman of Yr., Women's Direct Response Group and Westchester County Fedn. Women's Clubs, Hampton Roads Woman of Yr., So. New England Entrepreneur Yr., Bravo award YWCA; named to Acad. Women Achievers, YWCA, Direct Mktg. Assn. Hall of Fame. Mem. Am. Bus. Conf. (dir.), Am. Stock Exch. (listed co. adv. com.), Com. of 200, Women's Forum, Nat. Retail Fedn. (bd. dirs.), Lotos Club. Office: Lillian Vernon Corp 543 Main St New Rochelle NY 10801

VERPLANCK, EVA LOW, association volunteer, retired chemist; b. Vienna, Austria, Aug. 25, 1924; came to U.S., 1940; d. Arthur and Gertrude (Burger) Low; m. Vincent Verplanck, Aug. 26, 1950 (dec. 1986); children: Anne, Philip. BA, Radcliffe Coll., 1944; PhD, Yale U., 1947. Postdoctoral fellow Yale U., New Haven, Conn., 1946-47, instr. rsch., 1947-50; rsch. fellow Acad. Natural Scis., Phila., 1950-58; retired. Past bd. dirs., pres., current hon. bd. dirs. YWCA, Newcastle County, Del., 1962—; bd. dirs. YWCA of the USA, N.Y.C., 1974-86, v.p. eastern region, 1983-86; allocations chair, v.p., United Way of Del., 1979-88; bd. dirs., pres. Vis. Nurse Assn., Chester Co., Pa., 1986-93, fundraising vol., 1993—; bd. dirs., pres. Red Clay Valley Assn., Pa./Del., 1987—; mem. vestry Christ Ch., Del., 1987-89; bd. dirs., sec. Ingleside Homes, Wilmington, Del., 1988-93; mem., treas Kennett Area Park Authority, Kennett Square, Pa., 1988—; chair Coun. of Home Health Agencies, Chester County, Pa., 1988-90.

VERSCHOYLE, JULIA ANN, advocate, artist; b. San Antonio, July 17, 1954; d. Hubert Henry and Katherine Leota (Largent) V.; m. Herbert E. Jordan, Dec. 29, 1973; 3 children. Student, S.W. Tex. State U., 1972-73, 89. tchr. Carnegie Arts Ctr., Leavenworth, Kans., spring 1993, summer and fall, 1994; contractor as advocate, resource contact exceptional family mem. program (EFMP) Army Community Svcs. (ACS), 1993—; speaker Acad. Allergy and Immunology, Kansas City, Kans., 1994; various positions retail sales. Exhibited in San Antonio Area Art Shows, 1989, Kuntslerbund Cafe Art Guild Annual Show, Stuttgart, Germany, 1992, Gallery 93, Kansas City, Kans., 1993, Women Vision Art Show, Kansas City, Mo., 1993, Carnegie Arts Ctr., Leavenworth, 1993, 1995 Theme Show Muse Gallery, Kansas City. Vol. receptionist, newsletter editor/illustrator ACS, Ft. Bliss, Tex., 1981-83, parent rep. EFMP, Ft. Ord, Calif., 1983-84, Leavenworth 1992—; vol. Cystic Fibrosis Found., Tuscaloosa, Ala., 1984; coord. asthma support group, vol. EFMP office Brooke Army Med. Ctr., San Antonio, 1984-90; vol. parent speaker asthma seminars Am. Lung Assn., San Antoinio, 1984-90; den leader, treas., com. chmn. Boy Scouts Am., San Antonio, 1984-90, com. vol., Stuttgart, 1990-92; mayor U.S. mil. housing areas during Desert Storm, Stuttgart, 1990-92; facilitator med. care com. DA Family Symposium, Stuttgart, 1990-92; mem. DOD Families and Schs. Together, Stuttgart, 1990-92; bd. dirs. Army Cmty. Svcs., 6th Area Support Group, Robinson Barracks, Stuttgart, 1990-92; vol. Asthma & Allergy Found., Leavenworth, 1992—; coord. Leavenworth Asthma Network, 1992—; mem. parents adv. coun. Leavenworth Special Edn. Coop., 1992-94; del. as advisor for handicapped Pioneers of Change seminar, Leavenworth, 1993; parent advocate Children with Spl. Needs, Leavenworth, 1993-94; com. mem. Levenworth County Spl. Edn. Coop. Transition Coun.; mem. Leavenworth Area Coordinating Coun. Early Childhood Devel.; vol. early childhood devel. program compliance reviews State of Kans. Recipient VII Corps Desert Shield/Storm Vol. award U.S. Army, 1992. Home: PO Box 214 Leavenworth KS 66043-0214

VERSIC, LINDA JOAN, nurse educator, research company executive; b. Grove City, Pa., Aug. 27, 1944; d. Robert and Kathryn I. (Fagird) Davies; m. Ronald James Versic, June 11, 1966; children: Kathryn Clara, Paul Joseph. RN, Johns Hopkins Sch. of Nursing, 1965; BS in Health Edn., Ctrl. State U., 1980. Asst. head nurse Johns Hopkins Hosp., Balt., 1965-67; staff Nurse Registry Miami Valley Hosp., Dayton, Ohio, 1973-90; instr. Miami Jacobs Jr. Coll. Bus., Dayton, 1977-79; pres. Ronald T. Dodge Co., Dayton, 1979-86, chmn. bd., 1987—; chmn. bd. dirs. A-1 Travel, Inc. instr. Warren County (Ohio) Career Ctr., 1980-84, coord. diversified health occupations, 1984—. Coord. youth activities, mem. steering com. Queen of Apostles Cmty. Recipient Excellence in Tchg. award, 1992, award for Project Excellence, 1992. Active Miami Valley Mil. Affairs Assn., Glen Helen, Friends of Dayton Ballet, Dayton Art Inst., Cin. Art Mus. Mem. Ohio Vocat. Assn., Am. Vocat. Assn., Vocat. Indsl. Clubs Am. (chpt. advisor 1982—). Roman Catholic. Club: Johns Hopkins, Yugoslav of Greater Dayton. Home: 1601 Shafor Blvd Dayton OH 45419-3103 Office: Ronald T Dodge Co PO Box 630 Dayton OH 45459-0630

VERSTEEG, JEAN DOROTHY, retired librarian; b. Pitts., Feb. 1, 1921; d. Theodore Harry and Dorothy Helen (Geiselhart) Doehla; m. Frederick Byer Thompson, July 20, 1946 (div. 1950); m. John de Ruiter Versteeg, July 21, 1951; children: Theodore Pieter, Mark de Ruiter. Student, Duke U., 1939-40; BS with honors, U. Pitts., 1943, MLS with honors, 1968. Asst. to chief job analyst Nat. Tube Co., Pitts., 1943-46; librarian Northland Pub. Libr., Pitts., 1968-69, Pine Jr. High Sch., Mars, Pa., 1970-71, North Hills Pub. Libr., Pitts., 1971-81. Author: The History of Pittsburgh-Des Moines Corporation 1892-1981, 1982. Founding bd. dirs. Richland Pub. Libr., Gibsonia, Pa., 1959-60; mem. corp. bd. North Hills Passavant Hosp., Pitts., 1968-92; pres. Richland Aux. Passavant Hosp., 1960, treas. women's bd., 1961; mem., pres. North Hills Fine Arts League, Pitts., 1969; chair legis. campaign Rep. Women Aware, Vero Beach, Fla., 1990-92; mem. Pub. Libr. Adv. Bd. Indian River County, 1986—. Pa. Libr. Assn. grantee, 1980, 81; nominee Treasure Coast Woman of Yr., Fla., 1991. Mem. AAUW (pres. Vero Beach br. 1987-89, grantee 1987, chair libr. book revs. 1985-92), Beta Phi Mu. Presbyterian. Home: 4155 12th St SW Vero Beach FL 32968-4826

VERSTEGEN, DEBORAH A., education educator, finance educator; b. Neenah, Wis., Oct. 27, 1946; d. Gerald C. and Margaret A. (Lamers) V. BA, Loretto Heights Coll., 1969; EdM, U. Rochester, 1972; MS, U. Wis., 1981, PhD, 1983. Adminstr. Iditarod Area Sch. Dist., McGrath, Alaska, 1976-79; rsch. asst. Wis. Ctr. for Edn. Rsch., 1981-84; dir. asst. prof. mid-mgmt. program U. Tex., Austin, 1984-86; asst. prof. U. Va., Charlottesville, 1986-91, assoc. prof., 1992—; rsch. assoc. Oxford U., Eng., 1991; adv. bd. U.S. Dept. Edn., 1989-92. Author over 100 books, reports, chpts., articles and revs., latest being The Impacts of Litigation and Legislation on Public School Finance, 1990, Spheres of Justice in Education, 1991; editor Jour. Edn. Fin., 1990-93, editor edn. policy, 1993—. Treas. LWV, 1986. Mem. AAUP, Am. Ednl. Fin. Assn. (bd. dirs., disting. svc. award 1989), Am. Ednl. Rsch. Assn., Univ. Coun. on Ednl. Adminstrn. (disting svc. award 1991, adv. bd. fin. ctr.), Phi Delta Kappa, Phi Kappa Phi. Home: 2030 Lambs Rd Charlottesville VA 22901 Office: U Va Curry Sch Edn Ruffner Hall 405 Emmet St S Charlottesville VA 22903-2424

VERTS, LITA JEANNE, university administrator; b. Jonesboro, Ark., Apr. 13, 1935; d. William Gus and Lolita Josephine (Peeler) Nash; m. B. J. Verts, Aug. 29, 1954 (div. 1975); 1 child, William Trigg. BA, Oreg. State U., 1973; MA in Lingustics, U. Oreg., 1974; postgrad., U. Hawaii, 1977. Librarian Forest Research Lab., Corvallis, Oreg., 1966-69; instr. English Lang. Inst., Corvallis, 1974-80; dir. spl. svcs. Oreg. State U., Corvallis, 1980—, faculty senator, 1988—. Editor ann. book: Trio Achievers, 1986, 87, 88; contbr. articles to profl. jours. Precinct com. Rep. Party, Corvallis, 1977-80; adminstrv. bd. 1st United Meth. Ch., Corvallis, 1987-89, mem. fin. com., 1987-93, tchr. Bible, 1978—; bd. dirs. Westminster Ho., United Campus Ministries, 1994—; adv. coun. Disabilities Svc., Linn, Benton, Lincoln Counties, 1990—, vice chair, 1992-93, chair, 1993-94. Mem. N.W. Assn. Spl. Programs (pres. 1985-86), Nat. Coun. Ednl. Opportunities Assn. (bd. dirs. 1984-87), Nat. Gardening Assn., Alpha Phi (mem. corp. bd. Beta Upsilon chpt. 1990—). Republican. Methodist. Home: 530 SE Mayberry Ave Corvallis OR 97333-1866 Office: Spl Svcs Project Waldo 337 OSU Corvallis OR 97331

VERVILLE, ELIZABETH GIAVANI, federal official; b. N.Y.C., July 13, 1940; d. Joseph and Gertrude (Levy) Giavani. BA, Duke U., 1961; LLB, Columbia U., 1964. Bar: Mass. 1965, U.S. Supreme Ct. 1970, D.C. 1980. Assoc. Snow Motley & Holt, successor Gaston Snow & Ely Bartlett, Boston, 1965-67; asst. atty. gen. Commonwealth of Mass., Boston, 1967-69; atty. advisor for African affairs U.S. Dept. State, Washington, 1979-72, asst. legal adviser for East Asian and Pacific affairs, 1972-80, dep. legal adviser, 1980-89; dep. asst. sec. state Bur. Politico-Mil. Affairs Bur. Politico-Mil. Affairs, Washington, 1989-92; sr. coord. Bur. Politico-Mil. Affairs, 1992—. Recipient presdl. rank of meritorious exec., 1985, 90, presdl. rank disting. exec., 1988. Mem. Am. Soc. Internat. Law, Coun. on Fgn. Rels. Home: 3012 Dumbarton Ave NW Washington DC 20007-3305 Office: Dept of State Bur Polit Mil Affairs 2201 C St NW Washington DC 20520-0001

VESPER, CAROLYN F., newspaper publishing executive. Sr. v.p. and assoc. publisher USA TODAY, Arlington, Va. Office: USA Today 1000 Wilson Blvd Arlington VA 22229

VESPO, MARY ELIZABETH, office manager; b. Indpls., Aug. 23, 1963; d. Anthony Joseph and Margaret Cecilia (Winsor) V. Student, Manatee C.C., Bradenton, Fla., 1988; student, Ind. U.-Purdue U. at Indpls., 1993. Instr. ABC Nursery Sch., Bradenton, 1988; office and standards mgr. ARA Leisure Svcs., Indpls., 1983— (summers); sec./supr. Roselyn Bakeries, Indpls., 1989-93; office mgr. Signart, Indpls., 1993—. Activist Ind. chpt. Prevention Child Abuse, 1992-94, Parents Anonymous, 1993, Big Sisters, 1994, Asbury United Meth. Ch. soup kitchen, 1990—; vol. activist for ret. persons Parkway Villas, Bradenton, 1988. Roman Catholic. Home: 803 N Drexel Indianapolis IN 46201 Office: Signart Inc 2315 Spencer Ave Indianapolis IN 46218

VEST, GAYLE SOUTHWORTH, obstetrician and gynecologist; b. Duluth, Minn., Apr. 7, 1948; d. Russell Eugene and Brandon (Young) Southworth; m. Steven Lee Vest, Nov. 27, 1971; 1 child, Matthew Steven. BS, U. Mich., 1970. Diplomate Am. Bd. Ob-Gyn. Intern in ob-gyn. Milw. County Gen. Hosp., 1974-75, So. Ill. U. Sch. Medicine, 1975-78; pvt. practice Chapel Hill (N.C.) Ob-Gyn., 1978-80; asst. attending physician dept. ob-gyn. U. N.C. Sch. Medicine, Chapel Hill, 1978-80; clin. assoc. dept. ob-gyn. Duke U. Med. Ctr., Durham, N.C., 1978-80; pvt. practice Big Stone Gap (Va.) Clinic, 1980-88, Norwise Ob-Gyn. Assocs., Norton, Va., 1988—. Fellow Am. Coll. Obstetricians and Gynecologists; mem. Am. Fertility Soc., Va. Ob-Gyn. Soc., Va. Perinatal Assn., Med. Soc. Va., Wise County Med. Soc. Office: Norwise Ob-Gyn Assocs Med Arts Bldg 3 100 15th St NW Norton VA 24273

VEST, MARY ELIZABETH, marketing and sales specialist; b. Roanoke, Va., Nov. 19, 1954; d. Robert Ellsworth and Margaret (Taylor) V. Student, St. Andrew's Coll., Laurinburg, N.C., 1972-74, U. S.C., 1976. Mng. editor Richlands (Va.) News-Press, 1976-78, Delmarva News, Millsboro, Del., 1979-83; ops. mgr. Mer-Lou Transp. Inc., 1983-90; mktg. dir. QDS, Inc., 1990-94; sales dir. WSCL-FM, 1994—. part-time journalism tchr. Del. Tech. and Community Coll., 1981-83; profl. cons. sch. publs. Recipient awards for spot news, series, and photo story, Va. Press Assn., 1977; award for layout, design, photo series, feature series, and editorials Md.-Del.-D.C. Press Assn., 1980, 81, 82. Mem. Sigma Delta Chi. Roman Catholic. Home: 41C Blue Teal Selbyville DE 19975-9507 Office: Salisbury State U Salisbury MD 21801

VESTAL, JEANNE MARIE GOODSPEED, book publishing company executive; b. Ithaca, N.Y., Oct. 30, 1930; d. Alvin Francis and Margaret Josephine (Stoddart) Goodspeed; m. Fred Lowe Vestal, July 17, 1959. B.A., Nazareth Coll., 1952. Sec. G.P. Putman's Sons, N.Y.C., 1953-56; asst. editor Alfred A. Knopf, N.Y.C., 1956-60; editor-in-chief Dial Press, Inc., N.Y.C., 1960-63; v.p., editor-in-chief J.B. Lippincott, Inc., N.Y.C., 1963-73; sr. v.p., editorial dir. Franklin Watts, Inc., N.Y.C., 1975-91; pub. 21st Century Books divsn. Henry Holts & Co., N.Y.C., 1991—. Mem. Children's Book Council (pres. 1966-67). Home: 1161 York Ave New York NY 10021-7940 Office: Twenty First Century Books Div of Henry Holts & Co Inc 115 W 18th St New York NY 10011

VESTAL, YOLANDA C. MUÑOZ, nurse; b. El Paso, Tex., June 18, 1943; d. Emilio and Dorotha (Comer) Munoz; m. William Vestal, May 18, 1968; children: William, Joanna Sue. RN, Hotel Dieu Sch. Nursing, 1964; BS in Health Care Adminstrn., St. Joseph Coll., 1987. Cert. spl. edn. nurse; lic. health occupation. Public health nurse State of Tenn., Mountain City, Tenn.; charge nurse Sycamore Shoals Hosp., Elizabethton, Tenn.; spl. edn. nurse Carter County Bd. of Ed., Elizabethton, Tenn. Mem. Boy Scouts Am. Capt. USAF, 1967-69. Recipient Silver Beaver award Boy Scouts Am., 1991, Dist. award Merit (Pioneer award), 1982. Home: 1311 Lowe St Elizabethton TN 37643-3429

VETERE, COLLEEN MARIE, nurse; b. Washington, Sept. 10, 1957; d. Alphonse Louis and Margaret Hilda (Nolan) V. BA in Biology, U. Tex., 1980, BS in Nursing, 1982; MPH, U. Tex., Houston, 1993. RN, Tex. Nurse intensive care unit Brackenridge Hosp., Austin, Tex., 1983, nurse emergency room, 1984; quality rev. supr. Tex. Med. Found., Austin, 1985-86; asst. dir. Peer Rev. Orgn. Tex., Austin, 1986-87, asst. to exec. dir., 1987-88, dir. quality rev. statewide, 1988-90; nurse emergency rm. St. Luke's Hosp., Houston, 1990-91; nurse emergency room Brackenridge Hosp., 1991; clin. rsch. monitor Pharmaco, Austin, 1992-93; v.p. Peer Rev. Orgn. Ind., Terre Haute, 1993-94; dir. improvement svcs. VHA Tristate, Indpls., 1994—. Med. support organizer Area 13 Tex. Spl. Olympics, Austin, 1985-89, vol. support Area 4, Houston, 1990-91. 1st lt. Nurse Corps, USAR, 1983-93. Recipient Army Achievement medal USAR-ANC, 1986. Mem. NAFE, Tex. Nurses Assn. Democrat. Roman Catholic. Office: 8900 Keystone Crossing Ste 480 Indianapolis IN 46240

VETRI, KRISTI M., public relations consultant; b. Des Moines, June 18, 1954; d. Jack C. Reindl and Marilyn M. (Mungon) Reindl-Carlberg. BS in Polit. Sci., Frostburg State U., 1975; MPA, So. Ill. U., 1983; JD, St. Louis U., 1987. Store mgr. County Seat, Fairview Heights, Ill., 1975-80; area supr. Southland Corp., St. Louis, 1980-81; alderman City of O'Fallon, Ill., 1981-85, mayor, 1985-93; owner MediaLink, Inc., O'Fallon, 1993—. Gubernatorial appointee Southwestern Ill. Planning Com., Collinsville, 1986—; v.p. Southwest Ill. Coun. of Mayors, Belleville, 1991-93; bd. dirs. East-West Gateway Coordinating Coun., St. Louis, 1991-93; mem. St. Clair County Planning Com., Belleville, 1991-94. Named Miss Maryland, Miss Am. Pageant, 1973-74. Mem. Metro-East Profl. Women (pres. 1994—), O'Fallon Women's Club (v.p. 1994—).

VETTE, KIRSTEN ERICA, financial analyst; b. Detroit, Nov. 25, 1962; d. Harry and Melosine Louise (Becker) Gebert; m. Terry J. Vette, Aug. 22, 1992; 1 child, Erika Marie. BA in Acctg., Mich. State U., 1985, MBA, 1985. Cert. mgmt. acct. Systems analyst Whirlpool Corp., Benton Harbor, Mich., 1985-88, auditor, sr. auditor, 1988-89; auditor, audit specialist The Upjohn Co., Kalamazoo, Mich., 1989-92, pricing fin. analyst, 1992-94, project mgr., 1994—. Mem. NAA/IMA. Office: Upjohn Co 7000 Portage Rd Kalamazoo MI 49001

VEVON, KRISTIN MARY, publisher; b. N.Y.C., May 11, 1957; d. Gerald Nicholas and Ann Lois (Leonard) V.; m. Al Douglas Rapaport, Nov. 27, 1982; 1 child, Ryan Vevon Rapaport. BA in Bus. Mgmt., Marymount Manhattan Coll., 1979. Lic. realtor. Advt. dir. New Age Mag., 1981-82; mktg. dir. New Mass Media, Hatfield, Mass., 1982-86; owner Mind Over Media, Northampton, Mass., 1986—, The Real Estate Book of Pioneer, Northampton, Mass., 1987—, The Real Estate Book of Hampden City, Northampton, Mass., 1991—, The Real Estate Book of Charleston, Charleston, S.C., 1994—, The Western Mass. Comml. Real Estate Book, 1994—, The Western Mass. Apartment Book, 1994—. Bd. dirs. Northampton Ctr. for the Arts, 1992—. Mem. Downtown Bus. Assn. Home: 10 Jewett St Northampton MA 01060-2808 Office: Mind Over Media The Real Estate Book 369 Pleasant St Northampton MA 01060-3914

VIAULT, SARAH UNDERHILL, civic volunteer; b. Richmond, Va., Aug. 6, 1938; d. Gary Madison and Sarah Jane (Reed) Underhill; m. David Ashmun Dobbins, Aug. 12, 1961 (div. 1969); m. Birdsall Scrymser Viault, May 9, 1970. BA in Liberal Arts, Sweet Briar Coll., 1960; BS in Elem. Edn., U. Minn., 1962. Exec. sec. Harper & Row Pub., N.Y.C., 1960-61; tchr. Efland (N.C.) Elem. Sch., 1963-65; adminstrv. sec. to chief of neurology Duke U. Med. Ctr., Durham, N.C., 1967-70; dir. med./social svc., newsletter editor York Gen. Hosp., Rock Hill, S.C., 1971-72; exec. sec. Kelly Svcs., Charlotte, N.C., 1973; med. transcriptionist Charlotte Meml. Hosp., 1973-74; Uniforce temp. exec. sec. Spring Industries, Rock Hill, 1979-82; ind. proofreader Rock Hill, 1988—. Bd. dirs. Carolina Community Action, Rock Hill, 1974-76; bd. dirs., officer Fine Arts Assn. Rock Hill, 1975-79; phone bank organizer local Dem. campaigns, 1982; vol. Am. Cancer Soc. Support Group, 1982-92, past circle chmn., sec. Women of Oakland Ave. Presbyn. Ch.; charter officer, sec. York County Dem. Forum, 1991-93; pres. Ebinport precinct York County Dem. Party, 1994; del. to state S.C. Dem. Party Conv., 1994. Named Disting. Vol., Boys Club Mpls., 1962; recipient Cert. of Honor, York County Hospice, 1987, Outstanding York County Dem. Vols., S.C. Dem. Party, 1993. Mem. AAUW (bd. dirs., chmn. drama group 1990-92), Amelia Pride Book Club (pres. 1990-92), Town and Country Garden Club (sec.), Sierra Club, Swan Meadows Garden Club (pres. 1994). Home: 2186 Wentworth Dr Rock Hill SC 29732

VICAREO, MARIA, creative director; b. Astoria, N.Y., July 6, 1945; d. Howard T. and Maria (Pellegrinelli) Weber; m. Nickolas A. Dipetrillo, July 11, 1970 (div. Dec. 1983); 1 child, Tara Dipetrillo; m. Vincent Vicareo, Nov. 9, 1985. AAS, Fashion Inst. Tech., N.Y.C., 1965; BFA, Sch. Visual Arts, N.Y.C., 1989. Various assoc. art dir. positions Avon Products, Vogue Pattern Book Internat., Bergdorf Goodman, Gimbels, 1965-72; art dir. Seligman & Latz, 1972-74; co-owner, corp. sec. Intermezzo Creations, 1974-75; designer Germaine Monteil, 1977-78, George Gotlieb, 1978-79; art dir. Avon Products, 1979-85; prin. Maria Vicareo Design, 1985-87; creative dir. M Co., 1989-90; art dir. Tsumura Internat., 1990-92; cons. art dir. Lancaster Group USA, N.Y.C., 1992-94; creative dir. In Flight Duty Free Shop, N.Y.C., 1994—; ptnr. Huggy Bear Love & Friends, Cedarhurst, N.Y., 1994—. Fashion Inst. scholar Lord & Taylor, 1963. Mem. Am. Inst. Graphic Arts, Am. Watercolor Soc. Home: 38-16 220 St Flushing NY 11361 Office: In Flight Duty Free Shop 215 Lexington Ave New York NY 10016

VICK, FRANCES BRANNEN, publishing executive; b. Trinity, Tex., Aug. 14, 1935; d. Carl Andrew and Bess (courtney) B.; m. Ross William Vick Jr., June 23, 1956; children: Karen Lynn, Ross William III, Patrick Brannen. BA, U. Tex., 1958; MA, Stephen F. Austin State U., 1968. Teaching fellow Stephen F. Austin State U., Nacogdoches, Tex., 1966-68, lectr., 1968-69; lectr. Angelina Coll., Lufkin, Tex., 1969-71, Baylor U., Waco, Tex., 1974-75, 77-78; vice prin. Vanguard Sch., Waco, 1975-77; pres. E-Heart Press, Inc., Dallas, 1979-95; co-dir. UNT Press U. North Tex., Denton, 1987-89, dir., 1989—. Punlisher 103 books; editor 30 books. Leadership coun. Ann Richards Com., Austin, 1990; amb. Inst. Texan Cultures; mem. Tex. Commn. on Arts, Lit., 1991. Mem. AAUW, Book Pubs. Tex. (v.p. 1990—), Tex. Folklore Soc. (councillor 1991-93), Tex. Humanities Resource Ctr. (bd. dirs. 1990), Conf. Coll. Tchrs. English, Western Lit. Assn., Western Writers Am., Philos. Soc. Tex., Pen Ctr. U.S.A. West, Tex. State Hist. Assn. (life), East Tex. Hist. Assn., Western Writers Am., Western Lit. Assn., Soc. Scholarly Pub., Women in Scholarly Pub., Rocky Mountain Book Pubs. Assn., Leadership Tex., Leadership Am., Tex. Humanities Alliance, UNT League Profl. Women. Democrat. Episcopalian. Home: 3700 Mockingbird Ln Dallas TX 75205-2125 Office: U North Tex PO Box 13856 Denton TX 76203-6856

VICK, SUSAN, playwright, educator; b. Raleigh, N.C., Nov. 4, 1945; d. Thomas B. Jr. and Merle (Hayes) V. MFA, Southern Meth. U., 1969; PhD, U. Ill., 1979. Dir. residence Clebration Co. at Sta. Theatre, Urbana, Ill., 1979-80; prof. drama/theatre Worcester (Mass.) Poly. Inst., 1981—; dir., playwright Excuse Me For Living Prodns., Cambridge, Mass., 1989—; Playwright Ensemble Studio Theatre, N.Y.C., 1982; script cons. Clyde Unity Theatre, Glascow, Scotland and London, 1993-94. Editor: (2 vols.) Playwrights Press, Amherst, 1988—; playwright plays including When I Was Your Age, 1982, Ord-Way Ames-Gay, 1982, Investments, 1985, Half Naked, 1989; appeared in plays including Rip Van Winkle, 1979, Why I Live at The P.O., 1982, The Play Group, 1984-85, Present Stage, 1985, Sister Mary Ignatius Explain It All, 1986, Wipeout, Edinburgh, 1988, Bogus Joan, 1992, 93; dir. play Give My Love to Everyone But, 1990 (Edinburgh Festival). Dir., Women's Community Theatre, Amherst, 1981-84. Faculty fellow U. Ill., 1976-77. Mem. Dramatists Guild (assoc.), Soc. Stage Dirs. and Choreographers (assoc.), Alpha Psi Omega. Office: Worcester Poly Tech Inst 100 Institute Rd Worcester MA 01609-2280

VICKERS, AUDREY, county commissioner, journalist; b. Evergreen Park, Ill., Dec. 17, 1934; d. William Richard and Helen Sarah (Morrison) Banks; m. Marion Edward Vickers, Nov. 28, 1955; children: Nancy Adele Pyle, Kelly Ellen, John Julius, Marion Edward II. Attended, Palm Beach C.C., Lake Worth, Fla., U. Miami. Reporter Ft. Lauderdale News, Hollywood, Fla., 1952-54; women's editor Sun Tattler, Hollywood, 1954-56; columnist Sun Sentinel, Pompano Beach, Fla., 1960-68; bur. chief Palm Beach Post Times, West Palm Beach, Fla., 1968-73; reporter, columnist Orlando Sentinel, Sebring, Fla., 1974-78, News Sun, Sebring, 1978-87; editor, pub. Heartland Mag., Sebring, 1987-92; chair commn. Highlands County Commn., Sebring, 1990-94. Commr. Highlands Gen. Hosp., Sebring, 1974-84, Cmty. Devel. Assn., Sebring, 1988-92; bd. dirs. Fla. Trust Hist. Preservation, 1992-94, Fla. Assn. Counties Found., 1991-94; pres. Fla. Women's Network/Alliance, 1989-91. Recipient Pub. Svc. award Sebring C. of C. Republican. Methodist. Home: 1825 Wright Ln Lorida FL 33857

VICKERS, MARY LOUISE, executive assistant; b. Cleve., June 28, 1948; d. Paul Orland and Margaret Corrine (Wolfe) V. AA, Dyke Coll., 1968, BSBA, 1986. Traffic coord. Sta. WDBN-Radio, Inc., Medina, Ohio, 1968-73; exec. sec. Newspaper Enterprise Assn., Cleve., 1974-76; adminstrv. sec. Eaton Corp., Cleve., 1976-84, exec. sec., 1984-86, exec. asst., 1986—. Mem. Nat. Hemi Owners Assn. Home: 4343 N Miami Dr Parma OH 44134-6217 Office: Eaton Corp Eaton Ctr Cleveland OH 44114

VICKERY, BYRDEAN EYVONNE HUGHES (MRS. CHARLES EVERETT VICKERY, JR.), retired library services administrator; b. Belleview, Mo., Apr. 18, 1928; d. Roy Franklin and Margaret Cordelia (Wood) Hughes; m. Charles Everett Vickery, Jr., Nov. 5, 1948; 1 child, Camille. Student, Flat River (Mo.) Jr. Coll., 1946-48; BS in Edn., S.E. Mo. State Coll., 1954; MLS, U. Wash., 1964; postgrad. Wash. State U., 1969-70. Tchr. Ironton (Mo.) Pub. Schs., 1948-56; elem. tchr. Pasco (Wash.) Sch. Dist. 1, 1956-61, jr. high sch. libr., 1961-68, coord. librs., 1968-69; asst. libr. Columbia Basin Community Coll., Pasco, 1969-70, head libr., dir. Instructional Resources Ctr., 1970-78, dir. libr. svcs., 1979-87, assoc. dean libr. svcs., 1987-90, ret., 1990; owner Vickery Search & Research, 1990—; chmn. S.E. Wash. Libr. Svc. Area, 1977-78, 88-90. Bd. dirs. Pasco-Kennewick Community Concerts, 1977-88, pres., 1980-81, 87-88, Pasco-Kennewick Community Concerts, treas., 1991—; bd. dirs. Mid-Columbia Symphony Orch., 1983-89; trustee Wash. Commn. Humanities, 1982-85; bd. mem. Arts Coun. Mid-Columbia Region, 1991-93. Author, editor: Library and Research Skills Curriculum Guides for the Pasco School District, 1967; author (with Jean Thompson), also editor Learning Resources Handbook for Teachers, 1969. Recipient Woman of Achievement award Pasco Bus. and Profl. Women's Club, 1976. Mem. ALA, AAUW (2d v.p. 1966-68, corr. sec. 1969), Wash. Dept. Audio-Visual Instrn., Wash. Libr. Assn., Am. Assn. Higher Edn., Wash. Assn. Higher Edn., Wash. State Assn. Sch. Librs. (state conf. chmn. 1971-72), Tri-Cities Librs. Assn., Wash. Libr. Media Assn. (community coll. levels chmn. 1986-87), Am. Assn. Rsch. Libr., Soroptimist Internat. Assn. (rec. sec. Pasco-Kennewick chpt. 1971-72, treas. 1973-74, pres. 1978-80, v.p. 1989-90, treas. 1991), Columbia Basin Coll. Adminstrs. Assn. (sec.-treas. 1973-74), Pacific N.W. Assn. Ch. Libr., Women in Communications, Pasco Bus. and Profl. Women's Club, PEO, Beta Sigma Phi, Delta Kappa Gamma, Phi Delta Kappa (sec. 1981-82, Outstanding Educator award 1983). Home: 3521 S Fisher Ct Kennewick WA 99337-2559

VICTOR, LORRAINE CAROL, critical care nurse; b. Duluth, Minn., June 14, 1953; d. George E. and Phyllis M. (Pierce) Drimel; m. Robert G. Victor. BA in Nursing, Coll. St. Scholastica, 1975; MS in Nursing, U. Minn., 1984. Cert. regional trainer for neonatal resuscitation program. Staff nurse St. Mary's Hosp., Rochester, Minn., 1975-79, 80-81, U. Wis. Hosp., Madison, 1979-80, U. Minn. Hosps., Mpls., 1981-84, 85-86; clin. instr. neonatal ICU, Children's Hosp. Inc., St. Paul, 1984-86; clin. nurse specialist neonatal ICU, Orlando (Fla.) Regional Med. Ctr., 1986-88, Children's Hosp. St. Paul, 1988—. Mem. AACN (Critical Care Nurse of Yr. award Greater Twin Cities chpt. 1992), NAACOG (cert. in neonatal intensive care nursing), Nat. Assn. Neonatal Nurses, Sigma Theta Tau.

VICTOR-FASSMAN, JO ANN, psychiatric nurse clinician; b. Bklyn., June 30, 1948; d. Marcel James and Anna (Homyak) Victor; m. Sheldon Fassman, Oct. 16, 1988; 1 child, Jessica Rose. BS, Niagara U., 1970; MA, NYU, 1980. RN, N.Y. Temporary LPN Booth Meml. Hosp., Flushing, N.Y., 1969; staff nurse Lenox Hill Hosp., N.Y.C., 1970-80; psychiat. nurse Payne Whitney Clinic Cornell Med. Ctr., N.Y.C., 1980-83; psychiat. nurse clin. specialist Albert Einstein Coll. Medicine, Bronx, N.Y., 1983—; formerly assoc. prof. Adelphi U. Sch. Nursing. Contbr. articles to profl. jours. Mem. ANA (coun. specialists in psychiat. and mental health nursing 1984-93), Am. Group Psychotherapy Assn., Network N.Y. Clin. Specialists in Psychiat. and Mental Health Nursing, Sigma Theta Tau (chairperson projects com. 1982-87).

VIDAL, LINDA EMMA, artist, art educator; b. Bklyn., Oct. 8, 1924; d. Carlo Slovanovich Vidal and Aida (Sansone) Rizutto; m. Geroge Belt Schwindeman, Aug. 29, 1947 (div. July 1962); children: Carl W. Schwindeman, Paula Ann Schwindeman, Kirk V. Schwindeman; m. Edwin E. Lewis, Aug. 12, 1963 (dec. May 1976); m. Tarif Mohammad Sobhi Umari/Omary, March 27, 1979 (div. 1989). Student, NYU, 1947, Escuela de Pintura and Froscoe, Mexico City, 1949; BFA, Calif. Coll. Arts and Crafts, 1950. Cert. coll. tchr., Calif., 1962. Owner, dir. Lewis and Vidal Fine Art Gallery, Walnut Creek, Calif., 1961-62; co-prodr. Future's Child Iliad Prodns., Inc., Walnut Creek, Calif., 1972-76; publs. dir., spl. projects Art Well Mag., Benicia, Calif., 1984-85; creator J/G Jesting Gesture Artoons in Art Well Mag., 1984, Calif. Art Rev., Book Publ., 1990. Exhibited in group shows at Oakland (Calif.) Art Mus., 1952, Pageant of Arts, Walnut Creek (Hon. mention award), 1959, 60, 62, Benicia Art Explosion, 1984, Valencia Gallery, San Francisco, 1992, Open Studios, Benicia, 1994; represented in permanent collections including Am. Art Soc., 1994; current works include sculptural relief paintings. With U.S. Army WAC, 1943-46. TV documentary by David Howard of "Art Seen" was produced showing some of Vidal's art works and exhibit at Valencia Gallery, 1992. Office: Vidal PO Box 394 Benicia CA 94510

VIDERMAN, LINDA JEAN, paralegal, corporate executive; b. Follansbee, W.Va., Dec. 4, 1957; d. Charles Richard and Louise Edith (LeBoeuf) Roberts; m. David Gerald Viderman Jr., Mar. 15, 1974; children: Jessica Renae, April Mae, Melinda Dawn. AS, W.Va. No. Community Coll., 1983; Cert. income tax prep., H&R Block, Steubenville, Ohio, 1986. Cert. surg. tech.; cert. fin. counselor; lic. ins. agt. Food prep. pers. Bonanza Steak House, Weirton, W.Va., 1981-83; ward clk., food svcs. Weirton Med. Ctr., 1982-84; sec., treas. Mountaineer Security Systems, Inc., Wheeling, W.Va., 1983-86; owner, operator The Button Booth, Colliers, W.Va., 1985—; paralegal, adminstr. Atty. Dominic J. Potts, Steubenville, Ohio, 1987-92; gen. ptnr., executrix Panhandle Homes, Wellsburg, W.Va., 1988—; ins. agt. Milico, Mass. Indemnity, 1991-92, L&L Ins. Svcs., 1992-94; paralegal Atty. Fred Risovich II, Weirton, 1991-93; sec. The Hon. Fred Risovich II, Wheeling, 1993; paralegal atty. Christopher J. Paull, Wellsburg, W.Va., 1993—; owner Wellsburg Office Supply, 1993—; notary pub., 1991—. Contbr. articles numerous jours.; author numerous poems. Chmn. safety com. Colliers (W.Va.) Primary PTA, 1985-87; mem., sec. LaLeche League, Steubenville, Ohio, 1978-80; vol. counselor W.Va. U. Fin. Counseling Svc., 1990—; IRS vol. Vol. Income Tax Assistance Program, 1991—. Mem. W.Va. Writers Assn., Legal Assts. of W.Va., Inc., Am. Affiliate of Nat. Assn. Legal Assts., W.Va. Trial Lawyers Assn., Wellsburg Art Assn., Phi Theta Kappa. Jehovah's Witness. Home: 137R St Johns Rd Colliers WV 26035 Office: Panhandle Homes 3027 Pleasant Ave Wellsburg WV 26070-1138

VIGEN, KATHRYN L. VOSS, nursing administrator, educator; b. Lakefield, Minn., Sept. 24, 1934; d. Edward Stanley and Bertha C. (Richter) Voss; m. David C. Vigen, June 23, 1956 (div. 1977); children: Eric. E., Amy Vigen Hemstad, Aana Marie. BS in Nursing magna cum laude, St. Olaf Coll., 1956; MEd, S.D. State U., 1975; MS, Rush U., 1980; PhD, U. Minn., 1987. RN. Staff nurse various hosps., Mpls, Boston, Chgo., 1956-68; nursing instr. S.E.A. Sch. Practical Nursing, Sioux Falls, S.D., 1969-74; statewide coord. upward mobility in nursing Augustana Coll., Sioux Falls, S.D., 1974-78; cons./researcher S.D. Commn. Higher Edn., 1974-79; gov. appointed bd. mem. S.D. Bd. Nursing, 1975-79; RN upward mobility project dir./chair dir. div. of nursing Huron Coll. S.D. State U., 1978-79, mobility project dir., 1980-84; head dept. nursing, assoc. prof. Luther Coll., Decorah, Iowa, 1984-94; prof. nursing Graceland Coll., Independence, Mo., 1994—; cons. in field; governing bd. mem. Midwest Alliance in Nursing, 1984-92; founder Soc. for Advancement of Nursing, Malta, 1992; developer Health Care in the Mediterranean study abroad program, Greece and Malta, 1994; developer summer internship for Maltese nursing students Mayo Med. Ctr. and Luther Coll. Author: Role of a Dean in a Private Liberal Arts College, 1992; devel. and initiated 3 nursing programs in S.D., 1974-84 (named Women of Yr., 1982). Lobbyist Nursing Schs. in S.D., 1974-79; task force mem. Sen. Tom Harkin's Nurse's Adv. Com., 1986-94. Fellow to rep. U.S.A. ANA cand. in internat. coun. nursing 3M, St. Paul, 1978; recipient Leadership award Bush Found., St. Paul, 1979; tenure Luther Coll., 1986; Faculty fellow Minn. Area Geriatric Edn. Ctr. U. Minn., 1990-91; recipient Fulbright award Malta Coun. Internat. Exch. of Scholars, Washington, 1992—. Mem. AAUW, ANA, Am. Assn. Colls. Nursing (exec. devel. subcom. 1990—), Internat. Assn. Human Caring, Iowa Nurse's Assn. (bd. dirs. 1989-92, mem. nursing edn. com. 1989—, co-pres. 1989—), Midwest Alliance in Nursing (gov. bd. rep. Iowa 1989-92, chair membership com. 1989-92, S.D. gov. bd. rep. 1984-86, Rozella Schlotfeldt Leadership award 1993), Iowa Acad. Sci., Iowa Assn. Colls. Nursing Soc., Gerontol. Soc. Am., Rotary, Sigma Theta Tau. Democrat. Lutheran. Home: 4316 Northern Ave # 2633 Kansas City MO 64133-7249 Office: Graceland Coll Divsn Nursing 221 W Lexington Independence MO 64050-3720

VIGIL, DIANA GAIL, psychotherapist; b. Provo, Utah, Apr. 18, 1955; d. David and Virginia (Vigil) Gilner; m. John A. Moran, Jan. 1, 1983; children: Brennan Moran, Maura Moran. BS in Psychology, James Madison U., 1978; MA in Psychology, George Mason U., 1984; postgrad., Family Inst.

Ariz., Scottsdale, 1985-86, Ericksonian Clin. Hypnosis, Phoenix, 1991. Cert. counselor. Psychiat. counselor adolescent unit Psychiat. Inst. Washington, 1978-79; employment counselor Fairfax County Govt., Va., 1979; systems analyst SYSCON Corp., Washington, 1980-84; orgn. and staff devel. specialist CIGNA Healthplan Ariz., Inc., 1984-86, psychotherapist alcohol and drug dependency dept., 1986-87; employee assistance program specialist St. Luke's Health System, 1987-89; pvt. practice psychotherapy Scottsdale, Ariz., 1986—; contract psychotherapist sex offenders treatment program Parents United Maricopa County, Mesa, Ariz., 1986-89mem. Samartian Behavioral Health Allied Health Profl. Com., Credentialing Com., 1993—; nat. employee assistance program provider Priority Systems, Mountainside, N.J., 1988—, Nat. Resource Cons., San Diego, 1989—; cons. Cottonwood In-Patient Sexual Trauma program, Scottsdale, 1989-91, Phoenix Adolescent Recover Ctr., 1989—, Ariz. Children's Home, Phoenix, 1991—, Casey Family program, 1991—. Participant design com. Forensic Interviews Assn., Phoenix, 1994, Office Maricopy County Atty., Design Kids in Ct. Program, Phoenix, 1994. Mem. Am. Counseling Assn., Am. Profl. Soc. on Abuse of Children. Democrat. Unitarian. Office: 7426 E Camelback Rd Scottsdale AZ 85251

VIGIL, ROSE ANN, weaver; b. Espanola, N.Mex., Feb. 24, 1965; d. Lawrence Jr. and Regina (Trujillo) Bartlett; m. Eugene David Vigil, July 25, 1987. AAS in Fibert Arts, No. N.Mex. C.C., 1995. Clerical aide No. N.Mex. C.C., Espanola, 1983-84; office mgr. trainee Branch Realty, Santa Fe, N.Mex., 1984-85; word processor, receptionist Legis. Edn. Study Com., Santa Fe, 1985-87; case recorder Las Cumbles Learning Ctr., Inc., Espanola, 1989-90; owner Los Vigiles Handcrafted Products, Espanola, 1990—; instr. N.Mex. Vocat. Tech. and Adult Edn. Conf., Albuquerque, 1992; instr. The Art Boosters, Taos, N.Mex., 1993, Chimayo (N.Mex.) Youth Group, 1993; coord. Chimayo Arts and Crafts Festival, 1993—. Mem. Handweavers Guild Am., Mountain Valley Wool Assn., Taos Hispanic Arts Coun. (mem. bd. 1993—). Home: PO Box 1221 Espanola NM 87532-1221

VIGIL-GIRON, REBECCA D., former state official; b. Taos, N.Mex., Sept. 4, 1954; M. Rick Giron; 1 son: Andrew. Grad., New Mex. Highlands Univ. Formerly with Public Service Co. of N.Mex., sec. of state of N.Mex., Santa Fe, 1986-90; exec. dir. N.Mex. Commn. on Status of Women. Democrat. also: PO Box 2012 Albuquerque NM 87103

VIGUERA, LAUREL M., professional association executive; b. Washington, Apr. 25, 1961; d. Edward E. Viguera; m. Juan J. Vega, Dec. 2, 1988. BA cum laude, Smith Coll., 1983; postgrad., U. Cordoba, Spain, 1984, George Washington U. Cert. in mgmt. Dir. lang. program French Consulate, Cordoba; intercultural specialist Eurolingua, Cordoba, 1984-86; interpreter, translator NIBCO-ATCOSA, Inc., Cordoba, 1984-86; sr. rsch. assoc. Am. Coun. Life Ins., Washington, 1986-89; assoc. mgr. rsch. and info. Am. Soc. Assn. Execs., Washington, 1989-91; rsch. mgr. Treasury Mgmt. Assn., Bethesda, Md., 1992—. Mem. ASIS, Am. Mgmt. Assn., Nat. Archives Assn., Spl. Librs. Assn., Smith Club of Washington. Address: 4970 Battery Ln Apt 205 Bethesda MD 20814

VIKEN, LINDA LEA MARGARET, lawyer; b. Sioux Falls, S.D., Oct. 27, 1945; d. Carl Thomas and Eleanor Bertha (Zehnpfennig) Crampton; m. Jerry Lee Miller, June 10, 1967 (div. 1975); m. Jeffrey Lynn Viken, Feb. 2, 1980. BS in Bus. Edn., U. S.D., 1967, JD in Law, 1977. Bar: S.D. 1978, U.S. Dist. Ct. S.D. 1978, U.S. Ct. Appeals (8th cir.) 1981. Tchr. Yankton (S.D.) High Sch., 1967-69, Edison Jr. High Sch., Sioux Falls, 1969-75; pvt. practice law Sioux Falls, 1978; ptnr. Finch, Viken, Viken, & Pechota, Rapid City, S.D., 1978-92, Viken, Viken, Pechota, Leach & Dewell, Rapid City, 1992—; part-time instr. Nat. Coll., Rapid City, 1978-80; magistrate judge Seventh Jud. Cir., Rapid City, 1983-84; chair S.D. Commn. on Child Support, 1985, 88; mem. S.D. Bd. of Bar Examiners, 1987-88. Contbr. articles to profl. jours. State rep. D.S. Legislature Minnehaha County, 1973-76, Pennington County, 1988-92; state party vice chair D.S. Dem. Party, 1978-80, 92-94; chair Pennington County Dem. Party, Rapid City, 1985-87. Named Woman Atty. of Yr. Law Sch. Women, 1987. Fellow Am. Acad. of Matrimonial Lawyers; mem. ABA, S.D. Assn., S.D. Trial Lawyers Assn. Democrat. Roman Catholic. Home: 4760 Trout Ct Rapid City SD 57702-4751 Office: Viken Viken Pechota Leach and Dewell 1617 Sheridan Lake Rd Rapid City SD 57702-3483

VIKIS-FREIBERGS, VAIRA, psychologist, educator; b. Riga, Latvia, Dec. 1, 1937; d. Karlis and Annemarie (Rankis) V.; m. Imants F. Freibergs, July 16, 1960; children: Karlis Roberts, Indra Karoline. B.A., U. Toronto, 1958, M.A., 1960; Ph.D., McGill U., 1965; LLD, Queen's U., 1991. Clin. psychologist Toronto (Ont.) Psychiat. Hosp., 1960-61; asst. prof. dept. psychology U. Montreal, Que., Can., 1965-72; asso. prof. U. Montreal, 1972-77, prof., 1977—; pres. Social Sci. Fedn. Can., 1980; chmn. NATO (spl. program panel on human factors), 1980; dir. Latvian Youth Ethnic Heritage Seminars Divreizdivi, 1979; mem. Sci. Council Can., 1980-89, vice chmn., 1984-89. Author: Le Fréquence Lexicale au Quebec, 1974, The Amber Mountain, 1989, Against the Current, 1993; co-author: Latvian Sun Songs, 1988; editor: Linguistics and Poetics of Latvian Folk Songs, 1989; contbr. articles to profl. jours. Recipient Prof. A. Abele Meml. pirze, 1979, Disting. Contbn. prize World Assn. Free Latvians, 1989, Marcel-Vincent prize and medal Assn. Canadienne-Francaise pour l'avancement des scis., 1992; Can. Coun. leave fellow, 1974-75; Killam Rsch. fellow Can. Coun., 1993-95. Fellow Can. Psychol. Assn. (pres. 1980), Royal Soc. Can.; mem. Acad. Sci. Latvia (fgn.), Assn. Advancement Baltic Studies (pres. 1984-86), Assn. Canadienne Francaise pour l'Avancement des Scis. (Marcel-Vincent prize and medal 1992), Sigma Xi. Lutheran. Home: 444 Grenfell Ave, Town of Mount Royal, PQ Canada H3R 1G5 Office: U Montreal Dept Psychology, CP 6128, Succursale Centre-ville, Montreal, PQ Canada H3C 3J7

VILA, ADIS MARIA, corporate executive, former government official, lawyer; b. Cuba, Aug. 1, 1953; came to U.S., 1962; d. Calixto Vila and Adis C. Fernandez. BA with distinction, Rollins Coll., 1974; JD with honors, U. Fla., 1978; LLM with high honors, Institut Universitaire de Hautes Estudes Internationales, Geneva, 1981. Bar: Fla. 1979, D.C. 1984. Assoc. Paul & Thomson, 1979-82; White House fellow Office Pub. Liaison, Washington, 1982-83; spl. asst. to sec. state for inter-Am. affairs Dept. State, Washington, 1983-86; dir. Office of Mex. and Caribbean Basin, Dept. Commerce, Washington, 1986-87; sec. Dept. Adminstrn., State of Fla., 1987-89; asst. sec. for adminstrn. USDA, Washington, 1989-91; v.p. internat. devel. The Vigoro Corp., Chgo., 1994—; vis. asst. Fla. Internat. U., 1993-94, Nat. Def. U., Washington, 1992-93; trustee So. Ctr. for Internat. Studies, 1987—. Bd. dirs. Rollings Coll. Alumni Coun., Winter Park, Fla., 1979—. Named one of 100 Most Influential Hispanics, 1988, Paul Harris fellow Rotary Internat., 1983, U.S.-Japan Leadership fellow, 1991-92, Eisenhower Exch. fellow, Beca Fiore, Argentina, 1992. Mem. Dade County Bar Assn. (bd. dirs. young lawyers sect. 1979-87), Coun. Fgn. Rels. (term mem. 1987-92), Am. Coun. Young Polit. Leaders (bd. dirs. 1984—), Women Execs. in State Govt. (bd. dirs. 1987-89). Republican. Roman Catholic. Office: The Vigoro Corp 225 N Michigan Ave Ste 2500 Chicago IL 60601

VILARDEBO, ANGIE MARIE, management consultant, parochial school educator; b. Tampa, Fla., July 15, 1938; d. Vincent and Antonina (Fazio) Noto; m. Charles Kenneth Vilardebo, June 26, 1960; children: Charles, Kenneth, Michele, Melanie. BA, Notre Dame Md., 1960; postgrad., Rollins Coll., 1980. Cert. tchr., Fla. Tchr. Sea Park Elem. Sch., Satellite Beach, Fla., 1960-61; office mgr. Computer Systems Enterprises, Satellite Beach, 1973-76; artist Satellite Beach, 1976-79; employment counselor Career Cons., Melbourne, Fla., 1979-80; tchr. Our Lady of Lourdes Parochial Sch., Melbourne, 1980-89; pres. Consol. Ventures, Inc., Satellite Beach, 1989—, Versatile Suppliers, Inc., Satellite Beach, 1989—; prin. search com. Diocese of Orlando, Fla., 1989-90. Patentee personal grading machine. V.p. Jaycees, Satellite Beach, 1976-77, pres., 1977-78. Recipient 1st Place Art award Fla. Fedn. Woman's Clubs, 1978, 2nd Place Art award, 1979, Honorable Mention, 1980. Mem. Satellite Beach Woman's Club, Paper Chaser's Investment Club, Brevard Arts Ctr. & Mus., Space Coast Art League (social chmn. 1987—). Roman Catholic. Home: 606 Barcelona Ct Satellite Beach FL 32937

VILIM, NANCY CATHERINE, advertising agency executive; b. Quincy, Mass., Jan. 15, 1952; d. John Robert and Rosemary (Malpede) V.; m. Geoffrey S. Horner, Feb. 16, 1992; children: Matthew Edward Cajda, Megan Catherine Cajda, Margaret Horner. Student, Miami U., Oxford, Ohio, 1970-72. Media asst. Draper Daniels, Inc., Chgo., 1972-74; asst. buyer Campbell Mithun, Chgo., 1974-75; buyer Tatham, Laird & Kudner, Chgo., 1975-77; media buyer Adcom, Inc. div. Quaker Oats Corp., Chgo., 1977-79; media supr. G.M. Feldman, Chgo., 1979-81; v.p. media dir. Media Mgmt., 1981-83; v.p. broadcast dir. Bozell, Jacobs, Kenyon & Eckhardt, Chgo., 1983-88; v.p., media mgr. McCann-Erickson, Inc., 1989—; judge 27th Internat. Broadcast Awards, Chgo., 1987. Mem. Berwyn (Ill.) Parents Assn., Inc., 1988. Recipient Media All Star awards Sound Mgmt. Mag., N.Y.C., 1987. Mem. Broadcast Advt. Club Chgo., Mus. Broadcast Communications, NAFE. Office: McCann-Erickson Inc 625 N Michigan Ave Chicago IL 60611-3110

VILLA, MARIA J., physician; b. Mar. 19, 1962; d. Crisanto and Cira Caridad Villa. BS, Barry U., 1984; DO, Nova/Southea. U., 1990. Diplomate Am. Coll. Osteopathic Med. Examiners. Physician Family Health Ctrs., Ft. Myers, Fla., 1994—; bd. dirs. Everglades Area Health Ctr., West Palm Beach; assoc. mem. faculty Nova-Southea. U., North Miami Beach, 1992-94. Mem. AMA, Am. Osteo. Assn., Am. Coll. Osteo. Family Physicians, Fla. Osteo. Med. Assn. Republican. Roman Catholic. Office: Family Health Ctrs SW Fla 11020 C Rosemary Dr Bonita Springs FL 33902

VILLAGONZALO, AMPARO DE LA CERNA, management analyst; b. Cebu, Philippines, Oct. 30, 1939; came to U.S.A., 1970; d. Ignacio Carangue and Josefa (De La Cerna) V.; adopted children: Victor, Emerald. AA, U. Visayas, 1956, LLB magna cum laude, 1960; postgrad., U. Philippines, 1966-67. Bar: Philippines, 1961. Atty. Villagonzalo Law Offices, Cebu City, Philippines, 1960-62; mgmt. analyst Presdl. Com. on Adminstrn. Performance Efficiency, Manila, Philippines, 1962-65; mgmt. analyst II Commn. on Elections, Manila, Philippines, 1965-70; spl. correspondent Bankers Life Ins. Co., Chgo., 1970-74; from transit mgmt. analyst to assoc. mgmt. analyst N.Y.C. Transit Authority, 1974-80, mgr., materials mgmt. dept., 1980—. Scholar U. Visayas, 1954-60, U. Philippines, 1966-67. Roman Catholic. Home: 15811 86th St Jamaica NY 11414-3002

VILLA-KOMAROFF, LYDIA, molecular biologist; b. Las Vegas, N.Mex., Aug. 7, 1947; d. John Dias and Drucilla (Jaramillo) V.; m. Anthony Leader Komaroff, June 18, 1970. BA, Goucher Coll., 1970; PhD, MIT, 1975. Rsch. fellow Harvard U., Cambridge, 1975-78; asst. prof. dept. microbiology U. Mass. Med. Ctr., Worcester, 1978-81, assoc. prof. dept. molecular genetics micro, 1982-85; assoc. prof. dept. neurology Harvard Med. Sch., Boston, 1986—; sr. rsch. assoc. neurology Children's Hosp., Boston, 1985—, assoc. dir. mental retardation rsch. ctr., 1987-94; mem. mammalian genetics study sect. NIH, 1982-84, mem. reviewers rsch., 1989, mem. neurol. disorders program project rev. com., 1989-94. Contbr. articles and abstracts to profl. jours.; patentee in field. Recipient Hispanic Engr. Nat. Achievement award, 1992; Helen Hay Whitney Found. fellow, 1975-78; NIH grantee, 1978-85, 89—. Mem. Am. Soc. Microbiology, Assn. for Women in Sci., Soc. for Neurosci., Am. Coll. Cell Biology, Soc. for Advancement Chicanos and Native Ams. in Sci. (founding, bd. dirs. 1987-93, v.p. 1990-93). Office: Children's Hosp Enders 260 Longwood Ave Boston MA 02115-5720

VILLALON, DALISAY MANUEL, nurse, real estate broker; b. Angat, Bulacan, Philippines, Apr. 27, 1941; came to U.S., 1967; d. Federico Manuel and Librada (Garcia) Manuel; divorced; children: Ricky, May, Liberty, Derrick, Dolly Rose. BS in Nursing, Manila Cen. U., 1961; postgrad. in nursing, U. Ill., Chgo., 1972-74. RN, Ill. Instr. nursing Cen. Luzon Sch. Nursing, Philippines, 1966-67; staff nurse St. Alexis Hosp., Cleve., 1968-70, Augustana Hosp., Chgo., 1972-74; nurse mgr. Holy Child Med. Clinic, Chgo., 1976-80; nurse auditor 1st Health Care, Rosemont, Ill., 1982-83; dir. nurses North Shore Terr., Waukegan, Ill., 1983-90, Carlton House, 1992—. Columnist Philippine News. Bd. dirs. Filipino Am. Coun., Chgo., 1978-80, v.p., 1980-82; bd. dirs. Asian Human Svcs., Chgo.; pres. Am.-Filipino Profl. Civic Alliance, Chgo., 1984-90, Philipino-Am. United for Svc.-Oriental Objective, 1991—; chmn. Philippine Week Com., 1979; v.p. Filipino Ams. Concerned for Elderly; trustee Rizal-MacArthur Found.; v.p. Filipino Svc. League, 1989-91; exec. v.p. Asian Festival, Inc.; past chmn. various civic coms.; mem. Asian-Am. Adv. Coun. Mayor Daley, 1989—; mem. Filipino Am. Polit. Assn. Recipient Cert. Appreciation Rizal-MacArthur Found., 1977, Most Outstanding Filipino in Midwest award Cavite Assn. Am., 1980, Outstanding Community Svc. Appreciation award Filipino Am. Coun., 1981, 89, NGHIA Sinh Internat., Inc., 1989, Outstanding Svc. award Asian-Am. Coaliton, 1989, Outstanding Contrn. award Dirs. Nursing and Adminstrs. Conf., 1988. Mem. Ill. Nurses Assn. (bd. dirs., dist. senator 1989-91, human rights and ethics commn. 1990-91), Philippine Med. Assn. Aux. (pres. 1980, Outstanding Leadership award 1981), Chgo. Med. Soc. Aux. (v.p. 1980), Chgo. Philippine Lioness Club (prs. 1983-84, Outstanding Svc. award 1985), Filipino Woman's Club Chgo. (Outstanding Woman in Leadership 1992). Democrat. Roman Catholic. Home: 4840 N Sheridan Chicago IL 60640 Office: Alden Lakeland Nursing Ctr Carlton House Chicago IL 60640

VILLANUEVA, KIMBERLY JEAN, communications director; b. Winona, Minn., Oct. 5, 1963; d. A.B. and Joyce Marie (Altman) V. BS in Journalism, U. Ill., 1985. Comm. asst. Ill. Assn. Realtors, Springfield, Ill., 1985; pub. info. officer Ill. C.C. Trustees Assn., Springfield, 1985-93, dir. comm., 1993—. Newsletter editor Ctrl. Ill. Dem. Women, 1993—. Treas. Springfield Women's Polit. Caucus, 1991—; commr. U.S. Senate Jud. Nominations Commn., Springfield, 1993-94; active Ill. Attys. Gen. Women's Adv. Commn., 1993—. Recipient Pres. award Ill. NOW, 1994; named Vol. of Yr., Ill. Women's Founding Fedn., 1992. Mem. NOW (chair Ill. polit. action com. Springfield 1989-94, pres. 1989-91, treas. 1994—), Nat. Coun. Mktg. and Pub. Rels. (judge Paragon awards 1989). Home: 434 W Cook Springfield IL 62704 Office: Ill CC Trustees Assn 509 S 6th Ste 426 Springfield IL 62701

VILLECCO, JUDY DIANA, substance abuse counselor, director; b. Knoxville, Tenn., Jan. 19, 1948; d. William Arthur and Louise (Reagan) Chamberlain; m. Tucker, June 10, 1965 (div. 1974); children: Linda Louise (Tucker) Smith, Constance Christine; m. Roger Anthony Villecco, May 3, 1979. BA in Psychology, U. West Fla., 1988, MA in Psychology, 1992. Lic. mental health counselor, Fla.; cert. addiction profl., Fla.; internat. cert. alcohol and drug counselor. Counselor Gulf Coast Hosp., Ft. Walton Beach, Fla., 1986-87; peer counselor U. West Fla., Ft. Walton Beach, 1987-89; family and prevention counselor Okaloosa Guidance Clinic, Ft. Walton Beach, 1988-89; family svc. dir. Anon Anew of Tampa (Fla.), Inc., 1989-91; dir. Renew Counseling Ctr., Ft. Walton Beach, 1990-92; substance abuse dept. dir. Avalon Ctr., Milton, Fla., 1992-93; adult coord. Partial & Rivendell, Ft. Walton Beach, 1994—; pvt. practice Emerald Coast Psychiat. Care, P.A., Fort Walton Beach, 1994—. Named Outstanding Mental Health Profl. of Yr., Nat. Mental Health Assn., 1994. Mem. Internat. Assn. for Offender Counselors, Fla. Alcohol, Drug, Substance Abuse Assn. (bd. dirs., regional rep., Regional Profl. of Yr. 1992-93), Internat. Assn. for Marriage and Family Counseling, Phi Theta Kappa, Alpha Phi Sigma.

VILLEGAS, THERESE MARGARET, engineer; b. Manila, Mar. 24, 1966; came to U.S., 1972; d. Jose Kalaw and Norma Victoria Villegas. BS in Gen. Engring., U. Ill., 1988. Application engr. GM-Packard Electric Divsn., Warren, Ohio, 1989-90; elec. design engr. GM-Packard Electric Divsn., Warren, Mich., 1990-91, 92—; mfg. engr. GM-Packard Electric Divsn., Nuevo Laredo, Mex., 1991-92; sales engr., account mgr. GM-Packard Electric Divsn., Troy, Mich., 1994—. Mem. Berkley Libr. (Mich.) of Friends, 1993; vol. Children's Hosp., 1993—. Mem. Kappa Kappa Gamma (auction com. 1993—). Democrat. Roman Catholic. Office: GM Packard Electric Divsn 1117 W Long Lake Rd Troy MI

VILLOCH, KELLY CARNEY, art director; b. Kyoto, Japan, July 22, 1950; d. William Riley and stepdaughter Hazel Fowler Carney; m. Joe D. Villoch, Aug. 9, 1969; children: Jonathan Christopher, Jennifer. A in Fine Arts, Dade C.C., Miami, Fla., 1971; student, Metro Fine Arts, 1973-74, Fla. Internat. U., 1985-88. Design asst. Lanvin, Miami, 1971—, Fieldcrest, Miami, 1974-77; art dir. Advercolor, Miami, 1977-78; art dir. copywriter ABC, Miami, 1978-89; writer Armed Forces Radio & TV Network; multimedia dir. ADVITEC, 1989-91; art dir. writer Miami Write, 1979—; owner Beach Point Prodns., 1992—; lectr. Miami Dade C.C., cons. Studio Masters, North Miami, 1979-89. Prin. works include mixed media, 1974 (Best of Show 1974), pen and ink drawing, 1988 (Best Poster 1988); writer, dir., editor, prodr. (video film): Bif, 1988, Drink + Drive = Die, 1994; writer, dir., prodr. (pub. svc. announcement) Reading is the Real Adventure, 1990; film editor Talent Times Mag.; author: Winds of Freedom, 1994; art dir., exec. com. Miami Hispanic Media Conf., 1992, 93, 94. State of Fla. grantee LimeLite Studios, Inc., 1990, William Douglas Pawley Found. grantee, Frances Wolfson scholar, Cultural Consortium grantee, 1993. Mem. Am. Film Inst., Phi Beta Kappa.

VINCENT, SHARON KAY, nursing educator; b. Owosso, Mich., Sept. 13, 1946; m. Jerry Vincent, 1964; children: Tami Corley, Troy Matthew Grant, Shawn Patrick. ADN, Ea. Ky. U., 1974, BSN, 1977; MSN, Med. Coll. Ga., 1981. RN, Ga. Staff nurse, epidemiologist, supr. Pattie A. Clay Hosp., Richmond, Ky., 1974-77; staff nurse Student Health Ctr., Ea. Ky. U., Richmond, 1977; instr. Lexington (Ky.) Vocat. Sch., 1977-80; staff nurse VA Med. Ctr., Lexington, 1977-79; head nurse dept. urology VA Med. Ctr., Augusta, Ga., 1980-83; staff nurse nursing pool Humana Hosp., Augusta, 1983—; nurse educator Med. Coll. Ga. Hosp. and Clinics, Augusta, 1983-88; asst. prof. dept. nursing Augusta Coll., 1988—; del. to China Citizen Amb. Program, U. Calif., 1991; curriculum cons. Athens (Ga.) Area Tech. Inst., 1990; ednl. mgmt. cons. Hilton Head (S.C.) Hosp., 1988—; presenter AIDS awareness programs, 1986—; coord. workshops; presenter at profl. confs. Mem. ANA, ARC, Internat. Toastmaster Club, Sigma Theta Tau. Office: Augusta Coll 2500 Walton Way Augusta GA 30910

VINCI, JOANNE MARIA, brokerage house executive; b. Phila., Jan. 3, 1962; d. Angelo Vincent and Joanne (Brown) V. BA, LaSalle Coll., 1984. Various positions including adminstrv. asst. Merrill Lynch, Bala Cynwyd, Pa., 1984—. Vol. ARC, Phila., 1991-93. Democrat. Roman Catholic. Home: 7411 Lapwing Pl Apt 1 Philadelphia PA 19153 Office: Merrill Lynch 2 Bala Plaza Bala Cynwyd PA 19004

VINES, KIMBERLY KAY, home health nurse; b. Alexandria, La., June 5, 1961; d. Buddy Clay Fairbanks and Rebecca Ellen McClellan; m. Roy Mack Vines, June 26, 1982; children: Jessica Kay, Hannah Beth. ADN, Alcorn State U., 1983. RN, Miss. Staff nurse Jeff Davis Meml. Hosp., Natchez, Miss., 1983-85; chief admission nurse South Miss. Home Health, Natchez, 1985—. Mem. Miss. Nurses Assn. (pres. Dist. I 1990-94, dist. level mem. com., state level awards com.). Baptist. Home: 28 Honey Bee Ln Natchez MS 39120

VINKEMULDER, H. YVONNE, lawyer; b. Grand Rapids, Mich., Aug. 21, 1930; d. Arthur and Frances (DeWitt) V. Student, Calvin Coll., 1948-50, Blodgett Hosp. Sch. Nursing, 1950-52; BA, Trinity Coll., 1956; JD, U. Miami, Coral Gables, Fla., 1983. Bar: Wis. 1983. Staff nurse Little Traverse Hosp., Petoskey, Mich., 1952-53, Swedish Covenant Hosp., Chgo., 1953-55; campus nurse Trinity Coll., Chgo., 1955-57; head nurse Colo. Coll., Colorado Springs, 1957-61; sec. Inter-Varsity Christian Fellowship, Chgo., 1961-65; asst. to dir. devel. Inter-Varsity Christian Fellowship, Chgo. and Madison, Wis., 1965-74; dir. devel. Inter-Varsity Christian Fellowship, Madison, 1974-80, dir. planned giving, 1979-81, 1990—, gen. counsel, 1983—; cons. in devel. various orgns., 1976-80; lectr. internat. law Fgn. Language Inst., Tianjin, China, 1989. Columnist The Branch, 1976-79; contbg. author: A Guide to Wisconsin Non Profit Corporations, 1990; contbr. articles to mags. Bd. dirs. Internat. Fellowship of Evang. Students, Inc., Boston, 1975-85, Schloss Mittersill Christian Conf. Inc., Madison, 1985-93, 94—; clk. Faith Bapt. Ch., Madison, 1985—; mem. standards com. Evang. Coun. Fin. Accountability, 1989—; mem. steering com. Evang. Legal Forum, 1988-90. Mem. Wis. State Bar Assn., State Bar Wis. (nonprofit subcom.), Christian Legal Soc. Baptist. Home: 801 Acewood Blvd Madison WI 53714-3209 Office: InterVarsity Christian Fellowship 6400 Schroeder Rd PO Box 7895 Madison WI 53707-7895

VINSON, LEILA TERRY WALKER, retired gerontological social worker; b. Lynchburg, Va., July 28, 1928; d. William Terry and Ada Allen (Moore) Walker; m. Hughes Nelson Vinson, Aug. 11, 1951; children: Hughes Nelson, William Terry. Student, Agnes Scott Coll., 1946-48; BA, U. Ala., Tuscaloosa, 1950; postgrad., U. Ala., Birmingham, 1980-81, U. Va., 1950-51. Cert. gerontol. social worker, Ala. Tchr. English and Latin Marion County Bd. Edn., Hamilton, Ala., 1952-59; social worker I Marion County Dept. Pensions and Security, 1963-72, gerontol. social worker II, 1972-85; ret., 1985. Bd. dirs. Marion County Dept. Human Resources, 1985—; speaker on gen. subjects. Recipient Ala. Woman Committed to Excellence award Tuscaloosa coun. Girl Scouts U.S., 1987; named Mrs. Marion County, PTA, Gwin, Ala., 1969, Woman of Yr. Town of Hamilton, 1980, New Retiree of Yr. Ala. Ret. State Employees Assn., 1988, Woman of Yr. BPW, 1985; Gessener Harrison fellow U. Va., 1950-51. Mem. AAUW, DAR (flag chmn. Bedford chpt. 1988-90), UDC, Bus. and Profl. Women's Club (dist. dir. 1984-86, Outstanding Dir. award 1986), Ala. Fedn. Women's Club. Home: PO Box 1112 Hamilton AL 35570-1112 also: Military Rd Hamilton AL 35570

VIOLENUS, AGNES A., school system administrator; b. N.Y.C., May 17, 1931; d. Antonio and Constance Violenus. BA, Hunter Coll., 1952; MA, Columbia U., 1958; EdD, Nova U., 1990. Tchr. N.Y. State Day Care, N.Y.C., 1952-53, N.Y.C. Bd. Edn., 1953-66; asst. prin. N.Y.C. Elem. and Jr. High Sch., 1966-91; adj. instr. computer dept. continuing edn. div. York Coll., N.Y.C., 1985-88; adj. instr. tchr. mentor program grad. edn. div. CCNY, 1990-91; reviewer ednl. and instructional films. Co-author: LOGO: K-12, 1980; contbr. articles to profl. jours. Life mem. Girl Scouts U.S., N.Y.C.; mem. N.Y.C. Sch. Vol. Program, 1991—. Recipient Dedicated Svc. award Coun. Suprs. and Adminstrs. Mem. N.Y. Acad. Scis., Nat. Assn. Negro Bus. and Profl. Women's Clubs (scholarship com. 1989—), Nat. Black Child Devel. Inst. (bd. dir. 1991—, pub. policy com. 1991—), Pub. Edn. Assn. (mem. good schs. exch. com.), Schomburg Ctr. Rsch. in Black Culture (bd. trustee, co-chair corp. task force on African-Am. in math., sci., and tech. 1992—), Doctorate Assn. N.Y. Educators, N.Y. Alliance Black Sch. Educators, Hunter Coll. Alumni Assn. (bd. dirs. 1993—), Bank St. Alumni Coun. Greater N.Y. (asst. sec. 1991—), Wistarians Alumni Hunter Coll. (pres. 1990—). Democrat. Roman Catholic. Office: PO Box # 85 Canal St Sta 350 Canal St New York NY 10013-2502

VIOLETTE, DIANE MARIE, small business owner, consultant; b. Pontiac, Mich., Apr. 19, 1958; d. Bernard Desmond and Mary Virginia (Bartosh) V.; m. Glenn Martin Payette, Apr. 18, 1987. BA in Journalism, Mich. State U., 1980; cert. in govt. contracts and mgmt., UCLA, 1987; MBA summa cum laude, Calif. State U., Northridge, 1991. Contract adminstr. Def. Contract Adminstrn. Services Mgmt. Area, Van Nuys, Calif., 1980-84, adminstrv. contract officer, 1984-87; pres. govt. contracting Diane Violette & Assocs., Northridge, 1987—. Contbr. articles to profl. jours. Mem. Nat. Contract Mgmt. Assn.

VIORST, JUDITH STAHL, author; b. Newark, Feb. 2, 1931; d. Martin Leonard and Ruth June (Ehrenkranz) Stahl; m. Milton Viorst, Jan. 30, 1960; children: Anthony Jacob, Nicholas Nathan, Alexander Noah. BA, Rutgers U., 1952; grad., Washington Psychoanalytic Inst., 1981. Author: (children's books) Sunday Morning, 1968, I'll Fix Anthony, 1969, Try It Again Sam, 1970, The Tenth Good Thing About Barney, 1971 (Silver Pencil award 1973), Alexander and the Terrible Horrible No Good Very Bad Day, 1972, My Mama Says There Aren't Any Zombies, Ghosts, Vampires, Creatures, Demons, Monsters, Fiends, Goblins or Things, 1973, Rosie and Michael, 1974, Alexander, Who Used to Be Rich Last Sunday, 1978, The Good-Bye Book, 1988, Earrings!, 1990, The Alphabet from Z to A (with Much Confusion on the Way), 1994; (poetry) The Village Square, 1965-66, It's Hard to Be Hip Over Thirty and Other Tragedies of Married Life, 1968, People and Other Aggravations, 1971, How Did I Get to Be Forty and Other Atrocities, 1976, If I Were in Charge of the World and Other Worries, 1981, When Did I Stop Being Twenty and Other Injustices, 1987, Forever Fifty and Other Negotiations, 1989, Sad Underwear and Other Complications, 1995; (with Milton Viorst) The Washington Underground Gourmet, 1970, Yes Married, 1972, A Visit from St. Nicholas (To a Liberated Household), 1977, Love and Guilt and the Meaning of Life, Etc., 1979, Necessary Losses, 1986, Murdering Mr. Monti, 1994; columnist Redbook mag.(Penney-Mo. award 1974, Am. Acad. Pediatrics award 1977, Am. Assoc. Univ. Women 1980). Jewish. Home: 3432 Ashley Ter NW Washington DC 20008-3238

VIRET, MARGARET MARY, art educator; b. N.Y.C., Apr. 18, 1913; d. James Lawrence and Mary Agnes (Hawkes) Buchanan. Student bus. coll.,

N.Y.C. Art tchr. Dade County Adult Edn., Fla. Exhibited in Contemporary Am. Art Exhibit Four Arts Soc., Palm Beach, Fla., 1965; watercolors and oil paintings represented in numerous nat. and local permanent collections. Trustee Miami Art League, Inc., 1947—. Recipient Best-in-Florida award Richard's Dept. Store. Mem. Nat. League of Am. Pen Women, Miami Woman's Club. Home: 294 NE 55th Terr Miami FL 33137-2558

VIRGO, MURIEL AGNES, swimming school owner; b. Liverpool, Cheshire, Eng., Apr. 3, 1924; d. Harold Thornhill and Susan Ann (Duff) Franks; m. John Virgo, Aug. 13, 1942; children: John Michael, Angela Victoria, Barbara Ann, Collin Anthony, Donna Marie. Grad. parochial schs. Co-owner Virgo Swim Sch., Garden Grove, Calif., 1967—. Mem. Ancient Mystical Order Rosae Crucis, Traditional Martinist Order. Republican. Roman Catholic. Home: 12751 Crestwood Cir Garden Grove CA 92641-5250 Office: Virgo Swim Sch 12851 Brookhurst Way Garden Grove CA 92641-5205

VIRTUE, VIRGINIA MAY, real estate broker; b. Berlin, N.J., Aug. 17, 1926; d. Carl and Gertrude (Heinecke) Fabrizio; m. Harlan N. Virtue, Apr. 10, 1948; children: Wanda, Penny, Melodie. Cert. real estate broker. Mgr. Fine Arts Silver & China Co., Wilmington, Del., 1945-68; sales assoc. J.P. Stoltz Realtor, Wilmington, Del., 1968-75; pres. V Virtue, Inc., Wilmington, 1975—; bd. dirs. First State Bank, Wilmington. Chmn. ladies activities Immanuel Bapt. Ch., Wilmington, 1965-80; mem. legis. com. State Assn. Realtors, Dover, Del., 1980-88. Named Realtor of Yr. New Castle County Assn. of Realtors, 1978. Mem. Nat. Assn. Realtors (coord. fed. dist. Del. chpt. 1984-90), Del. Assn. Realtors (bd. dirs. 1978-88), New Castle County Assn. Realtors, Realtors Nat. Mktg. Inst. Home: 49 Michangelo Ct RD #6 Hockessin DE 19707 Office: V Virtue Inc 26 Honeysuckle Dr Wilmington DE 19804-3901

VIS, DEBRA L., accountant; b. Caldwell, Idaho, May 19, 1960; d. Leonard Albert and Lorraine Alice (Noteboom) V. BBA, Boise State U., 1983. CPA, Idaho. Plat rm. clk. Canyon County Assessor, Caldwell, Idaho, 1983-84; staff acct. Christensen & Jackson, CPAs, Caldwell, 1984-90, ptnr., 1991-94; ptnr. Christensen, Jackson, Miller and Co., Caldwell, 1995—. V.p. ARC, Caldwell, 1992-93. Mem. AICPAs, Am. Bus. Women (pres., treas. 1991-95, Woman of Yr. 1994), Idaho Soc. CPAs, Beta Gamma Sigma, Phi Kappa Phi. Office: Christensen & Jackson CPAs 1201 S Kimball Caldwell ID 83605

VISCELLI, THERESE RAUTH, materials management consultant; b. Bitburg, Fed. Republic Germany, Nov. 18, 1955; d. David William and Joyce (Kelly) Rauth; m. Eugene R. Viscelli, Feb. 4, 1978; children: Christopher, Kathryn, Matthew. BS, Ga. Inst. Tech., 1977; postgrad., So. Tech. Inst., 1977-78, Ga. State U., 1982-83. Mktg. engr. Hughes Aircraft Corp., Carlsbad, Calif., 1978-79; indsl. engr. Kearfott-Singer, San Marcos, Calif., 1979-80; product analyst Control Data Corp., Atlanta, 1981-84; dir. R&D Am. Software, Inc., Atlanta, 1984-92; acct. mgr. The Coca-Cola Co., 1992-93; dir. info. sys. Mizuno, USA, Norcross, Ga., 1993—. Mem. Am. Prodn. and Inventory Control Soc. (program chmn. 1982-83, v.p. 1983-84). Republican. Roman Catholic.

VISOCKI, NANCY GAYLE, infosystems design consultant; b. Dumont, N.J., May 13, 1952; d. Thomas and Gloria (Valle) V. BA in Maths., Manhattanville Coll., 1974; MS in Ops. Rsch. and Stats., Rensselaer Poly. Inst., 1977. Rsch. asst. Coll. Physicians and Surgeons Columbia U., N.Y.C., 1974-75; programmer analyst R. Shriver Assocs., Parsippany, N.J., 1977-79; sr. tech. rep. GE Info. Svcs. Co., East Orange, N.J., 1979-81; mgr. project office GE Info. Svcs. Co., Morristown, N.J., 1981-83, tech. dir., 1983-87, tech. mgr., 1988-89; area mgr. system devel. and consulting GE Info. Svcs. Co., Parsippany, 1989-92; area tech. mgr. system devel. and cons., Fin. Info. Systems GE Info. Svcs. Co., Parsippany, N.J., 1992-93, sr. cons. electronic commerce info. svcs., 1993—. Active Western Hills Christian Ch., Tranquility, N.J., 1986—; vol. Women's Ctr., Hackettstown, N.J., 1989-93; class fundraising and gift chmn. Rensselaer Poly. Inst., 1991-95; vol. Elfun Soc. Manhattanville Coll. grantee, Purchase, N.Y., 1970-71; tuition fellow Rensselaer Poly. Inst., Troy, N.Y., 1975-77. Mem. NAFE, Women of Accomplishment. Home: 140 E Linden Ave Dumont NJ 07628-1916 Office: GE Info Svcs Co 20 Waterview Blvd Parsippany NJ 07054-1219

VISSER, VALYA ELIZABETH, physician; b. Chgo., Oct. 2, 1947; d. Roy Warren and Tania Eugenia (Morozoff) Nelson; children: Kira Elizabeth Visser, Michael Philip Visser. BS, Iowa State U., 1968; MD, U. Iowa, 1973. Diplomate Am. Bd. Pediatrics, Sub-Bd. Neonatal-Perinatal Medicine. Resident pediatrics U. Iowa Hosps. and Clinics, Iowa City, 1976; fellow neonatology Children's Mercy Hosp., Kansas City, 1978; asst. prof. pediatrics U. Kans. Sch. Medicine, Kansas City, 1978-81; staff pediatrician U.S. Army Med. Corps., Ft. Bragg, N.C., 1981-83; attending neonatologist Carolinas Med. Ctr., Charlotte, 1983—; acting chair dept. pediatrics Carolinas Med. Ctr., Charlotte, 1992-94; conf. chair Extracorporeal Life Support Orgn., Ann Arbor, Mich., 1993—. Major Med. Corps., 1981-83. Fellow Am. Acad. Pediatrics; mem. Soc. for Critical Care Medicine. Mem. Unitarian-Universalist Ch. Office: Carolinas Med Ctr Dept Pediatrics PO Box 32861 Charlotte NC 28232-2861

VITAGLIANO, KATHLEEN ALYCE FULLER, secondary education educator; b. Oneida, N.Y., May 3, 1949; d. Allen Herbert and Phyllis Ann (Fearon) Fuller; m. Gene Angelo Vitagliano, Feb. 10, 1973; children: Marissa Ariana, Marc Anthony, Michael Allen. BA in English, SUNY, Buffalo, 1971, EdM in English Education, 1973; cert. Creative Studies, SUC, Buffalo, 1990. Cert. secondary English tchr. N.Y. Tchr. English grades 7-12 Buffalo Pub. Schs., N.Y., 1972-93; magnet sch. tchr. specialist Campus West Sch., Buffalo, 1993—; facilitator Creative Problem Solving, 1990—; workshop presenter Buffalo Tchr. Ctr., N.Y., 1992—. Singer Buffalo Philharm. Chorus, N.Y., 1978—; mem. Just Buffalo Literary Ctr., N.Y., 1991—; del. Buffalo Tchrs. Fedn., N.Y., 1992—; bd. mem., Parent, Tchr. and Student Cmty. Orgn. of City Honors Sch., 1993—, v.p., 1994—. Grantee NEH, 1985. Fellow Western N.Y. Writing Project (steering com., workshop presenter 1990—, instr. 1992—); mem. NEA, ASCD, N.Y. State English Coun. (Tchr. of Excellence award 1991), Nat. Coun. Tchrs. of English, Grad. Sch. Edn. Alumni Assn. SUNY Buffalo, Creative Edn. Found., Creative Studies Alumni Assn. SUC Buffalo (newsletter editor 1991—, v.p. 1992—), Advocacy for Gifted Talented Edn. of N.Y., Internat. Creativity Network, Phi Delta Kappa. Home: 207 Saranac Ave Buffalo NY 14216 Office: Campus West Sch 1300 Elmwood Ave Buffalo NY 14222

VITALE, CONCETTA, college administrator, nurse; b. New Kensington, Pa., May 21; m. Joseph Lewis Hlafcsak, Mar. 19, 1983; children—Susan, Judith. B.S., U. Pitts., 1973, M.S. in Nursing, 1975, PhD, 1995. Various clin. and teaching positions, 1960-95; dean instrn. Community Coll. Allegheny County, Pitts., 1995—.

VITERI, SILVIA M., electrical engineer; b. Chgo., May 29, 1959; d. Jaime E. and Elvia B. (Lema) V. BSEE, Ga. Inst. Tech., 1985, MSEE, 1986. Elec. engr. AT&T, Atlanta, 1986-87; staff elec. engr. Motorola, Inc., Boynton Beach, Fla., 1987—. U.S. patentee driver CKT for peizoelectric transducer and electroluminescent lamp, 1991, leadless resistors, 1992, programming system and pager for use therwith, 1993. Recipient Nat. Hispanic scholarship Nat. Hispanic Assn., Calif., 1983-85. Mem. NAFE, Soc. Women Engrs., Eta Kappa Nu, Tau Beta Pi. Office: Motorola Inc 1500 NW 22nd Ave Boynton Beach FL 33426-8221

VITETTA, ELLEN S., microbiologist educator, immunologist. BA, Conn. Coll.; MS, NYU, 1966, PhD, 1968. Prof. microbiology Southwestern Med. Sch., U. Tex., Dallas, 1976—; dir. Cancer Immunobiology Ctr., U. Tex., Dallas, 1988—; Sheryle Simmons Patigian Disting. chair in cancer immunobiology Southwestern Med. Sch., U. Tex., Dallas, 1989—; bd. sci. coun. NCI Cancer Treatment Bd., 1993; sci. adv. bd. Howard Hughes Med. Inst., 1992—; Kettering selection com. GM Cancer Rsch. Foun., 1987-88; task force NIAID in Immunology, 1989-90; mem. sci. bd. Ludwig Inst., 1983—. Editorial bd.: Advances in Host Defense Mechanisms, 1983—, Annual Review of Immunology, 1991—, Bioconjugate Chemistry, 1989-93, Cellular Immunology, 1984-93, Current Opinion in Immunology, 1992—, FASEB Journal, 1987—, International Journal of Onocology, 1992—, International Soc. Immunopharmacology, 1989—, Journal of Immunology, 1975-78, Molecular Immunology, 1978-93; Assoc. Editor: Cancer Research, 1986—; Immunochemistry Section Editor: Journal of Immunology, 1978-82; Co-Editor in Chief: Therapeutic Immunology, 1992—. Recipient Women's Excellence in Sci. award Fedn. Am. Soc. Expn. Biology, 1991, Taittinger Breast Cancer Rsch. award Komen Found., 1983, Pierce Immunotoxin award, 1988, NIH Merit award, 1987—, U. Tex. Southwestern Med. Sch. Faculty Teaching awards 1989, 91, 92, 93, FASEB Execellence in Sci. award, 1991, Abbot Clinical Immunology award Am. Soc. Microbiologists, 1992, Past State Pres. award Tex. Fed. Bus. Profl. Women's Club, 1993. Mem. Am. Assn. Immunologists (pres. 1993—), Nat. Acad. Scis., Internat. Soc. Immunopharmacology (councillor 1991—). Office: Univ of Texas Southwestern Medical Ctr Cancer Ctr 6000 Harry Hines Blvd Dallas TX 75235

VITTADINI, ADRIENNE, fashion designer; b. Gyor, Hungary; came to U.S., 1957; d. Alexander and Aranka (Langhiel) Toth; m. Gian Luigi Maria Vittadini, 1972; 1 stepchild, Emanuele. Ed., Moore Coll. Art, Phila. Designer Rosanna-Warneco, N.Y.C., 1970-76; v.p. for design Kimberly Knitwear-Gen. Mills, N.Y.C., 1976-78; chmn. bd. Adrienne Vittadini Inc., N.Y.C., 1979—. Recipient Design award Retail Fashion Authorities Am., 1979, Outstanding Phila. Fashion Designer award Council for Labor and Industry, Phila., 1984, Coty Am. Fashion Critics award, 1984. Office: Adrienne Vittadini Inc 575 7th Ave 29th fl New York NY 10018-1805*

VITTETOE, MARIE CLARE, retired medical technology educator; b. Keota, Iowa, May 19, 1927; d. Edward Daniel and Marcella Matilda (Peiffer) V. BS, Marycrest Coll., 1950; MS, W.Va. U., 1971, EdD, 1973. Staff technician St. Joseph Hosp., Ottumwa, Iowa, 1950-70; instr. Ottumwa Hosp. Sch. Med. Tech., 1957-70, St. Joseph Hosp. Sch. Nursing, Ottumwa, 1950-70; asst. prof. U. Ill., Champaign-Urbana, 1973-78; prof. clin. lab. scis., med. tech. U. Ky., Lexington, 1978-94. Contbr. articles to profl. jours. Recipient Kingston award for Creative Teaching; Recognition award for svc. to edn. Commonwealth of Ky. Coun. on Higher Edn.; named Ky. Col. Mem. Am. Soc. for Med. Tech. (chmn. 1986-89, Profl. Achievement award 1991, Ky. Mem. of Yr. award 1994), Am. Soc. Clin. Lab. Scis., Alpha Mu Tau, Phi Delta Kappa, Alpha Eta. Office: 122 Medical Center Anx # 2 Lexington KY 40536

VITTORIO-PHILLIPS, MARY LOU, educator, pediatric nurse; b. Phila., Dec. 9, 1957; d. Louis F. and Mary T. (Moss) Vittorio; m. David A. Phillips, May 3, 1980; children: Peter M., Daniel A., Mary K. Diploma, St. Joseph Hosp. Sch. Nursing, Reading, Pa., 1979; BSN, Kutztown (Pa.) U., 1991. Cert. neonatal intensive care nurse, neonatal resuscitation instr., BCLS instr., PALS provider, breast feeding educator. ICU-coronary care unit staff nurse Sacred Heart Hosp., Allentown, Pa., 1979-85, labor and delivery staff nurse, 1985-86, perinatal/neonatal/pediatric staff devel. instr., 1986-89, neonatal/pediatric ICU staff nurse, 1985-92; pediatric/critical care nursing instr. St. Luke's Hosp. Sch. Nursing, Bethlehem, Pa., 1992—. Mem. NAPNAP. Home: 6117 Schaller Ct Germansville PA 18053-2317

VITUNAC, ANN E., judge; b. 1949. BS, Univ. of Fla., 1970; JD, Stetson Coll. of Law, 1972. Chief trial atty. Fla. State Attorney's Office, West Palm Beach, 1973-85; magistrate judge U.S. Dist. Ct. (Fla. so. dist.), 11th circuit, West Palm Beach, 1985—. Recipient Moot Court award Stetson Coll. of Law, 1972, Robert Sykes award Stetson Coll. of Law, 1973. Mem. Phi Delta Phi Legal Frat., Palm Beach County Bar Assn. Office: US Courthouse 701 Clematis St Rm 423 West Palm Beach FL 33401-5101*

VIVALDO, DENISE LOIS, food consultant; b. San Francisco, May 28, 1951; d. John Francis and Doris Marie (Simpson) V.; m. Ken Meyer, July 4, 1993. Cert. as profl. chef, Calif. Culinary Acad., 1984. Exec. chef Calif. Celebration, Marina del Rey, 1985-88; cons., pres. Food Fanatics, L.A., 1988—. Author: How to Open & Operate a Home-Based Catering Business, 1993. Mem. adv. bd. UCLA Hospitality, 1993-94. Mem. So. Calif. Culinary Guild, Internat. Assn. Cooking Profls. Home and office: 1753 S Shenandoah St Los Angeles CA 90035

VIVELO, JACQUELINE JEAN, author, English language educator; b. Lumberton, Miss., Jan. 23, 1943; d. Jack and Virginia Olivia (Bond) Jones; m. Frank Robert Vivelo, June 19, 1965; 1 child, Alexandra J. BA, U. Tenn., Knoxville, 1965, MA, 1970. Caseworker N.Y.C. Dept. Welfare, 1965-66; instr. reading Knoxville Coll., 1968-70; instr. English Middlesex County Coll., Edison, N.J., 1970-72, U. Mo., Rolla, 1975-77, Middlesex County Coll., Edison, 1978-80; instr. English Lebanon Valley Coll., Annville, Pa., 1981-87, asst. prof. English, 1987-91. Author: Super Sleuth, 1985 (Best Book award), Beagle in Trouble, 1986, A Trick of the Light, 1987, Super Sleuth and the Bare Bones, 1988, Writing Fiction: A Handbook for Creative Writing, 1993, Reading to Matthew, 1993 (Best Book award), Mr. Scatter's Magic Spell, 1993, Chills Run Down My Spine, 1994, Have You Lost Your Kangaroo?, 1995; editor: College Education Achievement Project's Handbook for College Reading Teachers, 1969; co-editor: American Indian Prose and Poetry, 1974: contbr. articles/short stories to various publs. Recipient Best Book award Am. Child Study Assn., 1985, Young Book Trust, U.K., 1994, Pa. Coun. of the Arts Fellowship award for Lit., 1992; NIMH grantee, 1969-70. Mem. Children's Lit. Coun. Pa. (v.p. 1991), Soc. Children's Book Writers, Sigma Tau Delta (sponsor Omicron Omicron chpt. 1988-90), Pi Lambda Theta. Home: 1309 Half Moon Dr Wharton TX 77488

VIVIAN, LINDA BRADT, sales and public relations executive; b. Elmira, N.Y., Nov. 22, 1945; d. Lorenz Claude and Muriel (Dolan) Bradt; m. Robert W. Vivian, Apr. 5, 1968 (div. Sept. 1977). Student, Andrews U., 1963-66. Adminstrv. asst. Star-Gazette, Elmira, 1966-68; editor Guide, staff writer Palm Springs (Calif.) Life mag., 1970-75; dir. sales and pub. rels. Palm Springs Aerial Tramway, 1975—; sec. Hospitality and Bus. Industry Coun. Palm Springs Desert Resorts, 1989-91, vice-chmn., 1991-94, chmn., 1994—. Mem. Hotel Sales and Mktg. Assn. (allied nominating chmn. Palm Springs chpt. 1986-88), Am. Soc. Assn. Execs., Travel Industry Assn., Hospitality Industry and Bus. Coun. of Palm Springs Resorts (sec. 1989-91, vice-chmn. 1991-94, chmn. 1994—), Nat. Tour Assn. (co-chair Team Calif. promotions com. 1993—), Calif. Travel Industry Assn., Palm Springs C. of C. (bd. dirs. 1984-85). Republican. Office: Palm Springs Aerial Tramway One Tramway Rd Palm Springs CA 92262

VLACHOS-KEASTEAD, KONSTANTINA, lawyer; b. Jersey City, N.J., Oct. 29, 1960; d. George K. and Panagioula (Golematis) Vlachos; m. Scott Brion Keastead, Nov. 28, 1993. BA in Psychology and Criminial Justice, Moravian Coll., 1982; JD, Nova U., 1985. Bar: N.J. 1985. Pvt. practice atty. Kearny, N.J., 1985—. Former mem. St. George Greek Orthodox Ch., Clifton, N.J.; active First Presbyn. Ch. of Arlington, Kearny. Mem. ABA, N.J. State Bar Assn. Office: 824 Kearny Ave Kearny NJ 07032

VLAHOKOSTA, FRIDERIKI V., physician, scientist, health foundation executive; b. Trikala, Greece; d. Vissarion and Efthimia (Batagianni) V. Attended, Aristotelion U., Thessaloniki, Greece, 1968. Straight med. intern Doctor's Hosp., Washington, 1973-74, Walter Reed Army Med. Ctr., Washington, 1973-74; asst. resident internal medicine D.C. Gen. Hosp., 1974-76; resident internal medicine Walter Reed Army med. Ctr., 1974-76; clin. fellow in diabetes Joslin Diabetes Ctr., Boston, 1977-78; rsch. assoc. Harvard Med. Sch., 1979-82, instr. medicine, 1981-85, asst. prof. medicine, 1985—; founder, CEO, assoc. physician Mass. Gen. Hosp.; rsch. assoc. Brigham and Women's Hosp., Harvard Med. Sch., 1979-80, assoc. physician, 1980-83; rsch. assoc. E.P. Joslin Rsch. Lab., 1979-81, Joslin Diabetes Ctr., investigator, 1981-85; med. dir. Diabetes Treatment Ctr., Waltham (Mass.)-Weston Med. Ctr., 1985-86; cons. physician New Eng. Deaconess Hosp., 1985—, Brigham and Women's Hosp., 1983—; founder, chairperson, CEO Hippocrates Internat. Med. Found., 1988—; physician Pub. Health Svc., Greece, 1968-69; physician, investigator Mass. Gen. Hosp.; asst. prof. Harvard Med. Sch., Boston,. Contbr. over 50 med. articles to profl. jours. Exec. bd. dirs. New Eng. Hellenic Med. Soc., 1980-81. Mem. AMA, Am. Diabetes Assn., Am. Med. Women Assn., Am. Fedn. for Clin. Rsch., New Eng. Helennic Med. Soc. (exec. bd. dir. 1980-87), Mass. Med. Soc., N.Y. Acad. Scis., Diabetes Assocs. Ea. Mass. (bd. dirs. 1985-86, treas. 1985-86).

VLAMIS, DIANA, computer applications consultant; b. Stamford, Conn., July 14, 1966; d. George John and Dorothea (Goudas) V. BS in Computer Sci., U. Pa., 1988. Software engr. Digital Equipment Corp., 1988-93; applications cons. Easel Corp., Burlington, Mass., 1993—; cons. U. Pa. Med. Dept., Phila., 1987-90. Mem. Assn. Computing Machinery, Women of Note (program chair 1990-93), NAFE. Office: Easel Corp 25 Corporate Dr Burlington MA 01803

VLISSIDES, IRENE ANGELA, tax accountant; b. McLean, Va., Nov. 18, 1963; d. Matthew John and Sophia (Drakoulis) V. BS in Commerce, U. Va., 1986, MS in Acctg., 1987. CPA, Va. Sr. mgr. KPMG Peat Marwick, Washington, 1987-93; cons. Anne L. Stone, Atty.-at-law, McLean, Va., 1993—. Mem. AICPAs, D.C. Inst. CPAs. Home: 2281 Kings Garden Way Falls Church VA 22043

VOCE, JOAN A. CIFONELLI, elementary school educator; b. Utica, N.Y., Mar. 22, 1936; d. Albert and Theresa (Buono) Cifonelli; m. Eugene R. Voce Sr., Aug. 16, 1958; children: Eugene R. Jr., Lisa V. Stewart, Mark L., Daniel A. BS in Elem. Edn., Coll. St. Rose, Albany, N.Y., 1958; MS in Elem. Edn., SUNY, Cortland, 1981. 1st grade tchr. Utica (N.Y.) Pub. Schs., 1958-59, 61-62, 1964-67; tchr. 1st and 2nd grades Deerfield Elem. Sch., Utica, 1968-91. Active YWCA. Mem. AAUW (Mohawk Valley br.), N.Y. State United Tchrs., Whitesboro Tchrs. Assn., Am. Italian Heritage Assn., Am. Assn. Ret. Persons, Utica Area Ret. Tchrs. Assn., N.Y. State Ret. Tchrs. Assn., Coll. St. Rose Alumni Assn., Skenandoa Golf and Country Club, Alpha Delta Kappa (v.p. 1974-76, pres. 1976-78, corr. sec. 1976-78, rec. sec. 1986-88, 90-91), Ladies of St. Anne, St. Anne's Ch., Whitesboro, N.Y. Home: 18 Calais Dr Whitesboro NY 13492-2527

VOCHT, MICHELLE ELISE, lawyer; b. Detroit, Sept. 27, 1956. BA with honors, U. Mich., 1978; JD, Wayne State U., 1981. Bar: Mich., U.S. Dist. Ct. (ea. and we. dist.) Mich., U.S. Ct. Appeals (6th cir.), 1981. V.p., treas. Roy, Shecter & Vocht PC, Bloomfield Hills, Mich., 1981—; mem. pro bono teaching faculty Detroit chpt. Fed. Bar Assn.; mediator Mediation Tribunal Wayne County Cir. Ct., 1989—; pre-sentencing probation officer 48th Dist. Ct., 1989-90. Mem. com. for re-election of current Mich. Supreme Ct. Justice, 1986; mem. Rep. Assembly, Oak County, 1992—; exec. bd. Birmingham Women's Community Ctr., 1987-88; bd. dirs. Community Adv. Bd.-Arbor Clin. Group, Inc., 1989-91; mem. drug and alcohol abuse spl. task force County of Oakland, 1989—. Mem. Assn. Trial Lawyers Am., Am. Inns of Ct. (barrister 1984-87), Mich. Trial Lawyers Assn., Women Lawyers Assn. Mich., Oakland County Trial Lawyers Assn. (exec. bd. dirs. 1982-84, 88—, sec. 1990—, v.p. 1991-92, pres. 1992-95), State Bar Assn. Mich. (chmn. gen. practice sect. 1984-86, sec. 1982-83, vice-chmn. 1983-84, mem. civil procedure com. 1982-84, assoc. mem. lawyers and judges assistance com., 1988-89, hearing panelist atty. discipline bd., 1982—, labor and employment sect., domestic rels. sect., rep. 6th jud. cir. 1993—), Mich. Employment Law Assn., Internat. Platform Assn., Indsl. Rels. Rsch. Assn. Roman Catholic. Home: 901 N Adams Rd Birmingham MI 48009-5646 Office: Roy Shecter & Vocht PC 1400 Woodward Ave Ste 205 Bloomfield Hills MI 48304

VOELCKERS, GWENN, health care facility executive; b. Mineola, N.Y., Sept. 20, 1954; d. William Warner and Barbara Anne (Walters) V. BS in Mgmt., Nazareth Coll., Rochester, N.Y., 1976. Pub. relations asst. Arts Council, Rochester, 1976-77; dir. gallery Genesee Country Mus., Mumford, N.Y., 1977-79; dir. pub. relations Planned Parenthood, Rochester, 1979-83; exec. v.p. mktg., devel. Rochester United Meth. Home (RUMH), 1983-85; v.p. mktg., devel. Wesley-on-East (formerly RUMH), 1985—. Contbr. articles The Gleaner mag., 1975-76. Chmn. dist. United Way, Rochester, 1985-87; vol. companion Compeer, 1982; bd. dirs. polit. action com. Family Planning Advocates, 1981-82; officer Alzheimer's Assn., 1989—; mem. Brighton Planning Bd. Mem. Nat. Soc. Fundraising Execs. (chmn. Rochester chpt. 1989-90), Pub. Rels. Soc. Am. (prog. com. 1987—), Upstate N.Y. Hosp. Pub. Rels. Coun., Mktg. Communicators Rochester, Grantmakers Forum Rochester, C. of C. Women's Coun., Rochester Area Assn. Homes Svcs. for Aging (mktg. com. 1987—), Nazareth Coll. Alumni Assn. (bd. dirs. 1981), Am. Coll. Healthcare Adminstrs., AAUW, Rotary. Office: Wesley-on-East 630 East Ave Rochester NY 14607-2194

VOELKER, MARGARET IRENE (MEG VOELKER), gerontology, medical/surgical nurse; b. Bitburg, Germany, Dec. 31, 1955; d. Lewis R. and Patricia Irene (Schaffner) Miller; 1 child, Christopher Douglas. ASN, Tacoma C.C.; diploma, Clover Park Vocat.-Tech., Tacoma, 1975, diploma in practical nursing, 1984; AS in Nursing, Tacoma (Wash.) C.C., 1988; postgrad., U. Washington Tacoma, Tacoma, 1992—. Cert. ACLS. Nursing asst. Jackson County Hosp., Altus, Okla., 1976-77; receptionist Western Clinic, Tacoma, 1983; LPN, Tacoma Gen. Hosp., 1984-88, clin. geriatric nurse, 1988-90, clin. nurse post anesthesia care unit, 1990—, mem. staff nurse coun., 1990-91. Recipient G. Corydon Wagner endowment fund scholarship. Mem. PostAnesthesia Nurses Assn., Phi Theta Kappa.

VOGEL, H. VICTORIA, psychotherapist, educator. BA, U. Md., 1968; MA, NYU, 1970, 1975; MEd, Columbia U., 1982, postgrad., 1982—; cert., Am. Projective Drawing Inst., 1983. Art Therapist Childville, Bklyn., 1962-64; tchr., Montgomery County (Md.) Jr. High Sch., 1968-69; with High Sch. div. N.Y.C. Bd. Edn., 1970—, guidance counselor, instructor, psychotherapist in pvt. practice; clinical counseling cons. psychodiagnosis and devel. studies, art/play therapy, The Modern School, 1984—; art/play therapist Hosp. Ctr. for Neuromuscular Disease and Devel. Disorders, 1987—; employment counselor-adminstr. N.Y. State Dept. Labor Concentrated Employment Program, 1971-72; intern psychotherapy and psychoanalysis psychiat. div. Cen. Islip Hosp., 1973-75; with Calif. Grad. Inst., L.A.; Columbia U. Tchrs. Coll., N.Y. intern psychol. counseling and rehab. N.J. Coll. Medicine, Newark, 1979. Mem. com. for spl. events NYU, 1989; participant clin. and artistic perspectives Am. Acad. Psychoanalysis Conf., 1990. Mem. APA, AAAS, Am. Psychol. Soc., Am. Orthopsychiat. Assn., Am. Soc. Group Psychotherapy & Psychodrama (publs. com. 1984—), Am. Counseling Assn., N.Y.C. Art Tchrs. Assn., Art/Play Therapy, Assn. Humanistic Psychology (exec. sec. 1981), Tchrs. Coll. Adminstrv. Women in Edn., Phi Delta Kappa (editor chpt. newsletter 1981-84, exec. sec. Columbia U. chpt. 1984—, chmn. nominating com. for chpt. officers 1986—, nominating com. 1991, pub. rels. exec. bd. dirs. 1991, rsch. rep. 1986—), Phi Delta Kappa (v.p. programs NYU chpt. 1994—). Author: The Never Ending Story of Alcohol, Drugs and Other Substance Abuse, 1992, Variant Sexual Behavior and the Aesthetic Modern Nudes, 1992, Psychological Science of School Behavior Intervention, 1993.

VOGEL, JUDITH ANN, university administrator; b. N.Y.C., Nov. 16, 1943; d. Harold Aaron and Mary Mildred (Hiller) Hillson; m. Marc Stephen Vogel, Sept. 6, 1970 (div. Oct. 1984); children: Michele Lea, Eric Jason. BSc in Edn., Ohio State U., 1964, MA in Edn., 1967, postgrad., 1972. Lic. real estate agt. Tchr. math and German Met. Sch. Dist. of Washington Twp., Indpls., 1964-66; asst. editor Charles Merrill Publ. Co., Columbus, Ohio, 1967-69; actuarial asst. Ohio Med. Indemnity, Columbus, 1974-75; researcher II Pub. Utilities Commn. of Ohio, Columbus, 1975-77; program mgr. Gould Computer Systems, Plantation, Fla., 1978-83; tchr. math/computer Jewish High Sch. of South Fla., North Miami Beach, 1983-88; rsch. assoc. U. Miami, 1988-91; rsch. svcs. assoc. Nova U., Ft. Lauderdale, Fla., 1991-93; adj. prof. math. dept. Broward C.C., 1994—; cons. U. Miami, 1991-92; utilization analyst Humana, 1994—. Mem. Assn. of Institutional Reseacher. Democrat. Jewish. Home: 1761 NW 73d Ave Plantation FL 33313 Office: 5801 W Sunrise Blvd Plantation FL 33313

VOGEL, MALVINA GRAFF, video and infosystems specialist; b. N.Y.C., May 5, 1932; d. Daniel Louis and Rose Miriam (Kanarick) Graff; m. Seymour Vogel, Jan. 27, 1952 (div.); children: Howard Ferris, Hal Steven, Scott Leslie, David Michael, Lisa Gayle. AB, Hunter Coll., 1952, postgrad., 1953. Cert. tchr., N.Y., N.J. Tchr. Norwood (N.J.) Pub. Schs., 1952-53, Farmingdale (N.Y.) Pub. Schs., 1953-55; researcher, writer Sy Vogel Realty, Commack, N.Y., 1965-67; writer-editor E.D.L.-McGraw Hill, N.Y.C., 1967-73; writer ednl. programs Ednl. Concepts, Inc., Babylon, N.Y., 1973-75, Instructional Concepts, Inc., New Hyde Park, N.Y., 1973-75; editor-in-chief Waldman-Playmore Pub. Co., N.Y.C., 1976-83; v.p. creative services Kid Stuff/GameTek, Inc., North Miami Beach, Fla., 1983-90; owner, pres. MVP Writing/Editing Prodns., Sunrise, Fla., 1990-94; v.p. creative svcs. Herbko Internat., Hallandale, Fla., 1995—. Author short stories, reading and social studies programs; adaptor lit. classics for children; editor over 200 books for children and adults, over 50 computer software and video cartridge programs for preschoolers, children, teens and adults. Pres. Old Bethpage Elem. Sch. PTA, 1967-71; founder, pres. women's aux. Plainview, N.Y. Little League, 1968; scholarship chair Plainview-Old Bethpage Scholarship Fund, 1972-73. Scholarship for children's writing, Hofstra U., 1975. Mem. Nat. Assn. Female Execs., Soc. Children's Book Writers, Women in Communications, Soc. Preservation of English Lang. and Lit. Home: 9225 NW 45th St Fort Lauderdale FL 33351-5247

VOGEL, SALLY THOMAS, psychologist, social worker, educator; b. Joplin, Mo., July 3, 1925; d. Clyde Albert Thomas and Kathryn (Waite) Thompson; m. F. Lincoln Vogel, Sept. 4, 1946; children: Kathryn Duchin, Linda, Robert L. BA, Beaver Coll., 1947; MEd, North Adams State Coll., 1969; postgrad., Seton Hall U., 1987—. Case worker Pa. Dept. Welfare, Phila., 1947-48; high sch. tchr. Downington High Sch., Coatesville, Pa., 1969-71; sch. social worker Delaware Valley High Sch., Frenchtown, N.J., 1970-84; study team coord. Holland Twp. Sch., Milford, N.J., 1975-85, sch. social worker, 1975-90, guidance counselor, 1990-94; sch. psychologist intern Lake Shore Sch. Dist., St. Clair Shores, Mich., 1994—; instr. in Parent Effectiveness and Tchr. Effectiveness, Hunt County Adult Edn., N.J., 1975-84; advanced trainee Edn. Tng. Inst., Calif., 1984-89; presenter in field. Acting exec. dir. Big Bros./Big Sisters, Hunterdon County, N.J., 1976. Recipient Ed Kiley Svc. award Big Bros./Big Sisters, 1978. Mem. APA (student affiliate), Am. Assn. Counseling and Devel., N.J. Edn. Assn., N.J. Assn. Sch. Psychologists (student affiliate). Office: Lake Shore Sch Dist Rodgers Sch 21 601 L'Anse Saint Clair Shores MI 48081

VOGEL, SARAH, state agency administrator, lawyer; b. Bismarck, N.D., May 3, 1946; d. Robert and Elsa Marie (Mork) V.; 1 child, Andrew. BA, U. N.D., 1967; JD, NYU, 1970. Commr. N.D. Agrl. Dept., Bismarck, N.D. Office: ND Agrl Dept 600 East Blvd Bismarck ND 58505

VOGELGESANG, SANDRA LOUISE, federal government official; b. Canton, Ohio, July 27, 1942; d. Glenn Wesley and Louise (Forry) Vogelgesang; m. Geoffrey Ernest Wolfe, July 4, 1982. BA, Cornell U., 1964; MA, Tufts U., 1965, MA in Law and Diplomacy, 1966, PhD, 1971. With Dept. State, Washington, 1975—, policy planner for sec. state and European Bur., 1975-80, dir. Econ Analysis Office, Orgn. Econ. Coop. and Devel., 1981-82, econ. minister U.S. Embassy, Ottawa, Can., 1982-86, dep. asst. sec. Internat. Orgn. Affairs Bur., 1986-89; dep. asst. adminstr. Office Internat. Activities Environ. Protection Agy., Washington, 1989-92; with Dept. State, Washington, 1992; sr. policy advisor Agy. for Internat. Devel., 1993; U.S. amb. to Nepal Dept. State, Washington, 1994—; bd. dirs. Edward R. Murrow Ctr. for Pub. Diplomacy, Fletcher Sch., Medford, Mass., 1978-81; bd. advisors Am.'s Soc., N.Y.C., 1986-89. Author: Long Dark Night of the Soul, The American Intellectual Left and the Vietnam War, 1974, American Dream-Global Nightmare: The Dilemma of U.S. Human Rights Policy, 1980. Recipient Meritorious Service awards, 1973, 74, 82, 83, 86, Disting. Honor award, 1976 Dept. State, Pres.' Disting. Service award, 1985. Mem. Council on Fgn. Relations. Office: US Embassy Kathmandu Dept of State Washington DC 20521-6190

VOGELZANG, JEANNE MARIE, professional association executive, management consultant; b. Hammond, Ind., Apr. 15, 1950; d. Richard and Laura Ann (Vanderaa) Jabaay; m. Nicholas John Vogelzang, May 17, 1971; children: Nick, Adam, Tim. BA, Trinity Christian Coll., Palos Heights, Ill., 1972; MBA, U. Minn., 1981; JD, U. Chgo., 1987. Bar: Ill. 1987; CPA, Ill. High sch. algebra tchr. Timothy Christian High Sch., Elmhurst, Ill., 1972-74; teaching assoc. in fin. U. Minn., Mpls., 1980-81; fin. analyst Quaker Oats Co., Chgo., 1982-84; atty. Baker & McKenzie, Chgo., 1987-89, Jenner & Block, Chgo., 1989-91; pres., owner J. M. Vogelzang & Assocs., Western Springs, Ill., 1991—; exec. dir. Structural Engrs. Assn. Ill., Chgo., 1992—. Mem. judicial code com. Christian Reformed Ch. N.Am., Grand Rapids, Mich., 1991—; bd. dirs. Austin Christian Law Ctr., Chgo., 1989-92, Barnabas Found., Palos Heights, 1989—; com. mem. Western Springs Planning Commn., 1991—; mem. adv. bd. Coll. DuPage Internat. Trade Ctr., Glen Ellyn, Ill., 1992-94; bd. dirs., mem. acad. affairs com. and planning com. Trinity Christian Coll., 1992—. Mem. ABA, Ill. State Bar Assn., Chgo. Bar Assn., Women's Bar Assn. Mem. Christian Reformed Ch. Home: 5108 Fair Elms Ave Western Springs IL 60558-1808 Office: 203 N Wabash Ave Ste 1000 Chicago IL 60601-2412

VOGES, ALICE FURBY, retired educator, realtor; b. Brush, Colo., Jan. 14, 1930; d. Ross Andrew and Marie Margaret (Dreith) Furby; m. Kenneth O. Voges, Sept. 1, 1949; children: Jan Marie Voges Reaver, James Kenneth. BA in Speech Edn., Pacific U., 1952. Grad. Realtor Inst. Tchr. Shumway Jr. H.S., Vancouver, Wash., 1952-54, Banks (Oreg.) H.S., 1955-57; tchr. Tillamook (Oreg.) H.S., 1960-88, speech coach, 1964-88; realtor Schmidt Real Estate, Tillamook, 1979-82, Pete Anderson Realty, Inc., Tillamook, 1982—. Bd. dirs. Tillamook Sch. Dist. 9, 1989—; mem. state dist. Oreg. Sch. Bds. Assn. Dist. 5, 1993; pres. Aid Assn. of Luths. Br. 1553, 1993-95; mem. ch. choir, 1990—. Named to Speech Coach Hall of Fame, Oreg. H.S. Speech League, 1990. Mem. AAUW, Nat. Sch. Bds. Assn. (del. conv. Anaheim, Calif. 1993, San Francisco, 1995), Delta Kappa Gamma (v.p. Alpha Gamma chpt. 1994). Republican. Lutheran. Office: Pete Anderson Realty Inc Better Homes & Gardens 709 Pacific Ave Tillamook OR 97141

VOGL, CANDICE DAWN, accountant; b. Evansville, Ind., May 20, 1969; d. William John and Marsha Jean (Freihaut) Schlumpf; m. J. Phillip Vogl, June 29, 1991. BA in Acctg., N.C. State U., Raleigh, 1992. CPA, N.C.; CMA. Staff acct. Glaxo, Research Triangle Park, N.C., 1992-93, adminstrv. acct., 1992-94, budget and acctg. analyst, 1994—. Tutor Cmty. in Schs., Durham, N.C., 1992—. Mem. Inst. Mgmt. Accts., Durham F.O.P. Auxiliary. Office: Glaxo Inc 5 Moore Dr Research Triangle Park NC 27709

VOGLER, DIANE CLARK, elementary school principal; b. McGehee, Ark., Jan. 11, 1945; d. Stuart Emerson and Mamye Tompye (Campbell) Clark; m. Richard Joseph Vogler, June 16, 1968 (dec. Nov. 1979); children: Amy Diane, Jodi Leigh. BSE, Ark. A&M Coll., 1966; MSE, U. Ark., 1975, EdS, 1983. Cert. elem. adminstr., Ark. Tchr. 6th grade McGehee Pub. Schs., 1966-67; tchr. 5th grade North Little Rock (Ark.) Schs., 1967-68, tchr. 6th grade, 1970-73, tchr. math. grades 1-6, 1975-80; tchr. 6th grade Manhattan (Kans.) Pub. Schs., 1968-70; tchr. 1st grade Pulaski County Spl. Schs., North Little Rock, 1980-85, prin., 1985—; prin. Sylvan Hills Elem., Pulaski County Special Sch. Dist., Sherwood, Ark., 1990—. Mem., v.p. United Meth. Women of United Meth. Ch., North Little Rock, 1980—; del. Ark. Democratic Party, Little Rock, 1988; active Sylvan Hills Elem. PTA. Recipient Tchr. of Yr. award Ark. PTA Coun., 1985, Ednl. Excellence award Greater Little Rock C. of C., 1985; named Elem. Prin. of Yr. Pulaski County Spl. Sch. Dist. Mem. ASCD, Internat. Reading Assn., Nat. Assn. Elem. Sch. Prins., Ctrl. Ark. Reading Coun., Ark. Assn. Elem. Prins. (zone dir. 1990-93), Pulaski County Adminstrs. Assn. (pres. 1989-90), Sherwood Rotary Club, Delta Kappa Gamma (pres. 1981-82), Phi Delta Kappa. Democrat. Office: Pulaski County Spl Sch Dist 402 Dee Jay Hudson Dr North Little Rock AR 72120-2302

VOGT, SHARON MADONNA, author; b. St. Ann, Mo., June 12, 1963; d. Ralph Paul and Jane Louise (Sandberg) V. BS in Edn., Northeast Mo. State U., 1985; MAT, Webster U., 1989. Cert. tchr., Mo. Tchr., coord. math. St. Cletus Sch., St. Charles, Mo., 1986-88; writer, math. editor Ligature, Inc., St. Louis, 1989-90; tchr., math. adviser Pattonville Adult Edn., St. Ann, Mo., 1991-93; dir., cons. math. ednl. svcs. Connections, South Hadley, Mass., 1991—. Author: Math Review, 1991, Math Journal Writing and Problem Solving, 1991, vol. 2, 1995, Linking Math. and Literature, 1992, Multicultural Math., 1995, Middle School Multicultural Math. Activities, 1995, Geometry Activities, 1995, Middle School Journal Writing, 1995, Olympic Math, 1995, (activity books) Graphibg, 1992, Money Fun, 1993; creator math. activities for math. and physics day at Sic Flags Over Mid Am. Mem. Nat. Coun. Tchrs. Math., Alpha Phi Sigma. : 12 Grand St South HAdley MA 01075 Home and Office: 12 Grant St South Hadley MA 01075

VOIGHT, ELIZABETH ANNE, lawyer; b. Sapulpa, Okla., Aug. 6, 1944; d. Robert Guy and Garnetta Ruth (Bell) Voight; m. Bodo Barske, Feb. 22, 1985; children: Anne Katharine, Ruth Caroline. BA, U. Ark.-Fayetteville, 1967, MA, 1969; postgrad. U. Hamburg (W.Ger.), 1966-67; J.D., Georgetown U., 1978. Bar: N.Y. 1979. Lectr. German, Oral Roberts U., Tulsa, 1968-69; tchr. German, D.C. pub. schs., 1971-73; instr. German, Georgetown U., Washington, 1973-74, adminstrv. asst. to dean Sch. Fgn. Svc., 1974-77; law clk. Cole & Corette, Washington, 1977-78; atty. Walter, Conston, Alexander & Green, P.C., N.Y.C., 1978-88, Munich, 1990—. Translator articles for profl. jours. Chmn. regional screening Am. Field Svc., N.Y.C., 1981-86. German Acad. Exchange Program fellow, 1966-67. Mem. Assn. Bar City N.Y., ABA, Internat. Fiscal Assn., Internat. Bar Assn., Am. C. of C. in Germany, Phi Beta Kappa, Kappa Kappa Gamma.

VOIGHT, NANCY LEE (MRS. JAY VAN HOVEN), counseling psychologist; b. Kansas City, Mo., Nov. 24, 1945; d. Paul and Leona Alvina (Schultz) V.; m. Jay Van Hoven, June 27, 1975; children: Joshua, Janna, Lydia. BA, Wittenberg U., 1967; MA, Ball State U., 1971; PhD, Mich. State U., 1975. Tchr. lang. arts Ashland (Ohio) City Schs., 1967-68; tchr. English, Speedway (Ind.) City Schs., 1969; basic literacy instr. Army Edn. Ctr., Gelnhausen, W. Ger., 1969-70; individual assistance Bethel Home for Boys, Gaston, Ind., 1970-71; counselor Wittenberg U. Ohio, 1971-72; staff psychologist Ingham County Probate Ct., Lansing, Mich., 1972-74; asst. prof. U. N.C., Chapel Hill, 1975-79, counseling psychologist, 1976-79; psychologist for employee devel. Gen. Telephone Electronics, No. Region Hdqrs., Indpls., 1979-80; behavioral sci. coord. Family Practice Ctr., Community Hosp., Indpls., 1980-82; media psychologist Sta. WIFE, Indpls., 1981-82; asst. dir. Chapel Hill Counseling Ctr., 1980-86; dir. Behavior Therapy Ctr., Indpls., 1982-86; treas. Med. Specialty Disability Ins. Corp., Indpls., 1982-86; psychologist Alternatives to Boys Sch., 1983-85, Mich. Dept. Corrections, Kincheloe, 1986-88, Wasilewski & Assocs., Monroe, Mich., 1994—, Elliott and Assocs., Toledo, 1995—; staff psychologist Meth. Hosp. Ind., 1985-86; assoc. prof. psychology Lake Superior State U., Sault St. Marie, Mich., 1988-95; advisor Sex Info. and Counseling Ctr., Chapel Hill, 1977-79. Chmn. housing bd. U. N.C., 1976-79. Office Edn. grantee, 1977-78, 78-80; Spencer Found. young scholars grantee. Mem. Am. Psychol. Assn., Ind. Psychol. Assn., Mich. Psychol. Assn., Assn. Advancement Behavior Therapy, Inst. Rational Living, Soc. Behavioral Medicine, Am. Assn. Marriage and Family Therapists. Lutheran. Author: Becoming, 1978; Becoming: Leader's Guide, 1978; Becoming Aware, 1979; Becoming Informed, 1979; Becoming Strong, 1979; also articles. Home: 12270 N Suder Rd Erie MI 48133 Office: Lake Superior State U 708 S Monroe St Monroe MI 48161

VOIGT, CYNTHIA, author; b. Boston, Feb. 25, 1942; d. Frederick C. and Elise (Keeney) Irving; married, 1964 (div. 1972); m. Walter Voigt, Aug. 30, 1974; children: Jessica, Peter. B.A., Smith Coll., 1963. High sch. tchr. English Glen Burnie, Md., 1965-67; tchr. English Key Sch., Annapolis, Md., 1968-69, dept. chmn., 1971-79, tchr., chmn., 1981-1988. Author: Homecoming, 1981, Tell Me If Lovers Are Losers, 1982, Dicey's Song, 1982 (Newbery medal 1983), The Callender Papers, 1983 (Edgar award 1984), A Solitary Blue, 1983, Building Blocks, 1984, Jackeroo, 1985, The Runner, 1985 (Silver Pencil award 1988, Deutscher Jugend Literator Preis 1989, ALAN award 1989), Come a Stranger, 1986, Izzy, Willy Nilly, 1986 (Calif. Young Readers award 1990), Stories About Rosie, 1986, Sons From Afar, 1987, Tree By Leaf, 1988, Seventeen Against the Dealer, 1989, On Fortune's Wheel, 1990, The Vandemark Mummy, 1991, Orfe, 1992, Glass Mountain, 1991, David and Jonathan, 1992, The Wings of a Falcon, 1993, If She Hollers, 1994. *

VOLAN, WENDY TYSON, marketing professional; b. Phila., July 21, 1953; d. James Robert and Caroline Helen (Macintyre) Tyson; m. Gregory D. Volan, Jan. 21, 1978. Student, U. Colo., 1971-75. Customer svc. mgr. Pallas Photo Labs, Inc., Denver, 1976-79; prin., dir. grafic design Volan Design Assocs., Boulder, Colo., 1979—. Mem. mktg. com. Boulder County United Way. Mem. Am. Ctr. Design, Inst. Packaging Profls., Rock Mountain Writers Guild. Office: Volan Design Assocs 1800 38th St Boulder CO 80301-2622

VOLES, LORRAINE ANN, government administrator; b. N.Y.C., Jan. 15, 1959; d. Joseph and Marie Voles; m. Daniel E. Smith. BA, George Washington U. Press sec. Mondale for Pres. campaign, Des Moines, Iowa, 1984, Sen. Tom Harkin campaign, Washington, 1990-93, Harkin for Pres. campaign, Washington, 1992; dir. comms. Nat. Hospice Orgn., 1985-87; dep. press sec. Dukakis for Pres. campaign, Boston, 1987-88, Exec. Office of Pres., Washington, 1993; nat. coord. Mothers & Others, Washington, 1991; dir. comms. Office of the V.P., Washington, 1993—; membership coord. Employee Relocation Coun., Washington, 1981-84. Contbr. articles to Mobility Mag. Mem. Iowa Dem. Party. Roman Catholic. Office: Office of the VP Old Exec Office Bldg Washington DC 20501*

VOLKENING-QUARTERNIK, DEBRA LYNN, disc-jockey; b. St. Louis, Feb. 13, 1962; d. Anton R. and Loretta (McCracken) Volkening. BA in Communications, Maryville Coll., St. Louis, 1984. Reporter St. Louis & Jefferson County News, Fenton, Mo., 1984-85; writer, proofreader Maritz Travel Co., Fenton, 1986-87; mobile disc-jockey Travelin' Tunes, St. Louis, 1984—. Mem. Women in Communication (chpt. publicity chmn. 1985-86), Gateway Portable Disc-Jockey Assn. (pres. 1990—).

VOLKERING, MARY JOE, special education educator; b. Covington, Ky., Mar. 13, 1936; d. Everett Thomas and Edna Mae (Bohmer) Foley; m. Jack Lawrence Volkering, Aug. 19, 1961 (dec. Jan. 11, 1989); 1 child, Tara. BA, Thomas More Coll, 1961; MEd, U. Cin., 1977. Cert. educator of mentally handicapped, Ohio, Ky. Asst. engr. AT&T Co., Cin., 1956-63; tchr. severe & profound Comprehensive Care, Covington, Ky., 1970-76; tchr. mentally retarded Riverside Good Counsel Sch., Ft. Mitchell, Ky., 1976-79; tchr. trainable handicapped Covington (Ky.) Ind. Sch., 1979—; bd. dirs. No. Ky. Assn. for Retarded, Covington, 1980—; adj. prof. No. Ky. U., Highland Heights, 1987-88. Leader Girl Scout Troop, Ft. Wright, Ky., 1973. Named John Bauer Spl. Edn. Tchr. of the Yr. North Ky. Assn. Retarded, 1979, Tchr. of the Yr. G.O. Swing Sch., Covington Ind. Schs., 1986, Golden Apple Nominee Tchr., Ky. Post and Jaycees, 1988. Mem. No. Ky. Assn. Retarded (treas. 1984-86, sec. 1980-82). Democrat. Roman Catholic.

VOLKERT, SUSAN ENGELMAN, textile, chemical, pharmaceutical executive, lawyer; b. Trenton, N.J., Oct. 18, 1948; d. Jacob and Anita (Sklar) Feinsilber; m. Donald J. Volkert Jr.; children: Christine, Scott, Jamie, Elizabeth, Stephen, Michael. BA in English, U. Pa., 1969; JD, U. Toledo, 1962. Trial atty. U.S. Dept. Justice, Washington, 1973-75, asst. dir., 1980-81, dep. dir., 1981-83; dep. chief U.S. Atty.'s Office, N.J., 1975-80; assoc. gen. counsel Hoechst Celanese Corp., Somerville, N.J., 1983-88, v.p. environ. health and safety com., 1988—; bd. dirs. Chem. Industry Inst. Toxicology, Research Triangle Pk., N.C. Mem. exec. com. CIC N.J., Conf. bd. Environ. Heath and Safety Policy Affairs. Recipient Women Achieves award YWCA, 1991. Mem. Chem. Mfrs. Assn. (health and safety com. Washington chpt. 1989—), Fed. Bar Assn. Office: Hoechst Celanese Corp PO Box 2500 Somerville NJ 08876-1258

VOLKMANN, FRANCES COOPER, psychologist, educator; b. Harlingen, Tex., May 4, 1935; d. Edward O. and Elizabeth (Bass) C.; m. John Volkmann, Nov. 1, 1958 (dec.); children: Stephen Edward, Thomas Frederick. A.B. magna cum laude, Mt. Holyoke Coll., 1957; M.A., Brown U., 1959, Ph.D., 1961; DSci., Mt. Holyoke Coll., 1987. Research assoc. Mt. Holyoke Coll., South Hadley, Mass., 1964-65; lectr. U. Mass., Amherst, 1964-65, Smith Coll., Northampton, Mass., 1966-67; asst. prof. Smith Coll., 1967-72, assoc. prof., 1972-78, prof. psychology, 1978—, dean faculty, 1983-88, Harold E. Israel and Elsa M. Siipola prof. psychology, 1988—, acting pres., 1991; vis. assoc. prof. Brown U., Providence, 1974, vis. prof., 1978-82; vis. scholar U. Wash., Seattle, summer 1977. Contbr. articles to profl. jours. Trustee Chatham Coll., 1987—. USPHS fellow, 1961-62; NSF grantee, 1974-78; Nat. Eye Inst. grantee, 1978-82. Fellow APA, AAAS, Optical Soc. Am.; mem. Ea. Psychol. Assn., Soc. Neurosci. Psychonomic Soc., Assn. Rsch. in Vision and Ophthalmology, New Eng. Assn. Schs. and Colls. (vice chair commn. instns. higher edn. 1991-93, chair 1993—). Home: 40 Arlington St Northampton MA 01060-2003 Office: Smith Coll Northampton MA 01063

VOLL, SARAH POTTS, state agency administrator; b. Wilmington, Del., Nov. 13, 1942; d. Robert Curtis and Dorothy Ruth (Counahan) Potts; m. John Obert Voll, June 12, 1965; children: Sarah Layla, Michael Obert. BA, Goucher Coll., Towson, Md., 1964; AM, Harvard U., 1966; PhD, U. N.H., 1977. Exec. sec. N.H. Council on World Affairs, Durham, 1966-68; mem. N.H. Ho. of Reps., Concord, 1977-78; ind. econ. cons. U.S. Agy. Internat. Devel., Ford Found., Middle East Adv. Group, Cairo, Egypt, 1978-79; dist. mgr. U.S. Census Bur. 1st Congl. Dist. N.H., Portsmouth, 1979-80; asst. budget dir. Office of Gov., Concord, N.H., 1980-81; chief economist N.H. Pub. Utilities Commn., Concord, 1981-94, exec. dir., sec., 1994—; mem. rsch. adv. com. Nat. Regulatory Rsch. Inst., 1988-92, chair, 1990-92; mem. Durham Town Coun., 1988-93, chair, 1992-93; treas. United Campus Ministry to the U. N.H.; lectr. Regulatory Rsch. Program, 1987—. Author: Plough in Field Arable, 1980, N.H. Regulatory Handbook for Small Scale Electric Producers; co-author: The Sudan: Unity & Diversity, 1985; contbr. articles to profl. jours. Mem. Durham Budget Com., 197-78, 87-88; co-chmn. Pres. Jimmy Carter Primary campaign for Towns of Durham, Lee and Madbury, 1975-76; sec. Strafford County Dems., 1977-78; chmn. bd. stewards Cmty. Ch. of Durham, 1984-86; mem. staff subcom. on econs. and fin. Nat. Assn. Regulatory Utility Commrs., 1986-94, task forces on electric cost allocation, rate design and least cost planning, mem. staff subcom. on water, 1993—, mem. staff subcom. on exec. dirs., 1994—. Harvard U. fellow, 1964-65, Nat. Def. for Language fellow Harvard U., 1965-66. Mem. Internat. Assn. Energy Economists, Am. Econs. Assn. (transp. and pub. utilities group), Mid. East Studies Assn., Sudan Studies Assn. (co-exec. dir., treas. 1990-94), DAR (chpt. regent 1976-80, state sec. 1980-83, 93—, state treas. 1983-86), State Officers Club (v.p. 1988-90, pres. 1990-92), Phi Beta Kappa. Democrat. Mem. United Ch. of Christ. Home: 4 Croghan Ln Durham NH 03824-3027 Office: NH Pub Utilities Commn 8 Old Suncook Rd Concord NH 03301-7320

VOLLAND, CAROL TASCHER, financial services executive; b. Morris, Ill., Mar. 23, 1935; d. Murl Elvyn and Helen Marie (Lindquist) Tascher; m. George William Volland, Aug. 12, 1978. Student Monmouth Coll., 1953-55; B.S. in Interior Design, U. Ill., 1957; postgrad. Art Inst. Chgo. Evening Sch., 1959-62. Lic. real estate broker, ins. and securities broker, Colo., Ill. Archtl. and interior designer Peoples Gas Light & Coke Co., Chgo., 1957-65, consumer lectr., corp. architect and interior designer, 1965-70, dir. home planning bur., 1970-74; corp. fashion coord. Ozite Corp. div. Brunswick Corp., Libertyville, Ill., 1974-75, dir. pub. rels., 1975-77, contract sales mgr., 1977-78; pres. Volland & Assocs., Lakewood, Colo., 1982-88; pres. Asset Planning Svcs., Lakewood, 1989—; mem. corp. responsibilities bd. Brunswick Corp. Internat., 1976-77. Author: Creative Moneystretchers for the Home, 1973. Mem. Nat. Home Fashions League (exec. v.p. 1977-78), Am. Soc. Interior Designers, Women in Communications, LWV, Nat. Trust Hist. Preservation, Genesee Found. Republican. Methodist. Home: 1962 Montane Dr E Golden CO 80401-8096 Office: Asset Planning Svcs 143 Union Blvd Ste 900 Lakewood CO 80228-1829

VOLLENBERG, DARLENE HELEN, accountant; b. Jersey City, Nov. 20, 1965; d. James Robinson and Constance Emily (Trotman) Williams; m. Jacobus Johannes Vollenberg, July 11, 1992. BA in Econs., Oberlin (Ohio) Coll., 1987; postgrad., George Washington U., 1990-92. Mgmt. trainee Citizens Bank & Trust Co. of Md., Bethesda, 1988-89; contract staff acct. Ogden Corp./NIH, Bethesda, 1989-92; libr. and translator The Anti-Racism Info. Ctr., Rotterdam, The Netherlands, 1993; staff acct. The Prudential Ins. Co. of Am., Newark, 1993—; co-developer and cons. for Am. Cultural Studies sect. Anti-Racism Info. Ctr., 1993—. Author poetry, short stories Rain Mag., 1985-87, Echoes Lit. mag., 1979. Tutor Shule Program, Oberlin Coll., 1985-87. Recipient award for outstanding cmty. involvement Black Studies Dept., Oberlin Coll., 1987. Mem. Nat. Geog. Soc., Nat. Acad. Polit. Sci., Nat. Economists Club. Democrat. Roman Catholic.

VOLLMAN, KATHLEEN MARY, clinical nurse specialist; b. Pontiac, Mich., Nov. 15, 1958; d. George Anthony Vollman and Mary Jo (McGovern) Grochulski. BSN, Wayne State U., 1980; MSN, Calif. State U., Long Beach, 1989. Staff nurse, asst. head nurse various hosps., Detroit and Calif., 1980-89; clin. nurse specialist med. critical care svcs. Henry Ford Hosp., Detroit, 1989—; clin. faculty critical care master's program Wayne State U., Detroit, 1992—; pres. HosTech Inc., Dearborn, Mich., 1993—; nat. and internat. speaker and expert witness in field. Contbr. articles to profl. jours.; inventor patient prone positioner, 1989. Campaign worker various elections, Detroit, 1976-80. Mem. AACN, Soc. Critical Care Medicine. Roman Catholic. Home: 23613 Edward Dearborn MI 48128

VOLLMER, CATHY ANN, administrator; b. St. Louis, Oct. 12, 1961. Diploma, Mo. Bapt. Sch. Nursing, 1984; BSN, Maryville Coll., 1988; postgrad., Avila Coll., 1993—. Cert. CPR instr. Staff nurse St. Joseph Hosp., St. Louis; nurse, critical care DePaul Health Ctr., St. Louis; br. dir., v.p. corp. office Favorite Nurses, St. Louis; nat. dir. Travel Div. Kansas City. Vol. YMCA. Recipient Drs. scholar, Copeland award, Scholastic AU Am. Mem. St. Louis Critical Care Assn., Long Term Care Dirs. Assn., Supplemental Staffing Assn., Delta Epsilon Signa.

VOLPE, ELLEN MARIE, educator; b. Bronx, Aug. 2, 1949; d. George Thomas and Mary (Popadinecz) Soloweyko; m. Ronald Edward Volpe, May 22, 1971; children: Keith, Daniel, Christopher, Stephanie. BBA, Pace U., 1971; MA in Teaching, Sacred Heart U., 1986. Tchr. Conn. Bus. Inst., Stratford, 1979-80, Katherine Gibbs Sch., Norwalk, Conn., 1980-89; adj. instr. So. Cen. Community Coll., New Haven, 1986-87, Salt Lake C. C., Phillips Jr. Coll., Salt Lake City, 1992—; instr. Bryman Sch., Salt Lake City, 1990-92; tchr. Indian Hills Mid. Sch., Sandy, Utah, 1993—; mem. reaccreditation and tech. coms. Indian Hills Mid. Sch.; mem. curriculum rev. com. Katharine Gibbs Sch., 1989-90. Mem. ASCD, NEA, Am. Vocat. Assn., Nat. Bus. Edn. Assn., Western Bus. Edn. Assn. Home: 8390 Sublette Cir Sandy UT 84093-1164

VOLTZ, JEANNE APPLETON, author b. Collinsville, Ala.; d. James Lamar and Marie (Sewell) Appleton; m. Luther Manship Voltz, July 31, 1943 (dec. Aug. 1977); children: Luther Manship, Jeanne Marie; m. Frank B. MacKnight, Aug. 6, 1988 (div. Sept. 1994). AB, U. Montevallo, Ala., 1942. Corr., The Birmingham (Ala.) News, 1939-42; reporter The Press-Register, Mobile, Ala., 1942-45; reporter, feature writer The Miami Herald, 1947-53, food editor, 1953-60; food editor Los Angeles Times, 1960-73, Woman's Day, N.Y.C., 1973-84; free-lance writer, food cons., N.Y.C., 1984-88, Chapel Hill, N.C., 1988—; instr. wine and food in civilization UCLA, 1972-73; expert witness Senate Com. on Nutrition and Health, Ft. Lauderdale, Fla., 1980; adj. prof. Dept. Nutrition Hotel Mgmt. NYU, 1986—, Home Econs. Hotel Mgmt., 1987—; judge Hardee's Willow Creek Rib Cook-Off, Raleigh, N.C., 1993, 94, Blue Ridge Barbecue and Rib Festival, Tryon, N.C., 1994. Author: The California Cookbook, 1970 (Tastemaker award 1970), The Los Angeles Times Natural Foods Cookbook, 1974, The Flavor of the South, 1976 (Tastemaker award 1976), An Apple A Day, 1983, Barbecued Ribs and Other Great Feeds, 1985 (Tastemaker award 1985), Community Suppers, 1987, Barbecued Ribs, Smoked Butts and Other Great Foods, 1991; author: (with Burks Hainker) The L.A. Gourmet, 1971, (with Elayne Kleeman) How to Turn a Passion for Food into Profit, 1979, (with Caroline Stuart) The Florida Cookbooks, 1993. Mem. N.C. Mus. Art, Raleigh. Mem. adv. bd. James Beard Found., N.Y. Recipient Vesta award Am. Meat Inst., 1962-72; Alumni of Yr. award U. Montevallo, 1981. Mem. Les Dames d'Escoffier (dir. 1976, pres. 1985-86, internat. pres. 1986-87), Inst. Food Technologists, Women in Communication, Soc. Women Geographers, Internat. Assn. Culinary Profls., The Authors' Guild N.Y., Am. Inst. Wine and Food, Culinary Historians N.Y., Phi Tau Sigma. Democrat. Methodist.

VOLZ, ANNABELLE WEKAR, learning disabilities educator, consultant; b. Niagara Falls, N.Y., May 24, 1926; d. Fred Wekar and Margaret Eleanor (McGillivray) Treadwell; m. William Mount Volz, May 9, 1958; children: Amy D., William M. Jr. BA, Seton Hill Coll., 1948; MS in Elem. Edn., N.Y. State Univ. Coll., 1956. Cert. learning disabilities cons. N.J. Lab. technician Moore Bus. Forms Inc., Niagara Falls, 1948-50, Niagara Falls Health Dept., 1950-53; tchr. Niagara Falls Bd. Edn., 1953-56, Am. Dependent Sch., Ashiya, Japan, 1956-58, Mehlville Bd. Edn., St. Louis County, Mo., 1968-70, U.S. Dependent Schs. European Theatre, Weisbaden, Fed. Republic of Germany, 1970-74; para-profl. Medford (N.J.) Bd. Edn., 1978-81; learning disabilities tchr., cons. Southampton Bd. Edn., Vincentown, N.J., 1981-91. Mem. Womens Fin. Info. Program, Burlington County, 1990-91. Mem. NEA, LWV (sec. 1994—), AAUW (scholar chmn. 1984, publicity chmn. 1991-92, treas. 1994—), N.J. Assn. Learning Cons.,

West Jersey Reading Coun., Seton Hill Alumnae Assn., Kappa Delta Pi. Home: 5080 Mountain View Rd Winston Salem NC 27104-5110

VOMACKA, JILL ELIZABETH, adapted physical education specialist; b. Franklin Square, N.Y., July 30, 1954; d. John William and Elizabeth Jane (Kettel) V. BS, Cortland U., 1976; MA, Adelphi U., 1981. Cert. phys. edn. tchr., adapted phys. edn. specialist, N.Y. Water safety instr. ARC, Mineola, N.Y., 1976—; adapted aquatics instr. ARC, Mineola, 1989—; physical edn. tchr. Franklin Square (N.Y.) Sch. Dist., 1977—, adapted phys. edn. specialist, coordinator, 1977—; instr. N.Y. State Park Games for the Physically Challenged, L.I., 1986—; adapted phys. edn. coord., specialist, cons., Franklin Square Sch. Dist. 1976—; adapted phys. edn. specialist Hofstra U., Hempstead, N.Y., 1980—; adj. prof. adapted phys. edn. Hofstra U., Hempstead, N.Y., 1980—; swimming coord. N.Y. State Games for the Physically Challenged, 1991—. Asst. leader Girl Scouts of U.S., Floral Park, N.Y., 1976-78; first aid instr. ARC, Mineola, 1976-78. Recipient PTA award, Franklin Square Schs., 1974, '76, 93, Svc. award, N.Y. State Parks Games for the Physically Challenged, 1991. Mem. N.Y. State Alliance for Health, Phys. Edn., Recreation and Dance (pres. elect phys. edn. sect. 1994-95). Office: John St Elem Sch Nassau Blvd Franklin Square NY 11010

VON BEHREN, RUTH LECHNER, adult day health care specialist; b. Dubuque, Iowa, Apr. 10, 1933; d. Adolph J. and Elva M. (Fedeler) Lechner; m. Donald D. Von Behren, Dec. 16, 1952 (div. 1965); children: Debi, Jerry, LuAnn. BS, Ill. State U., 1965, MA, 1968; PhD, U. Calif., Davis, 1972. Tchr. Centennial Sch., El Paso, Ill., 1962-65; grad. asst. Ill. State U., Normal, 1967-68; assoc. in History U. Calif., 1968-71; rsch. asst. Calif. Health and Welfare Agy., Sacramento, 1972-74; asst. prof. Sacramento State U., 1970-71, 78-79; analyst Calif. Dept. Health Svcs., Sacramento, 1974-75, sect. chief adult day health care, 1975-80; project dir. State Health and Welfare Agy., Sacramento, 1980-82; adult day health care specialist On Lok Sr. Health Svcs., San Francisco, 1982—; cons. adult day health care various orgns. Author: Adult Day Care in America, 1986, Adult Day Care: A Program for the Functionally Impaired, 1989, (with others) Planning and Managing Adult Day Care, 1989; contbr. articles to profl. jours. Sec. Yolo County Hist. Soc., Woodland, Calif., 1976-80; dir. Yolo County Mus. Assocs., Woodland, 1980-82. Recipient Adult Day Health Care Tech. Assistance award Kaiser Found., 1983-86, Rural Adult Day Care Model award Sierra Found., 1988-89. Mem. Nat. Coun. on Aging, Inc., Nat. Inst. on Adult Day Care (chair 1988-90, Ruth Von Behren award for Outstanding Dedication to Growth and Devel. of Adult Day Care, Nat. Inst. on Adult Day Care, 1992), Phi Alpha Theta, Alpha Phi Gamma, Alpha Psi Omega, Kappa Delta Phi, Phi Kappa Phi. Office: On Lok Sr Health Svcs 1333 Bush St San Francisco CA 94109

VON BERGEN WESSELS, PENNIE LEA, state legislator; b. Sterling, Ill., Mar. 19, 1949; d. Donald LeRoy and Mary Lou (Hammerle) von Bergen; m. Michael J. Wessels, Aug. 23, 1969. AA, Sauk Valley Coll., 1969; BSEd in English and Theater, No. Ill. U., 1971; postgrad., So. Ill. U., 1972-73; JD magna cum laude, U. Ill., 1983. Bar: Ill., 1983; cert. tchr., Ill. English and theater tchr. various schs., Ill., 1971-80; pvt. practice law Morrison, Ill., 1984-85; mem. Whiteside County Bd., Morrison, 1984-88, Ill. Gen. Assembly, Springfield, 1993-95. Bd. dirs. Ill. Citizens Utility Bd., 1989-92; mem. Save Our Kids Schs., various other orgns.; del. candidate Dem. Nat. Convention, 1980, 92. Named Outstanding Working Woman of Ill. Ill. Bus. and Profl. Women, 1988; recipient Mounders Pride award Mt. Morris Sch. Dist., 1993, Friend of Agr. award Farm Bus. Activator Com., 1994, Outstanding Freshman Legislator award Ill. Edn. Assn., 1994. Mem. ABA, Ill. Bar Assn., Ill. Women in Govt., Women's Legis. Lobby. Unitarian. Home: 1300 Sinnissippi Rd Sterling IL 61081

VON BRANDENSTEIN, PATRIZIA, production designer. Prodn. designer films including Girlfriends, 1978, Heartland, 1979, Breaking Away, 1979, Ragtime, 1981 (Academy Award nomination for art direction 1981), Silkwood, 1983, Amadeus, 1984 (Academy Award for art direction 1984), Beat Street, 1984, A Chorus Line, 1985, The Money Pit, 1986, No Mercy, 1987, The Untouchables, 1987 (Academy Award nomination for art direction 1987), Betrayed, 1988, Working Girl, 1988, The Lemon Sisters, 1990, Postcards From the Edge, 1990, State of Grace, 1990, Billy Bathgate, 1992, Sneakers, 1992, Leap of Faith, 1993, Six Degrees of Separation, 1993, The Quick and the Dead, 1995, Just Cause, 1995; costume designer films including Between the Lines, 1977, Saturday Night Fever, 1977, A Little Sex, 1982. Address: 161 W 15th St Apt 7B New York NY 10011-6768 Office: care Lawrence Mirisch The Mirisch Agency 10100 Santa Monica Blvd Ste 700 Los Angeles CA 90067

VON BURG, MARY M., advocate, social services administrator; b. Montezuma, Ind., Feb. 13, 1937; d. Jesse and Gertrude (wilburn) Thomas.; m. Raymond E. Von Burg; 1 child, Raymond E. BS in Edn., Ind. U., Indpls., 1980; MS in Counseling and Student Personnel, Ind. U., 1984, postgrad., 1989—. Rsch. asst., faculty sec. Sch. Pub. & Environ. Affairs, Ind. U., Indpls., 1980-81; adminstrv. sec. Sch. Medicine, Ind. U., Indpls., 1981-85; counseling Marion County Prosecutor's Alternative Runaways Program, 1984-85; instr. Ind. U., Indpls., 1984-85; sec. Dept. Pediatrics; exec. sec. dept. pediatrics Sch. Medicine Ind. U., Indpls., 1985-88; project mgr. Regionalization Care for Abused Children, Indpls., 1988—; coord. Liaison Child Abuse Forum, Indpls., 1988—; mem. com. Child Advocacy Ind. U. Hosp., Indpls., 1989—; delegation to Russia and Lithuania Citizen Amb. Program People to People Internat., 1994. Recipient Glenn W. Irwin Jr. award Ind. U., Purdue U., 1992. Mem. Child Welfare League Am., Nat. Assn. Counsel Children, Am. Assn. Protecting Children, Nat. Com. Prevention Child Abuse and Neglect (Ind. chpt.), Sigma Pi Alpha. Office: Ind U Comm Child Abuse Projects 1001 W 10th St # BU 444 Indianapolis IN 46202-2859

VONDRUSKA, ELOISE MARIE, information specialist; b. Chgo., Sept. 13, 1950; d. George A. and Irene L. (Pionke) Klebba; m. Richard J. Vondruska, Aug. 11, 1972. BA, Loyola U., Chgo., 1972; MS, U. Ill., 1973. Acquisitions librarian Parkland Coll., Champaign, Ill., 1973-79, tech. svcs. librarian, 1979-83; serials cataloger Arlington Heights (Ill.) Meml. Library, 1983-85; authorities librarian Northwestern U., Evanston, Ill., 1985-87; rsch. adminstr. Dastrup/Vondruska Assocs., Chgo., 1987-91; head catalog dept. Northwestern U. Sch. Law Libr., 1989—; cons. Catalist, Champaign, 1983-85. Editor: The Microcomputer, 1983, jour. issue Ill. Libraries, 1983. Ill. State scholar, 1968-72, DePaul U. scholar, 1968; Katharine L. Sharp fellow, 1972. Mem. Ill. Libr. Assn. (bd. dirs. 1983, 85-86), AALL, ALA. Office: 357 E Chicago Ave Chicago IL 60611-3008

VON FRAUNHOFER-KOSINSKI, KATHERINA, bank executive; b. N.Y.C.; m. Jerzy Kosinski, Feb. 15, 1987 (dec. May 3, 1991). Student, St. Joseph's Convent, London, Clark's Coll., London. Various positions Robert W. Orr & Assocs., N.Y.C., 1954-55; with traffic dept. Compton Advt., Inc., N.Y.C., 1956-63; acct. exec. J. Walter Thompson Co., N.Y.C., 1963-69; product mgr. Natural Wonder line Revlon Co., N.Y., 1969-71; pres. Scientia Factum, Inc., N.Y.C., 1971—; co-founder Polish Am. Resources Corp., N.Y.C., 1988—, pres., CEO, 1992—; founder, CEO, pres. Polish Am. Techs., L.P., N.Y.C., 1992—; chmn. bd. dirs. AmerBank, Warsaw, 1991—. Co-founder Westchester Sports Club. Home: 60 W 57th St New York NY 10019

VON FURSTENBERG, BETSY, actress, writer; b. Neiheim Heusen, Germany, Aug. 16, 1931; d. Count Franz-Egon and Elizabeth (Johnson) von F.; m. Guy Vincent de la Maisoneuve (div.); 2 children.; m. John J. Reynolds, Mar. 26, 1984. Attended Miss Hewitt's Classes, N.Y. Tutoring Sch.; prepared for stage with Sanford Meisner at Neighborhood Playhouse. Made Broadway stage debut in Second Threshold, N.Y., 1951; appeared in Dear Barbarians, 1952, Oh Men Oh Women, 1954, The Chalk Garden, 1955, Child of Fortune, 1956, Nature's Way, 1957, Much Ado About Nothing, 1959, Mary Mary, 1965, Paisley Convertible, 1967, Avanti, 1968, The Gingerbread Lady, 1970 (toured 1971), Absurd Person Singular, 1976; off Broadway appearances include For Love or Money, 1951; toured in Petrified Forest, Jason and Second Man, 1952; appeared in Josephine, 1953; subsequently toured, 1955; What Every Woman Knows, 1955, The Making of Moo, 1958 (toured 1958), Say Darling, 1959, Wonderful Town, 1959, Season of Choice, 1959, Beyond Desire, 1967, Private Lives, 1968, Does Anyone Here Do the Peabody, 1976; appeared in Along Came a Spider, Theatre in the Park, N.Y.C., 1985; appeared in film Women Without Names, 1950; TV appearances include Robert Montgomery Show, Ed Sullivan Show, Alfred Hitchcock Presents, One Step Beyond, The Mike Wallace Show, Johnny Carson Show, Omnibus, Theatre of the Week, The Secret Storm, As the World Turns, Movie of the Week, Your Money or Your Wife, Another World; writer syndicated column More Than Beauty; contbr. articles to newspapers and mags. including N.Y. Times Sunday Arts and Leisure, Saturday Rev. of Literature, People, Good Housekeeping, Art News, Pan Am Travel; co-author: (novel) Mirror, Mirror, 1988. Office: care Don Buchwald 10 E 44th St New York NY 10017-3606

VON FURSTENBERG, DIANE SIMONE MICHELLE, fashion designer; b. Brussels, Belgium, Dec. 31, 1946; came to U.S., 1969; d. Leon L. and Liliane L. (Nahmias) Halfin; m. Eduard Egon von Furstenberg, July 16, 1969 (div.); children: Alexandre, Tatiana. Student, U. Madrid, 1965-66, U. Geneva, 1966-68. Founder, pres. Diane von Furstenberg Studio, N.Y.C., 1970—; pres. Diane Von Furstenberg Ltd., N.Y.C. Author: Diane Von Furstenberg's Book of Beauty and Beds, The Bath; contbg. editor Vanity Fair. Recipient Ellis Island Medal of Honor, 1986. Office: Diane Von Furstenberg Studio 745 5th Ave Fl 24 New York NY 10151-0127*

VON HAKE, MARGARET JOAN, librarian; b. Santa Monica, Calif., Oct. 27, 1933; d. Carl August and Inez Garnet (Johnson) von Hake;. BA, La Sierra U., 1955; MS in Library Sci., U. So. Calif., 1963. Tchr., librarian Newbury Park (Calif.) Acad., 1955-60; librarian Columbia Union Coll., Takoma Park, Md., 1962-67, library dir., 1967—. Mem. ALA, Md. Libr. Assn., Congress of Acad. Libr. Dirs. of Md., Md. Ind. Coll. and Univ. Assn. Libr. Dir.'s Roundtable, Assn. Seventh Day Adventist Librs. (newsletter editor 1982, 83, pres. 1989-90), Paul Hill Chorale. Republican. Office: Columbia Union Coll 7600 Flower Ave Silver Spring MD 20912-7794

VON HARSCHER, HEIDI MARGARETE, clinical psychologist; b. The Pas, Manitoba, Can., Aug. 24, 1962; came to U.S., 1986; d. Frederick Karl and Ilse Dora Anna (Kaufeld) von H. BA in Psychology with honors, Carleton U., Ottawa, Can., 1986; MS in Clin. Psychology, Miami Inst. Psychology, 1987, PhD in Clin. Psychology, 1991. Lic. psychologist, N.Y., Fla. Consulting therapist Harbour View Hosp., Miami, Fla., 1988-90; psychology intern Univ. Counseling Ctr. SUNY, Buffalo, 1990-91; sr. psychologist Coll. Counseling Ctr. State Univ. Coll. at Buffalo, 1991-94, adj. faculty psychology dept., 1993-94, coord. clin. svcs. Coll. Counseling Ctr., 1993-94; univ. psychologist Fla. Internat. U., Miami, 1994—; adj. prof. psychology Niagara (N.Y.) U., 1991—; workshop presenter in field. Contbr. articles to profl. jours. Coord. interpretors athletics World Univ. Games, 1993. Mem. APA. Home: 7136 Bonita Dr # 3 Miami Beach FL 33141 Office: Fla Internat U Student Counseling Ctr GC211 Miami FL 33199

VONNIEDA, JEAN LORAYNE, medical/surgical nurse; b. Reading, Pa., Aug. 27, 1952; d. Claude E. Sr. and Miriam K. (Mohn) Keim; m. Richard VonNieda, Feb. 27, 1981; 1 child, Jenny Beth Miller. Diploma, Reading Hosp., 1973; BSN summa cum laude, Kutztown (Pa.) U., 1991. Staff nurse Reading Hosp., 1973-74, staff nurse ICU/CCU, 1975-76; charge nurse ICU/Emergency Rm. Martin Luther Hosp., Anaheim, Calif., 1976-77; staff nurse ICU/CCU Phoenixville (Pa.) Hosp., 1979-80; staff nurse/patient edn. resource nurse Reading Hosp., 1980-92, nurse mgr. med./surg., infectious disease specialty, 1992—. Mem. Nat. League for Nursing, Kutztown U. Nursing Honor Soc. (past sec.). Home: 601 El Hatco Dr Temple PA 19560-1109

VON PRINCE, KILULU MAGDALENA, occupational therapist, sculptor; b. Bumbuli, Lushoto, Tanzania, Jan. 9, 1929; came to U.S., 1949; d. Tom Adalbert and Juliane (Martini) Von P. BA in Occupational Therapy, San Jose State U., 1958, MS in Occupational Therapy, 1972; EdD, U. So. Calif., 1980. Registered occupational therapist; cert. work evaluator, work adjustment specialist. Commd. 2d lt. U.S. Army, 1959, advanced through grades to lt. col.; staff asst. U.S. Army, Denver, 1959-62; hand rehab. asst., hand therapy Walter Reed Army Med. Ctr., 1962-65; hand rehab. asst. occupational therapist 97th Gen. Hosp., U.S. Army, Frankfurt, Fed. Republic Germany, 1965-68; occupational therapist Inst. Surg. Rsch. U.S. Army, Ft. Sam Houston, Tex., 1967-70; occupational therapy dir., cons. U.S. Army, Honolulu, 1972-75; adminstr. occupational therapy clinic, cons. LAMC U.S. Army, Presido, Calif., 1975; asst. evening coll. program San Jose (Calif.) C.C., 1976-77; postdoctoral fellow allied health adminstrn. SUNY, Buffalo, 1978, Commonwealth U., Richmond, Va., 1978-79; project dir. Ctr. of Design, Palo Alto, 1980; part-time staff project developing pre-retirement program older adults De Anza Coll., Cupertino, Calif., 1980-81; part-time instr. Stroke Activity Ctr. Cabrillo Coll., Santa Cruz, Calif., 1981; dir. occupl. therapy Presbyn. Med. Ctr., 1981-86; ptnr., mgr. retail store, 1986-89; dir. rehab. therapy Merrithew Meml. Hosp. Contra Costa Med. Ctr., Martinez, Calif., 1990-93; sculptor, 1993—; part-time activity program coord. Calif. Women's Detention Facility, Chowchilla, Calif., 1994—; researcher, presenter workshops and seminars in field. Co-author: Splinting of Burned Patients, 1974; producer videos: Elbow Splinting of the Burned Patient, 1970, Self-Instruction Unit: Principles of Elbow Splinting, 1971; contbr. articles to profl. jours. Decorated Legion of Merit; recipient Disting. Alumni Honors award San Jose State U., 1982; grad. scholar U.S. Surgeon Gen.; Kellogg Found. postdoctoral fellow, 1979. Mem. Am. Occupational Therapy Assn., Occupational Therapy Assn. Calif. (award of excellence 1986, v.p. 1981-84, state chair pers. 1981-84, state chair continuing edn. 1984-86, Lifetime Achievement award 1994), Am. Soc. Hand Therapists (hon., life). Home: 36141 Manon Ave Madera CA 93638 Office: Calif Women's Detention Facility Chowchilla CA 93610-1501

VON QUINTUS-DORN, LINDA KAYE, lawyer; b. Brownfield, Tex., Nov. 1, 1952; d. Jesse Lee Barnes and Bernice Mae (Urdy) Simon; m. Daryl M. Dorn, June 23, 1990; 1 child, Michael Dorn. BBA, U. Houston, 1980; JD, Tex. So. U., 1986. Bar: Tex. 1987. Asst. mktg. mgr. Geosource, Power Sys., Houston, 1977-79; office mgr. Petroleum Fuels, Houston; project coord. Bovay Engrs., Houston; chief clk. State Bd. of Ins., Austin, Tex., 1991-94; staff atty. Tex. Dept. Ins., Austin, 1987-88, supervising staff atty., 1988-89, sr. staff atty., 1989-91, dep. commr. regulation and safety, 1994—. Agy. liaison state agy. liaison group Gov.'s Commn. for Women, Austin, 1990, 94; vol. lawyer Capital Area AIDS Legal Project, Austin, 1991, 92, 93; treas. polit. investment fund Sojourner's Trust, Austin, 1991, 92; co-chair fin. com. Austin Women's Polit. Caucus, 1991, 92, pres.-elect, 1994; v.p. policy coun. Tex. Women's Polit. Caucus, 1994; alumna Leadership Am., 1994, Leadership Tex., 1993. Recipient Appreciation award San Antonio Assn. Health Underwriters, 1990, Top Ladies of Distinction, 1992, State Bar of Tex. Profl. Devel., 1993, Outstanding Svc. award Capital Area AIDS Legal Project, 1993, Outstanding Achievement award in the professions YWCA Leader Luncheon, 1994. Mem. ABA (vice-chair pub. ins. 1990-92), Exec. Women in Tex. Govt. (program dir. 1992, Appreciation award 1992), Travis County Bar Assn. (program com. 1991-92, bd. dirs. adminstrv. law sect. 1994). Baptist. Home: 2303 Lear Ln Austin TX 78745

VON RAFFLER-ENGEL, WALBURGA, linguist, lecturer, writer; b. Munich, Germany, Sept. 25, 1920; came to U.S., 1949, naturalized, 1955; d. Friedrich J. and Gertrud E. (Kiefer) von R.; m. A. Ferdinand Engel, June 2, 1957; children: Lea Maxine, Eric Robert von Raffler. DLitt, U. Turin, Italy, 1947; MS, Columbia U., 1951; PhD, Ind. U., 1953. Free-lance journalist, 1949-58; mem. faculty Bennett Coll., Greensboro, N.C., 1953-55, U. Charleston (formerly Morris Harvey Coll.), W.Va., 1955-57, Adelphi U., CUNY, 1957-58, NYU, 1958-59, U. Florence, Italy, 1959-60, Istituto Postuniversitario Organizzazione Aziendale, Turin, 1960-61, Bologna Center of Johns Hopkins U., 1964; assoc. prof. linguistics Vanderbilt U., Nashville, 1965-77, prof. linguistics, 1977-85, prof. emerita, sr. rsch. assoc. Inst. Pub. Policy Studies, 1985—; dir. linguistics program Vanderbilt U., 1978-86; chmn. com. on linguistics Nashville U. Ctr., 1974-79; Italian NSF prof. Psychol. Inst. U. Florence, Italy, 1986-87; prof. NATO Advanced Study Inst., Cortona, Italy, 1988; pres. Kinesics Internat., 1988—; vis. prof. linguistics Shanxi U., Peoples Republic China, 1985; vis. prof. U. Ottawa, Ont., Can., 1971-72, Lang. Scis. Inst., Tokyo, 1976; grant evaluator NEH, NSF, Can. Coun.; manuscript reader Ind. U. Press, U. Ill. Press, Prentice-Hall; advisor Trinity U., Simon Frazer U.; lectr. in field. Author: Il prelinguaggio infantile, 1964, The Perception of Nonverbal Behavior in the Career Interview, 1983, The Perception of the Unborn Across the Cultures of the World, Japanese edit., 1993, English edit., 1994 (transl. into Chinese); co-author: Language Intervention Programs, 1960-74, 75; editor, co-editor 12 books; author films and videotape; contbr. over 300 articles to scholarly jours., over 200 to profl. and popular publs. in various countries. Grantee Am. Coun. Learned Socs., NSF, Can. Coun., Ford Found., Kenan Venture Fund, Japanese Ministry Edn., NATO, UNESCO, Finnish Acad., Meharry Med. Coll., Internat. Sociol. Assn., Internat. Coun. Linguists, Tex. A&M U., Vanderbilt U., others. Mem. AAUP, Internat. Linguistic Assn., Linguistic Soc. Am. (chmn. Golden Anniversary film com. 1974, emerita 1985—), Internat. Assn. for Applied Linguistics (com. on discourse analyses, sessions chmn. 1978), Lang. Origins Soc. (exec. com. 1985—, chmn. internat. congress, 1987), Internat. Sociol. Assn. (rsch. com. for sociolinguistics, session co-chmn. internat. conf. 1983, session chmn. profl. conf. 1983), Internat. Assn. for Study of Child Lang. (v.p. 1975-78, chmn. internat. conf. 1972), Inst. for Nonverbal Communication Research (workshop leader 1981), Southeastern Conf. on Linguistics, 1980— (hon. mem. 1985—), Semiotic Soc. Am. (organizing com. Internat. Semiotics Inst. 1981), Sietar Internat., Kinesics Internat. (pres. 1988—). Home and Office: 116 Brighton Close Nashville TN 37205-2501

VON REIS CORNELL, SONJA MARGARETHA, artist; b. Gothenburg, Sweden, Nov. 19, 1925; came to the U.S., 1948; d. James Adolf Helmer and Iris Margaretha (Malmstrom) von R.; m. Lorain Dale Cornell, Oct. 29, 1949 (dec. Dec. 1988); children: Charles Peter, Susan Christina, Sonja Elizabeth. BA, Mich. State U., 1969, MA, 1970, MFA, 1975. Interpreter Gen. Motors Overseas, Detroit, 1948-49; tchr. art and humanities Dewitt (Mich.) Pub. Schs., 1970-88; instr. evening coll. Mich. State U., East Lansing, 1975-76; mem. Art Scholarships, Lansing, 1985-90; jurying Lansing Art Guild, Mich., 1990—, East Lansing Arts Orgn., 1991—. One person shows include Prints Ancient and Modern, East Lansing, Okemos (Mich.) Community Ch., Jacobsons', East Lansing, Creative Arts Gallery, Mt. Pleasant, Mich., Lansing Art Gallery, others; group shows include Art Now, Goteborg, Sweden, Katharine Rich Perlow Gallery, N.Y.C., Foster/White Gallery, Seattle, others; collections include Wharton Ctr., East Lansing, Phillips Petroleum Corp., Bartlesville, Okla., Ceco Corp., Chgo., Mich. Edn. Assn., East Lansing, others. Mem. Friend of Kresge Art Mus., East Lansing, 1975—. Mem. NEA, Swedish Internat. Edn. Assn., Mich. Edn. Assn., Detroit Swedish Coun., Jenny Lind Club Mich., Zonta Mich.

VON TAAFFE-ROSSMANN, COSIMA T., physician, writer, inventor; b. Kuklov, Slovakia, Czechoslovakia, Nov. 21, 1944; came to U.S., 1988; d. Theophil and Marianna Hajossy; m. Charles Boris Rossmann, Oct. 19, 1979; children: Nathalie Nissa Cora, Nadine Nicole. MD, Purkyne U., Brno, Czechoslovakia, 1967. Intern Valtice (Czechoslovakia) Gen. Hosp., 1967-68, resident ob-gyn, 1968-69; med. researcher Kidney Disease Inst., Albany, N.Y., 1970-71; resident internal medicine Valtice Gen. Hosp., 1972-73; gen. practice Nat. Health System, Czechoslovakia, 1973-74; pvt. practice West Germany, 1974-80; med. officer Baragwanath Hosp., Johannesburg, South Africa, 1984-85, Edendale Hosp., Pietermaritzburg, South Africa, 1985-86; pvt. practice Huntingburg, Ind., 1988—; med. researcher, 1966—. Contbr. articles on medicine to profl. jours.; inventor, patentee in field. Office: 2301 N Ashley St Valdosta GA 31602

VONTUR, RUTH POTH, elementary physical education educator; b. Beeville, Tex., Sept. 10, 1944; d. Robert Bennal and Ruth (Matejek) Poth; m. Robert F. Vontur, Aug. 8, 1964; children: Catherine Anne, Craig Robert, Cynthia Anne. BS in Edn., Southwest Tex. State U., 1966. Cert. health and phys. edn. tchr., biology tchr. Tex. Teachng asst. Blessed Sacrament Confraternity Christian Doctrine, Poth, Tex., 1958-64; phys. edn. tchr. Judson Ind. Sch. Dist., Converse, Tex., 1966-68; substitute tchr. St. Monica's Confraternity Christian Doctrine, Converse, 1971—; substitute tchr. Judson Ind. Sch. Dist., Converse, 1972-75, phys. edn. tchr., 1981—; county adv. bd. Am. Heart Assn., San Antonio, Tex., 1985-88, jump rope for heart coord., 1984—, heart ptnr., 1992—. Pres. St. Monica's Coun. Cath. Women, Converse, 1975. Mem. NEA, AAHPERD, Alamo Area Tex. Assn. Health, Phys. Edn., Recreation and Dance, Tex. Assn. Health, Phys. Edn., Recreation and Dance, Judson Tchrs. Assn. (exec. dir. 1993—), Tex. State Tchrs. Assn., Judson Athletic Booster Club. Roman Catholic. Home: 105 Norris Dr W Converse TX 78109-1905 Office: Judson Ind Sch Dist Converse Elem Sch 102 School St Converse TX 78109

VOORHESS, MARY LOUISE, pediatric endocrinologist; b. Livingston Manor, N.Y., June 2, 1926; d. Harry William and Helen Grace (Schwartz) V. BA in Zoology, U. Tex., 1952; MD, Baylor Coll., Houston, 1956. Diplomate Am. Bd. Pediatrics and Pediatric Endocrinology. Rotating intern Albany (N.Y.) Med. Ctr., 1956-57, asst. resident pediatrics, 1957-58, chief resident pediatrics, 1958-59; rsch. fellow pediatric endocrinology and genetics SUNY Health Sci. Ctr., Syracuse, 1959-61, asst. prof. pediatrics, 1961-65, assoc. prof. pediatrics, 1965-70, prof. pediatrics, 1970-76; prof. pediatrics SUNY Sch. Medicine and Biomed. Scis., Buffalo, 1976-91, prof. pediatrics emeritus, 1991—; co-chief div. endocrinology Children's Hosp. Buffalo, 1976-91; ad hoc reviewer Jour. Pediatrics, Pediatrics, Am. Jour. Diseases Children, other. Contbr. sci. articles to profl. jours., chpts. to books. Mem. adv. bd. Med. Pers. Pool Buffalo, 1991—; mem. devel. coun. Children's Hosp. Buffalo Found., 1991—; med. dir. Children's Growth Found., Buffalo, 1976—; community advisor Assn. for Rsch. Childhood Cancer, Buffalo, 1990—. Recipient rsch. career devel. award Nat. Cancer Inst., 1961-71, Dean's award SUNY Sch. Medicine and Biomed. Scis., 1991. Fellow Am. Acad. Pediatrics, AAAS; mem. Soc. Pediatric Rsch., Am. Pediatric Soc., Endocrine Soc., Lawson Wilkins Pediatric Endocrine Soc., Buffalo Pediatric Soc., Zonta Internat., Phi Beta Kappa, Alpha Omega Alpha. Presbyterian. Home: 325 Lincoln Pky Buffalo NY 14216-3120 Office: Children Hosp 219 Bryant St Buffalo NY 14222-2006

VORE, MARY EDITH, pharmacology educator, researcher; b. Guatemala City, Guatemala, June 27, 1947; came to U.S., 1962; d. Charles Schrater and Sammye (Smith) V.; m. Edgar Tadasu Iwamoto, Dec. 27, 1976; children: Kenneth Edgar, Daniel Vore. BA, Asbury Coll., Wilmore, Ky., 1968; PhD, Vanderbilt U., Nashville, Tenn., 1972. Postdoctoral fellow Hoffman-LaRoche, Nutley, N.J., 1972-74; asst. prof. U. Calif., San Francisco, 1974-78; asst. prof. pharmacology U. Ky., Lexington, 1978-81, assoc. prof., 1981-86, prof., 1986—, vice chmn. dept., 1983-94, dir. grad. ctr. for toxicology, 1994—; cons. NIH, Bethesda, Md., 1983-87. Contbr. numerous articles to profl. jours., chpts. to books. USPHS grantee, 1979—. Mem. Soc. Toxicology, Am. Assn. Study of Liver Disease, Am. Soc. Pharmacology and Exptl. Therapeutics (sec., treas. 1986-89), Nat. Adv. Environ. Health Scis. Coun. Office: U Ky Coll Medicine 800 Rose St Lexington KY 40536-0001

VOROUS, PATRICIA ANN MARIE, elementary school educator; b. Cleve., Sept. 12, 1951; d. Leon Jr. and Margaret (Cotter) V. BS Edn. in Elem. Edn., St. John Coll., Cleve., 1973; postgrad., Notre Dame Coll., Cleve., 1988, Baldwin-Wallace Coll., Berea, Ohio, summer 1979, 91. Cert. tchr., Ohio. Intermediate tchr. lang. arts, social studies St. Mel Sch., Cleve., 1973-74; grade 6 tchr. lang. arts, social studies and religion St. James Sch., Lakewood, Ohio, 1975-80; tchr. grades 5 and 6 Our Lady of the Angels Schs., Cleve., 1980—; supervisory tchr. for elem. edn. students Cleve. State U.; from asst. dir. to dir. Lakewood Recreation Dept. Summer Play Ctr., 1973-94; safety patrol coord. Our Lady of Angels, Cleve., 1985—. Craftsman animals, dolls, 3-D scenes for fall festivals and gifts. Roman Catholic.

VORTHERMS, MARGENE MARY, nurse; b. Slayton, Minn., July 5, 1954; d. Lawrence B. and Lorraine F. (Hoffman) Halbur; m. Michael A. Vortherms, Aug. 9, 1975; children: Mark, Matt. LPN, Austin (Minn.) Tech., 1973; ADN, Iowa Lakes C.C., Emmetsburg, Iowa, 1975. Nurse United Hosp., Blue Earth, Minn., 1973-74, Worthington (Minn.) Regional Hosp., 1975—. Adult leader St. Gabriel's Youth Group, 1992—. Mem. Minn. Nurses ASsn. (treas. 1984-86), Fulda Coun. Cath. Women (sec. 1984-86. Roman Catholic.

VOSBURGH, VICTORIA LYNN, rehabilitation services executive; b. Putnam, Conn., Aug. 7, 1965; d. Douglas Warren Vosburgh and Margaret Jean (Grenier) Baggetta; m. Michael R. DeNardis, Aug. 7, 1988. Paralegal diploma, Westchester Sch., 1985. Adminstrv. asst. Hospitality House T.C., Inc., Albany, N.Y., 1985-87; exec. adminstr. Hospitality House T.C., Inc., Albany, 1987-91; human immunodeficiency virus issues coord. Hospitality House T.C., Inc., Albany, N.Y., 1989-91, dir. adminstrn., 1991—. Mem.

North Shore Animal League, Divers Alert Network. Home: 203 Blue Barns Rd Burnt Hills NY 12027 Office: Hospitality House TC Inc 271 Central Ave Albany NY 12206-2611

VOS-FITZSIMMONS, NANCY ELLEN, public relations and public affairs professional; b. Plainfield, N.J., Feb. 20, 1954; d. Joseph Andrew and Marilyn Patricia (Bloom) Vos; m. John Joseph Fitzsimmons Jr., Nov. 10, 1990. Assocs., Lab. Inst. Merchandising, N.Y.C., 1976; BA, NYU, 1991. From asst. buyer to pub. rels. mgr. Abraham & Straus, Bklyn., 1976-80; mgr. pub. rels. Springs Mills, N.Y.C., 1980-81; from account exec. to v.p. and accounts supr. Burson Marsteller, N.Y.C., 1981-89; dir. mktg. com. Warner-Lambert Co., Morris Plains, N.J., 1989-90; dir. issues and media Warner-Lambert Co., Morris Plains, 1990—. Chair spl. events United Way, Morris County, N.J., 1992. Mem. Pharm. Ad Coun., Healthcare Bus. Womens Assn., Food and Drug Law Inst. Conf. Bd. Office: Warner-Lambert Co 201 Tabor Rd Morris Plains NJ 07950-2614

VOSLOW, REBECCA ALLEN ROGERS, congressional staff executive; b. Fredericksburg, Va., Apr. 5, 1961; d. Fred Allen and Patsy Louise (Stallard) Rogers; m. Michael Gene Voslow, Oct. 28, 1989; children: Olivia Louise, Harrison Allen. BA, Coll of William and Mary, 1983, MA, 1989. Staff asst. Rep. Senatorial Com., Washington, 1983; legis. corr. U.S. Rep. Stan Parris, Washington, 1984; account asst. Ann Stine & Assocs., Alexandria, Va., 1984-85; asst. to chief of staff to co-chmn. Rep. Nat. Com., Washington, 1985, project supr. polit. edn. dept., 1986; legis. asst. U.S. Senator Paul S. Trible, Washington, 1987-88; profl. staff mem. U.S. Senate Com. on Labor and Human Resources, Washington, 1988-91; speechwriter to dir. Office of Pers. Mgmt., Washington, 1992, sr. congl. rels. officer, 1991—. Active mem. Arlington Va. Cmty Svcs. Bd., 1990-91; bd. dirs Langley Nonprofit Housing Devel. Corp., 1992-94; treas. Jr. League Northern Va., 1993-94. Mem. Alpha Kappa Delta. Republican. Office: Office of the Personnel Mgmt 1900 E St NW Washington DC 20415

VOSS, ANNE COBLE, nutritional biochemist; b. Richmond, Ind., Aug. 22, 1946; d. James Richard and Helen Lucille (Hoyt) Coble; m. Harold Lloyd Voss, July 20, 1969; children: Daniel, Jordan Matthew, Sarah Georgette. BS, Ohio State U., 1968, PhD, 1984. Registered dietitian. Therapeutic dietitian Johns Hopkins Hosp., Balt., 1968-69; clin. instr. Ohio State U. Hosps., Columbus, 1969-70; clin. dietitian U.S. Army Med. Clinic, Rothwesten, Fed. Republic Germany, 1970-72; clin. rsch. assoc. Ross Labs., Columbus, 1978-79; rsch. asst. Ohio State U., Columbus, 1979-84, rsch. assoc., lectr., 1985-91; med. nutriton R & D Ross Labs., Columbus, Ohio, 1992—; adj. asst. prof. Otterbein Coll., Westerville, Ohio, 1990-93; nutrition advisor Ohio Dental Assn., Columbus, 1977-93, ADA, Chgo., 1987-93; cons. Ohio Bd. Dietetics, Columbus, 1989-93; vis. scientist Rikshospitalet, Oslo, Norway, 1992. Author: Polyunsaturated Fatty Acids and Eicosanoids, 1987; author, editor: Nutrition Perspectives, 1990, 91, 2d edit., 1993; contbr. articles to profl. jours. Mem. exec. bd Aux. to Ohio Dental Assn., Columbus, 1979—; bd. dirs. Ohio Dental Polit. Action Com., Columbus, 1989-92, YWCA, Columbus, 1990-93; Gov.'s appointee, vice chmn. Ohio Bd. Dietetics. Recipient award Clement Found., Westerville, 1991, Nutrition Edn. in Tng. grant Ohio Dept. Edn., Columbus, 1978; appt. by Gov. of Ohio to Bd. Dietetics. Mem. Am. Dietetic Assn., Ohio Dietetic Assn. (career devel. 1968—), Med. Dietetics Assn. (founding mem., pres., v.p., sec. 1978—), Ohio Coun. Against Health Fraud (founding mem., bd. govs. 1987—), Ohio Nutrition Coun. (exec. bd. 1987—), Columbus Dietetic Assn., Sigma Xi, Sigma Delta Epsilon (sec. 1985—). Methodist. Home: 1526 Bridgeton Dr Columbus OH 43220-3908 Office: Ross Labs 105640 RP3-2 625 Cleveland Ave Columbus OH 43215-1724

VOSS, KATHERINE EVELYN, management consultant; b. Cleve., Sept. 2, 1957; d. Wendell Grant and Ann Terry (Miller) Voss; m. James Everett Mathias, Oct. 6, 1984 (div. Dec. 1988). BS, Bowling Green State U., 1979, MBA, 1981. Sci. systems analyst Eli Lilly & Co., Indpls., 1981-83, systems tng. cons., 1983-84; customer liaison mgr. Ind. U., Bloomington, 1985; prodn. ops. mgr. Ind. U., Indpls., 1985-86; prin. systems cons. Wang Labs., Inc., Carmel, Ind., 1986-93; mgmt. cons. Tenex Ireland Ltd., Dublin, 1994—; cons. Ind. Univ., Bloomington, 1984-85, Allied Irish Bank, Dublin, Ireland, 1990-91. Contbr. (book) Introduction to Business, 1980, Introduction to Accounting, 1981, Computers and Data Processing, 1981. Presidental advisor Jr. Achievement, Indpls., 1982-83; pres. PEO Chpt. AM, Indpls., 1987-89. Mem. Assn. for Image and Info. Mgmt., Irish Computer Soc., Beta Beta Beta. Republican. Presbyterian. Home: Hill Cottage, Brennanstown Rd Cabinteely, Dublin 18, Ireland Office: Tenex Ireland Ltd Elm House, Leopardstown Office Park, Foxrock Dublin 18, Ireland

VOYLES, BARBARA JEAN, social worker, consultant; b. Desloge, Mo., Aug. 14, 1938; d. Walter Edward and Glena Mae (Moyer) V. AA, Flat River Jr. Coll., 1959; BS, Mo. Valley Coll., 1968; MSW, Washington U., 1980. Cert. tchr., Mo.; lic. clin. social worker, Mo. Social worker Family Svcs. Div. State of Mo., St. Genevieve, 1960-66; nurse Mo. Valley Health Svcs., Marshall, Mo., 1966-68, Fitzgibbon Hosp., Marshall, 1966-68; tchr. sci. Farmington (Mo.) Sch. Dist., 1968-72; tchr., sch. nurse, counselor R 14 Sch. Dist., Lonedell, Mo., 1972-75; social worker, clinician Family Svcs. Div. State of Mo., St. Louis, 1975-93; dir. social svcs. Mineral ARea Regional Med. Ctr., Farmington, Mo., 1993—; pvt. practice therapy, St. Louis, 1975—; cons. juvenile ct., St. Louis, 1980—. Mem. NASW, Acad. Cert. Social Workers, Mo. Assn. Social Workers, Mo. Assn. Prevention Adult Abuse, St. Louis County Juvenile Justice Assn., Washington U. alumni Assn., Order Ea. Star. Home: 353 Keith St Park Hills MO 63601 Office: Mineral Area Regional Med Ctr 1212 Weber Rd Farmington MO 63640

VRATIL, KATHRYN HOEFER, federal judge; b. Manhattan, Kans., Apr. 21, 1949; d. John J. and Kathryn Ruth (Fryer) Hoefer; children: Alison K., John A., Ashley A. BA, U. Kans., 1971, JD, 1975; postgrad., Exeter U., 1971-72. Bar: Kans. 1975, U.S. Dist. Ct. Kans. 1975, Mo. 1978, U.S. Dist. Ct. (we. dist.) Mo. 1978, U.S. Ct. Appeals (8th cir.) 1978, U.S. Ct. Appeals (10th cir.) 1980, U.S. Ct. Appeals (11th cir.) 1983, U.S. Dist. Ct. (ea. dist.) Mo. 1985. Law clk. U.S. Dist. Ct., Kansas City, Kans., 1975-78; assoc. Lathrop Koontz & Norquist, Kansas City, Mo., 1978-83; ptnr. Lathrop & Norquist, Kansas City, 1984-92; judge City of Prairie Village, Kans., 1991-92; bd. dirs. Kans. Legal Svcs. Bd. editors Kans. Law Rev., 1974-75, Jour. Kans. Bar Assn., 1992—. Mem. Kansas City Tomorrow (XIV); bd. trustees, shepherd-deacon Village Presbyn. Ch.; nat. adv. bd. U. Kans. Ctr. for Environ. Edn. and Tng., 1993—. Fellow Kans. Bar Found., Am. Bar Found.; mem. ABA, Am. Judicature Soc., Nat. Assn. Judges, Fed. Judges Assn., Kans. Bar Assn., Mo. Bar Assn., Kansas City Met. Area Bar Assn., Wyandotte County Bar Assn., Johnson County Bar Assn., Assn. Women Lawyers, Lawyers Assn. Kansas City, Supreme Ct. Hist. Soc., Kans. State Hist. Soc., U. Kans. Law Soc. (bd. govs. 1978-81), Kans. U. Alumni Assn. (mem. devel. com. 1985—, mem. Kansas City chpt. alumni bd. 1990-92, nat. bd. dirs. 1991—, bd. govs. Adams alumni ctr. 1992—, mem. learned club 1992—, mem. chancellor's club 1993—, mem. Williams ednl. fund 1993—, mem. Jayhawks for higher edn. 1993—), Homestead Country Club Prairie Village (pres.), Sons and Daus. of Kans. (life), Rotary, Jr. League Wyandotte and Johnson Counties, Kans. State Hist. Soc., Supreme Ct. Hist. Soc., Order of Coif, Kans. Inn. of Ct. (master 1993—), Overland Park Rotary, Univ. Club, Phi Kappa Phi. Republican. Presbyterian. Office: 511 US Courthouse 500 State Ave Kansas City KS 66101

VUCANOVICH, BARBARA FARRELL, congresswoman; b. Fort Dix, N.J., June 22, 1921; d. Thomas F. and Ynez (White) Farrell; m. Ken Dillon, Mar. 8, 1950 (div. 1964); children: Patty Dillon Cafferata, Mike, Ken, Tom, Susan Dillon Stoddard; m. George Vucanovich, June 19, 1965. Student, Manhattanville Coll. of Sacred Heart, 1938-39. Owner, operator Welcome Aboard Travel, Reno, 1968-74; Nev. rep. for Senator Paul Laxalt, 1974-82; mem. 98th-103rd Congresses from 2d Nev. dist., 1983—; mem. coms. interior and insular affairs, appropriations com., subcom. agrl., military construction, mining and natural resources com., Nat. Parks, Forests, Pub. Lands. Pres. Nev. Fedn. Republican Women, Reno, 1955-56; former pres. St. Mary's Hosp. Guild, Lawyer's Wives. Roman Catholic. Club: Hidden Valley Country (Reno). Office: 2202 Rayburn House Of Representativ Washington DC 20515

VUCKOVICH, CAROL YETSO (MRS. MICHAEL VUCKOVICH), librarian; b. East Liverpool, Ohio, Sept. 23, 1940; d. Stephen A. and Louise (Sever) Yetso; m. Michael Vuckovich, Sept. 24, 1970. BS, Geneva Coll., 1966; MLS, U. Pitts., 1968. Computation analyst Crucible Steel div. Colt Industries, Midland, Pa., 1958-62; library dir. Community Coll. Beaver County, Monaca, Pa., 1968—, instr. human anatomy and physiology, 1970—. Mem. Am. Library Assn., Pa. Library Assn., Spl. Libraries Assn., Am. Inst. Biol. Scis., Am. Anti-Vivisection Soc., Nat. Wildlife Fedn., Coll. and Research Libraries. Home: 21 Elm St Midland PA 15059-1615

VUCUREVICH, CONSTANCE LANE, investment executive; b. Lynchburg, Va., Nov. 9, 1946; d. Landon Bell and Frances Nelson (Mathews) Lane; m. James Wilson Stanfield, Feb. 2, 1968 (div. July 1980); children: James Wilson Stanfield III, Amanda Page Stanfield; m. John Thomas Vucurevich, Oct. 1, 1988. Student, Sweet Briar Coll., 1965-68; BSBA in Mktg./Mgmt., Nat. Coll., Rapid City, S.D., 1984. Registered securities broker. Investment exec. Piper Jaffray & Hopwood, Rapid City, 1984-87; investment executive Wheat First Securities, Richmond, Va., 1987-88; asst. v.p. Piper Jaffray, Inc., Rapid City, 1988—. Founder, dir., v.p., sec. L.B. Lane Family Found., Hickory, N.C., 1988—; bd. dirs. John T. Vucurevich Found., Rapid City, 1991—, Rapid City Boys Club, 1991—, Rapid City YMCA, 1994—, Rapid City Regional Hosp., 1994—; grad. Leadership Rapid City, 1985; mem. Mayor's Econ. Devel. Com., Rapid City, 1990; mem. choir Emmanuel Episc. Ch., 1982—. Recipient Philanthropist of Yr. award Gov. of S.D., Pierre, 1992. Mem. Womens Network. Republican. Episcopalian. Home: 1416 Flormann St Rapid City SD 57701 Office: Piper Jaffray Inc 726 St Joe St Rapid City SD 57701

VUJOVICH, CHRISTINE M., engine manufacturing company executive; b. 1951. BS in Eath Scis., U. Ill., 1974, MS in Environ. Engring. & Civil Engring., 1978. Asst. to hydrologist Ill. State Water Svc., 1977-78; environ. specialist Cummins Engine Co., Inc., Columbus, Ind., 1978-81, environ. mgr., 1981-83, dir. environ. and govtl. rels., 1983-85, chief application engr. customer accts. dept., then v.p., 1985—, customer engring. product planning and environ. mgmt., 1989—; bd. dirs. Irwin Union Bank, Columbus, Kimball Internat., Columbus. Office: Cummins Engine Co Inc 500 Jackson St PO Box 3005 Columbus IN 47202

VUKIN, GERRI PATRICIA, real estate relocation company executive; b. Sharon, Conn., Oct. 17, 1939; d. Edmond William and Nuala (Houston) Kearney; m. Richard L. Vukin, July 3, 1965 (div. June 1982); children: Greg, Nick. RN diploma, Hartford Hosp. Sch. Nursing, 1960; student, Columbia U., 1960-61; B.S.P.H.N., U. Mich., 1964; postgrad., County Coll. of Morris, Randolph, N.J., 1985-86. Pub. health nurse Wayne County Health Dept., Wayne, Mich., 1964-65; sch. nurse Houston Independent Sch. Dist., Houston, 1965-66; pres., communications cons. GNG Enterprises, Chatham, N.J., 1983-84; corp. account mgr. relocation dept. Burgdorff Realtors, Murray Hill, N.J., 1984—; mem. Employee Relocation Coun., 1985—; speaker Am. Assn. Personnel Adminstrn., N.J., 1988; developer assertiveness tng. course, 1983-84. Vol. Alanon, N.J., 1980-89, United Way, Chatham, N.J., 1984; treas. N.J. Task Force-COA, N.J., 1982-84. Grantee Profl. Edn. Orgn. (PEO), N.J., 1985. Mem. Nat. Assn. for Female Execs., Real Estate Assn., Sales Exec. Club, U. Mich. Club N.J., Fairmount Country Club (chmn. pool-social 1980), Gamma Phi Beta. Republican. Roman Catholic. Office: Burgdorff Realtors 560 Central Ave New Providence NJ 07974-1513

VULGAMORE, ALLISON, performing arts administrator. BMus, Oberlin Coll. Former gen. mgr., artistic adminstr., mgr. ops. Nat. Symphony Orch., Washington; former gen. mgr. N.Y. Philharm. Orch., N.Y.C.; pres. Atlanta Symphony Orch., 1993—; bd. dirs. Oberlin Coll.; mem. arts challenge panel in music NEH. Bd. dirs. Midtown Alliance; active Vision 2000 Econ. Devel. Collaborative. Am. Symphony Orch. League fellow, 1980. Mem. Atlnbta Rotary. Office: Atlanta Symphony Orchestra Robert W Woodruff Arts Ctr 1293 Peachtree St NE Ste 300 Atlanta GA 30309*

VULLO-PENCILLE, WENDI, environmental microbiologist; b. Buffalo, Jan. 14, 1962; d. Joseph John and Janet Marie (Panzica) Vullo; m. Timothy James Pencille, Nov. 11, 1989. BS, Cornell U., 1985. Asst. adminstr. Bassett Manor Adult Residence, Williamsville, N.Y., 1985-86, adminstr., 1986-88; environ. microbiologist Westwood Squibb Pharms., Buffalo, 1991—. Mem. Am. Soc. Microbiology, Nat. Wildlife Rehab. Assn., Internat. Wildlife Rehab. Coun. Democrat. Home: 11207 Ryan Rd Medina NY 14103-9532

VYAS, MARY PRESSLEY, investment company executive; b. Princeton, N.J., Mar. 26, 1964; d. Robert Joseph and Anne Lucille (Conaty) Pressley; m. Jay Pressley Vyas, Aug. 10, 1991. BA in Applied Math & Econs., U. Calif., 1987; MS in Ops. Rsch., MIT, 1992; PhD in Finance, Stanford U., 1994. Sr. programmer BARRA, Berkeley, 1987-90; rsch. asst. Internat. Fin. Svcs. Rsch. Ctr. MIT, Cambridge, Mass., 1990-92; asst. v.p. State Street Global Advisors, Boston, 1992-94.

WAARA, MARIA ESTHER, artist; b. Menahga, Minn., June 16, 1930; d. William Matt and Maria Matilda (Alajoki) Haataja; m. Hubert Frank Waara, Dec. 25, 1954. Student, U. Calif., 1975, Gogebic Coll., Ewen, Mich., 1976. Freelance artist Bruce-Crossing, Mich. Home: RR 2 Box 31 Bruce Crossing MI 49912-9802

WACHBRIT, JILL BARRETT, accountant, tax specialist; b. Ventura, Calif., May 27, 1955; d. Preston Everett Barrett and Lois JoAnne (Fondersmith) Batchelder; m. Michael Ian Wachbrit, June 21, 1981; children: Michelle, Tracy. AA, Santa Monica City Coll., 1975; BS, Calif. State U., Northridge, 1979; M in Bus. Taxation, U. So. Calif., 1985. CPA. Supervising sr. tax acct. Peat, Marwick, Mitchell & Co., Century City, Calif., 1979-82; sr. tax analyst Avery Internat., Pasadena, Calif., 1982-83; tax mgr., asst. v.p. First Interstate Leasing, Pasadena, 1983-88, Gibraltar Savs., 1988, Security Pacific Corp., L.A., 1988-92; tax mgr., acct. El Camino Resources Ltd., Woodland Hills, Calif., 1992—. Republican. Jewish.

WACHNER, LINDA JOY, apparel marketing and manufacturing executive; b. N.Y.C., Feb. 3, 1946; d. Herman and Shirley W.; m. Seymour Applebaum, Dec. 21, 1973 (dec. 1983). BS in Econs. and Bus., U. Buffalo, 1966. Buyer Foley's Federated Dept. Store, Houston, 1968-69; sr. buyer R.H. Macy's, N.Y.C., 1969-74; v.p. Warner divsn. Warnaco, Bridgeport, Conn., 1974-77; v.p. corp. mktg. Caron Internat., N.Y.C., 1977-79; chief exec. officer U.S. divsn. Max Factor & Co., Hollywood, Calif., 1979-82, pres., chief exec. officer, 1982-83; pres., chief exec. officer Max Factor & Co. Worldwide, 1983-84; mng. dir. Adler & Shaykin, N.Y.C., 1985-86; owner, pres., CEO, chmn. Warnaco Inc., N.Y.C., 1986—; chmn., CEO Authentic Fitness Corp., 1991—; bd. dirs. The Travellers, Inc., Castle & Cooke Homes, Inc. Presdl. appointee Adv. Com. for Trade, Policy, Negotiations; trustee U. Buffalo Found., Carnegie Hall, Aspen Inst. Recipient Silver Achievement award L.A. YWCA; named Outstanding Woman in Bus. Women's Equity Action League, 1980, Woman of Yr., MS. Mag., 1986, one of the Yr.'s Most Fascinating Bus. People, Fortune Mag., 1986, one of 10 Most Powerful Women in Corp. Am., Savvy Woman Mag., 1989, 90, Am.'s Most Successful Bus. Woman, Fortune Mag., 1992, Queen of Cash Flow, Chief Exec. Mag., 1994. Mem. Young Pres.'s Orgn., Am. Mgmt. Assn., Am. Apparel Mktg. Assn. (bd. dirs.), Bus. Roundtable. Republican. Jewish. Office: Warnaco Inc/Authentic Fitness Corp 90 Park Ave New York NY 10016-1302*

WACHSTEIN, JOAN MARTHA, dental hygienist; b. Phila., Nov. 12, 1941; d. Milton and Mabel Louise (Friedman) Hertzfeld; m. Mortimer Berwyn Wachstein, July 14, 1962 (dec. 1989); children: Lisa Beth, Esther Lynn. RDH, Temple U., Phila., 1961. Registered dental hygienist; cert. gerontology referral. Dental hygienist Dr. M.B. Wachstein, Newark, Del., 1970-89; campaign mgr. Milton and Hattie Kurtz Home for Capital Campaign, 1995—. Mem. allocations panel & mem. planning coms. United Way, Wilmington, Del., 1986-92, bd. dirs., 1994—, allocations panel chair, 1994—, mem. strategic planning com., ethics com., 1994-95; bd. dirs. Jewish Family Svcs., Del., 1983—, rec. sec., 1984-86, 88-91, pres., 1992-94, treas. 1989-91, Milton and Hattie Kutz Home, Inc., 1987—, v.p., 1988—; pres. Aux. Milton and Hattie Kutz Home, Inc., 1985-87; bd. dirs. Jewish Fedn. Del., 1983-89, 91-92, 94—, mem. exec. com., 1992-93, mem. Jewish Cmty. endowment com., Mid-Atlantic coun. Union Am. Hebrew Congregations, 1981—, vice chair biennial program com., 1990-92, chair 1992-94, bd. dirs., 1994—, v.p. 1992—, bd. trustees, 1994—, mem. com. on Jewish family, mem. commn. on religious living, mem. outreach commn. exec. com., mem. com. on older adults; mem. Women of Reform Judaism, Fedn. Temple Sisterhoods, 1975—, v.p. 1987-89, 89-91, 91-93, mem. at large bd. dirs., 1993—; pres. Beth Emeth Sisterhood, 1968-70; mem. jr. bd. Med. Ctr. Del., Inc.; apptd. commn adult entertainment establishments, State of Del., 1993—; mem. N.Am. bd. World Union Progressive Judaism; chair Women for Carper com. for Gov. State of Del. Recipient Community Builder award NCCJ, 1985, Keva cert. Ctrl. Conf. Am. Rabbis and NAFE. Mem. Am. Dental Hygienist Assn., Del. Dental Hygiene Assn., Aux. of ADA, Nat. Coun. Jewish Women, Orgn. for Rehab. and Tng., Temple U. Dental Hygiene Alumni Assn., B'nai B'rith, Hadassah. Jewish. Home: 3331 Silverside Rd Wilmington DE 19810-3306

WADDELL, JONI LOUISE, financial consultant; b. Columbus, Wis., Jan. 6, 1957; d. James Edward and Shirley Ann (Robertson) Kohl; m. Jay L. Waddell, Aug. 6, 1977; children: Zachary Alexander, Alexandra Lauren. BBA, U. Wis., Madison, 1983, MBA, 1985. Cert. fund specialist. Acctg. mgr. Clk. of Cts., Mauston, Wis., 1977-81; mktg. svcs. asst. Foremost Guaranty Corp., Madison, 1984; mktg. lectr. City of London Poly., London, 1985-86; med. mktg. cons. British Oxygen Corp., Windlesham, Eng., 1985-87; project mgr., mktg. cons. Rocky Mountain Trade Adjustment Assistance Ctr., Boulder, Colo., 1988-89; clin. sales specialist Fujisawa Pharm. Co., Deerfield, Ill., 1989-91; fin. planner Fin. Planning and Mgmt., Inc., Boulder, 1992—; registered rep. Fin. Network Investment Corp., Torrance, Calif., 1992—. Vol. Boulder Valley Sch. Dist., 1991-93, Am. Cancer Soc., Boulder, 1990-93. Mem. AAUW, Internat. Assn. for Fin. Planners, Inst. of Cert. Fin. Planners, Inst. of Cert. Fund Specialists, Bould C. of C. Home: 1979 Joslyn Ct Boulder CO 80304-1952 Office: Fin Planning and Mgmt 2995 Center Green Ct S Ste A Boulder CO 80301-5421

WADDINGTON, BETTE HOPE (ELIZABETH CROWDER), violinist, educator; b. San Francisco, July 27, 1921; d. John and Marguerite (Crowder) Waddington; BA in Music, U. Calif. at Berkeley, 1945, postgrad.; postgrad. (scholarship) Juilliard Sch. Music, 1950, San Jose State Coll., 1955; MA in Music and Art, San Francisco U., 1953; violin student of Joseph Fuchs, Melvin Ritter, Frank Gittelson, Felix Khuner, Daniel Bonsack, D.C. Dounis, Naoum Blinder, Eddy Brown. Violinist Erie (Pa.) Symphony, 1950-51, Dallas Symphony, 1957-58, St. Louis Symphony, 1958—. Cert. gen. elem. and secondary tchr., Calif.; life cert. music and art for jr. coll.; cert. in librarianship from elem. sch. to jr. coll., Calif. Toured alone and with St. Louis Symphony U.S., Can., Middle East, Japan, China, England, Korea, Europe, Africa; concert master Peninsula Symphony, Redwood City and San Mateo, Calif., Grove Music Soc., N.Y.C.; violinist St. Louis Symphony, 1958—; numerous recordings St. Louis Symphony, 1958—. Mem. Am. String Tchrs. Assn., Am. Musicians Union (St. Louis and San Francisco chpts. life), U. Calif. Alumnae Assn. (Berkeley, life), San Francisco State U. Alumni Assn. (life), Am. String Tchrs. Assn., San Jose State U. Alumni Assn. (life), Sierra Club (life), Alpha Beta Alpha. Avocations: travel, art and archeology history, drawing, painting. Office: St Louis Symphony Orch c/o Powell Symphony Hall 718 Grand Blvd Saint Louis MO 63103

WADE, BARBARA ANN, accountant; b. Addis Abbaba, Ethiopia, Sept. 13, 1963; came to U.S., 1969; d. Robert Norval and Mary Maxine (Legg) W. B in Acctg., San Diego State U., 1986; AS in Computer Sci., Mesa Coll., 1992. Acct. Allartic Fin. Svc., Calsbad, Calif., 1986-87, acctg. supr., 1987-89; acct. Sanyo Mfg. Corp., San Diego, 1989-90, acctg. supr., 1990-91, asst. acctg. mgr., 1991-93, acctg. mgr., 1993—. Named Teen Vol. of Yr. San Diego Health Care Assn., 1981. Mem. Inst. of Mgmt. Accts., Inst. of Internal Auditors (v.p. 1985-86), Aspen Condo Assn. (v.p. 1989—). Baptist. Home: 5885 El Cajon Blvd Apt 306 San Diego CA 92115-3758 Office: Sanyo Mfg Corp PO Box 439056 San Ysidro CA 92143-9056

WADE, MARGARET GASTON, real estate property manager, educator; b. Shreveport, La., Feb. 26, 1948; d. Leroy Evans and Helena (DeWitt) Gaston; m. William Burgess Wade, May 24, 1969; children: Helena Elizabeth, Catherine Frances. BA, Stephen F. Austin State U., 1969; MS, Tex. Tech U., 1971. Cert. tchr., Tex. Tchr. Redland (Tex.) Sch. Dist., 1969-70, Lubbock (Tex.) Ind. Sch. Dist., 1971-73, San Antonio Coll., 1974-75, Midland (Tex.) Coll., 1975-78; owner, mgr. real estate investments BHM Enterprises, Midland, 1977—; tchr. Odessa Coll., Midland Coll., 1989-90, Midland Coll., 1989—; tchr. Hillander Sch., Midland, 1980-81. Troop leader Girl Scouts U.S., Midland, 1983-89; bd. dirs. Planned Parenthood, Midland, 1980-83; chmn. teen ct. Midland Jr. League, 1985-87, bd. dirs., 1987-88. Mem. Chi Omega Alumnus Assn. (pres. Midland chpt. 1978-79). Republican. Methodist. Club: Midland Lawyer's Wives (corr. sec. 1986-87). Home and Office: 1000 Sinclair Ave Midland TX 79705-8747

WADEMAN, PATSY ANN, psychiatric, geriatrics nurse; b. Atlantic, Iowa, Nov. 20, 1943; d. Willie Hollesen and Annie Mae (Lewis) Hollesen Bennet; m. Fredrick N. Wademan, Sept. 11, 1966; children: Stephen, Linnea, Bethany. BGS, Mercy Hosp., Council Bluffs, Iowa, 1966; BS in Gerontology, U. Nebr., Omaha. Cert. psychiat. mental health nurse, gerontol. nurse. Rsch. nurse intern I U. Nebr. Med. Ctr., Omaha; nurse Nebraska City (Nebr.) Pub. Schs., 1966-68, St. Mary's Hosp., Nebraska City, 1973-74, 76-78; staff nurse Duffs Friendship Villa Nursing Home, Nebraska City, 1986-88; dir. nursing Nebraska City Manor, 1988-89; staff nurse Med. Ctr. U. Nebr. Med. Ctr., Omaha, 1989-95; health coord. Head Start, Tecumseh, Nebr., 1984-86; rsch. nurse intern I U. Nebr. Med. Ctr., Omaha, 1995—; instr. Southeast C.C., Lincoln, Nebr., 1976-84; mem. Nat. Coun. on Aging. Mem. Am. Psychiat. Nurses Assn., Am. Gerontol. Nurses Assn., Nebr. Gerontol. Nurses Assn., Golden Key Nat. Honor Soc.

WADLEY, SUSAN SNOW, anthropologist; b. Baltimore, Nov. 18, 1943; d. Chester Page and Ellen Snow (Foster) W.; m. Bruce Woods Derr, Dec. 28, 1971 (div. July 1989); children: Shona Snow, Laura Woods; m. Richard Olanoff, July 4, 1992. BA, Carleton Coll., Northfield, 1965; MA, U. Chgo., 1967, PhD, 1973. Instr. Syracuse U., 1970-73, asst. prof., 1973-76; dir. Fgn. and Comparative Studies Program, Syracuse, 1978-83; prof. Syracuse U., 1982; dir. So. Asia Ctr. Syracuse U., 1985—; chair anthropology dept. Syracuse U., 1990-95; trustee Am. Inst. Indian Studies, Chgo., 1984—, exec. com., 1991-94; mem. joint com. South Asia Social Sci. Rsch. Coun., 1982-89. Author: Shakti: Power in the Conceptual Structure of Karimpur Women, 1975, Women in India: Two Perspectives, 1978, revised, 1989, 94; editor: Powers of Tamil Women, 1980, Oral Epics in India, 1989, Struggling with Destiny in Karimpur, 1925-84, 1994. Pres. Edward Smith Parent Tchr. Orgn., Syracuse, 1988-89. Grantee Doctoral Diss. Research grant Nat. Sci. Found., Wash., 1967-69, Faculty Research grant U.S. Dept. Edn., 1983-84, Smithsonian Institute Research grant, 1983-84, Faculty Research grant Am. Inst. Indian Studies, 1989; Recipient Marc Perry Galler Prize for best doctoral dissertation in social scis. U. Chgo., 1974. Mem. Am. Anthropological Soc., Am. Folklore Soc., Soc. for Ethnomusicology, Assn. for Asian Studies. Home: 302 Carlton Dr Syracuse NY 13214-1906 Office: Syracuse U Maxwell Sch Syracuse NY 13244

WADLOW, JOAN KRUEGER, university chancellor; b. LeMars, Iowa, Aug. 21, 1932; d. R. John and Norma I. (IhLe) Krueger; m. Richard R. Wadlow, July 27, 1958; children: Dawn, Kit. B.A., U. Nebr., Lincoln, 1953; M.A. (Seacrest Journalism fellow 1953-54), Fletcher Sch. Law and Diplomacy, 1956; Ph.D. (Rotary fellow 1956-57), U. Nebr., Lincoln, 1963; cert., Grad. Inst. Internat. Studies, Geneva, 1957. Mem. faculty U. Nebr., Lincoln, 1966-79; prof. polit. scis. U. Nebr., 1964-79, assoc. dean Coll. Arts and Scis., 1972-79; prof. polit. scis., dean Coll. Arts and Scis., U. Wyo., Laramie, 1979-84, v.p. acad. affairs, 1984-86; prof. polit. sci., provost U. Okla., Norman, 1986-91; chancellor U. Alaska, Fairbanks, 1991—; cons. on fed. grants; bd. dirs. Key Bank Alaska; mem. Commn. Colls. N.W. Assn. Author articles in field. Bd. dirs. Nat. Merit Scholarship Corp., Lincoln United Way, 1976-77, Bryan Hosp., Lincoln, 1978-79, Washington Ctr., 1986—, Key Bank of Alaska; v.p., exec. commr. North Cen. Assn., pres., 1991; pres. adv. bd. Lincoln YWCA, 1970-71; mem. def. adv. com. Women in the Svcs., 1987-89; mem. community adv. bd. Alaska Airlines. Recipient Mortar Board Teaching award, 1976, Disting. Teaching award U. Nebr., Lincoln, 1979; fellow Conf. Coop. Man, Lund, Sweden, 1956. Mem. Internat. Studies Assn. (co-editor Internat. Studies Notes 1978-91), Nat. Assn. State Univs. and Land-Grant Colls. (exec. com. coun. acad. affairs 1989-91), Western Assn. Africanists (pres. 1980-82), Assn. Western Univs. (pres.-elect 1993—), Coun. Colls. Arts and Scis. (pres. 1983-84), Greater Fairbanks C. of

C., Gamma Phi Beta. Republican. Congregationalist. Home and Office: PO Box 900147 Fairbanks AK 99775*

WADSWORTH, BEVERLY JANE, nursing administrator; b. Flemington, Pa., Dec. 25, 1932; d. Charles B. and Esther L. (Bartley) Miller; m. Earl C. Wadsworth, June 8, 1957; children: Kerry Lee, Jay C. Diploma, Lock Haven Hosp. Sch. Nursing, 1953; cert. anesthetist, Williamsport Hosp. Sch., 1955. Cert. nurse adminstr., nurse practitioner. Nurse anesthetist Newton-Wellsley Hosp., Newton-Lower Falls, Mass., 1959-62; dir. nursing Justice Resource Inst., Framingham, Mass., 1982-84; supr. nurses Colonial House, Framingham, 1984-85. Troop leader Girl Scouts U.S., 1968-73. Recipient Am. Legion award, Awards in Nursing Proficiency, Jaycee awards. Mem. Am. Assn. Nurse Adminstrs., Mass. Assn. Nurse Practitioners, Blazers' Band.

WADSWORTH, JACQUELINE DORÈT, private investor, interior designer; b. San Diego, June 15, 1928; d. Benjamin H. Dilley and Georgia E. (Elliott) Dilley Waters; m. Charles Desmond Wadsworth Jr., June 16, 1954 (dec. 1963); 1 child, Georgia Duncan Wadsworth Barber. BS, U. Oreg., 1946-50; MA, San Diego State U., 1950-52. Cert. tchr. Calif., Oreg. Dir. Jr. Red Cross, San Diego County chpt. ARC, 1952-59; asst. dir. leadership ctrs. for 8 western states ARC, Calif., 1954-59; pvt. investor, comml. real estate and property devel., 1974—; interior designer J. Wadsworth Interiors, La Jolla, Calif., 1990-93. Vol. chairperson nat. conv. ARC, San Diego, 1966; fund raiser San Diego Symphony Orch. Orgn., 1974-83; friends mem., vol. San Diego Mus. Art, 1958—; mem. Scripps Found. for Medicine and Sci., 1990—; life mem., chairperson fundraisers and hosp. programs Mercy Hosp. Aux., 1965—; life mem., chairperson, bd. dirs. Social Svc. Aux., 1968—. Recipient Svc. awards Mercy Hosp. Aux., 1967, 70. Mem. Caridad Internat. Globe Gliders (activity chairperson 1966-85). Republican.

WAELDE, GAIL PATRICIA, recreation aid, music educator; b. Teaneck, N.J., July 14, 1953; d. Clinton Brewster and Eileen Florence (Kennedy) W. BA in Music Edn., Glassboro State Coll., 1976. Cert. educator, N.J. Music dir. Music Found. for Visually Handicapped, Ridgewood, N.J., 1982-87, v.p., 1990—; receptionist U.S. Customs, N.Y.C., 1979-81; recreation aid Bergen County Adult Day Care Ctr., Paramus, N.J., 1978-79, 81—. Author: (pamphlet) Word Pictures, (novella) In His Time; composer of 26 songs. Mem. Christian Overcomers. Democrat. Home: 474 Ottawa Ave Apt D39 Hasbrouck Heights NJ 07604-2648

WAELSCH, SALOME GLUECKSOHN, geneticist, educator; b. Danzig, Germany, Oct. 6, 1907; came to U.S., 1933, naturalized, 1938; d. Ilya and Nadia Gluecksohn; m. Heinrich B. Waelsch, Jan. 8, 1943; children: Naomi Barbara, Peter Benedict. Student, U. Konigsberg, Germany, U. Berlin, 1927-28; PhD, U. Freiburg, Germany, 1932; D of Sci. (hon.), Columbia U., 1995. Rsch. assoc. in genetics Columbia U., 1936-55; assoc. prof. anatomy Albert Einstein Coll. Medicine, 1955-58, prof., 1958-63, prof. molecular genetics, 1963—, chmn. dept. genetics, 1963-76; mem. study sects. NIH. Contbr. numerous articles on devel. genetics. Recipient Nat. Medal of Sci., Pres. Clinton, 1993. Fellow AAAS, Am. Acad. Arts and Scis.; mem. NAS, N.Y. Acad. Scis. (hon. life), Am. Soc. Zoologists, Am. Assn. Anatomists, Genetics Soc., Soc. Devel. Biology, Am. Soc. Naturalists, Am. Soc. Human Genetics, Sigma Xi. Office: Albert Einstein Coll Med Dept Molecular Genetics 1300 Morris Park Ave Bronx NY 10461-1975

WAGAMAN, JANICE HAKES, clinical psychologist; b. South Williamsport, Pa., Sept. 17, 1950; d. Foster Emerson and Dorothy Frances (Bender) Hakes; m. Frederick Charles Wagaman Jr., Mar. 17, 1990. BA, Lycoming Coll., 1972; MA, SUNY, Plattsburg, 1986. Lic. psychologist, Pa. Pvt. music tchr. Williamsport, Pa., 1972-84; journalist Grit Pub. Co., Williamsport, 1976-79; mental health unit program dir. Lancaster (Pa.) Gen. Hosp., 1986-88; therapist Poloni and Assocs., York, Pa., 1989-92; staff psychologist Ephrata (Pa.) Cmty. Hosp., 1989—; clin. psychologist pvt. practice Ephrata-Akron, Pa., 1992—. Editor: Chinese Autobiographies, 1985. Mem. APA, Pa. Psychol. Assn., Lancaster-Lebanon Psychol. Assn. Office: 18F S 7th St Akron PA 17501

WAGENHOFFER, MARY CUSHING, medical/surgical nurse, nursing educator; b. Bklyn., Jan. 21, 1956; d. James Joseph and Irene Kathleen (Hennessey) Cushing; m. John Joseph Wagenhoffer, Aug. 7, 1982; children: John J. Jr., Kelly M. BSN, Rutgers U., 1979, MS, 1985. Cert. med./surg. nurse. Staff med.-surg., critical care nurse Rahway (N.J.) Hosp., 1979-84; instr. lic. practical nurse program Middlesex County Vocat.-Tech. Sch., East Brunswick, N.J., 1985-86; patient care coord. med.-surg. unit Raritan Bay Med. Ctr., Perth Amboy, N.J., 1988—. Mem. N.J. Soc. Healthcare Edn. and Tng., Rutgers Alumni Assn. Roman Catholic. Home: 875 Pioneer Dr Brick NJ 08724-1058 Office: Raritan Bay Med Ctr 530 New Brunswick Ave Perth Amboy NJ 08861-3654

WAGENIUS, JEAN, state representative; b. 1941; m. Dwight Wagenius; children: Peter, Stuart. BA, George Washington U., 1963; JD, William Mitchell Coll., 1983. State rep. State of Minn., St. Paul, 1987—. Named Environmentalist of Yr., Sierra Club (North Star chpt.), 1992. Office: State of Minn Minn State House Rm 439 Saint Paul MN 55155

WAGER, DEBORAH MILLER, researcher, consultant; b. Phila., Sept. 5, 1938; d. Albert S. and Pauline (Goldberg) Miller; m. Robert J. Wager, July 3, 1966; 1 child, James M. BA, Skidmore Coll., 1960; MAT, Columbia U., 1963. Editor Toy Quality and Safety Report, Washington, 1972-88; cons. Wager Rsch., Washington, 1989—; devel. rschr. Sidwell Friends Sch., Washington, 1988-89, 92-93; trustee Sheridan Sch., Washington, 1978-84. Author: Good Toys, 1986. Mem. Am. Prospect Rsch. Assn. Office: Wager Rsch Consulting 4545 29 St NW Washington DC 20008

WAGER, PAULA JEAN, artist; b. Lansing, Mich., Dec. 19, 1929; d. Mervin Elihu and Cora Della (Raymer) Fowler; m. William Douglas Wager, May 4, 1952; children: Pamela Ann, Scott Alan. Student, Mich. State U., 1949-52. Music tchr. Toledo, Ohio, 1968-72, Union Lake, Mich., 1972-76; tchr. art, artist Paula Wager's Art Studio, Commerce Twp., Mich., 1984—; hostess Artistic Touch with Paula, Cable Comcast channel 44, Waterford, Mich., TCI West Oakland, Walled Lake, Mich., Channel 10. Exhbns. include Villlage Art Supplies, 1982-88, Pontiac Oakland Soc. Artists, 1983—, St. Patrick Ch., Commerce Twp., Mich., 1983, Pontiac Galleria, 1983, Oakland C.C., Commerce Twp., 1985, Red Piano Gallery, Hilton Head, S.C., 1985-89, Mich. State U., East Lansing, 1986, Silver Pencil Gallery, Pontiac, 1987-89, Wooden Sleight, Vestaburg, Mich., 1988-93, Art Pad, Keego Harbor, Mich., 1990-93, Local Color Gallery, Union Pier, Mich., 1992-94, others; represented in pvt. collections. Recipient Outstanding Achievement award in instructional programming Comcast Cable TV, Waterford, 1992, 1st place, Waterford Friends of the Arts Art Show, 1988, Pontiac Oakland Soc. Artists Cmty. Rm., 1990; Waterford Cable Commn. grantee, 1991, 93, Charter Twp. of Waterford grantee, 1991-94. Mem. Pontiac Oakland Soc. Artists, Waterford Friends of the Arts, Mich. Watercolor Soc., Birmingham Bloomfield Art Assn., Colored Pencil Soc. Am. Home: 3316 Greenlawn Ave Commerce Township MI 48382

WAGES, VIRGINIA ANNE SOBOL, pediatrics nurse; b. Memphis, June 20, 1962; d. John Andrew and Jean Duffy (Gordon) Sobol; m. David Paul Wages, June 2, 1986; children: Ashley Anne, Julie Nichole, David Paul, Sarah Catherine. Student, Memphis State U., 1980-82; BSN, U. Tenn., 1985. RN, Tenn.; cert. pediatric nurse. Grad. nurse intern LeBonheur Children's Med. Ctr., Memphis, 1985, med.-surg. pediatric nurse, 1985—, quality assurance coun., 1988—, recruitment retention com., 1990-92, chair unit clin. practice coun., 1992. Mem. Memphis Maternal Welfare League, 1992—, Memphis Mus. System, 1987—, Memphis Zool. Soc., 1987—, Lactation Edn. and Promotion, Memphis, 1992; mem. St. Luke's Meth. Ch., United Meth. Women's Group. Named one of Top 100 Nurses in Memphis, Celebrate Nursing, 1991. Mem. Alpha Lambda Delta, Phi Eta Sigma, Gamma Beta Phi, Alpha Delta Phi (Gamma Eta chpt.). Methodist. Home: 4558 Dearing Rd E Memphis TN 38117 Office: LeBonheur Childrens Med Ctr 848 Adams Memphis TN 38104

WAGGENER, SUSAN LEE, lawyer; b. Riverside, Calif., Oct. 21, 1951; d. Lee Richard and Alice Lillian (Fritch) W.; m. Steven Carl McCracken, July 29, 1979; children: Casey James McCracken, Scott Kevin McCracken. BA magna cum laude, U. So. Calif., 1973; JD magna cum laude, U. San Diego, 1976. Bar: Calif. 1977, Hawaii 1977. Law clk. to hon. Samuel P. King, Jr. U.S. Dist. Ct. Hawaii, Honolulu, 1976-77; assoc. Gibson, Dunn & Crutcher, Newport Beach, Calif., 1978-86; ptnr. Gibson, Dunn & Crutcher, Newport Beach, 1986—. Exec. editor U. San Diego Law Rev., 1975-76. V.p. 552 Club Hoag Hosp., Newport Beach, 1982-85. Mem. ABA, Orange County Bar Assn. Office: Gibson Dunn & Crutcher Jamboree Ctr 4 Park Plz Irvine CA 92714-8560

WAGGETT, JEAN MCMONIGLE, lawyer, corporate; b. Kansas City, Mo., May 20, 1941; d. Vivian Whitley and Ruth McMonigle. BS, U. Mo., 1963; JD, U. Mich., 1975. Bar: Conn. 1977. Atty. Health, Edn. and Welfare, Washington, 1975-77; counsel, v.p. Aetna Life & Casualty, Hartford, Conn., 1977—; gen. counsel, sr. v.p. Aetna Internat., Inc., Hartford, Conn., 1987-93, v.p. and corp. sec., 1993—. Trustee McCauley Home, West Hartford, Conn., 1990-92. Mem. ABA, Internat. Bar Assn., Am. Corp. Counsel Assn. Home: 14 Ledyard Rd West Hartford CT 06117-1708 Office: Aetna Life & Casualty 151 Farmington Ave Hartford CT 06156-0002

WAGGONER, SUSAN MARIE, electronics engineer; b. East Chicago, Ind., Sept. 1, 1952; d. Joseph John and Elizabeth (Monyok) Vasilak; m. Steven Richard Waggoner, July 31, 1976; children: Kenneth David, Michael Christopher. AS, Ind. U., 1975, BA in Journalism, 1976, BS in Physics, 1982, M in Pub. Affairs, 1991. Engring. technician Naval Surface Warfare Ctr., Crane, Ind., 1978-82, electronics engr. test and measurement equipment, 1982-91, electronics engr. batteries, 1991—. Mem. Am. Soc. Naval Engrs., Fed. Mgrs. Assn., Federally Employed Women, Am. Rose Soc., Am. Hort. Soc., Mensa, Indpls. Rose Soc., Theatre Circle of Ind. U., Sigma Pi Sigma. Home: RR 5 Box 387 Loogootee IN 47553-9337 Office: Naval Surface Warfare Ctr 300 Hwy 361 Crane IN 47522-5001

WAGLE, SUSAN, state legislator, small business owner; b. Allentown, Pa., Sept. 27, 1953; m. John Thomas Wagle, Apr. 3, 1980; children: Julia Marie, Andrea Elizabeth, John Timothy, Paul Thomas. BA in Elem. Edn. cum laude, Wichita State U., 1979, post grad., 1979-82. Tchr. Chisholm Trail Elem., Kans., 1979-80; tchr. emotionally disturbed, special edn. Price Elem., Kans., 1980-82; real estate investor Kans., 1980—; prin. Wichita Bus. Inc., Kans., 1983—; mem. Kansas Ho. Reps., 1990, 92, 94—, speaker pro tem, 1994—. Mem. Am. Legis. Exchange Coun. (Outstanding Legis. of the Yr. 1994), Farm Bur., Nat. Fedn. Ind. Bus., Nat. Restaurant Assn., Wichita Ind. Bus. Assn. Home: 14 N Sandalwood St Wichita KS 67230-6612 Office: Kans Ho of Reps Rm 330 N State Capitol Topeka KS 66612-1504

WAGNER, ANN PRENTICE, art historian; b. Washington, Aug. 17, 1961; d. John Prentice and Polly (Sweet) W. AA in Studio Art, Montgomery Coll., 1982; BA in Art History, George Washington U., 1985; MA in Art History, Boston U., 1987. Mus. asst., docent Phillips Collection, Washington, 1987-89; art historian Nat. Portrait Gallery, Washington, 1989—. Author: Hiram Merrill: Memories of a Wood Engraver, 1995; contbr. articles to profl. publs. Grad. scholar Boston U., 1985-86; grad. alumni fellow Boston U., 1985-86. Mem. Coll. Art Assn., Soc. Am. Wood Engravers, Washington Print Club (bd. dirs. 1993—). Democrat. Office: Nat Portrait Gallery 8th & F St NW # G St NW Washington DC 20560-0010

WAGNER, ANNICE MCBRYDE, judge. BA, Wayne State U., law degree. With Houston and Gardner; gen. counsel Nat. Capital Housing Authority; people's counsel D.C.; assoc. judge Superior Court D.C., 1977-90; assoc. judge D.C. Ct. Appeals, 1990—, now chief judge; mem. teaching team, trial advocacy workshop Harvard U. Office: Dist of Columbia Ct 500 Indiana Ave NW 6th Fl Washington DC 20001*

WAGNER, CHARLENE BROOK, middle school educator, consultant; b. L.A.; d. Edward J. and Eva (Anderson) Brook; m. Gordon Boswell Jr. (div.); children: Gordon, Brook, John. BS, Tex. Christian U., 1952; MEd, Sam Houston U., 1973; postgrad., U. Tex., Austin, 1975, Tex. A&M U., 1977. Sci. educator Spring Branch Ind. Sch. Dist., Houston, 1970—; cons. Scott Foresman Pub. Co., 1982-83; owner Scientific Instructional Systems Co., 1988—. Mem. Houston Grand Opera Guild, 1992, Houston Symphony League, 1992, Mus. Fine Arts, 1991, Mus. of Art of Am. West, Houston, 1989, Women's Christian Home, Houston, 1991; social chmn. Encore, 1988; mem. Magic Cir. Rep. Women's Club. Mem. NEA, NAFE, Nat. U. Women's Assn., Tex. State Tchrs. Assn., Spring Branch Edn. Assn., Internat. Platform Assn., The Wellington Soc. for Arts (Houston chpt.), The Shepherd Soc., Watercolor Arts Soc. Houston, Clan Anderson Soc., Heather and Thistle Soc., Houston Highland Games Assn. Episcopalian. Home: B54 2670 Marilee Ln Houston TX 77057-4264 Office: Spring Oaks Mid Sch 2150 Shadowdale Dr Houston TX 77043-2608

WAGNER, CHRISTINA BREUER, media company executive; b. N.Y.C., Sept. 29, 1954; d. Wesley Allen and Ingrid (Reichhold) W. BA, Princeton U., 1976; MBA, Columbia U., 1983. Asst. mgr. Chemical Bank, Seoul, Korea and N.Y.C., 1977-80; corp. fin. assoc. Morgan Guaranty Trust, N.Y.C., 1983-84; dir. planning Macmillan, Inc., N.Y.C., 1985-88; v.p. fin. sch. div. Macmillan Pub. Co., N.Y.C., 1988-89; v.p. ops. Macmillan, Inc., N.Y.C., 1989-90; CFO Macmillan Pub. Co., N.Y.C., 1990-91; CFO K-III Mags. Inc., N.Y.C., 1991-94, v.p., 1994-95; CEO Stagebill, Inc., N.Y.C., 1994-95; group v.p. K-III Media, N.Y.C., 1995—. Office: K-III Mags Inc 717 Fifth Ave New York NY 10022

WAGNER, CYNTHIA KAYE, business administration educator, consultant; b. Lincoln, Nebr., Jan. 29, 1957; d. Richard and Gloria Jean (Larsen) W. BS in Agronomy with honors, Ohio State U., 1979, MS in Agronomy, 1980; PhD in Bus. Adminstrn., U. Pa., 1986. Rsch. assoc. Physiology Lab., Ohio State U., Columbus, 1977-80; rsch. scientist Battelle Columbus Labs., 1980-82; rsch. asst. Mgmt. and Behavioral Sci. Ctr., Wharton Sch., U. Pa., Phila., 1983-85; cons. UN Devel. Program, N.Y.C., 1985-86; bus. mgr. Pioneer Hi-Bred Internat., Des Moines, 1987-90; asst. prof. bus. adminstrn. U. Pacific, Stockton, Calif., 1990—. Contbr. articles on mgmt. of tech. to profl. jours. Dean's fellow Wharton Sch., U. Pa., 1983-84. Mem. AAAS. Office: U Pacific Sch Bus-Pub Admin 3601 Pacific Cir Stockton CA 95211-0110

WAGNER, DIANE M(ARGARET), theology educator; b. Hancock, Mich., Apr. 22, 1943; d. Benjamin Philip and Eunice Rose (La Mothe) W. BA, Alverno Coll., Milw., 1965; MA, Mundelein Coll., Chgo., 1972; student, Clin. Pastoral Edn., Milw., 1979-80. Cert. advanced standing chaplain, 1982. Tchr. grade 1 St. Peter Sch., Skokie, Ill., 1964-65; tchr. grades 1 and 2 St. Cecelia Sch., Hubbell, Mich., 1965-67; tchr. grades 1, 2, 4-6 St. Joseph Sch., Wilmette, Ill., 1967-71; tchr. grade 5. middle grade coord. St. Mary Sch., Buffalo Grove, Ill., 1971-73; tchr. grade 5 St. Alphonsus Sch., Greendale, Wis., 1973-74; recruiter Sch. Sisters of St. Francis, Milw., 1974-79; chaplain, dir. pastoral care Tau Home Health Care Agy., Milw., 1980-88, dir. vols., 1981-88; chaplain, dir. pastoral care St. Mary's Hill Hosp., Milw., 1988-92; tchr. theology, assoc. chaplain Divine Savior Holy Angels High Sch., Milw., 1993—; mem. Chaplain Adv. Bd., Milw., 1982-88, pres., 1985-88. Author: (tape) College of Chaplains, 1986. Vice pres bd. dirs. Clare Towers, Inc., Milw., 1981-87. Recipient Cert. Appreciation, Clare Towers, Inc., 1987. Mem. Nat. Assn. Cath. Chaplains (sec. regional bd. dirs. 1986-88), Milw. Area Dirs. Pastroal Care Assn. (pres. 1987-88). Democrat. Roman Catholic. Home: 2619 N 39th St Milwaukee WI 53210-2503 Office: Divine Savior Holy Angels High Sch 4257 N 100 St Milwaukee WI 53222

WAGNER, FLORENCE ZELEZNIK, telecommunications executive; b. McKeesport, Pa., Sept. 23, 1926; d. George and Sophia (Petros) Zeleznik; BA magna cum laude, U. Pitts., 1977, MPA, 1981; m. Francis Xavier Wagner, June 18, 1946; children: Deborah Elaine Wagner Franke, Rebecca Susan Wagner Schroettinger, Melissa Catherine Wagner Good, Francis Xavier, Robert Francis. Sec. to pres. Tube City Iron & Metal Co., Glassport, Pa., 1944-50; cons. Raw Materials, Inc., Pitts., 1955; gen. mgr. Carson Compressed Steel Products, Pitts., 1967-69; ptnr. Universal Steel Products, Pitts., 1970-71; gen. mgr. Josh Steel Co., Braddock, Pa., 1971-78; owner Wagner's Candy Box, Mt. Lebanon, Pa., 1979-80; borough sec./treas. Borough of Pennsbury Village, Allegheny County, Pa., 1980-88; ptnr. Tele-Communications of Am., Burgettstown, Pa., 1984-86; trustee Profit-Sharing trust, Pension trust Josh Steel Co., 1986—, Consol, Inc., Upper St. Clair, Pa., 1989—; mem. Foster Parents, Jefferson Twp. Planning Commn., Washington County, Pa. Mem. AAUW, Pitts. Symphony Soc., Pitts. Ballet Theater Guild. Mem. Soc. Pub. Adminstrn. (founder U. Pitts. br.), Acad. Polit. Sci., U.S. Strategic Inst., Southwestern Pa. Sec. Assn., Alpha Sigma Lambda (past treas., sec., pres.). Republican. Roman Catholic. Home: 1611 Upper St Clair Dr Pittsburgh PA 15241

WAGNER, HAZEL ANN (HOLLY WAGNER), marketing executive, consultant; b. Chgo., Dec. 30; d. Hans and Hildegard (Ross) Freeman; m. David M. Marinello, June 1, 1984; children: Joy Bohl, Audrey Wancket, Keith. BA, Northwestern U., 1965, MA, 1968, PhD, 1975; MBA, DePaul U., 1983. Dir. Criterion reference testing Chgo. Bd. Edn., 1974-77; sales professional Gen. Electric Info. Sys., Chgo., 1977-78; sales and mktg. dir. Digital Equipment Corp., Chgo. and Marlboro, Mass., 1978-92; pres. B9D, Inc., Barrington, Ill., 1992-94; dir. worldwide svcs. mktg. Oracle Corp., Barrington, 1994—; adj. assoc. prof. Grad. Sch. Bus. DePaul U., Chgo., 1993—, Kellogg Grad. Sch. Mgmt. U. Ill., Evanston, 1993—. Counselor active corps execs. Svc. Corps Ret. Execs., Chgo., 1993-94. Mem. Nat. Assn. Women Bus. Owners (mem. com.). Office: 784 Sanday Ln Barrington IL 60010

WAGNER, HAZEL EDITH, medical/surgical and neurological nurse; b. San Jose, Calif., Aug. 26, 1931; d. LaRena Beall; m. Raymond Wagner, May 20, 1951; children: Randel Ray, Wes Lee. BSN, Wash. State U., 1984, M of Nursing, 1992. Staff nurse Deaconess Rehab. Inst. (formerly St. Luke's Meml. Hosp.), Spokane, Wash., 1985-87, charge nurse, 1987-89, adminstrv. supr., 1989-94, also coord. quality assurance, 1992-93; clin. mgr. St. Joseph Care Ctr., 1994—; mgr. health care Waterford on South Hill, 1992-94, clin. instr. Intercollegiate Ctr. for Nursing Edn., 1994. Mem. Wash. League Nursing (sec.), Assn. Rehab. Nurses, Sigma Theta Tau.

WAGNER, JEANETTE SARKISIAN, cosmetics company executive; m. Paul A. Wagner. BS cum laude, Northwestern U.; MBA, Harvard U. Former editor-in-chief internat. editions, dir. new ventures Hearst Corp.; former editor Saturday Evening Post; with Estee Lauder Cos., 1975—, from v.p., dir. mktg. internat. divsn. to sr. v.p. Estee Lauder and Prescriptives Internat., past corp. sr. v.p., now pres. Estee Lauder Internat.; chmn. bd. dirs. Fragrance Found.; mem. planning bd. Am. Women's Econ. Devel. Corp.; bd. dirs., mem. audit and compensation coms. Am. Greetings.; bd. dirs., audit and nominating coms. Stride Rite Corp.; v.p. bd. dirs. Bus. Coun. for Econ. Understanding;. Mem. Fashion Group Internat. (past pres. and chmn.), Cosmetic Exec. Women, Econ. Club, Harvard Bus. Sch. Club Greater N.Y. (past v.p., honor roll), Harvard Bus. Sch. Network Women Alumni, Womens Forum N.Y. (bd. dirs., exec. com.), Northwestern Coun. 100, Com. 200 (bd. dirs., chair long range planning), Asia Soc., China Inst., Japan Soc., Korean Soc. Office: Estee Lauder Cos 767 Fifth Ave New York NY 10153*

WAGNER, JUDITH BUCK, investment firm executive; b. Altoona, Pa. Sept. 25, 1943; d. Harry Bud and Mary Elizabeth (Rhodes) B.; m. Joseph E. Wagner, Mar. 15, 1980; 1 child, Elizabeth. BA in History, U. Wash., 1965; grad. N.Y. Inst. Fin., 1968. Registered Am. Stock Exchange; registered N.Y. Stock Exchange; registered investment advisor. Security analyst Morgan, Olmstead, Kennedy & Gardner, L.A., 1968-71; security analyst Boettcher & Co., Denver, 1972-75; pres. Wagner Investment Mgmt., 1975—; chmn., bd. dirs. The Women's Bank, N.A., Denver, 1977-94, organizational group pres., 1975-77; chmn. Equitable Bankshares Colo., Inc., Denver, 1980-94; bd. dirs. Equitable Bank of Littleton, 1983-88, pres., 1985; bd. dirs. Colo. Growth Capital, 1979-82; lectr. Denver U., Metro State, 1975-80. Author: Woman and Money series Colo. Woman Mag., 1976; moderator 'Catch 2' Sta. KWGN-TV, 1978-79. Pres. Big Sisters Colo., Denver, 1977-82, bd. dirs., 1973-83; bd. fellows U. Denver, 1985—; bd. dirs. Red Cross, 1980, Assn. Children's Hosp., 1985, Colo. Health Facilities Authority, 1978-84, Jr. League Community Adv. Com., 1979-92, Brother's Redevel., Inc., 1979-80; mem. Hist. Paramount Found., 1984, Denver Pub. Sch. Career Edn. Project, 1972; mem. investment com. YWCA, 1976-88; mem. adv. com. Girl Scouts U.S.; mem. agy. rels. com. Mile High United Way, 1978-81, chmn. United Way Venture Grant com., 1980-81; fin. chmn. Schoettler for State Treas., 1986; bd. dirs. Downtown Denver Inc., 1988—; bd. dirs., v.p., treas. The Women's Found. Colo., 1987-91; treas., trustee, v.p., Graland Country Day Sch., 1990—, pres. 1994; trustee Denver Rotary Found., 1990—. Recipient Making It award Cosmopolitan Mag., 1977, Women on the Go award, Savvy mag., 1983, Minouri Yasoui award, 1986, Salute Spl. Honoree award, Big Sisters, 1987; named one of the Outstanding Young Women in Am., 1979; recipient Woman Who Makes A Difference award Internat. Women's Forum, 1987. Fellow Assn. Investment Mgmt. and Rsch.; mem. Women's Forum of Colo. (pres. 1979), Women's Found. Colo., Inc. (bd. dirs. 1986-91), Denver Soc. Security Analysts (bd. dirs. 1976-83, v.p. 1980-81, pres. 1981-82), Colo. Investment Advisors Assn., Rotary (treas. Denver chpt. found., pres. 1993-94), Leadership Denver (Outstanding Alumna award 1987), Pi Beta Phi (pres. U. Wash. chpt. 1964-65). Office: Wagner Investment Mgmt Inc 410 17th St Ste 840 Denver CO 80202-4418

WAGNER, MARY ANN, human resources executive; b. St. Louis, May 24, 1947; d. John Gerard and Carmela Lucy (Cozza) Blethroad; 1 child, John Patrick. BA, Webster U., St. Louis, 1979, MA, 1982. Tchr. Our Lady of Fatima, St. Louis, Wetterau, St. Louis; personnel mgr. Venture, St. Louis, 1979-81; customer svc. coord. Venture, O'Fallon, Mo., 1981-84, personnel mgr., 1984-86; regional personnel mgr., 1986-88, dir. tng. and devel., 1988-92; adj. prof. Webster U., 1990—, divisional v.p. tng. and devel., 1992—. Chmn. United Way, O'Fallon, 1985, bd. dirs. Mem. AAIM Mgmt. Assn., Am. Soc. Tng. and Devel., Am. Mgmt. Assn. Roman Catholic. Home: 15525 Debridge Way Florissant MO 63034-3456

WAGNER, MARY KATHRYN, sociology educator, former state legislator; b. Madison, S.D., June 19, 1932; d. Irving Macaulay and Mary Browning (Wines) Mumford; m. Robert Todd Wagner, June 23, 1954; children: Christopher John, Andrea Browning. BA, U. S.D., 1954; MEd, S.D. State U., 1974, PhD, 1978. Sec. R.A. Burleigh & Assocs., Evanston, Ill., 1954-57; dir. resource ctr. Watertown (S.D.) Sr. High Sch., 1969-71, Brookings (S.D.) High Sch., 1971-74; asst. dir. S.D. Com. on the Humanities, Brookings, 1976-90; asst. prof. rural sociology S.D. State U., 1990—; mem. S.D. Ho. of Reps., 1981-88, S.D. Senate, 1988-92. Mem., pres. Brookings Sch. Bd., 1975-81; chair fund dr. Brookings United Way, 1985; bd. dirs. Brookings Chamber music Soc., 1981—, Advance and Career Learning Ctr. Named Woman of Yr., Bus. and Profl. Women, 1981, Legislator Conservationist of Yr., Nat. and S.D. Wildlife Fedn., 1988. Mem. Population Assn. Am., Midwest Sociol. Soc., Rural Sociol. Soc., Brookings C. of C. (mem. indsl. devel. com. 1988—), PEO, Rotary. Republican. Episcopalian. Home: 929 Harvey Dunn St Brookings SD 57006-1347

WAGNER, MARY MARGARET, library and information science educator; b. Mpls., Feb. 4, 1946; d. Harvey F.J. and Yvonne M. (Brettner) W.; m. William Moore, June 16, 1988; children: Lebohang Y.C., Nora M. BA, Coll. St. Catherine, St. Paul, 1969; MLS, U. Wash., 1973. Asst. libr. St. Margarets Acad., Mpls., 1969-70; libr. Derham Hall High Sch., St. Paul, 1970-71; youth worker The Bridge for Runaways, Mpls., 1971-72; libr. Guthrie Theater Reference and Rsch. Libr., Mpls., 1973-75; asst. br. libr. St. Paul Pub. Libr., 1975; assoc. prof. dept. info. mgmt. Coll. St. Catherine, St. Paul, 1975—; del. Minn. Gov.'s Pre-White House Conf. on Librs. and Info. Svcs., 1990; mem. Minn. Pre-White House Conf. Program Com., 1989-90, Continuing Libr. Info. and Media Edn. com. Minn. Dept. Edn., Libr. Devel. and Svcs., 1980-83, 87-94; mem. cmty. faculty Met. State U., St. Paul, 1980—; mem. core revision com. Coll. St. Catherine, 1992-93, faculty budget adv. com., 1992—, faculty pers. com., 1989-92. Contbr. articles to profl. jours. Bd. dirs. Christian Sharing Fund, 1976-80, chair, 1977-78. Grantee: U.S. Embassy, Maseru, Lesotho, Africa, Brit. Consulate, Maseru, various founds.; Upper Midwest Assn. for Intercultural Edn. travel grantee Assoc. Colls. Twin Cities. Mem ALA (libr. book fellows program 1990-91), Am. Soc. Info. Sci., Am. Soc. Indexers, Spl. Libr. Assn., Minn. Libr. Assn. (pres. 1981-82, chair continuing edn. com. 1987-90, steering com. Readers Adv. Roundtable, 1989-91), Minn. Ednl. Media Orgn., Twin Cities Women in Computing. Office: Coll St Catherine Dept Info Mgmt 2004 Randolph Saint Paul MN 55105

WAGNER, MURIEL GINSBERG, nutrition therapist; b. N.Y.C., Apr. 6, 1926; d. Irving A. and Anna Ginsberg; divorced; 1 child, Emily Lucinda Faith. BA, Wayne State U., 1948, MS, 1951; PhD, U. Mich., 1982. Registered dietitian, Mich. Nutritionist Merrill-Palmer Inst., Detroit, 19151-74; pvt. practice nutritional therapy Southfield, Mich., 1976—; cons. select com. on nutrition U.S. Senate, 1973-74, Ford Motor Co., Dearborn, Mich., 1975-78, Detroit Dept. Consumer Affairs, 1979—; adj. faculty mem. Wayne State U., Detroit, 1970-80, U. Mich., Dearborn, 1974-79. Author: (cookbook) Tun...ahhh, 1993; contbr. articles to profl. publs. Vol. Am. Heart Assn. of Mich., Southfield, bd. dirs., apptd. to various local and nat. govtl. groups. Recipient Outstanding Cmty. Svc. award Am. Heart Assn., 1990. Mem. Am. Dietetic Assn. (organizer Dial-A-Dietitian), Soc. Nutrition Edn. Office: 24901 Northwestern Ste 613C Southfield MI 48075

WAGNER, NANCY ANN, secondary education educator; b. Sheboygan, Wis., Feb. 28, 1950; d. Robert Walter and Eva Fern (Longwell) W. BS, Wheaton Coll., 1972. RN; life cert. tchr., Calif. Nurse Sharp Hosp., San Diego, 1980; tchr., head sci. dept. Christian H.S., El Cajon, Calif., 1972-74, 81—. Leader, chain reaction youth coun. March of Dimes, San Diego, 1992—, chair Salk symposium com., 1993-94. Mem. Nat. Sci. Suprs. Assn., Nat. Sci. Tchrs. Assn., Nat. Assn. Biology Tchrs., Assn. Women in Sci., Calif. Sci. Tchrs. Assn., San Diego Educator's Assn. Republican. Baptist. Office: Christian H S 2100 Greenfield Dr El Cajon CA 92019

WAGNER, PATRICIA H., lawyer; b. Gastonia, N.C., Feb. 1, 1936; d. Luther Boyd and Mildred Ruth (Wheeler) Hamm; married; children: David Marion, Michael Marion, Laura Marion. AB summa cum laude, Wittenberg U., 1958; JD with distinction, Duke U., 1974. Bar: N.C. 1974, Wash. 1984. Asst. univ. counsel Duke U., Durham, N.C., 1974-75, assoc. univ. counsel health affairs, 1977-80; atty. N.C. Meml. Hosp., 1975-77; assoc. N.C. Atty. Gen. Office, 1975-77; prin. Powe, Porter and Alphin, P.A., Durham, 1980-83; assoc. Williams, Kastner & Gibbs, 1984-86, Wickwire, Goldmark & Schorr, 1986-88; spl. counsel Heller, Ehrman, White & McAuliffe, 1988-90, ptnr., 1990—; arbitrator Am. Arbitration Assn., 1978—; arbitrator, pro tem judge King County Superior Ct., 1986—; tchr. in field. Mem. bd. visitors Law Sch. Duke U., 1992—; bd. dirs. Seattle Edn. Ctr., 1990-91, Metroctr. YMCA, 1991-94, Cmty. Psychiat. Clinic, Seattle, 1984-86; bd. dirs., sec.-treas. N.C. Found. Alternative Health Programs, Inc., 1982-84; bd. dirs., sec.-treas. N.C. Ctr. Pub. Policy Rsch., 1976-83, vice chmn., 1977-80; mem. task force on committment law N.C. Dept. Human Resources, 1978; active Def. Rsch. Inst., 1982-84; bd. dirs. Law Fund, 1992—, v.p., 1993—. Fellow Am. Bar Found.; mem. ABA (mem. ho. dels. Seattle-King County Bar Assn. 1991-94, mem. litigation sect.), Am. Soc. Hosp. Attys., Wash. State Bar Assn. (mem. domestic rels. task force 1991-93), Seattle-King Bar Assn. (mem. bd. trustees 1990-93, sec. bd. 1989-90, chair judiciary and cts. com. 1987-89, mem. King County Superior Ct. delay reduction task force 1987-89, mem. gender bias com. 1990-94, chair 1990-91), Wash. Def. Trial Lawyers (chmn. ct. rules and procedures com. 1987, co-editor newsletter 1985-86), Wash. State Soc. Hosp. Attys., Wash. Women Lawyers (treas. 1986, 87). Office: Heller Ehrman White & McAuliffe 6100 Columbia Ctr 701 5th Ave Seattle WA 98104-7016

WAGNER, SANDRA ANN, publication services director; b. Joplin, Mo., Feb. 24, 1937; d. Esther Joye and Ruth Cecilia (Conard) Dugan; m. Stanley Edward Wagner, June 1962 (div. 1969); children: Michael Conard, Kenneth Edward. Student, Okla. State U., 1955-57; BS in Edn., Northeastern State U., 1960. Tchr. elem. edn. Los Alamos (N.Mex.) Pub. Schs., 1960-61, Okla. City Pub. Schs., 1961-64, Dist. 624, White Bear Lake, Minn., 1966-68; creative dir. World Toy House, St. Paul, 1969-71; pub. rels. dir. Chimera Theatre Co. St. Paul Arts & Sci., 1971-74; catalog coord. Premium Corp. Am., Mpls., 1974-75; comm. dir. Bacone Coll., Muskogee, Okla., 1976-79, Am. Bapt. Assembly, Green Lake, Wis., 1979-80; dir. pubs. svcs. Northeastern State U., Tahlequah, Okla., 1980—; desktop pub., Tahlequah, 1982—. Editor bi-monthly newsletter S.W. Coll. Bookstore Assn., 1990—, Portfolio Mag., 1988—, art dir. and editor, 1988—. Chair evangelism com. St. Paul United Meth. Ch., Muskogee, 1987-89; tchr., Precept Bible study interdenominational, Tahlequah, Muskogee, 1984—. Recipient 6 Publ. award Okla. Coll. Pub. Rels. Assn. Mem. Okla. Collegiate Press Assn., Assoc. Collegiate Press, Coll. Media Advisers. Republican. Home: 2617 Elgin St Muskogee OK 74401-5346

WAGNER, SUSAN ELIZABETH, secondary education educator; b. Shelby, Ohio, Jan. 22, 1951; d. Joseph H. and Patricia A. (Shoup) W. BS, U. Dayton, 1973. Cert. tchr., Tex., Ohio. Tchr. health and phys. edn. Copperas Cove (Tex.) High Sch., 1973—, dept. chairperson, 1979—, head coach cross country and track, 1986—, girlst athletic coord., 1994; mem. bd. govs. Copperas Cove High Sch., 1993. Mem. AAHPERD, Am. Assn. Health Educators, Tex. Alliance Health, Phys. Edn., Recreation and Dance, Tex. Classroom Tchrs. Assn., Tex. Girls Coaches Assn., Athletic Congress USA (cert. official), Nat. Sports and Phys. Edn. Home: 701 N 19th St Copperas Cove TX 76522-1202 Office: Copperas Cove High Sch 400 S 25th St Copperas Cove TX 76522-2099

WAGNER, SUSAN JANE, sales and marketing consulting company executive; b. Englewood, N.J., Aug. 11; d. Jules A. and Florence I. (Froeba) W.; m. Mark E. McKenna, May 4, 1984. MusB with honors, Syracuse U., 1974; MPA with honors, Fairleigh Dickinson U., 1983. Dir. music, theater dependant sch. U.S. Dept. Def., Fed. Republic Germany, 1976-82; grad. asst. Fairleigh Dickinson U., Rutherford, N.J., 1982-83; account exec. Katz Radio/Katz Communications, Inc., N.Y.C., 1983-85; account mgr. network Katz Radio Group, N.Y.C., 1985-87, v.p., dir. mktg., 1987-90, sr. v.p. dir.mktg., 1990-91; v.p. corp. mktg. Katz Comm., Inc., N.Y.C., 1992-93; prin., ptnr. Exec. Dynamics Inc., Mahwah, N.J., 1993—. Mem. Am. Women in Radio and TV, Electronic Media Mktg. Assn., Am. Mktg. Assn., Promotion Mktg. Assn. Am., Broadcast Promotion Mktg. Execs., Sigma Alpha Iota, Gamma Phi Beta. Office: Exec Dynamics 2 James Brite Cir Mahwah NJ 07430-2527

WAGNER, TERESA LEE, training and organization consultant; b. Reading, Pa., Jan. 24, 1954; d. Fred LeRoy and Emily (Wiest) W. BA in Psychology magna cum laude, Alvernia Coll., 1977; postgrad., U. Nottingham, Eng., 1978; MS in Counseling and Human Rels., Villanova U., 1981; postgrad., Columbia U., 1985-86. Trainer Juvenile Justice Ctr. Nat. Tng. Inst., Phila., 1977-80; sr. indsl. rels. rep. missile and surface radar RCA, Moorestown, N.J., 1980-81; mgr. orgnl. devel. govt. systems divsn. RCA, Cherry Hill, N.J., 1981-84; mgr. orgn. planning and devel. RCA Global Comms., Inc., N.Y.C., 1984-88; pres. T. L. Wagner Assocs., Monterey, Calif., 1988—. Author: (tng. manuals) Recovering from Grief, 1990, Managing Job Loss, 1991, Grief Support Skills, 1993, (self-assessment instrument) Grief Support Skills Assessment Profile, 1990. Docent Point Lobos State Res., Carmel, Calif., 1990—; mem. beach and seal watch, Am. Cetacean Soc., Monterey, 1990—; bd. dirs. Friends of Monterey County Wildlife, 1993—, Horse Power Internat., Monterey, 1990—, Assisi Animal Inst., 1994—. Mem. ASTD, Orgn. Devel. Network, Assn. for Death Edn. and Counseling. Home and Office: T L Wagner Assocs PO Box 522 Monterey CA 93942

WAGNER-WESTBROOK, BONNIE JOAN, management professional; b. Watertown, N.Y., July 18, 1953; d. Elmer Ethan and Joan Eleanor (Niedermeier) Wagner; m. John Drewry Westbrook Jr., Aug. 21, 1982. BS, SUNY, Geneseo, 1975, MS, 1981; EdD, Rutgers U., 1989. Tchr. elem. Rochester (N.Y.) Sch. for the Deaf, 1975-80; instr. adult basic edn. Rochester City Sch. Dist., 1981-82; profl. interpreter Nat. Tech. Inst. for the Deaf, Rochester, 1981-83; instr., interpreter Henrietta (N.Y.) Cen. Sch. Dist., 1983-84; intern Middlesex County Vocat. Tech. Schs., New Brunswick, N.J., 1985; cons. on urban initiative for N.J. Dept. Edn. Rutgers U., New Brunswick, N.J., 1985-86, program specialist, 1987-88, rsch. assoc. for N.J. Commn. on Employment and Tng., 1988-89, also senator Grad. Sch. Edn., 1985-87; adminstr. Pub. Svc. Electric and Gas Co., Newark, 1990-91; program dir. Rutgers U., New Brunswick, N.J., 1991—; cons. Blueprint Project, Hudson County C.C., 1992-93, Pub. Svc. Electric & Gas Co., Newark, 1986-89. Vol. Rochester Sch. for the Deaf, 1977; mem. Rochester Oratorio Soc., 1978-81, SUNY Geneseo Chamber Singers, 1971-75. Rutgers U. scholar, 1986; Rutgers U. fellow, 1987. Mem. ASTD, Am. Ednl. Rsch. Assn., Am. Coun. on Edn. of Deaf, Am. Vocat. Assn., Am. Mgmt. Assn., Nat. Registry Interpreters for Deaf, Rochester Amateur Radio Assn., Rutgers Univ. Alumni Assn., Omicron Tau Theta. Republican. Home: 327 Becker St Highland Park NJ 08904-2522 Office: Rutgers U Sch Mgmt & Labor Rels Ctr Mgmt Devel PO Box 5062 New Brunswick NJ 08903-5062

WAGNON, JOAN, former state legislator, association executive; b. Texarkana, Ark., Oct. 17, 1940; d. Jack and Louise (Lucas) D.; m. William O. Wagnon Jr., June 4, 1964; children: Jack, William O. III. BA in Biology, Hendrix Coll., Conway, Ark., 1962; MEd in Guidance and Counseling, U. Mo., 1968. Sr. research technician U. Ark. Med. Sch., Little Rock, 1962-64; sr. research asst. U. Ark. Med. Sch., Columbia, Mo., 1964-68; tchr. No. Hills Jr. High Sch., Topeka, 1968-69, J.S. Kendall Sch., Boston, 1970-71; counselor Neighborhood Youth Corps, Topeka, 1973-74; exec. dir. Topeka YWCA, 1977-93; mem. Kans. Legislature, 1983-94. Mem. Health Planning Rev. Commn., Topeka, 1984-85. Recipient Service to Edn. award, Topeka NEA, 1979, Outstanding Achievement award, Kans. Home Econs. Assn., 1985; named Woman of Yr. Mayors Council Status of Women, 1983; named one of Top Ten Legislators Kans. Mag., Wichita, 1986. Mem. Topeka Assn. Human Svc. Execs. (pres. 1981-83), Topekans for Ednl. Involvement (pres. 1979-82), Women's Polit. Caucus (state chair). Democrat. Methodist. Lodge: Rotary. Home: 1606 SW Boswell Ave Topeka KS 66604-2729 Office: Kans Families for Kids 2209 SW 29th St Topeka KS 66611*

WAGSTAFF, ANN TAFT, religious organization executive; b. Meadow, Utah, July 30, 1939; d. Ellis Varvilla and Edith Loretta (Bushnell) Taft; m. David Jesse Wagstaff, Jan. 4, 1963; children: David, Andrew, Terry. AS in Nursing, Weber Coll., 1959. RN, Utah. Staff nurse Utah Valley Hosp., Provo, 1959-62, LDS Hosp., Salt Lake City, 1962-63; pvt. researcher Missing Heirs, Enid, Okla., 1973-80; sr. clk., genealogist Washington Temple, Kensington, Md., 1987—. Author, compiler: 1810 Kentucky Census Index, 1980. Fellow Am. Coll. Genealogists. Mem. LDS Ch. Office: Washington Temple 9900 Stoneybrook Dr Kensington MD 20895

WAHL, JOAN CONSTANCE, technical writer, editor; b. Phila., Dec. 23, 1921; d. Frank L. and Sara E. (Timoney) O'Brien; B.A., Rosemont Coll., 1943; postgrad. U. Calif., Los Angeles, 1960-61; m. John Carl Wahl, Jr., Dec. 31, 1943 (div. 1959); children—John, Mark, David, Lawrence, Thomas, Jeanne, Madeleine Sophie, Eugene. Substitute tchr. Los Angeles City Bd. Edn., 1961; editor, proofreader Renner/Cal-Data Corp., Los Angeles, 1962-63; editor, tech. writer Volt Tech. Corp., 1964-66; sr. tech. editor, writer, sr. project editor Aerospace Corp., El Segundo, Calif., 1966—. Sect. chmn. United Way, Los Angeles, 1963-64; mem. communications com. St. Paul the Apostle, Westwood, Calif., 1976-78. Recipient Outstanding Service award United Way, 1964. Mem. Soc. Tech. Communications (sr.), Aerospace Women's Com., Mental Health Assn. Los Angeles County, Kistler Honor Soc. Contbr. articles to profl. jours. Office: Aerospace Corp M3/377 2350 E El Segundo Blvd El Segundo CA 90245-4609

WAHL, ROSALIE E., state supreme court justice; b. Gordon, Kans., Aug. 27, 1924; children: Christopher Roswell, Sara Emilie, Timothy Eldon, Mark Patterson, Jenny Caroline. B.A., U. Kans., 1946; J.D., William Mitchell Coll. Law, 1967. Bar: Minn. 1967. Asst. state pub. defender Mpls., 1967-73; clin. prof. law William Mitchell Coll. Law, 1973-77; assoc. justice Minn. Supreme Ct., St. Paul, 1977-94. Fellow Am. Bar Foundl; mem. ABA (legal edn. and bar admissions, sect. jud. adminstrn., criminal justice sect., individual rights and responsibility sect.), Minn. State Bar Assn., Am. Judicature Soc., Nat. Assn. Women Judges, Minn. Women Lawyers Assn. Office: Minn Supreme Ct Mink Ln # 25 Saint Paul MN 55127-2574

WAILLY, MARY KATHRYN, data processing administrator; b. Terre Haute, Ind., Oct. 4, 1949; d. Louis Auguste Francois and Luella Christina (Paton) W. BS, Ind. State U., 1971. Claims rep. various ins. cos. Indpls., 1971-79; acct. exec. Automatic Data Processing, Indpls., 1979-80; client svc. mgr. Automatic Data Processing, Cin., 1980-82; mgr. Automatic Data Processing, Atlanta, 1985-88; systems cons. mgr. Automatic Data Processing, Toronto, Ont., Can., 1988-89; nat. acct. mgr. Automatic Data Processing, Clifton, N.J., 1989-90; project mgr. Automatic Data Processing, Roseland, N.J., 1990—; cons. Automatic Data Processing, U.S., Can., 1982-85. Vol. Spl. Olympics, No. N.J., 1994, Montclair (N.J.) Iris Festival, 1993, 94, Irish Heritage Soc., No. N.J., 1993, 94. Recipient Hoosier scholarship Ind. Scholarship Com., 1967. Mem. N.J. Chamber Music Soc., Bach Festival Newark, Nat. Sociol. Soc. Home: 410 Cornelia St # 4 Boonton NJ 07005 Office: Automatic Data Processing 1 ADP Blvd Roseland NJ 07006

WAIN, HAY WUN, executive; b. Korea, Apr. 8, 1959; came to U.S., 1970; d. Ki Joon and Youn Bok (Lee) Chang; m. David William Wain, May 16, 1987; children: Nicole Christine, Ashley Lauren. BS in Indsl. Engring., Ga. Inst. Tech., 1981; MS in Indsl. Engring., U. Pitts., 1985. Systems analyst Westinghouse Electric Corp., Pitts., 1982-84, materials mgr., 1984-88; teaching, rsch. asst. U. Pitts., 1988-90; quality cons. Westinghouse P&Q Ctr., Pitts., 1990-92; corp. dir. TQM Ametek, Inc., Pitts., 1992—. Mem. Am. Soc. Quality Control, Soc. Women Engrs., Inst. Indsl. Engrs. Republican. Office: Ametek Inc 150 Freeport Rd Pittsburgh PA 15238

WAINESS, MARCIA WATSON, legal management consultant; b. Bklyn., Dec. 17, 1949; d. Stanley and Seena (Klein) Watson; m. Steven Richard Wainess, Aug. 7, 1975. Student, UCLA, 1967-71, 80-81, Grad. Sch. Mgmt. Exec. Program, 1987-88, grad. Grad. Sch. Mgmt. Exec. Program, 1988. Office mgr., paralegal Lewis, Marenstein & Kadar, L.A., 1977-81; office mgr. Rosenfeld, Meyer & Susman, Beverly Hills, Calif., 1981-83; adminstr. Rudin, Richman & Appel, Beverly Hills, 1983; dir. adminstrn. Kadison, Pfaelzer, L.A., 1983-87; exec. dir. Richards, Watson and Gershon, L.A., 1987-93; legal mgmt. cons. L.A., 1993—; faculty mem. UCLA Legal Mgmt. & Adminstrn. Program, 1983, U. So. Calif. Paralegal Program, L.A., 1985; mem. adv. bd. atty. asst. tng. program, UCLA, 1984-88. Mem. ABA (chair Displaywrite Users Group 1986, legal tech. adv. coun. litig. support working group 1986-87), San Fernando Valley Bar Assn., Profl. Liability Underwriting Soc., Assn. Legal Adminstrs. (bd. dirs. 1990-92, asst. regional v.p. Calif. 1987-88, regional v.p. 1988-89, pres. Beverly Hills chpt. 1985-86, membership chair 1984-85, chair new adminstrn. sect. 1982-84, mktg. mgmt. sect. com. 1989-90, internat. conf. com.), Internat. Platform Assn., Calif. Women Bus. Owners. Office: 78 Coolwater Rd Canoga Park CA 91307-1005

WAINMAN, BARBARA WALDEN, legislative staff member; b. Washington, May 16, 1956; d. Charles Burwell and Dorothy Belle (Drinkard) Walden; m. Garth Michael Wainman, Aug. 2, 1980; children: Laura Channing Wainman, Matthew Nench Wainman. BA, Smith Coll., 1978. Reporter South Shore News Day, Rockalnd, Mass., 1978; legis. analyst Ho. Rep. Conf., Washington, 1979-81; legis. asst. appropriations com., Rep. Ralph Regula U.S. Ho. Reps., Washington, 1981—. Recipient Cert. Extraordinary Conservation Achievement Wilderness Soc., 1988. Republican. Episcopalian. Home: 4244 Brittany Ct Woodbridge VA 22192 Office: Rep Ralph Regula R-Ohio 2309 Rayburn House Office Bldg Washington DC 20515

WAINRYB, CECILIA, psychology educator; b. Buenos Aires, Oct. 7, 1956; came to U.S., 1982; BA, U. Haifa, Israel, 1980, MA, 1982; PhD, U. Calif., Berkeley, 1989. Post-doctoral fellow U. Haifa, 1989-92; asst. prof. U. Utah, Salt Lake City, 1993—. Contbr. articles to profl. jours. Mem. APA, Soc. Rsch. in Child Devel., Jean Piaget Soc. Office: Univ of Utah Dept of Psychology Salt Lake City UT 84112

WAINWRIGHT, CATHERINE MARIE, skincare business owner, clinical cosmetician, make-up artist; b. Buffalo, N.Y., Apr. 26, 1957; d. Sam James Gerardi and Geraldine Rose (Aquisto) Smith; m. Andrew David Wainwright, Sept. 25, 1956; children: Vincent John, Natalie Calandre, Tess Audrey. Student, Rogue C.C., Grants Pass, Oreg. Lic. esthetician, Calif. Esthetician, makeup artist House of Joseph, Torrance, Calif., 1981-82, Bullocks, Torrance, 1982-83, Panache Appearance Studios, Torrance, 1984-87, Helena Toulmet Inst., Torrance, 1987-88, Edna Colman Salon de Beaute, Redondo Beach, Calif., 1988, Venona for Skin Care, Torrance, 1988-90; owner, educator, newsletter pub. Catherine Wainwright Skincare, Torrance, 1993—, Catherine Wainwright Dermal Products & Skincare, Grants Pass, Oreg., 1993—; on-site examiner Nat. Accrediting Commn. Cosmetology Arts & Scis., Washington, 1992—. Home: 1931 NW Wendy Way Grants Pass OR 97526 Office: Catherine Wainwright Makeup and Skin Care Ctr 203 SE H St Grants Pass OR 97526

WAINWRIGHT, CHRISTINE, brokerage house executive; b. Bryn Mawr, Pa., Nov. 9, 1956; d. Nicholas Biddle and Christine (Henry) W.; m. Douglas Fernald Stone, May 21, 1988 (div. Oct. 1990). BA in Philosophy, Trinity Coll., Hartford, Conn., 1979; MBA in Fin., U. Pa., 1984. Registered rep. series 7 and 63, Nat. Assn. Securities Dealers. Trust officer U.S. Trust Co. N.Y., N.Y.C., 1979-82; assoc. Lehman Bros., Inc., N.Y.C., 1979-83, v.p., 1983-87, sr. v.p., 1987-93, mng. dir., 1993—, mem. recruiting com. Wharton Sch., U. Pa., 1984-87. Trustee Andalusia Found., 1992—; mem. Blue Hill Troup Ltd., 1979—. Hartford Sch. Music scholar, 1977-79. Mem. Nat. Wildlife Orgn., U. Pa. Club. Republican. Episcopalian. Office: Lehman Bros Inc 3 World Fin Ctr New York NY 10285

WAINWRIGHT, CLARA MACK, artist; b. Boston, Nov. 27, 1936; d. Harold Alonzo and Caroline Stevenson (Saltonstall) Mack; m. William Harvey Wainwright, Sept. 15, 1969; children: Caroline Lee, Dedalus Alonzo. BA in English, U. N.C., 1959. founder, artistic dir., coord. Gt. Boston Kite Festival, 1969-70, First Night celebration Boston, 1976-78; coord. Fellini's Basement fundraiser Boston Visual Artists' Union, 1975, Newbury St. Paseo Awards, 1993; initiator Somerville Garden Awards, 1990; coord., artist Inner City Arts Projects, 1989; founder, artistic dir. Boston St. Olympics, 1982; coord. banner constrn. Very Spl. Arts Festival, 1979-81. One-woman shows include Addison Gallery, Andover, Mass., 1977, Colloquium Gallery, Salem, Mass., 1979, Mugar Gallery, Colby-Sawyer Coll., New London, N.H., 1982, Clark Gallery, Lincoln, Mass., 1982, Thomas Segal Gallery, Boston, 1984, Trustman Gallery, Simmons Coll., Boston, 1989; exhibited in group shows, including Hayden Gallery, MIT, 1973, Fuller Mus. Art, Brockton, Mass., 1980, 83, 86, 91, Brickbottom Gallery, Somerville, Mass., 1991, 93, DeCordova Mus., Lincoln, Mass., 1989, others. Participant Teen Art project Youth Resources Ctr., Boston, 1988-89, Voices of Neighborhood Quilt project Somerville Community Partnership, 1992-93; artist-in-residence Fenway Mid. Coll. High Sch., Boston, 1991-92; participant various youth artistic activities, including prodn. of 3 large quilts for Jamaica Plain Art Ctr., Asian Youth Essential Svcs. and Fenway Mid. Coll. High Sch., 1992, quilt prodn. with students of East Somerville Community Sch., 1993. Recipient Grand Bostonian award City of Boston, 1976, Creativity award Bloomingdales, 1985, Kevin Lynch award Sch. Architecture and Planning, MIT, 1990, Massart award Mass. Coll. Art, 1988; Bunting Inst. fellow Radcliffe Coll., 1987. Mem. Boston Soc. Architects (hon., Commonwealth award 1986). Home: 57 Upland Rd Brookline MA 02146-7735

WAIT, CAROL GRACE COX, organization administrator; b. L.A., Dec. 20, 1942; d. Earl George Atkinson Sr. and Virginia Rose (Clanton) Boggs; m. David L. Edwards (div. 1974); children: Nicole Rose Smith, Alexandra Edwards; m. Gary G. Cox, Jan. 25, 1975 (div. 1982); m. Robert Atwood Wait, July 4, 1991. AA in Pre Law, Cerritos Coll., 1966; AB in History, Whittier Coll., 1969. Probation counselor Los Angeles County Probation Dept., Downey, Calif., 1967-69; corp. sec., mgr. Dennis and Dennis Personnel, Santa Ana, Calif., 1969-71; owner, pres. Cox Edwards & Assocs., Santa Ana, 1971-73; adminstrv. services officer County of Santa Cruz (Calif.), 1973-74; cons. State of Calif., Sacramento, 1974-75; project dir. Nat. Assn. Counties, Washington, 1975-77; legis. dir. U.S. Senate Com. on the Budget, Washington, 1977-81; pres. Com. for a Responsible Budget, Washington, 1981—, Carol Cox & Assocs., Washington, 1984—; cons. to bus. and other orgns. on the fed. budget, the budget process and other econ. issues; writer and speaker on the budget and budget process. Am. participant USIS/Brazilian Senate Symposium on Budget Process, Brazilia, Brazil, 1985—, Ampart speaker on 1990 budget agreement France, Ger., 1990. Named one of 150 Who Make a Difference Nat. Jour., 1986; recipient Nat. Disting. Svc. award Am. Assn. Budget and Program Analysis. Mem. Washington Women's Forum, Internat. Women's Forum (pres.). Republican. Episcopalian. Office: Com Responsible Fed Budget 220 1/2 E St NE Washington DC 20002-4923

WAITE, ELLEN JANE, library executive; b. Oshkosh, Wis., Feb. 17, 1951; d. Earl Vincent and Margaret (Luft) W.; m. Thomas H. Dollar, Aug. 19, 1977 (div. July 1984); m. Kent Hendrickson, Mar. 26, 1994. BA, U. Wis., Oshkosh, 1973; MLS, U. Wis., Milw., 1977. Head of cataloging Marquette U., Milw., 1977-82; head catalog librarian U. Ariz., Tucson, 1983-85; assoc. dir. libraries Loyola U., Chgo., 1985-86, acting dir. libraries, 1986-87, dir. libraries, 1987-94, v.p. acad. svcs., 1994—; cons. Loyola U., Chgo., 1984, Boston Coll., 1986, U. San Francisco, 1989; bd. trustees Online Computer Lib. Ctr., Dublin, Ohio, 1994—. Contbg. author: Research Libraries and Their Implementation of AACR2, 1985; author: (with others) Women in LC's Terms: A Thesaurus of Subject Headings Related to Women, 1988. Mem. ALA. Office: Loyola U 25 E Pearson St Chicago IL 60626

WAITE, KARLEEN LOUISE, financial analyst; b. Portland, Oreg., Sept. 16, 1965; d. Donald Day and Sharon Louise (Libby) W. BS in Fin., George Mason U., 1987, MBA, 1992. Ops. analyst Nat. Rural Utilities Cooperative Fin. Corp., Washington, 1987-92; fin. analyst Nat. Rural Utilities Cooperative Fin. Corp., Herndon, Va., 1992—. Home: 11732 Decade Ct Reston VA 22091 Office: NRUCFC 2201 Cooperative Way Herndon VA 22071-3025

WAITE, LINDA JOAN, educator; b. Ann Arbor, Mich., Oct. 25, 1947; d. Allan Edward and Barbara Joan (Bennett) W.; m. Ross Mark Stolzenberg, May 1974; children: Shana Anat, Nava Rachel. BA, Mich. State U., 1969; MA, U. Mich., 1970, PhD, 1976. Statistician U.S. Bur. of Census, Washington, 1973-76; asst. prof., assoc. prof. U. Ill., Urbana, 1976-80; sociologist, sr. sociologist The Rand Corp., Santa Monica, Calif., 1981-91; prof. U. Chgo., 1991—. Author: (with Fran Goldscheider) New Families, No Families? The Transformation of the American Home, 1991 (Duncan award 1993). Mem. Am. Sociol. Assn. (nominations com. 1990), Population Assn. Am. (pres.-elect 1994), Gerontological Soc. Am., Sociol. Rsch. Assn. Office: Population Rsch Ctr NORC 1155 E 60th St Chicago IL 60637

WAITES, CANDY YAGHJIAN, former state official; b. N.Y.C., Feb. 21, 1943; d. Edmund Kirken and Dorothy Joanne (Candy) Yaghjian; children: Jennifer Lisa, Robin Shelley. B.A., Wheaton Coll., Mass., 1965. Elected county councilwoman Richland County, S.C., 1976-88, mem. S.C. Ho., 1988-94; dir. external programs The Leadership Inst., Columbia Coll., 1993—; vice chmn. Adv. Commn. on Intergovtl. Relations, S.C., 1977-87; bd. dirs. Interagy. Council on Pub. Transp., S.C., 1977-85, Central Midlands Regional Planning Council, Columbia, S.C., 1977-84; dir. Wachovia Bank. Vice pres. bd. dirs. United Way of Midlands, 1977-89; trustee Columbia Mus. Art, 1982-88; bd. dirs. Rape Crisis Network, 1984-87; chmn. County Coun. Coalition; mem. C. of C. Leadership Forum, S.C. Fedn. of the Blind; mem. adv. bd. U. S.C. Hunanities and Social Scis. Coll., Family Shelter, Nurturing Ctr.; pres Trinity Housing Corp.; found. bd. Richland Meml. Hosp., 1995. Named Outstanding Young Career Woman, Columbia YWCA, 1980, YWCA Hall of Fame, 1993, Outstanding Young Woman of Yr., Columbia Jaycees, 1975, Pub. Citizen of Yr. Nat. Assn. Social Workers, hon. mem. Mortar Bd. Soc., 1994; recipient Ann. Legis. award Common Cause S.C., 1990, 91, Legis. Yr. award by S.C. Assn. Counties, 1992. Mem. S.C. Women in Govt. (vice chmn. 1984-86), S.C. Assn. Counties (bd. dirs. 1982-88 , Pres's award 1983), Network Female Execs., LWV (pres. 1973-76), Omicron Delta Kappa. Democrat. Episcopalian. Club: Univ. Assocs. (Columbia). Avocations: exercising, drawing, gardening, walking. Home: 3419 Duncan St Columbia SC 29205-2705 Office: Columbia Coll Leadership Inst 1301 Cola Coll Dr Columbia SC 29203

WAITS, PATRICIA DIANE, oncological nurse; b. Oklahoma City, July 23, 1945; d. John Aaron and Joyce Maxine (White) Flynn; m. Delbert Wayne Waits, Apr. 5, 1963; children: Kristin, Joseph, Michael. ADN, Tulsa (Okla.) Jr. Coll., 1989. Cert. oncological nurse. Staff nurse bone marrow unit St. Francis Hosp., Tulsa, 1990—, mem. coms., 1991—. Vol. Tulsa County Health Dept., 1990—, ARC, 1992—. Mem. Oncology Nursing Soc. Republican. Mem. Assembly of God Ch. Home: 6937 E 73 St Tulsa OK 74133

WAKE, MARVALEE HENDRICKS, biology educator; b. Orange, Calif., July 31, 1939; d. Marvin Carlton and Velvalee (Borter) H.; m. David B. Wake, June 23, 1962; 1 child, Thomas A. BA, U. So. Calif., 1961, MS, 1964, PhD, 1968. Teaching asst./instr. U. Ill., Chgo., 1964-68, asst. prof.,

1968-69; lectr. U. Calif., Berkeley, 1969-73, asst. prof., 1973-76, assoc. prof., 1976-80, prof. zoology, 1980-89, chmn. dept. zoology, 1985-89, chmn. dept. integrative biology, 1989-91, assoc. dean Coll. Letters and Sci., 1975-78, prof. integrative biology, 1989—. Editor, co-author: Hyman's Comparative Vertebrate Anatomy, 1979; co-author: Biology, 1978; contbr. articles to profl. jours. NSF grantee, 1978—; Guggenheim fellow, 1988-89. Fellow AAAS, Calif. Acad. Sci. (trustee 1982—); mem. Am. Soc. Ichthyology and Herpetology (pres. 1984, bd. govs. 1978—), Internat. Union Biol. Scis. (U.S. Nat. Com. 1986-95, chair 1992-95, sec. gen. 1994—). Home: 999 Middlefield Rd Berkeley CA 94708-1509 Office: U Calif Dept Integrative Biology Berkeley CA 94720

WALASH, EILEEN ROBIN, public relations consultant, freelance writer; b. Bklyn., Jan. 30, 1964; d. Myron and Marilyn Estelle (Rosner) W. BA, Miami U., Oxford, Ohio, 1986. Asst. editor Gralla Publs., N.Y.C., 1986-88; market editor Women's Wear Daily, N.Y.C., 1988-89; account supr. The Rowland Co., N.Y.C., 1989-92; pub. rels. cons., freelance writer N.Y.C., 1992—. Vol. N.Y. Cares, N.Y.C., 1993—. Mem. NAFE, Publicity Club of N.Y., N.Y. Alumni Assn. Miami U. (steering com.). Democrat.

WALCZAK, JOANNE CAROL, accountant; b. Buffalo, Feb. 8, 1959; d. Joseph Charles and Carol Dolores (Nicklas) Moorhouse; m. John T. Walczak, Aug. 2, 1980; 1 child, Bryan. BS in Acctg., SUNY, Geneseo, 1986; MBA in Fin. and Corp. Acctg., U. Rochester, 1991. CPA, N.Y. Staff acct. Genesee C.C., Batavia, N.Y., 1986-87; sr. acct. Strong Meml. Hosp., Rochester, N.Y., 1987-88; ptnr. J&L Assocs., Batavia, 1988-93, Landers & Walczak, Batavia, 1993—; adj. faculty Genesee C.C., 1988-92. Bd. dirs. YWCA Genesee County, Inc., Batavia, 1989-90; mem. bus. devel. com. Genesee County C. of C., 1992-95; v.p. Zonta Club of Batavia-Genesee, 1994-95. Roman Catholic. Home: 16 Linwood Ave Batavia NY 14020-3714 Office: Landers & Walczak 12 Center St Batavia NY 14020-1909

WALD, FRANCINE JOY WEINTRAUB (MRS. BERNARD J. WALD), physicist, academic administrator; b. Bklyn., Jan. 13, 1938; d. Irving and Minnie (Reisig) Weintraub; student Bklyn. Coll., 1955-57; BEE, CCNY, 1960; MS, Poly. Inst. Bklyn., 1962, PhD, 1969; m. Bernard J. Wald, Feb. 2, 1964; children: David Evan, Kevin Mitchell. Engr., Remington Rand Univac div. Sperry Rand Corp., Phila., 1960; instr. Poly. Inst. Bklyn., 1962-64, adj. research asso., 1969-70; lectr. N.Y. C.C., Bklyn., 1969, 70; instr. sci. Friends Sem., N.Y.C., 1975-76, chmn. dept. sci., 1976-94; instr. sci., chmn. dept. sci. Nightingale-Bamford Sch., N.Y.C., 1994—. NDEA fellow, 1962-64. Mem. Am. Phys. Soc., Am. Assn. Physics Tchrs., Assn. Tchrs. in Ind. Schs., N.Y. Acad. Scis., Nat. Sci. Tchrs. Assn., AAAS, Sigma Xi, Tau Beta Pi, Eta Kappa Nu.

WALD, MARY S., risk management and personal finance educator; b. Baker, Oreg., June 17, 1943; d. Paul H. and Mary Elsie (Bartshe) Stoner; m. Lance Albert Wald, June 22, 1968. BA in English, Coll. of Idaho, Caldwell, 1966; MBA in Fin., Temple U., 1984. Tchr. Salt Lake City Bd. Edn., 1967-74; office mgr. Montgomery County Homemaker-Home Health Aide Svc., Inc., Blue Bell, Pa., 1975-82; adj. lectr. risk mgmt. and personal fin. Temple U., Phila., 1984—. Co-author: Controlling Your Money, Step By Step, 1987. Named Outstanding Tchr. of Yr., Salt Lake City Bd. Edn., 1973-74. Mem. Am. Risk and Ins. Assn., Gamma Iota Sigma, Golden Key Nat. Honor Soc. (hon. mem.). Republican. Office: Temple U Ambler Campus 580 Meetinghouse Rd Ambler PA 19002-3923

WALD, PATRICIA MCGOWAN, federal judge; b. Torrington, Conn., Sept. 16, 1928; d. Joseph F. and Margaret (O'Keefe) McGowan; m. Robert L. Wald, June 22, 1952; children—Sarah, Douglas, Johanna, Frederica, Thomas. BA, Conn. Coll., 1948; LLB, Yale U., 1951; HHD (hon.), Mt. Vernon Jr. Coll., 1980; LLD (hon.), George Washington Law Sch., 1983, CUNY, 1984, Notre Dame U., John Jay Sch. Criminal Justice, Mt. Holyoke Coll., 1985, Georgetown U., 1987, Villanova U. Law Sch., Amherst Coll., N.Y. Law Sch., 1988, Colgate U., 1989, Hofstra Law Sch., 1991, New Eng. Coll., 1991, Hoffstra U., 1991. Bar: D.C. 1952. Clk. to judge Jerome Frank U.S. Ct. Appeals, 1951-52; asso. firm Arnold, Fortas & Porter, Washington, 1952-53; mem. D.C. Crime Commn., 1964-65; atty. Office of Criminal Justice, 1967-68, Neighborhood Legal Svc., Washington, 1968-70; co-dir. Ford Found. Project on Drug Abuse, 1970, Ctr. for Law and Social Policy, 1971-72, Mental Health Law Project, 1972-77; asst. atty. gen. for legis. affairs U.S. Dept. Justice, Washington, 1977-79; judge U.S. Ct. Appeals (D.C. cir.), 1979—, chief judge, 1986-91. Author: Law and Poverty, 1965; co-author: Bail in the United States, 1964, Dealing with Drug Abuse, 1973; contbr. articles on legal topics. Trustee Ford Found., 1972-77, Phillips Exeter Acad., 1975-77, Agnes Meyer Found., 1976-77, Conn. Coll., 1976-77; mem. Carnegie Council on Children, 1972-77. Mem. ABA (bd. editors ABA Jour. 1978-84), Am. Law Inst. (coun. 1979—, exec. com. 1985—, 2d v.p. 1988-93, 1st v.p. 1993—), Inst. Medicine, Am. Acad. Arts and Scis., Phi Beta Kappa. Office: US Ct Appeals US Courthouse 3rd & Constitution Ave NW Washington DC 20001

WALD, SYLVIA, artist; b. Phila., Oct. 30, 1915. Ed., Moore Inst. Art, Sci. and Industry. One-woman shows include U. Louisville, 1945, 49, Kent State Coll., 1945, Nat. Serigraph Soc., 1946, Grand Central Moderns, N.Y.C., 1957, Devorah Sherman Gallery, Chgo., 1960, New Sch., 1967, Book Gallery, White Plains, N.Y., 1968, Benson Gallery, Bridgehampton, L.I., 1977, Knoll Internat., Munich, Germany, 1979, Amerika Havs, Munich, 1979, Aaron Berman Gallery, N.Y.C., 1981, Hirschltadler Gallery, 1994, New Britain (Conn.) Mus., 1994; group shows include Nat. Sculpture Soc., 1940, Sculpture Internat., Phila., 1940, Chgo. Art Inst., 1941, Bklyn. Mus., 1975, Library of Congress, 1943, 52, 58, Smithsonian Instn., 1954, Internat. Print Exhbn., Salzburg and Vienna, 1952, 2d Sao Paulo Biennial, 1953, N.Y. Cultural Center, 1973, Mus. Modern Art, N.Y.C., 1975, Benson Gallery, Bridgehampton, L.I., 1982, Dumon-Landis Gallery, New Brunswick, N.J., 1982-83, Suzuki Gallery, N.Y.C., 1982, Sid Deutch Gallery, N.Y.C., 1983, Aaron Berman Gallery, N.Y.C., 1983, Full House Gallery, Kingston, N.J., 1984, Worcester Mus., 1991, Boston Mus. Fine Arts, 1991, Hirschl & Adler Gallery, N.Y.C., 1993, others; represented in permanent collections Aetna Oil Co., Am. Assn. U. Women, Ball State Tchrs. Coll., Bibliotheque Nationale, Paris, Bklyn. Mus., Howard U., State U. Iowa, Library of Congress, U. Louisville, Nat. Gallery, Mus. Modern Art, Phila. Mus., N.C. Mus., Rose Mus. Art at Brandeis U., Whitney Mus., N.Y.C., Finch Coll. Mus., N.Y.C., U. Nebr., Ohio U., U. Okla., Princeton, Victoria and Albert Mus., Walker Gallery, Worcester (Mass.) Art Mus., Guggenheim Mus., N.Y.C., Grunewald Mus., U.Calif. Los Angeles, Rutgers Mus., N.J., Aschenbach Collection Mus., San Francisco, Grunewald Coll. Mus. UCLA; Contbr. to profl. publs. Address: 417 Lafayette St New York NY 10003

WALDBAUM, JANE COHN, art history educator; b. N.Y.C., Jan. 28, 1940; d. Max Arthur and Sarah (Waldstein) Cohn. B.A., Brandeis U., 1962; M.A., Harvard U., 1964, Ph.D., 1968. Research fellow in classical archaeology Harvard U., Cambridge, Mass., 1968-70, 72-73; asst. prof. U. Wis.-Milw., 1973-78, assoc. prof., 1978-84, prof. art history, 1984—, chmn. dept., 1982-85, 86-89, 91-92; Dorot rsch. prof. W.F. Albright Inst. Archeol. Rsch., Jerusalem, 1990-91. Author: From Bronze to Iron, 1978; Metalwork from Sardis, 1983; author (with others), editor Sardis Report I, 1975; mem. editorial bd. Bull. Am. Schs. Oriental Rsch., 1994—; contbr. numerous articles to profl. jours. Bd. dirs. Milw. Soc. of Archaeol. Inst., 1973—, pres., 1983-85, 91—. Woodrow Wilson Found. fellow, dissertation fellow, 1962-63, 65-66, NEH post-doctoral rsch., Jerusalem, 1989-90; grantee Am. Philos. Soc., 1972, NEH, summer 1975, U. Wis.-Milw. Found., 1983. Mem. Am. Schs. Oriental Research, Soc. for Archaeol. Sci., Archaeol. Inst. Am. (exec. com. 1975-77, chmn. com. on membership programs 1977-81, nominating com. 1984, chmn. com. on lecture program 1985-87, acad. trustee 1993—, com. profl. responsibilities 1993—, fellowships com. 1993—, gold medal com. 1993—, Ancient Near East com. 1993—), Phi Beta Kappa. Office: U Wis Dept Art History PO Box 413 Milwaukee WI 53201-0413

WALDEN, BONNIE JEAN, public information specialist; b. Eau Claire, Wis., July 3, 1938; d. Miles F. and Edna Mae (Lowry) Mathieu; m. Paul R. Walden, June 10, 1961; children: Grant R., Matt F. AA, Clark Coll., 1958; BA, Western Wash. U., 1960; MEd, U. Portland, 1964. Cert. tchr., Wash. Tchr. Vancouver (Wash.) Sch. Dist., 1960-65; assoc. Hansen Consulting, Battle Ground, Wash., 1979-85; pub. rels. specialist Battle Ground (Wash.) Schs., 1984-88; pub. info. specialist Ednl. Svc. Dist., Vancouver, 1988—. Writer weekly column "In and Around", 1979—. Mem. Alki Jr. Women's Club, 1963-66, Silver Star Jr. Women's Club, 1966-72, Columbia Dist. Jrs., 1963-72, dist. dir., 1968-70; v.p. GFWC-Columbia Dist., 1980-82, pres., 1982-84; mem. Battle Ground City Pk. Bd., 1982-92, PTA, 1960-65, Wash. State Soc. for Prevention of Blindness, 1967-68; internat. membership chmn. Gen. Fedn. Women's Club, 1994-96. Named Battle Ground Citizen of Yr., 1984, Wash. State Vol. of Yr., 1984, Outstanding Young Woman of Am., 1967, Personality of West and Midwest, 1968. Mem. Vancouver Edn. Assn., Wash. Edn. Assn., Nat. Sch. Pub. Rels. Assn., Am. Volkssporting Club, Wash. State Fedn. Women's Clubs (sec. 1980-82, treas. 1984-86, 3rd v.p. 1986-88, 2d v.p. 1988-90, 1st v.p. 1990-92, pres. 1992-94). Republican. Methodist. Home: 101 W 8th Cir Battle Ground WA 98604

WALDEN, DANIA LEA, food service director; b. Panama City, Fla., Jan. 12, 1957; d. Kent Austin and Cora Ann (Parham) Ball; m. William A. Griffith, Aug. 21, 1976 (div. May 1988); children: William Jason Griffith, Christopher Ryan Griffith; m. Kenneth Wayne Walden Sr., Nov. 20, 1993; stepchildren: Shannon Zahn, Kenny Walden, Christian Walden, Jonathan Walden. BS in Home Econs. Edn., Lander Coll., 1982. Instr. Union County Vocat. Sch., Union, S.C., 1983-84, Greenwood County Vocat. Sch., Greenwood, S.C., 1984-89; dir. sch. food svc. Greenwood County Dept. Edn., Greenwood, 1989—. Methodist. Home: 500 Flatwood Rd Hodges SC 29653

WALDEN, LINDA L., lawyer; b. Dallas, Aug. 16, 1951; d. Leslie LaFayette Jr. and Neva Irene (McBee) W.; m. David Lee Finney, June 9, 1984. BA, Tex. Women's U., 1972; JD., St. Mary's U., 1975. Asst. city atty. City of Amarillo, Tex., 1976-77; asst. dist. atty. 84th Judicial Dist., Forger, Tex., 1977-79; asst. atty. gen. Office Atty. Gen. Tex., Austin, 1979-84; litigation atty. Friedman & Ginsberg, Dallas, 1984-86, Bradford & Snyder, Dallas, 1986-88; corp. counsel Occidental Chem. Co., Dallas, 1988—. Home: 2209 Greenview Dr Carrollton TX 75010 Office: Occidental Chem Corp 5005 LBJ Freeway Dallas TX 75244

WALDER, DEBBY JEAN, program director, quality manager, nursing service administrator, nurse, educator; b. Watertown, S.D., Nov. 25, 1947; d. James Russell and Gladys Elizabeth (Owen) W. BS in Nursing with honors, S.D. State U., 1970; MS in Nursing, U. Minn., 1977. Staff nurse VA Med. Ctr., Mpls., 1970-71, instr., 1971-75, coordinator, 1976-77, trainee-assoc. chief nursing service for edn., 1977; assoc. chief nursing service for edn. VA Med. Ctr., Wilmington, Del., 1977-80, Richmond, Va., 1980-83; chief nursing service VA Med. Ctr., Huntington, W.Va., 1983-85, VA Med. Ctr., Cin., 1985-87; quality mgmt. coord. VA Hosp., Madison, Wis., 1987-91; clin. program mgr., dir. risk mgmt. VA Ctrl. Office, Washington, 1991-93, dir. risk mgmt., 1993—; adj. faculty Med. Coll. Va., Richmond, 1980-82; basic cardiac life support instr.-trainer Am. Heart Assn., Richmond, 1980-83; clin. prof. Marshall U. Sch. Nursing, Huntington, 1983—. Mem. task force Richmond Area chpt. Am. Heart Assn. Recipient Outstanding Cardio-pulmonary Resuscitation Instr. award Richmond Area chpt. Am. Heart Assn., 1982, Achievement award VA Med. Ctr., Richmond, 1983, recognition award for excellence in mgmt. VA Med. Ctr., Huntington, 1983, Spl. Contbn. award, 1992, 93, 94, Unsung Heroes award, 1994; Bush Found. fellow, 1975-76. Mem. Nat. Assn. Quality Assurance Profls., Phi Kappa Phi, Sigma Theta Tau (Phi chpt. scholar 1969-70), Nat. Assn. Quality Assurance Profls., Pi Lambda Theta. Roman Catholic. Office: VA Cen Office Office Quality Mgmt 810 Vermont Ave NW Washington DC 20420

WALDHAUSER, CATHY HOWARD, financial services executive; b. St. Paul, Oct. 18, 1949; d. Jack Roger and Lois (Johnson) Howard; m. Stanley Jay Waldhauser, Feb. 3, 1973. BA in Math. and Econs., Gustavus Adolphus Coll., 1971. Various actuarial positions IDS Life Ins. Co., Mpls., 1971-81; v.p. IDS Life Ins. Co., 1981-91; chief acctg. officer IDS Fin. Svcs., 1991-93; dir. Fin. Instns. Group, 1993—. Trustee Gustavus Adolphus Coll., 1993—, mem. alumni bd. dirs., 1984-90; active Golden Valley (Minn.) LWV, 1986-89; sec., treas. Calvary Luth. Ch., Golden Valley, 1988-89; allocations vol. United Way, Mpls., 1988-90; mem. family selection com. Habitat for Humanity, 1993—. Fellow Soc. Actuaries (product devel. sect. coun. and rsch. com. 1985-88, edn. and exam. com. 1980-81, 83, panelist, lectr. 1980, 87-90), Am. Acad. Actuaries, Minn. Life and Health Guarantee Assn. (bd. dirs. 1984-92), Life Office Mgmt. Assn. (mgmt. rsch. com. 1987-90), Twin Cities Actuarial Club.

WALDHOF, SHARKA EVA, lawyer; b. Prague, Czech Republic, Aug. 8, 1962; came to U.S., 1966; d. Martin and Libuse Kral; m. Kenneth James Waldhof; children: Kevin, Brian. BA, L.I.U., 1985; JD, St. John's U., 1988. Bar: N.Y. 1989, Conn. 1989. Atty. European Am. Bank, Uniondale, N.Y., 1989-90, asst. counsel, 1990-92, sr. atty., 1992—; bd, dirs. First Class Child Care, Uniondale.. Active 1st Class Child Care Parent Adv. Coun., Uniondale, 1992—. Mem. ABA, N.Y. State Bar Assn., Nassau County Bar Assn. Office: European Am Bank 1 EAB Plz Uniondale NY 11555-2722

WALDHOLTZ, ENID GREENE, congresswoman; b. San Rafael, Calif., Oct. 5, 1958; m. Joe Waldholtz. BS in Pol. Sci., U. Utah, 1980; JD, Brigham Young U., 1983. Caseworker, rsch. asst. U.S. Rep. Dan Marriott, R., 1982; law clerk Andrew & Kurth, 1982; atty. Ray, Quinney & Nebeker, 1983-90; dep. chief of staff Gov. Norman H. Bangerter, 1990-92; corp. counsel Novell, Inc., 1993-94. Office: US House Reps 414 Cannon House Office Bldg Washington DC 20515-4402*

WALDMAN, BARBARA, mayor; b. Phila.; m. Mel Waldman; 4 children. BA in Polit. Sci./Pub. Adminstrn., San Jose State U.; JD, Golden Gate U. Dir. Sunnyvale (Calif.) Redevel. Agy., 1987—; mem. coun. City of Sunnyvale, 1987—, vice mayor, 1991-92, mayor, 1994—; mem. Sunnyvale Fin. Authority Bd., 1992—, Sunnyvale/Mountain View Moffett Field Task Force, Bay Vision Action Coalition; mem. congestion mgmt. adv. policy com. Santa Clara County, 1994, child support task force, cmty. devel. block grant local planning coun., 1992—, intergovtl. coun., 1987—, exec. com., 1988—, chair child care com., 1988—, airport land use commn., 1987-91; mem. Santa Clara Transp. Commn., 1991-92; mem. Sunnyvale Housing and Human Svcs. Com., 1984-87, chairperson, 1986-87; mem. Sunnyvale Housing and Cmty. Devel. Citizens' Adv. Com., 1985; mem. sub-element rev. com. Sunnyvale Dept. Pub. Safety. Troope sec. Boy Scouts Am.; leader Girl Scouts Am.; mem. allocations com. United Way, bd. dirs. Sunnyvale chpt.; mem. Sunnyvale Hist. Soc.; bd. dirs. Leadership Sunnyvale, 1987, Our Daily Bread, 1991-93; pres. bd. dirs. Family Planning Alternatives, Inc., 1991-93; steering com. Tomorrow's Leaders Today; bd. dirs. Fremont Union High Sch. Dist. Superschs. Found.; pres. Fremont High Sch. Site Coun., chairperson study skills com. Mem. AAUW (Woman of Achievement award 1991), LWV, NOW, League of Calif. Cities (housing and cmty. econ. devel. com. 1987—, econ. devel. sub-com. 1988-90, affordable housing sub com. 1988—, growth mgmt. com. 1993), Assn. Bay Area Govts. (del. 1987—, growth mgmt. task force 1993-94, legis. govt. orgn. com. 1992—, vice chair 1994), Santa Clara County Cities Assn. (bd. dirs. 1990—, founding pres. 1990-91, chair legis. task force 1991-93), Calif. Assn. Leadership Programs (bd. dirs. 1991—, treas. 1993-94). Office: PO Box 3707 Sunnyvale CA 94088-3707*

WALDMAN-CHANEY, NANCY SUE, vocational rehabilitation specialist; b. Scranton, Pa., May 30, 1960; d. Aaron Hirsch and Doris Elaine (Freedman) W. Student, Cornell U., 1977; BS, Syracuse U., 1982; MEd, U. Va., 1986. Dir. coll. age svcs. Jewish Community Ctr., Richmond, Va., 1986-89; rehab. specialist Intracorp, Richmond, 1989-92, Genex, Richmond, 1992-93, Cor Vel Corp., Richmond, 1993—. Mem. Jefferson scholar selection com. U. Va., Richmond, 1987-90; alumni rep. Syracuse (N.Y.) U., 1987—. Honored by Women Who Make A Difference, 1989. Jewish. Home: 11306 Lady Slipper Ln Richmond VA 23236

WALDO, KATITA, ballet dancer; b. Madrid. Student, Escuela de Danza Classica, San Francisco Ballet Sch. Apprentice San Francisco Ballet, 1987-88, mem. Corps de Ballet, 1988-90, soloist, 1990-94, prin. dancer, 1994—; tchr. summer programs Ithaca (N.Y.) Ballet, Modesto Ballet, 1993. Appeared in ballets The Sleeping Beauty, Swan Lake, Concerto in d: Poulenc, Ballet d'Isoline, Guiliani: Variations on a Theme, Beads of Memory, Aurora Polaris, Handel- a Celebration, Menuetto, Bugaku, The Four Temperaments, Who Cares?, Theme and Variations, Stars and Stripes, Agon, Ballo della Regina, Serenade, La Pavane Rouge, Calcium Light Night, The Concert, Interplay, Rodin, Dark Elegies, Tagore, Nutcracker, Romeo and Juliet, La Sylphide, In the middle, somewhat elevated, Pulcinella, In Perpetuum, Job, The Sons of Horus, The "Wanderer" Fantasy, Dreams of Harmony, The Comfort Zone, Scarlatti Portfolio, Vivaldi Concerto Grosso, Variations de Ballet, La Fill mal gardee. Office: San Francisco Ballet 455 Franklin St San Francisco CA 94102-4471*

WALDON, KAREN RENEE, asset manager; b. San Francisco, Dec. 10, 1960; d. Richard Allen and Dorothy Louise (Underhill) W. Masters, U. Hamburg, Germany, 1980. Project mgr. Balzhiser Group Archs., Seattle, 1980-83, Roebling Mgmt., Seattle, 1983-84; pres. Waldon, VanWaters & Tyler, Seattle, 1984-88; mng. officer Fed. Savs. and Loan Ins. Corp., Seattle and Atlanta, 1988-90; account officer Fed. Deposit Ins. Corp., Atlanta, 1990; mem. Atlanta Com. for Olympic Games, 1990-93; asset mgr. Mut. Benefit Life Ins. Co., Atlanta, 1993—. Vol. Habitat for Humanity, Atlanta, 1989—, Project Atlanta, 1993—; tchr. Literacy 2000, Atlanta, 1989—. Democrat.

WALDROP, ENID JOHNSON, nurse; b. Waco, Tex., Mar. 22, 1945; d. Elbert Medley and Agnes Lorraine (Fulbright) Johnson; m. George William Waldrop, Aug. 6, 1964; children: Suzanne Elaine, Charlotte Michelle, Christy Lynn. BS in Nursing, U. Mary Hardin-Baylor, Belton, Tex., 1980. RN, Tex.; cert. women's healthcare nurse practitioner, ANCC. Staff nurse Hillcrest Bapt. Med. Ctr., Waco, 1980-81, Waco-McLennan County Pub. Health Dist., Waco, 1981-93; women's health care nurse practitioner Scott and White Clinic, Temple, Tex., 1993—. Mem. Hist. Waco Found., 1987—. Mem. AWHONN, Tex. Nurse Practitioners, Am. Acad. Nurse Practitioners. Republican. Methodist.

WALDROP, LINDA M., medical administrator; b. Jefferson County, Ala., Oct. 24, 1942; d. Luther Grady Jr. and Anna Katherine (Gray) McGill; m. Bennie Lee Waldrop Jr., Mar. 14, 1961; children: Tracy L., Terry L. AS, Jefferson State Jr. Coll., 1971; BSN, Samford U., 1985; MA, U. Ala., Birmingham, 1989. Head nurse open heart ICU Bapt. Med. Ctr.-Montclair, Birmingham, 1976-82, head nurse telemetry unit, 1985-87, head nurse med. unit, 1983-85, head nurse oncology unit, 1987-90, edn. coord.; internal auditor Bapt. Med. Ctr.-Montclair, 1991; dir. med.-surg. telemetry nursing Shelby Med. Ctr., Alabaster, Ala., 1991—, dir. gastroenterol. svcs., 1993—, dir. women's svcs., nursing internal auditor, 1993—. Mem. ANA (cert. nursing adminstrn.), Oncology Nursing Soc., AACN, Nat. Mgmt. Assn.

WALENTIK, CORINNE ANNE, pediatrician; b. Rockville Centre, N.Y., Nov. 24, 1949; d. Edward Robert and Evelyn Mary (Brinskele) Finno; m. David Stephen Walentik, June 24, 1972; children: Anne, Stephen, Kristine. AB with honors, St. Louis U., 1970, MD, 1974, MPH, 1992. Diplomate Am. Bd. Pediatrics, Am. Bd. Neonatal and Perinatal Medicine. Resident in pediatrics St. Louis U. Group Hosps., 1974-76, fellow in neonatology, 1976-78; neonatalogist St. Mary's Health Ctr., St. Louis, 1978-79; co-dir. neonatal unit St. Louis City Hosps., 1979-83, dir. neonatal unit, 1983-85; dir. neonatology St. Louis Regional Med. Ctr., 1985—; asst. prof. pediatrics St. Louis U., 1980-94, assoc. clin. prof., 1994—; supr. nursery follow up program Cardinal Glennon Children's Hosp., 1979—. Contbr. articles to profl. jours. Mem. adv. com. Mo. Perinatal Program., 1983-86. Fellow Am. Acad. Pediatrics; mem. Mo. Perinatal Assn. (pres. 1983), Nat. Perinatal Assn. (coun. 1984-87), Mo. State Med. Assn., St. Louis Met. Med. Soc. Roman Catholic. Home: 7234 Princeton Ave Saint Louis MO 63130-3027 Office: St Louis Regional Med Ctr 5535 Delmar Blvd Saint Louis MO 63112-3005

WALES, SISTER PATRICE, school system administrator; b. Washington, Sept. 9, 1935; d. Robert Corning and Bernadette Mary (Dyer) W. BA, Dunbarton Coll. of Holy Cross, 1957; MTS, Cath. U. Am., 1978; PhD, U. Md., 1993. Cert. tchr., Md. Tchr. mid. sch. St. Marys, Laurel, Md., 1960-61; tchr. high sch. St. Vincent Pallotti High Sch., Laurel, Md., 1962-65; instr. nursing sch. St. Mary's Sch. Nursing, Huntington, W.Va., 1965-66; tchr. St. Vincent Pallotti High Sch., Laurel, 1967-76, adminstr., 1976—, chair sci. dept., 1962-80, dean students, 1976-87, sponsorship dir., 1988—; bd. dirs. St. Vincent Pallotti High Sch., Laurel, 1988—; dir. German Exch. Program, Laurel, Ahlen, Germany, 1976—. Senator Sisters Senate Archdiocese of Washington, 1993—. NSF grantee, 1967, 69, 71. Mem. ASCD, Nat. Cath. Edn. Assn. Roman Catholic. Home: 404 8th St Laurel MD 20707-4032 Office: St Vincent Pallotti High Sch 113 8th St Laurel MD 20707-4025

WALHOUT, JUSTINE SIMON, chemistry educator; b. Aberdeen, S.D., Dec. 11, 1930; d. Otto August and Mabel Ida (Tews) S.; m. Donald Walhout, Feb. 1, 1958; children: Mark, Timothy, Lynne, Peter. BS, Wheaton Coll., 1952; PhD, Northwestern U., 1956. Instr. Wright City Community Coll., Chgo., 1955-56; asst. prof. Rockford (Ill.) Coll., 1956-59, assoc. prof., 1959-66, 81-89, prof., 1989—, dept. chmn., 1987—; cons. Pierce Chem. Co., Rockford, 1968-69; trustee Rockford (Ill.) Coll., 1987-91. Contbr. articles to profl. jours. Mem. Ill. Bd. Edn., 1974-81. Mem. Am. Chem. Soc., AAUW (Ill. bd. mem. 1985-87), Rockford LWV (bd. dirs. 1983-85), Sigma Xi. Presbyterian. Home: 320 N Rockford Ave Rockford IL 61107 Office: Rockford Coll 5050 E State St Rockford IL 61108-2393

WALITZER, KIMBERLY SUE, psychologist, researcher; b. Medford, Mass., Aug. 16, 1962. BA in Psychology, U. Mo., 1984, MA in Clin. Psychology, 1987, PhD in Clin. Psychology, 1990. Lic. psychologist, N.Y. Intern in psychology VA Med. Ctr., Brockton, Mass., 1989-90; fellow Harvard U., Boston, 1989-90; rsch. scientist Rsch. Inst. on Addictions, Buffalo, 1990—. Contbr. articles to profl. jours. Grant application reviewer Nat. Inst. Alcohol Abuse and Alcoholism, Washington, 1993—. Grantee Rsch. Inst. on Addictions, 1992, Nat. Inst. Alcohol Abuse and Alcoholism, 1994—. Mem. APA, Assn. for Advancement Behavior Therapy, Rsch. Soc. Alcoholism. Office: Rsch Inst on Addictions 1021 Main St Buffalo NY 14203

WALKER, ALICE MALSENIOR, author; b. Eatonton, Ga., Feb. 9, 1944; d. Willie Lee and Minnie (Grant) W.; m. Melvyn R. Leventhal, Mar. 17, 1967 (div. 1977); 1 dau., Rebecca Walker Leventhal. B.A., Sarah Lawrence Coll., 1966; Ph.D. (hon.), Russell Sage U., 1972; D.H.L. (hon.), U. Mass., 1983. Wild Tree Press, Navarro, Calif., co-founder and pub. 1984-88; Writer in residence and teacher of black studies at Jackson State College, 1968-69, and Tougaloo College, 1970-71; lecturer in literature, Wellesley Coll. and U. Mass.-Boston, both 1972-73; distinguished writer in Afro-American studies dept., U. Calif. Berkeley, 1982; Fannie Hurst Prof. of Literature, Brandeis U., Waltham, Mass., 1982. Author: Once, 1968, The Third Life of Grange Copeland, 1970, Five Poems, 1972, Revolutionary Petunias and Other Poems, 1973 (National Book award nomination 1973, Lillian Smith award Southern Regional Council 1973), In Love and Trouble, 1973, (Richard and Hinda Rosenthal Found. award Am. Acad. and Inst. of Arts and Letters 1974) Langston Hughes: American Poet, 1973, Meridian, 1976, Goodnight, Willie Lee, I'll See You in the Morning, 1979, You Can't Keep a Good Woman Down, 1981, The Color Purple, 1982 (Pulitzer Prize for Fiction 1983, Am. Book Award 1983, National Book Critics Circle Award nomination 1982), In Search of Our Mothers' Gardens, 1983, Horses Make a Landscape Look More Beautiful, 1984, To Hell With Dying, 1988, Living By the Word: Selected Writings, 1988, The Temple of My Familiar, 1989, Her Blue Body Everything We Know: Earthling Poems (1965-90), 1991, Finding the Green Stone, 1991, Possessing the Secret of Joy, 1992, (with Pratibha Parmar) Warrior Marks, 1993, (with others) Double Stitch: Black Women Write About Mothers & Daughters, 1993, Everyday Use, 1994; editor: I Love Myself When I'm Laughing... And Then Again When I'm Looking Mean and Impressive, 1979. Bread Loaf Writer's Conference, scholar, 1966; first prize, American Scholar essay contest, 1967; Merrill writing fellowship, 1967; McDowell Colony fellowship, 1967, 1977-78; National Endowment for the Arts grant, 1969, 1977; Radcliffe Inst. fellowship, 1971-73; O. Henry Awd., 1986, for "Kindred Spirits"; Guggenheim Found award, 1977-78; Nora Astorga Leadership award, 1989; Bay Area Book Reviewers Assn. Fred Cody award for Lifetime Achievement, 1990; PEN Ctr USA West Freedom to Write award, 1990. Address: care Harcourt Brace 111 Fifth Ave New York NY 10003*

WALKER, ANGELITE BERNADINE, real estate and insurance broker; b. Mobile, Ala., July 27, 1936; d. William James and Lenice Ziobel (Doyle) Byrd; children: Anita Angelite Walker, Ferguson, Clarence Quentin, David William, Bernard Walkers, Joseph Edwin Ferguson. Student, Bklyn. Coll.,

1954-56; cert. Real Estate,, N.Y.U., 1973-77; cert., Life Underwriters Tng. Coun., 1980-83; Real Estate Broker, Bklyn. Coll., 1986-88. Lic. notary pub., real estate broker, life, health and accident ins. sales, N.Y. Advance mortgage clk. Freedom Nat. Bank, N.Y.C., 1975-77; real estate sales rep. Pinkey Harris Realty, Bklyn., 1980-88; real estate broker pvt. practice, N.Y.C., 1986—; real estate sales rep. Green and Spence Realty, Bklyn., 1977-80; life ins. sales broker Bankers Life and Casualty Co., 1979-81, Union Ctrl. Life Ins. Co., Inc., 1980—; dir. Property Tax Assistance Project, Bklyn., 1984-85. Pres. Aux. Bd. Woodhull Hosp., Bklyn.; mem. adminstrv. com., bd. trustees, usher Newman Meml. United Meth. Ch.; mem. at large ins. com. United Meth. Ch. Mem. Nat. Assn. Real Estate Brokers, Inc. (Region II, Women's Coun.), Bedford Stuyvesant Real Estate Bd., Inc. (past mem. bd. dirs.), Assn. LIfe Underwriters, Women Life Underwriters Conf., Order of Eastern Star (past worthy matron, youth supr.). Home: 1000 President St Apt 1E Brooklyn NY 11225-1367 Office: 555 5th Ave Ste 1400 New York NY 10017-2416

WALKER, ANN F., federal official. BA, Sarah Lawrence Coll. Account supr. Burson-Marsteller, N.Y.C.; sr. account supr. Hill and Knowlton, N.Y.C.; spl. asst. to pres., dir. comm. rsch. The White House, Washington, 1993—. Office: The White House Office Comm Rsch Washington DC 20503*

WALKER, ANNETTE, counseling administrator; b. Birmingham, Ala., Sept. 20, 1953; d. Jesse and Luegene (Wright) W. BS in Edn., Huntingdon Coll., 1976; MS in Adminstrn., Supervision, Troy State U., 1977, 78, MS in Sch. Counseling, 1990, AA in Sch. Adminstrn., 1992; diploma, World Travel Sch., 1990; diploma in Cosmetology, John Patterson Coll., 1992. Cert. tchr., adminstr., Ala.; lic. cosmetologist, Ala. Tchr. Montgomery (Ala.) Pub. Sch. System, 1976-89, sch. counselor, 1989—; gymnastics tchr. Cleveland Ave. YMCA, 1971-76; girls coach Montgomery Parks and Recreation, 1973-76; summer sch. sci. tchr. grades 7-9, 1977-88; chmn. dept. sci. Bellingrath Sch., 1987-90, courtesy com., 1987-88, sch. discipline com., 1977-84; recreation asst. Gunter AFB, Ala., 1981-83; calligraphy tchr. Gunter Youth Ctr., 1982; program dir. Maxwell AFB, Ala., 1983-89, vol. tchr. Internat. Officer Sch., 1985—, Ala. Goodwill Amb., 1985—, day camp dir., 1987, calligraphy tchr., 1988; leader of workshops in field. Mem. CAP; tchr. Sunday sch. Beulah Bapt. Ch., Montgomery; vol. zoo activities Tech. Scholarship Program for Ala. Tchrs. Computer Courses, Montgomery, Ala.; bd. dirs. Cleveland Ave. YMCA, 1976-80; sponsor Bell-Howe chpt. Young Astronauts, 1986-90, Pate Howe chpt. Young Astronauts, 1991-92; judge Montgomery County Children Festival Elem. Sci. Fair, 1988-90; bd. dirs. Troy State U. Drug Free Schs., 1992—; chmn. Maxwell AFB Red Cross-Youth, 1986-88, goodwill amb. sponsor to various families; active Civil Air Patrol, 1989—. Recipient Outstanding High Sch. Sci./Math. Tchr. award Sigma Xi, 1989, Most Outstanding Youth Coun. Leader award Maxwell AFB Youth Ctr., 1987, Outstanding Ala. Goodwill Amb. award, 1989, 95; named Tchr. of the Week, WCOV-TV, 1992, Ala. Tchr. in Space Program, summer 1989, Local Coord. Young Astronaut Program, 1988. Mem. NEA, Montgomery County Edn. Assn., Montgomery Sch. Counselors Assn., Nat. Sci. Tchrs. Assn., Ala. Sch. Counselors, Space Camp Amb., Huntingdon Alumni Assn. (sec.-treas.), Ala. Goodwill Amb., Montgomery Capital City Club, Young Astronauts, Eastern Star, Zeta Phi Beta, Chi Delta Phi, Kappa Pi. Home: 2501 Westwood Dr Montgomery AL 36108-4448 Office: Paterson Sch 1015 E Jefferson St Montgomery AL 36104-2712

WALKER, BRENDA JUNE, secondary school educator; b. McAlester, Okla., Aug. 26, 1955; d. Johnie H. and Theresa (Wilson) W. BS in Biology, Chemistry, Northeastern State U., Tahlequah, Okla., 1977; MA in Counseling, Northeastern State U., 1980. Physical sci. tchr. Tahlequah Pub. Schs., 1977—; tchr. gifted and talented Explorations in Creativity, Okla. City, 1990; curriculma adviser Holt, Rinehart and Winston, Orlando, Fla., 1993. Mem. Sequoyah High Sch. Bd., Tahlequah, 1988-94, Cherokee Nation Edn. Core Com., Tahlequah, 1993-94, Gifted and Talented Com., 1993-94, Miss Cherokee Adv. Bd., 1992-94. Named Sertoma Tchr. of Month, 1987, 88. Mem. AAUW, NEA, Okla. Edn. Assn., Tahlequah Edn. Assn., Okla. Acad. Sci. Democrat. Home: PO Box 72 Tahlequah OK 74465

WALKER, BRIGITTE MARIA, translator, linguistic consultant; b. Stolp, Germany, Sept. 20, 1934; came to U.S., 1957; d. Joseph Karl and Ursula Maria Margot Ehrler; m. John V. Kelley (div.); 1 child, John V. Jr.; m. Edward D. Walker, July 3, 1977. Grad., Erlangen Translator's Sch., Germany, 1956; grad. fgn. corres., Berlitz Sch., Germany, 1956. Bilingual sec., translator Spencer Patent Law Office, Washington, 1959-62; office mgr., translator I. William Millen, Millen and White, Patent Law, Washington, 1962-67; prin. Tech. Translating Bur., Washington, 1967-68, St. Petersburg Beach, Fla., 1968—; cons. for patent law offices, Washington, 1962—; ofcl. expert for ct. Paul M. Craig, Patent Atty., Rockford, Ill., 1981; cons. to sci. editor Merriam-Webster, Inc., Springfield, Mass., 1987—. Author: German-English/English-German Last-Resort Dictionary for Technical Translators, 1991, (poetry) The Other Side of the Mirror, 1992 (Poetry award Nat. League Am. Pen Women 1994); co-translator: The Many Faces of Research, 1980; holder of trademark in field. Evaluator fgn. textbooks Pinellas County Sch. Bd., St. Petersburg, 1987, German judge, 1988. Recognized for support of pub. edn. Pinellas County Sch. Bd., 1988; recipient Meritorious Pub. Svc. award City of St. Petersburg Beach, 1987, Poetry award Nat. Leage Am. Pen Women, 1994. Mem. Mensa. Democrat. Lutheran. Home and Office: 7150 Sunset Way Apt 1007 Saint Petersburg FL 33706-3650

WALKER, CAROLYN PEYTON, English language educator; b. Charlottesville, Va., Sept. 15, 1942; d. Clay M. and Ruth Peyton. BA in Am. History and Lit., Sweet Briar Coll., 1965; cert. in French, Alliance Francaise, Paris, 1966; EdM, Tufts U., 1970; MA in English and Am. Lit., Stanford U., 1974, PhD in English Edn., Stanford U., 1977. Tchr. Elem. and jr. high schs. in Switzerland, 1967-69; tchr. elem. grades Boston Sch. System, 1966-67, 69-70; Newark (Calif.) Unified Sch. System, 1970-72; instr. div. humanities Canada Coll., Redwood City, Calif., 1973, 76-78; instr. Sch. Bus., U. San Francisco, 1973-74; evaluation cons. Inst. Profl. Devel., San Jose, Calif., 1975-76; asst. dir. Learning Assistance Ctr., Stanford U., Calif., 1972-77, dir., 1977-84, lectr. Sch. Edn., 1975-84, dept. English, 1977-84, supr. counselors, tutors and tchrs., 1972-84; assoc. prof. dept. English, San Jose State U., Calif., 1984—; dir. English dept. Writing Ctr., 1986—, Steinbeck Rsch. Ctr., 1986-87; pres. Waverley Edn., Inc., Ednl. Cons., 1983-91; head cons. to pres. to evaluate coll.'s writing program, San Jose City Coll., 1985-87; cons. U. Tex., Dallas, 1984, Stanford U., 1984, 1977-78, CCNY, 1979, U. Wis., 1980, numerous testing programs; cons. to pres. San Diego State U., 1982, Ednl. Testing Svc., 1985-88, also to numerous univs. and colls.; condr. reading and writing workshops, 1972—; reviewer Random House Books, 1978—, Rsch. in the Teaching of English, 1983—, Course Tech., Inc., 1990—; cons. Basic Skills Task Force, U.S. Office Edn., 1977-79, Right to Read, Calif. State Dept. Edn., 1977-82, Program for Gifted and Talented, Fremont (Calif.) Unified Sch. Dist., 1981-82; bd. dirs. high tech. sci. ctr., San Jose, 1983-84; speaker numerous profl. confs. Author: (with Patricia Killen) Handbook for Teaching Assistants at Stanford University, 1977, Learning Center Courses for Faculty and Staff: Reading, Writing, and Time Management, 1981, How to Succeed as a New Teacher: A Handbook for Teaching Assistants, 1978, ESL Courses for Faculty & Staff: An Additional Opportunity to Serve the Campus Community, 1983, (with Karen Wilson) Tutor Handbook for the Writing Center at San Jose State University, 1989, (with others) Academic Tutoring at the Learning Assistance Center, 1980, Writing Conference Talk: Factors Associated with High and Low Rated Writing Conferences, 1987, Lifeline Mac: A Handbook for Instructors in the Macintosh Computer Classrooms, 1989, Communications with the Faculty: Vital Links for the Success of Writing Centers, 1991, Coming to America, 1993, Teacher Dominance in the Writing Conference, 1992, Instant Curriculum: Just Add Tutors and Students, 1993; contbr. chpts. to Black American Literature Forum, 1991; contbr. articles to profl. jours. Vol. fundraiser Peninsula Ctr. for the Blind, Palo Alto, Calif., 1982—, The Resource Ctr. for Women, Palo Alto, 1975-76. Recipient Award for Outstanding Contbns., U.S. HEW, 1979, award ASPIRE (federally funded program), 1985, two awards Student Affirmative Action, 1986, award Western Coll. Reading & Learning Assn., 1984; numerous other awards and grants. Mem. MLA, Coll. Reading & Learning Assn. (treas. 1982-84, bd. dirs. 1982-84), Nat. Coun. Tchrs. English, No. Calif. Coll. Reading Assn. (sec.-treas. 1976-78), Am. Assn. U. Profs., Jr. League Palo Alto (bd. dirs. 1977-78, 83-84). Home: 2350 Waverley St Palo Alto CA 94301-4143 Office: San Jose State U English Dept San Jose CA 95192

WALKER, DEBRA MAY, marketing professional; b. Flint, Mich., May 11, 1956; d. Vern Luke and Rosemary (Deanhofer) W.; m. Stephen Robert Strong, Aug. 14, 1982; 1 child, Evan Walker Strong. BA in Advt., Mich. State U., 1978, MA in Advt., 1979. Sr. bus. analyst Goodyear Tire & Rubber Co., Akron, Ohio, 1979-81, mgr. advt. rsch., 1981-82, mgr. market planning systems, 1982-85; mktg. strategy mgr. Europe Goodyear Tire & Rubber Co., Brussels, 1985-89; mktg. strategy mgr. U.S. Goodyear Tire & Rubber Co., Akron, 1989-90, mktg. mgr. retail stores div., 1990-91, gen. mktg. mgr. retail, 1991-92; mktg. mgr. auto tires Goodyear Tire & Rubber Co., 1992-94; mgr. dealer sales San Leandro, Calif., 1994—; speaker on mktg. and distbn. topics. Contbr. articles to various publs. Mem. Am. Mgmt. Assn. Office: Goodyear Tire & Rubber Co San Francisco Dist 1800 Merced St San Leandro CA 94577-3228

WALKER, E. ANN, association adminsitrator, workshop consultant; b. Avon Park, Fla., Aug. 3, 1951; d. Litton Meredith and Harriet Elizabeth (Williams) W. BA in Sociology, Lake Erie Coll., 1973; MS in Criminology, Fla. State U., 1975. Correctional counselor I Fla. Dept. Corrections, Tampa, 1976-79; renovation cons. Libbey Apts., Sebring, Fla., 1978-81; program dir. Heart of Fla. Coun. Girl Scouts, Lakeland, 1980-87; dep. dir. West Pacific Girl Scouts, Okinawa, Japan, 1988-91; exec. dir. Becky Thatcher Area Coun. Girl Scouts, Hannibal, Mo., 1991—; cons. USN Chaplains, CREDO, Okinawa, 1990-91, United Meth. Women Mo., 1993, Assn. Girl Scouts Exec. Staff, 1993. Officer Hannibal Arts Coun., 1992-94; lay speaker Mo. East conf. United Meth. Ch., 1993-94. Mem. Girl Scouts U.S.A. (life), AAUW (pres. 1993-95), Assn. Girl Scout Exec. Staff (sustaining mem.), Toastmasters Internat. (treas. 1992-94, Competent Toastmaster 1991, Able Toastmaster 1994). Office: Becky Thatcher Coun Girl Scouts 512 Church St Hannibal MO 63401-4324

WALKER, ELJANA M. DU VALL, civic worker; b. France, Jan. 18, 1924; came to U.S., 1948; naturalized, 1954; student Med. Inst., U. Paris, 1942-47; m. John S. Walker, Jr., Dec. 31, 1947; children—John, Peter, Barbara. Pres., Loyola Sch. PTA, 1958-59; bd. dirs. Santa Claus shop, 1959-73; treas. Archdiocese Denver Catholic Women, 1962-64; rep. Cath. Parent-Tchr League, 1962-65; pres. Aux. Denver Gen. Hosp., 1966-69; precinct committeewoman Arapahoe County Republican Women's Com., 1973-74; mem. re-election com. Arapahoe County Rep. Party, 1973-78, Reagan election com., 1980; block worker Arapahoe County March of Dimes, Heart Assn., Hemophilia Drive, Muscular Dystrophy and Multiple Sclerosis Drive, 1978-81; cen. city asst. Guild Debutante Charities, Inc. Recipient Distinguished Service award Am.-by-choice, 1966; named to Honor Roll, ARC, 1971. Mem. Cherry Hills Symphony, Lyric Opera Guild, Alliance Franciase (life mem.), ARC, Civic Ballet Guild (life mem.), Needlework Guild Am. (v.p. 1980-82), Kidney Found. (life), Denver Art Mus., U. Denver Art and Conservation Assns. (chmn. 1980-82), U. Denver Women's Library Assn., Chancellors Soc, Passage Inc., Frends of the Fine Arts Found. (life mem. Denver). Roman Catholic. Clubs: Union (Chgo.); Denver Athletic, 26 (Denver); Welcome to Colo. Internat. Address: 2301 Green Oaks Dr Greenwood Village CO 80121

WALKER, ELVA MAE DAWSON, health consultant; b. Everett, Mass., June 29, 1914; d. Charles Edward and Mary Elizabeth (Livingston) Dawson; m. John J. Spillane Jr. R.N., Peter Bent Brigham Hosp., Boston, 1937; student Simmons Coll., 1935, U. Minn., 1945-48; m. Walter Willard Walker, Dec. 16, 1939 (div. 1969). Supr. nursery Wesson Maternity Hosp., Springfield, Mass., 1937-38; asst. supr. out-patient dept. Peter Bent Brigham Hosp., Boston, 1938-40; supr. surgery and out-patient dept. Univ. Hosps., Mpls., 1945. Chmn. Gov.'s Citizens Coun. on Aging, Minn., 1960-68, acting dir., 1962-66, Econ. Opportunity Com. Hennepin County, 1964-69; v.p., treas. Nat. Purity Soap & Chem. Co., 1968-69, pres., 1969-76, chmn. bd., 1976—; cons. on aging to Minn. Dept. Pub. Welfare, 1962-67; mem. nat. adv. Coun. for Nurse Tng. Act, 1965-69, Com. Status on Women in Armed Svcs., 1967-70; dir. Nat. Coun. on the Aging, 1963-67, sec., 1965-67, 1986-88, chairperson, 1988-91; chmn. Minn. Bd. on Aging, 1982-91, Nat. Retiree Vol. Ctr., 1982-89; dir. Planning Agy. for Hosps. of Met. Mpls., 1963-67, United Hosp. Fund of Hennepin County, 1955-60, Nat. Coun. Social Work Edn., 1966-68; vice chmn. Hennepin County Gen. Hosp. Adv. Bd., 1965-68; sec. Hennepin County Health Coalition, 1973; chmn. bd. dirs. Am. Rehab. Found, 1962-68, vice chmn., 1968-70, chmn. Minn. Bd. On Aging, 1988-91, Sr. Resources, 1985-87; pres. bd. trustees Northwestern Hosp., 1956-59, Children's Hosp. Mpls., 1961-65; dir. Twin Cities Internat. Program for Youth Leaders and Social Workers, Inc., 1965-67; mem. community adv. coun. United Community Funds and Coun. Am., Inc., 1968, Nat. Assembly Social Policy and Devel., Inc., 1968-74, Minn. Action for Children Commn., 1989—, mem., 1991—; mem. priorities determination com. United Fund Mpls., 1971; vice chmn. govt. specifications com. Soap and Detergent Assn., 1972-76, vice-chmn. indsl. and instn. com., 1974-76, chmn., 1976-78, bd. dirs., 1974—; candidate for Congress, 3d Minn. Dist., 1966; trustee Macalester Coll., Archie D. and Bertha H. Walker Found.; chmn. St. Mary's Jr. Coll. Bd., 1970-74, 78-80; pres. U. Minn. Sch. Nursing Found., 1958-70; pres. Minn. Gerontological Soc., 1994-95; sec. Metro Area Agy. Aging Minn., 1995—. Mem. Am. Pub. Welfare Assn., Minn. Gerontol. Soc. (pres. 1994—), Mpls. Med. Research Found., Minn. League Nursing (pres. 1971-73), Jr. League Mpls. Democrat. Presbyterian. Home: 3655 Northome Rd Wayzata MN 55391-3020 Office: Nat Purity Soap & Chem Co 434 Lakeside Ave Minneapolis MN 55405-1529

WALKER, EVELYN, retired educational television executive; b. Birmingham, Ala.; d. Preston Lucas and Mattie (Williams) W.; AB, Huntingdon Coll., 1927; student Cornell U., 1927-28; MA, U. Ala., 1963; LHD, Huntingdon Coll., 1974. Speech instr. Phillips High Sch., Birmingham, 1930-34; head speech dept. Ramsay High Sch., Birmingham, 1934-52; chmn. radio and TV, Birmingham Pub. Schs., 1944-75, head instructional TV programming svcs., 1969-75; mem. summer faculty extension div. U. Va., 1965, 66, 67; former regional cons. ednl. TV broadcasting; Miss Ann, broadcaster children's daily radio program, Birmingham, 1946-57; prodr. Our Am. Heritage radio series, 1944-54; TV staff prodr. programs shown daily Ala. Pub. TV Network, 1954-75; past cons. Gov.'s Ednl. TV Legis. Study Com., 1953; nat. del. Asian-Am. Women Broadcasters Conf., 1966; former regional cons. Ednl. TV Broadcasting. Mem. emerita Nat. Def. Adv. Com. on Women in Svcs.; past TV-radio co-chmn. Gov.'s Adv. Bd. Safety Com.; past chmn. creative TV-radio writing competition Festival of Arts; past audio-visual chmn. Ala. Congress, also past mem. Birmingham coun. PTA; media chmn. Gov.'s Commn. on Yr. of the Child; bd. dirs. Women's Army Corps Mus., Fort MiClellen, 1960-93. Recipient Alumnae Achievement award Huntingdon Coll., 1958; Tops in Our Town award Birmingham News, 1957; Air Force Recruiting plaque, 1961; Spl. Bowl award for promoting arts through Ednl. TV. Birmingham Festival of Arts, 1962; citation 4th Army Corps., 1962; cert. of appreciation Ala. Multiple Sclerosis Soc., 1962; Freedoms Found. at Valley Forge Educator's medal award, 1963; Top TV award ARC, 1964; Ala. Woman of Achievement award, 1964; Bronze plaque Ala. Dist. Exch. Clubs, 1969; cert. of appreciation Birmingham Bd. Edn., 1975; Obelisk award Children's Theatre, 1976; 20-Yr. Svc. award Ala. Ednl. TV Commn.; key to city of Birmingham, 1966; named Woman of Yr., Birmingham, 1965; named Ala. Woman of Yr., Progressive Farmer mag., 1966; hon. col. Ala. Militia. Mem. Am. Assn. Ret. Persons, Ala. Assn. Ret. Tchrs., Huntingdon Coll. Alumnae Assn. (former internat. pres.), Former Am. Women in Radio and TV, Ala. Hist. Assn., Arlington Hist. Assn. (dir., pres. 1981-83), Magna Charta Dames (past state sec.-treas.), DAR (former pub. rels. com. Ala., TV chmn., state program chmn. 1979-85, state chmn. Seimes Microfilm com. 1985-88, state chmn. Motion Picture, Radio TV com. 1988-94, tricom. chmn. 1988-94), Colonial Dames 17th Century (chmn. pub. rels. com.), U.S. Daus. 1812 (past state TV chmn.), Daus. Am. Colonists (past 2d v.p. local chpt., past state TV and radio chmn.), Ams. Royal Descent, Royal Order Garter, Plantagenets Soc. Am., Salvation Army Women's Aux., Symphony Aux., Humane Soc. Aux., Eagle Forum, Nat. League Am. Pen Women, Womens's Com. 100 for Birmingham (bd. dirs.), Royal Order Crown, Women in Communications (past local pres., nat. headliner 1965), Birmingham-Jefferson Hist. Soc., Delta Delta Delta (mem. Golden Circle), Ladies Golf Assn., Birmingham Country Club, The Club. Methodist. Home: Mountain Brook 744 Euclid Ave Birmingham AL 35213-2538

WALKER, FLORENCE ANN, preschool educator, insurance underwriter; b. Magnolia, Miss., Nov. 23, 1939; d. Albert E. and Florence (Hunnicutt) Pardue; m. Charles Hickman Walker, June 24, 1961; children: Charles David (dec.), John Dwayne, Paul Douglas. BA, La. Coll., 1961. Cert. elem. tchr., La. Tchr. Cen. Elem., Baton Rouge, 1961, North Bayou Rapides Elem., Alexandria, La., 1961-64; tchr., asst. dir. Southside Bapt. Preschool, Baton Rouge, 1972-86, dir., 1986—; chief underwriter/adminstr. Starmount Life Ins. Co., Baton Rouge, 1986—. Mem. Parkview Eagle Backers, 1983-87, Parent, Tchr. and Friends, Baton Rouge. Mem. Assn. Life Ins. Underwriters, La. Assn. Educators, La. Assn. for Children Under Six, Nat. Assn. for Edn. of Young Children, So. Early Childhood Assn., Optimist Internat. Republican. Baptist. Office: Southside Bapt Presch 1700 Lee Dr Baton Rouge LA 70808-3831

WALKER, GLENDA CHITWOOD, mental health nurse; b. Fort Payne, Ala., Oct. 27, 1950; d. James R. and Imogene F. (Walker) Chitwood. BSN, Troy State U., 1973; MSN, U. Ala., 1978, DSN, 1983. Unit chief C.E.D. Mental Health Ctr., Gadsden, Ala., 1973-74, clin. specialist, 1975-76; asst. prof. Jacksonville (Ala.) State U., 1976-80; asst. prof. Vanderbilt U., Nashville, 1980-83, health major, 1983-85; assoc. dean U. N.D., Grand Forks, 1985-87; assoc. prof., assoc. dean for clin. and community affairs U. of Tex. Health Sci. Ctr., Houston, 1987-92; dir. divsn. nursing Stephen F. Austin State U., Nacogdoches, Tex., 1992—. Contbr. over 30 publs. to books, jours. and conf. proceedings. Recipient Hon. professorship Troy State U., 1987, Community Svc. award Houston Area Women Ctr.; named Leadership Tex., Found. for Women's Resources, 1990. Mem. Am. Orthopsychiat. Assn., Houston Area Psychiat. Nurses Assn. (bd. dirs. 1989, scholarship chair 1989), Houston Area Women's Ctr. (bd. dirs. 1990-920. Methodist. Home: RR 7 Box 5020 Nacogdoches TX 75961-9528 Office: PO Box 6156 Nacogdoches TX 75962

WALKER, HARRIETTE KATHERINE, religious administrator; b. Cad, Ga., Jan. 7, 1929; d. James Wilden and Eugie Arleen (Harton) Pack; m. William Daniel Walker, June 4, 1960. AA, Tenn. Wesleyan Coll., 1948; BA, U. Tenn., Chattanooga, 1953. Edn. dir. 1st United Meth. Ch., Copperhill, Tenn., 1953-55, Morristown, Tenn., 1955-57, Alcoa, Tenn., 1957-59; field exec. Citrus Coun. Girl Scouts, Inc., Orlando, Fla., 1968-85; program dir. United Meth. Ch., Satellite Beach, Fla., 1985-87; del. Fla. Ann. Conf., Lakeland, 1978-94, Meth. World Conf., Nairobi, 1986, Singapore, 1991; mem. Meth. World Coun., 1991; mem. exec. bd. Haitian Refugee Ministry, Ft. Pierce, Fla., 1988-94; United Meth. rep. Fla. Coun. Chs., Orlando, 1990—; mem. lay-clergy adv. coun. Bethune-Cookman Coll., 1994. Mem. Girl Scouts USA; mem. Daus. of the Nile, Shilah Temple No. 151, 1993, bd. lay ministry, 1993, Melbourne lay dist. leader, 1993, mem. Fla. conf. commn. on archives and history, 1992. Recipient Conf. Laity Christian Svc. award United Meth. Ch. Fla. Conf., 1988, Thanks Badge Citrus Coun. Girl Scouts U.S., 1988. Mem. AAUW, Nat. Assn. United Meth. Scouters Ministry, Missile, Space and Range Pioneers, Inc. (life), Fla. So. Coll. Pres. Coun., Pi Beta Phi. Home: 145 Allan Ln Melbourne Beach FL 32951

WALKER, JANE MARIE, women's health nurse; b. Portland, Maine, Jan. 19, 1959; d. Richard Herbert and Rose Marie (Renna) W.; 1 child, Amara. BSN, St. Joseph's Coll., Standish, Maine, 1981. Cert. in inpatient obstetrics; cert. BLS, neonatal resuscitation nurse. Nursing asst. St. Joseph's Manor, Portland, Maine, 1979-80; staff and charge nurse Maine Med. Ctr., Portland, Maine, 1981-82, staff nurse perdiem, 1988-89; staff nurse, resource person Brighton Med. Ctr., Portland, Maine, 1982—, profl. practice coun., 1991—, cons. quality assurance, 1992—. Musician, singer, educator chs. and ind. agys., Portland, 1985-92, 94—. Mem. Assn. Women's Health, Obstetric and Neonatal Nurses (cert.). Roman Catholic. Home: 21 Carlson St Westbrook ME 04092-4606

WALKER, JEWEL LEE, health facility administrator, consultant; b. Columbus, Ohio, Jan. 4, 1950; d. Zerold and Frieda Arlene (Tolliver) Sizemore; m. David Walker (div. Sept. 1984). AS, Mt. Vernon (Ohio) Nazarene Coll., 1970; diploma in Nursing, Mansfield (Ohio) Gen. Hosp., 1974; BSBA summa cum laude, Franklin U., 1983; postgrad., U. Dayton, 1985; MSA in Health Care Adminstrn., Cen. Mich. U., 1991. RN Ohio. Nurse Martin Meml. Hosp., Mt. Vernon, 1974-75, Ohio State U. Hosp., Columbus, 1974-78; chief registrar Nurses Profl. Registry, Columbus, 1978-82, cons., 1982-84; dir. nurses Bryden Manor Nursing Home, Columbus, 1982-83; health svcs. coord. Nat. Nursing Corp., Columbus, 1983-86, corp. dir. nursing svcs., 1986-88; pvt. practice nursing cons. Columbus, 1988—; shift dir. Columbus Community Hosp., 1991—. Active Columbus AIDS Task Force, 1988, Callvac, Columbus, 1988, Columbus Arthritis Found., 1988. Mem. NOW, ANA (cert. in nursing adminstrn. 1989), NAFE. Democrat. Home and Office: 1407 Royston Dr Columbus OH 43204-1532

WALKER, KATHRINE L., museum educational administrator; b. San Jose, Calif., Mar. 12, 1962; d. Paul D. and Barbara (White) W. BA with Honors, Stanford U., 1984; MA, Coll. William and Mary, 1985. Archaeologist Va. Rsch. Ctr. for Archaelogy, Newport, 1984-85; curatorial asst. Colonial Williamsburg Found., Va., 1985-86; asst. curator, coord. edn. Nantucket (Mass.) Historical Assn., 1986-88; dir. edn. Webb-Deane-Stevens Mus., Wethersfield, Conn., 1988-91, Lyman Allyn Art Mus., New London, Conn., 1991-94, Beach Mus. Art, Kans. State U., Manhattan, 1994—; mem. Mass. Arts Lottery Coun., Nantucket, 1988-89; chair diversity subcom. Regional Adv. Com. on Edn. Reform, 1994; adv. bd. Manhattan Arts Coun., 1995—. Author: (curriculum) The Outsiders, 1990, (gallery guide) From Distaff Side, 1992; author: (with others) Cultural Diversity in Literature, Art and Music, 1992. Vol. tchr. Nantucket Learning & Resource Ctr., 1988; mem. New London Culture and Tourism Alliance, 1991—. Grantee Inst. Mus. Svcs., Nantucket, 1987, 88, Rockefellor Found./Conn. Humanities Coun., New London, 1991-92; scholar Conn. Humanities Coun., 1989—. Mem. Am. Assn. Mus. (rep. bd. 1990-93, edn. com. 1988—, Excellence and Equity award), Nat. Art Edn. Assn., New England Mus. Assn. (edn. com. 1988—, chair 1991—), Conn. Art Docents Network (bd. dirs. 1991—), Alliance of Cultural Educators of Hartford. Office: Beach Mus Art 2323 Anderson Ave Ste 151 Manhattan KS 66502

WALKER, KRISTY LOU, sales executive; b. Austin, Tex., July 5, 1952; d. Joe Sidney and Mary Francis Louise (Engbloom) W.; 1 child, Jenny. BS in Criminal Justice, Southwest Tex. State U., 1983. Operator Southwestern Bell Tel. Co., Austin, 1970-77; mgr. Great Earth Vitamins, Austin, 1978-82; buyer Whole Foods Market, Austin, 1983-87; v.p. Sunbelt Organics, Inc., Austin, 1988-91, pres., 1991-93; nat. sales mgr. Herb Pharm, Williams, Ore., 1993—. Spiritual svcs. coord. ECKANKAR, Austin, 1984-85, pres., 1986-87, state comm. dir. 1989, local dir. 1992-93. Home: 1821 Westlake Dr # 114 Austin TX 78746 Office: Herb Pharm PO Box 116 Williams OR 97244

WALKER, LINDA ANN, financial planner; b. Denver, May 10, 1956; d. John Bruce Elmer and Ruth Evelyn (Rogers) Metsker; m. Sidney Carr Walker III, Feb. 9, 1992; 1 child. BA, U. Colo., 1978. CFP. Account exec. E.F. Hutton, Boulder, 1980-84; with Fin. Planning and Mgmt., Boulder, 1984-91, pres., 1989-91; pres. Premier Planning Assocs., Boulder, 1991—; cons. Lighting Co., Boulder, 1987-88. Actress (play) Shadow of a Gunman, 1991, La Ronde, 1992 (dancer) Who's There, 1991. Bd. dirs. Nancy Spanier Dance Theatre, Boulder, 1986—; mem. Win/Win, Boulder, 1989-91. Mem. Internat. Assn. of Fin. Planners, Inst. of CFP. Democrat. Office: Premier Planning Assocs 4730 Walnut St Ste 208 Boulder CO 80301-2558

WALKER, LINDA LEE, lawyer; b. Phila., Jan. 24, 1954; d. M. Lorenzo and Romaine Yvonne (Smith) W.; m. Bruce McIntyre, Sept. 16, 1981; children: Jessica Marie, Nicole Yvonne. BA with honors, U. Pa., 1975; JD, Yale U., 1978. Bar: N.Y. 1979, U.S. Dist. Ct. (so. and ea. dists.) N.Y. 1982, U.S. Ct. Appeals (1st cir.) 1982. Asst. regional atty. U.S. Dept. Health & Human Svcs., N.Y.C., 1978-82; assoc. Shea & Gould, N.Y.C., 1982-85; v.p., sr. assoc. counsel Chase Manhattan Bank, N.A., N.Y.C., 1985-89; v.p., assoc. gen. counsel Citicorp Credit Svcs., N.Y.C., 1989—. Mem. ABA, Phi Beta Kappa. Office: Citicorp Credit Svcs Inc 1 Court Sq Long Island City NY 11120

WALKER, LINDA WALESKA, educator; b. New Haven, Conn., June 19, 1952; d. Edward Lawrence and Waleska Katherine (Bussmann) W. BS, So. Conn. State Coll., 1974, postgrad., 1979. Tchr. 4th grade Union Sch., West HAven, Conn., 1974-75, tchr. 2d grade, 1975-76; tchr. 3d grade Washington Sch., West HAven, Conn., 1976-81; tchr. 1st grade Washington Magnet Sch., West HAven, Conn., 1981—; unit leader Washington Magnet Sch., 1991—; coop. tchr., mentor Conn. Dept. Edn., West Haven, 1987—. Mem. PTA (2d v.p. 1987—), Schooner Inc., New Haven, New Haven Preservation Trust.

Mem. Conn. Fedn. Tchrs., Vintage Truck Assn. Office: Washington Magnet Sch 369 Washington Ave West Haven CT 06516-5328

WALKER, MARGARET SMITH, real estate company executive; b. Lancashire, Eng., Oct. 14, 1943; came to U.S., 1964; d. Arthur Edward and Doris Audrey (Dawson) Smith; m. James E. Walker, Feb. 6, 1992. Lic. real estate agt., Hawaii. Broker Lawson-Worrall Inc. (now Worrall-McCarter), Honolulu, 1974-81; pres. Maggie Parkes & Assocs., Inc., Honolulu, 1981—. Bd. dirs. Hawaii Combined Tng. Assn., Honolulu, 1985—; dist. commr. Lio Lii Pony Club, Honolulu, 1980; com. chmn. Hist. Hawaii Found., Honolulu, 1990. Mem. Am. Horse Shows Assn., Hawaii Horse Shows Assn., Outrigger Canoe Club. Episcopalian. Office: PO Box 25083 Honolulu HI 96825-0083

WALKER, MARY ANN, lawyer; b. Anderson, S.C., Aug. 21, 1953; d. Ernest McCreary and Virginia (Selman) Glymph; m. Thomas M. Walker, Aug. 28, 1976. BS, U. Va., 1975; JD, U. Richmond, 1979. Bar: Va. 1979, U.S. Dist. Ct. (ea. dist.) Va. 1980, U.S. Ct. Appeals (4th cir.) 1980, U.S. Ct. Appeals (5th, 7th and D.C. cirs.) 1984, U.S. Ct. Appeals (10th cir.) 1987, U.S. Supreme Ct. 1987, D.C. 1988. Assoc. Wickwire, Gavin & Gibbs, P.C., Washington and Vienna, Va., 1980-86; ptnr. Wickwire, Gavin & Gibbs, P.C., Washington, 1986-89, Pepper, Hamilton & Scheetz, Washington, 1989-91, Shaw, Pittman, Potts & Trowbridge, Washington, 1992-94, Mudge Rose Guthrie Alexander & Ferdon, Washington, 1994—; bus. mgr. Energy Law Jour., Washington, 1986-88; sec. Cogeneration Coalition Am. Inc., Washington, 1985-87. Contbr. articles to profl. jours. Named Outstanding Atty. in Va. Met. Women's Bar Assn., Va. Womens Attys. Assn., 1986. Mem. ABA (chair ratemaking com. sect. of adminstrv. law and regulatory practice), Va. Bar Assn., Fairfax Bar Assn., Fed. Bar Assn., Fed. Energy Bar Assn. (vice chmn. practice and procedures com. 1985-86, vice chmn. phys. facilities com. 1987-88), Midwest Gas Assn. (exec. bd. legal affairs sect.). Presbyterian. Office: Mudge Rose Guthrie Et Al 2121 K St NW Ste 700 Washington DC 20037

WALKER, MARY DIANE, secondary school educator; b. Royal Oak, Mich., Sept. 11, 1955; d. Thomas Walker and Mary Jo Brown Stevenson. BS in Med. Records Adminstrn., U. Ctrl. Fla., 1979; postgrad., U. South Fla., 1992—. Registered records adminstr.; cert. secondary sci. and biology tchr., Fla. Tchr. Key Tng. Ctr., Lecanto, Fla., 1982-87; tchr. biologytechnology, ecology, environ. sci., and gen. sci. Lecanto High Sch., 1987—; dist. rep. Region II Svc. Project for Environ. Edn., U. Fla. Ctr. for Environ. Edn., Gainesville, 1990—; tchr. Withlacoochee Environ. Tng. Ctr., 1992, tchg. fellow, 1993, 94. Mem. NEA, Fla. Assn. Sci. Tchrs., Fla. Assn. Student Coun. Advisors, Phi Kappa Phi. Methodist. Home: PO Box 1121 Floral City FL 34436 Office: Lecanto High Sch 3810 W Educational Path Lecanto FL 34461-8052

WALKER, MARY ELLEN, family physician, health facility administrator; b. Seattle, May 21, 1953; d. Richard Battson and Helen Marie (Bramsch) W.; m. Ronald Lee Barnett, Apr. 10, 1982 (div. Dec. 1986). BA in Phys. Anthropology, U. Wash., 1974, MD, MPH, 1978. Diplomate Am. Bd. Family Practice. Family physician, tchr. Frontier Nursing Svc., Hyden, Ky., 1981-82; family physician, med. co-dir. Vashon Health Ctr., Vashon Island, Wash., 1982-86; family physician, clinic co-dir. Island Family Medicine, Vashon Island, 1991—. Bd. dirs., officer Blue Heron Arts Ctr., Vashon Island, 1990—. Mem. APHA, Am. Med. Women's Assn., World Orgn. Family Drs., King County Med. Soc. Home: PO Box 389 Vashon WA 98070

WALKER, MARY ERLINE, critical care nurse; b. Newport, R.I., June 4, 1951; d. Edgar Hergor and Doris Elizabeth (Allen) Sherman; m. Michael Robert Walker, Dec. 22, 1970; 1 child, Michael Robert II. AS in Nursing, Lake City (Fla.) Community Coll., 1971; AA, Santa Fe Community Coll., Gainesville, Fla., 1974; BS in Profl. Arts, St. Joseph's Coll., North Windham, Maine, 1980. RN; cert. critical care nurse, med./surg. nurse. Staff nurse Cape Fear Valley Hosp., Fayetteville, N.C., 1971-72, surg. staff nurse, 1975-76; staff nurse Alachua Gen. Hosp., Gainesville, 1972-74; staff nurse male medicine Womack Army Community Hosp., Ft. Bragg, N.C., 1976-81, staff nurse, 1986-87, inservice coordinator, 1987; staff nurse Reynolds Army Community Hosp., Ft. Sill, Okla., 1981-83, evening supr., 1983-84; staff nurse cardiology Lettermen Army Med. Ctr., San Francisco, 1984-85, clin. nurse specialist recovery room, 1985-86, charge nurse cardiac rehab., 1985; staff nurse, insvc. coord. Bayne Jones Army Hosp., Ft. Polk, La., 1988-90; staff nurse MICU Brooke Army Med. Ctr., Fort Sam Houston, Tex., 1990—. Pres. Bay Bandits Volksmarch, San Francisco, 1985-86; den leader Cub Scouts, 1993—. Mem. Am. Assn. Critical Care Nurses (North Cen. Fla. chpt. pres. 1974), Am. Nurses Assn., Am. Heart Assn., Nat. League Nursing, Phi Theta Kappa. Republican. Methodist. Home: 9719 Fortune Ridge Dr Converse TX 78109-2752 Office: Brooke Army Med Ctr San Antonio TX 78234

WALKER, MARY L., lawyer; b. Dayton, Ohio, Dec. 1, 1948; d. William Willard and Lady D. Walker; 1 child, Winston Samuel. Student, U. Calif., Irvine, 1966-68; BA in Biology/Ecology, U. Calif., Berkeley, 1970; postgrad., UCLA, 1972-73; JD, Boston U., 1973. Bar: Calif. 1973, U.S. Supreme Ct. 1979. Atty. So. Pacific Co., San Francisco, 1973-76; from assoc. to ptnr. Richards, Watson, & Gershon, L.A., 1976-82; dep. asst. atty. gen. lands div. U.S. Dept. Justice, Washington, 1982-84; dep. solicitor U.S. Dept. Interior, Washington, 1984-85; asst. sec. of energy, environment, safety and health U.S. Dept. Energy, Washington, 1985-87; spl. cons. to chmn. bd. Law Engring., Atlanta, 1988-89; v.p., West Coast and the Pacific Law Environ., Inc., San Francisco, 1989; ptnr., head environ. law dept. Richards, Watson & Gershon, San Francisco, 1989-91; ptnr. Luce, Forward, Hamilton & Scripps, San Diego, 1991-94; ptnr. and head San Diego Environ. Practice Group Brobeck, Phleger & Harrison, San Diego, 1994—; U.S. commr. InterAm. Tropical Tuna Commn., 1989—. Bd. dirs. Endowment for Community Leadership, 1987—; adv. coun. Adam Smith Inst., 1993—. Mem. Calif. Bar Assn., San Diego Bar Assn., San Diego BioCommerce Assn. (bd. dirs. 1991—, pres. 1994), World Affairs Coun., Renaissance Women. Republican.

WALKER, MILDRED LUCILE, small business owner; b. Dallas, Oct. 13, 1923; d. Henry Hubbard and Julia Orene (Henson) Dickerson; m. Ralph J. Walker, Apr. 5, 1942; children: Don Robert, Larry Ralph, Julie Cheryl. Lic. real estate broker. V.p. Walker's Sporting Goods, Inc., Grand Prairie, Tex., 1946—, No. Tex. Cir. Bd., Inc., Grand Prairie, 1979—; sec. treas. W-Tek, Inc., Irving, Tex., 1985—; chief exec. officer, ptnr. Lynn Creek Marina, Ltd., Grand Prairie, 1991—. Mem. bd. dirs., past chair Children First, Inc., Grand Prairie, 1986—, Dallas-Ft. Worth Med. Ctr. Found., Grand Prairie, 1984—; chmn. bd. dirs. Indsl. Rels. Commn., Grand Prairie, 1990—. Mem. Grand Prairie C. of C. (chmn. bd. dirs. 1990, recipient Citizen of Yr. award 1987, Athena award 1992), Woman's Club of Grand Prairie (pres. 1969), Jr. Woman's Club of Grand Prairie (founder). Presbyterian. Home: 2321 Little John Dr Grand Prairie TX 75050-2018 Office: Lynn Creek Marina Ltd 5700 Lake Ridge Pky Grand Prairie TX 75052-8514

WALKER, OLENE S., lieutenant governor; b. Ogden, Utah, Nov. 15, 1930; d. Thomas Ole and Nina Hadley (Smith) W.; m. J. Myron Walker, 1957; children: Stephen Brett, David Walden, Bryan Jesse, Lori, Mylene, Nina, Thomas Myron. BA, Brigham Young U., 1954; MA, Stanford U., 1954; PhD, U. Utah, 1986. V.p. Country Crisp Foods; mem. Utah Ho. of Reps. Dist. 24; lt. gov. State of Utah, 1993—. Mem. Salt Lake Edn. Found. bd. dirs. 1983-90; dir. community econ. devel.; mem. Ballet West, Sch. Vol., United Way, Commn. on Youth, Girls Village, Salt Lake Conv. and Tourism Bd. Mormon. Office: 203 State Capitol Salt Lake City UT 84114

WALKER, PEGGY JEAN, social work agency administrator; b. Carbondale, Ill., Aug. 9, 1940; d. George William and Lola Almeda (Black) Robinson; children: Edith Nell and Keith Alan. BA, So. Ill. U., 1962, PhD, 1986; MSW, Washington U., St. Louis, 1967. Lic. clin. social worker. Caseworker, casework supr. Ill. Dept. Pub. Aid, 1964-71; child welfare adminstr. Ill. Dept. Children and Family Svc., 1971-75; mem. faculty social work program So. Ill. U., 1975-79; exec. dir. Western divsn. Children's Home Soc. of Fla., Pensacola, 1979—; appointed to Fla. State Coord. Coun. for Early Childhood Devel., 1994—; adj. adv. bd. dept. social work U. West Fla., 1982—; appt. by Fla. Dept. Edn. to task force Edn. for Children of the Homeless, 1989—, Dept. of Health and Rehab. Svcs. Dist. Task Force on Child Abuse and Neglect Prevention, 1985—, chmn. 1988, 89. Bd. dirs. United Way Escombia County, Fla., 1992—; mem. Leadership Fla., 1988—. Mem. NASW (cert.), Acad. Cert. Social Workers. Presbyterian. Home: 613 Silverthorn Rd Gulf Breeze FL 32561-4625 Office: 5375 N 9th Ave Pensacola FL 32504-8725

WALKER, RUTH ANN, journalist; b. Elmhurst, Ill., June 22, 1954; d. Robert F. and Jeanne (Carsman) W. AB, Oberlin (Ohio) Coll., 1976. Staff reporter Aiken (S.C.) Standard, 1977-78; various editing and writing positions Christian Sci. Monitor, Boston, 1978-83, bus. corr., 1983-85, editorial writer, 1985-88, asst. editor editorial page, 1988, asst. mng. editor, 1988-90, dep. editor, 1990-94, assoc. editor, 1994—. Recipient Exceptional Merit Media award Nat. Women's Polit. Caucus, 1987. Christian Scientist. Home: 26 Waverly St #402 Brighton MA 02135

WALKER, SALLY BARBARA, retired glass company executive; b. Bellerose, N.Y., Nov. 21, 1921; d. Lambert Roger and Edith Demerest (Parkhouse) W. Diploma Cathedral Sch. St. Mary, 1939; AA, Finch Jr. Coll., 1941. Tchr. interior design Finch Coll., 1941-42; draftsman AT&T, 1942-43; with Steuben Glass Co., N.Y.C., 1943—, exec. v.p., 1959-62, exec. v.p. ops., 1962-78, exec. v.p. ops. and sales, 1978-83, exec. v.p., 1983-88, ret. 1988. Pres. 116 E. 66th St. Corp. Mem. Fifth Ave. Assn. Republican. Episcopalian. Clubs: Rockaway Hunting, Lawrence Beach, U.S. Lawn Tennis, Colony, English-Speaking Union. Home: 116 E 66th St New York NY 10021-6547

WALKER, SANDRA, mezzo-soprano; b. Richmond, Va., Oct. 1, 1946; d. Phillip Loth and Mary Jane W.; m. Melvin Brown, May 17, 1975; 1 child, Noel Christian Brown. MusB, U. N.C., 1969; postgrad., Manhattan Sch. Music, 1971-72. Artist-in-residence Ky. Opera Assn., 1980. Recorded Ned Rorem's song cycle King Midas on Desto Records, 1974; debut San Francisco Opera, 1972, re-engaged 1986, Chgo. Lyric Opera, 1973, 88, re-engaged 1988, Washington Opera Soc., 1973, Phila. Lyric Opera, 1973, Teatro Communale, Florence, Italy, 1985, Met. Opera, N.Y.C., 1986, re-engaged 1989, Opernhaus Zurich, 1987, Stadt Theater Wiesbaden, 1987, Rigoletto, Eugene-Onegin, Met. Opera. 1989, Netherlands Opera, 1989, Orlands Furioso, San Francisco Opera, 1989, Ring Cycle, 1990; leading mezzo soprano N.Y.C. Opera, 1974—, Stadt Theater, Würzburg, Germany, 1980-82, Stadt Theater Gelsenkirchen, Fed. Republic Germany, 1983-85, Stadt Theater Essen, Fed. Republic Germany, 1984, Frankfurt Opera, Fed. Republic Germany, 1985; soloist Orchestra Santa Cecilia Academia, Rome, 1987, New Orch. Paris, 1988; singer in major U.S. and European music festivals Tanglewood, Caramoor, Spoleto-U.S.A. and Spoleto Festival of Two Worlds in, Italy; soloist, Am. Symphony, San Francisco Symphony, 1980; appeared in: PBS nat. telecasts Manon, The Ballad of Baby Doe, Saint of Bleeker Street, 1981, on Great Performances: in The Consul and Eugene Onegin, 1986; Met. Opera nat. broadcast Samson, 1986, Eugene Onegin, 1989; orchestral appearances with Nat. Symphony, Washington, St. Louis Symphony, Chgo. Symphony, Richmond (Va.) Symphony, Houston Symphony, San Francisco Symphony, Charlotte Symphony, Cleve. Orch.; comml. video prodns. Eugene Onegin, Manon, Orlando Furioso; opera appearances include Falstaff, Calgary Opera, 1991, Mephistofiles, Chgo. Lyric Opera, 1991, Barber of Seville, Phila. Lyric Opera, 1991;. Recipient Nat. Endowment for Arts Affiliate Artist grant sponsored by Va. Opera Assn. and Sears Roebuck Co., 1978. Office: care Columbia Artists Mgmt Inc 165 W 57th St New York NY 10019-2201*

WALKER, SANDRA MORTON, accountant; b. Ft. Knox, Ky., July 30, 1967; d. Thomas Lee Morton and Eunice Yvonne (Christiensen) Pearson; m. Robert Marion Walker III, June 16, 1991; 1 child, Taylor Morgan. BS in Bus. Mgmt., U. N.C., 1992, M in Acctg., 1992. CPA, N.C. Acctg. mgr. Point South Investment Co., Asheville, N.C., 1992-94; fin. mgr. Q-Matic Corp., Asheville, 1994—. Mem. Inst. Mgmt. Accts. (treas. 1993-94, bd. dirs. meetings 1994—, Outstanding Svc. award 1994). Republican. Home: 51 Rex Dr Asheville NC 28806-2963

WALKER, VIRGINIA BOYD, elementary school educator; b. Tuskegee, Ala.; d. Johnnie Lee and Lucy (Bryant) Boyd; m. Johnny Bee Walker, Apr. 18, 1978; children: Carolyn Annette Walker Stone, Kevin Cordell, Kenneth Boyd. BS in Elem. Edn., Tuskegee U., 1975; MS in Reading Edn., Ala. State U., Montgomery, 1979; cert. K-12 sch. counseling, Troy State U., Montgomery, Ala., 1990. Chpt I reading tchr. Tuskegee (Ala.) Sch. System, 1976-81, chpt. I reading lab. tchr., 1983, classroom tchr., 1984—; mem. sch. adv. com., Tuskegee, 1986, 92-93, corod. for social studies subject area, 1992-93, grade level chair, 1985-86, mem. prin.'s adv. coun., 1990-91, student coun. advisor, 1993-94. Mem. Tuskegee Dem. Club, 1983—, Ala. Dem. Orgn., 1988—. Mem. NEA, Ala. Edn. Assn., Macon County Edn. Assn., Am. Legion, VFW Ladies Aux., Elks, Phi Delta Kappa. Home: PO Box 81 Tuskegee AL 36083

WALKER, WENDY K., marketing executive; b. Elizabeth, N.J., Nov. 11, 1961; d. William Henry Jr. and Catherine Lillian (Fulton) Knight; m. George Russell Walker Jr., Oct. 25, 1986; 1 child, Faith Corinne. Student, U. Warwick, Eng., 1981-82; BA, Duke U., 1983. Cert. ins. counselor, assoc. in risk mgmt. Underwriter Chubb & Son, Inc., N.Y.C., 1983-86; sr. underwriter Atlantic Mut. Ins. Cos., N.Y.C., 1986-87, producer specialist, 1987-88, underwriting supr., 1988; asst. brokerage mgr. Continental Ins. Cos. div. Nat. Brokerage Svcs., N.Y.C., 1988-90; mgr. comml. underwriting Gt. Am.-West, Inc., Salt Lake City, 1990-92; prodn. coord. TIG Ins. Group, 1992-94; mktg. exec. Rollins Hudig Hall of the Carolinas, 1994—; tchr. internship program Howard U., N.Y.C., 1986; bus. advisor internship program Inroads, Inc. Mem. NAFE, Assn. Profl. Ins. Women, Am. Biog. Inst. (mem. rsch. bd. advisors), Soc. Cert. Ins. Counselors, Young Profls. Coun., Wasatch Front Econ. Forum. Democrat. Episcopalian. Home: 800 Bundaberg Ln Rural Hall NC 27045

WALKER-DANIELS, KIMBERLY KAYNE, publishing company executive; b. Trenton, N.J., Feb. 18, 1958; m. Kenneth R. Walker-Daniels, June 23, 1982. BS, No. Ill. U., 1980. Asst. roadmaster C&NW Transp. Co., Chgo., 1980-82; account exec. Dean Witter Reynolds Inc., Schaumburg, Ill., 1982-84; InterCapital Mut. Fund coord. DWR, Inc., Schaumburg, Ill., 1983-84; product coord. mktg. Balcor/Am. Express, Skokie, Ill., 1984-85, mgr. new product devel., 1985; cons., ptnr. KW-D Ltd./AFAP Ent., Chgo., 1982—; product mgr. Longman Fin. Svcs. Inst., Chgo., 1986-87; exec. editor Dearborn Fin. Inst., Chgo., 1987—. Author 35 NASD/NYSE/MSRB/NASAA exam-prep. texts, 1986—; editor 40 exam-prep texts, 1986—; contbr. numerous articles to fin. jours. Pres. West Cook Dist. ARC, Chgo., 1986; v.p., bd. dirs. Mensa of Ill. Found., 1988-92. Mem. Am. Mensa, Mensa of Ill. (pres., chmn. 1987-88, 88-89, Life Achievement award 1988), Mensa of Wis. (exec. com., dir. pub. rels. 1991-92), Mensa Internat. (mng. editor Mensa World 1987-88, mng. editor Mensa Internat. Jour. 1991-94). Office: Dearborn Fin Inst 155 N Wacker Dr Chicago IL 60606-1719

WALKER-WRIGHT, ROXANNE BETH, radio news director; b. Marshall, Mich., Sept. 15, 1959; d. Dallas Edward and Leona Patricia (Kowalski) Seiler; m. Edward Phillip; 1 child, Benjamin Ross. Student, Western Ky. U., U. S.C., Spartanburg. Lic. FCC 3d class. News dir. Sta. WORD, Spartanburg, 1981-83; traffic coord. Sta. WHNS-TV, Greenville, S.C., 1984-85; nat. sales asst. Sta. WYFF-TV, Greenville, 1985; news anchor Sta. WCAW-WVAF, Charleston, W.Va., 1985-87, Sta. WWNC, Asheville, N.C., 1987; dir. news/pub. svc. Sta. WMYI, Greenville, 1987—. Vol. Guardian Ad Litem, Greenville, 1990—; sec., pres., v.p. St. Mary's Womens Club, Greenville, 1990—; bd. dirs. Pendleton Place Children's Shelter, Greenville, 1994—; mem. allocations com. United Way, Greenville, 1994. Named Cath. Woman of Yr., St. Mary's Ch., Greenville, 1993. Mem. NOW, Greenville Coalition for Women. Office: Sta WMYI Ste 801 Nations Banke Pla 7 N Laurence St Greenville SC 29601

WALKUP, CHARLOTTE LLOYD, lawyer; b. N.Y.C., Apr. 28, 1910; d. Charles Henry and Helene Louise (Wheeler) Tuttle; m. David D. Lloyd, Oct. 19, 1940 (dec. Dec. 1962); children—Andrew M. Lloyd, Louisa Lloyd Hurley; m. Homer Allen Walkup, Feb. 4, 1967. AB, Vassar Coll., 1931; LLB, Columbia U., 1934. Bar: N.Y. 1935, U.S. Supreme Ct. 1939, U.S. Dist. Ct. D.C. 1953, Va. 1954. Asst. solicitor Dept. Interior, Washington, 1934-45; asst. gen. counsel UNRRA, Washington and London, 1945-48; assoc. and cons. firms, Washington, 1953, 55, 60; atty., spl. asst. Office Treasury, Washington, 1961-65; asst. gen. counsel Dept. Treasury, Washington, 1965-73; cons. Rogers & Wells, Washington, 1975-86. Editor, Columbia Law Rev., 1933, 34. Pres. Alexandria Community Welfare Coun., 1950-52; bd dirs. Alexandria Coun. Human Rels., 1958-60, New Hope Found., 1977. Recipient Meritorious Svc. award Dept. Treasury, 1970, Exceptional Svc. award, 1973, Career Svc. award Nat. Civil Svc. League, 1973; named Hon. fellow Harry S. Truman Libr. Inst. Mem. Columbia U. Alumni Assn., Phi Beta Kappa. Democrat. Episcopalian. Home: 2501 Ridge Road Dr Alexandria VA 22302-2830

WALL, BARBARA WARTELLE, lawyer; b. New Orleans, Sept. 30, 1954; d. Richard Cole and Ruth Druhan (Power) W.; m. Christopher Read Wall, June 21, 1980; children: Christopher, Louisa. BA, U. Va., 1976, JD, 1979. Bar: N.Y. 1980, U.S. Dist. Ct. (so. and ea. dists.) N.Y. 1980. Assoc. Satterlee & Stephens, N.Y.C., 1979-85; asst. gen. counsel Gannett Co., Inc., Arlington, Va., 1985-90, sr. legal counsel, 1990-93, v.p., sr. legal counsel, 1993—. Mem. ABA (co-chair first amendment and media litigation com. of sect. litigation, mem. gov. bd. forum on comm. law), N.Y. State Bar Assn., Assn. of Bar of City of N.Y. Republican. Roman Catholic. Home: 5026 Tilden St NW Washington DC 20016-2334 Office: Gannett Co Inc 1100 Wilson Blvd Arlington VA 22209-2297

WALL, BETTY JANE, real estate consultant; b. Wichita Falls, Tex., Mar. 23, 1936; d. Albert Willis and Winnie Belle (Goodloe) Beard; m. Richard Lee Wall, Feb. 21, 1959; 1 child, Cynthia Lynn. BS, Vocat.Home Econs. Edn, U. Okla., 1958; MEd, Midwestern U., 1959. Lic. real estate salesperson, Tex. Tchr. San Diego County Schs., 1959-60, Long Beach (Calif.) City Schs., 1960-61, Norman (Okla.) Kindergarten Assn., 1961-65; real estate salesperson WestMark Realtors, Lubbock, Tex., 1983-85; now ind. real estate salesperson Lubbock; coll. adviser Nat. Panhellenic Conf., Tex., 1979-91; judge talent and beauty pageants, Tex. N.Mex., Okla., 1984—. Treas. Lubbock Symphony Guild, 1985-87, v.p. ways and means com., 1987-88, chmn. ball, 1990, pres. elect, 1993-94, pres., 1994—; bd. dirs. Miss Lubbock Pagaent, 1992—. Recipient Tex. Tech. U. Outstanding Greek Alumni award, 1994. Mem. Tex. Real Estate Assn., Jr. League Lubbock (treas. 1976-78, sustaining adviser fin. com. 1979-83, hdqrs. commn. advisor 1989—), West Tex. Mus. Assn. (bd. dirs. women's coun.), Nat. Platform Assn., Women's C. of C., Lubbock Women's Club, Tex. Tech. U. Faculty Women's Club (v.p. & pres. 1967-69), Alpha Chi Omega (nat. coun., nat. panjellenic del. 1978-83, 88-90, nat. v.p. membership 1985-88, nat. v.p. collegians 1990-92). Republican. Methodist. Home and Office: 3610 63rd Dr Lubbock TX 79413-5308

WALL, CATHERINE, writer, editor; b. China, Dec. 22, 1939; d. Tienhu and Gweisin (Wang) Ho; divorced; children: Mark, Diana, Roland. MEd in Music Edn., Columbia U., 1980, MA in Teaching of Singing, 1980, MEd in Teaching of Spanish Lit., 1990. Tchr. various schs. and univs.; mgr. China Worldwide Travel, 1980-85; Wall-to-Wall Press, N.Y.C. Contbr. poems to mags., newspapers and anthologies; writer, editor, translator books and mags. interpreter, artist La Follia ie N.Y., 1985—; innovator new method of teaching singing, voice placement, voice and speech therapy, voice interpretation. Mem. N.Y. Singing Tchrs. Assn., Nat. Assn. Singing Tchrs. Office: Wall-to-Wall Press 315 8th Ave Apt 19H New York NY 10001-4820

WALL, DONNA SUE, pharmacist; b. Linton, Ind., Mar. 25, 1955; d. Donald Joe and Wanda Mae (Miller) W. BS, Butler U., 1978; PharmD, Purdue U., 1993. Registered pharmacist, Ind. Staff pharmacist Wishard Meml. Hosp., Indpls., 1978-82; staff pharmacist St. Vincent Hosp., Indpls., 1982-90, staff pharmacist level II, 1990-94; clin. pharmacist surgery and critical care Ind. U. Med. Ctr., Indpls., 1994—. Recipient Clerkship award Sandoz Pharm., 1994. Mem. Am. Soc. Hosp. Pharmacists, Am. Coll. Clin. Pharmacists, Ind. Soc. Hosp. Pharmacists, Soc. Critical Care Medicine, Lambda Kappa Sigma. Office: Ind U Med Ctr 550 N University Blvd UH 1410 Indianapolis IN 46202

WALL, GLENNIE MURRAY, historic preservation professional; b. Roseburg, Oreg., Oct. 8, 1931; d. James Matheny and Emily Lenore (Aten) Corbin; m. Louis Samuel Wall, Jan. 3, 1975; 2 daus. BS, Portland (Oreg.) State U., 1965, postgrad., 1966; postgrad., U. Mo., Springfield, 1969, U. Mich., 1978, Practicing Law Inst., N.Y.C., 1980-82. Historian, Pipestone (Minn.) Nat. Monument Nat. Pk. Svc., 1966-68; historian, pk. supt. Herbert Hoover Hist. Site Nat. Pk. Svc., West Branch, Iowa, 1968-69; historian, landmark specialist western regional office Nat. Park Svc., San Francisco, 1969-72; div. chief Denver Svc. Ctr. Nat. Park Svc., 1974-83; mus. mgr. (maritime) Nat. Park Svc., San Francisco, 1983-89, cultural resources specialist, curator Presidio Project, 1989-90; prin. Hist. Preservation Planning, San Francisco, 1990—; instr., lectr. on preservation law and policy Nat. Pk. Svc., 1974-83; lectr. Nat. Trust for Hist. Preservation, washington, 1971-89; dir. Coun. Am. Maritime Mus., Phila., 1987-88, Nat. Maritime Mus. Assn., San Francisco, 1983-88; chair Equal Opportunity Com., Nat. Pk. Svc., Denver, 1979-81. Author, editor: Maritime Preservation, 1987, Agency Guidelines for Cultural resources Management, 1979-83; photographer: Pipes on the Plains, 1967; author, photographer numerous plans and studies. Treas. Colo. Corral of Westerners, Denver, 1974-76; mem. Com. for Green Foothills, San Mateo, Calif., 1984-88, Sta. KQED-TV, San Francisco, 1985—. Recipient spl. achievement awards Dept. Interior, 1969, 72, citation for excellence, 1976; Nat. Preservation award President's Adv. Coun., Washington, 1988., 72; Hoover scholar, 1993. Mem. Am. Decorative Arts Forum, Am. Assn. Mus., Internat. Coun. Mus., Internat. Congress Maritime Mus., Am. Assn. for State and Local History, NOW. Office: PO Box 370634 Montara CA 94037-0634

WALL, JACQUELINE JARDINE, art educator; b. Calcutta, India, Apr. 21, 1926; came to U.S., 1939; d. Geoffrey Owen and Olga Patricia (Bradlaugh) Jardine; m. Joseph Barrye Wall Jr., Nov. 1, 1952 (dec. Mar. 1972); children: Barrye Langhorne, Marjorie Lancaster, Geoffrey Hanes, Angus Alexander. BA in Psychology, Westhampton Coll., 1952; MA in Art Edn., Va. Commonwealth U., 1979. Feature writer, reporter The Farmville (Va.) Herald, 1953-57; art dir. Lab. Sch. Longwood Coll., Farmville, 1974-83; supr. art edn. Longwood Coll., 1974-83, instr. art, 1984; art specialist Prince Edward County Pub. Schs., Farmville, 1984-89; freelance sculpture Farmville, 1989—; adj. instr. art Longwood Coll., 1989—; dir. Va. Gov.'s Sch., Farmville, 1982, 83; co-dir. Regional Va. Gov.'s, Hampden-Sydney, 1986, 87; adjudicator Va. Gov.'s Sch., 1987-89, 93. Leader Girl Scouts Am., Farmville, 1960-72. Recipient prize for Innovative Programming Am. Assn. Summer Schs., 1978. Mem. Richmond Women's Caucus Art (past chair 1991-93, exhibit chair 1994—), Longwood Ctr. Visual Arts (edn. coord. 1992—), Mortar Board, Phi Beta Kappa. Office: Longwood Ctr Visual Arts Farmville VA 23909-1800

WALL, JACQUELINE REMONDET, industrial psychologist, rehabilitation counselor; b. Paris, Dec. 25, 1958; came to U.S., 1959; d. Jack Whitney and Hazel Aline (Riley) Hargett; m. Mel Dennis Remondet, Aug. 5, 1977 (div. Mar. 1984); m. David Gordon Wall, Jan. 27, 1990; 1 child, Jeanette Renee. BA, Southeastern La. U., 1978; MA, U. Tulsa, 1982, PhD, 1989. Lic. profl. counselor, Okla. Program coord. Hillcrest Med. Ctr., Tulsa, 1982-88; coord. psychol. svcs. Rebound Inc.-Cane Creek Hosp., Martin, Tex., 1989-90; psychologist Sea Pines Rehab. Hosp., Melbourne, Fla., 1990; indsl. psychology intern Morris & Assocs., Jackson, Miss., 1990-91; ind. cons. indsl. psychology, 1991-92; clinic coord. Ill. Inst. Tech., Chgo., 1992—, postdoctoral fellow clin. respecialization program, 1993-94; intern psychology dept. U. Miss. Med. Ctr., 1994; instr. Tulsa Jr. Coll., 1989; rsch. asst. U. Tulsa, 1981-82, 84-86, La. State U., Baton Rouge, 1980, Med. Sch., Tulane U., New Orleans, 1979-80; part-time instr. Wayne State U., 1991, IIT, 1994; presenter in field. Contbr. book chpts. and articles to profl. jours. Recipient rsch. grant U. Tulsa, 1982. Mem. APA, Soc. for Indsl.-Orgnl. Psychology, Southeastern La. U. Thirteen Club, Sigma Xi, Psi Chi, Phi Kappa Phi, Phi Lambda Pi. Office: U Miss Med Ctr Dept Psychiaty & Human Behavior 2500 N State St Jackson MS 39216

WALL, JOY MARIE, loan specialist, housing official; b. Gadsen, Ala., May 28, 1953; d. Willard William and Lois Rosella (Warsham) W. BS in Mgmt. Fin., Jacksonville State U., Alz., 1987. Asst. sec. First Fed. Savings & Loan Assn., Gadsen, 1974-87; bank examiner Fed. Deposit Ins. Corp., Birmingham, Shreveport, Ala., La., 1988-91; loan specialist Dept. Housing & Urban Devel., Birmingham, Ala., 1991—. Home: 213 Shalimar Cir Alabaster AL 35007 Office: Dept Housing & Urban Devel 600 Beacon Pkwy W Ste 300 Birmingham AL 35209

WALL, SONJA ELOISE, nurse, administrator; b. Santa Cruz, Calif., Mar. 28, 1938; d. Ray Theothornton and Reva Mattie (Wingo) W.; m. Edward Gleason Holmes, Aug. 1959 (div. Jan. 1968); children: Deborah Lynn, Lance Edward; m. John Aspesi, Sept. 1969 (div. 1977); children: Sabrina Jean, Daniel John; m. Kenneth Talbot LaBoube, Nov. 1, 1978 (div. 1989); 1 child, Tiffany Amber. BA, San Jose Jr. Coll., 1959; BS, Madonna Coll., 1967; student, U. Mich., 1968-70. RN, Calif., Mich., Colo. Staff nurse Santa Clara Valley Med. Ctr., San Jose, Calif., 1959-67, U. Mich. Hosp., Ann Arbor, 1967-73, Porter and Swedish Med. Hosp., Denver, 1973-77, Laurel Grove Hosp., Castro Valley, Calif., 1977-79, Advent Hosp., Ukiah, Calif., 1984-86; motel owner LaBoube Enterprises, Fairfield, Point Arena, Willits, Calif., 1979—; staff nurse Northridge Hosp., L.A., 1986-87, Folsom State Prison, Calif., 1987; co-owner, mgr. nursing registry Around the Clock Nursing Svc., Ukiah, 1985—; critical care staff nurse Kaiser Permanente Hosp., Sacramento, 1986-89; nurse Snowline Hospice, Sacramento, 1989-92; carepoint home care and travel nurse Hosp. Staffing Svcs. Inc., Placerville, Calif., 1992-94, interim home health nurse, 1994—; owner Royal Plantation Petites Miniature Horse Farm. Contbr. articles to various publs. Leader Coloma 4-H, 1987-91; mem. mounted divsn. El Dorado County Search and Rescue, 1991-93; docent Calif. Marshall Gold Discovery State Hist. Park, Coloma, Calif. Mem. AACN, NAFE, Soc. Critical Care Medicine, Am. Heart Assn. (CPR trainer, recipient awards), Calif. Bd. RNs, Calif. Nursing Rev., Calif. Critical Care Nurses, Soc. Critical Care Nurses, Am. Motel Assn. (beautification and remodeling award 1985), Nat. Hospice Nurses Assn., Soroptimist Internat. Calif., Am. Miniature Horse Assn. (winner nat. grand championship 1981-82, 83, 85, 89), DAR (Jobs Daus. hon. mem.), Cameron Park Country Club. Republican. Episcopalian. Home and Office: Around the Clock Nursing Svc PO Box 559 Coloma CA 95613-0559

WALL, TERESA LAURINE, nursing and healthcare administrator; b. Redmond, Oreg., May 22, 1951; d. Monroe James and Arlene (Manuel) W.; 1 child, Richard James. BSN, Ariz. State U., 1981; MPH in Health Adminstrn., U. Okla. Health Scis. Ctr., 1990. Pub. health nurse trainee Gila River Indian Community, Sacaton, Ariz., 1982, pub. health nurse, 1985-88; clin. nurse USPHS Indian Health Svc., Sacaton, 1982-85; pub. health nurse USPHS Indian Health Svc., Watonga, Okla., 1988-90; exec. dir. Gila River Indian Community Dept. Health Svcs., 1990—; bd. dirs. Gila River Care Ctr., treas., 1992—; alt. mem. Indian Health Svc., Phoenix Indian Med. Ctr. Instnl. Rev. Bd., 1993—; commn. mem. Ariz. Area Health Edn. Ctr., 1993—. Lt. USPHS, 1983-86. Mem. APHA, Am. Coll. Healthcare Execs. (assoc.), Okla. Coll. Pub. Health Alumni Assn., Arizonans for Prevention. Democrat. Home: 1762 W Mariposa Ct Chandler AZ 85224-6605

WALLACE, ALICEANNE, civic worker; b. Chgo., Sept. 28, 1925; d. Alexander and Mary (Zurek) Zalac; m. Henry Clay Wallace, Jr., Apr. 10, 1948; children: Laura Lillian Wallace Bergin, Christine Claire Wallace Stockwell. Student, St. Teresa Coll., Winona, Minn., 1944-45, DePaul U., 1946-48, North Tex. State U., 1971, 72. City sec. City of Southlake, Tex., 1969-77; pres. AZW, Inc., real estate sales, Roanoke, Tex., 1977-84. Mem. Trinity Valley Mental Health-Mental Retardation, Ft. Worth, 1971-72; chmn. ways and means Tex. Silver-Haired Legislature, Austin, 1986-90, parliamentarian, 1991-94, treas. TSHL Found., 1990-92, pres., 1992—; sec. Sr. Citizens Activities, Inc., Temple, Tex., 1989-90; sec. cit. CTCOG Area Agy. on Aging Citizens Adv. Coun., Belton, Tex., 1991; vice chmn. bd. Tex. Dept. on Aging, Austin, 1991—; congl. sr. intern U.S. Ho. of Reps., Washington, 1991; pres. Tri-County Tex. Dem. Women, 1990-94; elected State Dem. Exec. Com. Senatorial Dist. #24, 1994—. Mem. Am. Assn. Ret. Persons (legis chmn. Temple chpt. 1990-94, regional coord. VOTE 1991—), Tex. Fedn. Women's Clubs (state legis chmn. 1990-92, resolutions chmn. 1992-94, parliamentarian Capitol dist. 1990-92), North Ctrl. Tex. Secy. Assn. (pres. 1976), City Fedn. Women's Clubs (corr. sec. 1991-92, records custodian 1991—), Triangle Forum (pres. 1992-94), Daus. Republic Tex. (assoc.), Internat. Inst. Mcpl. Clks. (state cert.), Epsilon Eta Phi. Home: RR 2 Box 2585 Belton TX 76513-9611

WALLACE, BETTY JEAN, elementary school educator, lay minister; b. Denison, Tex., Dec. 5, 1927; d. Claude Herman and Pearl Victoria (Freels) Moore; m. Billy Dean McKneely, Sept. 2, 1950 (div. Nov. 1964); children: Rebecca Lynn, Paul King, David Freels, John Walker, Philip Andrew McKneely. Student, Tulane U., 1947; BA, Baylor U., 1949; postgrad., U. Houston, 1949-50, 74, 81, Rocky Mountain Bible Inst., 1959, U. Colo., 1969-70, U. No. Colo., 1965, 68, 72, U. St. Thomas, 1992, Autonomous U. Guadalajara, summer 1993; MEd, Houston Bapt. U., 1985. Cert. life profl. elem., high sch., life profl. reading specialist, secondary field ESL tchr., Tex. Tchr. Galena Park (Tex.) Ind. Sch. Dist., 1949-50, 52-53, 72—, Corpus Christi (Tex.) Independent Sch. Dist., 1950-51, Denver Pub. Schs., 1953-54, 63-72. Author: The Holy Spirit Today, 1989, Our God of Infinite Variety, 1991, God Speaks in a Variety of Ways, 1991. Sun. sch. tchr. So. Bapt. Conv. chs., Tex., 1946-50, Denver, 1952-56; tchr. kindergarten Emmanuel Bapt. Ch., Denver, 1956-59; missionary, Queretaro, Mex., 1977,78; mem. Rep. Senatorial Inner Circle, Washington, 1989-91, Round Table for Ronald Reagan, Washington, 1989-90; bd. advisors Oliver North; tchr. Kindergarten Ch., Denver, 1960-63; helper Feed the Poor, Houston, 1983-85; active Suicide Prevention, Houston, 1973-76, Literacy, Houston, 1978-81; rep. NEA, Denver, 1966-72; mem. Retirement Com., Denver, 1970-72; bd. advisors Oliver North, 1994. Recipient Rep. Senatorial medal of freedom, 1994; grantee NSF, 1969-70. Mem. Tex. Classroom Tchrs. Assn. (officer rep., pres. Galena Park chpt. 1988-91), Delta Alpha Pi (pres. Waco chpt. 1948-49), Alpha Epsilon Delta. Republican. Home: 14831 Anoka Dr Channelview TX 77530-3201 Office: North Shore Elem Sch 14310 Duncannon Dr Houston TX 77015-2514

WALLACE, BETTY LOUISE DOLLAR, religious educator; b. Glenwood, Ark., Aug. 6, 1935; d. James Herbert and Ora Lee (Yarbrough) Dollar; m. Robert Stanley Wallace, Oct. 7, 1965; children: David, Debra, Sarah. Diploma, Moore's Career Coll., Sacramento, 1959, Liberty Bapt. Coll., Lynchburg, Va., 1980; DD, Am. Bible Inst., Kansas City, Mo., 1983; cert., Jerusalem Ctr. for Biblical Studies, 1984-85; freelance salesperson, Campbell, Calif., 1960-65, freelance writer, speaker, 1965-83; ministry assoc., educator, Seventh Presbyn. Ch., Cin., 1983—. Pres. beauty salons and products. Author: Prayers for Mother and Child, 1970, Children's Prayers, Praises and Pledges, 1976, God in My Kitchen, 1977, (with others) Faith and Heritage, 1976; TV producer, hostess Children's Church, Noblesville, Ind., 1979-81. Mem. adv. com. Granby (Colo.) Elem. Sch., 1975-77; mem. Walnut Hlls Block Watch, Cin., 1984—; hon. life mem. Program Agy. United Presbyn. Ch., 1987. Recipient Jerusalem Pilgrim award Minister of Tourism and Mayor of Jerusalem, Israel, 1983, Interdenominational Clergy Achievement award, Korea, 1988, Cin. Jewish Welfare Fund medal, 1990, Citation, Beyer Mus. Soc., 1992; named Internat. Woman of Yr., 1992; Mayor's Proclamation "Betty Wallace" Day, Cin., 1992. Mem. NAFE, LWV, Nat. League of Am. Pen Women, Inc., Nat. Story League, Poetry Soc. Colo., Ch. Women United, Christian Writers' League Am., Nat. League Am. Pen Women Inc., Beyer Mus. Soc., Assn. Presbyn. Ch. Educators, World Found. of Successful Women (charter life). Home: 2726 Cleinview Ave Cincinnati OH 45206-1813 Office: Seventh Presbyn Ch 1721 Madison Rd Cincinnati OH 45206-1816

WALLACE, BONNIE ANN, biochemistry and biophysics educator, researcher; b. Greenwich, Conn., Aug. 10, 1951; d. Arthur Victor and Maryjane Ann W. BS in Chemistry, Rensselaer Poly. Inst., 1973; PhD in Molecular Biophysics and Biochemistry, Yale U., 1977. Postdoctoral rsch. fellow Harvard U., Boston, 1977-78; asst. prof. dept. biochemistry and molecular biophysics Columbia U., N.Y.C., 1979-86, assoc. prof. 1986; prof. dept. chemistry, dir. Ctr. for Biophysics Rensselaer Poly. Inst., 1987-92; reader in crystallography U. London, 1991—; vis. scientist MRC Lab. Molecular Biology, Cambridge, Eng., 1978; Fogarty sr. fellow Birkbeck Coll., U. London, 1990. Assoc. editor Peptide and Protein Letters; contbr. numerous articles to profl. jours. and books. Jane Coffin Childs fellow, 1977-79; recipient Irma T. Hirschl award, 1980-84; Camille and Henry Dreyfus tchr.-scholar, 1986; named Hot Young Scientist Fortune Mag., 1990; Subject of Documentary Film: New Insights in Hypertension, 1995. Fellow Royal Soc. Chemistry; mem. Aspen Ctr. for Physics Fellowship, 1986, Biophys. Soc. (nat. coun., Dayhoff award 1985), Am. Crystallographic Assn., Brit. Crystallographic Assn. (BSG award 1994), Biochem. Soc. Britain (coun. mem. peptides and proteins group), Sigma Xi, Phi Lambda Upsilon. Office: U London Birkbeck Coll, Dept Crystallography, London WC1E 7HX, England

WALLACE, CLARA ISABELLE MARINER, adult education educator, missionary; b. Northville, S.D., Apr. 15, 1904; d. Frank Converse and Merta Mary (Peterson) Mariner; m. John Elder Wallace, Dec. 30, 1949 (dec. Oct. 12, 1980); stepchildren: John Elder II, Mary Jane. AB, Park Coll., 1926; postgrad., San Francisco Theol. Sem., 1929-30, Landour (India) Lang. Sch., 1930-31, UCLA, 1940. Office sec. Nat. Missions Larger Parish, Hurley, Wis., 1926-29; headmistress Intermediate Girls' Sch., Farrukhabad, India, 1931-32; informal religious educator North India Mission, Mainpuri, 1932-36; office sec., youth work sec. Nat. Missions Larger Parish, Hurley, 1936-38; dormitory supr., math. tchr. Wasatch Acad., Mt. Pleasant, Utah, 1938-43; supr. village edn. North India Synodical Bd., 1944-59; social worker Head Start Community Action, Wooster, Ohio, 1967-69; office sec., insp. Palmer House Apts., Wooster, Ohio, 1969; coord., tchr. adult basic edn. Wayne County Joint Vocat. Sch., Wooster, Ohio, 1970-86, tchr. adult basic edn., 1986-94; mem. human rights study AAUW, Wooster, 1960-70; program chair HEW, Wooster, 1987-88. Treas. Presbyn. Ch., Mt. Pleasant, Utah, 1940-43; elder United Ch. of North India, Etah, 1945-48; mem. adult edn. com. First Presbyn. Ch., Wooster, 1962—, Christian edn. com., 1972-75; precinct committeeman Dem. Party, Wooster, 1968-71; bd. dirs. Wayne United Ministries, Wooster, 1973-92, jail chaplain support team, 1973—; bd. dirs. LWV, Wooster, 1987-94; family selection com. bd. Habitat for Humanity, Wayne County, Ohio, 1987-94; mem. Wayne County Housing Coalition, 1991-94. Recipient Old Hickory award Wayne County Dem. Party, 1981, Humanitarian award HEW, Ohio, 1991, Women of Achievement award Wooster Community Ctr., 1991, Outstanding Svc. award Wayne County Sheriff, 1990-, 92. Home and Office: 439 Bloomington Ave Wooster OH 44691-2309

WALLACE, CONSTANCE WOLYNIEC, photographer, marketing executive, artist, consultant b. N.Y.C., Jan. 17, 1954; d. Adolph B. and Marion (Jankowsky) W. BS cum laude in Bus. Adminstrn., Ithaca Coll., 1974; MBA, Babson Coll., 1978. Systems mktg. rep. Control Data Corp., Boston, 1974-78, sales trainer, Greenwich, Conn., 1978-80; dir. Strategic Projects, internat. market entry and devel. co., St. John, V.I., 1980-88; pres. The Clothing Studio Inc., Mongoose Jct., St. John, 1984—; gen. mgr. Maine Photographic Resource, 1992; photography represented by Island Fancy Gallery, St. John, V.I. Photographic exhibitions include Maine Photo Workshop, Rockport, Maine, 1992, Chase Manhattan Bank, St. John, V.I., 1992, 93, Island Fancy Gallery, St. John, 1993, 94, 95. Bd. dirs. St. John Community Found., chmn. mktg. and pub. rels. com.; govs. Tourism Policy Coun. Named Artist of Month St. John Sch. Arts, 1992, 93. Mem. Mongoose Junction Mcht. Assn. (advt. com.), Mensa. Lutheran. Home: PO Box 8301 Cruz Bay VI 00831-8301 Office: Strategic Projects PO Box 8301 Cruz Bay VI 00831-8301 also: PO Box 396 Camden ME 04843

WALLACE, DOROTHY ALENE, special education administrator; b. Wright County, Mo., Sept. 11, 1942; d. Stephen Foster and Lois Alene (Breman) Dudley; widowed; children: Michael Dean Huckaby, David Lee. BS in Edn., Drury Coll., 1975, MS in Edn., 1978; Specialist in Ednl. Adminstrn., Southwest Mo. State U., 1988. Cert. tchr. and adminstr., Mo. Tchr. 3rd grade Mansfield (Mo.) R-IV Schs., 1975-78, tchr. 1st grade, 1978-85, tchr. learning disabled, 1985-89, adminstr. spl. edn., 1989-92, adminstr. spl. svcs., 1992—; active sch. coms. on curriculum and nutrition Mansfield R-IV Schs., mem. sch./cmty. adv. coun., 1992—. Mem. Am. Salers Assn., Mo. State Tchrs. Assn., Mo. Coun. Adminstrs. of Spl. Edn., Coun. for Exceptional Children, Coun. Adminstrs. of Spl. Edn., Local Adminstrs. of Spl. Edn., Cmty. Tchrs. Assn. Home: 202 N Ash Ave Mansfield MO 65704

WALLACE, ELAINE WENDY, lawyer; b. Worcester, Mass., Feb. 16, 1949; d. Louis S. and Ida (Zeiper) W. BA, Yeshiva U., 1971; JD, John F. Kennedy Sch. Law, 1976. Sole practice Oakland, Calif. Home: 2430 Palmetto St # 1 Oakland CA 94602-2923 Office: # 2 2430 Palmetto St Oakland CA 94602-2923

WALLACE, GLADYS BALDWIN, librarian; b. Macon, Ga., June 5, 1923; d. Carter Shepherd and Dorothy (Richard) Baldwin; m. Hugh Loring Wallace, Jr., Oct. 14, 1941 (div. Sept. 1968); children: Dorothy, Hugh Loring III. BS in Edn., Oglethorpe U., 1961; MLS, Emory U., 1966; EdS, Ga. State U., 1980. Libr. pub. elem. schs., Atlanta, 1956-66; libr. Northside High Sch., Atlanta, 1966-87, Episc. Cathedral St. Philip. Author: The Time of My Life, 1994. Mem. High Mus. Art, Madison-Morgan Cultural Ctr. Ga. Dept. Edn. grantee, 1960, NDEA grantee, 1963, 65. Mem. AAUW, Atlanta Bonsai Soc., Inc., Nat. Audubon Soc., The Cousteau Soc., Atlanta Bot. Garden, Am. Assn. Ret. Persons, Ga. Conservancy, Ga. Geneal. Soc., Oglethorpe U. Nat. Alumni Assn., Emory U. Alumni Assn., Ga. State U. Alumni Assn., Atlanta Hist. Soc., Ga. Trust for Historic Preservation, Piedmont Health and Fitness Club. Home: NC 6 136 Peachtree Memorial Dr NW Atlanta GA 30309

WALLACE, HELEN MARGARET, physician, educator; b. Hoosick Falls, N.Y., Feb. 18, 1913; d. Jonas and Ray (Schweizer) W. AB, Wellesley Coll., 1933; MD, Columbia U., 1937; MPH cum laude, Harvard U., 1943. Diplomate Am. Bd. Pediatrics, Am. Bd. Preventive Medicine. Intern Bellevue Hosp., N.Y.C., 1938-40; child hygiene physician Conn. Health Dept., 1941-42; successively jr. health officer, health officer, chief maternity and new born div., dir. bur. for handicapped children N.Y.C. Health Dept., 1943-55; prof., dir. dept. pub. health N.Y. Med. Coll., 1955-56; prof. maternal and child health U. Minn. Sch. Pub. Health, 1956-59; chief profl. tng. U.S. Children's Bur., 1959-60, chief child health studies, 1961-62; prof. maternal and child health U. Calif. Sch. Pub. Health, Berkeley, 1962-80; prof., head divsn. maternal and child health Sch. Pub. Health San Diego State U., 1980—; Univ. Research lectr. San Diego State U., 1985—; cons. WHO numerous locations, including Uganda, The Philippines, Turkey, India, Geneva, Iran, Burma, Sri Lanka, East Africa, Australia, Indonesia, China, Taiwan, 1961—, traveling fellow, 1989—; cons. Hahnemann U., Phila., 1993, Ford Found., Colombia, 1971; UN cons. to Health Bur., Beijing, China, 1987; fellow Aiiku Inst. on Maternal and Child Health, Tokyo, and NIH Inst. Child Health and Human Devel., 1994; dir. Family Planning Project, Zimbabwe, 1984-87. Author, editor 10 textbooks; contbr. 325 articles to profl. jours. Mem. coun. on Disabled Children to Media, 1991; dir. San Diego County Infant Mortality Study, 1989—, San Diego Study of Prenatal Care, 1991. Recipient Alumnae Achievement award Wellesley Coll., 1982, U. Minn. award, 1985; Ford Found. study grantee, 1986, 87, 88; fellow World Rehab. Fund, India, 1991-92, Fulbright Found., 1992—, NIH Inst. Child Health and Human Devel., 1994, Aiiku Inst. of Maternal-Child Health, Tokyo, 1994. Fellow APHA (officer sect., Martha May Eliot award 1978), Am. Acad. Pediatrics (Job Smith award 1980, award 1989); mem. AMA, Assn. Tchrs. Maternal and Child Health, Am. Acad. Cerebral Palsy, Ambulatory Pediatric Assn., Am. Sch. Preventive Medicine. Home: 850 State St San Diego CA 92101-6046

WALLACE, JANE HOUSE, geologist; b. Ft. Worth, Aug. 12, 1926; d. Fred Leroy and Helen Gould (Kixmiller) Wallace; A.B., Smith Coll., 1947, M.A., 1949; postgrad. Bryn Mawr Coll., 1949-52. Geologist, U.S. Geol. Survey, 1952—, chief Pub. Inquiries Offices, Washington, 1964-72, spl. asst. to dir., 1974—, dep. bur. ethics counselor, 1975—, Washington liaison Office of Dir., 1978—. Recipient Meritorious Service award Dept. Interior, 1971, Disting. Svc. award, 1976, Sec.'s Commendation, 1988, Smith Coll. medal, 1992. Fellow Geol. Socs. Am., Washington (treas. 1963-67); mem. Sigma Xi (assoc.). Home: 3003 Van Ness St NW Washington DC 20008-4701 Office: Interior Bldg 19th and C Sts NW Washington DC 20240 also: US Geol Survey 103 National Ctr Reston VA 22092

WALLACE, JANE YOUNG (MRS. DONALD H. WALLACE), editor; b. Geneseo, Ill., Feb. 17, 1933; d. Worling R. and Margaret C. (McBroom) Young; m. Donald H. Wallace, Aug. 24, 1959; children: Robert, Julia. BS in Journalism, Northwestern U., 1955, MS in Journalism, 1956; LittD (hon.), Johnson and Wales U., 1990. Diplomate Nat. Restaurant Assn. Edn. Found., 1991. Editor house organ Libby McNeill & Libby, Chgo., 1956-58; prodn. editor Instns. Mag., Chgo., 1958-61; food editor Instns. Mag., 1961-65, mng. editor, 1965-68, editor-in-chief, 1968-85; editor Restaurants and Instns., 1970-85, editorial dir., 1985-89, assoc. pub., 1985-89, pub., 1989-94; pub. R & I Market Pl., 1989-94, v.p., editor/pub. emeritus, 1994—; editorial dir. Hotels and Restaurants Internat. Mag., 1971-89; v.p., editor/pub. emeritus Restaurants and Instns., 1994—; editorial dir. Foodservice Equipment Specialist Mag., 1975-89; v.p. Cahners Pub. Co. (Reed USA), 1982; mem. editorial quality audit bd. Reed USA, 1993—; cons. Nat. Restaurant Assn., dir., 1977-82; cons. Nat. Inst. for Food Svc. Industry; vis. lectr. Fla. Internat. U., 1980. Editor: The Professional Chef, 1962, The Professional Chef's Book of Buffets, 1965, Culinary Olympics Cookbook, 1980, 3d edit., 1988, Academy of American Culinary Foundation Cookbook, 1985, American Dietetic Associaton Foundation Cookbook, 1986; contbr. restaurant chpt. World Book Ency., 1975, 94, Food Service Trends, American Quantity Cooking, 1976. Mem. com. investigation vocat. needs for food svc. tng. U.S. Dept. Edn., 1969; mem. Inst. Food Editors' Conf., 1959-88, pres., 1967; mem. hospitality industry edn. adv. bd. Ill. Dept. Edn., 1976, mem. adv. bd. Ill. sch. foodsvc., 1978; mem. corp. adv. bd. Am. Dietetic Assn. Found., 1981—; trustee Presbyn. Ch., Barrington, Ill., 1983-85; bd. trustees Culinary Inst. Am., 1987—. Recipient Jesse H. Neal award for best bus. press editorial, 1969, 70, 73, 76, 77, 79, 82, 87, Diplomate award Nat. Restaurant Assn. Edn. Found., 1991; named Outstanding Woman Northwood Inst., 1983. Fellow Soc. for Advancement Foodservice Research (dir. 1975—, sec. 1980); mem. Internat. Foodservice Mfrs. Assn. (Spark Plug award 1979), Nat. Assn. Foodservice Equipment Mfrs., Am. Bus. Press Assn. (chmn. editorial com. 1978), Am. Inst. Interior Designers (asso.), Women in Communications (v.p. Chgo. 1957-58), Ivy Soc. Restaurateurs of Distinction (co-founder 1970—), Am. Dietetic Assn. (hon.), Roundtable for Women in Food Service (bd. dirs. 1980-84; Foodservice Woman of Yr. 1988, Lifetime Recognition award 1994), Les Dames d'Escoffier (charter mem.), Culinary Inst. of Am. (ambassador, trustee 1987), Brotherhood of Knights of Vine (Gentlelady award 1980, 81), Disting. Restaurateurs of N.Am. (Hall of Fame award 1994), Gamma Phi Beta, Kappa Tau Alpha. Home: 186 Signal Hill Rd Barrington IL 60010-1929 Office: Restaurants & Instns PO Box 5080 1350 E Touhy Ave Des Plaines IL 60018-3303

WALLACE, JEANNETTE OWENS, state legislator; b. Scottsdale, Ariz., Jan. 16, 1934; d. Albert and Velma (Whinery) Owens; m. Terry Charles Wallace Sr., May 21, 1955; children: Terry C. Jr., Randall J., Timothy A., Sheryl L., Janice M. BS, Ariz. State U., 1955. Mem. Los Alamos (N.Mex.) County Coun., 1981-82; cons. County of Los Alamos, 1983-84; chmn., vice chmn. Los Alamos County Coun., 1985-88; cons. County of Los Alamos, Los Alamos Schs., 1989-90; rep. N.Mex. State Legislature, 1991—; mem. appropriations & fin. govt. and urban affairs, N.Mex., 1991—, legis. fin. com., Indian affairs; co-chmn. Los Alamos County's Dept. Energy Negotiating Com., 1987-88; mem. legis. policy com. Mcpl. League, N.Mex., 1986-88. Bd. dirs. Tri-Area Econ. Devel., Pojoaque, N.Mex., 1987-92, Los Alamos Econ. Devel., 1988-94, Crime Stoppers, Los Alamos, 1988-92, Los Alamos Citizens Against Substance Abuse, 1989-94; mem. N.Mex. First, Albuquerque, 1989-93; legis. chmn. LWV, 1990; mem. Los Alamos Rep. Women, pres., 1989-90. Mem. Los Alamos Bus. & Profl. Women (legis. chmn. 1990), Los Alamos C. of C., Mana del Norte, Kiwanis. Methodist. Home: 146 Monte Rey Dr S Los Alamos NM 87544-3826

WALLACE, JOAN SCOTT, psychologist, international consultant; b. Chgo., Nov. 8, 1930; d. William Edouard and Esther (Fulks) Scott; m. John Wallace, June 12, 1954 (div. Mar. 1976); children—Mark, Eric, Victor; m. Maurice A. Dawkins, Oct. 14, 1979. A.B., Bradley U., 1952; M.S.W., Columbia U., 1954; postgrad., U. Chgo., 1965; Ph.D., Northwestern U., 1973; H.H.D. (hon.), U. Md., 1979; L.H.D. (hon.), Bowie State Coll., 1981; LLD (hon.), Ala. A&M U., 1990. Lic. social psychologist, social worker. Asst. prof., then assoc. prof. U. Ill.-Chgo., 1967-73; assoc. dean, prof. Howard U., Washington, 1973-76; v.p.-programs Nat. Urban League, N.Y.C., 1975-76; v.p. adminstrn. Morgan State U., Balt., 1976-77; asst. sec. adminstrn. USDA, Washington, 1977-81, adminstr. Office Internat. Cooperation and Devel., 1981-89; rep. to Trinidad and Tobago Inter Am. Inst. for Cooperation in Agr., USDA, 1989; internat. cons. U.S. Partnerships Internat., Ft. Lauderdale, 1993—; speaker in field. Contbr. articles, chpts. to profl. publs. Chair Binat. Agrl. Research and Devel. Fund, 1987. Recipient Disting. Alumni award Bradley U., 1978, Meritorious award Delta Sigma Theta, 1978, award for leadership Lambda Kappa Mu, 1978, award for outstanding achievement and svc. to nation Capital Hill Kiwanis Club, 1978, Links Achievement award, 1979, Presdl. Rank for Meritorious Exec., 1980, NAFEO award, 1989, Community Svc. award Alpha Phi Alpha, 1987, Pres.' award for outstanding pub. svc. Fla. A&M U., 1990. Mem. APA, NASW, AAAS, Am. Consortium for Internat. Pub. Adminstrn. (exec. com., governing bd. 1987), Soc. Internat. Devel. (Washington chpt.), Sr. Exec. Assn., Soc. for Internat. Devel., White House Com. on Internat. Sci., Engring. and Tech., Internat. Sci. and Edn. Coun. (chmn. 1981-89), Am. Evaluation Assn., Consortium Internat. Higher Edn. (adv. com.), Caribbean Studies Soc., Caribbean Assn. of Agriculture Economists, Assn. Polit. Psychologists, Pi Gamma Mu. Presbyterian. Home: 6010 S Falls Circle Dr Fort Lauderdale FL 33319-6900 Office: US Partnerships Internat 5557 W Oakland Park Blvd Fort Lauderdale FL 33313-1411

WALLACE, JOYCE IRENE MALAKOFF, internist; b. Phila., Nov. 25, 1940; d. Samuel Leonard and Henrietta (Hameroff) Malakoff; A.B., Queens Coll., City U. N.Y., 1961; postgrad. Columbia U., 1962-64; M.D, State U. N.Y., 1968; m. Lance Arthur Wallace, Aug. 30, 1964 (div. 1974); 1 dau., Julia Ruth; m. Arthur H. Kahn, Oct. 7, 1979 (div. 1986); 1 son, Aryeh N. Kahn. Intern, St. Vincent's Hosp. Med. Center, N.Y.C., 1968-70; resident Manhattan VA Hosp., N.Y.C. and Nassau County Med. Center, East Meadow, N.Y., 1972-73; practice medicine, N.Y.C., 1970-71, North Conway, N.H., 1974-75; practice medicine specializing in internal medicine, N.Y.C., 1976—; mem. attending staff Nassau County Med. Center, 1974, St. Vincent's Hosp. and Med. Center, N.Y.C., 1976—; asst. prof. medicine Mt. Sinai Med. Sch., N.Y.C.; pres. Found. for Research on Sexually Transmitted Diseases, Inc., 1986-89, exec. med. dir., 1989—. Diplomate Am. Bd. Internal Medicine. Fellow ACP, N.Y. Acad. Medicine; mem. Am. Med. Women's Assn., N.Y. County, N.Y. State med. socs. Office: 369 8th Ave New York NY 10001

WALLACE, JULIA DIANE, newspaper editor; b. Davenport, Iowa, Dec. 3, 1956; d. Franklin Sherwood and Eleanor Ruth (Pope) W.; m. Doniver Dean Campbell, Aug. 23, 1986; children: Emmaline Livingston Campbell, Eden Jennifer Dampbell. BS in Journalism, Northwestern U., 1978. Reporter Norfolk (Va.) Ledger-Star, 1978-80, Dallas Times Herald, 1980-82; reporter, editor News sect. USA Today, Arlington, Va., 1982-89, mng. editor spl. projects, 1989-92; mng. editor Chgo. Sun-Times, 1992—. Mem. Am. Soc. Newspaper Editors. Office: Chgo Sun-Times 401 N Wabash Ave Chicago IL 60611-3532*

WALLACE, KATHLEEN MARY, accountant; b. Everett, Mass., Sept. 23, 1964; d. George Anthony and Florence Margaret (Buist) Scheibert; m. Charles F. Wallace, Mar. 19, 1988; 1 child, Patrick Charles. BS in Accountancy cum laude, Northeastern U., 1990. Asst. acct. Whidden Meml. Hosp., Everett, Mass., 1983-84; sr. tax examiner Mass. Dept. Revenue, 1984-85; staff acct. Charles E. DiPesa and Co., CPA, Boston, 1985-88; fin. reporting acct. The Shareholder Svcs. Group, Boston, 1988—. Mem. Sigma Epsilon Rho. Home: 811 Shawsheen St Tewksbury MA 01876

WALLACE, LOUISE MARGARET, clinical coordinator; b. Norwich, Conn., June 15, 1942; d. Irving Clifford and Helen Lucille (Fain) Hayden; m. R.D. Wallace, Dec. 2, 1967; 1 child, Donald Orville. Grad., Joseph Lawrence Sch. Nursing, Conn., 1963; student, Miami-Dade (Fla.) Jr. Coll., 1966-67, Yavapai Coll., 1970. RN, Ariz., Mo., D.C., Fla., Conn., New Zealand. Nurse ICU and ob-gyn. dept. George Washington U. Hosp., Washington, 1964-65; nurse pediatrics dept. Jackson Meml. Hosp., Miami, Fla., 1965-66; nurse ICU Bapt. Hosp., Miami, 1966-67; nurse ICU and CCU N. Shore Hosp., Miami, 1967-71; nurse ICU and CCU VA Med. Ctr., Prescott, Ariz., 1971-84; nurse ICU and CCU VA Med. Ctr., Poplar Bluff, Mo., 1984-93, relief clin. coord., 1991-92; clin. coord., 1993—; instr. nursing Miami-Dade Jr. Coll., 1968-69; instr. basic CPR, Prescott, 1975-81. Mem. Am. Assn. Critical Care Nurses, Am. Diabetes Assn. Home: HC 1 Box 76 Grandin MO 63943-9602

WALLACE, MARY ELAINE, opera director, author; m. Robert House. BFA cum laude, U. Nebr., Kearney, 1940; MusM, U. Ill., 1954; postgrad., Music Acad. West, Santa Barbara, Calif., 1955, Eastman Sch. Music, 1960, Fla. State U., 1962. Prof. voice, dir. opera La. Tech. U., Ruston, 1954-62, SUNY-Fredonia, 1962-69, So. Ill. U.-Carbondale, 1969-79; dir. Marjorie Lawrence Opera Theatre, Opera on Wheels; adminstrv. adviser Summer Playhouse, Carbondale; stage mgr. Chautauqua Opera Co., N.Y.,

1963; asst. mus. dir., condr. Asolo Festival, Sarasota, Fla., 1961; music editor, critic The Chautauquan Daily; adjudicator Met. Opera auditions; exec. sec. Nat. Opera Assn., 1981-91. Co-author: Opera Scenes for Class and Stage, 1979, (with Robert Wallace) More Operas Scenes for Class and Stage, 1990, Upstage Downstage, 1992. Mem. Nat. Opera Assn. (pres. 1974, 75), Music Tchrs. Nat. Assn., Nat. Assn. Tchrs. Singing, AAUP, AAUW, Met. Opera Guild, Mortar Bd., Sigma Tau Delta, Pi Kappa Lambda, Phi Beta, Alpha Psi Omega, Delta Kappa Gamma. Address: 3106 Lakeside Rockwall TX 75087

WALLACE, PEGGY MARIE, state commissioner; b. Barbourville, Ky., Jan. 3, 1950; d. Chester and Katherine (White) W. BS, Union Coll., 1971; MSSW, U. Louisville, 1977. Eligibility worker Dept. Econ. Security, State of Ky., Barbourville, 1972-74; social worker Dept. Social Svcs., Barbourville, 1974-76; social svcs. trainer, cons. Dept. Social Svcs., Frankfort, 1977-78, budget analyst, 1978-80, adminstrv. asst., 1980-81, adminstrv. supr., 1981, exec. asst., 1981-85, prin. asst., 1985-88, dep. commr., 1988-92, commr., 1992—; mem. Ky. Atty. Gen's. Task Force on Child Sexual Abuse, Ky. Child Labor Task Force, Ky. Multi-Disciplinary Commn. on Child Sexual Abuse, Ky. Crime Commn. (mem. juvenile justice adv. com.), Ky. Children's Justice Act Task Force, Ky. Family Resource and Youth Svcs. Ctr. Task Force, Ky. Child Care Policy Coun., Ky. Adv. Coun. on the Homeless, Ky. Early Intervention System Interagy. Coord. Coun., Ky. Gender Fairness Standing Com. (mem. subcom. on domestic violence), Ky. Birth Surveillance Adv. Com., Ky. Long Range Juvenile Detention Planning Com., Ky. State Interagy. Coun. for Children and Youth; chair Am. Pub. Welfare Assn's. Children, Families and Adult Svcs. Com. Mem. NASW (mem. bluegrass chpt.), Nat. Forum for Black Pub. Adminstrs. Baptist. Office: Social Svcs Dept 275 E Main St Frankfort KY 40601

WALLACE, PERMELIA FRANKLIN, artist; b. Lexington, Tenn., Oct. 21, 1935; d. Hulon Woodard and Etta Mae (Wood) Franklin; m. Clifford Franklin Wallace; children: Linda Dianne Wallace Lodes, Randy DeWaine Wallace. Grad., Am. Sch., Chgo., 1954. One woman show includes Fall Art Show, Carnegie Ctr. for History and Arts, Jackson, Tenn., Jackson City Hall. Mem. Family Community Edn. (reporter 1990, Woman of Yr. 1994), West Tenn. Decorative Painters (pres. 1992), Jackson Art Assn. (reporter 1989), Jackson Bus. Women's Club, Order Ea. Star. Roman Catholic. Home: 175 Summar Dr Jackson TN 38301

WALLACE, ROANNE, hosiery company executive; b. Greenwood, Miss., Dec. 18, 1949; d. Robert Carter and Lois Anne (Vick) W. BM, U. Tenn., 1971; MA, U. N.C., 1976; MBA, Wake Forest U., 1982. Exec. dir. Am. Bd. Clin. Chemistry, Winston-Salem, N.C., 1977-78; adminstrv. officer Winston-Salem/Forsyth County Office Emergency Mgmt., 1978-79, sr. asst. dir., 1979-82; with Sara Lee Hosiery, Winston-Salem, 1982—, mktg. dir., 1988—; product mgr. L'eggs Products, Inc., Winston-Salem, 1986-88. Mem. adv. coun. Winston-Salem/Forsyth County Office Emergency Mgmt.; bd. dirs. Piedmont Opera Theatre, Inc. Miss U. Tenn., 1970. Home: 803 Devon Ct Winston Salem NC 27104 Office: L'Eggs Products Inc PO Box 2495 Winston Salem NC 27102

WALLACH, ANNE JACKSON See JACKSON, ANNE

WALLACH, BARBARA PRICE, classicist, educator; b. Roanoke, Va., Aug. 31, 1946; d. Benjamin Thomas and Geneva Mae (Bittinger) Price; m. Luitpold Wallach, Aug. 22, 1970 (dec. Nov. 1986). BA in Latin, Mary Washington Coll., 1968; MA in Classics, U. Ill., 1970, PhD in Classical Philology, 1974. Summer vis. lectr. U. Ill., Urbana, 1977; vis. asst. prof. U. Pitts., 1979-80; asst. prof. U. Mo., Columbia, 1980-85, assoc. prof., 1985—. Author: Lucretius and the Diatribe, 1976; contbr. articles to profl. jours. Mem. Am. Philol. Assn., Classical Assn. Middle West and South, Internat. Soc. for the History of Rhetoric, Soc. for Ancient Greek Philosophy, Vergilian Soc., Internat. Plutarch Soc., Phi Beta Kappa. Democrat. Office: U Mo Dept Classical Studies Columbia MO 65211

WALLACH, MAGDALENA FALKENBERG (CARLA WALLACH), writer; b. Brussels; d. Carl Albert and Renee Antoinette (Meunier) Falkenberg; m. Philip Charles Wallach, Mar. 5, 1950. Student, Columbia U., Hunter Coll., New Sch. for Social Rsch. Ptnr. Williams-Falkenberg Advt. Assocs., Inc., N.Y.C., 1951-55. Author: Reluctant Weekend Gardener, 1971, Interior Decorating with Plants, 1976, Gardening in the City, 1976, Garden in a Teacup, 1978; contbr. articles to N.Y. Times, Glamour, Working Woman, others. Former bd. dirs. ARC, N.Y.C.; active Bruce Mus., 1987—, chmn. spl. events, 75th anniversary gala, nominating com., mem. Renaissance Ball benefit com., long-range planning com., bd. dirs., also other fund raising activities; bd. dirs., v.p. Greenwich Adult Day Care Ctr. Mem. Nat. League Am. PEN Women (pres. Greenwich br. 1987-92), Authors Guild, Garden Writers Assn., English-Speaking Union (bd. dirs. Greenwich br.), Alliance Francaise, Nat. Inst. Social Scis. Roman Catholic. Home: 126 WestLyon Farm Dr Greenwich CT 06831

WALLACH, PATRICIA, mayor; b. Chgo.; m. Ed Wallach; 3 children. Grad., Pasadena City Coll. Mem. city coun. City of El Monte, Calif., 1990-92, mayor, 1992—; tchr.'s aide Mountain View Sch. Dist. Past trustee El Monte Union High Sch. Dist., L.A. County High Sch. for the Arts; chief amb. of goodwill Zamora, Michoacan, Mex., Marcq-en-Baroeul, France, Yung Kang, Hsiang, Republic of China, Minhang, Peoples Republic of China; mem. adv. com. L.A. Regional Libr.; mem. air quality com. West San Gabriel Valley; chairperson of bd. Cmty. Redevel. Agy.; chairperson El Monte Cmty. Access TV Corp.; mem. PTA, Little League Assns. Mem. League of Calif. Cities, San Gabriel Valley Assn. of Cities, Independent Cities Assn., Bus. and Profl. Women, U.S./Mex. Sister Cities Assn., Sister Cities Internat. Office: 11333 Valley Blvd El Monte CA 91731-3210

WALLACH, SHIRLEY SCHMONES (SHIRLEY SCHMONES), physician; b. N.Y.C., Nov. 29, 1920; d. Benjamin and Gertrude (Schwartz) Schmones; m. Morton B. Wallach, June 11, 1944 (div. 1971); children: Joelle Marsha, Lee Ann Wallach Saltzman. BA magna cum laude, NYU, 1941, MD, 1943; postgrad., Dartmouth Med. Sch., Taylor Manor Hosp., Mt. Sinai Sch. Medicine, So. Conn. State U. Diplomate Am. Bd. Psychiatry and Neurology, Am. Bd. Child Psychiatry. Intern The Jewish Hosp. of Bklyn., 1944; resident in internal medicine NYU, 1945-46; resident in psychiatry Hillside Hosp., Queens, N.Y., 1959-61; fellow in child psychiatry Mt. Sinai Hosp., N.Y.C., 1961-62, Albert Einstein Coll. Medicine, Bronx, N.Y., 1962-63; dep. unit chief Harlem Valley Psychiat. Ctr., N.Y., 1981-82; psychiatrist Queens Children's Hosp. Ctr., 1982-85; psychiatrist II Creedmoor State Hosp., 1985-86; sch. psychiatrist City of N.Y. Bd. Edn.; pvt. practice N.Y.C. and Forest Hills, N.Y., 1946-86; attending physician NYU-Bellevue Hosp., N.Y.C., 1946—, Beth Israel Hosp., N.Y.C., 1948, Mt. Sinai Hosp., N.Y.C., 1968; cons. psychiatrist Menorah Hosp., Ottilie Home for Children, 1963-64, Child Devel. Ctr.; supervising psychiatrist S.I. Children's Hosp.; dir. adolescent unit Fair Oaks Hosp., Summit, N.J., 1977-78; coord. resident tng. program dept. psychiatry divsn. child psychiatry Mt. Sinai Hosp., N.Y.C., 1963-77, Elmhurst Hosp., N.Y.C.; instr. Hunter Coll., N.Y.C., 1949-52; cardiac cons. N.Y.C. Dept. Health; asst. clin. prof. dept. psychiatry Mt. Sinai Sch. Medicine Appointment, 1969. Contbr. articles to profl. jours. Fellow Am. Psychiat. Assn., Am. Acad. Child Psychiatry, Acad. Psychosomatic Medicine, Am. Geriatrics Soc.; mem. AMA, Am. Med. Writers' Assn., Am. Assn. Psychiat. Clinics for Children, N.Y. Acad. Scis., Hastings Inst. Soc., Ethics and Life Scis. Office: 70-25 Yellowstone Blvd 11D Forest Hills NY 11375-3172

WALLACK-ROSELLI, RINA EVELYN, lawyer; b. Pitts.; d. Erwin Norman and Gloria A. (Schacher). AD in Nursing, Delta Coll., 1973; BS cum laude in Psychology, Eastern Mich. U., 1980; JD cum laude, Wayne State U., 1983. Registered nurse Mich.; bar: Calif. 1983. Psychiat. head nurse Ypsilanti (Mich.) State Hosp., 1973-77, instr., nursing educator, 1977-80; teaching asst. contracts Wayne State U., Detroit, 1981-83; legal asst. Wayne County Prosecutor's Office, 1982-83; atty. NLRB, L.A., 1983-86, dir. employee rels. legal svcs. Paramount Pictures Corp., L.A., 1986-89, v.p., 1989—. Contbr. articles to profl. jours. Instr. ARC, Mich., 1978-80. Recipient Am. Jurisprudence Book award, 1983. Mem. ABA, L.A. County Bar Assn., Am. Trial Lawyers Assn., Mich. Bar Assn., Calif. Bar Assn., Order of Coif. Avocations: shooting, movies, dancing, reading, photography.

WALLEN, ELEANOR ANDREA, podiatrist; b. Toronto, Ont., Can., Oct. 18, 1950; d. Irvin and Ruth Rose (Silverman) W. BA, U. Toronto, 1973; D of Podiatric Medicine, Ohio Coll., 1987. Diplomate Am. Bd. of Podiatric Orthopaedics and Primary Podiatric Medicine. Intern Ohio Coll. Podiatric Medicine, Huron Rd. Hosp., Cleve., 1987-88; resident Oakwood Down River Med. Ctr., Lincoln Park, Mich., 1988-89; asst. mgr. Karelia Ltd., Toronto, 1973-75; paralegal Toronto, 1975-82; podiatrist Burbank Podiatry Assoc. Group, 1989-93; pvt. practice Burbank, 1993—. Recipient Chi Hsuin U. Chu PhD Meml. award, 1987. Mem. C. of C., Am. Podiatric Med. Assn., Calif. Podiatric Med. Assn., L.A. County Podiatric Med. Assn., Am. Assn. of Women Podiatrists, Pi Delta. Office: Tri-City Podiatry 3322 W Magnolia Blvd Burbank CA 91505-2907

WALLEN, LINA HAMBALI, educator, consultant; b. Garut, West Java, Indonesia, Mar. 24, 1952; came to U.S., 1986; d. Mulyadi and Indra (Hudiyana) Hambali; m. Norman E. Wallen, Apr. 16, 1986. BA, IKIP, Bandung, Indonesia, 1975, DRA, 1984; PhD in Psychology, Columbia Pacific U., San Rafael, Calif., 1990; MA in Economics, San Francisco State U., 1993. Cert. tchr. Clk. PT Radio Frequency Communication, Bandung, 1972-74; adminstrv. mgr. CV Electronics Engring., Jakarta, Indonesia, 1974-76; exec. sec. PT Tanabe Abadi, Bandung, 1977-81; br. mgr. PT Ama Forta, Bandung, 1982-84; tchr. SMA Pembangunan, Bandung, 1976-83, Patuha Coll., Bandung, 1980-84.

WALLENBORN, JANICE RAE, elementary education educator; b. Chgo., Jan. 22, 1938; d. Ramon Joseph and Anne Joan (Seaquist) W. BEd, Beloit Coll., 1960; MEd, The George Washington U., 1966; postgrad., George Mason U., 1987-88, U. Va., 1965-85; Degree in Theol. Edn., U. of South, 1989. Cert. tchr. Va. Tchr. Quantico (Va.) Marine Base, 1960-62; elem. tchr. Pearl Harbor Elem. Sch., Honolulu, 1962-64, Quantico Dependents Sch. System, 1964—. Counselor Diet Ctr., Springfield, Va., 1979-89. Mem. NEA (life), Quantico Edn. Assn. (treas. 1968-72), Va. Edn. Assn., Pi Lambda Theta (life), Kappa Alpha Theta (treas. 1979-81, pres. North Va. chpt. 1981-85, alumni dist. pres. 1989—). Republican. Episcopalian. Home: 8576 Gwynedd Way Springfield VA 22153-3422 Office: Quantico Dependents Sch Sys WW Burrows 3308 John Quick Rd Quantico VA 22134-1702

WALLER, MARIE TUTTLE, executive secretary; b. La Junta, Colo., Mar. 24, 1923; d. George W. and Cora (Caldwell) White; m. Roy Waller, Mar. 19, 1958; children: Kenneth David Tuttle, Richard William Tuttle, Roy Waller, Ross Waller. Student, No. Va. Community Coll. Exec. sec. USAF-Wright Patterson AFB, Dayton, Ohio; sec. CAB, Washington; clk-stenographer Pentagon, Occupational Test Evaluation Agency, Washington; exec. sec. Pentagon, Washington. Mem. Profl. Secs. Inst., Gold Star Wives. Address: Bay Point 60 Bay Saint Louis MS 39520

WALLER, PATRICIA FOSSUM, transportation executive, researcher, psychologist; b. Winnipeg, Man., Can., Oct. 12, 1932; d. Magnus Samuel and Diana Isabel (Briggs) Fossum; m. Marcus Bishop Waller, Feb. 27, 1957; children: Anna Estelle, Justin Magnus, Martha Wilkinson, Benjamin Earl. AB in Psychology cum laude, U. Miami, Coral Gables, 1953, MS in Psychology, 1955; PhD in Psychology, U. N.C., 1959. Lic. psychologist, N.C. Psychology intern VA Hosp., Salem, Va., 1956; psychology instr. Med. Sch. U. N.C., Chapel Hill, 1957; USPHS postdoctoral fellow R.B. Jackson Lab., Bar Harbor, Maine, 1958-60; psychologist VA Hosp., Brockton, Mass., 1961-62; psychology lectr. U. N.C., Chapel Hill, Greensboro, 1962-67; assoc. dir. driver studies Hwy. Safety Rsch. Ctr. U. N.C., Chapel Hill, 1967-89, dir. Injury Prevention Rsch. Ctr., 1987-89; dir. Transp. Rsch. Inst. U. Mich., Ann Arbor, 1989—; bd. dirs. Intelligent Vehicle/Hwy. Soc. Am., Washington, 1991—, Traffic Safety Assn. Mich., Lansing, 1991—; bd. advisors Eno Transp. Found., Inc., Landsdowne, Va., 1994—; chair group 5 coun. Transp. Rsch. Bd. of Nat. Rsch. Coun., Washington, 1992—, chmn. Task Force Operator Regulations, 1974-76, mem. study com. devel. ranking rail safety r&d projects, 1980-82, chmn. group 3 coun. operation, safety and maintenance transp. facilities, 1980-83, mem. IVHS-IDEA tech. rev. panel, 1993—, chair workshop human factors rsch. in highway safety, 1992, chair ad hoc com. environ. activities, 1992, mem. task force on elderly drivers, 1990-93, mem. com. vehicle user characteristics, 1983-86, mem. com. planning and adminstrn. of transp. safety, 1986-92, mem. com. alcohol, other drugs and transp., 1986—, numerous other coms., mem. spl. coms. including Inst. Medicine Dana Award com., 1986-90, com. of 55MPH nat. maximum speed limit, 1983-84; mem. motor vehicle safety rsch. adv. com. Dept. Transp., Washington, 1991—; reviewer JAMA, Jour. Studies on Alcohol, Jour. of Gerontology, Am. Jour. Pub. Health; apptd. Pres. Coun. Spinal Cord Injury, 1981; apptd. advisor Nat. Hwy. Safety Adv. Com. to Sec. U.S. Dept. Transp., 1979-80, 80-83; author numerous reports on transp. to govtl. coms. and univs. Author: (with Paul G. Shinkman) Instructor's Manual for Mogan and King: Introduction to Psychology, 1971; author: (with others) Psychological Concepts in the Classroom, 1974, Drinking: Alcohol in American Society—Issues and Current Research, 1978, The American Handbook of Alcoholism, 1982, The Role of the Civil Engineer in Highway Safety, 1983, Aging and Public Health, 1985, Young Driver Accidents: In Search of Solutions, 1985, Alcohol, Accidents and Injuries, 1986, Transportation in an Aging Society: Improving the Mobility and Safety for Older Persons, 1988, Young Drivers Impaired by Alcohol and Drugs, 1988; mem. editorial bd. Jour. Safety Rsch., 1979—; assoc. guest editor Health Edn. Quar., 1989; assoc. editor Accident, Analysis, and Prevention, 1978-84, mem. editorial bd., 1976-87; contbr. articles to profl. jours. Grantee HHS, 1992, NIH. Mem. AAAS, APA (Harold M. Hildreth award 1993), APHA (injury control and emergency health svcs. sect., Disting. Career award 1994, transp. rsch. bd., Roy W. Crum award for rsch. contbns. 1995), Assn. for the Advancement of Automotive Medicine (chmn. human factors sect. 1978-80, bd. dirs. 1979-82, pres. 1981-82), Coun. Univ. Transp. Ctrs. (exec. com. 1991—), Transp. Rsch. Bd., Ea. Psychol. Assn., Sigma Xi. Democrat. Office: U Mich Transp Rsch Inst 2901 Baxter Rd Ann Arbor MI 48109-2150

WALLER, WILMA RUTH, retired secondary school educator and librarian; b. Jacksonville, Tex., Nov. 15, 1921; d. William Wesley and Myrtle (Nesbitt) W. BA with honors, Tex. Woman's U., 1954, MA with honors, 1963, MLS with honors, 1976. Tchr. English Dell (Ark.) High Sch., 1953-54, Jefferson (Tex.) Ind. Schs., 1954-56, Tyler (Tex.) Ind. Schs., 1956-68; librarian Wise County Schs., Decatur, Tex., 1969-71, Thomas K. Gorman High Sch., Tyler, 1971-74, Sweetwater (Tex.) Ind. Sch. Dist., 1974-86; ret.; lectr., book reviewer for various clubs. Active in past as vol. for ARC, U. Tex. Health Ctr. Ford Found. fellow, 1959. Mem. AAUW (past chmn. book, critique, drama and contemporary interests groups), UDC, Smith County Ret. Sch. Pers., Bible Study Group, Delta Kappa Gamma. Republican. Baptist. Home: 1117 N Azalea Dr Tyler TX 75701

WALLING, ESTHER MARIE, school counselor; b. Redding, Calif., June 12, 1953; d. Haskell Eugene and Flora Margaret (Hammon) W. MusB, U. So. Calif., 1976; MS, Calif. State U., Long Beach, 1990. Tchr. music Pilgrim Sch., L.A., 1977-78, St. Francis Xavier and Blessed Sacrament Schs., L.A., 1978-79, St. Joseph Sch., Redding, 1981-82, Johnson Intermediate Sch., Westminster, Calif., 1985-86; sec. Transam. Corp., L.A., 1979-81; substitute tchr. Irvine Unified Sch. Dist. and Fountain Valley Sch. Dist., Orange County, Calif., 1983-85, Bell Intermediate Sch., Garden Grove, Calif., 1984-85; tchr. music and English, Bret Harte Prep. Intermediate Sch., L.A., 1986-91; coll. counselor Bell (Calif.) High Sch., 1991-94, Thomas Jefferson High Sch., L.A., 1994—. Mem. Nat. Assn. Coll. and Admissions Counselors, L.A. Sch. Counselors Assn. Republican. Roman Catholic. Home: 1222 Princeton St # 12 Santa Monica CA 90404-1451 Office: Thomas Jefferson High Sch 1319 E 41st St Los Angeles CA 90011

WALLINGFORD, ANNE, writer, marketing consultant; b. Chgo., June 29, 1949; d. Lester Arlyn and Roseanne (Jones) W. BS in Edn., Chgo. State U., 1975. Cert. elem. and mid. sch. tchr., Ill. Profl. dressmaker Annie's Original's, Chgo., 1968-72; instr., asst. prin., St. Bonaventure Sch., Chgo., 1972-81; instr., chairperson sci. dept. Our Lady of Lourdes Sch., Chgo., 1981-88; product designer, catalog mgr. FSC Ednl., Inc., Mansfield, Ohio, 1988-91; freelance journalist, catalog mgr., sci. coord. A. Wallingford, Wordsmith, Mansfield and Chgo., 1981—. Contbr. bus. profiles to profl. publs., 1990—. Active The Vol. Ctr., Mansfield, 1992-93, steering com. Wright Community Ctr., 1991; treas. Wolfram St. Block Club, Chgo., 1975-78. Recipient Gold award Adler Planetarium, Chgo., 1985. Mem. NAFE, Nat. Writers Union, Chgo. Women in Pub., Soc. Tech. Communicators, Profl. Freelance Assn. (founder, pres. 1991-92), Mensa. Office: 6155 N Moody Chicago IL 60646

WALLIS, LORRINE KATHRINE, sales executive; b. Columbus, Ohio, Apr. 24, 1958; d. James William and Patricia Elaine (Becker) W.; m. Gary M. Short, May 25, 1985 (div. Jan. 1989). BA in Criminal Justice, U. Ctrl. Okla., 1980. Detention officer Oklahoma County Juvenile Bur., Oklahoma City, 1980-82; sales rep. Wesbanco, Oklahoma City, 1982-83, OtelCo, Oklahoma City, 1983-84; ter. mgr. Micro-Magic div. AMS, Inc., Bolivar, Mo., 1984—. Mem. Ill. Hunter and Jumper Assn., Reebok Alliance, Am. Mixed Breed Obedience Registration. Republican. Jewish. Home: 4404 Kensington Ct Gurnee IL 60031-6213 Office: AMS Inc Micro-Magic Div 1807 W Aldrich Rd Bolivar MO 65613-3305

WALLISON, FRIEDA K., lawyer; b. N.Y.C., Jan. 15, 1943; d. Ruvin H. and Edith (Landes) Koslow; m. Peter J. Wallison, Nov. 24, 1966; children: Ethan S., Jeremy L., Rebecca K. AB, Smith Coll., 1963; LLB, Harvard U., 1966. Bar: N.Y. 1967, DC 1982. Assoc. Carter, Ledyard & Milburn, N.Y.C., 1966-75; spl. counsel, div. market regulation Securities & Exchange Commn., Washington, 1975; exec. dir., gen. counsel Mcpl. Securities Rulemaking Bd., Washington, 1975-78; ptnr. Rogers & Wells, N.Y.C. and Washington, 1978-83; ptnr. Jones, Day, Reavis & Pogue, N.Y.C., and Washington, 1983—; mem. Govtl. Acctg. Standards Adv. Council, Washington, Nat. Council on Pub. Works Improvement, Washington; mem. environ. fin. adv. bd. EPA. Fellow Am. Bar Found.; mem. Nat. Council Govtl. Acctg., Nat. Assn. Bond Lawyers, N.Y.C. Bar Assn. Contbr. articles to profl. jours. Office: Jones Day Reavis & Pogue Ste 600 1450 G St NW Washington DC 20005-2088

WALLNER, MARY JANE, state legislator, director child care organization; b. St. Louis, Oct. 25, 1946; d. Arthur M. and Frances (Fulkerson) Bills; m. Nicholas Anthony Wallner, Mar. 10, 1967; children: Jenny, Jessy. BS in Child and Family, U. N.H., 1971; postgrad, Wheelock Coll., 1974-76. Child care worker Newmarket (N.H.) Day Care, 1967-69, dir., 1971-72; tchr. Exeter (N.J.) Head Start, 1969-70; dir. Merrimack Valley Day Care, Concord, N.H., 1973—; mem. N.H. Ho. of Reps., Concord, 1980—. VISTA vol. Jane Adams Hull House, Chgo., 1966; bd. dirs. N.H. Womens Lobby, Concord, 1991—, Meritorious Svc. award, 1988; bd. dirs. N.H. Task Force for the Prevention Child Abuse, Concord, 1985-91; trustee Trust Fund for the Prevention Child Abuse, Concord, 1987-91. Recipient Friend of Children award N.H. Group Home Assn., 1988, Commitment to Young Children award N.H. Assn. for the Edn. Young Children, 1989, Voice for Children award Child and Family Svcs., 1990. Mem. Zonta (sec. 1980—). Democrat. Office: Merrimack Valley Day Care Svcs 19 N Fruit St Concord NH 03301-2989 also: NH Ho of Reps State House Concord NH 03301*

WALLS, DARLENE CERETA, lawyer; b. Detroit, Dec. 1, 1960; d. James and Barbara Jean (Brown) W. BA, U. Mich., 1982; JD, U. West L.A., 1989. Bar: Calif. 1989. Atty. Calif. Pub. Defender Assn., L.A., 1991—. Episcopalian. Office: Law Office Pub Defender 210 W Temple St Los Angeles CA 90012-3210

WALLS, GLORIA JEANNE WILSON, computer consultant; b. Pitts., Nov. 12, 1963; d. James Oscar and Frances Rebecca (Brown) W. BS in Fin., Pa. State U., 1985; MBA, U. Pitts., 1986. Fin. analyst IBM Corp., Essex Junction, Vt., 1986-92; software support analyst Lotus Corp., Austin, Tex., 1992—. Supr. Teen Hotline/King St. Youth Ctr., Burlington, Vt., 1991-92. Mem. Fin. Mgmt. Assn., Bus. and Profl. Women's Club, Nat. Black MBA Assn. Home: 4807 Gypsy Cv Austin TX 78727-6816

WALLS, MARTHA ANN WILLIAMS (MRS. B. CARMAGE WALLS), newspaper executive; b. Gadsden, Ala., Apr. 21, 1927; d. Aubrey Joseph and Inez (Cooper) Williams; m. B. Carmage Walls, Jan. 2, 1954; children: Byrd Cooper, Lissa Walls Vahldiek. Student pub. schs., Gadsden. Pres., dir. Walls Newspapers, Inc., 1969-70; sec., treas., dir. Summer Camps, Inc., Guntersville, Ala., 1954-69; CEO, pres., dir. So. Newspapers, Inc., Houston, 1970—; v.p., dir. Scottsboro (Ala.) Newspapers, Angleton (Tex.) Times, Ft. Payne (Ala.) Newspapers, Inc.; sec.-treas., dir. Portales (N.M.) News Tribune Publ. Co., Quay County Sun Newspaper, Inc., Tucumcari, N.M.; v.p., dir. Bay City (Tex.) Newspapers, Inc.; bd. dirs. Liberal (Kans.) Newspapers, Inc., Monroe (Ga.) Newspapers, Inc., Moore Newspapers, Inc., Dumas, Tex., Jefferson Pilot Corp., Greensboro, N.C., Jefferson-Pilot Life Ins. Co., Jefferson Pilot Communications. Bd. dirs. Montgomery Acad., 1970-74. Mem. Soc. Profl. Journalists, The Houstonian. Episcopalian. Office: So Newspapers Inc 1050 Wilcrest Dr Houston TX 77042-1608

WALLS, SANDRA L., educational administrator; b. Milford, Del., Dec. 5, 1953; d. Thomas S. and Verna L. (Lodge) W.; m. Charles H. McKinney Jr., June 18, 1976 (div. Feb. 1980); 1 child, Charles H. McKinney III. BS, U. Del., 1975; MEd, Salisbury State U., 1978. Cert. prin. spl. edn., elem. and secondary adminstr., Del. Tchr. spl. edn. Indian River Sch. Dist., Frankford, Del., 1975-79, spl. edn. bldg. coord., 1979-85; tchr. spl. edn. Cape Henlopen Sch. Dist., Lewes, Del., 1985-86; program cooord. Sussex Vocat. Tech. Sch. Dist., Georgetown, Del., 1986-92; asst. prin. Sussex Tech. High Sch., Georgetown, 1992—; adj. prof. Del. State Coll., Georgetown, 1989-90; expert witness Pub. Defender's Office, Worcester, Snow Hill, Md., 1989; trainer Del. Learning Resource Ctr., Georgetown, 1986-88. Com. chair Dem. Polit. Party, Milford, 1975-78; mem. Gov.'s Coun. for Exceptional Citizens, Dover, Del., 1980-82; coach Rookie League, T-Ball League, Ocean City, Md., 1989-92. Spl. Edn. Tng. fellow Dept. Public Inst., 1977-78. Mem. ASCD, Nat. Assn. Sec. Sch. Prins., Nat. Coun. for Children with Behavioral Disorders, Nat. Coun. for Children with Learning Disabilities, Coun. for Exceptional Children (state pres. 1980-81, 86-87), Lower Del. Sch. Prin. Assn. (pres. 1990-91), Phi Delta Kappa (dist. rep. 1990—). Democrat. Methodist. Home: 72 Keenwik Selbyville DE 19975

WALRATH, PATRICIA A., state legislator; b. Brainerd, Minn., Aug. 11, 1941; d. Joseph James and Pansey Patricia (Drake) McCarvill; m. Robert Eugene Walrath, Sept. 1, 1961; children: Karen, Susan, David, Julie. BS, Bemidji State U., 1962; MS, SUNY, Oswego, 1975. Cert. secondary math. tchr., N.Y., Mass. Programmer analyst Control Data Corp., Mpls., 1962-65; crewleader dept. commerce U.S. Census, Middlesex County, Mass., 1979-80; selectman Town of Stow, Mass., 1980-85; tchr. math. Hale Jr. High Sch., Stow, 1981-82; instr. math. Johnson & Wale Coll. Hanscom AFB, Bedford, Mass., 1983-84; test examiner Hanscom AFB, Bedford, 1983-84; state rep. 3d Middlesex dist. State of Mass., Boston, 1985—; mem. House ways and means com., 1987-92, joint coms. on local affairs and pub. svc., 1993—. Chmn. Mass. Indoor Air Pollution Commn., Boston, 1987-88; mem. Stow Dem. Com., 1988—; merit badge counselor Boy Scouts Am., Stow and Hudson, Mass., 1990—; bd. dirs. Hudson Arts Alliance, 1991—. Recipient Disting. Svc. award Auburn N.Y. Jaycees, 1976. Mem. LWV (pres. 1973-76, dir. fin. 1977-78), Am. Legis. Exch. Coun., Mass. Legislators' Assn., Mass. Dem. Leadership Coun. (v.p. 1991-92, co-chmn. 1993-94), Mass. Women's Legis. Caucus (chair 1986). Roman Catholic. Home: 20 Middlemost Way Stow MA 01775-1363 Office: State Capital RM 275 Boston MA 02133

WALSER, VICKI LYNN, communications sales executive; b. Portland, Oreg., May 30, 1957; d. Daniel Stansel and Jeanne Inez (Barker) W.; m. Curtis Dee Sorensen, Nov. 19, 1976 (div. Feb. 1983); 1 child, C. Dane Sorensen. BS, City U., Bellevue, Wash., 1990; postgrad., Seattle U., 1991—. Data entry operator Signetics, Orem, Utah, 1980-82; data processing supr. Scott Wetzel Ins., Tukwila, Wash., 1982-83; office mgr. Interline Comms. (a U.S. West Co.), Renton, Wash., 1983-85; customer svc. rep. U.S. West Info. Sys., Bellevue, Wash., 1985-88; account rep. U.S. West Comms. Svcs., Inc., Seattle, 1988—. Mem. U.S. Coaches Assn. (mem. level I 1986-87), Profl. Ski Instrs. of Am. (ski instr., mem. level II 1983—). Republican. Mormon. Office: US West Comms Svcs Inc 1420 5th Ave Ste 1400 Seattle WA 98101-2341

WALSH, DIANA CHAPMAN, academic administrator, social and behavioral sciences educator; b. Phila., July 30, 1944; d. Robert Francis and Gwen (Jenkins) Chapman; m. Christopher Thomas Walsh, June 18, 1966; 1 child, Allison Chapman Walsh. AB, Wellesley Coll., 1966; MS, Boston U., 1971, PhD, 1983; LHD (hon.), Boston U, 1994. Mgr. spl. events Barnard Coll.,

N.Y.C., 1967-70; dir. info., edn. Planned Parenthood League, Newton, Mass., 1971-74; sr. program assoc. Dept Pub. Health, Boston, 1974-76; dir. program evaluations Boston U. Health Policy Inst., 1976-85; asst. prof. Sch. Pub. Health, Sch. Medicine, Boston U., 1982-84, assoc. prof., 1984-87, prof., 1987-93, assoc. dir. Health Policy Inst., 1985-93; pres. Wellesley Coll., 1993—; editorial bd. dirs. Bus. and Health; C.O. Sappington lectr. Am. Occupational Med. Assn. Nat. Conv., Phila., 1987. Author: (book) Corporate Physicians, 1987; editor (book series) Industry and Health Care, 1977-80; contbr. articles to profl. jours. Bd. dirs. Planned Parenthood League of Mass., 1974-79, 1981-85; trustee Occupational Physicians Scholarship Fund, 1987—. Kellogg Nat. fellow, 1987-90. Mem. AM. Pub. Health Assn., Am. Sociol. Assn., Soc. for Study of Social Problems. Home: 1720 Commonwealth Ave Newton MA 02165-2823 Office: Wellesley Coll Office of the Pres Roxbury MA 02181*

WALSH, DIANE, pianist; b. Washington, Aug. 16, 1950; d. William Donald and Estelle Louise (Stokes) W.; m. Henry Forbes, 1969 (div. 1979); m. Richard Pollak, 1982. MusB, Juilliard Sch. Music, 1971, MusM, Mannes Coll., 1982. Vis. assoc. prof. Hunter Coll. CCNY, 1991-92, Vassar College, 1992-93. N.Y.C. debut Young Concert Artists Series, 1974; founding mem. Mannes Trio, 1983-94; solo appearances include: Kennedy Ctr. for Performing Arts, Washington, 1976, Met. Mus., N.Y.C., 1976, Wigmore Hall, London, 1980, Merkin Concert Hall, 1989, Miller Theatre, 1994; with Mannes Trio: Lincoln Ctr.'s Alice Tully Hall, Library of Congress, 1987; appeared with maj. orchs. worldwide, including St. Louis Symphony, Indpls. Symphony, San Francisco Symphony, Bavarian Radio Symphony of Munich, Berlin Radio Symphony, Radio Symphony Frankfurt, Radio Symphony Stuttgart; has toured Europe, N.Am., S.Am., C.Am., former Soviet Union, Marlboro Festival, 1982, Bard Festival, 1990-95; recs. for Nonesuch Records, 1980, 82, Book-of-Month Records, 1985, Music and Arts, 1990, CRI, 1991, Koch, Biddulph Records, 1995; mem. piano and chamber music faculty Mannes Coll. Music, 1982—. Recipient 3d prize Busoni Internat. Piano Competition, Italy, 1974, 2d prize Mozart Internat. Piano Competition, Salzburg, Austria, 1975, 1st prize Munich Internat. Piano Competition, 1975, Naumburg Chamber Music award, 1986; NEA grantee, 1981.

WALSH, GERALDINE FRANCES, nursing administrator; b. Phila., July 3, 1946; d. Raymond S. and Marie Ruth (Lipsett) Lore; m. Harry G. Walsh, Jan. 29, 1966; children: Michael, Gregory. AA, No. Va. Community Coll., 1979; BS, St. Joseph's Coll., Windham, Maine, 1987, postgrad. Cert. in nursing adminstrn.; cert. instr. basic life support. Charge nurse, asst. head nurse Parkview Hosp., Phila., 1968-73; staff nurse JFK Med. Ctr., Edison, 1973-76; clin. nursing supr., charge nurse med.-surg. Loudoun Hosp. Ctr., Leesburg, Va., 1976-88; asst. dir. nursing Loudoun Long Term Care Ctr., Leesburg, 1988—. Recipient Nursing Achievement award. Mem. ANA, Nat. League Nursing, Va. League Nursing, Va. Nurses Assn., Am. Coll. Healthcare Execs. (student assoc. mem.), Nat. Assn. for Healthcare Quality, Assn. Healthcare Adminstrs. of Nat. Capitol Area. Address: 20380 Harmony Ct Ashburn VA 22011

WALSH, JEANNE See SINGER, JEANNE

WALSH, KATHERINE HERALD, state legislator; b. Pitts., May 1, 1944; m. James L. Walsh; children: Elizabeth, Sara. BA, U. Pitts., 1966; student, U. London, England, 1972-73; JD magna cum laude, Cleve. State U., 1976. Staff atty. Lorain County Legal Aid Soc., 1976-77; pvt. practice Oberlin, Ohio, 1977-91; mem. Ohio Legislature, 1989—; chmn. ethics and standards com Ohio Legis. Mem. exec. com. March of Dimes. Recipient award of Merit Ohio Probate Judge's Assn. for Legis. Action on Probate Legis., award of Distinction Ohio Assn. County Bds. Mental Retardation and Devel. Disabilities, Govtl. Leaders Against Drunk Driving award MADD (Ohio chpt.); named Outstanding Legislator of the Yr. Ohio Acad. Trial Lawyers, 1990. Home: 365 Edison Dr Vermilion OH 44089 also: 15 Hawthorne Dr Oberlin OH 44074 Office: Ohio Ho of Reps State House Columbus OH 43215*

WALSH, MARIE LECLERC, nurse; b. Providence, Sept. 11, 1928; d. Walter Normand and Anna Mary (Ryan) Leclerc; m. John Breffni Walsh, June 18, 1955; children: George Breffni, John Leclerc, Darina Louise. Grad., Waterbury Hosp. Sch. Nursing, Conn., 1951; BS, Columbia U., 1954, MA, 1955. Team leader Hartford (Conn.) Hosp., 1951-53; pvt. duty nurse St. Luke's Hosp., N.Y.C., 1953-57; sch. nurse tchr. Agnes Russel Ctr., Tchrs. Coll. Columbia U., N.Y.C., 1955-56; clin. nursing instr. St. Luke's Hosp., N.Y.C., 1957-58; chmn. disaster nursing ARC Fairfax County, Va., 1975; course coord. occupational health nursing U. Va. Sch. Continuing Edn., Falls Church, 1975-77; mem. disaster steering com. No. Va. C.C., Annandale, 1976; adj. faculty U. Va. Sch. Continuing Edn., Falls Church, 1981; disaster svcs. nurse ARC, Wichita, Kans., 1985-90; disaster svcs. nurse Seattle-King County chpt. ARC, Seattle, 1990—; rsch. and statis. analyst U. Va. Sch. Continuing Edn. Nursing, Falls Church, 1975; rsch. libr. Olive Garvey Ctr. for Improvement Human Functioning, Inc., Wichita, 1985. Sec. Dem. party, Cresskill, N.J., 1964-66; county committeewoman, Bergen County, N.J., 1965-66; pres., v.p., Internat. Staff Wives, NATO, Brussels, Belgium, 1978-80; election officer, supr. Election Bd., Wichita, 1987, 88. Mem. AAAS, AAUW, N.Y. Acad. Sci., Pi Lambda Theta, Sigma Theta Tau. Home: 13822 NE 37th Pl Bellevue WA 98005-1420

WALSH, MARY D. FLEMING, civic worker; b. Whitewright, Tex., Oct. 29, 1913; d. William Fleming and Anna Maud (Lewis) Fleming; B.A., So. Meth. U., 1934; LL.D. (hon.), Tex. Christian U., 1979; m. F. Howard Walsh, Mar. 13, 1937; children: Richard, Howard, D'Ann Walsh Bonnell, Maudi Walsh Roe, William Lloyd. Pres. Fleming Found.; v.p. Walsh Found.; partner Walsh Co.; charter mem. Lloyd Shaw Found., Colorado Springs; mem. Big Bros. Tarrant County; guarantor Fort Worth Arts Council, Scholar Cantorum, Fort Worth Opera, Fort Worth Ballet, Fort Worth Theater, Tex. Boys Choir; hon. mem. bd. dirs. Van Cliburn Internat. Piano Competition; co-founder Am. Field Service in Ft. Worth; mem. Tex. Commn. for Arts and Humanities, 1968-72, mem. adv. council, 1972-84; bd. dirs. Wm. Edrington Scott Theatre, 1977-83, Colorado Springs Day Nursery, Colorado Springs Symphony, Ft. Worth Symphony, 1974-81; hon. chmn. Opera Ball, 1975, Opera Guild Internat. Conf., 1976; co-presenter (with husband) through Walsh Found., Tex. Boys Choir and Dorothy Shaw Bell Choir ann. presentation of The Littlest Wiseman to City of Ft. Worth; granted with husband land and bldgs. to Tex. Boys Choir for permanent home, 1971, Walsh-Wurlitzer organ to Casa Manana, 1972. Sem. Recipient numerous awards, including Altrusa Civic award as 1st Lady of Ft. Worth, 1968; (with husband) Disting. Service award So. Bapt. Radio and Television Commn., 1972; Opera award Girl Scouts, 1977-79; award Streams and Valleys, 1976-80; named (with husband) Patron of Arts in Ft. Worth, 1970, 91, Edna Gladney Internat. Grandparents of 1972, (with husband) Sr. Citizens of Yr, 1985; Mary D. and Howard Walsh Meml. Organ dedicated by Bapt. Radio and TV Commn., 1967, tng. ctr. named for the Walshes, 1976; Mary D. and Howard Walsh Med. Bldg., Southwestern Bapt. Theol. Sem.; library at Tarrant County Jr. Coll. N.W. Campus dedicated to her and husband, 1978; Brotherhood citation Tarrant County chpt. NCCJ, 1978; Spl. Recognition award Ft. Worth Ballet Assn.; Royal Purple award Tex. Christian U., 1979; Friends of Tex. Boys Choir award, 1981; appreciation award Southwestern Bapt. Theol. Sem., 1981, B. H. Carroll Founders award, 1982, (with husband) Patrons of the Arts award, 1991; Outstanding Women of Fort Worth award City of Fort Worth, 1994, numerous other award for civic activities. Mem. Ft. Worth Boys Club, Ft. Worth Children's Hosp., Jewel Charity Ball, Ft. Worth Pan Hellenic (pres. 1940), Opera Guild, Fine Arts Found. Guild of Tex. Christian U., Girl's Service League (hon. life, hon. chmn. Fine Arts Guild Spring Ballet, 1985), AAUW, Goodwill Industries Aux., Child Study Center, Tarrant County Aux. of Edna Gladney Home, YWCA (life), Ft. Worth Art Assn., Ft. Worth Ballet Assn., Tex. Boys Choir Aux., Friends of Tex. Boys Choir, Round Table, Colorado Springs Fine Art Center, Am. Automobile Assn., Nat. Assn. Cowbelles, Ft. Worth Arts Council (hon. bd. mem.), Am. Guild Organists (hon., Ft. Worth chpt.), Rae Reimers Bible Study Class (pres. 1968), Tex. League Composers (hon. life), Children's Hosp. Woman's Bd. (hon. 1991), Chi Omega (pres. 1935-36, hon. chmn. 1986), others. Baptist. Clubs: The Woman's (Club Fidelite), Colorado Springs Country, Garden of Gods, Colonial Country, Ridglea Country, Shady Oaks Country, Chi Omega Mothers, Chi Omega Carousel, TCU Woman's. Home: 2425 Stadium Dr Fort Worth TX 76109-1055 also: 1801 Culebra Ave Colorado Springs CO 80907-7328

WALSH, MICHELE J., entertainment executive; b. Germantown, Pa., May 18, 1965; d. Michael Joseph and Erma Isabelle (Dougan) W. Receptionist Snow, Becker, Kroll, N.Y.C., 1984; employment counselor Friedman's Employment, N.Y.C., 1984-85; sales exec. Blank's Fabrics, Balt., 1987-88; proprietor Renaissance Romance, Woodbridge, Va., 1988-92; with WDC/Potomac Mills, Woodbridge, 1988-89; mgr. Frank's Nursery and Crafts, Manassas, Va., 1989-91; salesperson So-Fro Fabrics, Fairfax, Va., 1991-92; columnist Bloodlines, Hawaii, 1992-93; CEO Triad Entertainment, Inc., Manassas, 1993—; cons. Azure Pubs., Manassas, 1994, Bloodtypes, Manassas, 1994. Author mo. column: Bloodlines, 1993. Office: Triad Entertainment Inc 9855 Fairview Ave Manassas VA 22110-5827

WALSH, PATI LUNDE, speech and language pathologist; b. Lake City, Minn., May 10, 1950; d. J.W. and Evelyn (Schmidt) Lunde; m. Timothy Daniel Walsh, Aug. 3, 1974; children: Maggie, Kay Leigh. BA in Social Sci. cum laude, U. Calif., Irvine, 1972; MS in Communication Disorders, U. N.Mex., 1974. Cert. clin. competence. Speech pathologist Esperanza Para Nuestros Niños, Albuquerque, 1974-75, Newport Mesa Unified Sch., Newport Beach, Calif., 1975-77; speech and language pathologist Albuquerque Pub. Schs., 1984—, spl. edn. head tchr., 1985-87. Author: American Anthology of Poetry, 1984-85. Pres. PTA, Griegos Sch., 1986-87. Office of Edn. fellow U. N.Mex., 1972-74; named one of Internat. Leaders in Achievemnt, 1988. Home: 3021 San Patricio Pl NW Albuquerque NM 87107-2932 Office: Albuquerque Pub Schs 4040 San Isidro St NW Albuquerque NM 87107-2828

WALSH, PATRICIA ANN, aircraft company executive; b. Rome, N.Y., Sept. 26, 1938; d. Joseph Fazio and Ann Mary (Stosal) Kapinos; m. Jack Martin Walsh, Aug. 16, 1958; children: Thomas, John, Kellie, Jeffrey. Student, Mohawk Valley C.C., 1991. Adminstrv. asst. Hughes Aircraft Co., Rome, 1980—. Vol. Rome Family Counseling Svc., 1992-93, Parents Anonymous, Rome, 1993; mem. Nat. Women's Rep. Com., 1983-89. Mem. Armed Forces Comm. and Electronics Assn. (bd. dirs. 1991—, sec. 1983-91, Cert. of Appreciation 1991), Rome Def. Women's Assn. Roman Catholic. Home: 1407 Craig St Rome NY 13440 Office: Hughes Aircraft Co 1721 Black River Blvd Rome NY 13440

WALSH HANSEL, JEANETTA LYNN, home infusion nurse; b. Providence, June 14, 1947; d. Herman David and Carmela Rosemary (Coletta) Harris; m. R.J. Walsh, Dec. 16, 1967 (div. 1983); children: Robert A., Shawn M.; m. Robert Raymond Hansel, Mar. 21, 1991. AA, R.I. Jr. Coll., 1968; BSN, U. Tex., Arlington, 1981. RN, Tex., RNC; cert. chemotherapy nurse. Staff nurse Osteo. Med. Ctr., Ft. Worth, 1981-82; charge nurse Duncan Meml. Hosp., Ft. Worth, 1983; supr. Northwest Hosp., Ft. Worth, 1983-85; staff nurse St. Joseph Hosp., Ft. Worth, 1985-86; relief charge nurse All Saint's Hosp., Ft. Worth, 1986-87; staff nurse, asst. supr., staff devel. John Peter Smith Hosp., Ft. Worth, 1987-93; home infusion therapy nurse AACU Care Infusion, Burleson, Tex., 1993—; peripherally inserted ctrl. catheter line specialist John Peter Smith Hosp., Ft. Worth, 1992; mem. test devel. com. for gen. practice ANCC, 1995-98. Mem. ANA, NAACOG, INS, Tex. Nurse's Assn., Am. Paint Horse Assn., Pinto Horse Assn. Roman Catholic. Home and Office: 4501 Cross Timber Rd Burleson TX 76028-6723

WALSH-MCGEHEE, MARTHA BOSSE, conservationist; d. Leon and Lenore (Carter) Bosse; m. Leo S. Walsh, Sept. 30, 1972 (div. Oct. 1982); m. Donald B. McGehee, Aug. 6, 1992. Student, U. Mo., 1966, Baker U., 1966-67, Marymount-Manhattan, 1980-82. Flight attendant TWA, N.Y.C., 1967-78; pres. Island Conservation Effort, 1988—; trustee Rare Ctr. for Tropical Bird Conservation, Phila., 1987-91. Ptnr. in conservation World Wildlife Fund, Washington, 1986—; assoc. World Resources Inst., Washington, 1987—; mem. St. Croix (V.I.) Landmarks Soc., 1985—, Sherman (Conn.) Hist. Soc., 1986, Sherman Libr. Assn., 1986. St. Croix Environ. Assn., 1987—; mem. Saba Conservation Found. Nature Conservency. Mem. Caribbean Conservation Assn., St. Lucia Naturalists Soc., Cedam Internat., Soc. Caribbean Ornithology, Friends of Abaco Parrot, Assn. Parrot Conservation Tropical Audubon. Republican. Home: 90 Edgewater Dr Apt 901 Coral Gables FL 33133 also: Windwardside, Saba Netherlands Antilles

WALSTON, LOLA INGE, dietitian; b. Chgo., Jan. 26, 1943; d. Willy and Ingeborg (Smith) Neumann; m. Steven Ward Walston, Aug. 5, 1967; children: Bradley, Scott. BS, No. Ill. U., 1965; MS, U. Iowa, 1967. Registered, lic. dietitian. Asst. dietary dir. Alaska Hosp. Med. Ctr., Anchorage, 1975-78; cons. dietitian Mercer County Hosp., Coldwater, Ohio, 1979; profl. service cons. Health Care and Retirement Corp. Am., Lima, Ohio, 1981-84; dietary dir. Estes Health Care Ctr., Montgomery, Ala., 1979-80, Mercy Meml. Hosp., Urbana, Ohio, 1984-86, Dairy & Nutrition Council Mid East, Dayton, Ohio, 1987-89; cons. Sharonview Nursing Home, South Vienna, Ohio, 1987—; Miami Health Care Ctr., Troy, Ohio, Columbia House, Springfield, Ohio, SCOPE Nutrition Program for the elderly, Fairborn, Ohio, CLS Nutrition Program, Bellefontaine, Ohio, 1987-90, Preble County Home, Eaton, Ohio, 1988—; St. John's Nursing Home, Springfield, 1989—, Oakwood Village, Springfield, 1989—, Villa Springfield, Springfield, Ohio, 1990—, Covington (Ohio) Care Ctr., 1990-91, Champaign Nursing Home, 1993, Covenant House, 1993. Mem. com. Tecumseh council Boy Scouts Am., 1984, Tri-County Community Action Commn./CLS Nutrition, Bellefontaine, Ohio, 1987-90. Mem. Am. Dietetic Assn., Ohio Dietetic Assn., Ohio Cons. Dietitians Health Care Facilities (chmn. 1982-84), Dayton Dietetic Assn., AAUW. Club: Hilltoppers (Fairborn, Ohio) (pres. 1982-83). Avocations: camping, sewing, knitting, crocheting, cooking.

WALTER, ELIZABETH THOMAS, protective services official; b. Glencove, N.Y., Jan. 30, 1958; d. Robert Wheaton and Patricia Marie (Ward); m. Stephen Barnhill, Feb. 12, 1983 (Mar. 1986). Postgrad., Carleton Coll., Northfield, 1976-77; student, U. Denver, 1977. Sherrif's cadet Arapahoe County Sheriff's Dept., Englewood, Colo., 1975-79; retail security Assorted Major Dry Goods, Denver, 1977-80, patrol officer, 1980-85; detective Denver Police Dept., 1985-88, sgt., 1988-92, lt., 1992—; cadet advisor Denver Police Dept., 1981-83. Mem. Denver Police Protective Assn., Colo. Police Protective Assn., Neighborhood Watch & Crime Prevention Assn. (v.p. 1994—), Denver Assn. Women Police. Republican. Episcopalian. Office: Denver Police Dept 1331 Cherokee St Rm 206 Denver CO 80204

WALTER, HELEN JOY, executive director, teacher; b. Bronx, May 22, 1938; d. David and Frieda (Halpern) Presby; m. Wolfgang Walter, Feb. 4, 1962; children: Cheryl, Rochelle, Laurie. BA, Yeshiva U., 1961; MEd, Northeastern U., Boston, 1979. Tchr. Maimonides Day Sch., Brookline, Mass., N.Y.C. Pub. Schs.; counselor Northeastern U.; exec. dir. Brookline C. of C., 1979—. Office: Brookline C of C 1330 Beacon St Brookline MA 02146-3202

WALTER, KATHY LOU, farmer; b. Iowa City, Iowa, Oct. 4, 1950; d. Floyd and Louise Aldean (Miller) Brenneman; m. Michael Duayne Walter, Nov. 7, 1970; children: Andrea Lou, Jason Michael. Student, Goshen Coll., 1968-70, U. Iowa, 1986-88. Farmer Tipton, Iowa; meter reader Ea. Iowa Light and Power Corp., Wilton, Iowa, 1983-91; basketball coach Mt. Vernon (Iowa) Jr. High Sch., 1988-91. Dem. candidate for dist. 39 Iowa State Ho. of Reps., 1994. Mem. Nat. Farmers of Iowa, Nat. Corn Growers, Iowa Corn Growers, Am. Soybean Assn., Iowa Soybean Assn., Farm Bur. Democrat. Mennonite. Home: 357 210th St Tipton IA 52772

WALTER, MARILYN JOYCE, artist, art therapist; b. Burlington, Iowa, Aug. 3, 1941; d. Robert Ralph and Mary Florence (Moberly) La Mont; m. William Winton Weaver, Aug. 31, 1962 (div. Dec. 8, 1976); 1 child, Andrea Marie; m. Gary Steve Walter, Dec. 11, 1976; 1 child, Teresa Lynn. BS, Ctrl. Mo. State U., 1963; MS, Avila Coll., Kansas City, Mo., 1993. Engrng. asst. AT&T, Kansas City, Mo., 1963-64; tech. asst. Social Security Adminstrn., Kansas City, Mo., 1965-90; art therapist Spofford Home, Kansas City, Mo., 1993—. Mem. APA, Am. Art Therapy Assn., Kans. Art Therapy Assn., Mo. Art Therapy Assn., Psi Chi. Home: 17801 Sycamore St Holt MO 64048-8988 Office: Spofford Home 9700 Grandview Rd Kansas City MO 64137-1135

WALTER, SHERYL LYNN, lawyer; b. Morris, Ill., July 18, 1956; d. C. Frank and Margaret (Juhl) W. BA in History cum laude, Grinnell (Iowa) Coll., 1978; JD cum laude, U. Minn., 1984. Bar: Minn. 1984, U.S. Dist. Ct. Minn. 1987, U.S. Ct. Appeals (8th cir.) 1987, D.C. 1989, U.S. Dist. Ct. D.C. 1989, U.S. Ct. Appeals (D.C. cir.) 1989. Law clk. to presiding judge 3d Jud. Dist. of Minn., Rochester, 1984-85; law clk. to Chief Judge Donald P. Lay U.S. Ct. Appeals (8th cir.), St. Paul, 1985-87; assoc. Mayer, Brown & Platt, Washington, 1987-89; gen. counsel Nat. Security Archive, Washington, 1989-94, Assn. Records Review Bd., 1994—; cons. Amnesty Internat., Washington, 1988-89. Mem. ABA (vice chmn. adminstrv. law sect. govt. info. subcom. 1990—), D.C. Bar Assn. (steering com., adminstrv. law sect. 1990—), Am. Judicature Soc., Am. Soc. Access Profls. (bd. dirs. 1990—), Brit.-Am. Security Info. Coun. (bd. dirs. 1990—), Minn. Lawyers Internat. Human Rights Com., Internat. Lawyers Com. for Human Rights, Lawyers Alliance for World Security (bd. dirs. 1994—). Office: Assn Records Review Bd 600 E St NW Ste 209 Washington DC 20530

WALTERS, BARBARA, television journalist; b. Sept. 25, 1931; d. Lou and Dena (Selett) W.; 1 child, Jacqueline. Grad., Sarah Lawrence Coll., 1953; LHD (hon.), Ohio State U., Marymount Coll., Tarrytown, N.Y., 1975, Wheaton Coll., 1983. Former writer-producer WNBC-TV; then with Stas. WPIX and CBS-TV; joined Today Show, 1961, regular panel mem., 1964-74, co-host, 1974-76; moderator syndicated program Not For Women Only, 1974-76; newscaster ABC Evening News (now ABC World News Tonight), 1976-78; host The Barbara Walters Spls., 1976—; co-host ABC TV news show 20/20, 1979—. Contbr. to ABC programs Issues and Answers. Author: How To Talk With Practically Anybody About Practically Anything, 1970; contbr. to Reader's Digest, Good Housekeeping, Family Weekly. Recipient award of yr. Nat. Assn. TV Program Execs., 1975, Emmy award Nat. Acad. TV Arts and Scis., 1975, Mass Media award Am. Jewish Com. Inst. Human Relations, 1975, Hubert H. Humphrey Freedom prize Anti-Defamation League-B'nai B'rith, 1978, Matrix award N.Y. Women in Communications, 1977, Barbara Walters' Coll. Scholarship in Broadcast Journalism established in her honor Ill. Broadcasters Assn., 1975, Pres.'s award Overseas Press Club, 1988, Lowell Thomas award Marist Coll., 1990, Lifetime Achievement award Internat. Women's Media Found., 1992; named to 100 Women Accomplishment Harper's Bazaar, 1967, 71, One of Am.'s 75 Most Important Women Ladies' Home Jour., 1970, One of 10 Women of Decade Ladies' Home Jour., 1979, One of Am.'s 100 Most Important Women Ladies' Home Jour., 1983, Woman of Year in Communications, 1974, Woman of Year Theta Sigma Phi, Broadcaster of Yr. Internat. Radio and TV Soc., 1975, One of 200 Leaders of Future Time Mag., 1974, One of Most Important Women of 1979 Roper Report, One of Women Most Admired by Am. People Gallup Poll, 1982, 84, to Hall of Fame Acad. TV Arts and Scis., 1990. Office: 20/20 147 Columbus Ave Fl 10 New York NY 10023-5900 also: Barwell Productions The Barbara Walters Spls 825 7th Ave Fl 3 New York NY 10019-6014*

WALTERS, BETTE JEAN, lawyer; b. Norristown, Pa., Sept. 5, 1946. BA, U. Pitts., 1967; JD, Temple U., 1970, LLM in Taxation, 1974. Bar: Pa. 1970, U.S. Dist. Ct. (ea. dist.) Pa. 1971. Law clk., assoc. William R. Cooper, Lansdale, Pa., 1969-72; spl. asst. to pub. defender Montgomery County (Pa.), 1973; pvt. practice North Wales, Pa., 1972-73; assoc. counsel Alco Standard Corp., Valley Forge, Pa., 1973-79, group counsel mfg., 1979-83; v.p., gen. counsel, sec. Alco Industries, Inc., Valley Forge, 1983—, also bd. dirs., 1983—. Mem. corp. sponsors com. Zool. Soc. of Phila. Mem. ABA, DAR, Pa. Bar Assn., Montgomery County Bar Assn., Am. Corp. Counsel Assn., Licensing Execs. Soc.. Republican. Office: Alco Industries Inc PO Box 937 Valley Forge PA 19482-0937

WALTERS, CANDACE REBECCA, counselor, educator; b. Suffolk, Va., Feb. 20, 1947; d. John Derward and Eula (Farrar) W. BA in History, Fisk U., 1968; MEd in Elem. Edn., U. Va., 1970; MEd in Counseling, Regent U., 1989. Aide Head Start, Suffolk, summer 1967, 68; tchr. Suffolk Pub. Schs., 1970-71; tchr. Fairfax (Va.) County Pub. Schs., 1971-92, counselor, 1992—. Singles leader United Pentecostal Ch. Arlington, 1992—. Office: Deer Park Elem Sch 5775 Spindle Ct Centreville VA 22020

WALTERS, CATHY DARLENE, social sciences educator; b. Atlanta, Aug. 1, 1957; d. John H. and Harriet Jean (Buffington) W.; m. Kenneth Joseph Exum, May 26, 1984; children: Alana Michelle, Theresa Nicole. BA in Psychology, Agnes Scott Coll., 1978; MS in Nat. Security, Naval Postgrad. Sch., Monterey, Calif., 1988; MA in Psychology, Nat. U., 1990. Cert. C.C. instr., Calif. Commd. ensign USN, 1978, advanced through grades to lt., 1983; adminstrv. asst. USN, Yokusuka, Japan, 1978-80, counseling dir., 1980-82; with pub. rels. dept., recruiter USN, San Francisco, 1982-85; student/computer mgr. USN, Monterey, Calif., 1985-89; computer systems mgr. USN, Monterey, 1987-89; sub. tchr. Alameda (Calif.) Unified Sch. Dist., 1989-90; instr. Lawton Bus. Sch., Oakland, Calif., 1989-90, Coll. of Alameda, 1989-91, Diablo Valley Coll., Pleasant Hill, Calif., 1989-92; educator HIV, referral mgr. N.W. AIDS Found., 1992—; adj. faculty Columbia Coll. Ext., San Francisco, 1991-92; guest speaker personal devel., 1992. Mem. NAFE, U.S. Navy League, Nat. Naval Officers Assn. Democrat. Jewish.

WALTERS, DORIS LAVONNE, pastoral counselor; b. Peachland, N.C., Feb. 24, 1931; d. H. Lloyd and Mary Lou (Helms) W. BA cum laude, Carson-Newman Coll., 1961; MRE, Southwestern Bapt. Theol. Sem., 1963; MA in Pastoral Counseling, Wake Forest U., 1982; DMIn in Pastoral Counseling, Southeastern Bapt. Theol. Sem., 1988. Min. of edn. and youth First Bapt. Ch., Orange, Tex., 1963-66; assoc. prof. Seinan Jo Gakuin Jr. Coll., Japan, 1968-72; dir. Fukuoka (Japan) Friendship House, 1972-88, pastoral counselor, chaplain, 1983-86; Tokyo lifeline referral counselor (in English) Hiroshima-Shuto, Fukuoka, 1983-86; supr. Japanese and Am. staff Fukuoka Friendship House, 1972-86; with chaplaincy Med. Coll. Va., Richmond, 1976; resident chaplain N.C. Bapt. Hosp., Winston-Salem, 1981-82, counselor-in-tng. pastoral care dept., 1986-88; dir. missionary counseling and support svcs. Pastoral Care Found. N.C. Bapt. Hosp., Winston-Salem, 1989-93; dir. Missionary Family Counseling Svcs., Inc., Winston-Salem, 1993—; mem. Japan Bapt. Mission Exec. Com., Tokyo, 1973-76. Author: An Assessment of the Reentry Issues of the Children of Missionaries, 1991; translator: The Story of the Craft Dogs, 1983. J.M. Price scholar Southwestern Bapt. Theol. Sem., 1962; First Bapt. Ch. Blackwell grantee Southeastern Sem., 1986-88. Mem. Assn. for Clin. Pastoral Counselors (assoc.), Am. Assn. Pastoral Counselors (pastoral affiliate). Democrat. Home: 208 Oakwood Sq Winston Salem NC 27103-1914 Office: Missionary Family Counseling Svcs Inc Stratford Oaks Bldg Ste 420 514 S Stratford Rd Winston Salem NC 27103

WALTERS, ELAINE M., librarian; b. Somerville, N.J., Nov. 23, 1947; d. John A. and Helen M. (Lazor) Koval; m. Peter P. Walters, Jan. 17, 1970; children: Christina, Peter. BA in English, Douglass Coll., 1969; MLS, Rutgers U., 1972; MBA in Mktg., Fairleigh-Dickinson U., Madison, N.J., 1978. Cert. media specialist, K-12, N.J. Reference libr. East Brunswick (N.J.) Pub. Libr., 1968-69; sch. libr. Edison (N.J.) Bd. Edn., 1969-70; reference, children's libr. Somerset County Pub. Libr., Somerville, N.J., 1972-73; sch. libr. Manville (N.J.) Bd. Edn., 1973—. Mem. VFW Women's Aux. Office: 1100 Brooks Blvd Manville NJ 08835-1542

WALTERS, JUDITH RICHMOND, neuropharmacologist; b. Concord, N.H., June 20, 1944; d. Samuel Smith and Hazel Albertina (Stewart) Richmond; m. James Wilson Walters, Aug. 23, 1969 (div. 1992); children: James Richmond, Gregory Stewart, Douglas Powers. BA, Mt. Holyoke Coll., 1966; PhD, Yale U., 1972. Postdoctoral fellow dept. psychiatry Yale U. Med. Sch., New Haven, rsch. assoc. dept. pharmacology, asst. prof. dept. psychiatry; unit chief neurophysiol. pharmacology sect. exptl. therapeutics br. Nat. Inst. Neurol. Disease and Stroke, Bethesda, Md., 1976-81, sect. chief physiol. neuropharmacology sect. exptl. therapeutics br.; mem. sci. adv. bd. Hereditary Disease Found., L.A., 1977-80, 82-86, Tourette Syndrome Assn., 1992—; mem. bd. sci. counselors Nat. Inst. on Alcohol Abuse and Alcoholism, 1992—. Contbr. more than 100 articles on neuropharmacology and neurophysiology to profl. jours. Recipient NIH Dir.'s award, 1994. Mem. Am. Soc. Pharmacology and Exptl. Therapeutics, Soc. for Neuroscience. Home: 3615 Littledale Rd Kensington MD 20895-3435 Office: NIH Bldg 10 Rm 5C106 Bethesda MD 20892

WALTERS, LEANN, business analyst; b. Dallas, Nov. 6, 1955; d. Elza Carter and Cecilia Florence (Wildin) W.; m. Robert Theodore McCoy Jr., July 14, 1978. BS, Ind. U., 1977, Coleman Coll., 1980; MBA, Calif. Luth.

U., 1984. Software engr. Bunker Ramo Corp., Westlake Village, Calif., 1980-81; computer staff Hughes Rsch. Labs., Malibu, Calif., 1981-89; tech. analyst Rockwell Internat., Canoga Park, Calif., 1989-92; bus. analyst Amgen, Inc., Thousand Oaks, Calif., 1992—; pres., founder TRI-EDI Users Group, Thousand Oaks, 1993—; chair JD Edwards Focus SIG Group, Denver, 1993—; presenter in field. Mem. NOW. Home: 3964 Camphor Ave Newbury Park CA 91320-5202

WALTERS, MARYL KATHLEEN, public information administrator; b. Eldorado, Kans., Aug. 29, 1941; d. Joseph Wade and Martha Geneve (Gates) Watkins; m. David John Walters, Feb. 1, 1958 (div. 1984); children: Cynthia Louise Walters Obrist, Kristin Lynn, David Wade. BS in Elem. Edn., Okla. State U., 1962; MBA, U. N.C., 1983. Tchr. primary sch. Consolidated Sch. Dist. 561, Haysville, Kans., 1962-67; tchr. Romper Room Sta. WAND-TV, Decatur, Ill., 1968-69; prodr., talk show host Sta WXII-TV, Winston-Salem, N.C., 1977-79; store support mgr. Food Lion, Inc., Sailsbury, N.C., 1988-90; dir. pub. info. Rowan-Salisbury Schs., 1990—. Bd. dirs. Rowan County YMCA, Salisbury, 1991—, Salisbury City Parks and Recreation, 1991—, Rowan County Info. and Referral, Salisbury, 1993—, Residents Old Salisbury, 1994—; role and status of women com. 1st United Methodist Ch., 1992—. Mem. Rowan County C. of C. (bus. support com. 1990—, recognition com. 1992—). Home: 218 W Thomas St Salisbury NC 28144 Office: Rowan-Salisbury Schs 314 N Ellis St Salisbury NC 28144

WALTERS, NORMA LEE, educator, counselor; b. Checotah, Okla., Feb. 4, 1943; d. Roy J. And Eunice M. (Lane) Lawson; m. Neil A. Walters, Jan. 13, 1990; 1 child, Edward A. Turney. BS, U. Tulsa, 1970, MA, 1976; MA, Northeastern State U., Tulsa, 1988; postgrad., U. Tulsa, 1993. Cert. sch. counselor, Okla.; lic. profl. counselor. Instr. Tulsa Pub. Schs., 1970-82, coord. gifted programs, 1982-86, counselor, 1986—; cons. Orgnl. Systems, Tulsa, 1991—; advisor N.E. Network For Tchrs., Tulsa, 1984-86; coord. Adopt-A-School Program, Tulsa, 1986—. Author: (curriculum guide) Middle School Gifted Program, 1984. Coord. Red Ribbon Week, Okla. Fedn. Parents Against Drugs, Tulsa, 1991—. Mem. ASTD, NEA, ACA, Okla. Counseling Assn., Phi Delta Kappa. Home: 7614 E 54th Pl Tulsa OK 74145-7812

WALTERS, REBA NELLE, nursing educator, administrator; b. Lenox, Ga., Apr. 20, 1933; d. John Roy and Essie (Barton) Rowan; m. Charles Ray Walters, Sept. 3, 1955; children: Charles Ray, Jr., Nancy Walters Harman, J. Douglas. BSN, U. N.C., 1969; EdM., N.C. State U., 1973; MSN, East Carolina U., 1982, postgrad. Nova, 1989—. RN, N.C. Staff nurse Monongalia Gen. Hosp., Morgantown, W.Va., 1955-56, Vincent Pallotti, Morgantown, 1957; Kingston Hosp., N.Y., 1960-65; nursing instr. Rex Hosp., Raleigh, N.C., 1969-75, Wake Tech. Coll., Raleigh, 1975-82; chairperson health edn., dir. nursing edn. Vance Granville C.C., Henderson, N.C., 1982-87, chairperson, 1988—, health, human svcs., dir. nursing edu. Piedmont C.C.; active Assoc. Degree Nursing Coun. Recipient Best Ob Nurse award Crawford Long, 1955. Mem. ANA (pres. dist. 13 1979-80, bd. dirs. 1980-82), Am. Vocat. Assn. (v.p. c.c. and tech. edn. div. 1977-79), Assoc. Degree Nursing Dirs. (sec., treas 1989-91, mem. nominating com. 1994-95), Alpha Kappa Delta, Sigma Theta Tau. Democrat. Baptist. Avocation: gardening. Home: 1303 Country Club Dr Roxboro NC 27573 Office: Piedmont CC PO Box 275 Roxboro NC 27573

WALTERS, REBECCA RUSSELL YARBOROUGH, medical technologist; b. Lancaster, S.C., Mar. 9, 1951; d. William Peurifoy and Anna Beth (Cheatham) Yarborough; m. Thomas Edward Walters, Oct. 15, 1983; 1 child, Katherine Rebecca. BA, Winthrop Coll., 1972; postgrad. in med. tech., Bapt. Med. Ctr., Columbia, S.C., 1974; MA, Cen. Mich. U., 1978. Diplomate in Lab. Mgmt. ASCP. Teaching asst. in biology Winthrop Coll., Rock Hill, S.C., 1972-73; microbiology technologist Bapt. Med. Ctr., 1974-76, night shift supr., 1976-77, asst. adminstrv. dir., 1977—, tchr. Sch. Med. Tech., 1974—; article reviewer Med. Lab. Observer; mem. Nat. Cert. Agy. for Med. Lab. Personnel. Hycel, Inc. scholar, 1976, 77. Mem. Am. Soc. for Med. Tech. (scholar 1977), S.C. Soc. Med. Tech. (pres. 1979-80, scholar 1976), Am. Soc. Clin. Pathologists (assoc.), Clin. Lab. Mgmt. Assn., Beta Beta Beta, Alpha Mu Tau (scholar 1977). Republican. Presbyterian. Home: 155 Shawn Rd Chapin SC 29036-9215 Office: Bapt Med Ctr Taylor At Marion Columbia SC 29220

WALTERS-PARKER, KIMBERLY KAY secondary school educator; b. Mt. Sterling, Ky., Apr. 9, 1961; d. Robert Wendell and Lagene Kay (Stull) Walters; m. Steve Robert Parker, July 3, 1992. BA, Georgetown Coll., 1983; MA, Morehead State U., 1985; Rank I Cert., U. Ky., 1990. Cert. secondary English educator, reading specialist, Ky. Instr. Eastern Ky. U., Richmond, 1985-87; reading specialist Bryan Sta. High Sch. Fayette County Pub. Schs., Lexington, Ky., 1987—, dir. writing ctr., 1990—; co-owner Walters/Parker Learning Ctr., Inc., 1993—; cons. tech. writing and rsch. skills Ky. Sci. and Tech. Coun., 1993. Recipient Merit of Excellence award County of Fayette; grantee Ky. Dept. Edn., 1991-92, 93, Lexington Edn. Assistance Found., 1992. Mem. ASCD, Nat. Coun. Tchrs. English, Internat. Reading Assn., Ky. Coun. Tchrs. English. Home: 4201 Ridgewater Dr Lexington KY 40515

WALTHER, ZERITA, paralegal; b. N.Y.C., Nov. 22, 1927; d. James Alexander and Sarah Rebecca (Esperance) Potter; m. George P. Walther II; children: Joseph, Leona. BS in Edn., Met. Inst., London, 1973; cert. in labor studies, Cornell U., 1979; paralegal cert., Manhattanville Coll., 1984. Tchr. OEO, L.I. City, N.Y., 1966-69, Washington Bus. Inst., N.Y.C., 1969-70; editorial asst., feature writer N.Y. Times, N.Y.C., 1973-85; corp. legal asst. Kim Taylor Profls., White Plains, N.Y., 1988-92; casting cons., 1962-63; bd. dirs., cons. Rockingchair Press News Svc., Elmsford, N.Y., 1978-93. Soprano Westfair Chamber Singers, Westchester, Fairfield Counties, 1991-94, White Plains Coalition Singers, White Plains, Our Lady of Mount Carmel Adult Choir, Elmsford, 1989-94. Sec. Women of Westchester, 1978-80; mem. Westchester Black Women's Polit. Caucus, 1989-91; coord. Elmsford chpt. Women in Self Help, 1982—; mediator, vol. Better Bus. Bur., White Plains, 1983-85, Westchester Mediation Ctr., Yonkers, N.Y., 1988—; legis. asst. to 12th dist. Westchester County legislator, White Plains, 1984-92; cert. ombudson N.Y. State Office for the Aging, 1994—. Lily Endowment Found. and Smithsonian Inst. scholar Sarah Lawrence Coll., summer 1979. Democrat. Roman Catholic.

WALTON, AMANDA LORETTA, educator; b. Millen, Ga., Sept. 16, 1941; d. Willie (dec.) and Gussia (Wilson) Jones; m. Van L. Walton, July 3, 1966 (dec.); children: Myshiel Massa, Van Lawrence Walton Jr. AA in Liberal Arts, Manhatten Community Coll., 1975; BA in Polit. Sci., York Coll., 1980; M, City Coll. of N.Y., 1983, postgrad., 1985. Teacher asst. Pub. Sch. 200, Manhatten, 1970-73; aux. trainer Pub. Sch. 132, N.Y.C., 1974-81; tchr. Pub. Sch. 274, Bkyln., 1981—; ednl. cons., Queens, N.Y., 1981—; developer grant N.Y. Bd. Edn., 1989-90; adaptor grant N.Y. Bd. Edn., 1989-90 Calif. Books Across Am., 1991-92. Mem. legisl. adv. com., Albany, N.Y., 1981, Queens Village Bellrose Dems., Queens Village, 1983. Grantee Am. Heart Assn., Am. Cancer Soc., Cool Cats Don't Smoke, 1989-90, Nat. Diffusion Network, 1991-92. Mem. NAFE, Internat. Reading Assn., Manhattan Reading Coun. Democrat. Roman Catholic. Home: 22139 112th Ave Jamaica NY 11429-2510

WALTON, ANGELA DESHAE, management consultant; b. Duluth, Ga., Nov. 19, 1957; d. Jessie I. and Lorraine Hopson W. BA, Brandeis U., 1980. Sales rep. ITT, Atlanta, 1980-82, Allnet Comm., Atlanta, 1982-84; ter. mgr. Cook-Wave Labs., Atlanta, 1984-86; major accounts mgr. Minolta Corp., Atlanta, 1986-87; sr. account exec. Friden Alcate 1, Atlanta, 1987-88; pres. ADW & Assocs., Atlanta, 1988-95; mgmt. cons. Fred Pryor Resources, Kansas City, Kans., 1995—. Mem. resource devel. bd. Apex Mus., Atlanta, 1991; active Ga. Rep. Found., Atlanta, 1992—, United Way of Atlanta. Martin Luther King scholar Brandeis U., 1976; named Outstanding Vol., NAACP, 1994. Mem. ASTD, Sales and Mktg. Exexs. of Atlanta, V.I.P. Initiative, Alpha Kappa Alpha.

WALTON, CAROLE LORRAINE, clinical social worker; b. Harrison, Ark., Oct. 20, 1949; d. Leo Woodrow Walton and Arlette Alegra (Cohen) Armstrong. BA, Lambuth Coll., Jackson, Tenn., 1971; MA, U. Chgo., 1974. Diplomate Clin. Social Work, Acad. Cert. Social Workers; lic. clin. social worker. Social worker Community Mental Health, Flint, Mich., 1971-72; clin. social worker Community Mental Health, Westchester, Ill., 1974-76; dir. self-travel program Chgo. Assn. Retarded Citizens, 1973; coord. family svcs. Inner Harbors Psych. Hosp., Douglasville, Ga., 1976-83; sr. mental health clinician Northside Mental Health Ctr., Atlanta, 1983—. Mem. NASW, Ga. Soc. for Clin. Work (pres. 1981-82, pres. 1993-95). Office: Northside Mental Health Ctr 5825 Glenridge Dr Bldg 4 Atlanta GA 30328

WALTON, EILEEN ROWAN, lawyer; b. Bklyn., Jan. 29, 1948; d. Charles Thomas and Helen Bridget (McCormick) Rowan; m. David Richard Walton, Oct. 14, 1978; 1 child, Megan Bridget. BA, Hofstra U., 1969; JD, Fordham U., 1976. Bar: N.Y. Atty. Pfizer, Inc., N.Y.C., 1977-88, corp. counsel, 1988-91, corp. coun., asst. sec., 1991—. Office: Pfizer Inc 235 E 42d St New York NY 10017

WALTON, KATHLEEN ENDRES, librarian; b. Columbus, Ohio, Mar. 24, 1961; d. Kenneth Raymond and Mary Margaret (Brown) Endres; m. Thomas Walton, Dec. 7, 1985; children: Tristan James, Arden Siobhan. BA, U. Md., 1982; MLS, Cath. U. Am., 1985. Head engring./architecture/math libr. Cath. U. Am. Libr., Washington, 1985-87; libr. Congl. Quarterly Jour., Washington, 1987-90, head libr., 1991-92, libr. dir., 1992—. Mem. ALA, Am. Assn. Law Librs., D.C. Libr. Assn., Spl. Librs. Assn. Roman Catholic. Office: Congl Quarterly Inc 1414 22nd St NW Washington DC 20037

WALTON, PATTY ANN, writer, publicist; b. Balt., Apr. 9, 1962; d. Peter Paul and Vilma Marie (Zavacky) Kamysz; m. Douglas Craig Walton, June 10, 1983. BA in Journalism, San Jose State U., 1985. Cert. in mktg. comms. Trainer, supr., writer Precision Monoliths Inc., Santa Clara, Calif., 1980-89; pub. rels. account exec. Hayes Rothwell, Santa Clara, 1989-90; mktg. comms. specialist Varian Assocs., Palo Alto, Calif., 1990—. Mem. Bus. Mktg. Assn., Sierra Club (forest conservation chair Loma Prieta chpt. 1991-93). Home: 250 Acalanes Dr # 2 Sunnyvale CA 94086 Office: Varian Oncology Systems 2045 Hanover St Palo Alto CA 94304-1129

WALTON, VALLI YVONNE, insurance consultant; b. Bronx, N.Y., May 24, 1950; d. William Jackson Sr. and Addie Ruby (Scott) Foy; m. Haywood Walton Sr., May 23, 1981. BA magna cum laude, Barrington Coll., 1971; postgrad., New Sch. for Social Rsch., 1975; cert. small bus. mgmt., NYU, 1976; MA in Liberal Studies, SUNY, Stony Brook, 1980; postgrad., Rutgers U., 1980; DDiv (hon.), London Inst. Applied Rsch., 1992. Approver group health benefits Metro. Life Ins. Co., Hauppauge, N.Y., 1971-73; account analyst, sales agt., publs. specialist group benefits dept. Equitable Life Assurance Soc. of the U.S., N.Y.C., 1973-76, litigations specialist, 1980-82; supr. major med. and death benefits Program Planners Ins. Cons., N.Y.C., 1976-77; group health and disability benefits specialist Operating Engrs. Local 825 Welfare Fund, Newark, N.J., 1982-91; sr. cons. group ins. N.Y. Life, N.Y.C., 1991—; litigation specialist, sr. supr., mgr., dir. legis. svcs. Mut. of N.Y., Purchase; assoc. mem. Practising Law Inst., N.Y.C., 1985—, dep. gov. Am. Biog. Inst., 1989, rsch. bd. advisors, 1989. Mem. Nat. Com. to Preserve Social Security and Medicare, Rep. Nat. Com., Washington, 1986—; dir. Bklyn. Dist. Children; dir. Christian edn. Durham A.M.E. Zion Ch., 1972. Mem. NAFE (cert. 1987), N.Y. Acad. Scis. (assoc.). Home: 1 Fordham Hill Oval Bronx NY 10468-8002

WALZER, JUDITH BORODOVKO, university administrator, educator; b. N.Y.C., May 27, 1935; d. Isidore and Ida (Gins) Borodovko; m. Michael L. Walzer, June 17, 1956; children—Sarah, Rebecca. B.A., Brandeis U., 1958, M.A., 1960, Ph.D., 1967. Dir. office women's edn. Radcliffe Coll., Cambridge, Mass., 1974-77, assoc. dean., 1976-77; Allston Burr sr. tutor, asst. dean for co-edn. Harvard Coll., Cambridge, Mass., 1977-80; asst. to the pres. Princeton U., N.J., 1980-85; provost New Sch. for Social Research, N.Y.C., 1985—. Mem. alumni fund com. Brandeis U., Waltham, Mass., 1983—; mem. adv. com. Overseas Sch., Hebrew U. in Jerusalem, 1989—; bd. dirs. Woodrow Wilson Found., Princeton U., 1991—. Democrat. Jewish. Office: New Sch for Social Rsch 66 W 12th St New York NY 10011-8603

WAMBLES, LYNDA ENGLAND, educational sales consultant; b. Nashville, Dec. 30, 1937; d. Henry Russell and Doris Olivia (Stuart) England; m. Byron Adolph Wambles, Sept. 3, 1965; 1 child, Teri Leigh Moore Wambles Taylor. Student, U. Tenn., 1964-65, 73-74, Washington U., St. Louis, 1984-86. Cert. profl. sec. Exec. sec. Gen. Truck Sales, Knoxville, Tenn., 1972-74; asst. to dean Coll. Law U. Tenn., Knoxville, 1974-76; office mgr. Washington U. Sch. Bus., St. Louis, 1977-78, registrar, dir. info. systems, 1978-83, asst. dean for faculty and adminstrn. services, 1983-86; cons. in field St. Louis, 1978-86, Overland Park, Kans., 1986—; acct. rep. Met. Life and Affiliated Cos., Shawnee Mission, Kans., 1992-94; cons. in field St. Louis, 1978; lectr. divsn. continuing edn. Washington U., St. Louis, 1978-80. Author: (with others) Procedures Manual and Information for State Guaranty Associations, 1987. Active United Way of Greater Knoxville, 1973-74; leader lunch participant YWCA, St. Louis, 1981-83. Fellow Acad. Cert. Profl. Secs.; mem. Prof. Secs. Internat., Nat. Secs. Assn. (Sec. of the Yr. 1975). Republican. Presbyterian. Home and Office: 8425 W 113th St Shawnee Mission KS 66210-2437

WAMPLER, BARBARA BEDFORD, entrepreneur; b. New Bedford, Mass., July 23, 1932; d. William and Mary (Fitzpatrick) Bedford; m. John H. Wampler, Oct. 21, 1950; children: John H. Jr., William C., James B., Robert T. AS, Tunxis Community Coll., 1975. Lic. real estate agt., Mass. Counselor Wampler Counseling Rehab. Services, Farmington, Conn., 1975-85; owner, mgr. Wampler Mktg., Farmington, 1980-84, Earth Campgrounds I and II, Otis, Mass., 1984—; pres., mgr. Earth Works (name now Earth Enterprises), Otis, Mass., 1984—; founder, pres. Advt. Matters, Otis, 1989—; v.p. Mastery Books, Otis, 1989—; mem., clk. Zoning Bd. Appeals, Otis, Mass., 1988-92; notary pub., 1988; agt. Primerica Fin. Svcs., 1992—. Contbr. articles to profl. jours. Dir. music First Congl. Ch., Otis, trustee, 1994—; family counselor Berkshire Coun. Alcoholism and Addictions, 1994—, Berkshire Mediation Option, 1994—. Faculty scholar U. Hartford, 1976. Mem. Acad. Family Mediators, Bus. Mgrs. Assn., Kiwanis. Home and Office: Earth Enterprises RR 8 Box 690 Otis MA 01253

WANAMAKER, CAROL ANN, personnel director; b. Newark, Jan. 28, 1947; d. Charles Claude and Marjorie Nevins (Cain) W. Student, Eckerd Coll., 1965-66. Legal sec. State Atty.-17th Jud. Cir., Ft. Lauderdale, Fla., 1969-83; tng. supr. State Atty.-17th Jud. Cir., Ft. Lauderdale, 1984-91, pers. dir., 1991—; steering com. co-chair Broward County PC Users Group, Ft. Lauderdale, 1993-94. Author: (manual) Support Staff Tng. Manual, 1981—. Mem. Fla. Pers. Assn. Democrat. Office: State Atty 17th Jud Cir Ste 655 201 SE 6 St Fort Lauderdale FL 33301

WANAMAKER, ELLEN PONCE, tax specialist; b. Newark, June 27, 1956; d. Arthur Zachary and Charlotte Rhoda (Frisch) Ponce; m. William A. Wanamaker, Aug. 8, 1979; 1 child, Marlee Ann. AS in Dental Hygiene, Fairleigh Dickinson U., 1978, BS in Dental Hygiene, 1979; student, H&R Block tax tng. seminars, Wayne, N.J., 1984-90, William Paterson Coll., 1975-76 90—. Registered dental hygienist, N.J., dental hygiene specialist, N.J.; cert. dental asst. patient accounts mgr., inst. dental assisting; accredited tax perparer; accredited tax advisor; IRS licensure-enrolled agt. status. Dental hygienist, dental asst. Arthur Ponce, DDS, Bloomingdale, N.J., 1972-80; dental asst., dental hygienist various dentists, N.J., 1977-80; instr., dept. chmn. Berdan Inst., Totowa, N.J., 1980-83; prodn. coord., cons. performer These Days Prodns., Ltd., Pompton Lakes, N.J., 1981—; tax preparer H&R Block, Wayne, N.J., 1985-90; mgmr. William Paterson Coll., Bloomingdale, 1975-76, 90-91; pvt. practice tax advisor, tax preparer Bloomingdale, 1985—; pvt. instrn. dental assts. and dental hygienists, Ellen Wanamaker, Bloomingdale, 1981-83; instr. County Coll. of Morris, Randolph, N.J., 1979-80. Vol. dental asst. N.E. Regional Bd. Dental Licensing Exams., 1978-86, Head Start Program, 1979, Bloomingdale Saturday Sch. Bloomingdale Bd. of Health, 1981, Ann. Bloomingdale Health Fair, 1983-93. Recipient Gold cert. Music Educators Assn., 1967-69. Mem. NOW, Am. Speech and Hearing Assn., Am. Dental Hygiene Assn., Nat. Assn. Tax Practitioners, Nat. Soc. Pub. Accts., Nat. Assn. Dental Assts., N.J. Dental Assn., FDU Dental Hygiene Assn., FDU Alumni Assn., Phi Omega Epsilon. Office: William A Wanamaker DMD MS 14 Leary Ave Bloomingdale NJ 07403-1612

WANBAUGH, REBECCA BOWDEN HERRICK, history educator; b. Sargentville, Maine, Apr. 12, 1923; d. Chandler Hale and Lilla Estelle (McIntyre) Bowden; BA, U. Maine, Orono, 1945, MA, 1964, PhD, 1980; student (merit scholar) Andover-Newton Theol. Sch., 1957-58. Personnel/tng. supr. Sibley, Lindsay & Curr Co., Rochester, N.Y., 1946-49; vocat. rehab. counselor N.Y. State Dept. Edn., Rochester, 1958-59; instr. sociology U. Maine, Orono, 1959-62; dean of women U. Maine, Presque Isle, 1963-74, instr. social sci., 1963-71, asst. prof. sociology and history, 1971-74, asso. prof. sociology and history, 1974-82, prof. history, 1982—, faculty rep. to bd. trustees, 1979-81, bd. trustees acad. planning com. on student life, 1979-80; social sci. cons. State Dept. Ednl. and Cultural Svcs., 1987-92; mem. Women's Studies Consortium U. Main, 1989-92. Exec. council Alcohol Info. and Referral Services, 1976-82; bd. dirs. N.E. chpt. Audubon Soc., 1991—; active Central Aroostook Assn. Retarded Citizens, 1965—. Faculty Devel. grantee U. Maine, 1978-79, Women and Women's Issues in Victorian Eng. fed. grantee, 1983; Alumni Grad. scholar U. Maine, 1980. Mem. AAUW, NEA, Am. Sociol. Assn., Am. Hist. Assn., Phi Eta Sigma, Pi Beta Phi. Baptist. Home: 6 Haven Ct Presque Isle ME 04769-3113 Office: U Maine 181 Main St Presque Isle ME 04769

WAND, PATRICIA ANN, librarian; b. Portland, Oreg., Mar. 28, 1942; d. Ignatius Bernard and Alice Ruth (Suhr) W.; m. Francis Dean Silvernail, Dec. 20, 1966 (div. Jan. 19, 1986); children: Marjorie Lynn Silvernail, Kirk Dean Silvernail. BA, Seattle U., 1963; MAT, Antioch Grad. Sch., 1967; AMLS, U. Mich., 1972. Vol. Peace Corps, Colombia, S.Am., 1963-65; secondary tchr. Langley Jr. High Sch., Washington, 1965-66; asst. libr. Wittenberg U. Libr., Springfield, Ohio, 1967-69; secondary tchr. Caro (Mich.) High Sch., 1969-70; assoc. libr. Coll. of S.I. (N.Y.) Libr., 1972-77; head, access svcs. Columbia U. Librs., N.Y.C., 1977-82; asst. univ. libr. U. Oreg., Eugene, 1982-89; univ. libr. The Am. U., Washington, 1989—; cons. Bloomsburg (Pa.) U. Libr., 1990. Contbr. articles to profl. jours. Pres. West Cascade Returned Peace Corps Vols., Eugene, 1985-88; v.p. Friends of Colombia, Washington, 1990—; speaker on Peace Corps, 1965—, libr. and info. svcs., 1979—. Honors Program scholarship Seattle U., 1960-62, Peace Corps scholarship Antioch U., 1965-66; recipient Beyond War award, 1987, Fulbright Sr. Lectr. award Fulbright, 1989, Disting. Alumnus award Sch. of Info. and Libr. Studies, U. Mich., 1992. Mem. ALA, Assn. Coll. and Rsch. Librs. (chair budge and fin. bd. dirs. 1987-89; chair WHCLIS task force 1989-92, On-line Computer Libr. Ctr. Adv. com. on Coll. and Univ. Librs. 1991—), D.C. Libr. Assn. (bd. dirs. 1993—). Home: 4854 Bayard Blvd Bethesda MD 20816-1785 Office: Am Univ Libr 4400 Massachusetts Ave NW Washington DC 20016-8046

WANDERMAN, SUSAN MAE, lawyer; b. N.Y.C., Mar. 12, 1947; d. Leo and Muriel D. Wanderman. AB, Wheaton Coll., Norton, Mass., 1967; JD, St. John's U., 1970; LLM, NYU, 1976. Bar: N.Y. 1971, U.S. Dist. Ct. (ea. and so. dists.) N.Y. 1972, U.S. Ct. Appeals (2d cir.) 1973, U.S. Supreme Ct. 1974. Asst. legal officer, legal dept. Chem. Bank, N.Y.C., 1972-75; 2d v.p. legal dept. Chase Manhattan Bank N.A., N.Y.C., 1975-82; asst. gen. counsel Citicorp Services, Inc., N.Y.C., 1982-84, v.p. Citibank, N.A., N.Y.C., 1984—; instr. bus. law and law for the layman LaGuardia Community Coll., 1976-77; law day speaker Queens County Supreme Ct., 1979-83; mem. Community Bd. 6, Queens County, N.Y.C., 1987—. Contbr. articles to legal publs. Past vol. N.Y. State Bar Assn. Lawyers in the Classroom. Mem. ABA, N.Y. State Bar Assn., Queens County Bar Assn. Office: Citibank NA One Court Sq Long Island City NY 11120

WANDLING, MARILYN ELIZABETH BRANSON, artist, art educator; b. Alton, Ill., May 16, 1932; d. Ralph Marion and Mary Mildred (Branson) W.; children: Jeffrey W. Tedford, Douglas H. Tedford, Pamela Lee Seymour Bliss. Student, Monticello Coll., Godfrey, Ill, 1950-51, U. Ill. U-C Sch. Fine Arts, 1951-53; BA in Art, Webster U., St. Louis, 1968; MA Edn. in Art Edn., Washington U., St. Louis, 1975. Cert. tchr. art Kindergarten-Grade 12, Mo. 4th grade tchr. Alton (Ill.) Pub. Schs., 1961-62; with art buying dept. Gardner Advt. Co. Inc., St. Louis, 1962-63; art tchr. mid. sch. Lindbergh Sch. Dist., St. Louis, 1968-75; cons., designer V.P. Fair, Inc., St. Louis, 1982; adminstrv. asst. to headmaster, coll. counseling dept. John Burroughs Sch., St. Louis, 1979-82; dir. pub. rels. and advt. Dance St. Louis, 1983-85; freelance art and design St. Louis, 1970—; art tchr. mid. sch. St. Louis Pub. Schs., 1987-90, art tchr. Elem. Magnet Sch. for Visual & Performing Arts, 1990—; tchr. drawing and painting Summer Arts Inst., St. Louis Pub. Schs., 1992, graphic arts designer, cons. comty. affairs divsn., 1985—, sch. vol. divsn., 1990-92, Webster Groves (Mo.) Sch. Dist., 1989-90, Pub. Sch. Retirement Sys., St. Louis, 1991; implementer classroom multicultural art edn. projects, 1987—; summer participant Improving Visual Arts Edn., Getty Ctr. for Edn. in Arts, 1990; book illustrator for McGraw Hill Inter-Americana de Mexico, Mexico City, 1994-95. Designer Centennial Logo for St. Louis Pub. Schs. Sesquicentennial, 1988; painter, designer murals for Ctrl. Presbyn. Ch. Nursery, 1978-79, St. Nicholas Greek Orthodox Ch., 1980; designer two outdoor villages VP Fair, Arch Grounds, St. Louis, 1982. Recipient merit and honor awards Nat. Sch. Pub. Rels. Assn., 1990, 91, 92, 93, Mo. Sch. Pub. Rels. Assn., 1989-90, 91, 92, 93. Mem. Nat. Art Edn. Assn., St. Louis Art Mus., PEO Sisterhood, Nat. Soc. DAR, Chi Omega Alumnae. Office: Ames Magnet Elem Sch Adminstrv Office 2900 Hadley St Saint Louis MO 63107-3911

WANE, SARA DIAMOND, elementary education educator, reading specialist; b. Jersey City, Oct. 29, 1933; d. Benjamin Diamond and Fay Rachel (Singer) Diamond-Usenheimer; m. Leonard Sheldon Wane, Aug. 7, 1955; children: Edward Marc Wane, Marcia Lynn Wane-Spiess. BA, Douglass Coll., 1955; MA, Kean Coll., 1962. Cert. elem. educator, reading specialist, learning disabilities specialist, Mass., N.J. Tchr. Metuchen (N.J.) Pub. Schs., 1955-56, Elizabeth (N.J.) Pub. Schs., 1956-60; reading specialist Morristown (N.J.) Pub. Schs., 1966-70, Framingham (Mass.) Pub. Schs., 1970—; guest lectr. Lesley Coll., Cambridge, Mass.; guest lectr., supr., tchr. mentor for grad. students in reading Framingham State Coll. Contbr. articles to profl. jours. Elected officer, exec. bd. dirs., trustee, com. chair Temple Beth Am, Framingham, 1970—; bd. dirs. Community Concert Program, Framingham, 1970—. Grantee, Framingham Edn. Found., Juniper Hill PTO. Mem. NEA, Mass. Tchrs. Assn., Framingham Tchrs. Assn. (com. mem.), Internat. Reading Assn., Mass. Reading Assn. (com. mem.), Nobscot Reading Assn. (exec. bd., com. chair). Democrat. Jewish. Home: 70 Lanewood Ave Framingham MA 01701-3658 Office: Juniper Hill Sch 29 Upper Joclyn Ave Framingham MA 01701-4411

WANG, CHANG YI, biomedical company executive; b. Taipei, Taiwan, Dec. 19, 1951; came to U.S., 1973, naturalized, 1988; d. Cheng-Shen and Dyi-Fen (Shyu) W.; m. Nean Hu, Dec. 25, 1980; 1 child, Shih-ye. B.Sc., Nat. Taiwan U., 1973; Ph.D., Rockefeller U., 1979. Grad. fellow Rockefeller U., N.Y.C., 1974-79; research assoc. Meml. Sloan Kettering Cancer Ctr., N.Y.C., 1979-82; dir. Lab. Molecular Immunology, Meml. Sloan Kettering Cancer Ctr., N.Y.C., 1982-85; dir. Lab. Molecular Immunology, North Shore Univ. Hosp., Cornell U. Med. Sch., 1985-87; cons. Cooper Labs., 1981-83; founder, chief sci. cons. United Biomed. Inc., 1983-85, exec. v.p., dir. research and devel., 1985-89, chief exec. officer United Biomed Inc., 1989-92, chief sci. officer, 1992—; NIH grant reviewer, 1987—, ad hoc rev. com. 1987—. Contbr. over 80 articles to profl. jours., patentee biomedicals, NIH grantee, 1981—; Nat. Cancer Inst. grantee, 1982—. Mem. AAAS, N.Y. Acad. Sci., Am. Assn. Immunologists, Am. Soc. Microbiology, Am. Assn. Clin. Research. Office: United Biomed Inc 25 Davids Dr Hauppauge NY 11788-2035

WANG, JOSEPHINE L. FEN, physician; b. Taiwan, China, Jan 2, 1948; came to U.S., 1974; d. Pao-San and Ann-Nam (Chen) Chao; m. Chang-Yang Wang, Dec. 20, 1973; children: Edward, Eileen. MD, Nat. Taiwan U., Taipei, 1974. Diplomate Am. Bd. Pediatrics, Am. Bd. Allergy and Immunology. Intern Nat. Taiwan U. Hosp., 1973-74; resident U. Ill. Hosp., Chgo., 1974-76; fellow Northwestern U. Med. Ctr., Chgo., 1976-78, instr. pediatrics, 1978—; cons. Holy Cross Hosp., Chgo., 1978—, Meth. Hosp. Ind., 1979—, St. Anthony Hosp., 1985—. Fellow Am. Coll. Allergy; mem. AMA, Am. Acad. Allergy. Office: 9012 Connecticut Dr Merrillville IN 46410 also: 4901 W 79th St Burbank IL 60459

WANG, MARGARET CHING-FENG, graphic designer, writer; b. Providence, R.I., Nov. 9, 1954; d. Kung-Chih and Joan Ingersoll (Parsons) W. BA in Geology, Ind. U., 1982, MS in Edn., 1984. Advt. sales mgr. Ind. U. Daily Student newspaper, Bloomington, 1981-82; audio-visual subctr. mgr. Ind. U., Bloomington, 1983; newspaper advt. coord. Bambergers,

Newark, 1984; store mgr. Clancy-Paul Computers, Princeton, N.J., 1984-85; desktop pub. specialist Prodigy Computers, Iselin, N.J., 1985-86; owner, chief designer Mid. Mountain Designs, Flagstaff, Ariz., 1985—. Author, photographer, prodr. (slide/tape show), Ind. U. Dept. Geology, 1983; contbr. articles to N.J. Audubon Soc. Mag., 1990—. Vol. N.J. Audubon Soc., 1990—. Recipient USGS internship Nat. Assn. Geology Tchrs., 1982, Silver medal Neographics, 1991, award of excellence APEX, 1994. Mem. Sigma Gamma Epsilon.

WANG, SHUJEN, journalism educator; b. Tao-Yuan, Taiwan, Republic of China, May 9, 1963; d. Chieh and Chong-Hsiu (Kuo) W. BA in Journalism, Chinese Culture U., 1985; MS in Telecommunications, Ind. U., 1987; PhD in Journalism, U. Md., 1991. English instr. Perfect Lang. Sch., Taipei, Taiwan, 1984; grad. tutor athletic tutorial program Ind. U., Bloomington, 1987; grad. teaching asst. dept. radio-television-film U. Md., College Park, 1987-91; asst. prof. dept. communication and theater Southeastern La. U., Hammond, 1991-93; asst. prof. mass communication dept. Westfield (Mass.) State Coll., 1993—; freelance writer, News Mirror Weekly, Taipei, 1989—; editor: The Culture Weekly, 1984, reporter, 1983-84; reporter China Econ. News Agy., 1984-85; programming asst. Internat. Community Radio, Taipei, 1984. Contbr. articles to profl. jours. and chpts. to books; reviewer Jour. of Communication, 1993. Mem. Assn. for Edn. in Journalism and Mass Comm., Internat. Comm. Assn., Speech Comm. Assn. (sec. Asian Pacific Am. Caucus 1994—), Eastern Comm. Assn., Chinese Comm. Assn., Assn. Chinese Comm. Studies. Office: Westfield State Coll Dept Mass Communication Westfield MA 01086

WANG, VERA, fashion designer; b. 1950; d. Cheng Ching Wang; m. Arthur Becker; children: Cecilia, Josephine. Grad., Sarah Lawrence Coll., New York. Sr. fashion editor Vogue, N.Y.C.; design dir. Ralph Lauren Women's Wear, N.Y.C., 1987-89; prin. Vera Wang Bridal House Ltd., N.Y.C., 1990—. Office: Vera Wang Bridal House Ltd 980 Madison Ave New York NY 10021*

WANMAN, AGNES WHITE, state agency professional, dance educator, performer/entertainer; b. Statesville, N.C., May 1, 1945; d. Hugh Sylvanus and Margaret Elizabeth (Carrithers) White; m. Chris Arthur Wanman, 1967 (div. 1978). BA, Radford (Va.) Coll., 1968; student, W.Va. Wesleyan Coll., 1963-66; postgrad., Va. Polytech. Inst. & State U., 1974-75. Community planner N.C. Dept. Commerce, Fayetteville, N.C., 1975—. Artistic dir., choreographer Oasis Tapestry Middle Eastern Dance Troup. Bd. dirs. Arts Coun. Fayetteville/Cumberland County, 1986-93. Recipient Svc. award N.C. Dept. Natural Resources and Community Devel., 1986. Mem. Cumberland Photo Club (sec. 1980-82, v.p. 1983-84, pres. 1985-86, treas. 1987—), Zeta Tau Alpha. Home: 4804 Old Field Rd Fayetteville NC 28304-5190 Office: NC Dept Commerce 714 Wachovia Bldg Fayetteville NC 28301

WANZER, MARY KATHRYN, computer company executive, consultant; b. South Bend, Ind., Sept. 12, 1942; d. Cyril Joseph and Kathryn Alice (Dumke) Tlusty; m. Boyd Eugene Wanzer, May 30, 1964; children: Adam James, Christopher James. BS, Northland Coll., 1964; student, Am. U., Washington, 1972-75. Tchr. Montgomery Co. Md. Schs., Rockville, 1964-66; mathematician Johns Hopkins U., Silver Spring, Md., 1966-68; systems analyst ITT Fed. Elec. Corp., Kennedy Space Ctr., Fla., 1968-69; computer programmer Atlantic City (N.J.) Hosp., 1969-71; project leader Fairfax Hosp. Assn., Falls Church, Va., 1971-73; sr. systems analyst Xerox Corp., Leesburg, Va., 1973-76; software engr. E-Systems, Falls Church, Va., 1982-85; pres. Atlantic Office Svcs., Ltd., Bethany Beach, Del., 1988—; cons. Chesapeake Utilities, Dover, Del., 1990, Intervet., Millsboro, Del., 1990-92; MIS mgr. Thompson Pub. Group, Salisbury, Md., 1992-93; systems analyst Mountaire, Selbyville, Del., 1993—. Leader LaLeche League, Annandale, Va., 1980-83; v.p. No. Va. Hockey Club, Fairfax County, Va., 1986-87. Roman Catholic. Home: 941 Lake View Dr Bethany Beach DE 19930-9675 Office: Atlantic Office Svcs Ltd 5 Starboard Ct # 1 Bethany Beach DE 19930-9679

WARD, DENITTA DAWN, lawyer; b. Gardner, Kans., Apr. 29, 1963; d. Gerald Dee Ascue and Patricia Diane (Henderson) Ray; m.m Kent Alan Ward, July 6, 1991. BA, U. Kans., 1985; JD magna cum laude, Georgetown U., 1989. Bar: Md. 1989, U.S. Ct. Appeals (fed. cir.) 1990, D.C. 1991, U.S. Ct. Internat. Trade 1991. Rsch. asst. Georgetown U., Washington, 1988-89; jud. clk. U.S. Ct. Appeals for Fed. Cir., Washington, 1989-90; assoc. Donovan Leisure Rogovin Huge & Schiller, Washington, 1990-94; atty. Fed. Election Commn., Washington, 1994—. Mng. editor Law and Policy in Internat. Bus., 1988-89. Mem. ABA, Ct. of Appeals for Fed. Cir. Bar Assn., Ct. of Appeals of Fed. Cir. Former Jud. Clks. Assn., Order of Coif, Omicron Delta Kappa, Pi Sigma Alpha. Home: 5711 N 25th St Arlington VA 22207 Office: Fed Election Commn 999 E St NW Washington DC 20037

WARD, DIANE KOROSY, lawyer; b. Cleve., Oct. 17, 1939; d. Theodore Louis and Edith (Bogar) Korosy; m. S. Mortimer Ward IV, July 2, 1960 (div. 1978); children: Christopher LaBruce, Samantha Martha; m. R. Michael Walters, June 30, 1979. AB, Heidelberg Coll., 1961; JD, U. San Diego, 1975. Bar: Calif. 1977, U.S. Dist. Ct. (so. dist.) Calif. 1977. Ptnr. Ward & Howell, San Diego, 1978-79, Walters, Ward & Howell, A.P.C., San Diego, 1979-81; mng. ptnr. Walters & Ward, A.P.C., San Diego, 1981—; dir., v.p. Oak Broadcasting Systems, Inc., 1982-83; dir. Elisabeth Kubler-Ross Ctr., Inc., 1983-85; sheriff Ranchos del Norte Corral of Westerners, 1985-87; trustee San Diego Community Defenders, Inc., 1986-88; dir. Calif. State U. Found., San Marcos, 1990—. Pres. bd. dirs. Green Valley Civic Assn., 1979-80; dir. Poway Ctr. for the Performing Arts, 1990-93; trustee Palomar-Pomerado Hosp. Found., 1985-89; v.p. Endowment Devel., 1989-91; bd. dirs. Clean Found.; trustee Episc. Diocese of San Diego. Recipient Dove award Assn. Retarded Citizens, 1992. Mem. ABA, Rancho Bernardo Bar Assn. (chmn. 1982-83), Lawyers Club San Diego, Profl. and Exec. Women of the Ranch (founder, pres. 1982—), San Diego Golden Eagle Club, Soroptimist Internat. (pres. chpt. 1979-80, Woman of Distinction 1992), Phi Delta Phi. Republican. Episcopalian. Home: 16503 Avenida Florencia Poway CA 92064-1807 Office: Walters & Ward 11665 Avena Pl Ste 203 San Diego CA 92128-2498

WARD, DORIS ELIZABETH, career counselor, biologist, educator; b. Charlotte, N.C., Jan. 11, 1935; d. James Hopkins and Florie Kathryn Cofield; m. Eddie Eugene Ward, Sept. 18, 1954; children: Eddie Eugene, Tanya Devonne, Tracia Lynnore, Tamara Elizabeth. BS, Howard U., 1966, postgrad., 1967-70; MEd in Guidance and Counseling, Bowie State U., 1985; EdS, George Washington U., 1987, EdD, 1990. Cert. sci. tchr. and guidance counselor, Md.; nat. cert. counselor. Med. technician U.S. Dept. Agr., Washington, 1958-64; biol. lab. technician U.S. Dept. Agr., Bethesda, Md., 1964-65; histologic tech. lab. instr. Howard U., Washington, 1966-67; biologist (histopathology) NIH, Bethesda, 1969-71; tchr. Our Lady Queen of Peace Sch., Washington, 1972-74; program analyst/mgmt. analysis HHS, Washington, 1974-82; career counselor Prince Georges Community Coll., Largo, Md., 1985—; asst. prof. counseling and psychology Grad. Sch. Arts and Scis., Marywood Coll., Scranton, Pa., 1990-91; doctoral intern in counseling Career Devel. Ctr., U. Md., College Park, 1988-89; asst. prof. counseling and psychology Marywood Coll., Scranton, Pa., 1990-91; counselor assoc. prof. East Carolina U., 1991-93; profl. counselor, pvt. practice, Greenville, N.C., 1993—; pvt. practice, Upper Marlboro, Md., 1994—. Hospice vol.; developer, facilitator bereavement support ministry St. Joseph's Ch., Landover, Md., 1984; cons./vol., career counselor for transition and spl. needs populations Cerebral Palsy Assn. Prince Georges County, 1986. Mem. AACD, Am. Soc. Clin. Pathologists (assoc. mem.). Democrat. Roman Catholic. Home: 13003 Keverton Dr Upper Marlboro MD 20772-1839

WARD, ERICA ANNE, lawyer, educator; b. Okiyama, Japan, Oct. 20, 1950; d. Robert Edward and Constance Regina (Barnett) W.; m. Ralph Joseph Gerson, May 20, 1979; 1 child, Stephanie Claire. B.A., Stanford U., 1972; J.D., U. Mich., 1975. Bar: Calif. 1975, D.C. 1976, U.S. Ct. Appeals (5th and D.C. cirs.) 1977, Temporary Emergency Ct. Appeals 1983, Mich. 1989. Assoc. Wilmer, Cutler & Pickering, Washington, 1975-77; staff counsel U.S. Senate Ethics Com., Washington, 1977-78; exec. asst. gen. counsel Dept. Energy, Washington, 1978-79, counsellor to dep. sec., 1980; assoc. dir. energy and natural resources, domestic policy staff White House, Washington, 1980-81; of counsel Skadden, Arps, Slate, Meagher & Flom, Washington, 1981-87, ptnr., 1987—; adj. prof. law U. Mich., Ann Arbor, 1984-85. Editor Mich. Law Rev., 1975. Commr. Mackinac Island (Mich.) State Park Commn., 1989—; mem. adv. bd. Ctr. Edn. of Women U. Mich., Ann Arbor, 1989—; bd. trustees Cranbrook Ednl. Cmty., 1993—; mem. visitors com. U. Mich. Law Sch. Recipient Outstanding Svc. medal Dept. Energy, 1981. Mem. ABA, Fed. Energy Bar Assn., Women's Bar Assn. D.C. Democrat. Jewish. Office: Skadden Arps Slate Meagher Flom 1440 New York Ave NW Washington DC 20005-2111

WARD, IVA NELL BELL, special education educator; b. Grapeland, Tex., Aug. 29, 1949; d. Frenchie and Eunice (Smith) Bell; m. Edward K. Ward Jr., Sept. 1969 (div. 1972); children: Eric Kendrick, Edward Kelly III. BS, Tex. So. U., 1978. Cert. tchr., Tex. Tchr. spl. edn. Houston Ind. Sch. Dist., 1978-85, reading specialist, program coord., 1990—; mem. steering com. Mayor's Hearing on Children and Youth, 1990, steering com. for restructuring Houston Ind. Sch. Dist., 1991, shared decision making com. for Sch. Campus. Active City of Houston Task Force for Infant Mortality Rate, 1993. Mem. NAACP, Nat. Women of Achievement (youth advisor, spelling bee coord., VIP coord., Golden Apple award 1992), Assn. Tex. Profl. Tchrs., Houston Fedn. Tchrs. (svc. and recruitment com. 1985-86), Houston Area Alliance of Black Sch. Educators, Africa Am. Reclaiming Our Cmty., Ioto Phi Lambda (S.E. area coord., VIP). Home: 1660 W T C Jester Blvd Apt 511 Houston TX 77008-3265 Office: Houston Ind Sch Dist 3830 Richmond Ave Houston TX 77027-5864

WARD, JEANNE LAWTON, family counselor, consultant; b. Bklyn., Mar. 23, 1945; d. James Joseph and Grace Frances (Brennan) Lawton; m. Robert L. Bucher, June 11, 1966 (div. Aug. 1977); children: Barbara Anne, Laura Jeanne; m. Charles F. Ward Jr., Aug. 19, 1983. BA in Edn., St. Catherine's Coll., St. Paul, 1966; MA in Counseling and Psychology, Coll. St. Thomas, St. Paul, 1970. Elem. tchr. Cooper Elem. Sch., 1966-69; spl. edn. resource tchr. Susie Tolbert 6th Grade Ctr., Jacksonville, Fla., 1976-78, sch. counselor, Arlington Heights Elem. Sch., Jacksonville, Fla., 1978-83; instr. Fla. C. C., Jacksonville, 1978-88; pvt. practice family counseling, Jacksonville, 1984-88; dir. tng. staff devel. City of Jacksonville, Fla., 1987-88; adj. prof. U. North Fla., 1990-92; dir. legis. affairs Mayors Office Jacksonville, Fla., 1992—. cons. mktg. tng. design and devel. Am. Transtech, Jacksonville, 1985-87; cons. child care Community Coll. Jacksonville, 1990-92; founder, dir. Divorce Ministry Diocese of St. Augustine, Jacksonville, 1979-83; Fla. del. White House Conf. on Families, 1980; regular panelist Sta. WJXT, Jacksonville, 1982—, editorial writer, 1990-92. Author curriculum. Bd. dirs., chmn. pers. com. Child Guidance Clinic, Jacksonville, 1977—; bd. dirs. Girls Club of Jacksonville, 1981-83; chairperson Mayors Commn. on Status of Women, Jacksonville, 1985-87; bd. dir. tng. and staff devel. City of Jacksonville, 1986-87; chmn. task force Corp. Child Care, 1985—, founding dir., 1985—; cons. Fla. Community Coll., 1988—; bd. dirs. YWCA, Jacksonville Symphony, Hope Haven, Family Care Connections, Inc., Nutcracker Ballet; chmn. bd. dirs. Child Guidance Ctr.; mem. Literacy Coalition, Coalition for a Drug Free Jacksonville, Leadership Jacksonville. Recipient Eve award Fla. Times Union, 1990, Woman of Achievement award Bus. and Profl. Women. Mem. AAUW, NAFE, ASTD, Nat. Coun. of Family Rels., Phi Delta Kappa, N.E. Fla. Soc. Parents of Visually Impaired Children Club (program chmn. 1985—). Democrat. Roman Catholic. Home: 3523 Park St Jacksonville FL 32205-7726 Office: Office of the Mayor 220 E Bay St Jacksonville FL 32202-3429

WARD, JEANNETTE POOLE, psychologist, educator; b. Honolulu, June 19, 1932; d. Russell Masterton and Bessie Naomi (Hammett) Poole; children: John Russell Ward, Lisa Joy Ward. BA, Birmingham (Ala.) So. Coll., 1963; PhD in Psychology, Vanderbilt U., 1969. NSF summer rsch. asst. U. Iowa, Iowa City, 1962; NSF summer rsch. asst. Vanderbilt U., Nashville, 1963, NASA fellow, 1963-66, NIH postdoctoral fellow, 1966-67; spl. rsch. fellow Duke U., Durham, N.C., 1970-71; asst. prof. psychology Memphis State U., 1967-72, assoc. prof. psychology, 1972-77, prof. psychology, 1977—. Editor: Current Research in Primate Laterality, 1990, Primate Laterality, 1992; mem. editorial bd. Jour. Comparative Psychology, 1988—; contbr. chpts. to books and articles to profl. jours. Fellow Am. Psychol. Soc.; mem. Psychonomic Soc., Animal Behavior Soc., Am. Psychol. Assn., Am. Primatology Soc., Southeastern Psychol. Assn., Soc. for Neuroscis., Internat. Soc. for Comparative Psychology (treas. 1989-90), Sigma Xi (pres. Memphis State U. chpt. 1989-90, rsch. award 1985). Democrat. Office: Univ of Memphis Dept Psychology Memphis TN 38152

WARD, JENNIFER C., diplomat; b. Worcester, Eng., Jan. 29, 1944; 1 child. BA, Vassar Coll., 1965; MA, PhD, UCLA. Asst. to v.p. for acad. affairs, lectr. in social sci., Medgar Evers Coll. CUNY, 1971-73; dir. grad. admissions, lectr. in pub. and internat. affairs Princeton U., 1975-78; staff dir. House Fgn. Affairs Com., subcom. on Africa U.S. Congress, 1978-79; cons. Office of Asst. Sec. of Def. for Internat. Security Affairs for Africa, 1979; dep. dir. office of Inter-African affairs Bur. African Affairs, 1979-81; counselor for polit. affairs U.S. Embassy, Kinshasa, Zaire, 1981-83; sr. watch officer ops. ctr. U.S. Dept. State, 1983-84, dep. dir. office security assistance and sales, bur. politico-military affairs, 1984-86; dep. chief of mission U.S. Embassy, Dakar, Senegal, 1986-89; counselor for polit affairs U.S. Embassy, Kingston, Jamaica, 1989-91; U.S. amb. Niger, 1991-93; special asst. to the pres./sr. dir. for African affairs Nat. Security Council, Washington, D.C., 1993—. Office: Dept of State Niamey Embassy Washington DC 20521-2420*

WARD, JO ALICE, computer consultant, educator; b. Ft. Worth, Aug. 14, 1939; d. Boyd Wheeler and Frances Elizabeth (Wheeler) Patton; m. John Oliver Ward, Mar. 19, 1960 (div. Feb. 1976); children: Russell Scott, Pamela Joan Ward Watson. BA in Math., North Tex. State U., 1961, MA in Math., 1965, postgrad., 1969-72. Instr. math. North Tex. State U., Denton, 1965-67, grad. asst., 1968-72; instr. math. Tarrant County Jr. Coll., Ft. Worth, 1967-68; math. tchr. Aldine Ind. Schs., Houston, 1973-76; math. instr. U. Houston Downtown, 1974-80; sys. analyst Conoco Inc, Houston, 1981-93; computer cons. Quality First Computer Svcs., Houston, 1994—. Vol facilitator for family violence program Houston Area Women's Ctr., 1993-94. Mem. Am. Entrepreneurs Assn. Home: 11943 Briar Forest Dr Houston TX 77077-4132

WARD, JOAN GAYE, psychologist; b. Englewood, N.J.; d. James A. and Eda D. (Mullan) W. BA, Miami U., 1956; MA, New Sch. for Social Rsch., 1965; PhD, NYU, 1973, cert. psychotherapy and psychoanalysis, 1981. Rsch. assoc. Mktg. Survey & Rsch. Corp., N.Y.C., 1962-67; counselor, rsch. fellow NYU, N.Y.C., 1967-68, instr., 1970-71; psychologist Bur. Child Guidance, Sch. Bd. Support Teams, Bronx, 1969—; field trainer Sch. Bd. Support Teams, Bronx, 1989—; practicum supr. Fordham U., N.Y.C., 1989-90, 91-92; internship supr. L.I. U., Dobbs Ferry, N.Y., 1990-91; pvt. practice psychotherapy N.Y.C., 1969—; adjunct asst. clinical prof. NYU, 1992-93. Mem. APA, N.Y. State Psychol. Assn., Ea. Psychol. Assn., Nat. Assn. Sch. Psychologists, N.Y. Assn. Sch. Psychologists, Postdoctoral Soc. Home: 91 Schofield St City Island NY 10464-1533

WARD, JUDY KITCHEN, bank executive; b. Asheville, N.C., Jan. 19, 1940; d. Jesse Ernest and Mary Daisy (Pressley) Kitchen; m. Wayne Leigh; children: Robert Wayne, Shari Leigh, Rodney Victor; m. Jerry Ellsworth Ward; 1 child, Jerry E. Jr. Student, Thomas Nelson Community Coll., Hampton, Va., 1987. Bank teller 1st City Bank, Newport News, Va., 1977-82; adminstrv. asst. Va. Nat. Bank, Newport News, 1982-84; br. mgr. 1st Am. Bank Va., Newport News, 1984-91, asst. v.p., 1991—. Treas. Alternatives/Drug Abuse, Newport News and Hampton, 1986-88, bd. dirs., 1986—; cabinet mem. United Way, Newport News, 1988; mem. ways and means com. Dem. Orgn., 1987—; sec. Denbigh Little League, 1974-76; pres. local PTA, 1972-73, Block Mother's Prevention Against Child Abuse, 1967-69; bd. dirs. Dem. City Com., 1992. Recipient cert. United, 1984-88, Mar. of Dimes, 1982-88. Mem. Am. Inst. Banking (chief consul 1986, award 1987, v.p. 1990—, bd. dirs. 1991, chmn. child abuse 1992), Exch. Club (pres. James River chpt. 1990—). Episcopalian. Home: 193 Compton Pl Newport News VA 23606-1626 Office: 1st Am Bank Va 2901 Huntington Ave Newport News VA 23607-3917

WARD, JULIE MCDUFF, real estate marketing specialist; b. Birmingham, Ala., Mar. 26, 1946; d. Oliver Tabor and Julia Frances (Cooper) McDuff; m. David William Ward, Jan. 19, 1968; 1 child, Brian William. BS in Edn., U. Ala., 1968. Mgmt. trainee Bell Telephone Co., Birmingham, 1964-68; tchr. elem. edn. Huntsville (Ala.) City Schs., 1969-73; real estate agt. Frontier Better Homes and Gardens, Littleton, Colo., 1988—. Mem. pers. com. Ken Caryl Bapt. Ch., Littleton, 1992-95. Mem. Colo. Assn. Realtors (grad. realtor inst. designation), Jefferson County Assn. Realtors. Office: Frontier Better Homes 5944 S Kipling St # 100 Littleton CO 80127-2590

WARD, KATHERYN HOPE, marketing educator and administrator, consultant; b. Murphysboro, Ill., Jan. 6, 1941; d. Henry James and Cornelia (Spann) Hubbard; m. George Ward, Apr. 27, 1963; children: Christel D., Christopher L., Phillip M. A, Olive-Harvey Coll., 1979; BSBA, Roosevelt U., 1981, MS in Internat. Bus., 1983. Prose counselor Ill. Indsl. Commn., Chgo., 1979-81; grad. advisor Roosevelt U., Chgo., 1981-84; asst. prof. Chgo. State U., 1984-93, chair Mgmt. Mktg. and Info. Systems Dept., 1988-93; exec. dir. Ctr. for Internat. Devel., Inc., Chgo., 1993—; dir. Advance Internat. Mktg. Inc., Wood Dale, Ill., 1992—. Mem., com. chair Polit. Action Conf. of Ill., Chgo., 1981-83; sec.-treas. Bus. Hall of Fame, 1985—; bd. dirs. Positive Anti-Crime Thrust, 1990—; bd. dirs. Roseland Area chpt. Am. Cancer Soc., Chgo., 19916. Mem. NAFE, AAUW, Nat. Coun. Negro Women, Am. Mktg. Assn., Midwest Mktg. Assn., Assn. Black Women in Higher Edn. Inc., Sigma Gamma Rho, Beta Gamma Sigma. Office: Advance Internat Mktg Inc 317 N Central Ave Wood Dale IL 60191-1605

WARD, LESLIE ALLYSON, journalist, editor; b. L.A., June 3, 1946; d. Harold Gordon and Marilyn Lucille (Dahlstead) W.; m. Robert L. Biggs, 1971 (div. 1977); m. Colman Robert Andrews, May 26, 1979 (div. 1988). AA, Coll. San Mateo, 1966; BA, UCLA, 1968, MJ, 1971. Reporter, researcher L.A. Bur. Life mag., 1971-72; reporter, news asst. L.A. bur. N.Y. Times, 1973-76; sr. editor New West mag., L.A., 1976-78, 79-80; L.A. bur. chief US mag., 1978-79; Sunday style editor L.A. Herald Examiner, 1981-82, editor-in-chief Sunday mags., 1982-83, Olympics editor, 1984, sports editor, 1985-86, sr. writer, 1986; sr. editor L.A. Times Mag., 1988-90; travel editor L.A. Times, 1990—. Democrat. Office: LA Times Times Mirror Sq Los Angeles CA 90053

WARD, LILLIAN LOVETT, educator; b. Shepherd, Tex., Dec. 17, 1939; d. Charles Williard and Paralea (Lovett) Kirby; m. Cecil Don Ward, Jan. 29, 1959; children: Tammy, Don, JoLynn. BS, Butler U., 1971; MEd, Mid. Tenn. State U., 1974; EdS, Tenn. Tech. U., 1981. Lic. tchr. Tchr. Lebanon (Ind.) City Schs., 1971-72, Sumner County Bd. Edn., Gallatin, Tenn., 1972—. Grantee Joe David Found., Nashville, 1993. Mem. NEA, Tex. Edn. Assn., Tenn. Reading Assn. (pres. 1993-94, Outstanding Conf. award 1981-91), Mid. Tenn. Reading Assn. (pres. 1979-80), North Ctrl. Reading Assn. (pres. 1989-90). Baptist. Home: 542 Ward Ln Hendersonville TN 37075-8408

WARD, MARILYNN ITALIANO, Spanish language educator; b. N.J., Oct. 2, 1942; d. Felix M. and Philomena (Verderosa) Italiano; m. Richard J. Ward, June 25, 1965; children: Christopher L., Craig R. BA, Mich. State U., 1963, MA, 1964; PhD, U. Colo., 1974. Cert. Spanish, English and remedial reading tchr., Ohio. Migrant tchr. Eastwood Schs., Pemberville, Ohio, 1979-84; instr. Bowling Green (Ohio) State U., 1980; Spanish and reading tchr. Woodmore Local Schs., Elmore, Ohio, 1984-86; asst. prof. Spanish Findlay (Ohio) Coll., 1986—; assoc. prof. U. Findlay (formerly Findlay Coll.), 1989—; spkr. Hispanic Lits. Conf., 1987, 88, Gt. Decisions Spkr., 1988. Contbr. articles on women's studies to profl. jours.; reviewer bilingual books. Mem. NEA, TESOL, AAUW (edn. chmn. 1981-82, membership v.p. 1982-83), Delta Kappa Gamma, Phi Kappa Phi. Office: U Findlay Internat Ctr 1000 N Main St Findlay OH 45840-3653

WARD, MARTHA GAIL JOINER, adult education educator; d. Woffard Johnston and Tommie Lee Joiner; m. James Edward Ward; 1 child, Jonathan Calder. Student, Brunswick (Ga.) Jr. Coll., 1971; BFA in Art Edn., Valdosta State Coll., 1974; MEd in Early Childhood Edn., Ga. So. Coll., 1985, postgrad., 1987. Reading instr. Madison County (Fla.) Sch. Bd., 1974-76; tchr. David Emanuel Acad., Stillmore, Ga., 1976-78, Candler County Bd. Edn., Metter, Ga., 1979-87; learning svcs. coord. The Job Network Ctr., Ga. So. U., Statesboro, 1987-90; adult edn. instr. Swainsboro Tech. Inst., 1990—. Reviewer series of math books: Math Matters for Adults, 1992. Recipient Most Innovative Program of the Yr. award State of Ga.'s Job Tng. Partnership Act 8% Grant, 1989. Mem. Ga. Adult Literacy Assn., Profl. Assn. Ga. Educators (state student group liaison, Candler County chpt. pres. 1986), Ga. Adult Edn. Assn., Inc., Kappa Delta Pi (chpt. pres. 1989-90), Delta Kappa Gamma Soc. Internat. (Beta Beta chpt.). Home: RR 2 Box 110 Metter GA 30439-9548 Office: Swainsboro Tech Inst 201 Kite Rd Swainsboro GA 30401-1852

WARD, MARY JOHNSON, pediatrician; b. Harrogate, Tenn., Sept. 6, 1924; d. LeRoy and Willa Sarah (Mitchell) Johnson; m. Dennis Earl Ward, June 19, 1950; children: Dennis Earl Jr., Thomas Roy, Edward Haynes. BA, Lincoln Meml. U., 1944; MD, U. Tenn., 1952. Diplomate Am. Bd. Pediats. Intern Scott-White Hosp., Temple, Tex., 1952-53; resident in pediats. Ga. Bapt. Hosp., Atlanta, 1956-58, chief resident in pediats., 1958; mem. med. staff Magnolia Regional Med. Ctr., Corinth, Miss., 1961—. Pres. Theatre Arts Aux., Corinth, 1985; chmn. social com. Corinth Symphony, 1993; bd. trustees Corinth Concert Assn., 1994. Fellow Am. Acad. Pediats. (mem. Miss. chpt.); mem. AMA, DAR (Corinth-LaSalle chpt.), N.E. Miss. Med. Assn. Republican. Episcopalian. Home: 2701 Gaines Rd Corinth MS 38834 Office: Ward Clinic 3201 Gaines Rd Corinth MS 38834

WARD, OLLIE TUCKER, counselor, educator; b. St. Louis, June 14, 1930; d. George Thomas and Luevenia (Casey) Stewart; m. George O. Tucker, Dec. 25, 1950 (div. Apr. 1969); children: George Stewart, Jeffrey Terrance; m. John Henry Ward, 1974. Student, Stowe Tchrs. Coll., 1946-50; MA, Washington U., St. Louis, 1958; postgrad., Webster U., 1972, U. Mo., 1973. From reading instr. to mid. sch. counselor St. Louis Pub. Schs., 1950-90; adj. faculty Harris Stowe State Coll., St. Louis, 1974, 84, 90; field rep. Tucker Bus. Coll., St. Louis, 1950-66, Tucker Bus. Coll. Alumni Assn., 1987—. Recipient Disting. Svc. award Iota Phi Lambda, 1988, award Nat. Bd. for Cert. Counselors; named Coro finalist, Class 30, 1994. Mem. NAACP (life, 1st v.p. St. Louis County br. 1988-89), CORE (So. Christian Leadership award St. Louis br. 1986), St. Louis Pers. and Guidance Assn. (pres.-elect 1984), St. Louis Sch. Counselors Assn. (pres. 1987-88 svc. award 1990), Coalition 100 Black Women (charter mem., ad hoc chmn. 1984-85), Am. Cancer Assn., Abarasque (pres. 1977-78), Jack and Jill Am. (1st v.p., pres.-elect, assoc. 1968-91), Alpha Kappa Alpha. Democrat. Baptist. Home: 1513 Bredell Ave Richmond Heights MO 63117-2110

WARD, SANDRA LYNN ASHER, family nurse practitioner; b. Ft. Lauderdale, Fla., Dec. 7, 1961; d. Robert Lee and Linda Jo (Allen) Siler; m. Patrick C. Ward, Mar. 26, 1994. BSN, U. Fla., 1984, MSN, 1994. RN, Fla.; cert. intravenous nurse; cert. family nurse practitioner. Staff nurse, charge nurse Vets. Adminstrn., Gainesville, Fla., 1984-86, staff nurse ICU, 1986-87; staff nurse ICU Alachua Gen. Hosp., Gainesville, Fla., 1987, Cleve. Clinic Found., 1987-88; staff nurse home care ICU various agys., Cleve. & Gainesville, 1988-89; staff nurse Shands Hosp., Gainesville, 1989-90; nurse mgr., nurse clinician IV therapy Ceremark Inc., Orlando, Fla., 1990-92, Jacksonville, Fla., 1992—; family nurse practitioner Tri-County Family Health Care, Madison, Fla., 1993-94, Andrews Internal Medicine, 1994—. Lt. USN, 1990—. Mem. AACN, Intravenous Nursing Soc., Sigma Theta Tau. Home: Rt 1 Box 482 Marble NC 28905

WARD, SELA, actress; b. Meridian, Miss.; d. Granberry Holland and Annie Kate Ward. BA, U. Ala. Appearances include: (TV series) Emerald Point, N.A.S., 1983-84, Sisters, 1991— (Emmy award for Lead Actress in Drama Series 1994), (TV movies) Rainbow Drive, 1990, Double Jeopardy, 1993, (films) Nothing in Common, 1986, Hello Again, 1987, Rustler's Rhapsody, 1985, The Fugitive, 1993. Office: Somers Teitelbaum David 1925 Century Park E # 2320 Los Angeles CA 90067

WARD, SUE ELLEANORE FRYER, social worker, state agency administrator; b. Albuquerque, Oct. 28, 1935; d. E. Reeseman and Florence Ione (Pierce) F.; m. Archibald Floyd Ward, Nov. 3, 1959; children: Beth Ione, Lucille Elleanore. BA, Coll. William and Mary, 1957; MSW, U. Utah, 1961; postgrad., Am. U., Beirut, McGill U., Montreal, Can. Cert. social worker;

diplomate in clin. social work Am. Bd. Examiners in Clin. Social Work. Social worker, clin. social worker State Hosp. South, Blackfoot, Idaho, 1959-61; social worker Children's Convalescent Hosp., Washington, 1961-62; caseworker Children's Home Soc. N.C., Greensboro, 1967-68; social worker Mental Health Study Ctr., NIMH, Adelphi, Md., 1968-70; therapist in pvt. practice Annapolis, Md., 1970-74, Clinton, Md., 1973-77; dir. Charles County Children's Aid Soc., La Plata, Md., 1977; project coord. Regional Direction Ctr. for Handicapped, Upper Marlboro, Md., 1980; dir. spl. projects Viacom Cablevision of Md., Rockville, 1981-82; dir. Prince George's County Dept. Aging, Hyattsville, Md., 1982-91, dir. dept. family svcs., 1991-95; dir. Md. Office on Aging, Balt., 1995—; mem. faculty and adv. bd. U. Md. Leisure and Aging, Therapeutic Recreation Mgmt. Sch., 1984—; chmn. Elder Abuse and Neglect Project Oversight Com. Prince George's County; mem. Md. Gov.'s Task Force on Delivery Svcs. to Elderly, 1990. Contbr. articles to profl. jours. Mem., treas., chmn. bd. Hospice of Prince George's County, Md., 1983—; chmn. profl. adv. com. Prince George's Mental Health Assn., 1983-90; Dem. nominee from 4th Congl. dist., Md., 1978; bd. dirs. Md. Congress Parents and Tchrs., 1974-82; sec. Older Women's League, Prince George's County, 1988-90; pres. Women's Polit. Caucus, Prince George's County, 1986. Recipient Gladys Noon Spellman award for excellence in pub. svc., 1994; certs. for pub. svc. and awards. Mem. NASW, Acad. Cert. Social Workers, Nat. Assn. Area Agys. on Aging (bd. dirs., 2d v.p., pres. 1988-92), Md. Assn. Area Agys. on Aging (chmn. 1989-92). Home: 6109 Buckler Rd Clinton MD 20735-3417

WARD, SUSAN MARIE, consultant; b. Detroit, Jan. 29, 1954; d. Richard Guerin and Helen Marie (Stone) W. BA in Art History, Wayne State U., 1983; MA in Decorative Arts, Parsons Sch. Design/Cooper-Hewitt Mus., 1985. Intern Met. Mus. Art, N.Y.C., 1985; asst. curator Biltmore Estate, Asheville, N.C., 1985-86, curator, 1987-92; exec. dir. Travellers Rest, Nashville, 1992-94; founder, dir. Heritage Comm., Brentwood, Tenn., 1994—; sec. Biltmore Village Hist. Mus., Asheville, 1989-91; adj. prof. O'More Coll. Design, Franklin, Tenn. Author: The Gilded Age at Biltmore Estate, 1990. Vol. Big Bros. and Sisters, Asheville, 1988-92; com. mem. Bele Cher, Asheville, 1989; bd. dirs. Asheville Art Mus.; vol. cons. Jr. Achievement, 1994—. Mem. Am. Assn. State and Local History (state membership chmn. 1989), N.C. Mus. Coun. (chmn. computers and museums com.), Southeast Museums Conf. (chmn. intern staff devel. com.), Asheville Mus. of Art (bd. dirs. 1991-92).

WARD, SUZANNE MARY, librarian; b. Sydney, Australia, Apr. 28, 1956; came to U.S., 1958; d. John Robert and Cicely Marian (Kearns) W. BA, UCLA, 1978; MLS, U. Mich., 1981; MA, Memphis State U., 1985. Archivist Ctr. So. Folklore, Memphis, 1981; reference librarian, then engring. librarian Memphis State U., 1982-87; info. specialist Purdue U., West Lafayette, Ind., 1987-93; access svcs. libr., 1993—. Reader, West Tenn. Talking Library, Memphis, 1983-86. Mem. Spl. Libraries Assn. (pres. Mid-South chpt. 1985-86), ALA (group newsletter editor 1989-92). Office: Purdue Univ Stewart Ctr West Lafayette IN 47907

WARD, WANDA ELAINE, psychologist; b. Atlanta, June 27, 1954; d. Clifford R. Ward and Elaine (Phillips) Ward Jackson. BA in Psychology, Princeton U., 1976; PhD in Psychology, Stanford U., 1981. Asst. prof. psychology U. Okla., Norman, 1981-88, assoc. prof. psychology, 1988—, founding dir. Ctr. for Rsch. on Multi-Ethnic Edn., 1986-92; program dir. career access programs NSF, Washington, 1992-94; spl. asst. to the asst. dir. Directorate for Edn. and Human Resources, NSF, Washington, 1994—; vis. asst. prof. Ctr. for Study of Reading, U. Ill., Urbana, 1984-85; vis. scholar Ctr. for Social Orgn. of Schs., Johns Hopkins U., Balt., 1990; mem. joint legis. task force on literacy Okla. State Senate, Oklahoma City, 1987-88, mem. legis. task force on minority tchr. recruitment, 1989-90; mem. Okla. Scholar-Leadership Enrichment Program Adv. Coun., Norman, 1990-92; presenter workshops, seminars, symposia in field. Sr. co-editor: Key Issues in Minority Education: Research Directions and Practical Implications, 1989; contbr. articles to profl. publs. Mem.-at-large exec. com. alumni coun. Princeton U., 1989-91; bd. dirs. Support Ctr. of Okla., Oklahoma City, 1990-92; mem. minority adv. bd. KOCO-TV 5, Oklahoma City, 1989-92. Ford Found. fellow, 1976-81; recipient A.C. Hamilton Tribute of Appreciation and Commendation, 12th ann. conf. Nat. Black Caucus of State Legislators, 1988. Mem. APA, Am. Edni. Rsch. Assn., Assn. Black Psychologists, Western Psychol. Assn. Office: NSF 1800 G St NW Washington DC 20550-0001

WARD-SHAW, SHEILA THERESA, nurse; b. N.Y.C., June 20, 1951; d. Arthur and Cynthia Melba (Mapp) Jenkins; m. Howard J. Ward, Nov. 1977 (div. 1981); m. Thomas N. Shaw, Sept. 1988; children: Tanyatta, Barbara, Thomas. Student, Rockland Community Coll., 1973, U. Nev., Las Vegas, 1984, San Jose State U., 1994—. Charge nurse Hillcrest (N.Y.) Nursing Home, 1973-74; infirmary nurse St. Agatha's Home for Children, Nanuet, N.Y., 1974-75; temp. bldg. charge nurse Letchworth Village, Thiells, N.Y., 1976; charge nurse New Paltz (N.Y.) Nursing Home, 1977; non secure detention, foster bdg. parent St. Agatha's Home for Children, Nanuet, 1977-79; asst. nursing supr., inservice coord., infection control nurse So Nev. Mental Retardation, Las Vegas, 1979-84; psychiat. nurse II evening duty officer Harbor View Devel. Ctr., Valdez, Alaska, 1987-89; infection control, employee health nurse, unit coord. North Star Hosp., Anchorage, 1989-92; psychiat. nurse, infection control Oak Creek Hosp., San Jose, Calif., 1992-93, writer, producer OSHA precaution tng. staff video, 1993; psychiat. nurse VA Hosp. Menlo Park Divsn., Palo Alto, 1992—. Campaign worker Nev. Gov. Bryan Dem. Candidate, Las Vegas, 1983-84, Pearson for County Commn. Race, Las Vegas, 1984; pres. Clark County Health Educators, 1983; mem. APIC., 1980-85. Mem. Assn. for Practioners of Infection Control. Roman Catholic. Office: VA Hosp Palo Alto MPD 3801 Miranda Ave Palo Alto CA 94304-1207

WARDWELL, JEANNE KATHERINE, financial planner; b. Elko, Nev., Mar. 16, 1966; d. Gary H. and Ruth M. (Botsford) W. BS in Acctg., U. Utah, 1988. CPA, Calif. Pub. acct. KPMG Peat Marwick, L.A., 1988-91, Anderson, Behrenz & Co., Reno, Nev., 1991-92; fin. planner-analyst Internat. Game Tech., Reno, 1992—; tchr., instr. Nev. Self-Employment Trust Fund, Reno, 1994; cons. Jr. Achievement, Salt Lake City, L.A., Reno, 1987-94. Vol. Suicide Prevention & Crisis Call Ctr., Reno, 1993-94; treas. Good Tymes Country Dancers, Reno, 1992-94. Mem. Inst. Mgmt. Accts. (v.p. fin., pres., program booklet dir. 1992-94), Nev. Soc. CPAs. Office: Internat Game Tech 520 S Rock Blvd Reno NV 89502

WARE, BARBARA HENLEY, management consultant; b. Kingsville, Tex., Dec. 5, 1955; d. Albert Lowry and Jane Cavin (Deason) Henley; m. David Scott Ware, Sept. 10, 1983. BSBA in Acctg., U. Mo., 1978, MBA in Financial Mgmt., 1982. Cost acctg. supr. Orscheln Co., Moberly, Mo., 1978-80; mgmt. cons. Arthur Andersen & Co., St. Louis, 1982-86, Ernst & Young, St. Louis, 1986—. Active St. Louis Symphony Soc., 1992—, Mo. Botanical Garden, St. Louis, 1984—, St. Louis Orchid Soc., 1994—. Mem. Mo. Athletic Club. Office: Ernst & Young 701 Market St Saint Louis MO 63101-1850

WARE, PEARL CUNNINGHAM, educator; b. Greensboro, N.C., Aug. 18, 1939; d. Cyprian Reginald and Ida (Williams) Cunningham. BA summa cum laude, N.C. Agrl. and Tech. Coll., 1959; MA, Columbia U., 1962. Cert. English and spl. edn. tchr., N.Y. Tchr. Raleigh (N.C.) Pub. Schs., 1959-61; office worker Tchrs.' Coll., Columbia U., N.Y.C., 1961-62; hosp. tchr. N.Y.C. Pub. Schs., 1962—. Candidate for N.Y. State Assembly, N.Y. State Right-to-Life Party, 1980, 82, candidate for N.Y. State Senate, 1984. Recipient plaque Boy Scouts Am., Bklyn., 1984, Honor cert. N.Y.C. Alliance Pub. Schs., 1987. Mem. Nat. Honor Soc. Secondary Schs., Alpha Kappa Mu, Sigma Rho Sigma, Kappa Delta Pi, Nat. Sorority Phi Delta Kappa (Theta chpt., editor bimonthly publ. 1981-83). Home: 91 E 91st St Brooklyn NY 11212-1501 Office: Interfaith Hosp PS 403 Annex 1545 Atlantic Ave Brooklyn NY 11213-1166

WARE, PEGGY JENKINS, photographer, writer, artist, dancer; b. Santa Monica, Calif., Sept. 6, 1947; d. Stanley Lauder Mahony and Patricia Lou Chapman Covo; m. James Michael Jenkins, Feb. 5, 1966 (div. May 1982) 1 child, Cheryl Denise Jenkins; m. Wiley Neal Ware, Jan. 1, 1988. Dance student of Eugene Loring, U. Calif., Irvine, 1979; dance student Valentina Oumansky, Dramatic Dance Ensemble, North Hollywood, Calif., 1969-72; dance student, Jerry Bywaters Cochran, Dallas, 1972-75; photography student of James Baker, U. Tex., Dallas, Richardson, 1984-86; BA in English, U. Tex. at Dallas, Richardson, 1986, postgrad., 1987. Propr. Mahony/Jenkins & Assocs., Richardson, 1980-82; mng. editor, writer Happenings Mag., Dallas, 1983; prodn. supr. Publishing Concepts, Dallas, 1983-85; mem. book prodn. team David Marquis/Robin Sachs-Corp. for Edn., Dallas, 1990; freelance photographer and artist Dallas, 1984—; rsch. editor Prin. Fin. Securities, Dallas, 1994; dance rsch. interviewer Simon Semenoff, Ballet Russe, Sol Hurok, Impressario. Transcribing editor: I Am A Teacher, A Tribute to America's Teachers, 1990; photographer: Photo Essay of the Berlin Wall, 1988; contbr. articles and photos to mags. Exec. bd. Friends of Photography, Dallas Mus. Art, 1993-94; bd. dirs., trustee Dancers Unltd. Repertory Co., Dallas, 1990-91; contbr. photographer Lakewood Svc. League, Dallas, 1992; writer, video producer Women's Conf., Women's Caucus for Art, Dallas, 1986. Home: 6233 Belmont Ave Dallas TX 75214

WARGETZ, GEORGIA LYNN RANCE, accountant; b. Oklahoma City, Feb. 7, 1959; d. William and Ruth Virginia (Kemp) Rance; m. David John Wargetz, Jan. 2, 1981. BBA in Acctg., Baylor U., 1981. CPA, Tex. Revenue agt. asst. IRS, Dallas, 1980-81; tax acct. Computer Lang. Rsch., Inc. (Fast-Tax), Carrollton, Tex., 1982-83, sr. tax acct., 1983-84, tax acctg. supr., 1984-87, mgr. sales adminstrn., 1987-94, mgr. product support and system assurance testing, 1994—; pvt. practice acctg., Grapevine, Tex., 1983—. Mem. Nat. Arbor Day Found., Nebraska City, Nebr., 1984—, Wilderness Soc., Washington, 1985—; charter mem. Lone Star Composting Corps, master composter, 1993—. Recipient Star Performer Intensity award CLR-FAST-TAX, 1988, v.p. award, 1989. Mem. Am. Inst. CPA's, Tex. State Bd. Pub. Accountancy (Dallas chpt.), Baylor U. Alumni Assn., Tex. Enrolled Agts. Soc. (Metroplex chpt.). Republican. Baptist. Home: 1107 Silverlake Dr Grapevine TX 76051-3391 Office: Computer Lang Rsch Inc 2395 Midway Rd Carrollton TX 75006-2521

WARING, MARY LOUISE, social work administrator; b. Pitts., Feb. 15, 1928; d. Edith (McCallum) W. AB, Duke U., 1949; MSS, Smith Coll., 1951; PhD, Brandeis U., 1974. Lic. clin. social worker, Tenn. Dir. social svc. Cambridge (Mass.) Mental Health Ctr., 1965-70; assoc. prof. Sch. Social Work Fla. State U., Tallahassee, 1974-77; prof. Fordham U., N.Y.C., 1977-82; cons. Dept. Human Svc., N.J., 1983-84; cons., sr. staff mem. Family Counseling Svc. Bergen County, Hackensack, N.Y., 1984-86; dir. Step One Employee Assistance Program Fortwood Ctr., Inc., Chattanooga, 1986—; sr. supervising social worker Judge Baker Guidance Ctr., Boston, 1965-70. Contbr. articles to profl. jours. Mem. Citizen Amb. Program Human Resource Mgmt. Delegation to Russia, 1993. Recipient Career Tchr. award Nat. Inst. Alchohol and Alchohol Abuse, 1972-74; traineeship NIMH, 1949-51. Mem. NASW (charter), Acad. Cert. Social Workers, Nat. Mus. Women in Arts (charter), Smithsonian Assocs. Office: Fortwood Ctr Inc 1028 E 3rd St Chattanooga TN 37403-2170

WARLICK, KARLA JAN, school counselor; b. Levelland, Tex., Aug. 6, 1949; d. Milton Jr. and Mary Tom (Bradford) Tankersley; m. Philip Owen Warlick, Aug. 24, 1968 (div. Oct. 1994); children: Allyson Wynn, Philip Owen II. BS, Tex. Women's U., 1970; MA, U. Tex., Odessa, 1991. Tchr. Richardson (Tex.) Ind. Sch. Dist., 1970-72; agt. Irene Smith Realtors, Austin, 1977-79; broker Bohannan Realtors, Midland, Tex., 1979-80; broker in pvt. practice Midland, 1980-92; tchr. Hillander Sch., Midland, 1980-81; assessment coord. Midland Coll., Midland, 1988-90; therapist, substance abuse supr. Dept. Family Svcs., Midland, 1990-91; counselor Midland Ind. Sch. Dist., Midland, 1991—; counselor in pvt. practice Midland, 1992—; mem. gifted and talented com. Midland Ind. Sch. Dist., 1992—. Active Midland Symphony Guild; bd. dirs. Am. Heart Assn., Midland, 1982-85. Mem. Am. Counseling Assn., Tex. Counseling Assn., Permian Basin Counseling Assn. (mem. legis. com. 1992—), Zeta Tau Alpha. Methodist. Home: 3209 Elma Dr Midland TX 79707-5200

WARN, GRACE HELEN, city official; b. Chgo., Feb. 5, 1922; d. Fred Albert and Sophie (Kozakiewicz) Miller; m. Raymond B. Stosik, May 7, 1949 (div. Oct. 1968); children: Michael, Raymond, Patricia, Susan, David, Grace, James, Paul. Grad. high sch., Chgo. Cert. pub. housing mgr., Mich. Exec. dir. Alpena (Mich.) Housing Commn., 1952—. With WAC, 1943-45, PTO. Mem. Mich. Housing Dirs. Assn., Alpena Assn. for Retarded, VFW, DAV, Am. Assn. Ret. Persons, Am. Diabetes Assn., Elks. Roman Catholic. Home: 313 S 6th St Alpena MI 49707-2519 Office: Alpena Housing Commn 2340 S 4th St Alpena MI 49707-3017

WARNAT, WINIFRED L., federal agency administrator; b. Grosse Point, Mich., Feb. 8, 1943; d. Rudolf Paul Walter and Frieda (Lupp) W. BA, Fla. Atlantic U., 1965, MEd, 1967; PhD, Am. U., 1971. Dept. mgr., exec. trainee Burdine's Dept. Store, Miami, Fla., 1965-69; asst. dean Grad. Sch. Arts and Sci., clin. prof. Coll. of Medicine, chair, prof. Sch. of Edn. Howard U., Washington, 1969-77; dir. Adult Learning Potential Inst., rsch. prof. Sch. of Edn. Am. U., 1977-81; dir. Nat. Ctr. Teaching and Learning Eastern Mich. U., 1981-84; tech., trade and indsl. edn. specialist Dept. of Edn., Washington, 1984-88, dir. divsn. vocat.- tech. edn. Office of Vocat. and Adult Edn., 1988—; spl. edn. tchr. Deerfield Beach Jr. High Sch., Fla.; vocat. rehab. counselor Broward County, Fla.; career guidance and placement counselor Gallaudet Coll., Washington; disting. lectr. Mich. Dept. of Edn., 1983, 84. Contbr. articles to profl. jours., chpts. to books. Commr. Montgomery County Commn. on Women, Md., 1974-76; U.S. del. World Congress on Vocat. Edn., Sydney, Australia, 1988; U.S. del., U.S. Dept. of Edn. rep. to Conf. on Tech. Change and Human Resources Devel.: the Svc. Sector, Orgn. Econ. Coop. and Devel., Utrecht, Netherlands, 1989, U.S. study coord. Project on The Changing Role of Vocat. and Tech. Edn. and Tng. Office: Office of Vocational & Adult Edn Dept of Edn 330 C St SW Rm 4315 Washington DC 20202-7241*

WARNATH, MAXINE AMMER, organizational psychologist, educator; b. N.Y.C., Dec. 3, 1928; d. Philip and Jeanette Ammer; m. Charles Frederick Warnath, Aug. 20, 1952; children: Stephen Charles, Cindy Ruth. B.A., Bklyn. Coll., 1949; M.A., Columbia U., 1951, Ed.D., 1982. Lic. psychologist, Oreg. Various profl. positions Hunter Coll., U. Minn., U. Nebr., U. Oreg., 1951-62; asst. prof. psychology Oreg. Coll. Edn., Monmouth, 1962-77; assoc. prof. psychology, chmn. dept. psychology and spl. edn. Western Oreg. St. Coll., Monmouth, 1978-83, prof. 1986—, dir. organizational psychology program 1983—; pres. Profl. Perspectives Internat., Salem, Oreg., 1987—; cons., dir. Orgn. Rsch. and Devel., Salem, Oreg., 1983-87, seminar leader Endeavors for Excellence program. Author: Power Dynamism, 1987. Mem. APA (com. pre-coll. psychology 1970-74), ASTD, N.Y. Acad. Sci., Oreg. Acad. Sci., Oreg. Psychol. Assn. (pres. 1980-81, pres.-elect 1979-80, legis. liaison 1977-78), Western Psychol. Assn. Office: Profl Perspectives Internat PO Box 2265 Salem OR 97308-2265

WARNER, HEIDI C., community health nurse; b. Thomasville, NC, Nov. 7, 1962; d. Walter Vance and Virginia Ruth (Beck) Warner. BSN, N.C. U., Charlotte, 1985. RN, N.C.; cert. in audiometry. Clin. rsch. assoc. tng. The Blethen Group, Research Triangle Park, N.C.; audiometrist ELB & Assocs., Chapel Hill, N.C.; cmty. health nurse Tar Heel Home Health, Raleigh. Walter C. Teagle Found. nursing scholar. Exxon Co. USA. Mem. Nat. Honor Soc., Phi Eta Sigma. Republican. Methodist.

WARNER, JANET CLAIRE, software design engineer; b. Portland, Oreg., May 2, 1964; d. W. J. and Wendelyn A. (Twombly) W. Student, Clackamas Community Coll., 1982-85; BS in Computer Sci., U. Portland, 1987, MSEE, 1992. Systems asst. U. Portland, 1986-87, programmer Applied Rsch. Ctr., 1987; software design engr. Photon Kinetics, Inc., Beaverton, Oreg., 1987-92; software engr. FLIR Sys., Inc., Portland, 1993; ind. software cons., 1993—. Mem. IEEE, Assn. Computing Machinery (chmn. U. Portland chpt. 1986-87), Soc. Women Engrs. (treas. Oreg. sect. 1988-89), U. Portland Alumni Assn. (Portland programming bd. 1993—), Portland Rose Soc., Eta Kappa Nu (treas. chpt. 1991-92).

WARNER, JANET RENEE, nurse; b. Albany, Ga., Mar. 22, 1963; d. Ronald LeMoyne and Gail Patricia (Syno) W. AA, U. Iowa, 1981; ASN, Darton Coll., 1985; postgrad., SUNY. RN, Ga.; cert. neonatal intensive care nurse, NCC. Nurse pediats. ICU Phoebe Putney Meml. Hosp., Albany, Ga., 1985-87; nurse, patient rep. Pediat. Svcs. of Am., Atlanta, 1987-88; clin. supr., high tech specialist Vis. Nurse Svcs., Atlanta, 1988-90; quality improvement coord., charge nurse North Fulton Regional Hosp., Roswell, Ga., 1990—; expert witness Fulton County Med. Examiners Office, Atlanta, 1989-91. Mem. Assn. Women Health Nurses. Republican. Lutheran. Office: North Fulton Regional Hosp 3000 Hospital Rd Roswell GA 30076

WARNER, JUDITH (ANNE) HUSS, educator; b. Plainfield, N.J., June 15, 1936; d. Charles and Martha McMullen (Miller) Huss; m. Howard R. Warner, June 14, 1958; children: Barbara, Robert. BS in Elem. Edn., Russell Sage Coll., 1959. Elem. tchr. Pitts. Bd. Edn., 1959-60; home tchr. Napa (Calif.) Sch. Bd., 1974-77; substitute tchr. Allegheny Intermediate Unit, Pitts., 1977—. Leader Girl Scouts U.S.A., Pitts., 1966-70; vol. Children's Hosp., PItts., 1967-74, Jefferson Hosp., Pitts., 1977-88; pres., trustee Whitehall Libr., Pitts., 1984-92; pres., bd. dirs. Friends of Whitehall Libr., Pitts., 1969-94. Mem. AAUW, DAR. Republican. Methodist. Home: 4985 Wheaton Dr Pittsburgh PA 15236-2064

WARNER, LAVERNE, education educator; b. Huntsville, Tex., Aug. 14, 1941; d. Clifton Partney and Velma Oneta (Steely) W. BS, Sam Houston State U., 1962, MEd, 1969; PhD, East Tex. State U., 1977. Cert. elem. sch. tchr., Tex. First grade tchr. Port Arthur (Tex.) Ind. Sch. Dist., 1962-64; kindergarten tchr. Burlington (Vt.) Community Schs., 1964-66; first grade tchr. Aldine Sch. Dist., Houston, 1967-68; music tchr. Crawfordsville (Ind.) Community Schs., 1968-71; prof. early childhood edn. Sam Houston State U., Huntsville, 1975—, chmn. faculty senate, 1988-89; chair faculty senate Sam Houston State U., 1990-91, chair-elect, 1989-90. Author: (with P. Berry) Tunes for Tots, 1982, (with K. Craycraft) Fun with Familiar Tunes, 1987, Language in Centers: Kids Communicating, 1991, Theme Escapapdes, 1992, What If...Themes, 1993; contbg. editor Good Apple, Inc., Carthage, Ill., 1986-88, 91-93; contbr. over 60 articles to profl. jours. Mem. Huntsville Leadership Inst., 1986-88, chmn. adv. bd. 1987-88, chmn. 1987-88; Community Child Care Assn., Huntsville, 1988-90. Recipient Sam Houston State U. Excellence in Teaching award, 1992, Tchr. Educator of Yr. award Tex. Assn. for Edn. Young Children, 1992. Mem. Tex. Assn. Coll. Tchrs. (life, past pres.), Nat. Assn. for Edn. Young Children (life), Tex. Elementary-Kindergarten Nursery Educators (state pres. 1982-84), Tex. Assn. for Edn. Young Children (v.p. 1988-89, newsletter editor, 1991-93, Teacher Educator of Yr. 1992, pres.-elect 1993—, pres. 1995), Huntsville Leadership Inst. Alumni Assn. (pres. 1988-89), Phi Delta Kappa (area 3H coord. 1986-92, Svc. Key 1987), Sam Houston Assn. for Edn. Young Children (charter, pres-elect, 1991-92, pres. 1992-93), Sam Houston Univ. Women (pres. 1985-86), Huntsville High Sch. Ex-Students Assn. (charter, pres. 1989-91). Mem. Ch. of Christ. Office: Sam Houston State U Coll Edn and Applied Sci Huntsville TX 77341

WARNER, LOUISE OMAN, physician, researcher; b. Columbus, Ohio, Jan. 19, 1930; d. Galen Francis and Mary Caroline (Hills) Oman; m. E. Jackson Warner, Sept. 12, 1953; children: David O., Gale L. BSc, Ohio State U., Columbus, 1951; MD, Ohio State U., 1955. Diplomate Am. Bd. Anesthesiology. Staff anesthesiologist Children's Hosp., Columbus, 1960-85, dir. clin. anesthesia rsch., 1986—. Bd. dirs. Pickaway County YMCA, Circleville, Ohio, 1977—, Stratford Ecol. Ctr., Delaware, Ohio, 1990—, Innovative Farmers Ohio, Delaware, 1994—. Mem. AMA, Ohio Med. Assn., Pickaway County Med. Soc. (pres. 1976), Am. Women's Med. Assn. Home and Office: 5353 Williams Rd Ashville OH 43103-9647

WARNER, PATRICIA ANN, hospital administrator; b. Pontiac, Mich., Apr. 4, 1945. BE in Elem. Edn., U. Mich., 1967, MPH in Health Planning and Adminstrn., 1977. Tchr. 4th grade Lakewood Elem. Sch., Ann Arbor, Mich., 1967-68; program devel. planner VISTA, 1968-69; nat. exec. sec. Med. Com. Human Rights, Chgo., 1970-72; rsch. asst., spl. asst. to dir. divsn. Emergency Med. Svcs. and Hwy. Safety Ill. Dept. Pub. Health U. Ill. Sch. Pub. Health, 1972-74; asst. dir. Office of Emergency Med. Svcs. Mass. Dept. Pub. Health, 1974-76; adminstrv. mgr., disaster dir. emergency svcs. U. Mich. Hosps., Ann Arbor, 1977-80, ops. and policy analyst office of exec. dir., 1981-83, asst. hosp. adminstr. ambulatory care svcs., 1983-85, assoc. hosp. adminstr. ambulatory care svcs., 1985-87, interim assoc. dir. and adminstr., 1987-89, assoc. hosp. dir. and adminstr., 1989-94, assoc. hosp dir ops. and ambulatory sys., 1994—, adminstr. C.S. Mott Children's Hosp. and Svcs., Women's Svcs., Psychiat. Svcs., 1994—. Mem. editl. bd. Inside Ambulatory Care; contbr. articles to profl. jours. Mem. APHA (health adminstrn. sect. coun., chair women health adminstrs. network), Am. Hosp. Assn. (adv. bd. ambulatory care, mem. Am. Hosp. Assn.-Soc. for Hosp. Planning, bd. govs., pres. Am. Hosp. Assn.-Soc. Ambulatory Care Profls. 1994, quality assurance com.). Home: 1716 Morton Ave Ann Arbor MI 48104 Office: U Mich Hosps D-5202 MPB Box 0718 1500 E Medical Ctr Dr Ann Arbor MI 48109

WARNER, PATRICIA JOAN, psychotherapist; b. Greenville, N.C., Mar. 5, 1947; d. Joseph Ophir and Florence Genevieve (Jenkins) Teel; m. Richard Barr Cayton, May 21, 1971 (div. 1978); 1 child, Heather Jeanine; m. Michael Roy Warner, Jan. 9, 1987. BS in Elem. Edn., East Carolina U., 1968, MA in Guidance an Counseling, 1969. Lic. profl. counselor, Ga., Tenn.; nat. cert. counselor. Mental retardation counselor Pineland Mental Health, Jesup, Ga., 1983-85; mental health counselor Jesup, 1985-89; therapist, adolescence substance abuse Sci. Applications Internat., Nuernberg, Germany, 1989-92; therapist, adolescent Action for Youth, Clarksville, Tenn., 1992—; chairperson Troubled Childrens Com., Baxley, Ga., 1988; presenter Am. Women's Activities in Germany, 1989. Recipient Letter of Commendation Comdr. U.S. Army Europe, 1991. Mem. Am. Counseling Assn., Erlangen Amateur Radio Soc. (sec. 1990-92), Clarksville Amateur Transmitting Soc., Assn. of Specialists in Group Work. Democrat. Home: 447 Winding Way Rd Clarksville TN 37043-5191 Office: Harriett Cohn Mental Health Ctr 511 8th St Clarksville TN 37040-3093

WARNICK, CHRISTINA HOFFMANN, development officer; b. Aarau, Aargau, Switzerland, Jan. 19, 1963; came to the U.S., 1963; d. Charles Richard and Karin (Westling) H. BA, Haverford Coll., 1985; MSEd, U. Pa., 1990. Paralegal Pepper Hamilton & Scheetz, Phila., 1985-86; annual giving coord., dorm parent Westtown (Pa.) Sch., 1986-91, Spanish tchr., 1987-88, 89-90; dir. annual giving Nat. Cathedral Sch., Washington, 1991—. Mem. NOW, Nat. Abortion Rights League, Amnesty Internat., Potomac Pedlars. Democrat. Mem. Soc. of Friends. Office: Nat Cathedral Sch Mount Saint Alban Washington DC 20016

WARNICK, PATRICIA ANN, health care executive, nurse ethicist; b. Shenandoah, Pa., Sept. 30, 1948; d. Alfred Samuel and Anna Patricia (Knapp) W. Diploma in nursing, Coatesville (Pa.) Hosp., 1972; BS in Sociology, St. Joseph's U., 1980, MS in Health Adminstrn., 1982. RN, Pa.; CEN; cert. ACLS. Staff nurse Presbyn. Hosp.-U. Pa. Med. Ctr., Phila., 1972-75, 87—, asst. nurse mgr. ICU, 1975-76, staff nurse emergency dept., 1976-78, hospice nurse, 1978-80, asst. nurse mgr. emergency room, 1981-82, clin. specialist emergency dept. and ambulatory care, 1982-83, dir. hospice services and asst. dir. Presbyn. Home Health, 1983-87, nurse emergency dept., 1987—; clin. preceptor Villanova (Pa.) U., 1985-86; mem. steering com., treas. P.M.C. Founds. for the Advancement of Nursing; mem., sec. ethics com. Presbyn. Hosp.-U. Pa. Med. Ctr., 1986—, mem. nursing practice com., 1986-88. Vol. nurse ARC; chmn. svc. and rehab. com. Am. Cancer Soc., Phila., 1987-90; mem. Del. Valley Ethics Com. Network; mem. Phila. Gospel Seminar Choir, 1990—. Mem. NAAFA, Nat. League for Nursing, Nat. Hospice Orgn., Pa. Hospice Orgn. (ethics com.), Emergency Nurses Assn., Alpha Sigma Lambda. Democrat. Roman Catholic. Home: Washington Bldg Apt A214 3900 City Ave Philadelphia PA 19131-5606 Office: Presbyn U Pa Med Ctr 51 N 39th St Philadelphia PA 19104-2640

WARREN, AMY DIANE, veterinarian; b. Mt. Kisco, N.Y., Mar. 23, 1959; d. Bryan Pope and Jane (Walker) W. BS in Chemistry, Antioch Coll., 1982; DVM, U. Pa., 1986. Vet. Dr. Robert Weber, Mechanicsburg, Pa., 1986-87, Dr. Leonard Patrick, 1987-93, Stanton Equine Assocs., Phila. and Wilmington, Del., 1993—. Mem. Am. Vet. Med. Assn., Pa. Vet. Med. Assn., Internat. Vet. Acupuncture Soc. Home: 8319 Childs Rd Glenside PA 19038

WARREN, CAROLINE FRANKIL, association executive; b. Phila., Jan. 29, 1957; d. Gideon Alexander and Elaine May (Schlesinger) Frankil; m. Richard Fenton Warren, May 26, 1991. BS, Skidmore Coll., 1980. Mgr. La. Racquetball & Health Club, Kenner, 1980-81; tchr., dir. dance program St. Martin's Episcopal Sch., New Orleans, 1981-84; adminstrv. dir. Delta

Festival Ballet Co., New Orleans, 1984-87; dir. mktg. and edn. Fairfax (Va.) Symphony Orch., 1988-91; dir. membership Corcoran Gallery Art, Washington, 1991-92; mgr. mem. svcs. AAUW, Washington, 1992-95, assoc. dir. membership, 1995—; dancer Delta Festival Ballet, 1980-87; mem. faculty New Orleans Ctr. for Creative Arts, 1984-88; freelance choreographer Fairfax Ballet, 1989-90. Mem. artist's roster La. Div. Arts, Baton Rouge, 1986-87; del. La. Heritage Congress, 1987; bus. vol. for arts Cultural Alliance Greater Washington, 1992—. Ford Found. scholar Pa. Ballet Sch., 1973-74. Mem. Am. Soc. Assn. Execs. Home: 108 E Alexandria Ave Alexandria VA 22301-2013 Office: AAUW 1111 16th St NW Washington DC 20036-4873

WARREN, FAYE HANSON, banker; b. Grand Forks, N.D., Aug. 31, 1953; d. Charles Henry Hanson and Mary Zella (Ziegler) Starks; m. G. Daniel Warren, Nov. 18, 1978; children: Ross Hanson, C. Daniel. BSBA, U. Mont., 1976, MBA, 1983. Banker First Bank System, Missoula, Mont., 1976—; dir. adv. bd. Women's Econ. Devel. Group, Missoula, 1986—, St. Patrick Hosp., Missoula, 1989—; dir. gov. bd. No. Rockies Med. Svcs., Inc., Missoula, 1994. Steering com. mem. U. Mont. Found. Excellence Fund, Missoula, 1989—; bd. dirs. Missoula Area Econ. Devel Coun., 1995—. Mem. Internat. Women's Forum, Robert Morris Assocs. (pres. Western Mont. group 1992-93), C. of C. Rangers (Missoula), Rotary. Office: First Bank Missoula 2801 Brooks St Missoula MT 59801-7717

WARREN, JANET ELAINE, librarian; b. Lindsborg, Kans., Sept. 19, 1951; d. Jack Edward and Mildred Louise (Ahlstedt) Beebe; m. Perry DeLong Warren, July 6, 1974; children: Emily Louise, Britta Elizabeth. Student Stephens Women's Coll., 1969-70; BS in Edn., U. Kans., 1973; MLS, Emporia State U., 1974. Asst. dir. Goodland Pub. Library (Kans.), 1974-75, libr. dir., 1975—. Bd. dirs. Sherman County Jr. Miss Program, 1979; mem. exec. com. N.W. Kans. Library System, 1988—; pres. Chpt. Philantropic Edn. Orgn., 1992-94. Mem. ALA, Kans. Libr. Assn., Mountain Plains Libr. Assn., AAUW. Republican. Club: Thalia Women's (pres. 1982-83, 90-91). Home: PO Box 185 Goodland KS 67735-0185 Office: Goodland Pub Libr 812 Broadway Goodland KS 67735

WARREN, LESLEY ANN, actress; b. N.Y.C., Aug. 16, 1948. Studied ballet, N.Y.C.; studied acting, The Actors Studio, N.Y.C. TV appearances include Rodgers and Hammerstein's Cinderella, 1964, Fight for Jenny, 1986, 27 Wagons Full of Cotton, 1990, A Seduction in Travis County, 1991, In Sickness and in Health, 1991; Broadway debut in 110 in the Shade, 1963, Drat the Cat, 1964, Metamorphosis, Three Penny Opera; films include The Happiest Millionaire, 1967, Harry and Walter Go to New York, 1976, Victor/Victoria, 1982, Songwriter, Choose Me, Clue, Apology, 1986, Burglar, 1987, Cop, 1988, Baja Oklahoma, 1988, Worth Winning, 1989, Life Stinks, 1991, Pure Country, 1992, The Color of Night, 1994; TV mini-series include 79 Park Ave., 1977, Beulah Land, 1980, Pearl, Evergreen, 1985, Family of Spies, 1990; TV films include Seven in Darkness, 1969, Love Hate Love, 1971, Assignment Munich, 1972, The Daughters of Joshua Cabe, 1972, The Letters, 1973, The Legend of Valentino, 1975, Betrayal, 1978, Portrait of a Stripper, 1979, Beulah Land, 1980, Portrait of a Showgirl, 1982, A Flight for Jenny, 1986, Baja Oklahoma, 1988, Family of Spies, 1990, A Seduction in Travis County, 1991, In Sickness and Health, 1992, Willing to Kill: The Texas Cheerleader Story, 1992. *

WARREN, MARY ALICE, health science association administrator; b. Lorain, Ohio, Apr. 12, 1931; d. Howard Edson and Emma Grace (Warren) Dulmage; m. Grant Harland Muse, Oct. 21, 1950 (div. July 1963); children: Howard Lee, George Harland, Michele Adrienne; m. Joe Sherman Warren, Dec. 21, 1981. Ed. pvt. schs., Oberlin, Ohio and Berkeley, Calif. Dir. Midwest Celiac Sprue Assn., Des Moines, 1985-86, Celiac Sprue Assn., Omaha, 1986-89; dir., founder Celiacs of the Desert, Palm Springs, Calif., 1988-89; co-dir., founder Gluten Intolerance Group of Fla., Cocoa Beach, Fla., 1990—; founder Celiac Experience, Cocoa Beach, 1991—; facilitator Celiac Experience II, Cocoa Beach, 1992; co-facilitator Celiac Experience III, Cocoa Beach, 1994. Editor Celiac ActionLine, 1990—. Civic coord. Vols. Against Drugs and Alcohol, Palm Springs, 1988-89; campaign coord. Bono for Palm Springs Mayor, 1988; vol. hydrotherapist Crippled Children's Ctr., Merritt Island, Fla., 1989—. Mem. Celiac Disease Found., Can. Celiac Soc., Gluten Intolerance Group of N.Am. Home: 112 Saint Croix Ave Cocoa Beach FL 32931-3335

WARREN, MILDRED ELBERTA, banker; b. London, Oct. 17, 1944; d. Ira M. and Janie (Vandeventer) W. Student, Sue Bennett Coll., London, Ky., 1962-64, Am. Inst. Banking., Lexington, Ky., 1973-79, 89; diploma in interior decorating, LaSalle Extension U., 1974. Supr. book-keeping and proof 1st Nat. Bank, London, 1969-73, asst. cachier, 1973-76, asst. v.p., 1977-80; v.p. 1st Nat. Bank & Trust, London, 1981—. Mem. welfare chair Bus. and Profl. Women, Laurel County, Ky., 1986-88. Fellow Nat. Geographic Soc., World Changers Internat. (Inner Cir. award 1985); mem. Fin. Women Internat. Baptist. Office: 1st Nat Bank and Trust 202 S Main St London KY 40741-1865

WARRICK, MILDRED LORINE, library consultant, civic worker; b. Kellerton, Iowa, June 21, 1917; d. Webie Arthur and Bonnie Lorine (Hyatt) DeVries; m. Carl Wesley Warrick, Feb. 11, 1937 (dec. June 1983); children: Carl Dwayne, Arthur Will; m. John B. Irwin, Feb. 1, 1994. BS in Edn., Drake U., 1959; M of Librarianship, Kans. State Tchrs. Coll., 1970. Cert. tchr., libr., Iowa. Elem. tchr. Monroe Ctr. Rural Sch., Kellerton, Iowa, 1935-37, Denham Rural Sch., Grand River, Iowa, 1945-48, Grand River Ind. Sch., 1948-52, Woodmansee Rural Sch., Decatur, Iowa, 1952-55, Centennial Rural Sch., Decatur, 1955-56; elem. tchr., acting libr. Cen. Decatur Sch., Leon, Iowa, 1956-7l, media libr. jr. and sr. high sch., 1971-79; libr. Northminster Presbyn. Ch., Tucson, 1985-93, advisor, 1994—; media resource instr. Graceland Coll., Lamoni, Iowa, 1971-72; lit. dir. S.W. Iowa Assn. Classroom Tchrs., 1965-69. Editor (media packet) Mini History and Quilt Blocks, 1976, Grandma Lori's Nourishing Nuggets for Body and Soul, 1985, As I Recall (Loren Drake), 1989, Foland Family Supplement III, 1983; author: (with Quentin Oiler) Van Der Vlugt Family Record, 1976; compiler, editor Abigail Specials, 1991; compiler Tribute to Ferm Mills 1911-1992, 1992; co-editor: (with Dorothy Heitlinger) Milestones and Touchstones, 1993; contbr. articles to publs. Leader Grand River 4-H Club for Girls, 1954-58; sec. South Ctrl. Iowa Quarter Horse Assn., Chariton, 1967-68; chmn. Decatur County Dems., 1981-83, del., 1970-83; pianist Salvation Army Amphi League of Mercy Rhythm Noters, 1984-90; pianist, dir. Joymakers, 1990—; Sunday Sch. tchr. Decatur United Meth. Ch., 1945-54, 80-83, lay speaker, 1981-83, dir. vacation Bible sch., 1982, 83. Named Classroom Tchr. of Iowa Classroom Tchrs. Assn., 1962, Woman of Yr., Leon Bus. and Profl. Women, 1978, Northminster Presbyn. Ch. Women, 1990; English and reading grantee Nat. Dept. Edn., 1966. Mem. NEA (life), AAUW (chmn. Tucson creative writing/cultural interests 1986-87, 89-93, historian, 1994—, Honoree award for ednl. found. programs Tucson br., Svc. award 1991), Internat. Reading Assn. (pres. Clarke-Ringgold Decatur chpts. 1967-68), Cen. Community Tchrs. Assn. (pres. 1961-62), Pima County Ret. Tchrs. Assn. (pres. 1989-90), Decatur County Assn. (pres. 1961-63), Decatur County Ret. Tchrs. Assn. (historian 1980-83), Iowa Edn. Assn. (life), Presbyn. Women (hon. life 1990—), Luth. Ch. Libr. Assn. (historian Tucson area chpt. 1991-92, v.p. 1993-94, pres. 1994—), Delta Kappa Gamma (pres. Iowa Beta XI chpt. 1974-76, sec. 1984-85, historian Ariz. Alpha Gamma chpt. 1986-89). Democrat. Presbyterian. Home: 2879 E Presidio Rd Tucson AZ 85716-1539

WARRIS, ANNA CUMMINGS, religious organization executive; b. Phila., Aug. 8, 1912; d. James Emlen and Anna May (Mock) Cummings; widow; 1 child, Joseph Emlen. Student, Wheaton Coll., 1931-32, Albany Bible Inst., 1933-34, Pa. State U., 1934-35, U. Ariz., 1955-56, Temple U., 1958-59. Cert. SEC, Nat. Assn. Security Dealers. Soil conservationist USDA, 1941-42; acctg. clk. Lansdale (Pa.) Tube Co., 1943-48; office mgr. Clark and Co., Tucson, 1952-54; head acctg. dept. Philco (formerly Lansdale Tube Co.), Spring City, Pa., 1956-61; comptr., then exec. asst. to pres. De Moss Assocs., King of Prussia, Pa., 1961-66; field underwriter, pension trust work and estate planning N.Y. Life Ins. Co., Phila., 1966-91; pres. Bible Women Internat., 1974—; spkr. in field. Author: Foretaste of Glory, 1979, 2nd edit., 1982, Braille edit., 1994, Come Travel with Me, 1984, Seed of David...Son of God, 1985, Navajo transl., 1986, Portugese transl., 1992, Nest in a Rock, 1991, 2nd edit., 1993. Mem. ad hoc fin. com. Ariz. State Opera, 1975-76; active Montgomery County War Bd., 1941-42, So. Ariz. Estate Planning Com., 1975, 76. Recipient Kemper Merriam award U. Ariz., 1972; named Hon. Citizen of South Korea. Mem. Nat. Assn. Accts. (emeritus, bd. dirs. Tuscon chpt.), Nat. Women's Leaders Round Table (nat. pension leader). Republican. Mem. Brethren Ch. Home: 3941 Desmond Ln Tucson AZ 85712-3304 Office: Bible Women Internat 3941 Desmond Ln Tucson AZ 85712

WARSCHAUSKY, JUDITH SUE, clinical psychologist; b. Ann Arbor, Mich., May 29, 1957; d. Sidney Warschausky and Lorraine Nadelman; 2 children. BA cum laude, Brandeis U., 1979; MA, Boston U., 1983, PhD in Clin. Psychology, 1988. Lic. psychologist, Ill. Psychiat. counselor inpatient unit Cambridge (Mass.) Hosp., 1979-81; rsch. analyst Mass. Gen. Hosp., Boston, 1981-85; psychology trainee Douglas A. Thom Clinic, Boston, 1982-83; psychology fellow Danielsen Inst., Boston, 1984-85; assessment coord. House of Affirmation, Hopedale, Mass., 1986-87; mem. staff Ill. Masonic Med. Ctr., Chgo., 1987-92; pvt. practice, Chgo., 1987—. Vol. organizer Mothers-in-Touch, Evanston, Ill., 1990. Mem. APA. Democrat. Jewish. Office: 55 E Washington St Ste 3301 Chicago IL 60602-2207

WARSHAW, ROBERTA SUE, lawyer, financial specialist; b. Chgo., July 10, 1934; d. Charles and Frieda (Feldman) Weiner; m. Lawrence Warshaw, July 5, 1959 (div. June 1978); children: Nan R., Adam; m. Paul A. Heise, Apr. 2, 1994. Student, U. Ill., 1952-55; BFA, U. So. Calif., 1956; JD, Northwestern U., 1980. Bar: Ill. 1980. Atty., fin. specialist Housing Svcs. Ctr., Chgo., 1980-84, Chgo. Rehab. Network, 1985-91, 92—; dir. housing State Treas., State of Ill., Chgo., 1991; legal worker Sch. of Law, Northwestern U. Legal Clinic, Chgo., 1977-80; real estate developer, mgr., marketer, Chgo., 1961-77. Co-author: (manual) The Cook County Scavenger Sale Program and The City of Chicago Reactivation Program, 1991, (booklet) Fix the Worst First, 1989. Alderman 9th ward City of Evanston, Ill., 1985-93, mem. planning and devel., rules com., unified budget com., chair flood and pollution control com.; pres. Sister Cities Found.; mem. cmty. and econ. devel. policy Nat. League Cities, 1990-93; mem. Dem. Nat. Com.; bd. dirs. Dem. Ctrl. Com. Evanston, 1973—; elected committeeman Evanston Twp. Dem. Com., 1994—. Mem. ABA (affordable housing com.), Ill. State Bar Assn., Chgo. Bar Assn. (real estate coms.), Decalogue Soc. Lawyers, Chgo. Coun. Lawyers (housing com.). Home: 550 Sheridan Sq # 2G Evanston IL 60202

WARWICK, DIONNE, singer; b. East Orange, N.J., Dec. 12, 1940; m. Bill Elliott (div. 1975); children: David, Damon. Ed., Hartt Coll. Music, Hartford, Conn. As teen-ager formed Gospelaires and Drinkard Singers, then sang background for rec. studio, 1966; debut, Philharmonic Hall, N.Y. Lincoln Center, 1966; appearances include London Palladium, Olympia, Paris, Lincoln Ctr. Performing Arts, N.Y.C.; records include Don't Make Me Over, 1962, Walk On By, Do You Know The Way to San José, What The World Needs Now, Message To Michael, I'll Never Fall In Love Again, I'll Never Love This Way Again, Deja Vu, Heartbreaker, That's What Friends are For; albums include Valley of the Dolls and Others, 1968, Promises, Promises, 1975, Dionne, 1979, Then Came You, Friends, 1986, Reservations for Two, 1987, Greatest Hits, 1990, Dionne Warwick Sings Cole Porter, 1990; TV appearance in Sisters in the Name of Love, HBO, 1986; screen debut Slaves, 1969, No Night, So Long, also, Hot! Live and Otherwise; co-host: TV show Solid Gold; host: TV show A Gift of Music, 1981; star: TV show Dionne Warwick Spl. Founder Dionne Warwick Scholarship Fund, 1968, charity group BRAVO (Blood Revolves Around Victorious Optimism), Warwick Found. to Help Fight AIDS; spokeswoman Am. Sudden Infant Death Syndrome; participant U.S.A for Africa; Am. Amb. of Health, 1987. Recipient Grammy awards, 1969, 70, 80; NAACP Key of Life award, 1990. Address: Arista Records Inc 6 W 57th St New York NY 10019*

WARWICK, MARGARET ANN, health science facility administrator, consultant; b. Camden, N.J., June 7, 1931; d. Ralph Arthur and Margaret Wilson (Dilworth) W. BS, Fairleigh Dickinson U., 1955. Staff mem., med. tech. Jefferson Med. Coll. Hosp., Phila., 1955-61; clin. chemist West Jersey Health System, Camden, 1961-68; lab. supr. West Jersey Health System, Voorhees, 1968-80, mgr. clin. lab. services, 1980-85, quality assurance mgr. clin. lab svcs., 1985—; founder, pres. Clin. Lab. Cons. Services, Inc., Cherry Hill, N.J., 1985-94; mem. faculty chemist dept. Harcum Jr. Coll., Bryn Mawr, Pa., 1958-64; ednl. coordinator West Jersey Hosp. Sch. of Med. Tech., Voorhees, 1963-81. Vice pres. Wilderness Acres Civic Assn., Cherry Hill, 1980-81; chmn. com. Respond Inc. at Asbury United Meth. Ch., Camden, 1985-94, trustee, 1984-93. Mem. Am. Assn. for Clin. Chemists (secret treas. 1966-70, chmn. elect 1971-72, chmn. 1972-73 Phila chpt.), Clin. Lab Mgmt. Assn., Am. Soc. of Clin. Pathologist, Am. Soc. for Med. Tech., N.J. Soc. for Med. Tech. (bd. dirs. 1978-79). Republican. Presbyterian. Office: West Jersey Health Systems Evesham Rd Voorhees NJ 08043

WARWICK, SHARON BRENDA, art educator; b. El Paso, Tex., Dec. 18, 1946; d. George Clark and Charlene (Walker) W.; m. Alfonso Cortes, Sept. 14, 1978 (div. 1980); 1 child, Clark Lewis Cortes. BA, U. Tex., 1971; MEd, Tex. Woman's U., 1981, MFA, 1984. Cert. tchr. elem., art, secondary English., Tex. Art specialist Roger Williams Middle Sch., Providence, 1971-76; prof. English Instituto Allende, San Miguel de Allende, Mexico, 1977; tchr. English Krum (Tex.) High Sch., 1980-86; art specialist Borman Elem. Sch., Denton, Tex., 1986-92, Lakewood Elem. Sch., Euless, Tex., 1992-93, Shady Brook Elem. Sch., Bedford, Tex., 1993—; adj. instr. Cooke County Coll., Gainesville, Tex., 1984-85, Tex. Woman's U., Denton, 1985-86, U. North Tex., Denton, 1986-87; Cen. Jr. H.S., 1994-95; v.p. It Works Inc. Pub. Co., Denton, 1979-80; assoc. rep. Tex. State Tchrs. Assn., Denton, 1989-91; presenter in field. Solo exhbns. include Tex. Woman's U., Denton, 1984, Bath House Cultural Ctr., Dallas, 1989, Studio W Gallery, El Paso, Tex., 1991, Chilton Hall U. N. Tex., Denton, 1991, African Meth. Episcopal Ch., Denton, 1992; group shows include Saguarro Gallery, Denton, 1987, Lamar State U., 1989, Waterworks Gallery, 1989, Trammell Crow Ctr., Dallas, 1992, Trading Sisters Gallery, South Padre, 1993, others; solo slide/lectr. Dallas Mus. Art; contbg. author: Art Works, 1987, Spectra, 1988, Milagros, 1994. Hospitality chair Delta Kappa Gamma, Denton, 1992; exhbn. com. chair Greater Denton Arts Coun., 1987—; del. Tex. Dem. Conv., Dallas, Houston, 1985-86. Recipient Yellow Rose of Tex., Gov. Ann Richards, 1991, PTA Tchr. of Yr., Shady Brook PTA, 1993-94, various art awards, 1988—. Mem. Nat. Art Edn. Assn., Am. Craft Assn., Tex. Art Edn. Assn. (elem. div. chair 1989-91, newsletter editor, bus. mgr.), Dallas Womans Caucus for Art, Dallas Mus. Art, Modern Art Mus. Ft. Worth, North Tex. Inst. for Educators in the Visual Arts (leadership group, 1992), League United Latin Am. Citizens. Democrat. Unitarian. Home: 1003 Aileen St Denton TX 76201-2527 Office: Cen Jr H S 3191 W Pipeline Rd Evless TX 76040

WASCOU, ELLEN FERN, radio news and public service director; b. Lancaster, Pa., Jan. 12, 1950; d. Albert E. and Anne F. (Weil) W. AS in Fine Arts, Vernon Ct. Jr. Coll., 1969. With ad layouts Lancaster Newspapers, Inc., 1969-72; front office mgr. Host Resort Hotels, Lancaster, 1972-76; news broadcaster Sta. WLAN AM-FM Radio, Lancaster, 1976, Stas. WNOW AM & WQXA FM RADIO, York, Pa., 1977; news & pub. svc. dir. Sta. WLAN AM-FM Radio, Lancaster, 1977—; mem. radio com. Spanish Sta. WLCH. Dir., anchor: AP Outstanding Regularly Scheduled Newscast, 1982, 83, 86, 88, 89, AP Outstanding Pub. Affairs Program News, 1983, 90, Pa. Women in Communications - Hard News Coverage, 1988 (Best Regularly Scheduled Program News, 1989-90, Best News Series, 1991, Best Spot News, 1992). Bd. dirs. Crispus Attucks Community Ctr., Lancaster, Am. Heart Assn., Lancaster, Lancaster Dance Co.; com. mem. March of Dimes, Lancaster; mem. employment com. Lancaster City/County Human Rels. Commn. Recipient Commun. Spirit award United Way Lancaster, 1978, Friend of Edn. award Pa. State Edn. Assn., 1983, Patriotic Svc. award U.S. Dept. Treasury, 1984, Appreciation award NAACP Lancaster, 1986, Office of Impaired Driver Program, Ct. of Common Pleas of Lancaster County, 1991; Radio Sta. of Yr. honoree Pa. Am. Legion, 1992; named to Outstanding Young Women of Am., 1979. Mem. Radio & Television News Dirs. Assn., Pa. AP Broadcasters Assn. (bd. dirs. 1980—, pres. 1987-89, 1st Community Svc. award 1982), Pa. Assn. of Broadcasting. Office: WLAN AM/FM Radio 252 N Queen St Lancaster PA 17603-3588

WASH, LINDA THOMAS, sales professional; b. Shelby, N.C., Dec. 20, 1947; d. Herman Lee Jr. and Billie Jo (Carr) Thomas; m. Allen Gardner Wash, June 18, 1966 (div. Oct. 1985); children: Bradley Kevin, Jason Allen. Grad. high sch., North Augusta. Sec. Nationwide Ins. Co., North Augusta, 1966-69; tax preparer Lamar Baker, CPA, Belmont, N.C., 1981-82; corp. sec. Monroe Mobile Homes, Inc., Lowell, N.C., 1982-84; ptnr., sec. Family Choice Homes of Gaston County, Inc., Gastonia, N.C. and Clover, S.C., 1984—. Sec. Sweetwater Bapt. Ch., North Augusta, 1966-68. Home: 2467 Jacobs Rd Gastonia NC 28054-6501 Office: Family Choice Homes 1850 Us Highway 321 N Clover SC 29710-6649

WASHBURN, CARYL ANNE, occupational therapist; b. Los Cruces, N.Mex., May 3, 1943; d. Peyton Randolph Walmsley and Eleanor (Kellar) Walmsley Davis; m. Arlon Craig Washburn, Dec. 19, 1981. BS, Tex. Woman's U., 1983, MA, 1991. Registered occupational therapist. Flight attendant Am. Flyers Airline, Ardmore, Okla., 1969; libr. asst. Douglas County Libr., Roseburg, Oreg., 1970-71; clk. Forrest Industries, Roseburg, Oreg., 1971-73; adminstrv. asst. pers. Alaska Hosp., Anchorage, 1974-77; psychiat. occupational therapist Harris-H.E.B. Hosp., Bedford, Tex., 1983-84; self-contractor Multiple Home Health Agys., Dallas, 1984-87; prin. Caryls Clinic Occupational Therapy, Denton, Tex., 1987—; co-owner, operator Applied Therapeutic Scis., South Lake, Tex., 1994—; mentor O.T. students; condr. seminars for reversal of carpal tunnel syndrome without surgery (Washburn Technique). Contbr. articles to profl. jours. Vol. horseback therapy for handicapped Freedom Ride, 1983. Mem. Am. Occupational Therapy Assn., Am. Soc. Hand Therapists, Tex. Occupational Therapy Assn., South Lake C. of C., Phi Theta Kappa.

WASHBURN, DOROTHY A., entrepreneur; b. Detroit, Oct. 28, 1934; d. Dajad and Mary (Pevrenkjian) Katchadoorian; m. Floyd Donald Washburn, June 23, 1956; children: Mary Susan, Dorothy Ann, Sherry Lynn, Tina Marie. Addressograph and graphotype instr. Burrough's Corp., Detroit, 1952-54; sec. to wire divsn. mgr. Mich. Oven Co., Detroit, 1954-58; exec. sec. to pres. Walch Metal Products, Detroit, 1961-62; sec. and treas. Record Distbrs. Corp., Detroit, 1963-65; fundraiser and trip coord. Edison High Sch., Huntington Beach, Calif., 1972-90; pres. Sunset Sales, Huntington Beach, 1977—. Editor: Annual Assembly Booklet of Ladies Society of the Armenian Church of North America Western Diocese, 1993, 94. Campaign com. Gov. George Deukmejian, Doris Allen Campaign com.; chair band boosters Edison High Sch., 1975-77, chair choir boosters, 1988-90; vice chair parish coun. St. Mary Armenian Apostolic Ch., 1994, treas., social and entertainment com., 1993, advisor Ladies Soc., 1994—, advisor cultural com., 1993—, tchr. Sunday sch., 1992; corr. sec. Armenian ch. N.Am., Western Diocese, Ladies Ctrl. Coun., 1985—. Recipient Hon. Svc. award Calif. Congress of Parents, Tchrs. and Students, 1990. Armenian Orthodox.

WASHINGTON, ADANDE, clergywoman, educator; b. Mt. Clemens, Mich., Aug. 29, 1951; d. William L. and Myrtice E. (Mickens) Byrd. AB, Brown U., 1981; MATS, Gordon-Conwell Theol. Sem., South Hamilton, Mass., 1986; postgrad., UCLA, 1989—. Ordained elder African Meth. Episcopal Ch., 1990. Dir., founder Women's Shelter for Hope, Durham, N.C., 1988-89; pastor Kannapolis (N.C.) African Meth. Episcopal Ch., 1987-88; adminstr. Duke U. Office of Student Activities, Durham, 1985-89; teaching assoc. dept. anthropology UCLA, 1990-91, 92-93; advocate Sojourn Shelter for Battered Women, Santa Monica, Calif., 1991-93; dir. Ecumenical Black Campus Ministry, L.A., 1990-93; lectr. Dept. Anthropology U. Transkei, Umtata, Transkei, South Africa, 1994—; asst. pastor St. Mary's AME Ch., Umtata, South Africa, 1994—; founder, co-dir. Bldg. Bridges, Sacramento, 1992. Vol., R.I. Rape Crisis Ctr., Providence, 1980-81, Watts St. Bapt. Ch. Women's Shelter, Durham, 1985-86. Named to Outstanding Young Women of Am., 1986. Mem. AAUW, Soc. for Psychol. Study of Social Issues, Am. Acad. Religion, Transkei Assn. Univ. Women.

WASHINGTON, KATHERINE SITTON, accountant; b. Macon, Ga., Mar. 26, 1956; d. Thomas Myron and Norma Jean (Sapp) Sitton; divorced; children: Nate Lincoln, Laura Washington. BS in Acctg. and Bus. Adminstrn., Shorter Coll., 1981; MBA, Berry Coll., 1991. CPA, Ga. Acct. Ernest J. Rudert & Co., Rome, Ga., 1982-83, Gladney & Hemrick, CPA, Atlanta, 1983-87, Fisher and Co., CPA, Atlanta, 1987-88; dir. acctg. svcs. Floyd Coll., Rome, 1988—. Editor newsletter Tidings, 1994. Fellow AICPA, Ga. Soc. CPAs (chair continuing edn. 1985). Episcopalian. Home: 10 Wilson Dr Rome GA 30165

WASHINGTON, SHELLEY LYNNE, dancer; b. Washington, Nov. 3, 1954; d. Edward Freeman and Geraldine (Butler) W. Student, Interlochen Arts Acad., 1969-72, Juilliard Acad., N.Y.C., 1972-74. Dancer Martha Graham, N.Y.C., 1974-75, Twyla Tharp Dance Found., N.Y.C., 1975—, Am. Ballet Theatre, N.Y.C., 1988-91; ballet mistress and artistic assoc. dir. for Twyla Tharp, including repertory for Boston Ballet, Hubbard St. Dance Co., Martha Graham Dance Co. Dancer in film Hair, 1978; in Broadway show Singin in the Rain, 1985-86. Recipient Bessie Schonberg award for Outstanding Performing, 1987.

WASHINGTON, VALORA, foundation administrator; b. Columbus, Ohio, Dec. 16, 1953; d. Timothy Washington and Elizabeth (Jackson) Barbour; children: Omari, Kamilah. BA in Social Sci. with honors, Mich. State U., 1974; PhD, Ind. U., 1978; PhD (hon.), Bennett Coll., 1992. Assoc. instr. sch. edn. Ind. U., Bloomington, 1975-77; dir., cons. Urban League Ind., Indpls., 1977-78; substitute tchr. Indpl. Pub. Schs., 1978; dir. U. N.C., Chapel Hill, 1980-82; congrl. sci. fellow Soc. for Rsch. in Child Devel., Washington, 1981-82; prof. edn. U. N.C., Chapel Hill, 1978-83; asst. dean, assoc. prof. Howard U., Washington, 1983-86, Am. U., Washington, 1986-87; prof., v.p. Antioch Coll., Yellow Springs, Ohio, 1987-90; v.p. Kellogg Found., Battle Creek, Mich., 1990—; cons. Ford Found., N.Y.C., 1990; project evaluator Carnegie Corp., N.Y.C., 1989-90, Ohio Bd. Regents, Columbus, 1990—. Author: (with others) Creating New Linkages for the Adoption of Black Children, 1984, Project Head Start: Past, Present and Future Trends in the Context of Family Needs, 1987, Black Children and American Institutions: An Ecological Review and Resource Guide, 1988, Affirmative Rhetoric, Negative Action: The Status of Black and Hispanic Faculty in Higher Education, 1989; contbr. articles to profl. jours; contbr. chapters to numerous books. Recipient Capital U. award, 1990, award Springfield Alliance Black Educators, 1989; named one of Ten Outstanding Young Women Am., 1980, Outstanding Young Women N.C., 1980, one of 100 Young Women of Promise Good Housekeeping Mag., 1985. Mem. Nat. Coun. Negro Women (chmn. 1982-83), Am. Assn. for Higher Edn. (sec. black caucus 1989), Soc. for Rsch. in Child Devel. (pres. black caucus 1987-89), Nat. Assn. for the Edn. of Young Children (sec. of bd. dir. 1990—), Phi Delta Kappa, Delta Kappa Gamma.

WASHINGTON, VIVIAN EDWARDS, social worker, former government official; b. Claremont, N.H., Oct. 26, 1914; d. Valdemar and Irene (Quashie) Edwards; m. George Luther Washington, Dec. 22, 1950; 1 child, Valdemar Luther. AB, Howard U., 1938, MA, 1946, MSW, 1956; LHD (hon.), U. Balt., 1993. Tchr., guidance counselor, sch. social worker, asst. prin., prin. Edgar Allan Poe Sch. Program for Pregnant Girls, Balt., 1939-73; cons. Office Adolescent Pregnancy Programs, HEW, Washington, 1978-80, program devel. specialist, 1980-81; exec. dir. Balt. Coun. on Adolescent Pregnancy, Parenting and Pregnancy Prevention Inc., 1982-86, cons., 1986—; cons. to adolescent parents. Author: I Am Somebody, I Am Me, 1986; contbr. articles to profl. jours. Bd. dirs. Nat. Alliance Concerned with Sch.-Age Parents, 1970-76, pres., 1970-72; YWCA, Balt., 1966-69, United Way Central Md., 1971-80; mem. bd. visitors U. Balt., 1978-80, U. Balt. Ednl. Found., 1980, 92—, chair, 1992-94; adv. commn. on social services City of Balt., 1978-85, Govs. Coun. on Adolescent Pregnancy, 1986; chmn. Md. Gov.'s Commn. on Children and Youth, 1972-77, active 1987. Recipient Alumni award Howard U. Sch. Social Work, 1966, Clementine Peters award United Way, 1980, Sojourner Truth award Nat. Bus. and Profl. Women, 1979, Vashti Turley Murphy award Balt. chpt. Delta Sigma Theta, 1981, Balt.'s Best Blue and Silver award, 1983, Pvt. Sector Vol. Svc. award Pres. Reagan, 1984, United Way Community Svc. award, 1985, H. Mebane Turner Svc. award U. Balt. Alumni Assn., 1991, 94, Disting. Black Marylander award Towson State U., 1992, Cmty. Svc. award For Sister's Only, 1994; named to Balt. Women's Hall of Fame, 1989, Md.'s. Outstanding Ch. Woman Nat. Episc. Triennial, 1991; Paul Harris fellow Balt. Rotary, 1985. Mem. Nat. Assn. Social Work, LWV, Nat. Coun. Negro Women (life), Balt. Urban League (Equal Opportunity award 1987), Balt. Mus. Art, Delta Sigma Theta (nat. treas. 1958-63, Las Amigas Svc. award Balt. chpt. 1973),

Pierians Club. Democrat. Episcopalian. Home: 3507 Ellamont Rd Baltimore MD 21215-7422

WASHINGTON-PEEPLES, SAUNDRA L., minister; b. Highland Park, Mich., July 14; d. Andrew and Reatha (Gardner) Smith; m. Samuel Fitzgerald Peeples, Nov. 28, 1994. BSW, Marygrove Coll., Detroit, 1978; MA in Counseling Edn., Wayne State U., Detroit, 1981; MA in Theol. Studies, Ashland Theol. Sem., Ohio, 1986; DD (hon.), Tenn. Sch. Religion, 1992. Lic. to ministry AME Ch., 1971, ordained deacon, 1975, elder, 1977; lic. profl. counselor, Mich.; registered social worker, Mich.; nat. cert. counselor. Assoc. minister St. Stephens AME Ch., Detroit, 1971-73; youth pastor St. Paul AME Ch., Detroit, 1973-75; pastor Brown Chapel AME Ch., Detroit, 1975-78; asst. pastor New St. James AME Ch., Detroit, 1978-86, pastor, 1986-93; dir. pastoral bereavement and vol. svcs. Hospice of Southeastern Mich., Southfield, 1990-93; entrepreneur Grief Relief Inc., Detroit, Mich., 1994—; child care worker Barat Human Svcs., 1973-75; social worker, intern Detroit Assn. for Retarded Citizens, 1977-78; foster care worker Children's Aid Soc., 1978-81; cmty. health edn. specialist Southeastern Mich. Family Planning; social worker II Franklin Wright Settlement, 1983-85; substance abuse prevention coord. Eastwood Clinics, 1985-87; foster care supr. Spectrum Human Svcs., 1987-90. Named Ashland Sem. scholar, 1983, 84; recipient Svc. plaque Eastwood Clinics, 1986. Mem. NAACP, Greater Detroit Interfaith Roundtable, Am., Arabic and Jewish Friends Soc., Assn. of Death Edn. and Counseling, Am. Assn. Christian Counselors, Assn. of Christian Therapists, Greater Detroit Meml. Soc., Mich. Cath. Guidance Counsel, Mich. Counseling Assn. Home: 20520 Prevost St # 2C Detroit MI 48235-2165

WASHOW, PAULA BURNETTE, security company and investigation agency executive; b. Milw., Feb. 14, 1948; d. John W. and Darlene A. (Johnson) Hudson; children: Kimberly Anderson, Paul Washow. Cert. detective agy. owner, Wis.; cert. in advanced criminal interrogations and investigations, audio and CCTV surveillance and countermeasures,. Owner, pres. Alpha Omega Security, Milw., 1976—, Always Freight Inc., Franklin, 1980-85, Amrac Trucking, Franklin, Wis., 1985-91; pres. Amrac Distbrs., Inc., Franklin, Wis., 1985—, Angé, Ltd., 1994—; mem. adv. bd. Wis. Dept. Regulation and Licensing, 1992—. Vol., corp. sponsor Make-a-Wish Found. of Wis., 1989—; security chair Am. Cancer Soc. Ball, Milw., 1989; vol. Spl. Olympics Torch Run. Mem. Am. Soc. Indsl. Security, Nat. Assn. Chiefs Police, Wis. Chiefs Police Assn. (pvt. security liaison 1988—), Inter County Assn. Crime Prevention Practioners, World Assn. Detectives, Internat. Assn. Credit Card Investigators, Am. Assn. Handwriting Analysts, Wis. Narcotics Officers Assn., Internat. Chiefs of Police Assn., Wis. Juvenile Officers, Wis. Fire and Burglar Alarm Assn. (legis. com.), Wis. Women Entrepreneurs, Wis. Bus. Initiative Corp. Mentor Program. Office: 312 E Wisconsin Ave Ste 601 Milwaukee WI 53202-4305

WASICK, MARY ANN, librarian; b. Milw., July 19, 1946; d. Julius John and Florence Elizabeth (Brockway) W. BS in Edn., U. Wis., Milw., 1969; MA in Libr. Sci., U. Wis., Oshkosh, 1972; postgrad., U. Wis., 1969—. Tchr., libr. Milw. Pub. Schs., 1969-71; adminstrv. grad. asst. U. Wis., Oshkosh, 1971-72; libr. West Allis (Wis.) Pub. Libr., 1972—; reviewer in field. Bd. dirs. West Allis Hist. Soc., 1991-93; publicity chair Fountain Art Fair West Allis Art Alliance, 1991. Mem. ALA, Am. Classical League, Embroiderer's Guild Am (program chmn. 1989-90), Wis. Libr. Assn., Wis. Quilters Inc., U. Wis.-Oshkosh Alumni Assn. (life), U. Wis. Milw. Alumni Assn. (life). Home: 1310 S 98th St West Allis WI 53214-2641 Office: West Allis Pub Libr 7421 W National Ave West Allis WI 53214-4699

WASKO-FLOOD, SANDRA JEAN, artist, educator; b. N.Y.C., Mar. 12, 1943; d. Peter Edmund and Margaret Dalores (Kubek) Wasko; m. Michael Timothy Flood, June 28, 1969. BA, UCLA, 1965, postgrad., 1968-69; postgrad., Calif. State U., Northridge, summer 1968; student, Otis Art Inst., L.A., 1969, Marie Kaufman, Rio de Janeiro, 1970-72, Museo de Arte Moderno, Rio de Janeiro, 1970-73, Foothill Coll., Los Altos, Calif., 1973-74, Claremont (Calif.) Coll., 1975, U. Wis., Janesville, 1977, Beloit (Wis.) Coll., 1977-78, U. Wis., 1977-78; grad. etching student, Warrington Colescott. Instr. printmaking Washington Women's Arts Ctr., 1983; artist-in-residence U. Md., College Park, 1984; instr. printmaking Arlington (Va.) Arts Ctr., 1984-85; prof. St. Mary's (Md.) Coll., 1985; instr. printmaking Arlington County Lee Arts Ctr., 1989-95; workshop coord. cultural affairs div. Arlington County Parks, Recreation and Community Resources, 1989—. One woman shows include Wisconsin Women in the Arts Gallery, Madison, 1977, Mbari Art, Washington, 1981, Miya Gallery, Washington, 1981, Slavin Gallery, Washington, 1982, Stuart Mott House, Washington, 1983, Washington Printmakers Gallery, 1986, 88, 91, St. Peter's Ch., N.Y.C., 1989, Montana Gallery, Alexandria, Va., 1991, Montpelier Cultural Arts Ctr., Laurel, Md., 1992, Gallery 10, Washington, 1994; mus. and internat. shows include Boston Printmakers: The 39th North Am. Print Exhbn., Framingham, Mass., Jan.-Mar., 1986, Internat. Graphic Arts Found. and Silvermine Guild Arts Ctr., New Canaan, Conn., Feb., 1988, prints: Washington, The Phillips Collection, Washington, Sept.-Oct., 1988, Contemporary Am. Graphics, Book Chamber Internat., Moscow, 1990, Gallery 10 Artists of Washington D.C. Vartai Gallery, Lithuania, 1994. and numerous others; juried shows include Washington Women's Arts Ctr.: Printmakers VII show, 1985, Washington Women's Arts Ctr., 1981, 82, Seventh Ann. Faber Birren Color Show Nat. Juried Open Exhibit, Stamford, Conn., 1987, Acad. of the Arts 25th Ann. Juried Exhbn., 1989, Fla. Printmakers Nat., 1994, S.W. Tex. State U., 1995, and numerous others; invitational shows include Office of the Mayor, Mini Art Gallery, Washington, "Glimpses: Women Printmakers", 1981, Pyramid Paperworks, Balt., 1984, Gallery 10 "Nightmare Show", Washington, D.C., 1987, The Intaglio Process, The Benedicta Art Ctr. Gallery, St. Joseph, Minn., 1988, Women's Caucus for Art, Washington Artists in Perspective, Westbeth Gallery, N.Y.C., 1990, 91, Wesley Theol. Sem., 1992, Balt. City Hall, N.Am. Print Alliance, 1993, The Five Elements Women's Caucus For Art, 1994, and numerous others; galleries: Slavin Gallery, Washington, D.C., 1981-83, Washington Printmakers Gallery, Washington, 1985—, White Light Collaborative, Inc., N.Y.C., 1988-89, Montana Gallery, Alexandria, Va., 1989-91, Gallery 10, Washington, 1992—, and numerous others; collections include Nat. Mus. of Women in the Arts, Washington, Corcoran Gallery of Art, Washington, Am. Mus. of Art, Washington, Museo de Arte Moderno, Buenos Aires, Cultural Found., USSR, Coll. Notre Dame, Balt. Pres. Washington Area Printmakers, Washington, D.C., 1985-86; pub. rels. dir. Washington Women's Arts Ctr., 1980; bd. dirs. Washington Women's Arts Ctr., 1981-82. Grantee Friends of the Torpedo Factory Art Ctr., Alexandria, Va., 1989, Va. Commn. on the Arts, 1994; recipient Award of Honorable Mention Nat. Gallery of Art, 1989. Mem. Nat. Print Orgn., Pyramic Atlantic, So. Graphics Coun., Women's Caucus for Art, Coalition Washington Artists, L.A. Printmaking Soc., Washington Ctr. for Photography, Md. Printmakers, Calif. Printmakers, Calif. Printmaking Soc., Am. Print Alliance, Washington Project for the Arts, Washington Sculpture Group. Home: 8106 Norwood Dr Alexandria VA 22309-1331 Office: Lee Arts Ctr 5722 Lee Hwy Arlington VA 22207-1455 Studio: 57 N St NW Washington DC 20001-1254

WASS, HANNELORE LINA, educational psychology educator emeritus; b. Heidelberg, Germany, Sept. 12, 1926; came to U.S., 1957, naturalized, 1963; d. Hermann and Mina (Lasch) Kraft; m. Irvin R. Wass, Nov. 24, 1959 (dec.); 1 child, Brian C.; m. Harry H. Hisler, Apr. 13, 1978. B.A., Tchrs. Coll., Heidelberg, 1951; M.A., U. Mich., 1960, Ph.D., 1968. Tchr. W. Ger. Univ. Lab. Schs., 1958-60; mem. faculty U. Mich., Ann Arbor, 1958-60, U. Chgo. Lab. Sch., 1960-61, U. Mich., 1963-64, Eastern Mich. U., 1965-69; prof. ednl. psychology U. Fla., Gainesville, 1969-92; prof. emeritus, 1992—; faculty assoc. Ctr. for Gerontol. Studies U. Fla., Gainesville, 1986-92; cons., lectr. in thanatology. Author: The Professional Education of Teachers, 1974, Dying-Facing the Facts, 1979, 2d edit., 1988, 3d edit., 1994-95, Death Education: An Annotated Resource Guide, 1980, vol. 2, 1985, Helping Children Cope with Death, 1982, 2d edit., 1984, Childhood and Death, 1984; founding editor: (jour.) Death Studies, 1977—; cons. editor: Ednl. Gerontology, 1977— (book series) Death Education, Aging, and Health Care; contbr. approximately 200 articles to profl. jours. and book chpts. Mem. Am. Psychol. Assn., Gerontol. Soc., Internat. Work Group Dying, Death and Bereavement (bd. dirs.), Assn. Death Edn. and Counseling. Home: 6014 NW 54th Way Gainesville FL 32606-3265 Office: U Fla 1418 Norman Hall Gainesville FL 32611

WASSELL, IRENE MARTIN, food editor; b. Siloam Springs, Ark., Sept. 19, 1931; d. Leslie and Cora Etna (Jones) Martin; m. Bill J. Wassell, Mar. 29, 1953; children: Lisa Annette, Cynthia Lenore, Eric Lyndon. BA, U. Ark., 1978; MA, U. Ark., Little Rock, 1983. Woman's editor The Times of North Little Rock, 1978-80; staff features writer Ark. Gazette, Little Rock, 1980-90, food editor, 1990-91; food editor Ark. Dem.-Gazatte, Little Rock, 1992—. Office: Ark Dem Gazette 121 E Capitol Ave Little Rock AR 72201-3819

WASSERMAN, HELENE WALTMAN, art dealer, artist; b. Phila., Jan. 29, 1929; d. William T. and Bertha (Brener) Waltman; m. Richard M. Wasserman, June 23, 1950 (div. 1972); children: Ann Zelver, Ellen Rubinfield, Stephen; m. Mark C. Cooper, Jan. 22, 1988. BFA, U. Pa., 1951. Pvt. practice art dealer, 1972—; apptd. appraiser Supreme Ct., State of N.Y., 1978. One-woman shows at Philmont Gallery, Phila., 1964, Roko Gallery, N.Y., 1965; exhibited in group shows at Phila. Mus. Art, Pa. Acad. Fine Arts, Philbrook Mus., Tulsa, Woodmere Gallery, Roko Gallery, 1953-68. Active Nassau County Art Commn., 1968-72; trustee, Sculpture Ctr., N.Y.C., bd. dirs., 1991. Mem. Pvt. Art Dealers Assn., Cosmopolitan Club, Nature Conservancy.

WASSERMAN, KAREN BOLING, clinical psychologist, nursing consultant; b. Olney, Ill., July 29, 1944; d. Kenneth G. and Betty Jean (Varner) Boling; m. James M. Wasserman, Apr. 14, 1965; children: Nicole C., Michael B. RN, Barnes Hosp. Sch. Nursing, St. Louis, 1965; BA, Antioch Coll., 1977; Dr. of Psychology, Wright State U., 1986. Lic. psychologist, Miss., Ohio, Ind.; RN, Miss., Mo., Ohio. Staff nurse various med. facilities, 1965-76; instr. practical nurse program Ind. Vocat. Tech. Coll., Richmond, 1976-77; staff, float nurse Good Samaritan Hosp., Dayton, Ohio, 1977-78; pub. health nurse coord. Bur. Alcoholism Svcs., Dayton, 1978-79; alcoholism counselor IV Bur. Alcoholism Svcs., Dayton, Ohio, 1979-82; practicum student Wright State U. Sch. Profl. Psychology, Dayton, 1983-85; psychology intern Balt. VAMC Consortium, 1985-86; clin. psychologist Dayton VAMC, 1987-89; co-owner Fairhaven Pvt. Mental Health Clinic, Biloxi, Miss., 1989—; clin. psychologist Gulf Oaks Hosp., Biloxi, 1989—; Sand Hill Hosp., Gulfport, Miss., 1993—; psychiatric nursing cons. Mercy Hosp., Omaha, Council Bluffs, Iowa, 1987; instr. William Carey Coll. on the Coast, 1993. Chmn. cmty. svcs. Altrusa Internat., Biloxi, 1990—, treas., 1993-94; mem. Evangelism com. First United Meth. Ch., Gulfport, Miss., 1991-93, coun. on ministries, 1994; Friend of the Rainbow Warrior, Greenpeace, 1986-93. Recipient Alumnae award in Acads., Barnes Hosp. Sch. Nursing, 1965. Fellow Am. Acad. Psychologists Treating Addiction; mem. APA, Ohio Psychol. Assn., Miss. Psychol. Assn. (continuing edn. com. 1990—, chair 1994-95). Office: Fairhaven Pvt Mental Health Clinic 2635 Pass Rd Biloxi MS 39531-3722

WASSERMAN, KRYSTYNA, librarian, art historian; b. Lodz, Poland, Aug. 10, 1937; came to U.S., 1971; d. Henryk and Polina (Volk) Ostrowski; m. Paul Wasserman, Apr. 14, 1972. M in Journalism, U. Warsaw, Poland, 1963; MLS, Pratt Inst., Bklyn., 1972; MA, U. Md., 1981. Reporter Ekran-The Screen Mag., Warsaw, Poland, 1960-62; sec. edn. com. Inst. Sci., Tech. and Econ. Info., Warsaw, Poland and Internat. Fedn. for Documentation, The Hague, The Netherlands, 1962-71; ind. editor reference books College Park, Md., 1972-82; libr. Nat. Mus. Women in Arts, Washington, 1982—. Contbr. articles to profl. jours.; editor: A Guide to the World Training Facilities in Documentation and Information Work, 1965, 2nd edit., 1969. ASTEF fellow Govt. of France, 1967. Home: 4940 Sentinel Dr Apt 203 Bethesda MD 20816-3554 Office: Nat Mus Women in Arts 1250 New York Ave NW Washington DC 20005-3920

WASSERMAN, MARLIE P(ARKER), publisher; b. Chgo., Feb. 14, 1947; d. Theodore E. and Faye (Beller) Parker; m. Mark Wasserman, Nov. 24, 1968; children—Aaron David, Danielle Elizbeth. B.A., Duke U., 1969; M.A., Old Dominion U., 1970. Editor, U. Chgo. Press, 1970-78; sr. editor Rutgers U. Press, New Brunswick, N.J., 1978-83, asst. dir. and editor-in-chief, 1983-87, assoc. dir., editor-in-chief, 1987-94; exec. editor social sciences Routledge, N.Y.C., 1994—. Office: Routledge 29 W 35th St New York NY 10001-2299

WASSERMAN, ROSE, artist; b. Stamford, Conn., Jan. 23, 1921; d. Isadore and Esther (Slapin) W. BA, Pratt Inst., 1941. Pvt. practice as graphic designer, 1951-79; chair AOS dept. Pratt Inst., 1979-83, assoc. prof., 1983-85, adj. assoc. prof., 1985-94. Exhibited serigraphs and watercolor paintings in one-woman and groups shows, including Histadrut House, N.Y.C., 1975, Pratt-Manhattan Gallery, N.Y.C., 1986, 87, 88, Independence Savs. Bank, N.Y.C., 1987, Am. Artist's Profl. League, Great Neck, N.Y., Chelsea Manor, N.Y., 1993; watercolor paintings represented in pvt. collectins in N.Y., Conn., Mass., Calif. and N.J. Mem. Am. Artist's Profl. League (assoc.), Allied Artists Am. Home: 2404 Via Mariposa W # 3F Laguna Beach CA 92653

WASSERMAN, SUSAN VALESKY, accountant; b. St. Petersburg, Fla., June 5, 1956; d. Charles B. Valesky and Jeanne I. (Schulz) Morgan; m. Fred Wasserman III, May 19, 1990; 1 child, Sara Elisabeth. BS in Merchandising, Fla. State U., 1978; BA in Acctg., U. South Fla., 1983; ChFC, Am. Coll., 1991. CPA, Fla.; ChFC, Fla. Mgmt. trainee Burdines Dept. Stores, Miami, Fla., 1978-79; store mgr. Levi Straus Inc., San Francisco, 1979; pvt. practice St. Petersburg, Fla., 1980—. Paintings shown at Longboat Key (Fla.) Art Ctr. Watercolor 10 Art Show, 1993, Fla. Suncoast Watercolor Soc. Aqueous Show, Sarasota, 1994. Mem. Fla. Inst. CPAs, Am. Soc. CLUs and ChFCs (bd. dirs.). Office: 4830 49 St N Saint Petersburg FL 33709

WASSERSTEIN, WENDY, playwright; b. Bklyn., Oct. 18, 1950; d. Morris and Lola W. BA, Mt. Holyoke Coll., 1971; MA, CCNY, 1973; MFA, Yale Drama Sch., 1976. Author: (plays) Any Woman Can't, 1973, Happy Birthday, Montpelier Pizz-zazz, 1974, (with Christopher Durang) When Dinah Shore Ruled the Earth, 1975, Uncommon Women and Others, 1975 (Joseph Jefferson award, Dramalogue award, Inner Boston Critics award), Isn't It Romantic, 1981, Tender Offer, 1983, The Man in a Case, 1986, Miami, 1986, The Heidi Chronicles, 1988 (Pulitzer prize for drama 1989, Outer Critics Circle award for best Broadway play 1989, Tony award for best play 1989, New York Drama Critics Circle award 1989, Susan Smith Blackburn prize, 1989), The Sisters Rosensweig, 1993 (Outer Critics Circle award 1993); (essays) Bachelor Girls, 1990; (screenplays) Uncommon Women and Others, 1978, The Sorrows of Gin, 1979, (with Christopher Durang) House of Husbands, Isn't It Romantic, The Heidi Chronicles. Bd. dirs. Channel Thirteen, MacDowell Colony. Am. Playwrights Project grantee, 1988, Brit.-Am. Arts Assn. grantee, Hale Matthews Found. award, Commissioning Program Phoenix Theater grantee, Guggenheim fellow, 1983. Mem. British Am. Arts Assn., Found. of the Dramatists Guild. *

WASSON, BARBARA HICKAM, music educator; b. Spencer, Ind., Feb. 12, 1918. Student, DePauw U., 1937-38; BA, Vassar Coll., 1939; MusM, Chgo. Mus. Coll., 1944; postgrad., Ind. U., 1962-63. Founder, co-dir. Wasson Piano Studios, Dayton, 1946—; instr. Cedarville (Ohio) Coll., Dayton, 1970-72; adj. prof. Wright State U., Dayton, 1973-78; asst. prof. U. Cin., 1982-87. Mem. Ohio Music Tchrs. Assn. (pres. 1980-82), Dayton Music Club (pres. 1989-91), Mu Phi Epsilon (pres. Dayton alumnae chpt. 1986-88). Home: 5797 Paddington Rd Dayton OH 45459-1749

WATANABE, RUTH TAIKO, music historian, library science educator; b. Los Angeles, May 12, 1916; d. Kohei and Iwa (Watanabe) W. B.Mus., U. So. Calif., 1937, A.B., 1939, A.M., 1941, M.Mus., 1942; postgrad., Eastman Sch. Music, Rochester, N.Y., 1942-46, Columbia U., 1947; Ph.D., U. Rochester, 1952. Dir. Sibley Music Library Eastman Sch. of Music, Rochester, N.Y., 1947-84; prof. music bibliography Eastman Sch. of Music, 1978-85, historian, archivist, 1984—; adj. prof. Sch. Library Sci. State U. Coll. at Geneseo, 1975-83; coordinator adult edn. program Rochester Civic Music Assn., 1963-75; mem. adv. com. Hochstein Music Sch.; lectr. on music, book reviewer, 1966—; program annotater Rochester Philharmonic Orch., 1959—. Author: Introduction to Music Research, 1967, Madrigali-II Verso, 1978; editor: Scribners New Music Library, Vols. 2, 5, 8, 1973, Treasury of Four Hand Piano Music, 1979; contbr. articles to profl. jours., contbr. symphony orchs. of U.S., 1986, internat. music jours.; modern music librarianship, 1989; contbr. to Festschrift for Carleton Sprague Smith, 1989, De Mósica Hispana et aliis, 1990. Mem. overseers vis. com. Baxter Sch. Library Sci., Case Western Res. U., 1979-85, Alderman Book Com., 1986-89. Mem. ALA, AAUW (Pa.-Del. fellowship. 1949-50, 1st v.p. Rochester 1964-65, mem. N.Y. state bd. 1965-66, mem. nat. com. on soc.'s reflection on arts 1967-69, nat. com. Am. fellowships awards 1969-74, br. pres. 1969-71, hon. co-chair Capital Fund Drive, 1986-88, Woman of Yr. award 1990), Internat. Assn. Music Libraries (2d v.p. commn. on conservatory libraries, commn. research libraries), Am. Musicol. Soc., Music Library Assn. (v.p. 1968-70, citation 1986, mem. editorial bd. 1967—, pres. 1979-81), Music Library Assn./Internat. Assn. Music Libraries (joint com., 1986-87), Civic Music Assn. Rochester, Riemenscheider Bach Inst. (hon.), Hanson Inst. Am. Music (bd. mem. 1981—), Univ. Club, Century Club, Phi Beta Kappa (pres. Iota chpt. of N.Y. 1969-71), Phi Kappa Phi, Mu Phi Epsilon (gen. chmn. nat. conv. 1956, nat. librarian 1958-60, recipient citation 1977, Ora Ashley Lambke award 1989), Pi Kappa Lambda (sec. 1978—, treas. 1980—), Delta Phi Alpha, Epsilon Phi, Delta Kappa Gamma (parliamentarian 1986-88). Home: 111 East Ave Apt 610 Rochester NY 14604-2539 Office: Eastman Sch Music Rochester NY 14604

WATERER, BONNIE CLAUSING, home economics coordinator, child care occupations instructor; b. Toledo, Sept. 25, 1940; d. Kermit Henry and Helen Ethel (Waggoner) Clausing; m. Louis P. Waterer, June 17, 1961; children: Ryan, Reid. BS in Home Econs. Edn., Ohio State U., 1962; MA in Home Econs. Edn., San Jose State U., 1966. Cert. home economist. Tchr. James Lick High Sch., San Jose, 1963-67, 1973-76; adult edn. instr. Met. Adult Edn. Program, San Jose, 1968-75; home econs. dept. chair Independence High Sch., San Jose, 1976-81; home econs. coord. East Side Union High Sch. Dist., San Jose, 1981—; child care occupations instr. Independence High Sch., San Jose, 1989—. Named State Tchr. of Yr. Calif. Home Econs. Assn., 1994. Mem. Nat. Assn. Vocat. Home Econs. Tchrs., Am. Vocat. Assn., Am. Home Econs. Assn., Assn. Calif. Sch. Adminstrs., Calif. Home Econs. Assn. (mem. articulation com., Tchr. of Yr. 1994), Home Econs. Tchrs. Assn. Calif. (pres. 1989-91, Outstanding Tchr. award 1987), Omicron Nu, Delta Kappa Gamma. Republican. Methodist. Home: 3836 Suncrest Ave San Jose CA 95132-3204 Office: Eastside Union High Sch Dist 830 N Capitol Ave San Jose CA 95133-1316

WATERHOUSE, MONA ELISABETH, artist; b. Grangesberg, Dalarna, Sweden, June 9, 1942; came to U.S., 1966; d. Rolf Folke and Gunborg Sofia (Skog) Johansson; m. John Fredric Waterhouse, Aug. 17, 1961; 1 child, Andrew John. Student, Coventry (Eng.) Coll. Art, 1961-63; BFA summa cum laude, U. Mass., 1975, MAT, 1978. Cert. art instr., Mass., Wis. Tchr. art Covington (Va.) High Sch., 1968-70; art and critic tchr. Clarke Sch. for Deaf, Northampton, Mass., 1976-78; tchr. art John F. Kennedy Jr. High Sch., Florence, Mass., 1978, Westfield (Mass.) State Coll., 1979; instr. art U. Mass., Amherst, 1978-81; tchr. art Hadley (Mass.) Elem. Schs., 1979-81; asst. adminstr. Appleton (Wis.) Gallery Arts, 1981-84; instr. art St. Thomas More Sch., Appleton, 1983-89; free-lance artist Peachtree City, Ga., 1989—; art cons. Dignity of Man Found., San Francisco, 1975-81; art judge various art events; mem. Diocesan Art Curriculum Com., Green Bay, Wis., 1987-89; artist-in-residence Ga. Coun. for the Arts, 1991—, Fulton County Sch. Arts Program, 1991—. Exhbns. include Heter Gallery, U. Mass., Amherst, 1980, Hampshire Coll., Amherst, 1981, U. Wis., Oshkosh, 1984, Edna Carlsten Gallery U. Wis., Stevens Point, 1985, U. Wis., Menasha, 1985, Marquette Haggerty Mus., Milw., 1986, Dard Hunter Mus., Appleton, Wis., 1986, 87, The Arts Ctr., Iowa City, 1986, Neville Pub. Mus., Green Bay, Wis., 1986, 87, Milw. Inst. Art and Design, 1986, GEF Bldg., Madison, Wis., 1987, Edgewood Orchard Galleries, Fish Creek, Wis., 1987, No. Mich. U., Marquette, 1987, Fine Arts Gallery Ind. U., Bloomington, 1988, Wis. Women in the Arts, 1988-89 (travelling exhibit), Mindscape Gallery, Evanston, Ill., 1988, Milw. Art Mus., 1989, West Bend Gallery of Fine Arts, Wis., 1989, TAPPI's Internat. Paper Art Festival, Atlanta, 1990, Columbia Coll., Mo., 1991, Perspectives Gallery, Mpls., 1991, Arts Ctr., Athen, Ohio, 1991, Arts Ctr., Cartersville, Ga., 1992, Forum Gallery, Jamestown, N.Y., 1992, Hastings Seed Bldg., Atlanta, 1993, Univ. Milw. Art Gallery, 1993, Westbrook Gallery, Atlanta, 1993; publs. include Chgo. Art Rev., 1989, Fiber Arts Design Book 4, 1991. Active Amnesty Interant., Save the Children. Recipient Individual Artist grant Ga. Coun. for Arts and Fulton County Arts Coun., 1994. Mem. Nat. Art Edn. Assn., Internat. Assn. Paper Artists, Internat. Soc. Edn. through Art, Wis. Women in Arts, Friends Dard Hunter Paper Mus. Democrat. Home and Office: 102 Delbank Pt Peachtree City GA 30269-1184

WATERMAN, CAROLYN SUE, librarian, educator; b. McLouth, Kans., Oct. 29, 1941; d. Leland Leroy and Mildred Beatrice (Osborn) McPherson; m. Neil Albert Waterman, June 26, 1966; 1 child, Steven Neil. BS, McPherson Coll., 1963. Secondary bus. tchr. Greenleaf (Kans.) Rural High Sch., 1963-66, Morrowville (Kans.) High Sch., 1966-67; tchr. 2d and 3d grade Greenleaf Elem .Sch., 1967-68, tchr. 3d, 4th, and 5th grades, 1970-80; 3d grade tchr. Washington (Kans.) Elem. Sch., 1969-70, libr., 1980—. Mem. Washington Tchrs. Assn. (sec. 1986-88, 84-85), Kans. Assn. Sch. Librs. Home: RR 2 Box 212 Washington KS 66968-9331

WATERMAN, MIGNON REDFIELD, public relations executive, state legislator; b. Billings, Mont., Oct. 13, 1944; d. Zell Ashley and Mable Erma (Young) Redfield; m. Ronald Fredrick Waterman, Sept. 11, 1965; children: Briar, Kyle. Student, U. Mont., 1963-66. Lobbyist Mont. Assn. Chs., Helena, 1986-90; senator State of Mont., Helena, 1990—; with pub. rels. dept. Mont. Coun. Tchrs. Math., Helena, 1991—; mem. human svc. subcom., fin. and claims commn. Mont. Senate; chair interim com. on job tng. partnership act, 1991-92. Sch. trustee Helena (Mont.) Sch. Dist. 1, 1978-90; bd. dirs. Mont. Hunger Coalition, 1985—; pres. Mont. Sch. Bds. Assn., 1989-90; active Mont. Alliance for Mentally Ill (Mon Ami award 1991). Recipient Marvin Heintz award Mont. Sch. Bds. Assn., 1987, Friends of Edn. award Mont. Assn. Elem. and Middle Sch. Prins., 1989, Child Advocacy award Mont. PTA, 1991, award Mont. Alliance for Mentally Ill, 1991. Mem. Mont. Sch. Bds. Assn. (Marvin Heintz award 1988, pres.1989-90), Mont. Elem. Sch. Prins., Mont. Parent, Teacher, Student Assn. (child advocacy award 1991). Democrat. Methodist. Home and Office: 530 Hazelgreen Pl Helena MT 59601 Office: Mt State Senate State Capitol Helena MT 59620

WATERS, AMY JILL, critical care nurse; b. Titusville, Fla., Mar. 13, 1967; d. George Leroy and Jean Audry (Opland) W. ADN, Hillsborough C.C., Tampa, Fla., 1989. Cert. BLS, PALS provider and instr., ACLS, CCRN. Nurse technician Tampa Gen. Hosp., 1988-89, GN/RN, staff nurse, 1989-90, staff nurse, RN, 1990-92; staff nurse, RN All Children's Hosp., St. Petersburg, Fla., 1992—, charge nurse, 1994—; instr. PALS, Ctr. for Emergency Med. Edn., Tampa, 1991—. Home: 6401 31st St S Apt 408 Saint Petersburg FL 33712-5478 Office: All Childrens Hosp 801 6th St S Saint Petersburg FL 33701-4899

WATERS, BETTY LOU, newspaper reporter, writer; b. Texarkana, Tex., June 13, 1943; d. Chester Hinton and Una Erby (Walls) W. AA, Texarkana Jr. Coll., 1963; BA, East Tex. State U., 1965. Gen. assignment reporter Galveston County Pub. Co., Galveston and Texas City, 1965-68; news and feature writer Ind. and Daily Mail, Anderson, S.C., 1968-69; reporter Citizen-Times newspaper, Asheville, N.C., 1969-74; edn. and med. reporter News Star World Pub. Co., Monroe, La., 1974-79; reporter, writer Delta Democrat Times, Greenville, Miss., 1980-89; staff writer Tyler (Tex.) Morning Telegraph, 1990—. Recipient 1st place award for articles La. Press Women's Contest, 1978, 1st place for interview, 1979; news media award N.C. Easter Seal Soc., 1973; 3d place award for feature writing Miss. Press Assn., 1984, for gen. news, 1983, for investigative reporting, 1988, 1st place for best series of articles, 1990; hon. mentions Tex. AP, 1966. Mem. Sigma Delta Chi.

WATERS, CYNTHIA WINFREY, television show host, public service director; b. Atlanta, Feb. 25, 1951; d. Tommie Lee (Winfrey) W.; m. Leroy Hollaway Jr., June 7, 1970 (div. 1981); children: Marechalnelle, Geoffrey; m. Leamond Howard Waters, Sept. 1, 1985. Cert. in acctg., Atlanta Area Tech. Inst., 1982; cert. in human relations, Chattahoochee Tech. Inst., 1988. Customer svc. rep. Atlanta Gaslight Co., 1975-83; asst. mktg. mgr. Vorwerk, U.S.A., Atlanta, 1983-86; fg. sec. coordinator Focal Point Inc., Atlanta, 1986-91, safety facilitator, 1988-91; pub. svc. dir. Sta. WYZE Radio, Atlanta, 1991—; TV host A New Look in Gospel, Atlanta, 1991—; sec. Emory U.,

Atlanta, 1993—. Mem. Atlanta Prevention Connection, Edwin Hawkins Arts & Music Seminar Choir Metro Atlanta chpt. Home: 1306 Winchester Trl Smyrna GA 30080-6642 Office: Focal Point Inc PO Box 813056 Smyrna GA 30081

WATERS, ELLEN MAUREEN, publishing executive, writer; b. Liberty, Ill., Aug. 19, 1938; d. Charles Francis and Virginia Elizabeth (Robinson) Linker; m. Gerald Louis Waters, Jan. 18, 1957 (div. 1990); children: Tamara, Gerri-Layne, Christina, Andrea. Student, Baker U., 1977-82, 88—; grad. Women's Leadership Inst., Avila Coll., 1990, grad. Women's Entrepreneur Program, 1990. Typesetter, reporter Baldwin (Kans.) Ledger, 1967-73; editor Wellsville (Kans.) Globe, 1973-74; asst. registrar Baker U., Baldwin City, 1975-77, registrar, 1977-82; mng. editor Mag. Design and Prodn., editor Pre mag. Southwind Pub. Co., Prairie Village, Kans., 1985-92; editor Signature mag., 1992-94; freelance writer, Baldwin City, 1974—, Overland Park, 1984—; owner, operator Mentor Editl. Svc., Overland Park; lectr. on mentoring. Editor, publ. Mentor newsletter. Mentor, Women's Network for Entrerpeneurial Tng., SBA. Mem. Internat. Women's Writing Guild, Internat. Mentoring Assn. Office: PO Box 4382 Overland Park KS 66204-0382

WATERS, KAREN MARIE, journalist; b. Chgo., Jan. 9, 1968; d. Leon and Mary Ruth (Causey) W. BS in Comms., U. of Ill., Chgo., 1990; student, DePaul U., 1994—. Asst. comms. coord. dept. of ophthalmology U. of Ill., Chgo., 1988-89; staff assoc./intern Centel Corp., Chgo., 1989; assoc. producer Chgo. Cable Access Corp., 1991-92; editorial asst. Morningstar, Chgo., 1991-92; dir. coord. Pensions and Investments, Chgo., 1992—; cons. print journalism Black Media Coalition, Chgo., 1991-93, Chgo. Assn. Black Journalists, Chgo., 1993—. Mem. Pres.'s Leadership Coun., 1989; vol. Community Law Project, Chgo., 1994—, Blind Svc. Assn., Chgo., 1993—; vol./asst. chair spl. Projects Starlight Found., Chgo., 1992-93; bd. dirs. Habitat for Humanity, Chgo., 1992—. Legal scholar DePaul Sch. Law, Chgo., 1994, DePaul scholar, 1994, Mayor's Leadership 2000 scholar, 1994. Mem. Chgo. Assn. Black Journalists, Black Media Coalition. Roman Catholic. Office: Pensions and Investments 740 N Rush St Chicago IL 60611

WATERS, KRISTIN BENTON, philosophy educator, women's studies educator; b. Rome, N.Y., Oct. 10, 1951; d. George B. and Shirley B. (Barnard) W.; m. Edmund F. O'Reilly, Aug. 9, 1980; 1 child, Colin O'Reilly. BA, Bard Coll., 1973; MA, U. Conn., 1974, PhD, 1980. Asst. prof. philosophy Clark U., Worcester, Mass., 1980-87; lect. philosophy Bard Coll., Annandale-on-Hudson, N.Y., 1989; lect. women's studies Holy Cross Coll., Worcester, 1991—. Mem. Am. Philos. Assn., Nat. Assn. Women's Studies. Home: Laurel Hill Rd Wales MA 01081

WATERS, MARTHA MORGAN, media specialist; b. Cumming, Ga., July 4, 1949; d. Benjamin and F.L. (Wilbanks) Morgan; m. Edward Daniel Waters, Dec. 18, 1970; children: Richard David, Jeffery Michael. BA in French and Social Studies, Berry Coll., Rome, Ga., 1972; MEd in LS, West Ga. Coll., Carrollton, 1980; SEd in LS, Ga. State U., Atlanta, 1986. Cert. tchr., Ga. Tchr. Coosa High Sch., Rome, Ga., 1972-80, media specialist, 1980—. Mem. Soc. of Sch. Librs. Internat. (com. chair 1992, book award com. 1989-92). Democrat. Methodist. Home: 13 Donley Dr Rome GA 20165 Office: Coosa High Sch 4454 Alabama Hwy Rome GA 30165

WATERS, MARY BASKIN, state government official; b. Sumter, S.C., Aug. 31, 1945; d. Norwood Fleming and Nan Richardson (Rickenbaker) Baskin; m. Samuel C. Waters, Sept. 14, 1968. Cert. d'Etude, Sorbonne U., Vichy, France, 1966; BA, U. S.C., 1985, MA in Teaching, 1987, grad. cert., 1993. Instr. art Newberry (S.C.) Coll., 1987-92; instr. women's studies U. S.C., Columbia, 1988—; instr. art U. S.C., Lancaster, 1990-92; dir. S.C. Commn. on Women, A Divsn. of Gov.'s Office, Columbia, 1992—; vis. lectr. U. S.C., Columbia, 1988; art cons., broker Carolina Editions Gallery, Columbia, 1990; instr. art Midlands Tech. Coll., Columbia, 1991; exec. bd. Advs. for Women on Bds. and Commns., Columbia; adv. bd. Pathways for Women at Richland Meml. Hosp., Columbia; mem. Leadership Inst., Columbia (S.C.) Coll.; lectr. in field. Contbr. articles to profl. jours. Mem. S.C. Dept. Edn. Visual and Performing Arts Transition Com., Columbia, 1991; adv. com. Women in State Work Force Symposium, 1993; adv. bd. S.C. Women in Higher Edn. Adminstrn., 1994. Mem. Nat. Art Edn. Assn., Nat. Coun. for Rsch. on Women, Southeastern Women's Studies Assn., Nat. Assn. Commns. on Women, Richland County Legal Aux. (pres. 1982-83), Brennen Elem. Sch. PTO (pres. 1980-81), Golden Key Honor Soc., Gamma Beta Phi, Kappa Phi Kappa. Office: Office of Gov SC Commn on Women 2221 Devine St Ste 408 Columbia SC 29205-2418

WATERS, MAXINE, congresswoman; b. St. Louis, Aug. 15, 1938; d. Remus and Velma (Moore) Carr; m. Sidney Williams, July 23, 1977; children: Edward, Karen. Grad. in sociology Calif. State U., L.A.; hon. doctorates, Spelman Coll., N.C. Agrl. & Tech. State U., Morgan State U. Former tchr. Head Start; mem. Calif. Assembly from dist. 48, 1976-91, Dem. caucus chair, 1984; mem. 102nd-104th Congresses from Dist. 35, Calif., 1991—; mem. Banking, Fin., Urban Affairs com., Ho. subcom. on banking, capitol subcom. on banking, employment and tng. subcom. on vets., veterans affairs com. Mem. Dem. Nat. Com., Dem. Congrl. Campaign com.; del. Dem. Nat. Conv., 1972, 76, 80, 84, 88, 92, mem. rules com. 1984; mem. Nat. Adv. Com. for Women, 1978—; bd. dirs. TransAfrica Found., Nat. Women's Polit. Caucus, Ctr. Nat. Policy, Clara Elizabeth Jackson Carter Found. Spellman Coll., Nat. Minority AIDS Project, Women for a Meaningful Summit, Nat. Coun. Negro Women, Black Women's Agenda; founder Black Women's Forum. Office: US Ho of Reps 330 Cannon HOB Washington DC 20515

WATERS, PATTY DIANE, elementary educator; b. Great Bend, Kans., Aug. 5, 1948; d. Layton Strapman and Patricia Ieta (Shira) Roesler; m. Jame Andrew Waters Jr., Jul. 8, 1972; children: James Andrew, Joshua Layton. BA, Long Beach State Coll., 1970, teaching cert., 1971. Elem. tchr. Long Beach (Calif.) Unified Sch. Dist., 1971, Ventura (Calif.) Unified Sch. Dist., 1971-72, Moorpark (Calif.) Unified Sch. Dist., 1971-78; propr. Patty Waters Goldsmith, Moorpark, 1985—. Bd. mem. Moorpark Unified Sch. bd., 1985-91; pres., 1990; social chmn., past pres. Forty Leagues of Ventura County, 1972-87; pres. Moorpark Com. Complex Found., Inc., 1992, 93; bd. mem. Moorpark Boys & Girls Club, 1990—; bd. mem. Moorpark A.Y.S.O., 1983-85. Named Citizen of Yr., Moorpark C. of C., 1994. Office: Patty Waters Goldsmith 10865 Broadway Moorpark CA 93021

WATERS, SYLVIA, dance company artistic director. Prin. dance Alvin Ailey Am. Dance Theater, N.Y.C.; artistic dir. Alvin Ailey Repertory Ensemble, N.Y.C., 1974—. Office: Alvin Ailey Repertory Ensemble 1515 Broadway New York NY 10036-5702*

WATFORD, JAMIE DENISE (JAMIE DENISE JONES), mechanical engineer; b. Gadsden, Ala., Aug. 16, 1955; d. James A. and Jennie Ruth (Amberson) Jones; m. William Edward Reinecke, May 21, 1977 (div. Nov. 1981); 1 child, Jennifer Louise; m. Robert Michael Watford Jr., Aug. 14, 1982; 1 child, Robert James. Student, Jacksonville (Ala.) State U., 1975; BSME, U. Ala., 1977. With chem. div. PPG Industries, Lake Charles, La., 1976, summers 1977-79, mech. engr., 1979-80, design engr., mech., 1980-81, tech. asst. maintenance, 1981-85, design engr. mech., 1981-85; mech. engr. maintenance dept. Shawnee Fossil Plant TVA, West Paducah, Ky., 1986—. Seamstress Joan Crawford Sch. Dance, Paducah, 1990-91; pianist Music Makers Choir, Reidland Bapt. Ch., Paducah, 1990—, asst. dir. adult handbell choir, 1990—, dir. youth handbell choir, 1988; asst. Webelos den leader Cub Scouts, 1993—. Recipient one of Outstanding Young Women Am. award, 1979. Mem. TVA Engring. Assn., Capstone Engring. Soc., U. Ala. Nat. Alumni Assn., Pi Tau Sigma, Delta Gamma. Home: 1005 Tyree Rd Paducah KY 42003-9417 Office: TVA Shawnee Fossil Plant PO Box 2000 West Paducah KY 42086

WATFORD, PATTI EILEEN, accountant, payroll and computer specialist; b. Sumter, S.C., Mar. 16, 1961; d. Francis Brainard and Mildred Edna (Evans) W. Student, Sumter (S.C.) Area Tech., 1990—, Ctrl. Carolina Tech. Coll. (previously Sumter Area Tech.), 1992-94. Sec. McIntosh Mech., Manning, S.C., 1984-85, Glen Mfg., Sumter, 1985; office mgr. Hose & Equipment Indsl. Maintenance, Sumter, 1985-89; with sales Chromate Indsl. Sales, Sumter, 1989; sec. Associated Psychotherapists Chromate Indsl. Sales, 1989-90; records inventory clk. Laidlaw Environ. Svcs. Inc., Pinewood, S.C., 1990-91, purchasing asst., 1991, payroll clk., 1991-92, computer supr., 1991-92; office mgr., bookkeeper Whitaker's Inc. of Sumter, S.C., 1992; sec. People's Resources, Sumter, S.C., 1993-94; traffic coord. Cadco, Inc., Florence, S.C., 1994; sec. People's Resources at Ga. Pacific, Alcolu, S.C., 1994—. Sec.-treas. Brewington Presbyn. Ch., 1990—; sec.-treas. Watford Family Reunion, 1990—; v.p. Evans Family Reunion, 1993-94, pres., 1994-95. Office: Ga Pacific PO Box 267 Alcolu SC 29001

WATFORD, SUE ANN, mortgage company professional; b. South Bend, Ind., Nov. 20, 1956; d. Robert Joseph and Wanda Gene Zoller; m. James Michael Watford, Sept. 25, 1976 (div. June 1981). Br. mgr. Tower Fed. Savs. and Loan, South Bend, Ind., 1975-86; customer svc. rep. Transamerica Fin. Svcs., Phoenix, 1986-87; sr. loan processor Qualified Plan Investments, Phoenix, 1987-90; v.p. Hilton Fin. Corp., Phoenix, 1990—. Republican. Presbyterian.

WATHEN, KAREN DENISE, home health care nurse; b. Shelbyville, Ind., Oct. 12, 1953; d. James and Patsy Ruth (Bowman) Francis; m. Michael Joseph Wathen, Aug. 17, 1974; children: Christopher Michael, David Andrew. BSN, Ball State U., 1975. RN, Ind. Nurse ICU, critical care unit, med.-surg., obstetrics Greene County Gen. Hosp., Linton, Ind., 1976-79; nurse emergency rm. Greene County Gen. Hosp., Linton, 1979-85, relief evening supr., 1983-85; dir. Greene County Gen. Hosp. Home Care, Linton, 1985—; CPR instr. Am. Heart Assn., Linton, 1985—. Com. mem. Boy Scouts Am. Troop 450 and Pack 453, Linton. Named Young Careerist, Bus. and Profl. Women's Club, Linton, 1982. Mem. Ind. Assn. Home Health Agys. (ethics com., pub. rels. com., medicare com., program com.). Roman Catholic. Office: Green County Gen Hosp RR 1 Box 555 Linton IN 47441

WATKIN, VIRGINIA GUILD, lawyer; b. Clinton, Mass., July 28, 1925; d. George Cheever and Dorothy Louise (Springer) Guild; m. Donald M. Watkin, June 22, 1946; children—Henry M., Mary Ellen, Edward G., Ann Kymry. B.A., Wellesley Coll., 1946; LL.B., Columbia U., 1949, LLD (hon.) Norwich U., 1986. Bar: N.Y. 1949, D.C. 1952, U.S. Ct. Appeals (D.C. cir.) 1952, U.S. Supreme Ct. 1954, Mass. 1963, U.S. Dist. Ct. Mass. 1968, U.S. Ct. Appeals (1st cir.) 1968, U.S. Ct. Appeals (9th cir.) 1976, U.S. Ct. Appeals (4th cir.) 1980, U.S. Ct. Fed. Claims 1983, U.S. Ct. Appeals (5th cir.) 1993. Assoc., Covington & Burling, Washington, 1952-58; assoc. counsel Mass. Crime Commn., 1963-64; assoc. Herrick, Smith, Donald, Farley & Ketchum, Boston, 1966-72, ptnr., 1973-74; ptnr. Covington & Burling, Washington, 1974—. Bd. vis. Columbia U. Sch. Law; trustee Northfield (Mass.) Mount Hermon Sch. Bd. 1978-83, Norwich U., Northfield, Vt., 1977-90, emertia 1990—, Wellesley Coll., 1989—; bd. overseers Wellesley Coll. Stone Ctr. for Develop. Svcs. and Studies, 1989—, Wellesley Coll. Ctr. for Rsch. on Women, 1990—. Mem. Am. Law Inst., ABA, D.C. Bar (pres. 1993—), Soc. Woman Geographers, Columbia Law Sch. Alumni Assn. (regional v.p.), Wellesley Coll. Alumnae Assn. (bd. dirs. 1985-88). Club: Cosmos. Author: Taxes and Tax Harmonization in the Central American Common Market, 1967; contbr. articles to profl. jours. Home: 3001 Veazey Ter NW Washington DC 20008-5455 Office: Covington & Burling PO Box 7566 1201 Pennsylvania Ave NW Washington DC 20044-7566

WATKINS, CATHY COLLINS, corporate purchasing agent; b. Memphis, Sept. 20, 1952; d. Amos Verlyn and Ruby Etoile (Mayo) Collins; m. Lewis McGill Watkins Jr., May 21, 1988. AA, Clarke Coll., 1972; BMus, William Carey Coll., 1974. Sales assoc., mgr. inventory and receiving Waldoff's Inc., Hattiesburg, Miss., 1974-80; buyer Forrest Gen. Hosp., Hattiesburg, 1980-81; asst. mgr. Ward's Fast Food of Laurel (Miss.), Inc., 1981-82; buyer, sole purchasing agent Eagle Distbrs., Hattiesburg, 1982-85; inventory coord., purchasing agent Miss. Music, Inc., Hattiesburg, 1985—. Photographer campus yearbook Carey Crusader, 1974; editor: (newsletter) Mississippi Bandmaster, 1988—. Mem. Nat. Assn. Music Merchants. Baptist. Home: 105 Elaine Cir Hattiesburg MS 39402 Office: Miss Music Inc PO Box 1705 222 S Main Hattiesburg MS 39401

WATKINS, DONNA MARIE, school counselor, educator; b. Salt Lake City, Aug. 25, 1942; d. Leland Blair and Elverda Phyllis (Loge) Hughes; m. Tim Oliver, June 19, 1965 (div. Oct. 1974); 1 child, Tim; m. Gilbert Dean Watkins, Mar. 15, 1975; 1 child, Zach. BA in Edn., U. Oreg., 1964; MA in Counseling and Guidance, Pacific Luth. U., 1974; PhD in Coll. Student Pers. Adminstrn., U. No. Colo., 1982. Cert. sch. counselor, Colo.; lic. profl. counselor. Elem. tchr. Durham (N.C.) Pub. Schs., 1964-65, Honolulu Pub. Schs., 1965-66; tchr. English and history Durham Acad., 1967-70; rschr. judiciary com. Wash. Ho. of Reps., Olympia, 1970-71; counselor Youth Emergency Svc., Olympia, 1971-72; instr. sociology and psychology St. Martin's Coll., Olympia, 1972-74; dir. ext. program St. Martin's Coll., Ft. Lewis, Wash., 1974-75; counselor Milliken (Colo.) Middle Sch., 1975-79; asst. Placement Office, U. No. Colo., Greeley, 1979-80; coord. counseling Roosevelt High Sch., Johnstown, Colo., 1980-83, Smoky Hill High Sch., Aurora, Colo., 1983—; reviewer Wash. State Arts Commn., Olympia, 1970-72; instr. English and psychology Centralia (Wash.) C.C. Evening Sch., 1972-74;instr. MA degree program in counseling and guidance Western State Coll., Gunnison, Colo., summers 1987-89; adj. prof. MAEd program in counseling and guidance U. Phoenix, Denver, 1989—; presenter in field to profl. assn. convs. and leadership confs., counseling seminars and workshops, Colo., 1980—. Singer Cherry Creek Chorale, 1986—. Mem. ACA, Am. Sch. Counselors Assn. (membership chmn. 1986-88), Colo. Sch. Counselors Assn. (pres. 1986-87), Colo. Counselors Assn., Nat. Assn. Coll. Admissions Counselors. Democrat. Home: 9879 E Escalante Ct Parker CO 80134-5514 Office: Smoky Hill High Sch 16100 E Smoky Hill Rd Aurora CO 80015-1751

WATKINS, HORTENSE CATHERINE, middle school educator; b. St. Louis, Nov. 29, 1924; d. Isaiah S. and Katie M. (Phelps) W. BA, Harris-Stowe State Coll., St. Louis, 1946; MEd, U. Ill., 1953; postgrad. U. Chgo., InterAm. U., Saltillo, Coahuila, Mex.; postgrad., U. Seville, Spain, Webster U., St. Louis. Cert. life tchr., reading specialist, Mo. Coord. urban rural programs Carver-Dunbar Schs., St. Louis, 1975-76; adminstrv. asst. Shaw Visual Performing Arts Sch., St. Louis, 1978-82; team IV leader Woerner IGE, St. Louis, 1982-87; tchr., head lang. arts dept. Nottingham Mid. Sch., St. Louis, 1987-92; tutor fgn.-speaking religious, presenter, lectr. numerous workshops; curriculum advisor St. Louis Pub. Schs. Active numerous cmty. orgns.; bd. dirs. St. Louis Cathedral Sch.; bd. dirs. Concert Series of St. Louis Cathedral. Mem. ASCD, Nat. Coun. Tchrs. English, Mo. State Tchrs. Assn., Greater St. Louis Coun. Social Studies, Delta Sigma Theta (Golden life), Delta Kappa Gamma. Home: 5070A Enright Ave Saint Louis MO 63108-1008

WATKINS, JOAN FRANCES, educator; b. Linwood, N.J., Mar. 8, 1940; d. Francis Joseph and Alberta Catherine (Seabold) W. BS, St. Bonaventure U., 1967. Cert. elem. tchr., N.J. Tchr. various parochial schs., 1961-71, Atlantic City (N.J.) Pub. Schs., 1971—. Mem. Atlantic City Edn. Assn., N.J. Edn. Assn. Roman Catholic. Home: PO Box 714 Northfield NJ 08225-0714

WATKINS, JOAN MARIE, osteopath, occupational medicine physician; b. Anderson, Ind., Mar. 9, 1943; d. Curtis David and Dorothy Ruth (Beckett) W.; m. Stanley G. Nodvik, Dec. 25, 1969 (div. Apr. 1974). BS, West Liberty State Coll., 1965; Cert. of Grad. Phy. Therapy, Ohio State U., 1966; DO, Phila. Coll. Osteo., 1972; M of Health Professions Edn., U. Ill., Chgo., 1986; MPH, U. Ill., 1989. Diplomate Osteo. Nat. Bds., Am. Bd. Preventive Medicine. Emergency osteo. physician Cooper Med. Ctr., Camden, N.J., 1974-79, Shore Meml. Hosp., Somers Point, N.J., 1979-81, St. Francis Hosp., Blue Island, Ill., 1981-82; emergency osteo. physician Mercy Hosp. and Med. Ctr., Chgo., 1982-90, dir. emergency ctr., 1984-88; resident in occupational and preventive medicine U. Ill., 1988-90. Fellow Am. Coll. Preventive Medicine. Home: 4306 Harbor House Dr Tampa FL 33615 Office: U Community Hosp Occupational Health Svcs 3100 E Fletcher Ave Tampa FL 33613

WATKINS, KAREN J., librarian; b. Albuquerque, July 5, 1947; d. Clifford Ray and Glenys Bell (Frevert) Jurgensen; m. William Gray Watkins, May 15, 1976. BA magna cum laude, St. John's Coll., Santa Fe, 1967; MA, U. Denver, 1972; postgrad., U. Calif., Berkeley, 1980-82. Libr. Santa Fe Pub. Schs., 1972-78; libr. cons. N.Mex. State Libr., Santa Fe, 1978-84, adminstr., 1984-89, dir., 1989—. Mem. AAUW (pres. Santa Fe chpt. 1991), N.Mex. Libr. Assn. (pres. 1988-89), N.Mex. Libr. Found. (bd. dirs. 1994), Rotary (bd. dirs. 1994). Office: N Mex State Libr 325 Don Gaspar Ave Santa Fe NM 87501-2745

WATKINS, LINDA THERESA, educational researcher; b. York, Pa., Sept. 29, 1947; d. Nathan Franklin and Madelyn Marie (Mandl) W.; m. Hugh Jerald Silverman, June 22, 1968 (div. Apr. 1983); children: Claire Christine Silverman, Hugh Christopher Silverman; m. Patrick Grim. BA, Muhlenberg Coll., 1968; MA, San Jose (Calif.) State Coll., 1970; PhD, Stanford (Calif.) U., 1977; cert., Hofstra U., 1991. Rsch. asst. prof. L.I. Rsch. Inst., Stony Brook, N.Y., 1977-79; asst. prof. NYU, 1979-85; rsch. assoc. Psychiatry dept. SUNY, Stony Brook, 1985-87; rsch. analyst Bd. Coop. Ednl. Svcs. Eastern Suffolk, Patchogue, N.Y., 1987—; adj. lectr. SUNY Sch. Soc. Welfare, 1994; cons. Dowling Coll., Oakdale, N.Y., 1991, Tele-Niger Evaluation Project, Paris, 1972; survey cons. Redbook Mag., N.Y., 1987; interviewer Am. Inst. for Rsch., Kensington, Md., 1973. Contbr. articles to profl. jours. Rsch. grant Ronald McDonald Children's Charities, 1988, Am. Broadcasting Co., 1978, Dissertation rsch. grant Nat. Assn. of Broadcasters, 1974; NDEA fellowship, 1972. Mem. ASCD, Am. Psychol. Assn., Soc. for Rsch. in Child Devel., Am. Ednl. Rsch. Assn. Home: 99 Swezey St Patchogue NY 11772 Office: Bd Coop Ednl Svcs Suffolk 1 15 Andrea Rd Holbrook NY 11741

WATKINS, MARY POSTON, library information specialist; b. Wabash, Ind., Aug. 6, 1950; d. Bob E. and April C. (Ogle) Poston; m. Dan A. Watkins; children: Bari, Ben, Mike, Joshua. BA, Ball State U., Muncie, Ind., 1972, MLS, 1975. Libr. info. specialist Mt. Pleasant Community Schs., Yorktown, Ind.; pres., creative cons. Mary Poston-Watkins; workshop leader, humorist, prof. rsch., profl. storyteller, writer in field. Contbr. numerous articles to profl. jours. Founder libr. Ind. Ronald McDonald House; dir. devel. Life, Love and Laughter at Ball Meml. Hosp. Recipient Outstanding Literacy award ALA, Delaware County Outstanding Svc. to Young People award; Ball Found. grantee; Eli Lilly grantee. Mem. Internat. Platform Assn., AIME (Ester Burrin award), IASL. Home: 4438 N 850 W Middletown IN 47356

WATKINS, NANCY HOBGOOD, sales executive; b. Oxford, N.C., Mar. 7, 1949; d. Ruben Northington and Julia Clyde (Hobgood) W. AA, Vardell Hall Jr. Coll., Red Springs, N.C., 1967-68; student, Atlantic Christian Coll., 1968-71. Tchr. Granville County Schs., 1972-74; with Combined Ins. Co., 1974-76; dist. mgr. Investors Heritage Life Ins. Co., 1976-80; mfrs. rep. Jerry Elsher Co., N.Y.C., 1982-85, Down South, Atlanta, 1985-90; nat. sales mgr. Chang Seng, Inc., Charlotte, N.C., 1990-93; mfrs. rep. Good Ship, Atlanta, 1993—. Mem. Young Reps., Charlotte, 1985-91. Episcopalian.

WATKINS, SHERRY LYNNE, elementary school educator; b. Bloomington, Ind., Oct. 13, 1944; d. Quentin Odell and Velma Ruth W. BSEd, Ind. U., 1966, MSEd, 1968. Tchr. 4th grade North Grove Elem. Sch., Ctr. Grove Sch. Dist., Greenwood, Ind., 1966-68; tchr. 4th and 6th grades John Strange Sch., Met. Dist. of Wash. Twp., Indpls., 1968-91; tchr. 4th grade Allisonville Sch., MSD of Wash. Twp., Indpls., 1991—. Mem. People for Ethical Treatment of Animals. Mem. NEA (nat. del. 1978—), ACLU, AAUW, Ind. Tchrs. Assn. (state del. 1966—), Washington Twp. Edn. Assn. (pres. 1986-89), World Confedn. Orgn. of Tchg. Profls. (del. Costa Rica 1990), Delta Kappa Gamma (chpt. pres. 1992-94, chmn. coordinating coun. Indpls. area 1994—), Alpha Omicron Pi. Office: Allisonville Sch 4920 E 79th St Indianapolis IN 46250-1615

WATKINS, SUSAN GAIL, lawyer; b. Independence, Mo., May 17, 1962; d. Floyd L. and Judy G. (Bell) W.; m. Richard L. Davis, Jr., Jan. 10, 1992; children: Eva, Andrea. BA, Graceland Coll., 1983; JD, U. Mo., 1986. Bar: Mo. 1986, U.S. Dist. Ct. (we. dist.) Mo. 1986, U.S. Ct. Appeals 1990. Assoc. Les D. Wight, P.C., Independence, 1986-87; ptnr. Snoke & Watkins, Independence, 1987-90, Watkins Law Offices, 1990—; asst. prosecuting atty. Jackson County, Mo., 1991-94; instr. Draughon Bus. Coll., Independence, 1987-90; exec. dir. Independence Youth Ct., 1988—. Mem. ABA, Assn. Trial Lawyers Am., Kansas City Bar Assn. (young lawyers sect.), East Jackson County Bar Assn., Sertoma, L.E.A.D. Independence C. of C., Phi Alpha Delta. Mem. Reorganized Ch. of Jesus Christ of Latter-day Saints. Office: Watkins Law Offices 221 W Lexington Ave Ste 250 Independence MO 64050-3720

WATKISS, REGINA (REGINA MONKS), secondary school educator; b. Worcester, Mass., Apr. 21, 1952; d. Albin and Victoria (Babicz) Linga; m. G. Philip Watkiss. BA, Assumption Coll., 1974; MA, Western Md. Coll., 1980; postgrad., U. Ala.; MS, Western Md. Coll., 1992. Cert. sci. tchr., Ga., Colo. Sci. tchr. Randolph Sch., Huntsville, Ala.; sci. coord. Divine Redeemer Sch., Colorado Springs, Colo.; sci. curriculum cons. U.S. Space Found., Colorado Springs; head dept. sci. Heritage Sch., Newnan, Ga.; workshop presenter, curriculum author in field. Recipient Dreyfus Master Tchr. award in Chemistry, 1986, Colo. Sci. Tchr. of Yr.; Woodrow Wilson fellow, 1986; grantee State of Ala. Mem. NSTA, Colo. STA, Ga. AST. Home: 215 Creek View Trl Fayetteville GA 30214-7231

WATLINGTON, SARAH JANE, community volunteer, retired military officer; b. Denver, May 6, 1938; d. William Thomas and Margaret (Stewart) W. BS, Purdue U., 1960; MA, Naval Post Grad. Sch., 1970. Commd. ensign USN, 1960, advanced through grades to capt., 1979; social sec. Chief of Naval Operations, Washington, 1966-69; exec. officer Recruit Tng. Command, Bainbridge, Md., 1971-73; head officer student placement Bur. Naval Personnel, Washington, 1973-75; exec. officer NROTC Unit, Purdue U., West Lafayette, Ind., 1976-79; commanding officer Navy Manpower and Material Analysis Ctr., San Diego, 1979-82; dep. dir. manpower & tng. Office Chief of Naval Ops., Washington, 1982-83; ret., 1984; sec. Cmty. and Family Resource Ctr., Lafayette, Ind., 1990-91; mem. dean of liberal arts adv. coun., 1992—. Vol. YWCA, Lafayette, 1984—, bd. dirs., 1985-91, pres., 1988-90, v.p., 1994—; bd. dirs. YWCA Found., Lafayette, 1988-90, 93, Greater Lafayette Mus. Art, 1984-85; v.p. grants Greater Lafayette Cmty. Found.; mem. nat. nominating com. YWCA U.S.A., 1991-94; trustee, sec.-treas. Alpha Chi Omega Found.; pres. IN Coun. YMCAs, 1994—. Decorated Legion of Merit with gold star; recipient Jefferson award 1989, Disting. Alumna award Purdue Sch. Liberal Arts, 1990. Mem. Purdue U. Sch. Liberal Arts Alumni Assn. (pres. 1991-92), Purdue Pres. Coun., John Purdue Club, Gold Block Booster Club (sec. 1986-87, Girl Scout Woman of Distinction 1992), Boilermaker Network Booster Club (sec. 1991-94), Alpha Chi Omega (Disting. Alumna award 1980, Golden Gavel Woman of Distinction award 1994). Congregational. Home: 9 Elvernan Dr West Lafayette IN 47906-9424

WATMAN, CELESTE V., librarian; b. Queens, N.Y., Nov. 6, 1949; d. Herbert A. and Veronica D. Spoerer; m. William A. Watman, July 30, 1972. BA, L.I. U., 1971, MS, 1972. Cert. N.Y. state pub. libr. Libr. Plainedge Pub. Libr., Massapequa, N.Y., 1973-87; asst. libr. dir. Hicksville (N.Y.) Pub. Libr., 1987-91, dir., 1991—. Mem. Nassau County Libr. Assn., N.Y. Libr. Assn., ALA, Pub. Libr. Assn., Profl. Sculptors Guild, Kiwanis (asst. sec. Hicksville chpt. 1993—), Hicksville C. of C. (bd. dirs. 1989—), Town of Oyster Bay Arts Coun. (bd. dirs. 1989—). Office: Hicksville Pub Libr 169 Jerusalem Ave Hicksville NY 11801

WATSON, BEVERLY ANN, nurse; b. Springfield, Mass., Aug. 31, 1948; d. Paul Michael and Ann Theresa (Wheeler) Urekew; m. Kenneth A. Watson Jr., Dec. 17, 1977. Diploma in Nursing, Framingham Union Hosp., 1970. RN; cert. nursing supr., Ga. Staff nurse Hartford (Conn.) Hosp.; charge nurse Ridgeview Nursing Home, Springfield, Vespers Nursing Home, Wilkesboro, N.C.; asst. dir. nurses North Macon Health Care, Macon, Ga.; medical supr. Hospitality Care Ctr., Macon, Ga. Mem. ANA, Ga. Nurses Assn. Address: PO Box 13144 Macon GA 31208-3144

WATSON, CATHERINE ELAINE, journalist; b. Mpls., Feb. 9, 1944; d. Richard Edward and LaVonne (Slater) W.; m. Al Sicherman (div.); children: Joseph Sicherman, David Sicherman. B.A. in Journalism, U. Minn., 1967; M.A. in Teaching, Coll. of St. Thomas, 1971. Reporter Mpls. Star Tribune, 1966-72; editor Picture mag., 1972-78, Travel sect., 1978—; editor in chief Galena (Ill.) Gazette, 1990-91. Author: Travel Basics, 1984. Contbr. articles to newspapers and travel mags. Recipient Newspaper Mag. Picture Editor's award Pictures of Yr. Competition, 1974, 75; awards for writing and photography Soc. Am. Travel Writers, 1983, 84, 85,86, 87, 88, 89, 90, 91, 92, 93, Photographer of Yr. award, 1990; Lowell Thomas Travel Journalist of Yr., 1990. Mem. Am. Newspaper Guild, Soc. Am. Travel Writers, Phi Beta Kappa, Kappa Tau Alpha, Alpha Omicron Pi. Office: 425 Portland Ave Minneapolis MN 55488-0001

WATSON, CHRISTINE DONNA, financial consultant; b. Carmel, Calif., Dec. 20, 1958; d. Thomas Harold and Barbara Glee (Leedom) W. BBA, Suffolk U., 1980, MBA, 1981. CPA, Mass. Office acct. Deloitte Haskins & Sells, Boston, 1979-81; staff auditor Wolf & Co. Mass., Boston, 1981-82; controller Capron Lighting & Sound Co., Needham, Mass., 1982-83, BFC Enterprises, Inc., Boston, 1983-84; mgr. acctg. Hersey Products Inc., Dedham, Mass., 1984-87; acct. mgr. Pathfinder Internat., Watertown, Mass., 1988-92, Anderson Power Products, Boston, 1993—; cons. Boston Waterfront Realty, 1979-80, Grinnell Fire Protection System, Cleve., N.C., 1987, Ctr. Design Industry Schedule, 1981, 82, Harvard U., 1981-83, Brigham and Women's Hosp., 1983-84. Comdr. USARNG, 1977—. Recipient Mass. Medal Merit, 1987; fellow Suffolk U. 1980. Mem. ASQC, Nat. Speleological Soc., Tech Sqs. Club, Boston Grotto Club. Office: Anderson Power Products 145 Newton St Boston MA 02135-1598

WATSON, DARCIE ANN, speech pathologist; b. Van Nuys, Calif., July 22, 1965; d. Robert Jerome and Marie Eugene (Pryzbyla) Duba; m. John Michael Watson, Nov. 5, 1994. BS, U. Nev., 1987, MA, 1989. Cert. clin. competence. Sr. speech pathologist Sierra Rehab. Svc., Reno, Nev., 1989-92, Alameda (Calif.) Hosp., 1992-94; advanced clin. applications, speech pathologist Tolfa Corp., Mountain View, Calif., 1994—. Republican. Roman Catholic. Office: Tolfa Corp 1001 Ringstorff Mountain View CA 94043

WATSON, DEBORAH ROSZAK, quality engineer; b. Staunton, Va., Sept. 13, 1956; d. Walter Felix and Jean Viktoria (Wozniak) Roszak; m. Francis Marion Watson III, May 2, 1981; 1 stepchild, Leslie Cauvel. ASME, W.Va. Inst. Tech., 1977; BS in Mfg. Mgmt., Va. Commonwealth U., 1994. Sr. designer GE, Waynesboro, Va., 1977-78; from specialist to engr. B, project leader Philip Morris USA, Richmond, Va., 1978-90, quality engr., 1990—; v.p. programs Womens Resource Com., Richmond, 1986-87; quality assurance rep. Project BOB (Bldg. Our Bus.), Richmond, 1990-92. Mem. Lewis Ginter Bot. Garden, Fishing Bay Yacht Club, Golden Kay, Phi Kappa Phi. Home: 2121 Chepstow Ter Midlothian VA 23113-4190 Office: Philip Morris USA PO Box 26603 Richmond VA 23261-6603

WATSON, DENISE SANDER, medical products sales executive; b. Bellville, Tex., July 19, 1960; d. Charles Morris and Corinne Olive (Bakke) S. Assoc., S.W. Tex. State U., 1981, BS in Allied Health Mgmt., 1982. Cardiodiagnostician Katy Community Hosp., Katy, Tex., 1982-84; staff cardiodiagnostician Sharpstown Gen. Hosp., Houston, 1984-85; cardiodiagnostician, noninvasive lab. supr. W. Houston Med. Ctr., Houston, 1985-86; with Pro-Tech Med. Assocs., Houston, 1985-86; clinical applications specialist Hewlett-Packard Co., Houston, 1986-87; field application specialist Acuson, Houston, 1987-92; dist. medical product sales rep. Acuson, St. Louis, 1992—. Named Field Application Specialist of Yr., Western Cardiology Region, 1990. Fellow Am. Registry Diagnostic Med. Sonographers, Am. Soc. Diagnostics Med. Sonographers, Am. Soc. Echocardiography, Soc. Vascular Tech., Bluebonnet Soc. Bellville, Alpha Delta Pi. Republican. Episcopalian. Office: Acuson 1899 Powers Ferry Rd Ste 100 Atlanta GA 30339

WATSON, DIANE EDITH, state legislator; b. L.A., Nov. 12, 1933; d. William Allen Louis and Dorothy Elizabeth (O'Neal) Watson. A.A., L.A. City Coll., 1954, B.A., UCLA, 1956; M.S., Calif. State U., Los Angeles, PhD Claremont Grad. Sch., 1987. Tchr., sch. psychologist L.A. Unified Sch. Dist., 1960-69, 73-74; assoc. prof. Calif. State U., L.A., 1969-71; health occupations specialist Bur. Indsl. Edn., Calif. Dept. Edn., 1971-73; mem. L.A. Unified Sch. Bd., 1975-78; mem. Calif. Senate from dist. 28, 1978—, chairperson health and human svcs. com.; Legis. Black Caucus, mem. edn. com., judiciary com., ins. com., appropriations com.; del. Calif. Democratic Party; mem. exec. com. Nat. Conf. State Legislators. Author: Health Occupations Instructional Units-Secondary Schools, 1975; Planning Guide for Health Occupations, 1975; co-author; Introduction to Health Care, 1976. Del. Democratic Nat. Conv., 1980. Recipient Mary Church Terrell award, 1976, Brotherhood Crusade award, 1981, Black Woman of Achievement award NAACP Legal Def. Fund, 1988; named Alumnus of Yr., UCLA, 1980, 82. Mem. Calif. Assn. Sch. Psychologists, Los Angeles Urban League, Calif. Tchrs. Assn., Calif. Commn. on Status Women. Roman Catholic. Office: 4401 Crenshaw Blvd # 300 Los Angeles CA 90043-1200

WATSON, DOROTHY COLETTE, real estate broker; b. Boston, Oct. 26, 1938; d. Edward Vincent and Ethel May (Sanford) Walsh. Student, Regis Coll., 1957-59; BS, Harvard U., 1960; m. Gerald C. McDonald, May 23, 1959 (dec.); children: Gerald C., Deborah L. McDonald, Hermanson, Gregory Christopher (dec.); m. William G. Watson, May 29, 1993. Various secretarial positions, 1958-59. model, 1958-75; guidance counselor Newton High Sch., 1959-60; model, personal shopper Filene's, Chestnut Hill, Mass., 1974-78; designer program covers Boston Red Sox, 1974-76; TV facts girl for TV comml. T.V. Facts mag., 1974-75; real estate broker Channing Assocs., Inc., Wellesley, Mass., 1976-81, Boca Blossom Realty Co., Boca Raton, Fla., 1979-81, N.B. Taylor & Co., Inc., Sudbury, Mass., 1986—; fashion coord. Ava Botélle Fashions, Natick, Mass., 1988-90, mgr. Newton store, 1990-93. Roman Catholic. Home: 11 Saunders Rd Sudbury MA 01776-1282 also: 230 N Federal Hwy Deerfield Beach FL 33441-3627 Office: NB Taylor & Co Inc 356 Boston Post Rd Sudbury MA 01776-3007

WATSON, ELIZABETH LOUISE, publisher; b. Bakersfield, Calif., Jan. 13, 1968; d. Ray Stuart and Margaret Helen (Schell) W. BS in Animal Sci., U. Calif., Davis, 1989. Pres., owner Watson Enterprises, Roseville, Calif., 1985-92; advt. cons. Calif. Horse Rev., Rancho Cordova, 1990-91, advt. dir., 1991-93, assoc. publisher, 1993—. U.S. troop morale supporter Desert Dogs, Dhahran, Saudi Arabia, 1990; mem. Adventure Christian Ch. Mem. Am. Horse Show Assn., U.S. Dressage Fedn., Calif. Dressage Soc. Republican. Home: 1751 E Roseville Pkwy #1316 Roseville CA 95661 Office: Calif Horse Rev 11353 Sunrise Gold Cir # 1 Rancho Cordova CA 95742

WATSON, ELIZABETH MARION, protective services official; b. Phila., Aug. 25, 1949; d John Julian and Elizabeth Gertrude (Judge) Herrmann; m. Robert LLoyd Watson, June 18, 1976; children: Susan, Mark, David. BA in Psychology with honors, Tex. Tech. U., 1971. With Houston Police Dept., 1972-92, detective homicide, burglary and theft, 1976-81, lt. records div. northeast patrol div., 1981-84, capt. inspections div., auto theft div., 1984-87, dep. chief west patrol bur., 1987-90, police chief, 1990-92; with Austin, Tex. Police Dept., 1992—, police chief, 1992—; mem. editorial bd. S.W. Law Enforcement Inst., Richardson,Tex., 1990—. Mem. editorial bd. Am. Jour. Police, 1991—. mem. Internat. Assn. Chiefs of Police (bd. dirs. found., exec. com.), Police Exec. Rsch. Form, Tex. Police Chiefs Assn. Roman Catholic. Office: Police Department PO Box 1088 Austin TX 78767-8801*

WATSON, ELLEN I., library director, academic administrator; b. Sioux City, Iowa, Jan. 14, 1948; d. Homer V. and Elsie (Bertelsen) W. AB, Wellesley Coll., 1970; MLS, U. Md., 1973. Cataloger Eisenhower Libr. Johns Hopkins U., Balt., 1970-74; appointments sec. to mayor City of Balt., 1974-75; libr. Community Coll. Balt., 1975-82, acting dir. librs., 1982-83; dir. learning resources ctr. Ark. Coll., Batesville, 1983-88; dir. Cullom-Davis Libr. Bradley U., Peoria, Ill., 1988—; interim assoc. provost info. technologies and resources Cullom-Davis Libr. Bradley U., Peoria, Ill., 1995—; adv. bd. Ill. Valley Libr. System, Pekin, 1989—. Contbr. articles to profl. jours. and chpts. to books. Mem. ALA, Assn. Coll. and Rsch. Librs., Libr. Adminstrn. and Mgmt. Assn., Libr. and Info. Tech. Assn., Ill. Libr. Assn., Ill. Assn. Coll. and Rsch. Librs., Phi Kappa Phi. Office: Bradley U Cullom-Davis Library 1511 W Bradley Ave Peoria IL 61625

WATSON, EVELYN EGNER, guest scientist; b. Corbin, Ky., Dec. 15, 1928; d. Edgar Mattison and Bertha Mae (Mayfield) Egner; m. Earl Greene Watson, Nov. 10, 1953; children: Nancy Eileen, Philip Allen. Student, Lincoln Meml. U., 1947-48; BA, U. Ky., 1949; postgrad., U. Tenn., 1968; AA, Cumberland Coll., 1946. Math. and sci. tchr. Lynch (Ky.) High Sch., 1949-50; office mgr. Whitley County Sch. System, Williamsburg, Ky., 1950-53; sr. lab. tech. Radiation Internal Dose Ctr. Oak Ridge (Tenn.) Assoc. Univs., 1961-71, scientist, 1971-79, program mgr., 1979-89, program dir., 1989-94; lectr. in field; cons. USFDA, Rockville, Md., 1983-88. Assoc. editor Jour. Nuclear Medicine, 1981-86; editor newsletter Soc. Nuclear Medicine S.E. chpt., 1988—; co-author: MIRD Primer, 1988; contbr. articles to profl., chpts. to books. Bd. dirs. Youth Haven, Oak Ridge, Tenn., 1970-74, Clinch River Home Health, Clinton, Tenn., 1988-94. Recipient Excellence in Tech. Transfer award Fed. Lab. Consortium, 1985, Lifetime Scientific Achievement award Assn. Women in Sci., 1993. Mem. Soc. Nuclear Medicine (med. internal radiation dose com. 1980—, chmn. 1994—), Health Physics Soc. (Disting. Svc. award 1981, treas. 1976-77), European Assn. Nuclear Medicine, Nat. Coun. on Radiation Protection and Measurements (sci. com. 1986—), Sigma Xi. Mem. Ch. of Christ. Home: 104 New Bedford Ln Oak Ridge TN 37830-4228 Office: Oak Ridge Assoc Univs PO Box 117 Oak Ridge TN 37831-0117

WATSON, HEATHER ANNE, fashion sales manager; b. Springfield, Mass., July 14, 1968; d. Frank D. and Phyllis E. (McCombe) W. AS in Retail, Endicott Coll., 1988; BS in Mktg., Fashion Inst. Tech., 1990. Sales Rita Mitchell, N.Y.C., 1988, B. Altman, N.Y.C., 1988-89; beauty cons. Lancome @ B. Altman, N.Y.C., 1989; sales Ltd. Express, N.Y.C., 1989, Doral Tuscany Hotel, N.Y.C., 1989-90; fashion cons. Anne Klein II, N.Y.C., 1990-91, sample coord., 1991-92, asst. southeast sales mgr., 1992-94, west coast petite sales mgr., 1994—. Mem. NAFE. Republican. Home: 425 E 74th St # 4-B New York NY 10021 Office: Anne Klein II 530 7th Ave New York NY 10018

WATSON, HELEN RICHTER, educator, ceramic artist; b. Laredo, Tex., May 10, 1926; d. Horace Edward and Helen Mary (Richter) Watson. B.A., Scripps Coll., 1947; M.F.A., Claremont Grad. Sch. and U. Ctr., 1949; postgrad. Alfred U., 1966; Swedish Govt. fellow Konstfackskolan, Stockholm, 1952-53. Mem. faculty Chaffey Coll., Ontario, Calif., 1950-52; chmn. ceramics Mt. San Antonio Coll., Walnut, Calif., 1955-57; prof., chmn. ceramics dept. Otis Art Inst., Los Angeles, 1958-81; mem. faculty Otis-Parsons Sch. Design, 1983-88, ret. 1988 ; studio ceramic artist, Claremont, Calif. and Laredo, Tex., 1949—; design cons. Interpace, Glendale, Calif., 1963-64; artist-in-residence Clarement Men's Coll., 1977. Claremont Grad. Sch. fellow, 1948-49; Swedish Govt. grantee, 1952-53; recipient First Ann. Scripps Coll. Disting. Alumna award, Claremont, 1978. Mem. Artists Equity, Nat. Ceramic Soc., Am. Craftsmen's Council, Los Angeles County Mus. Art, Mus. Contemporary Art Los Angeles. Republican. Episcopalian. Address: 220 Brooks Ave Claremont CA 91711-4026 also: 1906 Houston St Laredo TX 78040-7709

WATSON, KATHARINE JOHNSON, art museum director, art historian; b. Providence, Nov. 11, 1942; d. William Randolph and Katharine Johnson (Badger) W.; m. Paul Luther Nyhus, Dec. 17, 1983; stepchildren: Kristina Victoria, Karen Ida, Katharine Ellen. BA, Duke U., 1964; MA, U. Pa., 1967, PhD, 1973. Teaching asst. U. Pa., 1966-67; instr., curator exhbns. U. Pitts., 1969-70; curator of art before 1800 Allen Meml. Art Mus., Oberlin, Ohio, 1973-77; lectr. Oberlin Coll., 1973-77; dir. Peary-MacMillan Arctic Mus. Bowdoin Coll., Brunswick, Maine, 1977-83, dir. Mus. of Art, 1977—; trustee Mus. Art of Ogunquit, 1977-89, Regional Art Conservation Lab., Williamstown, 1977-90, Surf Point Found., York, Maine; mem. Smithsonian Coun. Author: Pietro Tacca, 1983; author text for exhbn. catalogues; co-editor: Allen Meml. Art Mus. Bull, 1974-77; contbr. articles to profl. jours. Mem. profl. adv. com. Victoria Soc. Maine, 1988-93; mem. adv. coun. Archives of Am. Art, 1982-90. Kress Found. fellow, 1967-68, Chester Dale Fellow, 1970-71, Am. Coun. Learned Socs. fellow, 1977-78, Villa I Tatti fellow, 1977-78. Mem. Am. Assn. Art Mus. Dirs., Am. Assn. Museums, Coll. Art Assn. Office: Bowdoin Coll Mus Art Walker Art Bldg Brunswick ME 04011

WATSON, MARY ANN DIEVENDORF, music educator; b. Amsterdam, N.Y., Aug. 4, 1948; d. Anson S. and Rhoda Elaine (Longshore) Dievendorf; m. Thomas A. Bickerstaff, July 5, 1969 (div. 1988); children: Thomas A. Jr., David Anson; m. Stanley C. Watson, Aug. 14, 1992. BA, Chatham Coll., 1970; grad., U. Hartford, 1970-72; tchr. cert., Glassboro State Coll., 1985. Cert. music tchr., N.J. Tchr. gen. music Vineland (N.J.) Pub. Schs., 1986; tchr. vocal music Lower Camden County Bd. Edn., Tansboro, N.J., 1986-87, Glassboro (N.J.) Bd. Edn., 1987—. Pres. Woods Women's Club, Berlin, N.J., 1976-77; soloist, sect. leader Wethersfield (Conn.) First Ch. of Christ, 1972-75, Moorestown (N.J.) Presbyn. Ch., 1982-84, Trinity Presbyn. Ch., Cherry Hill, N.J., 1986—. Mem. Music Educators Nat. Conv., N.J. Music Educators Assn., Glassboro Edn. Assn.(bldg. rep. 1993-94), Choristers Guild. Home: 3 Villanova Ct Berlin NJ 08009

WATSON, MARY ELLEN, ophthalmic technologist; b. San Jose, Calif., Oct. 29, 1931; d. Fred Sidney and Emma Grace (Capps) Doney; m. Joseph Garrett Watson, May 11, 1950; children: Ted Joseph, Tom Fred, Pamela Kay Watson. Cert. ophthalmic med. technologist and surg. asst. Ophthalmic technician Kent W. Christoferson, M.D., Eugene, 1965-80; ophthalmic technologist, surg. asst., adminstr. I. Howard Fine, M.D., Eugene, 1980—; course dir. Joint Commn. Allied Health Pers. in Ophthalmolgy, 1976—, lectr., mem. faculty, 1983—, skill evaluator and site coord., Eugene, 1988—; internat. instr. advanced surgical techniques. Contbr. articles to profl. jours. Recipient 5-Yr. Faculty award Joint Commn. for Allied Health Pers. in Ophthalmology, 1989. Mem. Allied Tech. Pers. in Ophthalmology, Internat. Women's Pilots Assn. Home: 2560 Chaucer Ct Eugene OR 97405-1217 Office: I Howard Fine MD 1550 Oak St Eugene OR 97401-4042

WATSON, MARY JO, special education educator; b. Candandaigua, N.Y., May 7, 1947; d. Joseph William and Mary (Treble) W. BS, Pembroke State U., 1970; postgrad., U. N.C., 1970, East Carolina U., 1977; MS, SUNY, Geneseo, 1983. Cert. tchr. phys. edn., N.C., tchr. phys. edn. and spl. edn., N.Y. Tchr. 3rd grade Scurlock Elem. Sch., Raeford, N.C., 1970-71; tchr. phys. edn., tennis coach, creative dance instr. E.E. Smith Sr. High Sch., Fayetteville, N.C., 1971-73; tchr. social studies and art for gifted students Reilly Rd. Elem. Sch., Fayetteville, 1973-74, specialist elem. phys. edn. resource, 1974-78; devel. specialist Craig Devel. Ctr., Sonyea, N.Y., summer 1981; tchr. spl. edn. Naples (N.Y.) Ctrl. Sch., 1984—; mem. com. special edn. membership, Naples (N.Y.) Ctrl. Sch., special olympic com.- Cumberland County, Reilly Rd. Elem. Sch., Fayetteville, Curriculum Com. E.E. Smith Sr. High Sch., Fayetteville. Author, publisher (jour.) Teaching Exceptional Children, 1982, Learning Disabilities Advocacy Newsletter, The Advocator, 1993. Fellow ASCD, Coun. for Exceptional Children (presenter nat. conf. 1980, 81, Conn. and N.Y. state conf. 1981), N.Y. State United Tchrs., Naples Tchrs. Assn. Home: PO Box 277 Honeoye NY 14471-0277 Office: Naples Ctrl Sch 136 N Main St Naples NY 14512-9201

WATSON, PATRICIA L., library director; b. Jan. 15, 1939; m. Jack Samuel Watson, 1960; children: Bradley, Amanda. BA, Univ. Tenn., 1961, MS in Libr. and Info. Sci., 1975. Cataloging asst. tech. svcs. dept. Knoxville Pub. Libr., 1961-65; adminstrv. asst. Knoxville-Knox County Pub. Libr., 1975-78, head West Knoxville br. libr., 1978-85; dir. Knox County Pub. Libr. System, 1985—. Bd. dirs. Tanasi Girl Scout Coun., 1981-86; treas. Univ. Tenn. Grad. Sch. Libr. and Info. Sci. Alumni Orgn., 1983-84; elder Farragut Presbyn. Ch. Mem. ALA, Tenn. Libr. Assn. (v.p. 1991-92, pres. 1992-93), East Tenn. Libr. Assn. (pres. 1988-89). Office: Knox County Pub Libr System 500 W Church Ave Knoxville TN 37902-2505

WATSON, PATTI RAE, mental health counselor and psychotherapist; b. Phoenix, Oct. 3, 1958; d. Kenneth Wayne Watson and Janice Lee Schramke Motley; m. Donald Leo Miller, Jan. 4, 1994. BS in Psychology, Emporia State U., 1988; MA in Counseling and Guidance, U. Ariz., 1991; postgrad., No. Ariz. U., 1993—. Dir., vol. coord. Ariz. AIDS Info. Line, Phoenix, 1986; co-chair So. Ariz. Task Force on Domestic Violence, Tucson, 1990; psychotherapist-practicum Tucson Ctr. for Women and Children, 1990; psychotherapist intern Cath. Social Svcs., Tucson, 1990-91; psychotherapist in pvt. practice Tucson, 1991-92, Mayer, Ariz., 1993—; psychotherapist Wahkiakum County, Cathlamet, Wash., 1992-93; instr. No. Ariz. U., Flagstaff, 1993. Mem. Women's Ctr. of Yavapai County, Prescott, Ariz., 1993—. U. Ariz. Regent's scholar, 1986-87, Nesbit Agrl. scholar, 1989, U. Ariz. grad. tuition scholar, 1989-91, Ruth R. Cowden scholar, 1990. Mem. APA, Am. Counseling Assn., Emporia State U. Alumni Assn., Kiwanis, Psi Chi, Chi Sigma Iota. Office: PO Box 1230 Mayer AZ 86333-1230

WATSON, PATTY JO, anthropology educator; b. Superior, Nebr., Apr. 26, 1932; d. Ralph Clifton and Elaine Elizabeth (Lance) Andersen; m. Richard Allan Watson, July 30, 1955; 1 child, Anna Melissa. M.A., U. Chgo., 1956, Ph.D. in Anthropology, 1959. Archaeologist-ethnographer Oriental Inst.-U. Chgo., 1959-60, research assoc., archaeologist, 1964-70; instr. anthropology U. So. Calif., Los Angeles, 1961, UCLA, 1961, Los Angeles State U., 1961; asst. prof. anthropology Washington U., St. Louis, 1969-70; assoc. prof. Washington U., 1970-73, prof., 1973—; Edward Mallinckrodt Disting. univ. prof., 1993—; mem. rev. panel NSF, Washington, 1974-76; fellow Ctr. Advanced Study in Behavioral Scis., Stanford, Calif., 1981-82, 91-92. Author: The Prehistory of Salts Cave, Kentucky, 1969, Archaeological Ethnography in Western Iran, 1979; (with others) Man and Nature, 1969, Explanation in Archaeology, 1971, Archaeological Explanation, 1984, Girikihaciyan, A Halafian Site in Southeastern Turkey; author, editor: Archaeology of the Mammoth Cave Area, 1974, Prehistoric Archaeology Along the Zagros Flanks, 1983; co-editor: The Origins of Agriculture, 1992. Grantee NSF, 1959-60, 68, 70, 72-74, 78-79, NEH, 1977-78, Nat. Geog. Soc., 1969-75. Fellow Am. Anthropol. Assn. (editor for archaeology 1973-77), AAAS (chair sect. H 1991-92); mem. NAS, Soc. Am. Archaeology (exec. com. 1974-76, 82-84, editor Am. Antiquity 1984-87, Fryxell medal 1990), Cave Rsch. Found., Assn. Paleorient (sci. bd.), Nat. Speleological Soc. (hon. life, editorial bd. bull. 1979—). Office: Washington U Dept Anthropol Cb # 1114 Saint Louis MO 63130

WATSON, PAULA D., library administrator; b. N.Y.C., Mar. 6, 1945; d. Joseph Francis and Anna Julia (Miksza) De Simone; m. William Douglas Watson, Aug. 23, 1969; children—Lucia, Elizabeth. A.B., Barnard Coll., 1965; M.A., Columbia U., 1966; M.S.L.S., Syracuse U., 1972. Reference librarian U. Ill., Urbana, 1972-77, city planning and landscape architecture librarian, 1977-79, head documents library, 1979-81; asst. dir. gen. services U. Ill. Library, Urbana, 1981—, acting dir. gen. svcs., 1988-93, dir. ctrl. pub. svcs., 1989-93, asst. univ. libr., 1993—. Contbr. articles to profl. jours. N.Y. State Regents fellow Columbia U., N.Y.C., 1965-66; Council on Library Resources profl. edn. and tng. for librarianship grantee, 1983. Mem. ALA (sec. univ. librs. sect. ALA-Assn. Coll. and Rsch. Librs. 1989-91, mem. libr. adminstrn. mgmt. sect. com. on comparative libr. orgn. 1988-89, mem. conf. planning com. optical disk interest group 1988), Ill. Library Assn. Home: 715 W Delaware Ave Urbana IL 61801-4806 Office: U Ill 246 A Library 1408 W Gregory Dr Urbana IL 61801-3692

WATSON, SANDRA M., lawyer; b. Hillsboro, Ill., June 14, 1950; d. Harold Wayne Watson and Elizabeth Ann (Washut) Uhlry; m. Terrence J. Cullen, May 23, 1981; 1 child, Christopher John. BA, MacMurray Coll., Jacksonville, Ill., 1972; JD, U. Ill., 1977. Staff atty. Land of Lincoln Legal Assistance Found., Champaign, Ill., 1977-82, Puget Sound Legal Assistance Found., Tacoma, 1982-83; code compliance coord. Dept. Constrn. and Land Use City of Seattle, 1983-87, asst. city atty. Dept. Law, 1987—. Bd. dirs. MacMurray Coll. Alumni Bd., 1979-82, 92— (Young Alumni award, 1982); mem. St. Vincent de Paul Soc., Burien, Wash., 1992—; commr. Lawyers League Softball, Seattle, 1989—. Mem. Wash. Bar Assn. (land use and environ. sect., bd. dirs. 1993—), Ill. State Bar Assn., Wash. Assn. Mcpl. Attys. (bd. dirs. 1990—, 2d v.p. 1993-94, 1st v.p. 1994-95), N.W. Women's Law Ctr., Wash. Women Lawyers. Office: City of Seattle City Atty's Office 600 4th Ave Rm 1000 Seattle WA 98146

WATSON, SHARON GITIN, psychologist, executive; b. N.Y.C., Oct. 21, 1943; d. Louis Leonard and Miriam (Myers) Gitin; m. Eric Watson, Oct. 31, 1969; 1 child, Carrie Dunbar. B.A. cum laude, Cornell U., 1965; M.A., U. Ill., 1968, Ph.D., 1971. Psychologist City N.Y. Prison Mental Health, Riker's Island, 1973-74; psychologist Youth Services Ctr., Los Angeles County Dept. Pub. Social Services, Los Angeles, 1975-77, dir. clin. services, 1978, dir. Youth Services Ctr., 1978-80; exec. dir. Crittenton Ctr. for Young Women and Infants, Los Angeles, 1980-89, Assn. Children's Svcs. Agys. of So. Calif., L.A., 1989-92, L.A. County Children's Planning Coun., 1992—. Contbr. articles to profl. jours. Mem. Commn. for Children's Svcs. Family Preservation Policy Com., Mayor's Com. on Children, Youth and Families, L.A. Learning Ctrs. Design Team, Interagy. Coun. Child Abuse and Neglect Policy Com.; bd. dirs. L.A. Roundtable for Children, 1988-94, Adolescent Pregnancy Childwatch, 1985-89; trustee L.A. Ednl. Alliance for Restructuring Now; co-chmn. Los Angeles County Drug and Alcohol Abuse Task Force, 1990; mem. planning coun. Dept. Children's Svcs., 1986-88; mem. steering com. western region Child Welfare League Am., 1985-87. Mem. APA, Calif. Assn. Svcs. for Children (sec.-treas. 1983-84, pres. elect 1985-86, pres. 1986-87), Assn. Children's Svcs. Agys. So. Calif. (sec. 1981-83, pres. elect 1983-84, pres. 1984-85), Town Hall Calif., U.S. Figure Skating Assn. (bd. dirs. 1991-93, vice chair 1989-91, chair sanctions and eligibility com.), Pasadena Figure Skating Club (bd. dirs., pres. 1985-87, 89-90). Home: 4056 Camino Real Los Angeles CA 90065-3928 Office: LA County Children's Planning Coun 500 W Temple St Rm B-26 Los Angeles CA 90012-2713

WATSON, SUSAN BRADFORD, pharmacist; b. Henderson, N.C., June 6, 1958; d. James William and Glenna (Garrett) Bradford; m. Daniel Thomas Watson, Jan. 2, 1981; 1 child, Heather Danielle. BS in Pharmacy, U. N.C., 1981. Registered pharmacist. Asst. mgr., pharmacist Revco Drugs, Inc., Oxford, N.C., 1981-83; store mgr., pharmacist Peoples Drugs, Inc., Oxford, N.C., 1983-87; insvc. pharmacist Maria Raeham Hosp., Henderson, N.C., 1987-92; dir. pharmacy Chatham Hosp., Inc., Siler City, N.C., 1992—; mem. Chatham County Bd. Health, Pittsboro, N.C., 1992—. Mem. Chatham County Med. Soc. Democrat. Bpatist. Home: 1007 Parkwood Dr Siler City NC 27344-2353 Office: Chatham Hosp Pharmacy 3D W Ivey St Siler City NC 27344

WATT, LEANNE ELIZABETH, clinical psychologist; b. San Diego, June 5, 1961; d. Richard Edwin and Susan Rae (Greenberg) W. BA in Psychology, Biola U., 1984; MA in Theology, Full. Theol. Sem., 1990; PhD in Clin. Psychology, Fuller Grad. Sch., 1991. Lic. clin. psychologist. Asst. prof. Fuller Grad. Sch. Psychology, Pasadena, Calif., 1990-91; pre-doctoral intern U. So. Calif., L.A., 1990-91; postdoctoral fellow UCLA Med. Ctr., Torrance, 1991-92; NIH postdoctoral fellow Alzheimer's Disease Rsch. Ctr., L.A., 1992-93; clin. psychologist Psychiat. Hosp., Sylmar, Calif., 1993—; clin. psychologist pvt. practice Pasadena, 1993—. Mem. APA, Psi Chi Nat. Honor Soc. Office: 745 S Marengo Ave Pasadena CA 91106-3687

WATT, MOLLY LYNN, educational researcher; b. Danbury, Conn., Jan. 9, 1938; d. Paul Ross and Denise (Dryden) Lynn; m. Daniel Watt, Apr. 26, 1970; children: Robin Flanagan, Kristin Lynn Gustafson. MA, Antioch Coll., 1963; BS cum laude, Lesley Coll., 1970, cert. advanced study, 1979. Tchr. Brookline (Mass.) Pub. Schs., 1970-80; co-founder Tchr. Ctr., Brookline, 1971; adminstr. Amherst (Mass.) Pub. Schs., 1980-81; dir. Ednl. Alternatives, Antrim, N.H., 1980—; sr. assoc. Edn. Devel. Ctr., 1986—, dir. Action Rsch. Ctr.; dir. State Systemic Initiatives (Electronic) Network; mem. adj. faculty Lesley Coll., Keene State Coll., Union Coll.; assoc. prof. Antioch/New Eng. Grad. Sch. Edn. Union Coll., 1986-89; cons. to Computer Camps Internat., Bolt Beranek & Newman, Tech. Edn. Rsch. Ctrs. Nat. Hands-on Workshops; mem. edn. adv. com. Apple Co.; co-leader The Logo and Computers in Edn. workshop, Beijing, Peoples Republic of China, 1986; mem. N.D. Study Group on Edn.; mem. internat. steering com. Classroom Action Rsch. Network, East Anglia, Eng.; dir. Nat. Action Rsch. Ctr. Co-author: Teaching with Logo, 1984, Welcome to Logo, 1984, Assessing Learning, 1992, New Paradigms in Classroom Research, 1993; columnist Teaching and Computers mag.; mem. adv. bd. Internat. Action Rsch. Jour.; contbr. chpts. to books, articles to profl. jours. Bd. mem. N.H. Assn. for Computers in Edn., chmn. publs. com. Danforth grantee; grantee NSF. Mem. ASCD, ASTD, Am. Edn. Rsch. Assn., Nat. Assn. Elem. Sch. Prins., N.H. Assn. Elem. Sch. Prins., New Eng. Coalition Ednl. Leaders, Nat. Coun. Tchrs. of Math, Internat. Soc. Tech. Edn. Democrat. Mem. Soc. of Friends. Address: Gregg Lake Rd Antrim NH 03440

WATTERS, CHERYL MARI, instructional systems specialist; b. Cleve., Feb. 13, 1954; d. Herbert William and Gloria (Mendez) Bagg; m. Terry Ray Watters, Nov. 8, 1976; children: Rachel Monique, Katrina Mari. BA, U.

No. Iowa, 1978, MA, 1980; MS, Fla. State U., 1990. Cert. Spanish and French translator. Trilingual sec. U. No. Iowa, Cedar Falls, 1974-76, anthropology rsch. asst., 1976-78, lang. instr., 1979-85; supr., translator U.S. Army Civil Svc., Columbus, Ga., 1985-86; supr. instructional systems specialist U.S. Army Civil Svc., Columbus, 1986—; instructional designer Fla. Dept. Law Enforcement, Tallahassee, 1990. Com. mem. Alliance Française, Columbus, 1982—, HOLA Sponsorship Program, Columbus, 1986—. Mem. NAFE, Internat. Officers Assn. (spokesperson 1985-87). Roman Catholic. Home: 7161 Secretariet Dr Columbus GA 31909-1851

WATTERS, CYNTHIA ELLEN, preschool owner, operator; b. Milford, Mass., Feb. 1, 1944; d. John Donald Geake and Grace Virginia (Donahue) Barone; m. Mark Lynn Watters, Aug. 3, 1968 (div. Dec. 1981); children: Lynne Marie, Eric Robert. BA in Edn., U. Fla., 1966. Cert. secondary tchr. Tchr. Dade County Pub. Schs., Miami, Fla., 1966-68, Cen. Dauphin Sch. Dist., Harrisburg, Pa., 1968-69; tng. specialist Commonwealth of Pa., Harrisburg, 1969-70; direct distbr. Amway Corp., Harrisburg, 1970-72; office mgr. Doctor's Bldg., Miami, 1974-81; support svcs. supr. North Miami Found. for Sr. Citizens' Svcs., Inc., 1982-84, acting exec. dir., 1983; presch. owner, dir. 3 R.R.R.s Full Svc. Sch., Miramar, Fla., 1985—; pres., sec., treas. Cinderlyn, Inc., Miramar, 1985—; unit leader Art Finds Internat., 1993—; mem. numerous coms. Dade County Assn. Svc. Providers for the Aging, Miami, 1982-84, sec., 1983-84. Chmn. vol. svcs., mem. exec. bd. St. Stephen Sch. PTO, Miramar, 1986-88; team mother S.W. Broward Jr. Athletic Assn., Miramar, 1979-81; chmn. pub. relations com. St. Stephen Edn. Endowment Found., Miramar, 1987; active Embassy Cts. Homeowners Assn., 1991—. Mem. Fla. Assn. for Children Under Six, Broward County Assn. for Children Under Sic, Broward County Kindergarten and Nursery Sch. Assn. Democrat. Roman Catholic. Home: 11136 Long Boat Dr Cooper City FL 33026-4729

WATTERS, TERESA MARIE, health care administrator; b. Columbus, Ohio, Dec. 11, 1961; d. James Lilburn Banner and Eleanor Jane (Lewis) Smith; m. Jerome Wendell Watters, Sept. 9, 1989; 1 child, Ashley Lauren. BS, Howard U., 1984; M in Health Svc. Adminstrn., George Washington U., 1991. From adminstrv. asst. to exec. asst. for clin. ops. George Washington U. Med. Ctr., Washington, 1987-91; from exec. assoc. to dir. bus. ops. VITAS Healthcare Corp., Miami, Fla. and Ft. Worth, 1991-93; regional dir. bus. ops. VITAS Healthcare Corp., Dallas, Ft. Worth, 1993—. Coord. D.C. CARE Health Directory, 1989. Adminstrv. vol. Dept. Health and Human Svcs., Washington, 1987. Mem. Am. Coll. Healthcare Execs. (assoc. 1991—), Nat. Assn. Healthcare Exec., Nat. Hospice Assn., Tex. Hospice Assn. Home: 3924 Baylor Dr Bedford TX 76021

WATTERSON, JOYCE GRANDE, editor, publisher; b. Cleve., May 15, 1937; d. Anthony John Sr. and Helen Bernice (Kramer) Grande; m. Thomas Batchelor, Sept. 27, 1968; children: Sean Anthony, William Grande. BA, Notre Dame Ohio, 1960; Cert. Pratique, U. Paris, 1964; MA, Case Western Res., 1967. Cert. sales profl.; cert. tchr., Ohio. Tchr. Cleve. Bd. Edn., 1960-63, 64-65; asst. pers. dir. Cleve., Ohio Retail, 1965-66; tchr. Shaker Heights (Ohio) Bd. Edn., 1966-69, 71-72, 1983-85; lectr. Cleve. State U., 1987-88, Notre Dame Coll. Ohio, Cleve., 1990-91; adminstrv. dir. No. Ohio Acad. Pharmacy, Cleve., 1991-94. Author, editor, pub.; Cascade Valley Soups, 1989, Cascade Valley Beans, 1992; editor/pub. Concord Gazette, 1994—. Advisor Alateens, Cleve., 1970-73; pres. Parents of U. Sch., Hunting Valley, Ohio, 1986-87. Mem. Le Cercle des Conférences Françaises of Cleve. (pres. 1986-88, life). Republican. Roman Catholic. Home: 7067 Cascade Rd Concord OH 44077-9509 Office: GrandeLine Custom Comm 7067 Cascade Concord OH 44077

WATTLETON, (ALYCE) FAYE, association executive; b. St. Louis, July 8, 1943; d. George and Ozie (Garret) Wattleton; m. Franklin Gordon (div.); 1 child, Felicia. BS in Nursing, Ohio State U., 1964; MS in Maternal and Infant Health Care, Columbia U., 1967; LLD (hon.), Northeastern Univ. Law Sch., 1990; LHD (hon.), Long Island Univ., 1990, Univ. of Pa., 1990, Bard Coll., 1991; HHD (hon.), Oberlin Coll., 1991; LLD (hon.), Wesleyan Univ., 1991. Tchr. Miami Valley Hosp. Sch. Nursing, Dayton, Ohio, 1964-66; asst. dir. Montgomery County Combined Pub. Health Dist., Dayton, 1967-70; exec. dir. Planned Parenthood, Dayton, 1970-78; pres. Planned Parenthood Fedn. Am., Inc., N.Y.C., 1978-92; host syndicated TV show Tribune Entertainment, Chgo., 1992—. Author: How to Talk to Your Child About Sexuality, 1986. Bd. dirs. Kaiser Family Found., Calif. Wellness Found., WNET, Inst. for Internat. Edn., Quidel, Empire Blue Cross Blue Shield, Leslie Fay Cos. Recipient Claude Pepper Humanitarian award Internat. Platform Assn., 1990, Pioneer of Civil Rights and Human Rights award Nat. Conf. of Black Lawyers, 1990, Florina Lasker award N.Y. Civil Liberties Union Found., 1990, Whitney M. Young Jr. Service award Boy Scouts of Am., 1990, Ministry of Women award Unitarian Universalist Women's Fed., 1990, Spirit of Achievement award Albert Einstein Coll. of Med. Yeshiva Univ., 1991, 20th Anniversary Advocacy award Nat. Family Planning and Reproductive Health Assn., 1991, Women of Achievement award Women's Projects and Production, 1991, Margaret Sanger award, 1992, Jefferson Public Service award, 1992, Dean's Distinguished Service award Columbia Sch. of Public Health, 1992. Office: care Fischer-Ross Agy 250 W 57th St New York NY 10107

WATTS, BEVERLY L., civil rights executive; b. Nashville, Feb. 4, 1948; d. Willliam E. and Evelyn L. (Bender) Lindsley; 1 child, Lauren. BS, Tenn. State U., 1969; MS, So. Ill. U., 1973. Mgr., exec. sec. State of Ill. Minority and Female Bus. Enterprise Program, Chgo.; equal opportunity specialist U.S. Dept. of Health, Edn., and Welfare, Chgo.; reginal dir., civil rights/equal employment opportunity USDA, Chgo. Recipient Chgo Forum Gavel award, BEEP Gold Seal award; grad. Leadership Louisville, 1994. Mem. Nat. Urban Affairs Coun., Ky. Women's Leadership Network, Chgo. Forum, Affirmative Action Assn., Chgo. Urban Affairs Coun. (pres.), Coalition 100 Black Women. Office: Ky Commn on Human Rights 322 W Broadway St Fl 7 Louisville KY 40202-2130

WATTS, CAROLE JAYNE, real estate broker, interior designer; b. Orange, N.J., Jan. 6, 1938; d. William John and Irene Elizabeth (Kiss) Matzek; children: Colleen Lee, Kelley Jayne, John Craig; m. George Durnell Jr., Nov. 15, 1986. Student, Coll. William and Mary, 1958, Sch. Interior Design, Ft. Lauderdale, Fla., 1970, Marymont Coll., Boca Raton, Fla., 1971, Bert Rogers Sch. Real Estate, 1972, Sam Brown Sch. Real Estate, Tom Bermingham Sch. Real Estate. Lic. real estate broker, Fla. Pres. Jupiter Island Interiors, Hobe Sound, Fla., 1972—; pres., chmn. bd. dirs. Jupiter Island and Hobe Sound Properties, Inc., Hobe Sound, Fla., 1972—. Contbr. articles in field to local newspapers. Named one of 13 Top Realtors So. Fla. Mem. Nat. Assn. Realtors, Fla. Assn. Realtors, Nat. Multiple Listing Assn., Women's Council Realtors (pres. 1974), Jupiter Island Assn., Hobe Sound C. of C., Jupiter-Tequesta-Hobe Sound Bd. Realtors, Stuart Bd. Realtors. Republican. Catholic. Home: 3801 SE Fairway W Stuart FL 34997-6039 Office: Jupiter Island and Hobe Sound PropertiesInc Box 1083 PO Box 1083 Hobe Sound FL 33475

WATTS, DEBORAH DUDNEY, claims adjuster; b. Tuscaloosa, Ala., Feb. 26, 1956; d. Blonie Ezell and Mildred Irene (Messer) Dudney; m. Robert Tyler Watts Jr., Feb. 14, 1981. BA, Rhodes Coll., 1978. Casualty liability adjuster GAB Bus. Svcs., Memphis, 1978-81; multi-line adjuster GAB Bus. Svcs., Jackson, Miss., 1981-82; supr. adjuster GAB Bus. Svcs., Wilmington, N.C., 1985—; instr. continuing edn. N.C. Dept. Ins., Raleigh, 1991—. Vol. March of Dimes, Wilmington, 1986—. Mem. Nat. Assn. Ins. Women (Claims Woman of Yr. 1988), N.C. Adjusters Assn. (pres. 1994, Adjuster of Yr. 1987), N.C. Assn. Ins. Women, Wilmington Claims Assn. (pres. 1988, Adjuster of Yr. 1987), Wilmington Assn. Ins. Women (Woman of Yr. 1986, pres. 1986), Phi Beta Kappa. Episcopalian. Office: GAB Bus Svcs 5040 New Centre Dr Ste C Wilmington NC 28403

WATTS, ELIZABETH SWANSON, elementary educator; b. Summit, N.J., May 19, 1949; d. Martin and Elizabeth (Peters) Swanson; divorced; children: Jennifer Leigh, Julie Patrice. BS in Edn., Pembroke U., 1978; M in Human Devel. Learning, U. N.C., Charlotte, 1983. 5th grade tchr. Anson County Schs., Wadesboro, N.C., 1978—; chmn. Site Base Mgmt., 1992—; Model T math. tchr., 1994-95. Leader, chmn. svc. unit Anson County Girl Scouts U.S.A., Wadesboro, N.C., 1978-90, dir. day camp, 1978-89, bd. dirs. Hornets' Nest coun., 1983-90; mem. Anson County Arts Coun.; mem. Carolinas Leadership Program, Charlotte, N.C., 1993—. Mem. N.C. Assn. Educators (sch. rep. 1992-93). Methodist. Home: 103 Charlestown Pl Wadesboro NC 28170 Office: Wadesboro Mid Sch Box 939 Wadesboro NC 28170

WATTS, EMILY STIPES, English educator; b. Urbana, Ill., Mar. 16, 1936; d. Royal Arthur and Virginia Louise (Schenck) Stipes; m. Robert Allan Watts, Aug. 30, 1958; children: Benjamin, Edward, Thomas. Student, Smith Coll., 1954-56; A.B., U. Ill., 1958, M.A. (Woodrow Wilson Nat. fellow), 1959, Ph.D., 1963. Instr. English U. Ill., Urbana, 1963-67, asst. prof., 1967-73, assoc. prof., 1973-77, prof., dir. grad. studies dept. English, 1977—; bd. dirs. U. Ill. Athletic Assn., chmn., 1981-83; mem. faculty adv. com. Ill. Bd. Higher Edn., 1984—, vice chmn., 1986-87, chmn., 1987-88. Author: Ernest Hemingway and The Arts, 1971, The Poetry of American Women from 1632 to 1945, 1977, The Businessman in American Literature, 1982; contbg. editor: English Women Writers from the Middle Ages to the Present, 1990; contbr. articles on Jonathan Edwards, Anne Bradstreet to lit. jours. John Simon Guggenheim Meml. Found. fellow, 1973-74. Mem. MLA, AAUP, Midwest MLA, Authors Guild, Ill. Hist. Soc., Phi Beta Kappa, Phi Kappa Phi. Presbyterian. Home: 1009 W University Ave Champaign IL 61821-3317 Office: U Ill 208 English Urbana IL 61801

WATTS, HEATHER, ballerina; b. Long Beach, Calif., Sept. 27, 1953; d. Keith Nevin and Sheelagh Maud (Woodhead) W. Student, Sch. Am. Ballet, N.Y.C. Mem. corps de ballet N.Y.C. Ballet Co., 1970-78, soloist, 1978-79, prin., 1979-95, retired, 1995; dir. N.Y. State Summer Sch. of Arts Sch. of Dance, Saratoga Springs, from 1982; organized dance troupe, Dancers, 1986. Created roles in George Balanchine's Robert Schumann's Davidsbündlertänze, Peter Martin's Rossini Pas de Deux, Lille Suite, Suite from Histoire du Soldat, Calcium Light Night, Sonate di Scarlatti, Concerto for Two Solo Pianos, Tango, A Schubertiad, Song of the Auvergne, Ecstatic Orange, Jerome Robbins' Piano Pieces, Chamber Works, I'm Old Fashioned, & The Four Seasons; performed in N.Y.C. Ballet's Balanchine Celebration, 1993; PBS-TV appearances include Bournonville Dances, The Magic Flute, A Choreographer's Notebook (all Dance in America series), and Lincoln Center Special: Balanchine Celebrates Stravinsky. Recipient Dance Mag. award, 1985; L'Oreal Shining Star award, 1985, Lions of the Performing Arts award N.Y. Pub. Library, 1986. *

WATTS, HELENA ROSELLE, military analyst; b. East Lynne, Mo., May 29, 1921; d. Elmer Wayne and Nellie Irene (Barrington) Long; m. Henry Millard Watts, June 14, 1940; children—Helena Roselle Watts Scott, Patricia Marie Watts Foble. B.A., Johns Hopkins U., 1952, postgrad., 1952-53. Assoc. engr., Westinghouse Corp., Balt., 1965-67; sr. analyst Merck, Sharp & Dohme, Westpoint, Pa., 1967-69; sr. engr. Bendix Radio div. Bendix Corp., Balt., 1970-72; sr. scientist Sci. Applications Internat. Corp., McLean, Va., 1975-84; mem. tech. staff The MITRE Corp., McLean, 1985-94, ret., 1994; adj. prof. Def. Intelligence Coll., Washington, 1984-85. Contbr. articles to tech. jours. Mem. IEEE, AAAS, AIAA, Nat. Mil. Intelligence Assn., U.S. Naval Inst., Navy League of U.S., Air Force Assn., Assn. Former Intelligence Officers, Assn. Old Crows, Mensa, N.Y. Acad. Sci. Republican. Roman Catholic. Avocations: photography; gardening; reading. Home: 4302 Roberts Ave Annandale VA 22003-3508

WATTS, LINDA SIZER, technical information specialist; b. Washington, Aug. 4, 1957; d. Louis Garland and Lillian Bernice (Stewart) Sizer; m. Donald Sylvester Watts, July 17, 1981 (dec. July 1990); 1 child, Donald Sylvester. BA, Howard U., 1979. Lab. asst. Nat. Naval Med. Ctr. U.S. Navy Dept., Bethesda, Md., 1975-76; file clk. Passport Office U.S. Dept. State, Washington, 1978-79, tech. infor specialist Office of Info. Svcs., 1979-94; mgmt. analyst in info. support group Office of Info. Svcs., Washington, 1994—; musician, mgr. Marquees, Washington, 1979-80; musician, asst. mgr. Don Watts Band, Hyattsville, Md., 1981-90, musician, mgr., 1990—. Recorded album A Capital Christmas, 1989. Recipient Golden Poet award World of Poetry, 1992, cert. of achievement Billboard Mag., 1993. Home: 1900 Charleston Pl Hyattsville MD 20783-2818 Office: US Dept State Office of Info Svcs 2201 C St NW Rm B-264 Washington DC 20520-0001

WATTS, WENDY HAZEL, wine consultant; b. York, Pa., Oct. 9, 1952; d. Alphonso Irving and Daphne Jean (Gainsford) Watts; m. Frederic Joseph Bonnie, (div. 1986); m. Kenneth Scott Herron, Feb. 14, 1987 (div. Jan. 1992). BS, U. Cin., 1975. Store mgr. The Grapevine, Inc., Birmingham, Ala., 1978-81; sales rep. Supreme Beverage Co., Birmingham, 1981-84, Internat. Wines Co., Birmingham, 1984-90; nat. sales exec. Kermit Lynch Wine Mcht., Berkeley, Calif., 1990-91; on-premise mgr., fine wine mgr. Premier Beverage Co., Birmingham, 1991-94; key accounts mgr. Ala. Crown Distbg. Co., Birmingham, 1994—; speaker, instr. various groups, Birmingham; co-chmn. Sonoma Wine Tour of Birmingham, 1987-88, chmn. 1989-90; chmn. Wine Tour of France, Birmingham, 1988-89; mem. exec. com. Taste of the Nation, 1992—. Wine columnist Black and White, 1992—; wine radio show host, 1992—. Co-chmn. Multiple Sclerosis Wine Auction, 1992—, mem. exec. com., 1990—. Mem. Wine Educator's Soc., Tuesday Tasting Group. Democrat. Mem. United Ch. Christ.

WAVLE, ELIZABETH MARGARET, music educator, college official; b. Homer, N.Y., Jan. 18, 1957; d. John Andrew Jr. and Louise Hayford (Estey) W. BMus, SUNY, Potsdam, 1979; AM in Libr. Sci., U. Mich., 1980; MS in Edn., Elmira Coll., 1990. Sr. libr. asst. U. Mich., Ann Arbor, 1979-80; pub. svcs. libr. Elmira (N.Y.) Coll., 1980-84, instr. music, 1981—, head tech. svcs., 1984—, coord. women's studies, 1992; mem. South Ctrl. Rsch. Libr. Coun. Interlibr. Loan Adv. Com., Ithaca, N.Y., 1991-93; mem. South Ctrl. Rsch. Libr. Coun. Regional Automation Com., Ithaca, 1994—. Contbr. revs., essays to profl. publs. Mem. Ithaca Concert Band, 1st Unitarian Ch. of Ithaca. Mem. ALA. Democrat. Home: 700 Comfort Rd Spencer NY 14883-9622 Office: Elmira Coll PO Box 7023 Elmira NY 14901

WAX, NADINE VIRGINIA, retired banker; b. Van Horne, Iowa, Dec. 7, 1927; d. Laurel Lloyd and Viola Henrietta (Schrader) Bobzien; divorced; 1 child, Sharlyn K. Wax Munns. Student, U. Iowa, 1970-71; grad. Nat. Sch. Real Estate and Fin., Ohio State U., 1980-81. Jr. acct. McGladrey, Hansen, Dunn (now McGladrey-Pullen Co., CPAs), Cedar Rapids, Iowa, 1944-47; office mgr. Iowa Securities Co. (now Norwest Mortgage Co.), Cedar Rapids, 1954-55; asst. cashier Mchts. Nat. Bank, Cedar Rapids, 1956-75, asst. v.p., 1976-78, v.p., 1979-91; ret., 1991. Bd. dirs., v.p. Kirkwood C.C. Facilities Found., Cedar Rapids, 1970-94; bd. dirs., treas. Kirkwood C.C., 1984-91; trustee Indian Creek Nature Ctr., Cedar Rapids, 1974—; vol. St. Luke's Hosp. Aux., Cedar Rapids, 1981-85; mem. Linn County Regional Planning Commn., 1982-92, Cedar Rapids-Marion Fine Arts Coun., 1984—; bd. suprs. Compensation Commn. for Condemnation, 1987-92; bd. dirs. Am. Heart Assn., Cedar Rapids, 1983-94; mem. Iowa Employment and Tng. Coun., Des Moines, 1982-83. Recipient Outstanding Woman award Cedar Rapids Tribute to Women and Industry, 1984. Mem. Fin. Women Internat. (state edn. chmn. 1982-83), Am. Inst. Banking (bd. dirs. 1968-70), Soc. Real Estate Appraisers (treas. 1978-80), Linn. County Bankers Assn. (pres. 1979-80), Cedar Rapids Bd. Realtors, Cedar Rapids C. of C. (bus.-edn. com. 1986-91), Cedar Rapids Country Club. Republican. Lutheran. Home: 147 Ashcombe SE Cedar Rapids IA 52403-1700

WAX, ROSLYN PAULA, computer company executive; b. Chgo., June 5, 1963; d. Morton Irving and Lorraine Ruth (Borman) W. BBA in Mktg., U. Iowa, 1985. Inside sales rep. Micro Am., Schaumburg, Ill., 1985-86, inside sales mgr., 1986-88; area mgr. Micro Am., Moonachie, N.J., 1988-89; sr. dist. sales rep. Micro Am., Schaumburg, 1989-90; dist. mgr. Merisel, Woodale, Ill., 1990-91; major account exec. Merisel, El Segundo, Calif., 1991-92, dir. sales, 1992-93, dir. major accounts, 1993-94, dir. margin and market-share, 1994—. Home: 320 The Village Apt 207 Redondo Beach CA 90277 Office: Merisel 200 Continental Blvd El Segundo CA 90245

WAXLER, BEVERLY JEAN, anesthesiologist, physician; b. Chgo., Apr. 11, 1949; d. Isadore and Ada Belle (Gross) Marcus; m. Richard Norman Waxler, Dec. 24, 1972; 1 child, Adam R. BS in Biology, No. Ill. U., 1971; MD, U. Ill., Chgo., 1975. Diplomate Am. Bd. Anesthesiology, Am. Bd. Pathology. Intern dept. pathology Northwestern U., Chgo., 1975-76, resident, 1976-79; instr. Rush Presbyn. St. Luke's Med. Ctr., Chgo., 1979-81; asst. prof. pathology Loyola U., Maywood, Ill., 1981-84; resident dept. anesthesiology Cook County Hosp., Chgo., 1984-87, attending anesthesiologist, 1987—; clin. asst. prof. U. Ill., Chgo., 1988—. Contbr. papers to Tissue and Cell, British Jour. Exptl. Pathology, Biochem. Medicine, Calcified Tissue Internat., Jour. Lab. Clin. Med. Recipient B.B. Sankey Anesthesia Advancement award Internat. Anesthesia Rsch. Soc., 1989; Nat. Rsch. Svc. award fellow Nat. Cancer Inst., 1980; grantee Varlen Corp., 1982. Mem. AAAS, Internat. Anesthesia Rsch. Soc., Am. Soc. Anesthesiologists, Sigma Xi. Home: 7615 Church St Morton Grove IL 60053-1618 Office: Cook County Hosp Chicago IL 60612

WAXMAN, PEARL LATTERMAN, early childhood education educator; b. Montclair, N.J., June 7, 1936; d. Louis and Fannie (Schaeffer) Latterman; m. Ronald Waxman, June 19, 1955; children: David, Roberta, Benjamin. AA, Dutchess Community Coll., 1969; BA, Vassar Coll., 1972; MS, Yeshiva U., 1976. Cert. tchr. N.Y. Head tchr. Community United Meth. Ch. Nursey Sch., Poughkeepsie, N.Y., 1972-77; lectr. VandenBerg Learning Ctr., SUNY, New Paltz, 1977-78; dir. Task Force on Child Protection, Inc., Poughkeepsie, 1978-79; trainer Dutchess County Child Devel. Com., and Office Human Resources, Poughkeepsie, 1980; head tchr. NOVA Child Devel. Ctrs., Inc., Arlington, Va., 1980-81; dir., head tchr. DC Jewish Community Ctr. Day Care Ctr., Washington, 1982-86; dir. World Bank Children's Ctr., Washington, 1986-90; early childhood cons. U.S. Dept. Energy, Washington, 1990-91; adj. faculty early childhood edn. program No. Va. Community Coll., Alexandria, 1981-94; adj. faculty Sch. Edn. and Human Svcs. Marymount U., Arlington, 1991—; active No. Va. Early Childhood Adv. Com., Alexandria, 1981-94; workshop leader Montgomery County Child Care Assn., Kensington, Md., 1989—, Confs. Early Childhood Programs Businesses Orgn.; project coord. Model Comprehensive Ctr.-Based Early Childhood Tech. Assistance Project, Va. Coun. Child Day Care and Early Childhood Programs, Reston, 1992—; adj. prof. edn. dept. George Mason U., Fairfax, Va., 1993—. Mem. Va. Assn. for Early Childhood Edn. (pres. 1993—), Nat. Assn. for the Edn. Young Children (commr., mentor, validator), Acad. Early Childhood Programs, Nat. Assn. for the Edn. Young Children (reviewer), Dirs. Exch. Met. Washington. Home: 2369 Paddock Ln Reston VA 22091-2607

WAXMAN, R. ELAINE, managed health care administrator; b. Norfolk, Va., Feb. 12, 1963; d. Clarence Kenneth and Rhoda Anne (Gillespie) Peters; m. David Scott Waxman, Sept. 8, 1990. BA in English with honors, Ind. U., 1984; MA in Pub. Policy Studies with honors, U. Chgo., 1986. Sr. policy cons. Am. Hosp. Assn., Chgo., 1987-88; sr. cons. KPMG Peat Marwick, Chgo., 1988-90; sr. cons. and dir. Blue Cross and Blue Shield Assn., Chgo., 1990-93; v.p. mktg. and sales Green Spring Health Svcs., Chgo., 1993—; prin. staff Workgroup for Electronic Data Interchange, Chgo., Hartford, Conn., 1991-93, Am. Hosp. Assn. Spl. Com. on AIDS/HIV Infection Policy, Chgo., 1987-88. Co-author: Medicaid Options, 1987; contbr. articles to profl. jours. Chmn. AIDS svc. com. Chgo. Sinai Congregation, 1990—; route vol. Open Hand Chgo., 1990— (Vol. Svc. award 1992); bd. dirs. Lincoln-Belmont Pantry, Chgo., 1987-90. Am. Hosp. Assn./Blue Cross and Blue Shield Assn. fellow in health care policy and mgmt., 1986-87. Democrat. Home: 1356 W Fletcher St Chicago IL 60657 Office: Green Spring of Ill 233 N Michigan Ave #1708 Chicago IL 60601

WAY, BARBARA HAIGHT, dermatologist; b. Franklin, N.J., Dec. 27, 1941; d. Charles Padley and Alice Barbara (Haight) Shoemaker; m. Anthony Biden Way; children: Matthew Shoemaker Way, Sarah Shoemaker Way. AB in Music cum laude, Bryn Mawr Coll., 1962, postgrad., 1963-64; MD, U. Pa., 1968. Diplomate Am. Bd. Dermatology. Systems engr. IBM, Balt., 1962-63; mem. dean's staff Bryn Mawr (Pa.) Coll., 1963-64; med. intern U. Wis. Hosps., Madison, 1968-69, resident in dermatology, 1969-72; physician emergency rm. St. Francis Hosp., La Crosse, Wis., 1969-72; asst. prof. dept. dermatology Tex. Tech U. Sch. Medicine, Lubbock, 1972-73, from asst. clin. to assoc. clin. prof., 1973-74, asst. prof., assoc. chair, 1974-76, assoc. prof., chair, 1976-81; assoc. clin. prof. Tex. Tech U. Health Scis. Ctr. (formerly Tex. Tech U. Sch. Medicine), Lubbock, 1981-92, founder, dir. dermatology residency tng. program, 1978-81; pvt. practice Lubbock, 1973-74, 81—; acting dir. Lubbock City Health Dept., 1982-83; mem. exec. com. Lubbock Gen. Hosp., 1978-81, mem. credentials com., 1978-81, chmn., 1979-81; mem. presdl. search com. Tex. Tech U., 1979, mem. univ. fringe benefits com., 1980-81; chmn. exec. com. ambulatory clinics Tex. Tech U. Health Scis. Ctr., 1980-81, mem. MPIP-bus. affairs subcom., 1980-81, mem. space com., 1981, mem. anatomy search com., 1981; exec. dir., chmn. search com. Ambulatory Clinic, 1980-81; mem. active staff Meth. Hosp., Lubbock, mem. investigative rev. bd., 1989, subsection chief, 1992, 94; mem. active staff St. Mary of Plains Hosp., Lubbock, mem. credentials com., 1990, 92, 94, founding dir. phototherapy unit, 1990-91, 93, mem. exec. com., 1991, 93, chief dermatology sect., 1991, 93; cons., presenter, rschr. in field. Reviewer Archives Dermatology, Cutis, Pediatric Dermatology, Tex. Medicine; contbr. articles to profl. jours. Alumna admissions rep. Bryn Mawr Coll., 1972-75, 87—; pres. adult choir 1st Presbyn. Ch., 1974, mem. nominating com., 1975; mem. LEAP adv. bd. Lubbock Ind. Sch. Dist., 1979; mem. jud. hearing com. Lubbock Soccer Assn., 1980-82, chmn., 1981-82; mem. water safety com. Lubbock County chpt. ARC, 1982-83; chmn. fund raising com. soccer team Lubbock High Sch., 1986-87, mem. ad hoc parents' com. rev. closing of campus, 1988, sponsor cheerleading camp, 1989; active United Way Campaign, 1987-88; mem. adv. com. Lubbock Ind. Sch. Dist. for Re-Orgn. of Schs., 1990; mem. selection com. outstanding physician Lubbock chpt. Am. Cancer Soc., 1991-94, chmn., 1991; bd. dirs. Tex. Tech U. Med. Found., 1987-89, Double T Connection, 1988-90. Recipient Pathology Preceptorship award Pa. Hosp., 1966. Fellow Am. Acad. Dermatology (reviewer jour.); mem. AMA, Am. Soc. Dermatologic Surgery, Tex. Dermatol. Soc. (chmn. roster com. 1980), Tex. Med. Assn. (mem. sexually transmitted diseases com. 1986-90, mem. coun. pub. health 1990-92, vice councillor dist. III 1992—, chmn. reference com. fin. and orgnl. affairs ann. session 1992), Lubbock County-Garza County Med. Soc. (mem. various coms. 1980—, chmn. sch. and pub. health com. 1983, mem. bd. censors 1983-85, chair 1985, sec. 1986, v.p. 1987, liaison with Tex. Tech U. Health Scis. Ctr. com. 1988-91, co-chmn. pub. rels. com. 1988-89, alternate Tex. Med. Assn. del. 1988-89, del. 1990—, pres.-elect 1989, pres. 1990, chmn. ad hoc bylaws com. 1991-94, chmn. Hippocratic award 1991), Soc. Pediatric Dermatology, Women's Dermatologic Soc. (founding mem.). Office: 4102 24th St Ste 201 Lubbock TX 79410

WAY, CAROL JANE, non-profit organization administrator; b. Providence, Jan. 24, 1940; d. Wilfred Bartholomew and Lillian Elizabeth (Tainsh) Martineau; m. Paul Howard Way, June 28, 1958 (div. 1986); children: Laura L. Way Jordahl, P. Craig, Victoria L. Way Hermansen, J. Brent. EdB, R.I. Coll., 1960; postgrad., U. R.I., 1960; MPA, Mankato (Minn.) State U., 1978; postgrad., Universidad Internacional, Mexico City, 1985. Cert. in secondary edn.; lic. in real estate. Tchr. pub. secondary schs. Scotia, N.Y., 1962-64, 67-68, Schenectady, N.Y., 1968-69; reporter, freelance writer The Long Islander newspaper, Huntington, N.Y., 1969-71; tchr. pub. secondary schs. Avon, Conn., 1971-72; asst. to dir. Ret. Sr. Vol. program, Hartford, Conn., 1972-73; dir. pub. info. Mankato Schs., 1974-78; tchr. pub. secondary schs. Fairfield, Conn., 1979-80; assoc. dir. YWCA of Greater Bridgeport, Conn., 1980-81; dir. alumni relations Sacred Heart U., Fairfield, 1982-84; exec. dir. Westport (Conn.) C. of C., 1986-88, West Hartford (Conn.) C. of C., 1988-91, Greater Meriden (Conn.) C. of C., 1991—; bd. dirs. Child Guidance Ctr. of Greater Bridgeport, 1986—; participant English Inst. SUNY chpt. N.Y. State Tchrs. Assn., 1964. Contbr. articles to mags. and newspapers. Lt. gov. R.I. Girls' State, Providence, 1955; mem. Housewives for Rockefeller and Schenectady Reps., 1964; registered lobbyist various non-partisan groups, Minn. and Washington, 1975-78; chairwoman Blue Earth County (Minn.) Reps., 1975-78; town com. Fairfield Reps., 1980-83; bd. dirs. YMCA of West Hartford. Mem. Nat. Assn. Bus. Economists, Nat. Assn. Female Execs., AAUW (life, bd. dirs. 1963-81, nat. legis. com. 1976-78, 80-83), Women in the Arts (charter), Fairfield Network Exec. Women, Women in Mgmt., Farmington Woods Country Club. Episcopalian. Lodge: Rotary. Home: 48 Gate Ridge Rd Fairfield CT 06432-1164 Office: Greater Meriden C of C 290 Pratt St Meriden CT 06450

WAY, CATHERINE AGNES, librarian; b. Cooperstown, N.Y., Mar. 7, 1950; d. Charles Alanson and Helen Adeline (Morton) W. BA, Elmira Coll., 1972; MA in Librarianship, U. Denver, 1973. Children's libr. James Prendergast Libr., Jamestown, N.Y., 1973-75, gen. svcs. libr., 1975-76, asst. dir., 1976—. Sr. warden St. Luke's Episc. Ch., Jamestown, 1989-94; founder, organizer The Safe House, Jamestown, 1992. Mem. N.Y. Libr. Assn. (treas. 1979-82, v.p./pres.-elect 1983, pres. pub. libraries sect. 1984), YWCA, Embroiderers' Guild Am., Fenton Hist. Soc., Phi Beta Kappa, Beta Phi Mu. Office: James Prendergast Libr Assn 509 Cherry St Jamestown NY 14701

WAYMAN, VICKI KIM, psychotherapist; b. New Martinsville, W.Va., Apr. 16, 1954; d. Kenneth Marion and Mary Elizabeth (Boston) W.; m. Corinne Schoeb, Dec. 19, 1990. BA in Psychology with honors, Lynchburg Coll., 1976; MEd in Counseling, U. Del., 1981; MSW, Widener U., 1994. Cert. counselor; cert. clin. mental health counselor; lic. profl. mental health counselor. Psychiat. attendant Del. State Hosp., Wilmington, 1976-77; social worker II Del. Div. of Social Svcs., Wilmington, 1977-80; counselor U. Del., Newark, 1980-84; therapist, psychol. cons. Human Svcs., Inc., Downingtown, Pa., 1981-84; intern, temporary counselor Bowling Green Inn, Kennett Square, Pa., 1985-86; therapist, cons. Counseling Assocs., Inc., Newark, 1984-86; clin. supr. Open Door, Inc., Claymont, Del., 1987-88; exec. dir. Eugenia Counseling Ctr., Newark, 1988-93; intern Terry Childrens Psychiat. Hosp., New Castle, Del., 1993-94; pvt. practice psychotherapy Wilmington, 1993—; psychol. cons. PsycResource Assocs., Swarthmore, Pa., 1994—. Dir., cons. Gay and Lesbian/AIDS Hotline, Wilmington, 1983-85; counselor vol. Drug Info. Action Hotline, Wilmington, 1977-79; vol. Womens Task Force on Substance Abuse, Wilmington, 1989-91. Mem. Lic. Clin. Social Workers Del., Del. Mental Health Counselors Assn., Del. Assn. Alcoholism and Drug Abuse Counselors, Chi Beta Phi, Phi Kappa Phi. Office: 71 Hillside Rd Wilmington DE 19804

WAYNE, KYRA PETROVSKAYA, writer; b. Crimea, USSR, Dec. 31, 1918; came to U.S., 1948, naturalized, 1951; d. Prince Vasily Sergeyevich and Baroness Zinaida Fedorovna (Fon-Haffenberg) Obolensky; m. George J. Wayne, Apr. 21, 1961; 1 child, Ronald George. B.A., Leningrad Inst. Theatre Arts, 1939, M.A., 1940. Actress, concert singer, USSR, 1939-46; actress, U.S., 1948-51; enrichment lectr. Royal Viking Line cruises, Alaska-Can., Greek Islands-Black Sea, Russia/Europe, 1978-79, 81-82, 83-84, 86-87, 88. Author: Kyra, 1959; Kyra's Secrets of Russian Cooking, 1960, 93; The Quest for the Golden Fleece, 1962; Shurik, 1971; The Awakening, 1972; The Witches of Barguzin, 1975; Max, The Dog That Refused to Die, 1979 (Best Fiction award Dog Writers Assn. Am. 1980); Rekindle the Dreams, 1979, Quest for Empire, 1986, Li'l Ol' Charlie, 1989. Founder, pres. Clean Air Program, Los Angeles County, 1971-72; mem. women's council KCET-Ednl. TV; mem. Monterey County Symphony Guild, 1989-91, Monterey Bay Aquarium, Monterey Peninsula Mus. Art, Friends of La Mirada. Served to lt. Russian Army, 1941-43. Decorated Red Star, numerous other decorations USSR; recipient award Crusade for Freedom, 1955-56; award Los Angeles County, 1972, Merit award Am. Lung Assn. L.A. County, 1988. Mem. Soc. Children's Book Writers, Authors Guild, P.E.N., UCLA Med. Faculty Wives (pres. 1970-71, dir. 1971-75) UCLA Affiliates (life), Los Angeles Lung Assn. (life), Friends of the Lung Assn. (pres. 1988), Carmel Music Soc. (bd. dirs. 1992-94), Idyllwild Sch. Music, Art and Theatre Assn. (trustee 1987), Los Angelenos Club (life). Home: 25031 Hidden Mesa Ct Monterey CA 93940-6633

WEAKLAND, ANNA WU, artist, art educator; b. Shanghai, China, May 1, 1924; came to the U.S., 1947; d. Tse-Chien and Kwei-Ying (Sze) Wu; m. John H. Weakland, Feb. 11, 1950; children: Alan Wade, Lewis Francis, Joan. BA, U. Shanghai, China, 1943; MA, Columbia U., 1948; postgrad., Stanford U., 1953-55. art instr. U. Calif., 1968, 72, 78, 82, 84, Stanford (Calif.) U., 1990; vis. art prof. Zhejiang Acad. Arts, Hangzhou, China, 1991. One-woman shows include De Young Mus., San Francisco, 1959, San Francisco Mus. Modern Art, 1961, Chathan Gallery, Hong Kong, 1963, Seattle Art Mus., 1964, Ashmolian Mus., Oxford, Eng., 1964, Sale Internat./Palacio De Bellas, Mexico City, 1966, Downtown Gallery, N.Y., 1967, Victoria (Can.) Art Mus., 1967, Heritage Gallery, L.A., 1971, Wells Fargo Bank Hdqs., San Francisco, 1973, Macy's, Palo Alto, 1976, I. Magnin, Palo Alto, 1981, Tresidor Union Gallery, Stanfor U., 1982, Palo Alto (Calif.) Med. Found., 1984, Stanford (Calif.) Mus. Art, 1988, Hewlett-Packard Co. Art Gallery, Palo Alto, 1989, Gump's Art Gallery, San Francisco, 1990, Marin County Civic Ctr., San Rafael, Calif., 1994; represented in permanent collections including Ashmolean Mus., Oxford, Eng., U. B.C., Vancouver, Fukuoka (Japan) U., Stanford U., Seattle (Wash.) Art Mus., IBM Corp., others. Named Artist of the Yr., Friends of The Libr. award, Palo Alto, Calif., 1979, Artist of the Month, No. Calif. Home and Garden Mag., Redwood City, Calif., 1992. Mem. Am. Women Caucas for Art, Asian Am. Women Artists Assn. Home: 4245 Manuela Ct Palo Alto CA 94306-3731

WEAN, BLANCHE MCNEELY, accountant; b. Monroe County, Ind., Jan. 28, 1901; d. Homer Clark and Ruth Jane (Tutterrow) McNeely; m. Francis Willard Wean, June 16, 1926 (dec.); children: Jane, Doris, Ruth. BA, Ind. U., 1923, MA, 1932, postgrad., 1945-46. CPA, Ind. Tchr. Mt. Carroll (Ill.) High Sch., 1919-20, Bloomington (Ind.) High Sch., 1920-23, Jefferson High Sch., Lafayette, Ind., 1923-27; head bus. dept. Cen. Normal Coll., Danville, Ind., 1931-47; acct. Wean Acctg., Danville, 1947-80, Wean, Andrews & Co., Danville, 1980—. Mem. Danville Pub. Libr. Bd., 1969-82. Recipient John F. Jenner III Citizenship award, 1972. Mem. Nat. Assn. Pub. Accts., Ind. Pub. Acts. Assn. (pres. 1977-78, Hall of Fame), Danville C. of C. (sec. 1950-75), Bus. and Profl. Womens Assn., Beta Gamma Sigma. Republican. Home: 11 Orchard Ct Danville IN 46122-1166 Office: 249 S Wayne St Danville IN 46122-1925

WEAR, JEAN ANN, accountant; b. Wheeling, W.Va., Oct. 19, 1959; d. Robert J. and Bertha Ann (Beltz) Loth; m. Mark E. Wear, May 21, 1983; children: Sean Michael, Aaron Patrick. BSBA in Acctg., West Liberty State Coll., 1981. CPA. Staff auditor Wheeling Dollar Bank and Trust Co., 1981-84; asst. mgr. Citizens Fidelity Bank and Trust Co., Lexington, Ky., 1985; internal auditor, investment acct. Bradford Nat. Life Ins. Co., Lexington, Ky., 1985-87; v.p. fin., CFO Concordia Mutual Life Assn., Downers Grove, Ill., 1987-93; contr., sec. Zurich Life Ins. Co. Am., Schaumburg, Ill., 1993—. Mem. Oswego (Ill.) Jaycees, 1990-92. Mem. AICPA, Ill. Soc. CPAs, Inst. Mgmt. Accts., Inst. Internal Auditors, Am. Mgmt. Assn. Republican. Lutheran. Office: Zurich Life Ins Co Am 1400 American Ln 12th Fl Schaumburg IL 60173

WEATHERBEE, ELLEN GENE ELLIOTT, botanist, educator; b. Lansing, Mich., Sept. 16, 1939; d. Eugene Bradley and Wilma Alcott (Gardner) Elliott; m. Lee Weatherbee, Aug. 18, 1959; children: Anne Susan, Brent Robert, Julie Patricia. BA in Edn., U. Mich., 1960, postgrad., 1972-77; MA in English Lit., Eastern Mich. U., 1962. Cert. tchr. Tchr. adult edn. Schoolcraft Coll., Livonia, Mich., 1983-85; tchr. adult edn. lifelong learning program U. Mich./Wayne State U., Ann Arbor and Detroit, 1973-84; tchr. adult edn. Leelanau Schs./Sleeping Bear Nat. Lakeshore, 1982—; tchr., nature trip leader adult edn. program Matthaei Bot. Gardens, U. Mich., Ann Arbor, 1984—, dir., founder adult edn. program, 1984—; cons. botanist U. Mich., Ann Arbor, 1977—; cons. on plant and mushroom identification Mich. Hosps. Poison Control Ctr., 1978—; founder, dir. Weatherbee's Bot. Trips, 1990—; field worker for wetlands and threatened and endangered species Mich. Dept. Natural Resources and Army Corp of Engrs.; bot. cons. for wetlands permits, 1991—. Co-author: Edible Wild Plants, A Guide to Collecting and Cooking, 1982; mem. editorial bd. Mich. Botanist, 1978—; contbr. articles to profl. jours. Constable Dem. party,Ann Arbor Twp., Mich. Mem. Austrian Mountain Climbing Soc., British Canoe Union, Fedn. Ont. Naturalists, Great Lakes Sea Kayaking Club, Mich. Acad. Sci., Mich. Bot. Club, Nature Conservancy, N.Am. Mycological Assn., Pipsissewa Chamber Music Soc. Home: 11405 Patterson Lake Dr Pinckney MI 48169-9748 Office: U Mich Matthaei Bot Gardens 1800 N Dixboro Rd Ann Arbor MI 48105-9741

WEATHERFORD, CATHERINE J., state insurance commissioner; b. Miami, Okla., Jan. 26, 1955; d. Joseph E. and Norma J. (Hankins) Mountford; m. Stephen R. Weatherford, July 24; children: Holly Catherine, Allyson Taylor, Chelsey Elizabeth. BA in Polit. Sci., U. Ctrl. Okla., 1991. Exec. sec. Okla. Ins. Dept., Oklahoma City, 1976-79, life accident & health policy analyst, 1980-83, adminstrv. asst., 1983-85, asst. commr., 1985-90; exec. asst. to Gov. State of Okla., Oklahoma City, 1990-91, state ins. commr., 1991—; chmn. Okla. Real Estate Appraise Bd., Oklahoma City, 1991—, State Bd. Property and Casualty Rates, Oklahoma City, 1991—; state dir. Okla. Motor Vehicle Assigned Risk Plan, Oklahoma City, 1991—; active Oklahoma Police Pension & Retirement Bd., Oklahoma City, 1991—, Okla. Firefighters Pension & Retirement Bd., Oklahoma City, 1991—, Okla. Linked Deposit Rev. Bd., Oklahoma City, 1991, Oklahoma State and Edn. Employees Group Ins. Bd., Oklahoma City, 1991, Interagency Coordinating Coun. on Early Childhood Intervention, Oklahoma City, 1992—, Okla. Health Care Study Commn., Oklahoma City, 1992—; bd. trustees Okla. Pub. Employees Retirement Sys., Oklahoma City, 1991—. chmn. Okla. Real Estate Appraisal Bd., 1991—, State Bd. for Property and Casualty Rates; state dir. Okla. Motor Vehicle Assigned Risk Plan, 1991—; mem. Okla. Police Pension & Retirement Bd., 1991—, Okla. Firefighters Pension & Retirement Bd., Okla. Linked Deposit Review Bd., Okla. State and Edn. Employees Group Ins. Bd.; mem. bd. trustees Okla. Pub. Employees Retirement System; mem. Inter Agy. Coord. Coun. on Early Childhood Intervention, 1992—, Okla. Health Care Study Commn. Named Outstanding Young Oklahoman, Jaycees, 1994. Mem. Nat. Assn. Ins. Commrs. (zone chair 1993, treas. edn. and rsch. found. 1993). Democrat. So. Baptist. Office: Okla Ins Commr Office 1901 N Walnut Oklahoma City OK 73105

WEATHERFORD-BATMAN, MARY VIRGINIA, rehabilitation counselor, consultant; b. St. Louis, Mar. 28; d. John Ely and Virginia Louise (Cox) Weatherford; m. Aug. 28, 1965 (div. Jan. 1976); 1 child, Christopher James Batman. Cert. med. technologist, Jackson Meml. Hosp., Miami, Fla., 1966; BS, Barry U., 1984, MBA, 1986, EdS, 1992; postgrad., Union Inst. cert. rehab. counselor. Crossmatch technologist John Elliott Blood Bank, Miami, 1966-68; nurse D. E. Fortner MD, P.A. Gutlohn MD, Miami, 1969-75; allergy technologist Dadeland Allergy, Ear, Nose and Throat Assocs., Miami, 1975-78; tech. mgr. Morris Beck MD, Miami, 1978-86; sales rep. Glaxo, Inc., Research Triangle Park, N.C., 1987-88; med. ctr. specialist Wyeth Ayerst, Phila., 1988-90; hosp. rep. Allen & Hanburys, Div. Glaxo, Inc., Research Triangle Park, 1990; sales cons. Profl. Detailing Network, Princeton, N.J., 1991—; chief psychology intern Miami Heart Inst., 1994—; rehab. counselor Nat. Health & Rehab. Cons., Inc., Miami, 1991—; therapist Ctrs. for Psychol. Growth, 1994; chief psychology intern Miami Heart Inst., 1994—. Vocat. devel. vol. Jackson Meml. Hosp., U. Miami, 1991—; vol. Crippled Children's Soc., Miami, 1968-69, South Miami Hosp., 1959-63. Recipient award DAR, 1962; Training scholar NIH, 1962, Lucille Funk Keely Trust scholar, 1991. Mem. ACA, APA, Assn. for Adult Devel. and Aging, Am. Rehab. Counseling Assn., Fla. Counseling Assn., Fla. Assn. for Adult Devel. and Aging (pres.), Fla. Soc. Med. Technologists, Barry U. Counseling Assn., Miami Parrot Club, Country Club of Coral Gables, Delta Epsilon Sigma. Methodist. Office: PO Box 141196 Miami FL 33114-1196

WEATHERS, BARBARA HILLER, librarian; b. Mineola, N.Y., July 23, 1942; d. Raymond Archer and Marie (Toomey) H.; m. Lloyd Ray Weathers, Aug. 24, 1963; children: Jon, Elizabeth. BA, Tex. A&M, 1965; MA in Secondary Edn., U. Houston, 1982; student, Cambridge U., 1986. Rsch. asst. U. Houston, 1968-70; libr. Queen of Peace Sch., Houston, 1976-83; upper sch. libr. Duchesne Acad., Houston, 1983—; summer adj. prof. U. Houston, 1988—; cons. Villa de Matel, Houston, 1990. Editorial chair Cath. Libr. World, 1992—; contbr. articles to profl. jours.; presenter in field. Mem. Houston Mus. of Fine Arts, 1983—; vol. East End Progress Assn., Houston, 1985-86; mem. exec. bd. Cossaboom YMCA, Houston, 1987-92. Named Libr. of Yr. Catholic Libr. Assn., 1989. Mem. Texas Libr. Assn., Am. Libr. Assn. (com. mem.), Catholic Libr. Assn. (exec. bd. 1989—), Internat. Reading Assn., Greater Houston Area Reading Coun., Ind. Sch. Librs., Am. Assn. Sch. Librs. (mem. exec. bd. 1994—). Roman Catholic. Home: 6721 Wildwood Way Houston TX 77023-4023 Office: Duchesne Acad 10202 Memorial Dr Houston TX 77024-3299

WEATHERS, MARY BECKER, psychologist; b. L.A., Aug. 2, 1947; d. Richard Burton and Margaret Josephine (Komevak) Becker; m. Lawrence Ray Weather, Aug. 29, 1970. BA, U. Calif., Santa Barbara, 1969; MA, Mid. Tenn. State U., 1974; PhD, U. Miami, 1978. Diplomate Am. Bd. Med. Psychotherapists. Pre-sch. tchr. Santa Barbara (Calif.) Sch. Dist., 1970-71; parent advisor Inst. for Mental Retardation and Intellectual Devel., Nashville, 1972-73; psychologist II Divsn. Devel. Disabilities/Wash. State, Spokane, 1978-80; psychologist V Ea. State Hosp., Medical Lake, Wash., 1980-83; pvt. practice psychologist Lawrence R. Weathers, Spokane, 1981—. Sec. Action Women's Exch., Spokane, 1990; bd. dirs. Spokane Mountaineers, 1988-92. Mem. Wash. State Psychol. Assn. (pres. 1984-85), Am. Psychol. Assn. Democrat. Home: E 6921 Jamieson Spokane WA 99223 Office: Lawrence R Weathers Ste 1 W 1525 8th Ave Spokane WA 99204

WEATHERUP, WENDY GAINES, graphic designer, writer; b. Glendale, Calif., Oct. 20, 1952; d. William Hughes and Janet Ruth (Neptune) Gaines; m. Roy Garfield Weatherup, Sept. 10, 1977; children—Jennifer, Christine. B.A., U. So. Calif., 1974; Lic. ins. agt. Freelance graphic designer, desktop pub., Northridge, Calif. Mem. Nat. Assn. Female Execs., U. So. Calif. Alumni Assn., Alpha Gamma Delta. Republican. Methodist. Avocations: photography; travel; writing novels; computers. Home: 17260 Rayen St Northridge CA 91325-2919

WEAVER, BARBARA FRANCES, librarian; b. Boston, Aug. 29, 1927; d. Leo Francis and Nina Margaret (Durham) Weisse; m. George B. Weaver, June 6, 1951; 1 dau., Valerie S. Clark. B.A., Radcliffe Coll., 1949; M.L.S., U. R.I., 1968; Ed.M., Boston U., 1978. Head libr. Thompson (Conn.) Pub. Libr., 1961-69; dir. Conn. State Libr. Svc. Ctr., Willimantic, 1969-72; regional adminstr. Cen. Mass. Regional Libr. System, Worcester, 1972-78; asst. commr. of edn., state libr. State of N.J., Trenton, 1978-91; dir. R.I. Dept. State Libr. Svcs., Providence, 1991—; lectr. Simmons Coll., Boston, 1976-78. Mem. ALA, R.I. Libr. Assn., Chief Officers State Libr. Agys. Office: State Libr Svcs Dept Providence RI 02903-4222

WEAVER, CARRIE ETTA, sales executive; b. Brenham, Tex., Oct. 5, 1935; d. Arthur and Matilda Marietha (Atkinson) Correthers; m. Frank Jay Weaver, July 13, 1956; children: Deborah Lene Weaver Nash, Dianna Lynn Weaver Baronville. AS, Seminole Community Coll., 1978. With Emerson Electric Co., Sanford, Fla., 1976-88; buyer Emerson Electric Co., 1978-86, sr. buyer, 1986-88; beauty cons. Mary Kay Cosmetics, Inc., Winter Springs, Fla., 1982-89, sales dir., 1989—. Chmn. Winter Springs Bd. Adjustment, 1975-80; chmn. administrv. com. St. Augustine Cath. Ch., Casselberry, Fla., 1987-89; chmn. pers. policy, bd. dirs. Seminole Cmty. Vol. Program, Sanford, 1988—, Seminole County Ret. Srs. Vol. Program. Democrat.

WEAVER, CONNIE MARIE, foods and nutrition educator; b. LaGrande, Oreg., Oct. 29, 1950; d. Robert Chesley and Averil Jean (Harris) Shelton; m. Lloyd Rollin Weaver, Dec. 22, 1971; children: Douglas, Mark, Richard. BS, Oreg. State U., 1972, MS, 1974; PhD, Fla. State U., 1978. Teaching asst. Oreg. State U., Corvallis, 1973-74; instr. Grossmont Coll., El Cajon, Calif., 1974-75; rsch. assoc. U. R.I., Kingston, 1975; teaching asst. Fla. State U., Tallahassee, 1975-78, mem. adj. faculty, 1977-78; asst. prof. foods and nutrition Purdue U., West Lafayette, Ind., 1978-84, assoc. prof., 1984-88, prof., 1988—, head, 1991—; rsch. fellow Kraft, Inc., Glenview, Ill., 1988—. Contbr. articles to profl. jours. Mem. Inst. Food Technologists (exec. com. 1991—, Outstanding Svc. and Recognition award Ind. sect. 1984), Am. Chem. Soc., Am. Inst. Nutrition (treas. 1992—), Soc. for Exptl. Biology and Medicine, Sigma Xi, Gamma Sigma Delta. Office: Purdue U Foods-Nutrition Stone Hall West Lafayette IN 47907

WEAVER, DONNA RAE, company executive; b. Chgo., Oct. 15, 1945; d. Albert Louis and Gloria Elaine (Graffis) Florence; m. Clifford L. Weaver, Aug. 20, 1966; 1 child, Megan Rae. BS in Edn., No. Ill. U., 1966, EdD, 1977; MEd, De Paul U., 1974. Tchr. H.L. Richards High Sch., Oak Lawn, Ill., 1966-71, Sawyer Coll. Bus., Evanston, Ill., 1971-72; asst. prof. Oakton Community Coll., Morton Grove, Ill., 1972-75; vis. prof. U. Ill., Chgo., 1977-78; dir. devel. Mallinckrodt Coll., Wilmette, Ill., 1978-80, dean, 1980-83; campus dir. Nat.-Louis U., Chgo., 1983-90, dean div. applied behavioral scis., 1985-89; dean Coll. Mgmt. and Bus., 1989-90; pres. The Oliver Group, Inc., Kenilworth, Ill., 1993—; cons. Nancy Lovely and Assocs., Wilmette, 1981-84, North Ctrl. Assn., Chgo., 1982-90. Contbr. articles to Am. Vocat. Jour., Ill. Bus. Edn. Assn. Monograph, Nat. Coll. Edn.'s ABS Rev., Nat. View. Mem. Ill. Quality of Work Life Coun., 1987—, New Trier Twp. Health and Human Svcs. Adv. Bd., Winnetka, Ill., 1985-88; bd. dirs. Open Lands Project, 1985-87, Kenilworth (Ill.) Village House, 1986-87. Recipient Achievement award Women in Mgmt., 1981; Am. Bd. Master Educators charter disting. fellow, 1986. Mem. Nat. Bus. Edn. Assn., Delta Pi Epsilon (past pres.). Office: 505 N Lake Shore Dr Ste 4010 Chicago IL 60611-3408

WEAVER, LISA SAULS, accountant; b. Zwolle, La., Aug. 1, 1955; d. James Lane and Joyce (Dousay) Sauls; m. Jonathan Devere Sanson, Jan. 12, 1974 (div. Feb. 1978); 1 child, Brande Nanelle; m. Steve A. Weaver, June 29, 1981. BS in Acctg cum laude, U. Ark., Little Rock, 1979. CPA, Ark.; cert. internal auditor. Tutor Learning Devel. Ctr., U. Ark., 1976-78; acct., pension adminstr. Baxley & Assocs., Inc., Little Rock, 1978-80; auditor, audit supr. Ark. Pub. Svc. Commn., Little Rock, 1980-83, 86-88; rate analyst Ark. Western Gas Co., Fayetteville, 1983-85; ind. acctg. cons., Little Rock, 1985; sr. auditor quality control unit audit sect. Ark. Dept. Human Svcs., Little Rock, 1988—. Bd. dirs. Ark. chpt. Nat. Multiple Sclerosis Soc., Little Rock, 1991-93. Recipient Disting. Svc. award Ark. chpt. Nat. Multiple Sclerosis Soc., 1993. Mem. Inst. Internal Auditors, Inst. Cert. Mgmt. Accts. Democart. Home: 5502 A St Little Rock AR 72205-3402 Office: Ark Dept Human Svcs 7th And Main St Ste 900 Little Rock AR 72205

WEAVER, LOIS JEAN, physician, educator; b. Wheeling, W.Va., May 23, 1944; d. Lewis Everett and Ann (Novak) W. BA, Oberlin Coll., 1966; MD, U. Chgo., 1970. Pulmonary fellow Northwestern U., Evanston, Ill., 1975-77; trauma fellow U. Wash. Harborview Hosp., Seattle, 1977-79, research assoc., instr. medicine, 1979-81, clin. asst. prof. medicine, 1983—; clin. research fellow Virginia Mason Med. Research Ctr., Seattle, 1981-82; mem. med. staff Swedish Hosp., Seattle, 1984-92; pulmonary cons. Fred Hutchinson Cancer Research Inst., Seattle, 1984-86, regional med. advisor and med. cons., disability quality br. Social Security, Seattle, 1985—. Contbr. sci. articles to profl. jours. La Verne Noyes scholar U. Chgo., 1966; Parker B. Francis fellow Northwestern U., 1975. Mem. AMA, Am. Thoracic Soc., Wash. Lung Assn., Sigma Xi. Home: PO Box 2098 Kirkland WA 98083-2098 Office: 2201 6th Ave # 53 Seattle WA 98121-1832

WEAVER, MARGUERITE MCKINNIE (PEGGY WEAVER), plantation owner; b. Jackson, Tenn., June 7, 1925; d. Franklin Allen and Mary Alice (Caradine) McKinnie; children: Elizabeth Lynn, Thomas Jackson III, Franklin A. McKinnie. Student, U. Colo., 1943-45, Am. Acad. Dramatic Arts, 1945-46, S. Meisner's Profl. Classes, 1949, Oxford U., 1990, 91. Actress, 1946-52; mem. staff Mus. Modern Art, N.Y.C., 1949-50; journalist radio sta. WTJS-AM-FM, Jackson, Tenn., 1952-55; editor, radio/TV Jackson Sun Newspaper, 1952-55; columnist Bolivar (Tenn.) Bulletin-Times, 1986—; chmn. Ho. of Reps. of Old Line Dist., Hardeman County, Tenn., 1985-91, 94—. Founder Paris-Henry County (Tenn.) Arts Coun., 1965; pres. Assn. Preservation of Tenn. Antiquities, Hardeman County chpt., 1991—; charter mem. adv. bd. Tenn. Arts Commn., Nashville, 1967-74, Tenn. Performing Arts Ctr., Nashville, 1972—; chmn. Tenn. Libr. Assn., Nashville, 1973-74; regional chmn. Opera Memphis, 1979-91; mem. nat. coun. Met. Opera, N.Y.C., 1980-92, Tenn. Bicentennial Com., Hardeman County, 1993—. Mem. DAR, Nat. Soc. Colonial Dames Am., Am. Women in Radio and TV, Jackson Golf and Country, English Speaking Union (London chpt.), Summit (Memphis), Dilettantes (Memphis). Methodist.

WEAVER, MAURA MARISA, accountant; b. Chgo., Oct. 25, 1963; d. Mauro and Adriana (Trotta) Padovini; m. Brian Keith Weaver, Sept. 17, 1988. Student, St. Xavier U., 1981-83; grad., DePaul U., 1985, M, 1992. Ops. acct. Talent Ptnrs., Chgo., 1985-93; internal auditor Brian Weaver Appraisals, P.C., Chgo., 1993—; acct. Brian Weaver Apraisals, P.C., Evergreen Park, Ill., 1990—. DePaul U. scholar, Chgo., 1990. Republican. Roman Catholic. Office: Talent Ptnrs 303 E Ohio St Chicago IL 60611

WEAVER, MOLLIE LITTLE, lawyer; b. Alma, Ga., Mar. 11; d. Alfred Ross and Annis Mae (Bowles) Little; m. Jack Delano Nelson, Sept. 12, 1953 (div. May 1970); 1 dau., Cynthia Ann; m. 2d, Hobart Ayres Weaver, June 10, 1970. B.A. in History, U. Richmond, 1978; J.D., Wake Forest U., 1981. Bar; N.C. 1982, Fla. 1983; Cert. profl. sec.; cert. adminstrv. mgr. Supr., Western Electric Co., Richmond, Va., 1952-75; cons., owner Cert. Mgmt. Assocs., Richmond, 1975-76; sole practice, Ft. Lauderdale, Fla., 1982-86, Emerald Isle, N.C., 1986-89, Richmond, 1989—. Author: Secretary's Reference Manual, 1973. Mem. adv. council to Bus. and Office Edn., Greensboro, N.C., 1970-73, adv. com. to bus. edn. Va. Commonwealth U., Richmond, 1977. Recipient Key to City of Winston-Salem, N.C., 1963; Epps award for scholarship, 1978. Mem. ABA, N.C. Bar Assn., Fla. Bar Assn., Word Processing Assn. (v.p., founder Richmond 1973-75), Adminstrv. Mgmt. Soc. (com. chmn. Richmond, 1973-75), Phi Beta Kappa, Eta Sigma Phi, Phi Alpha Theta. Republican. Home: 12301 Renwick Pl Glen Allen VA 23060-6959

WEAVER, PAMELA ANN, hospitality research professional; b. Little Falls, N.Y., July 7, 1947; d. Floyd Aron Weaver and Norma May (Putnam) Hoyer; m. Ken Ward McCleary, Mar. 2, 1947; children: Brian Wilson, Blake McCleary, Ryan McCleary. AA, Fulton Montgomery Community Co, Amsterdam, NY, 1968; BA, SUNY, 1970; MA, U. S. Fla., 1973; PhD, Mich. State U., East Lansing, 1978. Mem. Mathematics Dept., Riviera Jr. High Sch., Miami, Fla., 1970-72; grad. asst. Office of Med., Edn. Research and Devel., Mich. State U., East Lansing, 1973-74, Dept. of Mktg., Mich. State U., East Lansing, 1974-75; instr. mktg. Mich. State U., East Lansing; asst. prof. mktg., hospitality svcs. administrn. Cen. Mich. State U.,, Mt. Pleasant, 1978-79, Cen. Mich. U., 1982-86; chair acad. senate Cen. Mich. U., Mt. Pleasant, 1985-86, prof. mktg., hospitality svcs. administrn., 1986-89; prof. Dept. Hospitality and Tourism Mgmt. Va. Poly. Inst. and State U., Blacksburg, 1989—. Contbr. articles to profl. jours. Mem. Coun. on Hotel, Restaurant and Instln. Edn., Acad. Mktg. Sci., Am. Mktg. Assn., So. Mktg. Assn. Office: Va Poly Inst and State U Wallace Hall Blacksburg VA 24061-0429

WEAVER, SIGOURNEY (SUSAN ALEXANDRA WEAVER), actress; b. N.Y.C., Oct. 8, 1949; d. Sylvester (Pat) Weaver and Elizabeth Inglish; m. James Simpson, 1984; 1 child, Charlotte. BA in English, Stanford U., 1971; MA in Drama, Yale U., 1974. First profl. theater appearance in The Constant Wife, 1974; other roles in Beyond Therapy, Hurlyburly, 1984, The Merchant of Venice, 1987; films include: Annie Hall, 1977, Alien, 1979, Eyewitness, 1981, The Year of Living Dangerously, 1982, Deal of the Century, 1983, Ghostbusters, 1984, Aliens, 1986 (Acad. award nomination for best actress), Half Moon Street, 1986, One Woman or Two, 1987, Working Girl, 1988, Gorillas in the Mist, 1988 (Golden Globe award 1989), Ghostbusters II, 1989, Alien 3, 1992, 1492: Conquest of Paradise, 1992, Dave, 1993, Death and the Maiden, 1994. Office: Internat Creative Mgmt care Sam Cohn 40 W 57th St New York NY 10019-4001*

WEAVER, SUSAN JEANNE, sociology educator; b. Huntington, W.Va., Dec. 11, 1950; d. John Francis and Sherley Rae (Wells) Marnell; m. Douglas W. Weaver, Jan. 28, 1970; children: Sarah Marnell, Nathaniel Heath. BA in Sociology, Marshall U., 1975, MA in Sociology, 1980. Instr. in sociology Marshall U., Huntington, 1985—, Ashland (Ky.) C.C., 1988—, Ky. Christian Coll., Grayson, 1993. Vol. Contact of Huntington, 1992—; leader Girl Scouts U.S., Proctorville, Ohio, 1985-92; cub scout den mother Boy Scouts Am., Proctorville, 1990-92. Mem. Am. Sociol. Assn., So. Sociol. Assn., W.Va. Sociol. Assn. (pres. 1993-94). Office: Marshall U Hal Greer & 3d Ave Huntington WV 25755

WEAVER, VELATHER EDWARDS (VAL WEAVER), small business owner; b. Union Hall, Va., Feb. 20, 1944; d. Willie Henry and Ethel (Smith) Edwards; m. Ellersn Fitzpatrick Weaver; children: Frankie Lawrence Mattox Jr., Terence Leon Mattox, Christopher Lamar Williams, Sharon, Shelley, Stephanie. Student, Sonoma State Coll., 1972, U. Calif., Berkeley, 1972; BA, Calif. State U., Hayward, 1973; MBA, St. Mary's Coll., Moraga, Calif., 1989. Coach, counselor Opportunities Industrialization Ctr., Oakland, Calif., 1967-69; tchr. Berkeley Headstart, 1969-70; instr., cons. external degree program Antioch Coll.-West, San Francisco, 1971-74; market analyst World Airways, Inc., Oakland, 1972-75, affirmative action adminstr., 1975-78; cons. A.C. Transit, Oakland, 1982; owner, mgr. Val's Designs and Profl. Svcs., Lafayette, Calif., 1980—; mgr. adminstrn., tng. supr. North Oakland Pharmacy, Inc., 1970—, also bd. dirs.; adv. bd. The Tribune, Oakland, 1982-88. Author RAPRO Self Mgmt. Program, 1985. Program coord., publicity Lafayette Arts and Sci. Found., 1982-83; mem. admission bd. grad. bus. sch. St. Mary's Coll., 1990; bd. dirs. Acalanes High Sch., Lafayette, 1980-82, Lafayette Elem. Sch., 1975-80; mem. City of Lafayette Econ. Devel. Task Force, 1994—. Mem. Calif. State Pharmacists Assn. Aux. (pres. Contra Costa Aux. 1980, pres. state aux. 1986-88, recognition award 1987), Calif. Pharmacists Polit. Action Com. (appreciation award 1988), Diablo Valley

Bus. and Profl. Women (pub. rels. com. 1986-87, best local orgn. award 1987, author yearbook 1987), No. Calif. Med., Dental and Pharm. Assn. Aux. (bd. dirs., com. chair 1975—, pres. elect 1991, pres. 1991-93), Internat. Platform Assn., Links, Inc. Office: North Oakland Pharmacy Inc 5705 Market St Emeryville CA 94608-2892

WEAVER, VIRGINIA DOVE, museum executive; b. Westerly, R.I.; d. Ronald Cross and Elva Gertrude (Burdick) Dove; m. Water Albert Weaver, Jr. (div. Apr. 1982); children—Marshall Gueringer, Claudia Cross, Leila Jane. B.A., Tulane U., 1973; M.A., 1977. Dir. vols.Hermann Grima Hist. House, New Orleans, 1976-77; adminstrv. analyst City Chief Adminstrv. Office, New Orleans, 1977-83; dir. pub. rels. New Orleans Mus. Art, 1983—. chmn. publicity 15th Triennial Vol. Commns. Art Mus. Internat. Conf., New Orleans, 1994. Coeditor: Letters From Young Audiences, 1971; contbr. articles to profl. jours. Bd. dirs. New Orleans chpt. Young Audiences, Inc., 1968-77; co-chmn. New Orleans Symphony Book Fair, 1973-74; mem. city coun. investigative panel SPCA, New Orleans, 1981-82; nat. pub. rels. chmn. Nat. Soc. Daus. of Founders and Patriots Am., 1985-88, publicity chmn. Spirit of 76 chpt., 1988-90. Nat. Coun. Jewish Women grantee, 1977. Mem. Pub. Rels. Soc. Am. (So. Classics anvil award 1985, 87, So. Classics award Excellence 1986), La. Press Assn. (assoc.), La. Travel and Promotion Assn., Deep South Hotel/Motel Assn. Episcopalian. Bd. dirs. Symphony Womens Com., 1982-86; mem. steering com. Mayors Arts Task Force, New Orleans, 1978-79. Clubs: Orleans (fine arts com., current events com., hist. com. 1990-92); Le Petit Salon (chmn. publicity for 150th anniversary 1988, co-chmn. programs 1989, 90—, chmn. summer programs 1994), France-Amérique de la Louisiane, Inc. (bd. dirs. 1992—), Vol. Commits. of Art Mus. (host. com. internat. triennial conf. 1994). Avocation: piano. Home: 7478 Hurst St New Orleans LA 70118-3641 Office: New Orleans Mus Art PO Box 19123 New Orleans LA 70179-0123

WEBB, ALICE MARY, artist, poet; b. Gatesville, Tex., Feb. 10, 1953; d. James Albert and Margaret Brookes (Amis) Dickie; m. Count Brooke Webb, Aug. 15, 1975 (div. 1989); children: James Christian, Marc Abraham Burney. BFA summa cum laude, U. N.Mex., 1993. One woman shows at Palisander Gallery, Taos, N.Mex., 1983, The Collector's Gallery, Nashville, 1987, New Directions Gallery, Taos, 1989, John Sommers Gallery, Albuquerque, 1993; permanent collections include The Shuck Corp., Ctrl. Bank Garden of the Gods, Colorado Springs, United Bank of Skyline, Denver, Diamond Shamrock Bldg., Dallas, Denver U. Hosp., Affiliated Bankshares, Denver, Deloitte-Haskins and Sells, Denver, North Denver Med. Ctr., White & Steel, Denver, others. Group exhbns. include E.S. Lawrence Gallery, Taos, 1987, Stables Art Ctr., Taos, 1988, Paperworks Artist Studio and Gallery, Taos, 1988, Kimo Gallery, Albuquerque, 1991, John Sommers Gallery, Albuquerque, 1992, Frameworks, Albuquerque, 1992, Albuquerque Pub. Libr., 1992, Phillip Bariess Gallery, Taos, 1993, others. U. N.Mex. scholar, 1992. Mem. Albuquerque United Artists. Democrat. Home: 537 Palomas SE # A Albuquerque NM 87108

WEBB, BERNICE LARSON, writer, consultant, press owner, publisher; b. Ludell, Kans.; d. Carl Godfred and Ida Genevieve (Tongish) Larson; m. Ralph Raymond Schear, Aug. 9, 1942 (div. July 1956); children: William Carl Schear, Rebecca Rae Schear Gentry; m. Robert MacHardy Webb, July 14, 1961 (dec. June 1983). BA, U. Kans., 1956, MA, 1957, PhD, 1961; postgrad., U. Aberdeen, Scotland, 1959-60. Asst. instr. English U. Kans., Lawrence, 1958-59, 60-61; asst. prof. U. Southwestern La., Lafayette, 1961-67, assoc. prof., 1967-80, prof., 1980-87; owner, publisher Spider Press, 1991—; vis. assoc. prof. S.S. Universe Campus/World Campus Afloat, 1972; coord. Poetry-in-the-Schs., Lafayette Parish, La., 1974; dir. grad. seminars NDEA Inst. Intellectual and Cultural History, Lafayette, summer 1966; poetry cons. Acadian Arts Coun., 1976-87, Lafayette Parish Schs., 1976-87; bd. dirs. Deep South Writers Conf., 1979—; acting dir. English reading-writing lab., U. Southwestern La., summers 1977, 78, 79, writing cons., 1987—. Author: The Basketball Man, 1973, transl. to Japanese, 1981, new edit., 1994, Beware of Ostriches, 1978, Poetry on the Stage, 1979, Lady Doctor on a Homestead, 1987, Two Peach Baskets, 1991 (with J. Allan) Born to Be a Loser, 1993, Spider Web, 1993; contbr. poetry and articles to various publs.; book reviewer Jour. Am. Culture, Jour. Popular Culture, 1980-87; actress Little Theater, La., 1969-83, off-off Broadway, 1980. Vol. Mayor's Commn. on the Needs of Women, City of Lafayette, 1976-86; vol. La. Talent Bank of Women, 1978-86; judge of writing contests for schs., clubs., profl. socs., La. and U.S., 1961—; newsletter editor Bayou Coun. Girl Scouts of U.S., 1964-66. Mem. AAUW (mem. br. bd. 1967-71, state editor 1967-71, grantee 1978-80, faculty rsch. support grant U. Southwestern La., 1980-81, 85-86), Soc. for Values Higher Edn., S. Ctrl. Coll. English Assn. (pres. 1986-87), S.W. Br. Poetry Soc. (pres. 1988), La. Poetry Soc. (pres. 1978-79, 81-82, editor 1970-90), S Ctrl. MLA, Coll. English Assn., Am. Folklore Soc., Conf. Christianity and Lit., Nat. Fedn. State Poetry Socs. Inc., (Queen of Poetry 1993), Phi Beta Kappa (pres. regional assn. 76-77, 83-84). Mem. AAUW (bd. dirs. br. 1967-71, state editor 1967-71, grantee 1978-80, faculty rsch. grant U. Southwestern La., 1980-81, 85-86), Soc. for Values in Higher Edn., South Ctrl. Coll. English Assn. (pres. 1986-87), S.W. Br. Poetry (pres. 1988—), La. State Poetry Soc. (pres. 1978-79, 81-82, editor 1970-90) South Ctrl. MLA, Coll. English Assn., Am. Folklore Soc., Conf. on Christianity and Lit., Nat. Fedn. State Poetry Socs., Inc. (Queen of Poetry 1993), Phi Beta Kappa (regional pres. 1976-77, 83-84). Democrat. Roman Catholic. Home: 159 Whittington Dr Lafayette LA 70503-2741

WEBB, ELLEN NAIRNE, elementary educator; b. Ann Arbor, Apr. 16, 1918; d. Ivan Norman Sr. and Minnie Almeda (Libey) Cuthbert; m. Kermit Melvin Webb, July 22, 1941 (dec. 1980); children: Frederick Norman, Douglas Melvin, Ronald Kermit, Barry William. BA, U. Mich., 1939. Cert. kindergarten tchr., Tex. Substitute tchr. Hampden (Mass.) Primary Sch., 1958-60; kindergarten tchr. Hampden Community Kindergarten, 1960-62, Dickinson (Tex.) Preparatory Sch., 1963-64; substitute tchr. Dickinson Primary Schs., 1964-65; kindergarten tchr. Easthaven Bapt. Sch., Houston, 1965-69; pre-kindergarten tchr. Paradise Valley (Ariz.) Sch., 1969-70; kindergarten tchr. Easthaven Bapt. Sch., Houston, 1970-72; dir. pre-kindergarten Brittanica Presch., Joliet, Ill., 1972-79; dir. prekindergarten and kindergarten Early Achievement Ctr., Joliet, 1980—; cons., workshop presenter Ency. Britannica Ednl. Corp., Chgo. Author: Britannica Early Childhood Program, 1975. Bible sch. dir., pianist First Presbyn. Ch., Dickinson, Tex., Westminster Presbyn. Ch., Joliet, outreach commn., 1978-79; mem. polit. action and lobbying group Joliet Area Ch., 1991—; cub scout den mother Boy Scouts of Am., 1959-67. Mem. AAUW, Joliet, Ill. and Nat. Assns. for the Edn. of Young Children (sec., publicity and enrichment), Will County Farm Bur. Office: Early Achievement Ctr 353 N Midland Ave Joliet IL 60435

WEBB, EMILY, retired plant morphologist; b. Charleston, S.C., Apr. 10, 1924; d. Malcolm Syfan and Emily Kirk (Moore) W.; m. John James Rosemond, Apr. 23, 1942 (div. 1953); 1 child, John Kirk; m. Julius Goldberg, Sept. 9, 1954; children: Michael, Judith. AB in Liberal Arts and Sci. with honors, U. Ill., Chgo., 1968, MS in Biol. Scis., 1972, PhD in Biol. Scis., 1985. Undergrad. fellow in bacteriology Med. Coll. S.C., Charleston, 1952-54; teaching asst. U. Ill., Chgo., 1969-72, 77-84, rsch. asst., 1977; teaching fellow W.Va. U., Morgantown, 1974, instr., 1974-75; rsch. in N.Am. bot. needlework art, 1986—. Author: Studies in Several North American Species of Ophioglossum, 1986; translator Nat. Transl. Ctr., Chgo., 1976; contbr. articles to profl. jours. James scholar U. Ill., 1968-69. Mem. DAR. Democrat. Episcopalian. Home and Office: 1356 Mandel Ave Westchester IL 60154-3433

WEBB, GLENDA JEFFERSON, nurse; b. Elberton, Ga., Jan. 6, 1954; d. James Ray and Regenia (Blackmon) Jefferson; m. Michael Ayers Webb, Dec. 15, 1974; children: Bridget Dawn, Derrick Michael. BSN in Nursing cum laude, Med. Coll. Ga., 1975. RN, Ga.; cert. PALS. Staff nurse Self Meml. Hosp., Greenwood, S.C., 1975-78; pub. health nurse Elbert County Health Dept., Elberton, Ga., 1978-80, divsn. dir. med./surg. area, 1978-87, emergency med. care first responder, 1980—. CPR instr., 1979-83; emergency room coord., 1987-90, asst. dir. nurses, 1990-91; infection control surveillance nurse, 1987-90, employee health nurse, 1987-90, staff nurse, 1991—; part-time RN, staff nurse 1st Am. Home Care Home Health, 1992—; mem. Emergency Med. Svc. Region 10 Coun., Athens, Ga., 1980-82. Mem. Am. Practitioners in Infection Control, Emergency Nurses Assn., Sigma Theta Tau. Home: 3022 Calhoun Falls Hwy Elberton GA 30635

WEBB, JILLA ROSE, small business owner; b. Detroit, July 26, 1923; d. Arthur Joseph and Rosaria (Mannino) Weber; div.; 1 child, Jilla Rosaria Robertson. Student pub. sch., Detroit. Dancer Jake Shubert, N.Y.C., 1941-42; singer Sonja Henie Ice Show, N.Y.C., 1943-45, MGM Record Co., N.Y.C., 1945-48, MGM Records, N.Y.C., 1948, Mercury Records, N.Y.C., 1948, Mario Lanzo Show, L.A., 1950, Tommy Dorsey Orchestra, N.Y.C., 1958, Jimmy Dorsey Orch., N.Y.C., 1958, Harry James, L.A., 1954-60; owner Jillas Sch. of Dance, Alpena, 1972-91; has taught singing and dancing throughout U.S.; students have won numerous state awards. Choreographer Jr. Miss Shows Awards in 1983, 84, 85, 88. Recipient Nat. award for best choreographer of Jr. Miss Shows, award for the Best in the Nation Young women of Yr. Show. Home: 22770 Pleasant Valley Rd Hillman MI 49746

WEBB, LINDA LOU, buyer; b. Rocky Mount, Va., Aug. 16, 1960; d. Tommy and Virginia P. Webb. AA, Ferrum Coll., 1980; BS, U. Md., Eastern Shore, 1982. Buyer Gardner Denver, Roanoke, Va., 1984-93; customer svc. rep. Blue Cross Blue Shield, Roanoke, 1993; with social svc. dept. City of Roanoke, 1993-94; buyer Va. Transformer, Roanoke, 1994—. Mem. NAACP (treas. 1989—, Support award 1991), Nat. Assn. Purchasing Mgmt. (pres. 1991-92), Delta Sigma Theta Sorority (co-chair polit. awareness 1994, chairperson social action 1994). Home: 2325 Ranch Rd NW Roanoke VA 24017

WEBB, LYNDAL MILLER, principal; b. Deerfield, Fla., Feb. 14, 1933; d. Bowling Dickinson Miller and Cerece Monique (Walker) Miller-Mahoney; m. Thomas Lavelle Webb, Feb. 11, 1951; children: Fredonia W. Ray, Nancy W. Nevil, Gay W. Davis, Susan W. Elsinger. BS in Edn., Valdosta State Coll., 1965, EdM in Elem. Edn., 1968, EdM in Adminstrn. and Supervision, 1971, ednl. specialist, 1982. Cert. adminstrn. and supervision in edn. Resource tchr., classroom tchr. Pine Grove Lowndes County, Valdosta, Ga., 1965-71; asst. prin. Pine Grove Primary, Valdosta, 1971-80, Pine Grove Elem., Valdosta, 1980-83; prin. Hahira Elem. Sch., Valdosta, 1984—. Supervisory chmn. Locoga Credit Union, Valdosta, 1979-93; dir. vacation bible sch. Bemiss United Meth. Ch., Valdosta, 1990-94. Mem. AAUW (v.p. 1986-88), NEA, Ga. Assn. Educators, Lowndes Assn. Educators (prs.), Ga. ASCD (bd. dirs. 1992-94), Internat. Reading Assn., Partnership 2000 (bd. dirs. 1994—), Phi Delta Kappa (prs.), Delta Kappa Gamma (prs. Sigma chpt. 1989-91). Republican. Methodist. Office: Hahira Elem Sch 350 Claudia Dr Hahira GA 31632

WEBB, LYNNE MCGOVERN, communications educator, consultant; b. Shamokin, Pa., Mar. 20, 1951; d. Charles Ralph and Ethel Elizabeth (Harris) McGovern; m. Ronald E. Webb, Sept. 28, 1978 (div. June 1981); m. Robert Blakely Moberly, Apr. 6, 1984; children: Laura Ellen, Richard Edward, Reed JeeMinSeo. BS, Pa. State U., 1972; MS, U. Oreg., 1975, PhD, 1980. Field rep. East Central Ill. Area Agy. on Aging, Campaign, Ill., 1972-74; grad. teaching asst. U. Oreg., Eugene, 1974-78; instr. Berea Coll., Berea, Ky., 1978-80; asst. prof. U. Fla., Gainesville, 1980-86, assoc. prof., 1986-90; vis. assoc. prof. U. Hawaii, Honolulu, 1990-91; assoc. prof. U. Memphis, 1991—; cons. Fla. Farm Bur., Gainesville, 1981, Clay County Electric Coop., Keystone Heights, Fla., 1987, Retirement Rsch. Found., Chgo., 1988. Mem. Fla. Speech Comm. Assn. (v.p. 1986-87), So. States Comm. Assn. (chair applied comm. divsn. 1989-90, chair gender studies divsn. 1992-93, chair membership 1993—, v.p. 1994, pres. 1995), Speech Comm. Assn. (chair com. on comm. and aging 1982-83, legis. coun. 1989-92, chair applied comm. sect. 1994—). Democrat. Methodist. Office: Univ Memphis 143 Theatre and Comm Arts Memphis TN 38152

WEBB, THEORA GRAVES, public relations executive; b. Norfolk, Va., July 21, 1941; d. Lemuel and Theora (Weaver) Graves. BA, Wilson Coll., 1962. Chmn. modern langs. dept. William Henry High Sch., Dover, Del., 1962-64; abstractor-indexer, Rockville, Md., 1966-67; owner RML Translations, Acton, Mass., 1969-70; asst. dir. communications and pub. relations, acting dir. publs. br., spl. asst. to dep. supt., cons.-expert, instr. adult edn. pub. schs. D.C., 1971-78; regional coordinator, cons. Nat. Energy Edn. Day, Cedar Rapids, Iowa, 1979; projects mgr. U.S. Com. for Energy Awareness, Washington, 1980-83; dir. office pub. affairs Internat. Trade Adminstrn., U.S. Dept. Commerce, Washington, 1983-86; pres. HSW Comm., 1986-92; dir. pub. affairs Duracell Internat., Bethel, Conn., 1992—. Mem. energy and econ. devel. com. nat. NAACP, 1980-83, energy task force Nat. Conf. Black Mayors, 1982-83; adv. council vol. services Dist. 7 Dept. Correctional Services, 1979-80; adv. bd. Linn County Jail Chaplaincy, 1979-80, Cedar Rapids YWCA, 1978-80; mem. bd. dirs. Wilson Coll., 1992-94. Mem. Am. Assn. Blacks in Energy, Md. State Right to Read Task Force, Nat. Sch. Pub. Relations Assn., Nat. Assn. Women's Bus. Owners. Council of 100, Nat. Press Club. Home: 2 Davis Ct Martinsville NJ 08836 Office: Duracell Internat Inc Berkshire Industrial Park Bethel CT 06801

WEBB, VERONICA, fashion model, journalist; b. Detroit, Feb. 25, 1965; d. Leonard Douglas and Marion (Stewart) W. Student, New Sch. Social Rsch., 1983; signed with, Ford Models, Inc., N.Y.C., 1992—. Contbg. editor, columnist Paper Mag., 1989—; contbg. editor features column Interview Mag., 1990—; spokesmodel Revlon, 1992—. First featured on cover of Vogue, 1988. First African-Am. to receive exclusive cosmetics contract. Mem. Lifebeat (bd. dirs. 1994—). Office: Ford Models Inc 344 E 59th St New York NY 10022

WEBBER, CATHERINE CARNEY, state legislator, lawyer, social worker, state official; b. New Bedford, Mass., Aug. 11, 1942; d. Henry D. Carney and Catherine (Breault) Richetson; m. William B. Webber, May 21, 1971 (div. 1981); 1 child, Carney. BA in Edn., U. Fla., 1964; MSW, U. Hawaii, 1971; M in Mgmt., Willamette U., 1985, JD, 1985. Bar: Oreg. Supr. social svcs. Dept. Pub. Welfare, Cambridge, Mass., 1966-73; program exec. Children's Svcs. Divsn., 1974-79; program mgr. Oreg. Advocacy Project, 1979-82; law clk.to Hon. Kurt Rossman Oreg. Ct. Appeals, 1985; adminstr./counsel joint interim task force liability ins. Oreg. State Legislature, Salem, 1986; assoc. William, Troutwine & Bowersox, Portland, Oreg., 1987-88; mem. parole bd. Oreg. Bd. Parole and Post Prison Supervision, 1989-91; sr. policy advisor, adminstr. Gov.'s Office, Criminal Justice Svcs. Divsn., 1991-93; mem. Oreg. Senate, 1993—, chair senate edn. com., co-chair joint legis. com. data processing, mem. various coms.; sr. counsel, adminstr. ho. judiciary com. Oreg. Legislature, 1987, sr. counsel, adminstr. senate judiciary com., 1989; mem. exec. bd. Oreg. Coun. Crime and Delinquency. Mem. citizens' budget com. Salem-Keizer Sch. Bd.; mem. citizens budget adv. com., cable regulatory commn. Marion County/City of Salem; mem. Marion County Juvenile Svc. Commn., Oreg. Commn. Hispanic Affairs; bd. dirs. Cath. Community Svcs. Found. Recipient Women of Achievement award YWCA, 1993. Mem. Ladies Aux. VFW. Democrat. Roman Catholic. Office: Oregon Senate State Capital # 215 Salem OR 97310*

WEBBER, POLLY ABBOTT, lawyer, sole practice; b. Pitts., Aug. 2, 1949. BA in Math., U. Calif. Berkeley, 1973; JD, U. Calif. San Francisco, 1976. Bar: Calif. 1977, U.S. Dist. Ct. Calif. 1977, U.S. Ct. Appeals (9th cir.) 1983, U.S. Supreme Ct. 1992. Atty. Park & Litwin, San Francisco, 1977-78, Warwick, Stahl, Gardenr & Webber, Oakland, San Jose, Calif., 1978-80; lectr. law U. Santa Clara (Calif.) Sch. Law, 1980-84; atty. Webber Law Offices, San Jose, 1980—; bd. dirs. Asian Law Alliance, San Jose, 1981—. Contbr. articles to profl. jours. Vol. supr. atty. Legal Aid Soc. Santa Clara County, 1987-91. Recognized Honoree Nat. Ctr. Immigrants' Rights, Inc., 1989; recipient Pro Bono award State Bd. Govs., 1984, 87-90, World of People award Girl Scouts Santa Clara County, 1992. Mem. Com. on Women Lawyers, Santa Clara County Bar Assn., Am. Immigration Lawyers Assn. (pres. 1989-90, officer 1985-89, bd. govs. 1982—, chair No. Calif. chpt. 1981-82). Office: Webber Law Offices 100 Park Ctr Plz Ste 530 San Jose CA 95113

WEBBER, SHERRON HILL, critical care pediatrics nurse; b. Montgomery, Ala., May 26, 1947; d. Florice Arnold and Frances Elizabeth (Kamykowski) Hill; m. John Henry Webber, Sept. 1, 1966 (div. 1989); children: John Henry Jr., Clennan Hill. ADN, Northampton Community Coll., 1984. RN, Ala., Pa., N.J., Wash., Maine; cert. enucleation technician Ala. Eye and Tissue Bank; cert. ACLS, Pediatric Advanced Life Support. Staff nurse in telemetry Warren Hosp., Philipsburg, N.J., 1984-85; staff nurse in CCU St. Margret's Hosp., Montgomery, Ala., 1985-86; staff nurse post anesthesia care unit, pediatrics specialist St. Joseph Hosp., Bellingham, Wash., 1986-89; staff nurse, supr. Humana Hosp. East Montgomery, 1989-90, 1991, staff nurse CCU, 1990-91, staff nurse emergency rm., 1991—; office nurse Pediatric Care Group, Montgomery, 1991—; staff nurse spl. care level II nursery Montgomery Regional Med. Ctr., 1992—; coord. organ and tissue procurement St. Joseph Hosp., Bellingham, 1988-89; technician Lions Eye Bank, Seattle, 1988-89; technician, educator Ala. Eye and Tissue Bank, Birmingham, 1990—; pediatric advanced life support instr. Am. Heart Assn., Montgomery, 1990—. Author ednl. materials for insvc. tng. programs. Democrat. Presbyterian. Home: 3336 Vaughn Rd Montgomery AL 36106

WEBER, ADELHEID LISA, former nurse, chemist; b. Cottbus, Germany, June 1, 1934; came to the U.S., 1958; d. Johannes Gustav Paul and Johanna Katinka (Askevold) Haertwig; m. Joseph Cotrell Weber (dec. 1986), Oct. 25, 1957; children: Robert Andreas, Miriam Lisa. RN, Stadtisches Hosp., Dortmund, Germany, 1956; BS in Distributive Sci., Am. U., 1983; MBA, U. Md., 1991. RN. Nurse Krankenhaus, Wuppertal, Germany, 1956-57; pvt. nurse Wellesley, Mass., 1969-74; lab. tech. Microbiol. Assoc., Bethesda, Md., 1979-84; switchboard operator Best Products Co., Bethesda, 1983-87; lab. tech. Uniformed Svcs. U. Health Scis., Bethesda, 1984-90; info. rsch. tech. Info. Rsch. Internat. Inc., Bethesda, 1987; chemist USDA, Beltsville, Md., 1990-93; ret., 1993. Vol. Sibley Meml. Hosp., Washington, 1991. Recipient Cert. award County of Montgomery, Md., 1988, Whitman Walker Clinic, 1987. Mem. NAFE, Soc. for Rsch. Adminstrs., Am. Chem. Soc., Nat. Assn. for Amputees, Soc. for Applied Spectroscopy, Nat. Trust for Historic Preservation, Hemlock Soc. Nat. Capital Area, Nat. Mus. for Women in Arts, Wash. Performing Arts Soc. Home: 20 A Sunset Ln Osterville MA 02655

WEBER, BECKY BENTSON, federal and state government lawyer; b. Dover, Del., Feb. 18, 1960; d. Rodney Emmanuel and Joan Lee (Campbell) Bentson; m. Luther Paul Weber, Oct. 20, 1990; 1 child, Paul. BA, Baylor U., 1982; JD, U. Kans., 1984. Bar: Kans. 1984. Honors atty. Dept. Transportation, Washington, 1984-86, atty. rsch. and special programs adminstrn., 1986-87, atty. office of gen. counsel, 1987-88; congressional intern to Senator Robert Dole, Washington, 1988—; minority counsel sub-com. on surface transportation Ho. Com. on Pub. Works and Transportation, Washington, 1988—. Mem. Jr. League of Washington, First Baptist Ch., Alexandria, Va. Mem. Coll. Rep., Christian Legal Soc., Gamma Beta Phi, Chi Omega, Pi Sigma Alpha. Office: Surface Transp Subcommittee B-375 Rayburn House Office Bldg Washington DC 20515*

WEBER, GAIL L., lawyer; b. Tacoma, June 14, 1955; d. Arthur Dean and Vera Martha (Grimm) Lundgren; AB cum laude, Vassar Coll., 1977; JD cum laude, U. Puget Sound., 1980. Bar: Wash. 1981. Legal intern Reed, McClure, Moceri & Thonn, Seattle, 1979, Burgess & Kennedy, Tacoma, 1979-80; legal intern Lee, Smart, Cook, Martin & Patterson, P.S., Inc., Seattle, 1980-81, assoc., 1981-92; prin. Law Offices Gail L. Weber, Bothell, Wash., 1992—. Vestry com. Queen Anne Luth. Ch., 1983-86, v.p. of congregation, 1988, 89, mem. worship and music com., 1982-83, 84-86, parish edn. com., 1983-84. Recipient Am. Jurisprudence Book award in Criminal Procedure, Corporations and Business Planning, 1980. Mem. ABA, Fed. Bar Assn., Am. Trial Lawyers Assn., Wash. State Bar Assn., King County Bar Assn., Wash. State Trial Lawyers Assn., Order of Barristers, Wash. State Vassar Club (chmn. alumni admissions 1983-85, rep. 1986-92). Democrat. Avocations: scuba diving, tennis, classical music, needlepoint and stitchery. Office: Law Offices Gail L Weber 19125 Northcreek Pky Ste 120 Bothell WA 98011

WEBER, GLORIA RICHIE, minister, retired, state representative; married; 4 children. BA, Washington U., St. Louis; MA, MDiv, Eden Theol. Sem., Webster Groves, Mo. Ordained to ministry Evang. Luth. Ch. Am., St. Louis, 1974;. Min. Am. Luth. Ch., St. Louis, 1974; family life educator Luth. Family & Children's Svcs. Mo.; state representative State of Mo., 1993—; mem. Ho. of Reps., Mo./com. high edn.; vice-chmn. fed.-state rels. and vets. affairs com., pub. health and safety and social svcs. com., Medicaid and the elderly com., 1993—. Exec. dir. Older Women's League. Recipient Woman of Achievement award St. Louis Globe-Dem., 1977, Unselfish Cmty. Svc. award St. Louis Sentinel Newspaper, 1985, Faith in Action award Luth. Svcs. St. Louis, 1994, Outstanding Woman award Coalition of St. Louis Labor Women, 1994; named Woman of Yr., Variety Club, 1978, Woman of Worth, Older Women's League, 1993. Democrat. Home and Office: 4910 Valley Crest Dr Saint Louis MO 63128 Office: Captiol Bldg House Post Office Jefferson City MO 65101

WEBER, JANET M., nurse; b. Lansdale, Pa., Mar. 12, 1936; d. Russell H. and Naomi (Moyer) W. Diploma in nursing, Washington County Hosp. Sch. Nursing, 1959; B.S. in Nursing, Grace Coll., 1960; M.Ed., Duquesne U., 1969. Staff nurse, supr. Murphy Med. Ctr., Warsaw, Ind., 1959-60; coll. nurse Grace Coll., Winona Lake, Ind., 1959-60; med. surg. nursing instr. Washington County Hosp. Sch. Nursing, Hagerstown, Md., 1961-64; pvt. duty nurse Washington County Hosp., Hagerstown, 1964; chmn. found. of nursing Presbyn. Univ. Hosp. Sch. Nursing, Pitts., 1964-72; curriculum coordinator Albert Einstein Med. Ctr. Sch. Nursing, Phila., 1972-73; assoc. dir. Albert Einstein Med. Ctr. Sch. Nursing, 1973-74, acting dir., 1974, dir., 1974-87; staff nurse ARC Penn-Jersey Blood Drive Donor Services, Phila., 1988-92, asst. nurse mgr., 1992—; nurse mgr. ARC Penn-Jersey Blood Drivce Donor Svcs., Phila., 1992—; cons. Md. Bd. Higher Edn., 1981-82. Author: The Faculty's Role in Policy Development, 1981, Assisting Students with Educational Deficiencies, 1975. Sec. coun. hosps. Schs. Nursing Washington County Hosp., 1979. Mem. Washington County Hosp. Nurses Alumni Assn. (pres. 1962-64), Grace Coll. Alumni Assn., Duquesne U. Alumni Assn. Republican. Home: 5640 Arbor St Philadelphia PA 19120-2502 Office: ARC Blood Donor Svcs 700 Spring Garden St Philadelphia PA 19123

WEBER, JEAN MACPHAIL, museum director; b. Boston, Apr. 2, 1933; d. Harold Percy and Dorothy Norma (Mutch) MacPhail; children: Julia Lee, Karin MacPhail, Laurie Stewart. Student, Brown U. and R.I. Sch. Design, 1950-52, Edinburgh U., Scotland, 1952-53; B.A. magna cum laude, Brown U., 1954; postgrad. Danforth scholar, State U. Iowa, 1954-55. Mgr. Lane Bryant Splty. Shop, Denver, 1956-57; campus advisor Saratoga Springs Council Chs., Skidmore Coll., N.Y., 1960-64; art dir. Our Lady of Peace Hosp., Louisville, 1964-65; dir. Jr. Art Gallery, Louisville, 1965-69, Parrish Art Mus., Southampton, N.Y., 1969-79, Rochester Mus., N.Y., 1979-80, Rochester Mus. and Sci. Ctr., N.Y., 1979-80, Mus. N.Mex., Santa Fe, 1981-85; co-dir. Mus. Mgmt. Inst., U. Calif.-Berkeley, 1981; dir. hist. sites State Hist. Soc. Wis., 1985-90; dir. Marine Maritime Mus., 1990-94, Mus. Art, U. Maine, 1994—; dir. Maine Maritime Mus., 1990-94; dir. U. Maine Mus. of Art, 1994; mem. mus. studies adv. com. Tufts U., Medford, Mass., 1993—; mem. Maine State Archives Commn.; mem. mus. panel Maine Arts Commn. Contbr. articles to profl. jours. Mem. cultural affairs adv. com. Suffolk County, N.Y., 1974—; trustee Brown U., 1983—, Inter Pueblo Cultural Ctr., 1981-82; bd. dirs. Maine Community Cultural Alliance, 1991—. Met. Mus. grantee, 1971. Mem. Am. Assn. Mus. (accreditation commn. 1976-85, chmn. 1982-85, mem. coun. 1979-81, v.p. 1985—, bd. dirs. 1993—), N.E. Mus. Conf. (v.p. 1978-79, pres. 1979-80), Internat. Coun. Mus., N.Y. State Assn. Mus. (coun. 1977-80), Phi Beta Kappa. Mem. Soc. of Friends. Home: Rt 1 Box 2090 Surry ME 04684 Office: U Maine Mus of Art 5712 Carnegie Hall Orono ME 04469-5712

WEBER, JOAN MARGERY, artist, educator; b. N.Y.C., Oct. 21, 1933; d. Arpad and Violet (Bernstein) Willheim; m. Harry Weber (div. 1965); children: Eliot, Anthony, Maria (dec.). BFA, UCLA, 1958; MA, Calif. State U., Northridge, 1967. Lectr. L.A. Pierce Coll., Woodland Hills, Calif., 1969-75; assoc. prof. West L.A. Coll., Culver City, Calif., 1970-89; lectr. UCLA, L.A., 1970-80; tchr. Pepperdine Coll., Malibu, Calif., 1975-77. One-woman shows include Gallery 428 West Broadway, Okayama, Japan, 1982, Orlando Gallery, Sherman Oaks, Calif., 1978, 89, 93, others; group shows include "Geng-Kai" Tokyo, 1984, Aesthetics of Graffiti, San Francisco Mus. Modern Art, 1978, Houston Soc. Illustrators, 1992; pvt. collections include Fluor Corp., Irvine, Calif., Laguna Mus. Art, Laguna Beach, Calif., San Francisco Mus. Modern Art, others. Workshop educator Aids Project L.A., 1988-90. Recipient Video grant Calif. C.C., 1978-80. Mem. Phi Beta Kappa. Home and Office: 4043-1/2 Cumberland Los Angeles CA 90027

WEBER, KATIE, special education educator; b. Delhi, La., Dec. 6, 1933; d. Sullivan and Teresa McClain Aytch; m. Hilliard Weber Jr., June 16, 1956;

children: Barrett Renwick, Sandra Anita, Dawna Lynn, Thaddeus Marc. BA, So. U., 1957; MEd, Tex. So. U., 1982. Cert. elem. and spl. edn. tchr., La., Tex. Elem. tchr. Port Arthur (Tex.) Ind. Sch. Dist., 1957-73, elem. spl. edn. tchr., 1974-85, secondary spl. edn. tchr., 1985—; part-time prin. Port Arthur Ind. Sch. Dist., 1976-83, interim prin., 1983-85; mem. Tex. assessment acad. skills test Tex. Edn. Agy., Austin, 1988-90, scorer master tchr. test, 1990; also curriculum writer. Candidate for city coun. City of Port Arthur, Tex., 1974; active Rock Island Bapt. Ch., Port Arthur, 1975—, Buchanan Cir., 1980—, Port Child Svc. League, Port Arthur, 1989—, Life PTA-Tex. PTA, 1985, Clean Cmty. Commn., Port Arthur, 1990—. Named One of Top 20 Tchrs. in Tex., Leadership Edn., 1984-85, Bus. Assoc. of Yr. plaque Energy City chpt. Am. Women Bus. Assn., 1984. Mem. Assn. Tex. Profl. Educators (Leadership cert. 1989), Zeta Phi Beta. Democrat. Home: 741 E 10th St Port Arthur TX 77640

WEBER, MARY E., lawyer; b. June 21, 1948; d. George H. and Arlis A. (Holleman) Weber; m. Robert Duggan, May, 1977; children: Sarah Duggan, Anne Duggan, Laurence Duggan. BA, Northwestern U., 1970; JD, U. Pa., 1973. Bar: Mass. 1973, Pa. 1973. Ptnr. Ropes & Gray, Boston, 1973—. Trustee Greater Boston Legal Svcs., 1985—, Mass. Continuing Legal Edn., Inc., Boston, 1987—, pres., 1989-92. Office: Ropes & Gray 1 Internat Plz Boston MA 02110

WEBER, NANCY WALKER, charitable trust administrator; b. Adrian, W.Va., Aug. 26, 1936; d. James Everett and Wanna Virginia (Alderman) Walker; m. J. Raymond Jacob, Jr., June 12, 1955 (div. 1967); children: Paul M., Sharon L.; m. George Harry Weber, Apr. 27, 1983. Student, Peabody Prep. Mus., 1946-53, Peabody Conservatory Mus., 1954-56. Asst. buyer cosmetics Hutzler's Dept. Store, Balt., 1967-69; exec. sec. to exec. v.p. Martin Marietta Corp., Bethesda, Md., 1969-75; asst. exec. to exec. dir. hosp. U. Utah, Salt Lake City, 1976-80; dir. program adminstrn. Lucille P. Markey Charitable Trust, Miami, Fla., 1983—. Pianist, organist Middle River Bapt. Ch., Balt., 1953-61. Named Mrs. Del. in Mrs. Del./Am. Pagent, 1966. Office: Lucille P Markey Charitable Trust 3250 Mary St Ste 405 Miami FL 33133-5232

WEBER, PATRICIA, speaker, human resources training executive; b. Glen Cove, N.Y., Mar. 19, 1949; d. Michael R. and Agnes P. (Abbondondolo) Pasucci; m. Boyd Martin Weber, June 28, 1970; 1 child, Christopher Lee. BS in Edn., SUNY, Plattsburgh, 1971; MS in Bus., Troy (Ala.) State U., 1976. European registrar Troy State U., Adana, Turkey, 1974-76; ter. mgr. Burroughs Corp., Newport News, Va., 1976-78; area sales mgr. CCH Computax (PSCI), Norfolk, Va., 1978-81; dept. mgr. Tandy Corp., Norfolk, 1981; sales mgr. Reams Computer Corp., Newport News, 1981-83; saleswoman ComputerLand in Hampton & Norfolk, Norfolk, 1983-85, store mgr., 1985-88, dir. sales and mktg., 1988-90; pres. Profl. Strategies, Inc., Newport News, 1990—. Mem. Chesapeake Bay Found., Md., 1989—. Recipient Tribute to Women in Industry and Bus., YWCA, Hampton, Va., 1985. mem. ASTD, Nat. Assn. Women Bus. Owners (founding pres. Tidewater chpt. 1991), Va. Peninsula C. of C. (Small Bus. Women Adv. 1992), Kiwanis. Office: Profl Strategies Inc Ste 305B 732 Thimble Shoals Blvd Newport News VA 23606-4218

WEBER, SUSAN, research organization executive; b. Freiburg, Germany, Dec. 7, 1941; d. Willie and Anna Marie (Herold) W.; children: Illeny Maaza, Seble-Wengale Maaza. Asst. dir. pub. rels. Ams. for Dem. Action, Washington, 1966-71; legal asst. Strout, Adams, Payson & Pellicani, Rockland, Maine, 1971-72; adminstrv. assoc. Fund for Neighborhood Devel., Washington, 1972-74; sr. assoc. Ct. Internat. Policy, Washington, 1976-78; dir. office of support projects Pub. Citizen Inc., Washington, 1978-79; dir. adminstrn. New Directions, Washington, 1979-80; exec. dir. Zero Population Growth, Washington, 1984—; dep. dir. Zero Population Growth, 1983-84, devel. dir., 1981-83. Editor: USA by Numbers, 1988; dir. study Urban Stress Test, 1988. Mem. Wider Opportunities for Women (treas. bd. dir. 1976-82), Global Tomorrow Coalition (treas. bd. dir. 1987-93), Natural Resources Coun. Am. (bd. dirs. 1984-86, 88—), Nat. Immigration, Refugee, & Citizenship Forum (treas. 1984-86), InterAction (exec. com. 1992—). Office: Zero Population Growth Inc 1400 16th St NW # 320 Washington DC 20036-2290

WEBSTER, CINDY ANN, customer service administrator. BBA, U. Minn., 1989. Asst. store mgr. Neatables, Roseville, Minn., 1989-90; br. adminstrn. trainee/adminstrv. sup. Manulife Fin., Edina, Minn., 1990-92; br. tng./comms. analyst Manulife Fin., Toronto, Ont., Can., 1992-93; customer svc. mgr. Manulife Fin., Bloomfield Hills, Mich., 1993—. Office: Manulife Fin 500 N Woodward Ave Ste 250 Bloomfield Hills MI 48304

WEBSTER, LOIS SHAND, association executive; b. Springfield, Ill., Sept. 25, 1929; d. Richings James and C. Odell (Gilbert) S.; m. Terrance Ellis Webster, Feb. 12, 1954 (dec. July 1985); children: Terrance Richings, Bruce Douglas, Andrew Michael. BA, Millikin U., 1951; cert. in libr. tech., Coll. Du Page County, Glen Ellyn, Ill., 1974; postgrad. libr. sci., No. Ill. U., 1977-82. Exec. asst. Am. Nuclear Soc., La Grange Park, Ill., 1973—. Contbr. articles and book chpts. to profl. pubs. Field dir. Springfield coun. Girl Scouts U.S., 1951-54; libr. advisor Du Page County coun. Girl Scouts U.S., 1973-74. Recipient Octave J. Du Temple award Am. Nuclear Soc., 1989. Mem. Spl. Librs. Assn. (divsn. chmn. 1984-85, chmn. by-laws com. 1987-89, bd. dirs. 1989-92, sec. 1990-91, visioning com. 1992—), Coun. Engring. and Sci. Soc. Execs., Am. Soc. Assn. Execs., Met. Chgo. Libr. Assembly (bd. dirs. 1982-85). Home: 560 Dorset Ave Glen Ellyn IL 60137-5703 Office: Am Nuclear Soc 555 N Kensington Ave La Grange Park IL 60525-5535

WEBSTER, SHARON B., economist; b. Wildwood, Fla., Aug. 23, 1937; d. James McWilliams and Marion (Hallbrook) Boen; BA in Polit. Sci., Econs. and Psychology, U. Fla., 1959; postgrad. (vis. doctoral fellow), Princeton U., 1964-65; PhD, U. Va., 1965. . Asst. prof. No. Mich. U., Marquette, 1962-64, U. Md., 1964-66, Hollins Coll., Roanoke, Va., 1966-71; prof. Fed. Exec. Inst., Charlottesville, Va., 1971-72; internat. program mgr. Dept. Treasury, Washington, 1972-74; economist Econs., Statistics and Coop. Svc., U.S. Dept. Agr., Washington, 1974-79; mem. Presdl. Commn. for Exec. Exchange, 1979-80; dir. internat. econs. Occidental Petroleum Corp., L.A., 1980-83; investment banker, account exec. Johnston, Lemon and Co., Inc., Washington, 1983-88; fin. cons. Shearson Lehman Hutton, 1988—. Mem. adv. bd. Pres.'s Carribbean Basin Initiative, 1982; chmn. bd. dirs. NATA, Inc.; bd. dirs. GENTA, Inc., NABE; pres., chief exec. officer A.A. Global; bd. advisors Sintal Communications USA, Inc., Internat. Trade Council, Patterson Sch. Diplomacy and Internat. Commerce, U. Ky., Consumer Health and Svcs. of Am., Inc. Contbr. articles to profl. jours. Recipient Presdl. award Pvt. Sector Initiative, 1982; NDEA fellow. Mem. AAUP, Internat. Policy Inst. (v.p. 1977—), Internat. Assn. Energy Economists, Am. Assn. Agrl. Economists, Am. Polit. Sci. Assn., Nat. Assn. Bus. Economists, Internat. Studies Assn., Soc. Internat. Devel., Nat. Council Career Women, Washington Soc. Money Mgrs., Assn. Polit. Risk Analysts, Pres.'s Exec. Exchange Assn., Fed. Exec. Inst. Alumni Assn., Capital Speakers Club, Army Navy Club, Internat. Club. Home: The Winthrop # 602 1727 Massachusetts Ave NW Washington DC 20036-2153 Office: AA Global 9039 Furrow Ave Ellicott City MD 21042-1841

WECHSBERG, WENDEE MARA, psychologist, substance abuse consultant; b. Miami, Fla., May 21, 1954; d. Henry and Florence (Orinosky) W.; children: Josh, Sarah. BA, U. South Fla., 1975; MS, Vanderbilt U., 1979; PhD, N.C. State U., 1993. Tchr., counselor Tenn. State Gov., Nashville, 1976-77; counselor Drug & Alcohol Abuse Ctr., Nashville, 1977-79, residential coord., 1979-80; pvt. practice Nashville, 1981-83; treatment dir. Drug Action, Raleigh, N.C., 1984-89; clinician, consultant Carolina Psychiatry, Raleigh, 1990—; rschr., cmty. psychologist Rsch. Triangle Inst., Rsch. Triangle Park, N.C., 1990—; cons. U. N.C. Med. Sch., Chapel Hill, 1990—; project dir. AIDS Outreach, 1987-89; prin. investigator women and HIV risk Nat. Inst. Drug Abuse, 1994—. Contbr. articles to profl. jours. Founder, mem. adv. bd. Jewish Cmty. Svcs., Raleigh, 1986—, AIDS Svc. Agy., Raleigh, 1988—; bd. dirs. Planned Parenthood, Raleigh, 1988-89. Recipient AIDS Svc. Appreciation award N.C. State Govt., 1989, Psychology Emeritus award for rsch. N.C. State U., 1990. Mem. APA, APHA, S.E. Psychology Assn., Addiction Profls. N.C. Democrat. Jewish. Office: Rsch Triangle Inst PO Box 12194 Research Triangle Park NC 27709-2194

WECHSLER, ELLEN, lawyer; b. Boston, Aug. 29, 1950. BA, Radcliffe Coll., 1972; JD, Pitts. Law Sch., 1978. Bar: Pa. Law clk. Allegheny County Pub. Defender's Office, Pitts., 1987-91. Home: PO Box 81810 Pittsburgh PA 15217-0810

WECHSLER, JESSICA See **JOSELL, JESSICA**

WECHSLER, MARY HEYRMAN, lawyer; b. Green Bay, Wis., Jan. 8, 1948; d. Donald Hubert and Helen (Polcyn) Heyrman; m. Roger Wechsler, Aug. 1971 (div. 1977); 1 child, Risa Heyrman; m. David Jay Sellinger, Aug. 15, 1981; 1 stepchild, Kirk Benjamin; 1 child, Michael Paul. Student, U. Chgo., 1966-67, 68-69; BA, U. Wash., 1971; JD, U. Puget Sound, 1979. Bar: Wash. 1979. Assoc. Law Offices Ann Johnson, Seattle, 1979-81; ptnr. Johnson, Wechsler, Thompson, Seattle, 1981-83, Mussehl, Rosenbert et al, Seattle, 1987-88; pvt. practice, Seattle, 1984-87; ptnr. Wechsler, Besk, Erickson, Ross & Rubik, Seattle, 1988—; presenter in field. Author: Family Law in Washington, 1987, rev. edit., 1988; contbr. articles to legal publs. Mem. Wash. State Ethics Adv. Com., 1992—; bd. dirs. Seattle LWV, 1991-92. Fellow Am. Acad. Matrimonial Lawyers (trustee Wash. state chpt.); mem. ABA (membership chmn. Wash. state 1987-88), Wash. State Bar Assn. (exec. com. family law sect. 1985-91, chair 1988-89, legis. com. 1991-94, Outstanding Atty. of Yr. family law sect. 1988), Wash. Women Lawyers, King County Bar Assn. (legis. com. 1985—, vice chmn. 1990-91, chair family law sect. 1986-87, chair domestic violence com. 1986-87, trustee 1988-90, policy planning com. 1991-92, 2d v.p. 1992-93, 1st v.p., 1993-94, pres. 1994—). Office: Wechsler Besk Erickson Ross & Rublik 701 5th Ave Seattle WA 98104-7016

WECHSLER, SUSAN LINDA, software design engineer; b. Burbank, Calif., Oct. 7, 1956; d. Robert Edward and Sharron Ilene Wechsler; m. Gary Daniel Grove, Aug. 24, 1975 (dec. Dec. 1980); m. Dane Bruce Rogers, Feb. 28, 1987; children: Shayna Marneen Rogers, Ayla Corinne Rogers. BA in Math., Calif. State U., Long Beach, 1979. R&D software engr. Hewlett-Packard Co., Corvallis, Oreg., 1980—; Presenter N.W. Software Quality Conf., 1984. Contbr. articles to profl. publs.; patentee in field; co-designer HP 200LX Palmtop PC/Organizer, 1993. Pres. Gifts for a Better World, Corvallis, Oreg., 1994; bd. dirs. Gifts for a Better World, Corvallis, 1990—. Democrat. Office: Hewlett-Packard 1000 NE Circle Blvd Corvallis OR 97330

WECHTER, CLARI ANN, paint manufacturing company executive; b. Chgo., June 1, 1953; d. Norman Robert and Harriet Beverly (Golub) W.; m. Gordon Jay Siegel, Feb. 10, 1980; 1 child, Alix Jessica. BA, U. Ariz., 1975; BE, Loyola U., Chgo., 1977. Cert. tchr., Ill. Saleswoman, v.p. sales Federated Paint Mfg. Co., Chgo., 1979—. Republican. Jewish. Home: 25 E Cedar St Chicago IL 60611-1151 Office: Federated Paint Mfg Co 1882 S Normal Chicago IL 60616

WECK, KRISTIN WILLA, savings bank executive; b. Elgin, Ill., Nov. 5, 1959; d. John Francis and Florence Elaine (Ebel) W. BBA, Augustana Coll., Rock Island, Ill., 1981. Lic. real estate broker, Ill., life/health ins. producer; registered securities rep. (series 7 and series 24). Intern with investment banking group First Chgo. Bank, London, 1980; intern Prudential-Bache Co., Ft. Lauderdale, Fla., 1981; residential appraiser Fox Valley Appraisal Counselors, Ltd., West Dundee, Ill., 1982-84; asst. real estate loan officer First Nat. Bank, Barrington, Ill., 1982-84; savs. and loan field examiner III Office of Thrift Supervision, Chgo., 1984-90; mng. agt. Resolution Trust Corp., Elk Grove Village, Ill., 1990-91; sr. v.p., treas., bd. dirs. Cardunal Savs. Bank, West Dundee, Ill., 1991—. Vice pres. Brandywine Condo Assn., Crystal Lake, Ill., 1983; Project Bus. cons. Jr. Achievement, 1992—. Recipient Outstanding Achievement award Fed. Home Loan Bank Bd., 1985. Mem. Nat. Assn. Securities Dealers (registered rep., registered prin.). Republican. Lutheran. Home: PO Box 930 Dundee IL 60118-0930 Office: Cardunal Savs Bank FSB 704 W Main St Box 97 Dundee IL 60118-0097

WEDDELL, LINDA ANNE, speech and language pathologist; b. Pitts., Nov. 21, 1946; d. Gilbert Eugene and Anna Margaret (Duffer) Everett; m. Charles Michael Weddell, Aug. 7, 1971; children: Michael Everett, Allison Joanne. BS, Purdue U., 1970; postgrad., Butler U., 1987. Speech pathologist Clermont County Sch. System, Batavia, Ohio, 1970-71, MSD Decatur Twp., Indpls., 1971-76; asst. dir. Mom's Day Out program Calvary United Meth. Ch., Brownsburg, Ind., 1983-86; speech pathologist Brownsburg Community Schs., 1989—. Vol. Am. Heart Assn., Indpls., 1988; com. mem. Calvary United Meth. Ch., Brosnwburg, 1976—; dir. Brownsburg Tennis Tournament, 1988; leader Girl Scouts U.S.A., Brownsburg, 1987-89. Continuing edn. grantee Brownsburg Fellowship, 1990. Mem. Ind. Speech & Hearing Assn., Purdue Alumni Assn. (life). Home: 3115 N 950th E Brownsburg IN 46112

WEDDINGTON, ELIZABETH GARDNER (LIZ GARDNER), actress, editor; b. N.Y.C., Oct. 13, 1932; d. A. Adolph and Anne Mary (Gardner) Blank; m. George Lee Weddington, Jr., Oct. 23, 1965; 1 child, Georgiana Marie. Actress TV, radio, telephone, N.Y./Calif, 1957—; editor comml. scripts N.Y., 1969—; freelance writer N.Y. City Tribune, various other publs., N.Y., nat., 1984—. Columnist polit. commentary, 1984—; appeared in over 300 TV commls., also TV and radio voice-overs. Mem. County Com., Conservative Party, N.Y.C., 1988-90, 94-96, 17th Precinct Comty. Coun., N.Y.C., 1974—; rep. Yorkville Area Cath. Coun., N.Y.C., 1986-93. Recipient Mayor's Vol. Action Ctr. award, N.Y.C., 1981-82, Cert. Recognition N.Y.C. Dept. Police Dep. Commr. Community Affairs, 1981. Mem. Screen Actors Guild, Am. Fedn. Radio and TV artists, Nat. League Am. Pen Women, Internat. Platform assn., Nat. Soc. Children of Am. Revolution - Fraunces Tavern Soc. (sr. pres. 1985-89), N.Y. State Soc. Children Am. Revolution (sr. historian 1988-90, sr. 2d v.p. 1990-92), Nat. Soc. DAR (chmn. com. Mary Washington Colonial chpt., corr. sec. 1992-94), Nat. Soc. U.S. Daughters of 1812 (organizing pres. Pres. James Madison Chpt. 360 1988—), N.Y. State Soc. Daughters 1812, N.Y. State Soc. Dames of Ct. of Honor (pres. 1984-88), United Daughters of Confederacy (pres. N.Y. div. 1988-90, nat. chmn. revision of gen. bylaws com. 1989-91, McMath Scholarship gen. com. 1991-92, nat. chmn. gen. bylaws com. 1992—), Daus. Colonial Wars (N.Y. State chpt.), Nat. Geneal. Soc., Colonial Dames of Am. (parent chpt. N.Y. claims com. 1993—). Conservative. Roman Catholic. Home and Office: 401 E 74th St Apt 6D New York NY 10021-3931

WEDEL, MILLIE REDMOND, secondary school educator; b. Harrisburg, Pa., Aug. 18, 1939; d. Clair L. and Florence (Heiges) Aungst; BA, Alaska Meth. U., 1966; MEd, U. Alaska, Anchorage, 1972; postgrad. in comm. Stanford U., 1975-76; m. T.S. Redmond, 1956 (div. 1967); 1 child, T.S. Redmond II; m. Frederick L. Wedel, Jr., 1974 (div. 1986). Lic. third class broadcasting, FCC. Profl. model Charming Models & Models Guild of Phila., 1954-61; public rels. staff Haverford (Pa.) Sch., 1959-61; asst. dir. devel. in charge public rels. Alaska Meth. U., Anchorage, 1966, part-time lectr., 1966, 73; comm. tchr. Anchorage Sch. Dist., 1967—; owner Wedel Prodns., Anchorage, 1976-86; pub. rels. staff Alaska Purchase Centennial Exhibit, U.S. Dept. Commerce, 1967; writer gubernatorial campaign, 1971; part-time instr. Chapman Coll., 1990-93; adj. instr. U. Alaska, Anchorage, 1972, 77-79, 89—; cons. Cook Inlet Native Assn., 1978, No. Inst., 1979; judge Ark. Press Women's Writing Contest, 1990-91; sec. exec. bd. Alaska Dept. Edn. Profl. Tchg. Practices Commn., 1993—. Bd. dirs. Sta. KAKM, Alaska Pub. TV, membership chmn., 1978-80, nat. lay rep. to Pub. Broadcasting Svc. and Nat. Assn. Pub. TV Stas., 1979; bd. dirs. Ednl. Telecom. Consortium for Alaska, 1979, Mid-Hillside Community Coun., Municipality of Anchorage, 1979-80, 83-88, Hillside East Community Coun., 1984-88, pres. 1984-85; rsch. writer, legal asst. Vinson & Elkins, Houston, 1981; mem. Valley Forge Freedoms Found., Murdoch Scholarships, Valley Forge; bd. dirs. Rev. Richard Gay Trust, Alaska and Pa., 1992—; commn. dept. edn. State Alaska, 1993-94, sec. exec. bd. 1993—; v.p. bd. dirs. Inlet View Cmty. Sch., 1994—. Recipient awards for newspapers, lit. mags.; award Nat. Scholastic Press Assn., 1968, 74, 77, Am. Scholastic Press Assn., 1981, 82, 83, 84; Alaska Coun. Econs., 1982, Merits award Alaska Dept. Edn., 1982, 93, Legis. commendation State of Alaska. Mem. NEA (AEA bldg. rep., state del. 70s, 80s, 94-95), Nat. Assn. Secondary Sch. Prins., Nat. Fedn. Interscholastic Speech and Debate Assn., Assn. Pub. Broadcasting (charter mem., nat. lay del. 1980), Indsl. TV Assn. (San Francisco and Houston 1975-81), Alaska Press Club (chmn. high sch. journalism workshops, 1968, 69, 73, awards for sch. newspapers, 1972, 74, 77), Alaska Fedn. Press Women (dir. 1978-86, 94-95, high sch. journalism competition youth projects dir., award for brochures, 1978), Internat. Platform Assn., World Affairs Coun., Alaska Coun. Tchrs. of English, Chugach Electric (chair 1990, nomination com. for bd. dirs. 1988-90), Stanford Alumni Club (pres. 1982-84, 90-92), Capt. Cook Athletic Club, Alaska (Anchorage), Edgewater Beach Club, Glades Country Club (Naples, Fla.), Delta Kappa Gamma. Presbyterian. Office: PO Box 730 Girdwood AK 99587-0730

WEDEMEYER, W. ANNE LITTLE, pediatric cardiologist, educator, lawyer; b. Mercer County, Pa., May 29, 1937; d. Frederick and Lois (Waldorf) Little; m. Phillips Wedemeyer, May 18, 1963 (div. Dec. 1979); children: William J., Hope S., Christian K. BS, U. Pitts., 1959, MD, 1962; JD, Duquesne U., 1988. Diplomate Am. Bd. Pediatrics, Am. Bd. Pediatric Cardiology; bar: Pa. 1989. Intern U. Minn. Hosp., 1962-63, resident, 1966-67, fellow in pediat. cardiology, 1967-69; pediatrician U.S. Army, Hanau, Germany, 1965-66; asst. prof. pediat. U. Pitts., 1969-71; rschr. with Dr. Jessica H. Lewis, 1971-73; dir. pediat. cardiology Mercy Hosp. Pitts., 1972-88, active, adj. staff, 1972-88, 88—; clin. asst. prof. pediat. U. Pitts., 1971—; pvt. practice pediat. cardiology Pitts., 1972—; active staff physician Children's Hosp. Pitts., 1969—; cons. staff Allegheny Gen. Hosp., Pitts., 1978—. Co-chair NCCJ, Pitts., 1991-93, bd. dirs., 1989—, sec.; chair edn. and med. com. Pitts. Friends of Tibet, Trafford, Pa., 1993—, bd. dirs., 1994—, legal and tax com., 1993. Recipient Rsch. award Paul S. and Faith S. Cardiac Fund, 1968-69; rsch. grantee Minn. Heart Assn., 1968-69, Beaver County Heart Assn., 1970-71, HEALTH Rsch. and Svcs. Found., 1973-74; rsch. support grantee U. Pitts., 1971-72. Fellow Am. Acad. Pediat., Am. Coll. Cardiology; mem. AMA, Pa. Med. Soc., Pa. Bar Assn., Allegheny County Med. Soc. (med.-legal sect. 1991—), Allegheny County Bar Assn. (health law sect. 1991—), Fox Chapel Golf Club, Rivers Club (charter). Office: 1501 Locust St Ste 229 Pittsburgh PA 15219

WEDGEWORTH, ANN, actress; b. Abilene, Tex., Jan. 21, 1935; m. Rip Torn (div.); 1 child, Danae; m. Ernest Martin; 1 child, Dianna. Attended, U. Tex.; B.A. in Drama, So. Methodist U. Broadway debut in Make A Million, 1958; other Broadway appearances Chapter Two (Tony award), Thieves, Blues for Mr. Charlie, The Last Analysis; off-Broadway appearances Line, Chapparal, The Crucible, Days and Nights of Beebee Fenstermaker, Ludlow Fair, The Honest to God Shnozzola, A Lie of the Mind; toured with nat. cos. of The Sign in Sidney Brustein's Window and Kennedy's Children; appeared: in TV series Three's Company, The Edge of Night, Another World, Somerset, Filthy Rich, Evening Shade; other TV appearances All That Glitters, The Defenders, Bronk, Evening Shade, Twilight Zone, Trapper John, M.D.; TV film The War Between the Tates, Bogey, Right to Kill, A Stranger Waits; movies Handle With Care (Nat. Soc. Film Critics award), Thieves, Bang the Drum Slowly, Scarecrow, Catamount Killing, Law and Disorder, One Summer Love, Dragon-Fly, Birch Intervals, Soggy Bottom, USA, No Small Affair, Sweet Dreams, Mens Club, A Tiger's Tale, Made in Heaven, Far North, Miss Firecracker, Green Card. Office: care Blake Agy 415 N Camden Dr Ste 121 Beverly Hills CA 90210*

WEDGWOOD, RUTH, law educator; b. N.Y.C.; d. Morris P. and Anne (Williams) Glushien; m. Josiah Francis Wedgwood; May 29, 1982. BA magna cum laude, Harvard U., 1972; fellow, London Sch. Econs., 1972-73; JD, Yale U., 1976. Bar: D.C., N.Y. Law clk. to judge Henry Friendly U.S. Ct. Appeals (2d cir.), N.Y.C., 1976-77; law clk. to justice Harry Blackmun U.S. Supreme Ct., Washington, 1977-78; spl. asst. to asst. atty. gen. U.S. Dept. Justice, Washington, 1978-80; asst. U.S. atty. U.S. Dist. Ct. (so. dist.) N.Y., N.Y.C., 1980-86; prof. law Yale U., New Haven, 1986—, faculty fellow Inst. for Social and Policy Studies, 1989—, faculty fellow Berkeley Coll., 1989—, faculty mem. Yale Internat. Security program, 1992—; mem. Sec. of State's Adv. Com. Internat. Law, 1993—; dir. Coun. Fgn. Rels. study group on UN and Regional Peacekeeping and Conflict Resolution, 1993—; sr. fellow, dir. Coun. Fgn. Rels. Project on Internat. Orgns. and Law, 1994—. Exec. editor Yale Law Jour., 1975-76. Prin. rapporteur U.S. Atty. Gen.'s Guidelines on FBI Undercover Ops., Informant Use and Racketeering and Gen. Crime Investigations, 1980; bd. dirs. Lawyers Com. for Human Rights, N.Y.C., 1988-94. Mem. ABA, Am. Law Inst., Am. Soc. Internat. Law (exec. com. 1995—, chmn. N.Y. Ctr. 1994—), Internat. Law Assn. (v.p. 1994—, program chmn. Am. br. 1992, exec. coun. 1992—), Assn. Am. Law Sch. (chmn.-elect sect. internat. law 1994—), Assn. Bar City N.Y. (arms control and internat. security affairs com., chmn. 1989-92, chmn. internat. affairs coun. 1992—, exec. com. 1995—), Union Internationale des Avocats, U.S.A. (chpt. bd. govs. 1993—, rep. to UN 1995—), Coun. on Fgn. Rels., Elizabethan Club, Yale Club (N.Y.C.), Mchts. Club (N.Y.C.). Office: Yale U Sch Law PO Box 208215 New Haven CT 06520-8215 also: Coun on Fgn Rels 58 E 68th St New York NY 10021

WEED, BARBARA ANN, medical technologist; b. Kansas City, Mar. 3, 1941; d. Olin Dewayne and Catherine Caroline (Kladusan) Myers; m. Thomas Walter Borchert, June 16, 1962 (div.); 1 child, Sherylin Sue Borchert Dakin; m. Ralph Dennis Weed, Feb. 14, 1976; children: Kathleen M., Wesley R. BS in Med. Tech., U. Mo., 1964. Registered med. technologist. Gen. med. technologist St. Margaret's Hosp., Kansas City, 1963-68, sr. chemist med. tech., 1968-75; unit supr. Providence Hosp., Kansas City, 1975-76; supr. stat lab. Providence St. MAargaret;s Health Ctr., Kansas City, 1976-78; med. technologist dept. microbiology Providence St. Margaret's Sch. of Med. Tech., Kansas City, 1978—, instr. med. tech., 1979-90. Office: Providence Med Ctr 8929 Parallel Pky Kansas City KS 66112-1636

WEEDEN, MARY ANN, organizational development executive; b. Troy, N.Y., July 23, 1948; d. John James and Antionette Catherine Foley; m. Paul Joseph Weeden, Aug. 31, 1968; 1 child, Eric Paul. BSBA, Russell Sage Coll., 1978. Corp. rels .rep. Ariz. Pub. Svc., Phoenix, 1983-85, contract adminstr., 1985-88, sr. trainer mgmt. devel., internal cons., 1988-91; organizational devel. adminstr. Data Mgmt. div. Ariz. Dept. Adminstrn., Phoenix, 1991; quality circle leader and facilitator Ariz. Nuclear Power Project, Phoenix, 1988-91; cons., trainer Inroads of Phoenix, 1988-91. Editor The Signature, 1973. Candidates' forum coord. LWV, Albany, 1975-80; coord. Project S.H.A.R.E., Phoenix, 1984-85; exec. advisor Jr. Achievement, Phoenix, 1985-87, Bus. Leader Advisor award, 1986, 87; environ. issues coord. Maricopa County Platform, Phoenix, 1986. Recipient Community Action award Salvation Army, 1985. Mem. Am. Mgmt. Assn., Am. Bus. Women's Assn. (exec. bd. mem., edn. com. chmn. 1984-86), World Affairs Coun.

WEEDN, TRISH, state legislator; b. Oklahoma City, May 10, 1950; d. Carl R. and Teddeline (Morrell) Throckmorton; m. James A. Weedn; children: Marnie, Mindy. Assessor McClain County, Okla., 1979-88; mem. Okla. State Senate, 1989—. Former chmn. McClain County Dem. Com; sect./treas. Purcell Pentacostal Holiness Ch. Mem. Okla. Assn. Assessing Officers, S.W. Coll. Ministry. Democrat. Pentacostal. Office: Okla State Senate State Capitol Oklahoma City OK 73105*

WEEKS, BRIGITTE, publishing executive; b. Whitchurch, Hants, Eng., Aug. 28, 1943; came to U.S., 1965; d. Jack and Margery May (Millett) W.; m. Edward A. Herscher, Sept. 6, 1969; children—Hilary, Charlotte, Daniel. Student, Univ. Coll. of North Wales, Bangor, 1962-65. Asst. editor Boston Mag., 1966-70; editor Kodansha Internat., Tokyo, 1969-72, Resources for the Future, 1973-74; asst. editor The Washington Post Book World, 1974-78, editor, 1978-88; sr. v.p., editor-in-chief Book-of-the-Month Club, N.Y.C., 1988-94; editor-in-chief Guideposts Assocs., N.Y.C., 1994—; pres. Nat. Book Critics Circle, 1984-86; bd. dirs. Nat. Book Found. Office: Guideposts Assocs 16 E 34th St New York NY 10016

WEEKS, DONNA RITA, human rights assistant executive, artist; b. Chgo., July 14, 1935; d. William Leroy and Rita Mary (Graham) Dubbs; m. Everette J. Weeks, Nov. 23, 1961 (div. Feb. 1983); children: David James, Joseph Everette, Mary Anne Weeks Collins. Exec. sec., Moser Bus. Sch., 1959; BA, U. Tenn., 1983; postgrad., Atlanta Inst. Art Therapy, 1983-85. Cert. paralegal, Tenn. Sec. Leo Burnett Advt. Agy., Chgo., 1959-61; sec. devel. dept. U. Tenn., Chattanooga, 1977-78, sec. art dept., 1978-83, sec. Engring. Sch., 1983-87; sec. Allied Arts, Chattanooga, 1987-90; adminstrv. asst. Chattanooga Human Rights/Human Rels. Commn., 1990-92, 93-94, interim dir., 1992—. One-woman show includes All Five Senses Used, 1989. Ballot chmn. Election Commn., Chattanooga, 1981-82; human rights activist Chattanooga Human Rights Commn., 1990-91; facilitator Creative Spirituality Classes, Chattanooga, 1989-91, Spl. Arts Festival Retarded, Chattanooga, 1984. Mem. Am. Bus. Women's Assn. (pres. 1985-86, bulletin chmn. 1989-90, sec. 1990-91, program chmn. 1991-92, scholarship chmn. 1992-94). Roman Catholic. Office: Chattanooga Human Rights Human Rels Commn 305 City Hall Anx Chattanooga TN 37402

WEEKS, M. J., international management consultant; b. N.Y.C., June 12, 1942; d. Kenneth James and Annette Jude (Williams) Altman; m. Robert S. Weeks, June 15, 1960; children: Sean Robert, Megan Elizabeth. BA cum laude, U. S.D., 1967, MA, 1969. Tchr. high sch. Orono Schs., Long Lake, Minn., 1970-74; mem. faculty Winona (Minn.) State U., 1976-82; mem. faculty Sioux Falls (S.D.) Coll., 1982—, dir. Ctr. Mgmt., 1985-89; pres. M.J. Weeks Seminars, Sioux Falls, 1982—; cons. to numerous Fortune 500 orgns.; mgmt. cons., Sioux Falls, 1982—; speaker at numerous nat. assns., seminars, workshops, and convs. throughout U.S., S.Am., Can., and Mexico. Author: Taking Control with Time Management, rev. edit., (cassette tapes) Listening: The Quiet Side of Communication, How To Deliver Unpopular Information; also videos on strategic communication. Bd. dirs. League of Women Voters, Sioux Falls, 1983-85; mem. Women's Network, S.D., 1984-86, Peace and Justice Ctr., 1984-86, Sioux Falls Leadership II. Mem. AAUW (bd. dirs. 1983-84), Am. Soc. Tng. and Devel., Nat. Council Tchrs. of English, Nat. Am. Soc. Tng., Sioux Falls Personnel Assn. Home and Office: 3505 Spencer Blvd Sioux Falls SD 57103-4654

WEEKS, ROBBIE C., elementary education educator, administrator; b. Mulga, Ala., Oct. 13, 1936; d. Jesse Lewis and Ruby Pearl (Miles) Jackson; m. Cleophus James Weeks, June 10, 1956; children: Cleophus, Reginald Darnell. BS, Daniel Payne Coll., Ala., 1966; MEd, Ala. State U., 1976; postgrad. in edn., U. Ala.-Birmingham, 1977. Cert. educator, administr., Ala.; cert instrn. supervision/curriculum K-8, 1988. Instr. J.A. Davis Elem. Sch., Bessemer, Ala., 1968—, coord. programs Bessemer City Sch. System, 1971—, supr. comm., 1979-83, coord. workshops, 1984-85, coord. in-svc. tng. tchrs., 1990-94, resource curriculum specialist; coord. creative writing, oratorical contests, sponsor Red Cross Club, 1985—. Contbr. articles to profl. jours., scripts for video presentations in edn.. Coord. programs Allen Temple AME Ch., Bessemer, 1970—, steward, 1985—; mem. Unserv Coun., Birmingham, Ala., 1984—; block capt. March of Dimes Mothers, Bessemer, 1986; pres. Bessemer Edn. Assn., 1985—, U.S. Postal Coun., 1993-94. Mem. NEA (mem. supervision/curriculum 1993-94), NAFE, Ala. Edn. Assn. (mem. supervision, curriculum 1993-94), Nat. Reading Assn. Democrat. Methodist. Club: Auxiliary (Bessemer). Lodge: Order Eastern Star. Avocations: writing; singing; speaking; sports; traveling. Home: 1314 21st Ave N Bessemer AL 35020-3943

WEEKS, SANDRA KENNEY, healthcare administrator; b. Akron, Ohio. BSN, Stockton State Coll.; postgrad., Trenton State Coll., 1995. RN, N.J., cert. rehab. registered nurse Assn. Rehab. Nurses. Staff nurse Akron (Ohio) Childrens Hosp., William Beaumont Hosp., Royal Oak, Mich.; elected pub. official Twp. of Cranford (N.J.); rehab. nurse Kessler Inst. Rehab., West Orange, N.J.; supr. HIP/HMO Ambulatory Care Ctr., Medford, N.J.; rehab. nurse mgr. Lourdes Rehab. Ctr., Camden, N.J.; rschr. in nursing. Contbr. articles to profl. jours. Bd. dirs. United Way; trustee pub. libr.; mem. Twp. Com. Bd. Health. Mem. Am. Nurses Assn., N.J. Nurses Assn., Assn. Rehab. Nurses, Sigma Theta Tau. Home: 3 Dewberry Ct Medford NJ 08055-9159 Office: Lourdes Regional Rehab Ctr 1600 Haddon Ave Camden NJ 08103-3101

WEEKS-CALANDER, SUSAN K., critical care nurse; b. Marysville, Kans., Nov. 17, 1955; d. Marvyn E. and Ruth (Rundus) Weeks; m. John J. Calander, Oct. 26, 1986. Diploma, Stormont Vail Sch. Nursing, Topeka, 1976; student, Ft. Hays U., Hays, Kans. Cert. emergency med. technician, trauma nurse, BLS instr., ACLS instr. ICU staff nurse Stormont Vail Regional Med. Ctr., Topeka, critical care charge nurse. Emergency med. technician, mobile intensive care technician/paramedic, fire fighter, tng. officer Mission Twp. Fire Dept. Mem. AACCN. Home: 3996 W 23d St Topeka KS 66614

WEEMS, JO LETA, retired school counselor; b. Walters, Okla., Oct. 13, 1932; d. Corneilous Rudolphous and Leta O'Reta (Wallen) Wilson; m. Thurman D. Weems, July 2, 1950; children: Deborah Sue, Robert Eugene, Consuella Weems Borgren. BS in English, East Ctrl. State Coll., 1968; M in Counseling, Emporia State U., 1973, Specialist in Edn. Counseling, 1985. Tchr. Calallen, Tex., 1966-67, Unified Sch. Dist. 454, Burlingame, Kans., 1967-68, Unified Sch. Dist. 330, Eskridge, Kans., 1968-75; sch. cmty. coord. Emporia State U./Unified Sch. Dist. 330, Emporia/Eskridge, Kans., 1975-77; tchr. behavior disorder Unified Sch. Dist. 501, Topeka, 1977-78; dir. guidance Unified Sch. Dist. 329, Alma, Kans., 1978-94; ret., 1994; mem. Kans. State Bd. Edn. Para Profl. Task Force, Topeka, 1976-76; mem. Kans. State Bd. Edn. Counseling Role and Function Task Force, Topeka, 1990—. Recipient awards Life Career Planning for Rural Schs. ASCA/ACDA, Washington, 1993, Star Sch. Project Video-Career Materials, Midlands Consortium, Manhattan, Kans., 1990. Mem. NEA, ACA, Sch. Counselor's Assn., Kans. Adult Aging Divsn. Assn. (pres./media chair 1990—), N.E. Kans. Counseling Assn. (media chair, past pres. 1978), Kans. Counseling Assn. (sec. 1978), Kans. Sch. Counselors Assn., Wabaunse East Tchrs. Assn., Kans. NEA. Home: Box 155 Harveyville KS 66431

WEERTMAN, JULIA RANDALL, materials science and engineering educator; b. Muskegon, Mich., Feb. 10, 1926. BS in Physics, Carnegie-Mellon U., 1946, MS in Physics, 1947, DSc in Physics, 1951. Physicist U.S. Naval Rsch. Lab., Washington, 1952-58; vis. asst. prof. dept. materials sci. and engring. Northwestern U., Evanston, Ill., 1972-73, assoc. prof., 1978-82, prof., 1982—, Walter P. Murphy prof., 1989, chmn. dept., 1987-92, asst. to dean grad. studies and rsch. Tech. Inst., 1973-76; mem. various NRC coms. and panels. Co-author: Elementary Dislocation Theory, 1964, 1992, also pub. in French, Japanese and Polish; contbr. numerous articles to profl. jours. Mem. Evanston Environ. Control Bd., 1972-79. Recipient Creativity award NSF, 1981, 86; Guggenheim Found. fellow, 1986-87. Fellow Am. Soc. Metals Internat., Minerals, Metals and Materials Soc.; mem. ASTM, NAE, Am. Phys. Soc., Materials Rsch. Soc., Soc. Women Engrs. (disting. engring. educator award 1989, achievement award 1991). Home: 834 Lincoln St Evanston IL 60201-2405 Office: Northwestern U Dept Material Sci & Engring 2225 N Campus Dr Evanston IL 60208-3108

WEESE, CYNTHIA ROGERS, architect, educator; b. Des Moines, June 23, 1940; d. Gilbert Taylor and Catharine (Wingard) Rogers; m. Benjamin H. Weese, July 5, 1963; children: Daniel Peter, Catharine Mohr. B.S.A.S., Washington U., St. Louis, 1962; B.Arch., Washington U., 1965. Registered architect, Ill. Pvt. practice architecture Chgo., 1965-72, 74-77; draftsperson, designer Harry Weese & Assocs., Chgo., 1972-74; prin. Weese Langley Weese Ltd., Chgo., 1977—; design critic Ball State U., Muncie, Ind., Miami U., Oxford, Ohio, 1979, U. Wis.-Milw., 1980, U. Ill.-Chgo., 1981, 85, Iowa State U., Ames, 1982, Washington U., St. Louis, 1984, U. Ill., Champaign, 1987-92, Kans. State U., 1992; dean sch. architecture Washington U., St. Louis, 1993—. Bd. regents Am. Architecture Found., 1990-93. Recipient Alpha Rho Chi award Washington U., 1965, Met. Chgo. YWCA Outstanding Achievement award, 1990. Mem. AIA (bd. dirs. Chgo. chpt. 1980-83, v.p. 1983-85, 1st v.p. 1986-87, pres. 1987-88, regional dir. 1990-92, Disting. Bldg. awards 1977, 81, 82, 83, 86, 91, Interior Architecture award 1981, 90, 92, nat. v.p. 1993), AIA/ACSA Coun. on Archtl. Rsch. (chair 1991-92), AIA Found. (pres. Chgo. chpt. 1988-89), Soc. Archtl. Historians (bd. dirs. 1992—), Chgo. Women Architecture, Chgo. Network, Nat. Inst. Archtl. Edn. (bd. dirs. 1988-90), Chgo. Archtl. Club (pres. 1988-89), Washington U. Sch. Architecture Alumni (nat. coun. 1988-93), Lambda Alpha. Democrat. Clubs: Arts, Chgo. Archtl. Office: Weese Langley Weese Ltd 9 W Hubbard St Chicago IL 60610-4605

WEESNER, BETTY JEAN, editor; b. Danville, Ind., Jan. 22, 1926; d. Edward Jabin and Ruth Leah (Daugherty) W. BA, Ind. U., 1951. Sports writer The Rep., Danville, 1940-44, reporter and advt., 1951-69, editor, 1969—; Pres., treas. Hendricks County Rep., Inc., Danville, 1974—. Mem. Ind. Rep. Editorial Assn., Hoosier State Press Assn., Ind. U. Alumni Assn., Women's Press Club Ind., DAR, Am. Legion Aux. Republican. Mem. Christian Ch. Office: The Rep 6 E Main St Danville IN 46122-1818

WEGENER, KRISTY ANN, medical/surgical nurse, homecare nurse; b. Greenville, S.C., Dec. 3, 1954; d. Gordon Wayne and Beverly Ann (Lewis) W. Lic. practical nurse diploma, 1975; ADN, North Iowa Area Community Coll., 1979; BSN, Buena Vista Coll., Ft. Dodge, Iowa, 1987. RN, Iowa, Minn., Colo., Calif. Nurse emergency room Boone County Hosp., Boone, Iowa; team nurse Wyo. Family Clinic, Casper; nursing assoc. Universal Nursing Svc., Des Moines; dir. nursing Cen. Iowa for Home Care, Colo.; asst. DON Ft. Dodge (Iowa) Villa Care Ctr.; home care nurse Cross County Nursing, 1992-93; adminstr. home care agy. Nurses House Call, Iowa City, Iowa, 1993—; home care nures IMMC, Cedar Rapids, 1994—; hightech. pediatrics home care Cross Country Nursing, Tucson, 1992. Founding mem. Am. Air Mus. in Eng. Capt. USAR. Mem. ANA, Smithsonian Soc., Ducks Unltd. (ladies com.).

WEGERT, MARY MAGDALENE HARDEL, special education director, consultant; b. Knox, Ind., Nov. 3, 1942; d. Adam Alford and Lucy (Fletcher) Hardel; m. Dennis Harold Wegert, Dec. 20, 1964. Student, Ball State U., 1960-61; BSE, Ark. State U., Jonesboro, 1964, MSE, 1967, postgrad., 1967-77; postgrad., U. S.W. La., 1972, U. Cen. Ark., 1977. Spl. edn. tchr. Knox (Ind.) Ctr. Washington Schs., 1964-65; 1st grade tchr. Jonesboro (Ark.) Pub. Schs., 1965-66; spl. edn. tchr. Dudley Sch. for Handicapped, Jonesboro, 1967-75; adult edn. tchr. Jonesboro Pub. Schs., 1970-75, spl. edn. tchr., 1975-77, spl. edn. dir., 1977—. Recipient Outstanding Alumnus award Coll. Spl. Edn. and Communicative Disorders Ark. State U., 1991. Mem. Ark. Assn. Edn. Adminstrs., Ark. Assn. Spl. Edn. Adminstrs. (various chairmanships 1977—), Ark. Assn. for Pub. Continuing and Adult Edn. (pres. 1971-72). Office: Jonesboro Pub Schs Dept Spl Edn 1307 Flint St Jonesboro AR 72401-3968

WEGNER, LAURA SHOWN, social services director; b. Ft. Lee, Va., Sept. 26, 1955; d. Edward R. and Laura Louise (Jones) Shown; m. Robert Carl Wegner, Aug. 29, 1975; children: Eamon Colin-Shown, Cyrus Sharpe. BA in Sociology, Mary Baldwin Coll., 1990. Social work aid eligibility worker Nottoway (Va.) Social Svcs., 1979-84; fraud investigator Lunenburg (Va.) Social Svcs., 1984-85; benefit programs specialist Va. Dept. Social Svcs., Lynchburg, 1985-89; benefit programs supr. Va. Dept. Social Svcs., Richmond, 1989-91; dir. social svcs. Charlotte County (Va.) Social Svcs., 1991—; cons. Piedmont Humanities Coun., Farmville, Va., 1992—; bd. dirs. Va. League Social Svcs. Execs. Vol. Nottoway County Emergency Squad, Crewe, Va., 1987—; bd. dirs. Nottoway Regional Arts Coun., Crewe, 1991—, Southside Va. Food Distbn. Ctr., Dolphin, Va., 1991—. Named Squadman of Yr., Nottoway County Emergency Squad, 1992. Democrat. Episcopalian. Home: RR 1 Box 143 Blackstone VA 23824-9763 Office: Charlotte County Social Svcs PO Box 440 Charlotte Court House VA 23923

WEHR, ALMA AMANDA, data services company manager; b. Milw., Jan. 3, 1946; d. Arthur and Janet (Stewart) Stephens; m. Clarence Edward Wehr, Sept. 6, 1969; children: Edward Lawrence, Steven Joseph, Joseph Michael, Elizabeth Anne. With computer ops. Marine Bank Svcs., Milw., 1966-78; supr. data processing Rexnord Data Systems, Milw., 1978-87; mgr. data processing Johnson Controls, Inc., Milw., 1988—; cons. Baxter, Inc., Waukegan, Ill., 1987. Mem. Assn. Records Mgrs. Adminstrs., Data Processing Mgrs. Assn., Am. Show Mgmt. (advt. bd. 1991—). Home: 2420 W Henry Ave Milwaukee WI 53221-4924 Office: Johnson Controls Inc 507 E Michigan St Milwaukee WI 53202-0423

WEHRLE, MARTHA GAINES, state legislator; b. Charleston, W.Va., Nov. 30, 1925; d. Ludwell Ebersole and Betty (Chilton) Gaines. AB, Vassar Coll., 1948; MA, Harvard U., 1954; m. Russell Schilling Wehrle, Oct. 16, 1954; children: Michael H., Ebersole Gaines, Katherine S., Philip N., Martha Chilton. Tchr., W.Va. schs., 1949-50, Belmont (Mass.) Day Sch., 1951-53; mem. W.Va. Ho. of Dels., 1974-84, vice chmn. edn. com., 1976, chmn. constl. revision com., 1977-84, mem. fin. com.; state senator W.Va. State Senate from Kanawha County dist., 1989-95; bd. dirs. United Bankshares, McJunkin Corp.; mem. adv. coun. W.Va. Woman's Commn. Mem. LWV, Garden Club Am. (chmn. nat. affairs and legis. 1987-89), Kanawha Garden Club, Charleston Jr. League Club. Democrat. Episcopalian. also: WVa Senate State Capitol Charleston WV 25305*

WEICKSEL, CHARLENE MARIE, principal; b. York, Pa., June 16, 1945; d. Edward A. and Mary Elizabeth (Hoffman) Debes; m. Stephen A. Weicksel, Aug. 27, 1967; children: Ann, Andrew. B Music Edn., Westminster Choir Coll., 1967; MEd, Trenton State Coll., 1986. Cert. tchr., prin., supr., N.J. Tchr. Hillsborough Twp. Bd. Edn., Neshanic, N.J., 1967-87, curriculum supr. fine and performing arts, 1987-93; prin. Triangle Rd. Elem. Sch., Hillsborough, N.J., 1993—. Bd. dirs. Lenape Swim Club, Skillman, N.J., 1990-93, Raritan Valley Chorus, Belle Mead, N.J., 1991-92. Mem. NEA, N.J. Edn. Assn., Nat. Art Educators Assn., Art Educators N.J., Jazz Educators. Democrat. Presbyterian. Home: 302 Sunset Rd Skillman NJ 08558-1628 Office: Hillsborough Twp Bd Edn 555 Amwell Rd Neshanic Station NJ 08853-3409

WEIDEMANN, CELIA JEAN, social scientist, international business and financial development consultant; b. Denver, Dec. 6, 1942; d. John Clement and Hazel (Van Tuyl) Kirlin; m. Wesley Clark Weidemann, July 1, 1972; 1 child, Stephanie Jean. BS, Iowa State U., 1964; MS, U. Wis.-Madison, 1970, PhD, 1973; postgrad. U. So. Calif., 1983. Advisor, UN Food & Agr. Orgn., Ibadan, Nigeria, 1973-77; ind. researcher, Asia and Near East, 1977-78; program coord., asst. prof., rsch. assoc. U. Wis., Madison, 1979-81; chief institutional and human resources U.S. Agy. for Internat. Devel., Washington, 1982-85, team leader, cons., Sumatra, Indonesia, 1984; dir. fed. econs. program Midwest Rsch. Inst., Washington, 1985-86; pres., CEO Weidemann Assocs., Arlington, Va., 1986—; cons. U.S. Congress, Aspen Inst., Ford Found., World Bank, Egypt, Nigeria, Gambia, Pakistan, Indonesia, AID, Kenya, Jordan, Poland, India, Egypt, Russia, Finnish Internat. Devel. Agy., Namibia, pvt. client, Estonia, Lativa, Russia, Japan, Internat. Ctr. Rsch. on Women, Zaire, UN Food and Agriculture Orgn., Ghana, Internat. Statis. Inst., The Netherlands, Global Exchange, 1986-87. Author: Planning Home Economics Curriculum for Social and Economic Development, Agricultural Extension for Women Farmers in Africa, 1990, Financial Services for Women, 1992, Egyptian Women and Microenterprise: The Invisible Entrepreneurs, 1992, Small Enterprise Development in Poland: Does Gender Matter?, 1994; contbr. chpts. to books and articles to profl. jours. Am. Home Econs. Assn. fellow, 1969-73 (recipient research grant Ford Found. 1987-89). Mem. Soc. Internat. Devel., Am. Sociol. Assn., U.S. Dirs. of Internat. Agrl. Programs, Assn. for Women in Devel. (pres. 1989, founder, bd. dirs.), Internat. Devel. Conf. (bd. dirs., exec. com.), Am. Home Econs. Assn. (Wis. internat. chmn. 1980-81), Internat. Fedn. Home Econs., Internat. Platform Assn., Pi Lambda Theta, Omicron Nu. Roman Catholic. Avocations: mountain trekking, piano/pipe organ, canoeing, photography, poetry. Home and Office: 2607 24th St N Arlington VA 22207-4908

WEIDEMANN, JULIA CLARK, principal, educator; b. Batavia, N.Y., May 21, 1937; d. Edward Thomas and Grace Eloise (Kenna) Clark; m. Rudolph John Weidemann, July 9, 1960; 1 child, Michael John. BA in English, Daemen Coll., 1958; MS in Edn., SUNY, Buffalo, 1961, MEd in Reading Edn., 1973, postgrad, 1985-86. Cert. sch. adminstr., supr. Tchr Buffalo Pub. Schs., 1958-61, 66-67; remedial reading tchr. West Seneca (N.Y.) Cen. Sch. Dist., 1972-79, coord. chpt. I reading program, 1974-79, reading coord., 1980-87; prin. Parkdale Elem. Sch. East Aurora (N.Y.) Union Free Sch., 1987—; adj. prof. edn. Canisius Coll., Medaille Coll.; tchr. cons. Scott Foresman Lang. Arts Textbooks; chmn. elem. com. staff devel. West Seneca Ctrl. Sch., 1985-87; mem. adv. coun. Medaille Coll.; chmn. various confs.; lectr. in field. Author numerous poems. Mem. West Seneca Dist. Computer Adv. Com., 1980-87, East Aurora Hist. Soc., 1990—; mem. community adv. coun. SUNY, Buffalo; pres. Roycroft Wordsmiths. Scholar Rosary Hill Coll., 1954, N.Y. State Regents, 1954; recipient Reading award Niagara Frontier Reading Coun., 1986. Mem. AAUW (life, Buffalo br., exec. bd. dir., named gift ednl. found.), Assn. Compensatory Edn. (pres. 1984-85, exec. bd. mem. Region VI 1983-87 1982-87, conf. chmn. Region VI 1985-87), Internat. Reading Assn. (acting chmn. 3d eastern regional reading conf. 1980), Niagara Frontier Reading Assn. (pres. 1979-80, fin. com. chmn., bd. dir. 1973—), Daemen Coll. Alumni Assn. (bd. govs. 1987-87, chmn. alumni reunion weekend, chmn. sr. reception, named Disting. Alumni, 1989), Assn. Supervision and Devel., Assn. Tchr. Educators, Roycrofters (pres. word smiths, East Aurora 1989—), Delta Kappa Gamma (pres., Ruth Fraser scholar 1986), Beta Zeta (pres.), Phi Delta Kappa (Buffalo-South chpt. 1989). Democrat. Roman Catholic. Home: 50 Boxwood Cir Hamburg NY 14075-4212 Office: Parkdale Elem Sch 80 Parkdale Ave East Aurora NY 14052-1699

WEIDENBRUCH, ANNA MAE, nurse; b. Owosso, Mich., July 26, 1926; d. Robert Harry and Della Jane (Gander) Thompson; m. Manley Lavern Nixon, Aug. 3, 1946 (div. 1961); children: Terry Lee, Douglas Kent, LaVerna Ann, Norma Jean; m. Donald F. Clewley, Aug. 27, 1961 (dec. 1973); m. Heinz Weidenbruch, 1984. ADN, Lansing (Mich.) C.C., 1983; BS in Health Studies, Western Mich. U., Kalamazoo, 1994. RN, Mich. Staff nurse Sparrow Hosp., Lansing, 1958-62, Ingham Med. Hosp., Lansing, 1962-64, Lansing Gen. Hosp., 1964-66, 77-88, Hazel I. Findlay Country Manor, St. Johns, Mich., 1987-89, Norrell Health Care, Okemos, Mich., 1990—. Democrat. Home: 2123 Northwest Ave Lansing MI 48906-3653

WEIDENFELD, SHARON FELICE, private investigator; b. Patterson, N.J., Feb. 26, 1962; d. Gil and Muriel Pearl (Pogarsky) W. AA in Criminal Justice, Prince George's C.C., 1984. Lic. pvt. investigator. Pvt. investigator Trace Am., Burtonsville, Md., 1983-87; pre-trial release counselor Prince George's County Jail, Upper Marlboro, Md., 1985; intake counselor Alexandria (Va.) Jail, 1987-89; pvt. investigator, prin. Investigative Enterprises, Greenbelt, Md., 1989—. Democrat. Jewish. Home: 408 Ridge Rd #7 Greenbelt MD 20770 Office: Investigative Enterprises PO Box 897 Greenbelt MD 20768

WEIDENFELD, SHEILA RABB, television producer, author; b. Cambridge, Mass., Sept. 7, 1943; d. Maxwell M. and Ruth (Cryden) Rabb; BA, Brandeis U., 1965; m. Edward L. Weidenfeld, Aug. 11, 1968; children: Nicholas Rabb, Daniel Rabb. Assoc. producer Metromedia, Inc., WNEW-TV, N.Y.C., 1965-68; talent coord. That Show with Joan Rivers, NBC, N.Y.C., 1968-71; coord. NBC network game programs, N.Y.C., 1968-71; producer Metromedia, Inc., WTTG-TV, Washington, 1971-73; creator/producer Take It From Here, NBC (WRC-TV), Washington, 1973-74; press sec. to first lady Betty Ford and spl. asst. to Pres. Gerald R. Ford 1974-77; mem. Pres.'s Adv. Commn. on Historic Preservation, 1977-81; TV producer, moderator On the Record, NBC-TV, WRC-TV, Washington, 1978-79; pres. D.C. Prodns., Ltd., 1978; producer, host Your Personal Decorator, 1987; mem. Sec. State's Adv. Commn. on Fgn. Service Inst., 1972-74; founding mem. Project Censured Panel of Judges, 1976—. Author: First Lady's Lady, 1979. Mem. U.S. Holocaust Meml. Council, 1987—; corporator, Dana Hall Sch., Wellesley, Mass; bd. dirs. Wolf Trap Found., Women's Campaign Fund, 1978-79; bd. dirs. D.C. Contemporary Dance Theatre, 1986-88, D.C. Rep. Cen. Com., 1984—, D.C. Preservation League, 1987-90; chmn. C&O Canal Nat. Hist. Park Commn, 1988—; bd. dirs. Am. Univ. Rome, 1988—. Recipient awards for outstanding achievement in the media AAUW, 1973, 74, Silver Screen award A Campaign to Remember for the U.S. Holocaust Meml. Coun., 1989, Bronze medal Internat. Film and Video Festival N.Y., 1990; named hon. consul gen. of Republic of San Marino to Washington; knighted by Order of St. Agatha, Republic of San Marino, 1986. Mem. NATAS (Emmy award 1972), Washington Press Club, Am. Newspaper Women's Club, Am. Women in Radio and TV, Cosmos Club, Consular Corps, Sigma Delta Chi. Home and Office: 3059 Q St NW Washington DC 20007-3081

WEIDENFELLER, GERALDINE CARNEY, speech and language pathologist; b. Kearny, N.J., Oct. 12, 1933; d. Joseph Gerald and Catherine Grace (Doyle) Carney; BS, Newark State U., 1954; postgrad. Northwestern U., summer 1956, U. Wis., summer 1960; MA, NYU, 1962; m. James Weidenfeller, Apr. 4, 1964; children: Anne, David. Lic speech/language pathologist, N.J. Speech pathologist Kearny (N.J.) Public Schs., 1954-61, North Brunswick (N.J.) Public Schs., 1961-65, Bridgewater (N.J.) Public Schs., 1969-72; speech therapist Somerset County Ednl. Commn., 1983-88; real estate agt., N.J., 1982-89; pvt. practice speech therapy, Somerville, N.J., 1980-92; speech therapist no. br. Midland Sch., 1989, No. Plainfield, N.J., 1989-90. V.p. Rosary Soc., Hillsborough, N.J., 1986—; Rep. county com. woman, 1989-90, 91—; chmn. fedn. of Rep. women program com., Somerset, program chmn. 1991—; dancer Hillsborough Rockettes, 1994—; tudor Literacy Vol. of Am., 1993-94; storyteller Cath. Charities, 1992-93. Mem. Am. Speech and Hearing Assn., N.J. Speech and Hearing Assn. Roman Catholic. Club: Toastmasters (winner dist. humorous speech contest 1984, sec. 1985, advanced Toastmaster 1986). Home: 3 Banor Dr Somerville NJ 08876-4501

WEIDENSAUL, REBECCA LOUISE, university official; b. Oct. 29, 1967; d. George Edward and Janet Kathryn (Praetorius) W. BA, Gettysburg Coll., 1989; MS, Drexel U., 1994. Admissions counselor Drexel U., Phila., 1989-91, acad. advisor, NCAA compliance coord., 1991—. Mem. Nat. Assn. Acad. Advisors Student Athletes, Nat. Assn. Compliance Ofcls. Republican. Lutheran. Office: Drexel U 32D And Chestnut St Philadelphia PA 19104

WEIDMAN, ANNA KATHRYN, publishing company financial executive; b. Redwood City, Calif., July 6, 1962; d. Ronald Frank and Jane (Cotton) W.; m. Charles Shaw Robinson, Nov. 1, 1993. BA, U. Calif., Berkeley, 1984, MBA, 1992. Asst. to dir. U. Calif. Press, Berkeley, 1985-91, exhibits/sales mgr., 1991-93, chief fin. officer, 1993—; bd. dirs. Mercury House Pubs.; ind. cons., Berkeley, 1991-93; treas., bd. dirs. Assocs. of U. Calif. Press, Berkeley, 1992—. Mem. vestry, bd. dirs. St. Mark's Episcopal Ch., Berkeley, 1993—. Democrat. Office: U Calif Press 2120 Berkeley Way Berkeley CA 94720

WEIDMAN, CATHERINE MARY, naval officer; b. Dansville, N.Y., Dec. 1, 1959; d. George Washington and Mary Louise (DePuy) W. BA in Anthropology cum laude, U. Buffalo, 1983. Archaeol. rsch. diver Tex. A&M U., 1983; ranger Nat. Park Svc., Salem, Mass., 1984; commd. USN, 1985, advanced through grades to lt., 1988, naval flight officer, 1987—. Vol. ARC, San Antonio, 1994. Recipient Nat. Def. Svc. medal Dept. Def., 1991, Humanitarian medal USCG, 1992, Joint Svc. Commendation medal U.S. Army, 1993, Peacekeeping medal UN, 1993. Mem. DAR, Am. Legion. Republican. Episcopalian. Home: 15607 E Country Cir San Antonio TX 78247

WEIDNER, GERDI, psychologist; b. Mainz, Germany, May 12, 1954; came to U.S., 1976; m. Edward J. Carpenter. BS, Justus Liebig U., 1976; MS, Kans. State U., 1978, PhD, 1981. Lic. psychologist, N.Y. Postdoctoral rsch. fellow Oreg. Health Scis. U., 1982-83, UCLA, 1983-84; asst. prof. psychology SUNY, Stony Brook, 1984-88, assoc. prof. psychology, 1989—; adv. coun. Pritikin Rsch. Found., Santa Monica, Calif., 1991—; adj. assoc. prof. med. psychology Oreg. Health Scis. U., 1990—; guest researcher Nat. Cancer Inst., Bethesda, Md., 1980, Karolinska Inst., Stockholm, 1990-91; NSF fellow in social psychophysiology Ohio State U., 1990. NIH grantee, 1984-91, Am. Heart Assn. grantee, 1985-89, NATO grantee, 1991—. Mem. APHA (epidemiology div.), APA (div. 38), Soc. Behavioral Medicine, Internat. Soc. Behavioral Medicine, Soc. Epidemiologic Rsch., Assn. Women in Sci., Am. Psychomatic Soc. Office: SUNY Dept Psychology Engring Dr Stony Brook NY 11794-2500

WEIGEL, BARBARA BROBACK, community activist; b. Orange, N.J., Nov. 26, 1935; m. Robert F. Weigel, June 3, 1961; children: Eric P., Dana E. BA in Art History, Wellesley Coll., 1957. With pub. rels. dept., exec. sec. NBC, N.Y.C., 1957-58; sec. to dir. pub. rels., compt. and curator Mus. Primitive Art, N.Y.C., 1958-62; teaching asst. libr. and spl. edn. Piscataway (N.J.) Bd. Edn., 1975-77; pvt. tutor spl. edn., reading, math., 1977; ind. sales rep. Avon, Piscataway, 1977-87. Polit. Cons. People for Whitman gabernatorial campaign, 1993, co-dir. New Market Residents Assn., 1986—; mem. Dist. Election Bd., Middlesex County, 1972-79; committeewoman Piscataway Rep. Orgn., 1986—, corr. sec., membership chair, 1988—; candidate Piscataway Twp. Coun., 1989, Piscataway Twp. Coun.-at-Large, 1992, N.J. State Assemby, 1991; mem. environ. adv. com. Congressman Jim Courter for Gov. campaign, 1989; vol. coord. Senator Dick Zimmer for Congress campaign, 1990; coord. Piscataway Rep. campaign, 1990, 94, campaign mgr. 17th dist. State Assembbly, 1993. Mem. AAUW (bd. dirs. Plainfield chpt., v.p. membership, chair pub. policy and legal advocacy, mem. scholarship com., Outstanding Young Woman of Am. award 1971), LWV, MADD, Women's Polit. Caucus (Leg. N.J. Rep. Task Force), Rep. Women of the90's (exec. bd.), Coun. for Citizens Against Gov. Waste, Registered Voters Organized to Limit Terms, Friends of Rutgers Ecol. Preserve, N.J. Wellesley Club.

WEIGEL, ELSIE DIVEN, publishing executive, writer, editor, public affairs officer; b. Phila., May 31, 1948; d. William Bleakley Diven and Elsie May (Betts) Darling; m. John C. Weigel, Dec. 19, 1970 (div. 1979); 1 Child, Kimberly Joy. BA, Am. U., 1970. Editorial asst. Water Pollution Control Fedn., Alexandria, Va., 1970-72; asst. dir. publs. Am. Speech, Hearing, and Lang. Assn., Rockville, Md., 1972-78; editor-in-chief Potato Chip/Snack Food Assn., Alexandria, 1978-79; dir. publs. Nat. Soc. Pub. Accts., Alexandria, 1979-80; editorial project dir. Energy Info. Adminstrn. U.S. Dept Energy, Washington, 1980-91; editorial project dir. NASA, Washington, 1991-93, pub. affairs officer, 1994—; guest speaker in field. Editor newsletter Rittenhouse Family Assn., Ednl. Horizons; coprodr. ednl. cable series on space; contbr. articles to profl. jours. Mem. Life Skills Ctr. (bd. dirs. 1987-91) Washington. Mem. Nat. Assn. Govt. Communicators (Blue Pencil award), Nat. Assn Female Execs., Sigma Delta Chi. Home: 11317 River Rd Mason Neck VA 22079-4221 Office: NASA 300 E St SW Washington DC 20546

WEIGHTMAN, JUDY MAE, lawyer; b. New Eagle, Pa., May 22, 1941; d. Morris and Ruth (Gutstadt) Epstein; children: Wayne, Randall, Darrell. BS in English, California U. of Pa., 1970; MA in Am. Studies, U. Hawaii, 1975; JD, U. Hawaii, 1981. Bar: Hawaii 1981. Tchr. Fairfax County Sch. (Va.), 1968-72, Hawaii Pub. Schs., Honolulu, 1973-75; lectr. Kapiolani Community Coll., Honolulu, 1975-76; instr. Olympic Community Coll., Pearl Harbor, Hawaii, 1975-77; lectr. Hawaii Pacific Coll., Honolulu, 1977-78; law clk. to atty. gen. Hawaii & Case, Kay & Lynch, Davis & Levin, 1979-81, to chief judge Intermediate Ct. Appeals State of Hawaii, 1981-82; dep. pub. defender Office of Pub. Defender, 1982-84; staff atty. Dept. Commerce & Consumer Affairs, State of Hawaii 1984-86; pres., bd. dirs. Am. Beltwrap Corp., 1986—; asst. prof. law, dir. pre-admission program, asst. prof. Richardson Sch. Law, U. Hawaii, 1987—, faculty senator; faculty senate exec. com. U. Hawaii Manua. Author: Days of Remembrance: Hawaii Witnesses to the Holocaust; producer (documentary) The Panel: The First Exchange, Profile of An Aja Soldier, Profile of a Holocaust Survivor; prodr., dir. From Hawaii to The Holocaust: A Shared Moment in History; patentee in field; mem. Richardson Law Rev., 1979-81. Mem. neighborhood bd. No. 25 City and County Honolulu, 1976-77; vol. Legal Aid Soc., Honolulu, 1977-78; bd. dirs. Jewish Fedn., Protection and Advocacy Agy.; parent rep. Wheeler Intermediate Adv. Coun., Honolulu, 1975-77; trustee Carl K. Mirikitani Meml. Scholarship Fund, Arts Coun. Hawaii; membership dir. ACLU, 1977-78, bd. dirs., Hawaii, 1988—, treas. Amicus; founder Hawaii Holocaust Project; trustee Jewish Fedn. Hawaii. Community scholar, Honolulu, 1980; Internat. Rels. grant Chaminade U., 1976; recipient Hawaii Filmmakers award Hawaii Internat. Film Festival, 1993, Golden Eagle award CINE, 1995. Mem. ABA, Afro-Am. Lawyers Assn. (bd. trustee), Hawaii Women Lawyers, Assn. Trial Lawyers Am., Hawaii State Bar Assn., Am. Judicature Soc., Richardson Sch. Law Alumni Assn. (alumni rep. 1981-82), Advocates for Pub. Interest Law, U. Hawaii Senate Faculty (senator), Phi Delta Phi (v.p. 1980-81), Hadassah Club, Women's Guild Club. Democrat. Jewish. Office: U Hawaii William S Richardson Sch Law 2515 Dole St Honolulu HI 96822-2328

WEIGLE, MARTA, folklorist, educator; b. July 3, 1944, Janesville, Wis.; d. Richard Daniel and Mary (Day) W. Student, St. John's Coll., Annapolis, Md., 1961-62; AB cum laude in Social Relations, Radcliffe Coll., 1965; MA, U. Pa., 1968, PhD, 1971. Asst. prof. anthropology and English U. N.Mex., Albuquerque, 1972-77, assoc. prof., 1977-83, prof. anthropology, English and Am. studies, 1983-87, prof. Am. studies and anthropology, 1987—, became chmn. dept. Am. studies, 1984; mgr., co-owner Abacus Books, Inc., 1973-74; rev. panelist NEH; cons. Hispanic heritage wing Mus. Internat. Folk Art, Sante Fe, 1986—; lectr. in field. Author: Follow My Fancy: The Book of Jacks and Jack Games, 1970, The Penitentes of the Southwest, 1970, Brothers of Light, Brothers of Blood, 1976, (with David Johnson) Lightning and Labyrinth: An Introduction to Mythology, 1979, At the Beginning: American Creation Myths, 1980, (with Kyle Fiore) Santa Fe and Taos: The Writer's Era, 1916-1941, 1982, Spiders and Spinsters: Women and Mythology, 1982, (with Peter White) The Lore of New Mexico, 1988, Creation and Procreation: Feminist Reflections on Mythologies of Cosmogony and Parturition, 1989; editor: Echoes of the Flute, 1972, Hispanic Villages of Northern New Mexico, 1975, A Penitente Bibliography, 1976, (with Charles L. Briggs) Hispano Folklife of New Mexico: The Lorin W. Brown Fed. Writers' Project Manuscripts, 1978, (with Claudia and Samuel Larcombe) Hispanic Arts and Ethnohistory in the Southwest, 1983, New Mexicans in Cameo and Camera, 1985, Two Guadalupes: Hispanic Legends and Magic Tales from Northern New Mexico, 1987, Indian Tales from Picuris Pueblo, 1989, Women of New Mexico: Depression Era Images, 1993; cons. editor: Chamisal and Penasco: The Farm Security Administration Photography of Russell Lee, 1985, Colonial Frontiers: Art and Life in Spanish New Mexico, 1982-83; assoc. editor Ancient City Press, 1972-74, ptnr., editor, 1981—; contbr. numerous articles to revs. and papers to profl. jours. Recipient award of honor Cultural Properties Rev. Com., State of N.Mex., 1976, Zia award N.Mex. Press Women, 1977, Twitchell award Hist. Soc. N.Mex., 1989; grantee Nat. Endowment for Humanities, 1979-81, Exxon Edn. Found., 1979. Bd. dirs. Santa Fe Hist. Soc., 1977-81, Spanish Colonial Arts Soc., 1979—; trustee Am. Folklife Ctr., 1987-89. Mem. N.Mex. Folklore Soc. (2d v.p. 1977-78, 1st v.p. 1978-79, pres. 1979-80, Roll of Honor 1978), Am. Folklore Soc. (editor Folklore Women's Communication 1977-79, editor publs., series, vols. 1-8, exec. bd. 1983-86, fellow 1987). Office: Univ of New Mexico Dept of Anthropology Albuquerque NM 87131*

WEIHE, STARR CULVER, biology educator; b. Salisbury, Md.; d. Frederick A. and Violet (Timmons) Culver; m. Rudolph George Weihe, Oct. 20, 1967. BA, Hood Coll., 1959; MA, Duke U., 1961; EdD, Nova U., 1978. Biology asst. Fla. Presbyn. Coll., 1961-62; prof. biology St. Petersburg Jr. Coll., Fla., 1963—, chair natural scis. dept., 1989-93. Contbr. articles profl. jours. Active St. Petersburg Symphony Guild, St. Petersburg Mus. Fine Arts. Hood Coll. scholar, 1958; recipient Nat. Tchg. Excellence award U. Tex., 1989. Mem. AAAS, AAUW, Am. Inst. Biol. Scis., Fla. Acad. Scis., Beta Beta Beta. Democrat. Methodist. Clubs: St. Petersburg Yacht, Lakewood Country. Avocation: piano. Home: 5108 Brittany Dr S # 901 Saint Petersburg FL 33715-1510 Office: St Petersburg Jr Coll Saint Petersburg FL 33710

WEIKERT, BARBARA RUTH, librarian; b. Kalispell, Mont., June 26, 1931; d. Austin D. and Ruth (Dinwiddie) W. Assoc. degree, John Muir Jr. Coll., Pasadena, Calif., 1951; BS, San Jose State U., 1954; MS, U. So. Calif., 1957. Tchr. elem. edn. Ashley Creek Elem. Sch., Kila, Mont., 1951-52; libr. Fall River Mills High Sch., McArthur, Calif., 1954-56; asst. libr. Spokane (Wash.) County Libr., 1961-62; br. libr. Pierce County Libr., Tacoma, Wash., 1962-66, coord. ext. svcs., 1966-76, coord. circulation and interloan, 1976-82, reference and supervising reference libr., 1982—. Mem. policy adv. com., LWV rep. Citizen's Land Use Policy Com., Tacoma, 1974; mem., citizen-at-large N.E. Tacoma Citizen's Adv. Com., 1977; com. mem. Land Use Mgmt. Plan, 1975, Land Use Planning N.E. Tacoma Plan, 1979; newsletter editor LWV, 1972-74; mem. dist. and conf. com. of ch. and women's orgn. United Meth. Ch., 1970—. Mem. AAUW (pres. 1966-68, state chair internat. rels. 1968-70), UN Assn. of U.S.A. (pres. 1977-79, state sec. 1984-88), Wash. Libr. Assn. (rep. to steering com. status 1980, mem. tech./energy cmty. forums 1980, interlibr. loan chpt. 1982-84), Pacific N.W. Libr. Assn. (circulation chair 1979-81, ref. chair 1993—). Office: Pierce County Libr 6300 Wildaire Rd SW Tacoma WA 98499

WEIL, DENIE SANDISON, foundation administrator; b. St. Louis, Mar. 16, 1931; d. James Calvin and Eliza (Tillman) Sandison; m. Frank A. Weil, Feb. 11, 1951; children: Deborah, Amanda, Sandison, William. AB, Radcliffe Coll., 1954. Dep. dir. rsch. Vera Inst., N.Y.C., 1974-77; program officer German Marshall Fund U.S., Washington, 1977-82; writer, cons., 1983-85; pres. Citizens' Participation Project, Washington, 1986-88; bd. dirs. Fiduciary Trust Co. Internat., N.Y.C. Contbr. articles on career mgmt. to Working Women. Trustee, v.p. Irvington (N.Y.) Inst. Med. Rsch., 1958-77, Abbott House, Irvington, 1965-75, Jewish Assn. for Svcs. for Aged, N.Y.C., 1969-77; trustee Arena Stage, Washington, 1984—, pres., 1991—; trustee Radcliffe Coll., Cambridge, Mass., 1972-83; bd. overseers Harvard U., Cambridge, 1981-87. Mem. Harvard Club (N.Y.C., bd. mgrs. 1987—), Cosmopolitan Club (N.Y.C.). Democrat. Home: 1516 28th St Washington DC 20007

WEIL, NANCY HECHT, psychologist, educator; b. Chgo., Apr. 15, 1936; d. Theodore R. and Jenice (Abrams) Hecht; children: Lynda Jo, Edward S.; m. John T. Newmark. Student Cornell U., 1954-57; M.Ed., Nat. Coll. Edn., Ill., 1974; Ph.D., Northwestern U., 1976; postgrad. Chgo. Inst. Psychoanalysis, 1972-74; attending staff Michael Reese Hosp., 1978—; clin. asst. prof. U. Chgo. Pritzker Sch. of Medicine, 1985-90; adj. asst. prof. psychiatry Coll. Medicine, U. Ill. at Chgo., 1990; med. staff, clin. asst. prof. psychiatry U. Ill. Abraham Sch. Medicine, Chgo., 1993—. mental health cons.; vice-chair Ill. Mental Health Planning Bd., 1973-75; cons. Ill. Comprehensive Health/Planning Agency, 1974; bd. trustees Chgo Inst. for Psychoanalysis, 1973—, faculty continuing edn., 1976, 87; asst. prof. Northwestern U. Med. Sch., 1976-77, assoc. prof., 1977-79; lectr. U. Chgo. Pritzker Sch. Medicine, 1978-85; chmn. adv. council Ill. Dept. Mental Health 5-Yr. Plan, 1975-80. Bd. dirs. Chgo. Focus. Fellow Am. Orthopsychiat. Assn.; mem. Am. Psychol. Assn., Ill. Psychol. Assn., Nat. Health Register Assn., Chgo. Assn. Psychoanalytic Psychology, AAUP. Contbr. articles to profl. jours.; lectr. applied psychoanalysis. Home: 200 E Delaware Pl Unit 24 C Chicago IL 60611-1757 Office: 180 N Michigan Ave Chicago IL 60601-7400

WEILAND, JULIETTE MARIE, public relations executive, freelance writer and photographer; b. St. Cloud, Minn., Oct. 5, 1944; d. Raymond Henry and Marie Julie (Fradette) Peterson; m. James Edward Weiland, Sept. 18, 1965; children: James Edward Jr., Timothy Paul, Kristin Juliette, Stephanie Marie. BS, U. Minn., 1967; student, U. Calif., Berkeley, 1978-83, Silvermine Sch. Art, New Canaan, Conn., 1987, Am. Mgmt. Assn., 1993. Cert. English tchr. Tchr. English Anoka Hennepin Sch. Dist., Coon Rapids, Minn., 1968-71; tutor ESL Anoka Hennepin Sch. Dist., Anoka, Minn., 1971-73, Cherry Creek Sch. Dist., Englewood, Colo., 1975-76; pvt. tutor ESL Bethel, Conn., 1976-78; ptnr., owner, author Pamphleteers & Co., Wilton, Conn., 1986—; pub. rels. dir. Nursing & Home Care, Wilton, Conn., 1988—; owner Breathe Easy Environ. Assocs., Wilton, Conn., 1991—; freelance writer, Acton, Mass., 1982-84. Author: (short story) Somewhere There's A Child Waiting For Me, 1984; newspaper columnist on polit. govt. issues, 1987-89; co-editor The Wilton Voter, Wilton LWV, 1994-95; photographer various newspapers, mags., reports; contbr. numerous articles to profl. jours. Co-chmn. Open Door Soc. for Adoptive Parents, Acton, 1980-83; pub. rels. dir. LWV Conn., Hamden, 1986-88, comm. cons., 1988-89; publicity dir. Crop Walk for Hungry, Wilton, 1987-88. Mem. Pub. Rels. Soc. Am., Internat. Freelance Photographers Orgn., Nat. Fedn. Press Women, Women in Comm. Inc., Fairfield County Pub. Rels. Assn., Inc., Conn. Press Club (3d prize external ann. report for non-profits 1990, 2d prize 1991, 3d prize news photo 1991). Democrat. Roman Catholic. Home: 67 Signal Hill Rd Wilton CT 06897-1930 Office: Nursing & Home Care 180 School Rd Wilton CT 06897-2527

WEILER, DOROTHY ESSER, librarian; b. Hartford, Wis., Feb. 21, 1914; d. Henry Hugo and Agatha Christina (Dopp) Esser; A.B. in Fgn. Langs., Wash. State U., 1935; B.A.L., Grad. Library Sch., U. Wash., 1936; postgrad. U. Ariz., 1956-57, Ariz. State U., 1957-58, Grad. Sch. Librarianship, U. Denver, 1971; m. Henry C. Weiler, Aug. 30, 1937; children—Robert William, Kurt Walter. Tchr.-librarian Roosevelt Elem. Schs., Dist. #66, Phoenix, 1956-59; extension librarian Ariz. Dept. Library and Archives, Phoenix, 1959-67; library dir. City of Tempe (Ariz.), 1967-79; assoc. prof., dept. library sci. Ariz. State U., 1968; vis. faculty Mesa Community Coll., 1980-84. Mem. public relations com. United Fund; treas. Desert Samaritan Hosp. and Health Center Aux., 1981, v.p. community relations Hosp., 1982, vol. asst. chaplain, 1988—, pastoral care vol. Named Ariz. Librarian of Yr., 1971; recipient Silver Book award Library Binding Inst., 1963. Mem. Tempe Hist. Soc., Ariz. Pioneers Hist. Soc., Am. Radio Relay League, Am. Bus. Women's Assn., ALA, Southwestern Library Assn., Ariz. State Libr. Assn. (pres. 1973-74), Ariz. Libr. Pioneer. Roman Catholic. Clubs: Our Lady of Mt. Carmel Ladies' Sodality, Soroptimist Internat. Founder, editor Roadrunner, Tumbling Tumbleweed; contbr. articles to mags. Home: PO Box 26018 Tempe AZ 85285-6018

WEIMER, FERNE LAURAINE, librarian; b. Valparaiso, Ind., May 28, 1950; d. John Junior and Helen Lorraine (Dillingham) W. AB in History, Wheaton Coll., 1972; MA in Libr. Sci., No. Ill. U., 1974. Cataloger, Lake County Pub. Library, Merrillville, Ind., 1974-77, Billy Graham Ctr. Libr., Wheaton (Ill.) Coll., 1977-79, dir., 1979— . Mem. ALA, Am. Theol. Libr. Assn. (chairperson bibliographic systems com. 1988-89), Assn. Christian Librs. (dir. at large 1991-92, treas. 1992—), Chgo. Area Theol. Libr. Assn. (v.p. 1985-86, pres. 1986-87), DuPage Libr. Assn. (sec. 1981-82, pres. 1982-83), Evang. Ch. Libr. Assn. (v.p. 1991—). Office: Wheaton Coll Billy Graham Ctr Libr Wheaton IL 60187

WEIMER, JEAN ELAINE, nursing educator; b. Denver, June 8, 1932; d. John and Marquerite Christina (Friehauf) Jacoby; m. James David Weimer, Aug. 5, 1956; 1 dau., Lisa Marie. Diploma in nursing Children's Hosp. Sch. Nursing, Denver, 1953; BS in Nursing, U. Denver, 1954; MA, NYU, 1962. RN, Colo., S.D., N.Y., Ill. Staff nurse Children's Hosp., Denver, 1953-54, head nurse, 1954-56; dir. nursing edn. Yankton (S.D.) State Hosp., 1956-60; instr. Mt. Sinai Hosp. Sch. Nursing, N.Y.C., 1962-63, curriculum coord., 1964-67; asst. prof. nursing City Colls. Chgo., 1968-78, assoc. prof., 1978-85, prof., 1985—; co-chmn. nursing dept. Truman Coll., 1984-93, chmn. 1993—; chmn. program com. RN Tutoring project, 1988-92. Deacon United Ch. of Christ, 1988-90. NIMH grantee, 1960-62. Mem. Am. Nurses Assn., Coun. Advanced Practioners Psychiat. Coun. of Dirs. of Assoc. Degree Nursing Programs, Nursing Truman Coll. Faculty Coun., City Coll. Faculty Coun., Kappa Delta Pi, Pi Lambda Theta. Home: 50 E Bellevue Pl Apt 904 Chicago IL 60611-1167 Office: Truman Coll 1145 W Wilson Ave Box 184 Chicago IL 60640-5691

WEINBERG, FLORENCE MAY, modern language and literature educator; b. Alamogordo, N.Mex., Dec. 3, 1933; d. Steven Horace and Olive Gladys (Edgington) Byham; m. Kurt Weinberg, May 8, 1955. PhD, U. Rochester, 1968. Instr. modern langs. St. John Fisher Coll., Rochester, N.Y., 1967, asst. prof. modern langs., 1967-71, assoc. prof. modern langs., 1971-75, prof. modern langs., 1975-89, dept. chmn. modern langs., 1972-79, dir. internat. studies, 1983-86; prof. French/Spanish, chair modern langs./lits. Trinity U., San Antonio, Tex., 1989—. Author: The Wine and the Will, 1972, Gargantua in a Convex Mirror, 1986, The Cave, 1986. Recipient grant-in-aid Am. Coun. Learned Socs., 1974-75, sr. fellowship NEH, 1979-80, grant NEH, 1983, Rsch. grant Ludwig Vogelstein Found., 1986. Mem. MLA, N.E. MLA (sec. French 16th century sect. 1978, chmn. 1979), South Ctrl. MLA, Am. Assn. Tchrs. French, Renaissance Soc. Am. Democrat. Home: 331 Royal Oaks Dr San Antonio TX 78209-1623 Office: Trinity Univ 715 Stadium Dr San Antonio TX 78212-3104

WEINBERG, HELEN ARNSTEIN, American art and literature educator; b. Orange, N.J., June 17, 1927; d. Morris Jerome and Jeannette (Tepperman) Arnstein; m. Kenneth Gene Weinberg, Sept. 12, 1949; children: Janet Sue Weinberg Strassner, Hugh Benjamin, John Arnstein. BA in English Lit., Wellesley Coll., 1949; MA in English Lit., Western Res. U., 1953, PhD in English Lit., 1966. Teaching fellow Ohio State U., Columbus, 1949-51, Western Res. U., Cleve., 1953-57; instr. to prof. Cleve. (Ohio) Inst. Art, 1958—; standing officer Coll. English Assn. Ohio, 1987-90; vis. tchr. NYU, 1985, Sch. Visual Art's, 1981; lecture tours Israel, 1968, 70, 71. Author: The New Novel in America: The Kafkan Mode in Contemporary Fiction, 1970. Recipient fellowship in art history NEH, Columbia U., N.Y.C., 1977-78; Recipient Am. Culture grantee NEH/Vassar Coll., 1993. Mem. AAUP, Modern Lang. Assn., Coll. Art Assn. Democrat. Jewish. Home: 3015 Huntington Rd Shaker Heights OH 44120-2407 Office: Cleve Inst Art 11141 East Blvd Cleveland OH 44106-1710

WEINBERG, LAURA A., marketing executive, financial analyst; b. Phila., Apr. 22, 1963; d. Robert Louis and Diana Hedy (Wilder) W.; m. Richard A. Aronow, Oct. 16, 1988. BA in History, Yale U., 1985; MBA in Mktg. and Fin., U. Pa., 1991. Market rsch. analyst Prentice Hall/Simon and Schuster, Englewood Cliffs, N.J., 1985-87; rsch. assoc. AC&R Advt., N.Y.C., 1987-89; mktg. intern Kraft Dairy Group, Phila., 1990; assoc. prof. rep. Merck & Co., Inc., West Point, Pa., 1991-92, mktg. analyst, 1992-94; sr. analyst Merck-Medco, Merck & Co., Inc., Montvale, N.J., 1994—. Office: Merck and Co Medco Containment Svcs 100 Summit Ave Montvale NJ 07645

WEINBERG, LORETTA, state legislator; b. N.Y.C., Feb. 6, 1935; d. Murray Issacs and Raya Hamilton; m. Irwon S. Weinberg, July 25, 1960; children: Daniel J. and Francine S. BA, UCLA, 1956. Vice chair N.J. State Dem. Com., Trenton. Recipient Legis. Leadership award No. N.J. Chiropractic Assn., 1992. Mem. Nat. Coun. Jewish Women (life). Democrat. Jewish. Address: 545 Cedar Ln Teaneck NJ 07666-1712

WEINBERG, LOUISE, lawyer, educator, author; b. N.Y.C.; m. Steven Weinberg; 1 child, Elizabeth. AB summa cum laude, Cornell U.; JD, Harvard U., 1969, LL.M., 1972. Bar: Mass. Sr. law clk. Hon. Chas. E. Wyzanski, Jr., Boston, 1971-72; assoc. in law Bingham, Dana & Gould, Boston, 1969-72; teaching fellow Harvard Law Sch., Boston, 1972-74; lectr. law Brandeis U., Waltham, Mass., 1974; assoc. prof. law Suffolk U., Boston, 1974-76, prof., 1977-80; vis. assoc. prof. law Stanford U., Palo Alto, Calif., 1976-77; vis. prof. law U. Tex., Austin, 1979; prof. law Sch. Law, U. Tex., Austin, 1980-84, Thompson prof., 1984-90, Andrews and Kurth prof. law, 1990-92; Fulbright and Jaworski regents rsch. prof. U. Tex., Austin, 1991-92, Angus G. Wynne, Sr. prof. civil jurisprudence, 1992—, Eugene R. Smith Centennial rsch. prof. law, 1993; vis. scholar Hebrew U., Jerusalem, 1989; Forum fellow World Econ. Forum, DAvos, 1995; lectr. in field. Author: Federal Courts: Judicial Federalism and Judicial Power, 1994, and ann. supplement; co-author: Conflict of Laws, 1990; contbr. chpts. to books and articles to profl. jours. Bd. dirs. Ballet Austin, 1986-88, Austin Coun. on Fgn. Affairs, 1985—. Mem. Am. Law Inst. (consultative com. complex litigation 1989-93, consultative com. enterprise liability 1990—), Assn. Am. Law Schs. (chmn. com. on conflict laws 1991-93, exec. coun. 1989-90), Maritime Law Assn., Scribes, Tuesday Club, Met. Club, Phi Beta Kappa, Phi Kappa Phi. Office: U Tex Sch Law 727 E 26th St Austin TX 78705-3224

WEINBERG, MARCY, psychologist; b. Detroit; m. Michael Eugene Weinberg, June 1, 1966. BA, Northeastern Ill. U., 1977; MA, Northwestern U., 1978; PhD, Nova Univ., 1989. Lic. psychologist. Psychology intern Broward Gen. Med. Ctr., Ft. Lauderdale, Fla., 1984-85; psychology resident U. Miami Sch. Medicine, 1989-90; psychologist Marcy Weinberg, Hollywood, Fla., 1991—; adj. prof. dept. psychiatry U. Miami, 1991-92; diagnostician Cen. Agy. for Jewish Edn., Miami, 1981-87; invited lectr., guest WLRN-TV, Miami, 1987, 90, Hollywood Meml. Hosp. Contbg. author: Pediatric Nephrology, 1991; author computer prog., 1985. Fundraiser Transplant Found. of South Fla., Miami, 1989—; invited speaker Dialysis/Organ Transplant Support Groups, Miami, Boca Raton, 1990. Recipient Svc. award Stratford Ctr. Sch., Highland Park, Ill., 1977. Fellow Am. Orthopsychiat. Assn.; mem. APA, Fla. Psychol. Assn. Office: 3990 Sheridan St Ste 204 Hollywood FL 33021-3656

WEINBERG, SYDNEY STAHL, historian; b. N.Y.C., Oct. 2, 1938; d. David Leslie and Berenice (Jarvis) Stahl; B.A., Barnard Coll., 1960; M.A., Columbia U., 1964; Ph.D., 1969; divorced; children: Deborah Sara, Elisa Rachel. Instr. history N.J. Inst. Tech., 1967-69, asst. prof., 1969-72; asso. prof. history Ramapo Coll. N.J., Mahwah, 1972-74, prof., 1974—dir. Master of Arts Program in Liberal Studies, 1994—; dir. Garden State Immigration History Consortium, 1987-89. Nat. Endowment for Humanities fellow, 1977-78; sec./treas. Berkshire Conf. Women Historians, 1994—. Mem. Inst. for Rsch. in History, Am. Hist. Assn., Orgn. Am. Historians, Am. Studies Assn., Jewish Studies Assn., Assn. of Graduate Liberal Studies Programs. Author: The World of Our Mothers: The Lives of Jewish Immigrant Women, 1988; contbr. articles to profl. jours. Home: 80 La Salle St 19F New York NY 10027-4711 Office: Ramapo Coll MA Liberal Studies Program Office Mahwah NJ 07430

WEINBRECHT, DONNA, Olympic athlete; d. Jim and Caroline W. Gold medalist, freestyle skiing, Women's moguls Albertville Olympic Games, 1992. Rookie of Yr. World Cup Circuit, 1988; World Cup champion 1990, 91, 92, 94; nat. champion 1988, 89, 90, 91, 92, 94. Address: US Olympic Committee 1750 E Boulder St Colorado Springs CO 80909

WEINER, ANNETTE B., university dean, anthropology educator; b. Philadelphia, Pa., Feb. 14, 1933; d. Archibald W. and Phyllis M. (Stein-Goldman) Cohen; m. Martin Weiner, 1953 (div. 1973); children: Linda Matisse, Jonathan Weiner; m. Robert Palter, 1979 (div. 1982); m. William E. Mitchell, 1987. B.A., U. Pa., 1968; Ph.D., Bryn Mawr Coll., 1974. Vis. asst. prof. Franklin and Marshall Coll., Lancaster, Pa., 1973-74; assoc. prof. Clare Hall, Cambridge, Eng., 1976; asst. prof. anthropology U. Tex., Austin, 1974-80, assoc. prof., 1980-81; prof., chmn. dept. anthropology NYU, N.Y.C., 1981-91; David B. Kriser prof. NYU, 1985—; dean Grad. Sch. Arts and Scis. NYU, N.Y.C., 1991—, dean Social Scis., 1993—; mem. adv. com. NRC, 1993—; bd. dirs. Social Sci. Rsch. Coun. Author: Women of Value: Men of Renown: New Perspectives in Trobriand Exchange, 1976, The Trobrianders of Papua New Guinea, 1989; editor (with J. Schneider) Cloth and Human Experience, 1989, (film, with D. Wason) The Trobriand Islanders of Papua New Guinea, Bilan du Film Ethnographique, Paris, 1991 (Grand Prix award), Inalienable Possessions: The Paradox of Keeping-While-Giving, 1992. Guggenheim fellow, 1980; grantee Wenner-Gren Found. Anthrop. Rsch., 1982, 85, 86, NEH, 1976, 85, Am. Council Learned Socs., 1976, NIMH, 1972-73. Fellow Am. Anthrop. Assn. (pres. 1991-93), Royal Anthrop. Inst. Gt. Britain and Ireland, Assn. Social Anthropology in Oceania, Soc. Cultural Anthropology (bd. dirs. 1985-87, pres. 1988-89), N.Y. Inst. of the Humanities; mem. Cibola Anthrop. Assn. (pres. 1977-79), Commn. Visual Anthropology, Nat. Rsch. Coun. (adv. com. 1993—), Social Sci. Rsch. Coun. (bd. dirs. 1993—). Office: NYU Dean Grad Sch 6 Washington Sq N New York NY 10003-6668

WEINER, CLAIRE MURIEL, freelance writer; b. Bronx, N.Y., Dec. 18, 1951; d. David and Norma (Berry) W. BA, U. Miami, Coral Gables, Fla., 1973; MA, U. Md., 1980. Pub. rels. specialist Hialeah Recreation Div., Hialeah, Fla., 1974-77; freelance writer North Miami Beach, 1977-78, Germantown, Md., 1989—, Montgomery County, Md., 1981—; govt. affairs liaison for new ednl. data base co. being formed, Montgomery County, 1982—. Contbr. articles to local newspapers; contbr. travel articles to profl. jours, mags. Active membership com. newsletter Greater Miami Jewish Fedn., 1974-77; charter mem. Women for Today chpt. B'nai B'rith Women, Washington, 1985-89. Named Hon. Citizen of Historic Williamsburg. Life fellow Am. Biog. Inst. Rsch. Assn., World Lit. Acad.; mem. NAFE, Pub. Rels. Soc. Am., Internat. Platform Assn., Nat. Trust for Hist. Preservation. Jewish. Home: 18828 Sky Blue Cir Germantown MD 20874-5398

WEINER, CLARE FRANCES, social worker, psychotherapist; b. Phila., Dec. 3, 1929; d. Jack and Jessie (Rosengarten) Weinbaum; m. George C. Wheeler, Jan. 21, 1978; children by previous marriage: Justin M., Kate J., Lucian J. BS, Temple U., 1951; MSW, U. Wis., 1967. Diplomate Am. Bd. Clin. Social Work. Social worker Ohio Valley Mental Retardation Evaluation Unit, Athens, Ohio, 1968-69; social worker inpatient psychiat. svc. VA Hosp., Albany, N.Y., 1969-70; chief social worker Schenectady County Outpatient Mental Health Clinic, 1970-76; adult treatment team leader, supervising social worker Saratoga County Mental Health Ctr., N.Y., 1976-81; pvt. practice psychotherapy individuals, couples, families Schenectady and Albany, 1975—. Bd. dirs. Hammond Halfway House, Saratoga Springs, N.Y., 1976-81, Mechanicville Civic Ctr., N.Y., 1978-81. Mem. Nat. Assn. Social Workers (diplomate), Gestalt Inst. Cleve., Thurs. Mus. Soc. Office: 29 Front St Schenectady NY 12305-1301

WEINER, DEBRA, private investigator; b. Belvidere, Ill., Apr. 21, 1962; d. Earl C. and Rosemary (Beggin) W. BAS, Western Ill. U., 1984. Registered and lic. pvt. investigator, real estate commn.; registered EMT. Investigator Angel & Brewer Ltd., Chgo., 1984-85; co-owner, investigator M&W Investigative Specialists, Atlanta, 1985-87; owner, investigator d/b/a Debra Weiner, Decatur, Ga., 1987-90, The Melrose Co., Marietta, Ga., 1990—. Vol. Neighborhood Watch Program, Marietta, 1993—; vol. various programs St. Ann's Cath. Ch., Marietta, 1994—. Office: The Melrose Co PO Box 72318 Marietta GA 30007-2318

WEINER, DEBRA A., federal official; b. Ann Arbor, Mich., July 11, 1952; d. Robert L. and Dora (Weidenbaum) W.; m. Hillel Weinberg, July 24, 1983; 1 child, Sarah Weinberg. BA with honors in History, Wellesley Coll., 1974; MA in City and Regional Planning, Harvard U., 1978; JD, Boston U., 1978. Bar: Mass. 1978, D.C. 1979. Honors atty. Office Gen. Counsel, Dept. Transp., 1979; atty. advisor Office Chief Counsel, Nat. Hwy. Traffic Safety Adminstrn., 1979-80; sr. trial atty. Office Asst. Gen. Counsel for Litigation, Dept. Transp., 1980-85; assoc. Pepper, Hamilton & Scheetz, Washington, 1985-88; chief of staff Office of Commr., ICC, Washington, 1988—; legis. fellow Office of Senator Alphonse D'Amato, 1983. Mem. FBA. Office: ICC ICC Bldg Rm 5124 12th St & Constitution Ave NW Washington DC 20423*

WEINER, DORIS L., artist; b. Boston, July 2, 1929; d. Max Robert and Sarah N. (Novick) Lehner; m. Sumner K. Weiner, June 8, 1952; children: Mark L., Alan David. Student, Decordova Mus. Sch., Lincoln, Mass., 1983-84, Bennington Coll., 1987-94, Mus. Sch. Fine Arts, 1990-91. Pres. Depot Sq. Gallery Co-op, Lexington, Mass., 1993-94. Exhbns. include Depot Sq. Gallery, Lexington, Mass., 1986-94, Diana Levine Fine Art, Boston, 1989-94, Wenninger Graphics Gallery, Rockport, Mass., 1993—, Mahlar Gallery, Washington, 1993—, Reece Gallery, N.Y.C., 1993—. Mem. Nat. League Am. PEN Women & Artists (bd. dirs. 1989-91, state art chmn., Best in Show award 1989), Concord (Mass.) Art Assn., New Eng. Watercolor Soc. (bd. dirs., chmn. open and winter shows 1988-94), Monotype Guild New Eng. Home: 12 Sagamore Rd Newton MA 02161

WEINER, KAREN COLBY (KAREN LYNN COLBY), psychologist, lawyer; b. Oak Park, Ill., Oct. 28, 1943; d. Leonard L. and Mildred Irene (Berman) Colby; m. J. Laevin Weiner, July 26, 1964; children: Joel Laevin, Doren Robin, Anthony Justin. BA, Mich. State U., East Lansing, 1964; JD, U. Detroit, 1977, MA, 1986, PhD, 1988. Bar: Mich. 1977, D.C. 1978. Speech therapist Oak Park Sch. Dist., 1965-68; law clk. justice G. Mennen Williams Mich. Supreme Ct., Lansing, 1977-79; assoc. Dickinson, Wright, Moon, Van Dusen & Freeman, Detroit, 1979-83; intern in psychology Detroit Psychiat. Inst., 1986-88; psychologist Northland Clinic, Southfield, Mich., 1987-88, Counseling Assocs., Southfield, 1988—; postdoctoral intern Wyandotte (Mich.) Hosp. and Health Ctr., 1988-90; dir. psychol. svcs., quality assurance coord. Counseling Assocs., Southfield, 1991—; hearing panelist Atty. Discipline Bd., Detroit, 1982—; hearing referee Mich. Civil Rights Commn., Detroit, 1983-91. Contbr. articles to profl. jours. Mem. adv. bd. Mich. chpt. Anti-Defamation League, 1981-90. Mem. APA, Mich. Psychol. Assn. (ethics com. 1992—, chmn. legis. com. 1993), Mich. Soc. for Psychoanalytic Psychology (sec. 1991-92, treas. 1992—), Assn. for Advancement Psychoanalysis, Women Lawyers Assn. Mich. (pres. 1981-82, pres. Found. 1982-83), Mich. Bar Assn. (chmn. spl. com. for expansion under represented groups in law 1980-83). Democrat. Jewish. Home: 1764 Alexander Dr Bloomfield Hills MI 48302-1201 Office: 29260 Franklin Rd Ste 115 Southfield MI 48034-1144

WEINER, MARIAN MURPHY, insurance executive, consultant; b. N.Y.C., Mar. 20, 1954; d. Stephen Patrick and Evelyn (McTiernan) Murphy; m. Joseph Longo, Feb. 15, 1975 (div. May 1977); m. Ira Elliott Weiner, Sept. 23, 1983; children: Joshua Stephen, Samantha Beth. BA, William Paterson Coll., 1984. CPCU, CIC. Bookkeeper RJT, Inc. trading as The Turner Group, Pine Brook, N.J., 1973-75; ins. broker RJT, Inc. T-A The Turner Group, Pine Brook, N.J., 1975-80, office mgr., 1980-82, exec. v.p., 1982—. Bd. dirs. Homeowners Assn., Vernon, N.J., 1989. Mem. Profl. Ins. Agts. Democrat. Roman Catholic. Home: 7 Curtis Dr Vernon NJ 07462 Office: The Turner Group 350 Main Rd Montville NJ 07045-9730

WEINER, PATRICIA HERMANN, performing arts administrator, concert manager, artist manager; b. Cape Town, Republic of South Africa, July 7, 1941; came to U.S., 1962; d. Gunther and Beatrice (Frankel) Hermann; m. Jay Joseph Weiner, Mar. 31, 1969; children: Jason Lee, Wendy Lynn. BA in Music and Communications, Western Conn. State U., 1986. Outreach coord. Aston Magna, Danbury, Conn., 1986-88; assoc. dir. Berkshire Friends of Baroque Music, Danbury, 1986-88; dir. concerts and press info. Sch. of Music Yale U., New Haven, 1988-91; mgr. New Music Consort, N.Y.C., 1991; prin. Weiner Mgmt. Co. Artist Mgmt., 1991—; bd. dirs. Music Mountain, Falls Village, Conn. assoc. prodr. (opera) Burning Bright Yale U., 1993. Founder Ives Festival Artists, Danbury, 1979; bd. dirs. Charles Ives Ctr., Danbury, 1979-80; publicity dir. Norwalk Youth Symphony, 1984-88; mgr., v.p. Western Conn. Symphony Orch., 1984-87; adminstr. Beth Israel Med. Ctr., N.Y.C., 1967 active pub. rels. devel. civic orgns. Address: 150 Brushy Hill Rd Danbury CT 06810-8431

WEINER, SANDRA JOAN, transportation company administrator; b. N.Y.C., Oct. 27, 1951; d. Louis and Rose (Rosansky) Kornbluth; m. Gerald Weiner, Feb. 14, 1992. BA magna cum laude, Queens Coll., 1973; MA in Romance Langs., Princeton U., 1975. Instr. French lang. Princeton (N.J.) U., 1973-77; mgr. cargo tariffs Air France, N.Y.C., 1977-82; mgr. internat. pricing Emery Worldwide, Wilton, Conn., 1982-86, dir. pricing, 1986-89; pres. Riverview Traffic Group, Trumbull, Conn., 1989-90; mgr. strategic sourcing, program mgr. Pitney Bowes, Shelton, Conn., 1990-94; mgr. quality and adminstrn. Entex Info. Svcs., Rye Brook, NY, 1994—; mem. adv. bd. Cargo Rate Services, Miami, Fla., 1984—. Bd. dirs. Literacy Vols. Greater Norwalk, 1987. Fullbright-Hayes scholar, 1973. Office: Entex Info Svcs 6 International Dr Rye Brook NY 10573

WEINER, SANDRA SAMUEL, critical care nurse, consultant; b. N.Y.C., Jan. 12, 1947; d. Herbert A. and Ruth (Wallerstein) Samuel; m. Neil D. Weiner, June 15, 1969 (div. June 1980); 1 child, Jaime Michelle. BS in Nursing, SUNY, Buffalo, 1968; cert. in critical care, Golden West Coll., 1982; postgrad. UCLA, U. West L.A. Sch. of Law, 1992. RN, Pa., Calif. Staff nurse N.Y. Hosp.-Cornell Med. Ctr., 1968-69; head nurse med.-surg. nursing Abington (Pa.) Hosp., 1969; assoc. prof. Sch. Nursing, U. Pa., Phila., 1970; instr. nursing Coll. of Med. Assts., Long Beach, Calif., 1971-72; surg. staff nurse Med. Ctr. of Tarzana, Calif., 1978-79, Cedar-Sinai Med. Ctr., L.A., 1979-81; supr. recovery room Beverly Hills Med. Ctr., L.A., 1981-92; PACU nurse Westside Hosp., 1992—; med. cons. RJA & Assocs., Beverly Hills, Calif., 1984-92; instr. CPR, L.A., 1986—. Mem. women's aux. Ctr. Theater Group Vols., L.A., 1986—, Maple Ctr., Beverly Hills, 1987—; mem. Friends of Joffrey Ballet, 1990—. Mem. Am. Nursing Assn., Am. Assn. Critical Care Nurses, Heart and Lung Assn., Post Anesthesia Nurses Assn., U.S. Ski Assn., AAU. Democrat. Jewish. Avocations: skiing, running, travel, theater, ballet. Home: 12633 Moorpark St Studio City CA 91604

WEINER, SUSAN S., mayor; b. Albany, N.Y., Feb. 5, 1946; d. Louis and Esther (Gellman) Scher; m. Albert B. Weiner, Mar. 2, 1972; children: Justin, Kate, Lucian. BS, SUNY, New Paltz, 1966. Owner Playback Network, Savannah, Ga., 1980-86, Weiner Assocs., Savannah, 1987—; mayor City of Savannah, Ga., 1992—. Co-prodr. TV show The Bo$$, 1990; appeared in And Ain't I A Woman, 1976, The First Barefoot Dancer, 1982. Co-chair Ga. Bush-Quayle Campaign, 1992; delegate to Nat. Rep. Convention, Houston, 1992; mem. Chatham County Rep. Women; active Savannah Hadassah, Keep Savannah Beautiful, Leadership Savannah, Jr. Achievement, Chatham County Bus.-Edn. Partnership, Local Coord. Coun. (chmn. 1990). Mem. Savannah-Chatham Pvt. Industry Coun. (chmn. 1989-90), Oglethorpe Bus. and Prof. Women (past officer, Ga. Pres.'s Life award 1989), Women Bus. Owners of Savannah (pres. 1990), Savannah Area C. of C. (bd. dirs. 1989—), Savannah Kiwanis (past bd. dirs.). Office: Office of the Mayor PO Box 1027 Savannah GA 31402-1027*

WEINER-HEUSCHKEL, SYDELL, theater educator; b. N.Y.C., Feb. 18, 1947; d. Milton A. and Janet (Kay) Horowitz; children: Jason, Emily; m. Rex Heuschkel, Sept. 3, 1992. BA, SUNY, Binghamton, 1968; MA, Calif. State U., L.A., 1974; PhD, NYU, 1986; postgrad. in acting, Yale U., 1968-70. Profl. acting coach The Studio, Fullerton, Calif., 1982-83; prof. in theater arts, dir. of honors program, dept. chair Calif. State U. Dominguez Hills, Carson, 1984—; guest lectr. Calif. Inst. Arts, 1988. Appeared in play Vikings, Grove Shakespeare Festival, 1988; dir. Plaza Suite, Brea (Calif.) Civic Theatre, 1982, Gypsy, Carson Civic Light Opera, 1990, Same Time Next Year, Muckehthaler, 1987, Slow Dance on the Killing Ground, Alternative Repertory Theatre, 1989; co-author: School and Community Theatre Problems: A Handbook for Survival, 1978, (software) Public Speaking, 1991. Yale U. fellow, 1969; recipient Lyle Gibson Disting. Tchr. award, 1989. Mem. Screen Actors Guild, Am. Fedn. TV and Radio Artists, Calif. State U. Women's Coun. (treas. 1989-91), Phi Kappa Phi.

WEINERT, FRITZIE JOHANNA, nurse administrator; b. N.Y.C., Dec. 27, 1933; d. William Gerders and Magda Agnes (Kalbhern) Strobach; m. Alfred C. Weinert, July 25, 1953 (div. 1979); children: Frederick Alexander, Suzanne Lorraine, Jeanette Christine. ASA, Orange County Community Coll., Middletown, N.Y., 1968. RN, N.Y. Mental hygiene therapy aide Middletown Psychiat. Ctr., 1957-68, staff nurse I, 1968-69, head nurse II, 1969-79, nurse adminstr., 1979—; nurse technician Horton Meml. Hosp., Middletown, 1968-69. Mem. ANA, N.Y. State Nurses Assn., Middletown Psychiat. Ctr. Nurses Assn., German Am. Club of Middletown. Republican. Lutheran. Home: Pine St And 1st Ave Wurtsboro NY 12790 Office: Middletown Psychiat Ctr Monhagen Ave Middletown NY 10940

WEINGART, CAROL JAYNE, university administrator; b. Schenectady, N.Y., Oct. 2, 1943; d. Clare James Murphy and Carolyn Marie (Jayne) Carroccio; m. Robert Edward Weingart, Apr. 2, 1966 (div. Feb. 1977); children: Julia M. Ashman, Anne E. Spencer, Kenneth L., Phillip M., Jayne E. Garro, Carolyn M. Garro; m. Prentiss E. Dwinell, May 29, 1992. Diploma in nursing, Parkview Meth. Sch. Nursing, 1965; BS, Defiance Coll., 1975; MA in Counseling, Norwich U., 1990; PhD, Summit U., 1995, Asst. Provost, 1995—. Psychiatric nursing instr. St. Joseph Hosp. Sch. Nursing, Ft. Wayne, Ind., 1975-76; nurse clinician Dr. Joseph Fiacable MD, Ft. Wayne, 1976-77, Wyo. State Hosp., Evanston, 1977, State Hosp. South, Blackfoot, Idaho, 1977-81; nurse supr. Bannock Meml. Hosp., Pocatello, Idaho, 1979-82; nurse Idaho Home Health, Blackfoot, 1982; nurse clinician Region I Mental Health, Coeur d'Alene, Idaho, 1983-88; nurse clinician, therapist Spokane (Wash.) Community Mental Health, 1988-89; crisis/intake therapist N.E. Kingdom Mental Health, Newport, Vt., 1989-94; asst. provost Summit U., 1995—; nurse Girl Scouts Day Camp, Kendallville, 1974-75; edn. chairperson Noble County Mental Health Assn., Kendallville, 1973; presenter N. Idaho Coll., Coeur d'Alene, 1988; lectr. Whitworth Coll., Spokane, 1989; ARC instr. expectant parents. Author: Childbirth with Hypnosis Expecting, 1970. Mem., pres. Assn. Retarded Citizens, Blackfoot, 1982-83; pres. Tiny Tots Games, Coeur d'Alene, 1983-89; mem. adv. bd. Orleans/Essex Home Health, Newport, 1989-93. Mem. P.E.O. (various offices). Quaker. Home: RR 2 Box 217 North Troy VT 05859-9711

WEINGARTEN, SHARON, advertising executive, consultant; b. Grosse Point, Mich., July 1, 1963; d. Cliffold Mark and Barbara (Ravinett) W. Hon. degree, Campaign Mgmt. Coll., 1992. Office mgr., pol. coord. Ray Adell Media Enterprises, Inc., Greenlawn, N.Y., 1980-85; acct. exec. Mktg. Design Concepts, Kings Park, N.Y., 1985; pres. Intermedia Rsch. Corp., Middle Island, N.Y., 1985-90, Image Profls., Inc., Middle Island, 1990—; distbr. Advtg. Specialty Inst., Langhorne, Pa., 1986—; cons. Rep./Cons. Party Candidates & Office Holders, 1985—. mem. adv. coun. Airport Joint-Use Feasability Study, Calverton, N.Y., 1992-93; mem. Suffolk County Legis. Commn. on Low Income Housing, Hauppauge, N.Y., 1992—. Republican. Jewish. Office: Image Profls Inc PO Box 217 Middle Island NY 11953

WEINKAUF, MARY LOUISE STANLEY, clergywoman; b. Eau Claire, Wis., Sept. 22, 1938; d. Joseph Michael and Marie Barbara (Holzinger) Stanley; m. Alan D. Weinkauf, Oct. 12, 1962; children: Stephen, Xanti. BA, Wis. State U., 1961; MA, U. Tenn., 1962, PhD, 1966; MDiv Luth. Sch. Theology, Chgo., 1993. Grad. asst., instr. U. Tenn., 1961-66; asst. prof. English, Adrian Coll., 1966-69; prof., head dept. English, Dakota Wesleyan U., Mitchell, S.D., 1969-89; instr. Columbia Coll., 1989-91; pastor Siloa Lutheran Ch., Ontonagon Faith, White Pine, Mich., Gowrie, Iowa. Mem. Mitchell Arts Council; bd. trustees, The Ednl. Found., 1986—. Mem. Nat. Council Tchrs. English, S.D. Council Tchrs. English, Sci. Fiction Research Assn., Popular Culture Assn., Milton Soc., AAUW (div. pres. 1978-80), S.D. State Poetry Soc. (pres. 1982-83), Delta Kappa Gamma (pres. local chpt., mem. state bd. 1972-89 , state v.p. 1979-83, state pres. 1983-85), Sigma Tau Delta, Pi Kappa Delta, Phi Kappa Phi. Republican. Lutheran.

WEINMAN, ROBERTA SUE, marketing and financial communications consultant; b. Bennington, Vt., Sept. 22, 1945. BA, U. Calif., Berkeley, 1967; MA, Stanford U., 1975, MLA, 1994; MBA, Pepperdine U., 1982. Tech. editor SRI Internat., Menlo Park, Calif.; adminstr. consumer affairs Fed. Home Loan Bank, San Francisco, 1977-79; legal research asst. Townsend and Townsend, San Francisco, 1979-80; pvt. practice mktg. and fin. communications cons. Palo Alto, Calif., 1981—. Editor, writer, developer various mktg., pub. relations and fin. documents, primarily for high-tech. industry. Home and Office: 99 Orchard Hills Menlo Park CA 94027

WEINMANN, BERT MILLICENT LANDES, artist; b. N.Y.C., July 20, 1924; d. Harry and Esther (Lurie) Landes; student Hunter Coll., 1941-43, Queens Coll., 1958-59, Bklyn. Mus. Art Sch., 1959. New Sch. for Social Research, 1963; grad. Fashion Inst. Tech., 1943; also pvt. student art; m. Richard A. Weinmann, Dec. 26, 1944; children—Harriet, Elaine. Fashion illustrator, designer with Mainbocher, Maurice Rentner, Tabin Picker, others, 1942-50; exhibited one-woman shows Six Trees Gallery, Edgartown, Mass., 1971, Kron Gallery, Mattituck, N.Y., 1972, Firehouse Gallery, Garden City, N.Y., 1975, Unicorn Gallery, N.Y.C., 1974, Gallery 33, N.Y.C., 1976, The Galery, N.Y.C., 1982; exhibited in group shows at Palazzo Vecchio, Florence, Italy, 1972, Nat. Acad. Art, 1969, 72, 73. Hecksher Mus., Huntington, N.Y., 1971, Salvator Rosa, Naples, Italy, 1972, Port Washington (N.Y.) Public Library, 1972, Fairfield (Conn.) U., 1973, Royal Acad., Stockholm, 1978, Sindin Gallery, N.Y.C., 1981, Suziki Gallery, N.Y.C., 1986, Discovery Gallery, 1987, Jehangar Art Gallery, Bombay, 1989, Sansker Kendra Mus., Ahmedebed, India, 1989, Fine Arts Mus. of the South, Mobile, Ala., 1989, Sabbeth Art Gallery, Glencove, N.Y., 1990, also numerous art galleries; works represented in numerous pvt. and corp. collections; tchr. drawing and painting North Shore Community Arts Center, Great Neck, N.Y., 1973-81, AIA, Great Neck, 1981-84. Recipient awards from numerous juried art exhbns., purchase award Nassau Coll. Assn., 1973. Mem. Nat. Assn. Women Artists (co-chmn. fgn. exhbns. com. 1973-74, Ziuta G. and Joseph James Akston prize 1972), Women in Arts, Profl. Artists Guild, Artists in Am. Home and Studio: 61 Franklin Pl Great Neck NY 11023

WEINSHIENK, ZITA LEESON, federal judge; b. St. Paul, Apr. 3, 1933; d. Louis and Ada (Dubov) Leeson; m. Hubert Troy Weinshienk, July 8, 1956 (dec. 1983); children: Edith Blair, Kay Anne, Darcy Jill; m. James N. Schaffner, Nov. 15, 1986. Student, U. Colo., 1952-53; BA magna cum laude, U. Ariz., 1955; JD cum laude, Harvard U., 1958; Fulbright grantee, U. Copenhagen, Denmark, 1959; LHD (hon.), Loretto Heights Coll., 1985; LLD (hon.), U. Denver, 1990. Bar: Colo. 1959. Probation counselor, legal adviser, referee Denver Juvenile Ct., 1959-64; judge Denver Mcpl. Ct., 1964-65, Denver County Ct., 1965-71, Denver Dist. Ct., 1972-79, U.S. Dist. Ct. Colo., Denver, 1979—. Precinct committeewoman Denver Democratic Com., 1963-64; bd. dirs. Crime Stoppers. Named one of 100 Women in Touch with Our Time Harper's Bazaar Mag., 1971, Woman of Yr., Denver Bus. and Profl. Women, 1969; recipient Women Helping Women award Soroptimist Internat. of Denver, 1983, Hanna G. Solomon award Nat. Coun. Jewish Women, Denver, 1986. Fellow Colo. Bar Found., Am. Bar Found.; mem. ABA, Denver Bar Assn., Colo. Bar Assn., Nat. Conf. Fed. Trial Judges (exec. com.), Dist. Judges' Assn. of 10th Cir. (past pres.), Colo. Women's Bar Assn., Fed. Judges Assn., Denver Crime Stoppers Inc. (bd.dirs.), Devner LWV, Women's Forum Colo., Harvard Law Sch. Assn., Phi Beta Kappa, Phi Kappa Phi, Order of Coif (hon. Colo. chpt.). Office: US Dist Ct 1929 Stout St Denver CO 80294-2900*

WEINSTEIN, DIANE GILBERT, federal judge, lawyer; b. Rochester, N.Y., June 14, 1947; d. Myron Birne and Doris Isabelle (Robie) Gilbert; children: Andrew, David. BA, Smith Coll., Northampton, Mass., 1969; postgrad., Stanford U., 1977-78, Georgetown U., 1978; JD, Boston U., 1979. Bar: D.C. 1979, Mass. 1979. Law clk. to judge D.C. Ct. Appeals, Washington, 1979-80; assoc. Peabody, Lambert & Meyers, Washington, 1980-83; asst. gen. counsel Office of Mgmt. and Budget, Washington, 1983-86; dep. gen. counsel U.S. Dept. Edn., Washington, 1986-88, acting gen. counsel, 1988-89; legal counselor to V.P. of U.S., White House; counsel Pres.'s Competitiveness Coun., Washington, 1989-90; judge U.S. Ct. Fed. Claims, Washington, 1990—. Recipient Young Lawyer's award Boston U. Law Sch., 1989. Mem. Fed. Am. Inn of Ct., Federalist Soc., Univ. Club. Republican. Home: 3927 Massachusetts Ave NW Washington DC 20016-5104

WEINSTEIN, JOYCE, artist; b. N.Y.C., June 7, 1931; d. Sidney and Rose (Bier) W.; student CCNY, 1948-50, Art Students League, 1948-52; m. Stanley Boxer, Nov. 28, 1952. Exhibited in one-women shows: Perdalma Gallery, N.Y.C., 1953-56, L.I. U., Bklyn., 1969, U. Calif.-Santa Cruz, 1969, T. Bortolazzo Gallery, Santa Barbara, Calif., 1972, Dorsky Gallery, N.Y.C., 1972, 74, Galerie Ariadne, N.Y.C., 1975, Gloria Cortella Gallery, N.Y.C., 1976, Meredith Long Contemporary Gallery, N.Y.C. 1978, 79, 88-90, Martin Gerard Gallery, Edmonton, Alta., Can., 1981, 82, 84, Galerie Wentzel, Cologne, W.Ger., 1982, Haber Theodore Gallery, N.Y.C., 1983, 85, Cologne, W.Ger., 1987, Gallery One, Toronto, Ont., Can., 1983, Paul Kuhn Gallery, Calgery, 1985, Eva Cohn Gallery, Highland Park, Chgo, Ill., 1985, Galerie Wentzell, Cologne, 1987, Meredith Long & Co., Houston, 1988, Alena Adlung Gallery, N.Y.C., 1989, Meredith Long & Co., Houston, 1990; group shows: Marlborough Gallery, N.Y.C., 1968, Bula Mus. Art, Calcutta, India, 1970, Phoenix Gallery, N.Y.C., 1988, 1988, Provident Nat. Bank, Phila., 1988, Alena Adlung Gallery, N.Y.C., 1989, 90, Edmonton Art Mus., 1989, Rose Fried Gallery, N.Y.C., 1970, Hudson River Mus., 1971, Dorsky Gallery, 1972, 94, Suffolk Mus., Stony Brook, N.Y., 1972, New York Cultural Center, 1973, Stamford (Conn.) Mus., 1973, Landmark Gallery, N.Y.C., 1974, Women's Interart Center, N.Y.C., 1974, 75, 78, New Sch. Social Research, N.Y.C., 1975, Bklyn. Mus., 1975, Galerie Areadne, N.Y.C., 1975, Edmonton Art Gallery Mus., Alta., Can., 1989, Mus. of Modern Art N.Y.C., 1980, The Queens Mus. N.Y., 1984, The Centre de Creacio Contemporania, Barcelona, Spain, 1987, Fairleigh Dickinson U., Hackensack, N.J., 1976, Gloria Cortella, Inc., 1976, Edmonton Art Gallery Mus., 1977, 77, 83, Northeastern U., Boston, 1977, Lehigh (Pa.) U., 1977, Meredith Long Contemporary Gallery, 1977, 78, 79, 80, Mus. Modern Art, N.Y.C., 1981, Galerie Wentzel, Cologne, W.Ger., 1981-85, Martin Gerard Gallery, Edmonton, 1981, Gallery One, Toronto, 1983, 84, Martin Girard Gallery, 1981-84, Haber Theodore Gallery, 1982-85, Queens Mus., N.Y.C., 1984, Jerald Melberg Gallery, Charlotte, N.C., 1984, Edmonton Art Gallery Mus., 1985, Richard Green Gallery, N.Y.C., Rosel Art Fair, Basel, Switzerland, 1986, Centre de Creacio, Barcelona, Spain, 1987, Meredith Long & Co. Gallery, Houston, 1988-90, Broome St. Gallery, N.Y.C., 1991, Andre Zarre Gallery, N.Y.C., 1990, Alena Adlung Gallery, N.Y.C., 1989-90, Cork Gallery, N.Y.C., 1990, Chgo. Internat. Art Expn., 1990, Queens Coll., N.Y.C., 1991, Miami Art Fair, 1993, Meredith Long & Co. Gallery, Houston, 1988, 89, 90, 93, Bklyn. Botanic Gardens, 1994; also numerous univs. and colls.; represented in permanent collections: Pa. Acad. Fine Arts, N.J. State Mus., Ciba-Geigy Corp., New Sch. Social Research, Bula Mus. Art, U. Calif., Mus. Modern Art, N.Y.C., McMullen Gallery, Edmonton, Ga., De Spisset Mus., U. Santa Clara, Edmonton Art Gallery Mus., Edmonton, The Hines Collection, Boston, others; represented by Hokin Gallery, Palm Beach and Miami, Fla., Galerie Wentzel, Cologne, W. Ger., Meredith Long and Co., Houston , Dorsky Gallery, N.Y.C., Gallery One, Toronto, Can., Smith Anderson Gallery, Palo Alto, Calif.; exec. coordinator Women in Arts Found., Inc., 1975-79, 81-82, coordinating bd., 1983-87. Recipient Lambert Fund award Pa. Acad. Fine Arts, 1955; Susan B. Anthony award NOW, 1983. Home and Studio: 46 Fox Hill Rd Ancramdale NY 12503-5311

WEINSTEIN, MARIE PASTORE, psychologist; b. N.Y.C., Oct. 3, 1940; d. Edward and Sarah (Mancuso) Pastore; children: Arielle Rebecca, Damon Alexander. BA in Polit. Sci. and Lit., Ind. U.; MS in Psychology, L.I. U.; PhD in Ednl. Psychology, CCNY, 1986. Cert. sch. psychologist; lic. psychologist, N.Y. Sch. psychologist evaluation unit Bd. Edn., N.Y.C., 1977-78; dir., adminstr. learning ctr. Guidance Ctr. Flatbush, Bklyn., 1978-82; clin. team coord./psychologist Lorge Upper and Lower Sch., N.Y.C., 1982-85; psychologist devel. disabilities ctr. Roosevelt Hosp., N.Y.C., 1985-87; chief psychologist Blueberry Treatment Ctrs., Bklyn., 1987-89; cons. psychologist Ctr. for Children & Families, St. Albans, N.Y., 1989—; cons. psychologist United Cerebral Palsy Hearst Presch., Bklyn., 1988-89, Charles Drew Day Ctr., Queens Village, N.Y., 1982-85, Warbasse Nursery Sch., Bklyn., 1981-85, YWCA Montessori Sch., 1993-94; adj. asst. prof. Baruch Coll. CUNY, 1989; pvt. practice, Bklyn.; rsch. cons. Children's TV Workshop, N.Y.C., 1979; clin. cons. Bedford Stuyvesant Mental Health Ctr., Bklyn., 1990, Youth Counseling League, N.Y.C., 1993; cons. dist. 2 N.Y.C. Bd. Edn., 1988; guest lectr. Met. Hosp. Dept. Psychiatry, N.Y.C., 1988, Dist. 3 Bd. Edn., 1993; edn. cons. Lit. Vols. N.Y., 1974-76. Contbg. author to children's ency., 1970. Bd. dirs. Artists in Search of. . . . Fellow Am. Orthopsychiat. Assn. (program com. 1990—); mem. APA, Internat. Congress on Child Abuse and Neglect, Manhattan Fedn. Child and Adolescent Svcs. Office: 26 Court St Ste 2112 Brooklyn NY 11242

WEINSTEIN, SHARON SCHLEIN, public relations executive, educator; b. Newark, Apr. 15, 1942; d. Louis Charles and Ruth Margaret (Franzblau) Schlein; m. Elliott Henry Weinstein, May 7, 1978. BA, U. Pa., 1964; MA, New Sch. for Social Rsch., N.Y.C., 1985. Researcher London Daily Express, N.Y.C., 1965-69; reporter Forbes mag., N.Y.C., 1969-72; sr. editor Merrill Lynch, N.Y.C., 1972-74; pub. rels. officer Chase Manhattan Bank, N.Y.C., 1974-79; v.p. pub. rels. and advt. Blyth, Eastman, Dillion, N.Y.C., 1979-80; mgr. corp. communication Sanford C. Berstein & Co., N.Y.C., 1980-83; v.p. corp. affairs Nat. Westminster Bancorp, N.Y.C., 1983—; adj. asst. prof. NYU, 1988—; bd. dirs. N.Y.C. Coun. Econ. Edn. Mem. Women Execs. in Pub. Rels. Home: 161 W 15th St New York NY 10011-6720 Office: Nat Westminster Bancorp 10 Exchange Pl Jersey City NJ 07302-3999

WEINSTOCK, CAROL ANN, manufacturing executive; b. San Francisco, July 19, 1946; d. Vernon A. and Kathleen (Taylor) Davison; D. Michael Romano, Apr. 4, 1971 (div. Mar. 1979); children: Michael G. Romano, Kimbely A. Romano; m. Ronald D. Weinstock, Jan. 12, 1984 (div.). BA in Edn., U. Ariz., 1964-70, grad. work, 1977-82; MS in Photography, Brooks Inst. Photography, 1982-84. Exhibits Shalom-Salaam Liese Communal Svcs. Bldg., Tucson, 1980; photographer Jews of Ethiopia, 1982, Nat. Jewish Community Rels. Adv. Coun., 1983, Jews of Ireland, 1985-87, Bet Hatefutsot Mus. of Diaspora, Tel Aviv, Israel, 1987-88, Westside Jewish Community Ctr., L.A., 1989, Irish Jewish Mus., Dublin, Ireland, 1992—; pres., owner EthnoGraphics Greeting Cards, 1987—. exec. bd., adv. com. Jewish Fedn. So. Ariz., 1979-82 chmn. Run for Soviet Jewry, 1983-84. Recipient Internat. Greeting Card awards, 1988, 91, 92, 93, Community Svc. award Jewish Fedn. So. Ariz., 1981, Simon Rockower award for excellence in Jewish journalism, Excellence in Photography mag. category, 1992. Mem. Am. Soc. Media Photographers, Greeting Card Assn. (bd. dirs. 1994—). Office: 417 Santa Barbara St # B 7 Santa Barbara CA 93101-2348

WEINSTOCK, GRACE EVANGELINE, librarian, retired educator; b. Currie, Minn., Dec. 16, 1904; d. Charles Clementine and Lydia Hannah (Halland) O'Neill; m. Joseph Marshall Weinstock, Sept. 1, 1945 (dec. July 1973). BA, Hamline U., 1925; AAS in Libr. Sci. Tech., Coll. Lake County, 1988. High sch. tchr. Latin, history, phys. edn. Bd. Edn., Grafton, N.D., 1925-27; high sch. tchr. Latin, history, phys. edn. Bd. Edn., Norwood, Minn., 1928-32; high sch. tchr. Latin, English, libr. Bd. Edn., Wells, Minn., 1932-38; interviewer I Minn. State Employment Svc., Redwood Falls, Minn., 1938-45; interviewer II U.S. Employment Svc., Mpls., 1938-45; substitute tchr. English and bus. depts. North Chicago (Ill.) High Sch. Dist. 123, 1956-72; contractual employment instr. typing U.S. Dept. Army 5th U.S. Army Edn. Ctr., Ft. Sheridan, Ill., 1959-71; mil. personnel clk. Dept. Def., USN, Great Lakes, Ill., 1972-86; part-time libr. Outboard Marine Corp., Waukegan, Ill., 1988-90; part-time clerical worker Highland Park (Ill.) Hosp., 1990-91. bd. dirs. Lake County Community Concert Orgn., Waukegan, 1990. Grantee Waukegan br. Ednl. Found., 1993. Mem. AAUW (program chmn. Waukegan br. 1960), Navy League U.S., Phi Theta Kappa, Alpha Kappa Delta, Pi Gamma Mu. Home: 450 Pine Ct Lake Bluff IL 60044-2433

WEINTZ, CAROLINE GILES, advertising executive, travel writer; b. Columbia, Tenn., Dec. 8, 1952; d. Raymond Clark Jr. and Caroline Higdon (Wagstaff) Giles; m. Walter Louis Weintz; children: Alexander Harwood, Elizabeth Pettus. AB, Princeton U., 1974; postgrad. diploma, U. London, 1976. Dir. advt. and promotion E.P. Dutton Pubs., N.Y.C., 1977-86; advt. cons. Assn. Jr. Leagues Internat., N.Y.C., 1986-91, advt. mgr., 1992-94, dir. of systems, 1994—. Author: The Discount Guide for Travelers over 55, 4th edit., 1988. Vol. researcher St. Paul's Nat. Hist. Site and Bill of Rights Mus., Westchester, N.Y., 1986—; treas. Soc. Nat. Shrine of The Bill of

Rights; mem. Jr. League, Pelham, N.Y. Mem. Authors Guild, Nat. Soc. Colonial Dames, Huguenot Soc. Am., Daus. Cin., Mensa. Episcopalian. Home: 444 Wolfs Ln Pelham NY 10803-2127

WEIR, RITA MARY, retail executive; b. Ft. Dix, N.J., Aug. 28, 1955; d. Rynart Barnabas and Teruko (Yokota) Haling; m. Mark Adrian Weir, Oct. 25, 1986. AA, Austin C.C., 1988; BA summa cum laude, Coll. of Lifelong Learning, 1990. Store mgr. KFC, El Paso and Austin, Tex., 1973-86; asst. mgr. Stuart Shaines, Portsmouth and Newington, N.H., 1989-90, Wal-Mart, Portsmouth, N.H., 1991—. Mem. NAFE, Am. Bus. Women's Assn. (pres. 1992-93, bull. chair 1993-94, hospitality com. 1993-94, 94-95, membership com. 1993-94, 94-95, Woman of Yr. 1993, v.p. 1994-95, chpt. del. 1994—), Phi Theta Kappa. Home: 44 Lamprey Ln Lee NH 03824-6552 Office: Wal-Mart 2460 Lafayette Rd Portsmouth NH 03801

WEIR, SONJA ANN, artist; b. Hazleton, Pa., Oct. 12, 1934; d. Stephen and Anna (Prehatny) Tatusko; m. Richard Clayton Weir, Jan. 14, 1956; children: Robert, Carl, Donna, Lisa, Nancy. Student of Mary Ellen Silkotch, 1963-83; student, Art Students League, N.Y.C., 1985-87. Artist Knickerbocker Toy Co., Middlesex, N.J., 1980; guest speaker career day Bridgewater High Sch., 1993, 94. One-person shows include Johnson & Johnson, Piscataway, N.J., 1992, Somerset County Libr., Bridgewater, N.J., 1992-94; Manville (N.J.) Pub. Libr., 1994; group shows include Raritan Valley Art Assn. 1982-83 (Best in Show award), Ariel Gallery, N.Y.C., 1991, Am. Artists Profl. League, 1991, Barren Art Ctr., Woodbridge, N.J., 1993; represented in permanent collections N.W.B. Bank of South Bound Brook, N.J. Mem. Nat. Mus. of Women in the Arts, Am. Artists Profl. League (v.p. N.J. chpt. 1988-91, pres. N.J. chpt. 1992-95, show chmn. 1989-91, publicity com. 1988-91), Internat. Platform Assn., Raritan Valley Arts Assn. (pres. 1982-84), Nat. Miniature Assn. (assoc.), Miniature Art Soc. Fla., Miniature Art Soc. Mont. Home and Studio: 25 Madison St South Bound Brook NJ 08880-1244

WEIS, JUDITH SHULMAN, biology educator; b. N.Y.C., May 29, 1941; d. Saul B. and Pearl (Cooper) Shulman; m. Peddrick Weis; children: Jennifer, Eric. BA, Cornell U., 1962; MS, NYU, 1964, PhD, 1967. Lectr. CUNY, 1964-67; asst. prof. Rutgers U., Newark, 1967-71, assoc. prof., 1971-76, prof., 1976—; Congl. sci. fellow U.S. Senate, Washington, 1983-84; mem. grant rev. panel NSF, Washington, 1976-82, program dir., 1988-90; mem. rev. panel EPA, 1984-92; vis. scientist EPA Lab., Gulf Breeze, Fla., 1992. Mem. marine bd. NAS, 1991—. Grantee NOAA, 1977—, N.J. EPA Rsch., 1978-79, 81-83, N.J. Marine Scis. Consortium Rsch., 1987—; NSF fellow, 1962-64. Mem. Am. Inst. for Biol. Scis. (bd. dirs. 1986-88, 89-91), Soc. Environ. Toxicology and Chemistry (bd. dirs. 1990-93), Estuarine Rsch. Fedn., Ecol. Soc. Am., NOW (pres. Essex County 1972), Sierra Club (bd. dirs. N.J. chpt. 1986-88). Office: Rutgers U Dept Biol Scis Newark NJ 07102

WEIS, SUSAN FURMINGER, education educator; b. Washington, Sept. 4, 1940; d. Carlos Paul and Gladys (Kanak) Furminger; m. K. Ronald Weis, Aug. 4, 1962; children: Marcus Dane, Kristian Djorn, Penn Ronson, Kael Janson. BS, The Penn State U., 1962, MS, 1966, PhD, 1969. Instr. Penn State U., University Park, Pa., 1967-69, asst. prof., 1969-76, assoc. prof., 1976—. Co-editor Directory-American Vocational Assn.-Home Econs. Div., 1982—; editor Yearbook-Occupational Home Economics, 1992—. Mem. Pa. Task Force for Home Econs., 1990—; pres. Nat. Assn. for Vocat. Home Econs., 1986-87; chairperson Pa. Adv. Coun. for Vocat. Edn., 1982-83; pres. Pa. Vocat. Assn., 1975-76. Named for Outstanding Contbn., Am. Vocat. Assn. Home Econs. Div., 1990. Mem. Am. Vocat. Assn., Am. Home Econs. Assn. Office: The Penn State U 102 Rackley Bldg University Park PA 16802-3202

WEISBERG, LYNNE WILLING, psychiatrist, consultant; b. N.Y.C., Apr. 11, 1948; d. Stanley S. and Pearl R. Willing. BA, Barnard Coll., 1969; PhD, U. Mich., 1972; MD, SUNY, Downstate, 1978. Diplomate Am. Bd. Psychiatry and Neurology, Am. Bd. Adolescent Psychiatry. Intern NYU Med. Ctr., 1978-79; resident in adult psychiatry Mt. Sinai Hosp., N.Y.C., 1979-81; fellow in child psychiatry Columbia Med. Ctr., 1981-83; staff psychiatrist Fair Oaks Hosp., Summit, N.J., 1983-85, asst. dir. child and adolescent psychiatry, 1985-88, assoc. dir. child and adolescent psychiatry, 1988-92; dir. child and adolescent outpatient psychiat. svcs. Psychiat. Assocs. N.J. at Fair Oaks Hosp., Summit, 1992—; pvt. practice Morristown, N.J., 1992—; cons. Bonnie Brae Sch., Millington, N.J., 1984-92. Author: When Acting Out Isn't Acting, 1991. Horace Rackham Prize fellow, 1972. Mem. AMA, Med. Soc. N.J. Office: 20 Community Pl Morristown NJ 07960

WEISBERG, RUTH MAXINE, radio reporter, television talk show host; b. Phila., May 31, 1956; d. William and Libby (Magness W.; 1 child, Talia Genevieve. BS in Spl. Edn. with honors, Pa. State U., 1977. Reporter Shadow Traffic Network, Phila., 1978-82; news dir., morning anchor Sta. WIFI-FM, Phila., 1982-83; features editor Sta. WPEN, Phila., 1983-85; arts and entertainment editor Sta. WSNI-FM, Phila., 1985-88; TV, radio talk show host CBS, Phila., 1988—; ind. filmmaker, voice over narrator. Nat. corr., contb. editor Single Mother mag. Miss Am. Pageant scholar, 1980; recipient Radio Features awards Phila. Press Assn., 1983, AP, 1983, Women in Comm., 1984. Mem. Internat. TV Assn. (contbg. editor monthly newsletter Phila. 1982—, Video Craft award for voiceover narration 1992, Mem. of Yr. 1994), Nat. Orgn. Single Mothers, Inc. Home: 37 Sabine Ave Narberth PA 19072-1740 Office: PO Box 903 Narberth PA 19072

WEISBERG-SAMUELS, JANET SUSAN, psychologist; b. N.Y.C., Mar. 21, 1940; d. Morris and Vivian (Wank) Weisberg; m. Richard Samuels, Jan. 16, 1983; children—Debra, David. B.B.A., CCNY, 1960; M.S., CUNY, 1966; Ph.D., Yeshiva U., 1984. Lic. psychologist; cert. sch. psychologist N.Y. State. Psychologist, Bklyn. Jewish Hosp., 1969-75;team leader N.Y. State Dept. Mental Hygiene, N.Y.C., 1977; cons. N.Y.C. Bd. Edn., 1977, Parent-Child Consultation Ctr., 1980—; psychologist Beth Israel Hosp., N.Y.C., 1975-87, acting chief psychologist dept. child psychiatry, 1982-83, dir. Enuresis Clinic, 1981-85; practice in psychology, N.Y.C.; program dir. Brotherhood Synagogue, N.Y.C., 1968-75; dir. tng. Interfaith Hosp., Bklyn., 1987—; clin. faculty Mt. Sinai Sch. Medicine, N.Y.C., 1979—. Pres. Singles div. Park Ave. Synagogue, N.Y.C., 1980-83, bd. dirs. Couples Club, 1986—, pres. 1988-90. Mem. Am. Psychol. Assn., N.Y. State Psych. Assn., Eastern Psychol. Assn., Manhattan Psychol. Assn. (exec bd. 1993—). Jewish. Avocations: opera, ballet, museums. Office: 160 E 89th St Rm 1B New York NY 10128

WEISBURD, ELLEN S., lawyer; b. Newark, Jan. 13, 1949; d. Harry Edward Weisburg and Ida (Taratoot) Weisburg Miller; m. Edward Wilson; children: Deborah, Kimberly. BA, Rutgers U., 1973; JD, Yeshiva U., 1979. History tchr. N.J. Dept. Edn., East Orange, N.J., 1973-76; pub. defender N.J. Office Pub. Defenders, East Orange, 1979-81; dep. atty. gen. N.Y. State Dept. Law, N.Y.C., 1981-83; asst. dir. legal affairs Anti-Defamation League, N.Y.C., 1983-85; gen. counsel Citibank, N.A., N.Y.C., 1985—. Home: 161 W 15th St New York NY 10011

WEISBURGER, ELIZABETH KREISER, retired chemist, editor; b. Greenlane, Pa., Apr. 9, 1924; d. Raymond Samuel and Amy Elizabeth (Snavely) Kreiser; m. John H. Weisburger, Apr. 7, 1947 (div. May 1974); children: William Raymond, Diane Susan, Andrew John. BS, Lebanon Valley Coll., Annville, Pa., 1944, DSc (hon.), 1989; PhD, U. Cin., 1947, DSc (hon.), 1981. Rsch. assoc. U. Cin., 1947-49; col. USPHS, 1951-89; postdoctoral fellow Nat. Cancer Inst., Bethesda, Md., 1949-51, chemist, 1951-73, chief carcinogen metabolism and toxicology br., 1972-75, chief Lab. Carcinogen Metabolism, 1975-81, asst. dir. chem. carcinogenesis, 1981-89, ret.; cons. in field; lectr. Found. for Advanced Edn. in Scis., Bethesda, 1980—; adj. prof. Am. U., Washington, 1982—. Asst. editor-in-chief Jour. Nat. Cancer Inst., 1971-87; mem. editorial adv. bd. Environ. Health Perspectives, 1993—; mem. editorial bd. Chem. Health and Safety, 1994—; contbr. articles to profl. jours. Trustee Lebanon Valley Coll., 1970—, pres. bd. trustees, 1985-89. Recipient Meritorious Service medal USPHS, 1973, Disting. Service medal, 1985; Hillebrand prize Chem. Soc. Washington, 1981. Fellow AAAS (nominating com. 1978-81); mem. Am. Chem. Soc. (Garvan medal 1981), Am. Assn. Cancer Research, Soc. Toxicology, Am. Soc. Biochem. and Molecular Biology, Royal Soc. Chemistry, Am. Conf. Govtl. Indsl. Hygienists, Grad. Women in Sci. (hon.), Iota Sigma Pi (hon.). Lutheran.

WEISE, JOAN CAROLYN, electronics company executive; b. Libertyville, Ill., Feb. 3, 1939; d. James Gardner McDearmid and Anne Louise (Quist) Nehls; m. James Edward Weise, Aug. 15, 1959; children: Renee, James, Laura. Student, U. Ill., 1956-58; BA in Edn., Carthage Coll., 1973; MBA, U. La Verne, 1994. Cert. tchr., Ill. Dir. nursery sch. Rosa Kahn Sch., Mundelein, Ill., 1971-73; tchr. Avon Sch., Round Lake, Ill., 1973-77; with customer service, contracts depts. AM Documentor, Santa Ana, Calif., 1978-81; mgr. customer service Plessey Semicondr., Irvine, Calif., 1981-84, mgr. ops. support, 1984-87; profl. beauty cons. Mary Kay Cosmetics, Irvine, 1987-89; sales office mgr. Newport Corp., Irvine, Calif., 1989-92, mgr. tng. and devel., 1992—; small bus. cons., 1991. chmn. Library Friends, Millburn, Ill., 1969-73, Citizen Sch. Adv., Millburn, 1974-75; leader 4-H, Millburn, 1972-77; vol., tutor Laubach Literacy, 1988—. Mem. NAFE, Am. Mfg. Excellence, Am. Mgmt. Assn., ASTD, Internat. Networking Assn.

WEISENFELD, MILDRED (MRS. ALBERT G. MOSLER), research organization executive; b. Bklyn.; d. David and Augusta (Kagen) W.; m. Albert G. Mosler, June 24, 1956. Student, Bklyn. Coll., 1939-42. Founder, exec. dir. Fight for Sight, Inc., N.Y.C., 1959—. Founder Nat. Coun. to COmbat Blindness, 1946; organizer eye rsch. testimony subcom. Com. Interstate and Fgn. Commerce, U.S. Ho. of Reps., 1949. Recipient Eleanor Roosevelt Community Svc. citation, 1954, Citizens Meritorious Svc. award Med. Soc. County N.Y., 1962, Spl. Honorary award Glaucoma Found., 1991; named 1st lay person to receive award Am. Acad. Ophthalmology, 1974. Mem. Assn. Rsch. Vision and Ophthalmology (hon., Ann. Mildred Weisenfeld Excellence in Ophthalmology award established in 1986). Office: Fight for Sight Inc 160 E 56th St New York NY 10022-3609

WEISGOLD, MYRA (MARCI), sculptor; b. Phila., Apr. 10, 1939; d. Samuel and Mae (Kaufman) Chernoff; m. Arnold Stanley Weisgold, June 14, 1959; children: Dean, Richard, Melissa. BA, U. Pa., 1961; studied with Ev Angelos Frudakis. Sculptures include (bronze bust) D. Walter Cohen, 1981, (bronze bas reliefs) Memorial: Robert Ravdin, 1982, Memorial: J. George Coslet, 1985, (bronze compositions) Stepping Stones, 1989, Testing the Waters, 1992, Middle States Tennis Found., 1994. Recipient Pietro and Alfreda Montana Meml. award Allied Artists of Am., 1982, Edwin and Theresa Richard Meml. award, 1987, Excalibur Bronze Sculpture Foundry award Pen and Brush, 1990. Helen G. Oehler Meml. award Am. Artists Profl. League, 1991, Margaret Sussman Meml. award Pen and Brush, 1993, Harriet Frishmuth Meml. award Catherine L. Wolfe Art Club, 1993. Mem. Nat. Sculpture Soc. (Mildred Victor Meml. prize 1994), Catherine L. Wolfe Art Club, Am. Artists Profl. League, Allied Artists Am. (assoc.), Pen and Brush Inc., Knickerbocker Artists (assoc.), Artists Equity, Internat. Sculpture Ctr., Phi Beta Kappa. Home: 150 Summit Ln Bala Cynwyd PA 19004 Office: Mill Artists Studios 123 Leverington Ave Philadelphia PA 19127

WEISMAN, ANN ELISABETH, city official, artist; b. Tulsa, July 26, 1948; d. William Israel and Gertrude (Blend) W.; m. James L. Roper, July 1981 (div. Jan. 1982). Student, Reed Coll., 1966-67, Monterey Inst. Fgn. Studies, Calif., 1970; BA, U. Tulsa, 1971; MFA, U. Mont., 1974. Poet in the schs. Mont. Arts Coun., Missoula, 1974-76; tchr. English Pikuni Cmty. Sch., Browning, Mont., 1976-78; poet in the cmty. Arts and Humanities Coun., Tulsa, 1978-80; mng. dir. Living Arts of Tulsa, 1984-85; tech. writer Cooper Mfg., Tulsa, 1981-84; mng. editor Coun. Oaks Books, Tulsa, 1985-88; arts coord. City of Lawton, Okla., 1988-90, adminstr. arts and humanities, 1990—. Author: Open Air, 1984, Eye Imagine, 1991; contbr. articles to profl. jours. Mem. Okla. Visual Arts Coalition (mem. bd. 1989—), Tulsa Artists Coalition (mem. bd. 1986-88), Alt. Roots. Office: Lawton Arts & Humanities Coun 103 SW 4th St Lawton OK 73501-4039

WEISMAN, JANA-LYN, lawyer; b. Phila., Nov. 25, 1949; d. Harvey and Matilda (Miller) W. BS, Syracuse U., 1971, JD, 1974. Bar: Pa. 1974. Atty. Cmty. Legal Svcs., Inc., Phila. Office: Cmty Legal Svcs Inc 3638 N Broad St Philadelphia PA 19140

WEISS, ANN, filmmaker, editor, writer, photographer, information specialist, consultant; b. Modena, Italy, July 17, 1949; came to U.S., 1951, naturalized, 1959; d. Leo and Athalie Weiss; children: Julia Emily, Rebecca Lauren. BA magna cum laude in English Lit. and Edn., U. Rochester, 1971; MA in Info. Sci. summa cum laude, Drexel U., 1973; MA in Comm., Annenberg Sch Comm., 1994; postgrad., U. Pa., 1992—, postgrad. in Edn., 1993—. Editor, chief cons. monographs, articles, freelance photographer, 1974—; cataloguer Drexel U., Phila., 1971-73; libr. Akiba Lower Sch., Merion, Pa., 1973; head children's dept. Tredyffrin Pub. Libr., Strafford, Pa., 1973-79, co-head reference dept., 1979-87; cons. in edn. and librs. Gulf Arab States Edn. and Rsch. Ctr. UNESCO, 1977—, cons. Rabbi Zalman Schachter-Shalomi, P'nai or Fellowship, 1987—; photojournalist in Ea. Europe, mainly Poland, Ukraine and Czechoslovakia, 1987—; mem. editl. bd. Studies of Shoah, 1991—; primary investigator Holocaust rsch. team U. Pa., Transcending Trauma: Psychological Mechanism of Survival, 1989—. Dir., producer (video documentary and archive creation) oral history project Inst. Pa. Hosp., (video documentary) The Institute: An Intimate History, 1992; dir., producer, writer, narrator, photographer (video documentary) Eyes From The Ashes, Archival Photographs from Auschwitz, 1989-90; dir., producer, writer, narrator, photographer (with D. Rosenberg) Auschwitz documentary Lighting Six Candles, 1992—; author, lyricist (with Thaddeus Lorentz/musical), Zosia: An Immigrant's Story; chief editorial cons. Puppetry and the Art of Story Creation, 1981, Puppetry in Early Childhood Education, 1982, Puppetry, Language and the Special Child: Discovering Alternative Language, 1984, Humanizing the Enemy...and Ourselves, 1986, Imagination, 1987, Celebrate! Holidays, Puppetry and Creative Dramatics, 1987; author: (CD-Rom) Archival Photos of Auschwitz; one-person photographic shows throughout U.S., Europe, Israel; represented in permanent collections including Martyr's Meml. Mus./Yad Vashem, Simon Wiesenthal Ctr./Mus. Tolerance. Active So. Poverty Law Ctr., Common Cause, promoting dialogue and understanding between Jews and Arabs, Jews and Poles; active Coun. for Soviet Jews, Internat. Network Children Holocaust Survivors; photographer Bob Edgar's Campaign U.S. Senate, 1985-86, David Landau's Congl. Campaign, 1986. Mem. ACLU, NOW, SANE, Free Wallenberg Alliance, Physicians for Social Responsibility Amnesty Internat., New Israel Fund, Sierra Club, Shefa Fund. Office: PO Box 1133 Bryn Mawr PA 19010-7133

WEISS, BILLIE ANN, music educator; b. Scott City, Kans., Mar. 29, 1928; d. William Ralph and Margaret Frances (Slaughter) Gorsuch; m. Harold David Weiss, July 1, 1951; children: David Spencer (dec.) Paul Dana. BA, Wheaton (Ill.) Coll., 1950. Cert. spl. secondary music tchr., Calif. Elem. music tchr. Midland Dist., Riverside, Calif., 1950-52; 3rd grade tchr. Crest Forest Dist., Crestline, Calif., 1952; organist Community Presbyn. Ch., Crestline, 1954-57; organist Lake Arrowhead (Calif.) Presbyn. Ch., 1962—, choir dir., cherubs, 1977—, choir dir. adults, music dir., 1980—, dir. handbell choir, 1984—; substitute tchr. Rim of the World Unified Schs., Lake Arrowhead, 1977—. Sec. Mountains Community Hosp. Aux., 1977-80; bd. dirs. Arrowhead Arts Assn., 1989-92; session clk. Lake Arrowhead Community Presbyn. Ch., 1972-74, elder 1958—; mem. Lake Arrowhead Arts Aux. Recipient Vol. Svc. award, Mountains Community Hosp. Aux., 1983, Vocat. Svc. award, Rotary Club Am., 1989. Mem. AAUW (pres. Rim of World br. 1983-85, Gift Honoree 1983, Woman of Yr. 1986), Rim of the World Interpretive Assn. Democrat. Home: PO Box 64 Cedar Glen CA 92321-0064 Office: Lake Arrowhead Community Presbyn Ch PO Box 340 Lake Arrowhead CA 92352-0340

WEISS, DEBRA S., marketing director; b. Three Rivers, Mich., Dec. 4, 1953; d. Harold E. and Winifred (Dunn) W. Student Albion Coll., 1972-73, Lake Superior State Coll., 1974-76; cert. Industrialized Housing Inst., Wausau, Wis., 1975. Lic. builder and mech. contractor, Mich. Sales mgr. Weiss Constrn., Inc., Alanson, Mich., 1976-80; owner, chmn. bd. dirs. Weiss Constrn., St. Ignace, Mich., 1980-91; corp. sec., supr. spl. projects Weiss Corp., St. Ignace, 1984; mktg. dir. First Nat. Bank of Gaylord, Mich., 1992—. Bd. dirs. Ea. Upper Peninsula Pvt. Industry Council, Sault Ste. Marie, Mich., 1984-92, treas., 1985-87, pres. 1987-89; mem. Downtown Devel. Authority, Mackinaw City, Mich., 1985-87; mem. St. Ignace Zoning Bd., 1984-92, vice chmn., 1990-92; mem. St. Ignace City Council, 1985-92; chmn. Utility Authority Task Force; conv. chmn. designate, 1993; pres., bd. dirs. Otsego County/Gaylord Friendship Shelter for Homeless, 1992—. Recipient Ruth Huston Whipple award, 1986, Garden City award, 1986. Mem. NOW, St. Ignace Bus. and Profl. Women (pres. 1980-81; Woman of Yr. 1980, Anna Howard Shaw award 1981, 82), Mich. Fedn. Bus. and Profl. Women (mem. strategic long range planning com. 1985-87, chmn. issues mgmt. com., named Outstanding Young Career Woman 1982, Woman of Achievement award 1987), Nat. Fedn. Bus. and Profl. Women (long range strategic planning comm., 1987-89), Silver Mountain Ski Assn. (bd. dirs. 1982-85), Mich. Fedn. of Bus. and Profl. Women, St. Ignace C. of C., St. Ignace Tourist Assn., Upper Peninsula Tourist and Recreation Assn., Silver Mountain Cross Country Club, Nat. Assn. Female Execs. Avocations: skiing, reading, water sports. Office: 1st Nat Bank Gaylord PO Box 310 Gaylord MI 49735-0310

WEISS, GAIL ELLEN, legislative staff director; b. N.Y.C., Apr. 11, 1946; d. Joseph and Elaine (Klein) W.; m. John A. Kelly. BA, U. Md., 1967. Staff asst. U.S. Office Econ. Opportunity/Job Corps, Washington, 1967-69; legis. asst. Hon. William L. Clay, Mem. Congress, Washington, 1969-72; rsch. asst. Rt. Hon. Roy Hattersley, Mem. Parliament, London, 1972-73; legis. asst. various coms. U.S. Ho. of Reps., Washington, 1973-90, staff dir. Com. on P.O. and Civil Svc., 1991-94, Dem. staff dir. Com. on Econ. and Ednl. Opportunities, 1995&; mem. working group Pres.'s Task Force on Nat. Health Reform, 1993. Democrat. Jewish. Office: Com on Econ and Ednl Opp 2100 Rayburn Ho Office Bldg Washington DC 20515

WEISS, JOAN RUTH, educator; b. Phila., Feb. 14, 1953; d. Fred and Sara (Ginsberg) Cantor; m. Fredric K. Weiss, Oct. 13, 1953; 1 child, Saul Aaron. BS, Pa. State U., 1974; MA in Teaching and Bus. Edn., Trenton State Coll., 1988. Retail buyer Lit Bros., Phila., 1974-77; real estate saleswoman Korman Corp., Trevose, Pa., 1980-81; retail mgr. Macy's (formerly Bambergers), Langhorne, Pa., 1981-83; prof. mktg. and retailing Bucks County C.C., Newtown, Pa., 1983—, also mem. adv. coun. to pres. V.p. Women's Am. Orgn. Rehab. and Tng., Richboro, Pa., 1985-87, Ohev Shalom Sisterhood, 1986—. Fellow Students in Free Enterprise, 1991-93. Mem. Fashion Group Phila., Delta Pi Epsilon. Republican. Office: Bucks County Community Coll Swamp Rd Newtown PA 18940-1525

WEISS, JOANNE MARION, writer; b. Wayne, N.J., Mar. 16, 1960; d. Henry Daniel and Florence Frances (Zaratkiewicz) W. BA, Bennington Coll., 1982; MA, U. Cambridge, Eng., 1988. Prodn. mgr. The Suburban News, N.J., 1982-83; gardener Artistic Landscaping, N.J., 1983; case mgr. Mid-Bergan Mental Health Ctr., N.J., 1985-86. Author, dir.; (play) The Gift, 1987, 88. Translator Solidarity, Poland, 1983; co-leader Vols. for Peace, 1986; mem., worker Pregnancy Adv. Svc., Cambridge, 1991-92. Recipient scholarship Inst. for Brit. and Irish Studies, Trinity Coll., Dublin, 1985, Chancellor's medal for poetry U. Cambridge, Eng., 1988, grants for Edinburgh, Sir John Gielgud, 1988, grant Judith Wilson Fund, U. Cambridge, Eng., 1988. Mem. British Heritage, Abyssinian Cat Assn., People for Ethical Treatment Animals. Home: 265 River Rd Allenstown NH 03275

WEISS, JUDITH MIRIAM, psychologist; b. Chgo., June 29, 1939; d. Louis and Annette (Frazin) Schmerling; m. Jon Howard Kaas, May 19, 1963 (div. Dec. 1984); children: Lisa Karen, Jon Michael; m. Stephen Fred Weiss, Dec. 22, 1988. AB in Liberal Arts, Northwestern U., 1961; PhD, Duke U., 1969. Lic. clin. psychologist, Tenn. Postdoctoral fellow U. Wis. Hosp., Madison, 1969-71; neuropsychologist Mental Health Assocs., Madison, 1971-72; asst. prof. George Peabody Coll., Nashville, 1972-77, Vanderbilt U., Nashville, 1972-77; neuropsychologist Comprehensive Clin. Svcs., Nashville, 1977—; advocate, cons. Tenn. Protection and Advocacy, Inc., Nashville, 1976—. Mem. CABLE, Nashville. Mem. APA, Tenn. Psychol. Assn., Internat. Neuropsychol. Assn., Nat. Acad. Neuropsychology, Tenn. Assn. Speech and Lang. Pathologists. Jewish. Home: 893 Stirrup Dr Nashville TN 37221 Office: Comprehensive Clin Svcs 102 Woodmont Blvd Ste 215 Nashville TN 37205

WEISS, LINDA WOLFF, health facility administrator; b. Albany, N.Y., Apr. 12, 1953; d. Charles Vincent and Hilda Bertha (Kitzman) Wolff; divorced; 1 child, Russell. A in Applied Sci., Hudson Valley C.C., Troy, N.Y., 1973; BS, Empire State Coll., 1983; MS in Health Sys. Mgmt., Union Coll., 1987. Staff nuclear medicine technologist VA Med. Ctr., Albany, 1973-83, chief technologist-nuclear medicine, 1983-84, asst. chief radiology/nuclear medicine svc., 1984-87, area mgr. emergency medicine preparedness office, 1987-94; area mgr. emergency medicine preparedness office U.S. Dept VA, Albany and Syracuse, N.Y., 1994—; mem. N.Y. State Disaster Preparedness Commn., Albany; charter mem. human needs in disaster standing com., 1989—, Albany County Local Emergency Preparedness Commn., 1987—, N.Y. State Vol. Orgns. Active in Disaster, 1989; mem. adj. faculty, tutor Empire State Coll, Albany; investigator Northridge Earthquake Epidemiology Study, 1995—. Contbg. editor Jour. Clin. Ultrasound, 1981-85, Med. Ultrasound, 1981-83; mem. editl. bd. EMPO News, 1992—. Recipient Dir.'s cert. Hurricane Andrew Response, 1992. Mem. Ptnrs. of the Ams. (W.K. Kellogg Found. fellow 1991-93, chair emergency preparedness com. 1991—), Albany County Hist. Soc., Barn Raisers. Lutheran. Avocations: travel, project devel., swimming, bungee jumping. Office: VA Med Ctr Emergency Med Preparedness Office 113 Holland Ave Albany NY 12208

WEISS, MAREDA RUTH, university administrator; b. Chgo., Sept. 23, 1941; d. William Arthur and Ruth Emily (Schauble) W. BBA, U. Wis., 1963. Acct., then supr. rsch. adminstrn./fin. U. Wis. System, Madison, 1964-69; specialist, asst. dean, now assoc. dean, dir. rsch. svcs. U. Wis., Madison, 1969—; univ. chair State Employees Combined Campaign, Madison, 1986. Treas. Wis. Cen. Ctr. Aux., Madison, 1971-73, 75-77, 79-81, Frineds of WHA-TV pub. tv, Madison, 1989-91; chair nominating com. U. Wis. Credit Union, 1982-88. Mem. Nat. Coun. Univ. Rsch. Adminstrs. (presenter workshops, sec.-treas. 1980-83, chair, vice-chair mid-Am. region 1989-91, Disting. Svc. award 1989), Univ. Ins. Assn. (bd. dirs. 1982—). Office: U Wis Grad Sch 500 Lincoln Dr Madison WI 53706-1380

WEISS, MYRNA GRACE, financial consulant; b. N.Y.C., June 22, 1939; d. Herman and Blanche (Stiftel) Ziegler; m. Arthur H. Weiss; children: Debra Anne Huddleston, Louise Esther. BA, Barnard Coll., 1958; MA, Hunter Coll., 1968; MPA, NYU, 1978; cert. in Mktg., U. Pa. Tchr. N.Y.C. and Vallejo, Calif., 1959-68; dir. admissions Columbia Prep. Sch., N.Y.C., 1969-72; dir. PREP counselling NYU, N.Y.C., 1973-74; dept. head Hewitt Sch., N.Y.C., 1974-79; mgr. Met. Ins. Co., N.Y.C., 1979-84; mktg. exec. Rothschild, Inc., N.Y.C., 1984-85; pres. First Mktg. Capital Group Ltd., N.Y.C., 1985—; mng. dir. Wrap Co. Internat. N.V., 1992—; ptnr. Lared Group, N.Y.C., 1987—; advisor Gov.'s Hwy. Safety Com., N.Y.C., 1985-88; pres. Fin. Women's Assn. N.Y., 1984-85. Bd. dirs. 92nd Y, N.Y.C., 1972-90, ARC, N.Y.C., 1989—, asst. treas., 1993—. Mem. Internat. Women's Forum (bd. dirs. 1990-92), Econ. Club N.Y., Women's Econ. Roundtable (bd. dirs. 1988-90). Office: 1st Mktg Capital Group Ltd 1056 Fifth Ave New York NY 10028-0112

WEISS, PEARL MILLER, transportation agency executive; b. Phila., Nov. 28, 1934; d. Benjamin P. and Anna (Blodstein) Miller; m. Norman Weiss, Aug. 22, 1966 (div.); children: Michael F., Marshall J. Grad., Olney High Sch., Phila., 1952. Inventory control clk. J. Maimon and Sons, Phila., 1952-57; credit mgr. Martil Clothing Co., Phila., 1957-61; sec. B'nai B'rith Voc. Svc., Phila., 1961-67; contract purchasing sec. Southeastern Pa. Transp. Authority, Phila., 1973-78, acting buyer, 1978-80, buyer, 1980-89, sr. buyer contract, purchasing/procurement, 1989—. Mem. Purchasing Mgmt. Assn. Phila., Am. Legion Ladies Aux., Jewish War Vets. Ladies Aux. (past pres.). Office: Southeastern Pa Transp 200 W Wyoming Ave Philadelphia PA 19140-1530

WEISS, RENÉE KAROL, editor, writer, musician; b. Allentown, Pa., Sept. 11, 1923; d. Abraham S. and Elizabeth (Levitt) Karol; m. Theodore Weiss. BA, Bard Coll., 1951; student, Conn. Sch. Dance; studied violin with, Sascha Jacobinoff, Boris Koutzen, Emile Hauser, Ivan Galamian. Mem. Miami U. Symphony Orch., 1941, N.C. State Sympnony, 1942-45, Oxford U. Symphony, Opera Orchs., Eng., 1953-54, Woodstock String Quartet, 1956-60, Bard Coll. Chamber Ensemble, 1950-66, Hudson Valley Philharmonic, 1960-66, Hudson Valley String Quartet, 1965, Princeton Chamber Orch., 1980-93; orchestral, chamber, solo work, 1966—; with Theodore Weiss poetry writing workshops, Princeton U., 1985, Hofstra Coll., 1985, Modern Poetry Cooper Union, 1988; tchr. modern dance to children Bard Coll., kindengarren Tivoli, N.Y. Pub. Sch., 1955-58. Author:

(children's books) To Win A Race, 1966, A Paper Zoo, 1968 (best books for children N.Y. Times, Book World 1968, N.J. Author's award 1968, 70, 88), The Bird From the Sea, 1970, David Schubert: Works and Days, 1984; co-editor, mgr. Quar. Rev. Lit., 1945—; contbr. poems to various jours.; poetry readings (with Theodore Weiss) at various colls. in U.S. and abroad, including China. Office: Q R L Poetry Series 26 Haslet Ave Princeton NJ 08540-4914

WEISS, RITA S., transportation executive; b. Phila., May 24, 1935; d. Jack J. and Cecelia (Alper) Brown; m. Irvin J. Weiss, Oct. 29, 1955; children: Brett David, Judith Weiss Bohn. BS in Edn., Temple U., 1955; MA in Edn., U. Md., 1976. Cert. elem. tchr., Md. Tchr. Solis-Cohen Elem. Sch., Phila., Va., 1955-59, Geneva Nursery Sch., Rockville, Md., 1966-71; dir. Har Shalom Nursery Sch., Potomac, Md., 1971-78; ednl. cons. Am. Automobile Assn., Falls Church, Va., 1978-88; program analyst Nat. Hwy. Traffic Safety Adminstrn. U.S. Dept. Transp., Washington, 1988-93, divsn. chief Nat. Hwy. Traffic Safety Adminstrn. Regional Ops., 1994—, mem. fellows program, 1993-94. Author numerous traffic safety publs. Dept. Transp. fellow, 1993-94; recipient Disting. Svc. to Safety award Nat. Safety Coun., 1994, Adminstr's Superior Achievement award NHTSA, 1995. Mem. NHTSA Profl. Women's Assn. (rec. sec., area rep., Adminstr.'s award for merit 1990, outstanding performance award 1989, 91, 92, 93, 94, superior accomplishment award 1988, performance award 1988), Nat. Safety Coun. (bd. dirs., chmn. edn. resources div., chmn. community agys. sect.), Md. Community Assn. for Edn. Young Children (pres., newsletter editor, historian), Childhood Edn. Internat. (assoc.), U. Md. Alumni Assn., Women's Transp. Seminar. Office: US Dept Transp NHTSA Regional Ops NRO-20 400 7th St SW Washington DC 20590-0002

WEISS, SHIRLEY F., urban and regional planner, economist, educator; b. N.Y.C., Feb. 26, 1921; d. Max and Vera (Hendel) Friedlander; m. Charles M. Weiss, June 7, 1942. BA, Douglas Coll., 1942; postgrad., Johns Hopkins U., 1949-50; M in Regional Planning, U. N.C., 1958; PhD, Duke U., 1973. Assoc. research dir. Ctr. for Urban and Regional Studies U. N.C., Chapel Hill, 1957-91, lectr. in planning, 1958-62, assoc. prof., 1962-73, prof., 1973-91, prof. emeritus, 1991—; research assoc. Inst. for Research in Social Sci., U. N.C., 1957-73; research prof. U. N.C., Chapel Hill, 1973-91, acting dir. women's studies program Coll. Arts and Scis., 1985, faculty marshal, 1988-91; mem. tech. com. Water Resources Rsch. Inst., 1976-79; mem. adv. com. on housing for 1980 census Dept. Commerce, 1976-81; cons. Urban Inst., Washington, 1977-80; mem. rev. panel Exptl. Housing Allowance Program, HUD, 1977-80; mem. adv. bd. on built environ. Nat. Acad. Scis.-NRC, 1981-83, mem. program coordinating com. fed. constrn. coun. of adv. bd. on built environ., 1982-83; mem. Planning Accreditation Bd., Site Visitation Pool, Am. Inst. Cert. Planners and Assn. Collegiate Schs. Planning, 1985—; mem. discipline screening com. Fulbright Scholar awards in Architecture and City Planning, Coun. for Internat. Exchange of Scholars, 1985-88. Author: The Central Business District in Transition: Methodological Approaches to CBD Analysis and Forecasting Future Space Requirements, 1957, New Town Development in the United States: Experiment in Private Entrepreneurship, 1973; co-author: A Probabilistic Model for Residential Growth, 1964, Residential Developer Decisions: A Focused View of the Urban Growth Process, 1966, New Communities U.S.A, 1976; co-author, co-editor: Urban Growth Dynamics in a Regional Cluster of Cities, 1962; co-editor: New Community Development: Planning Process, Implementation and Emerging Social Concerns, vols. 1, 2, 1971, City Centers in Transition, 1976, New Communities Research Series, 1976-77; mem. editorial bd.: Jour. Am. Inst. Planners, 1963-68, Rev. of Regional Studies, 1969-74, 82—, Internat. Regional Sci. Rev, 1975-81. Trustee Friends of Libr., U. N.C., Chapel Hill, 1988-94, Santa Fe Chamber Music Festival, adv. coun., 1990-91, trustee, 1991—; bd. dirs. Triangle Opera Theatre, 1986-89, 91—. Adelaide M. Zagoren fellow Douglass Coll., Rutgers U., 1994; recipient Mary Turner Lane award Assn. Women Faculty, 1994. Fellow Urban Land Inst. (sr., exec. group, community devel. coun. 1978—); mem. Am. Inst. Planners (sec., treas. southeast chpt. 1957-59, v.p. 1960-61), Am. Inst. Cert. Planners, Am. Planning Assn., Am. Econ. Assn., So. Regional Sci. Assn. (pres. 1977-78), Regional Sci. Assn. (councillor 1971-74, v.p. 1976-77), Nat. Assn. Housing and Redevelopment Ofcls., Interamerican Planning Soc., Internat. Fedn. Housing and Planning, Town and Country Planning Assn., Internat. Urban Devel. Assn., Econ. History Assn., Am. Real Estate and Urban Econs. Assn. (regional membership chmn. 1976-82, 84-85, dir. 1977-80), AAUP (chpt. pres. 1976-77, pres. N.C. Conf. 1978-79, mem. nat. council 1983-86, William S. Tacey award Assembly of State Confs.), Douglass Soc., Order of Valkyries, Phi Beta Kappa. Home: 155 N Hamilton Rd Chapel Hill NC 27514-5628

WEISSMAN, RHODA YVETTE, artist; b. Bklyn., July 27, 1929; m. Albert Weissman, Dec. 13, 1947; children: Jack (dec.), Richard. BA in Fine Art, Calif. State U., Northridge, 1976; MA in Art Therapy, Goddard Coll., 1980. Registered art therapist. Freelance artist L.A., 1965—; tchr. art L.A. Unified Schs.; art therapist Bridge Away Across, Burbank, Calif., 1978-88; pvt. practice art therapist Reseda, Calif., 1982-83; represented by LACMA Art Rental Gallery, L.A., 1994—; art instr. pvt. adult classes, L.A.; art adminstr. Sunland/Tujunga Cmty. Solo exhbns. include Environ. Home Furnishings Gallery, N.Y.C., 1964, Pacific Palisades (Calif.) Libr. Art Gallery, 1989, L.A. Artcore Gallery, 1991; numerous group shows including Vista del Mar Art Show, 1971, Santa Monica Libr., 1975, Beverly Hills Art League, 1976, Roberts Art Gallery, 1987, Mus. Contemporary Art, 1988, William Grant Sills Arts Ctr., 1989, Pacific Art Guild, 1989, Installations Gallery, 1990, Lancaster Mus., 1990, Minus Zero Gallery, 1991, U. Judaism, 1992, Downey Mus., 1992, Hippodrome Gallery, 1993, West Valley Jewish Ctr., 1993, Galerie Galerie, 1993, Joslyn Fine Arts Gallery, 1994, Artspace Gallery, 1994, U. Judaism, 1995, others. Mem. So. Calif. Women's Caucus for the Arts (exhibiting chairperson 1988-90), Am. Art Therapy Assn. Home: 2480 Angelo Dr Los Angeles CA 90077

WEISSMAN, SUSAN, social services professional; b. N.Y.C., Feb. 11, 1938; d. Samuel and Anne (Kunis) Miller; m. Irwin Weissman, June 2, 1957; children: Debra, Emily. BS, Queens Coll., 1976; MSW, Columbia U., 1978; DSW, CUNY, 1995. Lic. social worker, N.Y.; cert. elem. tchr. Pvt. practice clin. social worker N.Y.C., 1978-81; social worker L.I. (N.Y.) Jewish Hosp., 1978-80, psychoednl. therapist, 1979-80; founder, exec. dir. Park Ctr. Preschs. (4), N.Y.C., 1981-91; with Child Care Cons. Corp., N.Y.C., 1991-94; pvt. corp. child care cons. N.Y.C., 1985—; lectr. Learning Annex, N.Y.C., 1986-90, Borough of Manhattan C.C., CUNY, 1987; bd. dirs. Child Care, Inc., N.Y.C., 1986-88; pres. Child Care Cons. Corp., 1990-94; mem. bd. profl. advisors Mothers' Network, 1992—; mem. parents' adv. bd. Showtime TV Network, 1993—; spl. events chmn. Pearl Theatre, 1992—. Author: Parents Guide to DayCare, 1986; contbr. articles to Parent's Mag., Working Woman, Parent Guide, others. Mem. NAFE, Nat. Assn. Edn. Young Children, Early Childhood Edn. Soc., Nat. Assn. Child Care Mgmt., Nat. Assn. Social Workers. Home: 10 Leonard St New York NY 10013 Office: Susan Weisman Cons Corp 570 7th Ave New York NY 10018

WEISSMANN, HEIDI SEITELBLUM, radiologist, educator; b. N.Y.C., Feb. 4, 1951; d. Louis and June (Joseph) Seitel Bloom; m. Murray H. Weissmann, June 16, 1973; 1 dau., Lauren Erica. BS in Chemistry magna cum laude, Bklyn. Coll., CUNY, 1970; MD, Mt. Sinai Sch. Medicine, N.Y.C., 1974. Diplomate Nat. Bd. Med. Examiners. Intern Montefiore Med. Ctr. Bronx, N.Y., 1974-75, resident in diagnostic radiology, 1975-78; fellow in computerized transaxial tomography and ultrasonography N.Y. Hosp.-Cornell U. Med. Ctr., N.Y.C., N.Y., 1978-79; instr. in radiology and nuclear medicine Albert Einstein Coll. Medicine, Montefiore Med. Ctr., Bronx, N.Y., 1979-80; asst. prof. radiology and nuclear medicine Albert Einstein Coll. Medicine and Montefiore Med. Ctr., Bronx, N.Y., 1980-84, assoc. prof. nuclear medicine, 1984—, assoc. prof. radiology, 1986—; adj. attending physician Montefiore Med. Ctr., 1979-87; chmn. Nuclear Medicine Grand Rounds: Greater N.Y., 1980-87; physician coord. Nuclear Medicine Technologist In-Service Tng. Program, 1982-86; cons. NIH, 1984-86, NIH Diagnostic Radiology, 1985-86. Assoc. editor Nuclear Medicine Ann., 5 vols., 1979-84, editor, 5 vols., 1985—; contbr. chpts. to books, articles to jours.; reviewer Jour. of Radiology, 1981—, mem. editorial adv. bd., 1985-86, assoc. editor, 1986—; reviewer. Jour. of Nuclear Medicine, 1981—, Am. Jour. of Roentgenology, 1986—, Gastroenterology, 1986—, Western Jour. of Medicine, 1985—; contbr. audiovisual programs and films. Recipient Saul Horowitz, Jr., Meml. award (Disting. Alumnus award), Mt. Sinai Sch. Medicine, 1980, Pres.' award, Am. Roentgen Ray Soc., 1979, Berta Rubinstein, M.D., Resident award, 1978, others. Mem. Radiol. Soc. N.Am. (mem. subcom. for nuclear medicine of program com., 1981, 82, 83, chmn. 1984, 85, 86), Soc. Nuclear Medicine (trustee 1983-87, 88—, sec.-treas. Correlative Imaging Council 1979-82, exec. bd. 1982-84, pres. 1984-86, exec. bd. 1986—, mem. acad. council 1980—, task force on interrelationship between nuclear medicine and nuclear magnetic resonance 1983-85 , gov. Greater N.Y. chpt. 1983-85, treas., 1985-86, 86-87, 2d ann. Tetalman award of Edn. and Research Found. 1982, mem., vice chmn. coms. and subcoms.), Soc. Gastrointestinal Radiologists, Am. Inst. Ultrasound in Medicine, N.Y. Acad. Scis., Assoc. Alumni Mt. Sinai Med. Ctr., Nuclear Radiology Club (chmn. 1983—). Phi Beta Kappa.

WEISSMANN, REGINA ANN, pastoral associate, psychotherapist; b. Chgo., May 20, 1935; d. Henry Frances and Martha Rosalie (Walovich) W. BS in Psychology, Coll. St. Benedict, 1969; MA in Counseling Psychology, Loyola U., 1973; grad. studies, Gestalt Inst., 1979-80. Jr. high dept., tchr. Cmty. Cath. Schs., Lisle, Joliet, Ill., 1961-67; elem. sch. prin. Queen of Peace, Wichita Falls, Tex., 1967-68, Lady of the Mount, Cicero, Ill., 1969-71; psychotherapist Interfaith Counseling, Naperville, Ill., 1975-84; pastoral assoc. St. Scholastica Parish, Woodridge, Ill., 1984—; sch. therapist St. Scholastica, Woodridge, 1985-92; adv. bd. mem. Diocese Joliet, Romeoville, Ill., 1990—. Reporter: (periodical) Lisle Benedictine Women, 1993—. Recipient Religion award Kiwanis Club, Naperville, Ill., 1985. Mem. Am. Assn. for Counseling and Devel., Am. Sch. Counselor Assn., Assn. for Religious and Value Issues in Counseling. Home: 1910 Maple Ave Lisle IL 60532-2164 Office: St Scholastica Parish 7800 Janes Ave Woodridge IL 60517-3520

WEIST, JONE BARLOW, community association executive; b. Ft. Benning, Ga., Sept. 22, 1951; d. Don Adin and Phyllis M. (Casey) Barlow; m. John Albert Weist, Nov. 2, 1983 (dec. Feb. 1987). AA, Lorain C.C., 1975; BS, Oberlin Coll., 1978; postgrad., Baldwin-Wallace Coll., 1985. Lic. comty. assn. mgr., Fla. Pres. The Barlow Group, Inc., Sarasota, Fla., 1991—. Mem. Am. Comty. Assn. Mgrs., Comty. Assns. Inst. Democrat. Roman Catholic. Home: PO Box 1946 Sarasota FL 34230-1946 Office: The Barlow Group Inc PO Box 1946 Sarasota FL 34230-1946

WELBORN, CARYL BARTELMAN, lawyer; b. Phila., Jan. 29, 1951; d. Raymond C. and Helen Ann (Roach) Bartelman; m. Lucien Ruby, Apr. 11, 1987. AB, Stanford U., 1972; JD, UCLA, 1976. Bar: Ill. 1976, Calif. 1978. Assoc. Isham Lincoln & Beale, Chgo., 1976-78; from assoc. to ptnr. Morrison & Foerster, San Francisco and L.A., 1978—; lectr. real property law. Mem. ABA (chmn. com. on partnerships, real property sect. 1989-93), Am. Coll. Real Estate Lawyers (bd. govs. 1994). Office: Morrison & Foerster 345 California St San Francisco CA 94104

WELCH, ADELE MERRILL, psychiatric nurse; b. Cambridge, Mass., Dec. 3, 1938; d. Dudley and Katherine (Park) Merrill; m. Wilford Hitchcock Welch, June 11, 1966; children: Ashley Hitchcock, Alexandra Merrill. BA, Conn. Coll., 1960; BS, RN, Columbia U., 1963; MSN, U. Calif., San Francisco, 1966. RN, Mass.; clin. specialist in adult psychiat. and mental health nursing. Head nurse, staff nurse Montefiore Hosp., Bronx, N.Y., 1963-66; rsch. assoc. Georgetown U. Hosp., Washington, 1966-69; psychiat. nurse, case adminstr. Marlboro (Mass.) Hosp., 1987-89, Adolescent Day Treatment Program, Arlington, Mass., 1989-92; dir. nursing Choate Health Systems, Woburn, Mass., 1992-93; clin. specialist psychiat. nursing Spl. Care Home Health Svcs., Woburn, 1994—. Mem. ANA, Am. Holistic Nurse Assn., Mass. Nurses Assn., Sigma Theta Tau. Unitarian. Home: 34 Lincoln Rd Wayland MA 01778

WELCH, C. DEBRA, lawyer; b. West Palm Beach, Fla., Nov. 21, 1957; d. John M. and Lydia G. (George) W. BA, Stetson U., 1979; MEd, Ga. State U., 1981; JD cum laude, New England Sch. Law, 1992. Bar: Mass. 1992, Fla. 1993, U.S. Dist. Ct. Mass. 1993; cert. secondary tchr., Fla. Counselor student devel. Valdosta (Ga.) State Coll., 1981-85; assoc. dir. counseling and student devel. Bentley Coll., Waltham, Mass., 1985-91; legal asst. Commonwealth Mass., Boston, 1992; assoc. Houston & Shaloub P.A., West Palm Beach, 1993—; Ga. state chmn. Assn. Fraternity Advisors, 1983-84; area cons., presenter BACCHUS U.S., Inc., 1986-88, Brandeis U., 1987; presenter numerous papers. Intake counselor vol. parent-child study ctr., asst. counselor vol. tree-house inpatient facility Palm Beach Community Mental Health Ctr., 1978; mem. info. and evaluation com. Dist. 8-1 Teenage Pregnancy Prevention Program, Lowndes County, Ga., 1984-85. Mem. ABA, Mass. Bar Assn., Fla. Bar, ACA, Am. Mental Health Counselors Assn., Am. Coll. Pers. Assn. (Commn. XVIII task force on alcohol and other drugs 1988-91), Acad. Fla. Trial Lawyers, Fla. Assn. for Women Lawyers, Palm Beach County Bar Assn., Pi Beta Phi (alumnae, nat. legis. com. 1979-83).

WELCH, CAROL MAE, lawyer; b. Rockford, Ill., Oct. 23, 1947; d. Leonard John and LaVerna Helen (Ang) Nyberg; m. Donald Peter Welch, Nov. 23, 1968 (dec. Sept. 1976). B.A. in Spanish, Wheaton Coll., 1968; J.D., U. Denver, 1976. Bar: Colo. 1977, U.S. Dist. Ct. Colo. 1977, U.S. Ct. Appeals (10th cir.) 1977, U.S. Supreme Ct. 1981. Tchr. State Hosp., Dixon, Ill., 1969, Polo Community Schs., Ill., 1969-70; registrar Sch. Nursing Hosp. of U. Pa., Phila., 1970; assoc. Hall & Evans, Denver, 1977-81, ptnr., 1981-82; spec. 1993-94; mem. Miller & Welch, L.L.C., Denver, 1995—. mem. Colo. Supreme Ct. Jury Inst., Denver, 1982—; vice chmn. com. on conduct U.S. Dist. Ct., Denver, 1982-83, chmn., 1983-84; lectr. in field; speaker Women and Bus. Conf., Denver, 1982. Pres. Family Tree, Inc. Named to Order St. Ives, U. Denver Coll. Law, 1977. Mem. ABA, Internat. Soc. Barristers, Internat. Assn. Def. Counsel, Am. Coll. Trial Lawyers, Am. Bd. Trial Advs. (treas. Colo. chpt. 1991-92, pres. 1992-93), Colo. Def. Lawyers Assn. (treas. 1982-83, v.p. 1983-84, pres. 1984-85), Denver Bar Assn., Colo. Bar Assn. (mem. litigation sect. coun. 1987-90), Colo. Bar Found. (trustee 1992—), Def. Rsch. Inst. (chmn. Colo. chpt. 1987-90, regional v.p. 1990-93, bd. dirs. 1993—), William E. Doyle Inn. Office: Miller & Welch LLC 730 17th St #370 Denver CO 80202-3503

WELCH, EVIE JEAN ADAMS, university administrator; b. Lakeland, Fla., Apr. 9, 1936; d. Booker Taliferro and Mildred Rebecca (Shaw) Adams; m. Johnny Lee Welch, Aug. 19, 1960 (div. 1975). BA, Fla. A&M U., 1958; MA, Va. State U., 1969; PhD, Howard U., 1974. Tchr. Pinellas Sch. Bd., St. Petersburg, Fla., 1958-70; rschr. Nat. Fellowship Found., Africa and Europe, 1972-74; prof. Western Ill. U., Macomb, 1975-77; prof. Edward Waters Coll., Jacksonville, Fla., 1977-79, adminstr., 1989—; merchant/adminstr. Dafrique Internat. Export Mgmt. Co., Jacksonville, Fla., 1979—; steering com. U.S. Commerce Minority Ent. Devel., Jacksonville, 1990—. TV prodr.: Politics is Your Business, 1980-82. Woodrow Wilson fellow, 1972, Howard U. fellow, 1973; recipient Certificat d'Assiduite, Lettres de Grenoble, France, 1973. Mem. LAV (bd. dirs. 1971-73, TV prodr. 1980-82), Nat. Assn. for Colored People, Leadership Jacksonville, Delta Sigma Theta.

WELCH, JEANIE MAXINE, librarian; b. L.A., Jan. 22, 1946; d. Howard Carlton and Roberta Jean (Dunsmuir) W. BA, U. Denver, 1967, MA, 1968; M of Internat. Mgmt., Am. Grad. Sch. Internat. Mgmt., 1981. Asst. libr. Am. Grad. Sch. Internat. Mgmt., Glendale, Ariz., 1968-83; reference libr. Lamar U., Beaumont, Tex., 1983-85, head reference, 1985-87; reference unit head U. N.C., Charlotte, 1988—. Author: The Spice Trade; contbr. articles to profl. jours. Chpt. pres. NOW, Beaumont, 1985-87, state sec., Tex., 1986; exec. bd. Ariz. State Libr. Assn., 1976-80. Rsch. grantee Tex. Libr. Assn., 1986. Mem. AAUP, ALA, Southeastern Libr. Assn., Metrolina Libr. Assn., N.C. Libr. Assn., Spl. Librs. Assn. Democrat. Methodist. Office: U NC Atkins Libr Charlotte NC 28223

WELCH, JENNIFER DIANE, lawyer; b. Boston, Apr. 11, 1965; d. George P. and Margery Welch. BA, Vanderbilt U., 1987; JD, Emery U., 1990. Assoc. Drew, Eckl & Farnhan, Atlanta, 1990-93; corp. counsel RaceTrac Petroleum, Inc., Atlanta, 1993-95; mgr. regulatory and legis. affairs BellSouth Corp., 1995—. Active Legal Clinic Homeless, 1990—, Jr. League, 1994—; com. chair Cancer Soc., Atlanta, 1990—. Mem. ABA, Ga. State Bar, Ky. State Bar, Atlanta Bar Assn., PEO. Methodist. Home: 2222 Peachtree St NW A-S Atlanta GA 30304 Office: Racetrac Petroleum Inc 300 Technology Ct Smyrna GA 30082

WELCH, J(OAN) KATHLEEN, entrepreneur; b. Pensacola, Fla., Jan. 28, 1950; d. Leslie Peter and Frances Louise (Hughes) Morales. Salesperson with Arthur Murray Dance Studio, Colo., Fla., Pa. and N.J., 1970-81; sales rep. Warner-Lambert Co., Morris Plains, N.J., 1981-83; supr., mgr. Dance Club Internat., Chatham, N.J., 1983-90; dist. rep. Nat. Fedn. Ind. Bus., 1990—; developed sales program adopted nationwide by Dance Club Internat.; judge Nat. Dance Coun. Am., 1977-90; dance coach, 1975-90; coached winners U.S. Ballroom Championships Hustle divsn., 1978, choreographer, 1971-90, competitor, 1972-81; condr. New Age lectrs., seminars and workshops, 1994—. Co-prodr., promoter, talent scout for TV program: Astrology Today (formerly It's in the Stars), 1989-94; performed on nat. TV with leading personalities including George Raft, Donald O'Connor and Mike Douglas. Recipient awards Arthur Murray Studio, 1971-81, 1st place counselor award Arthur Murray All Star Tournament, 1977, 1st place Supr. award Dance Club Internat., 1st place Registrar award Dance Club Internat. in the Tournament of Champions, 1984; ranked No. 1 rep. in Profls. Corner, N.Y. div. Nat. Fedn. Ind. Bus., 1991, ranked No. 2 rep., 1992, named Internat. Woman of Yr., 1993. Mem. Imperial Soc. Tchrs. of Dancing (assoc. Ballroom br., Latin-Am. br.), Am. Dance Tchrs. Assn. Mem. Unity Ch. Home and Office: PO Box 1177 Elizabeth NJ 07207-1177

WELCH, KATHY JANE, information technology executive; b. San Antonio, Aug. 5, 1952; d. John Dee and Pauline Ann (Overstreet) W.; m. John Thomas Unger, Jan. 8, 1977. B.A.S. in Computer Sci., So. Meth. U., 1974; M.B.A. in Fin., U. Houston, 1978. Programmer, analyst Tex. Instruments, Houston, 1974-76, project leader, 1976-78, br. mgr., 1978-81; mgr. systems and programming Global Marine, Houston, 1981-84, mgr. office automation, 1984-85, mgr. user systems, 1985-88, dir. MIS, Advanced Tech. div. Browning-Ferris Industries, Houston, 1988-89, dir. Telecom. and Computer Svcs., 1989-93; v.p. info. tech. Talent Tree Svcs., Inc., Houston, 1993—. Mem. Mensa, Beta Gamma Sigma. Office: Talent Tree Svcs Inc 9703 Richmond Ave Houston TX 77042

WELCH, LINDA OGDEN, sales executive; b. Wabash, Ind., Apr. 3, 1958; d. Russell Devon and Nancy Rebecca (Bright) O.; m. Albert Darius Welch III. Jan. 31, 1990. BS, Oral Roberts U., 1980. Sales coord. Sta. KIRO, Seattle, 1980-81; account exec. Sta. KRAV/KGTO, Tulsa, 1981-84, Sta. KOTV-TV, Tulsa, 1984-86, Sta. KHOU-TV, Houston, 1986-87, Sta. KTXA-TV, Dallas, 1987-89, Sta. KATZ-TV, Dallas, 1989-90, Petry TV, Dallas, 1990-91; sales exec. IOPTEX Rsch., Inc., Irwindale, Calif., 1992-94; pres. Ogden-Welch Longhorn Co., 1992—; territory mgr. Allergan, Valley View, Tex., 1994—; cons. Synthes, Paoli, Pa., 1994—; pres. The Welch Group, Inc. Republican. Office: Synthes USA 1690 Russell Rd PO Box 1766 Paoli PA 19301

WELCH, MILDRED BAILEY, elementary school administrator; b. Bryson City, N.C., Aug. 1, 1944; d. Ezekiel H. and Ollie Mae (Parton) Bailey; m. Robert Lyle Welch, May 30, 1964; children: Derek Robert, Mark Lyle. BS, Bethel Coll., 1968; MEd, East Tenn. State, 1983, postgrad., 1988; postgrad., Lincoln Meml. U., 1990. Cert. tchr. elem. edn. 1-9, reading specialist K-8, 7-12, elem. guidance counselor, English tchr. 7-12, elem. adminstrn. and supervision K-8. 2nd grade tchr. Marion County Bd. of Edn., South Pittsburg, Tenn., 1965-66; 6th grade tchr. Marion County Bd. of Edn., Jasper, Tenn., 1967-69; 3d grade tchr. Hawkins County Bd. of Edn., Rogersville, Tenn., 1970-92, vice prin., 1992—. Recipient Outstanding Svc. award Local Edn. Assn., 1989, Human Rels. State award State Edn. Assn., 1990. Mem. Delta Kappa Gamma (pres. local chpt. 1983-85, Tenn. xi state coord. of workshops 1991-93, Tenn. xi state expansion chmn. 1993—, Lottye McCall State scholar 1982). Democrat. Baptist. Home: 143 N Johnson Rd Rogersville TN 37857

WELCH, RAQUEL, actress; b. Chgo., Sept. 5, 1940; d. Arm and Josepha (Hall) Tejada; m. James Westley Welch, May 8, 1959 (div.); children: Damon, Tahnee; m. Patrick Curtis (div.); m. Andre Weinfeld, July 1980 (div.). Actress: (films) including Fantastic Voyage, 1966, One Million B.C, 1967, The Biggest Bundle of Them All, 1968, Fathom, 1967, The Queens, 1967, 100 Rifles, 1969, Magic Christian, 1970, Bedazzled, 1971, Fuzz, 1972, Bluebeard, 1972, Hannie Caulder, 1972, Kansas City Bomber, 1972, Myra Breckinridge, 1970, The Last of Sheila, 1973, The Three Musketeers, 1974 (Golden Globe award for best actress), The Wild Party, 1975, The Four Musketeers, 1975, Mother, Jugs and Speed, 1976, Crossed Swords, 1978, L'Animal, 1979, (TV movies) The Legend of Walks Far Woman, 1982, Right to Die, 1987, Scandal in a Small Town, 1988, Trouble in Paradise, 1989, Torch Song, 1993, Naked Gun 33 1/3, 1993, (Broadway debut) Woman of the Year, 1982; author: The Raquel Welch Total Beauty and Fitness Program, 1984. Address: RWP Inc # 514 9903 Santa Monica Blvd Beverly Hills CA 90212

WELCH, SANDRA HOPPER, broadcasting executive; b. Lebanon, Ky., Jan. 9, 1946; d. William O. and Thelma (Ruby) Hopper; m. Brant Welch (div. 1983). AA, St. Catharine (Ky.) Jr. Coll., 1965; BA, U. Ky., 1967, MS in LS, 1974. Libr. Fayette County Pub. Schs., Lexington, 1967-69, Key West (Fla.) Pub. Schs., 1969-70; utilization specialist Ky. Ednl. TV, Lexington, 1971-73, dir. programming, 1973-76, exec. producer, 1976-80, dep. exec. dir., 1980-87; became chief oper. officer Ky. Ednl. TV, 1987; now exec. v.p. of education PBS, Alexandria; mem. PBS Adult Learning Svc. Adv. Com., 1982-84, Satellite Ednl. Resources Consortium, 1988—. Mem. Ky. Literacy Commn., Frankfort, 1985—; trustee St. Catharine Coll., 1987—; bd. dirs. Jr. Achievement, Lexington, 1988—. Recipient numerous grants, 1980—, including Corp. for Pub. Broadcasting, Nat. Endowment for Arts, NEH, Bell South Found., Hitachi Found. Mem. So. Assn. Colls. and Schs. Democrat. Office: PBS 1320 Braddock Pl Alexandria VA 22314*

WELCH-FREEDAIN, JUNE SHEILA, corporate and environmental lawyer; b. Jacksonville, Fla., June 9, 1939; d. Robert Paul and Carrie (Drawdy) W.; m. John A. Freedain, 1991; children by previous marriage: Stacy Lorraine Harker, Lisa Jane Harker, Carrie Bess McGonigle. BA, Calif. State U., Long Beach, 1960; JD, Western State U., 1974. Tchr. various pub. schs., So. Calif., 1961-71; ednl. cons. Western State U., Fullerton, Calif., 1972-74; account exec. Mass. Mut. Life Ins., Long Beach, 1975-77; sole practice Santa Ana, Calif., 1978-81; pres. Calista Petroleum Co., Paramount, Calif., 1982-92; corp. counsel Great West Car Wash, Inc., Culver City, Calif., 1992—; corp. counsel Bear Welding, Inc., Long Beach. Mem. U.S. Senate Inner Circle, Calif. Reps. Mem. L.A. County Bar Assn., Orange County Bar Assn., Calif. Women Lawyers, Am. Trial Lawyers Assn. Office: Calista Petroleum Co 6510 Alondra Blvd Paramount CA 90723-3727

WELCOME, CELESTINE FLORENCE, elementary education educator; b. Phila., Aug. 30, 1950; d. Craig Allen and Celestine (Williams) W. BS, Morgan State U., 1972; MEd, Antioch U., 1974. Tchr. Sch. Dist. Phila., 1972—; counselor, coord. Negro Trade Union Leadership Coun., Phila., 1977-82. Pres. 1900 Montrose St. Clean Block, Phila., 1978-83; mem. exec. bd. dirs. Southwest Ctr. City Citizens Coun., Phila., 1977-83, YWCA of Phila., 1980-93. Mem. Women in Edn. (sec. 1978-80, treas. 1980-82, plaque 1982), Delta Sigma Theta. (chairperson various coms. 1991-93). Baptist. Home: 819 Yeadon Ave Yeadon PA 19050-3620 Office: 17th and Tasker Sts Philadelphia PA 19146

WELDEN, MARY CLARE, nurse; b. Wichita, Kans., Mar. 4, 1943; d. Lee Henry and Betty Clare (Lansdowne) Pates; m. Francis Bernard Hacker, Apr. 18, 1964 (div. Apr. 1978); children: Stephen (dec.), Michael, William; m. Wetzel Allen Welden (div. June 1983). Diploma in nursing, St. Joseph Sch. Nursing, 1964. Staff nurse, supr. Richardson (Tex.) Gen. Hosp., 1968-70; supr., obstetrics supr. Collin Meml. Hosp., McKinney, Tex., 1970-77; staff nurse, charge nurse Presbyn. Hosp., Dallas, 1977-81; staff nurse Bapt. Med. Ctr., Oklahoma City, 1981-88, quality assurance nurse, 1988—. Mem. Compassionate Friends. Democrat. Roman Catholic. Home: 1752 Lionsgate Cir Bethany OK 73008-6167 Office: Bapt Med Ctr 3300 NW Expressway St Oklahoma City OK 73112-4481

WELDON, VIRGINIA V., corporate executive, physician; b. Toronto, Sept. 8, 1935; came to U.S., 1937; d. John Edward and Carolyn Edith (Swift) Verral; children: Ann Stuart, Susan Shaeffer. A.B. cum laude, Smith Coll., 1957; M.D., SUNY-Buffalo, 1962; L.H.D. (hon.), Rush U., 1985. Diplomate Am. Bd. Pediatrics in pediatric endocrinology and metabolism. Intern Johns Hopkins Hosp., Balt., 1962-63, resident in pediatrics, 1963-64; fellow pediatric endocrinology Johns Hopkins U., Balt., 1964-67, instr. pediatrics, 1967-68; instr. pediatrics Washington U., St. Louis, 1968-69, asst. prof., 1969-73, assoc. prof. pediatrics, 1973-79, prof. pediatrics, 1979-89, v.p. Med. Ctr., 1980-89, dep. vice chancellor med. affairs, 1983-89; v.p. sci. affairs Monsanto Co., St. Louis, 1989, v.p. pub. policy, 1989-93, sr. v.p. pub. policy, 1993—, 1993—; mem. gen. clin. rsch. ctrs. adv. com. NIH, Bethesda, Md., 1976-80, mem. rsch. resources adv. coun., 1980-84; bd. dirs. Gen. Am. Life Ins. Co., Security Equity Life Ins. Co., G.D. Searle & Co., The NutraSweet Co.; bd. dirs., advisor Monsanto Co., 1989—. Contbr. articles to sci. jours. Commr. St. Louis Zool. Park, 1983-93; bd. dirs. United Way Greater St. Louis, 1978-90, St. Louis Regional Health Care corp., 1985-91; mem. rsik assesment mgmt. commn. EPA, 1992—; mem. Pres.'s com. of Advisors on Sci. and Tech., 1994—. Fellow AAAS, Am. Acad. Pediatrics; mem. Inst. Medicine, Assn. Am. Med. Colls. (del., chmn. coun. acad. socs. 1984-85, chmn. assembly 1985-86), Am. Pediatric Soc., Nat. Bd. Med. Examiners (bd. dirs. 1987-89), Endocrine Soc., Soc. Pediatric Rsch., St. Louis Med. Soc., Sigma Xi, Alpha Omega Alpha. Roman Catholic. Home: 242 Carlyle Lake Dr Saint Louis MO 63141-7544 Office: Monsanto Co DIA 800 N Lindbergh Blvd Saint Louis MO 63167

WELDON-PETERSON, KAREN JEAN, school counselor; b. Jamestown, N.Y., Jan. 30, 1945; d. Donald Clair and Betty Ruth (Murbach) Schmonsky; divorced; children: Shellee L. Gard Weldon, Sherrie L. Gard Weldon; m. David R. Peterson, Dec. 23, 1994. AA in Liberal Arts, Jamestown Community Coll., 1964; BA in English, SUNY, Fredonia, 1966, MS in Edn., 1986; MS in Counseling, St. Bonaventure U., 1993. Cert. tchr., English tchr., N.Y., provisional sch. counselor. Kindergarten tchr. Dept. of Def. Schs., Clark AFB, The Phillippines, 1967-68; English tchr. Burkburnett (Tex.) Schs., 1968-69; English tchr. Jamestown Pub. Schs., 1970-92, counselor, 1992—; tchr. adult edn. GED program, Jamestown, 1978-79; facilitator E.P.I.C. Parenting Skills Workshops, Jamestown, 1993—. Author poems, articles Tier Drops, 1990, 91. program dir. Agnes Home for Battered Women, Jamestown, 1987-88; cand. Town Justice, town of Kiantone, N.Y., 1993. Recipient scholarship AAUW, 1962-66. Mem. AAUW, NEA, Am. Counseling Assn., Chautauque County Counselors Assn., Delta Kappa Gamma, Delta Epsilon Sigma. Democrat. Lutheran. Home: 2487 Donelson Rd Jamestown NY 14701-9349

WELKER, JANET REYNOLDS, health facility administrator; b. Washington, Pa., Sept. 7, 1948; d. Ray Woodard Reynolds and Helen Louise (Shipe) Miles; m. Richard Keith Baird, Nov. 2, 1968 (div. 1979); children: Jonathan Bruce, Justin Erik; m. Sherman Edward Welker, Aug. 10, 1985; children: Kendall Ashley, Jordan Lindsey. Diploma, Westmoreland Sch. Nursing, 1969; BSN, U. Pitts., 1983, MSN, 1987. RN 1969; cert. nurse adminstr. 1988. Head nurse med. ctr. Presbyn. U. Pa., Phila., 1970-74; owner Animal Med. Ctr., Uniontown, Pa., 1976-78; dir. Aid Health Svcs., Pitts., 1978-81; nursing supr. John J. Kane Hosp., Pitts., 1981-84; capt. U.S. Army, 1983-93; DON Friendship Village, Upper St. Claire, Pa., 1984-85; adminstrn. coord. Hebrew Rehab. Ctr., Boston, 1985-88; dir. Iowa Lutheran Med. Ctr., Des Moines, 1989-90; adminstr. Ctr. Family Medicine, Marshalltown, Iowa, 1990—; bd. dirs. Iowa Nurse Found., Des Moines, 1993—; active Iowa County Care Reform Coun., 1993. Mem. Am. Nurses Assn., Iowa Med. Group Mgmt. Assn., Med. Group Mgmt. Assn., Sigma Theta Tau. Republican. Home: 1205 W Main St Marshalltown IA 50158-5476 Office: Ctr Family Medicine 312 E Main St Ste 1000 Marshalltown IA 50158-1885

WELLBORN, DAWN LINNELL, company executive; b. Dalton, Ga., Apr. 5, 1971; d. Freddie Griffeth and Wendy Beth (Drozd) W. BBA in Mktg./Fashion Merchandising, Ga. So. U., 1993. Sales assoc. Clothworld, Albany, Ga., 1987-88, Feetfirst, Albany, 1988-89, Carmen's Fine Footwear, Albany, 1989-92; intern Belk, Albany, 1992, sales assoc., 1992-93; divisional mgr./buyer Belk, North Augusta, S.C., 1993—, exec. trainee exec. trainee devel. progam, 1993. Vol. Statesboro (Ga.) Humane Soc., The Heart Fund, Browns Nursing Home, Cancer Soc., Ronald McDonald House, Spl. Olympics, Statesboro, 1989-93; participant Exec. Leadership Seminar Ga. So. U., 1993. Mem. Phi Kappa Phi, Beta Gamma Sigma (pres. 1992—, Richard D. Irwin scholar 1992), Gamma Beta Phi, Alpha Delta Pi, Kappa Sigma (rush hostess 1991—). Republican. Home: 324 Napa Dr Augusta GA 30909

WELLER, JANE KATHLEEN, emergency nurse; b. Balt., May 26, 1948; d. Donald Boyd and Jane Lee (Collins) Sealing; m. Richard Earl Weller, Oct. 20, 1973 (div. Dec. 1978); 1 child, Jennifer Lee. AA in Nursing, Essex Community Coll., Balt., 1971; BS in Health, U. Md., 1983. RN, Md. Nurse, clin. dir. Liberty Med. Ctr., Balt., 1971—. Mem. Nat. Emergency Nurses Assn., Md. Emergency Nurses Assn., Md. Accident Injury Prevention Network. Lutheran. Home: 8737 Sicklebar Way Elliott City MD 21043-9999 Office: Liberty Med Ctr 2600 Liberty Heights Ave Baltimore MD 21215-7892

WELLER, JANET LOUISE, lawyer; b. Boston, Sept. 17, 1953; d. Thomas Huckle and Kathleen (Fahey) W.; m. John Lee Holloway; children: Kelly Brianna, Janine Fahey. BA, Harvard U., 1975; JD, U. Mich., 1978. Bar: D.C. 1978, U.S. Dist. Ct. D.C. 1978, U.S. Ct. Appeals (D.C. cir.) 1979. Assoc. Cleary, Gottlieb, Steen & Hamilton, Washington, 1978-86, ptnr., 1986—. Office: Cleary Gottlieb Steen et al 1752 N St NW Washington DC 20036-2806

WELLER, KAREN ANNE, marketing executive; b. Newton, Mass., Feb. 27, 1948; d. George Herbert and Alice Anne (Carey) Weller; children: Stacy Kimmons, Ronald Kimmons, David Weller-Fahy, Nellie Cayaditto, Johanna Weller-Fahy, Katherine Weller-Fahy. BA, St. Mary's Coll., Notre Dame, Ind., 1970; MA, U. Notre Dame, 1976; M Health Svcs. Adminstrn., U. Mich., 1985. Dir. Health Cen., Lansing, Mich., 1975-77; adminstrv. asst. U. Mich. Hosps., Ann Arbor, 1984-86; adminstr. Metro Med. Group, Livonia, Mich., 1986-88; v.p. managed care P.H.A.S.E., Wayne, Mich., 1988-90; dir. mktg. United Care, Wayne, 1988-90; dir. mktg. and planning Freeport (Ill.) Meml. Hosp., 1990—. Mem. mktg. com. United Way, Freeport, 1990—; coach Am. Youth Soccer Orgn. Fellow U. Notre Dame, 1970, U. Mich., 1984, Healthcare Forum's Healthier Cmtys., 1994-95; recipient Taggert award-Woman of Excellence in Bus. and Professions, YWCA, 1993, 8 nat. healthcare mktg. awards, 12 regional awards, 1994; McGraw Found. grantee, 1984. Fellow Healthcare Forum; mem. Am. Coll. Healthcare Execs. (diplomate 1994), Assn. Pub. Rels. and Mktg., Assn. Healthcare Planning and Mktg., Ill. Healthcare Pub. Rels. Assn., Group Health Assn. Am., Freeport Regional Health Alliance (pres., CEO bd.), Freeport Communicators, Rotary (chmn. internat. svc. com. Freeport 1991-93). Democrat. Roman Catholic. Office: Freeport Meml Hosp 1045 W Stephenson St Freeport IL 61032-4899

WELLER, PENNY SUE, pharmaceutical executive; b. Grand Rapids, Mich., Nov. 27, 1948; d. Joseph P. and Emma (Bridge) W.; children: Bridget Elizabeth, Lawrence Joseph. BBA, Western Mich. U., 1975, MBA, 1977; PhD in Adminstrn. & Mgmt., Walden U., 1993. Cert. mgmt. acct. Libr. Caledonia (Mich.) Community Schs., 1966-68; acctg. clk. Shakespeare Co., Kalamazoo, Mich., 1969-72; head Internat. Gen. Acctg., 1972-84; mgr. subs. gen. acctg. The Upjohn Co., Kalamazoo, 1984-91, mgr. corp. accounts payable & travel expense reporting, 1991—; adj. prof. managerial fin., Nazareth Coll., Kalamazoo; dir. Kalamazoo Chpt. Inst. Mgmt. Accts. Profl. Devel. Mem. Inst. Mgmt. Accts. Office: The Upjohn Co 7000 Portage Rd Kalamazoo MI 49001-0102

WELLER, RITA BARBARA SHEPLEY, elementary educator; b. Reading, Pa., Aug. 26, 1951; d. Albert Raymond and Rita Barbara (Olsehfski) Shepely; m. Sherwood Dale Weller, Dec. 13, 1969 (dec. July 1985; 1 child, Theresa Marie. BA in Elem. Edn., Alvernia Coll., 1990; MS in Ednl. Tech., Lehigh U., 1993. Cert. tchr., Pa. Computer tchr. Sacred Heart Sch., West Reading, Pa., 1990—. Roman Catholic. Home: 410 Pineland Rd Birdsboro PA 19508 Office: Sacred Heart Sch 701 Franklin St West Reading PA 19611

WELLES, FERNE BINGHAM MALCOLM, retired archivist; b. Fayetteville, Ark., June 2, 1921; d. William Thomas and Nellie E. (Coffey) Bingham; m. Eugene Glenn Malcolm, Sept. 5, 1940 (dec. 1975); children: Rebecca Malcolm Schubert, Rachel Malcolm Woods, Eugene Glenn Jr.; m. Edward Randolph Welles II, Nov. 2, 1984 (dec. 1991). AA, Penn Valley Coll., Kansas City, Mo., 1977; BA in Am. Culture, U. Mo., Kansas City, 1981, MA in History, 1986. Archival intern Regional Br. Nat. Archives, Kansas City, Mo., 1976; historian, archivist, hist. writer St. Luke's Hosp. Kansas City, 1975-85; archivist, historiographer, researcher Episc. Diocese West Mo., Kansas City, 1974-85; historian, archivist, writer Grace and Holy Trinity Cathedral, Kansas City, 1972-79, 86-87; supr. grad students Emporia (Kans.) State U., 1983; presenter paper at history conf. Contbr. to numerous hist. publs. Pres. Kansas City Bus. and Profl. Women's Guild, 1982-83; mem. Women's C. of C., Kansas City, 1980-83; vestry mem. Grace and Holy Trinity Cathedral, 1982-84. Mem. AAUW (chmn. ednl. found. program 1989-92), Kansas City Area Archivists (edn. com.), Woman's City Club, Nat. Episc. Historians Assn., Phi Alpha Theta. Republican. Episcopalian. Home: 4545 Wornall Rd Apt 1002 Kansas City MO 64111-3209

WELLES, MELINDA FASSETT, artist, educator; b. Palo Alto, Calif., Jan. 4, 1943; d. George Edward and Barbara Helena (Todd) W. Student, San Francisco Inst. Art, 1959-60, U. Oreg., 1960-62; BA in Fine Arts, UCLA, 1964, MA in Spl. Edn., 1971, PhD in Ednl. Psychology, 1976; student fine arts and illustration Art Ctr. Coll. Design, 1977-80. Cert. ednl. psychologist, Calif. Asst. prof. Calif. State U., Northridge, 1979-82, Pepperdine U., L.A., 1979-82; assoc. prof. curriculum, teaching and spl. edn. U. So. Calif., L.A., 1980-89; mem. acad. faculty Pasadena City Coll., 1973-79, Art Ctr. Coll. Design, 1978—, Otis Coll. Art and Design, L.A., 1986—, UCLA Extension, 1980-84, Coll. Devel. Studies, L.A., 1978-87, El Camino C.C., Redondo Beach, Calif., 1982-86; cons. spl. edn.; pub. adminstrn. analyst UCLA Spl. Edn. Rsch. Program, 1973-76; exec. dir. Atwater Park Ctr. Disabled Children, L.A., 1976-78; coord. Pacific Oaks Coll. in svc. programs for L.A. Unified Schs., Pasadena, 1978-81; active Southwest Blue Book, Freedom's Found. at Valley Forge, Friends of French Art, Costume Coun. L.A. County Mus. of Art., Assistance League of So. Calif. Author: Calif. Dept. Edn. Tech. Reports, 1972-76; editor: Teaching Special Students in the Mainstream, 1981, Educating Special Learners, 1986, 88, Teaching Students with Learning Problems, 1988, Exceptional Children and Youth, 1989; group shows include: San Francisco Inst. Art, 1960, U. Hawaii, 1978, Barnsdall Gallery, L.A., 1979, 80; represented in various pvt. collections. HEW fellow, 1971-72; grantee Calif. Dept. Edn., 1975-76, Calif. Dept. Health, 1978. Mem. APA, Calif. Learning Disabilities Assn., Am. Council Learning Disabilities, Calif. Scholarship Fedn. (life), Alpha Chi Omega. Office: 700 Levering Ave Apt 1 Los Angeles CA 90024-2795

WELLES, VIRGINIA CHRISMAN, land use planner; b. Denver, June 17, 1954; d. John Galt and Barbara Lee (Chrisman) W.; m. Dwight Lyman Gertz, Oct. 9, 1982. Student, Hampshire Coll., 1972-74; BA in Polit. & Econ. Systems, Yale Coll., 1976; M in City Planning, MIT, 1981. Planning cons. Sugarloaf Mountain Corp., Carrabassett Valley, Maine, 1982-84; regional dir. EIP/Northeast, Boston, 1984-85; project mgr. MetroWest Growth Mgmt. Com., Natick, Mass., 1985-88; planner & environ. analyst Exec. Office of Transp. and Costr. State Mass., 1988-89, Cen. Transp. Planning Staff, Boston, 1989-91; gen. ptnr. Welles Farms Partnership, 1991—. Chair Loon Preservation Com., 1991-93; trustee Squam Lakes Assn., 1988-91, Squam Lakes Conservation Trust, 1988-92, Audubon Soc., N.H., 1988-95, sec., 1993-95, chmn. edn. com. 1994-95; sec. Lincoln Nursery Sch. Bd. Named Public Policy Fellow MIT, 1979-81. Mem. Am. Planning Assn. (officer New Eng. chpt. 1987-89). Democrat.

WELLING, KATHRYN MARIE, editor; b. Ft. Wayne, Ind., Feb. 4, 1952; d. Arthur Russell Sr. and Genevieve (Disser) W.; m. Donald Robert Boyle, Oct. 21, 1978; children: Brian Joseph, Thomas Arthur. BS in Journalism, Northwestern U., 1974. Copy reader Dow Jones News Retrieval, N.Y.C., 1974-75; copy reader/reporter AP-Dow Jones, N.Y.C., 1975-76; copy editor Wall Street Jour., N.Y.C., 1976; reporter Barron's, N.Y.C., 1976-81, asst. to editor, 1981, mng. editor, 1982-92, assoc. editor, 1992—. Office: Barron's 200 Liberty St New York NY 10281-1003

WELLINGTON, CAROL STRONG, law librarian; b. Altadena, Calif., Jan. 30, 1948; d. Edward Walters and Elizabeth (Leonards) Strong; m. David Heath Wellington, May 27, 1978; 1 child, Edward Heath. BA, Lake Forest (Ill.) Coll., 1969; MLS, Simmons Coll., 1973. Libr. Hill & Barlow, Boston, 1973-88, Peabody & Arnold, Boston, 1988—. Mem. Am. Assn. Law Librs., Assn. Boston Law Librs. (v.p. 1979-80, pres. 1980-81), Spl. Librs. Assn., Law Librs. New England. Office: Peabody & Arnold 50 Rowes Wharf Boston MA 02110-3328

WELLINGTON, CHARMAINE EILEEN, language professional and educator English; b. Chgo., Feb. 2, 1950; d. William Oscar Wattling and Rita Eileen (Van Dyk) Williams; m. Fredrick Victor Wellington, Aug. 8, 1970 (div. Aug. 8, 1977). BS in English, Ill. State U., 1974; MA in English, U. Tulsa, 1976; PhD in English, U. Ill., 1986. Grad. teaching asst. English U. Tulsa, 1975-76, U. Ill., Champaign, 1976-83; sales and seminar dir. InterCom, Inc., Champaign, 1983-85; vis. asst. prof. English Idaho State U., Pocatello, 1985-86; asst. prof. English U. West Fla., Pensacola, 1986-91; mng. editor Stillpoint Pub., Walpole, N.H., 1991-93; lectr. English dept. Keene (N.H.) State Coll., 1993—; journalist Valley-Times Jour., Walpole, 1991-94; freelance writer, Walpole, 1991-94. Editor: (book) Emerald Coast Review 1990, 1989, Emerald Coast Review III, 1990; co-author: (book) Search for Justice, 1992; editor Planetary Citizen Mag., 1991-93; writer, dir.: (video) Fall Mountain Facilities, 1993. Sec. U. West Fla. Chpt. United Facultyof Fla., Pensacola, 1989-91; bd. dirs. West Fla. Literacy Fedn., Pensacola, 1989-91, Children of the Earth, Inc., Newfane, Vt., 1992-94. Mem. NOW (pres. Escambia chpt. 1989-91). Home: care Williams PO Box 52 Asotin WA 99402

WELLMAN, BONNIE WADDELL, school nurse, educator, substance abuse counselor; b. Phila., May 5, 1952; d. Russell and Arlene (Spencer) Waddell; m. Ned Allen Wellman, Sept. 14, 1974 (div. 1981); 1 child, Jeffrey Allen. BSN, Ohio State U., 1974; MA in Counseling, Trenton State Coll., 1991. RN, Pa. Sch. nurse Pennsbury Sch. Dist., Fallsington, Pa., 1985—. Bd. dirs. YWCA, Newtown, Pa., 1990; mem. Pennsbury Year Round Edn. Task Force. Mem. NEA, ACA, Pa. State Edn. Assn., Pennsbury Edn. Assn., Pa. Sch. Nurse Assn., Nat. Assn. Sch. Nurses, Bucks County Sch. Nurses Assn., Chi Sigma Iota. Republican. Presbyterian. Home: 131 Windham Ct Newtown PA 18940-1750 Office: Pennsbury Sch Dist Yardley Ave Fallsington PA 19058

WELLMAN, MARY MARGARET, psychologist; b. Bklyn., May 20, 1946; d. John F. and Anna H. Haunss; m. Robert J. Wellman. BS, SUNY, Geneseo, 1967; MA, SUNY, Stony Brook, 1970; PhD, U. Conn., 1980. Lic. psychologist, Mass., R.I. Tchr. elem. sch. Kings Park (N.Y.) Schs., 1967-74; reading cons. Thompson (Conn.) Pub. Schs., 1974-81; asst. prof. R.I. Coll., Providence, 1981—, dir. Sch. Psychology, 1984-89; adj. instr. psychology Anna Maria Coll., Paxton, Mass., 1980-82, Worcester (Mass.) State Coll., 1982-84; pvt. practice, Charlton, Mass., 1985-88, Uxbridge, Mass., 1988-93, holistic practitioner, 1994—; cons. psychologist Comprehensive Mental Health Svc., Waban, Mass., 1983-85; asst. attending child psychologist McLean Hosp., Belmont, Mass., 1986-88; ednl. psychology cons. Ednl. Testing Svc., Princeton, N.J., 1989. Contbr. articles to profl. jours. Pres. Charlton Hist. Soc., 1977-79; vol. librarian and grant writer AIDS Project, Worcester. 1987-90. Recipient Disting. Svc. award Southbridge (Mass.) C. of C., 1980, Outstanding Vol. award APW, 1988. Mem. New Eng. Psychol. Assn., R.I. Sch. Psychologists Assn. (bd. dirs. 1985-89), Nat. Assn. Sch. Psychologists. Office: RI Coll Adams Libr # 115 Providence RI 02908

WELLS, CAROLYN CRESSY, social work educator; b. Boston, July 26, 1943; d. Harris Shipman Wells and Marianne Elizabeth (Monroe) Glazier; m. Dale Reed Konle, Oct. 11, 1970 (div. Sept. 3, 1982); m. Dennis Alan Loefler, Sept. 29, 1990. BA, U. Calif., Berkeley, 1965; MSW, U. Wis., 1968, PhD, 1973. Cert. ind. clin. social worker, marriage and family therapist. Vol. VISTA, Espanola, N.Mex., 1965-66; social worker Project Six Cen. Wis. Colony, Madison, 1968, Milw. Dept. Pub. Welfare, 1969, Shorewood (Wis.) Manor Nursing Home, 1972; sch. social worker Jefferson (Wis.) County Spl. Edn., 1977-78; lectr. sociology and social work Marquette U., Milw., 1972-73, dir. social work program, 1973-90, 93—, assoc. prof. social work, 1981-94, prof. social work, 1994—; social work therapist Lighthouse Counseling Assocs., Racine, Wis., 1989-91, The Cambridge Group, 1991-92; Achievement Assocs., 1992—; vis. lectr. social work U. Canterbury, Christchurch, N.Z., 1983. Author: Social Work Day to Day, 1982, rev. edit., 1988, Social Work Ethics Day to Day, 1986; co-author: The Social Work Experience, 1991. Mem. NASW, Am. Assn. Profl. Hypnotherapists, Coun. on Social Work Edn. (publs. and media com. 1989-91, site vis. for accreditation 1987—), Acad. Cert. Social Workers, Assn. Baccalaureate Program Dirs., Wis. Coun. on Social Work Edn. (pres. 1980-82, sec. 1985-87, exec. com. 1993—). Democrat. Home: 4173 Sleeping Dragon Rd West Bend WI 53095 Office: Marquette U Social Work Program 526 N 14th St Milwaukee WI 53233-2211

WELLS, CHRISTINE, foundation executive; b. Grayling, Mich., Aug. 6, 1948; d. Chester John and Mary W. BA, Mich. State U., 1970, MLIR, 1982; MLS, U. Mich., 1976. Head libr. Lansing State Jour., E. Lansing, Mich., 1973-82; mng. editor libr. svcs. USA TODAY, Washington, 1982-87; libr. dir. Gannett Co., Inc., Washington, 1985-87, chief staff, chmn. and CEO office, 1988-89; v.p. adminstrn. Gannett Found., Washington, 1989-90; v.p. internat. The Freedom Forum, Washington, 1991—; exec. dir. The Newseum, 1993-94; sr. v.p. The Freedom Forum, 1994—. Recipient Dising. Alumni award U. Mich., 1991. Mem. ALA, Spl. Librs. Assn. (Profl. award 1994). Office: The Freedom Forum 1101 Wilson Blvd Arlington VA 22209-2248

WELLS, DEBORAH JANE, human resources and communication consultant; b. Bryn Mawr, Pa., Apr. 11, 1954; d. John Wesley Sr. and Gladys Elizabeth (Aust) W. BA in Math. and Secondary Edn., Eastern Coll., 1975. Cert. employee benefit specialist. Analyst, programmer actuarial svcs. dept. Towers Perrin, Phila., 1975-79, analyst, programmer personalized communication svcs. dept., 1977-79, cons. personalized communication svcs. dept., 1979-81; supr. employee benefit info. ctr. Towers Perrin, N.Y.C., 1981-83; prin., new bus. coord. personalized communication svcs. Towers Perrin, Phila., 1983-87, prin., dir. mktg., recruiting, staff devel., benefit adminstrn. svcs., 1987-90, prin., dir. mktg. and sales personalized communication svcs., 1990-92; prin., dir. spl. projects, health, welfare, human resource and comm. practices Towers Perrin, Washington, 1992-93, prin., leader human resource and communication consulting, 1993-94, prin. sr. nat. mktg., consulting and project mgmt. resources, human resources and comm. practices, 1994—. Co-developer computer software Flex Planner, 1991, Outlook, 1991. Asst. at polls Dem. Party, Arlington, Va., 1993; active Greenpeace, Va., 1993, Rosslyn (Va.) Renaissance, 1993, Nat. Mus. of the Am. Indian Smithsonian, Washington, 1993. Recipient Presidential scholarship Eastern Coll., 1972. Mem. ASTD, Internat. Soc. Cert. Employee Benefit Specialists, Internat. Assn. Bus. Communicators. Democrat. Office: Towers Perrin 1001 19th St N Ste 1500 Arlington VA 22209-1710

WELLS, DONNA JO, accounting educator; b. Waco, Tex., Jan. 2, 1966; d. Weldon Clay and Joann (Richards) W.; three children. AAS, McLennan Community Coll., Waco, 1989; BBA, Baylor U., 1992, MBA, 1993; post-grad., U. Tex., Arlington, 1994—. Tutor McLennan C.C., Waco, 1988-89; bookkeeper Assoc. Ct. Reporters, Waco, 1988-89; acctg. clk. Pattillo, Brown & Hill, CPAs, Waco, 1990; adminstrv. asst. honors program Baylor U., Waco, 1990-93; instr. acctg. Ctrl. Tex. Coll. Mem. coun. 1st Bapt. Ch., Woodway, 1988-89; exec. bd. Woodway PTA, 1994—; mem. exec. com. Cub Scouts Am., 1993-94; exec. bd. mem. Midway Coun. of PTAs. Recipient Student Scholar award Am. Assn. Cmty. and Jr. Colls. Mem. Phi Theta Kappa (reporter 1988-89, Student Scholar award, Outstanding Acctg. Student award 1988, Outstanding Svc. award 1989). Home: 458 Catalina Dr Woodway TX 76712-3916

WELLS, ELAINE LOUISE, state legislator, health care administrator; b. Emporia, Kans., May 26, 1951; d. Walter Lawrence and Ruth Maxine (Mangold) Laue; m. Richard Dean Wells, Sept. 24, 1967; children: Dane Eric, Daric Ean. Student, Washburn U., 1978-85. Asst. activities dir. Brookside Manor, Overbrook, Kans., 1975-76, adminstr., 1976-86; adminstr. Rolling Hills Health Ctr., Fairlawn Heights, Topeka, 1987-89; life and health agt. Bankers Life & Casualty, 1989—; mem. Ho. of Reps., Topeka, 1987—. Vice chair Osage County (Kans.) Dem. Com., 1982-86; bd. dirs. Osage County Farm Bur., 1986. Mem. Kans. Health Care Assn. (bd. dirs. 1985-87), Am. Bus. Women's Assn., Lyndon Bus. Profl. Women (vice chairperson 1989), Ins. Women of Topeka (legis. dir.). Home: RR 1 Box 166 Carbondale KS 66414-9801 Office: Kans State Senate State Capital Rm 155E W Topeka KS 66612*

WELLS, ELEANORE S., advertising executive; b. Washington, Nov. 26, 1955; d. Samuel David and Martha Alberta (Traylor) W. BA in Clin. Psychology, Am. U., Washington, 1978; MS in Mktg., CUNY, 1984. Mental health therapist Sibley Meml. Hosp., Washington, 1978-81; program dir. Nat. Urban League, N.Y.C., 1981-87, Meyers Rsch. Ctr., N.Y.C., 1987-88; assoc. rsch. dir. Young & Rubicam, N.Y.C., 1988-94; v.p., assoc. dir. strategic planning D'Arcy Musius Benton & Bowles, N.Y.C., 1994—. Editor: Feast to Your Soul's Delight, 1986. Mentor, big sister Cath. Big Bros., Inc., N.Y.C., 1993; tutor Literacy Vols. N.Y., 1985. George E. Haynes grad. fellow Revson Found., 1981-82. Mem. N.Y. Urban League (bd. dirs. 1989). Home: 200 W 20th St Apt 1007 New York NY 10011-3563

WELLS, JUDEE ANN, lawyer; b. Claremont, Okla., June 10, 1951. BS, S.W. Mo. State Coll., 1972; JD, U. Tex., 1977; LLM, NYU, 1985. Bar: Tex. 1977, Wash. 1978. Assoc. Strassburger & Price, Dallas, 1977-78; assoc. prof. Pacific Luth. U., Tacoma, Wash., 1978-79; tax atty. Exxon, Houston, 1979-81; assoc. Atlantic Richfield, Dallas, 1981-84; ptnr. Foster, Pepper & Shefelman, Seattle, 1985—; bd. dirs., officer Harrison Pub., Bellevue, Wash. Author: Real Estate Excise Tax, 1991. Mem. ABA, Wash. State Bar Assn., Tex. State Bar Assn. Office: Foster Pepper & Shefelman 1111 3rd Ave Ste 3400 Seattle WA 98101

WELLS, KAREN KAY, medical librarian; b. Petaluma, Calif., Jan. 9, 1956; d. Albert Lee and Miyoko (Kay) W.; m. John Edward Guth, Aug. 4, 1979 (div. 1986). BS with honors, U. Colo., 1977; MEd with honors, U. Ill., 1980, MS with honors, 1982. Cert. tchr., Colo., Ill. Grad. asst. grad. libr. U. Ill., Urbana, 1981-82; asst. prof. med. libr. svcs. sch. medicine Mercer U., Macon, Ga., 1982-83; libr., head Presbyn.-St. Luke's Med. Ctr., Presbyn.-Denver Hosp., 1983-84; libr., dept. head AMI-St. Luke's Hosp. Health Scis. Libr., Denver, 1984-88, instr., cons. dialog pharm. database, 1985-87; head libr. Manville Health, Safety and Environ. Libr., Denver, 1988-89; info. cons. Wells Info. Svc., Denver, 1989—; sr. rsch. analyst EG & G, Golden, Colo., 1990-94; sr. adminstrv. assessor, 1994—. Editor Infosource newsletter, 1983-88. Mem. ALA, Med. Libr. Assn., Colo. Coun. Med. Librs. (cons. med.-sci. databases 1984—), Denver Area Health Scis. Libr. Consortium, IBM PC XT Users Group, U. Colo. Alumni Assn., U. Ill. Alumni Assn., Beta Phi Mu, Kappa Delta Pi. Democrat. Presbyterian. Office: RFETS PO Box 464 Golden CO 80402-0464

WELLS, LESLEY BROOKS, judge; b. Muskegon, Mich., Oct. 6, 1937; d. James Franklin and Inez Simpson (Schallmo) W.; m. Arthur V.N. Brooks, June 20, 1959; (div.); children: Lauren Elizabeth, Caryn Alison, Anne Kristin, Thomas Eliot. BA, Chatham Coll., Pitts., 1959; JD cum laude, Cleve. State U., 1974; cert. Nat. Jud. Coll., Reno, 1983, 85, 87, 89. Bar: Ohio 1975, U.S. Dist. Ct. (no. dist.) Ohio 1975. Pvt. practice, Cleve., 1975; ptnr. Brooks & Moffet, Cleve., 1975-79; dir., atty. ABAR Litigation Ctr., Cleve., 1979-80; assoc. Schneider, Smeltz, Huston & Ranney, Cleve., 1980-83; judge Ct. of Common Pleas Cleve., 1983-93; judge, U.S. District Ct. (no. Ohio)6th Cir., Cleveland, 1994—; adj. prof. law and urban policy Cleve. State U., 1979-82. Editor, author: Litigation Manual, 1980. Past pres. Cleve. Legal Aid Soc.; legal chmn. Nat. Women's Polit. Caucus, 1981-82; chmn. Gov.'s Task Force on Family Violence, Ohio, 1983-87; Nat. Council Juvenile and Family Ct. Judges, 1985-88; mem. biomedical ethics com. Case Western Res. U. Med. Sch., 1985—; mem. com. of Ethics and Profl. Responsibility Jud. Adminstrn., 1986—, Northwest Ordinance U.S. Constitution Commn., Ohio, 1986-88; trustee Miami U., 1988-90, Urban League of Clevel., 1989-90, Rosemary Ctr., 1986-92, Chatham Coll., 1989—. Recipient Outstanding Alumna award Chatham Coll., 1988, Superior Jud. award Supreme Ct. of Ohio, 1983; J. Irwin award Womenspace, Ohio, 1984, award Womens City Club, 1985. Mem. ABA, Ohio Bar Assn., Cleve. Bar Assn. (Merit Svc. award 1983), Cleve. County Bar Assn., Nat. Conf. State Trial Judges (ethics and profl. responsibility com. 1986—), Nat. Assn. Women Judges. Home: 16926 E Park Dr Cleveland OH 44119-1309 Office: US Courthouse 201 Superior Ave Rm 400 Cleveland OH 44114*

WELLS, LINDA ANN, editor-in-chief; b. N.Y.C., Aug. 9, 1958; d. H. Wayne and Jean (Burchell) W.; m. Charles King Thompson, Nov., 1993. BA in English, Trinity Coll., 1980. Edit. asst. Vogue Mag., N.Y.C., 1980-83, assoc. editor beauty, 1983-85; style reporter New York Times, N.Y.C., 1985, beauty editor, food editor, 1985-90; founding editor, editor-in-chief Allure Mag., N.Y.C., 1990—; speaker Am. Womens' Econ. Devel., N.Y., 1988-89. Contbr. numerous articles to N.Y. Times Mag., Allure Mag., 1985—. Chmn. N.Y. Shakespeare Festival, 1993, 94. Recipient Fragrance Found. award, 1991, Nat. Mag. Design award, 1994, Legal Def. and Edn. Fund Equal Opportunity award NOW, 1994. Mem. Am. Soc. Mag. Editors (bd. dirs. 1993—). Office: Allure Mag Condé Nast Publs 360 Madison Ave New York NY 10017-3136

WELLS, MELISSA FOELSCH, foreign service officer; b. Tallinn, Estonia, Nov. 18, 1932; emigrated to U.S., 1936, naturalized, 1941; d. Kuno Georg and Miliza (Korjus) Foelsch; m. Alfred Washburn Wells, 1960; children: Christopher, Gregory. BS in Fgn. Service, Georgetown U., 1956. Fgn. svc. officer Dept. State, Washington, 1958-61; consular officer Dept. State, Trinidad, 1961-64; econ. officer mission OECD, Paris, 1964-66; econ. officer London, 1966-71; internat. economist, 1971-73; dep. dir. maj. export projects Dept. Commerce, 1973-75; comml. counselor Brazil, 1975-76; amb. to Guinea-Bissau and Cape Verde Dept. of State, 1976-77; U.S. rep. ECOSOC, UN, N.Y.C., 1977-79; resident rep. UNDP, Kampala, Uganda, 1979-81; dir. IMPACT program UNDP, Geneva, 1982-86; amb. to Mozambique, 1987-90; amb. to Zaire (Kinshasa), Kinshasa, 1991-93; under-sec.-gen. for adminstrn. and mgmt. UN, N.Y., 1993—. Mem. Am. Fgn. Service Assn. Office: UN Hdqrs State Dept Rm S-2700 New York NY 10017

WELLS, ROSALIND LEA, economist; b. N.Y.C., Dec. 31, 1936; d. Joseph A. and Goldie (Fader) Leifer; m. Martin I. Roth, June 24, 1956 (div. 1967); children: Andrew, Karen; m. Alfred Newburgh, Feb. 26, 1984. BA magna cum laude, Queens Coll., N.Y.C., 1958; MA, Columbia U., 1960. Econ. analyst Boni, Watkins, Jason, N.Y.C., 1958-61, Exxon, N.Y.C., 1965-67, Citibank, N.Y.C., 1967-68; economist Union Carbide Petroleum, N.Y.C., 1968-71; mgr. econs. Monsanto Textiles, N.Y.C., 1971-78; chief economist J.C. Penney, N.Y.C., 1978-88; pres. Wells & Assocs., N.Y.C., 1988-91; group supr. NPD Group, Port Washington, N.Y., 1991-94; with Mgmt. Horizons (div. Price Waterhouse LLP), N.Y.C., 1994—; chief economist Nat. Retail Mchts. Assn., N.Y.C., 1988-91. Mem. Nat. Assn. Bus. Economists, Nat. Bus. Econs. Coun., Retail Mktg. Soc., Textile Analysts Group, Forecasters Club (sec. N.Y. chpt. 1987). Home: 67-34 Juno St Forest Hills NY 11375 Office: Mgmt Horizons 1177 Ave of the Americas New York NY 10036

WELLS, TONI LYNN, accountant; b. Lexington, Ky., June 24, 1959; d. George Andrew and Noreta Florence (Collins) W. AA, Hinds Jr. Coll., 1979; BSBA in Fin., U. So. Miss., 1982, M in Profl. Acctancy, 1984. Internal auditor First Nat. Bank Co., New Orleans, 1984; staff auditor Touche Ross & Co., Jackson, Miss., 1984-85, semi-sr., 1985-87; staff auditor Occidental Petroleum Corp., L.A., 1987-88, sr. auditor, 1988, audit supr., 1988-92; gen. acctg. supr. Occidental Petroleum Corp., Corpus Christi, Tex., 1992—. Vol. jr. achievement Calallen High Sch.; alt. del. West Tex. Diocese, Episcopal. Ch. Coun., 1995. Mem. Am. Soc. Women Accts., U. So. Miss. Alumni Assn., U. So. Miss. Golden Eagles, Corpus Christi Plant Recreation Club (sec. bd. dirs.), Internat. Order of St. Luke, Scottish Heritage Soc. (advisor to treas.). Episcopalian. Office: Occidental Petroleum Corp 1501 McKinzie Rd Corpus Christi TX 78460

WELLS-PRINES, VESTA LYNN, music publishing executive, singer; b. Rapid City, S.D., Sept. 28, 1950; d. Ervin Haefs and Helen Eliza (Nelson) Wells; children: Jessica Feliz, Amanda Renee. Grad., Rapid City High Sch., 1968; student, U. S.D., 1992—. Profl. singer midwest U.S., 1973—; owner, mgr. Creative Communications Cos., Sioux Falls, S.D., 1977-93; owner Creative Cassette, Rapid City, 1993—; model, 1968—. Active PTA, Sioux Falls, 1984-92. Recipient Addy award, 1993-94; named Miss 16 of S.D. Sixteen Mag., 1966. Mem. S.D. Advt. Fedn., Sioux Falls C. of C. Home & Office: Creative Cassette 911 Explorer St Rapid City SD 57701-0524

WELNA, CECILIA, mathematics educator; b. New Britain, Conn., July 15; d. Joseph and Sophie (Roman) W. B.S., St. Joseph Coll., 1949; M.A., U. Conn., 1952, Ph.D., 1960. Instr. Mt. St. Joseph Acad., 1949-50; asst. instr. U. Conn., 1950-55; instr. U. Mass., Amherst, 1955-56; prof., chmn. dept. math. and physics U. Hartford, 1957-82, dean Coll. Edn., Nursing and Health Professions, 1982-91, prof. math., 1991—. Mem. Math. Assn. Am., Nat. Council Tchrs. Math., Assn. Tchrs. Math. Conn., Sigma Xi. Office: U Hartford Dana 295A Bloomfield Ave West Hartford CT 06117

WELSH, DIANE M., judge. BA in Polit. Sci. magna cum laude, Villanova U., 1976, JD, 1979. Bar: Pa. 1979, U.S. Dist. Ct. (ea. dist.) Pa. 1981, U.S. Ct. Appeals (3rd cir.) 1984, U.S. Supreme Ct. 1985. Legal counsel Pa. Senate Judiciary Com., 1980-81; dep. dist. atty. Bucks County Dist. Atty.'s Office, Pa., 1981-84; ptnr. Gold-Bikin Welsh & Assocs., 1984-94; magistrate judge U.S. Dist. Ct. (ea. dist.) Pa., Phila., 1994—. Contbr. articles to legal jours. Actove one-on-one mentor program Norristown (Pa.) High Sch.; trustee Manor Jr. Coll., 1981-83, Norristown State Hosp., 1987-90. Mem. ABA, Fed. Bar Assn., Fed. Magistrate Judge Assn., Nat. Assn. Women Judges, Pa. Bar Assn., Montgomery County Bar Assn., Phila. Bar Assn., Brehon Law Soc. Office: US Courthouse 601 Market St Rm 4613 Philadelphia PA 19106*

WELSH, STACEY LAU, investment banker; b. Honolulu, Nov. 30, 1960; d. Timothy Shao Yu and Violet Yuk Kung (Lee) Lau; m. John Anthony Welsh, May 15, 1993. BS, San Francisco State U., 1984; MBA, U. Chgo., 1989. CPA, Calif. Office mgr. Markle, Stuckey, Clark & Co., San Francisco, 1982-84, acct., 1984-87; v.p. Citicorp Securities, Inc., N.Y.C., 1989—; pres. Capajava, Stamford, Conn., 1992—. Sponsor, Student/Sponsor Partnership, N.Y.C., 1990—. Home: 186 Field Point Rd Greenwich CT 06830 Office: Citicorp Securities Inc 399 Park Ave 3d Fl New York NY 10043

WELSHIMER, GWEN R., state legislator, real estate broker, appraiser, tax consultant; b. Poughkeepsie, N.Y., Nov. 5, 1935; d. Freanor Ralph and Beulah M. (Reedy) Grant; m. Billy L. Blake (div. 1979); children: Donald E., Jerry A.; m. Robert E. Welshimer. Student, Kans. State U., 1953-54; cert., Jones Real Estate Coll., Colorado Springs, Colo., 1975. Cert. real estate appraiser, 1993. Exec. sec. Coll. Bd. Trustees, Bellevue, Wash., 1967-69; exec. sec. to chmn. bd. dirs. Garvey Industries, Wichita, Kans., 1969-73, adminstrv. asst. pers. and pub. affairs, 1969-73; copywriter Walter Drake & Sons, Colorado Springs, 1973-75; real estate agt. UTE Realty, Colorado Springs, 1975-76; newspaper pub., owner Black Forrest News, Colorado Springs, 1976-79; real estate broker, appraiser Gwen Welshimer Real Estate, Wichita, 1979—; coord. Epic Real Estate Sch., Wichita, 1988—; legislator Kans. Ho. of Reps., Topeka, 1990—, minority leader local govt. com., 1994-95. Dem. precinct committeewomen, Wichita; bd. dirs. United Meth. Urban Ministries, Wichita, 1990—. Mem. NOW, AAUW, Colo. Press Assn., Colo. Bd. Realtors, Nat. Fedn. Women, Women's Home Extension (past pres.), Nat. Order Women Legislators (state dir. 1994-95). Democrat. Methodist. Home: 6103 Castle Wichita KS 67218 Office: Kans Ho of Reps State Capitol Topeka KS 66612*

WELSOME, EILEEN, journalist; b. N.Y.C., Mar. 12, 1951; d. Richard H. and Jane M. (Garity) W.; m. James R. Martin, Aug. 3, 1983. BJ with honors, U. Tex., 1980. Reporter Beaumont (Tex.) Enterprise, 1980-82, San Antonio Light, 1982-83, San Antonio Express-News, 1983-86, Albuquerque Tribune, 1987-94. Recipient Clarion award, 1989, News Reporting award Nat. Headliners, 1989, John Hancock award, 1991, Mng. Editors Pub. Svc. award AP, 1991, 94, Roy Howard award 1994, James Aronson award, 1994, Gold Medal award Investigative Reporters and Editors, 1994, Sigma Delta Chi award, 1994, Investigative Reporting award Nat. Headliners, 1994, Selden Ring award, 1994, Heywood Broun award, 1994, George Polk award, 1994, Sidney Hillman Found. award, 1994, Pulitzer Prize for Nat. Reporting, 1994; John S. Knight fellow Stanford U., 1991-92.

WELTER, ELIZABETH J., accountant; b. Bluffton, Ohio, Mar. 27, 1950; d. Robert L. and Mary F. (Stambaugh) Bowden; m. Mark F. Welter, Jun. 22, 1984. BA, Ohio Northern U., 1972; MBA, U. Toledo, 1988. CMA. Payroll supr. Haughton Elevator Co., Toledo, 1975-76, supr., gen. acct., 1976-78, fin. analyst, 1978-79; svc. fin. mgr. Schindler Elevator Corp., Toledo, 1979-82, svc. adminstrn. and fin. mgr., 1982-84, field acctg. mgr., 1984-87, svc. divsn. contr., 1987-89; contr. corporate reporting Millar Elevator Co., Toledo, 1989-93; fin. acctg. mgr. Buckeye Cellulose Corp., Memphis, 1993—. Bd. dirs. treas. YWCA, Toledo, 1991. Mem. Inst. Mgmt. Acctg., Mgmt. Forum (sec. 1992-93). Office: Buckeye Cellulose Corp 1001 Tillman Memphis TN 38112

WELTON, JESSICA WHEAT, advertising executive; b. Richmond, Va., Sept. 25, 1953; d. Francis Conway and Catherine May (Murphy) W.; m. Steven Jake Ellerbroek, Mar. 17, 1973 (div. 1979); m. Patrick Siddall, July 6, 1985; children: Justin, Jeremy, Peyton, Jenny. BFA, Va. Commonwealth U., 1977. Finished artist The Martin Agy., Richmond, 1977-78; art dir. Morgan & Assocs., Richmond, 1978-79; art dir. Siddall, Matus & Coughter, Richmond, 1979-88, v.p., assoc. creative dir., 1988—. Active Goochland County Gifted Adv. Coun., Goochland County Commn. Future in Edn., Goochland County Sch. Renewal Com. Recipient over 100 nat. and internat. awards London Internat., 1990, One Show, CA, Print, Art Dirs., Athenas, Addies, MIRMS, Clios, Andys. Mem. Richmond Advt. Club (bd. dirs.), Va. Mus., Va. Hist. Soc., Peyton Soc. Va., Va. Mus. Friends of Art. Episcopalian. Home: Readers Br Farm 1737 Manakin Rd Manakin Sabot VA 23103-2650 Office: Siddall Matus & Coughter 801 E Main St Richmond VA 23219-2901

WELTY, EUDORA, author; b. Jackson, Miss.; d. Christian Webb and Chestina (Andrews) W. Student, Miss. State Coll. for Women; B.A., U. Wis., 1929; postgrad., Columbia Sch. Advt., 1930-31. Author: A Curtain of Green, 1941, The Robber Bridegroom, 1942, The Wide Net, 1943, Delta Wedding, 1946, Music From Spain, 1948, Short Stories, 1949, The Golden Apples, 1949, The Ponder Heart, 1954 (William Dean Howells medal Am. Acad. Arts and Letters 1955), The Bride of the Innisfallen, 1955, Place in Fiction, 1957, The Shoe Bird, 1964, Thirteen Stories, 1965, A Sweet Devouring, 1969, Losing Battles, 1970 (Nat. Book award nomination 1971), One Time, One Place, 1971 (Christopher Book award 1972), The Optimist's Daughter, 1972 (Pulitzer prize in fiction 1973), The Eye of the Story, 1978, The Collected Stories of Eudora Welty, 1980 (Notable Book award ALA 1980, Am. Book award 1981), One Writer's Beginnings, 1985 (Am. Book award 1984, Nat. Book Critics Circle award nomination 1984), Eudora Welty Photographs, 1989, A Writer's Eye: Collected Book Reviews, 1994, Monuments to Interruption: Collected Book Reviews, 1994; editor: (with Ronald A. Sharp) The Norton Book of Friendship, 1991; contbr.: New Yorker. Recipient O. Henry award, 1942, 43, 68, Creative Arts medal for fiction Brandeis U., 1966, Nat. Inst. Arts and Letters Gold Medal, 1972, Nat. Medal for Lit., 1980, Presdl. Medal of Freedom, 1980, Commonwealth medal MLA, 1984, Nat. Medal of Arts, 1987; Lit. grantee Nat. Inst. Arts and Letters, 1944; Guggenheim fellow, 1942; Chevalier de l'Ordre des Arts et Lettres (France), 1987. Mem. Am. Acad. Arts and Letters. Home: 1119 Pinehurst Pl Jackson MS 39202-1812*

WEMPLE-KINDER, SUZANNE FONAY, history educator; b. Veszprém, Hungary, Aug. 1, 1927; came to U.S., 1949; d. Ernest Fonay and Magda (Mihalyfy) Széchényi; m. George Barr Wemple, June 17, 1956 (dec. Apr. 1988); children: Peter, Stephen, Carolyn; m. Gordon T. Kinder, May 26, 1990. Student, English Sisters, Budapest, Hungary, 1945; BS, U. Calif., Berkeley, 1953; MLS, Columbia U., 1955, PhD, 1967. Reference asst. Columbia U. Libr., N.Y.C., 1955-58, Stern Coll., N.Y.C., 1963-64, Tchr.'s Coll., N.Y.C., 1964-66; prof. Columbia U., Barnard Coll., N.Y.C., 1966-92, prof. emeritus, 1992—. Author: Atto of Vercelli, Church, State and Society in the Tenth Century, 1979, Women in Frankish Society, Marriage and the Cloister, 1981 (Berkshire Book prize 1982); co-editor: Women in Medieval Society, 1983; contbr. essay to A History of Women Vol. II: Silences of the Middle Ages, 1992; contbr. articles to profl. jours., essays to books. Grantee NEH, 1975, 81-86, Fulbright Found., 1982, Spivak-Summer Barnard Coll., 1981. Home: 1717 Gulf Shore Blvd N Apt 704 Naples FL 33940-4939

WENDELL, BARBARA TAYLOR, retired real estate agent; b. Ames, Iowa, Jan. 30, 1920; d. Harvey Nelson and Ruby (Britten) Taylor; m. Donald Thomas Davidson Sr., May 22, 1942 (dec. Oct. 1962); children: Donald Thomas Jr., John Taylor, Ann Elizabeth Davidson Costanzo; m. Connell S. Wendell, Oct. 10, 1992. BS in Home Econs. Sci., Iowa State U., 1943. Assoc. tchr. Ames (Iowa) Pub. Schs., 1970-73; retail mgr. Gen. Nutrition Ctr., Ames, 1974-77; sales assoc. Century 21 Real Estate, Ames, 1978-82, Friedrich Realty, Ames, 1982-89. Pres. Ames City PTA Coun., 1950; leader, advisor Boy Scouts Am., Ames, 1952-58; chmn. Campfire Leaders' Assn., Ames, 1959-61; sec. bd. dirs. Campfire Girls, Ames, 1964-66; property com. United Meth. Ch., Ames, 1964-67; vol. Para-Legal Svcs. for Elderly; active Octagon for the Arts, Brunier Gallery, Med. Ctr. Aux., Art Gallery Com. Mem. Nat. Home Econs. in Homemaking (chmn. fgn. student rels. com.), Internat. Orch. Assn., Iowa State U. Meml. Union (life), Iowa State U. Alumni Assn. (life), Ames Community Arts Coun. Republican. Home: 1110 Johnson St Ames IA 50010-4206

WENDELL, MARIE ELLEN, retired special education educator; b. West Frankfort, Ill., May 28, 1928; d. James Chris and Albina (Pavlaskas) Nickoloff; m. Donald George Wendell, Dec. 18, 1954 (dec. Oct. 1988); children: Donald II (dec.), Nancy Marie (dec.). BS in Edn., So. Ill. U., 1954; postgrad., U. Louisville, 1961. Tchr. elem. schs. Springfield, Ill., 1954-56; tchr. spl. edn. Allentown, Pa., 1956-58; counselor edn. N.J. Commn. for the Blind, Newark, 1959-60; tchr. educable handicapped grades 7-12 Louisville, 1961-88. Mem. NEA, Ky. Edn. Assn. Roman Catholic. Home: PO Box 91533 Louisville KY 40291-0533

WENDELN, DARLENE DORIS, English language educator; b. Indpls., July 18, 1956; d. Robert Edward and Doris Mae (Brabender) W. BS, U. Indpls., 1978; MS, Ind. U., 1986. Lic. tchr., Ind. Secondary English tchr., coach Centerville (Ind.)-Abington Sch. Corp., 1978—; coach girls' tennis regional and sectional championships. Mem. NEA, Am. Volleyball Coaches Assn., Nat. Coun. Tchrs. English, Ind. High Sch Tennis Coaches Assn., Ind. Coaches of Girls' Sports Assn., U.S. Tennis Assn. Lutheran. Office: Centerville High Sch Willow Grove Rd Centerville IN 47330

WENDER, DEBORAH ELIZABETH, policy analyst, social worker; b. Sacramento, June 30, 1954; d. Joseph Andrew Sr. and Caroline Elizabeth (Wulff) Wender; adopted children: alexander Darius Andrew, Zodie Miriam Caroline. AA, American River Coll., Sacramento, 1974; BA, Calif. State U., Sacramento, 1980, MSW, 1988. Counselor coord. Sacramento Women's Ctr., 1980-81, rape crisis project dir., 1981-84; program coord. Rape Prevention Edn. Program, U. Calif., Davis, 1984-87; criminal justice specialist Calif. Office Criminal Justice Planning, Sacramento, 1988-89; assoc. health program advisor Office of AIDS Calif. Dept. Health Svcs., Sacramento, 1989-91, pub. health social work cons. maternal and child health, 1991-93, assoc. govtl. program analyst Medi-Cal Eligibility, 1993—. Bd. dirs. Child Sexual Abuse Treatment Ctr., Yolo County, Woodland, Calif., 1984-86, WomanKind Health Clinic, Sacramento, 1984-86; bd. dirs. Sacramento Women's Ctr., 1987-91, bd. pres. 1989-91. Democrat. Home: 8649 Glenroy Way Sacramento CA 95826-1743

WENDROW, SYLVIA DIANN, speech and language pathologist; b. Ann Arbor, Mich.; d. Barnaby Alex and Margaret (Myers) W. AB, U. Mich., 1959, MS, 1963. Speech pathologist Lenawee Intermediate Sch. Dist., Adrian, Mich., 1959—; critic tchr. U. Mich., Ann Arbor, Mich., 1966-69; guest lectr. Adrian Coll., 1984; speech cons. Adrian Community Nursery, 1969-70. Sec., bd. dirs., performer Lenawee Pops Orch., Adrian, 1970-74; bd. dirs. Lenawee Community Concert Assn., Adrian, 1969-78. Named Spl. Edn. Itinerant Tchr. of Yr., 1990. Mem. NEA, AAUW (pres. 1966-68, bd. dirs.), LWV (bd. dirs. Lenawee chpt. 1974-78), Am. Speech-Lang.-Hearing Assn. (Continuing Edn. award 1990, 92), Lenawee Intermediate Edn. Assn., Sigma Alpha Iota. Office: Lenawee Schs Spl Edn Ctr 2946 Sutton Rd Adrian MI 49221-9375

WENDT, SHEILA MARIE, accountant; b. Goliad, Tex., May 8, 1963; d. Kenneth Charles and Barbara Jean (Seidel) W. BS, Miss. Univ. Women, 1985. Staff acct. Dennis R. Switzer, CPA, Natchez, Miss., 1985-86, Altus Bank, Mobile, Ala., 1986-89; acct. II U. South Ala. Med. Ctr., Mobile, 1989-90; cost rate analyst U. So. Ala. Hosps., Mobile, 1990—. Fin. sec. St. Paul's Luth. Ch., Mobile, 1992-93, Sunday Sch. tchr., 1993—, chmn. altar guild, 1992. Mem. Inst. Mgmt. Accts., Healthcare Fin. Mgmt. Assn. Office: U So Ala Hosps 2451 Fillingim St Mobile AL 36617-2238

WENDTLAND, MONA BOHLMANN, dietitian, consultant; b. Schulenburg, Tex., Mar. 30, 1930; d. Willy Frank and Leona A. (Bruns) Bohlmann; m. Charles William Ewing, Mar. 8, 1953 (div. Sept. 1975); children: Charles William Jr., Deborah Susan Ewing Richmond; m. William Wolters Wendtland, Jan. 12, 1991. BS in Home Econs., U. Tex., 1952, postgrad., 1952-57. Registered dietitian, Tex. Dietitian sch. lunch program Port Arthur (Tex.) Ind. Sch. Dist., 1952-53; elem. tchr. Portsmouth (Va.) Sch. Dist., 1953-54; dietitian, mgr. lunch room E.M. Scarbrough Dept. Store, Austin, Tex., 1955-57; asst. chief adminstrv. dietitian John Sealy HOsp., Galveston, Tex., 1957-59; chief therapeutic dietitian USPHS Hosp., Galveston, 1959-60, asst. chief dietitian, 1960-62; cons. dietitian Sinton (Tex.) Nursing Home, 1963-65; dietary cons. Deaton Hosp., Galena Park, Tex., 1966-68; dir. food svcs. Nat. Health Enterprises, Houston, 1975-76; dietary cons. to nursing homes and retirement ctrs. Houston, 1976—. Del. Internat. Congress Arts & Comm., 1993. Mem. Am. Dietetic Assn. (registered), Tex. Dietetic Assn., South Tex. Dietetic Assn. (chmn. cons. interest group 1978-79), U. Tex. Home Econs. Assn., Dietitians in Bus. and Industry (nat. rep. to mgmt. practices group 1980-83, treas. Houston chpt. 1980-81, pres. 1981-82, advisor 1983-84), Tex. Gerontol Nutritionists (sec. 1994-95), Tex. Cons. Dietitians in Healthcare Facilities, Tex. Nutrition Coun., Dietary Mgrs. Assn. (advisor Houston dist. 1979-92). Republican. Methodist. Home and Office: 5463 Jason St Houston TX 77096-1238

WENGER, SHARON LOUISE, pediatrics educator, researcher, cytogeneticist; b. Washington, Sept. 25, 1949; d. William Fred and Lois Helen (Compton) W.; m. George E. Fromlak Jr., Jan. 10, 1976; children: Nicholas Edward, Holly Louise, Andrea Lee. BA in Biology, Thiel Coll., 1971; MS in Human Genetics, U. Pitts., 1973, PhD in Human Genetics, 1976. Asst. prof. Sch. of Medicine U. Pitts., 1980-89, assoc. prof. Sch. of Medicine, 1989—. Contbr. articles to profl. jours. Mem. Am. Soc. Human Genetics, Midwest Soc. for Pediatric Rsch. Office: Children's Hosp Pitts 3705 5th Ave Pittsburgh PA 15213-2583

WENGER, VICKI, interior designer; b. Indpls., Aug. 30, 1928. Ed., U. Nebr., Internat. Inst. Interior Design, Parsons in Paris. Pres. Vicki Wenger Interiors, Bethesda, Md., 1963-71, Washington, 1982—; pres. Beautiful Spaces Inc., Washington, 1982—; chief designer Creative Design, Capitol Heights, Md., 1969-84; lectr. Nat. Assn. Home Builders, 1983-88; mem. programs com. D.C. Assn. Home Builders, 1983-88. Author-host: (patented TV interior design show) Beautiful Spaces 1984; producer, host (cable TV show) Design Edition, 1988—. Designer Gourmet Gala, March of Dimes, Washington, 1986-88; decorator showcase Nat. Symphony Orch., Washington, 1983-94, chmn. women's com., 1991-92; decorator showcase Am. Cancer Soc., Washington, 1983, Alexandria Cmty. YWCA, 1990. Mem. Am. Soc. Interior Designers (profl., nat. bd. dirs. 1973-75, nat. examining com. 1977-78, pres. Md. chpt. 1976, bd. dirs. Washington Metro chpt. 1989-91, pres.-elect 1994, mem. president's barrier free com. 1980), Nat. trust Hist. Preservation, Smithsonian Instn. (sponsor), Nat. Press Club. Democrat. Presbyterian. Office: Vicki Wenger Interiors 2801 New Mexico Ave NW Washington DC 20007-3921

WENIG, MARY MOERS, law educator; b. N.Y.C.; d. Robert and Celia Lewis (Kauffman) Moers; m. Jerome Wenig, Dec. 19, 1946; children: Margaret Moers Wenig Rubenstein, Michael M. Wenig. BA, Vassar Coll., 1946; JD, Columbia U., 1951. Bar: N.Y. 1952, U.S. Ct. Appeals (2d cir.) 1954, U.S. Dist. Ct. (so. dist.) N.Y. 1956, Conn. 1977. Assoc. Cahill, Gordon, Reindel & Ohl, N.Y.C., 1951-57; assoc. Greenbaum, Wolff & Ernst, N.Y.C., 1957-60, Skadden, Arps, Slate, Meagher & Flom, N.Y.C., 1960-71; asst. prof. sch. law St. John's U., N.Y.C., 1971-75, assoc. prof. sch. law, 1975-78; rsch. affiliate Yale Law Sch., New Haven, 1978-79; prof. sch. law U. Bridgeport, Conn., 1978-82, Charles A. Dana prof. law, 1982-92; prof. sch. law Quinnipiac Coll., Bridgeport, 1992—; cons. The Merrill Anderson Co., Stratford, Conn., 1982—, Conn. Permanent Commn. on Status of Women, 1978-79; vis. prof. sch. law Pace U., White Plains, N.Y., 1979; bd. dirs. Tax Analysts/TAX NOTES, Fairfax, N.Y., 1980—; bd. dirs., pres. Conn. Women's Ednl. & Legal Fund, Inc., New Haven, 1973; commr. State of Conn. Permanent Commn. on Status of Women, 1985-91; mem. Conn. Gen. Assembly's Adv. Commn. to Study the Uniform Marital Property's Act., 1985-86; lectr. in field; bd. dirs. Tax Analysts. Editor: PLI Tax Handbooks, 1978-86; co-editor: Bittker, Fundamentals of Federal Income Taxation, 1983; co-authrl: (with Douthwaite) Unmarried Couples and the Law, 1979; contbr. tax, estate planning, trust and estates and marital property articles to profl. jours.; editorial adv. bd. Estate Planning for the Elderly & Disabled, 1987-90, Community Property Jour., 1986-88, Estate Planning, 1975—, Estates, Gifts & Trusts Jour., 1976—. Mem. probate com. Conn. Law Revision Commn., 1985—, com. to study the probate system Conn. Probate Assembly, 1988-91, task force on the legal rights of women in marriage NOW, 1987-91; 2nd cir. rep. Fedn. of Women Lawyers Jud. Screening Panel, 1979; bd. govs. Radcliffe Club N.Y., 1975-77; mem. 1st selectman's com. on taxation relief for the elderly Town of Westport, 1974-75; pres. bd. dirs. Conn. Women's Ednl. and Legal Fund, Inc., 1975-79, bd. dirs., 1973-79. Named Salute to Women honoree Outstainding Women of Conn., Greater Bridgeport YWCA, 1990, Women in Leadership honoree New Haven YWCA, 1979, honoree U. Bridgeport Sch. Law Women's Law Assn., 1990; Harlan Fiske Stone scholar Columbia U. Sch. Law, 1949; recipient Award for Equality United Nations Assn.-USA of Conn., 1987; Summer Stipend grantee NEH, 1984, rsch. grantee Conn. Bar Found., 1980. Fellow Am. Coll. Trust & Estate Counsel (bd. regents 1985-91); mem. ABA (advisor to NCCUSL 1980-84, sect. coun. mem. 1970-72), Internat. Acad. Estates & Trust Law (academician, exec. coun. mem. 1992-94), Conn. Bar Assn. (sects.' exec. econs., Disting. Svc. commendation 1977), Assn. Am. Law Schs., Assn. of Bar of City of N.Y., N.Y. State Bar Assn., Am. Law Inst. (hon.), Am. Coll. Tax Counsel (hon.). Democrat. Jewish. Home: 5 Lamplight Ln Westport CT 06880-6106 Office: Quinnipiac Coll School of Law 303 University Ave Bridgeport CT 06604-5795

WENNER, LETTIE MCSPADDEN, political science educator; b. Battle Creek, Mich., Apr. 9, 1937; d. John Dean and Isma Doolie (Sullivan) McSpadden; m. Manfred Wilhelm Wenner, Apr. 3, 1962; children: Eric Alexis, Adrian Edward. AB, U. Chgo., 1959; MA, U. Calif., Berkeley, 1962; PhD, U. Wis., 1972. Fgn. svc. officer Dept. State, Washington, 1961-63; rsch. assoc. Dept. HEW, Washington, 1965-67; asst. prof. polit. sci. U. Ill., Chgo., 1972-79, assoc. prof. polit. sci., 1979-88; prof. and chair dept. polit. sci. No. Ill. U., De Kalb, 1988—. Author: One Environment Under Law, 1976, The Environmental Decade in Court, 1982, United States Energy and Environmental Interest Groups, 1990. Mem. Am. Polit. Sci. Assn., Midwest Polit. Sci. Assn., Law and Society Assn., Pub. Policy Assn., Audubon Soc., Sierra Club. Democrat. Home: 3112 Fairway Oaks Dr De Kalb IL 60115-4925 Office: No Ill U Dept Polit Sci De Kalb IL 60115

WENNER, LINDA MARIE, payroll manager; b. Detroit, June 6, 1966; d. Wayne D. and Priscilla E. (Goedde) W. AS in Acctg. summa cum laude, Jones Coll., Jacksonville, Fla., 1986. Receptionist, sec. Hubsch & Aguilar, P.A., Jacksonville, 1984-86; full charge bookkeeper Coastal Plaines Ins. Assocs., Jacksonville, 1986-88; payroll mgr. The Stellar Group, Jacksonville, 1988—. Mem. steering com. From the Heart, Jacksonville, 1991-93. Mem. Am. Payroll Assn., Jacksonville Jaycees (dir. human svcs. 1992-94, Chmn. of Yr. 1993, Dir. of Quarter 1994), St. Josephs Singles Group. Republican. Roman Catholic. Office: The Stellar Group 2900 Hartley Rd Jacksonville FL 32257

WENNINGER, MARY KATHERINE, plant manager; b. Holyoke, Mass., Jan. 25, 1965; d. Ronald Joseph and Jane (Beausoleil) W.; m. Stephen James Everett, June 27, 1987. BS, Fitchburg (Mass.) State Coll., 1987. Lab. technician Scott Splty. Gases, Houston, 1988, lab. supr., 1989, lab. mgr., 1990, quality assurance mgr., 1991-92, plant mgr., 1993—; co-cons. Sci. Mgmt. for Scott Splty. Gases, 1992. Mem. Am. Chem. Soc., Am. Soc. Quality Control. Office: Scott Splty Gases 3714 Lapas Dr Houston TX 77023-6436

WENTS, DORIS ROBERTA, psychologist; b. L.A., Aug. 26, 1944; d. John Henry and Julia (Cole) W. BA, UCLA, 1966; MA, San Francisco State U., 1968; postgrad., Calif. State U., L.A., 1989-90, Claremont (Calif.) Grad.

Sch., 1990—. Lic. ednl. psychologist, credentialed sch. psychologist, Calif. Sch. psychologist Diagnostic Sch. for Neurologically Handicapped Children, L.A., 1969-86; pvt. practice Monterey Park, Calif., 1986—; instr. Calif. State U., L.A., 1977. Co-author: Southern California Ordinal Scales of Development, 1977. Mem. Western Psychol. Assn., L.A. World Affairs Coun., L.A. Conservancy, Zeta Tau Alpha (officer Santa Monica alumnae chpt. 1970—, Cert. of Merit 1979), Sigma Xi. Office: Claremont Grad Sch Dept Psychology Claremont CA 91711

WENTSLER, GERTRUDE JOSEPHINE, secondary history educator; b. Campbell, Ohio, July 16, 1943; d. John Tofil and Irene S. (Glass) Wallace; m. Lawrence L. Murray, Dec. 29, 1967 (div. 1978); 1 child, Carolyn E. Murray; m. Wm. Scott Wentsler, Mar. 4, 1989. BA, Miami U., Oxford, Ohio, 1964; MEd, Xavier U., Cin., 1967. Cert. secondary tchr., Ohio. Tchr. history Cin. Pub. Schs., 1964-71, Northwest Sch. Dist., Cin., 1974—. Dist. dir. College Hill Forum, Cin., 1972, mem. edn. com., 1970-73. Jennings scholar, 1986-87; recipient Journalism awards, 1987-89, Outstanding Tchr. award U. Chgo., 1989, Tchr. award Friends of Wm. Howard Taft Birthplace, 1992. Mem. NOW, N.W. Tchrs. Assn. (bldg. rep. 1975-77), Nat. Coun. Social Studies, Cin. Fedn. Tchrs. (membership chair 1968, bldg. rep. 1966-69). Home: 2075 Connecticut Ave Cincinnati OH 45224-2368

WENTWORTH, MALINDA ANN NACHMAN, former small business owner, real estate broker; b. Greenville, S.C.; d. Mordecai and Frances (Brown) Nachman; m. William A. Wentworth, June 22, 1964; children: William Allen Jr., Linda Ann. BBA, U. Miami, 1960. Registered rep. brokerage, real estate broker. Personnel Mgrs. Asst. Jordan March, Miami, 1960-61; stock broker Barron & Co., Inc., Greenville, 1961-64; real estate agt. Par Realty, Inc., Conyers, Ga., 1969-72; real estate broker Par Realty, Inc., Conyers, 1972-83; owner/ops. Rockdale Cablevision, Conyers, 1979-83; real estate broker Coldwell Banker, Conyers, 1983-85; owner, operator Wentworth's Gym & Fitness Ctr., Conyers, 1981-90; real estate broker First Realty, Conyers, 1981-89; ptnr. and dir. Santa Barbara (Calif.) Cellular Systems, Inc., 1986-89; v.p. Santa Barbara Cellular Systems, Inc., Atlanta, 1986-87; investor, Cocoa Beach, Fla., 1990—. Producer and dir.: local sport events on cable to sta., 1979, '80, '81, '87. Founding dir., past pres. Porterdale PTO, 1972-79; mem. Nat. Cable TV Assn., 1979-83, pres. Unity Ch. of Rockdale, Conyers, 1984-85, dir., 1984-89. Named Lt. Col.--Aide-De-Camp, Gov. Staff, state of Ga., Gov. George Busbee, 1979, Appreciation Plaque award, Rockdale County High Sch. Football, 1987. Mem. Nat. Health & Strength Assn., Rockdale County Bd. of Realtors, Cellular Telephone Industry Assn., Rockdale County C. of C.

WENTZEL, KAREN LYNN, secondary education educator; b. Granite City, Ill., May 22, 1949; d. Mike J. and Virginia L. (Prewett) Firtos; m. Joseph A. Wentzel Jr., June 2, 1967 (div. 1989); 1 child, David J. AA, St. Louis Community Coll., 1988; BA summa cum laude, Fontbonne Coll., 1990; MEd, U. Mo., St. Louis, 1994. Cert. secondary tchr., Mo. Instr. writing Meramec Coll., St. Louis, 1990-91; tchr. Div. of Youth Svcs., St. Louis, 1991; tchr. lang. arts North Kirkwood Mid. Sch., St. Louis, 1991—. Features editor newspaper Fontbanner, 1990; mng. editor newsletter Hogan Highlights, 1991. Recipient Meramec's Exemplary Svc. award, 1991. Mem. Mo. Mid. Sch. Assn., Nat. Coun. Tchrs. English, Phi Theta Kappa, Sigma Tau Delta, Phi Delta Kappa, Chi Sigma Iota, Phi Kappa Phi. Home: 4908 Fite Dr Imperial MO 63052-1412 Office: North Kirkwood Mid Sch 11287 Manchester Rd Saint Louis MO 63122-1122

WENZEL, SANDRA LEE ANN, pediatrics nurse; b. Peoria, Ill., July 4, 1940; d. Henry M. and Gertrude R. (Burchell) W. Diploma, St. Mary's Sch. Nursing, Kankakee, Ill., 1962; BSN, Bradley U., Peoria, 1966; cert. PNP, Wilford Hall Med. Ctr., San Antonio, 1972. RN, Ill., Tex.; cert. sch. health nurse. Asst. clin. instr. pediatrics St. Francis Sch. Nursing, Peoria, 1962-66; commd. 1st lt. USAF, 1966, advanced through grades to lt. col., 1981; staff nurse cardiology, ICU and pediatrics units, PNP, Wilford Hall Med. Ctr., 1966-68, 72-74; ret., 1986; charge nurse newborn nursery USAF Hosp., Lakenheath Air Base, Eng., 1968-72; PNP USAF Hosp., Goodfellow AFB, Tex., 1974-77; dir. nursing, part-time PNP USAF Clinic, Vance AFB, Okla., 1978-80; PNP USAF Hosp., Scott AFB, Ill., 1980-86; sch. health nurse Marissa, Ill., 1987-89; PNP Family Care Ctr. Corondolet, St. Louis, 1989—. Fellow Nat. Assn. Pediatric Nurse Assocs. and Practitioners (cert.); mem. Am. Diabetic Assn., Uniformed Mil. Practitioners Assn., Sigma Theta Tau.

WERBEL, DEBRA ELAINE, lawyer; b. Ann Arbor, Mich., Jan. 26, 1963; d. Leslie Morton and Phyllis Irene (Isaacson) W. BA, U. Mich., 1985; JD, Boston U., 1988. Bar: Calif. 1988. Dep. pub. defender L.A. County Pub. Defender's Office, L.A., 1989—. Mem. ABA, Calif. Pub. Defenders Assn. Office: L A County Pub Defenders Office 210 W Temple Los Angeles CA 90012

WERDEGAR, KATHRYN MICKLE, judge; b. San Francisco; d. Benjamin Christie and Kathryn Marie (Clark) Mickle; m. David Werdegar; children: Maurice Clark, Matthew Mickle. Student, Wellesley Coll., 1954-55; AB with honors, U. Calif., Berkeley, 1957; JD with distinction, George Washington U., 1962; JD, U. Calif., Berkeley, 1990. Bar: Calif. 1964, U.S. Dist. Ct. (no. dist.) Calif. 1964, U.S. Ct. Appeals (9th cir.) 1964, Calif. Supreme Ct. 1964. Legal asst. civil rights divsn. U.S. Dept. Justice, Washington, 1962-63; cons. Calif. Study Commn. on Mental Retardation, 1963-64; assoc. U. Calif. Ctr. for Study of Law and Soc., Berkeley, 1965-67; spl. cons. State Dept. Mental Hygiene, 1967-68; cons. Calif. Coll. Trial Judges, 1968-71; atty., head criminal divsn. Calif. Continuing Edn. of Bar, 1971-78; assoc. dean acad. and student affairs, assoc. prof. Sch. Law, U. San Francisco, 1978-81; sr. staff atty. Calif. 1st Dist. Ct. Appeal, 1981-85, Calif. Supreme Ct., 1985-91; assoc. justice Calif. 1st Dist. Ct. Appeal, 1991-94, Calif. Supreme Ct., San Francisco, 1994—. Author: Benchbook: Misdemeanor Procedure, 1971, Misdemeanor Procedure Benchbook, 1975, 83; contbr. California Continuing Education of the Bar books; editor-in-chief U. Calif. Law Rev.; editor: California Criminal Law Practice series, 1972, California Uninsured Motorist Practice, 1973, I California Civil Procedure Before Trial, 1977. Recipient Charles Glover award George Washington U., 5 Am. Jurisprudence awards. Mem. Nat. Assn. Women Judges, Calif. Judges Assn., Nev./Calif. Women Judges Assn., Calif. Women Lawyers Assn., Queen's Bench, Boalt Hall Alumni Assn. (bd. dirs.), Order of the Coif. Office: Calif Supreme Court South Tower 303 2nd St San Francisco CA 94107-1366

WERKMAN, ROSEMARIE ANNE, past public relations professional, civic worker; b. Washingtonville, N.Y., Apr. 21, 1926; d. Alexander and Michelina (Russo) Di Benedetto; m. Henry J. Werkman, June 29, 1947; children: Elizabeth, Kristine, Hendrik. Student, U. Miami, Fla. Billing clk. Stern's Dept. Store, N.Y.C., 1945; clk., typist Doubleday-Doran Book Pub., N.Y.C., 1945-46; receptionist Moser & Cotins Advt. Agy., Utica, N.Y., 1947-48, Washingtonville Sch., N.Y., 1960-75. Author: (biography/autobiography) Love, War and Remembrance, 1992; author short stories; poetry pub. in several anthologies. Mem. Dem. Com., Blooming Grove; bd. dirs. Blooming Grove Hist. Assn.; mem. com. Update: Blooming Grove Master Plan; mem. Orange County Coun. Disabled; bd. dirs. Rehab. Support Svcs. Named Poet of Merit, Am. Poetry Assn., 1989. Mem. Blooming Grove C. of C. (v.p.), Orange County Classic Choral Soc., Clearwater (Fla.) Chorus. Democrat. Roman Catholic.

WERMUTH, MARY LOUELLA, educator; b. Oakland County, Mich., May 2, 1943; d. Burt and Ila A. (Cole) W.; m. David J. Kohne, Dec. 28, 1975; 1 child, John B. BA, Oakland U., Rochester, Mich., 1965, MA, 1969, 81. Educator Rochester Community Schs., Rochester Hills, Mich., 1965—; farmer, 1964—; presenter various English confs., 1982, 84, 87; mem. bd. dirs. Mich. Future Problem Solving, 1992—. Author: Images of Michigan, 1981, Michigan Centennial Farm History, 1986. Pres. Horizons Residential Ctrs., Inc., New Baltimore, Mich., 1984—. Recipient Disting. Alumni award Oakland U., 1976. Mem. NEA, Rochester Edn. Assn., Mich. Edn. Assn., Mich. Coun. Tchrs. English (coms. 1985, 87), Oakland U. Alumni Assn. (pres. 1971-73), Mich. Centennial Farm Assn. (bd. dirs. 1979—), Mich. Assn. Gifted Edn. (v.p. 1991-93), Oakland County Tchrs. English (coms. 1985-93). Office: Rochester Sch 180 S Livernois Rd Rochester MI 48307-1840

WERNEKE, DIANE E., federal official; b. Washington, Sept. 5, 1946; d. John George and Mary Werneke. BA in Econs., U. Calif., Berkeley, 1968; MA in Econs., George Washington U., 1970. With FRS, Washington, 1968-77, Confedn. Brit. Industry, London, 1979-81, Office of Senator Paul Tsongas, 1982-84, Ho. Com. on the Budget, Washington, 1984-87; spl. asst. to bd. for congl. liaison Fed. Res. Bd. of Govs., Washington, 1987—. Office: Fed Res Bd of Govs 20th & C Sts NW Rm 2125 Washington DC 20551*

WERNER, DEBORAH LARNED, lawyer; b. Detroit, Mar. 23, 1954; d. Cortland K. and Evelyn (Adkins) Larned; m. Thomas J. Werner, May 16, 1987; 1 child, Barrett Larned Werner. BA, U. S. Fla., 1976; JD, Stetson Coll. of Law, 1983; postgrad., U. Oxford, 1983, U. Thessaloniki, Greece, 1983. Cert. tchr. in law, social scis., Fla. Claims rep. Social Security Adminstrn., Clearwater, Fla., 1973-81; assoc. Battagia, Ross, St. Petersburg, Fla., 1984, Anderson, Thorn, Grose, Quesada, Clearwater, 1984-86; pvt. practice Tampa, Fla., 1986—; active Tampa Bay Estate Planning Coun., 1994—. Bd. dirs. Alzheimer Assn., Tampa, 1991—; bd. overseers Stetson Coll. of Law, St. Petersburg, Fla., 1989—; adv. bd. U. S. Fla. Ctr. for Free Enterprise, Tampa, 1992—. Named to Outstanding Young Women of Am., 1983; recipient acad. scholarship Stetson Coll. of Law, 1981. Mem. Stetson Lawyer's Assn. (pres. 1989-91, v.p. 1988), Bus. and Profl. Women (chair various coms., Woman of Yr. 1994), ABA, Fla. Bar Assn., Hillsborough Bar Assn., Clearwater Bar Assn., Fla. Assn. Women Lawyers, Hillsborough Assn. of Women Lawyers. Office: 3804 N B St Tampa FL 33609

WERNER, GLORIA S., librarian; b. Seattle, Dec. 12, 1940; d. Irving L. and Eva H. Stolzoff; m. Newton Davis Werner, June 30, 1963; 1 son, Adam Davis. BA, Oberlin Coll., 1961; ML, U. Wash., 1962; postgrad. UCLA, 1962-63. Reference librarian UCLA Biomed Library, 1963-64, asst. head pub. services dept., 1964-66, head pub. services dept., head reference div., 1966-72, asst. biomed. librarian public services, 1972-77, asso. biomed. librarian, 1977-78, biomed. librarian, assoc. univ. librarian, dir. Pacific S.W. regional Med. Library Service, 1979-83; asst. dean library services UCLA Sch. Medicine, 1980-83; assoc. univ. librarian for tech. services, 1983-89, dir. libraries, acting univ. librarian, 1989-90, univ. librarian, 1990—; adj. lectr. UCLA Grad. Sch. Library and Info. Sci., 1977-83. Editor, Bull. Med. Library Assn., 1979-82, asso. editor, 1974-79; mem. editorial bd. Ann. Stats. Med. Sch. Libraries U.S. and Can., 1980-83; mem. accrediting commn. Western Assn. Schs. and Colls., N.W. Assn. Schs. and Colls. Mem. ALA, Assn. Rsch. Librs. (bd. dirs. 1993—). Office: UCLA Rsch Libr Libr Adminstrv Office 405 Hilgard Ave Los Angeles CA 90024-1575

WERNER, JOANNE LOUCILLE, financial executive; b. Midland, Mich., Jan. 20, 1940; d. Ewald George and Martha (Yuchlal) W. AAS, Ea. Nazarene Coll., Quincy, Mass., 1972; BAS, Boston U., 1977; MBA, Suffolk U., Boston, 1979. Prog. asst. Dept. Def., Washington, 1966-68, budget analyst, 1968-70; budget analyst Dept. of Navy, Washington, 1970-72; budget analyst GSA, Boston, 1972-77, sr. budget analyst, 1977-79; sr. fin. mgmt. specialist HUD, Boston, 1979-90; founder, dir., coord. Network Industry Leaders Internat., Quincy, Mass., 1990-93; ind. contractor courier svcs. courier svcs., 1994—. Editor newsletter Baystatement, 1980-81. With USNR. Sioux Falls Coll. grantee, 1959; named Sailor of Yr. USNR, 1985. Mem. Am. Soc. Women Accts. (bd. dirs. 1986-88, 90-91). Home and Office: 1449 Quincy Shore Dr Quincy MA 02169-2334

WERNER, LUCEILLE MARIE, early childhood educator; b. Streator, Ill., Oct. 26, 1925; d. Louis Lester and Ina Elizabeth (Sundberg) Gleim; m. Vincent Arthur Werner, Oct. 26, 1946; children: Philip Louis, John Vincent. BS, Ill. State U., Normal, 1959, MS, 1961; postgrad., Northwestern U., Columbia U. Tchr. LaSalle County Schs., Grand Ridge, Ill., 1944-47; instr. LaSalle (Ill.)-Peru Jr. Coll., 1952-55; tchr. Livingston Counties (Ill.) Elem. Schs., 1952-60; curriculum coord. Woodland Unit 5 Schs., Streator, Ill., 1960-67, Ill. State Office Edn., Springfield, 1967-74; nat. dir. nat diffusion network program Adminstrn. Dist. Peotone (Ill.) 207U, 1974—; asst. prof. Ill. State U., Normal, 1973-85; owner Farming Operation, Livingston and LaSalle Counties, 1974—. Mem. Streator Study Club, 1985—, past pres.; vol. Salvation Army & Food Pantry, Streator, 1994—. Mem. Internat. Profl. Orgn. (pres. 1989-92, cert. Merit 1992), Nat. Assn. Supervising and Curriculum Devel. (com. mem. 1976-77), Nat. Diffusion Network Profl. Orgn. (com. mem. 1985-93, Hon. award 1992), Ill. Assn. Supervision and Curriculum Devel. (pres., v.p. 1976-78, Pres. award 1978), LaSalle County Hist. Soc. (v.p. 1993-94, bd. dirs. 1992—). Office: Curriculum Svcs 114 N 2d St Box 956 Peotone IL 60468

WERNICK, SANDIE MARGOT, advertising and public relations executive; b. Tampa, Sept. 13, 1944; d. Nathan and Sylvia (Bienstock) Rothstein. BA in English, U. Fla., 1966. Tchr. English Miami Beach (Fla.) Sr. High Sch., 1967; adminstrv. asst. pub. rels. Bozell & Jacobs, Inc., N.Y.C., 1968-69; asst. to dir. pub. rels. Waldorf-Astoria, N.Y.C., 1969-70; dir. advt. and pub. rels. Hyatt on Union Square, San Francisco, 1974-82; pres. Wernick Mktg. Group, San Francisco, 1982—. Bd. mem. Nat. Kidney Assn., San Francisco, 1985-87; advisor Swords to Plowshares, San Francisco, 1988-89. Recipient Award of Merit, San Francisco Advt. and Cable Car Awards, 1979, Award of Excellence, San Francisco Art Dirs, 1978, awards Am. Hotel and Motel Assn., 1981, 82, awards of excellence San Francisco Publicity Club, 1990. Mem. Women in Commnunications (bd. mem. 1987-89), Am. Women in Radio and TV (bd. mem. 1989-90), Pub. Rels. Soc. Am., San Francisco Publicity Club (pres. 1989), Variety Club, Profl. Bus. Women's Assn., Calif. Pacific Med. Ctr. (aux. 1988—). Democrat. Jewish. Home: 1690 Broadway St Apt 705 San Francisco CA 94109-2419 Office: Wernick Marketing Group 444 Market St Ste 1125 San Francisco CA 94111

WERT, LINDA ARLENE, kindergarten educator; b. York, Pa., June 26, 1948; d. Daniel O. Sr. and Teresa M. (Phillips) Bumbaugh; m. Gregory L. Wert, May 23, 1970. BS, Elizabethtown Coll., 1970. Cert. tchr., Pa. Tchr. kindergarten Red Lion (Pa.) Area Sch. Dist., 1969—, elem. computer coord., 1985-86; mem. tchr. adv. bd. York campus Pa. State U., 1991—. Mem. Aldersgate United Meth. Ch., York, 1975—; mem. Fools for Christ clown ministry, 1989—. Recipient Presdl. award for Excellence in Sci. and Math. Teaching NSF, 1992, 93. Mem. ASCD, Pa. Coun. Tchrs. Math., Nat. Coun. Tchrs. Math., Red Lion Area Math. Com., York Quilters Guild, NEA, Pa. State Edn. Assn., Red Lion Area Edn. Assn. Home: 363 Holyoke Dr York PA 17402-5013 Office: North Hopewell Winterstown Elem Sch RR 3 Box 241 Red Lion PA 17356-9451

WERT, LUCILLE MATHENA, librarian, educator; b. Sioux City, Iowa, May 24, 1919; d. Arthur Edmund and Anna Sarah (Harrington) Mathena; m. Charles Allen Wert, Sept. 7, 1942; children: John Arthur, Sara Ann. B.A., Morningside Coll., 1942; B.S. in L.S, Simmons Coll., 1945; M.A., U. Ill., 1963, Ph.D., 1969. Asst. librarian elec. engring. library M.I.T., Cambridge, 1944-45; math., physics and astronomy librarian U. Iowa, Iowa City, 1946-48, U. Chgo., 1948-51; research asst. Grad. Sch. Library Sci., U. Ill., Urbana, 1964-65; research assoc. Grad. Sch. Library Sci., U. Ill., 1966-67, vis. lectr., 1968-69, research asst. prof., 1969-71, research assoc. prof., dir. library research center, 1971-75, assoc. prof., 1975-77, prof. library adminstrn., chemistry librarian, 1977-86, asst. dir. pub. svcs. for phys. scis. & engring., 1981-86, emeritus prof., 1986—; library cons. Council for Advancement of Small Colls. Editor: Jour. Edn. for Librarianship, 1976-80. Mem. U. Ill. Pres.'s Coun., 1993—; sustaining fellow Art Inst. Chgo., 1987—. Recipient Disting. Alumni award Morningside Coll., 1992; U.S. Office of Edn. small rsch. project grantee, 1968-69. Mem. ALA (com. on accreditation site visitors pool 1972-92), Assn. Coll. and Rsch. Librs., Libr. Adminstrn. and Mgmt. Assn., Assn. Libr. and Info. Sci. Edn. (dir. 1974-77), Am. Chem. Soc. (liaison to Spl. Libr. Assn., mem. editorial bd. CHEMTECH 1987—, chair 1992, chem. info. div awards com. 1988-91), Am. Soc. Info. Scis. (chmn. spl. interest group biology and chemistry 1985-86, spl. interest group steering com. 1987-89), Spl. Librs. Assn. (chmn. chemistry div. 1986-87), Beta Phi Mu. Presbyterian. Office: 1708 W Green St Champaign IL 61821-3721

WERTANEN, KAREN ESTHER MARIA, nurse, public health administrator; b. Ishpeming, Mich., Oct. 3, 1941; d. Everett A. and Elmi A. (Makela) Annelin; m. Richard E. Wertanen, July 21, 1962; children: Pamela Smith, Scott, Brenda Gelhar. Diploma in nursing, St. Luke's Hosp., 1962; B of Nursing, No. Mich. U., 1994. RN, Wis., Mich. Operating rm. nurse St. Luke's Hosp., Marquette, Mich., 1962-63, instr., 1963-64; staff nurse Florence (Wis.) Villa Nursing Home, 1971-73; dir. pub. health nursing Florence County Nurse's Office, 1973—. Sec./treas. Florence County unit Am. Cancer Soc., 1974—. Mem. Wis. Pub. Health Assn., Wis. Counties Pub. Health Affiliate, Sch. Nurses of Wis., Wis. Conf. Local Pub. Health Ofcls. (treas. no. region 1991—), Phi Kappa Phi. Presbyterian. Office: Florence County Health Dept PO Box 17 Florence WI 54121-0017

WERTHEIM, SALLY HARRIS, academic administrator, dean, education educator; b. Cleve., Nov. 1, 1931; d. Arthur I. and Anne (Manheim) Harris; m. Stanley E. Wertheim, Aug. 6, 1950; children: Kathryn, Susan B., Carole J. BS, Flora Stone Mather Coll., 1953; MA, Case Western Res. U., 1967, PhD, 1970. Cert. elem. and secondary edn. tchr., Ohio. Social worker U. Hosps., Cleve., 1953-54; tchr. Fairmount Temple Religious Sch., Cleve., 1957-72; mem. faculty John Carroll U., Cleve., 1969—, prof., 1980—, dean grad. sch., rsch. coord., 1986-93, acad. v.p., 1993-94; dean Grad. Sch., coord. faculty rsch. John Carrol U., Cleve., 1994—; cons. in field; cons. Jennings Found., Cleve.; chmn. sch. com. Cleve. Commn. on Higher Edn., 1987—. Contbr. articles to profl. jours. Sec. Cuyahoga County Mental Health Bd., Cleve., 1978-82; pres. Jewish Family Svc. Assn., Cleve. 1974-77, Montefiore Home for Aged, Cleve., 1987-90, bd. dirs. Mt. Sinai Med. Ctr., Cleve., 1984-93, Cleve. Edn. Fund, 1992-94; v.p. Jewish Cmty. Fedn., 1988-91, bd. trustees, 1992—; chairperson edn. com. Cleve. Found. Commn. on Poverty, 1988-93, pres. bd. trustees, 1994—, Cleve. Comty. Bldg. Initiative, 1993—, United Way Svcs., 1994—. Named One of 100 Most Influential Women, Cleve. mag., 1983; recipient award Jewish Community Fedn.; grantee Jennings Found., 1984-87, Cleve. and Gund Found., 1987-90, Lilly Found., 1988. Mem. Am. Assn. Colls. for Tchrs. Edn. (bd. dirs. 1982-85), Ohio Assn. Colls. for Tchrs. Edn. (pres. 1981-83), Coun. of Grad. Schs. Office: John Carroll U Grad Sch Cleveland OH 44118

WERTHEIMER, LINDA, broadcaster. Disting. grad., Wellesley Coll., 1965. Congl. corr. Nat. Pub. Radio, Washington, 1971-76, polit. corr., 1976-89, host All Things Considered newsmag., 1989—. Recipient Alfred I. duPond-Columbia U. spl. citation, 1978, Corp. Pub. Broadcasting award, 1988. Office: Nat Pub Radio All Things Considered 635 Massachusetts Ave NW Washington DC 20001

WERTS, JOSEPHINE STARR, artist; b. Osage, Iowa, Aug. 5, 1903; d. William Jessie and Edna Lavinia (Wheeland) Starr; m. Leo Robert Werts, June 15, 1929 (div. 1947); 1 child, Barbara Werts Blatt. BA in Phys. Edn., Iowa State Tchrs. Coll., 1926; postgrad., Art Inst. Chgo., 1945, 46, U. Chgo., 1945, 46; MA in Fine Arts, U. So. Calif., 1961. One-woman shows include Cambria (Calif.) Coast Gallery, Ten Directions Gallery, Baywood Park, Calif., San Luis Obispo (Calif.) Art Ctr.; group shows include San Luis Obispo Art Ctr., U. So. Calif., Oakland (Calif.) Art Mus., Pasadena (Calif.) Art Mus., M.H. de Young Meml. Mus., San Francisco, Richmond (Calif.) Art Mus., Otis Art Inst., L.A., Long Beach (Calif.) Mus. Art, La Jolla (Calif.) Art Ctr., Ten Directions Gallery, Baywood Park, Calif., 1994; represented in permanent collections Va. Mus. Fine Arts, Richmond, U. So. Calif. Fisher Gallery, also pvt. collections. Recipient award Palos Verdes Community Arts Assn., 1954, 57. Mem. Nat. Watercolor Soc. (bd. dirs. 1965, corr. sec. 1965, D'Arches award 1969), Watercolor U.S.A. Honor Soc. (Jurors award 1990), Ctrl. Coast Printmakers Soc., San Luis Art Assn. Democrat. Home and Studio: 2050 Emmons Rd Cambria CA 93428

WERTZ, ELIZABETH MARIE, critical care nurse, administrator; b. Ft. Worth, July 31, 1956; d. William B. and Helen Anne (Stiffler) Hodgson; m. Patrick L. Wertz, May 7, 1983; children: Patrick F., Amanda Elizabeth, Ashley Marie. Diploma, St. Francis Gen. Hosp., Pitts., 1980; BSN, Carlow Coll., Pitts., 1993; postgrad. in Pub. Mgmt., Carnegie Mellon U., 1993—. RN, Pa.; CCRN; cert. CPA, ACLS instr., PALS instr., ENPC instr., PHTLS instr., pre-hosp. RN, ACLS affiliate faculty. Med. sec., asst. Cardiovascular Assocs., Pitts., 1976-78; nurse on cardiovascular ICU St. Francis Gen. Hosp., 1980-84, 91-93; flight nurse Allegheny Gen. Hosp. Life Flight, Pitts., 1986-88; paramedic coord. Allegheny Gen. Hosp., 1984-87; mgr. office of prehosp. care Allegheny Gen. Hosp., 1987-93, mgr. life support tng. ctr., 1993—. Co-chair emergency med. svc. for children adv. com., nursing adv. com., mem. EMT-paramedic adv. com. Pa. Emergency Health Svcs. Coun., 1984; mem. Nat. Safe Kids Campagin; mem. profl. adv. bd. Epilepsy Found. Western Pa.; mem. aux. and various coms. Easter Seal Soc. Allegheny County; mem. Pa. Protection and Adv. Devel. Disabilities Coun.; bd. dirs. Allegheny County Emergency Med. Svc. Coun., Inc.; vol. Wilkins-Churchill Rescue One Ambulance Svc. Recipient Mildred K. Fincke, RN, Emergency Nursing award Pa. Emergency Health Svcs. Coun., 1990. Mem. AACN, Nat. Emergency Med. Technicians (chair nat. pre-hosp. trauma life support com., bd. dirs., bd. govs., Leadership award 1988), Nat. Flight Nurses Assn., Am. Trauma Soc., Emergency Nurses Assn., Emergency Med. Svcs. Inst., Pa. Emergency Med. Svcs. Assn., Keystone Safety Belt Network. Home: 828 Wellington Dr Mars PA 16046 Office: Allegheny Gen Hosp Life Support Tng Ctr 320 E North Ave Pittsburgh PA 15212-9986

WERTZ, JEAN LOUISE, artist, candy company owner; b. Lebanon, Pa., Sept. 15, 1953; d. William and Josephine Bessie (Seiger) W. AA in Liberal Arts, Wesley Coll., 1973; BS in Art Edn., Kutztown U., 1978; postgrad., Vt. Studio Sch., 1990. Image assembler Lebanon Valley Offset, Annville, Pa., 1980-84; candymaker, sec. Wertz Candies, Lebanon, 1984—; guest lectr. Harrisburg Area C.C., Lebanon, 1992-93, AAUW, 1994. Exhibited in one-woman shows at Lebanon Valley Coll., Annville, Pa., 1987, Tangerine Fine Arts, Harrisburg, 1989, Harrisburg Area C.C., 1992, York Art Assn., 1994; group shows include Lebanon Valley Coll., 1990, Tremellon Gallery, Lancaster, Pa., 1990, Aart Vark Gallery, Phila., 1990, Greater Harrisburg Juried Mus. Show at State Mus. Harrisburg, 1991, Art Assn. Harrisburg, 1989, Elizabethtown Coll., 1992, B&S Gallery, Williamsport, Pa., 1993; in collections at Fulton Bank, Tangerine Fine Art. Bd. dirs. Lebanon Valley Coun. on Arts, 1990—, chair artist lecture series, 1990-93, sec., 1994—; mem. Friends of Colonial Theatre, Lebanon, 1992—. Recipient 2 Grumbacher Gold medallions, 1991, 92, numerous other awards for art. Mem. Art Assn. Harrisburg (numerous 1st place and best of show awards). Home: 603 Canal St Lebanon PA 17046

WESALA, CONNIE LYNN, therapist; b. Enid, Okla., Nov. 20, 1945; d. Lewis J. and Wanda R. (Hughes) Poole; m. Wayne D. Wesala, Mar. 17, 1973 (div. Aug. 1989). BA, Cen. State U., 1967; MS, Winona State U., 1971. Cert. sch. tchr., counselor, community coll. tchr. Program mgr. YWCA, Rochester, Minn., 1971-73; counselor Rochester, 1979-81; sml. bus. owner Scottsdale, Ariz., 1988-91; counselor Scottsdale, 1988-90; counselor, trainer Scottsdale Prevention Inst., 1990—; mktg. profl. Scottsdale Prevention Inst., 1991-92. Contbr. articles to local publs. Vol. coord. Scottsdale Schs., 1989-90; mem. Visioning Process, City of Scottsdale, 1992; mem. and coms. Scottsdale Leadership, 1993—; mem. Scottsdale Symphony, 1992-94. Mem. Am. Counseling Assn., Am. Mental Health Assn. Democrat. Presbyterian. Office: Scottsdale Prevention Inst 7428 E Stetson # 215 Scottsdale AZ 85251

WESCHLER, ANITA, sculptor, painter; b. N.Y.C.; d. J. Charles and Hulda Eva (Mayer) W.; married. del. U.S. Com. Internat. Assn. Art, Fine Arts Fedn., N.Y. Exhibited Met. Mus. Art, Mus. Modern Art, Art Inst. Chgo., Phila. Mus. Internat., Am. Acad., Inst. Arts and Letters, Bklyn. Mus., Newark Mus., Hofstra Mus., U. Conn., Carnegie Inst. Internat., Whitney Mus. Annuals, Storm King Art Ctr., mus. and galleries throughout U.S. and Japan; represented in permanent collections U. Pa., Michael Wolfson Found., Miami, Fla., Met. Mus. Art, Syracuse U., Butler Art Inst., Whitney Mus., Norfolk Mus., Brandeis U., Middlebury Coll., Amherst Coll., Yale U., Wichita State Mus., SUNY-Binghamton, U. Iowa, U. Nebr., La Salle U., Pa. Acad. Fine Arts, Insts. for Achievement of Human Potential in Pa., Italy, and Brazil, Art Students League; one-man shows include Birmingham (Ala.) Mus. Art, Main Library, Winston-Salem, N.C., U. Wis., Milw., Miami Beach Art Ctr., Tel Fair Acad., Savannah, Ga., Columbia (S.C.) Mus., U. N.C.-Chapel Hill, Stover Mill Gallery, Erwinna, Pa., Suffolk Art Mus., N.Y., Stony Brook, N.Y., also 50 traveling and stationary shows in N.Y.C. and nationwide, 1993; exhibited in over 500 shows; creator plastic resins and fiberglass as sculpture medium (bonded bronze), synthetic glazes as painting medium; author: poetry book Nightshade, A Sculptor's Summary. Recipient prizes Corcoran Gallery, San Francisco Mus., Am. Fedn. Arts Traveling Show, Montclair Art Mus.; fellow MacDowell Colony, Yaddo. Mem. Archtl. League Sculptors Guild (past bd. dirs., treas.), Nat. Assn. Women

Artists, Nat. Mus. Women in the Arts, Artist Craftsmen N.Y., Fedn. Modern Painters and Sculptors. Address: 136 Waverly Pl New York NY 10014

WESELY, YOLANDA THEREZA, retired sociologist, marketing professional, researcher; b. São Paulo, Brazil, Nov. 9, 1927; came to U.S., 1946; d. Richard Milton and Etelvina (Pacheco E Silva) Pyles; m. Edwin Joseph Wesely, July 1, 1950 (div. 1990); children: Marissa C., Adrienne Lee. BA in Math., Barnard Coll., 1950; MA in Sociology, Columbia U., 1968, PhD in Sociology with honors, 1975. CLU, 1984. With The Equitable, N.Y.C., 1974-76, dir. spl. studies, 1976-78, exec. asst. to chmn. and vice chmn. of the bd., 1978-79, dir. market research, 1979-84, asst. v.p. market rsch., 1984-88, ret.; co-founder Sociologists in Bus. Bd. dirs. Westchester Older Women's League, 1989-92; vice chairperson bd. dirs. Union Theol. Sem., N.Y.C., 1980-88, chair nominating com., 1984, com. on divestiture of investments in South Africa; trustee Scarsdale Congl. Ch., 1989-91, moderator, 1992-94), dir. Westchester Civil Liberties Union, 1991-94. Mem. Older Women's League, Phi Beta Kappa. Democrat. Congregationalist. Home: Scarsdale Chateaux Apt 6-J Scarsdale NY 10583-4124

WESINGER, SUSAN BETH, advertising executive, small business owner; b. Mpls., Apr. 18, 1955; d. Shayel Morton and Sylvia (Glass) Hochman; m. Merritt Louis Weisinger, Sept. 10, 1978; childen: Aaron Jason, Ethan Merritt, Elizabeth Sue. BS, U. So. Calif., 1976; MBA, Pepperdine U., 1978. Cert. advt. specialist Specialty Advt. Assn. Internat., Irving, Tex., 1982. Mgmt. trainee Mercury Savs. and Loan Assn., Huntington Beach, Calif., 1975-76; pres. A.J. Products, Inc., Newport Beach, Van Nuys, Calif., 1974-85; acct. mgr. Creative Gift Svcs., Van Nuys, Calif., 1985-89; br. mgr. Walter W. Cribbins, Chatsworth, Calif., 1989-90; ind. rep. Geiger Bros., Northridge, Calif., 1990—; account mgr. A1 Mktg., 1994—; owner Art N Point. Author: Meeting Planner's Guide to Promotions. Mem. L.A. Bar Assn. (arbitrator 1988-92), Admark, Danville (Calif.) C. of C. Home: 34 Cameron Ct Danville CA 94506-2051 Office: Art 'N' Paint 105 E Town Country Danville CA 94506

WESLEY, RUBY LAVERNE, nursing educator, administrator, researcher; b. Detroit, Nov. 25, 1949; d. David Williams and Leatrice (Gragg) Williams; 1 child, Nathaniel Rogers Wesley III. Diploma, Providence Hosp. Sch. Nursing, Southfield, Mich., 1971; BS in Nursing, Wayne State U., Detroit, 1974, MEd, 1977; PhD, U. Md., Balt., 1987. Clin. instr. U. Tenn. Sch. Nursing, 1978-79; community health nursing instr. U. Md., Balt., 1984-85; assoc. prof. Bowie State U., 1985-89; asst. dean Coppin State Coll., Balt., 1989-90; asst. prof. Wayne State U., 1991—; nurse researcher Rehab. Inst. Mich., 1992; dir. nursing practice Rehab. Inst. Mich., Detroit, 1992-93, dir. nursing, 1993—. Henry C. Welcome fellow, 1986-87; Nat. Inst. Disability and Rehab. rsch. fellow, 1991-92. Mem. Am. Assn. Spinal Cord Injury Nurses (chair rsch. com.). Home: 2146 Bryanston Crescent St Detroit MI 48207-3818

WESLEY, VIRGINIA ANNE, real estate property manager; b. Seattle, Apr. 29, 1951; d. Albert William and Mary Louise (Heusser) W. BA in Speech, U. Hawaii, Hilo, 1978. Cert. property mgr. Mgr. office, traffic Sta. KIPA-Radio, Hilo, 1972-74; reporter West Hawaii Today, Kailua-Kona, Hawaii, 1974; mgr. office U. Hawaii, Hilo, 1975-78; dir. property mgmt. First City Equities, Seattle, 1978-88, Winvest Devel. Corp., Seattle, 1988-89; with Quadrant Corp, Bellevue, Wash., 1992—; instr. Bellevue (Wash.) Community Coll., 1982-85. Bd. dirs. Mayor's Small Bus. Task Force, Seattle, 1981-83, 1st Hill Improvement Assn., Seattle, 1982—; active Goodwill Games, Seattle, 1990, Kauri Investments, Ltd., Seattle, 1991-92. Mem. Inst. Real Estate Mgmt., Internat. Coun. Shopping Ctrs., Comml. Real Estate Women, Women's Bus. Exch., Seattle-King County Bd. Realtors, Big Island Press Club, Phi Kappa Phi. Home: 906 Lake Washington Blvd S Seattle WA 98144

WESOLOWSKI, KAREN SUSAN, physical therapist; b. Riverside, Calif., May 27, 1965; d. Joseph and Mary Helen (Greco) W. AA, Riverside City Coll., 1985; BS in Phys. Therapy, Loma Linda U., 1988. Phys. therapist Calif. Children Svcs. Riverside County Health Dept., 1988-92; co-owner A.D.L. Rehab. Svcs., Redlands, Calif., 1992-93; rehab. dir. Manor Care Nursing and Rehab. Ctr., Hemet, Calif., 1993—; owner Sunrise Rehab. Svcs., Corona, Calif., 1993—; physical therapist Circle City Fitness and Wellness Ctr., Corona, 1991-93. Mem. Am. Phys. Therapy Assn., Greenpeace, People for Ethical Treatment of Animals, World Vision, World Wildlife Fund. Democrat. Roman Catholic. Office: Manor Care Nursing & Rehab 1717 W Stetson Ave Hemet CA 92545-6882

WESOLOWSKI, SISTER LORRAINE MARY, religious order member; b. Pitts., Feb. 2, 1942; d. Anthony Paul and Laura G. (Wisniewski) W. BS in Edn., Carlow Coll., Pitts., 1964; MA in Montessori Edn., Xavier U., Cin., 1972; cert., Montessori Tchr. Edn. Ctr., Boston, 1978; postgrad., Loyola U., New Orleans, 1984. Joined Order of St. Francis, Roman Cath. Ch., 1959. Elem. tchr. Dioceses of Pitts. and Greensburg, Pa., 1963-76; tchr. Mt. Lebanon (Pa.) Montessori Sch., 1978-84; adminstrv. asst., writer Crosspoint Comm./The Comm. Works, Pitts., 1984-89; dir. comm. Adrian (Mich.) Dominican Sisters, 1989—. Contbr. articles to various religious papers and mags. Home: 1401 Argyle Dr Adrian MI 49221-1843 Office: Adrian Dominican Sisters 1257 E Siena Heights Dr Adrian MI 49221-1755

WESSENDORF KNAU, SUANA LE, special education educator; b. Storm Lake, Iowa, Nov. 3, 1953; d. Billie and Grace Arlene (Piercy) Wessendorf; m. Gregory Charles Knau, July 27, 1991. BS in Edn., U. S.D., 1975; MEd, U. Ariz., 1980, postgrad., 1983-87; postgrad., Iowa State U., 1990—. Cert. tchr., Iowa, Ariz. Spl. edn. tchr. Cherokee (Iowa) Sch. Dist., 1975-77, Ctrs. of Youth Devel. and Achievement, Tucson, 1978-79, Amphitheater Sch. Dist., Tucson, 1979-80, Tucson Unified Sch. Dist., 1980-89, Ames (Iowa) Sch. Dist., 1989—; dir. mktg. Mktg. Concepts, Tucson, 1977-78; master trainer Tucson Unified Sch. Dist., 1987-90; dir. Tucson Very Spl. Arts Festival, 1980-85; crisis interventionist, mem. Models of Teaching Cadre, Ames Sch. Dist.; mem. spl. edn. adv. bd. Iowa State U., 1993—. Mem., chair Tucson Commn. of Arts and Culture, 1980-84; mem. Tucson/Pima Arts Coun., 1984-89. Recipient Recognition for Women Who Care award Gov. of Ariz., 1985, Cert. of Appreciation, Pima County Juvenile Ct., 1986. Mem. Coun. for Exceptional Children (1st v.p. 1991-92, pres.-elect 1992-93, pres. 1993-94, immediate past pres. 1994—), Iowa Coun. for Exceptional Children (pres. 1991—, coord. Political Action Network Coord. 1993—), Iowa Coun. for Children with Behavioral Disorders (pres. 1991-92), Alpha Delta Kappa (pres. 1994—). Congregationalist. Home: 1208 Truman Pl Ames IA 50010-4260 Office: Ames Sch Dist 120 S Kellogg Ave Ames IA 50010-6719

WESSNER, DEBORAH MARIE, telecommunications executive, computer consultant; b. St. Louis, Aug. 15, 1950; d. John George and Mary Jane (Beetz) Eyerman; m. Brian Paul Wessner, Sept. 15, 1972; children: Krystin, David. BA in Math. and Chemistry, St. Louis U., 1972; M Computer Info. Sci., U. New Haven, 1980. Statistitian Armstrong Rubber Co., New Haven, 1972-74; programmer analyst Sikorsky div. United Techs., Stratford, Conn., 1974-77; project engr. GE, Bridgeport, Conn., 1977-79; software mgr. GE, Arlington, Va., 1979-81; mgr. software ops. Satellite Bus. Systems, McLean, Va., 1981-83; v.p. ops. DAMA Telecommunications, Rockville, Md., 1983-87; dir. network ops. and adminstrn. Data Gen. Network Svcs., Rockville, 1987-91; dir. bus. ops. Sprint Internat., Reston, Va., 1991-92; v.p. network adminstrn. Citicorp, Washington, 1992-93; v.p. network info. svcs. Citicorp, Reston, Va., 1994—; assoc., cons. KDB Assocs., Columbia, Md., 1986—. Mem. Am. Bus. Women's Assn., NAFE. Office: Citicorp Washington DC 20001

WEST, DELOURIS JEANNE, project management company executive; b. Durham, N.C., July 13, 1943; d. James Hayward and Daisy Lilly (Penwell) O'Neal; m. Larry Alexander West, Aug. 10, 1961; children: Gregory Alexander, Dedrea Lynne, Brandon James. Grad. high sch., Mebane, N.C. Inventory control clk. Avon Products, Inc., Atlanta, 1962-67; dir., tchr. United Meth. Kindergarten, Woodstock, Ga., 1972-77; owner, mgr. Gift Emporium, Roswell, Ga., 1977-79; exec. dir. North Fulton C. of C., Roswell, 1979-88; pres. Project Ptnrs., Inc., Roswell, 1988—; founder, dir. Environ. Edn. Ctr., Alpharetta, Ga., 1991; founder, adminstr. Project Ripple Water Quality Program, 1991, Green Sch. Program, 1990; mem. Fulton County Soil and Water Conservation Dist. Bd.; adv. bd. Alpharetta Greenways System, Ga. DNR/EPD Stream Watch. Author: The Acorn, 1972; editor Nova News, 1966, The Acorn, 1972, News and View, 1980-88, Clean and Green Report, 1990—; newspaper columnist Rainbows and Butterflies, 1973. Active numerous civic orgns., including mem. Fulton County Devel. Bd., Fulton County Metro Pvt. Industry Coun., Chattahoochee River Corridor Adv. Coun.; bd. dirs. YMCA, North Fulton Regional Hosp., 1983-86, Chattahoochee Theater, 1990-91; chmn. vocat. com. Milton H.S., Alpharetta, Ga., 1987; trustee Chattahoochee Nature Ctr., 1988-92; chmn., founder North Fulton Ednl. Consortium, 1987-90; candidate County Commn., 1986, Ga. Ho. of Reps., 1989; exec. dir. Alpharetta Clean & Beautiful Commn., 1990—. Recipient Outstanding Layman award Roswell Jaycees, 1982, Supt.'s award Fulton County Bd. Edn. 1983, Perserverance award Am. Med. Internat., 1982, Appreciation award Adopt-A-Sch., 1986, svc. Appreciation award North Fulton Regional Hosp., 1987, Community Builder award Masons Lodge 739, 1987, Keys to Cities of Roswell and Alpharetta, 1990, Appreciation award Dept. Natural Resources, 1994; named One of Atlanta's 100, Sta. WRMM, 1985, One of Ten Most Powerful People in North Fulton County, Atlanta Jour. and Constn., 1986. Mem. Am. Water Works Assn., Groundwater Found. (charter mem.), Nat. Coun. for Urban Econ. Devel., Ga. C. of C. Execs. Assn., Ga. Indsl. Developers Assn., Roswell Hist. Soc., Alpharetta Hist. Soc., Ga. Clean and Beautivul Exec. Dirs. Assn., Nat. Arbor Day Found., Civitans (co-founder, charter v.p. Roswell 1982-83, Pres.'s award 1983). Methodist. Office: EEC Ste A-1 131 Roswell St Alpharetta GA 30201

WEST, ELIZABETH PRYOR, guidance counselor, education specialist; b. Nashville, Mar. 27, 1964; d. Joseph Albert and Carol Ann (Collins) P.; m. William Feemster West, Aug. 6, 1988. BA in Psychology and Fine Arts, U. Miss., 1986, MEd in Guidance and Counseling, 1988. Rsch. asst. in dept. psychology U. Miss. Med. Ctr., Jackson, 1985, bd. dirs., 1991—; rsch. asst. VA Hosp., Jackson, 1985; asst. instr. effective studies U. Miss., Oxford, 1987-88, adminstrv. asst., counselor parent-student support program, 1987-88; student-peer vol. Bessie Speed Drug and Alcohol Ctr., Univ., Miss., 1986-88; coord. student workshops Student Devel. Ctr., University, Miss., 1987; coord student workshops Student Devel. Ctr., Univ., Miss., 1988; patient coord. Charter Hosp. Jackson, 1988; vocat. rehab. counselor II Miss. Methodist Rehab. Ctr., Jackson, 1988-89; mental health counselor, support group leader, cir. breakers program Family Innovations, League City, Tex., 1990-91; dist.-wide counselor, dist. test coord. Rankin County Sch. Dist., Brandon, Miss., 1991-94, drug edn. specialist, 1991-94, mem. alternative edn. ctr. enrollment selection bd., 1993-94; sr. edn. specialist Office of Student Assessment, Miss. State Dept. Edn., 1994—. Mem. Am. Counseling Assn., Am. Sch. Counselor Assn., Am. Assn. Counseling and Devel., Am. Coll. Personnel Assn., Nat. Head Injury Found., Nat. Rehab. Orgn., Miss. Head Injury Assn., Miss. Rehab. Orgn., Miss. Counseling Assn., Student Dental Spouses Auxiliary (v.p. 1992-93, sec. 1993-94), Jr. League of Jackson, The Symphony League of Jackson, Phi Mu Alumni Assn. Jackson (pub. rels., sec. 1991-92).

WEST, GLENDA MURL, bookkeeper; b. Kosciusko, Miss., Nov. 2, 1947; d. Dalton Elvis and Essie Murl (Thompson) Graham; m. Oscar David West Jr., June 23, 1963; children: Glynis June, David Antony, Timothy Dalton. A in Acctg., N.W. Coll., Senatobia, Miss., 1967; postgrad., Internat. Coll., 1980; BS in Acctg., N.W. Coll., Southaven, Miss., 1982, postgrad., 1982; postgrad., Northwest C.C., 1993. Lic. cosmotologist, Tenn., 1967; lic. realtor, Miss., 1993. Cosmetologist Whitehaven Coiffures, Memphis, 1968-73; bus. mgr. Imperial Mfg. Co., Memphis, 1973-88; bookkeeper Hess Environ. Svcs., Inc., Memphis, 1988-93; sr. acct. Thomas & Betts, Memphis, 1993—. Cons. Southaven Ban Booster Club, 1992—. Mem. NAFE, Am. Payroll Assn., Inst. Profl. Bookkeepers (Cert. Merit 1990). Republican. Office: Thomas & Betts 4800 Southridge Blvd Memphis TN 38141

WEST, KAREN SUSANNE, obstetrics nurse, consultant; b. Dayton, Ohio, Nov. 28, 1956; d. Ethel Mae (Martin) Hout; m. Bradley William West, June 12, 1974; children: Jeremie William, Kenneth Duane. AS, Marion (Ohio) Tech. Coll., 1988. RN, N.C., Ohio. RN labor and delivery high risk level II NICU Valdese (N.C.) Gen. Hosp., 1989-91; CNA labor and delivery Morrow County Hosp., Mt. Gilead, Ohio, 1987-88, RN labor and delivery low risk, 1988-89, 91—; mem. RN quality assurance ad. bd., quality improvement adv. bd., insvc. improvement bd. Morrow County Hosp., 1990—. Mem., past pres. Trinity United Meth. Womens Club, Mt. Gilead; past pres. Jubilation Meth. Club, Mt. Gilead; sec. Swim and Dive Commn., Mt. Gilead. Mem. Am. Acad. Pediatrics (lic.), Am. Heart Assn. (lic.), ARC (lic.). Home: 218 South St Mount Gilead OH 43338-1450 Office: Morrow County Hosp 650 W Marion Rd Mount Gilead OH 43338-1056

WEST, KIM DENISE, university administrator; b. Mar. 19, 1957; d. Vaughn Edward and Maryln Margaret (Shults) W. B.A., Skidmore Coll., 1979; M.A., Columbia U., 1983; PhD, U. So. Calif., 1994. Residence hall dir. SUNY-Stony Brook, 1979-81, acting quad dir., 1981-82, complex dir., 1982-83; area coordinator Hofstra U., Hempstead, N.Y., 1983-85; asst. dir. residential life U. So. Calif., L.A., 1985-89, assoc. dir., 1989-90; dir. residence life Calif. Inst. Tech., Pasadena, 1990—; mem. residential life staff devel. com. SUNY-Stony Brook, 1981-83, instr. psychology, 1982-83; instr. ednl. counseling U. So. Calif., 1985-90, mem. student affairs divsn. staff devel. com., 1985-87, chair, 1989-90, mem. AIDS awareness task force, 1988-89, mem. gay and lesbian assembly for student svcs. adv. bd., 1989-90, mem. univ. peer rev. appeals panel, 1989-90; mem. AIDS awareness task force, Calif. Inst. Tech., 1990—, mem. student affairs divsn. staff devel. com., 1991-93; coord. various confs. in field. Sec. Skidmore Coll. Class of 1979, Saratoga Springs, N.Y., 1990—, co-chair reunion com., 1993-94; vol. Spl. Olympics, SUNY-Stony Brook, 1980; vol. All Saints AIDS Svc. Ctr., Pasadena, 1991—; mem. alumni awards com. Skidmore Coll., 1992—; mem. Pasadena Area Colls. Drug and Alcohol Consortium, Pasadena, 1992—; active Check-Out L.A., UCC Tng. Presdl. fellow Leadership Inst. U. So. Calif., 1994-95. Mem. Nat. Assn. Student Pers. Adminstrs. (acad. new profls. 1987), U. So. Calif. Assocs., Phi Delta Kappa. Office: Calif Inst Tech Winnett 115-51 Pasadena CA 91125

WEST, LOIS JEAN, commmunity and public relations executive; b. Forest City, Iowa, June 16, 1939; d. Paul Wesley and Sylvia Hall (Bernice) Kuns; m. Gordon C. West, Aug. 31, 1959 (dec. Feb. 1983); children: Tracy G., Brady P., Ryan J. BS, Mankato (Minn.) State U., 1976; MPA, Harvard U., 1986. News editor Albert Lea (Minn.) Tribune, 1973-78; press asst. to U.S. Senator Dave Durenberger, Mpls., 1978-79; newswriter, editor AP, Mpls., 1980-81; dir. campaign com. Paul Overgard for Gov., Bloomington, Minn., 1982, Cal Ludeman for Gov., Bloomington, 1986; dir. state com. Ind. Reps. Minn., Mpls., 1983-85; press sec. Senator Dave Durenberger, U.S. Senate, Washington, 1987-88, 90; dir. nat. com. Prison Fellowship, Reston, Va., 1989-90; dir. community and pub. rels. Ecolab Inc., St. Paul, 1991—; cons. on politics, organizing, comm., St. Paul, 1992—; v.p. Ecolab Found., 1993—. Editor Centering, 1990; contbr. poems and articles to various publs. Mem. bd. Minn. Pollution Control Agy., St. Paul, 1981-85, chmn. hazardous waste com., 1983-84; exec. com. Justice Fellowship U.S.A., Washington, 1991-92; bd. dirs. Nepal (Kathmandu) Social Svc. Agy., Clarks Grove, Minn., 1992—, Union Gospel Mission, St. Paul, 1992—, United Arts, St. Paul, 1993—, Minn. State Arts Bd., 1994—, Tentmakers, 1994—. Mem. St. Paul Area C. of C. (vice chair pub. affairs 1995—). Office: Ecolab Inc Ecolab Ctr Saint Paul MN 55102

WEST, LORETTA MARIE, underwriter; b. N.Y.C., Feb. 2, 1950; d. James L. and Alice (Richardson) W. AB, Washington Coll., Chestertown, Md., 1972. CPCU; cert. profl. ins. woman. Disbursements cashier Middlesex Ins. Co., Concord, Mass., 1972-76, tech. asst., 1976-78, comml. lines underwriter, 1978-83; sr. comml. lines underwriter Sentry Ins. Co., Concord, 1983-86, large acct. underwriter, 1986-88, sr. large account underwriter, 1988-92; with Hoffman Ins. Svcs., Inc., Wellesley, Mass., 1992—. Mem. Framingham (Mass.) Rep. Town Com., 1988-92; sec. Mass. Fedn. Rep. Women, 1992-94; trustee Prescott Gardens Condos, 1984-88; pres. Greater Precinct 12 Neighborhood Assn., 1990-92; pres. Framingham Rep. Women's Club, 1990-92; co-founder Framington Condominium Coalition, 1992—. Mem. Soc. CPCU, Nat. Assn. Ins. Women, Mass. Assn. Ins. Women (treas. 1990-92, various coms. Middlesex and South Middlesex chpts., co-dir. South Middlesex chpt. 1986-88, bd. dirs. South Middlesex chpt. 1988-90, Woman of Yr. award 1980), Women's Rep. Club Mass., Middlesex Club. Roman Catholic. Home: 6 Prescott St Framingham MA 01701-7511 Office: Hoffman Ins Svcs 200 Linden St Wellesley MA 02181

WEST, MARGARET JEAN, compensation and benefits executive; b. Portsmouth, Ohio, Dec. 14, 1955; d. George Eugene and Bernadette (Ford) Diener; m. George Peter West, Sept. 27, 1980. BA, Miami U., 1978. Cert. employee benefits specialist. Asst. fin. dir. City of Englewood, Ohio, 1978-83, dir. personnel, 1983-87; compensation and benefits mgr. Grandview Hosp., Dayton, Ohio, 1987-89, Kettering Med. Ctr., Dayton, 1989-90, Spectra-Physics Laserplane, Inc., Dayton, 1991—. Fellow Internat. Soc. Cert. Employee Benefits Specialists; mem. Am. Compensation Assn., Dayton Area Compensation Assn. (pres. 1993-94, v.p. 1992-93, treas. 1991-92, sec. 1990-91), Soc. for Human Resources Mgmt. Office: Spectra-Physics Laserplane 5475 Kellenburger Rd Dayton OH 45424-1099

WEST, MAXINE MARILYN, psychologist; b. St. Thomas, Ont., Can., Apr. 25, 1945; came to U.S., 1945; d. James and Selma Laura (Khoury) Toms; m. Gordon James West, Jan. 8, 1966 (div. Nov. 1978); children: Gregory, Laura, Amy, Nicholas. BA, Oakland U., 1966; postgrad., Mpls. Community Coll., 1978; MA, St. Mary's Coll., Winona, Minn., 1982. Lic. psychologist, Minn. Chem. dependency counselor Chrysalis-A Ctr. for Women, Mpls., 1979-82; chem. dependency counselor Mpls., 1982-88, pvt. practice psychologist, 1988—. Author: Shame-Based Family Systems: The Assault on Esteem, 1991; co-author and producer: (video film) Shame: When it Happens to a Child, 1989; contbr. articles to Jour. of Couple Therapy. Mem. Am. Psychol. Assn. (assoc.). Office: 430 Oak Grove Ste 418 Minneapolis MN 55403

WEST, ROBERTA BERTHA, writer; b. Saline County, Mo., Sept. 7, 1904; d. Robert and Amanda Melvina (Driver) Baur; m. Harold Clinton West, Aug. 27, 1932; children: Arle Faith West Lohof, Lyda West Hyde, Danna West Burns. AB, William Jewell Coll., 1928; AM, U. Mo., 1930. Cert. tchr., Mo., Mont. Elem. and secondary sch. tchr. Mo. and Mont. Schs., 1922-47; supt. schs. Hogeland (Mont.) Schs., 1947-48; prof. fgn. langs. Will Mayfield Coll., Marble Hill, Mo., 1930; columnist Quad County Star, Viburnum, Mo., 1982—; writer and researcher ch. history, 1964-91; cons. Yellowstone Conf. Meth. Ch.; compiler Mont. list of Meth. Mins. 1784-1984. Author: Northern Montana Methodist History, 3 vols., 1974; editor: Brother Van by Those Who Knew Him, 1975, reprinted, 1989; also articles. Recipient 1st John M. Templeton prize, 1959. Democrat. Home: PO Box 583 Viburnum MO 65566 Office: Quad County Star Viburnum MO 65566

WEST, ROBIN LEA, psychology educator; b. Mpls., Jan. 28, 1951. BA with distinction, U. Nebr., 1973; MA in Psychology, Vanderbilt U., 1978, PhD in Psychology, 1980. Vis. asst. prof. psychology Memphis State U., 1980-83; postdoctoral rsch. fellow Aging and Devel. Lab. Washington U., St. Louis, 1983-84; vis. asst. depts. psychology and clin. health psychology U. Fla., 1984-87, asst. prof. psychology, 1987-90, assoc. prof., 1990—, dir. curriculum, assoc. dir. Ctr. Gerontol. Studies, 1986—; rsch. cons. Memory Assessment Clinics, Inc., 1988-92; lectr., participant, presenter in field to confs. and workshops. Mem. editorial bd. Aging and Cognition, Experimental Aging Research, Psychology and Aging; reviewer numerous publs. including Jour. Gerontology, Psychology and Aging, Exptl. Aging Rsch., Applied Cognitive Psychology, Memory, Aging and Cognition, Internat. Jour. Behavioral Development, Devel. Psychology; contbr., editor articles to profl. jours. Grantee U. Fla. Divsn. Sponsored Rsch., 1987, 88, 90, NIH, 1987, Nat. Inst. Aging, 1986; Brookdale Found. fellow, 1989. Fellow Gerontol. Soc. Am., APA, Nat. Coun. on Aging, Soc. Applied Rsch. in Memory and Cognition. Office: U Fla Dept Psychology Box 112250 Gainesville FL 32611-2250

WEST, SALLY ELEANOR, psychotherapist; b. Greenville, Miss., June 7, 1951; d. Chester and Annie Eleanor (Tanner) W. AA, Ctrl. Tex. Coll., Killeen, 1981; BS in Social Svcs. and Rehab., U. Ctrl. Tex., Killeen, 1982, MS in Counseling Psychology, 1984. Lic. profl. couselor, marriage and family therapist, alcohol and drug dependency counselor, social worker, Tex. Coord. student svcs. Ctrl. Tex. Coll., 1980-84, instr. psychology, 1984-90; assoc. clin. psychologist Tex. Dept. Corrections, Gatesville, 1984-91; psychotherapist Assoc. Counseling, Harker Heights, Tex., 1991; psychotherapist, dir. Care Counseling, Inc., Killeen, 1991—. Mem. ACA, Tex. Counseling Assn., Tex. Assn. for Counselor Edn. and Supervision, Tex. Mental Health Counselors Assn., Tex. Assn. Marriage and Family Counselors, Am. Technol. U. Alumni Assn., Alpha Phi Sigma, Beta Sigma Phi. Baptist. Office: Care Counseling Inc Ste 310 1711 E Central Tex Expy Killeen TX 76541

WEST, SUSAN DENICE, accountant; b. Columbus, Ga., July 13, 1964; d. Ronald and Nannie Sue (Gross) W. AA, Catonsville (Md.) C.C., 1987; BS, Morgan State U., 1990, MBA, 1994. Receptionist Alexander & Alexander, Towson, Md., 1984-85, acctg. clk., 1985-86, sr. collections coord., 1986-89; technical acctg. coord. Alexander & Alexander, N.Y.C., 1989-90; acctg. mgr. Alexander & Alexander, Greenwich, Conn., 1990-91; asst. v.p. Alexander & Alexander, Owings Mills, Md., 1991—. Active mentorship program Lake Clifton-Eastern H.S.-Acad. Fin., Balt., 1993—. Mem. Alpha Kappa Alpha. Democrat. Baptist. Office: Alexander & Alexander 10461 Mill Run Cir Owings Mills MD 21117

WESTALL, SANDRA THORNTON, special education educator; b. Rochester, N.Y., Jan. 31, 1940; d. William Heldrith and Janice (King) Thonrton; m. Thomas Keith Westall, Jan. 10, 1965 (div. 1980); children: William Thornton, Robert Theodore. AS in Bus., So. Va. Coll. Women, 1962; BA in Early Childhood Edn., Mars Hill Coll., 1982; MA in Spl. Edn., Appalachian State U., 1989; MA in Behavioral Emotional Edn., Western Carolina U., 1990. Cert. tchr. spl. edn., learning disabilities, emotional handicapped, N.C., Fla. Tchr.'s asst. spl. edn. Mitchell County Sch., Spruce Pine, N.C., 1964-70; tchr. Pine Ridge Sch. for Learning Disabilities, Williston, Vt., summer 1985, 88, Summit Acad. for Learning Disabled Students, Waynesville, N.C., 1986-88; resource tchr. Ire B. Jones Elem. Sch. and Asheville Jr. High Sch., N.C., 1988-89; tchr. Irene Worthem Sch. for Severe/Profound Mentally Retarded, Asheville, 1989-90; resource tchr. G. Holmes Braddock High Sch., Miami, Fla., 1990-91, Kelsey L. Pharr Elem. Sch., Miami, 1991-94; tchr. Tyrone Mid. Sch., St. Petersburg, Fla., 1994—; night tchr. Nova U., Ft. Lauderdale, Fla., 1992—, Fla. Meml. Coll., Miami, 1992—; tutor, counselor Black Mountain (N.C.) Correctional Ctr. for Women, 1988-90; trainer behavior disorders No. Colo. U., Breckenridge, 1989, Willie M. Workshop, Asheville, 1989; condr. workshops on left and right brain teaching, 1980-87; speaker on learning disabled adults Harvard U., 1989; tchr. day camps for handicapped students, 1983, 84; advocate for learning disabled students and adults; del. Citizen Amb. Program field of learning disabilities, Diagnostic Ctr., various schs., Vilnius, Siauliai Pedagogical Inst., Dept. Spl. Pedagogics, Lithuania, Inst. Defectology, Russian Acad. Pedagogical, Moscow, City Coun., Inst. Econ. Problem Studies, St. Petersburg, Russia, 1993. Vol. Dade County Helpline and Dade County Schs. (in aid of Hurricane Andrew victims), swimming courses for ARC, 1980—; bd. dirs. N.C. Advocacy Ctr. for Children's Edn. and Parent Tng., 1986-90. Grantee Creative Learning for Behavior Handicapped Students, 1989; honoree ARC, 1980. Mem. Am. Coun. on Rural Spl. Edn., Assn. for Children and Adults with Learning Disabilities, The Orton Dyslexia Soc., Coun. for Exceptional Children, Coun. for Behavior Emotionally Handicapped Children. Episcopalian. Home: 540 Carillon Pky Apt 1071 Saint Petersburg FL 33716 Office: Tyrone Mid Sch 6421 22nd Ave N Saint Petersburg FL 33710

WESTBROOK, SUSAN ELIZABETH, horticulturist; b. Canton, Ohio, Sept. 27, 1939; d. Walter Simon and Rosella Hunt Tolley; m. Edward D. Westbrook, July 2, 1966 (div. 1980); 1 child, Tyler Hunt. Student, Smithdeal-Massey, Richmond, Va., 1958-59; student in Spanish, U. Honduras, 1960; student biology/geology, Mary Washington Coll., 1960, 72, 73; student hort., Prince Georges Community Coll., 1987-88. Farm owner Spotsylvania, Va., 1972-83; office mgr. Tolley Investments, Inc., Fredericksburg, Va., 1980-83; real estate agt. Cooper Realty, Fredericksburg, Va., 1981-83; salesperson Meadows Farms Nursery, Chantilly, Va., 1986-93; student Geology Dept. Mary Washington Coll., Fredericksburg, Va., 1993—; master gardener Va. Poly. Inst., 1993. Author booklets: Japanese Maples, 1990, Fruit Trees, 1989; author radio format: Gardening in Virginia, 1960; co-author computer program: Plantscape, 1990. Sec. Rep. Party, Spotsylvania, 1972-83, Elko County, Nev., 1968; judge Bd. Elections, Spotsylvania, 1980-83, cand. bd. suprs., 1979. Named Master Gardener Va. Poly. Inst., Blacksburg, Va., 1993. Mem. Nat. Wildlife Fedn., Md. Nurserymen's Assn., Friends of the Nat. Arboretum. Home: 6110 S Virginia Ln PO Box 8 Dahlgren VA 22448

WESTCOTT, KATHLEEN MOTEL, alcoholism counselor; b. New Brunswick, N.J., Nov. 8, 1960; d. Theodore Robert and Jean Marie (Olaski) Motel; m. David A. Westcott, Aug. 16, 1986. BA, U. Denver, 1983; MS, U. Scranton, 1990. Cert. alcoholism counselor, N.Y. Compensation analyst E.F. Hutton, Inc., N.Y.C., 1984-85; benefits asst. Midlantic Nat. Bank, Edison, N.J., 1985-86; grad. asst. U. Scranton (Pa.), 1987-89; alcoholism counseling intern Alcoholism Ctr. Broome County, Binghamton, N.Y., 1989; alcoholism counselor Family Counseling Svcs., Cortland, N.Y., 1989-92; counselor So. Tier Alcoholism Rehab. Svcs., Elmira, N.Y., 1992-94; cons. employee assistance program Corning (N.Y.) Incorp., 1994—. Recipient Hornbeck Scholar award, U. Denver, 1982. Mem. ACA, Assn. Specialists Group Work, Golden Key Nat. Honor Soc. Office: Corning Inc 2-8 Denison Pky, MP-QX-00 Corning NY 13831

WESTER, MARTHA JANIE, art educator; d. Everett Clifton and Winnie Dell (Mathis) Martin; m. Donald Gray Wester, June 5, 1953; children: Donald Gray Jr., James Everett, John Michael, Thomas Daniel. BA, Baylor U., 1953; MA, U. Okla., 1974. Tchr. math., art Ft. Worth Pub. Schs., 1954-56, Tecumseh (Okla.) Pub. Schs., 1967-71; asst. prof. art Okla. Bapt. U., Shawnee, 1971—; presenter in field. Solo exhibitions include Okla. Bapt. U., 1975; exhibited in group shows at MacDowell Club Allied Arts, 1975, Tecumseh Sq., 1979-80, Shawnee Little Theatre, Shawnee Fine Arts Club., 1984, 86, Okla. Bapt. U., 1985, others. Recipient Outstanding Handwoven Garment award Fiberworks 91. Democrat. Baptist. Home: 46500 Hardesty Rd # B Shawnee OK 74801-9633 Office: Okla Bapt U 500 W University St Shawnee OK 74801-2558

WESTERFIELD, CAROLYN ELIZABETH HESS, city planner; b. New Haven, Conn., May 3, 1933; d. Orvan Walter and Carol Woodruff (Maurer) Hess; m. Holt Bradford Westerfield, Dec. 17, 1960; children: Pamela Bradford Bingham, Leland Avery. BA, Wellesley Coll., 1954; postgrad., Yale U., 1954-55, M of City Planning, 1959. Planner, office mgr. Tech. Planning Assocs., New Haven, 1955-57, 61-62; assoc. planner City Plan Dept., New Haven, Conn., 1956-59; planner, editor State of Conn. Devel. Commn., 1959-61; cons., 1962—; prin. planner South Cen. Conn. Planning Region, 1979-87; asst. plan dir. Town of Fairfield (Conn.), 1987; planning and zoning adminstr. Town of North Branford (Conn.), 1987-89; devel. pvt. programs New Haven Hosp.-Boston City Hosp., 1952-54; lectr. city planning U. New Haven, 1988—. Mem. alumni bd. Yale U. Sch. Architecture, 1964-76, 85—, pres., 1993—; bd. dirs. alumni orgns. Prospect Hill Sch., New Haven, St. Thomas Day Sch.; class officer Wellesley Coll.; mem. Econ. Devel. Commn. Consortium, Hamden, Conn., clk. design rev. com.; mem. Ethics Commn. Mem. Am. Planning Assn., Am. Inst. Cert. Planners, Conn. Women in Planning and Devel. (co-chmn. program com. 1987-89, future of Conn. com. 1989-91), New Haven Colony Hist. Soc., Jr. League New Haven (various exec. positions), Watch Hill Improvement Soc. (pres. 1971-73), Conn. Child Welfare Assn., Yale U. Women's Orgn. (various exec. positions). Home and office: 115 Rogers Rd Hamden CT 06517-3533

WESTERHAUS, CATHERINE K., social worker; b. Corydon, Ind., Oct. 13, 1910; d. Anthony Joseph and Permelia Ann (Mathes) Kannapel; m. George Henry Westerhaus, Apr. 15, 1950. BEd in Music, Kans. U., 1934; MSW, Loyola U., Chgo., 1949. Cert. Acad. Cert. Social Workers. Clin. social worker Friendly Acres Home of Aged, Newton, Kans.; county welfare dir., state adult svcs. supr. Newton-Harvey County, State of Kans.; vol. cert. social worker Newton. Contbr. articles to profl. jours. With USNR, 1945-46. Named Kans. Social Worker of Yr., 1975. Mem. NASW (cert.), Kans. Soc. Cert. Social Work, Am. Legion (comdr. Wayne G. Austin post 1981-82). Home: 313 W Broadway St Newton KS 67114-2631

WESTERMAN, DONNA DAY, artist; b. Detroit, June 22, 1940; d. James McAdam and Mary Elizabeth (McGibbon) Day; m. Jan Hendrik Westerman, Sept. 28, 1967; 1 child, Johanna Louise. Student, U. Mich., 1958-60; BFA, Boston Mus. Sch., 1962; MFA, Otis Art Inst., L.A., 1966. Tchr. art various mus. and schs., Mass. and Calif., 1960-76; prof. Orange Coast Coll., Costa Mesa, Calif., 1976—, dir. computer graphics program, 1979-90; owner Saltlick Press, Studio C, Newport Beach, Calif., 1987—; curator confs. and symposiums; spkr. in field. Author: One-Of-A-Kind Artists Books; author, reviewer mag. Bookways, 1993; artist, creator cast glass, cast bronze and carved wood, archtl. commns.; exhibited in various shows, 1954—. Dir., vol. art program Santiago Sch., Santa Ana, 1976-78; mem. support group Big Bros./Big Sisters, Orange County, Calif., 1987—; mem. edn. com. Bowers Mus., Santa Ana, 1975-80. Recipient Outstanding Calender Design award Printing Inst. Am., 1975; State of Calif. grantee, 1983-84. Mem. L.A. Printmaking Soc. (membership chair), L.A. Women Letterpress Printers, Alliance for Contemporary Book Arts, Orange County Arts Alliance (officer, bd. dirs.). Office: Orange Coast Coll 2701 Fairview Rd Costa Mesa CA 92626-5561

WESTERMAN, KATY DOROTHEA, former vocational education administrator; b. Swink, Colo., Feb. 16, 1930; d. Orval Ernest and Beatrice Alzina (Cloud) Krout; m. Hugh Abraham Westerman, Oct. 15, 1955 (div. Apr. 1971); children: Vincent Hugh, Theodore Lynn, Michael Darryl Dean, Christopher Wayne, Mark Alan. BA, U. No. Colo., 1954; MEd, Colo. State U., 1979. Tchr. Eagle (Colo.) County High Sch., 1954-57, Sangre De Cristo High Sch., Mosca, Colo., 1957-61, Sierra Grande High Sch., Ft. Garland, Colo., 1961-70; instr., coord. power sewing program San Luis Valley Area Vocat. Sch., Monte Vista, Colo., 1970-74; instr., coord. spl. coop. program Alamosa (Colo.) High Sch., 1974-81; coord. community edn., supervisory adult basic edn. and GED Alamosa Pub. Schs., 1981-84; asst. dir. San Luis Valley Area Vocat. Sch., 1984-87; dir. secondary vocat. edn. San Luis Valley, 1988-92; adminstr. Carl Perkins Consortium San Luis Valley Area Vocat. Sch., 1990-92; ret., 1992; instr. Ford Found. Rocky Mountain Area Small High Schs. Project, Mosca, 1957-61; mem. Gov.'s Coun. on Status of Women, Monte Vista, 1971-74; adminstr. Community Recreation Bd., Alamosa, 1981-84; cons. Chinese Spl. Needs Program, People's Republic of China, 1986; sec. Colo. Vocat. Hall of Fame Found., 1979-84, pres., 1988-92. Member Alamosa C. of C., 1986-90; precinct rep. Alamosa County Cen. Dem. Com., 1984-90. Inducted into Colo. Vocat. Hall of Fame, 1994. Mem. NEA, Am. Vocat. Assn., Colo. Vocat. Assn. (sec. new and related svcs. div. 1980-82, pres. elect new and related svcs. div. 1983, pres. 1984-85), Nat. Assn. Vocat. Spl. Needs Pers. (sec. Colo. chpt. 1980-82, pres. elect 1983, pres. 1984-85), Colo. Edn. Assn., Colo. Assn. Vocat. Adminstrs., Colo. Assn. Sch. Execs., Iota Lambda Sigma, Beta Sigma Phi (Woman of the Yr. 1986). Roman Catholic. Home: 8481A County Road 8 S Alamosa CO 81101-9193

WESTERMAN, ROSEMARY MATZZIE, nurse; b. Sewickley, Pa., May 20, 1949; d. Joseph Edward and Martha (Aquino) Matzzie; m. Philip M. Westerman, Aug. 7, 1971. BSN, Duquesne U., 1971, MSEd, 1975. RN, Pa. Head nurse Dept. Vet. Affairs VA Med. Ctr., Pitts.; assoc. chief, nursing svc., edn. W. S. Middleton Meml. VA Hosp., Madison, Wis., Dept. VA Affairs VA Med. Ctr. Chilicothe; assoc. chief nursing svc., long term. care Dept. VA Affairs VA Med. Ctr., Chilicothe; chief nurse VA Med. Ctr., Muskogee, Okla. Active Literacy Vol. of Am. Mem. ANA (cert. nursing adminstrn. advanced), Okla. Orgn. Nurse Execs., Nursing Orgn. of VA, Okla. Nurses Assn., Chief Nurses Assn. Va., Sigma Theta Tau. Home: 1409 E Concord St Broken Arrow OK 74012

WESTERMAN, SYLVIA HEWITT, journalist, university official; b. Columbus, Ohio; d. Harry James and Grace (Doyle) W. BA, Ohio State U., 1994. With Sta. WLW-C, WTVN and WBNS, Columbus, 1954-63; with CBS News, 1963-79, radio TV producer, 1964-67, producer Face the Nation, 1967-74, dep. dir. news, 1974-78, v.p. spl. events and polit. coverage, 1978-79; v.p., exec. asst. to pres. NBC News, N.Y.C., 1979-82; v.p. spl. projects UPI, N.Y.C., 1983-84; pres. Sylvia Westerman Enterprises, N.Y.C.; dir. planning and new programs Fordham Grad. Sch. Bus. Adminstrn., N.Y.C., 1989—. Recipient Emmy award Nat. Acad. TV Arts and Scis. 1974. Bd. dirs. Ohio State U. Devel. Fund; adv. bd. Critical Difference for Women; coun. advisors Ohio State U. librs.; mem. steering com. Acad. Quality Consortium. Mem. Jr. League Columbus, Cosmopolitan Club, Sigma Delta Chi, Theta Sigma Pi, Kappa Alpha Theta. Home: 220 E 63rd St Apt 5-a New York NY 10021-7648 Office: 113 W 60th St New York NY 10023-7404

WESTHEIMER, RUTH SIEGEL (KAROLA RUTH SIEGEL WESTHEIMER), psychologist, television personality; b. Frankfurt, Fed. Republic Germany; came to U.S., 1956; m. Manfred Westheimer; children: Miriam, Joel. Grad. psychology, U. Paris Sorbonne; Master's degree, New Sch. for Social Research, N.Y.C., 1959; EdD, Columbia U., 1970. Research asst. Columbia U. Sch. Pub. Health, N.Y.C., 1967-70; assoc. prof. Lehman Coll., Bronx, N.Y., 1970-77; with Bklyn. Coll., West Point Milit. Acad.; counsellor, radio talk show hostess Sexually Speaking Sta. WYNY-FM, N.Y.C., 1980—; hostess TV series Good Sex, Dr. Ruth Show, Ask Dr. Ruth, 1987—; pvt. practice N.Y.C.; adj. assoc. prof. NYU. Author: Dr. Ruth's Guide to Good Sex, 1983, First Love: A Young People's Guide to Sexual Information, 1985, Dr. Ruth's Guide for Married Lovers, 1986, (autobiography) All In a Lifetime, 1987, Sex and Morality: Who is Teaching Out Sex Standards?, 1988, Dr. Ruth's Guide to Erotic and Sensuous Pleasures, 1991, Dr. Ruth's Guide to Safer Sex, 1992, Dr. Ruth Talks to Kids, 1993, The Art of Arousal, 1993, Dr. Ruth's Encyclopedia of Sex, 1994; contbr. articles to mags.; appeared in film A Woman or Two, 1986; appeared on TV show Quantum Leap, 1993. Fellow N.Y. Acad. Medicine. Office: King Features Syndicate Inc 235 E 45th St New York NY 10017-3305 also: Lifetime TV 36-12 35th Ave Astoria NY 11106*

WESTLOCK, JEANNINE MARIE, healthcare consultant; b. Pitts., Mar. 14, 1959; d. Russell and Shirley Anita (Meredith) W. BS in Applied Math., U. Pitts., 1981. Cert. profl. ins. woman, health ins. assoc. Ch. organist St. Luke Roman Cath. Ch., Carnegie, Pa., 1981-92; actuarial analyst Blue Cross & Blue Shield Mut. of Ohio, Cleve., 1984-89, health benefits mgmt. specialist, 1989-92, sr. health cons., 1992—; Active campaign state sen. Gary Suhadolnik, Cleve., 1988—; organist and vocalist St. Elizabeth Ann Seton parish, Carnegie, Pa., 1992—. Active polit. campaign State Sen. Gary Suhadolnik, Cleve., 1988—. Mem. Nat. Assn. Ins. Women (local exec. bd. 1986-90, local pres. 1989-90, state dir., 1990-91, Achievement award 1988, Nat. Rookie of the Yr. 1987, State Ins. Women of the Yr. 1988), Ins. Women of Cleve. (Ins. Woman of the Yr. 1986), Cleve. Women's City Club, Nat. Assn. Health Underwriters, NAFE, Toastmasters (local pres. 1988), Alpha Delta Pi. Roman Catholic. Home: 12900 Lake Ave Apt 1703 Cleveland OH 44107-1556

WESTLUND, JANICE RUTH, advertising executive; b. Rochester, N.Y., Dec. 15, 1948; d. Walter William and Mary Ruth (Kalsbeek) Blakley; m. Steven Jon Westlund, Mar. 26, 1972; children: Elisabeth Sara, Katherine Claire. BA, Hope Coll., Holland, Mich., 1970. Mem. faculty Marion Adult Edn. and Career Tng. Ctr., Chgo., 1971-72; office mgr. AP, Chgo., 1972-74; sales svc. mgr. Marshall Field & Co., Cherry Valley, Ill., 1974-75; advt. dir., housewares buyer Bob's Ace Hardware and Home Ctrs., Rockford, Ill., 1975—; mem. Hardlines Industry Environ. Coun., Indpls., 1992—. Chair steering com. for Women's History Month, Rockford, 1984—; trustee, com. chair Keith Sch. Bd. Trustees, Rockford, 1990—; mem. Nat. Home Ctr. Leadership Coun., 1986-92. Mem. AAUW, Rockford Network, Rockford Soc. of Archeol. Inst. Am. (bd. dirs. 1993—, v.p.). Office: Bobs Ace Hardware & Home Ctrs 2710 20th St Rockford IL 61109

WESTMORELAND, BARBARA FENN, neurologist, electroencephalographer, educator; b. N.Y.C., July 22, 1940; d. Robert Edward and Wanda Helen (Zabawski) Westmoreland. BS in Chemistry, Mary Washington Coll., 1961; MD, U. Va., 1965. Diplomate Am. Bd. Psychiatry and Neurology and certification of added qualification in clin. neurophysiology. Intern Vanderbilt Hosp., Nashville, 1965-66; resident in neurology U. Va. Hosp., Charlottesville, 1966-70; fellow in electroencephalography Mayo Clinic, Rochester, Minn., 1970-71, assoc. cons. neurology, 1970-71; asst. prof. neurology Mayo Med. Sch., Rochester, 1973-78, assoc. prof., 1978-85, prof., 1985—. Co-author: Medical Neurosciences, 1978, rev. edit., 1986, first author 3d edit., 1994. Mem. Am. Epilepsy Soc. (treas. 1978-80, pres. 1987-88), Am. EEG Soc. (sec. 1985-87, pres. 1991-92), Cen. Assn. Electroencephalographers (sec.-treas. 1976-78, pres. 1979-80), Mayo History of Medicine Soc. (pres. 1990-91), Sigma Xi (pres. chpt. 1987-88).

WESTON, FRANCINE EVANS, secondary education educator; b. Mt. Vernon, N.Y., Oct. 8, 1946; d. John Joseph and Frances (Fantino) Pisanielo. BA, Hunter Coll., 1968; MA, Lehman Coll., 1973; cert., Am. Acad. Dramatic Arts, N.Y.C., 1976; PhD, NYU, 1991. Cert. elem., secondary tchr., N.Y. Tchr. Yonkers (N.Y.) Bd. Edn., 1968—; aquatic dir. Woodlane Day Camp, Irvington-on-Hudson, N.Y., 1967-70, Yonkers Jewish Community Ctr., 1971-75; creative drama tchr. John Burroughs Jr. H.S., Yonkers, 1971-77; stage lighting designer Iona Summer Theatre Festival, New Rochelle, N.Y., 1980-81, Yonkers Male Glee Club, 1981-89, Roosevelt H.S., 1980—; rsch. specialist Scholarship Locating Svc., 1992-94, Yonkers Civil Def. Police Aux., 1994—; master electrician NYU Summer Mus. Theatre, 1979-80. Actress in numerous community theatre plays including A Touch of the Poet, 1979; dir. stage prodns. including I Remember Mama, 1973, The Man Who Came to Dinner, 1975; author: A Descriptive Comparison of Computerized Stage Lighting Memory Systems With Non-Computerized Systems, 1991, (short stories) A Hat for Louise, 1984, Old Memories: Beautiful and Otherwise, 1984; lit. editor: (story and poetry collection) Beautifully Old, 1984. Steering com. chairperson Roosevelt High Sch.-Middle States Assn. of Schs. and Colls. Self-Evaluation, 1985-88. Named Tchr. of Excellence, N.Y. State English Coun., 1990; recipient Monetary award for Teaching Excellence, Carter Products, 1992; named to Arrid Tchrs. Honor Roll, 1992. Mem. U.S. Inst. for Theatre Tech., Nat. Coun. Tchrs. English, N.Y. State English Coun., N.Y. State United Tchrs. Assn., Yonkers Fedn. Tchrs., Kappa Delta Pi. Republican. Roman Catholic. Office: Roosevelt High Sch Tuckahoe Rd Yonkers NY 10710

WESTON, JANICE LEAH COLMER, librarian; b. Phila., Jan. 3, 1944; d. Robert Henry and Mildred Viola (Hale) Colmer; m. Stephen Paul Oksala, Aug. 21, 1965 (div. 1970); m. Leonard Charles Weston, Oct. 28, 1972. BA in History, U. Mich., 1966; MS in LS, Wayne State U., 1969; postgrad., Cath. U. Am., 1975, Brigham Young U., 1975. Cert. profl. libr., Va. Library clk. Edn. Libr., U. Mich., Ann Arbor, 1966-67; reference libr. John Tyler Community Coll., Chester, Va., 1969-70, Tech. Libr., Aberdeen Proving Ground, Md., 1971-72; br. libr. Chester Pub. Libr., 1969-70; libr. Gen. Equipment Test Activity, Ft. Lee, Va., 1970-71; chief libr. Army Ordnance Ctr. and Sch., Aberdeen Proving Ground, 1972-94; mem. job analysis task force Dept. Army, Washington, 1976; chmn. Aberdeen Proving Ground Media Svcs. Com., 1978, 83, 88. Author: Operating Procedures, 1988. Mem. James Buchanan Found., Lancaster, Pa., 1977—, Fulton Opera House Found., Lancaster, 1985—, Friends Libr. So. Lancaster County, Quarryville, Pa., 1985—; Humane League Friends, Lancaster, 1988—. Mem. Spl. Librs. Assn., Fed. Libr. and Info. Network, Tng. and Doctrine Command Libr. and Info. Network, Allemande Dance Club (Lancaster). Episcopalian. Home: 25 Oak Ridge Dr Quarryville PA 17566-9284

WESTON, JOAN SPENCER, production director; b. Barton, Vt., Aug. 11, 1943; d. Rolfe Weston and Dorothy Lena (Spencer) Schoppe. BA magna cum laude, U. Mass., 1965. Tchr. high sch. Gorham (Maine) Schs., 1965-66; tchr. Sherwood Hall Sch., Mansfield, Eng., 1966-67; tchr. middle sch. Meden Sch., Warsop, Eng., 1967-68; dept. head high sch. Goffstown (N.H.) Schs., 1968-82; dir. circulation T.H.E. Jour., Acton, Mass., 1982-83; prodn. mgr. The Robb Report, Acton, 1983-87, prodn. dir., 1988; prodn. dir. New Age Jour., Watertown, Mass., 1993—. Mem. Women in Prodn., Phi Beta Kappa. Office: New Age Jour 42 Pleasant St Watertown MA 02172

WESTON, PHYLLIS JEAN, art gallery director; b. Cleve.; d. Armin and Wilma H. (Wasserman) Hornstein; m. Leo F. Weston, Oct. 18, 1963; children: H. Todd Cobey, John Cobey. Ed., Yale U., 1949-50. Director AB Closson Jr. Co. Art Gallery, Cin., 1964—; art cons. Proctor & Gamble Co., Cin., 1983—; cons., lectr. in art. Named Woman of the Yr. Cin. Enquirer, 1987; recipient Post Corbett award, 1989. Chmn., founder Enjoy the Arts; founder Cin. Commn. on the Arts, The Post Corbett awards; bd. dirs., mem. numerous arts and civic orgns. including Internation Visitors Ctr., Inc., Friends of Cin. Parks, Cinn. Chamber Orch., C.A.S.A.; adv. judge Congl. Art Competition Sch. Creative and Performing Arts; mem. Citizens Against Substance Abuse, Internat. Visitors Ctr., Japan Am. Soc. Home: 4 Taft Road Ln Cincinnati OH 45206-1805 Office: 401 Race St Cincinnati OH 45202-2804

WESTROPE, MARTHA RANDOLPH, psychologist, consultant; b. Gaffney, S.C., May 19, 1922; d. Gordon Robert and Hannah (Brown) W.; 1 adopted child, Ashley Randolph. BS, Winthrop Coll., 1942; MA, U. N.C., 1944; PhD, State U. of Iowa, Iowa City, 1952. Lic. psychologist, S.C. Pvt. practice Greenville, S.C., 1960—, part-time pvt. practice, 1987—; part-time staff mem. Spartanburg (S.C.) Mental Health Clinic, 1971-73, Greenville Mental Health Ctr., 1974-85, Patrick B. Harris Psychiat. Hosp., Anderson, S.C., 1985-87; med. cons. S.C. Vocat. Rehab. Dept., Greenville, 1987-91, part-time med. cons., 1993—; cons. S.C. Parole Bd. for Psychol. Evaluation, S.C. Dept. Corrections, 1983-87. Mem. Am. Psychol. Assn., Southeastern Psychol. Assn., S.C. Psychol. Assn., Am. Assn. for Advancement of Psychology, Greenville County Mental Health Assn., Am. Group Psychotherapy Assn., Coun. for the Nat. Register of Health Svc. Providers in Psychology. Democrat. Presbyterian. Home: 11 Darien Way Greenville SC 29615-3236 Office: 506 Pettigru St Greenville SC 29601-3117

WEST-TAYLOR, JO RENE, county official; b. Lubbock, Tex., Feb. 27, 1950; d. Joseph William and Fannie Ruth (Wright) Bean; m. John King Taylor, July 26, 1991; children: Michael Robert West, Mary Ann West Bradley, Jesse Nicholas Taylor. Student, Henderson U., 1968-69, Garland County C.C., Hot Springs, Ark., 1976-77. Cert. treas., Ark. Delinquent credit collector Hot Springs Credit Bur., 1970-76; dep. tax collector Garland County, Hot Springs, 1976-83, chief-dep. treas., 1983-92, treas., 1993—. Local del. exec. bd. Garland County Dems., Hot Springs, 1992-94; state del. Ark. Dems., Little Rock, 1994. Mem. Ark. Treas.'s Assn. (mem. exec. bd. 1993-94), Hot Springs C. of C. (amb. Oktoberfest chmn. 1993-94), Virginia Clinton Kelley Dem. Womens Club, Hot Springs Emblem Club, Leola Hunting Club, Beta Sigma Phi (holder all exec. offices 1975-94). Methodist. Home: 319 Songer Ln Pearcy AR 71964 Office: Garland County Treas Courthouse 501 Ouachita Rm 206 Hot Springs National Park AR 71901

WESTWICK, CARMEN ROSE, nursing educator, consultant; b. Holstein, Iowa, Feb. 2, 1936; d. J. Alfred and Hazel C. (Lage) Armiger; m. Richard A. Westwick, Dec. 28, 1957; children: Timothy, Ann. BS in Nursing, U. Iowa, 1958; MS, U. Colo., 1960; PhD, Denver U., 1972. RN, Tenn. Instr. Sch. Nursing West Suburban Hosp., Oak Park, Ill., 1958-59, 60-62; nurse Navajo Presch., Carson's Trading Post, N.Mex., 1967; lectr. then prof. U. Colo., Denver, 1968-69, 72-77; program dir. Western Coun. on Higher Edn. in Nursing, Boulder, Colo., 1976-77; prof. nursing, dean U. N.Mex, Albuquerque, 1977-81, Boston U., 1982-85, S.D. State U., Brookings, 1988-91; NHC chair of excellence in nursing Middle Tenn. State U., Murfreesboro, 1993—; exec. dir. N.H. Bd. Nursing, Concord, 1986-87; case reviewer Joint Underwriters Assn., Boston, 1983-92; mem. publs. and rsch. com. Aberdeen (S.D.) Area Indian Health Svc., 1989-91; manuscript reviewer Midwest Alliance in Nursing, Indpls., 1989-92; manuscript reviewer Holistic Nursing Jour.; mem. adv. coun. S.D. Office of Rural Health, Pierre, 1989-91. Contbr. articles to profl. jours. Nurse trainee fellow Nursing div. Dept. Health and Human Svcs., 1959-60, Predoctoral fellow, 1969-72; Nat. Merit scholar, 1954-56. Fellow Am. Acad. Nursing; mem. Sigma Theta Tau (nat. 1st v.p. 1968), Phi Kappa Phi, Kappa Delta Phi. Lutheran.

WESTWOOD, DEBRA ANN, library coordinator, sign language interpreter; b. Seattle, June 9, 1955; d. Walter Lee and Minnie Eleanor (Hedstrom) W. AA cum laude, South Seattle Community Coll., 1975; AAS cum laude, Seattle Cen. Community Coll., 1978; BA cum laude, U. Wash., 1986. Bookkeeper, office mgr. N.W. Svc., Inc., Seattle, 1974-79; classroom interpreter Seattle Community Coll., 1979-84; instr. Am. sign lang. Everett (Wash.) Community Coll., 1981-86; pvt. practice Seattle, 1984—; coord. libr. svcs. for deaf and hard of hearing Seattle Pub. Libr., 1990—, coord. literacy outreach program, 1991-92, coord. Rock 'n Read program, 1991-93; performance interpreter Seattle Womens Ensemble, Seattle Repertory Theatre, Valley Community Players, 1978—; coord. interpreted performances Seattle Repertory Theatre, 1981-87; leader trainer Boy Scouts Am., Everett, 1982-85; v.p., pres., bd. dirs. Family Edn. and Counseling Ctr. on Deafness, Seattle, 1992-94. Recipient Advancement of Libr. Svc. award Wash. Libr. Assn., 1991, Assn. Specialized Cooperating Libr. Agys. and Nat. Orgn. on Disabilities award ALA, Chgo., 1991. Mem. ALA, Registry Interpreters for Deaf (cert.), Wash. State Registry of Interpreters for Deaf (sec.-treas. 1980-86), Assn. Specialized Cooperating Libr. Agys. Office: Seattle Pub Libr 1000 4th Ave Seattle WA 98104-1193

WETHERALD, MICHELE WARHOLIC, lawyer; b. Lakewood, Ohio, June 17, 1954; d. Michael and Veronica (Walkuski) Warholic; m. Gary R. Wetherald, Nov. 26, 1987. AAB, Lorain County C.C., Elyria, Ohio, 1977; BA, Hiram Coll., 1980; JD, U. Akron, 1985. Bar: Ohio, 1986; U.S. Dist. Ct. (no. dist.) Ohio, 1987. Sec., dispatcher State Highway Patrol Ohio Turnpike Commn., Berea, Ohio, 1973-77; pers. and employee benefits rep. Terex Div. Gen. Motors Corp., Hudson, Ohio, 1978-83; labor relations rep. Lordstown Assembly Div. Gen. Motors Corp., Warren, Ohio, 1984-86; supr. labor relations and hourly employment Inland Div. Gen. Motors Corp., Livonia, Mich., 1986-87; staff atty. Hyatt Legal Svcs., Niles, Ohio, 1987-89; mng. atty. Hyatt Legal Svcs., Boardman, Ohio, 1990; assoc. Newman, Olson & Kerr, Youngstown, Ohio, 1990—; instr. Hiram (Ohio) Coll. Mem. exec. bd. Hiram (Ohio) Coll. Alumni, 1990-93; mem. public affairs com., profl. connection YWCA; mem. Cath. Svc. League; trustee, exec. com. Ursuline Ctr. Bd. Mem. ABA, AAUW (pres. Warren Ohio Br.), Ohio State Bar Assn., Trumbull County Bar Assn., Mahoning County Bar Assn., The Pers. Assn. Roman Catholic. Home: 106 Diamond Way Cortland OH 44410-1372 Office: Newman Olson & Kerr 1200 Metropolitan Tower Youngstown OH 44503

WETHERELL, R. CLAIRE, state legislator; b. Flandreau, S.D., Feb. 18, 1919; d. Thomas James and Margaret (Hefron) H.; m. Robert Miles Wotherell (dec. 1943); children: Michael Edward, Dennis Hart, Ellen Ann Hermann, Robert Thomas. Student, U. Calif., Berkeley, 1937-39; RN, Mercy Hosp. Sch. Nursing, 1942. City councilwoman Mountain Home, Idaho, 1971-78; mem. Idaho State Senate. Dem. committeewoman Elmore County, 1955—; vice chmn. Idaho State Dem. Party, 1962-72. Served as ensign, Navy Nurse Corps, 1942-43. Named Disting. Citizen Idaho Daily Statesman, Boise, 1978. Mem. Mountain Home Com. of Fifty, Bus. and Profl. Women (named Woman of Progress, S.W. Idaho, 1976), C. of C. (pres. 1971-72), Idaho Land Title Assn. (pres. 1977-78). Roman Catholic. Home: 360 E 15th N Mountain Home ID 83647-1702 Office: Idaho State Senate State Capitol Boise ID 83720*

WETHERELL, VIRGINIA BACON, state legislator, state agency administrator, engineering company executive; b. Anniston, Ala., May 15, 1947; d. William Dennis and Mary (Perkins) Bacon; children: Virginia Blakely, Page Perkins. BA, Auburn U., 1968; MS, Jacksonville State U., 1971. Tchr. Biology and Physiology Anniston High Sch., 1968-72; planner East Ala. Regional Planning & Devel. Com., Anniston, 1974-82; exec. dir. City-County Drug Abuse Commn., Pensacola, Fla., 1976-82; dir., officer Coastal Transp., Pensacola, 1980-86; mem. Fla. Ho. of Reps., 1982-88; dir., officer Ammons, Bass, Bass & Boys, Pensacola, 1985-86, Gulf Coast Mortgage & Investments, Pensacola, 1985-86; mktg. adminstr. Baskerville-Donovan Engrs., Pensacola, 1986-91; exec. dir. Fla. Dept. Natural Resources, 1991-93; secy. Fla. Dept. Environ. Protection, 1993—; mem. exec. com. Gulf Coast Econs. Club, Pensacola, 1985—, Homeporting Commn., Pensacola, 1985—; chmn. internat. trade and econ. devel. Fla. Ho. of Reps., 1986-88; active Commn. Sustainable South Fla. Environ. Coun. States; bd. dirs. Bapt. Health Care Found., Pensacola. Bd. dirs. Fla. Council on Asian Affairs, 1985—, Fla. Com. on Future, 1987-88; mem. exec. com. Fla. Dem. Party, 1985—. Named Profl. Leader of Yr. Pensacola C. of C. and Pensacola News Jour., 1981, Fla.'s Outstanding Young Woman Fla. Jaycees, 1982, Woman of Yr. Pensacola Breakfast of Champions, 1983. Mem. Nat. Conf. State Legislatures, Council of State Govt., Fla. Chpt. of Dem. Leadership. Episcopalian. Clubs: Leadership Pensacola (founding mem., pres. 1981), Pensacola Heritage Found. (pres. 1980-82). Home: 3770 Bobbin Mills Rd Tallahassee FL 32312-1202

WETJEN, DIANNE KAY, reading, writing and math consultant; b. Butler, Pa., Oct. 21, 1940; d. Nelson Pattison and Gladys Dorothy Palmer; m. Alan Jay Wetjen, Aug. 21, 1960; 1 child, Eric. BA, Allegheny Coll., 1962; MS,

Fla. State U., 1965. Cert. reading specialist, N.Y. 6th grade tchr. Meadville (Pa.) Pub. Schs., 1962-65, reading cons., 1965-67; reading specialist Smithtown (N.Y.) Ctrl. Sch. Dist., 1968-77, 81-94; project dir. N.Y. State Edn. Dept., Albany, 1977-81; sec. policy bd. Smithtown Tchrs. Ctr., 1992-94, tchr. insvc. courses, 1993-94; internat. speaker in field. Mem. AAUW, Internat. Reading Assn., Nat. Coun. Tchrs. English. Home: 1690 Rainbow Ct Marco Island FL 33937-5127

WETLE, TERRIE TODD, gerontologist, health institute executive, educator; b. Bremerton, Wash., Nov. 7, 1946; d. Gerald Lee and Elinor Myrle (Martindale) Todd; m. Richard W. Besdine, July 2, 1981; children: Sarah, Molly. BS in Psychology, Portland State U., 1968, MS in Psychology, 1971, PhD of Urban Studies, 1976. Asst. prof. Portland (Oreg.) State U., 1976-78; social policy analyst Dept. Health, Edn. and Welfare, Washington, 1978-79; asst. prof. Yale U., New Haven, 1979-81, Harvard U., Boston, 1981-88; dir. Braceland Ctr., Hartford, Conn., 1988-95; dep. dir. Nat. Inst. Aging, NIH, Bethesda, Md., 1995—; assoc. prof. U. Conn. Health Ctr., Farmington, 1989—; bd. dirs. Armed Forces Retirement Home, Washington. Editor: Older Veterans, 1984, Handbook of Geriatric Care, 1982; contbr. articles to profl. jours. Pres. Alzheimer's Assn. Greater Hartford, 1993-95; apptd. Alzheimer's Coalition Conn., 1991-95. Fellow Gerontol. Soc. Am. (chair com.); mem. APHA (del., governing coun.), Am. Soc. Aging, Am. Health Care Assn. Office: Nat Inst Aging NIH Bethesda MD 20892-2292

WETSCH, PEGGY A., nursing informaticist, educator; b. San Diego; d. Harvey William Henry and Helen Catherine (Thorpe) Brink; m. Gearald M. Wetsch, June 26, 1971; children: Brian Gearald, Lynette Kirstiann Nicole. Diploma, Calif. Hosp. Sch. Nursing, 1971; BSN cum laude, Pepperdine U., 1980; MS in Nursing, Calif. State U., L.A., 1985. Cert. in nursing adminstrn., human resource devel. Clin. nurse Orange County Med. Ctr./U. Calif. Irvine Med. Ctr., Orange, Calif., 1971-75; pediatric head nurse U. Calif. Irvine Med. Ctr., 1975-79; clin. nurse educator Palm Harbor Gen./Med. Ctr. Garden Grove, Calif., 1980-81; dir. ednl. svcs. Med. Ctr. of Garden Grove, 1981-85; dir. edn. Mission Hosp. Regional Med. Ctr., Mission Viejo, Calif., 1986-92; coord. computer and learning resources L.A. Med. Ctr. Sch. Nursing, 1992—; assoc. part time faculty Saddleback Coll., 1990—; lectr. statewide nursing program Calif. State U., Dominguez Hills, 1986-92; ednl. cons. Author: (with others) Nursing Diagnosis Guidelines to Planning Care, 1993; contbr. articles to profl. jours. Treas. Orange County Nursing Edn. Coun., 1986-87, 88-90, pres., 1987-88. Mem. ANA, Nat. League for Nursing (mem. nursing informatics coun. 1994—), Am. Nursing Informatics Assn. (elections com. So. Calif. chpt. 1994, coord. continuing edn.), Calif. Nurses Assn. (regional mem.-at-large 1990-92), Am. Soc. Health Edn. and Tng., N.Am. Nursing Diagnosis Assn. (secondary reviewer Diagnostic Rev. 1989-90, expert adv. panel 1990—, mem. diagnostic rev. com. 1992-96), So. Calif. Nursing Diagnosis Assn. (membership chmn. 1984-92, pres. 1992-94), Nat. Am. Mgmt. Assn. (charter L.A. County, U. So. Calif. Med. Ctr. chpt.), Spina Bifida Assn. Am., Sigma Theta Tau (pres.). Home: 1520 San Clemente Ln Corona CA 91720-7949

WETTERHAHN, KAREN ELIZABETH, chemistry educator; b. Plattsburgh, N.Y., Oct. 16, 1948; d. Gustave George and Mary Elizabeth (Thibault) W.; m. Leon H. Webb, June 19, 1982; children—Leon Ashley, Charlotte Elizabeth. B.S., St. Lawrence U., 1970; Ph.D., Columbia U., 1975. Chemist, Mearl Corp., Ossining, N.Y., 1970-71; research fellow Columbia U., N.Y.C., 1971-75, postdoctoral fellow, 1975-76; asst. prof. chemistry Dartmouth Coll., Hanover, N.H., 1976-82, assoc. prof., 1982-86, prof., 1986—; assoc. dean faculty scis., 1990-94, acting dean faculty, 1995—. Contbr. articles to profl. jours. A.P. Sloan fellow, 1981. Mem. Am. Chem. Soc., Am. Assn. Cancer Research, AAAS, N.Y. Acad. Scis. Office: Dartmouth Coll Dept Chemistry 6128 Burke Lab Hanover NH 03755-3564

WETZEL, JODI (JOY LYNN WETZEL), history and women's studies educator; b. Salt Lake City, Apr. 5, 1943; d. Richard Coulam and Margaret Elaine (Openshaw) Wood; m. David Nevin Wetzel, June 12, 1967; children: Meredith (dec.), Richard Rawlins. BA in English, U. Utah, 1965, MA in English, 1967; PhD in Am. Studies, U. Minn., 1977. Instr. Am. studies and family social sci. U. Minn., 1973-77, asst. prof. Am. studies and women's studies, 1977-79, asst. to dir. Minn. Women's Ctr., 1973-75, asst. dir., 1975-79; dir. acad. affairs Women's Resource Ctrs. U. Denver, 1980-84, mem. adj. faculty history, 1981-84, dir. Am. studies program, dir. Women's Inst., 1983-84; dir. Women in Curriculum U. Maine, 1985-86; mem. coop. faculty sociology, social work and human devel. Met. State Coll. Denver, 1986—, dir. Inst. Women's Studies and Svcs., 1986—, assoc. prof., 1986-89, asso. prof. history, 1986-89, prof. history, 1990—; speaker, presenter, cons. in field; vis. prof. Am. studies U. Colo., 1985. Co-author: Women's Studies: Thinking Women, 1993; co-editor: Readings Toward Composition, 2d edit., 1969; contbr. articles to profl. publs. Del. at-large Nat. Women's Meeting, Houston, 1977; bd. dirs. Rocky Mountain Women's Inst., 1981-84; treas. Colo. Women's Agenda, 1987-91. U. Utah Dept. English fellow, 1967; U. Minn. fellow, 1978-79; grantee NEH, 1973, NSF, 1981-83, Carnegie Corp., 1988; named to Outstanding Young Women of Am., 1979. Mem. Am. Hist. Assn., Nat. Assn. Women in Edn., Am. Assn. for Higher Edn., Am. Studies Assn., Nat. Women's Studies Assn., Golden Key Nat. Honor Soc. (hon.), Alpha Lambda Delta, Phi Kappa Phi. Office: Met State Coll Denver Campus Box 36 PO Box 173362 Denver CO 80217-3362

WETZSTEIN, SANDRA LYNNE, elementary school educator; b. San Angelo, Tex., Mar. 28, 1944; d. Robert Hans and Arline Edwina (Milleville) Jensen; m. Merrell W. Wetzstein, July 17, 1966; children: Raechel, Joel, Rebecca. BA, Concordia Coll., River Forest, Ill., 1966; MEd, U. Okla., Norman, 1985. Cert. coop. learning trainer. Elem. tchr. St. Paul's Luth. Sch., West Point, Nebr., 1966-67; tchr. English Centro Cultural Brasil-Estados Unidos, Belem, Brazil, 1972-76; elem. tchr. St. Mary's Sch., Balboa, Republic Panama, 1981-82, Dept. Def. Dependent Sch., Howard AFB, Republic Panama, 1982—. Mem. ASCD, Nat. Coun. Math. Tchrs., Phi Delta Kappa. Home: PSC 07 Box 573 APO AA 34007

WEXLER, ANNE, government relations and public affairs consultant; b. N.Y.C., Feb. 10, 1930; d. Leon R. and Edith R. (Rau) Levy; m. Joseph Duffey, Sept. 17, 1974; children by previous marriage: David Wexler, Daniel Wexler. B.A., Skidmore Coll., 1951, LL.D. (hon.), 1978; D.Sc. in Bus. (hon.), Bryant Coll., 1978. Assoc. pub. Rolling Stone mag., 1974-76; personnel adviser Carter-Mondale transition planning group, 1976-77; dep. undersec. regional affairs Dept. Commerce, 1977-78; asst. to Pres. of U.S., Washington, 1978-81; pres. Wexler and Assocs., Washington, 1981-82; govt. relations and pub. affairs cons., chmn. Wexler, Reynolds, Harrison & Schule, Inc., Washington, 1981-90; vice chmn. Hill and Knowlton PA Worldwide, Washington, 1990-92; chmn. The Wexler Group, div. Hill & Knowlton, Washington, 1992—; bd. dirs. Alumax, Inc., NOVA, Nat. Park Found., Am. Cyanamid Co., New Eng. Electric System, Continental Corp., Comcast Corp., Dreyfus Index funds; mem. vis. com. J.F. Kennedy Sch. of Govt., Harvard U., pub. responsibility com. bd. advisors Carter Ctr., Emory U.; bd. visitors U. Md. Sch. Pub. Affairs. Named Outstanding Alumna Skidmore Coll., 1972, recipient most disting. alumni award, 1984, Bryce Harlow award, 1989. Mem. Council on Fgn. Relations., Com. of 200, Nat. Womens Forum. Jewish. Office: 1317 F St NW Ste 600 Washington DC 20004-1105

WEXLER, JACQUELINE GRENNAN (MRS. PAUL J. WEXLER), former association executive and college president; b. Sterling, Ill., Aug. 2, 1926; d. Edward W. and Florence (Dawson) Grennan; m. Paul J. Wexler, June 1, 1969; stepchildren: Wendy, Wayne. A.B., Webster Coll., 1948; M.A., U. Notre Dame, 1957; LL.D., Franklin and Marshall Coll., 1968, Phila. Coll. Textiles and Sci., 1987; D.H.L., Brandeis U., 1968; LL.D., Skidmore Coll., 1967, Smith Coll., 1975; HHD, U. Mich., 1967, U. Ohio, 1976; D.H.L., Carnegie Inst., 1966, Colo. Coll., 1967, U. Pa., 1979, U. South Fla., 1991; HHD (hon.), U. Hartford, 1987; DH, St. Ambrose Coll., 1981; DD, Lafayette Coll., 1990. Tchr. English and math. Loretto Acad., El Paso, Tex., 1951-54; tchr. English and math. Nerinx Hall, St. Louis, 1954-59; tchr. English Webster Coll., 1959-60, asst. to pres., 1959, v.p. devel., 1960, exec. v.p., 1962-65, pres., 1965-69; v.p., dir. internat. univ. studies Acad. for Ednl. Devel., N.Y.C., 1969; pres. Hunter Coll., City U. N.Y., 1969-79, Acad. Cons. Assoc., N.Y.C., 1982-90; ret., 1990; pres. NCCJ, 1982-90; writer, commentator, cons.; mem. Am. Council on Edn., Commn. on Internat. Edn., 1967; mem. adv. com. to dir. NIH, 1978-80; mem. exec. panel chief naval ops. U.S. Navy, 1978-81; bd. examiners Fgn. Service, Dept. State, 1981-83; dir. Interpublic Group of Cos., Inc., United Techs. Corp.; mem. Pres.'s Adv. Panel on Research and Devel. in Edn., 1961-65; mem. Pres.'s Task Force on Urban Ednl. Opportunities, 1967. Author: Where I Am Going, 1968; contbr. articles to profl. jours. Trustee U. Pa. Recipient NYU Sch. Edn. Ann. award for creative leadership in edn., 1968, Elizabeth Cutter Morrow award YWCA, 1978, Abraham L. Sachar Silver medallion Brandeis U.'s Nat. Women's Com., 1988, The Albert Einstein award Am. Soc. Technion, 1989; named One of Six Outstanding Women of St. Louis Area St. Louis chpt. Theta Sigma Phi, 1963, Woman of Achievement in Edn. St. Louis Globe-Democrat, 1964, Woman of Accomplishment Harpers Bazaar, 1967, one of Am.'s Most Important 100 Women Ladies Home Jour., 1988; Kenyon lectr. Vassar Coll., 1967. Mem. Mo. Acad. Squires, Kappa Gamma Pi.

WEXLER, NANCY SABIN, clinical neuropsychology educator; b. Washington, July 19, 1945; d. Milton and Leonore Wexler. AB cum laude, Radcliffe Coll., 1967; PhD in Clin. Psychology, U. Mich., 1974; DHL (hon.), N.Y. Med. Coll., 1991; DSc (hon.), U. Mich., 1991. Lic. psychologist, N.Y. Psychol. intern, teaching fellow U. Mich., 1968-74; asst. prof. psychology grad. faculty New Sch. Social Rsch., N.Y.C., 1974-76; pvt. practice psychology N.Y.C., 1974-76; health sci. adminstr. Nat. Inst. Neurol., Comm. Disorders and Stroke, NIH, 1978-83; pres. Hereditary Disease Found., Santa Monica, Calif., 1983—; assoc. prof. clin. neuropsychology Coll. Phys. and Surgeons, Columbia U., N.Y.C., 1985-92, prof. clin. neuropsychology, 1992—; mem. Ctr. for Brain and Behavior Coll. Phys. and Surgeons of Columbia U., 1985; mem. adv. com. Human Genome Ctr., Lawrence Berkeley Labs. and U. Calif., 1988—; mem. external adv. com. Ctr. for Human Genome Studies, Los Alamos Nat. Labs., 1990—; co-chairperson ethical, legal and social issues com. Human Genome Orgn., 1991—, mem. dir. search Nat. Ctr. for Human Genome Rsch., NIH, 1992; chairperson Joint NIH/Dept. of Energy Ethical, Legal, Social Issues Working Group on Human Genome, 1989—. Contbr. articles to profl. jours. Trustee Nat. Huntington's Disease Assn., 1983-85, Marine Biol. Lab., 1984-86, Eleanor Roosevelt Inst. Cancer Rsch., 1985-91, Found. for Care and Cure of Huntington's Disease, 1988—. Fulbright scholar U. West Indies, Jamaica, 1967-68; fellow The Hastings Ctr., 1990—; recipient award Robert J. and Claire Pasarow Found., 1987, Living Legacy award Women's Internat. Soc., 1988, Alumnae Athena award Alumnae Coun. U. Mich., 1989, award Gov.'s Office, Zulia, Venezuela, 1989, Venezuelan Presdl. award, 1990, Legis. Commendation N.Y. State, 1990, Disting. Svc. award Nat. Assn. Biology Tchrs., 1993, Nat. Med. Rsch. award Nat. Health Coun., 1993, Albert Lasker Pub. Svc. award, 1993. Mem. AAAS (bd. dirs. 1993—), APA, Am. Soc. Law and Medicine, Soc. Neurosci. (chairperson social issues com. 1988-90, organizing com. Neurobiology of Human Diesease Workshop 1980—), Am. Psychol. Soc., Am. Soc. Human Genetics, World Fedn. Nuerology, Rsch. Group on Huntington's Disease, Am. Neurol. Assn. Office: Columbia U Coll Physicians & Surgeons Dept Neuropsychology 630 W 168th St New York NY 10032 Office: Hereditary Disease Found 1427 7th St # 2 Santa Monica CA 90401 also: Columbia U Coll Phys & Surg NY State Psychiat Inst 722 W 168th St Box 58 New York NY 10032

WEXLER, SUSAN, artist; b. N.Y.C., July 17, 1937; d. Nathan and Betty (Stoop) Kent; m. Lewis Wexler, June 22, 1958; children: Jeffrey, Steven, Daniel. BA, Syracuse U., 1957; MA, Columbia U., 1958. apptd. Palo Alto (Calif.) Pub. Art Commn., 1990; adv. bd. San Jose (Calif.) Inst. Contemporary Art, 1991; presenter and spkr. on pub. art. One-woman shows include San Jose Mus. Art, 1982, Palo Alto (Calif.) Cultural Ctr., 1991, Smith Andersen Gallery, Palo Alto, 1991, 94, San Jose (Calif.) Inst. Contemporary Art, 1993, Sazama Gallery, Chgo., 1994; exhibited in group shows including Fresno Arts Ctr. and Mus., 1987, Soco Gallery and the Goethe Inst., Napa, Calif., 1990, de Anza Coll., Cupertino, Calif., 1990, Ind. U., Gary, 1991; represented in permanent collections AT&T, IBM, Continental Bank, The Landahl Group, Chgo., Kindman & Assocs., N.Y.C., Plaza Bank, San Jose, others. Studio: 805 Tolman Dr Stanford CA 94305-1025

WEXTON, JANE LESLIE, lawyer; b. N.Y.C., Sept. 20, 1943; d. Godfried and Beatrice (Eppsteiner) Jacob; m. Charles I. Wexton, June 3, 1962 (div. Sept. 1981); children: Nancy S., Andrew L. BA, CCNY, 1964; MA in Teaching, Fairleigh Dickinson U., 1974; JD, Hofstra U., 1983. Asst. dist. atty. N.Y. County Dist. Attys. Office, N.Y.C., 1983-87; assoc. Fried, Frank, Harris, Shriver & Jacobson, N.Y.C., 1987-89; v.p., sr. atty. litigation Citicorp/Citibank Legal Affairs Office, N.Y.C., 1989—; lectr. in field. Mem. ABA (white collar crime subcom. on corp. criminal sanctions and money laundering), Am. Bankers Assn. (task force on money laundering 1989—, fgn. trade task force on money laundering), Hogan Morganthan Assocs. Office: Citibank Legal Affairs 425 Park Ave New York NY 10022-3506

WEYAND, EDWINA WICKER, elementary school educator; b. Dublin, Ga., Jan. 20, 1964; d. Edgar Pete and Bettye Laverne (Holt) Wicker; m. Patrick John Weyand, June 15, 1985. BS in Edn., Valdosta State Coll., 1986; postgrad., West Ga. Coll., 1992—. Cert. tchr., Ga., La. Fitness instr. Gulfport (Miss.) YMCA, 1986-87, England AFB, Alexandria, La., 1987; recreation therapist Pinecrest State Sch., Alexandria, 1987-88; dir. youth programs, camp dir. YMCA Cen. La., Alexandria, 1988-89; camp dir. Girl Scout Camp Martha Johnston, Lizella, Ga., 1990; tchr. phys. edn. Griffin (Ga.)/Spalding County Sch. System, 1990-93; tchr. phys. edn., coach Henry County Sch. System, 1993-94; elem. phys. edn. tchr. Clayton County Sch. System, Ellenwood, Ga., 1994—. Coach cycling, event coord. Spl. Olympics, Griffin, 1990-93; vol. Dept. Family and Children's Svcs., 1994—. Seven-time state cycling champion U.S. Cycling Fedn., La. and Ga., 1989-92, Olympic trials competitor, 1992; named Amateur Cyclist of Yr. Atlanta Health and Fitness mag., 1991. Mem. Profl. Assn. Ga. Educators, Ga. Assn. Health, Phys. Edn., Recreation and Dance, Spalding Sprockets Bicycle Club, Outdoor Spltys., Inc. Bicycle Racing Tean, So. Bicycle League (safety and edn. dir.), Outward Bound Alumni Assn. Methodist. Home: 964 Spring Dr Jonesboro GA 30236 Office: East Clayton Elem Sch Ellenwood Rd Ellenwood GA 40436-2388

WHALEN, ALBERTA DEAN, community health nurse; b. Oakland, Calif., Apr. 27, 1929; d. Govie and Lula (Rutledge) Smith; m. Joseph T. Whalen, May 29, 1954; children: Michael, Joseph, William. RN, Providence Coll. Nursing, Oakland, 1951; postgrad., Chabot Coll., Las Positas Coll. RN, Calif. Surgical/recovery room nurse Peralta Hosp., Oakland, Calif., 1951-55; surg., recovery rm. nurse Providence Hosp., Oakland, 1956; recovery room nurse Eden Hosp., Castro Valley, Calif., 1957; pvt. duty nurse Valley Meml. Hosp., Livermore, Calif., 1966-68; doctor's office nurse Daphne M. Chisolm, MD, Livermore, 1984-86; home nursing Livermore, 1987—; part-time pvt. duty nurse Hacienda Care Ctr., Livermore, Calif., 1993—. Vol. ARC, 1976—, CPR and std. 1st aid instr., rep. in fair booths and 1st aid stas., disaster teams; vol. cmty. health nurse for Livermore Libr. sr. blood pressure clinics, 1984—; rec. sec. Cath. Nurses Assn., South Alameda County, 1958-60; found. mem. Newly Merged Summit Med. Group, Oakland, Calif.; active St. Rose Hosp. Found., Hayward, Calif.; mem. welcoming com. St. Michaels Cath. Ch., Livermore, 1962—, Golden Friends, 1988—, Eucharistic min., 1991—. Recipient ARC nursing pin. Mem. Providence Hosp., Valley Meml. Hosp. Founds., ARC.

WHALEN, LUCILLE, academic administrator; b. Los Angeles, July 26, 1925; d. Edward Cleveland and Mary Lucille (Perrault) W. B.A. in English, Immaculate Heart Coll., Los Angeles, 1949; M.S.L.S., Catholic U. Am., 1955; D.L.S., Columbia U., 1965. Tchr. elem. and secondary parochial schs. Los Angeles, Long Beach, Calif., 1945-52; high sch. librarian Conaty Meml. High Sch., Los Angeles, 1950-52; reference/serials librarian, instr. in library sci. Immaculate Heart Coll., 1955-58; dean Immaculate Heart Coll. (Sch. Library Sci.), 1958-60, 65-70; assoc. dean, prof. SUNY, Albany, 1971-78, 84-87; prof. Sch. Info. Sci. and Policy SUNY, 1979-83; dean grad. programs, libr. Immaculate Heart Coll. Ctr., Los Angeles, 1987-90; ref. libr. (part-time) Glendale Community Coll., 1990—; dir. U.S. Office Edn. Instn. Author, editor: (with others) Reference Services in Archives, 1986. author: Human Rights: A Reference Handbook, 1989. Mem. ACLU, Common Cause, Amnesty Internat. Democrat. Roman Catholic. Home: 320 S Gramercy Pl Apt 101 Los Angeles CA 90020-4542 Office: Glendale Community Coll 1500 N Verdugo Rd Glendale CA 91208-2894

WHALEN, MARGARET CAVANAGH, retired secondary school educator; b. Des Moines, Iowa, Mar. 9, 1913; d. Thomas J. and Ann Lenore (Paul) Cavanagh; m. George Hubert Whalen, Aug. 3, 1946; children: Michael T., Ann Whalen Carrillo, George Patrick (dec.), Cheryl. BS in Commerce, St. Teresa Coll., Winona, Minn., 1935. Head bus. dept. St. Augustine High Sch., Austin, Minn., 1935-36, Parochial High Sch., Caledonia, Minn., 1936-37; clk., typist U.S. Govt., Dept. Socicl Security, Des Moines, 1937-38; county investigator for old age asst., aid to blind Marion County, Knoxville, Iowa, 1938; hydro dept. U.S. Weather Bur. Regional Office, Iowa City, Kansas City, Mo., 1939-42; head bills/warrants dept. IRS, Des Moines, 1942-46; substitute tchr. Los Gatos High Sch., Calif., 1961-65, Saratoga High Sch., Calif., 1961-65. Vol. Girl Scouts U.S.A., Boy Scouts Am., Saratoga, 1957-62; poll insp. Santa Clara County Regional Voters, Saratoga; precinct insp. Saratoga for Santa Clara County Registrar of Voters; organizer, vol. Saratoga Area Sr. Coordinating Coun., 1979—; Eucharistic minister, lector, commentator Sacred Heart Ch., Saratoga, 1986—; charter pres. Oz chpt. Children's Home Soc., Saratoga; mem. Sacred Heart Women's Club, Our Lady of Los Gatos #197 Young Ladies Inst. Recipient Papal Bronze medal for Pub. Rels. Nat. Coun. Cath. Women, Saratoga, 1958, Merit award Friends of Saratoga Librs., 1975—, Merit award Saratoga Area Sr. Coord. Coun., 1981. Mem. AAUW (corr. sec. Los Gatos-Saratoga br., chmn. social arts, bridge, hospitality, Friday Matinee sect., book rev. sect.), Saratoga Hist. Found., Alumnae Assn. St. Theresa Coll., Montalvo Assn., Saratoga Foothill Club. Democrat. Roman Catholic. Home: 14140 Victor Pl Saratoga CA 95070-5425

WHALEN, PATRICIA THERESE, marketing professional; b. Columbus, Ohio, June 26, 1955; d. Daniel Edward and Rose Eileen (Callahan) W. BA in English, Ohio State U., 1977; MS in Bus. Adminstrn., Ind. U., 1981; postgrad. in mass media, Mich. State U., 1994—. Sales promotion specialist Clark Components Div., Buchanan, Mich., 1978-81, supr., advt. and pub. rels., 1981-82; mgr. corp. comm. Clark Equipment Co., Buchanan, Mich., 1982-84; dir. govt. affairs Clark Equipment Co., South Bend, Ind., 1984-86; dir. pub. rels. COMSAT World Systems Div., Clarksburg, Md., 1986-87; dir. mktg. communications COMSAT World Systems Div., Washington, 1987-90; dir. mktg. COMSAT Mobile Comm., Washington, 1990-94; seminar speaker in field. Bd. dirs. Tri-county Pvt. Industry Coun., St. Joseph County, Mich., 1983-85, Jr. Achievement, Niles, Mich. and South Bend, Ind., 1982-86; chmn. Clark PAC Polit. Action Com., South Bend, 1984-86. Mem. Pub. Rels. Soc. Am. (tech. com. 1982—, Silver Anvil award 1982), Internat. Assn. Bus. Communicators, Bus. and Profl. Advertisers Assn., Soc. Satellite Profls. (bd. dirs. 1990-93). Roman Catholic. Home: 10853 Shawnee Trail Stanwood MI 49346

WHALEY, ELIZABETH ARD, school district administrator; b. Kingstree, S.C., June 20, 1953; d. Richard Lee and Sadie Louise (Dukes) Ard; m. Curtis Renay Whaley, Apr. 12, 1974; children: Janet Louise, Curtis Renay Jr. BS in Edn., MEd, Winthrop Coll., 1973. Cert. tchr., S.C. County food svc. supr. Florence County (S.C.) Schs., 1973-77; dist. sch. food svc. dir. Florence Sch. Dist. 3, Lake City, S.C., 1977—. Mem. S.C. Sch. Food Svc. Assn. (area rep. 1991-93, chair certification 1986-93), Am. Sch. Food Svc. Assn. Baptist. Home: RR 2 Box 261-a-10 Lake City SC 29560-9573 Office: Florence Sch Dist 3 140 Westover St Lake City SC 29560-2300

WHALLEY-KILMER, JOANNE, actress; b. Manchester, England, Aug. 25, 1964; m. Val Kilmer. Actress (theater) Bows and Arrows, 1982, Rita, Sue, and Bob Too, 1982, The Genius, 1983, Kate, 1983, The Crimes of Vautrin, 1983, The Pope's Wedding, 1984, Saved, 1984, As I Lay Dying, 1985, Women Beware Women, 1986, Three Sisters, 1987, What the Butler Saw, 1989 (Theatre World award 1989), (films) Pink Floyd-The Wall, 1982, Dance With a Stranger, 1985, The Good Father, 19886, No Surrender, 1986, Willow, 1988, Popielusko, (To Kill a Priest), 1989, Scandal, 1989, Kill Me Again, 1989, Navy SEALS, 1990, Crossing the Rapture, 1994, Trial By Jury, 1994, A Good Man in Africa, 1995 (TV) A Christmas Carol, 1984, A Kind of Loving, A Quiet Life, The Gentle Touch, Reilly, Save Your Kisses, Will You Love Me Tomorrow?, (TV mini-series) Edge of Darkness, 1986, The Singing Detective, 1988, Channel Crossings, 1988, Scarlett, 1994. Office: Creative Artists Agency 9830 Wilshire Blvd Beverly Hills CA 90212*

WHAM, DOROTHY STONECIPHER, state legislator; b. Centralia, Ill., Jan. 5, 1925; d. Ernest Joseph and Vera Thelma (Shafer) Stonecipher; m. Robert S. Wham, Jan. 26, 1947; children: Nancy S. Wham Mitchell, Jeanne Wham Ryan, Robert S. II. BA, MacMurray Coll., 1946; MA, U. Ill., 1949; D of Pub. Adminstrn. (hon.), MacMurray Coll., 1992. Counsellor Student Counselling Bur. U. Ill., Urbana, 1946-49; state dir. ACTION program, Colo./Wyo. U.S. Govt., Denver, 1972-82; mem. Colo. Ho. of Reps., 1986-87; mem. Colo. Senate, 1987—, chair jud. com., 1988—; with capital devel. com., health, environ, welfare, instns., fin. appropriations, legal svcs. Mem. LWV, Civil Rights Commn. Denver, 1972-80; bd. dirs. Denver Com. on Mental Health, 1985-88, Denver Symphony, 1985-88. Mem. Am. Psychol. Assn., Colo. Mental Health Assn. (bd. dirs. 1986-88), Colo. Hemophilia Soc. Republican. Methodist. Lodge: Civitan. Home: 2790 S High St Denver CO 80210-6352 Office: State Capitol Rm 342 Denver CO 80203

WHARE, WANDA SNYDER, lawyer; b. Columbia, Pa., Nov. 5, 1959; d. William Sylvester and Dorothy Jacqueline (Luttman) W.; m. James Robert Snyder, Nov. 14, 1987; 1 child, Eric James. BA, Franklin & Marshall Coll., 1981; JD, Dickinson Sch. Law, 1984. Bar: Pa. 1984. Asst. counsel Pa. Dept. Labor and Industry, Harrisburg, 1984-87; assoc. Gibbel, Kraybill & Hess, Lancaster, Pa., 1987-89; corp. counsel Irex Corp., Lancaster, 1990—. Mem. parish-staff rels. com. 1st Meth. Ch., Lancaster, 1987-92, mem. com. on status and role of women, 1989—, chair 1992—. Democrat. Office: Irex Corp 120 N Lime St Lancaster PA 17602-2951

WHARTON, JANE MARIE, psychiatric aide; b. Darby, Pa., Nov. 5, 1946; d. James Morris Henson and Florence E. (Demby) Moore; m. William Mitchell Wharton, May 18, 1974 (div. Dec. 1984); children: Rena Denise, Mitchell James. Psychiatric aide Haverford State Hosp., Haverford, Pa., 1968—. Sec.-treas. Union Local 2346, 1991-93, mem. exec. bd., 1992-93, treas. activity com., 1992-93; mem. Town Watch, Brookhaven, 1994. Mem. Am. Assn. Psychiatric Technicians (Technician of the Yr. 1993, 94), Babcock (Babcock award Haverford State Hosp. 1988), Swarthmore Coll. Upward Bound Program Parent Club.

WHARTON, KAY KAROLE, special education educator; b. Butler, Pa., Nov. 19, 1943; d. Clarence Henry Jr. and Alberta Elizabeth (Yost) Gilkey; m. David Burton Wharton, Nov. 28, 1975 (dec. May 1987). BS in Edn., Geneva Coll., 1965. Cert. spl. edn. tchr., Md. Tchr. 2d grade Butler Area Sch., 1965-71; resource tchr. Queen Anne County Bd. of Edn., Centreville, Md., 1971—; facilitator sch. improvement team Centreville Mid. Sch., 1992—. Music dir. Diocese of Easton (Md.) Mid. Convocation Episcopal Cursillo, Old St. Paul's, Kent, 1989-91, St. Paul's, Hillsboro, 1993—; Sunday sch. supt. primary dept. St. Mark's Luth. Ch., 1966-71, St. Paul's Episcopal Ch., 1985-87; program dir. Queen Anne's County chpt. Am. Cancer Soc., Centreville, 1981-85; mem. PTA. Mem. NEA, Queen Anne County Edn. Assn., Md. State Tchrs. Assn., Coun. for Exceptional Children, Internat. Reading Assn., Upper Shore Reading Assn. (sec. 1985-91, 93—), Learning Disabled Am., Guardians Learning Disabled (sec. 1991-92), Internat. Wildlife Fedn., Smithsonian Assocs., Order Ea. Star (worthy matron Centreville 1977, sec. 1982-93), Nat. Geographic Soc., Town and Country Women's Club (pres. 1977, 79), Delta Kappa Gamma (Nu chpt. pres. 1992—, rsch. com. chairperson Alpha Beta State 1993—). Republican. Home: PO Box 237 Centreville MD 21617-0237 Office: Centreville Mid Sch 231 Ruthsburg Rd Centreville MD 21617-9702

WHATCOTT, MARSHA RASMUSSEN, elementary educator; b. Fillmore, Utah, Mar. 29, 1941; d. William Hans and Evangelyn (Robison) Rasmussen; m. Robert LaGrand Whatcott, Sept. 14, 1961; children: Sherry, Cindy, Jay Robert, Justin William. Assoc., So. Utah State U., 1962; BS, Brigham Young U., 1968. Cert. tchr. early childhood, Utah. 1st grade tchr. Provost Elem., Provo, Utah, 1968-84, kindergarten tchr., 1984-91, 3d grade tchr., 1991—; music specialist Provost Elem., 1984-87, 91-92, 93-94, art specialist, 1984-85, math. specialist, 1988-89, sci. specialist, 1994—; del. Utah Edn. Assn., 1989-90; bldg. rep. Provo Edn. Assn., 1993-94, 94—. Mem. polit. action com. Provo Sch. Dist., 1982, 90, mem. profl. devel. com., 1972-79; mem. profl. devel. com. Benniville Uniserve (Provo, Alpine and Nebo Sch. Dist.), 1994-95. Recipient Millard County Utah PTA scholarship, 1959-62, Golden Apple award Provo City PTA, 1984, Recognition Disting. Svc. in

Edn. award Utah State Legis., 1992; named Outstanding Educator in Utah Legis. Dist. # 64, 1992. Mem. Bonneville Uniserve (profl. devel. com.). Mem. LDS Ch. Office: Provost Elem Sch 629 S 1000 E Provo UT 84606-5204

WHATLEY, JACQUELINE BELTRAM, lawyer; b. West Orange, N.J., Sept. 26, 1944; d. Quirino and Eliane (Gruet) Beltram; m. John W. Whatley, June 25, 1966. BA, U. Tampa, 1966; JD, Stetson U., 1969. Bar: Fla. 1969, Alaska 1971. Cert. real estate law specialist. Assoc. Gibbons, Tucker, McEwen Smith & Cofer, Tampa, Fla., 1969-71; pvt. practice, Anchorage, 1971-73; ptnr. Gibbons, Tucker, Miller, Whatley & Stein, P.A., Tampa, 1973-81, pres., 1981—. Bd. dirs. Travelers Aid Soc.; trustee Humana Women's Hosp., Tampa 1987-93, Keystone United Meth. Ch., 1986-89. Mem. ABA, Fla. Bar Assn. (realestate cert. com. 1993—), Alaska Bar Assn., Tenn. Walking Horse Breeders and Exhibitors Assn. (v.p. 1984-87, dir. for Fla. 1981-87, 1990-93, adv. com. Tenn. Walking Horse Celebration 1994—), Tenn. Walking Horse (mem. nat. celebration adv. com.), Fla. Walking and Racking Horse Assn. (bd. dirs. 1988-89, pres. 1980-82), Athena Club (Tampa). Republican. Methodist. Home: PO Box 17595 Tampa FL 33682-7595 Office: 101 E Kennedy Blvd Ste 1000 Tampa FL 33602-5146

WHEALEY, LOIS DEIMEL, humanities scholar; b. N.Y.C., June 20, 1932; d. Edgar Bertram Deimel and Lois Elizabeth (Hatch) Washburn; m. Robert Howard Whealey, July 2, 1954; children: Richard William, David John, Alice Ann Whealey Dediu. BA in History, Stanford U., 1951; MA in Edn., U. Mich., 1955; MA in Polit. Sci., Ohio U., 1975. Tchr. 5th grade Swayne Sch., Owyhee, Nev., 1952-53; tchr. 7th grade Ft. Knox (Ky.) Dependent's Sch., 1955-56; tchr. adult basic edn. USAF, Oxford, 1956-57; tchr. 6th grade Amerman Sch., Northville, Mich., 1957-58; tchr. 8th grade English, social studies Slauson Jr. High Sch., Ann Arbor, Mich., 1958-59; adminstrv. asst. humanities conf. Ohio U., Athens, 1974-76, 83; part-time instr. Ohio U., Athens, 1966-68, 75. Contbr. articles to profl. jours. Mem. Athens County Regional Planning Commn., 1974-78, treas., 1976-78; bd. dirs. Ohio-Meadville Dist. Unitarian-Universalist Assn., 1975-81; mem. Ohio coord. com. Internat. Women's Yr., 1977; v.p. Black Diamond Girl Scout Coun., 1980-86; chair New Day for Equal Rights Amendment, 1982; mem. Athens City Bd. Edn., 1984-90, v.p., 1984, pres., 1985 ; mem. Tri County Vocat. Sch. Bd., Nelsonville, Ohio, 1984-90, v.p., 1988-89; mem. adv. com. Ohio River Valley Water Sanitation Commn., 1986—; bd. dirs. Ohio Environ. Coun., 1984-90, sec. 1986-90; bd. dirs. Ohio Alliance for Environ., 1993—. Recipient Unsung UU award Ohio-Meadville Dist. Unitarian Universalist Assn., 1984, Thanks badge Black Diamond Girl Scout Coun., 1986, named Woman of Achievement, 1987; recipient How to award Ednl. Press Assn. Am., 1990, Donna Chen Women's Equity award Ohio U., 1994. Mem. AAUW (pres. Athens br. 1969-70, 89-90, 93—), LWV (pres. 1975-77), Pi Lambda Theta (life). Democrat. Home: 14 Oak St Athens OH 45701-2605

WHEATLEY, BARBARA, marketing and sales professional; b. Newark, Oct. 2, 1951; d. Andrew Walter and Ann Barbara (Chulick) Liyana; m. Michael Owen Wheatley; 1 child, Joy Whitcomb. BS in Mgmt., Rensselaer Poly. Inst., 1973; MBA, U. Wis., 1975. CPA, Tenn.; cert. mgmt. acct. Acctg. supr. Koehring Co., Appleton, Wis., 1973-75, market analyst, 1975; fin. systems analyst Dobbs-Life Savers, Inc., Memphis, 1976-77, mgr. adminstrv. procedures, 1977-80; dir. adminstrv. control Dobbs Houses, Inc., Memphis, 1980-82, dir. ops. svcs., 1982-83; divsn. ops. mgr. Frito-Lay, Inc., Memphis, 1983-84, mgr. sales ops., Dallas, 1984-85, mgr. expense analysis, Dallas, 1985-86, mgr. mktg. performance analysis, 1986-89, product mgr., 1989-91; pres., mng. dir. SolVision, Inc., Dallas, 1991-94; mktg. and sales support analyst Am. Med. Electronics, Richardson, Tex., 1994—. Mem. AICPAs, Inst. Mgmt. Accts. Home: 16215 Meandering Way Dallas TX 75248-2350 Office: Am Med Electronics 250 E Arapaho Rd Richardson TX 75081

WHEATLEY, BARNARESE P. (BONNIE WHEATLEY), health services consultant; b. New Iberia, La., Nov. 6, 1942; d. Ervin and Elizabeth (Pierce) Politte; m. Horace Wheatley, Oct. 9, 1967; children: Adrienne K., Alanna M. BS, Calif. State U., Hayward, 1989; MPH, San Jose State U., 1994. Project coord. Summit Med. Ctr., Oakland, Calif., 1989-93; health svc. cons. Alameda County, Oakland, 1993—. Co-author: Wellness Perspective, 1993. Treas. Leadership Am., 1992-93; coord. Nat. Black Leadership No. Calif., 1992—; bd. dirs. Susan B. Komen Found., 1994—, Breast Cancer Action, 1994—, Nat. Breast Cancer Coalition, 1993—; adv. com. Cancer Info. Svc., 1993—. Recipient Community Svc. award Calif. Legislature, 1989, Outstanding Svc. award Nat. Assn. Bench and Bar Spouses, 1992. Mem. Women and Girls Against Tobacco (bd. dirs.). Democrat. Home: 42 LaSalle Ave Piedmont CA 94611-3549 Office: Alameda County Med Ctr 1411 E 31st St Oakland CA 94602

WHEATLEY, ROBERTA JEAN, postmaster; b. Chgo., July 18, 1951; d. Oscar Jerome and Mary Elizabeth (De Saeugher) Gorman; m. Robert Melson Wheatley, Mar. 4, 1969 (div.); children: Tabitha Jean, Robert Sean. Student, Northwestern Bus. Coll., Chgo., 1966-68; AAS, Carl Albert State Coll., 1978. Steno clk. II Ouachita Correctional Ctr., Hodgen, Okla., 1978-79; flexible clk. U.S. Postal Svc., Cameron, Okla., 1979-81; postmaster U.S. Postal Svc., Monroe, Okla., 1981-84, Howe, Okla., 1984-88, Pocola, Okla., 1988—; postmaster trainer U.S. Postal Svc., Tulsa, 1987—. Mem. Mgmt. Sectional Ctr. Women's Program, Muskogee, Okla., 1983-90. With U.S. Army Res., 1986—. Mem. Nat. Assn. Postmasters U.S. (v.p. 1989-90, pres. 1990-91).

WHEATON, ALICE ALSHULER, secretary; b. Burbank, Calif., Mar. 20, 1920; d. Elmore and Anzy Jeanette (Richards) Wheaton; m. Robert Edward Alshuler, Sept. 19, 1942 (div. 1972); children: John Robert, Katherine Dennis. BA in Edn., UCLA, 1942. Cert. profl. sec. Owner, dir. The Fitness Studio, Washington, 1974-85; staff asst. Pres. Coun. Phys. Fitness and Sports, Washington, 1980-89; coord. Fed. Inter Agy. Health Fitness Coun., Washington, 1986-89; expert advisor U.S. Office Pers. Mgmt., Washington, 1986-89; adminstrv. asst. North County Bank, Escondido, Calif., 1990-95; sec. Pala Mesa Village Homes Assn., 1994—; cons. Pres. Coun. Phys. Fitness and Sports. Editor: The Federal FitKit-Guidelines for Federal Agencies, 1988. Recipient Gold Key award L.A. Area United Way, 1966. Mem. Profl. Secs. Internat. (pres. Palomar chpt. 1993—), UCLA Gold Shield Hon. (pres.), UCLA Alumni Assn. (v.p., Disting. Com. Svc. award 1968), San Diego Hist. Soc., Kappa Kappa Gamma. Republican. Episcopalian.

WHEDON, MARGARET BRUNSSEN, television and radio producer; b. N.Y.C.; d. Henry and Anna Margaret (Nickel) Brunssen; m. G. Donald Whedon, 1942 (div. Sept. 1982); children: Karen Whedon Green, David Marshall. BA, U. Rochester, 1948; postgrad., CUNY-Hunter Coll., 1950. With ABC-TV and Radio News; asst. prodr. Coll. News Conf., 1952-60; prodr. This Week with David Brinkley, 1981-84. Prodr.: Issues and Answers, 1960-81, From the Capitol, ABC Radio, 1962-69; nres prodr. Pub. Affairs Satellite Sys., Inc., 1983—, Pubs at Pub. Affairs Satellite, Washington, 1986—; mem. Capitol Speakers, lectr., pub. speaker; commentator Flair Reports, 1962-64; music critic The Hill Rag; author: Always on Sunday, 1980, Dining in the Great Embassies, 1987. Recipient NCCJ award, 1968; nominee NATAS award, 1968. Mem. White House Corrs. Assn., Nat. Press Club, Am. Newspaper Women's Club (pres. 1983), Am. Women in Radio and TV, Radio-TV Corrs. Assn. Home: 4201 Cathedral Ave NW Apt 702E Washington DC 20016-4901

WHEELER, CATHY JO, government official; b. Birmingham, Ala., Feb. 14, 1954; d. Charles Edwin and Hazel Josephine (Hollis) W.; m. David Arthur Tate. BA, U. Montevallo, 1975; postgrad., U. Ala., 1982-84. With Social Security Adminstrn., Birmingham, 1975—, mgmt. analyst, 1991—, sr. employment devel. specialist, 1983-85, mgr. tech. tng. dept., 1985-91, mgmt. analyst, 1991—; v.p. Fed. Women's Program, Birmingham, 1984-85; treas., charter mem. Federally Employed Women, Birmingham, 1984-88. Mem. alumni bd. dirs. U. Montevallo, Ala., 1991-94, v.p. fin., 1994-96. Mem. ASTD (treas. 1987-88, pres. elect 1989, pres. 1990, asst. regional dir. 1991-92), Soc. Govt. Meeting Planners (chartered, v.p. 1989-90, sec. 1990-91), Jaycees (v.p. mgmt. devel. Hoover, Ala. chpt. 1988-89), Chi Omega Alumni Assn. (treas. 1991, advisor 1991—). Home: 1108 Columbiana Rd Birmingham AL 35209-7008 Office: Social Security Adminstrn 2001 12th Ave N Birmingham AL 35285-0002

WHEELER, ERIN RYAN, human resources administrator; b. Mobile, Ala., Sept. 18, 1940; d. Frederick Grant Sr. and Agnes Estelle (Ryan) W. BA, Maryville U., 1962; MSW, St. Louis U., 1966. Lic. cert. social worker. Case worker Mobile County Dept. Human Resources, 1962-63, child welfare worker, 1964-65; AFDC supr. Aid to Families with Dependent Children, 1966-68; child welfare supr. Mobile County Dept. Human Resources, 1968-71, asst. dir., 1973-76, dir., 1977—; reg. tng. supr. Ala. Dept. Human Resources, Montgomery, 1971-73; adj. faculty Sch. Social Work, U. Ala., Tuscaloosa, 1974-75; participant Kennedy Sch. Govt. program sr. execs. in state/local govt. Harvard U., 1985; participant Leadership Ala. Class II, Montgomery, 1991-92. Pres., bd. dirs. Leadership Mobile, 1990-93; pres. Ala. Conf. Child Cae, 1973; bd. trustees Leadership Ala., 1990-93, Mercy Med., 1984—, United Way of S.W. Ala., 1991—; active Pvt. Industry Coun., 1983—. Named Social Worker of Yr., Ala. chpt. NASW, 1980; recipient Disting. Leadership award Nat. Assn. Cmty. Leadership, 1985. Mem. Acad. Cert. Social Workers, Ala. Assn. County Dirs. Human Resources (pres. 1986-88), Mobile Rotary Club. Home: 257 Charles St Mobile AL 36604-3059 Office: Mobile Co Dept Human Res PO Box 1906 850 St Anthony St Mobile AL 36633-1906

WHEELER, EVELYN A., communications specialist; b. Cedartown, Ga., May 1, 1955; d. W.F. and Alta E. (Pierce) W. BS in Psychology, Biology and Journalism, Berry Coll., Rome, Ga., 1977. Editor, dir. publs. Precept Ministries, Chattanooga, 1977-83; editor Youth with a Mission, Tujunga, Calif., 1983-84; tchr. Cobb Christian Sch., Marietta, Ga., 1984-85; chief comm. officer Precept Ministries, 1985—. Home: 4120 Albermarle Ave Chattanooga TN 37411-5203 Office: Dept of State Liaison Offices in Dept of State 2201 C St NW Washington DC 20520

WHEELER, JANICE MARIE, communications company administrator; b. L.A., Dec. 9, 1931; d. Emil Edward and Gertie Mae (Allumbaugh) Ryer; m. Jack DeWilton Wheeler, Apr. 8, 1952 (div. Jan. 1970); children: Robert, Donald, James, Jon, Thomas, Jack, Janice H. BA in Bus. Mgmt., BA in Computer Scis., El Camino Coll., 1986. Operator GTE, Redondo, Calif., 1963-71; data control supr. GTE, Santa Monica, Calif., 1971-83; revenue requirements adminstr. GTE, Thousand Oaks, Calif., 1983-89, safety, indsl. hygiene adminstr., 1989—. Active Del Amo Christian Ch., Torrance, Calif. Named Vol. of Month, Calif. Mus. Sci. and Industry Found., 1992, 93. Mem. Calif. Telephone Assn., Road Runners, GTE People, Docents of Calif. Mus. Sci. and Industry (trainer 1987—), Am. Bus. Women's Assn., So. Bay Cities Geneal. Soc. (rec. sec. 1982—), Internat. Telephone Pioneers Am., Shropshire Family, GTE Fitness Ctr. Home: 21008 Victor # 20 Torrance CA 90503-2847 Office: GTE Telephone Ops 112 Lakeview Canyon Rd Thousand Oaks CA 91362-3802

WHEELER, JEANETTE NORRIS, entomologist; b. Newton, Iowa, May 21, 1918; d. David Ottis and Esther (Miles) Norris; widowed; 1 child, Ralph Allen. BA, U. N.D., 1939, MS, 1956, PhD, 1962. Tchr. Casselton (N.D.) High Sch., 1939-40; instr. U. N.D., Grand Forks, 1944-49, asst. prof., 1963-65, rsch. assoc., 1965-67; rsch. assoc. Desert Rsch. Inst., U. Nev., Reno, 1967-80. Co-author: The Ants of North Dakota, 1963, The Amphibians and Reptiles of North Dakota, 1966, Ants of Deep Canyon, Colorado, Desert, California, 1973, Ant Larvae: Review and Synthesis, 1976, The Ants of Nevada, 1986; contbr. over 100 articles to profl. jours. Recipient Sioux award U. N.D. Alumni Assn., 1989. Home: 3338 NE 58th Ave Silver Springs FL 34488-1867

WHEELER, JO ANN, pharmacist; b. Rawlins, Wyo., July 18, 1943; d. Daniel Monroe and Lois Eileen (Campbell) Simmons; m. Bill J. Wheeler, June 25, 1966; 1 child, Jerrod Daniel. BS, U. Wyo., 1966. Registered pharmacist. Pharmacist Osco Drug, Decatur, Ill., 1966-68, Elgin, Ill., 1968-71; pharmacist, owner Wheelers Valley Pharmacy, Cascade, Idaho, 1971—. Treas. Valley County Hosp. Bd., 1972—; vice-chair Shepherd of Mountains Luth. Ch., 1993-94. Mem. AAUW (treas., pres., com. chair), Valley County Hosp. Aux., Idaho Pharm. Assn. Office: Wheelers Valley Pharmacy PO Box 797 Cascade ID 83611-0797

WHEELER, KATHERINE FRAZIER (KATE WHEELER), writer; b. Tulsa, July 27, 1955; d. Charles Bowen and Jan Nette (Moses) W. BA in English Fine Arts, Rice U., 1977; MA in Creative Writing, Stanford U., 1981. News reporter The Miami (Fla.) Herald, 1977-79; tchr. English composition Middlesex C.C., Lawrence, Mass., 1991; tchr. meditation Insight Meditation Soc., Barre, Mass., 1991—. Author: (short stories) Not Where I Started From, 1993; editor: (essays) In This Very Life, 1990; translator: (poems) Borrowed Time/Lo Esperady Lo Vivido, 1987; contg. editor: Tricycle Mag. Buddhist nun Mahasi Sasana Yeiktha, Rangoon, Burma, 1988; vol. Pet Share, Somerville (Mass.) Hosp., 1994. Recipient Pushcart Press prize, 1983-84, Best Am. Short Stories award Houghton Miflin, 1992, O. Henry award Doubleday, Inc., 1982, 93; nominee PEN/Faulkner award, 1994, Whiting Found. award, 1994; grantee NEA, 1994. Home: 72 Rev Nazareno Properzi Wy Somerville MA 02143

WHEELER, KATHERINE N., urban planner; b. St. Louis, June 28, 1939; d. Hiram and Emily (Lewis) Norcross; m. W. Mark Wheeler III, Jan. 2, 1965; children: Tim, Andrew, Geoffrey, Beth. BA in History, Boston U., 1962; MA in English Lit., Portland (Oreg.) State U., 1970, MA in Urban Planning, 1978. Pvt. practice tour operator Portland, 1985—. Contbr. Scribe, 1986—, Pdx Bus. Jour., 1987—. Mem. Portland Oreg. Visitors Assn., City Club of Portland, Racquet Club, Multnomah Athletic Club. Democrat. Episcopalian. Home and Office: 745 NW Culpepper Ter Portland OR 97210-3122

WHEELER, KATHERINE WELLS, state legislator; b. St. Louis, Feb. 8, 1940; d. Benjamin Harris and Katherine (Gladney) Wells; m. Douglas Lanphier Wheeler, June 13, 1964; children: Katherine Gladney, Lucille Lanphier. BA, Smith Coll., 1961; MA, Washington U., St. Louis, 1966. Founder auction N.H. Pub. TV, Durham, 1973-76; pub. mem. N.H. Pub. Broadcasting Council, Durham, 1975-80; founding mem. bd. govs. N.H. Pub. TV, 1980-88; elected N.H. Ho. of Reps., Concord, 1988—; coord. internat. visitors program N.H. Coun. World Affairs, 1981—; bd. dirs. Planned Parenthood No. New Eng., Gt. Bay Sch. and Tng. Ctr., Newington, N.H. Vice chair Strafford County Legis. Delegation, 1993-94; active Commn. on Health, Human Svcs. and Elderly Affairs N.H. Ho. of Reps., Concord, 1988; bd. dirs. Devel. Svcs. Strafford County, Inc., 1991—. Named Woman of Yr. Union Leader Newspaper, 1984, Citizen of Yr. Homemakers of Strafford County, 1990, Legislator of Yr. N.H. Assn. of Social Workers, 1993, Legislator of Yr. N.H. NASW, 1993; recipient Elizabeth Campbell Outstanding Pub. TV Vol. award Nat. Friends Pub. Broadcasting, 1984, Meritorious Svc. award N.H. Women's Lobby, 1992, Dist. Contbn. award N.H. Psychol. Orgn., Inc., 1994, Cert. of Achievement for Outstanding Legis. Leadership N.H. Citizen Action, 1994. Mem. AAWU, AARP, LWV, Order of Women Legis., N.H. Smith Coll. Club (v.p. 1974-76, pres. 1976-78), N.H. Assn. Social Workers (legislator of yr. 1993), N.H. Psychol. Orgn. Inc. (disting. contbn. award 1994). Democrat. United Ch. Christ. Home and Office: 27 Mill Rd Durham NH 03824-3098

WHEELER, M. CATHERINE, organization executive; b. Plainfield, N.J., May 31, 1942; d. William R. and Josephine S. (Ford) W. BA in Politics, Hollins Coll., 1964; MA in Theatre, U. Kans., 1966. Asst. mgr. South Shore Music Circus, Cohasset, Mass., 1967; pub. rels. asst. Trinity Square Repertory Co., Providence, 1967-68; co. mgr. Acad. Playhouse, Wilmette, Ill., 1968; adminstrv. asst. Am. U. Theatre, Washington, 1968-71; pub. rels. asst. Winterthur Mus. and Gardens, Wilmington, Del., 1972-76, dir. pub. rels., 1976-84; dir. Del. Tourism Office, Dover, 1984-93; pub. rels. coord. New Castle County Bd. of Realtors, Wilmington, 1994-95, dir. polit. affairs and comm., 1995—; pub. rels. cons. Historic Deerfield, Mass., 1983, Tourism Coun. Frederick County, Md., Bristol Riverside Theatre, Pa., 1994; bd. dirs. U.S. Travel Data Ctr., 1989-93. Editor Winterthur Newsletter, 1972-84. Pub. rels. cons. Historic Deerfield, Mass., 1983, Bristol Riverside Theatre, Pa., 1994; mem. Del. Heritage Commn., 1984-93, Del. Coastal Heritage Greenways Coun., 1991-93. Mem. Nat. Coun. State Travel Dirs. (chmn. nominating com. 1987-89, chmn. edn. com. 1989-91, chmn. rsch. task force 1991-92), Travel Industry Assn. (bd. dirs. 1990-94, chmn. Mid-Atlantic U.S.A (1989-92). Office: New Castle Cty Bd Realtors 3615 Miller Rd Wilmington DE 19802-2523

WHEELER, MARY HARRISON (MARDY WHEELER), human resource development specialist, consultant; b. Easton, Md., May 9, 1938; d. Robert Butler and Elizabeth (Fontaine) Harrison; m. David Weymouth Wheeler, May 9, 1962; children: Paul Harrison, Marjory Butler. BA in English, U. Maine-Orono, 1968, cert. in mgmt., 1976; MS in Human Resource Devel., Am. U., 1982. Counselor/coordinator Neighborhood Youth Corps, Lewiston, Maine, 1967-69; adminstr. Foruma, U. Maine-Augusta, 1973; tng. supr. Liberty Mutual Ins. Co., Lewiston, 1974-78, asst. dir., supervisory tng., Boston, 1978-80, dir. edn., 1980-83, dir. career devel., 1983-85, dir. edn., 1985-89, mgr. orgn. devel., 1989-90, dir. internal tng. U.C. Loss Prevention, 1991-93; prin. Kendall & Wheeler, Natick, Mass., 1993—; cons. in field; mem. faculty Middlesex C.C., Bedford, Maine, 1981-84, Worcester State Coll., 1985, Bentley Coll., 1987—, Bryant Coll., 1989-90, U. N.H., 1991—. Author: (with Christine Bingaman and Ralph Graham) Communication Skills for Managers, 1983; (with J. Marshall) Training Type Inventory, 1986; (with R. Leeper) When it's Time to Say Goodbye, Northeast Training News, 1985, Whose Objectives Are They Anyway, Training Magazine, 1988. State bd. dirs. Maine League Women Voters, 1972-74; mem. Monmouth Sch. Bd. (Maine), 1974; mem. Androscoggin County Com. to Hire the Handicapped, Lewiston, 1975-78; mem. adv. bd. Bryant Coll. Ctr. for Mgmt. Devel., 1987-89. Mem. ASTD (mem. at large, chmn. career devel. subm com. Mass. chpt. 1984, bd. dirs. 1987-89, chmn. spring conf. 1988), Am. Personnel & Guidance Assn., Orgn. Devel. Network. Democrat. Episcopalian. Office: Kendall & Wheeler 45 High St Natick MA 01760-4825

WHEELER, PATRICIA ANN, realtor; b. Mt. Sterling, Ill., Nov. 25, 1931; d. Charles Maurice and Velma Lorene (Wright) Peters; m. Richard M. Mari, Sept. 1, 1950 (div. Jan. 1955); children: Pamela S., Deborah J., Richard M. Jr.; m. Kenneth Richard Wheeler, Jan. 1, 1956; 1 child, Patricia Ann Jr. Registered real estate agt., Ill. Realtor Ladley Real Estate, Springfield, Ill., 1981-82, Charles Robbins, Springfield, %, 1982-83, John B. Clark Realtors, Springfield, %, 1983-84, 90-92, Julie Davis Realtors, Springfield, %, 1984-90, Realty Exec., Springfield, %, 1992—. County Chmn. Bicentenial, Petersburg, Ill., 1974-76. Mem. Grad. Realtors Inst., Springfield. Episcopalian. Office: Realty Executives 2725 W Monroe St Springfield IL 62704-1323

WHEELER, SUSAN, poet, educator, university administrator; b. Pitts., July 16, 1955; d. Ray Barton and Grace Louise (Skeen) W.; m. Philip Furmanski, Aug. 23, 1991; children: Lisa, Jonathan. BA in Lit., Bennington Coll., 1977; postgrad., U. Chgo., 1979-81. Dir. pub. programs and info. Art Inst. Chgo., 1981-85; freelance cons., editor and writer, 1983-91; dir. pub. affairs arts and sci. NYU, 1989-95; CETA writer and instr. Vt. Coun. on the Arts, 1977-78; instr. liberal arts Sch. of Art Inst. Chgo., 1984-85; instr. Poets in Pub. Svc., N.Y.C., 1989-91; instr. New Sch. for Social Rsch., N.Y.C., 1994—; Thornton writer-in-residence Lynchburg Coll., 1995. Author: (poetry collection) Bag 'o' Diamonds, 1993 (winner Poetry Soc. Am. Norma Farber First Book award 1994); poems anthologized in The Best American Poetry, 1988, 91, 93 (Pushcart prize 1994), Roth's Poetry Annual, 1990; contbr. poems to various jours. including o.blek, Witness, Chelsea, New Am. Writing, Paris Rev.; contbr. articles and essays to jours. Recipient Grolier award for poetry, 1987, Prize for Poetry, Roberts Found., 1988; Vt. Coun. Arts grantee, 1978-79, Fund for Poetry grantee, 1990; N.Y. Found. for Arts fellow, 1993-95. Mem. Acad. Am. Poets, Poetry Soc. Am., Poetry Project at St. Mark's Ch., Poets & Writers, Nat. Writers Union. Home: 37 Washington Square W # 6C New York NY 10011-9120

WHEELER, VALERIE A. SYSLO, accountant; b. New Brunswick, N.J., Nov. 16, 1958; d. Joseph Jr. and Florence (Kulesa) Syslo; m. Ray J. Wheeler, Oct. 7, 1978. AAS in Acctg., Middlesex County Coll., 1979; BA in Acctg. and Econs., Rutgers U., 1993. Prodn. acctg. technician E. I. DuPont, Sayreville, N.J., 1981-86; import acctg. clk. Jeri-Jo Knitwear, Inc., Edison, N.J., 1986-87; cost acctg. clk. Neilson & Brainbridge, Edison, 1987-88; tax clk. Johnson & Johnson-CPI, Skillman, N.J., 1988-92; acct. mil. sales divsn. Johnson & Johnson-CPI, New Brunswick, 1992—. Fundraising chair Rugters U. Coll., 1990-91. Mem. Inst. Mgmt. Accts., Univ. Coll. Governing Assn. Roman Catholic. Home: 12 Oxford Rd East Brunswick NJ 08816

WHEELER, YVONNE MARIE (VONNIE WHEELER), marketing professional; b. Denver, Nov. 28, 1938; d. Herb and Anna Marie (Bunn) Names; m. Loren Wheeler, June 22, 1958 (div. 1971); children: Brian Murray, Eric Wayne, Valerie Lynn, Amy Kathleen. BA, U. Colo., 1974. V.p. First Interstate Bank, Denver, 1974-84; pres. Wheeler & Co. Inc., Denver, 1984—; mng. ptnr. White River Inst., Vail, Colo., 1992—; mem. adv. coun. Regis U., Denver, 1988—, Grad. Sch. Internat. Studies, Denver U., 1990—; mem. mktg. com. Am. Ctr. for Internat. Leadership, Balt., 1989-92, leader Am. delegation to Kazakhstan, 1992. Creator, developer tourism book Adventure Colo., 1985-86; creator program EXPLORE, 1992—; author How To Manage Events manual. Bd. dirs. Colo. Conv. and Visitors Bur., Denver, 1979-84, Colo. Rural Job Tng. Found., Inc., 1991-93; mem. adv. com. U.S. Olympic Com., 1980-84; instr., presenter Dept. Econ. Devel., Colo., 1990-92; developer anti-litter program City of Denver, 1989. Recipient Gold Coin award Am. Bank Mktg. Assn., 1985. Office: Wheeler & Co Inc 312 S Franklin Denver CO 80209

WHEELOCK, ELIZABETH SHIVERS, trade association executive, small business owner; b. Marion, Ala., Nov. 29, 1932; d. William Lewitt and Willie Mae (Perkins) Shivers; m. Hugh Franklin Wheelock, Aug. 23, 1955; children: Hugh Franklin Jr., Elizabeth McLaurin, Lewitt Shivers. Student, Judson Coll., Marion, 1951-53, Wallace Community Coll., Dothan, 1973-74, 80. Credit mgr. Ted's Jewelers, Dothan, 1975-79; with mktg. and spl. projects depts. City Nat. Bank, Dothan, 1979-81, new account adminstr., 1980-81; founder, sec. Art Gallery, City Nat. Bank Art Gallery, Dothan, 1980-83; exec. officer Home Builders Assn. Dothan and Wiregrass Area, 1981—; cons., tchr., designer Needle Arts, Dothan, 1970—; owner, mgr. Elizabeth's Needle, Dothan, 1973; ptnr. Magnolia Springs Antiques, Foley. Editor newsletteers Perri-Winkle, 1950-51, Tapeline, 1981—; designer, pattern maker needle work, 1970—. Mem. Vivian B. Adams Sch. Parents Orgn., Ozark, Ala., 1973—, Wiregrass Art Mus., 1989—, Shakespeare Theatre Found., Montgomery, Ala.; bd. dirs. March of Dimes, Dothan, 1987-89. Recipient award March of Dimes, 1989, Pres. award Home Builders Assn. Dothan, 1994; nominee Small Bus. Prson of Yr. Dothan-Houston C. of C., 1994. Mem. DAR, Nat. Trust for Hist. Preservation, Internat. Platform Soc., Zonta Internat. Episcopalian. Home: 1405 W Newton St Dothan AL 36303-3924 Office: Home Builders Assn Dothan and Wiregrass Area 2207B Denton Rd Dothan AL 36303-2219

WHEELOCK, MOIRA MYRL BREWER, real estate broker, educator, church musician; b. Kirkland, Tex.; d. William Cassius and Marjorie (Lindsey) Brewer; m. Robert Denton Wheelock, June 5, 1938 (dec. July 1993); children: John Robert, Mary Ann Wheelock Reynolds. BA, Tex. Tech U., 1938; MA, W. Tex. State U., 1951. Cert. tchr.; lic. real estate broker. Tchr. various schs., Tex., 1936-40, 51-78; owner, broker Wheelock Real Estate, Canyon, Tex., 1979—. Contbr. articles to local newspaper. Active Friends to Save Our Courthouse, Canyon, 1984-86; musician First Bapt. Ch.; pianist Canyon Sr. Citizens. Mem. NEA (life), Tex. State Tchrs. Assn. (life), Canyon Ret. Classroom Tchrs. Assn. llife), Tex. Ret. Tchrs. Assn. (life), Canyon Ret. Tchrs. Assn., Tex. Assn. Realtors, Nat. Assn. Realtors, Sue Hite Federated Club (past pres.), Order Eastern Star (organist), Dalta Kappa Gamma (past pres. Eta Phi chpt.). Democrat. Home and Office: PO Box 122 Canyon TX 79015-0122

WHELAN, WENDY, ballet dancer; b. Louisville; d. Rich and Kay Whelan. Student, Louisville Ballet Acad., Sch. Am. Ballet. Apprentice N.Y.C. Ballet, 1984-86, mem. corps de ballet, 1986-89, soloist, 1989-91, prin., 1991—. Appeared in feature roles in George Balanchine's ballets such as Apollo, Raymonda Variations, Swan Lake, Who Cares?, Symphony in Three Movements, Danses Concertantes, Episodes, Cortege Hongrois, The Four Temperaments, Brahms-Schoenberg Quartet, Divertimento # 15, A Midsummer Night's Dream, Bournonville Divertissements, The Nutcracker, Walpurgisnacht Ballet, Brahms-Schoenberg Quartet Pieces, Union Jack, The Cage; in Jerome Robbins' Antique Epigraphs and Glass Pieces; in Peter Martins' Ash, Jazz, Les Petits Riens, Sleeping Beauty; in William Forsythe's Behind the China Dogs and Herman Scherman; in Christopher D'Amboise's The Bounding Line in Richard Tanner's A Schubert Sonata; and performed in N.Y.C. Ballet's Balanchine Celebration, 1993. Office: NYC Ballet NY State Theater 20 Lincoln Ctr New York NY 10023*

WHELCHEL, BETTY ANNE, lawyer; b. Augusta, Ga., Dec. 22, 1956; d. John Davis and Charnell (Ramsey) W.; m. Douglas Charles Kruse, June 20, 1987. AB, U. Ga., 1978; JD, Harvard U., 1981. Bar: D.C. 1981, N.Y. 1984, gaikokuho-jimu-bengoshi (fgn. lawyer) Japan. Atty.-advisor U.S. Dept. Treasury, Washington, 1981-84; assoc. Shearman & Sterling, N.Y.C., 1984-87, 89-90, Tokyo, 1987-89; dep. dept. head Deutsche Bank AG, N.Y., 1990—; staff atty. deregulation com. Depository Instns., Washington, 1983-84. Mem. Am. Soc. Internat. Law, Assn. of the Bar of the City of N.Y. (mem. comparative law com.), Harvard Law Sch. Assn. Office: Deutsche Bank AG 31 W 52nd St New York NY 10019

WHIDDON, CAROL PRICE, writer, editor, consultant; b. Gadsden, Ala., Nov. 18, 1947; d. Curtis Ray and Vivian (Dooly) Price; m. John Earl Caulking, Jan. 18, 1969 (div. July 1987); m. Ronald Alton Whiddon, Apr. 13, 1988. Student, McNeese State U., 1966-68; BA in English, George Mason U., 1984. Flute instr. Lake Charles, La., 1966-68; flutist Lake Charles Civic Symphony, 1966-69, Beaumont (Tex.) Symphony, 1967-68; freelance editor The Washington Lit. Rev., 1983-84, ARC Hdqrs., Washington, 1984; writer, editor Jaycor, Vienna, Va., 1985-87; writer, editor Jaycor, Albuquerque, 1987-90, publs. mgr., 1990-91; writer, editor Proteus Corp., Albuquerque, 1991-92; owner Whiddon Editorial Svcs., Albuquerque, 1989—; mem. S.W. Writer's Workshop, 1991—. Co-author: The Spirit That Wants Me: A New Mexico Anthology, 1991; contbr. various articles to Albuquerque Woman and mil. dependent pubs. in Fed. Rpublic Germany. Bd. dirs. Channel 27-Pub. Access TV, 1991-93, exec. bd. sec., 1992, v.p., 1993; dep. mgr. Fed. Women's Program, Ansbach, Fed. Republic Germany, 1980-81; pres. Ansbach German-Am. Club, 1980-82; sec. Am. Women's Activities, Fed. Republic Germany, 1980-81, chairwoman, 1981-82. Recipient cert. of appreciation from Am. amb. to Germany Arthur T. Burns, 1982, medal of appreciation from comdr. 1st Armored Div., Ansbach, Germany, 1982. Mem. NAFE, Women in Comm. (newsletter editor 1989-90, 91-92, 94-95, v.p. 1990-91, pres.-elect 1992-93, pres. 1993-94, chair programs com. Nat. Profl. Conf. 1994), Soc. Tech. Comm. (membership dir. 1993-94), Nat. Assn. Desktop Pubs., Am. Mktg. Assn., Greater Albuquerque C. of C., N.Mex. Caucus Soc. (historian 1989-94, sec. 1991, newsletter editor 1992—, various show ribbons 1989-91). Republican. Home: 1129 Turner Dr NE Albuquerque NM 87123-1917

WHIPKEY-LOUDEN, HARRIET BEULAH, fine arts and theatre productions executive; b. Willmar, Minn., Mar. 9, 1932; d. Frank Leroy and Annetta Cecelia (Cafferty) Whipkey; m. James William Louden, Aug. 20, 1956; children: Liza Katherin, Cheryl Anne. BS, St. Cloud State U., 1954; MA, Montclair State Coll., 1978. English-speech tchr. Minn. Dept. Edn., Verndale, Sauk Centre, Sauk Rapids, Minn., 1954-57; English-speech tchr. Bd. of Edn., Marquette, Mich., 1958-62, Slinger, Wis., 1963-67; drama dept. chair Bd. Edn., Pattonville High, St. Louis, 1967-69; speech and theatre dept. chair Bd. of Edn., Westfield, N.J., 1969-85; v.p. Louden Enterprises, Phoenix, 1990—; dir.-producer The Scholarship Show, Marquette, Mich., 1960; drama cons. New Faces of Charleston, Charleston, N.C., 1986-89, Internat. Models Talent Competition, Scottsdale, Ariz., 1986-89; edn. cons. Nat. Assn. Restaurant Mgrs., Scottsdale, 1988. Co-founder, chair 1st All Upper Peninsula Art Show, 1960; founder, pres. Ariz. State U. Theatre Assn., 1985-88; creator, dir. Children's Touring Theatre, St. Louis, 1968, Westfield, N.J., 1971, Summer Theatre Workshop, Pine-Strawberry, Ariz., 1990; founding bd. mem. N.J. Theatre Forum, 1979; TV talk show host Channel 9 Cable, Scottsdale, 1986-88; bd. mem. Phoenix East Valley Cath. Charities. Grantee N.J. Dept. Edn., 1978; recipient Gov.'s Citation, State of Mich., 1960. Mem. AAUW (pres. Marquette chpt. 1960), Ariz. Arts Commn., Ariz. for Cultural Devel., Ariz. Theatre Edn. Assn., Ariz. State U. Toastmasters, Friends of Ariz. State U. Art Mus. Home and Office: 1903 E Sarah Ln Tempe AZ 85284-3460

WHIPPLE, JUDITH ROY, book editor; b. N.Y.C., May 14, 1935; d. Edwin Paul and Elizabeth (Levis) Roy; m. William Whipple, Oct. 26, 1963. AB, Mount Holyoke Coll., 1957. Head libr. Am. Sch. Lima (Peru), S.A., 1957-59; asst. editor children's books G.P. Putnam's Sons, N.Y.C., 1959-62; assoc. editor W.W. Norton & Co., Inc., N.Y.C., 1962-68; editor Four Winds Press, 1968-75; editor-in-chief Scholastic Gen. Book Divsn., 1975-77; pub. Four Winds Press subs. Scholastic Inc., N.Y.C., 1977-82; pub., v.p. Macmillan Pub. Co., N.Y.C., 1982-89, exec. editor, 1989-94; editl. dir. Benchmark Books, Marshall Cavendish Corp., Tarrytown, N.Y., 1994—. Mem. PEN, Children's Book Coun. (pres. 1977, bd. dirs. 1970-79), Women's Nat. Book Assn., Soc. Children's Book Writers and Illustrators. Office: Marshall Cavendish Corp 99 White Plains Rd Tarrytown NY 10591

WHISMAN, ARDITH HELMONDOLLAR, psychiatric technician; b. Pineville, W.Va., May 3, 1942; d. Wade C. and Perlina Ellen (Stevens) Helmondollar; m. William J. Whisman, Mar. 6, 1947. Student, Marshall U., Huntington, W.Va., 1979. Cert. Nat. Assn. Psychiat. Techs. Psychiat. tech. W.Va. Dept. Health, Huntington, 1968—. Vol. Hospice, Huntington. Recipient Psychiat. Tech. of Yr. award Am. Assn. Psychiat. Techs., 1994. Mem. 1199 Health Workers. Democrat. Office: Huntington State Hosp 1530 Norway Ave Huntington WV 25709

WHISNER, PEGGY JANELLE, administrator; b. Lovington, N.Mex., Aug. 28, 1966; d. Floyd Pleasant and Imogene (Gage) Green; m. Gregory David Hoskins, Aug. 13, 1988 (div. Apr. 1992); m. Charles Whisner, Jan. 27, 1995. Student, Wayland Bapt. U., 1984-86; BBA, Eastern N.Mex. U., 1988. Bookkeeper Gen. Welding Supply, Inc., Lovington, N.Mex., 1985, Manpower, Hobbs, N.Mex., 1987; cashier, bookkeeper Alco, Portales, N.Mex., 1989; bookkeeper Parson's Inc., Tatum, N.Mex., 1989-90; sales rep. Dunlaps, Hobbs, 1990-93; acctg. Lea County Treas., Lovington, 1993—. Mem. Nat. Trust Hist. Preservation, 1993—. Mem. NAFE, Delta Mu Delta. Republican. Baptist. Home: 4030 Calle Grande Hobbs NM 88240

WHITAKER, EILEEN MONAGHAN, artist; b. Holyoke, Mass., Nov. 22, 1911; d. Thomas F. and Mary (Doona) Monaghan; m. Frederic Whitaker. Ed., Mass. Coll. Art, Boston. Annual exhibits in nat. and regional watercolor shows; represented in permanent collections, Charles and Emma Frye Mus., Seattle, NAD, Hispanic Soc., N.Y.C., High Mus. Art, Atlanta, U. Mass., Norfolk (Va.) Mus., Springfield (Mass.) Mus. Art, Reading (Pa.) Art Mus., Nat. Acad. Design, U. Mass., Okla. Mus. Art, St. Lawrence U., Wichita State U., Retrospective show, Founders Gallery U. San Diego, 1988, invitational one-person show Charles and Emma Frye Art Mus., 1990; included in pvt. collections; featured in cover article of American Artist mag., Mar. 1987, in article Art of Calif. mag., July 1991; invitational Am. Realism Exhbn. Cir. Gallery, San Diego, 1992; author: Eileen Monaghan Whitaker Paints San Diego, 1986. Recipient numerous major awards, including Allied Artists Am., Am. Watercolor Soc., 1st prize Providence Water Color Club, Wong award Calif. Watercolor Soc., De Young award Soc. Western Artists, 1st award Springville (Utah) Mus., Ranger Fund purchase prize, Orbrig prize NAD, Walter Biggs Meml. award, 1987; silver medal Am. Watercolor Soc., Watercolor West; fellow Huntington Hartford Found., 1964. Academician NAD; mem. Am. Watercolor Soc. (Dolphin fellow), Watercolor West (hon.), San Diego Watercolor Soc. (hon.). Home and Studio: 1579 Alta La Jolla Dr La Jolla CA 92037-7101

WHITAKER, KATHLEEN K., gifted education facilitator; b. Kansas City, Mo., Mar. 26, 1940; d. Richard Ingram and Rosemary (Frost) Kidd; m. William P. Whitaker, Feb. 24, 1962 (div. 1971); children: Lorie Beth, Minda Corinne. BA, U. Mo., 1962; MS, Kans. U., 1982. Cert. learning disabilities, gifted edn. and social studies tchr.; cert. psychol. examiner. Tchr. learning disabilities Wyandotte County Spl. Edn. Coop., Kansas City, Kans., 1980-84; learning specialist diagnostic team Children's Rehab. Unit Kans. U. Med. Ctr., 1984-85; tchr. learning disabilities Turner Sch. Dist., Kansas City, Kans., 1985-89, tchr. gifted edn., 1988-89, 94—; facilitator underachieving gifted edn. Shawnee Mission (Kans.) Schs., 1989—; presenter, staff mem. Rimm Underachievement Inst., 1992; presenter, developer larning materials in field; tchr., designer materials for parenting classes. Chmn. worship com. Shawnee Mission Unitarian Soc., 1991, trustee, 1992-93. Mem. Assn. for Edn. Gifted Underachieving Students, Kans. Assn. for Gifted, Talented and Creative, Phi Delta Kappa. Home: 4406 W 70th Ter Shawnee Mission KS 66208-2562 Office: Old Mission Multi-Use Ctr 4901 Reinhardt Dr Shawnee Mission KS 66205

WHITAKER, RUTH REED, retired newspaper editor; b. Blytheville, Ark., Dec. 13, 1936; d. Lawrence Neill and Ruth Shipton (Weidemeyer) Reed; m. Thomas Jefferson Whitaker, dec. 29, 1961; children: Steven Bryan, Alicia Morrow. BA, Hendrix Coll., 1958. Copywriter, weather person KTVE TV, El Dorado, Ark., 1958-59; nat. bridal cons. Treasure House, El Dorado, 1959; bridal cons. Pfeifers of Ark., Little Rock, 1959-60; dir. of continuity S. M. Brooks Advt. Agy., Little Rock, 1960-61; layout artist C. V. Mosby Co., St. Louis, 1961-62; editor, owner Razorback Am. Newspaper, Ft. Smith, Ark., 1979-81; ret., 1981. Contbr. author indsl. catalog, 1979 (Addy award). State sec. Rep. Party of Ark., 1992-94; mem. Ben Geren Regional Park Commn., Sebastian County, Ark., 1984-89, pres., 1990; past pres. Jr. Civic League; mem. Ft. Smith Orchid Com.; mem. com. of 21 United Way; publicity chmn. Sebastian County Rep. Com., 1983-84; state press officer Reagan-Bush Campaign, 1984; pres. Women's Aux. Sebastian County Med. Soc., 1974; mem. Razorback Scholarship Fund; class agt. alumni fund Hendrix Coll., 1990, 91, 92; mem. Sparks Womans Bd.; 1st vice chmn. 3d Dist. Rep. Party; state committeewoman Rep. Party Ark. Recipient Disting. Vol. Leadership award Nat. Found. March of Dimes, 1973, Appreciation award Ft. Smith Advt. Fedn., 1977, 78, Hon. Parents of Yr. award U. Ark., 1984, Recognition award United Cerebral Palsy, 1980. Mem. AAUW, Alden Soc. Am. (life), Ft. Smith C. of C., Ark. Nature Conservancy, Am. Legion Aux., Frontier Rschrs. Soc. (chmn. ways and means com. 1991—), Daus. Union Vets. Presbyterian. Home: PO Box 178 Cedarville AR 72932-0178

WHITAKER, SHIRLEY ANN, telecommunications company marketing executive; b. Asmara, Eritea, Ethiopia, Oct. 13, 1955; (parents Am. citizens); d. Calvin Randall and Ruth (Ganeles) Peck; m. John Marshall Whitaker, June 16, 1973; 1 child, Kathryn Ann. AA, Tacoma Community Coll., 1974; BA, Wash. State U., 1977, MBA, 1978. Planning adminstr. for econ. rsch. GTE NW, Everett, Wash., 1978-80; specialist in demand analysis western region GTE Svc. Corp., Los Gatos, Calif., 1980-81; fin. analyst GTE Svc. Corp., Stamford, Conn., 1981-83, staff specialist demand analysis and forecasting, 1983-84; group mgr. for rate devel. Nat. Exch. Carrier Assn., Whippany, N.J., 1984-87; mgr. pricing strategy and migration GTE Calif., Thousand Oaks, 1987-88; mgr. market forecasting GTE Telephone Ops. Hdqrs., Irving, Tex., 1989-90, dir. revenue analysis, 1990-92, dir. market rsch., 1992-93, dir. process re-engring., 1993-94; dir. network and resource mgmt., 1994—. Mem. Am. Mktg. Assn. (membership com. 1984), Beta Gamma Sigma, Phi Kappa Phi. Office: GTE Telephone Ops Hdqrs HQW02B77 700 Hidden Ridge Irving TX 75038-3897

WHITAKER, SUSAN HUNT, communications executive; b. Alpena, Mich., July 19, 1964; d. Marvin Gary and Jane Marie (Smart) Hunt; m. Thomas Gilbert Whitaker, Aug. 18, 1991. BA in Comm., U. Mich., 1986. Promotion writer, prodr. WDIV-TV, Detroit, 1986-91, pub. svc. dir., 1990-91; pub. info. officer City of Ann Arbor, Mich., 1991—. Vol. St. Joe's Holiday Ball Com., Ypsilanti, Mich., 1993. Nominated Emmy award Detroit/Mich. Nat. Acad. TV Arts and Scis., 1989, 90. Mem. Ann Arbor Womens City Club. Office: City of Ann Arbor 100 N 5th Ave Ann Arbor MI 48107

WHITAKER, SUSANNE KANIS, veterinary medical librarian; b. Clinton, Mass., Sept. 10, 1947; d. Harry and Elizabeth P. (Cantwell) Kanis; m. Daniel Brown Whitaker, Jan. 1, 1977. A.B. in Biology, Clark U., 1969; M.S. in Library Sci., Case Western Res. U., 1970. Regional reference librarian Yale Med. Library, New Haven, 1970-72; med. librarian Hartford Hosp., Conn., 1972-77; asst. librarian Cornell U., Ithaca, N.Y., 1977-78; vet. med. librarian Coll. Vet. Medicine, Cornell U., 1978—; sec. SUNY Council Head Librarians, 1981-83. Mem. Med. Libr. Assn. (sec.-treas. vet. med. librs. sect. 1983-84, chmn. 1984-85), Med. Libr. Assn. (upstate N.Y. and Ont. chpt.), Acad. Health Info. Profls. Home: 231 Highgate Rd Ithaca NY 14850-1435 Office: Cornell U Coll Vet Medicine Flower-Sprecher Libr Ithaca NY 14853-6401

WHITAKER, VON BEST, nursing educator; b. New Bern, N.C.; d. Cleveland W. and Lillie (Bryant) Best; m. Roy Whitaker Jr., Aug. 9, 1981; 1 child, Roy Whitaker III. BS, Columbia Union Coll., 1972; MS, U. Md., 1974; MA, U. N.C., 1980, PhD, 1983. Lectr. U. N.C., Chapel Hill, 1981-82; asst. prof. U. Mo., Columbia, Mo., 1982-85; asst. prof. grad. sch. Boston Coll., Newton, Mass., 1985-86; asst. prof. U. Tex. Health Sci. Ctr., San Antonio, 1986—; mem. cataract guideline panel Agy. for Health Care Policy Rsch., 1990-93. Contbr. articles to profl. jours., chpts. to textbooks; presenter in field. Vol. to prevent blindness. Bush fellowship, 1979-81; recipient Cert. of Appreciation, Prevent Blindness South Tex., 1988, 89. Mem. ANA (cert. community health nurse), Am. Soc. Ophthalmic Nursing (chair rsch. com.), Am. Pub. Health Assn., Rsch. Assn. Minority Profs., Assn. Black Faculty in Higher Edn., Nat. Black Nurses Assn., Sigma Theta Tau. Home: 6606 Bavaria Ct San Antonio TX 78256-2021

WHITAKER, WILMA NEUMAN, college dean; b. Chgo., Aug. 18, 1937; d. August P. and Wilma M. (Kaiser) Neuman; m. G.D. Whitaker, Mar. 28, 1970; children: Brett Allan Karlsen, Karen J. Whitaker Laflin, Mark D. Whitaker, David R. Whitaker. BA in Math., DePauw U., 1959; MEd in Math., Francis Marion Coll., 1988. Cert. secondary tchr., Ill., Mich., S.C.; cert. realtor Mich. High sch. math tchr. Dist. 209, Hillside, Ill., 1959-61, Dist. 214, Mt. Prospect, Ill., 1961-65; apprentice pharmacist Karlsen Pharmacy, Mt. Prospect, 1961-67; realtor Durbin Co., Clarkston, Mich., 1977-81; substitute tchr. Clarkston (Mich.) Community Schs., 1979-80; math instr. Florence (S.C.)-Darlington Tech. Coll., 1981-85, math dept. head, 1985-87, dean arts and scis., 1987—. Stephen min. St. Lukes Luth. Ch., Florence, 1991—, coun., 1989-92, tchr., 1981—; founder, organizer Spring Cmty. Walk Along Rotary Beauty Trail, Florence, 1988, 89, 91. Named Faculty Mem. of Yr., Florence-Darlington Tech. Coll., 1987, Adminstr. of Yr., 1992, Exec. of Yr., Florence chpt. Profl. Secs. Internat., 1993. Mem. ASTD, AAUW, Am. Assn. Women in C.C.s, Am. Assn. C.C.s, S.C. Assn. Devel. Educators, S.C. Assn. Math. Tchrs. Two-Yr. Colls., S.C. Tech. Edn. Assn., S.C. Women in Higher Edn., Optimist Club of Florence (v.p. 1991-92, pres. 1992-93), Optimist Internat. (lt. gov. Zone 6 S.C. 1993-94, gov.-elect. 1994-95), Theta Sigma Phi, Delta Zeta. Office: Florence-Darlington Tech Coll PO Box 100548 Florence SC 29501-0548

WHITCOMB, HELEN E., writer, publicist; m. John Whitcomb, July 16, 1950; children: Claire Whitcomb Klein, Jonathan. BA, Ursinus Coll., Collegeville, Pa., 1946; postgrad., Columbia U., 1947-50. Asst. editor Chain Store Age, Lebhar-Friedman Publs., N.Y.C., 1947-51; mng. editor Today's Woman, McGraw-Hill Book Co., N.Y.C., 1951-55, co-author books, 1955-80; co-editor weekly newspaper Dispatch, New Providence, N.J., 1980-85; publicist, writer Helen Whitcomb Assocs., Berkeley Heights, N.J., 1985—; host, prodr. Cmtys. on Cable, Summit, N.J., 1986-93. Co-author: Strictly for Secretaries, 1957, 2d edit., 1965, Today's Woman, 1964, 3d edit., 1976, Charm for the Modern Woman, 1967, The Modern Ms, 1969, 2d edit., 1975; contbr. articles to Seventeen, Woman's Day, Bus. Edn. World, McCalls, Victoria, others. Publicity chmn. PTA, Berkeley Heights, 1975-76; advisor Teen Hotline, Berkeley Heights; trustee Berkeley Heights Edn. Found. Mem. N.J. Press Women, AAUW (steering com. Berkeley Heights br.), College Club (Summit, N.J., fellowship com.). Unitarian. Home and Office: 111 Timber Dr Berkeley Heights NJ 07922

WHITE, ALICE ELIZABETH, physicist, researcher; b. Glen Ridge, N.J., Apr. 5, 1954; d. Alan David and Elizabeth Joyce (Jones) W.; m. Donald Paul Monroe, Oct. 13, 1990; 1 child, Ellen Elizabeth Monroe. BA in Physics, Middlebury (Vt.) Coll., 1976; MA in Physics, Harvard U., 1978, PhD in Physics, 1982. Postdoctoral mem. tech. staff AT&T Bell Labs., Murray Hill, N.J., 1982-84, mem. tech. staff, 1984-88, dept. head, 1988—. Contbr. over 100 articles to profl. jours. Mem. Am. Phys. Soc. (Maria Goeppert-Mayer award 1991), Phi Beta Kappa. Office: AT&T Bell Labs PO Box 636 Murray Hill NJ 07974-0636

WHITE, ALICE VIRGINIA, state executive; b. Wichita, Kans., June 30, 1946; d. Harry Houston White and Margaret V. (Milligan) Gabbert. BA in Russian (hons.) and Spanish, U. Kans., 1967; PhD in Journalism, U. Tex., 1991. Tchr. Russian and Spanish Ingalls Sch. Dist., Kansas City, Mo., 1967-72; instr. Dodge City (Kans.) C.C., 1972-73, 84; tchr. Arrowhead West, Inc., 1984-85; asst. dir. Ctr. for Bus. & Industry Dodge City (Kans.) Community Coll., 1984-85, dir. community rels. and resource devel., 1985-87; co-founder, treas. Breitenbach Farms, Inc., Dodge City, 1970-79, pres., 1979-85; asst. to dean for devel. Coll. Comm., U. Tex., Austin, 1990-93, asst. instr. journalism, 1988-90, lectr. pub. rels., 1992; asst. immunization strategic coord. Tex. Dept. Health, Austin, 1993—; media judge Headliners Found., Austin, 1989, Tex. Hosp. Assn., 1990, 91; dir. job placement Kans. Elks Tng. Ctr. for Handicapped, 1984-85; mgr. dental office, 1973-83; bd. dirs. Dispute Resolution Ctr., 1992-93. Treas. Ford County Hist. Soc., 1972-77, Ofcl. Bicentennial Com. Ford County, 1975-77; active Leadership Kans., 1986, Leadership Austin, 1990-91; co-founder Leadership Dodge, 1987; founder Walk-a-Dog project Williamson County SPCA, Austin State Sch., 1991; media judge Tex. PTA, 1992, Tex. Med. Assn., 1993; mem. chancellors coun. U. Tex. Sys. Recipient Most Creative Vol. Project award Tex. Mental Health and Mental Retardation, 1992, Athena winner Women's C. of C., 1987, Kans. PRIDE honoree, 1988; U. Tex. fellow, 1987-89; named of one of 100 Best-Managed Farms in U.S., Farm Futures Mgr., 1983. Mem. AAUW (pres. Kans. 1979-81, gift honoree 1973, 81, 91), Pub. Rels. Soc. Am. (mentor, profl. advisor U. Tex.), Tex. Pub. Rels. Soc. (bd. dirs. 1993), Women in Comm. (liaison to student chpt. 1989-91), Tex. Exes Alumni Assn. (life), U. Kans. Alumni Assn. (nat. bd. dirs. 1977-82), Austin C. of C., U. Tex. Pres.' Assocs., U. Kans. Chancellor's Club, Austin-Travis County Humane Soc. (life), Phi Beta Kappa, Phi Kappa Phi. Home: 5914 Upvalley Run Austin TX 78731-3669 Office: Tex Dept Health Shots Across Tex 1100 W 49th St Austin TX 78756

WHITE, ANN WELLS, community activist; b. Kansas City, Mo., Mar. 16, 1927; d. William Gates and Annie Loretta (Morton) Wells; m. Norman E. White, Oct. 2, 1949 (div. Dec. 1977); children: Thomas Wells, Norman Lee. BJ, U. Mo., 1948. Asst. to pres. Cities in Schs., 1978-79. Lobbyist Common Cause, Atlanta, 1972-73; vol. Jimmy Carter's Peanut Brigade, 1976, Carter/Mondale campaign, 1980; bd. dirs., vice chair Atlanta Area Svcs. for the Blind, 1973-81; Gov.'s Commn. on the Status of Women, Atlanta, 1974-76; office mgr. Carter/Mondale Transition Office, Atlanta, 1976; chair evaluation com. United Way Met. Atlanta, 1980-90; bd. dirs. Mems. Guild, The High Mus. of Art, Atlanta, 1982-83, Hillside Hosp., Atlanta, 1989—, Ga. Forum, Atlanta, 1988—; bd. dirs. Planned Parenthood of Atlanta area, 1975-89, pres., 1978-81; bd. dirs. Planned Parenthood Fedn. Am., N.Y.C., 1980-86, chair ann. meeting, New Orleans, 1986; legis. chair, lobbyist Ga. Women's Polit. Caucus, 1984-90; convenor, founding chair Georgians for Choice, 1989. Democrat. Presbyterian. Home: Colony House 1237 145 Fifteenth St Atlanta GA 30309

WHITE, BETTY MAYNARD, retired social worker; b. N.Y.C., May 22, 1922; d. William and Madge (Hooks) Maynard; B.A., Hunter Coll., 1964; M.S.W., Columbia U., 1969; m. Charles E. White, Sept. 8, 1941; 1 child, Charles B. Case worker Bur. Child Welfare, Jamaica, N.Y., 1964-69; supr. foster care Spl. Services for Children, Jamaica, 1969-73, case supr. application sec., family services, group services, 1973-83, supr. III, borough coordinator for Manhattan and Bronx, Office Home Care Services, Div. Med. Rev., 1983-84, dir. div. Med. Rev., 1984; pvt. practice, 1986-90. Mem. Nat. Assn. Social Workers, Acad. Cert. Social Workers, Hunter Coll. Alumni Assn. Democrat. Roman Catholic. Home: 7864 S Leewynn Dr Sarasota FL 34240-9072

WHITE, BEVERLY HAWKINS, elementary school counselor; b. Gholsonville, Va., Nov. 19, 1956; d. Henry Clarence and Elmer (Jones) Hawkins; m. John Raymond White, Sept. 14, 1991. BS, Va. State U., 1979, MS, 1982. Cert. tchr., Va. Tchr. Mecklenburg County Pub. Schs., South Hill, Va., 1982-85; tchr. Brunswick County Pub. Schs., Lawrenceville, Va., 1979-80, 85-88, counselor, 1989—. Treas. So. Christian Leadership Conf., Emporia, Va., 1991—; active NAACP, Emporia, 1991—. Mem. ACA, NEA, Va. Counselor's Assn., Va. Edn. Assn., Brunswick Edn. Assn., Jazz 90. Democrat. Baptist. Office: Brunswick County Pub Schs PO Box 309 Lawrenceville VA 23868-0309

WHITE, BEVERLY J., cytogeneticist; b. Seattle, Oct. 9, 1938. Grad., U. Wash., 1959, MD, 1963. Diplomate Nat. Bd. Med. Examiners, Am. Bd. Pediatrics, Am. Bd. Med. Genetics; lic physician and surgeon, Wash., Va. Rsch. trainee dept. anatomy Sch. Medicine U. Wash., Seattle, 1960-62, pediatric resident dept. pediatrics, 1967-69; rotating intern Phila. Gen. Hosp., 1963-64; rsch. fellow med. ob-gyn. unit Cardiovascular Rsch. Inst. U. Calif. Med. Ctr., San Francisco, 1964-65; staff fellow lab. biomed. scis. Nat. Inst. Child Health and Human Devel. NIH, Bethesda, Md., 1965-67, sr. staff fellow, attending physician lab. exptl. pathology Nat. Inst. Arthritis, Metabolism and Digestive Diseases, 1969-74, acting chief sect. cytogenetics, 1975-76, rsch. med. officer, attending physician sect. cytogenetics lab. cellular biology and genetics, 1974-86, dir. cytogenetics unit, interinstitute med. genetics program clin. ctr., 1987—. vis. scientist dept. pediatrics divsn. genetics Sch. Medicine, U. Wash., 1983-84; intramural cons. NIH, 1975—; cons. to assoc. editor Jour. Nat. Cancer Inst., 1976; med. staff cons. dept. ob-gyn. Naval Hosp. Bethesda, 1988-89; lectr. and presenter in field. Recipient Mosby Book award, 1963, Women of Excellence award U. Wash. and Seattle Profl. chpt. Women in Comm., 1963, Reuben award Am. Soc. for Study Sterility, 1963. Fellow Am. Coll. Med. Genetics (founding), Am. Acad. Pediatrics; mem. AMA. Am. Soc. Human Genetics, Fed. Physicians Assn., Assn. Cytogenetic Technologists (program com. 1989). Home: 20630 Highland Hall Dr Gaithersburg MD 20879 Office: NIH Cytogenetics Unit Bldg 8 Rm 108 Bethesda MD 20892

WHITE, BONNIE YVONNE, management consultant, educator; b. Long Beach, Calif., Sept. 4, 1940; d. William Albert and Helen Iris (Harbaugh) W. BS, Brigham Young U., 1962, MS, 1965, EdD in Ednl. Adminstrn., 1976. Tchr., Wilson High Sch., Long Beach, Calif., 1962-63; grad. asst. Brigham Young U., Provo, Utah, 1963-65; instr., dir. West Valley Coll., Saratoga, Calif., 1965-76; instr., evening adminstr. Mission Coll., Santa Clara, Calif., 1976-80; dean gen. edn. Mendocino Coll., Ukiah, Calif., 1980-85; dean instrn. Porterville (Calif.) Coll., 1985-89, dean adminstrv. svc., 1989-93; rsch. assoc. SAGE Rsch. Internat., Orem, Utah, 1975—. Del. Tulare County Ctrl. Com. Rep. Party, 1993-94; pres. community adv. bd. Calif. Conservation Corps, 1989-93; v.p. Porterville Community Concerts, 1990-94; bd. dirs. United Way North Bay, Santa Rosa, Calif., 1980-85, St. Vincent de Paul, 1993—; mem. Calif. Commn. on Basic Skills, 1987-89, Calif. Commn. on Athletics, 1987-90. Mem. AAUW, Faculty Assn. Calif. Community Colls., Calif., Coun. Fine Arts Deans, Assn. Calif. Community Coll. Adminstrs. Assn. Calif. Community Coll. Adminstrs. Liberal Arts, Zonta (intern), Soroptimists (intern). Republican. Mormon.

WHITE, CAROL LEE WEIR, corporate accountant; b. Lonaconing, Md., Feb. 26, 1965; d. David Lee and Ruth Lee (Schramm) Weir; m. Robert Joseph White, Sept. 11, 1993. AA in Bus., Allegany C.C., Cumberland, Md., 1985; BS in Acctg., Frostburg (Md.) State U., 1987. CPA, Md. Staff acct. Lawrence H. Hohing & Assocs., Cumberland, Md., 1986-90, Smith Elliott Kearns & Co., Hagerstown, Md., 1990-92; corp. acct. West Mfg. Co., Hagerstown, 1992-93, Donald B. Rice Tire Co., Inc., Frederick, 1993—. Mem. AICPA, Md. Assn. CPAs, Inst. Mgmt. Accts., Nat. Soc. Tole and Decorative Painters, Internat. Order of Job's Daus. (treas., exec. coun. 1994—). Home: 18827 Preston Rd Hagerstown MD 21742-2715 Office: Donald B Rice Tire Co Inc 909 East St Frederick MD 21701

WHITE, CECILE RENEE KINGSBURY, dance educator; b. Mpls., Sept. 23, 1952; d. Cecil Richard and Evelyn Marie (Barland) K.; m. Robert William Johannessen, Feb. 13, 1970 (div.); 1 child, Tawnya Renee Johannessen; m. Thomas Alva White, Oct. 4, 1975; 1 child, Corey Thomas. Student, Cribo Dance Studio, Houston, 1962-68, Sonja Isham Sch. Dance, Houston, 1977, San Jacinto Jr. Coll., Pasadena, Tex., 1977, N.W. Houston Dance Acad., 1978-81, S.W. Jazz Ballet, Houston, 1980-82, Space/Dance Theatre, Houston, 1980; studies with Lea Geeslin, Terrance Karns, 1981. Dancer N.W. Houston Dance Acad., 1971-81, choreographer, 1981; tchr. Sonja Isham Sch. Dance, 1976; dancer S.W. Jazz Ballet Co., 1980-81; tchr. N.W. Houston Dance Dance Acad., 1980-81; tchr. Am. Acad. Dance, 1981—, choreographer, 1981—; dancer North Houston Dance Theatre, 1981, Glenn Hunsucker Dance Co., 1981-83; tchr. jazz and modern dance and aerobics N. Harris Montgomery County Coll., 1989—, Kingwood Coll. Choreographer, performer Walt Disney "Donald Duck Birthday Celebration 50 Years", 1984, The Nutcracker Ballet, 1984-91. Tex. Mother/Dau. Pageant finalist, 1990; recipient 1st place award for interpretation Cece's Competition

Dance; 1st place overall dance competition, 1993-94. Mem. Am. Coll. Sports Medicine, Aerobic Fitness Assn. Am., Internat. Dance Edn. Assn., Am. Coun. on Exercise. Home: Rt 10 Box 5960 Cleveland TX 77327-9019

WHITE, CHRISTINE, educator; b. Taunton, Mass., Apr. 1, 1905; d. Peregrine Hastings and Sara (Lawrence) W. Cert., Boston Sch. Phys. Edn.; BS, Boston U., 1935, MEd, 1939. Instr. Winthrop Coll., Rock Hill, S.C., 1927-29; instr., asst. prof. The Woman's Coll. U. N.C., Greensboro, N.C., 1929-41; assoc. prof., head dept. physical edn. Meredith Coll., Raleigh, N.C., 1941-43; assoc. prof., prof. chair dept. physical edn. Wheaton Coll., Norton, Mass., 1943-70, prof. emerita, 1970—. co-editor Taunton Architecture: A Reflection of the City's History, 1981, 89. Chmn. Hist. Dist. Study Com., 1975-78, Recreation Commn., 1972-81; mem. Hist. Dist. Commn., 1979—, sec., 1979-86, acting chair, 1992-94; mem. Park and Recreation Commn., 1982—; bd. dirs. Star Theatre for the Arts, Inc., 1993—. Fellow AAHPERD; mem. AAUP (pres. Wheaton Coll. chpt. 1960-61), AAUW, LWV, Nat. Assn. Phys. Edn. in Higher Edn., Pi Lambda Theta. Home: 40 Highland Ter Taunton MA 02780-4729

WHITE, CLARA JO, graphoanalyst; b. County Cherokee, Tex., June 26, 1927; d. William and Elmira (Johnson) Walker; m. Jeff Davis White, May 5, 1950; children: Anita, Jackie, Mona Lisa, Jeris, Gina. Cert., Ft. Worth Bus. Coll., 1947; AA, Riverside City Coll., 1986; cert. mgmt. and supervisory devel., U. Calif., Riverside, 1986, cert. counseling skills, 1990. Cert. Graphoanalyst 1977; cert. master graphoanalyst 1979; cert. mus. docent tng., 1977. Owner, pres. White Handwriting Analysis Svc., Riverside, Calif., 1982—; lectr., cons. Graphoanalysis, Riverside, 1977—; instr. Internat. Congress and Resident Inst. sponsored by Internat. Graphoanalysis Soc., 1989, discussion group leader, 1988; presented in field; mem. adv. coun. Internat. Biog. Centre, Cambridge, Eng., 1991; analyzed handwriting Lady Margaret Beauford, 1992, Mary Queen of Scots, 1993, Hillary Rodham Clinton, 1993. Asst. editor: (commemorative book) Reflections, 1986; contbr. poems to anthologies. Mem. YWCA, Riverside; mem. children's conf. planning com. Riverside Mental Health Assn., 1981—; mem. U.S. Olympic Com., 1984; v.p. Heritage House Mus., Riverside, 1981—, co-pres., 1985-86, pres. 1986-87; historian Riverside Juvenile Hall Aux., 1984—, pres., 1987—; vol. teacher's aide County of Riverside Juvenile Ct. Schs., 1979—; mem. Riverside Mus. Assocs., bd. dirs., 1985-87, vol. 1985-88, aux. historian 1984—, pres., 1987-88; mem. Met. Mus. Assocs., 1960—. Recipient Cert. of Appreciation vol. svcs. program Riverside County Probation Dept., 1986, County Riverside Suprs., 1988; award F.H. Butterfield Sch., 1980, Golden Poet award The Homer Honor Soc., 1987, 90; named Vol. of Yr., recipient community svc. cert. Riverside City Coll., 1982; named to Hall of Fame, Riverside Juvenile Hall Aux., 1984; recipient Cert. of Appreciation, Riverside Mental Health, 1990, First Pl. award writing-poetry Am. Biog. Rsch. Assn., 1991, Trophy award for Outstanding Svc. to Community Sta. KQLH-FM, Trophy Pl. Vol. Ctr. of Riverside, 1991, Trophy award and Individual Svc. award, Riverside County Juvenile Hall of Fame, 1990-91, Cert. Recognition Riverside County Probation Dept., 1991, Cert. Recognition Calif. Legis.-State Assembly, 1991, Cert. Appreciation So. Calif. Chpt. IGAS, 1990-91, Cert. Appreciation Riverside County Bd. Suprs. and Riverside County Probation Dept., 1993, Participation award 21st Internat. Congress Arts and Comm. in Scotland, 1994; her poem Peace included in Scottish Library Archives, 1994. Fellow Internat. Biog. Assn. Eng. (adv. coun.); mem. NAFE, Internat. Graphoanalysis Soc. (life, cert. master graphoanalyst, 2d and 1st v.p., pres. So. Calif. chpt., pres. excellence award 1982, 83, 84, cert. of merit 1981, pres. citation of merit 1988), Am. Biog. Inst. Rsch. Assn. (dep. gov. 1988, bd. advisor 1988), U.S. Olympic Soc., Smithsonian Inst. (assoc.), Riverside C. of C., The Rsch. Coun. of Scripps Clinic and Rsch. Found., Women's Networking Club (Riverside), Confederation of Chivalry (life, grand coun., dame officer). Club: Women's Networking (Riverside). Home and Office: 7965 Helena Ave Riverside CA 92504-3513

WHITE, CONSTANCE BURNHAM, state official; b. Ogden, Utah, July 2, 1954; d. Owen W. and Colleen (Redd) Burnham; m. Wesley Robert White, Mar. 18, 1977. BA in English magna cum laude, U. Utah, 1976, postgrad., 1977; postgrad., Boston Coll., 1979; JD, Loyola U., 1981. Law clerk Kruse, Landa, Zimmerman & Maycock, Salt Lake City, 1979; law clerk legal dept. Bell & Howell, Lincolnwood, Ill., 1980; clerk, assoc. Parsons, Behle & Latimer, Salt Lake City, 1981-82; assoc. Reynolds, Vance, Deason & Smith, Salt Lake City, 1982-83; chief enforcement sect. Utah Securities Divsn., Salt Lake City, 1984-87, chief licensing sect., 1988, asst. dir., 1989-90; legal counsel Utah Dept. Commerce, Salt Lake City, 1990-92, exec. dir., 1993—; mem. Gov.'s Securities Fraud Task Force, 1984; spl. asst. atty. gen., 1986-88; spl. asst. U.S. atty., 1986—. Mem. North Am. Securities Adminstrs. Assn. (vice chair market manipulation com. 1988-89, penny stock/telecom. fraud com. 1989-90, chair uniform examinations com. 1990-92, chair forms revision com. 1992), Utah State Bar (securities adv. com. 1991—, task force on community-based mediation 1991—, chair securities sect. 1992-93). Office: Utah Dept Commerce 160 E 300th S Salt Lake City UT 84103

WHITE, DORIS ANNE, artist; b. Eau Claire, Wis., July 27, 1924; d. William I. and Mary (Dietz) W. Grad., Art Inst. Chgo., 1950. One woman shows, IFA Galleries, Washington, Bergstrum Art Center and Museum, Neenah, Wis., Bradley Gallery, Milw.; exhibited in group shows, Ill. Mus., Springfield, 1963, Art Alliance, Phila., 1963, Museum Modern Art, N.Y.C., 1967, Pa. Acad. Fine Arts, Phila., 1963, 64, 66, Art Inst. Chgo., 1963, Met. Museum, 1966, N.A.D., N.Y.C., 1962, 63, 64, 65, 67, Butler Inst. Am. Art, Youngtown, Ohio, 1960, 61, 63, 64, 65, Smithsonian Instn., Washington, 1960, Walker Art Center, Mpls., 1963, 64, Madison (Wis.) Salon Art, 1958-63, 64, Spanish Internat. Pavilion, St. Louis, 1969, Utah State U., Logan, 1969, 70, Cleve. Inst. Art, Miami (Fla.) U., Chautauqua (N.Y.) Art Assn., Soc. Four Arts, Palm Beach, Fla., Instituto de arte de Mexico, others; represented in permanent collection, Butler Inst. Am. Art, Walker Art Center, Milw. Art Center. Recipient grand award Am. WWatercolor Soc., 1963, Grumbacker award, 1965, Paul Remmy award, 1964; medal of honor Knickerbocker Artists, 1963, Four Arts award Soc. Four Arts, 1963. Mem. NAD (Ranger fund purchase award 1965, Obrig award 1967).

WHITE, DURIE NEWMANN, federal agency administrator; b. Westerly, R.I., June 19, 1950; d. Reed Maurice Neumann and Alice M. (Victoria) Quinn; m. Donald L. White, Oct. 6, 1979; 6 stepchildren. BA, U. R.I., 1972. Supply clk. USAF/Europe, Mainz Kastel, Germany, 1972-73; adminstrv. asst. Pearson's Travel, Providence, 1973; contracting officer GSA, Washington, 1973-77; contract specialist AID, Washington, 1977-80; procurement analyst A/SDBU Dept. State, Washington, 1980-91, ops. dir. A/SDBU, 1991—; chair small bus. working group Subcom. Interagency Small Bus. Dirs. Group, Washington, 1993—; liaison planning com. White House Conf. on Small Bus. Roman Catholic. Office: Small/Disadvantage Bus Dept State Rm 633, SA-6 Washington DC 20522-0602

WHITE, F. MICHELLE, aeronautical engineer, consultant; b. Abilene, Tex., Apr. 5, 1958; d. Turner Ashby and Faye N. (Bravenec) W. BS, McMurry U., 1980; MBA, U. Dallas, Irving, Tex., 1992. designated engring. rep. FAA. Systems analyst LTV Aerospace Corp., Dallas, 1981-82; sr. engr., rsch. engr. Bell Helicopter Textron, Inc., Ft. Worth, 1982-93; dir. engring. and cert. Premier Aviation, Inc., Grand Prairie, Tex., 1993-94; aeronautical engr., pres. Airborne Tech., Inc., Hurst, Tex., 1994—. Home and Office: 610-B Bellaire Dr Hurst TX 76053

WHITE, FAITH, sculptor; b. N.Y.C., Apr. 7, 1950; d. Edward and Faith-Hope (Green) Kahn. BA summa cum laude, L.I. U., 1971; studied woodcarving, with Nathaniel Burwash, Cambridge, Mass., 1976, with Joseph Wheelwright, Boston, 1977—. Freelance sculptor Boston, 1971—, N.Y.C., 1995—; adminstrv. asst. to dean of students Grahm Jr. Coll., Boston, 1972-74; exec. sec. to New Eng. regional mgr. Bur. of Nat. Affairs, Inc., Boston, 1974-77; asst. to dir. New Eng. Aquarium, Boston, 1977-80, dir. pers., 1980-82; guest juror for travel grant Boston Visual Artists Union, 1994; show mgr. Sculpture and Large Works, The Copley Soc. of Boston, 1992; instr. woodcarving The Eliot Sch., Jamaica Plain, Mass., 1992-94; tchg. artist Very Spl. Arts program Mus. of Sci., Boston, 1992, 93; project coord. First Night, Boston, 1986, 87, 88; judge Sr. Panel Carving competition Belmont (Mass.) Hill Sch., 1985; docent Hands-On Sculpture show New Eng. Sculptors Assn. at Mus. of Sci., Boston, 1984. Solo exhbn. Mills Gallery, Boston, 1987; 2 person invitational The Copley Soc. of Boston, 1994; other exhbns. include Boston Ctr. for the Arts, 1984, 85, Boston Visual Artists Union Gallery, 1985, Concord Art Assn., 1985, Cambridge Art Assn., 1986, The Copley Soc. of Boston, 1984, 85, 88, 89, 91, 92, 93 (including holiday invitationals for award winners 1988, 91, 92), Fed. Res. Bank of Boston Gallery, 1989, with Copley Masters, 1994, Howard Yezerski Gallery, 1989, 90, 91, 92, 93, 94, Libr. Ctr., Newport, Mass., 1990, Landau Gallery, Belmont Hill Sch., 1991, Attleboro (Mass.) Mus., 1992, Gallery NAGA, Boston, 1992, others; permanent collection Sherrill House, Boston, 1990. Liaison between mission com. Trinity Ch., Boston and vol. program Sherrill House Nursing Home, 1987-94. Mem. The Copley Soc. of Boston (Copley Master 1992), New Eng. Sculptors Assn. (bd. dirs., mem.-at-large 1985-86, 88-89), Boston Visual Artists Union. Epsicopalian. Studio: 115 E 34th St New York NY 10016

WHITE, GAYLE COLQUITT, religion writer, journalist; b. Lamar County, Ga., Nov. 4, 1950; d. Albert Candler and Ethel Eugenia (Moore) Colquitt; m. Robert Eugene White, Jr., Apr. 9, 1972; children: Margaret Candler, Robert Eugene III. AB in Journalism, U. Ga., 1972. Reporter Atlanta Jour. & Constn., 1972—. Named Templeton Reporter of Yr., Religion Newswriters Assn., 1992. Presbyterian. Office: Atlanta Journal & Constitution 72 Marietta St NW Atlanta GA 30303-2804

WHITE, GRACE SHEARER, gourmet food and wine accessories dealer; b. Cross Keys, Pa., Dec. 21, 1940; d. Ralph Brooks and Juniata Mae (Burdge) Shearer; m. Thomas Edward Mahin, Dec. 29, 1962 (div. 1982); children: Derek Alexander Mahin, Trevor Brook Mahin; m. Steven Ramsey White, Sept. 24, 1984. BA, Pa. State U., 1962. Owner, pres. Grace Lines, Santa Maria, Calif., 1990—. Mem. Santa Barbara County Vintners Assn., Pa. State U. Alumni Assn., Order of Eastern Star. Democrat. Office: Grace Lines 4182 Lockford St Santa Maria CA 93455

WHITE, HELEN FRANCES PEARSON, language educator, real estate broker; b. Bucoda, Mo., Sept. 26, 1925; d. William Sidney and Ella Myrtle Isaccs) Pearson; m. Jewel Porter White, June 21, 1942; children: Sydney LaVergne, Betty Ann, John Patrick. BA, Ark. State U., 1955; postgrad., U. Toulouse, 1965, U. Okla., 1962-64, U. Mex., 1966, Tex. A&M U., 1969; credited study tour on Creole Lang., Tex. A&M, 1969. Life time teaching lic. Mo., Tex., lic. real estate broker, lic. 1st class radio engr., FCC. High sch. English tchr. Manila, Ark., 1955-57; high sch. English, French tchr. New Madrid, Mo., 1958-63; Spanish, French tchr. Hardin Jefferson High Sch., Sour Lake, Tex., 1964-71; cons., instr. Radio Stas. KKAS & KWDX, Silsbee, Tex., 1969—; broker Accent Corner Real Estate, Silsbee, 1981—; tour dir. Robbins Ednl. Tours, Marquand, Mo., 1957-64, Whites' Tours, Silsbee, 1968—; host family, S.E. Tex. area rep. Youth for Understanding, 1968-75; workshop participant, job tng. instr., Programs for Human Svcs., 1981-84; pvt. lang. tutor, Portageville, Mo., Silsbee. Preservationist Hist. Landmark, 1991 (Tex. Hist. Commn. award for Old Silsbee Ice House); mem. Concept of Care, Kountze, Tex., 1985-88, Hardin County Tourist Bur.; charter commr. S.E. Tex. Women's Commn., 1985-88; coun. mem. County Assn. for Retarded Persons, Silsbee, 1986-89; pres. Silsbee Libr. Adv. Bd., 1986; founder, pres. Hardin County Arts and Ednl. Found., 1987—; mem. First Meth. Ch. Grantee Tex. A&M U., 1969. Mem. AAUW (life, pres. Hardin County br. 1983-86), Hardin County Geneal. Soc., Alpha Delta Kappa. Home: 1300 White Meadows RR 6 Box 75 Silsbee TX 77656-9232 Office: Accent Corner Real Estate Highway 327 W Silsbee TX 77656

WHITE, IRENE, insurance adjustor, environmental consultant; b. Taumuning, Guam, Jan. 3, 1961; d. Antonio Gill and Irma Magdalena (Idrogo) Gill; m. William Paul Franck, Aug. 4, 1979 (div. July 1984); m. Richard Nelson White, May 12, 1989 (div. Dec. 1993). Cert. ins. adjuster, Tex. Ins. adjuster Gen. Accident Group, San Antonio, 1983-85, Crum & Forster Ins., San Antonio, 1985-89, Aetna Life & Casualty, San Antonio, 1979-83; adjuster, analyst Aetna Life & Casualty, Dallas, 1989—. Big sister Big Bros. and Sisters, San Antonio, 1987-89; vol. counselor March of Dimes, San Antonio, 1988-89. Republican. Roman Catholic. Office: Aetna Life & Casualty 2350 Lakeside Blvd Ste 280 Richardson TX 75082-4341

WHITE, JEAN TILLINGHAST, former state senator; b. Cambridge, Mass., Dec. 24, 1934; d. James Churchill Moulton and Clara Jean (Carter) Tillinghast; m. Peregrine White, June 6, 1970. B.A., Wellesley Coll., 1956. Supr., programmer Lumber Mut. Ins. Co., Cambridge, 1964-70; selectman, chmn. Town of Rindge (N.H.), 1975-80; clk. regulated revenues N.H. Ho. of Reps., Concord, 1978-80, vice chmn. regulated revenues, 1980-82; mem. N.H. Senate, 1982-88, chmn. fin. com.; v.p., treas. Perry White, Inc., Rindge, N.H., 1970—; dir. Peterborough Savings Bank (N.H.). Chmn., Rindge Friends of Library, 1972; pres. Nat. Order Women Legislators, 1990-91. Trustee Univ. System of N.H., 1989-92, Jaffrey/Rindge Sch. Bd., 1989—; commr. Cheshire County, 1995—. Republican. Unitarian. Office: Hampshire Rd Rindge NH 03461

WHITE, JILL CAROLYN, lawyer; b. Santa Barbara, Calif., Mar. 20, 1934; d. Douglas Cameron and Gladys Louise (Ashley) W.; m. Walter Otto Weyrauch, Mar. 17, 1973. BA, Occidental Coll., L.A., 1955; JD, U. Calif., Berkeley, 1972. Bar: Fla. 1974, Calif. 1975, D.C. 1981, U.S. Dist. Ct. (no. and mid. dists.) Fla., U.S. Ct. Appeals. (5th and 11th cirs.), U.S. Supreme Ct. Staff mem. U.S. Dept. State, U.S. Embassy, Rio de Janeiro, Brazil, 1956-58; with psychol. rsch. units Inst. Human Devel., Inst. Personality Assessment and Rsch., U. Calif., Berkeley, 1961-68; adj. prof. U. Fla. Criminal Justice Program, Gainesville, Fla., 1976-78; pvt. practice immigration and nationality law Gainesville, 1976—; appointed mem. Fla. Bar Inaugural Immigration and Nationality Certification Com., 1994—. Contbr. articles to profl. jours. Mem. ABA, Am. Immigration Lawyers Assn. (bd. dirs. Ctrl. Fla. chpt. 1985-94, chair Ctrl. Fla. chpt. 1988-89, co-chmn. So. Regional Liaison com. 1990-92, nat. bd. dirs. 1988-89), Fla. Assn. Women Lawyers (8th jud. cir. chpt.), Bar Assn. 8th Jud. Cir. Fla., Gainesville Area C. of C., Gainesville Area Innovation Network, Gainesville Area Women's Network, Altrusa Club Gainesville. Democrat. Office: 1330 NW 6th St Ste C Gainesville FL 32601-2213

WHITE, JOAN MICHELSON, artist; b. Hartford, Conn., Jan. 4, 1936; d. William Allen and Mitzi (Lurie) Michelson; m. Harvey Marshall White, June 28, 1958; children: Randi Lynn, Andrew Steven. BA, Ctrl. Conn. State U., 1958; postgrad., Wesleyan U., 1980. Cert. tchr., Conn. One woman shows include Canton (Conn.) Gallery on the Green, 1977, Saltbox Gallery, West Hartford, Conn., 1986, Key Gallery, N.Y.C., 1982, Hartford Jewish Cmty. Ctr., 1980; mem. Hartford Art Sch. Aux.; mem. adv. bd. U. Hartford Joseloff Gallery. Group shows include Silvermine Guild New Eng. Exhbn., 1977, 79, Springfield (Mass.) Art League Nat. Exhbn., 1980, 83, 86, The Galleries, Wellesley, Mass., 1983, Stephen Haller Fine Arts, N.Y.C., 1987, 88, Penrose Gallery, Nantucket, Mass., 1984, Conn. Artists Showcase, Conn. Commn. on the Arts, Hartford, 1986, Provincetown (Mass.) Art Assn. and Mus., 1986, Old Lyme (Conn.) Art Works, 1985, Greene Gallery, Guilford, Conn., 1986, Signature Gallery, West Hartford, Conn., 1986-94, Allan Stone Gallery, N.Y.C., 1984, Shippee Gallery, N.Y.C., 1984, Heritage State Park Mus., Holyoke, Mass., 1988, Southern Conn. State U., New Haven, 1989, Farmington Valley Arts Ctr., Avon, Conn., 1992, John Slade Ely House, New Haven, 1993, Ute Stebich Gallery, Lenox, Mass., 1994, North Coast Collage Soc., Seattle, 1994. Mem. Conn. Watercolor Soc. (bd. dirs. 1980-82), West Hartford Ctr. for Visual Arts, Conn. Women Artists, Conn. Acad. Fine Arts. Home: 73 Avondale Rd West Hartford CT 06117-1108

WHITE, KATE, editor-in-chief. Former editor-in-chief Child mag.; editor-in-chief Working Woman mag., N.Y.C., 1989-91, McCall's mag, N.Y.C., 1991-94, Redbook, N.Y.C., 1994—. Office: Redbook Hearst Magazines 224 W 57th St New York NY 10019-3299*

WHITE, KATHERINE PATRICIA, lawyer; b. N.Y.C., Feb. 1, 1948; d. Edward Christopher and Catherine Elizabeth (Walsh) W. BA in English, Molloy Coll., 1969; JD, St. John's U., 1971. Bar: N.Y. 1972, U.S. Dist. Ct. (ea. and so. dists.) N.Y., 1973, U.S. Supreme Ct. 1976. Atty. Western Electric Co., Inc., N.Y.C., 1971-79; sr. atty. AT&T Co., N.Y.C., 1979—; bd. dirs. First Security Benefit Life Ins. Co. N.Y., 1994—; adj. prof. law N.Y. Law Sch., N.Y.C., 1987-88, Fordham U. Sch. Law, 1988-91; bd. dirs. First Security Benefit Life Inst. Co. of N.Y. Vol. Sloan Kettering Inst., 1973, North Shore U. Hosp., 1975, various fed., state and local polit. campaigns; judge N.Y. State Bicentennial Writing Competition, N.Y.C., 1977-78; chmn. Com. to Elect Supreme Ct. Judge, N.Y.C., 1982. Mem. Am. Corp. Counsel Assn., N.Y. State Bar Assn. (bus. and banking law com. real estate law sect., corp. counsel sect.), Assn. Bar City N.Y. (adminstrv. law com. 1982-85, young lawyers com. 1976-79, judge nat. moot ct. competition 1979—), Cath. Lawyers Guild for Diocese of Rockville Centre (pres. 1980-81), St. John's U. Sch. Law Alumni Assn. (pres. L.I. chpt. 1986-88), Women's Nat. Rep. Club (bd. govs. 1988-91), Met. Club. Home: 1035 Fifth Ave Apt 14D New York NY 10028-0135 Office: AT&T 32 Ave of Americas New York NY 10013-2412

WHITE, KATHLEEN MERRITT, geologist; b. Long Beach, Calif., Nov. 19, 1921; d. Edward Clendenning and Gladys Alice (Merritt) White; m. Alexander Kennedy Baird IV, Oct. 1, 1965 (dec. 1985); children: Pamela Roberts, Peter Madlem, Stephen Madlem, Mari Afify. Attended Sch. Boston Mus. Fine Arts, Art Students League, 1940-42; BS in Geology, Pomona Coll., 1962; MS in Geochemistry, Claremont Grad. Sch., 1964. Rsch. asst. geology Pomona Coll., Claremont, Calif., 1940-62, rsch. assoc. geology, 1966-75; cons. geology Claremont, Calif., 1975-77; sr. scientist Jet Propulsion Lab./NASA, Pasadena, 1977-79, mem. tech. staff, 1979-86; ind. rschr. Claremont, 1986—; cons. Pangaea Inc., Santa Barbara, Calif., 1991-92; owner Kittie Tales, Videos and CDs for Children, Claremont, 1992—. Contbr. Geosat Report, 1986; contbr. articles to profl. jours. Grantee NASA, 1984, 85; Pomona Coll. scholar, 1963. Mem. Geol. Soc. Am. (invited paper 1994), Am. Geophys. Union, Pomona Coll. Alumni Assn. Republican. Home: 265 W 11th St Claremont CA 91711-3804

WHITE, KATHRYN CARLSON, critical care nurse; b. Yokosuka, Japan, Dec. 2, 1954; d. Edward C. and Julia Mae (Rebsamen) Carlson; m. Frederick D. White, Oct. 20, 1979; children: Heather Lynne, Kelly Julianne. Student, Wesley Passavant Sch. Nursing, 1975; BS, Coll. of St. Francis, 1979; MS, George Williams Coll., 1980; postgrad., Ga. State U., 1993—. Cert. ACLS instr., BLS affiliate faculty. Neurosurg. educator Skull Base Surgery; staff nurse clin. level III ICU West St. Joseph's Hosp., 1989—. Former chmn. Dekalb County CPR Com., 1985-89. Mem. AANN (exec. bd. dirs. Ga. chpt. 1992—), AACN, CCRN, Nat. League Nursing, Am. Heart Assn. (Vol. of Yr. 1989). Home: 1240 Rocky Rd Lawrenceville GA 30244 Office: 5665 Peachtree Dunwoody Rd NE Atlanta GA 30342-1701

WHITE, LAURA KAY, neuropsychologist; b. Canton, Ohio, June 23, 1961; d. Gilbert Leighton and Paulene Ann (Beeler) White. BA in Psychology, Ind. U., 1983, PhD in Clin. Psychology, 1991. Lic. clin. psychologist. Rsch. assoc. U. Pa., Pitts., 1983-84; clin. psychology intern U. Wash. Med. Ctr., Seattle, 1988-89, neuropsychology fellow, 1991-92; dir. neuropsychology HealthSouth Med. Ctr., Richmond, Va., 1992—. Wash. Inst. Mental Illness Rsch. & Tng. grantee, 1990-91. Mem. APA, Internat. Neuropsychology Assn., Richmond Acad. Clin. Psychology, Phi Beta Kappa. Democrat. Office: HelathSouth Med Ctr 7700 E Parham Rd Richmond VA 23294-4301

WHITE, LESLIE MARY, epidemiologist; b. Huntington, N.Y., July 22, 1954; d. John B. and Inez M. (Montecalvo) W. BS, Mary Washington Coll., 1976; MPH, Johns Hopkins U., 1990; postgrad., U. Md., 1993—. Microbiologist II Am. Type Culture Collection, Rockville, Md., 1980-83; analyst InterAm. Assocs., Rockville, Md., 1984-86; sr. assoc. Triton Corp., Washington, 1986-87; health analyst Row Scis., Inc., Rockville, 1987-88; rsch. analyst Nat. BioSystems, Rockville, 1988-90; sr. assoc. Clement Internat., Fairfax, Va., 1990-92; project dir. epidemiology Consultants in Epidemiology and Occupational Health, Washington, 1992-93; dir. epidemiology Scis. Internat., Inc., Alexandria, Va., 1993-94; pres. Epidemiology and Health Rsch., Inc., Bethesda, Md., 1994—. Mem. APHA, Soc. Epidemiologic Rsch., Soc. Occupational and Environ. Health. Home: 7401 Westlake Ter Ste 512 Bethesda MD 20817 Office: Epidemiology and Health Rsch Inc 7401 Westlake Ter Ste 512 Bethesda MD 20817

WHITE, LIBBY KRAMER, librarian; b. Boston, Sept. 30, 1934; d. Samuel and Ida (Drucker) Kramer; m. Gerald Milton White, June 6, 1956; children: Charles, Andrew, Judith, Abigail White D'Costa. BS in Social Sci., Simmons Coll., Boston, 1956; MLS, SUNY, Albany, 1972. Librarian Temple Israel, Albany, N.Y., 1966-73; bookmobile librarian Schenectady County Pub. Library, 1973, br. librarian, 1973-76, ref./YA librarian, 1976-85, ref./ethnic culture librarian, 1985—; chmn. Nat. Library Wk., Schenectady, 1985. Book reviewer Sch. Libr. Jour., 1980—, Libr. Jour., 1989, Assn. Jewish Librs. Newsletter, 1994—; cons. various encys., mags. Sec. bd. trustees Beth Israel Synagogue, Schenectady, 1986-94, Jewish Cmty. Ctr., 1979-88; resident advisor Summer Seminars in Judaic Studies, Skidmore Coll., Saratoga, N.Y., 1987—. Mem. N.Y. Library Assn., Hudson Mohawk Library Assn. (pres. 1989—). Jewish. Home: 1274 Hawthorne Rd Schenectady NY 12309-4609 Office: 99 Clinton St Schenectady NY 12305-2038

WHITE, LINDA DIANE, lawyer; b. N.Y.C., Apr. 1, 1952; d. Bernard and Elaine (Simons) Schwartz; m. Thomas M. White, Aug. 16, 1975; 1 child, Alexandra Nicole. AB, U. Pa., 1973; JD, Northwestern U., 1976. Bar: Ill. 1976. Assoc. Walsh, Case, Coale & Brown, Chgo., 1976-77, Greenberger & Kaufmann (merged into Katten, Muchin), Chgo., 1977-82; ptnr. Greenberger & Kaufmann (merged into Katten, Muchin), 1982-85, Sonnenschein Nath & Rosenthal, Chgo., 1985—. Mem. ABA (real property fin. com., comml. leasing com., real property, probate and trust law sect. 1987—), Ill. Bar Assn., Chgo. Bar Assn., Internat. Assn. Corp. Real Estate Execs. Office: Sonnenschein Nath & Rosenthal 8000 Sears Tower 233 S Wacker Dr Chicago IL 60606

WHITE, LINDA SUE, cardiology technician; b. Gary, Ind., Apr. 14, 1964 D. Ralph Warren and Anna Elizabeth (Chadourne) W. Cert., Ill. Med. Tng. Ctr., 1986, Commonwealth Coll., Merrillville, Ind., 1988; student, Internat. Corr. Schs., 1991-93. With Video King, Merrillville, 1983-85, Olan Mills, Portage, Ind., 1984-85; EKG tech. Porter Meml. Hosp., Valparaiso, Ind., 1986-87; med. asst. Dr. Brown, Crown Point, Ind., 1988-89; office mgr., med. asst., office nurse Dr. Pargaonker, Merrillville, 1989-92; med. asst. Dr. J. Timothy Ames, Valparaiso, 1992—. Mem. Contact Cares of N.E. Ind. Democrat. Baptist. Home: 399 Keystone Dr Valparaiso IN 46383-8829 Office: Dr J Timothy Ames 1101 E Glendale Blvd Valparaiso IN 46383-9999

WHITE, LORAY BETTY, writer, actress, producer; b. Houston, Nov. 27, 1934; d. Harold White and Joyce Mae (Jenkins) Mills; m. Sammy Davis Jr., 1957 (div. 1959); 1 child, Deborah R. DeHart. Student, UCLA, 1948-50, 90-91, Nichiren Shoshu Acad., 1988-92; AA in Bus., Sayer Bus. Sch., 1970; study div. mem. dept. L.A., Soka U., Japan, 1970-86. Editor entertainment writer L.A. Community New, 1970-81; exec. sec. guest rels. KNBC Prodns., Burbank, Calif., 1969-75; security specialist Xerox X10 Think Tank, L.A., 1975-80; exec. asst. Ralph Powell & Assocs., L.A., 1980-82; pres., owner, producer LBW & Assocs. Pub. Rels., L.A., 1980—; owner, producer, writer, host TV prodn. co. Pub. Pub. Rels., L.A., 1987—; dir., producer L.B.W. Prodn. Yesterday, Today, Tomorrow, L.A., 1981—. Actress (film) Ten Commandments, 1956, (Broadway) Joy Ride; appeared in the following endorsements including Budweiser Beer, Old Gold Cigarettes, Salem Cigarettes, TV commls. including Cheer, Puffs Tissue, Coca Cola, Buffern, others; entertainment editor L.A. Community News, 1970-73; writer (column) Balance News, 1980-82. Mem. Soka Gakkai Internat. Youth divsn. ARC, Urban League, Nat. Audubon Found., Nat. Parks Assn., Smithsonian Instn., Lupus Found. of Am. (so. Calif. chpt.), World Peace Cultural Festival '72, Bicentennial Celebration '76, United High Blood Pressure Telethon, Com. for Sr. Citizens, Beverly Hills-Westwood Sr. Citizen Cmty. Ctr. Recipient award ARC, 1955, Cert. of Honor, Internat. Orgn. Soka Gakkai Internat. of Japan, Cmty. Vols. of Am. award, 1994; named Performer of Yr. Cardella Demillo, 1976-77. Mem. ULCA Alumni Assn., Lupus Found. Am. (so. Calif. chpt.). Buddhist. Home and Office: 625 S Shelton St # A Burbank CA 91506

WHITE, LORNA LOUISE, underwriter; b. Klamath Falls, Oreg., Sept. 18, 1944; d. Louis Carroll Pratt and Islay Myrtle (Sewell) Pratt Bushman; m. Lewis A. White, Nov. 26, 1977; children: Corbyn Michael, Travis Walter. A in Underwriting, Linn-Benton Community Coll., 1977; student, Am. Inst. for Property and Casualty Underwriters, 1989—. Cert. in gen. ins.; cert. profl. ins. woman. Cashier, receptionist Pacific Fin., Klamath Falls, 1962-64; accounts payable clk. George Dugan Chevrolet, Klamath Falls, 1965-71; office mgr. Dunmire Datsun, Albany, Oreg., 1971-73, Merle Taylor Dodge, Albany, Oreg., 1975-77, Gary-Worth Chrysler Plymouth, Gladstone, Oreg., 1977; full cycle bookkeeper L.R. Swarthout, Burns, Oreg., 1978-79; property-casualty clk., bookkeeper, adminstr. pension plan R.L. Morris, Bend, Oreg.,

1979-80; dispatcher Risberg's Truck Line, Redmond, Oreg., 1980-81; sr. underwriter Valley Ins. Co., Albany, 1982—; tchr. Profl. Ins. Agts., Salem, Oreg., 1989; speaker in field. Author poems. Vol. Albany Jaycees, 1982-92, Vietnam Vets. Oreg. Meml., Portland, 1984-89, Linn County Humane Soc., Albany, 1991. Named Jaycee Congresswoman, Assoc. of Yr., Ins. Women Tualatin Valley, 1991. Mem. Nat. Assn. Ins. Women (state membership chmn., state coun., awards chmn. Willamette Valley chpt. 1991—, chmn. industry breakfast 1991—, Ins. Woman of Yr. award 1990, 91, winner state speakoff Oreg. coun. 1990, state dir. 1993-94), Women's Internat. Bowling Congress, VFW Aux., Am. Legion Aux., Linn County Vets. Coun. (treas.). Democrat. Home: 2281 22nd Pl SE Albany OR 97321-5470 Office: Valley Ins Co 2450 14th Ave SE Albany OR 97321-8523

WHITE, MARIE CALDERONE, public relations executive, sports broadcaster; b. White Plains, N.Y., Jan. 22; d. Philip and Mary (Rullo) Calderone; m. Raymond Joseph White, Oct. 8, 1960. BS cum laude, St. Lawrence U.; cert., Acad. Broadcasting Arts. Reg. Bus. Cert., self employed. Pub. rels. account exec. Sudler & Hennessey, N.Y.C., 1960-68; comml. copywriter, spokeswoman Sta. WVIP, Mt. Kisco, N.Y., 1969-71; sports broadcaster Sta. WGCH, Greenwich, Conn., 1973-76; owner, pres. MCW Enterprises, Chappaqua, N.Y., 1977—; pub. rels. dir. Sudler & Hennessey, N.Y.C., 1982—; broadcaster U.S. Open Golf, 1974, U.S. Open Tennis, 1974, Bergdorf-Goodman Gala, 1975; ednl. announcer Schloat Prodns., Inc., 1976. Editor-in-chief: (newsletter) S&H Highlights, 1982—; patentee Stemware Rack, 1980. Dir./v.p. Stornowaye Assn., Chappaqua, N.Y., 1970-74; campaign co-chmn. N.Y. State Assemblyman, Chappaqua, 1972; exec. com. Sts. John & Mary Parish Coun., Chappaqua, 1972-74, fin. com., 1980-84; fashion adv. bd. B. Altman & Co., White Plains, N.Y., 1975. Mem. NAFE, Westchester Country Club, Beta Chi Rho (hon.), Phi Beta Kappa. Republican. Roman Catholic. Home: 26 Stornowaye St Chappaqua NY 10514-2323 Office: MCW Enterprises PO Box 216 Chappaqua NY 10514-0216

WHITE, MARJORIE MARY, elementary school educator; b. LaCrosse, Wis., May 10, 1944; d. Knute Emil and Florence Catherine (Fredrich) Johnson; m. David James White, July 6, 1985; stepchildren: Christopher Howard, Wendy Marie White Ehert. BSE, Winona State U., 1966, MSEd, 1971. Cert. elem. tchr., Minn. Tchr. Lacrosse Cath. Schs., Wis., 1966-68, Winona County Schs., Dakota, Minn., 1968-72, Ind. Sch. Dist., Winona, Minn., 1972—. Mem. NEA, AAUW (treas. 1990-92), Minn. Edn. Assn., Winona Edn. Assn. (Faculty rep. 1970—, membership chmn. 1990—), Phi Delta Kappa (newsletter editor 1984-92, 94—, del. 1985-91, v.p. membership 1989-91, Svc. Key award 1991). Democrat. Roman Catholic. Home: 705 W Wabasha St Winona MN 55987-2764 Office: Ind Sch Dist 861 654 Huff St Winona MN 55987-3320

WHITE, MARTINE T., television and film location manager. Student, Sorbonne U., Paris, 1972, Am. U., 1973; BA in Mass. Comms. & Polit. Sci., U. Calif., Santa Barbara, 1977; postgrad., Metromedia Broadcast Eng. Sch., L.A., 1980. Location mgr.: (films) Father Hood, 1993, Edison Preamble, 1993, Sister Act II, 1993, Love in the Dark Ages, 1993, Under Siege II, 1994, Camp Nowhere, 1994; asst. location mgr.: (films) The Last to Go, 1990, Snoops, 1990, The Five Heartbeats, 1990, V.I. Warshawski, 1990, Unlawful Entry, 1991, Black Hope Horror, 1991, The Owl, 1991, American Me (Spanish prodn.), 1991, I'll Do Anything, 1992, Bound by Honor, 1992, Fatal Instinct, 1992, Street Knight, 1992, In the Line of Fire, 1993, (TV series) Shannon's Deal, 1991, Reasonable Doubts, 1991-93; line prodr., assoc. dir.: AAA comml., 1989; dir., prodr., writer: (promo., training video) Compact Disclosure, Phillips, 1989; location mgr., prodn. coord.: Asahi Beer comml., 1989, (documentary) Space Heroes, 1989; assoc. prodr., assoc. dir., writer: Herbalife teleconfs., documentaries, 1984; assoc. prodr., writer: (fin. series pilot) Moneymaker, 1984; prodr., writer, editor: WFTY-Channel 50, Washington; coord., writer: (music videos) KEEFCO/John Weaver Prodns., 1984-85; program coord. KTTV Fox/Metromedia, 1979-84; prodr., writer: Channel 11 Movie Club; assoc. dir.: Cerebral Palsy Telethon, Jerry Lewis MDA Telethon, Rose Parade Pre-parade show, Teen Scene, Good Day, L.A.; assoc. prodr., alt. host Open Line: rschr.: (documentary Dem. Nat. Conv.) Legacy, 1988; prodr., writer: (satellite teleconfs.) Worldnet, U.S. Info. Agy., 1987; French trans., prodn. coord.: Amazing World, France, 1980. Office: Multilingual Prodn Svcs 2025 4th St Santa Monica CA 90405

WHITE, MARY JO, prosecutor. Atty. U.S. Dept. Justice, Manhattan, 1993—; U.S. Atty. So. Dist. N.Y. Office: 1 Saint Andrews Plz New York NY 10007-1701

WHITE, MARY RUTH WATHEN, social services administrator; b. Athens, Tex., Dec. 27, 1927; d. Benedict Hudson and Sara Elizabeth (Evans) W.; m. Robert M. White, Nov. 10, 1946; children: Martha Elizabeth, Robert Miles, Jr., William Benedict, Mary Ruth, Jesse Wathen, Margaret Fay, Maureen Adele, Thomas Evan. BA, Stephen F. Austin State U., Nacogdoches, Tex., 1948. Chmn. Regional Drug Abuse Com., San Antonio, 1975-81, Met. Youth Council, San Antonio, 1976-78; state chmn. Citizens United for Rehab. Errants, San Antonio, 1978-91; sec. Bexar County Detention Ministries, San Antonio, 1979-88; chmn. Bexar County (Tex.) Jail Commn., 1980-82; chmn. com. on role of family in reducing recidivism Tex. Dept. Criminal Justice, Austin, 1985—; chmn. Met. Community Corrections Com., San Antonio, 1986-90; bd. dirs. Tex. Coalition for Juvenile Justice, 1975-93, Target 90 Youth Coordinating Coun., San Antonio, 1986-89; local chmn. vol. adv. bd. Tex. Youth Commn., 1986-87. Pres. San Antonio City Coun. PTA, 1976-78, Rep. Bus. Women Bexar County, San Antonio, 1984-86; bd. dirs. CURE, 1978-92; legis. chmn. Archdiocese of San Antonio Coun. Cath. Women, San Antonio Alliance Mental Illness; pres. North Urban Deanery; mem. allocation com. United Way, San Antonio, 1986-91. Named Today's Woman, San Antonio Light newspaper, 1985, Outstanding Rep. Woman, Rep. Bus. Women Bexar County, 1987; honoree Rep. Women Stars over Tex., 1992. Mem. Am. Corrections Assn., Assn. Criminal Justice Planners, LWV (pres. San Antonio chpt. 1984-86), Conservation Soc., Fedn. Women (bd. dirs. 1984-90), DAR (regent), Colonial Dames (pres.), Cath. Daus. Am. (registered parliamentarian, past regent Ct. of St. Anthony), Tex. Cath. Daus. Am. (state legis. chair). Home: 701 E Sunshine Dr San Antonio TX 78228-2516 Office: 7461 Callaghan Rd Ste 307 San Antonio TX 78229-2988

WHITE, MICHELLE JO, economics educator; b. Washington, Dec. 3, 1945; d. Harry L. and Irene (Silverman) Rich; m. Roger Hall Gordon, July 25, 1982. AB, Harvard U., 1967; MSc in Econs., London Sch. Econs., 1968; PhD, Princeton U., 1973. Asst. prof. U. Pa., Phila., 1973-78; from assoc. prof. to prof. NYU, N.Y.C., 1978-83; prof. econs. U. Mich., Ann Arbor, 1984—; dir. PhD program in econs. U. Mich., 1992-94; vis. asst. prof. Yale U., New Haven, 1978; vis. prof. People's U., Beijing, 1986, U. Warsaw, 1990, U. Wis., Madison, 1991, U. Munich, 1992, Catholic U. Brabant, The Netherlands, 1993, U. Chgo., 1993; cons. Pension Benefit Guaranty Corp., Washington, 1987; chmn. adv. com. dept. econs. Princeton U., 1988-90. Editor: The Non-profit Sector in a Three Sector Economy, 1981; contbr. numerous articles to profl. jours. Bd. dirs. Com. on Status of Women in Econs. Profession, 1984-86. Resources for Future fellow, 1972-73; grantee NSF, 1979, 82, 88, 91, 93, Sloan Found., 1984, Fund for Rsch. in Dispute Resolution, 1989; Fulbright scholar, Poland, 1990. Mem. Am. Econ. Assn., Am. Law and Econ. Assn. (bd. dirs. 1991-92), Am. Real Estate and Urban Econs. Assn. (bd. dirs. 1992-95), Social Scis. Rsch. Coun. (bd. dirs. 1994—). Office: Univ Mich 611 Tappan Ave Ann Arbor MI 48109-1220

WHITE, NORMA JANE, microcomputer administrator; b. York, Pa., June 4, 1966; d. John Franklin and Phyllis Romain (Snelbaker) Stoner; m. Lenny Alan White, Mar. 12, 1990; 1 child, Tyler Scott. BS in Acctg., York Coll. Pa., 1988. Staff asst. P.H. Glatfelter, Spring Grove, Pa., 1988-93; microcomputer adminstr. P.H. Glatfelter, Spring Grove, 1993—. Office: P H Glatfelter 228 S Main St Spring Grove PA 17362

WHITE, PATRICIA ANN, clinical nurse specialist; b. Indiana, Pa., Dec. 11, 1956; d. Darl J. and Virginia M. (Nealer) W. ADN, Erie C.C., 1978; BSN, U. Tex., Houston, 1989; MSN, U. Tex., 1991. Cert. critical care nurse, clin. nurse specialst, ACLS instr., ABLS provider. Staff nurse M.D. Anderson, Houston, 1978-81; agy. nurse Kimberly Agy., San Francisco, 1981-82; staff nurse U. Calif., Davis, 1982-83; nurse Travel Nurse Corp., Malden, Mass., 1984-87; critical care instr. Hermann Hosp., Houston, 1987-91; clin. instr. U. Tex. Health Sci. Ctr., Houston, 1991-92; edn. coord. Tampa Gen. Healthcare; presenter in field. Contbr. articles to profl. jours. Vol. St. Petersburg Free Clinic. Mem. ANA, Am. Coll. Cardiovascular Nursing (pres. 1993—), Am. Assn. Critical Care Nurses, Am. Heart Assn., Continuing Edn. League, Sigma Theta Tau. Presbyterian. Office: Tampa Gen Healthcare Davis Island Tampa FL 33602

WHITE, POLLY SEARS, religious organization administrator; b. Phila., Jan. 29, 1931; d. W. Heyward and Emily P. (Welsh) Myers; m. Peter White, June 13, 1953; children: Katharine, Peter, Jennifer, Jeffrey. AB, Smith Coll., 1953. Adminstrv. aide Inst. Local and State Govt., U. Pa., Phila., 1953-55; parish sec. St. Mary's Episcopal Ch., Wayne, Pa., 1977-85; program dir. Metro Toledo Chs. United, 1987—. Sec., treas. Friends Radnor Twp. Meml. Libr., Wayne, 1978-80; pres. Presbyn. Hosp. Med. Aux., Phila., 1983-85; bd. dirs. Wood County Planned Parenthood Coun., Bowling Green, Ohio, 1985-86, Perrysburg (Ohio) LWV, 1986-88; oper. com. 1st Call for Help of United Way, Toledo, vice chair, 1993—; mem. altar guild, flower guild St. Timothy's Episc. Ch., vestry, 1993—; trustee Hist. Perrysburg, 1990, bd. dirs., 1990—; mem. Perrysburg Landmarks Commn., 1992—. Democrat. Home: 525 E 6th St Perrysburg OH 43551-2223 Office: Metro Toledo Chs United 444 Floyd St Toledo OH 43620-1735

WHITE, REBECCA ANNE, pharmaceutical territory manager; b. Erie, Pa., Aug. 16, 1949; d. Francis Edward and Anne Frances (Schwartz) W.; children: Matthew John Swabb, Anne Catherine Swabb. BS, Gannon U., 1979; MA, Cleve. State U., 1988. Territory mgr. Hoffmann-LaRoche, Inc., Nutley, N.J., 1979-94; biosci. sales rep. Hoffman-LaRoche, Inc., Nutley, N.J., 1994—; counselor St. Vincent Health Ctr., Erie, 1978-79. Named Scholastic All Am. Achiever, 1988; recipient Pres.'s Achievement award, 1983. Mem. Phi Alpha Theta, Pi Gamma Mu.

WHITE, REBECCA (HUDSON), office manager; b. Columbus, Ind., Oct. 4, 1948; d. James Edward and Jacquelyn Kerr (Stevens) Hudson; m. Dennis Robert White, June 3, 1967; children: Eric Matthew, Benjamin Logan. Grad., Columbus (Ind.) High Sch., 1966. Office mgr. Hope Mission Tours, Hope, Ind., 1983-94, Dr. Jim Alward, Nashville, 1994—; founder, dir. girls gospel group, E. Columbus (Ind.) United Meth. Ch., 1964-66, youth fellowship leader, 1967-71; bible sch. music dir. Mt. Olive Meth. Ch., Columbus, summer, 1988, 92, 93, youth fellowship leader, 1991-93, founder and dir. choir, 1986—; musician, singer Hope Trio, 1989—; mem. Haiti Missions, Hope Mission Tours, 1983—. Singer recording cassette tapes, 1985, 87, 89. Co-founder White Wood Sch. of Hope, Haiti, W.I., 1984; bd. dirs. Mission of Hope Compound, Haiti, 1989—; adminstrv. asst. Bartholomew County CETA Program, Columbus, 1978-79. Home: 431 West Dr Nashville IN 47448 Office: Dr Jim Alward PO Box 1160 Nashville IN 47448-2231

WHITE, RENEE ALLYN, judge; b. Bronx, N.Y., Sept. 22, 1945; d. Lawrence and Ann (Kaufman) W.; m. Michael W. Moore, Oct. 23, 1993. BA, Hofstra U., 1966, JD, Bklyn. Law Sch., 1969. Bar: N.Y. 1969, U.S. Dist. Ct. (ea. and so. dists.) N.Y. 1977, U.S. Supreme Ct. 1978. Trial atty. Criminal Def. div. The Legal Aid Soc. N.Y.C., 1969-74; atty. in charge Criminal Justice sect. Office of Projects Devel. Appellate div. First Dept., N.Y.C., 1974-78; adminstrv. law judge City N.Y. Office Adminstrv. Trials and Hearings, 1978-84; judge N.Y.C. Civil Ct., 1984, Criminal Ct. City of N.Y., 1985-88; acting supreme ct. justice,, supervising judge of N.Y. County Criminal Ct., 1988-90, acting supreme ct. justice, criminal term, 1990—; lectr. in field, mem. criminal procedure law com. of the office of ct. adminstrn. Editor: Criminal Trial Advocacy, 1977; contbr. in field. Mem. ABA, N.Y. State Bar Assn. (chmn. criminal justice sect. 1985-87, mem. house of dels. 1985-88, 91—, elected nominating com. 1989-90, co-chair, spl. com. on AIDS and the law 1992—, chair continuing legal edn. com. of judicial sect., 1994—), Assn. of Bar of City of N.Y. (coun. on judicial adminstrn.) , N.Y. Women's Bar Assn.

WHITE, ROBERTA LEE, comptroller; b. Denver, Sept. 18, 1946; d. Harold Tindall and Araminta (Campbell) Bangs; m. Lewis Paul White, Jr., Jan. 23, 1973 (div. Sept. 1974). BA cum laude, Linfield Coll., 1976; postgrad., Lewis & Clark Coll. Office mgr. Multnomah County Auditor, Portland, Oreg., 1977-81; rsch. asst. Dan Goldy and Assocs., Portland, 1981-83; regional asst. Vocat. Rehab., Eugene, Oreg., 1983-85; internal auditor Multnomah County, Portland, Oregon, 1985-89; cons. Portland, 1989-91; fin. analyst City of Portland, 1991-93; comptroller Wordsmith Svcs., Portland, 1993—; mem. Com. for Implementation of the ADA, Portland, 1991-93. Treas. Mary Wendy Roberts for Sec. of State, Portland, 1992, Re-Elect Mary Wendy Roberts, Portland, 1990, Elect Hank Miggins Com., 1994; mem. Oreg. Women's Polit. Caucus, Portland, 1982-85, City Club, Portland, 1978-81. Democrat. Mem. Disciples of Christ. Home: 6605 W Burnside Apt 121 Portland OR 97210 Office: Wordsmith Svcs Ste 350 1500 NE Irving Ste 350 Portland OR 97232

WHITE, RUTH BRYANT, counselor, communications specialist, minister; b. Denver, May 6, 1955; d. Volleny Bryant Sr. and Ruth Ada (Washington) Smith; m. Steven Alan White, Nov. 21, 1980; children: Pershaun R., LeJeune B., LaVonda M. Ed. high sch., Denver. Ordained to ministry Christian Ch. With acctg. sect. U.S. Govt., Denver and L.A., 1972-81; remittance processor Auto Club So. Calif., L.A., 1981-84; with acctg. dept. various agys. L.A., 1984-91; sr. adminstrv. support specialist Infonet, L.A., 1991—. Author: Free Indeed: The Autobiography of an Interracial Couple, 1989. Founder A Place for Us Ministry, Gardena, Calif., 1984—. Mem. Assn. Multiethnic Ams. (charter mem., regional v.p. western U.S. 1991—). Office: A Place for Us PO Box 357 Gardena CA 90248-0357

WHITE, SARAH JOWILLIARD, counselor; b. Oxford, N.C., Sept. 1, 1921; d. John Hiriam and Emma (Redfern) Isham; m. Hamilton B. Carson, Sept. 20, 1945 (div. 1968); 1 child, Lynne Denise. Student, Bennett Coll., 1939-42, Cornell U., 1979-82; BA, CCNY, 1973. Clk. N.Y. Dept. Law, N.Y.C., 1948-53; adutior U.S. Fed. Govt. Svc., N.Y.C., 1955-62; postal clk. U.S. Govt., Mt. Vernon, N.Y., 1963-66; prin. N.Y. State Dept. Labor, Mt. Vernon, 1966-88, ret., 1988; youth organizer N.Y. State Careerists Soc., Inc., N.Y.C., 1989—; youth and employment counselor Women in Community Svc., Nat. Coun. Negro Women, Manhattan sect., N.Y.C., 1983—. Vol. Advanced Vocation Edn. Day, Albany, N.Y., 1988; vol., coord. Decade of the Youth, N.Y.C., 1989, 90; corres. sec. Lower East Side United Neighbors, N.Y.C., 1989. Recipient Youth award, 1987, Recognition award, 1987, Internat. Assn. Pers. Employees Youth award, Plaque for Women in Comty. Svcs., Outstanding Vol. Svc. award Gov. Mario Cuomo, 1994, Outstanding Vol. award, 1991, 92, Outstanding Vol. award Wics, 1994; named one of N.Y.'s Finest Vols. Wics Mag., 1994, Woman on the Move, Cable TV, 1994. Mem. NAFE, N.Y. Careerists Soc. (sec., Merit award 1988), Nat. Coun. Negro Women (chairperson, Achievement award 1988-90), Internat. Assn. Pers. Employees, Black Alumni CCNY (pub. rels. com.), Assn. U.S. Govt. Job Corps. Assn. Democrat. 7th Day Sabbath Keeper.

WHITE, SUSANNE TROPEZ, pediatrician, educator; b. New Orleans, Apr. 13, 1949; d. Maxwell Sterling and Ethel (Ross) Tropez; m. James Carnell White, Apr. 10, 1971 (div. 1992); children: Lisa, Janifer, James Carnell. BS, Bennett Coll., 1971; MD, U. N.C., 1975, M.P.H., 1982. Diplomate Am. Bd. Pediatrics. Resident in pediatrics N.C. Meml. Hosp., Chapel Hill, 1975-76, 77-79; pediatrician Darnell Army Hosp., Ft. Hood, Tex., 1976-77; acting dir. pediatric day clinic Wake County Med. Ctr., Raleigh, N.C., 1979-82, dir. pediatric day clinic, 1982-88, dir. teens with tots clinic, 1980-88; asst. prof. pediatrics U. N.C., Chapel Hill, 1982-88, assoc. prof. pediatrics La. State U., New Orleans, 1988—; dir. div. pediatric emergency rm., 1988-89; chief div. ambulatory care, 1989-92, clin. coord. maternal and child health units, 1992, chief divsn. community pediatrics and adolescent medicine, 1992—; pediatrician Shelly Child Devel. Ctr., Raleigh, 1981-88, child med. examiner program, Raleigh, 1979-88; chairperson sch. health com. local chpt. AAP, 1993; adminstrv. bd. chair Cornerstone U.M.C., 1993—, chairperson edn. com., 1991-92; mem. Nat. Com. Sch. Health, 1993—. Contbr. articles to profl. jours. Mem. United Meth. Women. Mem. Walnut Terr. Child Devel. Ctr., Raleigh, 1981-83, chmn., 1982-83; chmn. pastor of parish com. Longview Ch., Raleigh, 1982-84, 87-88, chmn. membership care com.; chmn. edn. com. Cornerstone UMC, 1989-90. Fellow preventive medicine, 1979-82, Faculty Devel. fellow U. N.C. Sch. Medicine, 1985-87. Fellow Am. Acad. Pediatrics (mem. sch. health com.); mem. N.C. Pediatric Soc. (com. child abuse and neglect, adolescent pregnancy), La Pediatric Soc., Ambulatory Pediatric Assn., Adolescent Pregnancy Coalition United Way, Bennett Coll. Alumnae Assn. Democrat.

WHITE, SUSIE MAE, school psychologist; b. Madison, Fla., Mar. 5, 1914; d. John Anderson and Lucy (Crawford) Williams; m. Daniel Elijah White, Oct. 20, 1958 (dec. Sept. 29, 1968). BS, Fla. Meml. Coll., St. Augustine, 1948; MEd, U. Md., 1953; postgrad., Mich. State U., 1955, Santa Fe Community Coll., 1988; Cert. Child Care Supervision, W.T. Loften Edn. Ctr., Gainesville, Fla., 1994. Elem. tchr. Grove Park (Fla.) Elem. Sch., 1943; tchr. Douglas High Sch., High Springs, Fla., 1944-55; sch. psychologist Alachua County Sch. Bd., Gainesville, Fla., 1956-69; coord. social svcs. Alachua County Sch. Bd., Gainesville, 1970; owner, dir. Mother Dear's Child Care Ctr., Gainesville, 1988—. Del. Bapt. World Alliance, Bapt. Conv. Fla., Tokyo, 1970; state dir. leadership Fla. Bapt. Gen. Conv., 1971-85. Recipient Cert. of Appreciation Fla. State Dept. Edn., Tallahassee, 1971, Appreciation for Disting. Svc. award Fla. Gen. Bapt. Conv., Miami, 1979, Hall of Fame award Martin Luther King Jr. Hall of Fame, 1994. Mem. Nat. Ret. Tchrs. Assn., Alachua County Tchrs. Assn., Fla. Meml. Coll. Nat. Alumni Assn., AAUW, Heroines of Jerico, Masons. Democrat. Office: Child Care Ctr 811 NW 4th Pl Gainesville FL 32601-5049

WHITE, SYLVIA FRANCES, gerontology and home care nurse, consultant; b. Dayton, Ohio, May 2, 1952; d. Arthur Francis and Eleanor Ida (Beach) Scarpelli; m. Alan Bruce White, Nov. 28, 1981. BSN, Loyola U., 1975; MPH, U. Ill., Chgo., 1984. Cert. gerontol. nurse; lic. nursing home adminstrn., Ill. Staff nurse Vis. Nurse Assn., Chgo., 1975-80, team leader, 1980-81, supr., 1981-83, dist. adminstr., 1984-86, mgr. North side, 1986-87, dir. patient svcs., 1987; dir. clin. svcs. Kimberly Quality Care, Evanston, Ill., 1987-89; pub. health nurse City of Evanston, Ill., 1989-90; geriatric nurse assoc. City of Evanston, 1990—; cons. surveyor Joint Commn. on Accreditation of Healthcare Orgns., Oakbrook Terrace, Ill., 1988—. Trainer The Arthritis Found., Chgo., 1991-92; mem. Panel Rev. State of Ill. Continuing Edn.; mem. profl. edn. com. Arthritis Found.; hospice vol. Mem. APHA, Nat. Assn. Home Care, Am. Soc. Aging, Ill. Pub. Health Assn., Ill. Nurses Assn., Ill. Home Health Coun., Ill. Alliance for Aging, Zonta (bd. dirs.). Roman Catholic. Home: 248 Valley View Dr Wilmette IL 60091 Office: Evanston Health Dept 2100 Ridge Ave Evanston IL 60201-2796

WHITE, VICKI LEE, bank service representative; b. Steubenville, Ohio, Feb. 18, 1960; d. Paul W.H. and Norma Jean (Thomas) Oxier; m. John Robert White, Apr. 12, 1980. Diploma, Am. Inst. Banking, 1986, Am. Banker's Assn., 1987; AS in Banking and Fin., Jefferson County Tech. Coll., 1991. Teller Miners and Mechs. Savs. and Trust Co., Steubenville, 1979-85, mgr. cen. reference files, 1985-91, fedline coord., security adminstr., 1992-94; br. svc. rep. Nat. City Bank N.E., Steubenville, 1994—; adv. bd. mem. Jefferson Tech. Coll., 1988—. Active Foster Parents Plan, Steubenville Urban Mission, People for the Ethical Treatment Animals; adminstrv. bd. mem. Richmond United Meth. Ch., 1987—. Mem. Am. Inst. Banking (sec. Steubenville chpt. 1985-93), Steubenville Art Assn., Order Eastern Star, Rosicrucians. Republican. Methodist. Home: Nat City Bank NE N 4th St Richmond OH 43944-0051 Office: Nat City Bank NE 124 N 4th St Steubenville OH 43952

WHITE, WENDY JUNE, environmental research director; b. Queens, N.Y., Nov. 20, 1958; d. Nathaniel and Trudy (Schwartz) W. BA with distinction, Columbia U., 1981. Rsch. asst. biochemistry Mt. Sinai Med. Sch., N.Y.C., 1974-78; lectr. Met. Mus., N.Y.C., 1977-81; asst. to comms. dir. Wildenstein & Co., N.Y.C., 1982-83; real estate agt. N.Y. Land Co., N.Y.C., 1983-84; editorial asst. Instnl. Investor Mag., N.Y.C., 1984-88; asst. dir. environ. rsch. N.J. Inst. Tech., N.Y.C., 1989—; curator Kraine Internat. Gallery, 1992-93. Author screenplay Roses are Blind, 1994; contbr. articles to profl. jours. Asst. dir. Wascon: Environ., Maastricht, Holland, 1991. Dept. Def. Environ. Scholarship Tng. grantee, 1995; scholar Columbia U., 1977-81. Mem. COLAB (v.p. 1989—). Home: 190 Cedar St Cliffside Park NJ 07010 Office: NJ Inst Tech 138 Warren St Newark NJ 07102

WHITE, YVONNE GAIL (REIFF), accountant; b. Holton, Kans., Nov. 26, 1960; d. Carl E. and Lila M. (Garner) Reiff; m. William G. White. BBA magna cum laude, Washburn U., 1984, MBA, 1993. CPA, Kans.; CMA. Acct. Orthopedic Assocs., P.A., Topeka, Kans., 1983-88; staff acct. Vince Schulte, CPA, Yuma, Ariz., 1992, 94—. Washburn U. Sch. Bus. scholar, 1991. Mem. AICPAs, Kans. Soc. CPAs, Ariz. Soc. CPAs, Inst. Mgmt. Accts., Phi Kappa Phi. Home: 29546 US Hwy 75 Netawaka KS 66516

WHITEAKER, RUTH CATHERINE, retired high school educator, counselor; b. Monte Vista, Colo., Mar. 3, 1907; d. Samuel sigel and Vina Catherine (Becraft) Heilman; m. George Henry Whiteaker, June 23, 1946. BA, U. Denver, 1930, MA, 1954; student, Columbia U., Ohio State, and others, 1933-66. cert. tchr. Tchr./drama coach Brighton (Colo.) High Sch., 1930-36; tchr. Meeker Jr. High Sch., Greeley, Colo., 1936-42; tchr. South High Sch., Denver, 1942-52, couselor, 1952-61; tchr. Thomas Jefferson High Sch., Denver, 1961-66; organizer first career day Greeley High Sch., 1939, Future Tchrs. Am. in Colo. High Schs. Colo. Edn. Assn., 1949-55; co-organizer Wyo. Future Tchrs. Am. Wyo. Edn. Assn., 1951; com. mem. Nat. Future Tchrs. Am. Adv. Bd., 1954. Author: (English speech units) Colo. English Guide, 1939, Denver K-12 Program, 1951; editor: (guidebook) South High Syllabus, 1952-60. Chmn. 50th reunion U. Denver Class 1930, 1980. Grantee U.S. Dept. Edn. and Ministry of Edn. Mex., Mexico City, 1945; recipient plaque Colo. Future Tchrs. Am., 1955, Student Nat. Edn. Assn., Colo., 1955; Yearbook dedication South Denver High Sch., 1958. Mem. AAUW, Bus. and Profl. Women's Club (pres. 1933, 38), Colo. Bus. and Profl. Women's Club (v.p. 1944), Columbia U. Women's Club Colo. (pres. 1975-77), Rep. Ladies Roundtable, PEO Sisterhood, Meth. Women's Assn., Terr. Daus., Columbia U. Alumni Club, Alpha Gamma Delta (regional sec.-treas. 1934-36, pres. 1936-40), Delta Kappa Gamma (v.p. Colo. chpt. 1959). Republican. Methodist. Home: 6930 E Girard Ave Apt 108 Denver CO 80224-2900

WHITED, LANA ANN, English language educator; b. Kingsport, Tenn., May 23, 1958; d. Paul Edwin and Mildred Joan (McDavid) W. BA, Emory and Henry Coll., Emory, Va., 1980; MA, William and Mary Coll., 1981, Hollins Coll., 1983; PhD, U. N.C., Greensboro, 1993. Instr. Christopher Newport Coll., Newport News, Va., 1981-82; teaching fellow U. N.C., Greensboro, 1983-88; instr. Louisburg (N.C.) Coll., 1988-90; asst. prof. Ferrum (Va.) Coll., 1990—. Author: (poem) Cargoes, 1983; book reviews and papers in field. Mem. Nat. Coun. Tchrs. English, Modern Lang. Assn., Franklin County Humane Soc. Democrat. Episcopalian. Home: RR 2 Box 133 Ferrum VA 24088-9635 Office: Lang Lit & Philosophy Divsn Ferrum College Ferrum VA 24088

WHITEHEAD, BARBARA ANN, secondary school educator; b. Shreveport, La., Apr. 25, 1941; d. Clifton John and Leona Elizabeth (Lemoine) W. BA, McNeese State U., 1963, 1967; postgrad., Centenary Coll., 1982-83; MEd, La. Tech. U., 1983, postgrad., 1983. Cert. secondary edn. tchr., La. Tchr. Calcasieu Parish Sch. System, Lake Charles, La., 1963-68, Caddo Parish Sch. System, Shreveport, 1968—; chair social studies dept. C.E. Byrd Math./Sci. Magnet High Sch., Shreveport, 1987—. Author: Teaching the Historical Origins of Nursery Rhymes and Folk Tales, 1982. Named La. Tchr. of Yr. DAR, 1983. Mem. NEA, La. Assn. Educators, Caddo Assn. Educators, Sigma Tau Delta. Roman Catholic. Office: CE Byrd Math Sci Magnet High Sch 3201 Line Ave Shreveport LA 71104-4298

WHITEHOUSE, PHYLLIS JEANNE, public relations executive; b. Chgo., Apr. 10, 1923; d. Philip Bernard II and Emily (Soravia) Stockhausen; m. Walter L. Forward Jr., Feb. 19, 1958 (div. 1963); m. Jack Pendleton Whitehouse, Mar. 6, 1964 (div. Nov. 1984); 1 child, Mark Philip. BS in Chemistry, U. Ill., 1944. Chemist Bell Tel. Labs., Murray Hill, N.J., 1944-46; flight attendant, then with sales dept. Am. Airlines, 1946-62; mem. sales staff, 1980—; pres. Whitehouse Enterprises, L.A. Mem. Internat. Visitors' Program, Rep. Club. Mem. Am. Assn. Individual Investors. Home: 424 Kelton Ave Apt 310 Los Angeles CA 90024-2095

WHITEHOUSE, SUSAN, bank executive, association executive; b. Oakland, Calif., Oct. 26, 1955; d. Robert C. and Mary Lou (Hinerman) Schoeneman; m. Charles R. Whitehouse, June 14, 1975 (div. Oct. 1987). Grad. high sch., Canton, Ohio, 1973. Clk. CrediThrift Am., Canton, 1976—; v.p. Soc. Nat. Bank, Canton, 1989-94. Pres. bd. trustees YWCA Canton, 1993—; trustee Timken Mercy Devel. Bd., 1987—. Mem. Jr. League Canton.

WHITEHURST, M. CANDACE, physician; b. Norfolk, Va., Jan. 7, 1954; d. Carlton Earl and Dorothy Mae (Stafford) W. BS, James Madison U., 1976; MS, Old Dominion U., 1978; MD, Ea. Va. Med. Sch., 1985. Diplomate Am. Bd. Internal Medicine. Tchg. asst. Old Dominion U., Norfolk, Va., 1976-78; rsch. asst. Ea. Va. Med. Sch., Norfolk, 1978-82, resident physician, 1985-88; staff physician VA Med. Ctr., Hampton, Va., 1988—, acting assoc. chief of staff for ambulatory care, 1991-92; BCLS instr. VA Med. Ctr., 1991-93; spkr. Norfolk Task Force on Aging, 1994. Mem. ACP, AMA, Med. Soc. Va. Office: VA Med Ctr Hampton VA 23667

WHITELAW, DIANA M., educational consultant; b. England, Aug. 4, 1943; d. Geoffrey and Marion (Nankivell) du Fosse; m. Michael, Aug. 22, 1964; 1 child, Nicholas. BA in Early Childhood, U. London, 1964; MA in Spl. Edn., St. Joseph Coll., West Hartford, Conn., 1972; 6th yr. diploma, U. Hartford, 1976; PhD, U. Conn., 1984. Cert. elem. edn., spl. edn., intermediate supr., adminstr. Dir. preschool program Knight Hall Sch.; instr. Ednl. Ctr. for Human Devel.; coord. compensatory edn. unit, cons. State Edn. Dept., Hartford; pres. Nat. Assn. State Coords. of Compensatory Edn., 1990; mem. adv. panel Nat. Assessment of Chpt. I, 1991. Mem. ASCD, Phi Delta Kappa.

WHITELEY, SANDRA MARIE, librarian, editor; b. May 24, 1943; d. Samuel Smythe and Kathryn Marie (Voigt) Whiteley; m. R. Russell Maylone, Jan. 8, 1977; 1 child, Cybele Elizabeth. BA, Pa. State U., 1963; MLS, Columbia U., 1970; MA, U. Pa., 1975; postgrad., Northwestern U., 1985—. Tchr. Amerikan Kiz Koleji, Izmir, Turkey, 1967-69; reference libr. Yale U., New Haven, Conn., 1970-74; head reference dept. Northwestern U., Evanston, Ill., 1975-80; asst. editor Who's Who in Libr. and Info. ALA, Chgo., 1980-81, editor Reference Books Bull., 1985—; lectr. Grad. Libr. Sch. U. Chgo., 1982-83; assoc. exec. dir. Assn. Coll. and Rsch. Librs., Chgo., 1981-85. Author: Purchasing an Encyclopaedia, 4th edit., 1992, The American Library Association Guide to Information Access, 1994. Mem. ALA (various coms. 1977-81), Beta Phi Mu. Democrat. Congregationalist. Home: 1205 Noyes St Evanston IL 60201-2635 Office: ALA 50 E Huron St Chicago IL 60611-2795

WHITERABBIT, RENÉ HELEN, public health service officer, consultant; b. Menomenie, Wis., May 31, 1962; d. Ronald D. and Roberta J. Whiterabbit; 1 child, Morgan J. BA in Theology, St. Olaf Coll., 1985; postgrad., United Theol. Sem. Cert. trainer substance abuse and AIDS issues, Nat. Inst. Drugs and Substance Abuse. Adminstrv. coord. New Visions Program, Inc., Mpls., 1985-86; vol. coord. Women Nations, St. Paul, 1987-88; youth educator Minn. AIDS Project, Mpls., 1987-89; community worker Neighborhood Justice Ctr., Inc., St. Paul, 1988-89; AIDS project coord. Indian Health Bd. Mpls., Inc., 1989—; interim AIDS project coord. Am. Indian Health Care Assn., St. Paul, 1993; mem. regional/nat. planning com. minority AIDS conf. Office Minority Health and Pub. Health Svc., 1989, 91, 93, co-chair 1994 nat. conf.; mem. 5 yr. initiative HIV/AIDS related svcs. planning com. Office Minority Health, 1990; mem. planning com. HIV/STD unit state svc. initiative through HRSA Minn. Dept. Health, 1991; mem. rev. panel devel. linkages and partnerships Ctr. Disease Control, 1993; spl. asst. Sec. Health; speaker in field. Author: (with others) A Manual for Native American Health, 1992, Mashkiki-Old Medicine, 1992, HIV Prevention with Natvie American Youth, 1995. Gov. appointee minority issues adv. com. Met. Coun., 1991. Recipient Svc. award Pub. Health Svc., 1991, Youth Svc. award Wis. Winnebago Tribe, 1991; named Exemplary Role Model by Hennepin County, 1994. Office: Indian Health Bd Mpls 1315 E 24th St Minneapolis MN 55404-3919

WHITESIDE, ANN BIRDSONG, university public relations director; b. Gallatin, Tenn., Dec. 3, 1955; d. Jack Johnson and Dethel (Key) Birdsong; m. Lee Frank Whiteside, Oct. 10, 1975; children: Erica Evette, Kelli Danielle. Student, Stephens Coll., 1989; AD, Vol. State C.C., 1991; BA cum laude, Trevecca Nazarene Coll., 1992; postgrad., U. Tenn. Keypunch operator Gallatin Aluminum Products, 1971-76; keypunch operator, computer operator, supr. Space Age Computer Sys., Madison, Tenn., 1976-79; PBX operator, receptionist Vol. State C.C., Gallatin, 1979-80, sec. humanities, 1982, exec. aide, 1982-83, asst. to dir., 1983-86, dir. community rels., 1986—; receptionist, accounts receivable Sumner County Mental Health Ctr., Gallatin, 1980-81; speaker Vol. State C.C. Speakers Bur., Gallatin, 1986—; instr. student journalism workshop Fisk U., Nashville, 1991. Editor publs. com. Tenn. Higher Edn. Commn., 1990-91. Mem. Tenn. Homecoming 86 Campaign Com., Sumner County, 1986; mem. Gov.'s 3 Star Com., Gallatin, 1988; mem. Leadership Sumner, Gallatin, 1990-91, coord., 1991-92; sec. bd. dirs. Gallatin Day Care Ctr., 1986-94; mem. Tenn. 2000. Recipient Leadership Support award, Challenge '92 award Returning Women Orgn., Vol. State C.C., 1988, 90, 91. Mem. Nat. Coun. Mktg. and Pub. Rels. (bd. dirs.-at-large 1988-92, treas.), Am. Assn. Women in Cmty. and Jr. Colls., Tenn. Higher Edn. Commn. (mem. publ. com.), Tenn. Coll. Pub. Rels., Gallatin C. of C. (mem. exec. bd. 1993—), Tenn. Alumni Rels. Coun., Gamma Beta Phi. Democrat. Mem. African Methodist Episcopal Ch. Home: 103 Canterbury Close Gallatin TN 37066-4546 Office: Vol State CC Nashville Pike Gallatin TN 37066

WHITESIDE, CAROL GORDON, state official, former mayor; b. Chgo., Dec. 15, 1942; d. Paul George and Helen Louise (Barre) G.; m. John Gregory Whiteside, Aug. 15, 1964; children: Brian Paul, Derek James. BA, U. Calif., Davis, 1964. Pers. mgr. Emporium Capwell Co., Santa Rosa, 1964-67; pers. asst. Levi Strauss & Co., San Francisco, 1967-69; project leader Interdatum, San Francisco, 1983-88; with City Coun. Modesto, 1983-87; mayor City of Modesto, 1987-91; asst. sec. for intergovtl. rels. The Resources Agy., State of Calif., Sacramento, 1991-93; dir. intergovtl. affairs Gov.'s Office, Sacramento, 1993—. Trustee Modesto City Schs., 1979-83; nat. pres. Rep. Mayors and Local Ofcls., 1990. Named Outstanding Woman of Yr. Women's Commn., Stanislaus County, Calif., 1988, Woman of Yr., 27th Assembly Dist., 1991. Republican. Lutheran. Office: Governor's Office 1400 10th St Sacramento CA 95814-5569

WHITE-VONDRAN, MARY ELLEN, retired stockbroker; b. East Cleveland, Ohio, Aug. 21, 1938; d. Thomas Patrick and Rita Ellen (Langdon) White; m. Gary L. Vondran, Nov. 25, 1961; children: Patrick Michael, Gary Lee Jr. BA, Notre Dame Coll., South Euclid, Ohio, 1960; postgrad., John Carroll U., 1960, U. Mass., 1961, U. S.C., 1969, San Jose State U., 1971-75, U. Santa Clara, Calif., 1972, Stanford U., 1989; MSL, Peninsula U., Mountain View, Calif., 1994. Cert. life secondary tchr., Calif.; lic. NACD series 7, 11 & 18 broker. Tchr. Cleve. Sch. Dist., 1960-61, East Hartford (Conn.) Sch. Dist., 1961-62, San Francisco Bay Area Sch. Dist., 1970-75; life and disability agt. Travelers Ins. Co. and BMA Ins. Co., San Jose, Calif., 1975-77; stockbroker Reynolds, Bache, Shearson, Palo Alto, Calif., 1977-78, Schwab & Co., San Francisco, 1980; adminstr. pension and profit Crocker Nat. Bank, San Francisco, 1980-82; stockbroker Calif. Fed./Invest Co., San Francisco, 1982-83; head trader, br. mgr. Rose & Co., San Francisco, 1983-84; ret., 1984; tchr. citizenship for fgn. born adult community edn. Fremont Union High Sch. Dist., Sunnyvale, Calif., 1988—. Author: Jo Mora-Renaissance Man, 1973, Visit of Imperial Russian Navy to San Francisco, 1974, John Franklin Miller, 1974, 1905 Quail Meadow Road. Sec. Quota Internat., Los Altos, Calif., 1987; constn. chairperson LWV, Los Altos, 1985—, lectr. speakers bur. 1987, moderator, co-producer TV programs; precinct capt. 1988 & 90 Elections, Los Altos; appointee ad hoc com. for transp. of mobility impaired Santa Clara County, 1988; vol. tchr. English in Action; usher lively arts Stanford U.; mem. tele com. Peninsula Dem. Coalition; active Internat. Vis. Com., Palo Alto, People for Accessible Health Care, Women in History Mus., Calif. History Ctr., Cupertino, Palo Alto Neighbors Abroad. Recipient Valley Cable Recognition award, 1988. Mem. AAUW, ACLU, NOW (speakers bur. coord.), World Affairs Forum, Women in History Assn., The Great War Soc., Am. Assn. Retired Persons, Older Women's League, Los Altos Women in Bus., Women's Internat. League for Peace & Freedom, Commonwealth Club (steering com., program com. Palo Alto/Midpeninsula chpt.), Kenna Club. Democrat. Roman Catholic.

WHITFIELD, REBECCA WAVRIN, art educator; b. Little Rock, July 9, 1946; d. Clarence Peter and Johnnie Lou (Regan) W.; m. Paul Douglas Whitfield, Sept. 17, 1968; children: Tracy Meredith, Michael Paul. BSE, U. Ctrl. Ark., 1969; MA, U. Ark., 1987, MAE, 1988. Tchr. math. Yale (Okla.) High Sch., 1973-75; chairperson art dept. Wilbur D. Mills U. Studies H.S., Little Rock, 1977—; visual arts instr. Ark. Gov.'s Sch., Conway, 1991—; instr. drawing Ark. Arts Ctr., Little Rock, 1987-90; visual arts program dir. AEGIS-Ark. Gifted Programs, Pine Bluff, 1988-90; art curriculum cons. State Dept. Edn., Little Rock, 1988—. One-woman show at Chroma Gallery, 1993. Recipient Outstanding Contbn. to Ark. Arts award Ark. Arts Coun., 1993. Mem. NEA, Nat. Art Educators Assn., Nat. Advocates for Gifted Children, Ark. Art Educators, Arkansans for Gifted and Talented Edn., Ark. Edn. Assn. Democrat. Methodist. Office: Wilbur D Mill Univ HS 1205 E Dixon Rd Little Rock AR 72206-4181

WHITING, LISA LORRAINE, video production educator, producer, director; b. Lansing, Mich., July 22, 1959; d. Lowell Stanton and Ruth Lorraine (Gregory) W. BS in Psychology, Mich. State U., 1981, BA in Telecommunication cum laude, 1984, MA in Telecommunication, 1988; AA in Dance magna cum laude, Lansing Community Coll., 1984. Instr. video prodn./producer, dir. Sta. WKAR-TV, Mich. State U., East Lansing, Mich., 1987—; producer, dir. (TV show) The Outreach Mass, East Lansing, 1984—; instr. Nancie Bauer Dance Studio, Holt, Mich., 1984—, Dance World, 1994—. Mem. Jr. League of Lansing. Office: Mich State U Sta WKAR 508 Communication Arts Sci East Lansing MI 48824-1212

WHITKO, JEAN PHILLIPS, academic administrator; b. Dover, Del., Oct. 31, 1940; d. Albert Leroy and Helen (Busch) Phillips; m. Donald A. Whitko, July 1, 1972; children: Lenore Ann, Wayne P., Donna J., Sheri L. BS, U. Del., 1962; MEd, Pa. State U., 1968, postgrad., 1968-72. Cert. tchr., Del., Pa. Tchr. Newcastle (Del.) Spl. Sch. Dist., 1962-68; rsch. asst. Pa. State U., University Park, 1969, instr. edn., grad. asst., 1969-72; substitute tchr. Jerusalem Lutheran Nursery Sch. and Day Care, Schwenksville, Pa., 1983-85; supr. student teaching Pa. State U., 1988—; evaluator fed. title I and III projects Pa. Dept. Edn., Harrisburg, 1970-72. Officer Women's Civ. Club Schwenksville, 1972—; vol. tchr. Perkiomen Valley Schs., Schwenksville, 1976-86; bd. dirs. Jerusalem Lutheran Nursery Sch. and Day Care, 1983-85. Named Friend of Edn., Perkiomen Valley Edn. Assn., 1983; recipient Commendation from Gov. Richard Thornburg, 1985. Mem. ASCD, Pa. Assn. Colls. and Tchr. Educators. Home: 623 Main St Schwenksville PA 19473 Office: Pa State Univ 172 Chambers Bldg University Park PA 16802

WHITLEY, JUANA LYNN, advertising executive; b. LaGrange, Ga., Aug. 11, 1964; d. John Hamilton and Lena Pearl (Knight) W. BA in Math. and Bus. magna cum laude, LaGrange Coll., 1986. Gen. mgr. Unique Advt. Specialties, LaGrange, 1985—. Neighborhood capt. Am. Cancer Soc.; mem. La Fayette Singers, 1st Bapt. Ch. Choir, 3 yr.-old choir dir., 4 yr.-old Sun. sch. tchr., co-dir.; mem. Rep. Presdl. Task Force; mem. adult choir First Bapt. Ch. Ty Cobb scholar, 1985, 86. Mem. NASE, NAFE, Omicron Delta Kappa, Alpha Omicron Pi (chair philanthropy com.). Home: 811 Wisteria Way La Grange GA 30240-1639 Office: Unique Advt Specialties 818 N Greenwood St La Grange GA 30240-1705

WHITLEY, NANCY LYNNE, public relations healthcare executive; b. McKeesport, Pa., Dec. 29, 1943; d. Harrison Scott and Betty Mae (Hammel) Reed; m. Alec Tyrrell Whitley, Jan. 25, 1969; children: John Harrison, Aaron Tyrrell. BA in Psychology, W.Va. Wesleyan Coll., 1967; MA in Ednl. Leadership, Western Mich. U., 1983. RN. Charge nurse Butterworth Hosp., Grand Rapids, Mich., 1978-80; patient health edn. specialist Allegan (Mich.) Gen. Hosp., 1980-87; project mgr. cons. Upjohn Healthcare, Kalamazoo, Mich., 1987-89; dir. community rels. Hospice Western Mich., Grand Rapids, 1989-94; dir. market devel. Hospice of Mich., 1994—. Dem. Nat. Campaign worker, Grand Rapids, 1992; fundraiser Wayland Area Com., 1991-94. Mem. Am. Soc. Health Edn. and Tng. (pres. 1985), Am. Cancer Soc. (bd. dirs., chair pub. edn. 1982-86, Pacesetter award Allegan County chpt. 1988), Nat. Hospice Orgn., Mich. Hospice Orgn. (pub. rels. com. 1993—). Mem. United Ch. Christ. Home: 12815 Sunrise Ct Wayland MI 49348-9201 Office: Hospice Western Mich PO Box 2427 750 Fuller NE Grand Rapids MI 49501-2427

WHITLEY, NANCY O'NEIL, retired radiology educator; b. Winston-Salem, N.C., Feb. 21, 1932; d. Norris Lawrence and Thelma Mae (Hardy) O'Neil; m. J.E. Whitley, Dec. 20, 1958; children—John O'Neil, Catherine Anne. Student, Duke U., 1950-53; M.D., Bowman Gray Sch. Medicine, 1957. Fellow in cardiology Bowman Gray Sch. Medicine, Winston-Salem, 1958-60; intern Jefferson Davis Hosp., Houston, 1957-58; resident in radiology Bowman Gray Sch. Medicine, 1966-69, instr., 1969-70, asst. prof., 1970-74, assoc. prof., 1974-78; prof. radiology U. Md. Sch. Medicine, Balt., 1978-92; prof. oncology U. Md. Cancer Ctr., Balt., 1988-92; prof. radiology Med. U. S.C., Charleston, 1992-94; ret., 1994. Author: (with J.E. Whitley) Angiopgraphy, Techniques and Procedures, 1971.

WHITLEY, SANDRA ANN, business educator; b. Pitts., Oct. 30, 1951; d. Frank J. and Maryann (Juran) Lynch; m. Dan E. Whitley, Mar. 10, 1973; children: Dan II, W. Brian. AA, Allegheny Community Coll., 1971; student, U. Pitts., 1972-73; BS, BA magna cum laude, Robert Morris Coll., 1991. Acctg. clk. Gen. Electric Credit, Charlotte, N.C., 1971-76; corp. acct. Mellon Bank, N.A., Pitts., 1976-79, investment analyst, 1979-80, asst. officer, 1980, capital mkts. acctg. supr., 1980-82, acctg. officer, 1982, mgr., 1983-86, cons./specialist, 1986-88; tchr. Charlotte (N.C.)-Mecklenburg Sch. Dist., 1994—; acct./cons. Whitley's Hair Design, Coraopolis, Pa., 1979—; instr. Allegheny C.C., 1992-94, Monroeville Sch. Bus., 1993-94; substitute tchr. Moon Area Sch. Dist., 1991-93. Mem. Springhill Civic League, Pitts., 1980-86. Recipient Outstanding Achievement award Credit Mgrs. Assn., 1971. Mem. ASCD, Pa. Assn. Notaries, Tri-State Bus. Educators, Alpha Kappa, Alpha Tau Sigma. Office: 6900 Democracy Dr Charlotte NC 28215

WHITLOCK, DENISE LUCILLE See DAVIS, DENISE WHITLOCK

WHITLOW, DONNA MAE, daycare and primary school administrator; b. Buffalo, S.D., May 23, 1933; d. Carl Axel and Esther Johanna (Wickman) Magnuson; married, June 13, 1953; children: Debra Diane Reasy, Cathleen Denise Corallo, Lisa Mae. Diploma, Eugene Bible Coll., 1956; BA in Religious Edn., Internat. Seminary, 1985, MA, 1986. Corp. sec. various orgns., 1953-56; asst. registrar, prof. child edn. Calif. Open Bible Inst., Pasadena, 1956-57; dir. religious edn. and music, sec. to gen. bd. Jamaica Open Bible Inst., 1958-59; dir. religious edn. and music, sec. to gen. bd.. prof. on staff, bus. mgr. Trinidad Open Bible Inst., 1960-65; asst. to full-charge bookkeeper Jennings Strouss Law Firm, 1966-68; dir. religious edn. and music., mem. gen. bd., assoc. pastor Biltmore Bible Ch., Phoenix, Ariz., 1967-93; founder, dir. Biltmore Bible Day Care & Kindergarten, Phoenix, 1977—; founder bible schs. in South Africa, Argentina, Ctrl. Am., Europe, Carribean. Author: How To Start a Daycare in the Local Church, 1986. Republican. Home: 2144 E Lamar Rd Phoenix AZ 85016-1147 Office: Biltmore Bible Ch 3330 E Camelback Rd Phoenix AZ 85018-2310

WHITMAN, CHRISTINE TODD, governor. Former freeholder Somerset County, N.J.; former pres. State Bd. Pub. Utilities; host radio talk show Sta. WKXW, Trenton, N.J.; gov. State of N.J., 1994—; chmn. Com. for an Affordable N.J. Columnist newspapers. Rep. candidate for senator State of N.J., 1990. Office: State House Office of Governor Trenton NJ 08625

WHITMAN, HELEN HERRICK, elementary educator; b. Brewer, Maine, Feb. 16, 1925; d. Carleton Sewall and Helen Frances (Petrie) Herrick; m. Dana Trask Jr., Oct. 25, 1946; children: Dana III, Christian, Matthew, Noel. BA, U. Maine, Orono, 1946, MA, 1949. Tchr. Tchr. teaching asst. in psychology U. Maine, Orono, 1946-47; tchr. Old Town (Maine) High Sch., 1948-49; rsch. assoc. U. Mich., Ann Arbor, 1949-52; dir. presch. YWCA, Newton, N.J., 1962-64; elem. tchr. Fredon (N.J.) Sch. System, 1964-68, Wethersfield (Conn.) Sch. System, 1968-92; retired, tutor, 1992—. Mem. NEA, Conn. Edn. Assn. Ret. Tchrs. Home and Office: 341 Pleasant Valley Rd Rocky Hill CT 06067-3807

WHITMAN, KATHY VELMA ROSE (ELK WOMAN WHITMAN), artist, sculptor; b. Bismarck, N.D., Aug. 12, 1952; d. Carl Jr. and Edith Geneva (Lykken) W.; m. Robert Paul Luger, Feb. 2, 1975 (div. Jan. 1982); children: Shannon, Lakota, Cannupa, Palani; m. Dean P. Fox (div. 1985); 1 child, Otgadahe. Student, Standing Rock C.C., Ft. Yates, N.D., 1973-74, Sinte Gleska Coll., Rosebud, S.D., 1975-77, U. S.D., 1977, Ariz. State U., 1992-93. Instr. art Sinte Gleska Coll., 1975-77, Standing Rock C.C., 1977-78; co-mgr. Four Bears Motor Lodge, New Town, N.D., 1981-82; store owner Nux-Baga Lodge, New Town, 1982-85; artist-in-residence N.D. Coun. on Arts, Bismarck, 1983-84, bd. dirs., 1985. One woman shows include Mus. of Am. Indian, N.Y.C., 1983, Charleroi Internat. Fair, Belgium, 1984, Heard Mus., Phoenix, 1987-92, Phoenix Gallery, Nurnburg, Germany, 1990, Lovena Ohl Gallery, Phoenix, 1990-94, Phoenix Gallery, Coeur d'Alene, Idaho, 1992, Turquoise Tortoise Gallery, Tubac, Ariz., 1992-93, Yah-ta-hey Gallery, New London, Conn., 1992-93, Silver Sun Gallery, Santa Fe, N.Mex., 1993, others; represented in permanent collections at Mus. of the Am. Indian, N.Y.C., Mesa (Ariz.) C.C. Bd. dirs. Ft. Berthold C.C., New Town, 1983-85; pres. Cannonball (N.D.) Pow-Wow Com., 1978; parent rep. Head Start, Ft. Yates, 1974. Recipient best craftsman spl. award Bullock's Indian Arts and Crafts, 1986, best of fine arts aaward No. Plains Tribal Arts, Sioux Falls, S.D., 1988, best of show award Pasadena Western Relic and Native Am. Show, 1991, 2 1st place awards Santa Fe Indian Market, 1993. Mem. Indian Arts and Crafts Assn., S.W. Assn. on Indian Affairs (life). Home and Studio: 11041 N 84th St Scottsdale AZ 85260

WHITMAN, MARINA VON NEUMANN, economist; b. N.Y.C., Mar. 6, 1935; d. John and Mariette (Kovesi) von Neumann; m. Robert Freeman Whitman, June 23, 1956; children: Malcolm Russell, Laura Mariette. BA summa cum laude, Radcliffe Coll., 1956; MA, Columbia U., 1959, PhD, 1962; LHD (hon.), Russell Sage Coll., 1972, U. Mass., 1975, N.Y. Poly Inst., 1975, Baruch Coll., 1980; LLD (hon.), Cedar Crest Coll., 1973, Hobart and William Smith Coll., 1973, Coe Coll., 1975, Marietta Coll., 1976, Rollins Coll., 1976, Wilson Coll., 1977, Allegheny Coll., 1977, Amherst Coll., 1978, Ripon Coll., 1980, Mt. Holyoke Coll., 1980; LittD (hon.), Williams Coll., 1980, Lehigh U., 1981, Denison U., 1983, Claremont U., 1984, Notre Dame U., 1984, Eastern Mich. U., 1992 . Mem. faculty U. Pitts., 1962-79, prof. econs., 1971-73, disting. pub. svc. prof. econs., 1973-79; v.p., chief economist Gen. Motors Corp., N.Y.C., 1979-85, group exec. v.p. pub. affairs, 1985-92; disting. vis. prof. bus. adminstrn. & pub. policy U. Mich., Ann Arbor, 1992-94, prof. bus. adminstrn. and pub. policy, 1994—; mem. U.S. Price Commn., 1971-72; sr. staff economist Coun. Econ. Advisers, Exec. Office of Pres., 1970-73; bd. dirs. Chemical Bank, ALCOA, Procter & Gamble Co., Browning-Ferris Industries, UNOCAL, Inst. Internat. Econs.; mem. Trilateral Commn.; mem. Pres. Adv. Com. on Trade Policy and Negotiations, 1987-93; mem. tech. assessment adv. coun. U.S. Congress Office of Tech. Assessment, 1990—, Dept. Treasury, from 1977; mem. Consultative Group on Internat. Econs. and Monetary Affairs, from 1979; trustee Nat. Bur. Econ. Rsch., 1993—. Bd. dirs. Inst. for Internat. Econs 1986, Eurasia Found, 1992—; bd. overseers Harvard U., 1972-78, mem. vis. com. Kennedy Sch., 1992—; trustee Princeton U., 1980-90. Fellow Earhart Found., 1959-60, AAUW, 1960-61, NSF, 1968-70, also Social Security Rsch. Coun.; recipient Columbia medal for excellence, 1973; George Washington award Am. Hungarian Found., 1975. Mem. Am. Econ. Assn. (exec. com. 1977-80), Am. Acad. Arts & Scis., Coun. Fgn. Rels. (dir. 1977-87), Phi Beta Kappa. Author: Government Risk-Sharing in Foreign Investment, 1965; International and Interregional Payments Adjustment, 1967; Economic Goals and Policy Instruments, 1970; Reflections of Interdependence: Issues for Economic Theory and U.S. Policy, 1979; also articles; bd. editors Am. Econ. Rev., 1974-77; mem. editorial bd. Fgn. Policy. Office: U Mich Inst Pub Policy Studies 411 Lorch Hall Ann Arbor MI 48109-1220

WHITMORE, BEATRICE EILEEN, publishing company official; b. Harrisonburg, Va., Mar. 15, 1935; d. Everett Dulaney and Beatrice M. (Shorts) Ott; m. William Eugene Taylor, Sept. 30, 1955 (div. Mar. 1965); children: John David, Mark Wayne; m. Dale Wilford Whitmore, May 3, 1967; 1 child, Theresa Ann. High sch. grad., Harrisonburg. Clk. typist USAF Civil Service, Eglin AFB, Fla., 1956-58, Clark AFB, Phillipines, 1958-60; sec. USAF Civil Service, Wright-Patterson AFB, Ohio, 1960-75, fire insp., 1975-85, sec.-treas. local F-88, 1977-83, pres. local F-88, 1983-85, pres. emeritus, 1985—; fed. staff rep. Internat. Assn. Fire Fighters, Washington, 1985-89; assn. sec. Nat. Coffee Svc. Assn., Fairfax, Va., 1989-90; sec. Nat. Assn. Rehab. Facilities, 1990-91; editorial asst. Army Times Pub. Co., Springfield, Va., 1992—; cons. Q&D Cons. Svc., Inc., 1989-91. Leader, organizer Little Sparkies, Wright-Patterson AFB, 1976-79; den mother Boy Scouts Am., New Carlisle, Ohio, 1963-65; mem. Staff Reps. Union. Served with USAF, 1953-55. Mem. NAFE, Staff Reps. Union, Internat. Platform Assn., Job's Daus. Lodge: Job's Daughters. Home: 104 Wrightwood Pl Sterling VA 20164

WHITMORE, MENANDRA M., librarian; b. Ancash, Peru; d. Rafael and Jacinta (Moreno) Mosquera; m. Jacob L. Whitmore III, Jan. 7, 1965; children: Jacqueline Grace, Michelle Jacinta. Degree in social work, U. Catolica del Peru, 1967; MLS, U. P.R., 1974, Catholic U. Am., 1984. Social worker Cornell U., Vicos, Peru, 1960-62, Servicio de Extension Agricola del Peru, 1962-63, Am. Friends Svc. Com., Mex. and Peru, 1963-65; libr. Colegio Maria Auxiliadora, P.R., 1971, Country Day Sch., San Jose, Costa Rica, 1975-76, Colegio San Ignacio, P.R., 1976-77; dir. libs. Am. Coll. P.R., 1977-80; libr. Lib. Gov. Printing Office, 1981-84; chief acquisitions sect., mgr. Hispanic employment program Pentagon Lib., Washington, 1984—. Author: (all pub. under name Menandra Mosquera) Bibliography on Hypsipyla, 1976, Bibliography of Forestry of Puerto Rico, 1984, Useful Trees of Tropical North America, 1988. Recipient commendation Dept. Def., 1987-90. Mem. ALA, Soc. for Acquisition Latin Am. Libr. Materials, Reforma (treas. Washington chpt. 1988, pres. 1989-91, nat. ways and means chair 1991-92).

WHITNER, JANE MARVIN, analyst, programmer; b. Oakland, Calif., Aug. 29, 1935; d. Chauncey Hill and Alice Belle (Cromwell) Whitner. BA in Biol. Sci., San Jose State U., 1958; MA in Biostatistics, U. Calif., Berkeley, 1960. EDP programmer San Mateo County EDP Ctr., Redwood City, Calif., 1962-65; sci. programmer Lockheed Missiles & Space Co., Sunnyvale, Calif., 1967-68, Stanford U. Med. Ctr., 1969-73; sci. sys. programmer Physics Internat. Co., San Leandro, Calif., 1980-84; analyst, programmer Syntex Rsch. Corp., Palo Alto, Calif., 1985—. Mem. ACM, AAUW, Astron. Soc. Pacific, Planetary Soc., Smithsonian Instn., U. Calif. Alumni Assn., Commonwealth Club of Calif.

WHITNEY, CAROL MARIE, securities sales professional; b. Torrington, Conn., Mar. 31, 1946; d. Charles Lester and Emily Mae (Orr) W. BA in French, Wells Coll., 1968; 5th yr. cert., So. Conn. State Coll., 1971; postgrad., N.Y. Inst. Fin., 1976; MS in Mgmt., Rensselaer Poly. Inst., 1992. Trainee/investment exec. Blyth-Eastman Dillon, Hartford, Conn., 1976-77; account exec./registered rep. Bache Halsey-Stuart Shields, Hartford, Danbury, Conn., 1977-81, Advest, Inc., Hartford, 1981-88; registered securities rep. West Hartford, Conn., 1988-91; internat. fin. con., investment analyst, pres. Ask My Assoc., Collinsville, Conn., 1988—; v.p. registered rep. E.T. Andrews & Co. Inc., Hartford, Conn., 1991-92; v.p. Conn. Fin. Network, 1991-92; v.p., registered prin. Buell Securities Corp., Wethersfield, Conn., 1992—, br. mgr. Torrington office, 1993—; sec. Internat. Assn. for Fin. Planning, Hartford, 1982-83, pub. rels. Conn. chpt., Hartford, 1983-85, ethics chairperson Conn. chpt., Hartford, 1985-86. Performing mem. Farmington Valley chpt. Sweet Adelines, Simsbury, Conn., 1976-82. Named for Effective Speaking and Human Rels., Dale Carnegie, West Hartford, 1985. Mem. Internat. Platform Assn., World Affairs, Hartford Stockbrokers Club. Republican. Episcopalian. Home: PO Box 462 Collinsville CT 06022-0462

WHITNEY, DIANA, laboratory manager; b. Benavides, Tex., July 10, 1952; d. Efrain and Olivia (Cuevas) Vela; m. Robert Lester Whitney, Dec. 29, 1969; 1 child, Cynthia Jeanne. BS in Biochemistry, U. Calif., Riverside, 1978; MBA, Calif. State U., San Bernardino, 1992. Lab. technician City of Riverside (Calif.) Water Quality Control Plant, 1978-83; asst. chemist City of Riverside (Calif.) WQCP, 1983-89, lab. mgr., 1989—. Democrat. Office: City of Riverside WQCP 5950 Acorn St Riverside CA 92504-1036

WHITNEY, MACY ANN, construction company executive; b. Pampa, Tex., May 12, 1956; d. Clifford C. and Bettye A. (Bruton) W. BS in Bldg. Constrn. cum laude, Tex. A&M U., 1978. Estimator Thos. P. Harkins Co., Silver Spring, Md., 1978-81; chief estimator Henry A. Knott Co., Silver Spring, Md., 1982-84; sr. estimator Gilbane Bldg. Co., Lanham, Md., 1985-

88; project mgr. Chas. H. Tompkins Co., Washington, 1988—. Recipient Award of Excellence J.A. Jones Group, 1991. Mem. Assn. Builders and Contractors (state bd. dirs. 1986-90). Office: Chas H Tompkins Co 13110 Briarcliff Ter # 609 Germantown MD 20874-2687

WHITNEY, PHYLLIS AYAME, author; b. Yokohama, Japan, Sept. 9, 1903; d. Charles J. and Lillian (Mandeville) W.; m. George A. Garner, July 2, 1925; m. Lovell F. Jahnke, 1950 (dec. 1973). Grad., McKinley High Sch., Chgo., 1924. Instr. dancing San Antonio, 1 yr; tchr. juvenile fiction writing Northwestern U., 1945; children's book editor Chgo. Sun, 1942-46, Phila. Inquirer, 1947, 48; instr. juvenile fiction writing N.Y.U., 1947-58; leader juvenile fiction workshop Writers Conf., U. Colo., 1952, 54, 56. Author: A Place for Ann, 1941, A Star for Ginny, 1942, (vocat. fiction for teenage girls) A Window for Julie, 1943, (mystery novel for adults) Red Is for Murder, 1943, The Silver Inkwell, 1945, Willow Hill, 1947, Writing Juvenile Fiction, 1947, Ever After, 1948, Mystery of the Gulls, 1949, Linda's Homecoming, 1950, The Island of Dark Woods, 1951, Love Me, Love Me Not, 1952, Step to the Music, 1953, A Long Time Coming, 1954, Mystery of the Black Diamonds, 1954, The Quicksilver Pool, 1955, Mystery on the Isle of Skye, 1955, The Fire and The Gold (Jr. Lit. Guild), 1956, The Highest Dream (Jr. Lit. Guild), The Trembling Hills (Peoples Book Club), 1956, Skye Cameron, 1957, Mystery of the Green Cat (Jr. Lit. Guild), 1957, Secret of the Samurai Sword (Jr. Lit. Guild), 1958, The Moonflower, 1958, Creole Holiday, 1959, Thunder Heights, 1960, Blue Fire, 1961, Mystery of the Haunted Pool, 1961 (Edgar award Mystery Writers Am.), Secret of the Tiger's Eye, 1961, Window on the Square, 1962, Mystery of the Golden Horn, 1962, Seven Tears for Apollo, 1963, Mystery of the Hidden Hand, 1963 (Edgar award Mystery Writers Am. 1964), Black Amber, 1964, Secret of the Emerald Star, 1964, Sea Jade, 1965, Mystery of the Angry Idol, 1965, Columbella, 1966, Secret of the Spotted Shell, 1967, Mystery of the Strange Traveler, 1967, Silverhill, 1967, Hunter's Green, 1968, Secret of Goblin Glen, 1968, Mystery of the Crimson Ghost, 1969, Winter People, 1969, Secret of the Missing Footprint, 1970, Lost Island, 1970, The Vanishing Scarecrow, 1971, Listen for the Whisperer, 1971, Nobody Likes Trina, 1972, Snowfire, 1973, Mystery of the Scowling Boy, 1973, The Turquoise Mask, 1974, Spindrift, 1975, Secret of Haunted Mesa, 1975, The Golden Unicorn, 1976, Secret of the Stone Face, 1977, The Stone Bull, 1977, The Glass Flame, 1978, Domino, 1979, Poinciana, 1980, Vermilion, 1981, Guide to Fiction Writing, 1982, Emerald, 1983, Rainsong, 1984, Dream of Orchids, 1985, Flaming Tree, 1986, Silversword, 1987, Feather on the Moon, 1988, Rainbow in the Mist, 1989, The Singing Stones, 1990, Woman Without a Past, 1991, The Ebony Swan, 1992, Star Flight, 1993, Daughter of the Stars, 1994; sold first story to Chgo. Daily News; later wrote for pulp mags., became specialist in juvenile writing, now writing entirely in adult field. Pres. Authors Round Table, 1943, 44; pres. exec. bd. Fifth Annual Writers Conf., Northwestern U., 1944; spent first 15 years of life in Japan, China and P.I. (father in shipping and hotel bus.). Recipient Friends of Lit. award for contbns. to children's lit., 1974; Reynal and Hitchcock prize in Youth Today contest for book Willow Hill; Today's Woman award Coun. Cerebral Palsy Auxs., 1983, Agatha award Malice Domestic, 1990, Rita award Romance Writers Am., 1990, Lifetime award Romance Writers Am., 1990. Mem. Mystery Writers Am. (pres. 1975, Grandmaster award for lifetime achievement 1988), Am. Crime Writers League, Sisters in Crime, Authors League of Am.

WHITNEY, RUTH REINKE, magazine editor; b. Oshkosh, Wis., July 23, 1928; d. Leonard G. and Helen (Diestler) Reinke; m. Daniel A. Whitney, Nov. 19, 1949; 1 son, Phillip. BA, Northwestern U., 1949. Copywriter edn. dept. circulation div. Time, Inc., 1949-53; editor-in-chief Better Living mag., 1953-56; assoc. editor Seventeen magazine, 1956-62, exec. editor, 1962-67; editor-in-chief Glamour mag., N.Y.C., 1967—. Recipient Nat. Mag. award gen. excellence, 1981, 91, Pub. Interest, 1992, Cosmetic Executive Women Achiever award, 1993, honor award Women's City Club N.Y.; honoree Gala 11 Birmingham, So. Coll., 1993. Mem. Fashion Group, Am. Soc. Mag. Editors (pres. 1975-77, exec. com. 1989-92), Women in Communication (Matrix award 1980), Women in Media, U.S. Info. Agy. (mag. and print com. 1989-93), Alpha Chi Omega. Office: Glamour Condé Nast Bldg 350 Madison Ave New York NY 10017-3704

WHITSELL, HELEN JO, lumber executive; b. Portland, Oreg., July 20, 1938; d. Joseph William and Helen (Cornwell) Copeland; m. William A. Whitsell, Sept. 2, 1960; 2 children. BA, U. So. Calif., 1960. With Copeland Lumber Yard Inc., Portland, 1960—, pres., chief exec. officer, 1973-84, chmn., chief exec. officer, 1984—; bd. dirs. First Interstate Bank of Orgn. Office: Copeland Lumber Yards Inc 901 NE Glisan St Portland OR 97232-2784

WHITSON, BARBARA LEE, psychologist, consultant; b. Marietta, Ohio, Aug. 15, 1943; d. Richard Howard and Jean Elizabeth (Fox) Sullivan; m. Lish Whitson, Sept. 16, 1965; children: Lish Richard, Kimberly Shawn. BA, Swarthmore (Pa.) Coll., 1965; MEd, U. Wash., Seattle, 1971, PhD, 1981. Nat. cert. sch. psychologist. Part time teaching asst. U. Wash., Seattle, 1971-74; sch. psychologist Seattle Pub. Sch., Mercer Island, Wash., 1973-75; instr. Seattle Pacific U., 1974, 81, 82, Seattle U., 1975, 77, U. Wash., Seattle, 1976; program specialist gifted and talented U.S. Office Edn., Seattle, 1976-77; program specialist gifted Edmonds Sch. Dist., Lynnwood, Wash., 1977-79; sch. psychologist Shoreline Sch. Dist., Seattle, 1984-90, 91—, program specialist, 1986-94. Mem. title IV adv. coun. Wash. Spt. Pub. Instrn., Olympia, 1979-82. U.S. Office of Edn. fellow, 1976-77. Mem. Wash. State Assn. Sch. Psychologists, Nat. Assn. Sch. Psychologists, N.W. Gifted Child Assn., Wash. Assn. Educators of Talented and Gifted, Nat. Assn. Gifted Children, N.W. Evaluation Assn., Wash. Ednl. Rsch. Assn., Wash. Athletic Club, Women's Univ. Club. Office: Shoreline Pub Schs 18560 1st Ave NE Seattle WA 98155-2148

WHITSON, DOROTHY MARIE, medical technologist; b. Denver, June 26, 1934; d. John Lewis and Nancy Cecellia (Bonella) Denbo; m. Frederick Arthur Whitson, Nov. 8, 1952; children: Michelle Marie Rousseve, David Frederick, Alice Denise, Todd Paul. BS in Biology, U. Calif., Riverside, 1975; BS of Med. Tech., Loma Linda U., 1980. Lic. nat. med. technologist; registered med. technologist, Calif. Rsch. asst. U. Calif., Riverside, 1971-75, rsch. assoc., 1975-80; lab. mgr. Riverside Oncology Group, 1981-91. Mem. AAUW (pres. 1993-95).

WHITT, MARY F., reading specialist, educator; b. Montgomery, Ala.; d. Clarence and Georgia W. BS, Ala. State U., 1958; MEd, U. Ariz., 1971; EdD, U. Ala., 1980; postgrad., various colls. ongoing. Camp counselor N.Y.C. Mission Soc., Port Jervis, summer 1956; recreation counselor Dayton (Ohio) Parks and Recreation Dept., summer 1963; adminstrv. asst. Wiley Coll./NDEA Inst., Marshall, Tex., summer 1965; tchr. Montgomery (Ala.) County Schs., 1958-62; coordinator sci. and math. Dayton (Ohio) pub. schs., 1962-67; reading and spl. edn. tchr. Vacaville (Calif.) Unified Sch. Dist., 1967-70; coordinator reading Dallas pub. schs., 1971-72; prof. reading Ala. State U., Montgomery, 1972—. Contbr. articles to profl. jurs. U.S. Office Edn. fellow, 1970, 76, 77, NSF fellow, 1961, 64, 66. Mem. Internat. Reading Assn., Capstone Coll. of Edn. Soc., AAUW, Phi Delta Kappa, Kappa Delta Pi. Home: 717 Genetta Ct Montgomery AL 36104-5701

WHITTAKER, JEANNE EVANS, former newspaper columnist; b. Detroit, Jan. 1, 1934; d. Alfred Heacock and Margaret (Evans) W.; m. Charles Martin Hines Jr., Sept. 29, 1962 (div. Feb. 1970); children: Charles M. Hines III, Margaret Helen Whittaker. Student, Northwestern U., 1952-53; BS in History, U. Mich., 1956. Clubmobile worker UN forces ARC, Korea, 1956-58; staff programmer ARC, Chaumont, Evreux, France, 1958-61; dir. Bexar County chpt. youth ARC, San Antonio, 1961-62; staff writer/columnist Detroit Free Press, 1970-75; editor Mich. Social Register, 1975-77; Lifestyle editor Observer and Eccentric newspapers, Birmingham, Mich., 1977-87; staff writer, columnist Detroit News, 1987-91. Contbr. articles to mags. Bd. dirs. Detroit chpt. ARC, 1989-92, Detroit Hist. Soc. Recipient Penney-Mo. award U. Mo., 1984; 1st place lifestyles/Family award Mich. Press Assn., 1982, 84, Gen. Excellence award 1982, 86; Gen. Excellence award Suburban Newspaper Assn., 1979. Mem. Detroit Press Club, Detroit Hist. Soc. (bd. dirs. 1986-91), Southeastern Mich. Chpt. ARC (bd. dirs. 1987-93). Episcopalian. Home: 552 Cadieux Rd Grosse Pointe MI 48230-1508

WHITTAKER, JUDITH ANN CAMERON, lawyer; b. N.Y.C., June 12, 1938; d. Thomas Macdonald and Mindel (Wallman) Cameron; m. Kent E. Whittaker, Jan. 30, 1960; children: Charles Evans II, Catherine Cameron. BA, Brown U., 1959; JD, U. Mo., 1963. Bar: Mo. 1963, U.S. Dist. Ct. (we. dist.) Mo. 1963, U.S. Ct. Appeals (8th cir.) 1965, U.S. Supreme Ct. 1980, D.C. 1987. Assoc. and ptnr. Sheffrey, Ryder & Skeer, Kansas City, Mo., 1963-72; asst. and assoc. gen. counsel, v.p. legal Hallmark Card Co., Kansas City, 1972—; dir., v.p., gen. counsel Univision Holdings, Inc., Kansas City, 1988—. Trustee Brown U. Providence, 1977-83, U. Mo. Law Found., Kansas City, 1977-90; dir. Kansas City (Mo.) Indsl. Devel. Authority, 1981-84, Legal Aid Kansas City, 1971-77. Mem. ABA, Mo. Bar Assn., Internat. Soc. Barristers. Episcopalian. Office: Hallmark Cards Dept 339 PO Box 419126 Kansas City MO 64141-6126

WHITTAKER, MARY FRANCES, educational and industrial company official; b. Portsmouth, Va., Jan. 27, 1926; d. Milton Ernest and Esther (Morgan) Claud; m. Edmund H. Whittaker, June 21, 1947; 1 child, Richard W. BS, Coll. of William and Mary, 1958; MEd, U. Fla., 1966. Tchr., curriculum asst. Duval County Sch. Bd., Jacksonville, Fla., 1958-67; elem. prin. Duval County Sch. Bd., Jacksonville, 1967-70, 76-79, elem. supr., 1970-71, elem. area dir., 1971-76, coordinator planning and constrn., 1979-80, dir. pupil acctg., 1980-85, prin. Sch. of Arts, 1985-86, facilities planner, 1986-88, project mgr., 1988-90; asst. prof., coord. of interns Edward Waters Coll., Jacksonville, Fla., 1990-92; v.p. Ednl. & Indsl. Inc., Jacksonville Beach, Fla., 1988—; asst. prof. Edward Waters Coll., Jacksonville, Fla., 1993—, dir. of interns, 1994—. Bd. dirs. Jacksonville regional devel. council So. Bapt. Fgn. Mission Bd., 1986. Mem. Nat. Assn. Tchrs. of Singing, Nat. League Am. Pen Women (sec. 1980-82), Assn. Tchr. Educators.

WHITTEN, ANN YATES, journalism educator, academic administrator; b. Hernando, Miss., Jan. 5, 1934; d. Henry James Lynn and Martha Conn (Kimbrough) Yates; m. Edward Lee Whitten Sr., Sept. 20, 1952; 1 child, Edward Lee Jr. AA with honors, Gulf Park Coll., 1951; BA, U. Miss., 1952, MA, 1958, MEd, 1967, PhD in Ednl. Adminstrn., 1984. Reporter, news editor The Oxford (Miss.) Eagle, 1955-58; English tchr. Coldwater (Miss.) High Sch., 1958-60; English tchr. Olive Br. (Miss.) High Sch., 1960-63, guidance counselor, 1964-71; English tchr. Hernando (Miss.) High Sch., 1963-64; title I evaluator, testing coord. DeSoto County Schs., Hernando, Miss., 1971-74; journalism instr. N.W. Miss. C.C., Senatobia, 1974—, dir. pub. rels., 1974-83, 84-86, dir. counseling and testing, 1986-87, dir. pub. rels., 1987—. Contbr. articles to profl. jours. Brochure designer Sycamore Arts Coun., Senatobia, 1992. Fellow U. Miss., 1956. Mem. Nat. Fedn. Press Women, Miss. Press Women, Coll. Pub. Rels. Assn. Miss. (pres. 1991-92, Cert. of Excellence 1976—), DAR, U. Miss. Alumni Assn., N.W. Investors Group (v.p. 1991-93), Hernando Woman's Club, DeSoto Geneal. Soc., Nat. Jr. Coll. Athletic Assn. (tournament dir. 1985), Very Spl. Arts Miss., Delta Kappa Gamma, Kappa Kappa Gamma (scholarship 1952), Phi Kappa Phi, Kappa Delta Phi, Theta Kappa Phi. Episcopalian. Office: NW Miss C C 510 N Panola St Senatobia MS 38668

WHITTINGTON, MARY ELLEN, perioperative nurse; b. Ilion, N.Y., June 5, 1944; d. Stanley Vincent and Eleanor Katherine (Easitis) Szapiel; m. Paul Stephen Camm, Mar. 29, 1969 (div. Aug. 1981); children: Sara Melissa, Seth Sebastian; m. Marquis E. Whittington, May 22, 1993. Student, Syracuse U., 1962-63; diploma in nursing, Johns Hopkins Hosp., 1966; student, Coll. Notre Dame, 1981-82, St. Mary's U., 1988. RN, Tex.; cert. profl. healthcare quality; cert. profl. achievement perioperative nursing practice. Asst. head nurse open heart surgery Johns Hopkins Hosp., Balt., 1966-69; staff nurse oper. rm. Stanford Hosp., Palo Alto, Calif., 1969, El Camino Hosp., Mountain View, Calif., 1969-71, 1976-83; asst. head nurse oper. rm. Good Samaritan Hosp., San Jose, Calif., 1973; asst. dir. oper. rm. gastroenterology lab. Luth. Gen. Hosp., San Antonio, 1983-90, dir. surg. svcs., 1990-91; dir. surg. svcs. Humana Women's and Children's Hosp., San Antonio, 1991-92; staff rsch. nurse Design Excellence Inc., San Antonio, 1991-93, dir. nursing rsch., 1993—; cons. law firms and attys., 1989-93. Editor, pub. monthly newsletter Physicians Report, 1987-91. Scholar Luth. Ch. div. Social Ministry Orgns., San Antonio, 1988. Mem. Assn. Oper. Rm. Nurses, Nat. Assn. for Health Care Quality, Johns Hopkins U. Alumni Assn. Home: 831 Wiltshire Ave San Antonio TX 78209 Office: Design Excellence Inc 7551 Callaghan Rd Ste 200 San Antonio TX 78229-2861

WHITTINGTON-COUSE, MARYELLEN FRANCES, education administrator; b. Waverly, N.Y., June 16, 1957; d. Philip John and Sheila (Dewey) Whittington; m. Daniel Couse, May 18, 1985; children: Kristen, Benjamin. BA, SUNY, Empire, 1983; M of Internat. Adminstrn., Sch. for Internat. Tng., Brattleboro, Vt., 1992. Adj. faculty Rockland C.C., 1983-85; cons. UN Non-Govtl. Liaison Svc., N.Y.C., 1987; adminstrv. asst. Manitoga Nature Ctr., Garrison, N.Y., 1987-88; coord. Intensive Tchr. Inst. Manhattanville and Coll. of New Rochelle Satellites, New Paltz, N.Y., 1990-92; dir. bilingual edn. tech. assistance ctr. Ulster BOCES, New Paltz, 1988—; adj. faculty SUNY, New Paltz, 1994—; co-chair PROSPAN; mem. Parent Edn. Adv. Coun., Ulster County, 1988—; local coord. World Learning Inc., 1993—. Editor: (curriculum) Teacher's Guide and Content Activities for Limited English Proficient Students, 1992; co-author video script for N.Y. State Edn. Dept., 1992. Mem. ASCD, Nat. Assn. Bilingual Edn., N.Y. Tchrs. of English to Speakers of Other Langs., Tchrs. of English to Speakers of Other Langs. Internat., State Assn. of Bilingual Edn. Home: PO Box 262 Tillson NY 12486 Office: BETAC Ulster Bd Coop Ednl Svcs 175 Rte 32 N New Paltz NY 12561

WHITTLE, MARY QUINNAN, artist; b. N.Y.C., Dec. 7, 1948; d. Joseph Thomas and Elinor Delores (Lynn) Quinnan; m. Robert Edwin Whittle, Nov. 29, 1975; children: Scott Joseph, Joseph Daniel. AA, Valencia C.C.; BFA, U. Ctrl. Fla., 1986. Master printer Hunter Printmaking Studio, Winter Park, Fla., 1988-92; owner Whittle Art Svcs., Orlando, Fla., 1986-92, Artworks, Spring City, Tenn., 1992—; tchr. Orange County Schs., Orlando, 1987-88; juror for competitions Spring City C. of C., Patterson & Taylor Advt., Orlando. Represented in permanent collectionsMaitland Art Gallery, Fla., The White House, Washington. Mem. Tenn. Arts and Crafts Assn., Foothills Craft Guild, Art Market, Phi Kappa Phi. Office: Artworks PO Box 931 337 Front St Spring City TN 37381-5196

WHITTLESEY, JUDITH HOLLOWAY, public relations executive; b. Bartlesville, Okla., Dec. 28, 1942; d. Harry Haynes and Suzanne (Arnote) Holloway; m. Dennis Jeffrey Whittlesey, Aug. 3, 1968; children: Kristin Arnote, Kevin Jeffrey. BA, U. Okla., 1964; postgrad., Tulsa U., 1965, U. Va., 1971-72. Staff aide Office of the V.P. of U.S., Washington, 1979-81, Com. for Future of Am., Washington, 1981-82; dep. dir. scheduling and advance Mondale-Ferraro Campaign, Washington, 1982-84; dir. media rels. The Susan Davis Cos., Washington, 1986-87, v.p., 1987-88, exec. v.p., 1988—. Bd. dirs. Cultural Alliance of Greater Washington, 1983-93, Washington Project for the Arts, 1987-93, Levine Sch. Music, 1993—, Food Rsch. and Action Ctr., 1993—; elder Chevy Chase Presbyn. Ch., Washington. Recipient numerous Mercury and Anvil awards. Office: The Susan Davis Cos 1146 19th St NW Washington DC 20036-3703

WHITTMAN, ALLISON, lawyer; b. Plainfield, N.J., Nov. 23, 1948; d. Joseph and Marion Conner; m. Terrence Whittman, Aug. 26, 1974; children: Tim, Kelly, Lindsay, David. BA, Columbia U., 1974, JD, 1978. Bar: N.Y., 1978; Wis., 1985. With Ernest, Ernest & Plaine, N.Y.C., 1979-81, assoc., 1981-83; ptnr. Cole, Cole & Whittman, N.Y.C., 1983-85; pvt. practice Bayside, Wis., 1985-89; with Wallick and Assocs., Bayside, 1989-91; ptnr. Werik Assocs., Bayside, 1991—. Bd. dirs. Wis. Opera Guild, 1988—, Bayside County Libr., 1989—. Mem. AAUW, NOW, ACLU, ABA, Am. Assn. Female Execs., Wis. Bar Assn. Office: Werik Assocs 8511 North Pelham Pkwy Milwaukee WI 53217-2444

WHITWORTH, KATHRYNNE ANN, professional golfer; b. Monahans, Tex., Sept. 27, 1939; d. Morris Clark and Dama Ann (Robinson) W. Student, Odessa (Tex.) Jr. Coll., 1958. Joined tour Ladies Profl. Golf Assn., 1959—; mem. adv. staff Walter Hagen Golf Co., Wilson Sporting Goods Co. Named to Hall of Fame Ladies Profl. Golf Assn., Tex. Sports Hall of Fame, Tex. Golf Hall of Fame, World Golf Hall of Fame; Capt. of Solhiem Cup, 1990-92. Mem. Ladies Profl. Golf Assn. (sec. 1962-63, v.p. 1965, 73, 88, pres. 1967, 68, 71, 89, 1st mem. to win over $1,000,000). Office: care Ladies Profl Golf Assn 2570 Volusia Ave Daytona Beach FL 32114-1119

WHYTE, HELENA MARY, chemist, educator; b. Albuquerque, Dec. 19, 1948; d. Alexander Peter and Helen (Mriz) Mozden; m. Kent Neil Whyte, July 6, 1973 (dec. 1994); children: Stacey Helene, Kurt Neil. BS in Chemistry with honors, N.Mex. Inst. Mining Tech., 1970; MA in Sci. Teaching, U. N.Mex., 1971. Lab. asst. N.Mex. Bur. Mines, Socorro, 1966-70; rsch. asst. Los Alamos (N.Mex.) Sci. Lab., 1970-71; tchr. chemistry Los Alamos High Sch., 1971-79; instr. chemistry U. N.Mex., Los Alamos, 1981-84; staff mem. Los Alamos Nat. Lab., 1979—; apptd. to women's com. Los Alamos Nat. Lab., 1986-88, sect. leader, 1988-90, apptd. div. affirmative action rep., 1992-94; mem. steering com. Trade IH Sig, 1994—. Mem. manuscript rev. panel Sci. Tchr. mag., 1987-89; contbr. articles to profl. publs. Fellow Am. Inst. Chemists (cert.; adv. bd. Nat. Cerification for Chemistry and Chem. Engring. 1991, women chemists com. 1993-94); mem. AAUW, (divsn. liaison legal advocacy fund 1988-92), Am. Chem. Soc., Nat. Sci. Tchrs. Assn., Nat. Environ. Trainers Assn., Women in Sci., Alpha Delta Kappa (local pres. 1979-80). Democrat. Roman Catholic. Office: Los Alamos Nat Lab K403 HS-5 K403 ESH-5 Los Alamos NM 87545

WIANT, SARAH KIRSTEN, law library administrator, educator; b. Waverly, Iowa, Nov. 20, 1946; s. James Allen and Eva (Jorgensen) W.; m. Robert E. Akins. BA, Western State Coll., 1968; MLS, U. North Tex., 1970; JD, Washington & Lee U., 1978. Asst. law librarian Tex. Tech. U., 1970-72; asst. law librarian Washington & Lee U., 1972—, dir., 1978—, asst. prof. law, 1978-83, assoc. prof. law, 1984-92, prof. law, 1993—. Co-author: Copyright Handbook, 1984, Librarians and Copyright Law in the 1990s, 1994 District of Columbia, Virginia and Maryland Legal Research Book, 1995; contbr. chpts. to books; mem. adv. bd. Westlaw, 1990-93. Mem. ABA (com. on libraries 1987-93), Am. Assn. Law Libraries (program chmn. for ann. meeting 1987, copyright office rep.), Am. Law Sch. (chmn. sec. on librs. 1990-92, accreditation com. 1991-94), Spl. Libraries Assn. (chair copyright com. 1990—), Maritime Law Assn., U.S. Trademark Assn. Office: Washington & Lee U Law Libr Lewis Hall Lexington VA 24450

WIATT, RANDIE LAINE, photographer; b. L.A., Sept. 19, 1954; d. Lou J. and Marilyn (Friedman) Hasson; m. James A. Wiatt, Mar. 7, 1981 (div. Dec. 1990). BS, U. Calif., Santa Barbara, 1976. Account exec. Hollywood (Calif.) Reporter, 1977-80, Parish, Carroll & Kerns Advt., L.A., 1980-82; editor, founder Paramount News Paramount Pictures, Hollywood, 1982-85, segment producer Entertainment Tonight, 1985-88; program devel. mgr. The Disney Channel Disney Studios, Burbank, Calif., 1988-92; freelance photographer Marina Del Rey, Calif., 1992—. Chair Pro-Celebrity Paddle Tennis Tournament to benefit abused children Calif. Med. Ctr.; chair Mr. Paddle Tennis award, 1987; bd. dirs. Mus. of Neon Art, L.A., 1988-92, Camp JCA, L.A., 1994—; mem. Hollywood Women's Polit. Com., 1991, Heal the Bay, Santa Monica, 1990-94. Democrat. Jewish. Home: # 308P 4344 Promenade Way Marina Dl Rey CA 90292-6293

WIBLE, CONNIE, state legislator; b. Tulsa, Oct. 13, 1943; d. Carl Prince Lattimore and Jimmie Bell (Henry) Tallon; m. John Howard Masters, May 27, 1966 (div. 1981); m. Jerry Craig Wible, Apr. 24, 1982 (div. 1993). Cert. in oral hygiene, Temple U., 1965; BA, Loyola Coll., 1975; JD, U. Md., 1980. Registered dental hygienist Dental Office, Bethlehem, Pa., 1965-66, Dr. Thomas P. Rutherford, Joppa, Md., 1966-77; law clk. Hon. Albert P. Close, Belair, Md., 1980-81; atty. Balt. Gas and Electric Co., 1981; spl. prosecutor Office of the Atty. Gen., Branson, Mo., 1982-83; pvt. practice Springfield, Mo., 1983-85; realtor Coldwell-Banker-Vanguard Realtors, Springfield, 1985-88, Carol Jones Realtors, Springfield, 1988-90; state rep. State of Mo., Jefferson City, 1990—; of counsel Law Firm of Woolsey, Fisher, Whiteaker & McDonald, Springfield, 1993—. Bd. dirs. North Springfield Betterment Assn., 1989; vocat. adv. bd., dir. house intern programs Nat. Conf. State Legislators. Named Outstanding Freshman Legislator on Health Care Issues, Mo. Rep. Caucus, 1992; recipient Mem. of Yr. award Springfield Women's Coun. Realtors, 1989, Excel award Mo. Women's Coun. Realtors, 1989. Mem. ABA, LWV (bd. dirs. Springfield 1989, treas., Nat. Order Women Legislators, Nat. Women's Polit. Caucus, Women Legislator's Mo., Mo. Bar Assn., Md. Bar Assn., Greene County Bar Assn., Forum-A Women's Network. Home: 2138 E Cambridge Springfield MO 65804-3933 Office: State of Mo Gen Assy State Capitol House Post Office Jefferson City MO 65101-6806 also: 300 S Jefferson St Ste 600 Springfield MO 65801

WICK, BARBARA DIEBOLD, insurance executive; b. Durham, N.C., July 22, 1942; d. William Diebold and Janet (Hart) Sylvester; m. Thomas Ashton Wick, June 15, 1964; children: Cynthia Anne, Kevin William, Kristine Elaine. BA in Zoology, Swarthmore Coll., 1964; MAT, U. Chgo., 1966; A.R.M., Ins. Sch. Chgo., 1988. Sr. v.p. agy. adminstrn. Condominium Ins. Specialists Am., Inc., Arlington Heights, Ill., 1981—; exec. v.p. Community Assn. Risk Mgmt. and Ins. Cons., Inc. (CARMIC), Arlington Heights, 1986—. Contbr. articles to profl. jours. Mem. N.W. Mcpl. Conf., 1978-89; election judge Cook County, 1976-83; pres. Village of Northfield, 1985-89, trustee, 1977-85, zoning commr., 1976-78; trustee Community Assns. Inst., 1983-90, pres. Ill. chpt. 1990-91, pres. Rsch. Found., 1984-86, chmn. pub. policy com., 1986-88, pub. ofcls. com., 1988-90, chmn. workshops com., 1989—; pres. Northfield Community Nursery Sch.; v.p. Winnetka-Northfield Family Svcs.; chmn. PTA-Northfield Art Festival. Mem. Phi Beta Kappa. Democrat. Home: 2044 Middlefork Rd Northfield IL 60093-1119 Office: CARMIC/CISA/CICUS 3930 Ventura Ste 450 Arlington Heights IL 60004

WICK, SISTER MARGARET, college administrator; b. Sibley, Iowa, June 30, 1942. BA in Sociology, Briar Cliff Coll., 1965; MA in Sociology, Loyola U., Chgo., 1971; PhD in Higher Edn., U. Denver, 1976. Instr. sociology Briar Cliff Coll., Sioux City, Iowa, 1966-71, dir. academic advising, 1971-72, v.p., acad. dean, 1972-74, 76-84, pres., 1987—; pres. Colls. of Mid-Am., 1985-87; bd. dirs. Boatmen's Bank, Sioux City. Bd. dirs. Mary J. Treglia Cmty. House, 1976-84, Marian Health Ctr., 1987—, Iowa Pub. TV—. Mem. North Ctrl. Edn. Assn. (cons.-evaluator for accrediting teams 1980-84, 89—), Siouxland Initiative (adv. bd.), Assn. Cath. Colls. and Univs. (bd. dirs.), Quota Internat., Rotary. Home: 75 W Clifton # 113 Sioux City IA 51104-1122 Office: Briar Cliff Coll Office of the President 3303 Rebecca St Sioux City IA 51104-2340

WICK, TAMARA, artist, writer; b. July 15, 1961; d. James Alan and Maxine Evelyn (Tankersley) W.; m. John E. Kulukundis, 1986. BA in Comm./Broadcasting, Ariz. State U., 1984. Adminstrv. asst. to sr. v.p. Altschiller Reitzfeld Advtg., N.Y.C., 1984-86; asst. to exec. prodr. video devel. Columbia Pictures Industries, N.Y.C., 1986-87; pub. rels. coord., asst. to Estée Lauder and Ida Stewart Estée Lauder Cos., N.Y.C., 1987-89. Active Met. Mus. Art, N.Y.C. Recipient Scholastic award Nat. Conf. Tchrs. English 1976, nominee writing award; Merit scholar U. Ariz., 1976. Mem. NAFE, U.S. Equestrian Team, N.Y. Women in Comm., N.Y. Zool. Soc., N.Y. Young Reps. Club, Ariz. State U. Alumni, Kappa Kappa Gamma Alumnae. Episcopalian. Home: 150 W 56th St New York NY 10019

WICKES, MARY, actress; b. St. Louis, June 13; d. Frank A. and Mary Isabella (Shannon) Wickenhauser. A.B., D.Arts (hon.), Washington U., St. Louis; postgrad., UCLA, 1972—. Lectr. seminars on acting in comedy Coll. William and Mary, Williamsburg, Va., Washington U. at St. Louis, Am. Conservatory Theatre, San Francisco. Debut at Berkshire Playhouse, Stockbridge, Mass.; appeared in: Broadway plays Stage Door, 1936, Father Malachy's Miracle, 1937, The Man Who Came to Dinner, 1939, Jackpot (musical), 1944, Hollywood Pinafore (musical), 1945, Town House, 1948, Park Avenue (musical), 1946, Oklahoma (revival), 1979, others; numerous appearances in dramatic and musical stock, including St. Louis Mcpl. Opera, Cape Playhouse, Dennis, Mass., Bucks County Playhouse, Pa., Alliance Theater, Atlanta, The Coconut Grove Playhouse, Miami, Fla., Burt Reynolds Theatre, Jupiter, Fla., Fox Theatre, St. Louis, Mark Taper Forum, Ahmanson Theater and Chandler Pavilion, Los Angeles, Am. Shakespeare Festival, Stratford, Conn., Am. Conservatory Theater, San Francisco, Berkshire Playhouse, Mass., 1937-78; film debut in The Man Who Came to Dinner, 1942; other film appearances include Now Voyager, 1942, Higher and Higher, 1943, June Bride, 1948, Anna Lucasta, 1949, On Moonlight Bay, 1951, By the Light of the Silvery Moon, 1952, The Actress, 1953, White Christmas, 1959, The Music Man, 1962, The Trouble with Angels, 1966, Where Angels Go, Trouble Follows, 1968, Touched by Love, 1979, Postcards from the Edge, 1990, Sister Act, 1992, Sister Act II, 1993, Little Women, 1994; TV debut as Mary Poppins: other TV appearances include Studio One, 1946; regular: TV series Doc, Halls of Ivy, Lucy shows, Dennis the Menace, The Canterville Ghost, Murder, She Wrote, Wonderworks (PBS), Twigs, Highway to Heaven, others; co-star ABC series Father Dowling Mysteries, 1989-91. Mem. aux. Hosp. Good Samaritan, L.A.; chmn. Nat. Crippled Children's Soc., Mo., 1969; bd. dirs. Med. Aux. Ctr. for Health Scis., UCLA, 1977—, St. Barnabas Sr. Ctr., L.A., 1994—. Recipient numerous awards including Outstanding Actress award Variety Clubs, 1967; awards for vol. work UCLA; Humanitarian award Masons; elected to St. Louis Mcpl. Opera Hall of Fame, 1987; 1st annual Starbiird lectr. Washington U., St. Louis, 1988; nominated best comedy supporting-actress for Sister Act Am. Comedy awards, 1993. Mem. AFTRA, NATAS (Emmy award nomination), SAG, Actors Equity Assn., Acad. Motion Picture Arts and Scis., Phi Mu. Republican. Episcopalian. Office: care Artists Agy 10000 Santa Monica Blvd Los Angeles CA 90067

WICKIZER, CINDY LOUISE, elementary school educator; b. Pitts., Dec. 12, 1946; d. Charles Sr. and Gloria Geraldine (Cassidy) Zimmerman; m. Leon Leonard Wickizer, Mar. 21, 1971; 1 child, Charlyn Michelle. BS, Oreg. State U., 1968. Tchr. Enumclaw (Wash.) Sch. Dist., 1968—. Mem. NEA, Wash. Edn. Assn., Enumclaw Edn. Assn., Buckley Ednl. Agrl. Coun., Buckley C. of C., Wash. Contract Loggers Assn., Am. Rabbit Breeders Assn. (judge, chmn. scholarship found. 1986-87, pres. 1988-94, dist. dir. 1994—, Disting. Svc. award 1987), Wash. State Rabbit Breeders Assn. (life, Pres.'s award 1983, 94), Vancouver Island Rabbit Breeders Assn. (life), Fla. White Rabbit Breeders Assn. (pres. 1984-88, 94—), Wash. State Rabbit and Cavy Shows, Inc., Wash. State Evergreen Rabbit Assn. (sec., v.p. pres.), Alpha Gamma Delta. Home: 26513 112th St E Buckley WA 98321-9258

WICKIZER, MARY ALICE See **BURGESS, MARY ALICE**

WICKLINE, MARIAN ELIZABETH, former chemical librarian; b. St. Louis, Feb. 18, 1915; d. William Anderson and Grace B. (Gooding) W. BA, Mills Coll., 1935; postgrad., U. Calif., Berkeley, 1935-37. Tech. files asst. Shell Devel. Co., San Francisco, 1938-45; libr. western div. Dow Chem. Co., Pitts. and Walnut Creek, Calif., 1945-75; ret., 1975. Mem. Planning Commn., Danville, Calif., 1982-86, El Dorado County Libr. Commn., Placerville, Calif., 1989-92, poicy adv. com. gen. plan, 1989-92, policy adv. com. gen. plan, 1989-92; bd. dirs. Greenstone Country Cmty. Svcs. Dist., 1994—. Named Woman of Yr. San Ramon Valley C. of C., Danville, Calif., 1983. Mem. AAUW (Gift Honoree 1982, 84), Am. Hort. Soc., Am. Chem. Soc., Spl. Libr. Assn. (pres. San Francisco Bay region chpt. 1973-74, chair chemistry divsn. 1970-71). Home: 5474 Comstock Rd Placerville CA 95667-8712

WICKS, LUCY JANE, enterostomal therapy nurse; b. Akron, N.Y., Mar. 10, 1935; d. Percy Frank and Bertha Edith (Crouch) Asher; m. Robert B. Wicks, Oct. 2, 1954; children: Audrey J., Geoffrey B., Jill E. Assoc. degree, Harrisburg Area Community Coll, Harrisburg, Pa., 1974; BSN, Lebanon Valley Coll., 1984; MSN, Villanova U., 1990. Bd. cert. Wound, Ostomy and Continence Nurses Soc. Staff nurse Carlisle (Pa.) Hosp., 1974-78; instr., enterostomal therapy nurse Harrisburg (Pa.) Hosp., 1978-80, assoc. dir. enterostomal therapy sch./svcs., 1980-83, program dir. enterostomal therapy nursing edn. program, 1983-89; nurse mgr. Carlisle Hosp., 1989; owner, sole proprietor Wicks Ednl. Assocs., Camp Hill, Pa., 1990-91, pres., 1991—; chairperson continuing edn. com. Capital Health System, 1986-89; presenter in field. Mem. editorial adv. bd. Jour. Enterostomal Therapy, 1988-90. Profl. edn. com. Dauphin County unit Am. Cancer Soc., Harrisburg, 1985. Mem. ANA, Pa. Nurses Assn., Internat. Assn. for Enterostomal Therapy (enterostomal therapy nursing edn. program dirs. com. 1983—, regional trustee NE region 1990, chairperson ethics com. 1989-90, chairperson early admission com. enterostomal therapy nursing edn. program dirs. com. 1984-87, chairperson enterostomal therapy nursing edn. program dirs. com. 1987-89, v.p. NE region 1981-83), Am. Urol. Assn. Allied. Office: Wicks Ednl Assocs Inc Ste 202 5012 Lenker Rd Mechanicsburg PA 17055

WICKWIRE, PATRICIA JOANNE NELLOR, psychologist, educator; b. Sioux City, Iowa; d. William McKinley and Clara Rose (Pautsch) Nellor; m. Robert James Wickwire, Sept. 7, 1957; 1 child, William James. BA cum laude, U. No. Iowa, 1951; MA, U. Iowa, 1959; PhD, U. Tex., Austin, 1971; postgrad. U. So. Calif., UCLA, Calif. State U., Long Beach, 1951-66. Tchr., Ricketts Ind. Schs., Iowa, 1946-48; tchr., counselor Waverly-Shell Rock Ind. Schs., Iowa, 1951-55; reading cons., head dormitory counselor U. Iowa, Iowa City, 1955-57; tchr., sch. psychologist, adminstr. S. Bay Union High Sch. Dist., Redondo Beach, Calif., 1962-82, dir. student svcs. and spl. edn.; cons. mgmt. and edn.; pres. Nellor Wickwire Group, 1981—; mem. exec. bd. Calif. Interagency Mental Health Coun., 1968-72, Beach Cities Symphony Assn., 1970-82; chmn. Friends of Dominguez Hills (Calif.), 1981-85. Lic. ednl. psychologist, marriage, family and child counselor, Calif. Mem. APA, AAUW (exec. bd., chpt. pres. 1962-72), Nat. Career Devel. Assn. (media chair 1992—), Am. Assn. Career Edn. (pres. 1991—), L.A. County Dirs. Pupil Svcs. (chmn. 1974-79), L.A. County Personnel and Guidance Assn. (pres. 1977-78), Assn. Calif. Sch. Adminstrs. (dir. 1977-81), L.A. County SW Bd. Dist. Adminstrs. for Spl. Edn. (chmn. 1976-81), Calif. Assn. Sch. Psychologists (bd. dirs. 1981-83), Am. Assn. Sch. Adminstrs., Calif. Assn. for Measurement and Evaluation in Guidance (dir. 1981, pres. 1984-85), ACA (chmn. Coun. Newsletter Editors 1989-91, mem. com. on women 1989-92, mem. com. on rsch. and knowledge, 1994—), Assn. Measurement and Eval. in Guidance (Western regional editor 1985-87, conv. chair 1986, editor 1987-90, exec. bd. dirs. 1987-91), Calif. Assn. Counseling and Devel. (exec. bd. 1984—, pres. 1988-89, jour. editor 1990—), Internat. Career Assn. Network (chair 1985—), Pi Lambda Theta, Alpha Phi Gamma, Psi Chi, Kappa Delta Pi, Sigma Alpha Iota. Contbr. articles in field to profl. jours. Home and Office: 2900 Amby Pl Hermosa Beach CA 90254

WIDENER, PERI ANN, public relations manager; b. Wichita, Kans., May 1, 1956; d. Wayne Robert and LuAnne (Harris) W. BS, Wichita State U., 1978; MBA, Fla. Tech., 1992. Advt. intern Associated Advt., Wichita, 1978; pub. rels. asst. Fourth Nat. Bank, Wichita, 1978-79; mktg. communications rep. Boeing Co., Wichita, 1979-83, pub. rels. rep., Huntsville, Ala., 1983-85, pub. rels. mgr., 1985-92; sr. pub. rels. mgr. Boeing Mil. Airplanes, Seattle, 1992—; mem. exec. devel. program Boeing Def. & Space Group, 1993—. Preston Huston scholar, Wichita State U., 1978; recipient Best Electronic Ad award Def. Electronics mag., 1982, Best Total Pub. Rels. Program award Huntsville Press Club, 1985, Huntsville Media awards, 1986, 87, 88, 89, 90, 91, Huntsville Advt. Fedn. Addys, 1988. Mem. Pub. Rels. Soc. Am. (Seattle chpt.), Women in Communications, Pub. Rels. Coun. Ala. (bd. dirs. 1985-92, state pres. 1992, officer Huntsville chpt. 1984-91, pres. No. Ala. chpt. 1989, Excellence award 1986-91, Achievement award 1986-91, Pres.'s award Huntsville chpt. 1985, State Practitioner of Yr. 1989, PRCA Medallion award excellence, numerous others), Internat. Assn. Bus. Communicators (D2 Silver Quills award 1985, 91, D6 Silver Quills 1993, 94), Pub. Rels. Soc. Am. (accredited 1989—), So. Pub. Rels. Fedn. (practitioner of yr. 1991, Excellence award 1986-91, Lantern award 1991), Huntsville-Madison County C. of C. (pub. rels. adv. com. 1987-92), Huntsville Press Club (bd. dirs. 1989-92), Sigma Delta Chi (pres.'s award 1991). Methodist. Office: Boeing Mil Airplanes MS 4C-98 PO Box 3707 # 14 Seattle WA 98124-2207

WIDNALL, SHEILA EVANS, federal official, air force officer, former aeronautical educator, former university official; b. Tacoma, July 13, 1938; d. Rolland John and Genievieve Alice (Krause) Evans; m. William Soule Widnall, June 11, 1960; children: William, Ann. BS in Aero. and Astronautics, MIT, 1960, MS in Aero. and Astronautics, 1961, DSc, 1964; PhD (hon.), New Eng. Coll., 1975, Lawrence U., 1987, Cedar Crest Coll., 1988, Smith Coll., 1990, Mt. Holyoke Coll., 1991, Ill. Inst. Tech., 1991, Columbia U., 1994, Simmons Coll., 1994, Suffolk U., 1994, Princeton U., 1994. Asst. prof. aeros. and astronautics MIT, Cambridge, 1964-70, assoc. prof., 1970-74, prof., 1974-93, divsn. head divsn. fluid mechanics, 1975-79; dir. Fluid Dynamics Rsch. Lab., MIT, Cambridge, 1979-90; chmn. faculty MIT, Cambridge, 1979-80, chairperson com. on acad. responsibility, 1991-92, assoc. provost, 1992-93; sec. USAF, 1993—; bd. dirs. Chemfab Inc., Bennington, Vt., Aerospace Corp., L.A., Draper Labs., Cambridge; trustee Carnegie Corp., 1984-92. Contbr. articles to profl. jours.; patentee in field; assoc. editor AIAA Jour. Aircraft, 1972-75, Physics of Fluids, 1981-88, Jour. Applied Mechanics, 1983-87; mem. editorial bd. Sci., 1984-86. Bd. visitors USAF Acad., Colorado Springs, Colo., 1978-84, bd. chairperson, 1980-82; trustee Boston Mus. Sci., 1989—. Recipient Washburn award Boston Mus. Sci., 1987. Fellow AAAS (bd. dirs. 1982-89, pres. 1987-88, chmn. 1988-89), AIAA (bd. dirs. 1975-77, Lawrence Sperry award 1972), Am. Phys. Soc. (exec. com. 1979-82); mem. ASME, NAE (coun. 1992—), Am. Acad. Arts and Scis., Soc. Women Engrs. (Outstanding Achievement award 1975), Seattle Mountaineers. Office: USAF Office of Sec 1670 AF Pentagon Washington DC 20330-1670

WIDNER, MARY FRANCES, government official; b. Washington, Dec. 23, 1950; d. James Henry and Bernice Catherine (Conneran) W. BA in Journalism, Marquette U., 1972. Staff asst. to pres. White House, Washington, 1972-77; various positions to v.p. legis. affairs AICPAs, Washington, 1979-89; chief staff Office Postsecondary Edn. U.S. Dept. Edn., Washington, 1990-92; chief staff Office Congl. Rels. GAO, Washington, 1992—. Home: 2410 S Ives St Arlington VA 22202 Office: GAO 441 G St NW Washington DC 20548

WIDNEY, MARILYN EDITH (MARILYN PERRY), international finance and real estate executive, television producer; b. N.Y.C., Feb. 11, 1939; d. Henry William Patrick and Edna May (Bown) Perry; m. Charles Leonidas Widney (dec. Sept. 1981). BA, Mexico City Coll., 1957. Pres. Marilyn Perry TV Prodns., Inc., N.Y.C., 1970—, C.L. Widney Internat., Inc., N.Y.C., 1977—; mng. dir. Donerail Corp., N.Y.C., 1980-88, Lancer, N.Y.C., 1980-88, Assawata, N.Y.C., 1980-88. Prodr., host (TV program) International Byline, series of over 90 documentaries on the UN. Bd. dirs. UN After Sch. Program; ambassadorial candidate Pres. Bush., 1989. Recipient U.S. Indsl. Film Festival award, CINE Golden Eagle award, Bronze medal Internat. Film & TV Festival of N.Y., Bronzenen Urkinde, Berlin, award for superior quality Intercom-Chgo. Internat. Film Festival, Knights of Malta Trophy award for superior programming from Min. of Tourism, Internationales Tourismus award Filmfestival, Vienna, Manhattan Cable Ten Year award for continuous programming, citations from former pres. Ford and Carter. Mem. Asia Soc., UN Corrs. Assn., Rep. Presdl. Task Force (charter mem.), Rep. Nat. Com., Harbour Club (S.C.). Home: 211 E 70th St New York NY 10021 Office: C L Widney Internat Inc 677 Fifth Ave New York NY 10022

WIEBELHAUS, PAMELA SUE, educator; b. Stanley, Wis., May 28, 1952; d. Wilbur Leroy and Marjorie Jean (Bernse) Thorne; m. Mark Robert Wiebelhaus, Apr. 27, 1985; 1 child, Sarah Jean. AS in Nursing, No. Ariz. U., 1973, BS in Gen. Home Econs., 1974. R.N. Ariz., Colo; cert. post secondary vocat. tchr., Colo. Nurse Flagstaff (Ariz.) Community Hosp., 1973-75, Children's Hosp., Denver, 1975, St. Joseph's Hosp., Denver, 1980; office nurse, surg. asst. OB-Gyn Assocs., P.C., Aurora, Colo., 1975-78; nursing coordinator perinatal services Community Hosp. Smaritan Health, Phoenix, 1978-79; nurse, mem. personnel pool Good Samaritan Hosp., Phoenix, 1979-80, J. Bains, MD, Phoenix, 1979-80; file clk. Pharm. Card Systems, Inc., Phoenix, 1979-80; office nurse S. Eisenbaum, MD, Aurora, Colo., 1980; instr., coordinator mem. office program T.H. Pickens Tech. Ctr., Aurora (Colo.) Pub. Schs., 1980—; med. supr. healthfair sites, Denver, 1982-85; mem. adf. com. Emily Griffith Opportunity Sch., Denver, 1984-90; mem. survey team North Ctrl. Bd. Edn., 1985, Colo. Bd. Edn., Denver, 1987; book reviewer proposal and new edit. ins. text-reference book W.B. Saunders, 1992—. Acad. scholar No. Ariz. U., 1970, nat. def. grantee, 1970-74; PTA and Elks Club scholar, 1970. Mem. Am. Assn. Med. Assts. (cert.; membership chmn. Capitol chpt. Colo. Soc. 1981). Lutheran.

WIEBENSON, DORA LOUISE, architectural historian, educator, author; b. Cleve., July 29, 1926; d. Edward Ralph and Jeannette (Rodier) W. BA, Vassar Coll., 1946; MArch, Harvard U., 1951; MA, NYU, 1958, PhD, 1964. Architect N.Y., 1951-66; lectr. Columbia U., 1966-68; assoc. prof. U. Md., 1968-72, prof., 1972-77; vis. prof. Cornell U., 1974; prof. U. Va., Charlottesville, 1977-92, prof. emerita, 1992—, chmn. div. archtl. history, 1977-79, assoc. fellow U. Va. Ctr. Advanced Studies, 1982-83; pres. Archtl. Publs., N.Y.C., 1982—. Editor: Marsyas XI: 1962-64, 1965, Essays in Honor of Walter Friedlaender, 1965; Architectural Theory and Practice from Alberti to Ledoux, 1982, rev., 1983, Spanish transl., 1988; Guide to Graduate Degree Programs in Architectural History, 1982, rev., 1984, 86, 88, 90; author: Sources of Greek Revival Architecture, 1969, Tony Garnier: The Cité Industrielle, 1969, Japanese transl., 1983, The Picturesque Garden in France, 1978, Mark J. Millard Architectural Collection, Vol. I: French Books: Sixteenth through Nineteenth Centuries, 1993; contbr. articles to profl. books. Student fellow Inst. Fine Arts, 1961-62, 62-63; grantee Am. Philos. Soc., 1964-65, 70, Samuel H. Kress Found., 1966, Gen. Rsch. Fund, U. Md., 1969, 74, 76, NEH, 1972-73, Samuel H. Kress Found., 1972-73, Am. Coun. Learned Socs., 1976, 81, 85, Ctr. Advanced Studies, U. Va., 1980, 81, Graham Found. Advanced Studies Fine Arts, 1982, 93; fellow Yale Ctr. Brit. Art, 1983; sr. rsch. fellow NEH, 1986-87. Mem. Soc. Archtl. Historians (bd. dirs. 1974-77, 80-83, chair edn. com. 1976-90), Coll. Art Assn., Am. Soc. Eighteenth Century (mem. exec. bd. 1991-94).

WIEBER, PATRICIA MCNALLY, medical, surgical nurse, orthopaedics nurse; b. Albany, N.Y., Oct. 4, 1952; d. Stephen A. and Catherine E. (Dyer) McNally; children: Stephen, James. Diploma, Physician's Hosp. Med. Ctr., Plattsburg, N.Y., 1973; student, St. Joseph's Coll., Windham, Maine, 1986. Cert. nursing adminstr., orthopaedic nurse cert. Staff nurse Albany Meml. Hosp., 1972; staff nurse West Volusia Meml. Hosp., Deland, Fla., 1975, asst. head nurse, 1981; head nurse, mgr. Meml. Hosp. West Volusia, Deland, Fla., 1982—. Mem. Nat. Assn. Orthopaedic Nursing, Fla. Orgn. Nurse Execs.

WIECHEL-TRAVIS, JANE MARIE, state educational official; b. Port Clinton, Ohio, Dec. 13, 1952; d. Richard R. and Irene (Hudak) Wiechel; m. George Y. Travis, Dec. 12, 1987. BS, Kent State U., 1970; MEd, Bowling Green State U., 1978; PhD, Ohio State U., 1988. Tchr. Continental (Ohio) Local Schs., 1974-77, Norwalk (Ohio) City Schs., 1978-81; grad. asst. Bowling Green (Ohio) State U., 1977-78, Ohio State U., Columbus, 1985-86; cons. Ohio Dept. Edn., Columbus, 1981-85, asst. dir., 1986-90, dir., 1990—; trainer Georgetown U., Washington, 1994. Editor: Longitudinal Research Study, 1992. Past pres., bd. dirs. Support Dogs for Handicapped, Columbus, 1987. Recipient Svc. award Ohio Sch. Psychologists Assn., 1991, Accomplished Grad. award Bowling Green State U., 1993, Svc. award Ohio Assn. for the Edn. of Young Children, 1994. Mem. Nat. Assn. Edn. Young Children, Nat. Head Start Assn., Coun. Exceptional Children, Zonta Club Columbus (exec. bd. 1993—), Kappa Delta Pi. Office: Ohio Dept Edn 65 S Front St Columbus OH 43215-4183

WIECZOREK, PATRICIA CHRISTINE, medical/surgical nurse; b. Balt., Mar. 17, 1961; d. John and Florence (Polek) W. BSN, U. Md., 1983. Cert. nurse operating rm. Nursing asst. Jenkins Meml. Home, Balt., 1981-82; staff nurse ICU Harbor Hosp. Ctr., Balt., 1983-84; sr. clin. nurse gen. operating room, cardiac surgery Johns Hopkins Hosp., Balt., 1984—; pub. speaker nursing practice. Contbr. articles to profl. jours. Mem. Assn. Operating Rm. Nurses. Office: Johns Hopkins Hosp Gen Oper Rms Meyer 7 Cardiac 600 N Wolfe St Baltimore MD 21287-0002

WIEDENHOEFT, ANN MARIE, psychotherapist, consultant; b. Ladysmith, Wis., Feb. 16, 1938; d. Anton John and Josephine (Calmes) Schmirler; m. Gilbert John Wiedenhoeft, Nov. 29, 1958; children: Susan, Frances, Nicholas, Mathew. BSW, U. Wis., 1984; MA, St. Mary's Coll., 1987. Lic. clin. social worker, Minn. Group facilitator Family Svc., St. Paul, 1984-87, psychotherapist, 1987-90; pvt. practice St. Paul, 1990—; cons. Parents Anonymous Minn., St. Paul, 1985-87, 91, Capitol Community Ctr., St. Paul, 1987-90. Active Girl Scouts U.S., Stevens Point, Wis., 1966-70; mem. LWV, Madison, Wis., 1972-76; pres. PTA, Madison, 1972-75. Mem. NASW, Minn. Women Psychologists, Phi Eta Sigma.

WIEGAND, SYLVIA MARGARET, mathematician, educator; b. Cape Town, South Africa, Mar. 8, 1945; came to U.S., 1949; d. Laurence Chisholm and Joan Elizabeth (Dunnett) Young; m. Roger Allan Wiegand, Aug. 27, 1966; children: David Chisholm, Andrea Elizabeth. AB, Bryn Mawr Coll., 1966; MA, U. Wash., 1967; PhD, U. Wis., Madison, 1972. Mem. faculty U. Nebr., Lincoln, 1967—, now prof. math.; vis. assoc. prof. U. Conn., Storrs, 1978-79, U. Wis., Madison, 1985-86; vis. prof. Purdue U., 1992-93. Editor Communications in Algebra jour., 1990, Rocky Mountain Jour. Math., 1991—; contbr. rsch. articles to profl. jours. Troop leader Lincoln area Girl Scouts U.S., 1988-92. Grantee NSF, 1985-88, 90-93, Vis. Professorship for Women, 1992. Mem. AAUP, Am. Math. Soc. (mem.-at-large, coun.), Assn. Women in Math., London Math. soc., Math. Assn. Am. Office: U Nebr Dept Math Lincoln NE 68588-0323

WIELE, PATRICIA GIORDANO, interior decorator; b. Houston, Aug. 29, 1947; d. Conrad Joseph and Ellen Patricia (Condon) Schoppe; m. Natale Joseph Giordano, Apra. 17, 1971 (dec. Sept. 1989); children: Keith Joseph, Michael David, Ryan Peter, Todd Christopher; m. Frederick John Wiele, Jan. 16, 1964; stepchildren: Scott, Robin, Brian, Craig, and Suzanne Wiele. Student, U. Houston, 1965-67, NYU, 1969. Prin. Patricia S. Giordano Interiors, Ridgefield, Conn., 1975—; pub. speaker various floral design and horticulture workshops. Bd. dirs. Family and Children's Aid, Inc., Danbury, Conn., 1976-78, program and rev. and nominating coms., 1978, head pub. rels. com., 1978-79, pres. aux., 1976-79; v.p. Twin Homeowner's Assn., Ridgefield, Conn., 1978-79, chmn., founder area beautification, 1978; pres. East Ridge Mid. Sch. PTO, 1988-89, PTA, 1991-92. Recipient award of Excellence Fed. Garden Clubs Conn., 1984, Tricolor award Nat. Council State Garden Clubs, 1984, Aboreal award Nat. Council State Garden Clubs, 1984, Hort. Excellence award Nat. Council State Garden Clubs, 1984. Mem. Allied Bd. Trade, Caudatowa Garden Club (v.p. 1987-89, 90-91, pres. 1991-93). Republican. Roman Catholic.

WIEMER-SUMNER, ANNE-MARIE, psychotherapist, educational administrator; b. Ger., Mar. 3, 1938; came to U.S., 1949, naturalized, 1956; d. Franz and Margaret (Neubacher) Wiemer; BA, Hunter Coll., 1963; MA, N.Y. U., 1965; PhD Union Inst., 1989; cert. Psychoanalytic Individual and Group Therapy, Washington Square Inst. Psychotherapy, 1975, 76; m. Eric Eden Sumner, May 24, 1974 (dec.); children: Erika, Trevor. Adminstrv. asst., counselor, asst. chmn. admissions N.Y. U., N.Y.C., 1956-69; asst. dean student Hunter Coll., N.Y.C., 1969-71; assoc. dean students Cooper Union Advancement Art and Sci., N.Y.C., 1971—; supr. Washington Sq. Inst. for Psychotherapy, N.Y.C., 1977-81; pvt. practice psychotherapy, N.Y.C. Trustee Grace Ch. Sch., 1985-91, Greenwich Village Soc. for Historic Preservation, 1991—; pres. Washington Sq. Assn., 1987—. Mem. Coun. Psychoanalytic Psychotherapists, Am. Psychol. Assn., Am. Group Psychotherapy Assn., Am. Orthopsychiat. Assn., Internat. Assn. Group Psychotherapy, Nat. Accreditation Assn. and Am. Exam. Bd. Psychoanalysis, N.Y. State Assn. Practicing Psychotherapists, Coll. Placement Council, Eastern Coll. Personnel Officers, Megantic Fish & Game Corp. Home: 7-13 Washington Sq N New York NY 10003 Office: Cooper Union Cooper Sq New York NY 10003

WIENER, ANNABELLE, United Nations official; b. N.Y.C., Aug. 2, 1922; d. Philip and Bertha (Wrubel) Kalbfeld; ed. Hunter Coll.; married, Jan. 1, 1941; children: Marilyn Grunewald, Marjorie Petit, Mark. Chmn. UN Dept. Pub. Info., Nongovtl. Orgns. Exec. Com., spl. adviser to sec. gen. Internat. Women's Year Conf.; mem. exec. bd. Nongovtl. Orgns. Com. on Disarmament UN, UN Dept. Pub. Info's NGO Exec. Com.; bd. dirs. World Fedn. UN Assns., also founder, dir. art and philatelic program; bd. dirs. N.Y. chpt. UN Assn.-USA; bd. dirs., chmn. UN Day Programme, So. N.Y. State Div., v.p. North Shore chpt.; mem. UN Dept. Pub. Info.'s Non-Govtl. Orgn. Exec. Com.; mem., bd. dir. Non-Govtl. Orgn. for UNICEF at UN Hdqrs. Recipient Diplomatic World Bull. award for Distinction in politics and diplomacy and svc. to high ideals of UN, 1989; apptd. dep. sec.-gen. World Fedn. UN Assns., 1991. Mem. Am. Fedn. Arts, Mus. Modern Art, Musee Nat. Message Biblique Marc Chagall, Am. Philatelic Soc., UN Philatelic Soc., UN Assn. U.S., UNO Philatelie, Fed. Republic Germany. Address: Dep Sec-Gen World Fedn UN Assns DC1-1177 United Nations New York NY 10017

WIENER, VALERIE, communications company owner; b. Las Vegas, Nev., Oct. 30, 1948; d. Louis Isaac Weiner and Tui Ava Knight. BJ, U. Mo., 1971, MA, 1972; MA, Sangamon State U., 1974; postgrad., McGeorge Sch. Law, 1976-79. Producer TV show "Checkpoint" Sta. KOMU-TV, Columbia, Mo., 1972-73; v.p., owner Broadcast Assocs., Inc., Las Vegas, 1972-86; pub. affairs dir. First Ill. Cable TV, Springfield, 1973-74; editor Ill. State Register, Springfield, 1973-74; producer and talent "Nevada Realities" Sta. KLVX-TV, Las Vegas, 1974-75; account exec. Sta. KBMI (now KFMS), Las Vegas, 1975-79; nat. traffic dir. six radio stas., Las Vegas, Albuquerque and El Paso, Tex., 1979-80; exec. v.p., gen. mgr. Stas. KXKS and KKJY, Albuquerque, 1980-81; exec. adminstr. Stas. KSET AM/FM, KVEG, KFMS and KKJY, 1981-83; press sec. U.S. Congressman Harry Reid, Washington, 1983-87; adminstrv. asst Friends for Harry Reid, Nev., 1986; press sec. U.S. Senator Harry Reid, Washington, 1987-88; owner Wiener Communications Group, Las Vegas, 1988—. Author: Power Communications: Positioning Yourself for High Visibility (Fortune Book Club main selection 1994); contbg. writer The Pacesetter. Sponsor Futures for Children, Las Vegas, Albuquerque and El Paso, 1979-83; mem. Exec. Women's Coun., El Paso, 1981-83; mem. VIP bd. Easter Seals, El Paso, 1982; appointee, media chair Gov.'s Coun. Small Bus., 1989-93, Clark Coun. Sch. Dist. and Bus. Cmty. PAYBAC Spkrs. and Partnership Programs, 1989-93; media dir. 1990 Conf. on Women Gov. of Nev.; media chair Congl. Awards Coun., 1989-93; media chair, nat. rep. Nat. Assn. Women Bus. Owners, So. Nev., 1990-91, appointee, vice chair Gov.'s Commn. on Postsecondary Edn.; bd. dirs. Better Bus. Bureau So. Nev. Named Outstanding Vol. United Way, El Paso, 1983, SBA Nev. Small Bus. Media Advocate of Yr., 1992; recipient Woman of Achievment in Media award, 1992, numerous 1st place Nev. Press Women Media awards, 1990—, Outstanding Achievement award Nat. Fedn. Press Women, 1991, Disting. Leader award Nat. Assn. for Community Leadership, 1993, Cir. of Excellence award Las Vegas C. of C., 1993, numerous other awards. Mem. NAFE, Nev. Press Women, Nat. Speakers Assn., Internat. Speakers Network, Nat. Assn. Women Bus. Owners (Nev. Advocate of Yr. 1992), Dem. Press Secs. Assn., El Paso Assn. Radio Stas., Am. Soc. Assn. Execs., U.S. Senate Staff Club, Las Vegas C. of C. (Circle of Excellence 1993), Soc. Profl. Journalists. Democrat. Office: 1500 Foremaster Ln Ste 2 Las Vegas NV 89101-1103

WIENKE, V. KAY, clinical nurse specialist; b. Nebr., Dec. 17, 1950; d. Edward and Maxine (Cook) W. BSN, U. Nebr., 1973; MS in Nursing, U. Colo., Denver, 1981. Staff devel. coord. Mt. Sinai Hosp., Hartford, Conn., 1982; nurse clinician, oncology Lawrence & Meml. Hosp., New London, Conn., 1982-86; orthopedic coord. Windham County Meml. Hosp., Willimantic, Conn., 1986-87; orthopedic clin. nurse specialist Columbia Hosp., Milw., 1988-93; staff nurse Vis. Nurse Assn., Milw., 1994—. Contbr. articles to profl. jours. Mem. Nat. Assn. Orthopaedic Nurses (N.E. dist. rep. 1985-87, v.p. 1988-90, pres.-elect 1990-91, pres 1991-92), Sigma Theta Tau.

WIER, PATRICIA ANN, publishing executive, consultant; b. Coal Hill, Ark., Nov. 10, 1937; d. Horace L. and Bridget B. (McMahon) Norton; m. Richard A. Wier, Feb. 24, 1962; 1 child, Rebecca Ann. B.A., U. Mo., Kansas City, 1964; M.B.A., U. Chgo., 1978. Computer programmer AT&T, 1960-62; lead programmer City of Kansas City, Mo., 1963-65; with Playboy Enterprises, Chgo., 1965-71; mgr. systems and programming Playboy Enterprises, 1971; with Ency. Britannica, Inc., Chgo., 1971—; v.p. mgmt. svcs. Ency. Britannica USA, 1975-83, exec. v.p. adminstrn., 1983-84; v.p. planning and devel. Ency. Britannica, Inc., 1985, pres. Compton's Learning Co. div., 1985; pres. Ency. Britannica (USA), 1986-91, Ency. Britannica N.A., 1991-92; exec. v.p. Ency. Britannica, Inc., 1986-91; pres. Ency. Britannica N.Am., 1991-94; mgmt. cons. pvt. practice, Chgo., 1994—; cons. pvt. practice, Chgo., 1994—; bd. dirs. NICOR, Inc., Golden Rule Ins., Enrich, Internat., Alcas Corp.; mem. coun. Northwestern U. Assocs. Mem. fin. Coun. Archdiocese of Chgo., Coun. of Grad. Sch. of Bus. U. of Chgo. Mem. Direct Selling Assn. (bd. dirs. 1984-93, chmn. 1987-88, named to Hall of Fame 1991), Women's Coun. U. Mo. Kansas City (hon. life) Com. 200, The Chgo. Network. Roman Catholic. Office: Patricia A Wier Inc 175 E Delaware Ste 8305 Chicago IL 60611

WIERSIG, LEANN, counselor; b. Cherokee, Okla., Mar. 12, 1957; d. Ronald Clay and Barbara Ann (Baltz) Brady; m. Jim Dene Wiersig, Dec. 18, 1976; children: Jessica Le, Cori Ann. BA in Edn., Northwestern Okla. State U., 1978, MEd, 1981. English tchr., libr. South Haven (Kans.) High Sch., 1978-79; English tchr. Newkirk (Okla.) High Sch., 1979-89, counselor, 1989—; mem. Curriculum Rev. Com., Newkirk, 1989—, Okla. Plan for Ednl. Improvement, Newkirk, 1989—, Attendance Rev. Com., Newkirk, 1991—, Pioneer Tech. Prep. Adv. Com., Ponca City, Okla., 1992—, Priority Acad. Student Skills Com., Newkirk, 1993—; chmn. Pioneer Area Vo-Tech. Guidance Adv. Com., Ponca City, 1992—; trainee Substance Abuse Subtle

Screening Inventory, 1992—; leader Developing Capable People, 1993—. Named Hon. Chpt. farmer Newkirk (Okla.) FFA, 1982, Tchr. of Yr., Newkirk (Okla.) Pub. Schs., 1985; recipient Tchr. award merit Albright Community Trust, Newkirk, 1988. Mem. ACA, Okla. Sch. Counseling Assn., Newkirk Okla. Edn. Assn. (pres. 1983-85, 93—), Newkirk Women's League (pres. 1984). Democrat. Methodist. Home: 713 W 12th St Newkirk OK 74647-5029 Office: Newkirk High Sch Ninth & Main Newkirk OK 74647

WIERSMA, SANDRA CARMELA BROWN, psychologist, consultant; b. Fostoria, Ohio, May 4, 1939; d. Michael Lucien and Clara Helen Brown; m. Darryl Jay Wiersma, Dec. 20, 1958; children: Linda Anne, Lisa Anne, Michael Adrian, Matthew Adrian. AA, Grand Rapids (Mich.) Jr. Coll., 1974; BA magna cum laude, Aquinas Coll., Grand Rapids, 1982; MA in Clin. Psychology, U. Detroit, 1984, postgrad. in clin. psychology. Ltd. lic. psychologist, Mich. Psychologist in pvt. practice Grand Rapids, 1986—; adj. faculty psychology Aquinas Coll., Grand Rapids, 1988—; cons. psychologist Cardiac Rehab. Dept., Blodgett Hosp., Grand Rapids, 1990-92. Bd. dirs. Extracare Home Health Care, Grand Rapids, Mich., 1989-93; cons. psychologist ARC Phone Friends, Grand Rapids, 1987-93; patient discharge interviewer for rsch. dept. Pine Rest Christian Hosp., Grand Rapids, 1981-82, author vol. manual, 1981. U. Detroit teaching scholar, 1982-84. Mem. AAUW, APA, Mich. Psychol. Assn., Mich. Soc. for Psychoanalytic Psychology, Psi Chi. Office: 2348 E Beltline Ave SE Grand Rapids MI 49546-5906

WIESE, DOROTHY JEAN, business educator; b. Chgo., Sept. 20, 1940; d. Charles Ennis Chapman and Evelyn Catherine Flizikowski; m. Wallace Jon Wiese, Oct. 10, 1959; children: Elizabeth Jean Wiese Christensen, Jonathan Charles. BS in Edn., No. Ill. U., 1970, MS in Edn., 1976, EdD, 1994. Tchr. bus. Hampshire (Ill.) High Sch., 1970-78; prof. bus. Elgin (Ill.) C.C., 1978—; cons. Gould, Inc., Rolling Meadows, Ill., 1984; instr. vocat. practicum McDonald's Hamburger U., Ofcl. Airline Guides, Oak Brook, Ill., 1986; speaker SIEC, Sweden and Austria, 1987-88, North Ctrl. Bus. Edn. Assn./Wis. Bus. Edn. Assn. Conv., 1992, Chgo. Area Bus. Edn. Assn., 1992, AAUW, Batavia and Geneva, 1993; facilitator small group Internat. Congress Mng. Human Capacity in 21st Century, U. Helsinki, Lahti, Finland, 1990; participant Internat. Consortium for Internat. Studies and Program Faculty Short-term Exch. with U.K., 1992; speaker, presenter, moderator in field in Leningrad, USSR, 1991, cons. St. Petersburg, Russia, 1992. Presented paper 34th annual Adult Edn. Rsch. Conf., Pa. State U., 1993. Mem., sec. N.W. Kane County (Ill.) Airport Authority, 1987-94; host family Am. Intercultural Student Exch., 1989-90; presenter women's seminar Trinity Luth. Ch., Roselle, Ill., 1992. Mem. Internat. Soc. Bus. Edn. (North Cen. Bus. Edn. Assn. rep. 1989-90), Societe Internationl pour l'Ensignement Commercial, Nat. Bus. Edn. Assn., Ill. Bus. Edn. Assn., Ill. Vocat. Assn., AAUW, Delta Pi Epsilon (past historian Alpha Phi chpt.), Kappa Delta Pi. Lutheran. Office: Elgin Community Coll 1700 Spartan Dr Elgin IL 60123-7193

WIESE, NEVA, critical care nurse; b. Hunter, Kans., July 23, 1940; d. Amil H. and Minnie (Zemke) W. Diploma, Grace Hosp. Sch. Nursing, Hutchinson, Kans., 1962; BA in Social Sci., U. Denver, 1971; BSN, Met. State Coll., 1975; MS in Nursing, U. Colo., Denvr, 1978; postgrad., U. N.Mex., 1986—. RN, N.Mex.; CCRN. Cardiac ICU nurse U. N.Mex. Hosp., Albuquerque; coord. critical care edn. St. Vincent Hosp., Santa Fe, charge nurse CCU, clin. nurse III intensive and cardiac care. Recipient Mary Atherton Meml. award for clin. excellence St. Vincent Hosp., 1986. Mem. ANA (cert. med. surg. nurse), AACN (past pres., sec. N.Mex. chpt., Clin. Excellence award 1991), N.Mex. League Nursing (past v.p., bd. dirs., sec., membership com. 1992—).

WIESEN, ANNE RHODA, civic worker; b. Medford, N.J., Nov. 27, 1926; d. George William and Mary Rebecca (Hattman) W. BS, U. N.H., 1948; MRE, Andover Newton Theol. Sch., 1950. Cert. community coll. instr., Calif. Dir. Christian edn. Bapt. chs., Mass., R.I., 1950-54; tchr., recreator World Coun. Chs., France, 1955; dir. Christian edn. Bapt. chs., Norristown, Wayne, Pa., 1956-62; recreation worker U.S. mil. hosps. ARC, 1962-64, recreation supr. U.S. mil. hosps. and bases, 1964-1976; field dir. ARC, Wright Patterson AFB, Ohio, 1976-79; sta. dir. ARC, Osan AFB, Republic of Korea, 1979-80; asst. dist. dir. ARC, Camp Zama, Japan, 1981-83, March AFB, Calif., 1983-84; sta. mgr. ARC, Camp Pendleton, Calif., 1985-86; vol. resource assoc. ARC, Stuttgart, Germany, 1986-88; sec. European Recreation Soc., Heidelberg, Germany, 1973-74. Author: Children Around the World, 1960. Bd. dirs. Project Pup, 1993-95. Recipient medal for civilian svcs. in Vietnam, U.S. Govt., 1968. Mem. AAUW (v.p. 1991-93), Tiger Bay Club (bd. dirs.). Democrat. Baptist.

WIESENBERG, JACQUELINE LEONARDI, lecturer; b. West Haven, Conn., May 4, 1928; d. Curzio and Filomena Olga (Turrinziani) Leonardi; m. Russel John Wiesenberg, Nov. 23; children: James Wynne, Deborann Donna. BA, SUNY, Buffalo, 1970, postgrad., 1970-73, 80—. Interviewer, examiner U.S. Dept. Labor, New Haven, 1948-52; sec. W.I. Clark Co., Hamden, Conn., 1952-55; acct. VA Hosp., West Haven, 1956-60; acct.-commissary U.S. Air Force Missle Site, Niagara Falls, N.Y., 1961-62; tchr. Buffalo City Schs., 1970-73, 79; acct. Erie County Social Svcs., Buffalo, 1971-73; lectr., 1973—. Contbr. articles to CAP, U.S. Air Force mag., 1954—. Capt., Nat. Found. March of Dimes, 1969—, com. mem. telethon, 1983-86; den mother Boy Scouts Am., 1961-68; chmn. Meals on Wheels, Town of Amherst, 1975-76; leader, travel chmn. Girl Scouts Am., 1968-77; mem. Nat. Congress Parents and Tchrs., 1957—; heart fund vol. Heart Assn., 1960-86; rep. Am. Diabetes Assn., 1994—, vol. Diabetes collection, 1994-95. Mem. AAUW, NAFE, Internat. Platform Assn., Nat. Parks and Conservation Assn., Am. Astrol. Assn., Western N.Y. Conf. Aging, Nat. Geographic Soc., The Wilderness Soc., Nat. Trust for Hist. Preservation, The Nature Conservancy, Epsilon Delta Chi, Alpha Iota. Home: 14 Norman Pl Amherst NY 14226-4233

WIESENFELD, BESS GAZEVITZ, business executive, real estate developer; b. Elizabeth, N.J., May 6, 1915; d. Morris and Rebecca (Sokolov) Gazevitz; m. Benjamin Wiesenfeld, Oct. 23, 1938 (dec.); children: Myra Judith Wiesenfeld Lewis, Elaine Phyllis Wiesenfeld Livingston, Ira Bertram (dec.), Sarah Ann Wiesenfeld Wasserman. BFA, N.Y. Sch. Design, N.Y.C., 1982. Pres. Anasarca Corp., 1958—; real estate devel. Colonia, N.J., 1961—; interior designer, 1961—; chair Bess & Co., Phila., 1982—; pres. Carolier Lns., Inc., 1986—. Patron Met. Opera Guild, Friends Music at Princeton; mem. pres.' coun. Norton Gallery and Sch. Art, Inc.; sustaining mem. N.J. Symphony Orch. Mem. AAUW, Nat. Trust for Hist. Preservation (assoc.), Am. Soc. Interior Designers (allied mem.), Met. Mus. Art, Mus. Modern Art, Smithsonian Inst., Victorian Soc. of Met. Opera Guild, Preservation, N.J., Inc., N.J. Symphony Orgn., Friends of Art Mus., Princeton, N.J., Friends of Music at Princeton. Republican. Jewish. Home: 374 New Dover Rd Colonia NJ 07067-2799 also: 2600 South Ocean Blvd Palm Beach FL 33480

WIEST, DIANNE, actress; b. Kansas City, Mo., Mar. 28, 1948. Student, U. Md. Appeared in numerous plays including Ashes (off-Broadway), 1976, Leave It to Beaver is Dead, The Art of Dining (Obie award, 1979, Theatre World award 1983), Bonjour La Bonjour, Three Sisters, Serenading Louie (Obie award, 1983), Othello, After the Fall, Heartbreak House, Our Town, and Hunting Cockroaches, 1987, In the Summer House, 1993, Blue Light, 1994; appeared in films including It's My Turn, 1980, I'm Dancing as Fast as I Can, 1982, Independence Day, 1982, Footloose, 1984, Falling in Love, 1984, The Purple Rose of Cairo, 1985, Hannah and Her Sisters, 1986 (Acad. award for Best Supporting Actress 1987), Radio Days, 1987, Lost Boys, 1987, September, 1987, Bright Lights, Big City, 1988, Parenthood, 1989 (Acad. award nominee), Cookie, 1989, Edward Scissorhands, 1990, Little Man Tate, 1991, Cops and Robbersons, 1994, The Scout, 1994, Bullets Over Broadway, 1994 (Golden Globe award Best Supporting Actress-Drama 1995, Acad. award for Best Supporting Actress 1995); TV appearances include The Wall, 1982, The Face of Rage, 1983. Office: care Paul Wolfowitz Internat Creative Mgmt 59 E 54th St Ste 22 New York NY 10022-4001

WIGFALL, EDNA LOUISE, personnel director; b. Charleston, S.C., July 3, 1955; d. James and Thelma (cox) W.; children: Lisana S. Gabriel, Sakina R. Gabriel. AS in Bus. Adminstrn., Bronx C.C., 1985; BA in Econs., Lehman Coll., 1994. Dir. personnel N.Y. State Harlem Urban Devel. Corp., N.Y.C.; sec. Family Support Systems, Inc., Bronx; chmn. Beck Community Devel. Corp., Bronx; mentor coord. N.Y. State Mentoring Program, N.Y.C. Adv. bd. Colgate Bright Smiles, Bright Futures. Recipient Ptnr. in Edn. Appreciation award N.Y.C. Pub. Sch., 1992-93, Vision award Family Support Sys. Unltd., 1993. Democrat. Presbyterian. Office: NY State Harlem Urban Devel 163 W 125th St New York NY 10027

WIGG, RITA AGNES, writer, public relations consultant; b. Milw., June 14, 1946; d. Frank P. and Claudia E. (Diel) Lesar; m. Larry W. Wigg, June 15, 1968; children: Morgan, Laura, Charles, Lawrence. BA in Journalism, Marquette U., 1968. Staff writer Wauwatosa (Wis.) News-Times, 1982-85; corr. Sheboygan (Wis.) Press, 1986-91; cons. pub. rels. Rehab. Ctr., Sheboygan, 1986-91; asst. to pres. Leadership Dynamics, Sheboygan, 1989-90; comms. asst. Lakeland Coll., Sheboygan, 1991-92, comms. coord., 1992-93, communications dir., 1993—. Contbr. articles to various newspapers. Mem., scholarship chair Wauwatosa Jr. Women's Club, 1984-85; mem., pub. rels. cons. TOSA-FEST Com., Wauwatosa, 1984-86. Recipient Cert. Appreciation, Office of Mayor, Wauwatosa, 1983, Cert. Appreciation, St. Bernard's Parish, 1984, Cert. Appreciation, Cub Pack #3804, 1987; named Jr. of Month, Wauwatosa Jr. Women's Club, 1984. Mem. Bus. and Profl. Women of Wis., Wis. Regional Writer's Assn., Sheboygan Area Writer's Club. Roman Catholic. Home: 1214 N 4th St Sheboygan WI 53081 Office: Lakeland Coll PO Box 359 Sheboygan WI 53083

WIGGERS, CHARLOTTE SUZANNE WARD, magazine editor; b. Cleve., Dec. 14, 1943; d. Raymond Paul and Irene Mary (Knapp) W.; m. John Houston Black, Feb. 1975 (div. 1980). AB, Smith Coll., 1966. Asst. editor The Hudson Rev., N.Y.C., 1966-76; assoc. editor The Print Collector's Newsletter, N.Y.C., 1977-79; copy editor Electronics mag., McGraw-Hill, N.Y.C., 1979-81; sr. copy editor Spectrum mag., N.Y.C., 1981-85; mng. editor Essence mag., N.Y.C., 1985—. Home: 50 W 85th St Apt 5 New York NY 10024-4572 Office: Essence Magazine 1500 Broadway New York NY 10036-4015

WIGGINS, NANCY BOWEN, real estate broker, market research consultant; b. Richmond, Va., Oct. 9, 1948; d. William Roy and Mary Virginia (Colson) Bowen; m. Samuel Spence Saunders, Aug. 16, 1969 (div. 1977); m. Edwin Lindsey Wiggins, Jr., Apr. 16, 1983; children: Neal Bowen, Mark Edwin. AA, St. Mary's Coll., Raleigh, N.C., 1968; postgrad., Trinity U., 1968-69; BA, U.S. Internat. U., San Diego, 1970; MA, U. Tex., Arlington, 1975; postgrad., Tulane U., 1976-77. Bank teller Bank of Am., San Diego, 1971-72; lectr. U. Tex., Arlington, 1974-76; instr. Johnson C. Smith U., Charlotte, N.C., 1977-78; human svcs. planner Centralina Coun. of Govt., Charlotte, 1978-80; mktg. rsch. analyst First Union Nat. Bank, Charlotte, 1980-81; mktg. rep. Burroughs Corp., Charlotte, 1981-83; ptnr., mktg. researcher George Selden & Assocs., Charlotte, 1983-84; pres., broker Bowen Wiggins Co., Charlotte, 1984-92; pres. WRB, Inc. (merger Bowen Wiggins Co. and W. Roy Bowen Co., Inc.), Charlotte, 1992—; instr. U. N.C., Charlotte, 1984-85, 87-90, Winthrop U., Rock Hill, S.C., 1985-86, 91-92; bd. dirs. Roy Bowen, Inc., Frogmore, S.C., v.p., sec., 1990. Contbr. articles to profl. jours. Vice chmn. United Cerebral Palsy Coun., Charlotte, 1984; chmn. bd. dirs. Carriage House Condominium Assn., Charlotte, 1980-82; mem. Charlotte Mayor's Budget Adv. Com., 1980-81, Charlotte-Mecklenburg Planning Commn., 1994—, mem. planning com., 1994-95; pres. Mecklenburg Dem. Women's Club, 1990; mem. state exec. com. N.C. Dem. Party, 1991-95; mem. Charlotte Women's Polit. Caucus, Mecklenburg County Solid Waste Adv. Bd., 1991-92, chmn. recycling com., 1991-94. Mem. Charlotte Metro Comml. Bd. Realtors, N.C. Assn. Appraisers (bd. dirs., pres. 1989-90), Tournament Players Club Piper Glen, Pi Sigma Alpha. Democrat. Episcopalian. Home: 6425 Felton Ct Charlotte NC 28277-3570 Office: WRB Inc 7621 Little Ave Ste 508 Charlotte NC 28226

WIGGS, SHIRLEY JOANN, educator; b. Johnston County, N.C., Nov. 6, 1940; d. William H. and Sallie P. (Barden) W.; BA, Atlantic Christian Coll., 1963; postgrad. Duke U., 1966, East Carolina U., 1979-80; grad. Newspaper Inst. Am. Tchr. public schs. South Hill, Va., 1963-64; tchr. lang. arts and social studies Glendale Chapel High Sch., Kenly, N.C., 1964-65, Benson (N.C.) High Sch., 1965—; tchr. advanced placement English, lang. arts, journalism South Johnston High Sch., Four Oaks, N.C., 1969—, chairperson lang. arts dept., 1971-86, coordinating adminstr. curriculum, 1974-76, student adv., 1978-80, coach Acad. Super Bowl, 1982-87; evaluator profl. books Allyn and Bacon, Inc., 1974, 79; yearbook judge Columbia Scholastic Press Assn., 1986-92, yearbook advisor, 1980-94. Sunday sch. tchr. 1st Bapt. Ch., Smithfield, N.C., 1964-66, asst. supt. young people's dept., 1964-67; scholarship chairperson 1st Bapt. Ch., 1987-91; chmn. Keep Johnston County Beautiful, 1979-81. Named Woman of Yr., Atlantic Christian Coll., 1962; recipient Keep Johnston County Beautiful Appreciation award, 1980, Internat. Cheerleading Found. award, 1972, Acad. Booster Club award, 1986. Mem. NEA, Nat. Council Tchrs. English, Assn. Supervision and Curriculum Devel., N.C. English Tchrs. Assn. (dir. dist. 12, 1980-85), Johnston County Assn. of Educators, N.C. Assn. Educators (past pres. Johnston County chpt.). Home: 102 E Sanders St Smithfield NC 27577-4211 Office: South Johnston High Sch RR 3 Four Oaks NC 27524-9803

WIGHT, JANET HOWELL, nurse; b. Elmira, N.Y., May 29, 1936; d. Wallace John and Katie Lee (Simmons) Howell; m. Leland Walter Wight Jr., June 21, 1958; children: Stephen, Pamela W. (Mrs. James Kirkpatrick), Julia W. (Mrs. Jonathan Coyle). AA, Elmira Coll., 1956; BSN, Columbia U., 1959; cert. pediat. nurse practitioner, U. Conn., 1973; MS, So. Conn. State U., 1980; postgrad., Yale Div. Sch., 1981-82. Ordained deacon Episcopal Ch., 1986. Staff nurse Vis. Nurse Svc., Rochester, N.Y., 1959-61; office nurse Pediatric Group, Chapel Hill, N.C., 1962-64; nurse practitioner Pediatric Assocs., New Haven, 1973-75; instr. pediatrics So. Conn. State U., New Haven, 1975-82; counselor Episcopal Social Svc., New Haven, 1982-85; pastoral counselor Pastoral Ctr., New Haven, 1985-88; supr. nurses New Haven Nursing Ctr., 1984-86; staff nurse Vis. Nurse Assn., New Haven, 1990—; chaplain New Haven Nursing Ctr., 1984-88; visitor, mem. steering com. Interfaith Vol. Caregivers, New Haven, 1985-90; vol. chaplain Yale New Haven Hosp., 1981-86. Vol. ARC, New Haven, 1968-78, Columbus House Soup Kitchen, New Haven, 1982-90; tutor Lit. Vols. Am., New Haven, 1991-92; breast cancer group leader Am. Cancer Soc., New Haven, 1987-88. Roman Catholic. Home: 332 Berwick Ln New Haven CT 06515

WIGHT, NANCY ELIZABETH, neonatologist; b. N.Y.C., Aug. 27, 1947; d. John Joseph and Gisela (Landers) Probst; m. Robert C.S. Wight, Oct. 1, 1988; 1 child, Robert C.S. II. Student, Cornell U., 1965-67; AB in Psychology, U. Calif., Berkeley, 1968; postgrad., George Washington U., 1971-72; MD, U. N.C., 1976. Diplomate Am. Bd. Pediatrics. Resident in pediatrics U. N.C., Chapel Hill, 1976-79; fellow in neonatal/perinatal medicine U. Calif., San Diego, 1979-81; clin. instr. Dept. of Pediatrics La. State U. Sch. of Medicine, Baton Rouge, 1982-86; neonatologist The Baton Rouge Neonatology Group, 1981-86; co-dir. neonatology, med. dir. respiratory therapy Woman's Hosp., Baton Rouge, 1981-85; med. dir. newborn svcs., neonatal respiratory therapy HCA West Side Hosp. Centennial Med. Ctr., Nashville, 1986-88; staff pediatrician, neonatologist Balboa Naval Hosp., San Diego, 1988-89; attending neonatologist Sharp Meml. Hosp., San Diego, 1990—, Children's Hosp.-San Diego, 1990—; asst. clin. prof. U. Calif. San Diego, 1991—; physician assoc. La Leche League. Contbr. articles to profl. jours. mem. exec. bd. Capital Area Plantation chpt. March of Dimes, Baton Rouge, 1981-86, chmn. health adv. com., 1982-86; mem. health com. Capital Area United Way, Baton Rouge, 1982-86; bd. mem. Baton Rouge Coun. for Child Protection, 1983-86, NICU Parents, Baton Rouge, 1981-86; mem. health adv. com. Nashville Area March of Dime, 1987-88. Recipeint Am. Med. Women's Assn. award. Mem. AMA, Am. Acad. Pediatrics, Calif. Med. Assn., So. Med. Assn., San Diego County Med. Assn., Calif. Perinatal Assn., So. Perinatal Assn., Nat. Perinatal Assn., La. Perinatal Assn. (past 1st v.p. and pres.), Internat. Lactation Cons. Assn. (cert.), Hastings Soc. Home: 3226 Newell St San Diego CA 92106 Office: Children's Assoc Med Group 8001 Frost St San Diego CA 92123

WIGHTMAN, ANN, lawyer; b. Dayton, Ohio, July 29, 1958; d. William L. and Mary Ann (Lamb) W. AB, Ohio U., 1980; JD, Case Western Res. U., 1984. Bar: Ohio 1984, U.S. Dist. Ct. (so. dist.) Ohio 1984, U.S. Ct. Appeals (6th cir.) 1991, U.S. Ct. Appeals (7th cir.) 1992, U.S. Supreme Ct. 1993. Assoc. Smith & Schnacke, Dayton, 1984-89; sr. assoc. Faruki Gilliam & Ireland, Dayton, 1989-91, ptnr., 1991—; adj. prof. U. Dayton Sch. Law, 1988-93; chmn. Artemis House, Inc., Dayton, 1988-90, bd. dirs., 1985—; arbitrator Am. Arbitration Assn. Mem. Vol. Lawyer's Project, Dayton, 1988—; mem. Challenge 95 Task Force, Dayton, 1989-90, Up and Comer, Dayton, 1990; vol. arbitrator Montgomery County Common Pleas Ct., 1989—; bd. dirs. ACLU of Ohio Found., 1991-94; mem. Leadership, Dayton, 1992. Mem. ABA (trial and environ. sects.), Am. Arbitration Assn. (arbitrator), Ohio Bar Assn. (alternative dispute resolution com. 1990—), Dayton Bar Assn. (unauthorized practice com. 1990-93, com. on the judiciary 1993—), Phi Beta Kappa. Home: 334 Marathon Ave Dayton OH 45406-4837 Office: Faruki Gilliam & Ireland 10 N Ludlow St Dayton OH 45402

WIGLEY-MORRISON, KAREN, accountant, paralegal, administrative assistant; b. Dallas, July 14, 1950; d. Willard Robert Jr. and Jerry (McDonald) Wigley; m. Jon Edwin Morrison, Jan. 30, 1982. Student, Dallas Bapt. Coll., 1968-69; BA, U. Okla., 1971; diploma, Exec. Secretarial Sch., Dallas, 1971. Profl. model Kim Dawson Model Agy., Dallas, 1962-72; legal sec. Gardere & Wynne, Dallas, 1972-76; paralegal, sec. Geary, Brice Law Firm, Dallas, 1983-84; v.p., sec.-treas. Astraea Co., Dallas, 1984-90; paralegal, sec. Geary, Bryce Law Firm, Dallas, 1983-84; paralegal Gardere & Wynne, Dallas, 1972-76; corp. sec. X Part, Inc., Dallas, 1987-90; pvt. cons. Dallas, 1990—, acct., 1992—. Vol. I Have a Dream Found., Dallas, 1988—, exec. vol. coun., 1990—; vol. Texans' War on Drugs, Austin. Mem. NAFE, Am. Bus. Women's Assn., North Dallas Network Career Women, Dallas Summer Musicals Guild, Dallas Symphony Assn., Arboretum and Botanical Gardens, Phi Beta Lambda. Republican. Episcopalian.

WIIG, ELISABETH HEMMERSAM, audiologist, educator; b. Esbjert, Denmark, May 22, 1935; came to U.S., 1957, naturalized, 1967; d. Svend Frederick and Ingeborg (Hemmersam) Nielsen; m. Karl Martin Wiig, June 10, 1958; children—Charlotte E., Erik D. B.A., Statsseminariet Emdrupborg, 1956; M.A., Western Res. U., 1960; Ph.D., Case Western Res. U., 1967; postgrad., U. Mich., 1967-68. Clin. audiologist Cleve. Hearing and Speech Center, 1959-60; instr. dept. phonetics Bergen (Norway) U., 1960-64; asst. prof., dir. aphasia rehab. program U. Mich., 1968-70; asst. prof. Boston U., 1970-73, asso. prof., chmn. dept., 1973-77, prof. dept. communication disorders, 1977-87, prof. emerita, 1987—; v.p. EDUCOM Assocs. Inc., 1992-93. Author: Language Disabilities in Children and Adolescents, 1976, Language Assessment and Intervention for the Learning Disabled, 1980, 84, CELF Screening Tests: Elementary and Secondary Levels, 1980, Clinical Evaluation of Language Fundamentals, revised, 1987, Test of Language Competence, 1985, expanded edit., 1989, Test of Word Knowledge, 1992, Clinical Evaluation of Language Fundamentals Preschool, 1992; editor: Human Communication Disorders: An Introduction, 1982, 86, 90, 94; contbr. articles to profl. jours. Recipient Metcalf Cup and Prize for excellence in teaching Boston U., 1967. Fellow Am. Speech and Hearing Assn. (cert. clin. competence in speech pathology and audiology); mem. Coun. for Learning Disabilities, Coun. for Exceptional Children, Internat. Assn. for Rsch. on Learning Disabilities, Am. Psychol. Soc. Address: 5211 Vicksburg Arlington TX 76017-4941

WIITA, KATHRYN CARPENTER, public relations company executive; b. Casper, Wyo., Sept. 15, 1961; d. Hugh Lewis and Kathryn Estelle (Pepper) Carpenter; m. Thomas A. Wiita, Sept. 1, 1991. BS in Mass Communications, U. Utah, 1983. Mcht. rep. Tracy Collins Bank & Trust, Salt Lake City, 1983-84; communications specialist Arthur Young & Co., Salt Lake City, 1984-88; officer, dir. pub. rels. lst Interstate Bank Utah, Salt Lake City, 1988-89; pres. KC Communications, Jackson, Wyo., 1989—; cons. Mountain West Venture Group, Salt Lake City, 1984-87, Catheter Tech. Inc., Salt Lake City, 1986-89, Sta. KTVX, Salt Lake City, 1986, Inter Therapy, Inc., Costa Mesa, Calif., 1990, Stop Gap, Santa Ana, Calif., Jackson Peak Outfitters, 1992—, M W Med., 1990—, Jacksoh Hole Cowboy Ski Challenge, 1994; mktg. cons.Wines & Spirits, 1992—. Mem. Pub. Rels. Soc. Am. (accredited; officer 1988-89), Pub. Rels. Soc. Am. Counselors Acad., Women in Comms. (officer 1988-89), Jr. League Orange County, Calif. Inc. (pub. rels. coord. 1991-92, dir. pub. rels. c992—), Kappa Kappa Gamma. Home and office: 1630 Woodland Terr Lake Oswego OR 97034

WIKARSKI, NANCY SUSAN, information technology consultant; b. Chgo., Jan. 26, 1954; d. Walter Alexander and Emily Regina (Wejnerowski) W.; m. Michael F. Maciekowich, Dec. 5, 1976 (div. Feb. 1985). BA, Loyola U., Chgo., 1976, MA, 1978; PhD, U. Chgo., 1990. Paralegal Winston & Strawn, Chgo., 1978-79; real estate analyst Continental Bank, Chgo., 1979-84; systems analyst, 1984-88, ops. officer, 1988-89, automation cons., 1989-92; systems mgr. PNC Mortgage Co. of Am., Vernon Hills, Ill., 1992-94; ind. cons. Lake Bluff, Ill., 1994—. Author: German Expressionist Film, 1990. Fellow U. Chgo., 1987-90. Mem. NAFE, Am. Mensa, Chgo. Computer Soc., Alpha Sigma Nu.

WIKE, D. ELAINE, business executive; b. Ridgecrest, Calif., Sept. 26, 1954; d. Robert G. and Jimmie Mae (Sallee) Field; student U. Houston, 1975-77; m. Mike Wike, Oct. 14, 1978; children: Mike II, Angelina Elaine, William V., Danielle Elizabeth, Edward Lawrence, Windy Gale. Legal sec. Morgan, Lewis & Bockius, Washington, 1977-78; legal asst. Alfred C. Schlosser & Co., Houston, 1972-77, 78-81, Jerry Sadler, atty., Houston, 1982-83; founder, owner DEW Profl. & Bus. Svcs., Houston, 1979—; office mgr. Law Offices Mike Wike, Houston, 1983—. Treas., Wilhelm Schole Parents Orgn., 1981-82; mem. Free, Inc.; vol. campaign worker, (Ron Paul for Congress and Reagan for Pres.), 1975, 76. Recipient 3d place Nassau Bay Tex. Christmas Boat Lane Parade First Ann. Photography Contest, 1990. Mem. Young Ams. for Freedom, Nat. Notary Assn., Nat. Assn. Female Execs., Am. Soc. Notaries, Nat. Paralegal Assn. Republican. Libertarian. Mem. Christian Ch. Office: 2421 S Wayside Dr Houston TX 77023-5318

WILBUR, BARBARA MARIE, elementary education educator; b. Homer City, Pa., Dec. 1, 1945; d. Nicholas and Ann (Bender) Hrebik; m. Samuel Scime, Nov. 21, 1970 (div. Jan. 1974); m. Frederick Layton Wilbur, June 21, 1986 (dec. June 1989). BS in Elem. Edn., SUNY, Buffalo, 1967, EdM in Guidance Counseling, 1971; postgrad., Harvard U., 1969; grad., John Robert Powers Modeling Sch., Buffalo, 1974. Cert. permanent elem. sch. tchr., N.Y. Elem. tchr. Buffalo Pub. Schs., 1967-70, 94—, Diocese of Ft. Lauderdale, Fla., 1971-72, Diocese of Buffalo, 1973-94. Mem. State U. Buffalo Alumni Assn., State U. Coll. Buffalo Alumni Assn. (Outstanding Svc. award 1982), Buffalo State Coll. Alumni Assn. (bd. dirs. 1980-87, active various coms.). Republican. Roman Catholic. Home: 301 Lowell Rd Tonawanda NY 14217-1236 Office: Buffalo Pub Schs Sch #18 118 Hampshire St Buffalo NY 14213

WILBURN, MARY NELSON, lawyer, writer; b. Balt., Feb. 18, 1932; d. David Alfred and Phoebe Blanche (Novotny) Nelson; m. Adolph Yarbrough Wilburn, Mar. 5, 1957; children: Adolph II, Jason David. AB cum laude, Howard U., 1952; MA, U. Wis., 1955, JD, 1975. Bar: Wis. 1975, U.S. Supreme Ct 1981. Lectr. U. Wis. Law Sch., 1975-77, 83, 84, 85; atty. adv. Bur. Prisons, Dept. Justice, 1977-82; chmn. Wis. State Parole Bd., Madison, 1986-87; gen. counsel D.C. Bd. Parole, 1987-89; commr. The Commn. to Restructure the Interstate Compact, 1988-89; mgr. Bethune Mus.-Archives, Inc., 1990; asst. regional counsel mid-atlantic region Fed. Bur. Prisons, 1990-93, atty. Affirmative Action Programs, 1993—; mem. Wis. Sentencing Commn., 1986-87; adj. lectr. seminar on parole Washington Coll. Law Am. U., 1991. Mem. Madison Met. Sch. Dist. Bd. Edn., 1975-77; assoc. mem. Schutz Am. Sch. Bd., Alexandria, Egypt, 1983-85; commr. Nat. Coun. of Negro Women Commn. on Edn., 1986—; treas. Women's Strategies for 21st Century, Inc. Mem. Internat. Assn. Paroling Authorities (exec. v.p. 1987-89), Nat. Assn. Black Women Attorneys (pres. Rolark chpt. 1989-93), Fedn. Internat. de Abogadas, Howard U. Alumni Assn., Links, Inc., Leadership (Am. Class 1991, bd. dirs. Greater Washington 1992-94), Alpha Kappa Alpha. Office: 320 1st St NW Rm 437 Washington DC 20534

WILCHER, LAJUANA SUE, lawyer; b. Danville, Ky., Sept. 16, 1954; d. Dwain LaRue and Juanita (Tungate) W. BS magna cum laude, Western Ky. U., 1977; postgrad., U. Louisville, 1978; JD, No. Ky. U., 1980. Bar: Ky. 1980, U.S. Dist. Ct. (we. dist.) Ky. 1980. Assoc. Reynolds Catron & Johnston, Bowling Green, Ky., 1980-83; spl. asst. to gen. counsel USDA, Washington, 1983; spl. asst. to gen. counsel EPA, Washington, 1983-85, asst. to dep. adminstr., 1985-86; assoc. Bishop Cook Purcell & Reynolds, Washington, 1986-88, ptnr., 1988-89; asst. adminstr. for water U.S. EPA, Washington, 1989-93; ptnr. Winson & Strawn, Washington, 1993—. Mem. ABA, Ky. Bar Assn. Republican. Presbyterian. Office: Winston & Strawn 1400 L St NW Washington DC 20005-3509

WILCOX, BARBARA MONTGOMERY, accountant; b. Corpus Christi, Tex., Dec. 23, 1939; d. Archie James and Jewel (Williams) Montgomery; m. William L. Wilcox, Nov. 7, 1958 (div. June 1966); 1 child, Lawrence Montgomery. Office mgr., acct. Cattleland Oil Co., Corpus Christi, 1966-68; acct. Sanford E. McCormick, Houston, 1968-69; sr. acct. Penn Cen.(formerly Bus. Funds Inc. and Marathon Mfg. Co.), Houston, 1969-74; treas., acct. Frame It Inc., Houston, 1974-76; owner Wilcox Fin. Reporting, Houston, 1976—; owner The Office Gallery, Houston, 1981—, Pocketwatch, Houston, 1985—; sec. to trustees Pauline Sterne Wolff Meml. Found., Houston, 1977-85; treas. Ouisie's Inc., Houston, 1993—. Author: Accounting Procedure Manual for Frame Shop Franchises, 1975. Vol. Mus. Fine Arts, 1988—, Tex. Agrl. Ext. Svc. Master Gardener Program, 1986. Mem. Beta Sigma Phi (Outstanding Woman 1964, 65). Republican. Home and Office: 8626 Oakford Dr Houston TX 77024-4604

WILCOX, CHARLENE DELORIS, elementary school educator; b. Muncie, Ind., Jan. 8, 1932; d. Otto Orlando and Leona Irene (Forrest) Long;m. Arnold Henry Wilcox, Apr.17, 1955; children: George H., Roberta Lynn Cooley, Arnold Long. BS in Edn., Ohio State U., 1954; student, Mexico City Coll., 1952. Tchr. 3d grade Jackson (Mich.) Pub. Schs., 1954-56; tchr. grades 2 and 3 Wyandotte (Mich.) Pub. Schs., 1956-60; tchr. grade 4 Consolidated Schs. of Salem, N.H., 1961-62; tchr. grades 1, 2 and 4 Jackson (Mich.) Pub. Schs., 1963-86; ret. Mem. AAUW (membership v.p. 1990-92, social chmn. 1992-93), NEA, Am. Assn. Ret. Persons, Mich. Edn. Assn., Jackson Edn. Assn., Assn. of Childhood Edn. (corres. sec. 1954-56), Mich. Assn. Ext. Homemakers, Ch. Women United, Peace Coun. (sec. 1991-92), United Meth. Women (v.p. 1990-92, pres. 1992-94), Job's Daus., Alpha Gmma Delta (pres. 1953-54). Methodist. Home: 806 W Michigan # 305E Jackson MI 49202

WILCOX, DEBRA KAY, lawyer; b. Colorado Springs, Colo., Sept. 7, 1955; children: Justin, Lauren. BA in English, U. No. Colo., 1977; JD, U. Denver, 1986. Bar: Colo. 1987, U.S. Dist. Ct. Colo. 1988. Rsch. analyst Colo. Legis. Coun., Denver, 1978-80, 81-83; govt. affairs staff Alliance of Am. Insurers, Chgo., 1980-81; law clk. and assoc. Rotole, Jaunarajs, Walker & Lumbye, Denver, 1986-88; of counsel Jay M. Finesilver, P.C., Denver, 1988-90, Cogswell & Eggleston, Denver, 1990, Kobayashi & Assocs., P.C., Denver, 1990-94, Pencom, Inc., Denver, 1994—; mem. jud. tchg. faculty Colo. Dept. Jud. Adminstrn., P.C., Denver, 1988, mem. state collection agy. bd., 1992. Co-author: A History of Colorado's Legislative Leaders, 1979. Recipient Arnold M. Chuktow award, U. Denver, 1986; named Outstanding Young Women in Am., 1976, 1986. Mem. ABA (mem. host com. young lawyers divsn. 1988), Colo. Bar Assn. (mem. availability of legal svcs. com.), Denver Bar Assn., Sigma Sigma Sigma (v.p. 1988-90, mem. nat. ednl. found. bd. 1990-92). Office: Pencom Inc 511 16th St # 400 Denver CO 80203

WILCOX, DIANE POU, guidance counselor; b. Dallas, July 10, 1947; d. Robert Louis Jr. and Phyllis E. (Carter) Pou; m. Donald E. Wilcox, May 25, 1968; children: Dana Erin, Deren Pou. BFA, So. Meth. U., 1969, MEd, 1972. Tchr. Dallas Ind. Sch. Dist., 1969-72, counselor, 1973, 87-90; guidance counselor Highland Park High Sch. Highland Park Ind. Sch. Dist., Dallas, 1990—; sec. bd. dirs. FOCAS, 1980; bd. dirs. Trinity River Mission, 1990-91. Former Duchess, chmn. Fiesta de Las Seis Banderas, Dallas, 1994, asst. Duchess chmn., 1995; mem. Dallas Symphony Orch. League, Jr. League Dallas; Symphony Assembly assoc., com. chmn. Jr. Symphony Ball. Recipient Eisenhower award North Tex. West Point Soc., 1992. Mem. ACA, Tex. Counseling Assn., Tex. Assn. of Coll. Admissions Counselors (presenter 1993), Nat. Assn. Coll. Admissions Counselors, Kappa Alpha Theta Alumni. Republican. Methodist. Office: Highland Park High Sch 4220 Emerson Ave Dallas TX 75205-1099

WILCOX, MARY L., systems project analyst; b. Lewisville, Ark., Sept. 22, 1959; d. George Harold and Thelma Rene (Burton) Wise; m. Michael Darnell Wilcox, Dec. 24, 1978; 1 child, Melissa Christina. BS, Fla. State U., 1982. Pharmacy tech. Tallahassee Meml. Regional Med. Ctr., Fla., 1982-84; lab. tech. Dept. Health and Rehabilitative Svcs., State of Fla., Tallahassee, 1984-85, biological scientist, 1985-89, sr. human svcs. program specialist, 1989-92; systems project analyst Agency for Health Care Adminstrn., State of Fla., Tallahassee, 1992—. Home: 407 Great Lakes St Tallahassee FL 32310-0100 Office: Agency for Health Care Adminstrn State of Fla Bld 8 Rm 226 2730 Blairstone Rd Tallahassee FL 32301-5902

WILCOX, MARY MARKS, Christian education consultant, educator; b. Madison, Wis., Apr. 23, 1921; d. Roy and Mary Celia (Leary) Marks; m. Ray Everett Wilcox, Nov. 28, 1942; children: Peter, Anne, Susan, Steven. BA, U. Wis., 1942; MRE, Iliff Sch. Theology, Denver, 1968. Cert. Christian educator. Cons. local chs., Lakewood, Littleton, Wheat Ridge, Colo., 1963-74; instr., leader numerous seminars throughout U.S. and Can., 1963—; interim parish cons. 1st Presbyn. Ch., Lakewood, 1988-90; profl. assoc. for faith devel. 1st Presbyn. Ch., Lakewood, Colo., 1993—; adj. prof. Iliff Sch. Theology, 1970—. Author: Developmental Journey, 1979; contbr. articles to various publs., chpts. to books. Former vol. instr., life guard YMCA, Lakewood; trustee, mem. exec. bd. Nat. Ghost Ranch Found., Abiquiu, N. Mex., 1962-93. Recipient award Iliff Alumni Assn., 1989. Mem. Assn. Profs. and Researchers in Religious Edn. (presentr), United Meth. Assn. Profs. Christian Edn., Religious Edn. Assn., Assn. Presbyn. Christian Educators (past mem. exec. bd.), Moral Edn. Assn. Democrat. Presbyterian. Home: 3590 Estes St Wheat Ridge CO 80033-5933

WILCOX, MAUD, editor; b. N.Y.C., Feb. 14, 1923; d. Thor Fredrik and Gerda (Ysberg) Eckert; m. Edward T. Wilcox, Feb. 9, 1944; children: Thor (dec.), Bruce, Eric, Karen. A.B. summa cum laude, Smith Coll., 1944; A.M., Harvard U., 1945. Teaching fellow Harvard U., 1945-46, 48-51; instr. English Smith Coll., Northampton, Mass., 1947-48, Wellesley Coll., Mass., 1951-52; exec. editor Harvard U. Press, 1958-66, humanities editor, 1966-73, editor-in-chief, 1973-89, ret.; freelance editorial cons. Cambridge, 1989—; cons., panelist NEH, Washington, 1974-76, 82-84; cons. Radcliffe Pub. Course, 1991. Mem. MLA (com. scholarly edits. 1982-86), Assn. Am. Univ. Presses (chair com. admissions and standards 1976-77, v.p. 1978-79, chair program com. 1981-82), Phi Beta Kappa. Democrat. Episcopalian. Home and Office: 63 Francis Ave Cambridge MA 02138-1911

WILCOX, RHODA DAVIS, educator; b. Boyero, Colo., Nov. 4, 1918; d. Harold Francis and Louise Wilhelmina (Wilfert) Davis; m. Kenneth Edward Wilcox, Nov. 1945 (div. 1952); 1 child, Michele Ann. BA in Elem. Edn., U. No. Colo., 1941; postgrad., Colo. Coll., 1955-65. Life cert. tchr., Colo. Elem. tchr. Fruita (Colo.) Pub. Sch., 1938-40, Boise, Idaho, 1940-42; sec. civil service USAF, Ogden, Utah, 1942-43, Colorado Springs, Colo., 1943-44; sec. civil service hdqtrs. command USAF, Panama Canal Zone; sec. Tech. Libr., Eglin Field, Fla., 1945-46; elem. tchr. Colorado Springs Sch. Dist. 11, 1952-82, mem. curriculum devel. com., 1968-69; lectr. civic, profl. and edn. groups, Colo.; judge for Excellence in Literacy Coldwell Bankers Sch. Dist. 11, Colo. Coun. Internat. Reading. Assn. Author: Man on the Iron Horse, 1959, Colorado Slim and His Spectackler, 1964, (with Jean Pierpoint) Changing Colorado (Social Studies), 1968-69, Founding Fathers and Their Friends, 1971, The Bells of Manitou, 1973, (with Ben Froisland) In the Footsteps of the Founder, 1993. Mem. hist. adv. bd. State Colo., Denver, 1976; mem. Garden of the Gods master plan rev. com. City of Colorado Springs, 1987—; mem. cemetery adv. bd. City of Colorado Springs, 1988-91; mem. adv. bd. centennial com., 1971; mem. steering com. Spirit of Palmer Festival, 1986; judge Nat. Hist. Day, U. Colo. Colorado Springs and Colo. Coll., Colorado Springs; hon. trustee Palmer Found., 1986—; mem. Am. the Beautiful Centennial Celebrations, Inc., 1992-93. Named Tchr. of the Yr., Colorado Springs Sch. Dist. 11, 1968. Mem. AAUW (Woman of Yr. 1987), Colo. Ret. Educators Assn., Colorado Springs Ret. Educators Assn., Helen Hunt Jackson Commemorative Coun. Home: 1620 E Cache La Poudre St Colorado Springs CO 80909-4612

WILCOXEN, JOAN HEEREN, fitness company executive; b. Flushing, N.Y., May 30, 1948; d. Paul Arnold and Helena Catherina (Laskowski) Heeren; m. Eddie Dean Wilcoxen, Dec. 31, 1981. BA, Long Island U., 1971; grad., Radford U. Karate Coll., 1994. Cert. referee AAU. Real estate broker Heeren Agy., Riverhead, N.Y., 1970-72; 2d v.p. Levitt House, Inc., Medford, N.Y., 1972-78; radio broadcaster Sta. KWHW Radio, Altus, Okla., 1979-84; exec. dir. Ironworks Family Gym and Heartland Health Club, Altus, Okla., 1984-94, Wilcoxen's Acad. of the Martial Arts, Altus, Okla., 1994—; lectr. martial arts; lectr. Shortgrass Arts and Humanities Coun., Altus, 1988—. Vol. United Way of Jackson County, Altus, 1989—, project co-chair, 1994; fundraiser Muscular Dystrophy Assn., Wichita Falls, Tex., 1987—; mem. Shortgrass Arts and Humanities Coun., 1988-93, Nat. Bd. Realtors, 1978-79; state coord., co-chair Sooner State Games Karate, Oklahoma City, 1989-93; bd. dirs. Am. Heart Assn. 1993-95; mem. Altus 2000 edn. task force. Named for civic leadership Okla. State U. Coop. Extension Svc., Altus, 1988, S.W. Bell Tel. Co., Altus, 1989, Rotary Club and March of Dimes, Altus, 1989, Jackson County Free Fair, Altus, 1988, 89; Okla. State AAU karate champion, 1990, black belt. Mem. AAUW (v.p. Altus chpt. 1990, pres. 1992-93), Altus C. of C. (amb. 1989-90), Am. Bus. Women's Assn., Biz Tips Women's Assn. (v.p. 1989-90, pres. 1991-92), Am. Heart Assn. (bd. dirs. Altus chpt. 1994), Altus C. of C., Air Force Assn. Cmty. Ptnrs., Am. Ind. Karate Instrs. Assn. (instr. Christiansburg, Va. chpt. 1986—). Home: 1100 N Main St Altus OK 73521-3122 Office: Wilcoxen s Acad Martial Art Altus Plz Shopping Ctr 1100 N Main St # 5B Altus OK 73521-3122

WILCOXSON, JOAN ELIZABETH, special education educator; b. Portsmouth, Ohio, Feb. 17, 1940; d. Robert Lewis and Bonnie Jeannette (Borders) Stearnes; m. George P. Boss, June 23, 1968 (div. Aug. 1978); children: Catherine Clark, Donna Jean Clark West, Carol Clark, Donald William Clark, Jr. B in Secondary Edn., Ohio U., 1972; M in Spl. Edn., Trenton State Tchrs. Coll., 1976. Cert. supr. spl. edn., elem. prin., secondary prin. Tchr. Lucasville (Ohio) Sch. Sys., 1966-69, Gallia (Ohio) Acad. H.S., 1969-71, Bristol Twp. Sch. Sys., Levittown, Pa., 1972-94; chair dept. spl. edn. Armstrong Jr. H.S., Fairless Hills, Pa., 1992—. Author: A Hot Body in a Cool Society, 1980. Mem. NEA, Pa. Ednl. Assn., Bristol Twp. Tchrs. Assn. (bldg. rep.). Home: 40 Mayflower Rd Levittown PA 19056-3607 Office: Armstrong Jr. H.S. 475 Wistar Rd Fairless Hills PA 19030-4101

WILD, BONITA MARIE, hospital services company executive; b. Chgo., Jan. 14, 1949; d. Edward and Veronica (Hlad) Orzechowski; m. Forrest Wild; 1 child, Monica. Student, U. Chgo., 1973-75; BS, Roosevelt U., 1977; MA, U. Ariz., 1984. Sales rep. and dist. trainer Ortho Pharm. Corp., Raritan, N.J., 1978-82; v.p. and mktg. dir. Golden Era, Phoenix, 1982-84; sales rep. Surgikos, Arlington, Tex., 1984-88, Johnson & Johnson Med., Inc., Arlington, 1988-90; profl. products mgr. Johnson & Johnson Internat., Johnson & Johnson Poland, Warsaw, 1991-92; account bus. mgr. Johnson & Johnson Hosp. Svcs., New Brunswick, N.J., 1990-91, corp. bus. mgr., 1993—; corp. dir. Johnson & Johnson Health Care Sys., 1995—; counsellor Mariposa Women's Ctr., Orange, Calif., 1984-89. Mem. Toastmasters, Franklin Honor Soc. at Roosevelt U. Republican. Roman Catholic. Home: 506 Nyes Pl Laguna Beach CA 92651

WILD, EILEEN ALESSANDRO, nurse consultant; b. Bklyn., Dec. 9, 1944; d. Ralph and Doreen Jutson; m. Frederick W. Wild, Nov. 19, 1988; children: Thomas Frederick, Thomas Charles Alessandro, Eileen Lillian Alessandro. Diploma, Kings County Hosp. Ctr. Sch., 1965; BSN, L.I. U., 1968; MA, Columbia U., 1971; EdD, Rutgers The State U., 1990. Corp. dir. nursing fin. Cath. Med. Ctr. Bklyn. and Queens, 1992—; clin. dir. Princeton (N.J.) Productivity Inst., 1986-87; faculty, curriculum coord. St. Joseph's Coll., Patchogue, N.Y., 1976-80; exec. dir. Assn. Diploma Schs. Nursing, Princeton, 1980-85; v.p. Jamaica (N.Y.) Hosp., 1987-92. Pilot, USCG Air Aux. Mem. ANA, Coun. Gerontol. Nursing, Nat. League Nursing, Assn. Nurse Execs., Health Fin. Mgmt. Assn. Home: 2112 Spruce St Baldwin NY 11510-2713

WILDE, DAWN JOHNSON, artist and educator; b. Phila., Feb. 1, 1934; d. John Gilbert and Ruth Ellen (Dunigan) Johnson; m. Jack Powell Bowman, June 29, 1957 (dec. Aug. 1964); 1 child, Jack Powell II; m. James Bradford Wilde, July 12, 1969. BA in Art and Drama, Baylor U., 1956; MEd in Curriculum and Instrn., Memphis State U., 1967; MFA in Painting, Am. U., 1977. Tchr. art pvt. practice, Bitburg, Germany, 1960-61, Kingsbury High Sch., Memphis, 1968-69; Tchr. art Bemis Art Sch., Colorado Springs, Colo., 1983, honorarium instr., 1983-89; instr. U. Colo., Colorado Springs, 1989-90, 92-95; mem. art commn. adv. bd. City of Colorado Springs and El Paso County, Colo., 1983-86. Exhibited in solo and group shows at Discovery Gallery, Santa Fe N.Mex., 1977, Rutherford-Barnes Collection, Inc., Denver, 1978-81, Sebastian-Moore Gallery, Denver, 1982-84, Carson-Sapiro Gallery, Denver, 1983, Arnesen Fine Arts Ltr., Vail, Colo., 1987-92, William Havu Fine Arts, Denver, 1988-90, Sandy Carson Gallery, 1990—, Colorado Springs Fine Arts Ctr., 1974, 81, 83, 85, 94, Gallery Contemporary Art U. Colo., 1985—; solo shows Lincoln Ctr., Ft. Collins, Colo., 1994, Tointon Gallery Union Colony Civic Ctr., Greeley, Colo., 1994. Recipient David Lloyd Kreeger award Dept. Art, Am. U., Washington, 1977. Mem. Nat. Assn. Women Artists, Soc. Layerists in Multi-Media. Office: U Colo Dept Art 1420 Austin Bluffs Pky PO box 7150 Colorado Springs CO 80933-7150

WILDE, PATRICIA, artistic director; b. Ottawa, Ont., Can., July 16, 1928; m. George Bardyguine; children: Anya, Youri. Dancer Am. Concert Ballet, Marquis de Cuevas Ballet Internat., N.Y.C., 1944-45, Ballet Russe de Monte Carlo, N.Y.C., 1945-49, Roland Petit's Ballet Paris, Met. Ballet Britain, London, 1949-50; prin. ballerina N.Y.C. Ballet, 1950-65; dir. Harkness Sch. Ballet, N.Y.C., 1965-67; ballet mistress, tchr. Am. Ballet Theatre, N.Y.C., 1969-77; dir. Am. Ballet Theatre Sch., N.Y.C., 1977-82; artistic dir. Pitts. Ballet Theatre, 1982—; tchr. Am. Ballet Theatre, 1969-77, Joffrey scholarship program, N.Y.C. Ballet, 1968-69; established Sch. of Grand Theatre of Geneva, 1968-69; adjudicator Regional Ballet in Am. S.E. and S.W., 1969-82; choreographer N.Y. Philharmonic; guest tchr. various ballet cos. and colls.; trustee Dance U.S.A.; panelist Nat. Choreographic Project. Recipient Leadership award in Arts and Letters, 1990, Pitts. Woman of the Yr. in the Arts award, 1993. Office: Pitts Ballet Theatre 2900 Liberty Ave Pittsburgh PA 15201-1511

WILDER, ANNE, retired journalist; b. Rochester, N.Y., Oct. 13, 1913; d. Edward Lyman and Anna Ruth (Johnston) W. BA, Mt. Holyoke Coll., 1935. Press bur. dir. Mt. Holyoke Coll., South Hadley, Mass., 1940-43; news dir. Sta. WIRA, Ft. Pierce, Fla., 1946-61; bur. chief Miami Herald, Ft. Pierce, 1961-80; prof. in journalism Indian River C.C., Ft. Pierce, 1980-87; columnist Miami Herald, Ft. Pierce and Miami, Fla., 1961-91, Ft. Pierce Tribune, Ft. Pierce and Miami, 1991—. Author: Fair and Wilder, 1981. Mem. bd. family self-sufficiency program Ft. Pierce Housing Authority, 1993—; mediator St. Lucie County States Atty. Office, Ft. Pierce, 1991—; bd. dirs. AE (Bean) Backus Art Gallery, Ft. Pierce, 1970—, Sports Hall of Fame, 1992. Lt. (s.g.) USN, 1943-46. Named Woman of Yr., Bus. and Profl. Women's Club, 1961, 73, Dem. Women's Club, 1994, Outstanding Journalist, Ft. Pierce Rotary, 1992; recipient Gold medals for internat. swimming competitions. Democrat. Christian Scientist. Home: 1705 York Ct Fort Pierce FL 34482

WILDER, ELEANOR MARIE (NORA ROBERTS WILDER), writer; b. Washington, Oct. 10, 1950; d. Bernard Edward Robertson and Eleanor Margaret Harris; m. Ronald Eugene Aufdem-Brinke, Aug. 17, 1968 (div. 1985); children: Daniel, Jason; m. Bruce Allen Wilder, July 6, 1985. Grad. high sch., Silver Spring, Md. Legal sec. Wheeler & Korpec, Silver Spring, 1966-68; sec. R&R Lighting, Silver Spring, 1972-75; writer, 1979—. Author: The Heart's Victory, 1982, Golden Medallion, 1982-89 (Rita award 1992), This Magic Moment, 1983, Untamed, 1983, A Matter of Choice, 1984, MacGregor Clan Series, 1985, Hot Ice, 1987, Brazen Virtue, 1988, O'Hurley Series, 1988, Sweet Revenge, 1989, Public Secrets, 1990, Genuine Lies, 1991, Carnal Innocence, 1991, Honest Illusions, 1992, Divine Evil, 1992, Private Scandals, 1993, Hidden Riches, 1994. First inductee Romance Writers of Am. Hall of Fame, 1986; recipient Waldenbooks award, 1985, 86, 88, 91, 92, 94, B. Dalton award, 1990, 91, 92. Mem. Washington Romance Writers, Romance Writers Am., Mystery Writers Am. Democrat. Roman Catholic. Avocations: dancing, reading, films.

WILDER, KAY MARIDEL, home economics educator; b. Seattle, July 23, 1945; d. John and Violet (Precious) Wordsworth; m. Dean B. Wilder, Aug 26, 1967 (div. Mar. 1981); 1 child, Anne Elizabeth. BA, N.W. Nazarene Coll., Idaho, 1967; MS, Simmons Coll., Mass., 1972; EdD, No. Ariz. U., 1986. Tchr. home econs. Fruitland (Idaho) High Sch., 1968, North Quincy High Sch., Quincy, Mass., 1968-72, West Windsor-Plainsboro High Sch., Princeton Junction, N.J., 1972-75, Maple Park Mid. Sch., Kansas City, Mo., 1979-81; instr. William Jewell Coll., Liberty, Mo., 1976-77; prof., chmn. dept. human environ. sci. Point Loma Nazarene Coll., San Diego, 1981—; cons. Fresh Produce Coun. Calif., L.A., 1988-89; seminar speaker Elderhostel, San Diego, 1989-92; chmn. Calif. Home Econs. Articulation Liaison Com., 1990-94; speaker Women's Day seminar, 1994, 95. Author: Season with Love, 1985. Speaker on child abuse Assn. Christian Schs., L.A., 1991, 92, AAUW, Poway, Calif., 1992. Mem. Am. Assn. Family and Consumer Scis., Internat. Fedn. for Home Econs., Calif. Home Econs. Assn. (bd. dirs. San Diego dist. 1988—, pres. 1991-93). Office: Point Loma Nazarene Coll 3900 Lomaland Dr San Diego CA 92106-2810

WILDER-SMITH, PETRA ELFRIDA ERNA BEATE, dentist, educator; b. Chgo., May 16, 1958; d. Arthur Ernest and Beate (Gottwaldt) Wilder-Smith; m. Marc Dale Allmeroth, June 29, 1991. BDS with honors and distinction, London U., 1983; D Med. Dentistry, Bern (Switzerland) U., 1984; LDS, Royal Coll. Surgeons G.B., 1983. Asst. house officer London U., 1983; asst. dental practice Hilterfingen, Hiltesfurger, Switzerland, 1983-85, Bern U., 1983-85; sr. house officer Edinburgh (Scotland) U., 1985-86; sr. asst. Heidelberg (Fed. Republic Germany) U., 1986-90; dir. dental program Beckman Lser Inst., U. Calif., Irvine, 1991—; asst. prof. endodontics Loma Linda U. Dental Sch., Calif., 1993—; cons. in field. Contbr. articles to profl. jours. Recipient Honors and Distinction, Bd. Dental Examiners U.K., 1983, Rsch. prize European Soc. Endodontology, 1987. Mem. ADA, Calif. Dental Assn., Orange County Dental Assn., Internat. Assn. Dental Rsch. Office: U Calif Irvine 1002 Health Scis Rd E Irvine CA 92715

WILDEY, BARBARA ANN, health facility administrator; b. Binghamton, N.Y., Sept. 22, 1940; d. Frederick and Dorothy (Leschorn) Marold; m. James A. Wildey, Sept. 10, 1966; children: J. Dane, Eric E. Grad., Ridley Sch. Bus., 1961. Lic. residential care facility adminstr., Calif. Dental asst. Dr. Kenneth Smith, Binghamton, 1961-67; sr. adminstrv. asst. Outreach, Inc., Lebanon, Pa., 1975-78; asst. to prin. Grace Christian Sch., Myerstown, Pa., 1978-83; owner, mgr. Maid-In-Fresno, Calif., 1984-87; exec. sec. Fresno E.V. Free Ch., 1987-92; sr. facility adminstr. Elim Pl., Fresno, 1992—. Bd. dirs. Fresno/Madera Alzheimers Assn., 1993-94. Home: 2390 Alluvial Ave Clovis CA 93611 Office: Elim Pl 1808 5th St Sanger CA 93657

WILDING, DIANE, marketing, financial and information systems executive; b. Chicago Heights, Ill., Nov. 7, 1942; d. Michael Edward and Katherine Surian; m. Manfred Georg Wilding, May 7, 1975 (div. 1980). BSBA in Acctg. magna cum laude, No. Ill. U., 1963; postgrad., U. Chgo., 1972-74; cert. in German lang., Goethe Inst., Rothenburg, Germany, 1984; cert. in internat. bus. German, Goethe Inst., Atlanta, 1994. Lic. cosmetologist. Systems engr. IBM, Chgo., 1963-68; data processing mgr. Am. Res. Corp., Chgo., 1969-72; system rsch. and devel. project mgr. Continental Bank, Chgo., 1972-75; fin. industry mktg. rep. IBM Can., Ltd., Toronto, Ont., 1976-79; regional telecommunications mktg. exec. Control Data Corp., Atlanta, 1980-84; gen. mgr. The Plant Plant, Atlanta, 1985-92; IBM; sys. engr. IBM, Atlanta, 1993—; pioneer installer on-line Automatic Teller Machines, Pos Equipment. Author: The Canadian Payment System: An International Perspective, 1977. Mem. Chgo. Coun. on Fgn. Rels.; bd. dirs. Easter House Adoption Agy., Chgo., 1974-76. Mem. Internat. Brass Soc., Goethe Inst., Mensa. Clubs: Ponte Verde (Fla.); Royal Ont. Yacht, Libertyville Racquet. Home: 1948 Cobb Pky #28J Smyrna GA 30080

WILDING, MARGARET H., chemist; b. Mobile, Ala., July 31, 1952; d. Adam Augustus and Marjorie June (Beaty) Hayes; m. Randy L. Wilding, July 29, 1978; children: David Nathaniel, Elizabeth Marie, Anna Katherine. BS, Belhave Coll., 1974. Rsch. chemist Miss. Chem. Corp., Yazoo City, 1974-81; technician quality assurance, quality control Niagara Wires, Quincy, Fla., 1990-91; chemist adminstr. Fla. Dept. Bus. & Profl. Regulation, Tallahassee, 1991—. Recipient Davis Productive award Fla. Tax Watch and Ptnrs. Productivity, 1993. Mem. Assn. Racing Commrs. Internat. (mem. chemist adv. com. 1992—). Republican. Presbyterian. Office: Fla Dept Bus and Profl Regulation 1940 N Monroe St Tallahassee FL 32399-1039

WILDISH, KAT, ballerina, choreographer, cultural ambassador; b. Sept. 21; d. Leroy Franklin Wildish; m. Christopher Greene Covell. Grad., Sch. Am. Ballet, N.Y.C. With Ballet Who Inc., N.Y.C.; with Am. Ballet Theatre, Ballett der Deutschen Oper Am Rhein, Eglevsky Ballet Co., Hamburg Ballet, N.Y.C. Ballet, Met. Opera Ballet, La Scala Opera Ballet, Zuerich Opera Ballet, others. Appeared in Apparitions, Brigadoon, Concerto Barocco, Le Corsaire, Cortege Hongrois, Daphnis and Chloé, Dying Swan, Giselle, A Midsummer Night's Dream, The Nutcracker, Rhapsody in Blue, Romeo and Juliet, Serenade, Swan Lake, West Side Story, others; studied with Dick Andros, George Balanchine, Mikhail Baryshnikov, Alexandra Danilova, Agnes De Mille, Placido Domingo, Sir Kenneth MacMillian, Rudolf Nureyev, Franco Zefferelli, Igor Youskovitch, Nicolei Orloff, others. Counselor, speaker, cultural ambassador against child abuse. Recipient Ford Found. Dance scholarships. Office: Ballet Who Inc 344 E 85th St Ste 1B New York NY 10028

WILE, JOAN, composer, lyricist, singer; b. Rochester, N.Y., July 17, 1931; d. Louis and Janet Louise (Wile) Meltzer; children: Ron Wasserman, Diana Wasserman McCloskey. BA, U. Chgo., 1952. Freelance compower, lyricist, singer, mus. book writer. Rec. artist Vanguard Records, 1954; singer Storyville, 1954, The Crystal Palace, 1957; mem. vocal-revue act The Neighbors performances include The Village Vanguard, Le Ruban Bleu, The Bon Soir and The Living Room ; singer, lyricist feature film The Happy Hooker, 1974; singer radio and TV jingles, movie sound tracks, supper clubs, hotels, TV music spls. and variety shows; lyricist, composer mus. Tobacco Road, 1974, Seven Ages of Woman, 1987 (named most promising new musical); writer, producer When They Turned on the Tap at the Watergate, The Truth Come Pourin' Out; lyricist songs for Romper Room, 1983; lyricist, composer, writer People is People, 1983; lyricist, composer script for children's albums for Golden and Peter Pan Records, others; lyricist, composer material in Julius Monk's Upstairs at the Downstairs, 1958; lyricist, composer, performer Nancy's Economic Plan, 1980; lyricist, composer Mothers and Daughters, 1984; lyricist, composer, author The Symposium, 1987; lyricist, composer From There to Here, 1987; writer Rhyme, Women and Song; lyricist, librettist, composer Museum of Natural Sex History, 1992. Organizer Women in Def. Eleanor Roosevelt, N.Y.C., 1989—. Runner-up Am. Song Festival, 1976. Mem. Dramatists Guild, SAG, Theatre Artists Workshop, AFTRA, ASCAP (Popular award 1970-88). Home and Office: 484 W 43rd St Apt 22B New York NY 10036-6326

WILENZICK, PHYLLIS GLASER, educational consultant; b. New Orleans, Mar. 27, 1941; d. Philip Schatz and Doris (Rosenbaum) Glaser; m. Raymond M. Wilenzick, Dec. 22, 1963; children: Marc Brian, Wendy Leigh, Lauren Lynn Wilenzick Sturisky. BA, Newcomb Coll., New Orleans, 1962; MEd, Tulane U., 1975. Cert. elem. tchr., La.; cert. ednl. cons., La. Tchr. 4th grade Orleans Parish Schs., New Orleans, 1963-66; tchr. 3d grade St. Martin's Episcopal Sch., Metairie, La., 1976-77; instr. reading dept. Xavier U., New Orleans, 1977-78; team leader La. State Dept. Edn., Baton Rouge, 1977-79; tchr. ednl. assessment Jefferson Parish Schs., Harvey, La., 1979-88; dir. Learning Assocs., Metairie, La., 1988—; cons. Nat. Assn. Secondary Sch. Prins., Reston, Va., 1984—. Founder, pres. Greater New Orleans Mothers of Twins, 1967; mem. exec. bd. Benjamin Franklin Sr. High Sch., New Orleans, 1980-85. Mem. Internat. Reading Assn. (exec. bd. Jefferson Parish coun. 1979-81), La. Reading Assn., Coun. for Exceptional Children, Children with Attention Deficit Disorders, Orton Dyslexia Soc., Phi Beta Kappa. Republican. Jewish. Home: 229 Jewel St New Orleans LA 70124-2516 Office: Learning Assocs 3349 Ridgelake Dr # 203 Metairie LA 70002-3851

WILES, BETTY JANE, accountant; b. Scott County, Ark., Dec. 21, 1940; d. Edd and Nellie Margaret (Richey) Staggs; m. Ralph A. Wiles, July 18, 1959; children: Ralph A. Jr., Penny Margaret. BBA magna cum laude, Henderson State Coll., 1983. CPA, Ark. Sec. Royalty Holding Co., Oklahoma City, 1959-65, Rector & Eubanks, Mena, Ark., 1966-69; paralegal Shaw & Shaw Attys., Mena, Ark., 1969-83; pvt. practice acctg. Mena, Ark.,

1984—. Cons. adv. bd. Mena H.S., 1985-86; cons. adv. bd. St. John Libr., Rich Mountain C.C., 1987-90, mem. svc. adv. com., 1988-90; mem. bd. trustees Mena Hosp. Com., 1991-95. Mem. AAUW (pres. Mena br. 1993-95), Ark. Soc. CPAs (mem. emergency assistance com., mem. govt. acct. and auditing com. 1993-95), Ouachita Chpt. CPAs (mem. emergency assistance com.), Mena Lioness, Quachita Writer's Guild. Baptist. Club: Mena Lioness. Home: PO Box 522 Mena AR 71953-0522 Office: 513 Mena St Mena AR 71953

WILEY, BONNIE JEAN, journalism educator; b. Portland, Oreg.; d. Myron Eugene and Bonnie Jean (Galliher) W. BA, U. Wash., 1948; MS, Columbia U., 1957; PhD, So. Ill. U., 1965. Mng. editor Yakima (Wash.) Morning Herald; reporter, photographer Portland Oregonian; feature writer Seattle Times; war correspondent PTO AP; western feature editor AP, San Francisco; reporter Yakima Daily Republic; journalism tchr. U. Wash., Seattle, Cen. Wash. U., Ellensburg, U. Hawaii, Honolulu; mem. grad. faculty Bangkok U., Thailand, 1991; mem. faculty journalism program U. Hawaii, Honolulu, 1992—; Adminstr. Am. Samoa Coll., Pago Pago; news features advisor Xinhua News Agy., Beijing. Mem. Women in Communications (Hawaii Headliner award 1985, Nat. Headliner award 1990), Theta Sigma Phi. Home: 1434 Punahou St Apt 722 Honolulu HI 96822-4729

WILEY, HANNAH CHRISTINE, dance educator, choreographer; b. Spokane, Wash., Aug. 21, 1950; d. Owen and Martha M. (Spille) W. BA, U. Wash., 1973; MA, NYU, 1981. Instr. in dance Cornish Inst. Allied Arts, Seattle, 1973-75; dancer, tchr. Ballet Folk Co., Moscow, Idaho, 1975-76; choreographer Empty Space Theatre, Seattle, 1975-77; asst. prof. dance Mt. Holyoke Coll., South Hadley, Mass., 1977-82, assoc. prof., 1982—; vis. prof. dance U. Wash., Seattle, summers 1980-86, assoc. prof., 1982-87, prof., chair of dance, 1987—; artistic dir. Chamber Dance Co., 1990—; artist in resident U. Idaho, Moscow, 1975-76; chairperson Five Coll. Dance Dept., Western Mass., 1982-87; coordinator New Eng. Coll. dance Festival, Amherst, Mass., 1983-84. Choreographer numerous original ballets, 1977—; manuscript reviewer Schirmer Books, N.Y.C., 1983. Mem. Council on Arts and Humanities, South Hadley, 1981-83. Recipient Research Materials award Capezio Ballet Markers and Ballet Internat., 1982; faculty grantee Mt. Holyoke Coll., 1978, 82, 85, faculty fellow, 1980; bd. dirs. Allegro! Performance Support Svcs. Mem. Am. Coll. Dance Festival Assn. (dir. 1983-84), Congress on Research in Dance. Democrat. Unitarian. Office: U Wash Meany Hall Ave # 10 Seattle WA 98195

WILEY, LISA ANN, accountant; b. Elmhurst, Ill., Oct. 14, 1963; d. Neil E. and Marlene (Snearly) W. BA in Econs., U. Calif., Santa Barbara, 1985. CPA; cert. mgmt. acct. Auditor Deloitte & Touche, Oakland, Calif., 1985-90; audit supr. Lindquist & Co., San Ramon, Calif., 1990-91; sole practitioner Walnut Creek, Calif., 1991-92; fin. analyst Discovery Toys, Martinez, Calif., 1992—; auditor Teamsters Alcohol and Drug Rehab. Program, Livermore, Calif., 1991-92. Pres. Youthhomes, Inc., Walnut Creek, 1993; sec. Ewatom, Walnut Creek, 1992. Mem. Inst. Mgmt. Accts., Calif. Soc. CPAs, AICPAs. Home: 1493 Marchbanks Dr 1 Walnut Creek CA 94598 Office: Discovery Toys Inc Ste 400 2530 Arnold Dr Martinez CA 94553

WILEY, LOIS JEAN, artist; b. West Mifflin, Pa., Sept. 17, 1928; d. Avery Lysle and Cordelia (Thompson) Vice; m. Roger P. Wiley, June 12, 1950; children: Roger P., Jr., Lee A. BA, Allegheny Coll., 1950; MFA, Edinboro U. of Pa., 1979. Tchr. bus. edn. Phila. Pub. Schs., 1959-61, Ft. LeBoeuf Sch. Dist., Waterford, Pa., 1961-89; artist L. Wiley Originals, Waterford, 1968—; art reviewer Showcase Times Pub. Co.; art juror of selection and awards at local art shows, Frie and Waterford, 1990—. Mem. Nat. Assn. Women Artists, N.W. Pa. Artists Assn. (publicity chmn. 1978-80). Home and Office: PO Box 816 917 High St Waterford PA 16441

WILEY, MARY O'LEARY, psychologist; b. Saint Paul, Minn., May 2, 1954; d. James Michael and Patricia (McCann) O'L.; m. Francis Russell Wiley, May 28, 1977; children: Jordan, Justin, Erica. BS, Pa. State U., 1976; MA, U. Md., 1979, PhD, 1982. Lic. psychologist. Psychologist, counseling ctr. Ithaca (N.Y.) Coll., 1982-85, dir. counseling ctr., 1985-88; staff psychologist U. Md., College Park, 1988-89; pvt. practice Gaithersburg, Md., 1989—. Mem. editorial bd. Profl. Psychology: Rsch. and Practice, 1992-94; contbr. articles to profl. jours. Recipient Outstanding Young Profl. award Am. Coll. Pers. Assn., 1986. Mem. Am. Psychol. Assn. (chair divsn. 17 ind. practice com. 1993-94), Adoption Therapy Coalition (pres. 1994—), Md. Psychol. Assn. Roman Catholic. Home: 12006 Clover Knoll Ct North Potomac MD 20878-2328 Office: 963 Russell Ave # D Gaithersburg MD 20879-3287

WILEY, MILLICENT YODER, retired secondary school educator, realtor; b. Mercedes, Tex., June 7, 1923; d. Frank and Grace Mae (Setter) Yoder; m. William Gregory Wiley, Mar. 25, 1946; children: Sandra Kay Wiley, Patti Gayle Wiley Diamond. BS, Tex. State Coll. Women, 1949; postgrad. U. Houston, 1950-53. Choral dir., music tchr. schs. in Tex. and La., 1945-60; tchr. Kingsville (Tex.) Ind. Sch. Dist., 1960-80, trustee 1981-87; choral dir. H.M. King High Sch., 1964-80, ret., 1980; area admissions adv., adminstr. Pacific Am. Inst., 1976-80; state dir. South Tex. for Am. Internat. Edn. and Tng., 1980-83; Tex. rep. Internat. Travel Study, Inc., 1983-90; adminstr. Travel Selections, 1990-94; pianist Kingsville Rotary Club, 1966—. Bd. dirs. Kingsville chpt. Am. Heart Assn., Community Concerts Assn., Helen Kleberg Community Ctr., 1994—, Kingsville Action Com.; adjudicator Tex. Choral Contests; mem. Tex. All-State Alumni Bd., 1995; active Mayor's City Com., Mayor's Future Com. Recipient various certs. appreciation. Mem. NEA, Am. Sch. Bd. Assn. (trustee 1980-87), Am. Choral Dirs. Assn., Music Educators Nat. Conf., Tex. Assn. Sch. Bds. (trustee 1980-87), Tex. Music Educators Assn. (dir. 1973-74), Tex. Choral Dirs. Assn. (state clinic condr. 1977), Tex. State Tchrs. Assn., Tex. Music Adjudicators Assn., Kingsville Bd. Realtors (bd. dirs. 1994-95), Tex. Assn. Realtors, Multiple Listing Service Kingsville, Nat. Bd. Realtors, Fgn. Study League (adv., adminstr. 1971-76), Music Club of Kingsville (pres. 1982-84, 3rd v.p. 1987-91), Nat. Ret. Tchrs. Assn., Kingsville Ret. Tchrs. Assn. (sec. 1986-88, 2nd v.p. 1988-89, 1st v.p. 1989-91), Tri-City Ret. Tchrs. (sec.), Kingsville C. of C., 36th Div. Assn. (1st v.p. nat. ladies aux. 1989-90, pres. 1990-91), Women's Club Kingsville, (chmn. As You Like It dept. 1988-90, 1st vice chmn. 1992-94), General Women's Club of Kingsville (parliamentarian 1992-94, pres. 1994—), Exxon Annuitant Club (bd. dirs. 1992-94), Rotary (pianist 1966—, 1st Woman mem. 1987—, past social chmn., program chmn., membership chmn. 1993-94, chmn. membership devel. com. 1994—), Kiwanis (pianist Kingsville club 1985—), Exxon Bridge Club, Monday Night Bridge Club, Kingsville Country Club. Republican. Methodist. Home: 229 Helen Marie Ln Kingsville TX 78363-7305

WILEY, MYRA, nurse counselor; b. Lexington, Ala., Jan. 20, 1938; d. Joseph Aaron and Annie Lura (Putnam) Haraway; m. Robert Harold Wiley, Sept. 17, 1960; children: Sonya, Robert, Marie. BSN, U. Ala., Huntsville, 1989. RN, Ala. Nursing asst., night-weekend coord. Upjohn Health Care, Huntsville, 1983-87; nursing asst. North Ala. Rehab. Hosp., Huntsville, 1987-89; staff nurse Humana Hosp., Huntsville, 1989-91; staff nurse counselor Bradford-Parkside, Madison, Ala., 1991—. Mem. ANA, Ala. State Nurses Assn., Madison County Nurses Assn. Baptist.

WILFONG, BRENDA ANN, telecommunications executive; b. Ashland, Ohio, Jan. 2, 1963; d. Edward Eugene and Barbara Ann (Butterfield) Bush; m. Duane Hubert Wilfong, Oct. 22, 1984 (dec. Sept. 1994); children: Jessie Leona, Christina Elizabeth. BBA, Kent State U., 1989. Asst. editor Ohio dir. Harris Pub. Co., Twinsburg, Ohio, 1983-84; accounts payable clerk M. O'Neil's Co., Akron, Ohio, 1984-85; network mgmt. asst. Alltel Corp., Hudson, Ohio, 1985-86, treasury asst., 1986-87, assoc. analyst treasury, 1987-92, carrier svcs. coord., 1992-93; sr. staff asst. Alltel Corp., Twinsburg, 1993-94, adminstr. carrier svcs., 1994—. Recipient Brownie Mother Vol. award Girl Scouts Am., Akron, 1994. Mem. Inst. Mgmt. Accts. (editor newsletter 1990-92, dir. ins. 1992-94). Baptist. Home: 1630 Goodyear Blvd Akron OH 44305 Office: Alltel Corp 2000 Highland Rd Twinsburg OH 44087

WILFORD, BONNIE BAIRD, health policy specialist; b. Chgo., Jan. 11, 1946; d. George Martin and Ruth Eleanor (Anderson) Baird; m. David Edward Wilford, Oct. 2, 1967; children: Heather Lynn, Edward Baird. BA, Knox Coll., 1967; postgrad., Roosevelt U., 1969-71. Staff assoc. Am. Hosp. Assn., Chgo., 1967-70; mgr. plan devel. Blue Cross & Blue Shield Assn., Chgo., 1970-79; dir. dept. substance abuse AMA, Chgo., 1979-91, dir. clin. sci., 1988-91; ptnr. Wilford & Assocs., healthcare consultants, 1991—; dir. Ctr. Continuing Edn. Substance Abuse, Chgo., 1990—; cons. Office Nat. Drug Control Policy, The White House, 1991-92; cons. Pres.'s Commn. on Model State Drug Laws, 1993-94; dir. Pharm. Policy Rsch. Ctr., Intergovtl. Health Policy Project, George Washington U., Washington, 1992—. Author: Handbook on Alcohol and Drug Abuse, 1991, Drug Abuse: A Guide for the Primary Care Physician, 1981; editor: Principles of Addiction Medicine, 1994, Balancing the Response to Prescription Drug Abuse, 1990; contbr. articles to profl. jours. Chair subcom. continuing med. edn. Physicians Consortium on Med. Edn. in Substance Abuse, Rockville, Md., 1987-91; coord. Community Drug Prevention Programs, Ill., 1988-91. Recipient Outstanding Svc. award Fla. Task Force on Alcohol and Drug Abuse, 1986, Merit award State of Mo., 1985. Mem. APHA, Internat. Narcotic Enforcement Officers Assn. (Award of Honor 1985), Assn. for Med. Edn. and Rsch. Substance Abuse, Nat. Drug Treatment Consortium, Informal Steering Com. Prescription Drug Abuse (bd. dirs.). Office: IHPP/George WashingtonU 2021 K St NW Ste 800 Washington DC 20006

WILHELM, KATE (KATY GERTRUDE), author; b. Toledo, June 8, 1928; d. Jesse Thomas and Ann (McDowell) Meredith; m. Joseph B. Wilhelm, May 24, 1947 (div. 1962); children: Douglas, Richard; m. Damon Knight, Feb. 23, 1963; 1 child, Jonathan. Writer, 1956—; co-dir. Milford Sci. Fiction Writers Conf., 1963-76; lectr. Clarion Fantasy Workshop, Mich. State U., from 1968. Author: (novels) More Bitter Than Death, 1962, (with Theodore L. Thomas) The Clone, 1965, The Nevermore Affair, 1966, The Killer Thing, 1967, Let the Fire Fall, 1969, (with Theodore L. Thomas) The Year of the Cloud, 1970, Abyss: Two Novellas, 1971, Margaret and I, 1971, City of Cain, 1971, The Clewiston Test, 1976, Where Late the Sweet Birds Sang, 1976, Fault Lines, 1976, Somerset Dreams and Other Fictions, 1978, Juniper Time, 1979, (with Damon Knight) Better Than One, 1980, A Sense of Shadow, 1981, Listen, Listen, 1981, Oh! Susannah, 1982, Welcome Chaos, 1983, Huysman's Pets, 1986, (with R. Wilhelm) The Hills Are Dancing, 1986, The Hamlet Trap, 1987, Crazy Time, 1988, Dark Door, 1988, Smart House, 1989, Children of the Wind: Five Novellas, 1989, Cambio Bay, 1990, Sweet, Sweet Poison, 1990, Death Qualified, 1991, And the Angels Sing, 1992, Seven Kinds of Death, 1992, Naming the Flowers, 1992, Justice for Some, 1993, The Best Defense, 1994, (multimedia space fantasy) Axoltl, U. Oreg. Art Mus., 1979, (radio play) The Hindenburg Effect, 1985; editor: Nebula Award Stories #9, 1974, Clarion SF, 1976; contbr. short stories to anthologies and periodicals. Mem. PEN, Nat. Writers Union, Mystery Writers Am., Sci. Fiction Writers Am., Authors Guild. Address: 1645 Horn Ln Eugene OR 97404-2957

WILHELM, MARILYN, private school administrator. Founder-dir. The Wilhelm Sch., Houston. Office: The Wilhelm Sch 3003 Richmond Ave Houston TX 77027-6839

WILHELM, SUSAN A., legislative staff director; b. Flint, Mich., Sept. 3, 1955. BA in Pol. Sci., U. Mich., 1976. Legis. aide Rep. Dale E. Kildee, 1977-85; staff dir. subcom. on human resources, 1985—. Office: Subcom Elementary Sec & Voc Edn B-345A Rayburn House Office Bldg Washington DC 20515*

WILHELMI, MARY CHARLOTTE, education educator, university administrator; b. Williamsburg, Iowa, Oct. 2, 1928; d. Charles E. and Loretto (Judge) Harris; m. Sylvester Lee Wilhelmi, May 26, 1951; children: Theresa Ann, Sylvia Marie, Thomas Lee, Kathryn Lyn, Nancy Louise. BS, Iowa State U., 1950; MA in Edn., Va. Poly. Inst. and State U., 1973, cert. advanced grad. studies, 1978. Edn. coord. Nova Ctr. U. Va., Falls Church, 1969-73; asst. adminstr. Consortium for Continuing Higher Edn. George Mason U., Fairfax, Va., 1973-78; adminstr., asst. prof. George Mason U., Fairfax, 1978-83; dir. coll. rels. and devel., assoc. prof. No. Va. C.C., Annandale, 1983—; bd. dirs. No. Va. C.C. Ednl. Found., Inc., Annandale, 1984—, Fairfax (Va.) Symphony, 1995—; vice chmn. Health Systems Agy. No. Va., Fairfax; mem. George Mason U. Inst. for Ednl. Transformation. Edtl. bd. Va. Forum, 1990-93; contbr. articles to profl. jours. Bd. dirs. Fairfax County ARC, 1981-86, Va. Commonwealth U. Ctr. on Aging, Richmond, 1978—, Fairfax Com. of 100, 1986-88, 90—, Hospice No. Va., 1983-88, No. Va. Mental Health Inst., Fairfax County, 1978-81, Fairfax Profl. Women's Network, 1981—, Arts Coun. Fairfax County, 1989—; mem. supt. adv. coun. Fairfax County Pub. Schs., 1974-86, No. Va. Press Club, 1978—; mem. Va. Forum Editl. Bd., 1990-93. Named Falls Church Bus. and Profl. Women's Group Bus. Woman of the Yr., 1993; recipient Woman of Distinction award Soroptomists Internat. of Fairfax, 1988. Mem. State Coun. Higher Edn. Va. (pub. affairs adv. com. 1985—), Greater Washington Bd. Trade, Fairfax County C. of C. (legis. affairs com. 1984—, Va. Women Lobbyists, 1991—, Leadership Fairfax Class 1992), No. Va. Bus. Roundtable, Internat. Platform Assn., Phi Delta Kappa (10-Yr. Continuous Svc. award 1991), Kappa Delta Alumni No. Va., Psi Chi, Phi Kappa Phi. Roman Catholic. Home: 4902 Ravensworth Rd Annandale VA 22003-5552 Office: No Va Community Coll 4001 Wakefield Chapel Rd Annandale VA 22003-3744

WILK, DIANE LILLIAN, architect, educator; b. L.A., July 14, 1955; d. Stefan Piotr and Wanda Helen (Harasimowicz) W. BS in Architecture, U. So. Calif., 1977; MArch, Yale U., 1981; postgrad., Stanford U., 1981-82. Registered architect, Calif., Colo.; cert. Nat. Coun. Archtl. Registration Bds. Project designer Daniel, Mann, Johnson & Mendenhall, L.A., 1981, Boyd Jenks Architect, Palo Alto, Calif., 1982-84; project arch. HED Architects, Redwood City, Calif., 1984-86; asst. prof. architecture U. Colo., Denver, 1986—, assoc. dir. architecture program, 1991-92. Contbg. author: The Avant Garde and The Landscape, 1991; editor: Avant Garde; contbr. articles to profl. jours. Cellist Redwood Symphony, Redwood City, 1982-85. Recipient faculty rsch. award U. Colo. Sch. Architecture, 1988, 92; grantee Graham Found., 1989. Mem. AIA, Soc. Archtl. Historians, Tau Sigma Delta (award student chpt. 1990), Alpha Rho Chi, Alpha Lambda Delta. Office: U Colo Campus Box 126 PO Box 173364 Denver CO 80217

WILKE MONTEMAYOR, JOANNE MARIE, patient care coordinator; b. Jerome, Ariz., Sept. 10, 1941; d. Karl Nickolas and Anna Linda (Worgt) Wilke; m. Casimiro L. Montemayor, Oct. 8, 1978. BS in Nursing, U. Colo., 1965; M in Nursing, U. Washington, 1974. Patient care coord. Vesper Hospice, San Leandro, Calif., 1989—. With USNR, 1959-79. Mem. Nat. Hospice Orgn. Democrat. Methodist.

WILKEN, CLAUDIA ANN, judge; b. Mpls., Aug. 17, 1949; d. Claudius W. and Dolores Ann (Grass) W.; m. John M. True, 1984; 1 child, Peter Wilken True. BA with honors, Stanford U., 1971; JD, U. Calif., Berkeley, 1975. Bar: Calif. 1975, U.S. Dist. Ct. (no. dist.) Calif. 1975, U.S. Ct. Appeals (9th cir.) 1976, U.S. Supreme Ct. 1981. Asst. fed. pub. defender U.S. Dist. Ct. (no. dist.) Calif., San Francisco, 1975-78, U.S. magistrate judge, 1983-93, dist. judge, 1993—; ptnr. Wilkin & Leverett, Berkeley, Calif., 1978-84; adj. prof. U. Calif., Berkeley, 1978-84; prof. New Coll. Sch. Law, 1980-85; mem. jud. br. com. Jud. Conf. U.S.; mem. edn. com. Fed. Jud. Ctr. Magistrate Judges, 9th Cir. Magistrate Judges; chair 9th cir. Magistrates Conf., 1987-88. Mem. ABA (mem. jud. adminstrn. divsn.), Calif. State Bar Assn., Alameda County Bar Assn. (judge's membership), Fed. Magistrates Judges Assn. (sec.), Nat. Assn. Women Judges, Order of Coif, Phi Beta Kappa. Office: US Dist Ct No Dist PO Box 36060 450 Golden Gate Ave San Francisco CA 94102*

WILKENING, LAUREL LYNN, university official, planetary scientist; b. Richland, Wash., Nov. 23, 1944; d. Marvin Hubert and Ruby Alma (Barks) W.; m. Godfrey Theodore Sill, May 18, 1974. BA, Reed Coll., 1966; PhD, U. Calif., San Diego, 1970. Asst. prof. to assoc. prof. U. Ariz., Tucson, 1973-80, dir. Lunar and Planetary Lab., head planetary scis., 1981-83, vice provost, prof. planetary scis., 1983-85, v.p. rsch., dean Grad. Coll., 1985-88; div. scientist NASA Hdqrs., Washington, 1980; prof. geol scis., adj. prof. astronomy, provost U. Washington, Seattle, 1988-93; chancellor U. Calif., Irvine, 1993—; dir. Seagate Tech., Inc., 1993—, Rsch. Corp., 1991—; vice chmn. Nat. Commn. on Space, Washington, 1984-86, Adv. Com. on the Future of U.S. Space Program, 1990; chair Space Policy Adv. Bd., Nat. Space Coun., 1991-92; co-chmn. primitive bodies mission study team NASA/European Space Agy., 1984-85; chmn. com. rendezvous sci. working group NASA, 1983-85; mem. panel on internat. cooperation and competition in space Congl. Office Tech. Assessment, 1982-83. Author: (monograph) Particle Track Studies and the Origin of Gas-Rich Meteorites, 1971; editor: Comets, 1982. U. Calif. Regents fellow, 1966-67; NASA trainee, 1967-70. Fellow Meteoritical Soc. (councilor 1976-80), Am. Assn. Advanced Sci.; mem. Am. Astron. Soc. (chmn. div. planetary scis. 1984-85), Am. Geophys. Union, AAAS, Planetary Soc. (dir. 1994—), Phi Beta Kappa. Democrat. Office: U Calif Chancellors Office 501 Adminstrn Bldg Irvine CA 92717

WILKERSON, ISABEL, journalist. With The N.Y. Times, N.Y.C.; now bureau chief The N.Y. Times, Chgo. Bureau, Chgo. Recipient Pulitzer Prize for feature writing, 1994. Office: The New York Times Chicago Bureau 122 S Michigan Ave Ste 1916 Chicago IL 60603*

WILKERSON, PINKIE CAROLYN, state legislator, lawyer; b. L.A., Feb. 8, 1948; d. Calvin and Dora (Garner) W.; 1 child, John David Barabin Jr. BA cum laude, Grambling (La.) State U., 1968; MA with honors, Ohio U., 1971; JD with honors, So. U., 1979; LLM, Tulane U., 1989. Bar: La., N.Y., U.S. Tax Ct., U.S. Supreme Ct. Asst. dist. counsel IRS, L.A.; asst. prof. law So. U. Sch. Law, Baton Rouge; asst. atty. gen. La. Dept. Justice, Baton Rouge; with Merrill Lynch, Pierce, Fenner & Smith, N.Y.C.; asst. dist. atty. for Lincoln and Union Parishes, 3d Jud. Dist., La.; pvt. practice, Grambling; mem. La. Ho. of Reps., Baton Rouge, 1992—. Mem. So. U. Law Rev., 1978-79. Mem. adv. bd. Grambling State U.; bd. dirs. Phillips Sch. Theology, Atlanta; past pres. United League Voters; past v.p. Ruston-Grambling LWV. Named to Hall of Fame, Grambling State U., 1993; recipient Significant Achievement award Ohio U., 1994. Mem. Nat. Bar Assn. (bd. dirs. 1985-89), La. Bar, N.Y. State Bar Assn., Grambling State U. Alumni Assn. (life), So. U. Alumni Assn. (life), Delta Sigma Theta. Democrat. Methodist. Home: 611 E Grand Ave Grambling LA 71245 Office: PO Box 893 Grambling LA 71245

WILKERSON, RITA LYNN, special education educator, consultant; b. Crescent, Okla., Apr. 22; Mem. ASCD, Coun. for Exceptional Children, OARC, OACLD, Phi Delta Kappa, Kappa Delta Pi. BA, Cen. State U., Edmond, Okla., 1963; MEd, Cen. State U., 1969; postgrad., U. Okla., 1975. Elem. tchr. music Hillsdale (Okla.) Pub. Sch., 1963-64; jr. high sch. music and spl. edn. Okarche (Okla.) Pub. Sch., 1965-71; cons. Title III Project, Woodward, Okla., 1971-72; dir. Regional Edn. Svc. Ctr., Guymon, Okla., 1972-81; dir., psychologist Project W.O.R.K., Guymon, 1981-90; tchr. behavioral disorders Unified Sch. Dist. 480, Liberal, Kans., 1990—; sch. psychologist Hardesty (Okla.) Schs., 1994; cons. Optima (Okla.) Pub. Schs., 1990, Felt (Okla.) Pub. Schs., 1990, Texhoma (Okla.) Schs., 1994; spl. edn. cons. Optima Pub. Schs., 1992—, Goodwell (Okla.) Pub. Schs., 1992—; diagnostician Tyrone (Okla.) Pub. Shcs., 1992—; home svcs. provider Dept. Human Svcs., Guymon, 1990; active Kans. Dept. Social and Rehab. Svcs., 1993—. Grantee Cen. State U., 1968-69, Oklahoma City Dept. Edn., 1988-89. Mem. ASCD, NAFE, NEA (liberal Kans. chpt.), Coun. Exceptional Children, Okla. Assn. Retarded Citizens, Okla. Assn. for Children with Learning Disabilities, Phi Delta Kappa. Republican. Home: 616 N Crumley St Guymon OK 73942-4341 Office: Unified Sch Dist 480 7th And Western Liberal KS 67901

WILKEY, MARY HUFF, investor, writer, publisher; b. Dayton, Ohio, Sept. 30, 1940; d. Charles Joseph and Frances Rose (Wintersteen) Huff; divorced; children: Christopher Tyson, Charles Cory, Jennifer Jo. Student, Sinclair C.C., Dayton, 1979-85. Pvt. sec. Dare, Inc., Troy, Ohio, 1962-63; legal sec. Smith & Schnacke, Dayton, 1963-68; adminstrv. asst. U.S. Magistrate, Dayton, 1971-74; legal technician Coolidge, Wall, Womsley & Lombard Co., L.P.A., Dayton, 1968-75, 81-85, Lair & Owen, Dayton, 1979-81; owner, operator Village Mill Country Store, Tipp City, Ohio, 1987-88; owner, mgr. Happy Days Hotel, Franklin, Ohio, 1989—; pres., owner KSL Enterprises, Franklin, Ohio, 1988—. Author, pub.: (directory) Your Personal Guide, 1988, 89. Phone support vol. Operation Golden Ring, Dayton, 1984-85; vol. Sta. WPTD Pub. TV, Dayton, 1983-85. Mem. NAFE, Internat. Platform Assn., Greater Dayton Real Estate Investor Assn. Office: PO Box 854 Franklin OH 45005

WILKIE, KIMBERLY ANN, podiatrist; b. Portland, Maine, Sept. 13, 1962; d. William Louis and Eleanor Jane (Myers) W. BS in Biology, Pa. State U., 1983; D in Podiatric Medicine, Pa. Coll. Podiatric Medicine, Phila., 1988. Diplomate Am. Bd. Podiatric Orthopedics. Preceptor Contemporary Footcare, Arlington, Mass., 1988-89; resident North Phila. Health Systems, 1990-91; assoc. podiatrist Abington Foot Surg. Assn., Glenside, Pa., 1989—; sec. podiatric divsn. Abington Meml. Hosp., 1991—, women's lead group, 1991—. Mem. Am. Podiatric Med. Assn., Pa. Podiatric Med. Assn. (del. 1988—), Soroptomists. Office: Abington Foot Surg Assn Ste E 2701 Blair Mill Rd Glenside PA 19038

WILKINS, BRENDA MARIE, controller; b. St. Johnsbury, Vt., June 30, 1959; d. Kenneth Edwin and Georgette Marie (Royer) W. A in Acctg., Champlain Coll., 1979; postgrad., Lyndon State Coll., C.C. Vt., 1985—. Staff acct. Barry A. McCormick, CPA, St. Johnsbury, 1979-81; fin. analyst Fairbanks Weighing Divsn. Colt Industries, St. Johnsbury, 1981-88; fin. analyst The Savers Bank, Littleton, N.H., 1988-89, Hanover, N.H., 1990; asst. contr. Passumpsic Savings Bank, St. Johnsbury, 1990-91, contr., 1992—; town auditor Town of St. Johnsbury, 1988—. Named Young Careerist of Yr. by Bus. and Profl. Womens Club, 1988. Roman Catholic. Office: Passumpsic Savings Bank 124 Railroad St Saint Johnsbury VT 05819

WILKINS, CAROLINE HANKE, consumer agency administrator, political worker; b. Corpus Christi, Tex., May 12, 1937; d. Louis Allen and Jean Guckian Hanke; m. B. Hughel Wilkins, 1957; 1 child, Brian Hughel. Student, Tex. Coll. Arts and Industries, 1956-57, Tex. Tech. U., 1957-58; BA, U. Tex., 1961; MA magna cum laude, U. Ams., 1964. Instr. history Oreg. State U., 1967-68; adminstr. Consumer Svcs. divsn. State of Oreg., 1977-80, Wilkins Assoc., 1980—; mem. PFMC Salmon Adv. subpanel, 1982-86. Author: (with B. H. Wilkins) Implications of the U.S.-Mexican Water Treaty for Interregional Water Transfer, 1968. Dem. precinct committeewoman, Benton County, Oreg., 1964-90; publicity chmn. Benton County Gen. Election, 1964; chmn. Get-Out-the-Vote Com., Benton County, 1966; vice chmn. Benton County Dem. Cen. Com., 1966-70; vice chmn. 1st Congl. Dist., Oreg., 1966-68, chmn. 1968; vice chmn. Dem. Party Oreg., 1968-69, chmn. 1969-74; mem. exec. com. Western States Dem. Conf., 1970-72; vice chmn. Dem. Nat. Com., 1972-77, mem. arrangements com., 1972, 76, mem. Dem. charter commn., 1973-74; mem. Dem. Nat. Com., 1972-77, 85-89, mem. size and composition com., 1987-89, rules com. 1988; mem. Oreg. Govt. Ethics Commn., 1974-76; del., mem. rules com. Dem. Nat. Conv., 1988; 1st v.p. Nat. Fedn. Dem. Women, 1983-85, pres., 1985-87, parliamentarian, 1993—; mem. Kerr Libr. bd. Oreg. State U., 1989—, pres., 1994—, Corvallis-Benton County Libr. Found., 1991—, sec., 1993, v.p., 1994—. Named Outstanding Mem., Nat. Fedn. Dem. Women, 1992. Mem. Nat. Assn. Consumer Agy. Adminstrs., Soc. Consumer Affairs Profls., Oreg. State U. Folk Club (pres. faculty wives 1989-90), Zonta (vice area bd. dirs. dist. 8 1992-94, area dir., bd. dist. 8 1994—). Office: 3311 NW Roosevelt Dr Corvallis OR 97330-1169

WILKINS, JOSETTA EDWARDS, state representative; b. Little Rock, July 17, 1932; d. James Wesley and Laura Birdgette (Freeman) Edwards; m. Henry Wilkins III, Oct. 30, 1954 (dec.); children: Calvin Tyrone, Henry IV, Cassandra Felecia, Mark Reginald, Angela Juanita. BS, A.M. & N Coll., 1961; MEd, U. Ark., 1967; EdD, Okla. State U., 1987. Lic. counselor, Ark. Dep. dir. manpower tng. Ark. Coun./Farmer Workers, Little Rock, 1967-73; dir. cooperative edn. U. Ark., Pine Bluff, 1973-85, interim dir. univ. rels. and devel., 1987-88, assoc. prof., 1988—, prof. edn.; tchr. elem. Lincoln Sch. Dist., Star City, Ark., 1961-63; high sch. counselor Dollarway Pub. Sch. Dist., Pine Bluff, 1963-66; tchr. elem. Pitts. Pub. Schs., 1966-67; rehab. counselor State of Ark., Pine Bluff, 1967-69. Campaign mgr. senatorial race Edwards, Pine Bluff, 1988; sec. Mayor's Bi-Racial Coun., Pine Bluff, 1973, Comprehensive Health Care Jefferson County, Pine Bluff, 1973; rep. S.E. Ark. Health Systems Agy., 1975-85; pres. PTA Merrill High Sch., Pine Bluff, 1971; elected mem. Ho. of Reps., 1991; bd. dirs. Ptnrs. for a Better Pine Bluff; co-chair Dollarway Drug Adv. Coun.; active Wesley Found., Ark. Dem. Com., Jefferson County Juvenile Detention Commn., episcopacy com. United Meth. Ch., others. State of Ark. fellow, 1985. Mem. Nat. Assn. Tchr. Educators, Am. Assn. for Adult and Continuing Edn., Coop. Edn.

Assn., Ark. Tchrs. Assn., Am. Assn. for Counseling and Devel., Ark. Assn. for Counseling Guidance and Devel., Ark. Personnel and Guidance Assn., Sorority Pub. Svc. Orgn., Delta Sigma Theta. Methodist. Home: 303 N Maple St Pine Bluff AR 71601-3346*

WILKINS, RITA DENISE, researcher, multimedia design consultant; b. Detroit, June 21, 1951; d. William H. and Alice L. (Hayes) Smith. Student, George Peabody Coll., 1969-70, Cleveland (Tenn.) State Community Coll., 1973-75, Vanderbilt U. Mgmt. coord., legal coord. Arlen Realty and Devel. Corp., Chattanooga, Tenn., 1973-76; asst. v.p., office mgr. Newburger Andes & Co., Atlanta, 1976-78, asst. v.p., project mgr., 1978-79; project mgr. Robinson-Humphrey, Atlanta, 1979-80; dept. head Office Properties Group Merrill Lynch Realty Comml. Svcs., Atlanta, 1980-83; acquisition devel. mgmt. rep. Cardinal Industries, Inc., Atlanta, 1983-86; pres., sr. cons. CPC/Foresite, Charleston, S.C., 1986—; guest lectr. Ga. State U. Contbr. articles to profl. jours. Mem. Indsl. Devel. Rsch. Coun. (devel. and edn. coms.), S.C. Real Estate Broker, S.C. Econ. Developers Assn., Am. Real Estate Soc., Comml. Real Estate Women of Ga. (founder), Charleston World Trade Ctr. (steering com., growth strategy sub-cm., facility sub-com.), Comml. Real Estate Women, Goodlettsville C. of C. (econ. devel. com.). Office: CPC/Foresite 115 Dorris Ave Goodlettsville TN 37072

WILKINS, SHARIE LEE, pilot; b. Rapid City, S.D., Dec. 2, 1962; d. William Adrian and Carolyn Gene (Habben) Taylor; m. R. Steven Wilkins, July 6, 1985; children: Levi Scott, Jake Steven. Student, Ctrl. State U., 1981, 82, 83, 84, Okla. State U., 1981-83; AAS in Aviation, Rose State Coll., 1992. Instr. Jazzercise Inc., Edmond, Okla., 1985-92; owner Oxford Pointe Jazzercise Ctr., Edmond, 1989-92; aviation tutor Rose State Coll., Midwest City, Okla., 1991-92; ground instr./instrument Bus. Air, Bethany, Okla., 1992; flight instr. Crabtree Sch. Aeronautics, Guthrie, Okla., 1992-94, S.W. Air, Wiley Post Airport, Bethany, 1994-95; pilot Travel Lear Charter Svc., Wiley Post Airport, Bethany, 1994-95, Wal-Mart Aviation, 1995—. Coord. benefit for Hope Ctr., Edmond, 1990; booth chmn. Jazzercise Student Conv., Oklahoma City, 1992. Recipient Cash award Women in Bus., 1989. Mem. Engrs. Flying Club (sec. 1994—), Alpha Chi Omega, Phi Theta Kappa, Delta Upsilon. Republican. Home: 5500 E 2nd St Edmond OK 73034

WILKINS, SHEILA SCANLON, management consultant; b. Oakland, Calif., Sept. 23, 1936; d. Michael Joseph and Joan (Daly) Scanlon; m. Thomas Wayne Wilkins, Aug. 14, 1965; children: Mary, John, Kathleen. BMusic, AB Liberal Arts maxima cum laude, Holy Names Coll., Oakland, 1958, MA in Music, 1972; MA in Ednl. Adminstrn., St. Mary's Coll., Moraga, Calif., 1983. Cert. tchr., Calif.; cert. in human resources mgmt., human resources tng. and devel. Tchr., dir. student activities Vallejo (Calif.) Unified Sch. Dist., 1962-63; tchr. Berkeley (Calif.) Unified Sch. Dist., 1963-66; pub. rels. asst. Alta Bates Hosp., Berkeley, 1973-74; tchr., adminstr. Walnut Creek (Calif.) Sch. Dist., 1974-80; dist. tchg. Moraga Sch. Dist., 1980-83; tech. tng. adminstr. Crocker Nat. Bank, Walnut Creek, Calif., 1984-85; tng. officer Wells Fargo Bank, Concord, Calif., 1985-86; tng. mgr. Fab 3 Intel Corp, Livermore, Calif., 1986-91; orgn. cons. CIS ops. Intel Corp, Folsom, Calif., 1991-92; mgr. profl. devel. corp. edn. Intel Corp, Santa Clara, Calif., 1992-94; prin. The Wilkins Group, Walnut Creek, Calif., 1994—. Contbr. articles to profl. jours. Chair parent com. Boy Scouts Am., Concord, 1977-80; pres. Parents Club of St. Francis Sch., Concord, 1978-79; v.p. Parents Club of Carondelet High Sch., Concord, 1983-84. Mem. ASTD, Nat. Soc. Performance and Instrn. (v.p. fin. 1988-89, pres. 1989-91), No. Calif. Human Resources Coun., Inst. Mgmt. Cons. Home: 2182 Gill Port Ln Walnut Creek CA 94598-1150 Office: 712 Bancroft Rd Ste 250 Walnut Creek CA 94598

WILKINSON, ANNE THÉRÈSE, lawyer, state official; b. Ayer, Mass., Dec. 17, 1958; d. George Albert Jr. and Mary Anne (Reilly) W.; m. Shrin Rajagopalan, Aug. 23, 1986; children: Nina, Sheila. BA, U. Md., 1980; JD, Duke U., 1986. Rsch. asst. N.C. Supreme Ct., Raleigh, 1986-87, U.S. Dist. Ct., Durham, N.C., 1990-92; asst. legal counsel Office of the Gov., Raleigh, 1987-89, assoc. gen. counsel, 1992-93; vol. Vol. Income Tax Assistance, Durham, 1986; rsch. asst. Duke Ctr. for Health Law Policy and Edn., Durham, 1985; co-chair Dean's Adv. Coun., Durham, 1984-86. Block leader Sunshares Recycling Program, Durham, 1990-93; vol. Raleigh Nursery Sch., 1993, Soc. St. Andrew, N.C., 1993. Recipient Goddard medal U. Md. Alumni Assn., 1980, others. Mem. N.C. State Bar, D.C. Bar, San Diego County Jr. League, Las Madres, Kappa Alpha Theta (chair adv. bd. 1987-93). Home: 1228 Lupine Hills Dr Vista CA 92083

WILKINSON, CYTHIA MARIE, federal and state government lawyer; b. Galveston, Tex., July 30, 1948; d. Covy Ceard Sr. and Frances (Anselmo) W. BA, Lamar U., 1970; JD with honors, Potomac Sch. Law, 1981. Bar: Ga., D.C. 1988; Supreme Ct., 1985, Superior Ct. Fulton County Ga., Ct. of Appeals Ga., Supreme Ct. of Ga., 1982. Staff asst. to Rep. Jack Brooks, Washington, 1970-71; exec. asst. to Rep. Mario Biaggi, Washington, 1971-79; rsch. asst. Sub-com. on Coast Guard and Navigation, Washington, 1979-81; chief counsel, sub-com. on merchant marine Ho. Com. on Merchant Marine and Fisheries, Washington, 1981-89, majority counsel, 1989-92, minority chief counsel, 1992—. Mem. Law Review. Mem. DAR, Kappa Delta, Delta Theta Phi. Office: Ho Com Merchant Marine & Fisheries 1337 Longworth House Office Bldg Washington DC 20515*

WILKINSON, DORIS YVONNE, medical sociology educator; b. Lexington, Ky., June 13, 1936; d. Howard Thomas and Regina Wilkinson. BA, U. Ky., 1958; MA, Case Western Res. U., 1960, PhD, 1968; MPH, Johns Hopkins U., 1985. Asst. prof. U. Ky., Lexington, 1968-70; assoc. prof., then prof. Macalester Coll., St. Paul, 1970-77; exec. assoc. Am. Sociol. Assn., Washington, 1977-80; prof. med. sociology Howard U., Washington, 1980-84; vis. prof. U. Va., 1984-85; prof. sociology U. Ky., Lexington, 1985—; chmn. panel women in sci. program NSF, Washington, 1976; rev. panelist Nat. Inst. Drug Abuse, Washington, 1978-79; mem. bd. sci. counselors Nat. Cancer Inst., Bethesda, Md., 1980-84; vis. scholar Harvard U., Cambridge, Mass., 1989-90, vis. prof., summers 1992, 93, 94. Author: Wookbook for Introductory Sociology, 1968; editor: Black Revolt: Strategies of Protest, 1969; co-editor: The Black Male in America, 1977, Alternative Health Maintenance and Healing Systems, 1987, Race, Gender and the Life Cycle, 1991; social history photographic exhbn. "The African American Presence in Medicine" Harvard Med. Libr., 1991, Pearson Mus.- So. Ill. U. Med. Sch., 1992, N.J. Coll. Medicine and Dentistry, 1993, Louisville Mus. History and Sci., 1994, U. Cin. Med. Sch. Libr., 1994, Albert Einstein Coll. of Medicine, 1995; contbr. articles to profl. jours. Bd. overseers Case Western Res. U., Cleve., 1982-87. Recipient Pub. Humanities award U. Ky., 1990, Midway Coll. Women's History Month award, 1991, Great Tchr. award Nat. Alumni Assn. U. Ky., Disting. Scholar award Assn. Black Sociologists, 1993; inducted into Hall of Disting. Alumni, U. Ky., 1989; fellow Woodrow Wilson Found. 1959-61, Ford Found.; grantee Social Sci. Rsch. Coun., 1975, Nat. Inst. Edn., 1978-80, Nat. Cancer Inst., 1986-88, Ky. Humanities Coun., 1988, Am. Coun. Learned Soc., 1989-90, NEH, 1991; Disting. Prof. in Coll. Arts and Scis. U. Ky., 1992-93. Mem. So. Sociol. Soc. (honors com. 1993-94), Am. Sociol. Assn. (exec. assoc., budget com. 1985-88, v.p. 1991-92, mem. coun. 1994—, Dubois-Johnson-Frazier award 1988), D.C. Sociol. Soc. (pres. 1982-83), Soc. for Study Social Problems (v.p. 1984-85, pres. 1987-88), Ea. Sociol. Soc. (v.p. 1983-84, pres. 1992-93, I. Peter Gellman award 1987), N.Y. Acad. Scis., Phi Beta Kappa, Alpha Kappa Delta. Unitarian.

WILKINSON, FRANCES CATHERINE, librarian, educator; b. Lake Charles, La., July 20, 1955; d. Derrell Fred and Catherine Frances (O'Toole) W.; div.; 1 child, Katrina Frances. BA in Communication with distinction, U. N.Mex., 1982, MPA, 1987; MLS, U. Ariz., 1990. Mktg. rsch. auditor Mktg. Rsch. N.Mex., Albuquerque, 1973-78; freelance photographer, 1974-75; libr. supr. gen. libr. U. N.Mex., Albuquerque, 1978-89, libr., asst. dept. head, 1989-90, libr., dept. head, 1990—; cons., trainer ergonomics univs. and govt. agys. across U.S., 1986—; bd. dirs. Friends of U. N.Mex. Librs., Aubuquerque, 1991—; mediator Mediation Alliance, 1991-94. Contbr. articles to profl. jours. Counselor, advocate Albuquerque Rape Crisis Ctr., 1981-84. Mem. ALA (mem. com. 1990—), N.Am. Serials Interest Group (mem. com. 1994—), N.Mex. Libr. Assn., N.Mex. Preservation Alliance, (vice chair 1995—), Phi Kappa Phi (chpt. treas. 1991-92, chpt. pres. 1992-94), Pi Alpha Alpha. Home: PO Box 8102 Albuquerque NM 87198-8102 Office: U NMex Gen Libr Acquisitions and Serials Dept Albuquerque NM 87131

WILKINSON, JANET WORMAN, advertising and marketing consultant; b. Mpls., July 18, 1944; d. James Russell and Virginia Hale (Murty) Worman; m. Benjamin Delos Wilkinson, Jan. 7, 1967; children: David Delos, Steven Edward, John Douglas. BA, Wells Coll., 1966. With Met. Life Ins. Co., N.Y.C., 1966-67; elem. tchr. pub. schs., Parkersburg, W.Va. and Orange, Tex., 1968-69; on-air prin. WTAV-TV, Parkersburg, 1969-70; corp. communications educator Delmarva Power Co., Wilmington, Del., 1979-83; market mgr. W.L. Gore & Assocs., Inc., Elkton, Md., 1983-85; advt. coord., promotion mgr. Views Mag., Chadds Ford, Pa., 1985-86; cons. mktg. communications, 1986—; mem. Bus.-Industry Ednl. Consortium, Wilmington, 1981-83; chmn. steering com. NE Utilities Educators, 1981-83; tutor Dyslexic Children and Adults. Contbg. editor Lattice News, 1984-85; editor Retailer newsletter, 1984-85. Chmn. publicity Wilmington Flower Market, 1984-85, Wells Coll. Capital Campaign Fund, Wilmington, 1983-84, Wilmington Christmas Shop, 1973-81; loaned exec. United Way, Wilmington, 1985; bd. dirs. Girls Clubs Del., 1983-84; founder, developer Help Stop the Hurt child abuse awareness program, 1983; dir. Christian edn. Trinity Ch., Wilmington, 1982-88. Republican. Episcopalian. Avocations: sketching, watercolor, writing. Home and Office: 1001 Westover Rd Wilmington DE 19807-3016

WILKINSON, LINDA CORNELIA PAINTON, retired city official; b. Painton, Mo., Aug. 21, 1927; d. Herbert James and Bess Carmen (Cobb) Painton; m. A. Scott Wilkinson, July 20, 1957; children: Jean Mary Wilkinson Martinis, Ann Elizabeth. BS in Edn., S.E. Mo. State U., 1951; postgrad., U. N.Mex., 1961, 67. Cert. tchr., Mo. Tchr. pub. schs., Mo., 1945-53; adminstrv. asst. real estate dept. Gulf Oil Corp., N.Y.C., 1953-56; sec., adminstrv. asst. Bklyn. Law Sch., 1956-58; co-owner, mgr. Music Mart, Albuquerque, 1961-68; owner, mgr. rental properties, Albuquerque, 1968-86; chief dep. county clk. Valencia County, Los Lunas, N.Mex., 1986-89; adminstr. Harvey House Civic Ctr., City of Belen (N.Mex.), 1989-90; mem. Valencia County Commn., 1993—. County commr., 1993—; mem. Valencia County Citizens Adv. Bd., 1985-90; sec., bd. dirs. Valencia County Hist. Soc., Belen, 1986-90; bd. dirs. Keep N.Mex. Beautiful, 1986-94, 1st v.p., acting pres., 1992, 93; bd. dirs. Shelter for Victims of Domestic Violence, Valencia County, 1988-94; elder 1st Presbyn. Ch., Belen, 1991—. Home: 8 Meadowlake Ln Los Lunas NM 87031-9448

WILKINSON, LOUISE CHERRY, psychology educator, dean; b. Phila., May 15, 1948; m. Alex Cherry Wilkinson; 1 child, Jennifer Cherry. B.A. magna cum laude with honors, Oberlin Coll., 1970; Ed.M., Ed.D., Harvard U., 1974. Prof., chmn. dept. ednl. psychology U. Wis., Madison, 1976-85; prof., exec. officer Grad. Sch. Ph.D. Program CUNY, N.Y.C., 1984-86; prof. II, dean Grad. Sch. Edn. Rutgers U., 1986—; mem. Nat. rev. bd. Nat. Inst. Edn., 1977, 85, 87; cons. Nat. Ctr. for Bilinqual Research, 1982, 84; adv. bd. Nat. Reading Rsch. Ctr., 1992—. Co-author: Communicating for Learning, 1991; editor: Communicating in Classroom, 1982, Social Context of Instruction, 1984, Gender Influences in the Classroom; mem. editorial bds. and contbr. articles to profl. jours. Fellow Am. Psychol. Assn., Am. Psychol. Soc., Soc. for Rsch. Child Devel., Internat. Assn. for Study Child Lang., Am. Edn. Rsch. Assn. (v.p. 1990-92). Home: 3 Andrews Ln Princeton NJ 08540 Office: Rutgers U Grad Sch Edn 10 Seminary Pl New Brunswick NJ 08901-1183

WILKINSON, REBECCA ELAINE, human resources application specialist; b. Dallas, Nov. 11, 1960; d. John Cephas and Mary Magdeline (Rhea) Bishop; m. Billy Don Wilkinson, July 31, 1982; children: Eric Tyler, Kristen Rhea. BEd, U. Dallas, 1982, MBA, 1995. Sec./AA IBM, Irving, Tex., 1982-85; equal opportunity coord. IBM, Irving, 1985-90; human resources data analyst IBM, Roanoke, Tex., 1990-94; human resources application specialist Westinghouse Security Systems, Irving, 1994—. Mem. NOW, Greenpeace, Sigma Iota Epsilon. Democrat. Episcopalian.

WILKINSON, SIGNE, cartoonist; b. Phila.. BA in English, 1972. Reporter West Chester (Pa.) Daily Local News, Academy of Natural Scis., Phila.; organizer for housing project Cyprus, 1974; freelance cartoonist Phila. and N.Y. publs.; cartoonist San Jose (Calif.) Mercury News, 1982-85, Phila. Daily News, 1985—. Recipient Pulitzer Prize for editorial cartooning, 1992. Office: Phila Daily News PO Box 8263 400 N Broad St Philadelphia PA 19101*

WILKINSON, SUZANNE, human services executive director; b. Dallas, Feb. 15, 1940; d. Jay F. and Iola Murphy; m. Ernest B. Wilkinson, July 23, 1960; children: Audree Clark II, Mike Elizabeth Wilkinson Kirkpatric. A, North Tex. U., 1960; Lic. Vocat. Nurse, Frank Phillips Coll., Borger, Tex., 1967; BS in Health Mgmt., Kennedy Western U., Augora Hills, Calif., 1990, MS in Health Adminstrn., 1991. Cert. I.V. therapy, case mgr. Nurse med. staff Higland Gen. Hosp., Pampa, Tex.; dir. fl. Pampa Nursing Home; exec. dir. Agape Health Svcs., Amarillo, Tex.; adminstr., exec. dir. case mgmt., owner, pvt. duty nursing staff Shepard's Crook Nursing Agy., Pampa, Amarillo, Borger, Wheeler and Shamrock, Tex.; pres. bd. dirs. Gray County Retarded Adults, Highland Hosp. Chmn. food bank dr.; mem. St. Matthew Episc. Ch; tchr. Sunday Sch.; mem. Alter Guides. Lt. Civil Air Patrol, 1980. Mem. Lic. Vocat. Assn. State Bd. Vocat. Nurse Examiners (pres. divsn. 14), Alzheimers Support Group (divsn. 14. L.V.N. Assoc.), AARP (chpt. pres.), Am. Heart Assn. (pres. bd. dirs.), Gold Coats of the Pampa C. of C.

WILKOMER, TINA, distribution manager; b. Chgo., June 10, 1955; d. Leonard Morton and Greta (Hoffman) W. BA magna cum laude, Tex. Woman's U., 1993; postgrad., So. Ill. U., 1994—. Circulation audit supr. Irving-Cloud Pubs., Chgo., 1973-75; courier Dept. Def./USN, London, 1980-82; midwest customer svc. mgr. Plantronics Inc., Elk Grove, Ill., 1982-85; warehouse mgr. Boeing Def. Electronics, Corinth, Tex., 1987-88; material control mgr. Texonics, Inc., Denton, Tex., 1989-90; self-employed distbn. mgr. Valley View, Tex., 1990. Alternate del. Tex. Dem. Convention, Houston, 1992, del., Ft. Worth, 1994. Sgt. USAF, 1975-79. Mem. NOW, DAV, Cooke County Humane Soc., U.S. Humane Soc., Golden Key, Alpha Chi, Omega Rho Alpha, Phi Kappa Phi, Pi Sigma Alpha, Sigma Tau Delta. Office: 1300 Bryant Rd Valley View TX 76272-9300

WILKS, DUFFY JEAN, counselor, educator; b. Spur, Tex., Feb. 15, 1936; d. Rub Lee Jay and Elizabeth Audenn (Simmons) Austin; children from previous marriage, Vicki, Juli, Randy, Rodney; m. W. B. Wilks, Oct. 22, 1986; stepchildren: Linda, Sherry. BA in Psychology, Tex. Tech. U., 1981, MEd in Psychology, 1984. Cert. substance abuse counsleor; lic. profl. counselor, Tex.; lic. marriage and family therapist, Tex. Editor writer Floydada (Tex.) newspaper, 1972-80; probation officer Adult/Juvenile Probation, Lubbock, Tex., 1982-86; pvt. practice Horseshoe Bay, Tex., 1986—; instr. in field. Mem. ACA, Tex. Assn. Counseling and Devel. (editorial bd. jour. 1989-91, author revs., editor Disting. Svc. award 1991), Tex. Counseling Assn., Internat. Assn. for Addictions and Offender Counselors. Home: 5400 College Ave # 116 Snyder TX 79549

WILL, JANE ANNE, psychologist; b. Evansville, Ind., Feb. 6, 1945; d. Edwin Francis and Frances Elizabeth (Patry) W. BA in Edn., St. Benedict's Coll., Ferdinand, Ind., 1968; MA in Edn., MS in Clin. Psychology, U. Evansville, 1973, 1987; MA in Christian Spirituality, Creighton U., 1979; D Psychology, Fla. Tech., Melbourne, 1991. Lic. psychologist, Ind.; joined Sisters of St. Benedict, Inc., Roman Cath. Ch. Tchr. Ireland (Ind.) Jr. High Sch., 1969-76, Meml. High Sch., Evansville, Ind., 1976-77; dir. recruitment and tng. Sisters of St. Benedict, Inc., Ferdinand, Ind., 1978-84; cons. admissions bd. Sisters of St. Benedict, Inc., Ferdinand, 1984—; tchr. Mater Dei High Sch., Evansville, 1984-88; therapist Osceola Ctr., Kissimme, Fla., 1989-90, Charter Hosp., Kissimme, Fla., 1989-90; intern VA Med. Ctr., St. Louis, 1990-91; clin. psychologist St. Mary's Med. Ctr., Evansville, 1991—; cons., bd. dirs. Kordes Enrichment Ctr., Ferdinand; adj. prof. Bresica Coll., Owensboro, Ky., 1978-80, St. Mary's of the Woods Coll., Terre Haute, Ind., 1980-84. Author jour. Ind. Reading Quarterly, 1973. Bd. dirs. Nat. Formation Dirs., Washington, 1982-84; chairperson region VII Formation Conf., Mich. and Ind., 1982-84. Luise Whiting Bell scholar, 1986. Mem. APA, Ind. Psychol. Assn. (women's issues group 1991—), Southwestern Ind. Psychol. Assn. (treas. 1992, sec. 1993, v.p. 1994), Vanderburgh County Mental Health Assn. (bd. dirs. 1994—). Roman Catholic. Home: 725 Wedeking Ave Evansville IN 47711-3861

WILL, JERRIE ANN, psychologist; b. Hazleton, Pa., Apr. 6, 1950; d. Gordon John and Doris Griffiths (Brown) W.; m. Gene G. Kuehneman, June 26, 1982 (div. Oct. 1984). BA, Bucknell U., 1971; MA, W.Va. U., 1974, PhD, 1977. Lic. psychologist, Maine. Teaching fellow W.Va. U., Morgantown, 1974-76; clin. psychology intern U. Md. Hosp., Balt., 1976-77; sr. child psychologist Michael Reese Hosp., Chgo., 1977-82; cons. psychologist Ridgeway Psychiat. Hosp., Chgo., 1982-83, Sanford Sch. Dept., Maine, 1983—; pvt. practice Sanford and Wells, Maine, 1984—; team and child psychologist York County Counseling Svcs., Sanford, 1983-85; owner, mgr. Sanford Psychol. Assocs., 1987—; panelist, reviewer NSF, 1976. Contbr. articles to profl. jours. NIMH Grantee, 1972-75. Mem. Am. Psychol. Assn., Maine Psychol. Assn., Nat. Assn. Sch. Psychologists. Mem. APA, NASP, Maine Psychol. Assn. Home: 314 Webhannet Dr Wells ME 04090 Office: Sanford Psychol Assocs 100 Main St Sanford ME 04073-3523

WILL, JOANNE MARIE, food and consumer services executive, communications consultant, writer; b. Mpls., Mar. 18, 1937; d. Lester John and Dorothea Amelia (Kuenzel) W. BS in Home Econs. and Journalism, Iowa State U., 1959. Food writer, editor food guide Chgo. Tribune, 1959-67; account supr., home econs. coordinator J. Walter Thompson Co., Chgo., 1967-73; assoc. food editor, then food editor Chgo. Tribune, 1973-81; dir. food and consumer services Hill and Knowlton, Inc., Chgo., 1981-87; dir., group mgr. food and consumer svcs. Selz, Seabolt & Assocs., Inc., Chgo. Mem. bd. govs. Iowa State U. Found., past mem. home econs. adv. bd.; bd. dirs., officer Sr. Ctrs. Met. Chgo. Recipient Alumnae Recognition medal Iowa State U., 1994; named Outstanding Young Alumnus Iowa State U., 1968. Mem. Home Econs. in Bus., Am. Home Econs. Assn., Ill. Home Econs. Assn. (past bd. dirs.), Chgo. Nutrition Assn. (pres.-elect 1993-94, pres. 1994—), Dames d'Escoffier (bd. dirs. Chgo. chpt., past v.p.), Chgo. Nutrition Assn. (pres. 1994-95).

WILLANS, JEAN STONE, religious organization executive; b. Hillsboro, Ohio, Oct. 3, 1924; d. Homer and Ella (Keys) Hammond; student San Diego Jr. Coll.; m. Richard James Willans, Mar. 28, 1966; 1 dau., Suzanne Jeanne. Asst. to v.p. Family Loan Co., Miami, Fla., 1946-49; civilian supr. USAF, Washington, 1953-55; founder, dir. Blessed Trinity Soc., editor Trinity mag., Los Angeles, 1960-66; co-founder, exec. v.p., dir. Soc. of Stephen, Altadena, Calif., 1967—, exec. dir., Hong Kong, 1975-81; lectr. in field. Republican. Episcopalian. Author: The Acts of the Green Apples, 1974; co-editor: Charisma in Hong Kong, 1970; Spiritual Songs, 1970; The People Who Walked in Darkness, 1977; The People Who Walked in Darkness II, 1992. Address: PO Box 6225 Altadena CA 91003

WILLARD, SHEILA DURAM, English language and humanities educator; b. Evanston, Ill., July 22, 1942; d. George Thomas and Eleanor Mae (Kent) Duram; m. Michael M. Gee Sr., 1964 (div. 1972); children: Dana Gee Sturge, Natalie Gee Sullivan, Michael M. Gee Jr.; m. John Morris Willard, 1985. BA, U. Conn., 1964, MA, 1976; MA, U. Mass., 1989. Cert. tchr. secondary edn., Conn. Asst. to dean St. Joseph's Coll. for Women, West Hartford, Conn., 1976-77, Asnuntuck C.C., Enfield, Conn., 1977-78; prof. Middlesex C.C., Bedford and Lowell, Mass., 1978—; adj. instr. Ea. Conn. State Coll., Willimantic, Conn., 1975-78, Springfield (Mass.) C.C., 1977, Univ. Mass., Lowell, 1994; lectr. Humanities' Orgn., Conn. and Mass., 1980—. Editorial asst.: This Hallowed Ground, 1963, Seventeen from Everywhere, 1976, Sharing Literature with Children, 1977; contbr. poetry to anthologies, articles to jours. Vol. Unitarian Universalist Social and Ednl. Activist Roles, Conn. and Mass., 1972—. Mem. MLA (del. assembly), Nat. Coun. Tchrs. English, Conf. on Coll. Composition and Comm., New Eng. Regional Tchrs. English, C.C. Humanities Assn., Nat. Collegiate Hons. Coun., Phi Beta Kappa, Phi Kappa Phi. Democrat. Unitarian Universalist. Home: 467 Lowell St Andover MA 01810-5304 Office: Middlesex C C 33 Kearney Sq Lowell MA 01852-1901

WILLARDSON, KIMBERLY ANN CAREY, editor, writer, publisher; b. Akron, Ohio, May 8, 1959; d. James David and Concetta Marie (Bonanno) Carey; m. Roger Michael Willardson, Oct. 4, 1980. Student, Kent State U., 1978-79, Akron U., 1979-80; BA in English summa cum laude, Wright State U., 1983, MA in English, 1987. Teaching asst. Wright State U., Dayton, Ohio, 1983-84; assoc. editor Nexus Lit. Mag., Dayton, Ohio, 1982, editor, 1982-83; features editor The Daily Guardian Newspaper, Dayton, 1983; editorial asst. communications Wright State U., Dayton, 1985-88; freelance editor Dayton, 1986-88; editor The Vincent Bros. Rev. Mag., Fairborn and Dayton, Ohio, 1988—; pub. Vincent Bros. Pub., Dayton, 1988—; mem. adj. staff Antioch Writer's Workshop, Yellow Springs, Ohio, 1990, 91, fellowship, 1993. Author: (poems) Overcast at the Cat Dance Cafe, 1989, The Missy May Hopnoodle Saga (2d pl. Creative writing award Conf. Cin. Women 1990), Birch Violins (1st pl. poetry prize Conf. Cin. Women creative writing awards 1991), Violets for the Martyred Playwright, Heat Lightning, Waiting for the Vision Train; mem. bd. editors Fountain of Youth Literary Anthology, 1983-84. Regional organizer March of Dimes, Cuyahoga Falls, Ohio, 1977; canvasser Am. Heart Assn., Fairborn, 1989-91; mem. SANE/FREEZE, Dayton Citizens for Global Security. Wright State U. grantee, 1989, 90, Orgn. Support grantee, 1991, 92, 93, 94; Antioch Writer's Workshop fellow, 1993; Individual Artist fellow Ohio Arts Coun., 1993, 94, Montgomery County Regional Arts and Cultural Dist., 1994. Mem. SANE/FREEZE. Roman Catholic. Home and Office: 4566 Northern Cir Riverside OH 45424-5733

WILLE, LOIS JEAN, retired newspaper editor; b. Chgo., Sept. 19, 1931; d. Walter and Adele S. (Taege) Kroeber; m. Wayne M. Wille, June 6, 1954. B.S., Northwestern U., 1953, M.S., 1954; Litt.D. (hon.), Columbia Coll., Chgo., 1980, Northwestern U., 1990, Rosary Coll., 1990. Reporter Chgo. Daily News, 1958-74, nat. corr., 1975-76, assoc. editor charge editorial page, 1977; assoc. editor charge editorial and opinion pages Chgo. Sun-Times, 1978-83; assoc. editor editorial page Chgo. Tribune, 1984-87, editor editorial page, 1987-91, ret., 1991. Author: Forever Open, Clear and Free: the Historic Struggle for Chicago's Lakefront, 1972. Recipient Pulitzer prize for public service, 1963, Pulitzer prize for editorial writing, 1989, William Allen White Found. award for excellence in editorial writing, 1978, numerous awards Chgo. Newspaper Guild, numerous awards Chgo. Headline Club, numerous awards Nat. Assn. Edn. Writers, numerous awards Ill. AP, numerous awards Ill. UPI. Home: 120 Charmont Dr Radford VA 24141-4205

WILLEMS, DEBORAH MARIE, company official; b. Green Bay, Wis., Dec. 17, 1965; d. Floyd Oscar Olson and Eyvonne Marie (Massicotte) Kennedy; m. Patrick James Willems, Jan. 25, 1985; children: Antone, Jacob, Tanya. Student, N.W. Tech. Coll., Green Bay, 1989. Receptionist Tape, Inc., Green Bay, 1984-85, stenographer, 1985-90, sr. adminstrv. svcs. rep., 1990—. Home: 1155 Grant St DePere WI 54115 Office: Tape Inc 2612 S Broadway Green Bay WI 54304-5306

WILLENBRINK, ROSE ANN, lawyer; b. Louisville, Ky., Apr. 20, 1950; d. J.L. Jr. and Mary Margaret (Williams) W. Student, U. Chgo., 1968-70; BA in Anthropology with honors, U. Louisville, 1973, JD, 1975. Bar: Ky. 1976, Ind. 1976, U.S. Dist. Ct. (we. dist.) Ky. 1976. Atty. Mapother & Mapother, Louisville, 1976-79; v.p., counsel Nat. City Bank, Louisville, 1980—. Mem. ABA, NAFE, Ky. Bar Assn., Louisville Bar Assn., Women Lawyers Assn., Corp. House Counsel Assn., Phi Kappa Phi. Home: 2356 Valley Vista Rd Louisville KY 40205-2002 Office: Nat City Bank 3700 Nat City Tower Louisville KY 40202

WILLENS, KAY LEE, artist, educator; b. L.A., July 8, 1952; d. Joseph J. and Julia (Handleman) Willens; m. Georg Heimdal, June 22, 1987. Student, U. Calif., Santa Cruz, 1970-72; BA, U. Calif., Berkeley, 1976; MFA, Cranbrook Acad. Art, Bloomfield Hills, Mich., 1983. Lectr. Ohio State U., Columbus, 1983-84, So. Ill. U., Carbondale, 1984-85, Ohio State U., Lima, 1986, U. R.I., Kingston, 1987-88; asst. prof. art Kenyon Coll., Gambier, Ohio, 1988-93, assoc. prof. art, 1993—; panelist Ohio Arts Coun., Columbus, 1991. One-woman shows include Ind. U. Gallery, 1987, Coll. Wooster Art Mus., 1990, Bowman and Penelec Galleries, Meadville, Pa., 1989, Montpelier (Md.) Cultural Arts Ctr., 1987, Pacific Basin Arts Gallery, Calif., 1981, Kent State U. Gallery, 1995; exhibited in group shows at The Riffe Gallery, Columbus, 1990, Cleve. Ctr. for Contemporary Art, 1990, Butler Inst. Am. Art, Youngstown, Ohio, 1991, Nat. Mus. of Women in the Arts, Washington, 1990, Contemporary Arts Ctr., Cin., 1991, Zolla/Lieberman Gallery,

1992, Akron Art Mus., 1993, Spaces Gallery, Cleve., 1995. Ohio Arts Coun. individual artists fellow, 1986, 90, 92, 94; recipient New Works award Contemporary Arts Ctr., 1990. Office: Kenyon Coll Dept Art Gambier OH 43022

WILLENZ, JUNE ADELE, writer, public affairs executive, playwright, screenwriter. BS, U. Mich., postgrad.; ABD in Philosophy, New Sch. for Social Rsch. Instr. English, Montgomery Coll., Md.; conf. organizer Women in and After War, Bellagio, Italy, Rape in Armed Conflicts, Istanbul; lectr. USIA; spkr. vets. conv. NAACP; radio and TV guest appearances; honored guest internat. vets. assns. Author: Women Veterans: America's Forgotten Heroines, 1983; editor, author: Dialogue on the Draft, 1967, Human Rights of the Man in Uniform, 1969; author chpt. to book; editor: AVC Bull.; presenter Am. Hist. Assn., Am. Polit. Sci. Assn.; contbr. articles to profl. publs. on vets., mil., women's and internat. issues; columnist Stars and Stripes. Mem. VA Adv. Com. on Women Vets.; mem. UN Decade for Women com., head of working group on refugee women; accredited rep. to UN; organizer Workshop on Refugee Women at UN; pub. mem. 19th Fgn. Officer Selection Bd., U.S. Info. Agy.; chmn. Task Force on Veterans and Mil. Affairs for Leadership Con. on Civil Rights; speaker Nat. Urban League, Ctr. for Policy Rsch., Nat. League of Cities Vets. Program, advisor; trustee Internat. Devel. Conf.; co-chmn. Coordinating Com. on Voluntary Nat. Svc., organized nat. conf. Dialogue on Nat. Svc., 1989; del. White House Conf. on Youth; exec. dir. Am. Vets. Com., 1965—; chairperson Standing Com. Women, World Vets. Fedn.; mem. planning com. 5th and 6th legis. confs. WVF; vice chmn., subcom. on disabled vets. Pres. Com. Employment of Persons with Disabilities, Inter-Univ. Seminar Armed Forces & Soc. Mem. Authors Guild, Dramatists Guild. Home: 6309 Bannockburn Dr Bethesda MD 20817-5403

WILLET, AVA HILL, realtor; b. Japan, May 10, 1951; d. Joseph Lorince; m. Richard Alan Hill, June 5, 1971 (div.); children: Joseph Alan, Jason Eric; m. John F. Willet, Aug. 22, 1986. Realtor Am. Dream Realty, Scotts Valley, Calif., 1986—. Home: PO Box 251 Los Gatos CA 95031-0251 Office: American Dream Realty 5523 Scotts Valley Dr Scotts Valley CA 95066-3423

WILLETT, ROSLYN LEONORE, public relations executive, food service consultant; b. N.Y.C., Oct. 18, 1924; d. Edward and Celia (Stickler) S.; m. Edward Willett (separated); 1 child, Jonathan Stanley. BA, Hunter Coll., N.Y.C., 1944; postgrad., Columbia U., 1944, CUNY, 1947-48, NYU, 1947-48, 52, New Sch., 1987-88. Dietitian YWCA, N.Y.C., 1944; tech. and patents libr. Stein Hall & Co., N.Y.C., 1944-46, food technologist tech. svcs. and devel. dept., 1946-48; editor McGraw-Hill, Inc., N.Y.C., 1949-50, Harcourt Brace Jovanovich, Inc., N.Y.C., 1950-54; pub. rels. writer Farley Manning Assocs., N.Y.C., 1954-58; cons. pub. rels. and food svc. Roslyn Willett Assocs., Inc., N.Y.C., 1959—; adj. prof. Hunter Coll., 1955-56, Polytech. Univ., N.Y., 1981-82; lectr. in field. Author: The Woman Executive in Woman in Sexist Society, 1971. chmn. Woman's Polit. Caucus, Inc., N.Y., N.J., Conn., 1971-73; v.p. Mid Hudson Arts and Sci. Ctr., Poughkeepsie, N.Y.; bd. dirs. Small Bus. Task Force, Assn. for Small Bus. and Professions, 1981-85, Regional Adv. Coun. Fed. SBA, 1976-78, Rhinebeck Chamber Music Soc., 1985-86, Will Inst. , New Paltz, 1980—. Mem. Pub. Rels. Soc. Am. (accredited), Food Svc. Cons. Soc. Internat., N.Y. Acad. Scis., Inst. Food Technologists, Paris Club. Home: Hunn's Lake Rd Stanfordville NY 12581 Office: 441 W End Ave New York NY 10024-5328

WILLETTE, SHARON MARIE, early childhood educator, consultant; b. Portland, Maine, Mar. 22, 1945; d. John F. and Phyllis I. (Day) DeCosta; m. Gary H. Willette, July 18, 1964 (div. Dec. 1985); children: Rus Willette, Kerri Willette. BS in Edn., Nyack Coll., 1968; M in Early Childhood Edn., U. So. Maine, 1985; EdD, Nova U., 1994. Cert. tchr. K-8. Owner, dir., tchr. Presch., Inc., Gray, Maine, 1973-81; bus. mgr. Knapp's Music Store, Portland, 1982-83; tchr. kindergarten, pre- and transitional kindergarten Cath. Parochial Schs. Portland, 1983-87; early childhood cons. Maine Sch. Adminstrv. Dist. # 6, Bar Mills, Maine, 1994—. Guest lectr. Project Maine Families, Portland, 1992-94, Bonny Eagle Parenting Ctr., Buxton, Maine, 1991-94, Careshare Network, Portland, 1992-94, Carelink, Windham, Maine, 1992-94; organist, pianist, group leader local ch., Gray, 1984—. Mem. ASCD. Home: 286 Shaker Rd Gray ME 04039

WILLHITE, IRENE ELAINE, state government administrator; b. Lynn, Mass., May 10, 1933; d. John Guy and Catherine Louise (Woodbury) Powell; m. Earnest T. Willhite, Oct. 6, 1952; children: David, Patricia, Stephen, Kenneth, James. BA, U. Ala., Huntsville, 1987, MA, 1989. Rschr. Madison County Legis. Office, Huntsville, 1985-91, exec. dir., 1991—; mem. adv. bd.-ASSETS Dept. Human Resources, Huntsville, 1990—; mem. adv. bd.-CITY Huntsville City Schs., 1991—. Recipient Outstanding Achievement award Ret. Mil. Officers Assn., 1991, Participation award Madicon County Med. Soc., 1992. Mem. AAUW, Monrovia Pks. & Recreation (charter), Monrovia Optimist Club (charter). Home: 143 Lovvorn Ln Huntsville AL 35806

WILLHOIT, MARILYN J., medical equipment manufacturing company executive; b. Paterson, N.J., Aug. 9, 1947; d. Robert and Eleanor Jean (Lewis) Houston; m. Robert Norval Willhoit, Mar. 29, 1969 (div. June 1975); m. Louis L. Rudt, Jan. 1, 1982. BA, Trenton State Coll., 1968; MA, U. Conn., 1969. Cert. clin. competence-audiology. Audiologist Hartford Hearing League, West Hartford, Conn., 1970-71; audiologist The Gaylord Hosp., Wallingford, Conn., 1971-73, dir. lang. and comm., 1973-78; dir. ednl. svcs. Am. Electromedics, Hudson, N.H., 1979-81, dir. sales and mktg., 1982-83; v.p. Micro Audiometrics, South Daytona, Fla., 1983-86, K & A Med., Port Orange, Fla., 1987-93, Visions In Endosurgery, Port Orange, 1994—; cons. Phelps-Stokes Fund, N.Y.C., 1972-75, Employees Ins. of Wausau, North Haven, Conn., 1973-78; legis. counselor Am. Speech & Hearing Assn., Washington, 1975-78. Producer: (ednl. video) Why Don't You Come When I Call You, 1983 (ITA award 1983); co-author: Guidelines for Speech and Hearing - State of Connecticut, 1975. Vol. Rape Crisis Ctr., Volusia County, Fla., 1991—, also bd. dirs.; judge Turn-Around Program, Futures, Volusia County Schs., 1991-94; mentor Adopt-A-Child Compact, Volusia County Schs., 1993-94; bd. dirs. Our Children First, Volusia/Flagler Counties, 1994—; endowment Mem. Mus. Arts and Scis., Daytona, Fla., 1991—. Recipient award of recognition Conn. Speech & Hearing Assn., 1977. Mem. Halifax Club. Home: 1617 Crescent Ridge Rd Daytona Beach FL 32118

WILLIAM, PAMELA S., librarian; b. Keyser, W.Va., Oct. 4, 1948; d. Joseph Earl and Madeline Talmadge (Clark) W. BA in English, St. Joseph Coll., 1970; MLS, Kent State U., 1974; MA in Modern Humanities, Frostburg State U., 1981. Tchr. Bruce High Sch., Westernport, Md., 1970-73; asst. libr. Potomac State Coll., Keyser, W.Va., 1974-85; head reference dept. Frostburg (Md.) State U., 1985—. Mem. ALA, Md. Libr. Assn., W.Va. Libr. Assn. Roman Catholic. Home: 325 Parkview Dr Keyser WV 26726-2314 Office: Lewis Ort Libr Frostburg State U Frostburg MD 21532

WILLIAMS, ALICE NOEL TUCKERMAN, foundation administrator; b. Bethesda, Md., Dec. 21, 1918; d. Walter Rupert and Edith (Abercrombie-Miller) Tuckerman; m. Robert High Williams, June 21, 1939 (dec. 1983); children: Sarah Fenno Williams Lord, Edith Tuckerman Williams Ward. Ladies bd. St. John's Child Devel. Ctr., Washington, 1960—; pres. ladies bd. St. John's Devel. Ctr., Washington, 1969-72, v.p., bd. of trustees, 1970-72. Mem. The Colonial Dames of Am. (pres. Washington chpt. 1970-74), Sulgrave. Republican. Episcopalian.

WILLIAMS, ANITA JEAN, elementary educator educator; b. Little Rock, July 14, 1959; d. Hoover and Clara Mae (Lewis) W. BS in Edn., Ark. State U., 1983, MS in Edn., 1989. Tchr. Carver Washington YMCA Day Care, Little Rock, 1978-79, Annie Nannies Day Care, Memphis, 1986-87; elem. tchr. Parkin (Ark.) Sch. Dist., 1983-84; tchr. kindergarten Hughes (Ark.) Pub. Schs., 1984-86; receipt and ctrl. clk. IRS, Memphis, 1987-90; elem. tchr. English, kindergarten and 3d and 4th grade tchr. Earle (Ark.) Sch. Dist., 1988—; sec., bookkeeper Lewis and Son Rice Processing Mill, Earle, 1977—; wedding dir. and coord., Earle, 1992—. coach/sponsor Cheerleading Squad. Recipient Ednl. award Nacerima Club, Forrest City, Ark., 1977, 83, 89, award Bulter Chapel Christian Meth. Episcopal Ch., Earle, 1991, 92, 93. Mem. NEA, Ark. Edn. Assn., Ark. Cheerleading Coaches Assn., Nat. Cheerleading Assn., (5 trophies for safety, most spirited, and most improved team award), Kappa Delta Pi. Methodist. Home: RR 1 Box 308 Earle AR 72331-9745 Office: Earle Sch Dist PO Box 637 Earle AR 72331-9745

WILLIAMS, ANN CLAIRE, federal judge; b. 1949; m. David J. Stewart. BS, Wayne State U., 1970; MA, U. Mich., 1972; JD, U. Notre Dame, 1975. Asst. U.S. atty. U.S. Dist. Ct. (no. dist.) Ill., Chgo., 1976-85; faculty mem. Nat. Inst. for Trial Advocacy, 1979—; judge U.S. Dist. Ct. (no. dist.) Ill., Chgo., 1985—; chief Crime Drug Enforcement Task Force North Ctrl. Region, 1983-85; chair ct. adminstrn. and case mgmt. com. Jud. Conf. U.S., 1993—; adj. prof., lectr. Northwestern U. Law Sch., Chgo., 1979—. Trustee U. Chgo. Lab Sch.; sec. bd. trustees U. Notre Dame, Mus. Sci. and Industry. Mem. Fed. Bar Assn. (treas.), Fed. Judges Assn., Women's Bar Assn. of Ill. Office: US Dist Ct 219 S Dearborn St Chicago IL 60604-1702

WILLIAMS, ANN MEAGHER, hospital administrator; b. Hull, Mass., May 28, 1929; d. James Francis Meagher and Dorothy Frances (Antone) Mullins; m. Joseph Arthur Williams, May 15, 1954; children: James G., Mara A., A. Scott (dec.), Gordon M., Mark J., Antoinette M., Andrea M. BS, Chestnut Hill Coll., 1950; MS, Boston Coll., 1952. Radioisotope biologist Air Force Cambridge Rsch. Ctr., Bedford, Mass., 1952-55; asst. mgr. Roxbury Businessmen's Exch., Boston, 1956-66; owner, operator Chatterlane, Osterville, Mass., 1961-66; realtor James E. Murphy Inc., Hyannis, Mass., 1968-77; dir. community affairs Cape Cod Hosp., Hyannis, 1977—. Bd. dirs. Community Coun., Mid Cape, Mass., 1977-88, Cape Cod Mental Health Assn., 1977-82, Ctr. for Individual and Family Svcs., Mid Cape, 1982-87, Am. Cancer Soc., Mid Cape, 1981—; mem. sch. com. Cape Cod Regional Tech. High Sch., 1978—, United Way of Cape Cod, 1988-89; chmn. fin. com. City of Barnstable, Mass., 1969-77. Named Woman of Yr. Bus./Profl. Women's Club, 1982; recipient Cert. Appreciation Am. Cancer Soc., 1983, 88, Pres. Recognition award United Way Cape Cod, 1989. Mem. Am. Soc. Hosp. Mktg. and Pub. Rels., New Eng. Hosp. Pub. Rels. Mktg. Assn., Southeastern Mass. Hosp. Pub. Rels. Assn., Nat. Assn. Hosp. Devel., Chestnut Hill Coll. Alumnae Assn., Rotary Club of Osterville (bd. dirs. 1992—), Hyannis Area C. of C. (bd. dirs. 1993—). Roman Catholic. Home: 8 E Bay Rd Osterville MA 02655-1909 Office: Cape Cod Hosp 27 Park St Hyannis MA 02601-5230

WILLIAMS, ANNA M., social worker; b. Ft. Meade, Md., Sept. 5, 1956; d. William Arthur and Jacqueline Rae (Hull) W. BSW, B in African Studies, U. Md., 1978; MSW, U. Pitts., 1981. Lic. social worker. Investigator child abuse Dept. Social Svcs., Balt., 1978-80; counselor, program coord., supr. girls unit Ward Home for Children, Pitts., 1981-86; mental health therapist Pace Sch., Pitts., 1986-89; program coord. Justice Resources Inc., Balt., 1989-94; therapist Union Meml. Hosp., Balt., 1993-94; v.p. resdl. svcs. Children's Home Wyoming Conf., Binghamton, N.Y., 1994—; cons. Youth Advocacy Program, Balt., 1992-94. Bd. dirs. Ward Home for Children, Pitts., 1986-88, South Balt. Youth Ctr., 1993-94; speaker Meth. Women; adv. bd. WSKG Pub. Broadcasting, 1994—. Mem. NASW, Nat. Girls Caucus (charter), Binghamton Kiwanis, Alpha Kappa Alpha (Lambda Phi chpt.). Democrat. Roman Catholic. Office: Childrens Home Wyo Conf 1182 Chenago St Binghamton NY 13901

WILLIAMS, ANNIE JOHN, educator; b. Reidsville, N.C., Aug. 26, 1913; d. John Wesley and Martha Anne (Walker) W. AB, Greensboro Coll., 1933; MA, U. N.C., Chapel Hill, 1939; postgrad., Appalachian State U., summer 1944, Duke U., summer 1936, Cornell U., summer 1961. Tchr. math. Blackstone (Va.) Coll., 1934-35; tchr. Hoke High Sch., Raeford, N.C., 1935-37, Massey Hill High Sch., Fayetteville, N.C., 1937-42, Alexander Graham Jr. High Sch., Fayetteville, 1942-43, Carr Jr. High Sch., Durham, N.C., 1943-53; supr. math. N.C. Dept. Pub. Instrn., Raleigh, 1959-62; tchr. math. Durham High Sch., 1953-59, 62-78, ret., 1978; vol. in math. and computer geometry N.C. Sch. Sci. and Math., Durham, 1980—; adj. asst. prof. dept. math. and sci. edn. N.C. State U., Raleigh, 1966-73; mem. 16th Internat. Congress on Arts and Communications, Washington, 1989, 19th, Cambridge, Eng., 1992, 20th Cambridge, Mass., 1993, 21st Edinburgh, Scotland, 1994. Author: (with Brown and Montgomery) Algebra, First Course, 1963, Algebra, Second Course, 1963. Recipient Shell fellow Cornell U.; cert. of recognition Dept. Math. and Sci. Edn. N.C. State U., 1979, Gov.'s award for outstanding vol. svc., 1986, Disting. Alumni award Greensboro Coll., 1989; named Vol. of Yr., Key Vol. Program co-sponsored by Vol. Svcs. Bur. and Durham Morning Herald, 1986. Mem. DAR (N.C. chpt. chair Am. History Month 1980-82, corr. sec. 1982-84, chaplain 1984-86, Gen. Davie chpt.), Nat. Coun. Tchrs. Math. (life, bd. dirs. 1957-60), Assn. Women in Math., Math. Assn. Am. (life), N.C. Council Tchrs. Math. (hon. life, W.W. Rankin Meml. award 1975), Internat. Platform Assn., The World Found. of Successful Women (life charter), Pierian Lit. Club (sec. 1979-80, pres. 1980-81), Durham Woman's Club (co-chmn. internat. affairs dept. 1985-87, chmn. 1989-92), Delta Kappa Gamma, Mu Alpha Theta (hon.). Methodist. Died Nov. 19, 1994. Home and Office: 2021 Sprunt Ave Durham NC 27705-3251

WILLIAMS, ATHANASIA MARIA, perinatal nurse specialist; b. Englewood, N.J., Nov. 15, 1950; d. Nicholas P. and Stella Thespina (Zaharias) W. BSN, Duke U., 1972. Staff nurse Columbia Presbyn. Hosp., N.Y.C., 1972-75, asst. head nurse, 1975-87, clin. nurse III, 1987—. Contbg. author: High Risk Pregancy, 1986; also articles. Greek Orthodox.

WILLIAMS, BARBARA ELAINE, design production company executive; b. Bartlesville, Okla., Aug. 12, 1952; d. B. Joe and Roy Marie (Smith) W.; m. Charles M. Ellertson, Apr. 20, 1985. B.A. cum laude, Duke U., 1974. Asst. to bus. mgr. Duke U. Press, Durham, N.C., 1974-75, prodn. asst., 1975-78, assoc. prodn. mgr., 1979-82, jours. mgr., 1982-84; prodn., design mgr. Menasha Ridge Press, 1984-88; owner B. Williams & Assocs. Design and Prodn. Studio, 1988—; instr. Carolina Pub. Inst, Chapel Hill, N.C., 1994-95; panelist Career Counseling Conf., Durham, 1983, 84, Conf. Editors Learned Jours., Modern Lang. Assn., 1985. Photographer Latent Image 3, 1976, Latent Image 4, 1978, Latent Image 5, 1980, N.C. Mus. Art Ann. Show, 1978, 79. Chair comm. com. St. Paul's Luth. Ch., 1992-94. Mem. Assn. Am. Univ. Presses (jours. com. 1983-85, Design award 1988), Women in Scholarly Pub., Am. Inst. Graphic Arts. Democrat. Home: 1412 Pennsylvania Ave Durham NC 27705-3544

WILLIAMS, BARBARA JEAN MAY, state official; b. Alphoretta, Ky., June 5, 1927; d. Andrew Jackson and Bess (Salisbury) May. A.B. in Spanish, Centre Coll., 1949; postgrad., Columbia U., 1957; M.S. in L.S., U. Ky., 1963. Librarian Midway Jr. Coll., 1960-62, Ky. Dept. Libraries, Frankfort, 1965-68; planning librarian Ky. Program Devel. Office, Frankfort, 1968-71, Ky. Exec. Dept. for Fin. and Adminstrn., Frankfort, 1972-76; asst. state librarian Ky. Dept. Libraries and Archives, Frankfort, 1976; state librarian Ky. Dept. Libraries and Archives, 1977-80; adminstr. Ky. suggestion system program Dept. Personnel, div. employee services State of Ky., Frankfort, 1980-91; retired; mem. Depository Library Council to Public Printer. Mem. ALA, Southeastern Library Assn., Ky. Library Assn. (sec. spl. library sect. 1976, chmn. sect. 1976), Chief Officers State Library Agys. (liaison com. office Edn. 1979-80), Assn. State Library Agys. (Index State Library Activities 1979-80), Council Planning Librarian (treas.), Ky. Council Archivists, Ky. Hist. Soc., J. B. Speed Museum Guild. Presbyterian. Clubs: Democratic Woman's, Filson, La Jardiniere Garden Club.

WILLIAMS, BARBARA LOU, library director; b. Seattle, Aug. 20, 1927; d. Lawrence Earl and LouElla Barbara (Eubank) W.; children: Chrstine Mikel, Patricia Hannum, Kathryn McLane, Douglas Alan Hannum. BA, U. Colo., 1948; MEd, U. Ariz., 1963, ednl. specialist, 1976; MLS, U. Okla., 1975. Tchr. Indian Oasis High Sch., Sells, Ariz., 1959-6l, Sahuarita Sch., Tucson, 196l-62; elem. libr. Tucson Sch. Dist., 1963-65, high sch. libr., 1965-77; dir. libr. Ariz. Western Coll., Yuma, 1977-82, Tarrant County Jr. Coll. Dist., Ft. Worth, 1982—. Co-author: History of Sheridan, Wyoming, 1956; editor: Directory of Libraries in Southern Arizona, 1972; contbr. to Nobel Prize Winners, 1987. Mem. ALA, Assn. Ednl. Communication and Tech., Tex. Libr. Assn., Tex. Assn. Ednl. Tech., Tex. Jr. Coll. Tchrs. Assn., Librs. Tarrant County (pres. 1990-91), Trinity Valley Quilters Guild, Ft. Worth Opera Guild. Home: 3003 Marigold Ave Fort Worth TX 76111-2629 Office: Tarrant County Jr Coll 4801 Marine Creek Pkwy Fort Worth TX 76179

WILLIAMS, BETTY OUTHIER, lawyer; b. Woodward, Okla., Sept. 11, 1947; d. Robert E. and Ethel M. (Castiller) Outhier; children: Amanda J., Emily Rebecca. BA, Oklahoma City U., 1969; JD, Vanderbilt U., 1972. Bar: Okla. 1972, U.S. Dist. Ct. (no. dist.) Okla. 1972, U.S. Dist. Ct. (ea. dist.) Okla. 1973, (U.S. Ct. Appeals (10th cir.) 1973, U.S. Supreme Ct. 1980, U.S. Dist. Ct. (we. dist.) Okla. 1988. Atty. Reginal Heber Smith Community Lawyer Fellowship, Tulsa, 1972-73; asst. U.S. atty. U.S. Dept. Justice, Muskogee, Okla., 1973-81, U.S. atty., 1981-82; ptnr. Robinson, Locke, Gage, Fite & Williams, Muskogee, 1982—. Mem. bd. editors Okla. Law Enforcement Ops. Bull., 1993-94. Pres. Bus. and Profl. Women, Muskogee, 1975-77, 83; pres., bd. dirs. YWCA, Muskogee, 1975-82; bd. dirs. Green Country Mental Health, Muskogee, 1986-88; trustee Frontier Heritage Found., 1990—; dir. WISH, 1990—. Named one of Outstanding Young Career Women Bus. and Profl. Womens, 1974. Fellow Okla. Bar Found. (bd. trustees 1989—, v.p. 1994); mem. ABA, Okla. Bar Assn., Muskogee County Bar Assn. (pres. 1984-85), Gamma Phi Beta, Soroptimists (pres. 1986-88). Republican. Methodist. Home: 4326 Oklahoma St Muskogee OK 74401-2351 Office: Robinson Locke Gage Fite & Williams PO Box 87 Muskogee OK 74402-0087

WILLIAMS, BRENDA JOAN, medical technologist, project manager; b. Clarinda, Iowa, June 9, 1965; d. Donald Lee and Brenda Joyce (Miller) W. BS, N.W. Mo. State U., 1988, MBA; AA, Iowa Western Community Coll., 1985. Registered med. technologist, 1988, clin. lab. scientist, 1988. Product mgmt. technician The Blood Ctr. of Cen. Iowa, Des Moines, 1987-88; med. technologist Heartland Health Systems, St. Joseph, Mo., 1988—; med. technologist, project mgr. Cerner Corp., Kansas City, Mo., 1990—. Recipient Bus. and Profl. Women award and scholarship, 1985. Mem. NAFE, Am. Soc. Med. Technologists. Republican. Baptist. Office: Cerner Corp 2800 Rock Creek Pky Kansas City MO 64117-2530

WILLIAMS, CAMILLA, soprano, voice educator; b. Danville, Va.; d. Booker and Fannie (Cary) W.; m. Charles T. Beavers, Aug. 28, 1950. BS, Va. State Coll., 1941; postgrad., U. Pa., 1942; studies with, Mme. Marian Szekely-Freschl, 1943-44, 1952, Berkowitz and Cesare Sodero, 1944-46, Rose Dirman, 1948-52, Sergius Kagen, 1958-62; MusD (hon.), Va. State U., 1986, D. (hon.), 1985. Prof. voice Bronx Coll., N.Y.C., 1970, Bklyn. Coll., 1970-73, Queens Coll., N.Y.C., 1974, Ind. U., Bloomington, 1977—; 1st black prof. voice Cen. Conservatory Music, Beijing, People's Republic China, 1983. Created role of Madame Butterfly as 1st black contract singer, N.Y.C. Ctr., 1946, 1st Aida, 1948; 1st N.Y. performance of Mozart's Idomeneo with Little Orch. Soc., 1950; 1st Viennese performance Menotti's Saint of Bleecker Street, 1955; 1st N.Y. performance of Handel's Orlando, 1971; other roles include Nedda in Pagliacci, Mimi in La Boheme, Marguerite in Faust; major tours include Alaska, 1950, London, 1954, Am. Festival in Belgium, 1955, tour of 14 African countries for U.S. Dept. State, 1958-59, Israel, 1959, concert for Crown Prince of Japan as guest of Gen. Eisenhower, 1960, tour of Formosa, Australia, New Zealand, Korea, Japan, Philippines, Laos, South Vietnam, 1971, Poland, 1974; appearances with orchs. including Royal Philharm., Vienna Symphony, Berlin Philharm., Chgo. Symphony, Phila. Orch., BBC Orch., Stuttgart Orch., many others; contract with RCA Victor as exclusive Victor Red Seal rec. artist, 1944—. Recipient Marian Anderson award (1st winner), 1943, 44, Newspaper Guild award as First Lady of Am. Opera, 1947, Va. State Coll. 75th anniv. cert. of merit, 1957, NYU Presdl. Citation, 1959, Gold medal Emperor of Ethiopia and Key to City of Taiwan during Pres. Johnson's Cultural Exchange Program, 1962, Art, Culture and Civic Guild award, 1962, Negro Musician's Assn. plaque, 1963, Harlem Opera and World Fellowship Soc. award, 1963; named Disting. Virginian Gov. of Va., 1972; inducted Danville (Va.) Mus. Fine Arts and History Hall of Fame, 1974; Camilla Williams Park designated in her honor, Danville, 1974; honored by Ind. U. Sch. Music Black Music Students' Orgn., 1979; named to Hon. Order Ky. Cols., 1979; honored by Phila. Pro Arte Soc., 1982; Disting. award of Ctr. for Leadership and Devel., 1983; Taylor-Williams student residence hall at Va. State U. named in Billy Taylor's and her honor, 1985. Mem. NAACP (hon. life), Internat. Platform Assn., Alpha Kappa Alpha. Office: Ind U Sch Music Bloomington IN 47401

WILLIAMS, CAROL JORGENSEN, social work educator; b. New Brunswick, N.J., Aug. 12, 1944; d. Einar Arthur and Mildred Estelle (Clayton) Jorgensen; m. Oneal Alexander Williams, July 4, 1980. BA, Douglass Coll., 1966; MS in Computer Sci., Stevens Inst. Tech., 1986; MSW, Rutgers U., 1971, PhD in Social Policy, 1981. Child welfare worker Bur. Children's Svcs., Jersey City, 1966-67, Outagamie County Dept. Social Svcs., Appleton, Wis., 1967-69; supr. WIN N.J. Div. Youth and Family Svcs., New Brunswick, 1969-70; coord. Outreach Plainfield (N.J.) Pub. Libr., 1972-76; rsch. project dir. County and Mcpl. Govt. Study Commn., N.J. State Legislature, 1976-79; assoc. prof. social work Kean Coll. N.J., Union, 1979—; assessment liaison social work program Kean Coll. of N.J., Union, 1987—; chmn. faculty senate gen. edn. com., Kean Coll. N.J., 1990-94, chmn. faculty senate ad hoc com. for 5 yr. review of gen. edn. program, 1991-93, mem. retention and tenure com. Sch. of Liberal Arts, 1988-94, vice chmn., 1992-94; cons. N.J. div. Youth and Family Svcs., 1979-93, Assn. for Children N.J., 1985-88; cons., evaluator Thomas A. Edison Coll., 1977—, mem. acad. coun. and others. Mem. NAFE, NOW, Coun. on Social Work Edn., Nat. Assn. Social Workers (chpt. com. on nomination and leadership identification 1990-92, co-chmn. 1991-92), Assn. for Computing Machinery, Am. Evaluators' Assn., Kean Coll. Fedn. Tchrs. Democrat. Clubs: Good Sam (Agoura, Calif.); Outdoor World (Bushkill, Pa.). Home: 32 Halstead Rd New Brunswick NJ 08901-1619 Office: Kean Coll of NJ Social Work Program Morris Ave Union NJ 07083-7117

WILLIAMS, CAROLE ANN, cytotechnologist; b. Duquesne, Pa., Apr. 14, 1934; d. Theodore Wylie and Dorothy Belle (Mehrmann) Williams; BS, Chatham Coll., 1956; postgrad. Case-Western Res. U., 1956-57; MS Calif. State U., 1989. Cytotechnologist, Clin. Path. Lab. of Paul Gross, Pitts., 1957-59; chief cytotechnologist, teaching supr. Presbyn. U. Hosp., Pitts., 1959-63; staff Pathology Lab. of Drs. Armanini & Wegner, Stockton, Calif., 1964; chief cytotechnologist, teaching supr. Hosp. of Good Samaritan, Los Angeles, 1964-89; dir. cytotechnology and cytology tng. program UCLA Med. Ctr., 1989—; conductor workshops in field. Mem. Am. Soc. Clin. Pathologists (cytotech. exam. com. bd. registry 1978, mem. bd. govs. 1990—), Calif. Assn. Cytotechnologists (pres. 1967-68, 72-73), Internat. Acad. Cytology, Am. Soc. Cytology (Technologist of Yr. award 1981). Republican. Presbyterian. Home: 2460 Stoner Ave Los Angeles CA 90064-1326 Office: 10833 Le Conte Los Angeles CA 90024

WILLIAMS, CAROLYN ELIZABETH, manufacturing executive; b. L.A., Jan. 24, 1943; d. George Kissam and Mary Eloise (Chamberlain) W.; m. Richard Terrill White, Apr. 9, 1972; children: Sarah Anne, William Daniel. BS, Ga. Inst. Tech., 1969; MM, Northwestern U., 1988. Saleswoman Ea. Airlines, Atlanta, Montreal (Can.) and Seattle, 1964-69; job analyst Allied Products Corp., Atlanta, 1969-70; mgr. Allied Products Corp., Frankfort, Mich., 1970-71; planning analyst, sr. planning analyst Allied Products Corp., Chgo., 1972-74, dir. planning, 1974-76, staff v.p. planning, 1976-79, v.p. planning and bus. research, 1979-86, v.p. corp. devel., chief planning officer, 1986-93; pres. White, Williams & Daniels, 1993—. Mem. Winnteka Yacht Club (dir. jr. sailing), Midwest Youth Sailing Assn. (bd. dirs., treas.).

WILLIAMS, CHARLOTTE EVELYN FORRESTER, civic worker; b. Kansas City, Mo., Aug. 7, 1905; d. John Dougal and Georgia (Lowerre) Forrester; student Kans. U., 1924-25; m. Walker Alonzo Williams, Sept. 25, 1926; children: Walker Forrester, John Haviland. Trustee, Detroit Grand Opera Assn., 1960-87 , dir., 1955-60; chmn. Grinnell Opera Scholarship, 1958-66; founder, dir., chmn. adv. bd. Cranbrook Music Guild, Inc., 1952-59, life mem., 1952—; bd. dirs. St. Peter's Home for Boys, Detroit, 1951-53, Detroit Opera Theater, 1959-61, Severo Ballet, 1959-61; Detroit dist. chmn. Met. Opera Regional Auditions, 1958-66; patron-mem. Met. Opera Nat. Coun.; mem. Central Opera Svc., Met. Opera Guild, Children's Mus., Boca Raton, Friends of Children's Mus. at Singing Pines, Boca Raton Hist. Soc., Greater Miami Opera Guild, Fla. Atlantic U. Found.; past pres. Friends of Caldwell Playhouse, Boca Raton. Mem. Debbie-Rand Meml. Svc. League (life), DAR, English-Speaking Union, Vol. League Fla. Atlantic U., PEO, Order Eastern Star, Opus Soc. Philharmonic Orch. of Fla. Home: 2679 S Ocean Blvd Apt 5C Boca Raton FL 33432-8353

WILLIAMS, COLETTE COPELAND, business consultant; b. Balt., Mar. 22, 1966; d. John W. Copeland and Camille (Copeland) Cash; m. Ian Clifford Williams, May 10, 1991; 1 child, Camille Copeland. BFA, Pratt Inst., 1988. Asst. showrm. mgr. Mimi Di N, Inc., N.Y.C., 1986; asst. fashion cons. Elida Olsen et Cie, N.Y.C., 1986-88; director N.Y. State Theater, N.Y.C., 1986-89; photography rep. Northlight Studios, N.Y.C., 1988-89; sales and bus. cons. Mobil Oil Corp., Fairfax, Va., 1990-94; bus. cons. The Sullivan Group, 1994—. Exhibited photographic works at Lincoln Ctr. Family Art Show, 1988, Bellelevine Art Ctr., 1991, 92, 93, 94, Country Bank, 1992, Crystal Gallery, 1992, 94; one-woman shows at Bldg. and Design Ctr., 1992, Mahopac Libr., 1993, Le Petit Museè. Recipient Display award Mus. Natural History, 1987, Best Photography Annual award Photographer's Forum Mag., 1992, 93. Mem. NAFE, World Found Successful Women, Photographic Eye, Light Works, Woodstock Ctr. for Photography, Internat. Ctr. Photography, Silver Eye Ctr. Photography, Morris Arts Coun., Putnam Arts Coun., Am. Wine Soc., Calif. Wine Club.

WILLIAMS, DALE (TILLIE STROTHER), educator; b. California, Mo., Nov. 12, 1908; d. Edgar Hamilton and MAggie Emaline (Dale) Strother; m. Alfred Williams, June 9, 1934. BS in Edn., U. Mo., 1934; MA, So. Ill. U., Carbondale, 1959; postgrad., U. Wis., 1953-54, Wash. U., St. Louis; PhD, Mo. Bapt. Coll., 1989. Dept. chmn. Brentwood (Mo.) High Sch., Fgn. Lang. Program., 1960-74; chmn. legis. com. Greater St. Louis AAUW, 1964-70, pres., 1979-81; bd. chmn. Internat. Relations Lectr. Svc., Clayton, Mo., 1982-84. Rep. to So. Bapt. Convention in Indpls., Kirkwood Bapt. Ch., 1992. Mem. Mo. State Tchrs. Assn. Democrat. Baptist. Home: 700 High Hampton Rd Saint Louis MO 63124-1018

WILLIAMS, DEBRA ARNEICE, computer engineer; b. Toledo, July 14, 1953; d. Albert M. and Doretha (Walls) Carter; m. Clarence Williams, Jr., Feb. 5, 1988; children: Latisha Doretha, El Christopher. Cert. Computer Sci., Davis Bus. Coll., Toledo; Cert. Computer Technology, Control Data Inst., Toledo. Clk. Toledo County Pub. Libr., 1979-85; computer engr. IBM/TSS, Toledo, 1988—. Methodist. Office: Daw Vending 39 W Alexis Rd Ste 103 Toledo OH 43612

WILLIAMS, DENISE, secondary education educator; b. St. Louis, Nov. 25, 1950; d. Archie and Ivory (Payne) W. BS in Edn., Eastern Ill. U., 1971; MS in Edn., So. Ill. U., 1979. Cert. secondary edn. tchr., Ill.; cert. counselor, Ill. Substitute tchr. Madison/Venice (Ill.) Pub. Schs., 1972-74; tchr., program and curriculum developer Madison County (Ill.) CETA Program, 1974-76; tchr. life sci. Centralia (Ill.) City Schs. #135, 1976—; sponsor, coach Cheerleaders, Centralia, 1977—, Sci. Fair, Centralia, 1977—, Just Say No Campaign, Centralia, 1977—; cons. excellence in edn. task force Ill. Edn. Assn., Springfield, 1986. Mem. NAACP, Madison, 1991—, Quad City Coun. of Ch. Women, Granite City, Ill., 1991—; mem. pianist Mt. Nebo Missionary Bapt. Ch., Madison, 1960—; clk. Woodriver Bapt. Dist. Assn., 1973—. Named one of Outstanding Tchr.'s, Masons Lodge # 86, 1989. Mem. NEA, AAUW, Nat. Sci. Tchrs. Assn., Ill. Sci. Tchrs. Assn., Centralia Edn. Assn., Ill. Edn. Assn., Eastern Ill. U. Alumni Assn., So. Ill. U. Alumni Assn. Democrat. Home: 1007 E 3rd St # 4 Centralia IL 62801-3664

WILLIAMS, DOLORES LOUISE, retired telecommunications executive; b. Rockford, Ill., Apr. 20, 1937; d. Arthur F. and Erma Lee (Johnson) Warner; divorced; 1 child, Leona Marie Williams. BE, Ottawa (Kans.) U., 1959. Cert. tchr., Kans., Tenn. Tchr., acting prin. Navajo Indian Reservation, N.Mex. and Ariz., 1959-62; svc. rep. Ill. Bell., Rockford, 1962-64; sr. svc. rep. Mich. Bell, Jackson, 1964-67, South Cen. Bell, Memphis, 1967-70; unit supr. bus. office South Central Bell, Memphis, 1974-81; asst. sales mgr. AT&T and South Cen. Bell, Nashville and Memphis, 1981-90; mem. Bellsouth tng. staff AT&T and South Central Bell, Nashville and Memphis, 1991; asst. dir. HWPC Child Care Tng. Program, Memphis, 1970-71; dir. Shelby County Headstart, Memphis, 1971-73. Recipient Outstanding Svc. award Warren Headstart Ctr., Memphis, 1973, Bell System Eagle award, 1981, Ops. Mgrs.' Coun. Excellence award, 1986, 87, 88, 89, 90,Disting. Leadership award Outstanding Svc. in Communications Industry, 1989, White House Communication Cert. of Appreciation, 1988, 89. Home: 500 Michele Dr Antioch TN 37013-4109

WILLIAMS, DONNA LEE H., state agency administrator; b. Wilmington, Del., Nov. 13, 1960; d. Ronald Lee and Loretta M. (Simonson) H.; m. John R. Williams, Oct. 8, 1988. AA, Wesley Coll., 1979; BA in Govt., Coll. William and Mary, 1981; JD, Widener U., 1984. Atty. Prickett, Jones, Elliott, Kristol & Shnee, Dover, Del., 1983-87, Bayard Handelman & Murdock, Dover, 1987-92; ins. commr. State Del., Dover, 1993—. mem. Del. Bd. Accts., Dover. Mem. Nat. Assn. Ins. Commrs. (v.p. N.E. zone), Del. Bar Assn., Kent County Bar Assn. (past pres.), Women Bus. Leaders (program dir., bd. dirs.), Women's Rep. Club Dover (pres. 1985-87). Methodist. Office: Del Dept Ins 841 Silver Lake Blvd Dover DE 19901

WILLIAMS, DORIS TERRY, business executive, education consultant; b. Middleburg, N.C., Oct. 26, 1951; d. Robert and Lucy (Hargrove) Terry; m. Thomas Williams, Aug. 29, 1981 (div. 1986); children: Adriel Lemuel, Ariel LaShawn. BA, Duke U., 1972; MEd, N.C. State U., 1976, PhD in Edn., 1983. Pub. relations N.C. Blue Cross/Blue Shield, 1972; tech. writer pub. relations Floyd B. McKissick Enterprises, Soul City, N.C., 1972-73; instr., counselor Vance-Granville Community Coll., Henderson, N.C., 1973-75, dir. adult basic edn., 1975-82, counselor, 1982-84; instr. Shaw U., Raleigh, N.C., 1978-83; assoc. dir. N.C. Health Manpower Devel. Co., U. N.C., Chapel Hill, 1984-87; founder, dir. N.C. Ctr. for the Study Of Black History, N.C. Cen. U., Durham, 1987—, dir. African-Am. Resources Ctr., N.C. Ctrl. U., 1991—, Office of Sch. Svcs., 1992—; founder The Leadership Acad.; prin., Pen & Press Inc., 1987—; owner Pen & Press United and Ednl. Cons. Contbr., editor Oracles of Truth, 1983-88, 91—; cons. in field. Sec. bd. dirs. Sound and Print United Sta. WVSP, 1973-88; vice chair Warren County Bd. Edn., 1988-92; chairperson Warren County Polit. Action Com. Subcom. on Edn.; mem. N.C. Black Leadership Caucus; bd. dirs. Freedom Riders Commemerative Found.; chmn. Warren County (N.C.) Bd. Edn., 1992—; founder The Leadership Acad., N.C. Ctrl. U., 1990; co-founder Friends of Bo Med. Centre, USA; bd. dirs. N.C. Minority Health Ctr., 1991—. Mem. Nat. Coun. Negro Women. Democrat. Mem. Apostolic Ch. Avocations: writing, travel, reading, acting. Home: PO Box 465 Manson NC 27553-0465 Office: Pen & Press United 304D Hillsboro St Oxford NC 27565-3214 other: NC Cen U Ctr for Study Black History 804 Fayetteville St Durham NC 27701

WILLIAMS, DOROTHY PUTNEY, elementary school educator; b. Richmond, Va., Sept. 18, 1952; d. Meriwether Vaughan and Dorothy Louise (Martin) Putney; m. Gary Davis Williams, July 24, 1982; children: Gary Davis, Michael Dale, Mark Vaughan. BA, Averett Coll., 1974. Cert. tchr., Va. Tchr. New Kent County Pub. Schs., Quinton, Va., 1974-79; 5th grade tchr. Chesterfield (Va.) County Pub. Schs., 1979—; tchr. Salem (Va.) Elem. Sch., 1979-90; tchr. fgn. langs. and cultures , social studies, English grade 6, 7 and 8th. Swift Creek Mid. Sch., Midlothian, Va., 1990—; mem. Fgn. Lang. Curriculum Coun., Chesterfield, 1992. Author: A Holistic Appraoch to Foreign Languages and Cultures in the Elementary School Classroom, 1992; author fgn. langs. global awareness program, 1990; author curriculum on ancient Egypt taught at Ctr. for Gifted Edn., Coll. William and Mary. Named Tchr. of Yr., 1990-91; recipient award for Tchr. Excellence, 1992. Mem. Nat. Coun. Tchrs. of English, Internat. Reading Assn., Va. State Reading Assn., Richmond Area Reading Coun., Alpha Delta Kappa, Phi Delta Kappa (educator of the year award 1993). Baptist. Home: 5118 Rock Harbour Rd Midlothian VA 23112 Office: Swift Creek Middle Sch 3700 Old Hundred Rd South Midlothian VA 23112

WILLIAMS, DOROTHY RHONDA, gifted education consultant and teacher; b. Grants, N.M., Aug. 20, 1957; d. Howard Lemuel and Betty Virginia (Bragg) Williams; m. John T. McGill, May 31, 1985. BS in Secondry Edn., U. Ark., 1979, MEd in Gifted Edn., 1985; postgrad studies in Anthropology, U. Ill., 1984-86. Cert. tchr., Class 1, Mont. High sch. tchr. Heber Springs (Ark.) Pub. Schs., 1979-80; math. theory instr. Ark. Gov. Sch. for Gifted, 1980; rsch. asst. U. Ark., 1981-84, U. Ill., Champaign-Urbana, 1984-86; tchr. reading and English Browning (Mont.) Pub. Schs., 1986-87, tchr. 8th grade reading, 1987-91, tchr. critical thinking, 1991-92, bilingual gifted and talented resource tchr., 1992—; instr. Gifted Inst. Carroll Coll., Helena, Mont., 1991—; instr. Satori Camp Ea. Washington U., Cheney, Wash., 1993—; presenter at peer ednl. confs., 1987—; project success enrichment trainer, 1994—, ednl. cons. 1993—; mem. curriculum writing project Mont. Office Pub. Instrn./law-related edn.; peer mediation and conflict mgmt. trainer Nat. Conf. on Peacemaking and Conflict Resolution, 1995—. Edge scholar Office of Pub. Instrn. Mont., 1990-92; Taft fellow, 1993. Mem. Assn. Gifted and Talented Edn. (planning com., presenter), Nat. Conf. on Gifted and Talented Edn. for Native People (presenter 1993, 94), Glacier Reading Coun. (presenter), Mont. Reading Coun. (presenter), Internat. Reading Assn. Home: PO Box 246 East Glacier Park MT 59434 Office: Browning Pub Schs PO Box 610 Browning MT 59417-0610

WILLIAMS, EDNA ALETA THEADORA JOHNSTON, journalist; b. Halifax, N.S., Can., Sept. 19, 1923; d. Clarence Harvey and Edna May (Lewis) Johnston; m. Albert Murray Williams, Apr. 16, 1949 (dec.); children: Murleta, Norma, Martin, Charla, Kerrick, Renwick, Julia. Student, Maritime Bus. Coll., 1943. Typist Dept. Treasury (Navy), Halifax, 1944-49; with Bedford (N.S.) Mag., Halifax br., 1954-55, Presbyn. Office, New Glasgow, N.S., 1965-67, Thompson and Sutherland, New Glasgow, 1967-69; family editor, columnist and reporter New Glasgow Evening News, 1969-88, ret., 1988. Bapt. rep. Pictou County Coun. of Chs., 1978-82, sec., 1980-82; pres. ch. aux. 2d United Bapt. Ch., 1979-83, organist, 1970—, chorus dir. Men's Choir, 1980—, hon. mem. ch. aux., v.p., 1993—; organist St. James Anglican Ch., 1983-85, provincial organist, 1994—; provincial pres. Women's Inst. of African United Bapt. Assn., 1983-86; mem. coun. Halifax YWCA; founding mem. Pictou County YM-YWCA, 1966—, bd. dirs., 1967-77, corr. sec., v.p., 1975-77, 1974-75; past pres., past provincial dir. Home and Sch.; provincial sec. African United Bapt. Assn. of Nova Scotia, 1988-90; sec. area IV Atlantic United Bapt. Conv., 1989-93; past officer local interracial com.; bd. dirs. Big Bros./ Big Sisters, 1984-86, Pictou County United Way, 1983—, Palliative Care Aberdeen Hosp., 1985—, Black United Front; reference person media and religion Black History Month. Recipient Honor award United Way, 1993; honored by Pictow County Music Festival, 1994. Mem. N.S. Sr. Secretate. Mem. Can. Press Assn. Home: 230 Reservoir St, New Glasgow, NS Canada B2H 4K4 Office: Evening News, 352 East River Rd, Glasgow, NS Canada B2H 5E2

WILLIAMS, EDNA DORIS, retired educational administrator; b. Bronson, Iowa, July 26, 1908; d. Franklin James and Sarah Jane (Hunt) W. BA, U. No. Iowa, 1939; MA, U. Minn., 1947; postgrad., U. S.D., 1955-60, U. Iowa, 1957, 59, 60, U. Minn., 1951, 67, 69. Cert. adminstr., guidance counselor. Rural sch. tchr. Eurikia # 8, Sac County Rural Schs., Schaller, Iowa, 1929-30; tchr. grades 5 and 6 Bronson (Iowa) Consolidated Sch., 1931-38; normal tng. and English tchr. Rockwell City (Iowa) High Sch., 1939-44; history and debate tchr. Ames (Iowa) High Sch., 1944-47; dramatics and English tchr. East High, Sioux City (Iowa) Community Sch. Dist., 1947-51; dean of girls Central High, Sioux City Community Sch. Dist., 1951-52, East High, Sioux City Community Sch. Dist., 1952-67; asst. prin. East Sioux City Community Sch. Dist., 1967-72, asst. prin. North, 1972-73; cons., chmn. course of study in Am. history Iowa State Dept. Pub. Instrn., Des Moines, 1947-48; demonstration tchr. State Dept. Pub. Instrn., 1957; demonstration tchr. Woodbury County Supt., 1958; student coun. workshop adviser, mem. staff Iowa Assn. Student Couns., Cedar Falls, 1960-63; rep. of dist. Coll. Entrance Exam. Bd., 1950-73; advisor N.W. Coun. Student Coun., 1960-64; mem. exec. bd. N.W. Guidance Coun., 1965-66. Editor: (course book and handbook, high schs.) Ednl. Opportunities, 1968-69; author, editor: Food for Thought Yesterday Today and Tomorrow, 1987; author choral reading plays. Tax aide vol. IRS, Sioux City, 1979-86, 87-91; vol. Iowa Commn. for the Blind; chmn. of com. Sioux City Women's Club, pres. Sioux City Adminstrn. Club, 1957-58; circle chmn. United Meth. Women, 1978. Named one of 100 Counselors in U.S. Selected as a Guest, MIT, 1958, 1 of 30 Counselors as Guest of 6 Minn. Colls., 1966; recipient Cert. of Appreciation, Dir. Student Couns. in Iowa, 1963, Gov.'s Vol. award State of Iowa, 1989, Cert. Dedicated Svc. Am. Assn. Retired Persons, 1990. Mem. NEA (life), Iowa Assn. Women Deans and Counselors (state pres. 1961-62), Iowa State Edn. Assn. (life), Nat. Ret. Tchrs. Assn. (award from Iowa div., Cert. of Appreciation 1986), Sioux City Ret. Educators (life, pres. 1985-88), AAUW (life, treas. 1981-82, v.p. 1984-85, Cert. for Significant Svc. to Ednl. Found. 1981-82, 82-83, chair career women study group), Northern Iowa Alumni Assn., U. Minn. Alumni Assn. (life mem.). Methodist.

WILLIAMS, ELEANOR JOYCE, government air traffic control specialist; b. College Station, Tex., Dec. 21, 1936; d. Robert Ira and Viola (Ford) Toliver; m. Tollie Williams, Dec. 30, 1955 (div. July 1978); children: Rodrick, Viola Williams Smith, Darryl, Eric, Dana Williams Jones, Sheila Williams Watkins, Kenneth. Student Prairie View A&M Coll., 1955-56, Anchorage Community Coll., 1964-65, U. Alaska-Anchorage, 1976. Clk./stenographer FAA, Anchorage, 1965-66, adminstrv. clk., 1966-67, pers. staffing asst., 1967-68, air traffic control specialist, 1968-79, air traffic contr. supr., San Juan, P.R., 1979-80, Anchorage, 1983-85, airspace specialist, Atlanta, 1980-83 ; with FAA, Washington, 1985-87; area mgr. Kansas City Air Rt. Traffic Control Ctr., Olathe, Kans., 1987-89, asst. mgr. quality Assurance, 1989-91, supr. traffic mgmt., 1991; supr. system effectiveness section, 1991-93, asst. air traffic mgr., 1993-94; air traffic mgr. Cleve. Air Route Traffic Control Ctr., FAA, Oberlin, Ohio, 1994—. Sec. Fairview Neighborhood Coun., Anchorage, 1967-69; mem. Anchorage Bicentennial Commn., 1975-76; bd. dirs. Mt. Patmos Youth Dept., Decatur, Ga., 1981-82; mem. NAACP; del. to USSR Women in Mgmt., 1990; mem. citizens amb. program People to People Internat. Recipient Mary K. Goddard award Anchorage Fed. Exec. Assn. and Fed. Women's Program, 1985, Sec.'s award Dept. transp., 1985, Pres. VIP award, 1988, C. Alfred Anderson award, 1991, Disting. Svc. award Nat. Black Coalition of Fed. Aviation Employees, 1991, Paul K. Bohr award FAA, 1994; A salute to Her Name in the Congl. Record 104th Congress, 1995. Mem. Nat. Coun. Negro Women, Bus. and Profl. Women U.S.A., Inc. (North to the Future club, charter pres. 1975-76), Blacks in Govt., Nat. Black Coalition of Fed. Aviation Employees (pres. cen. region chpt. 1987-92, Over Achievers award, 1987, Disting. Svc. award 1988), Profl. Women Contrs. Orgn., Air Traffic Contrs. Assn., Fed. Mgrs. Assn., Internat. Platform Assn., Women in Mgmt. (del. Soviet Union), Gamma Phi Delta. Democrat. Baptist. Avocations: singing; sewing. Home: 5770-D2 Great Northern Blvd North Olmsted OH 44070 Office: FAA 326 East Lorain Oberlin OH 44074

WILLIAMS, ELIZABETH EVENSON, writer; b. Sioux Falls, S.D., Sept. 25, 1940; d. A. Duane and Eleanor (Kelton) Evenson; m. Louis P. Williams Jr., Aug. 31, 1968; 1 child, Katherine. BS, S.D. State U., 1962; MA, U. Wis., 1964; postgrad., U. Minn., 1969-70; MA, S.D. State U., 1983, postgrad., 1992—. Dir. pubs. No. State Coll., Aberdeen, S.D., 1965-68; instr. journalism S.D. State U., Brookings, 1968-69, 85—; asst. editor Journalism Quar., Mpls., 1969-70; pub. info. specialist S.D. Com. on Humanities, Brookings, 1975-78; asst. and instr. speech dept. S.D. State U., Brookings, 1981-92; part-time dir. Women's Ctr., Brookings, 1988-90; reading series coord. S.D. Com. on Humanities, Brookings, 1986-91. Author: Emil Loriks: Builder of a New Economic Order, 1987, Reflections of a Prairie Daughter, 1989, More Reflections of a Prairie Daughter, 1993; weekly columnist Brookings Daily Register, 1985-92, RFD News, 1992—; contbr. articles to profl. jours. Vestry mem. St. Paul's Ch., Brookings, 1975-76, 84-86, 92—; pres. LWV of S.D., 1985-89, treas., 1990-92. S.D. Humanities Com. grantee, 1984, 87, 90. Mem. Nat. Fedn. Press Women (1st place nat. writing contest 1977), Phi Kappa Phi, Pi Kappa Delta, Alpha Kappa Delta. Episcopalian. Home: 1103 3rd St Brookings SD 57006-2230 Office: SD State U Sociology Dept Brookings SD 57007

WILLIAMS, ELLA D., engineering services executive; b. 1940; divorced; 2 children. AA in polit. sci., El Camino Coll., 1979. Delivery room asst. Harbor Gen. Hosp., Torrance, Calif., 1963-65; with finance dept. Hughes Aircraft, L.A., 1965-1981; pres. Aegir Systems, Oxnard, Calif., 1981—. Office: Aegir Systems 2051 Solar Dr Ste 200 Oxnard CA 93030*

WILLIAMS, ELYNOR ALBERTA, public affairs specialist; b. Baton Rouge, Oct. 27, 1946; d. Albert Berry and Naomi Theresa (Douglas) W. BS, Spelman Coll., 1966; MS, Cornell U., 1973. Home econs. tchr. Eugene Butler Jr.-Sr. High Sch., Jacksonville, Fla., 1966-68; publicist, pkg. editor, copy editor Gen. Foods Corp., White Plains, N.Y., 1968-71; writer, researcher Expanded Nutrition Edn. program Cornell U., summer 1972, tutor, com. on spl. edn. projects, 1972-73; communication specialist N.C. Agrl. Ext. Service, N.C. A & T State U., Greensboro and N.C. State U., Raleigh, 1973-77; sr. pub. rels. specialist Western Electric, Greensboro, 1977-83; dir. corp. affairs Hanes Group, Winston-Salem, N.C., 1983-86; dir. pub. affairs, Sara Lee Corp., Chgo., 1985-90, v.p. pub. responsibility, 1990—. Bd. dirs. Greensboro Drug Action Coun., 1977-83, v.p., 1983; mem. Carolina Theatre Commn., 1977-81; mem. steering com. Guilford County Women's Coalition, 1978; agy. bd. mem. solicitor United Way Campaign, 1977-82; issues chmn. Triad council Girls Scouts Am., 1979-82; mem. Mayor's Energy Conservation Commn., 1977-78; vice-chmn. adv. com. dept. communication arts Cornell U., 1978-79; bd. dirs. Leadership Greensboro Alumni Assn., 1980-81, Women's Aid, 1980, Guilford Tech. Coll., 1981-84; pres. Guilford County Women's Polit. Caucus, 1980-81, Friends of Greensboro Coll. Adv. Com., 1980-82, Greensboro Symphony's Audience Devel. Adv. Com., 1980-82; candidate N.C. Ho. of Reps., 1980; mem. adv. bd. Greensboro Daily News Summer Journalism Inst., 1981; vice chmn. 6th Congressional Black Leadership Caucus, 1980-81; mem. pub. rels. adv. bd. YWCA, 1980-81; trustee U. N.C., Greensboro, 1981-91; mem. steering com. N.C. 2000, 1982; mem. Nat. Women's Polit. Caucus; mem. policy coun. N.C. Women's Polit. Caucus, 1982; chmn. Employment Task Force, Gov.'s Assembly on Women and the Economy, 1981; deacon Chgo. United Ch., 1986—; bd. dirs. Hayes-Taylor YMCA, 1983-84, YWCA, Winston-Salem/Forsyth County, 1984-86; mem. adv. council Office of Women in Econ. Devel., N.C. Dept. Commerce, 1985; mem. exec. com. Nat. Women's Econ. Alliance, 1985—; mem. nat. tech. adv. com. OICs of Am., Inc., 1985—; mem. Greensboro Dialogue Task Force, 1983. Recipient Outstanding Svc. award Nat. Coun. Negro Women, 1988, Black and Hispanic Achievers Industry award, 1989, Silver Trumpet award Publicity Club of Chgo., 1990, Lifetime Achievement award Dollar and Sense mag., 1991; named to Black Women's Hall of Fame, 1988, Top Black Women in Corp. Am., Essence mag., 1989, one of 15 Women Who Make a Difference Minorities and Women in Bus. mag., 1989, one of 100 Best and Brightest Black Women in Corp. Am., Ebony mag., 1990, a Nat. Headliners Women in Communications, 1992, one of 50 Top Black Execs. in Corp. Am. Ebony mag., 1992; United Negro Coll. Fund scholar, 1962-66; Cornell U. Grad. Sch. fellow, 1972-73; regional finalist White House fellowship program, 1981-82. Mem. LWV, NOW (mem. corp. adv. bd. legal def. and edn. fund), NAACP (Unsung Heroine award 1989), Exec. Leadership Coun. (founder, bd. dirs. 1986), Internat. Assn. Bus. Communicators, Pub. Rels. Soc. Am., Cosmopolitan C. of C. (bd. dirs. 1988-89), Alpha Kappa Alpha. Democrat. Methodist. Office: Sara Lee Corp 3 1st Nat Plz Fl 46 Chicago IL 60602

WILLIAMS, ERIKA, company executive; b. La Paz, Bolivia, Mar. 28, 1947; came to U.S., 1965; BS, Boston U., 1974, MS, 1977; postgrad., MIT, 1978. Mgr. Amdahl Corp., Sunnyvale, Calif., 1978-82, dir., 1982-86, v.p., 1986—, corp. officer, 1990—, sr. v.p., gen. mgr., 1993—; bd. dirs. Cin. Microwave. Fellow Silicon Valley chpt. Am. Leadership Forum, Los Alton Hills, Calif., 1991—; bd. dirs. Emergency Housing Consortium, San Jose, 1994—. Office: Amdahl Corp 1250 E Arques Ave Sunnyvale CA 94086-4730

WILLIAMS, ERNESTINE, substance abuse counselor; b. Fayetteville, N.C., July 11, 1937; d. Ernest and Melarez (Drye) McDonald; m. Donald Douglas Williams, Sept. 27, 1958; children: Daral, Trina. BA, Coll. New Rochelle, 1984. Credentialed substance abuse counselor, N.Y. Paraprofl. Bd. Edn., Bklyn., 1969-72, parent program asst., 1972-88, substance abuse counselor, 1988—; substance abuse supr. Bd. Edn. Dist. 23, Bklyn., 1991—; coord. parental workshops Bd. Edn., Bklyn., 1978—, coord. Substance Abuse Conf., 1988-93. Recipient awards for leadership. Mem. Coalition of Labor Union Women, Bd. Edn. Employees Local 372 (exec. bd. sec.-treas. 1993—, sec. dist. coun. 1988-93), Goodie award 1989), Coalition Black Trade Unionists. Baptist. Office: Bd Edn Employees Dist Coun 37 125 Barclay St New York NY 10007

WILLIAMS, HARRIET CLARKE, retired academic administrator, artist; b. Bklyn., Sept. 5, 1922; d. Herbert Edward and Emma Clarke (Gibbs) W. AA, Bklyn. Coll., 1958; student, Art Career Sch., N.Y.C., 1960; cert., Hunter Coll., 1965, CPU Inst. Data Processing, 1967; student, Chineses Cultural Ctr., N.Y.C., 1973; hon. certs., St. Labre Sch./St. Joseph's, Ind. Sch., Mont., 1990. Adminstr. Baruch Coll., N.Y.C., 1959-85; mktg. researcher 1st Presbyn. Arts and Crafts Shop, Jamaica, N.Y., 1986—; tutor in art St. John's U., Jamaica, 1986—; founder, curator Internat. Art Gallery, Queens, N.Y., 1991—. Exhibited in group shows at Union Carbide Art Exhibit, N.Y.C., 1975, Queens Day Exhbn., N.Y.C., 1980, 1st Presbyn. Arts and Crafts Shop, N.Y.C., 1986, others; contbr. articles to profl. publs. Vol. reading tchr. Mabel Dean Vocat. High Sch., N.Y.C., 1965-67; mem. polit. action com. dist. council 37, N.Y.C., 1973-77; mem. negotiating team adminstrv. contracts, N.Y.C., 1975-78; mem. Com. To Save CCNY, 1976-77, Statue Liberty Ellis Island Found., Woodrow Wilson Internat. Ctr. Scholars, Wilson Ctr. Assocs., Washington, St. Labre Indian Sch., Ashland, Mont. Appreciation award Dist. Coun. 37, 1979; recipient Plaque Appreciation Svcs., Baruch Coll., Key award St. Joseph's Indian Sch., 1990, Key award in Edn. and Art, 1990, others. Mem. NAFE, AAUW, Women in Mil. Svc., Assn. Am. Indian Affairs, Nat. Mus. of Am. Indian, Artist Equity Assn. N.Y., Lakota Devel. Coun., Am. Film Inst., Bklyn. Coll. Alumni, Nat. Geographic Soc., Nat. Mus. Woman in the Arts, Statue of Liberty Ellis Island Found., Inc., Alliance of Queens Artists, U.S. Naval Inst., El Museo Del Barrio, Am. Mus. Natural History, Internat. Ctr. for Scholars-Wilson Ctr. Assocs., Arrow Club-St. Labre Indian Sch., Mus. of Television and Radio, Women in Military Meml. Found., Nat. Mus. of Am. Indian, U.S. Holocaust Mus., Navy Meml. (adv. coun.). Roman Catholic. Office: Baruch Coll 17 Lexington Ave New York NY 10010

WILLIAMS, HARRIETTE FLOWERS, retired school system administrator, educational consultant; b. L.A., July 18, 1930; d. Orlando and Virginia (Carter) Flowers; m. Irvin F. Williams, Apr. 9, 1960; children: Lorin Finley, Lori Virginia. BS, UCLA, 1952, EdD, (HEW fellow), 1973; MA, Calif. State U., L.A., 1956. Tchr. L.A. Unified Sch. Dist., 1952-59, counselor, 1954-59, psychometrist, 1958-62, faculty chmn., 1956-57, student activities coord., 1955-59, leader insts. and workshops, 1952-76, dir. counseling, 1960-65, supr. Title I programs Elem. Secondary Edn. Act, 1965-68, asst. prin., 1968-76, prin., 1976-82, dir. instrn. sr. high sch. div., 1982-85, adminstr. ops., 1985-92; profl. svcs. cons. Assn. Calif. Sch. Adminstrs., Culver City, Calif., 1992—; asst. dir. HEW project for high sch. adminstrn. UCLA, 1971-72; adj. prof. in Masters in Sch. Adminstrn. program Pepperdine U., L.A., 1974-78; ednl. cons. Teach for Am., 1991-94. Recipient Sojourner Truth award Nat. Assn. Negro Bus. and Profl. Women's Clubs, L.A., 1968, Life Membership Svc. award L.A. PTA, 1972-75, L.A. Mayor's Golden Apple award for ednl. excellence. Mem. Assn. of Adminstrs. of L.A. (pres. region 16), Assn. Calif. Sch. Adminstrs. (state chmn. urban affairs com. 1985-88, region pres. 1989-90), Nat. Assn. Secondary Sch. Prins., Sr. High Sch. Asst. Prins. Assn. of L.A. (bd. dirs. 1974-76, sponsor 1985—), Sr. High Sch. Prins. Orgn., Nat. Coun. of Negro Women (life mem.), Lullaby Guild of Children's Home Soc. L.A. (pres. 1987-89), UCLA Gold Shield (1st v.p. 1994—), L.A. PTA, NAACP, Urban League, Inglewood-Pacific cpt. Links Inc. (sec. 1984-86, treas. 1987-89), Jack and Jill of Am., Inc. (pres. L.A. chpt. 1980-82), UCLA Alumni Assn. (bd. dir., 1979-83, v.p. 1992-94), Delta Sigma Theta (pres. L.A. chpt. 1964-66, regional dir. 1968-72, nat. committeewoman 1966-94), Pi Lambda Theta, Kappa Delta Pi, Delta Kappa Gamma (treas. 1991-94). Baptist.

WILLIAMS, HELEN JOYCE, systems analyst; b. Monroe, La., July 19, 1950; d. Tom Henry and Gordia Jane (Watley) Carr; m. Nathan Williams Jr., July 17, 1971. AA, Wayne County C.C., 1981; B of Gen. Studies with high distinction, Wayne State U., 1985. Catalog order clk. Nat. Bella Hess, North Kansas CIty, Mo., 1968-70; keypunch oper. 1st Nat. Bank, Kansas City, Mo., 1970-71; keypunch oper. Blue Cross Blue Shield, Detroit, 1972, med. claims processor, scheduler, 1972-73, sr. claims processor, asst. supr., 1973-75, provider info. specialist, 1976-83, supr., 1984-85, project analyst, 1985-92, chief systems analyst, 1992-94, project coord., 1995—. Mem. Nat. Mgmt. Assn., Health and People Polit. Action Com. (pres. circle 1992), Golden Key Honor Soc. Office: Blue Cross Blue Shield Detroit MI 48226

WILLIAMS, HELEN MARGARET, accountant; b. Fresno, Calif., Mar. 16, 1947; d. James Ray Jr. and Barbara (LaRue) Franklin; m. Phillip Dean Bangs, Apr. 16, 1977; children: Aluvia, Adevia, Rodney. AA in Home Economics, Sacramento City Coll., 1969, AA in Acctg., 1971; BS in Acctg. and Fin. cum laude, Calif. State U., Sacramento, 1988. Acct. tech. Sacramento Regional Transit Dist., 1974-87, revenue rm. contr., 1987-88, acct. I,

1988, acct. II, 1988—; editor employee newsletter Sacramento Regional Transit Dist., 1986-90. Past mother and worthy adv. Rainbow for Girls; past host parent Am. Field Svc., past chair host family selection com. Mem. NAFE, AAUW, Am. Soc. Women Accts. (chair scholarship com. 1992-94, chair pub. com. 1993-94, bd. dirs. 1993-95, sec. 1994-95), Calif. State U.-Sacramento Alumni Assn., Order Ea. Star, Precious Moments Collectors Club (newsletter editor 1992—, treas. 1993-95). Office: PO Box 2110 Sacramento CA 95812-2110

WILLIAMS, HOLLY THOMAS, business executive; b. Pitts., Dec. 24, 1931; d. Andrew Matthew and Elizabeth (Kuklinca) Thomas; m. Donald Evan Williams, May 14, 1961. AA cum laude, Keystone Jr. Coll., LaPlume, Pa., 1978; BS magna cum laude, U. Scranton, 1981. Dancer Arthur Murray Studios, Pitts., 1953-60; franchise owner Arthur Murray Studios, Scranton, Pa., 1960-80; mgr. Nutri/System Weight Loss Ctr., Scranton, 1984-85, franchise owner, 1985—. Fund raiser United Cerebral Palsy of Lackawanna County, Scranton, 1970-79, St. Joseph's Children's Hosp., Scranton, 1962-76; exec. sec. Foxhowe Assn., Buck Hill Falls, Pa., 1984-85. Mem. AAUW (bd. dirs. 1985-86, 94—), Scranton Club. Republican. Christian. Home: PO Box 151 Buck Hill Falls PA 18323-0151 also: 213 Karen Dr Scranton PA 18505 Office: Nutri/System Weight Loss Ctr 216 Linden St Scranton PA 18503-1404

WILLIAMS, HOPE DENISE, academic administrator, business consultant; b. Chgo., Dec. 24, 1952; d. Welmon and Mary Ann (Brefford) Walker; children: Albert Lee, Ebony Emani Denise. Student Ill. State U., 1971-72. BA in Psychology, St. Ambrose Coll., 1975, postgrad. bus. adminstrn. 1985—; postgrad. Harvard U. Grad. Sch. Design, summer 1981. Social svc. dir. Friendly House, Davenport, Iowa, 1977-78; data collector, cons., 1978; supr. CETA/Summer Youth Employment Program, Davenport, 1978; lead organizer Central and Western Neighborhood Devel. Corp., Davenport, 1978-79; exec. dir. Inner City Devel. Corp., Davenport, 1980-83; owner Midwestern Internat. Mktg. Assocs., San Francisco, 1983; ops. mgr. Dramatic Mktg. Assn., San Francisco, 1983-85; adminstrv. asst. Parker Ross Assocs., 1984-85; crisis intervention counselor Cath. Social Svcs., 1985-86; adminstrv. intern Scott County Iowa, 1985-87; counselor Marycrest Coll., Davenport, 1986-87, asst. dean, 1987-90, dir. of advising, 1989-90; dir. spl. svcs. Augustana Coll., Rock Island, Ill., 1990, asst. dean of students svcs., 1991—; bus. cons. Incorporator, sec. bd. dirs. United Neighbors Inc., 1980; bd. dirs. Community Health Care, 1978-80; v.p., treas. Athletes Say More Edn., 1980; treas., exec. com. F&A Community Warehouse, 1982—; bd. dirs. HELP Legal Aid, 1987—, v.p., 1990, pres., 1991, allocations panel United Way, 1987—. Recipient cert. of appreciation Palmer Jr. Coll., Davenport, 1979, Personal Dedication plaque Jr. Achievement, 1988, 89, 90; cert. of merit Ch. Women United, 1983; NEH grantee, 1979; presdl. grantee Palmer Jr. Coll., 1978. Mem. NAFE, Assn. Black Women Higher Edn., Nat. Assn. Women Edn. (nat. treas. 1993, Dorothy Truex award for Emerging Profls. 1994), Quad Cities Career Womens Network (treas., exec. com.), Assn. Acad. Affairs Adminstrs. (bd. dirs. 1989—, award for new profls. 1989, treas. 1992—), Nat. Acad. Advisors Assn., Nat. Assn. Acad. Advisors (bd. dirs. 1988), Quad Cities Assn. Black Sch. Educators (founding, charter, treas. 1993), Quad City Negro Heritage Soc., Assn. Black Profls. (chairperson), Nat. Assn. Black MBAs, Alpha Kappa Alpha (chair connection com. Xi Eta Omega chpt. 1989, pres. 1990—, mem. internat. stds. com. 1994—), Quad Cities Strivers Inc. (bd. dirs.). Author narrative and final report for oral history project, 1979. Home: 1504 Chateau Knoll Bettendorf IA 52722 Office: 639 38th St Rock Island IL 61201-2210

WILLIAMS, IDA JONES, consumer and home economics educator, writer; b. Coatesville, Pa., Dec. 1, 1911; d. William Oscar and Ida Ella (Ruth) Jones; m. Charles Nathaniel Williams, Mar. 17, 1940 (dec. July 1971). BS, Hampton Inst., 1935; MA, U. Conn., 1965; cert. recognition, Famous Writers Sch., Westport, Conn., 1976, 78. Cert. high sch. tchr., English, sci., home econs., Va., Pa. Sci. and home econs. tchr. Richmond County High Sch., Ivondale, Va., 1935-36; English and home econs. tchr. Northampton County High Sch., Chesaepeake, Va., 1936-40; consumer and home econs. tchr. Northampton County High Sch., Machipongo, Va., 1940-71, Northampton Jr. High Sch., Machipongo, 1971-76. Author: Starting Anew After Seventy, 1980 (plaque 1980), News and Views of Northampton County High Principals and Alumni, 1981; editor: Fifty Year Book 1935-1985 - Hampton Institute Class, 1985, Favorite Recipes of Ruth Family & Friends, 1986. V.p. Ea. Lit. Coun., Melfa, Va., 1987-89; mem. Ea. Shore Coll. Found., Inc.,Melfa, 1988-94; mem. Gov.'s Adv. Bd. on Aging, Richmond, Va., 1992-94; instr. Ladies Community Bible Class, 1976-80 (Plaque 1980); sec., treas., v.p. Hospice Support of Ea. Shore, 1980-94; mem. Northampton/Accomack Adv. Counc., 1992-94. Recipient Nat. Sojourner Truth Meritorious Svc. award Nat. Assn. Negro Bus. and Profl. Women's Clubs, Gavel Ea. Shore Ret. Tchrs. Assn., 1994, Jefferson award Am. Inst. Pub. Svc., Wavy-TV-Bell Atlantic and Mattress Discounters, 1991, Gov.'s award for Vol. Excellence, 1994; named Home Econs. Tchr. of Yr., Am. Home Econs. Assn. and Family Cir., 1975. Mem. Progressive Women of Ea. Shore (pres. 1985-93, Gold Necklace 1993), C. of C., Univ. Women (v.p. Portsmouth br. 1985-87), Ea. Shore Ret. Tchrs. (pres. 1977-84), Dist. L Ret. Tchrs. (pres. 1989-91), Va. State Fedn. Colored Women's Club (pres. 1990-94), Am. Assn. Ret. Persons (Va. state legis. com. 1995—). Mem. Ch. of Christ. Home and Office: PO Box 236 14213 Langford Hwy Eastville VA 23347-0236

WILLIAMS, JESSIE WILLMON, lay worker, retired librarian; b. Boynton, Okla., Feb. 23, 1907; d. Thomas Woodard and Eliza Jane (Adams) Willmon; m. Austin Guest, Aug. 13, 1932 (div. 1945); m. Thomas Washington Williams, Dec. 12, 1946 (dec.). BA, East Tex. State U., 1930, MA, 1944. cert. English and Spanish tchr., Tex. Libr. Gladewater (Tex.) Pub. Libr., 1935-46; med. libr. VA Hosp., North Little Rock, Ark., 1946-58; base libr. Little Rock AFB, 1958-68; ret., 1968; lay worker 1st Bapt. Ch., Pecan Gap, Tex., 1988—. Mem. Delta Kappa Gamma, Phi Beta Kappa. Democrat. Mem. So. Bapt. Conv. Home: PO Box 43 Pecan Gap TX 75469-0043

WILLIAMS, JIMMIE GAY, nurse, graphics specialist; b. Paris, Ark., July 8, 1949; d. Dewey and Jimmie Lee (Lowe) W. Student, John Brown U., 1969-71; ADN, Westark C.C., 1971. RN, Ark. Office asst. Dr. Charles Chalfant, Booneville, Ark., 1970-71; ortho charge nurse St. Edward Mercy Hosp., Ft. Smith, Ark., 1971-74; evening supr. St. Edward Mercy Med. Ctr., Ft. Smith, Ark., 1974-77, educator, 1977-79, asst. dir. edn., 1979-92, graphics coord., 1992—. Dir. nursery Cavanaugh Free Will Bapt. Ch., Ft. Smith, 1985-90; mem. St. Edward Mercy Med. Ctr. Aux. Mem. Ark. Geneal. Soc. Office: St Edward Mercy Med Ctr PO Box 17000 7301 Rogers Ave Fort Smith AR 72917-7000

WILLIAMS, JOAN MARIE, international trade analyst; b. Dayton, Ohio, June 25, 1966; d. John Douglas and Maura Louise (Blankenship) W. Cert., Pushkin Inst., Moscow, 1987; BA, U. Ky., 1988, MA, 1989. Internat. trade analyst U.S. Internat. Trade Com., Washington, 1990-94; postgrad. Harvard Bus. Sch., 1994—. Author: Europe 1992, 1989. Vol., event hostess Rep. Nat. Com., Washington, 1990-94. Gaines fellow Gaines Ctr. for Humanities, 1986, Congl. Rsch. fellow Libr. Congress, 1990. Roman Catholic.

WILLIAMS, JOANNE MOLITOR, elementary education educator; b. Medford, Wis., Oct. 25, 1935; d. Lawrence John and Marie Catherine (Bach) Molitor; m. Jack Dean Williams, Dec. 30, 1953; children: Patricia Varma, Ralph (Skip), L. Bradley. BS in Elem. Edn., U. Wis., Whitewater, 1971, MS in Elem. Edn., 1980; postgrad., Leslie Coll., U. Colo. Cert. tchr. in elem. edn. and geography, Wis. Tchr. grades 4, 5 and 6 Lakewood Sch., Twin Lakes, Ill., 1971-82, 83—, tchr. 5th grade gifted, 1989-91; receptionist A.F. Glass Ins., Lake Geneva, Wis., 1982-83; dir. Resources for Children, Milw., 1982-83; mem. textbook selection com. for reading, social studies, sci., lang.; mem. Lakewood Blue Ribbon Com., 1991, Lakewood Discipline Com., 1990—; mem. Educators Consortium-Parkside, Kenosha, Wis., 1988—; co-developer Respect, Obedience, Attitude, Responsibility program for students with good behavior, 1990; mem. Social Studies Curriculum Com., 1990; mem. Kohl Scholarship Selection Com., 1990, 93; mem. Blue Ribbon Task Force Dept. Pub. Instrn. 1993. Audubon editor Chat, 1975, Slue Membersheet, 1988—. Phone bank organizer Friends of Channel 10/36 Milw., 1987, chair Walworth County portion of Fund Dr., 1989; mem. People for Am. Way, 1986—; mem. 1st Congl. Dist. Acad. Selection Bd., 1988-95; leader Badger coun. Girl Scouts U.S., 1960-82; mem. Walworth County Dem. Party, 1972—, vice chair, 1989-91; host for congl. aide, 1988-93; county organizer presdl. campaign, 1980; vol. coord. assembly campaign, 1992, 94; Statutory Party pollworker of Lake Geneva, 1984—; mem. Friends of Lake Geneva Libr., 1986—, Friends of Twin Lake/Randall Pub. Libr., 1992—, Assn. Preservation of Va. Antiquities; participant Rediscover Jamestown, 1994. Recipient Youth Leader award Am. Legion, 1976, award VA Bloomfield Twp., 1977, Nat. Girl Scout award for community svc., 1976; Herbert Kohl fellow, 1990. Mem. AAUW, NEA (Twin Lakes del. to representative assemblies, congl. contact team 1986-93), Wis. Edn. Assn. (regional pub. rels. com. 1990-92), So. Lakes United Educators (pres. 1979-82, treas. 1982-84, pub. rels. chair 1986—, editor Membersheet, 1987—), Twin Lakes Edn. Assn. (local negotiator), Nat. Assn. Learning Disabled, State and Nat. Coun. Social Studies (curriculum writing team 1991), So. Lakes Reading Coun., Crow Canyon Archaeology Ctr., Nat. Audubon Soc., Lakeland Audubon Soc., Tchr. Place and Parent Resources, Concerned Parents & Edn., Alpha Delta Kappa. Democrat. Home: 307 Water St Lake Geneva WI 53147-1521 Office: Lakewood Sch 1218 Wilmot Ave Twin Lakes WI 53181-9419

WILLIAMS, JOBETH, actress; b. Houston, 1953; m. John Pasquin; children: Nick, Will. Student, Brown U. Appeared in plays A Coupla White Chicks Sitting Around Talking, 1980, Gardenia, 1982, Idiot's Delight, 1986, Cat on a Hot Tin Roof, 1993; films include Kramer vs. Kramer, 1979, The Dogs of War, 1980, Stir Crazy, 1980, Poltergeist, 1982, Endangered Species, 1982, The Big Chill, 1983, American Dreamer, 1984, Teachers, 1984, Desert Bloom, 1986, Poltergeist II, 1986, Memories of Me, 1988, Welcome Home, 1989, Switch, 1991, Dutch, 1991, Stop! Or My Mom Will Shoot, 1992, Me, Myself and I, 1993, Wyatt Earp, 1994; TV movies include Fun and Games, 1980, The Big Black Pill, 1981, Adam, 1983 (Emmy award nominee, Golden Globe award nominee), The Day After, 1983, Kids Don't Tell, 1985, Adam: His Song Continues, 1986, Murder Ordained, 1987, Baby M, 1988 (Emmy award nominee, Golden Globe award nominee), My Name is Bill W., 1989, Child in the Night, 1990, Victim of Love, 1991, Jonathan: The Boy Nobody Wanted, 1992, Sex, Love and Cold Hard Cash, 1993, Chantilly Lace, 1993, Voices from Within, 1994, Lemon Grove, 1994, Parallel Lives, 1994, Voices from Within, 1994, Season of Hope, 1994; TV series include The Guiding Light, Somerset; contbr. voice to Fish Police; co-exec. prodr.: (TV movie) Bump in the Night, 1991; dir. film: On Hope, 1994 (Acad. award nominee for Best Live Action Short Film 1995). Office: William Morris Agy Inc 151 El Camino Beverly Hills CA 90212

WILLIAMS, JOJO MACASAET, office administrator; b. Talisay, Batangas, The Philippines, Sept. 18, 1948; came to U.S., 1970, naturalized, 1990; d. Andrew Ricafort Macasaet and Petra (Casal) Arriola; m. Ernest Thomas Williams, Jr., June 2, 1973; children: Andrew (dec.), Enrico, Maria Elena, Frederick Mac. BS in Psychology, U. Santo Tomas, Manila, 1968; postgrad., Arellano U., Manila, 1970; spl. grad. specialized study in Cytology, U. Chgo., 1972. Tchr. Talisay High Sch., 1968-70, San Guillermo Acad., Talisay, 1968; instr. Mabini Jr. Coll., Talaga, The Philippines, 1968-70; sr. cytotechnologist U. Chgo. Hosp., 1970-73, St. Francis Hosp., La Crosse, Wis., 1973-74, VA Hosp. and Fargo (N.D.) Clinic, 1974-78; sr. histocytotechnologist St. Ansgar Hosp., Moorhead, Minn., 1974-78; bus. mgr., optometric asst. Office Dr. E. Williams, Optometrist, Nashwauk, Minn., 1978—. Vice pres. Am. Cancer Soc., Hibbing, Minn., 1986-91, pres., 1993-94. Mem. AAUW (co-editor bull. Hibbing 1986-88, 3d v.p. 1988-90), Am. Assn. Clin. Pathologists, Am. Found. Vision Awareness (2d v.p. Minn affiliate 1992—, comm. trustee), Internat. Acad. Cytology, Am. Soc. Cytology, Minn. Optometric Assn. (3d v.p. scholarship chmn. 1988-90, corr. sec. 1987—, coord. Save Your Vision Week 1992-94), Nashwauk C. of C. (v.p. 1980-82, sec.-treas. 1984-87), Mesaba Athletic Club, Hibbing Groumet Club. Roman Catholic. Home: 802 Aspen Knl Hibbing MN 55746-3848 also: 2932 1st Ave Hibbing MN 55746

WILLIAMS, JUDITH LORRAINE, pediatric emergency nurse; b. Little Chute, Wis., Mar. 29, 1948; d. Joseph Leo and Mary Theresa (Bowers) Hermes; m. Robert John Van Eyck, Aug. 10, 1968 (div. 1970); m. William Clarence Williams, Sept. 6, 1975; children: Erin Brooke, Justin David. Diploma in Practical Nursing, Neenah-Menasha Vocat. Sch., Wis., 1968; BSN, Calif. State U., Fresno, 1989. ACLS, PALS, BLS, ENA, CEN, TNCC, Calif. Nurse's aide St. Elizabeth's Hosp., Appleton, Wis., 1966-68, LVN, 1970-71; LVN Newport (R.I.) Hosp., 1968-70, Country Care Convalescent Hosp., Atascadero, Calif., 1971-72, Appleton Meml. Hosp., 1972-73, Ross-Loss Med. Ctr., L.A., 1973-74, L.A. Children's Hosp., 1974-75, Valley Children's Hosp., Fresno, 1975-77, Milford (Iowa) Nursing Home, 1977-79; staff nurse Valley Children's Hosp., Fresno, 1989—; mem. career advancement program task force Valley Children's Hosp., 1991—, protocal and standards task force, 1990—. Bd. dirs. Sch. Site Coun., Pacific Union Sch., Bowles, Calif., 1982. Mem. Emergency Nurses Assn., Mid-Valley Emergency Nurses Assn. (edn. com. chair 1992, sec. 1993—), Sigma Theta Tau. Pentecostal Ch. Home: 4345 E Springfield Fresno CA 93725 Office: Valley Children's Hosp 3151 N Milbrook Fresno CA 93703

WILLIAMS, JULIE BELLE, psychiatric social worker; b. Algona, Iowa, July 29, 1950; d. George Howard and Leta Maribelle (Durschmidt) W. BA, U. Iowa, 1972, MSW, 1973. Lic. psychologist, ind. clin. social worker, marriage and family therapist, Minn.; lic. social worker, Iowa. Social worker Psychopathic Hosp., Iowa City, 1971-72; OEO counselor YOUR, Webster City, Iowa, 1972; social worker Child Devel. Clinic, Iowa City, 1973; therapist Mid-Eastern Iowa Community Mental Health Ctr., Iowa City, 1973; psychiat. social worker Mental Health Ctr. No. Iowa, Mason City, 1974-79, chief psychiat. social worker, 1979-80; asst. dir. Community Counseling Ctr., White Bear Lake, Minn., 1980-85, dir., 1985—; lectr., cons. in field. NIMH grantee, 1972-73. Mem. NASW (ACSW, QCSW, diplomate), NOW, Am. Orthopsychiat. Assn., Am. Assn. Sex Educators, Counselors and Therapists, Minn. Women Psychologists, Minn. Lic. Psychologists, Phi Beta Kappa. Democrat. Office: 1280 N Birch Lake Blvd White Bear Lake MN 55110-6708

WILLIAMS, JULIE FORD, mutual fund specialist; b. Long Beach, Calif., Aug. 7, 1948; d. Julious Hunter and Bessie May (Wood) Ford; m. Walter Edward Williams, Oct. 20, 1984; 1 child, Andrew Ford. BA in Econs., Occidental Coll., 1970. Legal sec. Kadison, Pfaelzer, Woodard, Quinn & Rossi, L.A., 1970-71, 74-77; legal sec. Fried, Frank, Harris, Shriver & Jacobson, N.Y.C., 1971-72, Pallot, Poppell, Goodman & Shapo, Miami, Fla., 1973-74; adminstrv. asst. Capital Research-Mgmt., Los Angeles, 1978-82; corp. officer Cash Mgmt. Trust Am., 1982—, Bond Fund Am., 1982—, Tax-Exempt Bond Fund Am., 1982—, AMCAP Fund, 1984—, Am. Funds Income Series, 1985—, Am. Funds Tax-Exempt Series II, 1986—, Capital World Bond Fund, 1987—, Am. High-Income Trust, 1987—, Intermediate Bond Fund Am., 1987—, Tax-Exempt Money Fund Am., 1989—, U.S. Treasury Money Fund Am., 1991—, Fundamental Investors, 1992—, Ltd. Term Tax-Exempt Bond Fund Am., 1993—, Am. High-Income Mcpl. Bond Fund, 1994—; v.p. fund bus. mgmt. group Capital Rsch. Mgmt., 1986—. Mem. alumni bd. govs. Occidental Coll., 1994—. Democrat. Episcopalian. Office: Capital Rsch and Mgmt Co 333 S Hope St Los Angeles CA 90071-1406

WILLIAMS, K. ELAINE, psychologist; b. Alexandria, Va., Sept. 20, 1952; d. C.P. (Jimmie) Jr. and Kathryn L. (Ogden) Talbert; m. Terrence J. Williams, Dec. 28, 1973; children: Brendan Kyle, Laura Allyson. BA, Mary Washington Coll., 1974; MA, George Mason U., 1978; PhD, Am. U., 1992. Counselor Rappahannock Alcoholism, Fredericksburg, Va., 1974-77; therapist Rappahannock-Rapidan Community Mental Health Ctr., Culpeper, Va., 1978-82; intern Child Devel. Ctr., Georgetown U., Washington, 1987-88; therapist Am. U., Washington, 1989-94; psychologist Family Counseling Ctr., McLean, Va., 1994—. Contbr. articles to profl. jours. Mem. APA, Assn. for Advancement of Behavior Therapy. Democrat.

WILLIAMS, KAREN HASTIE, lawyer; b. Washington, Sept. 30, 1944; d. William Henry and Beryl (Lockhart) Hastie; m. Wesley S. Williams, Jr.; children: Amanda Pedersen, Wesley Hastie, Bailey Lockhart. Cert., U. Neuchatel, Switzerland, 1965; BA, Bates Coll., 1966; MA, Tufts U., 1967; JD, Cath. U. Am., 1973. Bar: D.C. 1973. Staff asst. internat. gov. relations dept. Mobil Oil Corp., N.Y.C., 1967-69; staff asst. com. Dist. Columbia U.S. Senate, 1970, chief counsel com. on the budget, 1977-80; law clk. to judge Spottswood Robinson III U.S. Ct. Appeals (D.C. Cir.), Washington, 1973-74; law clk. to assoc. justice Thurgood Marshall U.S. Supreme Ct., Washington, 1974-75; assoc. Fried, Frank, Harris, Shriver & Kampelman, Washington, 1975-77, 1975-77; adminstr. Office Mgmt. and Budget, Washington, 1980-81; of counsel Crowell & Moring, Washington, 1982, ptnr., 1982—; Bd. dirs. Crestar Fin. Services Corp., Fannie Mae, Washington Gas Light Co., Continental Airlines, SunAmerica, Inc. Chair, trustee Greater Washington Research Ctr., chair. Mem. ABA (pub. contract law sect., past chair), Nat. Bar Assn., Washington Bar Assn., Nat. Contract Mgmt. Assn., NAACP (bd. dirs. legal defense fund). Office: Crowell & Moring Ste 1200W 1001 Pennsylvania Ave NW Washington DC 20004-2595

WILLIAMS, KAREN JOHNSON, federal judge; b. Orangeburg, S.C., Aug. 4, 1951; d. James G. Johnson and Marcia (Reynolds) Johnson Dantzler; m. Charles H. Williams, Dec. 27, 1968; children: Marian, Ashley, Charlie, David. BA, Columbia Coll., 1972; postgrad., U. S.C., 1973, JD cum laude, 1980. Bar: S.C. 1980, U.S. Dist. Ct. S.C. 1980, U.S. Ct. Appeals (4th cir.) 1981. Tchr. Irmo (S.C.) Mid. Sch., 1972-74, O-W High Sch., Orangeburg, 1974-76; assoc. Charles H. Williams P.A., Orangeburg, 1980-92; circuit judge U.S. Ct. Appeals (4th cir.), 1992—; mem. exec. bd. grievance commn. S.C. Supreme Ct., Columbia, 1983-92. Mem. child devel. bd. First Baptist Ch., Orangeburg; bd. dirs. Orangeburg County Mental Retardation Bd., 1986—, Orangeburg-Calhoun Hosp. Found; bd. visitors Columbia Coll., 1988-92; dir. Reg. Med. Ctr. Hosp. Found., 1988-92; mem. Orangeburg-Calhoun Tech. Coll. Adv. Bd., 1987-92; mem. Rotary Club Orangeburg, 1989—. Mem. ABA, S.C. Bar Assn., Orangeburg County Bar Assn. (co-chairperson Law Day 1981), Assn. Trial Lawyers Am., S.C. Trial Lawyers Assn., Bus. and Profl. Women Assn., Order of Wig and Robe, Order of Coif, Jr. Service League. Home: RR 2 Box 110 Orangeburg SC 29115-9604 Office: US Courthouse PO Box 2087 Orangeburg SC 29116-2087*

WILLIAMS, KAREN OLIVIA, nurse manager, maternal-child health nurse; b. Alexandria, La., Nov. 23, 1959; d. Edward and Calian (Jacobs) W.; 1 child, Edward DeSean Marquis Williams. AS, La. State U., Alexandria, 1980; BS with honors, Northwestern State U., 1991. RN, La.; cert. ACLS, BLS, neonatal resusciation provider, PALS, TNCCP; cert. nurse oper. rm. Nurse ob.-gyn. Huey P. Long Med. Ctr., Pineville, La., 1980-83, nurse labor and delivery, 1983-87, charge nurse oper. rm., 1987-91, emergency rm. supr., 1992-94; maternal child health mgr., 1994—; nurse ARC, 1991. Mem. ANA, Assn. Women's Health Obstet. and Neonatal Nurses, La. Assn. Nurse Practitioners, La. Nurse Polit. Action Com., Emergency Nurse Assn., Assn. Oper. Rm. Nurses (cert., bd. dirs. 1991-92), La. State Nurses Assn. (polit. action com.), Alexandria Dist. Nurses Assn. (bd. dirs. 1992-93, pres. 1993-95), Sigma Theta Tau. Republican. Roman Catholic. Home: 107 Navaho Pl Pineville LA 71360-5931 Office: Huey P Long Med Ctr Hospital Blvd Pineville LA 71360

WILLIAMS, KAREN RUSSELL, safety technician; b. Birmingham, Ala., Aug. 27, 1952; d. Walter Earl and Nancy Alice (Maze) Russell; m. Kent Michael Williams, Dec. 13, 1980. Sec. Protective Life Ins. Co., Birmingham, 1972-74; sec. Am. Cast Iron Pipe, Birmingham, 1974-79, billing clk., 1979-89, safety technician, 1989—. Mem. Nat. Mgmt. Assn. (chairperson 1989—), Am. Soc. Safety Engrs., Assn. Women in Metal Industry. Democrat. Office: American Cast Iron Pipe Co 2930 N 16th St Birmingham AL 35202

WILLIAMS, KATHERINE KNAPP, college official; b. Missoula, Mont., Apr. 5, 1952; d. Henry William and Cornelia (Grothe) Knapp; m. Brian Douglas Williams, Mar. 4, 1972; children: Jennifer, Nadia, Hans. BS in Edn., Appalachian State U., Boone, N.C., 1976; MA, Appalachian State U., 1980; EdD, Ball State U., Muncie, Ind., 1991. Instr. Asheville (N.C.) Buncombe Tech. Coll., 1977-78; instr. tchr. edn. Dominica (W.I.) Tchrs. Coll., 1981-84; instr. Wilberforce (Ohio) U., 1984; chmn. dept. gen. edn. Ind. Vocat.-Tech. Coll., Richmond, 1985-88; dir. student support svcs. Ind. U. East, Richmond, 1988-91; dir. Ednl. Opportunity Ctr., No. Mont. Coll., Havre, 1991—. Com. chmn. Mont. Baha'i Schs., 1992—; organizer Reach for Tomorrow, Advocacy for Girls, Havre, 1993—. Mem. Assn. Spl. Programs in Region Eight, AAUW, Phi Delta Kappa. Mem. Baha'i Faith. Office: No Mont Coll 11th St Havre MT 59501

WILLIAMS, KATHLEEN FRANCES, retired government administrator, association executive; b. Phila., Aug. 22, 1929; d. Gilbert and Cynthia Amelia (Waters) W. Degree in bus., U. Pa., 1973. Supr. supply technician Phila. Naval Shipyard, 1951-93. Sec. bd. dirs. Stephen Smith Towers, 1988—; mentor Intergenerational Learning Ctr. Temple U., 1993—; nat. v.p. Continental Soc. Inc., 1993—; pres. bd. dirs. YWCA, Phila., 1993—. Recipient Lillian Parks award Continental Soc. Inc., 1988. Republican. Episcopalian. Home: 4323 Haverford Ave Philadelphia PA 19104-1355

WILLIAMS, KATHRYN BLAKE, librarian; b. Lancaster, Pa., Mar. 20, 1923; d. Harry Leslie and Mary Kauffman (Strine) Blake; m. William George Williams Sr., June 1, 1945; children: Leslie Williams Aronson, William George Jr. BS in Edn., U. Pa., 1944; elem. cert., Shippensburg U., 1969, MLS, 1973. Home economist Pa. State Extension Svc., Carlisle, 1944-46; kindergarten tchr. Blind Assn. Harrisburg, Pa., 1955; asst. elem. tchr. Sweeney Day Sch., Harrisburg, 1955-57; week-day kindergarten tchr. Presbyn. Ch., Camp Hill, Pa., 1961-63; 1st grade tchr. West Shore Sch. System, Lemoyne, Pa., 1965-71; dir. Ralpho Twp. Pub. Libr., Elysburg, Pa., 1973-75; libr. Bloomsburg (Pa.) Univ. of Pa., 1979-80, Bloomsburg Hosp., 1980-81; mem. adv. coun. North Cen. Region Job Tng. of Pa., Ridgeway, 1991—; organizing dir. DuBois office, vista vol. Mid-State Literacy Coun., State College, Pa., 1987-88. Leader, day camp dir. Girl Scouts U.S., Harrisburg, 1957; field svc. coord. Am. Field Svc., Camp Hill, 1963-65; weekly radio panelist United Coun. of Chs., Harrisburg, 1963-65; vol. libr. DuBois (Pa.) Regional Med. Ctr., 1990—; story teller Bloomsburg Pub. Libr., 1974-83; commr. to gen. assembly Presbyn. Ch., 1983, elder, 1973—, deacon, 1994—, sec. of deacons, 1994—. Mem. AAUW (v.p. 1987-89), Pa. State Edn. Assn. (life), Friends of DuBois Pub. Libr. (pres. 1984-86), Presbyn. Women (resource coord. 1975-85, mission coord. 1992—). Home: 377 Treasure Lake Du Bois PA 15801-9008

WILLIAMS, KATHY KARA, insurance broker; b. Richmond, Calif., Jan. 10, 1966; d. William Leonard Koenig and Roberta Eleonore (Eller) Becker; m. Kathy Kara Koenig-Williams, Feb. 10, 1984; 1 child, Krista Rae. Grad. H.S., Pinole, Calif., 1984. Receptionist, mail clk. Bayly, Martin & Faye, Walnut Creek, Calif., 1984-86; word processor Morris & Assocs., Walnut Creek, 1986-87; comml. lines rater Travelers Ins. Co., Walnut Creek, 1987-88; asst. acct. mgr. Putnam, Knudsen & Wieking, Oakland, Calif., 1988-93; account mgr., corp. sec.-treas., bd. dirs. Peder D. Knudsen, Inc. Ins. Brokers, Walnut Creek, 1993—. Office: Peder D Knudsen Inc 2735 N Main St Walnut Creek CA 94596

WILLIAMS, KATHY MARGENE, real estate broker; b. Rinard Mills, Ohio, Oct. 16, 1940; d. Willis S. and Juanita B. (Gray) Dye; m. Paul D. Williams, June 21, 1959; children: Gregory, Christine. Grad., Realtors Inst., 1987. Sales assoc. Jack Croy Realty, Findlay, Ohio, 1976-79, Bishop-Kandel Realty, Findlay, 1979-83, Geyer Assocs., Findlay, 1983-85; broker, owner Re/Max Realty, Findlay, 1985—. Recipient Ohio award of excellence Ohio Assn. Realtors, Columbus, 1993, 94. Mem. Employee Relocation Coun. (CRP), Residential Sales Coun., Findlay C. of C. (bd. dirs. 1993-95). Office: Re/Max Realty/Findlay 1621 Tiffin Ave Findlay OH 45840

WILLIAMS, LA SHINA BRIGETTE, mechanical engineer; b. Houston, Oct. 22, 1957; d. C.K. Jr. and Myrtle Opal (Bouchum) Morrow; divorced; 1 child, Chase Michael. BSME, Prairie View (Tex.) A&M U., 1980; MBA, Atlanta U., 1984. Mech. engr. Phillips Petroleum, Sweeny, Tex., 1980-82; product planner, project mgr. IBM, Gaithersburg, Md., 1985—. Republican. Home: 11122 Cedar Bluff Ln Germantown MD 20876

WILLIAMS, LEONA RAE, lingerie retailer; b. Fairfield, Nebr., July 1, 1928; d. Melton M. and Helga D. (Sorensen) Brown; m. Eugene F. Williams, June 6, 1946; 1 child, Dennis D. Grad. high sch., Fairfield. Owner Alice Rae Apparel Shop, Tucson, 1953—, second location 1967—, Green Valley, Ariz., 1976-93, Sun City, Ariz., 1979—. Sponsor Distributive Edn. Program, 1978-82; coord. fashion shows Am. Cancer Soc., Tucson, 1987, 88, 89. Mem. Exec. Women's Internat. Assn. (chpt. pres. 1994), Mchts. Assn. (pres. 1987-89), Soroptomists, C. of C. Better Bus. Bur. Republican. Baptist.

Office: Alice Rae Intimate Apparel 2954 N Campbell Ave Tucson AZ 85719-2876

WILLIAMS, LESLIE ELIZABETH, nurse, education specialist; b. Berkeley, Calif., Dec. 5, 1953; d. Gordon Hulin and Elizabeth (Wulff) Smith; widow. BSN, Loretto Heights Coll., 1976; MNA, U. Phoenix, 1992. RN, Colo.; cert. emergency nurse. Clinic nurse Mountain Cmty. Med. Ctr., Idaho Springs, Colo., 1976-77; staff nurse, chairperson Kremmling (Colo.) Meml. Hosp., 1977-78; staff nurse emergency dept. Provenant St. Anthony Ctrl. Hosp., Denver, 1978-84, 85-88, program coord. med. edn., 1984-85, clin. II emergency dept., 1988-91, edn. specialist, 1991—; owner, outfitter Cirrus Corp., Denver, 1984—; cons. quality trauma and emergency Emergency Physicians Med. Group, Santa Rosa, Calif., 1984; cons. telemedicine Decision Sci. Applications, Inc., Colorado Springs, Colo., 1994; mem. adj. faculty Regis U., Denver, 1994; presenter in field. Pres. Golden Meadows Homeowners Assn., Morrison, Colo., 1989; vol. Nat. Sports Ctr. for Disabled, Winter Park, Colo., 1989-92. Mem. Nat. Nursing Staff Devel. Orgn., Emergency Nurses Assn. (chpt. pres. 1991). Office: Provenant St Anthony Ctrl Hosp 4231 W 16th Ave Denver CO 80204

WILLIAMS, LINDA BERGENDAHL, information specialist; b. Glen Cove, N.Y., June 1, 1946; d. Eigil and Lilliam Gertrude (Bettine) Bergendahl; children from previous marriage: Heidi, Garth; m. Arthur G. Williams, 1993. BA, L.I. U., 1969; MA, SUNY, Stony Brook, 1984. Asst. curator Nat. Pk. Svc., Mastic, N.Y., 1980-84; office mgr. Coogan, Swanson and Lange, Burlington, Vt., 1985-87; rsch. officer U. Vt., Burlington, Vt., 1987-93; pres. Impact Info., Burlington, 1991—. Founder Brookhaven Hist. Dists., Patchoque, N.Y., 1978, Community Connection Program, Burlington, 1988, Holiday Basket Program, Burlington, 1988. Mem. Soc. Competitive Intelligence Profls., Am. Prospect Rsch. Assn. Office: Impact Information PO Box 1044 Burlington VT 05402

WILLIAMS, LINDA JO, interior designer; b. Wichita Falls, Tex., Jan. 17, 1942; d. Cleburne Milton and Jonell (Acuff) Maier; m. James Legrand Williams, June 7, 1963 (div. 1987); children: Brent Legrand, Kent Milton. BA in English, U. Tex., 1964. Tchr. English, Speech Spring Branch (Tex.) Ind. Sch. Dist., 1963-65; prin. Designs by Linda, Houston, 1978-81; pres. Linda Williams--By Design Inc., Houston, 1981-87; art cons. Simic Art Galleries, Carmel, Calif., 1987-88, Coast Gallery, Pebble Beach, Calif., 1988-89; interior designer Linda Williams-By Design, Carmel, 1989—. Mem. March of Dimes Gourmet Gala, 1990; trustee Forest Theatre Guild. Mem. Am. Soc. Interior Design (allied), Soroptimists. Methodist. Home and Office: PO Box 4505 Carmel CA 93921-4505

WILLIAMS, LINDA LEE, clinical coordinator; b. Corinth, Miss., June 5, 1966; d. Harry Lee Williams and Linda Anniese (Carroll) Carpenter. BSN, U. Miss., 1989; MSN, U. Ala., Birmingham, 1992. Nursing extern Magnolia Hosp., Corinth, 1988; staff RN Miss. Bapt. Med. Ctr., Jackson, 1989-90, St. Vincent's Hosp., Birmingham, 1990-93, Bapt. Med. Ctr. Montclair, Birmingham, 1990-93; clin. coord. Anesthesia Pain Svc. Bapt. Med. Ctr., Birmingham, 1992—. Mem. Am. Soc. of Pain Mgmt. Nurses. Ch. of Christ.

WILLIAMS, LINDA MANGHAM, corporate executive; b. Atlanta, Feb. 23, 1945; d. Harvey R. and Bernice (O'Kelley) Mangham; m. Jimmy L. Smith, Dec. 21, 1963 (dec. Jan. 1964); 1 child, Kellie Smith Williams Stein; m. Maryon J. Williams, Jr., June 9, 1968; 1 child, Claire Elaine. Student, Augusta Coll., 1972; student, U. Pa., 1989; BSBA, Thomas Edison Coll., 1989. Exec. sec. Firestone Tire & Rubber Co., Atlanta, 1966-68; Exec. asst. P & I Co., New Brunswick, N.J., 1968-72; vol. Med. Coll. Ga. Faculty Wives, Augusta, Ga., 1972-77; owner Freelance Editorial Svc., Princton Junction, N.J., 1977-79; recording sec. West Windsor Twp., Princton Junction, 1979-81; acting office mgr. Fellows Read & Assocs., Princeton, N.J., 1980-81; dir. corp. communications The Hillier Group, Princeton, 1981-86; dir. pub. affairs N.J. Dept. Commerce, Energy and Econ. Devel., Trenton, 1986-90; pres. Entertainment Inc., Princeton Junction, 1989—; mem. Employer Support of Guard & Res., Trenton, 1985—; mem. econ. com. N.J. Bus. & Industry Assn., Trenton, 1985-87; chair meetings and conv. com. N.J. Alliance for Action, Edison, N.J., 1985-86. Contbr. articles to profl. jours. Past mem. Grover's Mill Pond Restoration Com., Princeton Junction; mem. Faculty Wives Club, Med. Coll. Ga., Augusta, 1972-77; scout master Girl Scouts U.S., Piscataway, N.J., 1970-71, asst. scout master, Augusta, 1972-74. Named one of Outstanding Women in Govt., Gov. of N.J., 1987. Mem. Pub. Relations Soc. Am., N.J. Bus. and Industry Assn., Princeton Area C. of C. Office: Entertainment Inc 21 Quaker Rd Princeton Junction NJ 08550-1615

WILLIAMS, LORI ELIZABETH, newspaper editor; b. Hammond, La., Aug. 18, 1957; d. Clinton Antoine and Eloise Cecilia (Cuevas) Guwang; m. John Barry Williams, Sept. 1, 1984; children: Walter Trace, August Burl. BJ, La. State U., 1979. Newspaper reporter Beaumont (Tex.) Enterprise, 1979-83, asst. city editor, 1983-84; gen. mgr. Miss. Bus. Newspaper, Jackson, 1985-88; editor Clear Lake Citizen, Houston, 1988—. Mem. Tex. Press Assn. (1st place Cmty. Svc. award 1992, editorial awards), Gulf Coast Newspaper Assn., Bay Area Profl. Communicators (bd. dirs., v.p. 1992). Home: 2021 Cortlandt St Houston TX 77008-2615 Office: Clear Lake Citizen 17511 El Camino Real Houston TX 77058-3031

WILLIAMS, LOUISE TAYLOR, assistant principal; b. Shreveport, La., Mar. 11, 1921; d. Bailey Taylor and Geneva (Arkansas) Jones; m. James Monroe Murphy, July 13, 1973 (dec. Sept. 1980); m. Andrew Jackson Williams, Aug. 6, 1987. BS, Tex. So. U., 1944; MS in Edn., Chgo. State U., 1972. Clin. lab. technician Houston Negro Hosp., 1943-44; med. rsch. asst. Michael Reese Hosp., Chgo., 1944-52; substitute tchr. Chgo. Pub. Sch., 1952-54; tchr. Chgo. Pub. Sch./Coleman Sch., 1954-63; tchr. 4th-6th grades Chgo. Pub. Sch./Neil Sch., 1963-71, acting asst. prin., 1971-73, asst. prin., 1973-85, ret., 1985; tchr. 5th grade Pirie Sch., Chgo., summer 1965, Hookway, Chgo., summer 1966; team leader in-svc. program Sch. Community Reps. 5, summer 1967. Mem. adv. bd. Chatham-Avalon Mental Health Clinic, 1983—, St. Joachim Elem. Sch., 1987-92; bd. dirs. Chgo. State U., 1984-88; bd. dirs., treas. Higgins Found., 1992-93. Recipient Outstanding Svc. award Chgo. State U., 1988. Mem. AAUW (mem. at large 1994—), Coun. for Exceptional Children, West Chesterfield Community Block Club (social sec. Chgo. chpt. 1980—), Phi Delta Kappa. Roman Catholic.

WILLIAMS, LULA AGNES, retired writer, retired educator; b. Bentonville, Ark., May 11, 1904; d. Thomas Andrew and Nellie Louella (Mason) Nichols; m. Esmond Leonidas Williams, June 12, 1927 (dec. Jan. 1961). BA, U. Ark., 1956. Cert. secondary tchr., cert. to teach English and social studies. Stenographer Benton County Hardware Co., Bentonville, Ark., 1922-25; tchr. country sch. Cross Lanes, Bentonville, 1925-26; stenographer-sec. Skelly Oil Co., El Dorado, Kans., 1926-27; asst. adminstr. Benton County Home, Bentonville, 1935-40; acting postmaster U.S. Post Office, Bentonville, 1944-45; tchr. Bentonville Schs., 1956-70; acting postmaster U.S. Post Office, Bentonville, 1961-62; writer Bentonville, 1985-88. Author, pub.: Hills Are for Climbing, 1988. Pres. Bates Meml. Hosp. Aux., 1972, Qui Vive, Gen. Fedn. Women's Clubs, Bentonville, 1973, Benton County Ret. Tchrs. Assn., 1976-77; worthy matron Order of Eastern Star, Bentonville, 1936. Named Woman of Yr., Bus. and Profl. Women's Club, Bentonville, 1981-82; recipient Svc. award AAUW, Bentonville, 1981, gift named in her honor AAUW 1987. Mem. Nat. Retired Tchrs. Assn. (life), Ark. Retired Tchrs. Assn. (life), U. Ark. Alumni Assn. (life). Democrat. Mem. Christian Ch. (Disciples of Christ). Home: 425 SE A St Bentonville AR 72712

WILLIAMS, MADONNA JO, accountant; b. Traverse City, Mich., Mar. 24, 1945; d. Harold Augustus and Josephine Annabelle (Dreves) Barratt; m. Jerry J. Williams, Dec. 28, 1963; children: Jerry J. Jr., Scott T. AAS with honors, Northwestern Mich. Coll., 1983; BS in Acctg. with highest distinction, Ferris State U., 1984. CPA, Mich. Mem. taxpayer svc. staff IRS, Traverse City, 1971-73; staff acct. Seidman & Seidman, Traverse City, 1973-75; mem. staff, mgr. Fuller, Somero & Black, CPAs, Traverse City, 1975-85; ptnr. Black & Williams, CPAs, Traverse City, 1985—. Mem. AICPA, Am. Assn. CPAs (Elijah Watt Sells award 1984), Mich. Assn. CPAs (William A. Paton award 1984), Zonta Club Traverse City. Home: 8871 N Long Lake Rd Traverse City MI 49684-9622 Office: Black & Williams CPAs 3050 Sunset Ln Traverse City MI 49684-4672

WILLIAMS, MARGARET, federal official. Asst. to Pres., chief of staff to First Lady The White House, Washington, 1993—. Office: Office of the First Lady The White House 1600 Pennsylvania Ave NW Washington DC 20500

WILLIAMS, MARSHA KAY, data processing executive; b. Norman, Okla., Oct. 26, 1963; d. Charles Michael and Marilyn Louise (Bauman) Williams; m. Dale Lee Carabetta, Dec. 13, 1981. Student, Metro. State Coll., Denver. Data processing supr. Rose Mfg. Co., Englewood, Colo., 1981-84, Mile High Equip. Co., Denver, 1984-88; supr. info. tech. Ohmeda Monitoring Sys., Louisville, Colo., 1988—. Mem. info. tech. adv. bd. Warren Tech. Sch., 1994—. Mem. Bus. and Profl. Women's Assn. (Young Careerist 1991). Home: 3302 W 127th Ave Broomfield CO 80020-5800 Office: Ohmeda Monitoring Systems 1315 W Century Dr Louisville CO 80027-9560

WILLIAMS, MARSHA RHEA, computer scientist, educator, researcher, consultant; b. Memphis, Aug. 4, 1948; d. James Edward and Velma Lee (Jenkins) W.; BS, Beloit Coll., 1969; MS in Physics, U. Mich., 1971; MS in Systems and Info. Sci., Vanderbilt U., 1976, PhD in Computer Sci., 1982. Cert. data processing (CDP). Engring. coop. student Lockheed Missiles & Space Co., Sunnyvale, Calif., 1967-68; asst. transmission engr. Ind. Bell Telephone Co., Indpls., 1971-72; systems analyst, instr. physics Memphis State U., 1972-74; computer-assisted instrn. project programmer Fisk U., 1974-76; mem. tech. staff Hughes Rsch. Labs., Malibu, Calif., 1976-78; assoc. systems engr. IBM, Nashville, 1978-80; rsch. and teaching asst. Vanderbilt U., Nashville, 1980-82, spl. asst. to dean Grad. Sch., spring 1981, minority engr. advisor, 1975-76; cons. computer-assisted instrn. project Meharry Med. Coll., Nashville, summer 1982; assoc. prof. computer sci. Tenn. State U., Nashville, 1982-83, 84-90, full, tenured prof., 1990—, univ. marshal, 1992—; assoc. prof. U. Miss., Oxford, 1983-84, faculty senator; assoc. program dir. Applications of Advanced Techs. Sci. and Engring. Edn., NSF, 1987-88, apptd. USRA Sci. and Engring. Edn. Coun., Advanced Design Program, 1992—; cons. on minority scientists and engrs. Univ. Space Rsch. Assn., Washington, 1988; vis. scientist CSNET-Minority Instn. Networking Project Bolt, Beranek & Newman, Cambridge, Mass., 1989; mem. tech. staff Bell Communications Rsch., Red Bank, N.J., 1990; presenter papers profl. meetings. Editor-in-chief newspaper Pilgrim Emanuel Bapt. Ch., 1975-76; adv. Chi Rho Youth Fellowship, Temple Bapt. Ch., 1975-81, adv. com. Golden Outreach Sr. Citizens Fellowship, 1979-80, 86-87, 89-93, Women's Day speaker, 1979, 81, Ebenezer Missionary Bapt. Ch., 1993; adviser Nat. Soc. Black Engring. Students, 1983-84; founder, coord. Tenn. State U. Assn. for Excellence in Computer Sci., Math. and Physics (AE-COMP), 1986-87, coord. Tech. Opportunites Fair, 1986, 87; dir. Tenn. State U. Minorities in Sci., Engring. & Tech. Rsch. Project-MISET, 1989—; child sponsor World Vision, 1981—; mem. Lake Providence Missionary Bapt. Ch. Recipient Disting. Instr. award 1984, Disting. Svc. citation Beloit Coll. Alumni Assn., 1994; grantee Digital Equipment Corp., 1989-92; faculty rsch. grantee Tenn. State U., 1993, 94. Mem. NAACP (nat. judge ACT-SO sci. olympics 1992), Assn. Computing Machinery, Data Processing Mgmt. Assn. (edn. chmn., bd. dirs. 1986), Tenn. Acad. Sci. Achievements include founding Assn. for Excellence in Computer Sci., Math., and Physics, research in database, network and human-computer interfacing for broadening minority participation in science, engineering and technology. Home: PO Box 270093 Nashville TN 37227-0093 Office: Tenn State U Dept Physics Math & Computer Sci 3500 Merritt Blvd Nashville TN 37209-1561

WILLIAMS, MARTHA ETHELYN, information science educator; b. Chgo., Sept. 21, 1934; d. Harold Milton and Alice Rosemond (Fox) W. B.A., Barat Coll., 1955; M.A., Loyola U., 1957. With IIT Rsch.Inst., Chgo., 1957-72, mgr. info. scis., 1962-72, mgr. computer search ctr., 1968-72; adj. assoc. prof. sci. info. Ill. Inst. Tech., Chgo., 1965-73, lectr. chemistry dept., 1968-70, rsch. prof. info. sci., coordinated sci. lab. Coll. engring.; also dir. info. retrieval research lab. U. Ill., Urbana, 1972—, affiliate, computer sci. dept., 1979—; chmn. large data base conf. Nat. Acad. Sci./NRC, 1974, mem. ad hoc panel on info. storage and retrieval, 1977, numerical data adv. bd., 1979-82, computer sci. and tech. bd., nat. rsch. network rev. com., 1987-88, chmn. utility subcom., 1987-88; mem. task force on sci. info. activities NSF, 1977; U.S. rep. review com. for project on broad system of ordering, UNESCO, Hague, Netherlands, 1974; vice chmn. Gordon Rshc. Conf. on Sci. Info. Problems in Rsch., 1978, chmn., 1980; mem. panel on intellectual property rights in age of electronics and info. U.S. Congress, Office of Tech. Assessment; program chmn. Nat. Online Meeting, 1980—; cons. to numerous cos., govt. agys. and rsch. founds.; invited lectr. Commn. European Communities, Industrial R&D adv. com., Brussels, 1992. Editor in chief Computer-Readable Databases Directory and Data Sourcebook, 1976-89, founding editor, 1989-92; editor Ann. Rev. Info. Sci. and Tech., 1976—, Online Rev., 1979-92, Online and CDROM Rev., 1993—, procs. nat. online meeting, 1981—; contbg. editor column on databases to Bull. Am. Soc. Info. Sci., 1974-78; mem. editorial adv. bd. Database, 1978-88; mem. editorial bd. Info. Processing and Mgmt., 1982-89, The Reference Libr.; contbr. more than 200 articles to profl. jours. Trustee Engirng. Info., Inc., 1974-87, bd. dirs., 1976-91, chmn. bd. dirs., 1982-91, v.p., 1978-79, pres., 1980-81; regent Nat. Libr. Medicine, 1978-82, chmn. bd. regents, 1981; mem. task force on sci. info. activities NSF, 1977-78; mem. nat. adv. com. ACCESS ERIC, 1989-91. Recipient best paper of year award H. W. Wilson Co., 1975; NSF travel grantee Luxembourg, 1972; NSF travel grantee Honolulu, 1973; NSF travel grantee Tokyo, 1973; NSF travel grantee Mexico City, 1975; NSF travel grantee Scotland, 1976. Fellow AAAS (elected, computers, info. and communication mem.-at-large 1978-81, nominating com. 1983, 85); hon. fellow Inst. Info. Sci., 1985; mem. Am. Chem. Soc., Am. Soc. Info. Sci. (councilor 1971-72, 87-89, chmn. networks com. 1973-74, chmn. spl. interest group on SDI 1974-75, pres. elect 1986-87, pres. 1987-88, past pres. planning com. 1988-89, chmn. 1989, nominations com. 1989, chmn. budget and fin. com. 1987-89, Award of Merit 1984, Pioneer Info. Sci. 1987), Assn. for Computing Machinery (pub. bd. 1972-76), Assn. Sci. Info. Dissemination Ctrs. (v.p. 1971-73, pres. 1975-77), Nat. Acad. Sci. (joint com. with NRC on chem. info. 1971-73), U.S. Nat. Com. for Internat. Fedn. for Documentation. Home: RR 1 Monticello IL 61856-9801 Office: U Ill 1308 W Main St Urbana IL 61801-3005

WILLIAMS, MARY ANN, guidance counselor; b. Lakeland, Fla., Sept. 16, 1946; d. Robert Paul DAvis and Mary Elizabeth Shipe Ross; m. Jerome George Williams, Oct. 24, 1970. AA, Polk C.C., Winter Haven, Fla., 1967; BA in Social Sci. Edn., U. West Fla., Pensacola, 1969; MA in Reading, Rollins Coll., 1981; MS in Guidance and Counseling, Nova U., 1994. Tchr. Escambia Sch. Bd., Pensacola, Fla., 1969-72; tchr. Lake Sch Bd., Tavares, Fla., 1972-91, counselor Leesburg High Sch., 1991—. Mem. Lake County Edn. Assn. (bd. dirs. 1983-85), Kappa Delta Phi. Democrat. Baptist. Home: 03410 Sailfish Ave Fruitland Park FL 34731-6300 Office: Leesburg High Sch 1401 Meadows St Leesburg FL 34748

WILLIAMS, MARY ANNE, elementary education educator; b. Aurora, Colo., Apr. 12, 1949; d. Leo A. and Dorotha Mae (Russell) Bruce; m. Stephen C. Williams, Aug. 19, 1973; children: Rebecca, Mark. BA, Simmons Coll., 1971; MA, Gallaudet Coll., 1973. Advanced profl. cert. Bd. Edn. Md. CFO Westbrook Constrn., Frederick, Md., 1979-89; tchr. Fred County Bd. Edn., Frederick, 1989—; tchr. Parent-Child Program, Frederick, 1981-87; integration cadre Fred County Bd. Edn., Frederick, 1992—, math cadre, 1992—; mem. Md. state assessments consortium Md. Dept. Edn., Frederick, 1993—; presenter in field. Creator, author, pub.: Frederick's Female Firsts, 1994. Chair Frederick (Md.) Women's Fair, 1989. Mem. AAUW (chair women's history project, chair edn. found., state pub. info. chair 1987-88, program v.p. 1989-93, named gift grant Frederick br. 1987). Home: 14 E Ninth St Frederick MD 21701

WILLIAMS, MARY ELEANOR NICOLE, writer; b. Atlanta, May 14, 1938; d. Edward King Merrell and Bernice I. (Pitts) Smith; m. Charlie Lloyd Williams, July 25, 1993; children: Mary Palmer, Susan Gober, Traci Cox. Student, Fla. Jr. Coll., 1974. Lic. real estate broker, Fla. Editor, writer, former owner Southwestern Advt. and Pub., Carrollton, Ga., 1991-94; freelance writer children's stories, 1992—. Author, editor: West Georgia Area Guide, 1991-93. Mem. Carroll County C. of C. Home: 103 Ferndale Rd Carrollton GA 30117

WILLIAMS, MARY ELLEN, counselor; b. Cin., Dec. 12, 1939; d. Mel and Mary Ross; m. William E. Williams, Dec. 27, 1974. AB, Coll. Mt. St. Joseph, 1961; MA, St. Louis U., 1970; MEd, Xavier U., 1989; postgrad., U. Cin., 1993—, The Union Inst. Lic. profl. counselor, social worker; cert. tchr. Tchr. St. Sebastian High Sch., Chgo., 1961-62, St. Vincent Acad., Albuquerque, 1962-68, Cath. Ctrl. High Sch., Springfield, Ohio, 1968-70; counselor U. Cin., 1970-72; tchr., counselor Moeller High Sch., Cin., 1972-89; counselor St. Xavier High Sch., Cin., 1989—, Cin. Counseling Svc., 1993—; adj. prof. Xavier U., Cin., 1992—; guest lectr. No. Ky. Counseling Assn., 1992, Xavier U., 1990—, various local high schs., Cin., 1982—; mem. Task Force Higher Edn. Info. Svc., Cin. Nat. Def. Edn. Act grantee, 1962. Mem. ACA, Ohio Counseling Assn. (exec. bd. dirs. 1991-92), Greater Cin. Counseling Assn. (pres.-elect 1990-91, pres. 1991-92). Roman Catholic. Office: St Xavier High Sch 600 N Bend Rd Cincinnati OH 45224

WILLIAMS, MARY ELMORE, English language and history educator, educational administrator; b. San Angelo, Tex., Sept. 19, 1931; d. Taylor and Florrine (Gee) Elmore; m. Mark B. Williams, Sept. 6, 1951; children: John Mark, Mary Jean. AA, San Angelo Coll., 1950; BS, Tex. Christian U., 1951; MS, Corpus Christi State U., 1983; postgrad. U. Chgo., 1954, Princeton U., 1961, Mansfield Coll., Oxford U., 1966. Tchr. 1st grade First Methodist Ch., Dallas, 1951-52; tchr. 8th grade Pleasant Grove Jr. High, Dallas, 1952-54; tchr. Bible Ray High Sch., Corpus Christi, 1957, tchr. history Hamlin Jr. High Sch., 1958; tchr. 6th grade St. Christopher's Episcopal Sch., Lubbock, Tex., 1968; tchr. English and history Hamlin Jr. High, Corpus Christi, 1974—, asst. prin., 1989—; coord. Adopt-a-School Program, 1983—; organizer of Vet.'s Day Patriotic Rally; cons. KEDT-TV Tex. History series The Lone Star, Corpus Christi, 1984-85; cons. textbook com. Corpus Christi Ind. Sch. Dist., 1983, 86, mem. curriculum writing team, 1985-86, chmn. supt.'s adv. com., 1991-92, chmn. Quincentennial Edn. Com., 1991-92. Mem. Animal Control Bd.; campaign coord. Ruth Gill for Mayor, Corpus Christi, 1979; del. Gov.'s Commn. for Women, San Antonio, 1985, Tex. Sch. Assembly Gov. Ann Richards, 1991; participant Leadership Corpus Christi XIX, 1990-91; mem. Corpus Christi Coun. for Women; chmn. Tchr. Task Force on Edn. for state rep. Ted Roberts, 1986-88, chmn. tchr. com. Better Sch. Program, 1987, chmn. tchr. Task Force Excellence Edn. for State Rep. Todd Hunter, 1988— . Named Outstanding Tchr. Am. History-Tex., DAR, 1986; recipient Robert A. Taft accolade for Excellence in Tchng. Govt. and Politics, 1986, Women in Careers Edn. award YWCA, 1991; named Tchr. of Yr. Corpus Christi Ind. Sch. Dist., 1990-91. Mem. AACD, Corpus Christi Council Social Studies (v.p. 1981-83, supt.'s adv. com. 1991—, co-chmn. children's com. A Kid's Place 1991—), Tex. Nat. Coun. Social Studies (conv. chmn. 1988, chmn. nominating com. 1990-91), Corpus Christi C. of C. (events chmn. 1983), PTA (life), YWCA (v.p., chmn. bldg. com. 1983-88), AAUW (v.p. 1983-85, pres. 1986-88), Phi Delta Kappa, Delta Kappa Gamma, Kappa Delta Pi. Avocations: tennis, reading. Home: 601 Barracuda Pl Corpus Christi TX 78411-2112 Office: Hamlin Mid Sch 3900 Hamlin Dr Corpus Christi TX 78411-2237

WILLIAMS, MARY IRENE, college administrator; b. Hugo, Okla., June 30, 1944; d. Primer and Hyler B. (Tarkington) Jackson; m. Lee A. Williams (div. June 1981); 1 child, Monica Ariane. BS in Bus. Edn., Langston U., 1967; MS in Bus., Emporia (Kans.) State U., 1973; EdS, U. Nev., Las Vegas, 1977; D of Bus. Adminstrn. in Internat. Bus., U.S. Internat. U., 1992. Instr. Spokane (Wash.) C.C., 1967-70; tchr. bus. Topeka Pub. Schs., 1970-73; instr. Clark County C.C., Las Vegas, Nev., 1973—; assoc. dean of bus. Clark County C.C., Las Vegas, 1978-93; dean acad. support svcs. C.C. So. Nev., 1993—. Named Educator of Yr. Nucleus Plaza Assn., 1985, New Visions, Inc., 1986. Mem. NAFE, AAUW, Internat. Assn. Bus. Communicators, Nat. Bus. Edn. Assn., Nat. Coun. on Black Affairs, Am. Assn. Cmty. and Jr. Colls., Nat. Assn. Instrnl. Adminstrs., Nat. Rainbow Coalition. Office: CC So Nev 3200 E Cheyenne Ave North Las Vegas NV 89030-4228

WILLIAMS, MARY JANE MONGILLO, nursing educator; b. New Britain, Conn., June 24, 1943; d. Lincoln C. and Alexandrina C. Mongillo; m. Michael J. Williams, Oct. 21, 1978; children: Michael John, Meredith Jane. Diploma, Middlesex Meml. Hosp., Middletown, Conn., 1964; BS, Central Conn. State U., New Britain, 1969; MS in Edn., So. Conn. State U., New Haven, 1976; MS in Nursing, U. Conn., 1982. Staff/head nurse Middlesex Meml. Hosp., Middletown, 1964-67; office nurse H.A. Kaufman MD, Middletown, 1967-69; head nurse Hosp. St. Raphael, New Haven, 1969-70, insr., 1970-74; rsch. assoc. Yale U., New Haven, 1974-76; asst. prof. Central Conn. State U., New Britain, 1976-81, assoc. prof. nursing, 1981-94, assoc. prof. dept health and human svcs., 1994—; cons., coord. patient edn. Hartford (Conn.) Hosp., 1986-90. Author: Needs Assessment of RNs, 1983, Pharmacological Knowledge of RNs, 1984, Persistence in RN-BSN Programs, 1989. Mem. ANA, N.E. Orgn. Nursing, Conn. Nurses Assn. (chair cabinet nursing edn. 1988-92, cabinet econs. practice and edn., 1992—), Nat. League Nursing, Conn. League Nursing, Sigma Theta Tau, Phi Kappa Phi, Phi Theta Lambda. Home: 108 Dayton Dr Southington CT 06489-2261 Office: Cen Conn State U 1615 Stanley St New Britain CT 06053-2439

WILLIAMS, MELISSA ANNE, county government official; b. Ft. Thomas, Ky., Mar. 30, 1957; d. Charles Johns and Jean Rae (Schroder) Melville; m. Michael L. Williams, Oct. 9, 1982; stepchildren: Christine, Brian. BS in Corrections, Ea. Ky. U., 1979; MPA, No. Ky. U., 1990; grad., No. Ky. Area Extension Leadership Program, 1991. Juvenile probation officer Campbell County Fiscal Ct., Newport, Ky., 1979-86, asst. dir. juvenile dept., 1986, exec. asst., pers. dir., 1986-88, dir. adminstrn., 1988—. Active Com. Kids, 1981-87, Children's Psychiat. Hosp. No. Ky. Rsch. and Evaluation Ctr., 1991—; United Way campaign coord. Campbell County Fiscal Ct., 1986, 87; chmn., bd. dirs. No. Ky. Mental Health and Mental Retardation Regional Bd., Inc., 1980-87. Mem. No. Ky. City and County Adminstrn. Assn. (pres. 1994), No. Ky. C. of C. Democrat. Roman Catholic. Office: Campbell County Fiscal Ct 24 W 4th St Newport KY 41071-1000

WILLIAMS, MILLIE JONES, city auditor; b. Johnson City, Tenn., Nov. 28, 1949; d. John H. and Leota H. Jones; children: Garrison Lyle, Kimberly Lane. Student, East Tenn. State U., U. Ala. Acctg. asst. McClenny & Patrick, CPA, Tuscaloosa, Ala., 1978-84; acctg. mgr. Quality Foods, Inc., Tuscaloosa, 1984-89; auditor City of Tuscaloosa, 1989—; spkr. in field. Vol. First Presbyn. Ch., Tuscaloosa, Cancer Soc., March of Dimes. Recipient Arts award Ala. Women's Fedn., 1983, Vol. award Tuscaloosa City Schs., 1983, 86. Mem. Ala Revenue Officers Assn. (cert.), Profl. Women's Club, Ala. Wildlife Fedn. Democrat. Home: 714 Shallow Creek Rd Tuscaloosa AL 35406

WILLIAMS, NANCY ANN, psychologist; b. Fond du Lac, Wis., July 17, 1954; d. Irvin Cornelius and Ruth Evelyn (Sackey) W.; m. Robert Bruce Handley, Oct. 14, 1982; children: Ian William, Elyse Marie. BS in Psychology and Comms., U. Wis., Stevens Point, 1977; MS in Counseling Psychology, Colo. State U., 1981, PhD in Counseling Psychology, 1983. Staff psychologist student counseling ctr. Ill. State U., Normal, 1983-84; postdoctoral fellow psychology N.Y. Hosp. and Cornell Med. Ctr., White Plains, 1984-86; staff psychologist Nat. Jewish Ctr. Immunology and Respiratory Medicine, Denver, 1987—; asst. prof. psychology U. Colo. Health Scis. Ctr., Denver, 1987—; dir. psychosocial svcs. Kunsberg Sch.-Beaumont Learning Ctr., Denver, 1991—. Contbr. articles to profl. jours. Organizer Babysitting Coop., Denver, 1991. Mem. APA, Assn. Women in Psychology, Neighborhood Watch. Office: Nat Jewish Ctr Immunology and Repiratory Medicine 1400 Jackson St # 103C Denver CO 80206-2762

WILLIAMS, NANCY CAROLE, nursing researcher; b. Conover, N.C., Dec. 22, 1953; d. Howard G. and Edith (Hager) W. Diploma nursing, Gaston Coll., Dallas, N.C., 1981; student, U. N.C., 1990—. Charge nurse critical care unit Lincoln County Hosp., Lincolnton, N.C., 1981-83; primary charge nurse N.C. Meml. Hosp., Chapel Hill, N.C., 1983-85; charge nurse U. N.C. Clin. Rsch., Chapel Hill, 1985—. Mem. Nat. Assn. Rsch. Nurses and Dietitians, Am. Nurses Assn., N.C. Nurses Assn. Home: Rt 7 Box 12 Hwy 15-501 S Chapel Hill NC 27516

WILLIAMS, PAMELA R., secondary school administrator; b. Tacoma, Feb. 9, 1950; d. Richard Bartle and Elaine Staab; m. Raymond L. Williams, 1972. BA in Edn. with distinction, Wash. State U., 1972; MA in Adminstrn., Washington U., St. Louis, 1983. Cert. tchr., Mo., Colo., adminstr., Colo. Tchr. Countryside Elem., DeSoto, Kans., 1972-77, U. Chgo. Lab Sch., 1977-78, Francis Parker Sch., Chgo., 1978-80; mid. sch. tchr., coord. English,

Mary Inst., St. Louis, 1980-88; elem. bilingual tchr. Boulder (Colo.) Valley Schs., 1988-91, asst. prin, 1991—. Mem. ASCD, NEA, Am. Assn. Sch. Adminstrs. (women's caucus), Nat. Assn. Secondary Sch. Prins., CORO Women in Leadership Alumnae Assn., Phi Delta Kappa. Office: Base Line MS 700 20th St Boulder CO 80302-7702

WILLIAMS, PATRICIA BIGHAM (PATTY WILLIAMS), state official; b. Jacksonville, Fla., Jan. 27, 1947; d. William Earl and Grace Lenora (Guest) Bigham; m. Kenneth M. Williams, Sept. 5, 1970 (div.); children: K. Michael Jr., A. Brooke. Student, Stetson U., 1965; AA, So. Ga. Jr. Coll., 1967; BS in Criminology, Fla. State U., 1970. Statistician, tng. mgr., EEO coord. Parole & Probation Commn., Tallahassee, 1971-77; EEO coord. Fla. Dept. Law Enforcement, Tallahassee, 1977; patient svcs. coord. Grady Meml. Hosp., Atlanta, 1978-79; pers. technician Dept. Agr., Tallahassee, 1980-85; dir. pers. Tallahassee Community Hosp., 1985-86, Water Mgmt. Dist., Tallahassee, 1987-91; bur. chief Dept. Mgmt. Svcs., Tallahassee, 1991—; cons. Suits Me, Tallahassee, 1992; pers. cons. N.W. Fla. Water Mgmt. Dist., 1990. Bd. dirs. Tallahassee Urban League, 1976-77; pres. singles class Methodist Ch., 1992-93, chmn. staff parish com., 1995. Mem. Fla. Pers. Assn. (v.p. 1993-94, pres. 1994), Human Resource Assn. Tallahassee (past sec., treas.), Extra Point Club. Methodist. Home: 6320 Loma Farm Ct Tallahassee FL 32308-6333 Office: Dept Mgmt Svcs Carlton Bldg 415 Tallahassee FL 32399

WILLIAMS, PATRICIA DAY, organization development consultant; b. Summit, N.J., Aug. 22, 1952; d. Roger Withrow Williams and Nancy Hevener (Bowman) Dukek; m. J. Robert Elliott, May 8, 1982; children: Ethan Elliott-Williams, Camden Elliott-Williams. BA, Yale U., 1973; MD, Harvard U., 1978. Cert. Am. Bd. Family Practice. Resident Montefiore Hosp. and Med. Ctr., Bronx, N.Y., 1978-79; family practice residency program Cen. Maine Med. Ctr., Lewiston, Maine, 1979-81; med. dir. Bethel (Maine) Area Health Ctr., 1981-86; clin. core faculty Maine-Dartmouth Family Practice Residency, 1984-89; instr. U. So. Maine, 1990—; assoc. cons. Maine Ctr. for Ednl. Svcs., 1991—; orgn. devel. cons., 1989—; asst. clin. prof. Dept. Pediatrics, Jefferson Med. Coll., Phila., 1993—; adj. asst. prof. Clin. Community and Family Medicine, Dartmouth Med. Sch., Hanover, N.H., 1983-92; staff physician Western Maine Family Practice, Norway, 1986-89; staff mem. health clinic San Martin Jilotepeque, Guatemala, 1977; cons. Soc. of Tchrs. of Family Medicine, Kansas City, 1993, U. Wis. Dept. Pediatrics, Sisters of Charity Health System, Lewiston, Med. Care Devel., Inc., Augusta, others. Reviewer Family Medicine, Archives of Family Medicine; contbr. articles to profl. jours. Mem. Am. Acad. on Physician and Patient Assn. for Psychol. Type, Maine Soc. for Tng. and Devel., Orgn. Devel. Network, Soc. of Tchrs. of Family Medicine, Women's Bus. Devel. Corp., Ea. Coop. Recreation Sch. Democrat. Unitarian. Home and Office: 83 Road Less Traveled Woodstock ME 04219

WILLIAMS, PAULETTE W., state agency administrator; b. Moulton, Ala., Oct. 21, 1944; d. Paul Price and Sallie Davis (Bass) Wiley; m. Robert Thomas Williams, Oct. 11, 1968; 1 child, Shannon Thomas. Student, Florence State Coll., 1963-64. Planning and ops. officer civil def Decatur (Ill.)/Morgan Co., 1964-74, planning and ops. officer emergency mgmt., 1975-77; planning and ops. officer, dep. dir. emergency mgmt. Mobile (Ala.) Co., 1977-89; emergency mgmt. area coord. I State of Ala., Clanton, 1989-94; dir. Ala. Emergency Mgmt. Agy., Clanton, 1994—; observer nuc. power plant Dept. Def., Romania, 1994; mem. gov. cabinet State of Ala., Clanton, 1994—. Mem. cmty. advisor coun. Occidental Chem. Co., Muscle Shoals, Ala., 1993—; mem. state disaster svcs. com. ARC, Ala., 1993—. Recipient Spl. Recognition award Ala. Police Acad., 1986, Appreciation cert. Mobile (Ala.) Police Acad., 1986, Outstanding Svc. and Dedication cert. and flag, 1988, Hon. Adm. cert. Mayor of Decatur, 1988, Outstanding Svc. and Contbns. Appreciation cert. Nat. Coordinating Coun. on Emergency Mgmt., 1988, Appreciation plaque Greater Mobile Indsl. Assn., 1989, Appreciation for Profl. Assistance plaque Kerr McGee Chem. Corp., 1989, Appreciation cert. State of Ala., 1989, Meritorious Svc. cert. City of Mobile, 1989, Appreciation for Help and Support plaque City of Mobile Police Dept. Hazardous Materials Unit, 1989, Outstanding Dedication and Svc. plaque Mobile County Local Emergency Planning Com., 1989, Appreciation cert. FEMA-Floods of 1990, 1990, Pub. Svc. award U.S. Dept. Commerce, NOAA, 1994. Mem. Ala. Emergency Mgmt. Coun. (pres., Sec.-treas. plaque 1986, Appreciation cert. 1986, Legis. Chmn. plaque 1987), Nat. Emergency Mgmt. Assn. (mem. recovery com.). Episcopal. Home: 2224 Marietta Ave Muscle Shoals AL 35661 Office: Ala Emergency Mgmt 5898 Co Rd 41 Clanton AL 35045

WILLIAMS, PEGGY RYAN, academic administrator; b. Montreal, Que., Can., May 27, 1947; d. Fred Smith and Carol (Kennedy) Ryan; m. David A. Williams, May 30, 1970. BA, U. Toronto, Can., 1968; MEd, U. Vt., 1976; EdD, Harvard U., 1983. Caseworker Monroe County Dept. Social Svcs., Rochester, N.Y., 1968-72; med. social worker Med. Ctr. Hosp. of Vt., Burlington, 1972; coord. instruction, project dir. Community Coll. of Vt., Lamoille County, 1973-75, 75-76; regional dir. Community Coll. of Vt., Montpelier, Vt., 1976-82; asst. to the pres. Johnson (Vt.) State Coll., summer 1981; dir. ednl. and pers. svcs. Vt. State Coll., Waterbury, 1982-85; dir. bus. programs Trinity Coll., Burlington, 1985-88, assoc. acad. dean, 1988-89; pres. Lyndon State Coll., Lyndonville, Vt., 1989—; bd. dirs. Vt. Community Found., Blue Cross/Blue Shield of Vt., Alumni Coun. Grad. Sch. Edn. Harvard U., Lyndon State Coll. Found.; past chair Am. Coun. on Edn. Commn. on Women. Mem. Am. Assn. Higher Edn., Am. Assn. State Colls. and Univs., Vt. Higher Edn. Coun., Am. Coun. on Edn. Office: Lyndon State Coll Office of the President Vail Hill Lyndonville VT 05851

WILLIAMS, PENNY, state legislator; b. N.Y.C., May 6, 1937; d. Peter and Polly Sheffield Potter Baldwin; children: Joseph Hill Jr., Peter Baldwin, James Chestnut. Student, Sarah Lawrence Coll., U. Tulsa. Mem. Okla. Ho. of Reps., 1981-89, Okla. State Senate, 1989—. Trustee St. Gregory's Coll.; mem. Tulsa Com. on Fgn. Rels. Mem. LWV, Tulsa C. of C. Democrat. Episcopalian. Home: 1366 E 25th St Tulsa OK 74114-2702

WILLIAMS, PETRA SCHATZ, antiquarian; b. Poughkeepsie, N.Y., Sept. 2, 1913; d. Grover Henry and Mayme Nickerson (Bullock) Schatz; m. J. Calvert Williams, Nov. 26, 1946; children: Miranda, Frederica, Valerie. AB, Skidmore Coll., 1936; JD, Fordham U., 1940. Founder Fountain House, Phoenix, 1953, Fountain House East, Jeffersontown, Ky., 1966. Author: Flow Blue China, An Aid to Identification, 1971, Flow Blue China II, 1973, Flow Blue China and Mulberry Ware, 1975, Staffordshire Romantic Transfer Patterns, 1979, Staffordshire II Romantic Transfer Patterns, 1986. Past pres. Meml. Hosp. Aux., Phoenix, Heard Mus. Guild, Phoenix; bd. dirs. Ky. Humane Soc. Mem. Nat. Soc. Interior Designers (nat. dir. for Ariz. 1957-58, Ky. 1968, pres. Ky. 1967-68), DAR, Ky. Hist. Soc., Flow Blue Internat. Collectors Club (hon.). Mem. Soc. of Friends. Club: Filson. Address: PO Box 99298 Jeffersontown KY 40269-0298

WILLIAMS, PHYLLIS CUTFORTH, retired realtor; b. Moreland, Idaho, June 6, 1917; d. William Claude and Kathleen Jessie (Jenkins) Cutforth; m. Joseph Marsden Williams, Jan. 21, 1938 (dec. 1986); children: Joseph Marlis, Bonnie L. Williams Thompson, Nancy K. Williams Stewart, Marjorie Williams Karren, Douglas C., Thomas Marsden, Wendy K. Williams Clark, Shannon I. Williams Ostler. Grad., Ricks Coll., 1935. Lic. realtor, Idaho. Tchr. Grace (Idaho) Elem. Sch., 1935-38; realtor Williams Realty, Idaho Falls, Idaho, 1972-77; mem. Idaho Senate, Boise, 1977; owner, mgr. river property. Compiler: Idaho Legisladies Cookbook, Cookin' Together, 1981. With MicroFilm Ctr., LDS Ch. Mission, Salt Lake City, 1989-90; block chmn. March of Dimes Soc.; active Idaho State Legisladies Club, 1966-84, v.p., 1982-84. Republican. Home: 1950 Carmel Dr Idaho Falls ID 83402-3020

WILLIAMS, RITA ANNE, financial editor; b. Eugene, Oreg., Jan. 5, 1953; d. John (Jack) Evans and Faye Naomi (Squires) W. BA in English, U. Calif., Berkeley, 1977. Project coord. Institutional Educator Mag., N.Y.C., 1984-85; finance editor E.F. Hutton, N.Y.C., 1985-87, Lehman Bros. (E.F. Hutton merger), N.Y.C., 1987-93, S.G. Warburg, N.Y.C., 1993-94.

WILLIAMS, RUTH ELIZABETH (BETTY WILLIAMS), retired educator; b. Newport News, Va., July 31, 1938; d. Lloyd Haynes and Erma Ruth (Goodrich) W. BA, Mary Washington Coll., 1960; cert. d'etudes, Converse Coll., 1961, U. Oreg., 1962. Cert. tchr., Va. French tchr. York High Sch., York County Pub. Schs., Yorktown, Va., 1960-65; French resource tchr. Newport News Pub. Schs., 1966-74, tchr. French and photography, 1974-81, tchr. French, Spanish, German and Latin, 1981-91, ret., 1991; pres. Cresset Publs., Williamsburg, Va., 1977-94; lectr. sch. edn. Coll. William and Mary, Williamsburg, 1962-65; French tchr., coord. fgn. langs. York County Pub. Schs., 1962-65; workshop leader dept. pub. instrn. State of Del., Dover, 1965; cons. Heath de Rochemont Co., Boston, 1962-71. Driver Meals on Wheels, Williamsburg, 1989-90; contbr. Va. Spl. Olympics, Richmond, 1987-94; charter mem. Capitol Soc. Colonial Williamsburg Found., Inc., 1994. Grantee Nat. Def. Edn. Act, 1961, 1962. Mem. AAAU, Fgn. Lang. Assn. Va., AARP (ret. tchrs. divsn.), Heritage Soc., Mary Washington Coll. Alumni Assn., Am. Assn. Tchrs. French, Mortar Bd., Women in the Arts, Alpha Phi Sigma, Phi Sigma Iota. Episcopalian. Home and Office: 471 Catesby Ln Williamsburg VA 23185

WILLIAMS, RUTH LEE, clinical social worker; b. Dallas, June 24, 1944; d. Carl Woodley and Nancy Ruth (Gardner) W. BA, So. Meth. U., 1966; M Sci.in Social Work, U. Tex., Austin, 1969. Milieu coordinator Starr Commonwealth, Albion, Mich., 1969-73; clin. social worker Katherine Hamilton Mental Health Care, Terre Haute, Ind., 1973-74; clin. social worker, supr. Pikes Peak Mental Health Ctr., Colorado Springs, Colo., 1974-78; pvt. practice social work Colorado Springs, 1978—; pres. Hearthstone Inn, Inc., Colorado Springs, 1978—; practitioner Jin Shin Jyutsu, Colorado Springs, 1978—; pres., v.p. bd. dirs. Premier Care (formerly Colorado Springs Mental Health Care Providers Inc.), 1986-87, chmn. quality assurance com., 1987-89, v.p. bd. dirs., 1992-93. Author, editor: From the Kitchen of The Hearthstone Inn, 1981, 2d rev. edit., 1986, 3d rev. edit., 1992. Mem. Am. Bd. Examiners in Clin. Social Work (charter mem., cert.), Colo. Soc. Clin. Social Work (editor 1976), Nat. Assn. Soc. Workers (diplomate), Nat. Bd. Social Work Examiners (cert.), Nat. Assn. Ind. Innkeepers, So. Meth. U. Alumni Assn. (life). Home: 11555 Howells Rd Colorado Springs CO 80908-3735 Office: 536 E Uintah St Colorado Springs CO 80903-2515

WILLIAMS, SANDRA KELLER, postal service executive; b. Bethesda, Md., Oct. 3, 1944; d. Park Dudley and Julia Mildred (Hunter) Keller; m. Tommy Allen Williams, Dec. 24, 1970; children: Chris Allen, Wakenna, Barbara. BA, U. Colo., 1966; MBA, U. Mo., Kansas City, 1971; MS, Ga. Inst. Tech., 1973. Mathematician Colo. State U., Ft. Collins, 1966; sr. scientist Booz-Allen Applied Rsch., Kansas City, Mo., 1967-68; computer sci. instr. Mo. Western Coll., St. Joseph, 1968-71; systems planning analyst Decatur (Ga.) Fed. Savs. and Loan Assn., 1972-73; planning analyst Fed. Res. Bank, Atlanta, 1974-75; indsl. engr. so. region hdqrs. U.S. Postal Svc., Memphis, 1975-79; nat. mgr. quality control U.S. Postal Svc., Washington, 1979-86; dir. city ops. so. Md. div. U.S. Postal Svc., Capital Heights, 1986-87, dir., oper. supt. so. Md. div., 1987-88; postmaster U.S. Postal Svc., Reading, Pa., 1988—; cons. Personal Bus., St. Joseph, 1968-69; grad. teaching asst. Ga. Inst. Tech., Atlanta, 1971-73; adj. faculty Dekalb C.C., Clarkston, Ga., 1973-75, Memphis State U., 1976-78; owner Custom Florals, 1995—. Chmn. Combined Fed. Campaign, Reading, 1988-95, U.S. Postal Svc.-Berks County Savs. Bond Program, 1988-95, United Way's Govt. divsn., 1989-90; bd. dirs. YWCA, Reading and Berks County, treas., 1990, pres., 1991. Mem. Nat. League Postmasters (legis. officer 1988-91), Berks County Women's Network (bd. dirs. 1994-95, treas. 1995). Republican. Home: 1514 Hill Rd Reading PA 19602-1410

WILLIAMS, SANDRA QUINLIN, librarian, educator; b. Longview, Wash., Oct. 21, 1944; d. Calvin Philip and Beatrice Victoria (Shahan) Quinlin; m. Steven Frank Williams, Aug. 21, 1966; 1 child, Robert Quinlin Williams. AA, Lower Columbia Coll., Longview, Wash., 1964; BA, We. Wash. U., 1966; MLS, Univ. Oregon, 1972; EdS, St. Cloud State U., 1993. 1st grade tchr. L.A. City Schs., 1966-68; peace corps vol. U.S. Govt., Valparaiso, Chile, 1968-70; grad. asst. Univ. Oreg. Sch. Libr. Sci., Eugene, 1970-71; sch. media specialist Lincoln County Schs., Waldport, Newport, Yachats, Oreg., 1972-74; cataloger, ref. libr. St. John's U., Collegeville, Minn., 1975-79, St. John's U., Coll. of St. Benedict, Collegeville, 1985-86; cataloger, ref. libr. St. Cloud (Minn.) State U., 1986-94, assoc. prof., 1994—. Mem. ALA, AAUW (br. pres. 1994-96), Minn. Ednl. Media Orgn. (program chmn. 1991), Ctrl. Minn. Reading Coun. (sec. 1989-93). Office: St Cloud State Univ Centennial Hall 105 720 4th Ave S Saint Cloud MN 56301

WILLIAMS, SERENA MARIA, legal educator; b. Augusta, Ga., Dec. 13, 1959; d. Tracy Evans Jr. and Willarena Marguerite (Lamar) W. BA, Smith Coll., 1981; JD, Georgetown U., 1984; LLM, George Washington U., 1992. Bar: Md., D.C. Atty. U.S. Dept. HUD, Washington, 1984-87; fin. economist D.C. Dept. Fin. and Revenue, Washington, 1989-90; instr. Howard U. Sch. Law, Washington, 1990-93; asst. prof. law U. Louisville Law Sch., 1993—. Contbr. articles to profl. jours. Bd. dirs., com. chair Smith Coll. Club of Washington, 1988-91; trustee Smith Coll., Northampton, Mass., 1981-83. George Washington U. Nat. Law Ctr. teaching fellow, 1987-89; Clark Found. scholar Georgetown U. Law Ctr., 1982-84. Mem. ABA (sect. legal edn. and bar admissions 1990—), Nat. Bar Assn. (com. chair greater Washington area chpt. Women Lawyers divsn. 1991-93), Assn. Am. Law Schs. (mem. sect. on minorities 1993—), Smith Coll. Alumni Assn. (nat. alumnae admissions com. 1992-93), New York Ave. Cmty. Club (tutor, tng. coord. 1985-93). Baptist. Office: U Louisville Sch Law Belknap Campus Louisville KY 40292

WILLIAMS, SHARON JOYCE, business development manager; b. Washington, Feb. 2, 1961; d. Harold and Evelyn Sue (Calhoun) W.; m. Michael Vern Darbyshire, Mar. 2, 1990 (div. Nov. 29, 1993). BA, High Point Coll., 1983; MLS, U. N.C., 1985. Archivist Blue Bell, Inc., Greensboro, N.C., 1985; libr. Zimmerman Assocs., Inc., Vienna, Va., 1985-87, systems analyst, 1987-88, asst. program mgr., 1988-90, project mgr., 1990-91, program mgr. libr. support svcs., 1990-94, bus. devel. mgr., 1994—. Presdl. scholar High Point Coll., 1979-83, H. W. Wilson scholar, 1983-85. Mem. Spl. Librs. Assn., Beta Phi Mu. Democrat.

WILLIAMS, SHIRLEY CADLE, public speaking consultant, theatrical coach, playwright; b. Charlotte, N.C., Jan. 19, 1933; d. Frederick Leonard and Elizabeth Speth (Matthews) C.; m. James Earl Williams, Mar. 27, 1965; children: James Michael, Elizabeth Dianne Williams Horton, Christopher Wesley, Stephen Cadle. BA, U. Fla., 1952; profl. degree, Am. Acad. Dramatic Arts, N.Y.C., 1955; MFA, U. Okla., 1959; PhD, U. Denver, 1969. Actress, model various prodns. and cos., N.Y.C., 1955-57; instr. theatre and speech Tex. Tech. Coll., 1959-61; teaching fellow, costume designer U. Theatre, U. Denver, 1961-63; asst. prof. dramatic arts, designer, theater dir. Mary Washington Coll. of U. of Va., 1963-65; adj. asst. prof. theatre Shenandoah U., 1987-93; adj. asst. prof. speech Lord Fairfax C. C., 1988—; pub. speaking cons., 1993—. Playwright: (children's plays) Seven Months of Blizzards, 1965 (1st pl. award Seattle Jr. Playwriting Competition), The Green Monkey, 1965, Fiesta in Tzintzuntzan, 1967 (mus.) Anatomy of a Musical, 1974. Co-founder Front Royal Little Theatre, 1974; pres. E.W. Morrison PTA, 1974; tchr. kindergarten class Calvary Episcopal Ch. Sch., 1974-77; v.p., pres. Ressie Jeffries Intermediate Sch. PTA, 1975-77; co-founder, installer PTA Leslie Fox Keyser Primary Sch., 1977; supt. ch. sch. Calvary Episcopal Ch., 1978-81, lay reader, eucharistic lay min., 1979—; mem. Warren County Sch. Bd., 1980-90, chair, 1982-90; treas., bd. dirs. Stonewall Hist. Assn., 1986—; co-chmn. fundraising drive Warren Women's Shelter/Warren County Coun. on Domestic Violence, 1987; tester, v.p., pres. Literacy Vols. Am., 1990—; active Habitat for Humanity. Recipient (with family) Outstanding Warren County Family award, 1984. Mem. Valley Garden Club (pres.), Parents Club James Madison U., Alpha Chi Omega (founder, 1st pres.), Club Shenandoah (treas. 1991-93). Home: PO Box 1408 243 Locust Dale Rd Front Royal VA 22630-4532

WILLIAMS, SHIRLEY JEAN OOSTENBROEK AKERS, former educator, writer; b. Kansas City, Kans., Feb. 18, 1931; d. James Ralph and Florence (Snodgrass) Akers; m. Raymond Gale Williams, Feb. 17, 1949; children: David Ray, James Ronald, Vickie Sue, Richard Gene, Randy Wayne. Tchr. Su-Z-Lu Ceramics, Kansas City, 1957-70, 78, 79; sch. bus. driver Argentine Transit Lines, Kansas City, 1959-69; ceramic tchr., owner Su-Z-Lu Ceramics, Tonganoxie, Kans., 1972-78; tchr. Ft. Leavenworth Army Post, Leavenworth, Kans., 1979-85; pres. Wagonettes Extension Homemakers Club, Forsyth, Mo., 1987-88; day-care provider for the elderly, 1990-93, 95—. Den mother Boy Scouts Am., Kansas City and Tonganoxie, 1955-66, instr., 1961; driver ARC, Kansas City, 1958-63, canteen chmn., campfire leader, 1961-64; contbr. Taney County Rep. newspaper, Forsyth, 1986-87, bd. dirs., 1987-91; mem. Univ.-Extension Coun. bd., 1988-91; vol., supt. ceramic divsn. Leavenworth County Fair, 1974-84; vol. tchr. Kester Found., 1956-57. Recipient 4-H Gold Clover, Taney County 4-H, 1987. Mem. Taney County Homemakers. Democrat. Home: 203 Willetta Dreyelm MO 64742

WILLIAMS, SUE DARDEN, library director; b. Miami, Fla., Aug. 13, 1943; d. Archie Yelverton and Bobbie (Jones) Eagles; m. Richard Williams, Sept. 30, 1989. B.A., Barton Coll., Wilson, N.C., 1965; M.L.S., U. Tex., Austin, 1970. Cert. librarian, N.C., Va. Instr. Chowan Coll., Murfreesboro, N.C., 1966-68; libr.'s asst. Albemarle Regional Libr., Winston, N.C., 1968-69; br. libr. Multnomah County Pub. Libr., Portland, Oreg., 1971-72; asst. dir. Stanly County Pub. Libr., Albemarle, N.C., 1973-76; dir. Stanly County Pub. Libr., 1976-80; asst. dir. Norfolk (Va.) Pub. Libr., 1980-83; dir., 1983-94. Mem. ALA (orientation com. 1990-92, chair 1991), Libr. Adminstrv. and Mgmt. Assn. (pub. rels. sec. 1985-87), Southeastern Libr. Assn. (staff devel. com. 1986-88, Rothrock award com. 1984-86, sec. pub. libr. sect. 1982-84), Va. Libr. Assn. (SELA rep. 1993—, coun. 1984, 88-91, 93—, ad hoc conf. guidelines com. 1985-86, chmn. conf. program 1984, awards and recognition com. 1983), Pub. Libr. Assn. (bd. dirs.-at-large Met. area 1986-89), Va. State Libr. (coop edn. com. 88-89). Home: 3534 Brest Ave Norfolk VA 23509-2143

WILLIAMS, SUE WINKLE, educator, administrator; b. Checotah, Okla., June 19, 1943; d. Herman Dalton and Faye Louise (Davidson) Winkle; m. James W. Williams, Aug. 14, 1965; 1 child, Joshua. BS, Okla. State U., 1965, EdD, 1980. Tchr. Jefferson County Pub. Schs., Wheat Ridge, Colo., 1965-66, Chicopee (Mass.) Pub. Schs., 1966-70; child devel. specialist Okla. State Dept. Health, Oklahoma City, 1972-75; child devel. specialist, child devel. assoc. pilot project Oscar Rose Jr. Coll., Midwest City, Okla., 1975-76; lectr. Cen. State U., Edmond, Okla., 1976-79; vis. asst. prof. U. Okla., Norman, 1980-81; asst. prof. U. Akron, Ohio, 1981-85; prof. Southwest Tex. State U., San Marcos, 1985—; presenter in field. Outside manuscript reviewer Home Econs. Rsch. Jour., 1984-87, A Child's World, 1988; contbr. articles to profl. jours. Tex. Dept. Human Svcs. grantee, 1986-93; secured numerous rsch. and pilot program grants. Mem. Nat. Assn. Edn. Young Children, Southwestern Psychol. Assn., Soc. Rsch. in Child Devel., Omicron Nu, Phi Kappa Phi. Unitarian. Office: Southwest Tex State U Dept Home Econs San Marcos TX 78666

WILLIAMS, TONDA, entrepreneur, consultant; b. N.Y.C., Nov. 21, 1949; d. William and Juanita (Rainey) W.; 1 child, Tywana. Student, Collegiate Inst., N.Y.C., 1975-78, C.W. Post Coll., 1981-83; BA in Bus. Mgmt., Am. Nat. U., Phoenix, 1983. Notary pub. N.Y. Asst. controller Acad. Ednl. Devel., N.Y.C., 1971-81; mgr. office Chapman-Apex Constrn. Co., Bayshore, N.Y., 1982-84; specialist computer RGM Liquid Waste Removal, Deerpark, N.Y., 1985-87; contr. LaMar Lighting Co., Freeport, N.Y., 1987—; owner, pres. Omni-Star, Bklyn., 1981—. Author: Tonda's Songs in Poetry, 1978, The Magic of Life, 1991; co-author: Computer Management of Liquid Waste Industry, 1986. Recipient Golden Poet award World of Poetry, 1992. Mem. Am. Mus. Natural History, Am. Soc. Notary Pubs. Home: 74 Cedar Dr Bay Shore NY 11706-2419

WILLIAMS, TRUDY ANNE, English language educator, college administrator; b. Winnipeg, Man., Can., Mar. 4, 1946; d. Herbert Francis and Melita French (Russell) Sly; m. Harry G. Williams, June 17, 1980; 1 child, David Langdon Jr. BA, U. Southwestern La., 1969, MA, 1970. Teaching asst. U. Southwestern La., Lafayette, 1968-72; instr. Gaston Coll., Dallas, N.C., 1980-83; asst. prof. English, St. Petersburg (Fla.) Jr. Coll., 1983—, also acting program dir., comm., program dir. acad. svcs.; program dir. acad. svcs. St. Petersburg (Fla.) Jr. Coll., Tarpon Springs Campus; adj. prof., cons. St. James Sch. Theology, Tarpon Springs, Fla., 1992—. Founding mem. Episcopal Synod of Am.; dir. Christian edn. St. Anne of Grace Episcopal Ch., Seminole, Fla. Mem. MLA, Nat. Coun. Tchrs. English, Southeastern Conf. on English in 2-Yr. Colls., Fla. Assn. Community Colls., Fla. Devel. Edn. Assn., Fla. Coll. English Assn., Pinellas County Tchrs. of English, South Atlantic Modern Lang. Assn., Fla. Coun. Instructional Affairs. Home: 8021 Bayhaven Dr Largo FL 34646-3320

WILLIAMS, UNA JOYCE, psychiatric social worker; b. Youngstown, Ohio, June 24, 1934; d. Samuel Wilfred and Frances Josephine (Woods) Ellis; children: Wendy Louise, Christopher Ellis, Sharon Elizabeth. BA, U. Ala., 1957; MSW, Adelphi U., 1963. Diplomate CSW, Am. Bd. Examiners in Clin. Social Work. Dir. Huntington Program for Sr. Citizens; psychiat. social worker-supr. N.Y. State Dept. Mental Hygiene, Suffolk Psychiat. Hosp., Central Islip; info.-referral counselor Mental Health Assn. Nassau County, Hempstead, N.Y.; therapist Madonna Heights Family Clinic, Dix Hills, N.Y.; med. and psychiat. social worker Northport (N.Y.) VA Med. Ctr., psychiat. social worker acute psychiat. treatment svs.; med. social worker dialysis svcs. Northport (N.Y.) Va. Med. Ctr. Chmn. Huntington Twp. Com. Human Rels., 1970; sec. bd. trustess Unitarian Universalist Fellowship Huntington, 1984. Named Mem. of Yr. Germany Philetelic Soc. Mem. NASW (cert.), Am. Assn. Family Counselors and Medicators, Germany Philetelic Soc. (pres. chpt. 30, 1990). Home: 316 Lenox Rd Huntington Station NY 11746-2640

WILLIAMS, VANESSA, recording artist, actress; b. Millwood, N.Y., 1963; m. Ramon Hervey II, 1988; children: Melanie, Jillian, Devin. Recording artist, 1988—. Stage appearances include: (Broadway) Kiss of the Spider Woman, 1994; film appearances include Another You, 1991, Harley Davidson and the Marlboro Man, 1991, The Drop Squad, 1994; albums: The Right Stuff, 1988, The Comfort Zone, 1991, The Sweetest Days, 1994; # 1 hit single Save the Best for Last. Recipient 8 Grammy award nominations; named one of 50 Most Beautiful People, People Mag. Office: Polygram Records Worldwide Plaza 825 8th Ave New York NY 10019-7416*

WILLIAMS, VERONICA ANN, management information systems marketing manager; b. Washington, Feb. 8, 1956; d. Vernon and Shirley Ann (Felton) W. BA, Brandeis U., 1977; MBA, Northwestern U., 1979. Systems mktg. rep. Control Data Corp., Chgo., 1979-81, mktg. rep., 1981-82; staff mgr. AT&T, Basking Ridge, N.J., 1982-84; nat. account exec. AT&T, N.Y.C., 1984-86; mgr. bus. planning AT&T, Berkeley Heights, N.J., 1986-87; product mgr. AT&T, Morristown, N.J., 1987-88; dist. mgr. Unisoft Corp., N.Y.C., 1988-89; acct. mgr. Lotus Devel. Corp., N.Y.C., 1989-90; dir. bus. devel., 1990-91, Software Corp. of Am., Stamford, Conn., 1990-91; pres. Absolute Computer Techs., Inc., N.J., 1985—. Mem. South Orange Planning Bd., 1985-87, South Orange Citizens Budget Adv. Com., 1983—. Mem. Nat. Black MBA Assn. (fin. chmn. Chgo. br. 1979-81, Performance award 1981). Home: 541 Scotland Rd South Orange NJ 07079-3009 Office: ACT Inc PO Box 978 76 S Orange Ave Ste 4 South Orange NJ 07079

WILLIAMS, VICKIE JUNE, counselor; b. Chesterfield, Mo., May 29, 1955; d. Leroy nad Peggy Ann (Fisher) Branion; m. Herman Alfred Williams, Jr., June 24, 1978 (div. 1983); children: Jessica Lynne. BA in Law Enforcement, Corrections, Psychology and Sociology, Northeast Md. State U., 1977, MA in Counseling and Guidance, 1978. Home vis. family counselor Ferguson-Florissant (Mo.) Sch. Dist., 1978-80; social svc. worker, relative foster care Mo. Divsn. Family Svc., St. Charles, 1980-85; counselor Washington U., St. Louis, 1985-87, Vol. Interdistrict Coord. Coun., St. Louis, 1987—. Mem. Am. Counseling Assn., Parkway West Parent Orgn. Bd. (bd. dirs. 1994), Delta Sigma Theta. Home: 2235 Bixley Dr Chesterfield MO 63017-8214 Office: Vol Interdistrict Coord Coun 10601 Clayton Rd Saint Louis MO 63131

WILLIAMS, VIRGINIA WALKER, journalist; b. Walker County, Ala., June 5, 1915; married; 1 child. BA in Elem. Edn., Ala. State U., 1945; MA in Journalism, Marquette U., 1979; postgrad., U. Wis., Milw. Cert. remedial reading specialist, Wis. Tchr. various elem. schs., Ala., 1933-56; reading specialist Milw. Pub. Schs., 1956-69, journalist, editor, 1969-79; journalist Milw. Fire and Police Commn., 1980-85; founder, dir. Echo Writer's Workshop, Milw.; pub. Echo mag.; freelance writer. Contbr. articles to Milw. Jour., Milw. Sentinel, Milw. Community Jour., Wis. Rep. Newspaper, Westside News, An Anthology of Black Writing, New Voices in Am. Poetry, 1985, Quill Book Anthology, 1987. Mem. Conservation Work Project Bd.,

Milw. Recipient Headliner award, Jack and Jill award, NAACP award, Service Club award, Advt. Club Milw. award. Mem. Nat. Press Women, Wis. Council Writers, Women in Communications, Soc. Profl. Journalists, Adminstrs. Suprs. Council, Phi Delta Kappa, Lambda Kappa Mu, Pi Lamba Theta. Methodist. Club: Milw. Press. Lodges: Zonta. Home: PO Box 2107 Milwaukee WI 53201-2107

WILLIAMS, VIVIAN LEWIE, college counselor; b. Columbia, S.C., Jan. 23, 1923; d. Lemuel Arthur Sr. and Ophelia V. (McDaniel) Lewie; m. Charles Warren Williams, Apr. 4, 1947 (div. Dec. 1967); children: Pamela Ann Williams-Coote, Charles Warren Jr. BA, Allen U., 1942; MA, U. Mich., 1946; MS, U. So. Calif., 1971, postgrad., 1971-72. Cert. marriage, family, child counselor, community coll. counselor. Asst. prof. psychology Tenn. State Agrl. and Indsl. U., Nashville, 1946-47; asst. prof. edn. Winston-Salem (N.C.) State U., 1947-50; asst. prof. edn., dir. tchr. edn. Allen U., Columbia, S.C., 1951-53; specialist reading, coord. lang. arts Charlotte (N.C.) Mecklenburg Schs., 1963-67, cons. for CSIP, 1967-69; asst. prof. edn., psychology Johnson C. Smith U., Charlotte, 1967-69; counselor, team leader Centennial, U. So. Calif. Tchr. Corps, L.A., 1970-73; counselor Compton (Calif.) C.C., 1973—, adv. fgn. student, 1975-85; co-developer Hyde Park Estates and The Moors, Charlotte, N.C., 1960-63. Pres. bd. dirs. Charlotte Day Nursery, 1956-59; bd. dirs. Taylor St. USO, Columbia, S.C., 1951-53; sec. southwest region Nat. Alliance Family Life, 1973-74; sec. bd. dirs. NCCJ, Charlotte, 1959-62. Recipient Faculty Audit Program award Ford/Carnegie Found., Harvard U., Cambridge, Mass., 1968, Pub. Svc. Achievement award WSOC Broadcasting Co.; fellow U. Mich., 1946. Mem. NAACP (life, Golden Heritage mem. 1992), AAUW (life), NEA (life), Am. Fedn. Tchrs., Faculty Assn. Calif. C.C., Nat. Acad. Counselors and Family Therapists (life, clin. mem., pres. S.W. region 1989), C.C. Counselors Assn., Links, Inc. (Harbor area chpt. historian 1985-87, chaplain 1990-94), Jack and Jill Am. (charter, organizer Charlotte chpt., pres. 1954-56), Women on Target, Calif. Tchrs. Assn., Delta Sigma Theta, Alpha Gamma Sigma (Golden Apple award 1981). Democrat. Methodist. Home: 6621 Caro St Paramount CA 90723-4755 Office: Compton Community Coll 1111 E Artesia Blvd Compton CA 90221-5393

WILLIAMS-BARNARD, CAROL LOU, mental health nurse; b. New Britain, Conn., Feb. 20, 1950; d. Robert L. and Charlotte L. (Manon) W.; m. Theodore P. Barnard Jr., Aug. 10, 1974; children: Lauren, Kaetryn. AS in Nursing, Vt. Coll., 1970; BSN, Cath. U. Am., 1973, MS in Nursing, DNSc, 1979. Vis. nurse Vis. Nurse Assn., Washington, 1973; asst. prof. nursing U. N.H., Durham, 1978-83, assoc. prof. nursing, 1984—. Mem. ANA, AAUP, Nat. League for Nursing, N.H. Nurses Assn., Alliance for Mentally Ill, Sigma Theta Tau, Phi Theta Kappa.

WILLIAMS-DALY, ANGELIA EVETTE, marketing executive, small business owner; b. Chattanooga, Apr. 17, 1960; d. Tedi (Chester) W. BS in Nursing, U. Tenn., Chattanooga, 1988. Mktg. dir. Echols Furniture Co., Chattanooga, 1979-91. Bd. dirs. La. Make-A-Wish Found. 1991-94; mem. Chattanooga Rep. Com. Mem. Chattanooga Apt. Assn. (bd. dirs. 1988-90), Chattanooga Hotel-Motel Assn. (bd. dirs. 1988-90), Chattanooga Jaycees (bd. dirs. 1985-86, v.p. 1986-88, pres. 1989-90, chmn. bd. dirs. 1990-91, Dir. of Yr. award 1986, Exec. of Yr. award 1988, Pres. of Yr. award 1990). Roman Catholic. Office: 1225 Carrollton Ave Baton Rouge LA 70806-8164

WILLIAMS JONES, ELIZABETH, financial planner, business consultant; b. San Francisco, Jan. 16, 1948; d. John and Myrtle Mary (Thierry) W.; children: Brian, Jonathan; m. Archie W. Jones Jr. Cert. in bus., U. Calif., 1979. Cert. computers loan processing. Manpower coord., fed. programs U.S. Govt., San Francisco; patient svc. rep. Health Care Svc., Oakland, Calif.; ins. and real estate cons.; pres. Investments Unlimited, Oakland, EWJ & Assocs. Mktg. Firm; v.p. A&E Catering Svcs.; CEO Ultimate Vacations Inc. Mem. NAACP. Recipient Pub. Speaking award; European Investment fellow. Mem. AAUW, NAFE, Nat. Real Estate Owners Assn., Nat. Notary Assn., Order Ea. Star, Heroines Jericho, Daus. Isis, Toastmistress Club.

WILLIAMS-LUCK, NAOMI CATHERINE, management analyst; b. Bridgeton, N.J.; d. Stitt Williams and Catherine E. (Veney) Williams; m. Jerry Ingram, June 29, 1968; 1 child, Katrina Allayne. BA, U. Colo., 1971. Dir. assistance profl. Mountain Bell Telephone, Denver, 1966-68; office mgr. Systems Rsch. and Svcs., Inc., Denver, 1968-71; office asst. guidance dept. Denver Pub. Schs., 1972; mgmt. analyst Denver Dept. Social Svcs., 1974—. Editor: Williams-Veney Family Newsletter, 1989-93. Mem. exec. bd. Centre Pointe Neighborhood Assn., Aurora, Colo., 1990-91; historian Black Genealogy Search Group, Denver, 1993; active Colo. Quilt Coun., 1993. Mem. Am. Bus. Women's Assn. (v.p. 1989-91), Colo. Geneal. Soc. (mem. computer interest group 1994), Alliance Info. and Referral Systems, Social Svcs. Tech. and Bus. Staff. United Methodist.

WILLIAMSON, CHRISTINE WILDER, educational consultant, small business owner; b. Sylvester, Ga., Jan. 1, 1929; d. Thomas Herman and Irene (Beverly) Wilder; m. James Bryant Williamson, Aug. 10, 1947; children: James Robert, Joseph Nathan, Janet Marie. BS, Tift Coll., Forsyth, Ga., 1972; MEd, Mercer U., 1973; D Ministry, Luther Rice Sem., Jacksonville, Fla., 1983. Tchr. Houston County Bd. Edn., Warner Robins, Ga., 1947-50, Kathleen Pape Kindergarten, Macon, Ga., 1963-66, Vineville Bapt. Kindergarten, Macon, 1966-71; elem. dir. Vineville Bapt. Ch., 1971-80; presch. specialist, cons. Ga. Bapt. and So. Bapt. Conv., 1970—; instr. Macon Tech. Inst., 1980-85; owner, founder Splendid Difference Ent., 1990—. Author: I Can Do It Myself, 1983, Creative Art Activities for Children, 1991. Fund raiser Ga. Cancer Assn., Macon, 1970-88; dir. Mission Friends, Macon Bapt. Women's Missionary Union, 1989—; dir. Royal Ambassadors. Mem. Nat. Assn. Edn. Young Children, So. Assn. Children under Six, Ga. Assn. Young Children, Ga. Presch. Assn. (pres. 1984-86, chaplain 1990—), Bibb County Presch. Assn. (pres. 1975-77, chaplain, treas. 1988—), MADD. Democrat. Home and Office: 577 Old Lundy Rd Macon GA 31210-4305

WILLIAMSON, CYNTHIA ANN, school system administrator, consultant; b. Ft. Worth, Oct. 30, 1958; d. Paul Wayne and Dora (Ray) Belew; m. James Michael Jamieson, Aug. 1, 1990 (div. Apr. 1992); m. Daniel Royce Williamson, July 23, 1994; 1 child, Jennifer. BS, Northeast Mo. State U., 1980; MS, So. Ill. U., 1991. Cert. Novell engr. Spl. edn. tchr. United Cerebral Palsy Assn., St. Louis, 1980-83; dir. recreation Jefferson County Commn. Handicapped, Hillsboro, Mo., 1983-84; spl. edn. educator Festus (Mo.) R-6 Schs., 1984-90; edn./tech. specialist Regional Consortium for Ednl. Tech., St. Louis, 1990-92; edn. specialist Edn. Svc. Ctr. XI, Ft. Worth, 1992-93; dir. tech. Glen Rose (Tex.) Ind. Sch. Dist., 1993—; ind. cons., Weatherford, Tex. Co-author: (manual) Multimedia Comes Alive, 1991; author: (software) Charlie Russell: American Artist, 1992; contbr. (software) St. Louis Zoo Display, 1992. With USNR, 1990—. Mem. Beta Sigma Phi (sec. 1993), Phi Kappa Phi. Office: Glen Rose Ind Sch Dist PO Box 2129 Glen Rose TX 76043-2129

WILLIAMSON, DAISY LEE SMITH, librarian, consultant, researcher; b. Turkey, N.C., Jan. 15, 1939; d. William Howard and Ethel (Hill) Smith; m. Samuel Lee Williamson, Oct. 1, 1960; children—Samuel Scott, Melanie Joy. B.S. in Math., N.C. Central U., 1960, also postgrad.; M.L.S., CUNY, 1972. Tchr. math. Queen St. High Sch., Beaufort, N.C., 1960-61, Johnsonville High Sch., Sanford, N.C., 1961-62, Jr. High 64, Bklyn., 1964-65; social investigator N.Y.C. Dept. Social Services, 1962-63; actuary N.Y.C. Tchrs.'s Retirement Systems, 1964; sch. librarian N.Y.C. Schs., 1966-76, 84-87; researcher Dazee Enterprises, Clinton, N.C. and N.Y.C., 1974—. Co-author Inst. Findings Ethnic Materials at Queens Coll., Sch. Library Sci., 1975; contbr. articles to profl. mags. NSF grantee, 1961, 62. Mem. N.Y.C. Sch. Librarians Assn., United Fedn. Tchrs., Am. Fedn. Tchrs., Delta Sigma Theta (treas. 1958-60). Democrat. Baptist. Avocations: reading; puzzles; travel; plays; movies.

WILLIAMSON, DEBRA CAMP, accounting administrator; b. Gaffney, S.C., July 30, 1956; d. William Edwin and Julia Annette (Petty) Camp; 1 child, Justin Bradley. BSBA, Limestone Coll., 1986. Accounts payable clk. Milliken & Co., Spartanburg, S.C., 1974-79, cost acctg. clk., 1979-86, cost acctg. mgr., 1986—. Team mother Boiling Springs Little League, 1991-94, Spartanburg County Soccer, 1993-94. Mem. Inst. Mgmt. Accts. (newsletter editor 1986-90). Baptist. Home: 303 Gardenview Dr Inman SC 29349

WILLIAMSON, DONNA MARIA, pastoral counselor; b. Oswego, N.Y., Feb. 26, 1944; d. Donald Carl and Helen Mary (Saber) Townsley; m. Patrick H. Williamson, July 7, 1962; children: Kevin Patrick, Michael Brian, Timothy Daniel. Grad. pub. schs., Fulton, N.Y. Cert. in clin. pastoral edn., pastoral care, weight loss counselor, N.Y. Chaplain Loretto Geriatric Ctr., Syracuse, 1981-82; hosp. chaplain St. Rose of Lima Parish, Syracuse, 1982-84, pastoral counselor, 1984—; weight loss counselor Nutri-System, Syracuse, 1988-91. Founding mem. Fulton Community Nursery Sch., 1967, Commn. on Women in Ch. and Society, Syracuse, 1984; mem. Alethea, Ctr. on Death and Dying, Inc., Syracuse, 1978. Mem. Menninger Found., Greenpeace. Roman Catholic. Office: St Rose of Lima Parish 409 S Main St North Syracuse NY 13212-2811

WILLIAMSON, JO ANN, psychologist; b. Wichita, Kans., Feb. 12, 1951; d. Howard T. Murray and Ferryl Arlene (Rumsey) Fleming; m. James Wallace Johnson, Apr. 5, 1984 (div. 1984); m. Michael R. Williamson, Dec. 21, 1990; children: Wesley, Wade. BA, U. Kans., 1973; MA in Psychology, U. Mo., 1974; PhD in Psychology, Auburn U., 1979. Lic. psychologist, Kans. Clin. asst. prof. Ohio State U., Columbus, 1979-80; asst. prof. Chgo. Med. Sch., 1980-81; psychologist U. Mo., Kansas City, 1981-82; psychologist II Rainbow Mental Health Ctr., Kansas City, 1982-83; pvt. practice Wichita, 1983-86; pres. Jo Ann Murray PL.O.P.A., 1986-89; psychologist Iowa Meth. Hosp., Des Moines, 1989-90, Hutchinson (Kans.) Correctional Facility, 1990, Cedarvale, Wichita, 1991, Cowley County Mental Health, Winfield, Kans., 1991; cons. Riverside Hosp., Wichita, 1991-92; mental health psychologist Cowley County, 1991-93; clin. dir. Cowley County Mental Health, 1993—. Contbr. articles to profl. jours. Mem. APA (div. clin. psychology).

WILLIAMSON, JOAN COPELAND (J. C. WILLIAMSON), art director; b. Olney, Md., Sept. 21, 1950; d. Harold Ellsworth and Margaret Dana (Burrage) W. AA, Marjorie Webster Coll., Washington, 1970; BS, U. Md., 1972. Jr. art dir. Weitzman & Assocs. Advt., Bethesda, Md., 1974-77; art dir. Earle Palmer Brown & Assocs., Bethesda, 1978-79; sr. art dir. Needham, Harper & Steers, McLean, Va., 1979-83; sr. art dir., supr., producer Rosenthal, Greene & Campbell, Bethesda, 1984-89; sr. art dir., supr. producer Demaine, Vickers Assocs., Alexandria, Va., 1989-94; freelance art dir., producer, 1994—. Recipient various nat. advt. awards, 1976-89; entry in Cannes Film Festival, 1988, Gold and Silver Telly awards, finalist local Emmy awards, 1989, Winner Ads Against AIDS, Nat. TV, 1991, Gold plaque Chgo. Internat. Film Festival, 1994, Merit award N.Y. Film Festival, 1994.

WILLIAMSON, JUDY DARLENE GRAHAM, secondary school educator, librarian; b. Gallipolis, Ohio, Nov. 10, 1948; d. Byron Jr. and Margaret Mae (Bush) Greenlee; m. Lannes Clay Williamson, Aug. 29, 1984. AB, Glenville State Coll., 1970; MA, Marshall U., 1973, postgrad., 1994. Librarian, tchr. Mason County Bd. Edn., Point Pleasant, W.Va., 1970—; acting dir. Mason County Pub. Library, Point Pleasant, 1986-87; cons. Found. for Library Research, Point Pleasant, 1983—. Created the Automated Library System computer software; contbr. articles to profl. jours. Treas. Point Pleasant Emergency Med. Svcs., 1976-82; mem. chpt. 2 com. Mason County Bd. Edn., 1983—, mem. computer com., 1984—; mem. bicentennial steering com. City of Point Pleasant, 1987. Grantee W.Va. Dept. Edn., 1981, 82. Mem. W.Va. Libr. Assn., W.Va. Edn. Assn., Mason County Reading Coun., W.Va. Ednl. Media Assn., Alpha Delta Kappa, Delta Kappa Gamma. Republican. Methodist. Home: 2764 Us Route 35 Southside WV 25187-9730 Office: Point Pleasant HS Rt 1 Box 4 Point Pleasant WV 25550-2096

WILLIAMSON, MARILYN LAMMERT, English educator, university adminstrator; b. Chgo., Sept. 6, 1927; d. Raymond Ferdinand and Edith Louise (Eisenbies) Lammert; m. Robert M. Williamson, Oct. 28, 1950 (div. Apr. 1973); 1 child, Timothy L.; m. James H. McKay, Aug. 15, 1974. BA, Vassar Coll., 1949; MA, U. Wis., 1950; PhD, Duke U., 1956. Instr. Duke U., Durham, N.C., 1955-56, 58-59; lectr. N.C. State U., Raleigh, 1957-58, 61-62; asst. prof. Oakland U., Rochester, Mich., 1965-68, assoc. prof., 1968-72; prof. English Wayne State U., Detroit, 1972-90, Disting. prof. English, 1990—, chmn. dept. English, 1972-74, 81-83, assoc. dean Coll. Liberal Arts, 1974-79; dir. women's studies Wayne State U., 1976-87; dep. provost Wayne State U., Detroit, 1987-91, sr. v.p. for acad. affairs, provost, 1991—; pres. Assn. Depts. English, 1976-77. Author: Infinite Variety, 1974, Patriarchy of Shakespeare's Comedies, 1986, British Women Writers 1650-1750, 1990; editor: Renaissance Studies, 1972, Female Poets of Great Britain, 1981; contbr. articles to profl. jours. Pres. LWV, Rochester, 1963-65. Recipient Detroit Disting. Svc. award, 1986, Faculty Recognition award Bd. Govs., Wayne State U., 1991; Bunting Inst. fellow, 1969-70, AAUW fellow, 1982-83, J.N. Keal fellow, 1985-86. Mem. MLA (exec. coun. 1977-80, mem. editorial bd. 1992-94), Renaissance Soc. Am., Coll. English Assn., Mich. Acad. (pres. 1978-79), Shakespeare Assn. Am., Mich. Coun. Humanities (chair 1991-93), Fed. State Humanities Coun. (bd. dirs. 1994—). Democrat. Home: 2275 Oakway Dr West Bloomfield MI 48324-1855 Office: Wayne State Univ Dept of English Detroit MI 48202

WILLIAMSON, MARY LOU, bank officer; b. Green Island, Iowa, May 25, 1930; d. Frank William and Alma Christine (Clausen) Behrens; divorced; 1 child, Guy Leander. Student, Wartburg Coll., 1949. Sec., bookkeeper Miles (Iowa) Savings Bank, 1949-65; receptionist, sec. Bank of Kalispel (Mont.), 1965-66; bookkeeper, sec. Carroll Johnson Atty., Clinton, Iowa, 1966-67; bookkeeper McGuire Shoes, Roanoke, Va., 1969-71; cashier, loan officer Miles Savings Bank, 1971—. Mem. Am. Legion Aux., Order of Eastern Star. Republican. Lutheran. Office: Miles Savings Bank PO Box 327 Miles IA 52064-0327

WILLIAMSON, MILDRED FREDA, health program administrator; b. Chgo., Apr. 23, 1953; d. Cleveland L. and Gladys (Moore) McDowell; m. Willie Joe Williamson, June 13, 1971; children: Najja Shakir, Camille Rashida. BA of Urban Ethnic Studies, Loyola U., 1975; MA of Social Work, U. Chgo., 1989. Adminstrv. asst. YWCA of Met. Chgo., 1978-79; vol. recruiter Safer Found., Chgo., 1979-80; asst. dir. of devel. Hull House Assn., Chgo., 1980-81; Chgo. coord. Nat. Alliance Against Racist and Polit. Repression, 1981-86; adminstr. women and children HIV program Cook County Hosp., Chgo., 1989—; mem. adv. com. Nat. Pediat./Family HIV/AIDS Evaluation, Washington, 1994—; mem. adv. bd. AIDSFILMS Project for Pub. TV, N.Y.C., 1993—; coun. mem. Chgo./Cook County HIV Planning Coun., Chgo., 1993—; mem. adv. bd. U. Chgo. Maternal Child Health Tng. Program, 1993—. Vol. registrar Chgo. Bd. Elections Commn., Chgo., 1982-87. Pediat./Family HIV/AIDS demo grantee Maternal Child Health Bur., 1991-94, High Risk Youth HIV Prevention grantee Chgo. Dept. Health, 1993-94, HIV Prevention grantee for women, 1989-94, HIV/AIDS conf. grantee Office of AIDS Rsch./NIH, 1994. Mem. APHA, Family and Children's AIDS Network (mem. family advocacy com. 1989—, Appreciation award 1993). Office: Cook County Hosp Women & Children HIV Prog 1835 W Harrison St Chicago IL 60612

WILLIAMSON, MYRNA HENNRICH, retired army officer, lecturer, consultant; b. Gregory, S.D., Jan. 27, 1937; d. Walter Ferdinand and Alma Lillian (Rajewich) H. BS with highest honors, S.D. State U., 1960; MA, U. Okla., 1973; grad., U.S. Army Command and Gen. Staff Coll., 1977, Nat. War Coll., 1980. Commd. 2d lt. U.S. Army, 1960, advanced through grades to brig. gen., 1985; bn. comdr. Mil. Police Sch. U.S. Army, Fort McClellan, Ala., 1977-79; chief plans policy and service div. Jl 8th Army U.S. Army, Korea, 1980-81; chief mgmt. support Office Dep. Chief Staff for Research, Devel. and Acquisition U.S. Army, Washington, 1981-82; brigade comdr. U.S. Army, Fort Benjamin Harrison, Ind., 1983-84; comdg. gen. 3d ROTC Region U.S. Army, Fort Riley, Kans., 1984-87; dep. dir. mil. personnel mgmt. U.S. Army, Washington, 1987-89, ret., 1989; U.S. del. com. on women in NATO Forces, 1986-89. Pres. S.D. State U. Found.; bd. dirs. Women in Mil. Svc. to Am. Found.; mem. bd. adv. Safe Streets. Recipient Disting. Alumnus award S.D. State U., 1984. Mem. Internat. Platform Assn., Assn. U.S. Army (trustee), United Svcs. Automobile Assn. (bd. dirs.), Exec. Women in Govt., Phi Kappa Phi.

WILLIAMSON, VIKKI LYN, finance executive; b. Huntington, W.Va., June 30, 1956; d. Ernest E. and Wanda C. (Cole) W. BA in Secondary Edn., English, Temple U., 1978; postgrad. in Acctg. and Fin., U. Cin., 1984-86. CPA, Ohio; cert. tchr., Tenn., Ohio. Tchr. Springfield Christian Acad., Tenn., 1978-79; acctg. asst. Children's Hosp. Med. Ctr., Cin., 1979-84; asst. dir. fin. svcs. U. Cin. Med. Ctr., 1984-85, dir. fin. svcs., 1985-88, dir. fin. and adminstrn., 1988-91, dep. dir., 1991—; bd. dirs. Contemporary Dance Theatre, 1987-90. Bd. dirs. Habitat for Humanity-Hamilton, 1991—, v.p., 1991, pres., 1992. Mem. AICPA, Healthcare Fin. Mgmt. Assn., Am. Assn. Blood Banks, Ohio Assn. Blood Banks (fin. co. 1986-90, treas. 1991—), Coun. Community Blood Ctrs. (fin. com. 1991—, alt. trustee 1991—), Assn. Women Adminstrs. (fin. com. 1987-90), Assn. Mid-Level Adminstrs. (bd. dirs. 1987-90), Alpha Epsilon Theta, Beta Gamma Sigma, Delta Mu Delta. Office: Hoxworth Blood Ctr Univ Cin Med Ctr 3130 Highland Ave ML 55 Cincinnati OH 45267

WILLIAMS-STEINWENDER, KARIN MAE, artist; b. Santa Monica, Calif., Oct. 14, 1948; d. Marion Glen and Margaret Grace (Long) Williams; m. Helmut Adolf Ludwig Steinwender, Aug. 17, 1985. BA with hons., Calif. State U., Dominguez Hills, Carson, 1983. Cert. tchr. art-dance, Calif.; cert. hypnotist; cert. Shiat-su therapist; cert. Cecchetti Ballet instr. Chmn. bd. South Bay (Calif.) Ballet Co., 1977-78, choreographer, 1976-77; gallery coord. F.O.T.A., Hermosa Beach, Calif., 1978-79; ballet instr. Act III Acad., Redondo Beach, Calif., 1976-83; self-employed ballet instr. South Bay, 1972-93; artist, painter Calif., N.Y., Oreg., 1972—; exhbns. include Art of 80's Gallery, Hermosa Beach, Calif., Barnsdale Mcpl. Gallery, L.A., Community galleries, South Bay, Calif., Ambiente', Redondo Beach, Calif., Everson Mus. exhbn., Syracuse, N.Y., Gallery Syracuse, 1972—; one-woman show Crackerjack Prodns.; interview and art filming South Bay News, Redondo Beach, Calif.; studio opening/exhbn., 1992. Author: Technique in Balance and Turning, 1985; writer, producer, choreographer (ballets) Woodcutter's Daughter, 1977, Power Plays, 1978; choreographer Midsummer Nights Dream, 1975, holiday and community programs, 1975-83. Vol. Rep. Party, Syracuse, 1988-89, Park Assn. Syracuse, 1990. Recipient honor for one-man exhbn. Crackerjack TV Prodns., Redondo Beach, 1983. Mem. ASPCA, World Wildlife Fund, Rodale Inst., Arbor Day Found., Sierra Legal Fund, Nature Conservancy, Nat. Wildlife Fedn., Greenpeace, Wilderness Soc., Nat. Resources Def. Coun., Environ. Def. Fund, Rosicrucians, In Def. of Animals.

WILLIAMS-TIMS, LILLIE ALTHEA, distribution administrator, genealogist; b. Laurens, S.C., Aug. 17, 1951; d. Hunter Nathenial and Alma Sue Peal (hunter) W.; m. Benny Woodrow Tims, Sept. 1, 1973 (div. 1987); 1 child, Eltaro. Assoc. in Gen. Bus., Piedmont Tech. Coll., Greenwood, S.C., 1988. Weaver Delta Woodside Mills, Fountain Inn, S.C., 1981-87; seamstress, data entry clk. Josten's Cap and Gown, Laurens, 1987-88; supr. Wal-Mart Distbn. Ctr., Laurens, 1988—. Asst. supt. Flat Ruff Bapt. Ch. Sch., Laurens, 1989-91; pres. Young Women Assn. for Flat Ruff Bapt. Ch., 1991—; founder, pres. African-Am. Hist. Found., Laurens. Mem. S.C. Geneal. Soc. (sec. Laurens chpt. 1992—), S.C. African Am. Heritage Coun. (assoc.). Democrat. Home: 42 Chateau Arms Laurens SC 29360

WILLIAMS-WENNELL, KATHI, human resources officer; b. Danville, Pa., Sept. 22, 1955; d. Raymond Gerald and Julia Dolores (Higgins) Williams; m. Mark Kevin Wennell, Apr. 3, 1982; children: Ryan Christopher, Lauren Ashley. BA, Immaculata Coll., 1977; MEd, Pa. State U., State College, 1978. Cert. rehabilitation counselor, Pa. From project dir. to coord. devel. activities Community Interactions, Blue Bell, Pa., 1978-83; from mgmt. trainee to coord. coll. recruiting and rels. Meridian Bancorp, Inc., Reading, Pa., 1983-86, mgmt. recruiter, compensation analyst, 1986-88, 89-93; recruiter, 1993—; cons. Norristown (Pa.) Life Ctr., 1981; instr. Immaculata (Pa.) Coll., 1981-83, Alvernia Coll., Reading, 1988-89. Meridian campaign coord. United Way Berks County, Reading, 1985. Named Recruiter of Yr. LaSalle U., Phila., 1986; recipient Excellence in Programming award Nat. Assn. Bank Women, Pa., 1986. Mem. Soc. Human Resources Mgmt. Republican. Roman Catholic. Home: 69 S Hampton Dr Wyomissing PA 19610-3108 Office: Meridian Bancorp Inc Meridian Ctr at Springridge 1 Meridian Blvd Wyomissing PA 19610-3200

WILLIE, ROBERTA, geriatrics nurse; b. Letcher, Ky., Jan. 5, 1939; d. Dewey Roscoe and Martha (Eldridge) Brown; m. Robert Gene Willie, Mar. 19, 1988. LPN, Appalachian Sch. of Practical Nursing, 1960. Staff nurse emergency rm. Appalachian Regional Hosp., Whitesburg, Ky., 1960-78; staff nurse JA Dosher Meml. Hosp., Southport, N.C., 1978-80; supr. Friendship Manor Convalescent Ctr., Roanoke, Va., 1980—. Democrat. Home: 4613 Daleville St NW Roanoke VA 24012 Office: Friendship Manor Convalescent Ctr 317 Hershberger Rd NW Roanoke VA 24012

WILLINGER, RHONDA ZWERN, optometrist; b. Bklyn., Apr. 26, 1962; d. Jerome Max and Jeanette (Zwern) Willinger; m. Wayne Ken Chan, Aug. 26, 1990. BS, U. Miami, 1983; OD with honors, New Eng. Coll. Optometry, 1987. Resident in optometry VA Med. Ctr., Bedford, Mass., 1987-88; pvt. practice, Burlington, Mass., 1988-89; pvt. practice specializing in contact lenses Framingham, Mass., 1989—. Scholar New Coll., U. South Fla., 1979-81; honors scholarship U. Miami, 1981-83. Mem. Am. Optometric Assn. (contact lens sect.), Mass. Soc. Optometrists. Home: 228 Lowell Ave Newton MA 02160 Office: 150 Worcester Rd Framingham MA 01701-5308

WILLINGHAM, JEANNE MAGGART, dance educator, ballet company executive; b. Fresno, Calif., May 8, 1923; d. Harold F. and Gladys (Ellis) Maggart. student Tex. Woman's U., 1942; student profl. dancing schs., worldwide. dance tchr. Beaux Arts Dance Studio, Pampa, Tex., 1948—; artistic dir. Pampa Civic Ballet, 1972—. Mem. Tex. Arts and Humanities, Tex. Arts Alliance, Pampa C. of C. (fine arts com.), Pampa Fine Arts Assn. Office: Pampa Civic Ballet Beaux Arts Dance Studio 315 N Nelson St Pampa TX 79065-6013

WILLINGHAM, MARY MAXINE, fashion retailer; b. Childress, Tex., Sept. 12, 1928; d. Charles Bryan and Mary (Bohannon) McCollum; m. Welborn Kiefer Willingham, Aug. 14, 1950; children—Sharon, Douglas, Sheila. BA, Tex. Tech U., 1949. Interviewer Univ. Placement Service, Tex. Tech U., Lubbock, 1964-69; owner, mgr., buyer Maxine's Accent, Lubbock, 1969—; speaker in field. Leader Campfire Girls, Lubbock, 1964-65; sec. Community Theatre, Lubbock, 1962-64. Named Outstanding Mcht., Fashion Retailor mag., 1971, Outstanding Retailer; recipient Golden Sun award Dallas Market, May 1985. Mem. Lubbock Symphony Guild, Ranch and Heritage Ctr. Club: Faculty Women's. Office: 10 Briercroft Ctr Lubbock TX 79412

WILLIS, CONNIE (CONSTANCE E. WILLIS), author; b. 1945. Tchr. elem. and jr. high schs. Branford, Conn., 1967-69. Author: (short stories/novels) Letter from the Clearys (Nebula award 1982), Lincoln's Dreams, 1987, Doomsday Book (Nebula award 1992, Hugo award 1993), Impossible Things, 1993/Uncharted Territory, 1994, Even the Queen (Nebula 1992, Hugo 1993), (novelette) Fire Watch (Nebula 1982, Hugo 1983), At the Rialto (Nebula 1990), The Last of the Winnebagos (Nebula 1988, Hugo 1989), Death on the Nile (Hugo 1994), (novel) Remake, 1995; (with Cynthia Felice) Water Witch, 1982, Light Raid, 1989. Address: 1716 13th Ave Greeley CO 80631-5418

WILLIS, DAWN LOUISE, paralegal, small business owner; b. Johnstown, Pa., Sept. 11, 1959; d. Kenneth William and Dawn Louise (Joseph) Hagins; m. Marc Anthony Ross, Nov. 30, 1984 (div.); m. Jerry Wayne Willis, Dec. 16, 1989. Grad. high sch., Sacramento, Calif. Legal sec. Wilcoxen & Callahan, Sacramento, 1979-87, paralegal asst., 1987-88; legal adminstr. Law Office Jack Vetter, Sacramento, 1989—; owner, mgr. Your Girl Friday Secretarial and Legal Support Svcs., Sacramento, 1991—; with Amway Distbr., 1992—. Vol. ARC, 1985. Mem. NAFE, Assn. Legal Adminstrs., Calif. Trial Lawyers Assn., Sacramento Legal Secs. Assn. Republican. Lutheran. Home: 8303 Walerga Rd # 17 Antelope CA 95843

WILLIS, DEBRA RUBUSH, public speaker; b. Haines City, Fla., May 14, 1955; d. Jack Everette and Shirley Ann (Carmichael) Rubush. Student, Polk C.C., Winter Haven, Fla., 1973-74. Cert. in crime and rape prevention, children's safety, neuro-linguistics programming tng., chem. def. sprays. Motivational speaker and singer Willis and Hill, Orlando, Fla., 1981-84; children's safety educator Citizens Against Crime, Winter Park, 1989—, crime and rape prevention educator, 1990—; mgmt. team Citizens Against

Crime, Orlando, Jacksonville, 1990—, regional trainer, 1991—. Mem. Stop Turning Out Prisoners, Orlando, 1993. Recipient Nat. Pioneer award for Children's Safety, Divsn. of Citizens Against Crime, 1990; inducted into Spkrs. Hall of Fame for Citizens Against Crime, 1992. Mem. Winter Park C. of C., Orlando C. of C., Nat. Victim Ctr., Nat. Orgn. for Victim Assistance, NAFE, Cen. Fla. Am. Soc. for Tng. and Devel. Methodist. Office: Citizens Against Crime Ste 1201-365 931 State Rd 434 Altamonte Springs FL 32714

WILLIS, ELEANOR LAWSON, university official; b. Nashville, Sept. 15, 1936; d. Harry Alfred Jr. and Helen Russell (Howse) Lawson; m. Alvis Rux Rochelle, Aug. 25, 1956 (div. Mar. 1961); 1 child, Alfred Russell Willis; m. William Reese Willis Jr., Mar. 7, 1964 (div. June 1994); children: William Reese III, Brent Lawson. BA cum laude, Vanderbilt U., 1957. Host children's syndicated TV show Sta. WSIX-TV, Nashville, 1961-64; tchr. head start program Metro Pub. Sch., Nashville, 1965-67; co-investigator cognitive edn. curriculum project Peabody Coll., Nashville, 1979-81; dir., founder Heads Up Child Devel. Ctr., Inc., Nashville, 1973-87; dir. Tenn. Vols. for Gore for Pres. Campaign, Nashville, 1987-88; dir. devel. Vanderbilt Inst. Pub. Policy Studies, Vanderbilt U., Nashville, 1988—; mem. task force on child abuse Dept. Human Svcs., Nashville, 1976; mem. mental health ctr. adv. bd. Vanderbilt U., 1978-80, bd. dirs. Vanderbilt Child Devel. Ctr.; mem. instrumental enrichment adv. bd. Peabody/Vanderbilt U., 1981-82. Author: (with others) I Really Like Myself, 1973, I Wonder Where I Came From, 1973. Pres. Nashville Bar Aux., 1967-68, Nashville Symphony Guild, 1984-85, W.O. Smith Nashville Community Music Sch., 1987-89; founder, active in Rochelle Ctr., Nashville, 1968-90; vice chmn. Century III Com., Nashville, 1978-80; chmn. so. region Am. Symphony Orch. League Vol. Coun., Washington, 1984-86, Homecoming 1986 Steering Com., Nashville, 1985-86; mem. Cheekwood Fine Arts Ctr., Nahville City Ballet, Nashville Symphony Assn., Dem. Women of Davidson County; appointed Metro Arts Commn., 1992; bd. dirs. Friends of Warner Park, 1994. Recipient Leadership Nashville award, 1982; Seven Leading Ladies award Nashville Mag., 1984; Eleanor Willis Day proclaimed by City of Nashville, 1987. Mem. Nashville C. of C., Tenn. Conservation League, Vanderbilt Alumni Assn. Presbyterian. Office: 50 Vaughn Rd Nashville TN 39221

WILLIS, GEORGIA MARIE, banker; b. Waynesburg, Pa., July 9, 1952; d. George Arthur and Della Marie (Bonnell) W.; m. James Arthur Lampman, May 22, 1983 (div. Aug. 1988). BS in Commerce, U. Va., 1983. Mgmt. intern Ctrl. Fidelity Bank, Lynchburg, Va., 1983-84, asst. br. mgr., 1984-85; mgr. br. Ctrl. Fidelity Bank, Lynchburg, 1987-91, Moneta, Va., 1985-87; regional sales mgr. Ctrl. Fidelity Bank, Culpeper, Va., 1991-93; sr. v.p., regional area mgr. Ctrl Fidelity Bank, Culpeper, Va., 1993—; owner GA's Boutique, Culpeper, 1980—. Bd. dirs. Germanna C.C. Found., 1993—, Shenandoah U. Byrd Sch. Bus., 1992—; bd. dirs. Piedmont United Way, chair pers. com., 1991—; mem. planned giving com. Culpeper Meml. Hosp., 1991—; trustee Culpeper Found., 1991—. Recipient Outstanding Alumni award Culpeper 4-H Club, 1992; named to Outstanding Young Women of Am., 1985. Mem. U. Va. Alumni Assn. (pres. 1993), Rotary Internat. (chair fellowship com. 1993). Republican. Home: 20121 Buck Run Ct Culpeper VA 22701 Office: Ctrl Fidelity Bank 151 N Main St Culpeper VA 22701

WILLIS, JANE B., artist; b. New Orleans, July 25, 1937; d. Vernon Alwyn and Agnes Rella (Roberts) Broome; m. John Ray Willis, Dec. 19, 1959; children: Jeffrey Scott, Matthew David. BS in Elem. Edn., La. State U., 1959. Upper elem. edn. tchr. W. Baton Rouge Parish, Brusly, La., 1959-61. Artist: Best of Colored Pencil 2, 1994. Mem. oper. com. Slidell (La.) Cultural Ctr., 1989-91, 92—. Recipient Artist's Mag. award of merit West Bank Art Guild, New Orleans, 1994. Mem. Nat. League Am. Pen Women (br. membership chair 1991—), Catharine Lorillard Wolfe Art Club, Artwave, Slidell Art League, Inc. (pres. 1989-90, show coord. 1990-91, publicity dir. 1992-93, Holly Hegeman award 1985, Artist of Yr. 1992), New Orleans Art Assn. (2d place award 1994). Mem. Asssembly of God Ch. Home: 859 Cross Gates Blvd Slidell LA 70461

WILLIS, JUDY ANN, lawyer; b. Hartford, Conn., July 7, 1949; d. Durward Joseph and Angeline Rachael (Riccardo) W.; m. William Peter Ross, Apr. 24, 1977. BA, Cen. Conn. State U., 1971; postgrad., U. Conn. Law Sch., 1976-77; JD, Boston Coll., 1979. Bar: Mass. 1979, U.S. Dist. Ct. Mass. 1980. Sr. atty. H.P. Hood Inc., Charleston, Mass., 1979-83; v.p. law Parker Bros., Beverly, Mass., 1983-89; v.p., asst. gen. counsel Mattel, Inc., El Segundo, Calif., 1989—. Trustee Schs. for Children, Arlington, Mass., 1981—. Mem. ABA, Mass. Bar Assn., Boston Bar Assn. Club: Austin-Healey. Home: 29 Montemalaga Plz Palos Verdes Peninsula CA 90274-1641 Office: Mattel Inc 333 Continental Blvd El Segundo CA 90245*

WILLIS, LOUISE MCKINNEY, retired petroleum company executive; b. Cooper, Tex., Nov. 12, 1924; d. Charles Martin and Birdie Floy (Griffin) McKinney; m. Glenn Harry Willis, May 7, 1948; children: Stephen Eric, Susan Renee, Mary Lynn, Glenda Ann. Student U. Okla., 1946-47. Instrument repair technician Tinker Field AFB, Okla., 1943-46; transit check clk. Fed. Res. Bank, Oklahoma City, 1948-50; sec. Southwestern Power Co., Tulsa, 1950-51, U.S. Govt. Agy., New Orleans, 1951-53; dist. mgr. World Book Encyclopedia, Dallas, 1972-78; v.p. Dor-Texan Petroleum, Inc., Dallas, 1980-87, ret., 1987. Mem. Dallas Opera Guild, 1984-85; pres. Dallas PTA, 1965-66, hon. life mem., 1975—; pres. St. Andrews Study Club, Dallas, 1968-69, 87-88; chmn. Cotillion Park Bd., Dallas, 1964-66. Mem. Dallas C. of C. Baptist. Clubs: Petroleum, Dallas Athletic. Lodge: Order of Rainbow Girls (chmn. bd. dirs. 1973-76).

WILLIS, SELENE LOWE, electrical engineer; b. Birmingham, Ala., Mar. 4, 1958; d. Lewis Russell and Bernice (Wilson) Lowe; m. André Maurice Willis, June 12, 1987. BSEE, Tuskegee (Ala.) U., 1980; postgrad. in Computer Programing, UCLA, 1993-94. Component engr. Hughes Aircraft Corp., El Segundo, Calif., 1980-82; reliability and lead engr. Aero Jet Electro Systems Corp., Azusa, Calif., 1982-84; sr. component engr. Rockwell Internat. Corp., Anaheim, Calif., 1984; design engr. Lockheed Missile & Space Co., Sunnyvale, Calif., 1985-86; property mgr. Penmar Mgmt. Co., L.A., 1987-88; aircraft mechanic McDonnell Douglas Corp., Long Beach, 1989-93; Unix system adminstrn. Santa Cruz Ops., 1994; mem. tech. staff Space Applications Corp., El Segunda, Calif., 1995; sr. component engr. Gen. Data Communications Corp., Danbury, Conn., 1984-85. Vol. Mercy Hosp. & Children's Hosp., Birmingham, 1972-74; mem. L.A. Gospel Messengers, 1982-84, West Angeles Ch. of God & Christ, L.A., 1990. Bell Labs. scholar, 1976-80; named one of Outstanding Women Young Women in Am., 1983-87, Outstanding Women in Am., 1994. Mem. IEEE, ASME, Aerospace and Aircraft Engrs., So. Calif. Profl. Engring. Assn., Tuskagee U. Alumni Assn., UCLa Alumni Assn., Eta Kappa Nu. Mem. Christian Ch.

WILLISCROFT, BEVERLY RUTH, lawyer; b. Conrad, Mont., Feb. 24, 1945; d. Paul A. and Gladys L. (Buck) W.; m. Kent J. Barcus, Oct. 1984. BA in Music, So. Calif. Coll., 1967; JD, John F. Kennedy U., 1977. Bar: Calif., 1977. Elem. tchr., Sunnyvale, Calif., 1968-72; legal sec., legal asst. various law firms, Bay Area, 1972-77; assoc. Neil D. Reid, Inc., San Francisco, 1977-79; sole practice, Concord, Calif., 1979—; exam. grader Calif. Bar, 1979—; real estate broker, 1980-88; tchr. real estate King Coll., Concord, 1979-80; lectr. in field; judge pro-tem Mcpl. Ct., 1981—. Bd dirs. Contra Costa Musical Theatre, Inc., 1978-82, v.p. adminstrn., 1980-81, v.p. prodn., 1981-82; mem. community devel. adv. com. City of Concord, 1981-83, vice chmn., 1982-83, mem. status of women com., 1980-81, mem. redevel. adv. com., 1984-86, planning commnr. 1986-92, chmn., 1990; mem. exec. bd. Mt. Diablo coun. Boy Scouts Am., 1981-85; bd. dirs. Pregnancy Ctrs. Contra Costa County, 1991—, chmn., 1993—. Recipient award of merit Bus. and Profl. Women, Bay Valley Dist., 1981. Mem. Concord C. of C. (bd. dir., chmn. govt. affairs com. 1981-83, v.p. 1985-87, pres. 1988-89, Bus. Person of Yr. 1986), Calif. State Bar (chmn. adoptions subcom. north, 1994), Contra Costa County Bar Assn., Todos Santos Bus. and Profl. Women (co-founder, pres. 1983-84, pub. rels. chmn. 1982-83, Woman of Achievement 1980, 81), Soroptimists (fin. sec. 1980-81). Office: 3018 Willow Pass Rd Ste 205 Concord CA 94519-2570

WILLMAN, EVIN JANE, advertising executive; b. Bklyn., Mar. 8, 1951; d. Hyman Dell and Bernice Edna (Starr) Rosenbaum; m. Warren P. Willman, May 28, 1972 (div. Dec. 1980); 1 child, Rebecca Kate. BA in English, Bradley U., 1972; postgrad., New Sch. for Social Rsch., 1974-75. Copywriter George B. Buck Cons., N.Y.C., 1972-74; comms. cons. Frank B. Hall & Co., N.Y.C., 1974-77; dir. mktg. comm. Comml. Credit Corp., Balt., 1979-83, advt. cons., mgr., 1983-85; v.p. mktg. Old Stone Credit Corp., Jacksonville, Fla., 1985-87; sr. v.p., co-owner Hubbard Agy., Jacksonville, 1987-92; pres., owner Willman & Co., Jacksonville, 1992—. Bd. dirs. Quigley House, Clay County, Fla., 1993—, YWCA of Jacksonville, 1994. Mem. Internat. Alliance (bd. dirs., 2d v.p. 1993-94, pres.-elect, 1st v.p. 1995), Women Bus. Owners of North Fla. (bd. dirs. 1988-91, pres. 1991-92), Jacksonville C. of C. (small bus. devel. com. 1994), Jacksonville Advt. Fedn., Fla. Women's Alliance. Democrat. Jewish. Office: Willman & Co 1809 Art Museum Dr Ste 103 Jacksonville FL 32207-2566

WILLNER, ANN RUTH, political scientist, educator; b. N.Y.C., Sept. 2, 1924; d. Norbert and Bella (Richman) W. B.A. cum laude, Hunter Coll., 1945; M.A., Yale U., 1946; Ph.D., U. Chgo., 1961. Lectr. U. Chgo., 1946-47, research assoc. Ctr. for Econ. Devel. and Cultural Change, 1954-56, 61-62; advisor on orgn. and tng. Indonesian Ministry for Fgn. Affairs, Jakarta, 1952-53; expert for small scale indsl. planning Indonesian Nat. Planning Bur., Jakarta, 1953-54; fgn. affairs analyst Congl. Reference Service, Library of Congress, 1960; asst. prof. polit. sci. Harpur Coll., Binghamton, N.Y., 1962-63; postdoctoral fellow polit. sci. and Southeast Asian studies Yale U., New Haven, 1963-64; research assoc. Ctr. Internat. Studies, Princeton U., 1964-69; assoc. prof. polit. sci. U. Kans., Lawrence, 1969-70, prof., 1970—; vis. prof. polit. sci. CUNY, 1975; cons. govt. agys. and pvt. industry. Polit. sci. editor: Ency. of the Social Scis., 1961; mem. editorial bd. Econ. Devel. and Cultural Change, 1954-57, Jour. Comparative Adminstrn., 1969-74, Comparative Politics, 1977—; author: The Neotraditional Accomodation to Political Independence, 1966, Charismatic Political Leadership: A Theory, 1968, The Spellbinders, 1984; also monographs, articles, chpts. to books. Grantee Rockefeller Found., 1965, Social Sci. Research and Am. Council Learned Socs., 1966. Mem. Am. Polit. Sci. Assn. (gov. council 1979-81). Home: 2112 Terrace Rd Lawrence KS 66049-2733

WILLNER, DOROTHY, anthropologist, educator; b. N.Y.C., Aug. 26, 1927; d. Norbert and Bella (Richman) W. Ph.B., U. Chgo., 1947, M.A., 1953, Ph.D., 1961; postgrad., Ecole Pratique des Hautes Etudes, U. Paris, France, 1953-54. Anthropologist Jewish Agy., Israel, 1955-58; tech. asst., adminstrn. expert in community devel. UN, Mexico, 1958; asst. prof. dept. sociology and anthropology U. Iowa, Iowa City, 1959-60; research assoc. U. Chgo., 1961-62; asst. prof. dept. sociology and anthropology U. N.C., Chapel Hill, 1962-63, Hunter Coll., N.Y.C., 1964-65; assoc. prof. dept. anthropology U. Kans., Lawrence, 1967-70; prof. U. Kans., 1970-90; professorial lectr. Johns Hopkins U. Sch. Advanced Internat. Studies, 1992. Author: Community Leadership, 1960, Nation-Building and Community in Israel, 1969. Contbr. numerous articles to profl. publs. Fellow Am. Anthrop. Assn., Soc. Applied Anthropology, Royal Anthrop. Inst.; mem. Cen. States Anthrop. Soc. (past pres.), Assn. Polit. and Legal Anthropology (past pres.). Home: 5480 Wisconsin Ave Bethesda MD 20815-3530

WILLS, CORNELIA, university official; b. Eastaboga, Ala.; d. Willie Jr. and Rosa Lee (Elston) W. BS, Austin Peay State U., 1974; MEd, Tenn. State U., 1992, postgrad., 1992—. Adminstrv. sec. Tenn. State U., Nashville, 1974-77, 79-81; office mgr., adminstrv. asst. Fisk U., Nashville, 1981-84; gift acctg. coord. Meharry Med. Coll., Nashville, 1984-88; rsch. analyst Tenn. Bd. Regents, Nashville, 1988-89; dir. instnl. rsch. Mid. Tenn. State U., Murfreesboro, 1989—; cons. faculty rsch. com., strategic planning com. Mid. Tenn. State U., 1989—; mem. Exec. Com. for Instnl. Effectiveness, 1992—; mem. Com. for Performance Funding, 1992—. Mem. Am. Assn. Instnl. Rsch., So. Assn. for Instnl. Rsch., Tenn. Assn. Instnl. Rsch., Women in Higher Edn. in Tenn., Delta Sigma Theta, Phi Delta Kappa. Baptist. Office: Mid Tenn State U 116 Cope Adminstrn Bldg Murfreesboro TN 37132

WILLS, KATHERINE VASILIOS TSIOPOS, English language educator, biology researcher; b. St. Louis, Sept. 30, 1957; d. Vasilios and Kalliope (Stratos) Tsiopos. BA, Washington U., 1979; MA, Ind. U., 1990. Rsch. dir. U. Chgo. (Ill.) Gynecology, 1980-82, Northwestern U., Chgo., 1982-86; pres. Port of Nashville (Ind.) Inc., retailer of nautical items and antiques, 1986—; pub. reader various orgns.; adj. faculty dept. English Indian and Purdue Univs., Indpls., 1991—, rsch. asst. dept. biology Alzheimers and Parkinsons disease studies, 1991—. Contbr. articles and poetry to jours. Vol. Women's Writers' Conf., Chgo.; fundraiser Am. Bar Assn.; greeter World Congress on Equality and Freedom, St. Louis; student worker on dig for Am. Indian artifacts Tenn. River Archeol. Project; debutant Am. Hellenic Progressgive and Ednl. Assn. Recipient essay award Scholastic Mag., Inc., 1973, award for acad. excellence and community svc. Am. Hellenic Progessvie and Ednl. Assn., A poetry award Wednesday Club of St. Louis, Mo., 1977, Roger Conant Hatch hon. mention for writing, Washington U., 1977. Mem. NAFE, Nat. Histotechnologie Soc., MLA, Assn. Writers and Poets, Conf. on Coll. Composition and Communication, Midwest Regional Conf., Nat. Coun. Tchrs. English Poets and Writers Inc. Greek Orthodox. Home: RR 2 Box 378 Nashville IN 47448-9642 Office: IUPUI Dept English PO Box 806 Indianapolis IN

WILLS, SUSAN, insurance broker; b. Grand Rapids, Mich., Sept. 23, 1956; d. Roger Edward and Ann Louise (Gallo) W. BA, U. Mich., 1978. Exec. v.p. Rollins Hudig Hall, 1980-93, Hogg Robinson of Mich., 1993—. Contbr. articles to profl. jours. Mem. Nat. Trust for Historic Preservation, People for the Ethical Treatment of Animals, Arts Coun. Grand Rapids, Grand Rapids C. of C. Office: Hogg Robinson Mich 125 Ottawa Ave NW Grand Rapids MI 49503-2898

WILLSON, MARY F., ecology researcher, educator; b. Madison, Wis., July 28, 1938; d. Gordon L. and Sarah (Loomans) W.; m. R.A. von Neumann, May 29, 1972 (dec.). B.A. with honors, Grinnell Coll., 1960; Ph.D., U. Wash., 1964. Asst. prof. U. Ill., Urbana, 1965-71, assoc. prof., 1971-76, prof. ecology, 1976-90; rsch. ecologist Forestry Scis. Lab., Juneau, Alaska, 1989—; adj. prof. zoology and botany Wash. State U., Pullman; prin. rsch. scientist, affiliate prof. biology Inst. Arctic Biology U. Alaska, Fairbanks; faculty assoc. divsn. biol. scis. U. Mont., Missoula. Author: Plant Reproductive Ecology, 1983, Vertebrate Natural History, 1984; co-author: Mate Choice in Plants, 1983. Fellow AAAS, Am. Ornithologists Union; mem. Soc. for Study Evolution, Am. Soc. Naturalists, Ecol. Soc. Am., Brit. Ecol. Soc. Office: Forestry Scis Lab 2770 Sherwood Ln Juneau AK 99801-8545

WILMOT, LOUISE C., charitable organization executive; b. Wayne, N.J., Dec. 31, 1942; d. W.J. Currie and Dorothy Murphy; m. James E. Wilmot. BA in History, Coll. St. Elizabeth, Convent Sta., N.J., 1964; student, Naval War Coll., Newport, R.I., 1977; M in Legis. Affairs, George Washington U., 1978. Commd. ensign USN, 1964; advanced through grades to rear adm., 1991; comm. watch officer, registered publs. custodian, women's barracks officer Naval Air Sta., Pensacola, Fla.; with NATO staff Allied Forces, So. Europe, 1966-68; officer recruiter Recruiting Area Seven, Dallas; Naval Senate liaison officer Office Legis. Affairs, Washington; head women's equal opportunity br. Bur. Naval Pers., 1974-76; exec. officer Navy Recruiting Dist., Montgomery, Ala., 1977-79; command of Navy Recruiting Dist., Omaha, 1979-82; dep. dir accession policy Asst. Sec. Def. for Manpower, Installations, and Logistics, Washington, 1982-85; comdr. Navy Recruiting Area Five, Gt. Lakes, Ill., 1985-87; exec. asst., Naval aide Asst. Sec. Navy for Manpower and Reserve Affairs, Washington, 1987-89; comdr. Naval Tng. Ctr., Orlando, Fla., 1989-91; vice chief Naval Edn. and Tng., Pensacola, 1991-93; comdr. Naval Base, Phila., 1993-94; ret. U.S. Navy, 1994; dep. exec. dir. Cath. Relief Svcs., Balt., 1994—. Decorated DSM, Def. Superior Svc. medal, Legion of Merit with 3 gold stars. Office: Cath Relief Svcs Baltimore MD 21201-3443

WILNER, JUDITH, journalist; b. Framingham, Mass., Mar. 30, 1943; d. John C. and Marjorie E. (Devonshire) Earley; m. David Alan Wilner, Aug. 27, 1964 (div. Aug. 1968); 1 child, Erica Susan; m. Fred Karp, July 28, 1991. BA in Letters, U. Okla., 1964. Wire editor, copy editor The Norman (Okla.) Transcript, 1967-72; news editor Loveland (Colo.) Reporter-Herald, 1972-73; editor of editl. page The Albuquerque Tribune, 1974-76, city editor, 1974-76; copy editor The Denver Post, 1976-77, copy desk chief, 1977-80, mgr. editl. sys., 1980-84; dep. tech. editor N.Y. Times, 1984-86, tech. editor, 1986—; women's editor The Norman Transcript, 1964-66. Mem. Newspaper Assn. of Am. (tech. com., chmn. wire svc. guidelines com. 1992—).

WILNER, LOIS ANNETTE, speech and language pathologist; b. Newark, Jan. 15, 1935; d. Benjamin and Ida (Schwam) Friedman; m. Sherman Wilner, July 6, 1957; children: Bonnie Joy, Robert Steven. BS, Newark State Tchrs. Coll., 1953-57; MA, Newark State Coll., 1969-73. Tchr. 5th grade Maplewood-South Orange Bd. Edn., South Orange, N.J., 1957-58; permanent substitute Parsippany (N.J.)-Troy Hills Bd. Edn., 1967-68, speech and language pathologist, 1968—; cons., speech and lang. pathologist Ctr. for Communication Disorders, Livingston, N.J., 1987-89. Mem. AAUW, NEA, N.J. Edn. Assn., Morris County Edn. Assn., N.J. Speech-Hearing Assn., Morris County Speech-Hearing Assn. (libr. 1987-90), B'nai B'rith Women (Roseland, Livingston and Suburban Essex chpt. pres. 1985-88), Alpha Delta Kappa (pres. chpt. 1990-92, N.J. state scholarship chmn. 1992-94). Home: 9 Riker Hill Rd Livingston NJ 07039-1216 Office: Parsippany Troy Hills Bd Beachwood Rd Parsippany NJ 07054

WILNER, MARION LEONARD, art educator; b. N.Y.C., Sept. 27, 1929; d. Jack Frank and Madeline (Leff) Leonard; m. Myron Wilner, May 28, 1950; children: Andrew, Matthew, David. BS, NYU, 1950, MA, 1952. Prof. of art, coord. art transfer program Bristol Community Coll., Fall River, Mass., 1966-89, prof. emerita, 1989—; advisor dean's adv. coun. coll. visual and performing arts U. Mass., Dartmouth, 1993; lectr. Sacred Hearts Convent, 1992, R.I. Jewish Hist. Soc., 1992, Brandeis U. Nat. Women's Com., 1991, 90, Universidade Nova, Lisbon, 1988, Universidade Dos Acores, 1987; vis. scholar U. Mass., Dartmouth, 1992; mem. Higher Edn. Nominating Coun., 1990; judge Ea. Edison Poster and Essay Contest, 1989, R.I. Regional Scholastic Art Awards, 1987, Ann. Regional Art Exhbn. Fall River Festival, 1985. Prin. works exhibited in numerous one-woman and group shows including DeBlois Gallery, Newport, R.I., 1992, 94, Bert Gallery, Providence, 1991, Dodge House Gallery, Providence, 1990, Fall River Hist. Soc., 1988, Newport Art Mus., 1987, Escola Superior de Belas Artes, Lisbon, 1986, Eastbourne Gallery, Newport, 1977, Facets Gallery, Fall River, 1993, New England Ctr. Gallery, U. N.H., 1992, Fed. Res. Bank Boston, 1992; prin. works represented in numerous collections including Duro Industries, Inc. Trustee Swain Sch. Design, New Bedford, Mass., 1977-91, Fall River Pub. Libr., 1978-91; active Fall River Cultural Commn., 1988—, Fall River Arts Lottery Coun., 1989—; mem. adv. bd. SMU Ctr. for Jewish Culture, 1983; visual arts dir. Festival '82; graphic designer for various community orgns. Gulbenkian grantee Lisbon, Portugal, 1986, 88. Home: 786 Madison St Fall River MA 02720

WILSEA, MARILYN JUNE MUNFORD, geriatrics nursing administrator; b. Cooperstown, N.Y., Feb. 9, 1935; d. Joseph John and June Marie (Baye) Munford; m. Eugene H. Wilsea Jr., Dec. 1968 (div. Dec. 1979); 1 child, Eugene H. III. Grad., Crouse-Irving Hosp Sch Nursing, Syracuse, N.Y., 1955; BSN, Pace U., 1977; MEd in Nursing Adminstrn., Tchrs. Coll., Columbia U., 1979, EdD in Nursing Orng. Exec. Role, 1988. Cert. nursing adminstrn. advanced ANA, RUGS (PRI) assessor, N.Y.; lic. nurse, N.Y. Various healthcare positions, 1956-62; dir. I.V. therapy Blood Bank, 1963-64; office nurse Urol. Assocs., White Plains, N.Y., 1964-65; home care adminstr. Phelps Meml. Hosp., North Tarrytown, N.Y., 1965-70; dir. nursing Tarrytown (N.Y.) Hall, 1973-74; office nurse, internist Ossining, N.Y., 1976-77; assoc. dir. nursing Park Crescent, N.Y.C., 1981-82; dir. nursing Placid Meml. Hosp., Lake Placid, N.Y., 1980-81; nursing supr. Park View Nursing Home, Riverdale, N.Y., 1983-88, dir. staff devel., quality assurance, infection control, 1988-93; assoc. dir. nursing Laconia Nursing Home, Bronx, N.Y., 1993—. Author: Identification of Nonnursing Activities of Medical-Surgical Staff Nurses: An Observational FieldStudy, 1989. Mem. ANA, N.Y. State Nurses Assn., Sigma Theta Tau. Home: 12 Tappan Landing Rd Tarrytown NY 10591 Office: Laconia Nursing Home 1050 East 230th St Bronx NY 10466

WILSON, ALICE BLAND, real estate consultant; b. Rainelle, W.Va., Apr. 1, 1938; d. Brady Floyd and Mildred Martha (George) Bland; m. Louis William Groves, Jr., Apr. 20, 1957 (div. 1981); children: Martha Rachel, Leonora Jayne; m. Glen Parten Wilson, Dec. 11, 1982. AB, W.Va. U., 1959, postgrad. in microbiology, 1975-78. Contract adminstr. Washington Plate Glass Co., Washington, 1979-80; mem. acctg. staff Forbes Co., Washington, 1981; customer relations rep. Stern's Co., Washington, 1982; real estate assoc. Prudential Preferred Properties, Washington, 1985—. Contbr. articles to Jour. Parasitology. Vol. coord. John Glenn for Pres. campaign, Washington, 1983-84; co-chmn. hospitality com. Women's Nat. Dem. Club, Washington, 1985—; mem. internat. adv. coun. ARC, Washington, 1985—; mem. exec. com. Nat. Symphony Orch., 1990—. Mem. Washington Assn. Realtors (mem. residential sales com. 1985—), Leading Edge Soc., Million Dollar Club. Avocations: flying, aerobatics, nature study. Home: 433 New Jersey Ave SE Washington DC 20003-4034 Office: Prudential Preferred Properties 2550 M St NW Washington DC 20037

WILSON, ALMA, state supreme court justice; b. Pauls Valley, Okla.; d. William R. and Anna L. (Schuppert) Bell; m. William A. Wilson, May 30, 1948 (dec. Mar. 1994); 1 child, Lee Anne. AB, U. Okla., 1939, JD, 1941, LLD (hon.), 1992. Bar: Okla. 1941. Sole practice Muskogee, Okla., 1941-43; sole practice Oklahoma City, 1943-47, Pauls Valley, 1948-69; judge Pauls Valley Mcpl. Ct., 1967-68; apptd. spl. judge Dist. Ct. 21, Norman, Okla., 1969-75, dist. judge, 1975-79; justice Okla. Supreme Ct., Oklahoma City, 1982—. Mem. alumni bd. dirs. U. Okla.; mem. Assistance League; trustee Okla. Meml. Union. Recipient Guy Brown award, 1974, Woman of Yr. award Norman Bus. and Profl. Women, 1975, Okla. Women's Hall of Fame award, 1983, Pioneer Woman award, 1985, Disting. Svc. Citation U. Okla., 1985. Mem. AAUW, Garvin County Bar Assn. (past pres.), Okla. Bar Assn. (co-chmn. law and citizenship edn. com.), Okla. Trial Lawyers Assn. (Appellate Judge of Yr. 1986, 89), Altrusa, Am. Legion Aux. Office: Okla Supreme Ct State Capitol Rm 245 Oklahoma City OK 73105*

WILSON, ANN ALLBRITTON, science and home economics educator; b. Urania, La., Feb. 22, 1943; d. Walter Roy and Emaline (Glidewell) Allbritton; m. Richard Joseph Wilson, Mar. 21, 1964 (div. Mar. 1991); children: James Michael, Richard Gardner, Kathleen JoAnn. BS, La. Tech. U., 1965; cert. sci., N.E. La. U., 1991. Cert. home econs. tchr., sci. secondary tchr., La.; lic. realtor, La. Tchr. clothing Jefferson Parish, Morrero, La., 1965-68; tchr. home econs., head dept. St. Mary Parish, Morgan City, La., 1968-70; tchr. home econs. St. Mary Parish, Morgan City, 1971-73; receptionist Office of Dr. C.C. Gaddis, Jena, La., 1977; pvt. practice Jena, 1978-85; tchr. bus. edn. LaSalle Parish, Jena, 1979; asst. interior decorator Justiss Interiors, Jena, 1980-82; realtor Carol Traver Real Estate, Alexandria, La., 1986-90; tchr. biology, chemistry, home econs. Catahoula Parish, Enterprise, La., 1987-93, dept. head., FHA advisor, 1987-93; tchr. biology Rapides Parish, Alexandria (La.) Sr. H.S., 1993—; cons. La. State Dept. Edn. Curriculum Guides, Baton Rouge, 1990-91. Mem. Morgan City Panhellenic Orgn., 1969-73, LaSalle Gen. Hosp. Ladies Aux., Jena, 1982-84; judge, asst. Miss Patterson (La.) Contest, 1971-75, Miss LaSalle Contest, Jena, 1971-75; den. mother Cub Scouts, Morgan City, Jena, 1973-74, 78; others. Named Parish Secondary Tchr. of Yr., 1991. Mem. NEA, Am. Home Econs. Assn., La. Real Estate Assn., La. Sci. Tchrs. Assn., La. Edn. Assn., Alpha Tau Delta, Phi Kappa Phi, Phi Mu. Methodist. Home: 1109 Ola St Alexandria VA 71303 Office: Alexandria Sr HS 800 Ola St Alexandria LA 71303

WILSON, ANN BERRY, controller; b. Seminole, Tex., Feb. 15, 1954; d. William Ernest and Gene Eloise (Hardy) Berry; m. Jimmie Charles Paquin, Nov. 24, 1972 (div. Apr. 1980); m. Larry Joe Wilson, Feb. 15, 1991; children: Jamie Adele, D'Artagnan, Dakota, Dalon. BBA, Tex. A&M U., 1984. Owner County Line Stores Inc., Big Spring, Tex., 1977-78; maintenance III City of Hobbs, N.Mex., 1978-80; owner Extermascapers, Austin, Tex., 1985-93; contr. Jamie's Constrn. Co., Austin, 1992-93, Austin Aero, 1990—. Home: 14922 Running Deer Austin TX 78734 Office: Austin Aero 1901 E 51st St Austin TX 78723

WILSON, ANNE PATNODE, public relations executive; b. Ilion, N.Y., Aug. 29, 1957; d. Edward Maurice Patnode and Arlene Dorothy Bull; m. Marc F. Wilson, Nov. 5, 1988. BA, SUNY, Potsdam, 1979. Prodr. Citihope Here's Life, N.Y.C., 1985-86; prodr., reporter Family Talk Covenant Ho., N.Y.C., 1986-89, N.J. comm. coord., 1989-90; v.p., assoc. dir. corp. comm. J. Walter Thompson, N.Y.C., 1991—. Mem. Pub. Rels. Soc. Am.,

Advt. Women N.Y. Office: J Walter Thompson 466 Lexington Ave New York NY 10017

WILSON, BARBARA JEAN, oncological nurse; b. Framingham, Mass., Jan. 29, 1955; d. Alcide and Florence Lois (Erickson) Belloli; m. Donald F. Parlin, Sept. 30, 1972 (div. Dec. 1987); children: Kara Parlin, Jennifer Parlin, Donald Parlin; m. Gerald J. Wilson, Apr. 20, 1991; children: Jimmy, Michael. Diploma in nursing, Framingham Union Hosp. Sch., 1985. Cert. RN in intravenous therapy; oncology cert. nurse; cert. childbirth educator. Staff nurse Marlboro (Mass.) Hosp., 1985—, staff nurse, resource nurse oncology clinic, 1987—; childbirth educator Framingham Union Hosp., 1988—; with Cancer Care Ctr. at Framingham Union Hosp., 1992—. Mem. Oncology Nursing Soc., Boston Oncology Nursing Soc., Intravenous Nursing Soc. Roman Catholic. Home: 40 Mcalee Ave Framingham MA 01701-7203 Office: Marlboro Hosp 57 Union St Marlborough MA 01752-1208

WILSON, BARBARA LOUISE, communications executive; b. Bremerton, Wash., Aug. 3, 1952; d. Algernon Frances and Dorothy Virginia (Martin) W.; m. Ashby A. Riley III, Feb. 7, 1979 (div. Dec. 1983). BA in Fin. and Econs., U. Puget Sound, 1974; MBA, U. Wash., Seattle, 1985. With Pacific N.W. Bell, Seattle and Portland, Oreg., 1974-86, divsn. mgr. pub. comm., 1983-85, asst. v.p., exec. dir. number svcs. mktg., 1985-86; v.p. implementation planning US West, Inc., Englewood, Colo., 1986-87; pres. US West Info. Systems, Englewood, 1987-89; v.p. govt. and edn. svcs. US West Comm., Englewood, 1989; v.p. human resources U.S. West Comm., Denver, 1989-92; v.p., chief exec. officer Idaho state U.S. West Communications, Boise, 1992—; bd. dirs. U.S. West New Vector Group, Bellevue, Wash., 1988-90, U.S. Bank Idaho, Idaho Bus. Coun.; audit com. chair U.S. Bank; chair nat. adv. com. Tel. Pioneers Am., N.Y.C., 1989; chair adv. bd. Coll. Bus. and Boise State U. Bd. dirs., mem. exec. com. Wash. Coun. for Edn., Seattle, 1985-86; team capt. major gifts com. Boys and Girls Club, Seattle, 1986; chairperson co. campaign United Way, Seattle, 1985; bd. dirs. Denver Arts Ctr. Found., 1989-91; bd. advisors U. Wash. Exec. MBA Program, 1991-93; mem. adv. bd. Boise State U. Sch. Bus.; mem. bd. Boise State U. Found. Bd. dirs., mem. exec. com. Wash. Coun. for Edn. Edn., Seattle, 1985-86; team capt. major gifts com. Boys and Girls Club, Seattle, 1986; chairperson co. campaign United Way, Seattle, 1985; bd. dirs. Denver Arts Ctr. Found., 1989-91; bd. advisors U. Wash. Exec. MBA Program, 1991-93; mem. adv. bd. Boise State U. Sch. Bus.; bd. mem. Mountain States Med. Rsch. Inst.; Bd. dir. Boise State U. Found. Mem. Idaho Bus. Coun. (bd. dirs., chair-elect), Idaho Assn. Commerce and Industry (vice chmn. bd. dirs. 1992—), Boise C. of C. (bd. dirs. 1992—), Arid Club Boise. Roman Catholic. Office: US West Communications 999 Main St Fl 11 Boise ID 83702-9001

WILSON, BETTY MAY, finance company executive; b. Moberly, Mo., Mar. 13, 1947; d. Arthur Bunyon and Martha Elizabeth (Denham) Stephens; m. Ralph Felix Martin, Aug. 22, 1970 (div. May 1982); m. Gerald Robert Wilson Sr., Mar. 3, 1984; stepchildren: Gerald Robert Jr., Heather Lynn, Jeffrey Michael. BS in Acctg. and Bus. Adminstrn., Colo. State U., 1969. CPA, Mo. Tax mgr. Arthur Andersen and Co., St. Louis, 1969-75; v.p., asst. sec., dir. taxes ITT Fin. Corp., St. Louis, 1975—; sr. v.p., bd. dirs. Lyndon Ins. Co., St. Louis, 1977—, ITT Lyndon Life Ins. Co., ITT Lyndon Property Ins. Co., St. Louis, 1977—. Mem. AICPA, Mo. Soc. CPA's (chmn. family issues com.), Am. Fin. Svcs. Assn. (chmn. tax com. 1987-88), Tax Execs. Inst. Inc. (chair corp. tax mgmt. com. 1993—, regional v.p., 1995—, bd. dirs. St. Louis chpt., past sec., past pres.), Mo. Girls Racing Assn. (pres. 1977-82). Baptist. Office: ITT Fin Corp 645 Maryville Ctr Dr Saint Louis MO 63141-5832

WILSON, BETTY S., investment broker; b. Kansas City, Jan. 18, 1948; d. Harvey W. and Margie M. (Masters) Spor; m. Danny E. Wilson, Aug. 18, 1967 (div. Mar. 1985); children: Jeffrey Todd, Amy Luper; m. Barry D. Yack, Aug. 12, 1987. Sec. United Coop., Liberty, Mo., 1966-70; acct. Desert Gold-Douglas Chem., Liberty, Mo., 1972-74, United Coop., Liberty, Mo., 1974-80; br. office adminstr. Edward D. Jones, Liberty, Mo., 1980-85, investment rep., 1985-92; investment broker A.G. Edwards, Liberty, Mo., 1992—. Treas., v.p., pres. Soroptimist Internat., Liberty, 1988-92; dir. Liberty Area C. of C., 1989-92. Republican. Methodist. Office: A G Edwards & Sons 9 Westowne St Liberty MO 64068-3516

WILSON, BLENDA JACQUELINE, university chancellor; b. Woodbridge, N.J., Jan. 28, 1941; d. Horace and Margaret (Brogsdale) Wilson; m. Louis Fair Jr. AB, Cedar Crest Coll., 1962; AM, Seton Hall U., 1965; PhD, Boston Coll., 1979; DHL (hon.), Cedar Crest Coll., 1987, Loretto Heights Coll., 1988, Colo. Tech. Coll., 1988, U. Detroit, 1989; LLD (hon.), Rutgers U., 1989, Ea. Mich. U., 1990, Cambridge Coll., 1991, Schoolcraft Coll., 1992. Tchr. Woodbridge Twp. Pub. Schs., 1962-66; exec. dir. Middlesex County Econ. Opportunity Corp., New Brunswick, N.J., 1966-69; exec. asst. to pres. Rutgers U., New Brunswick, N.J., 1969-72; sr. assoc. dean Grad. Sch. Edn. Harvard U., Cambridge, Mass., 1972-82; v.p. effective sector mgmt. Ind. Sector, Washington, 1982-84; exec. dir. Colo. Commn. Higher Edn., Denver, 1984-88; chancellor and prof. pub. adminstrn. & edn. U. Mich., Dearborn, 1988-92; pres. Calif. State U., Northridge, 1992—; Am. del. U.S./U.K. Dialogue About Quality Judgments in Higher Edn.; adv. bd. Mich. Consolidated Gas Co., Stanford Inst. Higher Edn. Rsch., U. So. Col. Dist. 60 Nat. Alliance, Nat. Ctr. for Rsch. to Improve Postsecondary Teaching and Learning, 1988-90; bd. dirs. Alpha Capital Mgmt.; mem. higher edn. colloquium Am. Coun. Edn., vis. com. Divsn. Continuing Edn. in Faculty of Arts & Scis., Harvard Coll., Pew Forum on K-12 Edn. Reform in U.S.; trustee Children's TV Workshop. Dir. U. Detroit Jesuit High School, Northridge Hosp. Med. Ctr., Arab Community Ctr. for Econ. & Social Svcs., Union Bank, J. Paul Getty Trust, Internat. Found. Edn. and Self-Help, Achievement Coun., L.A.; dir., vice-chair Met. Affairs Corp.; exec. bd. Detroit area coun. Boy Scouts Am.; bd. dirs. Commonwealth Fund, Henry Ford Hosp.-Fairlane Ctr., Henry Ford Health System, Met. Ctr. for High Tech., United Way for Southeastern Mich.; mem. Nat. Coalition 100 Black Women, Detroit, Race Rels. Coun. Met. Detroit, Women & Founds. (corp. philanthropy), Greater Detroit Interfaith Round Table NCCJ, Adv. Bd. Valley Cultural Ctr., Woodland Hills; trustee assoc. Boston Coll., trustee emeritus Cambridge Coll., trustee emeritus/bd. dirs. Found. Ctr.; trustee Henry Ford Mus. & Greenfield Village, Sammmy Davis Jr. Nat. Liver Inst. Mem. AAUW, Assn. Governing Bds. (adv. coun. of pres.'s), Edn. Commn. of the States (student minority task force), Am. Assn. Higher Edn. (chair-elect), Am. Assn. State Colls. & Univs. (com. on policies & purposes, acad. leadership fellows selection com.), Assn. Black Profls. and Adminstrs., Assn. Black Women in Higher Edn., Women Execs. State Govt., Internat. Women's Forum, Mich. Women's Forum, Women's Econ. Club Detroit, Econ. Club, Rotary. Office: Calif State Univ Office of President 18111 Nordhoff St Northridge CA 91330-8230

WILSON, BONNIE JEAN, investor, lawyer, educator; b. Alameda County, Calif.; d. August and Violet Adeline (Lockard) Ritzenthaler; m. Allan Nicholas Wilson (div.); children: Albert Clyde, Bruce Allan. BA, U. Calif., Berkeley, cert. in elem. tchg.; JD, Western State U., 1981. Bar: Calif.; cert. tchr., Calif. Elem. sch. tchr. Contra Costa and San Diego Counties; intern San Diego County Dist. Atty. Office, 1981; pvt. practice La Jolla, Calif., 1982—. Bd. dirs. La Jolla Presbyn. Ch. Women's Assn., 1969; mem. San Diego Opera Assn., San Diego Symphony Assn., Friends of the La Jolla Libr. Mem. Calif. State Bar Assn., San Diego County Bar Assn., San Diego Lawyers Club, La Jolla Newcomer's Club (bd. dirs. 1968-69), U. Calif. Berkeley Alumni Club (bd. dirs. San Diego chpt. 1961-62), U. Calif. San Diego Faculty Club. Home: 2235 Bahia Dr La Jolla CA 92037-7007

WILSON, CAROLYN ROSS, school administrator; b. Lake Charles, La., June 25, 1941; d. Charles Wesley and Lucille Gertrude (Payne) Ross; m. James David Wilson, Apr. 10, 1971; 1 child, Charlise. BS in Music Edn. cum laude, Xavier U., 1962; MMus in Music Edn., Cath. U., Washington, 1968; postgrad., U. D.C., 1985-86, George Washington U., 1987-88, Harvard U., 1989. Tchr. Xavier U. Jr. Sch. Music, New Orleans, 1960-61, Orleans Parish Schs., New Orleans, 1962-63; tchr. D.C. Pub. Schs., Washington, 1964-87, curriculum writer, summer 1984, 85, adminstrv. intern Ea. High Sch., 1987-88, asst. prin. Cardozo High Sch., 1988-89, asst. prin. Duke Ellington Sch. of Arts, 1989-93; acting prin. Duke Ellington Sch. Arts, Washington, 1993—; curriculum writer music dept. D.C. Pub. Schs., Washington, 1984-85, dir. All City High Sch. Chorus, 1973. Composer: A Dedication to Federal City Alumnae Chapter of Delta, Sigma Theta Sorority, Inc., 1973. Lector Immaculate Conception Ch., Washington, 1986—; named D.C. Tchr. of Yr., 1987. Recipient Cert. of Merit-Outstanding Tchr. and Prin. award D.C. Govt., 1994; U.S. Dept. Edn. Effective Schs. grantee, Washington, 1992. Mem. ASCD, Instn. for Devel. Ednl. Activities (6th yr. fellow, session chair 1988, seminar leader 1991, 92), Delta Sigma Theta (Fed. City Alumnae chpt.). Roman Catholic. Office: Duke Ellington Sch Arts 35th And R St NW Washington DC 20912

WILSON, CAROLYN TAYLOR, librarian; b. Cookeville, Tenn., June 10, 1936; d. Herman Wilson and Flo (Donaldson) Taylor; m. Larry Kittrell Wilson, June 14, 1957 (dec.); children: Jennifer Wilson Rust, Elissa Anne Wilson. BA, David Lipscomb Coll., 1957; MLS, George Peabody Coll., 1976. Tchr. English Fulton County Sch. System, Atlanta, 1957-59; serials cataloger Vanderbilt U. Libr., Nashville, 1974-77; asst. libr. United Meth. Pub. House, Nashville, 1978-80; collection devel. libr. David Lipscomb U., Nashville, 1980—; cons. and rschr. in field; project dir. Tenn.'s Lit. Legacy for Tenn. Humanities Coun., 1994—. Rsch. asst. Handbook of Tennessee Labor History, 1987-89. Adv. bd. So. Festival of Books, Nashville, 1988-90, 90—, vol. coord., 1989, 90—; project dir. Women's Words (summer grant program) for Tenn. Humanities Coun. Recipient Nat. Honor Soc. award Phi Alpha Theta, 1956, Internat. Honor Soc. award Beta Phi Mu, 1980, Frances Neel Cheney award Tenn. Libr. Assn., 1992; nominee Athena award, 1992. Mem. ALA, Tenn. Hist. Soc., Tenn. Libr. Assn. (Frances Neel Cheney award 1992), Southeastern Libr. Assn. (chmn. outstanding S.E. author award com. 1991-92, chmn. So. Books Competition 1992-94), Women's Nat. Book Assn. (pres., v.p., treas., awards chmn. 1980—). Democrat. Office: David Lipscomb U Univ Libr # 317 Nashville TN 37204

WILSON, CATHERINE ANN, critical care nurse, educator, health policy analyst; b. Portsmouth, Va., Dec. 26, 1957; d. John Louis and Mary Catherine (Bernat) Hostinsky; m. Don D. Wilson, Mar. 19, 1988; children: Bronwyn, Dewayne. BSN, The Cath. U. Am., 1979; MS in Mgmt., Golden State U., 1988; MS in Nursing, U. Md., 1990. Staff nurse ICU, lt. USN, Bethesda, Md., 1979-84; charge nurse surg., lt. USN, Phila., 1984-87; asst. charge nurse, educator USN, Guantanamo Bay, Cuba, 1987-88; lt. comdr. Bur. of Medicine & Surgery, Washington, 1988-94; comdr. sr. health policy analyst The Pentagon, Washington, 1994—. Named Outstanding Young Woman of Am. Mem. AACN, Navy Corps Assn., Soc. Trauma Nurses, Assn. Neurosci. Nursing, Sigma Theta Tau. Home: 730 Lexington Cir Newport News VA 23602

WILSON, CATHERINE COOPER (KITTY WILSON), communications executive, writer; b. Dallas, Sept. 17, 1955; d. William Edward and Suzanne (Blessington) Cooper; m. James Alan Wilson, Oct.17, 1981; children: Nicholas James, Gregory Cooper. BA in Journalism, Tex. Tech U., 1977. Pub. rels. asst. Dallas Market Ctr., 1972-75, 77; pub. rels. coord. Herman Blum Engrs., Dallas, 1977-80, coord. new bus. devel., 1980; acct. exec. Helen Holmes & Assoc., Dallas, 1980; mktg. and pub. rels. coord. EDI Architects, Dallas, 1980-82; pres. Catherine Wilson Comm., Dallas, 1982—; owner, v.p. Wilson Creative, Inc., Dallas, 1988—. Contbr. articles to trade mags. Mem. membership com. North Tex. Commn., Dallas, 1979-81; mem. pub. rels. com., bldg. com. St. Rita Cath. Ch., Dallas, 1984-87. Mem. Women in Comm. (programs co-chair 1989-90, Matrix finalist 1990), Greater Dallas Writers Assn. Roman Catholic. Home and Office: 6435 Sudbury Dr Dallas TX 75214-2435

WILSON, CATHERINE ELIZABETH, psychologist; b. Highland Park, Mich., Feb. 14, 1953; d. A. B. Douglas and Mary Catherine (Schroeder) W. BA, So. Ill. U., 1981; D in Psychology, Chgo. Sch. Profl. Psychology, 1991. Lic. clin. psychologist. ESL instr. Asian Human Svcs., Chgo., 1979-80; Indochinese program specialist Alternatives, Inc., Chgo., 1981-86; rsch. interviewer Travelers & Immigrants Aid, Chgo., 1986-87; psychology intern Chgo. (Ill.)-Read Mental Health Ctr., 1988-89; psychologist Cook County Juvenile Ct., Chgo., 1989—, dir. psychology tng., 1994—; pvt. practice psychologist Chgo., 1992—; cons. Maryville City of Youth, Chgo., 1993—. Campus coord. Paul Simon Presdl. Campaign, Chgo. Sch. Profl. Psychology, 1987; mem. Refugee Mental Health Task Force, Ill. Dept. Mental Health, 1989-90, Presdl. Search Com., 1994. Mem. APA, Ill. Psychological Assn. Office: Cook County Juvenile Ct 1100 S Hamilton Chicago IL 60612

WILSON, CHARLENE WILLA, industrial sales specialist; b. Jim Thoppe, Pa., Feb. 13, 1943; d. Charles Byron and Jennie Larue (Levis) Frehulfer; m. Arthur David Wilson, Oct. 13, 1962 (div. Dec. 1982); 1 child, Edward; m. Arthur David Wilson, Dec. 23, 1987. Student, E. Stroudsburg State Coll., Pa., 1961-62. Tchr. part-time Lourdesmont Sch., Clarks Green, Pa., 1973-81; seamstress Barbini Bridals, Scranton, Pa., 1981-82; credit corr. Tose Fowler, Inc., Scranton, 1982-84; sales rep. Challenge Industries, Inc., Sparta, N.J., 1984-85, asst. dist. mgr., 1985-86, product specialist, 1986-87, dist. sales mgr. for Pa. and N.Y., 1987-90; corp. liaison Challenge Industries, Inc., Sparta, 1990-92, key account exec., 1990-92; enroller Nat. Assn. for Self-employed, agt. PFL Life Ins. United Group Assocs., Irving, Tex., 1992—. Author poems. Mem. Chinchilla (Pa.) Fire Co. Women's Aux., 1963-83. Mem. NAFE, VFW (women's aux. Clarks Summit, Pa. chpt. 1977—), Abington Players (bd. dirs. Waverly, Pa. chpt. 1975-81), Keynotes (sec. Clarks Summit chpt. 1969-77), Pa. Interscholastic Athletic Assn. (track official, swimming official Lackawanna, Pa. chpt. 1975—). Republican. Episcopalian. Home and Office: RR 1 Box 117W Union Dale PA 18470-9747

WILSON, CHRISTINE DUDGEON, municipal management executive; b. Akron, Ohio, Jan. 27, 1957; d. Edward Kingston Dudgeon and Carol Kay (Weidenthal) Boyd; m. Lawrence Wilson, May 25, 1985. AA, Cottey Coll., Nevada, Mo., 1977; BA, U. Tulsa, 1979; JD, U. Kans., 1984, MPA, 1985. Bar: Kans. 1985. Admissions counselor Cottey Coll., 1970-81; adminstrv. asst. City of Ottawa, Kans., 1981-83; law clk. State of Kans., Topeka, 1983-84; adminstrv. asst., asst. village mgr. Village of Lincolnshire, Ill., 1984-94. Stewardship chair St. Augustine's Episcopal Ch., Wilmette, Ill., 1989, 90. Mem. ABA, Kans Bar Assn., Internat. City/County Mgmt. Assn. (mem. award com. 1988-91), Ill. City Mgmt. Assn., Rotary Club of Lincolnshire (bull. editor 1993-95).

WILSON, DIANE BAER, health educator, dietitian; b. Flint, Mich., Feb. 10, 1949; d. John Henry and Phyllis Mae (Noyle) Baer; m. Stephen Russell Wilson, Oct. 2, 1971; children: April Lynn, Robin Elaine. BS, U. Del., 1971; MS, La. State U., 1975; EdD in Health Edn. Adminstrn., U. S.C., 1991. Registered dietitian, S.C. Adj. instr. Fla. Internat. U., Miami, 1976-77; cons. Nutrition Cons. Svcs., Miami, 1977-79; dietitian Coral Reef Hosp., Miami, 1979-80; cons. dietitian Baker Hosp., Charleston, S.C., 1980-83; adj. asst. prof. dept. phys. edn. and health Coll. of Charleston, 1985-94; dir. MS in Health Professions Edn. Med. U. S.C., Charleston, 1994—; adj. asst. prof. Med. U. S.C., Charleston, fall 1984-87. Mem. exec. bd. PTA, George Fishburne Elem. Sch., 1990-93. Mem. Am. Dietetic Assn. (mem. S.C. nutrition coun. exec. bd. 1993-94), S.C. Dietetic Assn. (treas. 1981-83, pres. 1984-85), Otranto Civic Club Charleston, Omicron Nu, Gamma Sigma Delta, Phi Delta Kappa, Phi Upsilon Omicron. Republican. Office: Med U SC Coll Health Professions MS Program Health Prof Edn Charleston SC 29425

WILSON, ELIZABETH SAWIN, psychiatrist; b. Cambridge, Mass., Oct. 16, 1939; d. Horace John and Katherine Biddle (Rhoads) Sawin; m. Robert Woodrow Wilson, Sept. 4, 1958; children: Philip, Suzanne, Randal. BA with honors, USC, 1962; MD with honors, Ross U., Roseau, Dominica, 1987. Diplomate Am. Bd. Neurology and Psychiatry. Resident in psychiatry U. Medicine and Dentistry N.J., Piscataway, 1991; pvt. practice Hazlet, N.J., 1991—. Mem. Am. Psychiatric Assn., N.J. Psychiatric Assn. Home: 9 Valley Point Dr Holmdel NJ 07733 Office: 1 Bethany Rd Ste 38 Hazlet NJ 07730

WILSON, EMILY MARIE, sales executive; b. Aberdeen, Wash., Mar. 24, 1951; d. Charles Robert and Alice Adele (Robinson) W.; m. Michael A. Rich, July 1, 1976. Student, U. Puget Sound, 1969-71, Austro-Am. Inst., Vienna, 1971; BA in Polit. Sci., U. Wash., 1973. U.S. sales mgr. Clairol, Inc., Seattle, 1975-81, sales rep. N.W. Wash., drug-mass mdse. div., 1975-77, sales rep. Met. Seattle, 1977-78, dist. mgr. sales western Wash., 1978-81; trainer territorial sales reps., mgr. dist. dollar sales, and dist. sales mgr. of Wash., Oreg., Idaho and Mont., Clorox, Inc., Seattle, 1981-82, assoc. regional mgr. Western div. spl. markets, 1982-83; regional mgr. Olympic Stain Co., Bellevue, Wash., 1983-86; dir. sales Inscape Products The Weyerhauser Co., Tacoma, 1986-88; dir. ops. Wildland Journeys, Seattle, 1988-89; Traveller World Wide Explorations, 1989—; sales mgr. Adventures Abroad, Seattle, 1990-92; owner Emily Unltd. Organizational Svcs. and Mgmt., 1992—. Mem. Transcendental Meditation Soc., Oreg. Hist. Soc., Sons and Daus. of Oreg. Pioneers, Pioneer Assn. Wash., Seattle Hist. Soc., Sidha of the Age of Enlightenment World Govt. Assn., Grad. Sci. of Creative Intelligence, Women's Profl. Managerial Network. Office: 4417 54th Ave NE Seattle WA 98105-4942

WILSON, ESTHER ELINORE, technical college educator; b. Uehling, Nebr., Nov. 4, 1921; d. Lorenz John and Dorothea Emma Rosena (Schmidt) Paulsen; m. Billy LeRoy Wilson, Nov. 14, 1919; 1 child, Frances Ann Wilson Dellar. BS, Morningside Coll., 1950; postgrad., U. Nebr., 1947-80, U. S.D., 1954-83; MS, U. Minn., 1968. Cert. postsecondary tchr., Iowa. Tchr. Irvington (Nebr.) Pub. Schs., 1942-44, Immanuel Luth. Schs., Wichita, Kans., 1944-45, Winnebago (Nebr.) Pub. Schs., 1946-50, Nat. Bus. Coll., Sioux City, Iowa, 1950-51; tchr., asst. prin. Liberty Consol. Sch., Merrill, Iowa, 1951-55; mktg. tchr. coord. South Sioux City (Nebr.) Community Schs., 1955-86; adj. faculty prof. adult basic edn. Western Iowa Tech. Coll., Sioux City, 1989-94; real estate assoc. State Nat., Dakota City, Nebr., 1988-92, Century 21 Marketplace, Sioux City, 1987-88; advt. sales mgr. Auto Hotline, South Sioux City, 1986-87. Vol. tchr. N.E. Nebr. C.C., South Sioux City, 1987-90; supt. St. Paul's Luth. Sunday Sch., Sioux City, 1972-76; treas. Hope Luth. Ch., 1989—; co-pres. Friends of Libr., South Sioux City, 1986-88; fundraiser South Sioux City Pub. Libr., 1984-85; pres. Am. Cancer Soc., Dakota County, Nebr., 1979-88; state pres. Nebr. Bus. Edn. Assn., 1979, Distributive Edn. Tchrs. Assn., 1980. Recipient Outstanding Svc. to State Orgns., Nebr. Vocat. Edn. Assn., 1976. Mem. NEA (sec., treas., v.p., pres., Dedicated Svc. award 1986), South Sioux City Chamberettes (sec., v.p., pres.), Am. Federated Women's Club (sec., v.p., pres.). Democrat. Home: 435 Dixon Path South Sioux City NE 68776

WILSON, FRANCES EDNA, police sergeant; b. Keokuk, Iowa, Aug. 4, 1955; d. David Eugene and Anna Bell (Hootman) W. BA, St. Ambrose Coll., 1982; MA, Western Ill., 1990; cert. massage therapist, Shocks Ctr. for Edn., Moline, Ill., 1993. Trainer, defensive tactics Davenport (Iowa) Police, 1990—, police corporal, 1985-94; police sgt., 1994—; pres. Iowa Assn. Women Police, Davenport, 1989-92; cons., def. tactics Scott C.C., Bettendorf, Iowa, 1993—; speaker workshops. Bd. dirs. Scott County Family YMCA, Davenport, 1990—, instr., 1989—; instr. Davenport Community Adult Edn., 1991—; mem. Iowa SAFE KIDS Coalition, 1992—; mem. First Presbyn. Ch., Davenport, 1986—; vol. asst. Davenport Police Dept.'s Sgts. Planning Com. on Tng., 1991, K-9 Unit, 1990—. Mem. Iowa Assn. of Women Police (pres. 1989-92), Internat. Assn. of Women Police, Iowa State Police Assn., Am. Soc. of Law Enforcement Trainers, Law Enforcement Alliance of Am. Presbyterian. Office: Davenport Police Dept 420 N Harrison St Davenport IA 52801-1310

WILSON, HEATHER ANN, state agency administrator; b. Keene, N.H., Dec. 30, 1960; d. George Douglas Wilson and Martha Lou Wilson-Kernozicky. BS, USAF Acad., 1982; M. Philosophy, Oxford U., 1984, PhD, 1985. U.S. mission NATO, Brussels, 1987-89, Nat. Security Coun., Washington, 1989-91; pres. Keystone Internat., Inc., Albuquerque, 1991-95; cabinet sec. N.Mex. Dept. Children, Youth and Families, Albuquerque, 1995—; adj. prof. U. N.Mex.; mem. Def. Adv. Com. on Women in the Svcs. Contbr. articles to profl. jours. Mem. Coun. Fgn. Rels. Capt. USAF, 1982-89. Decorated Def. Meritorious Svc. medal, USAF Meritorious Svc. medal; Rhodes scholar, 1982. Republican. Office: Keystone Internat Inc Ste 480 1650 University Blvd NE Albuquerque NM 87102-9999

WILSON, JANIS KAY, marketing executive; b. Anamosa, Iowa, Dec. 28, 1939; d. Clyde S. and Irma L. (Davis) W. B.F.A., Drake U., 1962. Copywriter, Chase Manhattan Bank, N.Y.C., 1962-66; presentation mgr. Newspaper Advt. Bur., N.Y.C., 1966-71; mktg./promotion mgr. Metromedia, N.Y.C., 1971-74; sr. promotion writer N.Y. Times, 1974-78; dir. mktg. svc. Crain Communications, N.Y.C., 1978-83; promotion dir., Standard Rate & Data Svc. div. Macmillan Pub., Wilmette, Ill., 1984-88, circulation dir., 1988-89; sr. writer The Bradford Exchange, Niles, Ill., 1989—. Mem. Women's Design Group, Mag. Pubs. Assn., Internat. Newspaper Advt. and Mktg. Execs., Internat. Newspaper Pubs. Assn., Assn. Bus. Pubs. Republican. Roman Catholic. Home: 927 Suffolk Ct Libertyville IL 60048-5218 Office: The Bradford Exch 9333 N Milwaukee Ave Niles IL 60714-1303

WILSON, JEAN L., state legislator; b. Phila., June 13, 1928; d. Horace and Catherine (Lennox) Terry; widowed; children: Sheryl J. Gordon, Denise T. Munn. BS in Edn., Pa. State U., 1949. Tchr. Columbia Inst., Phila., 1949-50, Wilkes Coll., Wilkes Barre, Pa., 1950-51; office mgr., exec. sec. Camden Fibre MIlls, Warminster, Pa., 1968-80; mem. Pa. Ho. of Reps., 1988-92. Active Bucks County Coun. Rep. Women, North Pa. Coun. Rep. Women, Warminster Rep. Club, Pennridge Rep. Club. Home: 12 Far View Rd Chalfont PA 18914-2511 Office: 300 W Street Rd Warminster PA 18974-3209

WILSON, JEAN MARIE HALEY, civic worker; b. Dallas, Oct. 16, 1921; d. William Eldred and Helen Marie (Littlepage) Haley; BA, So. Meth. U., 1943; m. Edward Lewis Wilson, Jr., Mar. 19, 1943; children: Edward Lewis III, William Haley, Sarah. Bd. dirs. Dallas Symphony Orch. League, 1963-89, sec., 1964-68, 1st v.p., 1968-72, vice-chmn. spl. projects, 1977-78, rec. sec., 1984-85, 7th v.p., 1985-86, trustee, 1976-88, showhouse chmn., 1987, corresponding sec., 1987-88; v.p. activities, bd. dirs. Allegro Dallas, Inc., 1986-90; precinct chmn. Democratic Party, 1952-62; mem. Dallas County Dem. Exec. Com., 1952-62; bd. dirs. TACA (Com. for Fund Raising of the Arts), 1975-88; mem. Southwestern hospitality bd. Met. Opera; charter mem., bd. dirs., North Tex. Herb Club, 1974-78; mem. Grand Heritage Ball Com. of Old City Park, exec. com. 1992-94 exec. com. Les Femme du Monde-fundraising arm Dallas Coun. on World Affairs, 1992-95. Mem. Nat. Trust Hist. Preservation, Dallas Mus. Art/League, Decorative Arts Guild N. Tex., Herb Soc. Am. (life), Am. Hort. Soc., Pewter Collectors Club Am., Royal Hort. Soc., Le Cercle Francaise of Dallas (hon. chmn. 1985-94), Herb Soc. of Old City Park, Kappa Alpha Theta. Methodist. Home: 3501 Lexington Ave Dallas TX 75205-3914 Office: 2909 Maple Ave Dallas TX 75201-1443

WILSON, JEANNETTE SOLOMON, retired elementary education educator; b. Columbus, Ga., Sept. 5, 1915; d. John C. and Mary L. (Parham) Solomon (adoptive parents, aunt and uncle); m. Harvie L. Wilson, Aug. 9, 1952; 1 child, Katrina M. Deese Turner. BS, Ft. Valley (Ga.) Coll., 1947; MS, Tuskegee (Ala.) Inst., 1951; postgrad., Syracuse U., 1961, U. Alaska, 1967. cert. elem. tchr. Elem. tchr. Muscogee County Sch. Dist., Columbus, 1939-53, 1954-60, 1969-71, home/hosp. tchr., 1971-75; elem. tchr. Am. Dependent Schs., Heilbronn, Fed. Republic Germany, 1953-54; ret., 1975; cons. in field. Active Girls Scouts Columbus chpt. Named one of Women of Achievement Girl Scouts, Inc., 1989; recipient Outstanding Svc. award Am. Cancer Soc., 1983-84. Mem. AAUW, The Links Club (one of the founders Columbus, Ga. chpt. 1964), Urban League, Nat. Coun. Negro Women, Tuskegee Alumni Assn., Mr. and Mrs. Club (sec. 1960-64), Matrons Club (Gracious Lady of Ga. 1988), Alpha Kappa Alpha.

WILSON, JUDIE ELAINE, prevention consultant; b. Dayton, Ohio, Apr. 15, 1945; d. John Luther and Mona (Huff) Chandler; m. Ronnie Ray Wilson, June 6, 1964; 1 child, Brian Kent. BS in Health and Human Svcs., Columbia Pacific U., 1992. Office asst. OHC Advt., Dayton, 1967-76; sec. Dept. Edn., Somerset, Ky., 1976-78; asst. to pres. Farm Credit Svcs., Somerset, 1978-85; prevention cons. The Adanta Group, Somerset, 1985—; prevention dir. The Adanta Group, Somerset, Ky., 1994—; regional coord. Champions, Ky., 1986—; bd. mem. Ky. Prevention Rev. Bd., Frankfort, 1991—; chairperson Ky. Prevention Network, Frankfort, 1991-93; coord. Teen Leadership Conf., Ky., 1993-94; presenter Pride Conf., Atlanta, 1991, 92, 93, Nat. Peer Helper Assn. Conf., Boston, 1993. Author: Community Prevention Handbook. Mem. Russell County Dem. Women; bd. mem. Am. Cancer Soc., Ky., 1990—. Mem. Nat. Assn. Teen. Insts., Nat. Peer Helper Assn. Democrat. Home: 3512 W Highway 80 Nancy KY 42544 Office: The Adanta Group PO Box 3368 Somerset KY 42564-3368

WILSON, JUDY JEANETTE, special education educator; b. Dallas, Oreg., Feb. 22, 1945; d. Ralph Delano and Daisy Marie (Oleman) Henry; m. James Roy Wilson, Nov. 5, 1966 (div.); children: James C., Laura, Daniel. BS, U. Oreg., 1978; MS, Portland State U., 1982; cert. sch. psychology, Lewis Clark Coll., 1989. Cert. prin., sch. psychologist, spl. edn. tchr., reading and elem. edn. Vol. artist in schs. overseas, 1968-77; reading specialist Rainier (Oreg.) Mid. Sch. Columbia County Sch. Dist. # 13, 1978-81, spl. edn. tchr., cons., 1981-84, testing coord., team tchr., 1984-85; spl. edn. tchr. Globe Elem. Sch. Goble Elem. Sch., 1985-88; sch. psychology intern Ednl. Svc. Dist. 112, Vancouver, Wash., 1988-89; sch. psychologist White Salmon, Lyle & Mill A Dists. Ednl. Svc. Dist. 112, 1989-90; sch. psychologist/master tchr. Naselle Grays River Valley Sch. Dist., Naselle, Wash., 1990-91; sch. psychologist/behavior interventionist Ocean Beach Sch. Dist. 101, Long Beach, Wash., 1990-92; spl. edn. dir., sch. psychologist Toutle Lake Sch. Dist. 130, Toutle, Wash.; spl. educator Port Angeles (Wash.) Sch. Dist.; regional task force Spl. Edn. Dirs. of Cowlitz County for establishment of regional programs for children; alt. sch. adminstr. for juvenile boys; mem. child protection team and CHAPS com., 1990-92; instr. early childhood edn. Grays Harbor Coll., Ocean Beach, 1991-92. Mem. Nat. Assn. Sch. Psychologists, Wash. State Sch. Psychologist's Assn., Phi Kappa Phi. Home: 222 N Chambers Port Angeles WA 98362 Office: Port Angeles Sch Dist Port Angeles WA 98362

WILSON, JUDY L., company executive; b. Pitts., Mar. 13, 1952; d. Frank Robert and Mildred Luchini; m. Robert H. Nesbitt. BSN, U. Pitts., 1974, MSN, 1976; MPA, NYU, 1983. RN. Clin. nurse, 1974-80; assoc. dir. Columbia Presbyn. Med. Ctr., N.Y.C., 1980-83; sr. mgr. Ernst & Young, N.Y.C., 1983-86; exec. dir. St. Barnabas Outpatient Ctr., Livingston, N.J., 1986-88; v.p. HBO & Co., Atlanta, 1988-93; v.p., gen. mgr. AMS, a divsn. SRC, Dayton, Ohio, 1993—. Mem. Am. Coll. Healthcare Execs., Healthcare Info. and Mgmt. System Soc., Healthcare Fin. Mgmt. Assn. Office: AMS a divsn of SRC 820 Bear Tavern Rd Ste 107 West Trenton NJ 08628-1022

WILSON, JUDY VANTREASE, publishing executive; b. Old Hickory, Tenn., Apr. 8, 1939; d. Luther Benjamin and Ethel (Shepherd) Vantrease; m. Robert Roland Wilson, May 4, 1968; children: Robert Roland Jr., Hilary Shepherd. BA, Smith Coll., 1961. Project mgr. Ency. Britannica, Palo Alto, Calif., 1961-62; prodn. mgr. AICPA, N.Y.C., 1962-63; successively editorial asst., assoc. editor, editor, mgr. programmed instrn., editor profl. group, pub. John Wiley & Sons, N.Y.C., 1963-85; v.p., gen. mgr. Macmillan Pub. Co., N.Y.C., 1985-88, pres., gen. mgr., 1988-94. Recipient Presdl. citation Nat. Soc. for Programmed Instrn., 1985; named to Acad. Women Achievers, YWCA, 1983. Mem. Women in Comm., Assn. Booksellers for Children, Soc. Childrens Book Writers, Am. Assn. Pubs. (exec. coun. 1979-82, childrens pub. com. 1988-93, gen. pub. divsn. coun. 1993-94).

WILSON, KAREN LEE, museum curator; b. Somerville, N.J., Apr. 2, 1949; d. Jon Milton and Laura Virginia (Van Dyke) W.; m. Paul Ernest Walker, 1980; 1 child, Jeremy Nathaniel. AB, Harvard U., 1971; MA, NYU, 1973, PhD, 1985. Rsch. assoc., dir. excavation at Mendes, Egypt Inst. Fine Arts, NYU, 1979-81; coord. exhbn. The Jewish Mus., N.Y.C., 1981-82, adminstrv. cataloguer, 1982-83, coord. curatorial affairs, 1984-86; curator Oriental Inst. Mus. U. Chgo., 1988—. Author, editor: Mendes, 1982; contbr. articles to profl. jours. Mem. Am. Oriental Soc., Am. Rsch. Ctr. in Egypt. Office: Oriental Institute Museum 1155 E 58th St Chicago IL 60637

WILSON, KATHRYN TERESE, food service director; b. Milw., Mar. 7, 1959; d. George Charles and Mary Kathryn (Fink) Schuld; m. Russel Harold Wilson, Dec. 21, 1985; children: Thomas Lawrence, James Charles. BS in Dietetics, U. Wis.-Stout, Menomonie, 1981, MS in Food Sci. and Nutrition, 1984. Lic. food svc. dir./adminstr. Resident housing-bldg. dir. U. Wis.-Stout, Menomonie, 1983-85, substitute teaching staff, 1984-85; asst. food svc. dir. Onalaska (Wis.) Pub. Schs., 1987-90; food svc. dir. West Salem (Wis.) Schs., 1990—; cons. outreach Wis. Dept. Pub. Instrn., Madison, 1993—. Nutriton edn. grantee Wis. Dept. Pub. Instrn., Madison, 1992. Mem. Am. Sch. Food Svc. Assn. (legis. del. 1991-92, 93, 94, 95), Wis. Sch. Food Svc. Assn. (chpt. pres. 1991-93, v.p. 1992-93, pres.-elect 1993-94, state pres. 1994—, legis. com., dist. rep. 1990-93, cons. program of excellence 1992—, Gold awards 1991-93). Home: N2130 Sunset Ln Rt 2 LaCrosse WI 54601

WILSON, LAURA ELEANOR, landscape architect, sculptor; b. Columbus, Ohio, July 9, 1930; d. Russell Brown and Geraldine Gertrude (Rang) W. BS in Landscape Architecture, Iowa State U., 1953. Landscape architect Rose Greeley Landscape architect, Washington, 1953-55, Prentiss French Landscape Architect, San Francisco, 1955-57; landscape architect Nat. Park Svc., San Francisco, 1957-72, Santa Fe, New Mex., 1972-83; sculptor pvt. practice, Santa Fe, 1983—. Landscape architecture: designer and team capt. Visitor's Ctr. Cabrillo Nat. Monument, 1969, (Garden Club award 1972), Lehman Caves New Mex., 1966, Redwoods NewMex., Visitor's Ctr., 1971; sculptor: solo exhibitions include Cadmium Gallery, San Francisco, 1962, Art Assocs. W. San Francisco, 1969, 71. St.John's Coll. Santa Fe, New Mex., 1972, Concepts Gallery, Santa Fe, 1984, 86, 88, 90, 92; group show: New Mex. Sculptor's Guild Fuller Lodge Art Ctr., Los Alamos, 1992; invitational, juried incl. 1987's New Mexico Selections Coll. of Santa Fe, invitation to outdoor sculpture Coll. Santa Fe, 1991, 92, 93, 94. Mem. emeritus Am. Soc. Landscape Architects. Home: 1107 Don Cubero Ave Santa Fe NM 87501-4220

WILSON, LINDA, learning network administrator; b. Rochester, Minn., Nov. 17, 1945; d. Eunice Gloria Irene Wilson. BA, U. Minn., Morris, 1967; MA, U. Minn., 1968. Libr. rsch. svcs. U. Calif., Riverside, 1968-69, head dept. phys. scis. catalog, 1969-71; city libr. Belle Glade (Fla). Mcpl. Libr., 1972-74; instr. part-time Palm Beach Jr. Coll., Belle Glade, 1973; head adult-young adult ext. Kern County Libr. Sys., Bakersfield, Calif., 1974-80; dir. dist. libr. Lake Agassiz Regional Libr. System, Crookston, Minn., 1980-85; supervising libr. San Diego County Libr., 1985-87; county libr. Merced (Calif.) County Libr., 1987-93; learning network mgr. Merced Coll., 1994—. Active Leadership Merced, 1987-88; mem. East Site Based Corodinating Coun., Merced, 1990-92, Merced Gen. Plan Citizens Adv. Com., 1992—, Sister City Com., Merced, 1992—. Recipient Libr. award Eagles Aux., 1984, Woman of Achievement award Commn. on the Status of Women, 1990, Libr. award Calif. Libr. Trustees and Commrs., 1990, Woman of Yr. award Merced Bus. and Profl. Women, 1987. Mem. ALA (sec. pub. libr. systems sect. 1988-89), Calif. Libr. Assn. (sec. govt. rels. com. 1991-92, continuing edn. com. 1993-94), Minn. Libr. Assn. (pres. pub. libr. div. 1985), Merced County Mgmt. Coun. (pres. 1989), Bus. and Profl. Women (pres. 1988-89). Democrat. Lutheran. Home: 3000 Park Ave #8 Merced CA 95348

WILSON, LINDA SMITH, university administrator; b. Washington, Nov. 10, 1936; d. Fred M. and Virginia D. (Thompson) Smith; m. Paul A. Wilson, Jan. 22, 1970; 1 dau. by previous marriage: Helen K. Whatley, a stepdau., Beth A. Wilson. B.A., Newcomb Coll., Tulane U., 1957; Ph.D., U. Wis., 1962; HLD (hon.), Tulane U., 1993; DLitt, U. Md., 1993. Postdoctoral rsch. assoc. U. Md., College Park, 1962-64, rsch. asst. prof., 1964-67; vis. asst. prof. U. Mo.-St. Louis, 1967-68; asst. to vice chancellor for rsch., asst. vice chancellor for rsch., assoc. vice chancellor for rsch. Washington U., St. Louis, 1968-75; assoc. vice chancellor for rsch. U. Ill., Urbana, 1975-85; assoc. dean Grad. Coll., U. Ill., Urbana, 1978-85; v.p. for rsch. U. Mich., Ann Arbor, 1985-89; pres. Radcliffe Coll., Cambridge, Mass., 1989—; chmn. adv. com. office sci. and engring. pers. NRC, 1990—; mem. dir.'s adv. coun. NSF, Washington, 1980-89, adv. com. edn. and human resources, 1990—; mem. Nat. Commn. on Rsch., Washington, 1978-80; mem. com. on govt.-univ. relationships NAS, 1981-83, mem. coun. for govt.-univ.-industry rsch. roundtable, 1984-89; mem. rsch. resources adv. coun. NIH, Bethesda, Md., 1978-82, energy rsch. adv. bd. DOE, 1987-90; mem. sci., tech. and the states task force Carnegie Commn. on Sci., Tech. and Govt., 1991-92. Author book chpts.; contbr. articles to profl. jours. Bd. govs. YMCA, Champaign-Urbana, Ill., 1980-83; mem. adv. bd. Nat. Coalition for Sci. and Tech., Washington, 1983-87; trustee Mass. Gen. Hosp., 1992—. Recipient Centennial award Newcomb Coll., 1986; named One of 100 Emerging Leaders Am. Coun. Edn. and Change, 1978. Fellow AAAS (bd. dirs. 1984-88); mem. Am. Chem. Soc. (bd. coun. com. on chemistry and pub. affairs 1978-80), Soc. Rsch. Adminstrs. (Disting. Contbn. to Rsch. Adminstrn. award 1984), Nat. Coun. Univ. Rsch. Adminstrs., Assn. for Biomed. Rsch. (bd. dirs. 1983-86), Inst. Medicine (mem. coun. 1986-89), Nat. Acad. Scis. (coord. coun. for edn. 1991-93), Am. Coun. Edn. (commn. on women in higher edn. 19919-93, chair 1993), Phi Beta Kappa, Sigma Xi, Alpha Lambda Delta, Phi Delta Kappa, Phi Kappa Phi. Home: 76 Brattle St Cambridge MA 02138-3452 Office: Radcliffe Coll Office of Pres Fay House 10 Garden St Cambridge MA 02138

WILSON, LISA ALLEN, trade association executive; b. Okemos, Mich., Sept. 23, 1960; d. Jimmy Mastin and Brenda Evangeline (Whittaker) Allen; m. Robert McClintock Wilson, Dec. 30, 1982; children: Sarah Elizabeth, Aaron James, Daniel Freeman. BA, Mich. State U., 1982. Prodn. asst. WLNS-TV, Lansing, Mich., 1982-83, WZZM-TV, Grand Rapids, Mich., 1983-84; promotions asst. WZZM-TV, Grand Rapids, 1984-85; promotions mgr. WXMI-TV, Grand Rapids, 1985-87; pub. rels. mgr. Old Kent Bank & Trust Co., Grand Rapids, 1987-88; comms mgr. United Dairy Industry of Mich., Okemos, 1990-92, adminstr. systems planning, 1992-93, v.p. programs, 1993—. Sec. Silent Observer (Grand Rapids C. of C.), 1985-87; mem. Dunkers, Grand Rapids, 1985-87; pub. rels. chair Celebration on the Grand Com., Grand Rapids, 1986; bd. dirs. Oak Park YMCA, Okemos, 1990-92. Recipient Mercury award Internat. Acad. Comm. Arts and Scis., Drama scholarship Stuttgart (Germany) Am. H.S., 1978; Hugenot scholarship Hugenot Soc. Am., N.Y.C., 1978-82. Mem. Pub. Rels. Soc. Am. (bd. dirs. 1991-93, chair pub. svc. com. 1991-93, Crystal Award winner Ctrl. Mich. chpt. 1993), Lansing Advt. Club, Sigma Kappa. Office: United Dairy Industry Mich 2163 Jolly Rd Okemos MI 48864-3961

WILSON, LORRAINE M., medical, surgical nurse, nursing educator; b. Mich., Nov. 18, 1931; d. Bert and Frances Fern (White) McCarty; m. Harold A. Wilson, June 9, 1953; children: David Scott, Ann Elizabeth. Diploma in Nursing, Bronson Meth. Sch. Nursing, Kalamazoo, Mich., 1953; BS in Chemistry, Siena Heights Coll., 1969; MSN, U. Mich., 1972; PhD, Wayne State U., Detroit, 1985. RN, Mich. Staff nurse U. Mich. Med. Ctr., Ann Arbor, 1953-54, Herrick Meml. Hosp., Tecumseh, Mich., 1954-69; asst. prof. nursing U. Mich., Ann Arbor, 1972-78, Wayne State U., Detroit, 1978-79; assoc. prof. nursing Sch. of Nursing Oakland U., Rochester, Mich., 1986-89; assoc. prof. nursing Ea. Mich. U., Ypsilanti, Mich., 1989—; researcher in field; bd. advs. Profl. Fitness Systems, Warren, Mich., 1986—; cons. wellness and exercise program General Motors CPC Hdqs., Warren, 1986; cons. and faculty liaison nurse extern program in critical care Ea. Mich. U. Catherine McAuley Health Ctr., 1989—. Co-author (with Sylvia Price) Pathophysiology: Clinical Concepts of Disease Processes, 4th ed., 1992; contbr. articles profl. jours. Vol. Community Health Screening Drives, Tecumseh, 1960-70, leader Girl Scouts U.S., Tecumseh, 1960; sunday sch. tchr. Gloria Dei Luth. Ch., Tecumseh, 1960; mem. PTA. Grantee Mich. Heart Assn., 1984, 88, R.C. Mahon Found., 1988. Mem. ANA (various offices and com. chairs), Midwest Nursing Rsch. Soc. (v.p., sec.-treas., bd. dirs.), Mich. Nurses Assn. (del.), Nat. League Nursing, Nat. Orgn. Women, Sigma Theta Tau. Lutheran. Home: 1010 Red Mill Dr Tecumseh MI 49286-1145 Office: Ea Mich U 53 W Michigan Ave Ypsilanti MI 48197-5436

WILSON, MARIE HAMMOND, sales representative; b. Bryn Mawr, Pa., Feb. 11, 1948; d. Frederick George Jr. and Anneliese Cecelia (Mahler) Hammond; divorced; 1 child, Cherish Meredith. BS in Elem. Edn., Monmouth Coll., 1970. Tchr. elem. sch. Little Silver (N.J.) Bd. Edn., 1970-71; adminstrv. asst. to pres. Assocs. of Bell Co., Atlanta, 1979-81; sr. acct. exec. Comprehensive Health Sys., Atlanta, 1983-86; sr. sales rep. Air Touch Cellular (formerly Pac Tel Cellular), Atlanta, 1987—. Vol. Am. Cancer Soc., Duluth, Ga., 1991—, Grady Hosp. Rape Crisis Ctr., Atlanta, 1991-92, Altanta Symphony, 1991—, Navy Relief Soc., Jacksonville, Fla., 1974-75. Nat. Defense Student scholar, Washington, 1968, 69, Monmouth County Freeholders scholar, 1966, 67, Trustee scholar Monmouth Coll., West Long Beach, N.J., 1966-70. Presbyterian. Home: 325 Avebury Ct Alpharetta GA 30202

WILSON, MARILY SHARRONN, accountant; b. Seattle, May 27, 1942; d. Jack Edward Murphy and Cora Phyllis Toby; m. Ronald Duncan Nelson, May 5, 1961 (dec. 1966); children: Sharon Louise, Zeatra Corinne, Ronald Stanley; m. Lawrence William Wilson, Feb. 14, 1981. BA, Griffin Murphy Bus. Sch., 1968. Audit clk. Pay'n' Save Corp., Seattle, 1967; bookkeeper Chromium Co. Inc., Seattle, 1967-70, Sunderland's Wholesale Jewelry, Seattle, 1970-73; staff acct. Helwig, Bulter and Assocs., CPAs, Seattle, 1973-78, Otto R. Enger, Seattle, 1978-85; acct., controller, adminstr. Majiq, Inc., Redmond, Wash., 1985—; acct., owner Paradise Book-keeping and Tax Service, Mt. Vernon, Wash., 1985—; owner, operator Hermit's Cocker Kennels, Mt. Vernon, 1990—; treas. Wilson Maintenance and Constrn., Inc., 1987—. Home: 1869 Peter Burns Rd Mount Vernon WA 98273-9378 Office: Majiq Inc 8343 154th Ave NE Redmond WA 98052-3890

WILSON, MARJORIE PRICE, physician, medical commission executive. Student, Bryn Mawr Coll., 1942-45; M.D., U. Pitts., 1949. Intern U. Pitts. Med. Ctr. Hosps., 1949-50; resident Children's Hosp. U. Pitts., 1950-51, Jackson Meml. Hosp., U. Miami Sch. Medicine, 1954-56; chief residency and internship div. edn. svc. Office of Rsch. and Edn., VA, Washington, 1956, chief profl. tng. div., 1956-60, asst. dir. edn. svc., 1960; chief tng. br. Nat. Inst. Arthritis and Metabolic Disease NIH, Bethesda, Md., 1960-63, asst. to assoc. dir. for tng. Office of Dir., 1963-64, assoc. dir. program devel. OPPD, 1967-69, asst. dir. program planning and evaluation, 1969-70; assoc. dir. extramural programs Nat. Libr. Medicine, 1964-67; dir. dept. instl. devel. Assn. Am. Med. Colls., Washington, 1970-81; sr. assoc. dean U. Md. Sch. Medicine, Balt., 1981-86, vice dean, 1986-88, acting dean, 1984; pres., chief exec. officer Edl. Commn. Fgn. Med. Grads., Phila., 1988—; mem. Inst. Medicine Nat. Acad. Scis.,1974—; bd. visitors U. Pitts. Sch. Medicine, 1974—; mem. Nat. Bd. Med. Examiners, 1980-87, 89—; mem. adv. bd. Fogarty Internat. Ctr., 1991—. Contbr. articles to profl. jours. Mem. adv. bd. Robert Wood Johnson Health Policy Fellowships, 1975-87; trustee Analytic Services, Inc., Falls Church, Va., 1976—. Fellow Am. Coll. Physician Execs., AAAS; mem. Assn. Am. Med. Colls., Am. Fedn. Clin. Research, IEEE. Office: Ednl Commn Fgn Med Grads 3624 Market St Philadelphia PA 19104-2614

WILSON, MARTHA FARLOW, business consultant; b. Richmond, Ind., May 12, 1952; d. Phillip E. and Jean A. (Seikel) Farlow; m. R.A. Wilson, Sept. 2, 1979 (div. July 1985). BA in Spanish and French, Andrews U., 1975; MS in Mgmt., Purdue U., 1976. Internal cons. Mellon Bank NA, Pitts., 1977-79, Hallmark Cards, Kansas City, Mo., 1981-84; mem. purchasing and acctg. staff City of Richmond, Ind., 1985-86; mem. purchasing staff, cons. 10th Pan Am. Games, Indpls., 1986-87; asst. product mgr. Gibson Greetings, Cin., 1988-89; owner, cons. Wilson Mktg., Richmond, 1989-92; mem. customer svc. staff Henny Penny, Eaton, Ohio, 1991-92; owner, cons. MBA's At Your Svc., Richmond, 1993—. Bd. dirs. Jr. Achievement, Richmond, 1993-94; officer, divsn. leader Seventh Day Adventist Ch., Richmond, 1986, 88-94; bd. dirs., counselor Friends of the Battered, Richmond, 1984-85; mem. choir Richmond Symphony/Cmty. Chorus, 1990-93. Office: MBAs At Your Svc PO Box 8092 Richmond IN 47374-0092

WILSON, MARY ELIZABETH, physician; b. Indpls., Nov. 19, 1942; d. Ralph Richard and Catheryn Rebecca (Kurtz) Lausch; m. Harvey Vernon Fineberg, May 16, 1975. AB, Ind. U., 1963; MD, U. Wis., 1971. Diplomate Am. Bd. Internal Medicine, Am. Bd. Infectious Diseases. Tchr. of French and English Marquette Sch., Madison, Wis., 1963-66; intern in medicine Beth Israel Hosp., Boston, 1971-72, resident in medicine, 1972-73, fellow in infectious diseases, 1973-75; physician Albert Schweitzer Hosp., Deschapelles, Haiti, 1974-75, Harvard Health Svcs., Cambridge, Mass., 1974-75; asst. physician Cambridge Hosp., 1975-78; hosp. epidemiologist Mt. Auburn Hosp., Cambridge, 1975-79, chief of infectious diseases, 1978—; adv. com. immunization practices Ctrs. for Disease Control, Atlanta, 1988-92; acad. adv. com. Nat. Inst. Pub. Health, Mex., 1989-91; cons. Ford Found., 1988; instr. in medicine Harvard Med. Sch., Boston, 1975-93, asst. clin. prof., 1994—; asst. prof. depts. epidemiology and population and internat. health Harvard Sch. Pub. Health, 1994—; lectr. Sultan Qaboos U., Oman, 1991; chair Woods Hole Workshop, Emerging Infectious Diseases. Author: A World Guide to Infections: Diseases, Distribution, Diagnosis, 1991; co-editor: (with Richard Levins and Andrew Spielman) Disease in Evolution: Global Changes and Emergence of Infectious Diseases, 1994; mem. editl. bd. Current Issues in Pub. Health. Mem. Cambridge Task Force on AIDS, 1987—, Earthwatch, Watertown, Mass., Cultural Survival, Inc., Cambridge; bd. dirs. Horizon Communications, West Cornwall, Conn., 1990. Recipient Lewis E. and Edith Phillips award U. Wis. Med. Sch., 1969, Cora M. and Edward Van Liere award, 1971, Mosby Scholarship Book award, 1971. Fellow ACP, Infectious Diseases Soc. Am., Royal Soc. Tropical Medicine and Hygiene; mem. Am. Soc. Microbiology, N.Y. Acad. Scis., Am. Soc. Tropical Medicine and Hygiene, Mass. Infectious Diseases Soc., Peabody Soc., Internat. Soc. Travel Medicine, Wilderness Med. Soc., Soc. for Vector Ecology, Internat. Union Against Tuberculosis and Lung Disease, Sigma Sigma, Phi Sigma Iota, Alpha Omega Alpha. Office: Mt Auburn Hosp 330 Mt Auburn St Cambridge MA 02138-5502

WILSON, MIRIAM GEISENDORFER, physician, educator; b. Yakima, Wash., Dec. 3, 1922; d. Emil and Frances Geisendorfer; m. Howard G. Wilson, June 21, 1947; children—Claire, Paula, Geoffrey, Nicola, Marla. B.S., U. Wash., Seattle, 1944, M.S., 1945; M.D., U. Calif., San Francisco, 1950. Mem. faculty U. So. Calif. Sch. Medicine, L.A., 1965—, prof. pediatrics, 1969—. Office: U So Calif Med Ctr 1129 N State St Los Angeles CA 90033-1069

WILSON, MIRIAM JANET WILLIAMS, publishing executive; b. London, Ont., Can., July 13, 1939; d. Ralph George and Lillian Conn Williams; m. Carson Winnette, Nov. 20, 1960 (div. 1971); children: Barrie Carson Winnette, Rebecca Lynn Winnette; m. Charles Lindsay Wilson, Dec. 14, 1973; 1 child, Charles William Wilson; stepchildren: Kenneth M., Carol Ann, Catherine S., Nancy L., Patrick L. Diploma in nursing, Glendale (Calif.) Sanitarium & Hosp., 1960. RN, Calif., Va., Ohio, Md., W.Va. Head nurse emergency and med. fls. Glendale Sanitarium and Hosp., 1960-65; psychometrist Harding Hosp., Worthington, Ohio, 1969-73; biofeedback specialist in assn. Dr. Randolph P. Johnston, Winchester, Va., 1980-84; dir. Stress Ctr. for Children and Adults, Shepherdstown, W.Va., 1985-87; pres. Rocky River Pubs., Shepherdstown, 1987—; lectr. ednl., profl. and civic groups, 1984—. Author: Help For Children, 6 edits., 1987-91, Stress Stoppers, 2 edits., 1989; contbr. articles to profl. publs. Active Shepherdstown Women's Club, 1986-91. Mem. NAFE, Internat. Platform Assn., Am. Booksellers Assn., N.Y. Acad. Scis. Office: Rocky River Pubs PO Box 1679 Shepherdstown WV 25443-1679

WILSON, PATRICIA DIANE, psychologist; b. Wichita, Kans., Oct. 12, 1958; d. Guy and Wilma (DeVore) W.; m. Dale C. Garwood, Aug. 5, 1978 (div. Nov. 1981). Bof Gen. Studies, Wichita State U., 1981, M of Edn., 1985, postgrad., 1985-88. Registered psychologist, Kans. Psychologist Winfield (Kans.) State Hosp., 1986-88, Family Consultation Svc., Wichita, 1988-90; psychologist, coord. continuing edn. Wichita Child Guidance Ctr., 1990—; cons. Head Start, Wichita, 1992—. Mem. APA, Assn. for Play Therapy (Kans. area rep.). Democrat. Methodist. Office: Wichita Child Guidance Ctr 415 N Poplar St Wichita KS 67214-4529

WILSON, PATRICIA POTTER, library science and reading educator, educational and library consultant; b. Jennings, La., May 3, 1946; d. Ralph Harold and Wilda Ruth (Smith) Potter; m. Wendell Merlin Wilson, Aug. 24, 1968. BS, La. State U., 1967; MS, U. Houston-Clear Lake, 1979; EdD, U. Houston, 1985. Cert. tchr., learning resources specialist (librarian), Tex. Tchr., England AFB (La.) Elem. Sch., 1967-68, Edward White Elem. Sch., Clear Creek Ind. Schs., Seabrook, Tex., 1972-77; librarian C.D. Landolt Elem. Sch., Friendswood, Tex., 1979-81; instr./lectr. children's lit. U. Houston 1983-86; with U. Houston/Clear Lake, 1984-87, asst. prof. libr. sci. and reading, 1988-94, assoc. prof. learning resources and reading edn., 1994—, mem. faculty senate, 1992-93; cons. Hermann Hosp., Baywood Hosp., 1986-87, Bedford Meadows Hosp., 1989-90, Wetcher Clinic, 1989; v.p., sec. Potter Farms, Inc., 1994—. Trustee, Freeman Meml. Library, Houston, 1982-87, v.p., 1985-86, pres., 1986-87; trustee Evelyn Meador Libr., 1993-94; adv. bd. Evelyn Meador Libr., 1994—; bd. dirs. Bay Area Soc. Prevention Cruelty Animals, 1994—; mem. Armand Bayou Nature Ctr., Houston, 1980—, bd. dirs. 1989-94; bd. dirs. Sta. KUHT-TV, 1984-87; mem. Bay Area Symphony League. Editor A Rev. Sampler, 1985-86, 89-90; dir. Learning Resources Book Rev. Ctr., 1989-90. Author: HAPPENINGS: Developing Successful Programs for School Libraries, 1987; contbg. editor Tex. Library Jour., 1988-94; contbr. articles to profl. jours. Recipient Rsch. award Tex. State Reading Assn., 1993, Pres. award Tex. Coun. Tchrs. of English; grantee Tex. Libr. Assn., 1993. Mem. ALA, Am. Assn. Sch. Librarians, Internat. Reading Assn., Nat. Council Tchrs. English, (Books for You review com. 1985-88, Your Reading review com., 1993—), Tex. Council Tchrs. English, Antarctican Soc., Phi Delta Kappa. Methodist. Club: Lakewood Yacht (Seabrook). Home: 629 Bay Vista Dr Seabrook TX 77586-3001 Office: U Houston Clear Lake 2700 Bay Area Blvd Houston TX 77058-1002

WILSON, PAULA JEAN, human resources professional; b. Newman, Calif., Aug. 4, 1959; d. Wallace Leland and Luraine (Willis) W.; 1 child, Aimee Nicole. BS, William Woods Coll., 1981; MBA, Wash. U., 1984. Profl. recruiter Naval Weapons Ctr., China Lake, Calif., 1982-85, program analyst, 1985-86; employment rep. Northrop B-2, Palmdale, Calif., 1986-87, compensation and benefits analyst, 1987-89; mgr. human resources devel. Contel/GTE, Victorville, Calif., 1989-94; mgr. human resources Echo Bay Alaska, Inc., Juneau, 1994—; internal cons. Qaulity Contender Com., Victorville, 1992-93; trainer, cons. AAUW, Victorville, 1993; guest lectr. Redlands U., Riverside, Calif., 1989, Victor Valley C.C., 1992-93, Alaska Workers Comp. Bd., U. Alaska S.E. Author tng. classes in field. Recipient Sr. Profl. Human Resources award Soc. for Human Resources Mgmt., 1993. Mem. Am. Compensation Assn., ASTD. Office: Echo Bay AK Inc 3100 Channel Dr Juneau AK 99801

WILSON, PEGGY DELORIS, executive secretary, cosmetologist; b. Warsaw, Ind., Apr. 12, 1943; d. Orin Leo and Roxie Mae (Sausaman) Pike; m. Bernard Hal Wilson Sept. 30, 1961 (div. July 1986); children: Bernadine Wilson Waikel, Lori Wilson, Jodie Wilson Hall, Sean Wilson. Diploma in Cosmetology/Hairstyling, Warner's. Beautician and frame stylist Hair Hut & Dr. Carman, Warsaw, 1986; mgr. Elizabeth Ardens Uhlmans, Warsaw, 1986-87; receptionist Creighton Bros., Warsaw, 1987-88; receiving clerk Zimmers, Warsaw, 1988-89; exec. sec. Kimble Glass, Warsaw, 1989—; transcriber NLRB, South Bend, Ind., 1994; typist Union Local 614 Contract, Warsaw, 1993. leader 4H Club, 1965; vol. Cancer Drive, 1970-74, Hosp. Auxillary, 1979. Recipient Telephone Techniques award Fred Pryor, 1986, Secretarial award Keye, 1989, Exceptional Asst. award Fred Pryor, 1994. Mem. NAFE, Onized Club (sec. 1993—), Claypool Alumni (sec. 1991-92). Home: 1416 Fox Farm Rd Warsaw IN 46580 Office: Kimble Glass Inc PO Box 798 Center St Warsaw IN 46580

WILSON, PEGGY HENICAN, city official; b. New Orleans, June 24, 1937; d. C. Ellis and Elizabeth (Cleveland) Henican; m. Gordon Francis Wilson Jr., Dec. 10, 1932; children: Gordon, Alice, Peter, Carter. BA cum laude, Barat Coll., Lake Forest, Ill., 1959; postgrad., Tulane and Dominican Coll., 1960-75. Cert. tchr. Tchr. Mercy Acad., New Orleans, 1961-62, Acad. Sacred Heart, New Orleans, 1959-72; mgr. polit. campaigns Campaign Specialists, 1978-80; ptnr. Mason, Glickman, Wilson, New Orleans, 1981-82; owner Trolley Tours, 1975-85; pres. Peggy Wilson & Assocs., New Orleans, 1980-87; mem. city council dist. A New Orleans, 1986-94, coun. mem.-at-large, 1994—; chmn. fin. com. S&WB, mem. bd. liquidations. Author: Trolley Tours, 1982. Chmn. Alcoholic Beverage Control Bd., 1984-86; sec.-treas. Warehouse Dist. Devel. Assn., 1982-84, pres., 1984; bd. dirs. Carrollton-Hollygrove Community Ctr.; bd. dirs. YWCA, 1984-87; bd. dirs. City Park, New Orleans Mus. Art, Preservation Action; mem. mktg. com. City of New Orleans; mem. Cox Cable Comm.; chmn. Hist. Dist. Landmarks Commn., 1981, 82; mem. bd., exec. com. St. George's Episcopal Sch., 1980-82; mem. Housing Task Force, 1978-80; mem. Police Chief Selection Com., 1978-79. Inst. Politics fellow Loyola U., 1978. Mem. Alliance for Good Govt., LWV, Upper St. Charles Civic Assn., Warehouse Dist. Devel. Assn., AARP. Office: Office City Council City Hall Rm 2E09 1300 Perdido St New Orleans LA 70112-2114

WILSON, RACHEL SARA, accountant; b. Bridgeport, Conn., Feb. 5, 1959; d. John Allan and Arline Rose (Delaney) McCague; m. Frank Wilson, Dec. 2, 1983; 1 child, Brittany Ayn. Grad. jr. accountancy program, Butler Bus. Coll., 1978; student, Contra Costa Coll.; ed. tax preparation program, H & R Block, Walnut Creek, Calif., 1984; student, U. Calif., Berkeley, 1987—. Office clk. Kombi Ltd., Norwalk, Conn., 1978-79; sr. acctg. clk. Brinks, Inc., Darien, Conn., 1979-81; bookkeeper Safeway Tire Co., Inc., Stamford, Conn., 1977-81, Mil Corp., San Francisco, 1982-83; acct./mgr.

office of med. dir. Elkhart (Ind.) Gen. Hosp., 1990-92; office adminstr. Frank Wilson, MD, Inc., Richmond, Calif., 1983-85, v.p., sec., 1985—. Active Calhoun County Women's Aux. Mem. NAFE. Republican. Roman Catholic. Home and Office: 329 Jonesville Rd Coldwater MI 49036

WILSON, RITA DIANE, career counselor; b. Evansville, Ind., Oct. 6, 1946; d. Herschel Randolph and Dulcie Glenn (Gidcumb) Ferguson; m. Robert Leroy Wilson, Oct. 12, 1962 (dec. June 21, 1987); children: Bobby Lee, Timothy Eugene, Michael Randolph, Roy Gustus Glenn. Assoc. in Mgmt., Lockyear Coll., Evansville, Ind., 1989, BBA in Adminstrn., 1990. Cert. career counselor, Ind.; lic. CRP, Fed. Registrar. Sec. S.W. Ind. CETA Consortium, Evansville, 1981-82; intake specialist Pvt. Industry Coun., Evansville, 1982-83, info. specialist, 1983-84, Title III coord., 1984-92, CRU specialist, 1990-92; coord. Workforce Devel. Ctr., Evansville, 1992-93; counselor Ind. Workforce Devel. Ctr., Evansville, 1993—; vol. counselor Evansville Vanderburgh Sch. Corp., 1993—, tutor, 1989—; notary public. Author brochure: Information Resource Area Brochure, 1992. Bd. dirs. St. Anthony's Ctr. for Family Living, Evansville, 1991—. Mem. NAFE, Am. Counseling Assn., Nat. Employment Counselors Assn., Am. Bus. Women's Assn. (pres. 1990-91, 93-94, 94-95, Woman of the Yr. 1992), U.S. Trotting Assn. Home: 4928 E Morgan Ave Evansville IN 47715 Office: Ind Workforce Devel Ctr 160 S Third Ave Evansville IN 47708

WILSON, RITA P., insurance company executive. Sr. v.p. corp. rels. Allstate Ins. Co., Northbrook, Ill. Office: Allstate Ins Co Allstate Plz Northbrook IL 60062*

WILSON, RUBY LEILA, nurse, educator; b. Punxsutawney, Pa., May 29, 1931; d. Clark H. and Alda E. (Armstrong) W. BS in Nursing Edn., U. Pitts., 1954; MSN, Case Western Res. U., 1959; EdD, Duke U., 1969. Staff nurse, asst. head nurse Allegheny Gen. Hosp., Pitts., 1951-52; night clin. instr., adminstrv. supr. Allegheny Gen. Hosp., 1951-55; staff nurse, asst. head nurse Fort Miley VA Hosp., San Francisco, 1957-58; instr. nursing Duke U. Sch. Nursing, Durham, N.C., 1955-57; asst. prof. med. surg. nursing Duke U. Sch. Nursing, 1959-66, assoc. in medicine, 1963-66, prof. nursing, 1971—, dean sch. nursing., 1971-84, asst. to chancellor for health affairs, 1984—; asst. prof. dept. community and family medicine Duke U. Sch. Medicine, 1971—; cons., vis. prof. Rockefeller Found., Thailand, 1968-71; vis. prof. Case Western Res. U., 1982-84; mem. Gov.'s Commn. on Health Care Reform in N.C., 1994. Contbr. articles to profl. jours. Active N.C. Med. Care Commn., Gov.'s Commn. on N.C. Health Care Reform, 1994—. Fellow Am. Acad. Nursing, Inst. Medicine; mem. ANA, Am. Assn. Colls. Nursing, Am. Assn. Higher Edn., Nat. League Nursing, Assn. for Acad. Health Ctrs. (mem. inst. planning com.), Women's Forum N.C. (bd. dirs. 1984-88), N.C. Found. for Nursing (pres. 1990-94). Office: Duke U Med Ctr PO Box 3243 Durham NC 27715-3243

WILSON, SARA REDDING, lawyer; b. Washington, Feb. 20, 1950; d. Lawrence James III and Jane Elizabeth (Smith) Redding; m. Steven L. Myers, June 21, 1969 (div. 1979); children: Blythe Ann, Robert Lawrence; m. Claude Watson Wilson, May 24, 1986; stepchildren: David B., Jessica Leigh. BA, Hamilton Coll., 1972; JD, U. Richmond, 1977; postgrad., Columbia U., Duke U. Bar: Va. 1978, U.S. Dist. Ct. (ea. dist.) Va. 1980. Mgmt. cons. Bankers Trust Co., N.Y.C., 1972-75; corp. atty. Signet Banking Corp. (formerly Bank of Va.), Richmond, 1977-79, assoc. corp. atty., 1979-83, corp. counsel, 1983-84, sr. corp. counsel, 1984-93, exec. v.p., gen. counsel, 1994, exec. v.p., gen. counsel, corporate sec., 1995—; mem. bank counsel unit Am. Bankers Assn., 1985-94. Bd. dirs. Bank of Va. Vol. Orgn., Richmond, 1984-86, Dispute Resolution Ctr., 1989—; chmn. U. Richmond Law Alumni Fund, 1985-86; trustee Hamilton Coll., 1993—, U. Richmond, 1994—; bd. mgrs. Jackson-Feild Home for Girls. Mem. ABA, Va. Bar Assn., Richmond Bar Assn., Am. Corp. Counsel Assn., Va. Bankers Assn. (chmn. legal affairs 1986-88), U. Richmond Law Alumni Assn. (bd. dirs. 1986-94), Bull and Bear Club. Episcopalian. Home: 8857 River Rd Richmond VA 23229-7801 Office: Signet Banking Corp 7 N 8th St Richmond VA 23219-3301

WILSON, SHERRY DENISE, speech and language pathologist; b. Rutherford, N.C., Jan. 10, 1963; d. Morris William and Betty Jean (Hudgins) Wilson. AA, Isothermal Community Coll., 1981; BS, Cen. Mo. State U., 1985, MS, 1988. Speech pathologist DePaul Hosp. Home Health, Cheyenne, Wyo., 1987, 89; coord. handicap svcs., staff speech-lang. pathologist Laramie County Head Start, Cheyenne, 1987-89; speech pathologist, supr., coord., dir. inclusive pre-sch. Ednl. Svc. Unit # 13, Scottsbluff, 1989—; project dir. The Early Intervention Demonstration Project Endl. Svcs. Unit # 13, Scottsbluff, 1991—; planning region chair Interagy. coord. Coun. Presch. Spl. Edn., Scottsbluff, 1989-93, mem., 1993—; mem. health adv. bd. Head Start, Gering, Nebr., 1989-91; cons., trainer in field. Founding mem. S.E. Wyo. AIDS Project, Cheyenne, 1989; Odyssey of the Mind coach Gering Jr. H.S., 1989-93; project dir., mem. exec. bd. Cmty. Devel. Coalition, 1994. Named Outstanding Speech Pathologist of Yr., Sigma Alpha Eta, 1985. Mem. NEA, Am. Speech-Lang.-Hearing Assn. (cert. clin. competence, Cert. Excellence 1993), Nebr. State Edn. Assn., Coun. for Exceptional Children (early childhood div.). Office: Ednl Svc Unit #13 Scottsbluff NE 69361

WILSON, SHERYL A., pharmacist; b. Nashville, Apr. 6, 1957; d. Robert Lewis and Norma Anne (Cox) W. BS in Biology, David Lipscomb U., 1979; BS in Pharmacy, Auburn U., 1985. Lic. pharmacist, Tenn. Student extern/intern East Alabama Med. Ctr., Opelika, Ala., 1982-86; staff pharmacist Metro Nashville Gen. Hosp., 1987-95, PharmaThera, Inc., Nashville, 1995—. Flutist Nashville Community Concert Band, 1973—; preschool tchr. Donelson Ch. of Christ, 1988—. Mem. Am. Pharm. Assn., Am. Soc. Hosp. Pharmacists, Tenn. Soc. Hosp. Pharmacists, Nashville Area Pharmacists Assn., Am. Soc. Parenteral and Enteral Nutrition. Democrat. Home: 1439 Mcgavock Pike Nashville TN 37216-3231 Office: Metro Nashville Gen Hosp 72 Hermitage Ave Nashville TN 37210-2110

WILSON, SHERYL J., state agency administrator; b. Shelton, Wash., May 23, 1936; d. Kenneth F. and Bernice (Angell) Sturdevant; m. Daniel I. Stuckey, Sept. 8, 1956 (div. June 1967); children: Mark, Ann, David, Noni; m. Donald R. Wilson, Aug. 9, 1968. Student, Wash. State U., 1954-57; BA, Evergreen State Coll., 1985. Rsch. analyst Wash. Pub. Pension Commn., Olympia, 1967-75; budget analyst Wash. State Senate, Olympia, 1975-80; retirement and ins. officer U. Wash., Seattle, 1980-83; asst. dir. Wash. Dept. Retirement Sys., Olympia, 1983-89, dir., 1993—; exec. dir. Oreg. Pub. Employees Retirement Sys., Portland, 1989-93; mem. exec. com. Nat. Coun. Tchr. Retirement, Austin, 1992—; pres., mem. exec. com. Nat. Preretirement Edn. Assn., 1985-91; vice chair Wash. State Investment Bd., Olympia, 1993—; mem. steering com. cert. employee benefit specialist program U. Wash., 1983—. Chair Interagy. Com. Status of Women, Olympia, 1987-88. Mem. Nat. Assn. State Retirement Adminstrs. (legal com. 1989—), Women in Pub. Adminstrn. (founder Oreg. chpt. 1990), Govt. Fin. Officers (retirement and benefits adminstrn. com. 1992—), Zonta Internat.

WILSON, SUSAN BERNADETTE, psychologist; b. Pitts., May 3, 1954; d. Booker Talifero and Edna Jean (Marconi) W.; m. John C. Scott Jr., Feb. 1975 (div.); children: Sharmel D., Justin. BS cum laude, U. Pitts., 1974, MS, 1981, PhD, 1985. Lic. clin. psychologist, Mo. Teaching asst., fellow U. Pitts., 1979-81; intern VA Med. Ctr., Pitts., 1983-84; staff psychologist, fellow Menninger Found., Topeka, 1984-89; clin. dir. Crittenton Kansas City (Mo.) Clinic, 1989-90; asst. prof. Med. Sch. U. Mo., Kansas City, 1990—; cons. The Kaufmann Found., Kansas City, 1990; mem. faculty Karl Menninger Sch. Psychiatry, Topeka, 1986-89; asst. prof. Sch. Medicine, U. Mo., Kansas City, 1990—. Creator workshop: Being the Best You Can Be: A Psychoeducational Program for an Urban Workforce, 1989. Commr. Mayor's Commn. on Human Rights, Kansas City, 1992—; regional adv. com. Dept. Mental Health, Alcohol and Drug Abuse, 1992. Provost Devel. Fund fellow U. Pitts., 1977-79. Mem. Am. Psychol. Assn., Am. Group Psychotherapy, Jack and Jill of Am., Delta Sigma Theta. Democrat. Roman Catholic. Home: 7223 E 134th Cir Grandview MO 64030-3343 Office: Crittenton Kansas City 10918 Elm Ave Kansas City MO 64134-4108

WILSON, TAMMY LYNN, accountant, government revenue agent; b. Huntington, W.Va., July 17, 1960; d. Thomas Owen and Peggy Jane (Mayenschein) Galloway; m. Rodney Allen Wilson, Sept. 3, 1982. BSBA in Acctg. magna cum laude, Youngstown State U., 1987. CPA, Va., W.Va.; cert. mgmt. acct. Auditing clk. United Parcel Svc., Covington, Va., 1984-85; acctg. clk. to asst. contr. Youngstown (Ohio) State U., 1986-87; tax auditor IRS, Huntington, 1988, revenue agt., 1988-89; revenue agt. IRS, Richmond, Va., 1989—; vol. income tax preparer VITA, IRS, Youngstown, 1987; algebra and pre-calculus tutor Sch. Partnership Program, Open H.S., 1994—. Vol. asst. W.Va. Spl. Olympics, Huntington, 1988, 89; mem. Humane Soc., Washington, 1989—. Mem. AICPA, Inst. Mgmt. Accts., Assn. Govt. Accts., Va. Soc. CPA, Alpha Tau Gamma. Democrat. Baptist. Home: 301 Grinell Dr Richmond VA 23236 Office: IRS Exam Div 479 Southlake Blvd Richmond VA 23236

WILSON, TAMRA MCELROY, public relations executive; b. Pana, Ill., Aug. 14, 1954; d. Lynn and Enid (McKinley) McElroy: m. Tym Turner Wilson, May 26, 1979; 1 child, Lantz McKinley. Student, Ill. State U., 1972-74, Brighton (Eng.) Coll. Edn., 1974; BJ, U. Mo., 1976. Reporter Daily Union, Shelbyville, Ill., 1976-77; staff writer The Country Cos., Bloomington, Ill., 1978-79; account exec. Inform, Inc., Hickory, N.C., 1979-81; pub. rels. assoc. Centel, Hickory, 1981-84; conf. coord. J. H. Heafner Co., Lincolnton, N.C., 1985-86; comms. specialist Meredith/Burda, Newton, N.C., 1987-92; mktg. dir. Catawba Valley Area Girl Scout Coun., Hickory, 1992; dir. pub. rels. Lenoir-Rhyne Coll., Hickory, 1992—; instr. Catawba Valley C.C., Hickory, 1992—. Editor: (book) USS Cabot, 1986; editor The Register, 1987-92 (rate excellent 3 times by The Ragan Report), Profile, 1993—. Mem. steering com. Christ United Meth. Ch., Hickory, 1991, accompanist, 1992-93, March of Dimes, 1991, 92, 94, 95; chair publicity com. Follies fund raiser for Hickory Mus. Art.; chmn. pub. rels. Western Piedmont Sister Cities Assn., 1994—. Mem. Coll. News Assn. of the Carolinas, Western Piedmont Pub. Rels. Assn. (Communicator award 1992), Catawba County C. of C. (Leadership grad. 1993). Office: Lenoir-Rhyne Coll PO Box 7483 Hickory NC 28603

WILSON, THEDA MORRIS, school board administrator, educator; b. Newark, Jan. 15, 1922; d. William Boen and Maggie (Hall) Morris; m. Donald Octavio Wilson, June 26, 1947; children: Milagros Wilson Williams, Sylvia Wilson Collins, Juana Wilson Brown. BS in Elem. Edn., N.J. State Tchrs., 1943; MA in Guidance and Pers. Adminstrn., NYU, 1946. Elem. tchr. Oakwood Ave. Sch., Orange, N.J., 1944-48, Sumner Ave Sch. and Forest Pk., Springfield, Mass., 1948-51, Elbert Elem. Sch., Wilmington, Del., 1951-54; elem. prin. Elbert Elem. Sch., N.E. Elem. Sch., Wilmington, 1954-64; prin. Sch. # 138, Sch. #97 Collington Sq., Balt., 1964-74; regional supt. Cen. and N.E. Balt. Regions, 1974-84; instr. Johns Hopkins U., Balt., 1975-80; vice-chmn. Flagler County Sch. Bd., Fla., 1988-90, chmn., 1990—; founder Edn. Opportunities Found., Balt., 1984-90. Co-author: World of Language, 1969, rev. edit., 1974. Bd. dirs. Citrus coun. Girl Scouts U.S.A., Winter Park, Fla., 1991—, YWCA, Springfield, Mass., Wilmington, Del., Balt. Recipient Balt.'s Best award Mayor and City Coun., 1983. Mem. AAUW (v.p. 1992-94, pres. 1994—), Girl Friends Inc. (pres. Orlando, Fla. chpt. 1991—), Les Amies des Arts, Phi Delta Kappa. Episcopalian. Home and Office: PO Box 350768 Palm Coast FL 32135-0768

WILSON, VICTORIA JANE SIMPSON, farmer; b. Floresville, Tex., Nov. 30, 1952; d. Joseph Eugene and Eva Gertrude (Ferguson) Simpson; m. Richard Royce Wilson, May 15, 1976; children: Sarah Beth, Nathan Lawrence. BSN, U. Cen. Ark., 1977; MS in Nursing, Northwestern State U., 1981. Charge nurse surg. St. Vincent Infirmary, Little Rock; staff nurse ICU La. State U. Med. Ctr., Shreveport, La.; patient edn. coord. White River Med. Ctr., Batesville, Ark.; co-owner, chief exec. officer Health Plus, Stuttgart, Ark.; co-owner, mgr. Wilson & Son Fish Farm. Mem. Catfish Farmers Am., Catfish Farmers Ark., Sigma Theta Tau. Home: PO Box 310 Humphrey AR 72073

WILSON, VIRGINIA HAMPTON, reading educator; b. St. Matthews, S.C., Apr. 25, 1954; d. Isreal and Josephine (Pinckney) W.; children: Jarell Hampton, Tonya Hampton, Delsean Irick. BS, S.C. State U., 1976, MEd, 1990. Sec. S.C. State U., Orangeburg, 1979-90; coach volleyball and track Calhoun County High Sch., St. Matthews, S.C., 1991—; reading instr. Phi Delta Kappa, Orangeburg, 1990—; basketball coach John Ford Mid. Sch.; adult edn. instr. Calhoun County H.S., 1994—. Office: Calhoun County High Sch RR 4 Box 30 Saint Matthews SC 29135-9416

WILSON-SIMPSON, DOROTHY ANDREA, healthcare facility executive; b. Bremerton, Wash., July 27, 1945; d. Merritt Hampden Wilson and Eva Jane (Quaring) Daniell; m. Marion Ray Simpson, Mar. 11,1983; children: Kimberly Simpson Walter, Chad Mitchell. BA cum laude, La. Coll., 1967; MS, La. State U., 1970. Instl. counselor, social svcs. dept. Cen. La. State Hosp., Pineville, 1967-68, 70-74; psychiat. social worker dept. child psychiatry Western Mo. Mental Health Ctr., Kansas City, 1974-76; dir. child care, then dir. treatment The Spofford Home, Kansas City, 1976-82; interim exec. dir. The Spofford Home, 1983, pres., chief exec. officer, 1983—; mem. Spofford Ozanam Svcs., Inc., bd. dirs.; mem. adv. coun. Health Edn. Coalition; bd. dirs. Gillis Ozanam Spofford Consortium, Inc.; subcom. chair Gov.'s Com. on Children and Youth, Mo., 1980-81; mem. Western Mo. Psychiat. Adv. Coun., 1986, ad hoc com. Jackson County, Mo. Mental Health Levy Bd., 1991, Mo. State Task Force for Investigation of Instl. Abuse, 1991; treas. children, youth, and family sect. United Meth. Assn. Health and Welfare Ministries, Dayton, Ohio, 1988-90. Contbr. to various publs. Community adviser Kansas City Jr. League, 1988. Mem. Child Welfare League Am., Nat. Fellowship Child Care Execs., Mo. Child Care Assn. (bd. dirs. 1982—, sec. 1982-85, treas. 1985-87, pres.-elect 1987-89, pres. 1989-90, past pres. 1990), Greater Kansas City Assn. United Way Agys., Rotary (treas. Kansas City South Club 1991, v.p. 1993), Alpha Chi, Phi Kappa Phi. Democrat. Baptist. Office: Spofford Home 9700 Grandview Rd Kansas City MO 64137-1135

WILSON-WEBB, NANCY LOU, adult educational administrator; b. Maypearl, Tex., Jan. 20, 1932; d. Madison Grady and Mary Nancy Pearson (Haney) Wilson; m. John Crawford Webb, July 29, 1972. BS magna cum laude, Abilene (Tex.) Christian U., 1953; MEd with high honors, Tex. Christian U., 1985. Cert. tchr., supr./adminstr., Tex. Tchr. elem. grades Ft. Worth Ind. Sch. Dist., 1953-67, tchr., 1970-73; dir. adult edn. coop. for 38 sch. dists. Tex. Edn. Agy., 1973—; pres. Nat. Commn. on Adult Basic Edn., 1994—; pres. Tex. Adult Edn. Adminstrn., 1994; apptd. mem. Tex. State Literacy Coun., 1987—; mem. exec. bd. Tex. Coun. Co-op Dirs., 1989—; apptd. Tex. State Sch. Bd. Commn., 1994-95. Cons. to textbook: On Your Mark?, 1994. Pres. Jr. Woman's Club, Ft. Worth, 1969, Fine Arts Guild, Tex. Christian U., Ft. Worth, 1970-72, Ft. Worth Women's Civic Club Coun., 1970; mem. Exec. Libr. Bd., Ft. Worth, 1990—; apptd. bd. dirs. Literacy Plus in North Tex., 1988, Greater Ft. Worth Literacy Coun.; commr. Ed-16 Task Forces Tex. Edn. Agy., 1985-92, Gen. Dynamics Literacy Task Force; bd. dirs. Friends of Libr., 1967—, Opera Guild of Ft. Worth, 1965—, Johnson County (Tex.) Corrs. Recipient Bevy award City of Ft. Worth, 1968, award for leadership literacy Tex., DAR, 1985, 86, 87, 89, Proclamation Commr.'s Ct. Outstanding 40 Yr. Literacy Svc. to Tarrant County, 1994, Most Outstanding Dir. Program in Literacy Labor Dept., 1990, U.S. Dept. Edn., 1991; named one of the Most Outstanding Educators in U.S. Nat. Assn. Adult Edn., 1983, Most Outstanding Woman Educator of Ft. Worth, City of Ft. Worth, 1991, Most Outstanding Leader for Literacy in Tex., Tex. Internat. Reading Coun., 1991, Woman of Yr. Tarrant County, 1994-95; scholar Fed. Republic Germany, 1983. Mem. NEA, DAR (Nat. Most Outstanding Literacy award 1992), AAUW, Am. Assn. Adult and Continuing Edn. (v.p. 1987-89, chair 1993 internat. conv. 1992) Tex. Assn. Adult and Continuing Edn. (pres. 1985-86, Most Outstanding Adult Adminstr. in Tex. award 1984), Tex. Coun. Adult Edn. Dirs. (pres.), Coun. World Affairs (bd. dirs. 1980-92), Am. Bus. Women's Assn., Ft. Worth C. of C., Lecture Found., Internat. Reading Assn. (literacy challenge award 1991), Ft. Worth Adminstrv. Assn., Zonta, Ft. Worth Garden Club, Woman's Club of Ft. Worth, Petroleum Club, Carousel Dance Assn., Optimist Club (Ft. Worth), Met. Dinner and Dance Club, Ridglea Country Club, Crescent Club, Phi Beta Kappa, Alpha Delta Kappa, Phi Delta Kappa. Democrat. Home: 3716 Fox Hollow Fort Worth TX 76109 Office: 100 N University Fort Worth TX

WILSTED, JOY, elementary education educator, reading specialist, parenting consultant; b. St. Marys, Pa., Aug. 12, 1935; d. Wayne and Carrie (Neiger) Furman; m. Richard William Wilsted, Feb. 14, 1982; 2 children. BA, Fla. Atlantic U., 1970; MS in Edn., Old Dominion U., Norfolk, Va., 1975. Cert. reading specialist, elem. tchr., Mo.; cert. permanent tchr., N.Y. Tchr. creative dramatics Hillsboro Country Day Sch., Pompano Beach, Fla., 1966-68; tchr. PTA Kindergarten, Boca Raton, Fla., 1968-69; tchr. creative dramatics Wee-Wisdom Montessori Sch., Delray Beach, Fla., 1969-70; elem. tchr. Birmingham (Mich.) Pub. Schs., 1970-72; classroom and reading resource tchr. Chesapeake (Va.) Pub. Schs., 1972-79; reading coord. Harrisonville (Mo.) Pub. Schs., 1979-81; Chpt. I reading tchr., reading improvement tchr. North Kansas City Pub. Schs., Kansas City, Mo., 1981—; instr. continuing edn. U. Mo., Kansas City, 1980-87, Ottawa U., Overland Park, Kans., 1990—; cons. Young Authors' Conf., Oakland U., Rochester, Mich.. 1971; coord. fine arts Alpha Phi Alpha Tutorial Project, Chesapeake, 1973-75; presenter Chpt. I Summer Inst., Tech. Assistance Ctr., Mo., 1984; cons. on parenting Reading Success Unltd., Gallatin, Mo., 1987—; mem. adv. bd. Parents & Children Together, Ind. U. Family Literacy Ctr., Bloomington, 1990-93; keynote speaker ann. conf. Nat. Coalition. Author: Dramatics for Self-Expression, 1967, Now Johnny CAN Learn to Read, 1987, Reading Songs and Poems of Joy, 1987. Mem. Internat. Reading Assn. (mem. coun., pres. local coun. 1986-88, state chmn. parents and reading com. 1988-89, mem. nat. parents and reading com. 1989-92, keynote speaker Conv. Inst. 1990, Literacy award 1989). Office: Reading SUCCESS Unltd PO Box 215 Gallatin MO 64640-0215

WILT, CATHERINE CHESSER, library network executive, librarian; b. Portsmouth, Va., Oct. 3, 1954; d. William Rock and Barbara (Harris) Chesser; m. Charles F. Wilt, July 7, 1979. BA, James Madison U., 1976; MLS, U. Pitts., 1977; EdM, Temple U., 1983. Cert. strategic planning Am. Mgmt. Assn. Audiovisual libr. Ursinus Coll., Collegeville, Pa., 1978-83, acting libr. dir., 1983-84, asst. dir., 1984-85; resource ctr. mgr. Drexel U., Phila., 1985-86; exec. coord. RONDAC, Columbus, Ohio, 1987-89; dir. AMIGOS Bibliographic Coun., Inc., Dallas, 1989—; chief investigator FLIS Libr. Cons., Dallas, 1990-91; grant reviewer U.S. Dept. Edn. Coll. Libr. Tech., 1992, 94; adj. faculty Tex. Woman's U., Denton, 1991, 94; judge N.J. Libr. Assn., Atlantic City, 1986. Author: book chpt.) Microcomputers in Libraries, 1986, Advances in Library Resource Sharing, 1990; producer, dir.: (video) ACRL President's Program, 1986; co-editor: Resource Sharing and Information Networks, Vol. 10, No. 1. Musician Madison Coll. Cmty. Orch., Harrisonburg, Va., 1972-76, North Pa. Symphony Orch., Hatfield, 1978-86, Knox County Symphony Orch., Gambier, Ohio, 1986-89, Mesquite (Tex.) Symphony Orch., 1989-93, North Dallas Symphony, 1993—. Mem. ALA, Am. Soc. Info. Sci., Assn. Libr. and Info. Sci. Educators, Assn. Edn. Comms. and Tech., Online Audiovisual Catalogers (charter mem.), Tri-State Coll. Libr. Coop., Sigma Alpha Iota, Alpha Beta Alpha. Home: 2905 Country Place Dr Plano TX 75075-2120 Office: AMIGOS Bibliographic Coun 12200 Park Central Dr Ste 500 Dallas TX 75251-2104

WILT, ELLEN, retired educator; b. Pitts., Apr. 13, 1921; d. James Greig and Ann (Kennedy) Bonar; m. Richard Wilt, Feb. 21, 1943 (dec. Jan. 1981); 1 child, Robin Christine. BFA, U. Mich., 1968, MA, 1970. Assoc. prof. art Ea. Mich. U., Ypsilanti, 1969-85, prof. emeritus, 1985—. Prin. works exhibited in numerous one-person shows including Xochipilli Gallery, Birmingham, Mich., 1994, Madonna U., Livonia, Mich., 1992, Bobbitt Ctr. Gallery Albion (Mich.) U., 1992, Ford Gallery Ea. Mich. U., 1986, Detroit Focus Gallery, 1985, Mott C.C. Fine Arts Gallery, Flint, Mich., 1995, others; prin. works represented in numerous pub. and pvt. collections including Blue Cross/Blue Shield, Detroit, Midland (Mich.) Arts Ctr., Northwood Inst., Midland, Delta Coll., University Center, Mich., U. Mich. Dental Sch., Ann Arbor, many others. Fellow Ossabaw Island Found., Ga., 1982, Atlantic Ctr. for Arts, Fla., 1986; recipient first prize Holland Area Arts Coun. Mich. Arts Competition, 1993, All Mich. All Media Krasl Art Ctr., St. Joseph, Mich., 1993, Mich. Water Color Soc. Dennos Art Mus., Traverse City, Mich., 1993, Purchase award Mich. Art Battle CreeknArt Ctr., 1992, Merit award Fine Arts Competition Ella Sharp Mus., Jackson, Mich., 1992, Annie award for Excellence in Two-Dimensional Visual Arts Washtenaw Arts Coun., 1992. Home and Studio: 1328 Broadway St Ann Arbor MI 48105-1810

WIMER, ALICE H., association executive; b. St. Paul, July 3, 1920; d. Otis Hickman and Alice Julia (Flinn) Godfrey; m. William E. Wimer III; children: Allan, William, Alice. BA, Macalester Coll., 1942; postgrad., Yale U., 1942-43. Exec. dir. Girl Scouts, Norristown, Pa., 1954-57, Harrisburg, Pa., 1957-63, Bergen County, N.J., 1963-69; exec. dir. YWCA of City of N.Y., 1969-72; civil and religious liberty specialist Presbyn Ch. U.S.A., N.Y.C., 1972-73; internat. affairs dir. Nat. Coun. Chs., N.Y.C., 1974-80; exec. dir. San Francisco Bay Girl Scouts, 1981-85; liaison World Coun. Chs. Internat. Affairs Commn., Geneva, Switzerland, 1974-80;mem. exec. com. U.S. Commn. for UNESCO, Washington, 1974-80; v.p. Christian Peace Conf., Prague, Czechoslovakia, 1980-88. Bd. dirs. Health and Welfare Coun., Bergen County, N.J., 1964-69, San Francisco Bay United Way, 1978, 79, 80. Recipient Disting. Citizen award Macalester Coll., 1971. Democrat. Mem. United Ch. of Christ. Home: 3 Seal Harbor Rd Apt 136 Winthrop MA 02152-1086

WIN, KHIN SWE, anesthesiologist; b. Rangoon, Burma, Sept. 27, 1934; came to U.S., 1962; d. U Mg and Daw Aye (Kyin) Maung; m. M. Shein Win, May 28, 1959; children: Tha Shein, Thwe Shein, Maw Shein, Thet Shein, Htoo Shein. Intermediate of Sci. Degree, U. Rangoon, 1954, MB, BS, 1962. Intern Waltham (Mass.) Hosp., 1962-63; resident anesthesiology Boston City Hosp., 1963-65; fellow pediatric anesthesiology New Eng. Med. Ctr. Hosps., Boston, 1965-66; fellow anesthesiology Martin Luther King Jr. Gen. Hosp., L.A., 1978-79; pvt. practice anesthesiology Apple Valley, Calif., 1984—; asst. prof. anesthesiology Martin Luther King Jr./Charles R. Drew Med. Ctr., L.A., 1979-84. Republican. Buddhist. Home: 13850 Pamlico Rd Apple Valley CA 92307-5400 Office: St Mary Desert Valley Hosp Dept Anesthesiology 18300 Us Highway 18 Apple Valley CA 92307-2206

WINANS, ANNA JANE, dietitian; b. Freeport, Ill., June 13, 1939; d. Leo Dale and Gwendolyn Jane White; m. Roger Eugene Winans, Aug. 26, 1967; children: Robert, Jonathan. BS in Dietetics, Iowa State U., 1962. Registered dietitian. Clin. dietitian VA Hosp., Madison, Wis., 1963-67; coord. U. Wis. Hosp., Madison, 1967-69; instr. nutrition Madison Gen. Hosp., 1969-75, Madison Area Coll., 1976-81; nutritionist Women, Infants and Children Nutrition Program, USDA, Fremont, Nebr., 1981—; nutrition cons. area health care facilities, Madison, 1976-81, Nebr., 1985—. Sec. Chapel Hill Pool Bd., Elkhorn, Nebr., 1987-89; bd. dirs. Homeowner's Assn., Elkhorn, 1989-93; active Elkhorn Woman's Club, 1982—; pres. Elkhorn Libr. Bd., 1989-91, 94. Mem. Am. Dietetic Assn. (registered), Nebr. Dietetic Assn., Omaha Dietetic Assn., PEO, Omicron Nu, Psi Chi. Methodist. Home: 910 S 218th St Elkhorn NE 68022-1938 Office: WIC 626 N D St Fremont NE 68025-5054

WINBY, MARY BERNADETTE, marketing executive; b. N.Y.C., Sept. 16, 1958; d. John Joseph and Theresa Eunice (Schoeffler) Vasile; m. Allan Gerard Winby, July 21, 1990. BSBA, St. John's U., Jamaica, N.Y., 1980. V.p. mktg. IBM Mid-Hudson Employees Fed. Credit Union, Kingston, N.Y., 1989-92; officer, dir. mktg. Mid-Hudson Savings Bank, FSB, 1992—; pres., owner Freelance Advt. Co., Poughkeepsie, N.Y., 1982-88; cons., tchr. in field. Office: Mid Hudson Savings and First Inter Bancorp Inc Corp Hdqs 1 Summit Ct Fishkill NY 12524-1334

WINCENC, CAROL, concertizing flutist, educator; b. Buffalo, June 29, 1949; d. Joseph and Margaret (Miller) Wincenc; m. Douglas Webster; 1 child, Nicola Wincenc-Webster. Grad., Santa Cecilia Acad., Rome, 1967, Chigiana Acad., Siena, Italy, 1968; MusB, Manhattan Sch. Music, N.Y.C., 1971; MusM, Juilliard Sch. Music, N.Y.C., 1972. Concertizing flutist recs. with Deutsche, Gramaphon, Nonesuch, New World, Music Masters, and Decca records; soloist with major symphony orchs.; artist faculty Juilliard Sch., 1988—. Bd. dirs., v.p. Chamber Music Am., N.Y.C., 1990-91, 91—. Recipient Naumburg award, 1978. Mem. Nat. Flute Assn. (life). Home: 875 W End Ave Apt 14E New York NY 10025-4954 Office: The Juilliard Sch Lincoln Ctr New York NY 10023

WINCHELL, MARGARET WEBSTER ST. CLAIR, realtor; b. Clinton, Tenn., Jan. 26, 1923; d. Robert Love and Mayme Jane (Warwick) Webster; student Denison U., 1940, Miami U., Oxford (Ohio), 1947, 48; m. Charles M. Winchell, June 7, 1941; children—David Alan (dec.), Margaret Winchell

Boyle; m. 2d, Robert George Sterrett, July 15, 1977 (dec. 1982). Saleswoman Fred K.A. Schmidt & Shirmer real estate, Cin., 1960-66, Cline Realtors, Cin., 1966-70; owner, broker Winchell's Showplace Realtors, Cin., 1972—; ins. agt. United Liberty Life Ins. Co., 1966—, dist. mgr., 1967-70, 77-82, regional mgr., 1982—; stockbroker Waddell & Reed, Columbus, Ohio, 1972—, Security Counselors; ins. broker, 1984, gen. agent; dir. Fin. Consultants, 1984, 85, 86, 87, owner; instr. evening coll. Treas., v.p. Parents without Partners, 1969, sec., 1968; pres. PTA; dir. Children's Bible Fellowship Ohio, 1953-76; dir. Child Evangelism Cin.; nat. speaker Child Evangelism Fellowship and Nat. Sunday Sch. Convs., 1955-57; pres. Christian Solos, 1974, Hamilton Fairfield Singles; chaplain Bethesda N. Hosp.; leader singles groups Hyde Park Community United Meth. Ch.; dir. Financial Cons., Sr. Ctr. Dance Leader and Coord. Mem. Nat. Assn. Real Estate Bds. West Shell Realtors (v.p.), Womens Council Real Estate Bd. (treas.). Clubs: Alfonta, Travel go go, Guys and Gals Singles (founder, 1st pres.), Hamilton Singles (pres.). Home and Office: 8221 Margaret Ln Cincinnati OH 45242-5309

WINCHESTER, ELIZABETH YOUNG, interior designer, consultant, space planner; b. Elgin, Ill., Dec. 7, 1934; m. Charles A. Winchester; 1 child, Susan. BA, Northwestern U., 1957; cert., N.Y. Sch. Interior Design, 1974; student Grad. Sch. Design, Harvard U., 1976. Exec. in fashion, cosmetics, design, promotion various orgns., N.Y.C., 1957-73; prin. Winchester Design, N.Y.C., 1974—. Mem. The Fashion Group, Inc., The Archtl. League. Club: Apawamis (Rye, N.Y.). Home and Office: Winchester Design 400 E 55th St New York NY 10022-5133

WINDLE, PAMELA EVELYN, surgical nurse; b. Dumaguete City, Negros, The Philippines, Aug. 3; came to U.S., 1975; d. Lorenzo Sr. and Mary (Kho) Yang; m. David A. Windle, Jan. 12, 1980; children: Cynthia Ann, Michael Adam. BSN, Silliman U., Dumaguete City, 1973; MS in Nursing Adminstrn., Tex. Womans U., 1991. Cert. nursing adminstrn., cert. post anesthesia nurse. Staff nurse, charge nurse to asst. head nurse med.-surg. ICU Med. Ctr. Hosp., Tyler, Tex., 1975-81; staff nurse, unit tchr., nurse mgr. cardiovascular recovery room to nurse mgr. post-anesthesia care unit St. Luke's Episcopal Hosp., Houston, 1981-91, nurse mgr. day/ambulatory surgery, post-anesthesia care unit, 1991—. Mem. AACN, Am. Post Anesthesia Nurses (mem. rsch. com. edn., provider com. 1994-95), Tex. Assn. Post Anesthesia Nurses (mem. membership com. 1994-95, mem. govtl. affairs com. 1994-95), Houston Gulf Coast Assn. Post Anesthesia Nurses (v.p. 1992, pres. 1993-94), Houston Orgn. Nurse Execs., Philippine Assn. Met. Houston (v.p. 1986, bd. dirs. 1994—), Sigma Theta Tau (TNA Dist. 9 award 1992). Roman Catholic. Home: 5421 Valerie St Bellaire TX 77401-4708 Office: St Lukes Episcopal Hospital PO Box 20269 Houston TX 77225-0269

WINDSOR, MARGARET EDEN, writer; b. Flemington, Mo., Aug. 10, 1917; d. John Denny and Rhoda Belle (Morgan) Head; m. Eugene B. Windsor, Jan. 10, 1987. Ret. med. technologist, 1982. Author: Murder in St. James, 1990; editor: From Pandora's Box, 1993. Cpl. USAF, 1944-45. Mem. Columbia Chpt. Mo. Writers Guild (v.p. 1989-90). Democrat. Roman Catholic. Home: 2404 Iris Dr Columbia MO 65202-1265

WINE-BANKS, JILL SUSAN, lawyer; b. Chgo., May 5, 1943; d. Bert S. and Sylvia Dawn (Simon) Wine; m. Ian David Volner, Aug. 21, 1965; m. Michael A. Banks, Jan. 12, 1980. BS, U. Ill.-Champaign-Urbana, 1964; JD, Columbia U., 1968; LLD (hon.), Hood Coll., 1975. Bar: N.Y. 1969, U.S. Ct. Appeals (4th cir.) 1969, U.S. Ct. Appeals (6th and 9th cirs.) 1973, U.S. Supreme Ct. 1974, D.C. 1976, Ill. 1980. Asst. press. and pub. rels. dir. Assembly of Captive European Nations, N.Y.C., 1965-66; trial atty. criminal div. organized crime and racketeering sect. and labor racketeering sect. U.S. Dept. Justice, 1969-73; asst. spl. prosecutor Watergate Spl. Prosecutor's Office, 1973-75; lectr. law seminar on trial practice Columbia U. Sch. Law, N.Y.C., 1975-77; assoc. Fried, Frank, Harris, Shriver & Kampelman, Washington, 1975-77; gen. counsel Dept. Army, Pentagon, Washington, 1977-79; ptnr. Jenner & Block, Chgo., 1980-84; solicitor gen. State of Ill. Office of Atty. Gen., 1984-86, dep. atty. gen., 1986-87; exec. v.p., chief oper. officer ABA, Chgo., 1987-90; pvt. practice law, 1990-92; bd. dirs. Cenvill Devel. Corp., 1991-92; v.p. Motorola Wireless Network Ventures Ltd. and sr. mgr. bus. devel. Network Ventures Divsn., Motorola, 1992—; mem. EEC disting. vis. program European Parliament, 1987; bd. dirs. Cenvill Devel. Corp., 1991-92; mem. bd. assocs. program for the study of cultural values & ethics U. Ill. Recipient Spl. Achievement award U.S. Dept. Justice, 1972, Meritorious award, 1973, Cert. Outstanding Svc., 1975; decoration for Disting. Civilian Svc., Dept. Army, 1979; named Disting. Visitor to European Econ. Community. Mem. Internat. Women's Forum, The Chgo. Network, Econ. Club. Address: 425 N Martingdale Rd 18th fl Schaumburg IL 60173

WINEBRENNER, BETH ANN, social worker, college student affairs specialist; b. South Bend, Ind., Feb. 25, 1950; d. Jack Joseph and Marina Louise (Hudson) W.; m. Louis Attila Pierre Balázs, May 27, 1984. BS, Ball State U., 1972; MSW, Ind. U., Indpls., 1978; MS, Purdue U., 1991. Cert. clin. social worker; lic. sch. social worker. Case worker Clay County Dept. Pub. Welfare, Brazil, Ind., 1973, Monroe County Dept. Pub. Welfare, Bloomington, Ind., 1973-76; med. social worker Bloomington Hosp., 1978-79; assessment counselor Employment Devel. Systems, Inc., Frankfort, Ind., 1979-88; fin. planner Waddell & Reed, Inc., Lafayette, Ind., 1988-90; case worker Family Svcs. Inc., Lafayette, Ind., 1989-90; med. social worker Vis. Nurse Home Health Svc., Lafayette area, 1992; spl. asst. to dir. internat. student svcs. Purdue U., West Lafayette, Ind., 1992-93; program mgr./psychotherapist partial hospitalization program Charter Hosp. Lafayette, 1993—; tchr. Hong Kong Coll. Langs., Kowloon, summer 1977; asst. to v.p. Ind. Hosp. Assn., Indpls., summer 1978. Chmn. Com. Human Rights in USSR of Greater Lafayette, 1982-91; mem. Speaker's Corps Mayor's Commn. on Status of Women, Columbus, Ind., 1972, Internat. Awareness Task Force Greater Lafayette, 1991. Mem. ACA, NASW (student rep. to state bd. 1977), Assn. Specialists in Group Work, Am. Coll. Counseling Assn., Acad. Cert. Social Workers, Pi Gamma Mu, Kappa Delta Pi. Democrat. Roman Catholic. Home: 218 Trace 2 West Lafayette IN 47906-1869

WINEGARDNER, ROSE MARY, special education educator; b. Granite City, Ill., Feb. 4, 1933; d. Arthur Udell and Margaret Helen (Brown) Barco; m. Carl Norman Winegardner, July 23, 1954; children: Laura Helen, Thelma Rose Winegardner Czajkowski, Jacob Harrison. BS in Edn., Mo. U., Columbia, 1954; MA in Ednl. Adminstrn., Wyo. U., 1977; edn. specialist, Nebr. U., 1988. Cert. tchr., Nebr., Iowa, Mo. Tchr. Elem. Sch. Grandview & Belton, Mo., 1957-64; tchr. mid. sch. Schleswig (Iowa) Community Schs., 1978-82; spl. edn. resource tchr. Ednl. Svc. Unit #4, Auburn, Nebr., 1982-94, Kans. U. Inst. Rsch. Learning Disabilities strategy implementation model trainer, 1989—; spl. edn. resource tchr. Dawson-Verdon Consol. Schs., 1990—. Grantee Nebr. Dept. Edn., 1990-93. Mem. Internat. Reading Assn., Coun. for Exceptional Children (v.p. S.E. Nebr. chpt. 1990-92, pres. 1992-94, 94—), DAR, Phi Delta Kappa. Lutheran. Home: 2100 23d St Auburn NE 68305

WINFIELD, NOVALYN L., federal bankruptcy judge; b. 1950. BA, Coll. St. Elizabeth; JD, N.Y. Law Sch. Bar: N.J. 1981. Bankruptcy judge U.S. Dist. Ct. N.J., Newark. Office: US Bankruptcy Court Martin Luther King Jr Fed Bldg 50 Walnut St Newark NJ 07102*

WINFIELD, SUSAN REBECCA, judge; b. East Orange, N.J., June 13, 1948; children: Jessica, Heather. BA in Math., U. Pa., 1970; JD, Boston Coll., 1976. Assoc. atty. Law Office of Salim Shakur, Boston, 1976-77; staff atty. U.S. Dept. of Justice, Washington, 1978-79; asst. U.S. atty. U.S. Atty.'s Office, Washington, 1979-84; assoc. judge D.C. Superior Ct., 1984—; chair Benchbook Com., Washington, 1991—, Amenities & Misfortune Com., Washington, 1992—, Family Divsn. Rules Com., Washington, 1993—, Justice Systems Coord. Com., Washington, 1993—. Boston Coll. scholar, 1973-76; recipient letter of commendation Met. Police Dept., Washington, 1981. Mem. District of Columbia Bar, Bar Assn. D.C., Washington Bar Assn., Women's Bar Assn. Office: DC Superior Ct 500 Indiana Ave NW Washington DC 20001

WINFREY, DIANA LEE, lawyer; b. Kansas City, Mo., July 17, 1955; d. James William and Louise Augusta (Harrison) W. BA in Spanish, U. Mo., 1978, JD, 1984. Bar: Mo. 1984, Calif. 1985. Tchr. Pan-Am. Workshop, Mexico City, 1979; law clk. Mo. Ct. of Appeals, Kansas City, 1984-85; assoc. Early, Maslach, Leavy & Nutt, L.A., 1985-87, Wilson, Elser, et al, L.A., 1987-88, Wood, Lucksinger & Epstein, L.A., 1988-90, Coony & Bihr, Beverly Hills, Calif., 1990—. Asst. editor The Urban Lawyer Jour., 1983-84. Member Heal the Bay, Santa Monica, Calif., 1991—. Recipient Outstanding Achievement and Svc. award U. Mo., 1978. Mem. ABA, Calif. Bar Assn., Mo. Bar Assn., L.A. County Bar Assn., Beverly Hills Bar Assn., Am. Bd. Trial Attys., Inns of Ct. Democrat. Office: 21112 Ventura Blvd Woodland Hills CA 91364

WINFREY, OPRAH, television talk show host, actress, producer; b. Kosciusko, Miss., Jan. 29, 1954; d. Vernon Winfrey and Vernita Lee. BA in Speech and Drama, Tenn. State U. News reporter Sta. WVOL Radio, Nashville, 1971-72; reporter, news anchorperson Sta. WTVF-TV, Nashville, 1973-76; news anchorperson Sta. WJZ-TV, Balt., 1976-77, host morning talk show People Are Talking, 1977-83; host talk show A.M. Chgo. Sta. WLS-TV, 1984; host The Oprah Winfrey Show, Chgo., 1985—; nationally syndicated, 1986—; host series of celebrity interview spls. Oprah: Behind the Scenes, 1992—; owner, prodr. Harpo Prodns., 1986—. Appeared in films The Color Purple, 1985 (nominated Acad. award and Golden Globe award), Native Son, 1986, Throw Momma From the Train, 1988, Listen Up: The Lives of Quincy Jones, 1990; prodr., actress ABC-TV mini-series The Women of Brewster Place, 1989, also series Brewster Place, 1990, movie There Are No Children Here, 1993; exec. prodr. (ABC Movie of the Week) Overexposed, 1992; host, supervising prodr. celebrity interview series Oprah: Behind the Scenes, 1992, ABC Aftersch. Spls., 1991-93; host, exec. prodr. Michael Jackson Talks...to Oprah-90 Prime-Time Minutes with the King of Pop, 1993. Recipient Woman of Achievement award NOW, 1986, Emmy award for Best Daytime Talk Show Host, 1987, 91, 92, America's Hope award, 1990, Industry Achievement award Broadcast Promotion Mktg. Execs./Broadcast Design Assn., 1991, Image awards NAACP, 1989, 90, 91, 92, Entertainer of Yr. award NAACP, 1989, CEBA awards, 1989, 90, 91; named Broadcaster of Yr. Internat. Radio and TV Soc., 1988. Office: Harpo Prodns 110 N Carpenter St Chicago IL 60607-2101*

WING, ADRIEN KATHERINE, law educator; b. Oceanside, Calif., Aug. 7, 1956; d. John Ellison and Katherine (Pruitt) Wing; children: Che-Cabral, Nolan Felipe. A.B. magna cum laude, Princeton U., 1978; M.A., UCLA, 1979; J.D., Stanford Law Sch., 1982. Bar: N.Y. 1983, U.S. Dist. Ct. (so. and ea. dists.) N.Y. 1983, U.S. Ct. Appeals (5th and 9th cirs.). Assoc. Curtis, Mallet-Prevost, Colt & Mosle, N.Y.C., 1982-86, Rabinowitz, Boudin, Standard, Krinsky & Lieberman, 1986-87; assoc. prof. law U. Iowa, Iowa City, 1987-93, prof. law, 1993—; mem. alumni council Princeton U., 1983-85, trustee Class of '78 Alumni Found., 1984-87, v.p. Princeton Class of 1978 Alumni, 1993—; mem. bd. visitors Stanford Law Sch., 1993—. Mem. bd. editors Am. Jour. Comp. Law, 1993—. Mem. ABA (exec. com. young lawyers sect. 1985—), Nat. Conf. Black Lawyers (UN rep., chmn. internat. affairs sect. 1982—), Internat. Assn. Dem. Lawyers (UN rep. 1984-87), Am. Soc. Internat. Law (exec. council 1986-89, group chair So. Africa nom. com. 1993—), Black Alumni of Princeton U. (bd. dirs. 1982-87), Transafrica Scholars Forum Coun. (bd. dirs 1993—), Iowa City Foreign Rels. Coun. (bd. dirs. 1989-94), Iowa Peace Inst. (bd. dirs. 1993-95), Council on Fgn. Relations. Democrat. Avocations: photography, jogging, writing, poetry. Office: U Iowa Sch Law Boyd Law Bldg Iowa City IA 52242

WING, ELIZABETH SCHWARZ, museum curator, educator; b. Cambridge, Mass., Mar. 5, 1932; d. Henry F. and Maria Lisa (Gutherz) (dec.) Schwarz; m. James E. Wing, Apr. 18, 1957; children: Mary Elizabeth Wing-Berman, Stephen R. BA, Mt. Holyoke Coll., 1955; MS, U. Fla., 1957, PhD, 1962. Interim asst. curator Fla. Mus. Natural History, U. Fla., Gainesville, 1961-69, asst. curator, 1969-73, assoc. curator, 1973-78, curator, 1978—; chmn. dept. anthropology U. Fla., Fla. Mus. Natural History, Gainesville, 1990-92; U.S. rep. Internat. Congress Archaeozoology, 1981—. Author: (with A.B. Brown) Paleonutrition, 1979; editor (with J.C. Wheeler) Economic Prehistory of the Central Andes, 1988; contbr. articles to profl. jours. NSF grantee, 1961-64, 68-70, 70-73, 79-80, 84-85, 89-91. Mem. Soc. Ethnobiology (pres. 1989-91, trustee 1991—). Office: U Fla Fla Mus Natural History PO Box 177800 Museum Rd Gainesville FL 32611-7800

WINGATE, BETTYE FAYE, librarian, educator; b. Hillsboro, Tex., Oct. 31, 1950; d. Warren Randolph and Faye (Gilmore) W. BA summa cum laude, Baylor U., 1971, MA, 1975; MLS, Tex. Womans U., 1985. Cert. prov. sec., learning resources endorsement. English tchr. Mexia (Tex.) High Sch.; reading tchr. Connally Ind. Sch. Dist., Waco, Tex.; reading tchr., libr. Grapevine-Colleyville Ind. Sch. Dist., Grapevine, Tex.; libr. Crockett Jr. High Sch., Irving, Tex.; mem. librs. coms., Campus Action Planning Com., 1989-93, Irving Ind. Sch. Dist. Site Based Decision-Making Com., 1992-94, mem. staff devel. com., 1994—; speaker, presenter in field. Founding sponsor Challenger Ctr. Recipient Tex. Media awards, 1988, 89, 94. Mem. ALA, NEA, Am. Assn. Sch. Librs., Tex. State Tchrs. Assn. (assn. rep.), Tex. Libr. Assn. (chmn. state media awards com. 1989-91), Tex. Assn. Edn. Tech., Tex. Computer Edn. and Tech., Assn. Ednl. Comm. and Tech., Planetary Soc., Nat. Space Soc., Nat. Parks & Conservation Assn., Baylor Alumni Assn. (life), Beta Phi Mu, Delta Kappa Gamma (scholar 1985).

WINGATE, LEAH ANNE ACKLEY, information systems specialist; b. Winter Haven, Fla., Jan. 13, 1955; d. David G. Ackley and Nancy M. (McMullen) Ackley Cramer; m. William L. Wingate, Dec. 2, 1979 (div. Sept. 1985); children: Brianne Leigh, William Bradley. Degree in liberal arts, Polk C.C., Winter Haven, 1991. Publs. editor State Farm Ins. Co., Winter Haven, 1973-78; office mgr. Wingate Electric, Inc., Auburndale, Fla., 1978-81; mktg. specialist SunBank, Winter Haven, 1985-89; info. sys. specialist Summit Consulting, Inc., Lakeland, 1989—; pres., CEO Dixie Homes, Inc., Auburndale, 1991—, Biltmore-Fla., Inc., Auburndale, 1991—. Mem. Ctrl. Fla. Computer Users (newsletter editor 1993—), Phi Theta Kappa. Republican. Home: 604 E Derby Ave Auburndale FL 33823

WINGER, DEBRA, actress; b. Cleve., 1955; d. Robert and Ruth W.; m. Timothy Hutton, March 16, 1986 (div.); 1 child, Emanuel Noah. Student, Calif. State U., Northridge. Made 1st profl. appearance in Wonder Woman TV series, 1976-77; appeared TV film Spl. Olympics, 1977; appeared in films Thank God It's Friday, 1978, French Postcards, 1979, Urban Cowboy, 1980, Cannery Row, 1982, An Officer and a Gentleman, 1982, Terms of Endearment, 1983, Mike's Murder, 1984, Legal Eagles, 1986, Black Widow, 1987, Made in Heaven, 1987, Betrayed, 1988, Everybody Wins, 1990, The Sheltering Sky, 1990, Leap of Faith, 1992, Wilder Napalm, 1992, Shadowlands, 1993 (Academy award nominee, Best Actress, 1993), A Dangerous Woman, 1993. Office: care John West PMK Pub Rels Inc 955 S Carrillo Dr # 200 Los Angeles CA 90048*

WINGERT, HANNELORE CHRISTIANE, real estate sales executive, chemical company executive; b. Karlsbad, Czechoslavakia; came to U.S., 1962, naturalized, 1967; d. Andreas and Gisela Maria (Ciharz) Zwickel; m. Rudolf Wingert, Feb. 9, 1963; children: Angela Helene, Christopher Rudolf. I.B.A., Stadt. Berufsschule, Fed. Republic Germany, 1961; postgrad. in mgmt., Bergen Community Coll., 1983. Lic. real estate, N.J. Clk. various cos., N.J., 1963, bilingual sec., 1963-78; exec. sec., adminstrv. asst. Lurgi Corp., Hasbrouck Heights, N.J., 1978-81; sr. exec. sec. Degussa Corp., Teterboro, N.J., 1981-83, asst. product mgr. silica, 1983-85, asst. product mgr. H202, 1985-87, sales promotion coord., 1987; sales assoc. Schlott Realtors, Kinnelon, N.J., 1987—. Author real estate newsletter, 1992—, community newsletter, 1977-79. Mem. Bd. Realtors Morris and Passaic (N.J.) Counties; chmn. master planning com. High Crest Lake, West Milford, N.J., 1974-75; advisor Jr. Woman's Club Kinnelon-Butler (N.J.), 1973-74; tchr. computer classes Bd. Realtors, Passaic County, 1989-92. Mem. N.J. Fed. of Woman's Clubs (past pres.), High Crest Lake Woman's Club (pres. 1972-73) (West Milford, N.J.). Republican. Roman Catholic. Home: 204 High Crest Dr West Milford NJ 07480-3710 Office: Caldwell Banker Schlott Kinnelon 1450 State Route 23 Butler NJ 07405-1624

WINGFIELD, LAURA ALLISON ROSS, fraternal organization executive; b. Kansas City, Mo., June 8, 1954; d. John Joseph and Jean Marie Ross; m. Wesley Hughes Wingfield, May 13, 1989. BFA, William Woods Coll., 1972-76. Div. chmn. Beta Sigma Phi Sorority div. Walter W. Ross and Co., Inc., Kansas City, 1979-80, dir. rushing, v.p. and asst. dir. service, 1986—; dir. svc., 1991—. Pub. chmn. Kansas City Am. Diabetes Assn., 1985-87, pres., 1986-87; bd. dirs., mem. exec. com. Heart of Am. affiliate, 1986-87, sec. state bd., chmn. pub. rels. com. Mo. state affiliate, 1993-94, bd. dirs. Kansas City chpt., 1993 pub. chmn. Walk fest; reading tutor Project Literacy, 1986, Penn Valley C.C. Republican. Office: 1800 W 91st Pl Kansas City MO 64114-3243

WINGO, MARIAN LEE, counselor, therapist; b. Asheville, N.C., Sept. 16, 1944; d. Hugh Albert and Lee Ardis (English) W.; m. Harry C. Davis, Aug. 28, 1966 (div. Sept. 1988); children: Remi, Wade; ptnr. Chris Vinsonhaler, Jan. 22, 1994. BS, Fla. State U., 1966; MS, George Peabody Coll., 1978. Nat. cert. counselor. Owner, dir., trainer, cons. Marian Wingo & Assocs., Ocean Springs, Miss., 1983—; co-owner, dir. Family Counselors Affiliated, Ocean Springs, 1987—; agt./mgr. Chris Vinsonhaler, Ocean Springs. Author: Skills for Rich Living, 1980; columnist Gulf Coast Papers We Are Family. Recipient Outstanding Citizen award Bus. and Profl. Women, San Antonio, 1981, Profl. Devel. Leadership award ASTD, Alexandria, Va., 1984; Today's Woman selectee San Antonio Light, 1980; named Gulf Coast Woman of Achievement, AAUW/Mississippi Gulf Coast C.C., 1991. Mem. AAUW, Assn. Women in Psychology (archivist), Nat. Feminist Therapist Inst. Democrat. Methodist. Office: Family Counselors Affiliated 998 Robinson Ocean Springs MS 39564-4621

WINIGRAD, ETTA, sculptor, company executive; b. Lansdowne, Pa., July 25, 1936; d. Herman and Lee (Vernekoff) Zuritsky; m. Allen J. Winigrad, June 25, 1960; children: Michael A., David J., Jacob S., Daniel J. B Applied Arts, U. Pa., 1958; postgrad., Moore Coll., 1968-76, Phila. Mus. Art, 1968-76. One-woman shows Jewish Cmty. Ctr. So. N.J., Cherry Hill, 1976, Muse Gallery, Phila., 1992, 94; 2-person show Meml. Hosp., Mt. Holly, N.J., 1994; exhibited in numerous group shows including Mus. Am. Jewish History, Phila., 1981, 83, Muse Gallery, 1990, 92, 94, Nat. Mus. Ceramic Art, Balt., 1991, Wayne (Pa.) Art Ctr., 1992, 93, James A. Michener Art Mus., Doylestown, Pa., 1994; represented in permanent collections Holocaust Ctr. Kean Coll., N.J., pvt. collections; commd. Holocaust Meml. competition Jewish Fedn. Ctrl. N.J., 1981. Treas. Muse Gallery and Found., 1990—. Recipient hon. mention Jewish Y's and Ctrs., Phila., 1975, award Phila. Coll. Art, 1982; Best of Show award Abington Art Ctr., 1992, Richard Guggenheim award 1993; merit award Ctrl. Pa. Festival of Arts, 1994. Mem. Am. Crafts Coun., Internat. Sculpture Ctr., Woman's Caucus for Arts. Home: 159 N Mansfield Blvd Cherry Hill NJ 08034 Office: Parkway Corp 150 N Broad St Philadelphia PA 19102

WINIKOFF, BEVERLY, physician; b. N.Y.C., Aug. 26, 1945; d. Harry and Blanche (Tepper) W.; m. Michael Charles Alpert, July 15, 1973; children: Hilary Winikoff A., Lindsay Winikoff A. AB magna cum laude, Harvard U., 1966; MD, NYU, 1971; MPH, Harvard U., 1973, rsch. fellow Sch. Pub. Health, 1973-74. Diplomate Nat. Bd. Med. Examiners. Tchr. history, social studies Escola Americana do Rio de Janeiro, 1966-67; intern in mixed medicine Gen. Rose Meml. Hosp., Denver, 1971-72; physician East Side Neighborhood Health Ctr. Denver Dept. Health, 1972, Boston Evening Clinic, 1973-74; med. writer ambulatory care project Beth Israel Hosp., Boston, 1973-74; asst. dir. health scis. Rockefeller Found., N.Y.C., 1974-78; med. assoc. The Population Coun., N.Y.C., 1978-82, sr. med assoc., 1982—; cons. Congl. Office Tech. Assessment, 1976-77, 78, Senate Select Com. Nutrition and Human Needs, 1976-77, Internat. Vitamin A Consultative Group, 1977, Internat. Nutritional Anemia Consultative Group, 1978—, Nat. Inst. Aging Consultancy, 1977-78, NAS, 1978, 78-79, Rockefeller Found., 1978; lectr. to numerous profl. groups. Co-author, editor: Nutrition and National Policy, 1978, Feeding Infants in Four Societies: Causes and Consequences of Mothers' Choices, 1988, (with S. Wymelenberg) The Contraceptive Handbook, 1992; guest editor spl. issue Social Sci. and Medicine, 1980; editor spl. issue Studies in Family Planning, 1981, mem. editorial bd., 1978—; contbr. articles to profl. jours., chpts. to books. Mem. White House Spl. Task Force on Internat. Health, 1977, Mayor's Emergency Med. Svcs. Adv. Com., 1978—, Steering Com. to Promote Breastfeeding in N.Y.C. Office Pub. Health, N.Y. State Health Dept., 1982—. Recipient scholarships Radcliffe Coll., 1962-66, GM, NYU, 1967; fellowship USPHS, 1970. Mem. Harvard U. Sch. Pub. Health Alumni Assn. (councillor 1983-85, pres. 1989-91), Harvard U. Alumni Assn. (bd. dirs. 1991—). Office: Population Coun 1 Dag Hammarskjold Plz New York NY 10017-2201

WINK, DOREEN MUSTO, interior designer; b. Rochester, N.Y., Oct. 18; d. Nunzio Edward and Ann (Iaculli) Musto; m. Douglas L. Wink; 1 stepdaughter, Melissa Lynn; 1 child, Douglas III. AAS in Psychology cum laude, Monroe C.C., 1973; BSW cum laude, SUNY, Brockport, 1975. Social worker, dir. mental health Cobbs Hill Nursing Home, Rochester, N.Y., 1975-78; social worker Rochester, N.Y., 1980-89; interior designer for retail stores Washington, 1989-91; CEO Three-D-Wink Inc., Washington, 1991—. Mem. Peerless Rockville (Md.) Hist. Soc.; judge, mem. 4-H Orgn., 1985—; vol. White House, Washington, 1994—; head art dept. Young Reps. Club, Rochester, 1964-69; organizer, pres. Rockshire New Comers Club, Rockville, Md.; active nat., local politics; co-chmn. Rockshire Arch. Com. Named Most Popular High Schooler in City of Rochester, Times Union Newspaper, 1964. Mem. NOW, Nat. Trust for Hist. Preservation, White House Hist. Soc., Decorative Arts Trust (cons.), Nat. Mus. of Women in the Arts (charter), Tex. State Soc. (inaugural ball com. 1985-94), Nat. Italian Found., Smithsonian Instn., Md. Design, Space Planning and Props Soc. (dir., founder). Office: 2205 Newton Dr Ste 201 Rockville MD 20850

WINK, JUDITH ELAINE, systems accountant; b. Lakewood-Bellflower, Calif., Mar. 30, 1948; d. Wilbur Henry and Doris Maxine (English) W. AA in Data Processing, American River Coll., Sacramento, 1968, Cert. in Acctg, 1970; MS, U. No. Colo., Greeley, 1982. Acct. Acctg. and Fin., McClellan AFB, Calif., 1968-77; chief quality control sect. Morale, Welfare and Recreation Div. Acctg., Lowry AFB, Colo., 1977-79; auditor Air Force Audit Agy., Lowry AFB, 1979-80; acct. Air Force Acctg. and Fin. Ctr., Lowry AFB, 1980-89; fin. mgmt. officer Morale, Welfare & Recreation Div. Lindsey AS, Wiesbaden, Germany, 1989-90; acct. Air Force Acctg. and Fin. Ctr. Def. Fin. and Acctg. Svc., Security Assistance Acctg. Ctr., Denver, 1990—. Sunday sch. tchr., publicist, mem. choir Christ Community Ch., Carmichael, Calif., 1965-77; mem. choir Faith Community Ctr., Littleton, Colo., 1977-81, South Evan Presbyn. Ch., Denver, 1981-85. Recipient Presdl. Citation, 1981. Mem. Am. Soc. Mil. Comptrollers (photographer 1982-88), Assn. Govt. Accts., Assoc. Photographers Internat. Mem. Reformed Ch. in Am. Home: 4310 S Alkire Ct Morrison CO 80465-1112

WINKLE, SHARON LOUISE, library administrator; b. Cin., Nov. 29, 1950; d. John F. and Marguerite T. (Platt) W.; m. Clifford J. Smith, June 16, 1979. BS, Findlay Coll., 1972; MLS, U. Ky., 1973; MPA, U. Denver, 1984. Libr. Findlay (Ohio)-Hancock County Pub. Libr., 1973-74; deputy dir. Sandusky (Ohio) Libr., 1974-76, dir., 1976-79; libr. dir. Englewood (Colo.) Pub. Libr., 1979-89; dir. libr. and recreation svcs. City of Englewood, 1989-90; libr. dir. Mead Pub. Libr., Sheboygan, Wis., 1991—. Ohio State U. scholar, 1972; named Mktg. Student of Yr., Findlay Coll., 1972, Outstanding MPA Student U. Denver, 1984, Woman of Yr. Englewood Bus and Profl. Women, 1989. Mem. ALA, Wis. Libr. Assn., Sheboygan Rotary, Altrusa Club Sheboygan, Sheboygan C. of C. Home: 1810 N 5th St Sheboygan WI 53081-2840 Office: Mead Pub Library 710 N 8th St Sheboygan WI 53081-4505

WINKLER, AGNIESZKA M., advertising agency executive; b. Rome, Italy, Feb. 22, 1946; came to U.S., 1953, naturalized, 1959; d. Wojciech A. and Halina Z. (Owsiany) W.; children from previous marriage: children: Renata G. Ritcheson, Dana C Sworakowski.; m. Arthur K. Lund. BA, Coll. Holy Name, 1967; MA, San Jose State U., 1971; MBA, U. Santa Clara, 1981. Teaching asst., San Jose State U., 1968-70; cons. to ea. European bus., Palo Alto, Calif., 1970-72; pres./founder Commart Communications, Palo Alto, 1973-84; pres./founder, chmn. bd. Winkler McManus, Santa Clara, Calif., 1984—; bd. dirs. Supercuts, Inc., Reno Air. Trustee Santa Clara U., 1991—; trustee O'Connor Found., 1987-93, mem. exec. com., 1988—, mem. Capital Campaign steering com., 1989; mem. nat. adv. bd. Comprehensive Health Enhancement Support System, 1991—; mem. mgmt. west com. A.A.A.A. Agy., 1991—; project dir. Poland Free Enterprise Plan, 1989-92; mem. adv. bd. Normandy France Bus. Devel., 1989-92; mem. bd. regents Holy Names Coll., 1987—; bd. dirs. San Jose Mus. Art, 1987; mem. San Jose Symphony, Gold Baton, 1986; mem. nat. adv. com. CHESS, 1991—; dir. Bay Area Coun., 1994—. Recipient CLIO award in Advt., Addy award and numerous others; named to 100 Best Women in Advt., Ad Age, 1988, Best Woman in Advt., AdWeek and McCall's Mag., 1993. Mem. Family Svc. Assn. (trustee 1980-82), Am. Assn. Advt. Agys. (agy. mgmt. west com. 1991), Bus. Profl. Advt. Assn., Polish Am. Congress, San Jose Advt. Club, San Francisco Ad Club, Beta Gamma Sigma (hon.), Pi Gamma Mu, Pi Delta Phi (Lester-Tinneman award 1966, Bill Raskob Found. grantee 1965). Office: Winkler McManus 150 Spear St 16th Fl San Francisco CA 94105-1535

WINKLER, DOLORES EUGENIA, hospital administrator; b. Milw., Aug. 10, 1929; d. Charles Peter and Eugenia Anne (Zamka) Kowalski; m. Donald James Winkler, Aug. 18, 1951; 1 child, David John. Grad., Milw. Bus. Inst., 1949. Acct. Curative Rehab. Ctr., Milw., 1949-60; staff acct. West Allis (Wis.) Meml. Hosp., 1968-70, chief acct., 1970-78, reimbursement analyst, 1978-85, dir. budgets and reimbursement, 1985—; mem. adv. coun./fin. com. Tau Home Health Care Agy., Milw., 1981-83. Mem. Healthcare Fin. Mgmt. Assn. (pres. 1989-90, Follmer Bronze award 1980, Reeves Silver award 1986, Muncie Gold award 1989, medal of honor 1993), Inst. Mgmt. Accts. (pres. 1983-84, nat. dir. 1986-88, pres. Mid Am. Regional Coun. 1988-89, award of excellence 1989), Beta Chi Rho (pres. 1948). Home: 12805 W Honey Ln New Berlin WI 53151-2652 Office: West Allis Meml Hosp 8901 W Lincoln Ave West Allis WI 53227-2477

WINKLER, KATHERINE MAURINE, management consultant, educator; b. Louisville, Nov. 29, 1940; d. Myrick and Maurine (Holland) W. Cert. in foreign studies, Inst. for Am. Univs., 1961; BA, Transylvania U., 1963. Market rsch. field supr. Procter & Gamble, Cin., 1963-65; Eng. tchr. Louisville Ky. Sch. System, 1967-68; mgmt. and staff positions in sales, mktg., human resources, total quality mgmt. and edn. IBM, Louisville, Lexington, Ky., Mpls. and Westchester, N.Y., 1968-93; pvt. practice Scarsdale, N.Y., 1993—; adj. prof. NYU. Author: Leadership, 1982; contbr. articles to The Westchester Historian. Com. mem. Mpls. Cultural Affairs Com., 1970; com. mem. Village of Tarrytown (N.Y.) Main St. com., 1981-82; trustee, exec. com. mem. Westchester County Hist. Soc., Elmsford, N.Y., 1989—. Named Outstanding Young Woman of Am., 1972. Mem. ASTD, Am. Soc. Quality Control, Ky. Col., Assn. for Quality and Participation, Soc. for Human Resource Mgmt. Home: 74 Drake Rd Scarsdale NY 10583-6447

WINKLER, MARGARET A., geriatrics nurse, nursing administrator; b. Mo., June 6, 1957; d. John Harvey and Mary Ann (Honigfort) Stark; m. Karl H. Winkler, Mar. 25, 1979; children: Karyl, Kim, Karl. Diploma, Deaconess Hosp., 1978. RN, Mo.; cert. gerontol. nurse; lic. nursing home adminstr. Asst. dir. nursing Masonic Home, St. Louis, 1984-86; dir. nursing Grand Manor, St. Louis, 1986-88; dir. nursing, asst. adminstr. Gravois Health Care, St. Louis, 1988-90; asst. dir. nursing Sherbrook Village, St. Louis, 1990; adminstr. South County Manor, Arnold, Mo., 1990-91, St. Louis Hills Retirement Ctr., St. Louis, 1991-93, Birchway Health Care, St. Louis, 1993—. Mem. Mo. Assn. Dirs. Nursing Adminstrn. (past pres., founding mem.), Long Term Care Dirs. Nursing Assn. St. Louis (past pres.), Nat. Assn. Dirs. Nursing Adminstrn. (founding mem.).

WINLAND, DENISE LYNN, physician; b. Elizabeth, N.J., Aug. 9, 1951; d. James Edward and Audrey Anna (Hansen) W.; m. Charles F. Francke III, May 30, 1982; children: Shannon W. Francke, Eric W. Francke. BS with honors, Rutgers U., 1973; M in Phys. Therapy with honors, Baylor U., 1975; MD, U. Louisville, 1982. Phys. therapist Vis. Nurse Assn., Louisville, 1977; resident in psychiatry U. Louisville, 1982-83, 90-93, staff physician student health svc., 1983-89; resident Frazier Rehab. Ctr., Louisville, 1989-90; pvt. practice psychiatry Louisville, 1993—; emergency room physician North Clark Community Hosp., Charlestown, Ind., 1983-87; physician Immediate Care Ctrs., Louisville, 1983-86. With U.S. Army, 1974-77, maj. Res., 1977—. Teagle Found. scholar, 1978-82; named Outstanding Young Women Am., 1983, 84. Mem. AMA, APA, Ky. Psychiat. Assn., Ky. Med. Assn., Jefferson County Med. Assn., Res. Officers Assn., Am. Med. Women's Assn. Democrat. Mem. Unity Christian Ch. Home: 1103 Holly Springs Dr Louisville KY 40242 Office: 2120 Newburg Rd Louisville KY 40205

WINN, JANICE GAIL, food products administrator; b. Springfield, Mass., Nov. 2, 1954; d. John Thomas and Rose Eleanor (Draskawich) W. BA, Western New Eng. Coll., 1976. Gen. mdse. mgr. Mott's Shop-Rite, East Hartford, Conn., 1979-84; sr. merchandiser Imperial Distbrs., Auburn, Mass., 1984-85; dir. of gen. mdse. Waldbaums Food Mart, Holyoke, Mass., 1985-91; dir. health, beauty care and gen. mdse. Big Y Foods, Inc., Springfield, 1991—. Republican. Office: Big Y Foods Inc 280 Chestnut St Springfield MA 01104-3456

WINN, JILL KANAGA KLINE, management executive; b. Oakland, Calif., Jan. 20, 1944; d. Lawrence Wesley and Virginia Louise (Honold) Kanaga; m. Donald Gene Kline, May 30, 1964 (div. 1979); children: Christian Lawrence, Kirsten Michael. Student, Northwestern U., 1961-63, Stella Adler Theater Studio, N.Y.C., 1963-64, Columbia Coll., Chgo., 1970-71. Comml. actress N.Y.C., 1964-77; v.p. Mid-Continent Agys., Inc., Glenview, Ill., 1980-92, mgr. accouts receivable portfolio program, 1983-92, cons., 1985-92, v.p. ednl. svcs., 1987-92, dir. seminars, 1987-92; dir. mktg. S.E. Collection Co., Glenview, Ill., 1992-93; founder, mng. mem. Vivendi, L.L.C., Northbrook, Ill., 1994—. Recipient CLIO award Am. TV Comml. Festival, 1966. Mem. Kappa Kappa Gamma (v.p. Westport, Conn. chpt. 1996). Democrat. Home: 2050 Valencia Dr Northbrook IL 60062-7057

WINN, JULIE, state representative; b. Tucson, Ariz., Sept. 6, 1956; d. George Richard and Mary Kay (Behnke) W. AS, U. Maine, BS, MBA. Home: RR 4 Box 570 Bangor ME 04401-9512 Office: Maine House of Reps State House Augusta ME 04330*

WINNER, ANNE MOORE WINDLE, psychologist; b. West Chester, Pa., Sept. 4, 1921; d. Ernest Garfield and Sylvia Louise (Moore) Windle; BA in Philosophy, Swarthmore (Pa.) Coll., 1942; postgrad. scholar, Pa. Sch. Social Work, 1945-46; MA in Psychology (scholar), Bucknell U., Lewisburg, Pa., 1961; cert. of advanced study in communication disorders Johns Hopkins U., 1974; EdD, Pa. State U., 1988; cert. psychologist nat., Md. m. Drexel Winner, Apr. 15, 1944 (dec. 1967); children: Catherine Winner Salam, David R., Hanna Winner Dunleavy, Rebecca Winner Diehl (dec.). Sch. psychologist II, Balt. City Schs., 1963-91; cons. psychologist (pvt. practice) problems of children, pets, learning problems; Md. rep. Internat. Sch. Psychology Com., 1981-84; mem. Friends Pastoral Counseling Svc. Mem. Md. Psychol. Assn. (officer 1975-76), Balt. City Assn. Sch. Psychologists (pres., founder 1970-71), Pa. Assn. Sch. Psychologists, Md. Assn. Sch. Psychologists, Am. Psychol. Assn., Internat. Sch. Psychologists Assn. (presenter, rschr. acad. consequences early childhood lead poisoning). Author articles in field. Quaker. Address: 102 E Chestnut Hill Ln Reisterstown MD 21136-3307

WINNER, CHARYL ANN, machinery company executive; b. Bellefontaine, Ohio, May 29, 1948; d. Charles Lawrence and Joan Marie (Webb) Shawver; m. Gary Lee Weymouth, June 28, 1966 (div. Sept. 1968); 1 child, Brian Lee; m. Ronald Henry Winner, May 4, 1985; stepchildren: Keith, John, Mark, Matt, Ronald, Christina. AA, Ohio State U., 1982. Clk. Rockwell Internat., Bellefontaine, 1968-77, acct. rep., 1977-79; customer svc. supr. Rockwell Internat. Machinery, Bellefontaine, 1979-81; customer svc. mgr. Rockwell Internat. Machinery, Memphis and Tupelo, Miss., 1981-82; dist. sales mgr. Delta Internat. Machinery, Chgo., 1982-84; sales rep. Hopewell Ctr., Anderson, Ind., 1984-86; br. mgr. E. B. Mueller Co., Inc., Indpls., 1986-93; pres. Winner Woodworking Equipment and Supply, Inc., Indpls., 1993—. Mem. German Am. Klub (bd. dirs. 1992-95), Kiwanis. Republican. Methodist. Office: Winner Woodworking Equip 2719 E Troy Ave Indianapolis IN 46203

WINNER, DENISE JOY, money management systems engineer; b. Chgo., May 26, 1961; d. Myron and Joan Alberta (Carlin) Green; m. Andrew Jay Winner, June 1, 1961. BS in Econs., U. Pa., 1983; MS in Computer Sci., Brown U., 1984. Futures trader, programmer Drexel Burnham Lambert, Chgo., 1984-88; fin. engr. Hull Trading Co., Chgo., 1988-90; with I.A.C. Corp., L.A., 1990-91; fin. engr. Lor/Geske Bock, L.A., 1991-93; money mgr. Applied Financials Inc., Beverly Hills, Calif., 1993—. Organizer Inner City Arts Coun., L.A., 1993. Mem. L.A. Soc. Fin. Analysts, Wharton Club So. Calif., Wharton Club Chgo. (v.p. 1985-88). Home: 7411 W 82d St Westchester CA 90045 Office: Quintelligent Corp 222 N Canon Dr # 201 Beverly Hills CA 90210

WINNER, KARIN, newspaper editor. Exec. editor San Diego Union-Tribune. Office: Copley Press Inc 350 Camino De La Reina San Diego CA 92108-3003*

WINNER, LESLIE JANE, state legislator, lawyer; b. Asheville, N.C., Oct. 24, 1950; d. Harry and Julienne (Marder) W.; m. Kenneth L. Schorr, Dec. 20, 1987. AB, Brown U., 1972; JD, Northeastern U., Boston, 1976. Bar; N.C. 1976, U.S. Dist. Ct. (we. dist.) N.C. 1976, U.S. Ct. Appeals (4th cir.) 1976, U.S. Dist. Ct. (ea. and mid. dists.) 1981, U.S. Supreme Ct. 1985. Clk. to presiding judge U.S. Dist. Ct., Charlotte, N.C., 1976-77; mng. atty. Legal Services of So. Piedmont, Charlotte, 1977-81; ptnr. Ferguson, Stein, Watt, Wallas, Adkins and Gresham, P.A., Charlotte, 1981-92; mem. N.C. Senate, Raleigh, 1993—. Pres. N.C. Women's Employment Law Ctr., 1989-90; past chmn. Mecklenburg County Dispute Resolution Ctr., Charlotte, 1985-86; coun. mem. So. Regional Coun., Atlanta, 1989—; trustee Temple Israel, Charlotte, 1988-89; pres. Elizabeth Community Assn., Charlotte, 1980-81. Mem. U.S. Ct. Appeals (4th cir.) Adv. Com. (N.C. rep. 1989—), N.C. Assn. Women Attys. (pres. 1982-83, pub. service award 1985), N.C. Acad. Trial Lawyers (legis. com.), N.C. Bar Assn. (litigation sect. coun.), Mecklenburg County Bar Assn. (grievance com.). Democrat. Jewish. Office: NC Senate Legis Office Bldg Rm 409 Raleigh NC 27611-2808*

WINNIE, BETTY NABOURS, retired microbiologist; b. San Antonio, Oct. 9, 1926; d. Raymond H. and Mary Etta (Curtis) Nabours; m. William Warren Winnie, Jr., Mar. 21, 1951 (dec. 1988); children: William Warren III, Peggy Jane. BA, U. Tex., Austin, 1949; MA, U. Tex. Microbiologist U. Tex. Med. Br., Galveston, 1949-50, St. Joseph Hosp., Albuquerque, 1950-52; chemist USDA Tung Lab., Gainesville, Fla., 1952-56; microbiologist Tex. Health Dept. Lab., Austin, 1963-93. Mem. Am. Soc. Microbiology, Tex. Pub. Health Assn.

WINOGRAD, AUDREY LESSER, advertising executive; b. N.Y.C., Oct. 6, 1933; d. Jack J. and Theresa Lorraine (Elkind) Lesser; m. Melvin H. Winograd, Apr. 29, 1956; 1 child, Hope Elise. Student, U. Conn., 1950-53. Asst. advt. mgr. T. Baumritter Co., Inc., N.Y.C., 1953-54; asst. dir. pub. rels. and creative merchandising Kirby, Block & Co., Inc., N.Y.C., 1954-56; divsn. mdse. mgr., dir. advt. and sales promotion Winograd's Dept. Store, Inc., Point Pleasant, N.J., 1956-73, v.p., 1960-73, exec. v.p., 1973-86; pres. AMW Assocs., Ocean Twp., N.J., 1976—. Editor bus. newsletters. Bd. dirs. Temple Beth Am, Lakewood, N.J., 1970-72. Mem. NAFE, Jersey Pub. Rels. and Advt. Assn. (past pres., bd. dirs.), Retail Advt. and Mktg. Assn. Internat., Monmouth Ocean Devel. Coun., Monmouth County Bus. Assn. (bd. dirs. 1985—, pres. 1988-90, Woman of the Yr. 1992-93), N.J. Assn. Women Bus. Owners, Am. Soc. Advt. and Promotion, Ocean C. of C. (bd. dirs. 1994), Retail Advt. Conf., Soc. Prevention Cruelty to Animals, Animal Protection Inst. Am., Humane Soc., United Animal Nation U.S., Internat. Fund Animal Welfare, World Wildlife Fund, Friends of Animals, Animal Protection Inst, Defenders of Wildlife, Nat. Humane Edn. Soc. Office: AMW Assocs 10 Pine Ln Ocean NJ 07712-7242

WINOGRAD, SESSILE SARAH, psychotherapist, consultant; b. Providence, June 18, 1928; d. Benjamin and Freda (Shaulson) Mayberg; m. Seymore Winograd, May 27, 1956; children: Yeuhda Leib, Jeffrey Asher. BA in Psychology summa cum laude, U. R.I., 1974, cert. in drug counseling, 1976; MS, Barry U., 1979. Diplomate Am. Bd. Med. Psychotherapists; lic. mental health counselor; nat. cert. counselor; cert. clin. mental health counselor. Field interviewer Brown U., Providence, 1968-69, med. coder, 1969-71; student counselor continuing edn. for women U. R.I. Ext., Providence, 1970-74; student counselor The Talmudic Coll. Fla., Miami Beach, 1979-84; drug counselor Aleph Inst., Miami Beach, 1979-86; dir. social svcs. Jewish Outreach Project Greater Miami, Inc., Miami, Fla., 1992-93; coord. cancer activities Ctr. for Psychol. Growth, Miami, 1992—; coord. women's cancer recovery program family workshop Miami Heart Inst., Miami Beach, 1992-94; pvt. practice Miami Beach, 1979—, Bklyn., 1994—; cons. Reaching Out for Emergency Help, Brookline, Mass., 1980—, Caring and Sharing, Bklyn., 1984—; lectr. and workshop presenter in field, 1985—; mem. instnl. rev. bd. Guidelines, Inc., Miami, 1991—. Author: Get Help, Get Positive, Get Well: The Aggressive Approach to Cancer Therapy, A Resource Book, 1992, (chpt.) Times of Challenge, 1988. Vice pres. Beth Yeshaye Charities of Miami, Miami Beach, 1980—; cons. Jewish Community Coun. for Russian Immigrants, Miami Beach, 1988—; bd. dirs. Jewish Outreach of Greater Miami, Inc., Miami Beach, 1991—; mem. Neshei Chabad Miami Beach, 1981—. Recipient Pulitzer prize nomination, 1992; named to Barry U. Alumni Hall of Fame, 1994. Mem. ACA, Am. Mental Health Counselor Assn., Gestault-in-Action, Alumni Assn. Barry U., Phi Kappa Phi. Home and Office: 800 Ocean Pkwy Ste 5A Brooklyn NY 11230

WINSETT-YOUNG, VICTORIA LOUISE, advertising executive, public relations consultant; b. Dallas, Feb. 6, 1950; d. Milo Asa and Louise Love (Metcalfe) Winsett; m. Robert Miles Young, May 27, 1983; 1 son, Christopher Asa. A.A. in Merchandising, Wade's Coll., Dallas, 1970; student So. Methodist U., 1974-78. Copywriter Sugarman Internat., Dallas, 1969-71; promotion dir. Quandrangle, Dallas, 1971-74; account exec. Tracy-Locke, Dallas, 1974-78, account supr., 1978-80, mgr. pub. relations Tracy-Locke/BBDO, 1980-82; dir. pub. relations Cunningham & Walsh, Dallas, 1982-86; owner The Young Co., Dallas, 1986—; cons. pub. rels. Haggar Apparel Co., Big Fish Films, The Container Store, The Dallas Morning News, NorthPark Shopping Ctr., Mary Kay Cosmetics; vol. YMCA, OPEN, Inc., Assn. Retarded Citizens, Boys Clubs Am., Dallas Children's Adv. Ctr., Dallas Assn. Homeless. Mem. NAFE, Pub. Rels. Soc. Am. (assoc.), Tex. Pub. Rels. Assn., Women in Comm. (profl.). Episcopalian. Address: 10806 Colbert Way Dallas TX 75218-1807

WINSLOW, ANNE BRANAN, artist; b. Waynesboro, Ga., July 28, 1920; d. Walter Augustus and Rubie (Griffin) Branan; m. James Addison Winslow Jr., May 8, 1943; children: Lu Anne, Jan Renee. BS in Fine Art, Queens Coll., Charlotte, N.C., 1941; postgrad., U. South Fla., 1974-75. One-woman shows include Dunedin (Fla.) Art Ctr., 1980, Tampa (Fla.) Originals Gallery, 1982, Pub. Libr., St. Petersburg, Fla., 1982, Lee Scarfone Gallery, 1983, 84, Studio 1212, Clearwater, Fla., 1983, 87, 90, Gallery 600, Largo, Fla., 1986, Gallery of State Capitol, Tallahassee, 1987, Berghoff Gallery, Clearwater, 1988, 92, Anderson-Marsh Gallery, St. Petersburg, 1989, 92, Loveland (Colo.) Mus., 1990, Gallery at City Hall of Tampa, 1990, Lawrence Charles Gallery, Tampa, 1993, Gallery Contemporanea, Jacksonville, Fla., 1994; painting, oil painting, Fla. Series II, Images II, 1980, Amagedon, 1974, Eastern Series III, 1984, original handpulled serigraphs, 1991, 92. Mem. Studio 1212, Fla. Artist Group, Mus. Women in Arts, Fla. Printmakers Soc., Generator Gallery (founding). Republican. Home and Studio: 5224 W Neptune Way Tampa FL 33609-3639

WINSLOW, FRANCES EDWARDS, city official; b. Phila., Sept. 12, 1948; d. Harry Donaldson and Anna Louise (McColgan) E.; m. David Allen Winslow, June 6, 1970; children: Frances Lavinia, David Allen Jr. BA, Drew U., 1969, MA, 1971; M Urban Planning, NYU, 1974, PhD, 1978; cert. hazardous material mgmt., U. Calif., Irvine. Adminstrv. asst. Borough of Florham Park, N.J., 1970-73; instr. Kean Coll., Union, N.J., 1973-75; adminstrv. asst. Irvine (Calif.) Police Dept., 1984-86; coord. emergency svcs. City of Irvine, 1986-91; dir. emergency svcs. City of San Jose, Calif., 1991—; instr. U. Calif., Irvine Extension; commr. Calif. Seismic Safety Commn., 1991—, Calif. Hosp. Bldg. Safety Bd., 1994—. Editor NCEER Workshop Procs., 1990, 92; contbr. chpt. to book, articles to profl. jours. Vice pres. San Diego Chaplain's Wives, 1976-79; treas. Girl Scouts U.S.A., Yokohama, Japan, 1980-81; treas. Camp Pendleton Officer's Wives Club, 1982-83, pres., 1983-84; vice chmn. curriculum ARC Disaster Acad., 1989-90, chmn., 1991; mem. community disaster preparedness com. ARC, 1992—; del. Nat. Coordinating Com. on Emergency Mgmt., 1990—. Recipient Vol. Svc. award Navy Relief Soc., 1984; Lasker Found. fellow, 1972; named one of Women of Distinction, Soroptimists Internat., 1991. Mem. ASPA (program chmn. Orange County 1984-85, chmn. criminal justice sect. award com. 1988-92, bd. dirs. 1992—, co-chmn. mini-conf. 1993), Am. Planning Assn. (regional conf. planning com. 1989-90), Internat. City Mgrs. Assn., Assn. Environ. Profls., Assn. Police Planning and Res. Officers (past sec., v.p. Orange County 1984-90), Creekers Club (past pres. 1985-88), San Jose Mgmt. Assn. (bd. dirs. 1993—), Calif. Emergency Svcs. Assn. Republican. Methodist. Home: 20405 Via Volante Cupertino CA 95014 Office: City of San Jose 855 N San Pedro St # 404 San Jose CA 95110-1718

WINSLOW, LILLIAN RUTH, nurse; b. Laconia, N.H., Oct. 23, 1930; d. James Edwin and Clemency (Anstey) Burbank; m. John Herrick Winslow, Apr. 25, 1964; children: Alice Faith Winslow Gay, Ruth Ellen Tenpenny. Diploma, Laconia (N.H.) Hosp. Sch. Nursing, 1951; BA, Providence Barrington Bible Coll., 1956; postgrad., Escuela de Idiomas, San Jose, Costa Rica, 1959. Sch. RN emotionally disturbed and handicapped Bedell Sch., Apache Junction, Ariz.; sch. RN East Mesa (Ariz.) Christian Acad.; nurse Mesa (Ariz.) Gen. Hosp. Med. Ctr. Missionary RN, World Radio Missionary Fellowship, Inc., Quito, Ecuador, 1959-63; camp RN, Camp Good News, Camp Pinnacle, N.H.; mem., choir RN the Acapella Choir, Providence Barrington Bible Coll. Recipient Cert. of Appreciation for Devoted and Invaluable Svcs., Maranatha Christian Acad.. Home: 1981 W 10th Ave Apache Junction AZ 85220-6933

WINSTEAD, ELISABETH WEAVER, poet, writer, English language educator; b. Nashville, July 31, 1926; d. Charles Preston and Carrie Lawrence (Hadley) Weaver; m. George Alvis Winstead, July 18, 1945. BA, Vanderbilt U., 1946; MA, Peabody Coll. Vanderbilt U., 1947; postgrad., Trevecca Nazarene, 1975-79, Vanderbilt U., 1980-83. Cert. tchr. of lang. arts, bus. edn., social sci., English, Tenn., Va., Ind., Idaho, Ariz. Head bus. edn. dept. La Crosse (Ind.) High Sch., 1947-48, Franklin (Tenn.) High Sch., 1952-54, Belmont Coll., Nashville, 1954-56; with English dept. Boise (Idaho) High Sch., 1948-49; critical analyst Dept. Commerce, Washington, 1949-50; with bus. edn. dept. Averitt Coll., Danville, Va., 1950-52; elem. and high sch. tchr. Met. Nashville Schs., 1956-85; cons. Model Tchr. Program, Nashville Met. Sch., 1958-68, mem. faculty adv. coun., 1970-79, mem. profl. devel. coun., 1980-84. Author: Social Studies Curriculum Guide, 1970, Metro Beautiful Programs, 1976, Metro PTA School History, 1980; contbr. poetry to anthologies and popular mags. Chmn. TB Seal Drive, Franklin, 1956-60, March of Dimes Fund Drive, Nashville, 1982-84, Red Cross Blood Drive, Nashville, 1984-86; capt. Heart Fund Drive, Nashville, 1979-81. Recipient Tchr. Appreciation awrd Sta. WKDA, 1970, Galaxy of Stars award Nashville Met. Schs., 1982, Ednl. Appreciation award City of Nashville, 1983, Commendation for pub. svc. Tenn. Legislature, 1994; named to Honorable Order of Ky. Cols., 1988. Mem. NEA, Am. Childhood Edn. Internat., Tenn. Hist. Soc., Wisdom Soc., Kappa Delta Pi, Pi Omega Pi, Pi Gamma Mu. Baptist. Home: 3819 Gallatin Rd Nashville TN 37216-2609

WINSTON, ANNETTE EADS, banker, lawyer; b. Nashville, Feb. 14, 1955; d. James E. Eads and Mary Janet Binkley Tabor; m. Barry A. Winston, Apr. 12, 1981; children: Samuel A. and Alexander J. (twins). BS, Middle Tenn. State U., 1977; JD, U. Tenn., 1980, MBA, 1987. Bar: Tenn. 1981, U.S. Dist. Ct. Tenn. 1981. Trust officer United Am. Bank, Knoxville, 1980-81; assoc. atty. Ridenour , Ridenour, Ridenour, Bowers and Shumate, Knoxville, 1981-83; grad. teaching asst. U. Tenn., Knoxville, 1986-87, asst. prof. fin., 1988; v.p. First Tenn. Bank, Knoxville, 1987-88, First Knoxville Bank, Knoxville, 1988—. Corp. dir. Boys and Girls Clubs, Knoxville, 1989—; past pres. com. for future Children's Hosp., Knoxville; sec. bd. edn. Heska Amuna Synagogue, Knoxville, 1984—; chmn. maj. employers United Way of Greater Knoxville, 1992; treas. Jr. League of Knoxville, 1992-93; mem. Leadership Knoxville Class of 1993. Mem. Tenn. Bar Assn., Knoxville Bar Assn. (chmn. membership svcs. 1994—), Exec. Women's Assn. (treas. 1994-95), Beta Gamma Sigma. Jewish. Home: 586 Arrowhead Trail SW Knoxville TN 37919 Office: First Knoxville Bank 620 Market St Knoxville TN 37902

WINSTON, JANET MARGARET, real estate professional, civic volunteer; b. Binghamton, N.Y., Sept. 30, 1937; d. Cornelius Adrian and Vera Helene (Strohman) Salie; m. Edmund Joseph Winston, Nov. 29, 1958 (dec. July 1981); children: Mark Edmund, Deborah Ann. Student, SUNY, 1955-57, Bliss Coll., 1978. Sales assoc. HER Realtors, Worthington, Ohio, 1979—. Dist. chair women's div. Community Chest ARC, Kalamazoo, 1970; docent Indpls. Mus. Art, 1975, Columbus (Ohio) Mus. Art, 1976—, beaux art mem., 1976-87; docent Chinese Son of Heaven Exhibit, 1989, mus. fund drive 1986-87, '89—; trustee Worthington Resource Ctr., 1979-84, v.p. 1984, chair youth employment svcs. 1980-83; trustee, sec. Worthington Hills Civic Assn., 1986-89. Mem. Columbus Bd. Realtors (pub. rels. com. 1980, 82, 86, 88, sales adv. com. 1987, mem. svcs. task force 1989), Nat. Assn. Realtors, Ohio Assn. Realtors (pres.'s sales club, The Dozen Nat. Sales award), Worthington C. of C., Worthington Hills Country, Worthington Hills Womens Club, Worthington Hills Garden Club (bd. dirs. 1989). Republican. Episcopalian. Home: 8036 Golfview Ct Columbus OH 43235-1230 Office: HER Realtors 6902 N High St Worthington OH 43085-2510

WINSTON, JUDITH ANN, lawyer; b. Atlantic City, Nov. 23, 1943; d. Edward Carlton and Margaret Ann (Goodman) Marianno; B.A. magna cum laude, Howard U., Washington, 1966; J.D., Georgetown U., 1977; m. Michael Russell Winston, Aug. 10, 1963; children: Lisa Marie, Cynthia Eileen. Dir. EEO Project, Council Great City Schs., Washington, 1971-74; legal asst. Lawyers Com. for Civil Rights Under Law, Washington, 1975-77; admitted to D.C. bar, 1977, U.S. Supreme Ct. bar; spl. asst. to dir. Office for Civil Rights, HEW, Washington, 1977-79; exec. asst., legal counsel to chair U.S. EEO Commn., Washington, 1979-80; asst. gen. counsel U.S. Dept. Edn., 1980-86; dep. dir. Lawyers Com. for Civil Rights Under Law, 1986-88; dep. dir. pub. policy Women's Legal Def. Fund, Washington, 1988-90, chair employment discrimination com., 1979-88; ednl. cons., 1974-77; asst. prof. law Washington Coll. Law of Am. U., 1990-93. assoc. prof. law, 1993—; gen. counsel U.S. Dept. Edn., Washington, 1993—. Pres. bd. dirs. Higher Achievement Program. Mem. ACLU (pres. Nat. Capital Area, bd. dirs.), D.C. Bar Assn., Washington Council Lawyers, Washington Bar Assn., Nat. Bar Assn., Lawyers' Com. for Civil Rights Under Law (treas., bd. dirs.), Links Inc., Alpha Kappa Alpha, Phi Beta Kappa, Delta Theta Phi. Democrat. Episcopalian. Author: Desegregating Schools in the Great Cities: Philadelphia, 1970, Chronicle of a Decade 1961-1970, 1970, Desegregating Urban Schools: Educational Equality/Quality, 1970; contbr. articles to profl. jours. Home: 1371 Kalmia Rd NW Washington DC 20012-1444 Office: Dept Edn 600 Independence Ave SW Washington DC 20202-2100

WINSTON, KRISHNA RICARDA, dean, language professional, translator; b. Greenfield, Mass., June 7, 1944; d. Richard and Clara (Brussel) W.; 1 child, Danielle Billingsley. BA, Smith Coll., 1965; MPhil, Yale U., 1969, PhD, 1974. Instr. Wesleyan U., Middletown, Conn., 1970-74, asst. prof., 1974-77; assoc. prof. Wesleyan U., Middletown, 1977-84, prof., 1984—, acting dean, 1993-94; coord. Mellon Minority Undergrad. Program, 1993—. Author: O. v. Horváth: Close Readings of Six Plays, 1975; translator: O. Schlemmer, Letters and Diaries, 1972, S. Lenz, The Heritage, 1981, G. Grass, Two States, One Nation, 1990, C. Hein, The Distant Lover, 1989, G. Mann, Reminiscences and Reflections, 1990, J.W. v. Goethe, Wilhelm Meister's Journeyman Years, 1989, C. v. Krockow, The Hour of the Women, 1991, E. Heller, With the Next Man Everything Will be Different, 1992, R.W. Fassbinder, The Anarchy of the Imagination, 1992, G. Reuth, Goebbels, 1994, E. Lappin, Jewish Voices, German Words, 1994, P. Handke, Essay on the Jukebox, 1994. Vol. Planned Parenthood, Middletown, 1972-77; mem. Recycling Task Force, Middletown, 1986-87; chmn. Resource Recycling Adv. Coun., Middletown, 1989—. Recipient Schlegel-Tieck Translation prize; fellow German Acad. Exchange Svc. Mem. MLA, NEMLA., Soc. for Exile Studies, Am. Lit. Translators' Assn., Am. Assn. Tchrs. German, Phi Beta Kappa (pres. Wesleyan chpt. 1987-90). Home: 655 Bow Ln Middletown CT 06457-4808 Office: Wesleyan Univ German Dept Middletown CT 06459

WINSTON, MAXINE SPEARS, social worker; b. New Orleans, Feb. 12, 1954; d. Thomas Lee and Lovie (Clipps) Spears; m. Joseph M. Winston, July 16, 1983. BS, Southern U., 1975; MSW, U. Wis., Milw., 1985. Genetic counselor sickle cell ctr. Deaconess Hosp., Milw., 1976-77; mental health asst. Milw. County Mental Health Ctr., Milw., 1977-83; social worker adolescent health care MCCH Teach Program, Milw., 1986-88; social worker United Meth. Children's Svcs., 1988-93; social worker, case mgr. Milw. Pub. Schs., 1993—. Recipient Helen Carey Award for Acad. Excellence. Mem. NASW, Wis. Assn. Black Social Workers (treas.), Pi Gamma Mu. Home: 3291 N 36th St Milwaukee WI 53216-3715

WINTER, ELIZABETH H., educational administrator; b. Upper Darby, Pa., Nov. 9, 1950; d. Stanley Jackson and Thurley Lillian (Blanchard) Shurtleff; m. Gary Winter, Apr. 24, 1982; children: Elizabeth Jackson, Alexander Cameron. AA, Lasell Coll., 1970; BA, Newton Coll. of Sacred Heart, 1972; MBA, Babson Coll., 1975. Sales rep. Xerox Corp., Boston, 1975-77; admissions counselor Lasell Coll., Newton, Mass., 1977-78, dir. fin. aid, asst. dir. admissions, 1978-79, contr., 1979-80, dir. fin. affairs, 1980-83, dean of adminstrn., 1983-88, v.p. bus. and finance, 1988—. Bd. dirs. Newton Television Found., 1989—; treas. Williams Sch. PTA, Newton, 1991. Mem. Nat. Assn. Coll. and Univ. Bus. Officers, Eastern Assn. Coll. and Univ. Bus. Officers (small coll. com. 1990-92). Home: 69 Maple St Newton MA 02166-2324 Office: Lasell Coll 1844 Commonwealth Ave Newton MA 02166-2716

WINTER, JOAN ELIZABETH, psychotherapist; b. Aiken, S.C., Feb. 24, 1947; d. John S. and Mary Elizabeth (Caldwell) Winter. BS, Ariz. State U., 1970; MSW, Va. Commonwealth U., 1977; EdS, Coll. William and Mary, 1989, EdD, 1993. Lic. clin. social worker, AMFT bd. approved supr., clin. group worker. Va. Counselor Child Psychiatry Hosp., Phoenix, 1969-70, Ariz. Job Coll., Casa Grande, 1970-71; dir. Halfway House, Richmond, Va., 1971-73; state supr. resdl. treatment, Richmond, 1973-75; psycotherapist Med. Coll. Va., Richmond, 1975-76, Va. Commonwealth U., 1976-77; adj. prof., exec. dir. Family Rsch. Project, William and Mary Coll., Richmond, Va., 1979—; dir. Family Inst. Va., Richmond, 1980—; examiner, approved supr. Bd. Behavioral Scis., Commonwealth of Va., 1982—; mem. adj. faculty dept. psychology Coll. William & Mary, Med. Coll. Va.; mem. Avanta Network, Exec. Coun. and Faculty, Nat. Inst. of Drug Abuse, Rsch. Adv. Com. Author: The Phenomenon of Incest, 1977, The Use of Self in Therapy: The Person and Practice of the Therapist, 1987, Family Life of Psychotherapists, 1987 Enhancing the Marital Relationship: Virginia Satir's Parts Party, 1990, Enhancing the Marital Relationship: Virginia Satir's Parts Party, 1991, Family Therapy Research Outlaws: Bowen, Haley and Satir; editor Jour. Couple Therapy; contbr. articles to profl. jours. Diplomate Nat. Assn. Social Workers; mem. Am. Soc. Cert. Social Workers, Am. Family Therapy Assn., Am. Assn. Marriage and Family Therapy (approved supr.), Avanta Network Faculty. Address: 2910 Monument Ave Richmond VA 23221

WINTER, RUTH GROSMAN (MRS. ARTHUR WINTER), journalist; b. Newark, May 29, 1930; d. Robert Delmas and Rose (Rich) Grosman; m. Arthur Winter, June 16, 1955; children: Robin, Craig, Grant. B.A., Upsala Coll., 1951; MS, Pace U., 1989. With Houston Press, 1955-56; gen. assignment Newark Star Ledger, 1951-55, sci. editor, 1956-69; columnist L.A. Times Syndicate, 1973-78, Register and Tribune, syndicate, 1981-85; contbr. to consumer mags.; instr. St. Peters Coll., Jersey City.; vis. lectr. mag. writing Rutgers U. Author: Poisons in Your Food, rev. edits., 1971, 91, How to Reduce Your Medical Bills, 1970, A Consumers Dictionary of Food Additives, 1972, 3d rev. edit., 1994, Vitamin E: The Miracle Worker, 1972, So You Have Sinus Trouble, 1973, Ageless Aging, 1973, So You Have a Pain in the Neck, 1974, A Consumers Dictionary of Cosmetic Ingredients, 1974, 4th rev. edit., 1994, Don't Panic, 1975, The Fragile Bond: Marriage in the '70's, 1976, Triumph Over Tension, 1976, The Smell Book: Scent, Sex and Society, 1976 (N.J. Press Women's Book award), Scent Talk Among Animals, 1977, Cancer Causing Agents: A Preventive Guide, 1979, The Great Self-Improvement Sourcebook, 1980, The Scientific Case Against Smoking, 1980, People's Guide to Allergies and Allergens, 1984; co-author: The Lean Line One Month Lighter Program, 1985, Thin Kids Program, 1985, Build Your Brain Power, 1986, Eat Right: Be Bright, 1988, A Consumer's Dictionary of Household, Yard and Office Chemicals, 1992, A Consumer's Guide to Free Medical Information By Phone and By Mail, 1993, A Consumer's Dictionary of Medicines: Prescription, Over-the Counter and Herbal, 1994. Recipient award of merit ADA, 1966, Cecil award Arthritis Found., 1967, Am. Soc. Anesthesiologists award, 1969, Arthritis Found. award, 1970; named Alumnus of Year Upsala Coll., 1971, Woman of Year N.J. Daily Newspaper Women, 1971, Woman of Achievement Millburn Short Hills Profl. and Bus. Women's Assn., 1991. Mem. Soc. Mag. Writers, Authors League, Nat. Assn. Sci. Writers, Am. Med. Writers Assn. (Eric Martin Meml. award), N.J. Daily Newspaper Women (awards news series 1958, 70, named Woman of Achievement 1971, 83), Am. Soc. Journalists and Authors (pres. 1977-78, spl. service award 1983), N.J. Press Women (pres. 1982-84). Home and Office: 44 Holly Dr Short Hills NJ 07078-1318

WINTERFIELD, LYNN ANN, writer, counselor, educator; b. Jamaica Queens, N.Y., Jan. 31, 1958; d. Samuel and Mildred Helen (Connelly) W. AA, Sullivan County C.C., Lock Sheldrake, N.Y., 1978; BA in Psychology, SUNY, Oswego, 1980, MS in Counseling and Psychology, 1987. Substance abuse counselor Farnham Youth Devel. Ctr., Oswego, N.Y., 1981-83; alcohol counselor, educator North Essex Health Resource Ctr., Newburyport, Mass., 1985-87; adj. faculty N.H. Coll., Laconia, 1988-89; employment counselor State of N.H. Employment Security, Laconia, 1988-90; program coord. State of N.H. Employment Security, Concord, 1990-94; tech. writer State of N.H. Dept. Health and Human Svcs., Concord, 1994-95; program specialist N.H. Dept. Health and Human Svcs., and Employment Security, 1995—; part time DWI instr. State of N.Y. Coun. on Alcoholism, Oswego, 1982-83, State of N.H. Office of Alcohol and Drug Abuse, 1986-87; advocate for disable persons N.H. Vocat. Rehab., Concord, 1992; trainer N.H. Employment Security, Concord, 1992-94; facilitator Portsmouth (N.H.) Naval Shipyard, 1992-94. Program designer: Job Search Workshop and Accompanying Workbook, 1990, School to Work Transition, 1994. Mem. N.H. Humane Soc., Friends of Ferret (founder, pres. 1993—). Home: 39 Arlene Dr Belmont NH 03220

WINTERHALTER, DOLORES AUGUST (DEE WINTERHALTER), art educator; b. Pitts., Mar. 22, 1928; d. Joseph Peter and Helen August; m. Paul Joseph Winterhalter, June 21, 1947 (dec.); children: Noreen, Audrey, Mark; m. Marvin Bernard Hoeing, Mar. 26, 1988. Student, Yokohama, Japan, 1963-64, Paris, 1968-70. Cert. tchr. Japanese Flower Arranging, Kamakuri Wood Carving. Tchr. YWCA, Greenwich, Conn., 1978-84, Friends of the Arts and Scis., Sarasota, Fla., 1992—; lectr. Sarasota Art Assn., 1984—; tchr., workshop presenter, Bangkok, 1971; mem. staff Hilton Leech Art Studio and Gallery, Sarasota; events chmn. State of Fla. Watercolor Exhbn., Sarasota, 1995. Numerous works in watercolor, ink, oriental brushwork; paintings in numerous corp. collections. Pres., Am. Women's Club, Genoa, Italy, 1962; participant to help raise money for scholarships Collectors and Creators Tour of Fine ARts Soc. of Sarasota, 1994. Recipient numerous awards Old Greenwich (Conn.) Art Assn., 1971-84, Sarasota, 1985, Collectors and Creators Tour award Fine Arts Soc. Sarasota, 1994; named Artist of Yr., Fine Arts Soc. Sarasota, 1994. Mem. Nat. League Am. Pen Women (pres. Sarasota br. 1994-95), Suncoast Fla. Watercolor Soc. (life), Fla. Watercolor Soc., Long Boat Key Art Assn., Sarasota Art Assn., Sumi-e Soc. Am. Democrat. Roman Catholic. Home and Office: 3883 Spyglass Hill Rd Sarasota FL 34238

WINTERMUTE, MARJORIE MCLEAN, architect, educator; b. Great Falls, Mont., Sept. 15, 1919; d. Allan Edward and Gladys Pearl (Pelton) McLean; m. Charles Richard Wintermute, June 14, 1947 (div.); children: Lynne Wintermute, Lane. BA, U. Oreg., 1941; postgrad. Portland State U., 1969-72. Registered architect, Oreg. Archtl. draftsman Def. Projects, Portland and San Francisco, 1941-43; architect Pietro Belluschi, Portland, 1943-47; free-lance architect, Portland, 1948—; architect-in-residence Edn. Service Dist., Portland, 1978-91, ret.; instr. Portland State U., 1973—; architect-in-residence Dept. Def. Dependents Sch., Asian Region Hdqrs. Japan, 1981-83; with Upshur Group Collaborative, 1976-87; architect-in-residence program coord. Oreg. Arts Commn., 1987—, AIA; leader archtl. tours to Europe, 1969, 71, 73, Greece and Turkey, 1989, 91. Author: Students, Structures, Spaces, 1983, Blueprints: A Built Environment Education Program, 1984, Architecture As A Basic Curriculum Builder, 1987-90; editor: Pitter Patter (Gold medal 1965), 1960-69. Prin. archtl. works include comml. and residential bldgs. and restoration and mus. installation Timberline Lodge, Oreg., 1983, 2d Timberline Restoration project, 1993. Bd. dirs. Oreg. Heart Assn., Portland, 1960-70, pres. 1968-69; bd. dirs. Friends of Timberline, Creative Arts Community, pres. 1993—; program devel. cons. Am. Heritage Assn., Lake Oswego, Oreg., 1969-83, Mt. Angel Abbey, St. Benedict, Oreg., 1970-73; bd. dirs., com. chmn. Environ. Edn. Assn., Portland, 1978-85. Recipient Disting. Citizen award Environ. Edn. Assn., 1983; role model award area coun. Girl Scouts, 1994; Woman of Achievement award Inst. Profl. and Managerial Women, 1984; Woman of Distinction award Women in Arch., 1993, named Disting. Citizen Portland Hist. Landmarks Commn., 1988, fellowship in The Am. Inst. of Architects, 1978. Fellow AIA (pub. edn. com. 1970-80, chair 1972-73); mem. Women's Archtl. League (bd. dirs., com. chmn. 1980—), Fashion Group Internat. (facilitator 1983-84), Ednl. Futures Inc. (Western rep. 1978-83), Oreg. State Dept. Edn. (adv. bd. 1980-83). Republican. Presbyterian. Home: 6740 SW Canyon Ln # 1 Portland OR 97225-3606

WINTERROWD, SHIRLEY LAWRENCE, bank officer; b. Taylor, Tex., Oct. 5, 1935; m. Jack C. Winterrowd, Aug. 28, 1954; children: Jack C. Jr., Janet Winterrowd Daniell, Christy Winterrowd Pick, Cass Matthew. Grad. high sch., Thrall, Tex. Teller, customer svc. officer, tng. coord., secrecy officer Bank of West, Taylor, Am. Inst. Banking rep., 1990—; mem. system legis. initiatives for edn. com. Tex. A&M U. System. Sec. Thrall Ind. Sch. Dist. Bd. Edn., 1973-82, also mentor; bd. dirs. Williamson County Youth Fair Assn., 1981—; past chmn. Williamson County Extension Program Com.; leader 4-H Club, 1968—; pres. Williamson County A&M Mothers' Club, 1976-78, 82-83; mem. exec. bd. Fedn. Tex. A&M U. Mothers' Clubs, 1981-90, pres., 1988-89; mem. Tex. A&M U. Legis. Incentive for Edn.; treas. Bapt. Ch. Recipient Dist. 4-H Leader award Tex. 4-H Vol. Leaders Assn., 1981, Outstanding 4-H Leader award Dist. 10 4-H Leaders Assn., 1987. Mem. VFW Ladies Aux., Williamson County 4-H Adult Leaders Assn. Baptist. Home: RR 1 Box 177 Thrall TX 76578-9744

WINTERS, BARBARA JO, musician; b. Salt Lake City; d. Louis McClain and Gwendolyn (Bradley) W. AB cum laude, UCLA, 1960, postgrad., 1961; postgrad., Yale, 1960. Mem. oboe sect. L.A. Philharm., 1961-94, prin. oboist, 1972-94; ret.; clinician oboe, English horn, Oboe d'amore. Recs. movie, TV sound tracks. Home: 3529 Coldwater Canyon Ave Studio City CA 91604-4060 Office: 135 N Grand Ave Los Angeles CA 90012-3013

WINTERS, NOLA FRANCES, food company executive; b. Achilles, Kans., Aug. 27, 1925; d. Edward Earl and Mary Ruby (Mikesell) Ginther; divorced. Student, U. Kans., 1943-45; BA, U. Colo., 1972. Exec. sec. Holly Sugar Corp., Colorado Springs, Colo., 1953-66, asst. sec., 1966-84, dir. corp. rels., asst. sec., 1981-84, dir. corp. and pub. rels., asst. sec., 1984-90; asst. sec. HSC Export Corp., Colorado Springs, 1980-90, Imperial Holly Corp., Colorado Springs, 1988-90. Mem. Phi Beta Kappa. Republican. Methodist.

WINTERS, SHARON ANN, librarian, library educator; b. West Palm Beach, Fla., Mar. 4, 1955; d. Edward William and Ethel Virginia (Held) W.; m. Kendall Martin Reid, May 7, 1988. BA in History, Wake Forest U., 1977; MLS, U. N.C., Greensboro, 1985; MPA, George Washington U., 1992. Tech. svcs. libr. Morgantown (W.Va.) Pub. Libr., 1985-86; systems libr. Hampton (Va.) Pub. Libr., 1986-91, support svcs. mgr., 1991—; mem., chair budget subcom. City of Hampton (Va.) Employee Coun., 1992—; lectr. Sch. Libr. and Info. Sci., Cath. U. Am., Washington, 1993—. Bd. mem., pres. Greenspring Food Coop., Winston-Salem, 1982-84; reading tutor Hampton (Va.) Literacy Coun., 1989-93. Recipient Excellence in Info. award Dynix, Inc., Provo, Utah, 1992. Mem. ALA, Pub. Libr. Assn., Customers of Dynix, Inc. (sec. 1988-90, newsletter editor 1990-92, chair local arrangements ann. conf. 1993-94, v.p. and pres.-elect 1994-95). Office: Hampton Pub Libr 4207 Victoria Blvd Hampton VA 23669-4243

WINTERS, SHELLEY (SHIRLEY SCHRIFT), actress; b. St. Louis, Aug. 18, 1922; m. Vittorio Gassman (div.); 1 child, Vittoria; m. Anthony Franciosa, 1957 (div. Nov. 1960). Student, Wayne U. Began acting career in vaudeville, later played roles on legitimate stage; motion pictures include The Diary of Anne Frank, 1958 (Acad. award best supporting actress), Odds Against Tomorrow, Let No Man Write My Epitaph, Matter of Convictions, Lolita, 1962, Wives and Lovers, 1963, The Balcony, 1964, A House Is Not a Home, 1964, Patch of Blue, 1966 (Acad. award best supporting actress), Time of Indifference, 1965, Alfie, 1965, The Moving Target, 1965, Harper, 1966, Enter Laughing, 1967, The Scalp Hunters, 1968, Buona Sera Mrs. Campbell, 1968, Wild in the Streets, 1968, The Mad Room, 1969, How Do I Love Thee, 1971, What's the Matter with Helen, 1971, The Poseidon Adventure, 1972, Blume in Love, 1973, Cleopatra Jones, 1973, Something to Hide, 1973, Diamonds, 1975, Next Stop Greenwich Village, 1976, The Tenant, 1976, An Average Man, 1977, Tentacles, 1977, Pete's Dragon, 1977, King of the Gypsies, 1978, The Visitor, 1980, Looping, 1981, S.O.B., 1981, My Mother, My Daughter, 1981, Over the Brooklyn Bridge, Ellie, Deja Vu, 1985, The Delta Force, 1986, Marilyn Monroe: Beyond the Legend, 1987, Purple People Eater, 1988, An Unremarkable Life, 1989, Touch of a Stranger, 1990, Stepping Out, 1991, The Pickle, 1993; appeared in: TV films Revenge!, 1971, The Devil's Daughter, 1973, Double Indemnity, 1974, The Sex Symbol, 1974, Elvis, 1978, Alice in Wonderland; plays A Hatfull of Rain, 1955, Girls of Summer, 1957, Night of the Iguana, Cages, Who's Afraid of Virginia Wolf?, Minnie's Boys; TV miniseries The French Atlantic Affair, 1979; Author: play One Night Stands of a Noisy Passenger, 1971; autobiography Shelley: Also Known As Shirley, 1980, Shelley II: The Middle of My Century, 1989. Recipient Emmy award Best Actress, 1964, Monte Carlo Golden Nymph award, 1964, Internat. TV award as best actress Cannes Festival, 1965.

WINTERS, SUZANNE, biomedical scientist, researcher; b. Cleve., Feb. 10, 1954; d. William Ebersole and Mary Louise (Stough) W.; m. Robert Howard Ramsey, Mar. 15, 1986; 1 child, Robert William Ramsey. BS, Ohio Wesleyan U., 1976; PhD, U. Utah, 1986. Rschr. Battelle Columbus (Ohio) Labs., 1976-81; sr. sci. Symbion Inc., Salt Lake City, 1985-86; dir. biomatris/membranes CardioPulmonics, Inc., Salt Lake City, 1986-90; cons. Membrane & Coatings Cons., Salt Lake City, 1990-93; state sci. advisor State of Utah, Salt Lake City, 1993—. Office: Planning & Budget Office 116 State Capitol Bldg Salt Lake City UT 84114

WINTERS, WANDA DENISE, therapist; b. Charlotte, N.C., Nov. 2, 1964; d. John Andrew Edward and Esther Belle (Cline) Mital; m. Bruce Kendal Winters, Aug. 3, 1985 (div. Feb. 1994). BS, Evangel Coll., 1988; MA, Rollins Coll., 1993. Activities specialist Circles of Care, Inc., Rockledge, Fla., 1988-89; day program counselor Circles of Care, Inc., Rockledge, 1989, day program coord. asst., 1989-90, family svcs. coord., 1990-92, outpatient therapist, 1992—; pub. speaker Circles of Care, Inc., Rockledge, 1990-92. Mem. ACA (student mem.). Republican. Home: 1912 Woodhaven Cir Apt 47 Rockledge FL 32955-8057 Office: 1770 Cedar St Rockledge FL 32955-3133

WINTERSCHEIDT-HILER, LAURIE B., barge transportation executive; b. Seneca, Kans., July 12, 1957; d. Gerald K. and Mary C. (Bergman) Winterscheidt; m. Steven E. Hiler, Apr. 5, 1986; 1 child, Hattie Ann. B in Liberal Arts with distinction, U. Kans., 1979; postgrad., Washington U., St. Louis, 1994—. Freight merchandiser Consolidated Grain & Barge Co., St. Louis, 1980-84, freight dept. mgr., 1984-88, v.p. freight merchandising, 1988-93; gen. mgr. Clearwater Transp., St. Louis, 1993—. Active Jr. League, St. Louis, 1988—. Mem. Agri Bus. Club, St. Louis Merchants Exch. (com. mem.). Republican. Roman Catholic.

WINTER-SWITZ, CHERYL DONNA, travel company executive; b. Jacksonville, Fla., Dec. 6, 1947; d. Jacqueline Marie (Carroll) Winter; m. Frank C. Snedaker, June 24, 1974 (div. May 1976); m. Robert William Switz, July 1, 1981. AA, City Coll. of San Francisco, 1986; BS, Golden Gate U., 1990, MBA, 1992. Bookkeeper, agt. McQuade Tours, Ft. Lauderdale, Fla., 1967-69; mgr. Boca Raton (Fla.) Travel, 1969-76; owner, mgr. Ocean Travel, Boca Raton, 1976-79; ind. contractor Far Horizons Travel, Boca Raton, 1979-80; mgr. Tara/BPF Travel, San Francisco, 1981-84; mgr. travel. dept. Ernst & Whinney/Lifeco Travel, San Francisco, 1984-86; travel cons. Siemer & Hand Travel, San Francisco, 1989—; instr. Golden Gate U., 1986—, U. San Francisco. Mem. Amateur Trapshooting Assn., Hotel and Restaurant Mgmt. Club. Republican. Episcopalian. Home: 642 Brussels St San Francisco CA 94134-1902 Office: Siemer & Hand Travel 101 California St Ste 1750 San Francisco CA 94111-5894

WINTHROP, ELIZABETH AMORY, horse trainer; b. N.Y.C., Dec. 14, 1931; d. Robert and Theodora (Ayer) W.; m. Francis E. Baker, June 16, 1949 (div. 1953); m. Malcolm P. Ripley, Apr. 21, 1958 (div. 1974). Student, Bradford Jr. Coll., 1952, Columbia U., 1956. Registered horseshow judge. Horse trainer Morley Farms, Millbrook, N.Y., 1955-67; humane investigator Dutchess and Putnam Counties, 1969-86, peace officer; humane investigator, 1969-86. Bd. dirs. Fund for Animals, N.Y.C., 1974—, N.Y. State Humane Assn., New Paltz, N.Y., 1975—; pres. Winley Found., N.Y.C., 1967—; registered judge Am. Horseshow Assn., N.Y.C., 1966-88; mem. gen. adv. bd. Am. Inst. Life Threatening Illness and Loss, 1992—. Mem. Defenders Wildlife (life), Nat. Audubon Soc. (life), Wild Horse Organized Assistance (life), World Wildlife Fund, African Wildlife Found., Human Soc. U.S., Nat. Inst. Social Scis., Animal Welfare Inst., New Eng. Anti-Vivisection Soc. (life), Am. Horse Show Assn. (life), Colony Club, Lansdowne Club (London). Episcopalian. Home: RR 1 Box 40 Millbrook NY 12545-9720

WINTOUR, ANNA, editor; b. Eng., Nov. 3, 1949; came to U.S., 1976; d. Charles and Elinor W.; m. David Shaffer, Sept. 1984; children: Charles, Kate. Student, Queens Coll., 1963-67. Deputy fashion editor Harper's and Queen Mag., London, 1970-76; fashion editor Harper's Bazaar, New York, 1976-77; fashion and beauty editor Viva Mag., New York, 1977-78; contbg. editor fashion and style Savvy Mag., New York, 1980-81; sr. editor N.Y. Mag., 1981-83; creative dir. U.S. Vogue, N.Y., 1983-86; editor-in-chief British Vogue, London, 1986-87, House and Garden, N.Y., 1987-88, Vogue, N.Y., 1988—. Office: Vogue Mag Conde Nast Bldg 350 Madison Ave New York NY 10017-3704*

WINZER, P.J., lawyer; b. Shreveport, La., June 7, 1947; d. C.W. Winzer and Pearlene Hall Winzer Tobin. BA in Polit. Sci., So. U., Baton Rouge, 1968; JD, UCLA, 1971. Bar: Bar: Calif. 1972, U.S. Supreme Ct. 1986. Staff atty. Office of Gen. Counsel, U.S. HEW, Washington, 1971-80; asst. spl. counsel U.S. Office of Spl. Counsel Merit Systems Protection Bd., Dallas, 1980-82; regional dir. U.S. Merit Systems Protection Bd., Falls Church, Va., 1982—. Mem. Fed. Bar Assn., Calif. Bar Assn., Fed. Cir. Bar Assn., Delta Sigma Theta. Office: US Merit System Protection 5203 Leesburg Pike Ste 1109 Falls Church VA 22041

WIPPERMAN, WENDY JANE, budget director; b. Buffalo, Aug. 2, 1957; d. Howard George and Elizabeth Jane (Leone) W. Student, U. Tulsa, 1975-78; BA in Econs., U. Tex., 1981. Budget analyst Governor of Tex., Austin, 1981-83; planner Tex. Dept. Community Affairs, Austin, 1983-84; asst. budget dir. Tex. Dept. Agriculture, Austin, 1984-85; sr. cons. Arthur Young & Co., Austin, 1986-87; procurement officer Town of Fallsburg, N.Y., 1987-92; budget dir. Dutchess County, Poughkeepsie, N.Y., 1992—. Vice-chair City of Austin Maj. Employers, 1983-84; active City of Austin Com. on Spending and Svcs., 1986-87. Mem. N.Y. State Govt. Fin. Officers Assn. Hindu. Office: Dutchess County Budget Off 22 Market St Poughkeepsie NY 12601-3222

WIRTH, F(RANCES) JANE, psychologist; b. Logansport, Ind., Mar. 13, 1937; d. Thomas C. and Bess V. (Renberger) Bradfield; m. Wallace L. Wirth, June 6, 1965; children: Charles Edward, Todd Lindsay. BS in Edn., Eastern Ill. U., 1959; MS in Edn., Purdue U., 1964; postgrad., Ind. State U., 1966-67, U. Wis., 1992, 93-94. Cert. sch. psychologist. Tchr. elem. edn. Decatur (Ill.) Pub. Schs., 1959-61, River Trails Dist. #26, Mt. Prospect, Ill., 1961-62; tchr., rsch. asst. Purdue U., W. Lafayette, Ind., 1962-63, dir. grad. women's residence hall, 1962-64; guidance counselor Sch. Dist. # 218, Oaklawn, Ill., 1963-68; tchr. dance Orland Park (Ill.)/Oak Forest (Ill.) Sch. Dist., 1972-80; sch. psychologist Sch. Dist. #130, Blue Island, Ill., 1969-71, 79-93, Sch. Dist. #89, Melrose Park, Ill., 1993—; intern supr. Sch. Dist. # 130, Blue Island, 1980-84; nutritional cons. Apply A Diet, Schamburg, Ill., 1987-93. Coord. Art Awareness program Sch. Dist. 118, Palos Park, Ill., 1977-78; mem. Educators Cmty. Profl. Gender Equity Roundtable, AAUW Task Force, Maraine Valley Coll. Commn., 1993; ways and means chair Palos Orland Swim Assn., Palos Park, 1977-82; entertainment chair C. Sandburg H.S. "Drug Free" Graduation Party, 1990; mem. Palos Vollage Players Cmty. Theater, 1989-94. Mem. AAUW (sec., pres.-elect), Nat. Assn. Sch. Psychologists, South Metro. Sch. Psychologists Assn. (bd. dirs. 1980-81), Ill. Sch. Psychologists Assn. (charter), Blue Island Evening Women's Club (pres., sec. 1965-72), Assettes Investment Club (pres., sec. 1985—). Home: 12343 S 76th Ave Palos Heights IL 60463 Office: Sch Dist 89 1133 S 8th St Maywood IL

WIRTH, PATRICIA ELLEN, telecommunications engineer; b. Nebraska City, Nebr., Mar. 5, 1950; d. Austin Otto and Kathleen (McGowen) W.; m. Duane Sneddeker, May 20, 1972 (div. 1982). BA in Math., U. Nebr., 1971; MS in Systems Sci. and Math., Washington U., St. Louis, 1978, DSc in Systems Sci. and Math., 1980. Tchr. high sch. Gresham (Nebr.) Schs., 1971-72; rsch. asst. Med. Sch. Washington U., St. Louis, 1972-78; mem. tech. staff AT&T Bell Labs., Holmdel, N.J., 1981-85, supr., 1985-90, dept. head, 1990—. Contbr. articles to profl. jours. Sponsor Save the Children, 1990—; mem. N.J. Pub. Interest Rsch. Group, 1990—, Emily's List Majority Coun., Washington, 1994; contbg. mem. Dem. Nat. Com., Washington, 1993—; del. Internat. Teletraffic Congress, 1991—. AAUW fellow, 1979. Mem. Soc. Engring. Sci. (sec. 1980-83), Phi Beta Kappa, Sigma Xi. Democrat. Home: 14 Bradford Dr Old Bridge NJ 08857-3103 Office: AT&T Bell Labs 101 Crawfords Corner Rd Holmdel NJ 07733-1900

WIRTHS, CLAUDINE GIBSON, psychologist, author; b. Covington, Ga., May 9, 1926; d. Count Dillon and Julia (Thompson) Gibson; m. Theodore William Wirths, Dec. 28, 1945; children: William M., David G. AB, U. Ky., 1946, MA, 1948; MEd, Am. U., 1979. Program dir. N.C. League for Crippled Children, Chapel Hill, 1948-49; research psychologist Savannah River Urbanization Studies, Aiken, S.C., 1950-52; research psychologist, cons. various pub. and pvt. agys., S.C., D.C., Md., Bermuda, 1953-79; spl. edn. tchr. Montgomery Pub. Schs., Gaithersburg, Md., 1979-80, coordinator learning ctr., 1980-84; adj. faculty Frederick (Md.) Community Coll., 1985—. Author: I Need A Job, 1988, Where's My Other Sock?, 1989, Are You My Type?, 1992, How to Get Up When Schoolwork Gets You Down, 1993, Time to Be series, 1994, Upgrade, 1995; co-author: (with Williams) Lives Through the Years, 1968, (with Bowman-Kruhm) I Hate School, 1986 (Best Book award ALA 1987); contbr. articles to profl. jours. and popular press. Vice chair Def. Adv. Com. Women in Service, Washington, 1960-63, adv. com. Seneca Pk., Montgomery County, 1970-79; adv. bd. Soc. Nat. Resources, Md., 1976-79. Named Outstanding Citizen of County, Aiken, 1954; recipient award Montgomery County Environ. Trust, 1973, 1st pl. award for feature story, Md., D.C., Del. Press Assn., 1980. Mem. Soc. Children's Book Writers, Assn. Children with Learning Disabilities, Washington Ind. Writers, Phi Beta Kappa. Episcopalian. Home and Office: PO Box 335 Braddock Heights MD 21714-0335

WIRTSCHAFTER, IRENE NEROVE, tax consultant; b. Elgin, Ill., Aug. 5; d. David A. and Ethel G. Nerove; B.C.S., Columbus U., 1942; cert. tax profl.; enrolled agt. IRS; m. Burton Wirtschafter, June 2, 1945 (dec. 1966). Commd. ensign Supply Corps, USN, 1944, advanced through ranks to capt., 1975; comdg. officer Res. Supply Unit, 1974-75; ret., 1976; agt. office internat. ops. IRS, 1967-75, internat. banking specialist, now pvt. practice tax cons., Cocoa Beach, Fla.; sr. intern program U.S. Senate, 1981; mem. Sec. of Navy's Adv. Com. Ret. Personnel, 1984-86, VA Adv. Com. for Women Vets., 1987-90. Past troop leader Girl Scouts U.S.A.; cons. Jr. Achievement, 1989—; lt. col. and mission pilot CAP; comml. instrument pilot; founder Sr. Action Com. Brevard County, 1981; chmn. College Park Airport Johnny Horizon Day, 1975; Navy liason officer Commd.'s Retiree Coun. Patrick AFB, 1985-89; elected dir. Fla. Space Coast Philharmonic, 1985—, treas. 1986-92; mem. bd. dirs., adv. mgr. Cocoa Beach Citizens League, 1990-92; co-chmn. Internat. Women's Yr. Take Off Dinner, Washington, 1976; mem. Nat. Com. Internat. Forest of Friendship, Atchison, Kans., 1976—; 1st v.p. Friends of Cocoa Beach Libr., 1988-90, pres., 1990-92, bd. dirs., 1993—; mem. Cocoa Beach Bus. Improvement Coun., Fla.; elected senator Silver Haired Legislature, Fla., 1985—; advisor Women's Air & Space Mus., 1993—; vol., founding mem. Brevard Zoo; chmn. Cocoa Beach Enforcement Bd., 1989—; sr. adv. com. Cape Canaveral Hosp., co-chmn. 1994. Named hon. citizen of Winnipeg (Can.), 1966, Atchison, 1989 and New Orleans, 1988; Ky. col., La. col. Mem. AAUW, Naval Res. Assn. (nat. treas. 1975-77, nat. adv. com. 1985—, Nat. award of Merit 1992), Ninety Nines (past chpt. and sect. officer); 99 Achievement awards), Naval Order U.S. (treas. nat. capitol commandry), Assn. Naval Aviation (nat. trustee 1988—), Banana River Squadron (founder, comptr.), Assn. Enrolled Agts., Cocoa Beach Area C. of C., Internat. Platform Assn., Silver Wings (bd. dirs., nat. sec. 1986, Woman of the Year 1985), WAVES Nat. (bd. dirs. chpt. 75 1989—), Tailhook Assn., Daybreak Rotary Club. First female Supply Corps officer to be assigned sea duty, 1956. Avocations: aviation, golf, music. Home: 1825 Minutemen Cswy Apt 301 Cocoa Beach FL 32931-2033

WISCHERTH, MARGHERITA MIECNIKOWSKI, finance manager; b. Mineola, N.Y., Mar. 11, 1961; d. Stanley and Frances Marie (Ruggiero) Miecnikowski; m. Jeffrey Wischerth, Apr. 6, 1986; children: Matthew, Victoria. BA, SUNY, Oneonta, 1983; student, Fashion Inst. Tech., N.Y.C., 1984-85; MA, Adelphi U., 1993. Asst. Am. Assn. Advt. Agys., N.Y.C., 1983-90; office mgr. Guaranty Risk Svcs., N.Y.C., 1990-91; mgr. fin. and adminstrn. Partnership for a Drug-Free Am., N.Y.C., 1991—. Active Nat. Mus. Women in the Arts. Republican. Roman Catholic. Office: Partnership Drug-Free Am 405 Lexington Ave New York NY 10174-0001

WISDOM, LORI ANN, dental hygienist; b. Santa Monica, Calif., Mar. 7, 1967; d. Douglas Minnel and Caroline Frances (Kilfoil) W. AA, Montgomery County C.C., 1991. Sec. to pres. Gatti, Inc., Willow Grove, Pa., 1984-86; office mgr. Dr. Robert Masonis DDS, Maple Glen, Pa., 1986-88, Drs. Cherkas DMD, Horsham, Pa., 1989; clk. Prudential Ins. Co., Horsham, Pa., 1990-91; dental hygienist Dr. Michael Haas & Dr. William Jakavick DDS, Norristown, Pa., 1991—; dental hygienist Dr. John DiGiralomo, Ambler, Pa., 1994—. Mem. Am. Dental Hygienist Assn., Pa. Dental Hygienist Assn., Montgomery/Bucks Hygiene Assn. Roman Catholic.

WISE, BARBARA SUE, counselor educator; b. Stillwater, Okla., Apr. 20, 1940; d. Horace Maynard and Joanna Maureen (Rose) Haws; m. Robert Lawrence Wise, Aug. 21, 1959 (div. Dec. 1989); children: Robert Todd, Christopher Anthony, Matthew Tate, Traci Elizabeth. BS, U. Ctrl. Okla., 1971, MEd, 1972; postgrad., Menningers Hosp., Topeka, 1988, Pacifica Grad. Inst., 1994. Lic. profl. counselor; cert. counselor substance abuse; cert. elem. tchr., mental retardation and learning disabilities. Coll. tchr. Southwestern Okla. State U., Weatherford, Okla., 1973-80; counselor Family Life Ctr., Oklahoma City, 1981-87; owner, mgr. Wise Couseling Inc., Oklahoma City, 1987—; program facilitator, counselor for adolescent dept. Laureate Pscyhiat. Hosp., Tulsa, 1992-94; counselor adolescents, case mgr. CPC Southwinds Hosp., Oklahoma City, Okla., 1995—; cons. Addiction Mgmt., Santa Fe, 1989-90; cons., writer Morter Health System, Rogers, Ark., 1993-94. Mem. ACA. Home: 820 Mac Arthur Blvd Oklahoma City OK 73127 Office: CPC Southwinds Hosp Oklahoma City OK 73159

WISE, JANET ANN, college official; b. Detroit, Aug. 8, 1953; d. Donald Price and Phyllis (Licht) W.; m. Peter Anthony Eisenklam, Oct. 16, 1976 (div. Aug. 1982); m. Edward Henry Moreno, Mar. 31, 1984; 1 child, Talia. Student, U. N.Mex., 1971-73; BA in English, Coll. of Santa Fe, 1989. Editorial asst., writer The New Mexican, Santa Fe, 1975-77; press asst., press sec. Office of Gov. N.Mex., Santa Fe, 1979-82; dir. pub. relations City of Santa Fe, 1983-84, Coll. of Santa Fe, 1984—. Bd. dirs. Santa Fe Bus. Bur., 1984-87, Santa Fe Girl's Club, 1986-89. Recipient Exemplary Performance award Office Gov. of N.Mex., Santa Fe., 1981, Outstanding Service award United Way of Santa Fe, 1982. Mem. PRSA, N.Mex. Press Women, Santa Fe Media Assn. (pres. 1989-91), Infolink (bd. dirs.). Democrat. Unitarian. Home: 7 Conchas Ct Santa Fe NM 87505-8803 Office: Coll of Santa Fe 1600 Saint Michaels Dr Santa Fe NM 87505-7634

WISE, JOANNE HERBERT, artist representative; b. Bryn Mawr, Pa., Aug. 11, 1943; d. Charles Nugent and Carolyn (Le Maistre) Herbert; m. Douglas Wise, Nov. 26, 1976. Student, Acad. Fine Arts, Phila. Sec. to corp. v.p. Fawcett Publs., N.Y.C., 1964-66; sec. to promotion dir. Weightman Advt., Phila., 1966-70; assoc. media mgr. Scott Paper Co., Phila., 1970-75; promotion dir. Jimmy Carters Nat. Campaign, Atlanta, 1976; dir. The Wise Collection, Tokyo, Houston and N.Y.C., 1980—; curator Japan Hands, N.Y.C., 1987-89; coord. screen project Sculptor Jiro Okura, Roanoke, Va., 1990-91; moderator, presenter Shaker/Japanese League for N.H. Craftsmen, Concord, 1993. Pub.: (newsletter) Current Influences in Contemporary Art, 1986—. Pres. Tokyo (Japan)/Am. Club, 1980; founder Tex. Print Alliance, Houston, 1982, Japan Hands, N.Y.C., 1987. Office: The Wise Collection PO Box 286 Lyme NH 03768

WISE, KATHLEEN ROSE VERONICA, psychotherapist, researcher; b. Forest Hills, N.Y., July 10, 1947; d. Irwin Thomas and Rosemary (Bacchini) Doty; m. Helbert Wise, Mar. 1, 1983; children—Bruce Kenwood, Marc. B.A., Hofstra U., 1967; M.A., SUNY, 1969; Ph.D., Met. Coll. London, 1985; Ph.D. (hon.), Southwestern U., 1985. Staff counselor U.S. Systems, Dallas, 1976-80; psychotherapist Garland Ctr. for Behavioral Sci., Garland, 1982-84; pvt. practice psychotherapy, Irving, Tex., 1984—; cons. Dallas Med. Ladies Clinic, 1983-84. Active Dallas Alliance for Mental Recovery, 1985. Mem. Am. Assn. Profl. Hypnotherapists, AAUW, Menninger Found., Am. Assn. Counseling and Devel. Roman Catholic. Avocation: oil painting.

WISE, MAUREEN KAMEN, public relations executive, editor, educator; b. Los Angeles, Mar. 26, 1946; d. Murray Morton and Rosalyn Estelle (Horowitz) Kamen; m. Murray Jay Wise, Aug. 7, 1966; children: Stephanie Lauren, Tracey Meredith. BS, Elmira Coll., 1966; MS, Iona Coll., 1993. Cert. elem. and lang. tchr., N.Y. Tchr. elem. Horseheads (N.Y.) Cen. Sch. Dist., 1966-67, East Ramapo Sch. Dist., Spring Valley, N.Y., 1967-69, 91-92, Pearl River (N.Y.) Ctrl. Sch. Dist., 1994—; dir. pub. rels. United Jewish Appeal of Rockland, Spring Valley, N.Y., 1971-86; publicity coordinator recreation dept. Town of Ramapo, Suffern, N.Y., 1973; community resources dir. Planned Parenthood of Rockland, West Nyack, N.Y., 1979-82; owner, pres. Wise Promotions, Spring Valley, 1981—; pub. relations dir. Women's League for Conservative Judaism, N.Y.C., 1985-91; bd. dirs. United Jewish Community of Rockland, Rockland City, N.Y., 1976-91; mem. chancellor's com. Jewish Theol. Sem., N.Y.C., 1987; founding mem., v.p. Rockland County Tourism Bd., Suffern, 1983-85. Mng. editor Women's League Outlook mag., 1985-91; producer, dir. multimedia presentations, theatrical prodns. Mem. citizens adv. com. Rockland County, 1984; mem. Pomona Jewish Ctr. Recipient Woman of Achievement award, J.T. Sem. Torah Fund Campaign, 1986, Disting. Service award Rockland County, 1984. Mem. Rockland Women's Network (In Celebration of Women award for achievement in bus. 1984), Westchester-Rockland Women's League (past chmn. pub. rels.), Elmwood Playhouse, Hadassah, Phi Delta Kappa. Democrat. Home: 24 Fairway Oval Spring Valley NY 10977-1723

WISE, SANDRA CASBER, legislative director. BA, Macalester Coll., 1969; JD, U. Minn., 1972. Bar: Minn. 1972, D.C., 1986, W.Va., 1987. Legis asst. to Rep. Martha Keys, Washington, 1977-78; asst. to asst. to the pres. for women's issues Sara Weddington, The White Ho., Washington, 1979; staff sub-com. on pub. assistance Ho. Com. on Ways and Means, Washington, 1980, staff sub-com. on health, 1981-85; atty. White, Fine and Verville, 1986; staff dir. sub-com. on social security Ho. Com. on Ways and Means, Washington, 1987—. Office: Ho Com on Ways & Means B-316 Rayburn House Office Bldg Washington DC 20515*

WISE, SUSAN TAMSBERG, management and communications consultant, speaker; b. Memphis, Nov. 16, 1945; d. Joseph Lane and Mable Rosa (Koth) Tamsberg; m. Roy Thomas Wise, June 29, 1968; children: Kristin Rebecca, Mary Catherine. BA in Math., Columbia (S.C.) Coll., 1967; M in Edn., Ga. State U., Atlanta, 1986. Tchr. high sch. math. various pub. schs., N.C., S.C., and Ga., 1967-73; instr. Cen. Piedmont Community Coll., Charlotte, N.C., 1979; devel. dir. Classique, Inc., Kannapolis, N.C., 1979-81; asst. v.p. First Nat. Bank of Atlanta, 1981-87; Ga. dir. The Exec. Speaker, Inc., Atlanta, 1987-90; pres. TrimTime, Inc., Atlanta, 1988—, Wise Consulting Inc., Atlanta, 1990—; speaker Girl Scouts USA, Jr. League, numerous med. assns., Atlanta and S.E. area, 1985—. Tng. cons. Jr. League of Atlanta, 1988-89; bd. dirs. Incarnation Luth. Ch., Atlanta, 1984; mem. ch. coun., bd. dirs, Luth. Ch. of the Redeemer. Mem. ASTD (v.p., bd. dirs., Leadership award 1987), Kappa Delta Pi. Republican.

WISECUP, PATTY LYNN, critical care nurse; b. Olathe, Kans., Mar. 17, 1964; d. James Phillip and Helgie (Tarnowski) Craig; children: Christopher Marc, Matthew Robert; m. James P. Wisecup, Oct. 16, 1992. ADN, Ea. N.Mex. U., 1985. ACLS instr.; cert. nurse of oper. rooms. Operating rm. nurse Gerard Champion Meml. Hosp., Alamogordo, N.Mex., 1986-94; med. info./triage nurse Park Nicollet Med. Ctr., Mpls., 1994—. Mem. ENA, AORN.

WISECUP, SANDRA JEAN, accountant; b. Ft. Dodge, Iowa, Dec. 14, 1964; d. Donald Gene and Pauline Jean (Rusnak) Prokop; m. Wesley J. Wisecup, June 16, 1990; 1 child, Emily Jean. BBA, U. Iowa, 1987; postgrad., Wichita State U. Cert. mgmt. acct. Fin. mgmt. devel. trainee Raytheon Co., Addison, Ill., 1987-88; acctg. supr. Safeco Ins. Co., Seattle, 1989-91; cost acct. Raytheon Aircraft Co., Wichita, Kans., 1991-93; treas. Travel Air Ins. (subs. Raytheon), Wichita, 1993—. Vol. bus. cons. Jr. Achievement, Seattle, 1990-91, Wichita, 1992-93. Mem. Inst. Mgmt. Accts. (cert.). Roman Catholic. Office: Travel Air Ins 220 W Douglas Wichita KS 67202

WISEMAN, BROOKE MARYL, association administrator; b. Michigan City, Ind., May 16, 1949; d. Charles William and Marjorie Marie (Greening) W. BS in Social Work, Ball State U., 1971; MA in Comms., Mich. State U., 1979. Field exec. Mich. Capitol Girl Scouts, Lansing, 1971-74, program svcs. dir., 1974-81; exec. dir. Permian Basin Girl Scouts, Odessa, Tex., 1981-84, Girl Scouts of Du Page County, Naperville, Ill., 1984-92, Girl Scouts of Chgo., 1992—; 1st v.p. Assn. of Girl Scout Exec. Staff, 1974-93; nat. trainer Girl Scouts U.S., N.Y.C., 1989-94, certification of ex-dirs. task force, 1993—. Mem. hon. bd. Family Shelter Svc., Glen Ellyn, Ill., 1990-93, nominating com. Nat. Women's Polit. Caucus, Chgo., 1992-94; exec. adv. com. United Way of Chgo., 1992-93; bd. dirs. Naperville Heritage Soc., 1993-94. Named 1 of 100 Women to Watch in 1993, Today's Chgo. Women. Fellow Leadership Greater Chgo.; mem. Econ. Club of Chgo., Women in Charge (bd. dirs. 1993), Women in Philanthropy (bd. dirs. Chgo. 1993-94), Women in Mgmt. DuPage (pres. 1986-94, woman of Achievement 1989), Zonta Internat. (bd. dirs. Chgo. Loop 1993-94). Lutheran. Home: 6707 Pershing Ct Woodridge IL 60517-1602 Office: Girl Scouts of Chgo 55 E Jackson Blvd Ste 1400 Chicago IL 60604-4105

WISHARD, DELLA MAE, state legislator; b. Bison, S.D., Oct. 21, 1934; d. Ervin E. and Alma J. (Albertson) Preszler; m. Glenn L. Wishard, Oct. 18, 1953; children: Glenda Lee, Pamela A., Glen Ervin. Grad. high sch., Bison. Mem. S.D. Ho. of Reps., Pierre, 1984—. Columnist County Farm Bur., 1970—. Committeewoman state Rep. Cen. Com., Perkins County, S.D., 1980-84. Mem. Am. Legis. Exch. Coun. (state coord. 1985-91, state chmn. 1991—), Fed. Rep. Women (chmn. Perkins County chpt. 1978-84), S.D. Farm Bur. (state officer 1982). Lutheran. Home and office: PO Box 139 HC 1 Prairie City SD 57649-0367

WISHERT, JO ANN CHAPPELL, elementary and secondary education educator; b. Carroll County, Va., July 10, 1951; d. Joseph Lenox and Helen Alata (Wagoner) Chappell; m. Clarence Hinnant Wishert, Jr., June 10, 1987; 1 child, Kelly Marie Greco. BA, Oral Roberts U., 1974; MS, Radford U., 1977; Degree in Advanced Postgrad Studies, Va. Poly. Inst. and State U., 1981; postgrad., U. S.C., Spartanburg, 1990. Cert. elem. music supr., Va., elem. and secondary music tchr., S.C., music tchr., ednl. specialist, N.C. Head start tchr. Rooftop of Va., Galax, 1975; elem. music tchr. Carroll County Pub. Schs., Hillsville, 1975-78; grad. asst., supr., course advisor Coll. Edn., Va. Poly. Inst. and State U., Blacksburg, 1975-81, pregrad. interviewer placement svcs., 1981-83; music dir. Heritage Acad., Charlotte, N.C., 1984-85, fine arts specialist, 1985-86; choral dir. Chester County Schs., Chester, S.C., 1986—; guest condr. workshop Patrick County Schs., Stuart, Va., 1980; liaison for Chester County Schs. to S.C. Gov.'s Sch. for Arts, 1990-91. Soloist PTL TV Network, Charlotte, 1984-85. Guest spkr. on battered women and marital abuse to chs. and workshops; entertainer; co-dir. Chester City Schs. Choral Festival; active Arts Coun. Chester County, 1988—, S.C. Arts Alliance and Arts Advocacy. Named Tchr. of Yr., Chester Sr. High Sch., 1989, Chester County Schs., 1991, Educator of Yr., Chester County C. of C., 1992. Mem. ASCD, AAUW (by-laws com. Chester br. 1987—, sec. 1988-89), Music Educators Nat. Conf., S.C. Music Educators Assn. (del. pub. rels. network Chester County Schs. 1991), S.C. Edn. Assn., Am. Ednl. Rsch. Assn., Am. Assn. Choral Dirs., Chester County Edn. Assn., Nat. Assn. Secondary Music Edn. (team evaluator div. tchr. edn. cert. 1989, 91—), State Southern Assn. Schs. and Colls. (evaluation team), All USA Chorus Student Group (alumni), 4-H Club (life), Phi Delta Kappa. Republican. Baptist. Home: 1122 Virginia Dare Dr Rock Hill SC 29730-9669

WISHNICK, MARCIA MARGOLIS, pediatrician, geneticist, educator; b. N.Y.C., Oct. 10, 1938; d. Hyman and Tillie (Stoller) Margolis; m. Stanley Wishnick, June 12, 1960; 1 child, Elizabeth Anne. BA, Barnard Coll., 1960; PhD, NYU, 1970, MD, 1974. Diplomate Am. Bd. Pediatrics, Nat. Bd. Med. Examiners. Rsch. technician Lederle Labs./Am. Cyanamid, Pearl River, N.Y., 1960-66; postdoctoral fellow N.Y. Pub. Health Lab., N.Y.C., 1970-71; resident in pediatrics Bellevue Med. Ctr. NYU-Bellevue Med. Ctr., N.Y.C., 1974-77; asst. prof. pediatrics Bellevue Med. Ctr. NYU Med. Ctr., N.Y.C., 1977-82, clin. assoc. prof. pediatrics Bellevue Med. Ctr., 1982-87, clin. prof. pediatrics Bellevue Med. Ctr., 1987—; pvt. practice, N.Y.C., 1977—. Contbr. articles to profl. jours. Fellow Am. Acad. Pediatrics; mem. AMA, Am. Soc. Human Genetics, N.Y. Pediatric Soc., N.Y. Med. Soc., N.Y. Women's Med. Assn. Office: 157 E 81st St New York NY 10028-1844

WISMER, PATRICIA ANN, educator; b. York, Pa., Mar. 23, 1936; d. John Bernhardt and Frances Elizabeth Loreen Marie (Fry) Feiser; m. Lawrence Howard Wismer, Aug. 4, 1961. BA in English, Mt. Holyoke Coll., 1958; MA in Speech/Drama, U. Wis., 1960; postgrad., U. Oreg., 1962, Calif. State U., Chico, 1963-64, U. So. Calif., 1973-74. Tchr., co-dir. drama program William Penn Sr. High Sch., York, 1960-61; instr. English, dir. drama York Jr. Coll., 1961-62; assoc. church editor San Francisco Examiner, 1962-63; reporter, publicist News Bur. Calif. State U., Chico, 1963-64; chmn. English Dept. Chico Sr. H.S., 1964—; mentor tchr. Chico Sr. High Sch., Chico Unified Sch. Dist., 1983-93; judge writing awards Nat. Coun. Tchr. English, 1970—; cons. No. Calif. Writing Project, 1977—. Mem. Educators for Social Responsibility, Calif. Assn. for Gifted, Upper Calif. Coun. Tchrs. English (bd. dirs. 1966-85, pres. 1970-71), Calif. Assn. Tchrs. English, Nat. Coun. Tchrs. English, NEA, Calif. Tchrs. Assn., Chico Unified Tchrs. Assn. Democrat. Lutheran. Home: 623 Arcadian Ave Chico CA 95926-4504 Office: Chico Sr High Sch 901 The Esplanade Chico CA 95926

WISNER, CYNTHIA FICKE, lawyer, educator; b. Cin., Aug. 17, 1957; d. Howard William and Verna Lee (Schriever) Ficke; m. Neal R. Wisner, Jan. 5, 1980; children: April Leigh, Shelbi Lynn. BS, Kent State U., 1978; JD, U. Mich., 1981. Bar: Mich. 1981, U.S. Dist. Ct. (ea. dist.) Mich. 1981, U.S. Tax Ct. 1982. Assoc. Jaffe, Snider, Raitt and Heuer, Detroit, 1981-83; assoc. Honigman Miller Schwartz and Cohn, Detroit, 1983-86, ptnr., 1987-93; ptnr. Howard & Howard Attys., P.C., Bloomfield Hills, Mich., 1993-94; gen. counsel The Detroit Med. Ctr., 1994—; adj. prof. U. Detroit Mercy, 1987—;presenter at profl. confs. Co-editor Health Law Focus newsletter, 1991-93. Tchr. Sunday jr. ch., Wed. midweek ch. Trinity Evangel. Presbyn. Ch., Plymouth, Mich., 1990—. Mem. ABA (health law forum), Mich. Soc. Hosp. Attys., Nat. Health Lawyers Assn., Acctg. Aid Soc., Kent State U. Alumni Assn., U. Mich. Alumni Assn. Office: The Detroit Med Ctr 3990 John R Detroit MI 48201

WISNER, LINDA ANN, advertising agency executive, publishing company executive, interior designer; b. Sidney, N.Y., Apr. 28, 1951; d. Herbert and Ruth W. B.A. in Theatre and Art, Macalester Coll., 1973, postgrad. in journalism, 1974; postgrad. in graphic design Mpls. Coll. Art and Design, 1973-74; postgrad. in advtg. and mktg. U. Minn., 1974. Designer, publs. asst. Macalester Coll., St. Paul, 1973-76; designer Stretch & Sew Inc., Eugene, Oreg., 1976-78; free-lance designer, Eugene, 1978-79; owner, creative dir. Wisner Assocs., Eugene, 1979-87, Portland, 1987—, Interludes, Eugene, 1981—; ptnr. Instant Interiors, Eugene, 1979-88; design dir. Palmer/Pletsch Assocs., 1988—, v.p., 1992—; chmn. Bus. Images Exhibit, Eugene, 1983. Author: Creative Serging for the Home, 1991 (Best Sewing Book award 1991); designer/author, editor booklet series: Instant Interiors, 1979-83 (Woodie award 1980-83); designer, illustrator: Palmer/Pletsch Sewing Books, 1981—. Ambassador, City of Eugene, 1985-87; bd. dirs. Maude Kerns Art Ctr., Eugene, 1984-85, Oreg. Repertory Theatre, 1986-87, Oreg. Sales and Mktg. Exec., 1986, Lloyd Dist. Transportation Mgmt. Assn.; bd. dirs Portland Culinary Alliance, 1989—, pres., 1992-93. Nat. Merit scholar Macalester Coll., 1969. Mem. Designers' Forum (pres. 1983-84, Designer of Yr. 1983), Sales and Mktg. Execs., Graphic Artists Guild, Exec. Bus. Women (pres. 1983-84), Mid Oreg. Ad Club (numerous certs. and trophy 1980-85), Eugene C. of C. (M.V.P. Leadership Program award 1986), Sullivan's Gulch Neighborhood Assn. (chairperson land use planning com., 1993—, bd. dirs 1990—). Avocations: design, illustration, soft sculpture, event planning, catering.

WISNESKI, MARY JO ELIZABETH, reading specialist, educator; b. Saginaw, Mich., Dec. 18, 1938; d. Walter Frank and Hedwig Josephine (Borowicz) W. BS, Cen. Mich. U., 1961; MS, So. Ill. U., 1969; EdD, U. No. Colo., 1979; postdoctoral, U. Calif., Berkeley, 1980-81. Cert. elem. educator, elem. adminstr., reading specialist, Calif. Elem. educator various schs., 1960-75; instr. U. No. Colo., Greeley, 1976-78, 79; reading specialist Vacaville (Calif.) Unified Sch. Dist., 1980—; lectr. San Francisco State U., 1983-86; prof. Chapman Coll., Travis AFB, Calif., 1986-90; cons. in field. Author: Clifford Books Teacher Manual, 1981. Vol. ARC, Travis Air Mus., Travis AFB; bd. dirs. Polish Arts and Culture Found., San Francisco, 1988-91, Vistula Dancers; mem. Reading Del. to Vietnam, People-to-People Internat. Amb. Program, 1995. Recipient Tchr. in Space Certificate NASA, 1986, Outstanding Tchr. Commendation Dept. of Defense, 1973. Mem. AAUW, Nat. Women's Polit. Caucus, Nat. Reading Conf., Internat. Reading Assn., Western Coll. Reading Assn., Calif. Profs. Reading (v.p., treas.), Calif. Edn. Assn., Solano County Reading Assn. (pres., v.p., sec.), Lowiczanie Folk Dance Ensemble (pres. pro tem, treas.), Polish Am. Congress, Phi Delta Kappa, Phi Kappa Phi, Kappa Delta Pi, Pi Lambda Theta. Home: 314 Creekview Ct Vacaville CA 95688-5318

WISNESKI, SHARON M., critical care nurse, educator; b. Phila., June 22, 1952; d. Charles Edward and Hilda Marie (Riley) Ashley. AS, Wesley Coll., Dover, Del., 1979, BS, 1985; MSN, Widener U., Chester, Pa., 1991, cert. in nursing edn., 1993, postgrad., 1994—. ACLS. Charge nurse, med.-surg. ICU Milford (Del.) Meml. Hosp.; clin. instr. Wesley Coll., Del. Tech. and Community Coll., Dover; critical care per-diem nurse Med. Ctr. Del., Newark; instr. nursing Del. State U., Dover; part-time staff nurse med. ICU Med. Ctr. of Del., Newark; apptd. rev. bd. Del. Medicaid Drug Utilization Rev. Bd., 1993—; mem. Del. Bd. Nursing Practice Adv. Com., 1994—. Mem. ANA (rev. panelist ANA continuing edn. ind. study 1995—), AACCN (southeastern Pa. chpt.), AAUW, Assn. Black Nursing Faculty, Del. Nurses Assn. (chmn. nursing practice com. 1992, Del. Nurse of Yr. 1993), Inst. Constituent Mems. in Nursing Practice, Sigma Theta Tau, Chi Eta Phi. Home: 336 Pine Valley Rd Dover DE 19901-7113

WISSBAUM, DONNA CACIC, lawyer; b. Portage, Wis., Dec. 3, 1956; d. Donald Richard and Rita Margaret (Polcyn) Cacic; m. David Michael Wissbaum, Dec. 29, 1984; children: Nicholas David, Heather Noelle. BA in Am. Instns., U. Wis., 1979; JD, Gonzaga U., 1982. Bar: Wis. 1982, U.S. Dist. Ct. (ea. and we. dists.) Wis. 1983. Assoc. Bennett & Bennett Law Offices, Montello, Wis., 1983-85, Gregory R. Wright Law Offices, Montello, 1985-89; prin. Donna Cacic Wissbaum, Atty. at Law, Montello, 1989—. Mem. ABA, Wis. Bar Assn., Tri-County Bar Assn. (sec.-treas. 1986-88, v.p. 1988-90, pres. 1990-92), Marquette County Crimestoppers, Inc. (vice chmn. 1994—), Croatian Fraternal Union. Roman Catholic. Home: W5436 County Hwy P Pardeeville WI 53954 Office: 5 E Park St Montello WI 53949-9700

WISSLER-THOMAS, CARRIE, professional society administrator, artist; b. Ephrata, Pa., Nov. 2, 1946; d. Robert Uibel and Grace Urbane (Nicholas) Wissler; m. James Richard Gamber, June 12, 1968 (div. 1972); m. Scott Kerry Thomas, Mar. 3, 1972; 1 child, Dylan Crayton Llewellyn. BA, Hood Coll., 1968; MS, Temple U., 1986. Copywriter WGSA Radio, Ephrata, Pa., 1970-71, William Assocs., Harrisburg, Pa., 1977; correspondent Art Matters of Phila., Harrisburg, 1984-86; art columnist Pennsylvania Beacon, Harrisburg, 1983-85; writer Strictly Business, Harrisburg, 1985-86; painting instr. Art Assn. of Harrisburg, 1980-86; freelance artist freelance, Harrisburg, 1968—; exec. dir., pres. Art Assn. of Harrisburg, 1986—; mem. exhbn. panel Harrisburg City Govt. Ctr., 1983—; mem. art adv. panel Harrisburg Area C.C., 1985—; mem. gallery com. Univ. Ctr. at Harrisburg, 1988—; chmn. Easter Seals Art Show by Disabled Artists, Harrisburg, 1983-86; trustee Pa. Sch. Art & Design, 1989—; mem. Harrisburg Multi-Cultural Coalition, 1992—; chmn. Harrisburg Gallery Walk, 1989—; bd. dirs. Historic Harrisburg Assn., 1992—. Prin. work includes Broadway Babies oil painting, 1982 (Grumbacher Gold Medallion 1982); over 30 solo exhibitions. Mem. Hist. Soc. Cocalico Valley, Ephrata, 1982—, Dauphin County Hist. Soc., Harrisburg, 1986—; minority inspector Paxtang Election Bd., Harrisburg, 1977-79; mem. ACLU, Pa., 1988—; bd. dirs. Historic Harrisburg Assn., 1992—. Recipient Women Who Work award Communications and the Arts Pomeroy's, 1985, Disting. Svc. to Arts award Harrisburg Community Theatre, 1991. Mem. Pa. Soc. Assn. Execs., Am. Coun. on Arts, Art Assn. Harrisburg (pres. 1980-84), Rotary. Democrat. Anglican. Home and Studio: 2721 N 2nd St Harrisburg PA 17110-1205 Office: Art Assn of Harrisburg 21 N Front St Harrisburg PA 17101-1606

WISSMANN, CAROL RENEÉ, sales executive; b. Berkeley, Calif., July 9, 1946; d. Conrad Clayton and Carol Elizabeth (Ward) W. BA, Whittier Coll., 1968; Montessori Diploma, Coll. Notre Dame, Belmont, 1970. Dist. mgr. U.S. C. of C., Washington; sales rep. Nat. Write Your Congressman; div. mgr. Classified Yellow Pages Inc., Cookeville, Tenn., 1986; ind. contractor MacDonald Geary, Renton, Wash., 1986-88; pres. The BelleMann Corp., Gig Harbor, Wash., 1988—. Mem. AAUW, Women Bus. Owners. Republican. Home and Office: Ste E 305 5109 Point Fosdick Dr NW Gig Harbor WA 98335-1774

WISWALL, MAUREEN LERAE, adoption consultant; b. Cedar Rapids, Iowa, Mar. 13, 1942; d. Marvin L. and Valena M. (Elmore) Stoner; m. John P. Wiswall, June 26, 1965; children: Courtney, Matthew, Kyle, Kristin, Kara. BS, W.Va. U., 1965; postgrad., Seton Hall U., 1965. Cert. tchr., N.J. Tchr. Parsippany (N.J.) High Sch., 1965-66; adoption resource cons. Boonton, N.J., 1978—. Bd. dirs. Amigos de las Americas, Montclair, N.J., 1989—; v.p. Wilson Sch. Bd. Trustees, Mountain Lakes, N.J., 1980—, sec., 1994-95, co-chair Art '92 com., 1980-91, chair, 1992, chair Art '93 com., 1993, Art '94 com., 1994. Home and Office: 209 Old Beach Glen Boonton NJ 07005

WITCHER, ALLISON DRU, accounting manager; b. San Francisco, Jan. 2, 1963; d. Wayne Clinton and Linda Lee (Larsen) W. BS in Acctg., Southwest Mo. State U., 1986. CPA. Sr. acct. KPMG-Peat Marwick, Tulsa, 1986-88; sr. internal auditor The Marley Co., Mission Woods, Kans., 1989-93, internal audit supr., 1993-94; acctg. mgr. N.Am. Chem. Co., Overland Park, Kans., 1994—. Big sister Big Bros./Big Sisters, Tulsa, 1987-88. Mem. AICPA, Inst. Internal Auditors, Inst. Mgmt. Accts. Home: 11748 Oakmont Overland Park KS 66210 Office: 8300 College Blvd Overland Park KS 66210

WITCHER, PHYLLIS HERRMANN, secondary education educator; b. Wilmington, Del., Feb. 23, 1938; d. Carl Victor and Ruth Naomi (Ice) Herrmann; m. Murray H. Witcher, Apr. 8, 1961 (div. 1992); children: David, Stephanie Witcher Stewart. BS, U. Del., 1960; MEd, West Chester U., 1982. Cert. secondary tchr., Pa. Tchr. pub. schs. Pa., Tenn., Del., 1974—; textile analyst Sears Roebuck Labs., Chgo., 1977-79; ind. admissions counselor Coll. Selection Svcs., Chadds Ford, Pa., 1983—; bd. dirs. Unionville-Chadds Ford Sch. Dist., 1986-91, Chester County Intermediate Unit, Exton, Pa., 1988-91. Author, speaker No-Fault Div., 1990. Bd. dirs. Mental Health Assn. in Del., Wilmington, 1985-93; past pres. Del. Symphony League, Wilmington, 1985; founder, pres. Protecting Marriage, Inc., Chadds Ford, 1991. Recipient Giraffe Project Nat. Commendation, 1994. Mem. Pa. Sch. Bds. Assn. Republican. Roman Catholic. Home: 22 Mountainview Tr Chadds Ford PA 19317-9182 Office: Protecting Marriage Inc 22 Mountainview Trl Chadds Ford PA 19317-9182

WITH, GERDA BECKER, artist; b. Hamburg, Germany, Mar. 4, 1910; came to U.S., 1939; d. Ludwig and Martha (De Bruycker) Becker; m. Karl E. With, July 17, 1939 (dec. Dec. 1980); children: Christopher B., Nela W. Dwyer. M in Decorative Arts, Charlottenburg, Berlin, 1938. One woman shows include Otis Art Inst., Mus. St. Barbara, also pvt. galleries throughout Europe and U.S., 1958—; illustrator: (book) The Man Who Stole the Word "Beautiful", 1991, others. Home: 3045 Kelton Ave Los Angeles CA 90034

WITHAEGER, ROSEMARY ANNE, civic volunteer, flight attendant; b. Chgo., Oct. 2; d. Edwin Louis and Marjorie Louise (Montgomery) W. Degree in nursing, Cook County Hosp. Sch. Nursing, 1973. RN, Ill. Staff nurse Cook County Hosp., Chgo., 1973-76; charge nurse, staff nurse Northwest Community Hosp., Arlington Heights, Ill., 1976-80; flight attendant Northwest Airlines, Mpls., 1980—; model and product spokesperson, Chgo., 1980—. Vol., chmn. transitional living programs Ctr. for

Abused Children, Chgo., 1986-90; vol. Columbus-Maryville Children's Ctr., Chgo., Cabrini Alive Rehab., Chgo., Camp Action, 1991-93, Chgo. Lung Assn.; mem. bd. dirs. 4th Presbyn. Ch., Ctr. for Whole Life, 1994. Recipient Vol. award Transitional Living Programs, 1988. Mem. Chgo. Coun. Fgn. Rels., Chgo. Health and Tennis Club. Presbyterian. Home: 663 W Barry Ave Apt K Chicago IL 60657-4504 Office: Northwest Airlines 2700 Lone Oak Pky Eagan MN 55121-1534

WITHERINGTON, JENNIFER LEE, sales and marketing executive; b. Albuquerque, Sept. 8, 1960; d. Terrence Lee and Pamela Ann (Hoerter) W. BA in Polit. Sci., James Madison U., 1982. Asst. press sec. U.S. Senate, Washington, 1983-85; nat. sales mgr. Madison Hotels, Washington, 1986-88; dir. sales Madison Air Charter Svcs., Washington, 1987-88; nat. sales mgr. Ritz-Carlton Hotels, Palm Springs, Calif., 1988-90; dir. sales and mktg. Cappa and Graham, Inc., San Francisco, 1990—; spkr. in field. Contbr. articles to profl. jours. Vol. San Francisco Emergency Rescue Team, Yerba Buena Ctr. for Arts. Mem. Am. Soc. Assn. Execs., Profl. Conv. Mgmt. Assn., Hospitality Sales and Mktg. Assn. Internat. (pres. San Francisco chpt. 1994—), Meeting Profls. Internat., Health Care Exhibitors Assn. Republican. Roman Catholic. Home: 1565 Green St #304 San Francisco CA 94123 Office: Cappa and Graham Inc 401 China Basin St Ste 212 San Francisco CA 94107

WITHEROW, KRISTINE J., development administrator; b. Gettysburg, Pa., Feb. 27, 1965; d. Dale E. Witherow and Joanne M. Witherow Stull. BA, U. Pitts., 1987. Freelance photographer Gettysburg, Washington, 1993—; prodn. mgr. York (Pa.) Stenographic Svcs., 1987-88; sales assoc. Am. Print Gallery, Gettysburg, Pa., 1988-89; profl. asst. Price Waterhouse, Washington, 1989-90; advt. coord. Nat. Assn. Life Underwriters, Washington, 1990-92; temporary asst. Temps & Co., Washington, 1992-93; devel. dir. YWCA of Gettysburg, Pa., 1993—. Bd. dirs. Big Bros. and Sisters and York and Adams County, Gettysburg, 1993-94. Recipient Pearl award Big Bros. and Big Sisters of Washington, 1992. Mem. NAFE, Nat. Soc. Fund Raising Execs. Home: 1088 Baltimore Rd York Springs PA 17372 Office: YWCA of Gettysburg 909 Fairfield Rd Gettysburg PA 17325

WITHROW, LUCILLE MONNOT, nursing home administrator; b. Alliance, Ohio, July 28, 1923; d. Charles Edward Monnot and Freda Aldine (Guy) Monnot Cameron; m. Alvin Robert Withrow, June 6, 1945 (dec. 1984); children: Cindi Withrow Johnson, Nancy Withrow Townley, Sharon Withrow Hodgkins, Wendel Alvin. AA in Health Adminstrn., Eastfield Coll., 1976. Lic. nursing home adminstr., Tex.; cert. nursing home ombudsman. Held various clerical positions Dallas, 1950-72; office mgr., asst. adminstr. Christian Care Ctr. Nursing Home, Mesquite, Tex., 1972-76; head adminstr. Christian Care Ctr. Nursing Home and Retirement Complex, Mesquite, 1976-91; nursing home ombudsman Tex. Dept. Aging and Tex. Dept. Health, Dallas, 1991-93; legal asst. Law Offices of Wendel A. Withrow, Carrollton, Tex., 1993—; mem. com. on geriatric curriculum devel. Eastfield Coll., Mesquite, 1979, 87; mem. ombudsman adv. com. Sr. Citizens Greater Dallas; nursing home cons. Vol. Dallas Arboretum and Bot. Soc., Dallas Summer Musicals Guild; mem. Ombudsman adv. com. Sr. Citizens of Greater Dallas, Health Svcs. Speakers Bur.; charter mem. Stage Show Prodns. Recipient Volunteerism awards Tex. Atty. Gen., 1987, Tex. Gov., 1992. Mem. Tex. Assn. Homes for Aging, Am. Assn. Homes for Aging, Health Svcs. Speakers Bur., White Rock Kiwanis. Republican. Mem. Ch. of Christ. Home: 11344 Lippitt Ave Dallas TX 75218-1922 Office: Law Office of W A Withrow 1120 Metrocrest # 200 Carrollton TX 75006

WITHROW, MARY ELLEN, treasurer of United States; b. Marion, Ohio, Oct. 2, 1930; d. Clyde Welsh and Mildred (Stump) Hinamon; m. Norman David Withrow, Sept. 4, 1948; children: Linda Rizzo, Leslie Legge, Norma, Rebecca. Mem. Elgin Local Bd. Edn., Marion, Ohio, 1969-73, pres., 1972; safety programs dir. ARC, Marion, 1968-72; dep. registrar State of Ohio, Marion, 1972-75; dep. county auditor Marion County, Ohio, 1975-77, county treas., 1977-83; treas. State of Ohio, Columbus, 1983-94; treas. of the U.S. Dept. Treasury, Washington, 1994—; chmn. Ohio Bd. Deposits, 1983—, Anthony Commn. on Pub. Fin. Mem. exec. com. Ohio Dem. Com., mem. exec. com. women's caucus; mem. Dem. Nat. Com.; mem. Met. Women's Ctr.; pres. Marion County Dem. Club, 1976; participant Harvard U. Strategic Leadership Conf., 1990.; mem. Dem. Leadership Coun. Inducted Ohio Women's Hall of Fame, 1986; named Outstanding Elected Dem. Woman Holding Pub. Office, Nat. Fedn. Dem. Women, 1987, Advocate of Yr., SBA, 1988, Most Valuable State Pub. Ofcl., City and State newspaper, 1990; recipient Donald L. Scantlebury Meml. award, 1991, Women of Achievement award YWCA of Met. Columbus, 1993; fellow Women Execs. in State Govt., Harvard U., 1987. Mem. LWV (dem. leadership coun.), State Assn. County Treas. (legis. com. 1979-83, treas. 1982), Nat. Assn. State Treas. (pres. 1992, Jesse Unruh award 1993, chair long range planning com., mem. exec. com.), Nat. Assn. State Auditors Comtps. and Treas. (pres. 1990, strategic planning com., intergov. rels. com., chair state and mcpl. bonds com.), Coun. State Govts. (exec. com., internat. affairs com., orgnl. planning and coord. com., strategic planning task force), Women Execs. in State Govt. (chair fund devel. com.). Club: Bus. and Profl. Women's. Office: Dept Treasury 1500 Pennsylvania Ave NW Rm 2134 Washington DC 20220

WITHROW, SHEILA KAY, school nurse; b. Dayton, Ohio, Oct. 13, 1959; d. Robert and Shirley Elaine (McGuire) H.; m. James Laurence Withrow, Jr., Aug. 7, 1982; 1 child, Robert Laurence. AAS in Nursing, Miami U., Oxford, Ohio, 1982, BS in Nursing, 1987. RN, Ohio. Staff nurse Children's Hosp. Med. Ctr., Cin., 1982-84; staff nurse Middletown (Ohio) Regional Hosp., 1984-87, adminstrv. clin. coord., 1987-90; clin. coord. Middletown Regional Hosp., 1990-91; sch. nurse Franklin (Ohio) City Schs., 1991—; participant Nursing Grand Rounds The Total Hip Patient, 1986; mem. Patient Care task force, 1988. Mem. Ohio Assn. of Sch. Nurses, 1992—. Democrat. Baptist. Home: 205 Leland Ct Middletown OH 45042-3915 Office: Franklin City Schs 150 E 6th St Franklin OH 45005-2555

WITHROW-GALLANTER, SHERRIE ANNE, construction and audio company executive; b. Sacramento, Mar. 10, 1960; d. Jim and Ilene (James) Withrow; m. Michael Paul Gallanter, Jan. 7, 1990. Student, Diablo Valley Community Coll., Pleasant Hill, Calif., 1977, Tarrant County Jr. Coll., Ft. Worth, 1982-83, Coll. of Marin, Kentfield, Calif., 1988, Merritt Coll., Oakland, Calif., 1990; AA in Bus. Adminstrn. and Mgmt., St. Louis Community Coll., Florissant, Mo., 1981. Internal cashier AAA Automobile Club Mo., St. Louis, 1977-79; receiving clk. Dayton-Hudson Target Stores, Florissant and Ft. Worth, 1979-81; supr. credit and collection World Svc. Life Ins. Co., Ft. Worth, 1982-83; bank br. balancer, data processing div. Tex. Am. Bank Svcs., Inc., Ft. Worth, 1984-85; asst. to contr. Positive Video-Post Prodn., Orinda, Calif., 1985-87; with contractor's desk adminstrn. dept. Shell Oil Co., Martinez, Calif., 1987-88; asst. to chief fin. officer J.T. Thorpe & Son, Inc., Richmond, Calif., 1988-89; founder, gen. ptnr. HomeVisions Constrn. Svcs., El Sobrante, Calif., 1989—, AudioVisions Sound Co., El Sobrante, 1990—, AV Electric, El Sobrante, 1994—; project fin. cons. various constrn. cos., No. Calif., 1988—. Fundraiser Sr. Citizen Subsidized Housing Complex, Martinez, 1987, 88. David L. Underwood scholar Florissant Valley (St. Louis) C.C., 1980-81. Mem. NAFE, Internat. Platform Assn., Phi Theta Kappa. Democrat. Office: HomeVisions Constrn Co and AudioVisions Sound Co PO Box 20368 El Sobrante CA 94820-0368

WITHSTANDLEY, HARRIET FRANKEL, lawyer; b. Phila., Nov. 27, 1945; d. Max and Rose (Resnick) Frankel; m. Paul B. Withstandley II, May 5, 1978; children: Peter Robert, Oliver David Henry. BA, Ohio State U., 1966, MA, 1967; JD, Temple U., 1973. Bar: Pa. 1973, U.S. Dist. Ct. (ea. dist.) Pa. 1974, U.S. Ct. Appeals (3d cir.) 1975. Rsch. dir. alcohol study unit Boston City Hosp., 1968-69; rsch. assoc. Univ. City Sci. Inst., Phila., 1969-71; summer assoc. Wolf, Block, Schorr & Solis-Cohen, Phila., 1972, assoc., 1973-75; law clk. U.S. Dist. Ct. (ea. dist.), Phila., 1975-78; assoc. Fellheimer, Krakower & Eichen, Phila., 1978; atty./divsn. mgr. Bell Telephone of Pa., Phila., 1978-89; shareholder Griffith & Burr, P.C., Phila., 1989-91; litigation atty./mgr. ARA Svcs., Inc., Phila., 1990-92; examiner Pa. Bd. Law Examiners, Phila., 1993—; dep. chief counsel Pa. Med. Profl. Liability Catastrophe Loss Fund, Harrisburg, Rosemont, 1993—; vis. lectr. Newton Coll. of the Sacred Heart, Newton, Mass., 1968-69. Pres. Penn Valley (Pa.) Civic Assn., 1993—. Recipient Am. Jurisprudence award Contract Law, 1971. Fellow Acad. Advocacy; mem. Am. Corp. Counsel Assn., Nat. Assn. Health Lawyers, Pa. Bar Assn., Delaware County Bar Assn. Home: 422 Old Gulph Rd Narberth PA 19072 Office: Med Profl Liability Catastrophe Loss Fund 1062 E Lancaster Ave 15-F Bryn Mawr PA 19010

WITKIN, EVELYN MAISEL, geneticist; b. N.Y.C., Mar. 9, 1921; d. Joseph and Mary (Levin) Maisel; m. Herman A. Witkin, July 9, 1943 (dec. July 1979); children—Joseph, Andrew. AB, NYU, 1941; MA, Columbia U., 1943, PhD, 1947; DSc honoris causa, N.Y. Med. Coll., 1978. Mem. staff genetics dept. Carnegie Inst., Washington, 1950-55; mem. faculty State U. N.Y. Downstate Med. Center, Bklyn., 1955-71; prof. medicine State U. N.Y. Downstate Med. Center, 1968-71; prof. biol. scis. Douglass Coll., Rutgers U., 1971-79, Barbara McClintock prof. genetics, 1979-83; Barbara McClintock prof. genetics Waksman Inst. Microbiology, 1983-91; Barbara McClintock prof. emerita Waksman Inst. Microbiology, Rutgers U., 1991—. Author articles; mem. editorial bds. profl. jours. Postdoctoral fellow Am. Cancer Soc., 1947-49; fellow Carnegie Instn., 1957; Selman A. Waksman lectr., 1960; Phi Beta Kappa vis. scholar, 1980-81; grantee NIH, 1956-89; recipient Prix Charles Leopold Mayer French Acad. Scis., 1977, Lindback award, 1979. Fellow AAAS, Am. Acad. Microbiology; mem. NAS, Am. Acad. Arts and Scis., Environ. Mutagen Soc., Am. Genetics Soc., Am. Soc. Microbiology. Home: 1 Firestone Ct Princeton NJ 08540-5220 Office: Rutgers U Waksman Inst Microbiology Piscataway NJ 08854

WITKIN, MILDRED HOPE FISHER, psychotherapist, educator; b. N.Y.C.; d. Samuel and Sadie (Goldschmidt) Fisher; children: Georgia Hope, Roy Thomas, Laurie Phillips, Kimberly, Nicole, Scott, Joshua, Jennifer; m. Jorge Radovic, Aug. 26, 1983. AB, Hunter Coll., MA, Columbia U., 1968; PhD, NYU, 1973. Diplomate Am. Bd. Sexology, Am. Bd. Sexuality; cert. supr. Head counselor Camp White Lake, Camp Emanuel, Long Beach, N.J.; tchr. econs., polit. sci. Hunter Coll. High Sch.; dir., group leader follow-up program Jewish Vacation Assn., N.Y.C.; investigator N.Y.C. Housing Authority; psychol. counselor Montclair State Coll., Upper Montclair, N.J., 1967-68; mem., lectr. Creative Problem-Solving Inst., U. Buffalo, 1968; psychol. counselor Fairleigh Dickinson U., Teaneck, N.J., 1968, dir. Counseling Center, 1969-74; pvt. practice psychotherapy, N.Y.C., also Westport, Conn.; sr. faculty supr., family therapist and psychotherapist Payne Whitney Psychiat. Clinic, N.Y. Hosp., 1973—; clin. asst. prof. dept. psychiatry Cornell U. Med. Coll., 1974—; assoc. dir. sex therapy and edn. program Cornell-N.Y. Hosp. Med. Ctr., 1974—; sr. cons. Kaplan Inst. for Evaluation and Treatment of Sexual Disorders, 1981—; supr. master's and doctoral candidates, NYU, 1975-82; pvt. practice psychotherapy and sex therapy, N.Y.C., also Westport, Conn.; cons. counselor edn. tng. programs N.Y.C. Bd. Edn., 1971-75; cons. Health Info. Systems, 1972-79; vis. prof. numerous colls. and univs.; chmn. sci. com. 1st Internat. Symposium on Female Sexuality, Buenos Aires, 1984. Exhibited in group shows at Scarsdale (N.Y.) Art Show, 1959, Red Shutter Art Studio, Long Beach, 1968. Edn. legislation chmn. PTA, Yonkers, 1955; publicity chmn. United Jewish Appeal, Scarsdale, 1959-65; Scarsdale chmn. mothers com. Boy Scouts Am., 1961-64; mem. Morrow Assn. on Correction N.J., 1969-91; bd. dirs. Girl Scouts of Am. Recipient Bronze medal for svcs. Hunter Coll.; United Jewish Appeal plaque, 1962; Founders Day award N.Y. U., 1973, citation N.Y. Hosp./Cornell U. Med. Ctr., 1990. Fellow Internat. Coun. Sex Edn. and Parenthood of Am. U., Am. Acad. Clin. Sexologists; mem. AAUW, APA, ACA, Assn. Counseling Supervision, Am. Coll. Personnel Assn., Internat. Assn. Marriage and Family Counselors, Am. Coll. Sexuality (cert.), Women's Med. Assn. N.Y.C., N.Y. Acad. Sci., Am. Coll. Pers. Assn. (nat. mem. commn. II 1973-76), Nat. Assn. Women Deans and Counselors, Am. Assn. Sex Educators, Counselors and Therapists (regional bd., nat. accreditation bd., cert. internat. supr.), Soc. for Sci. Study Sex Therapy and Rsch., Eastern Assn. Sex Therapists, Am. Assn. Marriage and Family Counselors, N.J. Assn. Marriage and Family Counselors, Ackerman Family Inst., Am. Personnel and Guidance Assn., Am., N.Y., N.J. psychol. assns., Creative Edn. Found., Am. Assn. Higher Edn., Assn. Counselor Supervision and Edn., Profl. Women's Caucus, LWV, Am. Assn. counseling and Devel., Am. Women's Med. Assn., Nat. Coun. on Women in Medicine, Argentine Soc. Human Sexuality (hon.), Am. Assn. Sexology (diplomate), Pi Lambda Theta, Kappa Delta Pi, Alpha Chi Alpha. Author: 45-And Single Again, 1985, Single Again, 1994; contbr. articles to profl. jours. and textbooks; lectr. internat. and nat. workshops, radio and TV. Home: 9 Sturges Commons Westport CT 06880-2832 Office: 35 Park Ave New York NY 10016-3838

WITKOWSKI, KIM LOUISE, counselor; b. Winchester, Mass., June 24, 1949; d. Sam R. and Glorya (Sheehan) Macaione; m. Walter Joseph Witkowski, Feb. 7, 1981. BA, U. Mass., 1971; MEd, U. S.C., 1982; MA, Webster U., 1991; PhD, Walden U., 1993. Tchr. Horry County Sch. Dist., Conway, S.C., 1976-79; English resource tchr. Georgetown (S.C.) County Sch. Dist., 1980; tchr. profoundly mentally handicapped Horry County Sch. Dist., 1981-82, spl. edn. resource tchr., 1982-86; dir. edn., staff psychologist Coastal Carolina Psychiatric Hosp., Conway, 1986-90; intern individual and family therapy Navy Family Svcs., Charleston, S.C., 1991; sch. psychologist Horry County Sch. Dist., 1990-93; pvt. practice in family and individual therapy Myrtle Beach, S.C., 1991—; adj. faculty Coastal Carolina U., Conway, 1993; adj. prof. Webster U.; hosp. credentialing com. Coastal Carolina Hosp., quality assurance com., clin. adv. com., accreditation com., fire and safety com., master treatment plan com., child and adolescent program devel. com., mktg. com., infection control com.; multicultural com. Horry County Sch. Dist., 1993, homebound instruction policies and procedures com., 1990, Coastal Carolina Hosp. rep., 1990, Myrtle Beach primary sch. discipline com., 1986, Spl. Edn. Dept. Head, 1985-86. Edn. chair Horry Human Rels. Coun., exec. dir. Afro-Fest; mem. Horry County Dept. Social Svcs. Multidisciplinary Case Adv. Team, Children's Protective Svcs., 1989-91; v.p., bd. dirs. South Horry Med. Ctr. Rural Health Initiative, 1984-87; treas., bd. dirs. Community Vol Svcs., 1979-81; past S.C. Guardian Ad Litem Program, 1985—; governing bd. Horry Human Rels. Coun., 1994. Mem. AACD, Coun. for Exceptional Children, Assn. Children with Learning Disabilities, S.C. Assn. Sch. Psychologists, Orton Dyslexia Soc., Assn. Edn. Therapists. Avocations: reading, travel. Home: Briarcliffe Acres 12 S Gate Rd Myrtle Beach SC 29572-5621

WITORT, JANET LEE, lawyer; b. Cedar Rapids, Iowa, Mar. 10, 1950; d. Charles Francis Svoboda and Phyllis Harriet (Wilber) Miller; m. Stephen Francis Witort, Oct. 27, 1979. Student U. Colo., 1968-69, U. Iowa, 1971; BA, U. No. Colo., 1972; JD, Loyola U., 1979. Bar: Ill. 1979; U.S. Dist. Ct. (no dist.) Ill. 1979; U.S. Supreme Ct. 1987. Paralegal, Fed. Nat. Mortgage Assn., Chgo., 1973-75, Sidley & Austin, Chgo., 1975-76; assoc. Frankel, McKay & Orlikoff, Chgo., 1979-81; atty. Mut. Trust Life Ins. Co., Oak Brook, Ill., 1981-86; assoc. counsel, asst. sec. N.Am. Co. for Life and Health Ins., Chgo., 1986-88; sr. atty. AMA, Chgo., 1988-89, gen. counsel, sec., AMA Ins., Chgo., 1989-91; v.p., gen. counsel, sec. AMA Ins., 1991-93; asst. gen. counsel Prudential Ins. and Fin. Svcs., 1994—. Author: (with others) The Legal Assistant-A Self Statement, 1974, (with others) Requirements and Limitations Imposed by Corporate Law, 1989, updated 1992. Vol. Rep. Campaign, Chgo., 1974-76, 90-93, Children's Hosp. Guild, N. Oaks, Minn., 1993—, Sci. Mus. Minn., St. Paul, 1994—; v.p. Children's Hosp. Guild, 1994—; trustee Hinsdale Ill. Pub. Libr., 1987-93, v.p., 1991-93; bd. dirs. Suburban Libr. System, Burr Ridge, Ill., 1988-91, sec., 1990-91. Mem. ABA, Am. Soc. Med. Assn. Coun., Ill. Bar Assn., Chgo. Assn. Paralegal Assts. (sec. 1973-74), Chgo. Bar Assn. (chair life & health ins. subcom. 1992-94), Womans Bar Assn. of Ill. (mem. ins. com. 1987-93), Ill. Paralegal Assn. (v.p. 1975-76), Nat. Fedn. Paralegal Assns. (midwest regional dir. 1975-76), Am. Corp. Counsel Assn. (mem. membership com. 1988-90), Phi Alpha Delta, Student Bar Assn. (class rep. 1976-77). Republican. Avocations: golf, travel, skiing. Office: 13001 County Rd #10 Plymouth MN 55440 also: 515 N State St Chicago IL 60610-4320

WITT, DOREEN MARIE, sales training executive; b. Dubuque, Iowa, Apr. 28, 1960; d. John Dale and Janet Louise (Chunat) Kenkel; m. Carey Michael Witt, Oct. 4, 1986; 1 child, Zachariah Harding. Student, Loras Coll., 1979; BS in Mktg., Iowa State U., 1983. Asst. mgr. Sanger Harris, Dallas, 1983, sales mgr., 1983, area mgr., 1983-85; product devel. specialist County Seat Stores, Dallas, 1985; S.W. account exec. Perry Ellis Sportswear, Dallas, 1985-86; account exec. Radio Stas. KOKE, KKMJ, Austin, Tex., 1986-90; sr. acct. exec. Radio Sta. KKMJ, Austin, 1990-93; dir. sales tng. Radio Stas. KKMJ, KFGI, KJCE, Austin, 1993—. Vol. Volente (Tex.) Vol. Fire Dept., 1986—; voter registrar Williamson County, Leander, Tex., 1987. Mem. Am. Mktg. Assn., Austin Bus. Forum (sec. 1987-88, v.p. membership 1988-90, 92—), Am. Women in Radio and TV (v.p. membership 1986-88, membership co-chair 1992—, v.p. scholarship 1988-91, del. 1988, 90, Appreciation award 1986, 87-88, 89-91). Republican. Home: 213 Reed Dr Leander TX 78641 Office: KKMJ MAJIC 95.5 FM 4301 Westbank Dr B-350 Austin TX 78746

WITT, RUTH ELIZABETH, retired museum administrator; b. Clark, Mo., Oct. 17, 1922; d. James Barnett and Lottie Myrtle (Heying) Croswhite; m. Arthur Witt, Jan. 13, 1943; children—Eric Van, David Arnold, Judith Ann. Student, U. Ill., 1940-42; B.A., U. Mo., 1969, M.A, 1972. Draftsman constrn. co., Columbia, Mo., 1958-59; supr. lang. library Stephens Coll., Columbia, Mo., 1959-62; interim dir. Christian edn. First Presbyn. Ch., Columbia, Mo., 1972-73; sr. clk. Mus. U. Mo., Columbia, 1973-74, adminstrv. asst., 1974-76, registrar, 1976-77, asst. dir., 1977-83, interim dir., 1983-84, hon. research fellow, 1984—. Editor: (catalogue) Gandharan Scultpure, 1981; editor mag., newsletter Mus. Art and Archaeology; contbr. articles to profl. jours.; exhibited in group shows Columbia, 1986—, Sarasota and Longboat Key, Fla., 1987—. Recipient Byler adminstrv. award U. Mo., 1979, awards for paintings, 1986-94; grantee Mo. Arts Coun., 1980, 81, 83, U. Mo., 1980. Mem. Am. Assn. Mus., Assn. Coll. U. Mus. and Galleries, Mus. Assocs. (sec. 1976-79, bd. dirs. 1976-85), Phi Beta Kappa. Home: 351 Crown Pt Columbia MO 65203-2202 Office: Mus Art Archaeology 1 Pickard Hall Columbia MO 65211

WITT, SANDRA SMITH, federal agency official; b. Rockwood, Tenn., Aug. 27, 1944; d. William Perry and Imogene C. Smith; children: Whitney, Christian. Student, U. Chattanooga, 1966-67; AS in Nuclear Technology, Chattanooga State Tech. Coll., 1976; BS in Physics, U. Tenn., 1978; MS in Engring. Sci., U. Tenn. Space Inst., 1982. Cert. nuclear equipment qualification engr., Ala. Tech. writer, editor Tenn. Blue Cross-Blue Shield, Chattanooga, 1966-68; supr. editing dept. Corp. Law Firm, Chattanooga, 1968-77; asst. physics lab. U. Tenn., Chattanooga, 1977-78; oil field engr. Schlumberger Co., Houston, 1978; research assoc. U. Tenn. Space Inst., Tullahoma, Tenn., 1979-81; sr. project engr. Wyle Labs., Huntsville, Ala., 1981-82; sr. engr., br. chief U.S. Dept. Energy, Aiken, S.C., 1983-91; engr. mgr. Martin Marietta Energy Sys., 1991—. Recipient spl. svc. award Dept. Energy, 1986, 87, 90, career award Nat. Bus. and Profl. Women, 1977; Diuguid fellow, 1976. Mem. NAFE, Am. Nuclear Soc., Phi Theta Kappa (past v.p.), Sigma Pi Sigma.

WITTE, LOUISE W., former librarian; b. La Salle, Ill., Oct. 17, 1915; d. Stanley Wujek and Agnes (Olsztynski); m. Michael Witte, Dec. 21, 1940; children: Michael Steven, Janet Louise, Lois Jean, John Craig. BSEd, U. Ill., 1940; MLS, State U. N.J., 1965. Tchr. English and Polish So. Milw. (Wis.) High Sch., 1940-41; libr. Maxson Jr. High Sch., Plainfield, N.J., 1965-67, Westfield (N.J.) Sr. High Sch., 1967-77. Recipient Mayor's Trophy Chatham (N.J.) Pub. Libr., 1984. Home: 3674 N Laurelwood Loop Beverly Hills FL 34465-3305

WITTICH, BRENDA JUNE, religious organization executive, minister; b. Muncie, Ind., Dec. 19, 1946; d. Plano Brentie and Norma June (Huggins) Gossett; m. Chester Edward Wittich, Dec. 24, 1980; 1 child, September Leigh Noonan. Lic., Morris Pratt Inst. Assn., 1979, postgrad., 1983-86. Ordained minister Nat. Spiritualist Assn. of Churches, 1986. Pastor Fifth Spiritualist Ch., St. Louis, 1988—. Co-author, editor: National Spiritualist Association Churches Public Relations Handbook, 1992; co-author booklet: Spiritualism - Pathway of Light, 1992; contbr. articles to Nat. Spiritualist Mag. Mem. St. Louis Pub. Sch. Clergy Leaders Forum, 1991-92, Tchrs. for Nat. Spiritualist Assn. of Chs. Ednl. Ctr.-Psychology and Parlimentary Procedures. Mem. Nat. Hemlock Soc., Nat. Spiritualist Assn. of Chs. (trustee 1990-92, supt. pub. rels. 1990-94, v.p. bd. trustees 1992-94, pres. bd. trustees 1994), Inst. Noetic Scis. Home: 3903 Connecticut St Saint Louis MO 63116 Office: Nat Spiritualist Assn Chs 13 Cottage Row PO Box 217 Lily Dale NY 14752

WITTIG, GERTRAUDE CHRISTA, biological sciences educator; b. Glauchau, Germany, Oct. 4, 1928; came to U.S., 1958; d. Heinrich and Frida (Grünler) W. Student, U. Marburg, Germany, 1947-50; D of Rerum Naturarum, U. Tübingen, Germany, 1955, staatsexamen, 1955. Rsch. scholar, Deutsche Forschungsgemeinschaft U. Tübingen, Germany, 1956-58; rsch. fellow U. Calif., Berkeley, 1958-59; microbiologist USDA Agrl. Rsch. Svc., Beltsville, Md., 1959-62; rsch. microbiologist USDA Forest Svc., Corvallis, Oreg., 1962-68; adj. assoc. prof. Oreg. State U., Corvallis, 1962-68; faculty rsch. assoc. Argonne Nat. Lab., Lemont, Ill., summer 1972; assoc. prof. So. Ill. U., Edwardsville, 1968-75, prof., 1975—; cons. U. Ariz., Tucson, 1971. Author: Manual and Study Guide for the Introductory Electron Microscopy Laboratory, 1972; mem. editorial group; contbr. articles to profl. jours. State senate candidate Rep. Party, Madison County, Ill., 1975-76; dist. vice chmn. Rep. Party, Edwardsville, 1976-79, precinct committeeman, 1976-81. Fulbright travel grantee, 1958; NSF Instructional Sci. Equipment Program grantee, 1969-72; grantee Lalor Found., 1958, Deutscher Akad. Austauschdienst, 1958, 92, U. Kans. Ford Found. Rsch. Inst. on Women, 1980. Mem. NOW (pres., sec., treas. metro-east chpt. 1974-78), Oreg. Electron Microscopists (co-founder, sec., treas.), Cen. States Electron Microscopy Soc. (pres. 1974-75), Phi Kappa Phi. Lutheran. Office: So Ill U Dept Biol Scis Edwardsville IL 62026

WITTMAN, SANDRA MARIE, librarian; b. Cleve., Oct. 24, 1943; d. Russell Joseph and Sylvia Maria (Beerkircher) W. B.Ed., U. Wis., Whitewater, 1965; MA Libr. Sci., Rosary Coll., River Forest, Ill., 1975. English tchr. Brodhead (Wis.) High Sch., 1965-68, Verona (Wis.) High Sch., 1968-70, 71-75; media specialist Career Edn. Svc. Ctr., Arlington Heights, Ill., 1975-77; libr. Oakton Community Coll., Des Plaines, Ill., 1977—. Author: (bibliography) Writing About Vietnam: The Literature of the Vietnam Conflict, 1989. Mem. Beta Phi Mu. Lutheran. Office: Oakton Community Coll Libr 1600 E Golf Rd Des Plaines IL 60016-1258

WITTMANN, CATHERINE CLAUSS, insurance broker; b. Buffalo, Oct. 30, 1964; d. James Thomas and Imelda (Sheedy) Clauss; m. Werner John Wittmann, May 25, 1990. BS, Nazareth Coll. Rochester, N.Y., 1986. Lic. ins. broker, N.Y.; cert. ins. svc. rep., ins. counselor. Asst. customer svc. rep. Clauss & Co., Inc., Buffalo, 1986-88, customer svc. rep., 1988-92; br. mgr. Clauss & Co., Inc., West Seneca, N.Y., 1992-94, sales, mktg. dir., 1994—. Vol. PBS, Buffalo, 1992-93, World U. Games '93, Buffalo, 1993, UNIFEST, Buffalo, 1993, 94. Mem. Ins. Women Buffalo, Up-Downtown Buffalo. Office: ET Clauss & Co Inc 735 Delaware Ave Buffalo NY 14209

WIZMUR, JUDITH H., federal judge; b. 1949. BA, Rutgers U., 1971, JD, 1974. Law clk. Camden County Ct., 1974-75; mcpl. prosecutor Twp. of Berlin, N.J., 1976-78; atty. Lewis Katz, P.A., Cherry Hill, N.J., 1976-78; asst. dir. N.J. Div. Motor Vehicles, 1978-81; adminstrv. law judge State of N.J., 1982-85, worker's compensation judge, 1985; bankruptcy judge U.S. Dist. Ct. N.J., Camden, 1985—. Mem. ABA, N.J. Bar Assn., Camden County Bar Assn., Burlington County Bar Assn., Nat. Assn. Women Judges, Nat. Conf. Bankruptcy Judges, Tri-State Women Lawyers Assn. Office: US Dist Ct 15 N 7th St Camden NJ 08102-1104*

WLODARSKY, SHARON LEE, landscape designer; b. Memphis, Aug. 5, 1952; d. James Alvin and Freddie Lee (King) Hensley; m. Larry Lloyd Wlodarsky, July 2, 1978; children from previous marriage: Wendy, Dawn, Walt, Tiffany. Grad. high sch., Huran, Ohio. Owner K & L Mfg., Berlin Heights, Ohio, 1973—; co-owner, landscape designer, bookkeeper, sales K & L Nursery, Berlin Heights, Ohio, 1976—; co-woner, mgr. Rental Properties, Berlin Heights, Ohio, 1976—, Norwalk, Ohio, 1976—; owner Rainbow Fabrics & Gifts, Berlin Heights. Co-inventor K & L Karrier, 1991. Mem. LDS Ch. Home and office: 12211 Berlin Rd Berlin Heights OH 44814-9610

WLODYKA, SUSAN K., accountant; b. Westfield, Mass., Oct. 15, 1964; d. Duane Lee and Joanne Eleanor (Tucker) Wyman; m. Jeffrey M. Wlodyka, May 20, 1989 (div. Sept. 1993). BS in Mgmt. Adv. Svcs., N.H. Coll., 1986. CPA. Staff auditor Ernst & Whinney, Manchester, N.H., 1986-88; auditor, sr. auditor Price Waterhouse, Providence, 1988-92; mgr. gen. acctg. Delta Dental Plan Mass., Medford, 1992-94; ins. audit mgr. Price Waterhouse, Boston, 1994—. Treas. One Voice of N.H, A Non-Profit AIDS Benefit Orgn. Mem. AICPA. Office: Price Waterhouse 160 Federal St Boston MA 02110

WOBBLETON, JUDY KAREN, artist, educator; b. Williamston, N.C., Aug. 31, 1947; d. Lloyd Thomas and Lillian Edith (Hudson) Letchworth; m. Albert Virgil Wobbleton Jr., Apr. 7, 1968; children: Olivia Elizabeth, Virgil Alan. Clk. Beaufort County Hosp., Washington, N.C., 1965-68; ins. supr. Mercy Hosp., Sacramento, 1968-72; adminstrv. asst. hosp. svcs. Fairbanks (Alaska) Meml. Hosp., 1972-75; basketry artist Williamston, 1983—; instr. basketry N.C. Basketmakers, 1984-94, Wayne C.C., Goldsboro, N.C., 1986-91, Wayne County Arts Coun., Goldsboro, 1990-91. Contbg. artist: The Basket Book, 1988, Basketmaker's Baskets, 1990, Craft Works in The Home, 1990. Troop leader Girl Scouts U.S., Goldsboro, 1983-88, svc. unit mgr., 1987-91; active Roanoke Arts & Crafts Guild, 1991-94. Recipient 2d Pl. award Wilson Arts Coun., 1987, 3d Pl. award Martin County Arts Coun., 1992. Mem. N.C. Basketmakers Assn. (hon., bd. dirs. 1984-94, membership chmn. 1984-87, pres. 1990-94), Goldweavers Basketry Guild (hon.). Home and Office: Baskets By Judy 1325 Oakview Rd Williamston NC 27892

WOELFLING, MAXINE MARIE, state agency administrator; b. Sharon, Pa., Oct. 26, 1949; d. Max Frank and Mary Theresa (Koch) Tomczak; m. Frank Adam Woelfling, Aug. 17, 1974; children: Andrew, Peter. BS, U. Pitts., 1971; JD, U. Notre Dame, 1974. Bar: Pa. 1974, U.S. Dist. Ct. (mid. dist.) Pa. 1976, U.S. Ct. Appeals (3d cir.) 1976. Asst. atty. gen. Dept. Environ. Resources, Commonwealth Pa., Harrisburg, 1974-81, dir. Bur. Regulatory Counsel, 1981-85; chmn. Environ. Hearing Bd., Commonwealth Pa., Harrisburg, 1985—. Named one of Outstanding Young Women of Am., 1980. Mem. Pa. Bar Assn. (treas. 1986-87, vice-chmn. 1987-88, chmn. 1988, environ. mineral and natural resources law sect.). Democrat. Roman Catholic. Home: 306 Coppersmith Ln Strasburg PA 17579-1021 Office: Environ Hearing Bd 400 Market St 2nd Fl PO Box 8457 Harrisburg PA 17105-8457

WOEPPEL, PATRICE, rehabilitation counseling organization executive; b. Elmira, N.Y., Mar. 13, 1939; d. Oswald Joseph and Alice (O'Reilly) W.; m. Richard W. Berkeley, June 19, 1971 (div. July 1985); 1 child, S. Jamal. B.S., CCNY, 1966; M.S., Fordham U., 1980; postgrad. in edn., Nova U., 1985—. Cert. rehab. counselor Commn. on Rehab. Counselor Cert., Chgo., Fla., Pub. relations coordinator, office adminstr. Am. Mus. Natural History, N.Y.C., 1966; caseworker Westchester County Dept. Social Services, White Plains, N.Y., 1966-69; research asst. NYU Med. Ctr., N.Y.C., 1969-70; project dir. Van Etten drug treatment program Albert Einstein Coll. Medicine, Bronx, N.Y., 1970-76; program adminstr. Westchester County Dept. Community Mental Health, 1976-84; exec. dir., chief operating officer Early Childhood Devel. Assocs., Fort Lauderdale, Fla., 1984-86 ; chief operating officer Threshold Inc., Rochester, N.Y., 1986—; workshop presenter; mem. regional task force on children and youth N.Y. State Office Mental Health, 1977-84; mem. instrnl. rev. bd. N.Y. State Div. Substance Abuse Services, 1980-83; mem. steering com. Westchester County Task Force on Child Abuse/Neglect, 1980-84; bd. dirs. SCAN Am. of N.Y., Inc., 1982-84; v.p. Westchester Coalition on Teenage Pregnancy, Prevention and Parenting, 1982-84; mem. residential treatment facility adv. com. Hudson River region N.Y. State Office Mental Health, 1983-84; chmn. legis. com. Presch. Interagy. Council, 1985-86; co-chmn. ins. com. Fla. Child Care Provider's Forum, 1985-86; mem. Children's Prevention Task Force for State Health and Rehabilative Services, Dist. X, 1985—. Recipient achievement award Nat. Assn. Counties, 1980, 81; Ruth Benedict award for grad. study in anthropology, 1966; Edwin Michaelian scholar Pace U., 1984. Lodge: Rotary. Mem. Assn. Mental Health Adminstrs. (cert.), Fort Lauderdale C. of C. Democrat. Home: 14 Arnold Park Rochester NY 14607-2030 Office: 115 Clinton Ave S Rochester NY 14604-1802

WOFFORD, CYNTHIA DALE, biologist, laboratory technician; b. Oct. 11, 1957; d. Clyde Del and Dorothy (Melton) W. BS in Biology, U. S.C., Spartanburg. Pharm. technician Rite-Aid Pharmacy, Spartanburg, S.C., 1980-82; lead instrumentation lab technician Hoechst-Celanese Corp., Spartanburg, S.C., 1982—. Home: 113 Maulden St Spartanburg SC 29302

WOHLGELERNTER, BETH, organization executive; b. N.Y.C., Jan. 30, 1956; d. Maurice Nathaniel and Esther Rachel (Feinerman) W. BA, Barnard Coll., 1977. Exec. aide to pres. Barnard Coll., N.Y.C., 1977-80; spl. asst. to pres. The Commonwealth Fund, N.Y.C., 1980-81; asst. to chief exec. officer/pres. Mary McFadden, Inc., N.Y.C., 1981-84; exec. adminstr. The Donna Karan Co., N.Y.C., 1984-90; exec. dir. Hadassah, The Women's Zionist Orgn. Am., Inc., N.Y.C., 1990—; comm. adv. coun. AT&T, 1992—. Bd. dirs., v.p. N.Am. Conf. on Ethiopian Jewry, N.Y.C., 1981-85, bd. advisors, 1985—; bd. govs. Lincoln Sq. Synagogue, N.Y.C., 1988-94, bd. trustees, 1994—; bd. govs. United Israel Appeal, 1991—. Office: Hadassah The Women's Zionist Orgn Am Inc 50 W 58th St New York NY 10019-2590*

WOHLRABE, MARY DURKIN, journalism educator; b. Chgo., Apr. 10, 1948; d. Joseph E. and Eleanor M. (Lorkowski) Durkin; m. Kent P. Wohlrabe, June 14, 1978 (div. Feb. 1991). BS, No. Ill. U., 1970, MA, 1976; EdD, Ill. State U., 1991. City editor Williams Press, Chicago Heights, Ill., 1970-73; mng. editor Pioneer Press, Wilmette, Ill., 1973-75; asst. prof. Baker U., Baldwin, Kans., 1976-77, U. Wis., LaCrosse, 1977-81; assoc. prof. journsliam Ea. Ill. U., Charleston, 1981—; acting chair journalism dept. Ea. Ill. U., 1983-84, chair faculty senate, 1985-86, chair coll. assessment com., 1993-94. Editor: The Collegiate Journalist mag., 1985-87, 91-92, The Am. Legion Premier Boys State Yearbook, 1981-88, 89-94, Legion Aux. Illini Girls State Yearbook, 1984-88, 89-94. Mem. Assn. for Edn. in Journalism and Mass Comm., Am. Assn. Higher Edn., Soc. Collegiate Journalists (v.p. 1992). Home: 1048 9th St Charleston IL 61920-2814 Office: Journalism Dept Ea Ill U Charleston IL 61920

WOHLTMANN, HULDA JUSTINE, pediatric endocrinologist, diabetologist; b. Charleston, S.C., Apr. 10, 1923; d. John Diedrich and Emma Lucia (Mohrmann) W. B.S., Coll. Charleston, 1944; M.D., Med. U. S.C., 1949. Diplomate Am. Bd. Pediatrics. Intern Louisville Gen. Hosp., 1949-50; resident in pediatrics St. Louis Children's Hosp., 1950-53; mem. faculty Washington U. Sch. Medicine, St. Louis, 1953-65, instr., 1953-58, asst. prof., 1958-65, postdoctoral fellow biochemistry, 1961-63; assoc. prof. pediatrics, head pediatric endocrinology Med. U. S.C., Charleston, 1965-70, prof., 1970-90, prof. emeritus, 1990—. Bd. dirs. Franke Home, Charleston, 1975—, treas., 1989-91; mem. adv. bd. for ethics ctr. Newberry (S.C.) Coll., 1989—; trustee Luth. Theol. So. Sem., 1991—. Mem. Am. Pediatric Soc., Ambulatory Pediatric Assn., Endocrine Soc., Am. Diabetes Assn., Am. Acad. Pediatrics, Am. Fedn. Clin. Rsch., Midwest Soc. Pediatric Rsch., So. Soc. Pediatric Rsch., S.C. Diabetes Assn. (bd. dirs. 1970-86, pres. 1970-73, 84-85, v.p., 1982-83, Profl Svc. award 1977), Lawson Wilkins Endocrine Soc., Sugar Club. Lutheran. Contbr. articles to sci. jours. Home: 280 N Hobcaw Dr Mount Pleasant SC 29464-2562

WOJAHN, R. LORRAINE, state legislator; b. Tacoma, Wash.; m. Gilbert M. Wojahn (dec.); children: Mark C, Gilbert M. Jr. (dec.). Mem. Wash. State Ho. of Reps., 1969-76, Wash. State Senate, 1977—, pres. pro tempore; vice chmn. rules, health and human svcs. com.; mem. labor and commerce, ways and means coms. Bd. dirs. Allenmore Hosp.; trustee Comsumer Credit Counseling Svcs., Inc., Tacoma-Pierce County; active, past pres. mem. Eastside Boys' and Girls' Club, Tacoma-Pierce County; active Wash. State Hist. Soc. Democrat. Office: State Senate State Capital Olympia WA 98504 Other: 2515 S Cedar St Tacoma WA 98405-2323

WOJCIK, KATHLEEN LOUISE, state representative; b. Chgo., July 15, 1936; d. George Frederick and Anna Marie (Nowak) Zorger; m. Norbert Robert Wojcik Sr., Aug. 25, 1956; children: Norbert Robert Jr., Noreen Wojcik Gallagher. Student, William Rainey Harper Coll. Exec. sec. E.L. Reibold Sales Promotion Agy., Chgo., 1956-60; twp. clk., mgr. office Schaumburg Twp., Hoffman Estates, 1968-83; broker Quinlin & Tyson Realty, Schaumburg, Ill., 1970-75; owner, broker Kathleen L. Wojcik Realty, Schaumburg, 1976—; state rep. Ill. Gen. Assembly, Springfield, 1983—. Active Republican Orgn. Schaumburg Twp., 1960—; twp. coordinator Women for Reagan, Women for Percy, Schaumburg, 1984; co-chmn. Small Businessmen for Reagan/Bush, Cook and DuPage Counties, Ill, 1984. Named Best Legislator of Yr. Ill Small Bus. Adminstrn., 1985, Legislator of Yr. Ill Assn. Homes for the Aging, 1985; recipient Superior Rating Taxpayers' Fedn. Ill, 1985, Cert. Appreciation Chgo. Bar Assn., 1986, Meritorious and Distg. Service award VFW, 1987. Mem. DAR, VFW, Am. Legion, Nat. Conf. State Legislators, Am. Legis. Exchange Council (membership co-chair 1983), NW Suburban Assn. Commerce and Industry, Ill. Realtors Assn. (legis. chmn.), Twp. Clks. Assn. Ill. (pres. 1979), Twp. Clks. Assn. Cook County (bd. dirs. 1973-82, past pres.). Lodge: Moose. Home: 411 Redwood Ln Schaumburg IL 60193-2747 Office: 514 W Wise Rd Schaumburg IL 60193-3815*

WOJCIKEWYCH, JOAN HARRIS, principal; b. Roanoke Rapids, N.C., Dec. 13, 1947; d. John Britton and Virginia Belle (Crowder) Harris; m. Raymond Wojcikewych, Feb. 5, 1973; children: Andrea, Ray, Greg, Kevin, Matthew. AA, Richard Bland Coll., 1968; MA in English, James Madison U., 1970; postgrad. in ednl. adminstrn., Bradley U., 1987-91, M. Ednl. Adminstrn., 1991; postgrad, Ill. State U., 1990, 91. Cert. secondary English tchr., Ill. Tchr. Chesapeake (Va.) Sch. System, 1970-73, Centre Bus. Sch., State College, Pa., 1973-74, St. Mark Sch., Peoria, Ill., 1980-87; asst. prin. Father Sweeney Sch. for Academically Gifted, Peoria, 1988-90, prin., 1990—; literary contest judge Ill. Elem. Sch. Assn., Bloomington, 1989—; speech coach Peoria Diocese Schs., 1980—; sponsor yearbook, 1988—; co-founder, bd. dirs. Bishop O'Rourke Speech League and Contest. Chmn. St. Mark Sch. PTO, Peoria, 1980-91; active Notre Dame High Sch. PTO; judge Odyssey of the Mind, 1993—. Mem. ASCD, Nat. Cath. Educators Am., Internat. Soc. for Tech. in Edn., Nat. Coun. for Gifted, Ill. Assn. for Gifted Children, Bradley U. Women's Club, Bradley U. Inst. for Gifted and Talented Youth (bd. dirs.), Phi Delta Kappa, Pi Lambda Theta. Republican. Home: 2827 W Winterberry Ln Peoria IL 61604-1829 Office: Father Sweeney Sch 403 NE Madison Ave Peoria IL 61603-3719

WOJEWODZKI, CATHERINE, state legislator, reference librarian; b. Austin, Tex., July 8, 1948; d. Dudley Lipscomb and Miriam Eugenia (Szafir) Willis; m. Robert Stanley Wojewodzki; 2 children. BA, U. Del., 1970; MLS, Rutgers U., 1982. Libr. Del. Divsn. Librs., 1983-85; info. specialist DuPont Co., 1985; libr. Del. Tech. and C.C., 1985-86; ref. dept. assoc. libr. U. Del., Newark, 1986—; state legislator Del. Ho. of Reps., Wilmington, 1992—. Office: Del Ho of Reps Legislative Hall Dover DE 19901*

WOLANIN, SOPHIE MAE, civic worker, tutor, scholar, lecturer; b. Alton, Ill., June 11, 1915; d. Stephen and Mary (Fijalka) W. Student Pa. State Coll., 1943-44; cert. secretarial sci. U. S.C., 1946, BSBA cum laude, 1948; PhD (hon.), Colo. State Christian Coll., 1972. Clk., stenographer, sec. Mercer County (Pa.) Tax Collector's Office, Sharon, 1932-34; receptionist, social sec., nurse-technician to doctor, N.Y.C., 1934-37; coil winder, assembler Westinghouse Electric Corp., Sharon, 1937-39, duplicator operator, typist, stenographer, 1939-44, confidential sec., Pitts., 1949-54; exec. sec., charter mem. Westinghouse Credit Corp., Pitts., 1954-72, hdqrs. sr. sec., 1972-80, reporter WCC News, 1967-68, asst. editor, 1968-71, asso. editor, 1971-76; student office sec. to dean U. S.C. Sch. Commerce, 1944-46, instr. math., bus. adminstrn., secretarial sci., 1946-48. Publicity and pub. relations chmn., corr. sec. South Oakland Rehab. Council, 1967-69; U. S.C. official del. Univ. Pitts. 200th Anniversary Bicentennial Convocation, 1986; mem. nat. adv. bd. Am. Security Council; mem. Friends Winston Churchill Meml. and Library, Westminster Coll., Fulton, Mo.; active U. S.C. Ednl. Found. Fellow; charter mem. Rep. Presdl. Task Force, trustee; sustaining mem. Rep. Nat. Com.; permanent mem. Nat. Rep. Senatorial Com.; patron Inst. Community Service (life), U. S.C. Alumni Assn. (Pa. state fund chmn. 1967-68, pres. council 1972-76, ofcl. del. rep. inauguration Bethany Coll. pres. 1973); mem. Allegheny County Scholarship Assn. (life), Allegheny County League Women voters, AAUW (life), Internat. Fedn. U. Women, N.E. Historic Geneal. Soc. (life), Hypatian Lit. Soc. (hon.), Acad. Polit. Sci. (Columbia) (life), Bus. and Profl. Women's Club Pitts. (bd. dirs. 1963-80, editor Bull. 1963-65, treas. 1965-66, historian 1969-70, pub. relations 1971-76, Woman of Year 1972), Met. Opera Guild, Nat. Arbor Day Found., Kosciuszko Found. (assoc.), World Literary Acad., Missionary Assn. Mary Immaculate Nat. Shrine of Our Lady of Snows; charter mem. Nat. Mus. Women in Arts, Statue Liberty Ellis Island Found. Inc., Shenago Conservancy (life); supporting mem. Nat. Woman's Hall of Fame; Recipient numerous prizes Allegheny County Fair, 1951-56; citation Congl. Record, 1969; medal of Merit, Pres. Reagan, 1982; named WPIC Sweetheart-of-the-Day Mercer County's Info. and Entertainment Radio Sta. 790, 1991. Fellow Internat. Inst. Community Service (founder); mem. World Inst. Achievement (rep.), Liturgical Conf. N. Am. (life), Westinghouse Vet. Employees Assn., Nat. Soc. Lit. and Arts, Early Am. Soc., Am. Acad. Social and Polit. Sci., Societe Commemorative de Femmes Celebres, Nat. Trust Historic Preservation, Am. Counselors Soc. (life), Am. Mus. Natural History (asso.), Nat. Hist. Soc. (founding mem.), Anglo-Am. Hist. Soc. (charter), Nat. Assn. Exec. Secs., Internat. Platform Assn., Smithsonian Assos., Asso. Nat. Archives, Nat., Pa., Fed. bus. and profl. women's clubs, Mercer County Hist. Soc. (life), Am. Bible Soc., Polish Am. Numismatic Assn., Polonus Philatelic Soc., UN Assn. U.S., Polish Inst. Arts and Scis. Am. Inc. (assoc.), N.Y. Acad. Scis. (assoc.), Am. Council Polish Cultural Clubs Inc. Roman Catholic (mem. St. Paul Cathedral Altar Soc., patron organ recitals). Clubs: Jonathan Maxcy of U. S.C. (charter); Univ. Catholic of Pitts.; Key of Pa., Fedn. Bus. and Profl. Women (hon.); Coll. (hon.) (Sharon). Contbr. articles to newspapers. Home: 5223 Smith Stewart Rd Girard OH 44420-1341

WOLD, SHELLEY T., librarian; b. Evansville, Wis., Jan. 27, 1935; d. John S. and Alice M. (Reese) Thurman; m. Donald C. Wold, June 11, 1956; children: Sara, Steve, Sheila. BA, U. Wis., 1956, MA, 1957. Gifts libr. U. Wis. Meml. Libr., Madison, 1957; lectr. libr. sci. Panjab U., Lahore, Pakistan, 1959-62; circulation libr. Ind. U., Bloomington, 1964-68; lectr. libr. sci. U. Ark., Little Rock, 1970-75, gifts libr., 1976-80, serials libr., 1977-79, govt. documents libr., 1980—, reference libr., 1988—. Mem. AAUW (v.p. 1974, 82, treas. 1984-86, Ednl. Found. honoree 1985), Ark. Libr. Assn. (chair coll. and univ. divsn. 1988-89), Ctrl. Ark. Recorder Soc. (treas. 1983—), Phi Kappa Phi (exec. sec. 1976-88, Meritorious Svc. award 1990). Home: 38 Pine Manor Dr Little Rock AR 72207-5137 Office: U Ark 2801 S University Ave Little Rock AR 72204-1000

WOLF, ANNE K., marketing professional; b. Carlisle, Eng., July 16, 1959; came to U.S., 1963; d. John Killen and Maureen (Diamond) McRae; m. Jeffrey William Wolf, Dec. 9, 1989; children: Megan Anne, William Jeffrey. BA, Calif. State U., Long Beach, 1982. Asst. br. mgr. Orange Micro, Anaheim, Calif., 1982-83, br. mgr., 1983, internat. sales mgr., 1983-84, mktg. mgr., 1984-85; sales rep. Sperry Corp., Orange, Calif., 1985-86; account mgr. UNISYS (formerly Sperry Corp.), L.A., 1986-88; mgr. strategic programs Hughes Aircraft Corp., L.A., 1988-89; edn. devel. mgr. Apple Computer, Inc., Newport Beach, Calif., 1989-92; nat. higher edn. market mgr. Apple Computer, Inc., Irvine, Calif., 1992; market devel. exec. Apple Computer, Inc., Phoenix, Ariz., 1992-94; nat. sales mgr. Apple Computer, Inc., Phoenix, 1994—. Vol. Youth Motivation Task Force, L.A., 1988—, Make-A-Wish Found., L.A., 1987—; mem. Commn. on Child Pornography and Obscenity, L.A., 1988; marshall Fiesta Bowl Parade, 1993. Mem. Gamma Phi Beta (advisor 1984-85). Office: Apple Computer Inc 2425 E Camelback Rd Ste 1100 Phoenix AZ 85016-4216

WOLF, BARBARA LEGLER, theater educator, theater director; b. Las Vegas, N.Mex., July 31, 1960; d. Philip F. and Martha Jane (Prater) Legler; m. R. Craig Wolf, Aug. 13, 1991. BS, No. Mich. U., 1982; MA, San Diego State U., 1988; PhD, Bowling Green State U., 1991. Actor, 1982-86; instr. San Diego State U., 1991-93, Southwestern Coll., Chula Vista, Calif., 1993; edn. dir. San Diego Jr. Theatre, 1992, exec. dir., 1993—; teaching artist San Diego Inst. Arts Edn., 1991—. Recipient Meritorious Achievement award for directing Am. Coll. Theatre Festival, 1988; Bowling Green State U. rsch. grantee, 1991, non-svc. fellow, 1991. Mem. Ctrl. Balboa Park Coun., Balboa Park Educators Coun. Democrat. Home: 5166 Hastings Rd San Diego CA 92116-2132

WOLF, DEBORAH ANN, dance educator, choreographer, artistic director, dancer; b. Buffalo, July 6, 1951; d. Fred Warren DeWight Wolf and Marion Leola (Brown) Mathewson; m. Roger Tregelles Curtis. BA in Dance, SUNY, Brockport, 1973; studied with, James Payton, Daniel Nagrin, Richard Bull, Diane Woodruff, Susannah Payton-Newman, Nancy Deckard. Instr. dance, artist-in-residence, workshop leader Concert Dance Co., Boston, 1973-91, resident choreographer, 1979-91, artistic dir., 1983-91; instr. dance SUNY, Brockport, 1971-73, 83, Walnut Hill Sch. Performing Arts, 1974-78, Boston Ballet Summer Sch., 1976, 81, Newton Arts Ctr., 1977-78, 91, Dance Circle Boston, 1978, Joy of Movement Dancers Program, 1979-84, Harvard-Radcliffe U., 1982-86, Boston U. Theatre Inst., 1982, Repertory Ballet/Ballet Theatre Sch., 1982-85, Rhode Island Coll., 1984, 87, Cambridge Sch. of Ballet, 1984, The Boston Conservatory of Music, 1984, 86, The Dance Complex, 1991-92, Cornish Coll. of the Arts, 1992—; artistic dir. WOLFWORKS, 1991—; panelist New Eng. Found. for Arts, R.I. Arts Coun., R.I. Dance Alliance. Choreographer: Islands, 1975, Lapses, 1976, Time & Time Again, 1977, Footnotes, 1978, Strand, 1980, Mixed Doubles, 1980, Twilight Games, 1981, Without Interruptions, 1982, Downside Up, 1983, Holding Pattern, 1985, Straight Up, 1986, Baby, Baby, 1987, Triple Glance, 1989, Points of Departure, 1990, Tangled Up in Blue, 1992, Black Tie Affair, 1992, Break Up, 1993, Isadora Duncan Slept with the Russian Navy, 1993; performer with N.Y. Chambre Dance Ensemble, 1971-73, Brockport Resident Dance Co., 1972-73, Seachange Theater Ensemble, 1976, Concert Dance Co. Boston, 1973-91. Recipient Artist Recognition award Boston Globe, 1986; grantee Somerville Arts Lottery, 1986, 88, 89, 90, 91, Cambridge Arts Coun., 1983, Boston Arts Lottery Coun., 1991; choreography fellow NEA, 1976, Mass. Artists Found., 1986; commd. works for Wellesley Coll., 1977, Boston Ballet Internat. Choreographers Showcase, 1980, SUNY Brockport, 1981, Harvard Radcliffe Dance Co., 1984, Boston Dances, 1986, 87, Peanut Butter and Jelly Dance Co., 1987, Works Contemporary Dance, 1988, Cape Cod Community Dancers, 1989, Bridgewater State Coll., 1991, Cornish Dance Theatre, 1993-94. Mem. Boston Dance Alliance (panelist), Dance Complex (bd. dirs.), Dance Umbrella (artist mem.). Home: 910 NW 52d St Seattle WA 98107

WOLF, ELLEN WILKINS, art educator; b. Parsons, Kans., Jan. 9, 1945; d. Emmet H. and Daisy E. (Farran) Caress; 1 child, Jason C. BS in Edn., Pittsburg State U., 1967; MA in Art Edn., No. Ariz. U., 1985, MA in Studio Art, 1986. Art therapist Parsons (Kans.) State Hosp. & Tng. Ctr., 1967-68; art instr. Parsons High Sch., 1968-84; asst. prof. No. Ariz. U., Yuma, 1988—; represented by Elaine Horwitch Gallery, Sedona, Ariz., 1985-91, Edith Lambert Gallery, Santa Fe, 1986-90, Old Town Gallery, Flagstaff, Ariz., 1986—, Yuma Fine Arts Ctr. Gallery, 1988-90, Galleria Mixta, Yuma, 1989-90, Hillside Gallery, Sedona, 1991-93, Prickley Pear Gallery, Yuma, 1994—. One-woman show Ind. C.C. Art Gallery, 1982, Yuma (Ariz.) Fine Arts Ctr., 1995; exhbns. include Galeria Mesa (ariz.) Art Gallery, 1985, NAU Art Gallery, Flagstaff, Ariz., 1986, 92, Ariz. State U., Tempe, 1986, Yuma Fine Arts Assn., 1986, 89, 90, Prescott (Ariz.) Fine Arts Ctr., 1986, Old Town Gallery, Flagstaff, 1987, 99, 89, Internat. Gallery, San Diego, 1987, 88, Phoenix Art Mus. Libr., 1987, Elaine Horwitch Gallery, Scottsdale, Ariz., 1987, Hillside Gallery, Sedona, Ariz., 1992, Electronic Gallery, Balt., 1994, others. Mem. steering com. Yuma Strategic Planning Project, 1993—; bd. dirs. Yuma Fine Arts Assn., 1994—. Named Tchr. of Yr., Yuma Edn. Found.and Yuma Rotary Clubs, 1991-92. Mem. Nat. Art Edn. Assn., Ariz. Art Edn. Assn. (S.W. regional coord., NAEA Higher Edn. Divsn. Art Educator of Yr. 1992), Edn. Found. Yuma County, Cultural Coun. Yuma (bd. dirs. 1989-92). Office: No Ariz U at Yuma PO Box 6236 Yuma AZ 85366-6236

WOLF, JESSICA, mental health administrator, educator; b. Southampton, N.Y., Aug. 2, 1944; d. Saul and Anne (Nisenbaum) W.; m. Martin Chasin, Nov. 12, 1989; children: Jonah Benjamin Gelbach, Alexis Saul Chasin, Frederic Selim Chasin. BA, Wellesley Coll., 1965; MA, Yale U., 1966, MPhil, 1967, PhD with distinction, 1971. Planner Midstate-Connecticut River Estuary Comprehensive Health, Middletown, Conn., 1970-74, South Cen. Conn. Comprehensive Health Planning Agy., New Haven, 1974-75; acting regional mental health dir. Conn. Dept. Mental Health, Norwich, 1976; bus. office mgr. Meml. Hosp., Lufkin, Tex., 1977-78; exec. dir. Mental Health Needs Coun., Inc., Houston, 1978, The Mothering Ctr., Inc., Greenwich, Conn., 1978-79; dir. mental health Southwest Conn. Health Systems Agy., South Norwalk, 1979-81; coord. grad. programs, asst. prof. pub. adminstrn. U. New Haven, West Haven, Conn., 1981-82; regional mental health dir. Conn. Dept. Mental Health, Bridgeport, 1982-92; dir. Mental Health and Edn Resource Ctr., 1992—; dir. cert. program Conn. Dept. Mental Health, Housatonic Cmty. Tech Coll., A.J. Pappanikou Ctr., U. Conn., 1992—; dir. Ctr. for Learning, Conn. Dept. Mental Health, 1994—; tchr. Yale U., Mt. Holyoke Coll., U. New Haven, Norwalk Community Coll., Housatonic Cmty. Tech. Coll.; cons. Mental Health orgns., Okla., Tex., Va. and Conn., 1984—; mem. adv. com. Conn. Dept. Health Svcs., Hartford, 1988-89; co-chair mental health task force Govt. Commn. on Implementation of Fed. Health Care Legis., 1975. Editorial bd., reviewer New Eng. Jour. Human Svcs., 1984-86, Hosp. Cmty. Psychiatry Journal, 1986—; contbr. articles to profl. publs. Woodrow Wilson Found. fellow, 1965-66, Fulbright fellow, France, 1968-69, Wellesley Coll. fellow, 1968-69, Yale fellow, 1968-69; recipient Leonard D. White award Am. Polit. Sci. Assn., 1972, Disting. Managerial Svc. award State of Conn., 1989. Fellow Am. Orthopsychiat. Assn.; mem. Human Resource Assn. of Northeast (excellence in Human Resource Devel., 1994, chair, sterring com., 1993-94), Am. Assn. Psychosocial Rehab. Svcs., Am. Soc. Pub. Administration, Wellesley Coll. Stone Ctr., Phi Beta Kappa. Office: Dept Mental Health Ctr Learning 211 State St 3rd Fl Bridgeport CT 06604

WOLF, KATIE LOUISE, state legislator; b. Wolcott, Ind., July 9, 1925; d. John H. and Helen Munsterman; m. Charles W. Wolf, 1945; children: Mark, Marcia. Grad., Ind. Bus. Coll., 1944. Registration officer County of White, Ind., 1960, mgr. lic. bur., 1960-68; clk. 39th Jud. Cir. Ct., 1968-78; mem. Ind. Ho. of Reps., 1985-86, Ind. State Senate, 1987—; mem. Dem. Nat. Com., 1968-90; del. Dem. nat. convs., 1972, 76, 80, 84. Recipient Athens award, 1987; named Woman of Yr. Bus. and Profl. Women's Club, 1984, Outstanding Freshman Legislator, 1985. Lutheran. Home: PO Box 766 Monticello IN 47960-0766 also: State Senate State Capitol Indianapolis IN 46204

WOLF, LESLEY SARA, lawyer; b. N.Y.C., Jan. 15, 1953; d. Herbert and Ardelle (Brush) W.; m. Dhiya El-Saden; children: Jordan, Evan. BA, Sarah Lawrence Coll., 1975; JD, U. Va., 1978. Bar: Calif. 1978. Assoc. Gibson, Dunn & Crutcher, L.A., 1978-86, ptnr., 1987—. Bd. dirs. L.A. Arts Coun., 1990-91, Franciscan Health Ctr., 1992-94. Office: Gibson Dunn & Crutcher 333 S Grand Ave Los Angeles CA 90071-1504

WOLF, MARY CAHN, association volunteer; b. Chgo., Apr. 1, 1929; d. Morton David and Elizabeth (Hofeller) Cahn; m. Stephen Louis Wolf, Jan. 29, 1955; 1 child, Matthew Stephen. BA, Rockford Coll., 1951. Bd. dirs. YWCA, N.Y.C., 1966-73; nat. bd. dirs. YWCA U.S.A., 1973-85, asst. treas. nat. bd. dirs., 1976-79, 1st v.p. nat. bd. dirs., 1982-85, del. triennial convs., 1967-85; vis. del. World YWCA Coun., Singapore, 1983; UN NGO rep. World YWCA, 1985—. N.Y. State Dem. commiteewoman, 1960-64; mem. The Mt. Sinai Hosp. Aux. Bd., 1970—, pres., 1976-81; founding mem., pres. Playwrights Horizons, N.Y.C., 1974-76; active World Svc. Coun., 1980—; vol. NGO Forum, Decade Women, Nairobi, 1985; trustee Mt. Sinai Hosp., 1976-81; bd. dirs. New Alternatives Children, N.Y., 1982—. Named hon. mem. nat. bd. dirs. YWCA U.S.A., 1991. Mem. Cosmopolitan Club, Women's City Club. Reform Jewish.

WOLF, MARYANNE, child development educator; b. South Bend, Ind., Oct. 25, 1947; d. Frank Joseph and Mary Elizabeth (Beckman) W.; m. Gil Noam, July 26, 1985; children: Benjamin, David. BA in English Lit., St. Marys Coll., Notre Dame, Ind., 1969; MA in English Lit., Northwestern U., 1970; EdD in Human Devel., Harvard U., 1979. Lectr., rschr. Harvard U., Cambridge, Mass., 1977-79; rsch. scientist Harvarard U., Cambridge, Mass., 1992—; asst. prof. psychology Brandeis U., Waltham, Mass., 1979-80; assoc. prof. child devel. Tufts U., Medford, Mass., 1980—. Editor: Thought and Language/Language and Reading, 1986; contbr. articles to profl. jours. Cofounder Peace & Justice Studies Program, Medford, 1982-87. Recipient Alumna Achievement award St. Mary's Coll., 1994; Radcliffe fellow, 1978, Livingston fellow, 1979, Fulbright fellow, 1993. Mem. APA (Nat. Teaching Excellence award 1991), Mass. Psychol. Assn. (Disting. Tchr. of Yr. award 1991), New Eng. Child Lang. Assn. (co-chair 1980), Internat. Soc. for Study Behavioral Devel., Internat. Neuropsychol. Assn., Soc. Rsch. in Child Devel., Soc. Sci. Study Reading (charter), N.Y. Acad. Scis. Democrat. Roman Catholic. Office: Tufts U Dept Child Study College Ave Medford MA 02155

WOLF, NAOMI, writer; b. San Francisco, Nov. 12, 1962; d. Leonard and Deborah W.; m. David Shipley, Sept. 1993. BA, Yale U., 1984. Author: The Beauty Myth: How Images of Beauty Are Used Against Women, 1990,

Fire With Fire: The New Female Power and How It Will Change the 21st Century, 1993. Rhodes scholar, 1986. Office: care Royce Carlton Inc 866 UN Plz New York NY 10017 also: care John Brockman John Brockman Associates Inc 2307 Broadway New York NY 10024*

WOLF, RENITA DIANE, assistant treasurer; b. Newport, Tenn., Aug. 5, 1958; d. Robert Vernard and Anna Cleo (Teague) Poe; m. Andrew Thomas Wolf, July 14, 1979. BS in Acctg., U. Colo., Colorado Springs, 1983, MBA, 1990. Cert. mgmt. acct.; cert. prodn. and inventory mgmt. Cost acct. Current, Inc., Colorado Springs, 1981-86; fin. analyst Honeywell, Inc., Colorado Springs, 1986-88; asst. treas. Cray Computer Corp., Colorado Springs, 1988—. Alumnus Citizens' Goals Leadership Class, Colorado Springs, 1983; vol. Jr. Achievement of Colorado Springs, Inc., 1991-93; treas. Wagon Wheel coun. Girl Scouts U.S.A., Colorado Springs, 1992—. Mem. Inst. Mgmt. Accts. (v.p., pres.-elect). Methodist. Office: Cray Computer Corp 1110 Bayfield Dr Colorado Springs CO 80906-4634

WOLF, RUTH ELLEN, analytical chemist; b. Missoula, Mont., May 16, 1964; d. Paul G. and M. Ruth (Fellion) W. Student, U. Mont., 1982-85; BS in Chemistry, Colo. State U., 1986, PhD in Chemistry, 1991. Lab. asst. Colo. State U., Ft. Collins, 1985-86, teachng asst., 1986-90; sr. scientist Idaho Nat. Engring. Lab., Idaho Falls, 1991-92; inorganic sr. scientist Enseco-Rocky Mountain Analytical Lab., Arvada, Colo., 1992-93; inorganic tech. mgr. Rocky Mountain Analytical Lab., Arvada, Colo., 1993-94; sr. tech. specialist The Perkin Elmer Corp., Norwalk, Conn., 1994—; cons. insturment testing Hewlett-PAckard, Little Falls, Del., 1994—, Perkin-Elmer Corp., Norwalk, Conn., 1993-94. Mem. Am. Chem. Soc., Soc. Applied Spectroscopy. Office: Perkin Elmer Corp 14818 W 6th Ave Ste 6 Golden CO 80401

WOLFE, DEBORAH CANNON PARTRIDGE, government education consultant; b. Cranford, N.J.; d. David Wadsworth and Gertrude (Moody) Cannon; 1 son, Roy Partridge. BS, N.J. State Coll.; MA, EdD, Tchrs. Coll., Columbia U.; postgrad., Vassar Coll., U. Pa., Union Theol. Sem., Jewish Sem. Am.; hon. doctorates, Seton Hall U., 1963, Coll. New Rochelle, 1963, Morris Brown U., 1964, Glassboro/Rowan Coll., 1965, Bloomfield Coll., 1988, Monmouth Coll., 1988, William Paterson Coll., 1988; LLD (hon.), Kean Coll., 1981; LHD (hon.), Stockton State Coll., 1982; LLD (hon.), Jersey City State Coll., 1987, Centenary Coll., William Paterson Coll., 1989, Tuskegee U., 1989, Glassboro State Coll., 1985, Tuskegee U., 1989, St. Peter's Coll., 1989, Rider Coll., 1989, Georgian Court Coll., 1990; DSc (hon.), Stevens Inst. Tech., 1991; LLD (hon.), Rutgers U., 1992, Thomas Edison Coll., 1992. Former prin., tchr. pub. schs. Cranford, also Tuskegee, Ala.; faculty Tuskegee Inst., Grambling Coll., NYU, Fordham U., U. Mich., Tex. Coll., Columbia U.; supervision and adminstrn. curriculum devel., social studies U. Ill., summers; prof. edn., affirmative action officer Queens Coll.; prof. edn. and children's lit. Wayne State U.; edn. chief U.S. Ho. of Reps. Com. on Edn. and Labor, 1962—; Fulbright prof. Am. lit. NYU; U.S. rep. 1st World Conf. on Women in Politics; chair non-govtl. reps. to UN (NGO/DPI exec. com.), 1983—; editorial cons. Macmillan Pub. Co.; cons. Ency. Brit.; adv. bd. Ednl. Testing Service; assoc. minister First Bapt. Ch., Cranford, N.J.; mem. State Bd. Edn., 1964—; chairperson N.J. Bd. Higher Edn., 1967—; mem. nat. adv. panel on vocat. edn. HEW; mem. citizen's adv. com. to Bd. Edn., Cranford; mem. Citizen's Adv. Com. on Youth Fitness, Pres.'s Adv. Com. on Youth Fitness, White House Conf. Children and Youth, 1950, 60, White House Conf. Edn., 1955, White House Conf. Aging, 1960, White House Conf. Civil Rights, 1966, White House Conf. on Children, 1970, Adv. Council for Innovations in Edn.; v.p. Nat. Alliance for Safer Cities; cons. Vista Corps, OEO; vis. scholar Princeton Theol. Sem., 1989—; active Human Rels. Coun., N.J., 1994—; vis. prof. U. Ill., U. N.C., Wayne State U.; theologian-in-residence Duke U. Contbr. articles to ednl. publs. Bd. dirs. Cranford Welfare Assn., Community Center, 1st Bapt. Ch., Cranford, Community Center Migratory Laborers, Hurlock, Md.; trustee Sci. Service, Seton Hall U.; mem. Public Broadcasting Authority.; bd. regents Seton Hall U.; sec. Kappa Delta Pi Ednl. Found.; mem. adv. com. Elizabeth and Arthur Schlesinger Library, Radcliffe Coll.; trustee Edn. Devel. Center, Sci. Svc., 1965—. Recipient Nat. Achievement award Nat. Assn. Negro Bus. and Profl. Women's Clubs, 1958, Woman of Year award Delta Beta Zeta, Woman of Year award Morgan State Coll., Achievement award Atlantic region Zeta Phi Beta, Medal of Honor DAR, 1990, Disting. Svc. medal Nat. Top Ladies of Distinction, 1991, Disting. Svc. award Nat. Assn. State Bds. Edn., 1992, Disting. Svc. to Edn. award N.J. Commn. on Status of Women, 1993, Svc. to Children award N.J. Assn. Sch. Psychologists, 1993, Disting. Educator award Phi Delta Kappa, 1994; named Disting. Educator, Rider U., 1993; U. Medicine and Dentistry of N.J. Disting Svc. award Nat. Assn. State Bd. of Edn., 1994, Disting. Medal award U. Medicine and Dentistry N.J., Union Coll. Mem. Council Nat. Orgns. Children and Youth, Am. Council Human Rights (v.p.), NCCJ, Nat. Panhellenic Council (dir.), Nat. Assn. Negro Bus. and Profl. Women (chmn. speakers bur.), Nat. Assn. Black Educators (pres.), NEA (life), LWV, N.Y. Tchrs. Assn., Am. Tchrs. Assn., Fellowship So. Churchmen, AAUW (nat. edn. chmn.), AAUP, Internat. Reading Assn., Comparative Edn. Soc., Am. Acad. Polit. and Social Sci., Internat. Assn. Childhood Edn., Nat. Soc. Study Edn., Am. Council Edn. (commn. fed. relations), Assn. Supervision and Curriculum Devel. (rev. council), AAAS (chmn. tchr. edn. com.), Nat. Alliance Black Educators (pres.), NAACP, Internat. Platform Assn., Ch. Women (UN rep., mem. exec. com.), UN Assn.-U.S.A. (exec. com.), Delta Kappa Gamma Edn. Soc. (chmn. world fellowship com.), Kappa Delta Pi (chmn. ritual com., mem. ednl. found., 1980—, laureate 1990, scholarship named in her honor), Pi Lambda Theta, Zeta Phi Beta (internat. pres. 1954, chmn. edn. found. 1974—). Home: 326 E Nantucket Ln Jamesburg NJ 08831 Office: NJ State Bd Higher Edn 20 W State St Trenton NJ 08608-1206

WOLFE, HARRIET MUNRETT, lawyer; b. Mt. Vernon, N.Y., Aug. 18, 1953; d. Lester John Francis Jr. and Olga Harriet (Miller) Munrett; m. Charles Briant Wolfe, Sept. 10, 1983. BA, U. Conn., 1975; postgrad., Oxford U. (Eng.), 1976; JD, Pepperdine U., 1978. Bar: Conn. 1979. Assoc. legal counsel, asst. sec. Citytrust, Bridgeport, Conn., 1979-90; v.p., sr. counsel, asst. sec. legal dept. Shawmut Bank Conn., N.A., Hartford, 1990—; mem. govt. rels. com. Electronic Funds Transfer Assn., Washington, 1983—. Mem. Conn. Bar Assn. (mem. legis. com. banking law sect.), ABA, Conn. Bankers Assn. (trust legis. com.), Guilford Flotilla Coast Guard Aux., U.S. Sailing Assn., Phi Alpha Delta Internat. (Frank E. Gray award 1978, Shepherd chpt. Outstanding Student award 1977-78). Home: 26 Farm View Dr Madison CT 06443-1631 Office: Shawmut Bank Conn NA 777 Main St Hartford CT 06115-2001

WOLFE, JANE LEE, consultant, association executive; b. N.Y.C., July 4, 1939; d. Frederick Billings and Jane Pillow (Rightor) Lee; m. Townsend D. Wolfe, Aug. 28, 1968; 1 child, Zibilla. BA, N.Y.U., 1962, MA, 1963. Headstart tchr. trainer Ark. State U., Beebe, 1978-79; asst. to dean Trinity Cathedral, Little Rock, 1979-90; cons. Episcopal Ch. U.S.A., N.Y.C., 1991—; spl. asst. to dean St. George's Coll., Jerusalem, 1991—; cons. Episcopal Ch. U.S.A., N.Y.C., 1991—. Author: Sermonettes, 1982, Blue Book of Spiritual Growth, 1991, Soap & Water, 1992. Nat. bd. dirs. YWCA of U.S.A., 1982—; mem. exec. com. World YWCA, Geneva, 1990—. Home: 2102 Louisiana St Little Rock AR 72206

WOLFE, JANICE E., government executive; b. Racine, Ohio, Aug. 25, 1939; d. Donald Clark and Erline (Sargent) W. A.B. in Govt., Ohio U., 1961; J.D., Ohio State U., 1964. Bar: Ohio 1964. Atty. examiner Ohio Dept. Liquor Control, Columbus, 1964; asst. atty. gen., Columbus, Ohio, 1965-72; dist. counsel SBA, 1972-80, dep. dist. dir., Chgo., 1980-83, dist. dir., Washington, 1983-87, dep. assoc. adminstr. bus. devel., 1987—. Recipient SBA awards. Office: SBA 1441 L St NW Washington DC 20005-3512

WOLFE, JEAN ELIZABETH, medical illustrator; b. Newark, N.J., Oct. 3, 1925; d. Arthur Howard and Ethel (Harper) Wolfe; B.S., Russell Sage Coll., 1947; student Pratt Inst., 1949-50; diploma U. Rochester Sch. Medicine and Dentistry, 1955; postgrad. (W.B. Saunders fellow), U. Pa., 1955-56, U. Pa., 1980; M.F.A., U. Pa., 1973, M.A. (hon.), 1973. Exhibitor, Print Inst. Galleries, Bklyn., 1958, N.Y. Med. Coll., 1958, Assn. Med. Illustrators, 1961-86, 90, AMA, N.Y.C., 1965, Phila., 1965, A.C.S., Atlantic City, 1965, Rsch. Study Club L.A., 1966, Phila. Art Alliance, 1967, 73, U. Pa. Ophthal. Soc., 1967-68, N.J. Med. Soc., 1968, Cayuga Mus. History and Art, 1968, Pensacola Art Ctr., 1969, FAA Aero. Center, Oklahoma City, 1970, Scheie Eye Inst., 1972-75, Assn. Med. Illustrators Traveling Salon, 1978, Moore Coll. Art, 1985, Mus. of Am. Illustration Soc. of Illustrators, 1986, Mutter Mus., Phila. Coll. of Physicians, 1990-92; represented in permanent collections Archives of Med. Visual Resources, Francis A. Countway Med. Libr., Harvard Univ., Mutter Mus., Phila. Coll. Physicians; comprehensive collection of major work donated by Scheie Eye Inst., life history and papers housed in The Arthur and Elizabeth Schlesinger Libr. on the History of Women in Am., Radcliffe Coll.; contbg. illustrator Adler's Textbook Ophthalmology, 8th edit., 1969; illustrations in med. books, jours., pharm. house pubs.; instr. Pembroke Coll. Brown U., 1947-49; mem. faculty Kimberley Sch., Upper Montclair, N.J., 1950-52; free lance med. illustration Studio N.Y. Med. Coll., 1956-60; instr. Pratt Inst., 1958-59; assoc. in med. illustration U. Pa. Sch. Medicine, 1960-72, research asst. prof. med. art in ophthalmology, 1972-85; independent studio (fine art) painting and medical illustration, 1985—; guest lectr. Johns Hopkins Med. Sch., 1973, NIH; guest artist USAF, Air Force Acad. and NORAD, 1971. Recipient Merit certificate AMA; Appreciation certificate ACS; 1st prize Pensacola Art Center, Am. Heart Assn., 1969, Gold medal Graphic Arts Soc. of Del. Valley, 1973. Fellow Assn. Med. Illustrators (emeritus); mem. Assn. Med. Illustrators (Ralph Sweet, Tom Jones awards, gov. 1970—, chmn. nominating com. 1972-73, vice chmn. bd. govs. 1973-74, chmn. bd. 1974-75, selection com., Lifetime Achievement award 1989—, adv. coun. Vesalius Trust 1990—), Soc. Illustrators (cert. merit 1986), Coll. Art Assn., Women's Caucus for Art.

WOLFE, LISA ANN, electronic data processing auditor; b. New Kensington, Pa., Sept. 29, 1962; d. Otis Lawrence and Lois Ann (Smouse) Wolfe. BS, Ind. U. Pa., 1983; MBA, Duquesne U., 1992. Sr. internal auditor EDP Allegheny Power Svc. Corp., Greensburg, Pa., 1984—. Vol. Am. Cancer Soc. Mem. Assn. Mgmt. Info. Systems, Zeta Tau Alpha (v.p. Ind. U. Pa. chpt. 1982-83). Republican. Home: 420 Spring Run Dr Monroeville PA 15146-3357 Office: Allegheny Power Svc Corp 800 Cabin Hill Dr Greensburg PA 15601-1650

WOLFE, LISA HELENE, psychologist; b. Phila., Jan. 15, 1959; d. Stuart and Barbara Joyce (Blumenburg) W. BA, U. Pa., 1981; AM, Harvard U., 1985, PhD, 1989. Lic. psychologist. Teaching fellow Harvard U., 1983-88; psychology intern Mass. Mental Health Ctr., Boston, 1988-89; psychology fellow N.Y. Hosp./Cornell Med. Ctr., White Plains, 1989-91; sr. staff psychologist Met. Hosp., N.Y.C., 1991; staff psychologist Ctr. for Women's Devel. Human Resource Inst., Brookline, Mass., 1992—; pvt. practice psychology, Brookline, 1992—. Author: (with others) (book chpt.) The Cognitive Rehabilitation of Learning Disabilities, 1987. Mem. APA (divsns. 30, 39, 42), Am. Assn. Applied and Preventive Psychology, Pi Gamma Mu, Psi Chi. Office: Human Resource Inst 227 Babcock St Brookline MA 02146-3199

WOLFE, MARGARET RIPLEY, historian, educator, consultant; b. Kingsport, Tenn., Feb. 3, 1947; d. Clarence Estill and Gertrude Blessing Ripley; m. David Earley Wolfe, Dec. 17, 1966; 1 child, Stephanie Ripley. BS magna cum laude, East Tenn. State U., 1967, MA, 1969; PhD, U. Ky., 1974. Instr. history East Tenn. State U., 1969-73, asst. prof., 1973-77, assoc. prof., 1977-80, prof., 1980—. Author: Lucius Polk Brown and Progressive Food and Drug Control, Tennessee and New York City, 1908-1920, 1978, An Industrial History of Hawkins County, Tennessee, 1983, Kingsport, Tennessee: A Planned American City, 1987, Daughters of Canaan: A Saga of Southern Women, 1995; contbg. author: Appalachia: Family Patterns in Transition, 1975, The United States and Italy: The First Two Hundred Years, 1977, Research in Social Policy: Historical and Contemporary Perspectives, 1987, The Future South: An Historical Perspective for the Twenty-First Century, 1991, Tennessee in American History, 1991; contbr. articles to profl. jours. Mem. Tenn. Com. for Humanities, 1983-85, exec. coun. mem., 1984-85; mem. Women's Symphony Com., Kingsport; exec. com. Tenn. Commemorative Woman's Suffrage Commn., 1994—. Haggin fellow U. Ky., 1972-73; recipient Disting. Faculty award East Tenn. State U., 1977; East Tenn. State U. Found. rsch. award, 1979, Alumni cert. merit, 1984. Mem. AAUP, ACLU (exec. com. Tenn. 1991-92), NOW, Tenn. State Employees Assn., Am. Studies Assn. (John Hope Franklin Prize com. 1992), Am. Hist. Assn., Orgn. Am. Historians, So. Assn. Women Historians (pres. 1983-84, exec. com. 1984-86), So. Hist. Assn. (com. on the status of women 1987, program com. 1988, interim chair of program com. 1988, mem. com. 1993, 94, 95, nominating com. 1994, chair nominating com. 1995), Smithsonian Assocs., Tenn. Hist. Soc. (editorial bd., 1995—), Coordinating Com. for Women in Hist. Profession, East Tenn. Hist. Soc. (mem. editorial bd. Jour. East Tenn. History), Phi Kappa Phi. Office: ETSU/UT at Kingsport Kingsport TN 37660 also: East Tenn State U Dept History Johnson City TN 37614

WOLFE, VERDA NELL, pension consultant, financial planner; b. Sulphur Springs, Tex., Jan. 31, 1927; d. Marvin Alvin and Winnie Davis (Bass) Hamiter; m. James Braddy Wolfe, May 3, 1947; children: James Gordon, William Gregory, Charles Gary. Student, Baylor U., 1948-52, Tex. Tech U., 1974-76. CLU, CFP; cert. pension cons. Estate analyst Estate Fin. Planning Svc., Lubbock, Tex., 1973-76, Planning Cons., Lubbock, 1977-81; pres. DDRW Fin. Svcs., Lubbock, 1982-85, Pension Concepts and Administration, Lubbock, 1986—. Mem. Am. Soc. CLU and ChFC (chpt. pres. 1988-89), Inst. Cert. Fin. Planners, Am. Soc. Pension Actuaries and Cons. Home: 2125 57th St Lubbock TX 79412 Office: Pension Concepts & Adminstn 2811A 74th St Lubbock TX 79423

WOLFE NATALI, JANE LOUISE, food service administrator; b. Bellofonte, Pa., Sept. 28, 1953; d. Glenn Leon and E. Allene (Kensinger) Wolfe; m. Edward Paul Natali, Apr. 8, 1989; children: Paul Edward, Louise Jane. Assoc., Williamsport C.C., 1973; BS, Ind. U., 1978; postgrad., Pa. State U. Employee Williamsport (Pa.) C.C., 1972-73; food svc. dir. Muncy Valley Hosp., Muncy, Pa., 1973-74, Hemlock Girl Scout Coun., Harrisburg, Pa., 1979, 80, Montgomery (Pa.) Area Sch. Dist., 1974-81, Pennridge Sch. Dist., Perkasie, Pa., 1981—. Mem. Am. Sch. Food Svc. Assn., Pa. Sch. Food. Svc. Assn. Home: 151 W Cherry Ln Souderton PA 18964 Office: Pennridge Sch Dist 1506 N 5th St Perkasie PA 18944

WOLFERT, RUTH, Gestalt therapist; b. N.Y.C., Nov. 10, 1933; d. Ira and Helen (Herschdorfer) W. BS summa cum laude, Columbia U., 1967, postgrad., 1966-68. Pvt. practice N.Y.C., 1972—; dir. Action Groups, N.Y.C., 1974-76, Gestalt Groups, N.Y.C., 1976—; mem. faculty, mem. coordinating bd. Women's Interart Ctr., N.Y.C., 1971-75, also bd. dirs.; presenter Stockton (N.J.) State Coll., 1974-75; mem. faculty Inst. for Experiential Learning and Devel., 1988-92, Woodstock U., 1989-91, Gestalt Inst., Atlanta, 1989—; presenter in field. Contbg. author: (booklet) A Consumer's Guide to Non-Sexist Therapy, 1978. Mem. Assn. Humanist Psychology (bd. dirs. ea. regional network 1981-87, pres. 1985-87), N.Y. Inst. Gestalt Therapy (trainer 1979—, chair workshops program 1979-83, co-chair conf. 1983-85, brochure com. 1987—, interim exec. com. 1988-90, conf. com. 1989-91, v.p. 1993—), Assn. Transpersonal Psychology (co-chair N.Y. discussion group 1983-85), Common Boundery (chair N.Y. discussion group 1991-92), N.Y. Acad. Scis. Office: 200 East 32nd St New York NY 10016

WOLFF, ANITA ELOIS, art educator; b. Compton, Calif., Aug. 31, 1923; d. Richard William and Ella Maude (Keltner) Oberlander; m. Kurt Wolff, July 10, 1945; children: Annalee, Stephen. Student, Otis Inst., 1960, Brit. Artists Inst., London, 1989. Owner Belmont Gallery, Long Beach, Calif., 1968-76; tchr. art Cypress (Calif.) Coll., 1968, Virginia City (Nev.) Sch. of Art, 1968—, Long Beach City Coll., 1969, Evergreen Coll., San Jose, Calif., 1970, Carrizo Sch. of Art, Ruidoso, N.Mex., 1971-72; tchr. art Art Ctr. Anita Wolff, Placerville, Calif., 1976-94, dir., 1991-94; video tchr. Centerpoint Prodns., Santa Clara, Calif., 1989-94; print artist Rave Prodns., Placerville, 1992-94. Artist: (mag.) Am. Artist, 1989; artist, author: Southwest Art, 1990; contbg. author: Pastel Interpretations, 1993. Program dir. Long Beach Art Assn., 1970-73; pres. Fireman's Aux., So. Calif., 1965, PTA, Compton, 1966. Recipient Marjorie Close award Soc. of Western Artists, 1989. Mem. Internat. Platform Soc. (Gold medal 1992), Am. Inst. Fine Arts, Pastel Soc. Am. (Best of Show award 1991), Pastel Soc. West Coast (adv. bd. 1992, Disting. Pastellist, 1st Portrait award 1994), Knickerbocker Artists (Gold medal 1994). Republican. Baptist. Home: 3116 Cedar Ravine St Placerville CA 95667

WOLFF, CHERYL MAE, public relations executive; b. Tuscaloosa, Ala., Sept. 11, 1947; d. Murray and Charlene Tina (Gordon) Kitman; m. Roger Edward Wolff, Aug. 18, 1973 (div. 1990); children: Jordan Howard, Adam Spencer. BA in Edn., U. Fla., 1969, MEd, 1970. 2d grade tchr. Balt. City Pub. Schs., 1970-72; med. sec. cardiology Sinai Hosp., Balt., 1972-77, med. sec. radiol. therapy, 1978-80; tchr. Stratford Sch., Towson, Md., 1983-88; counselor Hillcrest Clinic, Balt., 1983-85, pub. rels. dir., 1985—. Campaign worker Mel Mintz for Councilman, Balt.; poll worker Md. for Choice, Balt., 1992; mem. presdl. task force Dem. Nat. Com., 1992. Recipient Citizenship award Balt. County Police Dept., 1979. Mem. Md. Commn. for Women, Marylanders for Right to Choose, NARAL, NOW, Sex Edn. Coalition, Phi Sigma Sigma (pledge trainer 1966). Jewish. Office: Hillcrest Clinic Inc 5602 Baltimore National Pik Baltimore MD 21228

WOLFF, CYNTHIA GRIFFIN, humanities educator, author; b. St. Louis, Aug. 20, 1936; d. James Thomas and Eunice (Heyn) Griffin; m. Robert Paul Wolff, June 9, 1962 (div. 1986); children—Patrick Gideon, Tobias Barrington; m. Nicholas J. White, May 21, 1988. B.A., Radcliffe Coll., 1958; Ph.D., Harvard U., 1965. Asst. prof. English Manhattanville Coll., Purchase, N.Y., 1968-70; asst. prof. English U. Mass., Amherst, 1971-74, assoc. prof., 1974-76, prof., 1976-80; prof. humanities MIT, Cambridge, 1980-85, Class of 1922 prof. lit. and writing, 1985—; mem. exec. com. for Am. lit. MLA, 1979-81; mem. selection bd. Literary Classics Am., 1981—; mem. exec. bd. for fgn. grants Am. Council Learned Socs., 1981-84. Author: (literary criticism) Samuel Richardson, 1972, (literary biography) A Feast of Words: The Triumph of Edith Wharton, 1977, Emily Dickinson, 1986; bd. editors Am. Quar., 1979-84. AAUW grantee, 1964-65; NEH grantee, 1975-76, 1983-84; Am. Council Learned Socs. grantee, 1984-85. Mem. MLA, Am. Studies Assn. Home: Apt 619 416 Commonwealth Ave Boston MA 02215 Office: MIT Dept Humanities 14N-226 Cambridge MA 02139

WOLFF, DEBORAH H(OROWITZ), lawyer; b. Phila., Apr. 6, 1940; d. Samuel and Anne (Manstein) Horowitz; m. Morris H. Wolff, May 15, 1966 (div.); children: Michelle Lynn, Lesley Anne; m. Walter Allan Levy, June 7, 1987. BS, U. Pa., 1962, MS, 1966; postgrad., Sophia U., Tokyo, 1968; JD, Villanova U., 1979; LLM, 1988. Tchr. Overbrook High Sch., Phila., 1962-68; homebound tchr. Lower Merior Twp., Montgomery County, 1968-71; asst. dean U. Pa., Phila., 1975-76; law clk. Stassen, Kostos and Mason, Phila., 1977-78; assoc. Spencer, Sherr, Moses and Zuckerman, Norristown, Pa., 1980-81; ptnr. Wolff Assocs., 1981—; lectr. law and estate planning, Phila., 1980—; Recipient 3d Ann. Community Svc. award Phila. Mayor's Com. for Women, 1984; named Pa. Heroine of Month, Ladies Home Jour., July 1984. Founder Take a Brother Program; bd. dirs. Germantown Jewish Ctr.; high sch. sponsor World Affairs Club, Phila., 1962-68; mem. exec. com., sec. bd. Crime Prevention Assn., Phila., 1965—; bd. dirs. U. Pa. Alumnae Bd., Phila., 1965—, v.p. organized classes; chmn. urban conf. Boys Club Am., 1987; active Hahnaman Brain Tumor Rsch. Bd. Mem. ABA, Pa. Bar Assn., Phila. Bar Assn., Montgomery County Bar Assn., Phila. Women's Network, Bus. Women's Network (pres.), Crime Prevention Assn. (sec. bd. dirs., v.p. of bd.), Cosmopolitan Club (membership com. Phila.), Lions Club (mem. chmn.). Home and Office: 422 W Mermaid Ln Philadelphia PA 19118-4204

WOLFF, ELEANOR BLUNK, actress; b. Bklyn., July 10, 1931; d. Sol and Bessie (Schultz) Blunk; m. William Howard Wolff, June 19, 1955; children: Ellen Jill, Rebecca Louise. BA in Edn., Speech & Theatre, Bklyn. Coll., 1972, MS in Spl. Edn., 1975; postgrad., Adelphi U., 1980-81. Cert. tchr., N.Y. Fashion model Garment Ctr., N.Y.C., 1949-50; sec. to v.p. out-of-town/export sales Liebmann Breweries Inc., Bklyn., 1950-58; tchr. N.Y.C. Bd. Edn., Bklyn., 1971-76; sec. to dir. environ. programs, pub. affairs officers, speakers bur. project leader Power Authority State of N.Y., N.Y.C., 1976-85; tchr. Hewlett-Woodmere (N.Y.) Sch. Dist., 1986-89; instr. adult edn. County of Nassau, N.Y., 1986—; actress/model, N.Y.C., 1992—. V.p. program devel. for youth ctr. Wavecrest Gardens Community Assn., Far Rockaway, N.Y., 1959-63; teen leader Far Rockaway Jewish Ctr. Youth Coun., 1965-68; pres. Parents Assn. P.S. 215Q, Far Rockaway, 1966-67; tutor N.Y. C. Bd. Edn. Sch. Vol. Program, Far Rockaway, 1969-71; chair civic affairs Dem. Club, Far Rockaway, 1961-63; committeewoman Dem. Ctrl. Com., Queens County, N.Y., 1963-64; v.p. membership, mem. constn. com. Nassau County Dem. Women's Caucus, 1988, 89; awards com. Bklyn Coll. Named Mother of Yr. Congregation Shaaray Tefila, Far Rockaway, 1968; recipient Merit award Wavecrest Gardens Community Assn., 1960, Theater Arts Trophy for disting. svc. Bklyn. Coll. Alumni, 1992. Mem. Nassau Assn. Community/Continuing Edn., Alumni Assn. Bklyn. Coll. (life mem.), AFTRA, Nat. Audubon Soc. (South Shore chpt.). Home: 29 Princeton Ave Hewlett NY 11557

WOLFF, SIDNEY CARNE, astronomer, observatory administrator; b. Sioux City, Iowa, June 6, 1941; d. George Albert and Ethel (Smith) Carne; m. Richard J. Wolff, Aug. 29, 1962. BA, Carleton Coll., 1962, DSc (hon.), 1985; PhD, U. Calif., Berkeley, 1966. Postgrad. research fellow Lick Obs, Santa Cruz, Calif., 1969; asst. astronomer U. Hawaii, Honolulu, 1967-71, assoc. astronomer, 1971-76; astronomer, assoc. dir. Inst. Astronomy, Honolulu, 1976-83, acting dir., 1983-84; dir. Kitt Peak Nat. Obs., Tucson, 1984-87, Nat. Optical Astronomy Observatories, 1987—; dir. Gemini Project Gemini 8-Meter Telescopes Project, 1992-94. Author: The A-Type Stars--Problems and Perspectives, 1983, (with others) Exploration of the Universe, 1987, Realm of the Universe, 1988, Frontiers of Astronomy, 1990; contbr. articles to profl. jours. Trustee Carleton Coll., 1989—. Rsch. fellow Lick Obs. Santa Cruz, Calif., 1967; recipient Nat. Meritorious Svc. award NSF, 1994. Mem. Astron. Soc. Pacific (pres. 1984-86, bd. dirs. 1979-85), Am. Astron. Soc. (coun. 1983-86, pres.-elect 1991, pres. 1992-94). Office: Nat Optical Astronomy Obs PO Box 26732 950 N Cherry Ave Tucson AZ 85719-4933

WOLFF, VIRGINIA EUWER, writer, secondary education educator; b. Portland, Oreg., Aug. 25, 1937; d. Eugene Courtney and Florence Evelyn (Craven) Euwer; m. Art Wolff, July 19, 1959 (div. July 1976); children: Anthony Richard, Juliet Dianne. AB, Smith Coll., 1959; postgrad., Goddard Coll., Warren Wilson Coll., L.I. U., Portland State U., Lewis & Clark Coll. Cert. tchr., Oreg. Tchr. The Miquon Sch., Phila., 1968-72, The Fiedel Sch., Glen Cove, N.Y., 1972-75, Hood River Valley (Oreg.) H.S., 1976-86, Mt. Hood Acad., Govt. Camp, Oreg., 1986—; 2d violinist Quartet con brio, Portland, 1989—. Author: Probably Still Nick Swansen, 1988, The Mozart Season, 1991, Make Lemonade, 1993. Violinist Mid-Columbia Sinfonietta, Hood River, 1976—, Oreg. Sinfonietta, Portland, 1988—. Recipient Child Study Children's Book award Bank St. Coll., 1994, Young Adult Book award Internat. Reading Assn., 1989, PEN U.S.A. Ctr. West, 1989, Oreg. Book award Oreg. Lit. Arts, 1994. Mem. Soc. Children's Book Writers/Illustrators (Golden Kite 1994), Chamber Music Soc. Oreg. Office: Curtis Brown Ltd care Marilyn E Marlow 10 Astor Pl New York NY 10003

WOLFGANG, BONNIE ARLENE, musician, bassoonist; b. Caribou, Maine, Sept. 29, 1944; d. Ralph Edison and Arlene Alta (Obetz) W.; m. Eugene Alexander Pridonoff, July 3, 1965 (div. Sept. 1977); children: George Randall, Anton Alexander, Stephan Eugene. MusB, Curtis Inst. Music, Phila., 1967. Soloist Phila. Orch., 1966; soloist with various orchs. U.S., Cen. Am., 1966-75; prin. bassoonist Phoenix Symphony, 1976—, with Woodwind Quintet, 1986—. Home: 9448 N 106th St Scottsdale AZ 85258

WOLFKILL, SHARON ELAINE, social worker; b. Pryor, Okla., Sept. 27, 1949; d. Roy Leon and Hazel Lilace (Mitchell) Timmons; m. Jimmy Foster Wolfkill, Aug. 23, 1969; children: Kristin Elaine, James Christopher. BS in Edn., Northeastern State U., Tahleguah, Okla., 1971; MSW, U. S.C., 1983. Acad. of Cert. Soc. Workers. Social worker Okla. State Dept. of Soc. and Rehab. Svcs. County, Bartlesville, Okla., 1971-72, Whitaker State Children's Home, Pryor, Okla., 1972-73, Santa Cruz (Calif.) Dept. of Soc. Svcs., 1973-78, Presbyn. Children's Home and Svc. Agy., Dallas, 1983-88; dir. social svcs. Arbor Creek Psychiatric Hosp., Sherman, Tex., 1990-92; social worker Richardson (Tex.) Med. Ctr., 1992-94, Baylor Sr. Health Ctr., Garland, Tex., 1994—; workshop presenter State Conf. on Adoption of Older Children, Austin, 1985. Bd. dirs. Plano (Tex.) Ind. Sch. Dist. Counseling Adv. Bd., 1986-89, Canyon Creek Presbyn. Ch. Youth Coun., Richardson, Tex., 1988-92; mem. choir Canyon Creek Presbyn. Ch. Choir, Richardson, 1985-92; tchr. bible sch. Canyon Creek Presbyn. Ch., Richardson, 1985-92. Mem. Nat. Assn. Social Workers (diplomate), Dallas Area Gerontological Soc., Collin County Coalition on Aging, Long Term Care Social Workers Assn.

(program com. 1994). Democrat. Presbyterian. Office: Baylor Sr Health Ctr 777 Walter Reed Blvd Ste 102 Garland TX 75042

WOLFMAN, BRUNETTA REID, education educator; b. Clarksdale, Miss., Sept. 4, 1931; d. Willie Orlando and Belle Victoria (Allen) Reid Griffin; m. Burton Wolfman, Oct. 4, 1952; children: Andrea, Jeffrey. BA, U. Calif., Berkeley, 1957, MA, 1968, PhD, 1971; DHL (hon.), Boston U., 1983; DP (hon.), Northeastern U., 1983; DL (hon.), Regis Coll., 1984, Stonehill Coll., 1985; DHL, Suffolk U., 1985; DET (hon.), Wentworth Inst., 1987; AA (hon.), Roxbury Community Coll., 1988. Asst. dean faculty Dartmouth Coll., Hanover, N.H., 1972-74; asst. v.p. acad. affairs U. Mass., Boston, 1974-76; acad. dean Wheelock Coll., Boston, 1976-78; cons. Arthur D. Little, Cambridge, Mass., 1978; dir. policy planning Dept. Edn., Boston, 1978-82; pres. Roxbury Community Coll., Boston, 1983-88, ACE sr. fellow, 1988—; assoc. v.p. acad. affairs George Washington U., Washington, 1989-92, prof. edn., 1992—; pres. bd. dirs. Literacy Vols. of Capitol Region; bd. dirs. Am. Coun. Edn., Harvard Community Health Plan. Author: Roles, 1983. Bd. overseers Wellesley (Mass.) Coll., 1981; bd. dirs. Boston-Fenway Program, 1977, Freedom House, Boston, 1983, Boston Pvt. Industry Coun., 1983, NCCJ, Boston, 1983, co-chmn.; bd. overseers Boston Symphony Orch.; trustee Mus. Fine Arts, Boston; councilor Coun. on Edn. for Pub. Health. Recipient Freedom award NAACP No. Calif., 1971, Amelia Earhart award Women's Edn. and Indsl. Union, Boston, 1983; Sr. scholar Nat. Assn. Women in Edn. Mem. Am. Sociol. Assn., Assn. Black Women in Higher Edn., D.C. Sociol. Soc., Greater Boston C. of C. (edn. com. 1982), Cosmos Club (Washington), Pi Lambda Theta, Alpha Kappa Alpha (Humanitarian award 1984), Phi Delta Kappa (pres. GW chpt.). Home: 2022 Columbia Rd NW Washington DC 20009-1352 Office: George Washington U 2134 G St NW Washington DC 20052-0001

WOLFORD, PATRICIA WEBER, management company executive; b. Bowling Green, Ky., July 31, 1940; d. James Freeman and Selina Grace (McLin) Jones; m. Bruce Dennis Weber, Aug. 8, 1959 (div. Aug. 1980); children: Tod Alan, Scott David; m. Joseph Theodore Wolford, Sr., Mar. 5, 1981. Student, Bryant Bus. Coll., 1959; mgmt. cert., Columbia U., 1981. Adminstrv. asst. U. Louisville Engring. Sch., 1959-60; asst. dir. Louisville Urban Renewal Agy., 1960-64; bus. relocation advisor Nashville Housing Authority, 1964-69; adminstr. S.E. Washington County Health Svcs., Keedysville, Md., 1976-80; exec. dir. Hancock (Md.) Health Care Corp, 1980-88; coord. property mgmt. Magnolia Mgmt., Inc., Hagerstown, Md., 1988-95; pres. Md. Primary Care Assn., Annapolis, 1984-86; chairperson Md. Health Systems Agy. Com., Cumberland, 1978. Author: Standard Performance Maintenance Manual, 1994, Standard Performance Housekeeping Manual, 1994, Standard Performance Safety and Health Manual, 1994. Pres. Washington County Cmty. Action Coun. Bd., Hagerstown, 1974-77, Washington County Coun. PTA, Hagerstown, 1976-78; chairperson/commr. Washington County San. Com., 1980-84; dist. chairperson United Way Area Campaign, Hancock, Md., 1983, United Way Hagerstown, 1992, 93; mem. bd. Am. Heart Assn., Hagerstown, 1984-87; mem. dist. staff Dist. 10 Little League, Hagerstown, 1976-78; mem. Correctional Instn. Citizens Adv. Com., 1994—; mem. outreach com. First Christian Ch., 1993-94; ch. rep. Wash. County Habitat for Humanity, 1993-94; gov. appointed mem. citizens adv. com. Correctional Instn., 1994—, chairperson, 1994—; mem. transition com. Gov. P. Glendening, State of Md., 1994-95. Recipient Spirit award United Way of Washington County, 1992, Gov.'s Citation Com. to Children and Youth, Annapolis, 1979, Cert. of Appreciation, Am. Lung Assn., Hagerstown, 1985. Mem. NAFE, LWV, Md. Congress PTA, Am. Legion Aux. Christian. Home: 13023 Lance Cir Hagerstown MD 21742-2939

WOLF-RAGATZ, MARILYN PATRICIA, visual arts educator; b. Chelmsford, Eng., May 22, 1945; came to U.S., 1946; d. Harry Albert and Rita (Jones) Wolf; m. Philip Lee Ragatz II, Oct. 19, 1985. BS in Art Edn., Ohio State U., 1968; MEd in Art Edn., Fla. Atlantic U., 1981; EdD, U. Ga., 1988. Cert. in art edn. P-12, Ga. Art tchr. middle sch. Broward County Sch. Dist., Ft. Lauderdale, Fla., 1968-71; day program dir. Prospect Hall Coll., Hollywood, Fla., 1973-81; owner Philip St. Art Gallery, Athens, Ga., 1987-89; instr. U. Ga., Athens, 1982-91; account exec. The Adsmith Ad Agy., Athens, 1985-90; art tchr. middle sch. Clarke County Sch. Dist., Athens, 1990—; critical thinking trainer Ga. Dept. Edn., 1993—. Bd. dirs. Lyndon Arts Found., Athens, 1993—; mem. com. Athens-Clarke Tomorrow, 1993. Found. for Excellence grantee, 1990-91, 91-92, 93-94; Ga. Coun. for the Arts grantee, 1992-93. Mem. Nat. Art Edn. Assn., Ga. Art Edn. Assn. (pres. Dist. II 1991—), Ga. Mus. Art, Athens Fibercraft Guild (v.p. 1986-88), Nat. Mus. for Women in the Arts, Handweavers Guild Am. Home: RR 1 Box 259 Carlton GA 30627-9622

WOLFSON, FREDA L., judge; b. Vineland, N.J., May 20, 1954; d. Samuel and Ida (Vetter) Linsenbaum; m. Douglas Wolfson, June 8, 1975; children: Brian Samuel, Matthew Bradley. BA, Douglass Coll., 1976; JD, Rutgers Law Sch., 1979. Bar: N.J. 1979, U.S. Ct. Appeals (3rd cir.). With Sullivan & Cromwell, N.Y.C., 1978; assoc. Lowenstein, Sandler, Brochin, Kohl, Fisher & Boylan, 1979-81, Clapp & Eisenberg, Newark, 1981-86; magistrate judge U.S. Dist. Ct. N.J., 1986—. Recipient Profl. Achievement award N.J. Bar Assn. Young Lawyers Div. Mem. Middlesex County Bar Assn. Office: US Post Office & Courthouse 402 East State St Rm 436 Trenton NJ 08608-0515*

WOLFZAHN, ANNABELLE FORSMITH, psychologist; b. N.Y.C., Jan. 23, 1932; d. Paul Phillip and Addie (Glassman) Forsmith; m. Herbert Eytan Wolfzahn, Feb. 4, 1956; children: Risa Wolfzahn Herskowitz, Felice, Orna. BA, Hunter Coll., 1953; MA in Counseling Psychology, Manhattan Coll., 1971; PhD in Clin. and Community Psychology, Union Inst., 1979. Cert. sch. psychologist, sch. counselor, N.Y. Counselor for handicapped children Bklyn. Tuberculosis Assn., 1952; social worker Child Placement Svcs., N.Y.C., 1953-58; fellow in social and community psychiatry Albert Einstein Coll. Medicine, 1977-79; intern Bronx (N.Y.) Devel. Svcs., 1977-79; intern head trauma program Rusk Inst., NYU Med. Ctr., 1979; psychologist Creedmore Psychiat. Ctr., 1980-82, Harlem Valley Psychiat. Ctr., 1982-87; clin. coord. of group homes Green Chimneys Children's Svcs., 1987-88; with Ulpan Akiva and Assaf Harofeh Med. Ctr., Tel Aviv U., Israel, 1988-89; nursing home cons., psychotherapist Bklyn. Ctr. for Psychotherapy, 1989-91; pres., coord. Westchester chpt. Vols. for Israel, 1992—; freelance psychologist, counselor, 1994—; mem. staff Assaf Harofeh Med. Ctr., Tel Aviv, U., 1988-89; mem. workshops in field; mem. staff Mother-Child Home Program of White Plains, n.Y., 1975-76; counselor with multiple sclerosis victims and their families. Contbr. articles to profl. publs. Vol. Vols. for Israel, 1988, 91-92, founder, pres., coord. Westchester Region chpt., 1993—; mem. archaeol. dig Bet Shaan, Israel. Recipient Vol. award White Plains Hosp., 1974-76, John C. Klein Meml. Writing award Newspaper Inst. Am., 1965; Alvin Johnson scholar, 1953. Mem. APA, Women's Internat. Zionist Orgn., Westchester County Psychol. Assn., N.Y. Neuropsychology Assn., Am. Mental Health Affiliates of Israel, N.Y. Acad. Scis., Nat. Coun. Jewish Women., Am. Orthopsychiat. Assn. Home and Office: 34 Springdale Rd Scarsdale NY 10583-7329

WOLKEN, E. TERESA, compensation administrator; b. Arnold, Pa., Apr. 11, 1948; d. Luigi and Domenica (Mattioda) Crestetto; m. Daniel F. Wolken, Mar. 23, 1974 (dec. July 1982); m. Cyril A. Koval, Jan. 2, 1988. BS in Math., U. Pitts., 1972, MBA, 1978. Compensation analyst Westinghouse Electric, White Westinghouse, Pitts., 1972-74, supr. wage/salary, 1974-74; mgr. compensation Pullman Swindell, Pitts., 1975-79, Allegheny Internat., Pitts., 1979-87, Fisher Sci., Pitts., 1988—; owner Mail Boxes Etc., Pitts., 1988—; cons. Timet & Allegheny Internat., Pitts., 1987-88. Candidate Boro Coun., Aspinwall, Pa., 1979. Mem. Am. Compensation Assn., Total Compensation Network of Western Pa. (founding mem., pres. 1993—), Pitts. Pers. Assn., Pitts. Survey Group (pres. 1986), Pitts. Bonsai Soc. (pub. rels. chair 1981-83), Mail Boxes Ad Assn. (treas. 1989-91). Democrat. Roman Catholic. Home: 4277 Forest Glen Dr Allison Park PA 15101-2649 Office: Fisher Sci 711 Forbes Ave Pittsburgh PA 15219-4729 Office: Mail Boxes Etc 7 Market Sq Pittsburgh PA 15222

WOLLERSHEIM, JANET PUCCINELLI, psychology educator; b. Anaconda, Mont., July 24, 1936; d. Nello J. and Inez Marie (Ungaretti) Puccinelli; m. David E. Wollersheim, Aug. 1, 1959 (div. June 1972); children: Danette Marie, Tod Neil; m. Daniel J. Smith, July 17, 1976. AB, Gonzaga U., 1958; MA, St. Louis U., 1960; PhD, U. Ill., 1968. Lic. psychologist, Mont. Asst. prof. psychology, asst. dir. testing and counseling ctr. U. Mo., 1968-71; prof. psychology U. Mont., Missoula, 1971—, dir. clin. psychology, 1980-87; chair Mont. Bd. Psychologists, 1977-78; cons. Mont. State Prison, 1971-85, Trapper Creek Job Corps, 1973—; pvt. practice, Missoula, 1971—. Author numerous rsch. articles. Bd. dirs. Crisis Ctr., Missoula, 1972-73; mem. profl. adv. bd. Head Start, Missoula, 1972-79. Recipient Disting. scholar award U. Montana, 1991. Fellow Am. Psychol. Assn. (bd. dirs. div. clin. psychology 1990-92); mem. Rocky Mountain Psychol. Assn. (pres. 1983-84), Nat. Council Univ. Dirs. Clin. Psychology (bd. dirs., 1982-88). Roman Catholic. Catholic. Home: 105 Greenwood Ln Missoula MT 59803-2401 Office: 900 N Orange St Ste 201 Missoula MT 59802-2998

WOLOSCHAK, GAYLE E., molecular and radiation biology scientist; b. Sharon, Pa., June 4, 1955; d. Michael and Frances (Pysh) W. BS, Youngstown State U., 1976; PhD, Med. Coll. Ohio, 1980. Postdoctoral fellow Mayo Clinic, Rochester, Minn., 1980-83, asst. prof., 1983-87; asst. scientist Argonne (Ill.) Nat. Lab., 1987-92, scientist, 1992—; mem. rsch. com. Am. Cancer Soc., Chgo., 1992—; mem. radiation rsch. com. study sect. NIH, Bethesda, Md., 1994—. Author: Challenge Questions on Orthodoxy for Students, 1994; contbr. over 50 articles to sci. jours. Mem. met. coun. Ukrainian Orthodox Ch. USA, 1992—; bd. dirs. Ukrainian Orthodox League U.S.A., 1980-93, pres., 1983-86. Grantee Dept. Energy, 1987—, NIH, 1994—. Mem. AAAS, Am. Assn. Immunologists, Am. Soc. Cell Biology, Am. Soc. Photobiology, Am. Assn. Cancer Rsch., Autumn Immunology Coun., Radiation Rsch. Soc. Office: Argonne Nat Lab 9700 S Cass Ave CMB-202 Argonne IL 60439

WOLOSZYK, HOLLY ARLENE, microbiologist; b. Chgo., Jan. 19, 1960; d. Leonard Benedict and Dorothy Elaine (Wegehenkel) W. BS, U. Ill., 1982. Quality control technician G.D. Searle Pharm., Mount Prospect, Ill., 1982-83, Am. Hosp. Supply, McGaw Park, Ill., 1983-84; sr. technician rsch. and devel. G.D. Searle, Skokie, Ill., 1984-86, microbiologist rsch. and devel., 1986-87, supr. microbiology svcs. rsch. and devel., 1987-89; sr. microbiologist Intermedics, Inc., Freeport, Tex., 1989-92; microbiologist Eli Lilly and Co., Indpls., 1992—. Mem. Am. Soc. Microbiology, Soc. Quality Assurance. Home: 4954 Brock St Apt 112 Indianapolis IN 46254-1735 Office: Eli Lilly and Co Lilly Corp Ctr Indianapolis IN 46285

WOLPERT, ETTA, artist, poet; b. Mpls., Dec. 6, 1930; d. Garrett and Gertrude G. (Gruenberg) W. BA, U. Minn., 1952, MA, 1954. Asst. to Allen Tate U. Minn., Mpls., 1952; tutor Harvard U. Bur. of Study Counsel, Cambridge, Mass., 1955-59; instr. English Emerson Coll., Boston, 1955-58; workshop leader in poetry Cambridge Ctr. for Adult Edn., Boston, 1956; asst. prof. English & Art No. Essex Community Coll., Haverhill, Mass., 1964-66; leader art history workshop Brandeis Study Group, Lexington, Mass., 1962; social worker Welfare Dept., Lowell, Mass., 1969-71; artist, poet freelance Lexington, Mass., 1975—. One-woman show includes Cary Meml. Libr., 1962; exhibited in shows at Habit Inst., 1991, Cambridge Art Assn., 1992, 4th Ann. Internat. Exhibit, 1989; author: (poems) Selections, 1973. Recipient Hon. Mention, World of Poetry, 1991, Hon. Mention in Poetry Contest, Harvard Summer Sch., 1965, Two First prizes New Eng. Poets Club, 1969. Mem. Ariel Gallery, Gallery of Art Investment, Cambridge Art Assn., New Eng. Poetry Club. Home: 4 Revere St Lexington MA 02173-4420

WOLTERING, MARGARET MAE, educational consultant; b. Trenton, Ohio, July 24, 1913; d. David Lindy and Nellie Stevenson; m. Elmer Charles Woltering, Apr. 9, 1938; 1 child, Eugene Anthony. Student, Mercy Sch. Nursing, Hamilton, Ohio, 1931-34; BS, Miami U., 1962, MEd, 1968, postgrad., 1975. RN, Ohio; cert. tchr., curriculum supr., Ohio. Pub. health nurse Ohio State Dept. Health, Butler County, 1936-49; supr. Swedish Hosp., Seattle, 1944-45; various high sch. teaching positions Cin., 1968-78; ednl. cons. Ohio, 1981—; cons., Ohio, 1981—; ednl. cons. specializing in curriculum devel., 1980—. Author spelling book, 1981; book reviewer Friends of Libr., 1991-93. Chmn. Hosp. Svc. for Children, Hamilton, 1981-85; lectr. Sr. Citizens Ctr., 1992-93; chmn. vol. tutorial program Hamilton High Sch., 1989-93, Audabon Tutorial Program, 1994. Mem. AAUW, Toastmasters. Democrat. Roman Catholic.

WOLTERS, DONITA SUE, human resources management; b. Kokomo, Ind., Feb. 12, 1952; d. Daniel Marlyn and Donna Mae (Mang) Hollingsworth; m. Paul A. Wolters, Sept. 1, 1973 (div. Apr. 1992); children: Nicolette Alissa, Danielle Rae. BA in Mgmt., Mich. State U., 1974; MBA, U. Mich., 1980. Employment rep. U. Mich., Ann Arbor, 1974-75, compensation analyst, 1975-80, personnel rep., 1980-82; compensation adminstrn. Martin Marietta Astronautics, Denver, 1982-86, personnel mgr., 1986-87, human resources cons., 1987-93; human resources mgr. JMM Operational Svcs., Denver, 1993—. Spl. events chair Colo. Spl. Olympics, Denver, 1985-86; sch. restructuring initiative project Colo. Alliance of Bus., 1993. Mem. Colo. Human Resource Assn. (pres. 1989-90, v.p. 1988-89, publicity dir. 1987-88), Soc. Human Resource Mgmt. (nat. com. mem. 1990—), Beta Gamma Sigma. Episcopalian. Office: JMM Operational Svcs Inc 1700 Broadway Ste 1100 Denver CO 80290

WOLTERSTORFF, NANCY EMILY, officer services administrator; b. St. Paul, Sept. 24, 1954; d. Robert Gust and Emily Elizabeth (McHattie) W. BA, Moorhead State U., 1976. Asst. mktg. mgr. Toltz, King, Duvall, Anderson & Assocs., Inc., St. Paul, 1976-79; editor U. Minn., Mpls., 1979-81; corp. comm. coord. Comserv Corp., St. Paul, 1981-83; adminstrv. svcs. supr. Higher Edn. Assistance Found., St. Paul, 1983-87; purchasing and office svc. mgr. Fortis Fin. Group, St. Paul, 1987—. Contbr. articles to profl. jours. Mem. Nat. Assn. of Purchasing Mgrs., Postal Customer Coun., Bus. Forms Mgmt. Assn. (bd. dirs. Internat. Orgn. dir. symposium, 1990-92, exec. v.p. 1992-94, pres. Minn. chpt. 1989-91, v.p. 1987-89), Minn. Mailers Assn. Home: 8932 Military Rd Woodbury MN 55125 Office: Fortis Companies 500 Bielenberg Dr Woodbury MN 55125

WOLTZ, MARY LYNN MONACO, management consultant; b. Columbus, Ohio, Mar. 11, 1951; d. Frank Guy and Mary Catherine (Montenaro) Monaco; m. James David Woltz, June 19, 1971; children: Joseph David, Bethany Anne. Student, Ohio State U., 1969-71. Tchr. Career Acad., Columbus, Ohio, 1971-72; supr., mgmt. Battelle Meml. Inst., Columbus, Ohio, 1973—; pub. spkr. schs., bus., clubs. and profl. orgns., Ohio, 1981; dir. mktg. The General's Books. Amb. Assn. World Affairs, Columbus, 1968; co-chmn. United Way, Columbus, 1976; committeewoman Ohio Crime Prevention Assn., Columbus, 1988; mem. founding bd. Ohio Crime Prevention Found., Columbus, 1989—; founding mem., pres. Parents Support Group, 1990-94; cons. Lao Mai Assn., Columbus, 1981-85. Named Ohio Crime Practitioner of the Yr., 1988; recipient Nat. Crime Prevention award Nat. Crime Prevention Coalition, Washington, 1988, Spotlight award Nat. Crime Prevention Coalition and Am. Dist. Telegraph, 1993. Mem. Am. Soc. Indsl. Security (sec. 1992-93, mem. exec. bd. 1993-94). Roman Catholic. Office: Battelle Meml Inst 505 King Ave Columbus OH 43201-2681

WOLVERTON, JANET BEAR, accountant, educator; b. Denver, July 11, 1942; d. Frank and Helen Agnes (Bartosch) Bear; children: Paul, Rob, Kevin. BS in Bus. Adminstrn., Ea. Mont. Coll., 1979; MS in Acctg. and Info. Sys., U. Colo., 1989. CPA, Mont. Pub. Acctg., Billings, Mont., 1979-82; Instr. Ea. Mont. Coll., Billings, 1983-87; lectr. European Divsn. U. Md., Würtzburg, Germany, 1989-91; prof. Ft. Lewis Coll., Durango, Colo., 1991-94, Oreg. Inst. Tech., Klamath Falls, 1994—; cons. acctg. and computer sys., Billings, 1983-88, Durango, 1991-94, Klamath Falls, 1995—; lectr. grad. outreach program Sch. Nursing U. Colo., 1992-93; vis. prof. U. Lethbridge, Alta., Can., summers 1992-94. Contbr. articles to profl. jours. Smart Program, Klamath Falls, 1994—; Healthy Families, Klamath Falls, 1994—; coord. Choices, Klamath Falls, 1994-95. Mem. Am. Acctg. Assn., Internat. Bus. Schs. Computing Assn., Western Decision Scis. Inst., Soc. Case Rsch., Inst. Mgmt. Accts. Office: Oreg Inst Tech Mgmt Techs Dept 3201 Campus Dr Klamath Falls OR 97601

WOLYNIES, EVELYN GRADO, clinical nurse specialist, educator; b. N.Y.C., Apr. 2, 1944; d. Joseph Frederick and Evelyn Marie (Ronning) Grado; m. Jon Gordon Wolynies, July 12, 1964; children: Jon Andrew, Kristine Elisabeth. AAS, Burlington County Coll., 1990; AS, Camden C.C., 1990; BSN cum laude, Thomas Jefferson U., 1991, MSN summa cum laude, 1992; PhD in Nursing Studies, Johns Hopkins U., 1993. RN, N.J., Pa., cert. clin. nurse specialist. Charge nurse Hampton Hosp., Westampton, N.J., 1990-92; adjunct clin. instr. psychiat. nursing Burlington County Coll., Pemberton, N.J., 1992-93; project leader Alzheimer's disease clin. drug study Olsten Health Care, Cherry Hill, N.J., 1992-95, psychiat. case mgr., 1992—; CNS neuropsych in Huntingtons Disease Dr. Allen Rubin, Camden, N.J., 1992; psychiat. case mgr. Moorestown (N.J.) Vis. Nurses Assn., 1992; charge nurse Friends Hosp., Phila., 1994—; pvt. practice hypnotherapy. Contbr. articles to nursing jours. Mem. Burlington County Coll. Alumni Bd.; founder, dir. Support Group for Adult Children with Aging Parents. Recipient Juanita Wilson award, 1991, Farber fellowship, 1991-92.; Nurse in Washington intern, 1992; named to Burlington County Coll. Hall of Fame, 1994. Mem. Am. Assn. of Neuroscience Nurses (health policy com.), Am. Psychiat. Nurses Assn., N.J. State Nurses Assn., Sigma Theta Tau (Delta Rho chpt.), Phi Theta Kappa. Home: PO Box 3604 Cherry Hill NJ 08034-0550

WOLZ, LYN ANN, librarian; b. St. Louis, June 2, 1951; d. Donald Warren and Margaret Mary Ann (Brandenberg) W. BA in English, U. Mo., 1973, MLS, 1975; MA in Folklore, U. N.C., 1983. Libr. Columbia (Mo.) Coll., 1976-78; archivist U. N.C., Chapel Hill, 1978-79; reference libr. Ferrum (Va.) Coll., 1979-85, head of pub. svcs., 1985—; cons. Blue Ridge Heritage Archives, Blue Ridge Inst., Ferrum, 1979—; faculty rep. Jessie Ball DuPont seminar Nat. Humanities Ctr., N.C., 1994. Contbg. author: (reference book) Dictionary of Virginia Biography, 1994, (jour. index) Missouri Folklore Society Jour., 1991. Music dir. Blue Ridge Folklife Festival, Ferrum College, Va., 1979—, Jack Tales Theater Troupe, Ferrum College, 1983-89; dir. Women's Group, Ferrum, 1988-93. Mem. NOW, S.W. Va. Interlibr. Network Group (editor SWING newsletter 1992—), Mo. Folklore Soc., Va. Folklore Soc., Roanoke Valley Libr. Assn. (bd. dirs. 1994—), Sierra Club. Office: Ferrum Coll Ferrum VA 24088

WONG, ANNA MAY See **WONG, JADIN**

WONG, ASTRIA WOR, cosmetic business consultant; b. Hong Kong, Oct. 23, 1949; came to U.S., 1970; B in Vocat. Edn., Calif. State U., Long Beach, 1976. Cert. coll. tchr. (life), Calif. West coast sales trainer Revlon Inc., N.Y.C, 1975-82; nat. tng. dir. diReniel Internat., Palm Springs, Calif., 1982; dir. Beauty Cons. Service Agy., Long Beach, Calif., 1983—; pres. Boutique Astria, Scottsdale, Ariz., 1994—. Author: The Art of Femininity, 1971; editor (newsletter) So. Calif. Cosmetic, 1983-86. Chair Cmty. Involvement Paradise Rep. Woman's Club. Named Salesperson of Yr., Revlon, Inc., N.Y.C., 1978. Mem. So. Calif. Cosmetic Assn. (correspondence sec. 1982—), Women's Coun., Cosmetologist Tchr. Assn., Bus. and Profl. (ind. devel. chair.), Fashion Group Internat. Republican. Office: Beauty Cons Service Agy 7121 E 1st Ave Scottsdale AZ 85251-4305

WONG, CORINNE HONG SLING, minister; b. Hong Kong, China, Nov. 24, 1930; came to U.S., 1940; d. William Hong Sling and Clara Grace (Low) Shen; m. Howard Marn Yung Wong, Sept. 16, 1953; children: Alison Marie Wong Noto, Mark David, Martin John. BS, Houghton Coll., 1951; MRE, N.Y. Theol. Sem., 1954; MDiv, Princeton Theol. Sem., 1986. ordained Am. Bapt. Chs., 1992. Asst. to pastor 1st Presbyn. Ch., Honolulu, 1986-87; min. Christian edn. Wahiawa (Hawaii) Korean Christian Ch., 1988-89; interim lay pastor St. Elizabeth's Episcopal Ch., Honolulu, 1989-90; min. adult ministries and outreach 1st Bapt. Ch. Honolulu, 1991-92; min. Diamond Head Fellowship, Honolulu, 1991—. Author: Studies in the Gospel of Mark, 1979, Studies in Colossians, 1984. Recipient grants for religious study Chinese Christian Assn., Honolulu, 1984-86, C.K. Ai Found., Honolulu, 1984-86, Presbyn. Ch. (U.S.A.), 1985-86. Office: 4203 Kaimanahila St Honolulu HI 96816-4751

WONG, GWENDOLYN NGIT HOW JIM, banking executive; b. Chgo., Oct. 9, 1952; d. Vernon K. S. and Yun Soong (Chock) Jim; m. Carey R. Wong, Nov. 10, 1979; children: Jacquelyn C., Brandon R. BEd in Secondary Math., U. Hawaii, 1974; MA in Secondary Math., Columbia U., 1975; postgrad., St. John's U., N.Y.C., 1975-77; MBA, U. San Francisco, 1979. Tng. and devel. analyst and instr. Chase Manhattan Bank, N.Y.C., 1975-77; human resources profl. Crocker Nat. Bank, San Francisco, 1978-82, staff credit rev. dept. contrs. divsn., 1982-85; comml. lender Calif. middle market Wells Fargo Bank/Crocker Nat. Bank, Palo Alto and San Mateo, Calif., 1985-88; mgr. credit dept. San Francisco (Calif.) internat. br. Algemene Bank Nederland N.V., 1988-90; v.p., mgr. credit and loan adminstrn. The Indsl. Bank of Japan, Ltd. San Francisco (Calif.) Agy., 1990—. Bd. dirs. San Francisco Bay coun. Girl Scouts U.S.A., 1992, mem. fund devel. com., coun. self-evaluation com., long range planning com., legis. liaison, internat. applicants selection com., chair Tri-City Assn., 1991-92, troop leader; sec. bd. dirs. United Way of Bay Area, 1994, mem. Bay Area strive for five-multicultural conf. com., mem. cmty. initiative on multiculturalism 1991-92; founding bd. dirs. Multicultural Initiative, 1991—, chair edn. tng., 1992—. Mem. AAUW (San Mateo br., bd. dirs. 1989-90, 94—, newsletter editor, cmty. programs com., chair couples gourmet interest group, others), Assn. Jr. Leagues Internat. Inc. (1st v.p., exec. com. 1993—, bd. dirs. 1992-93), Jr. League of San Francisco, Inc. (adv. mem. bd. dirs. 1992—, treas. 1990-91, exec. com., bd. dirs. 1990-91, endowment fund com. 1992, others).

WONG, JADIN (ANNA MAY WONG), dancer, actress, talent manager; b. Marysville, Calif., May 24, 1914; d. Charles and Pauline (Fong) W.; m. Edward Duryea Dowling, Feb. 17, 1964 (dec. Dec. 1967). Solo dancer Sir Francis Drake Hotel, San Francisco, 1936, Forbidden City, San Francisco, 1938-41, Golden Gate Theatre, San Francisco, 1941; dance team mem. El Rancho Casino, Las Vegas, 1943; featured dancer Folie Begere, N.Y.C., 1943; dance team mem. China Doll, N.Y.C., 1947, Carnegie Hall, N.Y.C., 1948; solo dancer Casino Della Rosa, Rome, 1951, Dunes Hotel, Las Vegas, 1955; owner Jadin Wong Talent Mgmt., N.Y.C.; producer Town Ranch Club, Seattle, 1943, Blue Lei Club, Honolulu, 1947, China Doll, N.Y.C., 1947, Teatro de Americas, Nuevo Laredo, Mex., 1948. Actress: (feature film) Mr. Moto Takes a Vacation, 1939, Irene, 1940, Carnival Story, 1951 (documentary) Forbidden City, USA, 1989. Recipient Plaque, Hist. Soc., 1993; named on Congrl. Record, House of Reps., 1985. Mem. Actor's Fund Am., Screen Actor's Guild. Office: Jadin Wong Talent Mgmt 442 W 57th St New York NY 10019

WONG, JANET S., financial executive; b. Shreveport, La., July 17, 1958; d. Joe S. and Mae (Ping) Wong; m. Ronald L. Mullins, Aug. 30, 1980. M in Profl. Accountancy, La. Tech. U., 1981; M in Taxation, Golden Gate U., 1993. CPA, La. Staff acct. Wilson, Bratlie and Thomas, Shreveport, La., 1981-83; mgr. tax Touche Ross & Co., Kansas City, Mo., 1983-85, Peat Marwick Main & Co., Shreveport, 1985-88; sr. mgr. KPMG Peat Marwick, San Francisco, 1988-94, nat. dir., 1994—; tax/fin. commentator KTBS-TV Inc., 1985, 87-88, 89. Contbr. articles to profl. jours. Bd. dirs. First Bapt. Ch., Shreveport, La., 1987-89, mem. fin. com., 1987-89. Mem. AICPA, Calif. Soc. CPAs, Nat. Assn. Accts. (bd. dirs. 1987—), World Affairs Coun., Asian Bus. League. Republican. Baptist. Office: KPMG Peat Marwick 3460 W Bayshore Rd Palo Alto CA 94303

WONG, NANCY HING, lawyer; b. Fairfield, Calif., Mar. 19, 1957; d. Won Yet and Chuck Hing (Chong) W. BA, U. Calif., Berkeley, 1979; JD, U. Calif., Davus, 1988. Youth counselor Chinatown Youth Ctr., San Francisco, 1979-82; adminstrv. asst. Found. Ctr., San Francisco, 1982-84; employment counselor Community Ednl. Svcs., San Francisco, 1984-85; asst. referral coord. Bar Assn. San Francisco, 1988-89; staff atty. Asian Law Alliance, San Jose, Calif., 1990; dep. city atty. San Francisco, 1990—. Chairperson Susan Jang Youth Leadership Fund/The Women's Found., San Francisco, 1990—; vol. Asian Immigrant Women Advocates, Oakland, Calif., 1993—, Asian Women's Shelter, San Francisco, 1990—. Paul R. Wada scholar Friends of Paul Wada, 1988; reciient Martin Luther King Jr. Svc. award Law Students Assn., 1988; recognized for svc. to community FIlipinos for Affirmative Action, 1988. Mem. Asian Am. Bar Assn. Office: City Attys Office Rm 206 City Hall San Francisco CA 94102

WONG-LIANG, EIRENE MING, psychologist; b. Nassau, Bahamas, Nov. 20, 1961; came to U.S., 1969; d. Menyu and Lim Ming (Chow) Wong. BA, Trinity U., San Antonio, 1984; PhD, Calif. Sch. Profl. Psychology, 1992. Crisis counselor United Way Crisis Hotline, San Antonio, 1983; lab. asst.

Trinity U., 1983; counselor Bayer County Women's Ctr., San Antonio, 1984, Turning Point Juvenile Diversion Project, Garden Grove, Calif., 1985-86; psychol. trainee Wolters Elem. Sch., Fresno, 1987, San Luis Obispo (Calif.) Youth Day Treatment, 1987-88, Calif. Sch. Profl. Psychology, Fresno, 1988—; staff psychologist 314th Med. Ctr., Little Rock, Ark., 1989-93; pvt. practice, clin. psychologist Houston, 1993—. Mem. APA, Am. Soc. Clin. Hypnosis, Internat. Soc. Clin. Hypnosis, Nat. Register Health Svc. Providers in Psychology, Tex. Psychol. Assn., Houston Psychol. Assn., Houston Assn. Clin. Hypnosis (charter), Psi Chi, Zeta Chi (charter mem. Trinity U. chpt.). Office: 10101 SW Freeway Ste 445 Houston TX 77074

WOO, FRANCES MEI SOO, lawyer; b. San Francisco, Feb. 23, 1949; d. On Lung and Lai Shou (Wong) W.; m. Gary Duane Hoppe, May 3, 1986. BA, Wash. State U., 1971; JD, U. Wash., 1975; LLM in Tax, NYU, 1977. Bar: Wash. 1975, U.S. Dist. Ct. (we. dist.) Wash. 1975, U.S. Tax Ct. 1977, N.Y. 1978, U.S. Dist. Ct. (so. and ea. dist.) N.Y. 1978, U.S. Supreme Ct. 1982. Assoc. Brown & Wood, N.Y.C., 1977-80; employee benefits, tax counsel Westvaco Corp., N.Y.C., 1980-83, SCM Corp., N.Y.C., 1983-87; employee benefits, cons. Mercer Meidinger Hansen, Inc., 1987-88; employee benefits, tax counsel CBS Records, Inc., N.Y.C., 1988-91; employee benefits counsel BASF Corp., Parsippany, N.J., 1991-93; employee benefits cons. N.Y.C., 1993—; bd. dirs. Gramont Owners Corp. Contbr. articles to profl. jours. Mem. ABA, WEB, Wash. State Bar Assn., N.Y. State Bar Assn., Assn. Bar City N.Y., Tax Execs. Inst. Home: 215 W 98th St Apt 10D New York NY 10025-5635 Office: 757 3rd Ave Ste 700 New York NY 10017

WOOD, BARBARA, author; b. Eng., Jan. 30, 1947; d. Alfons and Ruth (Pemberton) Lewandowski; m. George Wood, June 25, 1966. Student, U. Calif., Santa Barbara, 1964-66. Surg. technician Santa Monica (Calif.) Hosp., 1973-77. Author: The Magdalene Scrolls, 1978, Hounds and Jackals, 1978, Curse This House, 1978, Yesterday's Child, 1979, (with Gareth Wootton) Night Trains, 1979, The Watchgods, 1980, Childsong, 1981, Domina, 1983, Vital Signs, 1985, Soul Flame, 1987, Green City in the Sun, 1988, The Dreaming: A Novel of Australia, 1991, Virgins of Paradise, 1993; (as Kathryn Harvey) Butterfly, 1988, Stars, 1992, Emerald, 1994. Office: care Harvey Klinger Inc 301 W 53rd St New York NY 10019-5766*

WOOD, BARBARA LOUISE CHAMPION, state legislator; b. Swampscott, Mass., Jan. 10, 1924; d. John Duncan and Eva Louise (Moore) Champion; m. Newall Arthur Wood, June 12, 1948; children: Gary Duncan, Craig Newall, Brian Scott, Dennis Michael, Joan Wood Unger. Diploma in Nursing, Mary Hitchcock Meml. Hosp. Sch. Nursing, Hanover, N.H., 1945; student, Simmons Coll., 1947-48. RN. Rep., mem. ho. edn. com. Vt. Gen. Assembly, Montpelier, 1981—, vice chmn. edn. com., 1983-87; trustee Vt. State Colls., Waterbury, 1986-90, Gifford Meml. Hosp., Randolph, Vt., 1986—; commr., Vt. rep. Edn. Commn. of the States, Denver, 1981-86. Sch. dir. Bethel Sch. Bd., Vt., 1963-85; mem.-at-large Vt. Sch. Bds. Assn., Montpelier, 1982-85. Served to 2d lt. U.S. Army, 1945-46. Mem. Am. Legion, Vis. Nurse Alliance Vt.-N.H. (bd. dirs. 1991—). Republican. Congregationalist. Clubs: Bethel Woman's (pres. 1976-78); Vt. Fedn. Women's Clubs (dist. pres. 1978-80). Home: Woodland Rd Bethel VT 05032 Office: Vt House of Reps State House Montpelier VT 05602

WOOD, CHRISTIE ANN, software developer; b. Texas City, Tex., Dec. 6, 1955; d. Clarence Jefferson and Mary Ellen (Standley) W. BME, U. North Tex., 1978. Asst. ops. mgr. North Tex. State U. Computer Ctr., Denton, 1980-81, programmer, 1981; computer sci. tchr. La. Sch. Professions, Shreveport, 1981-82; computer analyst Bossier Parrish Sch. Bd., Bossier City, La., 1982-84; sr. mktg. support Unisys Corp., Dallas, 1984-87; mktg. mgr. Unisys Corp. WHQ, Blue Bell, Pa., 1987-91; product devel. mgr. Unisys Corp., Blue Bell, Pa., 1991-93; software devel. project leader Paramount Packaging, Chalfont, Pa., 1993—; awards chmn. Data Processing Mgmt. Assn., Dallas, 1985. Editor: The LINC Systems Approach, 1989, The LINC Systems Approach 3.0, 1992; composer cantata. Flutist Shreveport Symphony Orch., 1981-84, Canterbury Chamber Consort, 1989-91, Ensemble Pro Musica, 1991—; bd. dirs. Nehemiah's Way, 1992-93; publicity and youth com. chmn. St. Peter's Evangelical Luth. Ch., 1993—. Recipient Exemplary Action award Burroughs Corp., 1985. Mem. Ensemble Pro Musica. Democrat. Office: Paramount Packaging Corp 202 Oak Ave Chalfont PA 18914

WOOD, CONSTANCE DORIS, psychologist; b. Boston, June 3, 1929; d. Henry and Annie Lena (Miller) Rosen; m. Edwin C. Wood, Dec. 17, 1977; children—Marsha Lasker, Shelley Lasker, Jeffrey Lasker. B.A. in Psychology, Boston U., 1950; M.Ed. Psychol. Examiner, U. Hartford, 1960; Ph.D. in Psychology, Fordham U., 1975; cert. in Psychoanalytic Psychotherapy, Inst. for Study of Psychotherapy, 1977. Lic. psychologist, Tex., N.Y. Grad. asst. in psychology, Boston U., 1950-51; clin. psychologist Mass. Gen. Hosp., Boston, 1951-52, Hartford Health Dept., Conn., 1963; research psychologist Inst. of Living, Hartford, 1963-66; sch. psychologist Conn. Inst. for the Blind, Hartford, 1965-68; clin. psychologist New Rochelle Ctr. for Psychol. Services and Edn., N.Y., 1970-77; sch. psychologist Mt. Vernon Bd. Edn., N.Y., 1968-77; pvt. practice psychology, New Rochelle, 1977; dir. Ima Hogg Therapeutic Sch., Children's Mental Health Services, Houston, 1978-79; pvt. practice psychology, Houston, 1978—; psychol. cons. St. Luke's Hosp., Houston, 1983—, Methodist Hosp., Houston, 1984—, Tex. Children's Hosp., Houston, 1982—, Belle Park Hosp., Houston, 1983-93, Houston Internat. Hosp., 1982-90, West Oaks Hosp., 1985—, Med. Ctr. Del Oro Hosp., 1986—, Ami Bellaire Hosp., Houston, 1986—, Spring Shadows Glen Hosp., Houston, 1986—, Baywood Hosp., Webster, 1987-93, Orchard Creek Hosp., 1991—, Houston Day Hosp., 1982-88, Jefferson Davis Hosp., Houston, 1982-83; expert witness, 1980—. Contbr. articles to profl. publs. Mem. Am. Psychol. Assn., Tex. Psychol. Assn., Houston Psychol. Assn., Phi Delta Kappa, Kappa Delta Pi. Home: 2704 Glen Haven Blvd Houston TX 77025-2102 Office: 5300 San Jacinto St Ste 150 Houston TX 77004-6841

WOOD, DEBORAH CHRISTINE, critical care nurse, educator; b. Houston, Oct. 20, 1948; d. John Bud and Bettye (Miller) Lawson; m. Billy Ray Wood, May 24, 1977; children: Amy, Mike, John, Daniel. ADN, Trinity Valley Jr. Coll., 1987; BSN, U. Tex., Arlington, 1990; MSN, U. Tex., Tyler, 1994. RN, Tex.; cert. BLS, ACLS, pediatric advanced life support; CCRN. Telemetry/stepdown unit staff, charge nurse Mother Frances Hosp., Tyler, 1987-88, staff nurse cardiovasc. ICU, 1987-88, charge nurse cardiovasc. ICU, 1988—; critical care instr. Tyler Jr. Coll., 1992-93, instr. AD nursing program, 1993—. Mem. AACN (Greater East Tex. chpt. and nat. chpt., cons. spl. interest mgmt., NTI program rev. panel), Am. Heart Assn. (cardiovascular nursing coun.), Sigma Theta Tau. Roman Catholic.

WOOD, DIANE PAMELA, lawyer; b. Plainfield, N.J., July 4, 1950; d. Kenneth Reed and Lucille (Padmore) Wood; m. Dennis James Hutchinson, Sept. 2, 1978; children: Kathryn, David, Jane. BA, U. Tex.-Austin, 1971, JD, 1975. Bar: Tex. 1975, D.C. 1978. Law clk. U.S. Ct. Appeals (5th cir.), 1975-76, U.S. Supreme Ct., 1976-77; atty.-advisor U.S. Dept. State, Washington, 1977-78; assoc. law firm Covington & Burling, Washington, 1978-80; asst. prof. law Georgetown U. Law Ctr., Washington, 1980-81, U. Chgo., 1981-88, prof. law, 1988—, assoc. dean, 1989-92, Harold J. and Marion F. Green prof. internat. legal studies, 1990— (on leave); spl. cons. antitrust divsn. internat. guide U.S. Dept. Justice, 1986-87, dep. asst. atty. gen. antitrust divsn., 1993—.Bd. dirs. Hyde-Park-Kenwood Community Health Ctr., 1983-85. Mem. ABA (sec. antitrust and internat. law, chmn. internat. law sect. BIT com., co-chmn. internat. antitrust com., ILP coun. 1989-91, internat. legal scholar officer 1991-93, chmn., antitrust sec. subcom. on internat. unfair trade, vice-chair, sec. internat. antitrust com. 1991, standing com. on law and nat. security 1991-93), Am. Soc. Internat. Law, Am. Law Inst., Internat. Acad. Comparative Law. Democrat.

WOOD, EMMA S., nursing administrator; b. Lancaster County, Pa., June 20, 1945; d. Moses H. and Elizabeth M. (Shirk) Zimmerman; m. George Wood, Feb. 4, 1977 (dec. July 1989); 1 child, George William Jr. ADN, Edison Community Coll., 1979; BSN, U. South Fla., 1987, MSN, 1989. RN, Fla.; cert. psychiat. and mental health nurse, cert. profl. in health care quality, clin. specialist in psychiat. mental health. Agy. adminstr., home health nurse VNA of Desoto County, Arcadia, Fla., 1979-81; utilization rev. coord. G. Pierce Wood Meml. Hosp., 1981-85, sr. nurse supr., mgr., 1989—. Mem. ANA, Fla. Nurses Assn., Nat. Assn. for Health Care Quality, Fla. Assn. for Health Care Quality, Am. Psychiat. Nurses Assn., NLN, Sigma Theta Tau. Home: 2808 Caribbean Dr Punta Gorda FL 33982-4302

WOOD, EVELYN NIELSEN, reading dynamics business executive; b. Logan, Utah, Jan. 8, 1909; d. Elias and Rose (Stirland) Nielsen; m. Myron Douglas Wood, June 12, 1929 (dec. May 1987); 1 child, Carolyn Wood Evans. BA, U. Utah, 1929, MA, 1947; postgrad., Columbia U., 1956-57. Tchr. Weber Coll., Ogden, Utah, 1931-32; girls counselor Jordan High Sch., Sandy, Utah, 1948-57, tchr. jr. and sr. high schs., 1948-59; instr. U. Utah, 1957-59; founder, originator Evelyn Wood Reading Dynamics, 1959—; tchr. rapid reading U. Del., 1961; guest lectr. NEA, 1961, Internat. Reading Assn., Tex. Christian U., 1962; faculty Brigham Young U., research specialist for reading, 1973-74. Author, conductor radio programs, 1947; author: (With Marjory Barrows) Reading Skills, 1958, A Breakthrough in Reading, 1961, A New Approach to Speed Reading, 1962, Speed Reading for Comprehension, 1962, also articles. Home: 6024 E Wendrew Ln Tucson AZ 85711-2517

WOOD, GINA ELEANE, state agency program administrator; b. Springfield, Mo., Aug. 29, 1959; d. George Henry and Emma (Cook) W. BA in Comm., U. Mo., 1983. With pub. rels. and sales Portland (Oreg.) Observer Newspaper, 1983-85; legis. asst. State Rep. Margaret Carter, Salem, Oreg., 1985-86; exec. dir. Highland Cmty. Svcs./Yaun Youth Care Ctr., Portland, 1986; legis./ops. mgr. Adult and Family Svcs., Salem, 1987-88; mem. gov. staff Gov. Neil Goldschmidt, Salem, 1988-89; regional coord. Child & Youth Commn., Salem, 1989-94; fed. program dir. Commn. Child and Families, Salem, 1994—; cons. Cmty. Rsch. Assocs., Champaign, Ill., 1993—. Precinct com. person Washington County, Portland, Oreg., 1992—; active Oreg. Women's Polit. Caucus, Portland, 1985—, Gov. Task Force on Family Law, Salem, 1993—. Mem. Am. Corrections Assn., Nat. Assn. Blacks in Criminal Justice, Pvt. Industry Coun. (past chair youth com.), Urban League Portland (past chairperson). Democrat. Home: 8040-C SW Brookridge Portland OR 97225

WOOD, GLADYS BLANCHE, retired educator and journalist; b. Sanborn, N.D., Aug. 12, 1921; d. Charles Kershaw and Mina Blanche (Kee) Crowther; m. Newell Edwin Wood, June 13, 1943 (dec. 1990); children: Terry N., Lani, Brian R., Kevin C.; m. F.L. Stutzman, Nov. 30, 1991. BA in Journalism, U. Minn., 1943; MA in Mass Comm., San Jose State U., 1972. Cert. secondary tchr., Calif. Reporter St. Paul Pioneer-Dispatch, 1943-45; editor J.C. Penney Co., N.Y.C., 1945-46; tchr. English and journalism Willow Glen H.S., San Jose, Calif., 1968-87; freelance writer, photographer, 1947—; cons. in field. Named Secondary Journalism Tchr. of Yr. Calif. Newspaper Pubs. Assn., 1977. Mem. AAUW, Soc. Profl. Journalists, Journalism Edn. Assn., Calif. Tchrs. English, Calif. Ret. Tchrs. Assn., Women in Comm., Santa Clara County Med. Assn. Aux., Montalvo Assn., LWV, Friends of Libr., Delta Kappa Gamma, Alpha Omicron Pi. Republican. Methodist. Home: 14161 Douglass Ln Saratoga CA 95070-5535

WOOD, JACALYN KAY, educational consultant, university administrator; b. Columbus, Ohio, May 25, 1949; d. Carleston John and Grace Anna (Schumacher) W. BA, Georgetown Coll., 1971; MS, Ohio State U., 1976; PhD, Miami U., 1981. Elem. tchr. Bethel-Tate Schs., Ohio, 1971-73, Columbus Christian Sch., 1973-74, Franklin (Ohio) Schs., 1974-79; teaching fellow Miami U., Oxford, Ohio, 1979-81; cons. intermediate grades Erie County Schs., Sandusky, Ohio, 1981-89, presenter, tchr. insvc. tng. Mem. coun. Sta. WVIZ-TV, 1981-88; assoc. prof. Ashland U., Elyria, Ohio, 1989, dir. elem. edn., 1989—; mem. Lorain County 20/20, mem. strategic planning bd., 1992—; mem. Leadership Lorain County, 1994—; mem. exec. com. Perkins Community Schs., 1981-85; mem. community adv. bd. Sandusky Vols. Am., 1985-89, Sandusky Soc. Bank, 1987-88, vol. Firelands Community Hosp., 1986-87; active Leadership Lorain County, 1994—. Mem. AAUW, ASCD, Am. Businesswomen's Assn. (local pres. 1985), Internat. Reading Assn., Ohio Sch. Suprs. Assn. (regional pres. 1986, state pres. 1986-87), Phi Delta Kappa (local sec. 1985, 86, v.p. 1991-93, pres. 1993—), Phi Kappa Phi, Kappa Delta Pi (local adv. 1991-93). Baptist. Home: 35873 Westminster Ave N Ridgeville OH 44039-1380 Office: Ashland U at LCCC 1005 Abbe Rd N Elyria OH 44035-1613

WOOD, JANE SEMPLE, editor, writer; b. Easton, Pa., June 23, 1940; d. Royer Daniel and Wilhelmina Annette (Weichel) Semple; m. James MacPherson Wood, Sept. 8, 1961; children: James MacPherson Jr., Robert Semple. BA in Journalism, U. Calif., Berkeley, 1961. Reporter San Jose (Calif.) Mercury News, 1962; asst. dir. pub. rels. Nat. Symphony Orch., Washington, 1963-65; free-lance writer and editor Adoption Listing Svc. of Ohio, Cleve., 1976; freelance writer and editor AIA, Cleve., 1977; free-lance writer and editor City of Bedford Heights, Ohio, 1980-81; free-lance writer and editor City of Shaker Heights, Ohio, 1979-80, pub. info. officer, dir. publs., 1980-85, 92—; founding editor Shaker mag., Shaker Heights, Ohio, 1983—; free-lance writer Exec. Living, Cleve., 1990-91; contbg. editor Corp. Cleve., 1991-92; pub. rels. cons. Cable TV Com., Shaker Heights, 1978-85, Oak Park Exch. Congress, Shaker Heights, 1981. Vol. editor, columnist Friends of Shaker Sq., Cleve., 1979-82; vol. pub. rels. com. Cleve. Ballet, 1980, Cleve. Orch., 1983; vol. contbg. editor Univ. Hosps., Cleve., 1990-92. Recipient Grand award City Hall Digest, 1983, 85, 87, Excellence in Journalism award Soc. Profl. Journalists, 1988, 92, Woman of Profl. Excellence award Cleve. YWCA, 1986, Ace award of Merit, 1991, Hon. mention Blue Pencil Competition of Nat. Assn. Govt. Communicators, 1993. Mem. Press Club of Cleve., Cleve. Internat. Vol. Orgn., U. Calif. Alumni Assn. (permanent class sec. 1961). Office: Shaker Mag 3400 Lee Rd Cleveland OH 44120-3408

WOOD, JEANNINE K., state official; b. Dalton, Nebr., Apr. 22, 1944; d. Grover L. and Elsie M. (Winkelman) Sanders; m. Charles S. Wood, Dec. 7, 1968; children: Craig C., Wendi L. Wood Armstrong. Student, Boise State U. Exec. sec. Idaho Hosp. Assn., Boise, 1966-71; com. sec. Idaho State Senate, Boise, 1976-81, jour. clk., 1981-85, asst. to sec. of senate, 1985-91, sec. of senate, 1991—; pvt. practice typing svc. Boise, 1979-86. Precinct committeeman Rep. Party. Mem. Am. Soc. Legis. Clks. and Secs. (vice chmn. legis. adminstr. com.), Nat. Assn. Parliamentarians, Idaho Assn. Parliamentarians. Methodist. Home: PO Box 83720 Boise ID 83720-0081 Office: Idaho State Capitol Boise ID 83720

WOOD, JOAN KLAWANS, architect; b. Chgo., Dec. 24, 1932; d. Paul H. and Anne (Bronstein) Klawans; m. Henry Austin Wood III, Oct. 5, 1962 (div. Dec. 1982); children: Paul, Joshua, Daniel. BA, U. Chgo., 1953; postgrad., Harvard U., 1954-56; BArch, MIT, 1960. Registered arch., Mass.; cert. arch. Pres. Joan Wood Assocs.-Archs., Inc., Cambridge and Boston, Mass., 1962—; mem., vice-chair Designer Selection Bd., Mass., 1985-89; alt. mem. Zoning Bd. Appeals, Boston, 1987-93, 94—. Prin. works include Coolidge Ice House, WIC and Family Svcs. Bldg., 20 Years of Joan Wood Assocs., 1983, AIA Centennial/Women, Traveling Exhibit, 1988, Boston Soc. Archs. Women in Arch., 1987-91. Mem., former chair Ward 4 Dem. Com., Boston, 1976—, Park Plaza Civic Adv. Com., Boston, 1980-90; mem. Copley Square Design Rev. Com., 1991; active nat. and local Dem. party campaigns, 1960—. Mem. AIA (urban design com. 1979—), New Eng. Women in Real Estate, Boston Soc. Archs. (urban design and homeless com. 1979—), Boston Club. Office: Joan Wood Assocs Archs Inc 24 Rutland Sq Boston MA 02118

WOOD, KATHLEEN OLIVER, writer, editor; b. Mt. Kisco, N.Y., Sept. 17, 1921; d. Eli Leslie and Melba Antoinette (Gislason) Oliver; m. John Thornton Wood, June 1941 (div. 1947); children: Mark Thornton, Jonna Hinkle; m. Clifford Emanuel Huff, June 1948 (div. 1955); 1 child, Karen Weston. Student Swarthmore Coll., 1938-39, Antioch Coll., 1940-41, U. N.Mex., 1949, Cleve. Coll., 1960-61. Tech. sec. Gray Iron Founders Soc., Cleve., 1955-57; tchr. Whiting Bus. Coll., Cleve., 1957-62; editorial asst. Chem. Rubber Co., Cleve., 1966; editor, writer Jefferson Ency., World Pub. Co., Cleve., 1967-68; disc jockey, announcer Sta. WCLV-FM, Cleve., 1968-69; communications coord., writer, editor Highlights newsletter University Circle, Inc., Cleve., 1971-81; talk-show hostess, announcer Sta. WERE-AM, Cleve., 1972-73; free-lance writer, editor, cons., 1981—; editor Insideout Magazine, 1994—; publicity specialist Am. Assn. Retired Persons, Ohio, 1987-88; tchr. Project LEARN; tutor VIP program. Author: Greenwood, 1967; editor, pub. Frog in the Milk Pan (Marie Wallace), 1963; editor Graffiti Mag., 1967, Office Gal Mag., 1962-63, Smorgasbrain Mag., 1968. Hostess weekly radio show, CRRS, Cleve. Soc. for Blind; taper books for Libr. of Congress Svc. for Visually Handicapped; treas. Cleve. Beautiful Com., 1980, sec., 1982; v.p. Cleve. Cultural Garden Fedn., exec. sec. 1989-90, 90-91, acting pres., 1989—; trustee E. Cleve. Community Theatre. Mem. Pub. Rels. Soc. Am., Internat. Assn. Bus. Communicators, Advt. Women of Cleve. (past pres., editor Weathervane 1982-83), Women in Communication (editor Write-Up 1989—), World Assn. Women Journalists and Writers (congress coordinator 1982-83, v.p. U.S. chpt. 1988—), Mensa, Early Settlers. Quaker. Clubs: Zonta Internat. (pres. Cleve. chpt. 1991—, dir. Area 3 Dist. V, 1984-86), Women's City, Esperanto League of N.Am., Universal Esperanto Assn. Home: 3118 E Overlook Rd Cleveland OH 44118-2440 Office: PO Box 5612 Cleveland OH 44101-0612

WOOD, KIMBA M., judge; b. Port Townsend, Wash., Jan. 2, 1944. BA cum laude, Conn. Coll., 1965; MSc, London Sch. Econs., 1966; JD, Harvard U., 1969. Bar: U.S. Dist. Ct. D.C. 1969, U.S. Ct. Appeals D.C. 1969, N.Y. 1972, U.S. Dist. Ct. (ea. and so. dists.) N.Y. 1974, U.S. Ct. Appeals (2d cir.) 1975, U.S. Supreme Ct. 1980, U.S. Dist. Ct. (we. dist.) N.Y. 1981. Assoc. Steptoe & Johnson, Washington, 1969-70; with Office Spl. Counsel, OEO Legal Svcs., Washington, 1970-71; assoc., then ptnr. LeBoeuf, Lamb, Leiby & MacRae, N.Y.C., 1971-88; judge, U.S. Dist. Ct. (so. dist.) N.Y., N.Y.C., 1988—. Mem. ABA (chmn. civil practice, procedure com. 1982-85, mem. coun. 1985-88, jud. rep. 1989-91), N.Y. State Bar Assn. (chmn. antitrust sect. 1983-84), Fed. Bar Coun. (trustee from 1978, v.p., 1984-85), Am. Law Inst. Office: US Dist Ct US Courthouse Foley Sq New York NY 10007

WOOD, LARRY (MARY LAIRD), journalist, author, university educator, public relations executive, environmental consultant; b. Sandpoint, Idaho; d. Edward Hayes and Alice (McNeel) Small; children: Mary, Marcia, Barry. BA summa cum laude, U. Wash., 1939, MA summa cum laude, with highest honors, 1940; postgrad., Stanford U., 1941-42, U. Calif., Berkeley, 1946-47; cert. in photography, U. Calif., Berkeley, 1971; postgrad. journalism, U. Wis., 1971-72, U. Minn., 1971-72, U. Ga., 1972-73; postgrad. in art, architecture and marine biology, U. Calif., Santa Cruz, 1974-76, Stanford Hopkins Marine Sta., Santa Cruz, 1977-80. Lifetime secondary and jr. coll. teaching cert., Wash., Calif. Feature writer and columnist Oakland Tribune and San Francisco Chronicle, Calif., 1939—; archtl. and environ. feature and travel writer and columnist San Jose (Calif.) Mercury News (Knight Ridder), 1972-90; teaching fellow Stanford U., 1940-43; pub. rels. dir. 12-county East Bay Regional Park Dist., No. Calif., 1948-68; pres. Larry Wood Pub. Rels., 1946—; prof. (tenure) pub. rels., mag. writing, journalism and investigative reporting, San Diego State U., 1974, 75; disting. vis. prof. journalism San Jose State U., 1976; assoc. prof. journalism Calif. State U., Hayward, 1978; prof. sci. and environ. journalism U. Calif. Berkeley Extension grad. div., 1979—; press del. nat. convs. Am. Geophys. Union Internat. Conf., 1986—, AAAS, 1989—, Nat. Park Svc. VIP Press Tour, Yellowstone after the fire Nat. Pk. Svc. VIP Press Tour, 1989, Nat. Assn. Sci. Writers, 1989, George Washington U./Am. Assn. Neurol. Surgeons Sci. Writers Conf., 1990, Am. Inst. Biol. Scis. Conf., 1990, Nat. Conf. Sci. Writers Am. Heart Assn., 1995, Internat. Cardiologists Symposium for Med./Sci. Writers, 1995; EPA del. to USSR and Ea. Europe; mem. Am. Bd. Forensic Examiners, 1994; expert witness on edn., affirmative action, pub. rels., journalism and copyright; cons. sci. writers interne project, Stanford U., 1989—; spl. media guest Sigma Xi, 1990—; mem. numerous spl. press corps; selected White House Special Media, 1993—; internat. press guest Swiss Nat. Tourist Offices, Lake Geneva Region Celebration, 1994, Can. Consulate Gen. Dateline Can., 1995, Ministerio delle Risorse Agricole Alimentari e Forestali and Assocs. Conf., 1995; mem. Am. Bd. Forensic Examiners, 1994; appeared in TV documentary Larry Wood Covers Visit of Queen Elizabeth II. Contbr. over 5,000 articles on various topics for newspapers, nat. mags., nat. and internat. newspaper syndicates including L.A. Times, Times-Mirror Syndicate, Washington Post, Phila. Inquirer, Chgo. Tribune, Miami Herald, Oakland Tribune, Seattle Times, San Francisco Chronicle, Parade, San Jose Mercury News (Nat. Headliner award), Christian Sci. Monitor, L.A. Times/Christian Monitor News Syndicate, MonitoRadio, Sports Illus., Mechanix Illus., Popular Mechanics, Parents, House Beautiful, Am. Home (awards 1988, 89), National Geographic World, Travel & Leisure, Chevron USA/Odyssey (Calif. Pub.'s award 1984), Xerox Edn. Publs., Europe's Linguapress, PSA Mag., Off Duty, Oceans, Sea Frontiers, AAA Westways, AAA Motorland, Travelin', others. Significant works include home and garden columnist and editor, 5-part series Pacific Coast Ports, 5-part series Railroads of the West, series Immigration, Youth Gangs, Endangered Species, Calif. Lighthouse Chain, Elkhorn Slough Nat. Estuarine Reserve; author: Wonderful U.S.A.: A State-by-State Guide to Its Natural Resources, 1989; co-author over 21 books including: McGraw-Hill English for Social Living, 1944, Fawcett Boating Books, 1956-66, Fodor's San Francisco, Fodor's California, 1982-89, Charles Merrill Focus on Life Science, Focus on Physical Science, Focus on Earth Science, 1983, 87, Earth Science, 1987; contbr. Earth Science 1987; 8 works selected for use by Europe's Wolters-Nordoff-Longman English Language Texts, U.K., Netherlands, 1988; author: (with others) anthology West Winds, 1989; reviewer Charles Merrill texts, 1983-84; book rerofl. Communicator, 1987—; selected writings in permanent collections Oakland Pub. Libr., U. Wash. Main Libr.; environ. works included in Dept. Edn. State of Md. textbook; contbr., author Journalism Quar.; author script PBS/AAA America series, 1992. Nat. chmn. travel writing contest for U.S. univ. journalism students Assn. for Edn. in Journalism/Soc. Am. Travel Writers, 1979-83; judge writing contest for Nat. Assn. Real Estate Editors, 1982—; Italy; press del. 1st Internat. Symposium Volcanism and Aviation Safety, 1991, Coun. for the Advancement of Science Writing 1977—, Rockefeller Media Seminar Feeding the World-Protecting the Earth, 1992, Global Conf. on Mercury as Pollutant, 1992, Earth Summit Global Forum, Rio de Janeiro, 1992; invited Nat. Park Svc. Nat. Conf. Sci. Writers, 1985, Postmaster Gen.'s 1992 Stamps, 1991, Internat. Geophysical Union Cong., 1982-95, EPA and Dept. Energy Tech. Conf., 1992, Am. Soc. Photogammetry and Remote Sensing Internat. Conv. Mapping Global Change, 1992, N.Y. Mus. Mod. Art Matisse Retrospective Press Rev., 1992, celebration 150th anniversary Oreg. Trail 1993, coun. advancement sci. writing 1993, 94, Sigma Xi Nat. Conf. 1988—, PRSA Travel and Tourism Conf. 1993, Internat. Conf. Environment, 1994, 95, Quality Life Europe, Prague, 1994; press guest State of Conn., 1993; mem. Gov.'s Conf. Tourism N.C., 1993, 94, 95, Calif., 1976—, Fla., 1987—, Coun. for Advancement in Sci. Writing Nat. Conf., 1994. Numerous awards, honors, citations, speaking engagements including induction into Broadway Hall of Fame U. Wash., Seattle, 1984, citations for environ. writing from Nat. Park Service, U.S. Forest Service, Bur. Land Mgmt., Oakland Mus. Assn., Oakland C. of C., Chevron USA, USN plaque and citation, Best Mag. Articles citation Calif. Pubs. Assn., 1984; co-recipient Nat. Headliner award for Best Sunday Newspaper Mag.; co-recipient citation Oakland Mus. for archtl. features, 1983; honoree Nat. Mortar Bd. for Achievements in Journalism, 1988, 89; selected as one of ten V.I.P. press for Yellowstone Nat. Park field trip on "Let Burn" rsch., 1989; named one of Calif.'s top 40 contemporary authors for 1989 with citation for writings on Calif.'s Underwater Pks.; named nat. honoree Social Issues Resources Series, 1987; invited V.I.P. press, spl. press guest numerous events worldwide. Mem. Am. Bd. Forensic Examiners, Calif. Acad. Scis., San Francisco Press Club, Nat. Press Club, Pub. Rels. Soc. Am. (charter mem. travel, tourism, environment and edn. divs.), Nat. Sch. Pub. Rels. Assn., Environ. Cons. N.Am., Am. Assn. Edn. in Journalism and Comm. (exec. bd. nat. mag. div. 1978, panel chmn. 1979, 80, author Journalism Quar. jour.), Women in Comm. (nat. bd. officer 1975-77, book reviewer Prof. Communicator), Soc. Profl. Journalists (nat. bd. for hist. sites 1980—), Nat. Press Photographers Assn. (hon. life, cons. Bay Area interne project 1989—, honoree 1995), Investigative Reporters and Editors (charter), Bay Area Advt. and Mktg. Assn., Nat. Assn. Sci. Writers, Calif. Writers Club (state bd., Berkeley bd. 1989—, honoree ann. conv. Asilomar, Calif. 1990), Am. Assn. Med. Writers, Internat. Assn. Bus. Communicators, Am. Film Inst., Am. Heritage Found. (citation 1986, 87, 88), Soc. Am. Travel Writers, Internat. Oceanographic Found., Oceanic Soc., Calif. Acad. Environ. News Writers, Seattle Advt. and Sales Club (former officer), Nature Conservancy, Smithsonian Audubon Soc., Nat. Wildlife Fedn., Nat. Parks and Conservation Assn., Calif. State Parks Found., Fine Arts Mus., San Francisco, Seattle Jr. Advt. Club (charter), U. Wash. Comm. Alumni (Sch. Comm. alumni, life, charter mem. ocean scis. alumni, Disting. Alumni 1987), U. Calif., Berkeley Alumni (life, v.p., scholarship chmn. 1975-81), Stanford Alumni (life), Mortar Board Alumnae Assn. (life, honoree 1988, 89), Am. Mgmt. Assn., Nat. Soc. Environ. Journalists (charter), Phi Beta Kappa (v.p., bd. dirs. Calif. Alumni Assn., statewide chmn. scholarship awards 197 Lambda Theta, Theta Sigma Phi. Home: Piedmont Pines 6161 Castle Dr Oakland CA 94611-2737

WOOD, LESLIE ANN, retail administrator; b. Chgo., Apr. 9, 1957; d. Howard Arnold and Anita Eleanor (Andler) W. AA, Harper Coll., 1977; BS in Communication Scis., Ill. State U., 1979; postgrad., Olivet Nazarene U. Advt. asst. Harry Alter Co., Chgo., 1979-80; clk. typist Career Guild, Evanston, Ill., 1980-81; reporter Aparacor, Evanston, Ill., 1981-82; sales mgmt. trainee Prudential Ins. Co. Am., Millburn, N.J., 1983-84; fin. cons. Summit Fin. Resources, Livingston, N.J., 1984; mgr. Chgo. area Renault Inc. div. AMC/Jeep/Renault, Elk Grove Village, Ill., 1985-87; customer relations specialist Chrysler Motors, Lisle, Ill., 1987-88; dist. svc. and parts mgr. Chrysler, Lisle; dist. parts mgr. Subaru of Am., Addison, Ill., 1989-91, dist. fixed ops. mgr., 1992—. Mem. NAFE, Toastmasters (v.p. membership Daniel Wright club 1993). Home: 230 Brett Circle Unit D Wauconda IL 60084

WOOD, LINDA ANNE, correctional specialist; b. Plainfield, N.J., Jan. 17, 1962; d. Harry L. and Barbara A. (Schmidt) W. BS in Criminal Justice, Trenton State Coll., 1984; MPA, Temple U., 1991. Student asst. N.J. Dept. Corrections, Trenton, 1981-84, adminstrv. analyst II, 1984-92; correctional program specialist Nat. Inst. Corrections, Longmont, Colo., 1992—. Vol. Boulder County (Colo.) AIDS Project, 1992—. Mem. Am. Jail Assn., Am. Correctional Assn., Am. Parole & Probation Assn., Nat. Sheriff's Assn., N.J. Cert. Pub. Mgr. Assn. (Elsie Fritz scholar 1990), Phi Kappa Phi. Office: Nat Inst Corrections 1960 Indsl Cir Ste A Longmont CO 80501

WOOD, LINDA DRYGALSKI, police officer; b. Paw Paw, Mich., Mar. 26, 1964; d. Edward Bernard and Lucille (Szjerman) Drygalski; divorced; 1 child, Jaclyn Nicole. Cert. law enforcement officer. Secretarial asst. U. Wis., Stevens Point, 1984-85, Oshkosh (Wis.) U., 1985-86; police officer Charlotte (N.C.) Police Dept., 1986—; mem. dept. pub. rels. Charlotte Police Dept., 1986—. Republican. Home: 10024 Oak Run Dr Apt H Charlotte NC 28210 Office: Charlotte Mecklenburg Police Dept 825 E 4th St Charlotte NC 28202

WOOD, LISA GAYE, civil engineering design company executive; b. Tampa, Fla., Dec. 12, 1957; d. James W. and Sylvia (Rosello) W.; m. Robert Howell, Mar. 13, 1976 (div. Nov. 1979); 1 child, Kyle A. Howell. With svc. Sears, Tampa, 1975-80; with drafting Heidt & Assocs., Tampa, 1980-83, Landmark Engring., Tampa, 1983-85; permit coord. Genesis Profl. Svcs., Lutz, Fla., 1985-89; sec.-treas. Premiere Engring., Inc., Tampa, 1989—. Notary pub., Tampa, 1989-97. Mem. NAFE, Tampa Bay C.of C. (N.W. coun.), Tampa Bay Snow Skiers, Carrollwood Area Bus. Assn. (chair holiday tree lighting event 1993), Gaither High Sch. Booster Club. Office: Premiere Engring Inc 3750 Gunn Hwy Ste 1C Tampa FL 33624-4905

WOOD, MARGARET GRAY, dermatologist, educator; b. Jamaica, N.Y., May 23, 1918; d. C.W. Bromley and B. Eleanor (Niblack) Gray; m. Alfred Conard Wood, Mar. 24, 1950; children: Margaret Diana, M. Deirdre Harper, Moira Dorothy. BA, U. ALa., Tuscaloosa, 1941; MD, Med. Coll. Pa., 1948, DMS, 1989, D in Med. Scis. (hon.), 1990, emeritus prof. medicine, 1993. Diplomate Am. Bd. Dermatology, Am. Bd. Dermatopathology. Intern Phila. Gen. Hosp., 1948-50; resident U. Pa. Hosp., 1950-53; instr. dept. dermatology U. Pa. Sch. Medicine, Phila., 1952-53, assoc., 1953-67, asst. prof., 1967-71, assoc. prof., 1971-75, clin. prof., 1975-80, prof. and chmn. dept. dermatology, 1980-82, prof., 1982-88, prof. emeritus, 1988—; assoc. prof. grad. Sch. Medicine U. Pa., Phila., 1957-71, cons. Sch. Dental Medicine, Sch. Vet. Medicine U. Pa., Phila.; asst. prof. Med. Coll. Pa., Phila., 1957-93, prof. emeritus, 1993—, vice chmn. bd. dirs. 1984—; vice chmn. bd. dirs. Med. Coll. Hosps., Phila., 1991—, Hahnemann U. Hosp., 1993—; mem. exec. com. Am. Med. Women's Hosp. Svc. Com., Washington, 1970—; dir. Alleghany Health Systems, Pitts., 1987-91, Alleghany Health Edn. and Rsch. Found., 1991-94; bd. dirs. St. Christophers Hosp. for Children. Author (with others) 4 books; contbr. numerous articles to med. jours. Recipient Rose Hershfeld award Women's Dermatology Soc., 1989. Mem. AMA, Internat. Dermatology Assn., Internat. Dermatopathology Assn., Phila. Dermatology Soc. (pres. 1978-79), Alpha Omega Alpha. Republican. Episcopalian.

WOOD, MARIAN STARR, publishing company executive; b. N.Y.C., Mar. 30, 1938; d. Edward James and Betty (Starr) Markow; m. Anthony Stuart Wood, Mar. 21, 1963. B.A., Barnard Coll., 1959; postgrad., Columbia U., 1959-64. Teaching asst., lectr. Columbia U., N.Y.C., 1960-64; editor Praeger Pubs., N.Y.C., 1965-71; sr. editor Henry Holt & Co., N.Y.C., 1972-81, exec. editor, 1981—.

WOOD, MARJORIE ELLEN (PEGGY WOOD), construction company executive, interior designer, real estate executive/broker; b. Chgo., Oct. 30, 1961; d. Lawrence M. and Lorraine E. McKeigue; m. John D. Wood, Feb. 14, 1988; children: Dee A., Kay L. Student, St. Mary-of-the-Woods. Mgr. Security Fin. Corp., Kileen, Tex., 1982-85; sr. v.p. and sec./treas. John D. Wood Builder, Inc., Greencastle, Ind., 1987—; pres. Wood Interiors, Inc., Greencastle, 1990—; pres., prin. broker Wood & Assocs. Real Estate, Inc., Greencastle, 1994—; chmn. regional bd. advisors Ind./Ky. region Decorating Den. Bd. dirs., v.p. Putnam County Operation Life, 1993—; bus. cons. Jr. Achievement Project; mem. bldg./grounds com. and ladies guild treas. St. Paul The Apostle Cath. Cdh. With U.S. Army, 1979-82, with USAR, 1985-88. Mem. LWV, NAFE, Greencastle C. of C. (pres. 1992, pres. 1993), Bus. and Profl. Women, Putnam County Bd. Realtors (state rep. 1995), Kiwanis.

WOOD, MARTHA OAKWELL, obstetrics-gynecology nurse practitioner; b. Chester, Pa., Apr. 19, 1941; d. Albert Edward Jr. and Gertrude Cecelia (Morgan) Warburton; m. Lawrence Dakin Wood, Nov. 22, 1957; children: Lawrence Dakin Jr., Thomas C., Elizabeth W., Michael L., Kathryn M., Scott G. BSN, Neumann coll., 1981; MSN, U. Pa., 1987. RN, Pa. Staff nurse Sacred Heart Med. ctr., Chester, Pa., 1981-84, Crozer-Chester Med. Ctr., 1984-88; clin. instr. obstetrics Neumann Coll., Aston, Pa., 1988, adj. faculty, 1991; instr. maternal-child health Chester County Hosp. Sch. Nursing, West Chester, Pa., 1989-90; adj. clin. instr. Widener U., Chester, 1991; staff devel. specialist Episcopal Hosp., Phila., 1992-93; ob.-gyn. nurse practitioner Camcare Health Corp., Camden, N.J., 1993—; supr. women and children nursing Bryn Mawr (Pa.) Hosp., 1988-89; perinatal nursing support Home Care Obstetrics, Bryn Mawr, 1991-93; manuscript reviewer Lippincott Pub. Co., Phila.; lectr. in field. Educator women's health Women's Assn. for Women's Alternatives, Wawa, Pa., 1990-91; big sister Del. County Pregnancy Ctr.; deaconess North Chester Bapt. Ch., 1991-94. Mem. Pa. Perinatal Assn., Acad. Nurse Practitioners, Assn. Reproductive Health Profls., Assn. Women's Health, Obstetrics, Neonatal Nurses, Sigma Theta Tau (Delta Tau chpt.). Baptist. Home: 103 W Mowry St Chester PA 19103 Office: Camcare Health Corp 3 Cooper Plaza Ste 104 Camden NJ 08103

WOOD, NANCY ELIZABETH, psychologist, educator; d. Donald Sterret and Orne Louise (Erwin) W. B.S., Ohio U., 1943, M.A., 1947; Ph.D., Northwestern U., Evanston, Ill., 1952. Prof. Case-Western Res. U., Cleve., 1952-60; specialist, expert Dept. HEW, Washington, 1960-62; chief of research Pub. Health, Washington, 1962-64; prof. U. So. Calif., Los Angeles, 1965—; learning disabilities cons., 1960-70; assoc. dir. Cleve. Hearing and Speech Ctr., 1952-60; dir. licensing program Brit. Nat. Trust, London. Author: Language Disorders, 1964, Language Development, 1970, Verbal Learning, 1975 (monograph) Auditory Disorders, 1978, Levity, 1980, Stoneskipping, 1989, Bird Cage, 1994. Pres. faculty senate U. So. Calif., 1987-88. Recipient Outstanding Faculty award Trojan Fourth Estate, 1982, Pres.' Svc. award U. So. Calif., 1992. Fellow Am. Speech and Hearing Assn. (elected, legis. council 1965-68), Am. Psychol. Assn. (cert.), AAAS; mem. Internat. Assn. of Scientists. Republican. Methodist. Office: U So Calif University Park CA 90089

WOOD, PAULA DAVIDSON, lawyer; b. Oklahoma City, Dec. 20, 1952; d. Paul James and Anna Mae (Ferrero) Davidson; m. Andrew E. Wood; children: Michael Paul, John Roland. BS, Okla. State U., 1976; JD, Oklahoma City U., 1982. Bar: Okla. 1983, U.S. Dist. Ct. (we. dist.) Okla. 1983; cert. pub. mgr. Staff atty Chuck Moss Legal Svcs., Oklahoma City, 1983-84; pvt. practice Oklahoma City, 1984-85; ptnr. Davidson & Wood, Oklahoma City, 1985-88; child support enforcement counsel Okla. Dept. Human Svcs., Oklahoma City, 1987-92, child support aminstr., IV-D dir., 1992—; adj. instr. Tech. Inst. Okla. State U., Oklahoma City, 1985. Articles editor Oklahoma City U. Law Rev., 1982. Mem. Okla. Bar Assn. (sec. family law sect. 1987, Golden Gavel award 1987), Okla. Child Support Enforcement Assn. (pres. 1992), Nat. Child Support Enforcement Assn., Southwest Regional Child Support Enforcement Assn., Nat. Assn. State Child Support Enforcement Adminstrs., Western Interstate Child Support Enforcement Coun. (sec. 1995). Republican. Roman Catholic. Office: Okla Dept Human Svcs PO Box 53552 Oklahoma City OK 73152

WOOD, ROBERTA SUSAN, foreign service officer; b. Clarksdale, Miss., Oct. 4, 1948; d. Robert Larkin and Dorothy Eloise (Shelton) Wood. BA with distinction, Rhodes Coll., Memphis, 1970; postgrad. Nat. U. Cuyo, Mendoza, Argentina, 1970-71; MPA, Harvard U., 1980. Joined U.S. Fgn. Svc., 1972; svc. in Manila, Philippines, Naples and Turin, Italy, and Port-au-Prince, Haiti; mgmt. analyst Dept. State, Washington, 1980-84; U.S. consul gen., Jakarta, Indonesia, 1984-87, NATO Def. Coll., Rome, 1987-88; U.S. consul gen. Marseilles, France, 1988-91, Montreal, Que., Can., 1991-94; min., dep. chief of mission US Embassy, Quito, Ecuador, 1994—. Fulbright scholar, 1970-71. Home and Office: US Embassy Quito Unit 5302 APO AA 34039

WOOD, RUBY FERN, writer, retired elementary educator; b. Strauss, Kans., Aug. 17, 1922; d. John Elijah and Mildred Floy (Cole) Morrow; m. Leonard Edgar Wood, Oct. 18, 1942; children: Michael Wood, Sherry Wood Ruddell, Toni Wood Treaster. BS in Elem. Edn., Pittsburg (Kans.) State U., 1961, MS in Elem. Edn., 1965. Cert. tchr. elem. edn., secondary English, reading, lit., social studies, psychology, Kans. Tchr. grades 1-8 Cunningham Sch., Labette County, Kans., 1939-41, Centennial Sch., Montgomery County, Kans., 1941-42, Overfield Sch., Montgomery County, 1942-43, Foster Sch., Montgomery County, 1946-47, Racob-Wetzel Sch., Montgomery County, 1955-58; elem. tchr. Cherryvale (Kans.) Unified Sch. Dist. 447, 1961-87; pres. Cherryvale Tchrs. Assn., 1971-72; mem. selection panel Master Tchrs. Kans., Emporia, 1983-85. Author: (biography) Pop and Bud, 1981, (hist. fiction) The Benders-Keepers of the Devil's Inn, 1992; editor: 10-Year History of the SWC Region of AAUW, 1986, (anthology) Memories of a Country School, 1989; editor, contbg. author: Southeast Kansas: Land of Discovery, 1993. Coord. Heritage 200 Day, Cherryvale, 1976; guest White House briefing, Washington, 1984; coord. spl. exhibits Cherryvale Mus., 1980—. Recipient 1st prize Tulsa Professionalism in Writing Conf., 1991. Mem. AAUW (Kans. pres. 1983-85), Kans. Authors Club (pres. 3d dist. 1989-93, state v.p. 1993-94, 1st prize Eisenhower theme 1990), Kans. Coun. Women, Phi Theta Kappa. Democrat. Methodist. Home: Rte 2 Box 114 Cherryvale KS 67335

WOOD, RUTH DIEHM, artist, design consultant; b. Cleve., July 31, 1916; d. Ellis Raymond and Frances Helen (Peshek) Diehm; m. Kenneth Anderson Wood, Sept. 14, 1937. Student, Spencerian Bus. Coll., 1935-36, John Huntington Inst., 1936, Cleve. Inst. Art, 1934-37, 45. Legal sec. Klein, Diehm & Farber, Attys., Cleve., 1936-37; freelance graphic designer Bailey Meter Co., Wickliffe, Ohio, 1967; interior design cons., lectr. One-woman shows include Artist & Craftsmen Assn., Cleve., 1949, Art Colony, Cleve., 1953, Women's City Club, Cleve., 1955, Cleve. Inst. Art Alumni, 1954, Malvina Freedson Gallery, Lakewood, Ohio, 1965, Intown Club, Cleve., 1953, Studio Inn, Painesville, Ohio, 1955, Little Gallery, Chesterland, Ohio, 1961, Hospitality Inn, Willoughby, Ohio, 1965, Coll. Club Cleve., 1965, Lakeland Community Coll., Mentor, Ohio, 1979, Holden Arboretum, Mentor, 1981, Fairmount Fine Arts Ctr., Russell, Ohio, 1992; represented in 12 nat. juried shows, 28 regional and local mus., many pvt. collections. Recipient 1st prize Oil Still Life, Cleve. Mus. Art, 1945, Grumbacher Merit award Lakeland Fla. Internat., 1952, Artistic Achievement award Gates Mills, 1973, numerous other awards; certs. of award in Nyumon and Shoden, Ikenobo Sch. Floral Art, Kyoto, Japan. Mem. Cleve. Inst. Art Alumni, Artists and Craftsmen, Geauga Artists, Women in the Arts. Republican. Seventh-Day Adventist. Home and Studio: Kenwood Designers 11950 Sperry Rd Chesterland OH 44026-2225

WOOD, RUTH LUNDGREN WILLIAMSON See LUNDGREN, RUTH WILLIAMSON WOOD

WOOD, SALLY RAE, accountant; b. Olathe, Kans., June 18, 1960; d. Floyd Ray Haddox and Alice Bertha (France) Schroder; m. John Harvey Wood, Aug. 19, 1978. BA, U. Colo., Colorado Springs, 1987, MBA, 1990. CPA, Colo. Transmission and storage analyst Colo. Interstate Gas Co., Colorado Springs, 1984—. Mem. AICPA, Colo. Soc. CPAs, Inst. Mgmt. Accts. Office: Colo Interstate Gas Co PO Box 1087 Colorado Springs CO 80944

WOOD, SHARON, mountaineer; b. Halifax, N.S., Can., May 18, 1957; d. Stan and Peggy Wood. LLD (hon.), U. Calgary, 1987. Climbed peaks Mt. McKinley (Alaska), Mt. Logan (Can.), Mt. Aconcagua (Argentina), Mt. Makalu (Himalayas), Mt. Everest (Himalayas, 1st N.Am. woman to climb); Can. Light Everest Expedition, 1986; lectr. in field. Recipient Tenzing Norgay Trophy, 1987. Address: Box 1482, Canmore, AB Canada T0L 0M0

WOOD, SONJA KAY, insurance agent; b. Udall, Mo., May 1, 1950; d. Jean D. (Kirkland) Jones; m. Tom Wood Oct. 10, 1968; 1 child, Monique D. Student, Stephens Coll., Columbia, Mo., Life Underwriter's Tng. Coun., Washington. Property mgr. Aristek Corp., Denver, 1981-83, The Shelter Group, Westminster, Colo., 1983-85; dir. property mgmt. Lockwood Mgmt. Topeka (Kans.), Inc., 1986-87; mktg. cons. Lockwood Mgmt., Inc., St. Louis, 1988; ins. agt. Am. Family Mutual Ins. Co., Madison, Wis., 1988-94; mktg. rep. computer scis. corp. adminstering Nat. Flood Ins. Program, 1994—; mem. bus. adv. com. Lawrence Employment Ctr., 1994. Nominee Kans. Bus. Woman of Yr., 1993, 94; recipient Ams. with Disabilities Full Citizenship/Independence, Inc., Lawrence, Kans., 1992. Mem. Lawrence Life Underwriter's Assn. (chair cmty. svc. 1993, bd. mem. 1994). Democrat. Baptist. Office: 1014 Masschusetts Ste B Lawrence KS 66044-2922

WOOD, STEPHANNIE ANNE, lawyer; b. N.Y.C., Apr. 18, 1958; d. Charles D. and Joan (Darcey) W.; m. Dale Robert McHenry, June 19, 1993. BA, Wellesley Coll., 1980; JD, Georgetown U., 1985. Assoc. Tucker, Flyer, Sanger & Lewis, Washington, 1985-88; corp. counsel Cordant, Inc., Reston, Va., 1988—. Office: Cordant Inc 11400 Commerce Park Dr Reston VA 22091

WOOD, TINA LACHTERMAN, psychologist; b. Bklyn., Jan. 21, 1948; d. Phil and Lilliam Selma (Nires) L.; m. R. L. Wood, Oct. 20, 1990; children: Sandra Anne, Cynthia Lorraine. MS in Edn., Bklyn. Coll., 1974; PhD, U. Ga., 1978. Lic. psychologist, Ga. Sch. psychometrist Gwinnett County Pub. Schs., Lawrenceville, Ga., 1977-79, sch. psychologist, 1979-88; psychologist Affiliated Counseling Svcs., Marietta, Ga., 1988-92; pvt. practice Atlanta, 1992—. Mem. APA, Ga. Psychol. Assn., Phi Delta Kappa, Psi Chi. Home: 4950 Appaloosa Trail Norcross GA 30071 Office: 1780 Century Blvd NE Ste A Atlanta GA 30345

WOOD, VIVIAN POATES, mezzo soprano, educator, author; b. Washington, Aug. 19, 1923; d. Harold Poates and Mildred Georgette (Patterson) W.; studies with Walter Anderson, Antioch Coll., 1953-55, Denise Restout, Saint-Leu-La-Fôret, France and Lakeville, Conn., 1960-62, 64-70, Paul A. Pisk, 1968-71, Paul Ulanowsky, N.Y.C., 1958-68, Elemer Nagy, 1965-68, Vyautas Marijosius, 1967-68; MusB Hartt Coll. Music, 1968; postgrad. (fellow) Yale U., 1968; MusM (fellow), Washington U., St. Louis, 1971, PhD (fellow), 1973. Debut in recital series Internat. Jeunesse Musicals Arts Festival, 1953, solo fellowship Boston Symphony Orch., Berkshire Music Ctr., Tanglewood, 1964, St. Louis Symphony Orch., 1969, Washington Orch., 1949, Bach Cantata Series Berkshire Chamber Orch., 1964, Yale Symphony Orch., 1968; appearances in U.S. and European recitals, oratorios, operas, radio and TV, 1953-68; appeared as soloist in Internat. Harpsichord Festival, Westminster Choir Coll., Princeton, N.J., 1973; appeared as soloist in meml. concert, Landowska Ctr., Lakeville, 1969; prof. voice U. So. Miss., Hattiesburg, 1971—, asst. dean Coll. Fine Arts, 1974-76, acting dean, 1976-77; guest prof. Hochschule für Musik, Munich, 1978-79; prof. Italian Internat. Studies Program, Rome, 1986; Miss. coord. Alliance for Arts Edn., Kennedy Ctr. Performing Arts, 1974—; mem. Miss. Gov.'s Adv. Panel for Gifted and Talented Children, 1974—; mem. 1st Miss. Gov.'s Conf. on the Arts, 1974—; bd. dirs. Miss. Opera Assn. Author: Polenc's Songs: An Analysis of Style, 1971. Recipient Young Am. Artists Concert award N.Y.C., 1955; Wanda Landowska fellow, 1968-72. Mem. Miss. Music Tchrs. Assn., Nat. Assn. Tchrs. of Singing, Music Tchrs. Nat. Assn., Am. Musicology Soc., Golden Key, Mu Phi Epsilon, Delta Kappa Gamma, Tau Beta Kappa (hon.), Pi Kappa Lambda. Democrat. Episcopalian. Avocation: sailing. Office: U So Miss Sch Music South Pt # 8264 Hattiesburg MS 39406-9539

WOOD, WENDY DEBORAH, filmmaker; b. N.Y.C., Oct. 4, 1940; d. John Meyer and Marion Emily (Peters) W.; m. William Dismore Chapple, Dec. 7, 1963; 1 child, Samuel Eliot. BA cum laude, Vassar Coll., 1962; MA, Stanford U., 1964. Teaching asst. Stanford U., 1962-64; photographer, film editor Bristol (Eng.) U., 1964-66, asst. dir. Internat. Conf. Film Schs., 1966; rsch. asst. biology dept. U. Conn., Storrs, 1970-72; sr. media specialist Aetna Life & Casualty Co., Hartford, Conn., 1972-89; media writer, prodr., dir. U. Conn. Ctr. for Media and Tech., Storrs., 1989—; pres. Chapple Films, Inc., 1972—. Films include: Yankee Craftsman, 1972; Alcoholism, Industry's Costly Hangover, 1974; Draggerman's Haul, 1975; Flight Without Wings, 1977; Auto Insurance Affordability (2 awards), 1981; Where Rivers Run to the Sea (award), 1981; Our Town is Burning Down (6 awards), 1982; Wellness at the Worksite, 1984 (4 awards); Welcome to the Aetna Institute, 1985 (4 awards); Aenhance, 1989 (3 awards). Mem. peer rev. com. Conn. Commn. Higher Edn, 1992—. Recipient CINE Golden Eagle award Council on Internat. Non-theatrical Events, 1972, 76, 84, 1st Place award Indsl. Photography, 1974, cert. Outstanding Creativity U.S. TV Commls. Festival, 1974, EFLA award Am. Film Festival, 1974, 76, Dir's. Choice award Sinking Creek Film Festival, 1975, award Columbus Film Festival, 1975, award Excellence Life Ins. Advtrs. Assn., 1975, Silver Screen award U.S. Indsl. Film Festival, 1976, 81, 1st place award Conn. Film Festival, 1977, 1st prize Nat. Outdoor Travel Film Festival, 1978, 1st pl. Houston Film Festival, 1982, CINE Golden Eagle, 1982, 84, award Am. Film Festival, 1982, N.Y. Film Festival, 1982, 83, Silver CINDY award Assn. Visual Communicators, 1985, others. Bd. dirs. Windham Regional Arts Council, 1987, 88, 89; mem. jury N.Y. Internat. Video and Film Festival. Mem. Info. Film Producers Am. (nat. dir., pres. chpt. 1981-82, Cindy award 1971, 72, 81, 82, 85, 87), Internat. Quorum Motion Picture Producers, Audio Visual Communicators (pres. Conn. chpt. 1985, treas. 1988). Democrat. Quaker. Home: 604 Phoenixville Rd Chaplin CT 06235-2211 Office: U Conn Media Ctr # U-1 Storrs CT 06269

WOOD, YVONNE CULBREATH, state health administrator; b. Portland, Tenn., Mar. 18, 1938; d. Sherman Lee and Amanda (Kelley) Culbreath; m. Ishmael Murphy Wood, Nov. 17, 1956; children: Deborah Gayle, George Andrew, Lee Anne, Marc Alan. Student, Watkins Bus. Inst., 1958; BA in Polit. Sci., U. Tenn., 1982; MEd, Vanderbilt U., 1987. Cert. profl. sec. Asst. to pres. Dobson & Johnson Mortgage Bankers, Nashville, 1965-66; asst. to gov. Office of Gov., Nashville, 1966-70; adminstrv. asst. to exec. dir. Tenn. Higher Edn. Commn., Nashville, 1970-77, asst. dir. for govt. rels., 1977-79, assoc. dir. govt. rels., 1979-86; dir. divsn. quality control Dept. Health and Environ., Nashville, 1986-93; dir. managed care Bur. TennCare, 1994—; tchr. Draughton's Jr. Coll., 1982; exec. dir. Tenn. Student Assitance Corp., 1983-84; presenter in field. Author: The Importance and Impact of Three Significant Political Decisions Upon Higher Education in Tennessee, 1982, The Volunteer State: Readings in Tennesee Politics, 1983; author chpts. in books and reports. Mem. Nat. Assn. Dirs. Quality Control, Nat. Women's Polit. Caucus, Nat. Assn. SURS Ofcls. (pres. 1993-94), Nat Health Care Anti-Fraud Assn., Tenn. Pub. Health Assn. (v.p. for legislation 1993-94), Nashville Women's Polit. Caucus (pres. 1994-95), Vanderbilt Inst. Pub. Policy, USCG Aux. (vice comdr. 1990-94, comdr. 1991-93). Democrat. Home: 405 Westland Dr Lebanon TN 37087 Office: Tenn Dept Health Bur Medicaid 729 Church St Nashville TN 37219

WOODARD, ALFRE, actress; b. Tulsa, Nov. 8, 1953; m. Roderick Spencer; 2 adopted children. Student, Boston U. Appeared in (films) Remember My Name, 1976, Health, Cross Creek, 1983 (Acad. award nomination), Extremities, 1986, Scrooged, 1988, Mandela, 1988, Miss Firecracker, 1989, Grand Canyon, 1991, The Gun in Betty Lou's Handbag, 1992, Passion Fish, 1992, Heart and Souls, 1993, Rich in Love, 1993, Bopha!, 1993, Blue Chips, 1994, Crooklyn, 1994, How to Make an American Quilt, 1995, (TV series) Tucker's Witch, 1982-83, Sara, 1985, St. Elsewhere, 1985-87, Hill Street Blues (Emmy award for guest appearance in drama series 1984), L.A. Law (Emmy award for guest appearance in drama series 1987), (TV spls.) For Colored Girls Who Have Considered Suicide/When the Rainbow is Enuf, Trial of the Moke, Words by Heart, (TV films) A Mother's Courage: The Mary Thomas Story, Child Saver, Ambush Murder, Freedom Road, 1979, Sophisticated Gents, 1981, The Killing Floor, Unnatural Causes, 1986, Mandela, 1987, The Child Saver, Sweet Revenge, 1990, Blue Bayou, 1990, Bopho, 1993, (plays) For Colored Girls Who Have Considered Suicide, When the Rainbow is Enuf, (off-Broadway plays) A Map of the World, 1985, A Winter's Tale 1989, So Nice They Named Twice, Horatio. Recipient Emmy awards for guest appearance in drama series. Office: ICM 8942 Wilshire Blvd Beverly Hills CA 90211*

WOODARD, CAROL JANE, educational consultant; b. Buffalo, Jan. 19, 1929; d. Harold August and Violet Maybelle (Landsittel) Young; m. Ralph Arthur Woodard, Aug. 19, 1950; children—Camaron Jane, Carsen Jane, Cooper Ralph. BA, Hartwick Coll., 1950; MA, Syracuse U., 1952; PhD, SUNY, Buffalo, 1972; LHD (hon.), Hartwick Coll., 1991; postgrad., Bank St. Coll., Harvard U. Cert. tchr., N.Y. State. Tchr. Orchard Park, N.Y., 1950-51, Danville, Ind., 1951-52, Akron, N.Y., 1952-54; dir. Garden Nursery Sch., Williamsville, N.Y., 1955-65; tchr. Amherst (N.Y.) Coop. Nursery Sch., 1967-69; asst. prof. early childhood edn. SUNY, Buffalo, 1969-72; lab. demonstration tchr. and student teaching supr. SUNY, 1969-76, assoc. prof., 1972-79, prof., 1979-88, prof. emeritus, 1988—; co-dir. Consultants in Early Childhood, 1988—; cons. Lutheran Ch. Am., Villa Maria Coll., Buffalo Pub. Schs., Buffalo Mus. Sci., Headstart Tng. Programs, Erie Community Coll., N.Y. State Dept. Edn., numerous workshops.; cons. sch. systems, indsl. firms, pubs., civic orgns. in child devel.; vis. prof. The Netherlands and East China Univ., Shanghai, People's Republic of China; sci. trainer The Wright Group, 1995. Author 7 books for young children, 2 textbooks in field; co-author Physical Science in Early Childhood, 1987, 2d edit., 1995; co-author nat. curriculum for ch. sch. for 3-yr.-olds; author: (booklet) You Can Help Your Baby Learn; author/coord. TAKE CARE child protection project, 1987; contbr. chpt. to When Children Play, 1985; cons. EPIC Birth to Three Program, 1992; design cons. for indoor playground Noah's Ark, Jewish Ctr., Buffalo, 1992, sites project Buffalo Pub. Schs., 1994-95; contbr. numerous articles in field to profl. jours. Bd. trustees Hartwick Coll., Oneonta, N.Y., 1978-87. Mem. Nat. Assn. Edn. Young Children, Early Childhood Edn. Council Western N.Y., Assn. Childhood Edn. Internat., Phi Delta Kappa, Pi Lambda Theta. Home: 1776 Sweet Rd East Aurora NY 14052-3028

WOODARD, CLARA VERONICA, nursing home official; b. Bayonne, N.J.; d. William George and Lula (Langston) Yelverton; m. John Henry Woodard; children: John Michael, Stephen Jay. Grad., Bayonne Hosp. Sch. Nursing, 1951, Manhattan Sch. Radiology, 1953, NYU-Bellevue Med. Ctr., 1955, Valencia Community Coll., Orlando, Fla. RN, N.J., Fla. Head nurse Bayonne Hosp., 1949-50; office nurse Dr. D.G. Morris, Bayonne, 1951-52; pvt. duty nurse Christ Hosp and Bayonne Hosp., 1954-58; tchr. kindergarten, Nuremburg, Fed. Republic Germany, 1972-73; ICU-CCU nurse Holy Spirit Hosp., Camp Hill, Pa., 1973-74; head nurse Orlando Gen. Hosp., 1974-76, house supr., 1976-78; dir. nurses Winter Park (Fla.) Care Ctr., 1980-83; Medicare coord. Pinar Terrace Manor, Orlando, 1987—. Named Employee of Yr. and Employee of Month, Orlando Gen. Hosp., 1980, Employee of Month, Winter Park Care Ctr., 1983. Mem. NAFE, Nat. League Negro Women. Democrat. Roman Catholic. Home: 2931 De Brocy Way Winter Park FL 32792-4505 Office: Pinar Terrace Manor 7950 Lake Underhill Rd Orlando FL 32822-8202

WOODARD, DOROTHY MARIE, insurance broker; b. Houston, Feb. 7, 1932; d. Gerald Edgar and Bessie Katherine (Crain) Floeck; student N.Mex. State U., 1950; m. Jack W. Woodard; June 19, 1950 (dec.); m. Norman W. Libby, July 19, 1982 (dec. Dec. 1991). Ptnr. Western Oil Co., Tucumcari, N.Mex., 1950—; owner, mgr. Woodard & Co., Las Cruces, N.Mex., 1959-67; agt., dist. mgr. United Nations Ins. Co., Denver, 1968-74; agt. Western Nat. Life Ins. Co., Amarillo, Tex., 1976—. Exec. dir. Tucumcari Indsl. Commn., 1979—; dir. Bravo Dome Study Com., 1979—; owner Libby Cattle Co., Libby Ranch Co.; regional bd. dirs. N.Mex., Eastern Plains Council Govts., 1979—. Mem. NAFE, Tucumcari C. of C., Mesa Country Club. Home: PO Box 823 Tucumcari NM 88401-0823

WOODARD, NINA ELIZABETH, banker; b. L.A., Apr. 3, 1947; d. Alexander Rhodes and Harriette Jane (Power) Mathews; m. John David Woodard, Mar. 17, 1966 (div.); children: Regina M., James D. Grad. Pacific Coast Banking Sch., 1987; BS in mgmt., Calif. Coast U., 1993. Lifetime cert. sr. profl. in human resources. Dental asst. Donald R. Shire DDS, L.A., 1965-66; with Security Pacific Nat. Bank, Marina Del Rey, Calif., 1968-69; with First Interstate Bank, Casper, Wyo., 1971—, adminstr. asst. personnel, 1975-78, asst. v.p., asst. mgr. pers., 1978-82, v.p., dir. mktg. and pers., 1982-84, v.p., mgr. human resources, 1984-88; v.p., mgr. employee rels. First Interstate Bank Ltd., L.A., 1988-93, v.p. mgr. employee rels. Americas Region; instr. mktg. Am. Inst. Banking, 1983, Casper Coll., 1982. Mem. Civil Svc. Commn., City of Casper, 1983-88; bd. dirs. YMCA, 1984-87, Downtown Devel. Assn.; pres. Downtown Casper Assn. Named Bus. Woman of Yr., Bus. and Profl. Women, 1982, Young Career Woman, 1975. Mem. Nat. Assn. Bank Women, Bus. and Profl. Women (dist. dir.), Am. Soc. Pers. Adminstrn. (regional v.p., state coun. Wyo. 1987-88), Pers. and Indsl. Rels. Assn. (chmn. govt. affairs com. 1989-90, Fast Track award 1991, Pres.'s Achievement award 1993, conf. chmn. 1991, 92, dist. vice chair 1992, dist. chair 1993, 2d v.p. 1994), Fin. Women Internat. (Wyo. state chair 1986, regional edn. and tng. chair 1987, dist. coord. L.A. 1993, L.A. group chair 1994), St. Patrick's Parish Religious Edn. (instr. 1991-92, parish coun. 1993-94). Republican. Roman Catholic.

WOODBRIDGE, RUTH I., elementary education educator; b. Juneau, Alaska, Sept. 9, 1939; d. Ralph Pryor and Dorothy Zimmerman (Owen) Waggoner; children: Carol E. Haymaker, Melody. BA, San Francisco State U., 1963; MA, U. Nev., 1968; student, Westminster Choir Coll., Princeton, N.J., 1958; postgrad., Coll. of Idaho. Cert. K-12 music, choral and voice tchr., speech-drama, speech therapy, voice disorder therapy, N.M. Tchr. 5th grade, chorus MacArthur, Barcelona, Lavaland abd Duranes Elem. Schs., John Adams Mid. Sch., Jackson and Monroe Jr. High Schs., Albuquerque, Reno, Nev. Schs., Caldwell, Idaho Schs.; instr. voice and music edn., grad. asst. U. Nev., Reno; music supr. Dist 132 Schs., Caldwell, Idaho; elem. tchr., dir. chorus Albuquerque Pub. Schs.; dir. mus. theatre; pvt. tchr. voice. Soloist with choirs and orchs. Mem. Mu Phi Epsilon. Home: 1409 Granite Ave NW Albuquerque NM 87104-1339

WOODEN, JULIE, critical care nurse; b. Joplin, Mo., Sept. 13, 1957; d. J. Sheldon and Barbaline (Mathews) Dudley; children: April, Kent. LPN, Sch. Dist. Joplin, 1982; BSN, BA, William Jewell Coll., 1989; postgrad., U. Mo., Kansas City. CCRN. EMT S. Barry County Ambulance, Cassville, Mo., 1978-80; CNA Aurora (Mo.) Nursing Ctr., 1980-82, charge nurse, 1982-83; staff practical nurse St. Vincent's Hosp., Monett, Mo., 1982-83; charge nurse Lacoba Homes, Monett, 1983; prin. nurse Truman Med. Ctr. East, Kansas City, Mo., 1984-85, sr. nurse, 1985-89, staff nurse, 1989; emergency nurse critical care Mid Am. Heart Inst. St. Luke's Hosp., Kansas City, 1989—; staff nurse level III ICU Bapt. Med. Ctr., Kansas City, 1989—; ptnr.-cons. Health Care Resource Assocs., Kansas City, 1992—. Mem. adv. bd. organ tissue ARC, Kansas City, 1993-95. Mem. ANA (RN med./surg., Congress Nursing Practice 1994—, spring symposium com. 1993—), AACN (NTI proposal rev. panel), Mo. Nurses Assn. (bd. dirs. dist. 2 1991—, program chair 1992-93, state govt. mental affairs com., state coun. nursing practice, state med./surg. SIG chair), Greater Kansas City Assn. Critical Care Nurses (treas. 1991-92, mktg. dir. Spring Symposium 1993), Sigma Theta Tau (Mu Mu chpt.). Democrat. Methodist. Home: 4011 Harrison Ln Kansas City MO 64110

WOODEN, REBA FAYE BOYD, guidance counselor; b. Washington, Ind., Sept. 21, 1940; d. Lester E. and Opal M. (Burch) Boyd; m. N. Nuel Wooden, Jr., Dec. 23, 1962 (div. 1993); children: Jeffrey Nuel, Cynthia Faye. BA, U. Indpls., 1962; MS, Butler U., 1968, Ind. U., 1990. Cert. tchr., counselor, Ind. Tchr. Mooresville (Ind.) High Sch., 1962-66; tchr. Perry Meridian High Sch., Indpls., 1974-92, counselor, 1992—; part-time instr. Ind. U.-Purdue U. at Indpls., 1994—. Named Outstanding High Sch. Psychology tchr. APA, 1987. Mem. AACD, NEA, Ind. State Tchrs. Assn., Perry Edn. Assn. Methodist. Home: 113 Severn Dr Greenwood IN 46142-1880 Office: Perry Meridian High Sch 401 W Meridian School Rd Indianapolis IN 46217-4215

WOODEN, RUTH A., public service advertising executive; b. Madison, Wis., Aug. 4, 1946. BA, U. Minn., 1968, postgrad. Project dir. Lee Creative Rsch., St. Louis, 1970-72; project mgr. Ralston Purina, St. Louis, 1972-78; sr. v.p., account dir. N.W. Ayer, N.Y.C., 1978-88; pres. The Advt. Coun., Inc., N.Y.C., 1988—; bd. dirs. U.S. Trust Corp. Bd. dirs. CARE Inc., N.Y.C., 1980—, U.S. Trust Corp., 1994—; trustee Edna McConnell Clark Found., St. Luke's/Roosevelt Hosp. Ctr. Mem. Internat. Radio & TV Soc. (bd. dirs.). Office: The Advt Coun Inc 261 Madison Ave New York NY 10016-2303

WOODERSON, MARY LOUISE, medical transcriptionist; b. Yakima, Wash., Apr. 22, 1933; d. David Russell and Mary Magdeline (Funkhouser) Fairbanks; m. Marvin Lee Wooderson, Nov. 2, 1951; children: David Ray, Randall Lee, Debra Lynne. Grad. high sch., Yakima, Wash. Med. sec. The Dalles (Oreg.) Clinic, 1957-60; med. transcriptionist Osteo. Physician, The Dalles, 1966-69; clk. II Pub. Welfare Div., The Dalles, 1971-73; clk. III Motor Vehicles Div., The Dalles, 1973-75; dispatcher Oreg. State Police, The Dalles, 1975-76; med. transcriptionist Mid-Columbia Med. Ctr., The Dalles, 1978—. Mem. Am. Assn. Med. Transcriptionists, Eagles Aux. Democrat. Home: 850 Garden Ct The Dalles OR 97058-4404 Office: Mid Columbia Med Ctr 1700 E 19th St The Dalles OR 97058-4404

WOODHULL, NANCY JANE, publishing executive; b. Perth Amboy, N.J., Mar. 1, 1945; d. Harold and May (Post) Cromwell; m. William Douglass Watson, Sept. 24, 1976; 1 child, Tennessee Jane. Student, Trenton State Tchrs. Coll., 1963-64. Dept. editor News Tribune, Woodbridge, N.J., 1964-73; reporter Detroit Free Press, 1973-75; mng. editor Times-Union, Rochester, N.Y., 1975-80, Democrat & Chronicle, Rochester, 1980-82; mng. editor USA Today, Arlington, Va., 1982-83, sr. editor, 1983-87; pres. Gannett New Media, Washington, 1986-90, Gannett News Svc., Washington, 1988-90; exec. v.p., editor-in-chief So. Living Mags., Birmingham, Ala., 1990-92; pres. Nancy Woodhull & Assoc., Inc., Washington and Pittsford, N.Y., 1991—. Office: Nancy Woodhull & Assoc Inc 5 Durham Way Pittsford NY 14534

WOODHULL, PATRICIA ANN, artist; b. Gary, Ind., Nov. 24, 1924; d. John Joseph and Georgia Mildred (Voorhis) Harding; m. Bradley Allen Woodhull, May 8, 1948; children: Leslie, Marcia, Clarisse. BS in Clothing Design, Purdue U., 1946; life teaching credential, Calif. State U., Fullerton, 1978. Social worker County Dept. Lake County and Bartholomew County, Gary and Columbus, Ind., 1946-50; home demonstrator Pub. Svc. Co. Ind., Columbus, 1950-53; substitute tchr. Fullerton (Calif.) H.S. Dist., 1968-73; children's art and drama tchr. Fullerton Cmty. Svcs., 1973-85; children's pvt. art tchr. Fullerton, 1990-93; art tchr. Montessori Sch., Fullerton, 1990-91; art/drama tchr. creative arts program Fullerton Pub. Schs., 1972-89; founder, dir. Players Improv Theatre Group, Fullerton, Calif. One woman shows include Fullerton City Libr., 1992, William Carlos Gallery, Fullerton , 1992, 93, Whittier (Calif.) City Hall, 1993, Muckinthaler Ctr., Fullerton, 1993, Brookhurst Ctr., Anaheim, 1993, Whitier Libr. Show, 1994; exhibited in group shows at Whittier Art Gallery, 1991, Hillcrest Art Show, Creative Arts Ctr., Burbank, Calif., 1991, Bidge Gallery City Hall, L.A., 1992, The Art Store, Fullerton, 1992, Women Painters West, 1993, New England Fine Arts Inst., Boston, 1993; represented in pvt. collections. Recipient Spl. award Orange County Fair, Costa Mesa (Calif.) County Fair, 1985; 3rd pl. award Hillcrest Whittier (Calif.) Show, 1990, 2nd award West Coast Collage Show, Lancaster, Calif., 1989, Evelyn Nunn Miller award Women Painters West, Torrance, Calif., 1994. Mem. Nat. League Am. Pen Women (pres. Orange County 1993), Women Painters West, Pan Hellenic Orange County (pres. 1994), Alpha Chi Omega (pres. local chpt. 1993). Republican. Home: 1519 E Harmony Ln Fullerton CA 92631-2015

WOODLIFF, CAROL J., law office supervisor; b. Rockford, Ill., Jan. 23, 1961; d. Russell M. and Lucille A. (Mara) W. BA in Journalism cum laude, Marquette U., 1983. Sales mgr. Macy's Midwest, Kansas City, Mo., 1983-84; sr. info. analyst Shook, Hardy & Bacon, Kansas City, 1984-87; litigation coord. O'Melveny & Myers, L.A., 1987-89; legal asst. mgr. Skadden, Arps, Slate, Meagher & Flom, L.A., 1989-94, weekend supr., 1994—. Office: Skadden Arps et al 34th Fl 300 S Grand Ave Los Angeles CA 90071

WOODRING, MARGARET DALEY, architect, planner; b. N.Y.C., Mar. 29, 1933; d. Joseph Michael and Mary (Barron) Daley; m. Francis Woodring, Oct. 25, 1954 (div. 1962); m. Robert Bell, Dec. 20, 1971; children: Ward, Lissa, Gabrielle, Phaedra. Studnet, NYU, 1959-60; BArch, Columbia U., 1966; MArch, Princeton U., 1971. Registered architect; cert. planner. Architect, planner various firms, N.Y.C.; environ. design specialist Rutgers U., New Brunswick, N.J., 1966-68; programming cons. Davis & Brody, N.Y.C., 1968-71; planning cons. William H. Liskamm, San Francisco, 1971-74; mgr. planning Met. Transp. Commn., Oakland, Calif., 1974-81; dir. Internat. Program for Housing and Urban Devel. Ofcls. Ctr. for Environ. Design Rsch. U. Calif., Berkeley, 1981-89; prin. Woodring & Assocs., San Rafael, Calif., 1989—; adj. lectr. dept. architecture U. Calif., Berkeley, 1974-84; founder New Horizons Savs. Assn., San Rafael, 1977-79; cons. U.S. Agy. for Internat. Devel., Washington, 1981-89; mem. jury Nat. Endowment Arts, others. Chair Bicentennial Com., San Rafael, 1976; bd. dirs. Displaced Homemakers Ctr., Oakland, 1981-84; pres. Environ Design Found., San Francisco, 1984-90. William Kinne Travel fellow Columbia U., 1965-66; Richard King Mellon fellow Princeton U., 1968-70. Mem. AIA (chair urban design com. San Francisco chpt. 1980-81), Am. Inst. Cert. Planners, Urban Land Inst., Soc. for Internat. Devel. (pres. San Francisco chpt. 1980-83), World Affairs Coun., Internat. World Congress on Land Policy. Home: 226 Magnolia Ave San Rafael CA 94901 Office: Woodring & Assocs 938 B St San Rafael CA 94901

WOODRUFF, DARLENE G., nursing educator; b. Allentown, Pa., May 18, 1935; d. Niels Laurence and Winifred Caroline (Theyken) Nielson; m. Lester E. Woodruff, Dec. 22, 1960. ADN, U. Nev., Las Vegas, 1980, BSN, 1985; MSN, U. Nev., 1991. LPN Desert Hosp., Palm Spring, Calif., 1960-66; staff nurse ICU Humana Hosp. Sunrise, Las Vegas, 1966-90; nursing instr. N.W. Coll., Powell, Wyo., 1990—. With Women's Army Corp., 1953-55. Recipient Faculty Devel. grant N.W. Coll., Powell, 1992. Mem. AACN, Wyo. League Nursing (exec. bd. mem.), Sigma Theta Tau (rsch. grant). Home: 419 Sunlight Dr Powell WY 82435 Office: Northwest College Nursing Dept 231 W Sixth St Powell WY 82435

WOODRUFF, FAY, paleoceanographer, geological researcher; b. Boston, Jan. 23, 1944; d. Lorande Mitchell and Anne (Fay) W.; m. Alexander Whitehill Clowes, May 20, 1972 (div. Oct. 1974); m. Robert G. Douglas, Jan. 27, 1980; children: Ellen, Katerina. RN, Mass. Gen. Hosp. Sch. Nursing, Boston, 1965; BA, Boston U., 1971; MS, U. So. Calif., 1979. Rsch. assoc. U. So. Calif., L.A., 1978-81, rsch. faculty, 1981—; keynote spkr. 4th Internat. Symposium on Benthia Foraminiferi, Sendai, Japan, 1990. Contbg. author: Geological Society of America Memoir, 1985; contbr. articles to profl. jours. Life mem. The Nature Conservancy, Washington, 1992. NSF grantee, 1986-88, 88-91, 91-94. Mem. Am. Geophys Union, Geol. Soc. Am., Internat. Union Geol. Scis. (internat. commn. on stratigraphy, subcommn. on neogene stratigaphy 1991-92]), Soc. Women Geographers (sec. So. calif. chpt. 1990-96), Soc. Econ. Paleontologists and Minerologists (sec., editor North Am. Micropaleontology sect. 1988-90), Oceanography Soc. (chpt. mem.), Sigma Xi. Episcopalian. Office: Dept Geol Scis U So Calif Los Angeles CA 90089-0740

WOODRUFF, JANE, sales executive; b. Derby, Eng., July 20, 1945; d. George John Schwaegerman and Joyce (Robinson) Turnock; m. Charles Walter Woodruff, Aug. 1, 1964 (div. 1976); 1 child, Jon Bradley. BA, Purdue U., 1967, MS, 1968, MA, 1970. Tchr. Kansas City (Mo.) Schs., 1970-73; asst. dir. communicatons Skyline Corp., Elkart, Ind., 1974-77; market analyst Motor Wheel Corp. subs. Goodyear Tire and Rubber Co., Lansing, Mich., 1977-80, mgr. planning and research, 1980-82, mgr. car and light truck mktg., 1982-84; account exec. Motor Wheel Corp., Farmington Hills, Mich., 1984—. Chmn. Motor Wheel Svcs. Bond Drive, Lansing, 1980; fundraiser Capital Area United Way, Lansing, 1981; cons. bus. projects Jr. Achievement, Lansing, 1981-82. NDEA scholar U.S. Dept. Edn., 1967-68; teaching fellow Purdue U., 1968-70; recipient Cert. Achievement YWCA, Lansing, 1980. Mem. Indsl. Mktg. Group Am. Mktg. Assn. (treas.), Automotive Market Research Council, Soc. Automotive Engrs. Office: Motor Wheel Corp 28295 Bayberry Rd Farmington MI 48331-3317

WOODRUFF, JUDY CARLINE, broadcast journalist; b. Tulsa, Nov. 20, 1946; d. William Henry and Anna Lee (Payne) W.; m. Albert R. Hunt, Jr., Apr. 5, 1980; children: Jeffrey Woodruff, Benjamin Woodruff, Lauren Ann Lee. Student, Meredith Coll., 1964-66; B.A., Duke U., 1968. News announcer, reporter Sta. WAGA-TV, Atlanta, 1970-75; news corr. NBC News, Atlanta, 1975-76; White House corr. NBC News, Washington, 1977-83; anchor Frontline, PBS documentary series, 1983-90; corr. MacNeil-Lehrer News Hour, PBS, Washington, 1983-93; anchor and sr. corr. CNN, Washington, 1993—; mem. bd. advisors Henry Grady Sch. Journalism, U. Ga., 1979-82; bd. visitors Wake Forest U., 1982-89; mem. bd. advisors Benton Fellowship in Broadcast Journalism, U. Chgo., 1984-90, Knight Fellowship in Journalism, Stanford U., 1985—; trustee Duke U., 1985—; founding bd. dirs. Internat. Women's Media Found., 1989—. Author: This is Judy Woodruff at the White House, 1982. Mem. Commn. on Women's Health, The Commonwealth Fund. Recipient award Leadership Atlanta, Class of 1974, Atlanta chpt. Women in Communications, 1975, Edward Weintal award for excellence in fgn. policy reporting, 1987, Joan Shorenstein Barone award for series on def. issues, 1987, Helen Bernstein award for excellence in journalism N.Y. Pub. Libr., 1989, Pres.'s award Nat. Women's Hall of Fame, 1994, CableAce award for best newscaster, 1995. Mem. NATAS (Atlanta chpt. Emmy award 1975), White House Corrs. Assn. Office: Cable News Network 820 1st St NE Washington DC 20002

WOODRUFF, MARTHA JOYCE, home health agency executive; b. Unadilla, Ga., Jan. 3, 1941; d. Metz Loy and Helen (McCorvey) Woodruff. BA, Shorter Coll., 1963; MA, U. Tenn.-Knoxville, 1972. Tchr., Albany High Sch. (Ga.), 1963-69; instr. U. Tenn.-Knoxville, 1970-72; asst. prof. Valdosta State Coll. (Ga.), 1972-76; coord. Staff Builders, Atlanta, 1976-78; pres., owner Med. Personnel Pool, Knoxville, 1978-93; owner, pres. Priority Healthcare Svcs, Knoxville, 1993—, Pers. Pool of Knoxville, Inc., 1985-87; mem., adviser Owners Adv. Council, Pers. Pool of Am., Ft. Lauderdale, Fla., 1980-82. active Altzheimers Assn. Mem. Exec. Women Internat., East Tenn. Women's Polit. Caucus, Tenn. Assn. Home Care, Nat. Assn. Homecare, Knoxville C. of C. (com. for cost containment 1982-85), Blount County C. of C. (retirement com. 1983, mem. indsl. rels. com. 1983). Republican. Methodist.

WOODRUM, PATRICIA ANN, librarian; b. Hutchinson, Kans., Oct. 11, 1941; d. Donald Jewell and Ruby Pauline (Shuman) Hoffman; m. Clayton Eugene Woodrum, Mar. 31, 1962; 1 child, Clayton Eugene, II. BA, Kans. State Coll., Pittsburg, 1963; MLS, U. Okla., 1966. Br. libr. Tulsa City-County Libr. System, 1964-65, head brs., 1965-66, head reference dept., 1966-67, chief extension, chief pub. svc., 1967-73, asst. dir., 1973-76, exec. dir., 1976—; bd. dirs. Local Am. Bank Tulsa. Mem. editorial bd. Jour. of Library Administration. Active Friends of Tulsa Libr., Leadership Tulsa Alumni; trustee U. Ctr., Tulsa, chmn., 1992-94. Recipient Disting. Libr. award Okla. Libr. Assn., 1982, Leadership Tulsa Paragon award, 1987, Women in Comm. Newsmaker award, 1989, Outstanding Alumnus award U. Okla. Sch. Libr. Info. Studies, 1989; inducted into Tulsa City-County Libr. Hall of Fame, 1989, Okla. Womens Hall of Fame, 1993. Mem. ALA, Pub. Libr. Assn. (pres. 1993-94), Okla. Libr. Assn. (pres. 1978-79, Disting. Libr. award 1982), Tulsa C. of C. Democrat. Episcopalian. Office: Tulsa City-County Libr 400 Civic Ctr Tulsa OK 74103-3830

WOODS, BARBARA A. SHELL, psychotherapist; b. Banner Elk, N.C., June 11, 1939; d. Oscar Ketron and Mamie Maruja (Perry) Shell; m. James Wesley Woods, May 7, 1966; children: Jonathan Scott, Eric Jason. BS in Bus. Mgmt., East Tenn. State U., 1961; MA in Counseling and Devel., George Mason U., 1983, postgrad., 1985-88. Cert. clin. mental health counselor; nat. cert. counselor, nat. cert. career counselor; lic. profl. counselor, Va. Office asst. vet. affairs East Tenn. State U., Johnson City, 1958-61; sec. purchasing dept. U. Tenn., Knoxville, 1961-62; social worker I and II Tenn. Welfare Dept., Knoxville, 1962-66; daycare coord. Econ. Opportunity of Atlanta, 1966-67; child welfare worker Forsyth County Dept. of Welfare, Winston Salem, N.C., 1967-68; dir., tchr. Woodland Pre-Sch., Alexandria, Va., 1975-78; pers. mgmt. Woodward & Lothrup, Tyson's Corner, Va., 1983; career coord. Nat. Bd. for Cert. Counselors, Alexandria, 1984; dir., owner Change and Growth Cons., Tyson's Corner, 1984—, Woodbridge, Va., 1984—; counselor, trainer The Women's Ctr. of Northern Va., Vienna, Va., 1985-90; counseling dir. The Women's Health Connection, Vienna, 1990-92; trainer, counselor City of Falls Ch. Youth At Risk Program, Falls Church, 1993—. Zoning chairperson West Springfield (Va.) Civic Assn., 1980-82; citizen mem. Fairfax County Citizens Planning Task Force, Springfield, 1979-82. Scholarship Am. Legion, 1957. Mem. ACA, No. Va. Chpt. clin. Counselors (chairperson 1990-92, Appreciation award 1992), Va. Clin. Counselor (regional rep. 1990-92), Nat. EAP Assn. (sec. 1989-90), Met. Area Career/Life Planning Network (founder, Appreciation award 1985), Va. Counselors Assn. Methodist. Office: Change and Growth Cons 1334 G St Woodbridge VA 22191

WOODS, DEANNA GAEL, education educator, consultant; b. Lebanon, Oreg., Dec. 23, 1945; d. Arthur James and Norma Vera (Quaring) W. BA in Lang. Arts, Portland State U., 1968, cert., 1972. Cert. secondary edn. tchr., Oreg. Sec. North Bapt. Ch., Portland, Oreg., 1965-69; tchr. Portland Pub. Schs., 1968—; local site coord. ednl. rsch. and dissemination program Am. Fedn. Tchrs., Portland and Washington, 1985—, asst. dir. edn. issues dept., 1994—; mem. adv. panel New Am. Schs. Devel. Corp., Arlington, Va., 1991—; mem. adv. com. N.W. Regional Ednl. Lab., Portland, 1987—, Edn. Testing Svc., Princeton, N.J., 1989—. Editor: (newsletter) Trendsetter, 1993—. Mem. Citizens Adv. Com. to Legis. Edn., Oreg., 1986-87. Recipient Educator award Oreg. Dept. Edn./Milken Family Found., 1991. Mem. ASCD, Am. Ednl. Rsch. Assn., Oreg. Fedn. Tchrs. (lobbyist 1989, Outstanding Contbn. to Edn. Awareness 1992), Portland Fedn. Tchrs. (cert. field rep., exec. coun. 1974—). Democrat. Baptist. Home: 401 12th St S # 422 Arlington VA 22202 Office: Am Fedn Tchrs Edn Issues Dept 555 New Jersey Ave NW Washington DC 20001

WOODS, DONNA SUE, education educator, reading consultant; b. Springhill, La., Jan. 15, 1954; m. Raymond M. Woods, Nov. 24, 1973; children: Klaten A., Matthew M., Laura E., Gabriele E. BA, La. Tech U., 1975; MEd, La. State U., 1983; EdD, Okla. State U., 1992. Cert. English, social studies, gifted edn. tchr., La.; cert. English, gifted edn. and reading tchr., Okla. Tchr. English, Grawood (La.) Christian Schs., 1979-80; tchr. spl. edn. Bossier Parish Sch. Bd., Benton, La., 1981-83, curriculum developer, 1990; tchr. gifted Curtis Elem. Sch., Bossier City, La., 1983-88; tchr. lang. arts Elm Grove (La.) Jr. High Sch., 1988-90; teaching asst., univ. rep. Okla. entry yr. assistance Okla. State U., Stillwater, 1990-92, co-dir., instr. 13th ann. reading workshop, 1991, instr. Coll. Vet. Medicine, 1991, developer, dir. student tchr. seminar, 1992; asst. prof. Coll. Edn. Northwestern Okla. State U., Alva, 1992—; adj. instr. Oklahoma City C.C., 1991-92; curriculum developer Okla. State Dept. Edn., 1993; dir. Okla. Nat. Young Readers' Day, 1994—. Tutor YWCA, Shreveport, La., 1975; supt. youth Sunday schs. 1st Presbyn. Ch., Edmond, Okla., 1991, co-dir. youth choir, 1994—. Named Favorite Tchr. of Yr., Bossier C. of C., 1987; Centennial scholar Okla. State U. Coll. Edn. Alumni Assn., 1992. Mem. Internat. Reading Assn., (Alpha Upsilon Alpha hon. soc. faculty sponsor 1994—), Okla. Reading Assn. (conf. presenter 1993), Okla. Early Childhood Tchrs. Assn. (conf. presenter 1991), Kappa Delta Pi. Republican. Avocations: reading, collecting and repairing antiques, youth work, quilting, computers, music. Home: 3113 Talon Rd Edmond OK 73013-7409

WOODS, ELLEN LOUISE, paralegal; b. Greensboro, N.C., Aug. 23, 1960; d. Walter Scott and Dorothy (Goodwin) W.; m. John Early Edwards (div. Apr. 1986); 1 child, Jonathan Scott. Cert. in paralegal studies, So. Career Inst., 1991; student, Guilford Coll., 1992—. From teller to supr. Wachovia Bank and Trust, Burlington, N.C., 1980-88; exec. sec. Burlington Ins. Group, 1988-90; legal sec. Frederick J. Sternberg, P.A., Graham, N.C., 1990-91; legal asst. Flicks & Licks Video, Inc., Burlington, 1991—, Animal Rehabilitative Care, Burlington, 1991—; telecommunicator Burlington Police Dept., 1993—; bd. dirs. Animal Rehabilitative Care, Burlington. Member PTA, Alamance County, N.C., 1985. Republican. Mem. United Ch. of Christ. Home: 2516 Parrish St Burlington NC 27215-4424

WOODS, HARRIETT RUTH, state official; b. Cleve., June 2, 1927; d. Armin and Ruth (Wise) Friedman; student U. Chgo., 1945; B.A., U. Mich., 1949; LLD (hon.) Webster U., 1988; m. James B. Woods, Jan. 2, 1953; children: Christopher, Peter, Andrew. Reporter, Chgo. Herald-Am., 1948, St. Louis Globe-Democrat, 1949-51; producer Star. KPLR-TV, St. Louis, 1964-74; moderator, writer Sta. KETC-TV, St. Louis, 1962-64; council mem. University City, Mo., 1967-74; mem. Mo. Hwy. Commn., 1974, Mo. Transp. Commn., 1974-76; mem. Mo. Senate, 1976-84, lt. gov. State of Mo., 1985-89; pres. Inst. for Policy Leadership, U. Mo., St. Louis, 1989-91; pres. Nat. Women's Polit. Caucus, 1991-95; dir. Federal Home Loan Mortgage Corp., 1995—; fellow inst. politics J.F. Kennedy Sch. Govt., Harvard U., 1988. Bd. dirs. LWV of Mo., 1963, Nat. League of Cities, 1972-74; Dem. nominee for U.S. Senate, 1982, 86. Jewish. Office: 1211 Connecticut Ave NW Washington DC 20036

WOODS, JANE HAYCOCK, state legislator; b. Bethesda, Md., Oct. 10, 1946; d. Stephen Pineo and Ruth (Yanovsky) Haycock; m. James Richard Fitzalan Woods, July 14, 1973. BA in Edn., Am. U., 1968. Tchr. Fairfax (Va.) County Pub. Sch., 1968-74, 76-87; co-mgr. Comml. Real Estate, Fairfax, 1982-91; mem. Va. Ho. of Dels., Fairfax, 1988-92, Va. Senate, 1992—. Chair City of Fairfax (Va.) Rep. Com., 1983-88, 11th Congl. Rep. Dist. Com., 1992; bd. mem. Va. Fedn. Rep. Women, 1986—. Named Outstanding Woman, City of Fairfax Commn. on Women, 1987. Mem. Nat. Assn. Parliamentarians (Outstanding Tchr. 1990), Va. Girls State (bd. mem.), Annandale C. of C. (Citizen of Yr. 1990), Fairfax C. of C. (Outstanding Woman 1989), Am. Legion Aux., Phi Delta Kappa. Methodist. Office: 3932 Old Lee Hwy # B Fairfax VA 22030-2417 also: Va Senate House State Capitol Richmond VA 23219*

WOODS, JEANNIE MARLIN, theatre educator; b. Shreveport, La., Oct. 6, 1947; d. Charles Raymond and Orlando (Crossett) Smith; m. Daniel Carl Woods, Sept. 6, 1973. BA, U. Idaho, 1970; MA, Hunter Coll., 1987; MPh, CUNY, 1988, PhD, 1989. Actress Germinal Stage, Third Eye Theatre, Denver, 1971-80; stage dir. N.Y.C., 1982-84; asst. to prodr. ABC-TV, N.Y.C., 1982-84; rschr., assoc. project dir. WNET/13, N.Y.C., 1986; lectr. CCNY, 1987, Baruch Coll., 1988; asst. prof. theatre Winthrop U., Rock Hill, S.C., 1989—; artistic dir. New Stage Ensemble, 1993—. Author: Theatre to Change Men's Souls, The Artistry of Adrian Hall, 1993, Maureen Stapleton: A Bio-Bibliography, 1992; contbr. to book: Notable Women in American Theatre, 1989. CUNY fellow, 1988-89. Mem. AFTRA, AAUW, Assn. for Theatre in Higher Edn., Southeastern Theatre Assn., S.C. Theatre Assn. Office: Winthrop Univ Dept Theatre And Dance Rock Hill SC 29733

WOODS, MERILYN BARON, psychologist, consultant; b. Bklyn., July 8, 1927; d. David Theodore and Helen (Mintz) Baron; m. John Galloway Woods, Sept. 15, 1948; children: Anne Helen, Elizabeth Ruth. BS, Cornell U., 1948; MEd, Temple U., 1957; PhD, Bryn Mawr Coll., 1968. Lic. psychologist, Pa. Rsch. asst. psychiatry Temple U., Phila., 1958-59, instr., counselor students, 1960-64; clin. psychologist Gloucester County Guidance Ctr., Woodbury, N.J., 1959-60; seminar coord. Bryn Mawr Coll., 1966-67, lectr., 1968-70, asst. prof., 1970-73; dir. counseling and placement Jewish Employment and Vocat. Svc., 1973-75; assoc. dean students Rider Coll., 1975-77; dir. student svcs., clin. asst. prof. mental health scis. Hahnemann Med. U., Phila., 1978-83; dir. Ctr. for Pers. and Profl. Devel. Pa. Coll. Optometry, Phila., 1983-93; pvt. practice psychologist Phila., 1983-86; pres. pvt. practice, 1986—. Mem., pres. bd. mgrs. Sr. Employment and Ednl. Svc., Phila., 1983-95; bd. dirs. Awbury Arboretum Assn., 1986—; mem. Mayor's Sci. and Tech. Adv. Coun. divsn. Urban Affairs City of Phila., 1973-76. Tuition scholar Bryn Mawr Coll. Fellow Nat. Vocat. Guidance Assn., Pa. Psychol. Assn., Behavior Therapy and Rsch. Soc. (clin.); mem. APA, Ea. Psychol. Assn., Am. Counseling Assn., Am. Coll. Pers. Assn., Phila. Soc. Clin. Psychologists (bd. dirs. 1981-91), Cornell Alumni Club of Phila. (co-chair 1989-91).

WOODS, PHYLLIS MICHALIK, elementary school educator; b. New Orleans, Sept. 12, 1937; d. Philip John and Thelma Alice (Carey) Michalik; 1 child, Tara Lynn Woods. BA, Southeastern La. U., 1967. Cert. speech and English tchr., libr. sci., La. Tchr. speech, English and drama St. Charles Parish Pub. Schs., Luling, La., elem. tchr., secondary tchr. remedial reading, Chpt. I reading specialist; Wicat tchr. coord.; tchr. cons. St. Charles parish writing project La. State U. Writing Project. Contbr. articles and poems to River Parish Guide. Mem. ASCD, Internat. Reading Assn., St. Charles

Parish Reading Coun., Newspaper in Edn. (chmn., historian), La. Assn. Newspapers in Edn. (state com.).

WOODS, ROSE MARY, consultant, former presidential assistant; b. Sebring, Ohio, Dec. 26, 1917; d. Thomas M. and Mary (Maley) W. Ed. high sch.; L.D.H., Pfeiffer Coll., 1971. With Royal China, Inc., Sebring, 1935-43, Office Censorship, 1943-45, Internat. Tng. Adminstrn., 1945-47, Herter Com. Fgn. Aid, 1947, Fgn. Service Ednl. Found., 1947-51; sec. to senator, then v.p. Nixon, 1951-61; asst. Mr. Nixon with firm Adams, Duque & Hazeltine, Los Angeles, 1961-63, firm Nixon, Mudge, Rose, Guthrie, Alexander & Mitchell, N.Y.C., 1963-68; exec. asst. to former Pres. Nixon, 1969-75; now consultant. Named 1 of 10 Women of Year Los Angeles Times, 1961, 1 of 75 Most Important Women in Am. Ladies Home Jour., 1971. Home: 1194 W Cambridge St Alliance OH 44601-2169

WOODS, SANDRA KAY, manufacturing executive; b. Loveland, Colo., Oct. 11, 1944; d. Ivan H. and Florence L. (Betz) Harris; m. Gary A. Woods, June 11, 1967; children: Stephanie Michelle, Michael Harris. BA, U. Colo., 1966, MA, 1967. Personnel mgmt. specialist CSC, Denver, 1967; asst. to regional dir. HEW, Denver, 1968-69; urban renewal rep. HUD, Denver, 1970-73, dir. program analysis, 1974-75, asst. regional dir. community planning and devel., 1976-77, regional dir. fair housing, 1978-79; mgr. ea. facility project Adolph Coors Co., Golden Colo., 1980, dir. real estate, 1981, v.p. chief environ. health and safety officer, 1982—. pres. Industries for Jefferson County (Colo.), 1985. Mem. Exec. Exchange, The White House, 1980; bd. dirs. Golden Local Devel. Corp. (Colo.), 1981-82; fundraising dir. Coll. Arts and Scis., U. Colo., Boulder, 1982-89, U. Colo. Found.; mem. exec. bd. NCCJ, Denver, 1982-94; v.p. Women in Bus., Inc., Denver, 1982-83; mem. steering com. 1984 Yr. for All Denver Women, 1983-84; mem. 10th dist. Denver br. Fed. Reserve Bd., 1990—, chmn. bd., 1995—; bd. dirs Nat. Jewish Hosp. 1994—. Named one of Outstanding Young Women Am., U.S. Jaycees, 1974, 78, Fifty Women to Watch, Businessweek, 1987, 92, Woman of Achievement YWCA, 1988. Chmn. Greater Denver Corp., 1991—. Mem. Indsl. Devel. Resources Council (bd. dirs. 1986-89), Am. Mgmt. Assn., Denver C. of C. (bd. dirs. 1988—, Disting. Young Exec. award 1974, mem. Leadership Denver, 1976-77), Colo. Women's Forum, Nat. Assn. Office and Indsl. Park Developers (sec. 1988, treas. 1989), Committee of 200 (v.p. 1994-95), Phi Beta Kappa, Pi Alpha Alpha. Republican. Presbyterian. Club: PEO (Loveland, Colo.). Office: Coors Brewing Co BC 320 Golden CO 80401

WOODS, SUSANNE, university dean; b. Honolulu, May 12, 1943; d. Samuel Ernest and Gertrude (Cullom) W. BA in Polit. Sci., UCLA, 1964, MA in English, 1965; PhD in English and Comparative Lit., Columbia U., 1970; MA (hon.), Brown U., 1978. Staff Senator Daniel K. Inouye, 1963; asst. editor Rand Corp., Calif., 1963-65; instr. Ventura Coll., Calif., 1965-66; lectr. CUNY, 1967-69; asst. prof. U. Hawaii, 1969-72; asst. prof. English Brown U., Providence, 1972-77, assoc. prof., 1977-83, prof., 1983-93, dir. grad. studies, 1986-88, assoc. dean faculty, 1987-90; v.p., dean Franklin and Marshall Coll., Lancaster, Pa., 1991—; vis. assoc. prof. U. Calif., 1981-82; dir. NEH-Brown Women Writers Project, 1988—. Author: Natural Emphasis, 1984; gen. editor: Women Writers in English, 1350-1850, 1992—; editor: The Poetry of Aemilia Lanyer, 1993; contbr. numerous articles to profl. jours. and scholarly books; reviewer for various profl. jours., including Renaissance Quar., Jour. of English and Germanic Philology; reader for PMLA Jour., SEL Jour., also others; editorial bd. Hunting Libr. Quar., 1987-90, Ben Jonson Jour., Duquesne U. Press. Pres. Cultural Coun. of Lancaster County, 1993—, bd. dirs., 1990—; bd. dirs. Lancaster Gen. Hosp. Found., 1992—; active various polit. campaigns, 1960-64, 68-76, 84, 92. Bronson fellow, 1976, Huntington Library, 1979-80, 81, Clark Library, 1981, Huntington-NEH, 1984-85, Woodrow Wilson Found., 1968-70. Mem. Am. Council Edn. (R.I. women's coord. 1988-90), MLA (chmn. div. 17th Century English lit. 1982), N.E. MLA (chmn. English Renaissance sect. 1978, Milton sect. 1983), Am. Assn. Higher Edn., Nat. Women's Studies Assn., Renaissance Soc. Am., Milton Soc. (exec. com. 1987-89), Lyrica Soc. (pres. 1987-90), Alpha Gamma Delta. Democrat. Episcopalian. Home: 452 Race Ave Lancaster PA 17603-2629 Office: Franklin and Marshall Coll Dean Of The College Lancaster PA 17604

WOODS, WILLIE G., English language and education educator; b. Yazoo City, Miss.; d. John Wesley and Jessie Willie Mae W. BA, Shaw U., Raleigh, N.C., 1965; MEd, Duke U., 1968; postgrad., Pa. State U., 1970, 80-82, Temple U., 1972, U. N.H., 1978, NYU, 1979, Indiana U. of Pa., 1986-88. Tchr. schs. in N.C. and Md., 1965-69; mem. faculty Harrisburg (Pa.) Area Community Coll., 1969—, assoc. prof. English and edn., 1976-82, prof., 1982-94, sr. prof., 1994—, supr. Writing Ctr., 1975-78, coord. Act 101/Basic Studies Program, 1978-83, dir. Acad. Founds. program 1983-87, asst. dean academ. affairs Acad. Found. and Basic Edn. Div., 1987-89, asst. dean acad. affairs, chmn. social sci., pub. svcs. and basic edn. div., 1989-94, dean social sci., pub. svcs. and basic edn. divsn., 1994—, chmn. dirs. coun., 1981-82; tchr. Community Resources Inst., 1975—; moderator workshops, cons. in field. Asst. editor Black Conf. Higher Edn. Jour., 1980. Sec., exec. com. People for Progress, 1971-73; bd. mgrs., exec. com. Camp Curtin br. YMCA, 1971-79; bd. dirs. Alternative Rehab. Communities, 1978—; bd. mgrs. Youth Urban Svcs., Harrisburg Area YMCA, 1981-92; bd. dirs. Dauphin Residences, Inc., 1981-88. Recipient cert. of merit for community svcs. City of Harrisburg, 1971, Youth Urban Svcs. Vol. of Yr. award, 1983, Black Student Union award Harrisburg Area Community Coll., 1984. Mem. Pa. Assn. Devel. Educators (chmn. conf. 1980, sec. 1981-82, v.p. 1986-87, pres. 1987-88), Pa. Black Conf. Higher Edn. (Outstanding Svc. award 1980, Central Region award 1982), Nat. Coun. Tchrs. English, Pa. Edn. Assn., Am. Assn. Community and Jr. Colls., Nat. Coun. on Black Am. (instl. rep. 1983—), AAUP, Alpha Kappa Alpha (Outstanding Svc. award 1983, Basileus award 1984, Ida B. Wells Excellence in Media award 1994, Ivy Honor Roll of Clips award 1994), Alpha Kappa Mu, Phi Kappa Phi. Baptist. Home: 1712 Ft Patton Dr Harrisburg PA 17112-8511 Office: 3300 N Cameron Street Rd Harrisburg PA 17110

WOODSIDE, LISA NICOLE, academic administrator; b. Portland, Oreg., Sept. 7, 1944; d. Lee and Emma (Wenstrom) W. Student Reed Coll., 1962-65; MA, U. Chgo., 1968; PhD, Bryn Mawr Coll., 1972; cert. Harvard U. Inst. for Ednl. Mgmt., 1979; MA, West Chester U., 1994. Mem. dean's staff Bryn Mawr Coll., 1970-72; asst. prof. Widener U., Chester, Pa., 1972-77, assoc. prof. humanities, 1978-83, asst. dean student services, 1972-76, assoc. dean, 1976-79, dean, 1979-83; acad. dean, prof. of humanities Holy Family Coll., Phila., 1983—, v.p., dean acad. affairs, prof. humanities, 1990—; cons. State N.J. Edn. Dept., 1990; accreditor Commn. on Higher Edn., Middle States Assn., 1979-83, 94. Co-author: New Age Spirituality: An Assessment. City commr. for community rels. Chester, 1980-83; mem. Adult Edn. Council Phila. Am. Assn. Papyrology grantee Bryn Mawr Coll.; S. Maude Kaemmerling fellow Bryn Mawr Coll. Mem. Am. Assn. Higher Edn., Coun. Ind. Colls., Eastern Assn. Coll. Deans, Pa. Assn. Colls. and Tchr. Educators, AAUW (univ. rep. 1975-83), Nat. Assn. Women in C. of C., Am. Psychol. Assn., Transpersonal Assn., Audubon Soc., Del. Valley Orienteering, Phi Eta Sigma, Alpha Sigma Lambda, Psi Chi. Home: 360 Saybrook Ln # A Media PA 19086-6761 Office: Holy Family Coll Torresdale Philadelphia PA 19114

WOODSON-HOWARD, MARLENE ERDLEY, former state legislator; b. Ford City, Pa., Mar. 8, 1937; d. James and Susie (Lettrich) Erdley; m. Francis M. Howard; children: George Woodson, Bert Woodson, Robert Woodson, Daniel Woodson, David Woodson. BS, Ind. U. of Pa., 1958; MA, U. South Fla., 1968; EdD, Nova U., 1981. Prof. math. Manatee Community Coll., 1970-82, dir., Inst. Advancement, 1982-86; exec. dir. Manatee Community Coll. Foundation, 1982-86; pres. Pegasus Enterprises, Inc., 1986—; state senator Fla., 1986-90. Candidate for gov. of Fla., 1990; bd. dirs. New Coll. Libr. Assn.; past pres. Manatee Symphony. Mem. Nat. Assn. Women Bus. Owners, Women Owners Network, Manatee C. of C., Sarasota Tiger Bay Club, Kiwanis. Republican. Roman Catholic. Home: 12 Tidy Island Blvd Bradenton FL 34210-3301

WOODSON-JOHNSON, CHERYL ANNE, clinical psychologist, consultant; b. Bristol, Pa., Jan. 16, 1959; d. Benjamin Franklin Woodson and Lucille (Weeks) Woodson-Lewis; m. Keith Byron Coleman, Nov. 7, 1977 (div. Feb. 1980); m. Larry Thomas Johnson, Sept. 26, 1992. BS, Nova U., 1981, MS, 1983; PsyD, Fla. Inst. Tech., 1987. Lic. psychologist, Fla. Coord. chpt. 2 programs Dade County Pub. Schs., Miami, Fla., 1987-88; adminstr., asst. prof. Southeastern U. of the Health Scis., Miami, Fla., 1988-92; mem. psychology faculty Nova U., Ft. Lauderdale, Fla., 1993—; ptnr. Campbell, Hall & Woodson Psychol. Svcs., Ft. Lauderdale, 1991—; disability cons. Dept. Labor and Employment Security, Office of Disability Determination, Miami, 1991—. Resource officer Office of Minority Health, Washington, 1988—; bd. dirs. AIDS Substance Abuse and Edn. Program, 1991—. Named one of Outstanding Young Women of Am., 1987. Mem. APA. Office: Campbell Hall & Woodson 4699 N State Rd 7 Ste A-1 Tamarac FL 33319

WOODSWORTH, ANNE, university dean, librarian; b. Fredericia, Denmark, Feb. 10, 1941; d. Thorvald Ernst and Roma Yrsa (Jensen) Lindner; 1 child, Yrsa Anne. BFA, U. Man., Can., 1962; BLS, U. Toronto, Ont., Can., 1964, MLS, 1969; PhD, U. Pitts., 1987. Edn. libr. U. Man., 1964-65; reference libr. Winnipeg Pub. Library, 1965-67; reference libr. sci. and medicine dept. U. Toronto, 1967-68; med. librarian Toronto Western Hosp., 1969-70; research asst. to chief librarian U. Toronto, 1970-71, head reference dept., 1971-74; personnel dir. Toronto Pub. Library, 1975-78; dir. librs. York U., Toronto, 1978-83; assoc. provost for librs. U. Pitts., 1983-88, assoc. prof., 1988-91; dean Palmer Sch. Libr. and Info. Sci. L.I. U., 1991—; pres. Anne Lindner Ltd., 1974-83; bd. dirs. Population Rsch. Found., Toronto, 1980-83, Ctr. for Rsch. Libraries, 1987-88; mem. rsch. libraries adv. coun. OCLC, 1984-87. Author: The Alternative Press in Canada, 1972, Leadership and Research Libraries, 1988, Patterns and Options for Managing Information Technology on Campus, 1990, Library Cooperation and Networks, 1991, Managing the Economics of Leasing and Contracting Out Information Services, 1993, Reinvesting in the Information Job Family, 1993, The Future of Education for Librarianship: Looking Forward from the Past, 1994. Trustee Long Island Librs. Resources Coun., 1993-98. Can. Coun. grantee, 1974, Ont. Arts Coun. grantee, 1974, Coun. on Libr. Resources grantee, 1986, 88, 91, 93; UCLA sr. fellow, 1985. Mem. ALA (com. on accreditation 1990-94, councillor 1993—), Can. Assn. Rsch. Librs. (pres. 1981-83), Assn. Rsch. Librs. (bd. dirs. 1981-84, v.p. 1984-85, pres. 1985-86), Assn. Coll. and Rsch. Librs. (chmn. K.G. Saur award com. 1991-93), Assn. for Libr. and Info. Sci. Edn., N.Y. Libr. Assn., Internat. Soc., Am. Soc. Info. Sci., Archons of Colophon. Office: LI U CW Post Campus Brookville NY 11548

WOODWARD, ISABEL AVILA, educational writer, foreign language educator; b. Key West, Fla., Mar. 14, 1906; d. Alfredo and Isabel (Lopez) Avila; student Fla. State Coll. for Women, 1925, A.B. in Edn., 1938; cert. in teaching Spanish, U. Miami, 1961; summer study U. Fla., Eckerd Coll.; postgrad. St. Lawrence U., U. Miami; m. Clyde B. Woodward, June 6, 1944 (dec.); children: Joy Avis Ball, Greer Isabel Woodward Sucke. Tchr., Key West, 1927-42, remedial reading cons., 1941-42; reading tchr., asst. reading lab. and clinic St. Lawrence U., summer 1941; Spanish translator U.S. Office of Censorship, Miami, 1943; tchr. Central Beach Elem. Sch., Miami Beach, Fla., 1943-44, Silver Bluff Elem. Sch., 1943-50, Henry West Lab. Sch., Coral Gables, Fla., 1955-57, Dade Demonstration Sch., Miami, 1957-61; author 125 sch. radio lessons for teaching Spanish, Dade County Elem. Schs., 1961; tchr. Spanish Workshop for Fla.; speaker poetry and short story writing, 1977; guest lectr. on writing the short story Fla. Inst. Tech., Jensen Beach, 1981, Circle Bay Yacht Club, Stuart, Fla., 1994; freelance writer; contbr. to Listen Mag., Sunshine Mag., Lookout Mag., Christian Sci. Monitor, Miami Herald, Three/Four, Child Life, Wee Wisdom, Fla. Wildlife, Young World; sponsor Port St. Lucie Jr. Woman's Club, 1983. Recipient Honoris Causa award Alpha Delta Kappa, 1972-74, award Contra Costa Times, Calif., 1985, 1st prize for short story in nat. Ark. writers conf. contest, 1992; named one of 5 Outstanding Fla. Tchrs., 1972-74. Mem. Nat. League Am. Pen Women (1st v.p. Greater Miami br. 1974-76, historian 1978—, librarian 1978—, awards for writing 1973, 74, 77, 1st and 3d place state writing awards for adult and juvenile fiction 1983, state 1st prize short story 1985), AAUW, Alpha Delta Kappa, Psi Psi Psi. Address: 1950 Palm City Rd Apt 6-301 Stuart FL 34994

WOODWARD, JOANNE GIGNILLIAT, actress; b. Thomasville, Ga., Feb. 27, 1930; d. Wade and Elinor (Trimmier) W.; m. Paul Newman, Jan. 29, 1958; children: Elinor Terese, Melissa Stewart, Clea Olivia. Student, La. State U., 1947-49; grad., Neighborhood Playhouse Dramatic Sch., N.Y.C. First TV appearance in Penny, Robert Montgomery Presents, 1952; understudy broadway play Picnic, 1953; appeared in plays Baby Want a Kiss, 1964, Candida, 1982, The Glass Menagerie, Williamstown Theatre Festival, 1985, Sweet Bird of Youth, Toronto, 1988; motion pictures include Three Faces of Eve, 1957 (Acad. award Best Actress, Nat. Bd. Rev. award, Fgn. Press award), Count Three and Pray, 1955, Long Hot Summer, 1958, No Down Payment, 1957, Sound and the Fury, 1959, A Kiss Before Dying, 1956, Rally Round the Flag Boys, 1958, The Fugitive Kind, 1960, Paris Blues, 1961, The Stripper, 1963, A New Kind of Love, 1963, A Big Hand for the Little Lady, 1965, A Fine Madness, 1965, Rachel, Rachel, 1968, Winning, 1969, WUSA, 1970, They Might Be Giants, 1971, The Effect of Gamma Rays on Man-in-the-Moon Marigolds, 1972 (Cannes Film Festival award), Summer Wishes, Winter Dreams, 1973 (N.Y. Film Critics award), The Drowning Pool, 1975, The End, 1978, Harry and Son, 1984, Glass Menagerie, 1987, Mr. & Mrs. Bridge, 1990, Philadelphia, 1993; TV appearances include All the Way Home; TV-film appearances in Sybil, 1976, Come Back, Little Sheba, 1977, See How She Runs, 1978 (Emmy award), Streets of L.A., 1979, The Shadow Box, 1980, Crisis at Central High, 1981, Do You Remember Love?, 1985 (Emmy award), Blind Spot, 1993 (Emmy nomination, Lead Actress - Miniseries, 1993), Breathing Lessons, 1994 (Emmy nomination, Lead Actress - Special, 1994, Golden Globe award, Best Actress); narrator film documentary Angel Dust, TV documentary on Group Theatre, 1989. Co-recipient (with Paul Newman) Kennedy Ctr. Honors for Lifetime Achievement in the Performing Arts. Democrat. Episcopalian. *

WOODWARD, SUSAN ELLEN, economist, federal official; b. Loma Linda, Calif., June 14, 1949; d. Frank Colwin and Dollie Dorothy (O'Kane) W.; 1 child, Sonja Stenger Weissman. BA in Econs., UCLA, 1970, PhD in Mgmt./Fin., 1978. Instr. U. Wash., Seattle, 1975, U. Toronto, 1975-77, UCLA, 1976-83, 84-85, U. Calif., Santa Barbara, 1977-79, U. Rochester (N.Y.), 1983-84; sr. staff economist Coun. Econ. Advisers, Washington, 1985-87; dep. asst. sec., chief economist HUD, Washington, 1987-92; chief economist SEC, Washington, 1992—. Mem. Am. Econ. Assn. (editor 1983-87), Am. Fin. Assn. Home: 2122 California St NW # 252 Washington DC 20008-1803 Office: US SEC 450 5th St NW Washington DC 20549

WOODWORTH, MARGO DEANE, religious organization administrator; b. Tacoma, Sept. 28, 1941; d. Owen Reeves and Margaret (Lewis) Smith; m. James W. Woodworth, Jan. 27, 1965; children: Sherri, Shannon. BA, Tex. Christian U., 1963. Dir. parents' tng. Advance-Zales Found. Project, Dallas, 1975-76; dir. children's activities and membership devel. Casa View Christian Ch., Dallas, 1976-78; dir. adminstrn., treas. Nat. Evangelistic Assn. of Christian Ch., Lubbock, Tex., 1979—; meeting planner cons. for religious conf. Nat. Evangelistic Assn. and Workshop, Lubbock, 1979—. Chmn. publicity Dudley Strain Lectureship Contact, Lubbock, 1986-87. Named to hon. order Ky. Cols., 1987. Mem. Nat. Assn. of Ch. Bus. Adminstrn., Religious Conf. Mgmt. Assn., Christian Ministries Mgmt. Assn., Am. Soc. Assn. Execs. Democrat. Office: Nat Evangelistic Assn 5001 Avenue N Lubbock TX 79412-2917

WOODY, CAROL CLAYMAN, data processing executive; b. Bristol, Va., May 20, 1949; d. George Neal and Ida Mae (Nelms) Clayman; B.S. in Math., Coll. William and Mary, Williamsburg, Va., 1971; M.B.A. with distinction (IBM Corp. fellow 1978, Stephen Bufton Meml. Ednl. Found. grantee, 1978-79), Babcock Sch., Wake Forest U., 1979; m. Robert William Woody, Aug. 19, 1972. Programmer trainee GSA, 1971-72; systems engr. Citizens Fidelity Bank & Trust Co., Louisville, 1972-75; programmer/analyst-tng. coordinator Blue Bell, Inc., Greensboro, N.C., 1975-79; supr. programming and tech. services J.E. Baker Co., York, Pa., 1979-82, fin. design supr. bus. systems Lycoming div. AVCO, Stratford, Conn., 1982-83; project mgr. Yale U., 1984—; co-owner Sign of the Sycamore, antiques; mem. Data Processing Standards Bd., 1977, CICS/VS Adv. Council, 1975; speaker Nat. Fuse Conf., 1989, Aion expert systems nat. conf., 1990, bus. sch. Coll. William & Mary, 1994. Mem. Am. Bus. Woman's Assn. (chpt. v.p. 1978-79; Merit award 1978), Nat. Assn. Female Execs. (founder shoreline network 1993), Assn. for System Mgmt., Delta Omicron (alumni pres. 1973-75, regional chmn. 1979-82). Republican. Presbyterian. Author various manuals, contbr. article to profl. jour. Home: PO Box 1450 Guilford CT 06437-0550 Office: 155 Whitney Ave New Haven CT 06510-1246

WOODY, CLAUDIA LAVERGNE, telecommunications executive, consultant; b. Martinsville, Va., Jan. 30, 1955; d. N. Rees and LaVergne (Tuck) W. BA summa cum laude, Mary Baldwin Coll., 1977; MS, U. Tenn., 1979; MBA, U. Tex., 1989. Asst. basketball coach U. Tenn., Knoxville, 1977-79, asst. athletics dir., 1979-81; asst. athletics dir. U. Tex., Austin, 1981-88, dir. external affairs, asst. dean Coll. Bus., 1988-91; dir. mktg. San Marcos Telephone Co. and San Marcos Telecorp, 1991-93; v.p. mktg. Century Telephone Enterprises, Dallas, 1993—; cons. various univs., 1981—, MacGregor Sporting Goods, Berlin, Wis., 1984-86, Apple Computer, Inc., 1987—; dir., tournament mgr. NCAA Nat. Championships, 1981-88. Mng. editor: Texas: The Business School Mag. (Coun. Advancement and Support Edn. award 1990), 1987-91. Bd. dirs The Vol. Ctr., Austin, 1989-92, Greater Austin Sports Found., 1990-94; bd. dirs., v.p. The Artemis Found., Winter Park, Colo., 1990—; mem. adv. bd. Tex. Ctr. for Legal Ethics and Professionalism, 1994—, Legends of Golf, Austin, 1991-93, San Marcos Incubator, 1992-94, Bus. Sch. S.W. Tex. State U., 1991-94, Rotary Internat., 1994—; mem. Leadership Tex., 1993. Russell scholar, Mary Baldwin Coll., Staunton, Va., 1977; Hilton A. Smith grad. fellow, 1979; recipient The Kozmetsky award U. Tex., Austin, 1989. Mem. Exec. Women Tex. Govt., Coun. Advancement and Support Edn., Coun. Coll. Women Athletics Adminstrs., NAFE, Nat. Soc. Fundraising Execs., Phi Beta Kappa, Omicron Delta Kappa, Psi Chi, Pi Lambda Theta, Kappa Delta Pi, Phi Kappa Phi, Beta Gamma Sigma. Democrat. Home: 6206 Stonehill Dr Dallas TX 75240 Office: Century Bus Devel 7502 Greenville Ave Ste 360 Dallas TX 75231

WOODY, ELIZABETH LYNN, accountant; b. Balt., July 17, 1946; d. William Albert and Elinor (Levis) Himes; m. James Nelson Woody, June 19, 1966; children: Brian Worth, Scott Nelson. BSBA, Coll. of Charleston, 1980. CPA. Staff acct. McKnight, Frampton, Buskirk, Charleston, S.C., 1980-84; mgr. Thiem, Jackson & Pace, Charleston, 1984-87, shareholder, 1987—; owner Probill, Charleston, 1993—. Mem. Am. Inst. CPAs, S.C. Assn. CPAs, Trident C. of C. Home: 541 Oyster Rake Dr Johns Island SC 29455 Office: Thiem Jackson & Pace CPAs 145 King St Ste 303 Charleston SC 29401

WOODY, JULIE See WYATT, JULIE

WOOLF, PAULETTE RUTH, financial executive; b. N.Y.C., June 11, 1956; d. Frank and Rose (Tessler) R.; m. David Myles Woolf, July 2, 1978; children: Shira Michal, Aviva Judith, Elie Scott. BA, Boston Univ., 1977; MPA, N.Y.U., 1982. Cert. high sch. English tchr. Staff analyst Parking Violations Bur., 1981-83; dep. dir. mgmt. planning and analysis Dept. of Parks and Recreation, 1983-84; cons. Resource Mgmt. Systems, Inc., N.Y.C., 1984-87; dir. spl. projects Dept. Transp., 1987-89; audit mgr. Mayor's Office of the Auditor Gen., 1989-90; dir. Mayor's Office of Contract Audit, 1990—; dep. dir. Mayor's Office of Contracts, 1992—; exec. com. N.Y./N.J. Intergovernmental Audit Forum, N.Y.C., 1993—; founder N.Y.C. Audit Dirs. Forum, N.Y.C., 1993—. Vice pres. programming Hollis Hills J.C. Sisterhood, 1992. Recipient Woman of Valor Jewish Theol. Sem., 1993. Mem. Am. Jewish Congress, Commn. of Women's Equality. Office: Mayors Office of Contracts 17 John St 12th Fl New York NY 10038

WOOLFOLK, PHYLLIS HODGE, nurse; b. Jersey City, Apr. 10, 1958; d. Maude Lee Hodge; m. Phillip D. Woolfolk, Feb. 25, 1989. BSN, Fairleigh Dickinson U., 1981; C.P.M., Rutgers U., Newark, 1993. RN, N.J.; cert. pub. mgr., N.J. Nurse ICU, St. Michael's Med. Ctr., Newark, 1981-87; case mgr. Cmty. Health Care, West Orange, N.J., 1987-89; mgr. New Horizon Treatment Svcs., Inc., Trenton, N.J., 1989—; staff nurse Mercer Med. Ctr., Trenton, 1990—; real estate investor, Trenton, 1981—. Inventor device to assist baby's feeding. Mem. Alpha Kappa Alpha (chpt. founder). Home: PO Box 1236 Trenton NJ 08607-1236

WOOLLEY, CATHERINE (JANE THAYER), writer; b. Chgo., Aug. 11, 1904; d. Edward Mott and Anna L. (Thayer) W. AB, UCLA, 1927. Advt. copywriter Am. Radiator Co., N.Y.C., 1927-31; freelance writer, 1931-33; copywriter, editor house organ Am. Radiator & Standard San. Corp., N.Y.C., 1933-40; desk editor Archtl. Record, 1940-42; prodn. editor SAE Jour., N.Y.C., 1942-43; pub. relations writer NAM, N.Y.C., 1943-47; condr. workshop on juvenile writing Truro Ctr. for Arts, 1977, 78, 92, Cape Cod Writers Conf., 1965, 66, 92. Author: juvenile books (under name Catherine Woolley) I Like Trains, 1944, rev., 1965, Two Hundred Pennies, 1947, Ginnie and Geneva, 1948, paperback edit., 1988, David's Railroad, 1949, Schoolroom Zoo, 1950, Railroad Cowboy, 1951, Ginnie Joins In, 1951, David's Hundred Dollars, 1952, Lunch for Lennie, 1952 (pub. as L'Incontentabile Gigi in Italy), The Little Car That Wanted a Garage, 1952, The Animal Train and Other Stories, 1953, Holiday on Wheels, 1953, Ginnie and the New Girl, 1954, Ellie's Problem Dog, 1955, A Room for Cathy, 1956, Ginnie and the Mystery House, 1957, Miss Cathy Leonard, 1958, David's Campaign Buttons, 1959, Ginnie and the Mystery Doll, 1960, Cathy Leonard Calling, 1961, paperback edit., 1988, Look Alive, Libby!, 1962, Ginnie and Her Juniors, 1963, Cathy's Little Sister, 1964, paperback edit., 1988, Libby Looks for a Spy, 1965, The Shiny Red Rubber Boots, 1965, Ginnie and the Cooking Contest, 1966, paperback 1979, Ginnie and the Wedding Bells, 1967, Chris in Trouble, 1968, Ginnie and the Mystery Cat, 1969, Libby's Uninvited Guest, 1970, Cathy and the Beautiful People, 1971, Cathy Uncovers a Secret, 1972, Ginnie and the Mystery Light, 1973, Libby Shadows a Lady, 1974, Ginnie and Geneva Cookbook, 1975, adult book Writing for Children, 1990, paperback, 1990; (under name Jane Thayer) The Horse with the Easter Bonnet, 1953, The Popcorn Dragon, 1953, rev. edit. 1989, Where's Andy?, 1954, Mrs. Perrywinkle's Pets, 1955, Sandy and the Seventeen Balloons, 1955, The Chicken in the Tunnel, 1956, The Outside Cat, 1957, English edit., 1958, 83, Charley and the New Car, 1957, Funny Stories To Read Aloud, 1958, Andy Wouldn't Talk, 1958, The Puppy Who Wanted a Boy, 1958, rev., 1986, paperback edition, 1988, French translation Le Petit Chien Qui Voulait Un Garcon, 1991, The Second-Story Giraffe, 1959, Little Monkey, 1959, Andy and His Fine Friends, 1960, The Pussy Who Went To the Moon, 1960, English edit., 1961, A Little Dog Called Kitty, 1961, English edit., 1962, 75, The Blueberry Pie Elf, 1961, English edit., 1962, revised edit., 1994, Andy's Square Blue Animal, 1962, Gus Was a Friendly Ghost, 1962, English edit., 1971, Japanese edit., 1982, A Drink for Little Red Diker, 1963, Andy and the Runaway Horse, 1963, A House for Mrs. Hopper; the Cat that Wanted to Go Home, 1963, Quiet on Account of Dinosaur, 1964, English edit., 1965, 74, paperback edit., 1988, Emerald Enjoyed the Moonlight, 1964, English edit., 1965, The Bunny in the Honeysuckle Patch, 1965, English edit., 1966, Part-Time Dog, 1965, English edit. 1966, The Light Hearted Wolf, 1966, What's a Ghost Going to Do?, 1966, English edit. 1972, Japanese edit., 1982, The Cat that Joined the Club, 1967, English edit. 1968, Rockets Don't Go To Chicago, Andy, 1967, A Contrary Little Quail, 1968, Little Mr. Greenthumb, 1968, English edit., 1969, Andy and Mr. Cunningham, 1969, Curious, Furious Chipmunk, 1969, I'm Not a Cat, Said Emerald, 1970, English edit. 1971, Gus Was A Christmas Ghost, 1970, English edit. 1973, Japanese edit., 1982, Mr. Turtle's Magic Glasses, 1971, Timothy And Madam Mouse, 1971, English edit., 1972, Gus And The Baby Ghost, 1972, English edit. 1973, Japanese edit., 1982, The Little House, 1972, Andy and the Wild Worm, 1973, Gus Was a Mexican Ghost, 1974, English edit. 1975, Japanese edit., 1982, I Don't Believe in Elves, 1975, The Mouse on the Fourteenth Floor, 1977, Gus Was a Gorgeous Ghost, 1978, English edit., 1979, Where Is Squirrel?, 1979, Try Your Hand, 1980, Applebaums Have a Robot, 1980, Clever Raccoon, 1981, Gus Was a Real Dumb Ghost, 1982, Gus Loved His Happy Home, 1989; contbr. stories to juvenile anthologies in U.S., Great Britain, France, Germany, and Holland, sch. readers, juvenile mags. Trustee Truro Pub. Libraries, 1974-84; Mem. Passaic (N.J.) Bd. Edn., 1953-56, Passaic Redevel. Agy., 1952-53; pres. Passaic LWV, 1949-52. Named mem. N.J. Literary Hall of Fame, 1987; recipient Phantom Friends Lifetime Achievement award, 1992. Mem. Authors League Am., Friends of Truro Libraries, Truro Hist. Soc., Amnesty Internat. U.S.A., Kenilworth Soc. Democrat. Home: PO Box 71 Truro MA 02666-0071

WOOLLEY, DONNA PEARL, timber land management executive; b. Drain, Oreg., Jan. 3, 1926; d. Chester A. and Mona B. (Cheever) Rydell; m. Harold Woolley, Dec. 27, 1952 (dec. Sept. 1970); children: Daniel, Debra,

Donald. Diploma, Drain High Sch. Sec. No. Life Ins. Co., Eugene, Oreg., 1943-44; sec., bookkeeper D & W Lumber Co., Sutherlin, Oreg., 1944, Woolley Logging Co. & Earl Harris Lumber Co., Drain, 1944-70; pres. Woolley Logging Co., 1970—, Smith River Lumber Co., 1970—, Mt. Baldy Mill, 1970—, Drain Plywood Co., 1970—, Woolley Enterprises, Inc., Drain, 1973—, Eagle's View Mgmt. Co., Inc., Eugene, 1981—; bd. dirs. Douglas Nat. Bank, Roseburg, Oreg. Bd. dirs. Oreg. Cmty. Found., Portland, Oreg., 1990—, Wildlife Safari, Winston, Oreg., 1986; trustee emeritus U. Oreg. Found., Eugene, 1979—; trustee Linfield Coll. Found., McMinnville, Oreg., 1990—; v.p. Oreg. Trail coun. Boy Scouts Am., Eugene, 1981—; mem. Yoncalla Rodeo. Recipient Pioneer award U. Oreg., 1982, Econ. and Social Devel. award Soroptimist Club, 1991. Mem. Oreg. Women's Forum, Pacific Internat. Trapshooting Assn., Amateur Trapshooting Assn., Eugene C. of C. (bd. dirs. 1989-92), Arlington Club, Town Club (bd. dirs., pres.), Shadow Hills Country Club, Sunnydale Grange, Cottage Grove/Eugene Rod & Gun Club. Republican. Office: Eagle's View Mgmt Co Inc 1399 Franklin Blvd Eugene OR 97403-1979

WOOLLEY, MARGARET ANNE (MARGOT WOOLLEY), architect; b. Bangor, Maine, Feb. 4, 1946; d. George Walter and Anne Geneva (Collins) W.; m. Gerard F. Vasisko, June 22, 1985. BA, Vassar Coll., 1969; MArch, Columbia U., 1974. Registered architect, N.Y. Urban designer Mayor's Office Lower Manhattan Devel., 1974-76, Mayor's Office Devel., N.Y.C., 1976-78; project mgr. Office Econ. Devel., N.Y.C., 1978-81, dep. dir. design and engring., 1981-83; dep. dir. design N.Y.C. Pub. Devel. Corp., 1983-85, asst. v.p. design, 1985-86, v.p. design, 1986-91; v.p. design N.Y.C. Econ. Devel. Corp., 1991-94; mem. N.Y. State Licensing Bd. Architecture, 1994—. Mem. assoc. bd. regents L.I. Coll. Hosp., Bklyn., 1982-93, mem. planning and devel. com., 1983-93; pres. assoc. bd. regents, 1988-89. William Kinne Fellows scholar, 1973. Mem. AIA (bd. dirs. N.Y.C. chpt. 1988-90, nat. pub. architects steering com. 1993—), N.Y. State Assn. Architects (bd. dirs. 1990-92), Heights Casino Club, Vassar Club, Jr. League. Home: 135 Willow St Brooklyn NY 11201-2255

WOOLLS, ESTHER BLANCHE, library science educator; b. Louisville, Mar. 30, 1935; d. Arthur William and Esther Lennie (Smith) Sutton; m. Donald Paul Woolls, Oct. 21, 1953 (div. Nov. 1982); 1 son, Arthur Paul. A.B. in Fine Arts, Ind. U., 1958, M.A. in Library Sci., 1962, Ph.D. in Library Sci., 1973. Elem. libr. Hammond Pub. Schs., Ind., 1958-65, libr. coord., 1965-67; libr. coord. Roswell Ind. Schs., N.Mex., 1967-70; prof. libr. sci. U. Pitts., 1973—; exec. dir. Beta Phi Mu, 1981—. Author: The School Library Media Manager, 1994; editor: Continuing Professional Education and IFLA: Past, Present, and a Vision for the Future, 1993. Recipient Disting. Svc. award Pa. Sch. Librs. Assn., 1993. Mem. ALA (coun. 1985-89, 91-94), Am. Assn. Sch. Librs. (dir. 1983-86, pres. 1993-94), Pa. Learning Resources Assn. (pres. 1984-85), Internat. Assn. Sch. Librs. (bd. dirs. 1991—), Internat. Fedn. Libr. Assns. (standing com. sch. librs. sect. 1991—, editor newsletter). Office: U Pitts Sch Libr and Info Sci Pittsburgh PA 15260

WOOLSEY, KATHLEEN MARGARET, psychotherapist; b. Peoria, Ill., May 3, 1947; d. Bernard George and Margaret Helen (Moran) Maxwell; m. E. Baird Woolsey, July 13, 1969 (div. 1989); children: Nathan B., Alexandria B.; m. John Richard Enzminger, Apr. 18, 1992. BA, U. Iowa, 1969; MA, Bradley U., 1987. Pvt. practice Pekin, Ill., 1989—; AIDS counselor Peoria City/County Health Dept., 1994—, AIDS support group facilitator, 1987-91; grief counselor Woolsey Funeral Home, Pekin, 1988-89. Bd. dirs. YWCA, Pekin, 1972-75; pres. Pekin Meml. Hosp. League, 1978. Mem. Am. Psychol. Assn. (assoc.). Republican. Methodist. Home: 16875 Springfield Rd Pekin IL 61554 Office: 110 N 5th Ste 217 Pekin IL 61554

WOOLSEY, LYNN, congresswoman. Mem. 103rd Congress from 6th Calif. dist., 1993—. Office: US House of Reps 439 Cannon Washington DC 20515-0506

WOOLSTON-CATLIN, MARIAN, psychiatrist; b. Seattle, Jan. 20, 1931; d. Howard Brown and Katharine Nichols (Dally) Woolston; m. Randolph Catlin Jr., July 5, 1959; children: Laura Louise, Jennifer Woolston, Randolph III. BA cum laude, Vassar Coll., 1951; MD, Harvard U., 1955. Diplomate Nat. Bd. Medicine. Intern and resident in medicine Children's Hosp., Boston, 1956; resident in psychiatry Mass. Mental Health Ctr., Boston, 1957-59; fellow in child psychiatry Tavistock Clin., London, 1961; commonwealth fellow in child psychiatry Harvard U. at Gaebler Children's Unit, Waltham, Mass., 1975-78, clin. instr. psychiatry, 1978-79; pvt. practice Wellesley Hills, Mass., 1978-91, Medfield, Mass., 1991—; clin. instr. psychiatry Harvard U. at Mass. Mental Health Ctr., Boston, 1957-59, 78-82, Tufts U. at Mass. Mental Health Ctr., 1957-59; mem. exec. bd. Parents' and Children's Svcs., Boston, 1983-86. Designer H.H. Hunnewell Meml. Garden for New England Flower Show Mass. Hort. Soc., 1975 (Ames Cup award). Mem. exec. bd. Ext. Divsn. New Eng. Conservatory Music., 1972-75; charter mem. reuse com. Medfield State Hosp., 1992—. Fellow Am. Acad. Child and Adolescent Psychiatry; mem. AMA, Am. Psychiat. Assn., Mass. Psychiat. Assn., Mass. Med. Soc., Boston Vassar Club (exec. bd. 1963-75), Hills Garden Club Wellesley (exec. bd. and design chief 1973-75). Episcopalian. Home and Office: 314 North St Medfield MA 02052-1204

WOOTTON, BROOKII E., executive assistant; b. Uvalde, Tex., Mar. 4, 1965; d. Charles K. and Leona Agnus (Farley) W.; m. John J. Ferguson Jr.; 1 child, J. Grey Ferguson. BS, SW Tex. State U., 1988. Operator test floor Motorola, Austin, Tex., 1987-88; stockbroker's asst. Shearson Lehman Hutton, Austin, 1988-89; instr. office adminstrn. Devine (Tex.) Ind. Sch. Dist., 1989-91; asst. to chief exec. officer Turbeco, Inc., Houston, 1991—; rep. for Turbeco, Inc. N.W. C. of C. Active community and charitable orgns.; sponsor cheerleading and twirling; judge, contest dir. Am. Twirling Festival. Mem. NEA, NAFE, AAUW, VOTAT, Bus. Profls. Am. Club (sponsor), Tex. Tchrs. Assn., Tex. Bus. Educators Assn., Devine Educators Assn. (v.p.), N.W. Houston C. of C. (rep.), Jr. League N.W. Harris County, Tex. Computer Edn. Assn., Golden Key Nat. Alumni Soc., Order of Omega, Phi Theta Kappa, Alpha Phi, Phi Upsilon Omicron. Home: 4326 Flint Hill San Antonio TX 78230

WORBY, RACHAEL BETH, conductor; b. Nyack, N.Y., Apr. 21, 1949; d. Louis Lincoln and Diana (Zacharia) W.; m. David Obst, Sept. 7, 1986. BS in Music, Crane Sch. of Music, 1971; postgrad., Ind. U., 1971-72; ABD, Brandeis U., 1979. Music dir. N.H. Philharmonic, Manchester, 1979-82, New Eng. Conservatory Youth Orch., Boston, 1980-82; Exxon asst. conductor Spokane (Wash.) Symphony, 1982-84; asst. conductor L.A. Philharmonic, 1983-87; music dir. Carnegie Hall, N.Y.C., from 1984, Wheeling (W.Va.) Symphony, 1986—; instr. New Eng. Conservatory of Music, Boston, 1979-82, MIT, Boston, 1980-82; lectr. N.Y. Philharmonic, N.Y.C., 1978-86. Rockefeller Found. grantee, 1981, Exxon/NEA grantee, 1982. Office: Wheeling Symphony Orchestra Capitol Music Hall 1025 Main St Ste 307 Wheeling WV 26003*

WORDEN, ELIZABETH ANN, artist, comedy writer, singer; b. Karnes City, Tex., Nov. 8, 1954; d. Alan Walker and Mary Paralee (Long) W. BS in Comms., U. Tex., 1977. Disc jockey, newsperson KMMK Radio, McKinney, Tex., 1978, KPBC Radio, Irving, Tex., 1979-80, KDNT Radio, Denton, Tex., 1980-81, KJIM Radio, Ft. Worth, 1981-82, KPBC Radio, Irving, 1983, KRYS Radio, Corpus Christi, Tex., 1984; owner Worden Industries, Corpus Christi, Tex.; rep. by Abney Gallery, N.Y.C., 1995—. Executed paintings for Am. Embassy, Bogota, Colombia; one-woman shows include Art Ctr., Corpus Christi, 1990; exhibited in groups shows at Tex. A&M, Corpus Christi, 1986, 92, Galeria Chapparal, Corpus Christi, 1988, New Eng. Fine Art Inst., Boston, 1993; represented in permanent collections including Am. Embassy, Bogota, Columbia. Mem. Art Ctr. Corpus Christi. Mem. Toastmasters Internat. Home and Office: Worden Industries 3842 Brookhill Corpus Christi TX 78410

WORDEN, KATHARINE COLE, sculptor; b. N.Y.C., May 4, 1925; d. Philip Gillette and Katharine (Pyle) Cole; m. Frederic G. Worden, Jan. 8, 1944; children: Rick, Dwight, Philip, Barbara, Katharine. Student Potters Sch., Tucson, 1940-42, Sarah Lawrence Coll., 1942-44. Sculptor; works exhibited Royce Galleries, Galerie Francoise Besnard (Paris), Cooling Gallery (London), Galerie Schumacher (Munich), Selected Artists Gallery, N.Y.C., Art Inst. Boston, Reid Gallery, Nashville, Weiner Gallery, N.Y.C., Boston Athanaeum, House of Humor and Satire, Gabrovo, Bulgaria, 1983, Newport Bay Club, 1984; pvt. collections Grand Palais (Paris), Dakar and Bathurst, Africa; dir. Stride Rite Corp., 1980-85; occupational therapist psychopathic ward Los Angeles County Gen. Hosp., 1953-57; Headstart vol., Watts, Calif., 1965-67; tchr. sculpture Watts Towers Art Center, 1967-69; participant White House Women Doers Luncheon meeting, 1968; dir. Cambridgeport Problem Center, Cambridge, Mass., 1969-71; mem. Jud. Nominating Commn., 1976-79; bd. overseers Boston Mus. Fine Arts, 1980-83; bd. govs. Newport Seamens Ch. Inst., 1989-91; trustee Communication Research Inst., Miami, Fla., 1960-69, chmn. bd., 1966-69; trustee Newport Art Mus., 1984-86, 92-94, Newport Health Found., 1986-91, Hawthorne Sea Fund, 1990-93; bd. dirs. Boston Center for Arts, 1976-80, Child and Family Svcs. of Newport County, 1983-90, 91—. Mem. Common Cause (Mass. adv. bd. 1971-72, dir. 1974-75), Mass. Civil Liberties Union (exec. bd. 1973-74, dir. 1976-77). Home: 24 Fort Wetherill Rd Jamestown RI 02835-2908

WORDEN, SUE JANINE, engineer, scientist; b. Dallas, Feb. 24, 1956; d. Ithiel Murray and Irene Elizabeth (Krepkovich) W.; m. Bapi Masroor Ahmad, May 1983 (div. Dec. 1984). BSME, U. Tex., 1978, MSEE, 1981, PhD in Elec. Engring., 1994. Engring. co-op Vought Corp., Grand Prairie, Tex., 1975-77; rsch. asst. U. Tex., Arlington, 1977; mech. engr. E.I. DuPont de Nemours, Wilmington, Del., 1978-79; tchg. asst. U. Tex., Austin, 1979-80; engr., scientist II Tracor Aerospace, Austin, 1980-86; rsch. engr., scientist asst. Applied Rsch. Labs., Austin, 1986-90; instr. Austin C.C., 1990-92; systems analyst U. Tex., Austin, 1992—. Com. chair Expanding Your Horizons in Scis. and Math.; mentor Austin Ind. Sch. Dist. Mem. AAUW, IEEE, ACM, SIAM, Assn. for Women in Sci., Assn. of Women in Math., Soc. Women Engrs., Sigma Xi, Tau Beta Pi, Pi Tau Sigma. Home: PO Box 4932 Austin TX 78765 Office: U Tex at Austin Computation Ctr Mail Code G2700U Austin TX 78712

WORDEN, SUSANNE LEE, physical therapist, consultant; b. Rochester, N.Y., Dec. 26, 1954; d. Gordon Warren and Ruth Charlotte (Illingworth) W. BS in Phys. Therapy, Russell Sage Cll., 1976; MS in Social Gerontology, Ctrl. Mo. State U., 1987. Registered phys. therapist, Mo., Kans. Phys. therapist Healthcare Rehab. Svcs. Am., Kansas City, Mo.; dir. Kendallwood Home Health Agy., Shawnee Mission, 1993—. Mem. Am. Phys. Therapy Assn., Mo. Phys. Therapy Assn. (pub. rels. chmn. 1988-93, sec. 1993—, dist. chmn. 1988-92), Sigma Phi Omega. Office: Healthcare Rehab Svcs Am Meadowbrook Manor Kans City 12000 Wornall Rd Kansas City MO 64145-1117

WORK, JANE MAGRUDER, professional society administrator; b. Owensboro, Ky., Mar. 30, 1927; d. Orion Noel and Willie May (Stallings) Magruder; m. William Work, Nov. 26, 1960; children: Paul MacGregor, Jeffrey William. BA, Furman U., 1947; MA, U. Wis., 1948; PhD, Ohio State U., 1959. Dir. radio U. South Miss., Hattisburg, 1948-51; pub. relations assoc. Ohio Fuel Gas Co./Columbia Gas, Columbus, 1952-62; adj. prof. communications Pace U., N.Y.C., 1963-75; dir. speechmodule ERIC, Washington, 1975-76; mgr. orgn. liaison, dir. legis. analysis Nat. Assn. Mfgs., Washington, 1977-84, asst. v.p. legis. analysis, 1984-87, v.p. legis. analysis, 1987—; adv. bd. public affairs NYU Grad. Bus. Sch., 1983-87; adv. bd. Proedn. Mag., 1984-87; cons. IBM, Xerox, 1963-77. Contbr. articles to profl. jours. Transition team Consumer Product Safety Commn., Washington, 1979-80; mem., chmn. No. Va. Pvt. Industry Council, Fairfax County, 1979-85; co-chair Va. Gov.'s Employment & Tng. Task Force, Richmond, 1983; active in other civic activities. Named to Acad. Women Achievers YWCA, 1987. Mem. Future Homemakers of Am. (bd. dirs. 1985-88), Issue Mgmt. Assn. (bd. dirs. 1985-88), Nat. Assn. Industry-Edn. Coop. (bd. dirs. 1983—), Am. Soc. Assn. Execs. (rsch. adv. com. 1989—), Speech Communication Assn. (sect. chmn. 1980-82), The Planning Forum (bd. dirs. Capital chpt. 1990—), World Future Soc. (steering network 1993 Gen. Assembly), Alpha Psi Omega (hon.), Pi Kappa Delta (hon.). Republican. Presbyterian. Home: 6245 Cheryl Dr Falls Church VA 22044-1809 Office: Nat Assn Mfrs 1331 Pennsylvania Ave NW Ste 1 Washington DC 20004-1703

WORKMAN, GAYLE JEAN, physical education educator; b. Mt. Vernon, Ohio, Sept. 26, 1959; d. Willard L. Workman and Joyce (Pealer) Workman-Garvic. BS in Phys. Edn., Bowling Green State U., 1982; MS in Sport Studies, Slippery Rock U., 1991; PhD, Ohio State U., 1995. presenter in field, 1992—. Elem. phys. edn. tchr., coach East Knox Sch. Dist., Howard, Ohio, 1983-89; teaching asst. Slippery Rock (Pa.) U., 1989-91; adj. prof. Butler (Pa.) C.C., 1991; prof. Kutztown (Pa.) U., 1992; teaching asst. Ohio State U., Columbus, 1992-95; asst. prof. U. Akron, Ohio, 1995—; presenter Midwest Conv. of Adult Edn., Columbus, 1993. Mem. AAHPERD (presenter nat. conv. 1994,95). Home: 80 Webster Park Ave Columbus OH 43214-3513

WORKMAN, MARGARET LEE, state supreme court justice; b. May 22, 1947; d. Frank Eugene and Mary Emma (Thomas) W.; m. Edward T. Gardner III; children: Lindsay Elizabeth, Christopher Workman, Edward Earnshaw. AB in Polit. Sci., W.Va. U., 1969, JD, 1974. Bar: W.Va. 1974. Asst. counsel to majority, pub. works com. U.S. Senate, Washington, 1974-75; law clk. 13th jud. cir., W.Va. Ct., Charleston, 1975-76, judge, 1981-88; pvt. practice Charleston, 1976-81; justice W.Va. Supreme Ct. Appeals, Charleston, 1989—, chief justice, 1993. Advance person for Rosalyn Carter, Carter Presdl. Campaign, Atlanta, 1976. Democrat. Episcopalian. Office: State Supreme Ct 317 State Capitol Charleston WV 25305-0001*

WORLEY, CARY JUNE, firefighter, engineer; b. Redding, Calif., Aug. 10, 1962; d. Elden Leroy and Alvina Lee (Knox) W. BA in Liberal Arts, Bethany Coll., Santa Cruz, Calif., 1984. Calif. clear teaching credential. Adminstrv. aid C. of C., Anderson, Calif., 1979-80; bookstore clk. Bethany Bible Coll. Bookstore, Santa Cruz, Calif., 1980-85; substitute tchr. Pacheco Sch. Dist., Redding, Calif., 1986-88, Redding Sch. Dist., 1986-88; longterm substitute tchr. Enterprise (Calif.) Sch. Dist., 1988-90; vol. firefighter Calif. Dept. Forestry, Redding, 1987-89; firefighter I Calif. Dept. Forestry, Shasta County, 1984-89; firefighter II Calif. Dept. Forestry, Fresno County, 1989-90; fire apparatus engr. Calif. Dept. Forestry, Riverside County, 1990—; beauty cons. Mary Kay Cosmetics, Menifee, Calif., 1991—. Mem. Calif. Dept. Forestry Employees Assn. Republican. Pentacostal. Home: 29084 Deer Creek Circle Menifee CA 92584 Office: Calif Dept Forestry & Fire Protection 210 W San Jacinto Perris CA 92570

WORLEY, GRACE MARIE, financial planner; b. Indpls., Aug. 10, 1949; d. Donald H. and M. Helen (Niehoff) Struck; m. Scott E. Worley, July 13, 1971 (div. 1977); 1 child, Heather; m. Thomas J. Mouzakis, June 1, 1986; 1 child, Maria L. BA, Ind. U., 1971; MBA, Ind. U., Indpl., 1988. Cert. fin. planner. Mgr. pub. affairs Allstate Ins. Co., Indpls., 1973-85; fin. planner Creative Fin. Planning, Indpls., 1985, Fin. Strategies Group, Indpls., 1986, Worley Mouzakis Adv. Inc., Indpls., 1986-91, Worley Halter Adv., Inc., Indpls., 1991—; adj. instr. Ind. U., Indpls., 1986—, Coll. Fin. Planning, Denver, 1988—. Pres. Big Sisters Greater Indpls., 1980-81, treas. Big Sisters of Greater Indpls. Found. Bd., 1994. Mem. Internat. Assn. Fin. Planning (treas. Ind. chpt. 1987), Inst. Cert. Fin. Planners (v.p. Ind. chpt. 1988—), Network of Women in Bus. Exec. Club (founding chmn. 1987, Bus. Woman of Yr. 1987), Cen. Ind. Soc. Cert. Fin. Planners (pres. 1990-92). Office: Worley Halter Adv Inc 3830 W 96th St Indianapolis IN 46268-2907

WORLEY, JANE LUDWIG, lawyer; b. Reading, Pa., Sept. 4, 1917; d. Walter Schearer and Marion Grace (Johns) L.; m. Floyd Edwin Worley, Oct. 30, 1946 (dec. Jan. 1982); children: Laetitia Anne, Thomas Allen, Christopher Ludwig. AB, Bryn Mawr Coll., 1938; JD, Temple U., 1942. Bar: Pa. 1943, U.S. Dist. Ct. (ea. dist.) Pa. 1980, U.S. Supreme Ct. 1968. Assoc. Richardson Moss & Richardson, Reading, 1943-48; pvt. practice Wernersville, Pa., 1948—; sec., bd. dirs. Worley Lumber Co. Inc., Wernersville, 1955—. Sec. Friends of Reading Mus. Art, 1986-91; sec. Berks County chpt. ARC, 1986-87, v.p., 1987-91. Mem. ABA, Pa. Bar Assn., Berks County Bar Assn., DAR, Jr. League Reading. Republican. Mem. United Ch. of Christ. Home: RD # 1 Box 128 Meadowgrove Farm Rd Womelsdorf PA 19567 Office: 551 W Penn Ave Wernersville PA 19565-1417

WORLEY, KAREN BOYD, psychologist; b. Hot Springs, Ark., Apr. 23, 1952; d. Wayne Johnson and Lou (Hull) Boyd; m. Timothy Riker, Sept. 22, 1979; children: Travis, Tyler, Kaitlin, Kelsey. BA, Okla. State U., 1974; PhD, Tex. Tech. U., 1983. Lic. psychologist, Ark. Rsch. asst. Rsch. and Tng. Ctr. for Mentally Retarded Tex. Tech. U., Lubbock, 1974-77, teaching asst., 1977-78; psychology intern Kansas City (Mo.) VA Med. Ctr., 1978-79; psychologist Johnson County Mental Health Ctr., Shawnee Mission, Kans., 1979-81; pvt. practice Pleasant Valley Clinic, Little Rock, 1982—; instr. dept. of pediatrics U. of Ark. for Med. Scis., 1991—; mem. Gov.'s Task Force on Child Abuse in Arks., 1983-85, Pulaski County Child Abuse Task Force, 1985, Pulaski County Family Svcs. Rev. Com., 1986-87, Com. to Rev. Investigation Procedures Ark. Children and Family Svcs., 1986, Child Sexual Abuse Network, 1988—; bd. dirs. Ark. Child Sexual Abuse Edn. Commn., 1985-91, Suspected Child Abuse and Neglect, 1986-92, Ark. Commn. on Child Abuse, Rape and Domestic Violence, 1991—; cons. Mother's Support Group, Parent Ctr., Little Rock, 1983-92. Contbr. articles to profl. publs. Mem. APA, Ark. Psychol. Assn., Nat. Register Health Svc. Providers in Psychology (coun.), Am. Profl. Soc. on Abuse of Children, Phi Kappa Phi. Methodist. Office: Family Treatment Program 1120 Marshall St Little Rock AR 72202-4600 also: Pleasant Valley Clinic 12361 Hinson Rd North Little Rock AR 72113

WORLEY, MERRY PENELOPE, medical library director; b. Vicksburg, Miss., Feb. 26, 1949; d. Robert Daniel and Cecil Elizabeth (Davis) W. BS in Math., U. Ala., Tuscaloosa, 1970; MA in Libr. Sci., U. Mo., 1975. Automated info. retrieval staff Tex. Med. Ctr., Houston, 1971-74; info. svcs. staff Tex. Med. Ctr. Libr., Houston, 1976-81; medline, reference coord. Med. Sch. U. Nebr., Omaha, 1975-76; libr. svcs. coord. Exxon Prodn. Rsch. Co., Houston, 1981-86; dir. med. libr. Scott & White Meml. Hosp., Temple, 1986—; summer outreach libr. Unger Meml. Libr., Plainview, Tex., 1975. Mem. Acad. Health Info. Profls., Med. Libr. Assn., Kiwanis Club of Temple, Beta Phi Mu. Office: Scott & White Meml Hosp 2401 S 31st St Temple TX 76508

WORMLEY, LILLIAN DELORES, administrative secretary; b. Trenton, N.J., July 17, 1951; d. Ernest Daniel Sr. and Mildred Louise (Johnson) W. Clerk civilian pers. U.S. Army, Fort Dix, N.J., 1968; clerk Walson Army Hosp. U.S. Army, Fort Dix, 1969, clerk army supply, 1971-72; student aide United Cerebral Palsy Assn. N.J., E. Orange, 1970; sr. clerk typist City of Trenton Dept. Pub. Works, 1972-77, prin. clerk typist, 1977-87, adminstrv. sec., 1987—; sec. bd. dirs. City of Trenton Employees Credit Union, 1991—. Leader Campfire Girls, Trenton, 1975-76; choir dir. New Salem Bapt. Ch., Trenton, 1985—, sec. nurses unit, 1988—, pres. youth advisors, 1990—. Home: 218 Spring St Trenton NJ 08618-4611

WORNER, RUBY KATHRYN, textile technologist; b. Manito Twp., Ill., Nov. 22, 1900; d. Henry and Mary Elizabeth (Kiesling) W. BS, U. Chgo., 1921, MS, 1922, PhD, 1925. Assoc. prof. Okla. Coll. Women, Chickasha, 1925-27; asst. chemist USDA, Washington, 1927-29, Nat. Bur. Standards, Washington, 1929-40; assoc. textile technologist USDA, New Orleans, 1940-62; head textile testing investigations So. Regional Rsch. Ctr. USDA; tech. officer UN FAO, Cairo, 1963-65; bibliographer Am. Assn. Textile Chemists and Colorists, New Orleans, 1966-70; textile cons. Internat. Exec. Svc. Corps, Manila, 1970; Fulbright prof. U. Alexandria, Egypt, 1960-61. Contbr. articles to profl. jours. Recipient Disting. Alumni award Shimer Coll., 1967. Fellow ASTM (award of merit 1964), AAAS, ASTM; mem. Am. Chem. Soc., Am. Assn. Textile Chemists and Colorists, Orgn. Profl. Employees USDA (life), Sigma Xi (life). Presbyterian. Home: Riverview Apt 510 500 Centennial Dr East Peoria IL 61611-4903

WORRELL, CYNTHIA LEE, bank executive; b. Moncton, NB, Can., May 27, 1957; came to U.S., 1979; d. Ronald William and Audrey Helen (Crothers) Jones; m. Geoffrey H. Worrell, Sept. 1, 1979; children: Lindsay Andrea, Geoffrey Andrew, Ashley Taylor. Student, U. New Brunswick, Fredericton, 1979. Lic. real estate broker, Mass., Pa., Calif. Instr. New Brunswick C.C., Fredericton, N.B., Can., 1978-79, Massasoit C.C., Brockton, Mass., 1981-82, Brockton Cmty. Schs., 1981-82; regional mgr. and instr. Worldwide Ednl. Services, Clifton, N.J.; procedures and documentation analyst Capital Blue Cross, Harrisburg, Pa., 1985; v.p., br. mgr. Comfed Mortgage Co., Inc., Mass., 1985-90; sr. residential loan officer Bank of Am., Santa Clara, Calif., 1990-92; regional sales mgr., asst. v.p. Shearson Lehman Mortgage, San Jose, Calif., 1992-93; br. mgr. Cypress Fin., San Jose, 1993-94, PNC Mortgage Corp. Am., San Jose, 1994—; guest spkr. numerous trade shows, real estate bd. seminars, cmty. workshops; instr. mortgage banking Calif. State U., Hayward, 1994—; mem. adv. bd., instr., outside cons. Calif. State U. Ext. divsn., 1993-95; cert. trainer Carlson Learning Co., 1993—. Mem. editl. bd. Mortgage Originator, 1995; contbr. articles to profl. jours. Vol. Handi Kids, Bridgewater, Mass., 1985-90, Fremont/Newark YMCA youth basketball and soccer; mem. Forest Park PTA, Self-Def. Inst. Tae Kwon Do Club; donor Berwick Boys Club. Named to IBC 200 Women of Achievement, 1991-92, ABI 2000 Notable Women, 1991-92,ABI Personalities of Am., 1992, Internat. Order of Merit, 1992, The World Found. of Successful Women, 1992, Outstanding Young Women in Am., 1984, 88. Mem. NAFE, Mass. Mortgage Bankers Assn., Data Entry Mgmt. Assn., Middleboro C. of C., Wareham Bus. and Profl. Women's Club, Taunton Area C. of C., Toastmasters. Republican. Home: 7 Kingwood St Wareham MA 02571 Office: PNC Mortgage Corp Am 2025 Gateway Pl Ste 132 San Jose CA 95110

WORTH, IRENE, actress; b. Nebr., June 23, 1916. B.Edn., U. Calif. at Los Angeles, 1937; pupil, Elsie Fogarty, London, 1944-45. Formerly tchr. Debut as Fenella in: Escape Me Never, N.Y.C., 1942; Broadway debut as Cecily Harden in: The Two Mrs. Carrolls, 1943; London debut in The Time of Your Life, 1946; following roles, mostly on London stage, include Anabelle Jones in Love Goes to Press, 1946; Ilona Szabo in: The Play's The Thing, 1947; as Eileen Perry in: Edward my Son, 1948; as Lady Fortrose in: Home is Tomorrow, 1948; as Mary Dalton in: Native Son, 1948; title role in: LaCrece, 1948; as Olivia Raines in: Champagne for Delilah, 1949; as Celia Coplestone in: The Cocktail Party, 1949, 50; various roles with Old Vic Repertory Co., London, including Desdemona in Othello; Helena in Midsummer Night's Dream and Lady Macbeth in Macbeth; also Catherine de Vausselles in: on tours The Other Heart, S. Africa, 1952; as Portia in: The Merchant of Venice, 1953; joined, Shakespeare Festival Theatre, Stratford, Ont., Can., 1953; as Helena in: All's Well That Ends Well; Queen Margaret in: Richard III; appeared as Frances Farrar in: A Day by the Sea, 1953-54; leading roles in: The Queen and the Rebels, 1955, Hotel Paradiso, 1956; as Mary Stuart, 1957, The Potting Shed, 1958; appeared as Albertine Prine in: Toys in the Attic, 1960 (Page One award); mem., Royal Shakespeare Co., 1962-64; including world tour King Lear, 1964; star: including world tour Tiny Alice, N.Y.C., 1964, Aldwych, 1970; appeared in: Noel Coward trilogy Shadows of the Evening; also appeared as Hilde in: A Song at Twilight; Anna-Mary in: Come into the Garden Maud (Evening Standard award); Hesione Hushabye in: Heartbreak House (Variety Club Gt. Britain award 1967); Jocasta in: Oedipus, 1968; Hedda in: Hedda Gabler, 1970; with internat. Co., Theatre Research, Paris and Iran, 1971; leading role in: Notes on a Love Affair, 1972; Mme. Arkadina in: The Seagull, 1973; Gertrude in: Hamlet; Mrs. Alving in: Ghosts, 1974; Princess Kosmonopolis in: Sweet Bird of Youth, 1975-76 (Jefferson award, Tony award); Lina in: Misalliance, 1976; Mme. Ranevskaya in: The Cherry Orchard, 1977 (Drama Desk award); Kate in: Old Times, 1977, After the Season, 1978, Happy Days, 1979, Eyewitness, 1980, Coriolanus, 1988, Lost In Yonkers, (Tony award, 1991); films include: role of Leonie in: Orders to Kill, 1958 (Brit. Film Acad. award), The Scapegoat, 1958, King Lear, 1970, Nicholas and Alexandra, 1971, Rich Kids, 1979, Eyewitness, 1981, Death Trap, 1982, Fast Forward, 1985, Lost in Yonkers, 1993, also numerous radio, TV appearances, Eng., Can., U.S., including; Stella in: The Lake; Ellida Wangel in: The Lady from the Sea (Daily Mail Nat. TV award), also Candida, Duchess of Malfi, Antigone, Prince Orestes, Variations on a Theme, The Way of the World, The Displaced Person; (with Brit. Broadcasting Co.) Coriolanus, 1984; poetry recitals, recs.; (recipient Whitbread Anglo-Am. award outstanding actress 1967). Decorated comdr. Brit. Empire (hon.). Address: Internat Creative Mgmt care Sam Cohn 40 W 57th St Fl 6 New York NY 10019-4001*

WORTH, MARY PAGE, mayor; b. Balt., Jan. 23, 1924; d. Christian Allen and Margaret Pennington (Holbein) Schwarzwaelder; m. William James Worth, Nov. 4, 1947 (dec. May 1986); children: Margaret Page, William Allen, John David III. Student, Ladycliff Coll., Highland Falls, N.Y., 1941-42, Abbott Sch. Art, Washington, 1942-44. Selectman Town of Searsport, Maine, 1973-75; mayor City of Belfast, Maine, 1986—; recreation chmn.

Town of Searsport, 1970-72. Del. Rep. State Conv., Maine, 1970-94; pres. Searsport Reps., 1974-76; active ARC Overseas Assn., 1976—; pres. Searsport C. of C., 1976-79; mem. exec. bd. Waldo County Com. for Social Action, Belfast, 1986—; mem. Abnacki coun. Girl Scouts U.S.; tutor Literacy Vols. Am.; recreation specialist ARC, Camp Haugen, Japan, 1946-47; bd. dirs. RSVP-Waldo County, Head Start Waldo County; vol. tchr. Sch. for Blind, Cholon, Republic Vietnam, 1959-61, Am. School at Saigon, Republic Vietnam, 1959-61; club dir. USAF Spl. Services, Fort Meyer, Va., 1962-63, U.S. Army Spl. Services, Fort Belvoir, Va., 1963-64; mem. Congresswoman Olympia Snow's Mcpl. Adv. Bd.; town chair Rep. Party. Mem. DAR (officer Maine 1986—), Internat. Platform Assn., Ret. Officers Assn., 11th Airborne Assn./511th PIR Korea War Vets. Assn., Waldo County Humane Soc. (pres. 1990—), Waldo County Law Enforcement (v.p. 1990—), VFW Aux., Am. Legion Aux., Belfast Garden Club (parliamentarian 1984—), Rotary (bd. govs. com. Maine St. '90). Home: 16 Church St Belfast ME 04915-1661 Office: City of Belfast Mayor's Office 71 Church St Belfast ME 04915-1796

WORTHAM, DEBORAH LYNNE, school system director, principal; b. Chgo., May 13, 1949; d. Leon Cabot and Bessie (Summers) Smith; m. Chester Hopes Wortham, Jan. 29, 1972; children: Shelley Sharon, Chester Hopes III. BS, U. Wis., 1972; MS, Morgan State U., 1981. Tchr., reading tchr., support tchr. Balt. City Pub. Schs., 1972-87, asst. prin., 1988-90, prin. Samuel Coleridge Taylor Sch., 1990-94, dir. efficacy, 1994—; program facilitator Balt. Schs.-Johns Hopkins U., 1987-88; dean of edn. Higher Dimensions Learning Ctr., Balt., 1985—. Author: Teaching by Signs and Wonders, 1992. Recipient Mayor's Citation for Volunteerism, Balt., 1982, Am. Best Elem. Sch. for Significant Improvement award Redbook Mag., 1993; cited Administrator's Class Act, Channel 11 TV, Balt., 1991. Mem. ASCD, Phi Delta Kappa, Alpha Kappa Alpha. Democrat. Pentecostal. Office: Balt City Pub Schs Bd Edn 200 E North Ave Baltimore MD 21212

WORTHEY, CAROL, composer; b. Worcester, Mass., Mar. 1, 1943; d. Bernard Krieger and Edith Lilian (Cramer) Symonds; m. Eugene Worthey III, June 1969 (div. 1980); 1 child, Megan; m. Raymond Edward Korns, Sept. 21, 1980. BA in Music Composition, Columbia U., 1965; grad., Dick Grove Sch. Music., L.A., 1979; grad. filmscoring prog., UCLA, 1978; music studies with Darius Milhaud, Walter Piston, Elliot Carter, Vincent Persichetti, Grant Beglarian, Karl Korte, Otto Luening, Eddy Lawrence Manson, Dick Grove; studied, RISD, 1948-54, Columbia U., 1965. Sr. composer, arranger Celebrity Ctr. Internat. Choir, Hollywood, Calif., 1985—. Composer, arranger The Hollywood Chorale; composer ballets Athena, 1963, The Barren, 1965; composer, lyricist, librettist full-length musical The Envelope Please, 1988; composer piano works performed in France, Italy, Germany, Can., U.S. and Eng. by Mario Feninger, 1982; composer Pastorale performed in Mex., 1994, Neighborhood of the Heart, 1994, (choir) Unquenchable Light, 1993; composer film score The Special Visitor, 1992; compositions performed at Aspen Music Festival, 1963, Carnegie Hall, 1954, Dorothy Chandler Pavilion, 1986-89; appeared as singer-songwriter on L.A. Songwriter's Showcase, 1977; arranger Merv Griffin Show, 1981, The Night Before Christmas, L.A. Children's Theatre, 1988-91, Capistrano Valley Symphony, 1994; author: Treasury of Holiday Magic, 1992, (poems) The Lonely Wanderer Comes Home, 1994; art work exhibited RISD, 1952, Folk and Craft Mus., L.A., 1975, 1st Internat. Art Exhibit Celebrity Ctr. Pavillion, 1992. Vol. performer various childcare ctrs., old folks homes, etc. Recipient Silver Poet award World of Poetry, 1987, 2nd place winner, 1st BarComposers and Songwriters Competition for "Fanfare for Joy & Wedding March", 1990, Golden Poet award World of Poetry, 1992. Mem. Nat. Assn. Composers, USA, Broadcast Music Inc., Nat. Acad. Songwriters, Songwriters and Composers Assn., Toastmasters Internat. Jewish.

WORTHING, CAROL MARIE, minister; b. Duluth, Minn., Dec. 27, 1934; d. Truman James and Helga Maria (Bolander) W.; children: Gregory Alan Beatty, Graydon Ernest Beatty. BS, U. Minn., 1965; Master of Divinity, Northwestern Theol. Seminary, 1982; D of Ministry, Grad. Theol. Found., Notre Dame, Ind., 1988; MBA in Ch. Adminstrn., Grad. Theol. Found., Donaldson, Ind., 1993. Secondary educator Ind. (Minn.) Sch. Dist., 1965-78; teaching fellow U. Minn., 1968-70; contract counselor Luth. Social Svc., Duluth, 1976-78; media cons. Luth. Media Svcs., St. Paul, 1978-80; asst. pastor Messiah Luth. Ch., Fargo, N.D., 1982-83; vice pastor Messiah Luth. Ch., Fargo, 1983-84; assoc. editor Luth. Ch. Am. Ptnrs., Phila., 1982-84; editorial assoc. Luth. Ptnrs. Evang. Luth. Ch. Am., Phila. and Mpls., 1984—; parish pastor Resurrection Luth. Ch., Pierre, S.D., 1984-89; assoc. pastor Bethlehem Luth. Ch., Cedar Falls, Iowa, 1989-90; exec. dir. Ill. Conf. Chs., Springfield, 1990—; mem. pub. rels. and interpretation com. Red River Valley Synod, Fargo, 1984-86, mem. ch. devel., Pierre, 1986-87; mem. mgmt. com. office comm. Luth. Ch. in Am., N.Y.C., Phila., 1984-88; mem. mission ptnrs. S.D. Synod, 1988, chmn. assembly resolutions com., 1988; mem. preassembly planning com., ecumenics com., chmn. resolutions com. N.E. Iowa Synod, 1989-90; mem. ch. and society com. Cen. and So. Ill. Synod, 1990—; nat. edn. cons. Am. Film Inst., Washington, 1967-70; chaplain state legis. bodies, Pierre, 1984-89. Author: Cinematics and English, 1967, Peer Counseling, 1977, Tischrede Lexegete, 1986, 88, 90, Way of the Cross, Way of Justice Walk, 1987, Introducing Collaboration as a Leadership Stance and Style in an Established Statewide Conference of Churches, 1993. Co-facilitator Parents of Retarded Children, 1985; bd. dirs. Countryside Hospice, 1985; cons. to adminstrv. bd. Mo. Shores Women's Ctr., 1986. Mem. Nat. Assn. Ecumenical Staff (chair of site selection com. 1991-92, scholarship com. 1993-94, mem. profl. devel. com. 1993-94, program planning com. 1995, bd. mem. 1995—), Pierre-Ft. Pierre Ministerium (v.p. 1986-87, pres. 1987-88), NAFE. Democrat. Home: 1520 Seven Pines Rd Apt J Springfield IL 62704-6617 Office: Ill Conf Churches 615 S 5th St Springfield IL 62703-1604

WORTHINGTON, JANET EVANS, academic director, English language educator; b. Springfield, Ill., Jan. 30, 1942; d. Orville Ray and Helen May (Tuxhorn) Evans; m. Gary H. Worthington; children: Rachael Allene, Evan Edmund, Adam Nicholas Karl. Student, Blackburn Coll., 1960-62; BA in English Lang. and Lit., U. Chgo., 1965; MA in English, U. Iowa, 1969; PhD in English Edn., Fla. State U., 1977; postgrad., W. Va. Inst. Tech., 1981-82, Rensselaer Poly. Inst., 1984. Teaching. fellow Fla. State U., Tallahassee, 1971-72, grad. assistant, 1972-73; coord. lang. arts rsch. Piedmont Schs. Project, Greer, S.C., 1973-76; English instr. Woodrow Wilson High Sch., Beckley, W.Va., 1976-77; Reading specialist, adj. instr. in English W. Va. Inst. Tech., Montgomery, W.Va., 1977-78; asst. prof. W.Va. Inst. Tech., Montgomery, 1979-82, assoc. prof., 1983-87, prof. English, 1987-88; dir. W.Va. Inst. Tech., Oak Hill, 1988-90; tech. writing program coord. Community and Tech. Coll. W.Va. Inst. Tech., Montgomery, 1983-88; dir. continuing edn. Nicholls State U., Thibodaux, La., 1990—; tech. writing cons., various bus., 1986—, Dept. of Mines, State of W.Va., 1980-81; reading cons. Dept of Mines, 1980-81, Mt. Hope (W.Va.) High Sch., 1980-81, Reading Tchrs. Study Group, Kanawha County, W.Va., 1981-83; project mgr. Dept. of Mines, State of W.Va., 1981-83, Dept. of Nat. Resources, State of W.Va., 1984-85; involved in curriculum devel. for various depts., W.Va. Inst. Tech., 1973-90, Raleigh County Schs., Beckley, W.Va., Piedmont Schs. Project, Greer, S.C., English and reading instr. Upward Bound Program, W.Va. Inst. Tech., 1980-85; adj. instr. W.Va. Coll. Grad. Studies, 1979, 81, 83. Author (with William Burns): Practical Robotics: Systems, Interfacing, and Applications, 1986, (with A.B. Somers): Candles and Mirrors: Response Guides for Teaching Novels and Plays in Grades Six through Twelve, 1984, Response Guides for Teaching Children's Books, 1979; editorial bd.: W.Va. Community Coll. Jour.; reviewer: Macmillan Pub. Co. texts, 1985; editor: Diamond Shamrock, 1985; co-producer, host (TV series): About the Author; contbr. numerous articles to profl. jours.; participated in numerous presentations. Mem. W.Va. Community Coll. Assn.; bd.dirs., Curtain Callers, 1979-89, Fayette Fine Arts Coun., 1986-87; promotions chair, W.Va. Children's Book award com., 1984-85. Mem. AAUW (recording sec. 1983-85, pres. 1985—), Assn. for Tchrs. of Tech. Writing, Nat. Assn. for Devel. Edn., Soc. for Tech. Comm. Home: 112 E Garden Dr Thibodaux LA 70301-3750 Office: Nicholls State U Continuing Edn PO Box 2011 Thibodaux LA 70310

WORTMAN, MITZI LYNN, nurse, educator; b. Pendleton, Oreg., Dec. 31, 1953; d. Stanley Charles and Fern Francis (Garrett) W.; m. Robert Milton Benson, Aug. 29, 1983. AS in Nursing, Portland C.C., 1977; BS in Psychology, Portland State U., 1982; MFA in Photography, San Francisco State U., 1993. Nursing asst. Grand Ronde Hosp., LaGrande, Oreg., 1972-75; med. nurse Holladay Park Hosp., Portland, Oreg., 1977-80; alcohol counselor, nurse Oreg. Health Scis. Ctr., Portland, 1979-83; psychiat. nurse St. Vincent's Hosp., Portland, 1980-85, Sequoia Hosp., Redwood City, Calif., 1986-91; psychiat. utilization case mgr. CPC Belmont Hills Hosp., Belmont, Calif., 1987-93; clin. nurse instr. Mission C.C., Santa Clara, Calif., 1988—; nurse case mgr. utilization Seton Hosp., Daly City, Calif., 1993—. Author, performance artist (multi-media play) Desire, 1993. Active San Francisco Mus. Modern Art, 1992-93. Leo D. Stillwell scholar San Francisco State U., 1991. Mem. ANA (cert. psychiat. nurse), Assn. Cert. Educators, Continuing Care Nurse Assn., Calif. Nurse Assn. Democrat. Home: 369 Vista Grande Ave Daly City CA 94014-3837

WORTMANN, DOROTHY WOODWARD, physician; b. Easton, Pa., Mar. 14, 1945; d. Robert Simpson III and Esther (Thomas) Woodward; m. Robert Lewis Wortmann, June 14, 1969; children: Jonathan Thomas, William Lewis. BA, Mount Holyoke Coll., 1967; MD, U. Kans. Sch. Medicine, 1971. Diplomate Am. Bd. Pediatrics, subspecialty pediat. rheumatology. Clin. instr. pediatrics Med. Coll. Wis., Milw., 1979-80, instr. pediatrics, 1980-82, asst. prof. pediatrics, 1982-92; assoc. clin. prof. pediatrics East Carolina U. Sch. Medicine, Greenville, N.C., 1993—; med. dir. rheumatology Children's Hosp. Wis., Milw., 1980-92. chair for juvenile arthritis and mem. pub. and patient svcs. com. Arthritis Found., Milw., 1981-92; med. adv. bd. Lupus Found., Milw., 1983-92. Recipient Disting. Svc. award Arthritis Found., 1991. Fellow Am. Acad. Pediatrics (mem. exec. coun. for rheumatology 1993—), Am. Coll. Rheumatology (mem. sect. pediat. rheumatology); mem. N.C. Med. Soc. Office: East Carolina U. Sch Medicine Dept Pediatrics Brody Med Scis Bldg Greenville NC 27858

WOS, CAROL ELAINE, small business owner; b. Bremerton, Wash., Apr. 21, 1957; d. Standley Ralph and Janet Estele (Galber) Stocker; m. George Joseph Wos; children: Samuel Harrison, Bridget Monique. BS in Chem., Wash. State U., 1979. Mfg. engr. Internat. Bus. Machines, E. Fishkill, N.Y., 1979-80; process devel. engr. Sperry Corp., Eagan, Minn., 1980-83; sr. process devel. engr. Cray Rsch. Inc., Chippewa Falls, Wis., 1983-90, mem. cleanroom design and constrn. team, 1991-92, bump/tab process engr., 1993-94; owner, mgr. The Nature of Things, Eau Claire, Wis., 1995—. Bd. dirs. Eau Claire Regional Arts Coun. Mem. ASTM. Republican.

WOYSKI, MARGARET SKILLMAN, retired geology educator; b. West Chester, Pa., July 26, 1921; d. Willis Rowland and Clara Louise (Howson) Skillman; m. Mark M. Woyski, June 19, 1948; children: Nancy Elizabeth, William Bruno, Ronald David, Wendelin Jane. BA in Chemistry, Wellesley (Mass.) Coll., 1943; MS in Geology, U. Minn., 1945, PhD in Geology, 1946. Geologist Mo. Geol. Survey and Water Resources, Rolla, 1946-48; instr. U. Wis., Madison, 1948-52; lectr. Calif. State U., Long Beach, 1963-67; lectr. to prof. Calif. State U., Fullerton, 1966-91, assoc. dean Sch. Natural Sci. and Math., 1981-91, emeritus prof., 1991—. Contbr. articles to profl. jours.; author lab. manuals; editor 4 guidebooks. Fellow Geol. Soc. Am. (program chmn. 1982); mem. South Coast Geol. Soc. (hon. pres. 1974), Mineral Soc. Am. Home: 1843 Kashlan Rd La Habra CA 90631-8423

WOYTHAL, CONSTANCE LEE, psychologist; b. Milw., Nov. 6, 1954; d. Gerald Clarence and Shirley Estelle (Gross) W.; m. John Francis Neisius, Mar. 20, 1982; children: Adam, Abby. BS, U. Wis., Milw., 1976; MS in Edn., U. Wis., River Falls, 1978; postgrad., Alfred Adler Inst., Chgo., 1980, George Williams Coll., 1984, Marquette U., 1984, Cardinal Stritch Coll., 1987, Wis. Sch. Profl. Psychology, 1990. Lic. sch. psychologist, Wis.; nat. cert. sch. psychologist. Psychologist Sch. Dist. of Marshfield, Wis., 1978-81, Sheboygan County Handicapped Children's Edn. Bd., Sheboygan Falls, Wis., 1981-91; devel. coord. wellness program Sheboygan County Handicapped Children's Edn. Bd., Plymouth, Wis., 1984—; psychologist Plymouth (Wis.) Joint Sch. Dist., Plymouth, Wis., 1991—; workshop facilitator Marshfield Clinic, 1981; cons. wellness lifestyle program Sch. of Sheboygan County, 1985—; lectr. profl. groups; mem. profl. adv. bd. Children with Attention Deficit Disorder (ChADD), 1992-93. Bd. dirs. Family Connections, 1988-90. Mem. APA (student affiliate), NASP, Nat. Wellness Assn., N.Am. Soc. Adlerian Psychologists, Wis. Sch. Psychology Assn., Sheboygan Wellness Assn. (bd. dirs. 1982-88), Mental Health Assn. Home: 859 Chaplin Ct Plymouth WI 53073-1012 Office: Riverview Mid Sch Riverview Cir Plymouth WI 53073

WOZNIAK, DEBRA GAIL, lawyer; b. Rockford, Ill., Oct. 3, 1954; d. Richard Michael and Evalyn Louise (Pickett) W. BA, U. Nebr., 1976, JD, 1979. Bar: Nebr. 1980, Iowa 1980, Ill. 1982. Asst. legal counsel Iowa Ho. of Reps., Des Moines, 1980-81; mng. atty. Rapp & Gilliam, Des Moines, 1981; from asst. counsel to counsel and asst. dir. Alliance of Am. Insurers, Schaumburg, Ill., 1981-87; counsel StateFarm Ins. Cos., Bloomington, Ill., 1987—. Mem. Nebr. Bar Assn., Iowa Bar Assn. Office: State Farm Ins Cos One State Farm Plz Bloomington IL 61710

WOZNIAK, JOYCE MARIE, sales executive; b. Detroit, Aug. 3, 1955; d. Edmund Frank and Bernice (Liske) W. BA, Mich. State U., 1976; MA, Nat. U., San Diego, 1988; postgrad., U.S. Internat. U., 1989-90. Probation officer San Diego County Probation, 1979-81; prodn. engr. Tuesday Prodns., Inc., San Diego, 1981-85; nat. sales mgr. Advance Rec. Products, San Diego, 1986-88; account exec. Joyce Enterprises, San Diego, 1986—; sales exec. Audio-Video Supply Inc., San Diego, 1988—. Producer (video) Loving Yourself, 1987, southwest cable access program, 1986—, Registered Marriage, Family, and Child Counselor-Intern, California, 1989. Active Zool. Soc. San Diego. Mem. Art Glass Assn. So. calif., Calif. assn. Marriage and Family Therapists, Internat. TV Assn. (treas. San Diego chpt. 1990-91).

WOZNICA, JANET GRACE, psychologist; b. L.A., Nov. 1, 1957. BA in Psychology, UCLA, 1979; MA in Jewish Studies, U. Judaism, 1982; MA in Clin. Psychology, Calif. Sch. Profl. Psychology, 1982, PhD in Clin. Psychology, 1986. Lic. clin. psychologist Calif. Pvt. tutor Hebrew L.A., 1979-90; tchr. Adat Ari El Religious Sch., North Hollywood, Calif., 1980-85; clin. researcher Ind. Rsch., Encino, Calif., 1987—; clin. psychologist, supr. Hathaway Children's Svcs., Lakeview Terrace, Calif., 1988-91; clin. psychologist pvt. practice, Encino, 1986—; adj. faculty Antioch U., Marina del Rey, Calif., 1988—, Pepperdine U. Grad. Sch. Edn. and Psychology, Encino, 1989—; dir. Project Tikvah Jewish youth suicide prevention program, L.A., 1994—. Contbr. articles to profl. jours. Postdoctoral fellow Children's Hosp. L.A., 1986-87. Mem. Am. Psychol. Assn., Calif. Psychol. Assn., L.A. County Psychol. Assn. Office: 16055 Ventura Blvd Ste 1129 Encino CA 91436

WRAGG, JOANNA DICARLO, public relations executive, newspaper editor; b. Batavia, N.Y., Nov. 3, 1941; d. Anthony Joseph and Josephine (Ruffino) DiCarlo; m. Otis O. Wragg, III, Dec. 21, 1963; children—Otis O. IV, LaMae. B.A., Fla. State U., 1963. Journalist Lakeland Ledger, 1969-72; editorial writer, then chief editorial writer Miami News, 1972-78; editorial dir. Sta. WPLG-TV, Miami, 1978; editorial writer Miami Herald, 1978-80, assoc. editor, 1980-92; v.p. Wragg & Casas Pub. Rels., 1992—; pub. speaker Am. Press Inst. Contbr. articles newspapers. Recipient Pulitzer prize, 1983, Robert F. Kennedy award Robert F. Kennedy Journalism Found., 1971, Disting. Service award Sigma Delta Chi, 1971. Mem. Nat. Conf. Editorial Writers (pres. 1991), Women in Communications, Pub. Rels. Soc. Am. Unitarian. Clubs: Zonta, Miami Forum. Office: Wragg & Casas Pub Rels 1110 Brickell Ave Ste 302 Miami FL 33131-3106

WRAY, GERALDINE SMITHERMAN (JERRY WRAY), artist; b. Shreveport, La., Dec. 15, 1925; d. David Ewart and Mary Virginia (Hoss) Smitherman; m. George Downing Wray, June 24, 1947; children: Mary Virginia Hill, Deanie Galloway, George D. Wray III, Nancy Armistead. BFA with honors, Newcomb Art Sch., Tulane U., 1946. One woman shows include Don Batman Gallery, Kansas City, Mo., 1982, Gallery II, Baton Rouge, 1985, McNeese Coll., Lake Charles, La., 1987, Dragonfly Gallery, Shreveport, La., 1987, Barnwell Garden and Art Ctr., Shreveport, 1988, Southdown Mus., Houma, La., 1989, La. State U., Shreveport, 1991, WTN Radio Station, Shreveport, 1993, The Cambridge Club, Shreveport, 1993, Centerary Coll., 1993; Group shows include Waddell's Gallery, Shreveport, 1990, 91, Water Works Gallery, Dallas, 1990, Southwestern Watercolor Show, 1991 (D'Arches award), Masur Mus. Exhibition (honorable mention 91, 92), 1991, 92, Bossier Art Ctr., Bossier City, La., 1992, Barnwell Garden and Art Ctr., Shreveport, 1992, Irving Art Assn. (honorable mention), 1992, Leon Loard Gallery, Montgomery, Ala., 1993, Ward-Nasse Gallery, N.Y.C., 1993, Soc. Experimental Artists Internat. (1st. place, honorable mention), 1993, Palmer Gallery, Hot Springs, Ark., 1994. Art chmn. Jr. League, Shreveport, 1955-60; bd. dirs. Holiday-in-Dixie Cotillion, Shreveport, 1974-76. Mem. Nat. Watercolor Soc. (signature mem. 1994), Southwestern Watercolor Soc. (signature mem. 1991), La. Watercolor Soc. (signature mem. 1990), La. Artists Inc. (elected mem.). Episcopalian. Home: 573 Springlake Dr Shreveport LA 71106

WREGE, JULIA BOUCHELLE, tennis professional, physical education educator; b. Charleston, W.Va., Apr. 11, 1944; d. Dallas Payne and Mary Louise (Hagan) Bouchelle; m. Douglas Ewart Wrege, July 13, 1968; children: Dallas Ewart, Shannon Bouchelle. B.S. in Physics, Ga. Inst. Tech., 1965, M.S. in Physics, 1967. Systems analyst GE Apollo Systems, Daytona Beach, Fla., 1967-68; med. scientist Space Instruments Research, Atlanta, 1968-70; head tennis profl. Riverside Tennis Club, Atlanta, 1971-72, Am. Adventures, Roswell, Ga., 1972-75, Hampton Farms Tennis Club, Marietta, Ga., 1975-79; head women's tennis coach Ga. Inst. Tech., Atlanta, Ga., 1979-86, 91-92; v.p. Sirius Software, Inc., 1988—; instr. physics So. Coll. Tech., 1990—; stadium chmn., umpire, referee USTA, Atlanta, 1977—. Author: Tournament Manual, 1977, 3d edit., 1989; co-developer software TMS Tennis Tournament, 1989. Pres. Dickerson Mid. Sch. Parent-Tchr.-Student Assn., Marietta, Ga., 1982-85. Named Umpire of Yr., Ga. Tennis Assn., 1978, So. Tennis Assn., 1978; Ga. Tennis Coach of Yr., Assn. Intercollegiate Athletics for Women-Ga. Tennis Coaches Assn., 1981, 82, 83. Mem. U.S. Profl. Tennis Assn. (pres. 1980), U.S. Tennis Assn., Intercollegiate Tennis Coaches Assn., Ga. Tennis Assn. (pres. 1976-81, 94—, v.p. 1974-76, 91-92), Atlanta Lawn Tennis Assn., Atlanta Profl. Tennis Assn., Alpha Xi Delta, Sigma Pi Sigma. Republican. Episcopalian. Home: 1366 Little Willeo Rd Marietta GA 30068-2135

WREN, SHEILA ANN, art director; b. Lima, Ohio, July 2, 1959; d. Kenneth Aart and Erma Charlotte (Berry) Miller; m. Christopher Alan Wren, Jan. 23, 1983; children: Brock Edward, Cameron Kenneth, Tara Raquel. BFA, Miami U., Oxford, Ohio, 1981. Art dir. advt. agy. T.R. Stuckey & Assoc., Inc., Lima, Ohio, 1981-83, Mktg. and Creative Svcs., Inc., Richmond, Ind., 1985-89, Adman/Hold It Systems, Lima, 1992—. Republican. Lutheran. Office: Adman/Hold It Systems 768 N Main St PO Box 1869 Lima OH 45802

WRIGHT, ANTOINETTE GREEN, educator; b. New Haven, Conn., May 7, 1951; d. David Alexander Sr. and Marion (Baker) Green; m. Clinton L.A. Wright, Aug. 24, 1974 (dec. Mar. 1991); children: Nia, Challa, Calvin. BA, Brandeis U., 1973; MA, Wesleyan U., 1980. Sec. asst. Brandeis U., Waltham, Mass., 1972-73; tchr.'s aide New Haven (Conn.) Pub. Schs., 1973; tchr. M.L.K. Community Sch., Atlanta, 1973-75, lead tchr., 1975-76, acting dir., 1975-76; grad. teaching asst. Wesleyan U., Middletown, Conn., 1976-78; tchr. homebound New Haven Pub. Schs., 1988-91; asst. tchr. 1st grade St. Thomas Day Sch., New Haven, 1990-93, libr., tchr., 1993—. Contbr. articles to newspapers. Active St. Luke's Episc. Ch. Network. Mem. Jack and Jill Am., Inc. (Disting. Mother of Yr. 1993), Alpha Kappa Alpha. Democrat. Home: 25 Rock View Terr New Haven CT 06511-1619 Office: St Thomas Day Sch 830 Whitney Ave New Haven CT 06511-1316

WRIGHT, BARBARA CLARE, business librarian; b. Mt. Holly, N.J., Dec. 6, 1943; d. Charles Hodge and Charlotte Elizabeth (Brown) W. BA, Temple U., 1966; MS, Drexel U., 1972; MA, Temple U., 1985. Circulation asst. Temple U., Phila., 1967-72, asst. to dir., 1972-75, asst. to dir. of pub. svcs., 1975-77, reference libr., 1977-80, bus. libr., 1980—. Mem. ALA, Pa. Libr. Assn., Spl. Librs. Assn., Phila. Area Reference Librs. Info. Exch., Assn. Coll. and Rsch. Librs., Drexel U. Libr. Sch. Alumni Assn. Democrat. Office: Temple U Paley Libr 13th and Berks Sts Philadelphia PA 19122

WRIGHT, BARBARA EVELYN, microbiologist; b. Pasadena, Calif., Apr. 6, 1926; d. Gilbert Munger Wright and Leta Luella (Browne) Deery; m. Kenneth Fremont-Smith, May 25, 1974. AB, Stanford U., 1947, MA, 1948, PhD, 1951. Biologist NIH, Bethesda, Md., 1953-61; assoc. biochemist Mass. Gen. Hosp., Boston, 1961-69; asst. prof. microbiology Harvard Med. Sch., Boston, 1966-75, assoc. prof., 1975-82; rsch. dir. Boston Biomed. Rsch. Inst., 1967-82; rsch. prof. biol. scis. divsn. U. Mont., Missoula, 1982—; dir. Stella Duncan Rsch. Inst., Missoula, 1982—; cons. Miles Lab., Elkhart, Ind., 1980-84. Author: Critical Variables in Differentiation, 1973; editor: Control Mechanisms in Respiration and Fermentation, 1963; contbr. articles to profl. jours. Grantee NIH, NSF, 1961-95. Mem. AAAS (pres. Pacific div. 1984-85), Am. Soc. for Microbiology (divisional lectr. 1978), Am. Soc. of Biol. Chemists. Home: 1550 Big Flat Rd Missoula MT 59801-9220 Office: U Mont DBS Missoula MT 59812

WRIGHT, BONNIE MCLEAN, psychology educator; b. Tampa, Fla., Apr. 20, 1956; d. Thaddeus W. and Elizabeth (Jones) McLean; m. Jerry E. Wright, June 18, 1983; children: Heather L. and Nicole V. (twins). BS in Psychology, North Ga. Coll., 1978; MS in Psychology, U. Ga., 1981, PhD, 1983. Asst. prof. psychology Bluefield (Va.) Coll., 1984-85; asst. prof. Gardner-Webb U., Boiling Springs N.C., 1985-93, assoc. prof. psychology, 1993—; adj. prof. psychology Tex. Women's U., Denton, 1992-93; cons. in field. Contbr. articles to profl. jours. Bd. dirs. Life Enrichment Ctr., Shelby, N.C., 1985-87, ACCES, Shelby, 1990-92; leader Gurl Scouts U.S., Lewisville, Tex., 1992-93, Boiling Springs, 1993—. Mem. APA, Assn. Women in Psychology, Psi Chi, Sigma Phi Omega. Baptist. Office: Gardner-Webb U Dept Psychology Boiling Springs NC 28017

WRIGHT, CAROLE DEAN, reading specialist; b. Mt. Clemens, Mich., Aug. 18, 1943; d. Edward Lawrence and Alice Agnes (Roshinski) Hundt; m. David John Wright, Dec. 20, 1964 (div. Sept. 1984); 1 child, Amy Elizabeth. BA, Mich. State U., 1964, MA, 1967. Reading specialist Holt (Mich.) Pub. Schs., 1965-70, Ypsilanti (Mich.) Pub. Schs., 1970-71, Aurora (Colo.) Pub. Schs., 1972—; pres. Aurora Edn. Assn., 1978-80, Colo. Edn. Assn., Denver, 1982; mem. adv. com. Nat. Assessment of Ednl. Progress, Denver, 1975; chair unit accreditation bd. Nat. Coun. Accreditation of Tchr. Edn., Washington, 1990—; trustee Pub. Employees Retirement Assn. Colo., 1993—. Contbg. author to Idea's for Children's Literature, 1976. Mem. Colo. Commn. on Tchr. Edn. and Accreditation, Denver, 1976-82; vice chair Gov.'s Chpt. 2 Adv. Com., Denver, 1987-93. Named Outstanding Educator, Fed. Programs Adminstr. Coun. U.S. Dept. Edn., 1991. Mem. NEA (bd. dirs. 1984-87), Internat. Reading Assn., Colo. Edn. Assn. (v.p. 1980-84), Phi Delta Kappa. Home: 2268 Clermont St Denver CO 80207-3740

WRIGHT, CHRISTINE ALLEN, travel consultant; b. Greensboro, N.C., Oct. 30, 1921; d. James Noah and Willie Pauline (Kent) Allen; m. Thomas Archibald Wright Jr., June 18, 1943; children: Laurinda W. Porter, Thomas Archibald III, Cynthia W. Fiala. BS, U. N.C., 1942. Assoc. editor Simplicity Pattern Co., N.Y.C., 1942-44; pub. rels. Textron Inc., N.Y.C., 1944-46; travel cons. VIP Travel Agy., New Canaan, Conn., 1969-87, Travelworld of New Canaan, Conn., 1987—. Pres. Bull Valley Garden Club, Woodstock, Ill., 1961-63; bd. dirs. Women's Aux. Meml. Hosp., Woodstock, 1964-66, Woodstock Fine Arts Assn., 1965-67, McHenry County Easter Seal Aux., Woodstock, 1966-68. Mem. AAUW, Woman's Club New Canaan, Nutmeg Theater Group, New Canaan Hist. Soc., Wed. Book Club. Republican. Office: New Canaan Travelworld 12 E Maple St New Canaan CT 06840-5693

WRIGHT, DANA JACE, nurse, entrepreneur; b. Cleve., Apr. 20, 1952; d. William James and Murl Jean (White) Ewing; m. David Alan Samball, June 22, 1968 (div. Apr. 1971); 1 child, David; m. David M. Wright, July 11, 1981; children: William James, Karen Marie. Assoc. in Nursing, Valencia Community Coll., 1973, AA, 1973; BS in Respiratory Therapy, U. Cen. Fla., 1975; MEd, Auburn U., 1979; D in Nursing, Case Western Res. U., 1982. RN, Fla., Ohio, N.Y., Ga.; cert. emergency med. technician; cert. and registered respiratory therapist; cert. med.-surg. nurse; lic. real estate agt., N.Y. Nursing asst. Holiday Hosp., Orlando, Fla., 1970-71, staff nurse critical care unit, intensive care unit, 1973; pvt. duty nurse Med. Personnel Pool, Orlando, 1973-74; nurse critical care burn team Upjohn, Inc., Augusta, Ga., 1976-77; ednl. dir. dept. respiratory therapy U. Hosp., Augusta, 1975-76; mem. staff respiratory therapy VA Hosp., Augusta, 1976-77; clin. instr. respiratory therapy Med. Coll. Ga., Augusta, 1976-77, Columbus Coll., 1977-78; ednl. dir. respiratory therapy Med. Ctr. Hosp., Columbus, 1977-79;

staff nurse, relief supr. Kelly Health Care, Beachwood, Ohio, 1979-81; staff nurse Med. Staff, Inc., Cleve., 1981-83; dir. nursing S.R.T. Med. Staff Inc., Cleve., 1983; pres. Wright Properties, Buffalo, 1987-94, Med. Ctr. Vending, 1994—; part-time nurse Millard Fillmore Suburban Hosp., 1990-91. Treas. Ch. Women's Assn., Snyder, N.Y., 1985-86; mem. nursing resources panel North Ohio Lung Assn., 1981-82; mem. Profl. Parent Network, Buffalo, 1987—. Mem. ANA (alt. del. 1993-94), Am. Assn. Nurses Practicing Independently (assoc.), Nat. Nurses Bus., N.Y. State Nurses Assn. (nurse rsch. cons. 1991-92, 94, chair nurse entrepreneurs 1992-94, WNY regional review team 1992-94), Women's Dental Guild. Republican. Home and Office: 49 Colony Ct Buffalo NY 14226-3507

WRIGHT, DAPHNE BROWN, driver's education educator; b. St. Louis, July 16, 1952; d. James and Helen (Wren) Brown; divorced; 1 child, Mechelle Anise. BS in Home Econs., Ea. Ill. U., 1974; MS of Ednl. Adminstrn., So. Ill. U., 1976, cert. in ednl. specialist, 1988, postgrad., 1993—. Cert. tchr. K-12, Ill., prin. K-12. Instr. driver's edn. East St. Louis (Ill.) Sr. High Sch., 1975—; mem. student assitance program East St. Louis Sr. High Sch., 1990-91, 92-93, adminstrv. aide, 1989-90, dept. chair driver edn., 1991-95, sponsor varsity cheerleaders and pep club; parenting facilitator St. Clair County Mental Health, East St. Louis, 1991-92, 92-93; tchr. Ctr. Child/Behavior Disorders East St. Louis, summer 1993; substance abuse interventionist St. Clair County, Belleville, Ill. Mem. adv. coun. Drug Free Schs., 1992-93, 93-94; mem. cmmty. action bd. Sta. KSD-K-TV, 1993—. Named Miss East St. Louis, 1976. Mem. Ill. High Sch. and Coll. Driver's Edn. Assn., Greater Beauticians of East St. Louis, Delta Sigma Theta, Order Ea. Star (Queen Elizabeth chpt.). Office: East St Louis Sr High Sch 4901 State St East Saint Louis IL 62205-1356

WRIGHT, DIANE VRBA, insurance company executive; b. Dallas, July 9, 1950; d. Reynold G. and Agnes (Kriska) Vrba; m. John D. Huchingson (div.); 1 child, David Ray; m. Ronald Edward Wright, July 10, 1987. AA, El Centro Coll., Dallas, 1970; student, U. Dallas, Irving, Tex., 1971, North Tex. State U., 1972. Escrow sec. Hexter-Fair Title Co., Dallas, 1975-81; br. mgr. Chgo. Title Ins. Co., Mesquite, Tex., 1981—; pres., dir. Heritage Sq. Investments, Mesquite, Tex. Mem. Bd. Adjustment, Mesquite, 1982-92, Planning and Zoning Commn., Mesquite, 1992—; past pres. Mesquite Svc. League. Named Career Woman of Yr. Casual Corner, Mesquite, 1986. Mem. Women's Coun. Realtors (com. chair, chmn. bd. 1989, Chmn.'s award 1986, Bus. Person of Yr. 1989, Mesquite C. of C. (bd. dirs.), S.E. Dallas County Women's Coun. Realtors. Office: Chgo Title Ins Co 200 W Davis Mesquite TX 75149

WRIGHT, ELEANOR STRAUB, communications educator; b. St. Louis, June 25, 1923; d. Charles H. and Edna C. (Schulz) Straub; m. James Arden Wright, June 21, 1947; children: Carolyn L. Wright Whitton, Elizabeth A. Wright Tomlin. AA, Monticello Coll., 1943; BJ, MS, Northwestern U., 1945. Soc. reporter St. Louis Post-Dispatch, 1945-47; pub. rels. staff Community Chest, Trenton, N.J., 1947-50; columnist Webster News-Times, Webster Groves, Mo., 1955-60; asst. editor Barks Publs., St. Louis and Chgo., 1964-74; editor St. Louis County Observer, Maplewood, Mo., 1974-76; freelance cons. Bicentennial, St. Louis, 1976-77; assoc. in info. svc. Lawrence Inst. Tech., Southfield, Mich., 1978-79; assoc. prof. Ea. Mich. U., Ypsilanti, 1979-93; ret., 1993. Author book in edn. series Detroit Free Press. Sec., trustee Westwood Bd. Edn., Dearborn Heights, Mich., 1987-91, pres. 1993-95. Recipient Disting. Faculty Svc. award Ea. Mich. U., 1988. Mem. Women in Communications (past pres. St. Louis chpt., Headliner award Detroit chpt. 1986, Faculty Advisor of Yr. award 1988), Pub. Rels. Soc. Am., Golden Key. Democrat. Presbyterian. Home: 25576 Blossingham Dr Dearborn Heights MI 48125-1076

WRIGHT, FAITH-DORIAN, artist; b. Bklyn., Feb. 9, 1934; d. Abraham and Molly (Janoff) J.; m. Jordan Merritt, Igrid-beth. BS, NYU, 1955, MA, 1958; postgrad., Pratt and Parsons Sch. of Design. Works exhibited in Kathryn Markel Gallery, N.Y.C., 1981, 82, Cumberland Gallery, Nashville, 1981, 82, Barbara Gillman Gallery, Miami, 1982, Hand and Hand Gallery, 1985, 86, Suzanne Gross, Phila., 1986, 87, Gallery Four, Alexandria, Va., 1986, 87, 88, Henri Gallery, Washington, 1986, 87, 88, 89, 90, 91, 92, 93, 94, Benton Gallery, Southampton, N.Y., 1986, 87, 88, 89, 91, 92, 93, King Stephen Mus., Hungary, 1987, Nat. Gallery Women in the Arts, 1987, 88, 90, 90, 91, 92, Ruth Volid Gallery, Chgo., 1990, James Gallery, Pitts., 1990, Aart Vark Gallery, Phila., 1990, Merrill Chase Gallery, Chgo., 1990, 91, 92, Guild Hall Mus., East Hampton, N.Y., 1991, Joy Berman Gallery, Phila., 1992, Ctr. for Book Arts, N.Y.C., 1992, Barnard-Biederman Fine Arts, N.Y.C., 1994, Arlene Bujese Gallery, East Hampton, 1994, Stoney Brook U., 1994; permanent collections Nat. Postal Art Mus., Ottawa, Can., Nat. Inst. Design, Ahmedabad, India, Fine Arts Acad., New Dehli, India, Mus. Modern Art, N.Y.C., Nat. Mus. Women in the Arts, Washington, D.C., Israel Mus., Jerusalem, Brenau Coll., Grainsville, Ga., Blue Cross, Blue Shield, Phila., Mc Donald's, Oakbrook, Ill., The Hyatt Collection, Chgo., Guild Hall Mus.; contbr. critical essays to various periodicals. Mem. Women in Arts, Women's Caucus for Arts, Artists Equity, Visitation Bd. of Met. Mus.-Rockefeller Connection. Address: 300 E 74th St New York NY 10021

WRIGHT, FRANCES JANE, educational psychologist; b. Los Angeles, Dec. 22, 1943; d. step-father John David and Evelyn Jane (Dale) Brinegar. BA, Long Beach State U., 1965, secondary tchr. cert., 1966; MA, Brigham Young U., 1968, EdD, 1980; postgrad. U. Nev., 1970, U. Utah, 1972-73; postdoctoral Utah State U., 1985-86. Cert. tchr., adminstr. Utah. Asst. dir. Teenpost Project, San Pedro, Calif., 1966; caseworker Los Angeles County, 1966-67; self-care inservice dir. Utah State Tng. Sch., American Fork, Utah, 1968, vocat. project designer, 1968; tchr. mentally handicapped Santa Ana Unified Schs., Calif., 1968-69; state specialist intellectually handicapped State Office Edn., Salt Lake City, 1969-70; vocat. counselor Manpower, Salt Lake City, 1970-71; tchr. severely handicapped Davis County Schs., Farmington, Utah, 1971-73, diagnostician, 1973-74, resource elem. tchr., 1974-78; instr. Brigham Young U., Salt Lake City, 1976-83; resource tchr. jr. high Davis County Schs., Farmington, 1978-90; ednl. cons., Murray, Utah, 1973-90; chief ednl. diagnostician Ctr. for Evaluation of Learning and Devel., Layton, Utah, 1989-90; clin. dir. assessment and observation program Idaho Youth Ranch, 1990—, clin. dir. intake program, 1992—, supr. family preservation svc./aftercare teams, 1993—, co-ranch treatment dir., 1995—; cons. and lectr. in field. Author curriculums in spl. edn.; contbr. articles to profl. jours. Named Profl. of Yr., Utah Assn. for Children with Learning Disabilities, 1985. Mem. Assn. Children/Adults with Learning Disabilities (del. 1979-85, 87, nat. nominating com. 1985-86, nat. bd. dirs. 1988-91), Utah Assn. Children/Adults with Learning Disabilities (exec. bd. 1978-84, profl. adv. bd. 1985-90, coord. LDA orgn. Idaho 1991—), Coun. Exceptional Children (div. learning disabilities, ednl. diagnostics, behavioral disorders), Council Learning Disabilities, Assn. Supervisors and Curriculum Devel. (regional adv.), Windstar Found., Smithsonian Found., Cousteau Soc., Am. Biographical Inst. (life, hon. advisor rsch. bd. advisors nat. div.), Nat. Assn. Sch. Adminstrs. Democrat. Mormon. Lodge: Job's Daughters. Avocations: geneology research, horseback riding, sketching, crafts, reading. Home and Office: Idaho Youth Ranch Rupert ID 83350

WRIGHT, GALE MARKS, technology services executive, consultant; b. Bainbridge, Md., Aug. 5, 1954; d. John Anthony and Mary Elizabeth (Borys) Marks; m. Robert George Wright II, Aug. 31, 1974 (div. Dec. 1987); children: Lyndsay Greer, Lesley Gale, Lacey Gage. Student, Allegheny Coll., 1972-73. Savs. mgr. First Nat. Bank, Colorado Springs, Colo., 1973-74; mgr. comml. loans and discounts First City Nat. Bank-El Paso, Tex., 1974-78; assoc. account mgmt. Hemphill Wells, Lubbock, Tex., 1979-80; customer svc. mgr. Southwest Lubbock (Tex.) Nat. Bank, 1980-82; asst. v.p. First City Bancorp., Dallas, 1982-86; sr. account exec. Hogan Systems, Inc., Dallas, 1986-89; assoc./account mgr. Perot Systems Corp., Dallas, 1989—. Pres. All Our Children Guild, Dallas, 1992-94; bd. dirs., guild liaison All Our Children Charity, Dallas, 1992-94. Mem. Fin. Women Internat. Roman Catholic. Office: Perot Systems Corp 12377 Merit Dr Ste 1100 Dallas TX 75251

WRIGHT, GLADYS STONE, music educator, composer, writer; b. Wasco, Oreg., Mar. 8, 1925; d. Murvel Stuart and Daisy Violet (Warren) Stone; m. Alfred George Wright, June 28, 1953. BS, U. Oreg., 1948, MS, 1953. Dir. bands Elmira (Oreg.) U-4 High Sch., 1948-53, Otterbein (Ind.) High Sch., 1954-61, Klondike High Sch., West Lafayette, Ind., 1962-70, Harrison High Sch., West Lafayette, 1970-84; organizer, condr. Musical Friendship Tours, Cen. Am., 1967-79; v.p., condr. U.S. Collegiate Wind Band, 1975—; bd. dirs. John Philip Sousa Found. 1984—; chmn. Sudler Cup, 1986—, Sudler Flag, 1982; pres. Internat. Music Tours, 1984—, Key to the City, Taxco, Mex., 1975. Editor: Woman Conductor, 1986—; composer: marches Big Bowl and Trumpets and Tabards, 1987; contbg. editor: Infornusica (Spain). Bd. dirs. N. Am. Wildlife Park, Battleground, Ind. 1985. Recipient Medal of the order John Philip Sousa Found., 1988, Star of Order, 1991; 1st woman guest conductor U.S. Navy Band, Washington D.C., 1961, Goldman Band, N.Y.C., 1958, Kneller Hall Band, London, 1975, Tri-State Music Festival Massed Orch., Band, Choir, 1985; elected to Women Bd. Dirs. Hall of Fame, 1994. Mem. Am. Bandmasters Assn. (bd. dirs. 1993, 1st woman mem.), Women Band Dirs. Nat. Assn. (founding pres. 1967, sec. 1985, recipient Silver Baton 1974, Golden Rose 1990), Am. Sch. Band Dirs. Assn., Nat. Band Assn. (recipient citation excellence 1970), Tippecanoe Arts Fedn. (bd. dirs. 1986-90), Tippecanoe Fife and Drum Corps. (bd. dirs. 1984), Tau Beta Sigma (Outstanding Service to Music award 1970), Phi Beta Mu (1st hon. woman mem. 1972).

WRIGHT, HELEN KENNEDY, professional association administrator, publisher, editor, librarian; b. Indpls., Sept. 23, 1927; d. William Henry and Ida Louise (Crosby) Kennedy; m. Samuel A. Wright, Sept. 5, 1970; 1 child, Carl F. Prince II (dec.). BA, Butler U., 1945, MS, 1950; MS, Columbia U., 1952. Reference libr. N.Y. Pub. Libr., N.Y.C., 1952-53, Bklyn. Pub. Libr., 1953-54; reference libr., cataloger U. Utah, 1954-57; libr. Chgo. Pub. Libr.; asst. dir. pub. dept. ALA, Chgo., 1958-62, editor Reference Books Bull., 1962-85, asst. dir. for new product planning, pub. svcs., 1985—, dir. office for libr. outreach svcs., 1987-90, mng. editor yearbook, 1988—. Contbr. to Ency. of Careers, Ency. of Libr. and Info. Sci., New Book of Knowledge Ency., Bulletin of Bibliography, New Golden Book Ency. Recipient Louis Shores/Oryx Pr. award, 1991. Mem. Phi Kappa Phi, Kappa Delta Pi, Sigma Gamma Rho. Roman Catholic. Home: 1138 W 111th St Chicago IL 60643-4508 Office: ALA 50 E Huron St Chicago IL 60611-2795

WRIGHT, HELENE SEGAL, editor; b. L.A., Jan. 31, 1955; d. Alan and Lila E. (Hambro) Segal; m. David Scott Wright, May 6, 1979. Student, Calif. State U., Fullerton, 1973-75; BA in English, U. Calif., Santa Barbara, 1978. Library asst. ABC-CLIO, Santa Barbara, 1979-80, editorial asst., 1980-81, asst. editor, 1981-83; mng. editor ABC-CLIO, ABC POL SCI, Santa Barbara, 1983—. Mem. Am. Polit. Sci. Assn., Current World Leaders (adv. bd. 1989—). Home: 142 La Vista Grande Santa Barbara CA 93103-2817 Office: ABC-CLIO 130 Cremona Dr Santa Barbara CA 93117-3075

WRIGHT, IDA JOHNSON, state official; b. Cocoa, Fla., June 20, 1933; d. Walter Richard and Ruth Mildred (Fitch) Johnson; m. James Wellington Hunt, July 10, 1954 (div. 1964); 1 child, Mary Evelyn; m. Fred Hamilton Wright, Jr., Nov. 22, 1972 (dec. 1992). AS, Polk C.C., Winter Haven, Fla., 1978, AA, 1980; BS in Mgmt., St. Leo (Fla.) Coll., 1989; MPA, U. South Fla., 1995. Cert. profl. sec., 1976. Sec. U.S. Air Force Civil Svc., Patrick AFB, Fla., 1953-60; exec. sec. GE Co., Patrick AFB, Fla., 1958-63; part-time v.p. Hunt Constrn. Co., Eau Gallie, Fla., 1960-63; exec. sec. to dir. Saturn/Apollo program McDonnell Douglas, Kennedy Space Ctr., Fla., 1964-72; exec. sec. W.R. Grace & Co., Bartow, Fla., 1973-81; sr. exec. sec. to pres. AMAX Chem. Co., Lakeland, Fla., 1981-84; asst. to pres. Allen & Co., Lakeland, Fla., 1985; clk. of commn. Fla. Citrus Commn., Lakeland, 1985—; part-time real estate salesperson Realty World/Griffin Assocs., Bartow, 1981-84; adj. faculty Polk C.C., 1986. Mem. bus. adv. bd. Polk C.C., 1984-85; team leader Paint Your Heart Out-Bartow, 1993-94; vol. Lakeland Reg. Med. Ctr. Auxiliary, 1992—. Mem. Profl. Secs. Internat. (chpt. pres. 1978), Am. Soc. Pub. Adminstrs., Am. Mgmt. Assn., Missile and Space Pioneers, Mosquito Beaters, Pilot Club. Democrat. Baptist. Office: Fla Dept of Citrus 1115 E Memorial Blvd Lakeland FL 33801-2021

WRIGHT, IRENE, artist; b. Detroit, May 1, 1926; d. Joseph and Esther (Hydu) Mrazik; m. C. Russell Wright, Sept. 16, 1950; children: James Joseph, Cinthia Jean, Richard Russell. Student, Ind. U. of Pa., 1976-78. One-woman shows include Nat. Bank of the Commonwealth, 1993. Mem. Ind. Area Art Assn., Ford City (Pa.) Art Assn. (pres. 1972-74). Home: 2220 Elm Dr Ford City PA 16226-1510

WRIGHT, JEAN NORMAN, elementary education educator; b. Norristown, Pa., June 20, 1931; d. John Rich and Mildred (Hitchcock) Norman; m. John A. Wright (dec. Mar. 1979); children: Lori Wright Lutter, Larry. BA cum laude, Cedar Crest Coll., Allentown, Pa., 1953. Cert. tchr., Pa. Elem. tchr. Upson Sch., Euclid, Ohio, 1953-55; tchr. art and music Schuylkill Elem. Sch., Phoenixville, Pa., 1965-70, elem. tchr., 1970—. Mem. alumni bd. dirs. Cedar Crest Coll., 1980-84; mem. Phoenixville Community Concert Bd., 1986—. Mem. NEA, Pa. Edn. Assn., Cedar Crest Coll. Alumnae Club (pres. 1962-64), Delta Kappa Gamma (pres. 1990-92). Republican. Presbyterian. Office: Schuylkill Elem Sch Whitehorse Rd Phoenixville PA 19460

WRIGHT, JEANNE, counselor; b. Clanton, Ala., Aug. 27, 1952; d. Elvin V. and Sara Nell (Mims) W.; m. J. Craig Gravlee, July 24, 1976 (div. Oct. 1980). BS, U. Montevallo, 1974, MEd, 1980; PhD, U. Ga., 1987. Lic. prof. counselor, Tex. Freshman orientation counselor U. Ala., Tuscaloosa, 1980, counselor spl. svc. program, 1980-81; coord. career devel. program Brenau Coll., Gainesville, Ga., 1983; coord. dept. counseling Ctr. for Counseling and Evaluation/U. Ga., Athens, 1985-87; staff psychotherapist U. Ga. Counseling Ctr., Athens, 1987; dir. counseling svcs. Adams State Coll., Alamosa, Colo., 1988-89; asst. prof. counseling Southwest Tex. State U., San Marcos, 1989-94, St. Mary's U., San Antonio, 1994—; counselor/evaluator Vocat. Rehab., Columbiana, Ala., 1974-79; counselor Career Svcs., U. Montevallo, 1979-80. Editorial bd.; Jour. of Mental Health Counseling, 1994; contbr. articles to profl. jours. Cons. Austin (Tex.) Mental Health, 1994; instr. Jung Soc. Austin, 1994. Mem. Assn. for Humanistic Edn. and Devel. (v.p. 1994), Am. Counseling Assn., Tex. Counseling Assn., Tex. Assn. for Humanistic Edn. (pres. 1992), AAUW, N.Y. Acad. Scis., Phi Delta Kappa.

WRIGHT, JEANNE ELIZABETH JASON, advertising executive; b. Washington, June 24, 1934; d. Robert Stewart and Elizabeth (Gaddis) Jason; m. Benjamin Hickman Wright, Oct. 30, 1965; stepchildren: Benjamin (dec.), Deborah, David, Patricia. B.A., Radcliffe Coll., 1956; M.A., U. Chgo., 1958. Psychiat. social worker Lake County Mental Health Clinic, Gary, Ind., Psychiat. and Psychosomatic Inst., Michael Reese Hosp., Chgo., Jewish Child Care Assn., N.Y.C., 1958-70; gen. mgr. Black Media, Inc. (advt. rep. co.), N.Y.C., 1970-74; pres. Black Media, Inc. (advt. rep. co.), 1974-75; pres., exec. editor, syndicator weekly editorial features Black Resources, Inc., N.Y.C., 1975—. Mem. planning com. First Black Power Conf., Newark, 1966, Second Black Power Conf., Phila., 1967, First Internat. Black Cultural & Bus. Expn., N.Y.C., 1971; nat. bd. dirs. Afro-Am. Family & Community Svcs., Inc., Chgo., 1971-75; founding coun. mem. Nat. Assault on Illiteracy Program, 1980—; pres. Metro-N.Y. chpt. Nat. Assn. Media Women, Inc., 1986-89. Recipient Pres.' award Nat. Assn. Black Women Attys., 1977, 2d ann. Freedom's Jour. award Journalism Students and Faculty of U. D.C. Dept. Communicative and Performing Arts, 1979, Communication award Harlem Svc. Ctr., ARC, 1988, Spl. award Beta Omicron chpt. Phi Delta Kappa, 1982; named Disting. Black Woman in Industry, Nat. Coun. Negro Women, 1981. Mem. AAAS, Nat. Assn. Social Workers, Acad. Cert. Social Workers, Nat. Assn. Media Women (pres. Met. N.Y. chpt. 1986-89, Nat. Media Woman of Yr. award 1984, 86, Founders award 1986), Newswomen's Club N.Y., U. Chgo. Alumni Assn., NAACP, Radcliffe Club, Harvard Club, Alpha Kappa Alpha. Democrat. Office: 231 W 29th St Ste 1205 New York NY 10001-5209 Home and Office: 19620 W Saint Andrews Dr Hialeah FL 33015-2340

WRIGHT, JUDITH MARGARET, law librarian, educator; b. Jackson, Tenn., Aug. 16, 1944; d. Joseph Clarence and Mary Catherine (Key) Wright; m. Mark A. Johnson, Apr. 17, 1976; children—Paul, Michael. B.S., Memphis State U., 1966; M.A., U. Chgo., 1971; J.D., DePaul U., 1980. Bar: Ill. 1980. Librarian Oceanway Sch., Jacksonville, Fla., 1966-67; program dir. ARC, South Vietnam, 1967-68; documents and reference librarian D'Angelo Law Library, U. Chgo., 1970-74, reference librarian, 1974-77, dir., lectr. in law, 1980—; mem. adv. bd. Legal Reference Svcs. Quar., 1981—. Mem. ABA, Am. Assn. Law Libraries, Chgo. Assn. Law Libraries. Democrat. Methodist. Home: 5525 S Harper Ave Chicago IL 60637-1829 Office: U Chgo D'Angelo Law Libr 1121 E 60th St Chicago IL 60637-2745

WRIGHT, JUDITH RAE, accountant; b. Paoli, Ind., Feb. 16, 1929; d. Samuel Earl and Bernice Louise (Lomax) Hudelson; m. James Edward Walters, July 11, 1947 (div. June 1971); children—Jamie Jo, Jennifer Rae; m. 2d, George Ralph Wright, Feb. 20, 1972 (dec. Apr. 1977). Student Northwood Inst., West Baden, Ind., 1968-69, Ind.-U.-Purdue U., Indpls., 1972-77. Acct., Ind. Hwy. Commn., Indpls., 1969-75, Ind. Dept. Correction, Indpls., 1975-76, Ind. Dept. Pub. Welfare, Indpls., 1976-78, Ind. Office Social Services, Indpls., 1978-79; acct. supr. Ind. Dept. Pub. Welfare, Indpls., 1979-92. Recipient Gov.'s Spl. Achievement award, 1992; Mem. Assn. Govt. Accts., Am. Legion Aux., Kappa Kappa Kappa. Republican. Mem. Christian Ch.

WRIGHT, KARA-LYN ANNETTE, software engineer; b. Phila., Feb. 27, 1963; d. Javis Leon and O. Elizabeth (Seals) W. BS in Computer Sci., Drexel U., 1986, MS in Computer Sci., 1992. Intake worker Wheel's Inc., Phila., 1983; staff cons. computer ctr. Drexel U., Phila., 1984, sr. cons., 1984-85; programmer E. I. duPont, Phila., 1985; sr. programmer, computer scientist RMS Techs., Inc., Marlton, N.J., 1986-94, tech. mgr. Geophys. Scis. Lab.; sr. programmer analyst SHL Systemhouse, Inc., Robbinsville, N.J., 1994—. Author manual: AFCAD Revisited, 1984; co-designer, implementor software. Recipient Letter of Commendation, U.S. Naval Acad., 1990. Mem. IEEE, Assn. for Computing Machinery. Home: 42 Medford Ln Willingboro NJ 08046-3121 Office: SHL Systemhouse Inc 350 Corporate Blvd Robbinsville NJ 08691

WRIGHT, KATHLEEN MARY, psychologist; b. Washington, Jan. 11, 1948; d. Ferrer Bruno and Virginia Mary (Barrett) Picchi; m. Thomas Michael Saczynski, April 5, 1969 (div. 1986); 1 child, Michelle Debra Saczynski; m. Kevin Vallee Wright, Dec. 19, 1987. BA in Psychology, Coll. William and Mary, 1970; MS in Adminstrn., George Washington U., 1972; MA in Psychology, New Sch. Soc. Rsch., 1976; PhD, Cornell U., 1983. Rsch. fellow dept. psychology Cornell U., Ithaca, N.Y., 1977-81; clin. psychology assoc. VA Med. Ctr., West Haven, Conn., 1981-83; postdoctoral fellow clin. psychology NIMH Yale Psychiatric Inst., New Haven, Conn., 1983-85; rsch. psychologist dept. mil. psychiatry Walter Reed Army Inst. Rsch., Washington, 1985—, dir. traumatic stress rsch. program, 1989—, dep. chief for sci., 1990-94, dep. chief, 1994—; rsch. asst. prof. psychiatry Uniformed Svcs. U. Health Scis., Bethesda, Md., 1988—. Co-editor Jour. Applied Behavior Sci., 1993—; contbr. articles to profl. jours., chpts. to books. Recipient Cert. Appreciation USAF, 1991. Fellow Inter-Univ. Seminar on Armed Forces and Soc.; mem. AAAS, APA, N.Y. Acad. Scis., Internat. Soc. Trauma Studies (program com. 1991). Office: Walter Reed Army Inst Rsch Forest Gln Bldg 101 Washington DC 20307

WRIGHT, KATIE HARPER, educational administrator, journalist; b. Crawfordsville, Ark., Oct. 5, 1923; d. James Hale and Connie Mary (Locke) Harper; BA, U. Ill., 1944; MEd, 1959; EdD, St. Louis U., 1979; m. Marvin Wright, Mar. 21, 1952; 1 dau., Virginia K. Jordan. Elem. and spl. edn. tchr. East St. Louis (Ill.) Pub. Schs., 1944-65, dir. Dist. 189 Instructional Materials Program, 1965-71, dir. spl. edn. Dists. 188, 189, 1971-77, asst. supt. programs, 1977-79; interim supt. East St. Louis Sch. Dist. 189, 1993-94; adj. faculty Harris/Stowe State Coll., 1980; mem. staff St. Louis U., 1989—; interim supt. Dist. 189 Schs., 1994—; cons. to numerous workshops, seminars in field; mem. study tour People's Republic of China, 1984. Mem. Ill. Commn. on Children, 1973-85, East St. Louis Bd. Election Commrs.; pres. bd. dirs. St. Clair County Mental Health Center, 1970-72, 87— (award 1992); bd. dirs. River Bluff coun. Girl Scouts U.S., 1979—, nat. bd. dirs., 1981-84; bd. dirs. United Way, 1979—, Urban League, 1979—; pres. bd. trustees East St. Louis Pub. Library, 1972-77; pres., bd. dirs. St. Clair County Mental Health Ctrs., 1987; adv. bd. Magna Bank; charter mem. Coalition of 100 Black Women; mem. coordinating council ethnic affairs Synod of Mid-Am., Presbyn. Ch. U.S.A; charter mem. Metro East Links Group; charter mem. Gateway chpt. The Links, Inc.; Ill. Minority/Female Bus. Coun., 1991—; mem. State of Ill. Corrections Sch. Bd. Author: Delta Sigma Theta/East St. Louis Chapter History, 1992. Recipient Lamp of Learning award East St. Louis Jr. Wednesday Club, 1965, Outstanding Working Woman award Downtown St. Louis, Inc., 1967, Ill. State citation for ednl. document Love is Not Enough, 1974, Delta Sigma Theta citation for document Good Works, 1979, Girl Scout Thanks badge, 1982, award Nat. Coun. Negro Women, 1983, Community Svc. award Met. East Bar Assn., 1983, Journalist award Sigma Gamma Rho, Spelman Coll. Alumni award, 1990, A World of Difference award, 1990, 91, Edn. award St. Louis YWCA, 1991, SIU-E-Kimmel award, 1991, St. Clair County Mental Health award, 1992, Gateway East Metropolitian Ministry Dr. M.L. King award, 1993; named Woman of Achievement, St. Louis Globe Democrat, 1974, Outstanding Adminstr. So. region Ill. Office Edn., 1975, Woman of Yr. in Edn. St. Clair County YWCA, 1987, Nat. Top Lady of the Yr., 1988; named to Vashon High Sch. Hall of Fame, 1989. Mem. Am. Libraries Trustees Assn. (regional v.p. 1978-79, 92, nat. sec. 1979-80), Ill. Commn. on Children, Mensa, Council for Exceptional Children, Top Ladies of Distinction (pres. 1987-91, nat. editor 1991—, journalism award 1992, Media award 1992), Delta Sigma Theta (chpt. pres. 1960-62), Kappa Delta Pi (pres. So. Ill. U. chpt. 1973-74), Phi Delta Kappa (Service Key award 1984, chpt. pres. 1984-85), Iota Phi Lambda, Pi Lambda Theta (chpt. pres. 1985-87). Republican. Presbyterian. Club: East St. Louis Women's (pres. 1973-75). Contbr. articles to profl. jours.; feature writer St. Louis Argus Newspaper, 1979—. Home: 733 N 40th St East Saint Louis IL 62205-2138

WRIGHT, LAURALI R. (BUNNY WRIGHT), writer; b. Saskatoon, Sask., Can., June 5, 1939; d. Sidney Victor and Evelyn Jane (Barber) Appleby; m. John Herbert, Jan. 6, 1962 (separated 1985); children: Victoria Kathleen, Johnna Margaret. Student, U. B.C., Carleton U., Banff Sch. Fine Arts, U. Calgary, Simon Fraser U., Burnaby, B.C., Can. Reporter The Calgary Herald, 1968-77, Calgary Albertan, Can., 1969-70; reporter, columnist Calgary Herald, 1970-76, asst. city editor, 1976-77; freelance writer Calgary, 1977—. Author: (novels) Neighbours, 1979 (New Alta. Novelist award Alta. Culture and Multiculturalism 1978), The Favorite, 1982, Among Friends, 1984, The Suspect, 1985 (Edgar Allan Poe Best Novel award Mystery Writers Am. 1986), Sleep While I Sing, 1986, Love in the Temperate Zone, 1988, A Chill Rain in January, 1989 (Arthur Ellis Best Novel award Crime Writers Can. 1990), Fall from Grace, 1991, Prized Possessions, 1993, A Touch of Panic, 1994. Mem. Writers Union Can., Authors' Guild of U.S., Internat. P.E.N., Mystery Writers of Am., Authors League Am., Periodical Writers Assn. Can., Writers Fedn. B.C. Office: Virginia Barber Lit Agy Inc 101 Fifth Ave New York NY 10003-1008

WRIGHT, LEOLA MARIE, music educator; b. Alexandria, La., Nov. 14; d. James Hunter and Elnora (Boxter) Lofton; m. Francis Hawthorne Wright (dec. June 1974); children—Ted Hawthorne, Francine Elaine, Hugh Gilbert. B.A., Huston Tillotson Coll., 1935; M.A. in Edn., Howard U., 1952; postgrad. Catholic U. Am., Tex. A&I U., Del Mar Coll. All level permanent life teaching cert., Tex. Tchr. music Kingsville Ind. Sch. Dist., Tex., 31 yrs.; pianist ch. sch. King Star Baptist Ch., Kingsville. Organizer, pres. Afro-Am. Hist. and Cultural Com. of Kingsville, 1974—; mem. council Camp Fire, Inc., Kingsville. Recipient Leadership award Afro-Am. Hist. and Cultural Com. Kingsville, 1984; Service award Kingsville Ind. Sch. Dist., 1985, Outstanding Tchr. award, 1984-85; award for ch., community and sch. services King Star Bapt. Ch., 1985. Mem. Tex. Music Educators Assn., Tex. State Tchrs. Assn., NEA, AAUW, Assn. Study Afro-Am. Life and History (life), Community Concerts Kingsville, Howard U. Prestige Clubs, Alpha Kappa Alpha. Baptist. Avocation: community work, especially with young people. Home: PO Box 300 Kingsville TX 78364-0300

WRIGHT, LILYAN BOYD, physical education educator; b. Upland, Pa., May 11, 1920; d. Albert Verlenden and Mabel (Warburton) Boyd; B.S., Temple U., 1942, M.Ed., 1946; Ed.D., Rutgers U., 1972; m. Richard P. Wright, Oct. 23, 1942; 1 child, Nicki Wright Vanek. Tchr. health and phys. edn. Woodbury (N.J.) High Sch., 1942-43, Glen-Nor High Sch., Glenolden, Pa., 1944-46, Chester (Pa.) High Sch., 1946-54; chmn. women's dept. health and phys. edn. Union (N.J.) High Sch., 1954-61; with Trenton State Coll., 1961-90, head women's program health and phys. edn., 1967-77, chmn. dept. health, phys. edn. and recreation, 1977-86, adj. faculty mem. 1990-92, prof. emeritus, 1991—; mem. N.J. State Com. Div. Girls and Women's Sports,

1958-80; chmn. New Atlantic Field Hockey Sectional Umpiring, 1981-85; chmn. New Atlantic Field Hockey Assn., 1985-90; with recreation after sch. program Newport Counseling Ctrl, 1992-93. Active Chester United Fund; water safety, first aid instr.; vestry Ch. Epiphany, Newport, N.H., 1992—, St. Luke's Episcopal Ch., 1988-91; trustee Olive Pettis Libr., Goshen, 1992—. ARC Scholarship in her honor N.J. Athletic Assn. Girls, 1971; named to Hall of Fame, Temple U., 1976. Recipient U.S. Field Hockey Assn. award, 1989, named Nat. Honorary Field Hockey Umpire. Mem. AAHPERD (chmn. Eastern Dist. Assn. Div. Girls and Women's Sports, sec. to council for services Eastern dist. 1979-80, chmn. 1980-81, chmn. com. on aging and adult devel. of ea. dist. 1993—, N.J. rep. to council for convs. 1984-85, Honor Fellow award 1986), N.J. AHPER (pres. 1974-75, past pres. 1975-76, v.p. phys. edn. div., parliamentarian 1990—, Disting. Service and Leadership award 1969, 93, Honor Fellow award 1977, Presdl. Citation award 1993, 95, Disting. Leadership award 1994), N.J. Women's Lacrosse Assn. (umpiring chmn. 1972-76), Nat. Assn. Phys. Edn. in Higher Edn., Eastern Assn. Phys. Edn. Coll. Women, North Jersey, Ctrl. Jersey bds. women's ofcls., Am., Pa. (v.p. 1953-54), Chester (pres. 1949-54) fedns. tchrs., U.S. Field Hockey Assn. (exec. com., chair honorary umpire award com. 1992), North Jersey Field Hockey Assn. (past pres.), N.H. Field Hockey Umpires' Assn., No. New Eng. Lacrosse Officials Bd., U.S. Women's LaCrosse Assn. (Honorary and Emeritus Umpiring Rating award), Kappa Delta Epsilon, Delta Psi Kappa (past pres. Phila. alumni chpt.), Kappa Delta Pi. Home: PO Box 239 Goshen NH 03752

WRIGHT, LINDA ELLEN, nurse educator; b. Elmira, N.Y., Mar. 4, 1943; d. Marcus Alton and Helen Marie (Eaton) W. Diploma, Arnot-Ogden Meml. Hosp., 1964; BSN, Alfred U., 1987; MS, Syracuse U., 1990. Staff RN med.-surg. Arnot-Ogden Meml. Hosp., Elmira, 1964-67, charge nurse, 1967-72, charge nurse NICU, 1972-76, asst. ob.-gyn. coord., 1976-78, asst. instr. sch. nursing, 1978-87, nursing instr., 1987—; exch. RN Rainbow Babies Children's Hosp., Univ. Hosp., Cleve., 1971; vis. RN Med. Coll. Va., Richmond. Supporter, vol. Children's Miracle Network. Mem. NOW, Assn. Women's Health, Obstetrics and Neonatal Nurses, N.Y. State Nurses Assn., Am. Cancer Soc. (edn. com.), Colonial Dames XVII Century, Nat. Parks and Conservation Assn., Wilderness Soc., Nature Conservancy, Ctr. for Marine Conservation, World Wildlife Fund, Sigma Theta Tau. Presbyterian. Home: 915 Lincoln St Elmira NY 14901-1806 Office: Arnot Ogden Med Ctr Grove St Elmira NY 14905

WRIGHT, LINDA JEAN, government relations executive; b. Chgo., Dec. 14, 1949; d. Eugene P. and Rosemary Margaret (Kiley) Kemph; m. Kelly W. Wright, Jr., Feb. 1979 (div. 1984); m. Samuel Neuwirth Klewans, Aug. 28, 1986 (div. 1991). Student Loretto Heights Coll., 1967-69, U. Ill., 1970-71. Asst. to v.p. Busey 1st Nat. Bank, Urbana, 1969-72; spa mgr., supr. sales tng. Venus and Apollo Health Club, San Antonio, 1973-76; owner Plant Shop, San Antonio, 1976-77; with Enterprise Bank, Falls Church, Va., 1977-84, comml. lending officer, 1978-84, sr. v.p., 1979-84, corp. sec. of bd. dirs., 1980-84; pres., CEO Fairfax Savs. Bank, 1984-87, Bankstar, N.A. (formerly Bank 2000 of Reston, N.A.), 1988-90; v.p. Ryan-McGinn Inc., Arlington, Va., 1991—; bd. dirs. INOVA Inst. Rsch. and Edn., 1990-94. Apptd. pub. ofcl., chmn. Va. Small Bus. Fin. Authority, Richmond, 1984-88; trustee Inova Health System, 1992—; mem. exec. com. Fairfax-Falls Ch., United Way, United Way Capital Area, Washington, 1984-85; Fairfax County Spl. Task Force, 1986; bd. dirs. Fairfax Com. of 100, 1993—; mem., bd. dirs. Hospice No. Va., Arlington, 1985-86, chmn. No. Va. Local Devel. Corp., 1986; mem. oper. bd. Fairfax Hosp., 1987-94; pres. No. Va. Transp. Alliance, 1987-92; bd. dirs. Va. Found. for Rsch. and Econ. Edn., 1989-91, No. Va. coun. Am. Heart Assn., 1989-94. Mem. Fairfax County C. of C. (dir., v.p., pres. 1987-88), Nat. Assn. Bank Women (chmn. No. Va. group 1980-81), Fairfax Hunt Club, Tower Club (bd. govs. 1989—). Roman Catholic. Avocations: aviation, fox hunting.

WRIGHT, MAE A., engineering and emergency management specialist; b. Northampton, Mass., Nov. 14, 1956; d. Lawrence Sheperd and Caroline Mary (La Rose) Wright; m. Frederick Wright Damerow, Aug. 7, 1981 (div. 1991). BSME, Worcester Poly. Inst., 1980. Assoc. engr. nuclear safety Westinghouse Electric Corp., Monroeville, Pa., 1978-80, engr. nuclear safety, 1980, shift tech. advisor Salem nuclear plant, 1980-81, engr. info. program, 1981-84, sr. engr. info. program, 1984, mgr. info. program, 1984-86, mgr. bus. rels., 1987-88; mgr. community rels. West Valley (N.Y.) Demonstration Project, 1988—, mgr. community rels. and total quality, 1990-91, mgr. ops. support, 1991—; speaker Campus Am., nationwide, 1979-81; bd. dirs. Energy Source Edn. Coun., Washington, 1987, pres. bd. dirs., 1988-90; mem. mgmt. com. Electric Info. Coun., N.D., 1987-89; mem. program com. U.S. Com. for Energy Awareness, Washington, 1987-89; mem. publs. subcom. U.S. Coun. for Energy Awareness, 1988-89. Office: W Valley Demonstration Project Rock Springs Rd West Valley NY 14171

WRIGHT, MARCILE K., school system administrator; b. Valdez, Alaska, Nov. 20, 1935; d. Dwight and Signe Aurora Thomas; m. Don C. Wright II, Aug. 21, 1958 (div. 1968) children: Lisa, Kimberly. BS, Brigham Young U., 1958; MS in Sch. Adminstrn., Calif. State U., L.A., 1972; EdD in Orgn. and Leadership, U. San Francisco, 1987. Cert. adminstr., elem. tchr., secondary tchr, Calif. Tchr. grades 7,8,9 Glendale (Calif.) Unified Sch. Dist., 1959-74; adminstr., athletic dir. Lake Washington Sch. Dist., Kirkland, Wa., 1974-75; asst. prin. Sinaloa Jr. High Sch., Novato, Calif., 1975-77; prin. Rincon Valley Jr. High Sch., Santa Rosa, Calif., 1977-81; dir. instrn. Liberty Union High Sch. Dist., Brentwood, Calif., 1981-85; asst. supt. ednl. svcs. Desert Sands Unified Sch. Dist., Indio, Calif., 1985-89; asst. supt. secondary edn. Moreno Valley (Calif.) Unified Sch. Dist., 1989-92; supt. Nuview Unified Sch. Dist., Nuevo, Calif., 1992—; adj. prof. Calif. State U., San Bernadino, 1988, Chapman Coll., 1991. Contbr. articles to profl. jours. Active Moreno Valley Unified Sch. Dist. Found., La Quinta Art Festival Found., Desert Orch. Soc.; exec. bd. dirs. YMCA of Coachella Valley; vol. Palm Desert Cerebral Palsy Telethon; mem. Desert Community Drug Edn. Adv. Com. Fulbright scholar, 1985; fellow Inst. for Devel. of Edn. Activities Charles F. Kettering Found., 1980, 82, 83, 86-92; recipient Cert. of Recognition Nat. Orgn. Student Assistance Programs and Profls. for Excellence in Student Assistance Programming. Mem. ASCD, Calif. Assn. Supervision & Curriculum Devel., Assn. Calif. Sch. Adminstrs., Calif. Assn. for Gifted/Talented, Calif. Elem. Edn. Assn., Fulbright Found. Alumni Assn., Phi Delta Kappa.

WRIGHT, MARGARET TAYLOR, marketing consultant; b. Wilmington, N.C., Nov. 8, 1949; d. Thomas Henry and Margaret (Taylor) W. BA, U. N.C., 1972; MBA, Wake Forest U., 1978. Child advocacy specialist Child Advocacy Council Dept. Human Resources, Raleigh, N.C., 1973-74; region dir. N.C. Office for Children Dept. Human Resources, Winston-Salem, 1974-76; product mgr. food div. Am. Home Products, N.Y.C., 1978-80; account exec. Ted Bates Advt., N.Y.C., 1981; product mgr. C.F. Mueller div. McKesson, Inc., Jersey City, 1981-83; mgr. new products Popsicle div. Sara Lee Corp., Englewood, N.J., 1983-86; pres. Wright Mktg. Blueprint, N.Y.C., 1987—. Co-author: (pamphlets) Children--Helping Them Grow, 1973. Youth coord. Jim Holshouser Gubernatorial Campaign, New Hanover County, N.C., 1972; mem. Jr. League, N.Y. and N.C., 1972-84. Episcopalian. Office: Wright Mktg Blueprint 400 E 54th St Apt 2D New York NY 10022-5165

WRIGHT, MARIE ANNE, management information systems educator; b. Albany, N.Y., Oct. 21, 1953; d. Arthur Irving and Ethel (Knickerbocker) W. BS, U. Mass., Boston, 1981; MBA, Clarkson U., 1984; PhD, U. Mass., Amherst, 1989. Systems analyst St. Lawrence U., Canton, N.Y., 1983-84; instr. Bentley Coll., Waltham, Mass., 1984-85; computer cons. Amherst (Mass.) Police Dept., 1986-88; asst. prof. Elms Coll., Chicopee, Mass., 1986-89; assoc. prof. Western Conn. State U., Danbury, 1990—; cons. Ctr. for Human Devel., Springfield, Mass., 1986-87, Early Childhood Ctr., 1986-87. Contbr. articles to profl. jours. and mags. Recipient Teaching Assistantship, U. Mass., 1985, Rsch. Assistantship, 1986; Grad. Assistantship, Clarkson U., Potsdam, N.Y., 1982, MIS award U. Mass., 1981. Mem. AAUW, IEEE, ACM, Math. Assn. Am., Communications Security Assn., Nat. Computer Security Assn., Info. systems Security Assn., Assn. Women in Math., Boston Computer Soc., Beta Gamma Sigma. Democrat. Office: Western Conn State U MIS Dept Danbury CT 06810

WRIGHT, MARY BETH, special education educator; b. Madison, Wis., Jan. 3, 1952; d. Harry Wesley and Rita Cecelia (Schreier) W. AA, U. Wis., LaCrosse, 1972; BA, U. South Fla., 1980, MA, 1982; doctoral student, Nova Southeastern U., 1994—. Subsitute tchr. Hillsborogh Pasco County Schs., Tampa and Land O'Lakes, Fla., 1980-81; tchr. specific learning disabilities Lutz (Fla.) Elem., 1981-86; tchr. specific learning disabilities, soccer coach Thomas Jefferson High Sch., Tampa, 1986-87; head tchr. Downtown Alt., Tampa, 1987-88; math and sci. tchr. Brandon (Fla.) Alt., 1988-91; specific learning disabilities tchr. King and Chamberlain High Sch., 1991—; tutor Hillsborough County Schs., 1981-91; cons. Hillsborough Cmty. Coll., Tampa, 1984-91; aerobics instr. Shapes Health Fitness, Tampa, YMCA, 1985-94. Scout leader Girl Scouts U.S.A., Tampa, 1981. Mem. Fla. Assn. for Children with Learning Disabilities, Hillsborough Classroom Tchrs. Assn., NEA, ASCD, Women in Mil. Svc., Orton Dyslexic Soc. Republican. Lutheran. Home: 11822 Wildeflower Pl Tampa FL 33617-2720 Office: King High Sch 6815 N 56th St Tampa FL 33610

WRIGHT, MARY JAMES, instructional designer; b. Charlottesville, Va., Aug. 20, 1946; d. Harry Beech and Virginia Allen (Root) James; m. Paul Sims Wright, July 26, 1969; children: Christopher Brennan, Keith Allen. BA summa cum laude, Mary Washington Coll., 1968; MA, Northwestern U., 1969; postgrad., Trinity Coll., 1981, Gallaudet U., 1991. Instr. drama and speech Mary Washington Coll., Fredericksburg, Va., 1969-71, Charles County Community Coll., La Plata, Md., 1973-79; arts and media coord. Charles County Arts Coun., La Plata, 1973-82, Gen. Smallwood Mid. Sch., Indian Head, Md., 1980-82, No. Va. Community Coll., Annandale, 1982-84; computer-based learning specialist USDA Grad. Sch., Washington, 1984-85, U.S. Army Engr. Sch., Ft. Belvoir, Va., 1985-87, Battelle Meml. Inst., Columbus, Ohio, 1987-88; videodisc designer Kendrick & Co., Washington, 1988-90; instrnl. design mgr. The Discovery Channel, Bethesda, Md., 1990-93; multimedia resource mgr. Edunetics Corp., Arlington, Va., 1993—; interactive multimedia designer and developer Smart House, Ltd. Partnership, Upper Marlboro, Md., 1990; project mgr. Toby Levine Comms., Inc., 1990-94; multimedia resources mgr. Edunetics Corp., 1994—. Author, dir.: (children's plays) Story-Theatre for Children, 1979; contbr. articles to profl. jours.; publisher classroom guides for nat. media products, PBS, Discovery Channel, Nat. Geographic. Pres. Am. Christian Television System of No. Va., Action for Women, Charles County AAUW; sign lang. interpreter Deaf Ministry. Nat. Danforth fellow 1969; recipient Achievement award Dept. of Army, 1986, Kendrick & Co., 1989; recipient Outstanding Arts Programming award Md. Dept. Parks and Recreation, 1980, Silver and Bronze Cindy awards Cinema in Industry and Edn., 1992, Red Ribbon Am. Film & Video Assn. Festival, Special Jury award Houston Internat. Film Festival, 1992, Gold award Nebr. Interactive Media, 1993. Mem. ASCD, Internat. Interactive Courseware Soc. (Mark of Excellence award 1992), Assn. for Devel. Computer-Based Instrn. Systems (coord. spl. interest groups D.C. chpt. 1989-90), No. Va. Registry Interpreters for the Deaf, Mortar Bd., Alpha Psi Omega, Alpha Phi Sigma. Home: 4302 Rolling Stone Way Alexandria VA 22306-1225 Office: 1600 Wilson Blvd Arlington VA 22209

WRIGHT, MARY R., state park superintendent; b. Hartford, Conn., Jan. 12, 1949; d. J. William and Eileen J. (Walsh) Bigoness; m. Roy C. Gunter III, June 24, 1972 (div. Feb. 1988); m. Kenneth Ross Wright, Dec. 1, 1988. BA, Marquette U., 1970; MS, U. Mo., 1972. Prgram analyst State Calif. Dept. Health, Sacramento, 1972-76; tng. ctr. dir. State Calif. Dept. Parks and Recreation, Pacific Grove, 1976-81; visitor svcs. mgr. State Calif. Dept. Parks and Recreation, Monterey, 1981-83, Monterey dist. supr., 1983-92, dep. dir., 1992-93; Monterey dist. supt. Calif. Dept. Parks and Recreation, 1993—; hist. preservation commr. City of Monterey, 1984-92. Bd. dirs. Big Sur Health Ctr., 1993—. Office: Monterey Dist Calif State Parks 2211 Garden Rd Monterey CA 93940

WRIGHT, MAUREEN ELIZABETH, marketing and sales company executive; b. Oak Park, Ill., Nov. 7, 1954; d. John James and Mary Maxine (Elliott) Mulvey; m. Bruce David Wright, Mar. 27, 1988; stepchildren: David, Kenneth. BA, So. Ill. U., 1979, MBA, 1984. Cons. Solution Mktg./Wright & Assocs., Carbondale, Ill., 1978-94; internat. strategic planning and devel. mgr. GTE Airfone, Inc., Oak Brook, Ill., 1984-87; pres. Creditfone, Inc., Chgo. and L.A., 1987-88; dir. mktg. Met. Fiber Systems, Inc., Oakbrook Terrace, Ill., 1988-89; v.p. sales and mktg. Telular, Inc., Wilmette, Ill., 1989-91; cons. J&E Mktg. & Solution Mktg., Carbondale, 1978-84; tchr. mktg. So. Ill. U. Coll. Bus., Carbondale, 1983-84. Recipient Honors award Direct Mktg. Inst., 1986, Cert. of Achievement Entrepreneurship Inst., 1987. Mem. Alpha Mu Alpha. Mem. Christian Ch. Home: 14501 SE 78th Way Renton WA 98059

WRIGHT, MILDRED ANNE (MILLY WRIGHT), conservator, researcher; b. Athens, Ala., Sept. 9, 1939; d. Thomas Howard and Anne Louise (Ashworth) Speegle; m. William Paul Wright, Nov. 20, 1965; children: Paul Howard, William Neal. BS in Physics, U. Ala., Tuscaloosa, 1963. Researcher in acoustics Wyle Labs., Huntsville, Ala., 1963-64; tchr. physics, English Huntsville High Sch., 1964-67; ptnr. Flying Carpet Oriental Rugs, Florence, Ala., 1974—; adj. mem. faculty U. North Ala., Florence, 1988, lectr. Inst. for Learning in Retirement, 1991—. Columnist Times Daily, 1992—; photojournalist, writer River Views Mag., 1993—; contbr. articles to profl. jours. (1st pl. award 1986, 87). Pianist, organist Edgemont Meth. Ch., Florence, 1987-90 (Outstanding Svc. award 1990); mem. steering com. Melton Hollow Nature Ctr., Florence, 1990—, Design Ala., Florence, 1991, River Heritage Discovery Camp, 1993—; mem. River Heritage Com., Florence, 1991—; accompanist Shoals Boy Choir, Muscle Shoals, Ala., 1992-93; bd. dirs. Heritage Preservation, Inc., 1989—, Capital award 1992, pres., 1990-92, treas. 1995—, Tenn. Valley Hist. Soc., pres., 1991-95, Ala. Preservation Alliance, treas., 1993—, Florence Main Street program, 1992-94, Maud Lindsay Free Kindergarten, Frank Lloyd Wright Rosenbaum House Found., Inc. , 1992—, Gen. Joseph Wheeler Home Found., 1994—, treas. 1995—, Friends of the Ala. Archives, 1995—; mem. adv. coun. Human Environ. Scis. Dept.; mem. Coby Hall steering com. U. North Ala., 1992—. Recipient Disting. Svc. award Ala. Hist. Commn., 1991. Mem. AAUW, Ala. Writers' Conclave (Creative Works award 1986, 87), Ala. Hist. Assn., Ala. Archeol. Soc., Natchez Trace Geneal. Soc., Colbert County Hist. Landmarks Found., Nat. Trust for Hist. Preservation, Firenze Club, Optimist Club, Sigma Pi Sigma. Home: PO Box 279 Florence AL 35631

WRIGHT, NANCY HOWELL, interior designer; b. Detroit, Sept. 6, 1932; d. David Austin and Catherine (Bradley) Howell; BFA, Ohio Wesleyan U.; student, Parsons Sch. Design, 1977; m. Hastings Kemper Wright, June 19, 1954; children: Mark, Kenneth, Barbara, Donald. Interior decorator Country Manor of Branford (Conn.), 1971-75, design mgr., 1976—. Sec. Branford Art League, 1977; chmn. Harrison House Hist. House, Branford, Conn., 1983-84; mem. Rep. Town Com., Branford, 1990-92; recording sec. Branford Garden Club, 1991—. Mem. Am. Soc. Interior Designers (award for best Conn. retail store design, 1980, Conn. Coalition), Branford Garden Club (rec. sec. 1990-94, membership chmn. 1995), Delta Phi Delta. Republican. Episcopalian. Home: 35 Wood Rd Branford CT 06405-4935 Office: 312 E Main St Branford CT 06405

WRIGHT, OLGA, artist, aesthetician; b. Mangum, Okla., Feb. 6, 1932; m. George Wayne Polly, Jr., Aug. 21, 1956. Student, N.Y. Art Students League, 1959; BS, Arts and Industries U., Kingsville, Tex., 1962. Owner Olga Wright Aesthetics, Corpus Christi, Tex., 1937—. One-woman shows include Centenial Mus., 1978. Recipient Best of Show award Dimension Show, 1977, Best Oil of Show award, 1977, 79. Mem. Art Ctr. Corpus Christi. Home: 4238 Estate Dr Corpus Christi TX 78412-2429 Office: Olga Wright Aesthetics 4238 Estate Dr Corpus Christi TX 78412-2429

WRIGHT, PATRICIA, state legislator; b. South Bend, Ind., Feb. 28, 1931; m. Paul J. Wright, 1951; children: Timothy, Patrick M. Mem. Ariz. State Senate. Republican. Home: 5818 W Northern Ave Glendale AZ 85301-1337 Office: Ariz Senate State House Phoenix AZ 85007*

WRIGHT, ROSALIE MULLER, newspaper and magazine editor; b. Newark, June 20, 1942; d. Charles and Angela (Fortunata) Muller; m. Lynn Wright, Jan. 13, 1962; children: James Anthony Meador, Geoffrey Shepard. BA in English, Temple U., 1965. Mng. editor Suburban Life mag., Orange, N.J., 1960-62; assoc. editor Phila. mag., 1962-64, mng. editor, 1969-73; founding editor Womensports mag., San Mateo, Calif., 1973-75; editor scene sect. San Francisco Examiner, 1975-77; exec. editor New West mag., San Francisco and Beverly Hills, Calif., 1977-81; features and Sunday editor San Francisco Chronicle, 1981-87, asst. mng. editor features, 1987—; tchr. mag. writing U. Calif., Berkeley, 1975-76; participant pub. procedures course Stanford U., 1977-79; chmn. mag. judges at conf. Coun. Advancement and Support of Edn., 1980, judge, 1984. Contbr. numerous mag. articles, critiques, revs., Compton's Ency. Mem. Am. Assn. Sun and Feature Editors (treas. 1984, sec. 1985, 1st v.p. 1986, pres. 1987), Am. Newspaper Pub. Assn. (pub. task force on minorities in newspaper bus. 1988-89, Chronicle minority recruiter 1987—), Calif. Soc. Newspaper Editors, Internat. Women's Forum, Women's Forum West (bd. dirs. 1993—, sec. 1994). Office: Chronicle Pub Co 901 Mission St San Francisco CA 94103-2905

WRIGHT, SARA-ALYCE PARSON, retired association executive; b. Harrisburg, Pa., Jan. 25, 1918; d. Henry Edwin and Fannie Katherine (Jackson) Parson; m. Emmett Franklin Wright, July 18, 1951. B.S. in Edn, Westchester State Coll., Pa., 1939; MS, U. Pa., 1945; MSW, U. Pitts., 1951; postgrad., Columbia U. Tchrs. Coll., 1960-61; HHD (hon.), North Adams State Coll., 1980. Tchr. Oxford Public Schs., Pa., 1939-41, Harrisburg, Pa., 1941-45; dir. teenage program YWCA, Youngstown, Ohio, 1945-49; nat. cons. teenage programs nat. bd. YWCA, N.Y.C., 1951-63, correlator teenage program, 1963-65; assoc. exec. dir. YWCA, 1965-66; dir. Freeport Youth Service Project of Family Service Assn. of Nassau County, N.Y., 1966-70; sch. community officer Freeport Public Schs., 1970-71; dep. exec. dir. nat. bd. YWCA of the U.S.A., N.Y.C., 1971-74; exec. dir. YWCA of the U.S.A., 1974-84, now ret.; nat. adv. com. White House Conf. on Aging. Contbr. articles to profl. jours. Charter mem. bd. dirs. Ind. Sector., now ret.; trustee Am. Bible Soc., N.Y.C., United Neighborhood Ctrs. Am., N.Y.C. and Washington; mem. gen. bd. Am. Baptist Chs. in U.S.A.; bd. dirs., exec. com. Family Service Assn. Nassau County, N.Y. Named Disting. Pennsylvanian, 1975; recipient Candace award Nat. Coalition of 100 Black Women, 1982, Equal Opportunity award Nat. Urban League, 1984, Disting. Alumnus award Westchester State Coll. (now Univ.), 1981, Bicentennial Medal Distinction U. Pitts., 1987, Ambassador award YWCA of the U.S.A., 1993. Mem. Nat. Assn. Social Workers, Nat. Assembly of Nat. Vol. Health and Social Welfare Orgns. (past pres.), Nat. Conf. Social Welfare (past dir.), Nat. Center Vol. Action (past dir.), Council Social Work Edn. (ho. of dels.), Nat. Council Negro Women, Nat. Assn. Negro Bus. and Profl. Women, Lambda Kappa Mu (Public Service award 1975), Delta Sigma Theta (Public Service award 1974).

WRIGHT, STEPHANIE M.G., aerospace educator; b. Boulder, Colo., Apr. 9, 1948; d. Henry J. and Dorothy J. (Puvodnic) Gerjovich; m. Brian Harry, Aug. 23, 1975; children: Henry Gordon, Harry Charles. BA, U. Del., 1970, MEd, 1976; DEd, Temple U., 1987. Music educator Alexis I. DuPont Sch. Dist., Del., 1970-78, Red Clay Consol. Dist., Del., 1978-89; space ambassador NASA, Washington, 1985—; dir. aerospace edn. Del. Tchr. Ctr., Dover, 1989—; pres., dir. Del. Aerospace Edn. Found./Del. Aerospace Acad., 1990—; adv. bd. Bartol Rsch. Inst., Newark, 1991—; steering mem. Challenger Ctr., Alexandria, Va., 1988—. Contbr. articles to profl. jours. Block rep. Caravel Civic Assn., Bear, Del., 1983—. Tchr. in Space award Dept. Pub. Instruction, NASA, Del., 1985, Christa McAuliffe fellowship Dept. Edn., Women in Aerospace Edn. award, Washington, 1988, Aerospace Educator award, 1992, 5-Yr. Svc. pin Challenger Ctr. for Space Sci. Edn., Alexandria, Va., 1993. Mem. Alumni Assn. U. Del. (exec. bd. mem. 1990-93, Hall of Fame 1989), Edn. Alumni Assn./U. Del. (exec. bd., pres. 1986-94), Sci. Alliance (bd. dirs. 1992-95, Sci. Recognition award 1992), Air Force Assn. (exec. bd. dir., state v.p. 1991—, Premier Salute 1993), AAUW, Phi Delta Kappa. Home: 5 Essex Dr Bear DE 19701

WRIGHT, SUSAN WEBBER, federal judge; b. Texarkana, Ark., Aug. 22, 1948; d. Thomas Edward and Betty Jane (Gary) Webber; m. Robert Ross Wright, III, May 21, 1983; 1 child, Robin Elizabeth. BA, Randolph-Macon Woman's Coll., 1970; MPA, U. Ark., 1972, JD with high honors, 1975. Bar: Ark. 1975. Law clk. U.S. Ct. Appeals 8th Circuit, 1975-76; asst. prof. law U. Ark.-Little Rock, 1976-78, assoc. prof., 1978-83, prof., 1983-90, asst. dean, 1976-78; dist. judge U.S. Dist. Ct. (ea. dist.) Ark., Little Rock, 1990—; vis. assoc. prof. Ohio State U., Columbus, 1981, La. State U., Baton Rouge, 1982-83; mem. adv. com. U.S. Ct. Appeals 8th Circuit, St. Louis, 1983-88. Author: (with R. Wright) Land Use in a Nutshell, 1978, 2d edit., 1985; editor-in-chief Ark. Law Rev., 1975; contbr. articles to profl. jours. Mem. ABA, Ark. Bar Assn., Pulaski County Bar Assn., Ark. Assn. Women Lawyers (v.p. 1977-78). Episcopalian. Office: US Courthouse 600 W Capitol Ave Ste 302 Little Rock AR 72201-3329

WRIGHT, TAMELA JEAN (T.J. WRIGHT), disc jockey, entertainer; b. Webb City, Mo., Jan. 20, 1962; d. Eugene I. and Fay Marie (Regenwold) W.; m. John Beckmman. Student, Lindenwood Coll., 1980-82. With radio Sta. KSHE, St. Louis, 1982, Sta. KMJM, St. Louis, 1982-83, Sta. KHTR, Sta. KWK, St. Louis, 1985; with radio Sta. WKSS, Hartford, Conn., 1986, San Jose, Calif., 1986-87; with radio Sta. WPGC, Washington, 1987-88, Sta. WAVA, Washington, 1988, Sta. WDJY-FM, Washington, 1988-89, Sta. KHTK, St. Louis, 1989-90; KWTX, Waco, Tex., 1990, WMIX, Balt., 1991, WNFI, Daytona Beach, Fla., 1992; tchr. La Petite Presch., 1993—; with radio sta. WCBW, St. Louis; interviewee Nightwatch, CBS, All Things Considered, Nat. Pub. Radio, Washington, Dec., 1987; writer Parenting Network publ., 1993. Narrator local fashion shows, Vandalia, Mo., San Jose, 1983-86; appearances include nat. syndicated show Party Am., 1986-87, Music Machine Video Sta. WFTY-TV, Washington, 1988, Nightwatch CBS and All Things Considered Nat. Pub. Radio, Washington, 1987; announcer radio commls., St. Louis, 1989—; contbr. Student Voice newspaper, 1989—; subject articles in various publs. Telethon vol. Easter Seals, Washington, 1989, Muscular Dystrophy Assn., St. Louis, 1989; flood clean-up vol. St. Louis Family Ch., Chesterfield, Mo.; vol. homeless shelter, Thanksgiving 1993. Mem. AFTRA, Am. Women in Radio & TV, Friends of Kennedy Ctr. (assoc.). Home: 4066 Sir Bors Ct # 2 Saint Louis MO 63129 Office: WCBW 4121 Union Rd Ste 201 Saint Louis MO 63129-1070

WRIGHT, THERESA LOUISE, law educator; b. New Haven, Jan. 20, 1955; d. Christopher and Margaret L. (Knapp) W.; m. Philip Hornik, July 16, 1989. BA, Evergreen State Coll., 1977; JD, Willamette U., 1981. Bar: Oreg. 1981, Wash. 1987, U.S. Dist. Ct. Oreg. 1984. Bus. agt. Oreg. Sch. Employees Assn., Salem and Portland, 1980-84; mng. atty. Hyatt Legal Svcs., Portland, 1984-86; clin. prof. law Willamette U. Law Sch., Salem, 1986-90, Lewis and Clark Coll., Portland, 1990—. Sec. Cascade AIDS Project, 1986-92, vice-chair, 1992-93, pres., 1993—. Mem. Nat. Lawyers Guild (exec. v.p. 1993—), Portland Bar Assn. (com. mem. 1988—), Multnomah Bar Assn. Office: Lewis and Clark Legal Clin # 108 310 SW 4th Portland OR 97204

WRIGHT-WATKINS, CHERYL, air traffic controller; b. Louisville, Jan. 3, 1957; d. Walter Lee and Lois (Lockard) W.; m. James C. Watkins Jr., June 5, 1992. Sec., personnel clk. Readiness Region, Ft. Knox, Ky., 1976-80; adminstrv. asst. Readiness Ragion, Ft. Knox, Ky., 1980-82; air traffic specialist Memphis Air Traffic Control Ctr., 1982-89, air traffic control supr., 1989—. Recipient Meritorious Performance award, FAA, 1992, 93, Exceptional Performance award, 1990-91. Democrat. Episcopalian. Home: 9218 Rosalie Olive Branch MS 38654-1665 Office: Memphis Air Rate Traffic Control Ctr 3229 Democrat Rd Memphis TN 38118-1513

WRIGLEY, ELIZABETH SPRINGER (MRS. OLIVER K. WRIGLEY), foundation executive; b. Pitts., Oct. 4, 1915; d. Charles Woodward and Sarah Maria (Roberts) Springer; BA U. Pitts., 1935; BS, Carnegie Inst. Tech., 1936; m. Oliver Kenneth Wrigley, June 16, 1936 (dec. July 1978). Procedure analyst U.S. Steel Corp., Pitts., 1941-43; rsch. asst. The Francis Bacon Found., Inc., Los Angeles, 1944, exec., 1945-50, trustee, 1950—, dir. rsch., 1951-53, pres., 1954—, dir. Francis Bacon Libr.; mem. adv. coun. Shakespeare Authorship Roundtable, Santa Monica, Calif.; mem. regional Fine Arts adv. coun. Calif. State Poly. U., Pomona. Mem. ALA, Calif. Libr. Assn., Renaissance Soc. Am., Modern Humanities Rsch. Assn., Cryptogram Assn., Alpha Delta Pi. Presbyn. Mem. Order Eastern Star, Damascus Shrine. Editor: The Skeleton Text of the Shakespeare Folio L.A. (by W.C. Arensberg), 1952. Compiler: Short Title Catalogue Numbers in the Library of the Francis Bacon Foundation, 1958; Wing Numbers in the Library of the Francis Bacon Foundation, 1959; Supplement To Francis Bacon Library Holdings in the STC of English Books, 1967; (with David W. Davies) A

Concordance to the Essays of Francis Bacon, 1973. Home: 4805 N Pal Mal Ave Temple City CA 91780-4129 Office: Francis Bacon Libr 655 N Dartmouth Ave Claremont CA 91711-3979

WRISTON, KATHRYN DINEEN, lawyer, business executive; b. Syracuse, N.Y.; d. Robert Emmet and Carolyn (Bareham) Dineen; m. Walter B. Wriston, Mar. 14, 1968; 1 stepchild. Student, U. Geneva, 1958-59; BA cum laude, Smith Coll., 1960; LLB, U. Mich., 1963. Bar: N.Y.1964, U.S. Ct. Appeals (2nd cir.) 1964, U.S. Supreme Ct. 1968. Assoc. Shearman & Sterling, N.Y.C., 1963-68; bd. dirs. Northwestern Mut. Life Ins. Co., mem. ins. products and mktg. com., 1986-89, mem. audit com., 1989—, mem. investment and fin. policy com., 1989—; bd. dirs. Santa Fe Energy Resources, Inc., mem. audit com., 1990—, chmn., 1990-93, mem. nominating com., 1990—; trustee Fin. Acctg. Found., 1992—, mem. selection com., 1992—, mem. audit com., 1992—, chmn., 1993—, mem. fin. com., 1994—, mem. nominating com., 1994—; mem. task force on timely fin. reporting guidanace Fin. Acctg. Stds. Bd., 1982-83, mem. bd. agenda adv. com., 1981-85, mem. process and structure com., 1981-85, chmn., 1983-85; mem. exec. com. CPR Inst. for Dispute Resolution, 1994—. Mem. vis. com. U. Mich. Law Sch., 1973—; trustee Fordham U., Bronx, N.Y., 1971-77, 78-81, vice chmn. bd. trustees, 1980-81, mem. student affairs com., 1971-77, chmn., 1974-77, mem. faculty affairs com., 1978-81, mem. grievance com., 1971-77, 78-81, mem. com. on law sch., 1978-81; mem. ea. region selection panel Pres. Commn. on White House Fellowships, 1981-83, chmn., 1982-83; mem. bus. com. Nat. Ctr. for State Cts., 1982-88; bd. overseers Rand Inst. for Civil Justice, 1985-93; trustee John A. Hartford Found., 1991—, mem. grant com., 1991—, vice chmn., 1992—, mem. evaluation com., 1991—, mem. audit com., 1992—, chmn., 1993—; active Gov. Wilson's N.Y. Little Hoover Commn., 1974. Mem. ABA, Nat. Assn. Accts., Practicing Law Inst. (exec. 1976—, mem. programs and publs. com., chmn. 1979—, mem. membership com. 1976—, chmn. 1977-79, mem. nominating com. 1978, 81-85, mem. bar rev. courses 1978-79, mem. fin. com. 1989—, mem. Am. Law Inst./ABA subcom. on Am. law network 1989-91), Fin. Women's Assn. N.Y., N.Y. County Lawyers Assn. (legal aid com. 1972-76), N.Y. State Bar Assn., Assn. Bar City N.Y.

WROBLESKI, JEANNE PAULINE, lawyer; b. Phila., Feb. 14, 1942; d. Edward Joseph and Pauline (Popelak) W.; m. Robert J. Klein, Dec. 3, 1979. BA, Immaculata Coll., 1964; MA, U. Pa., 1966; JD, Temple U., 1975. Bar: Pa. 1975. Pvt. practice law, Phila., 1975—; ptnr. Kohn, Nast & Graf, P.C. Mem. Commn. on Women and the Legal Profession, 1986-89; v.p. Center City Residents' Assn. Eisenhower Citizen Amb. del. to Soviet Union. Rhea Liebman scholar, 1974; bd. dirs. South St. Dance Co.; bd. dirs., mem. exec. com. Temple Law Alumni; del. to Moscow con. on law and econ. coop., 1990; del. to jud. conf. for 3d cir. U.S. Ct. Appeals, 1991. Mem. AAUW, ABA, Pa Bar Assn., Phila. Bar Assn. (chmn. women's rights com. 1986, com. on jud. selection and reform 1986-87, chmn. appellate cts. com. 1992, bus. cts. task force), Pa. Acad. Fine Arts, Nat. Mus. Women in the Arts, Am. Judicature Soc., Jagiellonian Law Soc., Alpha Psi Omega, Lambda Iota Tau. Democrat. Clubs: Lawyers, Founders, Peale, Penn. Office: Kohn Nast & Graf PC 2400 One Reading Ctr 1101 Market St Philadelphia PA 19107-2934

WROBLOWA, HALINA STEFANIA, electrochemist; b. Gdansk, Poland, July 5, 1925; came to U.S., 1960, naturalized, 1970; M.Sc., U. Lodz (Poland), 1949; Ph.D., Warsaw Inst. Tech., 1958; 1 dau., Krystyna Wrobel-Knight. Chmn. dept. prep. studies U. Lodz, 1950-53; adj. Inst. for Phys. Chemistry, Acad. Scis., Warsaw, Poland, 1958-60; dep. dir. electrochemistry lab. Energy Inst., U. Pa., Phila., 1960-67, dir. electrochemistry lab., 1968-75; prin. research scientist Ford Motor Co., Dearborn, Mich., 1978-91; pvt. practice cons., 1991—. Served with Polish Underground Army, 1943-45. Decorated Silver Cross of Merit with Swords. Mem. Electrochem. Soc., Internat. Electrochem. Soc., Mensa, Sigma Xi. Contbr. chpts. to books, articles to profl. jours., patent lit.

WRUCKE-NELSON, ANN C., elementary school educator; b. Mankato, Minn., Nov. 5, 1939; d. G.F. and Dorothy (Thomas) Wrucke; children: Chris, Dor-Ella. BS, Mankato State U., 1961; MLA, So. Meth. U., 1974; postgrad., U. Minn., 1963, Tex. Woman's U.; EdD in Early Childhood Edn., Tex. Woman's U., 1992. Cert. elem., kindergarten, bilingual-ESL, history tchr., Tex. Tchr. Rochester (Minn.) Pub. Schs., Christ the King Sch., Dallas; dir., tchr. Norway Christian Presch., Dallas; Every Student Learns Lang. program kindergarten tchr. Dallas Ind. Sch. Dist.; tchr. summer session Tex. Woman's U., 1991; presenter in field. Producer video: A Year of Language Learning, 1990. Sunday sch. tchr. Holy Trinity Ch. Recipient Tchr. of Yr. award, 1989, Tex. TESOL scholarship, 1994; scholar Mankato State U., Bill Martin Literacy Conf.; named ESL Tchr. Yr., 1991. Mem. Assn. for Childhood Edn. Internat., So. Assn. on Children Under Six, Tchrs. English to Speakers Other Lang., Tex. Tchrs. English to Speakers Other Lang., Dallas Assn. for Edn. of Young Child.

WU, JIN ZHONG, theoretical computational solid state physicist; b. Chengdu, Sichuan, China, Jan. 5, 1945; came to U.S., 1981; d. Chieh Wu and Shuying Zhang; m. Yue Ping Lu, Feb. 18, 1976; 1 child, Ying Jie Lu. BS in Physics, Beijing U., 1967; MS, U. Sci. and Tech. of China, Beijing, 1981; MS in Physics, U. Cin., 1983, PhD in Physics, 1988. Assoc. engr. Beijing Semiconductor Devices Inst., 1970-79; rsch. assoc. Inst. of Semiconductors, Chinese Acad. Scis., Beijing, 1981; postdoctoral assoc. Quantum Theory Project U. Fla., Gainesville, 1988-91; asst. scientist U. Fla., Gainesville, 1991—. Contbr. articles to Phys. Rev. B., Nuclear Instruments and Methods in Physics Rsch. and Internat. Jour. of Quantum Chemistry. Mem. Am. Phys. Soc. Office: U Fla Quantum Theory Project Dept Physics Gainesville FL 32611

WU, NAN FAION, pediatrician; b. Malaysia, July 13, 1943; came to U.S., 1969; m. Chia F. Wu, June 22, 1969; children: Edwin, Karen. MD, Nat. Taiwan U., 1969. Diplomate Am. Bd. Pediatrics. Intern Atlantic City Med. Ctr., 1969-70; resident in pediatrics Martland Hosp. U. Medicine and Dentistry of N.J., N.J. Med. Sch., Newark, 1970-73; pvt. practice pediatrics West Orange, N.J. Fellow Am. Acad. Pediatrics. Office: 35 Park Ave West Orange NJ 07052-5526

WU, YING CHU LIN SUSAN, engineering company executive, engineer; b. Beijing, June 23, 1932; came to U.S., 1957; d. Chi-yu and K.C. (Kung) Lin; m. Jain-Ming Wu, June 13, 1959; children: Ernest H., Albert H., Karen H. BSME, Nat. Taiwan U., 1955; MS in Aero. Engring., Ohio State U., 1959; PhD in Aeros., Calif. Inst. Tech., 1963. Sr. engr. Elecro-Optical Systems, Inc., Pasadena, Calif., 1963-65; asst. prof. aero. engring. U. Tenn. Space Inst., Tullahoma, 1965-67, assoc. prof., 1967-73, prof., 1973-88; adminstr. Energy Conversion R&D Programs, Tullahoma, 1981-88; pres., chief exec. officer ERC, Inc., Tullahoma, 1987—; presdl. appointee adv. bd. Nat. Air and Space Mus., Smithsonian Inst., 1993—. Contbr. over 90 articles to profl. jours. Mem. Better Sch. Task Force, Tullahoma, 1985-86; founding mem. Tullahoma Edn. Found. for Excellence; trustee Rochester Inst. Tech., 1992—. Recipient Chancellor's Rsch. award U. Tenn., 1978, Outstanding Educator of Am. award, 1973, 75; Amelia Earhart fellow, 1958, 59, 62. Fellow ASME, AIAA (assoc., chmn. Tenn. sect., H.H. Arnold award 1984, Plasmodynamics and Lasers award 1994); mem. Soc. Women Engrs. (life mem., achievement award 1985), Rotary, Sigma Xi (chmn. U. Tenn. Space Inst. club). Home: 1451 Rocky Ridge Dr Apt 809 Roseville CA 95661-3006 Office: ERC Inc PO Box 417 Tullahoma TN 37388-0417

WUDUNN, SHERYL, journalist, correspondent; b. N.Y.C., Nov. 16, 1959; d. David and Alice (Mark) W.; m. Nicholas D. Kristof, Oct. 8, 1988. BA, Cornell U., Ithaca, N.Y., 1981; MBA, Harvard U., 1986; MPA, Princeton U., 1988. Lending officer Bankers Trust Co., N.Y.C., 1981-84; intern reporter Wall St. Jour., L.A., 1986; bus. reporter South China Morning Post, Hong Kong, 1987; corr. N.Y. Times, Beijing, 1989-93, Tokyo, 1995—. Co-author: China Wakes, 1994. Recipient Pulitzer prize for fgn. reporting, 1990, George Polk award L.I. U., N.Y., 1990, Hal Boyle award Overseas Press Club, 1990. Home: 35 W 89th St New York NY 10024 Office: NY Times 229 W 43rd St New York NY 10036-3913

WUEBKER, COLLEEN MARIE, librarian; b. LaCrosse, Wis., June 22, 1943; d. Harris M. and Mary Frances (Collins) Gruber; m. William Joseph Wuebker, Aug. 14, 1965; children: Jon Paul, Timothy William, Maree Jean. BA, Mount Mercy Coll., 1965; MS, Mankato State U., 1975. Cert. permanent profl. media specialist, tchr., Iowa. Secondary tchr. Luverne Community Sch., Minn., 1965-66; tchr. St. Mary's Sch., Larchwood, Iowa, 1966; secondary tchr. SEMCO Community Sch., Gilman, Iowa, 1966-67; substitute tchr. West Bend (Iowa) Community Schs., 1968-74, sch. media specialist, 1975—; tchr., libr. Mallard Community Schs. (Iowa), 1974-75; mem. selection com. Lakeland Area Edn. Agy., Cylinder, Iowa, 1977—; mem. Gov.'s Sch. Efficiency Task Force, West Bend, 1987; mem. sch. evaluation team Dept. Pub. Instrn., Des Moines, 1986. Mem. Sts. Peter and Paul Parish Coun., West Bend, 1987—, music coord., song leader, 1987—; speaker Marriage Encounter Movement, Sioux City Diocese, 1985—, Pre-Cana Workshops, Emmetsburg, 1985—; chmn. Parish Liturgy Com., West Bend, 1987—. Mem. NEA, Iowa Edn. Assn., Iowa Ednl. Media Assn., Cath. Daus. Am. (past v.p. West Bend). Roman Catholic. Home: Box 426 11 11 1st Ave SW West Bend IA 50597-5036 Office: West Bend Community Sch 3 D Ave W West Bend IA 50597

WUJCIAK, SANDRA CRISCUOLO, personnel executive; b. Newark, Nov. 26, 1949; d. Salvatore Michael Criscuolo and Maria (Agliata) Ventura; m. Alfred J. Wujciak Jr., Oct. 11, 1969; children: Kimberly, Joseph. Student, Morris County Coll., 1979-81. Parental cons. Lake Dr. Sch. Hearing Impaired, Mountain Lakes, N.J., 1975-83; mktg. rep. Accts. On Call, Livingston, N.J., 1981-84, Edison, N.J., 1984-85; br. mgr. Accts. On Call, Edison, 1985-87; area mgr. Accts. On Call, Edison, Princeton, N.J., Mpls., 1987-88; area v.p. Accts. On Call, Edison, Princeton, Atlanta, Cin., Miami, Fla., Mpls., 1988-90, Mpls., Edison, Princeton, N.J., 1990—; area v.p. Accts. on Call, Edison, Princeton, Mpls., 1988—. Pres. ad hoc com. Dodge Tract, Parsippany, N.J., 1979-80. Mem. N.J. Assn. Pers. Cons., Rockaway River Country Club (Denville, N.J.). Republican. Roman Catholic.

WULF, SHARON ANN, management consultant; b. New Bedford, Mass., Aug 23, 1954; d. Daniel Thomas and Norma Dorothy (McCabe) Vieira; m. Stanley A. Wulf, 1983. BS in Acctg. cum laude, Providence Coll., 1976; MBA, Northeastern U., 1977; PhD, Columbia Pacific U., 1984. Staff acct., intern Laventhol & Horwath, Providence, 1977; jr. fin. analyst Polaroid Corp., Waltham, Mass., 1977-78, fin. analyst, Freetown, Mass., 1978-79, Cambridge, 1979-81; sr. fin. cons., mktg. strategic planner Digital Equipment Corp., Stow, Mass., 1981-82, Maynard, Mass., 1982-83, mgr. fin. devel. program, 1983-84, strategic fin. cons. engring. div., 1984-86, group mgr. planning and strategic ops., Hudson, Mass., 1986-87, group mgr. strategic bus. planning, 1987-89, mktg. planning mgr. Digital Equipment Corp., Marlboro, 1989-90, new ventures bus. devel. mgr., 1990-92; lectr. in fin. acctg. Southeastern Mass. U., 1979-81; adj. prof. acctg., mgmt. and fin., Northeastern U., Boston, 1980—; exec. com. enterprise forum MIT, 1987-92; prin. Work Systems Assocs., Inc., Marlborough, Mass., 1992-93; pres. Enterprise Systems, Framingham, Mass., 1993—; instr. Nat. Tech. U., 1991—; bd. advisors Spaceball Tech., Inc., Lowell, Mass., Terasys, Inc.; cons. in field. Chairperson pub. support and fund raising ARC, New Bedford, Mass., 1974-84; bd. dirs. Vets. Outreach Ctr., Metrowest, Framingham, Mass., 1989-93; v.p. MIT Leadership Found., Cambridge, Mass., 1991-93; mem. exec. com. MIT Enterprise Forum, also co-chair stant up clinics, 1986-92. Mem. Black Alumni of MIT (bd. advisors 1989—), Univ. Coll. Faculty Soc., Phi Sigma Tau. Home: 902 Salem End Rd Framingham MA 01701-5532 Office: Enterprise Systems 1257 Worcester Rd Ste 301 Framingham MA 01701-5217

WULLE-DUGAN, KATHY ANN, theater educator, theater director, set designer; b. Chgo., Ill., Mar. 18, 1942; d. William Albert and Irene Rose (Erdman) W.; m. Robert Kerr Dugan, Nov. 1, 1975; step-children: Stephanie Dugan Sackman, Kelly Dugan Cuci, Vali Dugan. BA in Biology, Carleton, 1963; MA in English Lit., Am. U. Beirut, 1971; MA in Theater, Northwestern U., 1970; EdD in Curriculum and Instrn., Ill. State U., 1970. Tchr. Tarouhy Hagopian Sec. Sch. for Girls, Hazmieh, Lebanon, 1964-66; editorial asst. Sci. Rsch. Assocs., Chgo., 1966-68; admissions rep. Monticello Coll., Godfrey, Ill., 1968-69; prof., theater coord. Moraine Valley C.C., Palos Hills, Ill., 1970—. Author: (sound filmstrip) From Rebaba to Violin, 1974. Mem. AAUW, Nat. Assn. Humanities Edn., U.S. Inst. for Theater Technology (midwest section mem. bd. dirs. 1992—), Ill. Theater Assn. (mem. bd. dirs. 1994—), Assn. for Theater in Higher Edn. Episcopalian. Office: Moraine Valley CC 10900 S 88th Ave Palos Park IL 60465

WUNDER, HAROLDENE FOWLER, accounting educator; b. Greenville, S.C., Nov. 16, 1944; d. Harold Eugene Fowler and Sarah Ann (Chaffin) Crooks. BS, U. Md., 1971; M Acctg., U. S.C., 1975, PhD, 1978. CPA, Ohio. Vis. asst. prof. U. S.C., Columbia, 1977-78; asst. prof. U. Pa., Phila., 1978-81; vis. asst. prof. U. N.C., Chapel Hill, 1981-82; asst. prof. U. Mass., Boston, 1982-86; vis. assoc. prof. Suffolk U., Boston, 1986-87; assoc. prof. U. Toledo, 1987-93; prof. acctg. Calif. State U., Sacramento, 1993—. Contbr. articles to acad. and profl. publs. George Olson fellow, 1975. Mem. NAFE, AICPA, Calif. Soc. CPAs, Am. Acctg. Assn., Am. Taxation Assn., Nat. Tax Assn.-Tax Inst. Am., Beta Gamma Sigma. Office: Calif State U Sch Bus Adminstrn Sacramento CA 95819-6088

WUNDERMAN, JAN DARCOURT, artist; b. Winipeg, Man., Can., Jan. 22, 1921; d. Rene Paul and Georgette Marie (Guionet) Darcourt; m. Frank Joseph Malina, 1938 (div. 1945); m. Lester Wunderman (div. 1967); children: Marc, Geroge, Karen Renee. BFA, Otis Art Inst., L.A., 1942. One man show Easthampton Guild Hall, L.I., 1977; represented in numerous permanent pub., corp. and pvt. collections including Zimmerli Mus., Nat. Assn. of Women Artists, Rutgers U., 1994. Recipient Ohashi award Pan Pacific Exhbn., Tokyo and Osaka, 1962, Emily Lowe award 1965, J.J. Akston Found. prize, 1965, Canaday Meml. prize, 1979, Marian De Solo Mendes prize, 1981, Charles Horman Meml. prize, 1983, Amelia Peabody award Nat. Assn. Women, 1991, Grumbacher Gold medal of honor, 1992, Doris Kreindler award 1992. Mem. Nat. Assn. Women ARtists (medal of honor 1966, Marcia Brady Tucker award 1965, E. Holzinger prize 1966, Jane C. Stanley prize 1977, Marge Greenblatt award 1990, Amelia Peabody award 1991), Am. Soc. Contemporary Artists (corr. sec. 1977-78, Bocour award 1980, Elizabeth Erlanger Meml. award 1990, Kreindler award 1992), Contemporary Artists Guild. Studio: 41 Union Sq W Rm 516 New York NY 10003-3208

WUNNICKE, BROOKE, lawyer; b. Dallas, May 9, 1918; d. Rudolph von Falkenstein and Lulu Lenore Brooke; m. James M. Wunnicke, Apr. 11, 1940; (dec. 1977); 1 child, Diane B. BA, Stanford U., 1939; JD, U. Colo., 1945. Bar: Wyo. 1946, U.S. Dist. Cty. Wyo. 1947, U.S. Supreme Ct. 1958, Colo. 1969. Pvt. practice law, 1946-56; ptnr. Williams & Wunnicke, Cheyenne, Wyo., 1956-69; of counsel Calkins, Kramer, Grimshaw & Harring, Denver, 1969-73; chief appellate dep. atty. Dist. Atty's Office, Denver, 1973-86; of counsel Hall & Evans, Denver, 1986—; adj. prof. law U. Denver, 1978—; lectr. Internat. Practicum Inst. Denver, 1978—. Author: Ethics Compliance for Business Lawyers, 1987; co-author: Standby Letters of Credit, 1989, Supplement, 1994, Corporate Financial Risk Management, 1992, Legal Opinion Letters Formbook 1994, UCP 500 and Standby Letters of Credit-Special Report, 1994, How to Survive Derivatives, 1995; columnist Letters of Credit Report; contbd. articles to profl jours. Pres. Laramie County Bar Assn., Cheyenne, Wy., 1967-68; Dir. Cheyenne C. of C., Cheyenne, Wy., 1965-68. Recipient awards for Outstanding Svc., Colo. Dist. Attys. Coun., 1979, 82, 86, Disting. Alumni award U. Colo. Sch. of Law, 1986, 93, Lathrop Trailblazer award Colo. Women's Bar Assn., 1992. Fellow Colo. Bar Found. (hon.); mem. ABA, Wyo. State Bar, Denver Bar Assn. (trustee 1977-80), Colo. Bar Assn., Am. Arbitration Assn. (nat. panel, regional panel large complex cases), William E. Doyle Inn of Ct. (hon.), Order of Coif, Phi Beta Kappa. Republican. Episcopalian. Office: Hall & Evans L L C 1200 17th St Denver CO 80202-5800

WUNSCH, KATHRYN SUTHERLAND, lawyer; b. Tipton, Mo., Jan. 30, 1935; d. Lewis Benjamin and Norene Marie (Wolf) Sutherland; m. Charles Martin Wunsch, Dec. 22, 1956 (div. May 1988); children: Debra Kay, Laura Ellen. AB, Ind. U., 1958, JD summa cum laude, 1977; postgrad., Stanford (Calif.) U., 1977. Bar: Calif. 1977, U.S. Dist. Ct. (no. dist.) Calif. 1977. Assoc. Hunt and Hunt, San Francisco, 1977-89; ptnr. Wunsch and George, San Francisco, 1989-93; founder Kathryn Wunsch and Assoc. Counsel, San Francisco, 1993—. Articles editor Ind. U. Law Rev., 1975-76. Mem. ABA (bus. law, real property, and alternative dispute resolution sects.), Calif. Bar Assn. (bus. law com.), Bar Assn. San Francisco (alternative dispute resolution com.), Calif. Acad. Scis., Nat. Assn. Women Bus. Owners (pres. San Francisco chpt. 1992-93, bd. dirs.), San Francisco Opera Guild, Commonwealth Club, City Club, Phi Beta Kappa, Psi Chi. Republican. Office: 100 Pine St Fl 21 San Francisco CA 94111-5102

WURMSER, JEANNE HAHN, health facility executive, psychologist; b. Bellefontaine, Ohio, Aug. 6, 1943; d. Donald Randolph and Anna Lucille (Kreglow) Hahn; m. Eric Alan Wurmser, June 7, 1965 (div. July, 1979); 1 child, Kurt. BA in Chemistry, Miami U., 1965; PhD in Clin. Psychology, Columbia U., 1974. Counselor in residence Rutgers U., New Brunswick, N.J., 1966-68; psychologist Children's Psychiat. Ctr., Eatontown, N.J., 1971-74, dir. evaluation and rsch., 1974-79, asst. exec. dir., 1979-80, exec. dir., 1981—; pres. CPC Human Svcs., Inc., Eatontown, 1984—; tech. asst. project dir. region II Pub. Health Svc., N.Y.C., 1976-81; mem. adv. group biometry and epidemiology NIMH, Washington, 1979; bd. dirs. Nat. Coun. of CMHC, Washington, 1986-88; cons. Head Start region II Pub. Health Svc., N.Y.C., 1989—. Alliance mem. Holmdel (N.J.) Alliance for Substance Abuse Prevention, 1991-92; mem. Monmouth Ocean Devel. Coun., Monmouth County, N.J., 1991. Mem. APA (accreditation site visitor 1978—), N.J. Psychol. Assn., N.J. Assn. Mental Health Agys. (pres. 1982-83, '84-86), Mental Health Corp. Am. (bd. trustees, sec. 1985-89, vice-chair 1990-92, chmn. 1992—). Office: CPC Behavorial Healthcare One High Point Center Way Morganville NJ 07751

WUSTENBERG, WENDY WIBERG, public affairs specialist, consultant; b. Faribault, Minn., Sept. 30, 1958; d. George Lyman and Ruth Elizabeth (Morris) Wiberg; m. William Wustenberg, Nov. 11, 1989; children: Russell Morris, Lauren Ruth. BA in Journalism, U. Minn., 1977-83. Dir. comms., press sec. Office Gov. Quie, St. Paul, 1980-83; sr. prodr. news and pub. affairs Twin Cities Pub. TV, St. Paul, 1983-88; chief of staff Minn. House Reps., St. Paul, 1990; CFO, mng. ptnr. Issue Strategies Group, St. Paul, 1988-92; cons. Wustenberg and Assocs., Farmington, MN, 1992—; trustee Farmington Sch. Bd., 1993—; dir. Cmty. Action Coun., Apple Valley, Minn., 1991-93; pres. SOAR, Inc., Rosemount, Minn., 1990—; adj. prof. Metro. State U., St. Paul, 1986—; lobbyist State of Minn., St. Paul, 1992—. Author: Families and Sexuality, 1983; creative dir.: (avt. campaign) Environmental Trust Fund, 1988 (Assn. Trends award 1988); contbr. articles to profl. jours. Minn. exec. dir. Bush/Quayle Campaign, Bloomington, Minn., 1992; instr. Courage Ctr. Alpine Skiers, Welch, Minn., 1988. Recipient Nat. Promotion award Corp. for Pub. Broadcasting, Washington, 1986, 87, Local Documentary and Outreach award, 1987, J.C. Penney award U. Mo. Journalism Sch., 1987; finalist TV Acad. awards Nat. Acad. TV Arts and Scis., N.Y.C., 1986; named Adult Educator of Yr., Mo. Valley Assn. Adult Edn., 1986; named Disting. Alumni, U. Minn., 1994. Mem. Minn. Sch. Bds. Assn. (del.), No. Minn. Citizens League, Minn. Alumni Assn., Order Eastern Star. Republican.

WYATT, DORIS FAY CHAPMAN, English language educator; b. Del Rio, Tex., July 12, 1935; d. Cecil Cornelius and Lola Wade (Veazey) Chapman; m. Jimmy Trueman Wyatt, June 2, 1956 (div. Nov. 1977); children: Abra Natasha Smith, Kent Colin Wyatt, Garrett Bret Wyatt. BS in Edn., S.W. Tex. State U., 1956; MA in English, U. North Tex., 1969; MA in Counseling, East Tenn. State U., 1983. Cert. profl. tchr. career ladder III, Tenn.; cert. marriage and family therapist. Elem. tchr. Clover Pk. Pub. Schs., Tacoma, 1957-58; jr. high reading tchr. Levelland (Tex.) Pub. Schs., 1964-67; tchr. English Denton (Tex.) Pub. Schs., 1967-70; tchr. reading & English Vets. Upward Bound, East Tenn. State U., Johnson City, 1981-87; tchr. English Johnson City (Tenn.) Pub. Schs., 1970—; beauty cons. Mary Kay Cosmetics, Johnson City, 1971—; adj. faculty mem. Tusculum Coll., Greeneville, Tenn., 1993—. Area dir. People-to-People Student Ambassador Program, Washington County, Tenn., 1975-94, tchr.-leader, Johnson City, 1974-84. Named to Nat. Dean's list, 1982-83. Mem. NEA, AAUW, Johnson City Edn. Assn. (pres., bd. dirs. 1989-90), Tenn. Edn. Assn., Nat. Coun. Tchrs. English, Assembly on Lit. for Adolescents, Alpha Delta Kappa (pres. 1994-95), Phi Kappa Phi. Democrat. Methodist. Home: 1805 Sundale Rd Johnson City TN 37604-3023 Office: Johnson City Pub Schs Sci Hill High Sch John Exum Pky Johnson City TN 37604-4553

WYATT, EDITH ELIZABETH, educator; b. San Diego, Aug. 13, 1914; d. Jesse Wellington and Elizabeth (Fultz) Carne; m. Lee Ora Wyatt, Mar. 30, 1947 (dec. Jan. 1966); children: Glenn Stanley (dec.), David Allen. BA, San Diego State Coll., 1936. Elem. tchr. Nat. Sch. Dist., National City, Calif., 1938-76. Sec. San Diego County Parks Soc., 1986—; librarian Congl. Ch. Women's Fellowship, Chula Vista, Calif., 1980—; active Boy Scouts Am, 1959—. Recipient Who award San Diego County Tchrs. Assn., 1968, Silver Fawn award Boy Scouts Am. Mem. AAUW (sec. 1978-80, pub. rels. 1985—), Calif. Retired Tchrs. Assn. (scholarship com. 1985-90, 1992—), Starlite Hiking Club (sec.-treas. 1979—). Home: 165 E Millan St Chula Vista CA 91910-6255

WYATT, JULIE (JULIE WOODY), interior designer; b. Washington, Okla., Dec. 2, 1939; d. Henry Edward and Nora Lee (Blalock) Woody; m. Kenneth Lynn Wyatt, June 23, 1961; children: Robert Adam, Nora Lynn. BA in Interior Design, U. Okla., 1963. Interior designer N. Ray Interiors, Norman, Okla., 1961-64, Slosky's, Oklahoma City, Okla., 1965, Stewart's, Oklahoma City, 1966-70, Pendergraft's, Inc., Oklahoma City, 1970-76; prin. J. Wyatt Interiors, Oklahoma City, 1976—; bd. visitors U. Okla. Coll. Architecture, Norman, 1987-93. Mem. Am. Soc. Interior Designers (pres. 1986, nat. bd. dirs. 1987-91, regional v.p. 1989-91, nat. v.p. 1993-94, judge design competition Houston chpt. 1989-90, mem. nat. product jury 1991, nat. nominating com. chair 1991-92, design competition jury 1991, Pres.'s citation 1976, 1st pl. for cmty. svc. projecy award 1987, medalist 1989). Home: 7511 N Country Club Dr Oklahoma City OK 73116-4319 Office: 2638 NW 50th St Oklahoma City OK 73112-8050

WYATT, KATHRYN ELIZABETH BENTON, psychologist, educator; b. Danville, Va., May 11, 1928; d. Joseph Nelson and Margaret (Davis) Benton; B.A., Randolph Macon Woman's Coll., Lynchburg, Va., 1949; M.Ed., U. Va., 1952; M.A., U. N.C., Greensboro, 1974, Ph.D., 1977; m. Landon Russell Wyatt, Aug. 30, 1952; children—Margaret Wyatt Scott, Landon Russell, III, Elizabeth Wyatt Ashe. Instr., then asst. prof. psychology Stratford Coll., Danville, 1949-74, chmn. dept., 1963-74; prof. psychology Danville Community Coll., 1977—. Pres. Danville Concert Assn.; mem. Danville Sch. Bd.; deacon, tchr. 1st Bapt. Ch., Danville; pres. so. region Va. Sch. Bds. Assn. Mem. Am. Psychol. Assn., Soc. Research Child Devel., Southeastern Psychol. Assn., Va. Psychol. Assn., Va. Acad. Sci., The Center for the Book, Va. Clubs: Friends Danville Pub. Library (pres.), The Wednesday Club (pres.), Gabriella (pres.), Wayside Garden (bd. dirs.), Shakespeare (pres.). Author articles in field. Home: 301 Magnolia Dr Danville VA 24541-3631 Office: Danville Community Coll 1008 S Main St Danville VA 24541

WYATT, LENORE, civic worker; b. N.Y.C., June 12, 1929; d. Benedict S. Rosenfeld and Ora (Copel) Kanner; m. Bernard D. Copeland, May 17, 1953 (dec. March 1968); children: Harry (dec.), Robert (dec.); m. C. Wyatt Unger, Mar. 26, 1969 (dec. Feb. 1992); 1 child, Amy Unger; m. F. Lowry Wyatt, Sept. 12, 1992. Student, Mills Coll., 1946-48; BA, Stanford U., 1950, MA, 1952; postgrad., NYU, 1952-53. Instr. Stanford U., Palo Alto, Calif., 1952, Hunter Coll., N.Y.C., 1052-53, Calif. State U., Sacramento, 1056-60, U. Calif., Davis, 1965-69; property mgr. Unger, Demas & Markakis, Sacramento, 1974-83; former actress and model. Pres. Sacramento Opera Assn., 1972-73; treas. Sacramento Children's Home, 1990-92, v.p., 1992—; former mem. bd. dirs. Sutter Hosp. Aux., Sutter Hosp. Med. Rsch. Found., Sacramento Symphony League, Temple B'nai Israel Sisterhood, Sacramento chpt. Hadassah, Sacramento Children's Home Guild; active Sacramento Opera Assn., Crocker Soc. of Crocker Art Gallery, Sacramento Symphony Assn., Sacramento Reportory Theater Assn.; founding mem. Tacoma Communities Art Sch.; mem. Temple Beth El of Tacoma. Mem. Joint Adventure Investment Club, Am. Contract Bridge League, Sacramento Pioneer Assn., Stanford U. Alumni Assn. (past bd. dirs. Sacramento) Sutter Club, Kandahar Ski Club, Sutter Lawn Tennis Club, DelPaso Country CLub (capt. women's golf 1983), Tacoma Country and Golf Club, Maui Country Club, Orcas Island Yacht Club, Wash. Athletic Club, Tacoma Club. Republican. Jewish.

WYATT, LINDA LEE, career planning counselor; b. Kansas City, Kans., Jan. 8, 1952; d. Robert L. and Helen L. (Haxel) Ogburn; m. William D.

Wyatt, Jr., Nov. 20, 1971; children: Heather S. Wyatt Duwe, Bryan W., Dustin R. AA, Kansas City, Ks. C.C., 1987; BA, Ottawa U., 1989; MA in Counseling, Liberty U., 1992. Asst. to the coll. youth rep. Assemblies of God, Springfield, Mo., 1971-74; sec. Kansas City, Kans. C.C., 1984-87, profl. asst., 1987-89, coord. career planning, 1989—; counselor Wyandotte Christian Counseling Ctr., Kansas City, Kans., 1992—; presenter in field. Vol. ARC, Kansas City, 1989-92, Dist. 500, Kansas City, 1990-94; lay ministry Glad Tidings Assembly of God, Kansas City, 1984—; mem. Project Yes, KU Talent Search, Kansas City, 1992—. Mem. Nat. Employers Counseling Assn., Am. Counseling Assn., Midwest Assn. for Career Planning, Assn. Multi-Cultural Counseling, Nat. Career Devel. Assn. Assembly of God. Office: Kansas City Kans Comm Coll 7520 State Ave Kansas City KS 66112-2816

WYATT, M. MILDRED, public relations and advertising consultant; b. Gary, Ind., Aug. 11, 1922; d. Mark E. and Stella (Wuletich) Wajagich; A.B., Ind. U., 1946. Reporter, Logansport (Ind.) Pharos-Tribune, 1946-52; supr. press relations Ill. Inst. Tech. and Armour Research Found., Chgo., 1953-58; assoc. editor Electrical/Electronic Procurement Mag., Chgo., 1958-59; mng. editor Indsl. Research Mag., Beverly Shores, Ind., 1960-61; account exec. Donald Young Assocs., Chgo., 1961-63, Fulton-Morrissey Co., Chgo., 1963-65; account supr. Griswold-Eshelman, Chgo., 1965-68; v.p. pub. relations K&A Advt., Chgo., 1968-69; pres. Wyatt Communications, Inc., Chgo., 1969—; mem. steering com., chmn. communications Nat. Computer Conf. (chmn. special activities 1987), 1981, chmn. ofcl. activities, 1987. Bd. dirs. NCCJ, Chgo., 1975-85, mem. exec. com., 1980-85; bd. dirs. Met. Chgo. YWCA, 1970; mem. Loop Center Com., 1963-75. Mem. Pub. Relations Soc. Am. (v.p. 1982-83, treas., 1980-82), Women in Communications (pres. Chgo. chpt. 1970-71), Women's Advt. Club Chgo. (v.p. 1969, 74).

WYATT, MARY CATHERINE, public relations executive; b. Tauton, Mass., Mar. 30, 1958; d. Frederick John and Hilda (Nunes) W.; m. Frederick William Conery, Sept. 11, 1982; children: Megan Kathleen, Kaitlyn Erin. BA, U. Mass., 1980; postgrad bus. adminstrn., U. R.I., 1986—. Acct. exec. Leonard Monohan, Providence, 1980-83; asst. v.p. Fleet Fin. Group, Providence, 1983-89; sr. v.p., prin. Chaffee & Ptnrs., Providence, 1989—. Editor, Keep Providence Beautiful, 1983-87. Vice chmn. Jr. Achievement, Providence, 1991—, bd. dirs., 1992—; bd. dirs. Nat. Com. for Prevention Child Abuse, Pawtucket, R.I., 1984-87. Recipient Young Career Woman award North Providence chpt. Bus. and Profl. Women, 1985. Mem. Pub. Relations Soc. Am. (editor 1981-83), Internat. Assn. Bus. Communicators (pres. R.I. chpt. 1986, recipient Gold Quill, 1986), Southeastern New Eng. Pub. Relations Soc. (charter mem.), R.I. Bankers Assn. (chair pub. relations com. 1986-88), N.E. Publicity Club (bell ringer 1981, 84, 90—). Republican. Roman Catholic. Office: Chaffee & Ptnrs 196 Richmond St Providence RI 02903

WYATT, ROSE MARIE, clinical social worker; b. San Angelo, Tex., Feb. 16; d. James Odis and Annie LaVernia (Lott) W. BA, Fisk U., 1957; MS, U. So. Calif., 1963; MA, MSW, U. Chgo., 1972; postgrad., Ill. Inst. Tech., 1976—. Elem. tchr. Chgo. Bd. Edn., 1959-63, clin. social worker, 1979—; adult program dir. Chgo. YWCA, 1963-64; youth counselor Chgo. Commn. on Youth Welfare, 1964-66; supervising social worker for Head Start, Chgo. Com. on Urban Opportunity, 1966; social worker Chgo. Commn. on Youth Welfare, 1966-68, Jewish Vocat. Svc., 1968; social worker Sch. Community Rels., Detroit Pub. Schs., 1968-70; social worker United Charities, 1972-74; clin. social worker Rosman-Wyatt and Assocs., Chgo., 1980—, pres., 1981—; instr. dept. corrections Chgo. State U., 1977—. Adv. bd. United Charities, Calumet area, program com. chmn., 1974-80; vol. Assn. of Community Agts. 1968-70, Southside Sr. Citizens Coalition, Chgo., 1963-66, Roseland Health Planning Com., 1974-76, Teen Pregnancy Caucus, 1978-82; mem. social work adv. coun. Chgo. Bd. Edn., 1976. Recipient Outstanding Employee award for med.-social work svcs. Maternal and Child Health Svcs. div. HEW; 1971; Ford Found. scholar Fisk U., 1953-57, U. Chgo. scholar, 1970-72, United Charities scholar, 1970-72. Mem. Nat. Assn. Social Workers, Acad. Cert. Social Workers, Ill. Cert. Social Workers, Chgo. Psychol. Club, Ill Acad. Criminology, NEA, Ill. Assn. Sch. Social Workers, Am. Assn. Mental Deficiency, Qualified Mental Retardation Profls., Fisk U. Alumni Assn., Am. Bridge Assn., Civenos Bridge Club, Alpha Kappa Alpha.

WYCH, ELIZABETH LEE, guidance counselor; b. Rockford, Ill., Aug. 8, 1948; d. Clarence Curtis and Verna (Swain) Sisson; m. Robert Dale Wych, Aug. 16, 1971; children: Heidi Michele, Aaron Mathew. BS, Iowa State U., 1970; MEd, Pa. State U., 1971. Lic. K-6 counselor, elem. tchr., Iowa. Tchr. remedial reading Ft. Leonard Wood (Mo.) Sch., 1971-72, Esparto (Calif.) Sch. Dist., 1973-77; tchr. learning disabilities Marengo (Ill.) Cmty. Schs., 1972; instr. Des Moines Area C.C., 1985; guidance counselor Grimes (Iowa) Sch. Dist., 1991—. Author: A Study of Creativeness in German Kindergartens, 1968. Speaker Grimes PTO, 1993-94; amb. Iowa State U., Ames, 1989—; mem. parent adv. com. Johnston (Iowa) Mid. and H.S., 1987-94; Omnibus vol. tchr. Johnston Schs., 1984-89; advisor, chmn. fundraising Johnston Band Parents Assn., 1990—; mem. session St. Paul Presbyn. Ch., chmn. Christian edn., 1986-89. Mem. ACA, NEA, Iowa Counseling Assn. (sec. chpt. 11, 1990-94), Iowa Talented and Gifted Assn. (pres. Johnston chpt. 1987-92), Quilter's Guild, Phi Kappa Phi, Alpha Lambda Delta. Office: Grimes Elem Sch 500 SW James St Grimes IA 50111

WYCHE, MARGUERITE RAMAGE, realtor; b. Birmingham, Ala., May 30, 1950; d. Raymond Crawford and Marguerite Getaz (Taylor) Ramage; m. Madison Baker Wyche III, Aug. 7, 1971; children: Madison Baker IV, James Ramage. BA cum laude, Vanderbilt U., 1972. Lic. broker, S.C., also cert. real estate specialist, grad. Real Estate Inst. Real estate agt. Slappey Realty Co., Albany, Ga., 1973-76, McCutcheon Co., Greenville, S.C., 1973-76; real estate agt. Furman Co., Greenville, 1985-87, broker's assoc., 1987—. Bd. dirs. Christ Ch. Episcopal Sch., Greenville, 1979-82, 86-89, chmn. bd. visitors, 1992-93; bd. dirs., community v.p. Jr. League of Greenville, 1983, state pub. affairs chair S.C. Jr. League, 1984; mem. Greenville Community Planning Coun., 1983; bd. dirs., chmn. long range planning com. Meals on Wheels, Greenville, 1990-93; mem. Palmetto Soc.-United Way of Greenville, 1992—; mem. elves workshop com. Children's Hosp., Greenville, 1992-93. Mem. Greenville Bd. Realtors, Million Dollar Club (life), Vanderbilt Alumni Assn., Christ Ch. Episcopal Sch. Alumni Assn. (pres., bd. dirs. 1980-81), Mortar Board, Delta Delta Delta. Republican. Episcopalian. Home: 134 Rockingham Rd Greenville SC 29607 Office: The Furman Co 252 S Pleasantburg Dr Ste 100 Greenville SC 29607

WYLER, MARJORIE GOLDWASSER, producer; b. N.Y.C., Sept. 23, 1915; d. Israel Edwin and Edith (Goldstein) Goldwasser; m. Wilfred Wyler, June 23, 1938; children: Ruth Wyler Messinger, Barbara Wyler Gold. BS, Bryn Mawr Coll., 1936, MA, 1937; postgrad., U. in Exile New Sch., N.Y.C., 1937-38. With Jewish Theol. Sem., N.Y.C., 1938-93; cons., producer radio and TV Jewish Theol. Sem., 1985-93; cons. Jewish media programming. Mem. Am. Jewish Pub. Rels. Assn., Interfaith Broadcasting Commn., VISN Interfaith Communications Network (membership bd.). Democrat. Home: 333 Central Park W New York NY 10025-7145

WYLIE, ANN GILBERT, geology educator; b. Tulsa, Mar. 31, 1944; d. Charles Churchill Gilbert and Dorothy Jean McIntyre Banks; m. John Voorhees Wylie, Dec. 16, 1971; children: John Woorhees Jr., Alice Belle, Eva Ann, Annabelle Gilbert. BA, Wellesley Coll., 1966; PhD, Columbia U., 1972. Asst. prof. U. Md., College Park, Md., 1972-79, assoc. prof., 1979-92, prof., 1992—. Contbr. articles to profl. jours. Fellow Geol. Soc. Am.; mem. Mineral Soc. Can., Soc. Econ. Geologists, Geol. Soc. Washington (Bradley prize 1989). Episcopalian. Office: Dept Geology Univ MD College Park MD 20742

WYLIE, LAURIE JEAN, nursing administrator; b. Seattle, Mar. 13, 1951; d. Alexander James and Edna O. (Pulis) Wylie II; m. John W. Iverson, Sept. 21, 1974 (div.); children: Sara Jean, John Berger. BS in Nursing, U. Wash., Seattle, 1975, postgrad., 1977; MA in Nursing, Columbia U., 1990. Cert. sch. nurse practitioner, community health nurse, nursing administr. Nurse practioner Child Devel. & Mental Retardation Ctr., Seattle, 1975-76; EPSDT nurse coord. State of Wash., Seattle, 1976; sch. nurse Snohomish (Wash.) Sch. Dist., 1976-80; interim sch. nurse Lake Stevens (Wash.) Sch. Dist., 1980-81; cons. nurse Group Health Coop., Redmond, Wash., 1980-91; maternal infant nurse cons. Vis. Nurse Assn. Snohomish, 1986-88; nursing practice and govt. rels. coord. King County Nurses Assn., Seattle, 1987-90; exec. dir. Western Wash. Area Health Edn. Ctr., Seattle, 1990—. Mem. ANA (senatorial coord., congl. dist. coord., com. of examiners for sch. nurse practitioner cert.), Wash. State Nurses Assn. (PAC trustee, dist. pres.). Home: 923 N 195th St Seattle WA 98133

WYMAN, A. CAROL R., nurse, childbirth educator; b. Pitts., Nov. 16, 1943; d. Joseph Michael and Jean Reda (Austin) Evans; m. Bruce Dana Wyman, Oct. 22, 1966; 1 child, Bruce D. Jr. Diploma in nursing, Braddock Gen. Hosp., 1964. RN, Pa., Va.; cert. cesarean childbirth educator Cesarean Families Assn., cert. childbirth educator. Staff nurse We. Psychiat. Clinic, U. Pitts., 1964-65; asst. head nurse Phipps Clinic, Johns Hopkins Hosp., Balt., 1965-66; office nurse to pvt. practice orthopedist Norfolk, Va., 1966-68; childbirth educator ARC, Seattle, 1975; ind. cons., childbirth educator Cesarean Families Assn., Reston, Va., 1975-79; childbirth educator ASPO/Lamaze Virginia Beach, Va., 1979-81; field examiner, advanced supr. PMI mgr. and sales Equifax, Inc., McLean, Va., 1980—; sales assoc., then store mgr. J. Putnam, Inc., Fairfax, Va., 1981-83; sales assoc. The Orchard, Inc., McLean, Va., 1983-84; ind. cons., childbirth educator Burke, Va., 1981—; childbirth educator Fairfax Hosp., Falls Church, Va., 1991—; bd. dirs. Cesarean Families Assn., Washington, 1976-79. Contbr. articles on childbirth to topical publs. Fellow Am. Coll. Childbirth Educators; mem. No. Va. Life Underwriters Assn., No. Piedmont Assn. Life Underwriters (treas. 1988-94, Vol. of Yr. 1990), ASPO/Lamaze (pres. Washington chpt. 1982-85), Rotary Internat. (treas. Burke Centre chpt. 1990-91, sec. 1991). Home: 6147 Poburn Landing Ct Burke VA 22015-2535 Office: Equifax-PMI 8180 Greensboro Dr 3rd Fl Mc Lean VA 22102

WYMAN, JANE (SARAH JANE FULKS), actress; b. St. Joseph, Mo., Jan. 4, 1914; d. R. D. and Emme (Reise) Fulks; m. Myron Futterman, 1937; m. Ronald Reagan, 1940 (div. 1948); children: Maureen Reagan Revell, Michael; m. Fred Karger (div.). Student, U. Mo., 1935. Formerly radio singer, chorus girl in movie musicals, actress. Chorus girl: Gold Diggers of 1937; actress: (featured roles) films My Man Godfrey, 1936, Brother Rat, 1938, Lost Weekend, 1945 (Acad. award nomination), The Yearling, 1946 (Acad. award nomination), Johnny Belinda, 1948 (Acad. award winner), Stage Fright, 1950, The Glass Menagerie, 1950, The Blue Veil, 1951 (Acad. award nomination), Magnificient Obsession, 1954 (Acad. award nomination), All That Heaven Allows, 1956, Miracle in the Rain, 1956, Holiday for Lovers, 1959, Pollyanna, 1960, Bon Voyage, 1962, How to Commit Marriage, 1969; TV shows Fireside Theater, 1955, Jane Wyman Theater, Falcon Crest, 1981-90 (recipient Golden Globe awardBest Actress in Series-Drama, 1984). *

WYMAN, NANCY S., state legislator; b. Bklyn., Apr. 21, 1946; d. Arthur and Ann (Rosenzweig) Schmukler; m. Ronald Michael Wyman, Sept. 11, 1966; children: Stacey, Meryl. Student, L.I. Coll. Hosp., 1966. X-ray technician Bapt. Hosp., Miami, Fla., 1966-67, Baird Orthopedics, Miami, 1967-70, Rockville (Conn.) Orthopedics, 1975-83; legis. aide State of Conn., Hartford, 1983-87, state rep., 1987—. Named Legislator of Yr., NARAL, 1990, Arts Commn., 1992, Coun. Small Towns, 1992; recipient Friend of Edn. award Conn. Edn. Assn., 1990. Democrat. Jewish. Home: 18 Pilgrim Dr Tolland CT 06084-2906 Office: Edn Com LOB Hartford CT 06106*

WYNE, MARGARET MARY, sales representative; b. Seattle, Feb. 16, 1965; d. Wilbert Michael and Anne (Godefroy) W. BA in Sociology, U. Wash., 1987. Asst. mgr. Crown Books, Seattle, 1987-89, mgr., 1989-91; mgr. Benjamin Books, Seattle, 1991; sales rep. Penguin USA, Inc., Seattle, 1991—. mem. Snoqualmie Pass Ski Patrol, Wash., 1980—, jr. advisor, 1984—; Region Ski Patrol, Wash., 1987—. Home: 5558 29th Ave NE Seattle WA 98105-5520

WYNETTE, TAMMY, singer; b. Red Bay, Ala., May 5, 1942; d. William Hollis Pugh; m. George Jones, Sept. 1968 (div.); m. George Richey, 1978; children: Gwen, Jackie, Tina. Former beauty operator. Rec. artist Epic Records, 1967—; regular appearances on Grand Ole Opry; tours U.S., Can., Europe; recs. include: Womanhood, Stand By Your Man, Run Woman Run, 1970, Woman to Woman, 1974, Womanhood, 1978, Crying In The Rain, 1981, Sometimes When We Touch, 1985, From the Bottom of my Heart, 1986, Higher Ground, 1987, Next To You, 1989, Heart Over Mind, 1990, Best Loved Hits, 1991, (with others) Tears of Fire: The 25th Anniversary Collection, 1992; author autobiography Stand By Your Man, 1982. Named Female Vocalist of Year Country Music Assn., 1968, 69, 70. Office: care Epic/CBS Records Inc 51 W 52nd St New York NY 10019-6119*

WYNN, BRENDA SUE, veterinarian; b. Blackwell, Okla., Dec. 28, 1961; d. Robert Henry and Trini Kitty (Rodruquez) Fisher; m. David Douglass Wynn, Aug. 10, 1985. AS in Agrl. Prodn., No. Okla. Coll., 1982; B Animal Sci., Okla. State U., 1984, DVM, 1989. Lic. vet., Ohio. Veterinarian Milford (Ohio) Animal Hosp. Mem. AVMA, Ohio Vet. Med. Assn., Cin. Vet. Med. Assn., Greater Clermont County Vet. Med. Assn. (sec. 1993). Democrat. Roman Catholic. Home: 1367 Mountain Ash Amelia OH 45102 Office: Milford Animal Hosp Milford Shopping Ctr Milford OH 45150

WYNN, JEAN MARIE, marine pipefitter journeyman; b. Grosse Pointe Farm, Mich., Apr. 25, 1954; d. John Phillip Jr. and Marjorie Jean (Ball) Thomas; m. Terry Jay Eckles, July 1, 1972 (div. Sept. 1983); 1 child, Terry Jay Jr.; m. John Franklin Wynn III, Oct. 1, 1983. A Tech. Arts, Olympic Community Coll., Bremerton, Wash., 1988. Sales clk. Rexall Drugstore, Holly, Mich., 1970-72; sales clk. Navy Exch., Bremerton, 1976-77, Long Beach, Calif., 1979; Tupperwear dealer Summit Sales, Norfolk, Va., 1975; clk.-typist Naval Undersea Warfare Engring. Sta., Keyport, Wash., 1980-81; supply clk. Puget Sound Naval Shipyard, Bremerton, 1981-82, marine pipefitter apprentice, 1982-86, journeyman, 1986-88, insp. nuclear, mech. and structural ships system, 1988-93; marine pipefitter journeyman, 1993—; mem. com. Apprentice Assn., Bremerton, 1982-85; mem., sec. quality assurance div. EEO Com., Bremerton, 1990-92. Co-author: Marine Pipefitter Handbook, 1985. Vol. Long Beach Unified Sch. Dist., 1978-79; mem. parish com. Naval Sta. Base Chapel, Long Beach, 1979. Named Region X Tradeswoman of Yr., Women in Trades Com., 1989. Mem. Federally Employed Women, Puget Sound Naval Shipyard Women in Trades (sec. 1990-91). Roman Catholic. Office: Puget Sound Naval Shipyard S/56 Bremerton WA 98314

WYNN, KARLA WRAY, artist, agricultural products company executive; b. Idaho Falls, Idaho, Oct. 1, 1943; d. William and Elma (McCowin) Lott; m. Russell D. Wynn, June 7, 1963; children: Joseph, Jeffrey, Andrea. Student, Coll. of Holy Names, 1962-63, Providence Coll. Nursing, 1962-63; BFA, Idaho State U., 1989; postgrad., Alfred U., 1993. Co-owner R.D. Wynn Farms, American Falls, Idaho, 1963—, office mgr., 1975-84; co-owner Redi-Gro Fertilizer Co., American Falls, 1970—, office mgr., 1980-84; pres. Lakeside Farms, Inc. (name now Redi-Gro Fertilitzer Inc.), American Falls, 1975—; owner Blue Heron, Pocatello, Idaho, 1991—. Watercolor paintings and ceramics exhibited at various statewide art shows. Lutheran. Office: Redi Gro Fertilizer Co PO Box 202 American Falls ID 83211-0202

WYNNE, VICKI MITSU, realtor; b. L.A., May 13, 1952; d. Mikio and Joyce Nobuko (Kamiyama) Takeuchi; m. Stephen Arthur Wynne, Apr. 28, 1984; children: Thomas Mikio, Stephanie Joyce Asako. AB cum laude, Princeton U., 1974; MSW, UCLA, 1977. Realtor Re/Max Exec. Realty, Fremont, Calif., 1988—. Interviewer Princeton Alumni Schs., Fremont, L.A., 1974—; tchr. Unity Palo Alto (Calif.) Community Ch., 1989—. Grantee Asian Am. Community Mental Health Ctr., 1976-77. Mem. Suzume No Gakko Cultural Program (bd. dirs.). Office: Re/Max Exec Realty 47655 B Warm Springs Blvd Fremont CA 94539

WYNSTRA, NANCY ANN, lawyer; b. Seattle, June 25, 1941; d. Walter S. and Gaile E. (Cogley) W. BA cum laude, Whitman Coll., 1963; LLB cum laude, Columbia U., 1966. Bar: Wash. 1966, D.C. 1969, Ill. 1979, Pa. 1984. With appellate sect., civil div. U.S. Dept. Justice, Washington, 1966-67; TV corr.-legal news Stas. WRC, NBC and Stas. WTOP, CBS, Washington, 1967-68; spl. asst. Corp. Counsel, Washington, 1968-70; dir. planning and rsch. D.C. Superior Ct., Washington, 1970-78; spl. advisor White House Spl. Action Office for Drug Abuse Prevention, Washington, 1973-74; fellow Drug Abuse Coun., 1974-75; gen. counsel Michael Reese Hosp. and Med. Ctr., Chgo., 1978-83; exec. v.p., gen. counsel Allegheny Health Edn. and Rsch. Found., Pitts., 1983—; pres., chief exec. officer Allegheny Health Svcs. Provider's Ins. Co., 1989—; adj. prof. Sch. of Urban and Pub. Affairs Carnegie Mellon U., 1985—; assoc. prof. Med. Coll. Pa., 1991—; cons. to various drug abuse programs, 1971-78; bd. overseers Whitman Coll., 1993—. Mem. ABA, Nat. Health Lawyers Assn. (bd. dirs. 1985-91, chair publs. com. 1989-91, audit com. 1991-92, treas. 1992-93, exec. com. 1992—, edn. fund com., 1992-93, mem. nominating com. 1992-93, sec. 1993—), Am. Soc. Hosp. Attys., others. Presbyterian. Contbr. articles to profl. jours. Office: Allegheny Health Edn & Rsch Found 120 Fifth Ave Ste 2900 Pittsburgh PA 15222 •

WYRICK, PRISCILLA BLAKENEY, microbiologist; b. Greensboro, N.C., Apr. 28, 1940; d. Carnie Lee and Prestine (Blakeney) W. BS in Med. Tech., U. N.C., Chapel Hill, 1962; MS in Bacteriology, U. N.C., 1967, PhD in Bacteriology, 1971. Technologist Clin. Microbiology Lab., N.C. Meml. Hosp., Chapel Hill, 1962-64; asst. supr. Clin. Microbiology Lab., N.C. Meml. Hosp., 1964-65, supr., 1965-66; sci. staff fellow Nat. Inst. Med. Rsch., Mill Hill, London, 1971-73; asst. prof. dept. microbiology U. N.C. Sch. Medicine, Chapel Hill, 1973-79; assoc. prof. U. N.C. Sch. Medicine, 1979-88, prof., 1988—. Grantee, NIH. Mem. Am. Acad. Microbiology, Am. Soc. Microbiology (pres. N.C. br. 1981-82, chmn. div. gen. med. microbiology 1981-82), AAAS, Soc. Infectious Diseases, Sigma Xi. Office: U NC Sch Medicine CB 7290 816 FLOB Chapel Hill NC 27599

WYSE, BONITA W(ENSINK), nutrition educator, researcher; b. Lorain, Ohio, Oct. 2, 1945; d. Norbert B. and Ruth B.(DeChant) Wensink. BS, Notre Dame of Ohio, 1967; MS, Mich. State U., 1970; PhD, Colo. State U., 1977. Registered dietitian. Clin. dietitian St. Lawrence Hosp., Lansing, Mich., 1968-69; instr. nutrition Utah State U., Logan, 1970-73, asst. prof., 1973-77, assoc. prof., dir. coordinated undergrad. med. dietetics program, 1977-81, prof., 1981—, acting dean Coll. Family Life, 1984-86, dean, 1986—; bd. dirs. Gerber Products Co., Fremont, Mich.; cons. Met. Life Found., N.Y.C., 1983-86; mem. adv. bd. Heart, Blood, Lung Inst., NIH, Bethesda, Md., 1984-87. Author: Nutritional Quality Index of Foods, 1979; contbr. articles to profl. jours. Bd. dirs. Citizens Against Phys. and Sexual Abuse, Logan, 1984. Recipient Outstanding Alumna award Dept. Food Sci. and Nutrition, Mich. State U., 1982. Mem. Am. Dietetic Assn. (council on research 1982-87, bd. dirs. 1984-87, Frances E. Fischer Meml. Nutrition Lectr., 1984), Utah Dietetic Assn. (pres. 1976-77), Am. Inst. Nutrition, Am. Home Econs. Assn. (Borden award for research 1981). Republican. Roman Catholic. Office: Utah State U Dean's Office Family Life Logan UT 84322-2900

WYSE, LOIS, advertising executive, author; b. Cleve.; d. Roy B. Wohlgemuth and Rose (Schwartz) Weisman; m. Marc Wyse (div. 1980); m. Lee Guber (dec. 1988). Pres. Wyse Advt. Inc., N.Y.C., 1951—; bd. dirs. Consol. Natural Gas, Pitts. Author 54 books; contbg. editor Good Housekeeping; syndicated columnist Wyse Words. Trustee Beth Israel Med. Ctr., N.Y.C. Mem. Woman's Forum (bd. dirs.), Com. 200, PEN. Office: Wyse Advt Inc 22 W 23d St 5th Fl New York NY 10010

WYSOCKI, ANNETTE B., nurse scientist, educator; b. Raleigh, N.C., Dec. 31, 1954; d. Robert Jospeh and Frances (Overton) W.; m. John Nussbaum, May 2, 1987. BSN, East Carolina U., 1978, MSN, 1980; PhD, U. Tex., 1986. Cert. med.-surg. nurse. Staff nurse U. Va., Charlottesville, 1978-79, Seton Med. Ctr., Austin, Tex., 1981-86; rsch. and teaching asst. U. Tex., Austin, 1982-84; sr. rsch. assoc. U. Tex. Southwestern Med. Ctr., Dallas, 1986-87; NIH postdoctoral rsch. fellow U. Tex., Dallas, 1987-89, Cornell U. Med. Coll., N.Y.C., 1989-91; asst. prof. NYU, N.Y.C., 1991—; rsch. asst. prof., dir. nursing rsch. NYU Med. Ctr., N.Y.C., 1991—. Mem. editorial bd. Wounds: A Compendium of Clin. Rsch. and Practice; contbr. articles to profl. jours. Vol. Girl Scouts U.S.A. Am. Nurses Found. scholar; grantee NIH, 1988-91, 93—, Nat. Inst. Nursing Rsch., Am. Nurses Found., 1984-85. Mem. AAAS, Am. Soc. Cell Biology, N.Y. Acad. Scis., Wound Healing Soc. (nominating com.), Soc. Investigative Dermatology, Assn. Oper. Rm. Nurses, Sigma Theta Tau (reviewer collateral grant). Office: NYU Med Ctr 550 1st Ave # 855 New York NY 10016-6497

WYSOCKI, JO ANN, elementary education educator, librarian; b. Loup City, Nebr., Sept. 28, 1935; d. Mathew Robert and Evelyn Lucille (Dilla) W. BA, U. So. Calif., 1957, MLS, 1957; MA in History, Calif. State U., Long Beach, 1978. Cert. gen. elem., jr. high sch., gen. secondary, jr. coll., reading tchr., ESL credentials, Calif. Libr., jr. high sch. tchr. Compton (Calif.) Unified Sch. Dist., 1957-62; K-9 tchr. Erlangen (Fed. Republic Germany) Elem.-Jr. High Sch., 1962-63; elem. and jr. coll. libr., elem. tchr. gifted edn. Long Beach (Calif.) Unified Sch. Dist., 1963-73; libr. South Australian Sch. System, 1973-75; elem. tchr. L.A. Unified Sch. Dist., 1978—; libr. L.A. Pub. Librs., 1980—, Long Beach Pub. Librs., 1980-90. Pres. Harbor Coalition Against Toxic Waste, Wilmington, Calif., 1982—; v.p. Wilmington (Calif.) Home Owners, 1985-90, pres., 1991—; v.p. Friends Wilmington Br. Libr., 1985—, Family Fed. Credit Union, Wilmington, 1987—; vice chmn. 54th, 57th, 58th Assembly Dists., 1990-91, chmn., 1991—; mem. L.A. Citizens Adv. Com., 1985—; v.p., treas. Drumm Barracks Soc., 1988—; mem. Rep. Nat. Com., 1990—. Named hon. mayor City of Wilmington, 1987; recipient Amicus Collegii award L.A. Harbor Community Coll., 1989. Mem. Wilmington Bus. and Profl. Women (pres. 1982-83, publicity chmn. 1990—), Greenpeace, Sierra Club, Isaac Walton League, Am. Soc. Prevention Cruelty to Animals, Claremont Inst., Audubon Soc. Roman Catholic. Home: 1006 King Ave Wilmington CA 90744-3204 Office: Miles Avenue Elem Sch 6720 Miles Ave Huntington Park CA 90255-5012

WYSS, ARLENE ELIZABETH, computer programmer; b. Bloomington, Ill., Feb. 25, 1962; d. Robert Louis and Doris Elizabeth (Janssen) W. BS in Agr., U. Ill., 1984; BS in Applied Computer Sci., Ill. State U., 1987. Mkt. rep. Ill. Agrl. Svc. Co., Bloomington, 1984-85; programmer/analyst Advanced Systems Applications, Bloomingdale, Ill., 1987-89; bus. cons. Kraft USA, Glenview, Ill., 1990-93, Kraft Gen. Foods, Northfield, Ill., 1993—. Home: 127 Dunton Ct Mundelein IL 60060 Office: Kraft General Foods 3 Lakes Dr Northfield IL 60093-2753

WYSS, DIANNE DUNLOP, coal fuel company executive; b. Kingsport, Tenn., May 1, 1950; d. Donald D. and Maxine (Hooker) Dunlop; m. John Benedict Wyss, Aug. 12, 1978; children: John Christian, Kirsten Dunlop. BS in Phys. Therapy, U. Okla., 1973; MBA in Finance, Va. Poly. and State U., 1980. Chief fin. and adminstrv. officer Slurrytech Inc., Miami, Fla., 1980-83; pres. Fuels Mgmt. subs. Slurrytech Inc., Miami, Fla., 1982-83; v.p. Fuels Mgmt. Inc., Miami, 1983—; natural resources advisor Nat. Congress Am. Indians. Mem. fair share fundraising com. Sidwell Friends Sch., Washington, 1986-87; mem. steering com. for coal water slurry Dept. Energy; coord. native Am. pre-conf. to White House Conf. on Libr. and Info. Sci.; bd. dirs. Honor Our Neighbors Origins and Rights. Mem. Vis. Nurse Assn. (profl. adv. com. 1979—), D.C. LWV (treas. 1980-81, v.p. 1982-83, 86-87). Democrat. Mem. Soc. Friends. Club: Washington Coal. Office: FMI/Slurrytech 7027 SW 148th Ter Miami FL 33158-2127

WYSS, MARY PONDER, social worker; b. Memphis, Nov. 3, 1946; d. Robert Evan Ponder and Marcella Clara (Goetz) Seyer; m. Bernard O'Neill Wyss, Sept. 5, 1970; children: Shannon, Eric, Colleen, Mark. BS, St. Louis, 1968, MSW, 1970. Lic. clin. social worker. Social worker Cath. Charities, St. Louis, 1970-72; med. social worker Cardinal Glennon Hosp., St. Louis, 1988—; coord. conf. Share, St. Louis, 1987, Focus, Chesterfield, Mo., 1988; tchr. community edn. Cardinal Glennon Hosp., 1992—. Mem. parish coun. St. Anselms at the Priory, St. Louis, 1992—; mem. letter writing campaign Cardinal Glennon Hosp., 1993—. Named Vol. of Yr., St. Luke's Med. Ctr., 1988. Mem. NASW. Roman Catholic. Home: 413 Forsheer Dr Chesterfield MO 63017

XIONG, JEAN Z., artist, consultant; b. Beijing, China, Nov. 1, 1953; came to U.S., 1983.; d. Xian-Li and Zhang Yao (Zhu) Xiong; m. Charles C. Feng, Apr. 12, 1989. Grad., Shu Zhou (China) Inst., 1977; MFA, Acad Art Coll., San Francisco, 1986. Freelance artist/instr. Beijing, 1978-81; design artist First Impressions Advt., Reno, 1986; computer artist Visual Dynamics, San Francisco, 1988-89, Mediagenic, Menlo Park, 1989-91; leader artist Tecmagik Inc., Redwood City, Calif., 1992-94; cons. entertainment software devel., Calif., 1991-92, 94—. One-woman shows San Francisco, 1984, 85,

Monterey, Calif., 1984; exhbns. in Hong Kong, China, 1979, 80, 81. Recipient prize of Excellence Nat. Youth Artist Assn., 1980, Artist Assn., Hong Kong, 1981; scholar Acad. Art Coll., 1983-86. Mem. Mus. Modern Art, Tradtional Chinese Inst. (Beijing). Office: 1601 Maxine Ave San Mateo CA 94401

YACOBIAN, SONIA SIMONE, metals company executive; b. Cairo, Egypt, Feb. 13, 1943; came to U.S., 1966, naturalized, 1971; d. Simon and Lucy (Guendimian) Samsonian; divorced; children: Tatiana, Richard. BS, Lycee of Cairo, 1962; BBA, U. Cairo, Egypt, 1965; student Pace U., 1978-80. Asst. mgr. new accounts Lincoln Savs. & Loan, Los Angeles, 1973-77; sr. acct. U.S. Industries, N.Y.C., 1977-81; dep. mgr. French C. of C., N.Y.C., 1981-82; mgr. mktg. Samancor Metals, New Rochelle, N.Y., 1982-84; pres. NIDDAM Inc., Dix Hills, N.Y., 1984—. Mem. Assn. Profl. Women in Metal. Republican. Orthodox Christian. Home: 37 Wintergreen Dr Melville NY 11747-1812 Office: NIDDAM Inc PO Box 877 Melville NY 11747-0877

YACONETTI, DIANNE MARY, business executive; b. Chgo., Dec. 16, 1946; d. Anthony and Dora Marie (Mazzoni) Pontillo. Student, Mallinckrodt Coll., 1984-85; Advanced Mgmt. Program, Harvard U., 1990. Various positions Brunswick Corp., Skokie, Ill., 1964-80, mgr. legal support services, 1980-83, asst. sec., 1984-86, corp. sec., 1986-88, v.p. adminstrn., corp. sec., 1988—; bd. dirs. The Lambs, Libertyville, Ill. Mem. Am. Soc. Corp. Secs. Roman Catholic. Office: Brunswick Corp 1 N Field Ct Lake Forest IL 60045-4810

YACOVONE, ELLEN ELAINE, banker; b. Ithaca, N.Y., Aug. 4, 1951; d. Wilfred Elliott and Charlotte Frances (Fox) Drew; m. Richard Daniel Yacovone, June 2, 1979; stepchildren: Christopher Daniel, Kimberly Marie. Student Broome Community Coll., 1973-80; cert. Inst. Fin. Edn., Chgo., 1974. Sec. to exec. v.p. Ithaca Savs., N.Y., summer 1968; mortgage clk. Citizens Savs. Bank, 1968-69; with Lincoln Bank, Van Nuys, Calif., 1970-71; asst. bookkeeper Henry's Jewelers, Binghamton, N.Y., 1971-74; teller, br. supt., br. mgr. First Fed. Savs., Binghamton, N.Y., 1974-82, v.p., cen. regional sales mgr., 1982-86, dist. sales mgr., 1986-88; br. mgr. Great Western Bank, Pensacola, Fla., 1988-89, v.p., regional mgr. San Diego east region, 1989—. Mem. Gov.'s Commn. on Domestic Violence, Albany, N.Y., 1983-87; bd. dirs. S.O.S. Shelter, Inc., Endicott, N.Y., 1979-88, pres., 1982-83, treas., 1985-86; vol. United Way of Broome County, Binghamton, 1976-88, Sta. WSKG Pub. TV, Conklin, N.Y., 1974-88; mem. Found. State U. Ctr. at Binghamton; bd. dirs. Interfaith Shelter Network, San Diego, 1992—. Named Woman of Achievement, Broome County Status of Women Coun., 1981. Mem. Triple Cities Bus. and Profl. Women (pres. 1979-81, young careerist award 1977), Sales and Mktg. Execs., Broome County C. of C., Broome County Bankers Assn. (bd. dirs. 1979-88, pres. 1983-84), Inst. Fin. Edn. (bd. dirs. 1976-88, pres. 1984-85, winner N.Y. State speech contest 1984). Republican. Methodist. Avocations: exercise, camping, wood working, gardening, needlecrafts. Home: 602 Myra Ave Chula Vista CA 91910-6230 Office: Great Western Bank 707 Broadway Ste 1400 San Diego CA 92101

YAES, JOYCE IDELSON, educator, musician, artist; b. N.Y.C., July 18, 1944; d. William Johnson and Jean (Brander) Idelson; m. Robert Yaes, Nov. 16, 1986. BA, Bklyn. Coll., 1966, MA, 1972; postgrad., Juilliard Sch., 1971-75, Mannes Coll., 1975, Manhattan Sch. Music, 1974-75, U. Neuchatel, Switzerland, 1967, U. San Miguel, Mex., 1969. Cert. tchr., N.Y., Ky. Tchr. art and music N.Y.C., 1966-86; tchr. music Emerson Sch., N.Y.C., 1976-80; agt. ins. N.Y.C., 1982-87; tchr. Living Arts and Sci. Ctr., Lexington, Ky., 1987—; pvt. tchr. music; violinist various orchs., N.Y., Ky.; dir. various art shows. Author: Humanities and Arts Perspectives, Microphishe Education Perspectives; one-woman show U. Ky. Ctr. for Arts, Arts Club Washington, 1994; 2-woman show Lexington Art League; exhibited in group shows Paula Insel Gallery, Harrison Gallery, N.Y.C., Aspen (Colo.) Gallery, Bklyn. Mus., Lincoln Ctr. Cork Gallery, N.Y.C., Lexington Art League, ArtsPlace, Lexington, Monserrat Gallery, N.Y.C., Accents Gallery, Lexington, Guild Hall, East Hampton, N.Y., West Hampton (N.Y.) Gallery, also others. Mem. United Fedn. Tchrs., Music Tchrs. Assn. (mem. exec. com.), Music Educators Nat. Conf., Port Educators Assn., Nat. Assn. Female Execs., Lexington Art League, Federated Music Club, U. Ky. Woman's Club.

YAKURA, THELMA PAULINE, retired library director, consultant, writer; b. Wilmington, Del.; d. Michael J. and Bertha (Blanchfield) Masticola; m. James N. Yakura, Nov. 18, 1950 (dec. 1974); children: James Peter, Kristie. BA, U. Del., 1945; BLS, Drexel Inst. Tech., 1946. Reference asst. U. Pitts. Library, 1946; head engring. library Carnegie Mellon U. (formerly Carnegie Inst. Tech.), 1947-51; children's librarian, head adult bookmobile Cuyahoga County Pub. Library, Cleve., 1952-55; asst. head bookmobile dept. Westwood Br. Dayton (Ohio) Pub. Library, 1956-57, head librarian, 1957-64; dir. Wright Mem. Pub. Library, Dayton, 1964-89; libr. cons., freelance writer, 1989—; County rep. Miami Valley Libr. Orgn., Dayton; mem. creative writer's group Miamisburg (Ohio) Sr. Ctr. Active in Oakwood Hist. Soc. Mem. ALA, Ohio Library Assn., Oakwood Hist. Soc. (life). Home and Office: 1327 Carlwood Dr Miamisburg OH 45342-3517

YALMAN, ANN, judge; b. Boston, June 9, 1948; d. Richard George and Joan (Osterman) Y. BA, Antioch Coll., 1970; JD, NYU, 1973. Trial atty. Fla. Rural Legal Svcs., Immokalee, Fla., 1973-74; staff atty. EEO, Atlanta, 1974-76; pvt. practice Santa Fe, N.Mex., 1976—; part time U.S. Magistrate, N.Mex., 1988—. Commr. Met. Water Bd., Santa Fe, 1986-88. Mem. N.Mex. Bar Assn. (commr. Santa Fe chpt. 1983-86). Home: 441 Calle La Paz Santa Fe NM 87501-2821 Office: 304 Catron St Santa Fe NM 87501-1806

YALOW, ROSALYN SUSSMAN, medical physicist; b. N.Y.C., N.Y., July 19, 1921; d. Simon and Clara (Zipper) Sussman; m. A. Aaron Yalow, June 6, 1943; children: Benjamin, Elanna. A.B., Hunter Coll., 1941; M.S., U. Ill., Urbana, 1942, Ph.D., 1945; D.Sc. (hon.), U. Ill., Chgo., 1974, Phila. Coll. Pharmacy and Sci., 1976, N.Y. Med. Coll., 1976, Med. Coll. Wis., Milw., 1977, Yeshiva U., 1977, Southampton (N.Y.) Coll., 1978, Bucknell U., 1978, Princeton U., 1978, Jersey City State Coll., 1979, Med. Coll. Pa., 1979, Manhattan Coll., 1979, U. Vt., 1980, U. Hartford, 1980, Rutgers U., 1980, Rensselaer Poly. Inst., 1980, Colgate U., 1981, U. So. Calif., 1981, Clarkson Coll., 1982, U. Miami, 1983, Washington U., St. Louis, 1983, Adelphi U., 1983, U. Alta. (Can.), 1983, SUNY, 1984, Tel Aviv U., 1985, Claremont (Calif.) U., 1986, Mills Coll., Oakland, Calif., 1986, Cedar Crest Coll., Allentown, Pa., 1988, Drew U., Madison, N.J., 1988, Lehigh U., 1988; L.H.D. (hon.), Hunter Coll., 1978; DSc. (hon.), San Francisco State U., 1989, Technion-Israel Inst. Tech., Haifa, 1989; DSc (hon.), Med. Coll. Ohio Toledo, 1991; L.H.D. (hon.), Sacred Heart U., Conn., 1978, St. Michael's Coll., Winooski Park, Vt., 1979, Johns Hopkins U., 1979, Coll. St. Rose, 1988, Spertus Coll. Judaica, Chgo., 1988; D. honoris causa, U. Rosario, Argentina, 1980, U. Ghent, Belgium, 1984; D. Humanities and Letters (hon.), Columbia U., 1984; DSc (hon.), Fairleigh Dickinson U., Israel, 1992, Fairleigh Dickinson U., 1992, Conn. Coll., 1992, Smith Coll., Schenectady, 1994, Union Coll., Schenectady, 1994. Diplomate: Am. Bd. Scis. Lectr., asst. prof. physics Hunter Coll., 1946-50; physicist, asst. chief radiosotope service VA Hosp., Bronx, N.Y., 1950-70, chief nuclear medicine, 1970-80, acting chief radioisotope service, 1968-70; research prof. Mt. Sinai Sch. Medicine, CUNY, 1968-74, Disting. Service prof., 1974-79, Solomon A. Berson Disting. prof.-at-large, 1986—; Disting. prof.-at-large Albert Einstein Coll. Medicine, Yeshiva U., 1979-85, prof. emeritus, 1986—; chmn. dept. clin. scis. Montefiore Med. Ctr., Bronx, 1980-85; cons. Lenox Hill Hosp., N.Y.C., 1956-62, WHO, Bombay, 1978; sec. U.S. Nat. Com. on Med. Physics, 1963-67; mem. nat. com. Radiation Protection, Subcom. 13, 1957; mem. Pres.'s Study Group on Careers for Women, 1966-72; sr. med. investigator VA, 1972-92, sr. med. investigator emeritus, 1992—. Co-editor: Hormone and Metabolic Research, 1973-79; editorial adv. council: Acta Diabetologica Latina, 1975-77, Ency. Universalis, 1978—; editorial bd.: Mt. Sinai Jour. Medicine, 1976-79, Diabetes, 1976, Endocrinology, 1967-72; contbr. numerous articles to profl. jours. Bd. dirs. N.Y. Diabetes Assn., 1974. Recipient VA William S. Middleton Med. Research award, 1960; Eli Lilly award Am. Diabetes Assn., 1961; Van Slyke award N.Y. met. sect. Am. Assn. Clin. Chemists, 1968; award A.C.P., 1971; Dickson prize U. Pitts., 1971; Howard Taylor Ricketts award U. Chgo., 1971; Gairdner Found. Internat. award, 1971; Commemorative medallion Am. Diabetes Assn., 1972; Bernstein award Med. Soc. State N.Y., 1974; Boehringer-Mannheim Corp. award Am. Assn. Clin. Chemists, 1975; Sci. Achievement award AMA, 1975; Exceptional Service award VA, 1975; A. Cressy Morrison award N.Y. Acad. Scis., 1975; sustaining membership award Assn. Mil. Surgeons, 1975; Distinguished Achievement award Modern Medicine, 1976; Albert Lasker Basic Med. Research award, 1976; La Madonnina Internat. prize Milan, 1977; Golden Plate award Am. Acad. Achievement, 1977; Nobel prize for physiology/medicine, 1977; citation of esteem St. John's U., 1979; G. von Hevesy medal, 1978; Rosalyn S. Yalow Research and Devel. award established Am. Diabetes Assn., 1978; Banting medal, 1978; Torch of Learning award Am. Friends Hebrew U., 1978; Virchow gold medal Virchow-Pirquet Med. Soc., 1978; Gratum Genus Humanum gold medal World Fedn. Nuclear Medicine or Biology, 1978; Jacobi medallion Asso. Alumni Mt. Sinai Sch. Medicine, 1978; Jubilee medal Coll. of New Rochelle, 1978; VA Exceptional Service award, 1978; Fed. Woman's award, 1961; Harvey lectr., 1966; Am. Gastroenterol. Assn. Meml. lectr., 1972; Joslin lectr. New Eng. Diabetes Assn., 1972; Franklin I. Harris Meml. lectr., 1973; 1st Hagedorn Meml. lectr. Acta Endocrinologica Congress, 1973; Sarasota Med. award for achievement and excellence, 1979; gold medal Phi Lambda Kappa, 1980; Achievement in Life award Ency. Brit., 1980; Theobald Smith award, 1982; Pres.'s Cabinet award U. Detroit, 1982; John and Samuel Bard award in medicine and sci. Bard Coll., 1982; Disting. Research award Dallas Assn. Retarded Citizens, 1982, Nat. Medal Sci., 1988; Abram L. Sachar Silver Medallion Brandeis U., Waltham, Mass., 1989, Disting. Scientist of Yr. award ARCS, N.Y.C., 1989, Golden Scroll award The Jewish Advocate, Boston, 1989, spl. award Clin. Ligand Assay Soc., Washington, 1988, numerous others. Fellow N.Y. Acad. Scis. (chmn. biophysics div. 1964-65), Am. Coll. Radiology (asso. in physics), Clin. Soc. N.Y. Diabetes Assn.; mem. Nat. Acad. Scis., Am. Acad. Arts and Scis., Am. Phys. Soc., Radiation Research Soc., Am. Assn. Physicists in Medicine, Biophys. Soc., Soc. Nuclear Medicine, Endocrine Soc. (Koch award 1972, pres. 1978), Am. Physiol. Soc., (hon.) Harvey Soc., (hon.) Med. Assn. Argentina, (hon.) Diabetes Soc. Argentina, (hon.) Am. Coll. Nuclear Physicians, (hon.) The N.Y. Acad. Medicine, (hon.) Am. Gastroent. Assn., (hon.) N.Y. Roentgen Soc., (hon.) Soc. Nuclear Medicine, Phi Beta Kappa, Sigma Xi, Sigma Pi Sigma, Pi Mu Epsilon, Sigma Delta Epsilon, Tau Beta Pi. Office: VA Hosp 130 W Kingsbridge Rd Bronx NY 10468-3904

YAMAGUCHI, KRISTI TSUYA, ice skater; b. Hayward, Calif., July 12, 1971; d. Jim and Carole (Doi) Y. Gold medalist, Figure Skating Albertville Olympic Games, 1992; U.S. Skating champion, 1992, World Skating champion, 1991, 1992, World Junior champion, 1988. Recipient Women First award YWCA, 1993. Address: U.S. Figure Skating Assn. 20 First St. Colorado Springs CO 80906*

YAMANI, ELAINE REIKO, computer-peripherial company executive; b. Ogden, Utah, Apr. 2, 1945; d. Joe and Chieko (Kato) Yamani; m. Victor G. Sugihara, Aug. 10, 1970 (div. June 1973); 1 dau., Jo Ann Renae. B.S. in English and Psychology, Weber State U., 1965, A.A., 1967; M in Human Resource Mgmt., U. Utah, 1975-79. Personnel generalist Weber State U., Ogden, Utah, 1973-78; personnel specialist Cutter Lab., Ogden, 1978-81; human resource mgr. Iomega, Ogden, 1981-83, compensation and benefits mgr., 1983-85; dir. human resources Cericor Inc., 1983; personnel mgr., Hewlett-Packard, 1983—. Mem. Utah Personnel Assn. (pres. 1988), No. Utah Personnel Assn. (pres. 1980-81).

YAN, SAU-CHI BETTY, biochemist; b. Hong Kong, Nov. 25, 1954; d. Ming Yan and Choo-Chen Woo; m. Victor J. Chen, Feb. 29, 1980; 1 child, Heidi I. BS, Ctrl. Mo. State U., 1975; PhD, Iowa State U., 1980. Postdoctoral fellow St. Paul-Ramsey Med. Ctr., 1980-82; postdoctoral fellow med. sch. U. Tex., Houston, 1982-84; sr. biochemist Eli Lilly & Co., Indpls., 1985-88, sr. scientist, 1989-93, sr. rsch. scientist, 1993—. Patentee in field; contbr. articles to profl. jours. Bd. dirs. A Children's Habitat, Indpls., 1994. Mem. AAAS, Am. Soc. Biochemistry, Molecular Biology, Protein Soc., Soc. Chinese Bioscientists Am. Office: Eli Lilly & Co DC1543 307 E McCarty St Indianapolis IN 46240

YANAGITANI, ELIZABETH, optometrist; b. Ogden, Utah, Nov. 24, 1953; d. Katsuyoshi and Yaeko (Watanabe) Y. AS, Weber State Coll., Ogden, Utah, 1974; BA magna cum laude, U. Utah, 1976; OD, Pacific U., Forest Grove, Oreg., 1980. Externship Tripler Army Med Ctr., Schofield Barracks, Hawaii, 1979; staff optometrist Gen. Med., San Diego, 1984-89, San Ysidro Health Ctr., Calif., 1985-87, 91—, Logan Heights Family Health Ctr., San Diego, 1989-91; assoc. of pvt. office Chula Vista, Calif., 1985—; asst. instr. Am. Bus. Coll., San Diego, 1982. Recipient Gates Meml. award Nat. Eye Rsch. Found., 1980; scholar Weber State Coll., 1972-73, U. Utah, 1975, Project award Beta Sigma Kappa, 1980. Mem. San Diego County Optometric Soc. (v.p. 1985), Calif. Optometric Soc. (del. to leadership conf. 1985), Achievement Through Vision/COVD (pres. 1990), Phi Kappa Phi.

YANKEE, HELEN MARIE, educator, publishing executive; m. J.R. Yankee, June 6, 1956; children: Michael, David, Stephen, Jennifer. Diploma Montessori edn., Montessori Inst. Am., 1968; MS, Southeastern U., Greenville, S.C., 1980, PhD, 1981. Chief exec. officer The Fernhaven Studio, Los Angeles, 1966—, Montessori Ednl. Environment, Los Angeles, 1974—, Yankee Montessori Mfg., L.A., 1980-86; pres. Internat. Montessori Inst. Tchr. Ednl. Programs, Sage, Calif., 1980—; rsch. editor Edn. Systems Pub., L.A., 1982—; dir. EEI, Inc., L.A., 1987—; cons. Calif. pub. schs., 1976; prof. Univ. Coll. Vancouver. Author: Montessori Curriculum, 1985, Reading Program, 1981, Science for Preschool, 1981, Geography for Preschool, 1982. Mem. Am. Montessori Soc., Montessori Inst. Am. Home: 38395 Trifone Rd Hemet CA 92544 Office: Edn Systems Pub PO Box 536 Hemet CA 92546-0536

YANNELLO, KAREN MARIE, lawyer; b. Buffalo, May 8, 1952; d. Guy R. and Grace A. (Barone) Y. BA, Coll. William and Mary, 1974; JD, U. Va., 1977. Bar: Va. 1977, D.C. 1979. Sr. editor Michie-Bobbs Merrill Law Pub. Co., Charlottesville, Va., 1977-80; inspector gen., dep. gen. coun. Office of Gen. Counsel, U.S. Dept. Def., Washington, 1980—; pres. sr. profl. women's group Office of Sec. Def., 1983-86. Mem. ABA (pub. contracts sect.), Va. State Bar, D.C. Bar, Phi Beta Kappa.*

YANNUZZI, ELAINE VICTORIA, food and home products executive; b. Summit, N.J., Aug. 14, 1933; d. Emil and Alice (Vance) Y. BA, Seton Hall U., 1968. Pres. Expression Unltd., Warren, N.J., 1971-89; pvt. practice cons. pub. industry and small bus. Bedminster, N.J., 1989—; presenter seminar N.Y. Food and Wine Show, Splty. Food Show; lectr. NYU, Rutgers U.; moderator Am. Women's Econ. Devel., N.Y.C., 1985-87; speaker Women Bus. Owners N.J., Princeton, 1986; bd. dirs. Platypus Stores. Author: Gift Wrapping Food, 1985; editorial advisor Fancy Food mag., 1985—; editorial cons. Family Circle Gt. Ideas mag., 1987-89. Named Entrepreneur of Yr. N.J. Living mag., 1983, Woman of Yr. NYU, 1986. Mem. Roundtable for Women (bd. dirs. 1986-89, Pacesetter award 1985), Nat. Assn. for Splty. Food Trade (steering com. 1986). Home and Office: 612 Timberbrooke Dr Bedminster NJ 07921-2106

YARBOROUGH, JUDITH ANN, bookstore owner, librarian; b. Williamsport, Pa., Aug. 26, 1949; d. Fred Arlington and Ethel Mary (Parker) Bingaman; m. John Henry Yarborough, Aug. 24, 1972; 1 child, Wendy Renee. BA in English, U. Tex., Arlington, 1970; MLS, U. North Tex., 1973. Tchr. Parker Found., Dallas, 1971-72; saleswoman Sanger-Harris, Dallas, 1972; mgr. br. libr. Irving (Tex.) Pub. Libr. N.W., 1974-78; libr. cons. Vaughn & Yarborough Libr. Cons., Irving, 1980-81; owner, mgr. Young Ideas, Irving, 1981—; speaker various orgns., 1974—. Bd. dirs. Irving Arts Reach Com., 1988; vol. coord. travelling exhbn. Smithsonian Instn., Irving, 1988. Mem. Am. Bookseller's Assn., Assn. Booksellers for Children (charter) AAUW (life, chmn. Ednl. Foudn. Irving br. 1987-88, v.p. programming 1988-89, 91—, v.p. mem. 1992-93), Belles-Lettres Book Discussion Club (pres. 1987-88, 91, treas. 1992—), Acad. Performing Arts (bd. dirs. 1992), Irving Heritage Soc., Washington Irving Com., 1991; guest lectr. for tchr. tng. classes Northlake Coll. DCCD, Irving, 1993—. Democrat. Methodist. Office: Young Ideas 1105 Story Village Shopping Ctr Irving TX 75062

YARBROUGH, DENA COX, retired special education educator; b. Gorman, Tex., June 20, 1933; d. William Thomas and Imogene (Dunlap) Cox; m. James Edgar Yarbrough, June 20, 1950. BA, Nicholls State U., 1964, MEd, 1971, postgrad., 1978. Supr. profl. pers., prin. schs., elem. tchr. Terrebonne Parish Sch. Bd., Houma, La., 1964-79, dir. spl. edn. svcs., 1980-91; ret., 1991. Bd. dirs. Terrebonne Literacy Coun., Dulac Community Ctr.; mem. adv. bd. Terrebonne Guidance Ctr. Mem. Terrebonne Retired Tchrs. Assn., Coun. for Exceptional Children, La. Mental Health Assn., La. Retired Tchrs. Assn., Alcohol and Drug Abuse Coun. for South La., Phi Delta Kappa. Democrat. Methodist. Home: 303 Westview Dr Houma LA 70364-2537

YARBROUGH, JEAN MARY, political science educator; b. N.Y.C., Nov. 16, 1946; d. Ralph J. and Mary (Reiziz) Y.; m. Peter A. Stern, May 6, 1972 (div. Sept. 1990); children: James Yarbrough Stern, John Francis Sutherlin Stern. BA, Cedar Crest Coll., Allentown, Pa., 1968; MA, New Sch. for Social Rsch., 1970, PhD, 1974. Asst. prof. polit. sci. U. Conn., Groton, 1974-79; asst. prof. polit. sci. Loyola U., Chgo., 1979-85, assoc. prof., 1985-88; prof. govt. Bowdoin Coll., Brunswick, Maine, 1988—. Contbr. articles to profl. jours. Woodrow Wilson dissertation fellow, 1972-73; NEH Bicentennial fellow, 1984-85. Episcopalian. Home: 25 School St Brunswick ME 04011 Office: Bowdoin Coll Dept Govt/Legal Studies Brunswick ME 04011

YARBROUGH, KATHRYN DAVIS, public health nurse; b. Montrose, Colo., Aug. 31, 1947; d. L.O. and V. Jean (Dunn) Davis; m. James H. Yarbrough, Aug. 8, 1970; children: James, Jason. Diploma, Good Samaritan Hosp. Sch. Nursing, Phoenix, 1971; BSN, Kennesaw State Coll., 1995. RN, Ga.; cert. NAACOG. Supr. Cherokee County Health Dept., Canton, Ga., 1976—. Den mother Boy Scouts Am., Canton, 1986-87; bd. dirs. Cancer soc., Canton, 1987—, Cherokee County Violence Ctr., 1990, First Steps Bd., 1993—, Cherokee County Advocacy Ctr., 1994—; HIV cons. ARC, Canton, 1988—, disaster vol., Cherokee County, 1993—; co-chair Early Intervention Coun., Canton, 1991-93; mem. Leadership Cherokee, 1994, Interagy Coun., 1994; mem. Blue Ridge Jud. Cir. Domestic Violence Task Force. Mem. Svc. League Cherokee County. Methodist. Office: Cherokee County Health Dept 1219 Univeter Rd Canton GA 30115-8261

YARBROUGH, LINDA ELAINE, advertising executive; b. Coral Gables, Fla., Nov. 26, 1950; d. Luther Curtis and Dolores Juanita (Miller) Knight. Student, N. Tex. State U., 1968-69, U. Tex., Arlington, 1973-81. Asst. advt. dir. Shop Rite Foods, Inc., Ft. Worth, 1970-77; media supr. Tracy Locke Advt., Dallas, 1977-80; owner, media dir. The Media Mix, Dallas, Arlington, 1980-88; media dir. Tandy/Radio Shack, Ft. Worth, 1988-91; v.p. media dir. Regian Advertising, 1991—; cons. various advt. agencies, Dallas, 1980—; moderator Women at Work Conf., U. Tex., Arlington, 1987. Pres. Exchange Club of Arlington, 1988; dist. dir. Tex. Dist. Exchange Clubs, 1987-88; mem. budget com. League of Women Voters, Tex., 1983—. Recipient AD-Q award Harvey Research, 1981. Mem. Dallas Advt. League, Network of Exec. Women, Bus./Profl. Advt. Assn., Tex. Assn. of Realtors, Arlington C. of C. Club: Tennis Assn. (Arlington).

YARBROUGH, MARILYN VIRGINIA, lawyer, educator; b. Bowling Green, Ky., Aug. 31, 1945; d. William Ottoway Yarbrough and Merca Lee (Hardin) Toole; m. Walter James Ainsworth, Sept. 3, 1967 (div. Oct. 1980); children: Carmen Virginia, Carla Renee; m. David A. Didion, Dec. 31, 1987. BA, Va. State U., 1966; JD, UCLA, 1973. Bar: Calif. 1973, Kans. 1982. Instr. Boston Coll. Law Sch., Newton, Mass., 1975-76; prof. law U. Kans., Lawrence, 1976-87, assoc. vice chancellor, 1983-87; prof. Law Sch. U. Tenn., Knoxville, 1987-93; dean Law Sch U. Tenn., Knoxville, 1987-91; William J. Maier Jr. chair law W.Va. U., Morgantown, 1991-92; prof. U. N.C. Law Sch., Chapel Hill, 1992—, assoc. provost, 1994—. Editor in chief Black Law Jour. 1972-73; contbr. articles to profl. jours. Bd. dirs. Knox County Endl. Enrichment Fund, Knoxville, 1989-92, Knoxville Housing Partnership, 1989-92, United Way of Knoxville, 1990-92; trustee Law Sch. Admission Coun., pres., 1986-88; trustee Webb Sch. of Knoxville, 1988-91; mem. Pulitzer Prize Bd., 1990—. Mem. ABA (reporter Am. Law Inst.-ABA com. continuing profl. edn. 1988-90, sect. legal edn. and admissions to bar 1989-94), Poynter Inst. for Media Studies (adv. bd. 1984-90, bd. dirs. 1990-92). Democrat. Mem. United Ch. of Christ. *

YARBROUGH, MARTHA CORNELIA, music educator; b. Waycross, Ga., Feb. 8, 1940; d. Henry Elliott and Jessie (Sirmans) Y.; B.M.E., Stetson U., 1962; M.M.E., Fla. State U., 1968, Ph.D., 1973. Choral dir. Ware County High Sch., Waycross, Ga., 1962-64, Glynn Acad., Brunswick, Ga., 1964-70; asst. choral dir. Fla. State U., 1970-72; cons. in music Muscogee County Sch. Dist., Columbus, Ga., 1972-73; cons. in tchr. edn. Psycho-Edno. Cons., Inc., Tallahassee, 1972-73; asst. prof. music edn., dir. univs. choruses and oratorio soc. Syracuse U., 1973-76, assoc. prof. music edn., 1976-83, prof., 1983-86, acting asst. dean Coll. Visual and Performing Arts, 1980-82, acting dir. Sch. Music, 1980-82, chmn. music edn., 1982-86; prof. music La. State U., Baton Rouge, 1986—, coordinator music, edn., 1986—; artist in residence Sch. Music U. Ala., Tuscaloosa, 1989-90. Chair exec. com. Music Edn. Rsch. Coun., 1992-94. Mem. Music Educators Nat. Conf., N.Y. State Sch. Music Assn., Am. Ednl. Research Assn., Soc. Research Music Edn. (mem. exec. com. 1988-90, program chair 1990-92, chair, 1992-94), AAUP, Pi Kappa Lambda, Phi Beta, Kappa Delta Pi. Co-author: Competency-Based Music Education, 1980; mem. editorial com. Jour. Research in Music Edn.; contbr. articles to profl. jours., chpts. in books. Office: Sch Music La State U Baton Rouge LA 70803

YARBROUGH, SONJA DIANNE, marketing and public relations professional; b. Trenton, Fla., June 6, 1948; d. George Charlie and Dorothy Mae (Carver) Y. BA in English, U. Fla., 1971; MS in Pub. Rels., Boston U., 1980. Pub. rels. asst. Digital Equipment Corp., Maynard, Mass., 1979; interim editor, rsch. asst. Rehab. Rsch. Inst., Gainesville, Fla., 1980-81; bus. mgr. Dental Specialty Practice, Atlanta, 1982-84; asst. account exec. Grizzard Advt., Atlanta, 1984-86; pub. rels. mktg. cons. Atlanta, 1987-88; account exec. Northlake Typography, Atlanta, 1988-89, TypoGraphics Atlanta, 1989-90; mktg. coord. Future Aviation Profls., Atlanta, 1990-93; pub. rels./mktg. cons. Atlanta, 1993-94; pub. rels. dir. Tech. Coll. of the Lowcountry, Beaufort, S.C., 1994—. Scholarship in Communications Boston U., 1979; recipient Bernice McCullar award Exemplary Leadership, 1990-91. Mem. Women in Communications, Inc. (co-chairperson ACE Competition 1989-90, publicity guide 1989-90, v.p. programs 1990-91, pres. 1992-93, past pres. 1993-94). Democrat. Home: 3125 W University Ave Gainesville FL 32607-2575 Office: 100 S Ribaut Rd PO Box 1288 Beaufort SC 29901

YARD, MOLLY, social activist; d. James Maxon and Mabelle Merriam (Hickcox) Y.; m. Sylvester Garrett; 3 children. AB, Swarthmore Coll., 1933, Hon. LLD, 1988. Chmn. Am. Student Union; active in Dem. party politics, Pa. and Calif., 1940s and 50s; active in civil rights movement, Pa., 1960s and 70s; staff mem. VISTA, 1960s; active NOW, from 1970s, polit. dir., 1985-87, pres., 1987-91. *

YARDLEY, ROSEMARY ROBERTS, journalist, columnist; b. Albertville, Ala., Apr. 1, 1938; d. James Bailey Jr. and Mildred (Smith) Roberts; m. Jonathan Yardley, June 14, 1961 (div. 1975); children: James B., William W. II; m. Donald Arthur Boulton, Apr. 30, 1988. BA, U. N.C., 1960; MA, U. N.C., Greensboro, 1978. Staff writer The Charlotte (N.C.) Observer, 1960-61; editorial asst. The N.Y. Times, N.Y.C., 1962-64; staff writer The Greensboro (N.C.) News and Record, 1974-78, editorial writer, 1978-88, editorial columnist, 1988—; mem. faculty English dept. U. N.C., Greensboro, 1990—. Contbr. articles, book revs. to various publs. Bd. dirs. Weatherspoon Art Mus. U. N.C., Greensboro, 1986—, U. N.C. Journalism Found., 1985-93, Weatherspoon Art Found., 1989—, Friends U. Libr., Greensboro, 1988-90, Ea. Music Festival, Greensboro, 1984-88; bd. dirs. English Speaking Union Greensboro, 1995—. Recipient 2d prize N.C. Press Assn., 1976, 1st prize 1987, 2d prize 1995; John S. Knight fellow Stanford U., 1980-81; Bosch Found. travel fellow, 1990, Atlantik Bruke Found. travel fellow, 1988. Democrat. Presbyterian. Home: 223 Elmwood Dr Greensboro NC 27408-5829 Office: The Greensboro News and Record 200 E Market St Greensboro NC 27401-2910

YAROS, CONSTANCE LENORE GREENBERG, painter, sculptor; b. Phila., Aug. 3; d. Harry William and Dorothy (Hofberg) Greenberg; m. Irvin Yaros, June 17, 1950 (dec. Nov. 6, 1983); children: Michael J. Yaros, Aimee Y. Silverman, Nancy S. Yaros. Student, Temple U., Tyler Sch. of Art, 1957-60, Blai Studio, 1976-81, Pa. Acad. Fine Arts, 1978-79, 87, Schuler Sch. of Art, 1990. One-woman shows include Tyler Alumni Gallery, 1992; exhibited in group shows icluding Am. Artists Profl. League, N.Y., 1993, Oil Painters

Am., 1994, Art at the Armory, Phila., 1990-92, Artists Equity Assn. Triennial, 1984, 88, 91, Allied Artists of Am., 1988, Catherine Loriliard Wolfe Art Club, 1988, Salmagundi Art Club, 1988, Tyler Alumni Gallery-Diamond Club, Temple U., 1988-92, Phila. Sketch Club, 1987, Old York Rd. Art Guild, 1975; public collections at Temple U., Jefferson Park Hosp., Bd. City Trusts; pvt. collections include William Meehan, 1993, Meg and Lynn Strawbridge, 1989, Mary Austin Phipps Fox, 1986, Boris Blai, 1985, 83, Jack Weinstein, 1978. Mem. Am. Technion Assn., Greenpeace, Phila. Mus. Art, Allied Artists Am., Am. Soc. Portrait Artists, Am. Artist Profl. League, Knickerbocker Artists, Pa. Acad. Fine Arts, Oil Painters of Am., Artists Equity Assn., Woodmere Art Mus. Home and Office: 2401 Pennsylvania Ave Apt 4A5 Philadelphia PA 19130-3018

YARYAN, RUBY BELL, psychologist; b. Toledo, Apr. 28, 1938; d. John Sturges and Susan (Bell) Y.; m. John Frederick Buenz, Jr., Dec. 15, 1962 (div. 1968). AB, Stanford U., 1960; PhD, U. London, 1968. Lic. clin. psychologist; diplomate Am. Bd. Psychology. Rsch. dir., univ. radio and tv U. Calif., San Francisco, 1968-70; dir. delinquency coun. U.S. Dep. Justice, Washington, 1970-73; evaluation dir. Office of Criminal Justice Planning, Sacramento, Calif., 1973-76; CAO project mgr. San Diego (Calif.) County, 1977-92; dir. devel. svcs. Childhelp USA, Woodland Hills, Calif., 1992-94; rsch. coord. Neuropsychiat. Inst. and Hosp. UCLA, 1986-87; exec. dir. Centinela Child Guidance Clinic, Inglewood, Calif., 1987-89; clin. dir. Nat. Found. Emotionally Handicapped, North Hills, Calif., 1990-93; pvt. practice Beverly Hills, Calif., 1973—; cons. White House Conf. Children, Washington, 1970; mem. Nat. Adv. Com. Criminal Justice Standards and Goals, Washington, 1973; clin. affiliation UCLA Med. Ctr. Contbr. articles to profl. jours.; chpts. to books and monographs in field. Chair Human Svcs. Commn., City of West Hollywood, Calif., 1986; first vice-chair United Way/ Western Region, L.A., 1988; mem. planning-allocations-rsch. coun. United Way, San Diego, 1980-82. Grantee numerous fed., state and local govt. orgns. Mem. Am. Psychol. Assn., Western Psychol. Assn., Calif. Psychol. Assn., Am. Orthopsychiat. Assn., Am. Profl. Soc. on Abuse of Children, Phi Beta Kappa. Episcopalian. Office: 337 S Beverly Dr Ste 107 Beverly Hills CA 90212-4307

YASENKA, DEBRA ANN, software consulting company executive; b. Plainfield, N.J., June 16, 1950; d. Ronald Howard and Irene Quadt; m. Robert Charles Yasenka, Mar. 17, 1973; children: Nancy, Robby. BBA, Kent State U., 1972. Asst. supr. Ea. Air Lines, N.Y.C., 1972-77; account exec. Sales Cons., Inc., Southfield, Mich., 1985-86; br. mgr. Analytical Techs., Inc., St. Paul, 1986-88, regional mgr., 1988-90; v.p. Analytical Techs., Inc., Bingham Farms, Mich., 1990-94; pres. Visual Sys. Devel. Group, Troy, Mich., 1994—; cons., trainer in field. Com. chair Jr. Woman's League, Canfield, Ohio, 1984-85. Athena award finalist, 1992; named Profl. Woman of Yr. St. Paul Area C. of C. Mem. NAFE, Data Processing Mgmt. Assn., Forest Lake Country Club, Dellwood Hills Golf Club (social chmn. 1989-90). Home: 4611 Brightmore Rd Bloomfield Hills MI 48302-2123 Office: Visual Sys Devel Group Ste 200 100 W Big Beaver Rd Troy MI 48084

YASNYI, LINDA FAYE, advertising and public relations executive; b. New Orleans, Feb. 27, 1951; d. Ben and Berte (Michalove) Y. BA in Communications Arts and Sci., U. New Orleans, 1974. Traffic, sales service mgr. Sta. WVUE-TV, New Orleans, 1974-78; dir. pub. relations Hyatt Regency New Orleans, 1978-80; v.p. broadcast prodn., pub. relations Keating & Assoc., New Orleans, 1980-83; writer, prin. Yasnyi Copywriting , Prodn., Publicity, New Orleans, 1983—; part-time instr. Loyola U., New Orleans, 1986—; past faculty advisor Loyola Ad Club. Host, prodr. "Advertising Studio" talk radio. Mem. press rm. staff Pope's Visit to U.S., 1987; mem. clue caper com. Multiple Sclerosis, New Orleans, 1987; publicity chair bring out the best com. United Way; past mem. adv. bd. Covenant House, New Orleans. Recipient Gold Key award Am. Hotel and Motel Assn., 1979, Am. Creativity award, 1986. Mem. Advt. Club New Orleans (pres. 1983-84, Addy award, Ad Club Pres. of Yr. 1984), Press Club New Orleans (bd. dirs. 1990-92), Pub. Rels. Soc. Am., Internat. Assn. Bus. Communicators, Toastmasters. Home and Office: Yasnyi Copywriting Prodn Publicity 1636 Amelia St New Orleans LA 70115-4643

YASUTAKE-RONSTADT, DIANE KIKUE, professional sports team executive; b. Heidelberg, Germany, Oct. 24, 1964; d. Jack Tadeo and Ulrike Wilhemina (Stauber) Yasutake. Grad., Pearl City High Sch., 1982. Intern, adminstrv. asst. Hawaii Islanders Profl. Baseball Team, Honolulu, 1982-87; adminstr. DynCorp, Honolulu, 1985-88; contract coord. TRICIL Hazardous Waste Mgmt., Chattanooga, 1988-90; adminstrv. asst. Chattanooga Lookouts Profl. Baseball Team, 1989-90; dir. comm. rels. Tucson Toros Profl. Baseball Club, Inc., 1991-92; asst. gen. mgr. Tuscon Toros Profl. Baseball Club, Inc., 1992—. Cons., vol., fundraiser Ednl. Enrichment Found., Tucson Pub. Libr., Tucson Children's Mus., Ronald McDonald House, others, 1991—. Named Rawlings Female Exec. of Yr., Pacific Coast League, 1993. Mem. NAFE, Nat. Employees Svcs. and Recreation Assn. Republican. Roman Catholic. Office: Tuscon Toros Profl Baseball PO Box 27045 Tucson AZ 85726

YATES, DENISE CAROL ROBERTS, geriatrics nurse; b. Atlanta, Ga., Feb. 1, 1955; d. Phillip Lanier and Wilma Carolyn (Cochran) Roberts; m. James Edward Yates, June 13, 1973; children: Mark Edward, Carol Anne. A in Nursing, Dekalb Community Coll., 1976. Cert. BLS instr., CPR instr., gerontol. nurse ANA. Primary nurse Alzheimers Unit Wesley Woods Ctr., Atlanta; health care coord. DeKalb Community Coun. on Aging, Decatur, Ga.; DON Tucker (Ga.) Nursing Ctr.; primary care nurse, nurse investigator rsch. project VA Med. Ctr., Decatur. Mem. NOVA, Nat. League for Nursing.

YATES, DORIS DENISE, recreation educator; b. Oakland, Calif., Jan. 24, 1952; d. Doris J. (Harshaw) Riley. BS, Fed. City Coll., Washington, 1973; MA, Mich. State U., 1974, PhD, 1982. Asst. home economist N.C. State U., Sanford, 1975-76; human resource devel. Ctrl. Carolina C.C., Sanford, N.C., 1976-77; dir. adult edn .%, Sanford, N.C., 1977-79; grad. resident asst. Mich. State U., East Lansing, 1980-82, resident dir., 1982-83; lectr. Calif. State U., Hayward, 1983-85, asst. prof., 1985-88, assoc. prof., 1988-94, prof., 1994—; prin. YCS & Assocs., Cons. Svc. Contbr. articles to profl. jours. Juror Nat. Edn. Film and Video Festival, Oakland, Calif., 1984—. Fulbright scholar, 1994-95; grantee U.S. Info. Agy., 1993—, Calif. Park and Recreation Soc., 1991. Mem. NAFE, African-Am. Soc. Econ. Advancement (co-founder, bd. dirs.), Calif. Faculty Assn. (pres. Hayward chpt., membership com., contract devel. and barganining strategies com.), Calif. Soc. Park and Recreation Educators, Ethnic Minority Assn. Calif. Parks and Recreation, Nat. Coun. Higher Edn., Nat. Recreation and Parks Assn., Companions Alameda County (pres., bd. dirs.), Bus. and Profl. Women, Bay Area Big Ten Alumni Club. Home: 3 Athlone Ct, 3 Stocksfield Rd, Walthamstow, London E17 3LW, England

YATES, ELLA GAINES, library consultant; b. Atlanta, June 14, 1927; d. Fred Douglas and Laura (Moore) Gaines; m. Joseph L. Sydnor (dec.); 1 child, Jerri Gaines Sydnor Lee; m. Clayton R. Yates (dec.). A.B., Spelman Coll., Atlanta, 1949; M.S. in L.S, Atlanta U., 1951; J.D., Atlanta Law Sch., 1979. Asst. br. librarian Bklyn. Pub. Library, 1951-54; head children's dept. Orange (N.J.) Pub. Library, 1956-59; br. librarian E. Orange (N.J.) Pub. Library, 1960-69; med. librarian Orange Meml. Hosp., 1967-69; asst. dir. Montclair (N.J.) Pub. Library, 1970-72; asst. dir. Atlanta-Fulton Pub. Library, 1972-76, dir., 1976-81; dir. learning resource ctr. Seattle Opportunities Industrialization Ctr., 1982-84; asst. dir. adminstrn. Friendship Force, Atlanta, 1984-86; state librarian Commonwealth of Va., 1986-90; library cons. Price Waterhouse, 1991; adv. bd. Library of Congress Center for the Book, 1977-85; cons. in field; vis. lectr. U. Wash., Seattle, 1981-83; mem. Va. Records Adv. Bd., 1986-90; mem. Nagara Exec. Bd., 1987-91. Contbr. to profl. jours. Vice chmn. N.J. Women's Coun. on Human Rels., 1957-59; chmn. Friends Fulton County Jail, 1973-81; bd. dirs. United Cerebral Palsy Greater Atlanta, Inc., 1979-81 Coalition Against Censorship, Washington, 1981-84, YMCA Met. Atlanta, 1979-81, Exec. Women's Network, 1979-82, Freedom To Read Found., 1979-85, Va. Black History Mus., Richmond, 1990-91; sec., exec. dir. Va. Libr. Found. Bd., 1986-90. Recipient Meritorious award Atlanta U., 1977, Phoenix award City of Atlanta, 1980, Serwa award Nat. Coalition 100 Black Women, 1989, Black Caucus award, 1989, Disting. Svc. award Clark-Atlanta U., 1991, Ednl. Support Svc. award Tuskegee Airmen, 1993; named Profl. Woman of Yr. NAACP, N.J., 1972, Outstanding Chum of Yr., 1976, Outstanding Alumni Spelman Coll., 1977. Mem. ALA (exec. bd. 1977-83, commn. freedom and access to info.), NAACP, Southeastern Libr. Assn., Nat. Assn. Govt. Archives and Records Adminstrn. (exec. bd. 1987-91), Delta Theta Phi, Delta Sigma Theta. Baptist. Home and Office: 1171 Oriole Dr SW Atlanta GA 30311-2424

YATES, LINDA SNOW, communications executive; b. St. Louis, July 20, 1938; d. Robert Anthony Jerrue and June Alberta (Crowder) Armstrong; m. Charles Russell Snow, Nov. 26, 1958 (div. 1979); children: Cathryn Louise, Christopher Armstrong, Heather Highstone, Sean Webster; m. Alan Porter Yates, July 22, 1983. BBA, Auburn U., 1971, MEd, 1975, postgrad. Cert. profl. sec. Div. head placement div. Solutions Group, Atlanta, 1981-83; employment coord. Fulton Fed. Savs., Atlanta, 1983-84; owner, recruiter Data One, Inc., Atlanta, 1984-85; ops. mgr. Talent Tree Temporaries, Atlanta, 1985-87; legal asst., sec. Rice & Keene, Atlanta, 1987-90; legal word processing asst. Kilpatrick & Cody, Atlanta, 1990-94; pres., owner Power Comm., Hilton Head, S.C., 1994—; adj. instr. DeKalb C.C., Atlanta, 1980-84, Mercer U., Atlanta, 1981-82; instr. bus. So. Union State Jr. Coll., Valley, Ala., 1974-75; legal sec. Swift, Currie, McGhee & Hiers, Atlanta, 1979-80, Samford, Torbert, Denson & Horsley, Opelika, Ala., 1969-71. Columnist Neon News Flash, 1995. Mem. Paralegal Assn. of Beaufort Co. (charter mem., sec. 1993-94), Women Bus. Owners, Nat. Assn. Personnel Cons., Phi Delta Kappa. Republican. Episcopalian. Home: 6 Wood Duck Ct Hilton Head Island SC 29928-3010 Office: 33 Office Park Rd 4A-127 Hilton Head Island SC 29928

YATES, MARGERY GORDON, educator; b. Walton, N.Y., July 3, 1910; d. McClellan Gordon and Marcia Beulah (Ramsdell) Gordon-Strahl; m. James McKendree Yates, Aug. 11, 1933; 1 child, Sally. BS, U. Houston, 1943, MS, 1948; MA, Stanford U., 1952. Tchr. Baldwin (N.Y.) Sch. Dist., 1928-34, Houston Sch. Dist., 1943-48; supr. primary edn. Watsonville (Calif.) Sch. Dist., 1948-53; edn. cons. San Mateo County Office Edn., Redwood City, Calif., 1953-58; supr. primary edn. Jefferson Elem. Sch. Dist., Daly City, Calif., 1958-65; tchr. Hillsborough (Calif.) Sch. Dist., 1965-75; instr. U. Houston, 1956, San Jose State Coll., 1957. Mem. AAUW (edn. area rep. 1987-88, 89-90, 91-92, 92-93, 93-94, Fellowship award honoree 1991), Burlingame Music Club (pres. 1992-93, 1992-94), Alpha Delta Kappa (corr. sec. Calif. state bd. 1981-82, Gamma Beta chpt. pres. 1971-74, treas. 1985-89, 94—). Republican. Mem. Ch. Christian Sci. Home: 2731 Summit Dr Burlingame CA 94010-6039

YATES, MARY MITCHELL, lawyer; b. Summerville, Ga., Mar. 7, 1950; d. George William and Dorothy (Davis) Mitchell; m. Charles R. Yates, Jr., Mar. 29, 1980; children: Charles, Sarah. BA in History, Emory U., 1971; JD, U. Ga., 1977. Bar: Ga. 1977. Assoc. Sutherland, Asbill & Brennan, Atlanta, 1977-83, ptnr., 1984-86, 89-93; v.p., U.S. gen. counsel English China Clays, Inc., Atlanta, 1993—. Chair devel. com. bd. trustees Historic Oakland, Atlanta, 1992-93; mem. alumni bd. dirs. Leadership Atlanta, 1992-93, class of 1985-86. Mem. ABA, State Bar of Ga., Atlanta Bar Assn., Ga. Assn. Women Lawyers, Corp. Counsel Assn. Methodist. Office: English China Clays Inc Ste 200G 5775 Peachtree Dunwoody Rd NE Atlanta GA 30342-1507

YATES, MARYPAUL, textile company executive; b. Knoxville, Tenn., Nov. 24, 1957; d. Paul and Peggy Adelle (Bryan) Y.; m. Benjamin H. Weisgal, Jan. 1, 1960; 1 child, Bryan Asher Weisgal. Student, U. Ga., 1973-75; BFA magna cum laude, Syracuse U., 1977; AAS, Fashion Inst. Tech., N.Y.C., 1979. Designer, studio mgr. Jeffrey Aronoff Inc., N.Y.C., 1978-81; designer, cons. N.Y.C., 1981-82; stylist Gerli & Co., N.Y.C., 1982-83; dir. design Maharam, Hauppauge, N.Y., 1983-87; prin. Yates Weisgal Inc., N.Y.C., 1987—; adj. instr. CUNY-Hunter Coll., 1978-82, Fashion Inst. Tech. SUNY, N.Y.C., 1985, Parsons Sch. Design, N.Y.C., 1988-93; guest speaker various groups, lectr., condr. workshops in field, 1980—. Author: Textiles, A Handbook for Designers, 1986, revised, 1995; group exhibits include The Galleries, Fashion Inst. Tech., 1984, R.I. Sch. Design, 1985. Mem. Textile Mus., Washington, industry adv. coun. Fashion Inst. Tech., 1984—. Designer products awarded Coty award Fashion Critics Circle, 1980, Roscoe award Resource Coun., 1982, Product award Inst. Bus. Designers, 1986; grantee Ford Found., 1976. Mem. Assn. for Contract Textiles (industry standards com. 1986-88), Color Assn. U.S. (interior forecasting com. 1988—), Color Mktg. Group (color projections com. 1983—), Textile Study Group N.Y., Am. Craft Coun., Surface Design Assn. Office: 185 E 85th St Apt 20F New York NY 10028-2149

YATES, PATRICIA ANN HENNING, nursing director; b. French Camp, Miss., Aug. 11, 1939; d. Dotson Sidney and Elsie (Armstrong) Henning; m. Jesse Morris Yates; children: Gail, Jesse, Cynthia, Renee, Cristelle. LPN, N.W. Jr. Coll.; ADN, Miss. Delta Jr. Coll. RN, Miss.; CNA; lic. nursing home adminstr.; cert. BTLS, ACLS; cert. healthcare risk mgmt. Dir. nursing North Panola Hosp. & Nursing Home, Sardis, Miss., 1976-84, Montfort Jones Hosp., Kosciusko, Miss., 1987-88, Quitman County Hosp. & Nursing Home, Marks, Miss., 1989—. Mem. ANA, Am. Orgn. Nurse Execs., Miss. Hosp. Assn., orgn. Nurse Execs. (bd. dirs.), Soc. for Risk Mgmt. Democrat. Baptist. Home: Rte 3 Box 170 Batesville MS 38606 Office: Quitman County Hosp & Nursing Home 340 Getwell Marks MS 38646

YATES, PATRICIA ENGLAND, employment company executive; b. Sparta, Tenn., Sept. 18, 1958; d. Edsel and Gladys Mary (Garland) England; m. Dennis Eugene Yates, Nov. 30, 1990. BS in Home Econs., Tenn. Tech. U., 1982. Purchasing sec. Porelon, Inc., Cookeville, Tenn., 1982-87; buyer purchasing dept. Tenn. Tech. U., Cookeville, Tenn., 1987-88; dir. pers. J & S Constrn. Co., Inc., Cookeville, 1988-93; placement coord. Putnam Employment Svc. Inc., Cookeville, 1993—; projects asst. Nat. and Internat. Issues Rsch., Sparta, 1982—. Mc. Cookeville Adult Literacy Coun. Mem. Bus. and Profl. Women's Orgn. (treas. 1990, 2d v.p. 1992, Finalist Young Careerist 1994), Am. Bus. Women's Assn., U.C. Soc. Resource Mgmt. (treas. 1993), Internat. Platform Assn. Office: Putnam Employment Svc Inc 430 S Lowe Cookeville TN 38501

YATES, RENEE HARRIS, economist; b. Oct. 20, 1950; d. Marion and Betty Jane (Edgerton) Harris; m. Earl W. Yates, Sept. 6, 1980 (div. July 1991); 1 child, Clinton Harris Yates. BA, Western Coll. for Women, 1972; MA in Internat. Studies, Johns Hopkins U., 1974. Project devel. officer U.S. Agy. for Internat. Devel., Washington, 1975-81; internat. economist U.S. Treasury Dept./Office Sec. of Internat. Affairs, Washington, 1981-87; pres. World Trade Assocs., Inc., Washington, 1987—; pres. InterFuture, N.Y.C., 1984-87. Mem. TransAfrica, Washington, 1991. Mem. Thursday Luncheon Group. Office: World Trade Assoc Inc 7320 Carroll Ave Takoma Park MD 20912

YATES, SHIRLEY JEAN, educator; b. St. Louis, Oct. 3, 1949; d. Norman William and Wilma (Bratton) M.; m. Joseph Hans Sturm, June 24, 1972 (div. June 1980); m. Robert A. Yates, June 2, 1984 (dec. 1993). BA, Harris Tchrs. Coll., 1970; M in Bus. Mgmt., Webster U., 1981. Cert. adminstrv. specialist; cert. gifted tchr. Educator St. Louis Pub. Schs., 1970—; tchr. gifted lang. arts McKinley Classical Jr. Acad., St. Louis, Mo. vol. abused neglected infants Salvation Army, St. Louis, 1986-92; mem. Dem. Nat. Com., Washington, 1993—, St. Clair NOW, Belleville, Ill., 1991—. Scholarship Parson's Blewett, 1981, 86, 94; recipient Pub. Svc. award Dept. of Justice, 1991, 92. Mem. NOW. Democrat. Roman Catholic. Office: McKinley Classical Jr Acad 2156 Russell Blvd Saint Louis MO 63104

YATES, VIVIAN MARIE, nurse educator; b. Elyria, Ohio, July 15, 1952; d. James William and Nellie Sue (Corn) Shores; children: Andre, Eric and Leslie Board; m. Edward William Yates, Mar. 17, 1990. ADN, Lorain County Community Coll., 1980; BSN, U. Akron, 1987; MSN, Kent State U., 1994. Staff nurse, float nurse Elyria (Ohio) Meml. Hosp., 1980-87; nurse mgr. Lorain (Ohio) Community Hosp., 1987-88, nurse case coord., 1988-89; faculty practical nursing Lorain County C.C., 1989—; occupational health nurse GM Corp., Elyria, 1983-84. Mem. ANA, Ohio Nurses Assn., Midwest Nurses Rsch. Soc., Ohio Orgn. Practical Nurse Educators, Sigma Theta Tau. Democrat. Office: Lorain County CC 1005 Abbe Rd N Elyria OH 44035-1613

YATES-BUCKLES, JEANNETTE KEBER, prosthodontics educator; b. Hackensack, N.J., Dec. 22, 1942; d. Richard Sigmund and Jeannette Ida (Zweil) Keber; m. Edward Scott Yates, Mar. 18, 1961 (div. June 1979); m. Kenneth Peter Buckles, Oct. 17, 1987; children: Darlene Denise, Edward Scott Jr. A. Applied Sci., Union Coll., 1972; student, Fairleigh Dickinson U., 1972-74; DMD, U. Dentistry and Medicine N.J., Newark, 1977. Postgrad. resident Mt. Sinai Hosp., N.Y.C., 1977-78; assoc. dentist Wayne (N.J.) Dental Group, 1978, Fairfield (N.J.) Dental Group, 1978-79; pvt. practice dentistry Hackensack, 1979—; assoc. prof. prosthodontics Fairleigh Dickinson U. Dental Sch., Teaneck, N.J., 1979-90; attending dentist Hackensack Med. Ctr., 1979-89. Fellow Acad. Gen. Dentistry (award 1987); mem. N.J. Women Dentists Study Group (v.p. 1980-82), N.J. Network Bus. and Profl. Women (v.p. 1985-87, bd. dirs. 1984-92). Republican. Scientologist. Office: 67 Summit Ave Hackensack NJ 07601-1290

YAWMAN, CHERYL LYNN SHANK, executive recruiter, accounting educator; b. Rochester, N.Y., Sept. 3, 1965; d. Frederick A. and Josephine Marie (Mangione) Shank; m. Philip Henry Edward Yawman, May 29, 1993. BS in Acctg., St. John Fisher Coll., 1986. CPA, N.Y. Staff auditor Deloitte Haskins & Sells, Rochester and Woodbury, N.Y., 1986-88; corp. auditor May Dept. Stores, Rochester, 1988-89; acctg. mgr. Sibley Co. divsn. May Dept. Stores, Rochester, 1989-90; sr. placement mgr. Robert Half International, Inc., Rochester, 1990—; adj. prof. acctg. St. John Fisher Coll., Rochester, 1993—. V.p. alumnae bd. dirs. Nazareth Acad., Rochester, 1990—; bd. dirs. Inst. Mgmt. Accts., 1986—, chpt. sec., treas., various other positions. Mem. N.Y. State Soc. CPA's (asst. dir. publicity 1993—). Roman Catholic. Office: Robert Half Internat Inc 2 State St Ste 910 Rochester NY 14614-1305

YAWORSKI, JOANN, reading skills educator; b. Phillipsburg, N.J., Oct. 11, 1956; d. Michael and Cecilia (Ruchala) Y. BA, Pa. State U., 1977; MEd, Millersville U., 1982; postgrad., U. Houston, 1984, Lehigh U., 1988-90, SUNY, Albany, 1991—. Cert. tchr. Russian lang., Russian area studies, reading specialist, elem. edn., Tex., N.J., Pa. Reading tutor Ephrata (Pa.) Sr. High Sch., 1980-81; tchr. Am. History/World Cultures Linden Hall Sch., Lititz, Pa., 1981-82; tchr., Russian lang. Spring Branch Sch. Dist., Houston, Tex., 1982-85; dir. devel. reading Green Mountain Coll., Poultney, Vt., 1989—; presenter 28th ann. conf. Coll. Reading and Learning Assn., Tempe, Ariz., 1995. Mem. U.S. Figure Skating Assn. Democrat. Roman Catholic. Home: 31 York St Poultney VT 05764-1024 Office: Green Mountain Coll 16 College St Poultney VT 05764-1199

YEADON-MCGINNIS, PEARL, musician, educator; b. Missoula, Mont., Mar. 2, 1948; d. Ralph Yeadon and Helen Elizabeth (McKee) McGinnis; m. Douglas Edward Erny; 1 child, Pamela Ann Erny-Glasell. MusB, U. Mont., 1969, MusM, 1970; student, Cerritos Jr. Coll., 1973-74; DMA in Performance, Lit. and German, U. Ill., 1995. Substitute tchr. El Segundo (Calif.) Sch. System, 1970-71; pvt. vocal instrn. Kassel, Germany, 1980-85, Munich, Germany, 1985-89; grad. asst. U. Ill., Champaign-Urbana, 1989-91; asst. prof. Millikin U., Decatur, Ill., 1991-93, S.W. Mo. State U., Springfield, 1993—; vis. artist Ea. Ill. U., Charleston 1974, 77, judge Dist. Met. Opera auditions, 1993; judge dist. auditions Nat. Assn. Tchrs. of Singing, 1992, Springfield, 1993; judge vocal contest Drury Coll., 1993; judge S.W. Mo. State U. Honors Choir Outstanding Singer, 1993. Composer: From Bed to Breakfast, Op. 2, 1994; dir., producer, filmed, editor, graphic arts, publicity Lincoln: Thomas Lincoln's Goosenest Prairie Farm, A Visit with Lincoln; recordings include Sixteenth Mass (Haydn), 9 Lessons of Christmas (La Montaine), Christmas Oratorio (Bach), Chamber Mass (Vivaldi); performances on TV include Series 6: Great Tenors, Mario del Monaco, The Lincoln-Douglas Debates of 1858, 1994; opera performances in U.S. and Europe including Am. Opera Co., San Diego Opera, West Coast Opera, L.A. Opera Ensemble, Beverly Hills Opera, Theater Divadlo Czech Republic, 1992-93, Kassel State Theatre, 1980-85, others, concerts with orch., concerts with piano, recitals; guest European theatres including Wiesbaden, Saarbrücken, Kiel, Innsbruck, Munich, Ulm, Enskede, Zagreb; compiler, editor: The Collected Speeches of Ralph Y. McGinnis. Mem. Actor's Equity, Am. Guild Mus. Artists, German Musicians Union. Republican. Episcopalian. Office: SW Mo State U 901 S National Blvd Springfield MO 65804-0094

YEAGER, ANDREA WHEATON, editor; b. Baytown, Tex., Apr. 17, 1951; d. Virgil Jerry Jr. and Billy Ruth (Leslie) Wheaton; m. Danny Rhea Bowen, Feb. 21, 1976 (div. Sept. 1985); m. Hubert Allen Yeager, Jr., Dec. 21, 1985. BA in Teaching, Sam Houston State U., Huntsville, Tex., 1973. Assoc. editor The Houstonian, Sam Houston State U., Huntsville, Tex., 1970-73; reporter The Orange (Tex.) Leader, 1973-74, lifestyle editor, 1974-78; editor The Suburbia Reporter, Houston, 1978-79; copy editor The Houston Chronicle, 1979-81, features copy desk chief, 1981-85; copy editor The Sun Herald, Biloxi, Miss., 1986-88, features editor, 1988-91, mng. editor, 1991—. Pres. Altrusa Internat. of Biloxi, 1993—; bd. dirs. Boys & Girls Clubs of Gulf Coast, Biloxi, 1992—; crisis vol. Gulf Coast Women's Ctr., Biloxi, 1991—; mem. Leadership Gulf Coast Class 1991-92; mem. nutrition adv. bd. Gulfport Sch. Dist./Am. Cancer soc., 1993—; bd. dirs. Am. Heart Assn., Gulfport, 1990-92, Crimestoppers. Mem. La.-Miss. AP Mng. Editors (2d v.p. 1994—), Harrison County Home Econs. Coun. (v.p. 1991—), Miss. Press Assn., Pub. Rels. Assn. Miss., Gayfers Career Club. Republican. Methodist. Home: 12297 Windward Dr Gulfport MS 39503-5501 Office: The Sun Herald 205 Debuys Rd Gulfport MS 39507-2838

YEAGER, CAROLINE HALE, radiologist, consultant; b. Little Rock, Sept. 5, 1946; d. George Glenn and Crenor Burnelle (Hale) Y.; m. William Berg Singer, July 8, 1978; children: Adina Atkinson Singer, Sarah Rose Singer. BA, Ind. U., Bloomington, 1968; MD, Ind. U., Indpls., 1971. Diplomate Am. Bd. Radiology; med. lic. State of Calif. Intern Good Samaritan Hosp., Los Angeles, 1971-72; resident in radiology King Drew Med. Ctr. UCLA, Los Angeles, 1972-76; dir. radiology Hubert Humphrey Health Ctr., Los Angeles, 1976-77; asst. prof. radiology UCLA, Los Angeles, 1977-84; asst. prof. radiology King Drew Med. Ctr. UCLA, Los Angeles, 1977-85, dir. ultrasound, 1977-84; ptnr. pvt. practice Beverly Breast Ctr., Beverly Hills, Calif., 1984-87; cons. Clarity Communications, Pasadena, Calif., 1981—; pvt. practice radiology Claude Humphrey Health Ctr., 1991-93; dir. sonograms and mammograms Rancho Los Amigos Med. Ctr., 1993-94; trustee Assn. Teaching Physicians, L.A., 1976-81; cons. King Drew Med. Ctr., 1984, Gibraltar Savs., 1987, Cal Fed. Inc., 1986, Medical Faculty At Home Professions, 1989—, Mobil Diagnostics, 1991-92, Xerox Corp., 1990-91, Frozen Leopard, Inc., 1990-91. Author: (with others) Infectious Disease, 1978, Anatomy and Physiology for Medical Transcriptionists, 1992; contbr. articles to profl. jours. Trustee U. Synagogue, Los Angeles, 1975-79; mem. Friends of Pasadena Playhouse, 1987-90. Grantee for innovative tng. Nat. Fund for Med. Edn., 1980-81. Mem. Am. Inst. Ultrasound in Medicine, L.A. Radiology Soc. (ultrasound sect.), Nat. Soc. Performance and Instrn. (chmn. conf. Database 1991, publs. L.A. chpt. 1990, info. systems L.A. chpt. 1991, dir. adminstrn. L.A. chpt. 1992, Outstanding Achievement in Performance Improvement award L.A. chpt. 1990, bd. dirs. 1990-93, Pres. award for Outstanding Chpt. 1992, v.p. programs 1993), Stanford Profl. Women L.A. Jewish. Home and Office: 3520 Yorkshire Rd Pasadena CA 91107-5440

YEARWOOD, TRISHA, country music singer, songwriter; b. Monticello, Ga., 1964; m. Chris Latham (div.); m. Robert Reynolds, May 21, 1994. Degree in Music Bus., Belmont Coll. Intern MTM Records, demo singer, commercial jingles singer; recording artist MCA Records. Albums include Trisha Yearwood, 1991 (platnium), Hearts in Armor, 1992 (Grammy nomination: Best Country Female Vocal, 1994 for "Walkaway Joe"), The Song Remembers When, 1993; back-up vocalist Garth Brooks albums; opening act Garth Brooks Tour, 1991; TV appearances on TNN American Music Shop. Named Best New Country Artist by Am. Music Awards, 1992, Top New Female Vocalist by Acad. Country Music, 1992; first female in country music history to have debut single reach #1 on charts with She's in Love with the Love, 1991. Office: MCA Records Internat 70 Universal City Plaza Universal City CA 91608*

YEARY, RUTH ANN, arts administrator, artist; b. Apr. 3, 1944; d. Charles Doxey and Ruth (Mathews) Turek; m. Jerry D. Yeary, Aug. 11, 1967; children: Rebekah, Dean, Aaron. Student, Ill. State U., 1965-67; BA in Edn., Wichita (Kans.) State U., 1970. Tchr. St. Francis (Kans.) Unified Sch.

Dist., 1970-72; sch. lunch supr. Goodland (Kans.) Unified Sch. Dist., 1972-73; house remodeler, Winfield, Kans., 1976-89. Trustee Winfield Pub. Libr., 1988-91; bd. dirs. Winfield Community Theater, 1976-81. Recipient Hambone award Winfield Community Theater, 1979. Mem. Nat. League Am. Pen Women, Assn. Community Arts Agys. Kans. (bd. dirs.), Hypatia Study Club. Baptist. Office: Winfield Arts and Humanities Coun 700 Gary St Ste A Winfield KS 67156-3137

YEAZEL, JANET ARLENE, insurance agent; b. Dayton, Ohio, July 5, 1949; d. Rufford and Annetta Gertrude (Bridge) Mobley; m. Walter A. Yeazel, May 18, 1974 (div. Sept. 1992); 1 child, Randall Wayne. Attended, Wright State U., 1983-86, Sinclair C.C., Dayton, 1992-93. Claim supr. Aetna Life & Casualty, Dayton, 1967-87; ins. broker Profl. Brokerage Agy., Inc., Dayton, 1988—. Mem. Mut. Ins. Adv. Assn., Vandalia-Butler C. of C., Dayton C. of C. (membership com.). Republican. Mem. United Meth. Ch. Office: Profl Brokerage Agy Inc 301 E 6th St Dayton OH 45414

YEAZELL, RUTH BERNARD, English language educator; b. N.Y.C., Apr. 4, 1947; d. Walter and Annabelle (Reich) Bernard; m. Stephen C. Yeazell, Aug. 14, 1969 (div. 1980). BA with high honors, Swarthmore Coll., 1967; MPhil (Woodrow Wilson fellow), Yale U., 1970, PhD, 1971. Asst. prof. English Boston U., 1971-74, UCLA, 1975-77, assoc. prof., 1977-80, prof., 1980-91, Yale U, 1991—, dir. grad. studies, 1993—. Author: Language and Knowledge in the Late Novels of Henry James, 1976, Death and Letters of Alice James, 1981, Fictions of Modesty: Women and Courtship in the English Novel, 1991; assoc. editor Nineteenth-Century Fiction, 1977-80; editor: Sex, Politics, and Science in the 19th Century Novel, 1986, Henry James: A Collection of Critical Essays, 1994. Woodrow Wilson fellow, 1967-68, Guggenheim fellow, 1979-80, NEH fellow, 1988-89, Pres.'s Rsch. fellow U. Calif., 1988-89. Mem. MLA (exec. coun. 1985-88), English Inst. (supervising com. 1983-86). Office: Yale U Dept English New Haven CT 06524

YELLEN, LINDA, film director, writer, producer; b. Forest Hills, N.Y., July 13; d. Seymour and Bernice (Mittelman) Y. BA magna cum laude, Barnard Coll.; MFA in Film, Columbia U., PhD in Lang., Lit. and Communications. Mem. film faculty Columbia U., N.Y.C., Barnard Coll., Yale U., CUNY; prin. Chrysalis-Yellen Prodns., Inc., N.Y.C., 1982—; pres. The Linda Yellen Co., N.Y.C., 1988—; represented by William Morris Agy. Producer, dir.: (films) Prospera; Come Out, Come Out; Looking Up, 1978; exec. producer (film) Everybody Wins, 1989; producer, dir., co-writer (film) Prisoner Without a Name, Cell Without A Number, NBC-TV, 1984 (Peabody award, Writers Guild nominee for best screenplay); exec. producer, producer (CBS network spls.): Hard Hat and Legs, 1980; Mayflower: The Pilgrims Adventure, 1979; Playing For Time, 1981 (Emmy award for best dramatic spl., Peabody award, Christopher award); exec. producer, producer, co-writer (CBS network spl.) The Royal Romance of Charles and Diana, 1982; exec. producer, producer (TV movies): Second Serve: The Renee Richards Story, CBS-TV, 1986 (Luminous award), Liberace, CBS-TV, 1988; exec. producer Hunt for Stolen War Treasures, syndicated TV, 1989, Sweet Bird of Youth, NBC-TV, 1989; dir., writer, prodr. Chantilly Lace, 1993, Parallel Lives, 1994 (Showtime); contbr. articles to N.Y. Times, Village Voice, Interview, Hollywood Reporter. Mem. Dirs. Guild Am. (exec. council), Writers Guild Am., Acad. TV Arts and Scis., Women in Film.

YELLIN, JUDITH, electrologist; b. Balt., Feb. 21; d. Jack and Sarah (Grebow) Levin; m. Sidney Yellin, Jan. 1; children: David, Paul, Tamar. Student U. Md., Catonsville Community Coll. Mgr. credit dept. Lincoln Co., Balt.; office mgr. Seaview Constrn. Co.; owner, operator Yellin Telephone Soliciting Agy.; mgr. Liberty Antique Shop; owner, mgr. Judith Yellin Electrology, 1973—; creator jewelry; chief examiner Md. State Bd. Electrology, 1978-81; designer jewelry. Poet: New American Poetry Anthology, 1988, Great Poems of the Western World, Vol. II, 1990. Mem. Am. Electrolysis Assn., Md. Assn. Profl. Electrologists. Avocations: travel, reading, collecting Haitian, art deco, nouveau art and jewelry, poetry, inventing. Home: 6232 Blackstone Ave Baltimore MD 21209-3909 Office: Judith Yellin Electrology 1401 Reisterstown Rd Baltimore MD 21208-3807

YEN, MICHELE CALEN, accountant; b. Rockville Centre, N.Y., Nov. 13, 1962; d. Victor Michael and Kathleen Ann (Murphy) Calen; m. Henry Chin-Yuan Yen, Oct. 8, 1988; children: Andrew Paul Yean-Shang, Matthew Victor Yean-Jah. AS in Acctg., Nassau C.C., Garden City, N.Y., 1983; BS in Acctg., St. John's U., Jamaica, N.Y., 1985. CPA, N.Y. Acctg. asst. Continental Extrustion Corp.; bookkeeper Sids Pants, Garden City; field auditor Nassau County Comptr., Mineola, N.Y., 1985-87; supervising sr. KPMG Peat Marwick LLP, Jericho, N.Y., mgr., sr. mgr.; v.p., treas. The Galamery Co., 1989—; pres. Aegis Info. Sys. Inc., Hicksville, N.Y. Mem. AICPA, N.Y. State Soc. CPAs, Inst. Mgmt. Accts. (L.I. chpt., dir. cmty. svc. 1989-90, dir. program and roster 1990-91, v.p. comm. 1991-92, v.p. fin. and adminstrn. 1992-93, pres. 1993-94, mem. past pres. club, Ed Brown Meml. award), Cath. Daus. Am. Office: KPMG Peat Marwick LLP One Jericho Plz Jericho NY 11753

YEN, YI-MEI, clinic nurse; b. Kaohsiung, Taiwan, Republic of China, May 11, 1962; d. Chin-Chang Yen and Ai-Kuei Tsai; m. Pei-Yu Chou, Nov. 23, 1989; children: Gabriel Chou, Raphael Chou. BSN, Taipei (Taiwan) Med. Coll., 1985; MSN, U. Mo., 1993. Charge nurse Cathay Gen. Hosp., Taipei, 1985-87; clin. instr. Mei-Ho Jr. Coll. Nursing, Pingtung, Taiwan, 1987-88; clinic nurse Clark County Health Dept., Jeffersonville, Ind., 1993—; teaching asst. U. Mo., 1992. Baptist. Home: 107 Fenley Ave # G5 Louisville KY 40207

YENSON, EVELYN P., lottery official; b. Johannesburg, Republic of South Africa, Dec. 20, 1944; came to U.S., 1963; d. T. and P.F. Yenson; children: Megan Y. Sun, Elliot H. Sun. BA, Coll. New Rochelle, 1967; MA, U. Wis., Milw., 1968. Planner/evaluator Seattle Pub. Schs., 1971-73; dir. planning divsn., various other positions Dept. Cmty. Devel., Seattle, 1973-83; planning dir. Seattle Ctr., 1983-84; pvt. practice as cons. Seattle, 1984-85; dir., dep. commr. Expo '86, Vancouver, B.C., Can., 1985-86; dir. Wash. State Lottery, Olympia, 1987—; presenter in field. Mem. Mcpl. League Bd., Seattle, 1991-92; bd. dirs. Seattle Arts Commn., 1989-93, Camp Brotherhood, Seattle, 1994—; sec. bd. dirs. Sunhill, Inc., Seattle. Mem. N.Am. Assn. State and Provincial Lotteries (pres. 1991-93, past pres.). Roman Catholic. Home: 2350 34th St Seattle WA 98144 Office: Wash State Lottery PO Box 43001 Olympia WA 98504-3001

YEO, DALE E., primary education educator, administrator; b. Mnpls., Jan. 21, 1943; d. Earnest Gripp and Margaret (Berkey) Knauss; m. Robert Pickering Yeo, Aug. 23, 1963; 1 child, William Allen Yeo. BS, U. Minn., Duluth, 1965; MA, No. Mich. U., 1980. Permanent cert. primary, elem. and secondary edn. Tchr. jr. and sr. high English Calumet (Mich.) Pub. Schs., 1966-67; title 1/chpt. 1 tchr. and adminstr. Lake Linden (Mich.)-Hubbell Pub. Schs., 1968-94; Chpt. 1 dir. Lake Linden-Hubbell Pub. Sch., 1990-94. Charter mem. Copper Country Humane Soc., 1973—, numerous offices held; mem. Lake Linden-Hubbell PTO, 1991—, Lake Linden-Hubbell Sch. Improvement Com., 1992—, Copper Country LWV, 1994—. Named Outstanding Mem. of Yr. Copper Country Edn. Assn./Lake Linden-Hubbell Tchrs., 1985/86, 93/94. Mem. NEA, Internat. Reading Assn., Mich. Edn. Assn., Mich. Reading Coun., Copper Country Edn. Assn., Copper Country Reading Coun. (sec. 1990—), Lake Linden-Hubbell Edn. Assn. Protestant. Home: 739 7th St Laurium MI 49913-2401 Office: Lake Linden Hubbell Pub Schs 601 Calumet St Lake Linden MI 49945-1099

YERION, JUDITH MARIE, education director; b. Salem, Oreg., Sept. 11, 1941; d. George Russel and Jeannette May (Stanton) Graen; m. James Milton Yerion, Feb. 8, 1964; children: Jeannette Marie, Julienne Melea, Janine Melissa. BS in Edn., Oreg. Coll. Edn., 1963; MAT, Lewis and Clark Coll., 1977; postgrad., 1993—. Tchr. grade 5 Aumsville (Oreg.) Sch. Dist., 1964-65, Corbett (Oreg.) Sch. Dist., 1965-66; tchr., drama coach Centennial Sch. Dist., Portland, Oreg., 1966-80; tchr., tutor Back to Basics Tutoring, Portland, 1984—; dir., tchr. Eastside Edn. Ctr., Portland, 1990—. Sunday sch. instr. St. Aidan's Episcopal Ch., Gresham, Oreg., 1974-90, dir. religious edn., 1989-91; founder clown troupe ministry Rainbow Children, Gresham, 1979-83; lay minister Ch. of Holy Spirit, Portland, 1992—. Republican.

YERKES, ADELINE MEISMER, community health nurse; b. Aurora, Nebr., Mar. 25, 1943; d. Dennis LaVerne and Phyllis (Zehr) Meismer; m. Michael King Yerkes, Apr. 11, 1964; 1 child, David. BSN, U. Nebr., 1964; MPH, U. Okla., 1980. School nurse Omaha Pub. Schs., 1964-69; nursing supr. Tulsa City-County Health Dept., 1969-71; dist. nursing supr., cons. Omaha-Douglas County Vis. Nurses Assn., 1971-74; dist. nursing supr. Okla. State Dept. Health, Lawton, 1975-78; eldercare and home care cons. Okla. State Dept. Health, Oklahoma City, 1978-80, dir. chronic disease, home care and elder care, 1980-87, chief chronic disease, 1987—; adj. prof. Coll. Nursing Okla. U., Oklahoma city, 1983—, Coll. Pub. Health, 1985—; cons. case mgr. commn. child and youth Vis. Nurse Assn., Oklahoma city, 1983-86, home care Hospice Cen. Okla., Oklahoma City, 1984-87. Aging enabler Presbyn. Ch., Okla., 1990. Named Outstanding Chpt. Women Bus. and Profl. Women, 1981. Mem. ANA, Nat. League for Nursing (com. chair), Okla. League for Nursing, Am. Diabetes Assn. (pres. 1983-86, Outstanding Health Profl. 1986, com. chair legis., patiend edn. ann meeting), Assn. State and Territorial Chronic Disease (bd. dirs. program, treas., 1988-92, pres. 1995, Outstanding Ledership award with CDC 1992), Sigma Theta Tau. Republican. Office: Okla State Health Dept 1000 NE 10th St Oklahoma City OK 73117-1299

YERKES, SUSAN GAMBLE, columnist; b. Evanston, Ill., Sept. 5, 1951; d. Charles Anthony Yerkes and Darthea (Campbell) Higgins. BA, U. Tex., 1974; MA, Wichita State U., 1976. Anchor radio newsperson Sta. KAKE, Wichita, Kans., 1976; writer, anchor TV newsperson Sta. KAKE-TV, Wichita, 1976-80, dir. pub. affairs, 1977-81; freelance writer internat. and U.S. newspapers and mags., 1981-86; columnist San Antonio Light, 1986-93, San Antonio Express-News, 1993—; co-owner Y&S Comm., San Antonio and San Diego, 1987—; instr. comm. arts Incarnate Word Coll., San Antonio, 1989—; contbg. writer Tex. Monthly, Austin, 1989—; talk show host Sta. WOAI, 1993; restaurant reviewer Images mag., 1993—. Dir. Tex. Pub. Radio, San Antonio, 1986—, San Antonio's Opera Guild, 1986—, Bexar County Women's Ctr., San Antonio, 1989—, Communications in Schs., 1989—. Fellow Amundsen Inst. for U.S./Mexico Studies; mem. Nat. Press Women (1st place nat. column award 1987), Pub. Rel. Soc. Am., Internat. Women's Forum, Phi Beta Kappa (San Antonio chpt. bd. dirs.). Episcopalian. Home: 7711 Broadway St Apt 29B San Antonio TX 78209-3269 Office: San Antonio Express-News Ave E & 3rd San Antonio TX 78205-1987

YESH-PRIBOZIE, CONNIE, association executive. Exec. dir. YWCA, Johnstown, Pa. Office: YWCA 526 Somerset St Johnstown PA 15901-2689

YESLOW, ROSEMARIE, real estate professional; b. Detroit; d. Karl E. and Madeline E. (Paret) Norberg; widowed; children: Bradford (dec.), Tod, Eric (dec.), Mark. Student, U. Miami, 1947-49; AA in Journalism, Broward Jr. Coll., 1972; student, Fla. Atlantic U., 1973-75. Ins. agt. Wittenstein Ins. Agy., Hollywood, Fla., 1965-75; owner, operator The Karl Motel/Apartments, Hallandale, Fla., 1980—; realtor/assoc. The Keyes Co., Hollywood, 1990-93; realtor, assoc. Ebby Halliday Real Estate, Dallas, 1993—; real estate investor, Hollywood, 1960—. Contbr. articles to profl. jours. Edn. v.p. Nat. Coun. Jewish Women, Hollywood, 1960-66; unit and dept. chmn. LWV, Ft. Lauderdale, Fla., 1960-72; edn. chmn. Dem. Exec. Com., Broward County, Fla., 1976-78; mem. planning and zoning bd. City of Hallandale, 1988-92. Recipient Sch. Bell award Fla. Edn. Assn., 1966. Mem. Hollywood Bd. Realtors, Hallandale Adult Cmty. Ctr. (adv. com., Cert. of Appreciation 1989), Hallandale Citizens United, Hallandale C. of C. (bd. dirs. 1987-92, Small Bus. Person of Yr. award 1990), Sierra Club. Democrat. Jewish. Home: 4247 Throckmorton St Dallas TX 75219 Office: Ebby Halliday Real Estate 8333 Douglas Ave Ste 100 Dallas TX 75225-6632

YESMONT, GEORGIA ARIS, psychologist; b. Boston, Apr. 23, 1943; d. Aristides and Frances (Novello) Lucas; children: April Aris, Christopher Kenneth. EdM, SUNY, Buffalo, 1966; Sch. Psychology Cert. Degree, NYU, 1969; PhD, Hofstra U., 1991. Lic. psychologist, N.Y.State; cert. sch. psychologist, N.Y. State. Sch. psychologist Harrison (N.Y.) Sch. Dist., 1970-72, Garden City (N.Y.) Sch. Dist., 1975-79, Hewlett-Woodmere (N.Y.) Sch. Dist., 1982-84; psychotherapist Ocean Promenade Health Related Facility, Queens, N.Y., 1988-89; sch. psychologist Nassau BOCES, Massapequa, N.Y., 1989-90; rsch. health analyst Nassau-Suffolk Health Systems Agy., Plainview, N.Y., 1991-92; psychologist in pvt. practice L.I., N.Y., 1993—; sch. psychologist Massapequa Sch. Dist., 1992—; cons. psychologist Carillon Nursing Home, Huntington, N.Y., 1993—; conf. organizer/Hiv/AIDS rschs. Nassau-Suffolk Health System Agy., Plainview, 1991-92; progrma devel. com. South Nassau Cmty. Hosp. Mental Health Clinic, Oceanside, 1988; lectr. in field. Contbr. articles to profl. jours. Committeeperson Dem. Party, Huntington, 1992—. Recipient H. Alan Robinson Outstanding Doctoral Dissertation award Hofstra U. Grad. Faculty, 1992. Mem. APA, Nassau County Psychol. Assn. (social issues com. 1993-94), Ea. Psychol. Assn., Nat. Alliance for the Mentally Ill, Greek-Am. Women's Network, L.I. Women's Inst., L.I. Marriage and Family Therapy Assn. Greek Orthodox. Home and Office: 17 Richard Ln Huntington NY 11743-2353

YETMAN, LEITH ELEANOR, administrator, educator; b. Kellits, Clarendon, Jamaica, West Indies; came to U.S., 1967; d. 2nd child of 12 children of Percival Augustus and Grace Elizabeth (Anderson) Y.; m. Noel W. Miller, Apr. 8, 1961 (div. 1977); children: Donovan, Jo-Ann, Kirk, Lori-Anne; adopted children: LaFara, Samantha, Brandon Ryan. Attended, Bethlehem Teachers Coll., St. Elizabeth, Jamaica, 1960; BSC, Baruch Coll., 1976; MA, Columbia U., 1978. Cert. tchr., N.Y. Legal sec. various law firms, N.Y.C., 1969-76; instr. Taylor Bus. Inst., N.Y.C., 1977-79; founder, pres., dir. N.Y. Inst. Bus. Tech., N.Y.C., 1981—. Recipient Outstanding Achievement award Baruch Coll. Alumni Assn., 1989; Leith E. Yetman Day proclaimed June 1, 1994 by Manhattan Borough Pres. Mem. Better Bus. Bur. N.Y.C. Office: NY Inst Bus Tech 401 Park Ave S New York NY 10016

YETSO, KATHY, sales executive; b. Aliquippa, Pa., Feb. 28, 1959; d. John J. and Dorothy (Green) Y. Diploma in Math., Grove City Coll., 1981; MBA, U. N.C., 1988. Computer programmer Armstrong World Ind., Lancaster, Pa., 1981-83; systems analyst Thomasville (N.C.) Furniture, 1983-88, contract salesperson, 1989-92; salesperson, Ala. Lineage Home Furnishings, High Point, N.C., 1993—. Sunday Sch. tchr. various Cath. Chs., 1983—; vol. YMCA, High Point, 1983-93. Home and Office: 214 Chadwick Ln Helena AL 35080-4914

YIANNAKIS, LINDA C., speech-language pathologist; b. Phila., Feb. 13, 1952; m. Andrew Yiannakis. AB magna cum laude, U. Conn., 1975; MS, U. So. Fla., 1982. Clinician Albuquerque (N.Mex.) Hearing and Speech Ctr., 1982-84, N.Mex. Dept. Corrections, Albuquerque, 1982-84, Isleta (N.Mex.) Pueblo Head Start Program, 1982-84; clin. coord. S.E. Conn. Hearing and Speech Ctr., Norwich, 1984-88; bilingual speech pathologist Windham (Conn.) Pub. Schs., 1988—. Organizer Parent Edn. Group, Isleta (N.Mex.) Pueblo Head Start, 1983-84, Self-Def. for Disabled, CT TBI Assn., Hemlocks Ctr., Hebron, Conn., 1989-91, Community Svc. Program, Natchaug Sch., Willimantic, Conn., 1994. Recipient Outstanding Clin. Svcs. award Ctr. for Children with Spl. Needs, U. So. Fla., Tampa, 1981, Outstanding Vol. Svc. award Project Head Start, Isleta, 1984. Mem. Am. Speech, Lang., Hearing Assn. (CCC/SLP), Conn. Speech, Lang., Hearing Assn., U.S. Judo Assn. (3d degree black belt), Phi Beta Kappa. Democrat.

YIANNIAS, NANCY MAGAS, municipal official; b. Kalamazoo, Feb. 1, 1936; d. George A. and Irene (Callas) Magas; m. Andrew Chris Yiannias, Oct. 20, 1968; 1 child, Chris Andrew. BA, Wester Mich. U., 1957; MPH, U. Mich., 1963. Registered sanitarian, Ill. Health educator Stickney Pub. Health Dist., Burbank, Ill., 1966-72, Chgo. Heart Assn., 1972-73; health coord. Village of Elk Grove, Ill., 1974—. Bd. counselors Alexian Bros. Med. Ctr., Elk Grove Village, 1977-93. Mem. Am. Pub. Health Assn., Ill. Pub. Health Assn. (sec. 1981), Soc. Pub. Health Educators, Ill. Soc. Pub. Health Educators (program planning com. 1966), Ill. Environ. Health Assn., N.W. Suburban Access to Care Assn. Home: 1521 Manor Ln Park Ridge IL 60068-1541 Office: Elk Grove Village Dept Health 901 Wellington Ave Elk Grove Village IL 60007-3389

YIH, MAE DUNN, state legislator; b. Shanghai, China, May 24, 1928; d. Chung Woo and Fung Wen (Feng) Dunn; m. Stephen W.H. Yih, 1953; children: Donald, Daniel. B.A., Barnard Coll., 1951; postgrad. Columbia U., 1951-52. Asst. to bursar Barnard Coll., N.Y.C., 1952-54; mem. Oreg. Ho. of Reps. from 36th dist., 1977-83, Oreg. Senate from 19th dist., 1983—. Mem. Clover Ridge Elem. Sch. Bd., Albany, Oreg., from 1969-78, Albany Union High Sch. Bd., from 1975-79, Joint Legis. Ways and Means Com., Joint Legis. Audit Com., Senate Transp. Com., Western States Forestry Task Force, 1993, senate pres. pro-tempore, 1993. Episcopalian. Home: 34465 Yih Ln NE Albany OR 97321-9557 Office: Oreg State Senate 206 State St Salem OR 97301-3444

YILMAZCETIN, MURIEL JEAN, human resources and outplacement consultant; b. Bklyn., Nov. 9, 1946; d. Jerry Isaac and Blossom (Markowitz) Negrie; m. Neal Savitt, Apr. 29, 1967 (div. Jan. 1973); children: Gary, Jason, Matthew Keysor; m. Sevket Yilmazcetin, Apr. 4, 1982 (div. Aug. 1993). BA in Anthropology, Calif. State U., Northridge, 1968; MA in Applied Psychology, U. Santa Monica, 1991. Mgr. pers. and adminstrn. Kontron Electronics, Inc., Mountain View, Calif., 1980-86; corp. mgr. human resources Kabi Vitrum, Inc., Almeda, Calif., 1986-88, Nova Pharm. Corp., Balt., 1988-90; human resources cons. Mentor, Inc., Severna Park, Md., 1990-93; v.p. Exec. Asst. Search, Balt., 1992—, Dinte Resources, Inc., McLean, Va., 1992—; com. chmn., v.p. No. Calif. Tech. Pers. Com., Sunnyvale, 1985-86; com. mem. Entrepreneur's Exch., Inc., Annapolis, Md., 1990—. Pres. Turkish Am. Assn. Calif., San Francisco, 1987-89; com. mem. Alliance for Drug Free Am., Annapolis, 1990—, Anne Arundel County Trade Coun., Arnold, Md., 1990-91; com. chmn., bd. dirs. Greater Severna Park Coun., 1991—. Mem. Soc. Human Resource Mgmt., Am. Bus. Women (com. chmn. 1991, v.p. 1992), Dulles Soc. Human Resource Mgmt. (treas. 1994—), Severna Park C. of C. (com. 1990—), Toastmasters (sec. Dundalk, Md. 1990-91). Home: 63 Marnel Dr Severna Park MD 21146-2903 Office: 8300 Greensboro Dr Ste 880 Mc Lean VA 22102-3604

YIN, BEATRICE WEI-TZE, medical researcher; b. Taipei, Taiwan, Mar. 9, 1959; came to U.S., 1970; d. Chuan Keun and Ming Hsien (Huang) Y. BS, CUNY, Flushing, 1982, MS, 1988. Rsch. asst. Meml. Sloan-Kettering Cancer Ctr., N.Y.C., 1982—. Inventor Monoclonal antibodies to human gastrointestinal cancers, 1992. Office: Meml Sloan Kettering Cancer Ctr 1275 York Ave New York NY 10021

YIN, JOANNA MILBAUER, English language educator; b. Huntington, N.Y., Mar. 26, 1943. BA, U. Hawaii, 1985, MA, 1987, PhD, 1994. Speechwriter N.Y.C., 1962-70; lectr. U. Hawaii, Honolulu, 1992—. Author: The Emily Dickinson Jour., 1993. Mem. Am. Lit. Assn., Soc. Early Americanists, Conf. on Christianity and Lit., Emily Dickinson Internat. Soc., George Eliot Fellowship, 18th-Century Studies Soc. Office: U Hawaii English Dept Honolulu HI 96822

YITTS, ROSE MARIE, nursery school executive; b. Bridgeport, Conn., Apr. 29, 1942; m. Richard Francis Yitts, Dec. 28, 1963; children: Anthony Michael, Jennifer Lisa, Heather Michelle. BS, So. Conn. State Coll., 1963; MS, So. Conn. State U., 1983. Tchr. Trumbull (Conn.) Bd. Edn., 1963-69; substitute tchr. Seymour (Conn.) and Oxford (Conn.) Bd. Edn., 1970-79; tchr. aide spl. edn. Oxford (Conn.) Bd. Edn., 1979-82; dir., founding ptnr., pres. and treas. Strawberry Tyme Nursery Sch. and Day Care Ctr. Ltd., Seymour, 1983—. Corr. sec. student senate So. Conn. State Coll., 1963; den leader, com. chmn. Boy Scouts Am., Seymour, 1973-77; troop leader Girl Scouts USA, Seymour, 1978-80; chair fundraisers, coach George J. Hummel Little League, Seymour, 1982-86, 1st woman pres., 1987-88, player agt., 1990; tchr., spl. edn. curriculum developer Ch. of Good Shepherd, mem. parish coun., 1984-86; corr. sec., dir. Seymour Libr., bd. dirs., 1983-89. Recipient award of merit, honorable mention, Golden Poet award World of Poetry, 1987, Editor's Choice award Nat. Libr. Poetry, 1994. Mem. Nat. Assn. for Edn. Young Children, Oxford Bus. Assn. (membership com. 1993—), Woman's Coll. Club, Trumbull Edn. Assn. (corr. sec.), Chi Delta Sigma (founder, past pres.). Republican.

YLINIEMI, HAZEL ALICE, educational administrator; b. Rural Becker County, Minn., Jan. 30, 1941; d. Isacki and Aili Maria (Haanpaa) Y. BS in English Edn., Moorhead State U., 1967; MS in Media Edn., Mankato State U., 1973; postgrad., Tri-Coll. U., 1973—, U. N.D., 1980—. Clk. group ins. Northwestern Nat. Life, Mpls., 1959-60; cosmetologist Looking Glass Dayton's, Mpls., 1961-63; clk. group ins. N.Am. Life & Casualty, Mpls., 1963-64; English tchr. grades 10, 12 Hibbing (Minn.) High Sch., 1967-69; English tchr. grades 10, 11 Carlton (Minn.) High Sch., 1969-71; libr. media specialist Fargo (N.D.) South High Sch., 1973-80; dir. instrnl. resources Fargo Pub. Sch. System, 1980—; mem. program com. AECT/DSMS, 1990; reviewer video tapes; treas. 16th Plains Internat. Reading Conv., Fargo, 1988. Sch. rep. N.D. Centennial State Kick-Off Celebration, Fargo, 1989. Recipient Literacy award Valley Reading Coun., Fargo, 1989. Mem. ALA, Am. Assn. Sch. Librs. (del. affiliate assembly of AASL 1980-81, 84-90, 93, region IV coord. affiliate assembly 1988-90), Young Adult Libr. Svc. Assn. (media selection and usage com. 1989-93, selected films and videos for young adults com. 1993-95), Phi Delta Kappa, Delta Kappa Gamma (pres. Beta chpt. 1984-86). Lutheran. Home: 2116 27th Ave S Fargo ND 58103-6628 Office: Fargo Pub Schs 1104 2d Ave S Fargo ND 58103

YNTEMA, MARY KATHERINE, retired mathematics educator; b. Urbana, Ill., Jan. 20, 1928; d. Leonard Francis and M. Jean (Busey) Y. BA in Math., Swarthmore Coll., 1950; MA in Math., U. Ill., 1961, PhD in Math., 1965. Tchr., secondary math. Am. Coll. for Girls, Istanbul, Turkey, 1950-54, Columbus (Ohio) Sch. for Girls, 1954-57; computer programmer MIT Lincoln Lab., Lexington, Mass., 1957-58; tchr., secondary math Roundup (Mont.) High Sch., 1959-60; asst. prof. math U. Ill., Chgo., 1965-67; asst. prof. computer sci. Pa. State U., University Park, 1967-71; assoc. prof. to prof. math. Sangamon State U., Springfield, Ill., 1971-91; ret., 1991.

YOCHELSON, BONNIE ELLEN, museum curator, art historian; b. Buffalo, Nov. 6, 1952; d. Samuel and Kathryn (Mersey) Y.; m. Paul Lewis Shechtman, Sept. 3, 1972; children: Emily, Anna. BA in History, Swarthmore Coll., 1974; MA, NYU, 1979, PhD, 1985. Asst. curator dept. prints and drawings Nat. Gallery Art, Washington, 1979-81; lectr. dept. art history U. Pa.q, Phila., 1985-87; curator prints and photographs Mus. of the City of N.Y., 1987-91, cons. curator, 1991—; faculty M of Photography program Sch. Visual Arts, N.Y.C., 1988—; adj. assoc. prof. dept. art history NYU, 1987. Mem. Coll. Art Assn.

YOCHELSON, KATHRYN MERSEY, art researcher; b. N.Y.C., Oct. 22, 1910; d. Nathan and Esther Mary Mersey; m. Samuel Yochelson, June 21, 1930 (dec. Nov. 1976); children: John Norman, Bonnie Ellen. BA in Art Edn., New Haven Tchrs. Coll., 1930; postgrad., Yale U., Columbia U., Albright Art Sch., Am. U., U. Md. Tchr. art New Haven Sch. System, 1930-39; rschr. artistic roots of Jewish People, 1940—; organizer permanent art collection Buffalo Jewish Ctr., 1952; chmn. Seven Painters of Israeli exhbn. Albright Knox Art Gallery, Buffalo, 1953, 20 Artists for Israel exhbn. George Washington U., 1968; organizer hist. materials Personal Vision: Yochelson Collection of Israeli Art, 1987, now permanent collection at Brown U., Providence, 1994; lectr. Israeli art Inst. for Learning in Retirement Am. U., Washington, 1991; mem. scholar series com. Washington Hebrew Congregation, Washington. Contbr. articles to profl. jours. Life mem. Sunday Scholar Series com. Albright-Knox Art Gallery, vol. dept. edn., 1940-60; mem. internat. bd. govs. Tel Aviv Mus. Art, 1977; establisher Dr. Samuel and Kathryn Yochelson meml. lectureship Sch. Psychiatry Yale U., New Haven, 1980. Mem. Sunday Scholar Series Com., Albright-Knox Art Gallery (life), Brandeis Women's Com., Hadassah (life), Washington Watercolor Soc. (sec. 1971-72), Nat. Am. Pen Women. Home: 4201 Cathedral Ave NW Apt 824 Washington DC 20016-4901

YOCHEM, BARBARA JUNE, sales executive, lecturer; b. Knox, Ind., Aug. 22, 1945; d. Harley Albert and Rosie (King) Runyan; m. Donald A. Yochem (div. 1979); 1 child, Morgan Lee; m. Don Heard, Dec. 12, 1987. Grad. high school, Knox, Ind., 1963. Sales rep. Hunter Woodworks, Carson, Calif., 1979-84, sales mgr., 1984-87; sales rep. Comml. Lumber and Pallet, Industry, Calif., 1987-92; owner By By Prodns., Glendora, Calif., 1976—. Author: Barbara Yochem's Inner Shooting; contbr. articles to profl. jours. Head coach NRA Jr. Olympic Shooting Camp, 1989-94; foster parent, 1992-94.

Recipient U.S. Bronze medal U.S. Olumpic Com., 1976, World Bronze medal U.S Olympic Com., 1980; nominated Calif. Trapshooting Hall of Fame, 1994. Address: By By Prodns PO Box 1676 Glendora CA 91740-1676

YOCHIM, SUSAN LAUREL, psychologist; b. Oak Park, Ill., July 20, 1952; d. John Joseph and Ida Helene (Besler) Shea-Szczepaniak; m. Scott Albert Yochim; children: Jonathan, Allison. BSE cum laude, Northern Ill. U., 1974; postgrad., U. Chgo., 1976; MA in sch. psychology, Govs. State U., 1979. Elem. tchr. Forest Ridge Sch. Dist. 142, Oak Forest, Ill., 1974-79; sch. psychologist Atwood Heights Sch. Dist. 125, Oak Lawn, Ill., 1980-90, Downers Grove (Ill.) Sch. Dist. 58, 1990—. Author: Melvin and the Mysterious Moot, 1974 (unpublished). Mem. Oak Brook (Ill.) Civic Assn., 1988—, Brook Forest Homeowners Assn., Oak Brook, 1988—; soccer coach Am. Youth Soccer Assn., Oak Brook, 1989-90; food days coord. Brook Forest PTA, Oak Brook, 1991-92, room mother, 1988—, leader Great Books, 1994; mem. Oak Brook Caucus, 1994-95. Mem. NEA, NASP, AAUW (bd. dirs., officer 1990-92, newsletter editor 1990-92), Ill. Edn. Assn., Ill. Sch. Psychologists Assn., Oak Brook Women's Club (bd. dirs., officer 1989—, newsletter editor 1989-90, membership sec. 1990-92, v.p. activities 1992-93, pres. 1993-95), Infant Welfare Soc. Chgo. (Oak Brook chpt. 1992—). Lutheran. Home: 27 Concord Dr Oak Brook IL 60521-1735

YODER, ANNA A., educator; b. Beach City, Ohio, Sept. 5, 1934; d. Abram J. and Barbara D. (Miller) Y. BS, Ea. Mennonite Coll., 1966; MEd, Frostburg State Coll., 1974. Cert. elem. tchr., Ohio, recreational leader. Tchr. Garrett County Schs., Oakland, Md., 1966-70; prin. elem. sch. Garrett County Schs., 1970-74; tchr. E. Holmes Local Schs., Berlin, Ohio, 1974—; chairperson edn. com. German Culture Mus., Berlin, Ohio, 1987—; cons. bilingual edn. E. Holmes Local Schs., Berlin, Ohio, 1982—. Supporting mem. German Culture Mus., Berlin, Ohio, 1983—; mem. Killbuck (Ohio) Valley mus., 1988—, Holmes County Hist. Soc., Millersburg, Ohio, 1989—; life mem. Mennonite Info. Ctr., Berlin, Ohio, 1985—; sustaining mem. The Wilderness Ctr., Wilmot, Ohio, 1974—. Jennings scholar Martha Holden Jennings Found., 1983-84; Silver Poet award World of Poetry, 1986. Mem. AAUW (v.p. Holmes County chpt. 1994), Creative Arts Soc. (sec.-treas. 1987-89), Delta Kappa Gamma (sec. Beta Iota chpt. 1987-90, pres. 1990-92). Mennonite. Home: 6583 State Route 241 Millersburg OH 44654-8824

YODER, MARY JANE WARWICK, psychotherapist; b. Corryton, Tenn., Nov. 20, 1933; d. Harry Alonzo and Mary Luzelle (Furches) Warwick; m. Edwin Milton Yoder, Jr., Nov. 1, 1958; children: Anne Daphne, Edwin Warwick. BA, U. N.C., Chapel Hill, 1956; MFA, U. N.C., Greensboro, 1969; MSW, Va. Commonwealth U., 1987; cert. individual psychotherapy, Smith Coll., 1991. Lic. ind. clin. social worker, D.C.; lic. clin. social worker, Va. Editorial asst. Harper & Bros., N.Y.C., 1956-57; flight attendant Pan Am. Airlines, N.Y.C., 1957-59; adj. faculty mem. in ballet Guilford Coll., Greensboro, 1961-64; ballet tchr., adminstr. Jane Yoder Sch. of Ballet, Greensboro, 1964-75; homilitics listener Va. Theol. Sem., Alexandria, 1978-80; social worker, dance therapist Woodbine Nursing Ctr., Alexandria, 1983-87; staff psychotherapist D.C. Inst. Mental Health, 1987-92; pvt. practice Capitol Hill Ctr. Individual and Family Therapy, 1992—. Ballet and book critic Greensboro Daily News, 1961-75. Dancer, choreographer Greensboro Civic Ballet, 1961-75. Mem. Nat. Assn. Social Workers, Greater Washington Soc. for Clin. Social Work, Inc., Washington Sch. Psychiatry, Washington Soc. for Jungian Psychology, Jungian Venture, Army-Navy Country Club. Episcopalian. Office: Capitol Hill Ctr Individual and Family Therapy 530 Seventh St SE Washington DC 20003

YODER, PATRICIA DOHERTY, public relations executive; b. Pitts., Oct. 30, 1939; d. John Addison and Camella Grace (Conti) Doherty; children: Shari Lynn, Wendy Ann. BA, Duquesne U., 1961. Press sec. U.S. Ho. of Reps., 1965-69; dir. office of pub. info. City of Ft. Wayne, 1973-76; asst. mgr. pub. and corp. communications Mellon Bank N.A., Pitts., 1977-79; v.p. pub. affairs Am. Waterways Operators Inc., Washington, 1980-83; sr. v.p., gen. mgr. 1983-86, exec. v.p., dir. internat. banking, 1989-91, Hill and Knowlton Inc., Pitts.; sr. v.p. corp. and pub. affairs PNC Bank, Pitts., 1987-89; v.p., mgr. corp. pub. rels. and advt. GE Capital, 1991—. Trustee Shadyside Hosp., Pressley Ridge Sch., Pitts.; bd. dirs. Children's Mus., Civic Light Opera, Pitts. Ballet Theatre, Stamford, (Conn.) Symphony; mem. communications bd. visitors U. Pitts. Mem. Pitts. Field Club, Duquesne Club, Century Club of Disting. Duquesne U. Alumni. Roman Catholic. Home: 13 Brown House Rd Old Greenwich CT 06870 Office: 260 Long Ridge Rd Stamford CT 06927-0001

YODER WISE, PATRICIA SNYDER, nurse, educator; b. Wadsworth, Ohio, July 2, 1941; d. Belford Grant and Leona Cora (Mohler) Snyder; m. Robert Thomas Wise, Feb. 17, 1973; children: Doreen Ellen, Deborah Ann. BS in Nursing, Ohio State U., 1963; MS in Nursing, Wayne State U., 1968; EdD, Tex. Tech. U., 1984. Cert. gerontol. nurse and nursing adminstr., RN, Tex., Ohio. Rsch. asst. Wayne State U., Detroit, 1968; ednl. dir. Ohio Nurses' Assn., Columbus, 1968-72; asst. dir. nursing Mt. Clemens (Mich.) Gen. Hosp., 1972-73; assoc. prof., head of nursing Ferris State Coll., Big Rapids, Mich., 1975-77; asst. prof., assoc. prof., dir. continuing edn. U. Colo., Denver, 1977-79; assoc. dean, assoc. prof. Sch. Nursing, Tex. Tech U. Health Scis. Ctr., Lubbock, 1979-86, assoc. dean, prof., 1986-87, interim assoc. dean grad. program, 1988-89, exec. assoc. dean, prof. nursing, 1987-92, interim dean, prof., 1992-93; dean, prof. Sch. Nursing, 1993—; prin. Part Time Wylan Assocs., Lubbock, 1989—; mem. acad. adv. panel on nursing Health and Scis. Network, 1983-92, Nurses Coalition, 1982-92; bd. dirs RN Polit. Action Com., 1989-93. Editor Jour. Continuing Edn. in Nursing, 1986—. Recipient Teaching Excellence award Am. Nurses Found. Fellow Am. Acad. Nursing; mem. ANA (site visitor continuing edn. 1982-88), Tex. Nurses Assn. (bd. dirs. 1989-93, pres. 1995—, pres. dist. 18 1987-89), Coun. Continuing Edn., Tex. Nurses Found. (pres. 1992-95), Sigma Theta Tau (grantee). Home: 3713 95th St Lubbock TX 79423-3811

YOGEV, SARA, psychologist; b. Tel Aviv, May 23, 1946; came to U.S., 1975; d. Israel and Cila (Fink) Frankel; m. Ram Yogev, Oct. 2, 1967; children: Eldad, Shelly, Tomer. BA, Hebrew U., 1965-69, MA, 1970-73; PhD, Northwestern U., Evanston, Ill., 1976-79. Cert. clin. psychologist, Ill. Clin. experience dist. sch. psychologist Office Edn. and Culture, Jerusalem, Israel, 1968-71; intern. Beer Yaakov Psychiatric Hosp., Israel, 1971-72; asst. dir. Dept. Psychology, Hebrew U., Jerusalem, Israel, 1972-73; psychotherapist Mental Health Ctr., Hebrew U., Jerusalem, Israel; clin. psychologist Inst. Psychoanalysis, Jerusalem, Israel, 1973-75; psychotherapist, supr. Youth and Family Services, Ill., 1977-80; pvt. practice psychology Skokie, Ill., 1981—; academic experience instr. counseling psychology, 1977-79, asst. prof., Northwestern U., 1979-82, research psychologist at the rank asst. prof., 1983-86, visiting scholar, Ctr. Urban Affairs and Policy Research, 1987. Contbr. articles to profl. jours. and books. Mem. American Assn. for Marriage and Family Therapy, American Psyhological Assn., Nat. Register Health Service. Jewish. Office: 5225 Old Orchard Rd # 32 Skokie IL 60077-1027

YOHN, SHARON A., manufacturing executive; b. Altoona, Pa., Mar. 1, 1952. AS in Retail cum laude, Harcum Jr. Coll. (Pa.), 1972; BSBA, Villanova U., 1976. Dir. overseas ops. Europe and Africa Airwalk divsn. of Items Internat., Inc., Altoona, Pa. and Carlsbad, Calif., 1987—. Republican. Office: Items Internat Inc 1540 E Pleasant Valley Blvd Altoona PA 16602

YOHO, AUDREY MAYE, automotive executive; b. Stark, Ohio, July 21, 1953; d. Jerome E. and Ella Maye (Taggart) Y. Diploma, Carrollton H.S., 1971. Ops. officer Bank Ohio Nat. Bank, Carrollton, 1970-86; bus. mgr. George Waikem Ford, Canton, 1986—. Named to Pres. Club Bank Ohio Nat. Bank, 1986. Mem. Nat. Soc. Daughters of the Am. Revolution. Office: George Waikem Ford 4321 Lincoln Way E Massillon OH 44646

YONTZ, PATRICIA, executive director; b. Tampa, Fla., Mar. 19, 1953. BA, U. So. Fla., 1988; MFA, Fla. State U., 1991. Co-owner Backdoor Gallery, Clearwater, Fla., 1991-92; dir. gallery, exhbn. com. Fla. Ctr. Contemporary Art, Tampa, 1992-94. Recipient Honorarium of Art in Window Hills County Art Coun., Tampa, 1992. Home: 5112 N Suwanee Ave Tampa FL 33603-2148 Office: Fla Ctr Contemporary Art 1017 N Franklin St Tampa FL 33602

YONUSAITIS, LINDA SUSAN, special education educator, environmentalist; b. Bklyn., Dec. 23, 1954; d. Edward Joseph and Dorothy Virginia (Brestlin) Y. Student, Nassau Community Coll., 1973-75; BA in Child Study and Spl. Edn., St. Joseph's Coll., Brentwood, L.I., N.Y., 1977; MS in Deaf Edn. with Speech Pathology/Audiology/Edn. Emphasis, Adelphi U., 1986. Cert. early childhood, elem., spl. edn., multihandicapped, deaf/hearing impaired tchr., N.Y., C.E.D., early childhood, elem., multihandicapped profl. cert. for teaching the hearing impaired, Coun. on Edn. Deaf, Washington. Naturalist, instr. outdoor and environ. edn. Caumsett State Park and various ctrs., L.I., N.Y., 1978-84; direct care resident counselor, instr. EPIC House Hicksville of Epilepsy Found., L.I., 1981-87; substitute tchr. spl. edn., multihandicapped Rosemary Kennedy Ctr., Wantagh, N.Y., 1979-81, 87-90; tutor/cons. elem., secondary study skills, spl. edn., deaf and hearing impaired, Wantagh, 1978, 81, 84-86, 88, 90—; home instrn., spl. edn. biol. and earth sci., tutor, Creative Tutoring Inc., L.I., 1989; subs. tchr. deaf edn., early intervention and programs for hearing impaired Nassau Bd. Coop. Ednl. Svcs., Wantagh, Merrick and North Merrick, L.I., 1985-90; tchr. various extended yr. summer programs for multihandicapped James E. Allen Learning Ctr. Melville-Bd. Coop. Ednl. Svcs. III, 1983, elem. sci. tchr. physically disabled, mentally handicapped (with hearing impaired and language delayed) Nassau Bd. Coop. Ednl. Svcs., L.I., 1987, 89. Author: College Study Guide in Anatomy and Physiology on Speech/Hearing/Vocal Mechanism Questions and Answers, Methods Guide to Young Adult Meetings in Special Education: A Series of Applied Christian Living Skills, 1980-90; contbg. author studies of The Office of Mental Retardation and Devel. Disabilities, Horticulture Therapy: Organic Gardening, 1983, Treatment Modality; editor-in-chief Reflections Yearbook S.J.C.; founder Good Guys newsletter Let's Communicate, 1988; rsch. on hyperactivity-drugs vs. diet, and otitis media with cen. auditory processing disorders, language delay and Landau-Kleffner Syndrome; contbt. articles to profl. publs. Vol. fund raiser United Cerebral Palsy Assn. Nassau County, 1969-81, Forest City Community Assn., Wantagh, 1973-80; tutor Elem. Remedial Reading Club Parochial Sch., Deer Pk., 1976; spl. edn. tchr. St. Frances de Chantal Religious Edn. Program, Wantagh, 1979-82; dir. and spl. edn. instr. and program developer: Young Adult Evening Meetings, The Good Guys-Spl. Guides, Wantagh, Diocese of Rockville Ctr., L.I., 1982-92; horticulture and organic gardening program developer Community Based Intermediate Care Facility, EPIC House, 1982-86; participant various antinuclear rallies Shoreham, L.I., and N.Y.C., 1979; land protection petitioner for Mill Pond Wantagh, Bellmore; preservation advocate Suffolk County Farm and Edn. Ctr., Riverhead, L.I., 1989; rschr. to promote Horticulture Therapy, 1991-92. Recipient rsch. assistantship Dept. Speech Arts & Communicative Disorders, Adelphi U., 1984-85, scholarship Grad. Sch. Arts & Scis., 1984, Honorable Mention Interdisciplinary Team Excellence Nat. Epilepsy Found. Am. to EPIC House, 1982. Mem. MADD, AAUW, AAUW Environ. Network, Am. Assn. on Mental Retardation, Am. Hort. Therapy Assn., N.Am. Assn. for Environ. Edn., N.Am. Conf. on Christianity and Ecology, N.Y. State Outdoor Edn. Assn., Bicultural Exch., Conv. of Am. Instrs. of the Deaf, Talking Over and Understanding Children with Handicaps, Endometriosis Assn., Nat. Coun. Therapy and Rehab. through Horticulture, Nature Conservancy, Women's Sports Found., Sierra Club, Forest City Community Assn., Support Our Country's Mil.

YOPP, JOHANNA FUTCHS, management consultant; b. Wilmington, N.C., Sept. 6, 1938; d. Richard and Louise (Friedman) Futchs; m. James D. Yopp Jr., Dec. 26, 1959; children: Beverly, Lynn, James III, Sara Katherine. BA, U. N.C., Greensboro, 1960. Tchr. New Hanover County Schs., Wilmington, N.C., 1960-62, Winston-Salem (N.C.) Forsyth County Schs., 1962-68; mgr. James D. Yopp Jr. MD, Winston-Salem, 1971—. Vol. Winston-Salem/Forsyth County Schs., Winston-Salem Optimist Soccer Club, 1970-73; leader Girl Scouts U.S.A., Winston-Salem, 1970-73; pres. Mt. Tabor High Sch. PTA, Winston-Salem, 1986-88; mem. Forsyth-Strokes Med. Aux., Bowman Gray Med. Ctr., Aux., Winston-Salem; mem. centennial planning bd. U. N.C.; mem. alumni bd. trustees U. N.C., Greensboro, 1991-94. Mem. NAFE, Am. Mgmt. Assn. Republican. Lutheran. Home: 3410 Thoresby Ct Winston Salem NC 27104-1740 Office: 755 Highland Oaks Dr Ste 204 Winston Salem NC 27103

YORBURG, BETTY (MRS. LEON YORBURG), sociology educator; b. Chgo., Aug. 27, 1926; d. Max and Hannah (Bernstein) Gitelman; m. Leon Yorburg, June 23, 1946; children: Harriet, Robert. PhB, U. Chgo., 1945, MA, 1948; PhD, New Sch. Social Rsch., 1968. Instr., Coll. New Rochelle, 1966-67; lectr. City Coll. and Grad. Center, City U. N.Y., 1967-69, asst. prof., 1969-73, assoc. prof. sociology dept., 1973-77, prof., 1978—; rsch. asst. Prof. Clifford Shaw, Chgo. Area Project, 1946-47. Author: Utopia and Reality, 1969, The Changing Family, 1973, Sexual Identity: Sex Roles and Social Change, 1974, The New Women, 1976, Introduction to Sociology, 1982, Families and Societies, 1983, Family Relationships, 1993, Sociological Reality, 1995. Mem. AAAS, Am. Sociol. Assn., Ea. Sociol. Assn., Am. Coun. Family Rels., N.Y. Acad. Scis. Home: 20 Earley St Bronx NY 10464-1512 Office: CCNY Sociology Dept 138th Convent Ave New York NY 10031-9127

YORK, JANET BREWSTER, nurse, family and sex therapist, sculptor; b. N.Y.C., Mar. 5, 1941; d. Edward Cox and Janet Stone Brewster; AA with honors, Briarcliff Coll., 1961; RN with highest honors, U. Iowa, 1965; BA summa cum laude, Marymount Manhattan Coll., 1975; MA with honors, N.Y. U., 1978; m. Albert Thompson York, Mar. 31, 1962 (dec.); children: Clifton Gaston, Torrance Brewster; 1 adopted child, Justin Brigham. Nurse, Manhattan Eye, Ear and Throat Hosp., N.Y.C., 1966-74; nurse, counselor Washington Free Clinic, 1969-71; family therapist Ackerman Family Inst., N.Y.C., 1976-80; sex therapist N.Y. Med. Coll., Flower Fifth Ave Hosp., N.Y.C., 1976-80; individual practice family and sex therapy, N.Y.C., 1978—; supervisory staff grad. edn. program in human sexuality N.Y.U. Med. Ctr., 1982—; sculptor, 1988—. Bd. dirs. Spence/Chapin Adoption Agy., Manhattan Eye, Ear and Throat Hosp. Vita fellow Internat. Coun. of Sex Edn. and Parenthood, Am. U., 1981; recipient Evelyn Monte Sculpture award, 1988, 94, Ellsworth Howell Art Sculpture award, 1991, 93. Mem. Am. Soc. for Sex Therapy and Research, Am. Assn. Sex Edn., Counseling and Therapy, Soc. for Sci. Study Sex, Sex Info. and Edn. Council U.S., Am. Assn. Marriage and Family Therapists, Nat. Assn. Women Artist, Am. Medallic Soc., Nantucket Art Assn., Walker Art Ctr., Nat. Mus. Women in the Arts. Clubs: Lawrence Beach, Rockaway Hunting, N.Y.U, Millbrook. Represented in permanent collection The Dog Mus. of Am., St. Louis; contbr. articles to profl. jours.; also videotape Death as a Part of Life. Home: 155 E 72nd St New York NY 10021-4371

YORK, SHERRY WHITE, librarian; b. San Angelo, Tex., June 23, 1947; d. Owen White; m. Donnie E. York, Jan. 3, 1970. BA, Sul Ross State U., 1968, MA, 1971, MEd, 1980. Cert. edn. adminstr., supr., libr., tchr. Tchr. Crystal City (Tex.) Ind. Sch. Dist., 1970-74; editor Gamco Industries, Big Spring, Tex., 1974-75; supr., reading dir. Edcouch-Elsa Ind. Sch. Dist., Elsa, Tex., 1975-77; libr. La Joya (Tex.) Ind. Sch. Dist., 1977-82, Crockett County Sch. Dist., Ozona, Tex., 1982—; presentor area-wide in-svc. tng., Edinburg/McAllen, Tex., 1976, Ozona H.S. In-Svc., 1993, 94; founder lit. mag. La Joya H.S., 1980-82, Ozona H.S., 1987-93. Reviewer books, media Book Report Mag., 1983—. Bd. mem. Libr. Bd. Dirs., Elsa, 1976-77; founding mem., v.p., pres. Libr. Bd., Ozona, 1985-90; mem. Friends of Libr., Ozona, 1985-94. Mem. Tex. Libr. Assn., Tex. Assn. Sch. Librs. Methodist. Home: PO Box 3008 Ozona TX 76943 Office: Ozona HS PO Box 400 Ozona TX 76943

YORKE, MARIANNE, lawyer, real estate executive; b. Ridley Park, Pa., Nov. 4, 1948; d. Joseph George and Catherine Veronica (Friel) Y. BA, West Chester U., 1971; JD, Temple U., 1980; MS, U. Pa., 1987. Bar: Pa. 1981, N.Y. 1992. Real estate mgr. CIGNA Service Co., Phila., 1982-85, asst. dir., Phila., 1985-89; v.p. Chase Manhattan Bank, N.Y.C., 1989-92; dir. corp. real estate Johnson & Johnson, 1992—; real estate atty. Garfinkel & Volpicelli, Phila., 1980-82; prin., mng. ptnr. Yorke/Eisenman, Real Estate, Phila., 1976-89, prin., mng. ptnr. Yorke/Mac Lachlin Real Estate, Phila, 1989—; lectr. Women in the Arts, 1982-90; guest speaker Wharton Sch. Bus. Class of 1989, U. Pa., grad. sch. arts and scis. Class of 1990. Contbr. articles to profl. jours. Solicitor Pa. Ballet, Phila., 1983-90, United Way, Phila., 1983-90; mem. steering com. U. Pa., 1986-90, dir. alumni assn., 1987-90; mem. adv. com. for econ. devel. Luth. Settlement House Adv, 1986-88; bd. dirs. Hamilton Townhouse Assn., 1988-90, chmn. ins. com., 1989-90, 718 Broadway, Inc., 1990-94. Mem. ABA (forum on constrn. 1982-90), Pa. Bar Assn. (condominium and zoning coms. 1982-90), Assn. of Bar of City of N.Y. (sects. on internat. law and real property law 1992-94), Phila. Bar Assn., Phila. Women Real Estate Attys., Nat. Assn. Corp. Real Estate Execs. (internat. coun. 1984—, comml. coun. 1984—), Internat. Atty's Roundtable, Women's Law Caucus, Phi Alpha Delta. Independent. Roman Catholic. Office: Johnson & Johnson World Headquarters Ste 7135 1 Johnson & Johnson Pla New Brunswick NJ 08933

YOSHIDA, KAREN KAMIJO CATEEL, public relations professional; b. Honolulu, Sept. 18, 1964; d. William Francis and Masako (Kamijo) Cateel; m. Ken Yutaka Yoshida, Aug. 4, 1990. BSBA in Mktg., Hawaii Pacific Coll., 1989. Jour. editorial asst. Univ. Press, U. Hawaii, Honolulu, 1983; customer svc. rep. GTE Hawaiian Tel, Honolulu, 1988; account coord. Ogilvy & Mather Hawaii, Honolulu, 1989; pub. rels. asst. McCormick Communications, Honolulu, 1989-90; account dir. Joyce Timpson & Assocs., Honolulu, 1989-90; mgr. communications and pub. rels. Hawaii State Bar Assn., Honolulu, 1990—; tchr. spl. edn. Kahi Mohala Sch., 1994—; mng. mag. editor, dir. membership benefits Hawaii State Bar Assn., 1990—; mem. Pub. Radio Community Adv. Bd., 1993; instr. Honolulu C.C., 1993. Vol. Easter Seal Soc., Hawaiian Humane Soc., Lanakila Elem. Sch. State contest winner Exec. Women's Internat., 1982. Mem. Sons. and Daus. 442nd RCT (newsletter and membership coms. 1993), Hawaii Pacific U. Alumni Assn. (comm. com. 1993). Home: 2807 Pacific Heights Rd Honolulu HI 96813-1019 Office: Hawaii State Bar Assn 1136 Union Mall # 1ph Honolulu HI 96813-2711

YOSHIKAWA, VIVECA RUTH, library automation specialist; b. Lund, Sweden, Nov. 12, 1944; came to U.S., 1965; d. Walther Sigfried Gustav and Ruth Kerstin (Nilsson) Edenheim; m. Tetsuo Yoshikawa, Dec. 18, 1965; children: Miko Ingrid, Makoto Daniel, Akiko Kristina. AA in Latin, Malmö (Sweden) Latinskola, 1964; AS in Computer Sci., Hillsborough Community Coll., Tampa, Fla., 1988. Libr., cataloger Libr. Congress, Washington, 1968-72; libr. technician Hillsborough Community Coll., 1982-86, project leader libr. automation, 1986-88, libr. automation specialist, 1988—. Republican. Presbyterian. Home: 311 E Windhorst Rd Brandon FL 33510-2527 Office: Hillsborough Community Coll 1502 E 9th Ave Tampa FL 33605-3793

YOSHIUCHI, ELLEN HAVEN, childbirth educator; b. Newark, Apr. 15, 1949; d. Michael Joseph and Adeline V. (Lindblom) Haven; m. Takeshi Yoshiuchi, Dec. 1, 1973; children: Teri Takumi, Niki Noboru. BA summa cum laude, CUNY, 1980; M Profl. Studies in Human Rels., N.Y. Inst. Tech., 1991. Cert. bereavement svcs. counselor. Pvt. practice childbirth edn., 1983-89; program asst. parent/family edn. St. Luke's/Roosevelt Hosp. Ctr., N.Y.C., 1989-93, mem. faculty parent/family edn. program, 1990—; mem. faculty Family Ctr. at Riverdale Neighborhood House, Bronx, N.Y., 1991—; mem. perinatal bereavement com. St. Luke's/Roosevelt Hosp. Ctr., N.Y.C., 1989—. Editor ASPO/N.Y.C. News, 1983-86; contbr. articles to profl. jours. Fellow Am. Coll. Childbirth Educators; mem. ACA, Internat. Childbirth Edn. Assn., Assn. Specialists in Group Work, N.Y. State Perinatal Assn., Am. Soc. for Psychoprophylaxis in Obstetrics/Lamaze (cert. tchr., pres. N.Y.C. chpt. 1987-91, nominating com. 1991-93, dir. ednl. program 1991-93).

YOSHIWARA, KATHERINE ANNE, mathematics educator, author; b. Derby, Eng., Aug. 10, 1953; came to U.S., 1954; d. Hubert Paul and Irene May (Saxton); m. Harold Lowell Franklin, July 26, 1980 (div. 1991); m. Bruce William Yoshiwara, Jan. 24, 1991. BS, Mich. State U., 1974; MA, UCLA, 1977. Prof. math. L.A. Pierce Coll., Woodland Hills, Calif., 1979—. Co-author: Elementary Algebra for College Students, 1988, Intermediate Algebra, 1991, Modeling, Functions, and Graphs, 1991; bd. editors Coll. Math. Jour., 1989—. Mem. Math. Assn. Am., Nat. Coun. Tchrs. Math., Am. Math. Assn. Two-Yr. Colls., Calif. Math. Coun. Community Colls. Office: LA Pierce Coll 6201 Winnetka Ave Woodland Hls CA 91371-0002

YOST, BERNICE, detective agency owner; b. Houston; d. Kenneth Wayne and Georgia (Sampson) Cox; m. Matthew Yost. Student, L.A. Trade Tech, 1968-70, Compton Coll., 1974-76, Ariz. State U., 1983-85. Staff acct. Moultrie, Liggens, Terrel CPA's, L.A., 1969-72; spl. agt. IRS, L.A., 1972-79; supervisory spl. agt. IRS, Phoenix, 1979-91; program mgr. IRS, Washington, 1991-93; owner, operator Yost Detective Agy., Silver Spring, Md., 1994—. Recipient Albert Gallatin award for merit, 1993. Mem. Nat. Orgn. of Black Law Enforcement Execs. Democrat. Baptist.

YOST, ELLEN GINSBERG, lawyer; b. Buffalo, May 30, 1945; d. Irwin Arthur and Sylvia Ruth Ginsberg; children: Elizabeth Anne, Peter Andrew, Benjamin Lewis. AB, Mt. Holyoke Coll., 1966; JD, SUNY, Buffalo, 1983. Bar: N.Y., U.S. Dist. Ct. (we. dist.) N.Y. 1984. Assoc. Jaeckle, Fleischmann & Mugel, Buffalo, 1983-89, Saperston & Day, P.C., Buffalo, 1989—; ptnr. Griffith & Yost, Buffalo, 1991—. Pres. Buffalo Coun. on World Affairs, 1987-89; bd. dirs. Buffalo World Trade Assn., 1988-90, Legal Svcs. for Elderly, Disabled, Disadvantaged, 1984—; mem. Erie County Can. Commerce Task Force, 1988. Mem. ABA (co-chair Can. law com. of internat. law and practice sect. 1990-94, vice chair immigration and nationality law com. 1994—, co-chair task force N.Am. Free Trade Agreement 1991-94), N.Y. State Bar Assn. (chmn. U.S. Can. law com. 1987-89, mem. exec. com. internat. law and practice sect. 1987-89, sec. commn. in internat. trade and transactions 1984-87), Am. Immigration Lawyers' Assn. Jewish. Office: Griffith & Yost 50 Fountain Plz Ste 1320 Key Buffalo NY 14202-2212

YOST, KELLY LOU, pianist; b. Boise, Idaho, Aug. 10, 1940; d. Roy Daniel and Helen Roberta (Kingsbury) Frizzelle; m. Nicholas Peter Bond, Dec. 27, 1961 (div. 1973); 1 child, Brook Bernard; m. Samuel Joseph Yost, June 16, 1984. BA in Music, U. Idaho, 1962; postgrad., U. So. Calif., 1965-69. Pvt. tchr. classical piano Twin Falls, Idaho, 1962-88; rec. artist, co-owner ind. record label Channel Prodns., Twin Falls, 1986—; soloist U. Idaho Symphony Orch., Moscow, 1962; pianist, keyboardist Magic Valley Symphony Orch., Twin Falls, 1985, 86; touring guest piano soloist Vandaleer Concert Choir, Moscow, 1961. Recorded recent albums: Piano Reflections, 1987, Quiet Colors, 1991. Mem. NARAS, Nat. Assn. Ind. Record Distbrs., Music Tchrs. Nat. Assn., Idaho Music Tchrs. Assn. (sec. 1981-82), Magic Valley Community Concert Assn. (bd. dirs. 1964-87), Phi Beta Kappa. Office: Channel Prodns PO Box 454 Twin Falls ID 83303-0454

YOST, NANCY RUNYON, artist, designer, art educator; b. Eaton, Ohio, July 16, 1933; d. Stanley Everett and Treva (Geeting) Runyon; m. Kenneth John Yost, Aug. 17, 1952 (div. Dec. 1962); 1 child, Debra Colleen Yost Mayne. BS in Art Edn., Miami U., Oxford, Ohio, 1966, MEd in Art, 1970. Cert. profl. permanent tchr., Ohio. Sec. N.Am. Aircraft, Columbus, Ohio, 1957; sec. Miami U., Oxford, 1957-61, textile instr., 1978; textile instr. Living Arts Ctr., Dayton, Ohio, 1972-73; coord. art, music and phys. edn. Stewart Jr. High Sch., Oxford, 1981-86; art instr. Talawanda Sch. System, Oxford, 1965-90, dist. coord., 1986-90; owner, creator Allegro Adornments Bus., 1988—; postgrad. Sem. Charles Jeffrey, Cleve., Inst. Art, Miami U., 1973, David Van Dommelen Penn State at U. Tenn., 1975, Bill Helwig, N.Y., 1975, Nik Krevitsky, N.Y., 1976, Tom Shafer, Columbus, Ohio, 1982; mem. curriculum coun. Talawanda Sch. Dist., 1982—; rep. Amway Corp., 1980-81, World Book Co., Chgo., 1986-88; lectr. Miami U., 1986; invited workshop speaker, presenter Nat. Art Edn. Assn. Conv., Phoenix, 1992. Contbg. artist: Wall Hangings, 1971, Knotting, 1973; One-woman exhibit at Creative Fibers Studio, Buffalo, 1974; exhibited group show Dayton Art Inst., Invitational Fiber Artists Am., Ball State U., 1974, Christkindl Markt, Canton Art Inst. 1994 (hon. mention); designer Oxford Bicentennial Calender, 1976; guest jewelry designer Saks 5th Avenue. Supr. Community Artworks, 1986; mem. adv. bd. Miami U. Summer Theatre, 1991-93; mem. spl. events planning com. Miami U. Art Mus., 1993—. Recipient Winner Most Creative Costume Ohio Mart, 1992, 93, First Pl. awards Community Photo Contest. Mem. Southwestern Art Edn. Assn., Ohio Art Edn. Assn., Ohio Edn. Assn., Talawanda Edn. Assn., Ohio Designer Craftsmen, Ohio Arts and Crafts Guild, Oxford Arts Club, Kappa Delta Pi. Home and Studio: 6674 Fairfield Rd Oxford OH 45056-9707

YOTHER, MICHELE, publisher; b. Atlanta, Aug. 25, 1965; d. Carole (Spence) Marsh; m. Michael B. Yother, Mar. 17, 1990. BA in acctg. cum laude, Ga. State U., 1990. Asst. v.p. Bank Am., Atlanta, 1986-90; pres. Gallopade Pub. Group, Atlanta, 1990—; pres. Carole Marsh Family Interactive Multimedia, 1993—. Pub. over 2500 children's books, computer disks and activities. Equifax Bus. scholar Ga. State U., 1989. Mem. Bank Am. Club (pres. 1989), Golden Key. Methodist. Home: 359 Milledge Ave Atlanta GA 30312 Office: Gallopade Pub Group 359 Milledge Ave Ste 100 Atlanta GA 30312

YOTHERS, WENDY LOU, artist, silversmith; b. Grand Rapids, Mich., May 21, 1952; d. Lee W. and Winona (Lagen) Y.; 1 child, Douglas Emory Olds. BFA cum laude, U. Mich., 1974; cert., Nat. Coll. Goldsmithing, Lahti, Finland, 1984; MFA (Mgh) with distinction, Guldsmedehojiskolen, Copenhagen, 1987. Teaching asst. Tex. Tech. U., Lubbock, 1979-81; lectr. Nat. Coll. Goldsmithing, Lahti, 1982-84; silversmith Studio Torben Hardenberg, Copenhagen, 1987, Tiffany & Co., N.Y.C. and Parsipany, N.J., 1993—; silversmith Kirk Stieff & Co., Balt., 1988, prototype, model maker, 1989-92. Author: (textbook) Enameling, 1984; exhibited in group shows at Tex. Tech. Mus., Lubbock, 1980, Nat. Inst. Arts and Handcraft, Lahti, 1982, Mus. Applied Art, Hensinki, 1984, Bella Ctr., Copenhagen, 1986, Galleri Metal, Copenhagen, 1986, Gallery Fgn. Ministry, Houses Parliament, Copenhagen, 1986, Galleri Hummeluhre, Jutland, Denmark, 1986, Hotel Sheraton, Goteborg, Sweden, 1986, Frantz Hingelberg Gallery, Arhus, Denmark, 1987, Petur Tryggvi Hjalmarsson Gallery, Reykjavik, Iceland, 1987, Musee des Arts Decoratifs, Paris, 1987-88, Mus. Applied Art, Copenhagen, 1987, Soc. Am. Silversmiths and Soc. Arts and Crafts, Boston, 1990, Soc. Arts and Crafts, 1991, Pritam & Eames, East Hampton, N.Y., 1992, Nat. Mus. Ornamental Metalwork, Memphis, 1992, Worcester (Mass.) Ctr. Crafts, 1992, Nat. Ornamental Metal Mus., Memphis, 1993. Grad. rsch. grantee Tex. Tech. U., Lubbock, 1979-80; Rotary Internat. grad. fellow, 1981-82; recipient Cultural award Am. Women's Club, Denmark, 1986, Direcktor Ib Henrickson's Fond stipend, 1985-87. Fellow Soc. Am. Silversmiths. Roman Catholic. Home: 90 Oakwood Village # 3 Flanders NJ 07836 Office: Tiffany & Co 801 Jefferson Rd Parsippany NJ 07836

YOUNG, ALICE, lawyer; b. Washington, Apr. 7, 1950; d. John and Elizabeth (Jen) Y.; m. Thomas L. Shortall, Sept. 22, 1984; children: Amanda, Stephen. AB magna cum laude, Yale U., 1971; JD, Harvard U., 1974. Bar: N.Y. 1975. Assoc. Coudert Bros., N.Y.C., 1974-81; mng. ptnr. Graham & James, N.Y.C., 1981-87; ptnr. Milbank, Tweed, Hadley & McCloy, N.Y.C., 1987-93; ptnr., chair Asia Pacific Practice (U.S.) Kaye, Scholer, Fierman, Hays & Handler, N.Y.C., 1994—; mem. Coun. on Fgn. Rels., 1977—. Contbr. articles to profl. jours. Trustee Aspen (Colo.) Inst., 1988—, Pan-Asian Repertory Theatre, N.Y.C., 1987-90, Lingnan Found., N.Y.C., 1984-91; mem. bus. com. Met. Mus. Art, N.Y.C., 1989-94, Nat. Com. on U.S.-China Rels., 1993—, U.S.-China Bus. Coun., 1993—, Com. of 100, 1993—; mem. bd. overseers visitation com. to Law Sch., Harvard U., 1994—. Named one of 40 Under 40 Crain's Bus., N.Y.C., 1989; Bates fellow Yale U., 1970, NDFL fellow Harvard U., 1967-68; recipient Star award N.Y. Women's Agenda, 1992. Mem. ABA, N.Y. State Bar Assn. (fgn. investment com.), Assn. Bar City N.Y. (spl. com. on rels. with Japanese bar, Union Internat. des Avocats), Nat. Asian Pacific Am. Bar Assn., Asian Am. Bar Assn. N.Y., Harvard Law Sch. Assn. N.Y.C. (trustee 1990—), Japan Soc. (sec. 1989—), Asia Soc. (pres.'s coun. 1984—). Office: Kaye Scholer Fierman Hayes & Handler 425 Park Ave New York NY 10022-3598

YOUNG, ALINE PATRICE, controller; b. Sacramento, Nov. 8, 1957; d. Rene Francis and Patricia May (Taylor) LeFevre; m. Patrick Charles Young, Sept. 6, 1976 (div. Oct. 1979); 1 child, Daniel Alan Young. AA, Fullerton Coll., 1979; BA, Calif State U., Fullerton, 1981; MBA, Pepperdine U., 1988. Mgmt. devel. program Gen. Electric Credit, Anaheim, Calif., 1981-83; credit mgr. Kwikset/Emhart, Anaheim, Calif., 1983-88, Avery Dennison, Azusa, Calif., 1988-90; contr., fin. mgr. Avery Dennison, Monrovia, Calif., 1990-92, site mgr., contr., 1992—. Chairperson Vision 95 Lutheran High Sch., Orange, Calif., 1993. Mem. Am. Mgmt. Assn., Inst. Mgmt. Accts. Republican. Lutheran. Office: Avery Dennison 1616 S California Ave Monrovia CA 91016

YOUNG, AMY LOUISE, lawyer, artist, illustrator; b. Boston, Mar. 31, 1958; d. Raymond H. and Louisa (Breda) Y.; m. Paul Allen Merewether, Aug. 8, 1987. BA in Art magna cum laude, Yale U., 1980; MFA in Painting, Ind. U., 1984; JD cum laude, Harvard U., 1987. Law clk. Young & Bayle, Boston, summer 1984, Gorsuch & Kirgis, Denver, summer 1985, White & Case, Washington and N.Y.C., summer 1986; assoc. Warner, Norcross & Judd, Grand Rapids, Mich., 1987-90, Drew, Cooper & Anding, Grand Rapids, Mich., 1990—; freelance illustrator, 1990—. Mem. adv. bd. Very Spl. Arts, Grand Rapids, 1991-93; bldg. capt. food and clothing drive Young Lawyers Horn of Plenty, Grand Rapids, 1991-93. Mem. ABA, Mich. Bar Assn., Grand Rapids Bar Assn., Women Lawyers Assn. Mich. Office: Drew Cooper & Anding 125 Ottawa Ste 300 Grand Rapids MI 49503

YOUNG, ANN ELIZABETH O'QUINN, historian, educator; b. Waycross, Ga.; d. James Foster and Pearl Elizabeth (Sasser) O'Quinn; student Shorter Coll.; BA, MA, U. Ga., PhD, 1965; m. Robert William Young, Aug. 18, 1968; children: Abigail Ann, Leslie Lynn. Asst. prof. history Kearney (Nebr.) State Coll. (name now U. Nebr. at Kearney 1991), 1965-69, assoc. prof., 1969-72, prof., 1972—; participant Inst. on Islam, Middle East and World Politics, U. Mich., summer 1984, Coun. on Internat. Ednl. Exch., London, 1990, NEH Seminar NYU, 1993. Mem. NEA, PEO, Phi Alpha Theta, Delta Kappa Gamma (chpt. pres. 1978-79), Phi Mu. Republican. Presbyterian. Contbg. author Dictionary of Georgia Biography; contbr. articles to profl. revs. Office: U Nebr at Kearney Dept History Kearney NE 68849-1285

YOUNG, ANNA BETHEL, English language educator, consultant; b. Phila., July 18; d. Walter and Mary Hayley Fields; m. Henry Wren Bethel (dec. 1971); children: Wayne, Leonard; m. John Gilbert Young (dec. 1977). BS, Temple U., 1946, MEd, 1955; student, U. Pa., 1956, 61-62; DEd, Rutgers U., 1986. Cert. elementary and secondary edn. tchr., prin., Pa. English tchr. Phila. Sch. Dist., 1948-51, Vaux Jr. High Sch., Phila., 1951-58, Wanamaker Jr. High Sch., Phila., 1958-70; English tchr. Bartram High Sch., Phila., 1970-81, adminstr., 1978-80; adj. prof. Trenton (N.J.) State Coll., 1986-88, prof., 1989—; prof. Temple U., Phila., 1988-89; tutor Cheyney U. Urban Ctr., Phila., 1983-87; workshop dir. Ewing Sch. Dist., Trenton, 1989, Black Engrs. Assn., N.Y., N.J., 1991, Rouse Builders, Phia., 1991. Author: Relationship of Writing and Self Esteem, 1980, Case Studies of Development of Black Studies, 1986. Bd. dirs. ARC, Phila., 1986-94, YWCA, Allegheny East Conf. of SDA, Pine Forge, Pa.; vol. United Way, Phila., 1993—. Mem. NAUW (parliamentarian), AAUW, Nat. Coun. Tchrs. English (workshop panelist 1974—), Les Muses (pres.), Temple U. Coll. Alumni Assn. (pres. 1986-88). Mem. Seventh Day Adventist. Office: 117 N Sickels St Philadelphia PA 19139-2533

YOUNG, BETTYE JEANNE, secondary education educator; b. Chgo., Nov. 2, 1929; d. Frank M. Forbish and Mary Bernice (Phillips) Lunde; m. Dale Eugene Young, July 22, 1950; 1 child, Debra Jeanne. AA, Vallejo Jr. Coll., 1964; BA in History, Dominican Coll., 1968. Tchr. North Star Elem., Anchorage, 1978; tchr. Inlet View Elem., Anchorage, 1978-82, tchr.-in-charge, 1979-82; tchr. Ctrl. Jr. High Sch., Anchorage, 1982—; chairperson N.W. Accreditation for Ctrl. Jr. High Sch., 1983; mem. Supt.'s Apprasal Com., Anchorage, 1983-85, Anchorage Sch. Dist.'s Talent Bank, 1979-93, Social Studies Curriculum Com., 1979-93, exec. bd. State Coun. Social Studies, 1990-92; chair social study dept. Ctrl. Jr. H.S., 1994—, Ctrl. Sch. Sci., 1994—. Author: Thematic Approach to U.S. History, 1989 (Merit award Alaska State Dept.), Immigration Unit for U.S. History, 1988 (Merit award Alaska State Dept.), others in field. Voter registrar, Anchorage, 1984; del. Rep. Caucus, Fairbanks, Alaska, 1984; facilitator marriage seminars, Anchorage, 1989-90; mem. Ch. choir, music dept., Anchorage, 1978-93; mem. adv. bd. Law Related Edn., Anchorage, 1993-94; bd. dirs. Alaska Jr. Coll., 1993-94. Named Tchr. of Month Anchorage Sch. Dist., 1981; recipient Jr. Achievement Appreciation award, Project Bus., 1987-92, Support of Social Studies award, Alaska Dept. Edn., 1991, 92; grantee Law Related Edn. Fed. Govt., ABA, 1990-94. Mem. NEA, Anchorage Edn. Assn. (chair instrnl. profl. devel. 1984-85), Anchorage Area Social Studies Coun. (sec. 1983-84, v.p. 1988-90, pres. 1990-92), Nat. Coun. Social Studies, Alaska Coun. Social Studies (secondary tch. of the yr. 1991), Phi Delta Kappa (Cook Inlet chpt., v.p. 1990-92), Delta Kappa Gamma. Home: 18872 Mt Point Dr Eagle River AK 99577 Office: Ctrl Jr High Sch 1405 E St Anchorage AK 99501-5098

YOUNG, BEVERLY SUE, educational psychology educator; b. Oskaloosa, Iowa, Sept. 11, 1925; d. George Floyd and Alta Bernice (Stephens) Garner; m. Robert Lee Silvers, July 1945 (dec. Feb. 1959); m. William Thomas Young, Feb. 12, 1960; children: Rebecca, Rolfe, Thomas, David, Jennifer. BA, William Penn, 1961; MA, U. No. Iowa, 1964; PhD, U. Iowa, 1968. Elem. tchr. North Mahaska Ind. Sch. Dist., New Sharon, Iowa, 1943-64; reading supr. Oskaloosa (Iowa) Ind. Sch. Dist., 1964-65; sch. psychologist Poweshief County, Montezuma, Iowa, 1965-66; dir. learning ctr. Stephen F. Austin State U., Nacogdoches, Tex., 1968-91, prof., 1991—; cons. numerous sch. dists., 1980-94. Author: Reading: How and Why, 1970 (4 edits.), Remedial Reading, 1975 (5 edits.), Reading Instruction for the Total Inclusion Classroom, 1995. Grantee U.S. Govt., 1969-70, Stephen F. Austin State U., Nacogdoches, 1990. Mem. Tex. Assn. Improvement of Reading (pres. 1983, v.p. 1982, legis. co-chair 1988-94), Tex. State Reading Assn., Am. Psychol. Assn., Tex. Profl. of Reading, Stone Fort Coun. Methodist. Office: PO Box 13017 Nacogdoches TX 75962

YOUNG, CHARLITA LUCILLE, community and educational administrator; b. Chgo., Oct. 5, 1958; d. Bernarr Elbert and Janean Elizabeth (Romig) Y. AA, Palomar Community coll., 1974; M of Ednl. Adminstrn., Nat. U., Chico, 1994; MA, Calif. State U., Long Beach, 1981. Mgmt. trainee J.W. Robinson's Dept. Store, Los Angeles, 1977-78; screening coordinator Riverview Hearing, Speech and Lang. Ctr., Long Beach, 1978-81, speech pathologist, 1981-84; speech pathologist, dir. Speech Pathology Svcs., Carlsbad, Calif., 1984—; dir. comty. outreach and student/alumni rels. Kelsey-Jenney Coll., San Diego; mem. adv. com. for Developmentally Disabled, San Diego, 1985-91; coord. pub. svc. announcements for Disabilities Awareness Week, ABC-TV, 1986, Inside San Diego program, 1988. Producer (cable TV series), Communicative Disorders, 1983. Active Carlsbad Hist. Soc., 1993—. Mem. Am. Speech, Lang. and Hearing Assn. (cert. charter mem. adminstrn. and supervision divsn. 1990, augmentative and alternative comm. divsn. 1993, 94), Calif. Speech, Lang. and Hearing Assn. (divsn. rep. 1985-88, Outstanding Achievement award 1987), Calif. Speech Pathologists and Audiologists in Pvt. Practice, Nat. Assn. Hearing and Speech Action (chmn. Disney benefit 1983-84), Assn. for Retarded Citizens, Calif. Scholastic Fedn., Sierra Club, Zeta Tau Alpha, Phi Delta Gamma (sec. 1982-88, v.p. 1983-84). Republican. Home: Unit 9 1263 Robinson Ave San Diego CA 92103 Office: Kelsey-Jenney Coll 201 A St San Diego CA 92101-4003

YOUNG, DAISY ALMEDA, small business owner; b. Morgan Mill, Tex., May 16, 1932; d. Benjamin F. and Dollie Lenora (Earp) Laughlin; m. Don W. Young; 1 child, Robert L. Grad. high sch., Portland, Oreg. Owner Daisy's Employment Svc., Ft. Worth, 1969—. Patron Kimbell Art Mus., Ft. Worth; coord. tutors/adopt a sch. program All Saints Hosp./Daggett Mid. Sch., Ft. Worth, 1989-90. Mem. Bus. and Profl. Women (bd. dirs. Ft. Worth chpt. 1989—), Better Bus. Bur. (arbitrator Ft. Worth chpt. 1983—), Ft. Worth Botanical Soc. (life), Ft. Worth Zoo Soc., Tex. Heritage (life), Tristle Hill Dascent Guild, Internat. Communications Club (pres. Ft. Worth chpt. 1989—). Home: 1316 6th Ave Fort Worth TX 76104-4326 Office: Daisy's Employment Svc 609-5 Sinclair Bldg Fort Worth TX 76102

YOUNG, DARLENE, post office executive; b. Chicago Heights, Ill., Aug. 31, 1954; d. Jeff Sr. and Ruther Lee (Prince) Y. BA in Sociology, Lawrence U., 1976; postgrad., Bloomfield Coll., 1993; cert. in materials mgtm., Bloomfield (N.J) Coll., 1994. Cert. materials mgr. Dir. youth devel. Newark Inst.-Urban Programs, 1977-78; vocat. counselor Newark Comprehensive Manpower Rehab. Project Drug Abusers, 1979-80; supr. distbn. ops. U.S. Postal Svc., Newark, 1980-94, 1994—. Mem. NAFE, Am. Soc. Quality Control, Nat. Assn. Postal Suprs. Home: 51 Clifton Ave Newark NJ 07104-1880

YOUNG, DEBORAH ROHM, exercise and health promotion researcher; b. Orange, Calif., Mar. 17, 1955; d. John Henry and La Vonne Charlotte (Heitshusen) Rohm; m. David Curtis Young, May 16, 1981. BS, UCLA, 1978; MBA, Tex. Christian U., 1984; PhD, U. Tex., 1991. EKG/stress lab. technician Brookhaven Hosp., Dallas, 1978-80; sci. tech. I/II Tex. Coll. Osteo. Medicine, Ft. Worth, 1980-83; intern in health edn. Maricopa divsn. Am. Heart Assn., Phoenix, Ariz., 1983-84; dir., cardiac rehab. coord. Human Performance Inst./Valley View Comty. Hosp., Youngtown, Ariz., 1984-87; office adminstr., cardiac rehab. dir. Thunderbird Heart Ctr., Glendale, Ariz., 1987-88; teaching/rsch. asst. dept. kinesiology and health edn. U. Tex., Austin, 1988-91; postdoctoral rsch. fellow Stanford Ctr. Rsch. Disease Prev. Stanford U. Sch. Medicine, Palo Alto, Calif., 1991-93; Am. Heart Assn. rsch. fellow John A. Burns Sch. Medicine U. Hawaii-Manoa, Honolulu, 1993-94; health promotion rsch. assoc. Sch. Medicine, Johns Hopkins U, Balt., 1994—. Contbr. sci. studies to profl. jours. Mem. heart health edn. in the young com. Maricopa divsn. Am. Heart Assn., Phoenix, 1984-85, mem. speaker's bur., 1986-87, mem. coun. on epidemiology and prevention. Karl K. Klein scholar U. Tex., Austin, 1989. Mem. Am. Coll. Sports Medicine (mktg. com. 1992-94, Hawaii state rep. health people 2000 vol. network S.W. chpt. 1992-94), Soc. Behavioral Medicine, Phi Kappa Phi. Republican. Lutheran. Office: Johns Hopkins U Sch Medicine Ctr Health Promotion 1830 E Monument St Baltimore MD 21205

YOUNG, DONA DAVIS GAGLIANO, lawyer, insurance executive; b. Bklyn., Jan. 8, 1954; d. Vincent Joseph and Shirley Elizabeth (Davis) Gagliano; m. Roland F. Young III, Aug. 18, 1979; children: Meghan Davis, Wesley Davis, Taylor Davis. BA and MA in Polit. Sci., Drew U., 1976; JD, U. Conn., 1980. Bar: Conn. 1980, U.S. Dist. Ct. Conn. 1980. With Phoenix Home Life Ins. Co., Hartford, Conn., 1980—, ast. v.p. reinsurance adminstrn., 1983-85; 2d v.p., ins. counsel Phoenix Mut. Life Ins. Co., Hartford, Conn., 1985-87, v.p. and asst. gen. counsel, 1987-89; sr. v.p. and gen. counsel Phoenix Mut. Life Ins. Co., Hartford, 1989-94; exec. v.p. individual sales and mktg., gen. counsel, 1994—; bd. trustees Hartford Coll. Women. Mem. ABA, Am. Coun. of Life Ins. (com. on risk classification 1985-88, legis. com. 1989—), Hartford County Bar Assn., Conn. Bar Assn., Greater Hartford C. of C. (sr. adv. coun.). Republican. Congregationalist. Office: Phoenix Home Life Ins Co 1 American Row Hartford CT 06115

YOUNG, ERNESTINE JONES, retired postal clerk; b. Eudora, Miss., June 22, 1930; d. James Herron and Ollie (Jones) Holmes; m. Arnett Young Jr., Jan. 3, 1947; children: Davena L., Gwendolyn M., Ernestine, Thelma O., Arnett III, William O., Gloria L. Student, Internat. Acctg. Soc., Chicago, 1966-69, Owen-Lemoyne Coll., 1961-63, U. Tenn., 1963-64; BS, Liberty U., 1994. Clk., ins. and acctg. E.H. Crump Hosp., Memphis, 1963-64; clk., staff asst. U.S. Postal Svc., Memphis, 1964-77; cons. Am. Bapt., Area VI Women, Memphis, 1989—; guest facilitator Ch. Missionary Workshops, Memphis, 1992. Pres. 25th Ward Civic Club, Memphis, 1960-62; bd. dirs., co-chmn. Sch. for Illiteracy, Memphis, 1963; pres. Walker Elem. PTA, Memphis, 1961-63, Lincoln Jr. High Sch. PTA, Memphis, 1964-69; bd. dirs. March of Dimes, 1982-84, Memphis City Beautiful Commn., 1966-68; mem. com. on hypertension U. Tenn., 1978-79; vol. dir. Metro. Bapt. Ch., Memphis, 1983—; dir. Call for Action WDIA, Memphis, 1977-80; asst. to dir. So. Region Call for Action, N.Y.C., 1979-80; sch. dist. chmn. Am. Cancer Soc. & Heart Assn., Memphis, 1964-70; co-chmn. budget com. Nat. Congress of Colored Parents & Tchrs., Memphis, 1966-70. Recipient Outstanding Sch. & Community Svc. award, Lincoln Jr. High Sch., 1969, Leadership award Call for Action, 1980, Cert. Appreciation for Valuable Contbn., 1981, Dorothy M. Lofton award for Meritorious Svc., Metro Bapt. Ch., 1991, Key to City and Cert. Appreciation for Outstanding and Meritorious Svcs. to Community, Memphis, 1991, Proclamation for Accomplishments and Contbns., Congressman Harold Ford, 1991. Mem. NAFE, (charter) NAACP, Am. Bapt. Women (sec. 1982-84, pres. area VI 1984-89, Outstanding & Dedicated Svc. award), Nat. Coun. Negro Women, YMCA, Zeta Phi Beta (dir. Storks' Nest 1981-83). Home: 4458 Whitepine Cove Memphis TN 38109-5922

YOUNG, ESTELLE IRENE, dermatologist; b. N.Y.C., Nov. 2, 1945; d. Sidney D. and Blanche (Krosney) Young. BA magna cum laude, Mt. Holyoke Coll., 1963; MD, Downstate Med. Ctr., 1971. Intern, Lenox Hill Hosp., N.Y.C., 1971-72, resident in medicine, 1972-73; resident in dermatology Columbia Presbyn. Hosp., N.Y.C., 1973-74, NYU Med. Ctr., 1974-75, Boston U. Hosp., 1975-76; asst. dermatologist Harvard U. Health Services, Cambridge, Mass., 1975-76; assoc. staff mem. dermatology Boston U. Med. Ctr., 1976-77; practice medicine specializing in dermatology, Petersburg, Va., 1976—; mem. staff Poplar Springs Hosp., 1976—, Southside Regional Med. Ctr. (formerly Petersburg Gen. Hosp.), 1976—, Cen. State Hosp., 1984—; clin. instr. dept. dermatology Med. Coll. Va., 1976—, asst. clinic prof., 1988-94, assoc. clin. prof., 1994—; sec. med. staff Petersburg Gen. Hosp., 1982—. Fellow Am. Acad. Dermatology; mem. Va. Med. Soc., Va. Dermatology Soc., Tidewater Dermatology Soc. (pres. 1982-83), Physicians for Social Responsiblity Soc., Tidewater Physicians for Social Responsibility (pres. 1990—), Internat. Physicians for Prevention of Nuclear War, Southside Va. Med. Soc., Sigma Xi. Contbr. articles to profl. jours. Home: 2319 Monument Ave Richmond VA 23220-2603 Office: 612A S Sycamore Petersburg VA 23803

YOUNG, FREDDIE GILLIAM, educational administrator; b. Miami, Fla., Nov. 1, 1939; d. Thomas and Myrtle (Gibson) Gilliam. BS, Fla. A&M U., 1961; MS, Hunter Coll., 1970; postgrad., U. Ghana, 1970; EdD, Nova U., 1990; cert. Prin.'s Exec. Tng. Program, Dade County Pub. Schs. Cert. supervision and adminstrn., African studies, elem. and jr. coll. Tchr. Collier County Pub. Schs., Naples, Fla., N.Y.C. Pub. Schs., Bronx, N.Y.; tchr. Dade County Pub. Schs., Miami, prin.; adj. lead prof. Nova U.; presenter Am. Assn. Ethnic Studies Conf., Fla. Atlantic U., 1991, Assn. Carribean Studies Cairo, 1993, Georgetown, Guyana, 1994. Del. 19th congl. dist. Dem. conv., 1988; mem. Am. Jewish Com. Named Most Outstanding Black Woman, S. Fla., Women's C. of C., Educator of Yr. Zeta Phi Beta; recipient 50 outstanding svc. awards Prin. Ctr. Harvard U. Sch. Edn., 1989; finalist for Adminstr. of Yr., 1991, DCAA. Mem. AAUW, ASCD, Am. Jewish Com., Nat. Alliance Black Educators, S. Fla. Exec. Educators, Miami Alliance Black Educators, Dade County Adminstrs. Assn. (chair), Fla. Reading Assn., Dade Reading Coun., Fla. A&M U. Alumni Assn. (pres. Miami-Dade chpt.), Nova U. Alumni Assn. (sec. Miami chpt.), Phi Delta Kappa. Home: 12390 SW 144th Ter Miami FL 33186-7419

YOUNG, GLADYS EVELYN LAMBETH, physician, air force officer; b. Vernon, Tex., Nov. 6, 1948; d. Otha Banks and Tena Ruth (Adams) Lambeth; m. James Arthur Bryan, June, 1971 (div. Dec. 1974); m. Herbert Lee Young, Dec. 31, 1974; 1 child, Otha Benjamin. BSc in Biology magna cum laude, Midwestern U., 1970; MD, U. Tex., 1974. Instr. ACLS, ATLS, pre-hosp. trauma life support, EMT. Resident So. Ill. U. Sch. Med.-Carbondale Doctors Meml. Hosp., 1974-75; commd. 1st lt. USAF, 1975, advanced through grades to col., 1993, gen. med. officer, chief primary care, Altus AFB (Okla.) Hosp., 1975-77, emergency physician, Duncan (Okla.) Regional Hosp., 1977-79; flight surgeon active reserves 507 TAC Clinic USAF, Tinker AFB, Okla., 1977-79; chief AMIC Clinic GS-11, Reynolds Army Hosp. USAF, Malmstrom AFB, Mont., 1982-84; emergency physician, Columbus Hosp. USAF, Great Falls, Mont., 1981-83; chief aerospace medicine, Hosp. Malmstrom USAF, 1982-84; emergency physician, Jackson County Meml. Hosp. USAF, Altus, 1984-87; chief aeromed. svcs., Hosp. Altus USAF, 1984-87, chief hosp. svcs., Hosp. Altus, 1986-87; dir. base med. svcs. USAF, Suwon AFB, Korea, 1987-88; chief aerospace medicine, 43 Med. Group/SGP USAF, Malmstrom AFB, 1988-94, comdr. 341 AERMS 341 Med. Group, 1994—; mem. 1611th Aeromed. Evacuation Squadron, provisional, Desert Storm USAF, King Khalid Mil. City, Saudi Arabia, 1991; comdr. 1610 med. squadron provisional, Restore Hope USAF, Caro West AB, Egypt, 1993. Field dir. med. team Great Centennial Trail Drive, 1989. Decorated Meritorious Svc. medal with oak leaf cluster, Nat. Def. medal, South West Asia 1st device, Outstanding Unit 4 device with valor, Liberation of Kuwait medal. Mem. Am. Acad. Family Physicians (cert., fellow 1980), Order of Eastern Star, VFW (life). Republican. Baptist. Office: 341 AMS/SGPoup Malmstrom A F B MT 59402

YOUNG, HOLLY PEACOCK, lawyer, mediator; b. Indpls., Sept. 21, 1949; d. John Edward and Sylvia (Griffith) Peacock; m. Gregory Glenn Young, Sept. 2, 1972; children: Reagan Wheelock, Trevor Griffith. Student Dartmouth Coll., 1969-70; B.A., Conn. Coll., 1971; M.A., U. Tex., 1973; J.D., So. Meth. U., 1982. Bar: Tex. 1983; state water programmer EPA, Dallas, 1973-75, 75-77; asst. mgr. Menlo Sport, Menlo Park, Calif., 1977-79; assoc. Wald, Harkrader & Ross, Dallas, 1983-84; mediator Settlement Cons. Internat., Inc., Dallas, 1993—. bd. dirs. Hindostone Co., Indpls.; with Jour. Air Law and Commerce, 1980-82. Bd. dirs. Montessori Sch. of Park Cities, 1983-87; bd. advisors Cottonwood Gulch Found., 1982-89. Recipient Bronze medal EPA, 1974. Mem. ABA, Tex. Bar Assn., Dallas Bar Assn., Dyslexics CAN. Episcopalian. Home: 4711 Cherokee Trl Dallas TX 75209-1917

YOUNG, JACQUELINE EURN HAI, state legislator; b. Honolulu, May 20, 1934; d. Paul Bai and Martha (Cho) Y.; m. Harry Valentine Daniels, Dec. 25, 1954 (div. 1978); children: Paula, Harry, Nani, Laura; m. Everett Kleinjans, June 4, 1988. BS in Speech Pathology, Audiology, U. Hawaii, 1969; MS in Edn., Spl. Edn., Old Dominion U., 1972; advanced cert., Loyola Coll., 1977; PhD in Communication, Women's Studies, Union Inst., 1989. Dir. dept. speech and hearing Md. Sch. for the Blind, Balt., 1975-77; dir. deaf-blind project Easter Seal Soc. Oahu, Hawaii, 1977-78; project dir. equal ednl. opportunity programs Hawaii State Dept. Edn., Honolulu, 1978-85, state ednl. specialist, 1978-90; state rep. dist. 20 Hawaii State Legislature, Honolulu, 1990-92, state rep. dist. 51, 1992—; vice-speaker Hawaii Ho. of Reps., Honolulu; apptd. to U.S. Dept. Def. Adv. Commn. on Women in the Svc.; cons. spl. edn. U.S. Dept. Edn., dept. edn. Guam, Am. Samoa, Ponape, Palau, Marshall Islands, 1977-85; cons. to orgns. on issues relating to workplace diversity; adj. prof. comm., anthropology, mgmt. Hawaii Pacific U. Guest moderator Sta. KGMB-TV. 1st v.p. Nat. Women's Polit. Caucus, 1988-90; chair Hawaii Women's Polit. Caucus, 1987-89; bd. dirs. YWCA Oahu, Kalihi Palama Immigrant Svc. Ctr., Hawaii Dem. Movement, Family Peace Ctr.; appointee Honolulu County Com. on the Status of Women, 1986-87; mem. Adv. Coun. on Family Violence. Recipient OUtstanding Woman Leader award YWCA of Oahu, 1994, Pres.'s award Union Inst., 1993, Fellow of the Pacific award Hawaii-Pacific U., 1993, Headliner award Honolulu chpt. Women in Commn., 1993. Mem. Soroptimist Internat. (Kailua chpt.), Orgn. Women Leaders, Kailua C. of C., Korean C. of C., Kook Min Hur, Sierra Club, Korean Univ. Club. Home: 212 Luika Pl Kailua HI 96734-3237 Office: State Office Tower Rm 1309 Leiopapa A Kamehameha Bldg Honolulu HI 96813

YOUNG, JANET CHERYL, electrical engineer; b. Roanoke, Va., Oct. 3, 1960; d. Don Gordon and Barbara Hill (Mumpower) Y. BS in Physics, U. Tenn., Chattanooga, 1982; MSEE, Va. Tech. Inst., 1991. Engr. Sci. Applications Internat. Corp., Springfield, Va., 1982-91, UTC Svc. Corp., Washington, 1991-93; LCC, LLC, Arlington, Va., 1993—. Active in World Peace Mission Foundry United Meth. Ch., Washington, 1984, Community Band, Vienna, Va., 1985. Mem. IEEE (mem. Electromagnetic Compatibility Soc. 1987—, Comm. Soc. 1992—). Methodist. Home: 4044 Chetham Way Lake Ridge VA 22192-5079 Office: LCC LLC 1140 Connecticut Ave 2300 Clarendon Blvd Ste 800 Arlington VA 22201-3367

YOUNG, JOAN CRAWFORD, advertising executive; b. Hobbs, N.Mex., July 30, 1931; d. William Bill and Ora Maydelle (Boone) Crawford; m. Herchelle B. Young, Nov. 23, 1971 (div.). BA, Hardin Simmons U., 1952; postgrad. Tex. Tech. U., 1953-54. Reporter, Lubbock (Tex.) Avalanche-Jour., 1952-54; promotion dir. Sta. KCBD-TV, Lubbock, 1954-62; account exec. Ward Hicks Advt., Albuquerque, 1962-70; v.p. Mellekas & Assocs., Advt., Albuquerque, 1970-78; pres. J. Young Advt., Albuquerque, 1978—. Bd. dirs. N.Mex. Symphony Orch., 1970-73, United Way of Greater Albuquerque, 1985-89; bd. trustees N.Mex. Children's Found., 1994—. Recipient Silver medal N.Mex. Advt. Fedn., 1977. Mem. N.Mex. Advt. Fedn. (bd. dirs. 1975-76), Am. Advt. Fedn., Greater Albuquerque C. of C. (bd. dirs. 1984), Albuquerque Petroleum Club (membership chmn. 1992-93, bd. dirs. 1993—, sec. 1994—). Republican. Author: (with Louise Allen and Audre Lipscomb) Radio and TV Continuity Writing, 1962. Home: 1638 Tierra Del Rio NW Albuquerque NM 87107 also: 303 Roma NW Albuquerque NM 87102

YOUNG, KATHERINE ANN, education educator; b. Castleford, Idaho, Apr. 9, 1941; d. Ross and Norna (Scully) Stoner; m. Virgil Monroe Young, Dec. 20, 1964; 1 child, Susan Annette. BS in Elem. Edn., U. Idaho, 1965; MEd, Ea. Washington U., 1969; EdD, Utah State U., 1980. Cert. advanced elem. tchr., Idaho. Tchr. spl. edn. Coeur d'Alene (Idaho) Sch. Dist., 1965-66; tchr. elem. grades Coeur d' Aleue (Idaho) Sch. Dist., 1966-67, Boise (Idaho) Sch. Dist., 1967-88; assoc. prof. edn. Boise State U., 1988-93, prof., 1993—. Co-author: (resource book) The Story of Idaho Author's, 1977, The Story of Idaho Guide and Resource Book, 1993; author: The Utah Activity

Book, 1980, Constructing Buildings, Bridges, and Minds, 1993; cons., contbr. (nat. edn. jour.) Learning, 1991—. Named Idaho Tchr. of Yr., State Dept. of Edn., Boise, 1983; invited to luncheon at White House, Pres. Ronald Reagan, Washington, 1983; Recipient Outstanding Young Educator award Boise Jaycees, 1983; profiled in Idaho Centennial pub., 1990; travel to Japan grantee Rocky Mountain Region Japan Project, 1990. Mem. ASCD, Nat. Coun. for Social Studies, Idaho Law Found., Alliance Idaho Geographers (state coord.). Office: Boise State U Dept Tchr Edn 1910 University Dr Boise ID 83725-0001

YOUNG, KATHLEEN ANNE, environmental engineer; b. Pompton Plains, N.J., Apr. 5, 1966; d. William Vincent and Lois Mae (Hazel) G. BS in Mech. Engring., U. Rochester, 1988, MS in Biomed. Engring., 1989. Cert. in biomed. engring. Mech. technician U. Rochester (N.Y.) Lab. for Laser Energetics, 1986-87; teaching asst. dept. mech. engring. U. Rochester, 1988-89; nuclear/environ. engr. U.S. Dept. Energy, Schenectady, 1989-92; environ. engr. Dames & Moore Cons., Dallas, 1992-94; sr. project adminstr. Central & Southwest Svcs., Inc., 1994—; Job Fair rep. U.S. Dept. Energy, 1989. Folk music soloist St. Mary's Ch., Schenectady, 1985-91; active Big Bros./Big Sisters, Rochester, 1985; vol. Ellis Hosp., Schenectady, 1992. Rochester scholar, 1984-88. Mem. ASME, Soc. Women Engrs. (activity chairperson 1986-87), Air and Waste Mgmt. Assn., U. Rochester Alumni Assn. (com. mem. 1991—). Republican. Roman Catholic. Home: 1907 Golden Trail Carrollton TX 75010 Office: Central & SW Svc Inc 1616 Woodall Rodgers Fwy P O Box 660164 Dallas TX 75266-0164

YOUNG, KATHRYN JUNE, sales executive; b. Boaz, Ala., Aug. 15, 1932; d. Benjamin Franklin and Arti Jane (Luther) Upton; m. William Milwee, Dec. 25, 1951 (div. Jun. 25, 1964); children: William Jeffrey Milwee, Gary Stephen Milwee; m. William Mayron Young, July 12, 1965 (dec.). Saleswomen Tamarisk Country Club, Palm Springs, Calif., 1970; sales mgmt. Alameda Plaza Hotel, Kansas City, Mo., 1974-75; saleswoman Bermuda Dunes Country Club, Calif., 1975; waitress Eldorado Country Club, Palm Desert, Calif., 1980; saleswoman, cashier La Quinta Country Club, Calif.; saleswoman, set up Rotary Club, Palm Desert, Calif.; sales mgmt. Found. for Retarded, Palm Desert, Calif., 1988; saleswoman Host Internat., Las Vegas, Nev., 1989-90; gen. mgr. Hospice Thrift, Hemet, Calif., 1991-95. Mem. Assn. Female Execs., Nat. Assn. Retail Resale Shops. Home: 7100 W Alexander Rd # 1089 Las Vegas NV 89129

YOUNG, KAY LYNN, dance educator, small business owner; b. Decatur, Tex., Aug. 7, 1955; d. Cecil V. and Evelyn Jane (Cohron) Y. BS in Dance Edn., U. North Tex., 1977, MS in Dance Edn., 1981. Freelance instr. Dallas, 1977—; owner, dir. Kay Lynn's Studio of Dance, Carrollton, Tex., 1982—; choreographer, dir. in field. Hostess (cable TV) Kay Lynn's Aerobics, 1985-87, Dallas Dance News, 1989—. Member Metrocrest C. of C., Carrollton, 1982-87, Farmers Branch C. of C., 1985-87; mentor Carrollton Farmers Branch; key communicator Carrollton Farmers Branch Ind. Sch. Dist., 1982—. Named one of Outstanding Young Women of Am., 1983. Mem. AAUW (ednl. v.p. 1983-84, cultural v.p. 1987-88, membership v.p. 1991—), Dallas Dance Coun. (social v.p. 1988—), Nat. Assn. Dance and Affiliate Artists (sec., treas. 1988—). Baptist. Home and Office: 1713 Aurora Dr Richardson TX 75081

YOUNG, LENORA JEAN, nurse; b. Lafayette, Ind., Aug. 9, 1963; d. Jackie Lee Fink and Eleanor Louise Childress; m. James Atkinson Young, Jr., Sept. 20, 1985 (div. 1989). BSN, Purdue U., 1994. RN. Med. asst. Community Hosp., Williamsport, Ind., 1982-83; tax examiner U.S. Treasury Dept., Atlanta, 1986-88; travel counselor Travel Incorp., Atlanta, 1988-89; student nurse technician Lafayette (Ind.) Home Hosp., 1989-92; student nurse extern Meth. Hosp., 1993; staff nurse Nat. Naval Med. Ctr., Bethesda, Md., 1994—. With U.S. Army, 1983-86, mem. Res. ret.; ensign USNR, 1994. Mem. AAUW, Nat. Student Nurses Assn., Women in Mil. Svc. Am. (charter), Jr. Mil. Nurses Assn., Sigma Theta Tau (Delta Omicron chpt.). Methodist. Home: 3427 Gateshead Manor Way #304 Silver Spring MD 20904

YOUNG, LINDA IRENE, school district administrator; b. Fort Smith, Ark., Dec. 2, 1948; d. Charles Holt and Wanda Louise (Graves) Y.; children: Charles, Patrick. BS Edn., U. Ark., 1970, MEd, 1971. Cert. tchr., adminstr., supr., Ark. Tchr. Fayetteville (Ark.) Pub. Schs., 1970-72, Bauxite (Ark.) Pub. Schs., 1972-75; tchr. Pulaski Acad., Little Rock, 1975-76, elem. prin., 1976-78; asst. dir. summer reading program U. Ark.-Little Rock, 1985-88, instr., 1987-88; dir. restructuring/new futures liaison Little Rock Sch. Dist., 1988—; bd. mem. Ark. Mid. Level. Assn., 1989—; fellow Ctr. for Leadership in Sch. Reform, Louisville, 1990—; mem. adv. bd. Ctr. for Mid. Level. Edn., Fayetteville, 1992—, cons., 1993; bd. mem. Ark. Mid. Level Grade Task Force, 1991—. Mem. editorial bd. MidSouth Jour. Mid. Level Edn. Mem. Ark. Arts Ctr. Alumni Orgn., Little Rock, 1985—; pres. Ark. Symphony Orch. Guild, Little Rock, 1986-87; bd. dirs. Ark. Symphony Orch. Assn., 1986-87. Recipient Juvenile Justice Recognition award Div. Children and Family Svcs., State of Ark., 1990. Mem. ASCD, Nat. Assn. Secondary Sch. Prins., Nat. Mid. Sch. Assn., Phi Delta Kappa. Democrat. Methodist. Home: 2 Sunset Circle Little Rock AR 72207 Office: Little Rock Sch Dist 810 W Markham Little Rock AR 72201

YOUNG, LOIS CATHERINE WILLIAMS, university agency consultant; b. Wakeman, Ohio, Mar. 10, 1930; d. William McKinley and Leona Catherine (Woods) Williams; m. William Walton Young; children: Ralph, Catherine, William. BS, NYU, 1957; MS, Hofstra U., 1962, profl. diploma, 1967, EdD, 1981; M Pub. Adminstrn., Fla. Internat. U., 1988. Cert. tchr., sch. supr., N.Y., pub. mgmt., Fla. Tchr. Copiague (N.Y.) Schs., 1957-59; research assoc. Columbia and Hofstra Univs., Hempstead, N.Y., 1964-69; tchr. Half Hollow Hills Pub. Schs., Dix Hills, N.Y., 1970-72; instr. Conn. Coll., New London, 1972-73; tchr., supr., reading coordinator Hempstead (N.Y.) Pub. Schs., 1975-85; cons. South African project AID Fla. Meml. Coll., Miami, Fla., 1987-88; clinician Hofstra U., Hempstead, 1962-64; tchr. trainer Amityville (N.Y.) Pub. Schs., 1965, Hofstra Univ., 1982; key speaker Internat. Reading Assn., N.Y., Calif., Caribbean Islands, 1982-86. Author numerous poems. Sec. Nassau County (N.Y.) chpt. Jack and Jill of Am., 1960-62; pres. PTA, Uniondale, N.Y., 1962-68; active Boy Scouts Am., Uniondale, N.Y., 1963-65; bd. dirs. Miami chpt. UN Assn./USA, 1987-92, 1st v.p. 1989-91, Broward Fort Lauderdale chpt., 1993—; active multilateral project, 1987-90; contbr. Procs. South African Project, 1987. Recipient Lifetime Membership award PTA, 1964, rsch. grant N.Y. State Fed. Programs, 1978, Laurel Wreath award Doctoral Assn. of N.Y. Educators, 1982, Cert. of award UN Assn./USA, 1987, 88, Outstanding Achievement award Fla. Internat. U., 1988, Golden Poet award World of Poetry, 1990, 91; fellow Fla. Internat. U., 1987. Mem. Internat. Soc. Poets (life, lifetime adv. panel 1993—, award, Nat. Libr. of Poetry award 1994), Fla. Internat. U. Alumni Assn., NYU Alumni Assn. (bd. dirs. 1983-90, 2d v.p. 1986-87), Hofstra U. Alumni Assn., Tuskegee Airmen, Inc., Weston (Fla.) Toastmasters Club (charter), Toastmasters Internat., Kappa Delta Pi, Alpha Kappa Alpha, Theta Iota Omega (global affairs com. 1984-86), Phi Delta Kappa. Home: 1345 Sunset Spgs Fort Lauderdale FL 33326-2936

YOUNG, LORETTA (GRETCHEN YOUNG), actress; b. Salt Lake City, Jan. 6, 1913; M. Thomas Lewis (div.). Grad., Ramona Convent, Alhambra, Calif.; student, Immaculate Heart Coll., Hollywood, Calif. Motion picture appearances include Laugh Clown Laugh, 1928, Loose Ankles, 1929, The Squall, 1930, Kismet, 1930, The Devil to Pay, 1930, I Like Your Nerve, 1931, Platinum Blonde, 1932, The Hatchet Man, 1932, Big Business Girl, 1932, Life Begins, 1932, Zoo in Budapest, 1933, Man's Castle, 1933, The House of Rothschild, 1934, Midnight Mary, 1935, The Crusaders, 1935, Clive of India, 1935, Call of the Wild, 1935, Shanghai, 1936, Ramona, 1936, Ladies in Love, 1937, Wife, Doctor and Nurse, 1937, Second Honeymoon, 1938, Four Men and a Prayer, 1938, Suez, 1938, Kentucky, 1938, Three Blind Mice, 1938, The Story of Alexander Graham Bell, 1939, The Doctor Takes a Wife, 1939, He Stayed for Breakfast, 1940, Lady from Cheyenne, 1941, The Men in Her Life, 1941, A Night to Remember, 1942, China, 1943, Ladies Courageous, 1944, And Now Tomorrow, 1944, The Stranger, 1945, Along Came Jones, 1946, The Perfect Marriage, 1946, The Farmer's Daughter, 1947 (Acad. award 1947), The Bishop's Wife, 1948, Rachel and the Stranger, 1948, Come to the Stable, 1949, Cause for Alarm, 1951, Half Angel, 1951, Paula, 1952, Because of You, 1952, It Happens Every Thursday, 1953, others; appeared in TV series Loretta Young Show (Emmy awards 1954, 56, 59, Acad. Television Arts & Scis.), 1953-61, in TV films Christmas Eve (Golden Globe Award for best actress in a TV movie), 1986, Lady in a Corner, 1989; stage appearance in An Evening with Loretta Young, 1989. Active in Cath. charity orgns. Roman Catholic. Office: care Studio Fan Mail 1122 S Robertson Blvd Los Angeles CA 90035*

YOUNG, LORETTA ANN, accountant, financial analyst; b. Reading, Pa., Dec. 2, 1962; d. Milton and Delois Jean (Ridley) Y. BS, Towson State U., 1985. Auditor Irving Burton Assocs., Inc., Washington, 1984-88; tax technician Gen. Bus. Svcs., Germantown, Md., 1989; auditor Montgomery County Govt., Rockville, Md., 1989-90; dir. membership devel. Nat. Forum for Black Pub. Adminstrs., Washington, 1990-91; sr. acct.-analyst Cox & Assocs. CPAs, P.C., Hyattsville, Md., 1992; mgr. ops. LKA Computer Cons., Inc., Hyattsville, 1992-94; sr. auditor Office Specialists, Inc., Washington, 1994—. Mem. NAFE, Mid Atlantic Notary Assn. Home: 763 Quince Orchard Blvd Apt 24 Gaithersburg MD 20878-1661 Office: #419 1025 Connecticut Ave NW Washington DC 20036

YOUNG, LUCY CLEAVER, physician; b. Wheeling, W.Va., Aug. 8, 1943. B.S. in Chemistry, Wheaton Coll. (Ill.), 1965; M.D., Ohio State U., 1969. Diplomate Am. Bd. Family Practice, Bd. of Ins. Medicine. Rotating intern Riverside Meth. Hosp., Columbus, Ohio, 1969-70; resident Trumbull Meml. Hosp., Warren, Ohio, 1970-71; practice medicine specializing in family practice, West Chicago, Ill., 1971-73, Paw Paw and Mendota, Ill., 1973-78; co-founder and med. dir. Wholistic Health Ctr. of Mendota, 1976-78; asst. med. dir. Met. Life Ins. Co., Gt. Lakes Head Office, Aurora, Ill., 1979-80; med. dir. Commonwealth Life Ins. Co., Louisville, 1980-85; assoc. prof. U. Ill. Abraham Lincoln Sch. Medicine, 1976-79; faculty monitor MacNeal Meml. Hosp. Family Practice Ctr. (Ill.), 1979-80; faculty preceptor U. Louisville Family Practice Dept., 1981-85; Locum Tenens Family Practice for Kron Med. Corp. of Chapel Hill, N.C., 1986-89; physician Red Bird Mission & Med. Ctr., Beverly, Ky., 1989-90; family practice floater Ochsner Clinic satellites, New Orleans, 1990—; clin. faculty preceptor La. State U. Sch. Medicine, 1992—; mem. staffs Central DuPage Hosp., Winfield, Ill., 1971-73, Mendota Community Hosp., 1973-80. Vol. Red Bird Med. Ctr., 1985—. Fellow Am. Acad. Family Practice; mem. Am. Med. Women's Assn. (pres. New Orleans br. 1992-93, reg. V reg. gov. 1993-94), Christian Med. and Dental Soc. Home: PO Box 0730 Madisonville LA 70447-0730 Office: Ochsner Clinic 1514 Jefferson Hwy New Orleans LA 70121

YOUNG, MARGARET ALETHA MCMULLEN (MRS. HERBERT WILSON YOUNG), social worker; b. Vossburg, Miss., June 13, 1916; d. Grady Garland and Virgie Aletha (Moore) McMullen; BA cum laude, Columbia Bible Coll., 1949; grad. Massey Bus. Coll., 1958; MSW, Fla. State U., 1965; postgrad. Jacksonville U., 1961-62, Tulane U., 1967; m. Herbert Wilson Young, Aug. 19, 1959. Dir. Christian edn. Eau Claire Presbyn. Ch., Columbia, S.C., 1946-51; tchr. Massey Bus. Coll., Jacksonville, Fla., 1954-57, office mgr., 1957-59; social worker, unit supr. Fla. div. Family Svcs., St. Petersburg, 1960-66, dist. casework supr., 1966-71; social worker, project supr., program supr. Project Playpen, Inc., 1971-81, pres. bd., 1982-83, cons., 1986-89; pvt. practice family counselor, 1982—; mem. coun. Child Devel. Ctr., 1983-89; mem. transitional housing com., Religious Community Svcs., 1984-90. Mem. Acad. Cert. Social Workers, Nat. Assn. Social Workers (pres. Tampa Bay chpt. 1973-74), Fla. Assn. for Health and Social Services (pres. chpt. 1971), Nature Conservancy, Eta Beta Rho. Democrat. Presbyn. Rotary Ann (pres. 1970-71). Home: Presbyterian Home CMR 13 201 W 9th N St Summerville SC 29483

YOUNG, MARGARET BUCKNER, civic worker, author; b. Campbellsville, Ky.; d. Frank W. and Eva (Carter) Buckner; m. Whitney M. Young, Jr., Jan. 2, 1944 (dec. Mar. 1971); children: Marcia Elaine, Lauren Lee. BA, Ky. State Coll., 1942, MA, U. Minn., 1946. Instr. Ky. State Coll., 1942-44; instr. edn. and psychology Spelman Coll., Atlanta, 1957-60; dir. emeritus N.Y. Life Ins. Co.; alt. del. UN Gen. Assembly, 1973. Mem. pub. policy com. Advt. Coun. Trustee emerita Lincoln Ctr. for Performing Arts; chmn. Whitney M. Young, Jr. Meml. Found., 1971-92; trustee Met. Mus. Art, 1976-90; bd. govs. UN Assn., 1975-82; bd. visitors U.S. Mil. Acad., 1978-80; dir. Philip Morris Cos., 1972-91. Author: The First Book of American Negroes, 1966, The Picture Life of Martin Luther King, Jr., 1968, The Picture Life of Ralph J. Bunche, 1968, Black American Leaders-Watts, 1969, The Picture Life of Thurgood Marshall, 1970, pub. affairs pamphlet.

YOUNG, MARGARET CHONG, elementary education educator; b. Honolulu, May 8, 1924; d. Henry Hon Chin and Daisy Kyau (Tong) Chong; m. Alfred Y.K. Young, Feb. 21, 1948; children: Robert S.W., Richard S.K., Linda S.K. EdB, 5th yr. cert., U. Hawaii, 1945. Cert. tchr., Hawaii. Tchr. Waipahu (Hawaii) Elem. Sch., Manoa Housing Sch., Hawaii Dept. Edn., Honolulu, Pauoa Elem. Sch., Honolulu. Author: And They Also Came, History of Chinese Christian Association, Hawaii's People From China; contbr. numerous articles to profl. jours. Ch. sch. tchr., supt. United Ch. Christ-Judd St. Grantee San Francisco State Coll. Mem. NEA, Hawaii State Tchrs. Assn., Hawaii Congress of Parents and Tchrs. (hon. life mem.), Kappa Kappa Iota (Disting. Educator award 1986-87), Delta Kappa Gamma (internat.).

YOUNG, MARILYN RAE, school system adminstrative secretary, mayor; b. Muskegon, Mich., Dec. 29, 1934; d. Albert Henry Cribley and Mildred Ida (Johnson) Raby; m. Peter John Young, May 21, 1955; children: Pamela Lynn Young-Walker, Lane Allen. Grad. high sch., Calumet City, Ill., 1952. Dep. pub. fiduciary Yuma County, Ariz., 1979-83; adminstrv. sec. Yuma Sch. Dist. One, 1983—; councilman City of Yuma, 1990-93, mayor, 1993—. Pres. bd. dirs. Behavioral Health Svcs. of Yuma, 1979-90; vice chmn. Yuma Planning and Zoning Commn., 1985-89; v.p. bd. dirs. Children's Village, Yuma, 1983-89; lay leader Trinity United Meth. Ch., 1986—; grad. Yuma Leadership, Inc., 1985; treas. bd. dirs. Yuma Leadership, Inc., 1986-89; participant Ariz. Women's Town Hall, 1989, various Yuma County Town Halls, 1987-90; adv. bd. mem. Friends of KAWC; chmn Yuma Pub. Safety Police Bd., 1990—, Yuma Fire Pub. Safety Bd., 1990—, Yuma Youth Leadership Com., 1991-92; mem. allocation panel United Way, 1991-93; charter mem. Friends of Roxaboxen; active High Sch. Ad Hoc Com., 1991—; exec. bd. mem., Yuma Met. Planning Orgn., 1990—, Western Ariz. Coun. of Govts., 1990—; corp. bd. dir. Yuma Econ. Devel., 1990—; hon. chmn. Yuma County San Luis Rio Colo.Commn., 1990—; mem. Nat. League of Cities FAIR Com., 1990—, Binational Border Health Task Force, 1990—, resolution com. League of Ariz. Cities and Towns, 1990—, mem. com. U.S. Conf. of Mayors, 1990—. Mem. Yuma County C. of C. (mem. mil. affairs com. 1988-90). Home: 1288 W 18th St Yuma AZ 85364-5313 Office: City of Yuma 180 W 1st St Yuma AZ 85364-1495

YOUNG, MARY ELIZABETH, history educator; b. Utica, N.Y., Dec. 16, 1929; d. Clarence Whitford and Mary Tippit Y. B.A., Oberlin Coll., 1950; Ph.D. (Robert Shalkenbach Found. grantee, Ezra Cornell fellow), Cornell U., 1955. Instr. dept. history Ohio State U., Columbus, 1955-58; asst. prof. Ohio State U., 1958-63, assoc. prof., 1963-69, prof., 1969-73; prof. history U. Rochester, N.Y., 1973—; cons. in field. Author: Redskins, Ruffleshirts, and Rednecks: Indian Allotments in Alabama and Mississippi, 1830-1860, 1961; co-editor, contbr.: The Frontier in Americal Development: Essays in Honor of Paul Wallace Gates, 1969. Recipient Pelzer award Miss. Valley Hist. Assn., 1955, Award Am. Studies Assn., 1982, Ray A. Billington award, 1982; Social Sci. Research Council grantee, 1968-69. Mem. Am. Hist. Assn., Orgn. Am. Historians, Am. Studies Assn., Am. Soc. Ethnic History, Soc. for Historians of the Early Am. Republic, Am. Antiquarian Soc. Home: 2230 Clover St Rochester NY 14618-4124 Office: U Rochester Dept History Rochester NY 14627

YOUNG, MELANIE ANNE, public relations executive; b. Chattanooga, Jan. 1, 1959; d. Melvin Asher and Sonia Lee (Winer) Y. BA in Internat. Rels., Sophie Newcomb Coll., 1980. Account exec. Cohn & Wolfe, Atlanta, 1981-86; v.p. Ruder & Finn, N.Y.C., 1986-89; account supr. Burson & Marsteller, N.Y.C., 1989-90; prin., pres. M. Young Comms., N.Y.C., 1990—; program dir. The James Beard Awards, N.Y.C., 1990—; program mgr. N.Y. Restaurant Week, N.Y.C., 1992—. Spl. project dir. The James Beard Found., 1992—. Office: M Young Comms 77 Fifth Ave 2CD New York NY 10003

YOUNG, MEREDITH ANNE, marketing and advertising professional; b. Newark, Apr. 12, 1952; d. W. Edward and Lois E. (Velthoven) Y. BA, Caldwell Coll., 1974. Advt., pub. rels. asst. Congoleum Corp., Lawrenceville, N.J., 1974-77; account mgr. Saatchi & Saatchi Compton, N.Y.C., 1977-82; dir. advt., sales promotion Singer Sewing Co., Edison, N.J., 1982-86, dir. product mktg., 1986-88, dir. nat. accounts, 1988-90; sr. mktg. rep. Walt Disney World Co., Lake Buena Vista, Fla., 1990-91; div. mktg. rep. Vista Advt., Walt Disney World Co., Lake Buena Vista, Fla., 1991-92; mgr. advt. Walt Disney World Co., Lake Buena Vista, Fla., 1992-94, mgr. Fla. tourist mktg., 1994—. Contbr. articles to profl. jours. Vol. North Brunswick Dem. Orgn., 1985-87; pub. rels. mgr. Cultural Arts Com., North Brunswick, 1986-87; props chair Adult Drama Group, North Brunswick, 1986-87; mem. mktg. com. Vol. Ctr. Ctrl. Fla., 1993-94. Mem. Fla. Direct Mktg. Assn., Cen. Fla. Direct Mktg. Assn. (bd. dirs. 1990-92). Democrat. Episcopalian. Office: Walt Disney World Co PO Box 10000 Orlando FL 32830-1000

YOUNG, NANCY MING CHONG, arts administrator, artist; b. Taipei, Taiwan, Jan. 13, 1963; came to U.S., 1965; d. Peter T. and Mary F. (Lee) Y.; m. Donald Errol Robert Meyers, July 10, 1992. BA in English Lit., U. Calif., Berkeley, 1985; cert. pub. policy, Harvard U., 1986; MA in Internat. Affairs, Columbia U., 1988; MA in Asian Studies, U. Hawaii, 1988. Adminsrv. asst. Harvard Law Sch., Cambridge, Mass., 1980-83; sr. ESL Tutor U. Calif., Berkeley, 1984-86; rsch. assoc. East-West Ctr., Honolulu, 1987-89; assoc. program dir. San Francisco C. of C., 1990-92; mgr. instnl. support Yerba Buena Ctr., San Francisco, 1992; program officer Walter and Elise Haas Fund, San Francisco, 1992-94; dir. devel. The Mexican Mus., San Francisco, 1994—; prin. couns. Young & Assocs., San Francisco, 1990—; co-founder Arts Svcs. Round Table, San Francisco, 1991-92; com. mem. Strive for Five, San Francisco, 1992; guest lectr. San Francisco State U., 1991; guest speaker Golden Gate, San Francisco, 1993. Painter: landscapes (acrylic), San Francisco Tritych, 1993. Mem. grants rev. panel Calif. Arts Coun., Sacramento, 1994, City of San Jose Cultural Affairs Dept., 1994, Cultural Equity Fund San Francisco Arts Comm., 1994, Americorp, Washington, 1994. Chancellor's scholar UCLA, 1981-82, Alfred P. Sloan fellow, 1985-87, East-West Ctr. fellow, Honolulu, 1987-89. Mem. No. Calif. Grantmakers (chmn. subcom.), Asian Am. and Pacific Islanders in Philanthropy, Grantmakers in the Arts, Theatre Art (bd. dirs. San Francisco chpt.). Democrat. Home: 634 Powell St Apt 39 San Francisco CA 94108-3022

YOUNG, OLIVIA KNOWLES, retired librarian; b. Benton, Ark., Sept. 3, 1922; d. Wesley Taylor and Med Belle (Crawford) Knowles; m. Calvin B. Young, Oct. 6, 1951; 1 child, Brigham Taylor. BA, Tenn. Tech. U., 1942; BS in Libr. Sci., George Peabody Coll. for Tchrs., 1946. Head periodicals and documents dept. Peabody Coll. Library, Nashville, 1946-49; area librarian U.S. Army, Austria, 1949-51; librarian Cairo Pub. Library, Ga., 1955-57, Caney Fork Regional Library, Sparta, Tenn., 1957-58; chief librarian Fort Stewart Ft. Stewart (Ga.) U.S. Army, 1959-63; dir. Watauga Regional Library, Johnson City, Tenn., 1963-70; dir. devel. and extension Tenn. State Library and Archives, Nashville, 1971-82, state librarian and archivist, 1982-85; ret., 1985. Mem. Tenn. Library Assn. (treas. 1970, Honor award 1985), Southeastern Library Assn., ALA, Boone Tree Library Assn. (pres. 1968). Methodist. Club: Altrusa (sec. 1967). Home: PO Box 160444 San Antonio TX 78280-2644

YOUNG, PAMELA INDERFURTH, paralegal; b. Phila., July 12, 1943; d. Karl Henry and Frances (Seawell) Inderfurth; m. Barnett C. Young, July 3, 1961 (div. 1971); 1 child, Barnett C. Jr. Student, U. Md., 1981-83. Legal asst. Kelly & Meneely, Annapolis, Md., 1981-84, Manis, Wilkison & Snider, Annapolis, 1984-86, Bereano & Resnick, P.A., Annapolis, 1986—. Mem. ABA (assoc.), Bay Area Paralegal Assn. Democrat. Presbyterian. Home: 21 Upshur Ave Annapolis MD 21403-4506 Office: Bereano & Resnick PA 195 Duke Of Gloucester St Annapolis MD 21401-2533

YOUNG, PATRICIA JEAN HEDRICK, mental health nurse, educator; b. Fairmont, W.Va., June 2, 1952; d. Raymond and Mary Jean (Sapp) Hedrick; m. David Martin Young, Apr. 7, 1973; children: William Glen, Georgia Lynn. ADN, W.Va. No. Community Coll., Wheeling, 1977; AB in Edn., West Liberty State Coll., 1973, BSN, 1980; MS in Nursing, W.Va. U., 1987. Cert. in psychiat./mental health nursing. Staff nurse Ohio Valley Med. Ctr., Wheeling, W.Va.; instr. Washington (Pa.) Sch. Nursing. Mem. ofcl. bd., nurturance and outreach com. West Liberty Federated Ch. Mem. AAUW, NOW, W.Va. Nurses Assn. (dist. 1 co-editor newsletter), TriState Psychiat. Nurses Assn., Sigma Theta Tau. Home: PO Box 258 West Liberty WV 26074-0258

YOUNG, PAULA ERNESS, educational administrator; b. Memphis, Sept. 20, 1957; d. Ernest Leroy and Carrie Louise (Watson) Y. BS, Memphis State U., 1978; M in Pub. Adminstrn. Atlanta U., 1981; EdD in Edtl. Adminstrn. U. Cin., 1993. Asst. dir. grants, contracts clearinghouse and conf. exhibits mgr. Nat. Assn. for Equal Opportunity in Higher Edn., Washington, 1981-83; dir. rsch. and proposal devel. Clark Coll., Atlanta, 1984-87; asst. v.p. for devel. Johnson C. Smith U., Charlotte, N.C., 1987-88; v.p. instl. advancement Bennett Coll., Greensboro, N.C., 1988-90; spl. asst. to dean coll. arts & scis. N.C. Agrl. and Tech. State U., Greensboro. Mem. Women of Color Com., 1994, Greensboro Minority/Women Bus. Enterprise Adv. Bd., 1993, Greensboro Human Relations Commn., 1990; founder African Am. Atelier Art Gallery; vol. Girl Scouts U.S.A., 1985-86; active YWCA, NAACP. Woodrow Wilson fellow, 1981-83, 85-87. Mem. Nat. Assn. Negro Bus. and Profl. Women's Clubs, Nat. Soc. Fund Raising Execs., Alpha Kappa Alpha, Toastmasters Internat. Avocations: ceramic artwork, reading.

YOUNG, REBECCA LEE, special education educator; b. Muncie, Ind., June 22, 1950; d. Norman Lee and Evelyn Faye (Mann) Hofherr; m. James Paul Young, Feb. 21, 1974; children: Evelyn Kaye, Jason Paul. BS, Ball State U., 1975; MS, St. Francis Coll., Ft. Wayne, Ind., 1985. Tchr. severe and profound Carlin Park Elem. Sch., Angola, Ind., 1975-80; tchr. learning disabled Lakeland High Sch., La Grange, Ind., 1980—; tchr.-multi-categorical class Parkside Elem. Sch., La Grange, Ind., 1991—; tchr. presch. handicapped Sch. Opportunity, LaGrange, summer 1987; insvc. prsenter, 1987—; mem. Lakeland Technology Com., 1992—. Vol. instr. Lakeland Band Camp, 1986-88; bd. dirs. Lakeland Band Boosters, 1986-89, Human Rights Com., La Grange, 1987—; mem. Lakeland Tech. Com., 1992—. Mem. ASCD, Coun. for Exceptional Children, Ind. Tchrs. Assn., Ind. Computer Educators, Lakeland Edn. Assn. (tech. com. 1992), Delta Kappa Gamma (chmn. scholarship com. 1985—), Sigma Alpha Iota, Learning Disabilities Assn. (Parkside child study team 1990—). Home: 353 Parkway St Lagrange IN 46761-1603 Office: Parkside Elem Sch 1 LeMaster Cir Lagrange IN 46761

YOUNG, REBECCA LOU, nutrition program administrator; b. Litchfield, Minn., Dec. 26, 1957; d. Delmar Eugene and Mary Elizabeth (Ulrick) Taylor; m. Michael LeRoy Young, Mar. 25, 1977; children: Chad Eugene, Jon Jeremy. Student, U. No. Iowa, 1976-77, 89—. Cook, prep-cook Pirate's Den, Hudson, Iowa, 1984, mgr., 1984-86; baker Child Nutrition Program Hudson Community Sch., 1986-90, mgr, 1990—. Com. chmn. troop 60 Boy Scouts Am., 1992—. Mem. Iowa Sch. Food Svc. Assn. (cert. gen. asst. I, co-chair door prizes state conv. 1994), Bremer County Food Svc. (treas. 1989—). Democrat. Roman Catholic. Home: PO Box 648 Hudson IA 50643-0648

YOUNG, REBECCA MARY CONRAD, state legislator; b. Clairton, Pa., Feb. 28, 1934; d. Walter Emerson and Harriet Averill (Colcord) Conrad; m. Merwin Crawford Young, Aug. 17, 1957; children: Eve, Louise, Estelle, Emily. BA, U. Mich., 1955; MA in Teaching, Harvard U., 1963; JD, U. Wis., 1983. Bar: Wis. 1983. Commr. State Hwy. Commn., Madison, Wis., 1974-76; dep. sec. Wis. Dept. of Adminstrn., Madison, 1976-77; assoc. Wadsack, Julian & Lawton, Madison, 1983-84; elected rep. Wis. State Assembly, Madison, 1985—. Translator: Katanga Secession, 1966. Supr. Dane County Bd., Madison, 1970-74; mem. Madison Sch. Bd., 1979-85. Recipient Pub. Interest award Ctr. for Pub. Representation, 1980, Woman of Distinction award YWCA, 1981, Clean 16 Environ. award WI Environ. Decade, Inc., 1985-94, Outstanding Contbns. in Supporting Women Nat. Women's Polit. Caucus Wis., 1985, Exemplary Work award Congress for Working Am., 1986, Wis. Pro-Choice Community award, 1987, Community Bldg. award

Wis. Coalition for Advocacy, 1988, Legis. Leadership award Maternal & Child Health Coalition, 1988, 89, WISCAP Gaylord Nelson Human Svc. award, 1989, Outstanding Contbn. in Supporting Women's Right to Choice, Nat. Women's Polit. Caucus Wis., 1989, Support Network award Transitional Employment Program, 1989, Outstanding Community Svc. Recognition, Rainbow Project Child and Family Mental Health Clinic, 1989, NAACP award, 1990, Planned Parenthood of Wis., Inc. award, 1990, Wis. Alliance of Cities Cert. of Merit., 1990, Key to the City of Madison, 1990, Dane County Alliance for the Mentally Ill Disting. Svc. award, 1991, Wis. Dept. of Health and Social Svcs. Head Start Bur. cert., 1991, Legis. of Yr. award Fair Housing of Dane County, 1991, Best of Madison Legis. award Madison Mag., 1991, Met. Milw. Fair Housing Coun. honor, 1991, Bus. Forum Dane County Ann. award, 1992, Stateswoman of Yr. award Wis. Women's Network, 1992, Partnership award Wis. Coun. Community Corrections, 1993, Recovery Options for Mothers and Children award 1993, Legislator of the Yr. award Wis. Child Support Enforcement Assn., 1993, Golden Triangle award Wis. Farmers Union, 1993-94, Family Svcs. Madison Meml. Sch. Dist Parents commendation, 1994, Merit cert. Wis. Alliance of Cities, 1994. Mem. ABA. Democrat. Home: 639 Crandall St Madison WI 53711-1836 Office: State Legislature-Assembly PO Box 8953 Madison WI 53708-8953

YOUNG, REBECCA MOLLIE, criminal justice administrator; b. N.Y.C., Feb. 19, 1964; d. Paul and Selma Lillian (Sidel) Y. AB in Psychology, Harvard and Radcliffe Colls., 1988; postgrad., LBJ Sch. of Pub. Affairs. Rsch. supr., conf. coord. Dare Inst., Cambridge, Mass., 1984-87; freelance editor Cambridge, 1986-90; project mgr., policy analyst BOTEC Analysis Corp., Cambridge, 1988-92; rsch. asst. program in criminal justice Kennedy Sch. of Govt., Harvard U., Cambridge, 1990; rsch. assoc. Tex. Punishment Standards Commn., Austin, 1992; criminal justice cons. Austin, Cambridge, 1991-94; exec. dir. Citizens for Juvenile Justice, Boston, 1994—; bd. dirs. Mass. Citizens Against the Death Penalty, Boston, 1989—, Mass. Correctional Legal Svcs., Boston, 1994—. Active mem. Mass. Women's Polit. Caucus, Boston, 1994—; mem. Jamaica Plain Area Planning Action Coun., 1995—. Most Valuable Female Student scholar Elks Nat. Found., 1982, John Harvard scholar Harvard Coll., 1988; fellow LBJ Sch. of Pub. Affairs, 1991, 92. Democrat. Jewish. Home: 40 Evergreen St Apt 2 Jamaica Plain MA 02130 Office: Citizens for Juvenile Justice 95 Berkeley St Ste 202 Boston MA 02116

YOUNG, ROSABEL RIBARES, neurologist; b. Laredo, Tex., June 1, 1960; d. Arthur and Rosario Ribares; m. Anthony O. Young, Nov. 25, 1984. AB, U. Chgo., 1982, MS in Pharmacology and Physiology, 1984; MD, U. Ill., 1987. Diplomate Am. Bd. Psychiatry and Neurology; cert. Am. Bd. Electrodiagnostic Medicine. Intern in neurology The Nat. Hosp., London, 1987; intern in internal medicine UCLA-Wadsworth VA Med. Ctr., 1987-88; resident in neurology Ctr. for Health Scis., UCLA, 1988-91; neurologist CIGNA Health Care, L.A., 1991-94; fellow neurophysiology EEG, EMG Harbor-UCLA Med. Ctr., 1994—; attending neurologist UCLA Neurology Clinic; chair edn. com. CIGNA Health Care, L.A., 1993—, cons. pharmacy and therapeutics, 1991—, mem. instnl. rev. bd., 1991—; dir. Doctors-to-Schs. Sci. Advisors Program, Chgo. and L.A., 1989—. Contbr. articles to profl. jours. judge advisor L.A. County Schs., 1990—; judge and awards contbr. Calif. State Sci. Fair, L.A., 1992—. Rsch. fellow Pharm. Mfrs. Assn., UCLA, 1984-85, NIH, 1983, Epilepsy Found. Am., 1984; recipient scholarships Bertram Richardson Internat. Studies, 1987, Joseph K. Narat Found., 1985, U. Chgo. MacArthur Found., 1982-86, U. Chgo. Becker Warburg, 1978-82, U. Chgo. Joseph Blazek, 1980-81, Ill. Gen. Assembly, 1984-85, 85-86, Nat. Med. Fellowship, 1983, 85, Chgo. Edmondson Rsch. award, 1981. Mem. AMA (Leadership in Cmty. Svc. award 1989, 90, RPS resource com. rep. to AMA ho. dels. 1989-90), Am. Acad. Neurology (editor Women in Neurology News 1993—, subcom. on edn. of non-neurologists, chair Neurosci. Prize subcom., chair comms. and liaison com.), Calif. Med. Assn., L.A. County Med. Assn., L.A. Soc. for Neurol. Scis., Am. Epilepsy Soc. Office: UCLA Harbor Med Ctr 1000 W Carson St Torrance CA 90502-2004

YOUNG, SHELLEY, food products executive; b. Newark, July 4, 1963; d. Howard and Jane Beatrice (Edwards) Y. BA, Howard U., 1986; MBA, Am. U., 1990; postgrad., Beulah Heights Bible Coll., 1993. Subcontract specialist IBM, Gaithersburg, Md., 1986-88; sales rep. Hewlett-Packard, Rockville, Md., 1988-91; mktg. rep. Xerox Corp., Sacramento, 1991-92; assoc. mgr. Coca-Cola, USA, Atlanta, 1992—; mktg. cons. Enterprising Concepts, Sacramento, 1992. Author poems. Mentor Big Sisters Orgn., Gaithersburg, 1988; tchr. New Birth Missionary Bapt. Ch., Atlanta, 1993. Mem. NAFE, Nat. Black MBA Assn. Office: Coca-Cola PO Box 1734 Atlanta GA 30301-1734

YOUNG, SHERILYN BURNETT, lawyer; b. Providence, Nov. 7, 1953; d. Archie C. III and Hope (Westcott) Burnett; m. Gary Richard Young, Oct. 9, 1977; children: Garrett, Alanna, Valerie. BA, Cornell U., 1975; JD, Franklin Pierce Law Ctr., 1982. Bar: N.H. 1982, U.S. Dist. Ct. N.H. 1982, U.S. Tax Ct. 1983. Assoc. Orr & Reno, P.A., Concord, N.H., 1982-87; ptnr. Rath, Young, Pignatelli & Oyer, P.A., Concord, 1987—; bd. trustees Univ. Systems N.H.; bd. dirs. Horizon Banks, Inc., Concord; speaker in field; legis. coun. to Gov. Gregg, Concord, 1989-90; mem. adv. coun. to ins. commr., 1989-93. Legal counsel Rudman for U.S. Senate campaign, Concord, 1984-93; bd. dirs. Concord chpt. ARC, 1988-91; mem. N.H. adv. bd. New Eng. Legal Found., 1991—; pres. Concord Hosp. Assn., 1991—, bd. dirs. Mem. ABA, N.H. Bar Assn., New Eng. Coun., Concord C. of C. (bd. dirs. 1988-91), Bus. and Industry Assn., Cornell Club N.H. Republican. Office: 2 Capital Pla PO Box 854 Concord NH 03302-0854

YOUNG, SONIA WINER, public relations director, educator; b. Chattanooga, Tenn., Aug. 20, 1934; d. Meyer D. and Rose (Demby) Winer; m. Melvin A. Young, Feb. 24, 1957; 1 child, Melanie Anne. BA, Sophie Newcomb Coll., 1956; M in Ednl. Psychology, U. Tenn.-Chattanooga, 1966. Cert. speech and hearing specialist Am. Speech and Hearing Assn. Speech therapist Chattanooga-Hamilton County Speech and Hearing Ctr., 1961-66, ednl. psychology, 1966-78; staff psychologist Chattanooga Testing and Counseling Services, 1978-80; ins. rep. Mut. Benefit Life Ins. Co., Chattanooga, 1980-84; columnist Chattanooga Times, 1982-84; cmty. affairs reporter Sta. WRCB-TV, Chattanooga, 1983-84; pub. relations and promotions dir. Purple Ladies, Inc., Chattanooga, 1984—; cons. psychology Ga. Dept. Human Resources, also Cheerhaven Sch., Dalton, 1970-78; adj. prof. psychology U. Tenn.-Chattanooga, 1971-80, adj. prof. dept. theatre and speech, 1988—; bd. dirs. M. Young Comm. Contbg. editor Chattanooga Life and Leisure Mag. Pres. Chattanooga Opera Guild, 1973-74, Chattanooga Opera Assn., 1979-80; bd. dirs., sec. Chattanooga-Hamilton County Bicentenniel Library, 1977-79; pres. Little Theatre of Chattanooga, 1984-90, bd. dirs., 1974—; pres. Speakout; v.p. Girls Club, Chattanooga, 1979-80; bd. dirs. March of Dimes, 1988, Chattanooga Symphony Guild, Mizpah Congregation, Chattanooga Area Literacy Council, Chattanooga Cares, 1993—, Tourist Devel. Agy., 1990—; mem. alumni council U. Tenn.-Chattanooga; mem. selection com. Leadership Chattanooga, 1984-86; sec. Allied Arts Greater Chattanooga, 1978-80, residential campaign chmn., 1985; bd. dirs. Chattanooga Ctr. for the Dance, Ptnrs. for Acad. Excellence, 1987—, Chattanooga Mental Health Assn., 1988; chmn. March of Dimes Mother's March, 1988, One of a Kind-the Arts Against AIDS-Chattanooga Cares, 1993, 94; co-chair Am. Heart Assn. Gala, 1994—. Recipient Disting. Citizens award City of Chattanooga, 1975, Steakley award Little Theatre, Chattanooga, 1982, Pres. award, 1991, 92. Mem. Phi Beta Kappa (pres. Chattanooga chpt. 1978-79). Jewish. Home: 1025 River Hills Cir Chattanooga TN 37415-5611 Office: U Tenn Theatre & Speech Dept 615 McCalle Ave Chattanooga TN 37403

YOUNG, TAMRA ANN, pediatrics nurse; b. Bremerton, Wash., Jan. 9, 1959; d. Alexander Blanger and Dana D. (Magden) Park; m. Earl Thomas Young, Oct. 17, 1981; children: Christopher Michael, Jacob Adam. ADN, San Juan Coll., 1985; BSN, U. N.Mex., 1991; cert., Inst. Children's Lit. Cert. pediatric advanced life support Am. Heart Assn.; cert. newborn resuscitation, N.J.; cert. BLS Am. Heart Assn. Newborn nursery nurse San Juan Regional Med. Ctr., Farmington, N.Mex., 1985-90, pediatrics nurse, 1990—; instr. in field. Author: (book of study) NCLEX, 1992; developer Asthma Program for Kids, Parenting Classes; creator child abuse prevention mascot the "Hug Bug". Spkr. San Juan Coll., 1989; cmty. spkr. in parent edn. and child abuse, Pub. Schs.-Parent Edn., San Juan Coll.; mem. San Juan County for Prevention of Child Abuse Coun., Farmington, 1992—. Recipient Award of Merit, San Juan Coll., 1991, Award of Svc., San Juan Regional med. Ctr., 1986. Mem. Young Am. Bowling Alliance (bd. dirs. 1987), Women's Internat. Bowling Alliance (pres. 1991-92), U. N.Mex. Alumni Assn. Republican. Episcopalian. Home: 7 Rd 5759-3011 D Farmington NM 87401

YOUNG, TERI ANN BUTLER, pharmacist; b. Littlefield, Tex., Aug. 22, 1958; d. Doyle Wayne and Bettie May (Lair) Butler; m. James Oren Young, Aug. 1, 1981; children: Andrew Wayne, Aaron Lee. BS in Pharmacy, Southwestern Okla. State U., 1981. Staff pharmacist St. Mary of Plains Hosp., Lubbock, Tex., 1981-84; staff pharmacist West Tex. Hosp., Lubbock, 1984-85, asst. dir. pharmacy, 1985-86; pharmacist cons. for nursing homes Billy D. Davis & Assocs., Lubbock, 1986—; relief pharmacist Prescription Lab., Med. Pharmacy and Foster Infusion Care, Lubbock, 1987-89; staff pharmacist Univ. Med. Ctr., 1990—; relief pharmacist West Tex. Hosp., 1986-91, Highland Hosp., 1990—, Med. Infusion Technology, 1992—. Mem. Lubbock Area Soc. of Hosp. Pharmacists (sec., treas. 1982-83), Lubbock Area Pharm. Assn., West Tex. Pharm. Assn., Am. Soc. Hosp. Pharmacists, Pilot Internat., Lubbock Genealogical Soc. Republican. Baptist. Lodge: Eastern Star. Home: 7410 Toledo Ave Lubbock TX 79424-2214 Office: Univ Med Ctr 602 Indiana Lubbock TX 79415

YOUNG, TOMMIE MORTON, social psychology educator, writer; b. Nashville. BA cum laude, Tenn. State U., 1951; MLS, George Peabody Coll. for Tchrs., 1955; PhD, Duke U., 1977; postgrad. U. Okla., 1967, U. Nebr., 1968. Coord., Young Adult Program, Lucy Thurman br. YWCA, 1951-52; instr. edn. Tenn. State U., Nashville, 1956-59; instr., coord. media program Prairie View Coll. (Tex.), 1959-61; asst. prof. edn., assoc. prof. English, dir. IMC Ctr., U. Ark.-Pine Bluff, 1965-69; asst. prof. English and edn., dir. learning lab., N.C. Central U., Durham, 1969-74; prof., dir./chairperson libr. media svcs. and dept. ednl. media, dir. Afro-Am. Family Project, N.C. Agrl. and Tech. State U., Greensboro, 1975—; adj. prof. langs., lit. and philosophy, dir. schs. history project Tenn. State U., Nashville, 1994—; dir. workshops, grants; pres., dir. Ednl. Cons. Svcs. Author: Afro American Genealogy Sourcebook, 1987, Oral Histories of Former All-Black Public Schools, 1991, After School Programs for At-Risk Youth and Their Families, 1994; contbr. poem to Poetry: American Heritage; contbr. rsch. papers, articles to profl. jours. Nat. chmn. Com. to Re-Elect the Pres.; past sec. Fedn. Colored Women's Clubs; bd. dirs. Southwestern div. ARC, Nashville area, 1994—, dir. Volun-Teens; chairperson learning resources com. Task Force Durham Day Care Assn.; bd. dirs., chairperson schs. div. Durham County Unit Am. Cancer Soc.; past mem. adv. bd., bd. dirs. YMCA, Atlanta; chair Gilford County Commn. on Needs of Children; bd. advisors NIH, N.C. Coun. of the Arts; mem. Guilford County Involvement Coun.; chmn. N.C. adv. com. U.S. Civil Rights Com.; mem. exec. planning com. Greensboro. Recipient awards ARC, 1968, 73, NAACP, 1973, HEW, 1978, U.S. Commn. on Civil Rights, 1982; named Disting. Alumni Tenn. State U., 1994. Mem. AAUW (honor award 1983, pres. Greensboro br., chairperson internat. rels. com.), ALA (divsn. coll. and rsch. librs., past chair), NAACP (life, 1st v.p. Durham br., exec. bd. Greensboro br., dir. parent edn./child advocacy program, Woman of Yr. 1992), NEA, Assn. Childhood Ednl. Internat., Comparative and Internat. Edn. Assn., Archives Assoc., Internat. Platform Assn., Nat. Hist. Soc., Greensboro Jr. League (community adv. bd. 1991—), Zeta Phi Beta (chairperson polit. action com. eastern region, nat. grammateus, Polit. and Civic Svc. award 1974, Outstanding Social-Polit. Svc. award 1982, Woman of Yr. 1977), Commn. on Status of Women (Woman of Achievement 1991), Phi Kappa Phi (Disting. State U. Alumni award 1994, Disting Alumni NAFEO award, 1995, Carl Rowan-Oprah Winfrey lectr. Tenn. State U., 1995). Home: PO Box 17684 Nashville TN 37217

YOUNG, VERA LEE HALL, educational administrator, association executive; b. Natchitoches, La., Jan. 9, 1944; d. Sidney and Gertrude (Bell) H.; m. Willie L. Young, Aug. 21, 1965 (div. June 1971). BS, Grambling State U., 1967; MS, Bank St. Coll., 1977; PhD with distinction, Century U., 1985. Cert. tchr., La., N.J., N.Y. Ednl. cons. family day care program N.Y.C. Community Sch. Dist. 6; ednl. dir. Leslie Freeman Daycare Ctr., Bklyn., 1973-74; tchr. West N.Y. Bd. of Edn., 1978—; exec. dir., founder Operation Super Inst., Ft. Lee, N.J., 1986—; lectr., tchr., panelist and cons. in field; participant Statewide Child Care Adv. Coun. Conf., N.J., 1980, State Ill. Tchrs. Conf., 1987, U. S.C. Tchrs. Conf., Georgetown, 1989; discussant Speaking for Schools radio program, N.J., N.Y. Author: A Day Care Solution in America: The Learning Center, 1985; contbr. articles to field. Recipient Internat. Order of Merit award (# 320 of 500 world-wide), Internat. Biog. Ctr., Cambridge, Eng.; named Educator or Yr., Black Achievement and Awards, 1988; Dept. Labor grantee, Jerusalem, 1982-83. Mem. NEA, N.J. Edn. Assn. (conf. participant 1987), N.J. Women Bus. Ownership Orgn., Internat. Platform Assn., Internat. Reading Assn., Minority & Women Owned Bus. N.Y., Bank St. Coll. Alumni Assn., Gambling Coll. Alumni Assn. Mem. Dutch Reform Ch. Office: Operation Super 229 Main St # 1834 Fort Lee NJ 07024-9998

YOUNG, VIVIAN, advertising executive; b. Hanover, Germany, June 9, 1949; came to U.S., 1949; d. Julius and Ilona (Rosenthal) Y.; m. Paul Farhi, Apr. 22, 1993; children: Nicholas Farhi, Sam Farhi, Mariel Farhi. BA, Queens Coll., 1971; MA, U. Wis., 1972. Project dir. DKG, Inc., N.Y.C., 1973-75, Ogilvy & Mather, N.Y.C., 1975-77; rsch. acct. supr. Needham, Harper Worldwide, N.Y.C., 1977-79, v.p. assoc. dir. rsch., 1979-82, v.p. dep. dir. rsch., 1982-83; sr. v.p. dir. rsch. Ammirati & Puris, N.Y.C., 1984-89, exec. v.p., dir. strategic svcs., 1989—. Ford Found. fellow U. Wis., 1971. Mem. NOW, Sierra Club. Office: Ammirati & Puris Inc Ammirati & Puris/Lintas New York NY 10011-6903

YOUNGBERG, CHARLOTTE ANNE, education specialist; b. Hampton, Iowa, May 8, 1937; d. Sebo and Marion Bradford (Boutin-Clock) Reysack; m. Paul Gordon Neal, Mar. 29, 1969 (div. Jan. 1984); children: Rachel Elizabeth, Kory Bradford; m. Lyle Edwin Youngberg, June 30, 1990; children: Lynn Eugene Youngberg, Lori Ann Youngberg Dodson. BA, U. No. Iowa, 1958; MEd, DePaul U., 1966; postgrad. No. Ill. U. Tchr., 4th grade, Des Moines Ind. Sch. Dist., 1958-59; tchr., 3d grade Glenview (Ill.) Pub. Schs., 1959-61, tchr. 3d grade, psychol. ednl. diagnostic Schaumburg Dist. Schs., Hoffman Estates, Ill., 1961-69; supr. learning disabilities and behavior disorders Springfield (Ill.) Pub. Schs., 1969-73; psycho-ednl. diagnostician Barrington (Ill.) Sch. Dist. 220, 1973-77; ednl. strategist Area Edn. Agy. 7, Cedar Falls, Iowa, 1978-90; spl. edn. tchr., dir. spl. edn. Verona (Mo.) R7 Sch. Dist., 1990—; ednl. cons. Spl. Edn. Dist. Lake County, Gurnee, Ill., summer, 1968. Certified K-14 teaching and supervising in guidance, counseling, elementary supervisory K-9, elementary K-9 teaching, spl. K-12 learning disabilities. Mem. NEA, Iowa Edn. Assn., Phi Delta Kappa. Home: PO Box 147 Verona MO 65769-0147 Office: Verona R7 Sch Dist PO Box 98 Verona MO 65769-0098

YOUNG-BILLMYER, PAMELA RUTH, information services company executive; b. Mt. Kisco, N.Y., July 15, 1959; d. Robert L. and Darleen R. (Fischer) Young; m. Stewart L. Billmyer, Apr. 10, 1982. BS, George Mason U., 1981. Account exec. AT&T/C&P Telephone, Falls Church, Va., 1981-82; asst. mgr. Mt. Vernon Realty, Woodbridge, Va., 1982-89; legal asst. Trammell Coow/Mark Tenenbaum, McLean, Va., 1989-90; adminstr. United Info. Svcs., Danbury, Conn., 1990-93; contracts adminstr. Advanced Tech. Materials, Inc., Danbury, 1993—; freelance graphics Narmon Pub., Danbury, 1992—. Mem. Alpha Chi, Beta Epsilon Phi. Republican. Mem. LDS Ch. Home: Ste 30-3 166 Old Brookfield Rd Danbury CT 06811 Office: 7 Sherman Tpke Danbury CT 06810-4124

YOUNGBLOOD, BETTY J., academic administrator; b. Detroit; m. Ralph P. Youngblood; 1 child. BS in Political Sci., Oakland U., Rochester, Mich.; MA in South Asian Studies, U. Minn., PhD in Political Sci. Formerly mem. faculty West Ga. Coll., Tex. Tech U.; various adminstrv. positions Kennesaw State Coll., Marietta, Ga.; v.p. acad. affairs MacMurray Coll., Jacksonville, Ill., Wesley Coll., Dover, Del.; vice chancelllor acad. affairs, dean faculty, prof. polit. sci. U. Wis.-Superior, 1990-91, acting chancellor, 1991-92, chancellor, 1992—; cons., evaluator North Ctrl. Assn. Colls. and Schs. Contbr. articles to profl. jours. Bd. dirs. United Way, Superior. Rsch. grantee for study in N.W. India. Mem. Superior C. of C., Rotary. Office: U Wis-Superior Office of the President 1800 Grand Ave Superior WI 54880*

YOUNGDAHL, PATRICIA LUCY, psychologist, educator; b. Cape Girardeau, Mo., Sept. 8, 1927; d. George B. and Alta Mae (Crites) Lucy; m. James E. Youngdahl, June 13, 1948 (div. Apr. 1974); children: Jay, Kristi, Lincoln, Sara. AA, Stephens Coll., 1946; BA, Washington U. (Mo.), 1948, MA, 1950; PhD, Fla. Inst. Tech., 1985. Lic. psychologist, Ark. Assoc. exec. dir. Social Planning Coun., St. Louis, 1950-52; instr. psychology U. Ark., Fayetteville, 1958-59, psychol. examiner Med. Ctr., Little Rock, 1961-64, asst. prof. Med. Scis. Campus, Little Rock, 1975—, dir. child clin. psychology internship tng. program. Author: (with others) How to Use Transactional Analysis in the Public Schools, 1974, (with others) Arkansas Divorce Simplified, 1994. Mem. exec. com. Pulaski County Dem. Com., Little Rock, 1972—, State Dem. Party, 1980—; chmn. Ark. for Kennedy, 1979-80; del. Nat. Dem. Conv. 1976, 80, 84; chmn. Ark. Women's Polit. Caucus, 1973-83. Named to 100 Ark. Women of Achievement Ark. Press Women's Assn., 1980; apptd. by gov. to Pygmalion Commn. for Alternative Edn., 1993. Mem. Ark. Psychol. Assn., Am. Psychol. Assn. (assoc.). Unitarian-Universalist Ch. Home: 7108 Rockwood Rd Little Rock AR 72207-1708 Office: Childrens Hosp 800 Marshall St Little Rock AR 72202-3510

YOUNGER, BETTY NICHOLS, social worker; b. Cleve., 1927; d. Manson E. and Esther L. (McDonald) Nichols; m. Paul A. Younger, 1952 (dec. Mar. 1969); children: Deborah, Rebekah, Sarah, Martha. BA, Otterbein Coll., 1949; MS in Social Adminstrn., Western Res. U., 1951. Cert. social worker, Mich.; diplomate Am. Bd. Examiners in Clin. Social Work. Family and youth worker East Harlem Protestant Parish, N.Y.C., 1951-52; organizer, parent worker Fidelity Presch., Cleve., 1955, 58-60; community worker YWCA, Cleve., 1966-67; organizer, dir. Community United Headstart, Cleve., 1965; social worker Children's Hosp., Columbus, Ohio, 1968, Mt. Sinai Hosp., Chgo., 1972-73, Billings Hosp. U. Chgo., 1973; supr. Ill. Masonic Med. Ctr., Chgo., 1974-79; counselor Barry County Substance Abuse, Hastings, Mich., 1981-82; organizer, dir. Love, Inc., Barry County, Mich., 1983-84; therapist Family & Child Svcs., Jackson, Mich., 1986, Livonia (Mich.) Counseling Ctr., 1986-89; pvt. practice Shumard Counseling, Livonia, 1988-91, Cambridge Counseling, Livonia, 1991-93, Tapestry Counseling, Ann Arbor, 1991-93; tchr. Schoolcraft Coll., Livonia, 1989—; bus. ptnr. Creating Results, Ann Arbor, Mich., 1990—. Mem. NASW, Acad. Cert. Social Workers, ACLU, NOW, Women's Internat. League Peace and Freedom, Sierra Club.

YOUNGER, JUDITH TESS, lawyer, educator; b. N.Y.C., Dec. 20, 1933; d. Sidney and Kate (Greenbaum) Weintraub; m. Irving Younger, Jan. 21, 1955; children: Rebecca, Abigail M. B.S., Cornell U., 1954; J.D., NYU, 1958; LL.D. (hon.), Hofstra U., 1974. Bar: N.Y. 1958, U.S. Supreme Ct 1962, D.C. 1983, Minn. 1985. Law clk. to judge U.S. Dist. Ct., 1958-60; asso. firm Chadbourne, Parke, Whiteside & Wolff, N.Y.C., 1960-62; mem. firm Younger and Younger, and (successors), 1962-67; adj. asst. prof. N.Y. U. Sch. Law, 1967-69; asst. atty. gen. State of N.Y., 1969-70; assoc. prof. Hofstra U. Sch. Law, 1970-72, prof., assoc. dean, 1972-74; dean, prof. Syracuse Coll. Law, 1974-75; dep. dean, prof. law Cornell Law Sch., 1975-78, prof. law, 1975-85; vis. prof. U. Minn. Law Sch., Mpls., 1984-85, prof., 1985—; of counsel Popham, Haik, Schnobrich & Kaufman, Ltd., Mpls., 1989—; cons. NOW, 1972-74, Suffolk County for Revision of Its Real Property Tax Act, 1972-73; mem. N.Y. Gov.'s Panel To Screen Candidates of Ct. of Claims Judges, 1973-74; mem. Minn. Lawyers' Profl. Responsibility Bd., 1991-93. Contbr. articles to profl. jours. Trustee Cornell U., 1973-78. Mem. ABA (council legal edn. 1975-79), Am. Law Inst. (adv. restatement property 1982-84), AAUP (v.p. Cornell U. chpt. 1978-79), N.Y. State Bar Assn., Assn. of Bar of City of N.Y., Minn. Bar Assn. Home: 3520 W Calhoun Pky Minneapolis MN 55416-4657 Office: U Minn Law Sch Minneapolis MN 55455

YOUNG LIVELY, SANDRA LEE, nurse; b. Rockport, Ind., Dec. 31, 1943; d. William Cody and Flora Juanita (Carver) Thorpe; m. Kenneth Leon Doom, May 4, 1962 (div. 1975); children: Patricia, Anita, Elizabeth. AS, Vincennes U., 1979, student, U. So. Ind., 1987—. Nursing aide, nurse Forest Del Nursing Home, Princeton, Ind., 1975-80; charge nurse Welborn Bapt. Hosp., Evansville, Ind., 1979-80, 82-83; staff nurse Longview Regional Hosp., Tex., 1980-82; dir. home health Roy H. Laird Meml. Hosp., Kilgore, Tex., 1984-86; med. post-coronary nurse Mercy Hosp., Owensboro, Ky., 1987, Dept. of Corrections charge nurse, Branchville Tng. Ctr., Tell City, Ind, 1987-90; charge nurse dept. mental health Evansville (Ind.) State Hosp., 1990—; staff nurse, asst. dir. Leisure Lodge Home Health, Overton, Tex., 1983-84. Grantee Roy H. Laird Meml. Hosp., 1986. Mem. NAFE, Menniger Found., Vincennes U. Alumni Assn., Ind. Correctional Nurses Assn., Internat. Platform Assn. Avocations: writing, research, cake decorating, house plants. Home: PO Box 1032 7388 Brentwood Dr #G Newburgh IN 47629-1032 Office: Evansville State Hosp 3400 Lincoln Ave Evansville IN 47714-0147

YOUNG-MALLIN, JUDITH, writer; b. Mt. Vernon, N.Y., Aug. 10, 1937; d. Milton and Marion Ethel (Peterfreund) Young; m. Joel Mallin, Aug. 8, 1957 (div. 1985); children: Jennifer Young, Adam Young, Noah Young. Student, Syracuse U., 1955, NYU, 1956, 86, 1956. Researcher Conde-Nast, N.Y.C., 1957-58; lectr. Am. Crafts Mus., N.Y.C., 1986; ind. lectr. N.Y.C., 1986—; cons., innovator Surreal Eye Series, N.Y.C., 1986-87; lectr. London-Courtauld Inst. Surrealism in N.Y., 1991, Art Inst. Chgo., 1992, Sch. for Visual Arts, N.Y.C., 1992; cons. Am. Masters, N.Y.C., 1991; established Young-Mallin Archives. Author: M.F.K. Fisher, Virgil Thomson, 1990, Juliet Man Ray, 1991, Surrealism and Women, Eileen Agar, 1991, View Anth. Index Edn., 1991, Edward James, 1991. Mem. James Beard Soc. (profl. mem.). Home: 719 Greenwich St New York NY 10014

YOUNG-OSKEY, SUSAN MARIE, elementary education educator; b. Astoria, N.Y., July 30, 1964; d. Thomas Bernard and Carole Marion (Fleming) Y. AA, Suffolk Coll., 1987; BA, Dowling Coll., 1989; MA in Liberal Studies Edn., SUNY, Stony Brook, 1992. Kindergarten asst. tchr. First Steps Sch., East Setauket, N.Y., 1989-90, pre-kindergarten/toddler tchr., 1989-90; kindergarten/pre-kindergarten tchr. Our Lady of Lourdes Sch., West Islip, N.Y., 1990-94, tchr. 1st grade, 1994—. Vol. Rainbow Program Our Lady of Lourdes Parish, 1992—. Mem. Reading Specialists Coun. Suffolk (reading specialist 1990-91). Republican. Home: 865216 Broadway Ave # A Holbrook NY 11741

YOUNGREN, DELVANA HOPE, secondary school educator; b. L.A., Apr. 13, 1941; d. Herman Melvin and Betty Floy (England) Ferguson; m. Allan Morse Youngren, June 17, 1961; children: Erik Allan, Deanna Marie. BA, Calif. State Coll., Long Beach, 1963; MA, Calif. State Coll., 1968. Cert. secondary tchr., Calif. Tchr. Long Beach (Calif.) Unified Sch. Dist., 1963-70, Faith Christian Acad., Pasadena, Tex., 1975-80, Cherry Valley (Calif.) Brethren Christian Sch., 1980-86, Arrowhead Christian Acad., Redlands, Calif., 1985-87, New Life Christian Acad., San Bernardino, Calif., 1987-90, Mt. View Jr. H.S., Beaumont, Calif., 1990—; chmn. GATE, Gifted and Talented, Calif.; educator Drug, Alcohol & Tobacco Edn. Treas. San Gorgonio Pass Geneal. Soc., Banning, Calif., 1992-95; mem. Yucaipa Geneal. Soc., 1992-95. Mem. NEA, Calif. Tchrs. Assn., Beaumont Tchrs. Assn., Calif. Inland Area Math. Project. Republican. Home: 10640 Jonathan Ave Cherry Valley CA 92223 Office: Beaumont United Sch Dist PO Box 187 Beaumont CA 92223

YOUNGS, DIANE CAMPFIELD, learning disabilities specialist, educator; b. Margaretville, N.Y., Feb. 16, 1954; d. Richard Maxwell and Charlotte June (Rickard) Campfield; m. William H. Youngs, June 30, 1984. BS in Edn., SUNY, Geneseo, 1976, MS in Edn., 1977. Tchr. educable mentally retarded Tompkins-Seneca-Tioga Bd. Coop. Ednl. Svcs., Ithaca, N.Y., 1978-80; tchr. learning disabled Joint Svcs. for Spl. Edn., Mishawaka, Ind., 1980—; mem. Task Force for Reorgn. Spl. Edn., Mishawaka, 1990-91. Mem. Coun. for Exceptional Children, Learning Disabilities Assn., Coun. for Learning Disabilities, Kappa Delta Pi, Psi Iota Xi. Republican. Office: Walt Disney Sch 4015 N Filbert Rd Mishawaka IN 46545

YOUNGS, JUNE SUSAN, transportation executive; b. Plainfield, N.J., June 2, 1957; d. Gustave Slawinski and Julia (Stachnik) Sendlein; m. Heinz Bischof, May 2, 1986 (div. Nov. 1987); m. Todd Youngs, July 30, 1994. BA, Moravian Coll., 1979; transp. cert., Middlesex County Coll., 1982; import/export cert., World Trade Inst., 1986; postgrad., Fairleigh Dickinson U.

Consumer loan analyst 1st Nat. Bank Ctrl. Jersey, Bridgewater, N.J., 1979-80; inventory control analyst Tenneco Chems., Piscataway, N.J., 1980-81, adminstrv. asst. to dir. transp., 1981, rate analyst, 1981-83; sr. rate analyst RJR Nabisco, Nabisco Foods Group, E. Hanover, N.J., 1984-85, transp. analyst nat. programs, 1985-86, sr. transp. analyst nat./internat. programs, 1986-88, mgr. transp. and delivery svcs., 1988-91, mgr. transp. ops., 1991-93, dir. transp. svcs., 1993—; spkr. Nat. Forum Air Contractors and Carriers, 1987, Intermodal Expo, 1994, Nat. Indsl. Transp. League, 1994. Contbr. articles to profl. jours. Assoc. Cathedral Concert Series, Newark, N.J., 1992; vol. Acad. Decathlon N.J., Morris County, 1993; Nabisco chmn. United Way Campaign, Morris County, 1993. Mem. NAFE, Nat. Indsl. Transp. League (bd. dirs. 1994, 3d vice chair 1995—), Nat. Pvt. Truck Coun. (bd. dirs. 1988-90), Coun. Logistics Mgmt. Democrat. Roman Catholic. Office: RJR Nabisco/Nabisco Food Gp 100 DeForest Ave East Hanover NJ 07936

YOUNT, CHERYL FAYE, psychotherapist; b. Borger, Tex., Jan. 9, 1949; d. Gerald Edward and Doris Devonne (Davidson) Winget; m. John Alford Yount, June 13, 1968; children: Stephanie Gail, Gregory Bryan. BS, U. Houston, 1979, MA in Psychology, 1986, MA in Family Therapy, 1990. Lic. profl. counselor, marriage and family therapist, chem. dependency counselor. Educator Alvin (Tex.) Ind. Sch. Dist., 1984-90; exec. dir. Brazoria/Matagorda County Coun. Alcohol and Drug Abuse, Angleton, Tex., 1990—; pvt. practice Houston. Nanette Bruckner fellow U. Houston, 1986. Mem. Am. Assn. Marriage and Family Therapy (clin.). Office: Bay Area Family Psychiatry 16815 Royal Crest Ste B-1 Houston TX 77058

YOUNTS, KEMBERLY, mental health therapist, educator; b. Greenwood, S.C., Apr. 20, 1954; d. Norman Wade and Bette Louise (Adams) Y. AS, U. S.C., 1974; BA in Psychology, Augusta (Ga.) Coll., 1989, MS in Clin. Psychology, 1991, MEd in Counseling, 1993. Nat. cert. counselor Nat. Bd. Cert. Counselors; lic. profl. counselor, Ga. Front office mgr. Ramada Inn, Aiken, S.C., 1974-76; textile design artist Clearwater (S.C.) Finishing, 1976-79; investment art broker Art Works, Inc., Aiken, 1977-83; bus. mgr. One Way Bible Coll., Martinez, Ga., 1983-85; asst. crusade coord. Leighton Ford Crusade/Billy Graham Ministries, Augusta, 1985-87; rsch. asst. Eisenhower Army Med. Ctr., Ft. Gordon, Ga., 1989-91; clin. counselor Charter Hosp. of Augusta, 1987—; adj. faculty dept. psychology Augusta Coll., 1993—. Tutor, Laubach Literacy Assocs., Aiken, 1980-84; interpreter for deaf Ga. Sch. for the Deaf, Cave Springs, 1984. Mem. Psi Chi (pres. 1990-91). Republican. Baptist. Home: 3914 Casa Rosa Ave Martinez GA 30907-2328 Office: 3100 Perimeter Pky Augusta GA 30909-4583

YOUREE, BEVERLY B., library science educator; b. Jackson, Tenn., Mar. 29, 1948; d. Beverly Durward and Rebecca Wade B.; m. Mack Moore Youree, May 26, 1973; 1 child, Roderick Buford. BA, Union U., 1969; MLS, Peabody Coll., 1970; EdD, Vanderbilt U., 1984. Reserves circulation libr. Mid. Tenn. State U., Murfreesboro, 1970-74, instr. libr. sci., 1974—, mem. faculty senate, 1984-90, sec.-treas., 1987-88; chmn. vis. coms. So. Assn. Evaluation Teams, 1989—; pres. Concerned Faculty and Adminstrv. Women, 1986-90. Contbr. articles to profl. jours. State founder, coord. Tenn. Exhibitors' and Media Profls. Tour; mem. adv. bd. John Wiley & Sons Pub. Co., 1991—; active Middle Tenn. State U.; mem. faculty senate, 1984-90, sec.-treas., 1987-88, mem. univ. libr. com., 1981-83, sec. 1981-82; mem. ad hoc com. on edn., curriculum svc. and facilities, 1975-76; mem. faculty senate legis. com., 1980-83, sec. 81-83; mem. non-instructional assignment semester com., 1988-90, sec. 88-89, chair 89-90; mem. com. on status of women, 1988-94; mem. grad. coun., 1988-90; active So. Assn. Evaluation Teams, chair vis. coms., 1989, 90, 91, 92, 93, 94; pres. Concerned Faculty and Adminstrv. Women, 1986-90; chmn. Commn. on Status of Women, 1994—. Mem. ALA (mem. state liaison to young adult svcs. divsn. 1988—, mem. outstanding theatre for the college bound list revision com. 1988), NEA, Tenn. Libr. Assn. (chair libr. edn. sect. 1979-80, 88-89, chair vol. state book award com. 1980—, co-chair exhibits for state conv. 1985—, Frances Neal Cheney award 1993), Southeastern Libr. Assn. (sec. sch. libr. sect. 1986-88, chair-elect sch. libr. sect. 1988-90, chair, 1990-92, co-chair exhibits for conv. 1988-90, 90-92), Tenn. Edn. Assn. (sec. higher edn. dept. 1989-93, pres. 1993—, mem. instructional and profl. devel. commn. 1991-94, past pres. and sec. Middle Tenn. State U. chpt.), Tenn. Assn. Sch, Librs., Middle Tenn. Edn. Assn., Assembly Literature for Adolescents, Soc. Sch. Librs. Internat. (mem. legis. task force 1988-89), Kappa Delta Pi (mem. nominating com. mem. 1991-92, mem. Theta Omicron chpt., treas. 1981—, assoc. counselor 1983-86, counselor 1987-94, Svc. to Edn. award), Phi Delta Kappa. Democrat. So. Baptist. Home: 3567 Castlewood Dr Murfreesboro TN 37129-4605 Office: Middle Tenn State U Dept Ednl Leadership PO Box 184 Murfreesboro TN 37132-0184

YOURISON, KAROLA MARIA, information specialist, librarian; b. Berlin, Germany, June 30, 1937; came to U.S., 1962; m. James E. Yourison, Feb. 29, 1992. BA, U. Pitts., 1974, MLS, 1976. Libr. mgr. Siemens Rsch. & Tech. Lab., Princeton, N.J., 1983-85; mgr. libr. svcs. Software Engring. Inst., Carnegie Mellon U., Pitts., 1986—. Mem. IEEE, Spl. Librs. Assn. (chair duplicates exch. com. 1990—, chair sci. and tech. divsn.), Assn. Computing Machinery. Office: Software Engring Inst 5000 Forbes Ave Pittsburgh PA 15213

YOURMAN, GLADYS ROTH, pension association administrator; b. N.Y.C., Aug. 1, 1918; d. Paul and Blanche (Frankfort) Roth; m. Stanley J. Mayer, Jan. 25, 1940 (div. Aug. 1947); children: Bobette Lister, Leslie Wexler; m. Leonard Baron, Dec. 23, 1956 (div. Dec. 1959); m. Jack Yourman, Apr. 11, 1976. Degree in Costume Design/Illustration, Parsons Sch. Design, 1938; BS, NYU, 1951, MA, 1953. Tchr. fine arts Bd. Edn. City of N.Y., 1951-65; field rep. United Fedn. Tchrs., N.Y.C., 1965-77; legis. rep. Tchrs. Pension Assn., N.Y.C, Albany, 1983-86; pres. Tchrs. Pension Assn., N.Y.C., 1986—. Co-author (with William Withers): Tchrs. Pension Assn. Newsletters, 1986, author, 1987—; co-author PTA of Pub. Sch. 131 Queens newsletter, 1955-56. Organizer PTA sch. chpt. Jr. High Sch. 194, Queens, N.Y., 1960-65, sch. liaison, 1962-65. Recipient Piano Medal award N.Y. Music Week Assn., 1934. Mem. AAUW, Orgn. for Rehab. Tng., United Fedn. Tchrs. (chair William S. Carr sch. chpt. 1960-65, dist. rep. 1962-65, Queens Borough rep. 1963-65), Nassau Coalition Nat. Health Plan. Democrat. Jewish. Home: 15 Baker Hill Rd Great Neck NY 11023

YOURMAN, JUDITH, artist, educator; b. N.Y.C., Mar. 3, 1957; d. Jack and Eleanor (Kolbrener) Y.; m. Steven Kass, June 8, 1985. Student, U Pa., 1975-76, Edinburgh Coll. Art, 1977; BFA with highest honors, Pratt Inst., 1981; MFA, U. Minn., 1991. Design supr. McGraw-Hill Book Co., N.Y.C., 1981-83; graphic designer Judith Yourman Design, Boulder, Colo., 1984-86, St. Paul, 1986-89; lectr. U. Wis., Madison, 1991-92; asst. prof. St. Olaf Coll., Northfield, Minn., 1993—; vis. artist Coll. Charleston (S.C.), 1993, U. Nev., Reno, 1995; panelist Walker Art Ctr., Mpls., 1994, Soc. for Photographic Edn., Atlanta, 1995; mem. conf. com. 4th Internat. Symposium on Elec. Art, Mpls., 1993. One-woman shows include Mpls. Inst. Arts, 1992-93, COll. of Charleston, 1993, Wright State U., 1995, others; producer (video) Leona Descending..., 1993, Witness Tape, 1989; screenings include Internat. Audio Visual Experimental Festival, The Netherlands, 1993, Am. Film Inst. Video Festival, Calif., 1994, Walker Art Ctr., Minn., 1994, others. Visual Arts fellow Arts Midwest/Regional NEA, 1993, Visual Arts fellow MCAD/McKnight Found., Mpls., 1992, Photography fellow McKnight Found., Mpls., 1993, Artist fellow Art Matters, N.Y.C., 1992, others. Mem. SIGGRAPH, Nat. Graphic Artist Guild (nat. bd. dirs. 1986-89), Assn. Ind. Video and Filmmakers, Soc. Photographic Edn., Coll. Art Assn. Office: St Olaf Coll 1520 St Olaf Ave Northfield MN 55057

YOUSUFF, SARAH SAFIA, physician; b. Binghampton, N.Y., Dec. 8, 1960; d. Mohamed and Razia (Sivaramasastry) Y.; m. Donald John Sudy, Aug. 7, 1993. BA in Zoology, U. Tex., Austin, 1982; MD, U. Tex., 1988. Diplomate Am. Bd. Anesthesiology. Fellow in med. mgmt. U. N.C., Chapel Hill, 1992-93; resident in anesthesiology U. Wash., Seattle, 1988-92; staff anesthesiologist Krön Med., Research Triangle Park, N.C., 1992-94; med. dir. dept. anesthesiology Southwest Hosp., Little Rock, Ark., 1994—; pres. Southwest Anesthesia Assocs., 1994—. capt. USAR, 1990—. Mem. AMA, Am. Soc. Anesthesiology, Am. Coll. Physician Execs., Ark. Med. Soc., Pulaski County Med. Soc. Home: 18 Edenfield Cove Little Rock AR 72212 Office: Southwest Anesthesia Assocs Southwest Hosp 11401 Interstate 30 Little Rock AR 72209

YOZELL, SALLY J., federal agency administrator; b. Boston; d. Peter S. and Jeanne (Wolfe) Y. BA in Polit. Sci., U. Vt., 1982; MPA, Harvard U., 1993. Staff asst. to Rep. Robert F. Drinan, 1980; field dir. Jim Guest for U.S. Senate Campaign, 1982; local staff coord. Mass. Office of Lt. Gov., 1983; legis. affairs specialist Mass. Office Fedn. and State Rels., 1984; minority staff dir. Subcom. on Handicapped, Senate Com. on Labor and Human Resources, 1984-86; sr. legis. asst. for environ. and energy issues, dep. legis. dir. to Sen. John Kerry Washington, 1987-92; dir. Office Legis. Affairs for Nat. Oceanic and Atmospheric Adminstrn. U.S. Dept. Commerce, Washington, 1994—. Office: US Dept Commerce 14th St & Constitution Ave NW Washington DC 20230*

YRIZARRY, ADITA LIVIA, fitness instructor; b. Victorville, Calif.; d. Jose Mercedes and Ada Nivia (Carrasquillo) Y. Fitness instr. cert., U. Tex., 1983; exercise sci. cert., U. Miami, 1987. Cert. aerobic and fitness tng. and step Reebok Aerobic Fitness Assn. Am.; personal tng. crt. Am. Coun. Exercise; cert. group leader Cooper Inst. Aerobic Rsch. Program mgr. Purley Physical, San Antonio, 1980-83; club dir. Broadway Workout, San Antonio, 1983-86; pres., owner Profl. Fitness, Inc., San Antonio, Miami, Tex., Fla., 1986—; cons., step Reebok examiner Aerobic Fitness Assn. Am.; fitness cons. for Med. and Travel Related Fitness Programs; physical tng. dir. Biltmore Hotel Fitness Ctr. and Spa; guest lectr. on fitness and health Jr. High Schs. Tex., Fla.; judge of many aerobics competitions including AAU Team Aerobic Dance, Costa Rica Step Championship, Reebok Nat. Aerobic Championship, Chile Nat. Aerobic Championship; adv. bd. Reebok Internat. CORPS, Muscle Mixes Music Impact Team, Sesamo Prodns. , Santiago, Chile; CEU provider AFAA, Am. Coun. Exercise; spokesperson Exerbar, Spri Products. Presentations include Cen. Am. Conv. Costa Rica, Congress Internat. Aerobics, Valencia, Spain, Body Factory, Madrid, Ctrl. Sportu Bergamo, Italy, Univ Miami, 12th St Gym, Phila., Weston Athletic Club, Ft. Lauderdale, Fla., Fisher Island (Fla.) Spa, Univ. Met., Santiago, Chile. Chmn. Dance for Health Am. Heart Assn., San Antonio, 1983, Workout for Hope, City of Hope, Miami, 1993; vol. Am. Cancer Soc., Miami, 1992—. Recipient 1st place honor Fitness Sanctioning Body, San Antonio, Hon. mention, Am. Heart Assn., San Antonio, 1985, 88. Mem. Nat. Acad. Sports Medicine (cert. personal trainer, cert. instr.). Roman Catholic. Home and Office: 1717 N Bayshore Dr Ste 1635 Miami FL 33132-1180

YU, ELEANOR NGAN-LING, advertising company executive; b. Hong Kong, July 28, 1958; d. Seong Yoon and Esther (Lam) Chan; m. Kenneth P. Yu, July 11, 1980. Student, Oxford U., 1976; BA with honors, U. Ottawa, 1979; MBA, Golden Gate U., 1986. Copywriter, intern Ogilvy & Mather, Ottawa, Can.; asst. account exec. DDB, N.Y.C.; account exec. JWT, N.Y.C.; account supr. Mktg. Group, Phila.; chief exec. officer, pres. Adland, San Francisco; active San Francisco Econ. Vitality Com., 1994. Mem. com. San Francisco Grandprix Assn., 1988; bd. dirs. Chinatown Youth Ctr., San Francisco, 1986, United Way, San Francisco, 1986, San Francisco C. of C., 1994, Inter Assn. Advertising Agys., 1994; mem. San Francisco Econ. Vitality Com., 1994. Mem. NAFE, Asian Bus. Assn. (pres. 1985-86), Pacific Affairs Council (chmn. 1988—), San Francisco C. of C. (mem. bd. dirs. 1994), Golden Gate U. Alumni Assn. (bd. dirs. 1986—), Inter Assn. of Advt. Agy's. Office: Adland Advertising Inc 3000 Steiner St San Francisco CA 94123

YU, JULIE HUNG-HSUA, marketing educator; b. Taipei, Republic of China, Nov. 22, 1954; came to U.S., 1959; d. Wei-Wen and Yueh-Hsin (Wang) Y.; m. Holger Gossmann, Feb. 1989; 1 child, Fred. BA in Biol. Sci., U. Mo., 1975, MSEE in Biomed. Engring., 1977, MBA in Mktg., 1981, PhD in Mktg., 1983. Rsch. asst. U. Mo., Columbia, 1975-81, grad. instr., 1981-82; asst. prof. mktg. Wake Forest U., Winston-Salem, N.C., 1983-84, Hofstra U., Hempstead, N.Y., 1984-86, U. Hawaii at Manoa, Honolulu, 1986-88, Chinese U. Hong Kong, 1988—; rsch. cons. Mktg. Metrics, N.J., 1985-86. Mem. Am. Mktg. Assn. (doctoral consortium fellow 1982), Acad. Internat. Bus., Mu Kappa Tau. Office: Chinese U Hong Kong, Dept Mktg, Shatin New Territories, Hong Kong

YUE, AGNES KAU-WAH, otolaryngologist; b. Shanghai, Peoples Republic China, Dec. 1, 1947; came to U.S., 1967; d. Chen Kia and Nee Yuan (Ying0 ; m. Gerald Kumata, Sept. 25, 1982; children: Julie, Allison Benjamin. BA, Wellesley Coll., 1970; MD, Med. Coll. Pa., 1974; postgrad., Yale U., 1974-78. Intern Yale-New Haven Hosp., 1974-75, resident, 1975-78; fellow U. Tex. M.D. Anderson Cancer Ctr., Houston, 1978-79; asst. prof. U. Wash., Seattle, 1979-82; physician Pacific Med. Ctr., Seattle, 1979-90; pvt. practice Seattle, 1991—. Fellow Am. Acad. Otolaryngology, Am. Coll. Surgeons; mem. Northwest Acad. Otolaryngology. Office: 1801 NW Market St Ste 410 Seattle WA 98107-3909

YUEN, JANET, financial analyst; b. Hong Kong, Aug. 10, 1958; came to U.S., 1969; d. Chun Kong and Chi Ying (Wong) Y. BS, U. Calif., Berkeley, 1980; MBA, U. Pa. Wharton Sch. of Bus., 1985. Chartered Fin. Analyst. Fin. mgr. Anaior Inc., N.Y.C., 1980-82; sr. acct. Marine Midland Bank, N.Y.C., 1982-83; treasury analyst Goldman Sachs & Co., N.Y.C., summer 1984; sr. fin. analyst Bank of Am., San Francisco, 1985-87; mgr., sr. fin. analyst Citicorp/Citibank, N.Y.C., 1987-89; asst. v.p., bank analyst Chem. Banking Corp., N.Y.C., 1989-93, Thomson Bankwatch, N.Y.C., 1993-94; fixed-income analyst Lipper Analytical Securities Corp., N.Y.C., 1994—; bd. dirs. N.Y. State Coun. on Econ. Edn. N.Y.C. coord. N.Y.C. exhbn. art show Artists to End Hunger, Inc., 1987-91. Recipient Citation of Honor Young Careerist, Bus. and Profl. Women Inc., N.Y. League, N.Y.C., 1988; nominated Internat. Woman of Yr., 1992-93. Mem. AAUW (treas. 1982-83), Fin. Women's Assn. (coll. intern liaison 1988—), N.Y. Soc. Security Analysts (mem. program com. 1988—), Assn. Investment Mgmt. and Rsch., Calif. Alumni Assn., Toastmasters. Home: 300 E 46th St Apt 9K New York NY 10017-3013 Office: Lipper Analytical Securities 74 Trinity Pl New York NY 10006

YURCHENCO, HENRIETTA WEISS, ethnomusicologist, writer; b. New Haven, Mar. 22, 1916; d. Edward and Rebecca (Bernblum) Weiss; m. Basil Yurchenco, June 1936 (div. 1955); 1 child, Peter; m. Irving Levine, 1965 (div. 1979). Student, Yale U., 1935-36; student piano scholarship, Mannes Coll. Music, 1936-38. Radio producer WNYC, WBAI, others, 1939-69; writer, critic, tchr., folk music editor Am. Record Guide and Musical Am., 1959-70; prof. music Coll. City N.Y., 1962-86, Bklyn. Coll., 1966-69, New Sch. for Social Research, 1961-68; co-dir. project for study of women in music, Grad. Ctr. CUNY. Author: A Fiesta of Folk Songs From Spain and Latin America, 1967, A Mighty Hard Road: A Biography of Woody Guthrie, 1970, !Hablamos! Puerto Ricans Speak, 1971; contbr. articles to profl. jours.; 11 field recs. from Mexico, P.R., John's Island, S.C., Guatemala, Ecuador, Morocco, issued by Libr. Congress, Folkways, Nonesuch, Folkways/Smithsonian Global Village; collections in Libr. Congress, Discoteca Hebrew U., Jerusalem, Arais Montana Inst., Madrid, Inst. Nacional Indigenista, Mexico City. Recipient grants-in-aid Am. Philos. Soc., 1954, 56, 57, 65, 67, 89, grants-in-aid CUNY Faculty Research Fund, 1970, 83, 87; NEH grantee, 1984. Mem. Internat. Council Traditional Music (com. on women's studies), Soc. Ethnomusicology, Soc. Asian Music, Sonneck Soc., Internat. Assn. Study of Popular Music, Am. Musicologists Soc. Home: 360 W 22nd St New York NY 10011-2600 Office: 139th St And Convent Ave New York NY 10031

ZABEL, VIVIAN ELLOUISE, secondary education educator; b. Randolph AFB, Tex., July 28, 1943; d. Raymond Louis and Dolly Veneta (Lyles) Gilbert; m. Robert Lee Zabel, Feb. 18, 1962; children: René Lynne, Robert Lee Jr., Randel Louis, Regina Louise. BA in English and Speech, Panhandle State U., 1977; postgrad., U. Cen. Okla., 1987-92. Cert. tchr., Okla. Tchr. English, drama, speech, debate Buffalo (Okla.) High Sch., 1977-79; tchr. English, drama, speech Schulter (Okla.) High Sch., 1979-80; tchr. English Morris (Okla.) High Sch., 1980-81; tchr. speech, drama, debate Okla. Christian Schs., Edmond, 1981-82; tchr. English, drama, debate, speech/debate coach Braman (Okla.) High Sch., 1982-83; debate coach Pawhuska (Okla.) High Sch., 1983-84; tchr. English, French, drama, debate, debate coach Luther (Okla.) High Sch., 1984—; dir. drama Nazarene Youth Impact Team, Collinsville, Okla., 1979-81; tchr. high sch. Sunday sch. class Edmond Ch. of the Nazarene, 1992—; mem. community-sch. rels. com. Luther Pub. Schs., 1991-92, supt.'s adv. com., 1992—. Editor Potpourri mag., 1975-76; author poetry, short stories. Adult supr. Texas County 4-H, Adams, Okla., 1975-77; double diamond coach NFL. Recipient Disting. Svc. award NFL, 1994. Mem. Nat. Debate Coaches Assn., Nat. Fedn. Interscholastic Speech and Debate Assn., Okla. Speech Theatre Communications Assn. Republican. Nazarene. Home: 2912 Rankin Ter Edmond OK 73013-5344

ZACCONE, SUZANNE MARIA, sales executive; b. Chgo., Oct. 23, 1957; d. Dominic Robert and Lorretta F. (Urban) Z. Grad. high sch., Downers Grove, Ill. Sales sec. Brookeridge Realty, Downers Grove, 1975-76; sales cons. Kafka Estates Inc., Downers Grove, 1975-76; adminstrv. asst. Chem. Dist., Inc., Oak Brook, Ill., 1976-77; sales rep., mgr. Anographics Corp., Burr Ridge, Ill., 1977-85; pres., owner Graphic Solutions, Inc., Burr Ridge, 1985—. Recipient Supplier Mem. award Internat. Bottled Water Assn., 1987-88, Supplier award for excellence, 1990, Adminstrs. award for excellence U.S. Small Bus. Adminstrn., 1990, Eugene Singer award for best managed co. in small bus. category Graphic Solutions, 1992, Top Performer Supplier award Cutler Hammer Westinghouse Divsn., 1993, 94, Blue Chip Enterprise Initiative award, 1994; named Supplier of Yr., Gen. Binding Corp., 1988. Mem. NAFE, Tag and Label Mfrs. Inst. (chairperson pub. rels. and mktg. com., bd. dirs., Best Managed Co. award 1993), Women Entrepreneurs of Dupage County (past pres.), Inst. Packaging Profls., Women in Packaging (exec. bd.). Office: Graphic Solutions Inc 150 Shore Dr Hinsdale IL 60521-5819

ZACHARY, ROBIN BETH, art director; b. L.I., N.Y., Aug. 29, 1960; d. Eugene and Maxine Zachary. BA, SUNY, Binghamton, 1982. Assoc. art dir. Hair and Beauty Guide, N.Y.C., 1984-85, Better Health and Living Mag., N.Y.C., 1985-88; art dir. Expecting Mag., N.Y.C., 1988-91; prin. Robin Zachary Design, N.Y.C., 1991—; art dir. Fragrance Found., 1986—. Art. dir. Am. Cheerleader mag., 1994—. Recipient Ad Directions award Art Direction Mag., 1988. Home: 208 W 23d St Apt 1409 New York NY 10011

ZACHERT, MARTHA JANE, retired librarian; b. York, Pa., Feb. 7, 1920; d. Paul Rodes and Elizabeth Agnes (Lau) Koontz; m. Edward G. Zachert, Aug. 25, 1946; 1 child, Lillian Elizabeth. AB, Lebanon Valley Coll., 1941; MLS, Emory U., 1953; DLS, Columbia U., 1968. Asst. Enoch Pratt Free Library, Balt., 1941-46; head librarian Wood Research Inst., Atlanta, 1947; sch. librarian DeKalb (Ga.) County Schs., 1950-52; head librarian, prof. history of pharmacy So. Coll. Pharmacy, Mercer U., Atlanta, 1952-63; instr. Ga. State Coll., 1962-63, Emory U., summers 1955-59, 1956-57, 59-60; mem. faculty Library Sch., Fla. State U., 1963-78, prof., 1973-78; prof. Coll. Librarianship U. S.C., Columbia, 1973-74, 78-84; vis. fellow Brit. Library, 1980; cons. So. Regional Med. Library, Emory U., 1976-77, Nat. Library Medicine, 1977, others. Assoc. editor: Jour. Library History, 1966-71, 73-76; mng. editor, 1971-73; cons. editor: Jour. Library Adminstrn., 1979-86; contbr. numerous articles to profl. jours. Fellow Med. Libr. Assn.; mem. ALA, Spl. Librs. Assn. (past pres. Fla. chpt., spl. citation 1977, Hall of Fame 1985), Southwestern Libr. Assn. (Hall of Fame 1985), Am. Printing History Assn., Beta Phi Mu (pres. 1974-75). Home and Office: 2018 W Randolph Cir Tallahassee FL 32312-3349

ZACHERT, VIRGINIA, psychologist, educator; b. Jacksonville, Ala., Mar. 1, 1920; d. R.E. and Cora H. (Massee) Z. Student, Norman Jr. Coll., 1937; A.B., Ga. State Woman's Coll., 1940; M.A., Emory U., 1947; Ph.D., Purdue U., 1949. Diplomate: Am. Bd. Profl. Psychologists. Statistician Davison-Paxon Co., Atlanta, 1941-44; research psychologist Mil. Contracts, Auburn Research Found., Ala. Poly. Inst.; indsl. and research psychologist Sturm & O'Brien (cons. engrs.), 1958-59; research project dir. Western Design, Biloxi, Miss., 1960-61; self-employed cons. psychologist Norman Park, Ga., 1961-71, Good Hope, Ga., 1971—; rsch. assoc. med. edn. Med. Coll. Ga., Augusta, 1963-65, assoc. prof., 1965-70, rsch. prof., 1970-84, rsch. prof. emerita, 1984—, chief learning materials div., 1973-84, mem. faculty senate, 1976-84, mem. acad. coun., 1976-82, pres. acad. coun., 1983, sec., 1978; mem. Ga. Bd. Examiners of Psychologists, 1974-79, v.p., 1977, pres., 1978; adv. bd. Comdr. Gen. ATC USAF, 1967-70; cons. Ga. Silver Haired Legislature, 1980-86, senator, 1987-93, pres. protem, 1987-88, pres. 1989-93, rep. 1993—, speaker protem, 1993—; gov.'s appointee Ga. Coun. on Aging, 1988—; U.S. Senate mem. Fed. Coun. on the Aging, 1990-93. Author: (with P.L. Wilds) Essentials of Gynecology-Oncology, 1967, Applications of Gynecology-Oncology, 1967. Del. White House Conf. on Aging, 1981. Served as aerologist USN, 1944-46; aviation psychologist USAF, 1949-54. Fellow AAAS, Am. Psychol. Assn.; mem. AAUP (chpt. pres. 1977-80), Sigma Xi. (chpt. pres. 1980-81). Baptist. Home: 1126 Highland Ave Augusta GA 30904-4628 Office: Med Coll Ga Dept Ob-Gyn Augusta GA 30912

ZACHERY-HOPKINS, DONNA S., government tax examiner; b. Kansas City, Kans., Apr. 6, 1952; d. Jerome and Mabel Lee (Gooden) Zachery; m. John Wesley Hopkins, Dec. 22, 1979; children: Carlos and Christopher (twins). BA in Speech, Drama and English, Benedictine Coll., 1974; postgrad., U. Mo., Kans. City, 1975, U. N.Mex., 1976, U. Kans., 1979, Ctrl. Mich. U., 1992—. Libr. clk. Kansas City (Mo.) Pub. Libr., 1974, substitute acting libr., 1975; substitute tchr. Kansas City (Mo.) Sch. Dist., 1974-76, tchr., 1976-87; tchr. Hope Day Sch., Independence, Mo., 1987-89; tax examiner U.S. Dept. Treasury, Kansas City, Mo., 1989—; Libr. Kiddie Coll., Kansas City, Kans., 1986-88; creative dramatics Happy Heart Montessori Pre-Sch., Kansas City, 1972-74. Vol. religious edn. tchr. St. Mary's Cath. Ch., Independence, 1987-91. Recipient Mt. St. Scholastica award, 1974. Mem. Nat. Coun. Tchrs. English, Nat. Assn. Negro Bus. and Profl. Women (chaplain 1980-81, treas. 1981-82), NAACP (entertainment and tourism planner nat. conv., recognition award 1988), Assn. for Improvement Minorities in IRS, Nat. Coun. Accreditation Tchr. Edn. (life, award), Independence Neighborhood Couns.-Clermont Neighborhood Coun. (treas. 1983-88).

ZAFFIRINI, JUDITH, state senator; b. Laredo, Tex., Feb. 13, 1946; d. George and Nieves Pappas; m. Carlos Zaffirini, 1965; 1 child, Carlos Jr. BS, U. Tex., 1967, MA, 1970, PhD, 1978. Committeewoman Tex. State Dem. Exec. Com., 1978-84; mem. Tex. State Senate, 1987—; del. Dem. Nat. Conv., 1980, 84. Bd. dirs., dir. pub. relations Laredo Civic Music Assn., 1968—. Recipient Medal of Excellence Nat. League United Latin Am. Citizens, 1987, Jose Maria Morelos y Pavon Medal of Merit for leadership in strengthening U.S.-Mex. rels., 1987, George Washington Medal of Excellence for Individual Achievement Freedoms Found. at Valley Forge, 1988; named to Nat. Hispanic Hall of Fame, 1987; named Woman of Achievement Tex. Press Women, 1980. Democrat. Roman Catholic. Home: PO Box 627 Laredo TX 78042 Office: 1407 Washington St Laredo TX 78040-4411

ZAGON, LAURIE, artist, writer, color consultant; b. N.Y.C., Feb. 4, 1950; d. Jerome and Janet (Rabinowitz) Z.; m. Joseph Sorrentino, Dec. 21, 1991. BFA, Md. Inst. Coll. Art, 1971; MFA, Syracuse U., 1973. Asst. prof. Art CUNY, N.Y.C., 1973-87; color cons. Fieldcrest/Cannon, N.Y.C., 1987-88; nat. speaker Am. Soc. Interior Designers, Washington, 1993—. Illustrator (book) It's Never Too Late to Have a Happy Childhood, 1989; one-woman shows include The Nat. Arts Club, N.Y.C., 1989, Gallery 1757, Laguna Beach, Calif., 1991; group exhibits include John Szoke Gallery, N.Y.C., Helio Galleries, N.Y.C., CUNY Abstract Show of Shanghai, China, 1986, L.A. Mcpl. Gallery, 1993; co-author: Power of Color, 1995. Color/art therapist for AIDS Children, L.A. Childrens Hosp., 1994; color/art therapist for recovering addicts Capo by the Sea, Dana Point, Calif., 1991, Martin Luther Hosp., Anaheim, 1990. Ralph Wilson Plastics grantee, 1993. Mem. Interior Platform Assn. (speaker), Nat. Symposium on Healthcare Design (speaker).

ZAGOREN, JOY CARROLL, health facility director, researcher; b. N.Y.C., Oct. 31, 1933; d. Murray Morris and Celia (Donner) Rossman; m. Robert H. Zagoren, June 29, 1958 (div. 1988); children: Glenn, Robin; m. Robert Henry Chester, Apr. 1, 1988; children: Peter, Lisabeth, Melinda, Cecily, Kate. BS, NYU, 1957; MS, Adelphi U., 1969; PhD with distinction, NYU, 1981. Sec. sch. faculty Great Neck (N.Y.) Pub. Schs., 1957-71; rsch. scientist Inst. Psychobiol. Studies, Queens Village, N.Y., 1968-71; rsch. assoc. Albert Einstein Coll. Medicine, Bronx, N.Y., 1971-84; asst. prof. Sch. Medicine SUNY, Stony Brook, 1984-86; dir. Seriatum, N.Y.C., 1991—; ptnr. Winter Tree Collection; chmn. Esrath Nashim Hosp., 1986—; med. bd. dirs. Sarah Herzog Meml. Hosp., 1994—. Editor: The Node of Ranvier, 1984; contbr. articles to profl. jours. Chairperson Peace Corps Svc. Coun., Tri-State, 1965-75; pres. Kidney Found. L.I., N.Y., 1965-77; v.p. United Cmty. Fund. L.I., 1970-83; bd. dirs. Jerusalem Mental Health Ctr., N.Y.C., 1986—; mem. med. bd. dirs. Sarah Herzog Meml. Hosp. Recipient post doctoral fellowship NIH, 1982-84, svc. awards Kidney Found., Kiwanis, and others, 1970-87; named Disting. Alumnus of Yr., Adelphi U., 1986. Mem. AAAS, ACA, N.Y. Acad. Sci., Am. Assn. Neuropathology, Esrath Nashim Hosp. (chairperson 1986—, apptd. med. bd. dirs. 1994—), Kappa Delta Epsilon. Democrat. Jewish. Home: 405 E 82nd St New York NY 10028-6038 Office: Seriatum PO Box 396 Livingston Manor NY 12758-0371

ZAGORSKY, CAROL LACCI, information systems project director; b. N.Y.C., Nov. 19, 1942; d. Arthur and Evelyn Marie (Strang) Lacci; m. Eugene Dennis Zagorsky, Jr., May 21, 1983. BBA in Econs., St. John's U., Jamaica, N.Y., 1968. Cert. data processor, quality analyst. Programmer info. systems and services dept. N.Y. Life Ins. Co., N.Y.C., 1967-71, programmer analyst, 1971-74, project leader, 1974-78, project mgr., 1978—, div. head, 1988-89, project dir., 1989—; conf. spkr. Managing Computer Aided Software Engring. Implementation; lectr. NYU, Info. Technols. Inst., 1990-92; instr. Am. Mgmt. Assn.-Total Quality Mgmt. for Mgmt. Info. Sys., 1993-94. Trustee Murray Hill Com., N.Y.C., 1977-79, 85-86, v.p. 1979-85. Mem. Women in Data Processing, Quality Mgmt. Assn. N.Y. (pres. 1991—), Nat. Excelerator Users Group (profl. devel. com.), Met. N.Y. Computer Aided Software Engring. Users Group. Democrat. Episcopalian. Office: NY Life Ins Co 51 Madison Ave New York NY 10010-1603

ZAHASKY, MARY MARGARET, counselor, psychotherapist, educator; b. Rome, Ga., Nov. 23, 1954; d. Harold William Jr. and Louise (Malone) Emick; 1 child, Jessica Roseann Detton; m. James W. Zahasky Jr. BA, Western State Coll., 1980, MA, 1981. Cert. tchr., Colo. Outpatient psychotherapist, mental health worker Midwestern Colo. Mental Health Ctr., Montrose, 1981-82; counselor Rainbow Counseling Exch., Montrose, 1982-93; pvt. practice Okla. City, 1994—; co-host radio show Heart of the Matter, 1993; mediator Women's Resource Ctr., Montrose, 1990-93, bd. dirs. Mem. Am. Counseling Assn., Am. Coun. Hypnotist Examiners (cert. hypnotherapist), Internat. Assn. Marriage and Family Therapists, Internat. Found. Shamanic Studies, Colo. Hypnotist Coun., Alchem. Hypnotherapy Inst. Home: 1500 E Wilshire Blvd Oklahoma City OK 73111-8413

ZAHN, PAULA, newscaster; b. Feb. 24, 1956; m. Richard Cohen; 1 child, Haley. With Sta. WHDH, Boston, 1983-85; anchor, reporter Sta. KCBS, L.A., 1985-87; co-anchor World News Now ABC News, N.Y.C., 1987-90; co-anchor CBS This Morning CBS News, N.Y.C., 1990—; contbr. CBS news mag. 48 Hours; co-host CBS broadcast Winter Olympics, Albertville, France, 1992. Office: CBS News CBS This Morning 524 W 57th St New York NY 10019-2902*

ZAHNLEY, BRENDA JEAN, counselor supervisor; b. Sheldon, Iowa, Oct. 23, 1960; d. William and Nancy (Van Roekel) Sinkey; m. James Allen Zahnley, Sept. 8, 1984. BA in Sociology, Northwestern Coll., Orange City, Iowa, 1983; MS in Counseling, Wayne State (Nebr.) Coll., 1993. Social worker Colonial Manor Nursing Home, Correctionville, Iowa, 1983-86; case mgr. A.I.D. Ctr., Sioux City, Iowa, 1986-87; bereavement supr. Hospice of Siouxland, Sioux City, Iowa, 1987—; adj. faculty Wayne State Coll., 1993; keynote speaker Hospice-Sioux County, Sioux Ctr., 1993. Co-author: (manual) Helping the Hurting, 1993 (Nat. Hospice Award 1993); author: (bookmark for children) When a Parent or Pet Dies, 1993. Mem. Am. Counseling Assn., Am. Assn. Marriage and Family Therapy. Home: 490 Knotty Pine St Correctionville IA 51016-8188 Office: Hospice of Siouxland 500 11th St Sioux City IA 51105-1427

ZAHRLY, JANICE HONEA, management educator; b. Ft. Payne, Ala., Sept. 27, 1943; d. John Wiley and Lillian (McKown) Honea. BA, U. Fla., 1964; MBA, U. Ctrl. Fla., 1980; PhD, U. Fla., 1984. Tchr. Hope Mills (N.C.) H.S., 1964-65, Satellite Beach (Fla.) H.S., 1965-69; realtor-assoc. WD Webb Realty, Melbourne, Fla., 1969-70; realtor Aero Realty, Melbourne, 1970-72, Albert J. Tuttle, Realtor, Melbourne, 1972-74; mktg. mgr. Cypress Woods Devel., Orlando, Fla., 1974-76; regional campaign mgr. Pres. Ford Com., 1976; ednl. researcher Peace Corps, Korea, 1976-78; rsch. analyst, tech. writer Rsch. Sys. Inc., Orlando, 1979-80; rsch. asst., lectr. U. Fla., Gainesville, 1980-84; asst. prof. Wayne State U., Detroit, 1984-89; assoc. prof. Old Dominion U., Norfolk, Va., 1989-94, U. N.D., Grand Forks, 1994—; mem. Melbourne Bd. Realtors, 1969-76, orientation chair, 1972, pub. rels. chair, 1973, civic affairs chair, 1973, grievance com., 1975; cons. Wayne County Retarded Persons Assn., Detroit, 1985, Gov.'s Conf. on Women Entrepreneurs, Mich., 1986, Oakland County AAUW Conf. on Women, Mich., 1987, 88, Coll. Bus. and Pub. Adminstrn. Inst. of Mgmt., Old Dominion U., Norfolk, 1990, U.S. Army Corps Engrs., Norfolk, 1990; presenter in field. Contbr. chpts. to books, articles to profl. jours. and procs. Vol. Tidewater AIDS Crisis Task Force, Norfolk, 1990-93, bd. dirs., 1990-92, v.p., 1991, rec. sec., 1992; mem. occupational adv. com. Brevard County Mental Health Ctr., Fla., 1973-74; mem. Brevard County Libr. Bd., 1973-74; bd. dirs. Fla. Dist. 12 Mental Health Bd., 1973-74, sec. 1973-74; bd. dirs. Alachua County Crisis Ctr., Gainesville, 1982-84, chair, 1983-84; vol. Open Door, Detroit, 1986-89. Recipient Best Paper award Midwest Soc. for Human Resources/Indsl. Rels., 1989; rsch. fellow Fed. Mogul Corp., 1987-88; rsch. grantee Old Dominion U., 1990. Mem. AAUW (bd. dirs. 1974-75), Acad. Mgmt., Assn. for Rsch. on Nonprofit Orgns./Vols., Strategic Mgmt. Assn., Hampton Roads Gator Club (co-founder, treas. 1989-91), Alpha Omicron Pi (bd. dirs. alumnae chpt. 1969-73, v.p. 1969-73). Home: 3424 Cherry St # A1 Grand Forks ND 58201

ZAHUMENY, JANET MAE, secondary education educator; b. Rahway, N.J., Mar. 23, 1945; d. Richard Evans and Elsie Mae (Walling) Franklin; m. Edward Zahumeny, Dec. 21, 1966 (div. 1987); 1 child, Carole Ann. BA, Newark State Coll., 1967; MEd, William Paterson Coll., 1990; MA, Kean Coll., 1994. Cert. secondary tchr., N.J. Math. tchr. Hunterdon Cen. High Sch., Flemington, N.J., 1967-68; math., computer tchr. Roselle Park (N.J.) High Sch., 1968—; instr. computers Roselle Park Adult Sch., 1987-88; instr. computer tech. William Paterson Coll., 1993—; cons. Gray's Appraisal, Cranford, N.J., 1987; textbook editor Prentice Hall, 1989; computer group asst. Bell Labs., Whippany, N.J., summers 1972-73; chmn. Dist. Computer Study Com., 1988; presenter dist.-wide insvc. workshops, 1987—, out of dist computer workshops, 1992—, 8th grade computer coord., 1988-89; mem. Mid. States Evaluation Team, 1972, 82, 85; liason com. RPHS, 1985—, cooperating tchr. Kean Coll., 1990—; adminstrv. asst. to v.p. Alpha Wire, summer 1991—; participant Computing Inst., 1983, Woodrow Wilson Inst., 1991, NSF Inst., 1991. Active Cranford PTA, Roselle Park PTSA. Named Outstanding Acad. Tchr., Cittone Inst., 1988, Outstanding Tchr., N.J. Gov.'s Recognition program, 1989, Outstanding Computer/Math. Tchr. Tandy Technologies, 1991; recipient grad. scholarship Kean Coll., 1992, Presdl. award for Excellence in Sci. and Math. Tchg. state level NSF, 1994; computer grantee, 1993. Mem. Mem. NEA, Nat. Coun. Tchrs. Math., Assn. Math. Tchrs. N.J., N.J. Edn. Assn., Roselle Park Edn. Assn., Mensa, Kean Coll. Alumni Assn., William Paterson Coll. Alumni Assn., Ednl. Tech. Network, Pi Lambda Theta, Kappa Delta Pi, Phi Kappa Phi. Office: Roselle Park High Sch 185 W Webster Ave Roselle Park NJ 07204-1699

ZAIK, CAROL FORD, museum director, art historian, educator; b. Springfield, Mass., Aug. 11, 1955; d. Edward William and Margaret (Ford) Z. BA, U. Mass., 1978; MA in Art Edn., Springfield Coll., 1979; PhD, NYU, 1984. Docent, adminstr. Currier Mus., Manchester, N.H., 1984-88; creating one-man sch. house into fine arts mus., West Ossipee, N.H., 1988—; actor Mt. Tom Playhouse, Holyoke, Mass., 1965-68. Active Smithsonian Assn., 1965-87, Acad. Polit. Sci., 1983-92, Audubon Soc., 1986-94. Mem. Nat. Art Edn. Assn. (chairperson mus. divsn. 1987-90), Mass. Art Edn. Assn., Internat. Soc. Edn., Nat. Mus. Women in Arts, Amherst Fine Arts Assn., U.S. Soc. Edn. Through Art, Smithsonian Assocs. Democrat. Roman Catholic. Home: 1062 Worthington St Springfield MA 01109-4021

ZAJICEK, IVA MARIE, educator; b. Hastings, Nebr., June 19, 1925; d. Harold Loper and Laura Jean (Evans) Foreman; m. Jerome Robert Zajicek, Sept. 10, 1944; children: James Craig, Ashley Marie. BSc, U. Nebr., 1959, ME, 1960, EdD, 1978. Tchr. pub. schs. York, Nebr., 1956-57, Ceresco, Nebr., 1957-58; art/libr. pub. schs. Los Alamos, N.Mex., 1960-64; edn. advisor, Advance Tchrs. Coll. Ohio U./U.S.A.I.D./Nigeria Project, Kano, 1964-68; elem. edn. advisor Washington County Elem. Schs., Title III, Marietta, Ohio, 1968-70; prin. Fort Frye Schs., Beverly, Ohio, 1970-71; prof. Marietta (Ohio) Coll., 1971-81; edn. advisor Botswana U. Ohio U./U.S.A.I.D., Gaborone, Botswana, 1981-85; edn. advisor U. Swaziland/Ohio U., Mbabane, Swaziland, 1985-87; cons. in field. Mem. Nat. Soc. DAR, PEO. Republican. Methodist. Home: 4281 S Royal Lytham Ct Green Valley AZ 85614-5636

ZAJICEK, LYNN ENGELBRECHT, educational administrator; b. Newport News, Va., Mar. 25, 1950; d. Herbert Charles and Lois (Kohler) Engelbrecht; m. Jon M. Zajicek, June 6, 1970; children: Carlye Lynn, Kate Elizabeth. BA, Kearney State Coll., 1971; MEd, U. Nebr., 1973, EdS, 1988. Cert. profl. adminstr./supr., Nebr. Tchr. Lincoln (Nebr.) Pub. Schs., 1971-73; instr. U.S. Army PREP Program, Crailsheim, Fed. Republic of Germany, 1974-76; subs. tchr. Grand Island (Nebr.) Pub. Schs., 1976-77; mgr., owner rental property Grand Island, 1978—; asst. on survey project U. Nebr., Lincoln, 1987-88; adminstr., ednl. diagnostician Nebr. Ctr. for Evaluation of Devel. and Learning, Inc., Grand Island, 1988—; bd. dirs. Reorganized Mark V Mortgage Corp. Bd. mem. PTA, Grand Island, 1980—; supt. Bible Sch. St. Stephen's Ch., Grand Island, 1984-85; mem. Christian edn. com. St. Stephen's, 1985—, subcom. for adult and continuing edn. of strategic planning com. Grand Island Pub. Schs., 1987; coach Odyssey of the Mind Grand Island Pub. Schs., 1986—; active in heart and cancer funds in Grand Island; bd. dirs. Episc. Ch. Women; candidate cmpaign mgr. Rep. Women, 1978; bd. dirs., exec. com. Marque of Nebr., 1989—. Recipient Gen. Arnold scholarship USAF, 1967. Mem. AAUW, Assn. Supervision and Curriculum Devel., Nat. Assn. Secondary Sch. Prins., Nebr. Coun. Sch. Adminstrs., Nebr. Assn. Elem. Sch. Prins., Nebr. Dental Assn. Aux. (numerous offices including pres. 1981-82), Hall County Dental Aux. (sec., treas. 1976—), St. Francis Med. Aux., Nebr. Assn. for Children and Adults with Learning Disabilities, Phi Delta Kappa, Pi Delta Phi, Alpha Mu Gamma, Sigma Tau Delta, Xi Phi. Home: 1618 S Harrison St Grand Island NE 68803-6359 Office: Nebr Ctr for Evaluation of Devel and Learning Inc 2121 N Webb Rd Ste 305 Grand Island NE 68803-1751

ZAKHEIM, BARBARA JANE, international business company consulting executive; b. London, Jan. 31, 1953; d. David Sloma and Sarah Frances (Leifer) Portnoi; m. Dov Solomon Zakheim, Aug. 20, 1972 (div. 1990); children: Keith Samuel, Roger Israel, Scott Elisha; m. Ronald Kleinfeldt, Dec. 13, 1992. BA, Oxford U., Eng., 1974, MA, 1978. Economist Maxima Corp., Silver Spring, Md., 1979, U.S. Dept. Energy, Washington, 1979-80; sr. project analyst Applied Mgmt. Scis., Silver Spring, 1980-83, staff assoc., 1983-85; prin. analyst NUS Corp., Gaithersburg, Md., 1985-87, cons. analyst, 1987-89; pres. Keith R. Scott Assocs., Inc., 1989—, African Treasures, Inc., 1990-93; dir. policy and econ. studies Sanford, Cohen & Assocs., Inc., 1993—; U.S. rep. Coll. Petroleum Studies, Oxford, 1984-93; N.Am. rep. Twirltrade Internat. Ltd., London, 1985—; mem. adv. com. on women in bus. Theodore Roosevelt Nat. Bank, Washington, 1991-92; profl. team mem. Venture Ptnrs. Internat., Inc., N.Y.C., 1990—. Contbr. articles to profl. jours. Bd. dirs. SE Hebrew Congregation, Silver Spring, 1977-78. Mem. NAFE, Nat. Assn. Environ. Profls., Internat. Network for Women in Enterprise and Trade, Inc. Republican. Home and Office: 11247 Watermill Ln Silver Spring MD 20902-3439

ZALESKI, JEAN, artist; b. Birkirkara, Malta; d. John M. and Carolina (Micallef) Busuttil; children: Jeffrey, Philip, Susan Jean. Student, Art Students League, N.Y.C., 1955-58, New Sch., N.Y.C., 1967-69, Moore Coll. Art, Phila., 1970-71, Parsons Sch. Design, N.Y.C., 1974-75, Pratt Inst., N.Y.C., 1976-77. Dir. art Studio 733, Great Neck, N.Y., 1963-67; sr. art instr. Hussian Coll. Art, Phila., 1970-71; dir. Naples (Italy) Art Studio, 1972-74; corp. sec. Women in The Arts, N.Y.C., 1974-75, exec. coord., 1976-78; adj. lectr. Bklyn. Coll., 1974-75, Hofstra U., 1977-82, Cooper Union, 1986—. One-woman shows include: Adelphi U., 1975, Women in Arts Gallery, N.Y.C., 1975, Il Gabbiano Gallery, Naples, 1973, Wallnuts Gallery, Phila., 1971, Neikrug Gallery, N.Y.C., 1970, Alonzo Gallery, N.Y.C., 1979, 80, Va. Ctr. for Creative Arts, Sweet Briar, 1981, Hodgell Galleries, Sarasota, Fla., 1982, 83, Elaine Starkman Gallery, N.Y.C., 1986, Romano Gallery, Barnegat Light, N.J., 1987, 88, Citicorp Ctr., N.Y.C., 1988-89, Z Gallery, N.Y.C., 1991, Sweet Briar Coll., Va., 1993; group exhbns. include Art U.S.A., N.Y.C., 1969, Internat. Art Exhbn., Cannes, France, 1969, Frick Mus., Pitts., 1970, NAD, N.Y.C., 1970-71, Phila. Mus. Art, 1971, Am. Women Artists, Palazzo Vecchio, Florence, 1972, Internat. Women's Arts Festival, Milan, Italy, 1973 (Gold medal), Bklyn. Mus., 1975, Sweet Briar Coll., 1977, CUNY, 1978, Va. Ctr., 1988, Mus. Hudson Highlands, 1982, Pace U. Gallery, N.Y.C., 1982, Bayly Mus., Charlottesville, Va., 1986, Allbright Knox Mus., Buffalo, 1986, E. Starkman Gallery, N.Y.C., 1987, Nabisco, 1989, Queens Coll., N.Y., 1991-92, Mus. City of N.Y., 1993; coauthor COW/LINES, 1983; represented in permanent collections N.Y. Pub. Library, Met. Mus. Art, Va. Ctr. for Creative Arts, Nat. Mus. Women in Arts, Mus. of City of N.Y., Nat. Mus. Malta; vis. artist, critic various colls. and univs., 1976—. Ragdale fellow, 1986—, Va. Ctr. for Creative Arts fellow, 1976-95, Tyrone Guthrie Ctr. fellow, 1991; grantee NEA, 1982, Artists Space, 1988; recipient Susan B. Anthony award NOW, 1986. Mem. Artists Equity, Women in The Arts, Women's Caucus for Art, Manhattan Pl. Health Club. Democrat. Roman Catholic.

ZALESKI, MARY PATRICIA, accounting administrator; b. Chgo., Dec. 8, 1964; d. Leonard Patrick and Mary Patricia (Geary) Z. BS in Acctg., Northeastern Ill. U., Chgo., 1994. Staff acct. Raminiak, Piper & Co., Chgo., 1985; acctg. mgr. Chgo. Comm. Svc., Inc., Franklin Park, Ill., 1988-92, ALH Systems, Inc., Elk Grove Village, Ill., 1993—; pvt. practice tax preparer, Chgo., 1986—; account rep. Conviser Duffy, Chgo., 1986—; acctg. tutor Acctg. Club Northeastern Ill. U., Chgo., 1993—. Mem. NAFE. Roman Catholic. Home: 4904 N Rutherford Ave Chicago IL 60656-4034 Office: ALH Systems Inc 119 Lively Blvd Elk Grove Village IL 60007-1620

ZALOZNIK, ARLENE JOYCE, oncologist, military officer; b. Pitts., Jan. 30, 1948; d. Ernest and Frances Elizabeth (Augustin) Z. BS, Carlow Coll., 1969; MS, Duquesne U., 1972; MD, Med. Coll. PA, 1976. Diplomate Am. Bd. Internal Medicine, Am. Bd. Oncology. Commd. U.S. Army, 1976, advanced through grades to col.; intern then resident in hematology and oncology Madigan Army Med. Ctr., Tacoma, 1976-77; fellow in hematology and oncology Fitzsimons Army Med. Ctr., Aurora, Colo., 1979-81, staff oncology, 1981-82, asst. chief med. oncology, 1982-84, chief hematology and oncology, 1984-86; chief hematology and oncology Brooke Army Med. Ctr., Ft. Sam Houston, Tex., 1986—; clin. instr. dept. medicine U. Colo. Health Sci. Ctr., 1982-86. Contbr. articles to books and profl. jours. and publs. Active profl. edn. com. Aurora-Adams Unit Am. Cancer Soc., 1983-86, pres., 1983-86, also active Colo. div., 1984-86. Fellow Am. Coll. Physicians, Am. Coll. Chest Physicians; mem. AMA, Am. Soc. Clin. Oncology, Assn. Mil Surgeons, Am. Acad. Med. Dirs., Am. Soc. Hematology. Home: 4041A S Atchison Way Aurora CO 80014 Office: Dep Commdr Fitzsimons Army Med Ctr Aurora CO 80045

ZAMBONE, ALANA MARIA, special education educator; b. Vineland, N.J., Sept. 17, 1952; d. L. Alan and Joyce (Bernero) Z. AB in Spl. Edn., U. N.C., Chapel Hill, 1974; MS in Human Devel. Liaison, George Peabody Coll. Tchrs., 1978; PhD in Spl. Edn., Vanderbilt U., 1984. Cert. spl. edn., visual impairments, mental retardation, N.C. Tchr., counselor Orange County Assn. for Retarded Citizens, Chapel Hill, N.C., 1973-74; lead tchr. Shelbyville-Bedford (Tenn.) County Adult Svc. Ctr., 1974; program coord. Dickson (Tenn.) County Adult Svcs., 1974-75; dept. head, habilitative svcs. CloverBottom Devel. Ctr., Nashville, Tenn., 1975-76; exec. dir. Waves, Inc. Adult Svcs., Fairview, Tenn., 1976-77; from vocat. cons. to liaison, Peabody Tchrs. Coll. Vanderbilt U., 1977-80; chairperson, bd. dirs. Residential Svcs., Inc., Nashville, 1976-80; asst. prof., coord., dept. curriculum N.C. State U., Raleigh, N.C., 1981-84; coord. and asst. prof., div. spl. edn. Minot (N.D.) State U., 1984-86; coord. internat. outreach svcs. Hilton-Perkins Internat. Program Perkins Sch. for the Blind, Watertown, Mass., 1989-94; assoc. prof., dir. Inst. for Visually Impaired Pa. Coll. Optometry, Phila., 1994—; nat. cons. Am. Found. for the Blind, N.Y.C., 1986-89; adj. asst. prof. div. spl. edn., Columbia U., 1987—; co-dir. model infant/toddler program, sch. medicine, U. N.C., Chapel Hill, 1983-84; bd. dirs. N.D. Coun. for the Arts; adv. bd. Blind Babies Found.; mem. adv. com. Robert E. Miller, Inc., Community Residential Svcs. for Disabled Children; bd. dirs. Specialized Svcs. for Children, Inc.; sch. edn. rep. to fac. N.C. State U., sch. edn. fac. sec., among others. Grantee Busch Found., N.D. Coun. Arts, Nat. Coun. on the Arts, Dean's Grant Program, Burlington/No. Found., Kate B. Reynolds Found., Nat. Rural Spl. Edn. Consortium, U.S. Office Human Devel. Svcs., U.S. Office of Spl. Edn. Mem. Council for Exceptional Children (past dir. div. visual handicaps), Assn. for Retarded Citizens, Assn. for Persons with Severe Handicaps, Am. Assn. Mental Deficiency, Am. Assn. for Applied Behavior Analysis, Nat. Assn. for Parents of the Visually Impaired, Internat. Assn. for the Edn. of the Deaf-Blind, Assn. for the Edn. and Rehab. of the Blind and Visually Impaired (pre-sch. div., multihandicaps div., chairperson elect multiple disabilities div.). Office: Pa Coll Optometry 1200 W Godfrey Ave Philadelphia PA 19141-3339

ZAMBONI, HELEN ATTENA, lawyer; b. Tuxedo, N.Y., Oct. 29, 1951; d. Frank Joseph and Janet Edwards (Johnson) Z.; m. Steve I. Rosen, Jan. 2, 1982. BA cum laude, Mount Holyoke Coll., 1973; JD cum laude, Syracuse U. Coll. of Law, 1977. Title officer Ticor Title Guarantee, Rochester, N.Y., 1977-79; assoc. atty. Underberg & Kessler, Rochester, 1980-82, Phillips, Lytle, Hitchcock et al, Rochester, 1982-83; corp. atty. Rochester Telephone, Rochester, 1983-84, sr. corp. atty., 1984-85, mng. atty., 1985-93, acting gen. counsel, 1993-94, corp. counsel, 1994—. Dir. YMCA of Greater Rochester, 1986—, Career Devel. Svcs., 1992—; mem. capital campaign com. Syracuse U. Coll. of Law, 1994—. Mem. Am. Corp. Counsel Assn. (dir. cen. and we. N.Y. chpt.). Home: 25 Spring St Avon NY 14414 Office: Rochester Telephone Corp 180 S Clinton Ave Rochester NY 14646-0700

ZAMBRANO, DEBRA KAY, community health nurse; b. Salida, Colo., Jan. 1, 1955; d. George and Kathleen Elizabeth (Davidoff) Argys; m. George Luis Zambrano, Mar. 11, 1978; children: George Jr., Jennifer. BSN, U. No. Colo., 1980; BS, Adams State Coll., Alamosa, Colo., 1977. RN, Colo. Charge nurse obstetrics unit Alamosa Community Hosp., 1980-83; staff nurse labor and delivery Holy Cross Hosp., Salt Lake City, 1983-84; charge nurse La Junta (Colo.) Med. Ctr., 1984-86; clin. RN II women's care unit Poudre Valley Hosp., Ft. Collins, Colo., 1987-93; cmty. health nurse Alamosa County Nursing Svc., Alamosa, Colo., 1993—. Mem. Assn. Women's Health, Obstetric and Neonatal Nurses (cert. in inpatient obstetrics and low-risk newborn), Kiwanis (Alamosa chpt.).

ZAMORA, MARJORIE DIXON, retired political science educator; b. Farm Randolph, N.Y., Nov. 8, 1933; d. Wendell Hadley and Jessie (Mercer) Dixon; m. Cornelio Raul Zamora, Dec. 20, 1969; 1 child, Daniel Cornelio. BA, Earlham Coll., 1956; MA, U. Ill., 1968; postgrad., U. Ill., Chgo., 1989—. Tchr. Ridge, Sch., Godsman Sch., Stenson Sch., various cities, 1956-62; with U.S. Peace Corps, tchr. Palmares High Sch., Costa Rica, 1963-64; reporter Lerner Newspaper, Chgo., 1965; dormitory counselor, researcher Univ. Ill., Urbana, 1966-68, 86; instr. Chgo. City Coll., 1968-69; prof. polit. sci. Moraine Valley C.C., Palos Hills, Ill., 1969-94, prof. emeritus, 1994—; researcher, Univ. Ill., Chgo., 1985-88. Contbr. articles on Costa Rican polit. bus. cycle and economy, land reform to various publs. in U.S., Cen. Am. Campaign dir. Polit. State Legis., 1974-76. Mem. AAUW, Moraine Valley Community Coll. Faculty Assn., Am. Polit. Sci. Assn. (chair profl. and community coms.). Home: 3820 Lawn Ave Western Springs IL 60558-1141 Office: Moraine Valley CC 10900 S 88th Ave Palos Hills IL 60465-2175

ZAMORANO, WANDA JEAN, secondary education educator; b. Mertzon, Tex., Aug. 11, 1947; d. A.L. and Billie Louise (Byler) Sawyer; married; 1 child, Anna. BS, Sul Ross State Univ., 1970; MEd, Tex. Tech., 1974; EdD, Nova Southeastern U., 1994. Cert. tchr., Tex. Migrant edn. tchr. Balmorhea (Tex.) ISD, 1970-72; reading tchr. Hurst-Euless Bedford (Tex.) ISD, 1972-92; owner cons. firm WZ Enterprizes; cons. Tex. Tech. U., 1980-81; demonstration tchr. Ednl. Svcs. Ctr., Austin, 1975; instr. Richland Coll., Dallas, 1982; mem. nat. faculty Turner Ednl. Svcs. Inc.; instr. grad. class Tex. Woman's U., summer 1995; adj. prof. Tex. Woman's U.; presenter 6th Annual So. N.Mex. Tech. Conf., 1994. Contbr. articles to profl. jours. Active Bedford Jr. High PTA. Named Tchr. of Yr., Bedford, 1984, Most Prominent Educators Tex., 1983, Cable Tchr. of Yr., 1993, Tchr. of Month, Bronco News, 1994; TCI Cable grantee J.C. Sparkman Ctr. for Ednl. Tech., 1995. Mem. AAUW, NEA, Hurst-Euless-Bedford Tex. State Tchrs. Assn. (v.p. 1994-95), Internat. Reading Assn., Tex. State Tchrs. Assn. (exec. bd.), The Gov.'s Club (charter), Kappa Delta Pi. Democrat. Home: 2403 Finley Rd Apt 1107 Irving TX 75062-3348 Office: Bedford Jr High 325 Carolyn Dr Bedford TX 76021-4195

ZANDER, GAILLIENNE GLASHOW, psychologist; b. Bklyn., Apr. 7, 1932; d. Saul and Anna (Karasik) G.; m. A.J. Zander, Aug. 5, 1952; children: Elizabeth L., Caroline M., Catherine A. MusB, U. Wis., 1953, MS, 1970; PhD, Marquette U., 1984. Music tchr. Wis. Sch. Systems, 1953-65; psychol. asst. Vernon Psychol. Labs., Chgo., 1965-70; psychologist Milw. Pub. Schs., 1970-92, CESA 19, Kenosha, Wis., 1977-78; pvt. practice psychology Milw., 1980—. Fellow Am. Orthopsychiat. Assn.; mem. APA, Wis. Psychol. Assn., Psychologists Assn. in Milw. Pub. Schs. (rep., v.p., pres.), Am. Acad. Pain Mgmt. (diplomate). Home: 13750 Carson Ct Brookfield WI 53005-4989 Office: Performance Enhancement 12630 W North Ave Brookfield WI 53005-4626

ZANDER, JANET ADELE, psychiatrist; b. Miles City, Mont., Feb. 19, 1950; d. Adelbert William and Valborg Constance (Buckneberg) Z.; m. Mark Richard Ellenberger, Sept. 16, 1979; 1 child, Evan David Zander Ellenberger. BA, St. Olaf Coll., 1972; MD, U. Minn., 1976. Diplomate Am. Bd. Psychiatry and Neurology. Resident in psychiatry U. Minn., Mpls., 1976-79, fellow in psychiatry, 1979-80, asst. prof. psychiatry, 1981—; staff psychiatrist St. Paul (Minn.) Ramsey Med. Ctr., 1980—, dir. edn. in psychiatry, 1980—, dir. inpatient psychiatry, 1986—; vice chair Dept. Psychiatry St. Paul Ramsey Med. Ctr., 1991—; bd. dirs. Perry Assurance. Contbr. research articles to sci. jours. Sec. Concentus Musicus Bd. Dirs., St. Paul, 1981-89; mem. property com. St. Clement's Episcopal Ch., St. Paul, 1985. Mem. Am. Psychiat. Assn., Am. Med. Women's Assn., Minn. Psychiat. Soc. (ethics com. 1985-87, women's com. 1985-87, mem. coun. 1994—), Minn. Med. Assn., Ramsey County Med. Soc. (bd. dirs. 1994—). Democrat. Home: 230 Crestway Ln West Saint Paul MN 55118-4424 Office: St Paul Ramsey Med Ctr 640 Jackson St Saint Paul MN 55101

ZANDERS, PATTIE BALDWIN, computer specialist; b. Conway, S.C., July 2, 1951; d. Jesse Odell and Clara Bell (Etheredge) Baldwin; m. Melvin Zanders, July 8, 1983; 1 child, Monya Loleta Baldwin. BS, S.C. State Coll., 1974. Computer programmer Liberty Mut. Assurance Co., Boston, 1974-75; head bookkeeper Southview Apts., Oxon Hill, Md., 1976-77; community vol. Aiken County, Aiken, S.C., 1975; vol. tutor Univ. Yr. for Action, VISTA, Elloree, S.C., 1973-74; computer programmer Naval Communication Unit, Cheltenham, Md., 1977-78; computer analyst Bur. Alcohol Tobacco and Firearms, Washington, 1978-82; computer analyst fin. mgmt. svc. U.S. Dept. Treasury, Washington, 1982—. Vol. aide Kapitol Day Care, Capitol Heights, 1991-92. Democrat. Home: 4104 Byers St Capitol Hts MD 20743-5724 Office: US Dept Treasury Fin Mgmt Svc 3700 East-West Hwy Rm 900B Hyattsville MD 20782

ZANESKI, ANNE MARLA, healthcare/pharmaceutical marketing executive; b. Boston, Apr. 6, 1960; d. Chester Edward and Mary Nancy (Blume) Z. BA in Polit. Sci., Wellesley Coll., 1982. Paralegal Howard, Rice, Nemerovski, Canady, Robertson & Falk, San Francisco, 1983-86, Wilson, Sonsini, Goodrich & Rosati, Palo Alto, Calif., 1986-87; healthcare mktg., 1987-90, mktg. and FDA regulatory cons. to biosci. cos., 1990-91; mktg. and ops. exec. Parenteral Alimentation Providers Assn., Emeryville, Calif., 1991—. Editor profl. newsletter P.A.P.A. Pen, 1991—; contbr. articles to profl. jours. Mem. Kosciuszko Found., 1978—, Jr. LEague, 1986—; mem. Young Reps., 1988—; bd. dirs., profl. mem. coun. Fine Arts Mus. of San Francisco, 1991-93. Mem. Spinsters of San Francisco. Republican. Roman Catholic.

ZANETTA, MARY TERESA, state agency administrator, analyst, firearms dealer; b. Sacramento, July 15, 1951; d. Fernando and Patricia Ellen (Coughlin) Z.; 1 child, Noah Antonio. Cert. firearms dealer, basic firearms safety instr. Support State of Calif., Sacramento, 1971-74, investigator, 1974-90; prin. firearms dealer Folsom, Calif., 1988—; planning commr. City of Folsom, State of Calif., 1990-92; analyst State of Calif., Rancho Cordova, Calif., 1990—. Charter com. mem. City of Folsom, Calif., 1990, city coun. candidate, 1992. Mem. NRA. Republican. Roman Catholic. Office: State Calif 3215 Prospect Park Dr Rancho Cordova CA 95670

ZANGER, VIRGINIA VOGEL, bilingual educator; b. N.Y.C., Sept. 27, 1948; d. John H. and Helen (Wolff) Vogel; m. Mark Zanger, Dec. 5, 1976; children: Benjamin, Nina. BA, Harvard Coll., 1972; Masters, Antioch Coll., 1974; EdD, Boston U., 1987. Cert. bilingual tchr., Mass. Bilingual tchr. Boston Pub. Schs., 1972-81; ednl. cons. Cross-Cultural Strategies, Jamaica Plain, Mass., 1981—; ednl. rschr. MIT Project Lighthouse, Cambridge, Mass., 1988; instr. Boston U., 1987-91; dir. sci. program Hurley Sch., Boston, 1992—; mem. commn. Mass. Bilingual Study Com., 1994. Author (chpt.), editor: Literacy Across Languages and Cultures, 1994; author: (textbook) Face to Face, 1985; prodr. (video) How We Feel: Hispanic Students, 1991, Quality Bilingual Edn., 1992. Co-founder Jamaica Plain Com. on Ctrl. Am., 1981; bd. dirs. Oficina Hispana, Jamaica Plain, 1982-85. Recipient Ansin Intercultural award Bostn U. Sch. Edn., 1985, Award for Excellence Boston Plan for Excellence in Pub. Schs., 1994; Title VII fellow Boston U., 1984-87. Mem. Mass. Assn. for Bilingual Edn. (pres., v.p. 1989-94), Mass. Coalition for Bilingual Edn. (co-founder 1992). Jewish. Home: 10 Myrtle St Jamaica Plain MA 02130

ZARA-KOBYLT, DEBORAH, television news reporter; b. Summit, N.J., Dec. 22, 1965; d. Anthony John and Edith Ida (DeBenedictis) Zara; m. John Chester Kobylt, June 14, 1992. BA in English Lit. and Comm., Rutgers U., 1986. News writer Sta. WWOR-TV, N.Y.C., 1986-87, CBS Network News, N.Y.C., 1986-87; anchor/reporter Sta. WMGM-TV, Atlantic City, 1987-88; reporter Sta. WNET/NJN-TV, N.Y.C., Atlantic City, 1988-92; news and entertainment reporter CNN and Fox TV, L.A., 1993—; media image cons., Beverly Hills, Calif., 1993—. Nominated 2 Emmy awards N.Y. Press Club, 1990, 92. Mem. Screen Actors Guild, Writers Guild, Hollywood Arts Coun. Office: CNN 6430 Sunset Blvd Los Angeles CA 90210

ZARALEYA-HARARI, SARAH, psychologist, psychotherapist; b. Bklyn., Dec. 30, 1926; d. Phillip and Goldie (Simon) Kurzweil; m. Lawrence H. Strear, Aug. 24, 1947 (div. Sept. 1969); children: Peter M., Marcy Jana De Luca, K. Jody Cucolo; m. Carmi Harari, Dec. 31, 1979; stepchildren: Karen Tarnofsky, Michelle Chino. BA, Bklyn. Coll., 1948; MS, CUNY, 1961; EdD, Yeshiva U., 1969. Lic. psychologist, sch. psychologist; nat. cert. sch. psychologist. Psychologist Wyandanch (N.Y.) Pub. Schs., 1961-63, Uniondale (N.Y.) Pub. Schs., 1963-69; pvt. practice N.Y.C., 1969—; asst. prof. CUNY, 1970-75; mem. field faculty grad. program Goddard Coll., N.Y.C., 1977-78; cons. psychologist Greek-Woodycrest Children's Svcs., Pomona, N.Y., 1980-82; psychologist East Ramapo Cen. Sch. Dist., Spring Valley, N.Y., 1982-91; lectr. Nassau C.C., Garden City, N.Y., 1967-69, Coll. of New Rochelle, N.Y., 1977-78, Rockland C.C., Suffern, N.Y., 1977-80; lectr. spkr.'s bur. Rockland County Mental Health Assn., Pomona, 1977—; cons. drug rehab. Topic House, L.I., N.Y., 1965-69; clin. dir. homosexual walk-in ctr. Identity House, N.Y.C., 1972-76; bd. dirs. women's issues divsn. Humanistic Psychology Ctr., N.Y.C.; pres. Women Unltd.; med. staff Nyack (N.Y.) Hosp., 1974—. Contbr. articles to profl. jours., chpts. to books; creator Zaraleya psychoenergetic technique, 1972, Zaraleya Semester Based Self-Actualization Psychotherapy. Editor yearbook Bklyn. Coll., 1946-47; parent seminar leader New City (N.Y.) Libr., spring 1981; conf. presenter E. Ramapo Cen. Sch. Dist., 1982, 84, 87; newsletter editor Rocklan Ctr. for the Arts, W. Nyack, N.Y., 1986-88. Recipient Gold Key award Bklyn. Coll., 1947. Mem. APA (exec. bd. divsn. humanistic psychology, newsletter editor 1977-79, svc. award 1977), Nat. Assn. Sch. Psychologists, N.Y. Soc. Clin. Psychologists, Rockland County Psychol. Soc. (chmn. clin. com., svc. award 1981, 82), Nassau and Suffolk Psychol. Assn., Nat. Register Health Svc. Providers in Psychology, Internat. Coun. Psychologists, Inc., Internat. Assn. Applied Psychology, Internat. Assn. Cross-Cultural Psychology. Home and Office: 10 Wyndham Ln New City NY 10956-4527

ZARKY, KAREN JANE, newspaper editor; b. St. Louis, Jan. 20, 1948; d. Herbert Lee Lawrence and Alice Ruth (Harrison) Lawrence Robison; m. Robert Gerald McCoy, Feb. 15, 1964 (div. Feb. 1982); 1 child, Karen; m. A.A. Zarky, Aug. 29, 1986. BA, Maryville Coll., St. Louis, 1988. Asst. to dir. fin. Clayton Mark Corp., Chgo., 1966-68; office mgr. A.R. Musical Enterprises, Columbus, Ind., 1969-75; owner, pres. Antique Galleries Inc., Louisville, 1975-81; sales mgr. Rainbow Graphics and Displays, St. Louis, 1981-87; editor, pres. Senior Circuit, Inc., St. Louis, 1987—; tchr. St. Louis Community Coll., 1987-89. Bd. dirs. Greeley Community Ctr., St. Louis, 1988—; mem. reorgn. com. United Way, St. Louis, 1988—; sec. Housing Options Provided for the Elderly, 1991—; v.p. mktg. and comm. Women's Consortium, 1993. Mem. Nat. Assn. Women Bus. Owners, Women in Comm., Internat. Assn. Bus. Communicators, Mo. Press Women (pres. Gateway chpt. 1993—), Mid-Am. Mature Pubs. Assn. (sec.-treas.).

ZARRETT, MARY ANN, nursing educator; b. Big Clifty, Ky., July 8, 1949; d. Julius Forest and Gladys Mae (Hawkins) Duvall; m. Robert Warren Zarrett, Dec. 27, 1969 (div. Aug. 1983); children: Rob Warren, Elizabeth Duvall. BSN, U. Ky., 1971; MS in Counseling, Ctrl. Mo. State U., 1977. RN, N.D.; nat. cert. counselor. Rsch., cataloging and circulation asst. U. Ky. Med. Ctr. Library, Lexington, 1969-71; nurse aide Taylor Manor Nursing Home, Versailles, Ky., 1970; self-employed Burlington, Vt., 1971-74; per diem nurse psychiat. ward St. Luke's Hosp., Fargo, N.D., 1988-92; counselor, instr. Moorhead State U., Fargo, 1985-89, asst. prof., 1990—, dir. tng. Counseling Ctr., 1987-90, outreach coord., 1989-90, affirmative action officer, 1992; cons. Minn. Army N.G. through Met. State U., 1987; cons. Pathways/U.S. West, 1990—; orgnl. cons., 1990—. Adv. bd. mem. Compassionate Friends Fargo, N.D., 1986—; chmn. music Plymouth Congregational Ch., Fargo, 1986-88; chmn. Fargo Clinic Art Gallery, 1982-84. Mem. ACA, Minn. Assn. Specialists in Group Work, Am. Mental Health Counselors Assn., Nat. Orgnl. Devel. Network, Phi Kappa Phi. Republican. Congregationalist. Office: Moorhead State U Counseling Ctr Moorhead MN 56560

ZATZ, ARLINE, writer, photographer; b. Bklyn., May 2, 1937; d. Joseph and Belle Baer; m. Joel Leon Zatz, Nov. 4, 1956; children: Robert Jay, David Alan. BA in Journalism, Rutgers U., 1977. Consumer affairs officer Borough of Highland Park, N.J., 1970-72; asst. coord. N.J. Div. Consumer Affairs, Newark, 1972-75; writer, photographer A-Z Publs., Metuchen, N.J., 1977—. Author: 25 Bicycle Tours in New Jersey, 1988, New Jersey's Special Places, rev. edition 1994 (Best Book N.J. Press Women, Nat. Assn. Press Women), Best Hikes with children in New Jersey, 1992; contbr. articles to profl. jours. Bd. dirs. YMCA, Metuchen, 1984-86. Mem. Nat. Assn. Press Women, N.J. Press Women, Outdoor Writers Assn. Am., Author's Guild Am. Home: 77 Woodside Ave Metuchen NJ 08840-1629 Office: A-Z Publs 77 Woodside Ave Metuchen NJ 08840-1629

ZATZ, JANET SHARE, lawyer; b. Passaic, N.J., Oct. 9, 1954; d. Stanley and Adele (Weinstock) Share; m. Irving J. Zatz, Aug. 15, 1976; children: Jonathan Share, Eric Daniel. BA cum laude, Cornell U., 1976; JD, Rutgers U., 1979. Bar: N.J. 1979; cert. pub. mgr. State of N.J., 1985. Law sec. to hon. Leon S. Milmed N.J. Superior Ct., Appellate Divsn., Newark, 1979-80; dep. atty. gen. N.J. Divsn. Law, Dept. Law and Pub. Safety, Trenton, N.J., 1981-83; dep. dir. N.J. Dept. Pers., Trenton, 1983-92, dir. appellate practices and labor rels., 1992—. Editor-in-chief: (govt. periodical) Merit System Reporter, 1988—. Fellow Cert. Pub. Mgrs. Soc.; mem. N.J. Bar Assn. Home: 8 Huntington Dr Princeton Junction NJ 08550-2122 Office: NJ Dept Personnel Cn # 312 Trenton NJ 08625

ZAVACKY, LYNETTE MICHELE, women's health nurse; b. Wheeling, W.Va., Feb. 2, 1966; d. Sam J. and Linda L. (Cheroka) Z. ADN, Belmont Tech. Coll., 1986; BSN, Ohio U., 1989; MSN, W.Va. U., 1990. RN, Ohio; cert. child birth tchr., inpatient obstetric nurse. Staff nurse obstetrics Bellaire (Ohio) City Hosp.; part-time clin. instr. W.Va. No. Community Coll., Wheeling. Home: 67561 Elizabeth St Saint Clairsville OH 43950-9127

ZAWADA, SANDRA M., protective service official; b. Hartford, Conn., Aug. 12, 1961; d. Chester and Helen (Kywan) Z.; 1 child, Christopher. AS, Post Coll., 1981. Correctional officer Bridgeport Correctional Inst., Dept. Corrections, State of Conn., Bridgeport, 1986-89, Gates Correctional Inst., Dept. Corrections, State of Conn., Niantic, 1989-92; correctional lt. Garner Correctional Inst., Dept. Corrections, State of Conn., Newtown, 1992-94, correctional capt., 1994—. Office: Garner Correctional Inst 50 Nunnawauk Rd Newtown CT 06470

ZAYATZ, LAURA VOSHELL, mathematical statistician; b. Milford, Del., Jan. 28, 1965; d. Robert John and Joyce Lorraine (Argo) Voshell; m. Tim Alexander Zayatz, Mar. 23, 1991; children: Nicholas Aaron. BS in Math., U. Del., 1987; MS in Stats., Va. Tech., 1988. Math. statistician U.S. Bur. of Census, Washington, 1989—. Contbr. articles to profl. jours. Active Christ United Meth. Ch., Columbia, Md., 1992—. Mem. Am. Stats. Assn. (mem. com. on privacy and confidentiality 1994—, subcom. on disclosure methodology of Fed. Com. on Statis. Methodology 1992—), Phi Beta Kappa. Democrat. Home: 7224 Lasting Light Way Columbia MD 21045 Office: Commerce/Census ESMPD/3108-4 Washington DC 20233

ZAYDON, JEMILLE ANN, English language and communications educator, school system administrator; b. Peckville, Pa., Feb. 21, 1940; d. Joseph and Catherine Ann (Hazzouri) Z.; student Barry Coll. for Women, 1957-59; B.S., Marywood Coll., 1963; M.S. in Edn., Wilkes Coll., 1978; doctoral candidate Temple U. Tchr. St. Hugh Elementary Sch., Coconut Grove, Fla., 1963-64; Allapattah Elementary Sch., Miami, 1964-65, Columbus Elementary Sch., Westfield, N.J., 1965-66; communications instr. Keystone Job Corps, Drums, Pa., 1966-73; vol. instr. Keystone Rehab. Ctr., Scranton, Pa., 1970-71; curriculum cons. for mentally retarded, Vienna, Austria, 1974; prof. English and reading Lackawanna Jr. Coll., Scranton, 1974—, head dept. English, speech and reading, 1976—, chmn. dept. arts, humanities and social studies, 1977—; adj. prof. English, U. Scranton, 1980—; communications instr. Lackawanna County Vocat. Tech. Sch., 1974—. Supr. recreation program, Hazleton, Pa., summer 1968; founder, adviser Keystone Kourier, 1967-69. Sec. Fedn. Youth, William W. Scranton, 1963; coord. annual Christmas for Mentally Retarded Keystone City Residence, Scranton, 1975—; supr. students Heart Fund campaign, 1968-71; developer program mentally retarded Allied Svcs. for Handicapped Scranton, 1973; Class rep. Marywood Coll. Fund Dr., 1978; gen., 1980—; faculty coord. Am. Cancer Soc., 1990—; active ARC, March of Dimes, Heart Fund, Leukemia and United Fund drives, also Sickle Cell Anemia Found. Bd. dirs. Michael F. Harrity Meml. Fund., 1969-73; mem. exec. bd. Northeastern Pa. Environ. Council, also co-chmn. public edn. and funding. Recipient Faculty Mem. of Yr. award, Job Corps, 1969, Humanitarian award, 1980, Outstanding Educators award, 1992, Educators award Dade County, 1973, 75; named Tchr. of Yr., 1973, Tchr. We Will Never Forget, Dade County Allpattah Elem. Students, 1991, Northeast Woman by Scranton Sunday Times, 1993; Service scholar, Barry Coll., 1958. Mem. Nat. Edn. Assn., Pa. State Edn. Assn., Beta Lambda Tau, Sigma Tau Delta, Theta Chi Beta (charter pres. 1961-63), Lambda Iota Tau (life). Democrat. Roman Catholic (instr. Confraternity Christian Doctrine 1956-71). Editor Lebanese Am. Jour., 1957-63. Home: 608 N Main Ave Scranton PA 18504-1870

ZBIEGIEN, ANDREA, educator, consultant; b. Berea, Ohio, May 12, 1944; d. Leopold and Anna Meri (Voskovich) Z. BS in Edn., St. John Coll., 1969; MS in Edn., John Carroll U., 1973; MDiv, Grad. Theol. Union, 1986, D of Ministry, 1988. Tchr. jr. high sch. Diocese of Cleve. Elem. Schs., 1964-76; instr. Dept. Religious Edn. Diocese of Cleve., 1971-82; dir. religious edn. Diocese of Cleve., 1976-82; instr. Dept. Christian Formation Diocese of Savannah, Ga., 1987—; dir. religious edn. Diocese of Savannah, 1987—; substitute tchr. pub. schs., Cleve., Brunswick, Ga., 1976—; cons. Benziger Pub. Co., Ohio, 1971-78, Our Sunday Visitor Pubs., 1978-90, Silver, Burdett & Ginn, Savannah, Charleston, St. Augustine, 1988—; adj. prof. (summers) St. John U., Grad. Theol. Sem., 1978—. Author: RCIA: Parish Team Formation, 1987; producer, author: (videos) RCIA: Parish Team Formation, 1987; contbr. articles to profl. jours. Facilitator Bishop's Task Force Action for a Change, Cleve., 1969-72; advocate, facilitator Systematic Techniques of Effective Parenting, Huron County, Ohio, 1982-87; advocate Commn. on Children and Youth, Glynn County, Ga., 1989—. Recipient scholarship KC, Cleve., 1961-69. Mem. AAUW, ASCD, YWCA, Nat. Cath. Edn. Assn., Sisters for Christian Community, Ind. Order of Foresters, Golden Isles Fiberarts Guild. Home: 707A Newcastle St Brunswick GA 31520-8012 Office: SFX Christian Fomation Ctr 510 Howe St Brunswick GA 31520-7527

ZDANOWITZ, PAULINE MAY, counselor, educator; b. Van Dyke, Mich., Oct. 2, 1933; d. Caryl Walter and Margaret Fredricka (Rose) Kroneck; m. Lawrence Stanley Zdanowitz, Oct. 28, 1961; children: Christopher, Maria, David. BS, Ea. Mich. U., 1955, MA, 1961; cert. guidance and counseling, U. Mich., 1974, cert. specialist in aging, 1982. Cert. tchr. secondary edn.; lic. profl. counselor; cert. guidance counselor. Coord. sr. citizens, instr. N.W. Sch. Dist., Jackson, Mich., 1984—; program developer peer support program Jackson County Dept. on Aging, 1987-93; evening counselor Western schs. adult community edn. program Western Sch. Dist., Parma, Mich., 1985-87; instr. Jackson Recreation Dept., 1993—; workshop facilitator, instr., program developer, Jackson, 1982—; leader tng. session Respite Program of Jackson, 1989—. Author tng. manuals for peer support programs. Pres., v.p. Women of Evang. Luth. Ch. of Am., 1964—. Recipient Recognition award for disting. individual in field of counseling and devel. Nat. Disting. Svc. Registry, 1989-90; peer support grantee Region II Area Agy. on Aging, 1987, mini-grantee Ea. Mich. U. Alumni Assn., 1988. Mem. AAUW (bd. dirs. 1964—), ACA, Generations United of Mich., Mich. Counseling Assn., Mich. Soc. Gerontology, Mich. Assn. of Activity Profls., Jackson County Counseling Assn. Home: 3024 John Glenn Dr Jackson MI 49201

ZEANAH, ELOIS, mayor. Grad., Shelton State Bus. Coll. Mayor City of Thousand Oaks, Calif.; office head White House Office of Consumer Affairs; staff asst. to chmn. U.S. Consumer Product Safety Commn.; adminstrv. asst. U.S. Dept. of Commerce; office mgr. The Clorox Co.; former small bus. owner. Commr. Santa Monica Mountains Nat. Recreation Area; bd. mem. Santa Monica Mountains Conservancy, com. environ. quality League Calif. Cities; mem. Gen. Plan Rev. Com., open space com.; bd. dirs. Save Open Space; mem. Westlake Joint Bd.; pres. Conejo Hills/Lynn Estates HOA; founder/pres. Conejo League of Homeowners. Home: 1988 Oberlin Ave Thousand Oaks CA 91360 Office: 2150 W Hillcrest Dr Thousand Oaks CA 91320

ZEEMAN, JOAN JAVITS, writer, inventor; b. N.Y.C., Aug. 17, 1928; d. Benjamin Abraham and Lily (Braxton) Javits; m. John Huibert Zeeman III, Mar. 20, 1954; children: Jonathan Huibert, Andrea Zeeman Deane, Eloise Zeeman Scharff, Phoebe Zeemon Fitch, Merrily Margaret. BA, Vassar Coll., 1949; MEd, U. Vt., 1976. Pub. relations exec. Benjamin Sonnenberg, N.Y.C., 1949-51; freelance writer, 1952—. Trustee Theatreworks (formerly Performing Arts Repertory Theatre), N.Y.C., 1953-83, Profl. Childrens Sch., N.Y.C., 1980-89, Palmer Beach Sch. Arts Found., 1993—, Fla. Theatrical Assn., 1994—. Author: The Compleat Child, 1964. Lyricist musical plays: Young Abe Lincoln, 1961; Hotel Passionato, 1965; Author, lyricist: Young Columbus, 1992; song lyricist: Santa Baby, 1953. Patentee Alphocube. Mem. ASCAP, Dramatists Guild, Gilbert and Sullivan Soc., Vassar Club (sec. 1978-84, v.p. 1984-86) (Westchester, N.Y.). Home: 230 Palmo Way Palm Beach FL 33480-3135

ZEFF, OPHELIA HOPE, lawyer; b. Oak Park, Ill., Aug. 19, 1934; d. Bernard Allen and Esther (Levinsohn) Gurvis; m. David Zeff, Dec. 29, 1957 (div. 1983); children: Sally Lyn Zeff Propper, Betsy Zeff Russell, Ellen, Adam; m. John Canterbury Davis, Sept. 18, 1987. BA, Calif. State U., 1956; JD, U. Pacific, 1975. Bar: Calif. 1975. Reporter Placerville (Calif.) Mountain Dem., 1956-57, Salinas Californian, 1957-59; corr. Modesto (Calif.) Bee, 1962-64; atty. ALRB, Sacramento, 1975-76, Yolo County Counsel, Woodland, Calif., 1976-78, Law Office of O.H. Zeff, Woodland, 1978-85; employee rels. officer Yolo County, 1985-87; ptnr. Littler, Mendelson, Fastiff, Tichy & Mathiason, Sacramento, 1987—. Mem. Vallejo (Calif.) Sch. Bd., 1971-74, pres., 1974; mem. Woodland Libr. Bd., 1982; v.p. LWV, Vallejo, 1972; mem. LWV, Sacramento, 1987—. Recipient Am. Jurisprudence Lawyer Coop. Pub., 1974. Mem. Sacramento County Bar, Sacramento Women Lawyers, Indsl. Rels. Assn. No. Calif., Traynor Soc. (life). Democrat. Jewish. Office: Littler Mendelson Fastiff Tichy & Mathiason 16th Fl 400 Capitol Mall Sacramento CA 95814

ZEGIOB-DEVEREAUX, LESLIE ELAINE, clinical psychologist; b. Cleve., Oct. 17, 1948; d. Charles G. and Elinore Lois (Jones) Zegiob; m. James Michael Devereaux, July 11, 1981. Student Allegheny Coll., 1966-68; BA, Am. U., 1971; MS, U. Ga., 1974, PhD, 1976. Lic. psychologist, Ariz., Ind. Asst. prof. dept. psychology Ariz. State U., Tempe, 1976-78, dir. psychology clinic, 1977-78; dir. childrens svcs. Dogwood Village, Memphis, 1978; adj. prof. dept. psychology Notre Dame (Ind.) U., 1979-80; clin. psychologist dept. psychology and psychiatry The Med. Group, Michigan City, Ind., 1978—; cons. child protective svcs. LaPorte County Dept. Pub. Welfare, Headstart program, 1979-84, Michigan City schs., 1979-84; mem. adv. bd. Headstart, 1979-84. Contbr. articles to profl. jours. Ariz. State U. faculty grantee, 1978. Mem. APA, Assn. for Advancement Behavior Therapy, Sierra Club, Phi Kappa Phi, Phi Beta Kappa. Democrat. Office: 1225 E Coolspring Ave Michigan City IN 46360-6300

ZEHAGEN, BONNIE LEE, municipal government official; b. Ogdensburg, N.Y., May 30, 1947; d. James Rodger and Violet (Robinson) Cuthbert; m. Clayton Edward ZeHagen, June 23, 1974 (div.); 1 child, Bonnie-Marie. AA, St. Petersburg Jr. Coll., 1967. Cert. mcpl. clk. Sec. bldg. and pub. works City of Treasure Island, Fla., 1967-73, bd. coord., 1974-78, dep. city clk., 1978—. Mem. Sunset Beach Civic Assn., Treasure Island, 1967-89. Mem. Internat. Inst. Mcpl. Clks., Fla. Assn. City Clks., Treasure Island Hist. Soc. Inc. (pres. 1989-91), Pinellas County Clks. Assn. Republican. Mem. United Ch. of Christ. Office: City of Treasure Island 120 108th Ave Saint Petersburg FL 33706-4702

ZEHNER, CAROL RUTH, insurance agent; b. Paterson, N.J., Jan. 30, 1942; d. Andrew Everett and Ruth Elizabeth (Van Euwen) Van Antwerp; m. Donald Paul Zehner, Oct. 24, 1964 (div. Apr. 1991); 1 child, Jill Zehner Davis. BA, Drew U., 1963. Customer svc. rep. Donald P. Zehner Agy., Caldwell, N.J., 1983-90; mktg. rep. Schlott Ins., Clifton, N.J., 1990-91; account exec. Weichert Ins., Morris Plains, N.J., 1991—. Mem. Paper Mill Playhouse Guild, Millburn, N.J., 1989—, Adventure on a Shoestring. Mem. Nat. Assn. Ins. Women. Office: Weichert Ins Agy 1625 Rt 10 Morris Plains NJ 07950

ZEHNTER, RITA, health educator; b. N.Y.C., Oct. 27, 1934; d. Peter Joseph and Sarah Cecelia (McLaughlin) Murphy; m. Eric C. Zehnter, Sept. 6, 1958; children: Mary, Eric M., Karen, Kristin, Brian. BS in Health Care Mgmt., St. Francis Coll., Blkyn., 1981; MPA, L.I. U., 1985. RN, N.Y.; cert. sch. nurse tchr. Staff nurse Meml. Sloan-Kettering Hosp., N.Y.C., 1955-57, Met. Hosp., N.Y.C., 1957-58; asst. dir. edn. and svc. speakers bur. Am. Cancer Soc., Queens, N.Y., 1958-79; sch. nurse tchr. Syosset (N.Y.) Sch. Dist., 1980-86, Nassau Bd. Coop. Ednl. Svcs., 1980-86; adj. asst. prof. St. John's U., Jamaica, N.Y., 1986—. Home: 26 Evelyn Ln Syosset NY 11791-5805 Office: St John's U 8000 Utopia Pky Jamaica NY 11439

ZEHRING, KAREN, information executive; b. Washington, Dec. 5, 1945; d. Robert William Zehring and Gretchen (Lorenz) Proos; m. George Lang, 1970 (div. 1979); m. Peter Frank Davis, June 10, 1979; children: Jesse, Antonia. BA, U. Denver, 1967; postgrad., Yale U., 1967-68. Assoc. pub. mktg. and sales Instl. Investor Systems, Inc., N.Y.C., 1968-74; co-owner, co-creator Café des Artistes Restaurant, N.Y.C., 1975-79; owner, pub. The Corp. Fin. Letter, N.Y.C., 1976-78; group dir. planning and devel. Bus. Week mag., N.Y.C., 1977-78; owner, pub., exec. editor Corp. Fin. Sourcebook The Corp. Fin. Bluebook, N.Y.C., 1979-84; chmn., pres., pub., editor-in-chief Corp. Fin. mag., N.Y.C., 1986-90; cons. Karen Zehring & Assocs., Castine, Maine, 1990—. Mem. The Women's Forum, Am. Soc. Mag. Editors. Unitarian. Office: PO Box 600 Castine ME 04421-0600

ZEIBER, LINDA MARIE, English language educator, writer; b. Lancaster, Pa., July 30, 1948; d. William Joseph and Clara Louise (Allen) Covert; m. Gerald Owen Zeiber, Apr. 3, 1982. BA, Susquehanna U., 1970; edn. cert., Kutztown U., 1971. Tchr. English Reading (Pa.) Sch. Dist., 1972—; contbg. writer The County Mag., Reading, 1978; lectr. Albright Coll., Reading, 1988; freelance writer. Mem. Pa. Coun. Tchrs. English, Green Valley Country Club (Women's Aux.). Republican. Lutheran. Home: 739 Brownsville Rd Reading PA 19608-9799 Office: Reading Sch Dist 8th & Washington Sts Reading PA 19601

ZEIBERG, MONA CAROL, lawyer; b. Bronx, N.Y., May 23, 1961; d. Seymour Lawrence and Marilyn Sonia (Wolfson) Z. BA, Am. U., 1983; JD, Emory U., 1986. Bar: Ga. 1986, D.C. 1991. Law clk. Office Adminstrv. Law Judges, U.S. Dept. Labor, 1986-88; sr. labor counsel Litigation Ctr., U.S. C. of C., Washington, 1988—. Mem. Fed. Bar Assn., Am. Corp. Counsel Assn. Office: US C of C 1615 H St NW Washington DC 20062-0002

ZEID, PAULA KLEIN, metals broker; b. Chgo., Oct. 16, 1941; d. Arthur A. and Rosalyn (Davidson) Schwartz; student Mich. State U., 1959-60; B.A., Governors State U., 1974, M.A., 1975; m. Sanford David Klein, Dec. 18, 1960 (div. 1981); children—Gregory Scott, Julie Ann. Mem. editorial staff Okinawa Morning Star, Machinato, 1960-63; exec. dir. Bloom Twp. Com. on Youth, Chicago Heights, Ill., 1975-81; dir. fund devel. and pub. relations South Chgo. Community Hosp., 1981-84; v.p. South Chgo. Health Care Found., 1982-84; dir. devel. and pub. relations Chgo. Crime Commn., 1985-88; broker Universal Metals, Chgo., 1988—. Mem. Calumet Area Indsl. Commn. Mem. Nat. Soc. Fund Raising Profls., Nat. Assn. Prevention Profls., So. Suburban Youth Service Alliance, Criminal Def. Consortium, Nat. Assn. Hosp. Devel., Twp. Ofcls. Ill., Youth Network Council, Sierra Club. Jewish. Home: 1908 N Dayton St Chicago IL 60614-5029 Office: Universal Scrap Metals 2201 W Fulton St Chicago IL 60612-2205

ZEIGLER, JUDY ROSE, leadership, marketing and business consultant; b. Monte Vista, Colo., Aug. 26, 1946; d. Orville Edgar Zeigler and Kathryn Genevieve (Parsons) Duncan. BA, U. Oreg., 1968. Asst. v.p., mgr. staff planning and devel. Rainier Nat. Bank, Seattle, 1979-81, asst. v.p., mgr. staff devel., 1981-83; v.p., mgr. staff planning Blue Cross of Washington and Alaska, Seattle, 1983-85, mgr. market research, 1985-86; pres. Strategies Unltd., Seattle, 1986—; workshop presenter Gov.'s Conf. Women on the Move, Seattle, 1984, Women Plus Bus Conf., Seattle, 1984, 85, 86, 88, 89; pres. Natalie Skeels Meml. Found. Trustees, Seattle, 1987-90. Vice chair Blue Ribbon Citizens Task Force of King County Assessor's Office, Seattle, 1984; chair mktg. com. Bellevue Community Coll. Telecommunications Ctr. Task Force, Seattle, 1985-87; mem. Women's Polit. Caucus, Seattle, 1987-88, co-chair fundraising com. Mem. ASTD (pres. Puget Sound chpt. 1984-85), Women's Profl. and Managerial Network (pres. 1987-88), N.W. Women's Law Ctr. (bd. dirs. 1988-90, pres. Leadership Synthesis 1991-92, mem. adv. coun. 1988—), Internat. Women's Conf. (exec. bd. officer 1991—). Democrat. Home: 1523 11th Ave W Seattle WA 98119-3204 Office: Strategies Unltd 1218 3rd Ave Ste 1500 Seattle WA 98101-3021

ZEIGLER, VICKI LYNN, pediatrics nurse; b. Hampton, S.C., May 26, 1961; d. Richard Jackson and Miriam Banner (Smith) Z.; m. Paul Crawford Gillette, Feb. 1, 1992. BSN, Med. U. of S.C., 1982, MSN, 1991. RN, S.C.; cert. spl. competency in cardiac pacing for non-physicians N.Am. Soc. Pacing and Electrophysiology. Staff nurse pediatrics Med. U. S.C., Charleston, 1983-85, nurse clinician pediatric cardiology, 1985-91, pediatric arrhythmia/pacemaker case mgr., 1992-94, pediatric arrhythmia nurse specialist, 1994—; BLS instr. Am. Heart Assn., Columbia, S.C. Contbr. articles to profl. jours. Recipient Young Investigator award Sigma Theta Tau. Mem. AACN, Assn. for Care of Children's Health, North Am. Soc. of Pacing and Electrophysiology, Am. Heart Assn. Coun. of Cardiovascular Nursing, Sigma Theta Tau. Republican. Office: Med Univ of SC 612 CH 171 Ashley Ave Charleston SC 29425-0001

ZEILIG, NANCY MEEKS, magazine editor; b. Nashville, Apr. 28, 1943; d. Edward Harvey and Nancy Evelyn (Self) Meeks; m. Lanny Kenneth Fielder, Aug. 20, 1964 (div. Dec. 1970); m. Charles Elliot Zeilig, Jan. 6, 1974 (div. Dec. 1989); 1 child, Sasha Rebecca. BA, Birmingham-So. Coll., 1964; postgrad., Vanderbilt U., 1971-73. Editorial asst. Reuben H. Donnelley, N.Y.C., 1969-70; asst. editor Vanderbilt U., Nashville, 1970-74; editor U. Minn., St. Paul, 1975; asst. editor McGraw-Hill Inc., Mpls., 1975-76; mng. editor Denver mag., 1976-80; editor Jour. Am. Water Works Assn., Denver, 1981—; Editor, co-pub.: WomanSource, 1982, rev. edit., 1994; contbr. articles to consumer mags. Editor, co-pub.: WomanSource, 1982, rev. edit. 1984; editor: 100 Years, 1975; contbr. articles to consumer mags. Office: Jour Am Water Works Assn 6666 W Quincy Ave Denver CO 80235-3098

ZEILINGER, ELNA RAE, educator; b. Tempe, Ariz., Mar. 24, 1937; d. Clayborn Eddie and Ruby Elna (Laird) Simpson; m. Philip Thomas Zeilinger, June 13, 1970; children: Shari, Chris. BA in Edn., Ariz. State U., 1958, MA in Edn., 1966, EdS, 1980. Bookkeeper First Nat. Bank of Tempe, 1955-56; with registrar's office Ariz. State U., 1956-58; piano tchr., recreation dir. City of Tempe; tchr. Thew Sch., Tempe, 1958-61; elem. tchr. Mitchell Sch., Tempe, 1962-74, intern prin., 1976, personnel intern, 1977; specialist gifted edn. Tempe Elem. Schs., Tempe, 1977-86; elem. tchr. Holdeman Sch., Tempe, 1986-89; tchr. Zeilinger Tutoring Svc., 1991—; grad. asst. ednl. adminstrn., Iota Workshop coordinator Ariz. State U., 1978; presenter Ariz. Gifted Conf., 1978-81; condr. survey of gifted programs, 1980; reporter public relations Tempe Sch. Dist., 1978-80, Access com. for gifted programs, 1981-83. Author: Leadership Role of the Principal in Gifted Programs: A Handbook, 1980; Classified Personnel Handbook, 1977, also reports, monographs and paintings. Mem. Tempe Hist. Assn., liaison, 1975, Tempe Art League; Freedom Train com. Ariz. Bicentennial Commn., 1975-76. Named Outstanding Leader in Elem. and Secondary Schs., 1976' Ariz. Cattle Growers scholar, 1954-55; Elks scholar, 1954-55; recipient Judges award Tempe Art League, 1970, Best of Show, Scottsdale Art League, 1976. Mem. Coun. Exceptional Children, Ariz. Assn. Gifted and Talented, Ariz. Sch. Adminstrs., Scottsdale Artists League, Am. Bus. Women's Assn. (Woman of Yr. 1983), Order Ea. Star, Daus. of the Nile (Supreme Session vice chair of registration 1994), Phi Kappa Phi, Pi Lambda Theta, Kappa Delta Pi, Phi Delta Kappa, Kappa Delta. Democrat. Congregationalist.

ZEIT, RUTH MAE, foundation administrator; b. N.Y.C., May 13, 1945; d. Albert Joseph and Gertrude (Goldberg) Janover; children: Rachael Miriam, Rebecca Madeleine. BA, U. Pa., 1967, postgrad., 1969-70; postgrad., Temple U., 1967-69. Teaching fellow Temple U., Phila., 1967-69, U. Pa., Phila., 1969-70; dir. piano music studio Phila., 1969—; pres. Lupus Found. Del. Valley, Ardmore, Pa., 1983—; Mem. Winner's Ball com. Lupus Found. of Del. Valley, Ardmore, 1986-87, presiding officer, bd. dirs., med. adv. bd., 1983—, prin. organizer Ednl. Symposia, 1983—, prin. organizer patient support groups, 1983—; lectr. Prin. coordinator Lupus Found. of Del. Valley Newsletter, 1983—. Liaison with Phila. Mayor Ed Nendell, liaison between Julius Erving and Children's Hosp. of Phila.; coord. Julius Erving Lupus Rsch. Fund; target chmn. Undergrad. Admissions Secondary Sch. Com., U. Pa. Mem. Am. Coll. of Musicians, Sigma Delta Gamma, Music Tchrs. Nat. Assn., Pa. Music Tchrs. Assn. Democrat. Jewish. Home: 1610 Gerson Dr Narberth PA 19072-1232 Office: Lupus Found Delaware Valley 44 W Lancaster Ave Ardmore PA 19003-1339

ZEITLAN, MARILYN LABB, lawyer; b. N.Y.C., Sept. 17, 1938; d. Charles and Florence (Geller) Labb; m. Barrett M. Zeitlan, Apr. 14, 1957; children: Adam Scott, Daniel Craig. BA, Queens Coll., 1958, MS, 1970; JD, Hofstra U., 1978. Bar: N.Y. 1979. Tchr. N.Y.C., 1958-61; pvt. practice matrimonial law, Roslyn, N.Y., 1983—. Assoc. editor: Law Rev., Hofstra U., 1977-78; contbr. articles to profl. jours. Commr. East Hills Environ. Commn., 1971-75; co-founder Roslyn Environ. Assn., 1970; v.p. Roslyn LWV, 1974-75. Hofstra Law Sch. fellow, 1976. Mem. Nassau County Bar Assn., N.Y. State Bar Assn., Nassau-Suffolk Women's Bar Assn., Phi Beta Kappa. Avocation: horseback riding. Office: 1025 Northern Blvd Ste 201 Roslyn NY 11576-1506

ZEITLIN, EUGENIA PAWLIK, retired college administrator, educator, librarian; b. N.Y.C., Jan. 29; d. Charles and Pauline Pawlik; m. Herbert Zakary Zeitlin, July 3, 1949; children: Mark Clyde, Joyce Therese Zeitlin Harris, Ann Victoria, Clare Katherine. BA in English, Bklyn. Coll., 1945; MA in English, NYU, N.Y.C., 1951; MALS, Rosary Coll., 1968. Teaching credential N.Y., Ariz., Calif., Ill. English tchr. Sea Cliff, L.I., N.Y., 1945-47; English, math. tchr. Merrick (N.Y.) Sch. Dist., 1948-49; English tchr. Wilson Sch. Dist., Phoenix, 1949-50; counselor West Phoenix (Ariz.) High Sch., 1953-56; asst. prof. English Wright Coll., Chgo., 1965-66; asst. prof. English, asst. to v.p. curriculum and instrn. Oakton C.C., Des Plaines, Ill., 1970-76; libr. Pasadena City Coll., L.A. C.C. Dist., L.A., 1979-91. Contbr. articles to profl. jours. Named Northridge City Employee of Yr., 1986. Mem. AAUW (br. pres. Lancaster, Calif. 1958-60), Thoreau Soc. (life), Beta Phi Mu. Home: 20124 Phaeton Dr Woodland Hills CA 91364-5633

ZEITZ, AVA CLAIRE, environmental engineer; b. Montgomery, W.Va., May 24, 1949; d. Bill Joseph and Clara Ethel (Dillard) King; m. David Lawrence Zeitz, Aug. 20, 1972; children: Christina Annette, Alexander Ward. AS in Structural Engring., Morris Harvey Coll., 1975, BS in Math., 1977; BSCE, W.Va. Inst. Tech., 1977; MS in Environ. Engring., Va. Coll. Grad. Studies, 1981. Draftsman bridge dept. W.Va. Dept. Transp., Charleston, 1972-76, engr.-in-tng. bridge dept., 1976-78, dir. environ. affairs dept., 1978-84, asst. dir. planning divsn., 1984-87; asst. to chief waste mfg. divsn. W.Va. Dept. Natural Resources, Charleston, 1987-89; environ. coord. Columbia Gas Transmission Corp., Charleston, 1989-91, mgr. ops. environ. dept., 1991—; part-time assoc. prof., head engring. dept. W.Va. Coll. Grad. Studies, Institute, 1980-90. Contbr. articles to profl. publs. Pres. Putnam County Planning Commn., Winfield, W.Va., 1984-89, Putnam County Solid Waste Authority, Winfield, 1989-93; candidate Putnam County Bd. Edn., Winfield, 1994. Mem. Nature Conservancy. Democrat. Home: Rt 5/2 Jim Ridge Box 172A Liberty WV 25124

ZEKMAN, TERRI MARGARET, graphic designer; b. Chgo., Sept. 13, 1950; d. Theodore Nathan and Lois (Bernstein) Z.; m. Alan Daniels, Apr. 12, 1980; children: Jesse Logan, Dakota Caitlin. BFA, Washington U., St. Louis, 1971; postgrad, Art Inst. Chgo., 1974-75. Graphic designer (on retainer) greeting cards and related products Recycled Paper Products Co., Chgo., 1970—, Jillson Roberts, Inc., Calif.; apprenticed graphic designer Helmuth, Obata & Kassabaum, St. Louis, 1970-71; graphic designer Container Corp., Chgo., 1971; graphic designer, art dir., photographer Cuerden Advt. Design, Denver, 1971-74; art dir. D'Arcy, McManus & Masius Advt., Chgo., 1975-76; freelance graphic designer Chgo., 1976-77; art dir. Garfield Linn Advt., Chgo., 1977-78; graphic designer Keiser Design Group, Van Noy & Co., Los Angeles, 1978-79; owner and operator graphic design studio Los Angeles, 1979—. Recipient cert. of merit St. Louis Outdoor Poster Contest, 1970, Denver Art Dirs. Club, 1973.

ZELAYA, GIANNA ANNETTE, food service executive; b. Chgo., May 2, 1963; d. Alejandro N. and Myrna A. (Taylor) Z. BBA, Ill. Inst. Tech., 1987; MBA, U. Chgo., 1989. Design drafter Ill. Tool Works, Elmhurst, Ill., 1981-85; sr. assoc. Continental Bank, Chgo., 1989-90; corp. banking officer Continental Bank, Chgo., Ill., 1991; area mgr. Chgo. market Pizza Hut, Inc. subs. PepsiCo Inc., Lisle, Ill., 1991-93, divsn. fin. mgr., 1993—. Mem. alumni admissions com. Ill. Inst. Tech., Chgo., 1987—; rec. sec. Am. Soc. Women Accts., 1989-90, program co-chmn., 1990-91, corr. sec., 1991-92, bd. dirs., 1989-91. Recipient Alumni award Ill. Inst. Tech., 1993; Time, Inc. scholar, 1989. Mem. Nat. Hispanic Scholarship Fund (chairperson Chgo. Alumni chpt. 1991—, mem. Chgo. ptnrs. com. 1994), U. Chgo. Grad. Bus. Club. Office: Pizza Hut Inc Ctrl Divsn 4225 Naperville Rd Ste 300 Lisle IL 60532-3660

ZELBY, RACHEL, realtor; b. Sosnowiec, Poland, May 6, 1930; came to U.S., 1955; d. Herschel Kupfermintz and Sarah Rosenblatt; m. Leon W. Zelby, Dec. 28, 1954; children: Laurie Susan, Andrew Stephen. Student, U. Pa., 1955, Realtors' Inst., Norman, Okla., 1974; grad., Realtors Inst., Oklahoma City, 1978. Lic. realtor, broker, Okla.; cert. residential specialist, Okla. Realtor, broker, ptnr. Realty World Norman Heritage, 1973-81; realtor, broker Century 21 Parker Real Estate, Norman, 1981—, residential specialist, 1986—. Mem. Jr. Svc. League, Norman, 1980—; charter mem. Assistance League Norman, 1970—; bd. dirs. Juvenile Svcs., Inc., Norman, 1975-76. Mem. Nat. Assn. Realtors, Norman Bd. Realtors, Women's Coun. Realtors (treas. 1985), U. Okla. Women's Assn. (past pres.), Norman C. of C., LWV, Planned Parenthood Cen. Okla. Home: 1009 Whispering Pines Dr Norman OK 73072-6912 Office: Century 21 Bray-Parker Realtors 319 W Main St Norman OK 73069-1312

ZELENY, ANN DOUGLAS, sculptor; b. Tucson, Dec. 7, 1955; d. Charles Ellingson and Marjorie Ann (Pfeiffer) Zeleny; m. Arthur Jeffrey Munson, Dec. 22, 1974 (div. 1985); 1 child, Frederick Michael Munson Zeleny; m. Carl Douglas Anderson, Nov. 3, 1985; 1 child, Gwyneth Violet Zeleny Anderson. BFA, Va. Commonwealth U., 1977. Songwriter/vocalist Seventh Dawn, Richmond, Washington, 1973-80; archtl. sculptor Monumental Constrn. and Moulding Co., Washington, 1981-86; freelance sculptor, 1986—; co-creator, set designer, propmaster, puppeteer The Mondo Breakfast Show, Arlington, 1984-86; graphics cons. Gfx, Washington, 1991—. Sr. sculptor, sites of installation include: The Nat. Theatre, The Washington Times Bldg., The Hay-Adams Hotel, Phoenix Park Hotel, Phillips Collection Gallery, Casa Casuarina, Miami Beach; songwriter, performer (albums) Sunrise, 1976, Dreams, 1978; creator ceramic or cold cast sculptures including Poser, Reflection, Moonrise, Consort, Green Man Series; cameraperson Arlington Weekly News, 1980-85. Vol. graphics The Greens, 1989-92, The Common Market Food Coop., Frederick, Md., 1990-93; vol. set fabrication Beaux Artes Ball, Frederick, 1993. Recipient "Ammy" Craft Award for set design Arlington Community TV, 1985, Ammy for best variety program, 1985, Ammy for humor, 1986. Office: PO Box 13 Boonsboro MD 21713

ZELENY, MARJORIE PFEIFFER (MRS. CHARLES ELLINGTON ZELENY), psychologist; b. Balt., Mar. 31, 1924; d. Lloyd Armitage and Mable (Willian) Pfeiffer; B.A., U. Md., 1947; M.S., U. Ill., 1949, postgrad., 1951-54; m. Charles Ellington Zeleny, Dec. 11, 1950 (dec.); children—Ann Douglas, Charles Timberlake. Vocational counseling psychologist VA, Balt., 1947-48; asst. U. Ill. at Urbana, 1948-50, research asso. Bur. Research, 1952-53; chief psychologist dept. neurology and psychiatry Ohio State U. Coll. Medicine, Columbus, 1950-51; research psychologist, cons., Tucson, Washington, 1954—. Mem. Am., D.C. psychol. assns., AAAS, Southeastern Psychol Assn., DAR, Nat. Soc. Colonial Dames XVII Century, Nat. Soc. Descendants of Early Quakers, Mortar Bd., Delta Delta Delta, Sigma Delta Epsilon, Psi Chi, Sigma Tau Epsilon. Roman Catholic. Home: 6825 Wemberly Way Mc Lean VA 22101-1534

ZELEZNAK, SHIRLEY ANNE, psychotherapist; b. Ft. Dodge, Iowa; d. Melvin Peter and Illiah Mary (Olson) Hood; m. Donald John Zeleznak, June 14, 1969; children: Kristine Anne, Ryan John. BA, Briar Cliff Coll., 1967; MS in Clin. and Ednl. Psychology and Counseling, Winona State U., 1972. Cert. hypnotherapist, psychotherapist. Secondary tchr. Rochester, Minn., 1969-74; secondary tchr./counselor Mankato, Minn., 1974-77; task force dir. Heart Assn., Mankato, 1978-82; mental health counselor Scottsdale, Ariz., 1985—; tchr. Maricopa County C.C., Scottsdale, 1986-89; motivational speaker, Mankato, 1974-84; sch. cons. Paradise Valley/Scottsdale Sch. Dist., 1987—; bd. dirs. Home Base, Phoenix; psychotherapist St. Maria Goretti Ch., Scottsdale, 1986—; crisis intervention counselor, police dept., Phoenix, 1993—. Author: Series for Junior High Students, 1981 (books), 1982-83 (software programs). Chef A'La Heart, Minn. Heart Assn., Mankato, 1979-81; motivational speaker Gang Awareness, Scottsdale, 1992—. Recipient Appreciation award Minn. Heart Assn., 1981. Mem. Mental Health Counselors, Nat. Ctr. for Learning Disabilities, Am. Counseling Assn., Phoenix Scottish Rite Found., Inst. for Developmental and Behavioral Neurology. Roman Catholic.

ZELLER, BARBARA ANN, nun, health care facility administrator; b. Evansville, Ind., Aug. 18, 1945; d. Wilbert John and Dorothy Elizabeth (Tremor) Z. BA in Edn., St. Mary-of-the-Woods Coll., 1968; MA Studies in Aging, North Tex. State U., 1971. Dir. gerontology Sisters of Providence, St. Mary-of-the-Woods, Ind., 1971-76, 78-81; adminstrv. asst. archdiocesan social ministries Cath. Charities Archdiocese of Indpls., 1976-78; exec. dir. Maryvale, Inc., S. Mary-of-the-Woods, 1978-81; dir. social svcs. Pfister and Co., Inc., Terre Haute, Ind., 1981-82; exec. dir. Providence Retirement Home, Inc., New Albany, Ind., 1982-93; pres., CEO Mercy Long Term Care Initiatives, Inc., 1991-94; ministry cons. Sisters of Providence, 1994—; cons., Poor Handmaids of Jesus Christ, Donaldson, Ind., Little Company of Mary Sisters, Evergreen Park, Ill., Sisters of St. Francis, Joliet, Ill., numerous other orders and ednl. instns. in Ind., Ill., Ohio and Ky.; presenter courses, seminars and workshops on aging and retirement; speaker in field. Author materials and problem solving kits in field. Recipient George E. Davis award, Interfaith Fellowship on Religion and Aging,1985; named Ky. Col., 1988, Sagamore of the Wabash, Gov. of Ind., 1988, Disting. Hoosier Gov. of Ind., 1988. Mem. Ind. Assn. of Homes for Aging, Internat. Soc. Pre-Retirement Planners. Democrat.

ZELON, LAURIE DEE, lawyer; b. Durham, N.C., Nov. 15, 1952; d. Irving and Doris Miriam (Baker) Z.; m. David L. George, Dec. 30, 1979; children: Jeremy, Daniel. BA in English with distinction, Cornell U., 1974; JD, Harvard U., 1977. Bar: Calif. 1977, U.S. Ct. Appeals (9th cir.) 1978, U.S. Supreme Ct. 1989. Assoc. Beardsley, Hufstedler & Kemble, L.A., 1977-81; assoc. Hufstedler, Miller, Carlson & Beardsley, L.A., 1981-82, ptnr., 1983-88; ptnr. Hufstedler, Miller, Kaus & Beardsley, L.A., 1988-90, Hufstedler, Kaus & Ettinger, L.A., 1990-91, Morrison & Foerster, L.A., 1991—. Editor-in-chief: Harvard Civil Rights-Civil Liberties Law Rev., 1976-77. Vol. atty. ACLU of So. Calif., L.A., 1977—; bd. dirs. N.Y. Civil Liberties Union, 1973-74. Mem. ABA (chmn. young lawyers div. pro bono project 1981-83, delivery and pro bono projects com. 1983-85, subgrant competition-subgrant monitoring project 1985-86, chair standing com. on lawyers pub. svc. responsibility 1987-90, chair law firm pro bono project 1989-91, standing com. legal aid and indigent defendants 1991—, chair 1993—), Calif. Bar Assn., L.A. Bar County Assn. (trustee 1989-91, v.p. 1992-93, sr. v.p 1993-94, pres.-elect 1994—, mem. fed. cts. and practices com. 1984-93, vice chmn. 1987-88, chmn. 1988-89, chmn. judiciary com. 1991-92, chair real estate litigation subsect. 1991-92), Women Lawyers Assn. L.A., Calif. Women Lawyers Assn. Democrat. Office: Morrison & Foerster 555 W 5th St Ste 3500 Los Angeles CA 90013-1024

ZEMAN, CATHERINE LOUISE, university program manager; b. Alton, Ill., Oct. 12, 1962; d. Dixie Byrd-Hill. AAS in Registered Nursing, Lewis & Clark Coll., 1982, AS in Biology, 1986; BS in Anthropology, So. Ill. U., 1990, MS in Environ. Sci., 1992. Registered profl. nurse. Sci. tutor Lewis & Clark Coll., Godfrey, Ill., 1980-82; med. nurse/supr. Carlinville (Ill.) Hosp. and Rolings Manor, 1982-84; legal researcher Kardi's Law Office, Alton, Ill., 1987-92; wildlife rehabilitator Tree House Wildlife Ctr., Alton, 1987-92; ad hoc mem. Am. Bottoms Coalition, St. Louis, 1991; environ. rsch. assoc. Mo. Coalition for the Environment, St. Louis, 1992; waste reduction rsch. asst. Iowa Waste Reduction Ctr. U. No. Iowa, Cedar Falls, 1992-93, waste reduction specialist Iowa Waste Reduction Ctr., 1993-94, program mgr. Recycling and Reuse Tech. Transfer Ctr., 1994—; coord. closing the loop on wood waste study Reuse/Recycling Tech. Transfer Ctr., U. No. Ill., Cedar Falls., 1992—, vegetative filter strip tech. transfer project Iowa Waste Reduction Ctr., 1993—, project mgr. lithographic pollution prevention project Small Bus. Pollution Prevention Ctr., 1993—, researcher food processing pollution prevention project Small Bus. Pollution Prevention Ctr., 1994—. Author: (brochure) Your Nuclear Workplace, 1992; contbr. articles to profl. jours. Co-coord. N.E. Iowa NOW, Cedar Falls, 1993—. Mem. Nat. Assn. Environ. Profls., Am. Indians in Sci. and Engring. Soc.

ZEMANS, FRANCES KAHN, legal association executive; b. Chgo., May 1, 1943; married; 3 children. BA in zoology, U. Mich., 1965; MA in polit. sci., Northwestern U., 1966, Ph.D.in polit. sci., 1972. Instr. dept. politics Lake Forest (Ill.) Coll., 1973-74; instr. dept. polit. sci. Northwestern U., Evaston, Ill., 1974-75; asst. prof. depts. edn. and polit. sci. U. Chgo., 1975-80; dir. edn., rsch. Am. Judicature Soc., Chgo., 1983-85, asst. exec. dir. programs, 1985-87, exec. v.p., dir., 1987—; cons. ABA, 1980; mem. task force on judicial conduct and ethics of spl. commn. on administrn. of justice in Cook County, 1985-88; vis. lectr. Northwestern U., Chgo., 1986; bd. dirs. Cook County Criminal Justice Project, 1987-90; adjudication working group Bureau Justice Assistance, U.S. Dept. Justice, Washington, 1987, 88; mem. task force gender bias in courts, State of Ill., 1988-90;mem. Ill. Judicial Inquiry Bd., 1988-92. Contbr. articles to profl. jours.; mem. editorial bd. Justice System Journal, 1986-90; presenter in field. Bd. dirs. ACLU, Ill., 1978-87; mem. Police Bd. City of Chgo., 1980-87, chair budget com., office of profl. standards com., rules and regulations revision com.; mem. Chgo. crime survey planning com. Chgo. Community Trust, 1984-86, adv. com. govt. assistance project, 1990—; bd. visitors So. Meth. U. Sch. Law, 1987-90. Scholar ABF, 1974-83. Mem. Am. Polit. Sci. Assn., Law and Soc. Assn. (trustee 1980-83). Office: Am Judicature Soc 25 E Washington St Ste 1600 Chicago IL 60602-1805

ZEMM, SANDRA PHYLLIS, lawyer; b. Chgo., Aug. 18, 1947; d. Walter Stanley and Bernice Phyllis (Churas) Z. BS, U. Ill., 1969; JD, Fla. State U., 1974. Bar: Ill. 1975, Fla. 1975. With fin. dept. Sinclair Oil, Chgo., 1969-70; indsl. rels. advisor Conco Inc., Mendota, Ill., 1970-72; assoc. Seyfarth, Shaw, Fairweather & Geraldson, Chgo., 1975-82, ptnr., 1982—. Bd. dirs. Chgo. Residential Inc., 1993-97; mem. Art Inst. Round Table, Chgo., 1993-94. Mem. Ill. State Bar Assn., Fla. State Bar Assn., Univ. Club Chgo. (bd. dirs. 1991-94). Office: Seyfarth Shaw 55 E Monroe St Chicago IL 60603-5863

ZENDER, JO ANN, accountant; b. Cresco, Iowa, Dec. 21, 1933; d. William Paul and Mary Elizabeth (Culbert) Lusson; m. W. Joseph Zender, June 4, 1956; children: Julie, Jaime, Jennifer, Janaan. BA in Theatre, U. No. Iowa, 1955, MS, 1968; postgrad., U. Minn., 1971; MS in Acctg., U. Colo., 1990. CPA, Colo. Instr. speech St. Cloud, Minn., 1965-69; v.p. acctg. Flatiron Paving Co., Boulder, Colo., 1979-89; acctg. mgr. Stolte Inc., Denver, 1989-90; contr. SPM/Denver, 1991-94; controller Solid Systems Engring., Boulder, 1994—. Victim advocate Boulder County Sheriff's Dept., 1986-89. Bertha Martin scholar U. No. Iowa, 1954. Democrat. Home: 3844 Orion Ct Boulder CO 80304-1024

ZENO, JO ANN, sales executive; b. Akron, Ohio, Sept. 25, 1952; d. Ross and Mary Francis (Gerbec) Z. BA in French and Edn., BS in Spanish, U. Akron, 1975. Tchr. French, Spanish S.E. Local, Ravenna, Ohio, 1975-77, Akron Pub. Schs., 1977-80; sales rep. Xerox Corp., Akron, Cleve., 1980-83; cert. stapling technician U.S. Surg. Corp., Norwalk, Conn., 1983-88; rep. cardiovascular surg. products Medtronic Inc., 1988—. Home: 272 Somerset Rd Akron OH 44313-4533

ZENO, PHYLLIS WOLFE, association executive, editor; b. Cleve.; d. Oliver MacKenzie and Helen Virginia (Shipley) Wolfe; m. Norman Zeno, June 10, 1960 (dec. Feb. 1983); children: Richard Williams, Linda Williams Aber, Leslie Williams Metzler. Student, U. Wisconsin, 1943-45, New Sch. Social Rsch., N.Y.C., 1948. Staff writer Fred Waring Show, CBS-TV, N.Y.C., 1953-54; indsl. show writer MCA, N.Y.C., 1959-61, MCI, N.Y.C., 1959-74; editor Club Life mag., Manhasset, N.Y., 1970-74; promotion coord. Peninsula Motor Club, Am. Automobile Assn., Tampa, Fla., 1974-86; creative dir. AAA Auto Club South (formerly Peninsula Motor Club), Tampa, 1986—; editor-in-chief AAA Going Places. Composer This Is An Opening, 1975 (pop music award ASCAP 1976), How Do You Open a Show?, 1976, We Never Sing Opening Numbers, 1976. Recipient Silver award of excellence Fla. Mag. Assn., 1988, Bronze award of excellence, 1987, Charlie award 1st pl. for regular column, 1993, Addy award of merit Tampa Ad Fedn., 1986. Mem. ASCAP, SATW. Christian Scientist. Home: 8402 Cherrystone Ct Tampa FL 33615-4913 Office: AAA Auto Club South 1515 N Westshore Blvd Tampa FL 33607-4505

ZENT, KAREN MINICH, medical technologist; b. New Bethlehem, Pa., Oct. 25, 1950; d. Wallace Gene and Norma Jean (Shaffer) Minich; m. Rex Allen Zent, Dec. 2, 1978; children: Brian Robert, John Webster. BA in Biology, Queen's Coll., Charlotte, N.C., 1972, BS in Med. Tech., 1973. Med. technologist Greenville (S.C.) Meml. Hosp., 1973-75, Doctor's Hosp., Columbus, Ohio, 1977-79, ARC, Columbus, 1988-90, Roche Biomed. Lab., Dublin, Ohio, 1990—. Founder, trustee Indian Run Meadows Civic Assn., Dublin, 1986-90; charter mem. Dublin Presbyn. Ch. Mem. AAUW (charter mem., pres. Dublin br. 1989-93, program v.p. 1993—). Democrat. Presbyterian. Home: 7152 Fenian Ct Dublin OH 43017 Office: Roche Biomed Lab Wilcox Rd Dublin OH 43017

ZEPEDA, SUSAN GHOZEIL, county official; b. N.Y.C., Aug. 8, 1946; d. Harry S. and Anne (Golden) Kantor; m. Isaac Ghozeil, Jan. 29, 1967 (div. Oct. 1979); children: Daniel Jacob, Adam Leo; m. Fernando Zepeda, Jan. 2, 1983; children: Paloma Andrea, Sofia Elisa. BA, Brown U., 1967; MA, U. Ariz., 1971, postgrad., 1971-75; PhD, Internat. Coll., 1985. Rsch. assoc. div. bus. and econ. rsch. U. Ariz., Tucson, 1971-73, rsch. assoc. Coll. Medicine, 1975-76; assoc. dir. Pima Alcoholism Consortium, Tucson, 1976-79, exec. dir., 1979-80; dep. dir. pub. health Orange County Health Care Agy., Santa Ana, Calif., 1980-89; dir. policy, planning Orange County Health Care Agy., Santa Ana, 1989-90; dir. pub. fin. Orange County, 1990-92; dir. San Luis Obispo County Health Agy., 1993—; cons. Tucson Sch. Dist. No. 1, 1973-75, U.S. Dept. Labor, Washington, 1976-79, Indian Health Svc., Rockville, Md., 1984-85; ptnr. Zepeda Assocs., Fullerton, Calif., 1987-93; presenter confs. Mem. Fullerton Planning Commn., 1984-91, chmn., 1990-91; mem. Calif. Task Force on Comparable Worth, 1984-85, Calif. Dist. Appeal Bd. No. 510, L.A., 1986—. Recipient Woman of Achievement award Orange County Bd. Suprs., 1988, Disting. Achievement awards Nat. Assn. Counties, 1985, 86, 87, 89. Mem. APHA, County Health Execs. Assn. Calif. (exec. com.), U.S.-Mex. Border Health Assn., County Alcohol Program Adminstrs. Assn. Calif. (v.p. 1983, pres. 1984-85), Rotary (San Luis Obispo de Tolosa). Home: 127 Cerro Romauldo San Luis Obispo CA 93405 Office: San Luis Obispo County Health Agy 2191 Johnson Ave San Luis Obispo CA 93406

ZERFOWSKI, JEAN ANN, newsroom graphic artist, artist; b. Decatur, Ill., Dec. 23, 1964; d. William Joseph and Dolores Jean (Harrington) Brady; m. Jeffrey Lee Zerfowski, Sept. 10, 1988; 1 child, Jessica Brady. BFA, Millikin U., 1987. Newsroom graphic artist Decatur (Ill.) Herald & Review, 1986—. Recipient 1st Pl. Mission to Heal, Ill. Press Assn., 1993, 1st Pl. Lost Horizons, Edn. Writers Assn., 1991, 3rd Pl. Lifestyle Secnon, Assoc. Press., 1993. Roman Catholic. Home: 33 Whirlaway Dr Mount Zion IL 62549 Office: Herald & Review 601 E William St Decatur IL 62523

ZEVON, SUSAN JANE, editor; b. N.Y.C., July 23, 1944; d. Louis and Rhea (Alter) Z. BA, Smith Coll., 1966. Asst. editor trends and environments House & Garden, N.Y.C., 1970-80; account supr. Jessica Dee Communications, N.Y.C., 1981-84; editor architecture House Beautiful, N.Y.C., 1985—. Author: (with others) Decorating On The Cheap, 1984. Mem. Archtl. League N.Y., Smith Coll. N.Y. Club (v.p. 1987-88, pres. 1988-89). Office: House Beautiful 1700 Broadway New York NY 10019-5905

ZEWE, JUDITH LYNN, human resources professional; b. Monongahela, Pa., May 2, 1947; d. Norman Edward and Martha Ellen (Harkins) Kenny; m. Dennis Dale Zewe, Aug. 17, 1964; children: Dennis Dale Jr., Donna Lynn. BA in Mgmt., Mercyhurst Coll., 1979; cert. of mgmt., U. Colo., Denver, 1982, postgrad.; postgrad., Regis U. Dir. pers. Mercyhurst Coll., Erie, Pa., 1975-79; compensation mgr. Community Coll. of Denver System, 1979-83, dir. employee rels., 1983-85; founder, pres., career cons. Lynn Dale & Co., Southfield, Mich., 1985-88; dir. pers., affirmative action Colo. Sch. Mines, Golden, 1988-93; dir. human resources Arapahoe C.C., Littleton, Colo., 1993—; compensation cons. Colo. Bd. Community Colls., 1981. Author: Successful Job Search Strategies. Vol. Make-a-Wish Found. Colo., 1990—, Children's Hosp. Denver, 1990—. Named Outstanding Vol. Make-a-Wish Found. Colo., 1991. Mem. Coll. and Univ. Pers. Assn. (nat. benefits coun. 1983-84), Colo. Higher Edn. Affirmative Action Adminstrs., Coll. and Univ. Pers. Assn. Colo. (pres. 1992-93). Home: 10244 Owens St Broomfield CO 80021-6656 Office: Arapahoe C C 2500 W College Dr Littleton CO 80160-9002

ZGONC, JANICE ANN, technical information specialist; b. Greensburg, Pa., Apr. 8, 1956; d. Joseph and Jennie (Yaniszeski) Z. BA, Edinboro U. of Pa., 1979. Tech. info. specialist Dept. Def., Washington, 1981—. With U.S. Army, 1974-76. Mem. NAFE, Capital PC Users Group, Assn. Old Crows, Data Processing Mgmt. Assn., Armed Forces Communication and Electronics Assn. Home: 1304 S Thomas St Arlington VA 22204

ZHENG, LISA LIQING, computer programmer; b. Xian, China, May 11, 1966; came to U.S., 1990; d. Youzhong Zheng and Siuping Huang; m. Bo Xu, June 7, 1990. BSEE, Huazhong U. Sci. & Tech., 1988; MSEE, Purdue U., 1992. Asst. engr. Inst. Electronics Chinese Acad. Scis., Beijing, 1988-90; electronics engr., systems programmer Computer Graphics, Corp., Indpls., 1992-94; programmer Bertelsmann Music Group, Inc., Indpls., 1994—. Office: Bertlesmann Music Group Inc 6550 E 30th St Indianapolis IN 46219

ZHENG, MAGGIE (XIAOCI), materials scientist, vacuum coating specialist; b. Shanghai, China, Apr. 21, 1949; came to U.S., 1986; d. George and Helen (Chou) Cheng; divorced; 1 child, Dee. BS in Physics, Qutu Normal U., Shangdong, China, 1981; MSEE, U. Sci. and Tech. China, Beijing, 1984; MS in Materials Sci., U. Wis., 1988, PhD in Materials Sci., 1991. Lectr. Tsinghua U., Beijing, 1984-86; assoc. scientist United Techs., East Hartford, Conn., 1991-92; staff scientist Engineered Coatings, Inc., Rocky Hill, Conn., 1992-93; materials and coating process engr. Chromalloy Turbine Techs., Middletown, N.Y., 1993-94; coating engr. CES, Schenectady, N.Y., 1995—;

rsch. asst. U. Wis., Madison, 1986-91. Contbr. articles in profl. publs.; patentee in field. Mem. NAFE, Am. Metal Soc., Minerals, Metals & Materials Soc. Office: Chromalloy Turbine Techs 105 Tower Dr Middletown NY 10940-2034

ZHENG, YAEL, telecommunication product manager; b. Shanghai, China, Nov. 7, 1964; came to the U.S., 1981; d. Bei-Wei and Si-Cong (Gao) Z.; m. Winthrop Alan White, Nov. 21, 1993. BS, MIT, 1987; MBA, U. Calif., Berkeley, 1992. Process engr. Standard Microsystem Corp., Hauppauge, N.Y., 1987-90; product mgr. mktg. leadership devel. program No. Telecom, Santa Clara, Calif., 1992—; assessment mgr. Pacific Telesis Group, San Francisco, 1991; cons. Berkeley (Calif.) Consulting Group, 1992. Recipient AT&T Minority fellowship AT&T, Murray Hill, N.J., 1986.

ZICHEK, SHANNON ELAINE, secondary school educator; b. Lincoln, Nebr., May 29, 1944; d. Melvin Eddie and Dorothy Virginia (Patrick) Z. AA, York (Nebr.) Coll., 1965; BA, U. Nebr., Kearney, 1968; postgrad., U. Okla., Edmond, 1970, 71, 72, 73, 74, 75, U. Nebr., Kearney, 1980, 81, 82, 89, 92. Tchr. history and English, NW High Sch., Grand Island, Nebr., 1948—. Republican. Christian. Home: 2730 N North Rd Grand Island NE 68803-1143

ZIEGEL, BARI ANN, marketing professional; b. N.Y.C., Nov. 25, 1959; d. Leonard and Norma (Nemeth) Z.; m. Steven M. Rosman, Sept. 8, 1984; 1 child, Michal Sima Ziegel Rosman. BBA, Hofstra U., 1980. Ops., sales rep. Unitours, Inc., N.Y.C., 1980-82; adminstrv. asst. Bozell and Jacobs, Inc., N.Y.C., 1982-83, Parfums Stern, Inc., N.Y.C., 1983-85; mgmt. assoc. Citicorp Indsl. Credit, Inc., Harrison, N.Y., 1985-87; mktg. officer Citicorp Indsl. Credit, Inc., Rye, N.Y., 1987-88; area mgr. AT&T Credit Corp., Hawthorne, N.Y., 1988—. Mem. NAFE, Women in Equipment Leasing. Jewish. Office: AT&T Credit Corp 1st Fl 50 Broadway Hawthorne NY 10532

ZIEGLER, CHRISTINE BERNADETTE, psychology educator, consultant; b. Syracuse, N.Y., Mar. 22, 1951; d. Salvatore and Beverlie (Hopkins) Capozzi; m. Steven Jon Ziegler, Jan. 7,1979;1 child. Justin. Bs, SUNY, Brockport, 1978; MS, Syracuse U., 1980, PhD, 1982. Adj. asst. prof. SUNY, Cortland, N.Y., 1983-86, Syracuse (N.Y.) U., 1984-86, LeMoyne Coll., Syracuse, 1986-87; rsch. cons. Syracuse (N.Y.) U., 1982-86; assoc. prof. Kennesaw (Ga.) State Coll., 1987—; dean continuing edn. East Cobb Mid. Sch.; parent facilitator Ga. Coun. Child Abuse, Atlanta, 1990—; cons. Dissertation Rsch. UGA, Atlanta; cons. aggression reduction tng. N.W. Regional Hosp., Rome, Ga.; presenter numerous profl. confs. in field. contbr. articles to profl. jours. Mem. Juvenile Ct. Panel, Health Children's Initiative; mem. sch. adv. com., Marietta, Ga., 1989, mem. sch. bond com., 1989. Recipient fellowship Syracuse U., 1982. Mem. APA, AAAS, NAS, Ga. Psychol. Assn., Southeastern Psychol. Assn., Soc. Soc. Philosophy and Psychology, Soc. for Rsch. in Child Devel. Home: 1408 Dewberry Trl Marietta GA 30062-4013 Office: Kennesaw State College 3455 Steve Frey Rd Kennesaw GA 30144

ZIEGLER, DELORES, mezzo-soprano; b. Decatur, Ga.; children: Katie, Adam. Grad., Maryville Coll.; postgrad., U. Tenn. Operatic roles include Dorabella in Cosi Fan Tutti, Octavian in Der Rosenkavalier, Dulcinee in Don Quichotte, Cherubino in Le Nozze di Figaro, Rosina in Barber of Seville, Romeo, in I Capuleti e i Montecchi (first singer to sing the role of Romeo in Moscow and San Francisco), Idamante in Idomeneo, Charlotte in Werther, Adalgisa in Norma, Sextus in La Clemenza di Tito; performances with Atlanta Symphony, Bonn Theater der Stadt, Theater der Stadt Koln, La Scala Opera, Paris Opera, Bolshoi Opera, Moscow, Vienna Stattsopera, Phila. Orch., Met. Opera; recs. include Dorabella in Cosi Fan Tutti, EMI, Mozart Requiem, Mozart Great Mass, Atlanta Symphony, Mahler's 8th Symphony Telark Records, Beethoven 9th Symphony, Phila. Orch., EMI, Bach B Minor Mass, Teldek records, Margared in Le Roi d'ys, Erato Disque, title role in Bertoni's Orfeo, Frequenz records, Mozart's Kronenmesse, Deutsch Grammaphon; debut as Dorabella in Cosi fan Tutti, Lyric Opera Chgo., first Carmen at Atlanta Opera. Office: care Lynda Kay 2702 Crestworth Ln Buford GA 30519 Office: Côté Artists Mngmt Inc 157 W 57th St Ste 803 New York NY 10019

ZIEGLER, JAN, writer, media consultant; b. Hartford, Conn., Oct. 18, 1953; d. Richard T. and Margaret (Whinnem) Z. BA cum laude, U. Conn., 1975. Reporter, photographer, features editor The Norwich (Conn.) Bulletin, 1975-78; reporter UPI, Hartford, Conn., 1978-79; sci. writer, broadcast writer, New England weekend editor UPI, Boston, 1979-82; editor fgn. desk UPI, N.Y.C., 1982-83; sci. writer UPI, Washington, 1983-87; sci. editor, 1987-88; free-lance writer, media cons. Washington, 1989—; cons. nat. vaccine program USPHS; cons. White Ho. report to UNICEF on child health, Nat. Rsch. Coun. report on sharing lab resources, 1993. Contbr. Omni, National Geographic, The Scientist, Mirabella. Bd. dirs. Cleve. Park Hist. Soc., Washington, 1986-87. Mem. Women in Comm., Women in Film and Video. Office: 2724 Ordway St NW No 2 Washington DC 20008

ZIEGLER, LYNN ANN, community health nurse; b. Teaneck, N.J., Aug. 5, 1961; d. Albert William and Marie L. (Rinaldi) Z. RN, Holy Name Hosp., Teaneck, 1980; student, St. Peter's Coll., Englewood, N.J. RN, N.J., N.Y.; BLS, Vascular Disease Studies, Am. Heart Assn.; cert. vascular tech. program Medisonic Sch., Calif. Staff RN ICU, oncology Holy Name Hosp., 1983-91; with CAT scan dept. Beth Israel Hosp., Passaic, N.J., 1986-87; office mgr., vascular studies, inservice Diagnostic Study Vascular Studies, Teaneck, 1987-91; supplemental staff No. N.J., 1991—; home care assessment planner Optioncare, 1992—; mem. med. staff N.J. Special Olympics, 1984; family educator Kendall Compression Books Inc., Jersey City, 1990-91. Mem. ANA. Office: Optioncare Edgewater NJ 07020

ZIEGRA, ALICE STEVENSON, state legislator; b. Boston, Feb. 26, 1927; d. Thomas Milton and Ruth Elinor (Tisdale) Stevenson; m. Louis Richard Ziegra, May 23, 1953 (dec. June 1985); children: James Cornwell, Ames Fuller. BS in Nursing, Skidmore Coll., 1949. RN, N.H., Conn. Staff nurse Boston Vis. Nurse Assn., 1950-52, State Dept. Health, Hartford, Conn., 1952-55, Rural Dist. Health Coun., Farmington, N.H., 1975-90; legislator N.H Gen. Ct. (Ho. of Reps.), Concord, 1988—. Mem. Am. Nurses Assn., N.H. Nurses Assn. Republican. Home: New Durham Rd RR 1 Box 165 Alton NH 03809-9728

ZIELINKSI, BETH BABICH, marketing consultant; b. Columbus, Ohio, Nov. 29, 1947; d. Robert and Marilyn (Barnett) B.; m. Thomas Zielinski, June 11, 1989. B.A. in Psychology, Ohio State U., 1969; M.Internat.Mgmt., Am. Grad. Sch. Internat. Mgmt., 1977. Counselor, cons. Ohio Bur. Employment Services, 1969-73; propr. retail art gallery, Toronto, Ont., Can., 1973-75; mktg. and advt. mgr. Ellio's Frozen Pizza div. Purex, Inc., 1977-78; mktg. mgr. The Drop Shop Ltd., cable TV installation parts, Roselle, N.J., 1978-80; product mgr. cheese and butter products mfg. div. Atlantic & Pacific Tea Co. Inc., Montvale, N.J., 1980-82; mktg. mgr. pies and pie shells Mrs. Smith's Frozen Foods Co., Pottstown, Pa., 1982-83; product mgr. Respond Communications Software Software Synergy, New Rochelle, N.Y., 1984-85; mktg. mgr. Eventide, Inc., Little Ferry, N.J., 1986-92; sr. ptnr. Strategic Directions Inc., Burr Ridge, Ill., 1992—. mem. research com. Alzheimer's Disease Soc., 1980-81; founding mem. singles div. United Jewish Appeal, Fort Lee, N.J., 1978. Recipient Outstanding Creativity award Am. Dairy Assn., 1981. Mem. Nat. Assn. Female Execs., Am. Grad. Sch. Internat. Mgmt. Alumni Assn., Mensa, Phi Alpha Theta.

ZIENERT, LUCRETIA ANNE, management educator; b. Roanoke, Ala., May 18, 1958; d. Wyatt Earl Freeman and Frances Adele (Miles) Weathers; m. Keith Edwin Zienert, Sept. 1, 1980 (div. 1994). BA, Auburn U., 1980, MBA, 1985, PhD in Mgmt., 1994. Dept. mgr. Wal-Mart, Inc., Auburn, Ala., 1981-82; mgr. Schuster Enterprises, Auburn, 1982-84; grad. asst. Auburn U., 1984-85, instr., 1985-91; asst. prof. Francis Marion U., Florence, S.C., 1991-94. Author: (case study) Strategic Management Cases, 3d edit., 1989, 4th edit., 1992. Mem. Am. Info. Soc., Nat. Decision Scis. Inst., S.W. Decision Scis. Inst. Democrat. Lutheran. Home: 310 Lansdale Dr Florence SC 29506 Office: Francis Marion U Hwy 301 Florence SC 29501-0547

ZIENTARA, SUZANNAH DOCKSTADER, insurance company executive; b. Wichita, Kans., Oct. 1, 1945; d. Ralph Walter and Patricia Ann (Harvey) Dockstader; m. Larry Henry Zientara, Oct. 18, 1975; 1 child, Jillian Sue Zientara Cox. Student, U. Kans., 1963-64; BS in Bus. Edn., Ft. Hays State U., 1968; MEd in Secondary Guidance and Counseling, U. Mo., St. Louis, 1973. CLU. Sec. to supt. Wichita Pub. Schs., 1968-69; tchr. bus. edn. Wichita Heights High Sch., 1969-71, Lindbergh High Sch., St. Louis, 1971-72, Holman Jr. High Sch., St. Louis, 1972-75; guidance counselor Pattonville Heights Jr. High Sch., St. Louis, 1975-79; tchr. data processing Lawrence (Kans.) High Sch., 1979-85; ins. agt. State Farm Ins. Cos., Lawrence, 1985-90; agy. mgr. State Farm Ins. Cos., Tulsa, 1990—; mem. Regional Mgr. Coun., Tulsa, 1992-93; participant Purdue Profl. Mgmt. Inst., West Lafayette, Ind., 1993. Author: Introduction to Data Processing, 1983. Mem. Williams Edn. Fund, U. Kans. Named Outstanding Young Woman of Am., 1974. Mem. Am. Soc. CLU and ChFC, USTA, Am. Ski Assn., Broken Arrow C. of C., Indian Springs Country Club, Kansas Alumni Assn., Mortar Bd., PEO Sisterhood (internat. chpt.), Pi Omega Pi. Republican. Episcopalian. Home: 8348 S 4th St Broken Arrow OK 74011 Office: State Farm Ins Cos 709 N Aspen Broken Arrow OK 74012

ZIERATH, MARILYN JEAN, medical/surgical and pediatrics nurse; b. Centralia, Wash., Jan. 24, 1942; d. Lloyd and Lolita Jeneva (Francis) Reese; m. David William Zierath, Dec. 1963; children: Carolyn, Robert, Michael. Diploma in nursing, Tacoma Gen. Hosp., 1964; BSN, U. Puget Sound, 1965; MS in Nursing, Calif. State U., Fresno, 1975. RN, Wash.; cert. in enterostomal therapy; advanced nurse practitioner. Instr. nursing Calif. State U., Fresno, 1973-75; nursing supr. med.-surg. unit Good Samaritan Hosp., Puyallup, Wash., 1977; clin. instr. Pacific Luth. U., Tacoma, 1977-79; med.-surg. clin. specialist, enterostomal therapy nurse Tacoma Gen. Hosp., 1979-92, nurse surgery in oper. rm., 1992-95; educator, infection control nurse, enterostomal therapy nurse Bremerton Convalescent Ctr., 1995—. Contbr. articles to nursing jours. Mem. ANA (cert. med.-surg. clin. nurse specialist), Wound, Ostomy and Continence Nurses, Assn. Enterostomal Therapy Nurses, Puget Sound Enterostomal Nurses, Clin. Nurse Specialists Puget Sound, Phi Kappa Phi.

ZIESE, NANCYLEE HANSON, social worker; b. Sioux City, Iowa, July 26, 1938. BA in Sociology, Morningside Coll., 1960; MSW, U. Iowa, 1982, cert. in aging studies, 1986. Social worker Florence Crittenton Home, Sioux City, 1960-65, L.A. County, 1965; social worker, supr. Polk County Dept. Social Welfare, Des Moines, 1966-69; social worker, community liaison Tommy Dale Meml., Sioux City, Iowa, 1977-79; dir. internships Briar Cliff Coll., Sioux City, 1981-83; dir. continuing edn. Coe Coll., Cedar Rapids, Iowa, 1983-85; exec. dir. Profl. Women's Network, Cedar Rapids, 1985-87; pvt. practice WOMANPLACE Counseling, Cedar Rapids, 1985-87; adoption supr. Hillcrest Family Svcs., Cedar Rapids, 1987—; bd. mem. Young Parent's Network M.E.L.D., Cedar Rapids, 1988—, pres., 1995; cons. projects related to community improvement, recycling. Contbr. articles to newspapers. Bd. mem., v.p. Sioux City Sch. Bd., 1978-83; bd. mem., pres. Friends of Iowa Pub. TV, 1978-88, Family Svc., Boys and Girls Home, Sioux City, 1973-81; pres.-elect, steering bd. Iowa Women's Polit. Caucus, 1987-93, pres., 1992-93, chair, 1994; active Iowa Women's Caucus Rsch. and Edn. Ctr.; bd. dirs. commn. mem. Episcopal Diocese Iowa-Human Needs; chair Birth Defects Inst. Adv. Com., Iowa Inter-Agy. Adoption Coalition; bd. mem. Linn County Adolescent Pregnancy Prevention Coalition, treas. 1992—, Friends of Iowa Commn. on Status of Women; mem. steering com. ERA Iowa 1992, 1991—; mem. gov.'s com. adoption reform in Iowa, 1993, 94, lt. gov.'s com. spl. needs adoption in Iowa, 1994. Recipient Outstanding Svc. awards Sioux City C. of C., 1976, Siouxland Arts Coun., 1977. Mem. NASW, Profl. Women's Network Cedar Rapids (bd. mem.). Republican. Episcopalian. Office: Hillcrest Family Svcs 205 12th St SE Cedar Rapids IA 52403-4028

ZIGA, KATHLEEN, lawyer; b. Phila., 1947; m. John Ziga; children: John Strand, Jeffrey, Karen. BA magna cum laude, Mich. State U., 1969; MA, U. Mich., 1970, JD, 1977. Ptnr. Dechert, Price & Rhoads, Phila. Office: Dechert Price & Rhoads 4000 Bell Atlantic 1717 Arch St Philadelphia PA 19103-2793

ZIKMUND, BARBARA BROWN, minister, seminary president, church history educator; b. Ann Arbor, Mich., Oct. 16, 1939; d. Henry Daniels and Helen (Langworthy) Brown; m. Joseph Zikmund II, Aug. 26, 1961; 1 child, Brian Joseph. BA, Beloit Coll., 1961; BDiv, Duke U., 1964, PhD, 1969; D in Div (hon.), Doane Coll., 1984, Chgo. Theol. Sem., 1985, Ursinus Coll., 1989. Ordained to ministry United Ch. of Christ, 1964. Instr. Albright Coll., Reading, Pa., 1966-67, Temple U., Phila., 1967-68, Ursinus Coll., Collegeville, Pa., 1968-69; asst. prof. religion studies Albion Coll., Mich., 1970-75; asst. prof. ch. history, dir. studies Chgo. Theol. Sem., 1975-80; dean and assoc. prof. ch. history Pacific Sch. Religion, Berkeley, Calif., 1981-85, dean and prof. ch. history, 1985-90; pres. Hartford (Conn.) Sem., 1990—; chmn. United Ch. of Christ Hist. Coun., 1983-85, mem. coun. for ecumenism, 1983-89; mem. Nat. Coun. Chs. Commn. on Faith and Order, 1979-87, World Coun. of Chs. Programme Theol. Edn., 1984-91, Nat. Coun. Chs. Working Group on Inter-Faith Rels., 1992—, World Orgn. Confs. Theol. Instns., sec. treas. 1992—. Author: Discovering the Church, 1983; editor: Hidden Histories in the UCC, 1984, vol. 2, 1987; (with Manschreck) American Religious Experiment, 1976; mem. editorial bd. Jour. Ecumenical Studies, 1987—, Mid-Stream, 1991—; contbr. articles to profl. jours. Mem. City Coun., Albion, Mich., 1972-75; elector Wadsworth Atheneum, 1994—, corporator St. Francis Hosp., 1994—; pres. Greater Hartford Consortium for Higher Edn., 1994—. Woodrow Wilson fellow, 1964-66; NEH grantee, 1974-75; vis. scholar Schlesinger Libr. Women's History, Radcliffe Coll., 1988-89. Mem. Assn. Theol. Schs. (v.p. 1984-86, pres. 1986-88, issues implementation grantee 1983-84), Am. Soc. Ch. History (council 1983-85, pres. elect 1995—), Internat. Assn. Women Ministers (v.p. 1977-79), AAUW (v.p. 1973-75), Greater Hartford C. of C. (bd. dirs. 1992-95). Democrat. Office: Hartford Sem Office of Pres 77 Sherman St Hartford CT 06105-2260

ZIMET, CAROL, writer; b. Bklyn., May 2, 1922; d. Oscar and Anna (Marcus) Segal; m. Bernard Chesner, June 1945 (div. Nov. 1968); children: Tasha Garfield, Jeffrey Chesner; m. Jesse Zimet, Mar, 1969. Student, Adelphi Coll., 1960-62, Caton Rose Inst. Art, 1962-64. Interior designer Sachs, N.Y.C., 1966-77; cons. lighting 1962-70; lectr. interior design, N.Y., 1967-77. Author: So You Are Going to the Hospital, 1994; author (with others) World of Poetry, 1990, Poems That Will Live Forever, 1992, In the Desert Sun, 1993, Outstanding Poets of 1994, 1994. Vol. ARC, AHRC, IHB. Recipient numerous awards. Mem. Poetry Group of Rockville Ctr. (chair), Barnes and Noble of Carle Place Poetry Group (chair), Internat. Soc. Poetry, Rockville Ctr. Guild for the Arts. Home: 942 Stratford Ct Westbury NY 11590

ZIMMER, SHARON MAURA, lawyer; b. N.Y.C., May 23, 1949; d. Louis K. and Lillian R. (Rosenberg) Z.; m. Robert H. Mayer, Jan. 23, 1983; 1 child, Gregory Loren. BA, Bryn Mawr Coll., 1970; JD, U. Pa., 1973; LLM in Taxation, NYU, 1976. Bar: N.Y. 1974. Assoc. Hofheimer Gartlir Gottlieb and Gross, N.Y.C., 1973-79; ptnr. Hofheimer Gartlir and Gross, N.Y.C., 1979—. Mem. ABA, N.Y. State Bar Assn., N.Y.C. Bar Assn. Office: Hofheimer Gartlir & Gross 633 3d Ave New York NY 10017

ZIMMERMAN, ANNE E., public relations company executive; b. L.A., Jan. 11, 1942; d. Arthur John and Fanchon Hunter (Roberts) Eggenberger; m. Kent Topping Zimmerman, Feb. 14, 1975. BA, Northwestern U., Evanston, Ill., 1963; MA, UCLA, 1975. Youth coord. Bullock's, L.A., 1963-64; publicity dir. Rose Marie Reid Swimwear, L.A., 1964-65; asst. editor L.A. Herald-Examiner, L.A., 1965-68; fashion dir. Ohrbach's West Coast Stores, L.A., 1968-71; instr. Fashion Inst. Design, L.A., 1971-74; sr. v.p. The Pub. Rels. Bd., Chgo., 1975-84; asst. prof. Drake U., Des Moines, 1984-88; dir. comm. Office of Gov., Des Moines, 1988-91; pres. Anne Zimmerman/Pub. Rels., Des Moines, 1991—. Recipient several Golden Trumpet awards Publicity Club of Chgo. Mem. Pub. Rels. Soc. of Am. (Silver Anvil 1975), Women in Communications, The Fashion Group, Inc. Republican. Presbyterian. Home: 5440 Waterbury Rd Des Moines IA 50312-1926 Office: 312 8th St Ste 110 Des Moines IA 50309

ZIMMERMAN, CAROLE LEE, public relations professional; b. Roxboro, N.C., Aug. 28, 1948; d. Ray Richard and Annie Theresa (O'Briant) Z.; m. Richard A. Hoehn, Oct. 26, 1991; 1 child, Kristin Nicole Sizemore. BS in Edn., Fla. State U., 1970; publs. specialist cert., George Washington U., 1980; MA in Pub. Comm., Am. U., 1993. Tchr. Gadsden County Pub. Schs., Quincy, Fla., 1971-72, Am. schs., Kaiserslautern and Darmstadt, Germany, 1975-76; editor, writer USLICO Corp., Arlington, Va., 1980-84; dir. communications Bread for the World, Washington, 1984—. vol. homeless women's shelter Luther Pl. Meml. Ch., Washington, 1983—. Mem. Am. Soc. Assn. Execs., Internat. Assn. Bus. Communicators, Pub. Rels. Soc. Am., Washington Women in Comm., Washington Women in Pub. Rels. Democrat. Lutheran. Office: Bread for the World 1100 Wayne Ave Ste 1000 Silver Spring MD 20910-5603

ZIMMERMAN, DIANE LEENHEER, law educator, lawyer; b. Newton, N.J., Apr. 16, 1941; d. Adrian and Mildred Eleanor (Booth) Leenheer; m. Earl A. Zimmerman, Sept. 24, 1960 (div. Aug. 1982); m. 2d, Cavin P. Leeman, Feb. 18, 1984. BA, Beaver Coll., Glenside, Pa., 1963; JD, Columbia U., 1976. Bar: N.Y. 1977, U.S. Supreme Ct. 1983. Reporter, Newsweek mag., N.Y.C., 1963-71; spl. features writer N.Y. Daily News, N.Y.C., 1971-73; law clk. U.S. Dist. Ct. (ea. dist.) N.Y., Bklyn., 1976-77; asst. prof. law NYU, N.Y.C., 1977-80, assoc. prof., 1980-82, prof., 1982—; mem. faculty Practicing Law Inst., N.Y.C., 1979, 84, 90, 92; of counsel Skadden, Arps, Slate, Meagher & Flom. Articles and book rev. editor Columbia Law Rev., 1975-76. Mem. working group on women, censorship and pornography Nat. Coalition Against Censorship. Recipient citation of merit Columbia U. Sch. Journalism, 1972; Kent scholar and Stone scholar, 1973-76. Mem. ABA (vice chmn. tort liability study com. tort and ins. sect. 1986-87, chair 1st amendment rights com. 1989—), Am. Law Inst., Assn. of Bar of City of N.Y. (chairperson com. civil rights 1981-83), Copyright Soc. USA (trustee 1988-91, Soc. Am. Law Tchrs. Office: NYU Sch Law 40 Washington Sq S New York NY 10012-1005

ZIMMERMAN, HELENE LORETTA, business educator; b. Rochester, N.Y., Feb. 26, 1933; d. Henry Charles and Loretta Catherine (Hobert) Z. BS, SUNY, Albany, 1953, MS, 1959; PhD, U. N.D., 1969. Cert. records mgr. Bus. tchr., chmn. bus. dept. Williamson (N.Y.) Cen. Sch., 1953-69; asst. prof. U. Ky., Lexington, 1969-70; assoc. prof. bus. Cen. Mich. U., Mt. Pleasant, 1970-74, prof., 1974—. Author General Business, 1977; contbg. author to records mgmt. text book, 1987. Sec. Isabella County Christmas Outreach, Mt. Pleasant, 1983-94. Mem. Assn. Records Mgmt. and Adminstrn., Inst. Cert. Records Mgrs. (sec. 1985-89, exam. devel. com. 1993—), Internat. Soc. Bus. Edn. (internat. v.p. English speaking nations 1986-88), Nat. Bus. Edn. Assn., Mich. Bus. Edn. Assn. (bd. dirs. 1985-90, 95—, pres. 1988-89), AAUW (pres. 1984-86), Delta Kappa Gamma (state pres. 1987-89, internat. fin. com. 1990-94). Office: Ctrl Mich U Grawn # 337 Mount Pleasant MI 48858

ZIMMERMAN, JEAN, lawyer; b. Berkeley, Calif., Dec. 3, 1947; d. Donald Scheel Zimmerman and Phebe Jean (Reed) Doan; m. Gilson Berryman Gray III, Nov. 25, 1982; children: Charles Donald Buffum and Catherine Elisabeth Phebe (twins); stepchildren: Alison Travis, Laura Rebecca, Gilson Berryman. BSBA, U. Md., 1970; JD, Emory U., 1975. Bar: Ga. 1975, D.C. 1976, N.Y. 1980. Asst. mgr. investments FNMA, Washington, 1970-73; assoc. counsel Fuqua Industries Inc., Atlanta, 1976-79; assoc. Sage Gray Todd & Sims, N.Y.C., 1979-84; assoc. counsel J. Henry Schroder Bank & Trust Co., N.Y.C., 1984-85, asst. gen. counsel, 1986, assoc. gen. counsel, 1987; assoc. gen. counsel, asst. sec. IBJ Schroder Bank & Trust Co., N.Y.C., 1988-90, chief counsel, sec., 1991-93, sr. v.p., gen. counsel, sec., 1993—; asst. sec. IBJ Schroder Leasing Corp., N.Y.C., 1987-90, bd. dirs., sec., 1991—; asst. sec. IBJ Schroder Leasing Corp., N.Y.C., 1987-90; asst. sec. IBJ Schroder Banking Corp., N.Y.C., 1989-90, chief counsel, sec., 1991-93; asst. sec. IBJ Schroder Internat. Bank, Miami, Fla., 1989-90, sec., 1991—; asst. sec. IBJS Capital Corp., N.Y.C., 1988-90, sec., 1991—; sec. Bonaght Corp., N.Y.C., 1991—; chief legal officer, sec. Execution Svcs., Inc., N.Y.C., 1991-93. Founder, officer ERA Ga., Atlanta, 1977-79; bd. dirs. Ct. Apptd. Spl. Advs., 1988-94. Named one of Outstanding Atlantans, 1978-79. Mem. ABA, Assn. of Bar of City of N.Y., Ga. Assn. Women Lawyers (bd. dirs. 1977-79), Am. Soc. Corp. Secs., Inc., LWV, DAR. Democrat. Office: IBJ Schroder Bank & Trust Co 1 State St New York NY 10004-1505

ZIMMERMAN, JO ANN, health services and educational consultant, former lieutenant governor; b. Van Buren County, Iowa, Dec. 24, 1936; d. Russell and Hazel (Ward) McIntosh; m. A. Tom Zimmerman, Aug. 26, 1956; children: Andrew, Lisa, Don and Ron (twins), Beth. Diploma, Broadlawns Sch. of Nursing, Des Moines, 1958; BA with honors, Drake U., 1973; postgrad., Iowa State U., 1973-75. RN, Iowa. Asst. head nurse maternity dept. Broadlawns Med. Ctr., Des Moines, 1958-59, weekend supr. nursing svcs., 1960-61, supr. maternity dept., 1966-68; instr. maternity nursing Broadlawns Sch. Nursing, 1968-71; health planner, community rels. assoc. Iowa Health Systems Agy., Des Moines, 1978-82; mem. Iowa Ho. Reps., 1982-86; lt. gov., Senate pres. State of Iowa, 1987-91; cons. health svcs., grant writing and continuing edn. Zimmerman & Assocs., Des Moines, 1991—; ops. dir. Medlink Svcs., Inc., rehab. and work hardening co., Des Moines, 1992—. Contbr. articles to profl. jours. Mem. advanced registered nurse practitioner task force on cert. nurse mid-wives Iowa Bd. Nursing, 1980-81, Waukee, Polk County, Iowa Health Edn. Coordinating Coun., Iowa Women's Polit. Caucus, Dallas County Women's Polit. Caucus; chmn. Des Moines Area Maternity Nursing Conf. Group, 1969-70, task force on sch. health svcs. Iowa Dept. Health, 1982, task force health edn. Iowa Dept. Pub. Instruction, 1979, adv. com. health edn. assessment tool, 1980-81, Nat. Lt. Govs., chair com. on Agrl. and Rural Devel., 1989; Dallas County Dem. Cen. Com., 1972-84; bd. dirs. Iowa PTA, 1979-83, Waukee Community Sch. Bd., 1976-79, pres., 1978-79; chairperson Health Com., 1980-84; bd. dirs. Iowa Parent and Tchrs. Assn.; mem. steering com. ERA, Iowa, 1991, 92; founder Dem. Activist Women's Network (DAWN), 1992. Mem. ANA, LWV (health chmn. met. Des Moines chpt.), Iowa Nurses Assn., Iowa League for Nursing (bd. dirs. 1979-83), Family Centered Childbirth Edn. Assn. (childbirth instr., advisor), Iowa Cattleman's Assn., Am. Lung Assn. (bd. dirs. Iowa 1988-92), Dem. Activist Women's Network (founder 1992). Mem. Christian Ch. Office: Zimmerman & Assocs 7630 Ashworth Rd West Des Moines IA 50266-5859

ZIMMERMAN, JUDITH ROSE, art educator; b. Youngstown, Ohio, Jan. 17, 1945; d. Emery and Josephine Leona (Terlecki) Ference; m. William Carl Zimmerman, Jr., Nov 27, 1965; children: Shawn, William III. BFA in Art Edn., Kent State U., 1977, MEd in Curriculum and Instruction, 1992. Cert. art tchr., Ohio. Elem. art tchr. Sandy Valley Sch. Dist., Magnolia, Ohio, 1977—; instr. art Massillon (Ohio) Art Mus. Adv. com. Edn. Enhancement Partnership Coun., Canton, Ohio, 1992; active Little Art Gallery, 1992, Massillon Art Mus. Mem. NEA, Nat. Art Edn. Assn., Ohio Edn. Assn., Ohio Art Edn. Assn. (chairperson east central divsn. 1985-90, elem. divsn. 1989-91, Art Educator of Yr. 1983, Featured Art Tchr. of Month 1990), Ohio Alliance for Art Edn., Canton Art Inst. (Art Educator of Yr. 1992), Phi Delta Kappa. Roman Catholic. Home: 802 Lucille Ave North Canton OH 44720 Office: Sandy Valley Sch Dist Rt 2 Magnolia OH 44643

ZIMMERMAN, KATHLEEN MARIE, artist; b. Floral Park, N.Y., Apr. 24, 1923; d. Harold G. and Evelyn M. (Andrade) Z.; m. Ralph S. Iwamoto, Nov. 23, 1963. Student, Art Students League, N.Y.C., 1942-44, Nat. Acad. Sch. Fine Arts, N.Y.C., 1944-47, 50-54. tchr. drawing and painting Midtown Sch. Art, N.Y.C., 1947-52. Illustrator: (with Ralph S. Iwamoto) Diet for a Small Planet, 1971; one woman shows include Westbeth Gallery, N.Y.C., 1973, 74, St. Mary's Coll., St. Mary's City, Md., 1990; exhibited in group shows at Woodstock Art Gallery, N.Y., 1945, Nat. Arts Club, N.Y.C., 1948-56, 84, Emily Lowe Award Show, 1951, Contemporary Arts Gallery, N.Y.C., 1952, 60, Allied Artists Ann., N.Y.C., 1956, 78, 80-91, 93, Art USA, 1958, Village Art Ctr., 1956-61, ACA Gallery, 1958, 59, Studio Gallery, 1957-60, City Center Gallery, 1960, Janet Nessler Gallery, N.Y.C., 1961, Silvermine Guild, Conn., 1962, Pioneer Gallery, Cooperstown, N.Y., 1962, 63, Audubon Artists Anns., N.Y.C., (various shows) 1963-95, NAD, (15 shows) 1969-95, Nat. Assn. Women Artists Anns., N.Y.C., 1957-85, 87-94, Women Artists Award Winners Show, N.Y.C., 1974, Am. Watercolor Soc., N.Y.C., 1975-78, 80, Cheyenne (Wyo.) Western Galleries, 1975, 76, 77, Edward-Dean Mus., Cherry Valley, Calif., 1975, 76, 77, Frye Mus., Seattle, 1975, 76, 77, Boise Gallery Art, 1975, Central Wyo. Mus. Art, 1975, 76, Willamette U., 1975, Yellowstone Art Ctr., Billings, Mont., 1975, Utah State U., 1975, Applewood Art Gallery, Colo., 1976, Charleston Art Gallery,

W.Va., 1976, Kent State U., 1976, Cin. Art Club, 1976, Martello Mus., Key West, Fla., 1976, Buecker Gallery, N.Y.C., 1976, Anchorage Fine Arts Mus., 1976, Davis and Long Gallery, N.Y.C., 1977, Butler Inst. Am. Art, 1978, Washington Square East Gallery, NYU, 1979, Internat. Festival Women Artists, Copenhagen, 1980, City Gallery, N.Y.C., 1981, Bergen Community Mus., Paramus, N.J., 1983, Kenkeleba Gallery, N.Y.C., 1985, Adelphi Univ., Garden City, N.Y., 1987, Lotos Club, N.Y.C., 1987, Temperance Hall Gallery, Bellport, N.Y., 1987, Monmouth Mus., Lincroft, N.J., 1987, Marbella Gallery, N.Y.C., 1989, Knickerbocker Artists, 1990, Brownstone Gallery, N.Y.C., 1993; represented in permanent collections, Butler Inst. Am. Art, Youngstown, Ohio, Sheldon Swope Art Gallery, Terre Haute, Ind., Lauren Rogers Mus. Art, Laurel, Miss., U. Wyo. Art Mus., Laramie, U. Miami Lowe Art Mus., Coral Gables, Fla., N.C. Mus. Art, Raleigh, Swarthmore Coll., Pa., Erie Art Ctr. (Pa.), Nat. Acad. Design, N.Y.C.; bibiography James Mellow, N.Y. Times Art Review, 1973, Hilton Kramer, N.Y. Times Review, 1977; contbr. bibliography to Gerald F. Brommer's The Art of Collage, 1978, Christopher Schink's Mastering Color & Design in Watercolor, 1981, John and Joan Digby's The Collage Handbook, 1985, David Ferry's "Painting Without a Brush", 1992, Gerald F. Brommer's Collage Techniques, 1994. Mem. NAD (Henry Ward Ranger Fund purchase prize 1976, 82, cert. of merit, 1980, L.G. Sawyer prize 1988, Ogden Pleissner Meml. award 1991, William A. Paton prize 1993), Audubon Artists (John Wenger Meml. award 1978, Ralph Fabri medal, 1981, J&E Liskin Meml. award 1987, Dick Blick award 1994), Am. Watercolor Soc. (Barse Miller Meml. award 1976), Nat.Assn. Women Artists (13 prizes 1957-91), Allied Artists Am. (silver medal 1981, 91, Jane Peterson award 1985, Creative Watercolor prize 1989), N.Y. Artists Equity Assn. (John F. and Anna Lee Stacey scholar 1954, Dr. Maury Leibovitz award 1985). Home: 463 West St # 1110A New York NY 10014-2010

ZIMMERMAN, MURIEL ELAINE, educational administrator; b. Harper, Iowa, Sept. 26, 1942; d. Merlin Edwin and Lois Elizabeth (Jasper) Gibson; m. Jerome L. Zimmerman, June 11, 1966 (div. Nov. 1985); children: Angela Beth, Gregory Allen. BS, McPherson Coll., 1964; MS, Kans. State U., 1969; postgrad., U. Mo., 1980—, N.W. Mo. State U., 1980-87. County extension home economist Kans. State U., Eureka, 1964-67; dir. homemaker svc. demonstration project Kans. State U., Manhattan, 1968-70; instr. home econs. N.W. Mo. State U., Maryville, 1978-85; coord. adult and community edn. Maryville RII Schs., 1984—; instr., condr. workshops U. Mo., Maryville, 1981-85; presenter on balancing work and family programs at state, regional and nat. confs.; mem. Total Quality Productivity Inst., 1991—; coord. Sch. Age Child Care Program, 1990—; adv. com. Mo. Ednl. Satellite Network. Mem. Maryville Community Wellness Coun., 1986—, Parents as First Tchrs. Adv. Com., 1987—; participant Leadership Maryville, 1988—; mem. Mo. Adult and Community Edn. Adv. Commn., 1988—. Recipient vol. leadership award U. Mo. ext. Svc., 1983, Disting. Svc. Woman award Soroptimist, 1990, GAPP Educator Study Tour of Germany, 1994. Mem. AAUW (Elenor Roosevelt Found. Award 1991), Am. Home Econs. Assn. (cert.), Am. Vocat. Assn., Nat. Coun. Vocat. Adminstrs., Mo. Tchrs. Assn., Mo. Assn. Adult Continuing and Community Edn. (bd. dirs. 1986—, conf. chmn. 1988, Newcomer's award 1989, Outstanding Educator award 1994), Mo. Home Econs. Assn. (v.p., pres., treas. 1982—, state bd. dirs. 1990—), Missouri Valley Adult Edn. Assn. (regional bd. dirs., Spl. Achievement award 1994), Mo. Coun. Vocat. Adminstrs. (program chmn. 1987—), NCEA (conf. exec. steering com. 1991), Mo. Employment and Tng. Assn., Mo. Assn. for Customized Tng., Total Quality Productivity Inst., Maryville C. of C. (exec. bd.). Home: 1809 Village O Dr Maryville MO 64468-1222 Office: NW Tech Sch 1515 S Munn Ave Maryville MO 64468-2757

ZIMMERMAN, PAMELA LAYNE, insurance company executive; b. Winchester, Tenn., Apr. 4, 1949; d. Walter J. and Bettye (Martin) Z. BS in Bus. Edn., Mid. Tenn. State U., 1971. Legal sec. Gullett, Steele, Sanford, Robinson and Merritt, Nashville, 1971-74; instr. secretarial sci. Nashville State Tech. Inst., 1974-75; paralegal Gullett, Sanford and Robinson, Nashville, 1975-83, J. Murray Milliken, Nashville, 1983-84, Boult, Cummings, Conners and Berry, Nashville, 1985-86; asst. v.p. and Tenn. state agy. mgr. Commonwealth Land Title Ins. Co., Nashville, 1986—. Vol. and supporter Ronald McDonald House, Nashville. Mem. Am. Land Title Assn., Tenn. Land Title Assn. (sec.-treas. 1988-90), Mid. Tenn. Paralegal Assn., Nashville Bar Assn. (assoc.), Nashville Area C. of C., Fannie Battle Social Workers (life), Alpha Delta Pi (grand sec. 1993—).

ZIMMERMAN, PATRICIA ANN, sales specialist, consultant; b. Topeka, Kans., Mar. 1, 1962; d. William H. and Shirley Patricia (Phelan) Z. B in Gen. Studies, U. Kans., 1986. Pharm. sales The Upjohn Co., Kalamazoo, Mich., 1986-88; hosp. profl. sales Glaxo Inc. div. Allen and Hanburys, Research Triangle Park, N.C., 1988-91, med. liaison, 1991, hosp. corp. sales, 1991-92, dist. sales specialist, 1992-93; dist. sales specialist Alaska Cnt., Juneau, Alaska, 1994—; cons. in field N.Y. Acad. Sci., U. Ill., Green Coll., Chgo., 1993. Pres. Womens Polit. Brunch Club, Chgo., 1993—. Mem. Chimera Self Def. for Women (assoc.). Democrat. Roman Catholic. Home: 911 1st St Juneau AK 99824

ZIMMERMANN, CLAUDIA PATRICIA, neurologist; b. Lima, Peru, Mar. 1, 1963; d. Oscar J. and Nora (DeBaisi) Z.; m. Jamie Sandoval, May 6, 1988; 1 child, Karen. MD, U. San Marcos, 1988. Med. chief Peru III Med. Ctr., Lima, 1989-91; resident neurology E. Rebagliatti Hosp., Lima, 1990-91; resident LaGuardia Hosp., Forest Hills, N.Y., 1991-92; resident neurology L.I. Jewish Med. Ctr., New Hyde Park, N.Y., 1992—. Mem. AMA, Am. Acad. Neurology, Med. Coll. Peru. Office: LI Jewish Med Ctr New Hyde Park NY 11042

ZIMMERMANN, PAMELA SEMMENS, secondary education educator; b. Cleve., Jan. 8, 1953; d. Thomas Michael and Katherine (Tehan) Semmens; m. Ronald Howard Murrison, Feb. 28, 1992; 1 child, Geoffrey. BS, U. Ill., 1975; MS, No. Ill. U., 1981, postgrad., 1989—. Lic. tchr., sch. svc. pers., adminstrn., Ill. Tchr. West Chicago (Ill.) High Sch., 1975-80; tchr., gifted coord. Lisle (Ill.) High Sch., 1980-85; tchr. Hinsdale (Ill.) Ctrl. High Sch., 1985-92; dir. social studies/fgn. lang. Adlai Stevenson High Sch., Lincolnshire, Ill., 1992—; speaker Am. Studies Conf., 1988, 90, 92; coord., organizer Am. Studies Ann. Conf., 1991; mem. sch. improvement com. Hinsdale Ctrl. High Sch. Author thematic curriculum, world cultures curriculum project. Precinct committeeman Dem. party Milton Twp., DuPage County, Ill., 1986—. James scholar U. Ill. Mem. ASCD, Nat. Coun. Social Studies, Com. on Am. Studies Edn. (mem. steering com.), Phi Delta Kappa. Home: 825 W Hawthorne Blvd Wheaton IL 60187-3476 Office: 1 Stevenson Dr Lincolnshire IL 60069-2824

ZIMMET, JESSIE VERELYNN, nurse, trust manager, home designer; b. Garden City, Kans., May 26, 1955; d. Vere Edward and Jessie Nina (Harmon) Z. A in Gen. Sci., Garden City Coll., 1975, ADN, 1977; BSN, Ft. Hays State U., 1982. CCRN; ACLS, instr.; trauma nurse core course provider. Aide Garden Valley, Garden City, 1975; ICU technician St. Catherine's Hosp., Garden City, 1975-76; PRN flight nurse Life Watch, Wichita, Kans., Amarillo, Tex., 1985; instr. Ft. Hays (Kans.) State U., 1979-80; med. nurse Hadly Regional Med. Ctr., Hays, 1977-83; charge nurse, staff N.W. Tex. Hosp., Amarillo, 1984-94; unit mgr. med. specialty Integrated Health System, Amarillo, 1994—; PRN CCU High Plains Bapt. Hosp.; spkr. in field. Devel. ventilator wean unit. Mem. San Jacinto Bapt. Ch., Amarillo, 1994; mem. Ulysses (Kans.) 1st Bapt. Ch., 1966. Mem. AACN, Emergency Nurse Assn. Home: 6605 Dreyfuss Amarillo TX 77106

ZIMNY, MARILYN LUCILE, anatomist, educator; b. Chgo., Dec. 12, 1927; d. John and Lucile Ruth (Andryske) Z. BA, U. Ill., 1948; MS, Loyola U., Chgo., 1951, PhD, 1954. Asst. prof. anatomy La. State U. Med. Ctr., New Orleans, 1954-59, assoc. prof., 1959-64, prof., 1964-75, prof., acting head, 1975-76, prof., head, 1976—, acting dean sch. grad. studies, 1989-90, dean sch. grad. studies and vice-chancellor for academic affairs, 1990—; vis. prof. anatomy U. Costa Rica Sch. Medicine, 1961, 62. Grantee, NIH, 1958-72, 88-89, Arthritis Found., 1969-72, Schlieder Ednl. Found., 1972-75, Frost Found., 1975-78, NSF, 1982-83. Mem. AAAS, Am. Assn. Anatomists (mem. exec. com. 1981-85, program sec. 1990-94), Am. Physiol. Soc., Assn. Anatomy Chmn. (pres. 1983), Electron Microscopic Soc. Am., Am. Assn. Dental Schs. (sect. anat. scis.), Assn. Rsch. in Vision and Ophthalmology, Am./Internat. Assn. Dental Rsch., Omicron Kappa Upsilon, Alpha Omega Alpha. Home: 3330 Esplanade Ave New Orleans LA 70119-3132 Office: La State U Med Ctr Resource Ctr New Orleans LA 70112

ZINAMAN, HELAINE MADELEINE, gifted/talented education educator; b. N.Y.C., Sept. 11, 1951; d. Harold Joseph and Charlotte (Orenstein) Z. BA, Am. U., 1973; MEd, U. Md., 1979. Spl. edn. resource tchr. John Eager Howard Elem. Sch., Capitol Heights, Md., 1973-85; coord. talented and gifted program Glenarden Woods TAG Magnet, Lanham, Md., 1985—; coord. Owens Rd. Math., Sci. and Tech. Sch., Oxon Hill, Md., 1992-93, Walker Mill Mid. Sch., Capital Heights, Md., 1993-94; pvt. tutor, Washington, 1982-85, 92—; tchr. overview course GED, Bladensburg, Md., 1983; instr. creative thinking Prince George's Community Coll., Largo, Md., 1983, 85; instr. Thinktank, U. Md., College Park, 1989—; mem. Math., Sci. and Tech. Network, 1989. Asst. editor Sci. Bowl, 1990—. Judge Md. State Odyssey of the Mind Competition; talent on "Count on Us" Cable TV Math. Show. Washington Post grantee, 1989; recipient Bowie Excellence in Edn. award, 1991. Mem. Nat. Assn. for Gifted Children, Assn. for Supervision and Curriculum Devel., Md. State Tchrs. Assn., Nat. Educators Assn., Prince Georges County Educators Assn. Democrat. Jewish. Home: # A-409 3440 38th St NW # A-409 Washington DC 20016-3006 Office: Glenarden Woods Elem Glenarden Pky Lanham Seabrook MD 20706

ZINKON, LANA SUE, occupational health nurse; b. Dover, Ohio, Oct. 19, 1954; d. Jack Eugene and Virginia Louise (Brown) Z.; divorced; children: Amanda Elyse and Emily Suzanne (twins). Diploma, Grant Hosp. Sch. Nursing, Columbus, Ohio, 1976; student, Ashland U., 1991—. RN, Ohio. Supr. med. Cedar Point Amusement Park, Sandusky, Ohio, 1977-82; shift supr. Nursing Home, Port Clinton, Ohio, 1978-82; staff nurse Flying Nurses, Calif. La., 1982-83; camp nurse Camp Blue Star, Hendersonville, N.C., summer 1983; staff nurse Med. Pers. Pool, Hendersonville, 1983; occupational health nurse Rockwell Internat., Fletcher, N.C., 1984-88; staff/charge nurse Joel Pomerene Hosp., Millersburg, Ohio, 1988-89, off-shift supr., 1989-93, dir. occupational health, 1990-94; occupational health nurse The Timken Co., New Philadelphia, Ohio, 1989—; coord. on-site svc. for occupational medcine Ctr. of Tuscarawas County, New Philadelphia, 1995—; dir., creator On-the-Job Occupational Program, Joel Pomerene Meml. Hosp., Millersburg, 1990. Mem. Am. Assn. Occupational Health Nurses, Ohio Assn. Occupational Health Nurses, Stark Assn. Occupational Health Nurses, Am. Legion Aux., Ohio Eastern Star. Democrat. Methodist. Office: Med Ctr Tuscarawas County 306 W High New Philadelphia OH 44663

ZINMAN, RHEA, artist; b. N.Y.C.; d. Jacob and Celia (Cohen) Z. BA, Hunter Coll., 1934; postgrad., CCNY, Nat. Acad. Design, SUNY-Purchase, Lehman Coll., Art Students League, Greenwich House Pottery. Pub. info. specialist US Def. Dept., N.Y.C., Phila., 1944-57, USDA, N.Y.C., 1957-73. Exhibited in group shows at CCNY, Art 54 Gallery, 1988, Temple Shalom, Plainfield, N.J., 1988, House of Living Judaism, Union Am. Hebrew Congregations, N.Y.C., 1991, Krasdale Foods Gallery, White Plains, N.Y., 1992-93. Mem. Nat. Mus. Women Artists, Jewish Mus., U.S. Holocaust Mus., Orgn. Ind. Artists, Bronx Coun. of the Arts, Artists Equity, Golden Key Nat. Honor Soc. Home: 2121 Paulding Ave #3C Bronx NY 10462-2136

ZINS, MARTHA LEE, elementary education educator, media specialist; b. Mankato, Minn., Dec. 14, 1945; d. Hubert Joseph and Rose Marie (Johannes) Z. BA in History, Mankato State U., 1966, BA in English, 1967; MLS, Western Mich. U., 1971; postgrad., U. Minn. Tchr. history Worthington (Minn.) High Sch., 1966-67; sch. media generalist Hopkins (Minn.) West Jr. High Sch., 1967-83, Curren Elem. Sch., Hopkins, 1986—; mem. Hopkins Dist. Tech. Com., 1986—; co-chair Hopkins Elem. Sci. Com., 1991—. Contbr. articles to profl. jours.; presenter and speaker at confs. Pres. Saddlewood Patio Homes Assn. Inc., Minnetonka, 1991—, bd. dirs., 1987—; mem. various gov.'s task forces. Mem. NEA (bd. dirs. 1976-77, 91—, Woman Educator of Yr. 1975), ALA, ACLU, Minn. Edn. Assn. (bd. dirs. 1975-86, 91—, v.p. 1977-83, pres. 1983-86, Human Rels. award 1979), Minn. Civil Liberties Union (bd. dirs. 1982—), State of Minn. Tchrs. Retirement Assn. (bd. dirs. 1989—), Minn. Ednl. Media Orgn. (co-founder, v.p. 1990), Delta Kappa Gamma (Beta Beta chpt., co-founder, chpt. treas.), Beta Phi Mu, Phi Alpha Theta. Mem. Dem. Farm Labor Party. Roman Catholic. Home: 17509 Saddlewood Ln Minnetonka MN 55345-2663 Office: Curren Sch Dept Media 1600 Mainstreet Hopkins MN 55343

ZINSER, ELISABETH ANN, university president; b. Meadville, Pa., Feb. 20, 1940; d. Merle and Fae Zinser. BS, Stanford U., 1964; MS, U. Calif., San Francisco, 1966, MIT, 1982; PhD, U. Calif., Berkeley, 1972. Nurse VA Hosp., Palo Alto, Calif., 1964-65, San Francisco, 1969-70; instr. Sch. Nursing U. Calif., San Francisco, 1966-69; pre-doctoral fellow Nat. Inst. Health, Edn. and Welfare, 1971-72; adminstr. Sch. Medicine U. Wash., Seattle, 1972-75, Coun. Higher Edn., State of Ky., 1975-77; prof., dean. Coll. Nursing U. N.D., Grand Forks, 1977-83; vice chancellor acad. affairs U. N.C., Greensboro, 1983-89; pres. Gallaudet U., Washington, 1988, U. Idaho, Moscow, 1989—; cons. Ctr. Leadership Devel. Am. Coun. Edn., Washington, Boeing Aircraft Co., Seattle, Nat. Workshop Acad. Deans, Higher Edn. Exec. Assocs., Denver, Bush Found., St. Paul; chmn. commn. on outreach and tech. transfer Nat. Assn. State Univs. and Land Grant Colls., 1993—, mem. bd. dirs., 1994—. Author: (with others) Contemporary Issues in Higher Education, 1985, Higher Education Research, 1988; co-author: Nurse: A Changing Word in a Changing World, 1982. Bd. dirs. Humana Hosp., Greensboro, 1986-88; v.p., bd. dirs. Ea. Music Festival, Greensboro, 1987-89; trustee N.C. Coun. Econ. Edn., 1985-89, Greensboro Day Sch., 1987-89. Leadership fellow Bush Found., 1981-82. Mem. Am. Assn. Higher Edn., Assn. Am. Colls. (Coun. Liberal Learning), Am. Assn. Univ. Adminstrs., AAUP, AAUW, Rotary, Pi Lambda Theta, Sigma Theta Tau. Home: 1026 Nez Perce Dr Moscow ID 83843-4138 Office: U Idaho Office of the President Moscow ID 83843*

ZINSSER, JUDITH P., historian; b. N.Y.C., July 24, 1943; d. Hans H. and Anne S. (Drinker) Z.; 1 child, Sarah K. Lippmann. BA in History magna cum laude, Bryn Mawr Coll., 1964; MA in English History, Columbia U., 1969; PhD in Early Modern European History, Rutgers U., 1993. Tchr. history dept. The Brearley Sch., N.Y.C., 1964-68; tchr. humanities dept. UN Internat. Sch., N.Y.C., 1969-93; instr. social studies M.A. program Columbia U., N.Y.C., 1989-90; instr. part-time, teaching asst. history dept. Rutgers U., 1990-93; asst. prof. Miami U., Oxford, Ohio, 1993—; lectr. in field; Unesco rep. to Ad Hoc Working Group on Indigenous Populations, Geneva, 1993; U.S. rep. to UNESCO Associated Schs. Project Conf. "Human Rights Education", Kuopio, Finland, 1989, IBO rep. to UN End of Decade Conf. on Women, Nairobi, Kenya, 1985; cons. curriculum design and materials for various orgns. Author: A New Partnership: Indigenous Peoples and the United Nations System, 1994, History and Feminism: A Glass Half Full, 1993, Approaches to the Comparative History of the Americas, 2nd edit., 1989, Understanding the Universal Declaration of Human Rights, 1978, The Chronological History of the Negro in America, 1969; co-author: A History of Their Own: Women in Europe from Prehistory to the Present, 1988; contbr. numerous articles and revs. to profl. publs. Grad. fellow Rutgers Ctr. for Hist. Analysis, 1992-94, Scott Trust Vis. scholar Poly. Sch., 1990; recipient AAUW Rsch. grant, 1992, Schlatter Fund of Rutgers U. Rsch. and Travel grant, 1991, 92, Grad. fellowship Rutgers U., 1990-94, UN Internat. Sch. Travel and Project grant, 1988, Oaklawn Found. grant for Travel to Africa, 1985, IMPACT II Developer grant N.Y.C. Bd. Edn., 1984-85, Good Samaritan Found. Inc. Travel and Study Grant to South Am., 1977. Mem. Am. Hist. Assn. (mem. com. on women historians 1980-82, mem. James Harvey Robinson prize com. 1982-83, mem. ann. meeting program com. 1990), World History Assn. (mem. nat. conf. program com. 1992, v.p. and pres.-elect 1994—, mem. editorial bd. Jour. World History 1989—), Berkshire Conf. of Women Historians (mem. book award com. 1982-88, 90-92). Office: Miami U 254 Upham Hall Oxford OH 45056

ZIPPRODT, PATRICIA, costume designer. B.A., Wellesley Coll.; student, Art Inst. Chgo., Art Students League N.Y., Fashion Inst. Tech. Asst. to various theatre designers; Sch. for Scancal, Shakespeare Co., Washington, 1994; lectr., condr. master classes Yale U., Harvard U., others; vis. lectr. theatre arts NYU; prof. theatre arts Brandeis U., 1985-93; founding mem. Nat. Theater for the Deaf. Designer: (Broadway mus.) Fiddler on the Roof, 1964 (Tony award 1964), Cabaret, 1966 (Tony award 1966), Zorba, 1968 (Drama Desk award 1968), 1776, 1969 (Drama Desk award 1969, Joseph P. Maharam award 1970), Pippin, 1972 (Drama Desk award 1973), Mack and Mable, 1974, Chicago, 1975, King of Hearts, 1978, Alice in Wonderland, 1982 (Joseph P. Maharam award 1983), Smile, 1983, The Accidental Death of an Anarchist, 1984, Sweet Charity, 1985 (Tony award 1986), Big Deal, 1986, Shogun: The Musical, 1990 (Drama Desk award 1990, Joseph P. Maharam award 1990), My Fair Lady, 1993; (Broadway plays) A Period of Adjustment, 1962, Little Foxes, 1967, Plaza Suite, 1968, Scratch, 1971, All God's Chillun' Got Wings, 1975, Poor Murderer, 1976, Kingdoms, 1981, Fools, 1981, Brighton Beach Memoirs, 1983, The Glass Menagerie, 1983, Macbeth, 1988, Cat on a Hot Tin Roof, 1989, My Favorite Year, 1992; (off-Broadway plays) Our Town, 1960, The Balcony, 1960, Camino Real, 1961, Oh Dad Poor Dad Etc., 1962, A Man's a Man, 1963, The Blacks, 1962; (Guthrie Theatre) Waiting for Godot, 1973, Don Juan, 1982 (Joseph P. Maharam award 1983), The Bacchae, 1987; (Nat. Actors Theatre) The Crucible, 1991-92, Hotel Paradiso, 1991-92, The Master Builder, 1991-92; (Boston Opera) Madam Butterfly, 1962, Hippolyte E Aricie, 1966, The Rise and Fall of the City of Mahagonny, 1972; (New York City Opera) Katerina Ismailova, 1967, The Flaming Angel, 1968, Naughty Marietta, 1978; (Guggenheim Mus., N.Y.C.) The Mother of Us All, 1972; (Julliard Opera) Lord Byron, 1973; (Met. Opera) Tannhaüser, 1977, The Barber of Seville, 1982; (Am. Repertory Theatre, Cambridge, Mass.) The Fall of the House of Usher, 1988; (Am. Ballet Theatre) Les Noces, 1969, The Leaves are Fading, 1975, Estuary, 1982, Coppélia, 1991; (New York City Ballet) Watermill, 1972, Dybbuk Variations, 1974, The Sleeping Beauty, 1991; (Houston Ballet) Helgi Tommasen, 1985; (Ballet Hispanico) Cada Noche Tango Jnez de Castro Tres Cantos, 1988; (films) The Graduate, 1967; (television spls.) Anne Bancroft Spl., CBS, 1970, June Moon, WNET, 1973, The Glass Menagerie, ABC, 1973, Alice in Wonderland, WNET, 1983, Chrysler Skating, 1992; (nat. tours) Bette Midler, 1976, Ben Vereen, 1983; designer, advisor: The Seagull (St. Petersburg, Russia), Anna Christie (Beijing, China); exhibitor design sketches Wright-Hepburn, London, 1966, Capicorn Gallery, N.Y.C., 1968, Mus. City N.Y., 1972, U. Calif.-San Diego, 1974, Toneelmuseum, Amsterdam, The Netherlands, 1975, U.S. Internat. Theatre Inst. traveling exhibit, 1974-78, N.Y. City Ballet, 1994. Recipient award for spl. costumes NATAS, 1970, Alumna Achievement award Wellesley Coll., 1971, spl. award New Eng. Conf., 1973, Ritter award Fashion Inst. Tech., 1977, Disting. Career award S.E. Theatre Conf., 1985. Mem. United Scenic Artists, Costume Designers Guild, Motion Picture Acad. Arts and Scis. Inducted into Theatrical Hall of Fame, 1992. Address: 29 King St New York NY 10014-4944

ZISKIN, LAURA, film producer. Co-founder Frogwood Films. Films include: (assoc. prodr.) Eyes of Laura Mars, 1978; (prodr.) Murphy's Romance, 1985, No Way Out, 1987, D.O.A., 1988, Everybody's An American, 1988, The Rescue, 1988, What About Bob?, 1991, The Doctor, 1991, Hero, 1992; (exec. prodr.) Pretty Woman, 1990. Office: Laura Ziskin Prodns 10202 W Washington Blvd Culver City CA 90232-3195*

ZLOTLOW, SUSAN FRANCES, administrator; b. Huntington, N.Y., July 13, 1952; d. Moses Gideon and Guta (Friedman) Z.; m. Kevin Edward O'Grady, Sept. 2, 1979; children: Megan Leah, Caitlin Alyce. BA, U. Rochester, 1974; MA, U. Conn., 1977, PhD, 1979. Lic. psychologist Md. Asst. prof. Wheaton Coll., Norton, Mass., 1979-80; staff psychologist Albuquerque Child Guidance, 1980-83; clin. asst. prof. U. N.Mex., Albuquerque, 1982-83; sr. child psychologist North Charles Gen. Hosp., Balt., 1983-84; faculty rsch. assoc. U. Md., College Park, 1984-86, asst. to dean, 1989-91, asst. dean grad. studies & rsch., 1991—. Post-doctoral fellow U. Md., 1986-89; recipient Individual Nat. Rsch. Svc. award Nat. Inst. Mental Health, 1986. Mem. Am. Psychol. Assn. Office: Grad Studies & Rsch U Md College Park MD 20742

ZLOTNICK, DIANA SHIRLEY, newsletter publisher; b. L.A., Sept. 3, 1927; d. Harry Samuel and Rose Izen Grossman; m. Harry Zlotnick, July 2, 1955; children: Bonnie Zlotnick Yates, Marianne. BA, Calif. State U., L.A., 1952. Editor Newsletter on the Arts, North Hollywood, Calif., 1971—; pvt. arts mgmt. cons., L.A. Mem. acquisitions com. Laguna (Calif.) Art Mus., 1992—, donor, 1992-95, trustee, 1993-94, lectr., 1995. Named Leading L.A. Art Collector, San Francisco Mus. of Art, 1977.

ZOBEL, JAN ARLEEN, tax consultant; b. San Francisco, Feb. 8, 1947; d. Jerome Fremont and Louise Maxine (Purwin) Z. BA, Whittier Coll., 1968; MA, U. Chgo., 1970. Tchr. Chgo. Pub. Schs., 1969-70, San Francisco Pub. Schs., 1971-78; editor, pub. People's Yellow Pages, San Francisco, 1971-81; pvt. practice tax cons. San Francisco, 1978—; tchr. community coll. dist., San Francisco, 1986-91; tax lectr. U. Hawaii, 1989—, U. Calif., San Francisco State U., Marin C.C. Editor: People's Yellow Pages, 1971-81 (cert. of honor San Francisco Bd. Suprs. 1974), Where The Child Things Are, 1977-80. Com. mem. Bay Area Career Women's Fund. Named Acct. Advocate of Yr. SBA, 1987; presented with Key to Buffalo, 1970. Mem. Nat. Assn. Enrolled Agts., Calif. Assn. Enrolled Agts., Nat. Assn. Tax Preparers, Bay Area Career Women. Home: 3045 Holyrood Dr Oakland CA 94611-2541 Office: 1197 Valencia St San Francisco CA 94110-3026

ZOBEL, LOUISE PURWIN, author, educator, lecturer, writing consultant; b. Laredo, Tex., Jan. 10, 1922; d. Leo Max and Ethel Catherine (Levy) Purwin; m. Jerome Fremont Zobel, Nov. 14, 1943; children: Lenore Zobel Harris, Janice A., Robert E., Audrey Zobel Dollinger. BA cum laude, Stanford U., 1943, MA, 1976. Cert. adult edn. and community coll. tchr., Calif. Freelance mag. writer and author Palo Alto, Calif., 1942—; writer, editor, broadcastor UP Bur., San Francisco, 1943; lectr. on writing, history, travel No. Calif., 1964—; lectr., educator U. Calif. campuses, other colls. and univs., 1969—; writing cons. to pvt. clients, 1969—; editorial asst. Assn. Coll. Unions Internat., Palo Alto, 1972-73; acting asst. prof. journalism San Jose State U., 1976; keynote speaker, seminar leader, prin. speaker at nat. confs. Author: (books) The Travel Writer's Handbook, 1980, (paperback), 1982, 83, 84, 85, rev. edit., 1992; author, narrator (90 minute cassette) Let's Have Fun in Japan, 1982; contbr. articles to anthologies, nat. mags. and newspapers; writer advertorials. Bd. dirs., publicity chair Friends of Palo Alto Libr., 1985—; officer Santa Clara County Med. Aux., Esther Clark Aux., others; past pres. PTA. Recipient award for excellence in journalism Sigma Delta Chi, 1943, awards Writers Digest, 1967-75, 94, Armed Forces Writers League, 1972, Nat. Writers Club, 1976. Mem. Am. Soc. Journalists and Authors, Travel Journalists Guild, Internat. Food, Wine and Travel Writers Assn., Pacific Asia Travel Assn., Calif. Writers Club (v.p. 1988-89), AAUW (v.p. 1955-57, Nat. writing award 1969), Stanford Alumni Assn., Phi Beta Kappa. Home and Office: 23350 Sereno Ct Unit 30 Cupertino CA 95014-6543

ZOBEL, RYA WEICKERT, federal judge; b. Germany, Dec. 18, 1931. A.B., Radcliffe Coll., 1953; LL.B., Harvard U., 1956. Bar: Mass. 1956, U.S. Dist. Ct., Mass., 1956, U.S. Ct. Appeals (1st cir.) 1967. Assoc. Hill & Barlow, Boston, 1967-73; assoc. Goodwin, Procter & Hoar, Boston, 1973-76, ptnr., 1976-79; U.S. dist. judge of Mass. Boston, 1979—. Mem. ABA, Boston Bar Assn., Am. Bar Found., Mass. Bar Assn., Am. Law Inst. Home: 294 Jerusalem Rd Cohasset MA 02025 Office: US Dist Ct John W McCormack PO & Courthouse 90 Devonshire St Rm 1802 Boston MA 02109*

ZOCCO, ROSEANNE MARIE, nurse, educator; b. Sioux Falls, S.D., July 15, 1955; d. Rosemarie B. Faini. BS in Nursing, Coll. Mt. St. Joseph on Ohio, Cin., 1977; MSEd, Youngstown State U., 1989. RN, Ohio. Asst. head nurse, then head nurse SICU St. Elizabeth Hosp. Med. Ctr., Youngstown, Ohio; staff devel. coord. Greenville (Pa.) Reg. Hosp., dir. edn. svcs. Mem. ARC, AACN (pres. northeastern Ohio chpt. 1978, 81, sec. 1977), Am. Heart Assn., Am. Soc. Health Edn. and Trainers, Soc. Healthcare Edn. Leaders.

ZOELLNER, JAMIE L., critical care nurse; b. Cumming, Ga., Sept. 18, 1963; d. James H. and Reba (Mills) Z. AS and AA with honors, Polk Community Coll., 1989; BSN with honors, U. Fla., 1993; MSN, Duke U., 1994. RN, CCRN, Fla., N.D.; cert. ACLS, adult NP, critical care CNS. Formerly staff nurse surg. ICU Lakeland (Fla.) Regional Med. Ctr. Mem. ACCN, SCCM, Sigma Theta Tau, Phi Kappa Phi.

ZOLBER, KATHLEEN KEEN, nutrition educator; b. Walla Walla, Wash., Dec. 9, 1916; d. Wildie H. and Alice (Johnson) Keen; m. Melvin L. Zolber, Sept. 19, 1937. BS in Foods and Nutrition, Walla Walla Coll., 1941; MA,

Wash. State U., 1961; PhD, U. Wis., 1968. Registered dietitian. Dir. food service Walla Walla Coll., 1941-50, mgr. coll. store, 1951-59, asst. prof. food and nutrition, 1959-62, assoc. prof., 1962-64; assoc. prof. nutrition Loma Linda (Calif.) U., 1964-72, prof. nutrition, 1973-91, dir. dietetic edn., 1967-84, dir. dietetics Med. Ctr., 1972-84, dir. nutrition program, 1984-91; retired. Mead Johnson grantee, 1965-67; recipient Alumna of Yr. award Walla Walla Coll., 1977; Delores Nyhus award Calif. Dietetic Assn., 1978. Mem. Am. Dietetic Assn. (pres. 1982-83, Copher award 1992), Am. Pub. Health Assn., AAUP, Omicron Nu, Delta Omega. Home: PO Box 981 Loma Linda CA 92354-0981

ZOLLAR, CAROLYN CATHERINE, lawyer; b. Evanston, Ill., July 5, 1947; d. Maurice Adam and Alice S. (Kelm) Z. BA, Smith Coll., Northampton, Mass., 1969; MA, Columbia U., 1970; JD, Am. U., Washington, 1976. Bar: D.C., Va. Legis. asst. Congressman William Anderson U.S. Ho. of Reps., Washington, 1970-72; planning cons. Nat. Inst. Edn., Washington, 1972, legal asst., 1973, asst. for govt. and external rels., 1973-75; assoc. Joe W. Fleming II, P.C., Washington, 1975-82; gen. counsel Nat. Assn. Rehab. Facilities, Washington, 1982-86, gen. counsel, dir. med. rehab., 1986-94; gen. counsel, v.p. pub. policy Am. Rehab. Assn., Washington, 1994—; sec. Am. Rehab. Svcs., Inc., Washington, 1988-94; bd. adv. Ind. Living Mag., N.Y.C., 1988—; mem. Joint Commn. Accreditation Health Care Orgns. Task Force on Rehab. Svcs., 1988. Contbr. articles to profl. jours. Sec. bd. dirs. Rock Creek Found., Silver Spring, Md., 1983-90. Recipient legis. achievement award Nat. Assn. Rehab. Facilities, 1981, legis. advocacy award U. Buffalo, 1993, pub. svc. award Am. Acad. Phys. Medicine and Rehab., 1994. Mem. Am. Soc. Assn. Execs., Bar Assn. D.C. (health com., cert. of appreciation young lawyers sect.), Nat. Health Lawyers Assn., Va. Bar Assn., D.C. Bar, Women in Govt. Rels. Episcopalian. Office: Am Rehab Assn 1350 I St N W Ste 670 Washington DC 20005

ZOLLAR, JAWOLE WILLA JO, artistic director; b. Kansas City, Mo., 1951. Grad., Florida State. Founder, artistic dir. Urban Bush Women, N.Y.C., 1984—. Office: Urban Bush Women care St Mark's Church 131 E 10th St New York NY 10003 also: care IMG Artists 22 E 71st St New York NY 10021*

ZOLLAR, NIKKI MICHELLE, state agency administrator; b. Chgo., June 18, 1956; d. Lowell M. and Doris J. (Lowe) Z.; m. William A. Von Hoene, Jr., June 18, 1983; children: William Lowell Von Hoene, Branden Tracey. BA, Johns Hopkins U., 1977; JD, Georgetown U., 1980. Fed. jud. law clk. U.S. Dist. Ct. (no. dist.) Ill., Chgo., 1980-81; assoc. Lafontant, Wilkins, Jones & Ware, Chgo., 1981-83, Kirkland & Ellis, Chgo., 1983-85; chmn., sec. Chgo. Bd. Election Commrs., 1987-90; dir. Ill. Dept. Profl. Regulation, Chgo., 1991—. Bd. trustees Woodland Acad. of Sacred Heart, Cmty. Youth Creative Learning Experience; mem. Louis R. Lowe women's bd. United Negro Coll. Fund; mem. women's coun. Chgo. Heart Assn.; mem. Chgo. com. Solidarity with So. Africa; mem. women's bd. Jackson Park Hosp.; active Chgo. Urban League, Nat. Coalition of 100 Black Women. Recipient Outstanding Achievement award YWCA, Outstanding Achievement of Svc. to Cmty. award Washington Park YMCA, Youth Svc. award Beatrice Caffrey Found., David C. Hilliard award Chgo. Bar Assn., 1988-89, Kizzy award Revlon Corp./Kizzy Scholarship Fund, African-Am. Women's Achievement award Columbia Coll., Martin Luther King Jr. award for dedicated leadership Boy Scouts Am., Outstanding Young Profl. award Chgo. Urban Profls., Svc. and Leadership award United Negro Coll. Fund, Outstanding Achievement cert. Ill. State Atty. Appellate Svc. Commn.; named One of 100 Outstanding Black Bus. and Profl. Women in U.S., Dollars and Sense mag. Mem. Ill. Women in Govt., Women Execs. in State Govt., Alpha Gamma Pi. Mem. United Ch. of Christ. Office: Ill Dept Profl Regulation Nurse Sect 320 W Washington St Springfield IL 62786

ZOLOTOW, CHARLOTTE SHAPIRO, author, editor; b. Norfolk, Va., June 26, 1915; d. Louis J. and Ella F. (Bernstein) Shapiro; m. Maurice Zolotow, Apr. 14, 1938 (div. 1969); children: Stephen, Ellen. Student, U. Wis., 1933-36. Editor children's book dept. Harper & Row, N.Y.C., 1938-44; sr. editor Harper & Row, 1962-70; v.p., assoc. pub. Harper Jr. Books, 1976-81; editorial cons., editorial dir. Charlotte Zolotow Books, 1982-90; pub. emerita, advisor Harper Collins Children's Books, 1991—; tchr. U. Colo. Writers Conf. on Children's Books, U. Ind. Writers Conf.; also lectr. children's books. Author: The Park Book, 1944, Big Brother, 1960, The Sky Was Blue, 1963, The Magic Words, 1952, Indian Indian, 1952, The Bunny Who Found Easter, 1959, In My Garden, 1960, But Not Billy, 1947, 2d edit, 1983, Not a Little Monkey, 1957, 2d edit., 1989, The Man With The Purple Eyes, 1961, Mr. Rabbit and the Lovely Present, 1962, The White Marble, 1963, A Rose, A Bridge and A Wild Black Horse, 1964, 2d edit., 1987, Someday, 1965, When I Have a Little Girl, 1965, If It Weren't for You, 1966, 2d edit., 1987, Big Sister, Little Sister, 1966, All That Sunlight, 1967, When I Have A Son, 1967, My Friend John, 1968, Summer Is, 1968, Some Things Go Together, 1969, The Hating Book, 1969, The New Friend, 1969, River Winding, 1970, 79, Lateef and His World, 1970, Yani and His World, 1970, You and Me, 1971, Wake Up and Goodnight, 1971, William's Doll, 1972, Hold My Hand, 1972, 2d edit., 1987, The Beautiful Christmas Tree, 1972, Janie, 1973, My Grandson Lew, 1974, The Summer Night, 1974, 3d edit. 1991, The Unfriendly Book, 1975, It's Not Fair, 1976, 2d edit., 1987, Someone New, 1978, Say It, 1980, If You Listen, 1980, 2d edit. 1987, The New Friend, 1981, One Step, Two ..., 1981, The Song, 1982, I Know a Lady, 1984, Timothy Too!, 1986, Everything Glistens, Everything Sings, 1987, I Like to be Little, 1987, The Poodle Who Barked at the Wind, 1987, The Quiet Mother and the Noisy Little Boy, 1988, Something's Going to Happen, 1988, This Quiet Lady, 1992, The Seashore Book, 1992, Snippets, 1992, The Moon was the Best, 1993, Peter and the Pigeons, 1993, others; compiler An Overpraised Season, Early Sorrow. Recipient Harper Gold Award for Editl. Excellence Harper, 1974, Kerlan Award U. Minn., 1986, Corp. award for children's books LMP, 1990, Silver Medallion U. So. Miss., 1990, Tribute for Far Reaching Contbn. for Children's Lit. ALA, 1991. Mem. PEN, Authors League. Home: 29 Elm Pl Hastings Hdsn NY 10706-1703 Office: 10 E 53rd St New York NY 10022

ZOMBER, BEVERLY LOUISE, medical-surgical, geriatric and psychiatric nurse, educator; b. Evergreen Park, Ill., June 24, 1945; d. Louis and Irene (Cloud) Z. BA, DePaul U., 1967; MA, Northwestern U., 1969; ADN, Fla. Keys Community Coll., 1990. RN, Fla. Ins. claims specialist R.R. Retirement Bd., Chgo., 1969-77; Medicare specialist Social Security Adminstrn., Key West, Fla., 1979-88, L.A., 1979-88; mental health technician Guidance Clinic of Middle Keys, Marathon, Fla., 1988-90; staff/charge nurse Marathon Manor Convalescent Ctr., 1990-92; med.-surg. staff nurse, team leader Mariner's Hosp., Tavernier, Fla., 1992; staff nurse, counselor Marathon Comprehensive Psychiat. Clinic, 1992—; area dir. Nursing Unlimited, Inc., Marathon, 1993; mktg. dir., mem. adj. faculty, cons. Nursing Unltd., Miami, Fla., 1992; staff nurse Staff Builders, Inc., Monroe County, Fla., 1993—; owner, pres. Forms Inc., 1992—; instr. English lit., composition and creative writing Fla. Keys C.C., Marathon, 1993—; instr. in practical nursing Monroe County Sch. System, Fla. Keys, 1993—; DON Griswold Spl. Care, Marathon, 1993—. Former chmn. Inter-Agy. Coun. Monroe County, Fla. Ill. State scholar 1963-67, DePaul U. scholar, 1963-67. Mem. ANA, Fla. Nurses Assn., Marathon Bus. and Profl. Women.

ZONGOLOWICZ, HELEN MICHAELINE, education and psychology educator; b. Kenosha, Wis., July 22, 1936; d. Edmund S. and Helen (Ostrowski) Z.; EdB, Dominican Coll., 1966; MA, Cardinal Stritch Coll., 1973; EdD, U. No. Colo., 1977. Tchr. elem. schs. Kenosha, 1956-58, Center Line, Mich., 1958-59, Taft, Calif., 1960-61, Lake Wales, Fla., 1962-63, Albuquerque, 1963-65; tchr., asst. prin. St. Mary's Sch., Taft, 1965-69; asst. sch. supt. Diocese of Fresno, Calif., 1969-70; tchr. primary grades Greasewood Boarding Sch., Ganado, Ariz., 1970-72, coord. spl. projects, 1972-75, liaison to parent adv. coun., 1972-75, tchr. supr., 1972-76; ednl. specialist Ft. Defiance Agy., Navajo Area, Ariz., 1974-75, ednl. diagnostician, 1979-80; asst. prof. Auburn (Ala.) U., 1977-79; asst. prof. U. N.Mex.-Gallup, 1981-94, prof. edn. and psychology, 1994—, dir. child care ctr.; prin. Chuska Sch., 1980-93; vis. prof. U. Colo., 1976. Recipient Spl. Achievement award U.S. Dept. Interior, 1971, 73, Points of Light award, 1990, Superior Performance award, 1982, Achievement award Navajo Nation, 1993; named Prin. of Yr. Bur. of Indian Affairs, 1990; named Prin. of Yr. Navajo Area Sch. Bd. Assn., 1991. Mem. AAUW, AAUP, NAEYC, NSDC, Am. Assn. Mental Deficiency, Assn. for Supervision and Curriculum Devel., Coun. for Exceptional Children, Coun. for Basic Edn., Am. Ednl. Rsch. Assn., NAFE, Internat. Reading Assn., Assn. for Children with Learning Disabilities Nat. Coun. Tchrs. of English., Assn. Childhood Edn. Internat., Navajo Nation North Cen. Assn. (mem. exec. bd.), Kappa Delta Pi, Phi Delta Kappa. Address: 604 McKee Dr Gallup NM 87301

ZONKA, CONSTANCE Z., educational organization administrator; b. Evanston, Ill.; d. Herbert Edward and Agnes Irene (Turpin) Zipprodt; m. Robert F. Zonka, Aug. 5, 1970; children: Heidi Zapanta, Milo Matthew. BA, U. Fla., 1958; postgrad., U. Chgo., 1960. Account exec. Daniel J. Edelman, Inc., Chgo., 1964-68; pres. Connie Zonka Assocs., Chgo., 1974-89; dir. coll. rels. Columbia Coll., Chgo., 1970-89; sr. dir. univ. rels. Roosevelt U., Chgo., 1990-93; dir. office pub. affairs Gov.'s State U., University Park, Ill., 1993—. Mem. NAFE, Pub. Rels. Soc. Am., Publicity Club Chgo., Nat. Assn. Women Bus. Owners, Friends of WFMT (sec. 1989—), Friends of Downtown, Friends of the Parks. Democrat. Home: 901 S Plymouth Ct Apt 1205 Chicago IL 60605-2053

ZOOK, MARTHA FRANCES HARRIS, retired nursing administrator; b. Topeka, Nov. 15, 1921; d. Dwight Thacher and Helen Muriel (Houston) Harris; m. Paul Warren Zook, July 2, 1948; children: Mark Warren (dec.), Mary Elizabeth Zook Hughey. RN, Meriden (Conn.) Hosp. Sch. Nursing, 1947; student U. Kans., 1948-49, Kans. State U., 1960-61, Barton County Community Coll., 1970-73; BA, Stephens Coll., 1977; postgrad. Ft. Hays State U., 1978-79. Staff nurse Stormont Hosp., Topeka, 1947-48; staff nurse Watkins Meml. Hosp., Lawrence, Kans., 1948-49; nursing supr. Larned State Hosp., 1949-53, sect. supr., 1956-57, dir. nursing, 1958-61, 83-86; sect. nurse Sedgewick Sect., 1961-76, clin. instr. nursing edn., 1976-77, dir. nursing edn., 1977-83; clinic nurse for podiatrist; sect. supr. Dillon Bldg., Larned, 1957-58; Vol. Am. Cancer Soc., ARC, Welcome Inn, Sr. Citizens' Ctr. Pawnee County, Larned grade sch. children's drug info. program. Mem. AAUW, DAR, Sacred Heart Altar Soc. Democrat. Roman Catholic. Home: 1109 Johnson Ave Larned KS 67550-2232

ZOOK, THERESA FUETTERER, gemologist, consultant; b. Barberton, Ohio, Mar. 12, 1919; d. Charles Theodore and Ethel May (Knisely) Fuetterer; m. Donovan Quay Zook, June 21, 1941; children: Theodore Alan, Jacqueline Deborah Zook Cochran. AB, Ohio U., 1941; MA in Pub. Adminstrn., Am. U., 1946. Adminstrv. intern Nat. Inst. Pub. Affairs, Washington, 1941-42; mgmt. intern U.S. Dept. Agr., Washington, 1941-42; adminstrv. analyst Office Emergency Mgmt., Washington, 1942-43, Office Price Adminstrn., Washington, 1943-45; founder Zook and Zook Cons., Arlington, Va., 1945-47; tchr. ancient history and U.S. govt. Fairfax County (Va.) Pub. Schs., 1963-64; founder, pres. Associated Gem Consulting Lab., Alexandria, 1974—, Alpha Gate Crafts Ltd., Alexandria, 1977—; color cons. Internat. Com. on Color in Gems, Bangkok, Thailand, 1983. Author: Basic Machine Knitting, 1979, Directory of Selected Color Resources Annotated Guide, 1982, Reunion of Descendants of David and Magdalena (Blough) Zook, 1983; contbr. articles to profl. jours. Bd. dirs. Am. Embassy Com. on Edn., Montevideo, Uruguay, 1972; co-founder Workshop of Arts, Santiago, Chile, 1958; mem. Nat. Trust for Hist. Preservation, Nat. Mus. Women in Arts, Nat. Mus. Am. Indian, Textile Mus. Fellow Gemmological Assn. of Gt. Britain (diplomate); mem. AAUW, DAR, Nat. Geneal. Soc., Inter-Soc. Color Coun. (chmn. com. color in gemstones 1982-84, Appreciation cert. 1984), Accredited Gemological Assn. (co-founder, v.p.). Home: PO Box 6310 Alexandria VA 22306-0310

ZOON, KATHRYN EGLOFF, biochemist; b. Yonkers, N.Y., Nov. 6, 1948; d. August R. and Violet T. (Pollock) Egloff; BS, Rensselaer Poly. Inst., 1970; PhD Johns Hopkins U., 1975; m. Robert A. Zoon, Aug. 22, 1970; children: Christine K, Jennifer R. Interferon research fellow NIH, Bethesda, Md., 1975-77, staff fellow, 1977-79, sr. staff fellow, 1979-80; sr. staff fellow div. biochem. biophysics Bur. Biologics, FDA, Bethesda, 1980-83; rsch. chemist divsn. biochem. biophysics, 1983-84, rsch. chemist divsn. virology, 1984-88, rsch. chemist div. cytokine biology, Ctr. for Biologics Evaluation and Rsch., FDA, 1988—, div. dir., 1989-92; dir. Ctr. for Biologics Evaluation and Rsch., 1992—; lectr. NIH, 1994, Reigelman Lecturship, 1994. N.Y. State Regents fellow, 1970; Person of the Yr. award Biopharm, 1992, 95, Pub. Svc. award Genetic Engring. News, 1994. Mem. Am. Soc. Biochemistry and Molecular Biology, Internat. Soc. Interferon Research, Internat. Soc. Cytokine Rsch. Roman Catholic. Contbr. numerous articles on research in biol. chemistry to sci. jours.; sect. editor Jour. Interferon Research, 1980—. Office: CBER 1401 Rockville Pike Rockville MD 20852-1428

ZORDICH-LYNCH, JANICE MARIE, mental health counselor; b. Youngstown, Ohio, Oct. 31, 1960; d. Stephen Andrew and June Marie (Zordich) Scali; m. Edward Franklin Lynch, Sept. 18, 1993. BA in Psychology, Youngstown State U., 1982; MS in Edn., Yountstown State U., 1985, postgrad., 1992. Cert. floral designer; nat. cert. counselor; lic. profl. clin. counselor, Ohio. Intake therapist Parkview Counseling Ctr., Youngstown, 1985-88; outpatient counselor Valley Counseling Svcs., Inc., Warren, Ohio, 1988-93. Named Outstanding Young Woman in Am., 1988. Mem. ACA, Ohio Counseling Assn., Ea. Ohio Counseling Assn., Psi Chi, Chi Sigma Iota. Democrat. Roman Catholic.

ZORIE, STEPHANIE MARIE, lawyer; b. Walla Walla, Wash., Mar. 18, 1951; d. Albert Robert and L. Ruth (Land) Z.; m. Francis Benedict Buda, Apr. 18, 1981 (div. 1985). BA, U. Fla., 1974, JD, 1978. Bar: N.Mex. 1991, Fla. 1978, U.S. Dist. Ct. (so. and mid. dists.) Fla. 1979, U.S. Ct. Appeals (5th cir.) 1979, U.S. Tax Ct. 1980, U.S. Ct. Customs and Patent Appeals 1980, U.S. Customs Ct. 1980, U.S. Ct. Mil. Appeals 1980, U.S. Ct. Claims 1981, U.S. Ct. Internat. Trade 1981, U.S. Ct. Appeals (11th cir.) 1981, U.S. Ct. Appeals (fed. cir.) 1982, U.S. Supreme Ct. 1988. Assoc. Richard Hardwich, Coral Gables, Fla., 1978-79, Brown, Terrell & Hogan P.A., Jacksonville, Fla., 1979-80, Dorsey, Arnold & Nichols, Jacksonville, 1980-81; sole practice Jacksonville, 1981-84; ptnr. Blakeley & Zorie P.A., Orlando, Fla., 1985-86; sole practice Orlando, Fla., 1986—, Santa Fe; owner Coyote Cody Co., 1991. Recipient Rep. Claude Pepper award, 1978. Mem. ABA, Assn. Trial Lawyers Am., John Marshall Bar Assn., Spanish-Am. Law Students Assn., Phi Alpha Delta (local sec.-treas. 1978-79). Address: PO Box 2898 Santa Fe NM 87504-2898 also: PO Box 372118 Satellite Beach FL 32937-0118

ZORN, DONNA CHARLOTTE, physical therapist; b. Balt., Feb. 19, 1952; d. James Robert and Joanne Bessie (McElfresh) Z. BS in Phys. Therapy, Russell Sage Coll., 1974; MPH, U. S.C., 1993. Lic. phys. therapist, Fla., N.C. Staff phys. therapist Melbourne (Fla.) Easter Seal Ctr., 1975-78; phys. therapist Dr. W.J. Creel Elem. Sch., Melbourne, 1978-82; staff phys. therapist Wuesthoff Meml. Hosp., Rockledge, Fla., 1982-83; sr. phys. therapist North Fla. Regional Med. Ctr., Gainesville, 1986-88; staff phys. therapist SP.O.R.T. Clinic, Gainesville, 1988-89; instr. Med. Coll. Ga., Augusta, 1989-93; mgr. phys. therapy Meml. Mission Hosp., Ashville, N.C., 1993—. Capt. U.S. Army, 1983-86; maj. Res. Mem. Neurodevel. Treatment Assn., Am. Phys. Therapy Assn., Delta Omega Soc. Home: 14 Ascension Ct Apt G Asheville NC 28806-1948 Office: Meml Mission Hosp 509 Biltmore Ave Asheville NC 28801-4690

ZOTTNICK, LISA ISOBEL, educational therapist; b. Sacramento, Calif., May 9, 1958; d. James T. and Rhoda (VanAllen) McElree. BS, Calvary Bible Coll., 1980; MS, Clayton U., 1991. Cert. ednl. therapist, Calif. Learning disabilities program tchr. New Vistas Christian Sch., Pleasant Hill, Calif., 1981-83; jr. high sch. tchr. Bethel Christian Acad., El Sobrante, Calif., 1983-85; jr. high learning disabilities tchr. Anchor Acad., Pleasant Hill, 1985-91; adminstr. sch.-based day treatment Clipper Acad. for Pvt. Study, Concord, Calif., 1991; pvt. practice ednl. therapist Lifeline Testing and Counseling Svcs., Pleasant Hill, 1986—; speaker at seminars, workshops and convs. in field. Author: Understanding A.D.D., 1992. Mem. Calif. Adv. Bd. on Attention Deficit Disorders, Sacramento, 1992—, chair advocacy and info. com. Mem. Assn. Ednl. Therapists, Learning Disabilities Assn., Children and Adults with Attention Deficit Disorders (coord. Contra Costa County chpt. 1991-94), Orton Dyslexia Soc. Office: Lifeline Testing and Counseling Svcs 140 Gregory Ln Ste 250 Pleasant Hill CA 94523-3357

ZOUBAREFF, OLGA VLADIMIR, accounting adminstrative assistant; b. Hassalt, Belgium; d. Vladimir F. and Kataryna (Sarcov) Z. BA in Polit. Sci., Wayne State U.; postgrad., Ann Parsley Sch. Dance, Clinton Twp., Mich., 1990—; A in Gen. Studies, Drama, Macomb Community Coll.; fitness and nutrition cert., Internat. Corr. Schs. Ctr., Detroit; voice studies, Ctr. for Creative Studies, Detroit, 1994—; drama studies, Wayne State U., 1994—. Acct./adminstrv. asst. Univ. Orthopaedic Assocs. Detroit, P.C., 1990—; mem. Charles J. Givens Orgn., 1991—; actress, dancer, fashion, TV comml. and photographic model/film screen extra. Model, Renaissance Ctr. Fashion Panel, Detroit, 1989-91; rsch. bd. advisors Am. Biog. Inst.; mem. Internat. Biog. Centre Adv. Coun., 1992. Mem. Voice Ctr. for Creative Studies. Home: 38579 Delta St Clinton Township MI 48036-1711 Office: Univ Orthopaedic Assocs Detroit PC 4707 Saint Antoine St Detroit MI 48201-1427

ZOUCHA, SHARON LEA, counselor, educator; b. Albion, Nebr., July 27, 1957; d. Earl Parker and Kathleen Mildred (Mannlien) Stephens; m. Michael Adam Zoucha, Sept. 10, 1983; children: Jonathan Robert, Amanda Anne, Elizabeth Kathleen. BS in Community Counseling, Wayne State Coll., 1979, MS in Sch. Counseling, 1985, BS in Edn. Psychology and Sociology, 1985. Cert. elem. tchr. Dental asst. Drs. Brown and Houfek, Genoa, Nebr., 1976; social worker, child protective svc. worker Nebr. Dept. Social Svcs., Albion, 1980-84; substitute counselor Albion Pub. Schs., 1985-86; elem. tchr. St. Michael's Elem Sch., Albion, 1986-90; K-12 counselor, tchr. St. Edward (Nebr.) Pub. Sch., 1990—; cons. social worker Boone County Hosp., Albion, 1983. Mem. St. Edward Edn. Assn., Nebr. Edn. Assn. Office: Saint Edward Sch Dist 17 PO Box C Saint Edward NE 68660-0138

ZSCHAU, MARILYN, singer; b. Chgo., Feb. 9, 1944. Ed. Juilliard Sch. Music, also studied with John Lester. Toured with Met. Nat. Co., 1965-66; debut, Vienna Volksoper, in Die Tote Stadt, 1967, Vienna Staatsoper, in Ariadne auf Naxos, 1971; with N.Y.C. Opera from 1978; debut Met. Opera, in La Boheme, 1985, La Scala, in Die Frau ohne Schatten, 1986; has toured and sung in many countries. Office: Harrison Parrott, 12 Penzance Pla, London W11 4PA, England also: Los Angeles Music Ctr 135 N Grand Ave Los Angeles CA 90012-3013 Office: Columbia Artists Mngmt Inc Joyce Arbib Div 165 W 57th St New York NY 10019*

ZUBER, NORMA KEEN, career counselor, educator; b. Iuka, Miss., Sept. 27, 1934; d. William Harrington and Mary (Hebert) Keen; m. William Frederick Zuber, Sept. 14, 1958; children: William Frederick Jr., Michael, Kimberly, Karen. BS in Nursing, U. Southwestern La., 1956; MS in Counselling, Calif. Luth. U., 1984. Nat. cert. counselor, nat. cert. career counselor. Intensive care nurse Ochsner Found. Hosp., New Orleans, 1956-59; career devel. counselor BFC Counseling Ctr., Ventura, Calif., 1984-87; founder, prin., counselor Career & Life Planning-Norma Zuber & Assocs., Ventura, 1987—; instr. adult continuing edn. Ventura (Calif.) C.C., 1987—; instr. Calif. State U., Northridge, 1988-89, U. Calif., Santa Barbara, Antioch U.; mem. adv. coun. on tchr. edn. Calif. Luth. U., Thousand Oaks, 1984-87; mem. adv. bd. for development of profl. career counseling cert. program U. Calif., San Diego, 1991—. Co-author: The Nuts and Bolts of Career Counseling: Setting Up and Succeeding in Private Practice, 1992. Chmn. bd. dirs. women's ministries Missionary Ch., Ventura, 1987-90. Recipient profl. contbn. award H.B. McDaniel Found.-Stanford U. Sch. Edn., 1988, Govt. Rels. Com. Cert. of Appreciation, Am. Assn. for Counseling and Devel. Mem. NAFE, ACA, Nat. Career Devel. Assn., Calif. Assn. for Counseling and Devel. (chmn. legis. task force 1987-89, So. Calif. coord. area cons. for Calif. Career Devel. Assn. 1990, Jim Saum govt. rels. award 1989), Calif. Career Devel. Assn. (bd. dirs. 1985-91, membership dir. 1991-92, pres. 1992-93, Leadership and Professionalism award 1988, 89), Calif. Career Conf. (program chair 1993), Ventura County Profl. Women's Network (dir. membership 1990-91), Calif. Registry Profl. Counselors and Paraprofls. (vice chmn. bd. dirs. 1990—), Internat. Platform Assn., Nat. Career Devel. Assn. (we. regional trustee 1995—). Republican. Home: 927 Sentinel Circle Ventura CA 93003-3504 Office: Career and Life Planning 3585 Maple St Ste 237 Ventura CA 93003-3508

ZUCCHET, JANINE LEE, public relations specialist; b. Teaneck, N.J., Mar. 2, 1967; d. Walter and Lina (DeCandido) Z. BA, Rutgers U., 1989. Editorial asst. Child mag., N.Y.C., 1989-92; copy editor Troll Assocs., Mahwah, N.J., 1992; pub. rels. specialist Blenheim Group, Ft. Lee, N.J., 1992—. Mem. AAUW (newsletter editor 1989—), NAFE. Home: 545 Kearney Ave Cliffside Park NJ 07010-2224

ZUCCO, RONDA KAY, community relations representative; b. Peoria, Ill., Apr. 3, 1960; d. Richard Leon Zucco. BA, So. Ill. U., 1981. Cert. addictions profl.; internat. cert. alcohol and drug counselor. Counselor Spl. Supportive Svcs., So. Ill. U., Carbondale, 1981-83; substance abuse counselor Interventions, Chgo., 1984-86; addictions counselor Parkside at BroMenn, Bloomington, Ill., 1986-89; dir. continuing care Parkside Lodge of Fla., Kissimmee, 1989-93; sr. counselor Fla. Hosp. East (formerly Parkside Lodge of Fla.), Orlando, 1993-94; cmty. rels. rep. dept. psychiatry Fla. Hosp., Orlando, 1994—; tng. instr. for group facilitation Parkside Lodge of Fla., 1989-93, Fla. Hosp. East, 1993—; presenter seminars in field. Vol. crisis hotline Jackson County Cmty. Mental Health Ctr., Carbondale, 1981; vol. ARC, Carbondale, 1978-81. State of Ill. Gen. Assembly scholar, 1977-81. Mem. Am. Assn. for Counseling and Devel., Am. Mental Health Counselors Assn., Kappa Delta Pi, Chi Sigma Iota. Home: 10600 Bloomfield Dr Spt 311 Orlando FL 32825

ZUCK, WYNONA COLLEEN, editor; b. Kansas City, Mo., Sept. 30, 1939; d. Earl Albert and Bertha (Drake) Howell; m. James Daniel Bardwell (div. 1967); 1 child, John Albert; m. Willard Alonzo Zuck; step-children: Cathy, Dawn, Sherrie, Linda. AA, Longview Community Coll. Paste-up artist Western Auto, Kansas City, Mo., 1957-60; keyline artist Trainor, Christianson & Barclay, Kansas City, 1960-61, Art, Inc., Kansas City, 1961-62, Nat. Bellas Hess, N. Kansas City, Mo., 1965-69, Unity Sch. Christianity, 1969-72; assoc. editor Wee Wisdom, Unity Village, Mo., 1972, editor, 1977-85; assoc. editor Daily Word, Unity Village, 1985, editor, 1985—; mem. editorial adv. com. Unity Sch., Unity Village, 1986—. Mem. Phi Theta Kappa. Office: Daily Word Unity Sch of Christianity Unity Village MO 64065

ZUCKER, MARJORIE BASS, medical researcher, hematologist; b. N.Y.C., June 10, 1919; d. Murray H. and Agnes (Naumburg) Bass; m. Howard D. Zucker, June 25, 1938; children: Andrew A., Ellen Zucker Harrison, Joan, Barbara Zucker-Pinchoff. AB, Vassar Coll., 1939; postgrad., Columbia Coll. Medicine, 1943-45; PhD, Columbia U., 1944. Rsch. asst. Coll. Physicians and Surgeons Columbia U., N.Y.C., 1944-49; asst. to assoc. prof. physiology Coll. of Dentistry NYU, 1949-54; assoc. mem. Sloan Kettering Inst., N.Y.C., 1955-63; asst. rsch. dir. ARC Rsch. Lab NYU Med. Ctr., N.Y.C., 1963-70, assoc. prof. pathology, 1963-71, prof. pathology, 1971-92, prof. emeritus, 1992—; mem. various rev. coms. NIH, Bethesda, Md., 1971-85. Co-author: The Physiology of Blood Platelets, 1965; co-patentee composition containing platelet factor 4, 1988; contbr. numerous articles to prof. jours. Recipient award N.Y. Met. chpt. Am. Women in Sci., 1986. Mem. Internat. Soc. Thrombosis (mem. coun., Marian Barnhart Lecture award 1989), Soc. for Exptl. Biology and Medicine (pres. 1983-85), Choice in Dying (dir., v.p. 1990). Democrat. Address: 333 Central Park W New York NY 10025-7145

ZUCKER-FRANKLIN, DOROTHEA, medical scientist, educator; b. Berlin, Aug. 9, 1930; came to U.S., 1949; d. Julian and Gertrude (Feige) Zucker; m. Edward C. Franklin, May 15, 1956 (dec. 1982); 1 child, Deborah Julie. BA, Hunter Coll., 1952; MD, NYU, 1956. Diplomate Am. Bd. Internal Medicine. Intern Phila. Gen. Hosp., 1956-57; resident in internal medicine Montefiore Hosp., N.Y.C., 1957-59, postdoctoral fellow in hematology, 1959-61; with Med. Sch. NYU, N.Y.C., 1962—, prof. Med. Sch., 1974—, dir. lab., 1966—; asst. attending physician Montefiore Hosp., 1961-65; assoc. attending physician Univ. Hosp., 1968-74, attending physician, 1974—; assoc. attending physician Bellevue Hosp., 1968-74, attending physician, 1974—; cons. physician Manhattan (N.Y.) VA Hosp., 1970—, PHS Agy. for Healthcare Policy and Rsch., 1992—; sci. adv. bd., rev. panel Israel Cancer Rsch. Fund, 1982—; mem. U.S.-Israel Binat. Sci. Found., 1980—; bd. dirs. Henry M. and Lillian Stratton Found., Inc., 1987—; AID related Rsch. Rev. Com. NIHLB, 1986-90; mem. allergy immunol. com. NIH, 1974-80, pathological tng. com. NIH, 1971-74, Health Resource Coun., N.Y.C., 1971-74, blood products com. FDA, 1981-87. Mem. editorial bd. Blood, 1973-76, 80-86, Jour. Reticuloendothelial Soc., 1964-74, 80—, Am. Jour. Pathology, 1979—, Blood Cells, 1980—, Ultrastructural Pathology, 1979, Am. Jour. Medicine, 1981—, Hematology Oncology, 1982—, Jour. Immunology, 1986—; author: (with others) The Physiology and Pathology of Leukocytes, 1962, Atlas of Blood Cells, Function and Pathology, 1981, 2d edit., 1989, Amyloidosis, 1990. Recipient Career Devel. award NIH, 1965-70; NIH Rsch. grantee, 1970—. Fellow N.Y. Acad. Scis.; mem. Am. Fedn. Clin. Rsch., Am. Soc. Clin. Investigation, Am. Assn. Physicians, Am. Soc. Hematology (pres. 1995, chairperson subcom on leukocyte physiology 1977, chairperosn subcom. on immunohematology 1984, exec. coun. 1985—, advanced learning resources com. 1987—), Soc. Exptl. Biology and Medicine, Am. Soc. Exptl. Biology, Am. Soc. Immunologists, Am. Soc. Cell Biology, Reticuloendothelial Soc. (pres. program and nominatingcoms. 1984-85), N.Y. Soc. Electron Microscopists (pres. 1962, 84-85), N.Y. Soc. for Study Blood. Office: NYU Med Ctr 550 1st Ave New York NY 10016-6402

ZUCKERMAN, DIANA M., psychologist, congressional aide; b. Somerville, N.J., June 16, 1950; d. Leo and Anne Rachel (Bernstein) Zuckerman; m. Howard Dubowitz, Apr. 27, 1985; children: Nicole, Andrew. BA, Smith Coll., Northampton, Mass., 1972; MA, Ohio State U., 1975, PhD, 1977; postgrad., Yale U., 1979-80. Asst. prof. Vassar Coll., Poughkeepsie, N.Y., 1977-78; rsch. faculty Yale U., New Haven, 1978-79; dir. seven coll. study Harvard U., Cambridge, Mass., 1980-83; congl. sci. fellow U.S. Congress, Washington, 1983-84; nat. policy assoc. APA, Washington, 1984-85; congl. aide Subcom. on Human Resources & Intergovtl. Rels. U.S. Ho. of Reps., Washington, 1985-93; assoc. dir. Ctr. for Mental Health Svcs.-U.S. Dept. Health & Human Svcs., Washington, 1993; congl. aide VA Com., U.S. Senate, Washington, 1993—; lectr. in field; cons. in field; clin. psychotherapist for adults, children and families. Co-author: Teaching Television, 1981, Use TV to Your Child's Advantage, 1990, Big World, Small Screen, 1992 (APA Media award). Fellow APA (bd. profl. affairs 1990-92), Soc. for Psychol. Study of Social Issues (coun. 1990-92, co-chair pub. policy fellow com. 1992-94). Democrat. Jewish. Home: 4703 DeRussey Pkwy Chevy Chase MD 20815 Office: US Senate 202 Hart Bldg Washington DC 20510

ZUCKERMAN, RUTH VICTOR, sculptor; b. N.Y.C., Sept. 21, 1923; d. Benjamin and Sonia (Koshansky) Victor; m. Bernard A. Zuckerman, Feb. 1, 1946; children: Rowann Kay Gilman, Laura Bellon. Student, The Sch. Visual Arts, N.Y.C., 1967, The Arts Student's League, Woodstock, N.Y., 1968, The New Sch., N.Y.C., 1968, Ga. State U., 1972. Pvt. tchr. Atlanta, 1978-81; lectr. in field. Permanent collections include The Temple, Atlanta, The H.F. Johnson Mus., Ithaca, N.Y., Temple Beth Israel, Longbeat Key, Fla., So. Bell Telephone Ctr., Atlanta, The Ben Gurion Med. Ctr., U. Negev, Beersheva, Israel, the Alliance Theatre, Meml. Arts Ctr., Atlanta, The Carter Presdl. Ctr., Atlanta, No. Telecom. Hdqs., Nashville, The First Union Bank Ctr., Charlotte, N.Y., The Bill Breman Home for the Aged, Atlanta, Bauerfiend/Anton Corp., Leipzig, Germany. Bd. dirs. Art Festival of Atlanta, 1971-83; chairperson Sta WPBS Arts and Antiques Auction, Atlanta, 1982-87. Served USMCWR, 1944-46. Mem. Am. Soc. Contemporary Artists, N.Y. Artist's Equity, Museo de Bozzetti (Italy). Home: 722 Mill Walk NW Atlanta GA 30327 also: 601 Longboat Club Rd #S-402 Longboat Key FL 34228

ZUHLKE, MARYBETH, curriculum consultant, educator; b. Kenosha, Wis., Jan. 16, 1946; d. Charles Casmir and Elizabeth (Mulich) Safransky; m. Lee VanLunduyt, Aug. 24, 1968 (div. 1985); children: Kyle, Ravi; m. Tom Zuhlke, Sept. 9, 1990. Student, U. Dallas, 1965-67; BS, U. Wis., Whitewater, 1968; MS, U. Wis., Milw., 1973, postgrad., 1988-89; postgrad., Marquette U., 1978-81. Cert. elem. tchr., prin., coord. instruction, Wis. Tchr. second grade Kenosha Unified Sch. Dist., 1968-70, community liaison tchr., 1974-79, dissemination specialist, 1979-82, curriculum cons., 1982—; adj. assoc. prof. U. Wis., Kenosha, 1979—; cons. Conn. Facilitator, North Haven, 1984-86; coordinator Regional Staff Devel Ctr., Kenosha, 1986—. Co-author: Kenosha Model Kindergarten Manual, 1985, Kenosha Model Math. Manual, 1986; editor: Kenosha Model Language Experience, 1979. Mem. Racine (Wis.) Arts Coun., 1980-90. Mem. Internat. Reading Assn., Parent Edn. and Childhood Assn. (exec. bd. 1976-83), Wis. State and Fed. Specialists (newsletter editor 1986-87), Assn. Wis. Sch. Administrs., Assn. Supervision and Curriculum, Phi Delta Kappa. Democrat. Mem. Unitarian Universalist Ch. Home: 1419 Crabapple Dr Racine WI 53405-1703 Office: U Wis Parkside Kenosha WI 53142

ZUIDEMA, JULIE SMITH, public administrator; b. Madison, Wis., Oct. 25, 1952; d. Karl and Kay (Snyder) Ruff; m. Steven Douglas Smith, Oct. 21, 1978 (div. Nov. 1992); m. Byron Lee Zuidema, July 3, 1994. BS in Anthropology, U. Wis., 1974, EdM, 1982. Vista vol. Duluth (Minn.) Indian Action Coun., 1975-78; paramedical coord. Fond du Lac Reservation, Cloquet, Minn., 1978-80; employment tech. City of Duluth, Minn., 1980-82; Job Tng. Partnership Act planner II City of Duluth, 1982-85; exec. dir. Duluth (Minn.) Pvt. Industry Coun., 1985-94; dir. workforce devel. Minn. Dept. Econ. Security, St. Paul, 1994—; bd. dirs. Duluth Tech. Coll., 1986—, Gov.'s Edn. to Employment Coun., St. Paul, 1993—; chair Women's Commn., Duluth, 1986-92, Minn. Job Tng. Partnership, 1992-93. Office: Minn Dept Econ Security Workforce Devel 390 N Robert St Saint Paul MN 55101

ZULCH, JOAN CAROLYN, retired medical publishing company executive, consultant; b. Great Neck, N.Y., Apr. 10, 1931; d. Walter Howard and Edna Ruth (Howard) Z. B.S. in Biology, Allegheny Coll., 1952; postgrad., Hunter Coll., 1954. Med. sec. E.R. Squibb & Sons, N.Y.C., 1952; with Macmillan Pub. Co., N.Y.C., 1952-88, editorial asst. med. dept., 1952-56, asst. editor med. dept., 1956-58, editor med. dept., 1958-61, med. editor coll. and profl. div., 1961-75, sr. editor medicine, coll. and profl. div., 1975-78, exec. editor med. books, profl. books div., 1978-79, editor-in-chief, 1979-80, asst. v.p., editor-in-chief profl. books div., 1980-82; v.p., pub. med., nursing, health sci. dept. Macmillan Pub. Co., 1982-85, v.p., pub. med. books, sci., tech., med. dept., 1985-88, cons. med. pub., 1989—. Recipient Best Illustrated Med. Book award Assn. Med. Illustrators, 1977, Outstanding Book in Health Sci. award Assn. Am. Pubs., 1982. Mem. AAAS, AAUW, Post Libr. Assn., L.I.U. (rec. sec. 1990-93, exec. coun. 1990—), Friends of Locust Valley Libr. (pres. 1991-93, 94—, treas. 1993-94), Alpha Gamma Delta, Delta Sigma Rho. Republican. Home and Office: 36 Wood Ln Lattingtown PO Box 547 Locust Valley NY 11560-0547

ZUMO, BILLIE THOMAS, biologist; b. Cheyenne, Wy., Sept. 25, 1936; d. Thomas Elias and Katherine A. (Pappas); m. Charles Vincent, Aug. 21, 1959; 1 child, Dr. Thomas J. BA, U. Wyoming, Laramie, 1958; MA, U. N. Colo., Greeley, 1963; student, U. Wyoming, 1964, U. N. Colo., 1964. Cert. Educator. Tchr. Carey Jr. High Sch., Cheyene, Wy., 1958-61; English tchr. McCormick Jr. High, Cheyenne, 1961; tchr. Carey Jr. High Sch., Cheyenne, 1961-63; freshman biology Laramie Co. Community Coll., Cheyenne; tchr. Central High Sch., Cheyenne, 1963; exec. bd. Sch. Dist. curriculum adv., 1982-85; chmn. sci. dept., 1990—; mem. faculty adv. com. Central High Sch., 1988—, mem. prin. screening com., 1990-91. Author: Genetics Accepted by Sch. Dist. Football statis. Cen. Football Team, Cheyenne, 1976—; lay mem. rsch. com. of the Pharmacy Therapetics Com., 1985; judge sch. dist. sci. fair, Cheyenne, 1987-88; choir dir. ch. choir, Cheyenne, 1985. Named Wyoming Biology Tchr. of the Year Nat. Assn. of Biology Tchrs., 1976; Recipient Distinguished Service award Sts. Constantineo Helen Orthodox Ch., Cheyenne, 1979, Distinguished Service award as Choir Dir. Archbishop Iakovas, N.Y., 1988. Mem. Nat. Assn. Biology Tchrs. (state rep. 1992—), NEA, Cheyenne Tchrs. Edn. Assn., Who. Edn. Assn., Nat. Forum of Greek Orthodox Musicians, Ladies Philoptochos Soc. of Denver Diocese (treas. 1989-93, 1st v.p. 1993—), AAUW, Phi Delta Kappa. Democrat. Eastern Greek Orthodox. Home: 900 Ranger Dr Cheyenne WY 82009-2535 Office: Cen High Sch 5500 Education Dr Cheyenne WY 82009-4008

ZUMPE, DORIS, psychiatry researcher, educator; b. Berlin, May 18, 1940; came to U.S., 1972; d. Herman Frank and Eva (Wagner) Z. BSc, U. London, 1961, PhD, 1970. Asst. to K.Z. Lorenz, Max-Planck-Inst. für Verhaltensphysiologie, Seewiesen, Fed. Republic Germany, 1961-64; rsch. asst. and assoc., lectr. Inst. Psychiatry, U. London, 1965-72; rsch. assoc. Emory U. Sch. Medicine, Atlanta, 1972-74, asst. prof. psychiatry (ethology), 1974-77, assoc. prof., 1977-87, prof., 1987—; reviewer NSF, 7 sci. jours. Contbr. over 140 articles to profl. jours. NIMH grantee, 1971—. Mem. AAAS, Internat. Soc. Psychoneuroendocrinology, Internat. Primatological Soc., Internat. Soc. for Human Ethology, Soc. for Study of Reprodn., Am. Soc. Primatologists, N.Y. Acad. Scis., Earl Music Am., Viola da Gamba Soc. Am. Office: Emory U Sch Medicine Dept Psychiatry Atlanta GA 30322

ZUMPF, YORDIS ETHANA, nursing supervisor; b. Oakes, N.D., Aug. 24, 1941; d. Wesley Ralph and Yordis Frederika (Olsen) Spear; m. John Paul Zumpf, Sept. 1, 1963; children: Paul, Steven, Doreen. Diploma in Nursing, St. Lukes Sch. Nursing, Fargo, N.D., 1962. Asst. clin. instr. St. Luke's Sch. Nursing, Fargo, 1962-64; staff nurse St. Mary's Hosp., Rochester, Minn., 1964; office nurse, pvt. operating rm. tech. Garberson Clinic, Miles City, Mont., 1981-94, nursing supr., 1989—; task force Robert Johnson Wood/Pew Grant Holy Rosary Hosp., Miles City, 1992-93. Mem. Cmty. Concert Series, Miles City, 1989, 90, 92, 94; chair 1st Luth. Ch. Women, Miles City, 1987-90; lay communion com. 1st Luth. Ch., 1985—. Named Outstanding Young Woman of Am., 1977. Republican. Home: RR 2 Box 3042 Miles City MT 59301-9103 Office: Garberson Clinic 2200 Box Elder St Miles City MT 59301-2898

ZUNKER, SHARON JIENELL, commercial expediters company executive; b. Charleston, W.Va., July 28, 1943; d. Clifford W. and Iva A. (Neeley) Kenneway; m. Anthony F. Zunker, Sept. 19, 1980; children: Tibor Kreiter, Anthony Charles, Carl August, Melissa J., Anthony F. Jr. Diploma, Sprayberry High Sch., 1963. Various clerical positions N.Y. and Ga.; mgr. Winn Dixie, Ft. Lauderdale, Fla., 1973-76; owner, operator Union 76 Svc. Sta., Manistee, Mich., 1980-82; pres., owner Am. Comml. Expediters, Pompano Beach, Fla., 1988—; sec.-treas. Atlanta Envelope Co., 1962-64. Mem. Am. Legion, Odd Fellows, Rosecrucions, Internat. Platform Assn. U.S. C. of C., Smithsonian. Republican. Home: 6250 SW 6th St Pompano Beach FL 33068-1709 Office: Am Comml Expediters 1852 NW 21st St Pompano Beach FL 33069-1306

ZUPKUS, ELLEN CICCONE, clinical psychologist, consultant; b. Passaic, N.J., Oct. 28, 1954; d. Joseph Condoluro and Emma (Gash) Ciccone; m. Edward Walter Zupkus Jr., July 29, 1984; children: Maureen, Erin, Emily, Lauren. BA, Kean Coll. N.J., 1976; MA, Seton Hall U., 1978, PhD, 1985. Cert. sch. psychologist N.J.; Nat. cert sch. psychologist, group psychotherapist; lic. psychologist, N.J., N.Y. Adj. instr. Seton Hall U., South Orange, N.J., 1979-84; chairperson child study team Bergen County Spl. Svcs. Sch. Dist., Paramus, N.J., 1983-85; pvt. practice Holmdel, N.J., 1985—; adj. instr. Rider Coll., Lawrenceville, N.J., 1986; prin. clin. psychologist Marlboro (N.J.) Psychiat. Hosp., 1986-88; cons. psychologist Arthur Brisbane Child Treatment Ctr., Farmingdale, N.J., 1988-89; adj. instr. Monmouth Coll., West Long Branch, N.J., 1989; cons. psychologist Cedar Grove (N.J.) Residential Ctr., 1989—; cons. psychologist Adult Diagnostic and Treatment Ctr., Avenel, N.J., 1980-82; clin. psychologist Woodbridge Child Diagnostic Ctr., Avenel, 1980-83; presenter workshop on Millon Adolescent Personality Inventories, 1989. Author: (with others) Conference on the Millon Inventories, 1987; contbr. articles to profl. jours. Mem. Monmouth County Sexual Abuse Coalition, Monmouth County Child Sexual Abuse Com., Nat. Audubon Soc., Nat. Wildlife Fedn., Vienna, Va. Mem. APA (assoc.), N.J. Psychol. Assn., N.J. Assn. Sch. Psychologists, Monmouth Ocean County Psychol. Assn., Seton Hall U. Sch. Psychology Assn. (pres. 1981). Office: 702 N Beers St Holmdel NJ 07733

ZURAW, KATHLEEN ANN, special education and physical education educator; b. Bay City, Mich., Sept. 29, 1960; d. John Luke and Clara Josephine (Kilian) Z. AA with high honors, Delta Community Coll., 1980; BS with high honors, Mich. State U., 1984, MA, 1987. Cert. spl. edn., mentally impaired phys. edn. grade K-12, adaptive phys. edn. tchr., Mich. Summer water safety instr. Camp Midicha, Columbia, Mich., 1982, Bay Cliff Health Camp, Big Bay, Mich., 1983; summer spl. edn. tchr. Jefferson Orthopedic Sch., Honolulu, 1984, 85, 86, Ingham Intermediate Sch. Dist., Mason, Mich., 1987; spl. edn. tchr. Bay Arenac Intermediate Sch. Dist., Bay City, 1985-87, Berrien County Intermediate Sch. Dist., Berrien Springs, Mich., 1987—; mem. citizen amb program fitness delegation People's Republic China, 1991. Area 17 coach Mich. Spl. Olympics, Berrien Springs, 1987—; mem. YMCA, St. Joseph, Mich., 1987—, Y-Ptnrs., 1989, Coun. Exceptional Children; participant Citizen Ambassador Delegation to People's Republic of China, 1991. Mem. Am. Alliance Health, Phys. Edn., Recreation and Dance, Phi Theta Kappa, Phi Kappa Phi, Phi Delta Kappa. Roman Catholic. Home: 7306 W S Saginaw Rd Bay City MI 48706

ZUSSY, NANCY LOUISE, librarian; b. Tampa, Fla., Mar. 4, 1947; d. John David and Patsy Ruth (Stone) Roche; m. R. Mark Allen, Dec. 20, 1986. BA in Edn., U. Fla., 1969; MLS, U. So. Fla., 1977, MS in Pub. Mgmt., 1980. Cert. librarian, Wash. Ednl. evaluator State of Ga., Atlanta, 1969-70; media specialist DeKalb County Schs., Decatur, Ga., 1970-71; researcher Ga. State Libr., Atlanta, 1971; asst. to dir. reference Clearwater (Fla.) Pub. Libr., 1972-78, dir. librs., 1978-81; dep. state libr. Wash. State Libr., Olympia, 1981-86, state libr., 1986—; chmn. Consortium Automated Librs., Olympia, 1982—; cons. various pub. librs., Wash., 1981—; exec. officer Wash. Libr. Network, 1986-90; v.p. WLN (non-profit orgn.), 1990-93. Contbr. articles to profl. jours. Treas. Thurston-Mason Community Mental Health Bd., Olympia, 1983-85, bd. dir., 1982-85; mem. race com. Seafair Hydroplane Race, Seattle, 1986—, mem. milk carton derby team, 1994—. Mem. ALA, Assn. Specialized and Coop. Libr. Agys. (legis. com. 1983-86, chmn. legis. com. 1985-87, vice chmn. state libr. agys. sect. 1985-86, chmn. state ibr. agys. sect. 1986-87, chmn. govt. affairs com. Libr. Adminstrn. and Mgmt. Assn. 1986-87), Freedom to Read Found. (bd. dirs. 1987-91), Chief Officers of State Libr. Agys. (dir.-at-large 1987-90, v.p./pres. elect 1990-92, pres. 1992-94), Wash. Libr. Assn. (co-founder legis. planning com. 1982—, fed. rels. coord. 1984—), Fla. Libr. Assn. (legis. and planning com. 1978-81), Pacific N.W. Libr. Assn., Rotary, Phi Kappa Phi, Phi Beta Mu. Home: 904 E Bay Dr NE #404B Olympia WA 98506-3970 Office: Wash State Libr PO Box 42464 Olympia WA 98504-2464

ZWANG, SHIRLEY SHAPIRO, artist; b. N.Y.C., Apr. 28, 1924; d. Benjamin and Lana Shapiro; widowed; children: David, Robert, Jonathan. Grad. in Illustration, Pratt Inst., 1945; B of Profl. Studies in Studio Art, SUNY, Saratoga, 1979. Artist Danbury, Conn., 1974—. Represented in permanent collections Temple Emanu-El, Temple Beth El, Spring Valley, N.Y., Maimonides Acad., Danbury, Conn., Jewish Fedn. Danbury, Temple Israel, U.A.H.C., Cystic Fibrosis Found., and pvt. collections; exhibited in group shows at Brookfield (Conn.) Craft Ctr. Gallery, 1974, Westchester Art Assn., White Plains, N.Y., 1976, B'nai B'rith Klutznick Mus., Washington, 1977, 82, Skirball Mus., L.A., 1977, Jewish Fedn. Exhibit, Nashville, 1978, Yeshive U. Mus., 1978, 79, SUNY, 1979, 80, Mamaroneck, N.Y. Artist Guild Show, 1980, Nat. Coun. Art in Jewish Life, N.Y.C., 1983, Am. Jewish Congress, 1985, Jewish Community Ctr., Tampa, 1986, U.A.H.C. Biennial Conv., Chgo., 1987, Jewish Community Ctr., Richmond, Va., 1988. Bd. dirs. Jewish Fedn. Greater Danbury, 1992—. Mem. Synagogue Artists and Craftsmen of Union of Am. Hebrew Congregations, Am. Guild of Jewish Art. Home: 33 Alan Rd Danbury CT 06810-8362

ZWEIGENTHAL, GAIL, magazine editor; b. N.Y.C., Feb. 27, 1944; d. Joseph and Bessie (Lang) Z. B.A., Tufts U., 1965. Editorial asst. Gourmet mag., N.Y.C., then assoc. editor, sr. editor, mng. editor, exec. editor, now editor in chief. Office: Gourmet Mag 560 Lexington Ave New York NY 10022-6828*

ZWICK, SHELLY CRITTENDON, university official; b. Cin., Dec. 27, 1941; d. Kenneth Shelby and Rosa Henrietta (Ruda) Crittendon; m. Peter Ronald Zwick, July 6, 1963. BA, Stetson U., Deland, Fla., 1963; JD, La. State U., 1976. Bar: La. 1977, U.S. Dist. Ct. (mid. dist.) La. 1977, U.S. Ct. Appeals (5th cir.) 1979, (11th cir.) 1981, U.S. Dist. (ea. dist.) La. 1988, (we. dist.) La. 1988, U.S. Supreme Ct. 1990. Asst. U.S. atty. mid. dist. Dept. Justice, Baton Rouge, 1978-84, chief civil div., 1981-84; magistrate U.S. Cts., Baton Rouge, 1984-86; ptnr. Roy, Kiesel, Aaron, Tucker & Zwick, Baton Rouge, 1986-90; dir. affirmative action Calif. State U., San Marcos, 1992—; adj. prof. La. State U., Baton Rouge, 1987-90, lectr., 1979-90, La. State Police, Baton Rouge, 1980-84. Contbr. articles to profl. jour. Recipient Disting. Alumni award Stetson U., 1985. Mem. Fed. Bar Assn., La. State Bar Assn., Nat. Assn. Coll. and Univ. Attys., Am. Assn. for Affirmative Action, Calif. Concerns, Dean Henry George McMahon Inn of Ct. Episcopalian. Home: 845 N Rios Ave Solana Beach CA 92075 Office: Calif State U San Marcos CA 92096

ZWICKE, DIANNE LYNN, internist, cardiologist, educator; b. Marshfield, Wis., Oct. 27, 1952; d. Edward Raymond and Donna Mae (Erickson) Z. Diploma in nursing, St. Joseph's Hosp., Marshfield, 1973; BS in Nursing, Marquette U., 1975; MD, U. N.C., 1982. Diplomate Am. Bd. Internal Medicine, subspecialty cert. in cardiovascular diseases. Resident in internal medicine U. Wis.-Marshfield Clinic-St. Joseph's Hosp., 1982-84, chief resident, 1984-85; fellow in cardiology U. Wis. Clin. Campus-Sinai Samaritan Med. Ctr., Milw., 1985-87, assoc. prof. medicine, 1987—; mem. active staff in cardiology and emergency medicine U. Wis. Cliin. Campus-Sinai Samaritan Med. Ctr., Milw., 1987—; clin. instr. surgery emergency-trauma svcs. Med. Coll. Wis., Milw; attending staff St. Luke's Hosp., St. Francis Hisp., St. Michael's Hosp., West Allis Meml. Hosp., Milw.; bd. govs., mem. State Wis. Nat. Faculty Am. Heart Assn.; presenter in field. Contbr. articles and abstracts to med. jours. Recipient attending teaching award Sinai Samaritan Med. Ctr., 1988. Fellow Am. Coll. Cardiology, Am. Coll. Chest Physicians; mem. Soc. Critical Care Medicine, Wis Med. Soc. (chmn. on continuing med. edn. 1987), Milw. County Med. Soc., Sigma Theta Tau. Democrat. Lutheran. Office: U Wis Clin Campus 950 N 12th St Milwaukee WI 53233

ZWIEBEL, MARIE BEE, librarian; b. Berea, W.Va., Apr. 4, 1934; d. Ernest Kay and Lillian Tallulah (Bottoms) Bee; m. Doyle Keith Zwiebel, Aug. 20, 1955 (dec.); children: Kevin Vaughn (dec.), Hans Kent, Veronica Ileen Zwiebel Sperry. BA cum laude, Salem Coll., 1955; MA, W.Va. U., 1978; postgrad., Marshall U., 1981-82. Cert. tchr., W.Va. English tchr. Canisteo (N.Y.) Cen. Sch., 1956-57; sci. and math. tchr. Richburg (N.Y.) Cen. Sch., 1957-60; dir. edn. W.Va. Indsl. Home for Youth, 1967-79; libr. Norwood Jr. High Sch., Nutter Fort, W.Va., 1979-81; libr., head tchr. Van Horn Elem. Sch., Salem, W.Va., 1981—; mem. Elem. Classroom Instrn. Act Chpt. I Adv. Coun., Clarksburg, W.Va., 1980—. Author of poems; editor: Reference Skills (4-6), 1991. Sec. Camp Joy, Inc., Berea, 1990—; mem. Salem Bicentennial Com., 1991—; mem. Christian Social Action Com., Janesville, Wis., 1991—; mem. Salem-Tiekyo U. Auz., Salem, 1991—; bd. dirs. Highland (W.Va.) Sch., 1981—; chmn. Harrison County Mini-Grant Com., Clarksburg, W.Va., 1988—; mem. City of Salem Hist. Preservation Commn., 1992—. Grantee W.Va. Dept. Edn., 1990, Harrison County Bd. Edn., 1991. Mem. ALA, W.Va. Bus. and Profl. Women (pres. 1983-84, Woman of Yr. 1985), W.Va. Profl. Educators Assn., Harrison County Hist. Assn., Harrison County Cultural Found., Internat. Quilling Guild, Alpha Delta Kappa (historian 1990-92). Republican. Seventh Day Baptist. Home: 192 Liberty St Salem WV 26426 Office: Van Horn Sch 229 W Main St Salem WV 26426

ZWILICH, ELLEN TAAFFE, composer; b. Miami, Fla., Apr. 30, 1939; d. Edward Porter and Ruth (Howard) Taaffe; m. Joseph Zwilich, June 22, 1969 (dec. June 1979). MusB, Fla. State U., 1960, MusM, 1962; D Mus. Arts, Juilliard Sch., 1975; studies with Roger Sessions and Elliott Carter; MusD (hon.), Oberlin Coll., 1987, Converse Coll., 1994; LHD (hon.), Manhattanville Coll., 1991, Marymount Manhattan Coll., 1994. composer in residence Santa Fe Chamber Music Festival, 1990, Am. Acad., Rome, 1990; bd. dirs. MacDowell Colony. Premiere, Symposium for Orch., Pierre Boulez, N.Y.C., 1975, Chamber Symphony and Passages, Boston Musica Viva, Richard Pittman, 1979, 82. Symphony 1, Gunther Schuller, Am. Composers Orch., 1982; violinist Am. Symphony, N.Y.C., 1965-73; composer: Sonata in Three Movements, 1973-74; String Quartet, 1974; Clarino Quartet, 1977; Chamber Symphony, 1979; Passages (for Soprano and Chamber Ensemble), 1981; String Trio, 1982; Symphony 1:3 Movements for Orch., 1982 (Grammy nomination New World Records, 1987); Divertimento, 1983; Einsame Nacht, 1971; Emlekezet, 1978; Im Nebel, 1972; Passages for Soprano and Orch., 1982; Trompeten, 1974; Fantasy for Harpsichord, 1983; Intrada, 1983; Prologue and Variations, 1983; Double Quartet for Strings, Chamber Music Soc. of Lincoln Ctr., 1984; Celebration for Orch., Indpls. Symphony, John Nelson, 1984; Symphony #2 (Cello Symphony) San Francisco Symphony, Edo De Waart, 1985, Symphony #2 Louisville Orch. recording, L.L. Smith (Grammy nomination 1991); Concerto Grosso 1985, Handel Festival Orch., Steven Simon, 1986; Concerto for Piano and Orch., Detroit Symphony, Gunther Herbig, Marc-André Hamelin, 1986; Images for 2 Pianos and Orch., Nat. Symphony Orch., F. Machetti, 1987; Tanzspiel, Peter Martins N.Y.C. Ballet, 1987; Praeludium Boston chpt. AGO, 1987; Trio for piano, violin and cello; Kalichstein, Laredo, Robinson trio, 1987; Symbolon, Zubin Mehta and the N.Y. Philharm., Leningrad and Moscow (USSR), N.Y.C. (Koussevitsky Internat. Rec. award nominee 1990), 1988; concerto for trombone and orch. J. Friedman, Sir Georg Solti, Chgo. Symphony, 1989, concerto for trombone and orch. Christian Lindberg, James De Priest, Malmö Symphony, concerto for flute and orch. D.A. Dwyer, Seija Ozawa, Boston Symphony, 1990, quintet for clarinet and string quartet David Schiffrin, Chamber Music N.W., 1990; concerto for oboe and orch. John Mack, Christoph von Dohnanyi, Cleve. Orch., 1991; concerto for bass trombone strings, timpani and cymbals Chgo. Symphony Orch.Ch. Vernon, Daniel Barenboim, 1991; concerto for violin, violoncello and orch. Jaime Laredo, Sharon Robinson, Louisville Orch., L. Smith, 1991; Immigrant Voices Peter Leonard, St. Lukes Orch., N.Y. Internat. Festival ot the Arts Chorus, Ellis Island, 1991, concerto for flute and orch, D.A. Dwyer, J. Sedares, London Symphony Orch., 1992, Symphony # 3, J. Ling, N.Y. Philharmonic, 1993, concerto for bassoon and orch., Nancy Goeres, Lorin Maazel, Pitts. Symphony, 1993, concerto for horn and string Orch., David Jolley, Rochester Philharm., L.L. Smith., 1993, Fantasy for Orch., JoAnn Falletta, Long Beach Symphony Orch., 1994; New World Records: Music By Ellen Taaffe Zwilich; N.Y. Philharm. conducted by Zubin Mehta. Recipient Elizabeth Sprague Coolidge Chamber Music prize, 1974, Gold medal G.B. Viotti, Vercelli, Italy, 1975, citation Ernst von Dohnanyi, 1981, Pulitzer prize, 1983, Composers award Lancaster Symphony Orch., Arturo Toscanini Music Critics award, 1987, Alfred I. DuPont award, 1991; Martha Baird Rockefeller Fund rec. grantee, 1977, 79, 82, Guggenheim fellow, 1981. Mem. Am. Fedn. Mudicians (hon. life), Am. Music Ctr. (bd. dirs., v.p. 1982-84), Am. Composers Orch. (bd. dirs.), Am. Acad. and Inst. Arts and Letters (Academy award), Internat. League Women Composers, Am. Composers Alliance, Am. Composers Orch. (bd. dirs.), Fla. Artista Hall of Fame. Home: 600 W 246th St Bronx NY 10471-3611 Office: care Music Assocs Am 224 King St Englewood NJ 07631-3026

ZWIREN, JAN MARIE, advertising executive; b. Columbus, Ohio, May 22, 1944; d. Justin Bernard and Annabell Lee (Slyh) Reichert. A.S., Fashion Inst. Tech., 1965; student Wharton Sch. Bus., Phila., 1970, 71, 72, 75. Copywriter, Rike's Dept. Store, Dayton, Ohio, 1966-67; copywriter John Wanamaker, Phila., 1967-69; promotion dir. Menley & James Labs., Phila., 1969-74; v.p. mktg. Helen Curtis Industries, Chgo., 1974-79; pres. Jan Zwiren Agy., Chgo., 1979-82; chmn. Zwiren & Wagner Agy., Chgo., 1983-86, founder Zwiren, Collins, Karo & Trusk, 1986-89; CEO Zwiren Ayer (div. N.W. Ayer Worldwide), 1989-91; exec. v.p. strategic bus. devel. DDB Needham Worldwid, 1992-93, mng. ptnr. DDB Needham Chgo., 1993—; bd. dirs. Lake Forest Grad. Sch. Mgmt., Northwestern Family Inst. Contbr. articles to profl. jours. Named Ad Women of Yr., Chgo. Tribune, 1981; recipient awards Clio's, Addys, Comm. Arts, Chgo. Ad Club. Mem. Nat. Assn. Women Bus. Owners, Winter Club,(Lake Forest), Assn. Advt. Agencies, Chgo. Advt. Club, Am. Advt. Fedn., NOW, LWV. Methodist. Clubs: Chgo. Yacht, Carlton. Office: DDB Needham Chgo 303 E Wacker Dr Chicago IL 60601-5212

ZYDEK, SALLIE ANN, artist, illustrator, paralegal specialist; b. Buckley, Wash., Nov. 28, 1940; d. Fred Antone and June (Brown) Z.; m. Richard A. Skagen, June 5, 1959 (div. Dec. 1968); children: Rick L. Skagen, Tim L. Skagen. Criminal justice degree, Tacoma C.C., 1976, AAS, 1977; BA, Puget Sound U., 1979. One-woman shows include Antiquarium Gallery, Omaha, 1983-87, Local Artists Exch., Omaha, 1991; exhibited in group nat. art shows at Haymarket Art Gallery, Lincoln, 1985-93, Fontenelle Forest Assn., Omaha, 1987-90, Nebr. Artist Art Show, Seward, 1990, Omaha Artist Art Show, 1990, Seven State Regional Art Show, Cheyenne, Wyo., 1991, Surya Gallery, Lincoln, 1992, Stuhr Gallery, Grand Island, Nebr., 1992, Inst. Fine Art, Boston, 1993, Elder Gallery, Lincoln, 1993, 24 Yrs.-24 States Art Show, Cheyenne, 1993. Active Wildlife Rescue, Inc., Raptor Recovery Ctr., Lindoln, Preservations of Mountain Lions, Sacramento, Calif. Home: 530 N 72nd Ave Omaha NE 68114-3204

ZYGAS, EGLE VICTORIA, arts administrator; b. Cleve., Nov. 8, 1952. BA cum laude, Radcliffe Coll., 1974, MA, 1977; PhD, Ind. U., 1993. Folk arts coord. Ind. Arts Commn., Indpls., 1980-82; exec. dir. Peoples and Cultures, Cleve., 1982-83; dir. ethnic and folk arts programs Ill. Arts Coun.,

Chgo., 1983-87, asst. dep. dir., 1987-89; curator of edn. Mus. Am. Folk Art, N.Y.C., 1989-90, Am. Craft Mus., N.Y.C., 1990-92; program coord. Cooper-Hewitt Nat. Design Mus., Smithsonian Instn., N.Y.C., 1992—. Co-editor: Folklorica: Festschrift in Honor of Felix J. Oinas, 1982; editor N.Y. Folklore, 1992—. Office: Cooper-Hewitt Nat Design Mus 2 E 91st St New York NY 10128-9990

ZYLANOFF, PHILLIPA LOUISE, anesthesiologist; b. Indpls.; Feb. 2, 1943; d. Joseph David Zylanoff and Phillipa (Schreiber) Moore; divorced; children: Gwendolynn, Ann, Daniel, Aliza, Tamar. BS, Calif. State U., Hayward, 1966; MD, Med. Coll. Pa., 1972. Diplomate Am. Bd. Anesthesiology. Asst. prof. U. Calif., Davis, 1977-79; staff anesthesiologist New Iberia (La.) Parish Hosp., 1979-81; pvt. practice anesthesiology Moorehead, Ky., 1981-84; asst. prof. U. S. Ala., Mobile, 1985-87; dir. anesthesiology Randolph Hosp., Asheboro, N.C., 1987-90; pvt. practice anesthesiology Detroit, 1990—. Contbr. articles to profl. jours. Course dir. Mich. affiliate Am. Heart Assn. Mem. AMA, Mich. Soc. Anesthesiologists, Mich. State Med. Soc., Wayne County Med. Soc. (peer review com. 1991-93), Soc. Cardiovascular Anesthesiologists (presenter 1987). Republican. Jewish. Home: 17311 Beechwood Ave Franklin MI 48025-5523

ZYROFF, ELLEN SLOTOROFF, information scientist, classicist, educator; b. Atlantic City, N.J., Aug. 1, 1946; d. Joseph George and Sylvia Beverly (Roth) Slotoroff; m. Jack Zyroff, June 21, 1970; children: Dena Rachel, David Aaron. AB, Barnard Coll., 1968; MA, The Johns Hopkins U., 1969, PhD, 1971; MS, Columbia U., 1973. Instr. The Johns Hopkins U., Balt., 1970-71, Yeshiva U., N.Y.C., 1971-72, Bklyn Coll., 1971-72; libr., instr. U. Calif., 1979, 81, 91, San Diego State U., 1981-85, 94; prof. San Diego Mesa Coll., 1981—; dir. The Reference Desk Rsch. Svcs., La Jolla, Calif., 1983—; prin. libr. San Diego County Libr., 1985—; v.p. Archaeol. Soc. Am., Balt., 1970-71. Author: The Author's Apostrophe in Epic from Homer Through Lucan, 1971, Cooperative Library Instruction for Maximum Benefit, 1989. Pres. Women's Am. ORT, San Diego, 1979-81. Mem. ALA (chair divsn. coms. 1982—), Am. Philol. Assn., Calif. Libr. Assn. (elected to assembly 1993—), Am. Soc. Info. Sci., Am. Classical League, Toastmasters, Beta Phi Mu. Office: PO Box 12122 La Jolla CA 92039